D0962200

CASSELL'S ITALIAN DICTIONARY

CASSELL'S

ITALIAN DICTIONARY

ITALIAN-ENGLISH   ENGLISH-ITALIAN

COMPILED BY

PIERO REBORA

Late Professor of English, State University of Milan

formerly Professor of Italian, University of Manchester

WITH THE ASSISTANCE OF

FRANCIS M. GUERCIO

Lecturer in Italian, University of London

AND

ARTHUR L. HAYWARD

MACMILLAN PUBLISHING COMPANY

New York

Macmillan Publishing Company
866 Third Avenue, New York, N.Y. 10022

Library of Congress Cataloging in Publication Data
Main entry under title:
Cassell's Italian dictionary.
1. Italian language—Dictionaries—English.
2. English language—Dictionaries—Italian. I. Rebora, Piero, 1889- . II. Guercio, Francis Michael.
III. Hayward, Arthur Lawrence, 1885-1967.
PC1640.C33 1977 453'.21 77-7405
ISBN 0-02-522530-8 (standard)
ISBN 0-02-522540-5 (indexed)

15 14 13 12 11 10 9 8

Printed in the United States of America.

La plupart des occasions des troubles du monde sont grammairiennes.

—MONTAIGNE.

Ogni uomo sa che la parola è mezzo di rappresentare il pensiero; ma pochi si accorgono che la progressione, l'abbondanza e l'economia del pensiero son effetti della parola.—UGO FOSCOLO.

PREFACE

THE Preface to a dictionary must be the least likely of all human utterances to awaken interest, yet it is the only means by which the lexicographer can introduce himself and explain the lines upon which he has done his work. "Every other author," says Dr. Johnson, "may aspire to praise; the lexicographer can only hope to escape reproach, and even this negative recompense has been granted to very few."

CASSELL'S ITALIAN DICTIONARY now takes its place among those other Cassell Dictionaries that for ninety years and more have been in constant use by the public. It has had its vicissitudes in the course of preparation, yet what dictionary worth the name has not been the fruit of much anxiety, many disappointments, and years of drudgery? So far as any such work can claim to be new, this is a new lexicon. Though based on the extensive examination of previous dictionaries it is as up to date as the study of newspapers, magazines, and current works of literature and science can make it. It does not pretend to be in any sense a technical or specialist dictionary; it is intended for both the beginner in Italian and the more advanced student in search of the *mot juste*. The aim throughout has been to make it a dictionary of real Italian as spoken and written to-day, embodying current phrases and rejecting the ghost words that clank their chains unhelpfully through the pages of many of its predecessors. Archaisms have, so far as was possible, been omitted; whereas neologisms have been included where there seemed some likelihood of their becoming permanent additions to the language. It is, by the nature of things, impossible for any dictionary to keep abreast of all such new words, for every year brings inventions and discoveries in every branch of science and each of these demands and receives its own new term; in the following pages the best has been done according to the compiler's ability, and there it must be left.

There have been relatively few Italian-English dictionaries produced in this country. Apart from the early *World of Words* by John Florio (1598), the first modern dictionary was that of Giuseppe Baretti, published in 1760, which for a century and a half remained without a serious competitor. Until the middle of the last century Italian was the recognised language of humanism, poetry, and classical culture. There were in England many Italian political refugees, men of great culture and literary gifts, who were driven to earn a meagre living by teaching their native tongue. Baretti in hand, they took bevies of young ladies through *Le Mie Prigioni*, *I Promessi Sposi*, Metastasio, or Alfieri, and taught them to sing "Voi che sapete" and "Caro mio ben" with a sense of the pronunciation and meaning of the words. By the 1850s this gentle culture had yielded to the study of German and the more exciting aspects of the Industrial Revolution, and the demand for an Italian dictionary consequently diminished. In the last forty years or so, however, there has been a renewed interest in the language; war, politics, and commerce have induced or obliged many to study Italian, and two or three new dictionaries have appeared. CASSELL'S ITALIAN DICTIONARY will, it is hoped, serve the dual purpose of helping the English student interested in contemporary Italian life and literature, and the Italian who wants to perfect his knowledge of English.

Italian is enriched, or rather encumbered, with a number of synonyms and variants, due to the fact that, whereas the language became fixed as a literary medium at a very early date, the continuance of the dialects—many of them practically languages in their own right—within the Peninsula has lasted in full vigour to this day. Thus it happens that in the various regions of Italy different words may be used to indicate the same thing. As an example: for "honeysuckle" we find "caprifoglio", "madreselva", "lonicera", "abbracciabosco", "abbracciadonne", "vincibosco", and yet others. It would be manifestly impracticable to include all synonyms in a work of this size and scope, which after all makes no pretension to being a dialectal or etymological dictionary. Nor has it been considered advisable to include all the variant forms of spelling as, for instance, "ammelanconire", "ammalinconire", "immelanconire", "immalinconire", "rammelanconire", and so on. An endeavour has been made always to translate rather than define; explanation has been resorted to only when no truly equivalent word has been found. A special effort has been made to avoid the snares of "false friends," so frequently encountered in various Anglo-Italian dictionaries.

Italian-English Dictionary

Italian spelling being almost phonetic, no attempt has been made to indicate the pronunciation of each word. Only the correct use of the tonic accent has been taken into consideration, and a practical method of transcription has been adopted for the assistance of the student. An accent is used in written and printed Italian only: (a) when the stress falls on a final vowel; (b) when it is desired to differentiate between two words pronounced and spelled alike; (c) in certain foreign words.

The usual rule of the stress falling on the penultimate syllable has many exceptions. In this dictionary, exceptions of this kind are repeated in square brackets with the stressed vowel indicated by a capital letter, *e.g.* **abito** [Abito], **concedere** [concEdere]. This method has also been employed to indicate where *ia, io, uo,* for instance, are not diphthongized, *e.g.* [meteorologIa]. As for the phonic accents (which are not commonly indicated in written or printed Italian) we have shown the closed or open sound of E and O only in the few cases of ambiguity (homonyms, or rather homographs). A grave or acute accent will show the open or closed sound in such words as: pèsca (=peach), pésca (=fishing) or dótto (= duct), dòtto (= scholar) etc.

A full study of the Italian verb will be found in any good grammar, but for the quick reference of students a brief survey of the conjugations is given on pp. xiv–xxi.

English-Italian Dictionary

There is little to be said about this half of the book. English orthography being what it is, the pronunciation of main words has been given in the script of the International Phonetic Association, according to the symbols on p. x. It is hoped that the Italian student will thus be enabled to master the consonant and vowel sounds not found in his own language. This portion of the Dictionary owes much to the help of Dr. Constance Brooks, of Manchester University.

CASSELL'S ITALIAN DICTIONARY is naturally indebted to its forerunners, from Baretti onwards. It has also embodied much help from other sources. That none of these is acknowledged in particular implies no belittling of the value of their aid, without which not one page of the dictionary would exist. They have been studied and re-studied, read and re-read, and no words from the compiler could discharge his obligations to these unnamed coadjutors.

The compiling of this dictionary has been the work of several decades. Little could be done towards bringing it out during the second World War, and after 1945 the dictionary needed to be completely revised. The compiler has been diligently assisted in this work by Dr. F. M. Guercio of London University, and also by Mr. Arthur L. Hayward.

The preparation of this dictionary has been a long and arduous task, but one that afforded satisfaction, since we are all keenly aware that a new work of this kind was necessary, and in fact long overdue. In the rich and noble world of Anglo-Italian intellectual relations, even this modest contribution of an ordinary lexicon should serve a useful purpose. P.R.

Further Notes on the Pronunciation of Italian

In addition to the notes on page vi, careful attention to the table of sounds on page xi and to the following principles will yield an approximately correct pronunciation of Italian.

Italian vowels are short and clear-cut, and should not be slurred, as is common in many English words, e.g. *general*, which is frequently pronounced *gen-ral*. In the equivalent Italian word *generale*, every vowel is clearly enunciated—*ge-ne-ra-le*. The common tendency in English to "slide" vowels (e.g. *where*, pronounced *whay-er*) should be carefully avoided in Italian pronounciation.

The basic unit of Italian, the syllable, must be very cleanly enunciated, no matter how fast the rate of enunciation. A single consonant goes with the following vowel, and this vowel must not carry over into the following syllable, nor must it be colored by the initial consonant of the following syllable (*ca-ro*, not *car-o*). Double consonants are divided (*trop-po*) and have the effect of shortening the preceding vowel and prolonging the internal sound of the consonant before it is released.

If the first of two consonants is *l*, *m*, *n*, or *r*, they are divided. When the preceding vowel is stressed, such an *l*, *m*, *n*, or *r* will be prolonged (*tem-po* = *temm-po*). A syllable does not end in *s* unless followed by another *s* (*bas-so*); otherwise the *s* goes with the following syllable (*pre-sto*). A combination of two consonants, when the first is not *l*, *m*, *n*, or *r*, goes with the following syllable (*ma-dre*, *de-gno*). In combinations of three consonants, the first (with the exception of *s*) goes with the preceding syllable (*om-bra* BUT *fi-ne-stra*). *Cia*, *cio*, *ciu*, *gia*, *gio*, *giu* are single syllables in which the *i* is not heard (*cha*, *cho*, *chu*, *ja*, *jo*, *ju*); the *i* is written solely to indicate that the *c* and the *g* are pronounced respectively as *ch* and *j*, rather than with the hard sound as before *a*, *o*, and *u*. Similarly, the *h* in *ch* and *gh* serves only to indicate the hard sound before *e* and *i*, and is not heard. The *i* in *chia*, *chio*, *chiu*, *ghia*, *ghio* is heard as a *y* (*kya*, *kyo*, etc.), but these combinations are pronounced as one syllable.

Normally, *s* between vowels is pronounced as in *rose* (*ro-sa*); purists and most Tuscans except certain common words like *casa*, *cosa*, *così*, *naso*, *Pisa*, but there is very little hiss to this *s*. In all words and syllables beginning with *s* followed by *b*, *d*, *g*, *l*, *m*, *n*, *r*, or *v*, the *s* must be pronounced as in *rose*, or the Italians will mistake the sound for *sp*, *st*, etc. (*sbagliare*, as opposed to *spagliare*; *sdentare*, as opposed to *stentare*, etc.).

Of the two sounds of *z* given in the table, the *ts* is by far the more common; *ds*, or more accurately *dz*, is heard, however, in the verbs in *-izzare*, and in the following common words: *azzurro*, *bronzo*, *dozzina*, *magazzino*, *mezzo*, *pranzo*, *romanzo*, *zero*, *zona*, and *zoologia* [zoologIa], and their derivatives.*

The most difficult problem in Italian pronunciation is word stress, and for this there is no very good rule. Normal stress falls on the penultimate, or on a final vowel bearing the written accent (*sofà*). As noted on page vi, in this dictionary exceptions are repeated in square brackets, with the stressed vowel indicated by a capital letter, e.g. *abito* [Abito], *concedere* [concEdere]. Many verbs in the first (*-are*) conjugation have irregular stress, but frequently there may be a clue to this in the related noun, e.g. *dedica* [dEdica], *n. f.* Dedication, *dedicare*, *v. t.* To dedicate, hence [dEdico], I dedicate; *telefono* [telEfono] *n. m.* Telephone, *telefonare*, *v. t.* To telephone, hence [telEfonano], they telephone.

It is helpful to know that open *e* and *o* are always stressed. The same is true of the diphthongs *ie* and *uo*, where the *e* and *o* in these groups are always open and stressed.

***Aside from the above-mentioned words, z and zz are pronounced as *dz* in the following words and their derivatives, as well as in a number of uncommon words: *arzillo*, *barzelletta*, *bizza*, *brezza*, *donzella*, *frizzo*, *garzone*, *gazzella*, *gazzetta*, *gonzo*, *Lazzaro* [lAzzaro], *lazzaretto*, *lazzo*, *manzo*, *orizzonte*, *orzo*, *penzolo* [pEnzolo], *ribrezzo*, *ronzio* [ronzIo], *rozzo*, *zaffiro*, *zanzara*, *zebra*, *zeffiro* [zEffiro], *zelo*, *zenit*, *zeta*, *zinco*, *zodiaco* [zodIaco], *zolla*.**

CONTENTS

Letters and Symbols of the International Phonetic Association employed in the English-Italian section of the Dictionary

The consonants b, d, f, h, k, l, m, n, p, r, s, t, v, w, z, have their usual values.

Symbol	*English sound*	*Approximate Italian Equivalent*
ɑː	fAther	pAdre
æ	mAn	—
ai	fIne	mAI
au	crOWd	lAUdare
e	mEn	bEllo
ei	grAte	cEna
ə	fathEr, graciOUs	—
əː	sEArch	—
ɛə	hAIr	mEro
i	fInIsh	Immenso
iː	stEEd	vIno
iə	stEEr	vIa
o	dOmain	dOmani
ou	rOpe	sOle
ɔ	blOck	blOcco
ɔː	fAll	—
ɔi	jOInt	pOI
u	pUdding	appUnto
uː	mOOn	lUna
juː	spUE	rifIUtare
ʌ	mUch	—
j	Yellow	IEri
dʒ	JuDGe	GIudice
g	Gag	Gallo
ŋ	riNG	carliNGa
ʃ	Sure	SCIacca
tʃ	CHurCH	Centro
ð	boTHer	—
θ	THin	—
ɹ	sailoR	—
ʒ	viSIon	—

ˈ precedes the stressed syllable.

˜ occurring over a vowel symbol indicates that the vowel sound is nasalized, *e.g.* **aplomb** [əˈplɔ̃].

N.B. In southern England a final R preceded by a vowel (*e.g.* **writer, sailor**) and R preceded by a vowel and followed by a consonant (*e.g.* **argue, nurse**) are generally silent.

THE ITALIAN ALPHABET

Letter	*Name*	*Equivalent English pronunciation*
a	a	as in English fAther.
b	bi	as in English.
c	ci	before *e* and *i* as in CHurCH, CHief; before *a*, *o*, *u*, as in Cake, Carpet.
d	di	as in English.
e	e	this vowel has two sounds: Open as in pEt, mEt; Closed, as in gAte, mAte.
f	effe	as in English.
g	gi	before *e* and *i* as in English General, reGister; before *a*, *o*, *u*, as in English Goat, roGue.
h	acca	Always mute. It is employed in the Grouped Consonants with *c* and *g*; it also serves to distinguish a few words from others similarly pronounced, *e.g. hai, ho, ha* as distinguished from *ai, o, a.*
i	i	as in English machIne, dEEm.
j	i lunga	not now used, being replaced by *i.*
l	elle	as in English.
m	emme	as in English.
n	enne	as in English.
o	o	this vowel has two sounds: Open as in pOt, rOt; Closed as in pOst, hOst.
p	pi	as in English.
q	cu	see Grouped Consonants.
r	erre	as in English but trilled with the tongue against the upper teeth.
s	esse	this letter has two sounds: Voiced as in English vaSe, chaiSe; Unvoiced as in caSe, Safe.
t	ti	as in English.
u	u	as *oo* in English cOOl, bOOt.
v	vu	as in English.
z	zeta	this letter has two sounds: Voiced as *ds* in English maiDS; Unvoiced as in raTS, caTS.
k	cappa	these letters do not belong to the Italian alphabet and are found only in foreign words.
w	doppia vu	
x	ics, icchese	
y	ipsilon	

GROUPED CONSONANTS

ch	Employed only before *e* and *i* to retain the hard sound of *c*, *e.g. che, chi, chiamare, ciechi.*
gh	similarly employed to retain the hard *g*, *e.g. luoghi, laghi.*
gl	before *i* these two letters make a palatal resembling English *lli* in haLLIard, *e.g. gli, quegli.*
gn	before all vowels these grouped consonants resemble the English *ni* in oNIon, *e.g. ogni, ingegno.*
qu	has the value of the English *qu* in QUick, *e.g. qui, questo.*

ABBREVIATIONS

a.	adjective.
abbrev.	abbreviation.
adv.	adverb.
Agric.	Agriculture.
Am.	American usage.
Anat.	Anatomy.
Arch.	Architecture, Building, etc.
Archaeol.	Archaeology.
Arith.	Arithmetic.
art.	article.
Astron.	Astronomy.
Aviat.	Aviation.
Bot.	Botany.
Chem.	Chemistry.
colloq.	colloquial.
Comm.	Commerce, Finance, Business, etc.
conj.	conjunction.
cp.	compare, refer to.
Dial.	Dialect.
Eccles.	Ecclesiastical, Religion, etc.
Elect.	Electricity.
Eng.	Engineering.
esp.	especially.
f.	feminine.
facet.	facetious.
fig.	figuratively.
Geog.	Geography.
Geol.	Geology.
Geom.	Geometry.
Gram.	Grammar.
Hist.	History.
hum.	humorous.
inter.	interjection.
iron.	ironic.
Leg.	Legal.
Lit.	Literature, Literary.
m.	masculine.
Math.	Mathematics.
Mech.	Mechanics, Machinery, etc.
Med.	Medicine, Surgery, Pathology, Pharmacology.
Meteor.	Meteorology.
Mil.	Military.
Min.	Mineralogy.
Motor.	Motoring.
Mus.	Music.
Myth.	Mythology.
n.	noun.
n.f.	noun feminine.
n.m.	noun masculine.
n.m.a.	noun masculine with its adjectival form.
n.m.f.	noun employed for both genders; also *m.* and *f.* forms of a noun.
obs.	obsolete.
off.	offensive.
p.p.	past participle.
p.p.a.	past participle also used as adjective.

part.	participle.
Phil.	Philosophy.
Phot.	Photography.
Phys.	Physics.
Physiol.	Physiology.
pl.	plural.
Poet.	Poetry, Prosody, etc.
Pol.	Politics.
prep.	preposition.
pres.	present.
Print.	Printing, Typography.
pron.	pronoun.
Psych.	Psychology.
Rail.	Railway.
sing.	singular.
Tech.	Technical.
Teleg.	Telegraphy.
Theat.	Theatrical.
Typ.	Typography.
v.i.	verb intransitive.
v.r.	reflexive verb.
v.t.	verb transitive.
v.t.i.	verb used transitively and intransitively.
Vet.	Veterinary.
vulg.	vulgar.
Zool.	Zoology, including beasts, birds, reptiles, fishes, insects.

OUTLINE OF

AUXILIARY

Infinitive	*Present Participle*	*Past Participle*	*Indicative Mood*					
			Present		*Imperfect*		*Past Definite*	
Avere *to have*	avendo	avuto	ho hai ha	abbiamo avete hanno	avevo avevi aveva	avevamo avevate avevano	ebbi avesti ebbe	avemmo aveste ebbero
Essere *to be*	essendo	stato	sono sei è	siamo siete sono	ero eri era	eravamo eravate erano	fui fosti fu	fummo foste furono

FIRST

With the exception of the four irregular verbs *andare, dare, fare, stare* all verbs of the

Parlare *to speak*	parlando	parlato	parlo parli parla	parliamo parlate parlano	parlavo parlavi parlava	parlavamo parlavate parlavano	parlai parlasti parlò	parlammo parlaste parlarono
Andare *to go*	andando	andato	vado vai va	andiamo andate vanno	andavo andavi andava	andavamo andavate andavano	andai andasti andò	andammo andaste andarono
Dare *to give*	dando	dato	do dai dà	diamo date danno	davo davi dava	davamo davate davano	diedi *or* detti desti diede *or* dette	demmo deste diedero *or* dettero
Fare *to do*	facendo	fatto	fo *or* faccio fai fa	facciamo fate fanno	facevo facevi faceva	facevamo facevate facevano	feci facesti fece	facemmo faceste fecero
Stare *to stand*	stando	stato	sto stai sta	stiamo state stanno	stavo stavi stava	stavamo stavate stavano	stetti stesti stette	stemmo steste stettero

SECOND

Credere *to believe*	credendo	creduto	credo credi crede	crediamo credete credono	credevo credevi credeva	credevamo credevate credevano	credei credesti credè *or* credetti credesti credette	credemmo credeste crederono credemmo credeste credettero

The following partially irregular verbs of the Second Conjugation differ from the example given above only in the Past Participle and the Past Definite tense. In the Past Definite only the 1st person singular and the 3rd person singular and plural are irregular, *e.g.* accesi, accendesti, accese, accendemmo, accendeste, accesero.
It should further be noted that as a rule compound verbs are conjugated like their main verb, *e.g. affiggere* follows the conjugation of *figgere*.

Infinitive	*Past Participle*	*Past Definite*	*Infinitive*	*Past Participle*	*Past Definite*
accendere, *to light*	acceso	accesi	ascendere, *to ascend*	asceso	ascesi
accludere, *to include*	accluso	acclusi	ascondere, *to hide*	ascosto	ascosi
accorgersi, *to perceive*	accorto	accorsi	aspergere, *to sprinkle*	asperso	aspersi
affliggere, *to afflict*	afflitto	afflissi	assidersi, *to sit down*	assiso	assisi
alludere, *to allude*	alluso	allusi	assistere, *to assist*	assistito	assistei *or* assistetti
annettere, *to annex*	annesso	annessi			
appendere, *to hang*	appeso	appesi	assolvere, *to absolve*	assolto	assolvei *or* assolsi
apprendere, *to learn*	appreso	appresi			
ardere, *to burn*	arso	arsi	assumere, *to assume*	assunto	assunsi

ITALIAN VERBS

VERBS

Future		Conditional Mood		Imperative Mood		Subjunctive Mood: Present		Subjunctive Mood: Imperfect	
avrò	avremo	avrei	avremmo		abbiamo	abbia	abbiamo	avessi	avessimo
avrai	avrete	avresti	avreste	abbi	abbiate	abbia	abbiate	avessi	aveste
avrà	avranno	avrebbe	avrebbero	abbia	abbiano	abbia	abbiano	avesse	avessero
sarò	saremo	sarei	saremmo		siamo	sia	siamo	fossi	fossimo
sarai	sarete	saresti	sareste	sii	siate	sia	siate	fossi	foste
sarà	saranno	sarebbe	sarebbero	sia	siano	sia	siano	fosse	fossero

CONJUGATION

First Conjugation, with the infinitive ending in ***-are***, are conjugated like ***parlare.***

Future		Conditional Mood		Imperative Mood		Subjunctive Mood: Present		Subjunctive Mood: Imperfect	
parlerò	parleremo	parlerei	par- leremmo		parliamo	parli	parliamo	parlassi	parlassimo
parlerai	parlerete	parleresti	parlereste	parla	parlate	parli	parliate	parlassi	parlaste
parlerà	parleranno	par- lerebbe	par- lerebbero	parli	parlino	parli	parlino	parlasse	parlassero
andrò	andremo	andrei	andremmo		andiamo	vada	andiamo	andassi	andassimo
andrai	andrete	andresti	andreste	va'	andate	vada	andiate	andassi	andaste
andrà	andranno	andrebbe	andrebbero	vada	vadano	vada	vadano	andasse	andassero
darò	daremo	darei	daremmo		diamo	dia	diamo	dessi	dessimo
darai	darete	daresti	dareste	da'	date	dia	diate	dessi	deste
darà	daranno	darebbe	darebbero	dia	diano	dia	diano	desse	dessero
farò	faremo	farei	faremmo		facciamo	faccia	facciamo	facessi	facessimo
farai	farete	faresti	fareste	fa'	fate	faccia	facciate	facessi	faceste
farà	faranno	farebbe	farebbero	faccia	facciano	faccia	facciano	facesse	facessero
starò	staremo	starei	staremmo		stiamo	stia	stiamo	stessi	stessimo
starai	starete	staresti	stareste	sta'	state	stia	stiate	stessi	steste
starà	staranno	starebbe	starebbero	stia	stiano	stia	stiano	stesse	stessero

CONJUGATION

Future		Conditional Mood		Imperative Mood		Subjunctive Mood: Present		Subjunctive Mood: Imperfect	
crederò	crederemo	crederei	crede- remmo		crediamo	creda	crediamo	credessi	credessimo
crederai	crederete	crederesti	credereste	credi	credete	creda	crediate	credessi	credeste
crederà	crede- ranno	crede- rebbe	credereb- bero	creda	credano	creda	credano	credesse	credessero

Infinitive	*Past Participle*	*Past Definite*	*Infinitive*	*Past Participle*	*Past Definite*
attendere, *to wait*	atteso	attesi	connettere, *to connect*	connesso	connessi
attingere, *to attain*	attinto	attinsi	conoscere, *to know*	conosciuto	conobbi
cedere, *to yield*	cesso *or* ceduto	cessi *or* cedei	correre, *to run*	corso	corsi
chiedere, *to ask*	chiesto	chiesi *or* chiedei	crescere, *to grow*	cresciuto	crebbi
chiudere, *to shut*	chiuso	chiusi	difendere, *to defend*	difeso	difesi
cingere, *to gird*	cinto	cinsi	dipingere, *to depict*	dipinto	dipinsi
concidere, *to coincide*	coinciso	coincisi	dirigere, *to direct*	diretto	diressi *or* dirigetti
compiere, *to accomplish*	compito	compii	discutere, *to discuss*	discusso	discussi
comprendere, *to comprehend*	compreso	compresi	dissuadere, *to dissuade*	dissuaso	dissuasi
comprimere, *to compress*	compresso	compressi	distinguere, *to distinguish*	distinto	distinsi
concedere, *to concede*	concesso *or* conceduto	concessi *or* concedei	dividere, *to divide*	diviso	divisi
			eccedere, *to exceed*	ecceduto	eccedei
			elidere, *to elide*	eliso	elisi
			eludere, *to elude*	eluso	elusi

SECOND CON-

Infinitive	*Past Participle*	*Past Definite*	*Infinitive*	*Past Participle*	*Past Definite*
emergere, *to emerge*	emerso	emersi	inflettere, *to inflect*	inflesso	inflettei
emulgere, *to soften*	emulso	emulsi	infliggere, *to inflict*	inflitto	inflissi
ergere, *to stand upright*	erto	ersi			
erigere, *to erect*	eretto	eressi	infrangere, *to break*	infranto	infransi
escludere, *to exclude*	escluso	esclusi	intrudere, *to intrude*	intruso	intrusi
esigere, *to exact*	esatto	esigei	invadere, *to invade*	invaso	invasi
esistere, *to exist*	esistito	esistei	istruire, *to instruct*	istruito	istruii
espellere, *to expel*	espulso	espulsi	leggere, *to read*	letto	lessi
esplodere, *to explode*	esploso	esplosi	mettere, *to put*	messo	misi
estinguere, *to extinguish*	estinto	estinsi	mordere, *to bite*	morso	morsi
evadere, *to evade*	evaso	evasi	mungere, *to milk*	munto	munsi
fendere, *to split*	fesso *or*	fendei *or*	muovere, *to move*	mosso	mossi
	fenduto	fendetti	nascondere, *to hide*	nascosto	nascosi
figgere, *to fix*	fitto	fissi	negligere, *to neglect*	negletto	neglessi
fingere, *to feign*	finto	finsi	nuocere, *to injure*	nociuto	nocqui
fondere, *to cast, to mould*	fuso	fusi	offendere, *to offend*	offeso	offesi
frangere, *to smash*	franto	fransi	opprimere, *to oppress*	oppresso	oppressi
friggere, *to fry*	fritto	frissi	percuotere, *to strike*	percosso	percossi
giungere, *to arrive*	giunto	giunsi	perdere, *to lose*	perduto *or*	perdei *or*
illudere, *to deceive*	illuso	illusi		perso	persi
immergere, *to emerge*	immerso	immersi	persuadere, *to persuade*	persuaso	persuasi
impellere, *to impel*	impulso	impulsi	piangere, *to weep*	pianto	piansi
imprimere, *to print*	impresso	impressi	pingere, *to depict*	pinto	pinsi
incidere, *to engrave*	inciso	incisi	piovere, *to rain*	piovuto	piovve
indulgere, *to indulge*	indulto	indulsi			(3rd person)

SECOND CONJUGATION

Infinitive	*Present Participle*	*Past Participle*	*Indicative Mood*					
			Present		*Imperfect*		*Past Definite*	
Addurre* *to adduce*	adducendo	addotto	adduco adduci adduce	adduciamo adducete adducono	adducevo adducevi adduceva	adduce- vamo adducevate adducevano	addussi adducesti addusse	addu- cemmo adduceste addussero
Bere *or* Bevere *to drink*	bevendo	bevuto	bevo bevi beve	beviamo bevete bevono	bevevo bevevi beveva	bevevamo bevevate bevevano	bevvi bevesti bevve	bevemmo beveste bevvero
Cadere *to fall*	cadendo	caduto	cado cadi cade	cadiamo cadete cadono	cadevo cadevi cadeva	cadevamo cadevate cadevano	caddi cadesti cadde	cademmo cadeste caddero
Cogliere *to gather*	cogliendo	colto	colgo cogli coglie	cogliamo cogliete colgono	coglievo coglievi coglieva	coglievamo coglievate coglievano	colsi cogliesti colse	cogliemmo coglieste colsero
Cuocere *to cook*	cocendo	cotto	cuocio cuoci cuoce	cociamo cocete cuociono	cocevo cocevi coceva	cocevamo cocevate cocevano	cossi cocesti cosse	cocemmo coceste cossero
Dolere *to ache*	dolendo	doluto	dolgo duoli duole	dogliamo dolete dolgono	dolevo *etc.*		dolsi dolesti dolse	dolemmo doleste dolsero
Dovere *to be obliged to*	dovendo	dovuto	devo *or* debbo devi deve	dobbiamo dovete devono *or* debbono	dovevo *etc.*		dovei *or* dovetti dovesti dovè *or* dovette	dovemmo doveste doverono *or* dovettero

* All other verbs ending in "urre"

Infinitive	*Past Participle*	*Past Definite*	*Infinitive*	*Past Participle*	*Past Definite*
porgere, *to offer*	porto	porsi	scuotere, *to shake*	scosso	scossi
prendere, *to take*	preso	presi	seppellire, *to bury*	sepolto *or* seppellito	seppellii
presumere, *to presume*	presunto	presunsi			
proteggere, *to protect*	protetto	protessi	solvere, *to solve*	solto	solvei
pungere, *to prick*	punto	punsi	sorgere, *to rise*	sorto	sorsi
radere, *to shave*	raso	rasi	spandere, *to spread*	spanto	spansi
recidere, *to cut short*	reciso	recisi	spargere, *to disperse*	sparso	sparsi
redigere, *to draft*	redatto	redassi	spegnere, *to extinguish*	spento	spensi
redimere, *to redeem*	redento	redensi	spendere, *to spend*	speso	spesi
reggere, *to govern*	retto	ressi	spingere, *to push*	spinto	spinsi
rendere, *to give back*	reso	resi	stringere, *to press*	stretto	strinsi
repellere, *to repel*	repulso	repulsi	struggere, *to destroy*	strutto	strussi
rescindere, *to rescind*	rescisso	rescissi	svellere, *to uproot*	svelto	svelsi
ridere, *to laugh*	riso	risi	tendere, *to stretch*	teso	tesi
riflettere, *to reflect*	riflesso *or* riflettuto	riflessi *or* riflettei	tergere, *to wipe*	terso	tersi
			tingere, *to dye*	tinto	tinsi
rispondere, *to respond*	risposto	risposi	torcere, *to twist*	torto	torsi
rodere, *to gnaw*	roso *or* roduto	rosi *or* rodei	uccidere, *to kill*	ucciso	uccisi
			ungere, *to anoint*	unto	unsi
rompere, *to break*	rotto	ruppi	vincere, *to vanquish*	vinto	vinsi
scendere, *to descend*	sceso	scesi	vivere, *to live*	vissuto	vissi *or* vivei
scernere, *to discern*	scernuto	scernei			
scindere, *to separate*	scisso	scissi	volgere, *to turn round*	volto	volsi
scrivere, *to write*	scritto	scrissi			

IRREGULAR VERBS

Future	*Conditional Mood*	*Imperative Mood*	*Subjunctive Mood* — *Present*	*Subjunctive Mood* — *Imperfect*
addurrò addurremo addurrai addurrete addurrà addurranno	addurrei addurremmo addurresti addurreste addurrebbe addurrebbero	adduciamo adduci adducete adduca adducano	adduca adduciamo adduca adduciate adduca adducano	adducessi adducessimo adducessi adduceste adducesse adducessero
berrò berremo berrai berrete berrà berranno *or* beverò, *etc.*	berrei berremmo berresti berreste berrebbe berrebbero *or* beverei, *etc.*	beviamo bevi bevete beva bevano	beva beviamo beva beviate beva bevano	bevessi bevessimo bevessi beveste bevesse bevessero
cadrò cadremo cadrai cadrete cadrà cadranno	cadrei cadremmo cadresti cadreste cadrebbe cadrebbero	cadiamo cadi cadete cada cadano	cada cadiamo cada cadiate cada cadano *or* caggia, *etc.*	cadessi cadessimo cadessi cadeste cadesse cadessero
coglierò coglieremo coglierai coglierete coglierà coglieranno *or* corrò, *etc.*	coglierei coglieremmo coglieresti cogliereste coglierebbe coglierebbero *or* correi, *etc.*	cogliamo cogli cogliete colga colgano	colga cogliamo colga cogliate colga colgano	cogliessi cogliessimo cogliessi coglieste cogliesse cogliessero
cocerò coceremo cocerai cocerete cocerà coceranno	cocerei coceremmo coceresti cocereste cocerebbe cocerebbero	cociamo cuoci cocete cuoca cuocano *or* cuociano	cuocia cociamo cuocia cociate cuocia cuociano	cocessi cocessimo cocessi coceste cocesse cocessero
dorrò dorremo dorrai dorrete dorrà dorranno	dorrei *etc.*	dogliamo duoli dolete dolga dolgano	dolga dogliamo dolga dogliate dolga dolgano	dolessi *etc.*
dovrò dovremo dovrai dovrete dovrà dovranno	dovrei *etc.*	dobbiamo *or* doviamo devi dovete deva *or* debba debbano *or* devano	debba dobbiamo debba dobbiate debba debbano	dovessi *etc.*

are conjugated like Addurre.

SECOND CON-

Infinitive	*Present Participle*	*Past Participle*	*Indicative Mood*					
			Present		*Imperfect*		*Past Definite*	
Giacere *to lie down*	**giacendo**	**giaciuto**	**giaccio** **giaci** **giace**	**giacciamo** **giacete** **giacciono**	**giacevo** ***etc.***		**giacqui** **giacesti** **giacque**	**giacemmo** **giaceste** **giacquero**
Nascere *to be born*	**nascendo**	**nato**	**nasco** **nasci** **nasce**	**nasciamo** **nascete** **nascono**	**nascevo** ***etc.***		**nacqui** **nascesti** **nacque**	**nascemmo** **nasceste** **nacquero**
Parere *to seem*	**parendo**	**parso**	**paio** **pari** **pare**	**pariamo** **parete** **paiono**	**parevo** ***etc.***		**parvi** ***or*** **parsi** **paresti** **parve** ***or*** **parse**	**paremmo** **pareste** **parvero** ***or*** **parsero**
Piacere *to please*	**piacendo**	**piaciuto**	**piaccio** **piaci** **piace**	**piacciamo** **piacete** **piacciono**	**piacevo** ***etc.***		**piacqui** **piacesti** **piacque**	**piacemmo** **piaceste** **piacquero**
Porre *to put*	**ponendo**	**posto**	**pongo** **poni** **pone**	**poniamo** **ponete** **pongono**	**ponevo** **ponevi** **poneva**	**ponevamo** **ponevate** **ponevano**	**posi** **ponesti** **pose**	**ponemmo** **poneste** **posero**
Potere *to be able*	**potendo**	**potuto**	**posso** **puoi** **può**	**possiamo** **potete** **possono**	**potevo** ***etc.***		**potei** **potesti** **potè**	**potemmo** **poteste** **poterono**
Rimanere *to stay*	**rimanendo**	**rimasto**	**rimango** **rimani** **rimane**	**rimaniamo** **rimanete** **rimangono**	**rimanevo** ***etc.***		**rimasi** **rimanesti** **rimase**	**rimanemmo** **rimaneste** **rimasero**
Sapere *to know*	**sapendo**	**saputo**	**so** **sai** **sa**	**sappiamo** **sapete** **sanno**	**sapevo** ***etc.***		**seppi** **sapesti** **seppe**	**sapemmo** **sapeste** **seppero**
Scegliere *to choose*	**scegliendo**	**scelto**	**scelgo** **scegli** **sceglie**	**scegliamo** **scegliete** **scelgono**	**sceglievo** ***etc.***		**scelsi** **scegliesti** **scelse**	**scegliemmo** **sceglieste** **scelsero**
Sedere *to sit*	**sedendo**	**seduto**	**siedo** ***or*** **seggo** **siedi** **siede**	**sediamo** ***or*** **seggiamo** **sedete** **siedono** ***or*** **seggono**	**sedevo** ***etc.***		**sedei** ***or*** **sedetti** **sedesti** **sedè** ***or*** **sedette**	**sedemmo** **sedeste** **sederono** ***or*** **sedettero**
Solere *to be in the habit of*	**solendo**	**solito**	**soglio** **suoli** **suole**	**sogliamo** **solete** **sogliono**	**solevo** **solevi** **soleva**	**solevamo** **solevate** **solevano**	***not used***	
Spegnere *to extinguish*	**spegnendo**	**spento**	**spengo** **spegni** **spegne**	**spegniamo** **spegnete** **spengono**	**spegnevo** ***etc.***		**spensi** **spegnesti** **spense**	**spegnemmo** **spegneste** **spensero**
Tacere *to be silent*	**tacendo**	**taciuto**	**taccio** **taci** **tace**	**tacciamo** **tacete** **tacciono**	**tacevo** ***etc.***		**tacqui** **tacesti** **tacque**	**tacemmo** **taceste** **tacquero**
Tenere *to hold*	**tenendo**	**tenuto**	**tengo** **tieni** **tiene**	**teniamo** **tenete** **tengono**	**tenevo** ***etc.***		**tenni** **tenesti** **tenne**	**tenemmo** **teneste** **tennero**
Togliere *to take away*	**togliendo**	**tolto**	**tolgo** **togli** **toglie**	**togliamo** **togliete** **tolgono**	**toglievo** ***etc.***		**tolsi** **togliesti** **tolse**	**togliemmo** **toglieste** **tolsero**
Trarre *to draw*	**traendo**	**tratto**	**traggo** **trai** **trae**	**traiamo** **traete** **traggono**	**traevo** **traevi** **traeva**	**traevamo** **traevate** **traevano**	**trassi** **traesti** **trasse**	**traemmo** **traeste** **trassero**
Valere *to be worth*	**valendo**	**valso** ***or*** **valuto**	**valgo** **vali** **vale**	**valiamo** ***or*** **vagliamo** **valete** **valgono**	**valevo** ***etc.***		**valsi** **valesti** **valse**	**valemmo** **valeste** **valsero**

Future	*Conditional Mood*	*Imperative Mood*	*Subjunctive Mood* — *Present*	*Subjunctive Mood* — *Imperfect*
giacerò *etc.*	giacerei *etc.*	giacciamo giaci giacete giaccia giacciano	giaccia giacciamo giaccia giacciate giaccia giacciano	giacessi *etc.*
nascerò *etc.*	nascerei *etc.*	nasciamo nasci nascete nasca nasciano	nasca nasciamo nasca nasciate nasca nascano	nascessi *etc.*
parrò parremo parrai parrete parrà parranno	parrei *etc.*	*none*	paia pariamo paia pariate paia paiano	paressi *etc.*
piacerò *etc.*	piacerei *etc.*	piacciamo piaci piacete piaccia piacciano	piaccia piacciamo piaccia piacciate piaccia piacciano	piacessi *etc.*
porrò porremo porrai porrete porrà porranno	porrei *etc.*	poniamo poni ponete ponga pongano	ponga poniamo ponga poniate ponga pongano	ponessi *etc.*
potrò potremo potrai potrete potrà potranno	potrei *etc.*	*none*	possa possiamo possa possiate possa possano	potessi *etc.*
rimarrò rimarremo rimarrai rimarrete rimarrà rimarranno	rimarrei *etc.*	rimaniamo rimani rimanete rimanga rimangano	rimanga rimaniamo rimanga rimaniate rimanga rimangano	rimanessi *etc.*
saprò sapremo saprai saprete saprà sapranno	saprei *etc.*	sappiamo sappi sappiate sappia sappiano	sappia sappiamo sappia sappiate sappia sappiano	sapessi *etc.*
sceglierò sceglieremo sceglierai sceglierete sceglierà sceglie- ranno	sceglierei *etc.*	scegliamo scegli scegliete scelga scelgano	scelga scegliamo scelga scegliate scelga scelgano	scegliessi *etc.*
sederò *etc.*	sederei *etc.*	sediamo siedi sedete sieda *or* siedano *or* segga seggano	sieda *or* sediamo segga sieda *or* sediate segga sieda *or* siedano *or* segga seggano	sedessi *etc.*
not used	*not used*	*none*	soglia sogliamo soglia sogliate soglia sogliano	solessi *etc.*
spegnerò *etc.*	spegnerei *etc.*	spegniamo spegni spegnete spenga spengano	spenga spegniamo spenga spegniate spenga spengano	spegnessi *etc.*
tacerò *etc.*	tacerei *etc.*	tacciamo taci tacete taccia tacciano	taccia taciamo taccia taciate taccia tacciano	tacessi *etc.*
terrò terremo terrai terrete terrà terranno	terrei *etc.*	teniamo tieni tenete tenga tengano	tenga teniamo tenga teniate tenga tengano	tenessi *etc.*
toglierò *or* torrò *etc.*	toglierei *or* torrei *etc.*	togliamo togli togliete tolga tolgano	tolga togliamo tolga togliate tolga tolgano	togliessi *etc.*
trarrò trarremo trarrai trarrete trarrà trarranno	trarrei *etc.*	traiamo trai traete tragga traggano	tragga traiamo tragga traiate tragga traggano	traessi *etc.*
varrò varremo varrai varrete varrà varranno	varrei *etc.*	*none*	valga valiamo valga valiate valga valgano	valessi *etc.*

SECOND CON-

Infinitive	Present Participle	Past Participle	*Indicative Mood*					
			Present		*Imperfect*		*Past Definite*	
Vedere *to see*	vedendo	veduto *or* visto	vedo vedi vede *or* veggo vedi vede	vediamo vedete vedono veggiamo vedete veggono	vedevo *etc.*		vidi vedesti vide	vedemmo vedeste videro
Volere *to be willing*	volendo	voluto	voglio vuoi vuole	vogliamo volete vogliono	volevo *etc.*		volli volesti volle	volemmo voleste vollero

THIRD

Infinitive	Present Participle	Past Participle	Present		Imperfect		Past Definite	
Finire *to finish*	finendo	finito	finisco finisci finisce	finiamo finite finiscono	finivo finivi finiva	finivamo finivate finivano	finii finisti finì	finimmo finiste finirono

The majority of Third Conjugation verbs follow the pattern of *Finire*; a few (listed below) are conjugated on the mode of *Partire*, though those marked with an * may be conjugated in either way.

Infinitive	Present Participle	Past Participle	Present		Imperfect		Past Definite	
Partire *to start*	partendo	partito	parto parti parte	partiamo partite partono	partivo partivi partiva	partivamo partivate partivano	partii partisti partì	partimmo partiste partirono

*abborrire, *to abhor*
*adempire, *to fulfil*
*applaudire, *to applaud*
*assorbire, *to absorb*
*avvertire, *to warn*
*bollire, *to boil*
*compartire, *to distribute*
*compire, *to finish*
conseguire, *to obtain*
consentire, *to consent*
*convertire, *to convert*
cucire, *to sew*
*divertire, *to amuse*
dormire, *to sleep*
fuggire, *to flee*
*inghiottire, *to swallow*
*lambire, *to lap*
*languire, *to languish*

THIRD CONJUGATION

Infinitive	Present Participle	Past Participle	Present		Imperfect		Past Definite	
Apparire *to appear*	apparendo	apparso	apparisco apparisci apparisce *or* appaio apparisci appare	appariamo apparite appariscono appariamo apparite appaiono	apparivo *etc.*		apparii apparisti apparì *or* apparvi apparisti apparve *or* apparsi apparisti apparse	apparimmo appariste apparirono apparimmo appariste apparvero apparimmo appariste apparsero
Aprire *to open*	aprendo	aperto	apro apri apre	apriamo aprite aprono	aprivo *etc.*		aprii apristi aprì *or* apersi apristi aperse	aprimmo apriste aprirono aprimmo apriste apersero
Dire *to say*	dicendo	detto	dico dici dice	diciamo dite dicono	dicevo *etc.*		dissi dicesti disse	dicemmo diceste dissero
Morire *to die*	morendo	morto	muoio muori muore	moriamo morite muoiono	morivo *etc.*		morii moristi morì	morimmo moriste morirono
Salire *to go forth*	salendo	salito	salgo sali sale	saliamo salite salgono	salivo *etc.*		salii *etc.*	
Udire *to hear*	udendo	udito	odo odi ode	udiamo udite odono	udivo *etc.*		udii *etc.*	
Uscire *to go out*	uscendo	uscito	esco esci esce	usciamo uscite escono	uscivo *etc.*		uscii *etc.*	
Venire *to come*	venendo	venuto	vengo vieni viene	veniamo venite vengono	venivo *etc.*		venni venisti venne	venimmo veniste vennero

Future		*Conditional Mood*		*Imperative Mood*		*Subjunctive Mood* — *Present*		*Subjunctive Mood* — *Imperfect*	
vedrò *etc.*		vedrei *etc.*		 vedi veda	vediamo vedete vedano	veda veda veda vegga vegga vegga	vediamo vediate vedano *or* vediamo vediate veggano	vedessi *etc.*	
vorrò *etc.*		vorrei *etc.*		 vogli voglia	vogliamo vogliate vogliano	voglia voglia voglia	vogliamo vogliate vogliano	volessi *etc.*	

CONJUGATION

Future		*Conditional Mood*		*Imperative Mood*		*Subjunctive Present*		*Subjunctive Imperfect*	
finirò finirai finirà	finiremo finirete finiranno	finirei finiresti finirebbe	finiremmo finireste finirebbero	 finisci finisca	finiamo finite finiscano	finisca finisca finisca	finiamo finiate finiscano	finissi finissi finisse	finissimo finiste finissero
partirò partirai partirà	partiremo partirete partiranno	partirei partiresti partirebbe	partiremmo partireste partireb- bero	 parti parta	partiamo partite partano	parta parta parta	partiamo partiate partano	partissi partissi partisse	partissimo partiste partissero

*mentire, *to tell lies*
*muggire, *to bellow*
*nutrire, *to nourish*
pentirsi, *to repent*
*pervertire, *to pervert*
*plaudire, *to applaud*
proseguire, *to pursue*
*putire, *to stink*
*ruggire, *to roar*
seguire, *to follow*
sentire, *to feel*
servire, *to serve*
sortire, *to go out*
sovvertire, *to subvert*
*spartire, *to divide*
*tossire, *to cough*
*travestire, *to disguise*
vestire, *to dress*

IRREGULAR VERBS

Future		*Conditional Mood*		*Imperative Mood*		*Subjunctive Present*		*Subjunctive Imperfect*	
apparirò *etc.*		apparirei *etc.*		 apparisci apparisca *or* appaia	appariamo apparite appariscano *or* appaiano	apparisca apparisca apparisca appaia appaia appaia	appariamo appariate appariscano *or* appariamo appariate appaiano	apparissi *etc.*	
aprirò *etc.*		aprirei *etc.*		 apri apra	apriamo aprite aprano	apra *etc.*		aprissi *etc.*	
dirò *etc.*		direi *etc.*		 di' dica	diciamo dite dicano	dica dica dica	diciamo diciate dicano	dicessi *etc.*	
morrò morrai morrà	morremo morrete morranno	morrei *etc.*		 muori muoia	moriamo moriate muoiano	muoia muoia muoia	moriamo moriate muoiano	morissi *etc.*	
salirò *etc.*		salirei *etc.*		 sali salga	saliamo salite salgano	salga salga salga	saliamo saliate salgano	salissi *etc.*	
udirò *etc.* *or* udrò *etc.*		udirei *etc.* *or* udrei *etc.*		 odi oda	udiamo udite odano	oda oda oda	udiamo udiate odano	udissi *etc.*	
uscirò *etc.*		uscirei *etc.*		 esci esca	usciamo uscite escano	esca esca esca	usciamo usciate escano	uscissi *etc.*	
verrò *etc.*		verrei *etc.*		 vieni venga	veniamo venite vengano	venga venga venga	veniamo veniate vengano	venissi *etc.*	

ITALIAN–ENGLISH DICTIONARY

A

A, a, *n.f.* First letter of the Italian alphabet. **Dall'a alla zeta,** from beginning to end.
a, *prep.* (With definite article becomes **al, allo, alla, ai, agli, alle,** generally **ad** before words beginning with a vowel), at, to, by. **Andare a casa,** to go home; **a casa,** at home ; **andare a piedi,** to go on foot; **tiro a segno,** target practice; **a cavallo,** on horseback; **a mente, a memoria,** by heart; **a due a due,** two by two; **a volte,** at times; **a caso,** by chance, **a ragione, a torto,** rightly, wrongly; **nave a vela,** sailing boat; **a centinaia,** in hundreds.
A., *n.f.* (abbrev. **altezza**), Highness (title).
abaca, *n.f.* (*Bot.*) Manila hemp plant.
abacamento, *n.m.* Dotage.
abaco [Abaco], *n.m.* (*Arch.*) Abacus, first slab surmounting the pedestal.
abadessa, *n.f.* Abbess [cp. **badessa**].
abate, *n.m.* Abbot; abbé.
abavo, *n.m.* Ancestor.
abazia [cp. **abbazia, badia**], *n.f.* Abbey.
abbacare, *v.i.* To day-dream.
abbaccamento, *n.m.* Exaggeration.
abbaccare, *v.i.* (*obs.*) To reckon, to calculate; to exaggerate.
abbacchiamento, *n.m.* Beating.
abbacchiare, *v.t.* To knock down (esp. nuts or olives); to beat down in price; to humiliate; to make a poor match.
abbacchiato, *p.p.a.* (*colloq.*) In low spirits, run down physically or mentally.
abbacchio [abbAcchio], *n.m.* Lamb (killed). **Arrosto d'—,** roast spring lamb.
abbachino, *n.m.* First arithmetic book for beginners.
abbachista (*pl.* **abbachisti**), *n.m.* (*colloq.*) Accountant.
abbacinamento, *n.m.* Act of dazzling, blinding.
abbacinare, *v.t.* To dazzle, to blind with a bright light.
abbaco [Abbaco], *n.m.* Art of computing; abacus, counting frame; arithmetic book.
abbacone, *n.m.* Day-dreamer.
abbadare, *v.i.* To mind, to pay attention; to look after, to care for.
abbadessa, *n.f.* Abbess [cp. **badessa**].
abbagliaggine [abbagliAggine], *n.f.* Dazzle, shimmer.
abbagliamento, *n.m.* Dazzling.
abbagliante, *a.* Dazzling.
abbagliare, *v.t.* To dazzle, to blind with a light; (*fig.*) to deceive.
abbagliatamente, *adv.* Confusedly.
abbaglio [abbAglio], *n.m.* Dazzling; mistake; misunderstanding. **Cadere in —, prendere —,** to be mistaken, to misunderstand, to make a blunder.
abbaiamento, *n.m.* Barking.
abbaiare, *v.i.* To bark; to howl; (*fig.*) to reproach. **— alla luna,** to cry for the moon, to long in vain.
abbaiata, *n.f.* Barking; baying.
abbaiatore, *n.m.* (*fig.*) Malevolent critic; bawler.
abbaino [abbaIno], *n.m.* Dormer window, skylight; garret; attic.
abbaio [abbAio], *n.m.* Barking, bark.
abbaione, *n.m.* Noisy fellow.
abballare, *v.t.* To pack, to bale [cp. **imballare**].
abballinare, *v.t.* To air the bed; to turn the mattress.
abballottamento, *n.m.* Confusion, jumble.
abballottare, *v.t.* To muddle up, to jumble together; to mix.
abballottio [abballottIo], *n.m.* Confusion.
abbambolato, *p.p.a.* Heavy with sleep. **Occhi abbambolati,** half-closed eyes.
abbandonamento, *n.m.* Abandon; abandonment.
abbandonare, *v.t.* To abandon, to forsake; to give up; to surrender; to desert. **Le forze mi abbandonano,** my strength is failing; **— la partita,** to give up the game; **— gli affari,** to give up business; **— un'amicizia,** to drop a friendship; **— la famiglia,** to desert one's family.
abbandonarsi, *v.r.* To surrender; to give oneself up to, to indulge in. **— alle proprie passioni,** to give free course to one's passions; **— al bere,** to take to drink.
abbandonatamente, *adv.* With abandon.
abbandonato, *n.m.a.* Foundling; abandoned, forsaken; neglected; deserted.
abbandono, *n.m.* Abandonment, forsaking; renouncement. **In —,** in disorder, unprotected; (*Comm.*) **— d'un diritto,** waiving a right.
abbarbagliamento, *n.m.* Dazzling.
abbarbagliare, *v.t.* To dazzle, to stupefy.
abbarbagliatamente, *adv.* Dizzily.
abbarbagliato, *p.p.* Dazzled, dizzy.
abbarbaglio[abbarbaglIo], *n.m.* Continuous dazzling glare.
abbarbicamento, *n.m.* (*fig.*) Entanglement.
abbarbicare, *v.i.* To take root, to root; to fix firmly, to establish.
abbarbicarsi, *v.r.* To entwine, to cling, to become deeply rooted (*lit. and fig.*).
abbarbicato, *p.p.a.* Firmly rooted, established.
abbarcare, *v.t.* To heap up.
abbarcatura, *n.f.* Heaping.

abbaruffamento, *n.m.* Disorder; scuffle, affray, dispute.
abbaruffare, *v.t.* To embroil; to rumple.
abbaruffarsi, *v.r.* To quarrel; to scuffle.
abbaruffata, *n.f.* Disorder.
abbaruffio [abbaruffIo], *n.m.* Confusion, disorder.
abbassamento, *n.m.* Lowering; subsiding; diminution, abatement; decline; fall of temperature.
abbassare, *v.t.* To lower, to let down; to abate, to diminish; to lessen, to degrade, to debase; to reduce. **— la testa,** to bend one's head; **— gli occhi,** to lower one's eyes; **— i prezzi,** to reduce the prices; **— il livello,** (*fig.*) to lower the standard; (*Theat.*) **— il sipario,** to lower the curtain; **— la voce,** to lower the voice; (*fig.*) **— la cresta,** to sing small, to come down from one's perch.
abbassarsi, *v.r.* To go down, to subside, to sink, to stoop; to degrade oneself. **Le acque si sono abbassate,** the floods have subsided; **— per salire,** to stoop to conquer.
abbasso, a basso, *adv.* Down, below, downstairs.
abbasso! *inter.* Down with! (opposite of **evviva,** long live).
abbastante, *a.* Sufficient.
abbastanza, *adv.* Enough, sufficiently; plenty; rather, fairly. **Ne ho — di lui,** I am tired of him; **— interessante,** fairly interesting.
abbate, *n.m.* Abbot; abbé [cp. **abate**].
abbattere [abbAttere], *v.t.* To throw down, to cut down, to fell; to overthrow; to bring down; (*fig.*) to dishearten, to prostrate, to depress; (*Naut.*) to careen. **— alberi,** to fell trees; **— un aeroplano,** to shoot down an aeroplane; **— animali,** to destroy animals; **— i pregiudizi,** to sweep away prejudices; **— un pugilatore,** to knock down, to floor a boxer.
abbattersi, *v.r.* To lose heart, to be dejected, to be in low spirits.
abbattifieno, *n.m.* Trapdoor in a hay loft.
abbattimento, *n.m.* Overthrowing, felling; prostration, depression, despondency.
abbattuto, *p.p.a.* Knocked down, cut down, felled; killed; dejected, downhearted, prostrated.
abbatufolare, abbatuffolare, *v.t.* To mingle, to jumble up; to make into small balls.
abbazia [abbazIa], *n.f.* Abbey.
abbaziale, *a.* Pertaining to an abbey or an abbot.
abbecedario [abbecedArio], *n.m.* First reading book, primer.
abbellimento, *n.m.* Embellishment, ornament, decoration; (*Mus.*) grace notes.
abbellire, *v.t.* To embellish, to make beautiful; to adorn, to decorate.
abbellirsi, *v.r.* To grow beautiful; to adorn oneself; to boast. **— dei meriti altrui,** to deck oneself with borrowed plumes.
abbellito, *p.p.a.* Beautified, adorned, grown more beautiful.
abbellitura, *n.f.* Embellishment.
abbenchè, *conj.* Although [cp. **benchè**].
abbeveramento, *n.m.* Watering of animals.
abbeverare, *v.t.* To water, to take cattle to water.
abbeverarsi, *v.r.* (*lit. and fig.*) To go to water, to drink.
abbeverata, *n.f.* Watering of cattle.
abbeveratoio [abbeveratOio], *n.m.* Watering pool for cattle; horse trough.
abbiabbe, *n.m.* Start of learning. **Essere all'—,** to be starting school.
abbiadare, *v.t.* To feed on oats.
abbicare, *v.t.* (*Agric.*) To form stacks of corn, to pile up in sheaves or stooks.
abbicci [Abbicci], *n.m.* Rudiments, beginnings; ABC.
abbiente, *n.m.* Proprietor, owner.
abbiente, *a.* Well-off, moneyed.
abbiettamente, *adv.* Abjectly, basely.
abbiettezza, *n.f.* Baseness, abjectness.
abbietto, *a.* Vile, base, abject, despicable.
abbiezione, *n.f.* Abjection, baseness; humiliation, degradation, misery.
abbigliamento, *n.m.* Dress, attire, suit of clothes. **Mostra dell'—,** dress show, mannequin parade.
abbigliare, *v.t.* To dress, to clothe, to attire; to adorn.
abbigliarsi, *v.r.* To dress oneself; to adorn oneself.
abbigliatura, *n.f.* Clothing, costume, habiliment.
abbinamento, *n.m.* Combining, coupling.
abbinare, *v.t.* To couple; to combine; to link together. **Le due questioni sono abbinate,** the two problems are linked together.
abbindolamento, *n.m.* Winding; (*fig.*) trick, deception.
abbindolare, *v.t.* To wind the thread on a reel; (*fig.*) to swindle, to take in, to dupe.
abbindolato, *p.p.a.* Swindled, cheated.
abbindolatura, *n.f.* Entanglement, trick.
abbisognare [cp. **bisognare**], *v.i.* To want, to need, to require, to be necessary; to be obliged (to do something). **— di tutto,** to be in want of everything; **la casa abbisogna di riparazioni,** the house needs repairs.
abbisognevole [abbisognEvole], *a.* Needy, indigent. **— d'aiuto,** in need of help.
abbittare, *v.t.* (*Naut.*) To bitt a cable.
abboccamento, *n.m.* Interview, conference, conversation, talk. **Dopo un lungo — si separarono,** they separated after a prolonged interview; (*Comm.*) **riferendoci al nostro —,** with reference to our conversation.
abboccare, *v.t.* To bite (of fish); to fill to the brim; to place together the brims of two vessels. **— l'amo, — all'amo,** to be caught by bait, to be taken in, to be deceived.
abboccarsi, *v.r.* To have a private conversation, to confer, to meet with. **I due generali si abboccarono,** the two generals conferred.
abboccato, *p.p.a.* Full to the brim; of good appetite; palatable (of wines).
abboccatoio [abboccatOio], *n.m.* Mouth (of a furnace).
abboccatura, *n.f.* Opening, mouth [cp. **imboccatura**].
abbocchevole [abbocchEvole], *a.* (*Naut.*) Crank, liable to be upset.
abbominabile [abbominAbile], *a.* Abominable, hateful.
abbominare, *v.t.* To abhor, to abominate, to loathe.

abbominevole [abbominEvole], *a.* Abominable, hateful.
abbominazione, *n.f.* Abomination, detestation; shame.
abbominio [abbomInio], *n.m.* Abomination, detestation; shame.
abbominoso, *a.* Abominable.
abbonacciamento, *n.m.* (*Naut.*) Calm.
abbonacciare, *v.t.* To calm, to quiet down.
abbonacciarsi, *v.r.* To calm oneself. **Il mare si abbonaccia,** the sea is becoming calm.
abbonacciatamente, *adv.* Calmly, placidly.
abbonamento, *n.m.* Subscription (to newspapers etc.); contract. **Fare un — a,** to subscribe to; **— ferroviario,** season ticket.
abbonare, *v.t.* To cause to subscribe; to abate, to deduct. **L'oste ci ha abbonato parte del conto,** the landlord (or innkeeper) has made a reduction in the bill.
abbonarsi, *v.r.* To subscribe to; to join. **— ad una biblioteca circolante,** to join a lending library.
abbonato, *n.m.* Subscriber; contract holder; habitué.
abbondante, *a.* Plentiful, abundant, rich, copious. **Uno scrittore —,** a prolific writer.
abbondantemente, *adv.* Abundantly.
abbondanza, *n.f.* Plenty, abundance, copiousness. **Nuotare nell'—,** to roll in wealth.
abbondare, *v.i.* To abound in, to have plenty of; to have in excess.
abbondevole [abbondEvole], *a.* Abounding in.
abbondevolmente, *adv.* Aboundingly, abundantly.
abbonire, *v.t.* To appease, to pacify, to soothe.
abbonirsi, *v.r.* To calm down, to be appeased.
abbono [cp. **abbuono**].
abbordabile [abbordAbile], *a.* Approachable; accessible.
abbordaggio [abbordAggio], *n.m.* (*Naut.*) Boarding; falling foul of another ship.
abbordare, *v.t.* (*Naut.*) To board, to come alongside; to attack, to force a passage on board; to run into, to fall foul of; (*fig*). to approach, to accost.
abbordo, *n.m.* (*Naut.*) Laying a ship alongside another; readiness of speech or ease of manner. **Un uomo di facile —,** an affable, approachable man.
abbordone, *n.m.* Chatterbox, bore.
abborracciamento, *n.m.* Bungling, botching.
abborracciare, *v.t.* To botch, to make a clumsy patch; to bungle; to do work in haste.
abborracciato, *p.p.a.* Clumsily done; patched up.
abborracciatura, *n.f.* Bungle, careless work, botch.
abborrare, *v.t.* To stuff.
abborrire, *v.t.* To abhor, to loathe.
abbottonare, *v.t.* To button, to button up.
abbottonarsi, *v.r.* To button oneself up. **— l'abito,** to button one's coat.
abbottonato, *p.p.a.* Buttoned; (*colloq.*) noncommittal, reserved. **Una persona molto abbottonata,** a very reticent person.
abbottonatura, *n.f.* Buttoning; row of buttons.
abbozzacchiare, *v.i.* To scheme in a futile way.
abbozzamento, *n.m.* [cp. **abbozzo**].
abbozzare, *v.t.* To sketch, to outline; to draft; to rough out; to delineate. **— una statua,** to rough out a statue; **— un sorriso,** to smile faintly, to give the shadow of a smile.
abbozzatamente, *adv.* Sketchily, imperfectly.
abbozzato, *p.p.a.* Outlined, sketchy; malformed (of a person).
abbozzatura, *n.f.* Sketch, outline, rough draft.
abbozzo, *n.m.* Rough copy; sketch, outline; malformed person.
abbozzolarsi, *v.r.* To curl up.
abbracciaboschi, *n.m.* Honeysuckle.
abbracciamento, *n.m.* Embrace, hugging, accolade.
abbracciare, *v.t.* To embrace, to hug, to clasp in one's arms; (*fig.*) to include, to encompass, to comprehend; to survey; to adopt. **Abbracciate i vostri nemici,** embrace your enemies; **— una risoluzione,** to adopt a resolution; **— un vasto orrizzonte,** to embrace a vast horizon.
abbracciata, *n.f.* Embrace; ceremonial embrace given to a newly-made cardinal.
abbracciato, *p.p.a.* Embraced; (*fig.*) surrounded.
abbracciatutto, *n.m.* Factotum, man-of-all-work; busybody.
abbraccio [abbrAccio], *n.m.* Embrace, hug; accolade.
abbrancare, *v.t.* To grip, to clutch at, to grasp; to take hold.
abbrancarsi, *v.r.* To cling together, to clasp at. **Le due belve si abbrancarono,** the two animals came to grips.
abbreviamento, *n.m.* Abridgement.
abbreviare, *v.t.* To shorten, to cut short; to abbreviate, to abridge. **— un discorso,** to curtail a speech; **— la strada,** to shorten the route; **abbreviate, vi prego,** please be brief.
abbreviatamente, *adv.* In brief, briefly.
abbreviativo, *a.* Abbreviating.
abbreviatura, abbreviazione, *n.f.* Abbreviation, abridgement.
abbrivare, *v.i.* (*Naut.*) To make headway, to get under way.
abbrividire, *v.i.* To shiver, to shudder, to quiver.
abbrivo, *n.m.* (*Naut.*) Course; headway. **Prendere, pigliare l'—,** to make headway.
abbronciare, *v.i.* To pout.
abbronzamento, *n.m.* Bronzing, sunburn.
abbronzare, *v.t.* To bronze, to tan.
abbronzarsi, *v.r.* To get sunburnt, to tan.
abbronzato, *p.p.a.* Bronzed, sunburned, tanned.
abbronzatura, *n.f.* Getting tanned.
abbronzito, *a.* Sunburned, tanned, bronzed.
abbruciacchiamento, *n.m.* Scorching.
abbruciacchiare, *v.t.* To scorch, to burn on the surface; to parch.
abbruciamento, *n.m.* Burning [cp. **bruciare**].
abbruciare, *v.t.i.* To burn, to fire; to scorch; to inflame; to be on fire; to be burning hot; (*fig.*) to long for; to be impatient; to desire feverishly; to be consumed. **— le ultime cartucce,** to expend the last cartridge.
abbruciarsi, *v.r.* To burn oneself, to get scorched. **— le cervella,** to blow one's

brains out; **— lentamente,** to be consumed gradually.
abbruciaticcio [abbruciatIccio], *n.m.* Scorching, burning. **Odore d'—,** faint smell of burning.
abbruciato, *p.p.a.* Burned down, scorched; sunburned.
abbrucimento, *n.m.* Blackening, darkening.
abbrumare, *v.i.* To corrode, to become worm-eaten.
abbrunamento, *n.m.* Mourning.
abbrunare, *v.t.* To drape with crape.
abbrunarsi, *v.r.* To wear mourning.
abbrunato, *p.p.a.* In mourning. **Bandiera abbrunata,** draped flag.
abbrunire, *v.t.* To burnish; to brown.
abbrustiare, *v.t.* To singe.
abbrustolire, *v.t.* To toast, to broil, to scorch. **Pane abbrustolito,** toast.
abbrutimento, *n.m.* Brutishness, brutalizing, degradation.
abbrutire, *v.t.* To brutalize, to degrade, to besot. **Abbrutito dal bere,** besotted by drink.
abbrutirsi, *v.r.* To become brutalized.
abbuiamento, *n.m.* (*lit. and fig.*) Darkening, obscurity.
abbuiare, *v.t.* To darken, to obscure.
abbuiarsi, *v.r.* To grow dark. **Il cielo si abbuia,** the sky grows dark.
abbuiata, *n.f.* Darkening.
abbuono, *n.m.* (*Comm.*) Allowance. **— per ammanco,** allowance for shortage; **— per deficienza di peso,** allowance for short weight.
abburattamento, *n.m.* Bolting, sifting of flour. **Grado d'—,** proportion of flour and bran.
abburattare, *v.t.i.* To bolt, to sift flour; to machine; (*fig.*) to wrangle, to argue.
abburattata, *n.f.* Sifting; sieveful.
abburattatura, *n.f.* Sifting.
abbuzzire, *v.t.i.* To cram (with food); to be overcast (of weather).
abdicare, *v.i.t.* To abdicate. (*fig.*) **— ai propri diritti,** to renounce one's rights.
abdicazione, *n.f.* Abdication.
abduttore, *n.m.* (*Anat.*) Abductor muscle.
abecedario [abecedArio], *n.m.* Primer, reading-book.
aberrante, *a.* Aberrant, deviating.
aberrazione, *n.f.* Aberration; (*fig.*) deviation. **È un — del gusto,** it is an error in taste.
abetaia [abetAia], *n.f.* Fir plantation.
abete, *n.m.* Fir tree, fir; spruce. **— del Canada,** hemlock spruce.
abiatico [abiAtico], *n.m.* Grandson.
abietto, abiezione [cp. **abbietto, abbiezione**].
abigeato, *n.m.* Cattle-stealing.
abile [Abile], *a.* Skilful, able, capable, clever, fit. **— al servizio militare,** fit for military service; **— negli affari,** capable in business; (*Mil.*) **dichiarare —,** report fit for service.
abilità [-à], *n.f.* Ability, skill, capability. **Giuoco d'—,** game of skill; **Bella —!** How clever you are!
abilitare, *v.t.* To qualify, to enable; (*Law*) to empower.
abilitarsi, *v.r.* To qualify oneself for a profession.
abilitazione, *n.f.* Qualification; habilitation, recognized competence.
abilmente, *adv.* Skilfully, ably.
abiogenesi [abiogEnesi], *n.f.* Abiogenesis, spontaneous generation.
abissale, *a.* Unfathomable.
Abissinia [abissInia], *n.f.* Abyssinia, Ethiopia.
abissino, *n.m.a.* Abyssinian, Ethiopian.
abisso, *n.m.* Abyss, precipice, gulf; (*fig.*) depth, utmost degree (of knowledge, vice, etc.) **Quell'uomo è un — di scienza,** that man is a mine of knowledge.
abitabile [abitAbile], *a.* Habitable.
abitacolo [abitAcolo], *n.m.* Slum dwelling; (*Naut.*) binnacle.
abitante, *n.m.a.* Inhabitant, resident.
abitare, *v.t.i.* To inhabit, to dwell, to live, to reside. **— presso di me,** to live near me; **i popoli che abitano l'Asia,** the peoples who inhabit Asia; **— in una brutta città,** to live in an ugly city.
abitato, *n.m.* Inhabited area; houses.
abitato, *p.p.a.* Inhabited, peopled.
abitatore, abitatrice, *n.m.f.* Inhabitant, dweller.
abitazione, *n.f.* Dwelling-place, abode, residence, house. **Le abitazioni moderne sono comode,** modern houses are convenient; **la crisi delle abitazioni,** the housing problem.
abiti [Abiti], *n.m.pl.* Clothes.
abito [Abito], *n.m.* Coat, dress, garment; (*fig.*) aspect, habit; (*Med.*) constitution, complex. **— da sera,** evening dress; **— da società,** (men's) evening dress; **— da ballo,** ball dress; **— da lutto,** mourning; **— da uomo,** suit; **— da donna,** dress; **vestire l'—,** to take Holy Orders; **l'— non fa il monaco,** the cowl does not make the monk.
abituale, *a.* Customary, usual, habitual, wonted.
abitualmente, *adv.* Habitually.
abituare, *v.t.* To accustom, to inure, to habituate.
abituarsi, *v.r.* To get accustomed, to get used; to adapt oneself.
abituato, *a.* Accustomed, habituated.
abituazione, *n.f.* Custom, habituation.
abitudinario [abitudinArio], *a.* Habitual, following a routine.
abitudine [abitUdine], *n.f.* Habit, custom, use, habitude, practice. **D'—, per —,** usually; **non posso allontanarmi dalla mia —,** I cannot depart from my practice; **come d'—,** as usual; **derogare dall'—,** to depart from practice.
abituro, *n.m.* (*Poet.*) Cottage; humble dwelling.
abiura, *n.f.* Ceremonial abjuration; renunciation.
abiurare, *v.t.* To abjure; to disavow.
abiurazione, *n.f.* Abjuration.
ablativo, *n.m.* (*Gram.*) Ablative.
ablazione, *n.f.* (*Med.*) Extirpation; total removal of a part; (*Geol.*) erosion.
abluente, *a.* (*Med.*) Abluent.
abluzione, *n.f.* Ablution.
abnegare, *v.t.* To deny; to disown; to renounce.
abnegazione, *n.f.* Abnegation, self-denial.
abolire, *v.t.* To abolish; to repeal.
abolizione, *n.f.* Abolition, repeal, abrogation.

abolizionismo, *n.m.* Prohibition, especially of alcoholic drinks.
abominare [cp. **abbominare**].
aborigene [aborIgene], *a.* Aboriginal.
aborigeni [aborIgeni], *n.m.pl.* Aborigines.
aborrente, *a.* Abhorrent.
aborrevole [aborrEvole], *a.* Abhorrent.
aborrevolezza, *n.f.* Abhorrence, horror.
aborrimento, *n.m.* Execration, loathing.
aborrire, *v.t.* To abhor, to loathe.
abortire, *v.i.* To miscarry, to abort, to bring forth prematurely; (*fig.*) to fail, to end in nothing. **Il tentativo abortì,** the attempt failed; **far —,** to cause or procure abortion.
abortivo, *a.* (*Med.*) Abortive.
aborto, *n.m.* Abortion, miscarriage; monster; (*fig.*) failure.
Abramo, *n.m.* Abraham
abrasare, *v.t.* To erase, to blot out.
abrasione, *n.f.* Abrasion, lesion of the skin; erasure.
abrogare, *v.t.* To abrogate, to repeal. **— una legge,** to repeal a law.
abrogatorio [abrogatOrio], *a.* Abrogatory.
abrogazione, *n.f.* Abrogation, repeal.
abrostine [abrOstine], *n.m.* (*Bot.*) Wild grape.
abrotano [abrOtano], *n.m.* (*Bot.*) Southernwood, wormwood.
abrupto, *adv.* **Ex —,** suddenly.
abside [Abside], *n.f.* (*Arch.*) Apse, apsis.
abulia [abulIa], *n.f.* (*Med.*) Abulia, loss of will power.
abusare, *v.i.* To abuse, to misuse; to take advantage, to trespass on; to deceive. **— dell'ospitalità,** to abuse one's hospitality.
abusivamente, *adv.* Abusively; illegally; unjustly.
abusivo, *a.* Abusive; illegal.
abuso, *n.m.* Abuse, misuse; vexation; infringement. (*Law*) **— di fiducia,** abuse of confidence, abuse of trust; **— d'autorità,** abuse of authority; **reprimere un —,** to remove an abuse.
acacia [acAcia], *n.f.* (*Bot.*) Acacia.
acagiù [-ù], *n.m.* Mahogany.
acanto, *n.m.* (*Bot.*) Acanthus.
acca, *n.f.* Letter H. **Non capire un'—,** to understand absolutely nothing; **non ci capisco un'—,** I haven't a clue.
accademia [accadEmia], *n.f.* Academy; society; high school for certain arts and crafts; school ceremony. **— navale,** naval college; **— di ballo,** dancing academy.
accademicamente, *adv.* Academically, abstractly.
accademico [accadEmico], *n.m.* Academician.
accademico [accadEmico], *a.* Academic, academical.
accademista, *n.m.f.* Academist, member of a particular school.
accadere, *v.i.* To happen, to befall, to occur, to take place. **Gli accadde una disgrazia,** a misadventure befell him; **questo fatto accadde l'anno scorso,** this event took place last year; **accade che,** it happened that; **come accadde,** as it happens.
accadimento, *n.m.* (*obs.*) Happening, occurrence.
accaduto, *n.m.* Happening. **Gli raccontai l'—,** I told him what happened.
accagionare, *v.t.* To charge with, to impute.
accagliamento, *n.m.* Curdling (of milk).
accagliare, *v.t.* To curdle; to coagulate; to turn to curds.
accagliatura, *n.f.* Curdling, coagulation.
accalappiacani, *n.m.* Dog-catcher.
accalappiare, *v.t.* To entrap, to ensnare; to catch; to dupe.
accalappiatura, *n.f.* (*fig.*) Hoax, deception.
accalcarsi, *v.r.* To throng, to crowd, to press together.
accaldarsi, *v.r.* To get heated or excited.
accaldato, *p.p.a.* Hot, perspiring.
accaloramento, *n.m.* Heat, excitement.
accalorarsi, *v.r.* To get excited, inflamed, aroused.
accampamento, *n.m.* Encampment; camping.
accampare, *v.t.* To encamp, to camp, to place troops in camp; (*fig.*) to allege, to pretend. **— dei pretesti,** to bring forward excuses; **— diritti,** to lay claims; **— ragioni,** to allege motives (for).
accamparsi, *v.r.* To camp, to pitch camp.
accampionare, *v.t.* To register; to stamp as correct.
accanimento, *n.m.* Rabidness, fury; ruthless obstinacy; tenacity, pertinacity.
accanirsi, *v.r.* To be exasperated, to give vent to one's fury; to persist in; to insist on; to concentrate doggedly on something.
accanitamente, *adv.* Desperately, doggedly.
accanito, *a.* Fierce, ruthless; tenacious, relentlessly dogged.
accannellamento, *n.m.* Winding upon a spool; fluting.
accanto, *adv. prep.* Near, close by, at hand; close to, beside, by. **La casa —,** the next-door house.
accantonamento, *n.m.* Cantonment, billets.
accantonare, *v.t.* (*Mil.*) To billet, to provide with quarters; (*Comm.*) to set aside, to put in reserve.
accantonato, *a.* Angular; set aside.
accapacciatura, *n.f.* Heaviness of the head (from sleepiness, fatigue etc.)
accaparramento, *n.m.* Monopolizing; appropriation; cornering, forestalling.
accaparrare, *v.t.* To monopolize; to engross; to reserve; to buy up, to corner.
accaparrarsi, *v.r.* To secure for oneself.
accaparratore, accaparratrice, *n.m.f.* Monopolist; forestaller.
accapigliamento, *n.m.* Brawl; dispute.
accapigliarsi, *v.r.* To seize one another by the hair; to quarrel; to come to blows.
accapigliatura, *n.f.* Brawl.
accappatoio [accappatOio], *n.m.* Bathing-gown; dressing-gown.
accappiare, *v.t.* To tie with a noose.
accappiatura, *n.f.* Noose, slip-knot.
accapponare, *v.t.* To capon, to castrate. **— la pelle,** to make one's flesh creep, to give one goose-flesh.
accaprettare, *v.t.* To tie an animal by the leg, to hobble.
accarezzamento, *n.m.* Caress.
accarezzare, *v.t.* To caress, to fondle, to stroke; (*fig.*) to cherish. **— un progetto,** to cherish a plan.
accartocciamento, *n.m.* Shrinking; crumpling up.
accartocciare, *v.t.* To wrap up.

accartocciarsi, *v.r.* To crumple up, to shrivel.
accartocciatura, *n.f.* Shrinkage.
accasamento, *n.m.* Marriage.
accasare, *v.t.* To marry.
accasarsi, *v.r.* To get married; to settle down.
accasciamento, *n.m.* Prostration, exhaustion; despondency, low spirits.
accasciare, *v.t.* To prostrate, to cast down (*fig. and lit.*).
accasciarsi, *v.r.* To be disheartened; to be overthrown; to be dejected.
accasermare, *v.t.* (*Mil.*) To quarter troops in barracks.
accatastamento, *n.m.* Heap, mass, pile; accumulation.
accatastare, *v.t.* To pile up, to stack.
accattabrighe, *n.m.* Wrangler, quarrelsome fellow.
accattafieno, *n.m.* (*Agric.*) Reaping-machine, harvester and reaper.
accattamento, *n.m.* Borrowing, begging.
accattare, *v.t.i.* To borrow; to pick up, to collect; to beg, to ask alms.
accatto, *n.m.* Borrowing. **D'—,** not original, that has been borrowed.
accattonaggio [accattonAggio], *n.m.* Begging, beggary.
accattone, *n.m.* Beggar.
accavalcare, *v.t.* To ride; to sit astride.
accavalciare, *v.t.* To straddle.
accavalcioni, a cavalcioni, *adv.* Astride.
accavallamento, *n.m.* Crossing, surmounting, piling up, overlapping.
accavallare, *v.t.* To bestride; to span, to over-arch; to surmount, to cross; to heap up, to gather. **— le gambe,** to cross one's legs.
accecamento, *n.m.* Blindness; lack of perception, ignorance; recklessness; obstruction.
accecare, *v.t.* To blind, to dazzle (*lit. and fig.*).
accedere [accEdere], *v.i.* To enter; to accede; to draw nigh; to adopt. **Accediamo alla vostra proposta,** we adopt your proposal.
acceleramento, *n.m.* Quickening; (*Mech.*) acceleration.
accelerando, *adv.* (*Mus.*) Quickening the movement.
accelerare, *v.t.* To accelerate, to speed up, to quicken.
accelerato, *p.p.a.* Quickened, speeded up. **Servizio —,** fast service; **treno —,** fast local train.
acceleratore, *n.m.* (*Mech.*) Accelerator.
accelerazione, *n.f.* Acceleration.
accendere [accEndere], *v.t.* To light, to kindle; to inflame; to stir up; to fire; (*Motor.*) to ignite; (*Elec.*) to switch on, to turn on; (*Comm.*) to open. **— la luce,** to put on the light; **— le passioni,** to stir the passions; **— una candela,** to light a candle; **— il desiderio,** to kindle the desire; **— il fuoco,** to light the fire; (*Comm.*) **— un conto a,** to open an account with.
accendersi [accEndersi], *v.r.* To kindle, to catch fire, to get alight; to be fired, stirred. **— in viso,** to blush.
accendibile [accendIbile], *a.* Inflammable.
accendifuoco, *n.m.* Firelighter.
accendimento, *n.m.* (*Motor.*) Ignition.
accendisigaro [accendisIgaro], *n.m.* Cigar or cigarette lighter.
accenditore, *n.m.* Lighter; (*Motor.*) sparking plug.
accennamento, *n.m.* Nodding, beckoning.
accennare, *v.t.i.* To indicate, to point out; to nod; to hint at; to beckon. **Egli accennò di sì,** he nodded in assent; **accennò di no,** he shook his head; **— ad una questione,** to touch upon a matter.
accenno, *n.m.* Hint, nod, sign, beckon.
accensibile [accensIbile], *a.* Inflammable.
accensione, *n.f.* (*Motor.*) Ignition. **— a candela,** sparking-plug ignition.
accentare, *v.t.* To accent, to stress.
accentatura, *n.f.* Accentuation, stress.
accento, *n.m.* Accent, stress; intonation; pronunciation. **Avere un buon —,** to have a good accent; **accenti d'ira,** accents of anger.
accentramento, *n.m.* Centralization.
accentrare, *v.t.* To centralize.
accentuare, *v.t.* To emphasize.
accentuato, *p.p.a.* Accentuated; stressed upon.
accerchiamento, *n.m.* Encircling, encirclement, surrounding.
accerchiare, *v.t.* To encircle, to surround, to round up; (*fig.*) to circumvent.
accertabile [accertAbile], *a.* Ascertainable.
accertamento, *n.m.* Assurance; assessment, control. (*Comm.*) **Fare un — di cassa,** to make a cash inventory; **— di un conto,** settlement of an account; **giorno di —,** settling day.
accertare, *v.t.* To ascertain, to assure; to verify; (*Comm.*) to settle, to assess. **— un conto,** to settle an account; **— un danno,** to assess a damage.
accertarsi, *v.r.* To assure oneself (of something).
accertatamente, *adv.* Assuredly.
acceso, *p.p.a.* Lit, lighted; ignited; enflamed. **— in viso,** flushed.
accessibile [accessIbile], *a.* Accessible.
accessibilità [-à], *n.f.* Accessibility.
accessione, *n.f.* (*Law*) Accession.
accesso, *n.m.* Access; admission, admittance; fit; attack. **Via d'—,** means of approach; **libero —,** free admittance, free access.
accessori [accessOri], *n.m.pl.* Accessories, supplies, fittings.
accessorio [accessOrio], *n.m.a.* Accessory, secondary. **Spese accessorie,** additional charges; **operazioni accessorie,** subsidiary operations.
accetta, *n.f.* Hatchet.
accettabile [accettAbile], *a.* Acceptable.
accettabilità [-à], *n.f.* Acceptability.
accettabilmente, *adv.* Acceptably.
accettante, *n.m.* (*Comm.*) Acceptor.
accettare, *v.t.* To accept; to consent to; to agree to. (*Comm.*) **— una tratta,** to accept a draft.
accettata, *n.f.* Blow with a hatchet or axe.
accettazione, *n.f.* Acceptation; (*Comm.*) acceptance.
accetto, *a.* Welcome; accepted; (*Comm.*) honoured.
accezione, *n.f.* Accepted meaning (of words); acceptation.
acchetare, *v.t.* To calm, to appease, to lull.
acchiappanuvole [acchiappanUvole], *n.m.* Dreamer of dreams, woolgatherer.

acchiappare, *v.t.* To catch, to seize; to entrap.
acchiapparello, *n.m.* Trick question, quiz; catch.
acchiappatoio [acchiappatOio], *n.m.* Trap, booby-trap; practical joke.
acchito, *n.m.* Lead off (at billiards). **Di primo —,** at first sight.
acchiudere [cp. **accludere**].
accia [Accia], *n.f.* Linen or other coarse thread.
acciabattare, *v.t.* To cobble, to botch.
acciabattone, *n.m.* Bungler.
acciaccamento, *n.m.* Bruising, crushing.
acciaccare, *v.t.* To bruise, to batter, to ill-treat.
acciaccato, *p.p.a.* Battered; impaired; run down.
acciaccatura, *n.f.* Bruise; (*Mus.*) grace notes.
acciacchi, *n.m.pl.* Ailments, infirmities.
acciaccoso, *a.* Sickly, ailing.
acciaiare, *v.t.* To harden into steel.
acciaieria [acciaierIa], *n.f.* Steel-works.
acciaio [acciAio], *n.m.* Steel. **— crudo,** raw steel.
acciarino, *n.m.* Flint-lock, steel for tinderbox.
acciaro, *n.m.* (*Poet.*) Sword, blade.
acciarpare, *v.t.* To bungle.
acciarpatamente, *adv.* Clumsily, in a bungling manner.
acciarpatore, *n.m.* Bungler.
accidentale, *a.* Casual, accidental.
accidentalità [-à], *n.f.* Accidental happening; unevenness.
accidentalmente, *adv.* Accidentally, by chance, casually.
accidentato, *a.* Uneven; troubled; paralysed.
accidente, *n.m.* Accident, mishap; chance; (*colloq.*) apoplectic fit. **Per mero —,** by mere chance.
accidenti! *inter.* The devil! Damn!
accidenti, *n.m.pl.* (*Mus.*) Accidentals (sharp, flat or natural).
accidia [accIdia], *n.f.* Sloth, sluggishness; indolence.
accidioso, *a.* Slothful, indolent; lazy.
acciecare [cp. **accecare**].
accigliamento, *n.m.* Frown; knitting of the brows.
accigliarsi, *v.r.* To frown, to look sullen.
accigliato, *a.* Sullen, morose, gloomy.
accingersi [accIngersi], *v.r.* To get ready, to set about, to take steps, to prepare oneself. **— a fare una cosa,** to set about doing something.
accinto, *p.p.a.* Prepared, ready.
acciocchè, acciò che, *conj.* In order that, so that.
acciottolare, *v.t.* To pave with cobble stones.
acciottolato, *n.m.* Pebblework, pavement.
acciottolio [acciottolIo], *n.m.* Clash, clatter.
accipigliarsi, *v.r.* To frown.
acciucchito, *a.* Stupid, doltish, stupefied.
acciuffare, *v.t.* To seize by the hair; to catch. **Il ladro è stato acciuffato,** the thief has been caught.
acciuffarsi, *v.r.* To come to blows.
acciuga, *n.f.* Anchovy. **Star come le acciughe in un barile,** to be packed like sardines.
acciugata, *n.f.* Anchovies in oil; anchovy sauce.
accivettare, *v.t.* To entice, to decoy; to catch birds by means of an owl.
accivettato, *a.* Sharp, crafty, cunning.
acclamare, *v.t.* To acclaim, to applaud, to cheer; to proclaim, to hail. **La folla acclamò caldamente,** the crowd cheered enthusiastically.
acclamato, *p.p.a.* Applauded, celebrated. **Un — artista,** a celebrated artist.
acclamazione, *n.f.* Acclamation, ovation, applause. **Per —,** by acclamation, unanimously, without a vote.
acclimare, acclimatare, *v.t.* To acclimatize.
acclimatarsi, *v.r.* To become acclimatized, to adapt oneself.
acclimatazione, *n.f.* Acclimatization.
acclive, *a.* Steep, sloping.
acclività [-à], *n.f.* Acclivity, slope.
accludere [acclUdere], *v.t.* To enclose. **Ci pregiamo —,** we beg to enclose.
accluso, *p.p.a.* Enclosed. **La lettera qui acclusa,** the enclosed letter.
accoccare, *v.t.* To fit the arrow to the bow; to notch; (*fig.*) to take in, to dupe. **— un pugno,** to strike a blow.
accoccolarsi, *v.r.* To squat, to crouch down.
accodare, *v.t.* To tie head to tail; to cause to march at the end of a column, to place in the rear.
accodarsi, *v.r.* To form a queue, to follow.
accogliente, *a.* Welcoming, affable, hospitable.
accoglienza, *n.f.* Reception, welcome. **Fare buona —,** to give a hearty welcome.
accogliere [accOgliere], *v.t.* To receive; to accept; to welcome. **— con simpatia,** to receive with kindness; **— una proposta,** to agree to a proposal; **— la firma,** to honour the signature.
accogliticcio [accoglitIccio], *a.* Mustered at random.
accolito [accOlito], *n.m.* Acolyte, novice; follower.
accollare, *v.t.* To burden, to charge; to yoke; (*fig.*) **— una spesa,** to saddle with an expense.
accollarsi, *v.r.* To take upon oneself. **— tutto il lavoro,** to shoulder all the work.
accollatario [accollatArio], *n.m.* Contractor, tendering party.
accollato, *p.p.a.* Burdened; tight. **Un abito —,** a high-necked dress.
accollo, *n.m.* Overcharge; contract.
accolta, *n.f.* Meeting, gathering. **Una bellissima —,** a splendid gathering.
accoltellare, *v.t.* To stab, to knife.
accoltellatore, *n.m.* One who stabs, who uses the knife.
accomandante, *n.m.* (*Comm.*) **— socio,** limited partner.
accomandita [accomAndita], *n.f.* (*Comm.*) Commercial combine. **Società in —,** limited liability company.
accomiatare, *v.t.* To give leave; to dismiss, to disband; to bid adieu.
accomiatarsi, *v.r.* To take leave, to say good-bye; to withdraw. **Gli invitati si accomiatarono,** the guests took their leave.
accomodabile [accomodAbile], *a.* Adjustable.
accomodabilmente, *adv.* Adjustably, adaptably.
accomodamento, *n.m.* Arrangement, compromise, agreement, settlement; composition.

Venire ad un —, to come to a compromise; **i litiganti vennero ad un —,** the litigants reached a settlement.
accomodare, *v.t.* To arrange, to settle, to adjust, to mend; to touch up; to put in order. **Farsi — le scarpe,** to have one's shoes repaired; **— una lite,** to settle a dispute; (*fam.*) **lo accomoderò io quel biricchino,** I'll teach the young rascal; **non mi accomoda,** it does not suit me, it does not agree with me.
accomodarsi, *v.r.* To sit down, to take a seat. **Prego si accomodi,** pray take a seat.
accomodatamente, *adv.* Conveniently, opportunely.
accomodazione, *n.f.* Accommodation; arrangement.
accomodevole [accomodEvole], *a.* Adaptable; easy-going; unscrupulous.
accompagnamento, *n.m.* Accompaniment; suite, escort, retinue; concomitance; (*Mus.*) accompaniment.
accompagnare, *v.t.* To accompany, to escort, to be in attendance; to couple. **— le parole coi fatti,** to make good one's words with deeds.
accompagnarsi, *v.r.* To keep company with; to match; to join with.
accompagnato, *p.p.a.* Accompanied, escorted.
accompagnatore, accompagnatrice, *n.m.f.* Companion, escort, chaperon; (*Mus.*) accompanist.
accomunare, *v.t.* To have in common, to share.
accomunarsi, *v.r.* To fraternize.
acconciabile [acconciAbile], *a.* Adjustable.
acconciamente, *adv.* Suitably, becomingly.
acconciare, *v.t.* To arrange, to adjust; to put in order, to adorn; to handle roughly.
acconciarsi, *v.r.* To dress, to adorn, to attire oneself; to resign oneself, to submit. **— a qualunque lavoro,** to adapt oneself to any work.
acconciato, *p.p.a.* Attired; arranged.
acconciatura, *n.f.* Attire, array; mode of doing the hair.
acconcio [accOncio], *a.* Suitable, opportune, timely, seasonable. **In modo —,** suitably.
accondiscendenza, *n.f.* Condescension, acquiescence; affability.
accondiscendere [accondiscEndere], *v.i.* To condescend, to agree; to accede, to permit.
acconsentimento, *n.m.* Consent, approval, permission; assent.
acconsentire, *v.i., v.t.* To consent, to acquiesce, to agree, to approve. **Mentre parlavo egli acconsentiva,** as I talked he nodded assent; **chi tace acconsente,** silence gives consent.
accontare, *v.i.* To count, to reckon.
accontentare, contentare, *v.t.* To content, to satisfy, to please.
accontentarsi, *v.r.* To be contented, to be satisfied with. **Per accontentarti,** to please you.
acconto, *n.m.* Account, instalment, payment on account, advance (money). **In —,** in part payment; **dare un —,** to pay a deposit.
accoppare, *v.t.* To kill; to slaughter (cattle).
accoppiabile [accoppiAbile], *a.* Joinable.
accoppiamento, *n.m.* Coupling, junction; union, pairing; yoking; connection. (*Mech.*) **— a triangolo,** mesh connection.
accoppiare, *v.t.* To couple, to join; to pair, to marry; to yoke.
accoppiarsi, *v.r.* To get married; to unite; to mate. **Si sono accoppiati bene,** they are well matched.
accoramento, *n.m.* Grief, heart-ache, anguish, affliction; worry.
accorare, *v.t.* To grieve (a person), to afflict, to distress; to worry.
accorarsi, *v.r.* To be grieved, worried, afflicted; to worry oneself. **Non accorarti,** don't worry.
accoratamente, *adv.* Sadly.
accorato, *a.* Sad, sorrowful.
accoratoio [accoratOio], *n.m.* Butcher's knife for slaughtering pigs.
accorciabile [accorciAbile], *a.* Contractable, capable of abridgment or curtailment.
accorciamento, *n.m.* Curtailment, shortening, contraction.
accorciare, *v.t.* To shorten, to curtail, to abridge, to contract. **— un discorso,** to curtail a speech.
accorciarsi, *v.r.* To shorten, to shrink, to contract.
accorciatamente, *adv.* Contractedly, briefly.
accorciatoia [accorciatOia], *n.f.* Short-cut, by-way.
accorciatura, *n.f.* Curtailment, shortening, contraction.
accordabile [accordAbile], *a.* Admissible.
accordamento, *n.m.* Settlement, concordance.
accordare, *v.t.* To grant, to concede, to award; (*Mus.*) to tune. **Devo far — il piano,** I must have the piano tuned; (*Comm.*) **— un credito,** to open an account.
accordarsi, *v.r.* To agree, to reach an agreement, to come to an agreement; to be consistent with; to concur. **Essi si accordarono senza difficoltà,** they reached a speedy agreement; **questo non s'accorda coi tuoi principii,** this is not consistent with your principles.
accordatamente, *adv.* In agreement.
accordato, *p.p.a.* Agreed; (*Mus.*) tuned.
accordatore, *n.m.* Piano tuner.
accordatura, *n.f.* (*Mus.*) Tuning.
accordo, *n.m.* Agreement, arrangement; pact, accord, compromise; (*Mus.*) chord, tune. **D'amore e d'—,** in full agreement; **d'—,** granted, agreed; **essere d'—,** to be in agreement; **andare d'— con,** to get on well with, to agree with; **non andare d'—,** to disagree; **prendere accordi per,** to take steps, to make arrangements for; **di comune —,** by mutual consent.
accorgersi [accOrgersi], *v.r.* To notice, to become aware; to perceive.
accorgimento, *n.m.* Cleverness; device, expedient, stratagem.
accoro, *n.m.* (*Naut.*) Dog-shore; timber supporting a vessel on the slips or in dry dock.
accorrere [accOrrere], *v.i.* To run up, to rush, to hasten. **— in aiuto,** to rush to help.
accorrimento, *n.m.* Running up, rushing.
accortamente, *adv.* Shrewdly, ably, adroitly, cleverly.
accortezza, *n.f.* Cleverness, shrewdness, sagacity.

accorto, *p.p.a.* Noticed; shrewd, crafty, wise, wary. **Fare —,** to caution.
accor'uomo! *inter.* (*obs.*) Help!
accosciarsi, *v.r.* To crouch down, to squat, to lie down.
accostabile [accostAbile], *a.* Accessible, approachable.
accostamento, *n.m.* Approaching; union, coupling.
accostare, *v.t.* To approach, to go near, to accost; (*Naut.*) to board, to sheer.
accostarsi, *v.r.* To draw near, to approach to; to accost.
accosto, *adv. prep.* Near, beside, near at hand. **Stammi —,** keep close to me.
accostolato, *n.m.* (*Naut.*) Rib of a ship.
accostolatura, *n.f.* Wrinkle in pressed cloth.
accostumabile [accostumAbile], *a.* Easily trained.
accostumare, *v.t.* To accustom, to inure; to train.
accostumarsi, *v.r.* To get used, to be accustomed.
accostumatezza, *n.f.* (*obs*). Custom.
accotonare, *v.t.* (*Mech.*) To curl, to crisp cloth.
accotonatura, *n.f.* Curling of cloth.
accovacciarsi, *v.r.* To crouch, to squat, to cower; to nestle.
accovacciolarsi, *v.r.* To squat, to cower (of small animals).
accovonare, *v.t.* (*Agric.*) To pile sheaves of corn, to stook; to tie into sheaves.
accozzaglia [accozzAglia], *n.f.* Medley, confusion; mass, rabble; huddle.
accozzamento, *n.m.* Medley, miscellany.
accozzare, *v.t.* To mix together, to mingle; to amass.
accozzarsi, *v.r.* To butt, to fight.
accozzo, *n.m.* Medley, confusion.
accreditabile [accreditAbile], *a.* Creditable; trustworthy.
accreditamento, *n.m.* Credit.
accreditare, *v.t.* To credit; to accredit.
accreditarsi, *v.r.* To gain credit.
accreditato, *p.p.a.* Credited, accredited; esteemed; reliable.
accrescere [accrEscere], *v.t.* To increase, to augment, to add.
accrescersi [accrEscersi], *v.r.* To augment; to be increased.
accrescimento, *n.m.* Increase, growing.
accrescitivamente, *adv.* Augmentatively.
accrescitivo, *a.* (*Gram.*) Augmentative.
accresciuto, *p.p.* Increased.
accrespare, *v.t.* To curl; to crisp; to wrinkle.
accrespatura, *n.f.* Curl; wrinkle.
accrezione, *n.f.* (*Med.*) Intestinal accretion.
accubito [accUbito], *n.m.* Kind of divan, couch.
accucciarsi, *v.r.* To squat down; to curl up (of a dog).
accudire, *v.i.* To attend, to look after, to take care of, to mind. **— alle facende domestiche,** to attend to domestic matters.
acculare, *v.t.* To back against a wall (of animals).
accularsi, *v.r.* To squat on the haunches.
acculattare, *v.t.* To hold a person by arms and legs and bump him on the ground. **— le panche,** to sit idle.
accumulamento, *n.m.* Accumulation; hoarding.
accumulare, *v.t.* To accumulate, to heap up; to set in store.
accumularsi, *v.r.* To accumulate.
accumulativo, *a.* Accumulative; inclusive, total.
accumulatore, *n.m.* (*Elec.*) Accumulator, storage battery.
accumulazione, *n.f.* Accumulation; hoard, hoarding.
accuratamente, *adv.* Accurately; carefully.
accuratezza, *n.f.* Accuracy, exactness, care, precision.
accurato, *a.* Accurate, careful, attentive; searching.
accusa, *n.f.* Accusation, charge, indictment, impeachment; (*Comm.*) acknowledgment of receipt. **I capi d'—,** the counts of the indictment.
accusabile [accusAbile], *a.* Open to accusation.
accusabilità [-à], *n.f.* Liability to accusation.
accusamento, *n.m.* Accusation, imputation.
accusare, *v.t.* To accuse, to indict, to charge with, to arraign; to declare, to acknowledge. (*Comm.*) **— ricevuta,** to acknowledge receipt; **— uno di falso,** to charge someone with forgery; **— un malessere,** to plead indisposition.
accusata, *n.f.* (*Cards*) Call, declaration.
accusativo, *n.m.a.* (*Gram.*) Accusative case.
accusato, *n.m.* (*Law*) Defendant, prisoner, accused.
accusatore, *n.m.* (*Law*) Prosecutor, accuser.
acefalo [acEfalo], *a.* Headless; acephalous.
acerbamente, *adv.* Harshly, bitterly.
acerbezza, acerbità, *n.f.* Acerbity, bitterness.
acerbo, *a.* Unripe, green, sour; harsh, bitter; of tender age.
acereto, *n.m.* Wood of maple trees.
acero [Acero], *n.m.* (*Bot.*) Maple, maple tree.
acerrimo [acErrimo], *a. super.* (*fig.*) Very harsh; very bitter; fierce, implacable; (*colloq.*) tough. **Acerrimo nemico,** a bitter enemy.
acescente, *a.* Turning sour.
acetabolo [acetAbolo], *n.m.* Vinegar bottle; dice box.
acetare, *v.t.* To acetify, to convert into vinegar.
acetato, *n.m.* (*Chem.*) Acetate.
acetella, *n.f.* (*Bot.*) Sorrel.
acetico [acEtico], *a.* (*Chem.*) Acetic.
acetificare, *v.t.* To acetify, to convert into vinegar.
acetificazione, *n.f.* Acetification.
acetilene, *n.m.* Acetylene gas. **Lume ad —,** acetylene light.
acetini, *n.m.pl.* Gherkins; pickles.
aceto, *n.m.* Vinegar. **Sott'aceto,** seasoned with vinegar; pickles.
acetone, *n.m.* (*Chem.*) Acetone.
acetosità [-à], *n.f.* Acidity, acidness, sourness.
acetosa, *n.f.* Saline, chalybeate. **Acqua —,** water from a mineral well near Rome.
acetosella, *n.f.* (*Bot.*) Sorrel.
acetoso, *a.* Acid, sour, tart.
acheronteo, *a.* (*Class.*) Acherontean, pertaining to the infernal regions.
acicolare, *a.* (*Bot.*) Needle-shaped.

acidezza, *n.f.* Acidity, sourness, tartness.
acidificare, *v.t.* To acidify.
acidificazione, *n.f.* Acidification.
acidità [-à], *n.f.* Acidity, sourness, tartness.
acido [Acido], *n.m.a.* Acid, sour; (*Chem.*) acid.
acidulare, *v.t.* To acidulate.
acidulo [acIdulo], *a.* Acidulous.
acidume, *n.m.* Sourness, sour stuff.
acinesia [acinesIa], *n.f.* (*Med.*) Akenesia, moto-paralysis.
aciniforme, *a.* Grape-like.
acino [Acino], *n.m.* Acinus, grape.
acinoso, *a.* Fruiting in clusters, full of clusters.
acme, *n.f.* (*Med.*) Crisis of illness.
acne, *n.m.* (*Med.*) Acne, pimple.
acolito [cp. **accolito**].
aconito [acOnito], *n.m.* (*Bot.*) Aconite.
acoro [Acoro], *n.m.* (*Bot.*) Sweet sedge.
acotiledone [acotilEdone], *a.* (*Bot.*) Acotyledonous.
acqua, *n.f.* Water; rain; sea, lake, river; perspiration; urine; (*pl.*) waters, spas, watering-place. — **dolce,** fresh water; — **marina,** sea water; — **salsa,** salt water; — **di fonte,** — **sorgiva,** — **viva,** spring water; — **sudicia,** dirty water; — **santa,** holy water; — **potabile,** drinking, or fresh water; — **dura,** hard water; — **piovana,** rain water; — **morta,** still water; (*fig.*) — **cheta,** a reserved person; a dark horse; — **in bocca!** silence!; **sott'—,** underhand; **a fior d'—,** on the surface; **esser tutto in un'—,** to be in a bath of perspiration; **metter dell'— nel proprio vino,** to come down a peg or two; **affogare in un bicchier d'—,** to get lost in trifling difficulties; **far —,** to leak; to urinate; **prendere l'—,** to get wet; **a pane e —,** imprisoned; **attingere —,** to draw water; — **a catinelle,** raining cats and dogs; **pescar nell'— torbida,** to fish in troubled waters; **assomigliarsi come due gocce d'—,** to be as like as two peas; **aver l'— alla gola,** to be hard pressed, at the end of one's resources; **andare alle acque,** to go to a watering-place.
acquaforte, *n.f.* Nitric acid; (*Art*) etching; acid used in etching.
acquafortista (*pl.* **acquafortisti**), *n.m.* Etcher.
acquaio [acquAio], *n.m.* Kitchen sink.
acquaiolo [acquaiOlo], *n.m.* Water-carrier; seller of water.
acquamarina, *n.f.* Aquamarine, blue stone.
acquapendere [acquapEndere], *v.t.* To slope down to a river (of a mountain side).
acquare, *v.t.* To water.
acquarellista (*pl.* **acquarellisti**), *n.m.* Water-colour painter.
acquarello, acquerello, *n.m.* (*Paint*) Water-colour.
acquario [acquArio], *n.m.* Aquarium; (*Astr.*) Aquarius.
acquartieramento, *n.m.* (*Mil.*) Billet, cantonment.
acquartierare, *v.t.* (*Mil.*) To quarter troops.
acquartierarsi, *v.r.* (*Mil.*) To be billeted, to go into quarters.
acquarugiola [acquarUgiola], *n.f.* Drizzle.
acquasantiera, acquasantino, *n.m.* Holy water stoup.
acquata, *n.f.* Heavy shower, downpour; watering-place.
acquatico [acquAtico], *a.* Aquatic.
acquatinta, *n.f.* (*Art*) Aquatint.
acquattarsi, *v.r.* To squat down; to hide oneself.
acquavite, *n.f.* Brandy; gin.
acquazzone, *n.m.* Heavy shower, downpour, cloud-burst.
acquedotto, *n.m.* Aqueduct.
acqueo [Acqueo], *a.* Watery, aqueous. **Vapore —,** steam, aqueous vapour.
acquidoccio [acquidOccio], *n.m.* Aqueduct, canal, walled water-course.
acquiescente, *a.* Acquiescent.
acquiescienza, *n.f.* Acquiescence; consentment; submission.
acquiescere [acquiEscere], *v.i.* To acquiesce, to consent tacitly.
acquietamento, *n.m.* Quieting, quietening.
acquietare [cp. **quetare, quietare, chetare**], *v.t.* To pacify, to appease, to calm, to tranquillize.
acquietarsi, *v.r.* To become quiet, to be appeased, to calm down. **L'uragano si è acquietato,** the storm has passed away.
acquirente, *n.m.* Buyer.
acquisire, *v.t.* To acquire, to obtain; to purchase.
acquisito, *p.p.a.* Acquired, gained; (*Law*) **Diritto —,** an acquired right.
acquisività [-à], *n.f.* Acquisitiveness.
acquisizione, *n.f.* Acquisition.
acquistabile [acquistAbile], *a.* Procurable, acquirable; obtainable.
acquistare, *v.t.* To acquire, to obtain; to purchase, to buy; to conquer. — **fiducia,** to gain confidence; — **fama di,** to obtain a reputation for.
acquistarsi, *v.r.* To gain, to win over; to obtain, to acquire.
acquistato, *p.p.a.* Acquired, gained.
acquistevole [acquistEvole], *a.* Easily acquired.
acquisto, *n.m.* Purchase, bargain; acquisition; conquest; annexation. **Fare un ottimo —,** to get a good bargain; **l'— di Granada,** the conquest of Granada; **gli acquisti natalizi;** Christmas shopping; (*Comm.*) **potere d'—,** purchasing power.
acquitrino, *n.m.* Marsh, pond.
acquitrinoso, *a.* Marshy.
acquolina, *n.f.dim.* Fine rain, drizzle. (*fig.*) **Far venire l'— in bocca,** to make one's mouth water.
acquosità [-à], *n.f.* Aqueousness.
acquoso, *a.* Watery; aqueous; permeated with water; marshy.
acre, *a.* Acrid, pungent; sour; irritating; (*fig.*) harsh, cutting, sharp; piercing.
acredine [acrEdine], *n.f.* Acridity, sourness.
acremente, *adv.* Harshly.
acridio [acrIdio], *n.m.* Locust.
acrigno, *a.* Pungent, rather acrid.
acrimonia [acrimOnia], *n.f.* Acrimony, bitterness; resentment.
acrimonioso, *a.* Acrimonious, rancorous, resentful.
acrobata [acrObata], *n.m.* Acrobat, rope-dancer.
acrobatico [acrobAtico], *a.* Acrobatic.

acrobatismo, *n.m.* Acrobatism, acrobatics.
acromatico [acromAtico], *a.* Achromatic.
acromatismo, *n.m.* Achromatism.
acropoli [acrOpoli], *n.f.* Acropolis.
acrostico [acrOstico], *n.m.* Acrostic.
acuire, *v.t.* To sharpen, to whet; to give a point to; to irritate; to embitter; to stimulate. **— l'interesse, la curiosità,** to stimulate interest, curiosity.
aculeato, *a.* (*Zool.*) Sharp pointed sting.
aculeo [acUleo], *n.m.* (*Bot.*) Thorn, prickle; (*Zool.*) aculeus, sting.
acume, *n.m.* Acumen, discernment, penetration, insight. **— critico,** critical insight; **persona priva d'—,** person devoid of sagacity.
acuminare, *v.t.* To edge, to whet, to sharpen, to point.
acuminato, *a.* Pointed.
acumine [acUmine], [cp. **acume**].
acustica [acUstica], *n.f.* (*Physics*) Acoustics.
acustico [acUstico], *a.* Acoustic. **Cornetto —,** ear-trumpet.
acutamente, *adv.* Acutely, cleverly, subtly.
acutangolo [acutAngolo], *a.* (*Geom.*) With an acute angle.
acutezza, *n.f.* Sharpness, acuteness; subtlety; penetration, sagacity.
acutizzare, *v.t.* To make acute.
acutizzarsi, *v.r.* To become acute, to grow sharp.
acuto, *a.* (*lit. and fig.*) Acute, sharp, pointed, piercing, subtle. **Voce —,** shrill voice; **freddo —,** biting cold.
ad, *prep.* Usually used for **a** before a vowel. **Ad esempio,** for example.
adacquamento, *n.m.* Watering.
adacquare, *v.t.* To water [cp. **annacquare**].
adacquatura, *n.f.* Watering.
adagiamento, *n.m.* Placing; setting.
adagiare, *v.t.* To lay down, to place. **— un ferito nella barella,** to lay an injured person on a stretcher.
adagiarsi, *v.r.* To lie down, to subside into. **Si adagiò su una poltrona,** he subsided into an easy chair.
adagiato, *p.p.* Laid, stretched out; placed, situated.
adagino, *adv.* Softly, gently.
adagio [adAgio], *n.m.* Proverb, saying, adage.
adagio [adAgio], *adv.* Slowly, softly, smoothly, gently, peacefully. **Adagio adagio,** very slowly, little by little; **— Biagio!** take it quietly!
adagissimo, *a. super.* Very slowly; (*Mus.*) Slow movement, adagio.
adamante, *n.m.* (*Poet.*) Diamond.
adamantino, *a.* Adamantine; (*fig.*) strong, pure, lofty.
adamitico [adamItico], *a.* Naked, adamic. **In costume —,** naked.
Adamo, *n.m.* Adam.
adattabile [adattAbile], *a.* Adaptable, suitable.
adattabilità [-à], *n.f.* Adaptability.
adattamente, *adv.* Suitably.
adattamento, *n.m.* Aptness, adaptation.
adattare, *v.t.* To adapt, to suit, to fit, to adjust. **— un nuovo congegno,** to fit on a new mechanism.
adattarsi, *v.r.* To adapt oneself, to manage; to put up with, to resign oneself. **Bisogna —,** we must make the best of things.
adattatamente, *adv.* Suitably, aptly, conveniently.
adattato, adatto, *a.* Suitable, qualified for, fit for; proper. **Non sei adatto per questo lavoro,** you are not fit for this work; **la parola adatta,** the right word, *le mot juste*.
addarsi, *v.r.* To perceive; to devote oneself.
addaziare, *v.t.* To put an impost upon, to make dutiable.
addebbiare, *v.t.* (*Agric.*) To burn wood on ground for purposes of manuring.
addebitamento, *n.m.* (*Comm.*) Charge, debit.
addebitare, *v.t.* To debit, to charge; to impute; to place to one's debit.
addebito [addEbito], *n.m.* (*Comm.*) Debit, charge; imputation.
addensamento, *n.m.* Thickening, accumulation; increase.
addensare, *v.t.* To condense, to thicken; to amass, to increase.
addensarsi, *v.r.* To grow thick, to accumulate. **La tempesta si addensa,** the storm is gathering.
addentare, *v.t.* To bite, to seize with the teeth.
addentarsi, *v.r.* To bite each other.
addentatura, *n.f.* (*Mech.*) Dove-tailing; cogging; indenting.
addentellare, *v.t.* (*Mech.*) To dove-tail, to cog, to tooth; to link together; (*Arch.*) to leave toothing at a corner.
addentellato, *n.m.* (*Mech.*) Gear, cogged wheels; (*fig.*) connection, clue. **Cercare l'— d'una storia,** to look for the clue of a story.
addentrarsi, *v.r.* To enter in, to penetrate, to go deeply into. **— nello studio di,** to make a profound study of.
addentrato, *p.p.a.* (*fig.*) Very profound, specialized; versed.
addentro, *adv.* Within, inside. **Essere — nella questione,** to be well versed in the subject; **essere — a,** to be acquainted with.
addestrabile [addestrAbile], *a.* Capable of instruction or training.
addestramento, *n.m.* Training, practice; instruction; (*Mil.*) drilling.
addestrare, *v.t.* To train, to exercise; to instruct; (*Mil.*) to drill.
addestrarsi, *v.r.* To practise; to exercise, to train; to improve oneself.
addestrato, *p.p.a.* Trained, instructed; skilful.
addetto, *n.m.* Attaché. **— militare,** military attaché.
addetto, *a.* Attached, belonging to ; (*Comm.*) charged with. (*Comm.*) **— alla contabilità,** book-keeper; **— alla tenuta del mastro,** ledger-clerk; **— ai lavori,** employed on the work, on business.
addì, a dì, *adv.* This day of.
addiacciamento, *n.m.* Bivouacking; herding to the sheepfold.
addiacciare, *v.i.* To bivouac.
addiaccio [addiAccio], *n.m.* Sheepfold; (*Mil.*) bivouac. **Truppe all'—,** troops in temporary encampment.
addietro, *prep., adv.* Behind, to the rear, backward; ago. **Rimanere — (or in dietro),** to lag behind; **molti anni —,** many years ago; **dare —,** to recoil, to draw back.

addietro! *inter.* Back! Go back!
addimandare, *v.t.* [cp. **domandare**].
addio [addIo], *inter.* Farewell, adieu, good-bye. **Dire —,** to say good-bye; **— a domani,** good-bye until tomorrow.
addiritto, *adv.* By direct route; accurately.
addirittura, *adv.* Downrightly, absolutely, quite.
addirizzabile [addirizzAbile], *a.* Capable of being straightened.
addirizzamento, *n.m.* Straightening; making level a road.
addirizzare, addrizzare, drizzare, *v.t.* To straighten, to set right, to redress; to rectify.
addirizzarsi, *v.r.* To get upright, to stand erect.
addirizzatura, drizzatura, *n.f.* Straightening, parting (of the hair).
additamento, *n.m.* Indication.
additare, *v.t.* To indicate, to point at, to show; to designate.
addivenire, *v.i.* To come to, to arrive at. **— ad un accordo,** to come to an understanding.
addizionale, *a.* Additional, supplementary.
addizionare, *v.t.* To add up, to sum up.
addizione, *n.f.* (*Arith.*) Addition, adding up.
addobbamento, *n.m.* Ornament, decoration.
addobbare, *v.t.* To deck, to adorn, to decorate.
addobbato, *a.* Adorned, decorated.
addobbo, *n.m.* Ornament. **Gli addobbi sacri,** sacred ornaments.
addocciare, *v.t.* (*Mech.*) To groove.
addocilire, *v.t.* To tame; to appease; (*Tech.*) to soften (leather).
addolcimento, *n.m.* Sweetening, softening.
addolcire, *v.t.* (*fig. and lit.*) To sweeten; to mitigate, to soften; to relieve.
addolcirsi, *v.r.* To become mild, to soften; to relent.
addolcitivo, *n.m.* Softener, demulcent.
addoloramento, *n.m.* Pain [cp. **dolore**].
addolorare, *v.t.* To cause pain, to grieve, to vex, to afflict.
addolorarsi, *v.r.* To worry, to grieve, to be afflicted.
addolorata, *n.f.* (*Eccles.*) Our Lady in sorrow; Mater dolorosa.
addome, *n.m.* (*Anat.*) Abdomen.
addomesticabile [addomesticAbile], *a.* Domesticable, tractable.
addomesticare, *v.t.* To tame, to domesticate; to break in (animals); to subdue.
addomesticarsi, *v.r.* To grow tame, to become gentle, sociable.
addomesticatore, *n.m.* Tamer.
addomestichevole [addomestichEvole], *a.* Easily domesticated.
addominale, *a.* (*Med.*) Abdominal.
addoppiamento, *n.m.* Folding; doubling up.
addoppiare, raddoppiare, *v.t.* To double; to increase.
addoppio, raddoppio, *n.m.* Doubling; folding in two.
addormentare, *v.t.* To lull asleep, to send asleep; (*fig.*) to wheedle; to benumb; to weary; to deaden. **— un bambino,** to rock a child to sleep; **— per un'operazione,** to put under an anaesthetic.
addormentarsi, *v.r.* To fall asleep, to go to sleep, to slumber; (*fig.*) to become slow, lazy. **— sugli allori,** to rest on one's laurels.
addormentativo, *n.m.* Soporific.
addormentato, *a.* Asleep; numbed.
addormentatore, addormentatrice, *n.m.f.* One who puts to sleep; (*fig.*) bore, dull person; wheedler.
addossare, *v.t.* To burden, to charge upon, to lay on, to impute; to entrust. **Mi addossò tutta la responsabilità,** he saddled me with all the responsibility.
addossarsi, *v.r.* To stand massed together; to lean against; to burden oneself; to take upon oneself, to shoulder. **— le spese,** to shoulder all expenses; **si addossarono al muro,** they leaned against the wall.
addosso, *adv. prep.* On, upon, over. **Dare —,** to go for, to attack; **mettersi —,** to put on; **non venirmi —,** do not press me; **metter le mani — ad una persona,** to lay hands on a person.
addosso! *inter.* Forward! Come on! After him!
addotto, *p.p.a.* Adduced, alleged [cp. **addurre**].
addottoramento, *n.m.* Doctorate, degree.
addottorare, *v.t.* To confer an academic degree.
addottorarsi, *v.r.* To become a doctor, to obtain a university degree.
addottrinare, *v.t.* To instruct, to impart knowledge.
addottrinarsi, *v.r.* To learn, to become versed in.
addottrinatamente, *adv.* Learnedly, in a learned manner.
addottrinato, *a.* Well-informed, learned.
adducibile [adducIbile], *a.* Adducible.
addurre, *v.t.* To bring; to present; to allege. **— delle buone ragioni,** to produce good arguments; **— dei pretesti,** to find pretexts, to find excuses.
adduttore, *n.m.* (*Anat.*) Adductor muscle.
adeguabile [adeguAbile], *a.* Conformable, adaptable.
adeguamento, *n.m.* Adaptation; conformation; readjustment.
adeguare, *v.t.* To conform, to adapt; to readjust. **— alle circostanze,** to rise to circumstances.
adeguarsi, *v.r.* To conform oneself; to rise to.
adeguatamente, *adv.* Adequately, proportionately.
adeguato, *a.* Adequate, proportioned; suitable.
adempiere [adEmpiere], *v.t.* To fulfil, to accomplish, to execute, to effect, to achieve. **— una missione,** to perform a mission.
adempiersi, *v.r.* To come true, to be fulfilled.
adempimento, *n.m.* Fulfilment, execution.
adempire [cp. **adempiere**].
adempirsi, *v.r.* To come to pass; to be fulfilled.
adempito, adempiuto, *p.p.* Fulfilled, performed, carried out.
adenoide, *n.f.* (*Med.*) Adenoid.
adenzione, *n.f.* (*Law*) Revocation.
adepto, *n.m.* Initiate; follower; one of an inner circle.
aderente, *n.m.a.* Adherent, follower, supporter; tight, close-fitting (garment).

aderenza, *n.f.* Adherence; adhesion; *f.pl.* (*fig.*) influence, high connections.
adergere [adErgere], *v.t.* To raise.
adergersi [adErgersi], *v.r.* To rise.
aderire, *v.i.* To adhere; to acquiesce; to comply with; to take part, to join. — **ad un desiderio,** to consent to one's wish; — **ad un partito,** to join a party.
adescabile [adescAbile], *a.* Open to temptation, liable to enticement.
adescamento, *n.m.* Bait, allurement, enticement.
adescare, *v.t.* To bait; (*fig.*) to lure, to decoy, to attract; to beguile, to seduce. — **con false promesse,** to entice with false promises.
adescatore, adescatrice, *n.m.f.* Allurer, tempter, seducer.
adesione, *n.f.* Adhesion; (*fig.*) participation, solidarity, approval.
adesivo, *a.* Adhesive, sticky.
adeso, *a.* Attached, adherent.
adespoto [adEspoto], *a.* (*Lit.*) Anonymous.
adesso, *adv.* Now, at present; just now. **Fino —,** until now.
adiacente, *a.* Near, contiguous, next, adjacent.
adiacenza, *n.f.* Nearness, neighbourhood, vicinity; contiguity.
adiacenze, *n.f.pl.* Surroundings.
adianto, *n.m.* (*Bot.*) Maidenhair fern.
adibire, *v.t.* To destine, to use, to employ; to adapt. — **ad uso di,** to use as.
adinamia [adinamIa], *n.f.* Weakness.
adipe [Adipe], *n.m.* Fat.
adiposità [-à], *n.f.* Fatness, adiposity.
adiposo, *a.* Fatty, adipose.
adiramento, *n.m.* Anger; sulkiness.
adirare, *v.t.* To enrage, to make angry.
adirarsi, *v.r.* To get angry, to take offence. — **per un nonnulla,** to take offence without cause.
adiratamente, *adv.* Angrily, furiously.
adirato, *p.p.a.* Angry, enraged; morose.
adire, *v.t., v.i.* (*Law*) To present oneself. — **un'eredità,** to take possession of an inheritance; — **il tribunale,** to take legal proceedings.
adirevole [adirEvole], *a.* Easily angered, irascible.
adito [Adito], *n.m.* Access; (*fig.*) entrance, way; motive. **Dare — a lagnanze,** to give cause for complaint.
adiutore, *n.m.* Adjutor, assistant magistrate.
adiutorio [adiutOrio], *a.* Adjutory, helpful.
adizione, *n.f.* (*Law*) Acceptance (of an inheritance).
adnata, *n.f.* (*Anat.*) Conjunctiva.
adocchiamento, *n.m.* Ogling, glance; spying.
adocchiare, *v.t.* To glance, to ogle; to covet. — **la preda,** to catch sight of the prey.
adolescente, *n.m.a.* Adolescent, stripling, youth, teen-ager.
adolescenza, *n.f.* Adolescence; boyhood, girlhood.
Adolfo, *n.m.* Adolphus.
adombramento, *n.m.* Darkening, dullness; (*fig.*) suspicion, umbrage.
adombrare, *v.t.* To adumbrate, to shade; to delineate, to indicate faintly.
adombrarsi, *v.r.* To take umbrage, to be touchy.
adombrato, *a.* Shady, gloomy; foretold.
adombrazione, *n.f.* Adumbration; suggestion
Adone, *n.m.* Adonis, beau, dandy.
adonestare, *v.t.* To gloss over, to palliate.
adònio [adOnio], *n.m.* (*Lit.*) Adonic verse.
adontamento, *n.m.* Resentment, offence.
adontarsi, *v.r.* To take offence, to be offended; to feel hurt.
adoperabile [adoperAbile], *a.* Employable, practicable.
adoperamento, *n.m.* Use, employ.
adoperare, *v.t.* To use, to employ, to make use of. — **i mezzi adatti,** to employ the proper means.
adoperarsi, *v.r.* To exert oneself, to set about, to take the trouble, to busy oneself, to endeavour.
adoprare [cp. **adoperare**].
adorabile [adorAbile], *a.* Adorable.
adorabilmente, *adv.* Adorably.
adoramento, *n.m.* Adoration, homage.
adorare, *v.t.* To adore, to worship, to venerate; to love.
adoratore, adoratrice, *n.m.f.* Adorer, worshipper; admirer, lover.
adorazione, *n.f.* Adoration.
adornabile [adornAbile], *a.* Capable of embellishment.
adornamento, *n.m.* Decoration, ornament, embellishment.
adornare, *v.t.* To adorn, to deck, to decorate.
adornarsi, *v.r.* To adorn oneself, to deck oneself.
adornatamente, *adv.* Elegantly, gracefully.
adornato, *a.* Adorned, ornamented; embellished; dressed.
adorno, *n.m.a.* Ornament; adorned, embellished; dressed.
adottamento, *n.m.* Adoption.
adottare, *v.t.* To adopt, to accept; to use, to employ.
adottivo, *a.* Adoptive. **Figlio —,** adopted son.
adozione, *n.f.* Adoption; acceptance.
adrenalina, *n.f.* (*Chem.*) Adrenalin.
Adriano, *n.m.* Hadrian.
aduggiamento, *n.m.* Overshadowing.
aduggiare, *v.t.* To overshadow; (*fig.*) to dull, to oppress, to weigh down. **Non aduggiarmi con le tue lamentele,** don't bother me with your complaints.
aduggiato, *p.p.a.* Oppressed; sunless.
adulare, *v.t.* To flatter, to adulate; to fawn upon; to cajole, to blandish.
adulatore, adulatrice, *n.m.f.* Flatterer, adulator, cajoler, wheedler.
adulatoriamente, *adv.* Flatteringly.
adulatorio [adulatOrio], *a.* Flattering, blandishing, adulatory, fawning.
adulazione, *n.f.* Flattery, adulation; cajolery.
adultera [adUltera], *n.f.* Adulteress.
adulterabile [adulterAbile], *a.* Capable of adulteration.
adulteramento, *n.m.* Falsification.
adulterare, *v.t.* To adulterate, to debase, to falsify; (*fig.*) to distort, to misrepresent; to tamper with.
adulterazione, *n.f.* Adulteration.
adulterino, *a.* Adulterine; spurious.
adulterio [adultErio], *n.m.* Adultery.
adultero [adUltero], *n.m.* Adulterer.
adulto, *n.m.a.* Adult, grown-up.

adunabile [adunAbile], *a.* Collectable, assemblable.
adunamento, *n.m.* Assembly, assemblage.
adunanza, *n.f.* Assemblage, assembly, meeting. **Indire un'—,** to call a meeting; **— straordinaria,** special meeting.
adunare, *v.t.* To convene, to summon; to assemble; (*Mil.*) to muster.
adunarsi, *v.r.* To assemble, to join; (*Mil.*) to fall in, to take one's place in the line.
adunata, *n.f.* Rally; (*Mil.*) assembly, meeting. **Suonare l'—,** to sound the fall-in.
aduncare, *v.i.* To curve, to bend.
adunco, *a.* Hooked, bent. **Dal naso —,** hook-nosed.
adunghiare, *v.t.* To claw, to clutch.
adunque, *conj., adv.* Then, therefore, consequently.
adusare, *v.t.* To accustom.
adusarsi, *v.r.* To accustom oneself.
adustibile [adustIbile], *a.* Dry as tinder.
adusto, *a.* Adust, sunburnt, bronzed, tanned.
aedo, *n.m.* (*Poet.*) Poet, bard.
aerare, *v.t.* To air; to ventilate.
aerato, *p.p.a.* Aerated, aired; ventilated.
aerazione, *n.f.* Aeration.
aere [Aere], *n.m.* (*Poet.*) Air.
aeremoto, *n.m.* Whirlwind, hurricane.
aereo [aEreo], *n.m.* Aeroplane, aircraft.
aereo [aEreo], *a.* Aerial; of the air. **Veduta aerea,** air view; **comunicazioni aeree,** air communication.
aereolinea, *n.f.* Airline, aeroplane service.
aereolito [aereOlito], *n.m.* (*Geol.*) Aerolite, meteoric stone.
aerobomba, *n.f.* Aerial bomb, aerial torpedo.
aerodinamica [aerodinAmica], *n.f.* Aerodynamics.
aerodinamico [aerodinAmico], *a.* Aerodynamic; stream-lined. **Vettura aerodinamica,** stream-lined car.
aerodromo [aerOdromo], *n.m.* Aerodrome.
aerofaro [aerOfaro], *n.m.* (*Aviat.*) Air beacon.
aerolito [aerOlito], *n.m.* (*Geol.*) Aerolite.
aeronauta [aeronAuta], *n.m.* Aeronaut.
aeronautica [aeronAutica], *n.f.* Aeronautics.
aeronave, *n.f.* Airship, dirigible.
aeroplano, *n.m.* Aeroplane, airplane; flying machine. **— a reazione,** jet plane.
aeroporto, *n.m.* Air port, air station. **— d'imbarco,** out-going airport; **— di transito,** transit airport.
aeroscalo, *n.m.* Air station, aerodrome.
aerosilurante, *n.m.* Torpedo-carrying plane.
aerostatico [aerostAtico], *a.* Aerostatic.
aerostato [aerOstato], *n.m.* Aerostat, balloon.
aerotrasportato, *a.* Air-borne.
afa, *n.f.* Sultriness, closeness, stuffiness.
afasia [afAsia], *n.f.* (*Med.*) Aphasia.
afato, *a.* Stunted; puny; withered.
afelio [afElio], *n.m.* (*Astron.*) Aphelion.
aferesi [afEresi], *n.f.* (*Gram.*) Apheresis.
affabile [affAbile], *a.* Affable, courteous, polite, considerate.
affabilità [-à], *n.f.* Affability, courtesy.
affaccendamento, *n.m.* Bustle, business, agitation, fuss.
affaccendarsi, *v.r.* To bustle, to busy oneself; to take much trouble.
affaccendato, *a.* Busy, bustling.
affacchinarsi, *v.r.* To drudge, to fag.
affacciare, *v.t.* To indicate, to point out.
affacciarsi, *v.r.* To appear, to show, to present oneself (*e.g.* at a window). (*fig.*) to recall to call to mind.
affagottare, *v.t.* To bundle up [cp. **infagottare**].
affagottato, *a.* Ill-dressed; bundled up.
affaldare, *v.t.* To fold up closely; to fold over and over.
affamamento, *n.m.* Starvation.
affamare, *v.t.* To starve, to starve out, to deprive of food.
affamatamente, *adv.* Hungrily, in a hungry manner.
affamato, *p.p.a.* Starved, starving, hungry.
affamatore, affamatrice, *n.m.f.* Forestaller, profiteer, sweater.
affamatuccio [affamatUccio], *a.* Hungry, famished (of a child).
affamigliarsi, *v.r.* To become one of the family.
affannamento, *n.m.* Anxiety, worry, agitation.
affannante, *a.* Distressing; (*Med.*) asthmatic.
affannare, *v.t.* To weary, to bore; to worry; to excite.
affannarsi, *v.r.* To worry oneself; to bustle; to be anxious. **Non affannarti,** don't get excited, don't worry.
affannatamente, *adv.* Excitedly, worriedly.
affannato, *p.p.a.* Breathless; agitated; alarmed.
affannevole [affannEvole], *a.* Breathless; troubled [cp. **affannoso**].
affanno, *n.m.* Breathlessness; (*Med.*) asthma; (*fig.*) anxiety, anguish, pang; agitation.
affannone, *n.m.* Fussy fellow; busybody.
affannosamente, *adv.* Breathlessly, excitedly; painfully; anxiously.
affannoso, *a.* Gasping, breathless; anxious, excited, frenzied; hurried; difficult (in temper).
affaraccio [affarAccio], *n.m.* (*colloq.*) Nasty affair, sorry piece of work.
affardellare, *v.t.* To bundle up. (*Mil.*) **— lo zaino,** to pack up one's kit, to pack a kit-bag.
affare, *n.m.* Business; affair; bargain; matter. **Uomo d'affari,** business man; **è un altro —,** it is a different matter; (*colloq.*) **un — sballato,** a rotten business; (*iron.*) **un bell'—,** a pretty mess; **è un — serio,** it is a grave matter, it is no joke; **trattare un —,** to transact a piece of business; **fare un buon —,** to strike a bargain; **per affari,** on business; **affari in corso,** business on hand; **— urgente,** pressing business; **un buon — commerciale,** a paying proposition; (*colloq.*) **parlare d'affari,** to talk shop; **un — di nulla,** a trifling matter; **non è — mio,** it is none of my business; **persona di mal —,** disreputable person; **qui sta l'—,** there's the rub.
affaretto, *n.m.* Trifle, matter of no importance.
affari, *n.m.pl.* Business, affairs; bargains; trade. **— di banca,** bank business; **estendere gli —,** to extend one's business; **annodare relazione d'—,** to enter into business transactions; **interessare qualcuno negli —,** to give someone a share in the business; **cifra d'—,** amount of business; **gli — sono gli —,** business is business.

affarismo, *n.m.* Profiteering, speculation; greed of money.
affarista (*pl.* **affaristi**), *n.m.* Profiteer, speculator.
affarone, *n.m.* Bargain. **Fare un —,** to strike a good bargain.
affarsi, *v.r.* (*obs.*) To agree with, to accord.
affaruccio [affarUccio], *n.m.* Trifle; awkward affair, mess.
affascinamento, *n.m.* Fascination, charm, enchantment.
affascinante, *a.* Fascinating, charming, delightful, enchanting, bewitching.
affascinare, *v.t.* To fascinate, to enchant, to charm, to bewitch.
affascinatore, affascinatrice, *n.m.f.* Charmer, enchanter; seducer.
affastellamento, *n.m.* Heap, collection; bundle.
affastellare, *v.t.* To bundle up; to hoard up; to pile up; (*fig.*) to jumble up; to make a mess. **— delle corbellerie,** to pile up trash, to collect junk.
affastellio [affastellIo], *n.m.* Accumulation, heap; confusion, disorder.
affaticamento, *n.m.* Wearying, weariness.
affaticante, *a.* Fatiguing, wearisome, toilsome.
affaticare, *v.t.* To fatigue, to tire, to weary, to harass; to overwork. **— la mente,** to tire one's mind, to overwork.
affaticarsi, *v.r.* To toil; to weary oneself, to be jaded; to struggle hard.
affatto, *adv.* Quite, entirely. **Niente —,** not at all.
affattucchiare, *v.t.* [cp. **affatturare**].
affatturamento, *n.m.* Adulteration, corruption.
affatturare, *v.t.* To bewitch; (*fig.*) to adulterate, to debase, to defile; to tamper with.
affatturato, *p.p.a.* Adulterated.
affatturazione, *n.f.* Adulteration.
affazzonamento, *n.m.* Embellishment.
affazzonare, *v.t.* To arrange, to patch up; to embellish [cp. **raffazzonare**].
affazzonarsi, *v.r.* To bedizen oneself; to trick out.
affè!, *int.* (*obs.*) Faith!
afferente, *a.* (*Tech.*) Bringing, carrying.
affermabile [affermAbile], *a.* Affirmable.
affermamento, *n.m.* Affirming, act of affirmation.
affermare, *v.t.* To state, to assert, to aver, to affirm. **— i propri principi,** to assert one's principles.
affermarsi, *v.r.* To introduce oneself, to call attention to oneself.
affermativamente, *adv.* Affirmatively.
affermativo, *a.* Affirmative. **Dare una risposta affermativa,** to reply in the affirmative.
affermazione, *n.f.* Affirmation; statement; assurance. **Fare un'— arrischiata,** to make a bold statement.
afferramento, *n.m.* Clutch, grasp.
afferrare, *v.t.* To grasp, to seize, to get hold of; to catch, to snatch, to grip; (*fig.*) to grasp, to understand. **— un'occasione,** to seize an opportunity; **— una frase,** to understand a phrase.
afferrarsi, *v.r.* To catch hold of, to grip, to grasp at, to seize. **— all'ultima speranza,** to cling to the last hope.
affettante, *a.* Given to pretence or simulation.
affettare, (1), *v.t.* To slice, to cut off; to carve.
affettare (2), *v.t.* To affect, to feign; to pretend, to assume, to simulate. **— un'aria disinvolta,** to feign indifference; **— di sapere,** to pretend to know.
affettatamente, *adv.* Ostentatiously; affectedly.
affettato, *n.m.* Sausage cut in slices; sliced ham.
affettato, *a.* Mannered, affected.
affettatura, *n.f.* Affectation.
affettazione, *n.f.* Affectation, mannerism.
affettibile [affettIbile], *a.* Modifiable, susceptible to modification.
affettivo, *a.* Emotional, sentimental, affective.
affetto, *n.m.* Affection, fondness, tenderness; sentiment.
affetto, *a.* Affected; (*Med.*) affected, attacked, suffering from a disease.
affettuosamente, *adv.* Affectionately, lovingly, tenderly.
affettuosità [-à], *n.f.* Affectionateness, tenderness.
affettuoso, *a.* Affectionate, tender, loving.
affezionabilità [-à], *n.f.* Disposition to be affectionate.
affezionamento, *n.m.* Endearment.
affezionare, *v.t.* To endear, to win the love of, to secure the affections of.
affezionarsi, *v.r.* To love, to be fond of; to attach oneself to; to delight in.
affezionatamente, *adv.* Affectionately.
affezionato, *a.* Affectionate, devoted.
affezione, *n.f.* Affection, love, tenderness, attachment; (*Med.*) affection, disease.
affiancamento, *n.m.* Flanking.
affiancare, *v.t.* (*Mil.*) To flank.
affiancato, *p.p.a.* Flanked, in flank.
affiatamento, *n.m.* Harmony, concord, exact adaptation; combination.
affiatare, *v.t.* To bring together, to cause to agree; to mix together; (*Mus.*) to tune, to harmonize.
affiatarsi, *v.r.* To befriend; to get on together; to agree.
affibbiamento, *n.m.* Buckling, act of buckling (strap, etc.)
affibbiare, *v.t.* To buckle, to clasp; (*fig.*) to saddle with, to burden with; to shift, to lodge (a kick etc.). **Gli hanno affibbiato un bel grattacapo,** they have given him a rare tangle to clear up; **— un soprannome,** to give a nickname; **— un ceffone,** to slap in the face.
affibbiatura, *n.f.* Buckling, clasp.
affidamento, *n.m.* Confidence, trust, reliance. **Dare —,** to give assurances.
affidanza, *n.f.* Confidence.
affidare, *v.t.* To entrust, to commit, to charge with, to confide. **— un incarico,** to entrust with a charge.
affidarsi, *v.r.* To trust, to have confidence, to rely upon, to depend upon. **— alla sorte,** to rely on chance, to trust one's luck.
affidatamente, *adv.* Trustingly, confidingly.
affidato, *a.* Committed to trust.
affienare, *v.t.* To put out to hay; to feed on hay.

affievolimento, *n.m.* Weakening, dimness, attenuation.
affievolire, affievolirsi, *v.t.r.* To grow feeble, to weaken. **Le voci a poco a poco si affievolirono,** the voices gradually grew faint.
affiggere [affIggere], *v.t* To stick up, to paste up, to post, to placard.
affiggersi [affIggersi], *v.r.* To gaze at; to stare at.
affilamento, *n.m.* Sharpening.
affilare, *v.t.* To sharpen, to whet, to strop, to grind. **— il rasoio,** to strop the razor.
affilato, *p.p.a.* Sharpened, pointed. **Un viso —,** a lank face.
affilatura, *n.f.* Sharpening; edge.
affilettare, *v.t.* (*Arch.*) To point brickwork.
affiliare, *v.t.* To affiliate.
affiliato, *n.m.a.* Associate; affiliated.
affiliazione, *n.f.* Affiliation.
affinamento, *n.m.* Refinement, polishing.
affinare, *v.t.* To refine; to polish; to purify; to point. **— il gusto,** to refine one's taste.
affinarsi, *v.r.* To become refined, polished. **I costumi si affinano,** manners grow more gentle.
affinatoio [affinatOio], *n.m.* (*Metal.*) Refining machinery; refinery.
affinatore, *n.m.* (*Metal.*) Refiner.
affinatura, *n.f.* Refining, purification.
affinchè, *conj.* In order that, so that.
affine, *a.* Similar, akin, kindred. **Botanica e materie affini,** botany and kindred subjects.
affine di, *conj.* In order that, so that.
affinità [-à], *n.f.* Affinity, resemblance; relationship, congeniality; (*Chem.*) tendency to combine.
affiochimento, *n.m.* Hoarseness.
affiochire, affiochirsi, *v.i.r.* To become hoarse; to grow feeble. **Gli s'affiochì la voce,** his voice became hoarse; **i rumori s'affiochirono,** the noise grew faint.
affioramento, *n.m.* (*Min.*) Outcrop; appearing on the surface.
affiorare, *v.t.* To come to the surface; to crop out (of minerals etc.); to be level with, to be flush with.
affisamente, *adv.* Attentively.
affisare, *v.t.* (*Poet.*) To stare at.
affisamento, *n.m.* Application, close attention.
affissare, *v.t.* To affix, to fix.
affissatore, *n.m.* Bill-poster.
affissione, *n.f.* Posting up (bills, etc.); sticking. **È vietata l'—,** Post no bills.
affisso, *n.m.* Bill, placard, poster.
affittabile [affittAbile], *a.* Vacant, to let, open for hiring.
affittacamere [affittacAmere], *n.m.f.* Lodging-house keeper; landlord, landlady.
affittaiolo [affittaiOlo], *n.m.* Tenant; tenant farmer.
affittamento, *n.m.* Farming; lease (of land).
affittante, *n.m.f.* Landlord, landlady; tenant. **Un mio —,** a tenant of mine.
affittanza, *n.f.* Tenancy; lease; place to let.
affittare, *v.t.* To let; to rent, to lease; to hire. **— una casa,** to rent a house; **—** (for **dare in affitto**) **una casa,** to let a house; **— una carrozza,** to hire a cab; **da —,** or **affittasi,** to let, to be let.
affittire, affittirsi, *v.t.r.* To thicken; to increase; to grow thick [cp. **infittire**].
affitto, *n.m.* Rent, rental; lease; hire. **Pagare l'— di casa,** to pay the rent; **dare in —,** to let; **— alto,** high rental; **prendere in —,** to rent; **subaffitto,** sub-let.
affittuale, affittuario [affittuArio], *n.m.* Tenant, leaseholder; farmer.
affliggente, *pres.p.a.* Distressing, vexing, troublesome.
affliggere [afflIggere], *v.t.* To afflict, to trouble, to distress, to vex. **Non mi —,** don't bother me.
affligersi [afflIgersi], *v.r.* To worry, to grieve, to be troubled, to be distressed.
affliggitivamente, *adv.* Distressingly, vexingly.
afflitto, *a.* Afflicted, grieved; sorry; (*Med.*) affected.
afflizione, *n.f.* Affliction, distress; anguish, sorrow, grief.
affloscire, *v.i.* To become flabby; to be enervated, to lose nerve.
affluente, *n.m.a.* (*Geog.*) Affluent, tributary; well-off, affluent.
affluentemente, *adv.* Copiously.
affluenza, *n.f.* Affluence, abundance; concourse.
affluire, *v.i.* To flow into, to abound, to flock into.
afflussionato, *a.* Suffering with a cold.
afflusso, *n.m.* (*Med.*) Afflux.
affocare, *v.t.* To set on fire, to kindle.
affocarsi, *v.r.* To get hot (with rage).
affocato, *a.* Red-hot; flushed.
affogamento, *n.m.* Drowning; suffocation.
affogare, *v.t.i.* To drown; to submerge; to sink; (*fig.*) to stifle, to crush, to suppress; to poach (eggs). **— nei guai,** to be overwhelmed by troubles; **uova affogate,** poached eggs.
affogarsi, *v.r.* To get drowned; to drown oneself; to sink.
affollamento, *n.m.* Crowding; over-crowding; concourse.
affollare, *v.t.* To crowd, to throng, to press.
affollarsi, *v.r.* To throng, to crowd; to be crowded, to be packed.
affollatamente, *adv.* In crowds.
affondamento, *n.m.* Sinking, foundering.
affondare, *v.t.i.* To sink, to submerge, to founder, to go to the bottom, to send to the bottom; to thrust in.
affondarsi, *v.r.* To sink, to go down, to founder; to subside.
affondatore, *n.m.* (*Naut.*) Ram (for sinking vessels).
affortunato, *a.* Lucky [cp. **fortunato**].
afforzamento, *n.m.* (*Mil.*) Fortification; act of fortifying.
afforzare, *v.t.* To strengthen, to fortify, to invigorate.
afforzarsi, *v.r.* To fortify oneself, to grow strong.
affossamento, *n.m.* Ditching; excavation; cavity.
affossare, *v.t.* To ditch, to dig out; to sink (in the ground).
affossarsi, *v.r.* To subside; to become hollow.
affossatore, *n.m.* Grave-digger.
affossatura, *n.f.* Subsidence; excavation.
affralimento, *n.m.* Weakness; debility.
affralire, *v.t.i.* To weaken, to enfeeble, to impair the strength of.

affralirsi, *v.r.* To grow feeble, to decline, to fall away.
affrancamento, *n.m.* Release; liberation.
affrancare, *v.t.* To set free, to emancipate; to stamp (a letter).
affrancarsi, *v.r.* To free oneself; to be delivered; to become independent.
affrancato, *p.p.a.* Emancipated, delivered; stamped (of letters), post paid.
affrancatura, *n.f.* Postage (of a letter).
affrancazione, *n.f.* Enfranchisement, emancipation; exemption.
affranto, *a.* Exhausted, crushed, broken, worn out.
affratellamento, *n.m.* Fraternization, fellowship; intimacy.
affratellare, *v.t.* To cause to fraternize.
affratellarsi, *v.r.* To become comrades; to associate with; to unite with.
affrenare, *v.t.* To curb, to restrain.
affrescare, *v.t.* (*Art*) To fresco.
affresco, *n.m.* (*Art*) Fresco.
affrettamento, *n.m.* Hurrying, hastening.
affrettare, *v.t.* To hasten, to hurry, to speed up, to quicken. **— il passo,** to quicken one's step.
affrettarsi, *v.r.* To hurry, to hasten; to bustle. **Mi affretto a rispondere,** I hasten to reply; **affrettati,** make haste, hurry up! **bisogna —,** it is necessary to hurry.
affrettatamente, *adv.* Hurriedly.
affrettato, *a.* Hasty, hurried. **Un lavoro —,** done in haste, carelessly.
affrico [Affrico], *n.m.* South-westerly wind (blowing from Africa).
affrittellare, *v.t.* To fry (eggs); (*fig.*) to kill, to do in.
affrontamento, *n.m.* Facing, encounter.
affrontare, *v.t.* To face, to front; to defy, to brave; to attack. **— le conseguenze,** to face the consequences; **— la morte,** to face death.
affrontarsi, *v.r.* To stand face to face; to encounter; to fall upon.
affronto, *n.m.* Affront, insult, outrage. **Subire un —,** to suffer an affront.
affumato, *a.* Smoked [cp. **affumicato**].
affumicamento, *n.m.* Smoking, fumigation, blackening; curing (of meat).
affumicare, *v.t.* To smoke; to blacken; to fumigate; to fill with smoke.
affumicato, *p.p.a.* Smoked, smoky. **Occhiali affumicati,** smoked glasses.
affumicatoio [affumicatOio], *n.m.* Chamber for smoking or curing.
affumicatura, *n.f.* Smoking, fumigation [cp. **affumicamento**].
affusione, *n.f.* Affusion; pouring on.
affusolare, *v.t.* To taper.
affusolato, *p.p.a.* Tapered, slender; (*Motor.*) stream-lined.
affusto, *n.m.* (*Mil.*) Gun-carriage.
Afganistan [afgAnistan], *n.m.* Afghanistan.
afgano, *n.m.a.* Afghan.
afidi [Afidi], *n.m.pl.* (*Zool.*) Aphides.
afonia [afonIa], *n.f.* (*Med.*) Aphonia, loss of voice.
afono [Afono], (*Med.*) Aphonous, voiceless.
aforismo, *n.m.* Aphorism, maxim.
aforistico [aforIstico], *a.* Aphoristic.
afoso, *a.* Stuffy, close, sultry; ill ventilated. **Giornata afosa,** a stuffy day.
Africa [Africa], *n.f.* Africa. **— del Sud,** South Africa; **— occidentale,** West Africa; **— orientale,** East Africa; **— settentrionale,** North Africa.
africanista, *n.m.* Specialist on Africa.
africano, *n.m.a.* African.
afro, *a.* Rancid, with a sour smell.
afrodisiaco [afrodisIaco], *n.m.* Aphrodisiac; love philtre.
Afrodite, *n.f.* Aphrodite.
afrore, *n.m.* Odour, reek, stench, stink; stench of carbonic acid.
afroroso, *a.* Reeking, stinking.
afta, *n.f.* (*Med.*) Aphtha. **— epizootica,** foot and mouth disease.
Agamennone [agamEnnone], *n.m.* Agamemnon.
agamia [agamIa], *n.m.* (*Zool.*) Agamogenesis, sexual reproduction.
agarico [agArico], *n.m.* Kind of fungus, mushroom.
agata [Agata], *n.f.* (*Min.*) Agate.
agave [Agave], *n.f.* (*Bot.*) Agave.
agemina [agEmina], *n.f.* Damascening (steel).
ageminare, *v.t.* To damascene.
agenda, *n.f.* Diary, notebook, memorandum book.
agente, *n.m.* Agent; broker; representative. **— di polizia, — di questura,** constable, policeman; **— di cambio,** stock-broker; **— commissionario,** commission agent; **— marittimo,** shipping agent; **— consolare,** consular agent.
agenzia [agenzIa], *n.f.* Agency, agency-office. **— di viaggi,** tourist office; **— consolare,** consular agency; **— telegrafica,** telegraph office, news agency.
agevolamento, *n.m.* Facilitation.
agevolare, *v.t.* To facilitate, to further, to help forward, to make easy; to assist.
agevolazione, *n.f.* Assistance, help, facilitation, facilities.
agevole [agEvole], *a.* Easy, handy, smooth, comfortable, unconstrained; facile.
agevolezza, *n.f.* (*Comm.*) Facilitation; facilities.
agevolmente, *adv.* Comfortably, smoothly.
agganciare, *v.t.* To hook, to clasp; to hang up; (*Rail.*) to couple.
aggeggio [aggEggio], *n.m.* Gadget; trifle; worthless stuff.
aggettare, *v.i.* To jut out.
aggettivamente, *adv.* (*Gram.*) Adjectivally.
aggettivo, *n.m.* (*Gram.*) Adjective.
aggetto, *n.m.* Projection.
agghiacciamento, *n.m.* Freezing; congealment; frost.
agghiacciare, *v.t.i.* To freeze, to ice over, to congeal, (*fig.*) to paralyse.
agghiacciarsi, *v.r.* To freeze, to congeal.
agghiaiare, *v.t.* To gravel, to lay gravel.
agghindamento, *n.m.* Bauble; trinket.
agghindare, *v.t.* To dress up, to deck out, to bedizen.
agghindarsi, *v.r.* To bedizen oneself.
agghindatura, *n.f.* Bedizenment, gaudy attire.
aggiacciare, *v.t.* (*Naut.*) To handle the tiller.
aggina, *n.f.* Pasture; paddock.
aggio [Aggio], *n.m.* (*Fin.*) Agio; premium; money-changing.

aggiogare, *v.t.* To yoke, to couple; to link.
aggiornamento, *n.m.* Adjournment; bringing up to date. **Corso di —,** refresher course.
aggiornare (1), *v.t.* To bring up to date; to postpone, to adjourn, to defer.
aggiornare (2), *v.i.* To dawn, to break (day).
aggiotaggio [aggiotAggio], *n.m.* Agiotage, stock-jobbing.
aggiotatore, *n.m.* Stock-broker, speculator.
aggiramento, *n.m.* Circuit, surrounding, encirclement.
aggirare, *v.t.* To turn round, to encircle, to surround; (*fig.*) to dupe.
aggirarsi, *v.r.* To go about, to ramble, to roam, to rove; to loiter.
aggirata, *n.f.* Turn.
aggirato, *a.* Tortuous, twisting.
aggiudicare, *v.t.* To award, to grant; to decree.
aggiudicarsi, *v.r.* To claim for oneself.
aggiudicazione, *n.f.* Award; (*Law*) adjudication; contract.
aggiungere [aggiUngere], *v.t.* To add, to join; to adjoin, to increase. **— qualche parola,** Addition, to add a few words.
aggiungimento, *n.m.* Addition, joining, union.
aggiunta, *n.f.* Addition, increase; interpolation; (*Comm.*) rider.
aggiuntivo, *a.* Additional.
aggiunto, *p.p.a.* Added, attached.
aggiustabile [aggiustAbile], *a.* Adjustable.
aggiustaggio [aggiustAggio], *n.m.* (*Mech.*) Fitting.
aggiustamento, *n.m.* Adjustment, settlement, arrangement.
aggiustare, *v.t.* To adjust, to arrange; to settle; to mend; to repair; to aim at. **— una macchina,** to repair a machine; **— il colpo,** to aim a shot; **— un conto,** to settle an account; **— le cose,** to arrange matters; **vi aggiusterò io!** I'll pay you out!
aggiustarsi, *v.r.* To arrange oneself; to manage; to agree; to come to an agreement.
aggiustatamente, *adv.* Exactly, precisely.
aggiustatezza, *n.f.* Accuracy, precision; fitness.
aggiustatore, *n.m.* Fitter (mechanician).
aggiustatura, *n.f.* Repair; mending.
agglomeramento, *n.m.* Agglomeration; crowding, overcrowding. **— nelle città,** overcrowding in cities.
agglomerare, *v.t.* To agglomerate; to crowd; to gather.
agglomerazione, *n.f.* Agglomeration.
agglutinamento, *n.m.* Agglutination.
agglutinante, *a.* Agglutinate; sticky, gluey.
agglutinare, *v.t.* To agglutinate; to glue together.
agglutinativo, *a.* Agglutinative.
agglutinazione, *n.f.* Agglutination.
aggobbire, *v.t.i.* To render or become hunchbacked; to toil.
aggomitolare, *v.t.* To wind, to wind into a ball.
aggomitolarsi, *v.r.* To coil oneself up; to gather into knots.
aggomitolatura, *n.f.* Winding.
aggottamento, *n.m.* Draining.
aggottare, *v.t.* To drain (a pond, canal, etc.); to bale out a boat.**— una nave,** to pump a vessel dry.
aggottatura, *n.f.* Draining, pumping dry.
aggradare, *v.t.* To please. **Come vi aggrada,** as it pleases you.
aggradevole [aggradEvole], *a.* Pleasing, agreeable.
aggradevolmente, *adv.* Agreeably.
aggradimento, *n.m.* Approbation, approval, consent; pleasure, enjoyment; liking; agreement.
aggradire, *v.i.* To accept; to please, to like; to relish (taste). **Vi piaccia — i miei ringraziamenti,** please accept my thanks; **ciò non mi aggradisce,** I don't like it; **farò come vi aggrada,** I will do what you like.
aggraffare, *v.t.* To clasp; to pick up with the nails or with a hook.
aggraffignare, *v.t.* To claw, to seize with the claws.
aggranchiare, aggranchire, *v.i.* To become numbed (esp. of the fingers); to get stiff with cold.
aggrandimento, *n.m.* Enlargement, aggrandisement; (*fig.*) increase; elevation.
aggrandire, *v.t.* To enlarge; to exaggerate, to extend; (*fig.*) to elevate.
aggrandirsi, *v.r.* To grow larger, to increase; to advance.
aggrappare, *v.t.* To grapple, to hook. **— un nave,** to grapple a ship.
aggrapparsi, *v.r.* To cling to, to hold on tight, to stick to.
aggrappolato, *a.* Clustered, in a bunch.
aggraticciare, *v.t.* To twist together.
aggravamento, *n.m.* Becoming worse (of an illness); getting more serious; aggravation. (*Law*) **— di pena,** increased sentence.
aggravante, *pres.p.a.* Making worse; growing more serious; aggravating; compromising.
aggravare, *v.t.* To aggravate, to make worse; to overcharge. **— lo stato delle cose,** to make matters worse; **— la colpa,** to aggravate the guilt; (*Law*) **— la pena,** to increase the sentence; **— di lavoro,** to put too great a burden upon, to overwork.
aggravarsi, *v.r.* To become worse ; to overburden oneself; **— di vestiti,** to put on too many clothes. **— degli anni,** to feel the weight of one's years.
aggravazione, *n.f.* Worsening.
aggravio [aggrAvio], *n.m.* Burden (of taxes, etc.), charge; damage; imposition; inconvenience. **Essere di — a,** to be a burden upon.
aggraziare, *v.t.* To make graceful, to give grace to.
aggraziarsi, *v.r.* **— con qualcuno,** to gain someone's sympathy.
aggraziatamente, *adv.* Gracefully.
aggraziato, *a.* Graceful; pleasant tasting (of medicine).
aggredire, *v.t.* To attack, to assail.
aggregamento, *n.m.* Aggregation.
aggregare, *v.t.* To admit into a society or association; to join one thing to another.
aggregarsi, *v.r.* To become joined together; to join a society.
aggregato, *n.* Aggregate; an academical title, *e.g.* Fellow.
aggregazione, *n.f.* Aggregation; fellowship (of a society, etc.). **Forza di —,** molecular attraction.

aggressione, *n.f.* Aggression, attack. **Commettere un'— contro,** to commit an assault upon.
aggressività [-à], *n.f.* Aggressiveness.
aggressivo, *a.* Aggressive.
aggressore, *n.m.* Aggressor.
aggrinzamento, *n.m.* Wrinkling, frowning.
aggrinzare, aggrinzire, *v.i.* To wrinkle, to frown; to gather (needlework). **— le pelle,** to wrinkle the skin.
aggrinzarsi, aggrinzirsi, *v.r.* To wrinkle, to contract; to ripple; to shrivel.
aggrottamento, *n.m.* Knitting of the brows, frowning, frown.
aggrottare, *v.t.* To frown. **— le ciglia,** to knit the brows, to frown.
aggrovigliamento, *n.m.* Winding; entanglement.
aggrovigliare, *v.t.* To wind; to entangle.
aggrovigliarsi, *v.r.* To kink (of string, etc.); to get wound up in a ball; to become entangled.
aggrovigliato, *p.p.a.* Entangled; in kinks; intricate, obscure.
aggrumamento, *n.m.* Coagulation, clotting (of blood); curdling.
aggrumare, *v.t.* To collect; to clot; to curdle.
aggrumarsi, *v.r.* To coagulate; to form a crust; to clot; to curdle.
aggrumato, *p.p.a.* Coagulated; curdled; crusted.
aggruppamento, *n.m.* Grouping; knotting.
aggruppare, *v.t.* To group; to knot; to collect in a bunch.
aggrupparsi, *v.r.* To group, to form into groups; to collect in a group; to form into knots.
aggruzzolare, *v.t.* To collect savings; to scrape together (money); to save up.
agguagliabile [agguagliAbile], *a.* Capable of being made equal.
agguagliamento, *n.m.* Equalization; levelling.
agguagliare, *v.t.* To make equal; to make smooth, to level; to compare; *(Print.)* to justify.
agguaglio [agguAglio], *n.m.* Equality; comparison. **Non c'è — fra,** there is no comparison between.
agguantare, *v.t.* To catch forcibly; to seize; to grasp, to snatch; to steal. *(Naut.)* **Agguanta!** Hold on!
agguatare, *v.t.* To watch for; to lie in wait; to dog.
agguato, *n.m.* Ambush; snare; *(Mil.)* ambush, ambuscade. **Essere in —, tendere un —,** to lie in wait; **cadere in un —,** to fall into a snare; **stare in agguato,** to be on the lookout.
agguerrimento, *n.m.* Inuring to warfare; training for war.
agguerrire, *v.i.* To train for warfare; to inure to war hardships.
agguerrirsi, *v.r.* To become inured to hardships; to grow warlike.
agguindolamento, *n.m.* Wool-winding; reeling off.
agguindolare, *v.t.* To wind wool upon the bobbin.
aghetto, *n.m.* Tag of a bootlace; bootlace.
aghiforme, *a.* Needle-shaped (of crystals).
agiatamente, *adv.* In ease and comfort; commodiously. **Vivere —,** to be in easy circumstances.
agiatezza, *n.f.* Ease, comfort; easy circumstances. **Vive in —,** he is comfortably off.
agiato, *a.* Well-to-do, rich; deliberate in movement, sedate.
agile [Agile], *a.* Agile; light of foot.
agilità [-à], *n.f.* Agility, nimbleness.
agilmente,*adv.* With agility, nimbly.
agio [Agio], *n.m.* Ease, comfort; convenience; leisure. **A bell'—,** at one's convenience, at one's leisure; **trovarsi ad —,** to be at ease; **avere — di,** to be at leisure to; **dare —,** to offer the opportunity.
agiografia [agiografIa], *n.f.* Hagiography.
agire, *v.t.* To act, to behave; to work (of a machine); to proceed. **— per proprio conto,** to act on one's own account; **— nell'interesse di,** to act in the interests of, on behalf of; **meccanismo che non agisce,** mechanism that does not work.
agitare, *v.t.* To agitate, to shake, to stir, to toss; *(fig.)* to excite, to trouble; to discuss, to examine. **— una lite,** to carry on a law suit; **— la mano,** to wave one's hand in farewell; **— un liquido,** to stir a liquid.
agitarsi, *v.r.* To agitate oneself; to move about; to become agitated, to be troubled. **— nell'acqua,** to flounder in the water; **il mare si agita,** the sea is getting rough.
agitato, *p.p.a.* Agitated, shaken, stirred, tossed, waved; excited, troubled; examined.
agitatore, agitatrice, *n.m.f.* Political agitator; ringleader.
agitazione, *n.f.* Agitation, excitement; swell of the sea.
agli. At the, to the, on the [cp. **a**].
agliaio [agliAio], *n.f.* Vendor of garlic.
agliata, *n.f.* Garlic sauce.
aglio [Aglio], *n.m.* Garlic. **Mangiar l'—,** to fume, to rage in silence.
agnatizio [agnatIzio], *a.* *(Law)* Agnatic, agnate.
agnato, *n.m.a.* *(Law)* Agnate; allied.
agnazione, *n.f.* *(Law)* Agnation.
agnella, *n.f.* Ewe lamb.
agnellaio [agnellAio], *n.m.* Vendor, butcher of lamb.
agnellatura, *n.f.* Lambing season; lambing.
agnelletto, agnellino, *n.m.* Lambkin.
agnello, *n.m.* Lamb; *(fig.)* milksop; sheepish person.
agnellotto, *n.m.* Well-grown lamb; dumpling stuffed with meat or herbs.
agnizione, *n.f.* *(Law)* Agnition; recognition.
agnolo [cp. **angelo**].
agnosticismo, *n.m.* Agnosticism.
agnostico [agnOstico], *n.m.a.* Agnostic.
ago, *n.m.* Needle, hand (of a clock, etc.); spire; compass-needle; tongue (of a balance). **— per maglieria,** knitting-needle; **— da rammendo,** darning-needle; **cruna dell'—,** eye of the needle; **lavoro ad —,** needlework.
agognare, *v.t.* To covet; to desire eagerly, to hanker after; to long for.
agonale, *a.* Pertaining to the circus.
agone (1), *n.m.* Packing needle.
agone (2), *n.m.* Fight, battle, contest, struggle; wrestling match; arena, field. **Scendere nell'—,** to enter the lists.
agone (3), *n.m.* *(Zool.)* *Alosa vulgaris,* a fresh water fish.

agonia [agonIa], *n.m.* Agony, anguish; anxiety; torment. **Essere in —, nell'—,** to be at the point of death.
agonistica [agonIstica], *n.f.* Athletics.
agonizzante, *p.p.a.* Dying; agonizing.
agonizzare, *v.i.* To be at the point of death.
agostano, agostino, *a.* Of the month of August.
Agostino, *n.m.* Augustine.
agosto, *n.m.* The month of August.
agramente, *adv.* Bitterly; gruffly; harshly; sourly.
agrario [agrArio], *n.m.a.* Landowner; agrarian.
agrestamente, *adv.* Rustically, rurally.
agreste, *a.* Rural, rustic; wild.
agrestezza, *n.f.* Sourness, rusticity.
agrestino, *a.* Rather sour, sourish.
agresto, *n.m.* Verjuice. (*fig.*) **Fare —,** to get a rake-off.
agresto, *a.* Sour.
agrestume, *n.m.* Sourness.
agretto, *a.* Sourish, rather sour.
agrezza, *n.f.* Sourness, acidity; harshness.
agricolo [agrIcolo], *a.* Agricultural. **Prodotti agricoli,** farm produce.
agricoltore, *n.m.* Agriculturist, farmer.
agricoltura, *n.f.* Agriculture.
agrifoglio [agrifOglio], *n.m.* (*Bot.*) Holly.
agrigno, *a.* Sharp; bitter.
agrimensore, *n.m.* Land surveyor.
agrimensura, *n.f.* Land surveying.
agrimonia [agrimOnia], *n.f.* (*Bot.*) Agrimony.
agro, *n.m.* Rural surroundings of a town.
agro, *a.* Sour, acid, harsh, sharp, pungent, tart.
agrodolce, *n.m.* (*Bot.*) Woody nightshade, bitter sweet.
agrodolce, *a.* Sourish, rather bitter.
agronomia [agronomIa], *n.f.* Agronomy, rural economy.
agronomico [agronOmico], *a.* Agricultural.
agronomo [agrOnomo], *n.m.* Agriculturist.
agrumeto, *n.m.* Orange or lemon orchard.
agrumi, *n.m.pl.* Citrus fruits.
agucchiare, *v.t.* To sew, to sew up, to stitch.
aguglia [agUglia], *n.f.* Church spire; bar of magnet; compass needle.
agugliata, *n.f.* Needleful.
aguglione, *n.m.* Sting; prick.
aguzzamento, *n.m.* Sharpening, whetting.
aguzzare, *v.t.* To point; to sharpen, to whet; (*fig.*) to stimulate, to excite. **— l'appetito,** to sharpen the appetite.
aguzzarsi, *v.r.* To become pointed; (*fig.*) to quicken, to sharpen one's wits.
aguzzato, *p.p.a.* Pointed, sharpened; whetted.
aguzzatura, *n.f.* Sharpening, whetting.
aguzzino, *n.m.* Prison warder, jailer; tyrant. **Fare l'—,** to tyrannize.
aguzzo, *a.* Pointed, sharp.
ahi! *inter.* Oh! Oh dear!
ahimè!, *inter.* Alas!
ahibò!, *inter.* [cp. **oibò**].
ai. To the [cp. **a**].
aia [Aia] (1), *n.f.* Threshing-floor. **Menare il can per l'—,** to put off, to protract.
aia [Aia] (2), *n.f.* Governess.
Aia [Aia] (3), *n.f.* The Hague.
Aiace, *n.m.* (*Myth.*) Ajax.
aio [Aio], *n.m.* Tutor, teacher, coach.
aire, *n.m.* Flight; swing. **Dare l'— a,** to give a swing to, to give scope to.
airone, *n.m.* (*Zool.*) Heron.
aita, *n.f.* (*Poet.*) Help. **Aita! Help!**
aitante, *n.m.* Strong, robust, sturdy.
aiuola, *n.f.* Flower-bed.
aiuolo, *n.m.* Birdcatcher's net.
aiutante, *n.m.* Assistant, co-adjutor, helper, workmate; (*Mil.*) adjutant. **— di campo,** aide-de-camp.
aiutante, *a.* Aiding, helping, assisting.
aiutare, *v.t.* To aid, to help, to assist; to relieve; to lend a hand.
aiutarsi, *v.r.* To help oneself; to help one another. **Chi s'aiuta Dio l'aiuta,** God helps those who help themselves.
aiutato, *p.p.a.* Aided, assisted, helped; succoured.
aiutatore, aiutatrice, *n.m.f.* Helper, assistant.
aiuto, *n.m.* Aid, assistance, help; protection. **Chiamare —,** to call for help; **venire in —,** to lend help; **con l'— di,** by the help of; **Dio mi dia —!** So help me God! **Aiuto!** Help!
aizzamento, *n.m.* Instigation; provocation.
aizzare, *v.t.* To enrage, to irritate, to provoke; to excite; to instigate. **— i cani l'uno contro l'altro,** to set the dogs on one another.
al. At the, to the, on the [cp. **a**].
ala (*pl.* **ali**), *n.f.* Wing; blade (of an oar); yard (of ship); sail (of windmill); wing (of aeroplane; arm (of semaphore); (*fig.*) protection; aisle. **Far —,** to make room; **batter le ali,** to flutter the wings; (*Football*) **ala destra, sinistra,** right, left wing.
alabarda, *n.f.* Halberd.
alabardiere, *n.m.* Halberdier.
alabastraio [alabastrAio], *n.m.* Worker in alabaster.
alabastrino, *a.* Alabaster; (*fig.*) very white.
alabastro [alabAstro], *n.m.* Alabaster.
alacre [Alacre, alAcre], *a.* Active, brisk, busy, ready, expeditious, laborious.
alacremente, *adv.* Briskly; diligently; promptly.
alacrità [-à], *n.f.* Alacrity.
alaggio [alaggIo], *n.m.* Pulling, towing; warping.
alamaro, *n.m.* Loop of lace; frog (on uniform); braid.
alambicco, *n.m.* Still (for making spirits, etc.).
alano, *n.m.* Boar-hound; bull-dog.
alare, *v.t.* To haul, to heave; to tow. **— un bastimento,** to warp a vessel.
alare, *n.m.* Andiron, fire-dog.
alarsi, *v.r.* (*Naut.*) To haul to windward.
alata, *n.f.* Blow with the wing.
alato, *a.* Winged; fitted with wings.
alba, *n.f.* Daybreak, dawn. **All'—,** at daybreak.
albagia [albagIa], *n.f.* Conceit; haughtiness. **Gonfio di —,** puffed up with self-conceit.
albanese, *a.* Albanian. **Fare l'—,** to feign stupidity.
albaro, alberello [Albaro], *n.m.* (*Bot.*) White poplar.
albatro [Albatro], *n.m.* (*Bot.*) Arbutus; (*Zool.*) albatross.
albedine [albEdine], *a.* Whiteness.
albeggiamento, *n.m.* Break of day.
albeggiare, *v.i.* To dawn; (*fig.*) to be whitish.
alberare, *v.t.* To plant trees; (*Naut.*) to mast a vessel.
alberato, *a.* Planted with trees.

alberatura, *n.f.* (*Naut.*) Masting, masts and yards; rig.
alberella, *n.f.* (*Bot.*) Aspen tree.
alberello, *n.m.* Shrub; low tree, sapling; pot for toilet cream, etc.; paint-pot.
alberese, *n.m.* (*Geol.*) Limestone.
albereto, *n.f.* Plantation.
alberetto, *n.m.* Dwarf tree; shrub.
albergare, *v.t.i.* To harbour, to lodge, to shelter; to put up, to stay (at an inn); to dwell.
albergatore, albergatrice, *n.m.f.* Innkeeper, landlord, landlady, hotel-keeper.
albergo, *n.m.* Hotel, inn. **— per famiglie,** residential hotel; **— diurno,** public convenience.
alberino, *n.m.* Shrub.
albero [Albero], *n.m.* Tree; mast; pedigree; (*Mech.*) arbour, shaft. **— guasto,** tree-stump; **— sempreverde,** evergreen; (*Naut.*) **— di fortuna,** jury mast; **— di maestra,** mainmast; **— di trinchetto,** foremast; **— di mezzana,** mizenmast; **— di parrocchetto,** topmast; **— di bompresso,** bowsprit; (*Motor.*) **— a cardano,** cardan shaft; **— dei cammi,** cam-shaft; **— a manovella, a gomito,** crank-shaft.
alberone, *n.m.* Big tree.
albiccio [albIccio], *a.* Whitish.
albicocca, *n.f.* Apricot.
albicocco, *n.m.* Apricot tree.
albinismo, *n.m.* Albinism.
albino, *n.m.a.* Albino; whitish.
albo, *n.m.* Album; electoral register; bill board.
albo, *a.* White; (*Bot.*) having white bark.
albore, *n.m.* Brightness. **Ai primi albori,** at dawn.
album, *n.m.* Album.
albume, *n.m.* Albumen; white of an egg.
albumina, *n.f.* Albumin.
albuminoso, *a.* Albuminose.
alburno, *n.m.* (*Bot.*) Alburnum, sapwood.
alcaico [alcAico], *a.* (*Poet.*) Alcaic.
alcalescente, *a.* Alkalescent.
alcalescenza, *n.f.* Alkalescence.
alcali [Alkali], *n.m.* (*Chem.*) Alkali.
alcalinità [-à], *n.f.* Alkalinity.
alcalino, *a.* Alkaline.
alcalizzare, *v.t.* To alkalize.
alcalizzazione, *n.f.* Alkalization.
alcaloide [alcalOide], *n.m.* Alkaloid.
alcanna, *n.f.* Henna.
alce, *n.m.* (*Zool.*) Elk.
alchermes, *n.m.* Kermes; cochineal.
alchimia, *n.f.* Alchemy.
alchimico [alchImico], *a.* Pertaining to alchemy.
alchimista (*pl.* **alchimisti**), *n.m.* Alchemist.
alcione, *n.m.* Halcyon; (*Zool.*) kingfisher.
alcool [Alcool], *n.m.* Alcohol. **— denaturato,** methylated spirits.
alcoolico [alcoOlico], *a.* Alcoholic.
alcoolismo, *n.m.* (*Med.*) Alcoholism.
alcoolista, *n.m.* Alcoholic, victim of alcoholism.
alcoolizzare, *v.t.* To alcoholize.
alcoolizzato, *p.p.a.* Alcoholized.
alcoolizazzione, *n.f.* Alcoholization.
alcova, *n.f.* Alcove, recess.
alcunchè, *pron.* Anything, something.
alcuno, *a. pron.* Some, someone, somebody; anyone, anything; none, no one, not one, nobody. **Alcuni anni fa,** some years ago; **ho alcuni amici,** I have some friends; **non vi è — in casa,** there is nobody at home; **l'ho trovato senza alcuna difficoltà,** I found it without any difficulty.
alea [Alea], *n.f.* Chance, risk. **Correre l'—,** to run the risk.
aleatico [aleAtico], *n.m.* A sweet Tuscan grape; the wine made from this.
aleatorio [aleatOrio], *a.* Aleatory, depending on contingencies.
aleggiare, *v.i.* To flutter, to flap.
alerone, *n.m.* (*Aviat.*) Aileron.
alesaggio [alesAggio], *n.m.* (*Mech.*) Boring, drilling; bore (of cylinder).
alesare, *v.t.* To bore, to drill, to bore out, to ream.
Alessandria [alessAndria], *n.f.* Alessandria (in Italy). **Alessandria d'Egitto,** Alexandria (in Egypt).
alessandrino, *a.* (*Poet.*) Alexandrine.
Alessandro [alessAndro], *n.m.* Alexander.
aletta, *n.f.* Small wing; fin.
alfa, *n.f.* Alpha; (*Mech.*) float-board.
alfabettare, *v.t.* To alphabetize, to place in alphabetical order.
alfabeticamente, *adv.* Alphabetically.
alfabetico [alfabEtico], *a.* Alphabetical.
alfabeto, *n.m.* Alphabet.
alfiere, *n.m.* Standard-bearer; (*Chess*) bishop.
alfine, *adv.* At last, at length; in the long run; after all.
alga, *n.f.* Alga, seaweed.
algebra [Algebra], *n.f.* Algebra.
algebricamente, *adv.* Algebraically.
algebrico [algEbrico], *a.* Algebraical.
algebrista (*pl.* **algebristi**), *n.m.* Algebraist.
algente, *a.* *p.p.a.* Frozen, cold; freezing.
algere, *v.i.* (*Poet. obs.*) To be cold; to freeze.
Algeri [Algeri], *n.f.* Algiers.
Algeria [algerIa], *n.f.* Algeria.
algerino, *n.m.a.* Algerian.
algidità [-à], *n.f.* Intense cold.
algido [Algido], *a.* Cold as ice.
algore, *n.m.* Intense cold.
algoso, aligoso, *a.* Abounding in seaweed.
aliante, *n.m.* (*Aviat.*) Glider.
aliare, *v.i.* To flutter.
alibi [Alibi], *n.m.* (*Law*) Alibi. **Presentare un —,** to set up an alibi.
alice, *n.f.* (*Zool.*) Anchovy. **Alici sott'olio,** anchovies in oil.
alidada, *n.f.* Alidad.
alidezza, *n.f.* Dryness; aridity.
alidire, *v.i.* To dry out.
alido [Alido], *a.* Dry, arid; lean.
alidore, *n.m.* Aridity, dryness.
alienabile [alienAbile], *a.* Alienable.
alienabilità [-à], *n.f.* Alienability.
alienamento, *n.m.* Alienation; estrangement. **— mentale,** mental alienation.
alienare, *v.t.* To alienate; to estrange, to disaffect; to transfer; to sell.
alienarsi, *v.r.* To alienate, to drive away, to become alienated, to become estranged. **Si è alienata la mia amicizia,** he has estranged himself from me.
alienato, *n.m.* Lunatic. **Ospizio per gli alienati,** mental hospital.

alienato, *a.* Alienated; estranged, disaffected; deranged in mind, mad.
alienatore, *n.m.* (*Law*) Alienator.
alienazione, *n.f.* Alienation; estrangement; mental derangement.
alienista (*pl.* **alienisti**), *n.m.* Alienist, psychiatrist.
alieno, *a.* Alien, foreign; adverse, contrary.
alimentare, *v.t.* To feed, to maintain; to entertain; to feed on. **— le caldaie,** to stoke up the boilers.
alimentare, alimentario, *a.* Alimentary, nutritive. **Pensione —,** maintenance; **prodotti alimentari,** foodstuffs; **assegno —** alimony.
alimentarsi, *v.r.* To feed upon.
alimentatore, *n.m.* Nourisher; (*Mech.*) feeder.
alimentazione, *n.m.* Feeding.
alimenti, *n.m.pl.* (*Law*) Alimony; maintenance.
alimento, *n.m.* Aliment, food.
alinea [alInea], *n.m.* (*Print.*) New paragraph.
alipede [alIpede], *a.* (*Poet.*) With winged feet; speedy.
aliquota [alIquota], *n.f.* Aliquot part; rate.
aliquoto [alIquoto], *a.* Aliquot.
aliseo [alisEo], *n.m.* Trade wind.
alitare, *v.i.* To breathe; to pant.
alito [Alito], *n.m.* Breath; light breeze, puff of wind. **Riaver l'—**, to recover one's breath.
alla. At the, to the, on the [cp. **a**].
allacciabottoni, *n.m.* Button-hook.
allacciamento, *n.m.* Lacing, entwining; linking up (*e.g.* by telephone); (*Med.*) ligature. **Binario di —,** cross-over road.
allacciare, *v.t.* To lace; to twine; (*Med.*) to tie an artery; (*Naut.*) to make fast, to lash.
allacciarsi, *v.r.* To lace oneself up; to link.
allacciato, *p.p.a.* Laced, tied together; connected; entangled. **Scarpe allacciate,** laced shoes.
allacciatura, *n.f.* Lacing; linking up.
allagamento, *n.m.* Flood; inundation; overflow.
allagare, *v.t.* To flood, to inundate; to overflow; to submerge.
allagarsi, *v.r.* To be flooded.
allagato, *p.p.a.* Flooded, submerged.
allampanare, *v.i.* To grow lean with starvation; to get lean; to be very hungry, to be famished.
allampanato, *p.p.a.* Lean, emaciated; meagre.
allampare, *v.i.* To be very thirsty, to burn with thirst. **Ho una sete che allampo,** I am consumed with thirst.
allampato, *a.* Thirsty.
allappare, *v.t.* To set the teeth on edge, to be bitter.
allargamento, *n.m.* Enlargement; expansion.
allargare, *v.t.* To enlarge, to amplify, to widen, to let out (a garment); (*Naut.*) to put out, to put to sea; (*Meteor.*) to become calm. **— la mano,** to be open-handed; **— un vestito,** to let out a suit.
allargarsi, *v.r.* To be enlarged; to extend, to spread; (*Naut.*) to sheer off. **Il fuoco s'allarga,** the fire is spreading; **la città s'allarga** the city is spreading out; **l'imbarcazione s'allarga,** the boat puts off.
allargata, *n.f.* Enlargement.
allargatoio [allargatOio], *n.m.* (*Mech.*) Drill, borer.
allargatura, *n.f.* Enlargement, widening; extending.
allarmante, *adv.* Alarming.
allarmare, *v.t.* To alarm, to raise the alarm.
allarmarsi, *v.r.* To take alarm, to be alarmed.
allarme, *n.m.* Alarm; fright; tumult. **Segnale d'—,** alarm signal; **dare l'— aereo,** to give an air-raid warning; **cessato — !** All clear!
all'armi! *inter.* (*Mil.*) To arms! Stand to!
allarmista, *n.m.f.* Alarmist.
allato, a lato, *prep.* Near [cp. **accanto**].
allattamento, *n.m.* Suckling, giving suck to, nourishment; lactation.
allattare, *v.t.* To give suck to, to suckle, to nurse.
allattarsi, *v.r.* To suck (at the breast).
allattatrice, *n.f.* Wet nurse.
alle. To the, at the, on the [cp. **a**].
alleanza, *n.f.* Alliance, league; pact; union.
allearsi, *v.r.* To form an alliance; to unite.
alleato, *n.m.* Ally; confederate. **Gli Alleati,** the Allies.
allegabile [allegAbile], *a.* Adducible; (*Metal.*) alloyable.
allegamento, *n.m.* Setting the teeth on edge.
allegare, *v.t.* To adduce; to allege, to urge; to cite; to plead; to set on edge; (*Comm.*) to enclose; (*Metal.*) to alloy. **— un fatto,** to allege a fact; **— una scusa,** to plead an excuse.
allegato, *n.m.* Enclosure, document enclosed.
allegazione, *n.f.* Allegation; (*Metal.*) alloy.
alleggerimento, *n.m.* Lightening, easing, alleviation; relief.
alleggerire, *v.t.* To lighten; to alleviate, to ease; to mitigate. **— un carico,** to lighten a burden; **— uno,** to rob, or cheat someone.
alleggerirsi, *v.r.* To become lighter; to put on lighter clothing.
alleggerito, *p.p.a.* Lightened; alleviated, mitigated.
alleggiare, *v.t.* (*obs.*) To lighten.
alleggio [allEggio], *n.m.* (*Naut.*) Lighter, barge.
allegoria [allegorIa], *n.f.* Allegory.
allegoricamente, *adv.* Allegorically.
allegorico [allegOrico], *a.* Allegorical; rhetorical.
allegramente, *adv.* Cheerfully, gaily; easily (*colloq.*) **prendila —,** take it easy, don't strain yourself.
allegrare, *v.t.* To make glad, to gladden; to cheer up.
allegrarsi, *v.r.* To rejoice; to be delighted; to cheer oneself up, to cheer up; to congratulate. **Ci allegriamo pel vostro arrivo,** We are glad you have come.
allegretto, *a.* Rather jolly, (*Mus.*) somewhat brisk.
allegrezza, *n.f.* Cheerfulness; jolliness; merriment; gaiety.
allegria [allegrIa], *n.f.* Gaiety, merriment; cheerfulness, jolliness, mirth. **Far —,** to amuse oneself, to enjoy oneself.
allegro, *a.* Cheerful, gay, merry; good-humoured, lively; (*Mus.*) fast. **Stare —,** to be merry; **auguri allegri,** cheerful forecast.
alleluia [allelUia], *n.m.* Hallelujah; joyful praise.
allenamento, *n.m.* Training, keeping fit (of the body).

allenare, *v.t.* To train (athletically), to strengthen, to make fit.
allenarsi, *v.r.* To put oneself in training, to make oneself fit.
allenato, *p.p.a.* In training, in good trim physically.
allenatore, *n.m.* Trainer.
allenire, *v.t.* To soften, to alleviate.
allenirsi, *v.r.* (*obs.*) To get tired.
allentamento, *n.m.* Relaxation, slackening; slackening of speed. **— del freno,** release of the brake.
allentare, *v.t.* To loosen, to slacken, to relax. **— la disciplina,** to slacken the discipline; **— le redini,** to slacken the reins; **— la velocità,** to slacken the speed.
allentarsi, *v.r.* To become slack; to become relaxed; to work loose; (*Med.*) to rupture oneself.
allentato, *p.p.a.* Loose, loosened, slackened; worked loose; (*Med.*) ruptured. **Una fune allentata,** a slack rope; **la vite si è —,** the screw has worked loose.
allentatura, *n.f.* (*Med.*) Hernia, rupture.
allergia [allergIa], *n.f.* (*Med.*) Allergy.
allergico [allErgico], *a.* (*Med.*) Allergic.
allessamento, *n.m.* Boiling (in water).
allessare, *v.t.* To boil (in water).
allesso, *n.m.* Boiled meat. **Chi la vuole — e chi arrosto,** some want it one way and some another.
allestimento, *n.m.* Preparation; (*Naut.*) fitting out (of a ship).
allestire, *v.t.* To make ready, to prepare; (*Naut.*) to rig out a vessel, to equip her. **— il pranzo,** to get dinner ready.
allestirsi, *v.r.* To prepare oneself, to get ready.
allestito, *p.p.a.* Ready, prepared; dressed; (*Naut.*) rigged.
alletamare, *v.t.* (*Agric.*) To manure, to dung.
allettamento, *n.m.* Allurement (in all senses); attraction.
allettante, *a.* Alluring, charming; wheedling.
allettare, *v.t.* To allure (in all senses); to entice, to ensnare; to wheedle.
allettarsi, *v.r.* To take to one's bed, to keep one's bed; to be bedridden; to be flattened (of crops, by the wind).
allettativa, *n.f.* Allurement.
allettatore, allettatrice, *n.m.f.* Enticer, seducer.
alletterato, *a.* [cp. **letterato**].
allettevole [allettEvole], *a.* Attractive.
allevamento, *n.m.* Bringing up (of young), rearing; care of babies; lactation; breeding.
allevare, *v.t.* To rear (young); to bring up (a family); to breed; to nurse; to give early education.
allevato, *p.p.a.* Brought up, bred; educated. **Bene —,** well bred.
allevatore, *n.m.* Breeder. **— di bestiame,** cattle breeder.
alleviagione, *n.f.* **alleviamento,** *n.m.* Alleviation, relief, mitigation.
alleviare, *v.t.* To alleviate, to allay; to appease; to lighten; to relieve; to soothe. **— un bisogno,** to relieve a necessity; **— un dolore,** to relieve a pain, to soothe.
alleviarsi, *v.r.* (*obs.*) To be delivered (of a child).
allibbimento, *n.m.* Astonishment.
allibbire, allibire, *v.i.* To turn pale (with fear); to be taken aback; to be terrified.
allibramento, *n.m.* (*Comm.*) Booking, entering up (in ledger, etc.).
allibrare, *v.t.* (*Comm.*) To book, to enter.
allibratore, *n.m.* Bookmaker, bookie.
allicciare, *v.t.* To throw (in weaving).
allietare, *v.t.* To cheer (the spirits), to make happy; to delight; to enliven.
allietarsi, *v.r.* To become cheerful, to become light-hearted.
allievo, *n.m.* Pupil, schoolboy, student; apprentice; (*Mil. Naut.*) cadet; sucking calf or foal. **— di marina,** midshipman, apprentice at sea; **— ufficiale aviatore,** cadet in Air Force, Flying Cadet.
alligatore, *n.m.* (*Zool.*) Alligator.
allignare, *v.t.* (*Bot.*) To put forth, to take root; to thrive.
allineamento, *n.m.* Alignment, alinement; (*Print.*) ranging.
allineare, *v.t.* To aline, to set in a line; (*Mil.*) to form up, to put in ranks; (*Print.*) to range.
allinearsi, *v.r.* (*Mil.*) To dress (the ranks). **— a destra,** right dress.
allitterazione, *n.f.* Alliteration.
allivellare, *v.t.* To level.
allivellazione, *n.f.* Levelling, level.
allividire, *v.i.* To turn pale.
allo. To the, at the, on the [cp. **a**].
allocco, *n.m.* (*Zool.*) Owl; (*fig.*) silly, booby, ninny. **Fare l'—,** to play the booby.
alloccone, *n.m.* (*fig.*) Numskull, stupid, dolt.
allocuzione, *n.f.* Allocution; papal pronouncement.
allodola [allOdola], *n.f.* (*Zool.*) Skylark, lark.
allogamento, *n.m.* Location of, placing; allotting; (*Fin.*) investing, investment.
allogare, *v.t.* To place; to let out; to hire; to employ; (*Fin.*) to invest. **— una figlia,** to marry off a daughter.
allogarsi, *v.r.* To place oneself; to take employment; to get married.
allogazione, *n.f.* Employment.
allogeno [allOgeno], *n.m.* Alien; foreigner.
alloggiamento, *n.m.* Lodgings, rooms; (*Mil.*) quarters; encampment.
alloggiare, *v.t.i.* To lodge, accommodate; to live; (*Mil.*) to quarter, to billet. **— in stanze,** to live in rooms; **può alloggiarmi per questa notte?** can you put me up for the night?
alloggiato, *p.p.a.* Lodged, housed for a short time; (*Mil.*) billeted.
alloggiatore, alloggiatrice, *n.m.f.* Lodging-house keeper; innkeeper; host, hostess.
alloggio [allOggio], *n.m.* Lodging, lodgings; lodging-house; accommodation; quarters. **— ammobigliato,** furnished rooms; (*Mil.*) **maresciallo d'—,** quartermaster; **biglietto d'—,** billeting ticket; (*Naut.*) **— d'equipaggio,** crew's quarters, fo'csle.
allogliato, *a.* (*Agric.*) Full of tares or cockle.
allontanamento, *n.m.* Absence; removal to a distance; estrangement.
allontanare, *v.t.* To dismiss, to send away, to lead away, to drive away; to remove; to separate. **Fu allontanato dai suoi amici,** he was taken away by his friends; **allontanalo!** Send him off!

allontanarsi, *v.r.* To go away, to go off, to go far away; to stand aloof; to swerve (from one's duty, etc.); to be alienated or estranged. **S'allontanò dalla sua casa,** he left his house.
allopatia [allopatIa], *n.f.* (*Med.*) Allopathy.
allopatico [allopAtico], *a.* Allopathical, according to allopathy.
alloppiare, *v.t.* To put opium into, to drug with opium.
alloppiarsi, *v.r.* To go fast asleep, to sleep profoundly.
allora, *adv.* Then, at that time; in that case. **D'— in poi,** from that time, since then; **per —,** for the time being; **sino —,** until then; **—, rispondete!** answer, then! **— —,** in that moment.
allorchè, *adv.* When, whilst; at the moment that.
alloro, *n.m.* (*Bot.*) Laurel. **Cinto d'—,** crowned with laurels.
allorquando, *adv.* At the time when.
allotropia [allotropIa], *n.f.* (*Chem.,* etc.) Allotropy.
allottare, *v.t.* To allot; to put up to lottery, to raffle.
alluce [Alluce], *n.m.* Great toe.
alluciare, *v.t.* To stare about one.
allucignolare, *v.t.* To crumple (clothes, etc.), to wrinkle.
allucignolarsi, *v.r.* To get crumpled (of clothes).
allucinare, *v.t.* To dazzle; to bewitch; to hallucinate.
allucinarsi, *v.r.* To deceive oneself, to make a mistake.
allucinato, *n.m.* Delirious, wandering in mind; entranced.
allucinazione, *n.f.* Hallucination.
alluda, *n.f.* Soft leather, white kid.
alludere [allUdere], *v.i.* To allude, to refer to, to hint.
allumacare, *v.t.* To leave the mark of a snail, to make a shiny mark.
allumacatura, *n.f.* Shiny mark (on clothes, etc.).
allumare, *v.t.* To light, to illuminate; to dress in alum.
allumatura, *n.f.* Dressing with alum.
allume, *n.m.* Alum.
allumiera, *n.f.* Alum works.
allumina, *n.f.* Silicate of alumina; china clay.
alluminare, *v.t.* To illuminate; to illustrate; to colour; to treat with alum.
alluminio [allumInio], *n.m.* (*Metal.*) Aluminium.
alluminoso, *a.* Containing alum; furnishing china clay.
allungabile [allungAbile], *a.* Extensible.
allungamento, *n.m.* Lengthening, elongation, stretching out; delay, procrastination.
allungare, *v.t.* To lengthen, to elongate, to extend; to lodge (a kick, etc.); to quicken (the pace); to dilute; to stretch out. **— un vestito,** to lengthen a dress; **— il muso,** to pull a long face; **— una pedata,** to lodge a good kick; **— con acqua,** to dilute with water; **— le braccia,** to stretch out one's arms; (*Naut.*) **— un'ancora,** to carry out an anchor.
allungarsi, *v.r.* To stretch oneself; to get longer. **I giorni si allungano,** the days are drawing out.
allungato, *p.p.a.* Elongated, lengthened; diluted; stretched out, prolonged.
allungatura, *n.f.* Lengthening, prolongation.
allusione, *n.f.* Allusion, hint, reference to.
allusivamente, *adv.* Allusively.
allusivo, *a.* Allusive.
alluso, *p.p.a.* Alluded to, hinted at [cp. **alludere**].
alluviale, alluvionale, *a.* Alluvial.
alluvionati, *n.m.pl.* People made homeless by floods, flood victims.
alluvione, *n.f.* Inundation, flood, deluge.
alma, *n.f.* (*Poet.*) Soul.
almanaccare, *v.i.* To muse; to puzzle oneself; (*fig.*) to build castles in the air.
almanacchio [almanacchIo], *n.m.* Musing.
almanacco, *n.m.* Almanac, calendar.
almeno, *conj.* At least; however. **Dammi — di che vivere,** Give me at least enough to live on.
almo, *a.* (*Poet.*) Animating (spiritually); divine.
alno, *n.m.* (*Bot.*) Alder (tree).
alò! *inter.* Hallo!
aloe, aloè [Aloe, aloE], *n.m.* (*Bot.*) Aloe.
alogeno [alOgeno], *n.m.* (*Chem.*) Halogen.
alone, *n.m.* Halo.
alopecia [alopecIa], *n.f.* (*Med.*) Alopecia.
alpaca [Alpaca], *n.f.* (*Zool.*) Alpaca. **Lana di —,** alpaca wool.
alpacca, *n.m.* (*Metal.*) Britannia metal.
alpe, *n.f.* Alp, high mountain.
alpeggio [alpEggio], *n.m.* Mountain summer pasture.
alpestre, *a.* Alpine, mountainous; wild.
Alpi, *n.m.pl.* The Alps.
alpigiano, *n.m.a.* Man of the Alps; alpine.
alpinismo, *n.m.* Mountaineering, mountain climbing.
alpinista (*pl.* **alpinisti**), *n.m.* Mountain climber.
alpino, *n.m.a.* (*Mil.*) Soldier of a mountain regiment; alpine.
alquanti, *a.pl.* A good many; several.
alquanto, *a.* Somewhat; rather; a good deal. **— difficile,** rather difficult; **la ragazza è — graziosa,** the girl is rather pretty; **sta — meglio,** he is a bit better.
alt! *inter.* Halt!
altalena, *n.f.* See-saw; swing; (*fig.*) indecision.
altalenare, *v.i.* To see-saw; to swing; to be uncertain.
altamente, *adv.* Highly, greatly, remarkably; nobly.
altana, *n.f.* (*Arch.*) Belvedere (on the roof).
altare, *n.m.* Altar. **Altare maggiore,** high altar.
altarino, *n.m.* Small altar, side altar. **Scoprire gli altarini,** to clear up a mystery; to find someone out.
altea [altEa], *n.f.* (*Bot.*) Althea, marsh mallow.
alterabile [alterAbile], *a.* Alterable, changeable.
alterabilità [-à], *n.f.* Alterability, susceptibility to alteration.
alteramente, *adv.* Haughtily, loftily.
alteramento, *n.m.* [cp. **alterazione**].
alterare, *v.t.* To alter, to change, to impair; to falsify. **— l'amicizia,** to impair friendship;

— **i fatti**, to distort facts; — **una firma**, to forge a signature.
alterarsi, *v.r.* To be altered; (*fig.*) to get angry; to be perturbed; to get confused.
alterativo, *a.* Alterative, causing alteration.
alterato, *p.p.a.* Altered, changed; weakened; angry; counterfeited; adulterated.
alterazione, *n.f.* Alteration, change; forgery.
altercare, *v.i.* To dispute, to quarrel, to wrangle.
altercazione, *n.f.* Dispute, quarrel, argument.
alterco, *n.m.* Altercation; quarrel.
alterego, *n.m.* Representative; alter ego.
alterezza, *n.f.* Pride, dignity.
alterigia [alterIgia], *n.f.* Pride, haughtiness; arrogance; conceit.
alternamente, *adv.* Alternately.
alternare, *v.t.* To alternate. (*Agric.*) to farm with rotation of crops.
alternarsi, *v.r.* To alternate; to succeed one another.
alternativa, *n.f.* Alternative, choice, option.
alternativamente, *adv.* Alternatively.
alternativo, *a.* Alternative, alternating; (*Mech.*) reciprocating motion.
alternato, *p.p.a.* Alternate. (*Agric.*) **Coltivazione alternata**, rotation of crops; (*Elec.*) **corrente alternata**, alternating current.
alternatore, *n.m.* (*Elec.*) Alternator.
alternazione, *n.f.* Alternation.
alterno, *a.* Alternate.
altero, *a.* Haughty, proud.
altezza, *n.f.* Height, altitude; depth; (*Mus.*) loudness; highness (title) — **sul livello del mare**, height above sea level; — **meridiana**, meridian altitude; — **del mare**, depth of the sea; **doppia** —, double width (of cloth); — **di stile**, loftiness of style; **Altezza Reale**, Royal Highness.
altezzosamente, *adv.* Haughtily, proudly; loftily.
altezzoso, *a.* Haughty, proud; supercilious.
alticcio [altIccio], *a.* Tipsy, half-seas over.
altiero [cp. **altero**].
altimetria [altimetrIa], *n.f.* Altimetry.
altimetrico [altimEtrico], *a.* Altimetric.
altimetro [altImetro], *n.m.* Altimeter.
altipiano, *n.m.* Plateau; tableland.
altisonante, *a.* High-sounding; loud-sounding; resounding.
altissimo [altIssimo], *a.super.* Very high. **L'Altissimo**, the Most High God.
altitonante, *a.* Thundering from on high; loud thundering. **L'Altitonante**, Jove.
altitudine [altitUdine], *n.f.* Altitude.
alto, *n.m.* Height, top, summit; (*Mus.*) treble. **Guardare qualcuno dall'— in basso**, to look a person up and down haughtily; **vedere le cose dall'—**, to look at things generally; **alti e bassi**, ups and downs.
alto, *a.* High, lofty, tall; deep; (*fig.*) noble, great; (*Geog.*) upper, higher; (*Mus.*) high. **Ad alta voce**, aloud; **in — mare**, in the open sea; **a testa alta**, with one's head held high; **Alta Camera**, Upper Chamber; **qui il mare è —**, the sea is deep here; **egli è più — di me**, he is taller than I.
alto, *adv.* Highly; above, up. **In —**, upstairs.
alto! *inter.* Halt! Stop!
altoforno, *n.m.* Blast-furnace.
altolocato, *a.* High ranking, highly placed.
altoparlante, *n.m.* (*Radio*) Loudspeaker.
altore, **altrice**, *n.m.f.* (*Poet.*) One who provides food; nurse.
altorilievo [altoriliEvo], *n.m.* (*Art*) High relief sculpture.
altramente [cp. **altrimenti**].
altresì, *adv.* Also, likewise, too.
altrettale, *a.* Equal, identical, like, similar.
altrettanto, *a.adv.* As much, as many, as far, so much. **Due volte —**, twice as much; **vi erano molti soldati e altrettanti ufficiali**, there were many soldiers and as many officers; **è — buono che voi**, he is as good as you; **Altrettanto!** The same to you!
altri, *pron.pl.* Others; someone, somebody.
altrieri, *adv.* The day before yesterday.
altrimenti, **altramente**, *adv.* Otherwise, but for that, else. **Non posso fare —**, I cannot do otherwise.
altro, *n.m.* Another (person, thing); something else.
altro, *a.* Other; next; different; further. **L'— giorno**, the other day; **un'altra volta**, another time; **ho letto molti altri libri**, I have read many other books; **quest'altra volta**, the next time; **ogni altra cosa**, everything else; **ha un — libro che il mio**, he has a different book from mine; **datemi l'uno o l'— cane**, give me one dog or the other.
altro, *pron.* Someone, anyone; other. **Pochi altri**, a few others; **all'uno e all'—**, to each of them; **non questi ma gli altri**, not these but the others; **nient' —**, nothing else; **qualcun'—**, somebody else.
altro, *conj.* In short, except, but. **Per —**, nevertheless; **tutt'—**, on the contrary.
altro! *inter.* Certainly! No doubt! **Senz'—!** Certainly, of course!
altronde, *adv.* From elsewhere. **D'altronde**, on the other hand, however.
altrove, *adv.* Elsewhere.
altrui, *pron.* Others, of others.
altrui, *n.m.* The property of others. **Non desiderare l'—**, do not hanker after others' property.
altruismo, *n.m.* Altruism.
altruista (*pl.* **altruisti**), *n.m.* Altruist.
altruistico [altruIstico], *a.* Altruistic.
altura, *n.f.* Height. **Sulle alture**, on the heights.
alturiere, *n.m.* (*Naut.*) Pilot; sea pilot.
alunnato, *n.m.* Apprenticeship.
alunno, *n.m.* Pupil, scholar, student (at a university).
alveare, *n.m.* Beehive.
alveo [Alveo], *n.m.* River-bed.
alveolo [alvEolo], *n.m.* Socket of a tooth; (*Anat.*) alveolus; cell (*e.g.* in the lungs); cell of a honeycomb.
alvino, *a.* (*Med.*) Abdominal.
alvo, *n.m.* Belly, abdomen; womb, uterus.
alzabile [alzAbile], *a.* Raisable.
alzaia [alzAia], *n.f.* (*Naut.*) Hawser; tow-line; warp.
alzamento, *n.m.* Lifting, raising, heaving.
alzare, *v.t.* To lift, to raise; to heave; (*Cards*) to cut. — **la bandiera**, to hoist the flag; — **il braccio**, to lift an arm; — **la voce**, to raise one's voice; — **le carte**, to cut cards; — **un muro**, to raise or build a wall; **non posso alzarlo**, I cannot lift it.

alzarsi, *v.r.* To get up, to rise; to stand up. **Alzatevi!** Stand up! **— di buon mattino,** to get up early in the morning.
alzata, *n.f.* Rise, rising; lifting up; elevation; embankment, dam. **— del sole,** sunrise; **— di spalle,** shrug of the shoulders; **per — di mano,** by show of hands.
alzato, *n.m.* (*Arch.*) Elevation.
alzato, *p.p.a.* Risen, raised; cut (of cards); increased, augmented.
alzatura [cp. **alzata**].
alzo, *n.m.* (*Mil.*) Sight (of gun or rifle).
amabile [amAbile], *a.* Amiable, agreeable, attractive; lovable.
amabilità [-à], *n.f.* Amiability; affability; loveliness; lovableness.
amabilmente, *adv.* Amiably, kindly; affably.
amaca, *n.f.* Hammock.
amalgama [amAlgama], *n.m.* (*Min.*) Amalgam; amalgamation.
amalgamare, *v.t.* To amalgamate; to blend.
amalgamazione, *n.f.* Amalgamation.
amante, *n.m.f.* Lover, suitor, sweetheart; mistress.
amante, *a.* Loving; fond of. **— della libertà,** lover of liberty; **— del ballo,** fond of dancing; **— dei giuochi,** fond of games.
amanuense, *n.m.* Amanuensis; copyist.
amaramente, *adv.* Bitterly.
amaranto, *n.m.* (*Bot.*) Amaranth, love-lies-bleeding.
amarasca, *n.f.* (*Bot.*) Black cherry.
amaraschino, *n.m.* Maraschino; cherry wine.
amarasco, *n.m.* (*Bot.*) Black cherry tree.
amare, *v.t.* To love, to be fond of; to fancy, to like, to have an inclination for; to cherish. **— una donna alla follia,** to love a woman to distraction; **— l'equitazione,** to take pleasure in riding horseback; **ella non mi ama,** she does not love me.
amareggiare, *v.t.* To make bitter; (*fig.*) to chagrin; to grieve, to sadden; to make gloomy.
amareggiarsi, *v.r.* To afflict oneself; to grieve; to worry over.
amarena, *n.f.* (*Bot.*) Hard black cherry.
amaretto, *n.m.* Almond cake, macaroon.
amaretto, *a.* Rather bitter.
amarezza, *n.f.* Bitterness; grief, sadness; rancour.
amariccio [amarIccio], *a.* Somewhat bitter.
amarico [amArico], *n.m.* Amharic, language of Ethiopia.
amarilli, *n.m.* (*Bot.*) Amaryllis.
amarino, *a.* Slightly bitter.
amaritudine [amaritUdine] [cp. **amarezza**].
amaro, *n.m.* Resentment; hate; affliction; bitterness; bitters.
amaro, *a.* Bitter; (*fig.*) grievous, painful, sad; stinging; hateful.
amarognolo [amarOgnolo], *a.* Bitterish, rather bitter.
amarra, *n.f.* (*Naut.*) Mooring cable.
amarrare, *v.t.* (*Naut.*) to moor.
amarsi, *v.r.* To love oneself; to like one another, to be fond of each other [cp. **amare**].
amarume, *n.m.* Acerbity.
amata, *n.f.* The woman one loves; mistress.
amatista, *n.f.* (*Geol.*) Amethyst [cp. **ametista**].
amato, *n.m.* The man one loves.
amatore, amatrice, *n.m.f.* Lover; amateur, virtuoso.
amatorio [amatOrio], *a.* Amatory.
amaurosi, *n.f.* (*Med.*) Amaurosis; loss of sight.
amazzone [amAzzone], *n.f.* Amazon; horsewoman; woman of courage. **Abito da —,** riding-habit.
ambagi, *n.m.pl.* (*Rhet.*) Circumlocutions. **Senza —,** without dodging the point.
ambasceria, ambasciata [ambascerIa], *n.f.* Embassy; message.
ambascia [ambAscia], *n.f.* Shortness of breath; pain, agony; distress.
ambasciata, *n.f.* Embassy; message.
ambasciatore, ambasciatrice, *n.m.f.* Ambassador, ambassadress; messenger.
ambedue, *pron.* Both.
ambidestro [ambidEstro], *a.* Ambidextrous.
ambientare, *v.t.* To acclimatize.
ambientarsi, *v.r.* To become seasoned, to grow accustomed to the ways and habits of a place.
ambiente, *n.m.a.* Surroundings; atmosphere; (*fig.*) society; surrounding, ambient.
ambiguamente, *adv.* Ambiguously.
ambiguità [-à], *n.f.* Ambiguity, ambiguousness.
ambiguo [ambIguo], *a.* Ambiguous, equivocal.
ambio [Ambio], *n.m.* Amble (of a horse), pace. **Dar l'—** to send going, to send off.
ambire, *v.t.* To covet; to be longing for; to desire. **— onori,** to covet honours.
ambito [Ambito], *n.m.* Ambit; orbit; limit; compass.
ambivalenza, *n.f.* Ambivalence.
ambizione, *n.f.* Ambition.
ambiziosaggine [ambiziosAggine], *n.f.* Conceit.
ambiziosamente, *adv.* Ambitiously.
ambizioso, *a.* Ambitious; desirous; greedy.
ambo, *n.m.* Two numbers drawn in a lottery. **Che —!** What a pair! || *pron.* Both. **— le mani,** both hands; **— i sessi,** both sexes.
ambone, *n.m.* (*Arch.*) Ambone; pulpit.
ambra, *n.f.* Amber. **— grigia,** ambergris.
Ambrogio [ambrOgio], *n.m.* Ambrose.
ambrosia [ambrOsia], *n.f.* Ambrosia.
ambrosiano, *a.* Ambrosian. **Canto —,** Ambrosian chant.
ambulante, *a.* Itinerant; strolling; movable; travelling. **Biblioteca —,** travelling library; circulating library; **ospedale —,** ambulance, field hospital; **merciaio —,** pedlar.
ambulanza, *n.f.* Ambulance; surgery.
ambulare, *v.i.* To walk, to wander; to go away.
ambulatorio [ambulatOrio], *n.m.* Surgery, consulting room.
ambulatorio [ambulatOrio], *a.* Ambulatory.
ameba, *n.f.* Amoeba.
amen, *inter.* Amen.
amenamente, *adv.* Agreeably, amusingly, pleasantly.
amenità [-à], *n.f.* Amenity; pleasantness; pleasantry.
ameno, *a.* Agreeable, amusing; pleasing, pleasant; droll, funny. **Novelle amene,** amusing stories; **capo —,** funny chap.
amento, *n.m.* (*Bot.*) Catkin.
amenza, *n.f.* (*Poet.*) Madness.

americanata, *n.f.* American yarn or exploit; tall story; bravado.
americaneggiare, *v.i.* To ape American ways.
americanizzare, *v.t.* To Americanize.
americano, *n.m.a.* American.
ametista, *n.f.* Amethyst.
amianto, *n.m.* Asbestos.
amica, *n.f.* Lady friend, girl friend. **— mia!** my dear! my dear girl!
amicabile [amicAbile], *a.* Amicable.
amicamente, *adv.* In a friendly way.
amicare, *v.t.* To befriend, to be a friend to.
amicarsi, *v.r.* To become friends (with someone).
amichevole [amichEvole], *a.* Friendly. **Vendita —,** sale by private contract; **in via —,** in a friendly way.
amichevolezza, *n.f.* Friendliness.
amichevolmente, *adv.* In a friendly way.
amicizia [amicIzia], *n.f.* Friendship.
amico, *n.m.* Friend; protector; lover. **— di bottiglia,** boon companion; **trattare da —,** to treat one like a friend; **Amico mio!** My dear fellow!
amico, *a.* Friendly. **Voce amica,** friendly voice; **fortuna amica,** smiling fortune; **popoli amici,** friendly nations.
amicone, *n.m.* Intimate friend; bosom pal.
amido [Amido], *n.m.* Starch.
amidoso, *a.* Starchy.
amistà [-à], *n.f.* (*Poet.*) Friendship.
amitto, *n.m.* (*Eccles.*) Amice.
Amleto, *n.m.* Hamlet.
ammaccare, *v.t.* To bruise; to dent; to batter.
ammaccarsi, *v.r.* To get bruised, to be bruised.
ammaccatura, *n.f.* Bruise, lump, swelling.
ammaestrabile [ammaestrAbile], *a.* Teachable, trainable; ready to learn.
ammaestramento, *n.m.* Teaching; training or breaking of horses. **Servire da —,** to serve as a lesson.
ammaestrare, *v.t.* To teach, to train; to break (a horse).
ammaestrativo, *a.* Instructive.
ammaestratore, ammaestratrice, *n.m.f.* Teacher; trainer; tamer.
ammaestrevole [ammaestrEvole], *a.* Teachable; ready to learn; docile.
ammainare, *v.t.* (*Naut.*) To lower the sails. **— la bandiera,** to haul down or strike the flag.
ammalare, *v.i.,* **ammalarsi,** *v.r.* To fall sick; to get ill.
ammalaticcio [ammalatIccio], *a.* Sickly, infirm [cp. **malaticcio**].
ammalato, *n.m.* Sick person; patient. **Curare un —,** to nurse a sick man; **fare l'—,** to feign illness.
ammalato, *a.* Sick, ill; diseased. **Cader —,** to fall ill; **— a morte**; sick unto death; **aver l'aria ammalata,** to look ill; **essere — di cuore,** to have heart trouble ; **avere lo spirito —,** to have a disordered mind.
ammaliamento, *n.m.* Enchantment; bewitchment; charm; spell; witchcraft.
ammaliare, *v.t.* To bewitch, to charm; to enrapture.
ammaliato, *p.p.a.* Bewitched, charmed; enraptured. **Ne è —,** he is smitten with her.
ammaliatore, ammaliatrice, *n.m.f.* Bewitcher, charmer; seducer.
ammalinconire, *v.t.i.* To make gloomy; to become melancholy.
ammaliziare, *v.i.t.* To be malicious, to be sly; to make cunning.
ammaliziato, *p.p.a.* Malicious.
ammalizzire [cp. **ammaliziare**].
ammammolarsi, *v.r.* To fall asleep with one's head on one's breast.
ammanco, *n.m.* (*Comm.*) Deficit. **— di cassa,** misappropriation, defalcation; **— di pesi,** short weight.
ammandorlato, *p.p.a.* Almond-shaped; lozenge-shaped (of a wall built with the stones thus laid).
ammanettare, *v.t.* To handcuff; to shackle.
ammanieramento, *n.m.* Affectation, mannerism [cp. **affettazione**].
ammanierare, *v.t.* To embellish in an affected style; to show artificiality.
ammanierato, *p.p.a.* Affected; false.
ammaniatura, *n.f.* (*obs.*) Affectation; preciousness, preciosity.
ammanigliare, *v.t.* To handcuff, to shackle.
ammannare, *v.t.* (*Agric.*) To put in sheaves, to stook.
ammannellare, *v.t.* To make into small bundles or skeins.
ammannimento, *n.m.* Preparation; cooking; dressing (of salads, etc.).
ammannire, *v.t.* To prepare; to dress (food), to season. **— il pranzo,** to get dinner ready; **— l'insalata,** to dress the salad.
ammannitura, *n.f.* Preparation (of food, etc.)
ammansare, ammansire, *v.t.* To appease, to calm down, to quieten; to domesticate, to tame.
ammansarsi, ammansirsi, *v.r.* To be quieted, to be calmed; to be pacified; to become tamed. **Il lupo non si ammansisce facilmente,** the wolf is not easily tamed.
ammantare, *v.t.* To cloak, to wrap up; (*fig.*) to hide, to conceal.
ammantarsi, *v.r.* To put on a cloak; (*fig.*) to affect. **— di pietà,** to assume a cloak of piety.
ammantatura, *n.f.* Cloaking.
ammantellare, *v.t.* To cast a cloak over, to throw a cloak upon; (*fig.*) to shield.
ammanto, *n.m.* (*Poet.*) Cloak, mantle.
ammaraggio [ammarAggio], *n.m.* (*Aviat.*) Alighting (on water).
ammarare, *v.i.* To alight on the water (of a seaplane).
ammarraggio [ammarrAggio], *n.m.* (*Naut. Aviat.*) Mooring.
ammarrare, *v.t.* (*Naut. Aviat.*) To moor.
ammassamento, *n.m.* Heap, mass; crowd, throng.
ammassare, *v.t.* To amass, to collect; to heap up; to hoard.
ammassarsi, *v.r.* To gather together; to come together; to gather in a crowd.
ammassicciare, *v.t.* (*Techn.*) To place the ballast on a road.
ammasso, *n.m.* Heap, pile; accumulation; bulk, mass; government pool.
ammatassare, *v.t.* To skein.
ammatassarsi, *v.r.* (*fig.*) To become confused (in mind).

ammatassato, *p.p.a.* Wound in skeins; (*fig.*) mentally confused; intricate.
ammattimento, *n.m.* Annoyance; embarrassment; vexation; (*colloq.*) work.
ammattire, *v.i.* To go mad.
ammattirsi, *v.r.* To worry oneself; to get worked up.
ammattonare, *v.t.* To pave with bricks.
ammattonato, *n.m.* Brick pavement.
ammattonatura, *n.f.* Paving with bricks.
ammazzacani, *n.m.* Official dog-killer.
ammazzagatti, *n.m.* (*colloq.*) Useless gun; any sort of firearm.
ammazzamento, *n.m.* Killing; murder, assassination, slaughter.
ammazzare, *v.t.* To kill, to slaughter; to murder, to assassinate; (*fig.*) to tire out, to bore; to overpower, to overwhelm. **Il dispiacere la ammazzò,** she died of grief; **— il tempo,** to kill time; **il calore mi ammazza,** heat overpowers me.
ammazzarsi, *v.r.* To commit suicide, to kill oneself; to kill one another, to kill each other; (*fig.*) to work very hard. **Si è ammazzato cadendo dal muro,** he fell off the wall and killed himself.
ammazzasette, *n.m.* (*colloq.*) Bully; swaggerer.
ammazzatoio [ammazzatOio], *n.m.* Slaughter-house; poleaxe.
ammazzatore, ammazzatrice, *n.m.f.* Assassin, murderer, murderess; slaughterer, killer.
ammazzolare, *v.t.* To make bouquets, to bunch; to bind.
ammencire, *v.t.i.* To make flabby; to grow flabby.
ammenda, *n.f.* Amends; reparation; fine, penalty.
ammendabile [ammendAbile], *a.* Corrigible; repairable, reparable; liable to a fine.
ammendamento, *n.m.* Amendment.
ammendare, *v.i.* To make amends; to fine.
ammennicolare, *v.t.* To put forward paltry or foolish reasons; to split hairs.
ammennicolo [ammennIcolo], *n.m.* Paltry reason; trifle.
ammesso, *a.* Admitted into, received; taken for granted. **— a Corte,** received at Court; **— che,** taking for granted.
ammestare, *v.t.* To command imperiously; to lord it.
ammettere [ammEttere], *v.t.* To admit; to permit; to concede; to tolerate, to suffer; to acknowledge. **Quest'affare non ammette ritardo,** this business does not admit of delay; **— indulgenza verso i bambini,** to be indulgent to the very young; **non — indugio,** to suffer no delay; **— un fatto,** to admit a fact; **fu ammesso a difendersi,** he was permitted to defend himself.
ammezzamento, *n.m.* Halving.
ammezzare, *v.t.* To halve, to divide in two; to half fill or half empty; to half utter, to stop in the middle of a word.
ammezzato, *n.m.* (*Arch.*) Mezzanine floor.
ammezzire, *v.i.* To become over-ripe.
ammiccare, *v.i.* To wink. **Ammiccare ad una ragazza,** to wink at a girl.
ammicco, *n.m.* Wink; (*colloq.*) glad eye.
amminicolare, *v.i.* To trifle [cp. **ammennicolare**].
amministrante, *n.m.* (*Eccles.*) Priest administering the sacrament.
amministrare, *v.t.* To administer, to manage; to conduct (affairs of state).
amministrativamente, *adv.* Administratively.
amministrativo, *a.* Administrative.
amministratore, amministratrice, *n.m.f.* Administrator, administratrix; (*Comm.*) director (of a company); acting partner; **— delegato,** managing director.
amministrazione, *n.f.* Administration, management; (*Comm.*) management, board of directors.
ammirabile [ammirAbile], *a.* Admirable.
ammirabilità [-à], *n.f.* Admirableness.
ammirabilmente, *adv.* Admirably.
ammiraglia [ammirAglia], *n.f.* (*Naut.*) Flag ship.
ammiragliato, *n.m.* Admiralty.
ammiraglio [ammirAglio], *n.m.* Admiral. **Contra —,** rear admiral; **vice —,** vice-admiral; **grand'—,** high admiral, admiral of the fleet.
ammirando, *a.* Admirable.
ammirare, *v.t.* To admire.
ammirarsi, *v.r.* To admire oneself.
ammirativo, *a.* Pertaining to admiration. **Punto —,** exclamation mark.
ammirato, *p.p.a.* Admired.
ammiratore, ammiratrice, *n.m.f.* Admirer; suitor.
ammirazione, *n.f.* Admiration; surprise.
ammirevole [ammirEvole], *a.* Admirable.
ammiserire, *v.t.* To impoverish.
ammiserirsi, *v.r.* To become impoverished, to grow poor.
ammissibile [ammissIbile], *a.* Admissible, allowable. **È —,** it may be so.
ammissibilità [-à], *n.f.* Admissibility.
ammissione, *n.m.* Admission; admittance; acknowledgment; (*Motor.*) intake.
ammobiliamento, *n.m.* Furnishing, furniture.
ammobiliare, *v.t.* To furnish.
ammodernamento, *n.m.* Modernization, modernizing.
ammodernare, *v.t.* To modernize.
ammodo, a modo, *a.adv.* Discreet, prudent; carefully, properly, softly. **Un uomo —,** a man with tact, a discreet man.
ammogliare, *v.t.* To marry, to provide a wife for; to give a daughter in marriage; to match; to pair.
ammogliarsi, *v.r.* To get married (of a man); to wed.
ammogliato, *n.m.a.* Married man; married.
ammollamento, *n.m.* Drenching, soaking; steeping.
ammollare, *v.t.* To drench, to soak, to steep.
ammollarsi, *v.r.* To be drenched; to be steeped.
ammolliente, *n.m.* (*Med.*) Emollient.
ammollimento, *n.m.* Softening; slackening; (*fig.*) slackening (in character).
ammollire, *v.t.* To soften, to mellow; to enervate, to make effeminate.
ammollirsi, *v.r.* To soften, to grow tender; to become effeminate; to grow enfeebled.

ammollitivo, *a.* Mellowing, softening; (*Med.*) mollient.
ammoniaca [ammonIaca], *n.f.* (*Chem.*) Ammonia.
ammoniacale, *a.* Ammoniacal.
ammoniaco [ammonIaco], (*Chem.*) *a.* Ammoniac.
ammonico [ammOnico], *n.m.* (*Chem.*) Ammonium.
ammonimento, *n.m.* Admonition, caution, warning.
ammonio [ammOnio], *n.m.* (*Chem.*) Ammonium.
ammonire, *v.t.* To admonish, to counsel; to warn.
ammonito, *n.m.* One who has been warned by the police, or reprimanded.
ammonitore, ammonitrice, *n.m.f.* Monitor, admonisher.
ammonizione, *n.f.* Admonition, warning.
ammontare, *v.t.i.* To heap, to pile; to amount to. **Il debito ammonta a,** the debt amounts to.
ammontare, *n.m.* Amount. (*Comm.*) **— a credito,** amount to one's credit.
ammontarsi, *v.r.* To gather, to collect.
ammonticchiamento, *n.m.* Heaping up, piling up.
ammonticchiare, *v.t.* To heap up, to pile up.
ammonticchiarsi, *v.r.* To crowd; to close up.
ammorbamento, *n.m.* Stench, stink, bad smell; infecting, tainting.
ammorbare, *v.t.* To infect, to taint; to stink.
ammorbidamento, ammorbidimento, *n.m.* Softening.
ammorbidare, ammorbidire, *v.t.* To soften; to make supple.
ammorbidarsi, ammorbidirsi, *v.r.* To become soft; to grow supple.
ammorbidito, *p.p.a.* Softened.
ammorsellato, *n.m.* Hashed meat, mince.
ammortamento, *n.m.* (*Law, Comm.*) Amortization, redemption. **Fondo di —,** sinking fund, depreciation fund; **— del debito pubblico,** redemption of the public debt.
ammortimento, *n.m.* Weakening; abating; deadening.
ammortire, *v.t.* To allay, to soothe; to weaken; to deaden. **— la caduta,** to break the fall.
ammortirsi, *v.r.* To fade away; to faint; to allay; to cool off.
ammortizzabile [ammortizzAbile], *a.* (*Law*) Redeemable.
ammortizzamento [cp. **ammortamento**].
ammortizzare, *v.t.* To redeem, to pay off, to repay. **— un debito,** to pay off a debt.
ammortizzarsi, *v.r.* To be redeemed.
ammortizzazione [cp. **ammortamento**].
ammorvidire, *v.t.i.* To soften [cp. **ammorbidire**].
ammorzamento, *n.m.* Weakening, diminishing; deadening.
ammorzare, *v.t.* To allay, to moderate, to weaken; to abate; to cool off.
ammoscire, *v.i.* To become flabby; to fade (of colours, etc.)
ammosfera, *n.f.* Atmosphere [cp. **atmosfera**].
ammosferico [ammosfErico], *a.* Atmospheric.
ammostare, *v.t.* To tread down grapes.
ammostatoio [ammostatOio], *n.m.* Winepress; implement for pressing down grapes.
ammostatore, *n.m.* Man who presses down grapes.
ammostatura, *n.f.* Treading or pressing out of grapes.
ammucchiamento, *n.m.* Heaping up, piling up.
ammucchiare, *v.t.* To heap, to pile in heaps; (*fig.*) to hoard.
ammucchiarsi, *v.r.* To accumulate, to bunch up.
ammucidire, *v.i.* To get mouldy.
ammuffire, *v.i.* To grow mouldy, to get musty.
ammuffirsi, *v.r.* To become mouldy.
ammulinare, *v.t.i.* To raise a whirlwind (dust storm, water-spout, etc.); to turn (by wind or water) a mill; to fan away the chaff from the grains.
ammusarsi, *v.r.* To meet face to face.
ammusire, *v.i.* To become gruff, to be surly.
ammusonito, *a.* Looking gruff, appearing surly or sulky.
ammutinamento, *n.m.* Mutiny.
ammutinare, *v.t.* To cause to mutiny, to incite to mutiny.
ammutinarsi, *v.r.* To mutiny; to break into mutiny.
ammutinato, *n.m.* Mutineer.
ammutinato, *p.p.a.* Mutinied; in a state of mutiny, mutinous.
ammutinatore, *n.m.* (*Law*) Suborner.
ammutire, ammutolire, *v.t.i.* To hush, to silence; to become mute (with fear or shame); to keep one's mouth shut.
ammutolire, ammutolirsi, *v.i.r.* To be struck dumb (with astonishment, etc.)
ammutolito, *a.* Speechless.
amnesia [amnesIa], *n.f.* (*Med.*) Amnesia, loss of memory.
amnio [Amnio], *n.m.* (*Zool.*) Amnion.
amnistia [amnistIa], *n.f.* Amnesty.
amnistiare, *v.t.* To grant an amnesty, to pardon.
amo, *n.m.* Fish-hook.
amoerre [amoErre], *n.m.* Watered silk or cotton.
amorale, *a.* Amoral.
amoralità [-à], *n.f.* Lack of a moral sense.
amorazzo, *n.m.* Love (in a vicious sense) amour, shady love affair.
amore, *n.m.* Love; heat (of animals). **— proprio,** self-respect; **languire d'—,** to be love-sick; **fare l'— con,** to make love to, to woo; **nodo d'—,** love-knot; **Amore mio!** My darling! **filare il perfetto —,** to love long and faithfully; **che — di bambino!** what a lovely little fellow! **per — o per forza,** by hook or by crook; **essa è l'— mio,** she's my lady-love.
amoreggiamento, *n.m.* Love-making, love; flirtation.
amoreggiare, *v.i.* To make love; to flirt.
amoretto, *n.m.* Casual love affair, flirtation.
amorevole [amorEvole], *a.* Loving; lovely.
amorevolezza, *n.f.* Lovingness; tenderness.
amorfia [amorfIa], *n.f.* Amorphism.
amorfo, *a.* Amorphous.
amorino, *n.m.* Little darling; (*Bot.*) mignonette; (*Art*) a cupid.

amorosa, *n.f.* Lover, mistress; (*Theat.*) girl who plays the part of a lover.
amorosamente, *adv.* Lovingly.
amoroso, *n.m.* Lover, gallant, beau; admirer; suitor.
amoroso, *a.* Fond, loving, amorous. **— di,** in love with; **opera amorosa di carità,** labour of love.
amoruccio [amorUccio], *n.m.* Slight attachment; flirtation.
amoscino, *n.m.* (*Bot.*) Damson.
amovibile [amovIbile], *a.* Movable, removable.
amovibilità [-à], *n.f.* Removability.
ampelopraso, *n.m.* (*Bot.*) Wild leek.
amperaggio [amperAggio], *n.m.* (*Elect.*) Amperage.
ampère, *n.m.* (*Elect.*) Ampere.
amperometro [amperOmetro], *n.m.* (*Elect.*) Ammeter.
ampiamente, *adv.* Amply, abundantly; widely, extensively.
ampiezza, *n.f.* Amplitude, wideness, width. **— del pensiero,** breadth of thought.
ampio [Ampio], *a.* Ample, abundant, copious; spacious; diffuse.
amplesso, *n.m.* Embrace.
ampliamento, *n.m.* Amplification; enlargement; aggrandizement.
ampliare, *v.t.* To amplify, to enlarge, to extend; to dilate.
ampliativo, *a.* Causing amplification.
ampliazione, *n.f.* Amplification.
amplificamento, *n.m.* Amplification.
amplificare, *v.t.* To amplify; to exaggerate.
amplificativo, *a.* Causing amplification.
amplificatore, *n.m.* Amplifier.
amplificazione, *n.f.* Amplification.
amplio [Amplio], *a.* Ample (of clothes).
amplitudine [amplitUdine], *n.f.* Amplitude.
ampolla, *n.f.* Phial; (*Eccles.*) ampulla; cruets.
ampolliera, *n.f.* Cruets, cruet-stand.
ampollina, *n.f.* Small cruet, small bottle; sand-glass; (*Eccles.*) cruets.
ampollosamente, *adv.* Pompously.
ampollosità [-à], *n.f.* Pomposity, bombast.
ampolloso, *a.* Pompous, bombastic; redundant.
amputare, *v.t.* To amputate.
amputazione, *n.f.* Amputation.
amuleto, *n.m.* Amulet, talisman.
anabattista (*pl.* **anabattisti**), *n.m.* (*Eccles.*) Anabaptist.
anacardo, *n.m.* (*Bot.*) Cashew tree; cashew nut.
anace, anici [Anace, Anici], *n.m.* (*Bot.*) Anise; aniseed.
anaciato, *a.* Flavoured with aniseed.
anacini, *n.m.pl.* Aniseed drops.
anacoreta, *n.m.f.* Hermit, hermitess; anchorite.
anacoretico [anacorEtico], *a.* Hermit-like.
anacreontica [anacreOntica], *n.f.* (*Poet.*) Anacreontic.
anacreontico [anacreOntico], *a.* (*Poet.*) Anacreontic.
anacronismo, *n.m.* Anachronism.
anafora [anAfora], *n.f.* (*Gram.*) Anaphora.
anagallide [anagAllide], *n.m.* (*Bot.*) Pimpernel, chickweed.
anaglifo [anAglifo], *n.m.* (*Arch.*) Anaglyph.
anagogia [anagogIa], *n.f.* Anagogy; mystical interpretation.
anagogicamente, *adv.* Anagogically.
anagogico [anagOgico], *a.* Anagogical.
anagrafe [anAgrafe], *n.f.* Register office; registrar's office.
anagramma (*pl.* **anagrammi**), *n.m.* Anagram.
anagrammatico [anagrammAtico], *a.* Anagrammatic.
anagrammatizzare, *v.t.* To make anagrams.
anale, *a.* (*Med.*) Anal.
analfabeta, *n.m.f.* Illiterate.
analfabetismo, *n.m.* Illiteracy.
analgesia [analgesIa], *n.f.* (*Med.*) Analgesia.
analgesico [analgEsico], *a.* Analgesic.
analisi [anAlisi], *n.f.* Analysis; examination; testing. **In ultima —,** after all, in the last resort.
analista, *n.m.f.* Analyst.
analitica [analItica], *n.f.* Analytics.
analiticamente, *adv.* Analytically.
analitico [analItico], *a.* Analytical.
analizzabile, *a.* Susceptible of analysis.
analizzare, *v.t.* To analyse, to test.
analizzatore, *n.m.* Analyser; analyst.
analogamente, *adv.* Analogously.
analogia [analogIa], *n.f.* Analogy.
analogicamente, *adv.* Analogically.
analogico [analOgico], *a.* Analogical.
analogismo, *n.m.* Analogy.
analogo [anAlogo], *n.m.a.* Analogue; analogous.
ananasso, *n.m.* Ananas, pineapple.
anapesto, *n.m.* (*Poet.*) Anapaest.
anarchia [anarchIa], *n.f.* Anarchy.
anarchicamente, *adv.* Anarchically.
anarchico [anArchico], *n.m.a.* Anarchist; anarchistic, anarchic.
anarchismo, *n.m.* Anarchism.
anarchista, *n.m.f.* Anarchist.
anastigmatico [anastigmAtico], *a.* Anastigmatic.
anastrofe [anAstrofe], *n.f.* (*Gram.*) Anastrophe.
anatema [anatEma, anAtema], *n.m.* Anathema.
anatemizzare, *v.t.* To anathematize.
anatomia [anatomIa], *n.f.* Anatomy.
anatomicamente, *adv.* Anatomically.
anatomico [anatOmico], *a.* Anatomical.
anatomista (*pl.* **anatomisti**), *n.m.* Anatomist.
anatomizzare, *v.t.* To anatomize.
anatra, anitra [Anatra, Anitra], *n.f.* Duck.
anatraia [anatrAia], *n.f.* Duckpond.
anatrino, *n.m.f.* Duckling.
anatroccolo [anatrOccolo], *n.m.* Duckling; (*fig.*) short-legged person, rickety child.
anatrotto, *n.m.* Duckling.
anca, *n.f.* (*Anat.*) Haunch, hip; chicken leg; (*Naut.*) ship's quarter.
ancella, *n.f.* (*Lit.*) Maidservant.
anche, *adv. conj.* Also, too, even. **anch'io,** I too; **— più,** even more; **quand' —,** even if.
anchilosi, *n.f.* (*Med.*) Anchylosis.
anchina, *n.f.* Yellow cotton cloth.
ancia [Ancia], *n.f.* (*Mus.*) Reed.
ancillare, *a.* Ancillary; menial.
ancipite [ancIpite], *a.* Two-edged; (*fig.*) dubious.
anco [cp. **anche**].
ancona, *n.f.* (*Arch.*) Ancon.

ancora [Ancora], *n.f.* Anchor; pallet (clockwork). **Gettare l'—,** to drop the anchor; **levare l'—,** to weigh the anchor; **— di salvezza** or **di speranza,** sheet anchor; **l' — è impegnata,** the anchor is fouled.

ancora, *adv.* Again, yet, still, too, more. **— più facile,** still easier; **— un momento,** yet another moment; **provare —,** to try again; **non —,** not yet; **ciò è — meglio,** that is even better.

ancoraggio [ancorAggio], *n.m.* Anchorage; (*Naut.*) berth.

ancorare, *v.t.* To anchor, to drop the anchor.

ancorarsi, *v.r.* To anchor, to cast anchor.

ancorchè, *adv.* Even, though.

ancudine [ancUdine], *n.f.* Anvil [cp. **incudine**].

andamento, *n.m.* Walking; carriage, deportment; proceeding. **— degli affari,** course of business; **— di casa,** housewifery.

andana, *n.f.* Rope-walk.

andante, *p.p.a.* Going; current; cheap; (*Mus.*) moderately slow. **Il 17 —,** the 17th inst.; **articolo —,** cheap article.

andantino, *n.m.* (*Mus.*) Movement slightly quicker than andante.

andare, *v.i.* To go, to walk, to move; to happen. **Come è andata?** how has it gone? **— dietro,** to go after; **— contro,** to go against; **Come va?** How are you? **Va bene,** that will do, that's all right; **— fuor di strada,** to go astray; **— fuori,** to go out; **— a cavallo,** to go on horseback; **— a letto,** to go to bed; **— a gran passi,** to walk very fast; **a lungo —,** in the long run; **fare — un orologio,** to make a clock go; **— avanti,** to go ahead.

andare, *n.m.* Going; walk. **Con l'— del tempo,** with the passing of time.

andarne, *v.i.* To be at stake. **Ne va la vita,** my life is at stake.

andarsene, *v.r.* To go away, to be gone. **— a letto,** to get to bed.

andata, *n.f.* Going. **Biglietto di — e ritorno,** return ticket; (*Med.*) **— di corpo,** stool, defecation.

andato, *p.p.a.* Gone; elapsed, passed; lost, spoiled. **Il mese —,** last month.

andatura, *n.f.* Gait, way of walking. **Lo conosco dall'—,** I know him by his walk.

andazzo, *n.m.* Custom, fashion of the moment; bad custom; bad taste.

andirivieni [andiriviEni], *n.m.* Coming and going; labyrinth, maze; bustle.

andito [Andito], *n.m.* Corridor, passage.

Andrea [andrEa], *n.m.* Andrew.

andriolo [andriOlo], *n.m.* (*Agric.*) Kind of hard wheat.

androgino [andrOgino], *n.m.a.* Androgyne; androgynous; hermaphrodite.

androne, *n.m.* Entrance hall; passage.

aneddotico [aneddOtico], *a.* Anecdotal.

aneddoto [anEddoto], *n.m.* Anecdote.

anelante, *a.* Breathless, panting, gasping; (*fig.*) longing for.

anelantemente, *adv.* Breathlessly; (*fig.*) eagerly, avidly.

anelare, *v.t.i.* To pant, to gasp; (*fig.*) to be eager for.

anelato, *p.p.a.* Desired, eagerly awaited.

anelettrico [anelEttrico], *a.* Anelectric, non-electric.

anelito [anElito], *n.m.* Breath, breathing; (*fig.*) gasp; craving for.

anello, *n.m.* Ring; link; curl, ringlet. **— nuziale, matrimoniale,** wedding ring; (*Mech.*) **— di stantuffo,** piston-ring.

anelo, *a.* (*Poet.*) Breathless; longing.

anemia [anemIa], *n.f.* (*Med.*) Anaemia.

anemico [anEmico], *n.m.a.* (*Med.*) Anaemic; sufferer from anaemia.

anemografo [anemOgrafo], *n.m.* (*Meteor.*) Anemograph.

anemometro [anemOmetro], *n.m.* (*Meteor.*) Anemometer.

anemone [anEmone], *n.m.* (*Bot.*) Anemone, windflower.

aneroide [anerOide], *n.m.* Aneroid barometer.

anestesia [anestesIa], *n.f.* (*Med.*) Anaesthesia.

anestetico [anestEtico], *n.m.a.* (*Med.*) Anaesthetic; anaesthetic.

anestetizzare, *v.t.* (*Med.*) To anaesthetize.

aneto, *n.m.* (*Bot.*) Dill.

aneurisma, *n.m.* (*Med.*) Aneurism.

anfanamento, *n.m.* Bustling here and there; rambling in speech, aimless talk.

anfanare, *v.i.* To bustle; to repeat oneself endlessly; to talk at random.

anfanatore, anfanatrice, *n.m.f.* Prattler, chatterer.

anfibio [anfIbio], *n.m.a.* (*Zool.*) Amphibian; amphibious.

anfibologia [anfibologIa], *n.f.* Ambiguity, ambiguous statement.

anfiteatro, *n.m.* Amphitheatre.

anfitrione, *n.m.* Host, Amphitryon.

anfitrite, *n.f.* Amphitrite.

anfora [Anfora], *n.f.* Amphora.

anfratto, *n.m.* Winding passage; gorge, ravine.

anfrattuosità [-à], *n.f.* Windingness.

anfrattuoso, *a.* Winding, circuitous.

angar [angAr], *n.m.* (*Aviat.*) Hangar, shed.

angaria [angarIa], *n.f.* Exaction; vexation; oppression.

angariare, *v.t.* To vex; to oppress.

angela, angiola [Angela, Angiola], *n.f.* Angel.

angelica [angElica], *n.f.* (*Bot.*) Angelica.

angelicamente, *adv.* Angelically, like an angel.

angelico [angElico], *a.* Angelic, angelical.

angelino, *n.m.* Little angel.

angelo [Angelo], *n.m.* Angel. **— custode,** guardian angel; (*fig.*) military policeman.

angere [Angere] [cp. **affligere**].

angheria [angherIa] [cp. **angaria**].

angina, *n.f.* (*Med.*) Angina; quinsy.

anginoso, *n.m.* (*Med.*) Sufferer from angina.

angiola [Angiola] [cp. **angela**].

angioletta, *n.f.* Little angel.

angiologia [angiologIa], *n.f.* (*Med.*) Angiology.

angiosperme, *n.f.pl.* (*Bot.*) Angiosperms.

angiporto, *n.m.* Blind alley.

anglicanismo, *n.m.* Anglicanism.

anglicano, *n.m.a.* Anglican.

anglicismo, *n.m.* Anglicism.

anglofilo [anglOfilo], *n.m.* Anglophile.

anglofobia [anglofobIa], *n.f.* Anglophobia.

anglofobo [anglOfobo], *n.m.* Anglophobe.

anglomania [anglomanIa], *n.f.* Anglomania.

angolare, *a.* Angular. **Pietra —,** corner stone.

angolarmente, *adv.* Angularly.
angolato, *a.* Angled.
angolo [Angolo], *n.m.* Angle; corner. **— acuto,** acute angle; **— ottuso,** obtuse angle; **— retto,** right angle.
angoloso, *a.* Angulous; (*obs.*) forbidding.
angoscia [angOscia], *n.f.* Anguish (of mind or body).
angosciare, *v.t.* To cause anguish; to grieve.
angosciosamente, *adv.* Painfully.
angoscioso, *a.* Sorrowful, distressing.
angue [Angue], *n.m.* (*Poet.*) Serpent.
anguilla, *n.f.* (*Zool.*) Eel.
anguillaia [anguillAia], *n.f.* Eel-pond.
anguinaia [anguinAia], *n.f.* (*Anat.*) Groin.
anguria [angUria], *n.f.* Water-melon.
angustamente, *adv.* Narrowly, closely.
angustia [angUstia], *n.f.* Distress; narrowness; (financial) embarrassment.
angustiare, *v.t.* To distress.
angustiarsi, *v.r.* To distress oneself, to be distressed, to worry.
angustioso, *a.* Distressing.
angusto, *a.* Narrow, strait; (*fig.*) mean, close.
anice [Anice], *n.m.* (*Bot.*) Anis, aniseed.
anidride, *n.f.* (*Chem.*) Anhydride.
anile, *n.m.* (*Bot.*) Indigo plant.
anilina, *n.f.* (*Chem.*) Aniline.
anima [Anima], *n.f.* Soul, spirit; ghost; kernel, core. **Villaggio di cento anime,** hamlet of a hundred souls; **cura d'anime,** cure of souls; **pregare per l'— di mia madre,** to pray for my mother's soul; **anime gemelle,** twin spirits, soul mates.
animalaccio [animalAccio], *n.m.* Brute, nasty brute.
animale, *n.m.* Animal; (*fig.*) dolt, blockhead.
animale, *a.* Animal; (*fig.*) sensual.
animalescamente, *adv.* In an animal-like way.
animalesco, *a.* Beastly, like a beast.
animalità [-à], *n.f.* Animality.
animare, *v.t.* To animate, to cheer up; to enliven.
animarsi, *v.r.* To become animated; to take courage.
animatamente, *adv.* Animatedly.
animato, *p.p.a.* Animate, cheered, enlivened; brisk, buoyant.
animatore, animatrice, *n.m.f.* One who animates or cheers up; leader.
animazione, *n.f.* Animation; liveliness; briskness.
animella, *n.f.* Sweetbread.
animo [Animo], *n.m.* Mind, soul; courage, bravery; intention; disposition. **Farsi —,** to pluck up courage; **ho in — di andare a Roma,** it is my intention to go to Rome; **con — ben disposto,** in a favourable disposition.
animo! [Animo], *inter.* Courage!
animosamente, *adv.* Boldly, courageously; rancorously.
animosità [-à], *n.f.* Animosity, animus, spite.
animoso, *a.* Bold, brave, valiant; malevolent.
anisetta, *n.f.* Aniseed cordial.
anitra [Anitra], *n.f.* Duck (as opposed to a drake).
anitrotto, *n.m.* Duckling.
annacquamento, *n.m.* Watering, wetting; diluting.
annacquare, *v.t.* To water (esp. wine), to dilute; (*fig.*) to mitigate.
annacquata, *n.f.* Slight watering; shower of rain.
annaffiamento, innaffiamento, *n.m.* Watering.
annaffiare, *v.t.* To water, to sprinkle, to bedew.
annaffiata, *n.f.* Watering, sprinkling.
annaffiatoio [annaffiatOio], *n.m.* Watering-pot, watering-can.
annaffiatura, *n.f.* Watering, sprinkling.
annali, *n.m.pl.* Annals.
annalista (*pl.* **annalisti**), *n.m.* Annalist.
annasare, *v.t.* To smell [cp. **annusare**].
annaspare, *v.t.i.* To wind on a reel; to gesticulate; to grope; to bustle.
annaspatura, *n.f.* Reeling; bustle.
annaspio [annaspIo], *n.m.* Groping; gesticulation.
annaspo, *n.m.* Reel.
annaspone, *n.m.* Busybody, aimless person.
annata, *n.f.* Year, year's time. (*Comm.*) **Movimento di affari nell'—,** yearly turnover; **raccolta dell'—,** year's crop.
annate, *n.f.pl.* (*Eccles.*) Annates.
annatona, *n.f.* Year of plenty.
annebbiamento, *n.m.* Fogginess; dimness (of sight); (*Agric.*) blight, smut.
annebbiare, *v.t.i.* To be foggy; to fog; to mist over; to cloud (the sight).
annebbiarsi, *v.r.* To become foggy, to become dim; to grow dim (of sight).
annebbiato, *p.p.a.* Covered with fog or mist; become foggy; grown dim (of sight).
annegamento, *n.m.* Drowning; (*fig.*) ruin.
annegare, *v.t.i.* To drown, to be drowned.
annegarsi, *v.r.* To drown oneself; to be drowned.
annegato, *n.m.* Drowned person.
annegazione, *n.f.* Abnegation [cp. **abnegazione**].
anneghittimento, *n.m.* Idleness, laziness.
anneghittire, *v.t.i.* To make lazy; to be lazy.
anneghittirsi, *v.r.* To grow idle or lazy.
anneramento, annerimento, *n.m.* Blackening, making black.
annerare, annerire, *v.t.* To make black, to blacken; to turn black.
annerirsi, *v.r.* To turn black, to become black.
anneritura, *n.f.* Blackening, being black, blackness.
annessione, *n.f.* Annexation.
annessionista (*pl.* **annessionisti**) *n.m.* Annexationist.
annesso, *n.m.* Annex.
annesso, *p.p.a.* Annexed, connected with. **Annessi e connessi,** everything connected with.
annestamento, *n.m.* Grafting; inoculation. [cp. **innestamento**].
annestare, *v.t.* To graft, to inoculate [cp. **innestare**].
annettere [annEttere], *v.t.* To annex; to attach or enclose (documents); to include.
annetto, *n.m.* Period of about a year.
Annibale [annIbale], *n.m.* Hannibal.
annichilamento, *n.m.* Annihilation.
annichilare, annichilire, *v.t.* To annihilate.
annichilazione, *n.f.* Annihilation.
annichilimento, *n.m.* Annihilation.

annichilirsi, *v.r.* To annihilate oneself.
annidare, *v.t.i.* To harbour, to nest; (*fig.*) to harbour (in the mind).
annidarsi, *v.r.* To nest (of birds); to nestle; to hide.
annientamento, *n.m.* Annihilation; destruction.
annientare, *v.t.* To annihilate.
annientarsi, *v.r.* To debase oneself; to come to nothing.
anniversario [anniversArio]. *n.m.a.* Anniversary; birthday.
anno, *n.m.* Year, twelvemonth. **— bisestile,** leap year; **l'— prossimo,** next year; **l'— corrente**; the present year; **— di gestione,** trading year; **augurare un felice —,** to wish a happy new year; **essere avanti con gli anni,** to be getting on in years; **quanti anni hai?** how old are you? **ho dieci anni,** I am ten years old; **da molti anni,** for many years; **tutti gli anni,** every year; **due anni fa,** two years ago; **Capo d'—,** New Year's Day; (*Astron.*) **— luce,** light-year.
annobilimento, *n.m.* Ennobling, ennoblement.
annobilire, *v.t.* To ennoble, to raise to the peerage; (*fig.*) to elevate.
annobilitare, *v.t.* To ennoble.
annodamento, *n.m.* Knotting.
annodare, *v.t.* To knot, to tie a knot; (*fig.*) to entangle. **— un affare,** to fix up or settle a piece of business; **— relazioni,** to open relations (with).
annodarsi, *v.r.* To get knotted, to get entangled.
annodatura, *n.f.* Knotting, knot.
annoiamento, *n.m.* Weariness; tedium.
annoiare, *v.t.* To annoy; to tease; to weary, to tire, to bore.
annoiarsi, *v.r.* To be wearied, to be bored; to be annoyed. **— a morte,** to be bored to death.
annoiatore, annoiatrice, *n.m.f.* Bore; wearisome person.
annona, *n.f.* Year's provisions. **Ufficio d'—,** revictualling board; food office.
annonario [annonArio], *a.* Pertaining to provisions. **Carta annonaria,** ration card.
annoso, *a.* Old, full of years.
annotare, *v.t.* To annotate, to note.
annotariare, *v.t.* To train as a notary.
annotariarsi, *v.r.* To train oneself as a notary.
annotato, *p.p.a.* Taken note of; annotated.
annotatore, annotatrice, *n.m.f.* Annotator.
annotazione, *n.f.* Note; annotation. **— a margine,** marginal note; **— a piede,** footnote.
annottare, *v.i.* To grow dark, to become night.
annoveramento, *n.m.* Enumeration, numbering.
annoverare, *v.t.* To enumerate, to count, to number.
annuale, *n.m.a.* Annual; year; anniversary.
annualità [-à], *n.f.* Annuity.
annualmente, *adv.* Annually, yearly.
annuario [annuArio], *n.m.* Annual (book); year book; university calendar. **— commerciale,** trade directory.
annuente, *a.* Consenting.
annuenza, *n.f.* Consent.
annuire, *v.i.* To assent; to consent.
annuito, *p.p.a.* Assented, consented.
annullabile [annullAbile], *a.* Voidable.
annullamento, *n.m.* Annulment, cancellation; rendering void. **— di un contratto,** cancellation of a deal.
annullare, *v.t.* To annul, to render void, to cancel, to call off; to annihilate. **— un documento,** to invalidate a document.
annullativo, *a.* Annulative, cancelling.
annullatore, annullatrice, *n.m.f.* The annulling party.
annullazione, *n.f.* Annulment, cancellation.
annunciare, annuncio, see **annunz —.**
annunziare, *v.t.* To announce; to communicate; to inform; to advertise; to state; to foretell; to signal. **— sui giornali,** to advertise, to announce in the papers; **— l'arrivo,** to signal or announce the arrival.
Annunziata, *n.f.* Our Lady; the Annunciation.
annunziato, *a.* Announced; informed; foretold; signalled.
annunziatore, annunziatrice, *n.m.f.* Announcer; messenger; (*Theat.*) call-boy; (*Radio*) announcer.
Annunziazione, *n.f.* Feast of the Annunciation (Lady Day).
annunzio [annUnzio], *n.m.* Announcement; thing announced; advertisement; forecast.
annuo [Annuo], *a.* Yearly, annual. **Abbonamento —,** yearly subscription.
annusare, *v.t.* To smell; (*fig.*) to smell out, to discover.
annuvolamento, *n.m.* Clouding over; dimming.
annuvolare, *v.t.i.* To cloud, to obscure, to dim (of sight); to trouble.
annuvolarsi, *v.r.* To cloud over.
annuvolato, *p.p.a.* Clouded, dimmed, cloudy.
ano, *n.m.* (*Anat.*) Anus.
anodino, *n.m.a.* Anodyne.
anodo [Anodo, anOdo], *n.m.* (*Elect.*) Anode.
anofele [anOfele], *n.m.* (*Zool.*) Anopheles.
anomalia [anomalIa], *n.f.* Anomaly.
anomalo [anOmalo], *a.* Anomalous.
anonimamente, *adv.* Anonymously.
anonimo [anOnimo], *n.m.* Anonymous person; anonym.
anonimo [anOnimo], *a.* Anonymous. (*Comm.*) **Società anonima,** joint-stock company, limited company.
anormale, *a.* Abnormal.
anormalità [-à], *n.f.* Abnormality.
anormalmente, *adv.* Abnormally.
ansa, *n.f.* Handle; (*fig.*) pretext; (*Geog.*) bend (of a river).
ansare, *v.i.* To pant, to be out of breath; (*fig.*) to long for.
ansato, *p.p.a.* Handled, furnished with a handle; bent.
anseatico [anseAtico], *a.* Hanseatic.
ansia, ansietà [Ansia, -à], *n.f.* Anxiety, anxiousness; desire; restlessness.
ansima [Ansima], *n.f.* Shortness of breath.
ansimare, *v.i.* To pant.
ansiosamente, *adv.* Anxiously.
ansioso, *a.* Anxious; restless, uneasy.
ansito [Ansito], *n.m.* Panting, throb.
ansola [Ansola], *n.f.* Hook for a bell-clapper.
antagonismo, *n.m.* Antagonism.
antagonista (*pl.* **— isti**), *n.m.* Antagonist.

antartico [antArtico], *a.* (*Geog.*) Antarctic.
ante, *adv. prep.* Before.
antecedente, *n.m.a.* Antecedent; foregoing, previous; prior.
antecedentemente, *adv.* Antecedently, previously.
antecedenza, *n.f.* Antecedence, priority, precedence.
antecedere [antecEdere], *v.t.* To precede.
antecessore, *n.m.* Predecessor.
antecursore, *n.m.* Forerunner.
antedetto, *a.* Aforesaid.
antediluviano, *a.* [cp. **antidiluviano**].
antefatto, *n.m.* Antecedent fact.
anteguerra, *n.m.a.* Pre-war; pre-war period.
antelmintico, *n.m.* (*Med.*) Anthelmintic.
antelucano, *a.* Before the break of day.
antemurale, *n.m.* (*Mil.*) Rampart, defending wall; breakwater.
antenato, *n.m.* Ancestor, forefather.
antenna, *n.f.* (*Zool.*) Antenna; (*Radio*) aerial; (*Naut.*) lateen-yard.
anteporre, *v.t.* To prefer; to place before (someone else).
anteposizione, *n.f.* Preference (in a matter of precedence).
anteprima, *n.f.* Preview.
antera, *n.f.* (*Bot.*) Anther.
anteriore, *a.* Anterior; former, prior, previous. **Le gambe anteriori,** the forelegs; **impegno —,** prior engagement.
anteriorità [-à], *n.f.* Priority.
anteriormente, *adv.* Formerly, previously; in times past.
antesignano, *n.m.* (*Hist.*) Standard-bearer; leader; forerunner.
antiacido [antiAcido], *a.* (*Chem.*) Antacid.
antiaereo [antiaEreo], *a.* Anti-aircraft.
antialcoolico [antialcoOlico], *a.* Teetotal.
antiallergico, *a.* Antiallergic.
antibiotico [antibiOtico], *n.m.a.* (*Med.*) Antibiotic.
antibraccio [antibrAccio], *n.m.* (*Anat.*) Forearm.
anticaglia [anticAglia], *n.f.* Old curiosity; worthless antique.
anticamente, *adv.* Anciently; formerly, in times past; in olden days.
anticamera [anticAmera], *n.f.* Antechamber; entrance hall, lobby; (*fig.*) attendance. **Fare —,** to dance attendance, to be kept waiting.
anticarro, *a.* (*Mil.*) Anti-tank.
anticattolico [anticattOlico], *a.* Anti-Catholic.
anticheggiare, *v.i.* To affect an old style.
antichità [-à], *n.f.* Antiquity; antique. **Commerciante in —,** antique-dealer.
anticiclone, *n.m.* (*Meteor.*) Anticyclone.
anticipare, *v.t.i.* To anticipate, to advance (payment); to lend; to arrive before the time, to be too early. **— la data,** to advance the date; **— denaro,** to advance money.
anticipatamente, *adv.* In anticipation; prematurely.
anticipato, *p.p.a.* Anticipated; advanced (of money); premature.
anticipazione, *n.f.* Anticipation. **— in conto corrente,** advance on current account.
anticipo [antIcipo], *n.m.* Anticipation, advance. **Siete in —,** you are early; **dobbiamo pagare in —,** we must pay in advance.
anticivismo, *n.m.* (*Pol.*) Anticivism.
anticlericale, *n.m.f.a.* Anticlerical.
anticlericalismo, *n.m.* Anticlericalism.
antico, *n.m.* Antiquity.
antico, *a.* Old, ancient; antique; old-fashioned, obsolete. **L'Antico Testamento,** the Old Testament; **nei tempi antichi,** in ancient times; **gli antichi,** the ancients.
anticolerico [anticolErico], *a.* (*Med.*) Anticholeric; efficacious against cholera.
anticongelante, *n.m.*, (*Motor.*) Anti-freeze.
anticorte, *n.f.* Forecourt.
anticostituzionale, *a.* Anti-constitutional.
anticristiano, *a.* Antichristian.
anticristo, *n.m.* Antichrist.
antidata, *n.f.* Antedate.
antidatare, *v.t.* To antedate.
antidiluviano, *n.m.a.* Antediluvian.
antidoto [antIdoto], *n.m.* Antidote.
antifebbrile, *a.* (*Med.*) Antifebrile.
antifecondativo, *n.m.a.* Contraceptive.
antifona [antIfona], *n.f.* (*Eccles.*) Antiphon.
antifonario [antifonArio], *n.m.* (*Eccles.*) Antiphonary.
antifrasi [antIfrasi], *n.f.* (*Gram.*) Antiphrasis.
antigas [antigAs], *a.* Anti-gas, gas proof. **Maschera —,** gas-mask.
antilogia [antilogIa], *n.f.* Antilogy, contradiction.
antilope [antIlope], *n.f.* (*Zool.*) Antelope.
antimeridiano, *a.* Antemeridian, morning.
antimilitare, *a.* Antimilitary.
antimoniale, *a.* Antimonial.
antimonio [antimOnio], *n.m.* Antimony.
antimuro, *n.m.* (*Mil.*) Outward wall of defence, parapet.
antincendio, *a.* Fire-proof.
antinomia [antinomIa], *n.f.* Antinomy.
antipapa (*pl.* **antipapi**), *n.m.* Antipope.
antiparte, *n.f.* (*Law*) Preferential legacy; (*Comm.*) preferential share.
antipasto, *n.m.* Hors-d'œuvre, side-dish.
antipatia [antipatIa], *n.f.* Antipathy, dislike, aversion.
antipaticamente, *adv.* With dislike, with aversion.
antipatico [antipAtico], *a.* Disagreeable, antipathetic; unpleasant.
antipatriottico [antipatriOttico], *a.* Antipatriotic, unpatriotic.
antipenultimo [antipenUltimo], *a.* Antepenultimate, the last but one.
antipirina, *n.f.* (*Med.*) Antipyrine.
antipodi [antIpodi], *n.m.pl.* (*Geog.*) The Antipodes.
antiporta, *n.f.* Space between inner and outer gates or doors; (*Print.*) front ends, blank page before half-title.
antiquaria [antiquAria], *n.f.* Antiquities; study of the antique.
antiquario [antiquArio], *n.m.* Antiquary, antiquarian.
antiquato, *a.* Antiquated, old-fashioned; obsolete.
antiruggine [antirUggine], *a.* Rust-resisting.
antisala, *n.f.* Antechamber.
antisdrucciolevole [antisdrucciolEvole], *a.* (*Motor.*) Non-skid.
antisemita (*pl.* **antisemiti**), *n.m.* Antisemite.
antisemitico [antisemItico], *a.* Antisemitic.
antisemitismo, *n.m.* Antisemitism.

antisepsi, *n.f.* (*Med.*) Antisepsis.
antisettico [antisEttico], *n.m.a.* (*Med.*) Antiseptic.
antisismico, *a.* In use against earthquakes.
antisociale, *a.* Antisocial.
antistite [antIstite], *n.m.* (*Eccles.*) Bishop.
antitetico [antitEtico], *a.* Antithetical.
antitossina, *n.f.* (*Med.*) Anti-toxin.
antiurto, *a.* Shock-resisting.
antivedere, *v.t.* To foresee.
antivedutamente, *adv.* With foresight.
antiveggente, *a.* Foreseeing.
antiveggenza, *n.f.* Foresight; premonition.
antiveleno, *n.m.* Antidote for poison.
antivenire, *v.t.* To anticipate.
antivigilia [antivigIlia], *n.f.* Day before the vigil; two days before.
antologia [antologIa], *n.f.* Anthology.
Antonio [antOnio], *n.m.* Anthony.
antonomasia [antonomAsia], *n.f.* (*Gram.*) Antonomasia.
antracite, *n.f.* (*Min.*) Anthracite coal.
antro, *n.m.* Cave, cavern; den; grotto; (*Anat.*) antrum.
antropofagia [antropofagIa], *n.f.* Cannibalism.
antropofago [antropOfago], *n.m.* Cannibal.
antropologia [antropologIa], *n.f.* Anthropology.
antropologico [antropolOgico], *a.* Anthropological.
antropologo [antropOlogo], *n.m.* Anthropologist.
antropometria [antropometrIa], *n.f.* Anthropometry.
antropometrico [antropomEtrico], *a.* Anthropometric.
antropomorfismo, *n.m.* Anthropomorphism.
antropomorfo, *n.m.* Animal (such as a monkey) resembling man.
anulare, *n.m.* Ring finger, third finger.
anulare, *a.* Annular.
Anversa, *n.f.* Antwerp.
anzi, *adv.* On the contrary, rather, much more; even. **— che no,** rather than not; **— tempo,** before time.
anzianità [-à], *n.f.* Seniority. **Diritto di —,** right of seniority.
anziano, *n.m.a.* Doyen; aged person; senior; old; aged. **Gli anziani,** the old folk.
anzianotto, *a.* Getting old, on the old side.
anzichè, *conj.* Rather than.
anzidetto, *a.* Aforesaid, above-mentioned.
anzitutto, *adv.* First of all, in the first place.
aoristo, *n.m.a.* (*Gram.*) Aorist.
aorta, [aOrta], *n.f.* (*Anat.*) Aorta.
aortico [aOrtico], (*Anat.*) Aortic.
apatia [apatIa], *n.f.* Apathy.
apatico [apAtico], *a.* Apathetic, apathetical.
apatista, *n.m.* One suffering from apathy.
apatisticamente, *adv.* Apathetically.
apatistico [apatIstico], *a.* Apathetical.
ape, *n.f.* (*Zool.*) Bee. **— regina,** queen bee; **— operaia,** worker bee.
aperitivo, *n.m.* Aperitif, appetiser.
apertamente, *adv.* Openly; frankly.
aperto, *n.m.* Open air; open space. **Dormire all'—,** to sleep in the open.
aperto, *p.p.a.* Open, opened; unbarred; unsealed; (*fig.*) frank, sincere. **Una fronte —,** a broad forehead; **parlare a cuore —,** to speak frankly; **tenere gli occhi aperti su qualcuno,** to keep one's eye on someone; **a braccia aperte,** with open arms; (*Comm.*) **conto —,** running account; **all'aria aperta,** in the open air.
apertura, *n.f.* Aperture, opening; (*fig.*) overture; (*Mus.*) overture. **— di credito,** cash credit.
apetalo [apEtalo], *a.* (*Bot.*) Apetalous.
apiaio [apiAio], *n.m.* Beekeeper.
apiaria [apiAria], *n.f.* Bee-keeping, apiculture.
apiario [apiArio], *n.m.* Apiary.
apice [Apice], *n.m.* Apex; top, summit.
apicoltore, *n.m.* Beekeeper.
apicultura, *n.f.* Apiculture, beekeeping.
apio [Apio], *n.m.* (*Bot.*) Celery.
apiro [Apiro], *a.* Incombustible.
apocalisse, apocalissi, *n.f.* Apocalypse. The Book of the Revelation of St. John.
apocalittico [apocalIttico], *a.* Apocalyptic.
apocope [apOcope], *n.f.* (*Gram.*) Apocope, cutting off of the final sound; elision.
apocrifo [apOcrifo], *a.* Apocryphal.
apodo [Apodo], *a.* (*Zool.*) Apodal, footless.
apofisi [apOfisi], *n.f.* (*Med.*) Apophesis.
apoftegma, apoftemma, *n.m.* Apophthegm.
apogeo [apogEo], *n.m.* (*Astron.*) Apogee; (*fig.*) culminating point, pitch.
apolide, *a.* Stateless.
apolidi [apOlidi], *n.m.pl.* (*Pol.*) Persons deprived of their civic and political rights.
apolitico [apolItico], *a.* Uninterested in politics; non-political.
apologetica [apologEtica], *n.f.* Apologetics.
apologètico [apologEtico], *a.* Apologetic.
apologia [apologIa], *n.f.* Defence, apologia.
apologista (*pl.* **apologisti**), *n.m.* Apologist.
apologizzare, *v.i.* To write or make a defence.
apologo [apOlogo], *n.m.* Apologue, fable.
apoplessia [apoplEssia], *n.f.* (*Med.*) Apoplexy. **Colpo d'—,** apoplectic stroke.
apoplettico [apoplEttico], *a.* Apoplectic.
apostasia [apostasIa], *n.f.* Apostacy.
apostata [apOstata], *n.m.f.* Apostate.
apostatare, *v.i.* To apostasize, to become an apostate.
apostema, *n.f.* (*Med.*) Abscess [cp. **postema**].
apostemare, *v.i.* (*Med.*) To suppurate (of an abscess).
apostolato, *n.m.* Apostolate.
apostolicamente, *adv.* Apostolically.
apostolico [apostOlico], *a.* Apostolical. **Sede Apostolica,** Apostolic See.
apostolo [apOstolo], *n.m.* Apostle.
apostrofare, *v.t.* To apostrophize; to address; to put an apostrophe.
apostrofe [apOstrofe], *n.f.* (*Rhetoric*) Apostrophe.
apostrofo [apOstrofo], *n.m.* (*Print.*) Apostrophe.
apoteosi [apoteOsi], *n.f.* Apotheosis.
appaciare, appacificare, *v.t.* To pacify, to reconcile; to appease.
appaciarsi, appacificarsi, *v.r.* To become pacified, to make peace.
appagabile [appagAbile], *a.* That may be satisfied.
appagamento, *n.m.* Satisfaction; gratification; contentment.

appagare, *v.t.* To satisfy, to please, to content; to satiate, to glut; to cloy. — **la sete,** to quench one's thirst.
appagarsi, *v.r.* To satisfy oneself, to be satisfied.
appagliaiare, *v.t.* To get straw ready for stacking.
appaiamento, *n.m.* Coupling, yoking; matching (for colour, etc.)
appaiare, *v.t.* To couple, to pair (animals, objects, etc.), to yoke; to match. — **cavalli,** to match horses.
appaiarsi, *v.r.* To pair, to mate.
appaiatura, *n.f.* [cp. **appaiamento**].
appalesare, *v.t.* To make public.
appallare, appallottare, appallottolare, *v.t.* To make into balls or lumps.
appaltare, *v.t.* To let out (a contract, etc.)
appaltato, *p.p.a.* Let out, leased.
appaltatore, appaltatrice, *n.m.f.* Contractor.
appalto, *n.m.* Lease, contract (for work, etc.); undertaking; (*Tuscan*) salt and tobacco shop (in Italy government monopolies).
appanare, *v.t.* To make into loaves or cakes.
appannaggio [appannAggio], *n.m.* Apanage; (*fig.*) lot, prerogative.
appannamento, *n.m.* Dimming (with moisture).
appannare, *v.t.* To dim (with moisture), to dull, to deaden, to tarnish.
appannarsi, *v.r.* To become dim or dull.
appannato, *p.p.a.* Dull, dimmed; obscured; hoarse.
appannatoio [appannatOio], *n.m.* Cloth for rubbing down horses.
appannatura, *n.f.* Dimming; dulling; obscuring.
apparato, *n.m.* Apparatus (in all senses); decoration; (*fig.*) pomp.
apparecchiare, *v.t.* To prepare, to get ready; to dress; to cook. — **la tavola,** to lay the table.
apparecchiarsi, *v.r.* To get ready, to make oneself ready.
apparecchiatore, *n.m.* Dresser (of skins, etc.).
apparecchiatura, *n.f.* Preparation; dressing; apparatus.
apparecchio [apparEcchio], *n.m.* Apparatus, machine; (*Aviat.*) aeroplane, plane. — **radio,** radio set; — **da caccia,** fighter plane; — **da bombardamento,** bomber plane; **resti all'—,** hold the line (telephone).
apparcggiare, *v.t.* To level, to make equal.
apparentarsi, *v.r.* To become related by marriage.
apparente, *a.* Apparent, seeming.
apparentemente, *adv.* Apparently.
apparenza, *n.f.* Appearance, aspect; likelihood. **Salvar l'—,** to keep up appearances; **l'— inganna,** appearances are deceitful; **in —,** apparently.
apparigliare, *v.t.* To match.
apparire, *v.i.* To appear, to seem; to come forth; (*fig.*) to result. **Ciò appare strano,** that seems strange.
appariscente, *a.* Visible, remarkable; showy; pompous, ostentatious.
appariscenza, *n.f.* Appearance, look; showiness; bearing, carriage.
apparita, *n.f.* First appearance.
apparitore, *n.m.* Apparitor, beadle.
apparizione, *n.f.* Apparition.
apparso, *p.p.* [cp. **apparire**].
appartamento, *n.m.* Suite of rooms, flat. — **ammobiliato,** furnished flat.
appartare, *v.t.* To set apart, to set aside.
appartarsi, *v.r.* To stand aloof, to retire, to withdraw, to separate oneself.
appartatamente, *adv.* In a lonely way, separately.
appartato, *a.* Alone, set apart; remote; lonely. **Luogo —,** solitary place, secluded spot; **condurre vita appartata,** to keep oneself to oneself.
appartenente, *a.* Pertaining to, belonging to.
appartenenza, *n.f.* Appurtenance; belongings; competence.
appartenere, *v.i.* To belong to, to appertain to, to be a member (of); to be within one's competence. **Appartiene al prete di predicare bene,** it is a priest's job to preach well; **questo libro mi appartiene,** this book belongs to me.
appartenuto, *p.p.a.* Appertained; related.
appassimento, *n.m.* Fading; withering (of flowers, etc.).
appassionamento, *n.m.* Passion.
appassionare, *v.t.* To impassion, to inspire with passion.
appassionarsi, *v.r.* To be impassioned, to become impassioned; to become enamoured.
appassionatamente, *adv.* Passionately.
appassionato, *p.p.a.* Impassioned, passionate. **Essere appassionata per la musica,** to be passionately fond of music; **giudizio —,** biased judgment.
appassire, *v.i.* To fade, to wither (of flowers); to decay; to grow ripe (of fruit).
appassirsi, *v.r.* To fade, to wither.
appastellare, *v.t.* To gather into pellets or lumps.
appedare, *v.t.* [cp. **appiedare**].
appellabile [appellAbile], *a.* (*Law*) Susceptible of appeal, that may be appealed against.
appellabilità [-à], *n.f.* Power or right of appeal.
appellante, *n.m.f.* (*Law*) Appellant.
appellare, *v.t.i.* To appeal, to appeal against, to bring an appeal; to name, to summon by name.
appellarsi, *v.r.* To appeal, to appeal against.
appellativo, *a.* Appellative.
appellatorio [appellatOrio], *a.* (*Law*) Appellatory.
appellazione, *n.f.* Appellation, name.
appello, *n.m.* Call; muster; (*Law*) court of appeal. (*Mil.*) **Fare l'—,** to call the roll; **mancare all'—,** to be absent; **passare l'—,** to pass muster; (*Law*) **fare —,** to appeal.
appena, *adv.* Scarcely; as soon as; hardly. **Non —,** no sooner; — — **un po',** very little.
appendere [appEndere], *v.t.* To hang up, to suspend, to append. — **alla parete,** to hang on the wall; — **quadri,** to hang pictures.
appendice, *n.f.* Appendix; supplement; (*Med.*) appendix.
appendicite, *n.f.* (*Med.*) Appendicitis.
appendizie [appendIzie], *n.f.pl.* Extras (such as fowls, eggs, etc.) supplied by a tenant to his landlord.
Appennini, *n.m.pl.* (*Geog.*) The Apennines.
appesire, *v.i.* (*obs.*) To increase one's weight with age.

appeso, *p.p.a.* Hung up, suspended.
appestare, *v.t.i.* To infect (with disease, etc.); to taint; to stink.
appestato, *n.m.a.* Person infected with the plague; infected, tainted.
appetente, *a.* Appetizing.
appetenza, *n.f.* Appetence; craving for.
appetibile [appetIbile], *a.* Attractive, desirable.
appetibilità [-à], *n.f.* Attractiveness, desirability.
appetire, *v.t.i.* To desire greatly, to crave after; to stimulate the appetite.
appetito, *n.m.* Appetite. **Buon — !** good appetite! (an Italian phrase of politeness before a meal).
appetitosamente, *adv.* With appetite; appetizingly.
appetitoso, *a.* Appetizing, tempting.
appetto, a petto, *prep.* In comparison with, compared to; facing. **Stare — ad una persona,** to stand face to face.
appezzamento, *n.m.* Plot of land; piece of land.
appezzare, *v.t.* To piece together, to repair; to separate into pieces.
appezzatura, *n.f.* Piecing, repairing, patching; join (where two pieces are placed together).
appezzettare, *v.t.* To parcel out, to divide into portions.
appiacevolire, *v.t.* (*Lit.*) To make agreeable.
appianabile [appianAbile], *a.* Capable of being smoothed or planed; capable of settlement.
appianamento, *n.m.* Levelling, smoothing; (*fig.*) removal (of difficulties).
appianare, *v.t.* To smooth, to plane; to facilitate, to remove (difficulties).
appianato, *p.p.a.* Smoothed, level; (*fig.*) cleared up, settled.
appianatoio [appianatOio], *n.m.* Heavy roller for paths; steam roller.
appiastrare, appiastricciare, *v.t.* To plaster (a wall, etc.); to make sticky.
appiastricciarsi, *v.r.* To make oneself sticky, to get sticky.
appiattamento, *n.m.* Concealment.
appiattare, *v.t.* To hide, to conceal.
appiattimento, *n.m.* (*obs.*) Levelling (of prices, wages, etc.).
appiattire, *v.t.* To level; to flatten.
appiccagnolo [appiccAgnolo], *n.m.* Pretext; hook; peg.
appiccamento, *n.m.* Hanging.
appiccare, *v.t.* To hang, to hang up; to join. **— il fuoco,** to set fire to; **— la battaglia,** to give battle; **— un discorso,** to start a conversation [cp. **impiccare**].
appiccarsi, *v.r.* To hang oneself.
appiccaticcio [appiccatIccio], *a.* Sticky.
appiccativo, *a.* Contagious; sticky.
appiccatoio [appiccatOio], *n.m.* Hook.
appicciare, *v.t.* To join (with glue, paste, etc.); to string together; to light (candle, fire, etc.).
appicciatura, *n.f.* Joining together.
appiccicante, *a.* Sticky, clammy.
appiccicare, *v.t.* To join, to attach, to glue.
appiccicarsi, *v.r.* To adhere, to stick to.
appiccicaticcio [appiccicatIccio], *n.m.* Patchwork, hotchpotch of things stuck together.
appiccicaticcio [appiccicatIccio], *a.* Sticky; (*Med.*) contagious; (*fig.*) bothersome.
appiccicato, *p.p.a.* Glued, stuck together.
appiccicatura, *n.f.* Sticking, gumming; a thing badly stuck together.
appiccichino, *n.m.* Person who sticks to one; person one cannot get rid of.
appiccicoso, *a.* Sticky.
appiccinire, *v.t.* To belittle; to make smaller.
appiccinirsi, *v.r.* To belittle oneself.
appicco, *n.m.* [cp. **appiccagnolo**].
appiccolire, *v.t.* (*Lit.*) To reduce, to make smaller [cp. **impicciolire**].
appiè, *adv.* At the foot, at the bottom, below. **— del letto,** at the foot of the bed; **— della pagina,** at the foot of the page; **— delle scale,** downstairs.
appiedamento, *n.m.* (*Mil.*) Dismounting.
appiedare, *v.t.i.* (*Mil.*) To dismount.
appieno, *adv.* Completely, fully, entirely, quite, thoroughly.
appigionamento, *n.m.* Letting; renting, hiring.
appigionare, *v.t.* To lease, to let, to rent; to hire.
appigionarsi, *v.r.* (Of a house, etc.) To be let, to let.
appigionasi [appigiOnasi], *n.m.* (Notice) "House to let".
appigliarsi, *v.r.* To get hold of, to hold on to; to follow; to take a resolution; to have recourse to.
appiglio [appIglio], *n.m.* Support; pretext.
appinzare, *v.t.* To sting (of wasps, etc.).
appinzatura, *n.f.* Sting (both effect and cause).
appio [Appio], *n.m.* (*Bot.*) Celery.
appiolo [appiOlo], *n.m.* (*Bot.*) Rennet-apple tree.
appiombare, *v.t.* To apply the plumb-line to.
appiombo, *adv.* Perpendicularly.
appioppare, *v.t.* To deal (a blow), to fling; (rare) to train vines on poplars; to give something not wanted or of little value. **Gli appioppò un calcio,** he gave him a kick.
appisolarsi, *v.r.* To drop asleep, to nap.
applaudire, *v.t.i.* To applaud, to clap one's hands; (*fig.*) to approve.
applaudito, *p.p.a.* Applauded, cheered; commended.
applauditore, applauditrice, *n.m.f.* One who applauds.
applauso [applAuso], *n.m.* Applause, cheers.
applicabile [applicAbile], *a.* Applicable.
applicabilità [-à], *n.f.* Applicability.
applicare, *v.t.* To apply; to attribute; (*Law*) to enforce, to award. **— la legge,** to apply the law; **— una multa,** to impose a fine; **— la mente,** to apply one's mind.
applicarsi, *v.r.* To apply oneself; to devote oneself. **Questo ragazzo non vuole —,** this lad will not apply himself to his work.
applicato, *n.m.* Clerk in an inferior position.
applicazione, *n.f.* Application; close attention; (*Law*) enforcement; trimming (of a hat, etc.).
appo, *prep.* (*obs.*) Near, nearby; after, afterwards.
appoderamento, *n.m.* (*Agric.*) Farming.
appoderare, *v.t.* (*Agric.*) To cultivate, to farm.
appoderarsi, *v.r.* (*Agric.*) To settle on and work a farm.
appoggiacapo, *n.m.* Head-rest.
appoggiamano, *n.m.* Hand-rest.

appoggiare, *v.t.i.* To lean; to rest, to rest upon; to bear (to right or left); to back up; to support, to second. **ha degli amici che l'appoggiano,** he has friends to back him up; **— una mozione,** to second a motion.
appoggiarsi, *v.r.* To lean (upon); to rest (against); to trust. **— al braccio di un amico,** to lean on a friend's arm.
appoggiatoio [appoggiatOio], *n.m.* Rest, support; stair-rail.
appoggiatura, *n.f.* Leaning, resting; grace-note.
appoggio [appOggio], *n.m.* Support; staff; (*fig.*) help, protection; (*Comm.*) voucher.
appollaiarsi, *v.r.* To roost; to settle.
apponibile [apponIbile], *a.* Susceptible of being added or affixed.
apporre, *v.t.* To affix; (*fig.*) to impute, to assert; to ascribe. **— la firma,** to affix one's signature; **— un francobollo,** to stick on a stamp.
apporsi, *v.r.* To guess.
apportare, *v.t.* To bring; to carry; to bear, to yield; to contribute, to be the cause of, to occasion. **— gioia,** to be the cause of rejoicing; **— disturbo a qualcuno,** to cause someone trouble.
apportatore, apportatrice, *n.m.f.* Bearer; messenger.
appositamente, *adv.* Appositely; purposely.
apposito [appOsito], *a.* Apposite, suitable, proper. **Luogo —,** suitable site, proper place.
apposizione, *n.m.* Apposition; placing on; affixing. **— del sigillo,** affixing of the seal; **— della firma,** adding the signature.
apposta, *adv.* On purpose. **Lo ha fatto —,** he did it on purpose.
appostamento, *n.m.* Lying in wait; (*Mil.*) emplacement.
appostare, *v.t.* To lie in wait, to waylay; to watch.
appostarsi, *v.r.* To lie in wait, to lurk.
appostato, *a.* Concealed, hidden; in ambush.
apposto, *p.p.a.* Affixed, added, inserted. **La data apposta alla lettera,** the date on the letter.
appratire, *v.t.* To lay down in grass; to convert to meadow.
apprendere [apprEndere], *v.t.* To learn, to apprehend; to hear; to perceive; to teach.
apprendersi [apprEndersi], *v.r.* To attach, to cleave to; to take (fire).
apprendimento, *n.m.* Learning; perceiving.
apprendista (*pl.* **apprendisti**), *n.m.* Apprentice; beginner; junior clerk.
apprendistato, *n.m.* Apprenticeship.
apprensione, *n.f.* Apprehension, fear; understanding.
apprensionirsi, *v.r.* To become apprehensive.
apprensiva, *n.f.* (*Lit.*) Faculty of perception or apprehension.
apprensivo, *a.* Apprehensive, timid.
appreso, *p.p.a.* Learned, taught.
appressamento, *n.m.* Approach.
appressare, *v.t.* To approach, to bring closer.
appressarsi, *v.r.* To approach, to draw near, to come nearer. **— al fuoco,** to come nearer the fire.
appresso, *prep.adv.* Near, hard by, close to; after; as below, as follows. **Il giorno —,** the next day.
appressochè, *conj.* [cp. **pressochè**].
apprestamento, *n.m.* Preparation; outfit.
apprestare, *v.t.* To prepare, to get ready; to equip, to fit.
apprestarsi, *v.r.* To make oneself ready, to prepare oneself.
appretto, *n.m.* Finishing (of cloth).
apprezzabile [apprezzAbile], *a.* Appreciable.
apprezzamento, *n.m.* Valuation, appreciation, estimation.
apprezzare, *v.t.* To appreciate (value); to appraise; to estimate; to pass judgment.
apprezzato, *p.p.a.* Estimated, valued, esteemed; judged.
apprezzatore, *n.m.* Valuer, appraiser.
approcciare, *v.t.* (*Mil.*) To make approaches.
approccio [apprOccio], *n.m.* Approach.
approdare, *v.i.* (*Naut.*) To disembark, to land at; (*fig.*) to be of some purpose; (*Agric.*) to plant along the sides of a field. **Una discussione che non approda a nulla,** a discussion to no purpose.
approdato, *p.p.a.* Landed, disembarked.
approdo, *n.m.* (*Naut.*) Landfall, landing-place.
approfittare, *v.i.* To profit, to avail oneself of, to take advantage of.
approfittarsi, *v.r.* To avail oneself of.
approfondamento, approfondimento, *n.m.* Deepening, sinking lower; (*fig.*) search.
approfondare, approfondire, *v.t.* To deepen, to make deeper; (*fig.*) to search thoroughly.
approfondito, *p.p.a.* Deepened, made deeper; (*fig.*) thoroughly examined.
approntare, *v.t.* To make ready.
appropriabile [appropriAbile], *a.* That can be appropriated.
appropriamento, *n.m.* Appropriation.
appropriare, *v.t.* To adapt, to make suitable, to fit.
appropriarsi, *v.r.* To appropriate, to take for one's own; to embezzle.
appropriatamente, *adv.* Appropriately, opportunely.
appropriato, *p.p.a.* Suited, fitted; appropriate, proper.
appropriazione, *n.f.* Appropriation. **— indebita,** embezzlement.
approssimamento, *n.m.* Approach.
approssimare, *v.t.i.* To approach, to bring near, to draw near.
approssimarsi, *v.r.* To approach, to come near; to approximate. **Il tempo si approssima,** the time draws near.
approssimativamente, *adv.* Approximately, nearly.
approssimativo, *a.* Approximate, rough. **Calcolo —,** rough estimate.
approssimato, *p.p.a.* Near, drawn near.
approssimazione, *n.f.* Approximation.
approvabile [approvAbile], *a.* Deserving approval.
approvare, *v.t.* To approve, to approve of; to consent; to confirm. **— una legge,** to pass a law; **— un conto,** to approve or pass an account; **— una relazione,** to adopt a report; **essere approvato negli esami,** to pass one's exams.
approvativo, *a.* Approbatory.
approvato, *p.p.a.* Approved; passed, carried.
approvazione, *n.f.* Approval, approbation. **Ottenere l'— di,** to obtain the approval of.

approvvigionamento, *n.m.* Provisions, victualling, supply.
approvvigionare, approvvisionare, *v.t.* To victual, to supply with, to provision.
appruato, *a.* (*Naut.*) Down by the head.
appuntamento, *n.m.* Appointment, meeting, rendezvous. **Darsi un —,** To make an appointment.
appuntare, *v.t.* To point, to sharpen, to pin; (*fig*). to note; to accuse.
appuntato, *n.m.* (*Mil.*) Corporal.
appuntato, *p.p.a.* Pointed, pinned; noted. **Parlare —,** to talk in an affected manner.
appuntatura, *n.f.* Pointing, making pointed.
appuntellare, *v.t.* (*Arch.*) To shore up, to underprop [cp. **puntellare**].
appuntino, *adv.* Precisely. (*Colloq.*) **Signor Appuntino,** Mr. Know-all, Mr. Smartie.
appunto, *n.m.* Note, record, remembrance.
appunto, *adv.* Precisely, exactly, just so. **Per l'—,** that's so.
appuramento, *n.m.* Verification; settlement (of an account).
appurare, *v.t.* To ascertain, to verify, to examine.
appuzzare, *v.t.* To cause a foul smell, to stink; to infect.
aprico, *a.* (*Poet.*) Sunny, exposed to the sun.
aprilante, *a.* **Terzo — quaranta di durante,** as is the third of April so will the next forty days be (the Italian equivalent of St. Swithin prophecy).
aprile, *n.m.* April. **L'— degli anni,** the heyday of youth; **pesce d'—,** April Fool.
aprimento, *n.m.* Opening.
aprire, *v.t.* To open; to unlock; to unseal; to excavate; to unfold (wings); to unbosom (the feelings). **— un baule,** to unpack; **— le ali,** to spread the wings; **— la bocca,** to open one's mouth; **— le cortine,** to throw open the curtains; **— la radio,** to turn on the radio; **— un conto,** to open an account; **— gli occhi a qualcuno,** to open someone's eyes, to undeceive.
aprirsi, *v.r.* To open, to be opened; to unbosom oneself; to expand.
apriscatole [apriscAtole], *s.m.* Tin-opener, can-opener.
apritore, apritrice, *n.m.f.* Opener, attendant.
apritura, *n.f.* Opening, aperture.
aquario [aquArio], *n.m.* Aquarium.
aquila [Aquila], *n.f.* (*Zool.*) Eagle; standard (of the Romans); (*fig.*) man of master mind. **Occhi d'—,** sharp-sighted.
aquilifero [aquilIfero], *n.m.* (*Hist.*) Eagle-bearer.
aquilino, *a.* Aquiline.
aquilonare, *a.* Northern.
aquilone, *n.m.* North wind; large eagle; child's kite.
aquilotto, *n.m.* Eaglet.
Aquisgrana, *n.f.* Aix-la-Chapelle, Aachen.
ara, *n.f.* Altar; are (unit of metric land measurement, about 120 sq. yds.).
arabescare, *v.t.* To decorate with arabesques.
arabesco, *n.m.* Arabesque.
Arabia [arAbia], *n.f.* Arabia.
arabico [arAbico], *a.* Arab, Arabian, Arabic. **Cifra arabica,** Arabic numeral.
arabile [arAbile], *a.* Arable.
arabo [Arabo], *n.m.* Arab.
arachide [arAchide], *n.f.* Peanut, groundnut.
aracnidi [arAcnidi], *n.m.pl.* (*Zool.*) Arachnids.
aragno, *n.m.* (*obs.*) Spider. [cp. **ragno**].
aragosta, *n.m.* (*Zool.*) Lobster.
araldica [arAldica], *n.f.* Heraldry.
araldico [arAldico], *a.* Heraldic. **Consulta araldica,** (Italian) college of arms.
araldo, *n.m.* Herald.
aramento, *n.m.* Ploughing; tilling.
aranceto, *n.m.* Orange plantation, orange grove.
arancia [arAncia], *n.f.* Orange.
aranciata, *n.f.* Orangeade.
aranciato, *a.* Orange, orange-coloured.
aranciera, *n.f.* Orangery.
arancio [arAncio], *n.m.* (*Bot.*) Orange tree.
arancione, *a.* Orange (colour).
arare, *v.t.* To plough, to till.
arativo, *a.* Arable.
arato, *p.p.a.* Ploughed.
aratore, *n.m.* Ploughman.
aratro, *n.m.* Plough. (*fig.*) **Mettere l'— avanti ai buoi,** to put the cart before the horse.
aratura, *n.f.* Ploughing.
arazzeria [arazzerIa], *n.f.* Tapestry warehouse or factory.
arazziere, *n.m.* Tapestry weaver; upholsterer.
arazzo, *n.m.* Tapestry, hangings.
arbitraggio [arbitrAggio], *n.m.* Arbitration; (*Comm.*) calculation of the differences in values etc. between one country and another.
arbitrale, *a.* Concerning an arbitrator, arbitral.
arbitrare, *v.i.* To arbitrate.
arbitrariamente, *adv.* Arbitrarily, in an arbitrary manner.
arbitrario [arbitrArio], *a.* Arbitrary.
arbitrato, *n.m.* Arbitration.
arbitrio [arbItrio], *n.m.* Free will; an arbitrary action.
arbitro [Arbitro], *n.m.* Arbitrator; umpire, referee.
arbore [Arbore] [cp. **albero**].
arboreo [arbOreo], *a.* Arboreous.
arborescente, *a.* Arborescent.
arborescenza, *n.f.* Arborescence.
arboreto, *n.m.* Arboretum.
arboricoltore, *n.m.* Arboriculturist.
arboricultura, *n.f.* Arboriculture.
arboscello, *n.m.* Shrub, young tree.
arbusto, *n.m.* Shrub, bush.
arbuto, *n.m.* (*Bot.*) Arbutus.
arca, *n.f.* Ark; sarcophagus; tomb; place where many animals are gathered. **— dell'alleanza,** ark of the covenant; **— di scienza,** very learned man.
arcade [Arcade], *n.m.* Arcadian; member of the 17th-cent. Arcadian college in Italy.
arcadico [arcAdico], *a.* Arcadian; affected.
arcaico [arcAico], *a.* Archaic.
arcaismo, *n.m.* Archaism.
arcale, *n.m.* (*Arch.*) Arch (of a door); rafter (of roof).
arcanamente, *adv.* Mysteriously; occultly.
arcangelo, arcangiolo [arcAngelo, arcAngiolo], *n.m.* Archangel.
arcano, *n.m.a.* Arcanum, mystery; mysterious.
arcare, *v.t.* (*obs.*) To bend; to draw a bow, to shoot (an arrow); to throw a dart.

arcata, *n.f.* (*Arch.*) Arch of a bridge or other building; span of an arch; arcade; (*Mus.*) bowing (of violin, etc.).
arcavolo, arcavola [arcAvolo, arcAvola], *n.m.f.* Great-great-grandfather or mother.
arce, *n.f.* (*Lit.*) Rock; fortress, citadel.
archeggiare, *v.i.* (*Mus.*) To bow (violin, etc.).
archeggio [archEggio], *n.m.* (*Mus.*) Bowing.
archeologia [archeologIa], *n.f.* Archaeology.
archeologicamente, *adv.* Archaeologically.
archeologico [archeolOgico], *a.* Archaeological.
archeologo [archeOlogo], *n.m.* Archaeologist.
archetipo [archEtipo], *n.m.* Archetype.
archetto, *n.m.* (*Mus.*) Bow (of violin, etc.); (*Arch.*) small arch; kind of bird trap.
archiatro [archIatro], *n.m.* Principal physician (at court, etc.).
archibugiere, archibusiere, *n.m.* (*Hist.*) Arquebusier.
archibugio, archibusio [archibUgio, archibUsio], *n.m.* (*Hist.*) Arquebus.
archiepiscopale, *a.* Archiepiscopal.
Archimede *n.m.* Archimedes.
archipendolo, archipenzolo [archipEndolo, archipEnzolo], *n.m.* Plumb-line.
architettare, *v.t.* (*Arch.*) To design (a building), to lay out plans.
architetto, *n.m.* Architect.
architettonicamente, *adv.* Architecturally.
architettonico [architettOnico], *a.* Architectural.
architettura, *n.f.* Architecture.
architrave, *n.m.* (*Arch.*) Architrave; lintel.
archiviare, *v.t.* To place in the archives; to put on record; (*Comm.*) to file.
archiviatura, *n.f.* Recording; filing.
archivio [archIvio], *n.m.* Archive, record office; (*Comm.*) file.
archivista, *n.m.* Archivist.
arci-, *prefix.* First, principal, great, arch-; very.
arcibello, *a.* Very lovely.
arcidiacono [arcidiAcono], *n.m.* (*Eccles.*) Archdeacon.
arciduca, *n.m.* Archduke.
arciducato, *n.m.* Archduchy.
arciduchessa, *n.f.* Archduchess.
arciere, arciero, *n.m.* Archer, bowman; body-guard.
arcifanfano [arcifAnfano], *n.m.* Boaster, braggart.
arcignamente, *adv.* Gruffly, morosely, sourly.
arcignezza, *n.f.* Gruffness, surliness.
arcigno, *a.* Gruff, sulky, sullen, sour.
arcione, *n.m.* Saddle-bow; saddle.
arcipelago [arcipElago], *n.m.* (*Geog.*) Archipelago.
arciprete, *n.m.* (*Eccles.*) High priest.
arcivescovado, *n.m.* Archbishopric.
arcivescovile, *a.* Archiepiscopal.
arcivescovo [arcivEscovo], *n.m.* Archbishop.
arco, *n.m.* Bow; (*Math.*) arc; (*Arch.*) arch; (*Elec.*) arc; (*Mus.*) bow. **Tendere l'—,** to draw the bow; **a tiro d'—,** within bow-shot; (*Elec.*) **lampada ad —,** arc lamp.
arcobaleno, *n.m.* Rainbow.
arcolaio [arcolAio], *n.m.* Reel-winder, skein-winder; spinning-wheel.
arconte, *n.m.* (*Hist.*) Archon.
arcuare, *v.t.* To bend, to curve, to arch.
ardente, *a.* Burning; ardent; fiery; fervid. **Occhi ardenti,** burning eyes; **sole —,** scorching sun; **temperamento —,** fiery temper; **cavallo —,** spirited horse; **cappella —,** mortuary chapel.
ardentemente, *adv.* Ardently, passionately, hotly.
ardenza, *n.f.* Ardour; eagerness; impatience.
ardere [Ardere], *v.i.* To burn, to be on fire; (*fig.*) to be ardent, to be impatient; to shine. **— d'amore,** to burn with love; **spirito da —,** methylated spirit.
ardesia [ardEsia], *n.f.* (*Geol.*) Slate. **Cava di —,** slate quarry.
ardiglione, *n.m.* Tongue of a buckle.
ardimento, *n.m.* Boldness, hardihood, fearlessness, courage; impudence.
ardimentosamente, *adv.* Boldly, fearlessly.
ardimentoso, *a.* Bold, fearless, courageous.
ardire, *v.i.* To dare, to venture; to risk.
ardire, *n.m.* Boldness, courage; impudence, presumption.
ardirsi, *v.r.* To risk oneself, to take risks.
arditamente, *adv.* Boldly.
arditezza, *n.f.* Boldness.
arditi, *n.m.pl.* (*Mil.*) Scouts, shock troops; commandos.
ardito, *a.* Bold, daring, fearless.
ardore, *n.m.* Ardour, warmth; zeal.
arduamente, *adv.* Arduously, with difficulty; hardly.
arduo [Arduo], *a.* Arduous, hard, difficult.
area [Area], *n.f.* Area; surface.
arem, *n.m.* Harem.
arena, *n.f.* Sand; arena; amphitheatre.
arenaceo [arenAceo], *a.* Sandy, of a sandy nature.
arenamento, *n.m.* Stranding.
arenare, *v.t.i.r.* To get stranded; (*Naut.*) to beach (a vessel); to run aground.
arenaria [arenAria], *n.f.* (*Geol.*) Sandstone.
arenario [arenArio], *n.m.* (*Hist.*) Gladiator.
arenile, *n.m.* Sandy shore.
arenosità [-à], *n.f.* Sandiness.
arenoso, *a.* Sandy (of soil).
areodromo [areOdromo], *n.m.* Aerodrome.
areometro [areOmetro], *n.m.* Aerometer, hydrometer.
areonauta (*pl.* **areonauti**) [areonAuta], *n.m.* Aeronaut.
areonave, *n.f.* Airship.
areoplano, *n.m.* Aeroplane [cp. **aeroplano**].
areoscalo, *n.m.* Aerodrome, hangar.
areostato [areOstato], *n.m.* Balloon.
arfasatto, *n.m.* Clown, foolish fellow; cad.
arganetto, *n.m.* (*Naut.*) Windlass.
argano [Argano], *n.m.* Capstan, winch.
argentaio [argentAio], *n.m.* Silversmith.
argentana, *n.f.* German silver.
argentare, *v.t.* To silver, to plate, to silver-plate.
argentatura, *n.f.* Silvering, silver-plating.
argenteo [argEnteo], *a.* Silver; looking like silver.
argenteria [argenterIa], *n.f.* Silverware.
argentiera, *n.f.* Silver mine.
argentiere, *n.m.* Silversmith.
argentifero [argentIfero], *a.* Argentiferous.
argentino, *a.* Silvery (in colour); like silver. **Voce argentina,** silvery voice.
argento, *n.m.* Silver; silver money. **— vivo,** quicksilver.

argentone, *n.m.* German silver.
argilla, *n.f.* (*Geol.*) Clay.
argillaceo [argillAceo], *a.* Clayey.
argilloso, *a.* Clayey (of soil, etc.), loamy.
arginamento, *n.m.* Damming up.
arginare, *v.t.* To dam, to dyke; to embank; (*fig.*) to stem.
arginatura, *n.f.* Damming, embanking.
argine [Argine], *n.m.* Dam, dyke, embankment; (*fig.*) bar, barrier, obstacle.
Argo, *n.m.* (*fig.*) Very wide-awake person.
argomentare, *v.t.i.* To argue, to prove, to deduce, to infer.
argomentarsi, *v.r.* To exert oneself, to endeavour.
argomentato, *p.p.a.* Argued, proved; exerted, striven.
argomentatore, argomentatrice, *n.m.f.* Arguer, argufier.
argomentazione, *n.f.* Argumentation, argufying.
argomento, *n.m.* Argument, summary; subject, topic; proof, reason. **— della lezione**; subject of the lesson; **cambiamo —** let us change the subject; **ventilare un —** to ventilate a topic; **dare —,** to give cause.
argon, *n.m.* (*Phys.*) Argon.
argonauta [argonAuta], *n.m.* (*Zool.*) Argonaut; (*Hist.*) Argonaut.
arguire, *v.t.* To argue; to guess, to infer.
argutamente, *adv.* Acutely, keenly, subtly; wittily.
argutezza, *n.f.* Keenness, acuteness; wittiness.
arguto, *a.* Keen, acute; witty.
arguzia [arguzIa], *n.f.* Humour, wit; witticism.
aria [Aria], *n.f.* Air (in all senses); breeze; resemblance. **— aperta,** open air; **dare — ad una stanza,** to air a room; **corrente d'—,** a draught; **darsi l'— di,** to put on an air of; **cambiamento d'—,** change of air; **con — di protezione,** in a patronizing way; **avere l'— di,** to look like; **pompa ad —,** air-pump.
arianesimo [arianEsimo], *n.m.* Arianism.
ariano, *n.m.a.* (*Eccles.*) Arian; (*Ethnography*) Aryan, Indo-European.
aridamente, *adv.* Drily, aridly.
aridezza, aridità [-à], *n.f.* Aridity, dryness; barrenness.
arido [Arido], *a.* Arid, dry; barren; uninteresting; sterile.
arieggiare, *v.t.i.* To resemble, to have an air of; to air (a room, etc.). **Arieggia a grand'uomo,** he puts on the airs of a big man.
ariete, *n.m.* (*Zool.*) Ram; battering-ram; (*Astron.*) Aries.
arimmetica [cp. **aritmetica**].
aringa, *n.f.* (*Zool.*) Herring. **— affumicata,** bloater, kipper.
arioso, *a.* Airy.
arista (1), *n.f.* (*Bot.*) Beard of corn.
arista [Arista] (2), *n.f.* Chine of pork.
aristocraticamente, *adv.* Aristocratically.
aristocratico [aristocrAtico], *n.m.a.* Aristocrat; aristocratic.
aristocrazia [aristocrazIa], *n.f.* Aristocracy.
Aristofane [aristOfane], *n.m.* Aristophanes.
Aristotele [aristOtele], *n.m.* Aristotle.
aritmetica [aritmEtica], *n.f.* Arithmetic.
aritmeticamente, *adv.* Arithmetically.
aritmetico [aritmEtico], *n.m.a.* Arithmetician; arithmetical.
aritmico [arItmico], *a.* Arhythmic, without rhythm.
arlecchinata, *n.f.* Harlequinade.
arlecchinesco, *a.* Medley, motley, patch-work.
arlecchino, *n.m.* Harlequin.
arma, arme (*pl.* **armi**), *n.f.* Arm, weapon; branch of army; coat of arms. **Piazza d'armi,** drill ground; **arma aerea,** air force; **passare per le armi,** to shoot; **All'armi!** To arms!
armacollo, *adv.* **Ad —,** slung over the shoulder.
armadio [armAdio], *n.m.* Cupboard; wardrobe. **— a muro,** built-in wardrobe.
armaiolo, armaiuolo [armaiOlo, armaiuOlo], *n.m.* Armourer, (*Mil.*) artificer.
armamentario [armamentArio], *n.m.* Equipment, outfit, apparatus.
armamento, *n.m.* Armament (of troops, etc.); (*Mech.*) assembling (of parts, etc.); (*Naut.*) equipment of a vessel, rigging.
armare, *v.t.* To arm, to man; (*Mech.*) to assemble (parts, etc.); (*Naut.*) to rig. **— un fucile,** to cock a rifle; **— la linea ferroviaria,** to lay the railway line; **— una macchina,** to assemble or set up a piece of machinery; **— l'argano,** to man the capstan.
armarsi, *v.r.* To arm oneself; to take precautions; to provide oneself with. **— di pazienza,** to arm oneself with patience; **— fino ai denti,** to arm oneself to the teeth.
armata, *n.f.* Army; fleet. **Corpo d'—,** army corps.
armatamente, *adv.* By force of arms.
armato, *p.p.a.* Armed; equipped. **A mano armata,** by force of arms.
armatore, *n.m.* Shipowner.
armatura, *n.f.* Armour; (*Elec.*) armature; frame.
arme [cp. **arma**].
armeggiamento, *n.m.* Tournament, jousting, joust; plotting.
armeggiare, *v.i.* To joust; to fight; to manœuvre; to strive; (*fig.*) to fumble, to plot, to scheme.
armeggiatore, *n.m.* Jouster; schemer.
armeggio [armeggIo], *n.m.* Tournament; (*fig.*) bustle; plot.
armeggione, *n.m.* Bustler; busybody.
Armenia [armEnia], *n.f.* Armenia.
armeno, *n.m.a.* Armenian.
armento, *n.m.* (*Agric.*) Herd, flock, drove.
armeria [armerIa], *n.f.* Armoury, arsenal; the arms in an arsenal.
armiero, *n.m.* Squire to a jousting knight.
armigero [armIgero], *n.m.* (*Heraldry*) Armiger, bearer of arms.
armilla, *n.f.* (*Hist.*) Armlet, bracelet.
armillare, *a.* (*Astron.*) Armillary. **Sfera —,** armillary sphere.
armistizio [armistIzio], *n.m.* Armistice, truce.
armonia [armonIa], *n.f.* Harmony; concord; proportion; peace.
armonica [armOnica], *n.f.* (*Mus.*) Harmonica; harmonics.
armonicamente, *adv.* Harmoniously.
armonico [armOnico], *a.* Harmonical; (*fig.*) proportionate. **Cassa armonica,** sound-box.
armoniosamente, *adv.* Harmoniously.
armonioso, *a.* Harmonious; (*fig.*) proportionate.

armonium [armOnium], *n.m.* (*Mus.*) Harmonium.
armonizzamento, *n.m.* Harmonization.
armonizzare, *v.t.i.* To harmonize, to match (colours, etc.); (*Mus.*) to harmonize.
arnese, *n.m.* Implement, tool, utensil. **Male in —,** badly dressed; **— di polizia,** police spy, stool pigeon; **cattivo —,** thoroughly bad fellow.
arnia [Arnia], *n.f.* Beehive.
arniario [arniArio], *n.m.* Apiary.
arnica [Arnica], *n.f.* (*Bot. Med.*) Arnica.
arnione, *n.m.* (*Anat.*) Kidney (of animals only).
aro, *n.m.* Are (superficial measure) [cp. **ara**].
Aroldo, *n.m.* Harold.
aroma, *n.m.* Aroma, smell, flavour.
aromatico [aromAtico], *a.* Aromatic.
aromatizzare, *v.t.* To give an aroma to.
aromato, *a.* Aromatic.
aromi, *n.m.pl.* Spices.
arpa, *n.f.* (*Mus.*) Harp. **Suonare l'—,** to play the harp.
arpagone, *n.m.* (*Naut.*) Grappling iron.
arpeggiamento, *n.m.* Harping; long passage on the harp.
arpeggiare, *v.i.* (*Mus.*) To play arpeggios.
arpeggio [arpEggio], *n.m.* (*Mus.*) Arpeggio; chord in which the notes are played in rapid succession.
arpese, *n.m.* (*Arch.*) Cramp-iron.
arpia [arpIa], *n.f.* Harpy; (*fig.*) vixen, scold; usurer.
arpicordo, *n.m.* (*Mus.*) Harpsicord; spinet.
arpino, *n.m.* Boat-hook.
arpione, *n.m.* Hinge; pintle (of hinge, etc.); harpoon; grapple.
arpista, *n.m.f.* Harpist.
arra, *n.f.* Pledge, earnest, token.
arrabattarsi, *v.r.* To bestir oneself, to take great pains; to muddle through.
arrabbiamento, *n.m.* Raging, fury.
arrabbiare, *v.t.* To madden, to enrage, to exasperate. **Fare —,** to drive one mad, to vex.
arrabbiarsi, *v.r.* To get angry, to lose one's temper. **— con qualcuno,** to be enraged with someone.
arrabbiatamente, *adv.* Furiously; hastily. **Scrivere —,** to write in anger.
arrabbiatura, *n.f.* Raging, fury. **Prendere un'—,** to get angry, to be worried.
arraffare, *v.t.* To grasp, to seize, to snatch.
arrampicarsi, *v.r.* To climb, to scale, to clamber up, to shin up. **— su per un muro,** to shin up a wall; **— sui vetri,** to try to defend an untenable opinion.
arrampicatore, *n.m.* Mountain climber.
arrancare, *v.i.* To waddle; to plod along; (*Naut.*) to pull (at the oars). **Arranca!** Pull away!
arrandellare, *v.t.* To club, to strike with a club; (*fig.*) to undersell, to sell cheaply.
arrangiare, *v.t.* To manage; to make shift. **Arrangiatevi!** Do the best you can.
arrangiarsi, *v.r.* To be arrranged; to make shift.
arrapinarsi, *v.r.* To take great pains; to get furious.
arrecare, *v.t.* To bring; to cause, to occasion; to contribute; to yield, to bear. **— piacere,** to give pleasure.
arredamento, *n.m.* Furnishing; equipment.
arredare, *v.t.* To furnish, to equip, to rig out.
arredo, *n.m.* Vestments (esp. church); furnishings; décor.
arrembaggio [arrembAggio], *n.m.* (*Naut.*) Boarding (an enemy ship).
arrembare, *v.t.* (*Naut.*) To board (an enemy vessel).
arrembarsi, *v.r.* To tire oneself out.
arrembato, *a.* Tired out; jaded (of a horse).
arrenamento, *n.m.* (*Naut.*) Stranding.
arrenare, *v.i.* [cp. **arenare**].
arrendersi [arrEndersi], *v.r.* To surrender, to give oneself up; to submit to. **— al destino,** to yield to fate.
arrendevole [arrendEvole], *a.* Pliable, flexible, supple; (*fig.*) compliant.
arrendevolezza, *n.f.* Flexibility, suppleness; (*fig.*) docility.
arrendevolmente, *adv.* Compliantly, flexibly; (*fig.*) in a docile manner.
arrestare, *v.t.* To arrest, to stop; to staunch (blood); (*Mech.*) to throw out of gear; to draw up (of vehicles).
arrestarsi, *v.r.* To stop, to be stopped; (*Mech.*) to be thrown out of gear; to be allayed; to be at a standstill.
arrestato, *n.m.* Arrested person, prisoner.
arresto, *n.m.* Arrest; set-back, standstill; staunching (of blood). **Segnale d'—,** "stop" signal; **— della memoria,** failing of the memory.
arretare, *v.t.* To catch in a net, to net.
arretramento, *n.m.* Retirement, retiring, going back, withdrawal.
arretrare, *v.t.i.* To retire, to withdraw; to set back. **Essere in arretrato,** to be behindhand.
arretrarsi, *v.r.* To move back, to go back, to withdraw.
arretrati, *n.m.pl.* (*Comm.*) Arrears, back salary.
arri, arri la! *inter.* Gee up! (To horses in harness).
arricchimento, *n.m.* Enrichment.
arricchire, *v.t.i.* To enrich, to make rich; to grow rich; (*fig.*) to embellish.
arricchirsi, *v.r.* To enrich oneself, to grow rich.
arricciamento, *n.m.* Curling, curl, shagginess; (*Arch.*) rough-casting; preparing for plaster.
arricciare, *v.t.* To curl (hair, moustache, etc.); to ruffle (feathers). **— il naso,** to curl up the nose in contempt.
arricciato, *n.m.* (*Arch.*) Plaster-work.
arricciato, *p.p.a.* Curled, bristled, ruffled.
arricciatura, *n.f.* Curling (of the hair).
arricciolamento, *n.m.* Hair-curling.
arricciolare, *v.t.* To curl the hair.
arricordare, *v.t.i.* [cp. **ricordare**].
arridere [arrIdere], *v.i.* To smile on, to wish good, to favour. **La fortuna mi arride,** fortune smiles on me.
arriffare, *v.t.* To raffle something, to put up for raffle.
Arrigo, *n.m.* Harry, Henry.

arringa, *n.f.* Harangue, solemn public speech; (*Law*) pleading, defence.
arringare, *v.t.i.* To harangue, to deliver a speech; (*Law*) to plead. **— la folla,** to address the crowd.
arringatore, arringatrice, *n.m.f.* Haranguer, orator.
arringo, *n.m.* Arena, lists. **Scendere nell'—,** to enter the lists.
arrischiare, *v.t.* To risk, to venture, to hazard. **Chi nulla arrischia nulla rosica,** nothing venture nothing win.
arrischiarsi, *v.r.* To risk, to venture oneself. **Non —,** to be shy, to be diffident.
arrischiatamente, *adv.* Riskily, hazardously, venturesomely.
arrischiato, *p.p.a.* Risked, risky; bold; rash.
arrischievole [arrischiEvole], *a.* (Something) that may be risked.
arrivabile [arrivAbile], *a.* Attainable [cp. **raggiungibile**].
arrivare, *v.i.* To arrive, to reach; to understand; to attain. **La lettera non è arrivata oggi,** the letter has not come to-day; **— troppo tardi,** to get there too late; **non ci arrivo,** I can't make it out, I don't understand it; **— allo scopo,** to reach one's aim.
arrivato, *p.p.a.* Arrived, reached, attained. **Un nuovo —,** a newcomer; **ben —!** Welcome!
arrivederci, *inter.* Good-bye for the present; (*Am.*) so long!
arrivismo, *n.m.* Pushfulness.
arrivista (*pl.* **arrivisti**), *n.m.* Parvenu, an *arriviste*; a social thruster; careerist.
arrivo, *n.m.* Arrival.
arroccamento, *n.m.* (*Chess*) Castling. (*Mil.*) **linee d'—,** lines of communication.
arroccare, *v.t.* (*Chess*) to castle.
arrochire, *v.t.i.* To make or become hoarse.
arrogante, *a.* Arrogant, haughty.
arrogantemente, *adv.* Arrogantly, haughtily.
arroganza, *n.f.* Arrogance, haughtiness; presumption.
arrogare, *v.t.* To adopt (a child).
arrogarsi, *v.r.* To arrogate, to claim for oneself.
arrogazione, *n.f.* Adoption.
arrolamento, *n.m.* Enlistment, enrolment.
arrolare, *v.t.* To enlist, to enrol.
arrolarsi, *v.r.* To enlist, to enrol oneself.
arroncare, *v.t.* To cut with a bill-hook.
arroncigliare, *v.t.* To hook.
arroncigliarsi, *v.r.* To be caught out by one's own argument; to writhe.
arronzarsi, *v.r.* To work very hard, to labour.
arrossamento, *n.m.* Reddening.
arrossare, *v.t.i.* To make red, to redden.
arrossimento, *n.m.* Blush, redness; shame.
arrossire, *v.i.* To blush, to turn red, to flush; to be ashamed. **Non arrossisce di nulla,** nothing shames him.
arrostimento, *n.m.* Roasting.
arrostire, *v.t.* To roast, to bake, to grill, to toast.
arrostirsi, *v.r.* To get roasted, to be grilled.
arrostito, *p.p.a.* Roasted, broiled, grilled. **Poco —,** underdone.
arrostitura, *n.f.* Roasting.
arrosto, *n.m.* Roast, roast meat. **— di agnello,** roast lamb; **— di castrato,** roast mutton; **molto fumo e poco —,** great outcry but little to show for it.
arrotamento, *n.m.* Whetting, sharpening, grinding.
arrotare, *v.t.* To grind, to whet, to sharpen; to smooth. **— i denti,** to grind one's teeth.
arrotarsi, *v.r.* To work hard; to collide (of two vehicles).
arrotatura, *n.f.* Sharpening, whetting, grinding.
arrotino, *n.m.* Knife-grinder.
arrotolamento, *n.m.* Rolling-up.
arrotolare, *v.t.* To roll, to roll up.
arrotondare, *v.t.* To make round; (*Comm.*) to round off a sum of money.
arrotondato, *p.p.a.* Rounded. **Cifre arrotondate,** round figures.
arrovellarsi, *v.r.* To fly into a passion, to get enraged; to work very hard; to rack one's brains; to worry.
arroventare, *v.t.* To make red-hot.
arroventarsi, *v.r.* To become red-hot.
arroventato, *a.* Red-hot.
arroventatura, *n.f.* Making red-hot.
arroventamento, *n.m.* Red heat, the state of being red-hot.
arroventire [cp. **arroventare**].
arrovesciamento, *n.m.* Overturning, reversal, turning upside down.
arrovesciare, *v.t.i.* To reverse, to overturn, to turn upside down; to upset; to overthrow; to capsize.
arrovesciarsi, *v.r.* To capsize, to be capsized, to be turned upside down. **— le maniche,** to roll up one's sleeves.
arrovesciatura, *n.f.* Reversal; overthrow.
arrovescio, a rovescio [arrovEscio], *adv.* On the contrary. **Andar —,** to go wrong (morally); **capire —,** to misunderstand; **leggere —,** to read from right to left.
arrozzire, *v.t.i.* To make rough; to be rough (to the touch).
arruffamatasse, *n.m.* Mischief-maker; marplot.
arruffapopoli [arruffapOpoli], *n.m.* Ringleader; demagogue.
arruffare, *v.t.* To ruffle the hair; to turn topsy-turvy; to put in disorder.
arruffarsi, *v.r.* To ruffle one's hair; to get in a disordered state.
arruffatamente, *adv.* Topsy-turvy, in a state of disorder.
arruffio [arruffIo], *n.m.* Disorder, confusion.
arruffone, *n.m.* Blunderer, muddler.
arrugginire, *v.t.i.* To rust, to get rusty.
arrugginirsi, *v.r.* To become rusty; (*fig.*) to become impaired.
arrugginito, *a.* Rusty.
arruvidare, arruvidire, *v.t.i.* To roughen, to become rough.
arsella, *n.f.* Mussel.
arsenale, *n.m.* Arsenal, dockyard.
arsenalotto, *n.m.* Dockyard worker.
arseniato, *n.m.* (*Chem.*) Arsenate, arseniate.
arsenicale, *a.* (*Chem.*) Arsenical.
arsenico [arsEnico], *n.m.* (*Chem.*) Arsenic.
arsi, *n.f.* (*Lit., Mus.*) Arsis.
arsiccio [arsIccio], *a.* Scorched.
arsione, *n.f.* Parching thirst.
arso, *a.* Burnt.

arsura, *n.f.* Sultriness, high temperature; drought.
artatamente, *adv.* Craftily, artfully, cunningly.
arte, *n.f.* Art; skill, ability; artifice, cunning, deceit. **Belle arti,** fine arts; **ad —,** expressly, for the purpose; **chi ha — ha parte,** a man with a trade can always keep himself.
artefatto, *n.m.a.* Artefact; artificial; adulterated.
artefice [artEfice], *n.m.* Artificer, craftsman, artisan; (*fig.*) author.
Artemide [artEmide], *n.f.* (*Myth.*) Artemis.
arteria [artEria], *n.f.* (*Anat.*) Artery.
arteriale, *a.* Arterial.
arteriosclerosi, *n.f.* (*Med.*) Arteriosclerosis.
arterioso, *a.* (*Anat.*) Arterial.
artesiano, *a.* Artesian. **Pozzo —,** artesian well.
artico [Artico], *a.* Arctic.
articolare, *v.t.* To articulate (in all senses).
articolare, *a.* Articular, articulate.
articolatamente, *adv.* Articulately, distinctly.
articolato, *a.* Articulate; jointed, vertebrated.
articolazione, *n.f.* Articulation; (*Mech.*) working joint.
articolista, *n.m.f.* Writer of newspaper articles; columnist.
articolo [artIcolo], *n.m.* Article (in all senses); product. **— di fondo,** newspaper leader; **— di novità,** novelty in fancy goods; **— invendibile,** unsaleable article.
artiere, *n.m.* Artisan.
artificiale, *a.* Artificial.
artificialmente, *adv.* Artificially.
artificiere, *n.m.* (*Mil.*) Artillery artificer, gunner.
artificio, artifizio [artifIcio, artifIzio], *n.m.* Artifice; stratagem; device; deceit. **Fuochi d'—,** fireworks.
artificiosamente, artifiziosamente, *adv.* Artfully, cunningly, slyly.
artificiosità, artifiziosità [-à, -à], *n.f.* Artfulness, cunning; fraud.
artificioso, artifizioso, *a.* Artful, crafty, sly.
artigianato, *n.m.* Artisans as a body; handicraft.
artigiano, *n.m.* Artisan, craftsman, tradesman.
artigliare, *v.t.* To claw; to snatch; to clutch.
artigliere, *n.m.* (*Mil.*) Gunner.
artiglieria [artiglierIa], *n.f.* Artillery.
artiglio [artIglio], *n.m.* Claw; clutch. **Cadere negli artigli di qualcuno,** to fall into someone's clutches.
artista, *n.m.f.* Artist.
artisticamente, *adv.* Artistically.
artistico [artIstico], *a.* Artistic.
arto, *n.m.* (*Anat.*) Articulation; joint.
artrite, *n.f.* (*Med.*) Arthritis.
artritico [artrItico], *a.* (*Med.*) Arthritic.
artropodi [artrOpodi], *n.m.pl.* (*Zool.*) Arthropods.
Arturo, *n.m.* Arthur.
aruspice [arUspice], *n.m.* (*Hist.*) Haruspex, soothsayer.
arvicola [arvIcola], *n.f.* (*Zool.*) Vole.
arzente, *a.* Burning. **Acqua —,** fine brandy.
arzigogolare, *v.i.* To daydream, to muse; to trifle, to cavil.
arzigogolo [arzigOgolo], *n.m.* Evasion; trifle; quibble, cavilling.
arzigogolone, *n.m.* Trifler, pettifogger.
arzillo, *a.* Active, lively, brisk, nimble.
asbesto, *n.m.* Asbestos.
ascaride [ascAride], *n.m.* (*Zool.*) Ascarid.
ascaro [Ascaro], *n.m.* (*Mil.*) Askari, native African soldier.
ascella, *n.f.* (*Anat.*) Armpit.
ascendentale, *a.* Ascendant.
ascendente, *n.m.* Ascendancy, authority; ancestor; (*Astron.*) ascendant. **Gli ascendenti,** one's ancestors.
ascendente, *a.* Ascendant, ascending, rising upwards.
ascendenza, *n.f.* Ascendancy, influence; ancestors.
ascendere [ascEndere], *v.t.i.* To ascend, to rise, to mount; to climb; to amount to. **— una collina,** to climb a hill; **l'aerostato ascende,** the balloon rises, mounts up.
ascensionale, *a.* Ascensional.
ascensione, *n.f.* Ascension, ascent; increase (of temperature); (*Eccles.*) Ascension (of Our Lord).
ascensore, *n.m.* Lift, elevator.
ascesa, *n.f.* Ascent.
ascesso, *n.m.* (*Med.*) Abscess.
asceta, *n.m.* Ascetic.
ascetico [ascEtico], *a.* Ascetic.
ascetismo, *n.m.* Asceticism.
ascia [Ascia], *n.f.* Axe, hatchet; battleaxe. (*fig.*) **Fatto coll'—** clumsily made, botched.
asciare, *v.t.* To rough-hew; to chop.
asciata, *n.f.* Axe stroke.
asciolvere [asciOlvere], *v.i.* (*obs.*) To breakfast.
ascissa, *n.f.* (*Math.*) Abscissa.
ascite, *n.f.* (*Med.*) Ascites.
ascitico [ascItico], *a.* (*Med.*) Dropsical.
ascitizio [ascitIzio], *a.* Foreign, alien; borrowed.
asciugamano, *n.m.* Towel.
asciugamento, *n.m.* Drying.
asciugare, *v.t.i.* To dry, to wipe, to wipe away, to drain; to desiccate. **— le lagrime,** to dry one's tears; **— un fiasco,** to drain a flask.
asciugarsi, *v.r.* To dry oneself, to wipe oneself; to get dry. **— la faccia,** to dry one's face.
asciugatoio [asciugatOio], *n.m.* Towel.
asciugatura, *n.f.* Wiping, drying.
asciuttamente, *adv.* Drily, sharply, curtly.
asciuttezza, *n.f.* Dryness, aridity; sterility.
asciutto, *a.* Dry; arid; lean; dry (of wine); severe, sharp. **Avere la bocca asciutta,** to have a dry mouth; **essere all'—,** to be out of the rain; to be penniless; (*fig.*) **un cuore —,** a hard heart.
asciuttore, *n.m.* (*Agric.*) Dryness or barrenness of the soil.
ascoltante, *pres.p.a.* Listening.
ascoltare, *v.t.i.* To listen to, to hear, to harken; to overhear; (*Med.*) to auscultate. **— da un solo orecchio,** to pay little attention; **egli non ascolta alcuno,** he pays attention to no one.
ascoltatore, ascoltatrice, *n.m.f.* Listener; eavesdropper.
ascoltazione, *n.f.* (*Med.*) Auscultation.
ascolto, *n.m.* Hearing, listening; eavesdropping. **Dare —,** to give heed to; (*Radio*) **un buon —,** a good reception.
ascondere [cp. **nascondere**].
ascosamente, *adv.* (*Poet*). Secretly.

ascosto, *a.* Hidden.
ascritto, *p.p.a.* Ascribed, attributed; allotted.
ascrivere [ascrIvere], *v.t.* To ascribe, to attribute; to inscribe, to register; to allot; to impute.
ascriversi, *v.r.* To ascribe to oneself; to associate oneself.
asepsi, *n.f.* (*Med.*) Asepsis.
asessuale, *a.* Asexual.
asettico [asEttico], *a.* (*Med.*) Aseptic.
asfaltare, *v.t.* To asphalt.
asfaltatura, *n.f.* Asphalting.
asfaltico [asfAltico], *a.* Asphaltic.
asfalto, *n.m.* Asphalt.
asfissia [asfissIa], *n.f.* (*Med.*) Asphyxia.
asfissiante, *a.* Asphyxiating.
asfissiare, *v.t.* To asphyxiate.
asfissiarsi, *v.r.* To asphyxiate oneself; to suffocate oneself.
asfissiato, asfittico [asfIttico], *a.* Asphyxiated.
asfodelo, *n.m.* (*Bot.*) Asphodel.
Asia [Asia], *n.f.* Asia.
asiatico [asiAtico], *n.m.a.* Asiatic, Asian.
asilo, *n.m.* Refuge, shelter, asylum. **Diritto d'—,** right of sanctuary; **— infantile,** infant school, kindergarten.
asimmetria [asimmetrIa], *n.f.* Asymmetry, lack of symmetry.
asimmetrico, asimmetro [asimmEtrico], *a.* Asymmetrical.
asina [Asina], *n.f.* She-ass.
asinaggine [asinAggine], *n.f.* Stupidity, ignorance.
asinello, *n.m.* Ass foal.
asineria [asinerIa], *n.f.* Stupidity; nonsense; silly talk.
asinescamente, *adv.* Foolishly.
asinesco, *a.* Stupid, dull; boorish.
asininità [-à], *n.f.* Asininity, foolishness.
asinino, *a.* Asinine.
asino [Asino], *n.m.* Ass, donkey; (*fig.*) fool, stupid fellow. **Pezzo d'—,** stupid man; **testardo come un —,** as stubborn as a mule; **legare l'— dove vuole il padrone,** to obey one's boss; **lavare la testa all'—,** to do good to someone who is ungrateful; (*Zool*). **— selvatico,** onager.
asintote [asIntote], *n.f.* (*Geom.*) Asymptote.
asma, *n.f.* (*Med.*) Asthma.
asmatico [asmAtico], *n.m.a.* Sufferer from asthma, asthmatic, asthmatical.
asola [Asola], *n.f.* Button-hole, hem of button-hole.
asolare, *v.t.i.* To stir (of the wind); to air.
asolo [Asolo], *n.m.* Breath of wind, light breeze.
asparageto, *n.m.* Asparagus bed.
asparagio, asparago [aspAragio, aspArago], *n.m.* (*Bot.*) Asparagus.
asperge, *n.m.* (*Eccles.*) Asperges.
aspergere [aspErgere], *v.t.* To sprinkle; (*Eccles.*) to sprinkle with holy water.
asperità [-à], *n.f.* Roughness, asperity.
aspersione, *n.f.* Aspersion (with water); sprinkling.
asperso, *a.* Sprinkled.
aspersorio [aspersOrio], *n.m.* (*Eccles.*) Aspergillum, holy-water sprinkler.
aspettare, *v.t.i.* To wait for, to wait; to stay still; to go slowly; to expect. **Far —,** to keep waiting; **aspetta un momento,** wait a moment; **aspettare a braccia aperte,** to await with open arms; **lo aspettiamo a pranzo,** we expect him to dinner.
aspettarsi, *v.r.* To await, to look for, to expect, to hope for, to desire; to fear, to apprehend; to reckon on. **C'era d'aspettarsela,** it is what might have been expected; **vi aspettate troppo da lui,** you expect too much of him.
aspettativa, *n.f.* Anticipation, expectation, hope; confidence; temporary retirement. **Essere in —,** to be in expectation of; **essere posto in —,** to be granted leave of absence.
aspettato, *p.p.a.* Waited for, expected, looked for.
aspettazione, *n.f.* Expectation, expectancy.
aspetto, *n.m.* Appearance, aspect; point of view, standpoint. **Sala d'—,** waiting-room; **a primo —,** at first sight; **uomo di buon —,** good-looking man; **aver buon —,** to look well.
aspide [Aspide], *n.m.* (*Zool.*) Asp; (*fig.*) venomous person.
aspirante, *n.m.* Aspirant, candidate. **— di marina,** midshipman, cadet; **— ad un posto,** applicant for a job.
aspirante, *a.* Aspiring, aiming at; inhaling. **Pompa —,** suction pump.
aspirapolvere [aspirapOlvere], *n.m.* Vacuum-cleaner.
aspirare, *v.t.i.* To inhale, to sniff up; to aspirate (vowels); to aim at, to aspire to. **— alla grandezza,** to aim at greatness; **— l'aria della notte,** to breathe in the night air.
aspiratamente, *adv.* Aspiringly.
aspirato, *p.p.a.* Aspired after, aimed at; aspirated (of a vowel).
aspirazione, *n.f.* Aspiration, desire; (*Mech.*) suction; sump; intake; (*gram.*) aspiration (of a vowel).
aspirina, *n.f.* (*Med.*) Aspirin.
aspo, *n.m.* Skein-winder.
asportabile [asportAbile], *a.* Removable, transportable.
asportare, *v.t.* To remove, to transport; (*Med.*) to extirpate.
asportazione, *n.f.* Removal; (*Med.*) extirpation. **— delle tonsille,** tonsillotomy.
aspramente, *adv.* Harshly, severely; roughly.
aspreggiamento, *n.m.* Harshness, rough treatment.
aspreggiare, *v.t.* To treat harshly, to use roughly; to irritate; to produce an effect of roughness on the palate.
aspretto, *a.* Somewhat rough, tart or harsh.
asprezza, *n.f.* Harshness, rudeness; acrimony; tartness (of fruit, etc.).
asprigno, *a.* Sourish, rather tart.
asprino, *n.m.* A Neapolitan white wine.
aspro, *a.* (of taste) Harsh, rough, sour, tart; harsh (of voice); rough, rude; rigid. **Un uomo —,** a hard man; **una voce aspra,** a harsh voice; **parole aspre,** harsh words; **un'aspra gelosia,** a violent jealousy.
assaettante, *a.* Darting hither and thither; pungent.
assaettare, *v.t.* (*colloq.*) To be exceedingly unpleasant. **Un puzzo che assaetta,** an overpowering smell.
assaettarsi, *v.r.* To be enraged, to fly into a temper.

assafetida [assafEtida], *n.f.* Asafoetida.
assaggiare, *v.t.* To taste, to savour, to relish; (*fig.*) to attempt, to try.
assaggiatore, *n.m.* Taster (of wine, etc.).
assaggiatura, *n.f.* Tasting (of wine, etc.).
assaggio [assAggio], *n.m.* Tasting; testing.
assai, *adv.* Much, very much, copiously, in great numbers or quantity; enough. **— ricco,** very rich; **— volte,** very often; **avere — bambini,** to have lots of children; **ne ho avuto —,** I have had enough; **piove —,** it is pouring with rain.
assaissimo [assaIssimo], *a.adv.* Very much indeed; copiously.
assale, *n.m.* (*Mech.*) Axle; pole (of a carriage). (*Motor.*) **— motore,** driving-axle; **— anteriore,** front axle.
assalimento, *n.m.* (*obs.*) Assault.
assalire, *v.t.* To attack, to assail, to assault.
assalito, *p.p.a.* Attacked, assaulted.
assalitore, assalitrice, *n.m.f.* Assailant, aggressor.
Assalonne, *n.m.* Absalom.
assaltare [cp. **assalire**].
assalto, *n.m.* Assault, attack; (*fig.*) violence. **Un — di febbre,** an attack of fever; **prendere d'—,** to take by storm.
assaporamento, *n.m.* Savouring, relishing.
assaporare, *v.t.* To savour, to relish, to enjoy.
assaporire, *v.t.* To season, to flavour, to spice.
assassinamento, *n.m.* Assassination.
assassinare, *v.t.* To assassinate, to murder; to harm.
assassinio [assassInio], *n.m.* Assassination, murder; (*fig.*) waste.
assassino, *n.m.* Assassin, murderer; (*fig.*) rogue, rascal; waster.
assassino, *a.* Murderous.
asse, *n.m.f.* Board, plank; axis; axle. **— motore,** driving axle; (*Naut.*) **— dell'elica,** screw shaft; (*Law*) **— ereditario,** patrimony; **— della terra,** axis of the earth; (*Pol.*) **L'Asse,** the (Berlin-Rome) Axis.
assecchire, *v.i.* To grow thin.
assecondare, *v.t.* To second, to favour.
assediamento, *n.m.* Siege, besieging [cp. **assedio**].
assediante, *n.m.a.* Besieger; besieging. **L'esercito —,** the besieging forces.
assediare, *v.t.* To besiege; (*fig.*) to pester, to importune.
assedio [assEdio], *n.m.* Siege; (*fig.*) pestering, importunity; great crowd of people. **Mettere in stato d'—,** to proclaim martial law; **levare l'—,** to raise the siege.
assegnabile [assegnAbile], *a.* Assignable, transferable.
assegnamento, *n.m.* Allowance, allotment; reliance. **Fare —,** to rely on; **— di compiti,** allotment of tasks.
assegnare, *v.t.* To assign, to allot; to allow, to grant, to fix; to attribute. **— una somma,** to allot a sum; **— il tempo,** to fix the time; **— lo stipendio,** to fix the salary.
assegnatamente, *adv.* Particularly, peculiarly.
assegnatario [assegnatArio], *n.m.* Grantee.
assegnatezza, *n.f.* (*obs.*) Thriftiness.
assegnato, *p.p.a.* Allotted, allowed, granted; fixed; thrifty; unpaid. (*Comm.*) **Porto —,** carriage forward, postage unpaid.
assegnazione, *n.f.* Assignation, allotment, allowance. **— dei profitti,** allocation of profits.
assegno, *n.m.* Allowance; assignment; cheque. (*Comm.*) **Contro —,** cash on delivery; **— all'ordine,** cheque "to Order"; **— sbarrato,** crossed cheque; **— circolare,** bank draft; **emettere un —,** to give or write a cheque.
assemblaggio [assemblAggio], *n.m.* Assembly. **Linea di —,** assembly line.
assemblea, *n.f.* Assembly, meeting.
assembramento, *n.m.* Outdoor meeting, throng; mob.
assembrare, *v.t.* To assemble, to call a meeting; (*Mil.*) to muster.
assembrarsi, *v.r.* To assemble.
assennatamente, *adv.* Wisely, judiciously.
assennatezza, *n.f.* Wisdom, judiciousness, common sense.
assennato, *a.* Wise, prudent.
assenso, *n.m.* Assent.
assentarsi, *v.r.* To absent oneself, to be absent.
assente, *a.* Absent.
assenteismo, *n.m.* Absenteeism.
assenteista (*pl.* **assenteisti**), *n.m.* Absentee.
assentimento, *n.m.* Assent, approval.
assentire, *v.i.* To assent, to acquiesce, to approve.
assenza, *n.f.* Absence; (*fig.*) inattention, absent-mindedness.
assenziente, *a.* Assenting.
assenzio [assEnzio], *n.m.* (*Bot.*) Wormwood. **Liquore d'—,** absinthe.
asserella, *n.f.* Small plank; slat of wood.
asserire, *v.t.* To affirm, to assert, to maintain, to declare; to vindicate.
asserpolarsi, *v.r.* To writhe; to wriggle like a snake.
asserragliare, *v.t.* To barricade.
asserragliarsi, *v.r.* To barricade oneself.
assertivamente, *adv.* Assertively.
assertivo, *a.* Assertive.
asserto, *n.m.* Assertion.
assertore, *n.m.f.* One who asserts; defender.
assertorio [assertOrio], *a.* (*Law*) Assertive.
asservire, *v.t.* To enslave, to subject.
asserzione, *n.f.* Assertion.
assessorato, *n.m.* Office of assessor.
assessore, *n.m.* Alderman; municipal magistrate.
assestamento, *n.m.* Arrangement, adjustment; reconciliation. (*Pol.*) **— del bilancio,** balance of the budget.
assestare, *v.t.* To adjust, to arrange, to put in order, to settle; to strike. **— una faccenda,** to settle a matter; **— un colpo,** to strike a blow.
assestatamente, *adv.* In an orderly way.
assestatezza, *n.f.*, **assesto,** *n.m.* Order, exactness.
assestato, *a.* Arranged.
assetare, *v.t.* To cause thirst.
assetato, *a.* Thirsty.
assettamento, *n.m.* Adjustment, settlement, arrangement; economy.
assettare, *v.t.* To arrange, to put in order, to adjust, to settle; to adorn.
assettatamente, *adv.* With exactness, in good order.

assettatura, *n.f.* Adjustment, arrangement, settlement.
assetto, *n.m.* Order, adjustment. **Mettere in —,** to put in order.
asseverantemente, *adv.* With asseveration.
asseveranza, *n.f.* Assuredness, certainty.
asseverare, *v.t.* To asseverate, to affirm, to assert; to proclaim.
asseveratamente, *adv.* With certainty.
asseverativo, *a.* Affirmative, positive, certain.
asseverazione, *n.f.* Asseveration; affirmation [cp. **asseveranza**].
assiale, *a.* Axial.
assicella, *n.f.* Little board, small bit of wood.
assicurabile [assicurAbile], *a.* Insurable.
assicuramento, *n.m.* Assurance, confidence, promise.
assicuranza, *n.f.* Assurance, assuredness [cp. **assicurazione**].
assicurare, *v.t.* To assure, to give assurance, to certify; (*Comm.*) to insure, to assure, to effect insurance.
assicurarsi, *v.r.* To assure oneself, to make sure, to take precautions; to take courage; (*Comm.*) to insure oneself, to take out an insurance policy. **— sulla vita,** to take out a life assurance policy, to effect a life assurance.
assicuratamente, *adv.* With assurance, with confidence.
assicurato, *n.m.a.* Insured person, insurer; assured; (*Comm.*) insured, covered by insurance.
assicuratore, assicuratrice, *n.m.f.* Insurer; underwriter.
assicurazione, *n.f.* Assurance, confirmation; (*Comm.*) insurance, assurance. **— contro il fuoco,** fire insurance; **— contro gli infortuni,** accident insurance; **agente di —,** insurance broker or agent.
assideramento, *n.m.* Chill, frost-bite.
assiderare, *v.t.i.* To make chilly, to get chilled; to freeze; to congeal.
assiderarsi, *v.r.* To be chilled, to be congealed.
assiderazione, *n.f.* Chillness.
assidersi [assIdersi], *v.r.* To be seated (solemnly).
assiduamente, *adv.* Sedulously.
assiduità [-à], *n.f.* Assiduity, application, diligence.
assiduo [assIduo], *a.* Assiduous, sedulous, diligent.
assieme [cp. **insieme**].
assiepare, *v.t.* To fence in, to enclose with a fence.
assieparsi, *v.r.* To crowd.
assillare, *v.t.i.* To incite, to stir up, to egg on, to be stirred.
assillo, *n.m.* (*Zool.*) Horsefly, gadfly; (*fig.*) urge, disturbing thoughts; troublesome person.
assimilabile [assimilAbile], *a.* Assimilable.
assimilamento, *n.m.* Assimilation.
assimilare, *v.t.* To assimilate; (*fig.*) to absorb.
assimilarsi, *v.r.* To become similar to.
assimilativo, *a.* Assimilative.
assimilazione, *n.f.* Assimilation; comparison.
assiolo, *n.m.* (*Zool.*) Horned owl.
assioma, *n.m.* Axiom.
assiomaticamente, *adv.* Axiomatically.
assiomatico [assiomAtico], *a.* Axiomatic.
Assiria [assIria], *n.f.* Assyria.
assiro, *n.m.a.* Assyrian.
assisa, *n.f.* Dress, uniform; (*Hist.*) tax.
assise, *n.f.pl.* Assizes.
assiso, *a.* Seated; situated.
assistente, *n.m.a.* Assistant; assisting, helping; being a witness.
assistenza, *n.f.* Assistance, help; attendance, presence at.
assistere [assIstere], *v.t.i.* To assist, to help, to aid; to attend; to be present at; to be a witness; to cure.
assitare, *v.t.* To scent (of a dog).
assito, *n.m.* Fence; wooden partition; flooring.
assiuolo, *n.m.* (*Zool.*) Horned owl.
asso, *n.m.* Ace (of cards); champion (sports, etc.). **Lasciare in —,** to abandon, to leave in the lurch.
associamento, *n.m.* (*Agric.*) Lease of cattle on fifty-fifty terms.
associabile [associAbile], *a.* Associable.
associare, *v.t.* To associate, to take into partnership.
associarsi, *v.r.* To associate oneself, to join, to enter into partnership; to subscribe. **— ad un giornale,** to subscribe to a newspaper.
associato, *n.m.a.* Associate, partner; associated, taken into partnership.
associatore, *n.m.* Collector of subscriptions; (*Comm.*) Stock-exchange broker.
associazione, *n.f.* Association, partnership, confederacy; society.
assodamento, *n.m.* Consolidation, hardening, strengthening.
assodare, *v.t.i.* To harden, to consolidate, to ascertain.
assodarsi, *v.r.* To become hardened, to become firm (of flesh).
assoggettamento, *n.m.* Subjection.
assoggettare, *v.t.* To subject, to subdue. **— le passioni,** to subdue one's passions.
assoggettarsi, *v.r.* To subject oneself, to submit oneself.
assolare, *v.t.* To place in layers; to expose to the sun.
assolatio [assolatIo], *a.* Sunny.
assolcare, *v.t.* (*Agric.*) To furrow.
assoldamento, *n.m.* Enlistment, engagement, enrolment.
assoldare, *v.t.* To engage, to enlist.
assoldarsi, *v.r.* To enlist, to engage oneself.
assoldato, *a.* Recruited, enlisted.
assolto, *p.p.a.* Absolved, acquitted; forgiven [cp. **assolvere**].
assolutamente, *adv.* Absolutely.
assolutezza, *n.f.* Absoluteness.
assolutismo, *n.m.* (*Pol.*) Absolutism.
assoluto, *n.m.a.* Absolute, positive; arbitrary, despotic; (*Phil.*) the Absolute. **In tono —,** in a peremptory tone.
assolutore, *n.m.* Absolver.
assolutorio [assolutOrio], *a.* By way of absolution. **Sentenza assolutoria,** sentence of Not Guilty, acquittal.
assoluzione, *n.f.* Absolution; acquittal. (*Eccles.*) **Dare l'—,** to give absolution.
assolvere [assOlvere], *v.t.* To absolve, to acquit; (*Eccles.*) to give absolution; (*fig.*) to excuse; to pardon; to release. **— il proprio compito,** to perform one's duties.
assomigliante, *a.* Resembling.

assomigliare, *v.t.i.* To be like, to resemble; to liken, to compare. **A chi assomiglia?** who is he like?
assomigliarsi, *v.r.* To resemble one another; to be alike.
assommare, *v.t.* To compute, to add; to gather together.
assonante, *a.* Assonant.
assonanza, *n.f.* Assonance.
assonnacchiato, *a.* Half asleep.
assonnamento, *n.m.* Sleepiness.
assonnare, *v.i.t.* To be sleepy; to make sleepy.
assonnarsi, *v.r.* To fall asleep.
assonnato, *p.p.a.* Asleep, sleepy.
assopimento, *n.m.* Drowsiness; (*fig.*) laziness.
assopire, *v.t.* To make drowsy, to lull.
assopirsi, *v.r.* To become drowsy, to doze, to nap.
assopito, *a.* Drowsy.
assorbente, *n.m.a.* Absorbent. **Assorbenti igienici,** sanitary towels.
assorbimento, *n.m.* Absorption.
assorbire, *v.t.* To absorb, to engross, to take up; to exhaust; to swallow up.
assordamento, *n.m.* Deafness.
assordante, *a.* Deafening.
assordare, assordire, *v.t.i.* To deafen, to make deaf; to grow deaf. **— i remi,** to muffle the oars.
assordato, *p.p.a.* Deafened, deaf.
assorgere [assOrgere], *v.i.* To rise, to stand up; to soar.
assortimento, *n.m.* Assortment, selection; (*Comm.*) stock.
assortire, *v.t.* To assort, to sort; to choose, to match; (*Comm.*) to stock; to supply.
assortito, *p.p.a.* Assorted, sorted, matched, stocked.
assorto, *a.* Absorbed, immersed (in thought).
assottigliamento, *n.m.* Sharpening; making thin; refining.
assottigliare, *v.t.* To make thin, to sharpen; to make lean; to refine.
assottigliarsi, *v.r.* To grow thin; to become sharp.
assuefare, *v.t.* To accustom, to habituate.
assuefarsi, *v.r.* To accustom oneself, to get used to.
assuefatto, *a.* Accustomed, inured.
assuefazione, *n.f.* Being accustomed to.
assumere [assUmere], *v.t.* To assume; to undertake; to rise to; to raise. **— informazioni,** to make enquiries.
assumersi [assUmersi], *v.r.* To assume; to take upon oneself.
Assunta, *n.f.* (*Eccles.*) Our Lady; Feast of the Assumption.
assunto, *n.m.* Assumption; enterprise; assertion.
assunto, *a.* Assumed, taken over; undertaken.
assuntore, *n.m.* Contractor.
assunzione, *n.f.* Assumption; (*Eccles.*) Assumption of Our Lady; Feast of the Assumption.
assurdamente, Absurdly.
assurdità [-à], *n.f.* Absurdity.
assurdo, *n.m.a.* Absurdity; absurd; unreasonable, foolish.
assurgere [cp. **assorgere**].
asta, *n.f.* Pole; lance; public auction; stroke with a pen. **— di bandiera,** flag-staff; **vendere all'—,** to sell by auction.
astaco [Astaco], *n.m.* (*Zool.*) Crayfish.
astante, *n.m.a.* Person present, beholder, bystander, spectator; leg of compasses; (*Naut.*) boom; (*Med.*) doctor on duty (at hospital); present, standing by, looking on.
astanteria [astanterIa], *n.f.* First-aid post; duty staff (in hospital).
astatico [astAtico], *a.* Astatic.
astato, *a.* Armed with a spear or lance.
asteggiare, *v.t.* To make straight strokes in writing.
astemio [astEmio], *n.m.a.* Teetotaller; abstemious.
astenersi [astEnersi], *v.r.* To abstain; to forbear; to refrain from. **— dal fumo,** to refrain from smoking, to abstain from smoking; **— dal ridere,** to forbear laughing.
astenimento, *n.m.* (*obs.*) Abstention.
astensione, *n.f.* Abstention.
astensionismo, *n.m.* Abstentionism.
astensionista (*pl.* **astensionisti**), *n.m.* Abstentionist.
astergente, *a.* Cleansing.
astergere [astErgere], *v.t.* To cleanse.
asteria [astEria], *n.f.* (*Zool.*) Starfish.
asterisco, *n.m.* Asterisk, quotation mark.
asterismo, *n.m.* (*Astron.*) Asterism; constellation.
asteroide [asterOide], *n.m.* (*Astron.*) Asteroid.
astersione, *n.f.* (*Med.*) Abstersion.
astersivo, *a.* (*Med.*) Abstersive.
asterso, *a.* Clean, cleansed.
astice [Astice], *n.m.* (*Zool.*) Lobster.
astigiano, *a.* From Asti (Piedmont).
astigmatico [astigmAtico], *a.* Astigmatic.
astigmatismo, *n.m.* Astigmatism.
astinente, *a.* Temperate, sober, abstinent.
astinenza, *n.f.* Abstinence; fast.
astio [Astio], *n.m.* Hatred, grudge, rancour; envy; spite. **Avere — contro alcuno,** to bear a grudge against someone.
astiosamente, *adv.* Rancorously, with a grudge.
astioso, *a.* Rancorous, spiteful; envious.
astore, *n.m.* (*Zool.*) Goshawk.
astragalo [astrAgalo], *n.m.* (*Anat.*) Ankle-bone; knuckle-bone; (*Bot.*) *Astragalus*, milk-vetch; (*Arch.*) astragal.
astrale, *a.* Astral.
astrarre, *v.t.i.* To abstract, to eliminate; to distinguish.
astrattamente, *adv.* Abstractly.
astrattezza, *n.f.* Abstractness.
astratto, *n.m.a.* Abstract, indefinite; wrapt in thought. **In —,** in the abstract.
astrazione, *n.f.* Abstraction. **Fare — da,** to leave out of consideration.
astretto, *a.* Constrained; constricted. [cp. **astringere**].
astringente, *n.m.a.* (*Med.*) Astringent.
astringenza, *n.f.* Astringency.
astringere [astrIngere], *v.t.* To construct, to constrain, to coerce; to restrain; (*Med.*) to render costive.
astro, *n.m.* Star; planet; (*Bot.*) aster.
astrofisica [astrofIsica], *n.f.* Astrophysics.
astrolabio [astrolAbio], *n.m.* Astrolabe.
astrologamento, *n.m.* Astrologizing.
astrologare, *v.t.i.* To exercise the art of astrology, to cast horoscopes; to make wild guesses; to wander in one's mind.

astrologia [astrologIa], *n.f.* Astrology.
astrologicamente, *adv.* Astrologically.
astrologico [astrolOgico], *a.* Astrological.
astrologo [astrOlogo], *n.m.* Astrologer.
astronauta [astronAuta], *n.m.* Astronaut.
astronautica [astronAutica], *n.f.* Astronautics.
astronomia [astronomIa], *n.f.* Astronomy.
astronomicamente, *adv.* Astronomically.
astronomico [astronOmico], *a.* Astronomical, astronomic.
astronomo [astrOnomo], *n.m.* Astronomer.
astrusaggine [astrusAggine], *n.f.* Abstruseness.
astrusamente, *adv.* Abstrusely.
astruseria [astruserIa], *n.f.* Abstrusity; intricacy.
astruso, *a.* Abstruse; entangled, complex.
astucciaio [astucciAio], *n.m.* Maker or seller of sheaths, cases, etc.
astuccio [astUccio], *n.m.* Sheath, small box, case. — **di gioielli,** jewel-case; — **per aghi,** needle-case.
Asturie [astUrie], *n.f.pl.* Asturias.
astutamente, *adv.* Astutely.
astutezza, *n.f.* Astuteness, shrewdness.
astuto, *a.* Astute; crafty, wily.
astuzia [astUzia], *n.f.* Astuteness, shrewdness, cunning. trick, wile. **Usare —,** to practise deceit; to use a ruse.
atassia, *n.f.* (*Med.*) Ataxia, ataxy.
atavico [atAvico], *a.* Atavistic.
atavismo, *n.m.* Atavism.
atavo [Atavo], *n.m.* Great-great-grandfather.
ateismo, *n.m.* Atheism.
ateista, (*pl.* **ateisti**), *n.m.f.* Atheist [cp. **ateo**].
ateistico [ateIstico], *a.* Atheistic.
Atene, *n.f.* (*Geog.*) Athens.
ateneo, *n.m.* Athenaeum; university.
ateo [Ateo], *n.m.a.* Atheist, atheistical.
atlante, *n.m.* Atlas.
Atlantico [atlAntico], *n.m.a.* Atlantic.
atleta (*pl.* **atleti**), *n.m.* Athlete.
atletica [atlEtica], *n.f.* Athletics.
atletico [atlEtico], *a.* Athletic.
atmosfera, *n.f.* Atmosphere (in all senses).
atmosferico [atmosfErico], *a.* Atmospheric, atmospherical.
atollo, *n.m.* (*Geog.*) Atoll.
atomico [atOmico], *a.* Atomic. **Bomba atomica** atomic bomb, atom bomb.
atomismo, *n.m.* Atomism.
atomistica [atomIstica], *n.f.* Atomic theory.
atomo [Atomo], *n.m.* Atom.
atonia [atonIa], *n.f.* (*Med.*) Atony.
atono [Atono], *a.* (*Gram.*) Atonic.
atrabile *n.f.* Gloominess; irritability.
atrabiliare, atrabiliario [atrabiliArio], *a.* (*Med.*) Atrabilious.
atrio [Atrio], *n.m.* Hall, entrance hall; porch; vestibule; (*Hist.*) atrium.
atro, *a.* Black; (*fig.*) horrible, atrocious.
atroce, *a.* Atrocious, heinous, horrible, terrible.
atrocemente, *adv.* Atrociously.
atrocità [-à], *n.f.* Atrocity, atrociousness.
atrofia [atrofIa], *n.f.* Atrophy.
atrofico [atrOfico], *a.* (*Med.*) Atrophic.
atrofizzare, *v.t.i.* To atrophy.
atrofizzarsi, *v.r.* To atrophy, to waste away.
atropa [Atropa], *n.f.* (*Bot.*) Belladonna, deadly nightshade.
atropina, *n.f.* (*Med.*) Atropine.
attaccabile [attaccAbile], *a.* Attachable; assailable; liable to question.
attaccabottoni, *n.m.* Man who buttonholes one; bore.
attaccabrighe, *n.m.* Quarrelsome fellow.
attaccagnolo [attaccAgnolo], *n.m.* Peg, hook; (*fig.*) pretext.
attaccalite, *n.m.* Litigious man.
attaccamento, *n.m.* Attachment, love.
attaccante, *n.m.* Attacker; (*Football*) forward.
attaccapanni, *n.m.* Coat-stand; hat-rack; clothes-hanger; clothes-peg.
attaccare, *v.t.i.* To attach, to bind to, to tie; to chain; to nail; to hang up (clothes); to attack, to injure; (*Chem.*) to corrode; (*Mus.*) to strike a note clearly. — **i cavalli,** to put the horses to (the cart); — **un avviso,** to stick a bill; — **con colla forte,** to glue; — **un francobollo,** to affix a stamp; **non attacca!** it's no use! — **il nemico,** to attack the enemy; — **lite con uno,** to pick a quarrel with; — **discorso con,** to start a conversation with; — **un bottone,** to sew on a button; (*fig.*) to buttonhole.
attaccarsi, *v.r.* To adhere, to stick to; (*Med.*) to be catching; (*fig.*) to be fond of; to give one's mind to; to quarrel. — **a parole,** to come to words (with).
attaccaticcio [attaccatIccio], *a.* Sticky, gluey; (*Med.*) contagious.
attaccato, *p.p.a.* Attached, tied, joined; hung up; harnessed (of horses); (*fig.*) attached (of persons to one another).
attaccatura, *n.f.* Junction, point of union.
attacchino, *n.m.* Bill-poster, bill-sticker; quarrelsome fellow.
attacco, *n.m.* Attack (in all senses); access; carriage and horses together.
attagliarsi, *v.r.* To adapt oneself to; to fit; to suit; to conform.
attanagliare, *v.t.* To torture with red-hot pincers; (*fig.*) to grip tightly, to seize, to clutch.
attapinarsi, *v.r.* To live in a state of misery; to exert oneself.
attardarsi, *v.r.* To delay; to tarry, to be late.
attastare, *v.t.* To touch lightly, to feel [cp. **tastare**].
attecchimento, *n.m.* Taking hold; taking root; thriving.
attecchire, *v.i.* To take hold, to take root (of plants, etc.), to sprout; to thrive.
attediare, *v.t.* To weary, to bore [cp. **tediare**].
attediarsi, *v.r.* To grow bored, to be bored.
atteggiamento, *n.m.* Attitude, gesture, conduct, behaviour; posture, demeanour.
atteggiare, *v.t.* To pose; to give expression to; to shape. — **il volto al sorriso** to express by a faint smile.
atteggiarsi, *v.r.* To strike a posture, to assume *or* strike an attitude. — **a vittima,** to pose as a victim.
attemparsi, *v.r.* (*obs.*) To grow old, to get on in years.
attempatello, attempatotto, attempatuccio [attempatUccio], *a.* Oldish, getting on (in years).
attempato, *a.* Aged, old, elderly.

attendamento, *n.m.* Camp, encampment; pitching of tents.
attendarsi, *v.r.* To encamp (in tents), to pitch one's camp, to pitch tents.
attendente, *n.m.* (*Mil.*) Batman, orderly.
attendere [attEndere], *v.t.i.* To expect, to wait for; to apply oneself, to attend to, to look after. **Attendiamo istruzioni,** we await instructions; **— ai propri negozi,** to look after one's affairs, to mind one's own business.
attendibile [attendIbile], *a.* Reliable; trustworthy; worth attention.
attendibilità [-**à**], *n.f.* Certitude, certainty; likelihood; genuineness.
attenenza, *n.f.* Appurtenance; relationship (by blood), kinship.
attenere, *v.t.i.* To keep or maintain (a promise, etc.); to belong to.
attenersi, *v.r.* To cling, to hold on tight; to cling together; to adhere to a party; to hold to. **— agli ordini,** to adhere to instructions; **— ad un prezzo,** to keep to a price; **— al consiglio di,** to follow the advice of.
attentamente, *adv.* Attentively.
attentare, *v.i.* To attempt, to make an attempt on.
attentarsi, *v.r.* To dare, to venture.
attentato, *n.m.* Attempt, outrage; crime.
attentatorio [attentatOrio], *a.* Unlawful, criminal.
attenti! *inter.* Attention! (*Mil.*) **Mettersi sull'—,** to stand to attention.
attento, *a.* Attentive, diligent; watchful. **State —!** Look out! Be careful!
attenuamento, *n.m.* Attenuation, mitigation.
attenuante, *a.* Attenuating, mitigating. (*Law*) **Circostanze attenuanti,** extenuating circumstances.
attenuare, *v.t.* To attenuate, to minimize (difficulties, etc.); to extenuate.
attenuazione, *n.f.* Attenuation, mitigation.
attenzione, *n.f.* Attention, heed, care; consideration, courtesy, deference; application, study. **Fare —,** to pay attention; **colpire l'—,** to strike the attention; **non prestare —,** to pay no heed; **usare attenzioni ad un vecchio,** to show deference to an old man.
attepidire, attepidirsi, *now commonly used for* **attie-,** q.v.
attergare, *v.t.* To endorse (a document, etc.).
attergato, *n.m.* Docket; endorsed document.
atterraggio, atterramento, *n.m.* Landing (of aircraft), alighting, descent; demolition (of buildings, etc.), overthrowing; (*Naut.*) landfall. **— forzato,** forced landing.
atterrare, *v.t.i.* To land (of aircraft), to alight; to throw down, to knock down, to demolish, to pull down.
atterrimento, *n.m.* Terror, fright.
atterrire, *v.t.* To terrify.
atterrirsi, *v.r.* To be terrified, to be frightened. **— per nulla,** to be scared for nothing.
attesa, *n.f.* Expectation; waiting for; confidence. **Contro ogni mia —,** contrary to every expectation of mine; **sala d'—,** waiting-room.
atteso, *p.p.a.* Expected, longed for, waited for.
attesochè, atteso che, *prep.* In consideration of, considering, seeing that.
attestare, *v.t.* To testify, to witness; to certify. **Attesto in faccia a Dio,** I call God to witness.
attestarsi, *v.r.* (*Mil.*) To make a bridge-head.
attestato, *n.m.a.* Certificate; certified, attested. **Come — di,** as proof of, in evidence of.
attestatura, *n.f.* Joining together of two ends.
attestazione, *n.f.* Attestation, certificate; declaration.
atticamente, *adv.* In the Attic manner; elegantly, in perfect taste.
atticciato, *a.* Squat, dumpy; thick-set.
atticismo, *n.m.* Elegance of style (in writing).
atticista, *n.m.* Elegant writer.
atticizzare, *v.i.* To show perfect taste; to write elegantly.
attico [Attico], *n.m.a.* Attic; elegant, classic.
attiepidire, *v.i.* To cool, to make lukewarm [cp. **attepidire**].
attiepidirsi, *v.r.* To become cool, to cool off (in affection, etc.) [cp. **attepidirsi**].
attignere [cp. **attingere**].
attiguità [-**à**], *n.f.* Contiguity, adjacence.
attiguo [attIguo], *a.* Adjoining, adjacent, contiguous. **Nella stanza attigua,** in the next room.
attillarsi, *v.r.* To dress oneself in a close-fitting dress.
attillatezza, *n.f.* Close-fitting (dress).
attillato, *a.* Close-fitting, tight (of coat, etc.).
attimo [Attimo], *n.m.* Instant, moment. **In un —,** in an instant.
attinente, *a.* Appertaining, belonging; relating to.
attinenza, *n.f.* Relation, connection (of persons or things to one another).
attingere [attIngere], *v.t.* To draw (water, etc.); to reach; (*fig.*) to obtain information; to borrow (opinion, views, etc.).
attingimento, *n.m.* Drawing (water).
attingitoio [attingitOio], *n.m.* Siphon; implement for drawing liquids.
attingitore, attingitrice, *n.m.f.* Drawer of water; borrower.
attinico [attInico], *a.* (*Phys.*) Actinic (rays).
attinio [attInio], *n.m.* (*Metal.*) Actinium.
attinto, *p.p.a.* Drawn (of water from a well, or of wine from a cask).
attirare, *v.t.* To attract, to draw, to allure, to invite; to engage. **La calamita attira il ferro,** the magnet attracts iron; **— con carezze,** to wheedle; **— l'attenzione di,** to draw one's attention.
attirarsi, *v.r.* To attract to oneself, to draw upon oneself. **— addosso,** to bring upon oneself; **si è attirata la stima di tutti,** he won everyone's esteem.
attitudine [attitUdine], *n.f.* Disposition, aptitude, inclination; natural bent; ability; posture. **— per la musica,** aptitude for music.
attivamente, *adv.* Actively, industriously; (*Gram.*) in the active mood.
attivare, *v.t.* To make active, to bring into action. **— una macchina,** to start an engine.
attivazione, *n.f.* Execution, working. **Lavori in —,** works in process; (*Rail.*) **linea in —,** line working.

attivista (*pl.* **attivisti**), *n.m.* (*Polit.*) Factious agitator.
attività [-**à**], *n.f.* Activity, animation; (*Comm.*) credit account. (*Comm.*) — **e passivo,** assets and liabilities; — **negli affari,** animation in business; **essere in — di servizio,** to be in active service.
attivo, *n.m.* (*Comm.*) Assets; credit account. — **disponibile,** assets in hand; — **e passivo,** assets and debits.
attivo, *a.* Active, busy, diligent. (*Comm.*) **Debiti attivi,** outstanding credits.
attizzamento, *n.m.* Poking (of the fire); (*fig.*) excitement, arousing.
attizzare, *v.t.* To poke (the fire); (*fig.*) to stir up, to excite; to arouse.
attizzatoio [attizzatOio], *n.m.* Poker.
attizzatore, *n.m.* Inciter, one who excites; instigator.
atto, *n.m.* Act, action; gesture, attitude; function; appearance; (*Theat.*) act; (*Law*) deed, certificate, contract. **L'— di camminare,** the act of walking; — **di volontà,** act of the will; **in — di difesa,** in a posture of defence; **all'— di pagamento,** on payment; **stare in — di partire,** to be in the act of starting; **all'— pratico,** in practice; (*Comm.*) — **di costituzione,** act of incorporation; — **pubblico,** deed under seal; **all'— della consegna,** on delivery.
atto, *a.* Apt, fit, suitable, proper.
attonare, *v.t.* To strengthen, to invigorate.
attondare, *v.t.* To round, to make round.
attonitaggine [attonitAggine], *n.f.* Amazement, stupefaction, astonishment.
attonitamente, *adv.* Amazedly.
attonito [attOnito], *a.* Amazed, astonished.
attorcere [attOrcere], *v.t.* To twist; to wring.
attorcersi [attOrcersi], *v.r.* To twist round.
attorcigliamento, *n.m.* Twisting, winding.
attorcigliare, *v.t.* To twist round and round, to wind round.
attorcigliarsi, *v.r.* To twine round.
attorcimento, *n.m.* Twisting, twining, winding.
attore *n.m.* Actor; (*Law*) plaintiff.
attorniamento, *n.m.* Environment, surrounding.
attorniare, *v.t.* To surround, to encircle, to enclose; (*fig.*) to beset; to court; to deceive.
attorniarsi, *v.r.* To surround oneself.
attorniato, *p.p.a.* Surrounded, encircled; (*fig.*) beset; deceived.
attorno, *adv.prep.* About, round, around. — —, all round about; **là** —, thereabouts; — **alla persona,** about one's person; **andare** —, to stroll around, to saunter; **stare — a una cosa,** to attend to a thing; **darsi** —, to get busy; **levarsi d'— qualcuno,** to get rid of someone; **guardarsi** —, to look round.
attortigliamento, *n.m.* Twisting.
attortigliare, *v.t.* To twist; to twist up.
attortigliarsi, *v.r.* To twine around.
attortigliato, *a.* Twisted round and round.
attorto, *a.* Twisted, entangled, wound.
attossicamento, *n.m.* Poisoning [cp. **intossicazione**].
attossicare, *v.t.* To poison; (*fig.*) to corrupt; to embitter.
attossicatore, attossicatrice, *n.m.f.* Poisoner.
attossicazione, *n.f.* Poisoning [cp. **intossicazione**].
attraccare, *v.i.* (*Naut.*) To haul alongside (the quay).
attraente, *a.* Attractive, alluring, inviting, engaging.
attraentemente, *adv.* Attractively, alluringly, winningly.
attrappire [cp. **rattrappire**].
attrarre [cp. **attirare**].
attrattiva, *n.f.* Attraction, allurement, charm.
attrattivo, *a.* Attractive, alluring [cp. **attraente**].
attratto, *a.* Drawn, attracted; enticed.
attraversamento, *n.m.* Crossing, obstacle, impediment. — **per pedoni,** pedestrian crossing.
attraversare, *v.t.* To cross, to traverse; to pass through; to pierce; to thwart, to frustrate, to baulk. — **una strada,** to cross a road; — **i suoi disegni,** to thwart his plans.
attraversatore, attraversatrice, *n.m.f.* Opponent, one who thwarts plans, etc.
attraverso, *adv.prep.* Across, athwart, through; amongst. **Tutto va** —, everything is going wrong; **guardare qualcuno** —, to look askance at someone.
attrazione, *n.f.* Attraction.
attrezzare, *v.t.* (*Naut.*) To rig, to equip.
attrezzatore, *n.m.* (*Naut.*) Rigger, outfitter.
attrezzatura, *n.f.* (*Naut.*) Rigging; outfit, equipment; machinery.
attrezzista, *n.m.* Decorator; (*Theat.*) scene-painter; scene-shifter.
attrezzo, *n.m.* Utensil, tool, implement.
attribuibile [attribuIbile], *a.* Attributable.
attribuire, *v.t.* To attribute; to attach (importance); to ascribe; to impute; to award; to assign.
attribuirsi, *v.r.* To ascribe to oneself, to give to oneself, to arrogate.
attributivo, *a.* Attributive.
attributo, *n.m.* Attribute, property, emblem, symbol.
attribuzione, *n.f.* Attribution; authority, competence, power. **Non è nelle mie attribuzioni,** it is not in my competence.
attrice, *n.f.* Actress.
attristare, attristire, *v.t.* To sadden, to cause sadness.
attristirsi, *v.r.* To become sad; to lose one's strength.
attrito, *n.m.* Attrition; friction; (*fig.*) friction, dissension.
attrizione, *n.f.* Attrition.
attruppamento, *n.m.* Crowd, mob, throng.
attrupparsi, *v.r.* To assemble in a crowd, to throng.
attuabile [attuAbile], *a.* Feasible.
attuabilità [-**à**], *n.f.* Feasibility.
attuale, *a.* Current, real; effectual; present.
attualità [-**à**], *n.f.* Event of the day; novelty; topic.
attualmente, *adv.* At present.
attuare, *v.t.* To carry out; to perform; to keep (a promise).
attuariale, *a.* Actuarial.
attuariato, *n.m.* Actuary's office; recording office; registry office.

attuario [attuArio], *n.m.* Actuary; registrar.
attuazione, *n.f.* Fulfilment; working.
attuffamento, *n.m.* Diving; immersion.
attuffare, *v.t.* To dive, to plunge, to immerse.
attuffarsi, *v.r.* To dive.
attuffatura, *n.f.* Diving; immersion.
attutire, *v.t.* To soothe, to appease, to allay; to deaden (a noise, etc.)
attutirsi, *v.r.* To be appeased, to be allayed; to be soothed.
attutito, *p.p.a.* Allayed, soothed; deadened.
aucupio [aucUpio], *n.m.* Bird-snaring (with bird-lime).
audace, *a.* Bold, audacious.
audacemente, *adv.* Audaciously, boldly.
audacia [audAcia], *n.f.* Audacity, audaciousness; gallantry, courage.
auditivo, *a.* Pertaining to hearing.
auditore, *n.m.* Hearer, auditor, listener; (*obs.*) judge.
auditorio [auditOrio], *n.m.* Auditorium, concert-hall.
audizione, *n.f.* Audition; (*Radio*) reception; (*Theat.*) performance.
auge [Auge], *n.m.* Summit, apogee. **Essere in —,** to enjoy a great reputation, to live in style, to be at the zenith of one's career.
augello, *n.m.* (*Poet.*) Bird.
auggiare, *v.t.* [cp. **aduggiare**].
augnare, *v.t.* To clutch with the nails, to claw; (*Carp.*) to mitre.
augnatura, *n.f.* Clawing; (*Carp.*) mitring.
augurabile [augurAbile], *a.* To be wished for, desirable.
augurale, *a.* Of good augury; (*Hist.*) augural.
augurare, *v.t.* To wish, to desire; to predict, to forbode.
augurarsi, *v.r.* To hope to wish, to look forward to.
augurato, *p.p.a.* Wished, foreboded; happy. **Bene —,** fortunate.
augure [Augure], *n.m.* (*Hist.*) Augur.
augurio [augUrio], *n.m.* Wish, augury; omen, presage. **Gradite i miei auguri,** accept my best wishes; **uccello di mal —,** bird of ill omen.
augurosamente, *adv.* With (good or bad) omen.
auguroso, *a.* Of (good or bad) omen.
augustale, *a.* Imperial; Augustan.
augusto, *a.* August, majestic; venerable.
aula [Aula], *n.f.* Hall, main hall; council chamber; courtroom. **— magna,** public hall of a university; **— scolastica,** class-room.
aulente, *a.* (*Lit.*) Sweet-smelling.
aulico [Aulico], *a.* (*Lit.*) Aulic.
aulire, *v.i.* (*Lit.*) To smell.
aumentabile [aumentAbile], *a.* Augmentable.
aumentare, *v.t.i.* To augment, to increase, to raise; to grow; to enlarge. **— lo stipendio,** to raise the salary; **— i prezzi,** to raise the prices.
aumentativo, *a.* Augmentative.
aumentato, *p.p.a.* Increased, augmented; advanced, risen.
aumentatore, aumentatrice, *n.m.f.* One who increases or raises (prices, etc.).
aumento, *n.m.* Increase, advance, augmentation, rise (in prices).
auncinare, *v.t.* (*obs.*) To snatch, to grab with the claws.
aunghiare [cp. **augnare**].
aura [Aura], *n.f.* Gentle breeze
aurato, *a.* Golden; resplendent.
aureo [Aureo], *a.* Gold, golden; (*fig.*) noble, exalted; happy. **Secolo —,** golden age.
aureola [aurEola], *n.f.* Aureole; halo; (*fig.*) fame, glory.
auretta, *n.f.* Gentle breeze.
auricola [aurIcola], *n.f.* (*Anat.*) Auricle; (*Bot.*) auricula.
auricolare, *a.* Auricular; (*Eccles.*) **Confessione —,** auricular confession.
aurifero [aurIfero], *a.* Auriferous, gold-bearing.
auriga (*pl.* **aurighi**), *n.m.* (*Hist.*) Charioteer.
aurito, *a.* (*obs*). Eared (of vases, etc.).
auro [Auro], *n.m.* (*Poet.*) Gold, the colour of gold.
aurora, *n.f.* Day-break, sun-rise; (*fig.*) beginning. **Prima dell'—,** before dawn; **— della vita,** the dawn of life; **l'— boreale,** the aurora borealis.
auscultazione, *n.f.* (*Med.*) Auscultation.
ausiliare, ausiliario [ausiliArio], *n.m.a.* Auxiliary; assistant. **Verbo —,** auxiliary verb; **posizione —,** non-active service.
ausiliatore, ausiliatrice, *n.m.f.* Helper, protector, protectress.
ausilio [ausIlio], *n.m.* (*Lit.*) Help, aid.
ausonio [ausOnio], *a.* (*Lit.*) Italic.
auspicale, *a.* Auspicious.
auspicare, *v.t.* To augur; to portend; to look forward to, to hope for.
auspicato, *a.* Auspicious, boding well; fortunate, desired.
auspice [Auspice], *n.m.* Protector; (*Hist.*) Augur.
auspicio [auspIcio], *n.m.* Auspices; protection. **Sotto gli auspici di,** under the auspices of.
austeramente, *adv.* Austerely.
austerità [-à], *n.f.* Austerity.
austero, *a.* Austere, grave; sharp (of fruit, wine, etc.).
australe, *a.* Southern.
austriaco [austrIaco], *n.m.a.* Austrian.
austro, *n.m.* South; south wind.
autarchia [autarchIa], *n.f.* (*Pol.*) Self-sufficiency, autarchy.
autarchico [autArchico], *a.* (*Pol.*) Self-sufficient.
autentica [autEntica], *n.f.* Authentication; authenticity; authentic evidence.
autenticamente, *adv.* Authentically.
autenticare, *v.t.* To authenticate, to certify, to prove; to legalize.
autenticato, *p.p.a.* Authenticated, certified; legalized.
autenticatore, *n.m.* Certifier.
autenticazione, *n.f.* Authentication.
autenticità [-à], *n.f.* Authenticity, genuineness. **Mettere in dubbio l'—,** to question the genuineness.
autentico [autEntico], *a.* Authentic, genuine.
autista (*pl.* **autisti**), *n.m.* Chauffeur, paid driver of a motor vehicle.
auto, *n.m.f. abbrev.* Motor car; taxi cab [cp. **automobile**].
auto-, *prefix.* Auto-, self-, motor- (in one or other of these senses the prefix is applied to a

variety of words the principal of which are given herewith).
autoambulanza, *n.f.* Motor-ambulance.
autoavviatore, *n.m.* (*Motor.*) Self-starter.
autobiografia [autobiografIa], *n.f.* Autobiography.
autobiografico [autobiogrAfico], *a.* Autobiographical.
autobiografo [autobiOgrafo], *n.m.* Autobiographer.
autoblinda, *n.f.* (*Mil.*) Armoured car.
autobus [Autobus], *n.m.* Bus, motor coach.
autocarro, *n.m.* Motor-lorry.
autoclave, *n.f.* (*Med.*) Sterilizer (for instruments, etc.).
autocrate, autocrata [autOcrate, autOcrata], *n.m.f.* Autocrat, despot.
autocraticamente, *adv.* Autocratically.
autocratico [autocrAtico] *a.* Autocratic.
autocrazia [autocrazIa], *n.f.* Autocracy.
autoctono [autOctono], *n.m.* Autochthon, aboriginal.
autodecisione, *n.f.* Self-determination.
autodidatta, *n.m.f.* Self-taught person.
autodifesa, *n.f.* Self-defence.
autodromo [autOdromo], *n.m.* (*Motor.*) Speedway; motor track.
autogenesi [autogEnesi], *n.f.* Autogeny.
autogoverno, *n.m.* Self-government, home rule.
autografare, *v.t.* To autograph.
autografico [autogrAfico], *a.* Autographic.
autografo [autOgrafo], *n.m.* Autograph.
autointossicazione, *n.f.* Self-intoxication.
automa, *n.m.* Automaton.
automaticamente, *adv.* Automatically.
automatico [automAtico], *a.* Automatic.
automazione, *n.f.* Automation.
automezzo, *n.m.* Motor vehicle.
automobile [automObile], *n.m.f.* Automobile, motor-car. **Andare in —,** to motor, to go by car; **— da corsa,** racing car; **— da piazza,** taxi-cab.
automobile [automObile], *a.* Self-propelling.
automobilismo, *n.m.* Automobilism, motoring.
automobilista, (*pl.* **—isti**), *n.m.* Motorist.
automobilistico [automobilIstico], *a.* Concerning motors.
automotrice, *n.f.* (*Rail.*) Motor-driven railway vehicle; diesel-train.
autonomia [autonomIa], *n.f.* Autonomy, self-government.
autonomo [autOnomo], *a.* Autonomous.
autoparcheggio, *n.m.* (*Motor.*) Parking.
autoportato, *a.* Lorry-borne.
autopsia, autossia [autopsIa, autossIa], *n.f.* (*Med.*) Autopsy, post-mortem.
autoraduno, *n.m.* (*Motor.*) Motor rally.
autore, *n.m.* Author.
autorevole [autorEvole], *a.* Authoritative.
autorevolezza, *n.f.* Authoritativeness.
autorevolmente, *adv.* Authoritatively.
autorimessa, *n.f.* (*Motor.*) Garage.
autorità [-à], *n.f.* Authority, power; influence.
autoritariamente, *adv.* Authoritatively, imperiously.
autoritario [autoritArio], *a.* Authoritative, imperious; imperative.
autoritratto, *n.m.* (*Art*) Self-portrait.
autorizzare, *v.t.* To authorize, to empower.
autorizzazione, *n.f.* Authorization.
autoscafo *n.m.* (*Naut.*) Motor-vessel, motor-boat [cp. **motoscafo**].
autoscuola, *n.f.* (*Motor.*) School of motoring.
autostello, *n.m.*, Motel.
autostop, *n.m.* Hitch-hike.
autostoppista, *n.m.* Hitch-hiker.
autostrada, *n.f.* (*Motor.*) Motorway.
autosuggestione, *n.f.* Autosuggestion.
autotrasportare, *v.t.* To carry by motor lorry.
autotrasporto, *n.m.* Motor transport.
autotreno, *n.m.* Motor lorry with trailer.
autoveicolo [autovelcolo], *n.m.* Motor vehicle.
autrice, *n.f.* Author, authoress.
autunnale, *a.* Autumnal.
autunno, *n.m.* Autumn, fall.
ava, *n.f.* Grandmother.
avallante, *n.m.* Guarantor.
avallare, *v.t.* (*Comm.*) To back, to guarantee. **— una cambiale,** to back a bill.
avallo, *n.m.* (*Comm.*) Guaranty.
avambraccio [avambrAccio], *n.m.* (*Anat.*) Forearm.
avamposto, *n.m.* Outpost.
avana, *n.m.* Havana cigar.
avanguardia [avanguArdia], *n.f.* Vanguard.
avannotto, *n.m.* Fry (small fish).
avanscoperta, *n.f.* (*Mil.*) Scouting.
avanti, *adv.prep.* Before, forward, in the presence of, beforehand. **Il giorno —,** the day before; **farsi —,** to step forward; **— che,** sooner than; **piegarsi in —,** to lean forward; **Avanti!** Forward! Come in!
avantieri, *adv.* The day before yesterday.
avantreno, *n.m.* Limber (of a gun-carriage).
avanzamento, *n.m.* Advancement; promotion.
avanzare, *v.t.i.* To advance, to go forward, to proceed; to owe; to put forward; to put forth; to lend; to promote. **— pretese,** to make claims; **gli avanzo mille lire,** he owes me a thousand lire; **il mio orologio avanza,** my watch is fast; **— l'orologio,** to put the clock on.
avanzarsi, *v.r.* To advance, to push on. **Il nemico si avanza,** the enemy is advancing.
avanzata, *n.f.* Advance.
avanzaticcio [avanzatIccio], *n.m.* Refuse, scraps (of food, etc.).
avanzato, *p.p.a.* Gone ahead, advanced. **È notte avanzata,** it is late at night.
avanzo, *n.m.* Rest, remainder, residue; surplus; ruins. (*Comm.*) **— di cassa,** surplus, cash in hand; (*fig.*) **— di galera,** jail-bird, rascal; **averne d'—,** to have more than one needs.
avanzuglio, avanzume [avanzUglio], *n.m.* Left-over, remains.
avaraccio [avarAccio], *n.m.a.* Miser, mean fellow; very avaricious, miserly.
avaria [avarIa], *n.f.* (*Naut.*) Damage at sea; (*Comm.*) average.
avariare, *v.t.* To damage goods (at sea).
avariato, *p.p.a.* Damaged (at sea); spoiled, deteriorated.
avarizia [avarIzia], *n.f.* Avarice.
avaro, *n.m.a.* Miser; stingy man; avaricious, stingy, miserly.
ave! *inter.* Hail! **Ave Maria!** Hail Mary! [cp. **avemmaria**].
avellana, *n.f.* Cob, filbert or hazel nut.

avellano, *n.m.* Nut-tree (cob, hazel or filbert).
avello, *n.m.* (*Poet.*) Tomb, grave.
avemmaria, *n.f.* Prayer of Ave Maria; time of sunrise, noon and sunset when the bell of the Angelus is rung; bead of the rosary.
avena, *n.f.* (*Bot.*) Oats.
avente, *a.* (*Law*) Having. **L'— causa,** the rightful party.
avere, *v.t.* To have, to possess, to wear; to be. **— fame, freddo,** to be hungry, cold; **la ragazza ha dodici anni,** the girl is twelve; **— in pregio,** to esteem; **— per regola,** to make it a rule; **— a male,** to take offence; **— a cuore,** to have at heart; **che cosa avete?** What's the matter with you?
avere, *n.m.* Property; (*Comm.*) credit. (*Comm.*) **Il lato dell'—,** the credit side (of a ledger); **l'— del conto cassa,** the cash account.
averla, *n.f.* (*Zool.*) Shrike, butcher-bird.
aviatore, *n.m.* (*Aviat.*) Aviator, airman, pilot.
aviatorio [aviatOrio], *a.* Aircraft, aviation. **Medaglia al valore —,** medal for flying.
aviatrice, *n.f.* Airwoman.
aviazione, *n.f.* Aviation; aeronautics.
avicultore, *n.m.* Bird-fancier.
avidamente, *adv.* Avidly, greedily; eagerly.
avidità [-à], *n.f.* Avidity, greed, greediness; eagerness.
avido [Avido], *a.* Avid, eager, greedy.
aviere, *n.m.* Aircraftman.
aviolinea, *n.f.* (*Aviat.*) Air line; airway.
aviorimessa, *n.f.* (*Aviat.*) Hangar.
aviotrasportato, *a.* Air-borne.
avito, *a.* Hereditary, ancestral.
avo, *n.m.* Grandfather. **Gli avi,** the forefathers.
avocare, *v.t.* To assume, to take upon oneself; (*Law*) to remove to a higher court.
avocazione, *n.f.* (*Law*) Avocation.
avola [Avola], *n.f.* Grandmother.
avolo [Avolo], *n.m.* Grandfather.
avorio [avOrio], *n.m.* Ivory.
avulsione, *n.f.* Avulsion.
avulso, *a.* Forced away from; pulled off; eradicated.
avvalersi, *v.r.* To make use of; to profit by.
avvallamento, *n.m.* Valley, hollow (of ground); subsidence (of land), depression.
avvallarsi, *v.r.* To sink in; to subside.
avvallatura, *n.f.* subsidence, depression, hollow (of land).
avvaloramento, *n.m.* Improvement, strengthening.
avvalorare, *v.t.* To strengthen, to improve.
avvalorarsi, *v.r.* To grow strong, to increase in strength.
avvalorato, *p.p.a.* Strengthened, improved.
avvampamento, *n.m.* Blaze, flare, flame.
avvampare, *v.t.i.* To blaze, to flare up, to burst into flame. **— di collera,** to flare up in a temper.
avvantaggiamento, *n.m.* Advantage.
avvantaggiare, *v.t.* To advantage, to improve, to better.
avvantaggiarsi, *v.r.* To draw advantage from, to avail oneself of, to profit by.
avvantaggiato, *a.* Over measure; increased. **Un chilometro —,** a good kilometre, a kilometre and more.
avvantaggio [avvantAggio], *n.m.* (*obs.*) Advantage. **Non diro d'—,** I will say no more.
avvedersi, *v.r.* To notice, to perceive, to realize.
avvedimento, *n.m.* Cleverness, sagacity, shrewdness.
avvedutamente, *adv.* Cleverly, shrewdly.
avvedutezza, *n.f.* Sagacity, shrewdness, cleverness.
avveduto, *a.* Shrewd, cautious, clever.
avvelenamento, *n.m.* Poisoning.
avvelenare, *v.t.* To poison; (*fig.*) to embitter; to grieve.
avvelenarsi, *v.r.* To poison oneself, to take poison.
avvelenato, *p.p.a.* Poisoned; (*fig.*) spoiled, corrupted; saddened.
avvelenatore, avvelenatrice, *n.m.f.* Poisoner.
avvenente, *a.* Beautiful (of face), handsome, pretty.
avvenentemente, *adv.* Beautifully.
avvenenza, *n.f.* Beauty, handsomeness, grace, charm.
avvenimento, *n.m.* Event, incident, fact.
avvenire, *v.i.* To happen, to chance; to occur, to come to pass. **Avvenga che può,** come what may; **che cosa avvenne di lui?** what has become of him?
avvenire, *n.m.a.* Future. **Per l'—,** for the future; **nel tempo —,** in time to come.
avventamento, *n.m.* (*obs.*) Hurling; (*fig.*) pouring out (words).
avventare, *v.t.* To hurl; (*fig.*) to pour out (words, opinions, etc.); to menace; to rush at.
avventarsi, *v.r.* To throw oneself on, to rush at, to hurl oneself upon.
avventataggine [avventatAggine], *n.f.* Rashness, imprudence, lack of consideration.
avventatamente, *adv.* Rashly.
avventatezza, *n.f.* Rashness, recklessness, thoughtlessness.
avventato, *p.p.a.* Rash, inconsiderate, foolhardy.
avventiziato, *n.m.* Apprenticeship.
avventizio [avventIzio], *a.* Adventitious, casual, temporary. || *n.m.* day-labourer, hireling.
avvento, *n.m.* Advent; accession; (*Eccles.*) Advent. **— al trono,** accession to the crown.
avventore, *n.m.* Customer, client.
avventura, *n.f.* Adventure; luck, chance; risk. **Per —,** by chance.
avventurare, *v.t.* To venture.
avventurarsi, *v.r.* To venture, to engage in (speculation, etc.).
avventurato, *a.* Fortunate.
avventuriere, avventuriero, *n.m.* Adventurer; soldier of fortune.
avventurina, *n.f.* (*Min.*) Kind of quartz.
avventuroso, *a.* Adventurous, risky, hazardous, daring, adventuresome; lucky, favourable.
avvenuto, *p.p.a.* Happened, occurred, chanced.
avveramento, *n.m.* Assertion, confirmation; verifying.
avverare, *v.t.* To aver, to confirm, to verify.
avverarsi, *v.r.* To prove true, to come to pass; to be realized.
avverbiale, *a.* (*Gram.*) Adverbial.
avverbialmente, *adv.* (*Gram.*) Adverbially.
avverbio [avvErbio], *n.m.* (*Gram.*) Adverb.
avverdire, *v.i.* To turn green.
avversamente, *adv.* Adversely.
avversare, *v.t.* To oppose; to thwart, to obstruct, to withstand.

avversario [avversArio], *n.m.a.* Adversary, opponent; opposing; hostile.
avversativo, *a.* Showing opposition.
avversatore, avversatrice, *n.m.f.* Opponent, adversary.
avversione, *n.f.* Aversion; opposition; dislike.
avversità [-à], *n.f.* Adversity, misfortune, distress.
avverso, *a.* Adverse, contrary, hostile.
avvertente, *a.* (*obs.*) Cautious, prudent; admonishing.
avvertenza, *n.f.* Accuracy, prudence, precaution; preface (of a book).
avvertimento, *n.m.* Admonition, warning, caution; advice.
avvertire, *v.t.i.* To admonish, to warn, to caution, to advise; to inform, to acquaint; to pay attention, to heed; to observe. **Vi avverto,** I warn you, I inform you; **quando viene avvertimi,** when he comes let me know; **avverti di chiudere la porta,** take care to shut the door; — **un errore,** to discover a mistake.
avvertitamente, *adv.* Thoughtfully, carefully.
avvezzare, *v.t.* To accustom, to inure.
avvezzarsi, *v.r.* To become accustomed, to accustom oneself.
avvezzo, *a.* Accustomed.
avviamento, *n.m.* Beginning, introduction, start; (*Comm.*) good will, custom; (*Mech. Motor.*) starter, starting device.
avviare, *v.t.i.* To set going, to start, to set on foot.
avviarsi, *v.r.* To set out, to go forward.
avviato, *p.p.a.* Advanced; (*Comm.*) introduced (of custom).
avviatore, *n.m.* (*Mech. Motor.*) Starter, self-starter.
avviatura, *n.f.* Beginning of a task; embers (of a fire).
avvicendamento, *n.m.* Alternation; (*Agric.*) rotation (of crops).
avvicendare, *v.t.* To alternate; (*Agric.*) to farm on the system of rotation of crops.
avvicendarsi, *v.r.* To change by turns; to alternate.
avvicinamento, *n.m.* Approaching, approach.
avvicinare, *v.t.* To approach, to bring or draw near. — **la sedia alla tavola,** to draw the chair up to the table.
avvicinarsi, *v.r.* To approach, to get near, to come near. **La festa di Natale si avvicina,** Christmas is getting near.
avvicinato, *p.p.a.* Near, come nearer.
avvignare, *v.t.* (*Agric.*) To plant vines.
avvilimento, *n.m.* Humiliation, debasement; disgrace; discouragement. — **dello spirito,** dejection.
avvilire, *v.t.* To humiliate, to mortify, to degrade; to vilify, to revile; to humble.
avvilirsi, *v.r.* To degrade oneself; to humble oneself; to get discouraged, to be despondent, to lose hope.
avviluppamento, *n.m.* Envelopment; entanglement.
avviluppante, *a.* Enveloping.
avviluppare, *v.t.* To envelope, to fold, to wrap up; (*fig.*) to dupe.
avvilupparsi, *v.r.* To envelop oneself; to wrap oneself up; (*fig.*) to get entangled or embroiled.
avviluppatamente, *adv.* Confusedly.
avviluppatore, avviluppatrice, *n.m.f.* Cheat, swindler.
avviluppatura, *n.f.* Envelopment; entanglement.
avvinato, *p.p.a.* Tasting of wine; smelling of wine.
avvinazzamento, *n.m.* Slight tipsiness.
avvinazzare, *v.t.* To make fuddled or tipsy.
avvincere [avvIncere], *v.t.* To bind, to tie up; to captivate, to enthral. **È una storia avvincente,** it is an exciting story.
avvincersi [avvIncersi], *v.r.* To bind oneself, to bind one another; (*fig.*) to hug, to embrace.
avvincigliare, *v.t.* To bind tightly; to bind with thongs.
avvinghiare, *v.t.* To bind firmly.
avvinghiarsi, *v.r.* To embrace one another closely; to cling to one another.
avvinghiato, *p.p.a.* Entwined, clasped together.
avvio [cp. **avviamento**].
avvisaglia [avvisAglia], *n.f.* (*Mil.*) Skirmish.
avvisare, *v.t.* To give notice; to inform, to make acquainted, to bring to one's notice or knowledge; to send warning; to warn.
avvisatore, avvisatrice, *n.m.f.* Monitor, messenger; (*Theat.*) call-boy; (*Mech.*) annunciator. — **d'incendio,** fire-alarm.
avviso, *n.m.* Notice, announcement; advertisement; warning; preface (to a book); opinion. **A mio —,** in my opinion; **sono d'— che,** I am of the opinion that; **lettera d'—,** letter of advice; **stare sull'—,** to be on one's guard.
avvistare, *v.t.* To sight, to discover; to distinguish.
avvistarsi, *v.r.* To catch sight of one another.
avvistato, *p.p.a.* Sighted, perceived; shrewd.
avvitamento, *n.m.* Screwing; (*Aviat.*) spinning.
avvitare, *v.t.* To screw, to screw down.
avvitarsi, *v.r.* (*Mech.*) To be screwed; (*Aviat.*) to spin.
avviticchiamento, *n.m.* Twining, twisting, twist.
avviticchiare, *v.t.* To entwine.
avviticchiarsi, *v.r.* To twist round, to entwine; to embrace closely.
avviticciare, *v.t.* To twist (as a vine).
avvitire, *v.t.* (*Agric.*) To plant vines.
avvivamento, *n.m.* Vivification, animation.
avvivare, *v.t.* To vivify, to animate, to encourage.
avvivarsi, *v.r.* To recover strength, to take courage.
avvivato, *p.p.a.* Strengthened, encouraged.
avvivatoio [avvivatOio], *n.m.* (*Mech.*) Burnisher.
avvizzimento, *n.m.* Fading, withering, languishing.
avvizzire, *v.i.* To fade, to wither, to wilt.
avvocata, *n.f.* Protectress, mediatrix (applied to Our Lady).
avvocatare, *v.t.* To carry on the profession of the law; to give a law degree.
avvocatarsi, *v.r.* (*obs.*) To study law; to be admitted to the bar.
avvocateria [avvocaterIa], *n.f.* (*obs.*) Pettifoggery.
avvocatescamente, *adv.* In a pettifogging way.

avvocatesco, *a.* Pettifogging.
avocatessa, *n.f.* Woman lawyer.
avvocato, *n.m.* Lawyer (including barrister and solicitor); counsel.
avvocatorio [avvocatOrio], *a.* Pertaining to a lawyer.
avvocatura, *n.f.* Profession of the Law; legal practice; advocacy (in a law court).
avvolgere [avvOlgere], *v.t.* To wind; to twirl; to roll up, to entwine; to surround; (*fig.*) to implicate.
avvolgersi [avvOlgersi], *v.r.* To envelop oneself, to wrap oneself up; (*fig.*) to embroil oneself.
avvolgibile [avvolgIbile], *n.m.* Venetian blind; rolling shutter.
avvolgibile [avvolgIbile], *a.* Capable of being turned or twisted.
avvolgimento, *n.m.* Winding up; deception, intrigue. **Tendina ad —,** roller-blind.
avvoltare, *v.t.* To wrap round.
avvoltatura, *n.f.* Rolling up.
avvolticchiare, *v.t.* To wrap round and round.
avvolto, *p.p.a.* Enveloped, wrapped, enfolded, rolled up; (*fig.*) swindled.
avvoltoio [avvoltOio], *n.m.* (*Zool.*) Vulture.
avvoltolare, *v.t.* To roll up.
avvoltolarsi, *v.r.* To roll oneself up; to wallow.
avvoltolatamente, *adv.* With confusion, confusedly.
avvoltolatura, *n.f.* Wallowing; rolling up.
azienda, *n.f.* Business, concern; company; shop, factory, etc.
aziendale, *a.* Business. **Conti aziendali,** business accounts; **mensa —,** works canteen.
azimut, *n.m.* (*Astron.*) Azimuth.
azimuttale, *a.* Azimuth. **Bussola —,** azimuth-compass.
azionaccia [azionAccia], *n.f.* Bad deed, evil action.
azionamento, *n.m.* (*Mech.*) Drive.
azionare, *v.t.* (*Mech.*) To actuate, to drive; to put in action.
azionario [azionArio], *a.* (*Comm.*) Share. **Capitale —,** share capital.
azione, *n.f.* Action (in all senses), exploit, deed; (*Comm.*) share. (*Comm.*) **— al portatore,** transferable share; **— liberata,** paid-up share; **— ordinaria,** ordinary share; **— privilegiata,** preference share; **intentare un'—,** to sue at law; **mettere in —,** to put in motion; **essere in —,** to be in gear.
azionista, *n.m.* Shareholder.
azotato, *n.m.a.* (*Chem.*) Nitrate; nitrogenous.
azotico [azOtico], *a.* (*Chem.*) Nitric.
azoto, *n.m.* (*Chem.*) Nitrogen.
azza, *n.f.* Battle-axe.
azzampato, *a.* With well-shaped legs (of dogs, etc.).
azzannamento, *n.m.* Seizing with the teeth.
azzannare, *v.t.* To seize with the fangs, to gore with the tusks.
azzardare, *v.t.i.* To hazard, to risk.
azzardarsi, *v.r.* To hazard, to run risks.
azzardato, *p.p.a.* Hazarded, risky, bold.
azzardo, *n.m.* Hazard, risk. **Giuoco d'—,** game of chance; **colpo d'—,** lucky stroke; **quale —!** what cheek!
azzardoso, *a.* Hazardous, risky.
azzeccagarbugli, *n.m.* Pettifogger.
azzeccare, *v.t.* To guess; (*fig.*) to hit the nail on the head; to hit the mark. **Ho azzeccato un terno al lotto,** I picked three winning numbers in the lottery.
azzima [Azzima], *n.f.* Unleavened bread.
azzimare, *v.t.* To bedeck gaudily, to deck out, to perfume.
azzimarsi, *v.r.* To deck oneself out, to paint one's face, to perfume oneself.
azzimato, *p.p.a.* Decked out.
azzimella, *n.f.* Passover bread (of the Jews).
azzimo [Azzimo], *a.* Unleavened. **Gli azzimi,** Jewish Feast of Unleavened Bread.
azzittare, azzittire, *v.t.* To silence.
azzittarsi, azzittirsi, *v.r.* To keep silence, to hold one's tongue.
azzoppare, *v.t.* To lame.
azzoppire, *v.t.* To lame, to become lame; to be lame.
azzoppito, *a.* Lame.
Azzorre, *n.f.pl.* The Azores.
azzuffamento, *n.m.* Affray, feud.
azzuffarsi, *v.r.* To come to blows, to quarrel.
azzurreggiare, *v.i.* To be bluish in colour.
azzurriccio, azzurrigno [azzurrIccio, azzurrIgno], *a.* Light blue.
azzurrino, *a.* Clear blue.
azzurro, *a.* Blue.
azzurrognolo [azzurrOgnolo], *a.* Bluish.

B

B, b, Second letter of the Italian alphabet.
baba, babà [bAba, -à], *n.m.* A kind of sweet, usually soaked in rum.
babao, babau, *n.m.* (*colloq.*) Bugbear, bogey
babbaleo, babbalocco, babbeo, babbione, *n.m.* Simpleton, blockhead, booby.
babbo, *n.m.* (*colloq.*) Daddy, papa. **Fare da — a qualcuno,** to help; **a — morto,** post obit.
babbuaggine [babbuAggine], *n.f.* Stupidity.
babbuasso, *n.m.* Simpleton, stupid.
babbuccia [babbUccia], *n.f.* Bedroom slipper; Turkish slipper.
babbuino, *n.m.* (*Zool.*) Baboon; (*fig.*) dolt.
babele, *n.f.* Babel, confusion disorder. **Torre di Babele,** Tower of Babel, (*fig.*) scene of confusion.
babelico [babElico], *a.* In a state of confusion.
Babilonia, *n.f.* Babylon, Babylonia.
babordo, *n.m.* (*Naut.*) Port side, larboard.
bacare, *v.i.* To be worm-eaten.
bacaticcio [bacatIccio], *a.* Worm-eaten; (*fig.*) rather unwell.
bacato, *a.* Worm-eaten; maggoty (of fruit); (*fig.*) unwell; morally corrupt.
bacca, *n.f.* (*Bot.*) Berry.
baccalà [-à], *n.m.* Dried codfish; (*fig.*) lean person, fool.
baccalare, *n.m.* Know-all, wiseacre.
baccalaureato, *n.m.* (*obs.*) Bachelorship (of a university).
baccanale, *n.m.* (*Hist.*) Bacchanal; (*fig.*) rowdy orgy; racket.
baccano, *n.m.* Hubbub, uproar, din.
baccante, *n.f.* (*Hist.*) Bacchante.

baccarà [-**à**], *n.m.* Game of baccarat.
baccella, *n.f.* (*obs.*) Silly woman.
baccellaio [baccellAio], *n.m.* Beanfield. **Essere padrone del —,** to be cock of the walk.
baccellierato, *n.m.* Bachelorship (degree).
baccelliere, *n.m.* Bachelor (of arts, etc.).
baccellino, *a.* (*Bot.*) Descriptive of plants that form pods (*e.g.* peas).
baccello, *n.m.* Bean (in its pod); pod, husk; (*fig.*) simpleton.
baccellone, *n.m.* Large pod; (*fig.*) great fool.
baccheggiare, *v.i.* To revel.
bacchetta, *n.f.* Rod, stick, wand, drumstick. **Comandare a —,** to rule with an iron rod.
bacchettare, *v.t.* To beat, to thrash, to flog.
bacchettata, *n.f.* Blow with a stick.
bacchetto, *n.m.* Large stick; whip-handle.
bacchettone, *n.m.* Bigot, religious devotee.
bacchettoneria [bacchettonerIa], *n.f.* Bigotry.
bacchettonismo, *n.m.* Bigotry.
bacchiare, *v.t.* To knock down [cp. **abbacchiare**].
bacchiata, *n.f.* Blow with a stick.
bacchio, *n.m.* Pole; heavy stick, cudgel.
Bacco, *n.m.* Bacchus. **Per — !** By Jove!
bacheca, *n.f.* Glass show-case.
bacherozzo, bacherozzolo [bacherOzzolo], *n.m.* Maggot (esp. as bait for fishing).
bachicoltore, bachicultore, *n.m.* Breeder of silkworms.
bachicoltura, bachicultura, *n.f.* Silkworm breeding.
baciamano, *n.m.* Kissing the hand.
baciamento, *n.m.* Kissing.
baciapile, *n.m.* Bigot; (*fig.*) hypocrite.
baciare, *v.t.* To kiss.
baciarsi, *v.r.* To kiss one another.
bacile, *n.m.* Basin; washhand basin.
bacillo, *n.m.* (*Med.*) Bacillus.
bacinella, *n.f.* Basin (of glass or porcelain); (*Phot.*) developing tray.
bacinetto, *n.m.* (*Hist.*) Helmet; basinet.
bacino, *n.m.* Basin (in all senses); dock; (*Anat.*) pelvis; reservoir. **— di carenaggio,** dry dock; **— di raddobbo,** graving dock; **diritti di —,** dock dues.
bacio (1), *n.m.* Kiss. **Mandare un —,** to throw a kiss; **baci affettuosi da,** (in letters) love from.
bacio [bacIo] (2), *n.m.* Shady site facing north. **A —,** in the shade.
baciozzo, bacione, *n.m.* Hearty kiss, smack.
baciucchiare, *v.t.* To be always kissing, to keep on kissing.
baciucchiarsi, *v.r.* To be always kissing one another.
baciucchio [baciucchIo], *n.m.* Continual kissing.
baco, *n.m.* (*Zool.*) Caterpillar (esp. silkworm). **— del formaggio,** cheesemite.
bacolino, *n.m.* Small worm.
bacolo [bAcolo], *n.m.* Staff; bishop's crozier.
bacologia [bacologIa], *n.f.* The science of breeding silkworms, sericulture.
bacologico [bacolOgico], *a.* Pertaining to silkworms.
bacologo [bacOlogo], *n.m.* Breeder of silkworms, expert in sericulture.
bacterio [cp. **batterio**].
bada, *n.f.* Attention; delay. **Stare a —,** to dally; **tenere a —,** to detain, to check; to keep at bay.
badalone, *n.m.* (*Eccles.*) Lectern, reading-desk; (*fig.*) lounger, stroller.
badaluccare, *v.i.* (*obs.*) To skirmish.
badare, *v.i.* To mind, to pay attention to, to take care. **Bada!** Take care! **Senza — a spese,** regardless of expense; **— al bambino,** to baby-sit.
badarsi, *v.r.* To withdraw (from danger, etc.).
badessa, *n.f.* Abbess.
badia [badIa], *n.f.* Abbey [cp. **abbazia**].
badiale, *a.* (*colloq.*) Great, ample.
badile, *n.m.* Shovel.
baffi, *n.m.pl.* Moustache; whiskers (of animals). **Ridere sotto i —,** to laugh up one's sleeve; **coi —,** just as it should be; **arricciare i —,** to twirl one's moustache.
baffuto, *a.* With a moustache (esp. heavy).
bagagliaio [bagagliAio], *n.m.* Luggage van.
bagagliere, *n.m.* Baggage clerk.
bagaglio [bagAglio], *n.m.* Luggage; (*Am.*) baggage. **Fare i bagagli,** to pack; **con armi e bagagli,** with bag and baggage.
bagagliume, *n.m.* Heap of luggage.
bagarino, *n.m.* Forestaller; engrosser.
bagascia [bagAscia], *n.f.* Whore, harlot, strumpet.
bagattella, *n.f.* Trifle, bagatelle.
baggeo, *n.m.* Simpleton.
baggianata, *n.f.* Silly action, piece of foolery.
baggiano [cp. **babbeo**].
baglio [bAglio], *n.m.* (*Naut.*) Beam (supporting deck).
bagliore, *n.m.* Gleam, glimmer, beam, flash, ray. **Un — di speranza,** a ray of hope.
bagnino, bagnina, *n.m.f.* Bath attendant, bathing attendant.
bagnamento, *n.m.* Wetting, soaking.
bagnante, *n.m.f.* Bather; visitor to a bathing resort.
bagnare, *v.t.* To wet, to dip, to moisten; to steep, to wash (of rivers, seas, etc.).
bagnarsi, *v.r.* To get wet, to wet oneself; to bathe; to take a bath.
bagnato, *a.* Wet. **Tutto —,** wet through, soaked.
bagnatura, *n.f.* Bathing; course of curative bathing.
bagno, *n.m.* Bath, bathing; bathing place, bathroom; prison. **— penale,** convict prison; **— maria,** bain marie; **fare un —,** to take a bath.
bagnolo, bagnuolo, *n.m.* Hot fomentation.
bagordare, *v.i.* To revel, to carouse.
bagordo, *n.m.* Revelry, riotous feast; debauchery.
baia (1), *n.f.* Joke, pleasantry. **Dare la — a qualcuno,** to make fun of someone.
baia (2), *n.f.* (*Geog.*) Bay, inlet of the sea.
baiadera, *n.f.* Hindu dancing girl; bayadere.
baiata, *n.f.* Hooting, howling.
bailamme, *n.m.* Hubbub, uproar.
baio, *n.m.a.* Bay (horse and colour).
baiocco, *n.m.* Former Papal coin worth ½d. **Non vale un —,** it isn't worth a halfpenny.
Baiona, *n.f.* Bayonne.
baionetta, *n.f.* Bayonet. **Inastare la —,** to fix bayonets.

baionettata, *n.f.* Bayonet wound; bayonet thrust.
baita [bAita], *n.f.* Summer hut used by shepherds in the Alps.
balaustra, balaustrata, *n.f.* (*Arch.*) Balustrade.
balaustrato, *a.* (*Arch.*) Balustraded.
balaustro, *n.m.* (*Arch.*) Baluster.
balbettamento, *n.m.* Faltering, hesitation, stammering, stuttering.
balbettante, *a.* Stammering, stuttering; faltering.
balbettare, *v.t.i.* To stammer, to stutter, to lisp; to speak a language brokenly.
balbettio [balbettIo], *n.m.* Continual stammering or stuttering.
balbuzie [balbUzie], *n.f.* Stammer, stutter.
balbuziente, *n.m.* Stammerer, stutterer.
Balcani, *n.m.pl.* The Balkans.
balconata, *n.f.* Balcony, gallery.
balcone, *n.m.* French window opening on to a balcony; balcony.
baldacchino, *n.m.* (*Eccles.*) Baldachin, canopy.
baldamente, *adv.* Boldly, courageously; undauntedly.
baldanza, *n.f.* Boldness; self-confidence; self-reliance; dauntlessness.
baldanzosamente, *adv.* Boldly, with self-confidence, self-reliantly; haughtily.
baldanzoso, *a.* Bold, self-confident, self-reliant; haughty.
baldo, *a.* Gallant, bold.
baldoria [baldOria], *n.f.* Bonfire; (*fig.*) feasting, good-cheer, merrymaking. **Fare —,** to revel, to make merry, to go on a spree.
baldracca, *n.f.* Whore, strumpet.
balena, *n.f.* (*Zool.*) Whale. **Osso di —,** whale-bone.
balenamento, *n.m.* Lightning.
balenare, *v.i.* To lighten (storm); (*fig.*) to flash across one's mind.
baleniera, *n.f.* (*Naut.*) Whale-boat, whaler.
baleniere, *n.m.* Whaler.
balenio [balenIo], *n.m.* Continuous lighting.
baleno, *n.m.* Flash of lightning.
balenottera [balenOttera], *n.f.* (*Zool.*) Rorqual.
balenotto, *n.m.* (*Zool.*) Young whale.
balestra, *n.f.* Cross-bow, catapult.
balestraio [balestrAio], *n.m.* Maker or seller of cross-bow or catapult.
balestrare, *v.t.i.* To shoot with a cross-bow or catapult.
balestrata, *n.f.* Cross-bow or catapult shot.
balestriere, *n.m.* Cross-bowman.
balestruccio [balestrUccio], *n.m.* (*Zool.*) House-martin.
balì [-ì], *n.m.* (*Hist.*) Knight Commander (of a military order).
balia [balIa], *n.f.* Power, authority; (*obs.*) bench of magistrates. **Avere in —,** to have in one's power; **lasciare in —,** to leave at the mercy of; **in — di se stesso,** in his own power, uncontrolled.
balia [bAlia], *n.f.* Wet-nurse, children's nurse.
baliatico [baliAtico], *n.m.* Suckling; wet-nurse's wages.
balio [bAlio], *n.m.* Wet-nurse's husband, foster-father; (*Hist.*) title of honour, governor.
balipedio [balipEdio], *n.m.* (*Mil.*) Artillery firing-practice ground.
balista, *n.m.* (*Hist.*) Balista, heavy catapult.
balistica [balIstica], *n.f.* Ballistics.
balistico [balIstico], *a.* Ballistic.
balistite, *n.f.* Ballistite, smokeless powder.
balla, *n.f.* Bale, pack, package. (*fig.*) **A balle,** in great quantity.
ballabile [ballAbile], *n.m.* Dance; ballet; dance music; (*Lit.*) ballade.
ballabile [ballAbile], *a.* Fit for dancing, suitable for dancing.
ballare, *v.t.i.* To dance. (*fig.*) **Far —,** to make things hum, to stir things up; **quando siamo in ballo bisogna —,** when one has started a job one has got to finish it; **far — i quattrini,** to make the money fly.
ballata, *n.f.* Ballad; folk-song to accompany dancing; (*Lit.*) ballade.
ballatoio [ballatOio], *n.m.* (*Arch.*) Open gallery; perch in a birdcage.
ballatore, *n.m.* (*obs.*) Dancer.
ballerina, *n.f.* Professional dancer; ballet-girl; (*Zool.*) wagtail.
ballerino, *n.m.* Dancer, good dancer.
balletta, *n.f.* Small parcel.
ballettare, *v.i.* To walk with a dancing or mincing gait.
balletto, *n.m.* Ballet.
ballo, *n.m.* Ball, dance; dancing **— di San Vito,** St. Vitus's dance.
ballodole [ballOdole], *n.f.pl.* **Andare alle —,** (*colloq.*) to kick the bucket.
ballonzolare, *v.i.* To dance impromptu.
ballonzolo [ballOnzolo], *n.m.* Impromptu dance.
ballotta, *n.f.* Boiled chestnut; ballot ball.
ballottaggio [ballottAggio], *n.m.* Second ballot (between two highest candidates at first voting).
ballottare, *v.t.* To vote, to ballot.
balneare, balneario, *a.* Pertaining to bathing. **Stabilimento —,** bathing establishment; **stagione —,** bathing season.
baloccamento, *n.m.* Amusement, diversion.
baloccare, *v.t.* To amuse with toys; (*fig.*) to trifle.
baloccarsi, *v.r.* To toy, to dally, to waste one's time.
balocco, *n.m.* Toy, plaything; trifle.
baloccone, *n.m.* Booby, trifler.
balogio [balOgio], *a.* Unwell, indisposed; overcast (of sky), threatening to rain.
balordaggine [balordAggine], *n.f.* Dullness (of intellect), stupidity; stupid act.
balordamente, *adv.* Stupidly.
balorderia [balorderIa], *n.f.* Stupid act, piece of stupidity [cp. **balordaggine**].
balordo, *n.m.a.* Dull (through intellect or ill-health), stupid; blockhead, idiot.
balsamico [balsAmico], *a.* Balsamic.
balsamina, *n.f.* (*Bot.*) Balsam.
balsamo [bAlsamo], *n.m.* Balm, balsam.
balta, *n.f.* Upset (of vehicles), collision; shock. (*colloq.*) **dare — a,** to upset.
balteo [bAlteo], *n.m.* (*Hist.*) Baldric, belt.
Baltico [bAltico], *n.m.* The Baltic.
baluardo, *n.m.* Rampart, bastion; bulwark; (*fig.*) defence.

baluginare, *v.i.* To appear and disappear (like a flash of lightning); to blink.
balza, *n.f.* Ledge on a mountainside; cliff, precipice; flounce (of dress); white streak on a horse's foot.
balzana, *n.f.* White mark on horse's foot.
balzano, *a.* White-footed (of horse). **Cervello —,** queer, odd, mad person.
balzare, *v.i.* To bound, to leap; to start; to startle; to shrink. **— in piedi,** to start to one's feet, to rise; **— dal letto,** to leap out of bed.
balzellare, *v.i.* To hop; to skip.
balzello, *n.m.* Tax, duty, impost.
balzellone, *n.m.* Sudden leap, jump; start.
balzo, *n.m.* Bound, dash, leap, jump; precipice, cliff. **Prendere la palla al —,** to seize the opportunity.
bambagia [bambAgia], *n.f.* Cotton waste, cottonwool. **Tenere nella —,** to pamper.
bambagina, *n.f.* Cotton material.
bambagino, *a.* Cotton, of cotton.
bambina, *n.f.* Infant, baby, little girl (under 8 years of age).
bambinaggine [bambinAggine], *n.f.* Childishness.
bambinaia [bambinAia], *n.f.* Nurse, nursemaid.
bambinata, *n.f.* Childish talk, prattle; childish action.
bambineria [bambinerIa], *n.f.* Childishness; puerility; child's talk.
bambinesco, *a.* Childish.
bambino, *n.m.* Baby boy, little boy, baby.
bambocceria, bambocciata [bamboccerIa], *n.f.* Childishness, ingenuousness.
bamboccio [bambOccio], *n.m.* Fat child, chubby little fellow; puppet; (*fig.*) grown-up simpleton.
bambola [bAmbola], *n.f.* Doll; puppet.
bamboleggiamento, *n.m.* Childish romping.
bamboleggiare, *v.i.* To romp; to behave childishly.
bambolo [bAmbolo], *n.m.* Little boy.
bambolone, *n.m.* Chubby child.
bambù [-ù], *n.m.* Bamboo.
banale, *a.* Banal, common; trivial, commonplace.
banalità [-à], *n.f.* Banality, triviality, commonplace.
banana, *n.f.* Banana.
banano, *n.m.* (*Bot.*) Banana palm.
banca, *n.f.* Bank (in all senses). (*Comm.*) **— succursale,** branch bank; **affari di —,** banking business; **versare denari alla —,** to pay into the bank; **ritirare dalla —,** to draw out; **biglietti di —,** bank notes.
bancabile [bancAbile], *a.* (*Comm.*) Bankable, current.
bancaccio [bancAccio], *n.m.* Rough bench; settle.
bancarella, *n.f.* Street stall.
bancario [bancArio], *a.* (*Comm.*) Banking, bank. **Istituto —,** banking house; **ditta —,** banking firm; **operazione —,** banking operation; **valori —,** bank bills.
bancarotta, *n.f.* Bankruptcy, failure.
bancarottiere, *n.m.* Bankrupt.
banchettare, *v.i.* To banquet.
banchetto, *n.m.* Banquet.
banchiere, *n.m.* Banker.
banchina, *n.f.* Garden bench or seat; quay, wharf, pier; railway-station platform.
banco, *n.m.* Bench, counter; desk; counting-house; bank; sandbank. **— del lotto,** lottery office; **— degli accusati,** prisoner's dock; **— di ghiaccio,** ice-floe; **tenere il —,** to hold the bank (gaming).
bancogiro, *n.m.* (*Comm.*) Clearing; transfer of sum between customers in the same bank.
banconota, *n.f.* Banknote.
banda, *n.f.* Band (in all senses); banner; company, crew. **— civica,** municipal band; **mettere da —,** to put aside; **passare da — a —,** to run through and through; (*Naut.*) **alla —,** alongside.
bandella, *n.f.* Hinge.
banderaio [banderAio], *n.m.* Flag-maker.
banderola, banderuola, *n.f.* Streamer, pennant; weathercock; (*fig.*) a time-server, a weathercock.
bandiera, *n.f.* Flag, banner, colours, ensign. **Issare la —,** to hoist the flag; **a — spiegata,** with flying colours.
bandieraio [bandierAio], *n.m.* Flag-seller; flag-maker.
bandinella, *n.f.* Roller-towel.
bandire, *v.t.* To publish, to proclaim; to banish, to exile; to put aside. **Bandite questi pensieri,** banish such thoughts.
bandista (*pl.* **bandisti**), *n.m.* Bandsman.
bandita, *n.f.* Preserve (for fishing, hunting, etc.).
bandito, *n.m.* Bandit, outlaw; gangster.
bandito, *a.* Banished, exiled; advertised, proclaimed. **Tenere corte bandita,** to keep open house.
banditore, *n.m.* Town-crier; auctioneer.
bando, *n.m.* Proclamation, bann; exile, banishment. **— ai complimenti,** without compliments, without ceremony.
bandoliera, *n.f.* Bandoleer, cross-belt. **A —** worn over the shoulder.
bandolo [bAndolo], *n.m.* End of a skein; clue. **Il — della questione,** the clue for the solution of a problem.
bandone, *n.m.* Band iron, hoop iron.
bano, *n.m.* Ban (Hungarian governor).
bar, *n.m.* Bar (for serving liquors, etc.) **Gestore di —,** barman.
bara, *n.f.* Coffin, bier.
baracane, *n.m.* Barracan; cloth made from goat's hair.
baracca, *n.f.* Shack; hut, booth; (*fig.*) ill-managed or ill-established affair. (*fig.*) **Aiutare la —,** to help things along; **piantare — e burrattini,** to give up the whole thing; (*colloq.*) **far —,** to revel.
baraccone, *n.m.* Large tent (*e.g.* circus big top); pavilion; hangar.
baraonda, *n.f.* Hubbub, confusion, disorder; muddle.
barare, *v.i.* To cheat (at play).
barata, *n.f.* Cheat, trick; cheating.
baratro [bAratro], *n.m.* Abyss, chasm, gulf. **— infernale,** hell.
barattamento, *n.m.* Bartering, exchange.
barattare, *v.t.* To barter; to exchange.
barattarsi, *v.r.* To exchange with one another. **— delle ingiurie,** to exchange high words; to abuse one another.

barattatore, barattatrice, *n.m.f.* (*obs.*) Barterer, chafferer.
baratteria [baratterIa], *n.f.* (*Law*) Barratry.
barattiere, *n.m.* (*Law*) Barrator; swindler.
baratto, *n.m.* Barter, exchange, bartering; barratry.
barattolo [barAttolo], *n.m.* Medicine bottle; jampot, jam-jar, tin can.
barba, *n.f.* Beard; strength, virility; root (of plant or tooth); fin; wattle. **Farsi la —,** to shave oneself, to shave; **sapone da —,** shaving-stick; **vecchia —,** old man; **alla — di,** at the expense of; **fare la — a qualcuno,** to abuse someone; **in — a,** in spite of.
barbabietola [barbabiEtola], *n.f.* Beet, beet-root.
Barbablù, *n.m.* Bluebeard.
barbacane, *n.m.* Buttress; (*Mil.*) barbican.
barbaccia [barbAccia], *n.f.* Shaggy beard.
barbagianni, *n.m.* (*Zool.*) Barn owl, white owl; (*fig.*) stupid fellow, dolt.
barbaglio [barbAglio], *n.m.* Dazzle, glare of light, glaring.
barbaramente, *adv.* Barbarously.
barbare, *v.i.* To root, to take root.
barbareggiare, *v.i.* To write or speak in a crude fashion.
barbarescamente, *adv.* Barbarously, crudely.
barbaresco, *a.* Barbarian; from Barbary.
barbari [bArbari], *n.m.pl.* (*Hist.*) Barbarians.
barbarico [barbArico], *a.* Barbaric, barbarian.
barbarie [barbArie], *n.f.* Barbarity, lack of civilization; cruelty; ignorance.
barbarismo, *n.m.* Barbarism.
barbarità [-à], *n.f.* Barbarity, cruelty.
barbarizzare [cp. **barbareggiare**].
barbaro [bArbaro], *n.m.a.* Barbarian, uncivilized.
barbassoro, *n.m.* Wiseacre, pedant.
barbata, *n.f.* Roots, mass of roots.
barbatella, *n.f.* (*Agric.*) Layer (of strawberry, etc.); herb used in salads.
barbato, *a.* Bearded.
barbazzale, *n.m.* Curb chain; (*fig.*) check.
barbera, *n.m.* Piedmontese wine.
barberesco, *n.m.* Stableman (in charge of race-horses).
barbero [bArbero], *n.m.* Race horse; barbary horse, barb.
barbetta, *n.f.* Goatee; tuft of hair; barbette for a gun.
barbicamento, *n.m.* Rooting, taking root.
barbicare, *v.i.* To take root.
barbicella, *n.f.* Rootlet.
barbicone, *n.m.* Main root, tap-root.
barbiere, *n.m.* Barber, hairdresser.
barbificare, *v.i.* To spread roots; to root out for.
barbigi, *n.m.pl.* (*colloq.*) Whiskers, moustache.
barbino, *a.* Badly done, poorly made, second-rate. (*colloq.*) **Fare una figura barbina,** to cut a poor figure.
barbio [bArbio], *n.m.* (*Zool.*) Barbel.
barbitonsore, *n.m.* (*colloq.*) Barber.
barbiturici [barbitUrici], *n.m.pl.* drugs, narcotics.
barbo, *n.m.* (*Zool.*) Barbel.
barbogio [barbOgio], *n.m.a.* Dotard; foolish fellow; senile; foolish.
barbone, *n.m.* Long, luxuriant beard; man with this; poodle (dog); (*colloq.*) tramp, vagabond.
barbottare [cp. **borbottare**].
barbozza, *n.f.* Under part of horse's lower lip; chin-band of a helmet.
barbugliamento, *n.m.* Stammering, stuttering; mumbling.
barbugliare, *v.i.* To hesitate (in speech), to stutter, to mumble.
barbuglione, *n.m.* Stutterer.
barbuto, *a.* Bearded.
barca, *n.f.* Boat, bark; launch; heap, stack; (*fig.*) home, family. **A barche,** in great quantity; **mandar avanti la —,** to carry matters to a successful conclusion; to keep the ship afloat; **andare in —,** to go boating; **— a remi,** rowing boat.
barcaccia [barcAccia], *n.f.* Old boat; (*Theat.*) stage box on level with the stage.
barcaiolo, barcaiuolo, *n.m.* Boatman.
barcarmenarsi, *v.r.* To steer things through; to see-saw; to wangle.
barcarizzo, *n.m.* (*Naut.*) Gangway, entrance-port.
barcarola, *n.f.* (*Mus.*) Barcarolle.
barcata, *n.f.* Boat-load.
barcheggiare, *v.i.* To go boating.
barcheggiarsi, *v.r.* To wangle.
barcheggio [barchEggio], *n.m.* Boating.
barchetta, *n.f.* Small boat, dinghy.
barchetto, *n.m.* Small dinghy.
barchino, *n.m.* Punt (for wild-fowl shooting).
barcollamento, *n.m.* Tottering, staggering.
barcollare, *v.i.* To totter, to stagger; to vacillate.
barcollio [barcollIo], *n.m.* Continuous tottering.
barcollone, *n.m.* Tottering.
barda, *n.f.* Horse-armour.
bardamento, *n.m.* Harnessing (a saddle horse).
bardare, *v.t.* To harness (a saddle horse).
bardatura, *n.f.* Harness.
bardella, *n.f.* Cowboy's saddle; Mexican saddle.
bardellone, *n.m.* Large saddle (for breaking in young horses).
bardiglio [bardIglio], *n.m.* Marble streaked with blue and white.
bardo, *n.m.* (*Poet.*) Bard.
bardosso, *adv.* (Riding) bare-back.
bardotto, *n.m.* Mule, hinny; cattle-driver's mount, towing-horse; (*fig.*) apprentice, shopboy.
barella, *n.f.* Litter, stretcher; barrow.
barellare, *v.t.i.* To carry on a stretcher; to stagger, to reel.
barellata, *n.f.* Barrow-load.
barelliere, *n.m.* Stretcher-bearer.
bargello, *n.m.* (*Hist.*) Constable; chief of police; jail.
bargia [bArgia], *n.f.* Dewlap (of ox, etc.).
bargiglio, bargiglione, *n.m.* Wattle (of fowls, turkeys, etc.).
baricentro, *n.m.* (*Phys.*) Centre of gravity.
bariglione, *n.m.* Barrel.
barilaia [barilAia], *n.f.* Rack for barrels; vault for barrels.
barilaio [barilAio], *n.m.* Cooper.
barile, *n.m.* Barrel, cask; contents of either.
bariletto, barilotto, *n.m.* Keg, small cask.

barilozzo, *n.m.* Keg; marksman's target, bull's-eye.
bario [bArio], *n.m.* (*Metal.*) Barium.
barista, *n.m.f.* Barman, barmaid.
barite, *n.m.* (*Metal.*) Barytes.
baritonale, *a.* (*Mus.*) Baritone.
baritoneggiare, *v.i.* To imitate a baritone.
baritono [barItono], *n.m.* (*Mus.*) Baritone.
barlaccio [barlAccio], *a.* Bad (of an egg); (*fig.*) sickly, seedy.
barletta, *n.f.* Pocket flask.
barlume, *n.m.* Gleam, glimmer; (*fig.*) dim idea.
barnabita, *n.m.* (*Eccles.*) Barnabite; priest of that order.
baro, *n.m.* Cheat, swindler.
barocchismo, *n.m.* Oddness, queerness; baroque style.
barocciabile [barocciAbile], *a.* (*obs.*) Practicable for vehicles.
barocciaio [barocciAio], *n.m.* Carter, waggoner.
barocciata, *n.f.* Cartload, waggon-load. **A barocciate,** in quantities.
baroccino, *n.m.* Barrow, hand-cart.
baroccio [barOccio], *n.m.* Two-wheeled cart, tumbril.
barocco, *a.* Odd, queer; awkward, in bad taste; (*Arch.*, etc.) baroque.
barolo, *n.m.* Name applied to various red wines from Barolo, Piedmont.
barometrico [baromEtrico], *a.* Barometric.
barometro [barOmetro], *n.m.* Barometer. **Il — sale, scende,** the barometer is rising, falling.
baronale, *a.* Baronial.
baronata, *n.f.* Knavery, scurvy trick.
baronato, *n.m.* Baronage.
barone, *n.m.* Baron; dice game; (*fig.*) sharper, rogue.
baronesco, *a.* Baronial; (*fig.*) knavish.
baronessa, *n.f.* Baroness.
baronetto, *n.m.* Baronet.
baronia [baronIa], *n.f.* Barony.
baroscopio [baroscOpio], *n.m.* (*Phys.*) Baroscope.
barra, *n.f.* Bar, rod; (*Naut.*) tiller, helm. [cp. **sbarra,** *Law*].
barricare, *v.t.* To barricade.
barricarsi, *v.r.* To barricade oneself; to shut oneself up.
barricata, *n.f.* Barricade.
barriera, *n.f.* Barrier, gate; (*fig.*) obstacle, hindrance. (*Phys.*) **— del suono,** sound barrier.
barrire, *v.i.* To trumpet (of elephants).
barrito, *n.m.* Trumpeting (of elephants).
barrocciabile [cp. **barocciabile**].
barroccio [cp. **baroccio**].
Bartolomeo [bartolomEo], *n.m.* Bartholomew.
baruffa, *n.f.* Altercation, quarrel, affray. **Far —,** to scuffle, to start a row, to rag; to come to blows.
baruffare, *v.i.* To scuffle.
barzelletta, *n.f.* Jest, joke, witticism. **Dire barzellette,** to tell jokes.
barzellettare, *v.i.* To jest, to joke; to make sport of.
basalte, basalto, *n.m.* (*Geol.*) Basalt.
basaltico [basAltico], *a.* (*Geol.*) Basaltic.
basamento, *n.m.* (*Arch.*) Footings; base (of column).
basano, *a.* (*obs*). Dirty.
basare, *v.t.* To base, to found.
basarsi, *v.r.* To base oneself (on), to ground oneself (upon).
basato, *p.p.a.* Based (upon).
basco, *n.m.* Beret; (*Geogr.*) Basque.
basculla, *n.f.* Weigh-bridge; weighing-machine.
base, *n.f.* Base (in all senses), foundation; basis. **— aurea,** gold standard; **— aerea,** air base; **in — alle leggi,** under the law.
basetta, *n.f.* Side-whisker. **Portare basette,** to wear side-whiskers.
basico [bAsico], *a.* Basic.
Basilea [basilEa], *n.f.* Bâle, Basel.
basilica [basIlica], *n.f.* (*Arch.*) Basilica.
basilicale, *a.* Appertaining to a basilica.
basilico [basIlico], *n.m.* (*Bot.*) Basil.
basilisco, *n.m.* Basilisk; (*Zool.*) basilisk, lizard.
basimento, *n.m.* Faint, swoon.
basino, *n.m.* Bombazine.
basire, *v.i.* To faint, to swoon.
bassamente, *adv.* Basely, meanly, vilely; in a low voice; humbly.
bassetta, *n.f.* Card game of basset.
bassetto, *a.* Rather low (in all senses).
bassezza, *n.f.* Baseness, vileness; lowness.
bassifondi, *n.m.pl.* Underworld, criminal world.
basso, *n.m.* Bottom, lower part; foot; (*Mus.*) bass. **Il — delle scale,** the foot of the stairs; **gli alti e bassi della vita,** the ups and downs of life.
basso, *a.* Low, short (of stature); mean, abject; narrow. (*Comm.*) **Fatturare a — prezzo,** to invoice at a low price; **il — ventre,** the abdomen; **marea bassa,** ebb tide, low tide; **gente bassa,** lower classes; **parlare a bassa voce,** to speak in a low voice.
basso, *adv.* Down, downward. **Da —,** downstairs; **in —,** downwards; **dal —,** from below. **volar —,** to fly low.
bassofondo, *n.m.* (*Naut.*) Shallow water.
bassopiano, *n.m.* Lowland.
bassorilievo [bassoriliEvo], *n.m.* (*Art*) Bas-relief.
bassotto, *n.m.* Basset hound, dachshund; short man.
bassura, *n.f.* (*Geog.*) Low-land.
basta, *n.f.* Basting (needlework), tuck.
basta, *adv.inter.* Enough, sufficiently. That's enough! Nonsense! Silence!
bastaggio [bastAggio], *n.m.* (*obs.*) Carrying (by porters, etc.), portage.
bastaio [bastAio], *n.m.* Maker or seller of pack-saddles.
bastante, *a.* Sufficient, enough.
bastantemente, *adv.* Sufficiently, enough.
bastanza, *n.f.* Sufficience [cp. **abbastanza**].
bastardaggine [bastardAggine], *n.f.* Bastardy.
bastardella, *n.f.* Saucepan; casserole.
bastardo, *n.m.a.* Bastard; mongrel; foundling; (*fig.*) false, degenerate, hybrid; ill-proportioned.
bastardume, *n.m.* Bastardy; illegitimacy; collection of spurious things.
bastare, *v.i.* To be enough, to suffice, to satisfy. **Questa non basterà un mese,** this will not last a month; **più di quanto basta,** more than enough; **non gli basta il coraggio,** he lacks courage.
bastevole [bastEvole], *a.* Sufficient, enough.

bastevolezza, *n.f.* Sufficiency.
bastevolmente, *adv.* Sufficiently.
bastia [bastIa], *n.f.* (*Mil.*) Stockade, fort.
bastimento, *n.m.* Ship, vessel. **— a vela,** sailing ship.
bastina, *n.f.* (*obs.*) Light pack-saddle.
bastionare, *v.t.* (*Mil.*) To fortify with bastions.
bastione, *n.m.* (*Mil.*) Bastion.
basto, *n.m.* Pack-saddle; (*fig.*) load.
bastonamento, *n.m.* Thrashing, cudgelling.
bastonare, *v.t.* To beat with a stick, to thrash, to cudgel; (*fig.*) to ill-treat; to censure.
bastonata, *n.f.* Blow with a cudgel or stick.
bastonatore, *n.m.* Cudgeller.
bastonatura, *n.f.* Thrashing, beating.
bastone, *n.m.* Stick, walking-stick, cane; cudgel; golf club; (*Cards*) club. **— della bandiera,** flag-staff; **asso di bastoni,** ace of clubs.
batacchiata, *n.f.* (*obs.*) Blow with a pole.
batacchio [batAcchio], *n.m.* Pole; clapper of a bell.
batata, *n.f.* Sweet potato.
batiscafo, *n.m.* Bathyscaphe; submersible vessel for deep-sea observation.
batisfera, *n.f.* Bathysphere.
batista, *n.f.* Cambric, lawn.
batocchio [batOcchio], *n.m.* Clapper of a bell; blind man's stick.
batolo [bAtolo], *n.m.* (*Eccles.*) Cowl.
batosta, *n.f.* Severe blow (in health or fortune); defeat, discomfiture.
batrace, *a.* (*Zool.*) Batrachian.
battaglia [battAglia], *n.f.* Battle; (*Art*) battle scene; (*fig.*) struggle (in all senses). **Caval di —,** one's strong point.
battagliare, *v.i.* To battle; (*fig.*) to argue, to dispute.
battagliero, *a.* Pugnacious, warlike.
battaglio [battAglio], *n.m.* Clapper of a bell.
battaglione, *n.m.* (*Mil.*) Battalion.
battelliere, *n.m.* Boatman, waterman.
battello, *n.m.* Boat. **— a remi,** rowing-boat; **— di salvataggio,** life-boat.
battente, *n.m.* Leaf (of door, shutter, etc.); door-knocker; hammer (in striking clock).
battere [bAttere], *v.t.i.* To beat, to strike, to hit, to knock; (*fig.*) to defeat; to fly (a flag); to clap (hands); to coin (money); to strike (the hour). **— un luogo, una zona,** to go often to a place; **— gli occhi,** to blink; **— il tacco,** to run off.
batteria [batterIa], *f.* (*Mil.*) Battery; (*Elec.*) battery; outfit of cooking utensils; striking mechanism of a clock.
batterio [battErio], *n.m.* Bacterium.
batteriologia [batteriologIa], *n.f.* Bacteriology.
batteriologico [batteriolOgico], *a.* Bacteriological.
batteriologo [batteriOlogo], *n.m.* Bacteriologist.
battersi [bAttersi], *v.r.* To fight; to beat oneself. **— il petto,** to repent; **battersela,** to run away, to get off.
battesimale, *a.* Baptismal.
battesimo [battEsimo], *n.m.* Baptism, christening; blessing (of flag, etc.). **Tenere qualcuno a —,** to stand godfather to someone.
battezzando, *n.m.* Child (or person) to be christened.
battezzare, *v.t.* To baptize, to christen; (*colloq.*) to water (wine, etc.).
battezzatore, *n.m.* Baptizer, baptist.
battezzatorio [battezzatOrio], *n.m.* Font.
battezziere, *n.m.* Priest giving baptism.
battibaleno, *adv.* **In un —,** in a twinkling, in a moment.
battibecco, *n.m.* Bickering.
batticoda, *n.m.* (*Zool.*) Wagtail.
batticuore, *n.m.* Palpitation; heart-beat.
battifianco, *n.m.* Partition rail in a stable.
battifuoco, *n.m.* Steel for flint and steel.
battilana, battilano, *n.m.* Wool-carder.
battiloro, *n.m.* Goldbeater.
battimani, battimano, *n.m.* Clapping (of hands).
battipalo, *n.m.* Pile-driver.
battiporta, *n.m.* Door-knocker.
battiporto, *n.m.* Hatchway.
battiscarpa, *adv.* **A —,** in haste.
battisoffia [battisOffia], *n.m.* (*obs.*) Fright. **Avere la —,** to be scared.
battistero, battisterio [battistEro, battistErio], *n.m.* Baptistry.
battistrada, *n.m.* Outrider; tread of a tyre.
battito [bAttito], *n.m.* Heart-beat, palpitation.
battitoio [battitOio], *n.m.* Leaf (of folding door, etc.); door-knocker.
battitore, *n.m.* Beater (in all senses); (*Tennis*, etc.) server.
battitrice, *n.f.* (*Agric.*) Threshing-machine.
battitura, *n.f.* Beating; threshing.
battola [bAttola], *n.f.* Clapper (of a mill); (*Eccles.*) clapper.
battuta, *n.f.* Beat (in all senses); beating; (*Tennis*) service. **— di ali,** flapping of wings; **— spiritosa,** witty remark.
battuto, *p.p.a.* Beaten, struck; hammered (of metals); minced (of meat, etc.); frequented (of a path, road, etc.); **la strada battuta,** the beaten track.
batuffolo [batUffolo], *n.m.* Bundle (of rags, etc.), wad.
bau, *n.m.* Dog's bark; bogey.
baule, *n.m.* Trunk (for travelling). **Fare il —,** to pack; **disfare il —,** to unpack; **viaggiare come i bauli,** to travel without seeing or understanding anything.
bauletto, baulino, *n.m.* Travelling case.
bautta, *n.f.* Domino (garment).
bauxite, *n.f.* (*Metal.*) Bauxite.
bava, *n.f.* Dribble, slaver (from the mouth); floss (of silk); slime (of snails, etc.); rough edge of cast metal.
bavaglio [bavAglio], *n.m.* Gag. **Mettere il —,** to gag.
bavarese, *n.f.* Drink made of milk and chocolate.
bavarese, *a.* Bavarian.
bavella, *n.f.* Floss silk.
bavera [bAvera], *n.f.* Woman's tippet.
bavero [bAvero], *n.m.* Collar (of coat, etc.).
bavetta, *n.f.* Rough edge of cast metal.
bavettine, *n.f.pl.* Noodles.
Baviera, *n.f.* Bavaria.
bavoso, *a.* Slobbering.
bazar, *n.m.* Bazaar; market.
bazza, *n.f.* Long chin, turned-up chin; (*fig.*) bargain, good luck; (*Cards*) trick.

bazzana, *n.f.* Sheepskin leather; wash-leather.
bazzecola [bazzEcola], *n.f.* Trifle, gew-gaw, bagatelle.
bazzica [bAzzica], *n.f.* (*Cards*) Bezique; pool (billiards).
bazzicare, *v.t.i.* To frequent, to haunt, to resort to. **— cattive compagnie,** to frequent bad company.
bazzotto, *a.* Light-boiled (egg); inexperienced (person); unripe fruit.
be, *adv.* Well (*abbrev.* **bene**).
beare, *v.t.* (*Lit.*) To make happy.
bearsi, *v.r.* To delight in, to rejoice at.
beatamente, *adv.* Blissfully; in a state of beatitude.
beatificare, *v.t.* (*Eccles.*) To beatify.
beatificazione, *n.f.* (*Eccles.*) Beatification.
beatifico [beatIfico], *a.* Beatific.
beatitudine [beatitUdine], *n.f.* Beatitude. **Sua Beatitudine,** His Holiness (the Pope).
beato, *n.m.a.* Blessed one; blessed, beatified; supremely happy.
becca, *n.f.* (*obs.*) Corner of a handkerchief, etc.; garter.
beccaccia [beccAccia], *n.f.* (*Zool.*) Woodcock.
beccaccino, *n.m.* (*Zool.*) Snipe.
beccafico, *n.m.* (*Zool.*) Warbler.
beccaio [beccAio], *n.m.* Butcher.
beccamento, *n.m.* Pecking [cp. **beccatura**].
beccamorti, *n.m.* Grave-digger.
beccare, *v.t.* To peck; to pick up with the beak; (*fig.*) to pick up a scanty living; to pick up (an illness, etc.).
beccarsi, *v.r.* To peck at (one another), to tease. **— il cervello,** to rack one's brains; **— una malattia,** to catch an ailment.
beccastrino, *n.m.* Pick-axe for rocks.
beccata, *n.f.* Peck (of a bird), mouthful.
beccatello, *n.m.* (*Arch.*) Bracket to support a balcony, etc.; peg in a hatstand.
beccatoio [beccatOio], *n.m.* Feeding-trough in a birdcage.
beccatura, *n.f.* Pecking.
beccheggiare, *v.i.* (*Naut.*) To pitch.
beccheggio [becchEggio], *n.m.* (*Naut.*) Pitching.
beccheria [beccherIa], *n.f.* Butcher's shop.
becchime, *n.m.* Birdseed.
becchino, *n.m.* Grave-digger.
becco (1), *n.m.* Beak, bill; burner (gas, etc.); mouth-piece (of musical instrument; (*Naut.*) prow, bow; nib (of a pen). (*fig.*) **Metterci il —,** to speak without being wanted; to poke one's nose into; **ecco fatto il — all'oca,** well, that's done; **non avere il — d'un quattrino,** not to have a ha'penny in one's pocket; **dar di —,** to bite.
becco (2), *n.m.* He-goat; (*fig.*) cuckold.
beccuccio [beccUccio], *n.m.* Mouth of a jug, neck of bottle, spout.
beccuto, *a.* Beaked.
becerata, *n.f.* Ill-mannered action, caddish trick.
becero [bEcero], *n.m.* Boor; vulgarian; cad.
becerume, *n.m.* Low-down crowd.
beduina, *n.f.* Woman's long opera cloak.
beduino, *n.m.* Beduin.
befana, *n.f.* Feast of the Epiphany; old woman supposed by children to come down the chimney at Epiphany bringing presents; (*fig.*) ugly old woman.
beffa, *n.f.* Hoax; mockery, raillery; jest; practical joke, **Mettere in —,** to jeer at; **farsi beffe,** to ridicule, to sneer at.
beffardamente, *adv.* Mockingly.
beffardo, *n.m.a.* Mocker, railer; joker; mocking, railing.
beffare, *v.t.* To banter, to ridicule, to mock.
beffarsi, *v.r.* To laugh at; to ridicule; to make a fool of. **— di una cosa,** to hold of no account, to despise.
beffatore, beffatrice, *n.m.f.* Mocker.
beffeggiamento, *n.m.* Bantering, mocking.
beffeggiare, *v.t.* To keep on bantering or mocking; to make practical jokes.
bega, *n.f.* Dispute, quarrel, altercation.
beghina, *n.f.* Bigot; religious woman.
begli, bei, bel [cp. **bello**].
begliomini [begliOmini], *n.m.pl.* Balsam plant.
begonia, *m.f.* (*Bot.*) Begonia.
belamento, *n.m.* Bleating [cp. **belato**].
belare, *v.i.* To bleat.
belato, *n.m.* Bleating.
belga, *n.m.a.* Belgian.
Belgio [bElgio], *n.m.* Belgium.
belio [belIo], *n.m.* Prolonged bleating.
bella, *n.f.* Mistress, lover, beautiful woman [cp. **bello**].
belladonna, *n.f.* (*Bot.*) Belladonna, deadly nightshade.
bellamente, *adv.* Gently, gracefully; adroitly.
belletta, *n.f.* Slime; dirt.
belletto, *n.m.* Rouge, make-up.
bellezza, *n.f.* Beauty; charm. **Che —!** How beautiful! **Ho pagato la — di trenta mila lire,** I paid a cool thirty thousand lire; **è stato in Francia la — di tre anni,** he has been in France a good three years.
bellicista, *n.m.* War-monger.
bellico, *n.m.* (*Anat.*) Navel.
bellico [bEllico], *a.* Appertaining to war.
bellicosamente, *adv.* Martially, bravely, bellicosely.
bellicoso, *a.* Warlike, bellicose.
belligerante, *n.m.a.* Belligerent.
belligero [bellIgero], *a.* Warlike, belligerent.
bellimbusto, *n.m.* Dandy, fop, beau, coxcomb.
bellino, *a.* Pretty, nice.
bello, *n.m.* Beauty; the best thing; lover; right (opportune); fine (of weather). **Il —,** the finest, the fine thing; **capitare sul più —,** to arrive at the opportune moment; **il tempo si mette al —,** the weather is getting fine.
bello, *a.* Beautiful, fine, handsome, pretty nice, gracious; great. **Bel mondo,** the fashionable world; **bel sesso,** the fair sex; **belle parole,** soft, kind words; **scamparla bella,** to have a lucky escape; **una bella altezza,** a good height; **farsi — d'una cosa,** to take credit for something; **nel bel mezzo,** right in the middle; (*iron.*) **bel talento!** Doesn't he think he's clever! **fare una bella morte,** to die a peaceful *or* noble death.
bello, *adv.* **Bel —,** steadily, cautiously; **a — studio,** on purpose.
belloccio [bellOccio], *a.* Pretty, nice, rather handsome.

bellospirito [bellospIrito], *n.m.* Witty person, wit.
belluino, *a.* In a beast-like way.
bellumore, *n.m.* Jolly fellow, good-humoured wag.
belluria [bellUria], *n.f.* (*colloq.*) Superficial beauty; beauty skin-deep.
belo, *n.m.* (*Lit.*) Bleating.
beltà [-à], *n.f.* Beauty [cp. **bellezza**].
belva, *n.f.* Wild and ferocious beast; (*fig.*) cruel person.
belvedere, *n.m.* Turret, terrace, belvedere.
Belzebù, *n.m.* Devil, Beelzebub.
belzuino, *n.m.* [cp. **benzoino**].
bembè, *inter.* Well! (in ironical sense).
bemolle, *n.m.* (*Mus.*) Flat.
benaccetto, *a.* Welcome.
benallevato, *a.* Well brought up.
benalzato! *adv.* Good morning!
benamato, *a.* Well-beloved.
benanchè, *conj.* Although, still, yet.
benarrivato, *n.m.a.* Welcome.
benaugurato, *a.* Auspicious.
benchè, *conj.* Although; however.
bencreato, *a.* Well-bred [cp. **beneducato**].
benda, *n.f.* Bandage.
bendaggio [bendAggio], *n.m.* Bandaging, bandage.
bendare, *v.t.* To bandage; to bind up, to wrap up; to dress (a wound). — **gli occhi,** to blindfold.
bendatura, *n.f.* Bandaging, bandage.
bene, *n.m.* Good; (in pl.) goods, property. **Il Sommo Bene,** God; **ogni — di Dio,** all good things; **il — comune,** the common good; **beni immobili,** real estate.
bene, *adv.* Well. **Sto —,** I am quite well; **tutto va —,** all is well; **va —,** all right; **voler —,** to love, to like; **essere —,** to be convenient; **creder —,** to have reason to think; **promettere —,** to promise well, to give promise; **persona per —.** an honest, trustworthy person; **portarsi —,** to behave; **sono — stanco di questi affari,** I am heartily sick of this business.
benedettino, *n.m.* (*Eccles.*) Benedictine monk; a liqueur.
Benedetto, *n.m.* Benedict.
benedetto, *a.* Blessed, consecrated.
benedicente, *a.* Blessing; speaking well of.
benedicite [benedIcite], *n.m.* Grace (before meals).
benedire, *v.t.* To bless, to consecrate. (*fig.*) **Mandare a farsi —,** to send someone about his business.
benedizione, *n.f.* Benediction, blessing.
beneducato, *a.* Well-bred.
benefattore, benefattrice, *n.m.f.* Benefactor, benefactress.
beneficamente, *adv.* Beneficently.
beneficare, *v.t.* To benefit; to favour, to help.
beneficenza, *n.f.* Beneficence, charity. **Istituzione di —,** charitable institution; benevolent society.
beneficiare, *v.i.* To benefit, to profit, to gain; to take advantage.
beneficiario [beneficiArio], *n.m.a.* Beneficiary, beneficed priest; (*Comm.*) payee. **Azione beneficiaria,** dividend share.
beneficiata, *n.f.* (*Theat.*) Benefit.
beneficiato, *n.m.* (*Eccles.*) Incumbent.
beneficio [benefIcio], *n.m.* Benefit, good office, favour; profit, gain; (*Eccles.*) benefice. (*Comm.*) — **netto,** net profit; — **lordo,** gross profit; **chiedere a titolo di —,** to ask as a favour.
benefico [benEfico], *a.* Beneficent, charitable.
benefizio [benefIzio] [cp. **beneficio**].
benemerente, *a.* Deserving, meritorious.
benemerenza, *n.f.* Merit, good service.
benemerito [benemErito], *n.m.* Worthy person. **La benemerita arma,** the Italian carabineers.
beneplacito [beneplAcito], *n.m.* Consent, approval (of a superior); absolute power.
benessere [benEssere], *n.m.* Well-being, welfare, comfort.
benestante, *n.m.a.* Independent man (of means); well-to-do, comfortably off.
benestare, *n.m.* Consent, approval, sanction (of accounts, etc.).
beneviso, *a.* [cp. **benvisto**].
benevolenza, *n.f.* Benevolence, good-will.
benevolmente, *adv.* Benevolently, sympathetically.
benevolo [benEvolo], *a.* Benevolent, kindly, well-disposed.
benfatto, *a.* Well-made, handsome.
Bengala, *n.f.* Bengal; Bengal lights.
bengalese, *n.m.a.* Bengalese.
beni, *n.m.pl.* Goods [cp. **bene**].
beniamino, *n.m.* Favourite son, Benjamin.
benignamente, *adv.* Benignly, kindly.
benignità [-à], *n.f.* Benignity, kindliness.
benigno, *a.* Benign, benignant (in all senses).
benino, *adv.* Pretty well. **Per —.** nicely, properly.
benintenzionato, *a.* Well-meaning, well-intentioned.
beninteso, *adv.* Of course, well understood.
benna, *n.f.* (*Naut.*) Grab.
bennato, *a.* (*Lit.*) Well-born; generous.
benone, *adv.* Very well, all right.
benparlante, *n.m.* Correct speaker.
benpensante, *n.m.* A moderate.
benportante, *n.m.* Hale and hearty old man.
benservito, *n.m.* Testimonial (to employee, etc.). **Dare il —,** to dismiss.
bensì, *adv.* Rather; but; certainly. **Ma —,** but assuredly.
bentornato, *n.m.* Welcome. **Dar il —,** to welcome; **bentornato!** Welcome!
bentrovato, *n.m.* Greeting to someone met in the street.
benuscita, *n.f.* [cp. **buonuscita**].
benveduto, benvisto, *a.* Agreeable, viewed with pleasure; welcome.
benvenuto, *n.m.* Welcome. **Siate il —.** welcome!
benvolere, *v.t.i.* To like (a person), to love.
benvolere, *n.m.* Affection.
benvoluto, *p.p.a.* Liked, loved.
benzina, *n.f.* Benzine, petrol; (*Am.*) gasolene, gas. (*Motor.*) **Serbatoio della —,** petrol tank; **bidone per —,** petrol can.
benzoato, *n.m.* (*Chem.*) Benzoate.
benzoino, *n.m.* (*Chem.*) Gum benzoin, gum benjamin.
benzolo, *n.m.* (*Chem.*) Benzol.
beone, *n.m.* Drunkard, tippler, heavy drinker.
beota, *n.m.* Boeotian; (*fig.*) a stupid fellow.
bequadro, *n.m.* (*Mus.*) Flat, natural.

berbero [bErbero], *n.m.* (*Bot.*) Barberry.
berciare, *v.i.* To scream, to yell.
bercio [bErcio], *n.m.* Scream, yell, howl.
bere, *v.t.* To drink. **— un uovo,** to suck an egg; **— a centellini,** to sip; (*fig.*) **dare a —,** to make one believe; **questa non la bevo!** tell that to the marines!
bere, *n.m.* Drink, drinking.
bergamotta, *n.f.* Fruit of the bergamot orange.
bergamotto, *n.m.* (*Bot.*) Bergamot-orange tree; bergamot pear.
berillio [berIllio], *n.m.* (*Metal.*) Beryllium.
berillo, *n.m.* (*Min.*) Beryl.
beriolo, *n.m.* Water trough in a birdcage.
berlicche, *n.m.* (*colloq.*) The Devil. **Far — e berlocche,** to fall short of one's word.
berlina, *n.f.* Pillory; kind of parlour game; heavy travelling carriage; (*Motor.*) sedan.
berlingaccio [berlingAccio], *n.m.* Last Thursday of Carnival.
berlingozzo, *n.m.* Puff pastry; a rich cake.
Berlino, *n.m.* Berlin.
Bermude, *n.f.pl.* Bermuda, Bermudas.
Berna, *n.f.* Berne.
berneggiare, *v.i.* To write in a burlesque style (as the poet Berni).
bernesco, *a.* Burlesque, facetious (like Berni).
bernoccolo [bernOccolo], *n.m.* Bump, lump (on the head, etc., from a blow, etc.) (*fig.*) **Aver il — di qualcosa,** to have an aptitude for something.
bernoccoluto, *a.* Full of bumps.
berretta, *n.f.* Cap, biretta.
berrettaio [berrettAio], *n.m.* Cap-maker or seller.
berrettino, *n.m.* Child's cap.
berretto, *n.m.* Man's cap (with or without peak). **Levarsi il —,** to raise one's cap; **— basco,** beret.
bersagliare, *v.t.* To shoot at; (*fig.*) to harass.
bersagliere, *n.m.* Soldier of the crack corps in the Italian army.
bersaglio [bersAglio], *n.m.* Target, mark; (*fig.*) laughing-stock. **Tiro al —,** shooting range; target practice.
berta, *n.f.* Ram (for earth, etc.), rammer. **Dare la —,** to ridicule.
berteggiamento, *n.m.* Bantering, chaff; joke, jest.
berteggiare, *v.t.* To banter, to chaff; to deride.
bertesca, *n.f.* Scaffold platform for builders.
bertoldo, *n.m.* Blockhead, dolt.
bertuccia [bertUccia], *n.f.* (*Zool.*) Ape. (*fig.*) **Pigliar la —,** to get drunk.
bertucciata, *n.f.* Monkey trick.
bertuello, *n.m.* Bird-net; eel-net.
bestemmia [bestEmmia], *n.f.* Blasphemy, imprecation, oath, curse; (*fig.*) false judgment, false criticism.
bestemmiare, *v.i.* To blaspheme, to swear, to curse; (*fig.*) to criticize badly. **— come un turco,** to swear like a trooper; **— il francese,** to mangle French.
bestemmiatore, bestemmiatrice, *n.m.f.a.* Blasphemer.
bestia [bEstia], *n.f.* Beast, animal; (*fig.*) ignorant person, ignoramus; irreligious man. **Andare in —,** to fly into a rage.
bestiaccia [bestiAccia], *n.f.* Nasty beast; (*fig.*) brute (of a fellow).
bestiaio [bestiAio], *n.m.* Herdsman.
bestiale, *a.* Beastly, beast-like, brutal. **Uomo —,** brutal man.
bestialità [-à], *n.f.* Bestiality; (*fig.*) nonsense, foolishness.
bestialmente, *adv.* Brutally, in a bestial manner.
bestiame, *n.m.* Cattle, herd of cattle, etc. **Allevare —** to raise cattle.
bestiario [bestiArio], *n.m.* (*Lit.*) Bestiary; (*Hist.*) gladiator who fought with beasts.
bestiola, *n.f.* Small animal; (*fig.*) fool.
bestione, *n.m.* Dirty, nasty animal; (*fig.*) dirty brute; ignoramus.
betatrone, *n.m.* (*Phys.*) Betatron.
Betlemme, *n.f.* Bethlehem.
betoniera, *n.f.* Cement-mixer.
bettola [bEttola], *n.f.* Tavern, public-house.
bettolante, *n.m.* Frequenter of taverns, pub-crawler.
bettoliere, *n.m.* Tavern-keeper, landlord.
bettonica [bettOnica], *n.f.* (*Bot.*) Betony. **Conosciuto come la —,** known by everybody.
betulla [betUlla], *n.f.* (*Bot.*) Birch-tree.
beva, *n.f.* Time when wine is fit to drink. **A buona —, (wine)** worth drinking.
bevanda, *n.f.* Drink, beverage, potion.
beveraggio [beverAggio], *n.m.* Drink (esp. for cattle, etc.); drink-money, tip (for drivers, etc.).
beveratoio [beveratOio], *n.m.* Horse-trough.
bevere [bEvere] [cp. **bere**].
bevereccio [beverEccio], *a.* Drinkable [cp. **bevibile**].
beverello, beverino, *n.m.* Drinking trough in a birdcage.
beverone, *n.m.* Oatmeal and water (for horses, etc.); drench.
bevibile [bevIbile], *a.* Drinkable.
bevicchiare, *v.i.* To drink slowly and steadily, to tipple.
bevitore, bevitrice, *n.m.f.* Drinker, hard drinker.
bevone, *n.m.* Drunkard, hard drinker [cp. **beone**].
bevucchiare, *v.i.* To sip.
bevuta, *n.f.* Drinking; drink (of any liquid); drinking bout.
bezzicare, *v.t.* To peck at; (*fig.*) to pick on (with words).
bezzicarsi, *v.r.* To quarrel, to nag (at one another).
bezzicata, *n.f.* Peck (with the beak).
bezzicatura, *n.f.* (*obs.*) Peck (from a beak).
bezzo, *n.m.* Old Venetian coin worth less than a farthing. (*fig.*) **Aver dei bezzi,** to be rich, to be well off.
biacca, *n.f.* (*Metal*) White lead.
biacco, *n.m.* (*Zool.*) Grass-snake.
biada, *n.f.* Fodder. **Le biade,** *f. pl.*, crops.
biadaiolo [biadaiOlo], *n.m.* (*obs.*) Fodder merchant, corn-dealer.
biadare, *v.t.* To give fodder, to fodder, to feed.
Biagio [biAgio], *n.m.* Blaise.
Bianca, *n.f.* Blanche.
bianca, *n.f.* First sleep of silkworms.
biancana, *n.f.* Moorland; waste.
biancastro, *a.* Whitish, off white.
biancheggiamento, *n.m.* Whitening, turning white.

biancheggiare, *v.i.* To grow white; to turn white (of hair); to be snow-covered (of mountains).
biancheria [biancherIa], *n.f.* Linen or cotton clothing or material; anything for the person or household use made of cotton or linen (*e.g.* underclothing, sheets, etc.).
bianchetti, *n.m.pl.* Small fish like whitebait.
bianchetto, *n.m.* White lead; whitewash.
bianchezza, *n.f.* Whiteness.
bianchiccio [bianchIccio], *a.* Whitish.
bianchimento, *n.m.* Bleaching (esp. of salt, sugar, etc.).
bianchire, *v.t.* To bleach (salt, sugar, etc.), to blanch; to remove tarnish.
bianco, *n.m.a.* White; blank. **Il — dell'occhio,** the white of the eye; **il — dell'uovo,** white of egg; (*Comm.*) **cambiale in —,** blank bill; **assegno in —,** blank cheque.
biancone, *n.m.a.* Very pale-complexioned person; a variety of grape.
biancore, *n.m.* (*Poet.*) Whiteness.
biancospino, *n.m.* (*Bot.*) Hawthorn.
biancume, *n.m.* Quantity of white things, mass of white.
biascia [biAscia], *n.f.* Slobber, slaver (on the lips).
biasciamento, *n.m.* Mumbling.
biasciare, biascicare, *v.t.i.* To chew with the gums, to mumble, to munch.
biascicatura, *n.f.* Mumbling.
biascicotto, biasciotto, *n.m.* Piece of bread, paper, etc., chewed and spat out.
biasimabile [biasimAbile], *a.* Blameable, culpable [cp. **biasimevole**].
biasimare, *v.t.* To blame, to censure, to reprove.
biasimevole [biasimEvole], *a.* Censurable, culpable, blameworthy.
biasimevolmente, *adv.* Culpably.
biasimo [biAsimo], *n.m.* Blame; reproach; censure.
Bibbia [bIbbia], *n.f.* Bible.
bibita [bIbita], *n.f.* Drink, refreshments (liquid); draught (of medicine).
biblico [bIblico], *a.* Biblical.
bibliofilia [bibliofilIa], *n.f.* Bibliophily.
bibliofilo [bibliOfilo], *n.m.* Bibliophile.
bibliografia [bibliografIa], *n.f.* Bibliography.
bibliografo [bibliOgrafo], *n.m.* Bibliographer.
bibliomane [bibliOmane], *n.m.* Bibliomaniac.
biblioteca, *n.f.* Library (in all senses).
bibliotecario [bibliotecArio], *n.m.* Librarian.
bibulo [bIbulo], *a.* (*obs.*) Absorbent. **Carta bibula,** blotting-paper [cp. **carta assorbente**].
bica, *n.f.* Sheaf of corn; heap of cow-dung.
bicarbonato, *n.m.* Bicarbonate of soda.
bicchierata, *n.f.* Glassful, glass; toast (health); celebration party.
bicchiere, *n.m.* Glass, glass tankard; glassful. **— della staffa,** stirrup-cup; **— di vino,** glass of wine; **— da vino,** wine-glass
bicchierino, *n.m.* Small glass; tot.
bicchierotto, *n.m.* Largish glass.
bicicletta, *n.f.* Bicycle, **Andare in —,** to cycle; **— a due posti,** tandem.
biciclettare, *v.i.* To ride on a bicycle.
biciclettina, *n.f.* (Child's) fairy cycle.
biciclista, *n.m.f.* Cyclist.
biciclo, *n.m.* Penny-farthing bicycle.
bicipitale, *a.* Two-headed.
bicipite [bicIpite], *n.m.* (*Anat.*) Biceps.
bicipite [bicIpite], *a.* Two-headed, bicipital.
bicloruro, *n.m.* (*Chem.*) Bichloride.
bicocca, *n.f.* Small fortified tower or castle; hovel, hut.
bicolore, *a.* Two-coloured.
biconcavo [bicOncavo], *a.* Biconcave.
biconvesso, *a.* Biconvex.
bicorne, *a.* Two-horned; forked.
bicornia [bicOrnia], *n.f.* Anvil with two horns.
bicornuto, *a.* Two-horned.
bicromato, *n.m.* (*Chem.*) Bichromate.
bicuspide [bicUspide], *a.* Two-pointed, bicuspid.
bidè, *n.m.* Bidet.
bidello, *n.m.* Beadle, janitor.
bidente, *n.m.* Pitchfork; two-pronged fork.
bidone, *n.m.* Can, jug, drum. **— per benzina,** petrol-can.
biecamente, *adv.* Grimly; askance. **Guardare qualcuno —,** to look at someone askance.
bieco, *a.* Slanting; squinting; grim, sinister; angry (of a glance).
biella, *n.f.* (*Mech.*) Connecting rod; strut.
biennale, *a.* Biennial, two-yearly.
biennalmente, *adv.* Biennially.
bienne, *a.* Biennial.
biennio [biEnnio], *n.m.* Period of two years.
bietola [biEtola], *n.f.* (*Bot.*) Beet, beetroot.
bietolaggine [bietolAggine], *n.f.* (*obs.*) Foolishness, stupidity, silliness.
bietolone, *n.m.* Simpleton, booby.
bietta, *n.f.* Wedge, (*Mech.*) cotter.
bifase, *a.* (*Elec.*) Two-phase.
biffa, *n.f.* Surveyor's staff, measuring rod, levelling rod; builder's plumb.
biffare, *v.t.* To stake out, to peg out (a plot).
bifido [bIfido], *a.* Bifid.
bifolcheria [bifolcherIa], *n.f.* (*Agric.*) Ploughman's work.
bifolco, *n.m.* (*Agric.*) Ploughman; (*fig.*) rustic, boor.
biforcamento, *n.m.* Bifurcation; branching off.
biforcarsi, *v.r.* To be forked, to bifurcate, to fork off, to branch off.
biforcatura, *n.f.* Place where branching-off takes place.
biforcazione, *n.f.* Bifurcation, forking, branching off.
biforme, *a.* Biform.
bifronte, *a.* With two fronts; (*fig.*) double-faced.
biga, *n.f.* (*Hist.*) Chariot; (*colloq.*) carriage. (*Naut.*) **Bighe,** shears.
bigamia [bigamIa], *n.f.* Bigamy.
bigamo, bigama [bIgamo, bIgama], *n.m.f.a.* Bigamist; bigamous.
bigattiera, *n.f.* Silkworm nursery.
bigattiere, *n.m.* Silkworm breeder.
bigatto, *n.m.* Silkworm.
bighellonaggine [bighellonAggine], *n.f.* (*obs.*) Lounging.
bighellonare, *v.i.* To lounge, to walk listlessly.
bighellone, *n.m.* Lounger, idler.
bigherino, *n.m.* Lace (esp. for trimming).
bigio [bIgio], *a.* Grey. **Pane —,** brown bread.
bigiognolo [bigiOgnolo], *a.* Greyish.
bigiotteria [bigiotterIa], *n.f.* Trinket.

biglia, *n.f.* Billiard ball; billiard pocket [cp. **bilia**].
bigliardo [cp. **biliardo**].
bigliettaio, bigliettario [bigliettAio, bigliettArio], *n.m.* Booking-clerk, (*Theat.*) box-office attendant; tram conductor; ticket collector.
biglietteria [bigliettèrIa], *n.f.* Booking-office; (*Theat.*) box-office.
biglietto, *n.m.* Ticket; note (epistolary); bank-note. **— di visita,** visiting-card; **— galante,** love letter; (*Rail.*) **— d'andata e ritorno,** return ticket; **— di corsa semplice,** single ticket; (*Comm.*) **— all'ordine,** promissory note; **— di banca,** bank-note.
bigoncia [bigOncia], *n.f.* Tub, vat; reading desk, pulpit, rostrum. **Piove a —,** it's raining cats and dogs.
bigoncio [bigOncio], *n.m.* Large tun with handles for slinging on a pole.
bigonciolo [bigonciOlo], *n.m.* Pail, bucket.
bigotta, *n.f.* Female bigot; (*Naut.*) dead-eye.
bigotteria [bigotterIa], *n.f.* Bigotry.
bigottismo, *n.m.* Bigotry.
bigotto, *n.m.* Bigot.
bigutta, *n.f.* Iron pot or stew-pan; the soup or stew cooked therein.
bilancere [bilancEre] [cp. **bilanciere**].
bilancia [bilAncia], *n.f.* Balances, scales; whipple-tree (of a carriage). **— del commercio,** balance of trade; **dare il tracollo alla —,** to weigh down the scales.
bilanciaio [bilanciAio], *n.m.* Maker or seller of scales.
bilanciamento, *n.m.* Balancing; (*fig.*) weighing up (in one's mind).
bilanciare, *v.t.* To weigh, to balance; to weigh one thing against another.
bilanciarsi, *v.r.* To balance, to be in equilibrium; to be equal.
bilanciatamente, *adv.* In equilibrium.
bilanciere, *n.m.* Balance, beam; pendulum, balance-wheel (of watch).
bilancino, *n.m.* Trace-horse; extra help (on a job).
bilancio [bilAncio], *n.m.* (*Comm.*) Balance, balance-sheet. **— statale,** budget; **mettere in —,** to estimate; **— preventivo,** budget estimate; **— di verificazione,** trial balance; **— fallimentare,** statement of affairs.
bilaterale, *a.* Bilateral.
bile, *n.f.* Bile, gall; (*fig.*) ill-temper.
bilia [bIlia], *n.f.* Pocket of a billiard-table.
biliardo, *n.m.* Billiards; billiard-table; billiard-room. **Stecca da —,** cue.
biliare, *a.* Bilious; (*Med.*) biliary
bilicare, *v.t.* To keep in balance.
bilico [bIlico], *n.m.* Equilibrium; (*fig.*) **stare in —,** to be in equilibrium; to counterpoise; to be wavering, to reel.
bilingue [bilIngue], *a.* Bilingual.
bilione, *n.m.* Billion (in Italy this is a thousand million and not a million million).
bilioso, *a.* Bilious; irrascible.
bilustre [bilUstre], *a.* Ten years old.
bimbo, bimba, *n.m.f.* Baby, infant.
bimensile, *a.* Bimonthly, twice in a month.
bimestrale, *a.* Every two months.
bimestre, *n.m.* Period of two months.
bimetallismo, *n.m.* Bimetallism.
bimmolle, bimolle, *n.m.* (*Mus.*) Flat [cp. **bemolle**].
bimotore, *n.m.* (*Aviat.*) Twin-engined aeroplane.
binario [binArio], *n.m.* Railway-track, railway line. **— morto,** dead-end, siding; (*fig.*) **stare in —,** to toe the line.
binario [binArio], *a.* (*Chem. Math.*) Binary.
binascenza, *n.f.* Birth of twins.
binato, *n.m.a.* Twin; coupled.
binda, *n.f.* (*Mech.*) Jack (for lifting).
bindolare [cp. **abbindolare**].
bindoleria [bindolerIa], *n.f.* (*obs.*) Habit of swindling.
bindolo [bIndolo], *n.m.* Chain-pump, wheel with buckets attached for raising water; (*fig.*) swindler, bilker.
bindolone, *n.m.* Cheat.
binoccolo, binocolo [binOccolo, binOcolo], *n.m.* Binoculars, field-glasses.
binomio [binOmio], *a.* (*Math.*) Binomial.
bioccolo [biOccolo], *n.m.* Lock of wool; candle-drip; flock, tuft; (*fig.*) snowflake.
bioccoluto, *a.* In locks (of wool).
biodo, *n.m.* (*Bot.*) Rush, bulrush.
biografia [biografIa], *n.f.* Biography.
biografico [biogrAfico], *a.* Biographical.
biografo [biOgrafo], *n.m.* Biographer.
biologia [biologIa], *n.f.* Biology.
biologico [biolOgico], *a.* Biological.
biologo [biOlogo], *n.m.* Biologist.
bionda, *n.f.* Blonde (woman) [cp. **biondo**].
biondeggiante, *a.* Ripening, growing yellowish.
biondeggiare, *v.i.* To be fair (of complexion); to turn yellow (of corn, etc.).
biondezza, *n.f.* Fairness, blondness.
biondiccio [biondIccio], *a.* Fairish, rather blond.
biondino, *n.m.* Fair person (of complexion).
biondo, *n.m.a.* Fair of complexion, blond, fair-haired; fair man, fair youngster.
bioscia [biOscia], *n.f.* Melting snow; (*fig.*) tasteless soup, dishwater.
biossido [biOssido], *n.m.* (*Chem.*) Dioxide.
bipartire, *v.t.* To halve, to cut in two.
bipartizione, *n.f.* Division in two.
bipede [bIpede], *n.m. a.* Biped.
bipenne, *n.f.* Two-edged axe.
biplano, *n.m.* (*Aviat.*) Biplane.
bipolare, *a.* (*Elect.*) Bi-polar.
biposto, *n.m.* (*Motor.*) Two-seater.
biqquadro, biquadro, *a.* (*Mus.*) Natural [cp. **bequadro**].
birba, *n.f.* Young rascal, scapegrace; thoroughly bad young fellow.
birbaccione, *n.m.* Scoundrel.
birbante, *n.m.* Rogue, rascal.
birbanteria [birbanterIa], *n.f.* Rascality, roguery.
birbantescamente *adv.* Knavishly.
birbantesco, *a.* Knavish.
birbonata, *n.f.* Piece of roguery; thing ill-performed.
birbone, *n.m.* Rogue, rascal, knave, scamp.
birbone, *a.* Great, excessive. **Un caldo —,** a frightful heat.
birboneggiare, *v.i.* To act as a knave.

birboneria [birbonerIa], *n.f.* Bad action, unworthy deed.
birbonesco, *a.* Roguish, knavish.
bircio [bIrcio], *a.* Short-sighted.
bireme, *n.f.* (*Hist.*) Galley with two banks of oars, bireme.
biribissi, *n.m.* Game of chance played with counters.
biricchinata, birichinata, *n.f.* Boyish trick, roguish trick; prank.
biricchino, birichino, *n.m.* Little rascal, street urchin, mischievous boy, cheeky youngster; rogue (of adults).
birillo, *n.m.* Skittle. **Giuoco dei birilli,** skittles.
Birmania [birmAnia], *n.f.* Burma.
birmano, *n.m.a.* Burman, Burmese.
biroccino, *n.m.* Horse cab, cabriolet.
biroccio [cp. **baroccio**].
birra, *n.f.* Beer, ale.
birraglia [birrAglia], *n.f.* (*obs.*) Posse of police; gang of spies.
birraio [birrAio], *n.m.* Brewer.
birreria [birrerIa], *n.f.* Beer-shop, public-house, pub, ale-house.
birro, *n.m.* Police-agent, "nark" [cp. **sbirro**].
bis, *adv.* Twice, encore (at theatres, concerts, etc.). **Chiedere un —,** to call for an encore.
bisaccia [bisAccia], *n.f.* Bag; knapsack; wallet.
Bisanzio [bisAnzio], *n.m.* (*Hist.*) Byzantium.
bisarcavolo, bisarcavola [bisarcAvolo], *n.m.f.* Great-great-grandfather(mother).
bisavo, bisavolo, bisava, bisavola [bisAvolo], *n.m.f.* (*obs.*) Great-grandfather (mother).
bisbetico [bisbEtico], *a.* Crabbed, difficult to please, cross-grained. **Nome —,** name difficult to pronounce.
bisbigliamento, *n.m.* Whispering, whisper.
bisbigliare, *v.i.t.* To whisper.
bisbiglio [bisbIglio] (1), *n.m.* Whisper.
bisbiglio [bisbiglIo] (2), *n.m.* Continual whispering.
bisboccia [bisbOccia], *n.f.* Revelry, feasting; spree.
bisbocciare, *v.i.* To go on the spree.
bisboccione, *n.m.* Reveller, gay dog.
bisca, *n.f.* Gaming den, gambling house.
Biscaglia [biscAglia], *n.f.* Biscay. **Golfo di —,** Bay of Biscay.
biscaiuolo [biscaiuOlo], *n.m.* Gambler, frequenter of gambling dens.
biscazzare, *v.i.* (*obs.*) To frequent gambling dens.
biscazziere, *n.m.* Gambling-den keeper; billiard marker.
bischero [bIschero], *n.m.* (*Mus.*) Peg (for violin string); (*vulg.*) dolt, fool.
bischetto, *n.m.* Shoemaker's bench.
biscia [bIscia], *n.f.* (*Zool.*) Grass snake, slow worm.
bisciola [bIsciola], *n.f.* Fruit of the wild cherry.
bisciolo [bIsciolo], *a.* Lisping.
biscottare, *v.t.* To bake twice over, to bake again; to toast.
biscotteria [biscotterIa], *n.f.* Biscuit shop; biscuit factory; the biscuits.
biscottino, *n.m.* Little biscuit, sweet biscuit; (*fig.*) snap of the fingers.
biscotto, *n.m.* Biscuit.
biscroma, *n.f.* (*Mus.*) Demi-semiquaver.
biscugino, *n.m.* Second cousin.
bisdosso, *adv.* **A —,** (to ride) bareback.
bisdrucciolo [bisdrUcciolo], *n.m.* (*Gram.*) Word in which the accent is on the fourth syllable from the end.
bisecante, *a.* (*Math.*) Bisecting.
bisessuale, *a.* Bi-sexual.
bisestile, *a.* **Anno —,** leap-year.
bisesto, *n.m.* Leap-year [cp. **bisestile**].
bisettimanale, *a.* Bi-weekly.
bisezione, *n.f.* Bisection.
bisillabo [bisIllabo], *n.m.* (*Gram.*) Dissyllable.
bislaccheria [bislaccherIa], *n.f.* Oddness, extravagance (of quality, not money); clownishness [cp. **bizzarria**].
bislacco, *n.m.a.* Odd fellow, clown; extravagant, odd. **Mente bislacca,** capricious mentality.
bislungo, *a.* Oblong.
bismalva, *n.f.* (*Bot.*) Marsh-mallow.
bismuto, *n.m.* (*Metal. Med.*) Bismuth.
bisnipote [bisnipOte], *n.m.f.* Great-nephew or -niece; great-grandchild.
bisnonno, bisnonna, *n.m.f.* Great-grandfather, great-grandmother.
bisogna, *n.f.* (*Lit.*) Affair, business.
bisognare, *v.i.* To need, to want, to occur, to be necessary. **Bisogna lavorare,** one must work; **mi bisogna denaro,** I need money; **cose che bisogna sapere,** things one must know; **bisognava avvertirmi,** I should have been told; **bisogna bene!** of course, there's no help for it! **bisogna partire,** we must leave.
bisognatario [bisognatArio], *n.m.* (*Comm.*) Referee.
bisognevole [bisognEvole], *n.m.* Needful. **Il — per vivere,** the necessaries of life; **fare il —,** to do what is needed.
bisognevole [bisognEvole], *a.* Needful, necessary; poor, in want.
bisogno, *n.m.* Need, want; living expenses; necessaries, opportunity; distress, poverty. **Non abbiamo — di voi,** we don't need you; **avere tutto il suo —,** to have all he wants; **non c'è — che egli venga,** there's no need for him to come; **in caso di —,** in case of need.
bisognoso, *n.m.a.* Pauper, destitute person; needy, necessitous.
bisolfato, *n.m.* (*Chem.*) Bisulphate.
bisolfito, *n.m.* (*Chem.*) Bisulphite.
bisonte, *n.m.* (*Zool.*) Bison.
bissare, *v.t.* To encore; to call for an encore.
bisso, *n.m.* Byssus.
bistecca, *n.f.* Beef-steak.
bisticciamento, *n.m.* Wrangling, quarrelling.
bisticciare, bisticciarsi, *v.i.r.* To wrangle, to quarrel, to bicker; to argue.
bisticcio [bistIccio], *n.m.* Quarrel, jar; play on words sounding alike.
bistondo, *a.* (*obs.*) Oval; roundish.
bistorto, *a.* Crooked; very twisted.
bistrattare, *v.t.* To ill-treat, to treat badly; to snub.
bistro, *n.m.* Bistre (pigment).
bisturi [bIsturi], *n.m.* (*Med.*) Bistoury.

bisulco, *a.* Cloven-hoofed.
bisunto, *a.* Very greasy. **Unto e —,** filthy.
bitorzolo [bitOrzolo], *n.m.* Pimple, wart.
bitorzoluto, *a.* Pimply, covered with warts.
bitte, *n.f.pl.* (*Naut.*) Bitts.
bittone, *n.m.* (*Naut.*) Bollard.
bitume, *n.m.* Bitumen.
bituminare, *v.t.* To bituminize.
bituminoso, *a.* Bituminous.
bivaccare, *v.i.* To bivouac.
bivacco, *n.m.* Bivouac.
bivalve, *n.m.a.* (*Zool.*) Bivalve.
bivio [bIvio], *n.m.* Parting (of two roads, etc.), cross-roads; (*fig.*) uncertainty (of choice or decision).
bizantino, *n.m.a.* Byzantine.
bizza, *n.f.* (Passing) anger, (momentary) anger; caprice. **Fare le bizze,** to be in a bad temper.
bizzarramente, *adv.* Oddly, whimsically.
bizzarria [bizzarrIa], *n.f.* Oddness, whimsicality; freak.
bizzarro, *a.* Odd, original; fantastic; eccentric; spirited (of a horse).
bizzeffe, *adv.* **A —,** in abundance, abundantly.
bizzocco, *n.m.* Bigot.
bizzosamente, *adv.* Passionately (in anger).
bizzoso, *a.* Irritable ; wayward (of child).
blandamente, *adv.* Blandly, affably.
blandimento, *n.m.* Blandishment.
blandire, *v.t.* To fondle; to soothe; to flatter.
blandizie [blandIzie], *n.f.pl.* Flattery; caresses.
blando, *a.* Bland, soft, mild; feeble; gentle in action.
blasfema, *n.f.* (*Lit.*) Blasphemy.
blasfemo, *n.m.* Blasphemer.
blasonare, *v.t.* To blazon (heraldic arms).
blasonato, *a.* Gentle (with coat of arms); noble.
blasone, *n.m.* Coat of arms; scutcheon.
blateramento, *n.m.* Chattering.
blaterare, *v.i.* To chatter, to gossip.
blaterone, *n.m.* Chatterer, prater.
blatta, *n.f.* (*Zool.*) Cockroach.
blenda, *n.f.* (*Metal.*) Blende.
blenorragia [blenorragIa], *n.m.* (*Med.*) Blennorrhoea.
bleso, *n.m.a.* One who lisps; lisping.
blindaggio [blindAggio], *n.m.* (*Mil.*) Armour (for cars, etc.).
blindare, *v.t.* (*Mil.*) To armour (with metal plates, etc.).
blindato, *p.p.a.* (*Mil.*) Armoured. **Carro —,** armoured car.
blindatura, *n.f.* (*Mil.*) Armour, armouring.
bloccare, *v.t.* To blockade; to block up (**una strada,** a road); (*Comm.*) to freeze (prices, etc.).
blocco, *n.m.* Blockade; block (of wood, etc.); (*Rail.*) block. **In —,** in mass, in block, in bulk; (*Billiards*) **fare un —,** to hole a ball; (*Rail.*) **— automatico,** automatic blocking system.
blu, *a.* Blue.
bluastro, *a.* Bluish.
blusa, *n.f.* Blouse.
boa, *n.m.* (*Zool.*) Boa; *n.f.* (*Naut.*) buoy; boa (for the neck).
boario [boArio], *a.* Pertaining to cattle.
boaro, *n.m.* Cowherd.
boato, *n.m.* Roar, thunder, rumbling.
bobina, *n.f.* Spool, coil, bobbin; (*Cinema.*) reel; (*Phot.*) spool.
bocca, *n.f.* Mouth; opening, orifice; victuals; muzzle. **— da fuoco,** gun, cannon; **in casa siamo tre bocche,** our household consists of three; **munizioni di —,** rations; **turare la — ad uno,** to silence someone; **— dello stomaco,** pit of the stomach; **tener uno a — dolce,** to lead someone up the garden path; **lavarsi la — d'uno,** to speak of someone in bad terms; **acqua in —!** Hush! **— scelta,** dainty; **— d'incendio,** fire-plug; **— d'oro,** eloquent; **a mezza —,** by hints, in a vaguely allusive way.
boccaccia [boccAccia], *n.f.* Ugly mouth; (*fig.*) **essere una —,** to be calumnious, to be spiteful; **far le boccacce,** to make faces.
boccale, *n.m.* Mug, jug, pot, jar.
boccaporto, *n.m.* (*Naut.*) Hatchway.
boccata, *n.f.* Mouthful.
boccetta, *n.f.* Phial, medicine bottle.
boccheggiamento, *n.m.* Gasping (for breath).
boccheggiare, *v.i.* To gasp.
bocchetta, *n.f.* Small orifice; plate (of lock); (*Mus.*) mouthpiece of a wind instrument; tongue (of a boot).
bocchino, *n.m.* Mouthpiece; cigar or cigarette holder. **Fare il —,** to screw up one's mouth.
boccia [bOccia], *n.f.* Decanter; bud (of a flower); wood (in game of bowls). **Giocare alle boccie,** to play at bowls; (*colloq.*) **gli gira la —,** his head turns.
bocciare, *v.t.* (*Bowls*) To knock away the opponent's wood; (*fig.*) to fail at an exam.
boccino, *n.m.* (*Bowls*) Jack.
boccio [cp. **boccia**].
bocciolo, *n.m.* Bud; internode (on a cane); socket (on a candlestick).
boccione, *n.m.* Large decanter.
bocco, *n.m.* Nut thrown in certain boys' games; (*fig.*) good-for-nothing fellow.
boccola [bOccola], *n.f.* Nave ring (of a wheel), socket; buckle.
bocconata, *n.f.* Mouthful.
bocconcello, bocconcino, *n.m.* Tit-bit, morsel. **Un —,** just a little.
boccone, *n.m.* Mouthful. **Tutto in un —,** in one mouthful; **— amaro,** a bitter pill; **in due o tre bocconi,** in one or two bits.
bocconi, *adv.* Face downwards, flat on the face. **Cadere —,** to fall flat on one's face.
boccuccia [boccUccia], *n.f.* Dainty person. **Far —,** to turn up one's nose (at something).
bociare, *v.i.* To bawl, to shout [cp. **vociare**].
bocio [bocIo], *n.m.* Continual bawling [cp. **vocio**].
bocione, *n.m.* Bawler; brawler.
bodino, *n.m.* Pudding [cp. **budino**].
bodola [bOdola], *n.f.* Trap-door [cp. **botola**].
bodoniano, *a.* After the manner of the printer Bodoni. **Legato alla bodoniana,** bound in boards.
Boemia [boEmia], *n.f.* Bohemia.
boemme, *n.m.a.* (*obs.*) Bohemian, unconventional.
boemo, *n.m.a.* Bohemian.
boffice [bOffice], *a.* Soft, puffy, spongy; (*fig.*) plump (of a person).
bofonchiare, *v.i.* To grumble ; to snort.

bofonchio [bofOnchio], *n.m.* (*Zool.*) Bumble-bee.
bogia [bOgia], *n.f.* Spot (on the skin).
boia [bOia], *n.m.* Executioner, hangman; (*fig.*) villain, cruel fellow.
boicottaggio [boicottAggio], *n.m.* Boycott, boycotting.
boicottare, *v.t.* To boycott.
boldrone, *n.m.* Fleece (of a sheep).
bolero, *n.m.* Bolero (dance and music).
boleto, *n.m.* (*Bot.*) Boletus.
bolgetta, *n.f.* Attaché-case, portfolio.
bolgia [bOlgia], *n.f.* (*obs.*) Large pocket; bag; valise; hell (Dante).
bolide [bOlide], *n.m.* (*Astron.*) Shooting-star, asteroid.
bolina, *n.f.* (*Naut.*) Bowline.
bolla, *n.f.* Bubble; (*Med.*) boil, pimple, pustule; (*Eccles.*) bull. **— di sapone,** soap-bubble.
bollandista (*pl.* **bollandisti**), *n.m.* Bollandist (Jesuit hagiographer).
bollare, *v.t.* To seal, to stamp, to brand.
bollario [bollArio], *n.m.* (*Eccles.*) Collection of papal bulls.
bollato, *p.p.a.* Sealed, stamped. **Carta bollata,** stamped paper.
bollatore, *n.m.* Stamper; sealer.
bollatura, *n.f.* Stamping, sealing; branding.
bollente, *pres.p.a.* Boiling, hot; (*fig.*) ardent, impetuous, passionate.
bolletta, *n.f.* Bill; receipt. (*Comm.*) **— d'accompagnamento,** way bill; **— d'imbarco,** shipping bill; (*facet.*) **essere in —,** to be penniless.
bollettario [bollettArio], *n.m.* Receipt-book, book with counterfoils.
bollettino, *n.m.* Bulletin. (*Comm.*) **— commerciale,** trade report; **— dei cambi,** exchange list; **— di spedizione,** consignment note.
bollimento, *n.m.* Boiling [cp. **bollore**].
bollire, *v.t.i.* To boil, to bubble; to cause to boil; to ferment; (*fig.*) to be angry.
bollita, *n.f.* Boil, boiling. **Dare una —,** to give a boiling.
bollitore, *n.m.* Kettle.
bollitura, *n.f.* Act of boiling; time taken in boiling; water in which a thing has been boiled.
bollo, *n.m.* Stamp; seal; postage stamp; post-mark. **Marca da —,** receipt stamp; **esente da —,** exempt from stamp-duty; **data del — postale,** date of post-mark.
bollone, *n.m.* Bolt; large nail [cp. **bullone**].
bollore, *n.m.* Gurgling of water beginning to boil; ebullition; (*fig.*) excessive heat (of summer); excitement; agitation, tumult.
bolloso, *a.* Pimply.
bolo, *n.m.* Sort of clay; (*Med.*) bolus.
bolsaggine [bolsAggine], *n.f.* Broken-windedness (of horses).
bolscevico [bolscevIco], *n.m.a.* Bolshevik, Bolshevist.
bolscevismo, *n.m.* Bolshevism.
bolscevizzare, *v.t.* To Bolshevize.
bolso, *a.* Broken-winded (of a horse).
bomba, *n.f.* Bomb; prisoner's base, touch-wood (games); (*fig.*) tall story, lie. **Gettar bombe,** to drop bombs, to bomb; **— atomica,** atomic bomb; (*fig.*) **a prova di —,** bomb-proof, proof against anything (*colloq.*) **tornare a —,** to get back to the subject.
bombarda, *n.f.* (*Hist. Mil.*) Bombard.
bombardamento, *n.m.* Bombardment, shelling, bombing. (*Aviat.*) **Apparecchio da —,** bomber.
bombardare, *v.t.* To bombard, to shell, to bomb (from the air).
bombardiera, *n.f.* (*Mil.*) Embrasure for throwing bombs; (*Naut.*) vessel armed with guns.
bombardiere, *n.m.* Bombardier; (*Aviat.*) bomber.
bombardone, *n.m.* (*Mus.*) Bombardon.
bombetta, *n.f.* (*colloq.*) Bowler (hat).
bombice [bOmbice], *n.m.* (*Zool.*) Bombyx, silkworm grub.
bombola [bOmbola], *n.f.* jug, bottle, **— per gas,** gas bottle; **—d'ossigeno,** oxygen cylinder.
bombone, *n.m.* Liar, teller of tall stories.
bomboniera, *n.f.* Chocolate box, sweetmeat-box.
bompresso, *n.m.* (*Naut.*) Bowsprit.
bonaccia [bonAccia], *n.f.* Calm (of sea), flat calm, dead calm, still weather; (*fig.*) tranquillity, prosperity.
bonaccione, *n.m.* Good-natured man.
bonalana, *n.f.* Scoundrel.
bonamano, *n.f.* Tip (to waiter, etc.).
bonamorte, *n.f.* Prayers for the dying.
bonariamente, *adv.* Simply, plainly, frankly, friendlily.
bonarietà [-à], *n.f.* Candour, simplicity (of mind); affability.
bonario [bonArio], *a.* Good-natured, gentle, kindly.
bongustaio [bongustAio], *n.m.* Connoisseur; gourmet, epicure.
bonifica [bonIfica], *n.f.* Reclamation (of land); drainage or irrigation (of land); (*fig.*) cleaning; improvement.
bonificare, *v.t.* To reclaim (land); (*Comm.*) to allow a discount; to refund.
bonificazione, *n.f.* Reclamation (of land); (*Comm.*) abatement, discount. **— concessa per i pagamenti in contanti,** cash discount.
bono, *n.m.a.* Cheque; bill; good [cp. **buono**].
bonomia [bonomIa], *n.f.* Good-nature.
bonomo, *n.m.* Easy-going man.
bontà [-à], *n.f.* Goodness, kindness, generosity, benignity. **— del clima,** mildness of climate; **avere la — di,** to be so good as to; **quanta —!** How kind you are!
bontempone, *n.m.* Jolly fellow; man about town.
bonzo, *n.m.* Bonze.
bora, *n.f.* North-east wind.
borace, *n.m.* (*Chem.*) Borax.
boracico [borAcico], *a.* (*Chem.*) Boracic.
borbogliare, *v.i.* To murmur, to gurgle.
borbonico [borbOnico], *a.* (*Hist.*) Concerning the Bourbons.
borbottamento, *n.m.* Muttering, mumbling.
borbottare, *v.t.i.* To mutter, to mumble; to grumble; to speak a language badly. **— l'italiano,** to speak broken Italian.
borbottio [borbottIo], *n.m.* Continual mumbling or muttering; grumbling.
borbottone, *n.m.* Mutterer, mumbler, grumbler.

borchia [bOrchia], *n.f.* Metal boss (on harness, furniture, armour, etc.).
bordaglia [bordAglia], *n.f.* Mob, rabble.
bordare, *v.t.i.* To knock hard, to cudgel; to work hard; (*Naut.*) to plank.
bordata, *n.f.* (*Naut.*) Tack; broadside.
bordatino, bordato, *n.m.* Ticking (cloth).
bordatura, *n.f.* Hemming (of cloth).
bordeggiare, *v.i.* (*Naut.*) To tack, to beat against the wind.
bordeggio [bordEggio], *n.m.* (*Naut.*) Tacking.
bordello, *n.m.* Uproar; brothel.
borderò [-ò], *n.m.* Memorandum, specification.
bordino, *n.m.* Flange (of railway wheel, etc.).
Bordò, *n.m.* (*Geog.*) Bordeaux.
bordo, *n.m.* (*Naut.*) Side (of a ship, above the water); border, margin. **Andare a —,** to go on board; **gente di —,** the crew; **persona d'alto —,** high-ranking person, V.I.P.; (*Comm.*) **carte di —,** ship's papers; **giornale di —,** log-book; **franco a —,** free on board.
bordone, *n.m.* Pilgrim's staff; sprouting feather (of a young bird). (*fig.*) **Venir i bordoni, rizzare i bordoni,** to have one's hair stand on end; **tener — a qualcuno,** to lend someone a hand (usu. to do something bad).
borea [bOrea], *n.m.* (*Poet.*) North wind; the north.
boreale, *a.* Northern.
borgata, *n.f.* Suburban tenement district.
borghese, *n.m.a.* Person of the middle class; burgess; middle-class, bourgeois; civilian (clothes).
borghesia [borghesIa], *n.f.* Middle classes, bourgeoisie.
borghigiano, *n.m.* Villager.
borgo, *n.m.* Small town; village.
borgomastro, *n.m.* Burgomaster, mayor.
boria [bOria], *n.f.* Arrogance, haughtiness; ostentation.
boriarsi, *v.r.* To be arrogant, conceited; to swagger, to show off.
borico [bOrico], *a.* (*Chem*). Boracic.
borione, *n.m.* Swaggerer.
boriosamente, *adv.* Arrogantly, haughtily; ostentatiously.
boriosità [-à], *n.f.* Arrogance, vanity.
borioso, *a.* Arrogant, haughty, ostentatious, swaggering.
boro, *n.m.* (*Chem.*) Boron.
borotalco, *n.m.* Talcum powder.
borra, *n.f.* Stuffing (for upholstery, etc.); flock; worthless stuff; (*fig.*) poor writing, trash.
borraccia [borrAccia], *n.f.* Water-bottle, flask.
borraccina, *n.f.* (*Bot.*) Moss.
borraggine, borragine, borrana [borrAggine], *n.f.* (*Bot.*) Borage.
borro, *n.m.* Ditch, deep ditch.
borrone, *n.m.* Gully, ravine (worn by action of water).
borsa, *n.f.* Purse; bag, pouch; (*Comm.*) exchange. **— di tabacco,** tobacco pouch; **stringere la —,** to become mean; **con la — degli altri,** with other folk's money; **— Valori,** Stock Exchange; (*Univ.*) **— di studio,** scholarship, bursary, grant.
borsaiolo, borsaiuolo [borsaiOlo, borsaiuOlo], *n.m.* Pickpocket.
borsanera, *n.f.* Black market.
borsanerista, *n.m.f.* Black market merchant.
borseggiare, *v.t.* To pick pockets.
borseggio [borsEggio], *n.m.* Pocket-picking.
borsellino, *n.m.* Purse (for money); money-bag.
borsetta, *n.f.* Little purse, handbag.
borsista (*pl.* **borsisti**), *n.m.* Stock-broker.
borzacchino, *n.m.* Blucher boot.
boscaglia [boscAglia], *n.f.* Woody district, forest land.
boscaiolo, boscaiuolo [boscaiOlo, boscaiuOlo], *n.m.* Woodman, forester.
boschereccio [boscherEccio], *a.* Woody, sylvan.
boschetto, *n.m.* Thicket, grove.
boschivo, *a.* Planted with trees, wooded.
bosco, *n.m.* Wood, forest; silkworm cocoonery; (*fig.*) confusion, muddle. **— ceduo,** deciduous tree; **— inglese,** shrubbery.
boscoso, *a.* Woody, wooded.
Bosforo [bOsforo], *n.m.* Bosphorus.
bosso, bossolo [bOssolo], *n.m.* (*Bot.*) Box-tree; small wooden box; dice-box; cartridge-case.
bossola [bOssola], *n.f.* Horse-brush.
botanica [botAnica], *n.f.* Botany.
botanico [botAnico], *n.m.a.* Botanist; botanical. **Orto —,** botanic garden.
botola [bOtola], *n.f.* Trapdoor.
botolo [bOtolo], *n.m.* Snapping cur; (*fig.*) irascible but weak man.
botro, *n.m.* (*Lit.*) Ditch (with stagnant water).
botta, *n.f.* (*Zool.*) Toad; blow, stroke; fall; discharge (of a firearm); (*fig.*) dumpy man or woman; smart rejoinder; serious damage. **Ricevere una mala —,** to get a nasty blow; **— e risposta,** sharp reply to the point; repartee, witty retort.
bottacciata, *n.f.* Water in a mill-dam.
bottaccino, *n.m.* Small barrel, cask; squat, dumpy person.
bottaccio [bottAccio], *n.m.* Mill-pond; small barrel; bottle of wine given to carters for each barrel they carry.
bottaio [bottAio], *n.m.* Cooper.
bottame, *n.m.* Assemblage of casks or bottles.
bottarga, *n.f.* Variety of caviar.
bottata, *n.f.* Smart retort, quip.
botte, *n.f.* Cask, barrel; culvert (under a stream); horse-cab (in Rome). (*Arch.*) **A mezza —,** semi-circular; **— che canta,** empty barrel; **essere in una — di ferro,** to be out of harm's way.
bottega, *n.f.* Shop, store; warehouse; business premises, office (usu. *colloq.*). **— bene assortita,** well-stocked shop; **mettere a —,** to apprentice; **ferri di —,** implements for one's work; **essere ad uscio e —,** to live near one's shop; **questo proviene dalla vostra —,** this is your doing.
bottegaio [bottegAio], *n.m.* Shopkeeper (esp. of food-stuffs); tradesman; customer.
bottegante, *n.m.* Shopkeeper.
botteghino, *n.m.* Booth; lottery-office; (*Theat.*) box-office.
botticello, *n.m.* Small cask, keg.
bottiglia [bottIglia], *n.f.* Bottle, flask; wine (in the bottle). **Ho bevuto una buona —,** I've drunk a good bottle of wine.
bottiglieria [bottiglierIa], *n.f.* Wine-cellar; wine-shop; bar.
bottinaio [bottinAio], *n.m.* Sewer man.

bottino, *n.m.* Booty, loot, spoils; reservoir (of an aqueduct); cess-pool, sewage.
botto, *n.m.* Blow, stroke, toll (of a bell). **Di —,** suddenly; **in un —,** in a twinkling.
bottonaio [bottonAio], *n.m.* Button-maker, vendor.
bottoncino, *n.m.* Little button, stud; (*Bot.*) bud.
bottone *n.m.* Button, stud; knob; branding iron; (*Bot.*) bud. **— da collo,** collar-stud; **bottoni da polsino, bottoni gemelli,** cuff-links; **— automatico,** press-stud; (*Mech.*) **— di una manovella,** crank-pin.
bottoniera, *n.f.* Row of buttons.
botulismo, *n.m.* (*Med.*) Botulism.
bovaro, *n.m.* Ox-driver, drover.
bove, *n.m.* Ox [cp. **bue**].
bovina, *n.f.* Cow-dung.
bovini, *n.m.pl.* Cattle.
bovino, *a.* Bovine.
bozza, *n.f.* Swelling, tumour; draft, copy; sketch; (printer's) proof. **— di stampa,** galley-proof.
bozzacchio, bozzacchione [bozzAcchio], *n.m.* Withered plum.
bozzello, *n.m.* (*Naut.*) Block.
bozzettista, *n.m.* Sketcher; story teller.
bozzetto, *n.m.* Sketch, outline; draft; model; (*Lit.*) novelette.
bozzima [bOzzima], *n.f.* (*obs.*) Size (for dressing cloth); (*fig.*) confused, muddled affair.
bozzo, *n.m.* (*obs.*) Pool.
bozzolaio [bozzolAio], *n.m.* Vendor of silk-worm cocoons.
bozzolaro, *n.m.* (*obs.*) Vendor of buns.
bozzolo [bOzzolo], *n.m.* Cocoon; lump (in wool, cotton, paste, etc.).
bozzoloso, bozzoluto, *a.* Lumpy.
bozzone, *n.m.* Lamb (alive); (*obs.*) duffer, simpleton; (*Print.*) galley-proof.
braca, *n.f.* Sling, tackle; baby's nappy; trouser-leg; (*pl.*) **brache,** trousers, drawers, pants.
bracalone, *n.m.* Careless fellow (his trousers are always slipping down).
bracare, *v.i.* To tattle, to gather and repeat gossip.
bracato, *a.* Trousered. (*obs.*) **Grasso —,** very fat man.
braccare, *v.t.* To search for, to scent; to hunt down.
braccetto, *adv.* **A —,** arm in arm.
braccheggiare, *v.t.* [cp. **braccare**].
braccheggio [bracchEggio], *n.m.* Beating (shooting, etc.), searching, scenting (of hounds).
bracchiere, *n.m.* Huntsman, whipper-in.
braccia [brAccia], *n.f.pl.* Hands (workmen).
bracciale, *n.m.* Armlet (in game of pallone); arm-rest.
braccialetto, *n.m.* Bracelet.
braccianti, *n.m.pl.* Workmen, hands.
bracciare, *v.t.* (*Naut.*) To brace (yards), to trim (sails).
bracciata, *n.f.* Armful; stroke (in swimming).
bracciatura, *n.f.* Measure (of arm's length); yards (in length of cloth); fathom; sounding (in fathoms).
braccio [brAccio], *n.m.* (Human) arm (in the pl. this becomes **braccia** and is *f.*); (in following senses pl. is **bracci,** *m.*) arm, wing (of building); flight (of steps); neck (of land); crosspiece (of cross); yard (length). **— di terra,** promontory; **— di mare,** inlet; **— di ferro,** strong man; **tagliar le braccia a uno,** to ruin a man; **cascar le braccia,** to lose courage.
bracciolo, bracciuolo, *n.m.* Arm (of an easy chair).
bracco, *n.m.* Setter, foxhound, beagle; (*fig.*) detective, sleuth.
brace, bracia, bragia [brAcia, brAgia], *n.f.* Embers, live coal.
brachetta, *n.f.* Trouser-flap.
brachettone, *n.m.* (*Arch.*) Ornaments on an arch.
brachiale, *a.* (*Anat.*) Brachial.
brachicefalo [brachicEfalo], *a.* Brachy-cephalic.
brachieraio [brachierAio], *n.m.* Truss-maker.
brachiere, *n.m.* (*Med.*) Truss.
brachino, *n.m.* (*obs.*) Tattler, gossiper.
bracia [cp. **brace**].
braciaiolo [braciaiOlo], *n.m.* Charcoal burner.
braciere, *n.m.* Brazier, warming-pan.
bracino, *n.m.* Charcoal-seller; (*fig.*) dirty fellow.
braciola, braciuola, *n.f.* Cutlet, chop.
bracone, *n.m.* (*obs.*) Inquisitive person, "nosey-parker".
bradipo [brAdipo], *n.m.* (*Zool.*) Sloth.
brado, *a.* Wild (of animals), untamed.
bragia [cp. **brace**].
brago, *n.m.* Mud, slime.
bragozzo, *n.m.* (*Naut.*) Type of small fishing-boat.
brama, *n.f.* Longing for, hankering after, desire.
bramabile [bramAbile], *a.* Very desirable.
bramare, *v.t.* To long for, to covet, to hanker after.
bramino, *n.m.* Brahmin.
bramire, *v.i.* (of animals) To roar, to bellow, to sound, to bell.
bramito, *n.m.* (of animals) Roaring, belling, bellowing.
bramosamente, *adv.* Eagerly, ardently, longingly.
bramosia, [bramosIa], **bramosità [-à],** *n.f.* Longing, covetousness, avidity, greed.
bramoso, *a.* Eager, covetous, greedy.
branca, *n.f.* Claw, paw, branch (of learning); flight (of stairs).
brancata, *n.f.* Handful.
branchia [brAnchia], *n.f.* Gill (of fish).
brancicamento, *n.m.* Handling, feeling.
brancicare, *v.t.* To handle, to finger (usu. roughly).
brancicatura, *n.f.* Handling; finger-mark.
brancichio [brancichIo], *n.m.* Handling, fingering, pawing.
branco, *n.m.* Drove, flock, herd; crowd. **Un — di pecore,** a flock of sheep; **a branchi,** in numbers.
brancolamento, *n.m.* Groping, feeling (one's way).
brancolare, *v.i.* To grope, to feel one's way.
brancolone, brancoloni, *adv.* **A —,** gropingly.
branda, *n.f.* Folding-bed, camp-bed.

brandello, *n.m.* Rag, shred, tatter; (*fig.*) fragment.
brandimento, *n.m.* (*obs.*) Brandishing.
brandire, *v.t.* To brandish.
brando, *n.m.* (*Poet.*) Sword.
brano, *n.m.* Rag, tatter, shred; (*fig.*) extract (from a letter, book, etc.).
branzino, *n.m.* (*Zool.*) Bass (fish).
Brasile, *n.m.* Brazil.
brattea [brAttea], *n.f.* (*Bot.*) Bract.
bravaccio [bravAccio], *n.m.* Swaggerer, bully.
bravamente, *adv.* Bravely; cleverly.
bravare, *v.t.i.* To defy; to bluster, to threaten.
bravata, *n.f.* Bravado, threatening attitude.
bravazzata, *n.f.* Boast, showing-off.
bravazzare, *v.i.* To brag [cp. **braveggiare**].
bravazzo, *n.m.* Swaggerer, bully.
bravazzone, *n.m.* Boaster.
braveggiare, *v.i.* To act the bully, to swagger; (of a horse) to be frisky.
braveria [braverIa], *n.f.* Defiance; bluster; excellence [cp. **bravata**].
braviere, *n.m.* (*Zool.*) Corn-bunting.
bravo, *n.m.* Cut-throat, bully.
bravo, *a.* Able, clever, skilful; capable; honest; plucky.
bravo ! *inter.* Bravo! Fine! **Da —!** Courage!
bravura, *n.f.* Skill; cleverness, capability; bravery.
breccia [brEccia], *n.f.* Breach, gap; metal (for roads); (*Geol.*) breccia. **Far —,** to convince, to make an impression.
brecciame, *n.m.* Metal (for roads).
brefotrofio [brefotrOfio], *n.m.* Foundling hospital.
Brema, *n.f.* Bremen.
brenna, *n.f.* Old horse, jade, hack.
brenta, *n.f.* Wine cask; measure of about 100 litres.
brentina, *n.f.* Wine measure (100 litres).
bresciana, *n.f.* Small iron stake.
Bretagna, *n.f.* Brittany; Britain. **Gran Bretagna,** Great Britain.
bretelle, *n.f.pl.* Men's braces; (*Am.*) suspenders.
bretone [brEtone]. *n.m.a.* Breton.
breve, *n.m.* (Papal) brief; (*Mus.*) breve.
breve, *a.* Short, brief; concise; (*Gram.*) unaccented. **Fra —,** shortly; **in —,** in short; **entro il più — termine possibile,** as soon as possible.
brevemente, *adv.* Shortly.
brevettare, *v.t.* To patent.
brevetto, *n.m.* Patent; diploma; licence. **Prendere un —,** to take out a patent; **— d'invenzione,** patent (for an invention).
breviario [breviArio], *n.m.* Breviary.
breviloquente, *a.* Concise (in speech and writing).
breviloquenza, *n.f.* Conciseness (in speech and writing).
breviloquio [brevilOquio], *n.m.* Concise speaking.
brevità [-à], *n.f.* Brevity; conciseness.
brezza, *n.f.* Breeze.
brezzeggiare, *v.i.* To blow a breeze.
brezzolina, *n.f.* Gentle breeze.
briaco, *n.m.a.* Drunken man; drunk, intoxicated.
briacone, *n.m.* Drunkard.
briccica [brIccica], *n.f.* Trifle, bagatelle.
briccicare, *v.i.* To trifle.
bricco, *n.m.* Coffee-pot; kettle; tea-pot; jug.
bricconata, *n.f.* Roguery, knavery, trick.
briccone, *n.m.* Knave, rogue, rascal.
bricconeggiare, *v.i.* To cheat.
bricconeria [bricconerIa], *n.f.* Knavery, roguery.
briciola [brIciola], *n.f.* Crumb.
briciolo [brIciolo], *n.m.* Morsel, bit.
briga, *n.f.* Care, trouble, vexation; (*obs.*) tempest. **Attaccare — con,** to pick a quarrel with; **darsi la —,** to exert oneself.
brigadiere, *n.m.* (*Mil.*) Brigadier; sergeant (of Carabinieri, etc.).
brigantaggio [brigantAggio], *n.m.* Brigandage; robbery.
brigante, *n.m.* Brigand; (*fig.*) sharper, bad character.
brigantesco, *a.* Appertaining to a brigand.
brigantino, *n.m.* (*Naut.*) Brig. **— goletta,** brigantine; **— a palo,** barque.
brigare, *v.t.i.* To solicit, to canvass for; to intrigue.
brigata, *n.f.* Company, party of friends; (*Mil.*) brigade; covey (of birds).
brighella, *n.m.* One of the masks in Italian comedy; (*fig.*) silly ass, fool.
Brigida [brIgida], *n.f.* Bridget.
brigidinaio [brigidinAio], *n.m.* Maker or vendor of brigidini.
brigidino, *n.m.* Spiced biscuit of cake, flavoured with aniseed.
briglia [brIglia], *n.f.* Bridle (harness); (*Naut.*) bobstay; (*Building*) buttress, stay. **A — sciolta,** at full speed.
briglie [brIglie], *n.f.pl.* Reins; brake.
brilla, *n.f.* Rice-mill.
brillamento, *n.m.* Glitter, splendour, glare; explosion.
brillantare, *v.t.* To cut facets on diamonds, etc.; to ice (cakes).
brillante, *n.m.a.* Brilliant (diamond); brilliant, shining, glittering; witty, clever.
brillantemente, *adv.* Brilliantly.
brillantina, *n.f.* Brilliantine.
brillare, *v.i.* To glitter, to sparkle, to glare; to explode; to hull rice. **Far — una mina,** to explode a mine; **le stelle brillano,** the stars are twinkling.
brillatoio [brillatOio], *n.m.* Rice-mill; polishing mill (for rice).
brillatura, *n.f.* Hulling (rice).
brillo, *a.* Tipsy, "half-seas over".
brina, *n.f.* Hoar-frost, rime.
brinata, *n.f.* (Fall of) hoar-frost, rime.
brinato, *a.* Frosty; (*fig.*) grizzled, turning grey (hair).
brincello, *n.m.* Bit, morsel [cp. **briciolo**].
brindare, *v.i.* To toast, to drink a health.
brindello, *n.m.* Rag, tatter.
brindellone, *n.m.* Tatterdemalion.
brindisi [brIndisi], *n.m.* Toast, health. **Fare un —,** to drink a health, to give a toast.
brio, *n.m.* Vivacity, sprightliness, spirit, animation.
brionia [briOnia], *n.f.* (*Bot.*) Bryony.
briosamente, *adv.* With vivacity, spiritedly.
briosità [-à], *n.f.* Vivaciousness.
brioso, *a.* Vivacious, sprightly, spirited, animated.
briscola [brIscola], *n.f.* Kind of card game; trump in that game; (*colloq.*) blow.

Britannia, *n.f.* Britain.
britannico [britAnnico], *a.* British. **Le Isole Britanniche,** the British Isles.
brividio [brividIo], *n.m.* Continual shivering, shuddering.
brivido [brIvido], *n.m.* Shiver, shudder.
brizzolare, *v.i.* To speckle; to turn grey (of hair).
brizzolato, *a.* Speckled, grizzled (of hair).
brizzolatura, *n.f.* Speckling, grizzling.
brocca, *n.f.* Pitcher, jug, pot; sprout (of a plant).
broccatello, *n.m.* Kind of marble; kind of light brocade.
broccato, *n.m.* Brocade.
brocchetto, *n.m.* Small jug, ewer.
brocco, *n.m.* Sprout, shoot; curl.
broccolo [brOccolo], *n.m.* (*Bot.*) Broccoli; (*obs.*) nincompoop.
broda, *n.f.* Vegetable stock, wishy-washy soup; muddy water.
brodetto, *n.m.* Broth with fish.
brodicchio [brodIcchio], *n.m.* Weak, thin broth; (*fig.*) liquid mud.
brodiglia [brodIglia], *n.f.* Thin, washy broth.
brodo, *n.m.* Broth, soup (from water in which meat has been boiled). **— lungo,** watery broth; **— ristretto,** rich broth.
brodolone, *n.m.* Slovenly fellow.
brodoso, *a.* Very thin (of soup).
brogliare, *v.i.* To intrigue.
brogliaccio, brogliazzo [brogliAccio], *n.m.* (*Comm.*) Day-book.
broglio [brOglio], *n.m.* Intrigue, scheming (to get a job, etc.). **— elettorale,** corruption at elections.
brolo, *n.m.* Garden, enclosed garden.
bromatologia [bromatologIa], *n.f.* Dietetics.
bromo, *n.m.* (*Chem.*) Bromine.
bromuro, *n.m.* (*Chem.*) Bromide.
bronchi, *n.m.pl.* (*Anat.*) Bronchia.
bronchiale, *a.* (*Anat.*) Bronchial.
bronchite, *n.f.* (*Med.*) Bronchitis.
broncio [brOncio], *n.m.* Pout, wry face; grudge; ill-temper.
bronco, *n.m.* Stump, stem, trunk.
broncopolmonite, *n.f.* (*Med.*) Bronchial pneumonia.
brontolamento, *n.m.* Murmuring, grumbling, complaining [cp. **brontolio**].
brontolare, *v.t.i.* To murmur, to grumble, to mutter; to gurgle (internally).
brontolio [brontolIo], *n.m.* Murmuring, grumbling; (internal) gurgling.
brontolone, *n.m.* Grumbler.
bronzare, *v.t.* To bronze.
bronzatura, *n.f.* Bronzing.
bronzeo [brOnzeo], *n.m.* (*Metal.*) Bronze.
bronzina, *n.f.* (*Mech.*) Bearing.
bronzino, *a.* Bronzed; sunburnt.
bronzista (*pl.* **bronzisti**), *n.m.* Bronze-founder, worker in bronze.
bronzo, *n.m.* (*Metal*) Bronze. **Una faccia di —,** a brazen face; **i sacri bronzi,** church bells; **ha un cuore di —,** he is hard-hearted.
broscia [brOscia], *n.f.* Thin, tasteless broth.
brossura, *n.f.* paper-back (book).
brucare, *v.t.* To strip off leaves; to browse (esp. of goats)
brucatura, *n.f.* Browsing (on leaves).
brucente, *a.* [cp. **bruciante**].
bruciabile [bruciAbile], *a.* Burnable.
bruciacchiare, *v.t.* To scorch.
bruciacchiatura, *n.f.* Scorching.
bruciamento, *n.m.* Burning; scalding.
bruciapelo, *adv.* **A —,** point-blank.
bruciare, *v.t.i.* To burn, to set on fire; to be on fire; to cauterize. **La casa brucia,** the house is on fire; **— la scuola,** to play the truant; **questa lampada brucia bene,** this lamp burns well.
bruciarsi, *v.r.* To burn oneself. **— le cervella,** to blow one's brains out.
bruciata, *n.f.* Roast chestnut.
bruciataio [bruciatAio], *n.m.* Hot-chestnut seller.
bruciaticcio [bruciatIccio], *n.m.* Burning, burnt matter; smell of burning.
bruciato, *p.p.a.* Burned, burnt. **Ora bruciata,** hot spell; **— dal sole,** sunburnt.
bruciatura, *n.f.* Burning, cauterizing, cauterization; the scar left by this.
bruciore, *n.m.* Burning sensation, smart. **— di stomaco,** heartburn.
bruco, *n.m.* (*Zool.*) Caterpillar, grub, maggot. **Ignudo —,** naked, poor.
brughiera, *n.f.* Moor, heath.
brulicame, *n.m.* Swarm, swarming (with insects).
brulicare, *v.i.* To swarm (of insects); to swarm with people.
brulichio [brulichIo], *n.m.* Swarm. **— di gente,** swarm of people.
brullo, *a.* Naked, bare; barren. **Albero brullo,** bare tree; destitute (person).
brulotto, *n.m.* (*Naut.*) Fire-ship.
brum, *n.m.* Brougham, carriage.
bruma, *n.f.* (*Lit.*) Mist; depth of winter; (*fig.*) old age.
brumale, *a.* Wintry.
brunello, brunetto, *a.* Brownish.
brunezza, *n.f.* Brownness.
brunimento, *n.m.* Polishing; burnishing.
brunire, *v.t.* To polish, to burnish.
brunitoio [brunitOio], *n.m.* Burnisher, polisher (implement).
brunitore, *n.m.* Burnisher, polisher (person).
brunitura, *n.f.* Burnishing, polishing.
bruno, *a.* Brown; dark; mourning band. **Notte bruna,** dark night; **abito —,** suit of mourning.
brunotto, *a.* Brownish, rather dark.
brusca, *n.f.* Horse-brush.
bruscamente, *adv.* Abruptly, brusquely, bluntly.
bruscare, *v.t.* To prune (trees, etc.) [cp. **potare**].
bruschetta, *n.f.* Child's game of drawing the longest straw.
bruschetto, *a.* Tart, sourish.
bruschezza, *n.f.* Tartness, sourness, sharpness.
bruschino, *n.m.* Horse-brush.
brusco, *a.* Sour, sharp (in taste); brusque; cloudy; unexpected; rapid. **Vino —,** sour wine; **con le brusche,** bluntly; **una brusca decisione,** a sudden decision.
bruscolo [brUscolo], *n.m.* Mote (in the eye), speck; (*fig.*) doubt, suspicion.
brusio [brusIo], *n.m.* Hubbub, noise of many voices; bustle.
Brusselle, (*Geog.*) *n.f.* Brussels. **Cavolini di —,** Brussels sprouts.

brutale, *a.* Brutal (in all senses).
brutalità [-à], *n.f.* Brutality.
brutalmente, *adv.* Brutally.
Bruto, *n.m.* Brutus.
bruto, *n.m.a.* Brute, animal; brutal, irrational, violent. **Materia bruta,** inert matter.
bruttamente, *adv.* In an ugly way; unbecomingly.
bruttare, *v.t.* To soil.
bruttezza, *n.f.* Ugliness; filth.
brutto, *a.* Ugly, ill-favoured; deformed; bad; sad, troubled; confused. **Alle brutte,** at the worst; **vederne di brutte,** to come on hard times; **che brutto tempo,** what nasty weather.
bruttura, *n.f.* Filth; shamefulness, baseness; a base deed.
bruzzico, bruzzolo [brUzzico, brUzzolo], *n.m.* Daybreak, dawn.
bua, *n.f.* Hurt, pain (childish expression).
buaccio [buAccio], *n.m.* Blockhead, dolt.
buacciolata, *n.f.* Foolish (acts or words).
buacciolo, *n.m.* Young fool, silly young idiot.
buaggine [buAggine], *n.f.* Foolishness, stupidity.
bubbola [bUbbola], *n.f.* Trifle, silly thing; fib; white lie; story.
bubbolare, *v.t.i.* To shiver (with cold); to rumble, to growl; to cheat, to swindle.
bubbolata, *n.f.* Silly talk, tall story.
bubboliera, *n.f.* Horse-collar with bells on it.
bubbolo [bUbbolo], *n.m.* Bell for horse-collar.
bubbolone, *n.m.* Fibber, humbugger, teller of tall stories.
bubbone, *n.m.* (*Med.*) Bubo.
bubbonico [bubbOnico], *a.* (*Med.*) Bubonic. **Peste bubbonica,** bubonic plague.
bu bu, *n.m.* Bow-wow (dog's bark).
buca, *n.f.* Hole; pit; cave, cavern; ditch; grotto; (*fig.*) grave. **— del carbone,** coal-cellar; **— delle lettere,** letter-box, pillar-box; **— del biliardo,** pocket (in billiard table); (*Theat.*) **— del suggeritore,** prompter's box.
bucacchiare, *v.t.* To bore small holes.
bucaneve, *n.m.* (*Bot.*) Snowdrop.
bucare, *v.t.* To bore, to pierce, to perforate, to puncture.
bucarsi, *v.r.* To prick oneself; to be bored or punctured.
bucataia [bucatAia], *n.f.* Washerwoman.
bucataio [bucatAio], *n.m.* Laundryman.
bucato, *n.m.* Washing, laundry. **Panni di —,** clean linen; **mettere in —,** to send to the laundry.
bucato, *p.p.a.* Bored, pierced, perforated, riddled. **Aver le mani bucate,** to be a spendthrift.
bucatura, *n.f.* Hole, piercing, puncture (of a tyre).
buccellato, *n.m.* Sort of sweet cake.
buccia [bUccia], *n.f.* Peel, rind, skin, bark, crust. **Togliere la —,** to peel (a fruit); (*fig.*) **rivedere le bucce a,** to find fault with.
buccicata, *n.f.* **Non saper —,** to know nothing.
buccina [bUccina], *n.f.* Roman trumpet.
buccinare, *v.i.* To murmur, to mutter; to divulge.
buccino [bUccino], *n.m.* (*Zool.*) Whelk.
buccola [bUccola], *n.f.* Ear-ring.
bucefalo [bucEfalo], *n.m.* (*colloq.*) Sorry nag.
bucherare, bucherellare, *v.t.* To riddle with small holes.
bucherellato, *a.* Riddled with little holes.
bucherello, *n.m.* Little hole.
bucicare, bucicarsi, *v.i.r.* To budge, to stir.
bucinamento, *n.m.* Humming, whispering, buzzing.
bucinare, *v.i.* To spread a report, to noise abroad; to murmur, to whisper.
bucinarsi, *v.r.* To be rumoured, to be reported.
bucine [bUcine], *n.m.* Kind of fishing-net; net for catching partridges.
bucintoro, *n.m.* (*Hist.*) Bucentaur, the old Venetian state barge.
buco, *n.m.* Hole, orifice, aperture; cavity; small room. (*Aviat.*) **— d'aria,** air-pocket; **fare un — nell'acqua,** to fail, to have one's labour in vain; **tappare un —,** to pay a debt.
bucolica [bucOlica], *n.f.* (*Poet.*) Bucolic (poem); (*colloq.*) food.
bucolico [bucOlico], *a.* (*Poet.*) Bucolic; pastoral.
buddismo, *n.m.* Buddhism.
buddista, *n.m.* Buddhist.
budellame, *n.m.* Entrails, guts, bowels.
budello, *n.m.* (*pl.* **budella,** *f.*) Bowel, intestine, gut.
budino, *n.m.* Pudding.
bue, *n.m.* (*pl.* **buoi**) Ox; (*fig.*) dunce, dolt. **— salato,** salt beef, corned beef; **carne di —,** beef; **mettere il carro avanti i buoi,** to put the cart before the horse.
buetta, *n.f.* (*obs.*) Packet of tobacco.
bufalo [bUfalo], *n.m.* (*Zool.*) Buffalo; (*fig.*) blockhead.
bufare, *v.i.* To snow with wind, to blow a blizzard.
bufera, *n.f.* Squall with snow, blizzard; (*fig.*) sudden, unexpected disaster.
buffa, *n.f.* (*obs.*) Gust of wind; hood, lower part of the visor (of a helmet).
buffare, *v.t.i.* To blow, to puff (of the wind); to huff (at draughts).
buffata, *n.f.* Gust of wind; huff (at draughts).
buffè [-è], *n.m.* Buffet, sideboard.
buffetto, *n.m.* Buffet; flip with the fingers.
buffo, *n.m.a.* Buffoon; comedian; puff of wind; funny, comical; (*fig.*) queer, odd. **Opera buffa,** comic opera.
buffonaggine [buffonAggine], *n.f.* Buffoonery [cp. **buffonata**].
buffonata, *n.f.* Piece of buffoonery, comical word or action.
buffone, *n.m.* Buffoon; (*Hist.*) jester, fool; (*fig.*) unreliable person.
buffoneggiare, *v.i.* To play the fool.
buffoneria [buffonerIa], *n.f.* Buffoonery, tom-foolery.
buffonescamente, *adv.* Ridiculously, comically.
buffonesco, *a.* Ridiculous, comical.
buffonchiare, *v.i.* To grumble [cp. **bofonchiare**].
bugia [bugIa], *n.f.* Lie, falsehood; flat candlestick. **Una — pietosa,** a white lie; **dire una —,** to tell a lie.
bugiarderia [bugiarderIa], *n.f.* Fib, white lie.
bugiardo, *n.m.a.* Liar; lying, false. **Far — qualcuno,** to prove someone a liar.

bugigattolo [bugigAttolo], *n.m.* Small, dark room, closet.
bugliolo, bugliuolo, *n.m.* Bucket, pail. — **d'incendio,** fire-bucket; boil.
bugna, *n.f.* (*Arch.*) Ashlar; boss; (*Naut.*) clew (of a square sail).
bugno, *n.m.* Bee-hive; restricted place.
bugnola [bUgnola], *n.f.* Straw-plaited basket for carrying corn, etc.
bugnolo [bUgnolo], *n.m.* Small basket (for fruit, etc.).
buio [bUio], *n.m.* Darkness (in all senses); night; (*fig.*) prison. **Essere — pesto,** to be pitch dark.
buio [bUio], *a.* Dark; obscure.
bulbo, *n.m.* (*Bot.*) Bulb. **Il — dell'occhio,** the eye-ball.
bulboso, *a.* (*Bot.*) Bulbous.
Bulgaria [bulgarIa], *n.f.* Bulgaria.
bulgaro [bUlgaro], *n.m.a.* Bulgarian; Russia leather.
bulicare, *v.i.* To bubble up, to seethe (of water).
bulinare, *v.t.* To engrave.
bulino, *n.m.* Burin, graving-tool.
bulletta, *n.f.* Tin-tack, tack; stud; ticket (torn from counterfoil).
bullettaio [bullettAio], *n.m.* Maker *or* vendor of nails.
bullettame, *n.m.* Quantity of nails, tacks, etc.
bullettario [bullettArio] [cp. **bollettario**].
bullettinaio [bullettinAio], *n.m.* Ticket-seller (for theatres, etc.).
bullettino, *n.m.* Bulletin, summary of news (in a newspaper); entrance ticket to theatre, etc. [cp. **bollettino**].
bullettone, *n.m.* Large tack; upholsterer's tack.
bullone, *n.m.* Bolt (for nut).
bulo, bullo, *n.m.,* Ruffian; bully; (*fig.*) Teddy boy.
buon [cp. **buono**].
buonaccordo, *n.m.* (*Mus.*) Harpsichord.
buonalana, *n.m.* Rascal.
buonamano, *n.m.* Tip, gratuity.
buonanima [buonAnima], *a.* Late (deceased). **Mio fratello —,** my late brother.
buonavoglia [buonavOglia], *n.m.* Volunteer (for a job, etc.).
buondì, *inter.* Good morning.
buonentrata, *n.f.* Gratuity.
buongustaio [buongustAio], *n.m.* Connoisseur; gourmet.
buongusto, *n.m.* Good taste, taste.
buono, *n.m.* Good, good (person or thing); (*Comm.*) bond, obligation, Treasury bill; debenture, cheque. **— di cassa,** cheque; **— d'incasso**; money-order; **— di consegna,** delivery order.
buono, *a.* Good (in all senses); wholesome, salutary, sound; kind, nice; fine; right, fit, proper; profitable. **Buon mercato,** cheap; **a buon diritto,** rightly; **alla buona,** simply; **di buon'ora,** early; **— a nulla,** good-for-nothing; **con le buone,** gently; **tempo —,** fine weather; **vedere di buon occhio,** to look favourably on; **far di —,** to be in earnest; **Dio ce la mandi buona,** let us hope for the best.
buonpeso, *n.m.* (Put in for) good weight.
buonsenso, *n.m.* Common sense.
buonuscita, *n.f.* Indemnity; compensation.
buonuomo, *n.m.* Good fellow.
burattare [cp. **abburattare**].
burattinaio [burattinAio], *n.m.* Puppet showman; Punch and Judy showman.
burattinata, *n.f.* Puppet show; (*fig.*) foolish action.
burattino, *n.m.* Marionette, puppet; person who does foolish things; man with nothing to say for himself.
buratto, *n.m.* Sieve, implement for bolting flour.
burbanza, *n.f.* Arrogance.
burbanzosamente, *adv.* Arrogantly.
burbanzoso, *a.* Arrogant, haughty.
burbera [bUrbera], *n.f.* Windlass.
burberamente, *adv.* Rudely.
burbero [bUrbero], *a.* Gruff, rough, rude. **Un aspetto —,** a forbidding countenance.
burchiellesco, *a.* (*Poet.*) In the style of Burchiello, Florentine satirist.
burchiello, burchio [bUrchio], *n.m.* (*Naut.*) Canal barge; wherry.
bure, *n.f.* (*Agric.*) Plough-handle.
buriana, *n.f.* Storm, gale.
buricco, *n.m.* (*colloq.*) Ass, donkey.
burina, *n.f.* (*Naut.*) Bowline. **Andar di —,** to sail fast [cp. **bolina**].
burla, *n.f.* Jest, hoax, joke. **Per —,** in fun; **mettere in —,** to treat as a joke.
burlare, *v.t.i.* To ridicule; to jest; to mock, to jeer at.
burlarsi, *v.r.* To laugh at, to make fun of.
burlatore, burlatrice, *n.m.f.* Joker, banterer.
burlescamente, *adv.* Comically, in a burlesque fashion.
burlesco, *a.* Comical, burlesque.
burletta, *n.f.* Joke, farce; (*Theat.*) farce, vaudeville.
burlevole [burlEvole], *a.* Comical, farcical.
burlone, *n.m.* Joker, jester.
burocrate [burOcrate], *n.m.* Bureaucrat.
burocraticamente, *adv.* Bureaucratically.
burocratico [burocrAtico], *a.* Bureaucratic.
burocrazia [burocrazIa], *n.f.* Bureaucracy.
burraia [burrAia], *n.f.* Dairy.
burraio [burrAio], *n.m.* Dairyman.
burrasca, *n.f.* Storm, squall; (*fig.*) misfortune.
burrascosamente, *adv.* Stormily.
burrascoso, *a.* Stormy, squally.
burrato, *n.m.* Ravine, gorge.
burrato, *a.* Buttered.
burrificio, *n.m.* Butter factory.
burro, *n.m.* Butter.
burrona, *n.f.* Kind of pear.
burrone, *n.m.* Ravine, gorge.
burroso, *a.* Buttery; (*fig.*) delicate, tender.
busca, *n.f.* Quest, search. **Andare in —,** to go in search.
buscare, *v.t.* To get, to procure, to catch; to find (after searching). **— la giornata,** to earn one's daily bread; **buscarne,** to get a thrashing.
buscarsi, *v.r.* To earn, to procure, to catch.
buscherare, *v.t.* To deceive, to swindle, to do in.
buscherata, *n.f.* Nonsense; deception.
buscherio [buscherIo], *n.m.* Noise, hubbub; crowd.
busecca, *n.f.* Tripe (cooked with onions).
busecchia [busEcchia], *n.f.* Tripe, sausage-meat.

busillis [busIllis], *n.m.* **Qui sta il —**, here lies the difficulty.
bussa, *n.f.* Blow, knock.
bussamento, *n.m.* Knocking, beating.
bussare, *v.t.i.* To knock (at the door); to thrash.
bussata, *n.f.* Blow, knock.
busse, *n.f.pl.* Blows, beating; (*fig.*) damage.
bussola [bUssola], *n.f.* (Mariner's) compass; magnetic needle; inner door, screen (against draught); horse-brush. **Perdere la —**, to lose one's bearings (morally); **— giroscopica,** gyro compass; **rilevamento —** compass bearing.
bussolo [bUssolo], *n.m.* (*obs.*) Alms-box.
bussolotto, *n.m.* Dice-box; conjuror's box of tricks. **Giuoco di bussolotti,** jugglery.
busta, *n.f.* Envelope; folder for papers.
busto, *n.m.* Corset; (*Anat.*) bust; (*Art*) bust.
butano, *n.m.* (*Chem.*) Butane.
butirro, *n.m.* Butter [cp. **burro**].
butirroso, *a.* Buttery.
buttafuori, *n.m.* (*Theat.*) Call-boy.
buttalà [-à], *n.m.* Clothes-horse.
buttare, *v.t.* To throw, to cast, to hurl, to fling; to squander; to vomit. **— via,** to throw away; **— indietro,** to throw back; **— in faccia,** to throw in one's face; **— giù,** to overthrow, to ruin, to put down.
buttarsi, *v.r.* To throw oneself down, to lie down; to settle (of birds, etc.).
buttasella, *n.m.* (*Mil.*) Order to saddle.
buttata, *n.f.* Shoot (of a plant).
butterato, *a.* Pock-marked.
buttero [bUttero], *n.m.* Pock-mark; herdsman.
buzzicare, *v.i.* To stir, to move slightly [cp. **bucicare**].
buzzo, *n.m.* Paunch, belly (of beasts). **Di — buono,** with eagerness.
buzzone, *n.m.* Pot-belly, paunch (of a man).
buzzurro, *n.m.* Hawker of chestnuts : (*colloq*). boor.

C

C, c. Third letter of the Italian alphabet.
cabala [cAbala], *n.f.* Clique, cabal, cabbala; intrigue.
cabalare, *v.i.* To plot.
cabaletta, *n.f.* (*Mus.*) Short melodic air.
cabalista (*pl.* **cabalisti**), *n.m.* Diviner; believer in charms.
cabalistico [cabalIstico], *a.* Cabalistic, mysterious, occult.
cabalone, *n.m.* Intriguer.
cabina, *n.f.* Cabin; (*Aviat.*) cockpit. **— telefonica,** telephone call-box; **— di spiaggia,** beach-hut; **— di ascensore,** lift-car; (*Cinema*) **— di proiezione,** projection room; **— stagna,** air-tight chamber; **— di prima classe,** first-class cabin.
cablogramma (*pl.* **cablogrammi**), *n.m.* Cablegram.
cabotaggio [cabotAggio], *n.m.* (*Naut.*) Coasting, coasting trade.
cabotiera, *n.m.* (*Naut.*) Coasting vessel.
cabrare, *v.i.* (*Aviat.*) To ascend, to rise.
cacao, *n.m.* Cocoa; cocoa-palm. **Una tazza di —**, a cup of cocoa.
cacaloro, *n.m.* Man who brags of his wealth.
cacapensieri, *n.m.* One who hesitates, who raises difficulties.
cacare, *v.i.* (*vulg.*) To evacuate, to defecate; to dung (of animals).
cacasenno, *n.m.* Conceited puppy, wiseacre.
cacastecchi, *n.m.* Miser.
cacata, *n.f.* (*vulg.*) Motion of the bowels, stool.
cacatoio [cacatOio], *n.m.* (*vulg.*) Water-closet.
cacatua, *n.m.* (*Zool.*) Cockatoo.
cacatura, *n.f.* (*vulg.*) Motion of the bowels; excrement of insects.
cacca, *n.f.* (*vulg.*) Excrement, dung.
caccabaldole [caccabAldole], *n.f.pl.* Wheedling *or* coaxing words.
caccao [cp. **cacao**].
caccia [cAccia], *n.f.* Hunt, hunting, hunting party, chase. **— riservata,** private shoot; **— di frodo,** poaching; **— grossa,** big-game shooting; **licenza di —**, shooting licence; **pallini da —**, small shot; **far la — a uno,** to be on the look-out for someone; **mettere alla —**, to set someone in pursuit.
caccia [cAccia], *n.m.* (*Aviat.*) Scout, fighter; (*Naut.*) destroyer. **— a reazione,** jet fighter; **— bombardiere,** fighter-bomber.
cacciabuoi, *n.m.* (*Rail.*) Cowcatcher.
cacciachiodo, *n.m.* Claw-hammer; implement for extracting nails from horse's hoof.
cacciadiavoli [cacciadiAvoli], *n.m.* Exorcist.
cacciaffanni, *n.m.* Something that drives away care.
cacciagione, *n.f.* Game, venison; game preserve.
cacciamosche, *n.m.* Fly-whisk.
cacciapassere [cacciapAssere], *n.m.* Scarecrow.
cacciaperni, *n.m.* Cold chisel.
cacciare, *v.t.i.* To hunt, to chase, to pursue, to drive away; to eject, to banish; to thrust. **— via,** to chase away; **— di casa,** to eject, to turn out of the house; **— un grido,** to scream out; **— fuori la lingua,** to stick out one's tongue; **— dentro,** to drive in, to thrust in; **un diavolo caccia l'altro,** one care drives out another.
cacciarsi, *v.r.* To intrude, to insinuate oneself. **— in capo,** to take it into one's head.
cacciata, *n.f.* Expulsion, driving out; hunt, hunting expedition.
cacciatoia [cacciatOia], *n.f.* Cold-chisel; wedge; punch.
cacciatora, *n.f.* Hunting-jacket. **Alla —**, huntsmanlike; **pollastro alla —**, chicken ragout.
cacciatore, *n.m.* Hunter, huntsman. **— di frodo,** poacher.
cacciasommergibili [cacciasommergIbili], *n.m.* (*Naut.*) Submarine chaser.
cacciatorpediniere, *n.m.* (*Naut.*) Destroyer.
cacciatrice, *n.f.* Huntress, sportswoman.
cacciavite, *n.f.* Screwdriver.
cacciù [-ù], *n.m.* (*Bot.*) Catechu, cachou.
cacciucco, *n.m.* Fish soup.
caccola [cAccola], *n.f.* (*vulgar*) Mucus of the nose, snot; rheum in the eye; dirt in wool on a sheep.
caccoloso, *a.* Blear-eyed, dirty.
cacherello, *n.m.* Droppings (of rats, sheep, etc.).
cacheroso, *a.* (*vulgar*) Tiresome.

cachessia [cachessIa], *n.f.* (*Med.*) Cachexy.
cachettico [cachEttico], *a.* (*Med.*) Cachetic.
cachi, *n.m.* Khaki.
cachinno, *n.m.* (*Lit.*) Cachinnation, immoderate laughter; guffaw.
caciaia [caciAia], *n.f.* Cheese-room (in a dairy).
caciaio [caciAio], *n.m.* Cheese-maker.
caciaiuolo, *n.m.* Cheesemonger.
caciato, *a.* Sprinkled with grated cheese.
cacimperio, *n.m.* Cheese and meat omelette.
cacio [cAcio], *n.m.* Cheese. **— fresco,** new cheese; **— grattato,** grated cheese; **essere pane e —,** to be great friends; **come il — sui maccheroni,** (to suit) down to the ground; **essere alto come un soldo di —,** to be a little fellow.
caciocavallo, *n.m.* Southern Italian cheese.
cacioso, *a.* Cheesy.
cacofonia [cacofonIa], *n.f.* Cacophony.
cacofonico [cacofOnico], *a.* Cacophonic.
cacto, *n.m.* (*Bot.*) Cactus.
cacume, *n.m.* (*Poet.*) Mountain-top.
cadauno, *pron.* Each, each one, every one [cp. **ciascuno, ciascheduno**].
cadavere [cadAvere], *n.m.* Corpse. **— ambulante,** walking skeleton; ghost.
cadaverico [cadavErico], *a.* Cadaverous.
cadente, *pres.p.a.* Weak, feeble, frail. **Un vecchio —,** a very feeble old man; **stelle cadenti,** shooting-stars.
cadenza, *n.f.* Cadence, modulation; (*Mus.*) cadenza.
cadenzato, *a.* Rhythmical. **Passo —,** rhythmical step.
cadere, *v.i.* To fall, to fall down; to befall; to happen, to drop. **Lasciar —,** to let fall; **— di mente,** to slip from one's memory; **— dalla padella nelle braci,** to fall out of the frying-pan into the fire; **— in disgrazia,** to fall into disgrace; **— in un'imboscata,** to fall into an ambush; **— in deliquio,** to faint; **— per terra,** to fall on the ground; **la sorte cadde su di me,** the lot fell to me; **il Natale cadde di martedì l'anno scorso,** Christmas fell on a Tuesday last year; **— dalle nuvole,** to be taken aback, to be astonished; **— dal sonno,** to be overcome with sleep; **lasciar — l'argomento,** to let the matter drop; **cade la sera,** night is falling; **— ammalato,** to be taken ill, to fall sick; **— in proposito,** to come seasonably, to be appropriate; **— in ginocchio,** to fall upon one's knees.
cadetto, *n.m.* Cadet (in all senses).
cadì, *n.m.* Cadi, Turkish magistrate.
Cadice [cAdice], *n.f.* Cadiz.
cadmio [cAdmio], *n.m.* (*Min.*) Cadmium.
caducamente, *adv.* Frailly, fleetingly.
caduceo, *n.m.* (*Hist.*) Caduceus.
caducità [-à], *n.f.* Frailty, caducity. **La — delle umane cose,** the transitoriness of human things.
caduco, *a.* Frail fleeting, transitory, decaying, declining. **Mal —,** epilepsy.
caduno [cp. **cadauno**].
caduta, *n.f.* Fall, falling; (*Comm.*) slump; downfall, ruin, decline, failure.
caduto, *n.m.* Fallen (soldier). **Monumento ai Caduti,** war memorial.
caendo, *pres.p.* (*obs.*) **Andar —,** to go seeking.
cafaggiaio [cafaggiAio], *n.m.* (*obs.*) Head forester.
cafarnao, *n.m.* (*colloq.*) **Andare in —,** to get lost; **mandare in —,** to gulp down, to swallow.
caffè [-è], *n.m.* Coffee; coffee-house, café. **Chicchi di —,** coffee-berries; **— nero,** black coffee; **— tostato,** roasted coffee; **— macinato, — in polvere,** ground coffee; **caffelatte,** café-au-lait; **— della stazione,** station refreshment room; (*Theat.*) **— concerto,** music-hall.
caffeina, *n.f.* (*Chem.*) Caffeine.
caffettiera, *n.f.* Coffee-pot.
caffettiere, *n.m.* Coffee-house keeper, café proprietor.
caffo, *a.* (*obs.*) Odd, uneven. **Giuoco a pari e —,** to play at odds and evens.
cafone, *n.m.* Peasant; rustic boor; cad, vulgar fellow.
cafro, *a.* Kaffir.
cagionamento, *n.m.* Cause [cp. **cagione**].
cagionare, *v.t.* To cause, to occasion.
cagionatore, cagionatrice, *n.m.f.* (*obs.*) Causer, one who causes.
cagione, *n.f.* Cause, motive, reason. **A cagione di,** on account of.
cagionevole [cagionEvole], *a.* Sickly, ailing, weakly. **Essa è di salute —,** she is delicate; she is in indifferent health.
cagionevolezza, *n.f.* Frailty, infirmity.
cagionoso, *a.* Sickly, infirm.
cagliare, *v.t.i.* To curdle; to become curdled.
caglio [cAglio], *n.m.* Curd, rennet.
cagna, *n.f.* Bitch.
cagniaia [cagniAia], *n.f.* (*obs.*) Barking of dogs, uproar.
cagniaio [cagniAio], *n.m.* (*obs.*) Disorderly conduct; uproar, row.
cagnara, *n.f.* (*colloq.*) Barking of dogs; uproar.
cagnazzo, *n.m.* (*obs.*) Cur.
cagnesco, *a.* Surly. **Guardare in —,** to look askance, surlily.
cagnetta, cagnettina, cagnolino, *n.m.f.* Puppy; lapdog.
cagnotto, *n.m.* Bully, spy; hanger-on.
caicco, *n.m.* (*Naut.*) Long-boat; caique.
caimano, *n.m.* (*Zool.*) Cayman, caiman.
Caina, *n.f.* Ninth circle of Dante's Inferno.
Caino, *n.m.* Cain; traitor, murderer.
cala, *n.f.* Cove, creek, bay.
calabrese, *n.m.a.* Calabrian.
calabrone, *n.m.* (*Zool.*) Hornet; bumble-bee.
caladeposito [caladepOsito], *n.m.* Bin.
calafataggio [calafatAggio], *n.m.* (*Naut.*) Caulking.
calafatame, *n.m.* (*Naut.*) Caulking operations.
calafatare, *v.t.* (*Naut.*) To caulk.
calafato, calafatore, *n.m.* (*Naut.*) Caulker.
calafatura, *n.f.* (*Naut.*) Caulking (as an operation).
calamaio [calamAio], *n.m.* Inkstand, ink-well.
calamaro, calamaio [calamAio], *n.m.* (*Zool.*) Cuttlefish.
calamina, *n.f.* (*Min.*) Calamine.
calaminta, *n.f.* (*Bot.*) Catmint.
calamistro, *n.m.* Curling-tongs.
calamita, *n.f.* Magnet; loadstone. **Elettrocalamita,** electro-magnet.
calamità [-à], *n.f.* Calamity.
calamitare, *v.t.* To magnetize.

calamitarsi, *v.r.* To be magnetized.
calamitato, *a.* Magnetized. **Ago —,** magnetic needle.
calamitosamente, *adv.* Calamitously.
calamitoso, *a.* Calamitous, distressing.
calamo [cAlamo], *n.m.* Joint of a cane; pipe of a reed; (*fig.*) pen; arrow.
calanco, *n.m.* (*Geol.*) Argillaceous ground worn by erosion.
calando, *a.* (*Mus.*) Gradually diminishing.
calandra, *n.f.* (*Zool.*) Wood-lark; (*Mech.*) calender.
calandrino, *n.m.* Simpleton.
calante, *pres.p.a.* Diminishing, lowering; setting (of sun, etc.). **Marea —,** ebbing tide.
calappio [calAppio], *n.m.* Slip-knot; snare.
calapranzi, *n.m.* Dumb-waiter, service lift; tray.
calare, *v.t.i.* To lower, to let down; to fall; go down, to drop; to swoop down, to set (of sun, etc.); to diminish, to decline, to fall off; to descend (upon), to fall (upon). **I barbari calarono in Italia,** the barbarians overran Italy; **il sole cala,** the sun is setting; **al calar del sole,** at sunset; **— le vele,** to lower the sails; **— a fondo,** to sink; **i prezzi calano,** prices are falling; **cala il sipario,** the curtain falls.
calastra, *n.f.* Seating for a cask, barrel, etc.; trail of a gun-carriage.
calata, *n.f.* Descent, lowering, setting (of sun, etc.); slope; (*Naut.*) wharf, quay, landing-stage; invasion. **La — del sipario,** the fall of the curtain.
calatrone, *n.m.* (*obs.*) Large bucket.
calaverna, *n.f.* (*Naut.*) Leather band on an oar.
calca, *n.f.* Throng, crowd, press.
calcabile [calcAbile], *a.* That may be trodden (of a path, etc.).
calcafogli, *n.m.* Paper-weight.
calcagnata, *n.f.* Kick (with the heel).
calcagno (*pl.* **calcagni,** *m.*, **calcagna,** *f.*), *n.m.* Heel. **Stare alle —,** to be at one's heels, to pester.
calcalettere [calcalEttere], *n.m.* Letter-weight, paper-weight.
calcamento, *n.m.* Pressure; trampling.
calcare, *v.t.* To press, to trample upon, to tread upon; to lay stress upon; to trace. (*Theat.*) **— le scene,** to walk the boards; **— la mano,** to overdo a thing.
calcare [cAlcare], *n.m.* (*Geol.*) Limestone.
calcareo [calcAreo], *a.* (*Geol.*) Calcareous.
calcarsi, *v.r.* To crowd together.
calcata, *n.f.* Trampling; pressure.
calcatoio [calcatOio], *n.m.* Tracing-board; (*Mil.*) ramrod.
calce, *n.f.* Lime. **— viva,** quick-lime; **— spenta,** slaked lime.
calce, *adv.* **In —,** at the foot of the page.
calcedonio [calcedOnio], *n.m.* (*Min.*) Chalcedony.
calceolaria [calceolAria], *n.f.* (*Bot.*) Calceolaria.
calcese, *n.m.* (*Naut.*) Mast-head.
calcestruzzo, *n.m.* (*Arch.*) Concrete.
calcetto, *n.m.* (*obs.*) Sock; slipper.
calchino, *n.m.* Paper-weight.
calciante, *n.m.* [cp. **calciatore**].
calciare, *v.t.* To kick.
calciatore, *n.m.* Football player.
calcina, *n.f.* Lime, mortar. **Fornace di —,** lime-kiln.
calcinaccio [calcinAccio], *n.m.* Scrap of old mortar; piece of plaster.
calcinaio [calcinAio], *n.m.* Lime pit.
calcinare, *v.t.* To calcine.
calcinazione, *n.f.* Calcination.
calcio (1) [cAlcio], *n.m.* Kick; butt-end, butt; football. **Il giuoco del —,** the game of football; **una partita di —,** a game of football; **— d'inizio,** kick-off; **— d'angolo,** corner kick; **— di rigore,** penalty kick; **— di punizione,** free kick; (*Mil.*) **il — del fucile,** the rifle-stock; **appioppare un —,** to give a kick.
calcio (2) [cAlcio], *n.m.* (*Chem.*) Calcium.
calcistico [calcIstico], *a.* Pertaining to football. **Società —,** football club.
calcitrare, *v.i.* To kick, to be restive [cp. **ricalcitrare**].
calco, *n.m.* (*Art*) Cast; tracing, drawing.
calcografia [calcografIa], *n.f.* Engraving (on copper or other metal).
calcografo [calcOgrafo], *n.m.* Engraver (on copper, etc.).
calcola [cAlcola], *n.f.* Treadle (of a loom).
calcolabile [calcolAbile], *a.* Calculable.
calcolare, *v.t.* To calculate, to reckon, to estimate, to compute; to reflect upon.
calcolatore, calcolatrice, *n.m.f.* One who calculates; *n.f.* calculating machine, computer.
calcolazione, *n.f.* (*obs.*) Calculation.
calcolo [cAlcolo], *n.m.* Calculation, reckoning, computation; (*Med.*) calculus; gravel stone. **Fare un —,** to estimate; (*Med.*) **— biliare,** gall-stone; (*Math.*) **— differenziale,** differential calculus; **— integrale,** integral calculus.
calcomania [calcomanIa], *n.f.* Transfers (children's game).
calda, *n.f.* Heating (of iron, etc., in a furnace).
caldaia [caldAia], *n.f.* Kettle; copper; boiler (of steam engine). **Esplosione della —,** boiler explosion.
caldallesse, *n.f.pl.* Chestnuts boiled in their skins.
caldamente, *adv.* Warmly.
caldana, *n.f.* Stuffiness, heat, wave of heat; flush of anger.
caldarrostaio [caldarrostAio], *n.m.* Roast-chestnut man.
caldarroste, *n.f.pl.* Roast chestnuts.
caldeggiare, *v.t.* To favour, to support, to back. **— una causa,** to support a cause.
caldeggiato, *p.p.a.* Supported, backed-up.
calderaio [calderAio], *n.m.* Coppersmith; tinker.
calderotto, *n.m.* Small kettle.
caldezza, *n.f.* Warmth; affection.
caldino, *n.m.* Hand-warmer [cp. **scaldino**].
caldino, *a.* Warmish, fairly warm.
caldissimamente, *adv.* With the utmost warmth; with the greatest urgency.
caldo, *n.m.* Heat, warmth. **Fa un gran —,** it is very hot; **il — estivo,** the summer heat; **non mi fa nè — nè freddo,** it is quite immaterial to me.
caldo, *a.* Hot, warm. **Una testa calda,** a hot-tempered person, a hot-head; **tinta calda,** warm colour; **prendersela calda,** to take it to heart.

calduccio [caldUccio], *a.* Warm, pleasantly warm.
caldura, *n.f.* Heat, hot weather.
calefacente, *a.* (*Med.*) Calefacient.
calefazione, *n.f.* Calefaction; heating.
caleffo, *n.m.* (*obs.*) Joke; laughter.
caleidoscopio [caleidoscOpio], *n.m.* Kaleidoscope.
calendario [calendArio], *n.m.* Calendar.
calende, *n.f.pl.* Kalends. **Mandare alle — greche,** to postpone indefinitely.
calendimaggio [calendimAggio], *n.m.* (*Hist.*) May Day celebration.
calendula [calEndula], *n.f.* (*Bot.*) Marigold.
calenzolo, *n.m.* (*Zool.*) Greenfinch.
calepino, *n.m.* Dictionary.
calere, *v.i.* (*Poet.*) To care for, to mind. **Non mi cale,** I don't mind, it doesn't matter to me; **mettere in non cale,** to disregard (advice); **che te ne cale?** what is it to you?
calessabile [calessAbile], *a.* (Road) suitable for a carriage [cp. **carrozzabile**].
calessaccio [calessAccio], *n.m.* Tumble-down carriage, "one-horse shay".
calessata, *n.f.* Carriageful of people.
calesse, *n.m.* Calesh, phaeton; gig.
calessina, *n.f.* Cabriolet, cab.
caletta, *n.f.* (*Mech.*) Tenon.
calettare, *v.t.* (*Mech.*) To connect, to fit in, to tenon, to dovetail.
calettatura, *n.f.* Dovetailing, tenoning; coupling.
calia [calIa], *n.f.* Gold dust, (*obs.*) bauble; (*fig.*) old stuff.
calibrare, *v.t.* To calibrate.
calibratoio [calibratOio], *n.m.* Instrument for calibrating.
calibro [cAlibro], *n.m.* Calibre; (*fig.*) character, standing.
calice [cAlice], *n.m.* Goblet; chalice; (*Bot.*) calyx.
calicò [-ò], *n.m.* Calico.
calido [cAlido], *a.* (*obs.*) Calid, warm, balmy.
califfo, *n.m.* Caliph.
caliga [cAliga], *n.f.* (*Hist.*) Footwear of Roman soldier.
caligamento, *n.m.* (*obs.*) Darkening.
caligare, *v.i.* (*obs.*) To darken, to grow dim.
caligine [calIgine], *n.f.* Mist, dimness, darkness.
caliginosità [-à], *n.f.* Mistiness.
caliginoso, *a.* Misty, clouded.
calissa, *n.f.* Serge (fabric).
callaia [callAia], *n.f.* Path; passage (through hedges, snow, etc.).
calle, *n.f.* (*Poet.*) Path, way; narrow street in Venice.
callido [cAllido], *a.* (*obs.*) Astute, smart.
callifugo [callIfugo], *n.m.* Corn-killer, corn-plaster.
calligrafia [calligrafIa], *n.f.* Calligraphy, penmanship, handwriting.
calligrafo [callIgrafo], *n.m.* Calligrapher, handwriting expert.
callista (*pl.* **callisti**), *n.m.* Chiropodist.
callo, *n.m.* (*Med.*) Corn, callus. **Fare il — a,** to get inured to, to get accustomed to.
callosità [-à], *n.f.* (*Med.*) Callosity, callus.
calloso, *a.* Hard, hardened; callous.
callotta [cp. **calotta**].

calma, *n.f.* Calm, tranquillity, quietness, stillness; (*Comm.*) stagnation (in business).
calmante, *a.* Soothing. || *n.m.* sedative.
calmare, *v.t.* To calm, to soothe, to quiet, to appease, to tranquillize. **— il dolore,** to relieve the pain; **— la febbre,** to allay the fever.
calmarsi, *v.r.* To become calm, to abate, to quiet down. **La tempesta si calma,** the storm is dying down; **si calmi!** be calm!
calmeria [calmerIa], *n.f.* (*obs.*) (*Naut.*) Doldrums, perpetual calm.
calmierare, *v.t.* To fix the price of.
calmiere, *n.m.* (*Comm.*) Decree fixing the prices of commodities.
calmo, *a.* Calm quiet, still, tranquil, peaceful; (*Comm.*) dull, flat. **Mantenersi —,** to keep calm.
calo, *n.m.* (*Comm.*) Reduction or fall (of prices); diminution; consumption; short measure, short weight.
calomelano, *n.m.* (*Med.*) Calomel.
calore, *n.m.* Heat, warmth; eagerness; vehemence; ardour; (*Med.*) rash. **Resistere al —,** to stand heat; **— bianco,** white heat; **— elettrico,** electric heat.
caloria [calorIa], *n.f.* (*Phys.*) Calorie.
calorico [calOrico], *a.* (*Phys.*) Caloric.
calorifero [calorIfero], *n.m.* Heating apparatus, radiator.
calorimetro [calorImetro], *n.m.* (*Phys.*) Calorimeter.
calorosamente, *adv.* Warmly.
calorosità [-à], *n.f.* Warmth, heat.
caloroso, *a.* Warm. **Una dimostrazione calorosa,** a warm reception.
caloscia [calOscia], *n.f.* Overshoe, galosh.
calotta, *n.f.* Skull-cap; (*Eccles.*) calotte; (*Mech.*) cap. **— dell'orologio,** watch-case; **— cranica,** brain-pan, brain-case; **— polare,** polar cap.
calpestamento, *n.m.* Trampling down.
calpestare, *v.t.* To trample on, to trample down, to tread upon; to vilify.
calpestatore, calpestatrice, *n.m.f.* Oppressor.
calpestio [calpestIo], *n.m.* Trampling; pattering of feet.
calta, *n.f.* (*Bot.*) Marsh marigold, kingcup.
calterire, *v.t.* (*obs.*) To spill, to waste.
caluggine, calugine [callUgine], *n.f.* Down (of young birds).
calumare, *v.t.* (*Naut.*) To pay out a cable.
calumarsi, *v.r.* To lower oneself by a rope.
calumo, *n.m.* (*Naut.*) Length of cable.
calunnia [calUnnia], *n.f.* Libel, calumny, slander. **Sparger calunnie,** to spread calumnies, to publish libels.
calunniamento, *n.m.* (*obs.*) Libelling, slandering.
calunniare, *v.t.* To slander, to libel; to backbite, to malign, to calumniate.
calunniato, *p.p.a.* Slandered.
calunniatore, calunniatrice, *n.m.f.* Slanderer, calumniator.
calunniosamente, *adv.* Libellously, slanderously.
calunnioso, *a.* Calumnious, libellous, slanderous.
calura, *n.f.* Great heat; stuffiness.
calvario [calvArio], *n.m.* Calvary; series of troubles.
calvezza, *n.f.* Baldness [cp. **calvizie**].

calvinismo, *n.m.* Calvinism.
calvinista (*pl.* **calvinisti**), *n.m.* Calvinist.
calvinistico, *a.* Calvinistic.
calvizie [calvIzie], *n.f.* Baldness.
calvo, *n.m.a.* Bald man; bald, bald-headed.
calza, *n.f.* Stocking, long hose; sock; wick (of a lamp). **Un paio di calze di nailon,** a pair of nylon stockings; **calze da uomo,** men's socks.
calzaiolo [calzaiOlo], *n.m.* Hosier.
calzamento, *n.m.* (*obs.*) Covering for foot or leg collectively.
calzante, *a.* Suitable, fitting; tight; (*fig.*) pertinent, to the point.
calzare, *v.t.i.* To put on (shoes or gloves); to fit, to suit. **Questi guanti calzano bene,** these gloves are a perfect fit.
calzare, *n.m.* (*Poet.*) Stocking, hose; shoe. **Andare coi calzari di piombo,** to proceed with caution.
calzato, *p.p.a.* Shod. **Asino vestito e —,** an ignoramus.
calzatoio [calzatOio], *n.m.* Shoehorn.
calzatura, *n.f.* Footwear.
calzaturificio [calzaturifIcio], *n.m.* Shoe factory.
calzerotto, *n.m.* Sock.
calzetta, *n.f.* Stocking, sock.
calzettaio [calzettAio], *n.m.* Hosier.
calzetteria [calzetterIa], *n.f.* Hosiery.
calzino, *n.m.* Sock. (*colloq.*) **Tirare il —,** to die, to kick the bucket.
calzo, *n.m.* (*obs.*) Style of shoemaking, of footwear. **Un bel —,** a good style of shoe.
calzolaio [calzolAio], *n.m.* Shoemaker.
calzoleria [calzolerIa], *n.f.* Shoeshop.
calzoncini, *n.m.pl.* Children's drawers; (*Sport*) shorts.
calzoni, *n.m.pl.* Trousers; slacks.
camaleonte, *n.m.* (*Zool.*) Chameleon.
camarilla, *n.f.* Clique; cabal.
camarlinga, *n.f.* Nun acting as bursar of her convent.
camarlingheria [camarlingherIa], *n.f.* Bursar's office.
camarlingo, *n.m.* Steward, bursar, treasurer (of a convent, etc.).
camauro [camAuro], *n.m.* The pope's cap.
cambiabile [cambiAbile], *a.* Mutable, changeable; exchangeable.
cambiale, *n.f.* (*Comm.*) Bill (of exchange), promissory note. **— a vista,** bill payable at sight; **— pagabile al portatore,** bill payable on demand; **— a breve scadenza,** short-dated bill; **— protestata,** dishonoured bill; **scontare una —,** to discount a bill; **girare una —,** to endorse a bill; **avallare una —,** to back a bill.
cambiamento, *n.m.* Change, mutation, alteration. (*Mil.*) **— di fronte,** change of front; (*Motor.*) **— di marcia,** reversing gear.
cambiamonete, *n.m.* [cp. **cambiavalute**].
cambiare, *v.t.i.* To change, to exchange, to alter, to transform. **— (di) casa,** to move (house); **— vita,** to turn over a new leaf; **— idea,** to change one's mind; **— di colore,** to turn pale; **il vento cambia,** the wind is shifting; **cambiamo discorso,** let us drop the subject.
cambiario [cambiArio], *a.* Of exchange. **Effetto —,** bill of exchange.
cambiarsi, *v.r.* To change. **— il vestito,** to change one's dress; **— in viso,** to change colour.
cambiavalute, *n.m.* Moneychanger.
cambio [cAmbio], *n.m.* Change, exchange; (*Comm.*) rate of exchange; (*colloq.*) small change; barter. **In — di,** instead of; **fare un —,** to exchange; **non ho —,** I have no small change; (*Comm.*) **— marittimo,** bottomry; **agente di —,** stock-broker; **lettera di —,** bill of exchange; **— alto,** high rate of exchange; (*Motor.*) **— di velocità,** change of gear, gear-box.
cambista (*pl.* **cambisti**), *n.m.* Money-changer.
cambrì [-ì], *n.m.* Cambric (fabric).
cambusa, *n.f.* (*Naut.*) Galley; store-room.
cambusiere, *n.m.* (*Naut.*) Steward.
camelia [camElia], *n.f.* (*Bot.*) Camellia.
camelopardo, *n.m.* (*obs.*) Giraffe.
camene, *n.f.pl.* The (Nine) Muses.
camera [cAmera], *n.f.* Chamber, room; bedroom. **— di Commercio,** Chamber of Commerce; **— dei Pari, dei Comuni,** House of Lords, Commons; **— dei Deputati,** Chamber of Deputies; **— del Lavoro,** Labour exchange; **— di Compensazione,** clearing-house (for banks); **— ammobigliata,** furnished room; **camere d'affittare,** rooms to let; (*Phot.*) **— oscura,** dark room; (*Naut.*) **— di poppa,** after-cabin; **— di custodia,** strong-room.
camerale, *a.* Pertaining to State administration.
camerata, *n.m.* Comrade, companion, chum.
camerata, *n.f.* Dormitory, barrack-room; (*Hist.*) club, society.
cameratismo, *n.m.* Fellowship, companionship.
cameretta, *n.f.* Small room.
cameriera, *n.f.* Chambermaid; waitress.
cameriere, *n.m.* Waiter.
camerino, *n.m.* (*Theat.Sport*) Dressing-room; box-office; water closet.
camerlengo, *n.m.* Treasurer (of Holy See); bursar (of convent) [cp. **camarlengo**].
camerotto, *n.m.* (*Naut.*) Steward.
camice [cAmice], *n.m.* (*Eccles.*) Surplice; (*Med.*) gown; smock.
camiceria [camicerIa], *n.f.* Shirt factory.
camicetta, *n.f.* Blouse.
camicia [camIcia], *n.f.* Shirt, shift; (*Tech.*) cover, case, wrapper. **— di forza,** strait-jacket; **in maniche di —,** in shirt-sleeves; **— da donna,** chemise; **è nato con la —,** he was born with a silver spoon in his mouth; (*Mech.*) **— d'acqua,** water jacket.
camiciaio [camiciAio], *n.m.* Shirt-maker.
camiciola, *n.f.* Bodice; flannel, vest.
camiciotto, *n.m.* Overall.
caminetto, Fireplace, chimney.
caminiera, *n.f.* Chimney-piece, mantelpiece; fire-guard.
camino, *n.m.* Chimney, fireplace. **Gola di —,** flue.
camionabile [camionAbile], *a.* Suitable for heavy traffic (of a road).
camionale, *n.f.* Road suitable for lorries.
camione, *n.m.* Lorry, motor lorry; truck.
camionetta, *n.f.* Jeep.
camionista (*pl.* **camionisti**), *n.m.* Lorry-driver, truck-driver.
camma, *n.f.* (*Tech.*) Cam.
cammelliere, *n.m.* Camel-driver.

cammello, *n.m.* (*Zool.*) Camel.
cammeo [cammEo], *n.m.* Cameo.
camminamento, *n.m.* (*Mil.*) Communication trench.
camminante, *n.m.* Wayfarer, tramp.
camminare, *v.i.* To walk, to march; to go on, to step out, to go on foot. **— a gran passi,** to stride along; **cammina!** Go on! (*Motor.*) **la macchina cammina bene,** the car goes well.
camminare, *n.m.* (Style of) walking. **L'ho conosciuto al —,** I knew him by his walk.
camminata, *n.f.* Walk, stroll, ramble; gait.
camminato, *p.p.a.* Trodden (of a path).
camminatore, camminatrice, *n.m.f.* Pedestrian, walker.
camminatura, *n.f.* Gait.
cammino, *n.m.* Path, pathway, road; journey; course. **— facendo,** on the way; **mettersi in —,** to set out; **a metà del —,** half way.
camomilla, *n.f.* (*Bot.*) Camomile.
camorra, *n.f.* Camorra, Neapolitan criminal association.
camorrista (*pl.* **camorristi**), *n.m.* Member of the Camorra.
camosciare, *v.t.* To prepare shammy leather.
camosciatura, *n.f.* Preparation of shammy leather.
camoscino, *n.m.* Shammy leather.
camoscio [camOscio], *n.m.* (*Zool.*) Chamois. **Pelle di —,** shammy leather.
camozza, *n.f.* (*Zool.*) Female chamois.
campagna, *n.f.* Country, countryside; the fields; (*Naut.*) open sea; (*Mil.*) campaign. **Casa di —,** country house; **andare in —,** to go to the country (for a holiday); (*Mil.*) **artiglieria da —,** field artillery; **— elettorale,** electoral campaign; **Campagna Romana,** open country round Rome; **far —,** to take one's holidays.
campagnolo, campagnuolo, *n.m.a.* Countryman, peasant; farmer; rural, rustic.
campale, *a.* (*Mil.*) Pitched; decisive, pertaining to the battlefield. **Battaglia —,** pitched battle; (*fig.*) **giornata —,** field-day, decisive day, hard day's work.
campamento, *n.m.* Victuals, rations.
campana, *n.f.* Bell; glass case. **Suonar le campane,** to ring the bells; **essere di campane grosse,** to be hard of hearing; **far —,** to put one's hand to one's ear; **— da palombaro,** diving-bell; **boa a —,** bell-buoy.
campanaccio [campanAccio], *n.m.* Cow-bell, cattle-bell.
campanaio [campanAio], *n.m.* Bell-ringer; campanologist.
campanario [campanArio], *a.* Pertaining to the art of bell-founding; pertaining to bells. **Torre campanaria,** belfry.
campanaro, *n.m.* Bell-ringer.
campanella, *n.f.* Small church bell; (*Bot.*) bluebell.
campanello, *n.m.* Hand-bell; doorbell. **Suonare il —,** to ring the bell.
campaniforme, *a.* Bell-shaped.
campanile, *n.m.* Bell-tower, belfry; steeple.
campanilismo, *n.m.* Parochialism, provincialism.
campanilista, *n.m.* Village pump politician; chauvinist.
campanula [campAnula], *n.f.* (*Bot.*) Canterbury bell.
campare, *v.t.i.* To live, to live upon; to save oneself, to escape. **Non camperà molto,** he won't live long; **— la vita,** to earn one's living with difficulty; **— d'aria,** to live on nothing; **campare bene,** to get on all right; **si campa,** one just manages to exist.
campata, *n.f.* (*Arch.*) Span of a bridge.
campeggiamento, *n.m.* (*Mil.*) Encampment.
campeggiare, *v.t.* To camp, to encamp; to take the field; to set off; to stand out. **Lo scudo campeggia sulla bandiera,** the shield stands out on the standard.
campeggiatore, campeggiatrice, *n.m.f.* Camper.
campeggio [campEggio], *n.m.* Camping, camping out; (*Bot.*) logwood.
campestre, *a.* Rural, countrified, rustic.
campestremente, *adv.* Rurally, in a rustic way.
campicello, *n.m.* Small-holding.
campicchiare, *v.i.* To live from hand to mouth.
campidoglio [campidOglio], *n.m.* Capitol (in Rome).
campiello, *n.m.* Small city square in Venice.
campionario [campionArio], *n.m.a.* Book of patterns or samples; sample. **Fiera campionaria,** sample fair.
campionato, *n.m.* Championship.
campionatura, *n.f.* Sampling.
campione, *n.m.* Pattern, sample, specimen, model; champion (esp. in sport); defender. **— mondiale,** world champion.
campo, *n.m.* Field; space; ground; camp; time, opportunity; (*Her.*) field. (*Mil.*) **— trincerato,** entrenched camp; **— delle corse,** racecourse; **dar —,** to give the opportunity; **scendere in —,** to take the field; **— di giuoco,** playing-ground; **— di tennis,** tennis-court; (*Aviat.*) **— d'aviazione,** airfield; (*Radio*) **— d'onda,** wave-length.
camposanto, *n.m.* Cemetery, churchyard.
campucchiare, *v.i.* To live in privation, in abject poverty.
camuffare, *v.t.* To disguise, to camouflage.
camuffarsi, *v.r.* To disguise oneself.
camuso, *a.* Snub-nosed.
Canada [canadA], *n.m.* Canada.
canadese, *n.m.a.* Canadian.
canaglia [canAglia], *n.f.* Rabble, canaille.
canagliata, *n.f.* Action of the rabble; base trick.
canagliesco, *a.* Rowdy.
canagliume, *n.m.* Rowdy crowd.
canaio [canAio], *n.m.* Dog-fancier.
canaiuolo, *n.m.* Dark variety of grape.
canale, *n.m.* Canal, (artificial) water-course; channel; pipe, gutter; tube; duct. **— della Manica,** English Channel; **— per lubrificazione,** oil groove; **— di scolo,** drain, sewer.
canaletto, canalino, *n.m.* Small canal.
canalizzare, *v.t.* To canalize.
canalizzazione, *n.f.* Canalization.
canalone, *n.m.* Deep gulley down a mountainside.
canapa, canape [cAnapa, cAnape], *n.f.* (*Bot.*) Hemp. **Treccia di —,** hemp twist.
canapaia [canapAia], *n.f.* Field of hemp.
canapaio [canapAio], *n.m.* Dealer in hemp; hemp field.

canapè [-è], *n.m.* Sofa, settee.
canapificio [canapifIcio], *n.m.* Hemp mill.
canapino, *n.m.a.* Hemp-dresser; hempen.
canapo [cAnapo], *n.m.* Cable, rope. **Passare il —,** to pass all bounds.
Canarie [canArie], *n.f.pl.* Canary Islands.
canarino, *n.m.* (*Zool.*) Canary.
canavaccio [canavAccio], *n.m.* Coarse linen cloth; canvas; duster; (*Lit.*) plot (of a story), scenario.
cancan [cancAn], *n.m.* Cancan; fuss, bustle; scandal. **Fare un —,** to make a fuss.
cancellabile [cancellAbile], *a.* Capable of being cancelled.
cancellamento, *n.m.* Cancelling, cancellation.
cancellare, *v.t.* To cancel, to cross out, to strike out, to delete, to erase.
cancellata, cancellato, *n.f.m.* (Iron or wood) railing.
cancellatura, *n.f.* Erasure; effacement; deletion.
cancellazione, *n.f.* Annulment, cancellation.
cancelleresco, *a.* Chancery. **Scrittura cancelleresca,** chancery hand.
cancelleria [cancellerIa], *n.f.* (*Law*) Chancellery, Chancery; stationery. **Oggetti di —,** writing materials.
cancellierato, *n.m.* Clerkship in a tribunal; chancellorship.
cancelliere, *n.m.* Chancellor.
cancello, *n.m.* Railing; barred gate, gate.
canceroso, *a.* Cancerous.
canchero [cAnchero], *n.m.* (*obs.*) Cancer; (*colloq.*) pest, pesterer.
cancrena, *n.f.* (*Med.*) Gangrene.
cancrenoso, *a.* (*Med.*) Gangrenous.
cancrenarsi, *v.r.* To become gangrenous.
cancro, *n.m.* (*Med.Astron.*) Cancer. **Ricerche sul —,** cancer research.
candeggio [candEggio], *n.m.* Bleaching process.
candela, *n.f.* Candle; (*Motor.*) sparking-plug.
candelabro, *n.m.* Chandelier; candelabrum.
Candelaia [candelAia], *n.f.* [cp. **candelora**].
candelaio [candelAio], *n.m.* Candlemaker.
candeliere, *n.m.* Candlestick.
candelora, *n.f.* (*Eccles.*) Candlemas.
candelotto, *n.m.* Short candle; icicle.
candescente, *a.* Incandescent [cp. **incandescente**].
candidamente, *adv.* Candidly.
candidato, *n.m.* Candidate.
candidatura, *n.f.* Candidature.
candidezza, *n.f.* Whiteness; purity, righteousness.
candido [cAndido], *a.* Candid; white, clean, pure, innocent.
candire, *v.t.* To candy.
candito, *n.m.a.* Candy; candied. **Frutto —,** crystallized fruit.
candore, *n.m.* Whiteness; candour, innocence, sincerity.
cane, *n.m.* Dog; trigger (of a gun). **— da caccia,** hunting dog; **— da punta,** pointer; **— barbone,** poodle; spaniel; **— da fermo,** setter; **— di Terranova,** Newfoundland dog; **— da pastore,** sheepdog; **— randagio,** stray dog; (*fig.*) **— grosso,** bigwig; **azione da —,** disreputable action; **— che abbaia non morde,** barking dog seldom bites; **menare il can per l'aia,** to beat about the bush; **tempo da —,** foul weather; **fare una vita da —,** to lead a dog's life; **essere solo come un —,** to be lonely.
canea, *n.f.* Pack of hounds; uproar; (*fig.*) rabble.
canestra, *n.f.* Basket, hamper; wicker-work carriage.
canestraio [canestrAio], *n.m.* Basket-maker.
canestrata, *n.f.* Basketful.
canestro, *n.m.* Basket (with handle).
canettiere, *n.m.* Dog-breeder.
canevaccio, *n.m.* Duster; (*Lit.*) plot [cp. **canavaccio**].
canfino, *n.m.* Spirit of turpentine (used as illuminant).
canfora [cAnfora], *n.f.* Camphor.
canforato, *a.* Camphored; camphorated.
cangevole, cangiabile [cangEvole, cangiAbile], *a.* Changeable, mutable.
cangiamento, *n.m.* Change, alteration.
cangiante, *pres.p.a.* Changing. **Seta —,** shot-silk.
cangiare, *v.t.* To change, to alter [cp. **cambiare**].
cangiarsi, *v.r.* To transform oneself, to change.
canguro, *n.m.* (*Zool.*) Kangaroo.
caniccio [cp. **canniccio**].
canicola [canIcola], *n.f.* Dog-days; extreme heat (of summer).
canicolare, *a.* Very hot, canicular.
canile, *n.m.* Dog-kennel; hovel.
caninamente, *adv.* Dog-like.
canino, *n.m.* Puppy.
canino, *a.* Canine. **Dente —,** eye-tooth; **tosse canina,** whooping-cough; **fame canina,** ravenous hunger; **mosca canina,** horse-fly.
canizie [canIzie], *n.f.* Grey hairs, hoariness; old age. **— precoce,** premature grey hairs.
canizza, *n.f.* (*Lit.*) Insistent barking (of dogs); (*fig.*) snarling (of critics).
canna, *n.f.* Cane, reed, pipe. **— di fucile,** barrel of a gun; **— d'organo,** organ pipe; **— da pescare,** fishing-rod; **— da zucchero,** sugar cane; **— d'India,** bamboo; **essere povero in —,** to be abjectly poor.
cannamele, *n.m.f.* Sugar cane.
cannata, *n.f.* Blow with a cane or stick.
canneggiare, *v.t.* To measure land with a rod.
cannella, *n.f.* (*Bot.*) Cinnamon; small tube, small water-pipe; tap; plug. **Bere a —,** to drink from the tap; **color —,** hazel colour.
cannello, *n.m.* Tube, pipe, syphon; (*Mech.*) **— da saldare,** blow-lamp.
cannelloni, *n.m.pl.* Large macaroni.
cannelloso, *a.* Tubular.
canneto, *n.m.* Cane-brake.
cannetta, *n.f.* Small metal tube; (elegant) walking-stick.
cannibale [cannIbale], *n.m.* Cannibal.
cannibalismo, *n.m.* Cannibalism.
cannicciata, *n.f.* Trayful; hurdle.
canniccio [cannIccio], *n.m.* Tray made of reeds (for drying fruits, etc.).
cannocchiale, *n.m.* Binoculars, field-glasses; opera glasses.
cannonata, *n.f.* Discharge of a cannon; gunshot; gun-fire.
cannoncino, *n.m.* Small cannon; gun of small calibre; cream horn.

cannone, *n.m.* Cannon, gun. **— di stufa,** stove-pipe; **puntare un —,** to lay a gun, to aim.
cannoneggiamento, *n.m.* Cannonade, bombardment.
cannonneggiare, *v.t.* To bombard, to shell.
cannoniera, *n.f.* (*Naut.*) Port-hole (for a gun); gun embrasure; gun-boat.
cannoniere, *n.m.* Gunner.
cannuccia [cannUccia], *n.f.* Small reed, cane; drinking-straw; penholder.
canoa [canOa], *n.f.* (*Naut.*) Canoe.
canocchiale [cp. **cannocchiale**].
canone [cAnone], *n.m.* Canon, church law, rule; rent. **— della Messa,** Canon of the Mass; **i sacri canoni,** the holy laws; (*Mus.*) **— aperto, chiuso, sciolto,** open, close, free canon; **— annuo,** yearly rent.
canonica [canOnica], *n.f.* Presbytery, clergy house.
canonicale, *a.* Canonical.
canonicamente, *adv.* Canonically, regularly, according to the rites of the Church.
canonicato, *n.m.* Canonry.
canonichessa, *n.f.* Canoness.
canonico [canOnico], *n.m.a.* Canon; canonical. **Diritto —,** canon law.
canonista (*pl.* **canonisti**), *n.m.* Canonist.
canonizzare, *v.t.* To canonize.
canonizzazione, *n.f.* Canonization.
canoramente, *adv.* Harmoniously.
canorità [-à], *n.f.* Harmony.
canoro, *a.* Canorous, melodious. **Uccello —,** song-bird.
Canossa, *n.f.* (A castle in the Emilia.) **Andare a Canossa,** to humiliate oneself, to surrender.
canottaggio [canottAggio], *n.m.* Boating, rowing.
canottiere, *n.m.* Oarsman, rower. **Società dei canottieri,** rowing-club.
canotto, *n.m.* (*Naut.*) Ship's boat, rowing-boat; dinghy; canoe.
canova [cAnova], *n.f.* Provision store; cellar, larder.
canovaccio [cp. **canavaccio**].
canovaio [canovAio], *n.m.* Store-keeper; butler; (conventual) cellarer.
canoviere, *n.m.* Seller of wines; innkeeper.
cansare, *v.t.* To remove; to shirk (work).
cansarsi, *v.r.* To get out of the way.
cantabile [cantAbile], *a.* (*Mus.*) Singable; song-like.
cantafavola [cantafAvola], *n.m.* Cock-and-bull story.
cantaiolo, cantaiuolo [cantaiOlo, cantaiuOlo], *n.m.* Decoy bird-call; decoy bird.
cantaiolo, *a.* Singing, chirping.
cantambanco [cp. **saltimbanco**].
cantante, *n.m.f.* Singer.
cantare, *v.t.i.* To sing; to chant; to celebrate (in song); to carol; to warble; to crow; to chirp. **— a orecchio,** to sing by ear; **— intonato, stonato,** to sing in tune, out of tune; (*fig.*) **— chiaro,** to speak plainly; **cantarla a qualcuno,** to speak one's mind; **— da cane,** to bawl.
cantare, *n.m.* Singing, song; verse, canto. **I cantari,** epic songs.
cantarellare [cp. **canterellare**].
cantaride [cantAride], *n.f.* (*Zool.*) Cantharis.
cantaridina, *n.f.* (*Med.*) Cantharides, Spanish fly.
cantaro, *n.m.* Former Neapolitan measure of weight (about 100 lb.).
cantastorie [cantastOrie], *n.m.* Bard, ballad-singer.
cantata, *n.f.* (*Mus.*) Cantata. **Messa —,** High Mass.
cantatore, cantatrice, *n.m.f.* Singer.
canterano, *n.m.* Chest of drawers.
canterellamento, *n.m.* Humming.
canterellare, *v.t.i.* To hum (a tune).
canterellio [canterellIo], *n.m.* Continuous humming.
canterino, *n.m.a.* Singer; ballad singer; singing, warbling.
cantero [cAntero], *n.m.* Night-stool, basin (in commode).
cantica [cAntica], *n.f.* Poem, song; narrative poem; one of the three divisions of Dante's *Divine Comedy*.
canticchiare, *v.t.* To hum (a tune).
cantico [cAntico], *n.m.* Canticle, hymn. **— dei Cantici,** Song of Solomon.
cantiere, *n.m.* (*Naut.*) Shipyard, dockyard; yard, factory. **In —,** on the stocks.
cantilena, *n.f.* Sing-song, monotonous song; refrain; lullaby.
cantimplora, *n.f.* Ice pail, wine-cooler.
cantina, *n.f.* Cellar; canteen.
cantiniere, *n.m.* Butler; vintner.
cantino, *n.m.* (*Mus.*) Highest string on a violin; chanterelle.
canto (1), *n.m.* Singing, song, chant; warbling. **Il — del gallo,** cock-crow; **maestro di —,** singing master; **— fermo,** plain chant; **— funebre,** dirge; **— a cappella,** vocal church music; **— cromatico,** singing in semitones; **— popolare,** folk song; (*fig.*) **— del cigno,** swan-song.
canto (2), *n.m.* Corner, angle; side; part. **In un —,** in a corner; **dal — mio,** for my part; **dall'altro —,** on the other hand; **a —,** by the side of; (*Naut.*) **— di sopravvento,** weather side.
cantonale, *a.* Cantonal.
cantonata, *n.f.* Corner, street corner; angle (of building); (*fig.*) great blunder. **Prendere una —,** to make a ludicrous blunder or howler.
cantone, *n.m.* Corner; (*Pol.*) (Swiss, etc.) canton.
cantoniera, *n.f.* (*Rail.*) Signal-box; corner cupboard. **Casa —,** roadman's cabin or cottage.
cantoniere, *n.m.* Roadman, road-mender; (*Rail.*) signalman; man in charge of the line.
cantore, *n.m.* (*Eccles.*) Cantor, precentor; singer.
cantoria [cantorIa], *n.f.* (Church) choir, chantry.
cantorino, *n.m.* Service book (for the choir).
cantuccio [cantUccio], *n.m.* Internal corner (of a room, etc.); confined space; sort of biscuit.
canutamente, *adv.* Like a grey-beard, hoarily.
canutezza, *n.f.* Hoariness, greyness (of hair).
canutiglia [canutIglia], *n.f.* Gold or silver ribbon, tinsel.
canuto, *a.* Hoary, white, old.
canzonaccia [canzonAccio], *n.f.* Coarse song.

canzonare, *v.t.* To mock, to quiz, to laugh at, to twit, to make fun of, to jeer, to ridicule. **Tutti lo canzonano,** everybody laughs at him; **lui non canzona,** he is in earnest; **che si canzona?** Are we serious?
canzonatore, *n.m.* Mocker, joker, hoaxer.
canzonatoriamente, *adv.* Mockingly, jokingly.
canzonatorio [canzonatOrio], *a.* Mocking, scoffing, derisive.
canzonatura, *n.f.* Mockery, raillery, derision; hoax.
canzoncina, *n.f.* Little song.
canzone, *n.f.* Song; ballad; (*Lit.*) canzone.
canzonella, *n.f.* Joke. **Metter in —,** to make light of.
canzonetta, *n.f.* Short song; comic song.
canzonettina, *n.f.* Music-hall song; popular air.
canzonettista, *n.m.f.* Vocalist; comedian.
canzoniere, *n.m.* Collection of lyrics; song-book.
caolino, *n.m.* (*Min.*) Kaolin.
caos, *n.m.* Chaos, confusion.
caotico [caOtico], *a.* Chaotic.
capaccia [capAccia], *n.f.* Pork brawn.
capaccina, *n.f.* Headache.
capaccio [capAccio], *n.m.* Blockhead, dullard.
capacciuto, *a.* Big-headed (of vegetables, etc.).
capace, *a.* Capable, able, clever; ample, roomy, capacious.
capacità [-à], *n.f.* Capacity; ability, skill, talent; capability; competency; roominess, capaciousness; (*Comm.*) tonnage. **Misure di —,** measures of capacity; (*Law*) **— giuridica,** legal position.
capacitante, *a.* Persuasive.
capacitare, *v.t.* To persuade, to convince.
capacitarsi, *v.r.* To convince oneself; to make out. **Non posso capacitarmi perchè egli non sia riuscito,** I can't make out why he hasn't succeeded.
capale, *n.m.* Horse-bonnet.
capameno, *n.m.* Joker, wag, practical joker.
capanna, *n.f.* Hut, cabin; cottage.
capannello, *n.m.* Group of people. **Formar capannelli,** to gather in small groups.
capanno, *n.m.* Thatched hut.
capannone, *n.m.* Shed, hangar.
capannuccia [capannUccia], *n.f.* Hut, cabin; crib, manger (model for Christmas).
caparbiaggine [caparbiAggine], *n.f.* Obstinacy [cp. **caparbietà**].
caparbiamente, *adv.* Obstinately, stubbornly.
caparbieria [caparbierIa], *n.f.* (Act of) obstinacy, laziness.
caparbietà [-à], *n.f.* Obstinacy, stubbornness; headstrong behaviour.
caparbio [capArbio], *a.* Obstinate, stubborn; headstrong.
caparra, *n.f.* Earnest, earnest-money; pledge.
caparrare, *v.t.* To monopolize; to give earnest-money [cp. **accaparrare**].
capata, *n.f.* Butting (with the head). **Dare una —,** to peep in, to put in an appearance; (*colloq.*) to butt in.
capatina, *n.f.* Brief visit, call. **Dare una —** to drop in, to peep in; to put in a fleeting appearance.
capecchio [capEcchio], *n.m.* Tow, oakum. **Baffi di —,** sandy moustache.
capellame, *n.m.* Shock of hair.
capellatura, capelliera, *n.f.* Head of hair; false hair, wig [cp. **capigliatura**].
capellino, *n.m.* Fine hair, thin hair.
capello, *n.m.* Hair. **I miei capelli,** my hair; **capelli posticci,** false hair; **in capelli,** bare-headed; **a —,** exactly, perfectly; **fino ai capelli,** to the extreme limit; **mettersi le mani nei capelli,** to be desperate, to be at one's wit's end; **averne fin sopra i capelli di,** to have more than enough of.
capelluto, *a.* Long-haired. **Cuoio —,** scalp.
capelvenere [capelvEnere], *n.m.* (*Bot.*) Maidenhair fern.
capestreria [capestrerIa], *n.f.* Freak; odd action, caprice.
capestro, *n.m.* Halter, rope; capital punishment. **Gente da —,** gallows-birds.
capetto, *n.m.* Little head; capricious person.
capezzale, *n.m.* Bolster; bedside. **Essere al — di un ammalato,** to be at a sick person's bedside.
capezzolata, *n.f.* (*Arch.*) Coping (of a wall).
capezzolo [capEzzolo], *n.m.* Nipple, teat (of an animal).
capidoglio [capidOglio], *n.m.* (*Zool.*) Sperm whale.
capiente, *a.* Containing.
capienza, *n.f.* Capacity, size; content.
capifoco, *n.m.* Trestle.
capifosso, *n.m.* (*Mil.*) Main defence ditch.
capigliatura, *n.f.* Head of hair.
capilargo, *a.* Larger at the top.
capillare, *a.* Capillary. **Vaso —,** capillary vessel.
capillarità [-à], *n.f.* Capillarity.
capinera, *n.f.* (*Zool.*) Blackcap (bird).
capino, *n.m.* Little head; (*fig.*) scapegrace.
capire, *v.i.t.* To understand, to realize, to make out; to hold, to contain. **Non — più in sè dalla gioia,** to be beside oneself with joy; **si capisce benissimo che,** it is quite clear that; **non si capisce perchè,** one cannot make out why; **farsi —,** to make oneself understood; **si capisce,** certainly, of course; (*fig.*) **— il latino,** to understand the allusion.
capirosso, *n.m.* (*Zool.*) Red-crested duck; redpoll.
capistero, *n.m.* Tray or basket for carrying on the head.
capitagna, *n.f.* (*Agric.*) Headland (of a ploughed field); uncultivated land on the edge of a field.
capitale (1), *n.m.* Capital, fund, stock; riches. (*Comm.*) **— versato,** paid-up capital; **— a fondo perduto,** sunk capital; **— d'esercizio,** working capital; **— azionario,** share capital; **— di maneggio,** trading capital.
capitale (2), *n.f.* Capital (city).
capitale, *a.* Capital, chief, main; principal. **Pena —,** capital punishment; **peccati capitali,** mortal sins; **nemico —,** deadly enemy.
capitalismo, *n.m.* Capitalism.
capitalista (*pl.* **capitalisti**), *n.m.* Capitalist.
capitalistico [capitalIstico], *a.* Capitalistic.
capitalizzare, *v.t.* To capitalize; to economize; to treasure.

capitalizzazione, *n.f.* (*Comm.*) Capitalization.
capitalmente, *adv.* Capitally, principally.
capitana, *n.f.* (*Naut.*) Flagship.
capitananza, *n.f.* Captaincy, rank of captain.
capitanare, *v.t.* To lead, to command; to guide.
capitaneggiare, *v.t.* To act as a captain, to lead.
capitaneria [capitanerIa], *n.f.* Captaincy; residence of the captain; (*Naut.*) office of the harbour-master.
capitano, *n.m.* Captain; chief; commander, leader. **— di lungo corso,** captain of ocean-going vessel; **— di vascello,** (naval) captain; **— di corvetta,** (naval) lieutenant commander; **— di fregata,** (naval) commander; **— di porto,** harbour-master; **— d'armamento,** ship's husband; (*Hist.*) **— di ventura,** commander of mercenaries; **— d'industria,** captain of industry.
capitare, *v.t.i.* To arrive, to come to; to come to pass, to happen, to befall. **Capitò all'improvviso,** he came unexpectedly; **son capitato male,** I have been unlucky; **mi è capitata bella,** a strange thing has happened to me.
capitazione, *n.f.* (*obs.*) Capitation; poll-tax.
capite [cApite], *n.m.* **Generale in —,** general officer commanding; **parola in —,** word in large type in head-line of a book.
capitello, *n.m.* (*Arch.*) Capital.
capitolante, *n.m.* One who capitulates.
capitolare, *v.i.* To capitulate, to surrender; to come to terms.
capitolare, *n.m.* (*Hist.*) Capitulary, decree.
capitolare, *a.* Capitular; capitulary; belonging to cathedral chapter.
capitolarmente, *adv.* (*Eccles.*) By decree of the chapter.
capitolazione, *n.f.* Capitulation, surrender. **Le capitolazioni,** the capitulations.
capitolino, *a.* Capitoline, of the Capitol.
capitolo [capItolo], *n.m.* Chapter (of a book); cathedral chapter. **Non ha voce in —,** he has no say in the matter.
capitombolare, *v.i.* To fall headlong; to fall from top to bottom.
capitombolo [capitOmbolo], *n.m.* Headlong fall.
capitomboloni, *adv.* Head over heels, headlong.
capitondolo [capitOndolo], *n.m.* (*obs.*) Somersault.
capitone, *n.m.* (*Zool.*) Variety of eel.
capitoso, *a.* Headstrong.
capitozza, *n.f.* Pollarded tree.
capitozzare, *v.t.* To pollard, to lop.
capo, *n.m.* Head; chief, leader; top, end; article, object; (*Geog.*) cape. **— ameno,** wag; **— sventato,** feather-brain; **mal di —,** headache; **— scarico,** devil-may-care; **— d'anno,** New Year's Day; **— d'opera,** masterpiece; **— di casa,** head of the house; **— officina,** foreman of workshop; **— ufficio,** head of a department; **capi di bestiame,** head of cattle; **al — della via,** at the top of the road; **a — capotavola,** at the head of the table; **a — all'ingiù,** head downward; **a — fitto,** headlong; **da — a piedi,** from head to foot; **da —,** over again; **da — a fondo,** from beginning to end; **in — al mondo,** at the end of the world; **in — alla pagina,** at the top of the page; **in — a tre anni,** in three years' time; **— per —,** article by article; **nè — nè coda,** neither rhyme nor reason.
capobanda (*pl.* **capibanda**), *n.m.* Ringleader; (*Mus.*) bandmaster.
capobrigante (*pl.* **capibriganti**), *n.m.* Brigand chief.
capocaccia (*pl.* **capicaccia**) [capocAccia], *n.m.* Head keeper.
capocchia [capOcchia], *n.f.* Head (of match, pin, etc.).
capoccia [capOccia], *n.m.* Foreman; head of the house.
capocomico (*pl.* **capocomici**) [capocOmico], *n.m.* (*Theat.*) Leading comedian.
capocuoco (*pl.* **capicuochi**), *n.m.* Chef.
capodanno, *n.m.* New Year's Day.
capodoglio [cp. **capidoglio**].
capodopera (*pl.* **capidopera**) [capodOpera], *n.m.* Masterpiece.
capofabbrica (*pl.* **capifabbrica**) [capofAbbrica], *n.m.* Foreman (in a factory).
capofitto, *adv.* **A —,** head foremost, headlong.
capogiro (*pl.* **capogiri**), *n.m.* Giddiness, dizziness. **Avere il —,** to feel giddy.
capoguardia (*pl.* **capiguardia**) [capoguArdia], *n.m.* Head of local constabulary.
capolavoro (*pl.* **capolavori**), *n.m.* Masterpiece.
capolinea (*pl.* **capilinea**) [capolInea], *n.m.* (*Rail.*) Terminus.
capolino (*pl.* **capolini**), *n.m.* Little head. **Far —,** to peep (for curiosity); to put in a fleeting appearance.
capolista (*pl.* **capilista**), *n.m.* Head of a list, first name on a list.
capoluogo (*pl.* **capoluoghi**), *n.m.* Chief town (of province, etc.).
capomastro (*pl.* **capomastri, capimastri**), *n.m.* Foreman bricklayer, master builder.
caponaggine [caponAggine], *n.f.* Stubbornness, obstinacy.
capopagina (*pl.* **capipagina**) [capopAgina], *n.m.* (*Typ.*) Head-piece; running head.
capoparte (*pl.* **capiparte**), *n.m.* Party leader.
capopopolo (*pl.* **capipopolo**) [capopOpolo], *n.m.* Demagogue.
capoposto (*pl.* **capiposto**), *n.m.* (*Mil.*) Head of a guard-post.
caporale, *n.m.* (*Mil.*) Corporal.
caporione, *n.m.* Ringleader.
caporiparto (*pl.* **capiriparto**), *n.m.* Head of a department (in a shop).
caporovescio [caporovEscio], *adv.* Head down.
caposaldo (*pl.* **capisaldi**), *n.m.* Stronghold; base; bench-mark; (*Mil.*) **— della difesa,** key position.
caposcalo (*pl.* **capiscalo**), *n.m.* (*Aviat.*) Station commander.
caposcuola (*pl.* **capiscuola**), *n.m.* Founder of a movement (in art, letters, etc.).
caposezione (*pl.* **capisezione**), *n.m.* Head of a (Government) section.
caposquadra (*pl.* **capisquadra**), *n.m.* Squadron leader.
capostazione (*pl.* **capistazione**), *n.m.* (*Rail.*) Station-master.
capostipite (*pl.* **capistipiti**) [capostIpite], *n.m.* Founder of a family; fountain-head.

capotamburo (*pl.* **capotamburi**), *n.m.* Drum major.
capotamento, *n.m.* (*Aviat.*) Capsizal.
capotare, *v.i.* (*Aviat.*) To capsize.
capotondo, *n.m.* (*Zool.*) Species of dog-fish.
capotorto, *n.m.* (*Zool.*) Wryneck.
capotreno (*pl.* **capitreno**), *n.m.* (*Rail.*) Guard.
capoverso (*pl.* **capoversi**), *n.m.* (*Typ.*) Paragraph.
capovoga (*pl.* **capivoga**), *n.m.* (*Sport*) Stroke (rowing).
capovolgere [capovOlgere], *v.t.* To turn upside down, to upset, to reverse.
capovolgersi [capovOlgersi], *v.r.* To turn upside down; (*Naut.*) to capsize; to be reversed.
capovolta, *n.f.* Upset, capsizal, sommersault.
capovolto, *p.p.a.* Upset, capsized, reversed.
cappa, *n.f.* Letter "k"; cloak, cape, mantle, gown. — **del camino,** chimney cowl.
cappalunga, *n.f.* (*Zool.*) Razor-shell.
cappamagna, *n.f.* (*Eccles.*) State cloak worn by cardinals and bishops.
cappeggiare, *v.i.* (*Naut.*) To reef sail; to lie to (in a storm).
cappella, *n.f.* Chapel; benefice, choir. — **ardente,** mortuary chapel; **maestro di —,** choir-master; **musica a cappella,** singing to the accompaniment of the organ.
cappellaio [cappellAio], *n.m.* Hatter.
cappellania [cappellanIa], *n.f.* Chaplaincy.
cappellano, *n.m.* Chaplain.
cappellata, *n.f.* Hatful. **A cappellate,** in plenty.
cappelleria [cappellerIa], *n.f.* Hat-shop.
cappelletti, *n.m.pl.* Kind of soup; (*Hist.*) cavalrymen.
cappelliera, *n.f.* Hatbox.
cappellinaio [cappellinAio], *n.m.* Hatstand.
cappellino, *n.m.* Woman's hat, bonnet.
cappello, *n.m.* Hat, bonnet; covering; lid; (*Mech.*) cap, cross-head. — **di feltro,** felt hat; — **di paglia,** straw-hat; — **a cilindro,** top-hat; — **duro,** bowler; **mettersi il —,** to put on one's hat; **levarsi il —,** to take off one's hat; **far di —,** to raise one's hat (in greeting); **amico di —,** bowing acquaintance; **giù i cappelli!** hats off! (*colloq.*) **prendere —,** to take offence.
cappellotto, *n.m.* (*Mil.*) Percussion cap.
capperi! [cApperi], *inter.* By Jove!
cappero [cAppero], *n.m.* (*Bot.*) Caper.
cappio [cAppio], *n.m.* Knot.
capponaia [capponAia], *n.f.* Fatting coop for capons.
capponare, *v.t.* To capon, to castrate.
cappone, *n.m.* Capon; (*Naut.*) cat-head. **Far venir la pelle di —,** to make the flesh creep.
cappotta, *n.f.* Long mantle; woman's capote.
cappotto, *n.m.* Overcoat; soldier's tunic.
cappuccina, *n.f.* (*Eccles.*) Capuchin nun.
cappuccino, *n.m.* (*Eccles.*) Capuchin friar; white coffee; (*Bot.*) variety of cabbage.
cappuccio [cappUccio], *n.m.* Hood, cowl.
capra, *n.f.* Goat, nanny-goat; (*Eng.*) trestle, derrick. **Salvar — e cavoli,** to manage to have it both ways.
capraio [caprAio], *n.m.* Goatherd.
capretto, *n.m.* Kid.
capriata, *n.f.* (*Arch.*) Truss.
capriccio [caprIccio], *n.m.* Fancy, caprice, whim; temper; (*Mus.*) fanciful composition. **A —,** according to one's fancy; **per —,** through caprice; **capricci ne ha tanti,** he is full of whims.
capricciosamente, *adv.* Capriciously.
capricciosità [-à], *n.f.* Capriciousness.
capriccioso, *a.* Whimsical, fickle; unruly.
capricorno, *n.m.* (*Astron.*) Capricorn.
caprificare, *v.t.* (*Bot.*) To graft wild fig on a garden fig-tree.
caprifico, *n.m.* (*Bot.*) Wild fig.
caprifoglio [caprifOglio], *n.m.* (*Bot.*) Honeysuckle.
caprile, *n.m.* Goat house.
caprino, *n.m.* Goats' dung; smell of a billy goat.
caprino, *a.* Goatlike, goatish. **Questioni di lana caprina,** trifling matters, absurd arguments, quibbles.
capriola, *n.f.* Caper, jump, somersault. **Fare le capriole,** to cut capers.
capriolo, *n.m.* (*Zool.*) Roe-buck.
capro, *n.m.* Billy goat, he-goat. — **espiatorio,** scapegoat.
capruggine [caprUggine], *n.f.* Groove (in the stave of a barrel).
capsico [cApsico], *n.m.* (*Bot.*) Capsicum.
capsula [cApsula], *n.f.* Capsule; (*Mil.*) percussion cap.
captare, *v.i.* To seek to obtain; (*Radio*) to detect, to pick up stations.
capziosamente, *adv.* Captiously.
capzioso, *a.* Captious.
cara, *n.f.* Darling, beloved.
carabattole [carabAttole], *n.f.pl.* Baubles. **Pigliar le —,** to pack up one's belongings (for a journey).
carabina, *n.f.* Carbine; rifle, shot-gun.
carabinata, *n.f.* Shot from a gun.
carabiniere, *n.m.* Carabineer; Italian gendarme.
carabo [cArabo], *n.m.* (*Zool.*) Scarab beetle.
carabottino, *n.m.* (*Naut.*) Grating.
caracca, *n.f.* (*Naut.*) Carrack; galleon.
caracollare, *v.i.* To caracole, to wheel about (on horseback).
caraffa, *n.f.* Decanter, carafe.
Caraibi, *n.m.* Caribbean. **Mare dei Caraibi,** Caribbean Sea.
carambola [carAmbola], *n.f.* (*Billiards*) Cannon.
carambolare, *v.i.* (*Billiards*) To cannon.
caramella, *n.f.* Caramel, toffee; monocle.
caramellaio [caramellAio], *n.m.* Vendor of caramels.
caramellare, *v.t.* To candy.
caramente, *adv.* Dearly, cordially.
carantano, *n.m.* Old Austrian copper coin.
carapace, *n.m.* (*Zool.*) Carapace (of turtle. etc.).
caratare, *v.t.* To weigh in carats; to examine minutely.
caratello, *n.m.* Small barrel, keg.
caratista, *n.m.* Part-owner.
carato, *n.m.* Carat.
carattere [carAttere], *n.m.* Character, disposition, mark; letter (in print or handwriting); literary portrait. **Avere un bel —,** to have a good disposition; **il — di una**

lingua, the genius of a language; **un uomo di —**, a man of high principles; **fonderia di caratteri**, type foundry.
caratterista (*pl.* **caratteristi**), *n.m.f.* (*Theat.*) Leading comedian; character actor.
caratteristica [caratterIstica], *n.f.* Characteristic, peculiarity.
caratteristico [caratterIstico], *a.* Characteristic, typical.
caratterizzare, *v.t.* To characterize.
caratura, *n.f.* (*Comm.*) Share; partnership.
caravana [cp. **carovana**].
caravanserraglio [caravanserrAglio], *n.m.* Caravanserai.
caravella, *n.f.* (*Naut.*) Galley, caravel.
carbonaia [carbonAia], *n.f.* Coal cellar; coal bunker.
carbonaio [carbonAio], *n.m.* Coalman; dealer in charcoal; (*Naut.*) collier.
carbonarismo, *n.m.* (*Hist.*) Political views of the Carbonari.
carbonaro, *n.m.* (*Hist.*) Member of the Carboneria.
carbonata, *n.f.* (*obs.*) Grilled pork cutlet.
carbonato, *n.m.* (*Chem.*) Carbonate.
carboncello, carbonchio [carbOnchio], *n.m.* (*Med.*) Carbuncle; (*Min.*) ruby.
carbonchioso, *a.* (*Med.*) Susceptible to, or suffering from carbuncles.
carboncino, *n.m.* Charcoal (used by artists).
carbone, *n.m.* Coal; charcoal; carbon. **— fossile**, mineral coal, pit coal; **— di legno**, charcoal; **— bianco**, hydraulic or hydro-electric power; (*Naut.*) **far —**, to coal.
carbonella, *n.f.* Charcoal (in sticks).
carboneria [carbonerIa], *n.f.* (*Hist.*) Secret political society in Italy in the early 19th century.
carbonico [carbOnico], *a.* (*Chem.*) Carbonic. **Acido —**, carbon dioxide.
carboniera, *n.f.* (*Naut.*) Collier; coal cellar.
carbonifero [carbonIfero], *a.* (*Chem.*) Carboniferous.
carbonili, *n.m.pl.* Coal bunkers.
carbonio [carbOnio], *n.m.* (*Chem.*) Carbon.
carbonizzare, *v.t.* To carbonize, to char.
carbonizzazione, *n.f.* Carbonization.
carburante, *n.m.* (*Aviat.*) Fuel, aviation spirit. **Rifornirsi di —**, to refuel.
carburare, *v.t.* (*Chem.*) To carburize.
carburatore, *n.m.* (*Motor.*) Carburettor.
carburazione, *n.f.* (*Motor.*) Carburation.
carburo, *n.m.* (*Chem.*) Carbide.
carcame, *n.m.* Carcass; carrion.
carcassa, *n.f.* Carcass; (*Naut.*) skeleton (of a ship); derelict vessel; (*Elect.*) framework. **— della dinamo**, framework of the dynamo.
carceramento, *n.m.* Imprisonment.
carcerare, *v.t.* To imprison.
carcerario [carcerArio], *a.* Prison. **Guardia carceraria**, warder.
carcerato, *n.m.* Prisoner.
carcerazione, *n.f.* Imprisonment.
carcere [cArcere], *n.m.f.* Prison, gaol, jail; cell. **Le carceri**, prison.
carceriere, *n.m.* Gaoler, jailer.
carcinoma, *n.m.* (*Med.*) Carcinoma, cancer.
carciofaia [carciofAia], *n.f.* Artichoke bed.
carciofaio [carciofAio], *n.m.* Artichoke grower.
carciofo, *n.m.* (*Bot.*) Artichoke; (*fig.*) simpleton.
carco, *a.* (*Poet.*) Loaded, laden, burdened.
carda, *n.f.* Carding machine (for wool).
cardamomo, *n.m.* (*Bot.*) Cardamum.
cardanico [cardAnico], *a.* (*Mech.*) Cardan. **Giunto cardanico**, cardan joint.
cardano, *n.m.* (*Mech.*) Gimbal, shaft-drive; (*colloq.*) bowler hat.
cardare, *v.t.* To card, to comb (wool).
cardata, *n.f.* Quantity of carded wool.
cardatore, *n.m.* Wool-carder.
cardatura, *n.f.* Carding.
cardellino, cardello, *n.m.* (*Zool.*) Goldfinch.
cardenia [cp. **gardenia**].
cardeto, *n.m.* Field of thistles.
cardias [cArdias], *n.m.* (*Anat.*) Cardia, upper orifice of the stomach.
cardiaco [cardIaco], *a.* (*Anat.*) Cardiac. **Male —**, heart disease.
cardialgia [cardialgIa], *n.f.* (*Med.*) Cardialgia, heartburn.
cardinalato, *n.m.* Cardinalate.
cardinale, *n.m.a.* Cardinal; cardinal, principal. **I punti cardinali**, the cardinal points (of the compass); **numeri cardinali**, cardinal numbers.
cardinalesco, cardinalizio, *a.* Pertaining to a cardinal.
cardine [cArdine], *n.m.* Hinge, pivot. **Essere fuori dai cardini**, to be off the hinges.
cardio [cArdio], *n.m.* (*Zool.*) Cockle.
cardiografia [cardiografIa], *n.f.* (*Med.*) Cardiography.
cardiografo [cardiOgrafo], *n.m.* Cardiograph.
cardiogramma, *n.m.* Cardiogram.
cardiopalmo, *n.m.* (*Med.*) Palpitation (of the heart).
cardite, *n.f.* (*Med.*) Carditis.
cardo, cardone, *n.m.* (*Bot.*) Thistle.
carena, *n.f.* (*Naut.*) Keel; bottom (of a boat).
carenaggio [carenAggio], *n.m.* (*Naut.*) Careening; dry dock.
carenare, *v.t.* (*Naut.*) To careen; to clean the bottom (of a ship).
carenza, *n.f.* Dearth, privation.
carezza, *n.f.* Caress; stroking, fondling; coaxing; costliness. **Fare delle carezze**, to fondle, to pet, to stroke affectionately; **la — dei viveri**, the high cost of living.
carezzare, *v.t.* To caress, to fondle, to pet, to stroke.
carezzevole, carezzoso [carezzEvole], *a.* Sweet, mellifluous, gentle, caressing.
carezzevolmente, *adv.* Caressingly, gently, sweetly.
carfologia [carfologIa], *n.f.* (*Med.*) Carphology, plucking at bedclothes.
cariare, *v.t.* To decay (of teeth, bones, etc.).
cariarsi, *v.r.* To become decayed, to be decayed.
cariatide [cariAtide], *n.m.* Caryatid.
cariato, *a.* Decayed, carious.
carica [cArica], *n.f.* Charge; appointment, office, employment; dignity; (*Elect.*) charge. **— alla baionetta**, bayonet charge; **— onoraria**, honorary appointment; **entrare in —**, to take office; **tornare alla —**, to make a fresh attempt; (*Elect.*) **capacità di —**, charging capacity.
caricamento, *n.m.* Loading, the act of loading.
caricare, *v.t.* To charge, to load, to burden; to overload; (*Comm.*) to debit. **— un orologio**, to wind up a watch; **— una pipa**, to fill

a pipe; — **le merci,** to load the goods; — **un bastimento,** to load a vessel; — **le vele,** to reef the sails; (*fig.*) — **le tinte,** to exaggerate, to overdo; — **la mano,** to increase the dose; — **di busse,** to administer a sound thrashing.

caricarsi, *v.r.* To overburden oneself. — **lo stomaco,** to overload one's stomach; — **di debiti,** to plunge into debt.

caricatamente, *adv.* Affectedly.

caricato, *p.p.a.* Charged, loaded; (*fig.*) affected. **Uno stile —,** an affected style.

caricatore, *n.m.* Loader; (of gun) clip, cartridge case; (*Comm.*) freighter; shipper; coal-heaver.

caricatura, *n.f.* Caricature; an affected person.

caricaturista (*pl.* **caricaturisti**), *n.m.* Caricaturist.

carice [cArice], *n.f.* (*Bot.*) Sedge.

carico [cArico], *n.m.* Load, cargo, burden; charge, blame, reproach; expense; accusation. (*Naut.*) **Nave da —,** cargo-boat; **far — a,** to lay the blame on; — **di legnate,** a sound beating; **le spese saranno a vostro —,** the expenses will be charged up to you; **parlare a — di,** to speak against; **segnare a —,** to debit.

carico [cArico], *a.* Loaded, full, charged. — **di debiti,** burdened with debts; **rosso —,** deep red.

Cariddi, *n.m.* Charybdis.

carie, *n.f.* Decay; (*Med.*) caries.

cariglione, *n.m.* Carillion.

carina, *n.f.* Darling, sweetheart, loved one.

carino, *a.* Pretty, dear, kind.

Carinzia [carInzia], *n.f.* Carinthia.

cariola, *n.f.* Wheelbarrow [cp. **carriuola**].

cariolante, *n.m.* Barrow-boy, barrow-pusher.

carisma, *n.m.* (*Theol.*) Holy grace. **I carismi,** the gifts of the Holy Spirit.

carità [-à], *n.f.* Charity; love, benevolence; alms; compassion, pity. — **di patria,** love of one's country; **mancanza di —,** uncharitableness; **per —!** for goodness sake! **dama di —,** district visitor; **Suore della Carità,** Sisters of Charity; **ospizio di —,** almshouse.

caritatevole [caritatEvole], *a.* Charitable, merciful, compassionate.

caritatevolmente, *adv.* Charitably.

carlina, *n.f.* (*Bot.*) Carline thistle.

carlinga, *n.f.* (*Aviat.*) Cockpit.

carlino, *n.m.* (*Hist.*) Ancient Neapolitan coin worth about 4d.

carlista, *n.m.* (*Hist.*) (Spanish) Carlist.

Carlo, *n.m.* Charles.

Carlomagno, *n.m.* Charlemagne.

carlona, *adv.* **Alla —,** carelessly, haphazard.

carme, *n.m.* (*Poet.*) Poem, ode.

Carmelita, Carmelitano, *n.m.a.* Carmelite friar. — **scalzo,** discalced Carmelite.

carminare, *v.t.* To card (wool).

carminativo, *a.* (*Med.*) (*obs*). Carminative.

carmine [cArmine], *n.m.* Carmelite convent.

carminio [carmInio], *n.m.* Carmine, red.

carnagione, *n.f.* Complexion. — **fresca,** rosy complexion.

carnaio [carnAio], *n.m.* Charnel-house; carnage, massacre.

carnale, *a.* Carnal, sensual.

carnalità [-à], *n.f.* Carnality, lust.

carnalmente, *adv.* Carnally; in the flesh

carname, *n.m.* Mass of putrified flesh, carnage.

carnasciale, *n.m.* Carnival [cp. **carnevale**].

carnascialesco, *a.* Carnival. **Canti carnascialeschi,** songs sung in Carnival time (in old Florence).

carne, *n.f.* Flesh; meat; pulp (of fruit). — **macellata,** butcher's meat; — **di manzo, vitello,** beef, veal; — **salata,** corned beef; — **in scatola,** tinned, canned meat; — **congelata,** frozen meat; — **tritata,** minced meat, mince; — **stufata,** stewed meat, stew; **essere in —,** to be plump; **rimettersi in —,** to put on flesh; **sono io in — ed ossa,** here I am in person; **tagliare fino alla —,** to cut to the quick; **metter troppa — al fuoco,** to undertake too many things; (*Theol.*) **la resurrezione della —,** the resurrection of the body.

carnefice [carnEfice], *n.m.* Hangman, executioner; (*fig.*) brutal fellow.

carneficina, *n.f.* Carnage, slaughter, massacre.

carneo [cArneo], *a.* Fleshy.

carnevalata, *n.f.* Carnival revelry.

carnevale, *n.m.* Carnival.

carnevalesco, *a.* Pertaining to Carnival.

carnevalone, *n.m.* Four extra days of Carnival peculiar to Milan.

carniccio [carnIccio], *n.m.* Inner side of a hide; scraps of skin, etc., used for making glue.

carnicino, *a.* Flesh-coloured.

carniera, carniere, *n.f.m.* Game-bag.

carnivoro [carnIvoro], *n.m.a.* (*Zool.*) Carnivore; carnivorous.

carnosità [-à], *n.f.* Plumpness, obesity.

carnoso, *a.* Fleshy; muscular.

carnovale [cp. **carnevale**].

carnume, *n.m.* (*Med.*) Excrescence.

caro, *n.m.* Loved one, darling. **I nostri cari,** our loved ones; **scusami, mia cara,** excuse me, darling.

caro, *a.* Dear (in all senses), beloved; expensive, precious. **È un — ragazzo,** he's a dear boy; — **Lei,** my dear sir; **aver —,** to value, to esteem; **mi sarebbe più —,** I should prefer; **costa troppo —,** it is too dear.

caro, *adv.* Dearly, dear. **Le costerà —,** it will cost you dear.

carogna, *n.f.* Carrion; (*fig.*) disreputable fellow, rotter.

carola, *n.f.* (*Lit.*) Ballad; dance in a ring.

carolare, *v.i.* To dance in a ring.

carolina, *n.f.* Variety of billiards, played with five balls.

carolingio [carolIngio], *n.m.a.* Carolingian.

carolo, *n.m.* (*Agric.*) Disease of the rice plant.

Caronte, *n.m.* (*Myth.*) Charon.

carosello, *n.m.* Circus merry-go-round; (*Hist.*) tournament.

carota, *n.f.* (*Bot.*) Carrot; (*fig.*) lie. **Piantare carote,** to lie, to tell untruths.

carotaio [carotAio], *n.m.* Carrot-seller.

carotide [carOtide], *n.f.* (*Anat.*) Carotid.

carovana, *n.f.* Caravan; fleet (of vehicles); convoy. **Carro —,** caravan (house on wheels).

carovaniera, *n.f.* Caravan route.

carovaniere, *n.m.* Man who leads beasts in a caravan.

carovita, caroviveri [carovIveri], *n.m.* High cost of living.
carpa, *n.f.* (*Zool.*) Carp.
carpare, *v.i.* (*obs.*) To go on all fours.
Carpazi, *n.m.pl.* Carpathians.
carpenteria [carpenterIa], *n.f.* Carpentry; carpenter's shop.
carpentiere, *n.m.* Carpenter; joiner.
carpine, carpino [cArpine, cArpino], *n.m.* (*Bot.*) Hornbeam.
carpio, carpione [cArpio], *n.m.* (*Zool.*) Carp.
carpire, *v.t.* To snatch away, to seize, to extort.
carpita, *n.f.* (*obs.*) Kind of blanket.
carpo, *n.m.* (*Anat.*) Wrist, carpus.
carpone, carponi, *adv.* On all fours. **Andare carponi,** to go on all fours.
carradore, *n.m.* Cartwright, cart builder; wheelwright.
carraia [carrAia], *n.f.* Carriage road.
carraio [carrAio], *n.m.* Wheelwright.
carrata, *n.f.* Cartload.
carreggiabile [carreggiAbile], *a.* Practicable for vehicles. **Strada —,** carriage-way; cart-road.
carreggiare, *v.t.* To convey in a cart.
carreggiata, *n.f.* Cartway, wheel-track. (*fig.*) **Tornare in —,** to go right again; to return to the subject; **uscir di —,** to go astray; to wander from the subject.
carreggio [carrEggio], *n.m.* Cartage, freight; convoys, wagons.
carreggio [carreggIo], *n.m.* Continual passing of carts.
carrello, *n.m.* (*Rail.*) Trolley; (*Aviat.*) carriage. (*Aviat.*) — **d'atterraggio,** under-carriage.
carretta, *n.f.* Small cart, tumbril. **Tirare la —,** to drudge, to slave.
carrettaio [carrettAio], *n.m.* Carter.
carrettata, *n.f.* Cartload.
carrettiere, *n.m.* Carter, wagoner.
carretto, *n.m.* Barrow, hand-cart.
carrettone, *n.m.* Covered wagon.
carriaggio [carriAggio], *n.m.* Cartage, carriage (*Mil.*) train, baggage (of an army).
carriera, *n.f.* Career; course, race, speed. **Far —,** to succeed in one's profession; **a gran —,** at full speed; **scegliere una —,** to choose a career; (*Comm.*) — **fallimento,** bankruptcy.
carrista (*pl.* **carristi**), *n.m.* (*Mil.*) Driver (of armoured car or tank).
carriuola, *n.f.* Wheelbarrow.
carro (pl. **carri,** *m.*, **carra,** *f.*) *n.m.* Cart, car; van, wagon; lorry, truck; (*Typ.*) case. **A carra, a carri,** in large quantities; (*Rail.*) — **bagagli,** luggage van; — **merci,** goods truck; — **di scorta,** (engine) tender; — **caravana,** caravan (on wheels); (*Mil.*) — **blindato,** armoured car; — **armato,** tank; — **funebre,** hearse; — **rimorchiato,** trailer (to motor vehicle); — **di Tespi,** travelling theatre; **mettere il — avanti ai buoi,** to put the cart before the horse; (*Astron.*) **il Gran Carro, il Piccolo Carro,** the Great Bear, the Little Bear.
carroccio [carrOccio], *n.m.* (*Hist.*) War chariot of the Italian Communes.
carronata, *n.f.* Carronade.
carrozza, *n.f.* Carriage, coach, cab; railway carriage. (*Rail.*) — **diretta,** through coach; — **letto,** sleeping-car; — **ristorante,** dining-car; — **da nolo,** hired carriage.
carrozzabile [carrozzAbile], *a.* Practicable for vehicles.
carrozzaio [carrozzAio], *n.m.* Carriage-builder.
carrozzata, *n.f.* Coachful; drive in a carriage.
carrozzella, *n.f.* Cab (Neapolitan); bath-chair.
carrozzeria [carrozzerIa], *n.f.* Carriage-works; body of a motor-car.
carrozziere, *n.m.* Coachman; coach-builder; (*Motor.*) body **repairman**.
carrozzetta, *n.f.* (*Motor.*) Small car. **Moto —,** side-car.
carrozzina, *n.f.* Perambulator, pram.
carrozzino, *n.m.* Light carriage; bath-chair; pram.
carrozzone, *n.m.* Large car, heavy wagon; caravan.
carruba, *n.f.* Carob (fruit).
carrubo, *n.m.* (*Bot.*) Carob (tree).
carruccio [carrUccio], *n.m.* Baby's go-cart.
carrucola [carrUcola], *n.f.* (*Mech.*) Pulley. (*fig.*) **Ungere la — a qualcuno,** to flatter or bribe someone.
carrucolare, *v.t.* To raise with a pulley, to employ a pulley.
carta, *n.f.* Paper; card (in all senses); document; map. — **da lettere,** notepaper; — **da disegno,** drawing-paper; — **moneta,** paper money, currency; — **bollata,** stamped paper; — **protocollo,** — **ministro,** foolscap; — **velina,** tissue paper; — **marezzata,** marbled paper; — **smerigliata,** emery-paper; — **vetrata,** glass-paper, sandpaper; — **igienica,** toilet-paper; — **lucida,** tracing-paper; — **carbone,** carbon paper; (*Comm.*) — **breve,** short bill; **mettere le carte in tavola,** to put one's cards on the table; **dare le carte,** to deal (at cards); **mischiar le carte,** to shuffle; **dare — bianca,** to give carte-blanche; **cambiar le carte in mano,** to mislead wilfully.
cartabello, *n.m.* (*obs.*) Pamphlet.
cartaccia [cartAccia], *n.f.* Waste paper, litter.
cartaceo [cartAceo], *a.* Paper. **Moneta cartacea,** paper money.
Cartagine [cartAgine], *n.f.* (*Hist.*) Carthage.
cartaginese, *n.m.a.* Carthaginian.
cartagloria [cartaglOria], *n.f.* (*Eccles.*) Altar-card.
cartaio [cartAio], *n.m.* Paper-maker.
cartamo [cArtamo], *n.m.* (*Bot.*) Safflower, bastard saffron.
cartapecora [cartapEcora], *n.f.* Sheepskin parchment, vellum.
cartapesta, *n.f.* Papier-mâché.
cartasciuga, cartasciugante, *n.f.* Blotting-paper.
cartastraccia [cartastrAccia], *n.f.* Packing-paper [cp. **carta assorbente**].
cartata, *n.f.* Paperful.
carteggiare, *v.i.* To keep up a correspondence.
carteggio [cartEggio], *n.m.* Correspondence, documents, papers.
cartella, *n.f.* Sheet of paper; brief-case; (*Comm.*) share certificate, bond; lottery ticket; portfolio, satchel, bag. — **da scrittoio,** writing-pad; — **da scolaro,** school satchel; **Cartelle del Debito Pubblico,** Government bonds.

cartellaccio [cartellAccio], *n.m.* Defamatory notice.
cartelliera, *n.f.* Cabinet for papers.
cartellino, *n.m.* Label, ticket; business card.
cartello, *n.m.* Placard, poster, bill; notice, label; name above shop; (*Comm.*) trust, combine, cartel. — **di sfida,** challenge.
cartellone, *n.m.* Placard, wall-poster.
carter, *n.m.* (*Motor.*) Crank case; gear case
cartesiano, *a.* (*Phil.*) Cartesian.
carticino, *n.m.* Inserted pages in a book.
cartiera, *n.f.* Paper-mill.
cartiglio, *n.m.* (*Arch.*) Ornamental scroll.
cartilagine [cartilAgine], *n.f.* Cartilage.
cartilaginoso, *a.* Cartilaginous.
cartina, *n.f.* Scrap of paper; (*Med.*) powder; dose. — **d'aghi,** packet of needles.
cartocciata, *n.f.* Bagful.
cartoccio [cartOccio], *n.m.* Paper bag; small parcel; (*Arch.*) cartouche.
cartografia [cartografIa], *n.f.* Cartography.
cartografo [cartOgrafo], *n.m.* Cartographer.
cartolaio [cartolAio], *n.m.* Stationer.
cartoleria [cartolerIa], *n.f.* Stationer's shop; stationery.
cartolina, *n.f.* Post-card, card. — **illustrata,** picture post-card.
cartomanzia [cartomanzIa], *n.f.* Cartomancy.
cartonaggio [cartonAggio], *n.m.* Cartoon work; packing in cardboard.
cartoncino, *n.m.* Thin card; correspondence or invitation card.
cartone, *n.m.* Cardboard; cartoon. **I cartoni di Raffaello,** Raphael's cartoons.
cartuccia [cartUccia], *n.f.* Cartridge; round (of ammunition). — **a salve,** blank cartridge.
cartucciera, *n.f.* Cartridge-belt; bandolier.
caruncola [carUncola], *n.f.* (*Med.*) Caruncle; wattle.
caruso, *n.m.* Youth employed in Sicilian sulphur mines; young man.
carvi, *n.m.* (*Bot.*) Caraway.
casa, *n.f.* House, home, household; dynasty; hostel; establishment; business firm. — **di campagna,** country house; — **di commercio,** business house, firm; — **di correzione,** reformatory; — **di salute,** nursing home; — **Reale,** royal household; — **editrice,** publishing house; **amico di —,** friend of the family; **faccende di —,** household matters; **essere di —,** to be like one of the family; **fare gli onori di —,** to receive guests; **fatto in —,** home-made; **andare a —,** to go home; **andare di — in —,** to go from door to door; **stare in —,** to stay at home; **governo di —** housekeeping; **donna di —,** housewife; **Dove sta di —?** Where do you live? **È a — il signor X?** Is Mr. X at home? **a — mia non si fa,** this is by no means the thing to do; **sta a — del diavolo,** he's a long way off; **metter su —,** to set up house; (*Football*) **in —,** at home; **fuori —,** away.
casacca, *n.f.* Great-coat. (*fig.*) **Un volta —,** a turncoat.
casacchino, *n.m.* Woman's cape.
casaccio [casAccio], *n.m.* Unpleasant affair. **A —,** at random, heedlessly.
casale, *n.m.* Hamlet, village.
casalingo, *a.* Homely, domestic, home-made. **Alla casalinga,** in a homely way.
casamatta, *n.f.* (*Mil.*) Casemate.
casamento, *n.m.* Tenement house.
casare, casarsi, *v.t.r.* (*obs.*) To marry (a husband) [cp. **accasare**].
casaro, *n.m.* Cheesemaker.
casata, *n.f.* Lineage; illustrious family.
casato, *n.m.* Surname; birth, origin.
cascaggine [cascAggine], *n.f.* Weakness; drowsiness; (*fig.*) mawkishness.
cascame, *n.m.* Shred; waste. **Cascami di cotone,** cotton-waste.
cascamorto, *n.m.* Mawkish fellow; nincompoop. **Fare il —,** to make sheep's eyes, to dangle after.
cascante, *a.* Falling; feeble, mawkish.
cascare, *v.i.* To fall, to stumble; to fall into ruins; to tumble down. — **dal sonno,** to be dying for want of sleep; — **dalla fame,** to be dying of hunger; (*fig.*) **è cascato ritto,** he has fallen on his feet; **Dove andrà a —?** What will become of him? **chi casca, casca,** I don't care what happens; **i denti gli cascano uno a uno,** he is losing his teeth one by one; **cascai dalle nuvole!** I was astounded! **ci è cascato,** he has been caught; — **morto su una cosa,** to be mad to get a thing.
cascata, *n.f.* Fall; waterfall, cascade.
cascatella, *n.f.* Small waterfall, cascade.
cascaticcio, cascatoio [cascatIccio, cascatOio], *n.m.* Ready to fall (of fruit); weak, frail.
cascatura, *n.f.* (*obs.*) Siftings.
caschetto, *n.m.* Casque, small helmet.
cascimirra, *n.f.* Cashmere (wool).
cascina, *n.f.* Farm; dairy. **Le Cascine,** park in Florence.
cascinaio [cascinAio], *n.m.* Farmer, dairyman farmer.
cascinale, *n.m.* Large farm, farmstead.
cascino, *n.m.* Cheese-mould.
casco, *n.m.* Helmet, pith helmet. — **coloniale,** topee.
cascola [cAscola], *n.f.* (*Agric.*) Wheat grown for its straw (for hat-making).
caseggiato, *n.m.* Block of houses.
caseificio [caseifIcio], *n.m.* Cheese-factory, dairy.
caseina, *n.f.* (*Chem.*) Casein.
casella, *n.f.* Pigeon-hole; compartment in a cabinet or desk. — **postale,** post-office box.
casellante, *n.m.* (*Rail.*) Linesman, ganger; keeper of level crossing.
casellario [casellArio], *n.m* Nest of pigeon-holes; filing cabinet.
casellista, *n.m.* Owner of a post-office box.
casello, *n.m.* (*Rail.*) Linesman's box; gate-keeper's house.
caseo [casEo], *n.m.* Curds, cheese.
caseoso, *a.* Caseous.
casereccio [caserEccio], *a.* Homely, home-made.
caserma, *n.f.* Barracks.
casermaggio [casermAggio], *n.m.* Furniture of a barracks; bedding.
casetta, *n.f.* Little house.
casetto, *n.m.* Comical incident, curious occurrence; queer situation.
casiere, casiera, *n.m.f.* Caretaker.
casigliano, *n.m.* Fellow-lodger; inmate (of the same house).
casimirra, *n.f.* Cashmere.
casina, *n.f* Cottage; villa type of house.

casino, *n.m.* Casino; country club; brothel.
casipola [casIpola], *n.f.* Hovel [cp. **casupola**].
casista, *n.m.f.* (*Theol.*) Casuist.
casistica [casIstica], *n.f.* Casuistry.
caso, *n.m.* Case; accident; occurrence, event, happening; chance; fate; possibility. **A —,** by chance; at random; **per —, in ogni —,** at all events; **in un — simile,** in such a case; **— mai,** in case; **puta — che,** supposing that; **dato il — che,** should it happen that; **far —,** to matter; **fare — di una cosa,** to value a thing; **fare una cosa a —,** to do a thing heedlessly; **ti fa —?** does it surprise you? **se del —,** if necessary; **pensare ai casi propri,** to attend to one's own business; **vedi se c'è il — di riuscire,** see if there's any chance of success.
casolare, *n.m.* Isolated cottage; hovel, cabin.
casona, *n.f.* Large house.
casone, *n.m.* Large, ugly house; tenement house.
casotto, *n.m.* Sentry-box; (*Naut.*) **— del timone,** wheelhouse.
Caspio [cAspio], *n.m.* Caspian Sea.
caspita! [cAspita], *inter.* Good gracious! By Jove!
cassa, *n.f.* Box, trunk, case, coffer; (*Motor.*) body; cupboard; bank, cashier's desk; water-tank (of submarine); sounding-box (of gramophone). **— dell'orologio,** watch-case; **— del violino,** violin-case; **— del fucile,** stock of a gun; **— da morto,** coffin; **gran —,** big drum; **— di risparmio,** savings bank; **fondo di —,** reserve fund; **tener la —,** to be cashier; (*Typ.*) **— di caratteri,** case; **bassa —,** lower case; **alta —,** upper case, caps.; **batter —,** to collect money.
cassaforte, *n.f.* Safe, steel safe; strong-room.
cassaio [cassAio], *n.m.* Box-maker; packing-case-maker.
cassamadia [cassamAdia], *n.f.* Kneading-trough.
cassamento, *n.m.* Packing.
cassapanca, *n.f.* Settle, chest; bench-locker.
cassare, *v.t.* (*Law*) To cancel, to abrogate, to rescind.
cassata, *n.f.* Cream tart, cream cake; Neapolitan ice.
cassato, *p.p.a.* (*Law*) Annulled.
cassatura, *n.f.* Cancellation, annulment.
cassazione, *n.f.* (*Law*) Abrogation. **Corte di Cassazione,** Supreme Court of Appeal.
cassero [cAssero], *n.m.* (*Naut.*) Quarter-deck.
casserola, casseruola, *n.f.* Saucepan, stew-pan, casserole.
cassetta, *n.f.* Small case, box; collection box, alms box; coach-box. **— postale,** letter-box; **— della spazzatura,** dustbin; **— di sicurezza,** safe; **stare a —,** to drive a coach.
cassettina, *n.f.* Small box.
cassetto, *n.m.* Drawer; till (in shop counter). **Tirare il —,** to open the drawer.
cassettone, *n.m.* Chest of drawers; (*Arch.*) caisson.
cassia [cAssia], *n.f.* (*Med.*) Cassia.
cassiere, cassiera, *n.m.f.* Cashier; treasurer.
cassinese, *a.* Of the monastery of Montecassino, Benedictine.
cassino, *n.m.* Dust-cart.
cassone, *n.m.* Large case, trunk; (*Mil.*) ammunition wagon; (*Naut.*) chain locker.
cassula [cAssula], *n.f.* Capsule [cp. **capsula**].
casta, *n.f.* Caste; class, rank.
castagna, *n.f.* Chestnut; (*Mech.*) pawl.
castagnaccio [castagnAccio], *n.m.* Chestnut cake.
castagnaio [castagnAio], *n.m.* Gatherer or seller of chestnuts.
castagneto, *n.m.* Copse or wood of chestnut trees.
castagnetta, *n.f.* (*Mus.*) Castanet.
castagnino, *a.* Chestnut, chestnut brown.
castagno, *n.m.* (*Bot.*) Chestnut-tree.
castagno, *a.* Brown. **Capelli castagni,** auburn hair [cp. **castano**].
castagnola, *n.f.* Petard, cracker, firework.
castalda, *n.f.* Bursar (in a nunnery).
castalderia [castalderIa], *n.f.* Stewardship, agency.
castaldia [castaldIa], *n.f.* Office or residence of steward.
castaldo, *n.m.* Steward (of a manor); bailiff; factor, land-agent.
castamente, *adv.* Chastely, modestly.
castano, *a.* Chestnut brown.
castellana, *n.f.* Lady of the manor.
castellania [castellanIa], *n.f.* Governorship of a castle; lordship of a manor.
castellano, *n.m.* Governor of a castle, lord of the manor.
castellare, *n.m.* (*obs.*) Ruined castle.
castelletto, *n.m.* Small castle; (*Comm.*) credit register.
castellina, *n.f.* Pile (of fruit, nuts, etc.).
castello, *n.m.* Castle, fortress, citadel; country seat, mansion; water tower; train (of a watch, etc.). (*Naut.*) **— di prua,** forecastle; **— di poppa,** quarter-deck; **— del sopporto,** pedestal (of bust, statue, etc.); **— dei burattini,** puppet booth; **far castelli in aria,** to build castles in the air.
castigamatti, *n.m.* Castigator; whip.
castigamento, *n.m.* (*obs.*) Chastisement, punishment [cp. **castigo**].
castigare, *v.t.* To punish, to chastise; to reform, to correct.
castigatamente, *adv.* Soberly, moderately.
castigatezza, *n.f.* (*Lit.*) Sobriety, dignity; restraint.
castigato, *a.* (*fig.*) Sober, austere, restrained.
Castiglia [castIglia], *n.f.* Castile.
castigo, *n.m.* Punishment, chastisement; pain, torment.
castimonia [castimOnia], *n.f.* Chastity; continence.
castità [-à], *n.f.* Chastity, purity. **Voto di —,** vow of chastity.
casto, *a.* Chaste, pure, modest.
castone, *n.m.* Bezel (of a ring).
Castore [cAstore], *n.m.* (*Myth.*) Castor. (*Astron.*) **— e Polluce,** Castor and Pollux.
castoro, *n.m.* (*Zool.*) Beaver.
castracani, *n.m.* (*colloq.*) Unskilful surgeon.
castrametazione, *n.f.* (*Mil.*) Castrametation; fortification.
castrapensieri, *n.m.* Narrow-minded censor.
castraporci, *n.m.* Pig-gelder; (*colloq.*) unskilful surgeon.
castrare, *v.t.* To castrate, to geld, to emasculate.
castrato, *n.m.* Mutton; eunuch. **Costolette di —,** mutton chops.

castratoio [castratOio], *n.m.* Castrating knife.
castratore, *n.m.* Castrator.
castratura, *n.f.* (The operation of) castration.
castrazione, *n.f.* (The effect of) castration.
castrense, *a.* Pertaining to the army.
castrino, *n.f.* Small knife (for cutting open chestnuts, etc.).
castronaggine [castronAggine], *n.f.* Stupidity.
castrone, *n.m.* Wether, gelding; blockhead, dolt.
castroneria [castronerIa], *n.f.* Stupidity, nonsense.
casuale, *a.* Casual, uncertain. **Spese casuali,** unforeseen expenses; sundry expenses.
casualità [-à], *n.f.* Casuality.
casualmente, *adv.* Casually.
casuario [casuArio], *n.m.* (*Zool.*) Cassowary.
casuccia, casuccola, casupola [casUccia, casUccola, casUpola], *n.f.* Hovel, slum dwelling.
cataclisma, *n.m.* Cataclysm; ruin, disaster, catastrophe.
catacomba, *n.f.* Catacomb.
catacresi, *n.f.* (*Lit.*) Catachresis.
catafalco, *n.m.* Catafalque.
catafascio [catafAscio], *adv.* **A —,** topsy-turvy, upside down, in confusion.
catafratta, *n.f.* (*Hist.*) Roman armour.
catafratto, *n.m.* (*Hist.*) Roman soldier (in armour).
catalano, *a.* Catalan.
catalessi, catalessia [catalEssia], *n.f.* (*Med.*) Catalepsy.
catalettico [catalEttico], *a.* (*Med.*) Cataleptic; (*Poet.*) catalectic.
catalisi [catAlisi], *n.f.* (*Chem.*) Catalysis.
catalizzatore, *n.m.* (*Chem.*) Catalyst.
catalogare, *v.t.* To catalogue, to file.
Catalogna *n.f.* Catalonia.
catalogo [catAlogo], *n.m.* Catalogue; list. **— per materie,** subject catalogue.
catapecchia [catapEcchia], *n.f.* Hovel, dilapidated house; slum.
cataplasma (*pl.* **cataplasmi**), *n.m.* (*Med.*) Plaster, poultice.
catapulta, *n.f.* Catapult.
catapultare, *v.t.* (*Aviat.*) To catapult.
cataraffio, *n.m.* (*Naut.*) Caulking-iron.
cataratta, cateratta, *n.f.* Cataract (in all senses); weir. (*Med.*) **Operare di —,** to operate for cataract.
catarro, *n.m.* (*Med.*) Catarrh.
catarsi, *n.f.* Purification, expiation; (*Drama*) catharsis.
catartico [catArtico], *a.* (*Med.*) Cathartic, purgative.
catarzo, *n.f.* Floss silk.
catasta, *n.f.* Pile, heap (esp. of firewood, etc.); (*obs.*) stage or rack for torture.
catastale, *a.* Cadastral.
catastare, *v.t.* To pile up [cp. **accatastare**].
catasto, *n.m.* Register of landed property.
catastrofe [catAstrofe], *n.f.* Catastrophe, ruin, disaster.
catastrofico [catastrOfico], *a.* Catastrophic.
catechismo, *n.m.* (*Theol.*) Catechism.
catechista, *n.m.* (*Theol.*) Catechist.
catechizzare, *v.t.* To catechize; (*fig.*) to canvass.
catecumenato, catecumeno [catecUmeno], *n.m.* (*Theol.*) Catechumen.
categoria [categorIa], *n.f.* Category, class, kind.
categoricamente, *adv.* Categorically.
categorico [categOrico], *a.* Categorical, explicit, outspoken.
categorizzare, *v.t.* To categorize, to class.
catellone, *adv.* (*obs.*) **Catellon catelloni,** stealing along, as quiet as a mouse.
catena, *n.f.* Chain, linking; (*fig.*) bond, tie, impediment; range (of hills, etc.); (*Naut.*) cable; succession. (*Naut.*) **— dell'ancora,** anchor chain; **pozzo della —,** cable locker; **perno della —,** link pin; **— dei forzati,** convicts' chains, fetters; **a —,** in succession; **pazzo da —,** stark mad; **punto a —,** chain stitch; (*Mech.*) **— motrice,** driving-chain.
catenaccio [catenAccio], *n.m.* Bolt, padlock.
catenare, *v.t.* To chain [cp. **incatenare**].
catenaria [catenAria], *n.f.* Catenary.
catenella, *n.f.* Small chain, watch-chain.
catera [cAtera], *n.f.* Green almond.
cateratta, *n.f.* Cataract [cp. **cataratta**].
caterva, *n.f.* Multitude, mass, great number.
catetere [catetEre], *n.m.* (*Med.*) Catheter.
cateto, *n.m.* (*Geom.*) One of the shorter sides of right-angled triangle.
catilinaria [catilinAria], *n.f.* Catilinarian speech; invective.
catinaio [catinAio], *n.m.* Vendor of crockery.
catinella, *n.f.* Small basin, washhand basin. **Piovere a catinelle,** to rain very hard, to rain cats and dogs.
catinellata, *n.f.* Basinful.
catino, *n.m.* Basin, bowl, wash-tub.
catione, *n.m.* (*Elect.*) Kation, cation.
catodico [catOdico], *a.* Cathodic.
catodo [cAtodo], *n.m.* (*Elect.*) Cathode.
Catone, *n.m.* Cato; censor.
catoneggiare, *v.i.* To moralize.
catoniano, *a.* Catonian.
catorcio [catOrcio], *n.m.* Door-bolt.
catorzolo [catOrzolo], *n.m.* Knot (in a plank).
catorzoluto, *a.* Knotty (of wood).
catramare, *v.t.* To tar [cp. **incatramare**].
catrame, *n.m.* Tar.
catramato, *p.p.a.* Tarred.
catriosso, *n.m.* Carcass of a fowl; (*fig.*) very thin person.
cattabrighe, *n.m.* Quarrelsome fellow [cp. **accattabrighe**].
cattedra [cattEdra], *n.f.* Rostrum, (professorial) chair; professorship. **— ambulante,** travelling lectureship; **Cattedra di San Pietro,** the Holy See; (*fig.*) **salire in —,** to sermonize.
cattedrale, *n.f.a.* Cathedral.
cattedrante, *n.m.* Pedant; professor.
cattedraticamente, *adv.* Professorially, didactically.
cattedratico [cattedrAtico], *a.* Professorial; authoritative; pedantic. **Tono —,** authoritative tone.
cattivaccio [cattivAccio], *a.* Naughty; (*colloq.*) **il —,** the villain of the piece.
cattivamente, *adv.* Wickedly, maliciously, naughtily.
cattivarsi, *v.r.* To captivate, to gain, to win. **— la stima di un amico,** to win a friend's esteem.
cattivato, *a.* (*obs.*) Captive.

cattivello, *n.m.a.* Young rascal, scamp; naughty.
cattiveria [cattivEria, cattiverIa], *n.f.* Wickedness, badness; malice; naughtiness.
cattività [-à], *n.f.* Captivity, bondage; (*obs.*) wickedness.
cattivo, *n.m.* Bad man, wretch, villain.
cattivo, *a.* Bad, naughty, wicked; poor (in quality); wrong. **Con le cattive,** harshly; **aria cattiva,** bad air; — **soggetto,** a nasty fellow.
cattolicamente, *adv.* According to Roman Catholic doctrine.
cattolicismo, cattolicesimo, *n.m.* Roman Catholicism.
cattolicità [-à], *n.f.* Catholicity.
cattolico [cattOlico], *a.* Roman Catholic.
cattura, *n.f.* Capture, arrest, seizure. **Mandato di —,** warrant of arrest.
catturare, *v.t.* To capture, to seize, to arrest; (*Naut.*) — **una nave,** to seize a vessel.
Caucaso [cAucaso], *n.m.* Caucasus.
caucciù [-ù], *n.m.* Indiarubber.
caudale, *a.* Caudal; tail-like.
caudatario [caudatArio], *n.m.* (*Eccles.*) Trainbearer; (*fig.*) toady.
caudato, *a.* Caudate, tailed.
caudisono [caudIsono], *n.m.* (*Zool.*) Rattlesnake.
caule [cAule], *n.m.* (*Bot.*) Stalk.
cauri, *n.m.* Cowry shell.
causa [cAusa], *n.f.* Cause, motive, reason, grounds; origin; fault; (*Law*) action, suit. **A — della nebbia,** owing to the fog; **dare — di lagnanze,** to give cause for complaint; **dar — vinta,** to give in; **entrare in —,** to come into play; **parlare con cognizione di —,** to speak from experience; **per — mia,** through my fault; **in — propria,** for oneself; (*Law*) **far —,** to bring an action against; **essere in —,** to be carrying on a lawsuit; **patrocinare una —,** to plead a cause; **chiamare uno in —,** to make one a party to a suit.
causale, *n.m.* (*Law*) Suit, case.
causale, *a.* Causal. (*Law*) **Ragioni causali,** motives.
causalità [-à], *n.f.* Causality.
causare, *v.t.* To cause, to occasion; to determine; to produce.
causativo, *a.* Causative.
causatore, causatrice, *n.m.f.* Causer, occasion of.
causidico [causIdico], *n.m.* Legal adviser, lawyer.
caustica [cAustica], *n.f.* (*Phys.*) Caustic curve.
causticità [-à], *n.f.* Causticity; sarcasm.
caustico [cAustico], *n.m.a.* (*Med.*) Caustic; burning; (*fig.*) biting, sarcastic.
cautamente, *adv.* Cautiously, prudently.
cautela, *n.f.* Caution, precaution, circumspection, prudence.
cautelare, *v.t.* To secure, to make safe; to caution.
cautelarsi, *v.r.* To guarantee oneself, to protect oneself; to cover oneself against.
cautelatamente, *adv.* With caution, cautiously [cp. **cautamente**].
cautelato, *a.* Prudent, assured. **Esser — contro,** to be guaranteed against.
cauterio [cautErio], *n.m.* (*Med.*) Cautery.
cauterizzare, *v.t.* (*Med.*) To cauterize.
cauterizzazione, *n.f.* Cauterization.
cautezza, *n.f.* Cautiousness [cp. **cautela**].
cauto [cAuto], *a.* Cautious, prudent, wary, circumspect; thoughtful, sly, artful. **Andar —,** to go warily, to be prudent.
cauzionale, *a.* Cautionary.
cauzione, *n.f.* Security, bail, deposit. **Prestar —,** to give bail.
cava, *n.f.* Quarry, pit, mine. — **di marmo,** marble quarry.
cavadenti, *n.m.* (*colloq.*) Dentist.
cavafango, cavafondo, *n.m.* (*Naut.*) Dredger.
cavagno, *n.m.* Basket, pannier.
cavaiolo [cavaiOlo], *n.m.* Quarryman.
cavalcabile [cavalcAbile], *a.* Riding (horse); bridle (road).
cavalcamento, *n.m.* [cp. **cavalcata**].
cavalcante, *n.m.* Postillion, outrider.
cavalcare, *v.t.i.* To ride (a horse); to go on horseback; to be astride.
cavalcata, *n.f.* Ride, riding; cavalcade.
cavalcatura, *n.f.* Mount, riding-horse.
cavalcavia [cavalcavIa], *n.m.* Bridge over roadway; fly-over bridge.
cavalcioni, *adv.* **A cavalcioni,** astride.
cavalierato, *n.m.* Knighthood.
cavaliere, *n.m.* Horseman, rider; knight, cavalier; gentleman; dance partner; (*Chess*) knight. — **della Giarrettiera,** Knight of the Garter; — **errante,** knight-errant; — **d'industria,** swindler, sharper; **il castello sta a — della valle,** the castle overlooks the valley; — **servente,** lady's man.
cavalla, *n.f.* Mare.
cavallaio [cavallAio], *n.m.* Horse-dealer.
cavallaro, *n.m.* Horse-keeper; horse-dealer; leader of a train of pack-horses.
cavallata, *n.f.* (*obs.*) Horsemen, cavalry.
cavalleggiero, *n.m.* (*Mil.*) Trooper. **Cavalleggieri,** light cavalry.
cavallerescamente, *adv.* Generously, gallantly.
cavalleresco, *a.* Chivalrous, noble, gallant. **Ordine —,** order of knighthood; **poema —,** chivalric poem.
cavalleria [cavallerIa], *n.f.* Chivalry; (*Mil.*) cavalry.
cavallerizza, *n.f.* Riding-school.
cavallerizzo, *n.m.* Rider; riding-master.
cavalletta, *n.f.* (*Zool.*) Grasshopper; locust.
cavalletto, *n.m.* Easel, trestle.
cavallina, *n.f.* Filly, young mare. **Correre la —,** to live a lewd life, to go the pace; **saltar la —,** to play leap-frog; to go the pace.
cavallino, *n.m.* Colt; pony.
cavallino, *a.* Equine, horsy. **Mosca cavallina,** horse-fly. **Tosse —,** whooping-cough.
cavallo, *n.m.* Horse. — **restio,** restive horse; — **ombroso,** shying horse; — **da carrozza,** carriage-horse; — **da sella,** saddle-horse; — **di razza,** thoroughbred; — **da caccia,** hunter; — **da tiro,** draught-horse; — **da corsa,** race-horse; **mediatore di cavalli,** horse-dealer; **ferro di —,** horseshoe; **finimenti di cavalli,** horse trappings; — **a dondolo,** rocking-horse; — **da giostra,** vaulting-horse; **cavalli di Frisia,** chevaux-de-frise; **montare a —,** to mount; **smontare da —,** to dismount; **attaccare i cavalli,** to put

the horses to; (*Mech.*) — **vapore,** — **motore,** horse-power (h.p.); **motore da cento cavalli,** 100 h.p. motor; (*Elect.*) **energia in cavalli,** horse-power; **andare con il — di San Francesco,** to go on foot; **essere a —,** to be safe.

cavallone, *n.m.* Big horse; (*Naut.*) breaker, "white horses"; swell, heavy sea.

cavallotto, *n.m.* Medium-sized horse.

cavalluccio [cavallUccio], *n.m.* Pony; nag.

cavalocchio [cavalOcchio], *n.m.* (*Zool.*) Hornet; (*fig.*) pettifogging lawyer.

cavamacchie [cavamAcchie], *n.m.* Stain-remover.

cavapietre, *n.m.* Stone-quarrier.

cavapozzi, *n.m.* Well-digger.

cavare, *v.t.* To take off, to extract, to remove; to dig, to excavate; to pull up; to obtain, to derive; to wrest, to wring out of. — **un dente,** to draw a tooth; — **sangue,** to bleed (patient); **cavar acqua,** to draw water; — **le macchie,** to remove the stains; — **la fame,** to appease hunger; — **la sete,** to quench thirst; — **di bocca un segreto,** to wrest a secret out of someone; — **denari da qualcheduno,** to get money out of some-one; — **di capo qualcosa a qualcuno,** to persuade a person not to do something; **cavarsi il cappello,** to take off one's hat.

cavarsela, *v.r.* To get off, to rid oneself. — **a buon mercato,** to get out of a thing cheaply, to get off lightly.

cavarsi, *v.r.* To get oneself out, to free oneself from; to appease, to satisfy. — **la voglia,** to satisfy one's longing; — **un capriccio,** to satisfy a fancy; — **d'impiccio,** to get out of a difficulty.

cavastivali [cavastivAli], *n.m.* Bootjack.

cavata, *n.f.* Extraction; (*Mus.*) touch of a violinist. (*Med.*) — **di sangue,** blood-letting.

cavatappi, *n.m.* Corkscrew.

cavatesòri, *n.m.* Treasure-diviner.

cavatina, *n.f.* (*Mus.*) Melodious air.

cavatore, *n.m.* Miner, digger.

cavatura, *n.f.* Hollow.

cavaturaccioli [cavaturAccioli], *n.m.* Cork-screw.

cavazione, *n.f.* (*Fencing*) Disengage.

cavedio [cavEdio], *n.m.* (*Arch.*) Passage, corridor.

caverna, *n.f.* Cavern, cave; den.

cavernosità [-à], *n.f.* Depth; cavity.

cavernoso, *a.* Cavernous. **Voce —,** deep voice.

cavezza, *n.f.* Halter (of horse); (*fig.*) **Pagare sulla —,** to pay on the nail; **tenere a —,** to curb, to keep in hand.

cavia [cAvia], *n.f.* (*Zool.*) Guinea-pig, cavy.

caviale, *n.m.* Caviar.

cavicchio [cavIcchio], *n.m.* Peg, bolt, rung (of a ladder); (*Agric.*) dibble.

caviglia [cavIglia], *n.f.* (*Anat.*) Ankle; (*Tech.*) peg, pin, plug (in wall).

cavillare, *v.i.* To cavil, to quibble.

cavillatore, *n.m.* Quibbler, caviller.

cavillazione, *n.f.* Quibbling.

cavillo, *n.m.* Cavilling, cavil, quibble, sophistry.

cavillosamente, *adv.* Captiously.

cavilloso, *a.* Quibbling, captious.

cavità [-à], *n.f.* Cavity, hole, hollow.

cavo, *n.m.* Cable, rope; mould, hollow. **Il — della mano,** the hollow of the hand; — **di rimorchio,** tow-rope; (*Elect.*) — **aere,** over-head cable; — **principale,** main cable.

cavo, *a.* Hollow, empty, void.

cavolaia [cavolAia], *n.f.* Cabbage-bed; cabbage patch.

cavolaio [cavolAio], *n.m.* Market-gardener, cabbage-grower.

cavolfiore, *n.m.* Cauliflower.

cavolo [cAvolo], *n.m.* Cabbage. — **marino,** sea-kale; — **riscaldato,** a worn-out subject, a twice-told tale; **questo c'entra come i cavoli a merenda,** this has nothing whatever to do with the case; **non m'importa un —,** I don't care a fig, two hoots, a straw, etc.

cavolrapa, *n.m.* Kohlrabi.

cavriolo, *n.m.* (*Zool.*) Roe-buck [cp. **capriolo**].

cazza, *n.f.* (*Mech.*) Ladle for casting metal.

cazzare, *v.t.* (*Naut.*) To haul the cable; to draw home a sheet.

cazzascotte, *n.f.* (*Naut.*) Large cleat.

cazzola, cazzuola, *n.f.* Bricklayer's trowel.

cazzottare, *v.t.* (*vulg*). To strike, to thump, to pummel.

cazzotto, *n.m.* Blow with the fist, punch, thump, **Fare a cazzotti,** to punch one another.

ce, *pron.* To us (used instead of **ci** before other pronouns **lo, li, gli, la, le** and **ne**). **Ce lo mostra,** he shows it to us.

ce, *adv.* Here, there (instead of **ci** as above).

cecaggine [cecAggine], *n.f.* Blindness; drowsiness, heaviness of the eyelids.

cecamente, *adv.* Blindly.

cecca, *n.f.* (*Zool.*) Magpie. **Far —,** to miss fire.

ceccherino, *n.m.* Skinny fowl.

Cecco, *n.m.* (*abbrev.*) Francesco.

cece, *n.m.* (*Bot.*) Chickpea. **Color —,** fawn.

cecia [cEcia], *n.f.* Flat footwarmer.

ceciato, *a.* Fawn (colour).

cecità [-à], *n.f.* Blindness; (*fig.*) folly, reckless-ness.

ceco, *n.m.a.* Czech.

cecoslovacco, *n.m.a.* Czechoslovakian.

cedente, *n.m.* (*Comm.*) Assignor, transferer.

cedente, *a.* Flexible, yielding.

cedere [cEdere], *v.t.i.* To yield, to give way, to submit, to give in; to give up, to surrender, to cede; to collapse, to subside; to hand over; to assign, to transfer. — **il passo a,** to give precedence to; — **i propri diritti,** to give up one's rights; — **ad un impulso,** to yield to an impulse; **non — in nulla,** not to give way; **il terreno cede,** the land sub-sides; **cedi il posto a quella signora,** give your seat to that lady.

cedevole [cedEvole], *a.* Yielding, pliable, supple.

cedevolezza, *n.f.* Flexibility, suppleness.

cedibile [cedIbile], *a.* Assignable, transfer-able.

cedibilità [-à], *n.f.* Transferability.

cediglia [cedIglia], *n.f.* (*Gram.*) Cedilla.

cedimento, *n.m.* Yielding; sinking, subsidence (of ground, etc.).

ceditore, ceditrice, *n.m.f.* (*Comm.*) Ces-sionary.

cedola [cEdola], *n.f.* Card, bill; (*Comm.*) coupon, dividend warrant.

cedoletto, *n.m.* Slip (from a writing-pad).

cedolone, *n.m.* (*Eccles.*) Papal document summoning Councils, etc.
cedraio [cedrAio], *n.m.* Plantation of citron trees.
cedrare, *v.t.* To flavour with citron.
cedrina, *n.f.* (*Bot.*) Lemon-scented verbena.
cedro (1), *n.m.* (*Bot.*) Citron tree; citron (fruit).
cedro (2), *n.m.* (*Bot.*) Cedar tree; cedar (wood). — **del Libano,** cedar of Lebanon.
cedrone, *a.* Lemon-coloured, lemon yellow.
cedronella, *n.f.* (*Bot.*) Balm.
ceduo [cEduo], *a.* Woody. **Bosco —,** copse, coppice.
ceduto, *p.p.* Given up, surrendered [cp. **cedere**].
cefaglioli, cefaglione, *n.m.* (*Bot.*) Fan-palm.
cefalalgia [cefalalgIa], *n.f.* Severe headache.
cefalea [cefalEa], *n.f.* Headache.
cefalico [cefAlico], *a.* (*Anat.*) Cephalic.
cefalite, *n.f.* (*Med.*) Cephalitis.
cefalo [cEfalo], *n.m.* (*Zool.*) Mullet.
cefalometria [cefalometrIa], *n.f.* Craniometry.
cefalopodi [cefalOpodi], *n.m.pl.* (*Zool.*) Cephalopoda.
ceffata, *n.f.* Slap (on the face).
ceffo, *n.m.* Snout, muzzle. (*fig.*) **Un brutto —,** an ugly face.
ceffone, *n.m.* Slap (esp. on the face).
Ceilan, *n.m.* Ceylon.
celamento, *n.m.* Concealment.
celare, *v.t.* To conceal, to hide; to hush up.
celarsi, *v.r.* To hide oneself, to conceal oneself.
celata, *n f.* (*Hist.*) Helmet, visor; (*Mil.*) ambush.
celatamente, *adv.* Secretly, obscurely.
celeberrimo [celebErrimo], *a.* Very celebrated, notorious.
celebrabile [celebrAbile], *a.* Praiseworthy.
celebramento, *n.m.* Celebration, act of celebrating [cp. **celebrazione**].
celebrante, *n.m.* (*Eccles.*) Celebrant (at Mass or other service).
celebrare, *v.t.* To celebrate, to exalt, to honour; to solemnize (marriage); to officiate (at Mass, etc.). — **l'ufficio divino,** to celebrate divine service.
celebrato, *a.* Celebrated.
celebrazione, *n.f.* Celebration, commemoration.
celebre [cElebre], *a.* Renowned, celebrated, famous.
celebremente, *adv.* Famously.
celebrità [-à], *n.f.* Celebrity; noted person.
celere [cElere], *n.m.* (*Rail.*) Express; (*Police*) **La Celere,** flying squad.
celere [cElere], *a.* Quick, fast, swift.
celerimetro [celerImetro], *n.m.* Speedometer.
celerità [-à], *n.f.* Celerity, rapidity, speed.
celermente, *adv.* Quickly, swiftly.
celeste, *a.* Celestial, heavenly; (of colour) sky-blue, azure.
celestialmente, *adv.* Celestially, in a heavenly manner.
celestino, celestrino, *a.* Bluish; light blue.
celia [cElia], *n.f.* Jest, joke, fun. **Fare per —,** to do a thing for fun.
celiare, *v.i.* To joke to jest, to trifle with, to play with.
celiatore, celiatrice, *n.m.f.* Jester, joker.
celibatario [celibatArio], *n.m.* Old bachelor.
celibato, *n.m.* Celibacy.
celibe [cElibe], *n.m.a.* Bachelor; single, unmarried, celibate.
celidonia [celidOnia], *n.f.* (*Bot.*) Celandine, swallow-wort.
celione, *n.m.* Joker, jester.
cella, *n f.* Cell (in convent, prison, etc.); small room.
cellaio [cellAio], *n.m.* Cellar, canteen; cellarette.
cellula [cEllula], *n.f.* Cell (in all senses). — **comunista,** Communist cell.
cellulare, *n.m.* Prison, jail.
cellulare, *a.* Cellular (in all senses). **Segregazione —,** close or solitary confinement; **tessuto —,** cellular tissue.
celluloide [cellulOide], *n.f.* Celluloid.
cellulosa, *n.f.* (*Chem.*) Cellulose.
celluloso, *a.* Cellulose.
celo, *n.m.* Heaven [cp. **cielo**].
celsitudine [celsitUdine], *n.f.* (*obs*). Highness (as title).
Celti, *n.m.pl.* Celts.
celtico [cEltico], *a.* Celtic. **Malattie celtiche,** venereal diseases.
cembalista (*pl.* **cembalisti**), *n.m.* (*Mus.*) Harpsichord-player.
cembalo [cEmbalo], *n.m.* (*Mus.*) Cymbal; tambourine; spinet, harpsichord. **Andare col — in colombaia,** to blurt out secrets.
cembro, *a.* **Pino —,** a coniferous tree (*Pinus cembra*).
cementare, *v.t.* To cement. — **l'amicizia,** to cement a friendship.
cementazione, *n.f.* Cementing.
cemento, *n.m.* Cement, — **armato,** reinforced concrete.
cena, *n.i.* Supper. **Far —,** to take supper; **L'Ultima Cena,** the Last Supper.
cenacolo [cenAcolo], *n.m.* Refectory; supper-room; (*fig.*) literary or artistic clique, circle; (*Art*) The Last Supper.
cenare, *v.i.* To sup, to take supper.
cenata, *n.f.* Supper.
cenciaia [cenciAia], *n.f.* Heap of rags.
cenciaiuolo [cenciaiuOlo], *n.m.* Rag-picker.
cenciata, *n.f.* Flick with a duster; "a lick and a promise".
cencio [cEncio], *n.m.* Rag, duster; dish-cloth; (*fig.*) poverty; ill-health. **Non ha trovato un — di marito,** she has never had a hint of a proposal; **non sono nei miei cenci,** I'm feeling out of sorts; **mettere nei cenci,** to throw away (old rags, etc.).
cencioso, *n.m.a.* Tatterdemalion, ragamuffin; in rags and tatters.
cencro, *n.m.* (*Zool.*) Speckled snake; viper.
ceneraccio [cenerAccio], *n.m.* Ashes for making lye.
ceneraio [cenerAio], *n.m.* Ash-tray.
cenerario [cenerArio], *n.m.* Ash-pan.
cenerario [cenerArio], *a.* Cinerary [cp. **cinerario**].
cenerata, *n.f.* Ashes boiled to make lye.
cenere [cEnere], *n.f.* Ash, ashes, embers; cinders. **Mercoledì delle Ceneri, Le Ceneri,** Ash Wednesday; **ridurre in —,** to burn to

ashes; **covar sotto le ceneri,** to smoulder; **le ceneri di,** the ashes or remains (of one dead).
Cenerentola [cenerEntola], *n.f.* Cinderella.
cenericcio, cenerino, cenerognolo [cenerIccio, cenerOgnolo], *a.* Ashen, pale.
ceneroso, *a.* Covered with ashes.
cenetta, *n.f.* Light supper.
cengia [cEngia], *n.f.* (*Mountaineering*) Ledge, shelf-like ridge.
Cenisio [cenIsio], *n.m.* **Monte —,** Mont Cenis.
cennamella, *n.f.* (*Mus.*) Bagpipe.
cennare, *v.i.t.* [cp. **accennare**].
cenno, *n.m.* Sign, signal; nod, allusion; wave (of hand); wink; hint; order, instruction; (*Comm.*) acknowledgment (of receipt). **Far —,** to make a sign, to mention; **far — di una cosa,** to touch upon a matter; (*Comm.*) **— di ricevimento,** acknowledgment of receipt; **egli non ne fece —,** he did not mention it; **far — di sì,** to nod assent.
cenobiarca, *n.m.* (*Eccles.*) Abbot.
cenobio [cenObio], *n.m.* Monastery, convent.
cenobita (*pl.* **cenobiti**), *n.m.* Coenobite.
cenotafio [cenotAfio], *n.m.* Cenotaph.
cenozoico, *a.* (*Geol.*) cainozoic, caenozoic.
censimento, *n.m.* Census. **Fare il —,** to take the census.
censire, *v.t.* To take a census.
censito, *n.m.* Tax-payer.
censo, *n.m.* Wealth; income; national revenue; census. **Uomo di alto —,** a very wealthy man.
censorato, *n.m.* Censorship.
censore, *n.m.* Censor; critic.
censorio [censOrio], *a.* Censorious; pertaining to a censor.
censuare, *v.t.* To tax; to assess.
censuario [censuArio], *n.m.* Tax-payer.
censuazione, *n.f.* (*obs.*) Assessment.
censura, *n.f.* Censure; censorship.
censurabile [censurAbile], *a.* Censurable, reprehensible.
censurare, *v.t.* To censure, to reprehend.
centaurea [centAurea], *n.f.* (*Bot.*) Centaury.
centauro [centAuro], *n.m.* Centaur.
centellinare, *v.t.i.* To sip, to take in sips; (*fig.*) to savour, to relish.
centellino, *n.m.* Sip.
centenario [centenArio], *n.m.a.* Centenary; centenarian.
centenne, *a.* Centennial, centenary.
centesima [centEsima], *n.f.* Usury, rate of interest.
centesimale, *a.* Centesimal.
centesimo [centEsimo], *n.m.* Centime; hundredth, hundredth part. **Non ha un —,** he is penniless.
centigrado [centIgrado], *a.* Centigrade.
centigrammo, *n.m.* Centigramme.
centilitro [centIlitro], *n.m.* Centilitre.
centimetro [centImetro], *n.m.* Centimetre.
centina [cEntina], *n.f.* (*Arch.*) Centre-piece, keystone.
centinaio [centinAio], *n.m.* Hundred. **A centinaia,** by hundreds.
centinato, *a.* (*Arch.*) Arched.
cento, *a.* Hundred. **Ad un tanto per —,** at so much per cent; **al — per —,** a hundred per cent, entirely.
centofoglie [centofOglie], *n.m.* (*Bot.*) Yarrow.
centogambe, *n.m.* (*Zool.*) Centipede.
centomila, *a.* One hundred thousand.
centonchio [centOnchio], *n.m.* (*Bot.*) Chickweed.
centone, *n.m.* Patchwork; medley.
centopelle, *n.m.* Third stomach of a ruminant.
centrale, *n.f.* Central office, head office. (*Elect.*) **— elettrica,** power plant, power station; **— idroelettrica,** hydro-electric station.
centrale, *a.* Central. **Riscaldamento —,** central heating; **stazione —,** central station.
centralino, *n.m.* Telephone exchange; substation.
centrare, *v.t.* To hit in the centre; to centre.
centralità [-à], *n.f.* Centrality.
centralizzare, *v.t.* To centralize.
centralizzazione, *n.f.* Centralization.
centravanti, centrattacco, *n.m.* (*Football*) Centre forward.
centrico [cEntrico], *a.* Centric, central.
centrifugo [centrIfugo], *a.* Centrifugal.
centrina, *n.f.* (*Zool.*) Dogfish.
centripeto [centrIpeto], *a.* Centripetal.
centro, *n.m.* Centre, middle; interior; hub, heart; point of concentration; town; (*Pol.*) middle or moderate party. **Il — di gravità,** the centre of gravity; **essere nel proprio —,** to be in one's element: (*Football*) **— avanti, — attacco,** centre forward; **— mediano, — sostegno,** centre half-back; **— del bersaglio,** bull's-eye (target).
centuplicare, *v.t.* To multiply by a hundred.
centuplo [cEntuplo], *n.m.a.* Hundredfold.
centuria [centUria], *n.f.* (*Hist.*) Century (company of 100 men); a hundred people.
centurione, *n.m.* Centurion.
ceppa, *n.f.* (*Bot.*) Underground stem of a tree.
ceppaia [ceppAia], *n.f.* Stump of underwood.
ceppo, *n.m.* Stump, block, log; fetter; stock (of anchor, etc.); (*Mech.*) brake-block, shoe; (*fig.*) origin. **— vecchio,** old stock (family); **in ceppi,** in chains, fettered; **— di Natale,** Yule log.
cera (1), *n.f.* Look, face, mien, complexion. **Far buona —,** to welcome; **aver buona —,** to look well.
cera (2), *n.f.* Wax, beeswax. **— da scarpe,** boot-polish; **— da calzolaio,** cobbler's wax; **esser di —,** to look waxen, to be very pale.
ceraiolo [ceraiOlo], *n.m.* Candle-seller (in churches).
ceralacca, *n.f.* Sealing-wax. **Cannello di —,** stick of sealing-wax.
cerambice [cerAmbice], *n.f.* (*Zool.*) Stag-beetle.
ceramica [cerAmica], *n.f.* Ceramics, pottery.
ceramista (*pl.* **ceramisti**), *n.m.* Expert in ceramics.
cerasta, *n.f.* (*Zool.*) Cerastes, horned viper.
cerato, *a.* Waxed. **Tela cerata,** oilcloth.
Cerbero [cErbero], *n.m.* (*Myth.*) Cerberus; (*fig.*) tyrant; harsh custodian.
cerbiatto, *n.m.* (*Zool.*) Fawn, young deer.
cerboneca, *n.f.* Sour wine.
cerbottana, *n.f.* Blow-pipe, pea-shooter; speaking-tube for the deaf.
cerca, *n.f.* Search, inquiry, quest. **Andare in — di qualcuno,** to look for someone; **andara alla —,** to go on a quest; to go begging.

cercabile [cercAbıle], *a.* Searchable.
cercamento, *n.m.* Search [cp. **cerca**].
cercare, *v.t.* To seek, to look for; to search; to try, to attempt; (*Radio*) to tune in. — **brighe,** to look for trouble; — **di fare una cosa,** to try to do something; — **cogli occhi,** to look around for; — **un posto,** to look for a job; **chi cerca trova** who seeks finds. **Cercasi** (in advertisements) Wanted; **cercasi giovane stenografo,** Wanted, young shorthand writer.
cercata, *n.f.* Search.
cercatora, cercatrice, *n.m.f.* (*Eccles.*) Postulant (for a religious order).
cerchia [cErchia], *n.f.* Circle, range, sphere, limit. **La — delle mura,** the city walls; **nella nostra —,** in our (social) circle; **far —,** to stand in a circle; (*Comm.*) — **di affari,** line of business.
cerchiare, *v.t.* To circle, to encircle, to ring round; to hoop.
cerchiatura, *n.f.* Hooping (round a cask, etc.).
cerchiello, cerchietto, *n.m.* Ring, earring. **I cerchietti,** quoits.
cerchio [cErchio], *n.m.* Circle, ring, hoop. (*Aviat.*) — **della morte,** looping the loop.
cerchione, *n.m.* Tyre; hoop; rim (of a wheel).
cercine [cErcine], *n.m.* Pad (for bearing burdens on the head); porter's knot.
cereale, *n.m.* Cereal.
cerebrale, *a.* (*Anat.*) Cerebral; (*colloq.*) high-brow.
cerebralità [-à], *n.f.* Intellectualism.
cerebro [cErebro], *n.m.* (*Anat.*) Cerebrum, brain.
cerebrospinale, *a.* (*Med.*) Cerebro-spinal.
cereo [cEreo], *n.m.a.* (*Bot.*) Cactus; (*Eccles.*) Paschal candle; waxen; pallid.
Cerere [cErere], *n.f.* (*Myth.*) Ceres.
cereria [cererIa], *n.f.* Wax-chandler's shop.
cerfoglio [cerfOglio], *n.m.* (*Bot.*) Chervil.
cerimonia [cerimOnia], *n.f.* Ceremony, celebration; formality. **Far cerimonie,** to stand on ceremony.
cerimoniale, *n.m.a.* Ceremonial; protocol.
cerimonialmente, *adv.* Ceremonially.
cerimoniere, *n.m.* Master of ceremonies.
cerimoniosamente, *adv.* Ceremoniously.
cerimoniosità [-à], *n.f.* Ceremoniousness.
cerimonioso, *a.* Ceremonious.
cerinaio [cerinAio], *n.m.* Match-seller.
cerino, *n.m.* Wax match; taper.
cerna, *n.f.* Choice, selection; separation, division.
cernecchio [cernEcchio], *n.m.* Ruffled hair; stray wisp of hair.
cernere [cErnere], *v.t.* To choose, to select.
cerniera, *n.f.* Hinge, articulation. **A —,** hinged; — **lampo,** zip.
cernita [cErnita], *n.f.* Choice, selection.
cernitura, *n.f.* Choice. **Fare una —,** to make a selection.
cero, *n.m.* Altar-candle; taper. **Dritto come un —,** bolt upright.
cerone, *n.m.* (*Theat.*) Make-up (materials).
ceroso, *a.* Waxen; (*fig.*) affable.
cerotto, *n.m.* Plaster; taper; (*fig.*) sickly person; grumbler. — **adesivo,** sticking-plaster.
cerretano, *n.m.* Quack, charlatan.
cerro, *n.m.* (*Bot.*) Turkey oak.
certame, *n.m.* (*Poet.*) Combat. **Singolar —,** duel.
certamente, *adv.* Certainly, assuredly.
certezza, *n.f.* Certainty, certitude, assurance.
certificamento, *n.m.* Certification.
certificante, *a.* Certifying.
certificare, *v.t.* To certify; to attest, to declare; to confirm.
certificato, *n.m.* Certificate, testimony; warrant, voucher. (*Comm.*) — **d'azione,** share certificate; — **di nascita, di morte,** birth, death certificate; — **sanitario,** certificate of the Board of Health; (*Naut.*) — **d'avaria,** certificate of damage.
certificazione, *n.f.* (Act and result of) certification.
certo, *n.m.a.* Certainty, certain thing, certain person. **Un — Cecchi,** a certain person named Cecchi.
certo, *a.* Certain, assured, sure; undetermined.
certo, *adv.* Certainly, of course. **Ma certo!** of course!
certosa, *n.f.* Carthusian monastery, Charterhouse.
certosino, *n.m.* Carthusian monk.
certuno, *pron.* Someone, somebody.
certuni, *pron. pl.* Some people, some folk.
ceruleo, cerulo [cerUleo, cErulo], *a.* Blue, sky-blue.
cerume, *n.m.* Ear wax, cerumen.
cerusico [cerUsico], *n.m.* (*obs.*) Surgeon.
cerussa, *n.f.* (*Metal.*) White lead.
cerva, *n.f.* (*Zool.*) Hind, doe.
cervato, *a.* Dapple-grey.
cervellaccio [cervellAccio], *n.m.* Eccentric person; hot-head.
cervellaggine [cervellAggine], *n.f.* Caprice; stupid thing.
cervellata, *n.f.* Saveloy, sausage.
cervelletto, *n.m.* (*Anat.*) Cerebellum.
cervellino, *n.m.* Hare-brained fellow.
cervello (*pl.* **cervelli,** *m.*, **cervella,** *f.*), *n.m.* Brain; brains, intellect, understanding; sense, judgment. — **balzano,** crank, odd fellow; **stillarsi il —,** to rack one's brains; **bruciarsi le cervella,** to blow out one's brains; **mettere il — a partito,** to settle down, to turn over a new leaf.
cervellone, *n.m.* Dullard; pundit.
cervelloticamente, *adv.* Extravagantly, recklessly.
cervellotico [cervellOtico], *a.* Extravagant, reckless, hair-brained; absurd.
cervicale, *a.* (*Anat.*) Cervical.
cervice, *n.f.* Back of the neck, nape of the neck, neck. **Di dura —,** stubborn.
cerviere, *n.m.* (*Zool.*) Lynx.
cerviero, *a.* Lynx-like.
cervino, *a.* Cervine, pertaining to deer. **Monte Cervino,** the Matterhorn.
cervo, *n.m.* (*Zool.*) Stag; stag-beetle. **Cervo volante,** kite (for flying).
cervogia [cervOgia], *n.f.* Beer.
cerziorare, *v.t.* (*Law*) To inform; to ascertain.
cerziorazione, *n.f.* (*Law*) Information, notice.
Cesare [cEsare], *n.m.* Caesar. **Giulio Cesare,** Julius Caesar.
cesareo [cesAreo], *a.* Caesarian. (*Med.*) **Taglio —,** Caesarian operation; **poeta —,** poet laureate.

cesarie [cesArie], *n.f.* (*obs.*) Head of hair.
cesellamento, *n.m.* Chiselling.
cesellare, *v.t.* To chisel; to emboss.
cesellatore, *n.m.* Sculptor, engraver.
cesellatura, *n.f.* (Result of) chiselling.
cesello, *n.m.* Chisel.
cesena, *n.f.* (*Zool.*) Fieldfare.
cesio [cEsio], *a.* (*Poet.*) Blue; blue-eyed.
cesoiata, *n.f.* Snip or clip with scissors.
cesoie [cesOie], *n.f.pl.* Shears, scissors.
cespo, cespite [cEspite], *n.m.* Tuft, tuft of grass; shrub, bush; (*fig.*) source of income.
cespuglio [cespUglio], *n.m.* Bush, thicket.
cespuglioso, *a.* Bushy.
cessare, *v.t.i.* To cease; to interrupt, to leave off; to discontinue; to subside, to die down. **— di vivere,** to die; **— di piovere,** to stop raining; **— le relazioni,** to break off relations; **la tempesta cessa,** the storm is dying down; **— l'azienda,** to settle the business.
cessazione, *n.f.* Cessation, discontinuance.
cessino, *n.m.* Cess-pit.
cessionario [cessionArio], *n.m.* Cessionary, assignee.
cessione, *n.f.* Cession, assignment, transfer. **Fare una —,** to make a surrender.
cesso, *n.m.* Water-closet, latrine, lavatory.
cesta, *n.f.* Large basket, hamper.
cestaio [cestAio], *n.m.* Basket-maker.
cestello, cestellino, *n.m.* Basket, hand-basket.
cestinare, *v.t.* To throw into the waste-paper basket.
cestino, *n.m.* Small basket; waste-paper basket. **— da viaggio,** lunch basket, picnic basket.
cestire, *v.t.* To bush (of plants).
cesto, *n.m.* Basket, hamper; tuft (of growth); (*Hist.*) cestus; boxing-glove. **Far —,** to become bushy (of plants).
cestola [cEstola], *n.f.* Basket trap for bird-catching.
cestone, *n.m.* Hamper. **Aver il capo come un —,** to feel as if one's head were bursting (because of noise).
cesura, *n.f.* (*Poet.*) Caesura.
cetaceo [cetAceo], *n.m.* (*Zool.*) Cetacean.
cetera [cEtera], *n.f.* [cp. **cetra**].
ceto (1), *n.m.* Class, rank, distinction; order. **— medio,** middle class; **d'ogni —,** of all ranks; **— commerciale,** business people.
ceto (2), *n.m.* (*Zool.*) Whale.
cetologia [cetologIa], *n.f.* Cetology.
cetonia [cetOnia], *n.f.* (*Zool.*) Rose-chafer (beetle).
cetra, *n.f.* (*Hist.*) Zither, lyre.
cetriolo [cetriOlo], *n.m.* Cucumber; gherkin; (*fig.*) ninny, stupid, silly ass.
che, *n.m.* Thing. **Un gran che,** a fine thing; **un bel che!** a nice thing! **che è che non è,** in a moment, unexpectedly.
che, *rel. pron.* Who, whom; that; which, what. **L'uomo che parla,** the man who is speaking; **la signora che vedemmo,** the lady whom we saw; **il cane che era nel giardino,** the dog which was in the garden; **non so che dite,** I don't know what you are saying.
che, *interr. pron.* What? **Che fai?** What are you doing? **Che c'e di nuovo?** What's the news?
che, *conj.* That, than. **Senza che egli se ne avveda,** without his perceiving it; **più presuntuoso che bravo,** more presumptuous than clever; **gli dica che aspetti,** tell him to wait.
che, *adv.* When (as soon as), after until, but (only). **Tosto che arriva, dimmelo,** as soon as he arrives tell me; **aspettate che io venga,** wait till I come; **non ho che una sorella,** I have only one sister; **più bello che mai,** finer than ever.
chè, *conj.* Because; why (contraction of **perchè**).
che! *inter.* What! **Macche! Ma che!** Not at all! **Che! Che!** No! No!
checchè, *pron.* Whatever.
checchessia [checchessIa], *pron.* Whatsoever.
checchia [chEcchia], *n.f.* (*Naut.*) Ketch.
chele, *n.f.pl.* (*Zool.*) Chelae, claws.
cheliceri, *n.m.pl.* (*Zool.*) Palpae (of scorpions. etc.).
chelidro [chElidro], *n.m.* (*Zool.*) Water snake.
chellerina, *n.f.* Barmaid; waitress.
chelonite, *n.f.* (*Min.*) Toad-stone.
chepi, cheppi [-ì], *n.m.* (*Mil.*) Shako, peaked cap.
cheppia [chEppia], *n.f.* (*Zool.*) Shad.
chercuto, *a.* Tonsured [cp. **chiercuto**].
cherica, *n.f.* Tonsure.
chermes, *n.m.* (*Zool.*) Kermes, cochineal.
chermesi, *n.m.* Crimson.
chermesino, *a.* Crimson.
cherubico [cherUbico], *a.* Cherubic.
cherubino, *n.m.* Cherub; (*fig.*) lovely child.
chetamente, *adv.* Quietly.
chetare, *v.t.* To calm, to pacify.
chetarsi, *v.r.* To grow calm; to abate.
chetichella, *adv.* **Alla —,** noiselessly, secretly; underhand; **andarsene alla —,** to steal away; to take French leave.
cheto, *a.* Quiet, tranquil, calm; silent. **Starsene —,** to keep quiet; **— —,** perfectly still; **acqua cheta rovina i ponti,** still waters run deep.
chi, *rel. pron.* Who, whom, whoever, he who, one who. **Chi . . . chi,** some . . . others; **chi parlava, chi rideva,** some were talking, others laughing; **chi ha detto ciò si sbaglia,** whoever said that is wrong; **chi tace consente,** silence is consent; **egli aveva chi l'aiutava,** he had someone to help him.
chi, *interr. pron.* Who? Whom? **Chi c'è di sopra?** Who is upstairs? **Chi hai tu veduto?** Whom did you see? **Chi c'è?** Who's there?
chiacchiera [chiAcchiera], *n.f.* Chat, chatter, talk; gossip, chit-chat.
chiacchieramento, *n.m.* Chattering, cackling.
chiacchierare, *v.i.* To chatter, to prate; to gossip; to talk nonsense.
chiacchierata, *n.f.* Chatter, talk, tittle-tattle.
chiacchiere! *inter.* Nonsense!
chiacchiericcio [chiacchierIccio], *n.m.* Prating; nonsense.
chiacchierino, *n.m.* Chatterbox (child); talkative person.
chiacchierio [chiacchierIo], *n.m.* Constant chattering.
chiacchierone, *n.m.* Great talker, inveterate gossip; (*colloq.*) gas-bag.
chiama, *n.f.* Call; cry, appeal; roll call. **La — degli scolari,** school roll call [cp. **appello**].
chiamare, *v.t.* To call, to name; to cry, to appeal; to summon. **— aiuto,** to call for help; **— in disparte,** to call aside; **— le**

cose col loro nome, to call a spade a spade; **— in testimonio,** to call to witness; **mandar a —,** to send for; *(Mil.)* **— alle armi,** to call up; **— in giudizio,** to sue, to take legal proceedings; **— il medico,** to send for the doctor; *(Theat.)* **— alla ribalta,** to call before the curtain; **— al telefono,** to ring up.
chiamarsi, *v.r.* To be named, to be called. **Come si chiama quest'oggetto?** What is this thing called? **Come vi chiamate?** What is your name?
chiamata, *n.f.* Call, appeal, summons; cross-reference (in a book); *(Theat.)* curtain call; *(Mil.)* call-up. **— telefonica,** telephone call; **fare la —,** to call the roll.
chiana, *n.f.* *(obs.)* Marshy place.
chianti, *n.m.* Kind of wine (from a Tuscan district of that name).
chiappa, *n.f.(colloq.)*Buttock; *(obs.)* hold, grasp.
chiappamosche, *n.m.* Fly-paper, fly-trap.
chiappanuvole [chiappanUvole], *n.m.* Wool-gatherer, day-dreamer.
chiappare, *v.t.* To catch, to seize [cp. **acchiappare**].
chiapparello, *n.m.* Trap (in speech, examinations, etc.).
chiappo, *n.m.* *(obs.)* Gain, unexpected advantage.
chiappola [chiAppola], *n.f.* *(obs.)* Object of no value; matter of no importance.
chiara, *n.f.* White of (uncooked) egg.
chiaramente, *adv.* Clearly, plainly.
chiarata, *n.f.* Poultice made with beaten-up white of egg.
chiareggiare, *v.t.* To make clear, to clarify; to explain [cp. **chiarificare**].
chiaretto, *n.m.* Claret; light wine.
chiaretto, *a.* Clearish.
chiarezza, *n.f.* Clearness, brightness; distinctness; evidence, plainness.
chiarificare, *v.t.* To clarify; to clear up; to explain.
chiarificazione, *n.f.* Clarifying, clarification; explanation.
chiarimento, *n.m.* Explanation.
chiarina, *n.f.* *(Mus.)* Clarion.
chiarire, *v.t.* To make clear; to explain; to illustrate, to show.
chiarirsi, *v.r.* To make oneself clear; to ascertain.
chiarissimo, *a.* Very clear; illustrious. **— signore,** Dear Sir (in letters).
chiarità [-à], *n.f.* Clarity, terseness; splendour; lucidity, cleanness.
chiaritoio [chiaritOio], *n.m.* Implement (and place where it is used) for clarifying oil, etc.
chiaritura, *n.f.* (Operation of) clarification of oil, etc.
chiaro, *n.m.* Clearness, brightness, light. **Comincia a far —,** it begins to dawn; **— di luna,** moonlight; **mettere in —,** to clear up, to make clear, to explain.
chiaro, *a.* Clear, bright; evident, plain, manifest; distinct; noble, distinguished, illustrious. **È — che,** it is clear that.
chiarore, *n.m.* Glimmer, (increasing) brightness. **— dell'alba,** the first glimmer of dawn.
chiaroscuro, *n.m.* *(Art)* Chiaroscuro, light and shade.
chiaroveggente, *n.m.f.* Clairvoyant; clear-sighted person.
chiaroveggenza, *n.f.* Clairvoyance; clear-sightedness, perspicacity.
chiasmo, *n.m.* *(Gram.)* Chiasmus; *(Anat.)* chiasm.
chiassare, *v.i.* *(obs.)* To create an uproar.
chiassata, *n.f.* Uproar, row, racket.
chiassetto, *n.m.* Blind alley, lane.
chiasso (1), *n.m.* Noise, bustle; uproar; jest, joke. **Far —,** to make a noise; **l'ho fatto per —,** I did it as a joke.
chiasso (2), *n.m.* Lane, alley.
chiassolino, chiassolo, chiassuolo, *n.m.* Alley, back street, lane.
chiassone, *n.m.* Blusterer, noisy fellow.
chiassosamente, *adv.* Noisily, rowdily; showily.
chiassoso, *a.* Noisy, boisterous; gaudy, showy.
chiatta, *n.f.* *(Naut.)* Barge, lighter. **Spese di —,** lighterage. **Ponte di chiatte,** bridge of boats; pontoon bridge.
chiattaiuolo, *n.m.* *(Naut.)* Lighterman.
chiatto, *a.* Flat; dwarfish.
chiavaccio [chiavAccio], *n.m.* Bolt (of a door).
chiavaio [chiavAio], *n.m.* Custodian, holder of keys.
chiavarda, *n.f.* Iron pin; bolt.
chiavardare, *v.t.* To fasten with a bolt; to bolt.
chiave, *n.f.* Key; spanner, wrench; clue (to puzzle, etc.); plug; *(Mus.)* clef, key. **La — di casa,** the latch-key; **— falsa,** skeleton key; **buco della —,** key-hole; **— regolabile, — inglese,** monkey-wrench, adjustable spanner; **chiudere a —,** to lock; **tener sotto —,** to keep under lock and key; *(Mus.)* **— di do,** C clef.
chiavetta, *n.f.* Small key; tap (water, gas, etc.), cock; switch (light, etc.).
chiavica [chiAvica], *n.f.* Covered drain; sluice-gate (of a sewer).
chiavistello, *n.m.* Padlock; latch; door-bolt.
chiazza, *n.f.* Spot, stain, speck.
chiazzare, *v.t.* To speck, to stain, to spot.
chiazzatura, *n.f.* Blotchiness, spottiness.
chicca, *n.f.* Sweet, sweetmeat. **Chicche,** sweets (in general).
chicchera [chIcchera], *n.f.* Teacup; coffee-cup.
chicchessia [chicchessIa], *pron.* Whoever, whomsoever.
chicchiriata, *n.f.* Crowing of a number of cocks.
chicchirichì [-ì], *n.m.* Cock-crowing, cock-a-doodle-do.
chicco, *n.m.* Grain, coffee-bean, grape-stone, hailstone.
chichingero [chichIngero], *n.m.* *(Bot.)* Winter cherry.
chiedente, *n.m.* Applicant, petitioner.
chiedere [chiEdere], *v.t.* To ask, to demand; to request, to beg; to inquire, to implore. **— in moglie,** to ask in marriage; **bisogna —,** you must ask; **— una grazia,** to beg a favour; **— notizie di qualcuno,** to inquire (after someone); **— venia,** to apologize; **— perdono, — scusa,** to beg pardon.
chiedibile [chiedIbile], *a.* That may be asked for.
chiercuto, *n.m.a.* Priest, monk; tonsured.
chierica [chiErica], *n.f.* Tonsure.
chiericale, *a.* Clerical [cp. **clericale**].

chiericalmente, *adv.* Clerically, ecclesiastically.
chierichetto, *n.m.* Altar-server; choirboy.
chierico [chiErico], *n.m.* Cleric, ecclesiastic.
chiericuto, *a.* Tonsured.
chiesa, *n.f.* Church (in all senses); parish. **Andare in —,** to go to church.
chiesastico [chiesAstico], *a.* Ecclesiastical.
chiesetta, chiesina, *n.f.* Little church, chapel.
chiesola,chiesuola, *n.f.* Small country church; (*Naut.*) binnacle; (*fig.*) clique (artistic, etc.).
chiesta, *n.f.* (*obs.*) Request, petition.
chifel, *n.m.* Crescent-shaped pastry.
chiglia [chIglia], *n.f.* (*Naut.*) Keel.
chilificare, *v.i.* (*Physiol.*) To chylify, to form chyle.
chilo (1), *n.m.* (*Physiol.*) Chyle. (*fig.*) **Fare il chilo,** to have a short rest after a meal.
chilo (2), **chilogrammo,** *n.m.* Kilogramme.
chilociclo, *n.m.* (*Radio*) Kilocycle.
chilolitro [chilOlitro], *n.m.* Thousand litres.
chilometro [chilOmetro], *n.m.* Kilometre.
chilowatt [chilowAtt], *n.m.* (*Elect.*) Kilowatt. **Chilowattore,** Kilowatt hours.
chimera, *n.f.* Chimera; illusion.
chimericamente, *adv.* Chimerically.
chimerico [chimErico], *a.* Chimerical.
chimica [chImica], *n.f.* Chemistry.
chimicamente, *adv.* Chemically.
chimico [chImico], *n.m.a.* Chemist; chemical.
chimificazione, *n.f.* (*Physiol.*) Formation of chyme, chymification.
chimismo, *n.m.* Chemism.
chimo, *n.m.* (*Physiol.*) Chyme.
chimono, *n.m.* Kimono.
chimosi, *n.f.* (*Physiol.*) Chymification.
china (1), *n.f.* Slope, declivity, descent. **Lasciar andar l'acqua per la sua —,** let things take their course; (*fig.*) **essere su una cattiva —,** to be on slippery ground.
china (2), *n.f.* (*Bot.*) Peruvian bark; quinine. **Decotto di —,** tincture of quinine.
chinare, *v.t.* To incline, to bend, to bow; to lower, to droop. **— la testa,** to bow one's head.
chinarsi, *v.r.* To stoop, to bow down, to incline oneself; to submit.
chinata, *n.f.* Declivity; slope, descent.
chinato, *a.* With quinine.
chincaglie [chincAglie], *n.f.pl.* Knick-knacks.
chincagliere, *n.m.* Seller of nick-nacks.
chincaglieria [chincaglierIa], *n.f.* Nick-nacks, trifles, fancy goods.
chinea [chinEa], *n.f.* (*obs.*) Hackney horse.
chineseria [chineserIa], *n.f.* Chinoiserie.
chinino, *n.m.* Quinine.
chino, *a.* Bent, inclined, stooping. **A capo —,** with bowed head.
chinotto, *n.m.* (*Bot.*) Kind of citron.
chioccare, *v.t.* To crack a whip; to snap the fingers [cp. **schioccare**].
chioccia [chiOccia], *n.f.* Broody hen. || *a.* hoarse (of voice).
chiocciare, *v.i.* To cluck.
chiocciata, *n.f.* Brood of chickens.
chiocciola [chiOcciola], *n.f.* (*Zool.*) Snail; (*Mech.*) female screw. **Scala a —,** winding staircase, spiral staircase.
chiocciolaio [chiocciolAio], *n.m.* Vendor of (edible) snails.
chiocco, *n.m.* Crack (of a whip) [cp. **schiocco**].
chioccolare, *v.i.* To sing like a bird, to whistle, to trill.
chioccolio [chioccolIo], *n.m.* Whistling.
chioccolo [chiOccolo], *n.m.* Bird whistle.
chiodaiolo, *n.m.* Nail-maker or vendor.
chiodame, *n.m.* Nails, nailware.
chiodare, *v.t.* To nail [cp. **inchiodare**].
chiodato, *p.p.a.* Nailed. **Scarpe chiodate,** hobnailed shoes, spiked shoes.
chiodatura, *n.f.* Riveting; nailing. **— ermetica,** tight-riveting; **— a sovrapposizione,** lap-riveting [cp. **inchiodatura**].
chiodetto, *n.m.* Small nail, tack.
chiodo, *n.m.* Nail; hobnail (for boots); (*Mech.*) rivet, pin, clinch. **Conficcare un —,** to drive in a nail; **cavare un —,** to pull out a nail; **— da ribadire,** rivet; **passaggio da —, tracciato da —,** studded road-crossing; **avere un —,** to have a fixed idea; **roba da chiodi,** absurd or vile things; **piantar chiodi,** to run into debt.
chioma, *n.f.* (*Poet.*) Head of hair, long hair; mane (of lion); tail (of a comet).
chiomante, *a.* With luxuriant tresses.
chiomato, *a.* Hairy, with flowing hair; fibrous, leafy.
chiosa, *n.f.* Gloss, explanatory note.
chiosare, *v.t.* To comment, to expound, to gloss, to annotate.
chiosatore, chiosatrice, *n.m.f.* Annotator, expounder.
chiosco, *n.m.* Kiosk, stall. **— dei giornali,** bookstall.
chiostra, *n.f.* Precinct, boundary; round, circle.
chiostro, *n.m.* Cloister; monastery, convent.
chiotto, *a.* Silent and motionless. **Chiotto chiotto,** perfectly silent and still.
chiozzo, *n.m.* (*Zool.*) Gudgeon.
chiozzotta, *n.f.* (*Naut.*) Rig of vessel (used at Chioggia).
chiozzotto, *a.* Of Chioggia.
chiragra, *n.f.* (*Med.*) Gout of the hands.
chirografario [chirografArio], *a.* (*Comm.*) Book. **Debito —,** book debt.
chirografo [chirOgrafo], *n.m.* Written agreement, private agreement.
chirologia [chirologIa], *n.f.* Chirology, speaking with the hands.
chiromanzia [chiromanzIa]. *n.* Fortune-telling; palmistry.
chirotteri [chirOtteri], *n.m.pl.* (*Zool.*) Chiroptera, the bats (order of mammals).
chirurgia [chirurgIa], *n.f.* Surgery.
chirurgicamente, *adv.* Surgically.
chirurgico [chirUrgico], *a.* Surgical.
chirurgo, *n.m.* Surgeon.
chisciottesco, *a.* Quixotic. **Don Chisciotte,** Don Quixote.
chissisia [chissisIa], *pron.* Whosoever it may be.
chitarra, *n.f.* Guitar.
chitarrino, *n.m.* Small guitar; (*fig.*) bad music.
chitarrista (*pl.* **chitarristi**), *n.m.* Guitar-player.

chitarronata, *n.f.* Long-winded, dreary poem; a wearisome screed.
chitina, *n.f.* (*Zool.*) Chitin.
chiù [-**ù**], *n.m.* (*Zool.*) Horned-owl.
chiudenda, *n.f.* Enclosure; hedge, fence, palisade.
chiudere [chiUdere], *v.t.* To shut, to close, to lock, to bolt, to bar; to turn off (gas, etc.); to stop up (a hole); to clench (the fist); to conclude, to finish; (*Comm.*) to balance (books). **— la porta,** to close the door; **— a chiave,** to lock; **— il discorso,** to conclude the speech; **— la via,** to bar the road; **— un occhio,** to shut one's eyes (to another's defects), to wink at; (*Comm.*) **— i conti,** to close the accounts.
chiudersi, *v.r.* To shut oneself up; to be closed; to close; to be overcast (of weather). **Il museo si chiude alle sei,** the museum closes at six; **— in camera,** to shut oneself up in one's room.
chiudimento, *n.m.* Closing, closure [cp. **chiusura**].
chiunque, *pron.* Whoever; anybody.
chiurlare, *v.i.* To hoot (as an owl); to whistle (like a curlew).
chiurlo, *n.m.* (*Zool.*) Curlew.
chiusa, *n.f.* Enclosure, barrier; conclusion (of speech, letter, etc.); weir, dam, lock (of canal).
chiusamente, *adv.* Hiddenly, covertly.
chiusino, *n.m.* Cover or lid (of a hole); oven door; secret drawer.
chiuso, *n.m.* Enclosure; sheep-fold, pen.
chiuso, *a.* Locked, closed, shut, bolted; hidden, reserved; overcast (of weather); (*Comm.*) balanced, settled.
chiusura, *n.f.* Closing, closing down, shutting; fastening, lock, bolt. (*Elect.*) **— del circuito,** closing of the circuit; **— lampo,** zip-fastener; (*Comm.*) **— dei conti,** closing of the accounts; **registrazione di —,** closing entry in making up an account.
ci, *pron.* Us, to us, ourselves; of it; to it. **Ci diede,** he gave us; **ci lavammo,** we washed ourselves; **non ci ho mai pensato,** I have never thought of it; **ci ho proprio gusto,** I am very glad of it.
ci, *adv.* There, here. **Non ci sono gitanti,** there are no tourists; **veniteci quando volete,** come here whenever you like; **ci siamo,** here we are.
ciabare, *v.i.* (*obs.*) To jabber; to chat.
ciabatta, *n.f.* Down-at-heel slipper; broken shoe.
ciabattare, *v.i.* To shuffle along.
ciabattata, *n.f.* Spank with a slipper.
ciabatterie [ciabatterIe], *n.f.pl.* Rubbish, nonsense.
ciabattino, *n.m.* Cobbler.
ciabattone, *n.m.* Down-at-heel fellow; shuffler, bungler.
ciabone, *n.m.* (*obs.*) Chatterer, gossiper.
ciaccherino, ciacchero [ciAcchero], *n.m.* (*obs.*) Rascal; fellow with hoggish manners.
ciacciare, *v.i.* (*obs.*) To act the busybody.
ciaccione, *n.m.* (*obs.*) Busybody, meddler.
ciacco, *n.m.a.* (*fig.*) glutton; swinish, dirty.
ciaccona, *n.f.* (*Mus.*) Chaconne (dance and tune).
cialda, *n.f.* Wafer, waffle.
cialdone, *n.m.* Rolled wafer, cornet.
cialtrona, *n.f.* Slut, slattern.
cialtrone, *n.m.* Rascal, rogue; slovenly fellow.
cialtroneria [cialtronerIa], *n.f.* Rascality, blackguardism.
ciambella, *n.f.* Ring-shaped bun; air-cushion; (child's) teething-ring. **Non tutte le ciambelle riescono col buco,** not every undertaking is crowned with success.
ciambellaio [ciambellAio], *n.m.* Pastrycook.
ciambellano, *n.m.* Chamberlain.
ciambola [ciAmbola], *n.f.* Gossip, mischief-maker; slut.
ciambolare, *v.i.* To talk big, to brag; to prate.
ciambolio [ciambolIo], *n.m.* Bragging
ciambolone, *n.m.* Braggart.
ciampanelle, *n.f.pl.* (*slang*) **Dare in —,** to blunder, to act foolishly.
ciampicare, *v.i.* To shuffle along, to drag one's feet.
ciampichino, *n.m.* Slow worker.
ciampicone, *n.m.* Shuffler, one who shuffles when he walks; dawdler.
ciana, *n.f.* Slut, slattern.
cianata, *n.f.* Ill-bred act or word.
cianca, *n.f.* (*colloq.*) Leg, shank.
ciancanella, *n.f.* Bandy-legged person.
ciancia [ciAncia], *n.f.* Gossip, tittle-tattle; nonsense. **Ciancie!** Nonsense! Rubbish!
cianciafruscola [cianciafrUscola], *n.f.* (*colloq.*) Trifle, foolishness.
cianciamento, *n.m.* Chatter, twaddle.
cianciare, *v.i.* To chatter, to talk idly, to talk nonsense.
cianciatore, cianciatrice, *n.m.f.* Tatler, gossip.
ciancicare, *v.i.* To mouth (one's words), to mumble; to eat slowly.
ciancione, *n.m.* Gossip; boaster.
cianciosamente, *adv.* Noisily (with chatter).
cianciosο, *a.* Noisy, babbling.
cianciugliare, *v.i.* To mumble.
cianesco, *a.* Low, vulgar.
cianfruglione, *n.m.* Bungler.
cianfrusaglia [cianfrusAglia], *n.f.* Trifle, bric-a-brac; trash.
ciangola [ciAngola], *n.f.* (*obs.*) Chatter.
ciangottare, *v.i.* To speak badly (swallowing r's and l's); to lisp (as a child); to twitter (of a bird).
ciangottio [ciangottIo], *n.m.* Twittering.
cianico [ciAnico], *a.* (*Chem.*) Cyanic.
cianidrico [cianIdrico], *a.* (*Chem.*) Hydrocyanic.
cianina, *n.f.* (*Chem.*). Cyanin.
ciano, *n.m.* (*Bot.*) Cornflower; blue.
cianogeno [cianOgeno], *n.m.* (*Chem.*) Cyanogen.
cianosi, *n.f.* (*Med.*) Cyanosis.
ciantella, *n.f.* Old shoe.
cianuro, *n.m.* (*Chem.*) Cyanide. **— di potassio,** potassium cyanide.
ciao, *inter.* (*colloq.*) Hello ! So long! Cheerio!
ciappola [ciAppola], *n.f.* Graving-tool.
ciaramella, *n.f.* (*Mus.*) Bag-pipe [cp. **cennamella**].
ciarla, *n.f.* Tittle-tattle, idle talk, gossip.
ciarlare, *v.i.* To gossip; to chat.
ciarlatanesco, *a.* Like a charlatan, clownish.
ciarlatanata, *n.f.* Humbug, quackery, buffoonery.

ciarlatanismo, *n.m.* Charlatanry, quackery; humbug.
ciarlatano, *n.m.* Charlatan, quack; clown.
ciarlatore, ciarlatrice, *n.m.f.* Chatterer; bore.
ciarleria [ciarlerIa], *n.f.* Chatter, empty talk.
ciarliero, *a.* Talkative.
ciarlio [ciarlIo], *n.m.* Gossip, chatter.
ciarlone, *n.m.* Chatterer, "gas-bag"; tell-tale.
ciarpa, *n.f.* Scarf [cp. **sciarpa**].
ciarpame, *n.m.* Trash, rubbish; heap of scraps and rags.
ciascuno, ciascheduno, *pron.a.* Everyone, everybody; every one, each.
cibamento, *n.m.* Aliment, nourishment.
cibare, *v.t.* To feed, to nourish.
cibarie, *n.f.pl.* Victuals, foodstuff, provisions.
cibarsi, *v.r.* To feed upon; to live upon. (*fig.*) **— d'illusioni,** to cherish illusions.
cibazione, *n.f.* Nourishment, spiritual nourishment [cp. **cibo**].
cibo, *n.m.* Food, nourishment; diet; dish, meal. **— quotidiano,** daily bread; **prender —,** to take food.
ciborio [cibOrio], *n.m.* (*Eccles.*) Pyx, ciborium.
cibreo [cibrEo], *n.m.* Fricassee of eggs and giblets; (*fig.*) medley, muddle.
cica, *n.f.* Bagatelle, mere nothing.
cicala, *n.f.* (*Zool.*) Cicada.
cicalamento, *n.m.* Chattering, noisy talking.
cicalare, *v.i.* To chatter, to talk nonsense.
cicalata, *n.f.* Idle talk; long-winded speech.
cicaleccio, cicalio [cicalEccio, cicalIo], *n.m.* Chatter, prattle.
cicalone, *n.m.* Gossip, tell-tale.
cicatrice, *n.f.* Cicatrix, scar.
cicatrizzare, *v.t.i.* To skin over.
cicatrizzarsi, *v.r.* To cicatrize, to heal over, to skin over.
cicatrizzazione, *n.f.* Skinning over; cicatrization.
cicca, *n.f.* (*colloq.*) Cigar butt, cigarette end, fag-end; quid (tobacco). **— da masticare,** quid.
ciccaiolo, *n.m.* Picker-up of fag-ends.
ciccare, *v.i.* To chew tobacco.
cicchettare, *v.i.* (*colloq.*) To drink a drop, "to have one".
cicchetto, *n.m.* Nip (of brandy, etc.); (*colloq.*) rebuke.
ciccia [cIccia], *n.f.* Meat; (human) flesh, fat. **È tutto —,** he's all fat.
cicciola [cIcciola], *n.f.* (*Bot.*) Kind of edible fungus.
cicciolo [cIcciolo], *n.m.* Fatty meat to be rendered down for lard.
ciccione, *n.m.* Fat person; (*Med.*) boil.
ciccioso, cicciuto, *a.* Fleshy, fat, plump.
cicerbita [cicErbita] *n.f.* (*Bot.*) Sow-thistle.
cicerchia [cicErchia], *n.f.* (*Bot.*) Vetch.
Cicerone, *n.m.* Cicero.
cicerone, *n.m.* Guide (round a town, etc.).
cicisbeismo, *n.m.* Cicisbeism.
cicisbeo [cicisbEo], *n.m.* Cicisbeo; married woman's gallant, gigolo.
ciclamino, *n.m.* (*Bot.*) Cyclamen.
ciclico [cIclico], *a.* Curved; (*Astron.Lit.*) cyclic. **Poeti ciclici,** epic poets.
ciclismo, *n.m.* Cycling; bicycling.
ciclista (*pl.* **ciclisti**), *n.m.* Cyclist.
ciclistico [ciclIstico], *a.* Cycling. **Giro —,** cycling tour.
ciclo, *n.m.* Cycle (in all senses); bicycle.
cicloidale, *a.* Cycloidal.
cicloide [ciclOide], *n.f.* (*Geom.*) Cycloid.
ciclomotore, *n.m.* Autocycle, motor-bike.
ciclone, *n.m.* Cyclone, tornado.
ciclonico [ciclOnico], *a.* Cyclonic.
Ciclope, *n.m.* (*Myth.*) Cyclops.
ciclopico [ciclOpico], *a.* Cyclopean.
ciclostile, *n.m.* Cyclostyle.
ciclotrone, *n.m.* (*Phys.*) Cyclotron.
cicogna, *n.f.* (*Zool.*) Stork.
cicoria [cicOria], *n.f.* (*Bot.*) Chicory.
cicuta, *n.f.* (*Bot.*) Hemlock.
cieca [ciEca], *n.f.* Blind woman; recess cut for a screwhead.
cieca, *adv.* **Alla —,** blindly, thoughtlessly.
ciecamente, *adv.* Blindly.
cieco, *n.m.* Blind man.
cieco, *a.* Blind; dark, gloomy, obscure; concealed; without exit; doorless and windowless; inconsiderate, thoughtless. **— d'ira,** blind with anger; **vicolo —,** blind alley; **mosca cieca,** blindman's buff; (*Anat.*) **intestino —,** caecum.
cielo, *n.m.* Sky, Heaven, heavens; air; climate. **Per amor del —,** for Heaven's sake; **volesse il —,** would to Heaven; **il — me ne guardi,** Heaven forbid; **toccare il — col dito,** to be overjoyed at; to have unexpected luck; **egli ha mosso — e terra,** he has moved Heaven and earth, he has left no stone unturned; **non star nè in — nè in terra,** to be absurd; **portare ai sette cieli,** to extol to the skies.
cifra, *n.f.* Initials; cipher; number; figure, **In — tonda,** in round figures; **telegramma in —,** cipher telegram; (*Comm.*) **— di affari,** turnover; **—-indice,** index number.
cifrare, *v.t.* To cipher; to initial; to mark (linen, etc.).
cifrario [cifrArio], *n.m.* Key to cipher.
ciglio (pl. **ciglia,** *f.*; **cigli,** *m.*) [cIglio], *n.m.* Eyebrow; eyelash (of eyelid); brink, edge (of precipice, etc.); verge (of road, etc.). **Inarcar le ciglia,** to raise the brows (in surprise); **senza batter —,** without stirring.
cigliuto, *a.* With bushy eyebrows.
cigna [cp. **cinghia**].
cignale, *n.m.* Wild boar [cp. **cinghiale**].
cignersi, *v.r.* [cp. **cingere**].
cigno, *n.m.* (*Zool.*) Swan. **Il canto del —,** swan-song.
cigolamento, *n.m.* Clattering, rattling.
cigolare, *v.i.* To creak; to clatter; to grate; to hiss (of green wood burning).
cigolio [cigolIo], *n.m.* Creaking; clattering; hissing.
cilecca, *n.f.* Failure, baulking; disappointment. **Far —,** to miss fire, to fail, to fall through.
cilestro, *a.* Blue.
cilicio [cilIcio], *n.m.* Sackcloth.
ciliegeto, *n.m.* Cherry orchard.
ciliegia [ciliEgia], *n.f.* Cherry. **Ratafia di ciliegie,** cherry brandy.
ciliegio [ciliEgio], *n.m.* (*Bot.*) Cherry-tree; cherry wood.
cilindrare, *v.t.* To roll (smooth); to press; to mangle; to calender.
cilindrata, *n.f.* (*Motor.*) Capacity of a cylinder, cylinder displacement.

cilindratoio [cilindratOio], *n.m.* Roller, calender; mangle.
cilindricamente, *adv.* Cylindrically.
cilindrico [cilIndrico], *a.* Cylindrical.
cilindro, *n.m.* Cylinder, roller; mangle; barrel; drum; (*colloq.*) top-hat.
cilizio [cilIzio], *n.m.* Sackcloth; hair-shirt; (*fig.*) anything troublesome.
cima, *n.f.* Top, summit, peak; (*colloq.*) top of the tree. **Da — a fondo,** from beginning to end; **in —,** at the top; **— d'uomo,** eminent man; **non è una —,** he's by no means a genius.
cimare, *v.t.* To pollard, to lop; to shear (cloth).
cimasa, *n.f.* (*Arch.*) Finial; ogee.
cimata, *n.f.* (Operation of) clipping.
cimatore, *n.m.* Tailor's cutter.
cimatura, *n.f.* Clippings, clipping.
cimbalo [cImbalo], *n.m.* (*Mus.*) Cymbal [cp. **cembalo**].
cimberli [cImberli], *n.m.pl.* **Essere in —,** to be jolly (with drink), half-seas-over.
cimelio [cimElio], *n.m.* Relic; curio. **Cimeli di guerra,** war relics.
cimentare, *v.t.* To try, to put to the test, to risk. **— la propria riputazione,** to jeopardize one's reputation.
cimentarsi, *v.r.* To risk, to run a risk, to expose oneself (to danger); to venture upon, to dare.
cimento, *n.m.* Trial, test, experience; provocation; danger, risk.
cimice [cImice], *n.f.* (*Zool.*) Bug, bed-bug.
cimiciaio [cimiciAio], *n.m.* Nest of bugs.
cimicioso, *a.* Bug-infested.
cimiero, *n.m.* Crest of a helmet.
ciminiera, *n.f.* Funnel (of a steamer), smoke-stack.
cimino, *n.m.* (*Bot.*) Cumin.
cimiteriale, *a.* Pertaining to a cemetery.
cimitero, *n.m.* Cemetery.
cimmerio [cimmErio], *a.* Cimmerian, dark, gloomy.
cimosa, *n.f.* Selvedge; rag for cleaning a slate.
cimurro, *n.m.* Glanders (of horse); distemper (of dog).
Cina, *n.f.* China.
cinabro, *n.m.* Cinnabar, vermilion.
cincia, cinciallegra, cinciarella [cIncia], *n.f.* (*Zool.*) Tit, tom-tit, titmouse.
cinciazzurra, *n.f.* (*Zool.*) Blue tit.
cinciglia [cincIglia], *n.f.* (*Zool.*) Chinchilla.
cincinno, *n.m.* (*obs.*) Curl (of hair).
cincischiare, *v.t.i.* To gash, to hack; to trifle, to dawdle. **— le parole,** to clip one's words.
cincischio [cincischIo], *n.m.* Gash; trifling.
cincischione, *n.m.* Dawdler.
cincona, *n.f.* (*Bot.*) Cinchona.
cine, cinema [cInema], *n.m.* Cinematograph, picture-house, show; motion pictures, (*Am.*) movies. **Andiamo al —,** let's go to the pictures.
cineasta (*pl.* **cineasti**), *n.m.* Movie-man; film artist.
cinedo, *n.m.* Male prostitute.
cinegetica [cinegEtica], *n.f.* Cynegetics, the art and lore of hunting with dogs.
cinegiornale, cinemagiornale, *n.m.* Newsreel.
cinematografare, *v.t.* To film, to shoot a film
cinematografia [cinematografIa], *n.f.* Cinematography; film, pictures.
cinematografico [cinematogrAfico], *a.* Cinematographic, film. **Attrice cinematografica,** film actress.
cinematografista (*pl.* **cinematografisti**) *n.m.* Movie-man, film operator.
cinematografo [cinematOgrafo], *n.m.* Cinematograph, cinema, picture-house; the pictures.
cineraria [cinerAria], *n.f.* (*Bot.*) Cineraria.
cinerario [cinerArio], *a.* Cinerary.
cinereo [cinEreo], *a.* Ashy, ash-coloured.
cinese, *a.* Chinese.
cinetica [cinEtica], *n.f.* Kinetics.
cingallegra, *n.f.* (*Zool.*) Tit. [cp. **cincia**].
cingere [cIngere], *v.t.* To enclose, to encircle, to surround, to gird; to border; to clasp. **— di una siepe,** to hedge round.
cingersi [cIngersi], *v.r.* To gird oneself. **— la spada,** to gird on one's sword.
cinghia [cInghia], *n.f.* Strap, belt, girdle, girth (of harness); braces; (child's) leading-strings. (*Mech.*) **— di trasmissione,** driving-belt.
cinghiale, *n.m.* (*Zool.*) Wild boar.
cinghiata, *n.f.* Thrashing with a strap.
cinghio [cInghio], *n.m.* (*obs.*) Circle.
cingolo [cIngolo], *n.m.* Girdle, belt; cordon. (*Mech.*) **Catena a cingoli,** endless chain.
cinguettare, *v.i.* To chirp, to twitter; to chatter.
cinguettata, *n.f.* Confused noise of chattering.
cinguettio [cinguettIo], *n.m.* (Continual) chirping, twittering; chattering.
cinicamente, *adv.* Cynically.
cinico [cInico], *n.m.a.* Cynic; cynical.
cinigia [cinIgia], *n.f.* Ember; hot ash.
ciniglia [cinIglia], *n.m.* Chenille.
cinismo, *n.m.* Cynicism.
cinnamomo, *n.m.* Cinnamon [cp. **canella**].
cinocefalo [cinocEfalo], *n.m.* (*Zool.*) Baboon; (*Archaeol.*) dog-faced man of Egyptian monuments.
cinofilo [cinOfilo], *n.m.* Dog-fancier.
cinquanta, *a.* Fifty.
cinquantenario [cinquantenArio], *n.m.* Man aged fifty; fiftieth anniversary.
cinquantenne, *a.* Fifty years old.
cinquantennio [cinquantEnnio], *n.m.* Period of fifty years.
cinquantesimo [cinquantEsimo], *a.* Fiftieth.
cinquantina, *n.f.* About fifty.
cinque, *a.* Five.
cinquecentista, *n.m.f.* Writer or artist of the 16th century.
cinquecento, *a.* Five hundred; 16th century.
cinquefoglie [cinquefOglie], *n.m.* (*Bot.*) Cinquefoil.
cinquemila, *a.* Five thousand.
cinquina, *n.f.* Set of five; five winning numbers in State lottery; soldier's pay.
cinta, *n.f.* Enclosure; belt; town wall, circuit.
cinto, *n.m.a.* Enclosure, belt; girdle; girdled, surrounded. **— erniario,** medical truss.
cintola [cIntola], *n.f.* Girdle; band. **Stare colle mani alla —,** to stand idle.
cintolo [cIntolo], *n.m.* Small band.
cintura, *n.f.* Belt, girdle, sash; waist; enclosure. **— di salvataggio,** life-belt.

cinturino, *n.m.* Strap-belt; belt.
cinturone, *n.m.* Sword-belt; rifle-sling.
Cinzia [cInzia], *n.f.* (*Poet.*) The Moon; Cynthia.
ciò, *pron.* That, this, it. **Ciò che,** that which; **senza di ciò,** without it; **a ciò,** for this purpose; **oltre a ciò,** moreover; **con tutto ciò,** for all that; **essere da ciò,** to be fit for that.
ciocca, *n.f.* Lock of hair; bunch of flowers.
cioccia [ciOccia], *n.f.* (Mother's) breast.
ciocciare, *v.i.* To suckle.
ciocco, *n.m.* Log of wood.
cioccolata, *n.f.* Chocolate.
cioccolataio, cioccolatiere [cioccolatAio], *n.m.* Maker, vendor of chocolate.
cioccolatiera, *n.f.* Chocolate-pot.
cioccolatini, *n.m.pl.* Chocolates, chocolate drops.
ciocia, *n.f.* Shoe worn by Roman peasants.
ciociaro, *n.m.* Peasant of the Roman Campagna.
cioè, *adv.* That is, namely, to wit.
ciompo, *n.m.* (*Hist.*) Wool-carder; plebeian. **Il tumulto dei Ciompi,** the Florentine Carders' Riot (1378).
cioncare, *v.t.* To tipple, to booze.
cioncatore, *n.m.* Boozer, tippler.
cionco, *a.* Slovenly; drunk.
ciondolamento, *n.m.* Lounging, hanging about.
ciondolare, *v.i.* To dangle (round someone); to hang loosely.
ciondolo [ciOndolo], *n.m.* Pendant, trinket; (*colloq.*) medal, decoration, "gong".
ciondolone, *n.m.* Idler, lounger.
ciondoloni, *adv.* Dangling, swaying.
ciotola [ciOtola], *n.f.* Bowl, cup, basin.
ciotolata, *n.f.* Cupful.
ciotto, *a.* (*obs.*) Lame.
ciottolare, *v.t.* To pave with cobbles.
ciottolato, *n.m.* Cobbled pathway; crazy pavement.
ciottolo [ciOttolo], *n.m.* Pebble, flint, stone.
ciottoloso, *a.* Pebbly, flinty.
cipai, *n.m.* (*Mil.*) Sepoy.
cipero [cIpero], *n.m.* (*Bot.*) Sedge.
cipiglio [cipIglio], *n.m.* Frown, angry look, scowl. **Guardar con —,** to frown at, to look askance at, to scowl.
cipiglioso, *a.* Frowning.
cipolla, *n.f.* Onion; bulb; rose (of watering-can). **Egli è doppio come una —,** he is a double-dealer; **mangiar pane e —,** to fare badly.
cipollaio [cipollAio], *n.m.* Onion-bed; onion-seller.
cipollata, *n.f.* Dish of onions and other vegetables.
cipollato, *a.* Layered (like an onion). **Legno —,** knotty wood.
cipollatura, *n.f.* Hard knot (in wood).
cipollino, *n.m.* (*Geol.*) Kind of veined marble; cipolin.
cippilimerli, *n.m.pl.* (*vulg.*) **Far —,** to thumb one's nose.
cippo, *n.m.* (*Arch.*) Cippus.
ciprea [cIprea], *n.f.* Cowrie shell.
cipressa, *n.f.* (*Bot.*) Dwarf cypress.
cipressaia, cipresseto [cipressAia], *n.f.m.* Cypress grove.
cipresso, *n.m.* (*Bot.*) Cypress.
cipria [cIpria], *n.f.* Face-powder. **Portacipria,** *n.m.* powder-box.
ciprigna, *n.f.* (*Poet.*) Cyprian; Venus.
cipriota, *a.* Cypriot.
cipripedio [cipripEdio], *n.m.* (*Bot.*) Lady's-slipper (orchid).
cipro, *n.m.* Variety of wine (from Cyprus).
circa, *adv.* About, nearly, approximately.
circa, *prep.* About, regarding; concerning, as to. **— i di lui antecedenti nulla vi so dire,** I can tell you nothing about his antecedents.
circasso, *n.m.a.* Circassian.
circe, *n.f.* Enchantress, Circe.
circense, *a.* Pertaining to the Roman circus.
circo, *n.m.* Circus. **— equestre,** riding-ring, manege.
circolante, *a.* Circulating. **Biblioteca —,** circulating library.
circolare, *v.i.* To circulate, to get about, to travel, to move on; to be current (of money). **Circolate!** Move on!
circolare, *a.* Circular. **Una lettera —,** a circular; **biglietto —,** circular ticket, return ticket.
circolarmente, *adv.* Circularly, in a circular manner.
circolazione, *n.f.* Circulation; traffic; currency. **Ritirare dalla —,** to withdraw from circulation; **— cartacea,** paper currency; **vietata la —,** no thoroughfare; (*Comm.*) **in —,** outstanding.
circolo [cIrcolo], *n.m.* Circle (in all senses); club, group, party; district, region.
circoncidere [circoncIdere], *v.t.* To circumcise.
circoncisione, *n.f.* Circumcision.
circonciso, *a.* Circumcised.
circondabile [circondAbile], *a.* Encirclable.
circondamento, *n.m.* Encircling.
circondare, *v.t.* To surround, to encircle, to gird, to encompass.
circondurre, *v.t.* To lead around, to lead (by the nose).
circonferenza, *n.f.* Circumference.
circonflesso, *a.* Circumflex (accent).
circonfondere [circonfOndere], *v.t.* To spread around, to diffuse.
circonfuso, *p.p.a.* Spread around, surrounded.
circonlocuzione, *n.f.* Circumlocution.
circonvallare, *v.t.* (*Mil.*) To entrench (round a camp).
circonvallazione, *n.f.* (*Mil.*) Circumvallation. **Linea di —,** circular route of trams or trains (round a city).
circonvenire, *v.t.* To circumvent; to outwit.
circonvenzione, *n.f.* Circumvention; plot.
circonvicino, *a.* Neighbouring; surrounding.
circonvoluzione, *n.f.* Circumvolution.
circoscritto, *p.p.a.* Circumscribed, restricted.
circoscrivere [circoscrIvere], *v.t.* To circumscribe, to limit, to restrict.
circoscrivimento, *n.m.* Reduction, restriction.
circoscrizione, *n.f.* Circumscription; area. **— elettorale,** electoral constituency.
circospettamente, *adv.* Circumspectly.
circospetto, *a.* Circumspect; cautious.
circospezione, *n.f.* Circumspection, caution.
circostante, *a.* Surrounding, neighbouring.
circostanza, *n.f.* Circumstance, occasion, opportunity; particularity. **Secondo le circostanze,** according to circumstances; **si diede la — che,** it happened that.

circostanziare, *v.t.* To circumstantiate, to detail.
circostanziatamente, *adv.* Circumstantially.
circuire, *v.t.* To surround, to go round; (*fig.*) to entice, to take in.
circuito [circUito], *n.m.* Circuit (in all senses); circumference; race track. (*Elect.*) **— chiuso, aperto, corto,** close, open, short circuit.
circumcirca, *adv.* Thereabouts, more or less.
circumnavigazione, *n.f.* Circumnavigation.
Cirenaica [cirenAica], *n.f.* Cyrenaica.
cireneo [cirenEo], *n.m.* (*fig.*) Scapegoat.
ciriegia [ciriEgia], *n.f.* Cherry [cp. **ciliegia**].
Ciro, *n.m.* Cyrus.
cirriforme, *a.* Cirriform (of clouds).
cirro, *n.m.* Cirrus (cloud), fleecy cloud.
cirrosi, *n.f.* (*Med.*) Cirrhosis.
cisalpino, *a.* Cisalpine.
ciscranna, *n.f.* Armchair; piece of lumber.
cisoia [cp. **cesoia**].
cispa, *n.f.* Rheum, blearedness.
cispadano, *a.* South of the River Po.
cispellino, *a.* Blear-eyed.
cispicoso, *a.* Full of rheum.
cisposità [-**à**], *n.f.* Blearedness.
cisposo, *a.* Blear-eyed.
ciste, cisti, *n.f.* (*Med.*) Cyst.
cistercense, *a.* (*Eccles.*) Cistercian.
cisterna, *n.f.* Cistern, tank. (*Naut.*) **Nave —,** tanker; **acqua di —,** soft water, rain water.
cistite, *n.f.* (*Med.*) Cystitis.
citabile [citAbile], *a.* Quotable, citable.
citante, *n.m.* (*Law*) Plaintiff.
citare, *v.t.* To quote, to cite; (*Law*) to summon, to sue. **— il testo,** to quote the text; **— per danni,** to sue for damages.
citaredo, citarista, *n.m.* (*Poet.*) Lutanist.
citazione, *n.f.* Quotation; (*Law*) summons; allegation, statement.
Citerea [citErea], *n.f.*(*Myth.*) Cytherea, Venus.
citeriore, *a.* Hither, on this side.
citiso [cItiso], *n.m.* (*Bot.*) Laburnum.
citologia [citologIa], *n.f.* Cytology.
citoplasma, *n.m.* Cytoplasm.
citrato, *n.m.* Citrate.
citrico [cItrico], *a.* Citric.
citrino, *a.* Citrine; lemon-coloured.
citrullaggine [citrullAggine], *n.f.* Stupidity.
citrulleria [citrullerIa], *n.f.* Silliness.
citrullo, *n.m.* Stupid, blockhead.
città [-**à**], *n.f.* City, town. **— giardino,** garden city; **andare in —,** to go to town.
cittadella, *n.f.* Citadel; fortress.
cittadina, *n.f.* Small town; country town; woman citizen.
cittadinanza, *n.f.* Citizenship; freedom of a city; citizens of a city, population.
cittadinatico [cittadinAtico], *n.m.* Right of citizenship.
cittadinescamente, *adv.* Civically.
cittadinesco, *a.* Urban, civic.
cittadino, *n.m.a.* Citizen; civic, municipal.
ciuca, *n.f.* She-ass.
ciucaggine [ciucAggine], *n.f.* Stupidity, doltishness.
ciucaio [ciucAio], *n.m.* Donkey-driver.
ciucata, *n.f.* Donkey cavalcade; donkey ride; stupidity.
ciucheria [ciucherIa], *n.f.* Silliness, asininity.
ciuciare, *v.i.* To hiss [cp. **sibilare**].
ciuco, *n.m.* Ass, donkey. [dims. **ciuchetto ciucarello, ciuchino, ciuchettino**].
ciuffare, *v.t.* To seize by the forelock; to take by force [cp. **acciuffare**].
ciuffo, *n.m.* Forelock; tuft (of hair, grass, etc.) [dims. **ciuffetto, ciuffettino**].
ciuffole [ciUffole], *n.f.pl.* Baubles; trifles.
ciuffolotto, *n.m.* (*Zool.*) Bullfinch.
ciuffone, *n.m.* Man with tousled hair.
ciurlare, *v.i.* To caper. (*colloq.*) **— nel manico,** to be shifty; to take in (someone).
ciurlo, *n.m.* Pirouette; spin round on the toes.
ciurlotto, *n.m.* Dolt, fool.
ciurma, *n.f.* Crew (of a galley); mob.
ciurmadore, ciurmatore, *n.m.* Swindler; quack.
ciurmaglia [ciurmAglia], *n.f.* Rabble.
ciurmare, *v.t.* To swindle, to cheat.
civada, *n.f.* (*Naut.*) Spritsail.
civaie [civAie], *n.f. pl.* Peas, beans, etc.; legumes.
civetta, *n.f.* (*Zool.*) Screech-owl; (*fig.*) coquette. **Far la —,** to flirt.
civettaccia [civettAccia], *n.f.* Arrant flirt.
civettare, *v.t.* To flirt, to coquet.
civetteria [civetterIa], *n.f.* Coquettishness, flirtatiousness, coquetry.
civettuolo, *a.* Flirtatious; piquant, saucy.
civico [cIvico], *a.* Civic. **Guardia civica,** municipal guard.
civile, *a.* Civil (in all senses); civilized; refined. **Diritti civili,** civil rights; **abito —,** plain clothes, "civvies"; **coraggio —,** moral courage, public spirit; (*Law*) **parte —,** plaintiff; **stato —,** register of births, deaths and marriages.
civilista (*pl.* **civilisti**), *n.m.* Jurist.
civilizzare, *v.t.* To civilize.
civilizzatore, *a.* Civilizing.
civilizzazione, *n.f.* Civilization.
civilmente, *adv.* Civilly; courteously.
civiltà [-**à**], *n.f.* Civilization; civility, courtesy.
civismo, *n.m.* Public spirit; patriotism.
clamare, *v.i.* (*Poet.*) To cry aloud.
clamide [clAmide], *n.f.* (*Hist.*) Chlamys, soldier's cloak.
clamore, *n.m.* Clamour, outcry, noise. **Sollevare —,** to raise an outcry.
clamorosamente, *adv.* Clamorously, noisily.
clamoroso, *a.* Clamorous, noisy.
clandestinamente, *adv.* Clandestinely, surreptitiously, stealthily.
clandestino, *a.* Clandestine, secret, surreptitious.
clangore, *n.m.* (*Lit.*) Clangour.
claretto, *n.m.* Claret [cp. **chiaretto**]
clarificare [cp. **chiarificare**].
clarinettista (*pl.* **clarinettisti**), *n.m.f.* Clarinet-player.
clarinetto, clarino, *n.m.* (*Mus.*) Clarinet.
clarissa, *n.f.* (*Eccles.*) Nun of the order of St. Clare.
classare, *v.t.* [cp. **classificare**].
classazione, *n.f.* [cp. **classificazione**].
classe, *n.f.* Class (in all senses); order, rank, position; standard (at school); (*Mil.*) year of birth. **Lotta di —,** class war; **di —,** of good quality; **fuori —,** of superlative quality; **le classi medie,** the middle classes.
classicamente, *adv.* Classically.
classicismo, *n.m.* Classicism; classic learning.

classicista, *n.m.f.* Classical scholar.
classico [clAssico], *n.m.a.* Classic, one of the Classics, classical. **I Classici,** the Classics.
classificabile [classificAbile], *a.* Classifiable; possible to classify.
classificare, *v.t.* To classify; to class.
classificato, *a.* Classified. (*Naut.*) **Nave —,** vessel classed A 1 at Lloyds.
classificazione, *n.f.* Classification; mark (in schools).
claudia [clAudia], *a.* **Susina —,** greengage.
claudicare, *v.i.* To limp.
claudicazione, *n.f.* Limping, limp.
clausola [clAusola], *n.f.* Clause, stipulation, reserve.
claustrale, *a.* Monastic, claustral.
claustro [clAustro], *n.m.* Cloister.
claustrofobia [claustrofobIa], *n.f.* (*Med.*) Claustrophobia.
clausura, *n.f.* Claustration, seclusion (of nuns).
clava, *n.f.* Club, bludgeon.
clavicembalo [clavicEmbalo], *n.m.* (*Mus.*) Harpsichord; clavichord.
clavicola [clavIcola], *n.f.* (*Anat.*) Clavicle, collar-bone.
clavicordio [clavicOrdio], *n.m.* (*Mus.*) Clavichord.
claviforme, *a.* Club-shaped.
clematide [clemAtide], *n.f.* (*Bot.*) Clematis, virgin's-bower.
clemente, *a.* Clement, mild, merciful.
clementemente, *adv.* Clemently, mildly.
clementino, *a.* (*Eccles.*) Pertaining to the Clementine popes.
clemenza, *n.f.* Clemency, mildness, mercifulness.
cleptomane [cleptOmane], *n.m.f.* Kleptomaniac.
cleptomania [cleptomanIa], *n.f.* Kleptomania.
clericale, *n.m.a.* Cleric, priest; clerical, priestly.
clericalismo, *n.m.* Clericalism.
clericalmente, *adv.* Clerically.
clericato, *n.m.* Holy Orders.
clero, *n.m.* Clergy.
clessidra, *n.f.* Clepsydra, water-clock; hour-glass.
cliente, *n.m.f.* Client, customer; (*Med.*) patient.
clientela, *n.f.* Clientele, connexion; patronage; (*Med.*) practice; (*Comm.*) customers, goodwill. **Farsi una —,** to form a connection; **avere una larga —,** to have a good practice.
clima (*pl.* **climi**), *n.m.* Climate; region.
climaterico [climatErico], *a.* Climacteric, critical. **Giorno —,** decisive day.
climatico [climAtico], *a.* Climatic.
clinica [clInica], *n.f.* Clinical surgery; nursing-home.
clinicamente, *adv.* Clinically.
clinico [clInico], *n.m.a.* Clinical surgeon; clinical.
clinometro [clinOmetro], *n.m.* Clinometer, level.
clipeo [clIpeo], *n.m.* (*Poet.*) Shield.
clistere, *n.m.* (*Med.*) Enema, clyster.
Clitennestra, *n.f.* Clytemnestra.
clitoride [clitOride], *n.f.* (*Anat.*) Clitoris.
clivaggio [clivAggio], *n.m.* (*Min.*) Cleavage.
clivo, *n.m.* Hillock, rise in the ground.
cloaca, *n.f.* Sewer, drain; cesspool.
cloralio [clorAlio], *n.m.* (*Chem.*) Chloral.
clorato, *n.m.* Chlorate.
clorico [clOrico], *a.* Chloric.
cloridrico [clorIdrico], *a.* Hydrochloric.
cloro, *n.m.* (*Chem.*) Chlorine.
clorofilla, *n.f.* (*Bot.*) Chlorophyll.
cloroformio [clorofOrmio], *n.m.* (*Med.*) Chloroform.
cloroformizzare, *v.t.* To chloroform; to put under chloroform; to give gas (to).
clorosi, *n.f.* (*Med.*) Chlorosis.
cloruro, *n.m.* (*Chem.*) Chloride.
club, *n.m.* Club, society.
co', *n.m.* (*Poet.*) Head [from **capo**]. **In co' de ponte,** at the bridge-head.
coabitare, *v.t.* To cohabit; to live together (in the same house).
coabitazione, *n.f.* Cohabitation.
coaccademico [coaccadEmico], *n.m.* Fellow-collegian.
coaccusato, *n.m.* Co-defendant, fellow-prisoner.
coacervare, *v.t.* (*obs.*) To heap up.
coaderente, *a.* Adherent together.
coaderire, *v.i.* To stick together; to adhere to one another.
coadesione, *n.f.* Cohesion.
coadiutorato, *n.m.* Coadjutorship.
coadiutore, *n.m.* (*Eccles.*) Coadjutor. **Vescovo —,** suffragan bishop.
coadiuvare, *v.t.* To help, to assist, to co-operate with.
coadunare, *v.t.* To muster, to collect together.
coagulante, *a* Coagulative.
coagulare, coagularsi, *v.i.r.* To coagulate.
coagulazione, *n.f.* Coagulation.
coagulo [coAgulo], *n.m.* Blood-clot; curd of milk.
coalescenza, *n.f.* Coalescence.
coalizione, *n.f.* Coalition; league.
coalizzare, coalizzarsi, *v.t.r.* To coalesce, to combine, to form a coalition.
coarmatore, *n.m.* Joint owner of ship.
coartare. *v.t.* To coerce, to force.
coartazione, *n.f.* Coercion.
coattivo, *a.* Coercive.
coatto, *a.* Forced, compelled, coerced. (*Law*) **Domicilio —,** internment, forced residence (in a given place).
coazione, *n.f.* Compulsion.
cobalto, *n.m.* (*Min.*) Cobalt.
coboldo, *n.m.* Hobgoblin.
cobra, *n.m.* (*Zool.*) Cobra.
coc, *n.m.* Coke.
coca, *n.f.* (*Bot.*) Coca.
cocaina, *n.f.* Cocaine.
cocainismo, *n.m.* (*Med.*) Cocainism.
cocainizzare, *v.t.* To cocainize.
cocainomania [cocainomanIa], *n.f.* Insanity caused by addiction to cocaine.
cocca, *n.f.* Notch (of an arrow); tip (of a spindle); hen; pet (child). **La — d'un fazzoletto,** the corner of a handkerchief.
coccarda, *n.f.* Cockade.
cocchiere, *n.m.* Coachman; groom.
cocchio [cOcchio], *n.m.* Coach, carriage.
cocchiume, *n.m.* Bung-hole.
coccia [cOccia], *n.f.* Shell, husk, pod; hilt (of a sword).
coccige [cOccige], *n.m.* (*Anat.*) Coccyx.
coccinella, *n.f.* (*Zool.*) Ladybird.

coccinello, *n.m.* (*Naut.*) Toggle.
coccineo [cocclneo], *a.* (*obs.*) Purple.
cocciniglia [coccinlglia], *n.f.* (*Zool.*) Cochineal; cochineal dye.
coccio [cOccio], *n.m.* Potsherd; fragment; (*fig.*) sickly person, crock. **Cocci,** crockery.
cocciutaggine [cocciutAggine], *n.f.* Obstinacy.
cocciuto, *a.* Pig-headed, obstinate, headstrong.
cocco (1), *n.m.* (*Bot.*) Coco palm. **Noce di —,** coconut.
cocco (2), *n.m.* Darling, loved one, love.
coccodè [-è], *n.m.* Clucking (of a hen).
coccodrillo, *n.m.* (*Zool.*) Crocodile. **Lagrime di —,** crocodile tears.
coccola [cOccola], *n.f.* Pip; berry.
coccolarsi, *v.r.* To make oneself comfortable, to snuggle.
coccolino, *n.m.* Fat, healthy child; darling.
coccolo [cOccolo], *n.m.* Chubby little fellow; little darling.
coccoloni, *adv.* **Star coccoloni,** to squat.
cocente, *a.* Burning; (*fig.*) smarting; bitter (in speech), sarcastic; vehement. **Sotto il sole —,** under the scorching sun.
cocentemente, *adv.* Ardently, burningly.
cocere [cp. **cuocere**].
cocimento, *n.m.* Cooking.
Cocincina, *n.f.* Cochin-China.
cociore, *n.m.* Burn, scald, smart.
cocitura, *n.f.* Cooking, boiling, stewing.
coclea [cOclea], *n.f.* (*Anat.*) Cochlea; (*Arch.*) spiral ornament; (*Mech.*) screw-nut.
cocolla, *n.f.* (*Eccles.*) Cowl.
cocomeraio [cocomerAio], *n.m.* Melon-seller; melon-bed.
cocomero [cocOmero], *n.m.* Water-melon; (*fig.*) blockhead.
cocuzza, *n.f.* (*colloq.*) Pate, top of the head.
cocuzzolo [cocUzzolo], *n.m.* Crown of hat; summit.
coda, *n.f.* Tail, queue, train (of dress), retinue; rear, end; rider (to an expressed opinion or judgment); (*Mus.*) coda. **Far —,** to form a queue; **pianoforte a —,** grand piano; **la — di un treno,** the rear end of a train; **abito a — di rondine,** dress coat, tails, swallow-tails.
codardamente, *adv.* In cowardly fashion
codardia [codardIa], *n.f.* Cowardice.
codardo, *n.m.a.* Coward, poltroon; cowardly.
codato, *a.* Tailed.
codazzo, *n.m.* Long queue, train, retinue. **Far —,** to follow in the train (of).
codeina, *n.f.* (*Med.*) Codeine.
codesto, *a.pron.* This, that; that one.
codetta, *n.f.* (*Mus.*) Short coda.
codibianco, *n.m.* (*Zool.*) Wheatear.
codibugnolo [codibUgnolo], *n.m.* (*Zool.*) Long-tailed tit.
codice [cOdice], *n.m.* Code, statute-book (*pl.* **codici**); codex, manuscript (*pl.* **codices**). **— civile, penale,** civil, penal code; **— stradale,** highway code.
codicillare, *v.t.* To add a codicil.
codicillo, *n.m.* Codicil.
codificare, *v.t.* To codify.
codificazione, *n.f.* Codification.
codilungo, *n.m.* (*Zool.*) Long-tailed tit.
codimozzo, *a.* (*obs.*) Docked (tail).
codino, *n.m.* Pigtail, queue; (*fig.*) reactionary, die-hard.
codinzola [codInzola], *n.f.* (*Zool.*) Wagtail.
codinzolo [codInzolo], *n.m.* Stumpy tail.
codione, *n.m.* Rump (of a bird).
codirosso, *n.m.* (*Zool.*) Redstart.
coditremola [coditrEmola], *n.f.* (*Zool.*) Wagtail.
codolo [cOdolo], *n.m.* Stump, tang (of a knife); handle (of knife or fork).
coefficiente, *n.m.* (*Math.*) Coefficient. (*Mech.*) **— di attrito,** coefficient of friction.
coefficienza, *n.f.* Coefficiency.
coeguale, *a.* Co-equal.
coegualità [-à], *n.f.* Co-equality, parity.
coegualmente, *adv.* Co-equally.
coenzione, *n.f.* (*obs. Law*) Coemption.
coercibile [coercIbile], *a.* Coercible.
coercitivo, *a.* Coercive; compulsory.
coercizione, *n.f.* Coercion; compulsion.
coerede, *n.m.f.* Co-heir, co-heiress.
coerente, *a.* Coherent, consistent.
coerentemente, *adv.* Coherently.
coerenza, *n.f.* Coherence.
coesercizio [coesercIzio], *n.m.* (*Comm.*) Joint-working.
coesione, *n.f.* Cohesion.
coesistente, *a.* Co-existent.
coesistenza, *n.f.* Co-existence.
coesistere [coesIstere], *v.i.* To co-exist.
coetaneo [coetAneo], *n.m.a.* Contemporary; of the same age. **Sono nostri coetanei,** they are our contemporaries.
coevo, *a.* Coeval, contemporary.
cofanetto, *n.m.* Casket.
cofano [cOfano], *n.m.* Coffer, chest, casket; (*Motor.*) bonnet (of a car), (*Am.*) hood.
coffa, *n.f.* (*Naut.*) Top; main-top.
cogerente, *n.m.* (*Comm.*) Joint-manager.
cogitabondo, *a.* Thoughtful, musing.
cogitare, *v.i.* To ponder, to meditate.
cogitativa, *n.f.* Thinking faculty.
cogitativo, *a.* Thoughtful.
cogitazione, *n.f.* Cogitation, deep consideration.
cogli. With the [cp. **con**].
coglia [cOglia], *n.f.* (*Anat.*) Scrotum.
cogliere [cOgliere], *v.t.* To gather, to reap, to collect; to take, to grasp, to pluck, to pick; to hit; to befall, to surprise, to understand. **Stanno cogliendo ulive,** they are gathering olives; **coglie il frutto delle proprie fatiche,** he is reaping the fruits of his labour; **— l'occasione,** to seize the opportunity; **non ho colto il senso della frase,** I did not catch the meaning of the words; **— in flagrante,** to catch in the very act; **se mi avesse a — qualche disgrazia,** should any misfortune befall me; **— allori,** to gather one's laurels; **— nel segno**, to hit the target.
coglionare, *v.t.* (*colloq.*) To hoax, to take in; to mock, to make fun of.
coglionatura, *n.f.* Trick, hoax.
coglione, *n.m.* Testicle; (*vulg.*) blockhead.
coglioneria [coglionerIa], *n.f.* Foolishness; silly talk, nonsense.
coglitura, *n.f.* Gathering, collection.
cognac, cognacche, *n.m.* Cognac, brandy.
cognata, *n.f.* Sister-in-law.
cognatizio [cognatIzio], *a.* (*Law*) Cognate, proceeding from the same stock.

cognato, *n.m.* Brother-in-law.
cognato, *a.* Cognate, kin.
cognito [cOgnito], *a.* (*Law*) Known.
cognizione, *n.f.* Knowledge, notion; cognizance. **Sono venuto a — che,** I have been informed that.
cognizioni, *n.f.pl.* Attainments; knowledge, learning.
cogno, *n.m.* (*Agric.*) Oil given in payment for use of oil-press; cask, barrel.
cognome, *n.m.* Surname.
cognominarsi, *v.r.* To take the name (of); to name oneself.
cogolo [cOgolo], *n.m.* Pebble.
cogoma [cOgoma], *n.f.* Venetian coffee-pot [cp. **cuccuma**].
coguaro, *n.m.* (*Zool.*) Cougar, puma.
coi. With the [cp. **con**].
coiaio [coiAio], *n.m.* Tanner [cp. **cuoiaio**].
coiame, *n.m.* Hides.
coiattolo [coiAttolo], *n.m.* Scrap of leather.
coibente, *n.m.* (*Phys.*) Non-conductor (of heat, electricity, etc.).
coibenza, *n.f.* Non-conductivity.
coieria [coierIa], *n.f.* Saddler's shop.
coimputato, *n.m.* (*Law*) Co-defendant.
coincidente, *a.* Coincident.
coincidenza, *n.f.* Coincidence; (*Rail.*) connection. **Ho perso la —,** I have missed the connection.
coincidere [coincIdere], *v.i.* To coincide; to clash. **Le due conferenze coincidono,** the two lectures clash.
cointeressato, *a.* Jointly interested; associate.
cointeressenza, *n.f.* Co-interest, mutual interest; share of profit.
coinvolgere [coinvOlgere], *v.t.* To involve.
coio [cp. **cuoio**].
coire, *v.i.* To copulate, to have sexual connection (with).
coito, *n.m.* Coition, sexual intercourse.
col. With the [cp. **con**].
cola, *n.f.* (*obs.*) Strainer.
colà, *adv.* There, in that place, over there.
colabrodo, *n.m.* Colander, strainer.
colaggio [colAggio], *n.m.* Leakage.
colaggiù, *adv.* Down there.
colamento, *n.m.* Filtering.
colare, *v.t.i.* To strain (liquids), to filter, to sieve; to trickle, to leak; to cast (metals); to sink; to flow, to drain; to drop, to drip; to gutter (a candle). **— a fondo,** to founder, to sink; **gli cola il naso,** his nose is dripping; **— sudore,** to sweat.
colascionata, *n.f.* Third-rate verse; bad poetry.
colascione, *n.m.* (*Mus.*) Kind of lute. **Poeta di —,** poetaster.
colassù, *adv.* Up there, up yonder.
colata, *n.f.* Cast (metal); flow of molten lava; lava stream.
colaticcio [colatIccio], *n.m.* Drippings, dregs. **— di candela,** candlegrease.
colato, *p.p.a.* Strained, filtered; cast (of metals); sunk. **Oro —,** pure gold.
colatoio [colatOio], *n.m.* Sieve, filter, colander.
colatura, *n.f.* Filtering; dripping.
colazione, *n.f.* Breakfast; lunch, luncheon. **Far —,** to lunch.
colbac, colbacco, *n.m.* (*Mil.*) Busby.
colcare, *v.t.* To lay down; to put to bed [cp. **coricare**].
colchico, *n.m.* (*Bot.*) Colchicum.
colecisti, *n.f.* (*Anat.*) Gall-bladder.
colei [colEi], *pron.* She who; that woman.
colendissimo [colendIssimo], *a.* (*obs.*) Most revered, most respected.
coleottero [coleOttero], *n.m.a.* (*Zool.*) Coleopter; coleopterous.
colera, *n.m.* (*Med.*) Cholera.
colere [cOlere], *v.t.* (*Poet.*) To revere.
colerico [colErico], *a.* Pertaining to cholera.
colerina, *n.f.* (*Med.*) British cholera.
coleroso, *a.* Stricken with cholera.
colettare, *v.t.* (*Agric.*) To sieve (corn).
coletto, *n.m.* Sieve.
colibrì, colibri [colibrI, cOlibri], *n.m.* (*Zool.*) Humming-bird.
colica [cOlica], *n.f.* (*Med.*) Colic, gripes.
colimbo, *n.m.* (*Zool.*) Grebe.
colino, *n.m.* Strainer (for milk, tea, soup, etc.).
colio [colIo], *n.m.* Continuous dripping, leaking.
colite, *n.f.* (*Med.*) Colitis.
colla, *n.f.* Glue, paste. **— di pesce,** isinglass.
colla. With the [cp. **con**].
collaborare, *v.i.* To collaborate; to contribute (to a newspaper, etc.).
collaboratore, collaboratrice, *n.m.f.* Collaborator, co-worker; contributor (to the papers).
collaborazione, *n.f.* Collaboration; contribution; assistance to an occupying enemy.
collaborazionista, *n.m.f.* Collaborationist; quisling.
collana, *n.f.* Necklace collar ; (*fig.*) anthology; series (of books).
collare, *n.m.* Collar (in all senses); bands (clerical). **— dell'Annunziata,** Order of the Annunciation.
collaressa, *n.f.* Horse-collar.
collaretto, *n.m.* Shirt-collar, lace collar; neckband.
collarino, *n.m.* Neck-band; (*Arch.*) collar (in capital of a column).
collasso, *n.m.* (*Med.*) Collapse, breakdown, prostration.
collata, *n.f.* Blow on the neck; accolade.
collaterale, *a.* Collateral.
collateralmente, *adv.* Collaterally.
collaudare, *v.t.* To test, to try; to approve.
collaudatore, *n.m.* Inspecting engineer; tester; (*Aviat.*) test-pilot.
collaudazione, *n.f.* Approval; trial, test; certificate of fitness.
collaudo [collAudo], *n.m.* Test, trial; approval; **Un volo di —,** a trial flight; **passare il —,** to stand the test.
collazionamento, *n.m.* Collating, comparing; checking, proving.
collazionare, *v.t.* To collate, to compare; to check (accounts, etc.).
collazionatura, *n.f.* Collation.
collazione, *n.f.* Collation; (*Eccles.*) bestowal of a benefice.
colle, *n.m.* Hill; mountain pass.
colle. With the [cp. **con**].
collega (*pl.* **colleghi**), *n.m.* Colleague, partner.
collegamento, *n.m.* Binding, union, connection, junction. **Ufficiale di —,** liaison officer; (*Mech.*) **— a vite,** bolted joint.

colleganza, *n.f.* League, union, fellowship.
collegare, *v.t.* To bind, to connect, to unite.
collegarsi, *v.r.* To associate, to confederate.
collegatamente, *adv.* Firmly united.
collegatario [collegatArio], *n.m.* Co-legatee.
collegato, *n.m.* Associate, confederate.
collegatura, *n.f.* Bond; connecting link.
collegiale, *n.m.f.a.* Boarding-school boy or girl; collegian; collegiate.
collegialità [-à], *n.f.* Rights of a college.
collegialmente, *adv.* By decision of a college; jointly, in a body.
collegiata, *n.f.* (*Eccles.*) Collegiate church.
collegiato, *a.* Belonging to a college.
collegio [collEgio], *n.m.* College; boarding school, public school; professional body; committee. — **universitario,** college; — **femminile,** boarding school for girls; — **elettorale,** constituency; — **degli avvocati,** the Bar; — **giudicante,** the Bench.
collera [cOllera], *n.f.* Anger, rage, wrath, passion, temper. **Andare in —,** to fly into a passion; **essere in —,** to be angry; **accesso di —,** fit of anger.
collericamente, *adv.* Cholerically, biliously; angrily.
collerico [collErico], *a.* Choleric.
colletta, *n.f.* Collection. **Fare una —,** to make a collection, to collect money (for charity); (*Naut.*) **caricare a —,** to load a mixed cargo.
collettame, *n.m.* Parcels.
collettare, *v.t.* To collect.
collettarsi, *v.r.* To join in a guarantee.
collettivamente, *adv.* Collectively.
collettivismo, *n.m.* Collectivism.
collettivista, *n.m.* Collectivist.
collettività [-à], *n.f.* Collectivity.
collettivo, *a.* Collective, joint.
collettizio [collettIzio], *n.m.* Haphazard gathering (of people).
colletto, *n.m.* Shirt-collar, collar. — **molle,** soft collar; — **duro,** stiff collar.
collettore, *n.m.* Collector; (*Eng.*) drain, irrigating ditch.
collettoria [collettorIa], *n.f.* Tax-collector's office.
collezione, *n.f.* Collection (of books, stamps, etc.).
collezionista (*pl.* **collezionisti**), *n.m.* Collector.
collidere [collIdere], *v.t.* To collide; to clash, to rush into.
colligiano, *n.m.* Hill-dweller.
collimare, *v.i.* To coincide, to tally; to harmonize, to agree with.
collimazione, *n.f.* (*Phys.*) Collimation.
collina, *n.f.* Hill.
collinetta, *n.f.* Hillock.
collinoso, *a.* Hilly.
colliquamento, *n.m.* Liquefaction.
colliquare, *v.t.* To liquefy, to melt.
collirio [collIrio], *n.m.* Collyrium, eye-salve.
collisione, *n.f.* Collision; clash.
collo (1), *n.m.* Neck; throat (of an anchor); kink; hitch. — **del piede,** instep; **a rotta di —,** at breakneck speed; **rompersi il —,** to break one's neck; **fra capo e —,** unexpectedly; **avere il braccio al —,** to have one's arm in a sling; **bere a —,** to drink from the bottle; **mezzo —,** half-hitch (knot); **tirare il —,** to wring (a fowl's) neck; **prendere per il —,** to collar.
collo (2), *n.m.* Package, parcel; pack; piece of luggage.
collo. With the [cp. **con**].
collocabile [collocAbile], *a.* Disposable, placeable.
collocamento, *n.m.* Settlement, position; sale, investment; laying down; giving (in marriage); employment. **Agenzia di —,** employment agency; — **a riposo,** pensioning off.
collocare, *v.t.* To place, to put; to dispose of, to sell; to fit, to arrange; to invest; to give (in marriage). — **denaro,** to invest money; — **una ragazza,** to give a girl in marriage; — **a riposo,** to pension off.
collocarsi, *v.r.* To get oneself a job; to settle down.
collocazione, *n.f.* Arrangement, disposition, placing.
collodio [collOdio], *n.m.* (*Chem.*) Collodion.
colloidale, *a.* Colloidal.
colloidi [collOidi], *n.m.pl.* (*Chem.*) Colloids.
colloquio [collOquio], *n.m.* Conversation, interview, conference, colloquy.
collosità [-à], *n.f.* Stickiness, viscosity.
colloso, *a.* Sticky, viscous; glutinous.
collotorto, *n.m.* Hypocrite; (*Zool.*) wryneck.
collottola [collOttola], *n.f.* Nape (of the neck).
colludere [collUdere], *v.i.* To connive, to act in collusion.
collusivamente, *adv.* Collusively.
collusivo, *a.* Collusive.
collusore, *n.m.* Conniver.
collutorio [collutOrio], *n.m.* (*Med.*) Mouthwash.
colluttarsi, *v.r.* To come to blows, to fight.
colluttazione, *n.f.* Brawl, scuffle, fray.
colluvie [collUvie], *n.f.* Colluvies; rabble.
colmare, *v.t.* To fill to the brim; to fill up; to overwhelm, to load (with honours); to raise the level (of the soil). — **di gentilezze,** to overwhelm with kindness; — **una lacuna,** to fill a gap.
colmata, *n.f.* Silting up, levelling up; embankment; bank, ridge.
colmatura, *n.f.* Summit, top.
colmeggiare, *v.i.* To rise, to slope upwards (of landscape).
colmo, *n.m.* Top, summit, highest point; climax; depth; extremity. **La mia pazienza ha raggiunto il —,** my patience is exhausted; **per — di sventura,** to crown one's misfortunes; **questo è il —!** this is the limit!
colmo, *a.* Brimful; full.
colo, *n.m.* Sieve; (*Anat.*) colon.
colofonia [colofOnia], *n.f.* Colophony, resin.
colomba, *n.f.* Dove.
colombaia [colombAia], *n.f.* Dove-cot; pigeon-house, loft.
colombaccio [colombAccio], *n.m.* Wood-pigeon.
colombana, *n.f.* Variety of sweet, white grape.
colombario [colombArio], *n.m.* Columbarium, niche for cinerary urn.
colombella, *n.f.* Woodpigeon, stock-dove.
colombina, *n.f.* Small pigeon; prudish young woman; pigeon's droppings.
colombino, *a.* Concerning pigeons; of Colombo.
colombo, *n.m.* Pigeon. — **viaggiatore,** carrier-pigeon; **pigliare due colombi a una fava,** to kill two birds with one stone.

colon, *n.m.* (*Anat.*) Colon.
colonia [colOnia] (1), *n.f.* Colony, settlement. **— agricola,** farm settlement.
colonia [colonIa] (2), *n.f.* (*Law*) Farm lease.
Colonia [colOnia] (3), *n.f.* Cologne.
coloniale, *a.* Colonial.
coloniali, *n.m.pl.* Colonial goods (coffee, spices, etc.).
colonico [colOnico], *a.* Farming; pertaining to agriculture. **Casa colonica,** farmhouse.
colonizzabile [colonizzAbile], *a.* Ripe for colonization.
colonizzare, *v.t.* To colonize.
colonizzatore, *n.m.* Colonizer, pioneer, settler.
colonizzazione, *n.f.* Colonization.
colonna, *n.f.* Column (in all senses), pillar; post; support. (*Anat.*) **— vertebrale,** spine; (*Cinema.*) **— sonora, — di suono,** sound-track.
colonnato, *n.m.* Colonnade.
colonnello, *n.m.* (*Mil.*) Colonel.
colonnino, *n.m.* Small pillar, baluster.
colono, *n.m.* Farmer, tenant-farmer; settler.
colorabile [colorAbile], *a.* Colourable.
coloramento, *n.m.* Colouring.
colorante, *n.m.a.* Dye-stuff, dye; colouring. **Sostanza —,** colouring-matter.
colorare, *v.t.* To colour; (*fig.*) to give colour to, to make appear plausible.
coloratamente, *adv.* With simulation.
colorato, *a.* Coloured, painted, tinted.
coloratura, *n.f.* Colouring; (*Mus.*) ornamental passages.
colorazione, *n.f.* Colouring.
colore, *n.m.* Colour, colouring, hue; dye, paint; appearance; pretext; complexion. **"Colore fresco",** "Wet Paint"; **— solido,** fast dye; **colori ad olio,** oil paints; **colori ad acquarello,** water-colours; **sotto — di,** under colour of, on the pretext of; **vetrate a colori,** stained-glass windows; **mutar —,** to change one's political views; **farne di tutti i colori,** to commit every kind of folly.
colorire, *v.t.* To colour, to paint; to heighten the colour of.
colorista (*pl.* **coloristi**), *n.m.* Colourist.
colorito, *n.m.a.* Colouring; complexion; coloured.
coloro, *pron.* They; those who.
colossale, *a.* Colossal, gigantic.
Colosseo [colossEo], *n.m.* (*Hist.*) Colosseum.
colosso, *n.m.* Colossus, giant.
colpa, *n.f.* Fault, error; guilt, offence, crime; blame. **È — sua,** it's his fault; **dar la — a,** to lay the blame upon; **che — ha lui?** who can blame him? **per — di,** through the fault of.
colpabile [colpAbile], *a.* Culpable, blameworthy, guilty.
colpabilità [-à], *n.f.* Culpability, fault, guilt.
colpevole [colpEvole], *n.m.a.* Culprit, offender; culpable, at fault.
colpevolmente, *adv.* Culpably.
colpire, *v.t.* To hit, to strike, to beat, to shoot (with firearms); to slap, to knock; to stamp, to impress. **— nel segno,** to strike home, to hit the mark; **rimaner colpito,** to be impressed.
colpo, *n.m.* Blow, stroke, hit; thump, knock; impression, sensation; shot, report, bang; dig, stab; clap, flap, peal; tap, touch; kick, pitch; drive (tennis, etc.); turn; glance. **— mortale;** deadly blow; **— di cannone,** cannon shot; **— di vento,** gust of wind; **— di folgore,** lightning-stroke; **— di scena,** unexpected happening; **— apoplettico,** apoplectic stroke; **— di mano,** surprise action; **— d'aria,** cold (caught by sitting in a draught); **— di mare,** breaker; **— di sole,** sun-stroke; **di —,** all at once; **un bel —,** a lucky hit; **a — sicuro,** to a certainty; **a — d'occhio,** at a glance; **— di fortuna,** windfall, piece of luck; **sul —,** instantaneously; (*Mech.*) **— di stantuffo,** piston stroke; **— di stato,** coup d'état; **— di teatro,** stage trick, sensational happening.
colposamente, *adv.* Culpably.
colposo, *a.* (*Law*) Culpable. **Omicidio —,** manslaughter.
colta, *n.f.* Gathering, collection.
coltella, *n.f.* Large knife.
coltellaccio [coltellAccio], *n.m.* Large knife; (*Naut.*) studding-sail; (*Agric.*) ploughshare.
coltellame, *n.m.* Cutlery.
coltellata, *n.f.* Knife wound, stab; knifing.
coltellato, *a.* (*Arch.*) (Wall) built with bricks on edge.
coltelleria [coltellerIa], *n.f.* Cutlery; collection of knives.
coltellesca, *n.f.* Sheath (for a knife).
coltelliera, *n.f.* Knife-box; case of cutlery.
coltellinaio [coltellinAio], *n.m.* Cutler.
coltello, *n.m.* Knife (in all senses). **— per trinciare,** carving-knife; **— a serramanico,** clasp-knife; **affilare un —,** to sharpen a knife; **a —, per —,** edgewise (of bricks).
coltellone, *n.m.* Carving-knife.
coltivabile [coltivAbile], *a.* Tillable, for cultivation.
coltivabilità [-à], *n.f.* Suitability for cultivation.
coltivamento, *n.m.* Cultivation; act of cultivating.
coltivare, *v.t.* To till, to cultivate, to farm; to grow, to improve, to develop, to exploit. **— l'amicizia,** to cultivate the friendship; **— le arti,** to cultivate the arts.
coltivatore, *n.m.* Husbandman, farmer, grower; **— diretto,** smallholder.
coltivazione, *n.f.* Cultivation, husbandry, farming.
colto, *p.p.a.* Caught, gathered, reaped. **— sul fatto,** caught in the act; **— dalla notte,** benighted, overtaken by night [cp. **cogliere**].
colto, *a.* Cultured, cultivated, learned, educated [cp. **coltivare**].
coltrare, *v.t.* To plough.
coltratura, *n.f.* Ploughing.
coltre, *n.f.* Pall (on a coffin); counterpane.
coltrice, *n.f.* Featherbed.
coltro, *n.m.* Coulter; ploughshare.
coltroncino, *n.m.* Light quilt; bedspread.
coltrone, *n.m.* Padded quilt, quilt; eiderdown.
coltura, *n.f.* Culture, cultivation, tillage, farming; intellectual attainments. **— di bacilli,** culture of bacilli; (*Agric.*) **media —** ordinary farming; **piccola —,** cultivation by spade work alone [cp. **cultura**].
colturale, *a.* Cultural.
colubrina, *n.f.* (*Mil.*) Culverin.
colubro, *n.m.* (*Zool.*) Snake; viper.
colui [colUi], *pron.* He; he who.

coluro, *n.m.* (*Astron.*) Colure.
colza, *n.f.* (*Bot.*) Rape; rape seed. **Olio di —,** colza oil.
coma, *n.f.* (*Med.*) Coma; lethargy, stupor.
comandamento, *n.m.* (*Eccles.*) Commandment, precept. **I dieci Comandamenti,** the Ten Commandments.
comandante, *n.m.* Commandant, commander, commanding officer. **— di porto,** harbour-master; **— di marina,** naval commander.
comandare, *v.t.* To order, to command, to bid; to rule; to direct, to control; to bespeak. **— a bacchetta,** to rule with a high hand; **comanda altro?** do you want anything else? **egli comandava un battaglione,** he was in command of a battalion.
comandata, *n.f.* (*Mil.*) Fatigue; fatigue party.
comandi! *v.t. imp.* What can I do? At your service!
comando, *n.m.* Command, order; injunction; (*Mil.*) headquarters; (*Mech.*) drive, driving gear; control. (*Comm.*) **I vostri comandi ambiti,** your esteemed order; (*Mech.*) **leva di —,** gear lever.
comandolo [comAndolo], *n.m.* Thread (for repairing warp).
comare, *n.f.* Godmother; gossip, crony; (*obs.*) midwife.
comasco, *a.* Of Como.
comatoso, *a.* Comatose.
comatula [comAtula], *n.f.* Variety of seaweed.
comba, *n.f.* Dale, combe.
combaciamento, *n.m.* Point of contact; tallying; placing together.
combaciare, *v.i.* To tally, to fit closely together.
combattente, *n.m.* Combatant, fighter. **Ex-combattente,** ex-service man.
combattere [combAttere], *v.t.i.* To fight, to combat, to struggle, to battle; to oppose, to withstand. **— corpo a corpo,** to fight hand to hand.
combattimento, *n.m.* Fight, battle, combat, encounter; contest, match. **Messo fuori —,** disabled.
combattività [-à], *n.f.* Pugnacity, combativeness.
combattivo, *a* Pugnacious, combative, fighting.
combinabile [combinAbile], *a.* Combinable; possible to settle (of an arrangement).
combinare, *v.t.* To arrange, to settle, to fix up; to combine, to plan; to contrive; to match (colours). **— un buon affare,** to do a good stroke of business.
combinarsi, *v.r.* To agree, to come to terms; to unite, to combine. **Quei due non si combinano,** these two do not agree (with one another).
combinazione, *n.f.* Combination; coincidence, chance; agreement. **Per combinazione,** by chance; **per una curiosa —,** by a strange coincidence; **per pura —,** by a mere chance.
combriccola [combrIccola], *n f.* Cabal, clique; gang (of rogues).
combriccolone, *n m.* Schemer; frequenter of bad company.
comburente, *n.m.a.* Fuel; combustible matter; burning.
combustibile [combustIbile], *n.m.a.* Fuel; combustible.
combustione, *n.f.* Combustion. **— interna,** internal combustion.
combusto, *a.* Burnt.
combutta, *n.f.* Crowd, confused throng. **In —,** hand in hand, hand in glove.
come, *n.m.* The reason, the manner in which, the way.
come, *adv.* How, as, like; as soon as, when. **Non è così ricco — si crede,** he is not as rich as people think; **è — suo fratello,** he is like a brother to him; **— arrivò,** as soon as he arrived; **— sta?** How do you do? **non so —,** I don't know how; **— mai?** How can it be? How is it? **— fare?** What's to be done?
come! *inter.* What! Indeed! **Come! Non siete partito?** What! Haven't you gone?
comecchè, *conj.* However, although.
comecchessia [comecchessIa], *adv.* However, anyway.
comedia, comento, etc. [cp. **commedia, commento,** etc.].
cometa, *n.f.* Comet.
comica [cOmica], *n.f.* Gesticulation (in recitation, acting, etc.).
comicamente, *adv.* Comically, humorously.
comicità [-à], *n.f.* Comicality.
comico [cOmico], *n.m.a.* Actor, comedian; comical, funny, ludicrous, droll.
comignolo [comIgnolo], *n.m.* Gable, ridge (of roof), ridge-tile; chimney coping.
cominciamento, *n.m.* Commencement, beginning, start.
cominciare, *v.t.i.* To start, to begin, to commence.
cominciatore, *n.m.* Originator, founder.
comino, *n.m.* (*Bot.*) Cumin.
comitale, *a.* Pertaining to the rank of count.
comitato, *n.m.* Committee. **Far parte di un —,** to be on a committee; **nominare un —,** to appoint a committee; **— permanente,** standing committee.
comitiva, *n.f.* Party, company, group.
comito [cOmito], *n.m.* (*Naut.*) Boatswain.
comiziale, *a.* Electoral.
comiziante, *n.m.* One taking part in political meetings.
comizio [comIzio], *n.m.* Meeting, assembly; society. **— elettorale,** voters' meeting; **indire un —,** to call a meeting; **tenere un —,** to hold a meeting.
comma (*pl.* **commi**), *n.f.* Paragraph, paragraph heading; clause (between commas), comma.
commedia, comedia [commEdia, comEdia], *n.f.* Comedy; comic situation; make-believe. **Far la commedia,** to simulate; **Commedia dell'Arte,** professional improvised comedy of 16th and 17th centuries.
commediante, *n.m.f.* Actor, actress, comedian.
commedietta, *n.f.* Short comedy; curtain-raiser.
commediografo [commediOgrafo]. *n.m.* Playwright, writer of comedies.
commediola, *n.f.* Short comedy, farce.
commemorabile [commemorAbile]. *a.* Worth commemorating.
commemorare, *v.t.* To commemorate.
commemorativo, *a.* Commemorative.

Lapide commemorativa, memorial stone, tablet.
commemorazione, *n.f.* Commemoration.
commenda, *n.f.* Commandery, order of knighthood; (*Eccles.*) commendam.
commendabile [commendAbile], *a.* Commendable.
commendare, *v.t.* To commend, to praise; to recommend.
commendatizia [commendatIzia], *n.f.* Letter of recommendation.
commendatore, *n.m.* Commander or knight of an Italian order of chivalry.
commendazione, *n.f.* Commendation, praise.
commendevole [commendEvole], *a.* Commendable, praiseworthy.
commendevolmente, *adv.* Commendably.
commensale, *n.m.* Table companion (at an inn); fellow-boarder; (*Biol.*) commensal.
commensurabile [commensurAbile], *a.* Commensurable.
commensurare, *v.t.* To measure together; to commensurate.
commensurazione, *n.f.* Commensuration.
commentare, *v.t.* To comment on; to annotate; to expound, to set forth.
commentario [commentArio], *n.m.* Commentary.
commentatore, commentatrice, *n.m.f.* Commentator, annotator, expositor.
commento (1), *n.m.* Comment, remark, exposition, criticism.
commento (2), *n.m.* (*Naut.*) Seam (to be caulked).
commerciabile [commerciAbile], *a.* Marketable, negotiable.
commerciale, *a.* Commercial; mercantile; business.
commercialmente, *adv.* Commercially.
commerciante, *n.m.* Trader, dealer, business man, merchant; tradesman.
commerciare, *v.i.* To trade, to deal.
commercio [commErcio], *n.m.* Commerce, trade, business; intercourse; dealings; traffic. **Questo genere è in —,** this article is on the market; **fuori —,** not on sale; **— all'ingrosso,** wholesale trade; **— al minuto,** retail trade.
commessa, *n.f.* Shop assistant, shop-girl; a business order. **Le commesse americane,** American orders for goods.
commesso, *n.m.* Clerk, employee, shop assistant. **— viaggiatore,** commercial traveller.
commesso, *p.p.a.* Committed; joined together, coupled.
commessura, *n.f.* Joint, seam; (*Anat.*) commissure.
commestibile [commestIbile], *a.* Eatable, edible.
commestibili, *n.m.pl.* Foodstuffs, eatables, provisions. **Bottega di —,** provisions store.
commestione, *n.f.* (*Eccles.*) Single meal permitted on a fast-day.
commettere [commEttere] (1), *v.t.* To commit (in all senses); to entrust; to commission. **— il male,** to do ill; **— un'ingiustizia,** to do a wrong; **— una cosa ad uno,** to entrust someone with something; **— una mala creanza,** to be guilty of a breach of good manners.
commettere [commEttere] (2), *v.t.i.* To join together, to couple; (*Mech.*) to assemble.
commettitura, *n.f.* Joining, joint, seam; (*Anat.*) commissure.
commiato, *n.m.* Leave, discharge, dismissal; (*Poet.*) envoi. **Prendere —,** to take leave.
commilitone, *n.m.* Fellow-soldier, comrade-in-arms.
comminare, *v.i.* (*Law*) To threaten (with a sentence, penalty, etc.); to inflict.
comminatoria [comminatOria], *n.f.* (*Law*) Threat (uttered by a judge); warning.
comminatorio [comminatOrio], *a.* (*Law*) Threatening.
comminazione, *n.f.* Commination, threatening.
comminuto, *a.* (*Med.*) Comminuted.
commiserabile [commiserAbile], *a.* Pitiable.
commiserare, *v.t.* To commiserate, to pity.
commiserazione, *n.f.* Commiseration, pity.
commissariato, *n.m.* (*Mil.*) Commissariat; commissioner's office. **— di polizia,** police station.
commissario [commissArio], *n.m.* Commissary; commissioner, representative; (*Naut.*) purser, paymaster; (*Sport*) steward; (*Police*) inspector.
commissionare, *v.t.* To place on order, to commission.
commissionario [commissionArio], *n.m.* Commission agent; messenger; factor.
commissione, *n.f.* Commission, errand, charge, message; order; mandate; committee. **— d'inchiesta,** committee of inquiry; **far delle commissioni,** to go on errands, to go shopping; **fatto su —,** made to order.
commistione, *n.f.* Mixture, commixture.
commisto, *a.* Mixed.
commistura, *n.f.* Mixture.
commisurare, *v.t.* To compare, to measure (one thing with another); to adapt.
committente, *n.m.* (*Comm.*) Purchaser, customer, buyer; client; consigner.
commodoro, *n.m.* (*Naut.*) Commodore.
commosso, *a.* Moved, affected, stirred, touched.
commovente, *a.* Touching, moving, affecting, pitiful.
commovimento, *n.m.* Commotion, disturbance.
commozione, *n.f.* Commotion; emotion, agitation; shock; (*Med.*) concussion, shell-shock. **— cerebrale,** concussion of the brain.
commuovere, commovere [commuOvere, commOvere], *v.t.* To move, to touch, to affect; to agitate, to excite.
commuoversi [commuOversi], *v.r.* To be moved, to be affected, to be touched.
commutabile [commutAbile], *a.* Commutable, exchangeable, reversible.
commutare, *v.t.* To change, to commute, to reverse.
commutatore, *n.m.* (*Elect.*) Commutator; switch.
commutazione, *n.f.* Commutation; exchange. (*Law*) **— di pena,** commutation of punishment.
comò [-ò], *n.m.* Chest of drawers.
comodaccio [comodAccio], *n.m.* Comfort (at the expense of others). **Fa il — suo,** he suits his own convenience.

comodamente, *adv.* Comfortably, leisurely.
comodare, *v.i.* To suit [cp. **accomodare**].
comodato, *a.* (*Law*) Gratuitous lending.
comodino, *n.m.* Bedside table; (*Theat.*) drop-curtain. **Fare, servire da —,** to serve as a stop-gap.
comodità [-à], *n.f.* Convenience, comfort, ease; opportunity. **Per maggior —,** for greater convenience.
comodo [cOmodo], *n.m.* Convenience, comfort, ease, leisure; opportunity; service. **Questa cosa mi fa —,** this thing will come in useful; **a suo —,** at your convenience; **fare il proprio —,** to do as one pleases; (*Comm.*) **cambiale di —,** accommodation bill.
comodo [cOmodo], *a.* Comfortable, convenient, easy, handy; comfortably off; easy-going. **Stia —,** don't move, don't get up.
compadrone, *n.m.* Partner.
compaesano, *n.m.* Fellow-countryman, compatriot; man from the same district.
compagine [compAgine], *n.f.* Compages, complex structure; framework; connection, contexture.
compagna, *n.f.* (Female) companion; wife; girl-friend.
compagnevole [compagnEvole], *a.* Sociable, companionable.
compagnevolmente, *adv.* Sociably.
compagnia [compagnIa], *n.f.* Company (in all senses); society, partnership. **Dama di —,** lady-in-waiting; **far — a uno,** to keep one company; (*Comm.*) **— anonima,** limited or joint-stock company; **— di assicurazione,** insurance company.
compagno, *n.m.* Companion, comrade, mate, fellow; associate, partner; husband. **— di studi,** fellow student; **— di giuoco,** playmate.
compagno, *a.* Similar, like, equal. **Questi libri sono compagni,** these books are exactly alike; **questi guanti non sono compagni,** these gloves are not a pair.
compagnone, *n.m.* Good companion, jolly fellow.
companatico [companAtico], *n.m.* Anything (*e.g.* butter) eaten with bread.
comparabile [comparAbile], *a.* Comparable.
comparabilità [-à], *a.* Comparability.
comparabilmente, *adv.* Comparably.
comparare, *v.t.* To compare, to liken.
comparatico [comparAtico], *n.m.* Relationship of godparents.
comparativamente, *adv.* Comparatively.
comparativo, *a.* Comparative.
comparato, *p.p.a.* Comparative, compared. **Anatomia comparata,** comparative anatomy.
comparazione, *n.f.* Comparison.
compare, *n.m.* Godfather; crony; partner; accomplice.
comparente, *n.m.* (*Law*) Party appearing in court.
comparino, *n.m.* Godchild.
comparire, *v.t.* To appear, to show oneself, to come out; to attend (court). **— in giudizio,** to attend in court, to answer a summons.
compariscente, *a.* Handsome, of fine appearance.
compariscenza, *n.f.* Fine appearance.
comparita, *n.f.* Good appearance; good show; parade.
comparizione, *n.f.* (*Law*) Appearance (in court). **Mandato di —,** summons.
comparsa, *n.f.* Appearance, show; sudden arrival; nonentity; (*Theat.*) super; (*Law*) summons. **Far da —,** to act as a dummy.
compartecipare, *v.t.* To share with, to share in, to participate in. **— agli utili,** to share in the profits.
compartecipazione, *n.f.* Participation.
compartecipe [compartEcipe], *a.* Participatory.
compartimento, *n.m.* Compartment, division, department. **— stagno,** water-tight, air-tight compartment; **— delle macchine,** engine-room.
compartire, *v.t.* To partition, to divide off, to distribute.
compartizione, *n.f.* Division, distribution, partition.
compassare, *v.t.* To measure with compasses; to speak or act deliberately.
compassatamente, *adv.* Deliberately, cautiously.
compassato, *a.* Measured, restrained, controlled; precise, stiff. **Con modo —,** in a stiff, formal manner.
compassionamento, *n.m.* Sympathy, compassion.
compassionare, *v.t.* To pity, to compassionate, to commiserate.
compassione, *n.f.* Compassion, pity, commiseration; mercy. **Per —,** out of pity; **senza —,** mercilessly; **mi fece —,** I took pity on him; I felt sorry for him.
compassionevole [compassionEvole], *a.* Compassionate.
compassionevolmente, *adv.* Compassionately.
compasso, *n.m.* Compass; pair of compasses. **— a balaustro,** bow-compasses; **— di via,** steering-compass; **avere il — negli occhi,** to be a good judge of size.
compatibile [compatIbile], *a.* Compatible, consistent with; excusable.
compatibilità [-à], *n.f.* Compatibility, consistency.
compatibilmente, *adv.* Compatibly, consistently.
compatimento, *n.m.* Pity, indulgence; forbearance; sympathy.
compatire, *v.t.i.* To regard with indulgence, to pity, to sympathize with, to excuse. **Lo compatisco, ha avuto tanti grattacapi,** I sympathize with him, he is so worried; **Non farti —!** Don't make an exhibition of yourself!
compatirsi, *v.r.* To bear with one another.
compatrino, *n.m.* Fellow-godfather.
compatriota, compatriotta, compatriotto, *n.m.f.* Compatriot, fellow-countryman.
compatrono, *n.m.f.* (*Eccles.*) Joint patron (of a benefice).
compattezza, *n.f.* Compactness, solidarity, solidity.
compatto, *a.* Compact, solid; united.
compaziente, *a.* Compassionate.
compendiare, *v.t.* To abridge, to summarize, to epitomize.

compendiatamente, *adv.* In an abridged style.
compendio [compEndio], *n.m.* Epitome, compendium, abridgment, outline. **In —,** in brief, in outline.
compendiosità [-à], *n.f.* Compendiousness.
compendioso, *a.* Compendious, abridged, succinct.
compenetrabile [compenetrAbile], *a.* Penetrable.
compenetrabilità [-à], *n.f.* Penetrability.
compenetrare, *v.t.* To interpenetrate; to permeate, to pervade.
compenetrazione, *n.f.* Permeation.
compensabile [compensAbile], *a.* Remunerable; reparable.
compensare, *v.t.* To compensate; to reward; to offset; to indemnify.
compensativo, *a.* Remunerative.
compensato, *a.* **Legno —,** plywood.
compensatore, compensatrice, *a.* Counterbalancing, compensating.
compensazione, *n.f.* Compensation, reparation. (*Comm.*) **Stanza, camera di —,** clearing-house.
compenso, *n.m.* Reward, compensation, recompense. **In —,** in compensation.
compera [cOmpera], *n.f.* Purchase; bargain [cp. **compra**].
comperabile [comperAbile], *a.* Buyable.
comperare, *v.t.* To buy, to purchase [cp. **comprare**].
competente, *a.* Competent, qualified; suitable. **È persona —,** he is a qualified person; **mancia —,** suitable reward.
competentemente, *adv.* Competently.
competenza, *n.f.* Competence, competency; (*Law*) jurisdiction; honorarium, fee. **Di — di,** pertaining to.
competere [compEtere], *v.i.* To compete, to rival, to emulate; to be due, to belong. **Nulla le compete,** nothing is due to you.
competitore, competitrice, *n.m.f.* Competitor, rival.
competizione, *n.f.* Competition; rivalry; emulation.
compiacente, *a.* Polite, obliging; indulgent.
compiacentemente, *adv.* Politely, deferentially.
compiacenza, *n.f.* Kindness, politeness, complacence; satisfaction, pleasure. **Abbia la —,** have the kindness, be so kind as.
compiacere, *v.t.* To please, to comply with, to humour.
compiacersi, *v.r.* To take pleasure in, to delight in, to have the kindness to.
compiacimento, *n.m.* Satisfaction; gratification; complacence, complacency. **Le esprimo il mio —,** I express my satisfaction to you.
compiangere [compiAngere], *v.t.* To pity, to commiserate, to be sorry for; to deplore, to regret; to condole (with).
compianto, *n.m.a.* Pity, grief; regret; lamentation, complaint; lamented, regretted, mourned. **Esprimere il —,** to express one's sympathy; **il — artista,** the late lamented artist.
compicciare, *v.t.* To manage to get through a job with difficulty.
compiegare, *v.t.* To enclose; (*Comm.*) to enclose herewith.
compiere [cOmpiere], *v.t.* To accomplish, to fulfil, to complete, to end; to discharge. **— il proprio dovere,** to fulfil one's duty; **— una cattiva azione,** to accomplish an evil deed; **— gli studi,** to complete one's studies; **ha compito dieci anni,** he is ten years old.
compieta, *n.f.* (*Eccles.*) Compline.
compilare, *v.t.* To compile, to draw up.
compilatore, compilatrice, *n.m.f.* Compiler.
compilazione, *n.f.* Compilation.
compimento, *n.m.* Fulfilment, accomplishment; completion, conclusion. **Dar — a un lavoro,** to bring a work to completion.
compire, *v.t.* To complete, to accomplish, to bring to an end; to fulfil.
compitamente, *adv.* Politely.
compitare, *v.i.* To spell (out); to pronounce letter by letter.
compitazione, *n.f.* Spelling.
compitezza, *n.f.* Politeness, good breeding, refinement.
compito [cOmpito], *n.m.* Task, duty; homework (of school children).
compito, *a.* Polite, accomplished, well-bred.
compiutamente, *adv.* Completely, thoroughly.
compiuto, *a.* Fulfilled, completed, accomplished. **Fatto —,** accomplished fact.
compleanno, *n.m.* Birthday.
complementare, *a.* Complementary, auxiliary.
complemento, *n.m.* Complement (in all senses). (*Mil.*) **Ufficiale di —,** officer on the reserve; **complementi,** drafts.
complessionato, *a.* Constituted. **Ben —,** of a good constitution.
complessione, *n.f.* Constitution (health), temperament.
complessità [-à], *n.f.* Complexity.
complessivamente, *adv.* Inclusively, collectively, in the aggregate.
complessivo, *a.* Inclusive, total, aggregate.
complesso, *n.m.* Complex, totality, whole; combination. **In —,** in the main, as a whole.
complesso, *a.* Complex, complicated; compound; well-built. **Uomo —,** well-built man.
completamente, *adv.* Completely.
completamento, *n.m.* Completion.
completare, *v.t.* To complete, to finish, to perfect.
completo, *n.m.* (Man's) suit.
completo, *a.* Complete, whole, full, entire; perfect. **Al —,** in full; **"Completo",** "Full up" (of trams, buses, etc.).
completorio [completOrio], *a.* Supplementary.
complicanza, *n.f.* Complication.
complicare, *v.t.* To complicate, to entangle.
complicarsi, *v.r.* To become complicated, to get entangled; to become worse (in illness).
complicatezza, *n.f.* Complicatedness.
complicato, *a.* Complicated; elaborate; intricate, entangled.
complicazione, *n.f.* Complication. **Evitare ulteriori complicazioni,** to avoid further complications.
complice [cOmplice], *n.m.a.* Accomplice, partner (in crime), accessory; accessory, privy, a party to.
complicità [-à], *n.f.* Complicity.
complimentare, *v.t.* To compliment; to congratulate.

complimentario [complimentArio], *n.m.* (*obs.*) Bearer of congratulations.
complimento, *n.m.* Compliment; respects, regards; ceremony. **Non faccia complimenti,** do not stand on ceremony; **fare un —,** to pay a compliment; **senza complimenti,** without ceremony; frankly; **tanti complimenti,** kind regards.
complimentosamente, *adv.* Ceremoniously.
complimentoso, *a.* Ceremonious.
complottare, *v.t.* To plot.
complotto, *n.m.* Plot, conspiracy.
componente, *n.m.* Component.
componimento, *n.m.* Composition, essay; settlement; (*Law*) adjustment, arrangement. **— amichevole,** amicable arrangement.
comporre, *v.t.* To compose, to compound; to shape, to form; to write; to arrange, to settle. **— una lite,** to settle a lawsuit.
comporsi, *v.r.* To consist of, to be composed of. **La commissione si compone di quattro membri,** the committee is composed of four members.
comportabile [comportAbile], *a.* Tolerable.
comportabilmente, *adv.* Tolerably.
comportamento, *n.m.* Deportment, conduct, behaviour; action.
comportare, *v.t.* To tolerate, to afford, to allow; to endure, to resist (cold, heat, etc.). **Se le mie finanze lo comportano,** if my means allow it.
comportarsi, *v.r.* To behave, to conduct oneself. **Comportati bene,** behave properly; **— da,** to behave like.
comporto, *n.m.* Delay; (*Comm.*) respite, (days of) grace.
composito [compOsito], *a.* Composite.
compositoio [compositOio], *n.m.* (*Print.*) Compositor's stick.
compositore, *n.m.* (*Mus.*) Composer; (*Print.*) compositor.
composizione, *n.f.* Composition (in all senses).
compossessione, *n.f.* Joint-ownership.
compossessore, *n.m.* Joint-owner.
composta, *n.f.* Mixture; stewed fruit, compote.
compostamente, *adv.* Decorously, sedately.
compostezza, *n.f.* Dignity, self-possession; sedateness; modesty.
compostiera, *n.f.* Dish for stewed fruit.
composto, *n.m.* Compound, mixture.
composto, *p.p.a.* Composed, calm, sedate, modest; self-possessed; arranged. **Stai —,** sit still; behave yourself; **modi composti,** quiet, sedate behaviour; **interesse —,** compound interest.
compra, *n.f.* Purchase. **— ferma,** cash purchase.
comprare, *v.t.* To buy, to purchase. **— a contanti,** to pay cash for; **— a buon mercato,** to buy cheaply; **— all'asta,** to buy at auction; **— all'ingrosso,** to buy wholesale.
compratore, compratrice, *n.m.f.* Buyer, purchaser.
compravendita [compravEndita], *n.f.* (*Law*) Deed of sale; exchange; bargain.
comprendere [comprEndere], *v.i.* To understand; to comprehend; to include, to contain; to cover. **Non si comprende la ragione,** one cannot understand the reason.
comprendibile [comprendIbile], *a.* Understandable.
comprendimento, *n.m.* Comprehension, understanding.
comprendonio [comprendOnio], *n.m.* Judgment, gumption. **Duro di —,** slow-witted, slow in the uptake.
comprensibile [comprensIbile], *a.* Understandable.
comprensibilmente, *adv.* Understandably.
comprensione, *n.f.* Comprehension, understanding.
comprensivamente, *adv.* Comprehensively.
comprensivo, *a.* Comprehensive.
comprensorio [comprensOrio], *n.m.* District, limited area.
compreso, *a.* Understood; full (of); included, comprised. **Essere — di una cosa,** to be fully aware of; **essere — in,** to be included in; **servizio —,** service included; (*Comm.*) **nolo —,** including freight.
compressa, *n.f.* (*Med.*) Compress; tabloid, pill.
compressibile [compressIbile], *a.* Compressible.
compressibilità [-à], *n.f.* Compressibility.
compressione, *n.f.* Compression.
compressivo, *a.* Compressory.
compresso, *p.p.a.* Compressed, compacted; dense, thick, close.
compressore, *n.m.* (*Mech.*) Compressor, roller. **— stradale, rullo —,** steam-roller.
comprimario [comprimArio], *n.m.* (*Theat.*) Junior lead, second part.
comprimere [comprImere], *v.t.* To compress, to press, to squeeze, to stint; to restrain.
comprimibile [comprimIbile], *a.* Compressible, restrainable.
compromesso, *n.m.a.* Compromise, mutual concession; arbitration; compromised. **Mettere in —,** to risk, to hazard.
compromettente, *a.* Compromising.
compromettere [compromEttere], *v.t.* To put to arbitration; to compromise, to risk, to jeopardize, to imperil.
compromettersi [compromEttersi], *v.r.* To compromise oneself, to expose oneself; to take upon oneself; to become involved.
compromissario [compromissArio], *n.m.* (*Law*) Arbitrator, referee.
comproprietà [-à], *n.f.* Joint-ownership.
comproprietario [comproprietArio], *n.m.* Joint-owner, partner.
comprovabile [comprovAbile], *a.* Provable.
comprovare, *v.t.* (*Law*) To prove (by evidence); to bring evidence in support of.
comprovazione, *n.f.* Legal proof, evidence.
compulsare, *v.t.* To examine, to look through, to inspect; to consult (books, etc.); (*Law*) to compel; to summon (to appear).
compulsione, *n.f.* Constriction, compulsion.
compulsivo, *a.* (*Law*) Citing for judgment.
compulsoria [compulsOria], *n.f.* (*Law*) Order for payment.
compungere [compUngere], *v.t.* (*obs.*) To afflict.
compungimento, *n.m.* Compunction.
compuntamente, *adv.* With compunction.
compunto, *p.p.a.* Afflicted, grieved; conscience-stricken; demure. **Aria compunta,** contrite appearance.

compunzione, *n.f.* Compunction, contrition, remorse.
computabile [computAbile], *a.* Computable.
computare, *v.t.* To compute, to reckon, to calculate, to estimate.
computazione, *n.f.* Reckoning, computation.
computista (*pl.* **computisti**), *n.m.* Book-keeper, accountant.
computisteria [computisterIa], *n.f.* Book-keeping; accountancy.
computo [cOmputo], *n.m.* Calculation, reckoning; account.
comunale, *a.* Communal, civic, municipal. **Consiglio —,** city council.
comunanza, *n.f.* Community, society; identity. **In —,** in common; **— d'interessi,** community of interests.
comunardo, *n.m.* (*Hist.*) Communard.
comune, *n.m.f.* Commune, municipality, corporation; town; town hall; townsfolk. **Camera dei Comuni,** House of Commons. **La Commune,** the Paris Commune (of 1871).
comune, *a.* Common, ordinary, habitual, usual; mutual. **Il bene —,** the common good; **in —,** in common; (*Comm.*) **conto —,** joint account.
comunella, *n.f.* Clique. **Far —,** to form a clique, to associate with.
comunemente, *adv.* Commonly; communally, together, in common.
comunicabile [comunicAbile], *a.* Communicable.
comunicabilità [-à], *n.f.* Communicability.
comunicando, *n.m.* (*Eccles.*) Communicant; one prepared for First Communion.
comunicante, *n.m.* Communicant; celebrant of Communion.
comunicante, *a.* Communicating, communicant. **Camere comunicanti,** communicating rooms.
comunicare, *v.t.i.* To communicate, to inform; to connect; (*Eccles.*) to communicate, to administer or receive Communion; (*Med.*) to transmit a complaint; to infect with.
comunicarsi, *v.r.* To share with; (*Eccles.*) to receive Communion.
comunicativo, *a.* Communicative; (*Med.*) catching, infectious.
comunicato, *n.m.* (*Eccles.*) One who has received Communion; (*Pol.*) communiqué, official statement, bulletin.
comunicatorio [comunicatOrio], *a.* Communicating.
comunicazione, *n.f.* Communication (in all senses). **Mezzi di —,** means of communication; (*Teleph.*) **mettere in —,** to put through; **— intercomunale,** trunk call.
comunichino, *n.m.* (*Eccles.*) Wafer.
comunione, *n.f.* Communion (in all senses).
comunismo, *n.m.* Communism.
comunista (*pl.* **comunisti**), *n.m.f.* Communist.
comunità [-à], *n.f.* Community.
comunque, *adv.* However. **— sia,** however that may be.
con, *prep.* With, by, to. (Combined with the definite articles it makes **col, collo, colla, coi, cogli, colle,** which are all varying forms of **with the**). **Con mio dispiacere,** to my regret; **con tutto ciò,** for all that.
conato, *n.m.* Effort, attempt; impulse.

conca, *n.f.* Basin, cavity, hollow; wash-tub; shell; (*Anat.*) concha; (*Eng.*) lock, sluice.
concaio [concAio], *n.m.* Potter (of earthenware).
concambiare, *v.t.* To exchange.
concambio [concAmbio], *n.m.* (*Law*) Exchange.
concatenamento, *n.m.* Linking together, concatenation.
concatenare, *v.t.* To link together (in argument), to concatenate.
concatenatura, *n.f.* Juncture.
concatenazione, *n.f.* Concatenation.
concausa [concAusa], *n.f.* (*Law*) Concomitant cause, contributory cause; aggravation of guilt.
concavità [-à], *n.f.* Concavity.
concavo [cOncavo], *n.m.a.* Hollow; concave.
concedere [concEdere], *v.t.* To concede, to grant, to allow, to permit; to admit.
concedibile [concedIbile], *a.* Allowable.
concedimento, *n.m.* Concession, conceding.
concento, *n.m.* (*Poet.*) Harmony, melody.
concentramento, *n.m.* Concentration. **Campo di —,** concentration camp.
concentrare, *v.t.* To concentrate; to condense.
concentrarsi, *v.r.* To ponder over, to concentrate (one's thoughts).
concentrazione, *n.f.* Concentration.
concentricamente, *adv.* Concentrically.
concentrico [concEntrico], *a.* Concentric.
concepibile [concepIbile], *a.* Conceivable, imaginable.
concepimento, *n.m.* Conception, idea; imagination.
concepire, *v.t.* To conceive (in all senses); to devise, to imagine, to formulate (an idea, etc.).
conceria [concerIa], *n.f.* Tannery.
concernere [concErnere], *v.i.* To concern, to relate, to affect. **Per quanto concerne,** with regard to, as to.
concertare, *v.t.* To concert, to settle, to adjust, to plan; to conduct (music); to hatch (a plot).
concertarsi, *v.r.* To act in concert, to be agreed (upon).
concertato, *p.p.a.* Concerted, arranged. (*Mus*). **Pezzo concertato,** concerted piece (esp. finale of act or scene in opera).
concertatore, *n.m.* (*Mus.*) Conductor.
concertista, *n.m.f.* (Professional) pianist, violinist, etc.
concerto, *n.m.* Concert (in all senses), harmony. **Dare un —,** to give a concert; **agire di —,** to act in agreement with; **di —,** unanimously.
concessionario [concessionArio], *n.m.a.* Grantee, concessionaire; concessionary. **Unico —,** sole agent.
concessione, *n.f.* Concession; grant; adjudication; permission.
concessivo, *a.* Conceding.
concesso, *p.p.a.* Conceded, granted, allowed. **Dato e non —,** granting, for the sake of argument.
concettino, *n.m.* Affected wit.
concettismo, *n.m.* (*Lit.*) Euphuism, concettism, use of fanciful phraseology; preciosity, affectation.

concettizzare, *v.i.* (*Lit.*) To affect verbal conceits.
concetto, *n.m.* Conception, concept; thought, notion, idea; opinion; meaning; fancy, reputation; verbal conceit. **Formarsi un —,** to form an opinion; **essere in buon —,** to enjoy a good reputation; (*Comm.*) **impiegato di —,** managing clerk.
concetto, *a.* Pregnant; conceived.
concettosamente, *adv.* Thoughtfully.
concettoso, *a.* Pregnant, thoughtful; pithy, concise; sententious.
concettuale, *a.* Conceptual.
concezione, *n.f.* Conception. **L'Immacolata Concezione,** the Immaculate Conception.
conchifero [conchIfero], *a.* (*Zool.*) Conchiferous; full of shells.
conchiglia [conchIglia], *n.f.* Sea-shell; shell-fish.
conchiudere [conchiUdere], *v.t.* To conclude, [cp. **concludere**].
concia [cOncia], *n.f.* Tan, tanning, dressing (leather); tannery.
conciacaldaia [conciacaldAia], *n.m.* Tinker.
conciaia [conciAia], *n.f.* Manure-pit.
conciaio, conciaiolo [conciAio], *n.m.* Tanner.
concialana, *n.m.* Mattress-maker.
conciapelli, *n.m.* Tanner.
conciare, *v.t.* To tan, to dress skins; to repair; to spoil (by careless use), to ill-use; to thrash. **Guarda come son conciati quei libri,** see what a state those books are in.
conciarsi, *v.r.* To get dirty, to become soiled.
conciatetti, *n.m.* Tiler, roof-mender, slater.
conciato, *p.p.a.* Tanned; badly used.
conciatore, *n.m.* Tanner.
conciatura, *n.f.* Tanning, leather-dressing; mending.
conciliabilmente, *adv.* Compatibly; in a conciliatory manner.
conciliabolo [conciliAbolo], *n.m.* Conventicle; secret meeting.
conciliamento, *n.m.* Reconcilement; conciliation.
conciliare, *v.t.* To conciliate; to reconcile; to induce; to win over. **Il vino concilia il sonno,** wine induces sleep.
conciliarsi, *v.r.* To captivate, to gain (affection, etc.); to agree with.
conciliativo, *a.* Conciliating.
conciliatore, conciliatrice, *n.m.f.a.* Conciliator; peace-maker; conciliatory. **Giudice —,** justice of the peace.
conciliazione, *n.f.* Reconcilement, reconciliation.
concilio [concIlio], *n.m.* Council, assembly.
concimaia [concimAia], *n.f.* Manure-pit; dunghill.
concimare, *v.t.* To manure, to dung, to fertilize.
concimatura, *n.f.* Manuring, fertilizing.
concime, *n.m.* Manure, dung; organic fertilizer. **Concime chimico,** chemical manure.
concinnare, *v.t.* To make elegant.
concinnità [-à], *n.f.* (*Lit.*) Elegance, harmony (of style).
concinno, *a.* Harmonious; appropriate.
concino, *n.m.* Tan.
concio [cOncio], *n.m.* Dung; manure.
concio [cOncio], *a.* Tanned; bruised.
concionalmente, *adv.* In a haranguing manner; pompously.
concionare, *v.t.i.* To harangue, to declaim; to speechify; to preach
concionatore, *n.m.* Tub-thumper, mob-orator.
concionatura, *n.f.* Haranguing, tub-thumping.
concione, *n.f.* Harangue; declamation; tirade.
conciossiachè, *conj.* (*obs.*) As, because.
concisamente, *adv.* Concisely, briefly.
concisione, *n.f.* Conciseness.
conciso, *a.* Concise.
concistoriale, *a.* (*Eccles.*) Consistorial.
concistoro, concistorio, *n.m.* (*Eccles.*) Consistory.
concitamento, *n.m.* Emotion, perturbation; tumult; excitement.
concitare, *v.t.* To stir up, to arouse, to excite.
concitatamente, *adv.* Excitedly.
concitazione, *n.f.* Emotion; excitement.
concittadinanza, *n.f.* Fellow-citizenship
concittadino, *n.m.* Fellow-citizen.
conclamare, *v.t.* To proclaim, to acclaim; to hail.
conclamazione, *n.f.* Acclamation; funeral rite in which the defunct is summoned by name.
conclave, *n.m.* (*Eccles.*) Conclave.
conclavista (*pl.* **conclavisti**), *n.m.* (*Eccles.*) Cardinal summoned to a conclave; servant employed in a conclave.
concludenza, *n.f.* Conclusion.
concludere [conclUdere], *v.t.i.* To conclude, to finish, to bring to an end; to decide; to carry out, to effect. **Bisogna —,** we must come to a decision.
conclusionale, *a.* (*Law*) Concluding. **Comparsa —,** recapitulation of the case.
conclusione, *n.f.* Conclusion, close, end.
conclusivamente, *adv.* Conclusively, finally.
conclusivo, *a.* Conclusive, decisive.
concluso, *a.* Concluded, brought to an end.
concocimento, *n.m.* Concoction (in cooking).
concoide [concOide], *n.f.* (*Geom.*) Conchoid.
concologia [concologIa], *n.f.* Conchology.
concolore, *a.* (*Lit.*) Of the same colour.
concomitante, *a.* Concomitant, simultaneous.
concomitanza, *n.f.* Concomitance.
concordabile [concordAbile], *a.* Capable of agreement.
concordamento, *n.m.* Act of concord.
concordante, *a.* Concordant; consonant.
concordanza, *n.f.* Concordance, agreement.
concordare, *v.t.i.* To reconcile; to agree.
concordarsi, *v.r.* To agree together, to come together.
concordatario [concordatArio], *a.* (*Comm.*) Having come to, or, concerning, an agreement with one's creditors.
concordato, *n.m.* (*Eccles.*) Concordat; compact, convention; (*Comm.*) composition with creditors.
concorde, *a.* Concordant; agreeing; like-minded.
concordemente, *adv.* Unanimously.
concordevole [concordEvole], *a.* Concordant.
concordia [concOrdia], *n.f.* Concord, harmony, agreement, peace, unanimity.
concorrente, *n.m.* Competitor; candidate, applicant (for a job).
concorrente, *a.* Concurrent; competing.

concorrenza, *n.f.* Concourse; rivalry; competition. **Far —,** to compete with; **— accanita,** keen competition.

concorrere [concOrrere], *v.i.* To concur; to assemble; to contribute, to share in; to compete; to converge.

concorso, *n.m.* Concourse, meeting; competition, competitive examination; (*Comm.*) creditors' meeting **Bandire un —,** to advertise a post, to open a (State) competition; (*Comm.*) to make a tender; **mettere a —,** to call for tenders; **coprire un posto per —,** to fill a post by open competition.

concotto, *a.* Baked.

concozione, *n.f.* Concoction.

concreare, *v.t.* To create together.

concrescenza, *n.f.* Concretion [cp. **concrezione**].

concretamente, *adv.* Concretely.

concretare, *v.t.* To make concrete, to conclude, to settle, to determine.

concretezza, *n.f.* Concreteness.

concreto, *n.m.a.* The concrete; concrete, real, positive, definite. **Non c'è nulla di — ancora,** nothing has been decided yet.

concrezione, *n.f.* Concretion (in all senses).

concubina, *n.f.* Concubine.

concubinario [concubinArio], *n.m.* Man living in concubinage.

concubinato, *n.m.* Concubinage.

concubito [concUbito], *n.m.* Act of coition.

conculcamento, *n.m.* Oppression.

conculcare, *v.t.* To trample upon, to oppress.

conculcazione, *n.f.* Oppression.

concuocere [concuOcere], *v.t.* To digest.

concuocersi [concuOcersi], *v.r.* To mature (land) by action of frost and heat.

concupire, *v.t.* To lust after, to covet.

concupiscente, *a.* Concupiscent, lustful.

concupiscenza, *n.f.* Concupiscence, lust.

concupiscibile [concupiscIbile], *a.* Desirable (sexually).

concussionario [concussionArio], *n.m.* Extortioner, blackmailer.

concussione, *n.f.* Extortion, blackmail; peculation.

condanna, *n.f.* Condemnation; penalty; sentence; blame. **Pronunciare una —,** to pass sentence; **subire una —,** to suffer judgment, to be condemned; **— a morte,** death sentence; **scontare una —,** to serve a sentence

condannabile [condannAbile], *a.* Condemnable, blameworthy, censurable.

condannare, *v.t.* To condemn, to convict, to sentence; to blame, to censure.

condannato, *n.m.a.* Condemned criminal, convict; convicted, sentenced. **Quel malato è —,** that sick man is beyond hope of recovery.

condannazione, *n.f.* Condemnation.

condebitore, *n.m.* (*Law*) Joint-debtor.

condecente, *a.* Decent, proper.

condecentemente, *adv.* Decently, with propriety.

condegno, *a.* Condign; adequate, suitable, worthy.

condensabile [condensAbile], *a.* Condensable, liable to condensation.

condensabilità [-à], *n.f.* Condensability.

condensamento, *n.m.* Condensation, condensing.

condensare, *v.t.* To condense; to shorten, to abbreviate.

condensatore, *n.m.* (*Mech.*) Condenser.

condensazione, *n.f.* Condensation.

condicevole [condicEvole], *a.* (*Lit.*) Convenient.

condilo [cOndilo], *n.m.* (*Anat.*) Condyle.

condimento, *n.m.* Condiment, sauce, dressing.

condire, *v.t.* To season, to dress (salad); to pickle; (*fig.*) to improve.

condirettore, *n.m.* Co-editor (of a newspaper); co-director.

condiscendente, *a.* Condescending, indulgent.

condiscendentemente, *adv.* Condescendingly.

condiscendenza, *n.f.* Condescension, indulgence, compliance.

condiscendere [condiscEndere], *v.i.* To condescend; to comply with, to be indulgent; to yield to.

condiscendimento, *n.m.* Condescension.

condiscepolo [condiscEpolo], *n.m.* Schoolfellow; class-mate.

condito, *n.m.a.* Condiment; seasoned, tasty; pickled.

condito [cOndito], *a.* (*obs.*) Built; founded.

conditore, *n.m.* (*obs.*) Founder.

conditura, *n.f.* Flavouring.

condividere [condivIdere], *v.t.* To share (with), to participate in; to divide (among several). **Essa condivise gioie e dolori con lui,** with him she shared her joys and sorrows.

condizionale, *n.m.a.* Conditional (in all senses).

condizionalmente, *adv.* Conditionally.

condizionare, *v.t.* To condition; to qualify; to impose a condition; to dispose; to season.

condizionatamente, *adv.* On condition, with reservation.

condizionato, *a.* Conditioned; seasoned, dressed. **Con aria condizionata,** air-conditioned; **ben —,** in good condition.

condizione, *n.f.* Condition; state, station, situation, rank; proviso. **— implicita,** implied condition; **persona di bassa —,** person of humble birth; **di — sarto,** a tailor by trade; **si trova in brutta —,** he is in a sad plight; **a — che,** on condition that; **pongo per — che,** I must stipulate that.

condizioni, *n.f.pl.* (*Comm.*) Terms. **— di pagamento,** conditions of payment; **— del mercato,** state of the market.

condoglianza, *n.f.* Condolence, sympathy; expression of sympathy. **Vi esprimiamo le nostre sentite condoglianze,** we wish to express our most sincere sympathy.

condolente, *a.* Sympathetic.

condolersi, *v.r.* To condole with, to express sympathy with.

condominio [condomInio], *n.m.* Condominium; (*Law*) joint-ownership.

condomino [condOmino], *n.m.* (*Law*) Co-owner.

condonabile [condonAbile], *a.* Condonable, excusable.

condonare, *v.t.* To condone, to pardon, to excuse, to remit.

condonazione, *n.f.* Condonation, pardon.

condono, *n.m.* Remission, pardon; amnesty.

condore, *n.m.* (*Zool.*) Condor.

condotta, *n.f.* Conduct, behaviour; administration, management; conduit; driving (a vehicle). **— medica,** doctor's practice.
condottiero, condottiere, *n.m.* Soldier of fortune, captain, condottiere.
condotto, *n.m.* Conduit; water-pipe, duct, channel.
condotto, *p.p.a.* Conducted, led. **Medico —,** panel doctor; municipal doctor.
conducente, *n.m.* Driver; conductor; manager; (*Comm.*) contractor. (*Motor.*) **Proprietario —,** owner-driver.
conducibile [conducIbile], *a* Amenable, conducive.
condurre, *v.t.* To lead, to guide, to conduct; to manage, to direct; to escort; to persuade; to perform; to drive (a car, etc.) **— a buon fine,** to bring to a successful conclusion.
condursi, *v.r.* To behave oneself, to conduct oneself; to betake oneself, to go.
conduttanza, *n.f.* (*Elec.*) Conductance.
conduttività [-à], *n.f.* (*Elect.*) Conductivity.
conduttore, *n.m.* Conductor (in most senses); driver; guard; manager [cp. **direttore**].
conduttura, *n.f.* Conduit, water-pipe. **La — dell'acqua,** the water system.
conduzione, *n.f.* (*Law*) Contract of lease, tenancy; ducting of water; conduction.
conestabile [conestAbile], *n.m* (*Hist.*) Constable; former knightly rank.
confabulare, *v.t.* To confabulate; to chat.
confabulazione, *n.f.* Confabulation.
confacente, *a.* Suitable, convenient, agreeable to, proper.
confacentemente, *adv.* Suitably.
confacevole [confacEvole], *a.* Suitable, proper.
confarsi, *v.r.* To suit, to agree, to be proper, to fit. **Questo clima non mi si confa,** this climate does not suit me.
confarreazione, *n.f.* (*Hist.*) Confarreation.
confederamento, *n.m.* (Act of) confederating.
confederarsi, *v.r.* To unite, to form a confederation, to confederate.
confederativo, *a.* Tending to confederation.
confederato, *n.m.* Ally, confederate.
confederazione, *n.f.* Confederation, confederacy, league, union.
conferente, *n.m.* Member of a conference.
conferenza, *n.f.* Conference; lecture, discourse; conversation; interview. **Tenere una —,** to give a lecture.
conferenziere, *n.m.* Lecturer.
conferimento, *n.m.* Bestowal, conferment.
conferire, *v.t.i.* To grant, to confer, to bestow; to confer with, to consult (together); to have an interview. **— un onore,** to confer an honour; **egli sta conferendo con,** he is conferring with.
conferma, *n.f.* Confirmation; assurance; sanction. **A —,** in confirmation.
confermare, *v.t.* To confirm, to reaffirm; to corroborate; to sanction; to ratify.
confermativamente, *adv.* In confirmation.
confermativo, *a.* Confirmative, confirming.
confermazione, *n.f.* Confirmation.
confessare, *v.t.* To confess, to admit, to acknowledge, to avow; (*Eccles.*) to hear confession of (someone), to confess.
confessarsi, *v.r.* To confess oneself; to go to confession.
confessionale, *n.m.* (*Eccles.*) Confessional.
confessione, *n.f.* Confession; declaration; creed.
confesso, *p.p.a.* Confessed, acknowledged, convinced. (*Law*) **Reo —,** prisoner who pleads guilty.
confessore, *n.m.* (*Eccles.*) Confessor.
confettare, *v.t.* To preserve (fruit, etc.), to candy; to sweeten; (*fig.*) to make up to, to fawn upon.
confetteria [confetterIa], *n.f.* Confectionery.
confettiera, *n.f.* Sweet-meat box.
confettiere, *n.m.* Confectioner.
confetto, *n.m.* Sweet, sweetmeat; sugared almond. **Far mangiare i confetti,** to celebrate a wedding.
confettura, *n.f.* Jam; sweetmeat.
confettureria [confetturerIa], *n.f.* Sweet-shop; sweet factory.
confetturiere, *n.m.* Seller or maker of sweets.
confezionare, *v.t.* To make up, to form, to prepare, to compound; to manufacture, to parcel. **— su misura,** to make to measure.
confezionato, *a.* Ready-to-wear. **— su misura,** made to measure.
confezione, *n.f.* Mixture (medicine); made-up or compounded thing; completion.
confezioni, *n.f.pl.* Ready-to-wear clothes; outfits. **— uomini,** men's tailoring.
conficcamento, *n.m.* Driving in, knocking in; fixing.
conficcare, *v.t.* To nail, to knock in, to drive in (with hammer); (*fig.*) to fix (in the memory).
conficcarsi, *v.r.* To be thrust in; to be driven in.
conficcatura, *n.f.* Nailing, driving in.
confidare, *v.i.* To trust, to confide, to rely upon; to entrust to. **Confidiamo che farete del vostro meglio,** we trust you will do your best.
confidarsi, *v.r.* To confide in, to unbosom oneself.
confideiussore, *n.m.* (*Law*) Joint-bail.
confidente, *n.m.f.a.* Confidant; trusty friend; confiding.
confidentemente, *adv.* Confidingly.
confidenza, *n.f.* Confidence, trust, assurance; intimacy, familiarity; secret; disclosure. **Parlare in —,** to talk privately; **prendersi troppe confidenze,** to take too many liberties; **in —,** in confidence.
confidenziale, *a.* Confidential.
confidenzialmente, *adv.* Confidentially.
configgere [confIggere], *v.t.* To nail, to nail up, to knock in, to fix in.
configurare, *v.t.* To give shape to, to shape; (*fig.*) to symbolize.
confinante, *n.m.f.a.* Neighbour; adjacent, contiguous.
confinare, *v.t.i.* To confine; to intern; to limit; to banish; to adjoin, to border on. **È confinato a letto,** he is confined to his bed; **l'Italia confina con la Svizzera,** Italy and Switzerland have a common frontier.
confinarsi, *v.r.* To confine oneself, to limit oneself. **Si è confinato in casa,** he has shut himself up in his house.
confinazione, *n.f.* Demarcation of a frontier.
confine, *n.m.* Frontier; border, boundary; limit. **Stazione di —,** frontier station.

confino, *n.m.* Internment, banishment. **Mandare al —,** to intern, to send to a place of confinement.
confisca, *n.f.* Confiscation, forfeiture; distraint, distress.
confiscabile [confiscAbile], *a.* Distrainable.
confiscare, *v.t.* To confiscate, to seize, to forfeit; to distrain.
confitemini [confitEmini], *n.m.* (*colloq.*) **Essere al —,** to be on the point of death.
confitto, *p.p.a.* Nailed, fixed, fastened; driven in. **— in croce,** nailed to the Cross.
conflagrare, *v.i.* To burn, to blaze.
conflagrazione, *n f.* Conflagration.
conflitto, *n.m.* Conflict, fight, collision; clash, contest.
confluente, *n.m.* Confluent, tributary stream.
confluenza, *n.f.* Confluence, junction.
confluire, *v.t.* To flow together, to unite, to join.
confondere [confOndere], *v.t.* To confound, to confuse, to mix, to mingle; to abash, to disconcert, to embarrass.
confondersi [confOndersi], *v.r.* To get mixed, to become confused; to be perplexed; to get flurried; to become apprehensive.
confondibile [confondIbile], *a.* Liable to be confused.
confondimento, *n.m.* Confusion.
confonditore, confonditrice, *n.m.f.* One who causes confusion or perplexity.
conformabile [conformAbile], *a.* Conformable, adaptable; similar to.
conformare, *v.t.* To conform, to adapt, to accommodate, to assimilate.
conformarsi, *v.r.* To conform oneself, to adapt oneself, to comply with.
conformativo, *a.* Adaptable, conforming.
conformazione, *n.f.* Conformation, disposition, form, structure.
conforme, *a.* Consonant, consistent, suitable, conformable; similar. **Copia —,** certified copy; **— al vostro desiderio,** in compliance with your wishes.
conforme, *adv.* Conformably, in conformity (with). (*colloq.*) **Conforme!** That depends!
conformemente, *adv.* Conformably, in accordance.
conformismo, *n.m.* Spirit of conformity.
conformista (*pl.* **conformisti**), *n.m.* Conformist.
conformità [-à], *n.f.* Conformity. **In —,** in compliance with.
confortabile [confortAbile], *a.* Capable of being comforted; consolable; provable.
confortabilmente, *adv.* Comfortably.
confortante, *a.* Consoling, comforting.
confortare, *v.t.* To comfort, to console; to relieve; to corroborate; to fortify; to encourage. **Ha confortato la sua tesi con esempi,** he supported his thesis with examples.
confortativo, *a.* Comforting.
confortatore, confortatrice, *n.m.f.* Comforter; (*Eccles.*) prison chaplain.
confortevole [confortEvole], *a.* Comforting, comfortable.
confortino, *n.m.* Iced cake; snack; pick-me-up.
conforto, *n.m.* Comfort, relief, consolation. **Conforti religiosi,** spiritual consolation; **gli estremi conforti,** extreme unction.
confratello, *n.m.* Fellow-member, confrère.
confraternita [confratErnita], *n.f.* Confraternity, brotherhood.
confricamento, *n.m.* Rubbing.
confricare, *v.t.* To rub, to rub together.
confricazione, *n.f.* Friction, rubbing.
confrontare, *v.t.i.* To compare, to liken; to confront, to collate; to agree.
confronto, *n.m.* Comparison, comparing; (*Law*) confrontation. **In — a lui,** compared with him; **senza —,** incomparably, without comparison; **mettere a — i testimoni,** to confront witnesses.
confuciano, *n.m.a.* Confucian.
confuggire, *v.i.* (*Poet.*) To take refuge in flight.
confusamente, *adv.* Confusedly.
confusionario [confusionArio], *n.m.a.* Bungler, muddler; mischief-making.
confusione, *n.f.* Confusion, disorder; bustle, disturbance.
confuso, *a.* Confused, vague, muddled, obscure. **Idee confuse,** foggy notions.
confutabile [confutAbile], *a.* Refutable, confutable.
confutamento, *n.m.* Confutation, refutation.
confutare, *v.t.* To confute, to refute, to disprove.
confutazione, *n.f.* Confutation, refutation.
congedabile [congedAbile], *a.* Liable to dismissal.
congedamento, *n.m.* (Act of) dismissal.
congedare, *v.t.* To discharge, to dismiss; to give leave to; to disband.
congedarsi, *v.r.* To take leave (of); to take one's leave.
congedo, *n.m.* Leave, leave of absence, permission; discharge, "the sack". **Prendere —,** to take one's leave; **dar —,** to dismiss; (*Mil.*) **essere in —,** to be on leave.
congegnamento, *n.m.* Mechanism, device; gadget; artifice.
congegnare, *v.t.* To devise, to contrive, to set up.
congegnatura, *n.f.* Contrivance.
congegno, *n.m.* Mechanism, apparatus; device, contrivance, gadget; method of assembling parts.
congelamento, *n.m.* Congelation, congealment; freezing. **Punto di —,** freezing point.
congelare, *v.t.* To congeal, to freeze.
congelarsi, *v.r.* To be frozen, to become congealed, to freeze.
congelato, *p.p.a.* Congealed, frozen. **Carne —,** frozen meat.
congelatore, *n.m.* Refrigerator.
congelazione, *n.f.* Refrigeration.
congeneo [congEneo], *a.* Born together.
congenerato, *a.* Congenital.
congenere [congEnere], *a.* Similar, of the same kind.
congenito [congEnito], *a.* Congenital, constitutional; innate.
congerie [congErie], *n.f.* Congeries, heap, mass.
congestionare, *v.t.* To congest; to overcrowd.
congestionarsi, *v.r.* To be congested; to be overcrowded.
congestione, *n.f.* Congestion (in all senses); accumulation.

congesto, *a.* Crowded, thronged; congested.
congettura, *n.f.* Conjecture, supposition
congetturalmente, *adv.* Conjecturally.
congetturare, *v.i.* To conjecture, to surmise.
congio [cOngio], *n.m.* (*Hist.*) Liquid measure of ancient Rome.
congioirsi, *v.r.* To rejoice together.
congiungere [congiUngere], *v.t.* To join, to connect, to link up, to unite.
congiungersi [congiUngersi], *v.r.* To join, to couple, to match. **— in matrimonio,** to get married.
congiungimento, *n.m.* Junction, union.
congiuntamente, *adv.* Conjointly.
congiuntiva, *n.f.* (*Anat.*) Conjunctiva.
congiuntivite, *n.f.* (*Med.*) Conjunctivitis.
congiuntivo, *n.m.* (*Gram.*) Subjunctive (mood).
congiunto, *n.m.a.* Relative, relation; joined, connected; related.
congiuntura, *n.f.* Conjuncture, circumstance, occurrence; joint, seam.
congiunzione, *n.f.* Conjunction; union, connection, junction.
congiura, *n.f.* Plot, conspiracy.
congiurare, *v.i.* To plot, to conspire. **Tutto sembrò — contro di noi,** everything seemed to conspire against us.
congiurato, *n.m.* Conspirator.
conglobare, *v.t.* To roll into a ball; (*fig.*) to sum up, to summarize.
conglobazione, *n.f.* Abridgment.
conglomerare, *v.t.i.* To conglomerate, to gather into a heap, to mass together.
conglomerato, *n.m.a.* (*Geol.*) Conglomerate, conglomerate rock.
conglomerazione, *n.f.* Conglomeration, mass.
conglutinamento, *n.m.* Conglutination; sticking together with glue, etc.
conglutinare, *v.t.* To glue together.
conglutinazione, *n.f.* Adhesion, conglutination.
congratularsi, *v.r.* To congratulate, to felicitate, to compliment upon. **Mi congratulo con Lei per il suo successo,** I congratulate you on your success.
congratulatorio [congratulatOrio], *a.* Congratulatory.
congratulazione, *n.f.* Congratulation.
congrega, *n.f.* Assembly, gathering, society; gang.
congregamento, *n.m.* Aggregation, herding.
congregare, *v.t.* **congregarsi,** *v.r.* To congregate, to assemble, to gather.
congregazione, *n.f.* (*Eccles.*) Congregation; religious fraternity, institution.
congressista (*pl.* **congressisti**), *n.m.* Member of a congress, delegate.
congresso, *n.m.* Congress, meeting, assembly, conference.
congro, *n.m.* (*Zool.*) Conger eel [cp. **grongo**].
congrua [cOngrua], *n.f.* Stipend of a priest (paid by the State); benefice.
congruamente, *adv.* Conveniently, suitably.
congruente, *a.* Congruent, consistent.
congruentemente, *adv.* Conveniently.
congruenza, *n.f.* Congruence, agreement, consistency; adequacy.
congruo [cOngruo], *a.* Congruous, adequate, fair, suitable. **— compenso,** adequate compensation.
conguagliare, *v.t.i.* To equalize; (*Comm.*) to adjust or balance (accounts).
conguagliatamente, *adv.* Equally.
conguaglio [conguAglio], *n.m.* Equalization, balancing; compensation.
conia [cOnia], *n.f.* Joke, piece of fun. **Reggere alla —,** to take a joke in good part.
coniare, *v.t.* To coin, to mint, to strike (a medal); (*fig.*) to invent.
coniatore, *n.m.* (Legitimate) coiner, worker in the mint.
coniatura, *n.f.* Coinage.
coniazione, *n.f.* (Act of) coining.
conicamente, *adv.* Conically.
conico [cOnico], *a.* Conical, conic. **Tenda conica,** bell-tent.
conifero [conIfero], *n.m.* (*Bot.*) Conifer.
conigliera, *n.f.* Rabbit-hutch; warren.
coniglio, conigliolo [conIglio], *n.m.* Rabbit, cony; (*fig.*) coward.
conio [cOnio], *n.m.* Coin, brand, stamp; coinage. **Essere dello stesso —,** to be of the same stamp; **di nuovo —,** brand new; **sono tutti d'un —,** they are all alike; **femmina da —,** harlot.
coniugabile [coniugAbile], *a.* (*Gram.*) Capable of being conjugated.
coniugale, *a.* Conjugal.
coniugalmente, *adv.* Conjugally.
coniugare, *v.t.* **coniugarsi,** *v.r.* (*Gram.*) To conjugate, to inflect; to get married; to join together.
coniugazione, *n.f.* Conjugation.
coniuge [cOniuge], *n.m.f.* Consort, spouse. **I coniugi X,** Mr. and Mrs. X.
coniugio [coniUgio], *n.m.* (*Lit.*) Marriage.
conlegatario [conlegatArio], *n.m.* Joint-legatee.
connaturale, *a.* Innate, of like nature; apt, appropriate.
connaturalità [-à], *n.f.* Innateness; appropriateness.
connaturare, *v.t.* To acclimatize.
connaturato, *a.* Congenital; ingrained. **Abitudini connaturate,** habits that have become second nature.
connazionale, *n.m.* Fellow-countryman.
connessamente, *adv.* Connectedly.
connessione, *n.f.* Connection, union.
connesso, *a.* Connected.
connessura, *n.f.* Joint.
connettere [connEttere], *v.t.* To connect, to join, to link.
connettiva, *n.f.* Joint.
connettivo, *a.* Connecting, connective. **Tessuto —,** connective tissue.
connivente, *a.* Conniving.
connivenza, *n.f.* Connivance.
connotato, *n.m.* Description; personal marks. **I connotati in un passaporto,** (personal) description in a passport; (*colloq.*) **cambiare i connotati,** to give a black eye.
connubiale, *a.* Connubial.
connubio [connUbio], *n.m.* Marriage, union; blend. **Un felice — di razze,** a happy blending of races.
cono, *n.m.* (*Geom.*) Cone. (*Mech.*) **Innesto a —,** cone coupling.
conocchia [conOcchia], *n.f.* Distaff.
conoidale, *a.* (*Geom.*) Conoidal.
conoide [conOide], *n.m.* (*Geom.*) Conoid.

conopeo [conopEo], *n.m.* Mosquito-net; (*Eccles.*) veil for ciborium and chalice.
conoscente, *n.m.f.* Acquaintance.
conoscenza, *n.f.* Knowledge, notion, learning; acquaintance (in all senses); intelligence; (*Phil.*) cognition. **Far la — di,** to make the acquaintance of; **portare a — di,** to inform; **perdere la —,** to lose consciousness; **è una mia —,** he is an acquaintance of mine.
conoscere [conOscere], *v.t.* To know, to be acquainted (with), to make the acquaintance (of), to recognize; to take cognisance of. **Non conosce ragioni,** he is unreasonable; **lo conobbi alla voce,** I recognized his voice; **— a fondo,** to be thoroughly acquainted with; **— di nome,** to know by name; **— una lingua,** to know a language; **farsi —,** to make oneself known.
conoscibile [conosclbile], *a.* Knowable, recognizable.
conoscibilità [-**à**], *n.f.* Possibility of being known.
conoscimento, *n.m.* Discernment, knowledge; judgment.
conoscitivo, *a.* Cognitive.
conoscitore, *n.m.* Connoisseur, judge (of wine, pictures, etc.), expert.
conosciutamente, *adv.* Knowingly.
conosciuto, *p.p.a.* Known; noted, famous, well-known.
conquassare, *v.t.* To shake violently; to smash up [cp. **sconquassare**].
conquasso, *n.m.* Shock, crash. **Mettere a —,** to put things in great disorder; to smash things up.
conquibus, *n.m.* (*colloq.*) Cash, the wherewithal, the needful, money.
conquidere [conquIdere], *v.t.* (*Poet.*) To subdue, to vanquish.
conquiso, *p.p.a.* (*Lit.*) Subdued, vanquished.
conquista, *n.f.* Conquest; acquisition.
conquistabile [conquistAbile], *a.* Conquerable.
conquistare, *v.t.* To conquer, to subdue; to acquire; to win over; to gain.
conquistatore, *n.m.* Conqueror.
conregnare, *v.i.* To reign together.
consacrando, *n.m.a.* (*Eccles.*) One about to be ordained priest; to be consecrated.
consacrante, *n.m.* (*Eccles.*) Officiating priest (at Mass).
consacrare, *v.t.* To consecrate; to dedicate, to devote to; (*Eccles.*) to ordain; (*fig.*) to render valid.
consacrarsi, *v.r.* To devote oneself.
consacrazione, *n.f.* Consecration; ordination; devotion.
consanguineità [-**à**], *n.f.* Consanguinity.
consanguineo [consanguIneo], *a.* Related by blood.
consapente, *a.* Aware, conscious of.
consapevole [consapEvole], *a.* Conscious, aware. **Fare —,** to inform.
consapevolezza, *n.f.* Consciousness; knowledge, cognizance.
consaputo, *a.* Known.
conscio [cOnscio], *a.* Conscious, aware, cognizant.
consecutivamente, *adv.* Consecutively.
consecutivo, *a.* Consecutive, following, ensuing.
consegna, *n.f.* Consignment, delivery; trust, custody, care; (*Mil.*) confinement to barracks; instructions. (*Comm.*) **Pagare alla —,** to pay on delivery; **dare in — del denaro,** to entrust money; **venir meno alla —,** to disregard orders; **consegne,** orders.
consegnamento, *n.m.* Consignment.
consegnante, *n.m.* Consigner.
consegnare, *v.t.* To consign, to hand over, to deliver; to deposit; (*Mil.*) to confine to barracks. **— merci,** to deliver goods; **— una lettera,** to deliver a letter.
consegnatario [consegnatArio], *n.m.* Consignee; trustee.
consegnatore, *n.m.* Consigner.
conseguente, *a.* Consequent, following, ensuing.
conseguentemente, *adv.* Consequently.
conseguenza, *n.f.* Consequence; effect, result. **Affrontare le conseguenze,** to face the consequences.
conseguenziale, *a.* In consequence, consequent.
conseguibile [consegulbile], *a.* Attainable.
conseguimento, *n.m.* Attainment.
conseguire, *v.t.i.* To attain, to reach, to achieve, to obtain; to follow, to happen, to result. **— il proprio intento,** to attain one's object; **— un prezzo elevato,** to obtain a high price; **ne consegue che,** it follows that, in consequence.
conseguitare, *v.t.i.* To result, to happen.
consenso, *n.m.* Consent, assent, agreement; concurrence, approbation.
consensuale, *a.* By mutual consent.
consentaneo [consentAneo], *a.* In accordance, unanimous, accordant; adequate.
consentimento, *n.m.* Consent, agreement, acquiescence.
consentire, *v.t.i.* To consent, to agree; to approve; to permit, to allow; to yield to pressure.
consentitamente, *adv.* By consent.
consenziente, *a.* Consentient, consenting.
consequenziale, *a.* Consequential.
consertamento, *n.m.* Intertwining.
consertare, *v.t.* To intertwine; to fold.
conserto, *a.* Intertwined, interwoven, folded. **Le braccia conserte,** with folded arms.
conserva, *n.f.* Preserve, jam, marmalade; store, storage, storeroom; (*Naut.*) convoy. **— di pomodoro,** tomato purée; **— alimentari** canned, tinned foods; **carne in —,** canned meat; **andare di —,** to act in common accord.
conservabile [conservAbile], *a.* Conservable, preservable.
conservamento, *n.m.* Conserving, preserving.
conservare, *v.t.* To preserve, to conserve, to keep, to maintain. **Conservò sempre la sua calma,** he kept cool all the time.
conservarsi, *v.r.* To preserve oneself; to carry one's years well; to take care of oneself. **Si conservi!** Take care of yourself!
conservativo, *a.* Conservative, preservative.
conservatore, conservatrice, *n.m.f.* Guardian, curator; warden, ranger; (*Pol.*) Conservative, Tory. **— delle ipoteche,** registrar of mortgages.
conservatorio [conservatOrio], *n.m.* College of music, conservatoire.

conservazione, *n.f.* Preservation, maintenance. **Spirito di —,** instinct of self-preservation.
conservo, *n.m.* (*Lit.*) Fellow-servant.
consesso, *n.m.* (*Lit.*) Meeting, assembly. **— di professori,** an assembly of professors.
considerabile [considerAbile], *a.* Considerable.
considerabilmente, *adv.* Considerably.
considerando, *n.m.* (*Law*) Preamble; reasons for judgment; grounds for judgment.
considerare, *v.t.i.* To consider, to observe, to remark, to regard, to reflect; to value, to esteem. **— un affare regolato,** to consider a bargain as settled; **non considera che se stesso,** he thinks of nothing but himself; **non è considerato nulla,** he is a nonentity.
consideratamente, *adv.* With consideration.
consideratezza, *n.f.* Regard, prudence; considerateness.
considerato, *p.p.a.* Considered, considerate; esteemed. **— che,** considering that.
considerazione, *n.f.* Consideration, regard, reputation, esteem; attention; importance.
considerevole [considerEvole], *a.* Considerable, notable, remarkable.
considerevolmente, *adv.* Considerably.
consigliabile [consigliAbile], *a.* Advisable, expedient.
consigliare, *v.t.* To advise, to counsel, to recommend.
consigliarsi, *v.r.* To take advice, to take counsel, to consult.
consigliatamente, *adv.* Advisedly.
consigliato, *p.p.a.* Counselled, advised, exhorted, persuaded; prudent.
consigliatore, consigliatrice, *n.m.f.* Counsellor, adviser.
consigliere, consigliero, *n.m.* Counsellor; councillor. (*Comm.*) **— delegato,** managing director.
consiglio [consIglio], *n.m.* Advice, counsel; council. **Domandare —,** to seek advice; **— dei ministri,** cabinet council; (*Comm.*) **— d'amministrazione,** board of directors.
consiliare, *a.* Advisory; pertaining to a council.
consimile [consImile], *a.* Nearly alike, alike, similar; bearing a resemblance.
consimilmente, *adv.* Similarly.
consistente, *a.* Consistent, firm, solid.
consistenza, *n.f.* Consistency, firmness, stability, durability. (*Comm.*) **— di cassa,** cash in hand; **— di magazzino,** stock in hand.
consociante, *n.m.* Partner.
consociarsi, *v.r.* To join, to associate with.
consociazione, *n.f.* League, confederation.
consocio [consOcio], *n.m.* Partner; associate.
consolabile [consolAbile], *a.* Consolable.
consolante, *a.* Consoling.
consolare, *v.t.* To console, to comfort, to cheer; to relieve.
consolare, *a.* Consular. **Agente —,** consular agent.
consolarità [-à], *n.f.* Consulship.
consolarsi, *v.r.* To comfort oneself, to console oneself, to take comfort; to rejoice.
consolatamente, *adv.* Comfortingly, consolingly.
consolato, *n.m.* Consulate.
consolatore, consolatrice, *n.m.f.* Consoler, comforter.
consolatoria [consolatOria], *n.f.* Letter of condolence.
consolatorio [consolatOrio], *a.* Consolatory.
consolazione, *n.f.* Consolation; alleviation, relief. **Premio di —,** consolation prize.
console [cOnsole], *n.m.* Consul (in all senses).
consolida [consOlida], *n.f.* (*Bot.*) Comfrey.
consolidamento, *n.m.* Strengthening, consolidation.
consolidare, *v.t.* To consolidate, to strengthen.
consolidarsi, *v.r.* To become solid; to take root.
consolidato, *n.m.a.* (*Fin.*) Consols; consolidated.
consolidazione, *n.f.* Consolidation; funding (of interests, etc.).
consolle, *n.f.* Side-table, console-table.
consonante, *n.f.a.* Consonant (in all senses); harmonious.
consonantemente, *adv.* Harmoniously.
consonanza, *n.f.* Consonance; (*Mus.*) concord.
consonare, *v.i.* To harmonize, to accord.
consono [cOnsono], *a.* Adapted to, consonant with.
consorella, *n.f.* Sister (esp. *Eccles.*).
consorte, *n.m.f.* Spouse, husband, wife; companion, mate; associate. **Principe —,** prince consort.
consorteria [consorterIa], *n.f.* Faction, clique.
consortile, consorziale, *a.* Pertaining to a syndicate. **Decreto —,** order of the board (of directors).
consorzio [consOrzio], *n.m.* Society, trust, union, syndicate, association, partnership. **— agricolo,** agricultural union.
consostanziale, *a.* (*Theol.*) Consubstantial.
consostanziazione, *n.f.* (*Theol.*) Consubstantiation.
constare, *v.i.* To consist; to result; to be within one's knowledge. **Non consta che,** it does not appear that; **mi consta che,** it has come to my knowledge that; **consta di,** it consists of.
constatare, *v.t.* To establish, to ascertain; to note; to authenticate, to verify.
constatazione, *n.f.* Proof, evidence, authentication. **Fare la — che,** to establish that.
consuddito [consUddito], *n.m.* Fellow-subject (of a country).
consuetamente, *adv.* According to habit, customarily.
consueto, *n.m.a.* Custom, habit; usual, customary, habitual. **Secondo il —,** as usual, as is wont.
consuetudinario [consuetudinArio], *a.* Habitual, customary.
consuetudine [consuetUdine], *n.f.* Habit; practice, custom, usage.
consulente, *n.m.a.* Consultant, adviser. **— legale,** legal adviser.
consulenza, *n.f.* Advice, consultation.
consulta, *n.f.* Council, consultation; consulting room; council chamber. **— municipale,** municipal council; **Sacra Consulta,** administrative council of the Papal State.
consultare, *v.t.* To consult, to seek advice of; to refer to; to examine.
consultarsi, *v.r.* To take counsel with, to seek advice, to consult together, to confer.

consultativo, *a.* Consultative.
consultatore, *n.m.* Consultor.
consultazione, *n.f.* Consultation.
consultivo, *a.* Consultative.
consulto, *n.m.* Consultation (with doctors, lawyers, etc.).
consultore, *n.m.* (*Eccles.*) Consultor; adviser.
consultorio [consultOrio], *n.m.* (Doctor's) consulting room.
consuma, *n.f.* (The act of) consuming. **Andare alla —,** to ruin oneself; **aver la — in corpo,** to be ravenously hungry.
consumabile [consumAbile], *a.* Consumable.
consumamento, *n.m.* Consuming; (*fig.*) burning desire.
consumare, *v.t.* To consume, to waste, to wear out, to use up, to dissipate; to complete, to finish, to perfect. **— un delitto,** to commit a crime.
consumarsi, *v.r.* To wear oneself out; to waste away. **Si consuma col lavoro eccessivo,** he is wearing himself out with over-work.
consumato, *n.m.* Soup, consommé.
consumato, *a.* Accomplished, consummate; thin; wasted, exhausted.
consumatore, *n.m.* Consumer.
consumazione, *n.f.* Consumption, expense; consummation; refreshments (in a café).
consumo, *n.m.* Consumption; waste; wear and tear; food (for family daily use); provisions, commodities. **Per —,** for everyday use; **— interno,** home consumption; **cooperativa di —,** co-operative store.
consuntivo, *n.m.* (*Comm.*) Final balance.
consunto, *p.p.a.* Consumed, wasted, worn out.
consunzione, *n.f.* Consumption, waste; (*Med.*) consumption, phthisis.
consussistente, *a.* Existing together, co-existent.
consussistenza, *n.f.* Co-existence.
contabile [contAbile], *n.m.* Accountant, book-keeper.
contabilità [-à], *n.f.* Book-keeping; accounts department.
contachilometri, [contachilOmetri], *n.m.* (*Motor,* etc.) Speedometer.
contadina, *n.f.* Peasant woman, country woman; country dance.
contadiname, *n.m.* Crowd of peasants.
contadinata, *n.f.* Sort of thing a peasant would do.
contadinello, contadinella, *n.m.f.* Peasant boy, girl.
contadinesco, *a.* Like a peasant, rustic.
contadino, *n.m.* Peasant, countryman; farmer.
contado, *n.m.* Rural area (round a city); country district.
contafili, *n.m.* (*Mech.*) Glass for counting threads in material.
contagiare, *v.t.* To infect, to contaminate.
contagio [contAgio], *n.m.* Contagion, plague; infection.
contagioso, *a.* Contagious, catching.
contagiri, *n.m.* Speedometer.
contagocce, *n m.* Medicine dropper, dropping-tube.
contaminare, *v.t.* To contaminate; to sully, to defile; to corrupt.
contaminarsi, *v.r.* To become contaminated.
contaminatore, *n.m.* Contaminator.
contaminazione, *n.f.* Contamination; defilement.
contaminoso, *a.* Unclean, contaminating.
contanti, *n.m.pl.* Cash, ready money. **Pagar in —,** to pay cash.
contapassi, *n.m.* Pedometer.
contare, *v.t.* To count, to reckon, to calculate; to rely upon; to value, to esteem. **Contiamo su Lei,** we rely upon you; **conto di passar l'inverno in Italia,** I intend to spend the winter in Italy; **i suoi giorni son contati,** his days are numbered.
contata, *n.f.* Rapid counting.
contatore, *n.m.* Meter. **— del gas,** gas-meter.
contatto, *n.m.* Contact (in all senses); touch. **Stare in —,** to keep in touch; (*Elect.*) **— a spina,** two-(three-) pronged plug.
conte, *n.m.* Count, earl.
contea, *n.f.* Earldom, countship; county.
conteggiamento, *n.m.* Computing, reckoning.
conteggiare, *v.t.* To compute, to keep accounts; to enter in an account.
conteggiarsi, *v.r.* To make up accounts (between two persons).
conteggio [contEggio], *n.m.* Computation, calculation; keeping of accounts.
contegno, *n.m.* Demeanour, behaviour; appearance, aspect; dignity, reserve. **Darsi un —,** to keep one's countenance; to give oneself airs; **stare in —,** to be reserved.
contegnosamente, *adv.* With dignity, stiffly.
contegnoso, *a.* Reserved, stiff; demure; dignified.
contemperamento, *n.m.* Moderating, moderation.
contemperanza, *n.f.* Temperateness, moderation.
contemperare, *v.t.* To temper, to moderate, to proportion; to blend.
contemplamento, *n.m.* Contemplation.
contemplare, *v.t.* To contemplate, to behold, to regard; to meditate; to foresee.
contemplativo, *a.* Contemplative; ecstatic.
contemplazione, *n.f.* Contemplation, meditation.
contempo, *adv.* **Nel —,** in the meanwhile.
contemporaneamente, *adv.* Simultaneously.
contemporaneità [-à], *n.f.* Contemporaneity.
contemporaneo [contemporAneo], *n.m.a.* Simultaneous; contemporary, contemporaneous, belonging to the same period.
contendente, *n.m.* Rival, antagonist.
contendere [contEndere], *v.t.i.* To contend, to contest, to dispute; to prevent, to hinder; to ban; to refuse.
contenente, *n.m.a.* Container; containing.
contenere, *v.t.* To hold, to contain, to include; to repress.
contenersi, *v.r.* To behave (well); to refrain from; to restrain oneself. **Non potei contenermi dal ridere,** I could not help laughing.
contentabile [contentAbile], *a.* Capable of contentment.
contentare, *v.t.* To satisfy, to gladden; to gratify, to please; to satisfy.
contentarsi, *v.r.* To be satisfied, to be pleased; to consent to. **Chi si contenta gode,** a contented mind is a perpetual feast.
contentatura, *n.f.* Ability to be satisfied. **È di facile —,** he is easily pleased.

contentezza, *n.f.* Contentment, satisfaction; joy, gladness.
contentino, *n.m.* Make-weight; stop-gap.
contento, *n.m.* (*Lit.*) Contentment, satisfaction, pleasure.
contento, *a.* Glad, satisfied, content, happy. **— come una pasqua,** as happy as can be.
contentone, *a.* More than content.
contenuto, *n.m.* Contents, subject, tenor. (*Comm.*) **Abbiamo preso nota del —,** we have noted the contents (of your letter).
contenuto, *p.p.a.* Contained, included; restrained, repressed.
contenzione, *n.f.* Contention, dispute.
contenziosamente, *adv.* Contentiously.
contenziosità [-à], *n.f.* Contentiousness.
contenzioso, *n.m.* (*Law*) Tribunal.
contenzioso, *a.* Contentious.
conterello, *n.m.* Little account or bill.
conterie [conterIe], *n.f.pl.* Glass beads, fancy glassware.
conterminale, *a.* Conterminal.
conterminare, *v.i.* To end together, to be conterminous.
contermine [contErmine], *a.* Conterminous, conterminal.
conterraneo, [conterrAneo], *n.m.* Countryman, fellow-countryman.
contesa, *n.f.* Contention, strife, dispute, quarrel.
contessa, *n.f.* Countess.
contessere [contEssere], *v.t.* To interweave, to intertwine.
contessimento, *n.m.* Intertwining.
contessina, *n.f.* Count's daughter.
contestabile [contestAbile], *a.* Disputable, debatable.
contestare, *v.t.* To contest, to dispute; to oppose, to challenge; to notify.
contestazione, *n.f.* Contradiction, dispute; objection; litigation.
conteste, contestimone, *n.m.* Fellow-witness.
contestimonianza, *n.f.* Corroborative evidence.
contesto, *n.m.a.* Context; body (of a document); put together, composed.
contestuale, *a.* (*Law*) Contextual.
contezza, *n.f.* (*Lit.*) Knowledge, cognizance, information. **Dar —,** to inform; **avere —,** to be informed; **non ho — di quando è avvenuto,** I have no knowledge as to when it happened.
conti, *n.m.pl.* (*Comm.*) Accounts.
conticino, *n.m.* Little bill, trifling account.
contigiato, *a.* (*obs.*) Richly adorned.
contiguamente, *adv.* Contiguously.
contiguità [-à], *n.f.* Contiguity.
contiguo [contIguo], *a.* Contiguous, adjoining, neighbouring.
continentale, *a.* Continental.
continente, *n.m.* Continent.
continente, *a.* Continent, chaste.
continentemente, *adv.* Continently, chastely.
continenza, *n.f.* Continence, moderation, chastity.
contingentamento, *n.m.* (*Comm.*) Quota.
contingentare, *v.t.* To impose in quotas; to restrict by rationing.
contingente, *n.m.a.* Contingent, quota, share; contingent, incidental, accessory; (*Mil.*) a military contingent.
contingentemente, *adv.* Contingently.
contingenza, *n.f.* Contingency, eventuality, occasion; emergency.
continuabile [continuAbile], *a.* Continuable.
continuamente, *adv.* Continually.
continuare, *v.t.i.* To continue, to go on, to last; to persevere.
continuatamente, *adv.* Continuously.
continuazione, *n.f.* Continuation.
continuità [-à], *n.f.* Continuity.
continuo [contInuo], *a.* Continuous, continual, unbroken. **Di —,** without stopping, continuously; (*Elect.*) **corrente continua,** direct current.
conto, *n.m.* Account, bill; reckoning, calculation; esteem, regard; notice, information; value. **In fin dei conti,** in conclusion; **a buon —,** in any case; **per nessun —,** on no account; **per — mio,** so far as I'm concerned; **fare i conti,** to do one's accounts; **render — di,** to give an account of; **tener di —,** to take care of; (*Comm.*) **— corrente,** current account; **il — torna,** the account is correct; **far i conti addosso,** to meddle in other folks' affairs; **mettere in —,** to put to one's account; **non mi mette —,** it doesn't pay me; **saldare il —,** to settle the account; **conti chiari, amici cari,** short reckonings make long friends; (*Comm.*) **— passivo,** debit side of account; **— scoperto,** overdraft; **rendersi —,** to understand.
conto, *a.* (*Poet.*) Clear, manifest, known; ornate.
contorcere [contOrcere], *v.t.* To contort, to writhe, to twist.
contorcersi [contOrcersi], *v.r.* To writhe, to twist the body (as in pain).
contorcimento, *n.m.* Contortion, twisting.
contornare, *v.t.* To go round, to surround; to outline; to trim.
contornarsi, *v.r.* To surround oneself with; to associate with.
contorno, *n.m.* Outline, contour; trimming, dressing. **Carne con —,** meat and vegetables.
contorsione, *n.f.* Contortion, twisting.
contorto, *p.p.a.* Twisted, contorted.
contra, *prep.* Against. **Il pro e il —,** the pros and cons [cp. **contro**].
contrabbandare, *v.t.* To smuggle.
contrabbandiere, contrabbandiera, *n.m.f.* Smuggler; bootlegger.
contrabbando, *n.m.* Contraband, smuggling, smuggled goods. **Di —,** clandestinely, surreptitiously.
contrabbassista, *n.m.* Double-bass player.
contrabbasso, *n.m.* (*Mus.*) Double-bass.
contrabbietta, *n.f.* (*Naut.*) Counter-wedge.
contrabbilanciare, *v.t.* To counterbalance.
contrabbordo, *n.m.* (*Naut.*) Sheathing of the hull.
contraccambiare, *v.t.* To reciprocate; to requite. **Contraccambio di cuore i gentili auguri,** I heartily reciprocate your good wishes.
contraccambio [contraccAmbio], *n.m.* Return, exchange. **In — della sua gentilezza,** in return for his kindness; **rendere —,** to return like for like.
contraccarico [contraccArico], *n.m.* Counterweight.
contracchiave, *n.f.* Key for double-locking; skeleton key.

contraccolpo, *n.m.* Counter-stroke; repercussion; (*Motor.*) back-fire; reaction.
contraccorrente, *n.f.* Cross-current.
contraccusa, *n.f.* (*Law*) Counter-accusation.
contrada, *n.f.* District (of a town); stretch of country; country region; open road.
contraddanza, *n.f.* Folk dance; square dance.
contraddetto, *a.* Contradicted.
contraddicente, contradicente, *a.* Contradictory.
contraddire, contradire, *v.t.* To contradict, to disapprove, to oppose.
contraddirsi, contradirsi, *v.r.* To contradict oneself (inadvertently).
contraddistinguere, contradistinguere [contraddistInguere], *v.t.* To mark, to label; to contradistinguish; to characterize.
contraddistinto, *p.p.a.* Characterized.
contradditore, *n.m.* Opposer.
contraddittoriamente, *adv.* In a contradictory fashion.
contraddittorio [contradittOrio], *a.* Contradictory, opposing, heckling.
contraddizione, *n.f.* Contradiction; discrepancy; denial.
contraddote, *n.f.* Marriage settlement.
contraente, *a.* (*Law*) Contracting. **Parti contraenti,** contracting parties.
contraerea [contraErea], *n.f.* Anti-aircraft artillery.
contraereo [contraEreo], *a.* Anti-aircraft.
contrafagotto, *n.m.* (*Mus.*) Double bassoon.
contraffacente, *pres.p.a.* Counterfeiting.
contraffare, *v.t.* To counterfeit, to forge; to imitate, to ape; to adulterate.
contraffatto, *p.p.a.* Counterfeit, counterfeited; adulterated.
contraffattore, *n.m.* Forger, counterfeiter.
contraffazione, *n.f.* Counterfeit, forgery, falsification; imitation; (literary) piracy.
contrafforte, *n.m.* Buttress; bar (to secure a window or door); spur (of a mountain).
contraggenio [contraggEnio], *n.m.* Dislike, antipathy, aversion. **A —,** against the grain.
contralbero, *n.m.* (*Mech.*) Countershaft.
contraltare, *n.m.* Rival project. **Fare da —,** to vie with, to rival.
contralto, *n.m.* (*Mus.*) Contralto.
contrammandare, *v.t.* To countermand.
contrammiraglio [contrammirAglio], *n.m.* Rear-admiral.
contrappasso, *n.m.* Retaliation.
contrappelo, *n.m.* Wrong way of the hair, against the nap. **A —,** against the grain.
contrappesare, *v.t.* To counterbalance; to weigh carefully (one thing against another).
contrappeso, *n.m.* Counterpoise, counterbalance.
contrapponibile [contrapponIbile], *a.* Open to opposition.
contrapporre, *v.t.* To oppose, to contrast.
contrapposizione, *n.f.* Antithesis, contrast.
contrapposto, *n.m.a.* Opposite, antithesis; opposed, placed against.
contrappuntista, *n.m.* (*Mus.*) Contrapuntist.
contrappunto, *n.m.* (*Mus.*) Counterpoint.
contrariamente, *adv.* Contrarily, in opposition. **— a,** contrary to.
contrariare, *v.t.* To contradict, to oppose; to disappoint; to vex, to annoy.
contrariato, *a.* Disappointed, vexed.
contrarietà [-à], *n.f.* Opposition, contrariety; disappointment; misfortune, untoward event; impediment, obstacle. **— del tempo,** unseasonable weather.
contrario [contrArio], *n.m.a.* Contrary, reverse, opposite, adverse, contradictory, opposed; untoward, hostile, unfavourable. **Al —,** on the contrary; **in caso —,** in the contrary case; otherwise.
contrarre, *v.t.* To contract, to stipulate; to incur. **— cattive abitudini,** to contract bad habits; **— debiti,** to incur debts, to run into debt; **— amicizia,** to form a friendship; **— una malattia,** to catch an illness, to contract a disease.
contrarsi, *v.r.* To shrink, to contract.
contrasaluto, *n.m.* (*Naut.*) Answering signal (of salute).
contrassegnare, *v.t.* To countersign, to mark.
contrassegno, *n.m.* Countersign, mark, token; indication; password.
contrastabile [contrastAbile], *a.* Doubtful, disputable.
contrastare, *v.t.i.* To contrast; to contest, to oppose, to resist, to struggle against.
contrastarsi, *v.r.* To quarrel, to wrangle.
contrasto, *n.m.* Contrast; strife, opposition, conflict (of ideas). **Quei due son sempre in —,** those two are always at loggerheads; **senza —,** without opposition.
contrattabile [contrattAbile], *a.* Negotiable, ripe for negotiation.
contrattaccare, *v.t.i.* (*Mil.*) To counter-attack.
contrattacco, *n.m.* (*Mil.*) Counter-attack.
contrattamente, *adv.* By contraction.
contrattare, *v.t.* To negotiate, to bargain, to stipulate.
contrattazione, *n.f.* Bargain, dealing; haggling.
contrattempo, *n.m.* Disappointment; mischance, hitch; (*Mus.*) syncopation.
contrattile [contrAttile], *a.* Contractile, self-contracting.
contrattilità [-à], *n.f.* Contractibility.
contratto, *n.m.* Contract; agreement, deed; articles; bond; deal. **Redigere un —,** to draw up a contract.
contratto, *a.* Contracted, shrunken.
contrattuale, *a.* Contractual.
contravveleno, *n.m.* Antidote.
contravvenire, *v.i.* To contravene, to infringe, to transgress, to violate.
contravventore, *n.m.* Contravener, transgressor.
contravvenzione, *n.f.* Contravention, infraction, breach (of regulations, etc.); fine (for such breach). **Pagare una —,** to be fined; to pay a fine.
contravviso, *n.m.* Countermand.
contravvite, *n.f.* Female screw.
contrazione, *n.f.* Contraction (in all senses).
contribuente, *n.m.* Contributor; taxpayer; ratepayer.
contribuire, *v.i.* To contribute, to have part in; to aid, to help.
contributivo, *a.* Contributory.
contributo, *n.m.* Contribution; quota, share; (literary) contribution.
contributore, *n.m.* Contributor.

contribuzione, *n.f.* Contribution; participation, share, quota; tax, levy.
contristare, *v.t.* To grieve, to sadden, to afflict.
contristarsi, *v.r.* To be grieved.
contritamente, *adv.* Contritely, with contrition.
contrito, *a.* Contrite, repentent; afflicted.
contrizione, *n.f.* Contrition.
contro, *prep.* Against, opposite to. **Dar —,** to oppose, to criticize; **— il muro,** against the wall; **— assegno,** cash on delivery; **— pagamento,** against payment.
controavviso, *n.m.* Counterorder, countermand.
controbatteria [controbatterIa], *n.f.* (*Mil.*) Counter-battery.
controbilanciare, *v.t.* To counterbalance.
controcassa, *n.f.* Outer casing; case (of a watch, etc.).
controcolpo, *n.m.* [cp. **contraccolpo**].
controdado, *n.m.* (*Mech.*) Lock nut.
controdichiarazione, *n.f.* Counter-declaration.
controffensiva, *n.m.* (*Mil.*) Counter-offensive.
controfinestra, *n.f.* Double window.
controflocco, *n.m.* (*Naut.*) Flying jib.
controfirma, *n.f.* Counter-signature, endorsement.
controfirmare, *v.t.* To countersign, to endorse.
controfodera [controfOdera], *n.f.* Inner lining.
controfondo, *n.m.* False bottom.
controleva, *n.f.* Counter-lever.
controllare, *v.t.* To control, to test; to audit. **— i conti,** to audit the books.
controllo, *n.m.* Control, inspection; audit. (*Radio*) **— di volume,** volume control.
controllore, *n.m.* Controller, surveyor; (*Rail.*) ticket-collector; inspector.
controluce, *adv.* Against the light, back to the light.
controlume, *adv.* Against the light.
contromandare, *v.t.* To countermand.
contromarca, *n.f.* (*Theat.*) Pass-out check.
contromarcia [contromArcia], *n.f.* (*Mil.*) Countermarch; (*Motor.*) reverse gear.
contronota, *n.f.* (*Pol.*) Note in reply.
controparte, *n.m.* (*Law*) Opposite party; opposite number.
controporta, *n.f.* Double door; outside door; screen-door.
controprogetto, *n.m.* Counterplan.
controproposta, *n.f.* Counter-proposal.
controprova, *n.f.* Further evidence, counter-evidence; recount (of votes).
controquerela, *n.f.* Countercharge.
controrrdinare, *v.t.* To countermand.
controrrdine [contrOrdine], *n.m.* Counter-order.
controriforma, *n.f.* (*Hist.*) Counter-reformation.
controrivoluzione, *n.f.* Counter-revolution.
controrotaia [controrotAia], *n.f.* (*Rail.*) Counter-rail.
controscena, *n.f.* (*Theat.*) By-play.
controscritta, *n.f.* (*Law*) Indenture.
controsenso, *n.m.* Misconstruction, misinterpretation; misconception; nonsense, absurdity.
controspionaggio [controspionAggio], *n.m.* Counter-espionage.
controstallia [controstallIa], *n.f.* (*Comm.*) Demurrage.
controstimolante, *n.m.* (*Med.*) Sedative.
controstimolo [controstImolo], *n.m.* (*Med.*) (Action of) sedative.
controstomaco [controstOmaco], *adv.* **A —** with repugnance.
controtorpediniera, *n.f.* (*Naut.*) Destroyer.
controvento, *adv.* Against the wind.
controversia [controvErsia], *n.f.* Controversy, debate, disputation.
controversista, *n.m.f.* Controversialist.
controverso, *a.* Debated, disputed, controversial.
controvertere [controvErtere], *v.t.* To controvert, to dispute.
controvertibile [controvertIbile], *a.* Disputable, doubtful.
contumace, *a.* Contumacious; (*Law*) absconding.
contumacia [contumAcia], *n.f.* Contumacy, default; (*Med.*) quarantine. (*Law*) **Condannare in —,** to sentence by default; **processo in —,** judgment by default.
contumelia [contumElia], *n.f.* Contumely, abuse, insult, obloquy.
contundente, *a.* Bruising, blunt. **Corpo —,** blunt instrument.
contundere [contUndere], *v.t.* To bruise, to contuse.
conturbamento, *n.m.* Disturbance, perturbation, trouble.
conturbare, *v.t.* To disturb, to perturb, to trouble.
conturbarsi, *v.r.* To be perturbed.
conturbatamente, *adv.* In perturbation.
conturbatore, *n.m.* Disturber.
conturbazione, *n.f.* Perturbation.
contusione, *n.f.* Contusion, bruise.
contuso, *p.p.a.* Bruised.
contutore, *n.m.* Joint guardian.
contuttochè, *conj.* Although.
contuttociò, *adv.* Nevertheless.
conuro, *n.m.* (*Zool.*) Parakeet.
convalescente, *n.m.a.* Convalescent.
convalescenza, *n.f.* Convalescence.
convalidare, *v.t.* To ratify, to confirm, to validate.
convalidazione, *n.f.* Ratification.
convallaria [convallAria], *n.f.* (*Bot.*) Lily of the valley.
convalle, *n.f.* Long, wide valley, dale.
convegno, *n.m.* Meeting; meeting-place, rendez-vous; appointment.
convenevole [convenEvole], *a.* Convenient, suitable.
convenevolezza, *n.f.* Propriety, decency, decorum; opportuneness.
convenevoli, *n.m.pl.* Compliments, regards; greetings; ceremony. **Fare i —,** to pay one's respects; **stare sui —,** to stand on ceremony.
convenevolmente, *adv.* Suitably.
conveniente, *a.* Convenient, suitable, advantageous, profitable; cheap.
convenientemente, *adv.* Conveniently.
convenienza, *n.f.* Convenience, opportunity, suitability, suitableness; advantage, profit; propriety; expediency. **Non ho la —,** it doesn't pay me.

convenire, *v.i.* To come together; to agree; to admit, to confess; to suit; to be necessary; to be expedient; to be requisite; to be convenient; to be profitable, to pay. **Non mi conviene,** it does not suit me, "it's not my cup of tea"; **conviene che io resti,** I must needs stay; **non convenimmo sul prezzo,** we did not agree about the price; **conviene andare,** it is better to go; **convennero da tutte le parti,** they came from all parts.
convenirsi, *v.r.* To be agreed upon; to be established.
conventicola [conventIcola], *n.f.* Conventicle; secret meeting; clique.
convento, *n.m.* Convent; monastery
conventuale, *a.* Conventual.
conventualista (*pl.* **conventualisti**), *n.m.* (*Eccles.*) Conventual friar.
convenuto, *n.m.* (*Law*) Defendant; agreement.
convenuto, *p.p.a.* Agreed, settled, agreed upon.
convenzionale, *a.* Conventional.
convenzionalismo, *n.m.* Conventionalism
convenzionalità [-à], *n.f.* Conventionality.
convenzione, *n.f.* Convention, covenant, agreement, pact, contract.
convergente, *a.* Convergent.
convergenza, *n.f.* Convergence.
convergere [convErgere], *v.i.* To converge, to tend to one point.
conversa, *n.f.* (*Eccles.*) Lay sister in a convent.
conversare, *v.t.* To converse, to talk.
conversativo, *a.* (*obs.*) Companionable; talkative.
conversazione, *n.f.* Conversation; (*obs*). evening party.
conversevole [conversEvole], *a.* Sociable.
conversione, *n.f.* Conversion (in all senses); (*Mil.*) wheeling movement.
converso, *n.m.* (*Eccles.*) Lay brother.
converso, *p.p.a.* Turned. **Per —,** conversely, vice versa.
convertibile [convertIbile], *a.* Convertible.
convertibilità [-à], *n.f.* Convertibility.
convertire, *v.t.* To convert, to change.
convertirsi, *v.r.* To be converted, to become a convert.
convertito, *n.m.a.* Convert; converted. **Predicare a un —,** to preach to the converted.
convessità [-à], *n.f.* Convexity.
convesso, *a.* Convex.
convezione, *n.f.* (*Elect.*) Convection.
convincente, *a.* Convincing, forceful.
convincere [convIncere], *v.t.* To convince, to persuade.
convincersi, *v.r.* To be convinced, to convince oneself.
convincibile [convincIbile], *a.* Persuadable, convincible, open to conviction.
convincimento, *n.m.* Convincement, conviction.
convinzione, *n.f.* Conviction.
convitare, *v.t.* To invite (to a meal), to entertain.
convitato, *n.m.* Guest.
convito, *n.m.* Banquet. **Sacro Convito,** the Lord's Supper.
convitto, *n.m.* Boarding-school, public school.
convittore, *n.m.* Boarder (at school).
conviva, *n.m.f.* Fellow-guest.
convivale, *a.* [cp. **conviviale**].
convivente, *a.* Living with; cohabiting.
convivenza, *n.f.* Life (in common); cohabitation. **L'umana —,** human society.
convivere [convIvere], *v.i.* To live together, to cohabit.
conviviale, *a.* Convivial.
convivio [convIvio], *n.m.* Banquet
convocamento, *n.m.* (Act of) convoking *or* convening.
convocare, *v.t* To convoke, to convene, to call together.
convocazione, *n.f.* Convocation; summoning (of committee, etc.); (*Football*) selection of team.
convogliare, *v.t.* To escort, to convoy; to carry away, to collect (of waters, etc.).
convoglio [convOglio], *n.m.* Convoy, escort; (*Rail.*) train. **— funebre,** funeral procession.
convolare, *v.i.* To fly together, to hasten; (*colloq.*) **— a giuste nozze,** "to get spliced".
convolgere [convOlgere], *v.t.* To entwine.
convoluto, *a.* Convolute, entwined.
convolvolo [convOlvolo], *n.m.* (*Bot.*) Convolvulus.
convulsamente, *adv.* Convulsively
convulsione, *n.f.* Convulsion, commotion; fit, spasm. **Esser preso dalle convulsioni,** to be taken with convulsions.
convulsivamente, *adv.* Convulsively.
convulsivo, *a.* Convulsive.
convulso, *n.m.a.* Twitch; convulsed, agitated; fitful.
coobbligarsi, *v.r.* (*Law*) To enter jointly into an obligation.
coobbligato, *n.m.* (*Law*) Joint security.
coonestamento, *n.m.* Palliation.
coonestare, *v.t.* To palliate, to gloss over; to give an air of justice to some action.
cooperante, *n.m.* Co-operator.
cooperare, *v.i.* To co-operate.
cooperativa, *n.f.* Co-operative society; co-operative stores.
cooperativo, *a.* Co-operative. **Società cooperativa,** co-operative society.
cooperazione, *n.f.* Co-operation.
coordinamento, *n.m.* Co-ordination.
coordinare, *v.t.* To co-ordinate, to correlate, to arrange.
coordinazione, *n.f.* Co-ordination.
coorte [coOrte], *n.f.* Cohort, band, troop.
coperchio [copErchio], *n.m.* Lid; cover, covering.
coperta, *n.f.* Cover, lid; blanket, rug, counterpane; envelope; (*Naut.*) deck. **— da letto,** quilt; **— da viaggio,** travelling rug; **— di lana,** blanket; **alla —,** covertly; **sopra —,** on deck.
copertamente, *adv.* Covertly, secretly, by stealth.
copertina, *n.f.* Cover (of books, etc.), jacket, wrapper.
coperto, *n.m.* Cover (place at table), shelter, covered place. **Al —,** under cover.
coperto, *a.* Covered, hidden; overcast (of weather); (*Mil.*) protected, masked.
copertoio [copertOio], *n.m.* Large rug; lid (of big pot).
copertone, *n.m.* Thick rug; tarpaulin; (*Motor.*) tyre.
copertura, *n.f.* Roofing, roof, cover; (*Comm.*) cover, security. **Lettera di —,** covering letter; (*Mil.*) **truppe di —,** covering troops.

copia (1), *n.f.* Copy, transcription, duplicate; example, specimen. **Cattiva —,** rough draft; **bella —,** fair copy; **— conforme,** true copy.
copia (2), *n.f.* Abundance, plenty. **In gran —,** in great abundance.
copiafatture, *n.f.* (*Comm.*) Invoice book.
copialettere [copialEttere], *n.m.* (*Comm.*) Letter-book; copying-press.
copiare, *v.t.* To copy, to imitate; to transcribe.
copiativo, *a.* Copying. **Inchiostro —,** copying-ink; **carta copiativa,** carbon paper.
copiatore, copiatrice, *n.m.f.* Copier, imitator.
copiatura, *n.f.* Transcription, copying.
copiglia [copIglia], *n.f.* (*Mech.*) Linchpin, bolt.
copione, *n.m.* (*Theat.*) Script (of a play); actor's part (copied out).
copiosamente, *adv.* Copiously.
copioso, *a.* Abundant, copious.
copista, *n.m.f.* Copyist; typist.
copisteria [copisterIa], *n.f.* Typing-office, typing agency.
coppa, *n.f.* Cup, goblet; tumbler; (*Sport*) cup, trophy; event for which this is awarded; suit of Italian playing-cards; kind of sausage.
coppaia [coppAia], *n.f.* (*Mech.*) Mandrel (of lathe).
coppaiba, coppaive [coppAiba], *n.m.* (*Bot.*) Copaiba.
coppale, *n.m.* (*Bot.*) Copal; patent leather.
copparosa, *n.f.* (*Chem.*) Copperas.
coppella, *n.f.* Cupel (for assaying metal). **Oro di —,** pure gold; (*fig.*) person of integrity.
coppetta, *n.f.* (*Med.*) Cupping-glass.
coppia [cOppia], *n.f.* Couple, pair. **A coppie,** in pairs.
coppiere, *n.m.* Cup-bearer; wine waiter.
coppiglia, *n.f.* (*Mech.*) Linchpin, cotter pin [cp. **copiglia**].
coppiola, *n.f.* Discharge from both barrels (of a double-barrelled gun).
coppo, *n.m.* Large earthenware jar; tile.
copribusto, *n.m.* Bodice, camisole, undervest.
copricapo, *n.m.* Headgear, hat.
coprifuoco, *n.m.* Curfew.
coprimento, *n.m.* Covering.
coprimiserie [coprimisErie], *n.m* Coat (worn to cover shabby garments); overall.
copripiatti, *n.m.* Dish-cover.
copripiedi, *n.m.* Coverlet (for the feet).
copripneu, *n.m.* (*Motor.*) Tyre cover.
coprire, *v.t.* To cover (in all senses); to defend, to protect, to shelter; to hold, to keep; to muffle up, to drown (noise). **— un ufficio,** to occupy a position; **— le spese,** to cover expenses.
coprirsi, *v.r.* To cover oneself, to wrap oneself up. **Si copra,** put on your hat; **il tempo si copre,** it is getting overcast; (*Comm.*) **ci siamo coperti,** we have covered ourselves.
copriruota, *n.f.* Wheel-case, guard for wheel.
copritavola [copritAvola], *n.f.* Table-cloth.
copriteiera, *n.m.* Tea cosy.
copritura, *n.f.* Covering, coverlet.
coprivivande, *n.m.* Dish-cover.
coprolito, *n.m.* (*Geol.*) Coprolite.
copto, *n.m.a.* Coptic.
copula [cOpula], *n.f.* (*Gram.*) Copula, conjunction.
copulare, *v.t.* To copulate; to join together.
copulazione, *n.f.* Copulation.
cor, *n.m.* (*Poet.*) Heart [cp. **cuore**].
coraggio [corAggio], *n.m.* Courage, bravery; fearlessness, pluck; (*fig.*) effrontery, **Farsi —,** to pluck up courage; **far —,** to encourage, to urge, to incite.
coraggiosamente, *adv.* Courageously.
coraggioso, *a.* Courageous, fearless, brave, plucky.
corale, *n.m.* Plain chant; book of anthems.
corale, *a.* Choral.
corallino, *a.* Coralline. **Labbra coralline,** ruby lips.
corallo, *n.m.* Coral.
corame, *n.m.* Leather, hides.
Corano, *n.m.* Koran.
corata, coratella, *n.f.* Offal, liver and lights; pluck.
corazza, *n.f.* Cuirass; armour-plating; breast-plate; (*Zool.*) carapace.
corazzare, *v.t.* To armour; to plate (with steel); to harden, to steel.
corazzarsi, *v.r.* To protect oneself; to harden oneself.
corazzata, *n.f.* (*Naut.*) Battleship, warship, ironclad.
corazzato, *a.* Armour-plated.
corazzatura, *n.f.* Armour-plating.
corazziere, *n.m.* (*Mil.*) Cuirassier.
corba, *n.f.* Basket, hamper; (*Naut.*) rib.
corbame, *n.m.* (*Naut.*) Ribs of a vessel.
corbellaio [corbellAio], *n.m.* Maker or vendor of baskets; basket-maker.
corbellare, *v.t.* To mock, to hoax; to ridicule, to rally.
corbellatore, *n.m.* Jester, mocker.
corbellatura, *n.f.* Jest, hoax.
corbelleria [corbellerIa], *n.f.* Nonsense, silliness, foolishness, silly jest.
corbello, *n.m.* Basket, trug; (*fig.*) silly fellow; (*colloq.*) testicle.
corbezzoli! [corbEzzoli], *inter.* Good gracious!
corbezzolo [corbEzzolo], *n.m.* (*Bot.*) Arbutus.
corbo, *n.m.* (*Zool.*) Raven [cp. **corvo**].
corcarsi, *v.r.* To lie down, to repose [cp. **coricarsi**].
corcontento, *n.m.* Easy-going man.
corda, *n.f.* Rope, string, cord; chord. **Strumenti a —,** stringed instruments; **— di pianoforte,** piano wire; **scala di —,** rope ladder; **dar —,** to encourage one to do something; **tenere uno sulla —,** to keep one on tenter-hooks; **danzatore di —,** rope-walker; **mettere la — al collo ad uno,** to make someone do what he doesn't want to do; **tagliare la —,** to escape, to decamp; **tirare troppo la —,** to overdue, to exaggerate.
cordaio [cordAio], *n.m.* Ropemaker.
cordame, *n.m.* Cordage.
cordata, *n.f.* Roped party of mountaineers.
cordellina, *n.f.* Fine, braided silk.
corderia [corderIa], *n.f.* Ropemaking; rope-walk; rope factory.
cordiale, *n.m.a.* Cordial (drink); cordial, hearty.
cordialità [-à], *n.f.* Cordiality, heartiness.
cordialmente, *adv.* Cordially.
cordialone, *n.m.* Warm-hearted man; good-natured fellow.

cordicella, *n.f.* Fine cord, pack-thread.
cordiera, *n.f.* (*Mus.*) Nut (of a violin).
cordigliero, *n.m.* (*Eccles.*) Cordelier, Franciscan friar.
cordiglio [cordIglio], *n.m.* Girdle; rope girdle.
cordino, *n.m.* Thin rope.
cordite, *n.f.* Cordite.
cordoglio [cordOglio], *n.m* Grief, anguish, sorrow.
cordonare, *v.t.* To surround, to girdle, to gird; (*fig.*) to take in, to deceive.
cordonata, *n.f.* Mountain road rising in shallow steps.
cordonatura, *n.f.* (*colloq.*) Jest, hoax.
cordoncino, *n.m.* String, twist; braid; watch-guard.
cordone, *n.m.* Cordon; braid, cord; (*Arch.*) string course; (*Mil.*) line of forts. **— sanitario,** sanitary cordon; **— umbilicale,** umbilical cord; **— del campanello,** bell-pull.
cordoneria [cordonerIa], *n.f.* jest.
cordovano, *n.m.* Cordovan leather.
core [cp. **cuore**].
corea [corEa], *n.f.* St. Vitus's dance.
coreggia [corEggia], *n.f.* Leather belt, strap; (*vulg.*) fart.
coreggiato, correggiato, *n.m.* (*Agric.*) Flail, threshing machine.
coreggiolo, *n.m.* Leather thong, strap.
coreografia [coreografIa], *n.f.* Choreography.
coreografo [coreOgrafo], *n.m.* Choreographer.
coriaceo [coriAceo], *a.* Tough, leathery.
coriambo, *n.m.* (*Poet.*) Choriamb.
coriandolo [coriAndolo], *n.m.* (*Bot.*) Coriander seed; bit of confetti.
coriandro, (*Bot.*) Coriander.
coribante, *n.m.* Corybant.
coricamento, *n.m.* (Act of) lying down.
coricare, *v.t.* To put to bed, to lay down.
coricarsi, *v.r.* To go to bed, to lie down.
coricino, *n.m.* (*colloq.*) Darling.
corifeo [corifEo], *n.m.* Coryphaeus; dancer; leader (of a party, etc.).
corindone, *n.m.* (*Metal.*) Corundum.
corintio, corinzio [corIntio, corInzio], *a.* Corinthian.
corista, *n.m.f.* Chorister; singer in a chorus; dancing girl; tuning-fork.
cormorano, *n.m.* (*Zool.*) Cormorant.
cornacchia [cornAcchia], *n.f.* (*Zool.*) Crow, rook; (*fig.*) bird of ill omen.
cornaggine [cornAggine], *n.f.* Obstinacy.
cornalina, *n.f.* Cornelian.
cornamusa, *n.f.* (*Mus.*) Bagpipes.
cornare, *v.i.t.* To tingle (in the ears); to butt (with the horns).
cornata, *n.f.* Blow or butt (with horns).
cornea [cOrnea], *n.f.* (*Anat.*) Cornea.
corneo [cOrneo], *a.* Horny.
cornetta, *n.f.* (*Mus.*) Cornet, bugle; hooter.
cornettista, *n.m.f.* (*Mus.*) Cornet-player.
cornetto, *n.m.* Postman's horn. **— acustico,** ear-trumpet.
cornice, *n.f.* Picture-frame; cornice, ledge (on mountainside). **Mettere in —,** to put in a frame, to frame; **far — a,** to stand round (in a group).
corniciaio [corniciAio], *n.m.* Picture-frame maker.
corniciare, *v.t.* To frame.
corniciatura, *n.f.* Framing.
cornicione, *n.m.* (*Arch.*) Projection, entablature.
corniola, corniuola, *n.f.* (*Min.*) Cornelian, (*Bot.*) cornel berry.
corno (pl. **corni,** *m.*, **corna,** *f.*), *n.m.* Horn horny matter; projection; point (of flame); corn (on the foot); mountain peak; branch (of a river). **— da caccia,** hunting-horn; **suonare il —,** to blow the horn; **— di lumaca,** snail's horn; **corni della luna,** horns of the moon; (*fig.*) **abbassare le corna,** to sing small; **avere sulle corna qualcuno,** to dislike someone; **fiaccar le corna,** to take (one) down a peg; **fare le corna,** to make a gesture against the evil eye; to cuckold (a man); **dir corna di,** to speak evil of; **me ne importa un —,** I don't care a fig; **un —!** nonsense! **— da scarpe,** shoe-horn.
Cornovaglia [cornovAglia], *n.f.* Cornwall.
cornucopia [cornucOpia], *n.f.* Horn of plenty, cornucopia.
cornuto, *n.m.* Cuckold.
cornuto, *a.* Horned. **Argomento —,** dilemma.
coro, *n.m.* Chorus; choir. **Far —,** to be in entire agreement; to join in, to chime in; **cantare in —,** to sing in chorus.
corografia [corografIa], *n.f.* Chorography, topography.
corografo [corOgrafo], *n.m.* Chorographer, topographer.
coroide [corOide], *n.m.* (*Anat.*) Choroid.
corolla, *n.f.* (*Bot.*) Corolla.
corollario [corollArio], *n.m.* (*Math.*) Corollary.
corollifero [corollIfero], *a.* (*Bot.*) Corolliflorous, corollate.
corona, *n.f.* Crown; coronet, diadem; wreath; top (of buildings, etc.); (*Mil.*) driving-band (of bullet or shell); (*Eccles.*) rosary; (*Astron.*) halo, corona. **— di sonetti,** cycle of sonnets; **far —,** to form a circle; **deporre una —,** to lay a wreath; **discorso della Corona,** speech from the throne; (*Mech.*) **— dentata,** rim of gearwheel.
coronaio [coronAio], *n.m.* Maker or seller of rosaries.
coronale, *n.m.* (*Anat.*) Frontal bone.
coronamento, *n.m.* Crowning, completion; coronation; (*Naut.*) taffrail.
coronare, *v.t.* To crown; to complete, to perfect; to fulfil.
coronario [coronArio], *a.* (*Anat.*) Coronary.
coronazione, *n.f.* Coronation.
coroncina, *n.f.* Small wreath.
coronella, *n.f.* Sore on the finger; hang-nail.
corpacciata [cp. **scorpacciata**].
corpacciuto, *a.* Pot-bellied, paunchy.
corpetto, *n.m.* Waistcoat, vest.
corpo, *n.m.* Body, trunk; main part; substance, material; mass; corps; corpse; (*Naut.*) hull. **— di leggi,** code of laws; **— del delitto, — di reato,** material evidence (of crime); **— di guardia,** guard; guard-room; **a — morto;** desperately; **dolore di —,** stomach-ache, **andare di —,** to evacuate (the bowels); **combattere — a —,** to fight hand to hand; **Corpo di Bacco!** What the deuce! **— insegnante,** teaching staff; (*Mil.*) **— d'armata,** army corps; **corpi celesti,** celestial bodies.
corporale, *n.m.* (*Eccles.*) Corporal; (*Mil.*) corporal.
corporale, *a.* Corporeal, bodily, corporal.

corporalmente, *adv.* Corporeally.
corporativo, *a.* Corporate, corporative; *(Pol.)* **stato —,** corporative State.
corporatura, *n.f.* Bodily structure; build, physique; size.
corporazione, *n.f.* Corporation, company, guild, association.
corporeamente, *adv.* Corporeally.
corporeo [corpOreo], *a.* Corporeal.
corpulento, *a.* Corpulent, stout; massive.
corpulenza, *n.f.* Corpulence.
corpuscolare, *a.* Corpuscular.
corpuscolo [corpUscolo], *n.m.* Corpuscle.
Corpus Domini, *n.m. (Eccles.)* Corpus Christi.
corre, *v.t. (Poet.)* To gather, to reap [cp. **cogliere**].
corredare, *v.t.* To equip, to furnish, to supply, to adorn; to furnish with a trousseau; to accompany, to enclose.
corredato, *p.p.a.* Attached (to a letter, etc.), enclosed.
corredino, *n.m.* Baby linen, layette.
corredo, *n.m.* Trousseau; outfit, household goods, equipment; *(fig.)* wealth.
correggere [corrEggere], *v.t.* To correct; to amend, to rectify, to revise; to put right; to modify; to purify (wines, etc.).
correggia [corrEggia], *n.f.* Leather-belt, girdle.
correggibile [correggIbile], *a.* Corrigible.
correggiola [corrEggiola], *n.f.* Leather thong, strap.
corregionale, *a.* Of the same region.
correità [-à], *n.f.* Complicity.
correlativamente, *adv.* Correlatively.
correlativo, *a.* Correlative.
correlazione, *n.f.* Correlation, mutual relation.
correligionario [correligionArio], *n.m.* Co-religionist.
corrente, *n.f.* Current (in all senses), stream; draught (of air); trend (of opinion). **— elettrica,** electric current; **— d'aria,** draught; **andar contro —,** to go against the stream; *(Elect.)* **— alternata, continua,** alternating, direct current.
corrente, *a.* Current, running, flowing; general, usual, common. **Secondo l'uso —,** according to custom; **a posta —,** by return of post; **essere al —,** to be well informed; to be in the swim; *(Comm.)* **conto —,** current account; **il 24 —,** on the 24th inst.
correntemente, *adv.* Fluently. **Parla italiano —,** he speaks Italian fluently.
correntezza, *n.f.* Ease, fluency, facility; easy-going disposition.
correntia [correntIa], *n.f. (Lit.)* Stream (of a river).
correntista, *n.m.f. (Comm.)* Person with a current account, depositor.
correo [corrEo], *n.m.* Accomplice.
correre [cOrrere], *v.i.* To run, to run about; to hasten; to flow; to travel rapidly; to be current (of money). **Egli ha corso un gran pericolo,** he had a narrow escape; **— a rotta di collo,** to run at breakneck speed; **corre voce che,** they say that; **lascia —,** never mind, don't bother; **corre differenza,** there is a difference; **Ci corre!** There is a great difference! **ci corre l'obbligo,** we are in duty bound; **— dietro,** to run after; **coi tempi che corrono,** as times go.
correspettivamente, *adv.* Correspondingly.
correspettività [-à], *n.f.* Relation, correspondence (to).
correspettivo, *n.m.a.* Equivalent, corresponding; corresponding amount; compensation.
corresponsabile [corresponsAbile], *a.* Jointly responsible.
corresponsabilità [-à], *n.f.* Joint responsibility.
corresponsione, *n.f.* Payment; response.
correttamente, *adv.* Correctly, in the right manner; loyally.
correttezza, *n.f.* Correctness, accuracy; decency; honesty.
correttivo, *a.* Corrective.
corretto, *a.* Correct, corrected, right, exact, accurate.
correttore, correttrice, *n.m.f.* Corrector, emendator; *(Print.)* reader.
correzionale, *n.m.a.* Reformatory; correctional.
correzione, *n.f.* Correction, rectification; alteration, revision; emendation.
corrida, *n.f.* Bull-fight.
corridoio [corridOio], *n.m.* Corridor, lobby.
corridore, *n.m.* Runner, racer; race-horse.
corriera, *n.f.* Mail coach, mail van; motorbus, charabanc.
corriere, *n.m.* Courier, messenger; forwarding agent; mail, post; daily correspondence. **A volta di —,** by return of post.
corrigendo, *n.m.* Juvenile offender (in an institution or reformatory).
corriggibile [corriggIbile], *a.* Corrigible, open to correction.
corrispettivo, *n.m. (Comm.)* Corresponding amount; compensation.
corrispondente, *n.m.a.* Correspondent; corresponding, relating to; proportionate.
corrispondenza, *n.f.* Correspondence (in all senses); relation, intercourse. **Mettersi in —,** to enter into correspondence with; **biglietto di —,** return or through ticket; **— di oltremare,** overseas mail; **— per l'estero,** foreign mail.
corrispondere [corrispOndere], *v.t.i.* To correspond, to be in relation to; to reciprocate, to return; to harmonize; to fit; to be conformable; to answer; to repay with. **Gli corrisponde cento sterline all'anno,** he remits him £100 a year; **il mio amico mi corrispose male,** my friend made a poor return for all I did.
corrispondersi [corrispOndersi], *v.r.* To correspond with one another.
corrisposto, *p.p.a.* Returned, repaid, requited, reciprocal. **Amore non —,** unrequited love.
corrivamente, *adv.* Easily, indulgently.
corrivo, *a.* Easy-going, indulgent; careless, hasty, inconsiderate.
corroboramento, *n.m.* Strengthening, corroborating.
corroborante, *n.m. (Med.)* Tonic.
corroborante, *a.* Supporting, strengthening, corroborating.
corroborare, *v.t.* To strengthen, to corroborate; to support.
corroborativo, *a.* Corroborative.
corroborazione. *n.f.* Corroboration, support.

corrodere [corrOdere], *v.t.i.* To corrode, to wear away; to consume.
corrodimento, *n.m.* (Act of) corroding, corrosion.
corrompere [corrOmpere], *v.t.* To corrupt, to bribe; to taint, to defile, to infect; to seduce.
corrompersi [corrOmpersi], *v.r.* To become corrupt, to deteriorate.
corrompimento, *n.m.* Corruption.
corrosione, *n.f.* Corrosion.
corrosivo, *a.* Corrosive.
corroso, *p.p.a.* Corroded.
corrottamente, *adv.* Corruptly.
corrotto, *n.m.* Corrupt person; (*obs.*) mourning, dirge.
corrotto, *p.p.a.* Corrupt, corrupted, depraved, polluted, foul.
corrucciare, *v.t.* To torment, to vex, to grieve, to afflict; to enrage.
corrucciarsi, *v.r.* To be vexed; to get into a rage; to worry.
corrucciatamente, *adv.* Angrily.
corruccio [corrUccio], *n.m.* Anger; vexation.
corrugamento, *n.m.* Corrugation; wrinkling, knitting (of the brows).
corrugare, *v.t.* To wrinkle, to corrugate, to knit (the brows). **— le ciglia,** to frown.
corrugazione, *n.f.* Corrugation.
corruscare, *v.i.* To flash, to glitter, to sparkle, to corruscate.
corrusco, *a.* Flashing, shining, sparkling, corruscating.
corruttela, *n.f.* Corruption, depravity.
corruttibile [corruttIbile], *a.* Corruptible.
corruttibilità [-à], *n.f.* Corruptibility.
corruttivo, *a.* Corruptive.
corruttore, corruttrice, *n.m.f.* Corruptor.
corruzione, *n.f.* Corruption, depravity; pollution; bribery; deterioration.
corsa, *n.f.* Run; running, race; trip, excursion; haste; (*Mech.*) piston-stroke; (*Rail.*) train service. **Andare alle corse,** to go to the races; **cavallo da —,** race-horse; **di —,** hastily; **a tutta —,** in great haste; **fare una —,** to run on an errand; **— compensata,** handicap; **perdere la —,** to miss (train etc.); **prezzo della —,** fare.
corsaletto, *n.m.* Corslet.
corsaresco, *a.* Piratical.
corsaro, *n.m.* Pirate, corsair.
corseggiare, *v.i.* To go a-pirating; to plunder.
corsello, corsetto, *n.m.* Space between a bed and the wall or between two beds.
corsetto, *n.m.* Corset.
corsia [corsIa], *n.f.* Gangway, passage; ward (in a hospital); dormitory.
corsiero, *n.m.* Charger, steed, warhorse.
corsivo, *a.* Cursive (handwriting); (*Print.*) italics.
corso (1) [córso], *n.m.* Course; flow, stream; main street; studies, lessons, classes; space of time; run, running; (*Fin.*) currency. **— legale,** legal tender; **— del cambio,** rate of exchange; **— d'acqua,** water-course; **anno in —,** current year; **mettere in —,** to put into circulation; **affari in —,** current affairs; **seguire un —,** to attend a course of lectures; **la malattia deve fare il suo —,** the illness must take its course.
corso (2) [còrso], *n.m a.* Corsican.
corso (3), [córso], *a.* Passed, circulated.
corsoio [corsOio], *a.* Slipping, sliding. **Nodo —,** slip-knot [cp. **scorsoio**].
cortamente, *adv.* Shortly, in brief.
corte, *n.f.* Courtyard, court; law court, tribunal; courtship. **Dama di —,** lady-in-waiting; **far la —,** to pay court to; **tener — bandita,** to keep open house; (*Mil.*) **— marziale,** court martial.
corteccia [cortEccia], *n.f.* Bark (of tree), rind; crust.
corteggiamento, *n.m.* Courtship, courting; wooing.
corteggiare, *v.t.* To court, to pay court to, to woo; to flatter.
corteggiatore, *n.m.* Suitor.
corteggio [cortEggio], *n.m.* Retinue, cortege.
corteo [cortEo], *n.m.* Procession; train, cortege.
cortese, *a.* Courteous, kind, polite. **Di modi cortesi,** of engaging manners.
cortesemente, *adv.* Courteously, kindly; (*fig.*) liberally.
cortesia [cortesIa], *n.f.* Courtesy, politeness, kindness; favour, liberality. **Abbia la — di,** be good enough to.
cortezza, *n.f.* Shortness, brevity.
corticale, *a.* (*Bot.*) Cortical.
cortice [cOrtice], *n.m.* (*Bot*) Bark.
cortigiana, *n.f.* Courtesan, harlot.
cortigianeria [cortigianerIa], *n.f.* Obsequiousness, flattery; courtliness.
cortigianesco, *a.* Courtier-like; servile, cringing.
cortigiano, *n.m.* Courtier; flatterer.
cortile, *n.m.* Courtyard; farmyard.
cortina, *n.f.* Curtain; screen; blind. (*Pol.*) **— di ferro,** Iron Curtain; (*Mil.*) **— di fumo,** smoke screen.
cortinaggio [cortinAggio], *n.m.* Bed-hangings; curtain.
corto, *a.* Short, brief; limited; deficient, insufficient. **Tagliar —,** to cut short; **di vista corta,** short-sighted; **di intelligenza corta,** of limited intelligence; **per farla corta,** to make a long story short; **essere a — di moneta,** to be short of cash; **andare per le corte,** to go straight to the point; (*Elect.*) **— circuito,** short circuit; **alle corte!** in short!
cortometraggio [cortometrAggio], *n.m.* (*Cinem.*) Short-length film.
corvetta, *n.f.* (*Naut.*) Corvette; curvet (of a horse).
corvettare, *v.i.* To curvet.
corvino, *a.* Black, raven. **Capigliatura corvina,** raven-black hair.
corvo, *n.m.* (*Zool.*) Raven; crow.
cosa, *n.f.* Thing; affair, matter, fact, item; property, possessions. **— da nulla,** trifle; **Che — avete?** What is the matter with you? **Che — ti fa?** What does it matter to you? **è un'altra —,** it is a different thing; (**Che**) **— ne dici?** What do you say of this? **appianare le cose,** to smooth matters; **Signor Coso,** Mr. What's-his-name. (dims. **cosetta, cosina, cosettina, coserella, coserellina**).
cosaccia [cosAccia], *n.f.* Bad thing, rubbish; good-for-nothing man.
cosacco, *n.m.a.* Cossack.
cosare, *v.t.* (*Tuscan slang*) To do.

coscetto, *n.m.* Leg (of lamb, mutton, etc.).
coscia [cOscia], *n.f.* Thigh; haunch; leg (of mutton, etc.). **— di pollo,** leg of chicken.
cosciente, *a.* Conscious, aware.
coscienza, *n.f.* Conscience, scruple; knowledge; consciousness. **— larga,** accommodating conscience; **senza —,** unscrupulous; **in —,** honestly.
coscienziosamente, *adv.* Conscientiously.
coscienzioso, *a.* Conscientious, scrupulous.
cosciotto, *n.m.* Haunch. **— di selvaggina,** haunch of venison.
coscrivere [coscrIvere], *v.t.* To conscript.
coscritto, *n.m.* Conscript, recruit.
coscrizione, *n.f.* Conscription.
cosecante, *n.f.* (*Geom.*) Co-secant.
coseno, *n.m.* (*Geom.*) Cosine.
così, *adv.* Thus, so, therefore. **Così così,** pretty well, not so bad; **— ricco come Lei,** as rich as you are; **e — via,** and so forth; **— come,** just as; **è un uomo — fatto,** that is his nature; **— detto,** so called; **per — dire,** so to speak; **— sia,** amen; **e — di seguito,** and so forth; **proprio —,** just so.
cosicchè, *adv.* So that.
cosiddetto, *a.* So-called.
cosiffatto, *a.* Made in that way.
cosmetico [cosmEtico], *n.m.a.* Cosmetic.
cosmico [cOsmico], *a.* Cosmic.
cosmo, *n.m.* Cosmos.
cosmogonia [cosmogonIa], *n.f.* Cosmogony.
cosmografia [cosmografIa], *n.f.* Cosmography.
cosmologia [cosmologIa], *n.f.* Cosmology.
cosmopolita, cosmopolitano, *n.m.a.* Cosmopolite; cosmopolitan.
coso, *n.m.* (*colloq.*) Thing; fellow; bloke; what's-his-name, what-d'ye-call-it [cp. **cosa**].
cospargere [cospArgere], *v.t.* To strew, to sprinkle. **— di fiori,** to strew with flowers.
cosparso, *p.p.a.* Strewn.
cospergere [cospErgere], *v.t.* To sprinkle; to smear.
cosperso, *p.p.a.* Sprinkled.
cospetto, *n.m.* Presence, sight, view. **Al — di,** in the presence of.
cospetto! *inter.* Good heavens!
cospicuamente, *adv.* Conspicuously.
cospicuità [-à], *n.f.* Conspicuousness.
cospicuo [cospIcuo], *a.* Conspicuous, eminent. **Una somma cospicua,** a considerable amount.
cospirare, *v.i.* To conspire, to plot.
cospiratore, cospiratrice, *n.m.f.* Conspirator, plotter.
cospirazione, *n.f.* Conspiracy, plot.
costa, *n.f.* Slope, hillside; coast, shore; rib (in all senses). **Di —,** sideways; **a mezza —,** half-way up (a hill); **La Costa d'Oro,** the Gold Coast.
costà, costì, *adv.* There, yonder. **Dateci notizie di costà,** give us news of your town, place, etc.
costaggiù, *adv.* Down there (near the person spoken to).
costale, *a.* (*Anat.*) Costal; coastal.
costante, *a.* Constant, stable, firm; enduring.
costantemente, *adv.* Constantly, firmly.
Costantinopoli [costantinOpoli], *n.m.* Constantinople, Istanbul.
costanza, *n.f.* Constancy, steadiness, firmness; perseverance.
costare, *v.i.* To cost; to be worth. **— un occhio,** to be exceedingly dear; **costi quello che costi,** whatever the cost; **gli è costata cara,** he had to pay dearly for it; **quanto costa?** what's the price?
costassù, *adv.* Up there (near the person addressed).
costata, *n.f.* Cutlet, chop.
costato, *n.m.* Ribs, chest, side.
costeggiare, *v.i.* To skirt; (*Naut.*) to coast, to hug the coast.
costei, *pron.* She, that woman.
costellare, *v.i.* To constellate; to spangle.
costellazione, *n.f.* Constellation.
costernare, *v.t.* To consternate, to affright; to dismay, to stagger.
costernazione, *n.f.* Consternation.
costì, *adv.* There [cp. **costà**].
costiera, *n.f.* Stretch of coast.
costiere, *n.m.* (*Naut.*) Coasting vessel; coastal pilot.
costiero, *a.* Coasting; coastal.
costipare, *v.t.* To heap up; to condense; (*Med.*) to constipate.
costiparsi, *v.r.* To have a cold (in the head); to get constipated.
costipato, *a.* Having a cold; constipated.
costipazione, *n.f.* Cold, catarrh; constipation.
costituente, *n.f.* Constituent assembly.
costituire, *v.t.* To constitute, to form; to nominate, to elect; to establish, to settle (money on someone). (*Comm.*) **— una società,** to form a company.
costituirsi, *v.r.* To form oneself, to constitute oneself; to appoint oneself; (*Law*) to give oneself up.
costituito, *p.p.a.* Constituted, appointed. **Governo —,** established government.
costitutivo, *a.* Constituent.
costituto, *n.m.* (*Law*) Cross-examination.
costituzionale, *a.* Constitutional.
costituzione, *n.f.* Constitution, statute; habit or temperament of body; appointment. (*Comm.*) **Atto di —,** act of incorporation.
costituzionalmente, *adv.* Constitutionally.
costo, *n.m.* Cost, price; expense. **Ad ogni —, a tutti i costi, a qualunque —,** at any price at any cost; **a prezzo di —,** at cost price.
costola [cOstola], *n.f.* (*Anat.*) Rib; back; spine (of a book). **Stare alle costole di qualcuno,** to be always at someone's elbow.
costoletta, *n.f.* Cutlet.
costolone, *n.m.* (*Arch.*) Rib (of a vault).
costoro, *pron.* Those, those people, they.
costosamente, *adv.* Expensively.
costoso, *a* Expensive, costly, dear.
costretto, *p.p.a.* Obliged, compelled, forced.
costringere [costrIngere], *v.t.* To force, to compel, to oblige; to press; to compress; to constrain.
costringimento, *n.m.* Compulsion.
costrittivo, *a.* Compelling; restrictive; (*Med.*) retentive.
costrittore, *n.m.* (*Med.*) Constrictor.
costrizione, *n.f.* Constriction; constraint; compulsion.
costruire, costrurre, *v.t.* To construct, to build; (*Gram.*) to construe.

costrutto, *n.m.* (Grammatical) construction; advantage; interpretation; result.
costruttore, *n.m.* Builder, constructor.
costruttura, *n.f.* Structure, fabric.
costruzione, *n.f.* Construction, building; build; structure.
costui, *pron.* That man, that fellow.
costuma, *n.f.* (*obs.*) Custom, habit, usage.
costumanza, *n.f.* Custom, habit, usage, politeness.
costumare, *v.t.i.* To accustom; to be usual; to be in use; to be customary. **Ciò non si costuma in Italia,** that is not customary in Italy; **quest'abito non costuma più,** this kind of dress is no longer worn.
costumatamente, *adv.* Politely; in the usual manner.
costumatezza, *n.f.* Good manners, civility.
costumato, *a.* Well-mannered, well-bred; polite; honest; accustomed.
costume, *n.m.* Custom, usage; costume, dress. **Aver per —,** to be in the habit of; **come è il —,** as is customary; **uomo di buoni costumi,** a man of good morals; **— da bagno,** bathing-costume; **— da ballo,** fancy-dress.
costura, *n.f.* Seam.
costurino, *n.m.* Rib (in a stocking).
cotale, *pron.* Such, such a one, such.
cotangente, *n.f.* (*Geom.*) Cotangent.
cotanto, *a. adv.* So much, so very, so long.
cote, *n.f.* Hone, whetstone.
cotechino, coteghino, *n.m.* Kind of highly-spiced sausage.
cotenna, *n.f.* Pig-skin; rind; (*Agric.*) sod, turf; (*fig.*) thick-skinned person.
cotennoso, *a.* (*colloq.*) Thick-skinned, insensitive.
cotesto, *a. pron.* That, that one (near the person addressed). **Cotesti, coteste,** those; those ones there; such.
cotica [cOtica], *n.f.* Pig-skin [cp. **cotenna**].
cotidianamente, *adv.* Daily.
cotidiano, *a.* Daily [cp. **quotidiano**].
cotila [cOtila], *n.f.* (*Anat.*) Socket (of a bone).
cotiledone [cotilEdone], *n.m.* (*Bot.*) Cotyledon.
cotogna, *n.f.* Quince (fruit).
cotognata, *n.f.* Quince marmelade.
cotognino, *a.* Quince (smell and taste).
cotogno, *n.m.* (*Bot.*) Quince-tree.
cotoletta, *n.f.* Cutlet.
cotonami, cotonati, *n.m.pl.* Cotton goods, soft goods.
cotone, *n.m.* Cotton. **— filato,** cotton yarn; **refe di —,** sewing cotton; **tessuto di —,** cotton (cloth); **— idrofilo,** cotton-wool; **— fulminante,** gun-cotton.
cotonerie [cotonerIe], *n.f.pl.* Cotton goods.
cotoniere, *n.m.* Cotton-spinner; (cotton) mill-owner.
cotoniero, *a.* Cotton. **Industria cotoniera,** cotton industry.
cotonificio [cotonifIcio], *n.m.* Cotton-mill.
cotonina, *n.f.* Cotton cloth (for clothes).
cotonoso, *a.* Cottony, downy, fluffy.
cotta (1), *n.f.* (*Eccles.*) Cotta, surplice. **— d'arme,** surcoat.
cotta (2), *n.f.* Cooking, baking; (*fig.*) infatuation; drunkenness. **Prendere una —,** to fall head over heels in love; **un birbante di tre cotte,** an arrant knave.
cotticcio [cottIccio], *a.* Half-cooked, half-done; (*fig.*) half-seas over.
cottimista, cottimante, *n.m.* Piece-worker.
cottimo [cOttimo], *n.m.* Piece-work; job, contract. **Lavorare a —,** to do piece-work.
cotto, *n.m.* (*Arch.*) Red brick, terra-cotta.
cotto, *a.* Cooked, baked; (*fig.*) drunk; in love.
cottura, *n.f.* Cooking, baking (*esp.* method, conditions, etc.).
coturno, *n.m.* (*Hist.*) Buskin. (*Theat.*) **Calzare il —,** to tread the boards, to act in a tragedy.
cova, *n.f.* Nesting-place; brooding, sitting (on eggs).
covaccio, covacciolo [covAccio, covAcciolo], *n.m.* Lair; (*colloq.*) bed.
covare, *v.t.* To brood, to hatch; to smoulder; to sicken (for an ailment). **Gatta ci cova,** I smell a rat; **— odio,** to cherish a secret hatred.
covata, *n.f.* Brood, hatching, nestful.
covatura, *n.f.* (Act of) brooding.
coverta, *n.f.* (*Naut.*) Deck [cp. **coperta**].
covile, covo, *n.m.* Lair, burrow, den, hare's form; hovel. **Covo di ladri,** den of thieves.
covone, *n.m.* Sheaf, shock (of corn); bundle (of hay).
covrire, *v.t.* To cover [cp. **coprire**].
cozione, *n.m.* (*obs.*) Concoction.
cozza, *n.f.* (*Zool.*) Mussel.
cozzare, *v.t.i.* To butt, to butt against; to clash, to collide with; to dash. **— contro un albero,** to crash against a tree.
cozzata, *n.f.* Collision; butting into.
cozzatura, *n.f.* (Act and effect of) butting.
cozzo, *n.m.* Clash, collision; shock, conflict. **Dar di —,** to dash against; **dal — delle opinioni,** from the clash of opinions.
cozzone, *n.m.* Horse-breaker; horse-dealer.
crac, *n.m.* Financial crash, failure, bankruptcy; collapse.
Cracovia [cracOvia], *n.f.* Cracow.
crampo, *n.m.* (*Med.*) Cramp.
cranico [crAnico], *a.* (*Anat.*) Cranial.
cranio [crAnio], *n.m.* (*Anat.*) Skull, cranium.
craniologia [craniologIa], *n.f.* Craniology.
craniometro [craniOmetro], *n.m.* Craniometer.
craniotomia [craniotomIa], *n.f.* (*Med.*) Craniotomy.
crapula [crApula], *n.f.* Excess (eating or drinking), guzzling; debauch.
crapulare, *v.i.* To guzzle, to revel.
crapulone, *n.m.* Guzzler, debauchee.
crasi, *n.f.* (*Gram.*) Crasis.
crassamente, *adv.* Crassly.
crassezza, *n.f.* Crassitude, crassness.
crasso, *a.* Thick, gross, crass. **Ignoranza crassa,** crass ignorance.
crastino, *a.* (*obs.*) Pertaining to tomorrow.
cratere, *n.m.* Crater, large bowl.
cravatta, *n.f.* Tie, necktie, cravat.
cravattaio [cravattAio], *n.m.* Maker or vendor of ties.
crazia [crAzia], *n.f.* (*Hist.*) Tuscan coin, worth about $\frac{1}{2}$d.
creanza, *n.f.* Breeding, politeness, training, education. **Buona —,** good breeding; **mala —,** vulgarity, rudeness, uncouthness; **ti insegnerò io la —!** I'll teach you how to behave! **non conosce le buone creanze,** he has no manners.

creanzato, *a.* Well-bred, polite.
creare, *v.t.* To create, to produce, to beget; to appoint, to institute; to establish. **— difficoltà,** to raise difficulties.
crearsi, *v.r.* To win for oneself; to be formed.
creativo, *a.* Creative, constructive.
creato, *n.m.* The universe, the world, creation; nature.
creato, *p.p.a.* Created, formed. **Ben —,** well-bred.
creatore, *n.m.* Creator, God; maker.
creatura, *n.f.* Creature; child; favourite.
creaturina, *n.f.* Infant, babe.
creazione, *n.f.* Creation, formation, foundation.
credente, *n.m.* Believer (in a religion).
credenza (1), *n.f.* Belief, faith; credit, credence. **Far —,** to give credit; **comprare a —,** to buy on credit; **lettere di —,** credentials.
credenza (2), *n.f.* Sideboard; (*Eccles.*) credence table.
credenziale, *n.f.* Credentials, letter of credit.
credenziere, *n.m.* Butler.
credenzone, *n.m.* Credulous person, "sucker".
credere [crEdere], *v.t.i.* To believe, to think, to suppose; to trust, to confide; to consider. **Dare a —,** to make believe; **credo di sì,** I think so; **Lo credo!** I should think so! **a mio —,** in my opinion; **non credo,** I don't think so.
credersi [crEdersi], *v.r.* To believe in oneself. **Egli si crede un grand'uomo,** he thinks himself somebody.
credibile [credIbile], *a.* Credible.
credibilità [-à], *n.f.* Credibility.
credibilmente, *adv.* Credibly.
credito [crEdito], *n.m.* Credit, trust, reputation. (*Comm.*) **A —,** on credit; **lettera di —,** letter of credit; **sono in — di venti sterline,** I am owed £20; **— a breve scadenza,** short credit; **— arretrato,** outstanding credit; **scuotere il —,** to shake one's credit.
creditore, *n.m.* Creditor. (*Comm.*) **— garantito,** secured creditor; **accomodarsi coi creditori,** to make a composition.
credo, *n.m.* Creed, article of faith
credulità [-à], *n.f.* Credulity.
credulo [crEdulo], *a.* Credulous.
credulone, *n.m.* Credulous person, gull.
crema, *n.f.* Custard; cream. **— per toeletta,** cold cream.
cremagliera, *n.f.* Rack-railway.
cremare, *v.t.* To cremate.
crematoio [crematOio], *n.m.* Furnace (for cremating).
crematorio [cremat Orio], *n.m.* Crematorium.
cremazione, *n.f.* Cremation.
cremisi, cremisino [crEmisi], *n.m.* Crimson.
Cremlino, *n.m.* (*Geog.*) Kremlin.
cremore, *n.m.* Essence, extract. **— di tartaro,** cream of tartar.
cremoso, *a.* Creamy.
crena, *n.f.* (*obs.*) Notch.
crenato, *a.* Notched.
creolo [crEolo], *n.m.a.* Creole.
creosoto, *n.m.* (*Chem.*) Creosote.
crepa, *n.f.* Crack, fissure.
crepacciato, *a.* Creviced, full of crevices.
crepaccio [crepAccio], *n.m.* Large crevice, crevasse.
crepacuore, *n.m.* Heartbreak.
crepamento, *n.m.* Cracking, splitting, fissuring.
crepapelle, *adv.* Immoderately. **Mangiare a —,** to eat enormously; **ridere a —,** to laugh immoderately.
crepare, *v.i.* To crack, to split; to die; (*fig.*) to do (anything) to excess. **— dalla rabbia,** to burst with rage; **— dalle risa,** to explode with laughter.
crepatura, *n.f.* Crack; (*Med.*) hernia.
crepitare, *v.i.* To crackle.
crepitio [crepitIo], *n.m.* Crackling.
crepuscolare, *a.* Crepuscular.
crepuscolo [crepUscolo], *n.m.* Twilight, gloaming, dusk.
crescendo, *n.m.* (*Mus.*) Crescendo; progress (toward a climax), increase.
crescente, *a.* Increasing, growing. **Luna —,** crescent moon.
crescenza, *n.f.* Growth, increase; (*Med.*) excrescence.
crescere [crEscere], *v.i.* To grow, to increase; to advance; to augment; to rise. **— di prezzo,** to increase in price; **— a vista d'occhio,** to grow apace, to grow visibly.
crescimento, *n.m.* Growth, increase, advance.
crescione, *n.m.* (*Bot.*) Water-cress; cress.
crescioneto, *n.m.* Water-cress bed.
crescita, cresciuta [crEscita], *n.f.* Increase, growth, expansion.
cresciuto, *n.m.* Increase (in knitting).
cresima [crEsima], *n.f.* (*Eccles.*) Chrism; sacrament of Confirmation.
cresimando, *n.m.* Candidate for Confirmation.
cresimare, *v.t.* (*Eccles.*) To confirm, to anoint.
Creso, *n.m.* (*Myth.*) Croesus; wealthy man.
crespa, *n.f.* Pleat, wrinkle, ripple.
crespare, *v.t.* To pleat.
crespo, *n.m.* Crape.
crespo, cresposo, *a.* Pleated, curled, wrinkled, frizzled; curly (hair). **Capelli crespi,** frizzled or curly hair.
cresta, *n.f.* Crest (in all senses), comb (of cock); mountain ridge, peak; (*fig.*) pride. **Alzar la —,** to grow cocky; **abbassare la —,** to be crestfallen, to sing small.
crestaia [crestAia], *n.f.* (*obs.*) Milliner.
crestato, *a.* Crested.
crestomazia [crestomazIa], *n.f.* Chrestomathy.
creta, *n.f.* Clay, chalk.
cretaceo [cretAceo], *a.* Clayey, cretaceous, chalky.
cretese, *n.m.a.* (*Geog.*) Cretan.
cretineria [cretinerIa], *n.f.* Nonsense, stupidity.
cretinismo, *n.m.* Idiocy, cretinism.
cretino, *n.m.* Idiot, cretin; stupid, dunce.
cretoso, *a.* Clayey, chalky.
crettare, *v.t.* To crack, to chap.
cretto, *n.m.* Crack (in a wall).
cria, *n.m.* Smallest bird in a nest; sickliest member of a family.
criare, *v.t.* (*Lit.*) To create.
cribrare, *v.t.* To sift.
cribro, *n.m.* Sieve.
cric, cricche, *n.m.* Creak; sound of glass breaking; grasshopper's chirp.

cricca, *n.f.* The ace, the two and the three (of a suit of cards); clique; ring.
cricchetto, *n.m.* Wrench, monkey-wrench.
cricchiare, *v.i.* To creak, to crack.
cricchio [crIcchio], *n.m.* Creak, creaking; whim.
cricco, *n.m.* (*Mech.*) Jack (for lifting). **Coltello a —,** jack-knife.
crimenlese, *n.m.* (*Law*) High treason, lese-majesty.
criminale, *n.m.a.* Criminal.
criminalista (*pl.* **criminalisti**), *n.m.* Criminologist; criminal lawyer.
criminalità [-à], *n.f.* Criminality.
criminalmente, *adv.* Criminally.
criminare, *v.t.* To charge with a crime [cp. **incriminare**].
crimine [crImine], *n.m.* Crime, offence, wrong-doing.
criminosità [-à], *n.f.* Criminality.
criminoso, *a.* Criminal, heinous, flagitious.
crinale, *n.m.* Crest (of a mountain); watershed; hair-comb.
crine, *n.m.* Horsehair; mane; (human) hair, locks; (vegetable) fibre.
criniera, *n.f.* Horse's mane; tail of a comet.
crinito, *a.* Hairy, long-haired. **Cometa crinita,** tailed comet.
crino, *n.m.* Horsehair stuffing; fibre.
crinoidi [crinOidi], *n.m.pl.* (*Zool.*) Crinoidea.
crinolina, *n.f.* Crinoline.
cripta, *n.f.* Crypt.
cripto, *n.m.* (*Chem.*) Krypton.
crisalide [crisAlide], *n.f.* (*Zool.*) Chrysalis.
crisantemo, *n.m.* (*Bot.*) Chrysanthemum.
crisaora [crisAora], *n.f.* (*Zool.*) Medusa; jelly-fish.
crisi, *n.f.* Crisis; slump; attack, fit. **— finanziaria,** financial crisis; **— ministeriale,** political crisis.
crisma, *n.m.* (*Eccles.*) Chrism.
crisolito, *n.m.* (*Min.*) Chrysolite.
crisoprazio, *n.m.* (*Min.*) Chrysoprase.
cristallaio [cristallAio], *n.m.* Glass-blower; dealer in glass-ware.
cristallame, *n.m.* Glass-ware, glass.
cristalleria [cristallerIa], *n.f.* Glass-ware, crystal-ware; glass works.
cristallino, *a.* Crystalline; clear, transparent.
cristallizzare, *v.t.* To crystallize. **Zucchero cristallizzato,** crystallized sugar.
cristallo, *n.m.* Crystal, rock-crystal; glass-ware; window-pane. **— a punta,** cut glass.
cristallografia [cristallografIa], *n.f.* Crystallography.
cristallografo [cristallOgrafo], *n.m.* Crystallographer.
cristalloide [cristallOide], *n.m.* Crystalloid.
cristianamente, *adv.* In a Christian spirit.
cristianesimo [cristianEsimo], *n.m.* Christianity (as a religion).
cristianità [-à], *n.f.* Christianity; Christendom.
cristianizzare, *v.t.* To christianize, to convert (to Christianity).
cristiano, *n.m.a.* Christian; (*fig.*) human being; decent, civilized; pious, religious.
Cristo, *n.m.* Christ; (*fig.*) a crucifix. **Gesù Cristo,** Jesus Christ.
Cristoforo [cristOforo], *n.m.* Christopher.
criterio [critErio], *n.m.* Criterion, standard; discernment, sense; principle. **Farsi un — di qualcuno,** to weigh up, to size up someone; **senza —,** senseless, rash.
critica [crItica], *n.f.* Criticism; review, critique; blame, censure; (*Philos.*) critique. **— d'arte,** art criticism.
criticabile [criticAbile], *a.* Open to criticism, disputable.
criticamente, *adv.* Critically.
criticare, *v.t.* To criticize; to censure; to examine.
critico [crItico], *n.m.* Critic, reviewer, censor.
critico [crItico], *a.* Critical, pertaining to criticism; censorious; risky. **Edizione critica,** critical edition; **una situazione critica,** an embarrassing situation.
crittogamo [crittOgamo], *n.m.a.* (*Bot.*) Cryptogam; cryptogamous.
crittografia [crittografIa], *n.f.* Cryptography.
crittografico [crittogrAfico], *a.* Cryptographic.
crittogramma (*pl.* **crittogrammi**), *n.m.* Cryptogram.
crivellare, *v.t.* To riddle, to sift. **— di palle,** to riddle with bullets.
crivellatura, *n.f.* Sifting; sifted matter.
crivello, *n.m.* Sieve, riddle.
croato, *n.m.a.* Croatian.
croccante, *n.m.* Almond sweetmeat, almond cake.
croccante, *a.* Crisp (of pastry), crackling.
croccare, *v.i.* To sound cracked, to creak, to crunch.
crochetta, *n.f.* Croquette.
crocchia [crOcchia], *n.f.* Chignon.
crocchiare, *v.i.* To cluck (as a hen); to crack (one's joints); to creak, to sound cracked.
crocchio [crOcchio], *n.m.* Group, circle, gathering, knot (of persons); crackling sound. **Stare in —,** to sit together and gossip.
croccia [crOccia], *n.f.* Cassock worn by a cardinal in conclave.
croccolare, *v.i.* To cluck (like a hen).
croccolone, *n.m.* (*Zool.*) Snipe.
croce, *n.f.* Cross; (*Print.*) dagger; (*fig.*) trial, trouble. **La Croce Rossa,** Red Cross; **in —,** crosswise; **a occhio e —,** judging roughly, at a rough guess; **punto a —,** cross-stitch; **avere la sua —,** to have one's trials; **gettare la — addosso a qualcuno,** to revile somebody; **farsi il segno della —,** to cross oneself, to make the sign of the cross.
croceo [crOceo], *a.* Saffron-coloured, saffron yellow.
crocesignato, *a.* Signed with a cross.
crocetta, *n.f.* Little cross; (*Naut.*) cross-tree; (*Print.*) dagger.
crocevia [crocevIa], *n.m.* Cross-roads.
crociare, *v.t.* To mark with a cross.
crociata, *n.f.* Crusade.
crociato, *n.m.* Crusader.
crocicchio [crocIcchio], *n.m.* Crossroads, crossing.
crocidamento, *n.m.* Croaking.
crocidare, *v.i.* To croak.
crociera, *n.f.* (*Naut.*) Cruise; cross-piece, cross-bar; intersection; (*Aviat.*) long-distance flight. **Andare in —,** to go on a cruise.
crocierista, *n.m.f.* Person taking a cruise.

crocifero [crocIfero], *n.m.* (*Eccles.*) Crucifer, cross-bearer.
crocifiggere [crocifIggere], *v.t.* To crucify; to torment.
crocifissione, *n.f.* Crucifixion.
crocifisso, *n.m.* Crucifix.
crociforme, *a.* Cruciform.
croco, *n.m.* (*Bot.*) Crocus; saffron.
crogiolare, *v.t.* To cook on a slow fire; to cook slowly; to anneal (glass); (*fig.*) to bubble over with satisfaction; to bask.
crogiolarsi, *v.r.* To make oneself comfortable; to snuggle. **— al sole,** to bask in the sun.
crogiolo [crOgiolo], *n.m.* Slow cooking, simmering.
crogiuolo, *n.m.* Crucible, melting-pot.
croio [crOio], *a.* (*Poet.*) Hard, stiff.
crollamento, *n.m.* Crumbling, ruin; collapse; downfall.
crollare, *v.t.i.* To shake, to crash, to collapse, to give way, to tumble down, to crumble. **— il capo,** to shake one's head; **— le spalle,** to shrug one's shoulders; **tutto l'edificio crollò,** the whole building collapsed.
crollata, *n.f.* Shake, toss, jolt.
crollo, *n.m.* Shake; fall, downfall, crash; ruin; (*Comm.*) failure.
croma, *n.f.* (*Mus.*) Quaver.
cromaticamente, *adv.* Chromatically.
cromatico [cromAtico], *a.* Chromatic.
cromatina, *n.f.* (*Chem.*) Chromatin.
cromato, *n.m.a.* (*Chem.*) Chromate; chromium-plated.
cromo, *n.m.a.* Chrome yellow, chrome; chromium.
cromolitografia [cromolitografIa], *n.f.* Chromo-lithography.
cromosomo, *n.m.* Chromosome.
cromotipia [cromotipIa], *n.f.* Colour-printing; colour-print.
cronaca, cronica [crOnaca, crOnica], *n.f.* Chronicle; current gossip (in a newspaper); news of the day; newspaper diary of events.
cronicamente, *adv.* Chronically.
cronicità [-à], *n.f.* (*Med.*) Chronic condition.
cronico [crOnico], *n.m.a.* (*Med.*) Chronic; incurable.
cronista, *n.m.f.* Chronicler, reporter.
cronistoria [cronistOria], *n.f.* Chronicle (of events).
cronografia [cronografIa], *n.f.* Chronography.
cronografo [cronOgrafo], *n.m.* Chronographer.
cronologia [cronologIa], *n.f.* Chronology.
cronologico [cronolOgico], *a.* Chronological.
cronologista, *n.m.f.* Chronologist.
cronometria [cronometrIa], *n.f.* Chronometry.
cronometrico [cronomEtrico], *a.* Chronometrical.
cronometrista, *n.m.* (*Sport*) Time-keeper.
cronometro [cronOmetro], *n.m.* Chronometer.
cronometraggio, *n.m.* Timing.
cronometrare, *v.t.* To time.
crosciare, *v.i.* To rain in torrents, to pour; to gurgle; to roar (with applause, etc.).
croscio [crOscio], *n.m.* Splash, gurgle, downpour [cp. **scroscio**].
crosta, *n.f.* Crust, rind; shell; incrustation; (*Med.*) scab; surface.
crostaceo [crostAceo], *n.m.* (*Zool.*) Crustacean.
crostata, *n.f.* Pie, tart.
crostino, *n.m.* (Piece of) toast, buttered toast.
crostoso, *a.* Crusty; (*Med.*) scabby.
crotalo [crOtalo], *n.m.* (*Zool.*) Rattlesnake.
cruccevole [cruccEvole], *a.* Easily vexed.
crucciamento, *n.m.* Grave torment, affliction.
crucciare, *v.t.* To trouble, to worry; to irritate, to vex.
crucciarsi, *v.r.* To be vexed, to get irritated; to fret, to worry.
crucciatamente, *adv.* Vexedly, offendedly.
crucciato, *p.p.a.* Worried; vexed, angered.
cruccio [crUccio], *n.m.* Worry; vexation; grief; anger.
crucciosamente, *adv.* Angrily.
cruccioso, *a.* Angry, quick-tempered; sulky.
cruciale, *a.* Crucial, decisive; cross-shaped.
cruciare, *v.t.* To torment.
cruciforme, *a.* Cruciform.
crudamente, *adv.* Harshly, severely; crudely, roughly.
crudele, *a.* Cruel, merciless; grievous, sore, bitter; ferocious.
crudelmente, *adv.* Cruelly.
crudeltà [-à], *n.f.* Cruelty, inhumanity; atrocity.
crudezza, crudità [-à], *n.f.* Crudity, crudeness; rawness, unripeness, harshness.
crudo, *a.* Raw, uncooked, unripe; severe, cruel. **Seta cruda,** raw silk.
cruento, *a.* Bloody, sanguinary; blood-stained; (*fig.*) horrible, dreadful.
crumiro, *n.m.* Black-leg, scab (in strikes).
cruna, *n.f.* Eye of a needle.
cruore, *n.m.* (*Anat.*) Haemoglobin.
crup, cruppe, *n.m.* (*Med.*) Croup.
crurale, *a.* (*Anat.*) Pertaining to the leg or thigh, crural.
crusca, *n.f.* Bran, chaff. **La Crusca,** the Florentine Academy of Letters, founded in 1582.
cruscaio [cruscAio], *n.m.* Affected person; purist; "high-brow".
cruscante, *n.m.* One who affects to speak and write pure Tuscan.
cruschello, *n.m.* Fine bran.
cruscherella, *n.f.* Children's game with bran-tub.
cruscotto, *n.m.* (*Motor.*) Instrument panel, dash-board.
cubare, *v.t.* (*Math.*) To cube.
cubatura, *n.f.* (*Math.*) Cubature, measurement (of volume).
cubebe, *n.m.* (*Bot.*) Cubeb.
cubia [cubIa], *n.f.* (*Naut.*) Hawse-hole.
cubico [cUbico], *a.* Cubic.
cubicolo [cubIcolo], *n.m.* Cubicle, cell.
cubiforme, *a.* Cubiform.
cubismo, *n.m.* (*Art*) Cubism.
cubista, *n.m.f.* Cubist.
cubitale, *a.* (*Anat.*) Cubital. **In caratteri cubitali,** in huge letters.
cubito [cUbito], *n.m.* (*Anat.*) Elbow; cubit.
cubo, *n.m.a.* Cube; cubic. **Metro —,** cubic metre.
cuboide [cubOide], *a.* Cuboid.
cuccagna, *n.f.* Abundance, plenty; good fortune; godsend. **Paese di —,** land of

Cockaigne; (*Sport*) **albero della —**, greasy pole. **Che cuccagna!** What luck!

cuccare, *v.t.* (*colloq.*) To take in, to humbug.

cuccetta, *n.f.* Bunk, berth (in train or ship).

cucchiaia [cucchiAia], *n.f.* Ladle: scoop of a dredge; trowel.

cucchiaiata, *n.f.* Spoonful.

cucchiaino, *n.m.* Teaspoon.

cucchiaio [cucchiAio], *n.m.* Spoon; spoonful. **— da tavola,** tablespoon; **— da frutta,** dessert spoon.

cucchiaione, *n.m.* Large spoon, ladle; soup ladle.

cuccia [cUccia], *n.f.* Shake-down (bed); dog's bed; couch.

cucciarsi, *v.r.* (Of a dog) to curl round and lie down.

cuccio, cucciolo [cUccio, cUcciolo], *n.m.* Puppy.

cucco, *n.m.* Pet, darling, favourite (child).

cuccù, cucù [-ù, -ù], *n.m.* (*Zool.*) Cuckoo. **Orologio a —,** cuckoo clock [cp. **cuculo**].

cuccuma [cUccuma], *n.f.* (*colloq.*) Coffee-pot. **Non mi far girare la —,** don't put me out, don't provoke me.

cuccuruccù [-ù], *n.m.* Cock's crow; cock-a-doodle-doo.

cuccuveggia [cuccuvEggia], *n.f.* Owl.

cucicchiare, *v.t.* To sew poorly.

cucina, *n.f.* Kitchen; cooking; cookery; stove, range. **Far —,** to cook; **— casalinga,** plain cooking; **— a gas,** gas cooking; **— economica,** kitchen range; **libro di —,** cookery book.

cucinare, *v.t.i.* To cook; to dress (a fowl, etc.); to arrange, to deal with in a summary fashion.

cucinatura, *n.f.* (Practice of) cooking.

cuciniere, cuciniera, *n.m.f.* Cook; cookery book.

cucire, *v.t.i.* To sew, to stitch, to tack; (*fig.*) to cheat, to double-cross. **Macchina da —,** sewing-machine; **ago da —,** needle; **— una ferita,** to stitch a wound.

cucito, *n.m.* Sewing, needlework; stitching.

cucitrice, *n.f.* Seamstress.

cucitura, *n.f.* Seam; sewing; (*Med.*) suture.

cuculiare, *v.t.* To mock, to jeer at; to cry cuckoo.

cuculo, cuculio, *n.m.* (*Zool.*) Cuckoo. **Fior di —,** cuckoo-flower, ragged robin.

cucurbita [cucUrbita], *n.f.* Gourd, pumpkin; (*colloq.*) head.

cucuzza, *n.f.* (*colloq.*) Pate, top of the head.

cuffia [cUffia], *n.f.* Bonnet (of a child), cap; nightcap; coif; caul; (*Radio*) head-phones; (*Theat.*) prompter's box; (*Photo.*) dark cloth. **— da bagno,** bathing cap; **uscirne per il rotto della —,** to escape by the skin of one's teeth.

cugina, cugino, *n.f.m.* Cousin. **Cugino in secondo grado,** second cousin.

cui, *pron.* (after prep.) Whom, which; (with def. art.) whose, of which. **Il signore il cui libro hai trovato,** the gentleman whose book you found; **la signora a cui Lei ha dato la lettera,** the lady to whom you gave the letter.

culatta, *n.f.* Breech (of gun, etc.); seat (of trousers); rump.

culbianco, *n.m.* (*Zool.*) Stonechat, wheatear.

culinaria [culinAria], *n.f.* Culinary art; cookery. **Scuola —,** school of cookery.

culinario [culinArio], *a.* Culinary.

culla, *n.f.* Cradle, cot; (*fig.*) birthplace.

cullamento, *n.m.* Rocking, lulling.

cullare, *v.t.* To rock, to lull; to sway; to dandle; to delude.

cullarsi, *v.r.* To delude oneself; to cherish illusions. **— in dolci speranze,** to indulge in fond hopes.

culminante, *a.* Culminating.

culminare, *v.i.* To culminate, to reach the summit.

culmine [cUlmine], *n.m.* Apex, top, summit, climax.

culmo, *n.m.* (*Bot.*) Stalk (of wheat).

culo, *n.m.* (*colloq.*) Backside, arse; buttocks; rump (of animals).

culto, *n.m.a.* Cult, worship, creed; cultivated (in all senses); learned [cp. **colto**].

cultore, *n.m.* Cultivator; erudite person. **Cultori delle lettere,** men devoted to letters.

cultro, *n.m.* (*obs.*) Sacrificial knife.

cultura, *n.f.* Culture, education, scholarship, learning, erudition; agriculture, farming; crop [cp. **coltura**].

culturale, *a.* Cultural.

cumolo, cumulo [cUmolo, cUmulo], *n.m.* Heap, pile; store; lot; excess; cumulus cloud. **— di circostanze,** series of circumstances.

cumulare, *v.t.* To accumulate, to heap up [cp. **accumulare**].

cumulativamente, *adv.* Cumulatively.

cumulativo, *a.* Cumulative; inclusive. **Biglietto —,** party ticket.

cumulazione, *n.f.* Accumulation; heaping up.

cuna, *n.f.* Cradle.

cuneato, *a.* Wedge-shaped.

cuneiforme, *a.* Cuneiform.

cuneo [cUneo], *n.m.* Wedge.

cunetta, *n.f.* Gutter (in road); gulley; ditch.

cunicolo [cunIcolo], *n.m.* (*Mil.*) Mine; underground passage for mining.

cuoca, *n.f.* (Female) cook.

cuocere [cuOcere], *v.t.i.* To cook (by every method); to fire (bricks, etc.); (*fig.*) to smart; to vex. **Lascialo — nel suo brodo,** let him stew in his own juice; **— il pane,** to bake the bread.

cuocersi, *v.r.* To be cooked; to get vexed.

cuoco, *n.m.* Cook. **Capo —,** chef, head cook.

cuoiaio [cuoiAio], *n.m.* Leather-seller; saddler.

cuoiame, *n.m.* Leather, leather goods; dressed hide.

cuoio [cuOio] (pl. **cuoi,** *m.*, **cuoia,** *f.*) Leather, skin, hide; (*fig.*) limbs. **Stender le cuoia,** to stretch one's legs, to go to bed; **tirar le cuoia,** to die; **cuoio capelluto,** scalp.

cuore, *n.m.* Heart; love, affection; generosity; courage; centre; (*Cards*) heart. **Nel — della notte,** in the dead of night; **nel — dell'inverno,** in the depth of winter; **senza —,** heartless; **col — in mano,** sincerely; **mi sta a — il suo successo,** I have his welfare at heart; **di tutto —,** most heartily; **farsi —,** to take courage; **a —,** heart-shaped

cuoricino, *n.m.* Darling, sweetheart.

cupamente, *adv.* Sombrely, drearily.

cupè [-è], *n.m.* Coupé, private compartment; brougham.

cupezza, *n.f.* Darkness, gloom; depth.
cupidamente, *adv.* Covetously, greedily.
cupidigia, cupidità [cupidIgia, **-à**], *n.f.* Covetousness, cupidity, greediness, greed.
cupido [cUpido], *a.* Covetous, desirous, greedy.
Cupido [cupIdo], *n.m.* Cupid; love.
cupo, *a.* Dark, gloomy, sombre; hollow; taciturn; deep. **Verde —,** dark green.
cupola [cUpola], *n.f.* Dome, cupola. **A —,** dome-like.
cupolino, *n.m.* Summer-house, arbour.
cupolo [cUpolo], *a.* Very full, heaped up.
cupone, *n.m.* Coupon.
cupreo [cUpreo], *a* Cupreous, copper-coloured.
cura, *n.f.* Care, diligence, carefulness; solicitude, anxiety; (*Med.*) treatment, remedy, healing, cure; (*Eccles.*) parish, church. **Aver — di una cosa,** to take care of a thing; **a Lei ne commetto la —,** I leave it in your care; **lavorare senza —,** to work carelessly; **essere in —,** to be under medical treatment; **far una —,** to follow a treatment; **la — del sole,** sunbathing cure; **a — di,** edited by; **— d'anime,** cure of souls; **casa di —,** nursing-home.
curabile [curAbile], *a.* Curable.
curabilità [**-à**], *n.f.* Curability.
curandaio [curandAio], *n.m.* Bleacher.
curante, *a.* Attending, attentive, careful. **Medico —,** doctor in attendance; **non —,** careless [cp. **noncurante**].
curare, *v.t.* To care, to mind, to pay heed to; (*Med.*) to treat, to cure, to heal; (*Lit.*) to revise, to edit.
curarsi, *v.r.* To mind, to pay heed to; to take care of oneself. **Non mi curo di lui,** I don't take any notice of him; **— la salute,** to look after one's health.
curaro, *n.m.* (*Med.*) Curare.
curatela, *n.f.* (*Law*) Guardianship; (*Comm.*) **— di fallimento,** receivership (in bankruptcy).
curativo, *a.* Curative.
curato, *n.m.* Parish priest; curate. **Andar davanti al —,** to get married.
curatore, curatrice, *n.m.f.* Guardian, trustee, administrator; curator; (*Law*) official receiver.
curia [cUria], *n.f.* (*Eccles.*) Court, tribunal; legal profession. **La Curia Romana,** the Holy See; **—vescovile,** bishop's court.
curiale, *n.m.a.* Lawyer; curial; legal; of the Papal Court. **Linguaggio —,** legal phraseology.
curialescamente, *adv.* In legal style; formally.
curialesco, *a.* Lawyer-like; formal.
curiosamente, *adv.* Curiously; with curiosity.
curiosare, *v.i.* To pry into, to be curious about, to be inquisitive, to eavesdrop; to listen.
curiosità [**-à**], *n.f.* Curiosity, inquisitiveness; oddness, peculiarity.
curioso, *a* Curious, inquisitive; odd, peculiar; sight-seer, onlooker. **È —!** That's odd!
curricolo [currIcolo], *n.m.* Curriculum, course of study
curro, *n.m.* Roller (for moving weights); course, movement.
cursore, *n.m.* Messenger; (*Law*) tipstaff, messenger; (*Mech.*) slide-rule.
curule, *a.* Curule.
curva, *n.f.* Curve, bend, turn. **— pericolosa,** dangerous bend; **— a forcella,** hairpin bend; **— occulta,** concealed turning.
curvamento, *n.m.* Curvature, curving.
curvare, *v.t.* To curve, to bend.
curvarsi, *v.r.* To stoop, to bend down, to bow down.
curvatura, *n.f.* Curving, bending, curvature; convexity.
curvilineo [curvilIneo], *a.* Curvilinear.
curvità [**-à**], *n.f.* Curvature, curvedness.
curvo, *a.* Curved, bent, crooked. **Spalle curve,** round shoulders.
cuscinetto, *n.m.* Small cushion; pin-cushion; pillion; (*Mech.*) bearing. **— a sfere,** ball-bearings; **— di spinta,** collar-thrust; (*Pol.*) **stato —,** buffer state.
cuscuta [cUscuta], *n.f.* (*Bot.*) Bindweed.
cuspidale, *a.* (*Arch.*) Cuspidal.
cuspide [cUspide], *n.f.* Cusp, point; spire, pinnacle.
custode, *n.m.* Keeper, guardian, watchman; door-keeper; warder.
custode, *a.* Guardian. **Angelo —,** guardian angel; (*facet.*) policeman.
custodia [custOdia], *n.f.* Custody, care, protection; charge; safe-keeping; box, case (for violin). **Camera di —,** strong-room,
custodimento, *n.m.* Keeping, safeguarding.
custodire, *v.t.* To keep, to guard, to preserve; to overlook, to protect, to take care of.
cutaneo [cutAneo], *a.* Cutaneous.
cute, *n.f.* (Human) skin.
cuticagna, *n.f.* Scalp; nape.
cuticola [cutIcola], *n.f.* Cuticle.
cutrettola [cutrEttola], *n.f.* (*Zool.*) Wagtail.
czeco, *a.* Czech.

D

D, d, *n.m.f.* Fourth letter of the Italian alphabet.
da, *prep.* (With **il, lo, la, i, gli, le** becomes **dal, dallo, dalla, dai, dagli, dalle**). From, by, to, at, for; like, as a; for the purpose of; because of. **Venire da Roma,** to come from Rome; **uscire dal palazzo,** to go out of the palace; **amato da tutti,** loved by all; **vado da mia madre,** I'm going to my mother's; **andiamo da lui,** let's go to his house; **agire da eroe,** to act like a hero; **fare da padre,** to act as a father; **saltare dalla gioia,** to jump for joy; **macchina da cucire,** sewing-machine; **punta da disegno,** drawing-pin; **una commedia da ridere,** an amusing play; **un problema da risolvere,** a problem to solve; **aver da fare,** to have to do; **non scrive da due anni,** he hasn't written for the last two years; **da oltre un anno,** for over a year; **da oggi in poi,** from to-day on; **da capo,** over again; **da banda,** aside; **da lontano,** from afar; **da presso, da vicino,** nearby; **da senno,** seriously; (*colloq.*) **da bravo,** like a good boy; **da burla,** as a joke; **da dentro,** from within; **da fuori,** from outside; **da canto,** aside, apart.

dabbasso, da basso, *adv.* Downstairs, down below.
dabbenaggine [dabbenAggine], *n.f.* Simple-mindedness, artlessness; dullness, stupidity.
dabbene, *a.* Honest, respectable, upright; well-bred. **Gente —,** honest folk; **uomo —,** a good man, an honest fellow; **— uomo,** simpleton.
daccanto, *adv.* Near by, close to.
daccapo, da capo, *adv.* Again, over again, once more.
dacchè, da che, *conj.* Since, since when, as.
daccordo, d'accordo, *adv.* Agreed; in harmony.
daddolo [dAddolo], *n.m.* Coaxing manner; mincing way; childish grimace or gesture.
dadeggiare, *v.i.* To throw dice.
dado, *n.m.* Die (in game of dice); cube; pedestal; (*Mech.*) nut (for screw or bolt). **Il — è tratto,** the die is cast; **a dadi,** checked (pattern).
daffare, da fare, *n.m.* Work occupation, business. **Il — cotidiano,** the daily grind.
dafila [dAfila], *n.f.* (*Zool.*) Pin-tail duck.
Dafne, *n.f.* (*Myth.Bot.*) Daphne.
daga, *n.f.* Dagger, dirk, poniard.
dagherrotipia, dagherrotipo [dagherrotipIa, dagherrOtipo], *n.f.m.* (*Phot.*) Daguerrotype.
dagli, dai [cp. **da**].
daina [dAina], *n.f.* (*Zool.*) Doe.
daino [dAino], *n.m.* (*Zool.*) Deer, buck. **Pelle di —,** buckskin.
dalia [dAlia], *n.f.* (*Bot.*) Dahlia.
dallato, da lato, *adv.* Beside, by the side of; close to, near.
dalmatica [dalmAtica], *n.f.* (*Eccles.*) Dalmatic.
dalmatico [dalmAtico], *a.* Dalmatian.
daltonico [daltOnico], *a.* Colour-blind.
daltonismo, *n.m.* Colour-blindness, daltonism.
d'altronde, *adv.* On the other hand, besides, moreover.
dama, *n.f.* Lady, noblewoman, gentlewoman; dame; (game of) draughts; king (in draughts); dance-partner; sweetheart. **Giuocare a —,** to play at draughts.
damare, *v.t.* To crown (at draughts); to make a queen (at chess).
damascare, *v.t.* To damask.
damascatura, *n.f.* Damasking.
damaschinare, *v.t.* To damascene (a sword blade).
Damasco, *n.f.m.* (*Geog.*) Damascus; damask.
damerino, *n.m.* Dandy, beau, fop, coxcomb.
damiere, *n.m.* Draught-board.
damigella, *n.f.* Young woman; maid-of-honour; damsel.
damigello, *n.m.* (*Hist.*) Squire, young nobleman.
damigiana, *n.f.* Demijohn, carboy.
damina, *n.f.* Pretty young woman.
damma, *n.f.* (*obs.*) Deer.
dammara [dAmmara], *n.f.* Amber-yellow resin.
damo, *n.m.* (*colloq.*) Gallant, wooer, lover, beau; paramour.
danaro [cp. **denaro**].
danaroso, *a.* Moneyed, rich, wealthy.
danda, *n.f.* Leading-string (for children), brace-band. **Dande,** braces.
danese, *n.m.a.* Dane; Danish; Great Dane(dog).
Daniele, *n.m.* Daniel.
Danimarca, *n.f.* Denmark.
dannabile [dannAbile], *a.* Damnable; blameable.
dannabilmente, *adv.* Damnably.
dannamento, *n.m.* Damning, blaming.
dannare, *v.t.* To damn, to condemn, to doom; to blame; to torment.
dannato, *n.m.* One that is damned. **Urlare come un —,** to shriek like one of the damned.
dannazione, *n.f.* Damnation.
danneggiamento, *n.m.* Damaging, damage, injury.
danneggiare, *v.t.* To damage, to harm, to injure, to impair.
danneggiarsi, *v.r.* To suffer damage.
danneggiato (1), *n.m.* Injured person; wronged person.
danneggiato (2), *p.p.a.* Injured, damaged. **Merci danneggiate,** damaged goods.
danno, *n.m.* Damage, harm, havoc; injury; loss; prejudice. **A mio —,** to my cost; **avere il — e le beffe,** to have all kicks and no ha'pence; **risarcire i danni,** to pay damages; **subire un —,** to suffer a damage; **accertare i danni,** to assess damages.
dannosamente, *adv.* Hurtfully, harmfully, to disadvantage.
dannoso, *a.* Hurtful, noxious, injurious.
dante, *n.m.* **Pelle di —,** buckskin.
danteggiare, *v.i.* To imitate the style of Dante.
dantesco, *a.* Dantean, Dantesque
dantista, *n.m.f.* Dante scholar.
danubiano, *a.* Danubian.
danza, *n.f.* Dance, ball; dance music.
danzante, *a.* Dancing. **Tè —,** tea-dance.
danzare, *v.t.i.* To dance.
danzatore, danzatrice, *n.m.f.* Dancer; ballet-dancer.
dape, *n.f.* (*obs.*) Banquet, feast; spiritual food.
dappertutto, *adv.* Everywhere; on all sides.
dappiede, dappiè, *adv.* At the foot, below.
dappocaggine [dappocAggine], *n.f.* Unfitness, ineptitude, worthlessness; stupidity.
dappoco, *a.* Incapable, inept; good-for-nothing; worthless.
dappoi, dappoichè, *adv.* After, then; since.
dappresso, *adv.* Near, close by.
dapprima, *adv.* At first, firstly.
dapprincipio [dapprincIpio], *adv.* From the first, in the beginning; to start with.
Dardanelli, *n.m.pl.* The Dardanelles.
dardeggiare, *v.t.* To dart; to throw darts; to shoot forth; to dart rays (of the sun).
dardo, *n.m.* Dart, arrow.
dare, *v.t.i.* To give; to bring, to present, to offer; to bestow, to confer upon; to bring, to yield, to produce; to look out upon; to break out. **— il buon giorno,** to say "good morning"; **— a credere,** to make believe; **— fuoco a,** to set on fire; **— assicurazione,** to give assurance; **— del tu,** to address familiarly (in the 2nd pers. s.); **— a vedere,** to show, to hint; **— piacere,** to give pleasure; **gli do cinquantanni,** I take him to be fifty;

— **sui nervi,** to get on one's nerves; — **delle busse,** to beat, to thrash; — **contro qualcuno,** to be hostile to someone; — **nell'occhio,** to catch one's eye; **non mi è dato di,** I am not allowed to; **il balcone dà sul fiume,** the balcony overlooks the river; — **di cozzo,** to knock against; — **del ladro a qualcuno,** to call someone a thief; — **gli esami,** to sit for exams; — **in prestito,** to lend; **darsela a gambe,** to take to one's heels; — **in riso,** to burst out laughing; — **torto a,** to blame.
dare, *n.m.* (*Comm.*) Debit. — **e avere,** debit and credit; **passare al —,** to pass to the debit side.
darsena [dArsena], *n.f.* Dock, basin; small harbour; boat-house.
darsi, *v.r.* To give oneself up to, to surrender; to devote oneself; to be given to; to happen. — **intorno,** to look about; — **d'attorno,** to take pains to, to exert oneself; **può —,** it may be so, possibly; — **la briga di,** to take the trouble to; — **il caso,** to happen; — **pace,** to resign oneself; — **per vinto,** to give in; — **al commercio,** to go into business; — **alla fuga,** to take to flight.
dartro, *n.m.* (*Med.*) Rash; skin eruption.
darvinismo, *n.m.* Darwinism.
dasiuro, *n.m.* (*Zool.*) Dasyure.
dassai, *a.* Much.
data, *n.f.* Date; (*Eccles.*) church benefice; deal (cards); service (tennis). **Di vecchia —,** old; **di fresca —,** recent; — **del bollo postale,** date of post-mark.
datare, *v.t.* To date.
datariata, *n.f.* Bursar's office or post.
datario [datArio], *n.m.* (*Eccles.*) Bursar of the Vatican.
dativo, *n.m.* (*Gram.*) Dative.
dativo, *a.* **Tutore —,** guardian (appointed by parent or the court).
dato (1), *n.m.* Datum, fact; element; quantity; hint. **Voglio dati,** I want facts; **raccogliere dati,** to collect data.
dato (2), *p.p.a.* Given, established; addicted, inclined to; determined. — **che,** seeing that, supposing that, since.
datore, *n.m.* Donor, giver. — **di lavoro,** employer; — **di una cambiale,** drawer of a bill; — **di ogni bene,** God.
dattero [dAttero], *n.m.* (*Bot.*) Date-palm; date (fruit).
dattilico [dattIlico], *a.* (*Poet.*) Dactylic.
dattilo [dAttilo], *n.m.* (*Poet.*) Dactyl.
dattilografia [dattilografIa], *n.f.* Typewriting.
dattilografo, dattilografa [dattilOgrafo -a], *n.m.f.* Typist.
dattilologia [dattilologIa], *n.f.* Deaf-and-dumb language.
dattiloscopia [dattiloscopIa], *n.f.* Examination of finger-prints.
dattiloscritto, *n.m.a.* Typescript; typewritten.
dattorno, d'attorno, *adv.* Around, round about. **Levarsi — qualcuno,** to get rid of someone; **qui —,** hereabouts.
davanti, *adv. prep. n.m.a.* Before, in front of; front. **I denti —,** the front teeth; **il — della casa,** the front of the house.
davanzale, *n.m.* Window-sill.
davanzo, *adv.* In abundance, superabundantly. **Io ne ho —,** I have more than enough of it.
Davide [dAvide], *n.m.* David.
davidico [davIdico], *a.* Of David. **Canti davidici,** psalms of David.
davvantaggio [davvantAggio], *adv.* (*obs.*) Overmuch.
davvero, *adv.* Indeed, really, in truth. **Fare per —,** to mean it, to be in earnest; **Davvero?** Is it so? Really?; **non è — giusto che,** it is not fair that.
daziabile [dazıAbile], *a.* Liable to duty.
daziare, *v.t.* To tax, to lay an impost on, to levy duty.
daziario [daziArio], *a.* Pertaining to duties or imposts. **Cinta daziaria,** city boundaries, toll-gates; **tariffa daziaria,** customs rates.
daziere, *n.m.* Customs officer.
dazio [dAzio], *n.m.* Duty, municipal toll, impost. — **di consumo,** excise duty; **vendere fuori —,** to sell in bond; **magazzino fuori —,** bonded warehouse; — **d'entrata, d'uscita,** import, export duty; — **di consumo,** food-tax, excise.
de', (abb. of **dei**) Of the.
dea, *n.f.* Goddess.
dealbare, *v.t.* (*obs.*) To whiten.
deambulare, *v.i.* To walk about, to walk round.
debbiare, *v.t.* (*Agric.*) To manure with wood ash.
debbio [dEbbio], *n.m.* Ashes (for manure); place fertilized with such ashes.
debellamento, *n.m.* Defeat, rout.
debellare, *v.t.* To conquer, to subdue, to defeat.
debellatore, *n.m.* Conqueror.
debile [dEbile], *a.* (*Poet.*) Weak.
debilità [-à], *n.f.* Weakness, debility.
debilitante, *a.* Enervating, weakening, enfeebling.
debilitare, *v.t.* To weaken, to enfeeble, to debilitate.
debilitazione, *n.f.* Weakness; (the act of or result of becoming) crippled; infirmity in any limb.
debitamente, *adv.* Duly, regularly, properly, justly.
debito (1) [dEbito], *n.m.* Debt; due; obligation; deficit; duty. (*Comm.*) **mettere, porre, scrivere a —,** to debit; **uscire di —,** to get out of debt; — **ipotecario,** mortgage debt; **avere un —,** to be in debt; — **pubblico,** national debt.
debito (2) [dEbito], *a.* Due, proper. **A tempo —,** in due time; **con le debite maniere,** in the proper manner.
debitore, debitora, debitrice, *n.m.f.* Debtor. **Debitori diversi,** sundry debtors.
debituccio [debitUccio], *n.m.* Petty debt.
debole [dEbole], *n.m.* Weakness; weak person; foible. **Avere un — per,** to have a weakness for; **conosco il suo —,** I know his weakness.
debole [dEbole], *a.* Weak, feeble; faint (image); (*Comm.*) dull; (*fig.*) ineffective, pointless.
debolezza, *n.f.* Weakness, feebleness, debility; foible. **Le debolezze umane,** human failings.
debolmente, *adv.* Feebly, faintly, languidly.
deboscia [debOscia], *n.f.* Debauchery.
debosciato, *a.* Profligate; debauched.

debraiare, *v.t.* (*Motor*) To declutch.
debuttante, *n.m.f.* (*Theat.*) Actor making a first appearance on the stage.
debuttare, *v.i.* To make a first appearance or attempt.
debutto, *n.m.* (*Theat.*) First appearance (on the stage), debut.
deca, *n.f.* (*Hist.*) Group of ten books in Livy's history.
decade [dEcade], *n.f.* Decade (ten years or ten days).
decadente, *a.* Decadent.
decadenza, *n.f.* Decadence, decay, decline; forfeiture.
decadere, *v.i.* To decay, to decline, to fall off; to perish; to become obsolete, to lapse. **— da una carica,** to end a term of office.
decadimento, *n.m.* Decay, fall off, decline.
decaduto, *p.p.a.* Decayed, declined; impoverished.
decaedro, *n.m.* (*Geom.*) Decahedron.
decagono [decAgono], *n.m.* (*Geom.*) Decagon.
decagrammo, *n.m.* Decagram, 10 grammes.
decalcomania [decalcomanIa], *n.f.* Transfer (of coloured designs to paper, glass, etc.).
decalitro, *n.m.* Measure of 10 litres.
decalogo [decAlogo], *n.m.* Decalogue.
decametro [decAmetro], *n.m.* Distance of 10 metres.
decampare, *v.i.* To decamp; (*fig.*) to recede.
decana, *n.f.* (*Eccles.*) Mother superior.
decanato, *n.m.* (*Eccles.*) Dean; deanery; seniority.
decano, *n.m.* Senior, oldest member, doyen; (*Eccles.*) dean.
decantare, *v.t.* To praise, to extol, to exalt, to laud, to celebrate; to decant (liquor).
decantazione, *n.f.* Pouring off (liquor); decanting.
decapetalo [decapEtalo], *n.m.* (*Bot.*) Flower with ten petals.
decapitare, *v.t.* To behead, to decapitate.
decapitazione, *n.f.* Decapitation, beheading.
decapodi [decApodi], *n.m.pl.* (*Zool.*) Decapoda.
decarburare, *v.t.* To decarbonize.
decarburazione, *n.f.* Decarbonization.
decasillabo [decasIllabo], *n.m.* (*Poet.*) Decasyllable.
decedere [decEdere], *v.i.* To die.
deceduto, *p.p.* Deceased, dead.
decembre, *n.m.* December [cp. **dicembre**].
decembrino, *a.* Decemberish, wintry.
decemvirato, *n.m.* Decemvirate.
decennale, *n.m.a.* Tenth anniversary; recurring every ten years.
decenne, *a.* Ten years old; decennial.
decennio [decEnnio], *n.m.* Period of ten years.
decente, *a.* Decent, proper, respectable; passable.
decentemente, *adv.* Decently, decorously.
decentramento, *n.m.* Decentralization.
decentrare, *v.t.* To decentralize.
decenza, *n.f.* Decency, propriety, decorum. **Gabinetto di —,** water-closet.
decernere [decErnere], *v.i.* (*obs.*) To discern.
decesso, *n.m.a.* Decease, death; dead, deceased. **Atto di —,** death certificate.
dechinare, *v.i.* To bow down, to bend down.
decidere [decIdere], *v.t.* To decide, to settle (quarrels, etc.); to resolve.
decidersi, *v.r.* To decide, to resolve, to come to a decision, to make up one's mind.
decidimento, *n.m.* (Act of) deciding.
deciduo [decIduo], *a.* (*Bot.*) Deciduous falling off.
decifrabile [decifrAbile], *a.* Decipherable.
decifrare, *v.t.* To decipher; to explain.
decifrazione, *n.f.* Decipherment, decifering; explanation.
decigrammo, *n.m.* Decigramme.
decilitro, *n.m.* Tenth of a litre.
decima [dEcima], *n.f.* Tenth part; tithe. **Imporre una —,** to impose a tithe.
decimale, *n.m.a.* Decimal. **Sistema metrico decimale,** decimal system.
decimare, *v.t.* To decimate; to destroy a tenth part.
decimazione, Decimation.
decimetro [decImetro], *n.m.* Decimetre, tenth of a metre.
decimo [dEcimo], *n.m.a.* Tenth part, tithe, tenth. **Luigi decimo,** Louis the Tenth.
decimoprimo, decimosecondo, decimoterzo, etc., *n.m.* Eleventh, twelfth, thirteenth, etc.
decina, *n.f.* Ten, half-score.
decisamente, *adv.* Decidedly, resolutely, definitely.
decisione, *n.f.* Decision; conclusion; resolution; decree.
decisivamente, *adv.* Decisively, finally, conclusively.
decisivo, *a.* Decisive, conclusive, final. **Voto —,** casting vote.
deciso, *p.p.a.* Decided, resolved, settled.
decisorio [decisOrio], *a.* Decisive (in an argument, etc.).
declamare, *v.t.* To declaim, to recite; to utter, to inveigh.
declamatore, *n.m.* Orator, declaimer.
declamatorio [declamatOrio], *a.* Declamatory; oratorical.
declamazione, *n.f.* Declamation, harangue.
declassare, *v.t.* To underclass; to lose caste.
declinabile [declinAbile], *a.* Declinable.
declinare, *v.t.i.* To decline, to decay, to sink, to fall off; to deteriorate; to refuse, to reject; (*Gram.*) to decline, to inflect. **Il sole declina,** the sun sets; **— un incarico,** to decline an office.
declinatorio [declinatOrio], *a.* Declining. **Ago —,** dipping needle.
declinazione, *n.f.* (*Gram.*) Declension; declination, deviation; gradient, slope; (*Astron.*) declination.
declino, *n.m.* Decline, setting; falling off.
declive, declivo, *a.* Declining, sloping.
declivio [declIvio], *n.m.* Slope, declivity.
declività [-à], *n.f.* Declivity, slope; steepness.
decoesione, *n.f.* (*Elec.*) Decoherence.
decollaggio [decollAggio], *n.m.* (*Aviat.*) Taking-off.
decollare (1), *v.i.* (*Aviat.*) To take off.
decollare (2), *v.t.* To decapitate, to behead.
decollazione, *n.f.* Decollation; beheading (esp. of St. John Baptist).
decollo, *n.m.* (*Aviat.*) Take-off.
decolorante, *n.m.* Decolorant, bleaching substance.
decolorare, *v.t.* To discolour, [cp. **discolorare**].

decolorazione, *n.f.* Discoloration; loss of colour.
decomponente, *a.* Decomposing.
decomponibile [decomponIbile], *a.* Decomposable.
decomporre, *v.t.* To decompose, to separate; to dissolve. **— un numero,** to find the prime factors of a number.
decomporsi, *v.r.* To become decomposed, to putrefy.
decomposizione, *n.f.* Decomposition, putrefaction.
decomposto, *p.p.a.* Decomposed, rotten.
deconto, *n.m.* (*Comm.*) **Libretto di —,** bank pass-book.
decorare, *v.t.* To decorate, to adorn; to confer a distinction; to honour with a medal.
decorativo, *a.* Decorative.
decorato, *n.m.a.* Possessor of a medal, etc.; decorated.
decoratore, *n.m.* House decorator, decorator.
decorazione, *n.f.* Decoration, embellishment, ornamentation; act of decorating, badge of honour, medal.
decoro, *n.m.* Decorum, propriety, dignity, honour ; pomp, etiquette.
decorosamente, *adv.* Decorously, decently, with propriety.
decoroso, *a.* Decorous, dignified; fair; seemly.
decorrenza, *n.f.* Coming into force, dating; beginning; expiration.
decorrere [decOrrere], *v.i.* To elapse, to date, to run, to come into force (of laws, etc.); to expire.
decorso (1), *n.m.* Course, development; period, lapse. **Il — d'una malattia,** the course of an illness.
decorso (2), *p.p.a.* Elapsed; dated.
decorticare [cp. **scorticare**].
decotto, *n.m.a.* Decoction; cooked, boiled.
decozione, *n.f.* Decoction; bankruptcy.
decremento, *n.m.* Decrease, decrement.
decrepitare, *v.t.* (*Chem.*) To decrepitate (a salt).
decrepitezza, *n.f.* Decrepitude (of old age), senility.
decrepito [decrEpito], *a.* Decrepit; worn out, decayed.
decrescendo, *a.* (*Mus.*) Decreasing.
decrescente, *a.* Decreasing, diminishing, waning, abating.
decrescere [decrEscere], *v.i.* To decrease, to wane, to lessen, to abate.
decrescimento, *n.m.* Decrease, decline, diminution, abatement.
decretali, *n.m.pl.* (*Eccles.*) Decretals.
decretare, *v.t.* To decree, to enact, to ordain; to award, to grant.
decreto, *n.m.* Decree, edict, law, ordinance.
decretorio [decretOrio], *a.* Having the force of a decree.
decubito [decUbito], *n.m.* Prone (in bed); position of patient in bed. **I decubiti, piaghe da —,** bed-sores.
decuplicare, *v.t.* To increase tenfold.
decuplo [dEcuplo], *n.m.* Tenfold, ten times greater.
decuria [decUria], *n.f.* (*Hist.*) Squad of ten men.
decurione, *n.m.* (*Hist.*) Decurion.
decurtare, *v.t.* To diminish, to curtail.
decusse, *n.f.* The letter X representing 10 in Roman numerals; Roman coin.
dedaleo [dedAleo], *a.* Skilfully worked, complicated.
dedalo [dEdalo], *n.m.* Maze, labyrinth.
dedica [dEdica], *n.f.* Dedication; inscription, address.
dedicare, *v.t.* To dedicate, to consecrate; to inscribe (a literary work).
dedicarsi, *v.r.* To devote oneself, to give oneself up to.
dedicatore, *n.m.* Dedicator.
dedicatoria [dedicatOria], *n.f.* Dedication.
dedicatorio [dedicatOrio], *a.* Dedicatory.
dedicazione, *n.f.* Consecration, dedication; inscription.
deditamente, *adv.* Eagerly, solicitously.
dedito [dEdito], *a.* Addicted to, given to; engrossed in.
dedizione, *n.f.* Self-denial, abnegation; surrender, yielding.
dedotto, *p.p.a.* Deducted; derived, deduced.
deducibile [deducIbile], *a.* Deducible.
dedurre, *v.t.* To deduce, to infer; to deduct, to subtract; (*Law*) to state a case in Court.
deduttivamente, *adv.* Deductively.
deduttivo, *a.* Deductive. **Metodo —,** deductive reasoning.
deduzione, *n.f.* Deduction, inference, consequence; abatement.
defalcamento, *n.m.* Defaulting.
defalcare, *v.t.* To deduct, to diminish [cp. **diffalcare**].
defalcazione, *n.f.* Defalcation.
defecare, *v.t.i.* To defecate, to evacuate (the bowels); (*Chem.*) to free a liquid from impurities.
defecazione, *n.f.* Defecation, motion (of the bowels); excrement.
defenestrare, *v.t.* To throw (someone) out of the window; (*fig.*) to drive from office, to dismiss.
defensionale, *a.* (*Law*) Defensive, pleading in justification; for the defence.
deferente, *pres.p.a.* Deferential, complying; (*Physiol.*) deferent.
deferenza, *n.f.* Deference, respect, regard, compliance.
deferimento, *n.m.* Deferring.
deferire, *v.t.* To defer, to refer, to submit; (*Law*) to administer; to lodge (an accusation). **— all'autorità giudiziaria,** to commit to Court.
defettibile [defettIbile], *a.* Capable of defection, liable to fail; faulty.
defezionare, *v.t.i.* To desert, to betray; to fall off or away.
defezione, *n.f.* Defection, desertion, apostacy.
deficiente, *n.m.f.a.* Idiot, mentally deficient person; deficient, wanting; lacking; backward (at lessons).
deficienza, *n.f.* Deficiency, insufficiency, lack.
deficit [dEficit], *n.m.* (*Comm.*) Deficit. **Colmare il —,** to make up the deficit.
defilare, *v.i.* (*Mil.*) To defile; to march past.
defilato, *p.p.* Sheltered.
definibile [definIbile], *a.* Definable.
definire, *v.t.* To define, to explain, to determine; to settle.

definitivamente, *adv.* Definitively.
definitivo, *a.* Definitive, conclusive; definite.
definitore, *n.m.* (*Eccles.*) Assessor to a religious order.
definizione, *n.f.* Definition; delimitation; conclusion, decision. (*Comm.*) **Arrivare ad una —**, to come to a settlement.
deflagrare, *v.i.* To undergo combustion, to deflagrate.
deflagrazione, *n.f.* Combustion, explosion.
deflazione, *n.f.* (*Comm.*) Deflation.
deflemmare, *v.t.* (*Chem.*) To remove water from a composite liquid.
deflessione, *n.f.* Deflection, deviation.
deflettere [deflEttere], *v.i.* To deflect, to deviate, to bend, to swerve.
deflettore, *n.m.* (*Aviat.*) Deflector.
deflorare, *v.t.* To strip of flowers; to ravish, to violate.
deflorazione, *n.f.* Ravishing, violation, rape.
defluente, *a.* Flowing down, defluent.
defluire, *v.i.* To flow down.
deflusso, *n.m.* Down-flow, down-flowing; (*Med.*) defluxion.
deformamento, *n.m.* Deformation, deforming.
deformare, *v.t.* To deform, to disfigure, to distort (in all senses); (*Mech.*) to strain.
deformarsi, *v.r.* To become deformed; (*Mech.*) to warp, to buckle.
deformazione, *n.f.* (Action and result of) deformation, disfigurement.
deforme, *a.* Deformed, disfigured, misshapen; mutilated.
deformità [-à], *n.f.* Deformity, disfigurement, malformation.
defraudare, *v.t.* To defraud, to deprive; to cheat.
defraudatore, defraudatrice, *n.m.f.* Defrauder, cheat.
defraudazione, *n.f.* Defrauding, deceit.
defunto, *n.m.a.* Deceased. **I defunti,** the dead.
degenerare, *v.i.* To degenerate, to decay, to deteriorate; to become critical (of illness).
degenerato, *n.m.a.* Degenerate, profligate, wastrel.
degenerazione, *n.f.* Degeneration, deterioration; degradation; degeneracy; change of state.
degenere [degEnere], *a.* Fallen, corrupted; dissimilar, different from the normal.
degente, *n.m.a.* Hospital patient, in-patient; bed-ridden.
degenza, *n.f.* Period spent by a patient in hospital. **Certificato di —,** certificate of sickness.
degli. Of the [cp. **di**].
deglutire, *v.t.* To swallow.
deglutizione, *n.f.* Deglutition, swallowing.
degnamente, *adv.* Worthily, properly.
degnare, *v.i.* To deign; to deem worthy; to grant.
degnarsi, *v.r.* To condescend, to deign; to be pleased to do.
degnazione, *n.f.* Condescension, complaisance, kindness, honour, reputation.
degnità [-à], *n.f.* Dignity; (*Phil.*) axiom.
degno, *a.* Worthy, worth, deserving; dignified, noble-minded, honest; adequate. **È una degna persona,** he is a worthy fellow.
degradamento, *n.m.* Degradation; deprivation of office or dignity.
degradare, *v.t.* To degrade, to reduce in rank; to debase, to lower; to disgrace.
degradarsi, *v.r.* To degrade oneself, to demean oneself; to disgrace oneself.
degradazione, *n.f.* Degradation, debasement.
degustare, *v.t.* To taste; to relish, to savour; to sample (wines, etc.).
degustazione, *n.f.* Tasting, sampling, sipping.
deh! *inter.* Ah! Oh! For pity's sake! Pray!
dei. Of the [cp. **di**].
deiettore, *n.m.* Object put into a kettle to prevent furring.
deiezione, *n.f.* Evacuation of the bowels; faeces.
deificare, *v.t.* To deify, to make a god of; to idolize.
deificazione, *n.f.* Deification.
deifico [deIfico], *a.* Divine.
deiforme, *a.* Godlike (in form).
Deipara, *n.f.* (*Eccles.*) Mother of God, the Blessed Virgin Mary.
deiscente, *a.* (*Bot.*) Dehiscent.
deismo, *n.m.* Deism.
deista, *n.m.f.* Deist.
deità, *n.f.* Deity, Supreme Being.
del. Of the [cp. **di**].
delatore, *n.m.* Spy, informer.
delazione, *n.f.* Secret accusation, delation; espionage.
delebile [delEbile], *a.* Delible, erasable.
delega [dElega], *n.f.* Proxy; delegation. **Per —,** by proxy.
delegante, *n.m.* Delegate.
delegare, *v.t.* To delegate, to depute; to appoint (as representative); to assign.
delegato, *n.m.* Delegate, deputy, representative. **— di polizia,** superintendent of police.
delegatorio [delegatOrio], *a.* (*Eccles.*) Of the letters given by the Pope in reference to certain stated matters.
delegazione, *n.f.* Delegation; body of delegates; commission.
deleterio [deletErio], *a.* Deleterious, noxious, hurtful.
Delfinato, *n.m.* (*Geog.*) The Dauphiné (France).
delfino, *n.m.* (*Zool.*) Dolphin; (*Hist.*) Dauphin (of France); (*colloq.*) favourite, protégé.
Delfo, *n.m.* (*Geog.*) Delphi.
delibamento, *n.m.* Tasting, savouring; sampling.
delibare, *v.t.* To taste, to sample, to relish, to savour; (*Law*) to allude to; to touch upon.
delibazione, *n.f.* Tasting, savouring; (*Law*) consideration of documents and judgment in a case heard by a foreign court of law.
delibera [delIbera], *n.f.* (*Law, Pol.*) Decision, resolution.
deliberare, *v.t.i.* To deliberate, to decide, to ponder, to weigh, to take counsel; to assign.
deliberarsi, *v.r.* To decide upon; to resolve, to settle.
deliberatamente, *adv.* Deliberately, purposely.
deliberatario [deliberatArio], *n.m.* (*Comm.*) Highest bidder; successful tenderer.
deliberativa, *n.f.* Deliberative faculty; authority to make decisions.

deliberativamente, *adv.* Deliberately, after consideration.
deliberativo, *a.* Deliberative, after due consideration.
deliberato, *n.m.a.* (*Law, Pol.*) Decision, resolution; deliberate, resolved upon, resolute.
deliberatorio [deliberatOrio], *a.* Deliberative, acting with deliberation.
deliberazione, *n.f.* Deliberation, decision, resolution.
delicatamente, *adv.* Delicately.
delicatezza, *n.f.* Delicacy, sensitiveness; discretion, tact; fineness; gentleness; fragility.
delicato, *a.* · Delicate, sensitive, refined, fastidious; soft; gentle, dainty; smooth; fragile, weak, feeble; pleasing; scrupulous. **Un bambino —,** a delicate child.
delicatura, *n.f.* Daintiness, excessive refinement; extreme delicacy. **Delicature,** delicacies (cooking).
delimare, *v.t.* To corrode.
delimitare, *v.t.* To delimit, to fix the boundaries of, to define.
delimitazione, *n.f.* Delimitation.
delineamento, *n.m.* Delineation.
delineare, *v.t.* To delineate, to sketch out, to describe, to outline.
delinearsi, *v.r.* To take shape.
delineatore, *n.m.* Delineator.
delineatura, *n.f.* Delineation, thing delineated.
delineazione, *n.f.* Delineation; description; summary.
delinquente, *n.m.a.* Delinquent, criminal; offender, culprit.
delinquenza, *n.f.* Delinquency, criminality, crime.
delinquere [delInquere], *v.t.* (*Law*) To commit an offence. **Associazione a —,** criminal association.
deliquescente, *a.* Deliquescent, melting away.
deliquescenza, *n.f.* Deliquescence; (*fig.*) corruption, decay.
deliquio [delIquio], *n.m.* Faint, fainting fit, swoon. **Cadere in —,** to faint.
delirante, *a.* Delirious, raving, frenzied; furious.
delirare, *v.i.* To rave, to wander (in mind), to be delirious. (*fig.*) **— d'amore,** to be madly in love.
delirio [delIrio], *n.m.* Delirium, raving, frenzy; (*fig.*) rapture, ecstasy.
delitto, *n.m.* Crime, offence, misdeed; sin. **Corpo del —,** material evidence of a crime.
delittuoso, *a.* Criminal.
delizia [delIzia], *n.f.* Delight, pleasure; charm. **Queste fragole sono una —,** these strawberries are a sheer delight.
deliziare, *v.t.* To delight, to charm; to render delightful.
deliziarsi, *v.r.* To enjoy, to take pleasure in, to delight in.
delizioso, *a.* Delightful, delicious. **Quel bambino è —,** that child is delightful.
deliziosamente, *adv.* Delightfully, deliciously.
della, dello, delle, Of the [cp. **di**].
delta, *n.m.* (*Geog.*) Delta; 4th letter of Greek alphabet.
deltoide [deltOide], *n.m.* (*Anat.*) Deltoid.
delubro, *n.m.* (*Poet.*) Temple; shrine.
delucidare, *v.t.* To explain, to clarify.
delucidazione, *n.f.* Explanation, clarification.
deludente, *a.* Delusive, deceptive.
deludere [delUdere], *v.t.* To delude, to disappoint, to deceive, to frustrate; to escape.
deludimento, *n.m.* (Act of) deluding.
delusione, *n.f.* Delusion, disappointment, deception.
deluso, *a.* Deluded, deceived; frustrated.
delusoriamente, *adv.* Deceptively.
delusorio [delusOrio], *a.* Deceptive.
demagogia [demagogIa], *n.f.* Demagogy.
demagogico [demagOgico], *a.* Demagogic.
demagogo, *n.m.* Demagogue, agitator.
demandare, *v.t.* To delegate, to entrust, to assign.
demaniale, *a.* Pertaining to state territory.
demanio [demAnio], *n.m.* Crown lands, state property; demesne. **Ufficio del —,** public office dealing with state property; **— pubblico,** public domain.
demarcare, *v.t.* To delimit, to fix the boundaries of.
demarcazione, *n.f.* Demarcation.
demarrare, *v.i.* (*Naut.*) To weigh anchor; (*Aviat.*) to take off from the sea.
demente, *n.m.a.* Crazy person; demented, crazy.
demenza, *n.f.* Insanity, madness.
demeritare, *v.i.* To forfeit esteem, to lose esteem.
demeritevole [demeritEvole], *a.* Undeserving.
demerito [demErito], *n.m.* Demerit, unworthiness.
demeritorio [demeritOrio], *a.* Unworthy.
demersione, *n.f.* Immersion.
demiurgo, *n.m.* (*Hist.*) Demiurge.
demo, *n.m.* The people (as a whole), plebs.
democraticamente, *adv.* Democratically.
democratico [democrAtico], *n.m.a.* Democrat; democratic.
democratizzare, *v.t.* To democratize.
democrazia [democrazIa], *n.f.* Democracy.
democristiano, *n.m.* (*Pol.*) Christian Democrat.
demografia [demografIa], *n.f.* Demography.
demografico [demogrAfico], *a.* Demographic. **Problema —,** problem of the movement of population.
demolire, *v.t.* To demolish, to destroy, to raze; to overthrow.
demolitore, demolitrice, *n.m.f.* Destroyer.
demolizione, *n.f.* Demolition, destruction.
demone [dEmone], *n.m.* Demon, daemon.
demonetare, *v.t.* (*Fin.*) To demonetize.
demoniaco, demonico [demoniAco, demOnico], *n.m.a.* Demoniac, demoniacal.
demonio [demOnio], *n.m.* Demon, daemon; devil; evil spirit; imp; (*fig.*) very clever person. **Sterco del —,** money; **un — incarnato,** a devil incarnate.
demonologia [demonologIa], *n.f.* Demonology.
demopsicologia [demopsicologIa], *n.f.* Race psychology.
demoralizzare, *v.t.* To demoralize, to subvert, to dishearten.
demoralizzazione, *n.f.* Demoralization.
Demostene [demOstene], *n.m.* Demosthenes.
demotico [demOtico], *a.* (*Hist.*) Demotic.

denaro, danaro, *n.m.* Money, cash; diamonds (cards). **L'asso di denari,** the ace of diamonds; **fare denari,** to make money; **— contanti,** ready money.
denaroso, *a.* Wealthy.
denaturante, *n.m.* (*Chem.*) Denaturant.
denaturare, *v.t.* (*Chem.*) To denature. **Alcool denaturato,** methylated spirit.
denegamento, *n.m.* Disavowal.
denegare, *v.t.* To disavow; to deny.
denegazione, *n.f.* Denial, disavowal; disclaimer.
denicotinizzare, *v.t.* To denicotinize.
denigrare, *v.t.* To disparage, to detract from, to run down; to defame, to denigrate; to revile. **— le merci,** to undervalue goods.
denigratore, denigratrice, *n.m.f.a.* Defamer, traducer, slanderer; defamatory.
denigrazione, *n.f.* Defamation, denigration, detraction; traducement.
denodare, *v.t.* To unknot, to loosen.
denominare, *v.t.* To denominate, to name.
denominarsi, *v.r.* To be named, to be called.
denominativo, *a.* Denominative.
denominatore, *n.m.* (*Arith.*) Denominator.
denominazione, *n.f.* Denomination, title, description.
denotare, *v.t.* To denote, to signify, to indicate.
denotativo, *a.* Denoting.
denotazione, *n.f.* Denotation, indication, meaning.
densamente, *adv.* Densely, thickly.
densare, *v.t.* To condense.
densato, *a.* Cloudy.
densezza, densità [-à], *n.f.* Density, thickness.
denso, *a.* Dense, thick, compact.
dentale, *n.m.* Ploughshare; (*Gram.*) dental (consonant).
dentale, *a.* Dental.
dentame, *n.m.* Complete denture; teeth (of a comb, etc.).
dentarolo, *n.m.* Baby's coral.
dentata, *n.f.* Bite; mark of a bite.
dentato, *a.* Toothed, notched; cogged; (*Bot.*) dentate.
dentatrice, *n.f.* (*Mech.*) Machine for cutting teeth in a wheel.
dentatura, *n.f.* Set of (natural) teeth; (*Mech.*) teeth, cogs; teeth of a saw. **— sana,** set of sound teeth.
dente, *n.m.* Tooth; fang, tusk; cog, notch; fluke (of anchor); prong (of fork). **Mettere i denti,** to cut one's teeth; **mal di denti,** toothache; **denti di latte,** first teeth; **denti del giudizio,** wisdom teeth; **— canino,** eye-tooth; **strappare un —,** to extract a tooth; **otturare un —,** to stop a tooth; **i denti d'elefante,** tusks; **denti d'un ingranaggio,** cogs of a gear; **denti d'una sega,** teeth of a saw; **parlare tra i denti,** to mutter; **parlare fuori dei denti,** to be outspoken; **avere i denti lunghi,** to be greedy; **rimanere a denti asciutti,** to be left hungry; **non è pane per i miei denti,** it's not my cup of tea.
dentellare, *v.t.* To notch, to indent.
dentellatura, *n.f.* Indentation, notching.
dentello, *n.m.* (*Mech.*) Tooth, notch; (*Arch.*) dentil.
denticchiare, *v.t.* To nibble.
dentice [dEntice], *n.m.* (*Zool.*) Dentex.
dentiera, *n.f.* (Artificial) denture; dental plate.
dentiforme, *a.* Dentiform.
dentifricio [dentifrIcio], *n.m.* Dentifrice, tooth-paste, tooth-powder.
dentista (*pl.* **dentisti**), *n.m.* Dentist.
dentizione, *n.f.* Dentition, teething.
dentro, *adv., prep.* Within, inside, in; within, during. **— a, — di,** inside of. **— aprile,** within the month of April; **metter —,** to put inside, (*fig.*) to put in prison; **dal di —,** from within.
denudamento, *n.m.* (Act of) stripping, laying bare.
denudare, *v.t.* To lay bare, to strip, to denude, to divest.
denudarsi, *v.r.* To undress; to divest oneself.
denudazione, *n.f.* Stripping, denudation.
denuncia, denunzia [denUncia, denUnzia], *n.f.* Denunciation, denouncement; information; declaration, statement; banns of marriage.
denunciare, denunziare, *v.t.* To denounce, to impeach; to state, to declare; to inform against; to revoke. **— il reddito,** to declare one's income; **— una nascita,** to report a birth.
denunziatore, denunziatrice, *n.m.f.* Informer.
denutrito, *a.* Ill-fed, starved, underfed.
denutrizione, *n.f.* Under-nourishment.
deodara, *n.f.* (*Bot.*) Deodar.
deodorante, *n.m., a.* Deodorant; deodorizer
deodorare, *v.t.* To deodorize.
deostruente, *a.* (*Med.*) Aperient.
deostruire, *v.t.* (*Med.*) To loosen the bowels.
depauperare, *v.t.* To impoverish.
depauperazione, *n.f.* Impoverishment.
depennare, *v.t.* To erase, to cancel, to cross out.
deperibile [deperIbile], *a.* Perishable (of goods, etc.).
deperimento, *n.m.* Decline, decay, exhaustion, waste, loss of strength; (*Comm.*) depreciation. **— nervoso,** nervous exhaustion.
deperire, *v.i.* To pine away, to waste away, to be run down, to decay; to deteriorate.
depilare, *v.t.* To remove hair, to depilate.
depilatorio [depilatOrio], *n.m.a.* Depilatory.
depilazione, *n.f.* Depilation.
depletivo, *a.* (*Med.*) Depletive.
deplorabile [deplorAbile], *a.* Deplorable, lamentable, pitiable.
deplorabilmente, *adv.* Deplorably.
deplorare, *v.t.* To deplore, to regret, to lament over; to complain of; to blame.
deplorazione, *n.f.* Complaint, lamentation; rebuff, reprimand.
deplorevole [deplorEvole], *a.* Deplorable, pitiable; objectionable.
deponente, *n.m.* (*Law*) Deponent, witness.
deporre, *v.t.* To deposit, to place, to lay down; to dismiss, to depose, to remove (from post); (*Law*) to depone, to bear witness, to testify, to give evidence. **— un'idea,** to give up an idea; **— le armi,** to lay down one's arms; **— ad un processo,** to give evidence in Court.
deportare, *v.t.* To deport, to banish, to relegate; to remove.

deportato, *n.m.* Deportee, convict.
deportazione, *n.f.* Banishment, deportation.
deporto, *n.m.* (*Fin.*) Backwardation.
depositante, *n.m.* (*Comm.*) Depositor (in a bank).
depositare, *v.t.* To deposit, to lay down, to consign, to lodge (for safety). **— denaro,** to deposit money; **— la valigia,** to leave one's luggage (in the cloakroom).
depositario [depositArio], *n.m.* (*Comm.*) Depositary, trustee.
deposito [depOsito], *n.m.* Deposit; warehouse; (*Rail.*) left-luggage office, cloakroom; (*Mil.*) depot; (*Chem.*) sediment. (*Comm.*) **— vincolato,** deposit account; **pagare un —,** to pay a deposit; **— doganale,** bonded warehouse.
deposizione, *n.f.* Removal, deposition; (*Law*) deposition, evidence. (*Eccles.*) **La Deposizione,** the Descent from the Cross.
deposto, *n.m.* (*Law*) Written evidence; deposition.
deposto, *p.p.a.* Deposed, unseated, displaced, dismissed.
depravare, *v.t.* To deprave, to corrupt.
depravazione, *n.f.* Depravation, corruption.
deprecabile [deprecAbile], *a.* Avoidable, avertible.
deprecare, *v.t.* To deprecate, to argue against; to exorcise.
deprecativamente, *adv.* Deprecatingly.
deprecatorio [deprecatOrio], *a.* Deprecatory.
deprecazione, *n.f.* Deprecation.
depredamento, *n.m.* Depredation.
depredare, *v.t.* To ravage, to plunder, to loot; to lay waste.
depredatore, *n.m.* Ravager, looter; despoiler.
depredazione, *n.f.* Plunder, looting.
depressamente, *adv.* Dispiritedly.
depressione, *n.f.* Depression (in all senses).
depressivo, *a.* Depressing.
depresso, *a.* Depressed; dispirited; weak, feeble. **Polso —,** feeble pulse; (*Comm.*) **mercato —,** dull market.
deprezzamento, *n.m.* Depreciation, fall in value; shrinkage.
deprezzare, *v.t.* To depreciate; to disparage, to undervalue, to discredit.
deprimente, *a.* Depressing; depleting; boring, bothersome, tiresome.
deprimere [deprImere], *v.t.* To depress, to abase, to humble; to undervalue; to dishearten.
deprofundis, *n.m.* Opening words of the 129th Psalm (Vulgate) for the dead.
depuramento, *n.m.* Depuration, purifying.
depurare, *v.t.* To purify, to purge; to deduct.
depurativo, *a.* Purifying, purging.
depurazione, *n.f.* Purifying, depuration, purification.
deputare, *v.t.* To depute, to delegate; to appoint, to assign.
deputato, *n.m.* Deputy (in all senses); delegate; member of parliament.
deputazione, *n.f.* Deputation, delegation, committee.
deragliamento, *n.m.* (*Rail.*) Derailment.
deragliare, *v.i.* (*Rail.*) To run off the rails, to leave the rails.
derapare, *v.i.* (*Aviat.*) To side-slip.
derattizzare, *v.t.* To exterminate rats; to rid of rats.
derelinquere [derelInquere], *v.t.* To abandon.
derelitto, *n.m., a.* Abandoned child, waif; abandoned; forsaken, derelict. **Ospizio dei derelitti,** home for lost children.
deretano, *n.m.* Buttocks, backside, arse.
deridere [derIdere], *v.t.* To deride, to mock, to laugh at, to ridicule; to banter.
derisibile [derisIbile], *a.* Ridiculous, laughable.
derisione, *n.f.* Derision, mockery, ridicule, scorn.
derisivamente, *adv.* Derisively, mockingly.
derisivo, derisorio [derisOrio], *a.* Derisory.
deriva, *n.f.* (*Naut.*) Drift, leeway. **Andare alla —,** to go adrift.
derivare, *v.t.i.* To derive from, to proceed; to accrue; to originate; to draw, to trace; to divert (a stream, etc.); (*Aviat.*) to drift; (*Naut.*) to make leeway.
derivata, *n.f.* (*Math.*) Derivative equation.
derivativo, *a.* Derivative.
derivazione, *n.f.* Derivation; deflection.
derma, *n.m.* (*Anat.*) Derm, skin.
dermatite, *n.f.* (*Med.*) Dermatitis.
dermatologia [dermatologIa], *n.f.* Dermatology.
derno, *a.* (*Naut.*) **Bandiera in —,** flag rolled up and hoisted as a signal of distress.
derobare, *v.t.* To jib (of a horse).
deroga [dEroga], *n.f.* Repeal, abrogation; derogation; transgression.
derogare, *v.i.* To derogate, to depart from; to detract. **— a,** to contravene.
derogativo, *a.* Derogatory.
derogato, *a.* Annulled, lessened.
derogatoria [derogatOria], *n.f.* (*Law*) Cautionary clause; caution.
derogatorio [derogatOrio], *a.* Derogatory, detracting.
derogazione, *n.f.* Repeal, cancellation (of a previous decision, etc.); reprieve.
derrata, *n.f.* (*Comm.*) Commodity, merchandise; victuals, provisions, agricultural products (for the market). **— alimentare,** foodstuff.
derubare, *v.t.* To rob, to plunder, to despoil.
derubato, *n.m.* Victim of a robbery.
dervigio, dervis [dervIgio], *n.m.* Dervish.
deschetto, *n.m.* Little table, bench, cobbler's bench, stool.
desco, *n.m.* Table, dinner-table; meal on the table; table laid for meal; bench. **Sedere al —,** to sit down to dinner.
descrittivamente, *adv.* Descriptively.
descrittivo, *a.* Descriptive.
descritto, *a.* Described in detail.
descrittore, *n.m.* Describer.
descrivere [descrIvere], *v.t.* To describe, to give an account, to relate.
descrivibile [descrivIbile], *a.* Describable.
descrizione, *n.f.* Description, account, word-picture.
deserto, *n.m.a.* Desert, wilderness; desert, deserted; wild, solitary, bare; abandoned. **Predicare al —,** to preach to the winds.
deserzione, *n.f.* Desertion; (*Law*) failure to appeal.
desiante, *a.* (*Lit.*) Desirous.
desianza, *n.f.* (*Lit.*) Desire.
desiare, *v.t.* To desire.

desiderabile [desiderAbile], *a.* Desirable.
desiderabilmente, *adv.* Desirably.
desiderante, *a.* Desirous, desiring.
desiderare, *v.t.* To wish, to desire, to long for; to hanker after; to covet. **Farsi —,** to keep others waiting; **lascia molto a —,** there is much room for improvement; **desidero parlargli,** I want to speak to him; **desiderate qualche altra cosa?** do you want anything else?
desiderata, *n.m.pl.* Requirements, desiderata.
desideratamente, *adv.* In the desired way.
desiderativamente, *adv.* Desirously.
desiderativo, *a.* Expressing desire, desirous.
desiderato, *n.m.* (Person or thing) desired. **I desiderati,** what is desired, the aim.
desiderio [desidErio], *n.m.* Desire, wish, longing, eagerness. **È un pio —,** it is a vain hope; **ho conseguito il mio —,** I have fulfilled my wish.
desiderosamente, *adv.* Desirously, desiringly.
desideroso, *a.* Desirous; desirable.
designare, *v.t.* To designate, to point out, to specify; to select, to appoint.
designazione, *n.f.* Designation, nomination.
desinare (1), *v.i.* To dine, to take dinner.
desinare (2), *n.m.* Dinner. **Dopo—,** after dinner.
desinata, *n.f.* Banquet, feast.
desinenza, *n.f.* (*Gram.*) Termination, ending.
desio [desIo], *n.m.* (*Poet.*) Desire; object of desire.
desiosamente, *adv.* Desirously, eagerly.
desioso, *a.* Desirous, longing.
desipiente, *a.* (*obs.*) Fatuous, vain, stupid.
desipienza, *n.f.* (*obs.*) Stupidity, foolishness.
desire, desiro, *n.m.* (*Poet.*) Desire.
desistenza, *n.f.* Cessation, desisting; (*Law*) dropping of an action.
desistere [desIstere], *v.i.* To desist, to cease; to give up, to abandon; to abstain.
desolante, *a.* Distressing, grievous, afflicting.
desolare, *v.t.* To desolate, to lay waste; to distress, to grieve.
desolarsi, *v.r.* To be afflicted, to be distressed, to grieve.
desolatamente, *adv.* Desolately.
desolato, *a.* Desolate, waste; afflicted, disconsolate, forlorn. **Sono — ma non è possibile,** I'm sorry but it can't be done.
desolatore, *n.m.* Desolater, waster.
desolazione, *n.f.* Desolation, affliction, grief; ruin.
desolino, *n.m.* East wind in the Adriatic.
despota [dEspota] (*pl.* **despoti**), *n.m.f.* Despot, tyrant.
despotico [despOtico], *a.* Despotic.
despumare, *v.t.* (*Chem.*) To scum.
desquamazione, *n.f.* (*Med.*) Desquamation.
dessa, desso, *pron.* (*obs.*) She, he, she herself, he himself. **È —!** It's he himself!
destare, *v.t.* To awake, to rouse; to revive, to stir.
destarsi, *v.r.* To wake up, to rise.
destato, *a.* Awake, lively, keen.
destatoio [destatOio], *n.m.* Alarm clock.
destinare, *v.t.* To destine; to determine to a use, to devolve; to fix, to appoint; to allot; to decree; to address (letters). **Era destinato a perire,** he was doomed to perish; **quel-l'ufficiale è stato destinato a Roma,** that officer has been appointed to Rome.
destinatario [destinatArio], *n.m.* Addressee, consignee, receiver. **A rischio e pericolo del —,** at receiver's risk.
destinazione, *n.f.* Destination; purpose.
destino, *n.m.* Destiny, fate; fatality; doom; destination. **Pare un —,** it seems fated to happen.
destituire, *v.t.* To dismiss, to remove (from office), to discharge.
destituito, *a.* Dismissed; destitute; abandoned; devoid of; groundless. **— di senso morale,** devoid of moral sense.
destituzione, *n.f.* Dismissal, removal (from office).
desto, *a.* Wide awake; lively, quick, sharp.
destra, *n.f.* Right hand; right side; (*Pol.*) Right Wing. **Tenete a —,** keep to the right; **la — di un fiume,** the right bank of a river.
destramente, *adv.* Dexterously, cleverly.
destreggiamento, *n.m.* Dexterity, shrewdness.
destreggiare, destreggiarsi, *v.i.r.* To exert oneself, to contrive, to manage cleverly; to juggle (with figures, etc.).
destrezza, *n.f.* Dexterity, skill, cleverness, ability.
destriere, destriero, *n.m.* War-horse, steed.
destro (1), *n.m.* Opportunity, chance. **Cogliere il —,** to seize the opportunity.
destro (2), *a.* Right (side); dexterous, skilful; quick, agile; wide awake.
destrorso, *a.* Right-handed; from left to right; clock-wise.
desueto, *a.* (*Lit.*) Out of use; unusual.
desuetudine [desuetUdine], *n.f.* Desuetude, disuse.
desumere [desUmere], *v.t.* To deduce, to infer, to derive, to draw.
desumibile [desumIbile], *a.* Deducible, inferable.
desunto, *p.p.a.* Inferred, deduced; derived.
detenere, *v.t.* To detain, to retain, to keep; to hold in arrest. **— un incarico,** to hold a job, to keep a post.
detentore, *n.m.* Detainer; (*Sport*) holder of a title; receiver (of stolen goods).
detenuto, *n.m.a.* (*Law*) Prisoner; held in custody, imprisoned.
detenzione, *n.f.* Imprisonment, detention, confinement; possession of stolen property.
detergente, *n.m.a.* Detergent; polisher.
detergere [detErgere], *v.t.* To cleanse.
deteriorabile [deteriorAbile], *a.* Perishable.
deterioramento, *n.m.* Deterioration.
deteriorare, *v.t.* To impair, to cause to deteriorate.
deteriorarsi, *v.r.* To deteriorate, to degenerate, to decay; to get damaged.
deteriorato, *a.* Deteriorated, grown worse; damaged.
deteriorazione, *n.f.* Deterioration, decay.
determinabile [determinAbile], *a.* Determinable.
determinabilità [-à], *n.f.* Determinability, possibility of being determined.
determinante, *a.* Determining. **Causa —,** determining factor.
determinare, *v.t.* To determine, to ascertain, to fix; to define, to specify; to cause, to bring about.

determinarsi, *v.r.* To make up one's mind, to resolve.
determinatamente, *adv.* With determination.
determinatezza, *n.f.* Determination, resolution, strength of mind.
determinativo, *a.* Decisive, determinative.
determinato, *a.* Definite, determined, resolute, decided; resolved, fixed, stated.
determinazione, *n.f.* Decision, determination; resolve, conclusion.
determinismo, *n.m.* (*Phil.*) Determinism.
determinista, *n.m.* Determinist.
detersione, *n.f.* Cleansing.
detersivo, *n.m.a.* Detergent; polisher.
deterso, *a.* Cleansed, purified; clean.
detestabile [detestAbile], *a.* Detestable.
detestare, *v.t.* To detest, to hate, to abhor.
detestazione, *n.f.* Detestation, abhorrence, hatred.
detettore, *n.m.* (*Radio*) Detector.
detonante, *a.* Detonating.
detonare, *v.t.* To detonate.
detonatore, *n.m.* Detonator.
detonazione, *n.f.* Detonation, explosion.
detrarre, *v.t.* To deduct, to take away; to detract, to belittle, to speak ill of, to slight.
detrattore, *n.m.* Detractor, slanderer.
detrazione, *n.f.* Deduction; depreciation, slander.
detrimento, *n.m.* Detriment, loss, damage, injury.
detrito, *n.m.* Debris, detritus, waste; rubble.
detronizzare, *v.t.* To dethrone.
detruso, *a.* (*Med.*) Forced down, thrust down.
detta, *n.f.* Words, opinion. **A — di tutti,** according to the general opinion; **a — sua,** according to him.
dettafono [dettAfono], *n.m.* Dictaphone.
dettagliante, *n.m.* (*Comm.*) Retailer, retail dealer.
dettagliare, *v.t.* To detail, to set forth in detail, to relate minutely; to sell retail.
dettagliatamente, *adv.* Bit by bit, by degrees, in detail.
dettaglio [dettAglio], *n.m.* Detail, particular; (*Comm.*) retail. **Vendita al —,** sale by retail.
dettame, *n.m.* Precept, rule, dictate.
dettare, *v.t.* To dictate, to indicate; to determine, to fix; to write (a book, etc.).
dettato, *n.m.* Dictation; style.
dettatura, *n.f.* Dictation, diction, style. **Scrivere sotto —,** to write from dictation.
detto, *n.m.a.* Saying, maxim, proverb; word, witticism; said, named, called. **Pietro — Il Falegname,** Peter known as The Carpenter; **— fatto,** no sooner said than done.
detumescenza, *n.f.* (*Med.*) Reduction of a swelling.
deturpamento, *n.m.* Disfigurement, defilement; foulness.
deturpare, *v.t.* To disfigure, to soil, to defile.
deturpatore, *n.m.* Disfigurer.
deturpazione, *n.f.* Disfigurement; foulness.
Deuteronomio [deuteronOmio], *n.m.* (Book of) Deuteronomy.
devalutazione, *n.f.* (*Fin.*) Devaluation.
devastamento, *n.m.* (Act of) devastation.
devastare, *v.t.* To devastate, to lay waste, to ravage.
devastazione, *n.f.* Devastation, waste, ruin, havoc.
devenire, *v.i.* (*Law*) To arrive at a conclusion; to proceed on a certain line.
devenuto, *a.* Admitted (as an argument); come to a conclusion.
deviamento, *n.m.* Deviation; aberration; (*Rail.*) derailment; shunting.
deviare, *v.t.i.* To deviate, to swerve; to err; to diverge, to turn aside; (*Rail.*) to derail; to shunt.
deviatore, *n.m.* (*Rail.*) Pointsman, shunter.
deviazione, *n.f.* Deviation, error; deflection.
devio [dEvio], *a.* Devious, rambling.
devolutivo, *a.* Devolving.
devoluto, *a.* Devolved, transferred.
devoluzione, *n.f.* Devolution, transfer.
devolvere [devOlvere], *v.t.* To devolve, to assign, to transfer.
devolversi, *v.r.* To turn; to pass from one to another (cash, etc.).
devotamente, *adv.* Devotedly.
devotissimo, *a.* Most faithfully, very truly. **Suo —,** Yours faithfully (at conclusion of letters).
devoto, *n.m.a.* Devout man, devotee; pious, devout; devoted, attached; destined.
devozione, *n.f.* Devotion, piety; affection, reverence, attachment, loyalty. **Far le proprie devozioni,** to perform one's devotions.
di, *prep.* (With definite article becomes **del, dello, della, dei, degli, delle**). Of, made of, on account of, concerning; from, for, with, at, about, by; any, some. **Esempio di virtù,** example of virtue; **più grande di lui,** greater than he; **il popolo di Roma,** the people of Rome; **egli è di Milano,** he is from Milan; **di notte, di giorno,** by night, by day; **fremere di rabbia,** to fume with anger; **mangiar del pane,** to eat some bread; **poco di buono,** not much good; **ringraziare di una cosa,** to thank for something; **parlar di politica,** to talk politics; **una tavola di quercia,** an oak table; **di tempo in tempo,** from time to time; **dare dell'imbecille a qualcuno,** to call somebody an idiot; **dire di sì,** to say yes; **di solito,** usually; **d'un tratto,** suddenly; **di fretta,** in haste; **di cuore,** heartily; **di senno,** sensible; **di troppo,** in excess, too much; **di sopra,** upstairs, above; **di passo,** at a walking pace; **uccello di passo,** migrant, bird of passage.
dì, *n.m.* Day. **Buon dì,** good day; **sul far del dì,** at dawn; **mezzodì,** midday; **al dì d'oggi,** nowadays.
diabase, *n.f.* (*Geol.*) Diabase.
diabete, *n.m.* (*Med.*) Diabetes.
diabetico [diabEtico], *a.* Diabetic.
diabolicamente, *adv.* Diabolically.
diabolico [diabOlico], *a.* Diabolic, diabolical, devilish.
diacaustico [diacAustico], *a.* (*Phys.*) Diacaustic.
diacciare, *v.t.* (*Tuscan*) To freeze, to congeal [cp. **ghiaccio**].
diacciatura, *n.f.* Freezing.
diaccio [diAccio], *n.m.a.* Ice; icy, frozen; chilly.
diacciolo, *n.m.a.* Icicle; brittle (as ice); sensitive to cold..
diaconale, *a.* (*Eccles.*) Diaconal.
diaconato, *n.m.* (*Eccles.*) Diaconate.
diaconessa, *n.f.* Deaconess.

diaconia [diaconIa], *n.f.* (*Eccles.*) Diaconate, deaconship.
diacono [diAcono], *n.m.* (*Eccles.*) Deacon.
diacritico [diacrItico], *a.* (*Gram.*) Diacritic, diacritical.
diadema, *n.m.* Diadem.
diademato, *a.* Crowned with a diadem.
diafanità [-**à**], *n.f.* Transparency, diaphanousness.
diafano [diAfano], *a.* Diaphanous, transparent.
diafonia [diafonIa], *n.f.* Dissonance.
diaforesi, *n.f.* Sweat, (*Med.*) diaphoresis.
diaforetico [diaforEtico], *a.* (*Med.*) Diaphoretic, sudatory.
diaframma (*pl.* **diaframmi**), *n.m.* Diaphragm.
diagnosi [diAgnosi], *n.f.* Diagnosis.
diagnosticamente, *adv.* By diagnosis.
diagnosticare, *v.t.* To diagnose.
diagnostico [diagnOstico], *n.m.a.* Diagnostician; diagnostic.
diagonale, *n.m.a.* Diagonal.
diagonalmente, *adv.* Diagonally.
diagramma (*pl.* **diagrammi**), *n.m.* Diagram.
diagrammatico [diagrammAtico], *a.* Diagrammatic.
dialettale, *a.* Dialectal.
dialettica [dialEttica], *n.f.* Dialectics.
dialetticamente, *adv.* Dialectically.
dialettico [dialEttico], *a.* Dialectical, logical.
dialetto, *n.m.* Dialect.
dialettologia [dialettologIa], *n.f.* Study of dialects.
dialisi [diAlisi], *n.f.* Dialysis.
dialogare, *v.t.* To hold a dialogue; to put into dialogue form.
dialogismo, *n.m.* Use of dialogue; rhetorical figure.
dialogista (*pl.* **dialogisti**), *n.m.f.* Writer of dialogues.
dialogizzare, *v.t.* To hold a dialogue; to write in form of dialogue.
dialogo [diAlogo], *n.m.* Dialogue, conversation.
diamagnetico [diamagnEtico], *a.* (*Elect.*) Diamagnetic.
diamante, *n.m.* Diamond.
diamantifero [diamantIfero], *a.* Diamantiferous, diamond-bearing.
diamantino, *a.* Adamantine.
diametrale, *a.* Pertaining to a diameter, diametral.
diametralmente, *adv.* Diametrically. **Idee — opposte,** diametrically opposite ideas.
diametro [diAmetro], *n.m.* Diameter.
diamine! [diAmine], *inter.* The Deuce!
Diana, *n.f.* Diana; morning star; (*Mil.*) reveille. **Batter la —,** to sound the reveille.
dianzi, *adv.* Not long ago, just since.
diapason [diApason], *n.m.* Diapason, pitch; compass (of voice, etc.); tuning-fork.
diapositiva, *n.f.* (*Photo.*) Lantern slide.
diaria [diAria], *n.f.* (*Comm.*) Daily expense allowance; travelling allowance.
diario [diArio], *n.m.a.* Diary; daybook, journal; daily, lasting a day.
diarista, *n.m.f.* Diarist.
diarrea [diarrEa], *n.f.* (*Med.*) Diarrhoea.
diascolo [diAscolo], *n.m.* (*colloq.*) Devil.
diaspro, *n.m.* (*Min.*) Jasper.
diastasi, *n.f.* (*Chem.*) Diastase; (*Med.*) diastasis.
diastole [diAstole], *n.f.* (*Anat.*) Diastole.
diatermico [diatErmico], *a.* Diathermic.
diatesi [diAtesi], *n.f.* (*Med.*) Diathesis.
diatonico [diatOnico], *a.* (*Mus.*) Diatonic.
diatriba, *n.f.* Diatribe; dispute, quarrel; denunciation, invective.
diavolaccio [diavolAccio], *n.m.* **Un buon —,** a good fellow.
diavoleria [diavolerIa], *n.f.* Devilry, deviltry; muddle, tangle.
diavolesco, *a.* Devilish, in a devilish fashion.
diavolessa, *n.f.* She-devil, termagant.
diavoleto, *n.m.* Uproar, din, confusion.
diavoletto, *n.m.* Naughty little fellow.
diavolino, *n.m.* Little devil.
diavolio [diavolIo], *n.m.* Uproar, din, confusion, pandemonium.
diavolo [diAvolo], *n.m.* Devil; Satan; wicked or cunning person; wretch; (*fig.*) lively or mischievous child. **Buon —,** good fellow; **povero —,** poor devil; **avvocato del —,** devil's advocate; **mandare al —,** to send to hell; **aver il — addosso,** to be full of mischief; **fare il — a quattro,** to make a terrible mess, to make a fuss; **la farina del —,** an ill-gotten thing; **diavolo!** The deuce!
dibarbare, dibarbicare, *u.t.* (*Agric.*) To uproot.
dibassare, *v.t.* To lower.
dibattere [dibAttere], *v.t.* To debate, to argue, to discuss. **— i prezzi,** to discuss prices.
dibattersi [dibAttersi], *v.r.* To flounder, to struggle, to strive. **Si dibatteva nelle acque,** he was floundering in the water.
dibattimento, dibattito, *n.m.* Dispute, argument, debate, discussion; legal hearing; proceeding; beating, struggling. (*Law*) **— a porte chiuse,** case heard in camera.
dibattuto, *p.p.a.* Debated, discussed; controversial. **Una questione dibattuta,** an open question.
diboscamento, *n.m.* Deforestation.
diboscare, *v.t.* To deforest, to clear of forest; to make a clearing.
dibrucare, *v.t.* To prune.
dibrucatura, *n.f.* Pruning.
dibucciare, *v.t.* To peal off (rind, skin, etc.).
dicace, *a.* Garrulous, loquacious, sarcastic, satirical; petulant.
dicacità [-**à**], *n.f.* Loquacity; sarcasm, sarcastic manner.
dicastero, *n.m.* Department, ministry (of state). **Il — degli esteri,** the Foreign Ministry.
dicembre, *n.m.* December.
dicente, *n.m.f.* Speaker, person speaking.
dicentramento, *n.m.* Decentralization.
dicentrare, *v.t.* To decentralize.
diceria [dicerIa], *n.f.* Chatter, gossip; hearsay, rumour.
dicervellare, *v.t.* To bewilder.
dicervellarsi, *v.r.* To rack one's brains.
dicevole [dicEvole], *a.* Becoming, suitable.
dicevolezza, *n.f.* Decorum.
dicevolmente, *adv.* Becomingly.
dichiarante, *n.m.* (*Comm. Law*) Declarant.
dichiarare, *v.t.* To declare, to state, to explain, to make known, to certify; to announce; to nominate.
dichiararsi, *v.r.* To declare oneself, to propose (marriage).

dichiaratamente, *adv.* Openly, decidedly.
dichiarativo, *a.* Explanatory, declaratory.
dichiarato, *p.p.a.* Declared. **Valore —,** value declared.
dichiaratorio [dichiaratOrio], *a.* Declaratory.
dichiarazione, *n.f.* Declaration, proclamation; statement, notification; certificate.
dichinare, *v.i.* To slope down.
dichiocciarsi, *v.r.* (Of a hen) to abandon eggs.
diciannove, *a.* Nineteen.
diciannovenne, *a.* Nineteen years old.
diciannovesimo [diciannovEsimo], *a.* Nineteenth.
diciassette, *a.* Seventeen.
diciassettenne, *a.* Seventeen years old.
diciassettesimo [diciassettEsimo], *a.* Seventeenth.
dicibile [dicIbile], *a.* Speakable, that can be told.
dicioccare, *v.t.* To thin foliage (of trees).
diciottenne, *a.* Eighteen years old.
diciottesimo [diciottEsimo], *a.* Eighteenth.
diciotto, *a.* Eighteen.
dicitore, *n.m.* Speaker, orator, lecturer; reciter.
dicitura, *n.f.* Elocution, pronunciation, delivery; wording, form of wording; reading as. **Avere una bella —,** to have a good delivery; **la — è la seguente,** the wording is as follows.
dicotiledone [dicotilEdone], *n.f.* (*Bot.*) Dicotyledon.
dicotomia [dicotomIa], *n.f.* Dichotomy.
dicromatico [dicromAtico], *a.* Of two colours.
dicrotismo, *n.m.* (*Med.*) Dicrotism, double-beating of pulse.
didascalie [didascalIe], *n.f.pl.* (*Theat.*) Stage directions; cues; (*Cinem.*) running commentary; captions.
didascalica [didascAlica], *n.f.* Art of instruction.
didascalico [didascAlico], *a.* Didactic.
didattica [didAttica], *n.f.* Didactics.
didattico [didAttico], *a.* Didactic. **Direttore —,** local director of education.
didentro, *adv.* Within, inside.
didiacciare, *v.i.* (*Tuscan*) To melt.
Didone, *n.f.* Dido.
dieci, *n.m.a.* Ten. **Il —,** the tenth (of the month); **le —,** ten o'clock.
diecimila, *a.* Ten thousand.
diecimillesimo, *a.* Ten thousandth.
diecina, *n.f.* Ten, half a score.
diecino, decino, *n.m.* (*colloq.*) Ten centesimi.
diedro, *n.m.* (*Geom.*) Dihedron.
dielettrico [dielEttrico], *a.* (*Elect.*) Dielectric, non-conducting.
dieresi [diEresi], *n.f.* Diaeresis.
diesire, *n.m.* (*colloq.*) Day of death, or sentence in court (from Lat. *dies irae*).
diesis, *n.m.* (*Mus.*) Sharp.
dieta, *n.f.* Diet, regimen; abstinence from food; (*Hist.*) diet, assembly.
dietetica [dietEtica], *n.f.* Dietetics.
dietetico [dietEtico], *a.* Dietetic.
dietro *adv. prep.* Back, backwards, behind; after; against, upon. **Andar —,** to follow; **tener — a,** to follow, to keep pace with; **per di —,** from behind; (*colloq.*) **esser — a fare,** to be about to do; (*Comm.*) **— accettazione,** upon acceptance; **— ricevuta,** against receipt; **— versamento di,** on payment of; **— richiesta,** on application.
dietrobottega, *n.m.* Back shop; room behind the shop.
dietrocamera [dietrocAmera], *n.f.* Backroom.
dietrofront! *v.i.* (*Mil.*) About turn!
dietroguardia [dietroguArdia], *n.f.* (*Mil.*) Rearguard.
difatti, *adv.* In fact.
difendente, *n.m.* Defendant, defender.
difendere [difEndere], *v.t.* To defend, to protect, to screen, to shield; to guard against; to support; (*Law*) to defend, to plead on behalf of.
difendersi [difEndersi], *v.r.* To defend oneself.
difendibile, difensibile [difendIbile, difensIbile], *a.* Defendible, tenable.
difenditrice, *n.f.* Defender, protectress.
difensiva, *n.f.* Defensive. **Stare sulla —,** to be on the defensive.
difensivo, *a.* Defensive.
difensore, *n.m.* Defender, protector; (*Law*) counsel for the defence.
difesa, *n.f.* Defence; justification, excuse, apology; protection, safeguard; fender, screen; shield, shelter; (*Law*) defence. **Legittima —,** self-defence; **prendere la —,** to take somebody's part; **— contraerea,** anti-aircraft defence; **linea di —,** line of defence; **senza —,** defenceless.
difeso, *a.* Sheltered, protected. **Sono ben — dal freddo,** I am well protected from the cold.
difettare, *v.i.* To be wanting, to be lacking, to be deficient, to be short of. **— di buona volontà,** to lack good will.
difettivamente, *adv.* Defectively, imperfectly.
difettivo, *a.* (*Gram.*) Defective.
difetto, *n.m.* Defect, fault, flaw, blemish, shortcoming; default, want, lack. **La memoria gli fa —,** his memory is failing; **un — fisico,** a physical defect; **essere in —,** to be at fault.
difettosamente, *adv.* Faultily.
difettoso, *a.* Faulty, imperfect, defective.
difettuccio [difettUccio], *n.m.* Minor fault, slight defect.
diffalcare, *v.t.* To abate, to reduce, to deduct [cp. **defalcare**].
diffalta, *n.f.* (*obs.*) Fault.
diffamare, *v.t.* To defame, to slander, to libel.
diffamativo, *a.* Defamatory, slanderous.
diffamatore, *n.m.* Defamer, calumniator, libeller, slanderer.
diffamatorio [diffamatOrio], *a.* Defamatory.
diffamazione, *n.f.* Defamation, aspersion, calumny.
differente, *a.* Different, dissimilar, unlike; diverse.
differentemente, *adv.* Differently, diversely.
differenza, *n.f.* Difference, diversity, disparity; dissension. **A — di,** unlike.
differenziale, *n.m.a.* Differential; (*Motor.*) differential gear. **Ruota del —,** differential wheel; **calcolo —,** differential calculus.
differenziare *v.t.* To differentiate, to discriminate; to make different.
differenziarsi, *v.r.* To make oneself different.

differibile [differIbile], *a.* That may be deferred.
differimento, *n.m.* Postponement, adjournment, deferment.
differire (1), *v.t.* To put off, to postpone, to defer. — **la partenza,** to postpone one's departure.
differire (2), *v.i.* To differ, to vary, to be dissimilar. — **nelle opinioni,** to differ in opinion.
difficile (1) [diffIcile], *n.m.* Difficult thing. **Il — è questo,** this is the difficulty; **non fare il —!** don't be difficult!
difficile (2) [diffIcile], *a.* Difficult, hard, arduous. **Una persona —,** a person hard to please; **tempi difficili,** hard times.
difficilmente, *adv.* With difficulty, unlikely, hardly.
difficoltà [-à], *n.f.* Difficulty; obstacle, hindrance, impediment; objection, misunderstanding. **Far delle —,** to raise objections; **superare una —,** to overcome a difficulty.
difficoltoso, *a.* Difficult.
diffida, *n.f.* (Public) notice, warning, intimation.
diffidare, *v.t.i.* To distrust, to have no confidence in, to doubt; (*Law*) to warn, to intimate; to give notice of.
diffidente, *a.* Diffident, suspicious, distrustful.
diffidentemente, *adv.* Diffidently.
diffidenza, *n.f.* Diffidence, distrust, mistrust, suspicion.
diffilare, *v.t.* (*Mil.*) To defile.
diffondere [diffOndere], *v.t.* To spread, to disseminate, to diffuse, to circulate; to broadcast, to divulge, to propagate. — **notizie,** to spread news.
diffondersi, *v.r.* To spread, to expound, to enlarge upon.
diffondimento, *n.m.* Diffusion.
diffonditore, diffonditrice, *n.m.f.* Disseminator (of news, etc.).
difformare, *v.t.* To deform.
difforme, *a.* Diverse, dissimilar; shapeless.
difformità [-à], *n.f.* Diverseness, diversity; deformity.
diffrangere [diffrAngere], *v.t.* To diffract.
diffrazione, *n.f.* Diffraction.
diffusamente, *adv.* Abundantly.
diffusibile [diffusIbile], *a.* Easily diffused.
diffusione, *n.f.* Diffusion, prolixity; spreading (of news, etc.); circulation (of books); (*Radio*) broadcasting.
diffusivo, *a.* Diffusive.
diffuso, *a.* Diffuse, spread out; copious, prolix; (*Radio*) broadcast.
diffusore, *n.m.* (*Radio*) Broadcaster.
difilare, *v.i.* To go straight ahead; (*Mil.*) to march in file.
difilatamente, *adv.* Quickly, straightly, directly.
difilato, *adv.* Straight; at once, immediately.
difrenare, *v.t.* To release the brake, to unbrake.
difterico [diftErico], *a.* (*Med.*) Diphtheric.
difterite, *n.f.* (*Med.*) Diphtheria.
diga, *n.f.* Dyke, bank, dam, breakwater; (*fig.*) obstacle.
digamia [digamIa], *n.f.* Bigamy.
digerente, *a.* Digestive.
digeribile [digerIbile], *a.* Digestible.
digeribilità [-à], *n.f.* Digestibility.
digerire, *v.t.* To digest, to assimilate; (*fig.*) to tolerate, to bear, to brook.
digerito, *a.* Digested.
digestione, *n.f.* Digestion.
digestivo, *a.* Digestive.
digesto, *n.m.* (*Law*) Digest.
digestore, *n.m.* Pressure cooker.
dighiacciare, *v.i.* To thaw.
digiogare, *v.t.* To unyoke.
Digione, *n.m.* Dijon.
digitale, *n.f.a.* (*Bot.*) Digitalis, fox-glove; digital. **Impronta —,** finger-print.
digitare, *v.t.* To use the fingers in playing a musical instrument.
digitato, *a.* (*Zool.*) Digitate.
digitatura, *n.f.* Digitation.
digitazione, *n.f.* (*Zool.*) Digitation; (*Mus.*) fingering.
digito [dIgito], *n.m.* Digit.
digiunante, *n.m.* One who is fasting.
digiunare, *v.i.* To fast.
digiunatore, digiunatrice, *n.m.f.* Person who is fasting.
digiuno, *n.m.* Fasting, fast. (*Eccles.*) **Giorni di —,** fast days.
digiuno, *a.* Fasting, hungry, empty; ignorant.
dignità [-à], *n.f.* Dignity, worth; rank, estimation; self-respect.
dignitario [dignitArio], *n.m.* Dignitary.
dignitosamente, *adv.* Decorously, in a dignified manner.
dignitoso, *a.* Dignified, decorous, noble, lofty; self-respecting.
digradamento, *n.m.* Descent by degrees.
digradante, *a.* Sloping, diminishing.
digradare (1), *v.i.* To slope down, to descend gradually, to decline; to diminish.
digradare (2), *v.t.* [cp. **degradare**].
digradazione, *n.f.* Descent; loss of rank.
digrassare, *v.t.* To remove grease or fat, to skim; to scour.
digredire, *v.i.* To digress, to deviate.
digressione, *n.f.* Digression, deviation. **Fare delle digressioni,** to digress, to wander from the subject.
digressivamente, *adv.* Diffusely.
digressivo, *a.* Diffuse, digressive.
digrignamento, *n.m.* Baring the teeth.
digrignare, *v.i.* To gnash the teeth, to grind the teeth.
digrossamento, *n.m.* Whittling down, rough-hewing.
digrossare, *v.t.* To whittle down, to rough-hew; (*fig.*) to instruct.
digruma, *n.f.* Voracity.
digrumale, *n.m.* (*Zool.*) Rumen, first paunch in ruminants.
digrumare, *v.t.* To chew the cud; (*fig.*) to ruminate; to eat greedily.
diguazzamento, *n.m.* Paddling, dabbling.
diguazzare, *v.t.i.* To paddle, to splash about; to stir up (mud, etc.).
dilacerare, *v.t.* To tear, to rend, to lacerate; (*fig.*) to torment.
dilagare, *v.i.* To overflow, to flood; to spread.
dilagarsi, *v.r.* To flood, to form a lake.
dilagatamente, *adv.* Furiously.
dilaniare, *v.t.* To lacerate, to tear to pieces, to rend.
dilapidamento, *n.m.* Squandering, wasting.

dilapidare, *v.t.* To dilapidate, to squander, to waste. — **una sostanza,** to squander a patrimony.
dilapidazione, *n.f.* Wasting, dilapidation.
dilatabile [dilatAbile], *a.* Dilatable, elastic.
dilatare, *v.t.* To dilate, to expand, to enlarge, to spread.
dilatarsi, *v.r.* To expand, to swell, to be enlarged.
dilatato, *p.p.a.* Enlarged, swollen, blown out.
dilatazione, *n.f.* Dilatation, amplification, expansion.
dilatometro [dilatOmetro], *n.m.* Dilatometer.
dilatorio [dilatOrio], *a.* Dilatory, procrastinating.
dilavamento, *n.m.* Washing away.
dilavare, *v.t.* To wash away, to wash out.
dilazionare, *v.t.* To postpone, to procrastinate; to defer.
dilazione, *n.f.* Postponement, delay, respite. **Concedere una —,** to grant a respite.
dilegato, *n.m.* (*Eccles.*) Legate, papal envoy.
dileggiare, *v.t.* To mock, to scoff at, to deride, to ridicule.
dileggiatore, *n.m.* Mocker, scoffer.
dileggio [dilEggio], *n.m.* Mockery, derision; jeer.
dileguamento, *n.m.* Vanishing.
dileguare, *v.t.* To scatter, to disperse; to melt.
dileguarsi, *v.r.* To disappear, to vanish, to fade away; to melt.
dileguo [dilEguo], *n.m.* Distance. **Mandare in —,** to send far away; to melt.
dilemma (*pl.* **dilemmi**), *n.m.* Dilemma. **I corni di un —,** the horns of a dilemma.
dilettante, *n.m.* Amateur; dabbler. **Compagnia di dilettanti,** amateur company.
dilettantesco, *a.* Amateurish; superficial.
dilettantismo, *n.m.* Dilettantism, amateurism.
dilettare, *v.t.* To amuse, to delight, to charm.
dilettarsi, *v.r.* To take delight in; to take pleasure in.
dilettazione, *n.f.* Delight, delectation.
dilettevole [dilettEvole], *a.* Pleasant, pleasing, agreeable, delightful.
dilettevolmente, *adv.* Pleasantly, delightfully.
diletto, *n.m.* Delight, pleasure.
diletto, *n.m.a.* Beloved.
dilettosamente, *adv.* Delightfully, with delight.
dilettoso, *a.* Delightful, enchanting, charming.
dilezione, *n.f.* Love, affection.
diligente, *a.* Diligent; accurate, careful; sedulous, painstaking.
diligentemente, *adv.* Diligently.
diligenza (1), *n.f.* Diligence, care, accuracy, sedulity, application.
diligenza (2), *n.f.* Diligence, stage-coach.
diloggiare, *v.t.* To dislodge [cp. **sloggiare**].
dilogia [dilogIa], *n.f.* Double meaning.
dilombarsi, *v.r.* To strain one's back.
dilombato, *a.* Nerveless, feeble; broken-backed (of a horse).
dilucidare, *v.t.* To explain, to elucidate.
dilucidazione, *n.f.* Elucidation, explanation.
dilucolo [dilUcolo], *n.m.* Dawn, daybreak.
diluente, *a.* (*Med.*) Diluent.
diluire, *v.t.* To dilute, to water down; to weaken, to dissolve.
dilungamento, *n.m.* Removal to a distance.
dilungare, *v.t.* To remove to a distance; to prolong.
dilungarsi, *v.r.* To move away; to digress, to wander from the subject; to expatiate. **— nei particolari,** to dwell on the details.
dilungo, *adv.* Straight on, along, continuously. **Tirare —,** to pass on, to go on.
diluviale, *a.* Torrential.
diluviare, *v.i.* To rain in torrents, to pour with rain; (*fig.*) to eat voraciously.
diluvio [dilUvio], *n.m.* Deluge, flood; downpour, heavy rain. **— universale,** the Flood; **— di botte,** shower of blows; **— di gente,** crowd of people.
diluzione, *n.f.* Dilution.
dimacchiare, *v.t.* To clean (woodland).
dimagramento, *n.m.* Thinning, wasting away, emaciation.
dimagrante, *n.m.a.* Weight-reducer, slimmer; thinning. **Dieta —,** slimming diet.
dimagrare, dimagrire, *v.i.* To grow thin, to lose weight; to slim; to become lean, to emaciate.
dimandare, *v.t.* To demand [cp. **domandare**].
dimane, dimani, *adv.* Tomorrow [cp. **domani**].
dimembrare, *v.t.* To dismember [cp. **smembrare**].
dimenare, *v.t.* To agitate, to wag, to shake, to toss. **— la coda,** to wag the tail; **— le ganasce,** to eat voraciously.
dimenarsi, *v.r.* To keep tossing about, to wriggle, to flounder; to fumble, to fidget.
dimenio [dimenIo], *n.m.* Tossing, agitation, wriggling, fidgeting, constant shaking.
dimensione, *n.f.* Dimension, size; area; volume.
dimenticaggine [dimenticAggine], *n.f.* Carelessness; inadvertence; forgetfulness.
dimenticanza, *n.f.* Forgetfulness; oversight, inadvertence, omission, slip. **È stata una —,** it was an oversight.
dimenticare, dimenticarsi, *v.t.r.* To forget; to neglect, to omit. **Dimentichiamo il passato,** let bygones be bygones; **dimenticarsi di una cosa,** to forget a thing.
dimenticatoio [dimenticatOio], *n.m.* (*colloq.*) Oblivion. **Mettere nel —,** to consign to oblivion; **cadere nel —,** to fall into oblivion.
dimentico [dimEntico], *a.* Forgetful, careless, oblivious.
dimessamente, *adv.* Humbly, submissively, modestly. **Vestito —,** poorly dressed.
dimesso, *p.p.a.* Resigned, dismissed; lowly, humble; neglected.
dimesticare, *v.t.* To domesticate, to tame [cp. **addomesticare**].
dimestichezza, *n.f.* Familiarity, intimacy; fellowship.
dimestico [dimEstico], *a.* Intimate, familiar.
dimettere [dimEttere], *v.t.* To dismiss, to remove (from a job); to give up, to cease, to renounce; (*Eccles.*) to pardon.
dimettersi, *v.r.* To resign, to withdraw from office. **Dovrà —,** he will have to resign.
dimezzamento, *n.m.* Halving.

dimezzare, *v.t.* To halve, to divide into two; to share equally.
diminuendo, *adv.* Diminishingly.
diminuibile [diminuIbile], *a.* Diminishable.
diminuimento, *n.m.* Diminution; diminishing
diminuire, *v.t.* To lessen, to diminish, to lower, to reduce, to decrease, to abate.
diminuirsi, *v.r.* To degrade oneself.
diminutivamente, *adv.* Diminutively.
diminutivo, *a.* Diminutive.
diminuzione, *n.f.* Diminution, reduction, falling off.
dimissionario [dimissionArio], *n.m.a.* One who has resigned; resigning, withdrawing.
dimissione, *n.f.* Resignation; dismissal. **Dare, chiedere, accettare le dimissioni,** to tender, ask for, accept one's resignation.
dimissorio dimissOrio], *a.* (*Eccles.*) Dimissory.
dimodochè, *conj.* So that.
dimoiare, *v.i.* To thaw, to liquefy.
dimolto, *adv. a.* Very much.
dimora, *n.f.* Dwelling; residence, abode, sojourn; delay. **Senza fissa —,** without fixed abode; **prender —,** to take up one's residence.
dimorante, *a.* Dwelling, living.
dimorare, *v.i.* To dwell, to live, to stay; to delay.
dimostrabile [dimostrAbile], *a.* Demonstrable.
dimostrabilità [-à], *n.f.* Demonstrability.
dimostramento, *n.m.* Demonstrating; supplying evidence.
dimostrante, *n.m.* Demonstrator; demonstrating.
dimostrare, *v.t.* To demonstrate; to prove, to make evident; to bring evidence; to show, to manifest; to solve. **Egli non dimostra la sua età,** he doesn't look his age; **dimostra più anni del vero,** he looks older than he really is.
dimostrarsi, *v.r.* To show oneself; to prove oneself. **S'è dimostrato vero amico,** he has proved himself a true friend.
dimostrativamente, *adv.* Demonstratively.
dimostrativo, *a.* Demonstrative (in all senses).
dimostrazione, *n.f.* Demonstration, proof, evidence; public meeting, public demonstration.
dimozzare, *v.t.* (*Agric.*) To cut off, to lop.
dina, *n.f.* (*Phys.*) Dyne.
dinamica [dinAmica], *n.f.* Dynamics.
dinamico [dinAmico], *a.* Dynamic, dynamical; energetic, active.
dinamismo, *n.m.* Dynamism, energy.
dinamitardo, *n.m.* Dynamiter; thrower of bombs, dynamitard.
dinamite, *n.f.* Dynamite.
dinamo (pl. **dinamo**) [dInamo], *n.f.* Dynamo.
dinamometro [dinamOmetro], *n.m.* Dynamometer.
dinanzi, *adv.prep.* Before, in advance, in front; formerly; facing. **— a me,** in front of me, facing me; **— a suo padre,** in his father's presence.
dinasta (*pl.* **dinasti**), *n.m.* Dynast.
dinastia [dinastIa], *n.f.* Dynasty, ruling family.
dinastico [dinAstico], *a.* Dynastic.
dindo, *n.m.* (*Zool.*) Turkey.
dindon, *n.m.* Ding-dong (of bells); chime.
dinegare, *v.t.* To deny, to refuse.
dinegazione, diniego, *n.f.m.* Denial, refusal, negation.
dinervare, *v.t.* To unnerve.
dinoccolato, *a.* Slouchy, listless, indifferent; slovenly; awkward.
dinosauro [dinosAuro], *n.m.* Dinosaur.
dintorni, *n.m.pl.* Surroundings, environs; outskirts; neighbourhood, vicinity.
dintorno, d'intorno, *adv.prep.* Around, round about, on every side.
dinunziare, *v.t.* To denounce; to protest [cp. **denunziare**].
Dio, *n.m.* God. **Per l'amor di Dio,** for God's sake; **grazie a Dio,** thank God; **quanto ben di Dio,** what an abundance; **Dio guardi, Dio liberi,** God help me; **un'ira di Dio,** a confusion; **sta come Dio vuole,** God's will be done; **gli dei,** the (pagan) gods.
diocesano, *n.m.a.* Diocesan.
diocesi [diOcesi], *n.f.* Diocese.
diomedea [diomedEa], *n.f.* (*Zool.*) Albatross.
Dionigi, *n.m.* Dionysius.
dionisiaco [dionisIaco], *a.* Dionysiac.
diorama, *n.m.* Diorama.
diottra, *n.f.* Theodolite.
diottrica [diOttrica], *n.f.* (*Phys.*) Dioptrics.
dipanare, *v.t.* To wind into a ball; to unravel, to disentangle. **Dipanare la matassa,** to unravel the skein; (*fig.*) to clear up the difficulty.
dipanatura, *n.f.* Unravelling.
dipartenza, *n.f.* Departing, departure. **Far le dipartenze,** to say goodbye.
dipartimento, *n.m.* Department.
dipartire, *v.t.* To part, to divide.
dipartirsi, *v.r.* To depart, to leave, to go away; to differ; to digress. **— da una consuetudine,** to depart from a custom.
dipartita, *n.f.* Departure, quitting; (*fig.*) death.
dipendente, *n.m.a.* Dependant, inferior, subordinate; depending, dependent; inferior.
dipendenza, *n.f.* Dependence, dependency; employ. **Essere alle dipendenze di,** to be under orders from; **in —,** in consequence, in relation to.
dipendere [dipEndere], *v.i.* To depend, to proceed, to originate; to be dependent, to be subject; to be contingent, to be conditional. **Non dipende da me,** it does not rest with me; **— dagli altri,** to depend upon others (for support, etc.); **ciò dipende dalle circostanze,** that depends upon circumstances; **se fosse dipeso da me,** if it depended on me.
dipianare, *v.t.* To level.
dipingere [dipIngere], *v.t.* To paint; to depict; to portray; (*fig.*) to represent, to describe. **— dal vero,** to paint from nature.
dipingersi [dipIngersi], *v.r.* To rouge or paint oneself.
dipingimento, *n.m.* (Act or process of) colouring.
dipinto, *n.m.* Painting, picture; mural painting.
dipintore, *n.m.* (*Lit.*) Painter, artist.
dipintucchiare, *v.t.* To daub, to paint poorly.
dipintura, *n.f.* Painting, picture; description.

diploma (*pl.* **diplomi**), *n.m.* Diploma; certificate; charter.
diplomare, *v.t.* To confer a diploma.
diplomarsi, *v.r.* To graduate, to receive a degree.
diplomatica [diplomAtica], *n.f.* Diplomatics.
diplomaticamente, *adv.* Diplomatically.
diplomatico [diplomAtico], *n.m.a.* Diplomat, diplomatist; diplomatic.
diplomazia [diplomazIa], *n.f.* Diplomacy; (*fig.*) tact, adroitness.
dipoi, di poi, *adv.* Afterwards, after.
diportamento, *n.m.* Demeanour, deportment, behaviour.
diportarsi, *v.r.* To conduct oneself, to behave; to amuse oneself.
diporto, *n.m.* Recreation, sport, diversion, amusement. **Andare a —,** to go walking, to take recreation; **per —,** for sport, for one's own amusement.
dipresso, *adv.* Nearby, near. **A un —,** about so much, roughly, approximately.
dipsomane [dipsOmane], *n.m.f.* Dipsomaniac.
dipsomania [dipsomanIa], *n.f.* (*Med.*) Dipsomania.
diradamento, *n.m.* Thinning out, diminution; rarefication.
diradare, *v.t.* To thin out, to diminish; to do something rarely.
diradarsi, *v.r.* To become less dense, to rarefy; to clear (of the weather). **Le sue visite si diradarono,** his visits became less frequent.
diradato, *a.* Rarefied.
diradicamento, *n.m.* Uprooting, eradication.
diradicare, *v.t.* To uproot [cp. **sradicare**].
diragnare, *v.t.* To sweep away cobwebs.
diramare, *v.t.* To prune, to lop, to cut away branches; to circulate, to distribute. **— gli inviti,** to send out invitations.
diramarsi, *v.r.* To branch out, to ramify. **Una strada si dirama,** a road branches off.
diramazione, *n.f.* Ramification, branching off; crossroads; (*rare*) pruning, thinning out.
dirazzare, *v.i.* To degenerate.
dire (1), *v.t.* To say, to speak, to tell; to recite, to declaim; to mean; to signify; to harmonize. **A — il vero,** to speak the truth; **che vuole — ciò?** What does this mean? **vale a —,** that is to say; **aver a che — con uno,** to bear a grudge against someone; **— pane al pane,** to call a spade a spade; **lasciate —,** let folk talk; **ho sentito —,** I've been told; **trovare a —,** to find fault; **è tutto —,** this is the limit; **non c'è che —,** there's nothing to be said against it; **— per burla,** to speak jokingly; **far — una messa,** to have a Mass said; **dirsela con qualcuno,** to get on with someone; **mandare a — a,** to send word to; **— sciocchezze,** to talk nonsense; **per così —,** so to speak; **si dice,** they say, it is said; **il giuoco mi dice,** the game is in my favour; **voler —,** to mean. [cp. **dirsi**].
dire (2), *n.m.* Speech, words; assertion. **L'arte del —,** rhetoric; **oltre ogni —,** beyond all description; **avete un bel —,** it's all very well to say that; **al — di tutti,** in the general opinion; **un continuo — e disdire,** an unceasing shilly-shally.
direnare, *v.t.* To break the back of, to weary.
direnarsi, *v.r.* To break one's back; to be over-fatigued.
direttamente, *adv.* Directly, by the nearest way; immediately.
direttario [direttArio], *n.m.* (*Law*) Owner of an estate.
direttissimo [direttIssimo], *n.m.* (*Rail.*) Express, through train.
direttiva, *n.f.* Directive; rules for action. **Dare le direttive,** to give instructions.
direttivo, *a.* Managing, leading, directive. **Consiglio —,** board of managers.
diretto, *n.m.* (*Rail.*) Fast train.
diretto, *a.* Directed; addressed; direct, straight; (*Rail.*) through (carriage). **La via diretta,** the direct route, the shortest way.
direttore, *n.m.* Director, manager; editor (of a newspaper); headmaster; conductor (of an orchestra).
direttorio [direttOrio], *n.m.* Directory; board of managers.
direttrice, *n.f.* Manageress; head mistress.
direzione, *n.f.* Direction (in all senses); superintendence, management; directorship; director's office; editorial office.
dirigente, *n.m.a.* Director; directing, ruling, governing. **Classi dirigenti,** ruling classes.
dirigere [dirIgere], *v.t.* To direct, to manage, to lead, to conduct; to address. **— una lettera,** to address a letter; **— la propria attenzione,** to turn one's attention (to).
dirigersi [dirIgersi], *v.r.* To direct oneself; to direct one's steps; to make for.
dirigibile [dirigIbile], *n.m.a.* Airship; dirigible.
dirimente, *a.* (*Law*) Nullifying, invalidating, diriment.
dirimere [dirImere], *v.t.* To annul, to invalidate; to separate. **— una lite,** to settle a quarrel.
dirimpettaio [dirimpettAio], *n.m.* (*colloq.*) Vis-à-vis.
dirimpetto, *adv.prep.* Opposite, facing; face to face; in comparison.
diritta, *n.f.* Right hand, right side. **Tenere la —,** keep to the right.
dirittamente, *adv.* Straight, directly.
dirittezza, *n.f.* Straightness; rectitude.
diritto, *n.m.* Right, law, justice, equity; privilege, claim, title; fee. **A buon —,** with good reason; **— delle genti,** the law of nations; **studiare —,** to study for the law; **— canonico,** canon law; **a torto o a —,** wrongly or rightly; **— d'autore,** copyright; **il — di un tessuto,** the right side of a material; **a maggior —,** with all the more reason; **a — o a rovescio,** by hook or by crook; **diritti di riproduzione,** rights (film, etc.).
diritto, dritto, *a.adv.* Straight, direct, upright; right, honest, good. **Rigare —,** to keep to the straight and narrow path, to toe the line; **star su —,** to stand erect; **andate sempre —,** walk straight on; **nel — mezzo,** right in the middle.
dirittura, *n.f.* Straightness, rectitude, honesty; the straight (of a racecourse); **A dirittura, addirittura,** entirely, absolutely, completely.
dirizzamento, *n.m.* Directing, direction.
dirizzare, *v.t.* To direct, to straighten; to put right. **— le orecchie,** to prick up one's ears.

dirizzarsi, *v.r.* To rise, to stand up, to stand erect; to address oneself to.
dirizzatura, *n.f.* Parting (of hair).
dirizzone, *n.m.* (Bad) habit; a crotchet, a fad; thoughtless action.
dirlindana, *n.f.* Long fishing-line.
diro, *a.* Dire, cruel, atrocious.
diroccamento, *n.m.* Demolition.
diroccare, *v.t.i.* To demolish, to dismantle; to crumble down.
diroccarsi, *v.r.* To fall with a crash.
dirocciare, *v.i.* To descend by leaping down from rock to rock.
dirompere [dirOmpere], *v.t.* To break; to crush, to shatter. **— in lagrime,** to burst into tears; **bomba dirompente,** demolition bomb.
dirompersi [dirOmpersi], *v.r.* To break oneself in to; to crash.
dirompimento, *n.m.* Breaking in; crashing.
dirottamente, *adv.* Out of all bounds, excessively; in torrents (rain). **Piangere —,** to shed floods of tears.
dirottamento, *n.m.* Diverting the course.
dirottare, *v.t.* To divert, to turn aside.
dirotto, *a.* Pouring, pelting. **Pioggia dirotta,** pouring rain; **pianto —,** bitter weeping.
dirozzamento, *n.m.* (*fig.*) Polishing up, refining, civilizing.
dirozzare, *v.t.* To polish, to educate, to refine; to rough-hew.
dirsi, *v.r.* To style oneself [cp. **dire**].
dirugginio [diruggInIo], *n.m.* Scraping sound; grinding of the teeth.
dirugginire, dirugginare, *v.t.* To clean the rust off, to polish.
dirupamento, *n.m.* Falling down, sliding down.
dirupare, *v.t.i.* To hurl down; to fall rolling down; to precipitate.
dirupatamente, *adv.* Precipitously.
dirupato, *a.* Precipitous, rocky, abrupt.
dirupo, *n.m.* Crag; ravine, gorge; precipice.
diruto, *a.* Ruined, dismantled, dilapidated.
disabbellire, *v.t.* To disfigure, to spoil the beauty of.
disabbigliare, *v.t.* To undress; to divest of ornament.
disabile [disAbile], *a.* Unfit, incapable.
disabilità [-à], *n.f.* Disability, insufficiency, incapacity.
disabitato, *a.* Uninhabited, depopulated; deserted.
disabituare, *v.t.* To disaccustom.
disabituato, *a.* Unaccustomed; out of the way of.
disaccentare, *v.t.* To omit the accent.
disaccentrare, *v.t.* To decentralize.
disaccetto, *a.* Ill-received.
disacciaiare, *v.t.* To decarbonize steel.
disacconciamente, *adv.* Unsuitably.
disacconcio [disaccOncio], *a.* Unsuited, unsuitable; unbecoming.
disaccoppiare, *v.t.* To uncouple.
disaccordare, *v.t.* To disagree; to make discord.
disaccordo, *n.m.* Disagreement, contention; (*Mus.*) discord. **Essere in —,** to disagree.
disaccreditato, *a.* Discredited.
disacerbare, *v.t.* To make less bitter; to assuage, to mitigate.
disacrare, *v.t.* To desecrate.
disadattamente, *adv.* Unsuitably.
disadattezza, *n.f.* Unsuitability.
disadatto, *a.* Unfit, unsuitable, unfitted, incapable; unbecoming.
disadornare, *v.t.* To strip of ornament, to disfigure.
disadorno, *a.* Unadorned, plain, bare. **Uno stile —,** a bald style.
disaffezionare, *v.t.* To disaffect; to estrange, to alienate.
disaffezionarsi, *v.r.* To lose one's affection for.
disaffezione, *n.f.* Disaffection, alienation of feeling; want of sympathy, estrangement.
disagevole [disagEvole], *a.* Fatiguing, hard, uneasy, difficult, uncomfortable, rough.
disagevolezza, *n.f.* Hardness, difficulty.
disagevolmente, *adv.* With difficulty, hardly.
disaggio [disAggio], *n.m.* (*Comm.*) Discount of exchange.
disaggradevole [disaggradEvole], *a.* Disagreeable, unpleasing.
disaggradevolmente, *adv.* Disagreeably.
disaggradire, *v.t.* To dislike, to receive unkindly.
disagguagliare, *v.t.* To make unequal.
disagiatamente, *adv.* Uncomfortably; needily.
disagiato, *a.* Uncomfortable; needy.
disagio [disAgio], *n.m.* Uneasiness, discomfort; want, hardship. **Trovarsi a —,** to feel uneasy.
disaiuto, *n.m.* (*rare*) Impediment, hindrance.
disalberare, *v.t.* (*Naut.*) To dismast.
disalbergare, *v.i.* To move, to leave one's residence.
disamabile [disamAbile], *a.* Unamiable, dislikeable.
disamare, *v.t.* To cease to love.
disamenità [-à], *n.f.* Unpleasantness.
disameno, *a.* Unpleasant, disagreeable.
disamina [disAmina], *n.f.* Investigation, examination. **Fare un'attenta —,** to go thoroughly into, to examine minutely.
disaminato, *a.* Considered, weighed.
disamorare, *v.t.* To disaffect, to estrange, to alienate.
disamorarsi, *v.r.* To lose affection, to fall out of love.
disamoratamente, *adv.* Without affection.
disamore, *n.m.* Aversion, indifference, dislike.
disancorare, *v.i.* (*Naut.*) To weigh anchor.
disanimare, *v.t.* To dishearten, to discourage, to dispirit.
disappaiare, *v.t.* To uncouple.
disappariscente, *a.* Invisible, without any appearance.
disappassionarsi, *v.r.* To free oneself from a passion; to lose interest in.
disappetenza, *n.f.* Lack of appetite.
disapplicarsi, *v.r.* To disregard, to neglect.
disapplicazione, *n.f.* Lack of application, neglect.
disapprendere [disapprEndere], *v.t.* To forget, to unlearn.
disapprovare, *v.t.* To disapprove, to blame.
disapprovazione, *n.f.* Disapproval, censure, disapprobation.
disappunto, *n.m.* Disappointment, vexation. **Con mio grande —,** to my great disappointment.

disarcionare, *v.t.* To unsaddle.
disargentare, *v.t.* To unsilver.
disarmamento, *n.m.* Disarmament.
disarmare, *v.t.* To disarm; to dismantle; (*Naut.*) to unrig, to lay a vessel up; (*fig.*) to tame, to subdue.
disarmo, *n.m.* Disarmament. (*Naut.*) **Nave in —,** ship laid up.
disarmonia [disarmonIa], *n.f.* Discord, disharmony; disagreement.
disarmonico [disarmOnico], *a.* Discordant.
disarticolare, *v.t.* To disjoint.
disarticolarsi, *v.r.* To be dislocated.
disassociare, *v.t.* To disassociate, to dissociate.
disassociarsi, *v.r.* To dissociate oneself.
disassuefare, *v.t.* To disaccustom.
disastro, *n.m.* Disaster, accident, calamity, misfortune. **— ferroviario,** railway accident.
disastroso, *a.* Disastrous, ruinous, calamitous.
disattento, *a.* Inattentive, heedless; negligent, careless.
disattenzione, *n.f.* Inattention, negligence, carelessness.
disattrezzare, *v.t.* (*Naut.*) To unrig.
disavanzo, *n.m.* Deficit, loss, deficiency. **Colmare un —,** to make up a deficit.
disavvantaggiarsi, *v.r.* To place oneself at a disadvantage.
disavvantaggio [disavvantAggio], *n.m.* Disadvantage [cp. **svantaggio**].
disavvedutamente, *adv.* Inadvertently, heedlessly.
disavvedutezza, *n.f.* Inadvertence, heedlessness.
disavveduto, *a.* Inconsiderate, heedless.
disavvenente, *a.* Unattractive, unpleasant, undesirable.
disavventura, *n.f.* Mishap, accident, misadventure; bad luck.
disavventurato, *a.* Unlucky, unfortunate.
disavvertenza, *n.f.* Inadvertence, oversight, inattention; neglect.
disavvezzare, *v.t.* To disaccustom, to dissuade, to wean.
disavvezzarsi, *v.r.* To give up the habit (of).
disavvezzo, *a.* Unaccustomed.
disbandare, *v.t.* To disband.
disbarcare, *v.t.* To disembark.
disborsare, *v.t.* To disburse, to pay out.
disborso, *n.m.* Disbursement, paying out; advance; laying out (money). **Trovarsi in —,** to be out of pocket.
disboscare [cp. **diboscare**].
disbracare, *v.t.* (*Mech.*) To disengage gear.
disbramare, *v.t.* To satisfy (a wish).
disbrigare, *v.t.* To disengage, to disembarrass; to disentangle; to expedite, to despatch.
disbrigarsi, *v.r.* To get rid of, to clear oneself of; to get oneself out of a difficulty; to make haste.
disbrigo, *n.m.* Despatch, clearing up, settlement. **Il — degli affari,** the despatch of business; **— dell'affare,** settlement of a deal.
discacciare, *a.* To expel, to drive away.
discapitare, *v.i.* To suffer loss.
discapito [discApito], *n.m.* Detriment; damage, loss. **Con mio —,** to my own detriment.
discarica [discArica], *n.f.* Unloading.
discaricare, *v.t.* To unload, to disburden.
discarico [discArico], *n.m.* Unloading; acquittal, release, justification, excuse. **A mio —,** to ease my conscience.
discaro, *a.* Disagreeable, unpleasant, unacceptable. **Non vi sia — accettare,** please accept.
discendente, *n.m.a.* Descendant; descending. **Linea —,** line of descent.
discendenza, *n.f.* Descent, lineage, extraction, origin.
discendere [discEndere], *v.i.* To descend, to go down; to sink; to derive from, to spring from; to fall (of prices); to alight, to land. **I barbari discesero in Italia,** the barbarians came down into Italy; **— ad un albergo,** to put up at an hotel; **— dal treno,** to alight from the train; **— sempre più,** to descend lower and lower; **— a terra,** to land, to disembark.
discendimento, *n.m.* (Act and result of) descending.
discensione, *n.m.* Descent, derivation, origin.
discente, *n.m.* Pupil, scholar.
discentrare, *v.t.* To decentralize.
discepolo [discEpolo], *n.m.* Disciple, follower, pupil, scholar.
discernere [discErnere], *v.t.* To discern, to distinguish, to judge between, to discriminate.
discernibile [discernIbile], *a.* Discernible, visible.
discernimento, *n.m.* Discernment, discrimination, judgment, sense. **Egli non ha —,** he has no sense.
discernitivo, *a.* Discerning.
discervellare, *v.t.* To brain.
discervellarsi, *v.r.* To puzzle, to rack one's brains.
discervellato, *a.* Rash, hare-brained, foolish.
discesa, *n.f.* Descent, declivity, slope; declining, fall, abatement; (*Radio*) lead-in. (*Aviat.*) **— in picchiata,** nose-dive; (*Ski-ing*) **— a Cristiania,** Christiania turn; **una strada in —,** a descending road, a downhill road; **una forte —,** a steep descent; **— dei prezzi,** fall in prices.
disceverare, *v.t.* To sever, to part; to separate.
dischiodare, *v.t.* To unnail.
dischiomare, *v.t.* (*Lit.*) To deprive of hair.
dischiudere [dischiUdere], *v.t.* To disclose, to reveal; to open.
dischiuso, *a.* Disclosed, opened. **Le labbra dischiuse al sorriso,** a smile on the lips.
discingere [discIngere], *v.t.* To untie, to ungird, to loosen the girth, to undo.
discinto, *a.* Ungirt, untied, undressed.
disciogliere [disciOgliere], *v.t.* To untie, to loosen, to unbind, to undo; to dissolve; to break; to release, to pardon.
disciogliersi [disciOgliersi], *v.r.* To dissolve, to melt.
discioglimento, *n.m.* Dissolving, dissolution (in all senses).
disciolto, *p.p.a.* Dissolved, loose; melted; unfettered, free.
disciplina, *n.f.* Discipline; training, rule; order, obedience; teaching, doctrine, subject of learning; penance; (*Eccles.*) whip used for self-mortification.
disciplinabile [disciplinAbile], *a.* Amenable to discipline.
disciplinante, *n.m.* One undergoing penance, penitent.

disciplinare, *v.t.* To discipline; to train, to drill; to control, to direct; to enforce.
disciplinare, *a.* Disciplinary. **Misure disciplinari,** disciplinary measures.
disciplinata, *n.f.* (*Eccles.*) Stroke with a discipline.
disciplinatamente, *adv.* In accordance with the rules of discipline.
disciplinatezza, *n.f.* Discipline; docility, obedience.
disciplinato, *p.p.a.* Disciplined, orderly, well-trained; educated.
disco, *n.m.* Disk; quoit; gramophone record; railway signal. **— sul ghiaccio,** ice hockey; **— volante,** "flying saucer."
discoide [discOide], *a.* Discoid.
discolo [dIscolo], *n.m.a.* Young rascal, scamp, rogue, good-for-nothing; idle, undisciplined, wild.
discoloramento, *n.m.* Discolouring.
discolorare, *v.t.* To discolour, to bleach.
discolorazione, *n.f.* Discoloration.
discolorito, *a.* Wan, colourless.
discolpa, *n.f.* Justification, excuse, exculpation. (*Law*) **Testimoni a —,** witnesses for the defence.
discolpare, *v.t.* To exculpate, to clear (from blame).
discolparsi, *v.r.* To exonerate oneself, to excuse oneself; to prove one's innocence.
discompagnarsi, *v.r.* To part company.
disconoscente, *n.m.* Ingrate.
disconoscenza, *n.f.* Ingratitude, lack of appreciation.
disconoscere [disconOscere], *v.t.* To refuse to recognize, to slight, to ignore, to snub; to be ungrateful for.
discontentare, *v.t.* To dissatisfy, to discontent.
discontinuare, *v.t.* To discontinue; to interrupt.
disconvenevole [disconvenEvole], *a.* Inconvenient, unbecoming.
disconvenire, *v.t.* To be unsuitable, to be inconvenient, to disagree.
discoperta, *n.f.* Discovery.
discoperto, *p.p.a.* Open, unprotected. **A —,** in the open (air).
discoprire, *v.t.* To discover [cp. **scoprire**].
discoraggiamento, *n.m.* Discouragement.
discoraggiare, *v.t.* To discourage [cp. **scoraggiare**].
discordante, *a.* Discordant, jarring.
discordanza, *n.f.* Discordance, disagreement; (*Mus.*) discord.
discordare, *v.i.* To disagree, to be at variance; to make discord; to clash, to jar.
discorde, *a.* Discordant, conflicting; dissonant.
discordia [discOrdia], *n.f.* Discord, disagreement; contention, strife.
discorrere [discOrrere], *v.i.* To talk, to chat, to converse, to discourse, to hold forth. **— del più e del meno,** to discuss things in general; **discorriamo d'altro,** let's talk of something else; **e via discorrendo,** and so forth, and so on.
discorritore, *n.m.* Talker, conversationalist.
discorsa, *n.f.*(*colloq*). Gabble, long-winded talk.
discorsivo, *a.* Talkative; sociable.
discorso, *n.m.* Discourse, talk, address, speech; lecture; treatise. **Pronunciare un —,** to make a speech; **senza tanti discorsi,** abruptly, in a brusque manner; **che discorsi son questi?** what do you mean by that? **bei discorsi!** fancy that! (incredulously); **pochi discorsi!** hold your tongue!
discosceso, *a.* Steep.
discostare, *v.t.* To remove; to detach.
discostarsi, *v.r.* To move (oneself) to a distance; to detach oneself.
discosto, *adv.a.* Distant, far off, removed, at some distance; detached.
discoteca, *n.f.* Gramophone record library.
discredenza, *n.f.* Disbelief, unbelief.
discredere [discrEdere], *v.i.* To disbelieve.
discredersi [discrEdersi], *v.r.* To change one's mind, to alter one's opinion [cp. **ricredersi**].
discreditare, *v.t.* To discredit, to speak ill of.
discredito [discrEdito], *n.m.* Discredit, disrepute, disgrace; bad reputation.
discrepanza, *n.f.* Discrepancy, difference; variance.
discretamente, *adv.* Tolerably, sufficiently; discreetly. **— bene,** fairly well.
discretezza, *n.f.* Discretion, moderation; prudence.
discretiva, *n.f.* (*Law*) Power of discrimination.
discretivamente, *adv.* Discriminatingly.
discretivo, *a.* Discretionary.
discreto, *a.* Moderate, fairly good, reasonable; discreet, prudent, considerate. **È un — stipendio,** it's a pretty good salary; **un albergo —,** a fairly good hotel; **è un vino —,** the wine is not so bad.
discrezionale, *a.* Discretionary.
discrezione, *n.f.* Discretion, moderation, prudence, consideration; free choice. **A —,** at choice; **l'età della —,** the age of discretion; **senza —,** immoderately; **rendersi a —,** unconditional surrender.
discriminante, *a.* Distinguishing, causing a difference. (*Law*) **Circostanza —,** extenuating circumstance.
discriminare, *v.t.* To discriminate, to distinguish.
discriminatura, *n.f.* Parting of the hair, hair-parting.
discriminazione, *n.f.* Discrimination.
discussione, *n.f.* Discussion, debate.
discusso, *a.* Discussed, examined. **È una questione molto discussa,** it is a very moot point.
discutere [discUtere], *v.t.* To discuss, to debate; to argue about.
discutibile [discutIbile], *a.* Arguable, discussible, debatable, questionable.
disdegnare, *v.t.* To disdain, to scorn, to despise, to contemn.
disdegno, *n.m.* Disdain, contempt, scorn; indignation.
disdegnosamente, *adv.* Disdainfully, scornfully.
disdegnoso, *a.* Disdainful, scornful.
disdetta, *n.f.* Bad luck, misfortune; (*Comm.*) termination of contract; notice to leave (from either side); settlement or calling in of a loan. **Dar la —,** to give notice; **che —!** what hard luck!
disdetto, *p.p.a.* Cancelled, retracted, revoked; withdrawn [cp. **disdire**].
disdicente, *a.* Unbecoming, indecent.

disdicevole [disdicEvole], *a.* Unseemly, unbecoming, unsuitable.
disdicevolmente, *adv.* Unbecomingly.
disdicimento, *n.m.* Retraction, withdrawal (of something said).
disdire, *v.t.* To deny, to revoke, to retract, to cancel; to denounce; to recant; to take back words; to be unbecoming.
disdirsi, *v.r.* To contradict oneself, to retract (something said).
disdoro, *n.m.* Dishonour, disgrace, discredit.
disegnare, *v.t.* To draw, to design; to describe; to outline; to project, to lay plans, to resolve.
disegnatore, disegnatrice, *n.m.f.* Designer, draughtsman.
disegno, *n.m.* Design, drawing; (*fig.*) project, plan, scheme, intention, purpose. (*Pol.*) **— di legge,** parliamentary Bill; **far — su qualcuno,** to rely on someone; **punta da —,** drawing-pin, thumbtack.
diseguale, *a.* Unequal, unlike, dissimilar.
disellare, *v.t.* To unsaddle.
disenfiare, *v.t.* To reduce a swelling; to deflate.
disensatamente, *adv.* Insensately.
disensato, *a.* Insensate [cp. **insensato**].
disequilibrare, *v.t.* To upset the balance.
disequilibrarsi, *v.r.* To lose one's balance; to be unbalanced.
disequilibrio [disequilIbrio], *n.m.* Lack of balance, disequilibrium.
diseredare, *v.t.* To disinherit.
disertamento, *n.m.* Destruction, devastation.
disertante, *a.* Deserting.
disertare, *v.t.* (*Mil.*) To desert; to quit, to abandon, to lay waste.
diserto, *a.* (*Lit.*) Abandoned, deserted; eloquent.
disertore, *n.m.* Deserter.
diserzione, *n.f.* Desertion.
disfacimento, *n.m.* Disintegration, dissolution, decomposition; ruin.
disfacitura, *n.f.* Breaking up, demolition; materials resulting from demolition, rubble.
disfamare, *v.t.* To appease one's hunger.
disfare, *v.t.* To undo, to disentangle; to unpack; to dissolve; to demolish, to give up (house); to wear out. **—i nodi,** to undo the knots; **— un baule,** to unpack a trunk.
disfarsi, *v.r.* To be dissolved, to melt; to get rid of, to dispose of. **Voglio disfarmi di quest' auto,** I want to dispose of this car; **vorrei disfarmi di questo seccatore,** I should like to get rid of this bore.
disfatta, *n.f.* Defeat, rout, overthrow; ruin.
disfattista (*pl.* **disfattisti**), *n.m.* Defeatist.
disfatto, *a.* Decomposed, reduced to powder; ruined; defeated.
disfavore, *n.m.* Disfavour.
disfavorevole [disfavorEvole], *a.* Unfavourable, contrary.
disfavorevolmente, *adv.* Unfavourably.
disferrare, *v.t.* To unshackle; to unshoe a horse.
disfida, *n.f.* Challenge, defiance; duel.
disfidante, *a.* Challenging.
disfidare, *v.t.* To defy, to challenge (to combat).
disfigurare, *v.t.* To disfigure.
disfiorare, *v.t.* To deflower; to dishonour.
disformamento, *n.m.* Alteration.
disformare, *v.t.* To deform.
disformarsi, *v.r.* To become deformed; to be wasted.
disformatamente, *adv.* In a deformed way.
disformazione, *n.f.* Deformity; diversity.
disforme, *a.* Different, of a different shape.
disformità [-à], *n.f.* Diversity of form; difference.
disfrenare, *v.t.* To let loose, to unchain; to unbridle.
disfunzione, *n.f.* (*Med.*) Disorder; derangement; irregularity (in any function).
disgelare, *v.i.* To thaw.
disgelo, *n.m.* Thaw.
disgiungere [disgiUngere], *v.t.* To detach, to separate, to disjoin, to disconnect.
disgiuntivo, *a.* (*Gram.*) Disjunctive.
disgiunto, *p.p.a.* Parted, separated, disjoined.
disgiunzione, *n.f.* Disjunction, separation.
disgradare, *v.t.* To degrade, to ungrade; to discredit, to put in the shade; to put to shame.
disgradevole [disgradEvole], *a.* Unpleasant, disagreeable.
disgrado, *n.m.* Dislike. **A —,** unwillingly, grudgingly. **Avere a —,** to dislike, not to care for.
disgravare, *v.t.* To relieve from a burden; to disburden.
disgravio [disgrAvio], *n.m.* Disburdening, relief.
disgrazia [disgrAzia], *n.f.* Misfortune, ill luck; accident, disaster, mishap; disgrace. **Cadere in —,** to fall into disgrace (with someone); **per —,** unfortunately; **portar —,** to bring ill luck; **per colmo di —,** to complete the disaster, to cap it all.
disgraziatamente, *adv.* Unfortunately; unhappily.
disgraziato, *n.m.a.* Unfortunate fellow, poor devil; unfortunate, unlucky; miserable, wretched.
disgregabile [disgregAbile], *a.* Breakable, liable to dissolution, liable to be broken.
disgregamento, *n.m.* Disjointing; disunion, disintegration.
disgregare, *v.t.* To disintegrate, to disjoint; to disconnect, to dissolve.
disgregatamente, *adv.* Disjointedly, disunitedly.
disgregativo, *a.* Disintegrating.
disgregazione, *n.f.* Disintegration, dissolution.
disguido, *n.m.* Miscarriage (of parcel, etc.); postal error.
disgustare, *v.t.* To disgust, to displease; to sicken; to vex.
disgustarsi, *v.r.* To become disgusted with; to quarrel, to be at variance with. **Quelle due persone si sono disgustate,** those two persons are at variance with one another.
disgusto, *n.m.* Disgust, aversion, repugnance, dislike.
disgustosamente, *adv.* Disgustingly.
disgustoso, *a.* Disgusting, loathsome; shocking; vexatious.
disianza, *n.f.* (*Poet.*) Desire.
disillabo [disIllabo], *n.m.* (*Gram.*) Disyllable.
disilludere [disillUdere], *v.t.* To disillusion, to undeceive; to disenchant.
disilludersi [disillUdersi], *v.r.* To undeceive oneself.

disillusione, *n.f.* Disillusion, disillusionment, disenchantment; disappointment.
disilluso, *a.* Disillusioned, disappointed.
disimballare, *v.t.* To unpack.
disimbastire, *v.t.* To unstitch, to untack.
disimpacciare, *v.t.* To disengage, to disentangle, to free from embarrassment.
disimpacciarsi, *v.r.* To free oneself (from difficulties).
disimparare, *v.t.* To unlearn, to forget.
disimpegnare, *v.t.* To disengage, to release; to redeem (a pledge); to fulfil (an obligation); (*Naut.*) to clear (an anchor, etc.). **— un incarico,** to fulfil a task.
disimpegnarsi, *v.r.* To extricate oneself; to be rid of; (*fig.*) to acquit oneself.
disimpegno, *n.m.* Disengagement, disentanglement; release. (*colloq.*) **Abito di —,** presentable dress *or* suit.
disimpiegare, *v.t.* To throw out of work.
disincagliare, *v.t.* (*Naut*). To refloat (after grounding).
disincaglio [disincAglio], *n.m.* Floating.
disincantare, *v.t.* To disenchant.
disincantato, *a.* Disenchanted, disillusioned.
disincarnato, *a.* Discarnate.
disincatenare, *v.t.* To unchain.
disinclinazione, *n.f.* Disinclination.
disinfettante, *n.m.a.* Disinfectant.
disinfettare, *v.t.* To disinfect.
disinfezione, *n.f.* Disinfection.
disinfiammare, *v.t.* To lessen inflammation.
disingannare, *v.t.* To undeceive, to disenchant.
disinganno, *n.m.* Disenchantment, disillusionment; disappointment.
disingranare, *v.t.* (*Mech.*) To throw out of gear.
disinnamorare, *v.t.* To disaffect, to estrange.
disinnamorarsi, *v.r.* To fall out of love.
disinnescare, *v.t.* (*Motor.*) To declutch.
disinnestare, *v.t.* (*Mech.*) To disconnect, to disengage. (*Motor.*) **— la frizione,** to declutch.
disinserire, *v.t.* (*Elect.*) To disconnect.
disintegrare, *v.t.* (*Phys.*) To disintegrate, to split. **— l'atomo,** to split the atom.
disintegrazione, *n.f.* Disintegration.
disinteressamento, *n.m.* Indifference, lack of interest.
disinteressare, *v.t.* To make one lose all interest; (*Comm.*) to buy out (a person's) interest in a business, etc.
disinteressarsi, *v.r.* To become indifferent, to lose interest.
disinteressatamente, *adv.* Disinterestedly.
disinteresse, *n.m.* Disinterestedness; unselfishness.
disinvitare, *v.t.* To cancel an invitation; to ask someone not to come.
disinvoltamente, *adv.* Easily, frankly; with aplomb; impudently.
disinvolto, *a.* Jaunty, unconstrained, self-possessed; free and easy, spontaneous; cheeky.
disinvoltura, *n.f.* Ease, simplicity of manners; aplomb; coolness, cheek, impudence.
disio [disIo], *n.m.* (*Poet.*) Desire.
disistima, *n.f.* Lack of esteem, discredit; contempt.
disistimare, *v.t.* To slight, to despise.
dislacciare, *v.t.* To unlace, to untie.
disleale, *a.* Disloyal; false.
dislealmente, *adv.* Disloyally [cp. **slealmente**].
dislealtà [-à], *n.f.* Disloyalty [cp. **slealtà**].
dislegare, *v.t.* To untie, to loosen.
dislegarsi, *v.r.* To free oneself; (*fig.*) to exonerate oneself.
dislivello, *n.m.* Gradient, incline; unevenness; variation (in height or level); drop. **C'è un forte —,** there is a big drop.
dislocamento, *n.m.* Dislocation; (*Naut.*) displacement.
dislocare, *v.t.* To dislocate; to put out of joint [cp. **slogare**]; to displace; to dispatch.
dislocazione, *n.f.* Dislocation; (*Mil.*) dispatch (of troops).
dismagare, *v.t.* (*obs.*) To diminish, to perturb.
dismembrare, *v.t.* To dismember.
dismenorrea [dismenorrEa], *n.f.* (*Med.*) Dysmenorrhoea, irregular menstruation.
dismesso, *p.p.a.* Obsolete, out of use [cp. **smesso**].
dismettere [dismEttere], *v.i.* To cast off, to dismantle; to stop [cp. **smettere**].
dismisura, *n.f.* Excess, superfluity, redundancy. **A —,** exceedingly, excessively.
dismontare, *v.i.* To alight, to dismount.
disnodare, *v.t.* To untie [cp. **snodare**].
disnudare, *v.t.* To denude; to unsheathe.
disobbedire [cp. **disubbidire**].
disobbligare, *v.t.* To release from an obligation.
disobbligarsi, *v.r.* To disengage oneself from an obligation.
disobbligazione, *n.f.* Discharge, release from an obligation.
disoccupare, *v.t.* To disoccupy, to cease occupation; to leave vacant.
disoccuparsi, *v.r.* To cease work, to give up employment.
disoccupato, *n.m.a.* Unemployed, out of work.
disoccupazione, *n.f.* Unemployment; idleness.
disonestà [-à], *n.f.* Dishonesty, fraud, bad faith, cheating; lewdness.
disonesto, *a.* Dishonest, fraudulent; indecent, shameless.
disonorante, *a.* Dishonouring.
disonorare, *v.t.* To dishonour, to disgrace; to violate, to ravish.
disonorarsi, *v.r.* To disgrace oneself.
disonoratamente, *adv.* Dishonourably.
disonorato, *a.* Shameless, without honour.
disonore, *n.m.* Shame, dishonour, infamy.
disonorevole [disonorEvole], *a.* Dishonourable, shameful.
disopra, di sopra, *adv.* Upstairs; above, over. **Al — di,** above; **per —,** into the bargain; **andare —,** to go upstairs; **prendere il —,** to get the upper hand.
disordinatamente, *adv.* Inordinately; untidily, carelessly.
disordinare, *v.t.* To disorder, to derange, to disarrange, to confuse.
disordinato, *a.* Confused, disorderly; inordinate, extravagant.
disordine [disOrdine], *n.m.* Disorder, confusion; disturbance; tumult; excess, debauchery; (*Med.*) disorder, disease. **Essere in —,** to be untidy.

disorganizzare, *v.t.* To disorganize, to throw into confusion.
disorganizzazione, *n.f.* Disorganization.
disorientamento, *n.m.* Disorientation; confusion.
disorientare, *v.t.* To confuse, to make one lose one's bearings, to throw out of one's reckoning; (*fig.*) to disconcert, to bewilder.
disorientarsi, *v.r.* To lose one's bearings; to become bewildered.
disorientato, *a.* Disconcerted, flurried; lost, astray.
disormeggiamento, *n.m.* (*Naut.*) Unmooring.
disormeggiare, *v.t.* (*Naut.*) To unmoor, to cast off.
disossare, *v.t.* To bone (a fowl, fish, etc.); to fillet.
disossato, *a.* Boned, filleted.
disossidare, *v.t.* (*Chem.*) To deoxidize.
disotto, di sotto, *adv.prep.* Under, below. beneath; downstairs. **Al —,** down beneath, below.
dispaccio [dispAccio], *n.m.* Dispatch, telegram.
dispaiare, *v.t.* To unpair.
disparatamente, *adv.* Disparately, differently.
disparatezza, *n.f.* Dissimilarity.
disparato, *a.* Different, dissimilar, disparate.
disparecchiare, *v.t.* To clear the table (after a meal) [cp. **sparecchiare**].
disparente, *a.* Disappearing, vanishing.
disparere, *n.m.* Difference of opinion; variance, dissension.
dispari [dIspari], *a.* Odd (number); unequal. **Numero —,** odd number.
disparire, *v.i.* To disappear, to vanish.
dispariscente, *a.* Disappearing.
disparità [-à], *n.f.* Disparity, inequality. **— di opinione,** difference of opinion.
disparizione, *n.f.* Disappearance.
disparte, *adv.* Aside, apart. **Tenersi in —,** to hold aloof; **in —,** on one side.
dispendio [dispEndio], *n.m.* Expense, cost; wear, waste.
dispendiosamente, *adv.* Expensively.
dispendioso, *a.* Costly, expensive.
dispensa, *n.f.* Distribution; pantry, larder; cupboard; sideboard; exemption; number (of a serial publication); (*Eccles.*) dispensation (for marriage).
dispensabile [dispensAbile], *a.* Distributable.
dispensare, *v.t.* To distribute, to deal out, to dispense; to exempt; to excuse, to suspend. **— da un obbligo,** to relieve from an obligation.
dispensario [dispensArio], *n.m.* Dispensary, pharmacy.
dispensarsi, *v.r.* To be exempted, to be excused.
dispensazione, *n.f.* Dispensation.
dispensiere, *n.m.* Steward, butler; housekeeper; distributor.
dispepsia [dispepsIa], *n.f.* (*Med.*) Dyspepsia.
dispeptico [dispEptico], *a.* Dyspeptic.
disperabile [disperAbile], *a.* Hopeless.
disperamento, *n.m.* [cp. **disperazione**].
disperare, *v.i.* To despair, to give up hope; to be worried, to become desperate. **Far —,** to drive mad.
disperarsi, *v.r.* To abandon hope, to give way to despair. **— inutilmente,** to worry needlessly.
disperatamente, *adv.* Desperately, hopelessly.
disperato, *n.m.* Desperado, desperate fellow; one who is penniless. **Urlare come un —,** to yell like a madman; **alla disperata,** in a reckless manner.
disperato, *a.* Desperate, afflicted, hopeless. **Un'impresa disperata,** a hopeless task.
disperazione, *n.f.* Desperation, despair; hopelessness.
disperdere [dispErdere], *v.t.* To disperse, to scatter, to break up; to disseminate; to waste, to squander.
disperdersi [dispErdersi], *v.r.* To lose one's way, to be wasted.
disperdimento, *n.m.* Dispersion, waste.
dispersione, *n.f.* Dispersion, scattering, dissemination; loss, waste.
disperso, *a.* Dispersed, scattered, squandered; (*Mil.*) missing.
dispetto, *n.m.* Spite, scorn, malice; vexation, annoyance; resentment. **Per —,** out of spite; **fare un —,** to do an ill turn; **a — di tutti,** in spite of all; **avere in —,** to despise.
dispettosamente, *adv.* Spitefully, scornfully.
dispettoso, *a.* Spiteful, scornful.
dispettuccio [dispettUccio], *n.m.* Mean *or* petty provocation.
dispiacente, *a.* Sorry, displeasing. **Sono — di,** I am sorry to.
dispiacenza, *n.f.* Displeasure, disgust.
dispiacere, *v.i.* To displease; to regret, to be sorry; to mind. **Ti dispiace venire con noi?** do you mind coming with us? **mi dispiace d'essere in ritardo,** I'm sorry to be late; **sono cose che dispiacciono,** these are unpleasant things; **se non le dispiace,** if you don't mind, if you please; **me ne dispiace,** I'm sorry about it.
dispiacere, *n.m.* Displeasure, regret; trouble, misfortune, grief. **Dare dei dispiaceri,** to cause grief; **con — vi annuncio,** I regret to inform you.
dispiacevole [dispiacEvole], *a.* Displeasing, causing displeasure.
dispiacevolezza, *n.f.* Displeasingness.
dispiacimento, *n.m.* Displeasure, regret.
dispiaciuto, *p.p.a.* Displeased.
dispiccare, *v.t.* [cp. **spiccare**].
dispiccarsi, *v.r.* [cp. **spiccarsi**].
dispiegare, *v.t.* To display, to spread out.
dispietato, *a.* Pitiless, cruel [cp. **spietato**].
displuvio [displUvio], *n.m.* Watershed.
dispnea [dispnEa], *n.f.* (*Med.*) Dyspnoea, difficulty of breathing.
dispogliamento, *n.m.* Spoliation, despoilment.
dispogliare, *v.t.* To despoil.
dispogliatore, *n.m.* Despoiler.
dispolpare, *v.t.* To strip off, to remove flesh from.
disponente, *n.m.* (*Law*) Testator.
disponibile [disponIbile], *a.* Available, vacant, at hand.
disponibilità [-à], *n.f.* Availability. (*Comm.*) **Non ho —,** I have no available funds; (*Mil.*) **mettere in —,** to place (officers) on the reserve; to put on half-pay; **— di munizioni,** supply of ammunition.
disponimento, *n.m.* Disposal, order, decree.

disporre, *v.t.* To dispose, to prepare, to arrange, to set in order; to regulate, to fix; to place. — **ogni cosa con criterio,** to arrange everything with judgment; — **di molti mezzi,** to have ample means at one's disposal; — **per testamento,** to bequeath; — **di,** to dispose of by will.
disporsi, *v.r.* To place oneself, to prepare oneself, to get ready; to resolve.
disposare, *v.t.* (*Lit.*) To marry.
dispositiva, *n.f.* (*Law*) Operative words of a judgment.
dispositivamente, *adv.* By preparation, by arrangement.
dispositivo, *n.m.* Apparatus, contrivance, device; (*Law*) disposition. (*Elect.*) — **di commando,** control device; — **di sicurezza,** safety-catch.
dispositivo, *a.* Regulating, providing.
disposizione, *n.f.* Disposition, arrangement; disposal; propensity, inclination; ordinance, regulation, decree, provision. **In una buona — d'animo,** favourably disposed; **una — testamentaria,** a testamentary disposition; **prendere le proprie disposizioni per partire,** to make all one's arrangements for leaving.
dispossessare, *v.t.* To dispossess.
dispostamente, *adv.* By arrangement, in an orderly way.
dispostezza, *n.f.* (Orderly) disposition; composure, attitude.
disposto, *n.m.* (*Law*) Provision, decree.
disposto, *p.p.a.* Disposed, inclined; willing; arranged. **Come —,** as ordered.
dispoticamente, *adv.* Despotically.
dispotico [dispOtico], *a.* Despotic, absolute.
dispotismo, *n.m.* Despotism.
dispregevole [dispregEvole], *a.* Despicable, contemptible [cp. **spregevole**].
dispregevolmente, *adv.* Despicably, contemptibly.
dispregiabile [dispregiAbile], *a.* Despicable, worthless.
dispregiare, *v.t.* To despise, to value lightly.
dispregiativo, *a.* Contemptuous, disparaging.
dispregio [disprEgio], *n.m.* Contempt, scorn, slighting. **Avere in —,** to despise.
disprezzabile [disprezzAbile], *a.* Contemptible; despicable; negligible.
disprezzare, *v.t.* To despise, to disdain, to scorn; to under-value.
disprezzatamente, *adv.* Disparagingly.
disprezzo, *n.m.* Contempt, scorn; disdain; defiance; neglect.
disprigionare, *v.t.* To set free (from prison).
disproporzione, *n.f.* Disproportion.
disputa [dIsputa], *n.f.* Difference, dispute, debate, discussion; quarrel, altercation.
disputabile [disputAbile], *a.* Disputable; open to discussion, arguable.
disputante, *n.m.a.* Disputant.
disputare, *v.t.i.* To dispute, to debate, to discuss; to quarrel; to contend, to compete, to contest.
disputarsi, *v.r.* To contend for.
disputatore, *n.m.* Disputant.
disputatorio [disputatOrio], *a.* Disputable.
disputazione, *n.f.* Disputation, discussion.
disquilibrio [disquilIbrio], *n.m.* Lack of balance, unbalance [cp. **squilibrio**].
disquisizione, *n.f.* Disquisition, systematic discussion.
dissanguamento, *n.m.* Loss of blood, exhaustion; blood-letting.
dissanguare, *v.t.* To bleed, to impoverish.
dissanguarsi, *v.r.,* To ruin oneself by spending.
dissanguatore, dissanguatrice, *n.m.f.* (*fig.*) Blood-sucker, leech.
dissanguato, *a.* Bloodless, drained of blood; impoverished.
dissapore, *n.m.* Dissension, disagreement, discord.
dissaporito, *a.* Insipid.
dissecare, *v.t.* To dissect.
disseccare, *v.t.* To dry up, to parch.
disseccarsi, *v.r.* To become parched *or* dry.
disseccazione, *n.f.* Desiccation, drying-up.
disselciare, *v.t.* To unpave.
disseminare, *v.t.* To disseminate, to scatter abroad, to diffuse.
disseminazione, *n.f.* Dissemination.
dissennare, *v.t.* To deprive of one's senses, to drive crazy.
dissennatamente, *adv.* Foolishly, crazily, madly.
dissennatezza, *n.f.* Madness; foolishness, stupidity.
dissennato, *a.* Mad, crazy, foolish.
dissensione, *n.f.* Dissension, discord, disagreement; strife.
dissenso, *n.m.* Dissent, disagreement, difference. **Dissensi di famiglia,** family differences.
dissentaneo [dissentAneo], *a* Dissentient, dissenting.
dissenteria [dissenterIa], *n.f.* (*Med.*) Dysentery.
dissentimento, *n.m.* Dissent, disagreement; disapproval.
dissentire, *v.t.* To dissent, to differ, to disagree.
dissenziente, *n.m.* Dissident, one who disagrees.
disseppellimento, *n.m.* Disinterment.
disseppellire, *v.t.* To disinter, to exhume.
disseppellitore, *n.m.* One who exhumes or disinters.
disserrare, *v.t.* To unclose, to unlock, to open.
dissertare, *v.i.* To discourse, to expatiate, to argue.
dissertativo, *a.* Discursive, expatiatory.
dissertazione, *n.f.* Dissertation, disquisition; (academic) thesis.
disservire, *v.t.* To render a disservice.
disservizio [disservIzio], *n.m.* Disservice; bad service. **Il — ferroviario,** the bad railway service.
dissestare, dissestarsi, *v.t.r.* To derange, to unsettle; to break down, to get into (financial) trouble.
dissestato, *p.p.a.* Embarrassed (financially), in a bad way.
dissesto, *n.m.* Financial difficulty; failure.
dissetante, *n.m.* Thirst-quencher.
dissetare, *v.t.* To quench thirst.
dissetarsi, *v.r.* To quench one's thirst.
dissettore, *n.m.* Dissector.
dissezione, *n.f.* Dissection.
dissidente, *n.m.a.* Dissident.
dissidenza, *n.f.* Dissent, disagreement.

dissidio [dissIdio], *n.m.* Dissention, discord, disagreement. **Comporre un —**, to compose a quarrel.
dissigillare, *v.t.* To unseal, to break the seals.
dissimiglianza, *n.f.* Dissimilarity.
dissimigliare, *v.i.* To be unlike, to differ (in nature or appearance). [cp. **dissomigliare**].
dissimilare, *a.* Unlike, dissimilar, different.
dissimile [dissImile], *a.* Dissimilar, different, unlike. **— per indole, per educazione,** different by nature, by upbringing.
dissimilitudine [dissimilitUdine], *n.f.* Dissimilarity.
dissimulare, *v.t.* To dissimulate, to dissemble, to conceal.
dissimulatore, dissimulatrice, *n.m.f.* Dissembler, dissimulator.
dissimulazione, *n.f.* Dissimulation, dissembling.
dissipare, dissiparsi, *v.t.r.* To dissipate, to squander; to scatter, to disperse, to dispel. **— tutti i sospetti,** to dispel all suspicions; **— un patrimonio,** to squander a patrimony.
dissipatamente, *adv.* Dissolutely.
dissipatezza, *n.f.* Dissipation, dispersion; waste, extravagance; dissoluteness, vice, corruption.
dissipatore, dissipatrice, *n.m.f.* Squanderer, waster, wastrel.
dissipazione, *n.f.* Dissipation, dispersal; waste; dissoluteness.
dissociare, *v.t.* To dissociate, to separate.
dissociarsi, *v.r.* To dissociate oneself, to break apart, to separate oneself.
dissodamento, *n.m.* Tillage, cultivation.
dissodare, *v.t.* To till, to plough, to break (ground); to cultivate.
dissolubile [dissolUbile], *a.* Dissoluble.
dissolubilità [-à], *n.f.* Dissolubility.
dissolutamente, *adv.* Dissolutely, wantonly.
dissolutezza, *n.f.* Depravity, lewdness.
dissoluto, *n.m.a.* Profligate, wanton.
dissoluzione, *n.f.* Dissolution, disintegration, separation.
dissolvente, *n.m.a.* Dissolvent.
dissolvenza, *n.f.* (*Cinema.*) Fade-out.
dissolvere [dissOlvere], *v.t.* To dissolve, to decompose, to break up, to disperse; to annul.
dissolversi, *v.r.* To disperse, to fade away, to melt, to vanish.
dissolvimento, *n.m.* Dissolving, dissolution, annulling.
dissolvitore, *n.m.* Dissolver, disintegrator.
dissomigliante, *a.* Unlike, dissimilar.
dissomigliantemente, *adv.* Dissimilarly.
dissomiglianza, *n.f.* Dissimilarity, unlikeness.
dissomigliare, *v.i.* To be unlike, to differ.
dissonante, *a.* Dissonant.
dissonanza, *n.f.* Dissonance, discord.
dissonare, *v.t.* To make discord; to be out of tune, to sound discordantly.
dissonnare, *v.t.* (*obs.*) To awaken, to wake up.
dissono [dIssono], *a.* Dissonant.
dissotterrare, *v.t.* To disinter, to exhume; to excavate, to unearth.
dissuadere, *v.t.* To dissuade, to advise against.
dissuasione, *n.f.* Dissuasion.
dissuasivamente, *adv.* Dissuasively.
dissuasivo, *a.* Dissuasive.
dissueto, *a.* Disused, unaccustomed.
dissuetudine [dissuetUdine], *n.f.* Desuetude, unfamiliarity.
dissuggellare, *v.t.* To unseal.
distaccamento, *n.m.* (Act of) detaching; (*Mil.*) detachment, body of troops; reparation; (*Naut.*) fleet, squadron.
distaccare, *v.t.* To detach, to separate, to cut off, to disconnect; to alienate.
distaccarsi, *v.r.* To part, to sever, to separate, to become detached.
distacco, *n.m.* Separation, detachment, parting, severance; estrangement.
distante, *a.adv.* Distant, remote, far away.
distanza, *n.f.* Distance; range; interval; coolness, unfriendliness. **Tenere a rispettosa —**, to keep at a proper distance; **tener le distanze,** to keep at a distance (socially), to hold at arm's length; **percorrere una grande —**, to cover a great distance.
distanziare, *v.t.* To out-distance, to out-step.
distanziato, *a.* (*Racing*) Also-ran.
distare, *v.i.* To be distant, to be far off. **Roma dista poco dal mare,** Rome is not far from the sea.
distemperare, *v.t.* To dilute, to dissolve, to melt.
distendere [distEndere], *v.t.* To spread out, to extend, to stretch out; to draw up (a document); to develop (an argument). **— i panni al sole,** to hang out clothes to dry.
distendersi [distEndersi], *v.r.* To stretch oneself, to extend; (*fig.*) to expatiate.
distendimento, *n.m.* Stretching out, extending.
distensione, *n.f.* Distension, stretching; relaxation (of tension).
distesa, *n.f.* Extension, extent, expanse; length. **A —**, continuously; **la gran — del mare,** the great expanse of sea; **suonare (le campane) a —**, to ring a peal (of bells).
distesamente, *adv.* At length, minutely, amply; continuously; in detail; diffusedly.
disteso, *p.p.a.* Extended, spread out; spacious, extensive; flowing. **Cadere lungo —**, to fall full-length; **narrare una cosa per —**, to tell something in detail; **scrivere il proprio nome per —**, to write out one's name in full.
distico [dIstico], *n.m.* (*Poet.*) Distich.
distillamento, *n.m.* (Act of) distilling.
distillare, *v.t.* To distil, to extract the essence of; to fall in drops.
distillatoio [distillatOio], *n.m.* Still.
distillazione, *n.f.* Distillation.
distilleria [distillerIa], *n.f.* Distillery.
distinguere [distInguere], *v.t.* To distinguish, to discriminate, to differentiate. **— un oggetto a occhio nudo,** to distinguish an object with the naked eye.
distinguersi [distInguersi], *v.r.* To distinguish oneself; to make oneself conspicuous.
distinguibile [distinguIbile], *a.* Distinguishable.
distinta, *n.f.* List, bill; schedule. **— dei prezzi,** list of prices.
distintamente, *adv.* Distinctly; respectfully.
distintivo, *n.m.* Badge. **Portare il — di,** to wear the badge of.
distinto, *a.* Distinct; distinguished, gentlemanly. **Una voce distinta,** a clear voice; **una persona distinta,** a refined person; **posto —**, reserved seat (in theatre).

distinzione, *n.f.* Distinction (in all senses). **La — delle maniere,** refinement of manners.
distogliere [distOgliere], *v.t.* To divert, to dissuade, to distract from.
distolto, *p.p.a.* Distracted, removed.
distorcere [distOrcere], *v.t.* To twist, to distort.
distorcimento, *n.m.* Distortion.
distornamento, *n.m.* Deviation.
distornare, *v.t.* To divert, to deviate, to distract from.
distorsione, *n.f.* Distortion (in all senses).
distortamente, *adv.* Distortedly.
distorto, *a.* Twisted, distorted.
distrarre, *v.t.* To distract, to divert, to draw away; to misapply.
distrarsi, *v.r.* To take relaxation, to amuse oneself, to relax the mind; to divert one's attention; to be absent-minded.
distrattamente, *adv.* Distractedly, absent-mindedly; carelessly.
distratto, *p.p.a.* Distracted, abstracted (in thought), absent-minded. **Un'aria distratta,** a vacant air.
distrazione, *n.f.* Distraction, relaxation, diversion; absent-mindedness, absence of mind, heedlessness.
distretta, *n.f.* Straits, difficulties; imminent danger.
distretto, *n.m.* District, region; (*Mil.*) administrative area.
distrettuale, *a.* Pertaining to a district. **Magistrato —,** district magistrate.
distribuimento, *n.m.* [cp. **distribuzione**].
distribuire, *v.t.* To distribute; to deliver (letters, etc.); to allocate, to apportion, to assign.
distributivo, (*Gram. etc.*) Distributive.
distributore, distributrice, *n.m.f.* Distributor. **— automatico,** slot-machine; **— di benzina,** petrol pump.
distribuzione, *n.f.* Distribution, apportionment, sharing; arrangement; delivery (of letters, etc.); (*Mech.*) valve gear. (*Theat.*) **— delle parti,** casting of roles; the cast.
districare, distrigare, *v.t.* To disentangle, to disengage.
distruggibile [distruggIbile], *a.* Destructible.
distruggere [distrUggere], *v.t.* To destroy, to undo; to pull down, to demolish; to lay waste, to ruin; to consume.
distruggersi [distrUggersi], *v.r.* To pine away, to wear oneself out.
distruggitore, *n.m.* Destroyer.
distruttibile [distruttIbile], *a.* Destructible.
distruttivo, *a.* Destructive.
distrutto, *p.p. a.* Destroyed, ruined, wasted, consumed, melted.
distruzione, *n.f.* Destruction, demolition; ruin, waste; overthrow.
disturbare, *v.t.* To disturb, to trouble, to cause inconvenience; to unsettle, to hinder, to interfere with. (*Colloq.*) **Non mi disturba affatto,** it is no trouble.
disturbarsi, *v.r.* To trouble oneself, to put oneself out, to take trouble. **Non si disturbi,** don't trouble, don't put yourself out.
disturbatore, disturbatrice, *n.m.f.* Disturber.
disturbo, *n.m.* Trouble, inconvenience, annoyance; disorder. **Recare —,** to cause inconvenience; **non si dava alcun —,** he did not take any pains; (*Radio*) **disturbi atmosferici,** atmospherics.
disubbidiente, *a.* Disobedient.
disubbidientemente, *adv.* Disobediently.
disubbidienza, *n.f.* Disobedience, non-compliance.
disubbidire, *v.t.i.* To disobey; to violate, to transgress; to be disobedient.
disuguaglianza, *n.f.* Inequality, disparity dissimilarity.
disuguagliare, *v.t.* To make unequal.
disuguale, *a.* Unequal, uneven; irregular. **Terreno —,** broken ground.
disugualmente, *adv.* Unequally.
disumanamente, *adv.* Inhumanly.
disumanare, *v.t.* To brutalize, to render inhuman.
disumanarsi, *v.r.* To become inhuman.
disumano, *a.* Inhuman, cruel; savage.
disumare, *v.t.* To exhume, [cp. **esumare**].
disumazione, *n.f.* Exhumation.
disungere [disUngere], *v.t.* To remove grease from.
disunione, *n.f.* Dissension, division, secession, discord.
disunire, *v.t.* To disunite, to disjoin, to put at variance.
disunirsi, *v.r.* To become disunited, to get divided.
disunità [-à], *n.f.* Disunity, disharmony.
disusare, *v.t.* To disuse, to cease to use.
disusatamente, *adv.* In an unaccustomed or obsolete manner.
disusato, *a.* Disused, obsolete.
disuso, *n.m.* Disuse. **Andare, cadere in —,** to fall into desuetude.
disutile [disUtile], *n.m.* Good-for-nothing fellow or thing; loss.
disutile [disUtile], *a.* Useless, vain, good-for-nothing; harmful.
disutilmente, *adv.* Uselessly, vainly.
disvantaggio [disvantAggio], *n.m.* Disadvantage [cp. **svantaggio**].
disvelare, *v.t.* To unveil, to reveal.
disvellere [disvEllere], *v.t.* To uproot, to pluck out [cp. **svellere**].
disviare, *v.t.* To lead astray, to mislead.
disviarsi, *v.r.* To go astray, to wander.
disviatore, disviatrice, *n.m.f.* One who makes others go astray.
disvio, *n.m.* Wandering, leading astray, going astray.
disviluppare, *v.t.* To disentangle.
disvilupparsi, *v.r.* To free oneself.
disviticchiarsi, *v.r.* To untwist, to disentangle oneself.
disvolere, *v.i.* To wish no longer; to change one's mind. **Egli vuole e disvuole,** he will and he won't.
disvolere, *n.m.* Change of mind.
ditaiuolo, *n.m.* (*obs.*) Sore finger; hangnail.
ditale, *n.m.* Thimble; finger-stall.
ditata, *n.f.* Finger-mark; flick with the finger.
Dite, *n.m.* (*Myth.*) Dis, Pluto. **Città di Dite,** lower hell.
diteggiare, *v.t.* (*Mus.*) To finger.
diteggiatura, *n.f.* (*Mus.*) Fingering.

ditello, *n.m.* Armpit; piece of armour covering this [cp. **ascella**].
dito (pl. **diti,** *m.*, **dita,** *f.*), *n.m.* Finger (of hand), toe (of foot); inch, finger's breadth. — **indice,** forefinger; — **grosso,** thumb, big toe; — **medio,** middle finger; — **anulare,** ring-finger; — **mignolo,** little finger; **mostrare a** —, to point out; **essere a un — dal fare una cosa,** to be within an ace of doing something; **conoscere una cosa sulla punta delle dita,** to have a thing at one's finger-tips; **un — di vino,** a drop of wine; **mettere il — sulla piaga,** to touch the spot; **tra moglie e marito non mettere il —,** don't interfere between husband and wife.
ditta, *n.f.* (*Comm.*) Firm, house, company.
dittafono [dittAfono], *n.m.* Dictaphone.
dittamo [dIttamo], *n.m.* (*Bot.*) Dittany.
dittatore, *n.m.* Dictator.
dittatoriale, dittatorio [dittatOrio], *a.* Dictatorial.
dittatura, *n.f.* Dictatorship.
ditteri [dItteri], *n.m.pl.* (*Zool.*) Diptera.
dittico [dIttico], *n.m.* Diptych.
dittongo, *n.m.* Diphthong.
diurnamente, *adv.* Daily.
diurnista (*pl.* **diurnisti**), *n.m.* Clerk engaged by the day.
diurno, *a.* Diurnal, daily, by day, during day-time. **Albergo —,** day-hostel; public baths and lavatories.
diuturnamente, *adv.* Continuously, for a long time.
diuturnità [-à], *n.f.* Duration, lastingness.
diuturno, *a.* Lasting, of long duration, continuous.
diva, *n.f.* Goddess; operatic singer; film star.
divagamento, *n.m.* Divagation, rambling, distraction.
divagare, *v.i.* To ramble, to digress, to divagate.
divagarsi, *v.r.* To relax one's mind, to amuse oneself.
divagazione, *n.f.* Divagation; distraction; relaxation, diversion.
divallare, *v.i.* To slope down, to decline.
divampare, *v.i.* To blaze, to burn, to shine; to burst into flames.
divano, *n.m.* Sofa, settee; divan.
divaricare, *v.t.* To divaricate, to spread apart; to straddle.
divaricarsi, *v.r.* To divide into branches.
divario [divArio], *n.m.* Variety, difference, diversity.
divedere, *v.i.* Used only in the phrase **Dare a —,** to give clearly to understand.
divellere [divEllere], *v.t.* To uproot, to eradicate.
diveltare, *v.t.* (*Agric.*) To trench, to dig around.
divelto, *n.m.* (*Agric.*) Trenching.
divenire, *v.t.* To become, to grow; to change.
divenire, *n.m.* Becoming. **Il —,** the process of becoming.
diventare, *v.t.* To become, to grow; to change. **Si diventa vecchi,** one grows old; **che cosa diventeremo**? what will become of us? — **rosso, pallido,** to turn red, to turn pale.
diverbio [divErbio], *n.m.* Altercation, row, noisy quarrel.
divergente, *a.* Divergent.
divergenza, *n.f.* Divergence, divergency; difference.
divergere [divErgere], *v.i.* To diverge, to branch off.
diversamente, *adv.* Differently, otherwise.
diversi, *n.m.pl.* (*Comm.*) Sundries.
diversificare, *v.i.* To diversify, to vary; to be different.
diversificazione, *n.f.* Diversification, variety.
diversione, *n.f.* Diversion (in all senses); digression, turning aside; (*Mil.*) diversion, feigned attack.
diversità [-à], *n.f.* Diversity, unlikeness, difference, variety.
diversivo, *n.m.* Diversion, change, distraction (for the mind). **Ho bisogno d'un —,** I need a change.
diversivo, *a.* Diverting, causing to turn aside.
diverso, *a.* Different; diverse, unlike; sundry, divers, several, various. **Sono venute diverse persone,** several people have come; **è una cosa diversa**, that's another matter, that is a different thing.
divertente, *a.* Amusing, pleasant.
diverticolo [divertIcolo], *n.m.* Side road, lane.
divertimento, *n.m.* Amusement, entertainment, recreation, pastime. **Fare una cosa per —,** to do something for fun.
divertire, *v.t.* To amuse, to divert, to entertain; to turn aside.
divertirsi, *v.r.* To enjoy oneself, to amuse oneself. **Vi siete divertiti?** did you enjoy yourselves?
divetta, *n.f.* Starlet.
divettare, *v.t.* To lop (trees).
divezzamento, *n.m.* Weaning; (*fig.*) breaking of a habit.
divezzare, *v.t.* To wean; to break a custom.
divezzarsi, *v.r.* To break oneself of a habit.
diviato, *a.adv.* Quick, prompt; quickly, at once.
dividendo, *n.m.* Dividend, share. (*Comm.*) **Stabilire il —,** to declare a dividend; **— provvisorio,** interim dividend; **tagliando del —,** dividend warrant.
dividere [divIdere], *v.t.* To divide, to sever, to separate, to part; to distribute; to share, to allot, to assign; to participate.
dividersi [divIdersi], *v.r.* To be parted, to be disunited, to separate; to share. **Il partito si divise in tre,** the party was split into three.
dividucolo [dividUcolo], *n.m.* (*Arch.*) Water-tower, tower of an acqueduct.
divietare, *v.t.* To forbid [cp. **vietare**].
divieto, *n.m.* Prohibition. **— di transito,** no thoroughfare; **— di parcheggio,** no parking.
divinamento, *n.m.* Divination, foretelling.
divinare, *v.t.* To divine, to presage, to foresee, to predict.
divinatore, divinatrice, *n.m.f.* Diviner, foreteller, fortune-teller.
divinatoria [divinatOria], *n.f.* Art of divination.
divinazione, *n.f.* Divination, omen, augury, prediction; divining.
divincolamento, *n.m.* Wriggling, floundering, contortion.
divincolare, *v.t.* To twist.
divincolarsi, *v.r.* To wriggle, to flounder, to writhe, to struggle to free oneself.
divincolazione, *n.f.* Wriggling.

divincolio [divincolIo], *n.f.* Continuous writhing.
divinità [-à], *n.f.* Divinity; God.
divinizzare, *v.t.* To deify.
divinizzazione, *n.f.* Deification.
divino, *n.m.a.* The divine; divine essence; divine, godlike, sacred; religious; heavenly, celestial. **Per diritto —,** by divine right; **il poeta —,** the divine poet (Dante); **una bellezza divina,** a heavenly beauty.
divisa, *n.f.* Uniform, attire, livery; device, motto; coat of arms; parting (of the hair); (*Comm.*) bills of exchange, foreign currency. **— ordinaria,** service uniform; (*Comm.*) **— estera,** foreign bills.
divisamente, *adv.* Separately, bit by bit.
divisamento, *n.m.* Plan, project, scheme, design.
divisare, *v.i.* To plan, to devise, to project, to scheme, to intend; to decide.
divisatamente, *adv.* Distinctly, in an ordered manner.
divisibile [divisIbile], *a.* Divisible.
divisibilità [-à], *n.f.* Divisibility.
divisionale, *a.* Divisional.
divisionario [divisionArio], *n.m.* (*Mil.*) Divisional commander.
divisione, *n.f.* Division (in all senses); separation; distribution; dissension; department. (*Math.*) **Fare una —,** to divide; **capo —,** head of a department; **— del lavoro,** division of labour.
divisionismo, *n.m.* (*Art*) Pointillism.
diviso, *p.p.a.* Divided.
divisore, *n.m.* (*Math.*) Divisor.
divisorio [divisOrio], *n.m.a.* Partition; separating, dividing. **Muro —,** party wall.
divo, *n.m.* Male film star.
divo, *a.* Divine; (*fig.*) excellent.
divoramento, *n.m.* Devouring.
divorare, *v.t.* To devour, to swallow, to eat up, to consume; to destroy. **Un'auto che divora la strada,** a motor that eats up the road; **— i libri,** to devour books.
divorarsi, *v.r.* To devour each other; to consume oneself; to be consumed. **— dalla rabbia,** to be consumed with rage.
divoratore, divoratrice, *n.m.f.* Devourer.
divorziare, *v.i.* To divorce.
divorziarsi, *v.r.* To be divorced.
divorzio [divOrzio], *n.m.* Divorce.
divotamente, *adv.* Piously, devoutly.
divoto, *a.* Devout, pious.
divozione, *n.f.* Devotion.
divulgare, *v.t.* To divulge, to spread abroad, to make known; to broadcast.
divulgarsi, *v.r.* To become known, to spread abroad.
divulgatamente, *adv.* Publicly.
divulgazione, *n.f.* Publication, disclosure; vulgarization.
divulso, *a.* Disjoined.
dizionario [dizionArio], *n.m.* Dictionary. **— geografico,** gazetteer.
dizionarista, *n.m.f.* Lexicographer.
dizione, *n.f.* Diction, mode of expression; wording.
do, *n.m.* (*Mus.*) Note C.
doario [doArio], *n.m.* Widow's pension or allowance.
dobletto, *n.m.* Cotton, fustian.
doblone, *n.m.* (*Hist.*) Doubloon.
doccia [dOccia], *n.f.* Water-pipe, spout; douche; shower-bath. (*fig.*) **Dare una — fredda,** to throw cold water upon; **bere a —,** to pour into the mouth; **fare una —,** to take a shower.
docciare, *v.t.* To douche, to shower, to pour water upon.
docciatura, *n.f.* Douche, shower; shower-bath.
doccione, *n.m.* Large water-pipe.
docente, *n.m.* Teacher. **Libero —,** recognized university teacher not on the regular staff.
docile [dOcile], *a.* Docile, tame, obedient, tractable.
docilità [-à], *n.f.* Docility, tractability.
docilmente, *adv.* Docilely, submissively.
dock, *n.m.* (*Naut.*) Dock.
documentale, *a.* Documentary, concerned with documents.
documentare, *v.t.* To document; to prove by documents.
documentario [documentArio], *n.m.a.* Documentary (film); documentary.
documentato, *a.* Documentary. **Credito —,** documentary credit.
documentazione, *n.f.* Documentation.
documento, *n.m.* Document; proof, voucher.
dodecaedro, *n.m.* (*Geom.*) Dodecahedron.
dodicenne, *a.* Twelve years old.
dodicennio [dodicEnnio], *n.m.* Period of twelve years.
dodicesimo [dodicEsimo], *a.* Twelfth.
dodici [dOdici], *n.m.a.* Twelve. **Il —,** the twelfth (of the month).
dodicimila, *a.* Twelve thousand.
dodicina, *n.f.* Dozen [cp. **dozzina**].
doga, *n.f.* Stave (of a barrel).
dogale, *a.* Pertaining to a doge.
dogana, *n.f.* Custom-house; customs, custom-duties. **Pagare la —,** to pay duty; **guardia di —,** customs officer.
doganale, *a.* Pertaining to customs. **Visita —,** customs inspection; **imposta —,** duty; **barriera —,** customs barrier.
doganare, *v.t.* To impose customs duties.
doganiere, *n.m.* Customs officer.
dogare, *v.t.* To fit staves (of a barrel).
dogaressa, *n.f.* (*Hist.*) Wife of a doge.
dogato, *n.m.* Doge's office or dignity; period of his office.
doge, *n.m.* (*Hist.*) Doge (of Venice or Genoa).
doglia [dOglia], *n.f.* Ache, pain. **Le doglie del parto,** labour pains.
doglianza, *n.f.* Complaint, lament; regret.
dogliosamente, *adv.* Sorrowfully, painfully.
doglioso, *a.* Sorrowful, painful, sad.
dogma (*pl.* **dogmi**), *n.m.* Dogma, tenet.
dogmatica [dogmAtica], *n.f.* Dogmatics.
dogmaticamente, *adv.* Dogmatically.
dogmatico [dogmAtico], *a.* Dogmatic, doctrinal; authoritative; arrogant.
dogmatismo, *n.m.* Dogmatism.
dogmatizzare, *v.i.* To dogmatize.
dolce, *n.m.* Sweetness, sweet; mildness, gentleness, grace. **I dolci,** sweets, sweet-meats, cakes.
dolce, *a.* Sweet, pleasant, charming; mild, kindly; smooth, pleasant; fresh (of water). **Acqua —,** fresh water; **il tempo è molto —,** the weather is very mild; **parole dolci,** kind words; **maniere dolci,** kindly manners; **un**

— pendio, a gentle slope; **una — brezza,** a gentle breeze; (*Gram.*) **consonante —,** soft consonant.
dolcemente, *adv.* Sweetly, affectionately.
dolcezza, *n.f.* Sweetness; mildness; gentleness, grace. **La — del clima,** the mildness of the climate; **trattare con —,** to treat gently.
dolcia [dOlcia], *n.f.* Pig's blood (used in making sausages).
dolciamaro, *a.* Bittersweet.
dolciastro, *a.* Sickly sweet; mawkish; sweetish.
dolciere, *n.m.* Confectioner.
dolcificare, *v.t.* To sweeten.
dolcigno, *a.* Sweetish, rather sweet.
dolciloquo [dolcIloquo], *n.m.* Mealy-mouthed person.
dolcisonante, *a.* Sweet-sounding.
dolciume, *n.m.* Sweet-stuffs; overpowering sweetness.
dolciumi, *n.m.pl.* Sweets, sweetmeats, candies.
dolco, *n.m.a.* Damp weather; mild, warm and moist (of weather).
dolente, *a.* Sorry; sad, afflicted, painful. **Sono molto — di dirvi,** I very much regret to inform you.
dolentemente, *adv.* Sorrowfully, sadly.
dolere, *v.i.* To suffer pain; to ache. **Mi duole,** it grieves me, I'm sorry.
dolersi, *v.r.* To complain, to be sorry, to regret; to ache. **Mi duole il capo,** I have a headache; **mi duole di non poter venire,** I am sorry I cannot come.
dolicocefalo [dolicocEfalo], *a.* Long-headed; dolichocephalous.
dolio [dOlio], *n.m.* Barrel, vat; kind of whelk.
dollaro [dOllaro], *n.m.* Dollar.
dolo, *n.m.* Fraud, guile, deceit. **Con dolo,** fraudulently.
dolomite, *n.f.* (*Min.*) Dolomite. **Le Dolomiti,** the Dolomites.
dolone, *n.m.* (*Naut.*) Bowsprit.
dolorante, *a.* Aching.
dolorare, *v.i.* To feel pain, to suffer; to moan.
dolore, *n.m.* Sorrow; pain, grief, affliction, regret; suffering; ache, sore, pang. **Acuto — fisico,** acute physical suffering; **apprendo con — che,** I learn with regret that; **— di stomaco,** stomach ache; (*Eccles.*) **I Sette Dolori,** The Seven Sorrows (of Our Lady).
dolorosamente, *adv.* Painfully, grievously.
doloroso, *a.* Painful, grievous; sore, smarting; sorrowful.
dolosamente, *adv.* Fraudulently.
doloso, *a.* Fraudulent. **Incendio —,** arson; **fallimento —,** fraudulent bankruptcy.
dolzaina [dolzAina], *n.f.* Variety of oboe.
domanda, *n.f.* Question, query; request, demand, petition; application; price asked or offered. **Rivolgere una —,** to address a question; **rivolgere una — a qualcuno,** to ask someone a question; **fare una —,** to put a question; **presentare una —,** to send in a request; **— di impiego,** application for a job; **dietro —,** on application.
domandare, *v.t.* To ask, to beg, to request; to question; to demand, to require; to inquire. **— di uno,** to ask news of someone; **— un favore,** to ask a favour; (*colloq.*) **domando e dico!** I say!
domandarsi, *v.r.* To ask oneself, to wonder. **Io mi domando se,** I wonder whether.
domandata, *n.f.* (*obs.*) Demand, question.
domani, *n.m.adv.* Tomorrow; next day, morrow; **Da oggi a —,** immediately; **— l'altro,** the day after tomorrow; **da — a otto,** tomorrow week; **da — in poi,** from tomorrow on.
domare, *v.t.* To tame, to break in (of horses); to subdue, to conquer, to overpower. **— un incendio,** to get a fire under control.
domatore, domatrice, *n.m.f.* (Animal) trainer.
domattina, *adv.* Tomorrow morning.
Domeneddio [domeneddIo], *n.m.* God, Our Lord.
domenica [domEnica], *n.f.* Sunday. **Domenica delle Palme,** Palm Sunday; **osservare la —,** to observe Sunday.
domenicale, *a.* Of Sunday; of the Lord. **Scuola —,** Sunday school; **orazione —,** the Lord's Prayer.
domenicano, *n.m.a.* (*Eccles.*) Dominican.
Domenico [domEnico], *n.m.* Dominic.
domestica [domEstica], *n.f.* Maidservant, servant, housemaid. **Domestica a tutto fare,** maid-of-all-work.
domesticamente, *adv.* Familiarly.
domesticare, *v.t.* To tame, to domesticate; to subdue; to cultivate (plants).
domestichevole [domestichEvole], *a.* Tameable.
domestichezza, *n.f.* Familiarity, friendliness, intimacy.
domestico [domEstico], *n.m.* Manservant, valet.
domestico [domEstico], *a.* Domestic, familiar; tame; cultivated (plant). **Un animale —,** a tame animal; **economia domestica,** domestic economy; **le pareti domestiche,** the home, home, the four walls of home; **le cure domestiche,** home duties; **alla domestica,** familiarly.
domiciliare, *v.t.* (*Comm.*) **— una cambiale,** to make a bill payable at.
domiciliare, *a.* Domiciliary. **Perquisizione —,** house search.
domiciliarsi, *v.r.* To take up residence, to settle at.
domiciliatario [domiciliatArio], *n.m.* (*Comm.*) Referee.
domiciliato, *p.p.a.* Dwelling, resident, living at.
domicilio [domicIlio], *n.m.* Domicile, residence, abode, dwelling; address. (*Law*) **Violazione di —,** house-breaking; **servizio a —,** delivery (of goods) at the house; **d'ignoto —,** of unknown address; (*Law*) **— coatto,** internment, confinement.
dominante, *n.f.* (*Mus.*) Dominant.
dominante, *a.* Dominant, dominating, predominant, overshadowing; prevailing. **Il pensiero —,** the predominant thought; **la religione —,** the prevailing creed.
dominare, *v.t.* To dominate, to rule, to master; to sway, to predominate (over); to control; to govern, to subdue; to domineer; to overlook. **La torre domina la pianura,** the tower overlooks the plain.
dominarsi, *v.r.* To control oneself, to master one's emotions. **Egli non sa —,** he has no self-control.
dominatore, dominatrice, *n.m.f.* Ruler.

dominazione, *n.f.* Domination, rule, sway, power.
Domineddio [dominedd*I*o], *n.m.* God, the Lord.
dominicale, *n.m.* (*Eccles.*) Corporal-cloth used when carrying the Host to the sick.
dominicale, *a.* Proprietary.
dominio [dom*I*nio], *n.m.* Rule, sway, domination; dominion, domain, property. **Una cosa di — pubblico,** a matter of common knowledge; **questo è fuori del mio —,** this is out of my province; **il — delle passioni,** the control of the passions.
domino [d*O*mino], *n.m.* The game of dominoes; domino (mask).
domma (*pl.* **dommi**), *n.m.* Dogma.
dommatico [domm*A*tico], *a.* Dogmatic [cp. **dogmatico**].
domo, *a.* Tamed, subdued.
Don, *n.m.* Title of honour for priests and noblemen.
donabile [don*A*bile], *a.* Suitable for giving.
donamento, *n.m.* Donation; donating.
donante, *n.m.* Donor.
donare, *v.t.i.* To give, to make a gift, to present, to bestow; to suit (of clothes, etc.). **Più ha chi più dona,** he who gives more has more; **quest'abito le dona molto,** this dress suits her admirably.
donatario [donat*A*rio], *n.m.* Donee, recipient.
donatismo, *n.m.* (*Hist.*) Donatism.
donativo, *n.m.* Donative; gift, gratuity.
donato, *p.p.a.* Presented, bestowed upon, given. **A caval — non si guarda in bocca,** never look a gift horse in the mouth.
donatore, donatrice, *n.m.f.* Donor, giver.
donazione, *n.f.* Donation, present, gift.
donchisciottesco, *a.* Quixotic.
donde, *adv.* Whence, from where; for which reason, wherefore. **— vieni?** where do you come from? **averne ben —,** to have good reasons for it.
dondola [d*O*ndola], *n.f.* Rocking-chair.
dondolamento, *n.m.* Rocking, swinging.
dondolare, *v.t.i.* To rock, to swing, to sway, to reel. **— la testa,** to shake one's head.
dondolarsi, *v.r.* To rock oneself, to swing (oneself); to lounge.
dondolio, dondolo [dondol*I*o, d*O*ndolo], *n.m.* Rocking, swinging, swaying. **Sedia a —,** rocking-chair; **cavallo a —,** rocking-horse.
dondolone, *n.m.* Dangler, loiterer.
donna, *n.f.* Woman; womankind; lady, mistress; title of honour; (*Cards*) queen. **— di casa,** good housewife; (*Theat.*) **prima —,** leading singer or lady; **gentildonna,** gentlewoman; **— di grosso, — a mezzo servizio, — in giornata,** charwoman; **— di servizio,** domestic servant; **prender —,** to take a wife.
donnaccia [donn*A*ccia], *n.f.* Bad-tempered woman; loose woman.
donnaiolo, *n.m.* Ladies' man.
donnescamente, *adv.* In a womanly way.
donnesco, *a.* Pertaining to woman, feminine.
donnetta, *n.f.* Common little woman.
donnicciuola, *n.f.* Weak and stupid woman; simple woman.
donnicida, *n.m.* (*colloq.*) Lady-killer.
donnina, *n.f.* Good woman; clever girl. **— allegra,** woman of easy virtue.
donnino, *n.m.* Womanly girl.
donno, *n.m.* (*obs.*) Master, lord, patron.
donnola [d*O*nnola], *n.f.* (*Zool.*) Weasel.
donnona, *n.f.* Big woman, tall girl; virago.
donnone, *n.m.* Tall, imposing woman.
donnotta, *n.f.* Well-formed woman; buxom woman.
dono, *n.m.* Gift, present; donation, presentation. **— naturale,** natural gift; **dare in —,** to give as a gift; **fare un —,** to make a present.
donzella, *n.f.* Damsel, maid.
donzelletta, *n.f.* Maid, country girl.
donzello, *n.m.* Page, valet; usher, messenger.
dopo, *prep.adv.* After, afterwards, then. **Poco —,** shortly after; **il giorno —,** the following day; **— pranzo,** in the afternoon; **— tutto,** after all; **— di ciò,** after that; **e —?** what next? **a —,** later, for a later time; **— che,** since.
dopodomani, *n.m.* The day after tomorrow.
dopoguerra, *n.m.a.* Post-war; post-war period.
dopolavoro, *n.m.* (*Pol.*) Fascist institution for providing recreation after work hours.
dopopranzo, *n.m.* Afternoon.
doposcuola, *n.m.* Institution for providing play and amusement for children out of school.
doppia [d*O*ppia], *n.f.* (*Hist.*) Lining at the foot of a skirt; doubloon.
doppiamente, *adv.* Doubly.
doppiamento, *n.m.* Doubling.
doppiare, *v.t.* To double; (*Cinema*) to make a sound-track in a different language, to dub; (*Naut.*) to sail round or by, to double (a cape, etc.).
doppiato, *n.m.* (*Cinema*) Sound-track, dubbing.
doppiatura, *n.f.* Doubling, folding.
doppiere, *n.m.* Candelabrum, candlestick.
doppietta, *n.f.* Double-barrelled gun.
doppiezza, *n.f.* Duplicity, double-dealing, dissimulation.
doppio [d*O*ppio], *n.m.* Double, twice as much; duplicate; fold. **A cento doppi,** a hundred times as much; **fare un atto in —,** to draw up a deed in duplicate.
doppio [d*O*ppio], *adv.a.* Double, two-fold; duplicate; ambiguous, deceitful, double-faced. **— senso,** double meaning; (*Aviat.*) **— controllo,** dual control; (*Naut.*) **— fondo,** false bottom; **vedere —,** to see double.
doppiogiochista, *n.m.* Double-dealer, double-crosser.
doppiogioco, *n.m.* Double-dealing.
doppione, *n.m.* Duplicate; exact copy; (*gram.*) doublet.
dorare, *v.t.* To gild; to brighten. **— la pillola,** to gild the pill.
doratore, *n.m.* Gilder.
doratura, *n.f.* Gilding, gilt.
doricismo, *n.m.* Doricism.
dorico [d*O*rico], *a.* (*Arch.*) Doric. **Stile —,** Doric order.
dormente, *a.* Sleeping, dormant. **La bella — nel bosco,** the Sleeping Beauty.
dormi, *n.m.* Sleeper. **Fare il —,** to be inattentive; to feign ingenuousness.
dormicchiare, *v.i.* To doze, to nap.
dormiente, *n.m.* Sleeper, one who slumbers. **I Sette Dormienti,** the Seven Sleepers.
dormiente, *a.* Sleeping, dormant; (*Naut.*) fast at one end (of a rope).

dormiglione, dormigliona, *n.m.f.* Late riser, lazy creature.
dormire, *v.i.* To sleep, to be asleep; to rest, to be dormant, to be inactive. **Mettere a —,** to put to bed; to shelve, to put aside; **— della grossa, come un sasso, come un ghiro,** to sleep like a top; **— fra due guanciali,** to feel quite safe; **— con gli occhi aperti,** to be on one's guard.
dormire, *n.m.* Sleep.
dormita, *n.f.* A long, sound sleep.
dormitina, *n.f.* Nap. (*colloq.*) **Fare una —,** to snatch forty-winks.
dormitona, *n.f.* Long, refreshing sleep.
dormitorio [dormitOrio], *n.m.* Dormitory.
dormitura, *n.f.* Long sleep (esp. of silk-worms).
dormiveglia [dormivEglia], *n.m.* Dozing, drowsiness, half asleep half awake.
dormosa, *n.f.* Settee, sofa.
Dorotea [dorotEa], *n.f.* Dorothy.
dorsale, *a.* Dorsal, of the back. **Spina —,** backbone, spine.
dorso, *n.m.* Back; summit; mountain ridge, crest (of hill or mountain); spine (of a book). **Piegare il —,** to bend one's back (in all senses); **volgere il —,** to run away; **a dorso do mulo,** on a mule's back; **sul —,** on one's back.
dosaggio [dosAggio], *n.m.* Dosing, dosage, proportioning.
dosamento, *n.m.* Dosing.
dosare, *v.t.* To dose; to distribute.
dosatura, *n.f.* Dosing, dosage.
dose, *n.f.* Dose; ration. **In buona —,** in a good quantity; **rincarar la —,** to aggravate the matter.
dossale, *n.m.* (*Arch.*) Reredos; (*Eccles.*) cover for a missal; altar frontal.
dossiere, *n.m.* Dossier, collection of papers; back-rest.
dosso, *n.m.* Back; ridge (of hills, etc.), hill-top. **Voltare il —,** to turn one's back; **levarsi da —,** to get rid of.
dossologia [dossologIa], *n.f.* (*Eccles.*) Doxology.
dotale, *a.* Concerned with a dower. (*Comm.*) **Assicurazione —,** endowment assurance.
dotare, *v.t.* To endow, to dower, to give a dowry (to a daughter). **— la città di buone scuole,** to give the town some good schools.
dotazione, *n.f.* Endowment; grant; outfit; rates, taxes, etc., allotted to a fixed purpose.
dote, *n.f.* Dowry, marriage portion; gift, quality, merit. **Sposar la —,** to marry for money; **un giovane di alte doti,** a highly-gifted young man.
dottamente, *adv.* Learnedly.
dottato, *n.m.* (*Bot.*) Variety of early fig.
dottifico [dottIfico], *a.* (*colloq.*) Making one learned.
dotto [dòtto], *n.m.a.* Scholar, learned man; learned, scholarly, erudite.
dotto [dótto], *n.m.* Duct, conduit.
dottora, *n.f.* Learned woman; bluestocking.
dottoraggine [dottorAggine], *n.f.* Pedantry.
dottorale, *a.* Doctoral.
dottoralmente, *adv.* In a doctoral manner.
dottorame, *n.m.* Body of doctors.
dottorato, *n.m.* Doctorate.
dottore, *n.m.* Doctor, university graduate; (*Med.*) physician, doctor; (*Eccles.*) father of the Church. **Chiamare un —,** to send for a doctor.
dottoreggiare, *v.i.* To be overwise; to theorize; to assume a learned air.
dottoreria [dottorerIa], *n.f.* Ostentation of learning.
dottorescamente, *adv.* In a doctor's manner.
dottoresco, *a.* Like a doctor.
dottoressa, *n.f.* Woman doctor, woman graduate (in any faculty).
dottrina, *n.f.* Doctrine; knowledge, scholarship, erudition, learning; (*colloq.*) catechism. **Andare alla —,** to go to church (to learn the catechism).
dottrinale, *a.* Doctrinal.
dottrinalmente, *adv.* Doctrinally.
dottrinario [dottrinArio], *n.m.a.* Doctrinaire, theorizer; theoretical, visionary, unpractical.
dove, *n.m.* Place. **Per ogni —,** everywhere.
dove, *adv.* Where. **Da —,** whence, from where.
dovecchessia [dovechessIa], *adv.* (*obs.*) Wherever, in whatever place.
doventare [cp. **diventare**].
dovere, *v.t.i.* To owe, to be indebted; to be obliged to, to be bound to, to have to; shall, should, must, ought. **Io devo andare,** I must go; **egli mi deve tre mila lire,** he owes me 3,000 lire; **fa ciò che devi,** do your duty; **dovrei partire,** I ought to be leaving; **egli deve tutto a sè stesso,** he is a self-made man; **se dovessi abitar qui,** if I were to live here; **voi dovrete andarvene,** you will have to go.
dovere, *n.m.* Duty, task; what is necessary; (*pl.*) respects, compliments. **Compiere il proprio —,** to perform one's duty; **farsi un — di,** to make a point of (doing something); **presentare i propri —,** to pay one's respects to; **far stare a —,** to bring to heel; to bring to reason; **è mio — di,** I am bound in duty to.
doveroso, *a.* Dutiful, rightful, proper; fair.
dovizia [dovIzia], *n.f.* Wealth, plenty, abundance. **A —,** in plenty, copiously; **tempi di —,** times of plenty.
dovizioso, *a.* Rich, wealthy, moneyed; plentiful.
dovunque, *adv.* Everywhere, wherever; anywhere. **— io vada,** wherever I go.
dovutamente, *adv.* Duly, rightfully.
dovuto, *n.m.a.* Due; debt; due, rightful; accountable; owed. **Dare a ciascuno il —,** to give everyone his due.
dozzina, *n.f.* Dozen, twelve; board and lodging. **A dozzine,** by dozens; **mezza —,** half a dozen; **da —,** worthless; **stare a —,** to board with; **tenere a —,** to take boarders.
dozzinale, *a.* Plain, ordinary, common; clumsy; vulgar, cheap.
dozzinalità [-à], *n.f.* Vulgarity.
dozzinante, *n.m.* Boarder.
dracena, *n.f.* (*Bot.*) Dragon-tree.
draconiano, *a.* Draconian, inflexible, severe.
draga, *n.f.* Dredge, dredger, dredging-machine.
dragaggio [dragAggio], *n.m.* Dredging, sweeping (for mines, etc.).
dragamine, *n.m.* (*Naut.*) Mine-sweeper.
dragare, *v.t.* To dredge, to sweep (for mines, etc.).

draglia [drAglia], *n.f.* (*Naut.*) Stay; (*Rail.*) rail.
drago, *n.m.* Dragon. **Pallone —,** kite-balloon.
dragomanno, *n.m.* Dragoman, interpreter.
dragona, *n.f.* (*Mil.*) Sword-knot.
dragone, *n.m.* Dragon; (*Mil.*) dragoon.
dragonessa, *n.f.* She-dragon.
draia [drAia], *n.f.* Dredge, dredge-net.
dramma, *n.f.* Drachma, drachm. **A —,** little by little.
dramma (*pl.* **drammi**), *n.m.* Drama; dramatic literature; stage, theatre.
drammatica [drammAtica], *n.f.* Dramatic art.
drammaticamente, *adv.* Dramatically.
drammatico [drammAtico], *a.* Dramatic
drammatizzare, *v.t* To dramatize.
drammaturgia [drammaturgIa], *n.f.* Dramatic literature.
drammaturgo, *n.m.* Dramatist, playwright.
drappare, drappeggiare, *v.t.* To drape.
drappeggiarsi, *v.r.* To drape oneself; to strike an attitude.
drappeggio [drappEggio], *n.m.* Draping; drapery, draping (of a figure in art).
drappella, *n.f.* (*Herald.*) Knot, ribbon.
drappello, *n.m.* (*Mil.*) Troop, company, squad, platoon.
drappellonare, *v.t.* To decorate a church for a festival, etc.
drappellone, *n.m.* Hangings for church festival; curtain.
drapperia [drapperIa], *n.f.* Drapery; draper's shop; cloth warehouse.
drappiere, *n.m.* Draper.
drappo, *n.m.* Cloth, stuff, material; drapery. **— inglese,** sticking-plaster.
drastico [drAstico], *a.* Drastic.
drenaggio [drenAggio], *n.m.* Drainage; drain; (*Med.*) drainage tube. **Tubo di —,** drain-pipe.
Dresda, *n.f.* Dresden.
driade [drIade], *n.f.* Dryad, nymph of the woods.
drillo, *n.m.* (*Zool.*) Mandrill [cp. **mandrillo**].
dritta, *n.f.* Right hand (side); (*Naut.*) starboard. **Dar la —,** to place on one's right hand (as a sign of distinction).
drittamente, *adv.* Upright, straight.
drittezza, *n.f.* Straightness, uprightness; perpendicularity; rectitude.
dritto, *n.m.* Right side, top side; law, right.
dritto, *a.* Right, upright, straight; exact, proper. **Alla mano dritta,** on the right-hand side; **a —,** vertically.
drittorovescio, *adv.* Upside down.
drittura, *n.f.* Right, justice; rectitude.
drizza, *n.f.* (*Naut.*) Halyard.
drizzare, *v.t.* To raise, to set up, to erect; to direct, to turn; to straighten (*Naut.*) to trim. **— lo sguardo,** to turn one's gaze (on).
drizzarsi, *v.r.* To raise oneself
droga, *n.f.* Spice; drug.
drogare, *v.t.* To spice, to season with spice; to drug.
drogato, *p.p.a.* Spicy, piquant.
drogheria [drogherIa], *n.f.* Grocery, grocer's shop; delicatessen shop.
droghiere, *n.m.* Grocer.
dromedario [dromedArio], *n.m.* (*Zool.*) Dromedary.
dromo, *n.m.* (*Naut.*) Buoy or post marking a channel.
dromografo [dromOgrafo], *n.m.* (*Naut.*) Log (for measuring speed, distance, etc.).
dronte, *n.m.* (*Zool.*) Dodo.
druda, *n.f.* (*obs.*) Lover, mistress, paramour; sweetheart.
drudo, *n.m.* Lover, gallant, paramour.
druidico [druIdico], *a.* Druidical.
druido [drUido], *n.m.* Druid.
drupa, *n.f.* (*Bot.*) Drupe.
druscia [drUscia], *n.f.* (*obs.*) Caress.
drusciolente, *a.* Slippery.
drusiana, *n.f.* Slut, quean, harlot.
duale, *a.* Dual, two-fold.
dualismo, *n.m.* Dualism.
dualistico [dualIstico], *a.* Dualistic.
dualità [-à], *n.f.* Duality.
dualmente, *adv.* Dually.
dubbiamente, *adv.* Doubtfully, dubiously.
dubbietà, dubbiezza [-à], *n.f.* Doubt, doubtfulness, uncertainty.
dubbio [dUbbio], *n.m.* Doubt, uncertainty; suspicion; indecision, apprehension, suspense. **Mettere in —,** to call in question; **senza —,** without doubt, no doubt; **ho dei dubbi,** I have some doubts; **lasciare in —,** to leave in suspense; **chiarire un —,** to clear up a doubt.
dubbio [dUbbio], *a.adv.* Doubtful, uncertain, dubious. **Di dubbia fede,** of dubious faith; **è — ch'egli venga,** it's doubtful whether he will come.
dubbiosamente, *adv.* Dubiously, doubtfully
dubbiosità [-à], *n.f.* Dubiousness, doubtfulness.
dubbioso, *a.* Doubtful, dubious, uncertain, questionable.
dubitabile [dubitAbile], *a.* Open to doubt.
dubitabilmente, *adv.* Doubtfully, doubtingly.
dubitante, *n.m.* Doubter.
dubitanza, *n.f.* Doubt, hesitation.
dubitare, *v.t.i.* To doubt, to hesitate, to waver; to distrust, to question, to suspect. **Ne dubito,** I have my doubts; **— di,** to distrust.
dubitativo, *a.* Open to doubt, questionable.
dubitazione, *n.f.* Doubtfulness, hesitation.
dubitoso, *a.* Dubious, uncertain.
duca (*pl.* **duchi**), *n.m.* Duke.
ducale, *a.* Ducal.
ducato, *n.m.* Duchy, dukedom; ducat.
duce, *n.m.* Leader, chief.
duchessa, *n.f.* Duchess.
duchessina, *n.f.* Duke's daughter.
duchino, *n.m.* Duke's son; petty duke.
due, *n.m.a.* Two. **Star fra —,** to hesitate, to dilly-dally; **tutti e —** both; **— volte,** twice; **— a —,** two by two; **una delle —,** one or the other; **i casi sono —,** there are two alternatives.
duecentista, *n.m.* Artist or author of the 13th century.
duecento, *a.* Two hundred; 13th century.
duellante, *n.m.a.* Duellist; duelling.
duellare, *v.i.* To fight a duel.
duellista (pl. **duellisti**), *n.m.* Duellist; fencing master.
duello, *n.m.* Duel, single combat. **Sfidare a —,** to challenge (to a duel).

duemila, *a.* Two thousand.
duetto, *n.m.* Duet; dialogue; couple.
dugento, *a.* Two hundred [cp. **duecento**].
duglia [dUglia], *n.f.* (*Naut.*) Coil of rope.
Duina, *n.f.* Dwina.
dulcamara, *n.f.* (*Bot.*) Bittersweet; (*fig.*) quack doctor (from Donizetti's opera "Elisir d'amore").
dulcinea, *n.f.* Sweetheart, lover (from "Don Quixote").
dulia [dulIa], *n.f.* (*Eccles.*) Reverence paid to angels and saints.
dumo, *n.m.* (*Bot.*) Bramble.
duna, *n.f.* Sand dune, dune.
dunque, *adv.* Then; so; consequently. **Vieni —!** Come then! **penso, — sono,** I think, therefore I am.
duo, *a.* Two; (*Mus.*) duet.
duodecimo [duodEcimo], *a.* Twelfth
duodenale, *a.* (*Med.*) Duodenal.
duodeno, *n.m.* (*Anat.*) Duodenum.
duolo, *n.m.* Grief, sorrow, pain.
duomo, *n.m.* Cathedral; dome.
duplica [dUplica], *n.f.* (*Law*) Rejoinder.
duplicare, *v.t.* To duplicate, to double.
duplicato, *n.m.a.* Duplicate.
duplicazione, *n.f.* Duplication.
duplice [dUplice], *a.* Two-fold, double. **La questione è —,** the problem is two-fold.
duplicità [-à], *n.f.* Duplicity, double-dealing.
duplo, *n.m.a.* Double.
durabile [durAbile], *a.* Durable, lasting.
durabilità, *n.f.* Durability.
durabilmente, *adv.* Durably.
duracino [durAcino], *a.* Clingstone (of fruits). **Pesca duracina,** clingstone peach.
duralluminio [durallumInio], *n.m.* (*Metal*). Duraluminium, duralumin.
duramadre, *n.f.* (*Anat.*) Dura mater.
duramente, *adv.* Hardly, sternly; with difficulty; harshly.
duramento, *n.m.* Durability.
durante, *a.* Lasting, enduring. (*Law*) **Vita natural —,** for the term of one's natural life.
durante, *prep.* During. **— tutta la notte,** throughout the night, during the whole night.
durare, *v.t.i.* To last, to continue; to resist, to hold out, to endure; to stick to. **— fatica,** to make a great effort; **chi la dura la vince,** it's dogged as does it; **sono scarpe che durano,** they are shoes that will wear well; **— a lungo,** to last long; **— in carica,** to stay in office; **che la duri!** long may it last!
durata, *n.f.* Duration, length of time; resistance. **Fare una buona —,** to wear well (of clothes); **per la — di un anno,** for the duration of one year; **articolo di breve —,** perishable article; **colore di lunga —,** fast colour; (*Comm.*) **la — di una polizza,** the currency of a policy.
duraturo, *a.* Lasting, durable, resistant.
durevole [durEvole], *a.* Durable, lasting.
durevolezza, *n.f.* Durableness, durability.
durevolmente, *adv.* Durably.
durezza, *n.f.* Hardness, toughness; harshness; insensibility.
duriccio [durIccio], *a.* Rather hard.
duro, *a.* Hard; harsh, cruel; firm, steady; difficult, arduous; painful; stubborn, stupid. **Tener —,** to hold out, to stick to it; **muso —,** intractable person; **— d'orecchi,** hard of hearing; **testa dura,** dull or obstinate fellow; **pane —,** stale bread.
duttile [dUttile], *a.* Ductile; yielding, pliant.
duttilità [-à], *n.f.* Ductility; adaptability.

E

E, e, *n.f.* Fifth letter of the Italian alphabet. The vowel has two sounds, open, as in "cielo" and closed, as in "cena".
e (**ed** before vowels), *conj.* And; then; very well. **Tutti e due,** both; **tutti e tre,** all three; **e mio padre e mia madre,** both my father and my mother.
e', *pron.* He (abbreviation of **egli**).
è (*3rd sing. pres. indic.* of **essere**), is.
ebanista (*pl.* **ebanisti**), *n.m.* Cabinet-maker.
ebanisteria [ebanisterIa], *n.f.* Cabinet-making; cabinet-maker's workshop.
ebanite, *n.f.* Ebonite.
ebano [Ebano], *n.m.* Ebony, ebony-tree.
ebbene, *adv.* Well, well then. **—, che fai?** Well then, what are you up to?
ebbrezza, *n.f.* Drunkenness, intoxication; (*fig.*) enthusiasm, elation.
ebbrietà [-à], *n.f.* Drunkenness.
ebbro, *a.* Drunk, intoxicated; (*fig.*) enraptured.
ebdomada [ebdOmada], *n.f.* Week.
ebdomadario [ebdomadArio], *a.* Weekly, hebdomadal.
Ebe, *n.f.* (*Myth.*) Hebe.
ebetaggine [ebetAggine], *n.f.* Idiocy; stupidity, doltishness.
ebetazione, *n.f.* Mental obtuseness.
ebete [Ebete], *a.* Doltish, stupid; weak-minded.
ebetismo, *n.m.* Stupidity, silliness; weak-mindedness.
ebetudine [ebetUdine], *n.f.* Stupidity, dullness (of intellect).
ebollizione, *n.f.* Ebullition, effervescence (in all senses), ebullience.
ebraicamente, *adv.* In Hebraic style.
ebraico [ebrAico], *a.* Hebrew; Jewish. **La lingua ebraica,** Hebrew; **ristorante —,** kosher restaurant; **la questione ebraica,** the Jewish question.
ebraista, *n.m.* Hebrew scholar.
ebreo [ebrEo], *n.m.a.* Jew; Jewish, Hebrew. **— errante,** the Wandering Jew.
ebrezza [cp. **ebbrezza**].
ebrietà [cp. **ebbrietà**].
ebulliente, *a.* Ebullient, boiling.
eburneo [ebUrneo], *a.* Of ivory, white as ivory.
ecatombe, *n.f.* Hecatomb; (*fig.*) slaughter.
ecatostilo [ecatOstilo], *a.* (*Arch.*) With a hundred columns.
eccedente, *a.* Exceeding, excessive, surplus.
eccedentemente, *adv.* Exceedingly, surpassingly.
eccedenza, *n.f.* Surplus, excess.
eccedere [eccEdere], *v.t.i.* To exceed, to transcend; to go beyond; to go too far. **— la velocità permessa,** to exceed the speed limit.
eccellente, *a.* Excellent, very good.

eccellentemente, *adv.* Excellently.
eccellenza, *n.f.* Excellence, pre-eminence; perfection. **Per —,** pre-eminently; especially; **Sua —,** His Excellency.
eccellere [eccEllere], *v.t.i.* To excel; to surpass, to outdo; to stand out (above others).
eccelsamente, *adv.* In the highest degree; sublimely.
eccelso, *a.* High, lofty, sublime.
eccentrica [eccEntrica], *n.f.* (*Geom.*) Eccentric; (*Rail.*) switch-point.
eccentricamente, *adv.* Eccentrically (in all senses).
eccentricità [-à], *n.f.* Eccentricity; extravagance, queerness.
eccentrico [eccEntrico], *n.m.a.* Eccentric (in all senses). **Egli è molto —,** he is a crank.
eccepibile [eccepIbile], *a.* Objectionable; exceptionable.
eccepire, *v.i.* To object, to take exception; to allege.
eccessivamente, *adv.* Excessively, immoderately.
eccessività [-à], *n.f.* Excessiveness, excess.
eccesso, *n.m.* Excess, surplus; superfluity, exaggeration; intemperance, riot, abuse. **— di peso,** excess weight; **dare in eccessi,** to break out in excesses; **per — di zelo,** through excess of zeal; **andare all'—,** to go to extremes.
eccetera [eccEtera], *n.m.* Et cetera; and so forth, and so on.
eccetto, *prep.conj.* Except, save; unless, but. **— ch'egli venga,** unless he comes; **— una volta,** but for once; **— che,** unless.
eccettuabile [eccettuAbile], *a.* Exceptable.
eccettuare, *v.t.* To except, to leave out, to exclude; to exempt.
eccettuazione, *n.f.* Exclusion, exception.
eccezionale, *a.* Exceptional, unusual. **Misura —,** emergency measure.
eccezione, *n.f.* Exception (in all senses). **— alla regola,** exception to the rule; **l'— conferma la regola,** the exception proves the rule.
ecchimosi [ecchImosi], *n.f.* (*Med.*) Ecchymosis, bruise.
eccidio [eccIdio], *n.m.* Slaughter, massacre; bloodshed.
eccitabile [eccitAbile], *a.* Excitable, irritable.
eccitabilità [-à], *n.f.* Excitability.
eccitamento, *n.m.* Excitement, commotion.
eccitante, *n.m.a.* (*Med.*) Excitant, irritant; stimulant; exciting, stirring.
eccitare, *v.t.* To excite, to stir; to incite; to stimulate, to rouse; to inflame. **— la curiosità,** to arouse one's curiosity.
eccitarsi, *v.r.* To get excited; to get angry.
eccitativo, *a.* Exciting.
eccitatore, eccitatrice, *n.m.f.* Exciter, one who excites.
eccitazione, *n.f.* Excitement, commotion; incitement.
Ecclesiaste, *n.m.* Bible book of Ecclesiastes.
ecclesiastico [ecclesiAstico], *n.m.a.* Ecclesiastic, priest, divine; ecclesiastical, clerical.
ecco, *adv.* Here is, here are; there is, there are; behold, look. **Eccomi,** here I am; **eccoci arrivati,** here we are; **— fatto,** that's done; **— tutto,** that's all; **eccolo che viene,** here he comes; **eccone uno,** here's one; **ecco!** look!
echeggiante, *a.* Resounding, rumbling, echoing.
echeggiare, *v.t.i.* To resound, to echo.
echide [Echide], *n.f.* (*Zool.*) Kind of viper.
echino, *n.m.* (*Zool.*) Echinus, sea-urchin.
eclettico [eclEttico], *a.* Eclectic.
eclettismo, *n.m.* Eclecticism.
eclissare, *v.t.* To eclipse; to obscure; to outshine (another person).
eclissarsi, *v.r.* To disappear, to vanish, to make off.
eclisse, eclissi, *n.m.f.* Eclipse. **— lunare, solare, totale, parziale,** lunar, solar, total, partial eclipse.
eclittica [eclIttica], *n.f.* (*Astron.*) Ecliptic.
ecloga, *n.f.* Eclogue [cp. **egloga**].
eco, *n.m.f.* Echo. **Far —,** to echo; to second; **farsi — di,** to repeat, to voice; **— della stampa,** press-cutting agency.
ecologia [ecologIa], *n.f.* Ecology.
economato, *n.m.* Bursarship; stewardship; administrative department.
economia [economIa], *n.f.* Economy, saving, thrift; management, arrangement; economics. **Fare —,** to put by money, to save; **un trattato d'—,** a treatise on economics; **— politica,** political economy.
economica [econOmica], *n.f.* Economics.
economicamente, *adv.* Economically, thriftily.
economico [econOmico], *a.* Economical, frugal, thrifty. **Cucina economica,** kitchen range, fuel-saving stove.
economista (*pl.* **economisti**), *n.m.* Economist.
economizzare, *v.t.* To economize, to save, to spare, to put by.
economizzatore, *n.m.* Economizer.
economo (1) [ecOnomo], *n.m.* Bursar, steward.
economo (2) [ecOnomo], *a.* Economical, thrifty.
ectoplasma, *n.m.* Ectoplasm.
ecumenico [ecumEnico], *a.* Ecumenical.
eczema, *n.m.* (*Med.*) Eczema.
ed, *conj.* And [cp. **e**].
edace, *a.* Voracious, devouring.
edacità [-à], *n.f.* Voracity.
edema, *n.m.* (*Med.*) Oedema.
edematoso, *a.* (*Med.*) Oedematous.
eden, *n.m.* Eden. **L'Eden,** the Garden of Eden.
edera [Edera], *n.f.* Ivy.
ederoso, *a.* Ivied, ivy-mantled.
edicola [edIcola], *n.f.* Newspaper kiosk, news-stand, book-stall; public convenience; (*Arch.*) tabernacle, pavilion.
edificamento, *n.m.* Building, (act of) erecting.
edificante, *a.* Edifying.
edificare, *v.t.* To build, to erect, to construct; to edify, to build up spiritually, to enlighten.
edificazione, *n.f.* Building; edification.
edificio, edifizio [edifIcio, edifIzio], *n.m.* Building, edifice, structure, fabric.
edile, *n.m.* (*Hist.*) Aedile. || *a.* **Perito —,** contractor, master-builder.
edilizio [edilIzio], *a* Pertaining to building. **Impresa edilizia,** building contractor.
Edimburgo, *n.f.* Edinburgh.
edito [Edito], *a.* Published, printed.
editore, editrice, *n.m.f.* Publisher; editor, editress.
editore, *a.* Publishing. **Casa editrice,** publishing house, publisher.
editoria [editorIa], *n.f.* Publishing trade.

editoriale, *n.m.a.* Newspaper leader, editorial; editorial, publishing.
editto, *n.m.* Edict, proclamation, decree.
edizioncina, *n.f.* Small pocket edition; choice edition.
edizione, *n.f.* Edition; publication. **— riveduta e corretta,** revised edition; **— a tiratura ristretta,** limited edition; **— tascabile,** pocket edition.
edonismo, *n.m.* Hedonism.
edonista (*pl.* **edonisti**), *n.m.* Hedonist.
edotto, *a.* Informed, instructed. **Render —,** to inform.
edredone, *n.m.* (*Zool.*) Eider-duck.
educanda, *n.f.* Girl at boarding-school.
educandato, *n.m.* Institute for girls.
educare, *v.t.* To educate, to bring up, to rear, to train, to instruct.
educativo, *a.* Educational.
educato, *a.* Polite, well-bred.
educatore, educatrice, *n.m.f.* Teacher, educator.
educazione, *n.f.* Education, manners, good breeding. **Senza —,** ill-bred, without manners, ill-mannered.
edule [edUle], *a.* Edible.
efebo, *n.m.* (*Lit.*) Youth, adolescent.
efelide [efElide], *n.f.* Freckle, ephelis.
Efeso [Efeso], *n.m.* (*Geog.*) Ephesus.
effe, *n.f.* Letter F.
effemeride [effemEride], *n.f.* Diary, journal; calendar.
effeminare, *v.t.* To make effeminate.
effeminarsi, *v.r.* To grow effeminate.
effeminatezza, *n.f.* Effeminacy; weakness, softness.
effeminatamente, *adv.* Effeminately.
effeminato, *a.* Effeminate, womanish, unmanly.
efferatamente, *adv.* Inhumanly, cruelly.
efferatezza, *n.f.* Cruelty, barbarity, atrocity.
efferato, *a.* Inhuman, cruel, dastardly, brutal.
efferente, *a.* (*Med.*) Efferent. **Vasi efferenti,** blood-vessels.
effervescente, *a.* Effervescent, sparkling.
effervescenza, *n.f.* Effervescence, ferment; (*fig.*) unrest. **Essere in —,** to be all agog.
effetti, *n.m.pl.* Effects, goods, belongings. **— personali,** personal effects.
effettivamente, *adv.* In reality, truly, indeed.
effettività [-à], *n.f.* Reality, actuality.
effettivo, *n.m.a.* Real, actual; substantial, effective. (*Mil.*) **Ufficiali effettivi,** officers on active list.
effetto, *n.m.* Effect; result, consequence; bill. **Fare —,** to have an effect; **per — di,** as a consequence of; **mandare ad —,** to carry out, to effect; **fare un bell'—,** to show well, to make a good showing; **un — di luce,** a play of light; (*Comm.*) **un — bancario,** a bill of exchange.
effettone, *n.m.* Boom, success. **Fare un —,** to make a splash.
effettuabile [effettuAbile], *a.* Practicable, feasible, workable.
effettuabilità [-à], *n.f.* Practicability.
effettuale, *a.* Real, actual, effectual.
effettualmente, *adv.* Effectually.
effettuare, *v.t.* To effectuate, to carry out, to accomplish, to perform, to effect. **— una commissione,** to carry out an order.
effettuazione, *n.f.* Effectuation, accomplishment, execution, completion.
efficace, *a.* Efficacious, effectual, effective.
efficacemente, *adv.* Efficaciously.
efficacia [efficacIa], *n.f.* Efficacy, effectiveness.
efficiente, *a.* Efficient, effective, active; able.
efficientemente, *adv.* Efficiently.
efficienza, *n.f.* Efficiency; effectiveness. **Mantenere in —,** to keep in working order.
effige, effigie [effIgie], *n.f.* Effigy; portrait, picture, image. **Bruciare in —,** to burn in effigy.
effigiare, *v.t.* To portray, to picture, to paint.
effimera [effImera], *n.f.* Ephemera, May fly.
effimero [effImero], *a.* Ephemeral, transient, short-lived.
efflorescente, *a.* Efflorescent.
efflorescenza, *n.f.* Efflorescence.
effluente, *a.* Outflowing, effluent.
efflusso, *n.m.* Efflux, outflow, effusion.
effluvio [efflUvio], *n.m.* Effluvium, emanation; (*fig.*) outburst.
effondere [effOndere], *v.t.* To pour out, to shed, to emit, to effuse.
effondersi [effOndersi], *v.r.* To give vent to.
effondimento, *n.m.* Effusion, outpour.
effossorio [effossOrio], *a.* (*Naut.*) Dredging.
effrazione, *n.f.* (*Law*) House-breaking, burglary.
effumazione, *n.f.* Evaporation; fumes arising from a volcanic crater.
effusione, *n.f.* Effusion, overflowing, flow. **Senza — di sangue,** without bloodshed; **accogliere con grande —,** to receive demonstratively.
effuso, *p.p.a.* Outpoured, shed.
efimera [efImera], *n.f.* [cp. **effimera**].
eforo [Eforo], *n.m.* (*Hist.*) Ephor, Spartan magistrate.
egagro, *n.m.* (*Zool.*) Wild goat of Persia.
egemone [egEmone], *n.m.* Leader, chieftain.
egemonia [egemonIa], *n.f.* Hegemony, supremacy, predominance.
egemonico [egemOnico], *a.* Predominant, prevailing.
Egeo, *n.m.* (*Geog.*) The Aegean Sea.
egestione, *n.f.* (*Physiol.*) Excretion; excreta.
egida [Egida], *n.f.* Aegis, shield; protection. **Sotto l'— di,** under the aegis of.
egipane [egIpane], *n.m.* (*Myth.*) Faun, satyr.
egira, *n.f.* (*Hist.*) Hegira.
Egitto, *n.m.* (*Geog.*) Egypt.
egittologia [egittologIa], *n.f.* Egyptology.
egittologo [egittOlogo], *n.m.* Egyptologist.
egiziaco, egiziano [egizIaco], *n.m.a.* Egyptian.
egizio [egIzio], *a.* (Ancient) Egyptian.
eglantina, *n.f.* (*Bot.*) Eglantine, sweet briar.
egli, *pron.* He, it.
eglino [Eglino], *pron.pl.* (*obs.*) They.
egloga [Egloga], *n.f.* (*Poet.*) Eclogue.
egocentrico [egocEntrico], *a.* Egocentric.
egoismo, *n.m.* Egoism, selfishness.
egoista (*pl.* **egoisti**), *n.m.* Egoist.
egoistico [egoIstico], *a.* Egoistic, selfish.
egotismo, *n.m.* Egotism.
egregiamente, *adv.* Splendidly, very well.
egregio [egrEgio], *a.* Notable, eminent, distinguished. **— signore,** Dear Sir (in letters).
egresso, *n.m.* (*obs.*) Egress, way out.
egretta, *n.f.* (*Zool.*) Egret.

egro, *a.* (*Poet.*) Ill, infirm.
eguagliamento, *n.m.* Equalization, levelling, standardization.
eguaglianza, *n.f.* Equality, parity; evenness, uniformity.
eguagliare, *v.t.* To equal; to make equal, to standardize; to level down.
eguale, uguale, *a.* Equal, like; even, uniform, smooth, level. **Senza l'—,** unequalled.
egualità [-à], *n.f.* Equality, parity.
egualizzare, *v.t.* To standardize, to level, to make uniform.
egualmente, *adv.* Equally, alike.
eh! *inter.* Ah! Well! **Bello, eh?** beautiful, isn't it?
ehi! *inter.* Hello, I say! Here, I say!
ehm! *inter.* Ahem!
ei, *pron.* (*Poet. obs.*) He.
eia [Eia], *inter.* Hurrah.
eiaculare, *v.t.* To ejaculate (fluid).
eiaculazione, *n.f.* Ejaculation (of fluid).
eiettore, *n.m.* (*Mech.*) Ejector.
eira, *n.f.* (*Zool.*) Small species of puma.
elaborare, *v.t.* To elaborate, to work out, to develop in detail.
elaboratezza, *n.f.* Fineness, delicacy of workmanship.
elaborazione, *n.f.* Elaboration.
elape [Elape], *n.m.* (*Zool.*) Elaps, coral-snake.
elargire, *v.t.* To lavish, to bestow munificently, to make a donation of; to grant.
elargizione, *n.f.* Donation; bestowal, generous gift, present.
elasticamente, *adv.* Elastically.
elasticità [-à], *n.f.* Elasticity, springiness; adaptability, suppleness.
elastico [elAstico], *n.m.a.* Elastic band, rubber band; elastic material; elastic.
elatere, *n.m.* (*Zool.*) Elater; skip-back beetle.
elce, *n.m.* (*Bot.*) Holm-oak, ilex.
elefante, *n.m.* (*Zool.*) Elephant; bull elephant.
elefantesco, elefantino, *a.* Elephantine.
elefantessa, *n.f.* Cow elephant.
elefantiasi [elefantIasi], *n.f.* (*Med.*) Elephantiasis.
elegante, *a.* Elegant, graceful, neat; smart, fashionable; (*colloq.*) spruce.
elegantemente, *adv.* Elegantly.
elegantire, *v.t.* To make elegant.
elegantone, *n.m.* Dandy, beau.
eleganza, *n.f.* Elegance, smartness, neatness.
eleggente, *n.m.* Elector, voter.
eleggere [elEggere], *v.t.* To elect, to choose, to appoint. (*Law*) — **domicilio,** to take up one's abode.
eleggibile [eleggIbile], *a.* Eligible.
eleggibilità [-à], *n.f.* Eligibility.
elegia [elegIa], *n.f.* Elegy.
elegiaco [elegIaco], *a.* Elegiac, mournful.
elementare, *a.* Elementary; simple, rudimentary; elemental. **Scuola —,** elementary school.
elementarmente, *adv.* In an elementary way.
elemento, *n.m.* Element, principle, unit; cell (in scientific sense). **Elementi,** rudiments, elements (of a science etc.); **il tale è un buon —,** Mr. So-and-so is a reliable person, a capable man.
elemosina [elemOsina], *n.f.* Alms, charity. **Chieder l'—,** to beg (for alms); **cassetta per l'—,** alms-box.
elemosinare, *v.i.* To beg for alms; to solicit, to implore.
elemosiniere, *n.m.* Alms-giver; almoner.
elencare, *v.t.* To list, to draw up a list of, to inventory, to catalogue; to enumerate, to reckon up one by one; to tabulate.
elenco, *n.m.* List, inventory, catalogue, index. **— telefonico,** telephone directory.
eletta, *n.f.* Choice, selection; a collection of chosen persons.
elettamente, *adv.* Elegantly, with distinction.
elettivamente, *adv.* By election.
elettivo, *a.* Elective. **Affinità elettiva,** elective affinity.
eletto, *a.* Chosen, elect, select.
elettorale, *a.* Electoral. **Scheda —,** ballot-paper; **urna —,** ballot-box; **campagna —,** electoral campaign.
elettorato, *n.m.* Electorate; franchise.
elettore, elettrice, *n.m.f.* Elector, voter.
elettricamente, *adv.* Electrically.
elettricista (pl. **elettricisti**), *n.m.* Electrician.
elettricità [-à], *n.f.* Electricity.
elettrico [elEttrico], *a.* Electric, electrical. **Scossa elettrica,** electric shock; **luce elettrica,** electric light; **centrale elettrica,** power-station; **corrente —,** electric current.
elettrificare, *v.t.* To electrify, to make work by electricity.
elettrificazione, *n.f.* Electrification. **L'— delle ferrovie,** the electrification of the railways.
elettrizzante, *a.* Thrilling, stirring.
elettrizzare, To electrify, to thrill, to excite.
elettrizzarsi, *v.r.* To become excited, to excite oneself.
elettro, *n.m.* Yellow amber.
elettrobiologia [elettrobiologIa], *n.f.* Electro-biology.
elettrocalamita, *n.f.* Electro-magnet.
elettrochimica [elettrochImica], *n.f.* Electro-chemistry.
elettrocuzione, *n.f.* Electrocution.
elettrodinamica [elettrodinAmica], *n.f.* Electro-dynamics.
elettrodo [elEttrodo], *n.m.* Electrode.
elettrodomestici [elettrodomEstici], *n.m.pl.* Electrical household appliances.
elettro-esecuzione, *n.f.* Electrocution (as method of execution).
elettrolisi [elettrOlisi], *n.f.* Electrolysis.
elettromagnetico [elettromagnEtico], *a.* Electromagnetic.
elettrone, *n.m.* Electron.
elettronico [elettrOnico], *a.* Electronic.
elettrotecnica [elettrotEcnica], *n.f.* Electrical engineering.
elettroterapia [elettroterapIa], *n.f.* Electro-therapy.
elettrotreno, *n.m.* Electric fast train.
eleusino, *a.* (*Myth.*) Eleusinian.
elevamento, *n.m.* Raising, elevation, uplifting.
elevare, *v.t.* To lift up, to raise, to elevate; to erect; to promote, to exalt. **— il tono della voce,** to raise the pitch of the voice; **— i prezzi,** to raise prices.
elevarsi, *v.r.* To rise, to tower; to raise oneself, to be elevated, to be lofty; to soar. **Il duomo si eleva sulla città,** the cathedral towers above the city.
elevatamente, *adv.* Elevatedly, loftily.

elevatezza, *n.f.* Loftiness, eminence, sublimity, nobility.
elevato, *a.* High, elevated; noble, lofty. — **alla carica di,** appointed to the office of; **ferrovia elevata,** overhead railway.
elevatore, *n.m.* Lift, elevator; (*Anat.*) elevator muscle.
elevazione, *n.f.* Elevation; height, eminence, rising of ground; raising; loftiness, sublimity; (*Eccles.*) elevation of the Host.
elezione, *n.f.* Election, polling; choice, appointment. **Il giorno delle elezioni,** polling day; **ciò non è di mia —,** this is none of my choosing.
elfo, *n.m.* Elf.
eliaco [elIaco], *a.* (*Astron.*) Heliacal.
elianto, *n.m.* (*Bot.*) Helianthus, sunflower.
elica, elice [Elica, Elice], *n.f.* (*Naut.*) Propeller, screw; (*Aviat.*) propeller, air-screw; spiral. **Scala a —,** spiral stairway; **pala dell'—,** propeller blade; **vapore a un'—,** single-screw steamer.
elicoidale, *a.* Helicoidal.
eliconio [elicOnio], *a.* Of Mt. Helicon.
elicottero [elicOttero], *n.m.* (*Aviat.*) Helicopter.
elidere [elIdere], *v.t.* (*Gram.*) To elide; to cut off. **Le due forze si elidono,** the two forces cancel or neutralize each other.
eligibile [eligIbile], *a.* Eligible.
eligibilità [-à], *n.f.* Eligibility.
eliminare, *v.t.* To eliminate, to remove to dismiss; to strike out, to delete; to weed out.
eliminatoria [eliminatOria], *n.f.* (*Sport*) Heat; semi-final.
eliminazione, *n.f.* Elimination, expulsion, rejection; removal, dismissal.
elimosina, *n.f.* Alms [cp. **elemosina**].
elio [Elio], *n.m.* Helium.
eliocentrico [eliocEntrico], *a.* (*Astron.*) Heliocentric.
eliografia [eliografIa], *n.f.* (*Astron.*) Heliography.
eliografo [eliOgrafo], *n.m.* Heliograph (signalling apparatus).
elioscopio [elioscOpio], *n.m.* Helioscope.
eliostata, *n.m.* Heliostat.
elioterapia [elioterapIa], *n.f.* (*Med.*) Heliotherapy, sunlight treatment.
eliotipia [eliotipIa], *n.f.* (*Print.*) Heliotype.
eliotropio [eliotrOpio], *n.m.* (*Bot., Min.*) Heliotrope.
elisio [elIsio], *a.* Elysian. **I campi elisi,** the Elysian fields.
elisione, *n.f.* Elision.
elisir, elisire, *n.m.* Elixir, cordial; quintessence.
Eliso, *n.m.* (*Myth*). Elysium.
eliso, *p.p.a.* Elided.
ella, *pron.* She (**Ella** or **Lei** used in polite address for "you").
elle, *n.m.f.* The letter L.
elleboro [ellEboro], *n.m.* (*Bot.*) Hellebore.
ellenico [ellEnico], *a.* Hellenic.
ellenismo, *n.m.* Hellenism.
ellenista (*pl.* **ellenisti**), *n.m.* Hellenist, Greek scholar.
ellera [Ellera], *n.f.* (*colloq.*) Ivy [cp. **edera**].
ellisse, *n.f.* (*Geom.*) Ellipse.
ellissi, *n.f.* (*Gram.*) Ellipsis.
ellitticamente, *adv.* Elliptically.
ellittico [ellIttico], *a.* Elliptical, elliptic.
ello (*pl.* **elli**), *pron.* (*obs.*) He, they (for **egli, essi**).
elmetto, *n.m.* Tin hat, steel helmet (in modern warfare).
elminti, *n.m.pl.* (*Med.*) Helminth.
elmintologia [elmintologIa], *n.f.* Helminthology.
elmo, *n.m.* Helmet.
elocuzione, *n.f.* Elocution, utterance, delivery; clearness of expression.
elogiare, *v.t.* To commend, to praise, to eulogize.
elogiativo, *a.* Eulogistic.
elogiatore, elogiatrice, *n.m.f.* Eulogizer.
elogio [elOgio], *n.m.* Praise ; commendation; eulogy, panegyric, encomium. **Fare l'— di qualcuno,** to sing someone's praises; **— funebre,** funeral oration.
elogista (pl. **elogisti**), *n.m.* Eulogist.
elogistico [elogIstico], *a.* Eulogistic.
elongare, *v.t.i.* (*obs.*) To remove to a distance.
elongazione, *n.f.* (*Astron.*) Elongation.
eloquente, *a.* Eloquent; powerful, forceful.
eloquentemente, *adv.* Eloquently.
eloquenza, *n.f.* Eloquence, oratory.
eloquio [elOquio], *n.m.* (*Lit.*) Speech, discourse.
elsa, *n.f.* Hilt, sword-hilt.
elucidare, *v.t.* To explain, to elucidate, to make clear.
elucubrare, *v.t.* To ponder over, to muse upon.
elucubrazione, *n.f.* Lucubration, pondering.
eludere [elUdere], *v.t.* To evade, to shun, to elude; to shirk. **— la legge,** to evade the law; **— la vigilanza,** to escape the vigilance.
elusivo, *a.* Elusive, baffling.
elusorio [elusOrio], *a.* Elusory.
elvetico [elvEtico], *a.* Swiss, Helvetic. **Confederazione elvetica,** Swiss Confederation.
elzeviriano, *a.* Pertaining to Elzevir editions and type.
elzeviro, *n.m.* (*Typ.*) Elzevir.
emaciamento, *n.m.* Emaciation.
emaciarsi, *v.r.* To become emaciated, to waste away.
emaciato, *p.p.a.* Emaciated, wasted, lean.
emaciazione, *n.f.* Emaciation.
emanare, *v.i.t.* To emanate, to proceed from; to issue, to publish, to spread abroad.
emanazione, *n.f.* Emanation; enactment (of a law).
emancipare, *v.t.* To emancipate, to set free; to enfranchise.
emanciparsi, *v.r.* To gain one's liberty, to free oneself; to become independent.
emancipazione, *n.f.* Emancipation.
emarginare, *v.t.* To write on the margin, to annotate, to write up.
ematite, *n.f.* (*Min.*) Haematite.
ematosi, *n.f.* (*Med.*) Haematosis.
emazia [emazIa], *n.f.* (*Anat.*) Red blood corpuscle.
emblema (*pl.* **emblemi**), *n.m.* Emblem, symbol, attribute.
emblematicamente, *adv.* Emblematically.
emblematico [emblemAtico], *a.* Emblematic.
embolia [embolIa], *n.f.* (*Med.*) Embolism.
embolismo, *n.m.* (*Astron.*) Embolism.

embolo [Embolo], *n.m.* (*Med.*) Embolus; embolism.
embrice [Embrice], *n.m.* Roof tile. **Scoprire un —**, to reveal a secret.
embriciato, *a.* Tiled.
embriologia [embriologIa], *n.f.* Embriology.
embriologo [embriOlogo], *n.m.* Embriologist.
embrionale, *a.* Embryonic, rudimentary.
embrione, *n.m.* Embryo; germ. **In —**, in embryo.
embrocazione, *n.f.* Embrocation; rubbing with a lotion.
emenda, *n.f.* Correction, emendation.
emendabile [emendAbile], *a.* Amendable, capable of improvement.
emendamento, *n.m.* Amendment. **Proporre un —**, to propose an amendment.
emendare, *v.t.* To amend, to emend, to correct; to reform, to improve.
emendarsi, *v.r.* To amend (one's behaviour), to correct one's faults.
emendatore, emendatrice, *n.m.f.* Emendator.
emendazione, *n.f.* Emendation, correction.
emergente, *a.* Emergent. (*Comm.*) **Danno —**, consequential damage.
emergenza, *n.f.* Emergency; occurrence; pressing necessity.
emergere [emErgere], *v.i.* To emerge, to stand out; to come afloat; to crop up. **Uno scrittore che emerge,** an author who stands out.
emerito [emErito], *a.* Distinguished; emeritus. **Professore —**, emeritus professor.
emeroteca, *n.f.* Reading-room for periodicals.
emersione, *n.f.* Emersion, coming afloat, emergence; (*Astron.*) emersion.
emerso, *p.p.a.* Arisen, emerged; emitted, issued.
emetico [emEtico], *n.m.a.* Emetic.
emettere [emEttere], *v.t.* To issue, to emit, to send out, to utter, to express, to put into circulation. (*Comm.*) **— nuovi biglietti,** to issue new paper money.
emiciclo, *n.m.* Semicircle.
emicrania [emicrAnia], *n.f.* Headache; megrim, migraine.
emidattilo [emidAttilo], *n.m.* (*Zool.*) Species of small lizard.
emigrante, *n.m.* Emigrant.
emigrare, *v.i.* To emigrate, to migrate.
emigrato, *n.m.* Refugee; political exile.
emigratorio [emigratOrio], *a.* Migratory.
emigrazione, *n.f.* Emigration.
eminente, *a.* Eminent, lofty; distinguished, prominent.
eminentemente, *adv.* Eminently.
eminenza, *n.f.* Eminence, height. **Sua Eminenza,** His Eminence (mode of address for a cardinal); **— grigia,** power behind the throne.
emiplegia [emiplegIa], *n.f.* (*Med.*) Hemiplegia.
emiro, *n.m.* Emir.
emisferico [emisfErico], *a.* Semicircular, hemispheric.
emisfero, *n.m.* Hemisphere.
emissario [emissArio], *n.m.* Emissary; outlet (from a lake, etc.), drain; spy, informer.
emissione, *n.f.* Emission; issue (of currency, etc.); discharge (of gas, etc.); uttering. **— di banconote,** issue of bank-notes; **data d'—**, date of issue; (*Mech.*) **valvola d'—, valvola di scarico,** exhaust valve.
emistichio [emistIchio], *n.m.* (*Poet.*) Hemistich.
emittente, *n.m.* (*Comm.*) Drawer, issuer; *n.f.* (*Radio*) transmitting station.
emittente, *a.* Emitting, issuing. **La banca —**, the issuing bank.
emitteri [emItteri], *n.m.pl.* (*Zool.*) Hemiptera.
emme, *n.m.* Letter M.
emofilia [emofilIa], *n.f.* (*Med.*) Haemophilia.
emoglobina, *n.f.* Haemoglobin.
emolliente, *a.* Emollient, softening.
emolumento, *n.m.* Emolument, remuneration.
emorragia [emoraggIa], *n.f.* (*Med.*) Haemorrhage.
emorroidi [emorrOidi], *n.f.pl.* (*Med.*) Haemorrhoids, piles.
emostatico [emostAtico], *n.m.a.* Styptic, haemostatic.
emotività [-à], *n.f.* Excitability, sensibility, emotionalism.
emotivo, *a.* Emotional; apprehensive.
emotrasfusione, *n.f.* Blood-transfusion.
emozionabile [emozionAbile], *a.* Excitable, emotional.
emozionare, *v.t.* To excite emotion; to affect.
emozionarsi, *v.r.* To become excited, to be moved (emotionally).
emozione, *n.f.* Emotion, agitation, feeling; excitement.
empetiggine [empetIggine], *n.f.* (*Med.*) Impetigo.
empiere [Empiere] [cp. **empire**].
empietà [-à], *n.f.* Impiety, godlessness, impiousness.
empifondo, *n.m.* (*Naut.*) High tide (due to direction of wind); flood.
empimento, *n.m.* Filling up, stuffing, cramming.
empio [Empio], *a.* Impious, godless, irreligious, heathen; pitiless; wicked.
empire, empiere, *v.t.* To fill, to fill up; to cram, to stuff; to crowd, to throng; to load (with benefits); to satisfy.
empireo [empIreo], *n.m.* (*Lit.*) Empyrean.
empiricamente, *adv.* Empirically.
empirico [empIrico], *a.* Empiric, empirical; quack; rule-of-thumb. **Medico —**, quack doctor.
empirismo, *n.m.* Empiricism, quackery.
empirsi, *v.r.* To fill oneself, to cram oneself. **— di gente,** to become crowded.
empito [Empito], *n.m.* Impetus, rush, fury, violence (of motion).
empito, *p.p.a.* Crammed, filled.
empitura, *n.f.* Filling up, cramming, stuffing.
emporio [empOrio], *n.m.* Emporium, mart; trade centre.
emulare, *v.t.* To vie with, to emulate, to compete with, to seek to rival.
emulatore, emulatrice, *n.m.f.* Emulator; rival, competitor.
emulazione, *n.f.* Emulation; competition.
emulo [Emulo], *n.m.a.* Rival, competitor; emulous; rival, competing.
emulsione, *n.f.* Emulsion.

emungere [emUngere], *v.t.* (*obs.*) To drain, to dry up.
emunto, *a.* Worn out, emaciated.
emuntorio [emuntOrio], *a.* (*Med.*) Emunctory.
enarmonico [enarmOnico], *a.* (*Mus.*) Enharmonic.
encaustica [encAustica], *n.f.* Art of encaustic painting.
encaustico [encAustico], *a.* Encaustic.
encausto [encAusto], *n.m.* Encaustic (painting).
encefalico [encefAlico], *a.* (*Anat.*) Encephalic.
encefalite, *n.f.* (*Med.*) Encephalitis.
enciclica [encIclica], *n.f.* (*Eccles.*) Encyclical (letter).
enciclopedia [enciclopedIa], *n.f.* Encyclopedia.
enciclopedico [enciclopEdico], *a.* Encyclopedic.
enciclopedista (*pl.* **enciclopedisti**), *n.m.* Encyclopedist.
enclitica [enclItica], *n.f.* (*Gram.*) Enclitic.
encomiabile [encomiAbile], *a.* Laudable, praiseworthy, commendable.
encomiare, *v.t.* To praise, to commend, to eulogize.
encomiastico [encomiAstico], *a.* Encomiastic, laudatory.
encomio [encOmio], *n.m.* Encomium, praise, eulogy, high commendation.
endecasillabo [endecasIllabo], *n.m.* (*Poet.*) Hendecasyllable, line of eleven syllables.
endemico [endEmico], *a.* Endemic.
endice [Endice], *n.m.* Nest-egg.
endocardite, *n.f.* (*Med.*) Endocarditis.
endocrino, *a.* (*Anat.*) Endocrine. **Glandole endocrine,** endocrine glands.
endogeno [endOgeno], *a.* Endogenous.
endosmosi [endOsmosi], *n.f.* Endosmosis.
eneo [Eneo], *a.* (*Poet.*) Bronze.
energetico [energEtico], *a.* (*Med.*) Giving energy (to the system); tonic; energetic.
energia [energIa], *n.f.* Energy; force, strength, vigour, power; resolution. **— elettrica,** electric power; **— atomica,** atomic energy.
energicamente, *adv.* Vigorously, forcibly.
energico [enErgico], *a.* Vigorous, forcible, energetic; strong, powerful.
energumeno [energUmeno], *n.m.* Energumen, one possessed by a devil; desperado; enthusiast, fanatic.
enfasi [Enfasi], *n.f.* Emphasis, stress; bombast, pomposity.
enfaticamente, *adv.* Bombastically, pompously.
enfatico [enfAtico], *a.* Emphatic; pompous, bombastic.
enfiagione, *n.f.* Swelling; tumour.
enfiamento, *n.m.* Puffing out; swelling.
enfiare, enfiarsi, *v.i.r.* To swell, to inflate, to puff up; to get swollen.
enfiato, *p.p.a.* Swollen, inflated; bloated.
enfiatura, *n.f.* Swelling.
enfio [Enfio], *a.* (*colloq.*) Swollen, inflated.
enfiore, *n.m.* (*colloq.*) Swelling.
enfisema, *n.f.* (*Med.*) Emphysema.
enfiteusi [enfitEusi], *n.f.* (*Law*) Long lease (tenant paying only ground rent).
enfiteuta [enfitEuta], *n.m.* Tenant on this long lease.
enigma, enimma (*pl.* **enigmi, enimmi**), *n.m.* Riddle, conundrum, puzzle; enigma. **Sciogliere un —,** to solve a riddle.
enigmaticamente, enimmaticamente, *adv.* Enigmatically.
enigmatico, enimmatico [enigmAtico, enimmAtico], *a.* Enigmatic, obscure.
enigmatizzare, enimmatizzare, *v.i.* To speak in riddles.
enne, *n.m.f.* Letter N.
ennesimo [ennEsimo], *a.* (*Math.*) *n*th term; indefinite number.
ennico [Ennico], *a.* Ethnic [cp. **etnico**].
enofila [enOfila], *n.f.* (*Zool.*) Species of moth that breeds in wine-barrels.
enofilo [enOfilo], *a.* Concerned with the improvement of wines. **Circolo —,** wine-growers' club.
enologia [enologIa], *n.f.* Oenology, the science of wines.
enologico [enolOgico], *a.* Concerned with wines.
enologo [enOlogo], *n.m.* Wine expert.
enometro [enOmetro], *n.m.* Oenometer, instrument for measuring the alcohol in wine.
enorme, *a.* Enormous, immense, huge; (*fig.*) outrageous, ridiculous.
enormemente, *adv.* Enormously.
enormità [-à], *n.f.* Enormousness, hugeness, enormity; absurdity, nonsense. **Commettere un'—,** to commit a crime or blunder.
ensiforme, *a.* Sword-shaped.
entasi [Entasi], *n.f.* (*Arch.*) Entasis.
ente, *n.m.* Being; society, corporation; board, council, bureau. **— supremo,** God; **— morale, — giuridico,** officially recognized body or institution; **erigere in — morale,** to charter, to grant a charter to; **— autonomo,** autonomous board, board of governors.
entelechia [entelechIa], *n.f.* (*Phil.*) Entelechy.
enterico [entErico], *a.* (*Med.*) Enteric.
enterite, *n.f.* (*Med.*) Enteritis.
enteroclisma, *n.m.* (*Med.*) Clyster, enema.
entimema, *n.m.* (*Phil.*) Enthymeme.
entità [-à], *n.f.* Entity; importance, value. **Di nessuna —,** of no importance.
entomata [entOmata], *n.m.* (*Poet.*) Insect.
entomologia [entomologIa], *n.f.* Entomology.
entomologico [entomolOgico], *a.* Entomological.
entomologo [entomOlogo], *n.m.* Entomologist.
entrambi, entrambe, *pron. pl. m.f.* Both.
entrante, *a.* Entering, incoming, next. **Il mese —,** next month.
entrare, *v.i.* To enter, to go in, to come in; to penetrate; to be contained. **— in gioco,** to come into play; **— in possesso,** to take possession; **qui non s'entra,** no admittance here; **entrate pure!** come in! **questo non c'entra per niente,** this has nothing whatever to do with it; **— a far parte di,** to join; (*Law*) **— in vigore,** to come into force; **— in porto,** to come into port; **— in carica,** to take up a job; (*colloq.*) **questa cosa non gli entra,** he cannot take this in; **io non c'entro,** I have nothing to do with it.

entrata, *n.f.* Entrance, entering, coming in; entry; admittance; income; access; inlet. **— libera,** free admission; **vivere d'—,** to have a private income; (*Comm.*) **— e uscita,** debit and credit.

entratura, *n.f.* Entrance, admission; opening; entrance fee; intimacy. **Avere — con qualcuno,** to be on good (business) terms with someone; **diritto d'—,** right of entry.

entro, *prep.* Within, in the course of. **— un mese,** within a month.

entropia [entropIa], *n.f.* Entropy.

entusiasmare, *v.t.* To enrapture, to carry away (with delight), to arouse enthusiasm.

entusiasmarsi, *v.r.* To go into raptures, "to enthuse"; to gush.

entusiasmo, *n.m.* Enthusiasm; rapture; inspiration; ardour.

entusiasticamente, *adv.* Enthusiastically.

entusiasta (*pl.* **entusiasti**), *n.m.* Enthusiast.

entusiastico [entusiAstico], *a.* Enthusiastic.

enumerare, *v.t.* To enumerate, to count, to reckon up; to specify.

enumerazione, *n.f.* Enumeration, numbering.

enunciare, *v.t.* To enunciate, to state; to express.

enunciazione, *n.f.* Enunciation, utterance; expression.

enzima (*pl.* **enzimi**), *n.m.* Enzyme.

eolico [eOlico], *a.* Aeolian. **Arpa eolica,** Aeolian harp.

eolio [eOlio], *a.* Aeolian.

eoo [eOo], *a.* (*Poet.*) Eastern, of the Orient. **Vento —,** east wind.

epa, *n.f.* (*Lit.*) Paunch, belly.

epatico [epAtico], *a.* (*Med.*) Hepatic, concerned with the liver.

epatite, *n.f.* (*Path.*) Hepatitis.

epatta, *n.f.* Epact.

epentesi [epEntesi], *n.f.* (*Gram.*) Epenthesis.

eperlano, *n.m.* (*Zool.*) Smelt.

epica [Epica], *n.f.* Epic, epic poetry.

epicamente, *adv.* Epically.

epicedio [epicEdio], *n.m.* Elegy, dirge.

epiceno, *a.* Epicene, common to both sexes; of either sex.

epiciclo, *n.m.* (*Astron.*) Epicycle.

epico [Epico], *n.m.a.* Epic.

epicratico [epicrAtico], *a.* (*Med.*) Gradual, graduated (of remedies).

epicureismo, *n.m.* Epicurism, Epicureanism.

epicureo [epicurEo], *n.m.a.* Epicure; epicurean, pertaining to Epicurean philosophy.

epidemia [epidemIa], *n.f.* Epidemic.

epidemico [epidEmico], *a.* Epidemic, epidemical; catching, infectious.

epidermide [epidErmide], *n.f.* Epidermis, skin.

epidiascopio [epidiascOpio], *n.m.* Epidiascope.

Epifania [epifanIa], *n.f.* (*Eccles.*) Epiphany; Twelfth Night.

epifonema, *n.m.* Sententious peroration.

epigastrio [epigAstrio], *n.m.* (*Anat.*) Epigastrium.

epiglottide [epiglOttide], *n.f.* (*Anat.*) Epiglottis.

epigoni [epIgoni], *n.m.pl.* (*Hist.*) Descendants, followers, adherents.

epigrafe [epIgrafe], *n.f.* Epigraph, inscription.

epigrafia [epigrafIa], *n.f.* Epigraphy, study of ancient inscriptions.

epigramma (*pl.* **epigrammi**), *n.m.* Epigram.

epigrammatico [epigrammAtico], *a.* Epigrammatic.

epilatorio [epilatOrio], *a.* Depilatory.

epilessia [epilessIa], *n.f.* (*Med.*) Epilepsy, falling sickness.

epilettico [epilEttico], *n.m.a.* Epileptic.

epilogare, *v.t.* To sum up, to recapitulate.

epilogo [epIlogo], *n.m.* Epilogue, recapitulation, conclusion.

epinicio [epinIcio], *n.m.* (*Lit.*) Song of victory.

episcopale, *a.* Episcopal.

episcopato, *n.m.* Episcopate, bishopric; episcopacy [cp. **vescovato**].

episodico [episOdico], *a.* Episodic, episodical.

episodio [episOdio], *n.m.* Episode, incident.

epistassi, *n.f.* (*Med.*) Nose-bleeding.

epistemologia [epistemologIa], *n.f.* Epistemology.

epistola [epIstola], *n.f.* Epistle, letter.

epistolare, *a.* Epistolary.

epistolario [epistolArio], *n.m.* (*Lit.*) Correspondence, collected letters.

epistolarmente, *adv.* By means of letters.

epitaffio [epitAffio], *n.m.* Epitaph, inscription.

epitalamio [epitalAmio], *n.m.* Epithalamium, nuptial song.

epiteto [epIteto], *n.m.* Epithet.

epitomare, *v.t.* To epitomize.

epitome [epItome], *n.f.* Epitome, summary, abridgment.

epizootico, *a.* (*Vet.*) Epizootic. **Afta epizootica,** foot and mouth disease.

epoca [Epoca], *n.f.* Epoch, era, period, time. **Fare —,** to mark an epoch; **è un avvenimento che fa —,** it's an epoch-making event; **da quell'—,** from that time; **un'— remota,** an early or remote period.

epodo, *n.m.* (*Poet.*) Epode.

epopea [epopEa], *n.f.* Epic poetry, epopee, epos.

eppure, *conj.* And yet, and still, nevertheless, however. **Eppur si muove,** and yet it moves.

epsomite, *n.f.* Epsom salts.

eptacordo, *n.m.* (*Mus.*) Heptachord.

epulone, *n.m.* (*Lit.*) Rich feaster (Dives of the parable).

epuramento, *n.m.* Cleansing, purification, purging.

epurare, *v.t.* To cleanse, to purify, to purge; (*Polit.*) to purge, to expel

epurazione, *n.f.* Purging, cleansing; (*Polit.*) purge.

equabile [equAbile], *a.* (*Law*) Equable; uniform.

equabilità [-à], *n.f.* Equability.

equabilmente, *adv.* Equably.

equamente, *adv.* Justly, equitably, fairly.

equanime [equAnime], *a.* Impartial; calm, serene, equanimous.

equanimemente, *adv.* Impartially, with equanimity.

equanimità [-à], *n.f.* Equanimity, serenity, impartiality.

equatore, *n.m.* Equator. **Passare l'—,** to cross the Line.

equatoriale, *n.m.* Equatorial telescope.

equatoriale, *a.* Equatorial.

equazione, *n.f.* (*Math.*) Equation.
equestre, *a.* Equestrian. **Ordine —,** order of knighthood; **circo —,** circus.
equiangolo [equiAngolo], *a.* (*Geom.*) Equiangular.
equidistante, *a.* Equidistant.
equidistanza, *n.f.* Equidistance.
equilatero [equilAtero], *a.* (*Geom.*) Equilateral.
equilibrare, equilibrarsi, *v.t.r.* To balance, to poise, to equilibrate. **Le forze si equilibrano,** the forces counterbalance one another.
equilibrato, *p.p.a.* In equilibrium, counterpoised; (*fig.*) sensible, well-balanced (in mind and judgment).
equilibrazione, *n.f.* Balancing.
equilibrio [equilIbrio], *n.m.* Equilibrium, balance, equipoise, poise; (*Pol.*) balance of power. **— instabile,** unstable equilibrium; **stare in —,** to keep one's balance; **perder l'—,** to lose one's balance.
equilibrista (*pl.* **equilibristi**), *n.m.* Rope-walker, acrobat, equilibrist.
equino, *a.* Equine.
equinoziale, *a.* Equinoctial.
equinozio [equinOzio], *n.m.* Equinox.
equipaggiamento, *n.m.* Equipage, equipment; accoutrement; outfit, fitting out.
equipaggiare, *v.t.* To equip, to fit out, to furnish; (*Naut.*) to rig, to man. **Partì ben equipaggiato,** he left well fitted out.
equipaggio [equipAggio], *n.m.* (*Naut.*) Crew; (*obs.*) equipage, carriage. **L'— d'una nave,** the crew of a ship.
equiparare, equipararsi, *v.t.r.* To make equal, to standardize.
equipollente, *a.* (*Law*) Equivalent, equipollent, of equal force.
equiseto, *n.m.* (*Bot.*) Catkin, mare's-tail.
equità [-à], *n.f.* Equity, impartiality, justice.
equitativo, *a.* Equitable, impartial.
equitazione, *n.f.* Horsemanship, riding, equitation. **Maestro d'—,** riding-master.
equivalente, *n.m.a.* Equivalent, corresponding amount; tantamount, corresponding to.
equivalenza, *n.f.* Equivalence.
equivalere, *v.i.* To be equivalent, to correspond.
equivocamente, *adv.* Equivocally.
equivocare, *v.i.* To equivocate.
equivocazione, *n.f.* Equivocation.
equivoco [equIvoco], *n.m.* Equivocation, misunderstanding. **A scanso d'—,** to avoid misunderstanding.
equivoco [equIvoco], *a.* Equivocal, ambiguous, doubtful; deceitful.
equo [Equo], *a.* Equitable, just, fair, impartial.
era, *n.f.* Era, epoch, age.
eradicare, *v.t.* To uproot, to root out, to eradicate.
erariale, *a.* Of the Treasury, fiscal. **Avvocato —,** Crown counsel, Treasury counsel.
erario [erArio], *n.m.* Exchequer, Treasury. **— pubblico,** public treasury.
erba, *n.f.* Grass; herb, plant. **Filo d'—,** blade of grass; (*fig.*) **in —,** unfledged, immature; potential; **— trastulla,** trifles; **color —,** green; **tagliar l'—,** to mow the grass; **coperto d'—,** grass-grown, grassy.
erbaccia [erbAccia], *n.f.* Weed.
erbaceo [erbAceo], *a.* Herbaceous.
erbaggi, *n.m.pl.* Vegetables, greens.
erbaiuolo, *n.m.* Street greengrocer, costermonger.
erbario [erbArio], *n.m.* Herbarium.
erbetta, *n.f.* Short grass, new-mown or cropped grass.
erbivendolo [erbivEndolo], *n.m.* Greengrocer.
erbivoro [erbIvoro], *n.m.a.* Herbivore, herbivorous.
erborare, *v.t.* To collect plants.
erborista (*pl.* **erboristi**), *n.m.* Botanist, herbalist.
erborizzare, *v.t.* To botanize.
erboso, *a.* Grassy, grass-grown. **Tappeto —,** lawn.
Ercole [Ercole], *n.m.* (*Myth.*) Hercules.
erculeo [ercUleo], *a.* Herculean.
Erebo [Erebo], *n.m.* Erebus, hell.
erede, *n.m.f.* Heir, heiress. **Erede legittimo,** lawful heir.
eredità [-à], *n.f.* Inheritance; heritage; (*Biol.*) heredity. **Ricevere in —,** to inherit; **fare un'—,** to come into an inheritance.
ereditare, *v.t.i.* To inherit; to derive from, to succeed to.
ereditario [ereditArio], *a.* Hereditary. **Principe —,** crown prince.
ereditiera, *n.f.* Heiress of great wealth.
eremita, *n.m.f.* Hermit, anchorite; recluse.
eremitaggio [eremitAggio], *n.m.* Hermitage; retreat.
eremitano, *n.m.* (*Eccles.*) Augustinian Friar, Hermit of St. Augustine.
eremitico [eremItico], *a.* Like a hermit.
eremo [Eremo], *n.m.* Hermitage, place of retirement, retreat.
eresia [eresIa], *n.f.* Heresy, unorthodox opinion.
eresiarca (*pl.* **eresiarchi**), *n.m.* Heresiarch.
ereticale, *a.* Heretical [cp. **eretico**].
ereticalmente, *adv.* Heretically, in a heretical way.
ereticamente, *adv.* Heretically (from a doctrinal point of view).
eretico [erEtico], *n.m.a.* Heretic; heretical.
eretto, *a.* Erect, upright; erected.
erettore, *n.m.* Erector.
erezione, *n.f.* Erection; setting upright, constructing, building; establishment.
erg, *n.m.* (*Phys. Elec.*) Erg, ergon.
ergastolano, *n.m.* Convict, gaol-bird.
ergastolo [ergAstolo], *n.m.* Prison, penitentiary, long-term convict gaol; penal settlement.
erica [Erica], *n.f.* (*Bot.*) Heather.
erigere [erIgere], *v.t.* To raise, to erect, to build up.
erigersi [erIgersi], *v.r.* To set oneself up; to pretend to be. **— a giudice,** to presume to judge, to pass (unasked) judgment on.
erigibile [erigIbile], *a.* Capable of erection.
eringio [erIngio], *n.m.* (*Bot.*) Fleabane.
erisipela [erisIpela], *n.f.* (*Med.*) Erysipelas.
eritema, *n.m.* (*Med.*) Erythema; rash.
eritreo [eritrEo], *a.* Eritrean. **Mare —,** Red Sea.
erma, *n.f.* (*Arch.*) Herm, column surmounted by bust of Hermes.
ermafrodito, *n.m.a.* Hermaphrodite.
ermellino, *n.m.* (*Zool.*) Ermine; fur of ermine.

ermeneutica [ermenEutica], *n.f.* Hermeneutics.
ermeticamente, *adv.* Hermetically.
ermetico [ermEtico], *a.* Hermetic; air-tight; obscure.
ermetismo, *n.m.* (*Lit.*) Symbolical of allegorical method of expression; doctrine of Hermes Trismegistus.
ermisino, *n.m.* Light silk material, sarsenet.
ermo, *a.* (*Poet.*) Lonely, solitary, desert.
ernia [Ernia], *n.f.* (*Med.*) Hernia, rupture. **— strozzata,** strangulated hernia.
erniario [erniArio], *a.* Concerned with hernia. **Cinto —,** truss.
ernioso, *n.m.* Sufferer from hernia.
erniotomia [erniotomIa], *n.f.* (*Med.*) Herniotomy.
Ero, *n.m.* (*Myth.*) Hero.
Erode, *n.m.* Herod.
erodente, *a.* Corroding.
eroe [erOe], *n.m.* Hero; protagonist, hero, leading character. **Comportarsi da —,** to act like a hero.
erogabile [erogAbile], *a.* Available for donation.
erogare, *v.t.* To bestow, to donate, to give, to allocate (for charitable purposes), to lay out.
erogazione, *n.f.* Donation, bequest; distribution.
eroicamente, *adv.* Heroically.
eroicità [-à],*n.f.*(*rare*) Heroism [cp. **eroismo**].
eroicizzare, *v.t.* To make into a hero.
eroico [erOico], *a.* Heroic, heroical.
eroicomico [eroicOmico], *a.* Mock-heroic.
eroina, *n.f.* Heroine; (*Theat.*) leading lady; (*Med.*) heroin.
eroismo, *n.m.* Heroism.
erompere [erOmpere], *v.i.* To burst forth, to rush out, to break forth, to erupt.
erosione, *n.f.* Erosion.
erosivo, *a.* Erosive.
eroso, *p.p.a.* Eroded. **Moneta erosa,** coin with a minimum of silver.
erotico [erOtico], *a.* Erotic, amatory.
erotismo, *n.m.* (*Lit.*) Amorousness; sensualism.
erotomania [erotomanIa], *n.f.* (*Med. Psych.*) Erotomania.
erpete [Erpete], *n.m.* (*Med.*) Herpes, shingles.
erpicamento, *n.m.* (*Agric.*) Harrowing.
erpicare, *v.t.* (*Agric.*) To harrow.
erpicatura, *n.f.* (*Agric.*) Harrowing.
erpice [Erpice], *n.m.* (*Agric.*) Harrow.
errabondo, *a.* Wandering, roving, rambling, errant.
errante, *a.* Errant, wandering; vagabond. **Cavaliere —,** knight errant; **Ebreo —,** Wandering Jew.
errare, *v.i.* To roam, to wander, to rove; to go astray; to mistake, to blunder, to err. **Senza tema d'—,** without fear of being mistaken.
errata-corrige [errAta-cOrrige], *n.f.* (*Lit.*) Errata, errata slip.
erraticamente, *adv.* Mistakenly, erroneously.
erratico [errAtico], *a.* (*Geol., Med.*) Erratic, wandering; straying.
errato, *a.* Mistaken, wrong, erroneous.
erre, *n.m.f.* Letter R. **Aver l'— moscio,** to swallow one's Rs.
erro, *n.m.* (*obs.*) Error [cp. **errore**].
erroneamente, *adv.* Erroneously, by mistake.
erroneo [errOneo], *a.* Erroneous, incorrect, mistaken.
errore, *n.m.* Mistake, error, blunder; fallacy. **Per —,** by mistake; **— di stampa,** misprint; **cadere in —,** to fall into error; **trarre in —,** to lead into error; **salvo —,** if I'm not mistaken; **scoprire un —,** to detect a mistake; (*Comm.*) **— per difetto,** error below the true figure; **salvo — od omissione (S.E. od O.),** errors and omissions excepted (E. and O.E.).
erta, *n.f.* Ascent, incline, steep gradient. **Stare all'—,** to be on one's guard; **all'erta!** look out! beware! take care!
ertezza, *n.f.* Steepness.
erto, *a.* Steep, up-hill, rising; arduous; erect, upright.
erubescente, *a.* Reddish.
erubescenza, *n.f.* Redness, reddishness.
erudimento, *n.m.* [cp. **insegnamento**].
erudire, *v.t.* To instruct, to teach.
eruditamente, *adv.* Learnedly.
erudito, *n.m.a.* Scholar, man of learning; erudite, learned.
erudizione, *n.f* Learning, scholarship, erudition.
eruttamento, *n.m.* Eruption, belch.
eruttare, *v.t.i.* (Of a volcano) to belch forth, to erupt, to throw out (lava, etc.); to belch, to eruct.
eruttazione, *n.f.* Eructation, belching; eruption.
eruttivo, *a.* Eruptive.
eruzione, *n.f.* Eruption; (*Med.*) rash.
ervo, *n.m.* (*Bot.*) Vetch.
esacerbamento, *n.m.* Embitterment, aggravation.
esacerbare, *v.t.* To embitter, to irritate, to exacerbate, to aggravate.
esacerbarsi, *v.r.* To worry; to become embittered.
esacerbazione, *n.f.* Exacerbation, aggravation; embitterment.
esacordo, *n.m.* (*Mus.*) Hexachord.
esaedro, *n.m.* (*Geom.*) Hexahedron.
esagerare, *v.t.* To exaggerate; to magnify, to amplify; to over-state; to over-do.
esageratamente, *adv.* Exaggeratedly, in an exaggerated fashion.
esagerativo, *a.* Tending to exaggeration.
esagerazione, *n.f.* Exaggeration, over-statement; nonsense.
esagerone, *n.m.* (*colloq.*) One who exaggerates; "gas-bag".
esagitare, *v.t.* To agitate, to stir, to excite.
esagonale, *a.* (*Geom.*) Hexagonal.
esagono [esAgono], *n.m.* (*Geom.*) Hexagon
esalamento, *n.m.* Exhalation.
esalare, *v.t.i.* To exhale, to emit, to breathe forth; to reek with (a smell). **Esalare l'anima,** to breathe one's last.
esalatoio [esalatOio], *n.m.* Air-vent, air-hole.
esalazione, *n.f.* Exhalation, fume, vapour; effluvium.
esaltamento, *n.m.* Exaltation, excitement.
esaltare, *v.t.* To exalt, to extol, to cry up.
esaltarsi, *v.r.* To become excited, to be elated; to exalt oneself.
esaltato, *n.m.* Hot-head, fanatic, infatuated person.

esaltazione, *n.f.* Exaltation, glorification; excitement, infatuation; over-excitement.
esame, *n.m.* Examination; survey, inspection, investigation, research, scrutiny. **Prendere in —,** to investigate, to take into consideration; **dare un —,** to sit for an exam; **passare un —, superare un —,** to pass an examination; **esami orali o scritti,** viva voce or written exams; **cadere in un —,** to fail in an exam; (*Law*) **— dei testi e delle parti,** cross-examination.
esametro [esAmetro], *n.m.* (*Poet.*) Hexameter.
esaminando, *n.m.* Examinee, candidate (for an exam).
esaminare, *v.t.* To examine; to inspect, to survey, to search into, to investigate; to verify, to test. **— la faccenda,** to look into the matter.
esaminato, *n.m.* Person or thing that has been examined.
esaminatore, esaminatrice, *n.m.f.* Examiner, tester.
esaminatore, *a.* Examining. **Commissione esaminatrice,** board of examiners.
esamone, *n.m.* Examination very successfully passed.
esangue, *a.* Bloodless, pale; exhausted, worn-out; languid.
esanime [esAnime], *a.* Inanimate, lifeless; dead.
esantema, *n.m.* (*Med.*) Eruption.
esarca, *n.m.* (*Hist.*) Exarch.
esasperamento, *n.m.* Exasperation, irritation.
esasperare, *v.t.* To exasperate, to irritate.
esasperarsi, *v.r.* To become exasperated; to grow worse (of an illness).
esasperazione, *n.f.* Exasperation.
esattamente, *adv.* Exactly, precisely.
esattezza, *n.f.* Exactness, exactitude; accuracy; punctuality, precision; carefulness.
esatto, *a.* Exact, accurate, careful, precise, correct; (*Comm.*) cashed, collected.
esattore, *n.m.* Tax-collector, excise officer; extortioner.
esattoria [esattorIa], *n.f.* Tax-collector's office.
esaudibile [esaudIbile], *a.* Permissible.
esaudimento, *n.m.* Concession, granting; consent; satisfaction.
esaudire, *v.t.* To concede, to grant; to satisfy, to hear (a prayer).
esaudizione, *n.f.* [cp. **esaudimento**].
esauriente, *a.* Exhaustive. **Prova —,** exhaustive proof.
esaurimento, *n.m.* Exhaustion, collapse. **— nervoso,** nervous break-down.
esaurire, *v.t.* To exhaust, to consume, to use up; (*Comm.*) to sell out (stock).
esaurirsi, *v.r.* To wear oneself out, to spend one's strength.
esaurito, esausto [esAusto], *p.p.a.* Exhausted, worn-out; (*Comm.*) sold out. **Sentirsi —,** to feel run-down; **un libro —,** a book out of print; **il teatro era —,** the theatre was sold out.
esautorare, *v.t.* To deprive of authority, to weaken.
esautorazione, *n.f.* Depriving of authority, superseding.
esazione, *n.f.* Collection (of taxes, etc.); exaction; taxation.
esborso, *n.m.* (*Comm.*) [cp. **sborso**].
esca, *n.f.* Bait (in all senses); allurement; tinder; fuse (of a bomb). **Metter — al fuoco,** to add fuel to the fire.
escandescente, *a.* Bursting with rage.
escandescenza, *n.f.* Outburst of anger; rage, fury; frenzy. **Dare in —,** to fly into a passion, to lose one's temper, "to go off the deep end".
escara, *n.f.* (*Med.*) Eschar, slough.
escatologico [escatolOgico], *a.* Eschatological.
escavare, *v.t.* To excavate [cp. **scavare**].
escavatore, *n.m.* (*Agric.*) Excavator.
escavazione, *n.f.* Excavation [cp. **scavo**].
eschio [Eschio], *n.m.* (*Bot.*) Species of oak.
escire, *v.i.* To go out [cp. **uscire**].
escita, *n.f.* Exit, way out; issue [cp. **uscita**].
esclamare, *v.i.* To exclaim, to cry out, to utter.
esclamativo, *a.* Exclamatory. **Punto —,** exclamation mark.
esclamazione, *n.f.* Exclamation; cry, clamour.
escludere [esclUdere], *v.t.* To exclude, to debar, to reject, to shut out; (*Elec.*) to cut out.
esclusione, *n.f.* Exclusion, rejection. **Ad — di,** to the exclusion of.
esclusiva, esclusività [-à], *n.f.* (*Comm.*) Monopoly, sole agency, sole rights, patent; (*Eccles.*) right of veto; exclusiveness.
esclusivamente, *adv.* Exclusively.
esclusivismo, *n.m.* Exclusiveness; exclusivism.
esclusività [-à], *n.f.* Exclusiveness [cp. **esclusiva**].
escogitare, *v.t.* To excogitate, to think out, to devise.
escogitazione, *n.f.* Excogitation.
escoriare, *v.t.* To graze, to abrade.
escoriarsi, *v.r.* To graze oneself.
escoriazione, *n.f.* Grazing, excoriation, abrasion.
escreato, *n.m.* Expectoration, spitting.
escrementizio [escrementIzio], *a.* Excremental, pertaining to excrement.
escremento, *n.m.* Excrement.
escrescenza, *n.f.* Excrescence, outgrowth.
escretore, *a.* (*Physiol.*) Excretory.
escrezione, *n.f.* Excretion, ejection.
esculento, *a.* Edible.
escursione, *n.f.* Excursion, trip, tour. **Fare un'—,** to make an excursion; **— a piedi,** walking tour, hike.
escursionismo, *n.m.* Hiking.
escursionista (*pl.* **escursionisti**), *n.m.* Tripper, hiker; tourist.
escussione, *n.f.* (*Law*) **— dei testi,** cross-examination of witnesses.
escutere [escUtere], *v.t.* (*Law*) To examine (witness), to interrogate.
esecrabile [esecrAbile], *a.* Execrable, detestable, abominable.
esecrabilità [-à], *n.f.* Execrability, abominableness.
esecrabilmente, *adv.* Execrably, abominably.
esecrare, *v.t.* To execrate, to abhor, to loathe.
esecratorio [esecratOrio], *a.* Pertaining to an oath to the truth of which God has been called to witness.
esecrazione, *n.f.* Execration, hatred, detestation.

esecutivamente, *adv.* Executively.
esecutivo, *a.* Executive; (*Law*) executory. **Il potere —,** the executive.
esecutore, esecutrice, *n.m.f.* Executor, executrix; performer; executant (of music). **— testamentario,** executor (of a will).
esecutoria [esecutOria], *n.f.* (*Law*) Writ of execution.
esecuzione, *n.f.* Execution, performance, fulfilment, completion; (*Theat.*) performance; (*Law*) execution, capital punishment. **Mettere in —,** to carry out, to put in execution; **l'— d'una musica,** the performance of a piece of music.
esedra, *n.f.* (*Arch.*) Exedra, portico.
esegesi, *n.f.* Exegesis, interpretation.
esegeta (*pl.* **esegeti**), *n.m.* Exegetist, expounder.
esegetico [esegEtico], *a.* Exegetic.
eseguibile [eseguIbile], *a.* Practicable, feasible.
eseguibilità [-à], *n.f.* Practicability.
eseguire, *v.t.* To execute, to effect, to accomplish; to perform, to achieve. **— un ordine,** to carry out an order; **— al violino,** to play on the violin.
esempigrazia [esempigrAzia], *adv.* For instance, for example; e.g.
esempio [esEmpio], *n.m.* Example, instance; model, pattern; illustration. **Per —,** for instance; **dare un —,** to set an example; **senza —,** unexampled, unparalleled.
esemplare, *n.m.* Model, pattern, exemplar, copy (of a book).
esemplare, *a.* Exemplary, model.
esemplificare, *v.t.* To exemplify, to illustrate.
esemplificazione, *n.f.* Exemplification.
esentare, *v.t.* To exempt, to excuse, to dispense with; to discharge, to relieve (of a duty, etc.) **— da un esame,** to exempt from an exam.
esente, *a.* Exempt, free; excluded.
esenzione, *n.f.* Exemption, dispensation, immunity.
esequiare, *v.t.* To perform the obsequies (for).
esequie [esEquie], *n.f.pl.* Obsequies, funeral, burial.
esercente, *n.m.a.* Shop-keeper; practising a craft or profession; carrying on a business, keeping a shop.
esercire, *v.t.* To conduct (a business), to carry on (a trade); to practise (a profession).
esercitare, *v.t.* To exert, to exercise; to practise; to drill, to train. **Esercita la medicina,** he practises medicine.
esercitazione, *n.f.* Exercise; drill, training.
esercito [esErcito], *n.m.* Army, forces, troops; a great quantity. **— permanente,** standing army; (*fig.*) **un — di libri,** a great quantity of books.
esercizio [esercIzio], *n.m.* Exercise, practice, use; business, shop; drill, training; working, function, office; (*Comm.*) financial year, period. **— fisico,** physical exercise; **stare in —,** to practise; **esser fuori d'—,** to be out of practice; **scrivere un —,** to write an exercise; **esercizi di salvataggio,** boat-drill; (*Comm.*) **diritto d'—,** licence (to open a shop); **durante l'— finanziario,** during the financial year; **capitale d'—,** working capital.
esfogliazione, *n.f.* (*Med.*) Exfoliation.
esibire, *v.t.* To exhibit, to display; to show, to parade; to offer, to tender; to produce (documents, etc.).
esibirsi, *v.r.* To come forward, to offer one's services; (*Theat.*) to take part in a show.
esibitore, esibitrice, *n.m.f.* Exhibitor.
esibizione, *n.f.* Exhibition, show, ostentation.
esibizionismo, *n.m.* Ostentation; (*Med.*) exhibitionism.
esibizionista, *n.m.f.* (*Med.*) Exhibitionist.
esigente, *a.* Exacting, exigent, strict, severe.
esigenza, *n.f.* Exigency; need, necessity; requirement. **Troppe esigenze!** too many pretensions!
esigere [esIgere], *v.t.* To exact, to claim, to insist upon; to require; to collect (taxes, etc.). **Esigo obbedienza assoluta,** I demand absolute obedience.
esigibile [esigIbile], *a.* Exactable, payable.
esiglio, *n.m.* Exile [cp. **esilio**].
esiguità [-à], *n.f.* Smallness, exiguity; slightness, scantiness.
esiguo [esIguo], *a.* Exiguous, small, slight, slender; petty.
esilaramento, *n.m.* Exhilaration.
esilarante, *a.* Exhilarating, cheering. **Bevanda —,** exhilarating beverage.
esilarare, *v.t.* To exhilarate, to cheer.
esilararsi, *v.r.* To rejoice.
esile [Esile], *a.* Slender, thin, frail.
esiliare, *v.t.* To exile, to banish.
esiliarsi, *v.r.* To exile oneself voluntarily; to leave a place voluntarily.
esiliato, *n.m.* Exile (person).
esilio [esIlio], *n.m.* Exile, banishment; place of exile. **Andare in —,** to go into exile; **mandare in —,** to banish.
esilità [-à], *n.f.* Slenderness, thinness.
esimere [esImere], *v.t.* To exempt, to relieve from, to dispense.
esimersi, *v.r.* To evade, to shrink from; to refrain from. **Non posso esimermi dal farlo,** I cannot get out of doing it, I must do it; **egli cerca di esimersi da,** he is trying to shirk.
esimio [esImio], *a.* Excellent, notable, distinguished.
esistente, *a.* Existing, living, extant, in force.
esistenza, *n.f.* Existence, life; (*Comm.*) stock; cash balance, cash in hand. **La lotta per l'—,** the struggle for existence.
esistenzialismo, *n.m.* (*Phil.*) Existentialism.
esistere [esIstere], *v.i.* To exist, to be, to live; to be extant. **Non esiste alcun manoscritto di Dante,** no Dante MS. is extant; **non esiste più traccia,** no trace is left; **non esiste più,** it has ceased to exist.
esistito, *a.* Once existing.
esitabile [esitAbile], *a.* Saleable, marketable.
esitante, *a.* Hesitating, wavering, uncertain.
esitanza, *n.f.* [cp. **esitazione**].
esitare, *v.i.* To hesitate, to waver; to be in doubt, to be in suspense; to sell. **Non c'è da —,** one cannot hesitate, there is nothing to hesitate about.
esitazione, *n.f.* Hesitation, suspense, perplexity.
esito [Esito], *n.m.* Result, issue, outcome, end; outlet; (*Comm.*) sale; (*Theat.*) denouement (of a play). **Giudicare dall'—,** to judge from results; **l'— d'una malattia,** the outcome of an illness; **con — felice,** with happy results;

(*Comm.*) **questa merce ha poco —**, these goods have not much sale.
esiziale, *a.* Fatal, ruinous, disastrous; mortal.
esizialmente, *adv.* Fatally, disastrously.
eslege, *n.m.* (*Law*) Outlaw; bandit.
esodo [Esodo], *n.m.* Exodus, flight; emigration. **L'Esodo**, the Book of Exodus.
esofago [esOfago], *n.m.* (*Anat.*) Oesophagus, gullet.
esogeno [esOgeno], *a.* (*Biol*) Exogenous.
esonerare, *v.t.* To exempt, to exonerate, to discharge, to release; to dismiss (from employment).
esonerarsi, *v.r.* To exonerate oneself, to excuse oneself.
esonerazione, *n.f.* [cp. **esonero**].
esonero [esOnero], *n.m.* Exemption, exoneration, dispensing (from); removal, discharge (from employment).
esorbitante, *a.* Exorbitant, excessive, extravagant.
esorbitantemente, *adv.* Excessively, exorbitantly.
esorbitanza, *n.f.* Excess, extravagance, exorbitance.
esorbitare, *v.i.* To exceed (the limits, etc.); to go beyond (what is needed).
esorcismo, *n.m.* Exorcism.
esorcista (*pl.* **esorcisti**), *n.m.* Exorcist.
esorcizzare, *v.t.* To exorcize.
esorcizzazione, *n.f.* (Act and result of) exorcizing.
esordiente, *n.m.f.* Beginner; (*Theat.*) débutant, débutante.
esordio [esOrdio], *n.m.* Preamble, beginning, exordium; (*Theat.*) first appearance (of actor or actress).
esordire, *v.i.* To begin, to start; to begin speaking; (*Theat.*) to make one's début.
esornare, *v.t.* To embellish (with metaphors, etc., when speaking) [cp. **ornare**].
esornativo, *a.* Ornamental; florid (in speech).
esortamento, *n.m.* Exhcrtation.
esortare, *v.t.* To exhort, to urge; to admonish, to warn.
esortativo, esortatorio [esortatOrio], *a.* Exhortatory.
esortazione, *n.f.* Exhortation, admonishment, warning.
esosità [-à], *n.f.* Hatefulness; meanness.
esoso, *a.* Hateful, odious; mean, grasping, stingy.
esoterico [esotErico], *a.* (*Phil.*) Esoteric.
esoticità [-à], *n.f.* Exoticism.
esotico [esOtico], *a.* Exotic, foreign.
espandere [espAndere], *v.t.* To expand, to spread out; to distend; to extend.
espandersi [espAndersi], *v.r.* To be spread out, to expand (oneself).
espansibile [espansIbile], *a.* Expansible, capable of expansion.
espansione, *n.f.* Expansion; spreading, enlargement.
espansionismo, *n.m.* (*Pol.*) Expansionism.
espansività [-à], *n.f.* Expansiveness, effusiveness.
espansivo, *a.* Expansive (in all senses); effusive.
espatriare, *v.i.t.* To expatriate oneself, to emigrate; to banish, to exile.
espatrio [espAtrio], *n.m.* Expatriation.
espediente, *n.m.* Expedient, device, contrivance, makeshift. **Vivere di espedienti,** to live from hand to mouth.
espediente, *a.* Expedient, advisable.
espedire, *v.t.* To expedite [cp. **spedire**].
espellere [espEllere], *v.t.* To expel, to eject, to drive out.
Esperia [espEria] (1), *n.f.* (*Hist.*) Italy.
esperia [espEria] (2), *n.f.* (*Zool.*) Skipper butterfly, Hesperidia.
Esperidi [espEridi], *n.f.pl.* The Hesperides.
esperienza, *n.f.* Experience; experiment. **Fare —**, to learn by experience; **sapere per —**, to know by experience; **avere —**, to be experienced.
esperimentale, *a.* Experimental.
esperimentare, *v.t.* To experiment, to experience.
esperimentato, *p.p.a.* Experienced, skilful.
esperimentatore, *n.m.* Experimenter.
esperimento, *n.m.* Experiment, trial, test, proof.
esperire, *v.t.* To try, to make trial of; to carry out. **— le pratiche necessarie,** to perform the necessary formalities.
Espero [Espero], *n.m.* Hesperus; the evening star.
espertamente, *adv.* Expertly.
esperto, *n.m.a.* Expert, specialist; skilful, experienced.
espettibile [espettIbile], *a.* (*obs.*) Desirable.
espettazione, *n.f.* (*Lit.*) Expectation.
espettorante, *a.* Expectorant, spitting.
espettorare, *v.t.* To expectorate, to spit.
espettorazione, *n.f.* Expectoration.
espiabile [espiAbile], *a.* Expiable.
espiare, *v.t.* To expiate, to atone for. **— la colpa**, to expiate a fault.
espiatorio [espiatOrio], *a.* Expiatory. **Capro —**, scapegoat.
espiazione, *n.f.* Expiation, atonement.
espilare, *v.t.* (*obs*). To swindle (out of money, etc.).
espilazione, *n.f.* (*obs.*) Swindling.
espirare, *v.t.* To exhale, to breathe out.
espirazione, *n.f.* Exhaling.
espletare, *v.t.* To fulfil, to carry out, to perform.
espletivo, *n.m.a.* Expletive.
esplicare, *v.t.* To explain, to unfold; to display. **— molta attività,** to display great activity.
esplicarsi, *v.r.* To explain oneself, to unfold, to develop [cp. **spiegarsi**].
esplicativo, *a.* Explanatory.
esplicazione, *n.f.* Explanation; display; development, course.
esplicitamente, *adv.* Explicitly.
esplicito [esplIcito], *a.* Explicit, outspoken. definite, clear, plain.
esplodente, *n.m.a.* Explosive.
esplodere [esplOdere], *v.t.i.* To explode, to burst; to discharge (firearms); to go off (with a bang). **Far —**, to blow up.
esplorabile [esplorAbile], *a.* Open to exploration.
esplorare, *v.t.* To explore, to search, to investigate; to probe; (*Mil.*) to reconnoitre.
esploratore, esploratrice, *n.m.f.* Explorer; (*Mil.*) scout. **Giovane —**, Boy Scout; **giovane esploratrice**, Girl Scout.

esplorazione, *n.f.* Exploration (in all senses); (*Naut.*) sounding; (*Mil.*) reconnaissance.
esplosione, *n.f.* Explosion, bursting, burst; blowing up; report (noise); (*fig.*) outburst (of temper).
esplosivo, *n.m.a.* Explosive.
espoliazione [cp. **spoliazione**].
esponente, *n.m.* Exponent, representative; (*Math.*) exponent.
esponibile [esponIbile], *a.* Capable of being expounded.
esporre, *v.t.* To expose, to exhibit, to display; to unfold, to expound, to declare, to disclose; to risk, to endanger, to venture. — **al sole,** to expose to the sun; — **la vita,** to risk one's life; — **le proprie condizioni,** to state one's terms; — **una dottrina,** to expound a doctrine; — **un'ambasciata,** to deliver a message.
esporsi, *v.r.* To expose oneself, to run a risk; to make oneself liable. — **al pubblico,** to make oneself known.
esportabile [esportAbile], *a.* Exportable.
esportare, *v.t.* To export.
esportatore, *n.m.a.* Exporter; exporting. **Paese —,** exporting country.
esportazione, *n.f.* Exportation, export. **Dazio d'—,** export duty; **commercio d'—,** export trade.
espositivamente, *adv.* In an explanatory manner.
espositivo, *a.* Explanatory.
espositore, espositrice, *n.m.f.* Expositor.
esposizione, *n.f.* Exhibition; statement, exposition; aspect, frontage; (*Phot.*) exposure. — **d'arte,** art exhibition.
esposto (1), *n.m.* Statement, account; formal declaration.
esposto (2), *n.m.* Foundling child.
esposto (3), *p.p.a.* Liable, subject, exposed. — **a soffrir danni,** liable to be damaged; **la casa è — al settentrione,** the house faces north.
espressamente, *adv.* Expressly, on purpose.
espressione, *n.f.* Expression (in all senses); utterance, manifesto.
espressionismo, *n.m.* Expressionism.
espressiva, *n.f.* The faculty of expression (in writing or speech).
espressivamente, *adv.* Expressively.
espressivo, *a.* Expressive, significant, vivid, pregnant (with meaning).
espresso, *n.m.* Express train; express (postal) delivery, express letter; specially made black coffee.
espresso, *a.* Express, special; expressed; clear, definite. **Caffè —,** specially made black coffee.
esprimere [esprImere], *v.t.* To express, to signify, to utter, to declare; to word, to voice.
esprimersi [esprImersi], *v.r.* To express oneself.
esprimibile [esprimIbile], *a.* Expressible.
espropriare, *v.t.* (*Law*) To expropriate, to dispossess, to distrain, to eject.
espropriazione, *n.f.* Expropriation, distraint.
espugnabile [espugnAbile], *a.* Liable to be taken by storm.
espugnare, *v.t.* To take by storm, to conquer, to subdue.
espugnazione, *n.f.* Storming, taking by assault, conquest.
espulsione, *n.f.* Expulsion, ejection.
espulsivo, *a.* Expulsive.
espulso, *p.p.a.* Expelled.
espulsore, *n.m.* (*Mech.*) Ejector.
espungere [espUngere], *v.t.* To delete, to cancel.
espurgare, *v.t.* To expurgate, to purge. **Edizione espurgata,** bowdlerized edition.
esquimese, *n.m.a.* Eskimo.
essa, *pron.* She, it. — **stessa,** she herself.
esse, *n.f.m.* Letter S.
esse, *pron.* They (*fem.*).
essendochè, *conj.* Since, as.
essenza, *n.f.* Essence, main point, pith; essential oil. — **di rose,** attar of roses.
essenziale, *n.m.* Essential, main point.
essenziale, *a.* Essential, main, chief, principal.
essenzialità [-à], *n.f.* Essentiality.
essere [Essere], *v.i.aux.* To be, to exist; to stand, to become, to be situated; to happen, to be probable. **Chi è? Son io,** who's there? It is I; **sono di Roma,** I'm a native of Rome; **tu non sei da tanto,** you are not up to it; **c'è, v'è, ci sono, vi sono,** there is, there are; **che è stato?** what's the matter? **sia pure,** let it be so; **così sia,** so be it; **egli era per partire,** he was about to leave; **che c'è di nuovo?** what is the news? **s'è fatto il possible,** all that can be done has been done; **s'è pagato troppo,** we have paid too much; **può essere,** it may be; **cosa c'è?** what's the matter? **sarà!** it may be! **che è che non è,** all at once, suddenly; **sia come si sia,** at all events, in whichever way; **cosa sarebbe a dire?** what do you mean? **per essere uno straniero parla bene italiano,** he speaks Italian well for a foreigner; **i tempi che furono,** times past; — **in ribasso,** to be on the downgrade; (*colloq.*) — **a spasso,** to be out of work; **è tutto suo padre,** he is like his father; **questo è quanto,** that's all; **non son chi sono se non riesco a far ciò,** I'm not up to much if I can't do that; **come se nulla fosse,** indifferently, as if it meant nothing; **è ora!** it's time! **è tanto che aspetto,** I've been waiting long enough; **a che punto siete col dizionario?** how far have you got with the dictionary? **siamo alle solite!** again! as usual! — **da più, da meno,** to be far superior, inferior; (*colloq.*) — **dietro a,** to be about to; **egli era fuori di sè,** he was beside himself; **c'era una volta,** once upon a time; **quanto c'è da Milano a Roma?** how far is it from Milan to Rome, how long does it take from Milan to Rome? **non ce n'è più,** there's none left; **non c'è che dire,** there's nothing to be said; **quello che è stato è stato,** let bygones be bygones; **la signora non è in casa,** my mistress is not at home; — **di,** to belong to; — **in grado di,** to be able to; **sono quaranta anni che lavoro,** I've been working for forty years.
essere [Essere], *n.m.* Being, state, condition; creature. **Un piccolo —, un esserino,** a poor little creature; **contentarsi del proprio —,** to be contented with one's lot.
essi, *pron.* They (*m.*).
essiccamento, *n.m.* Drying up.
essiccare, *v.t.* To dry up, to dessicate. — **al forno,** to kiln-dry.
essiccativo, *a.* Desiccative.

essiccatoio [essiccatOio], *n.m.* Drying-shed, drying-room, drying-stove.
essiccatore, *n.m.* Drying apparatus.
essiccazione, *n.f.* Desiccation.
essilon [Essilon], *n.m.f.* Greek letter epsilon.
esso, *pron.* He, it. **— stesso,** he himself.
essoterico [essotErico], *a.* (*Phil.*) Exoteric.
essudare, *v.t.* To exude.
essudazione, *n.f.* Exudation.
est, *n.m.* East, eastward. **Verso est,** eastwards.
estasi [Estasi], *n.f.* Ecstasy, rapture; frenzy. **Andare in —,** to go into raptures.
estasiare, *v.t.* To enrapture, to charm.
estasiarsi, *v.r.* To go into raptures, to be enraptured.
estatare, *v.i.* To summer, to pass the summer (in a place).
estate, *n.f.* Summer. **Dove passi l'— ?** Where do you spend the summer? **vestirsi da —,** to wear light clothes; **in estate,** in summer time; **— di San Martino,** Indian summer.
estaticamente, *adv.* Ecstatically.
estatico [estAtico], *a.* Ecstatic, enraptured, ravished, entranced.
estemporaneamente, *adv.* Extemporaneously. extemporarily. **Parlare —,** to speak extempore.
estemporaneità [-à], *n.f.* Extemporaneousness.
estemporaneo [estemporAneo], *a.* Extemporary, improvised; impromptu, off-hand. **Un discorso —,** an impromptu speech.
estempore [estEmpore], *a.* Extempore.
estendere [estEndere], *v.t.* To extend, to expand, to prolong, to enlarge, to stretch.
estendersi [estEndersi], *v.r.* To extend (oneself), to expand; to expatiate.
estendibile [estendIbile], *a.* Extensible.
estense, *a.* (*Hist.*) Pertaining to the ducal family of Este.
estensibile [estensIbile], *a.* Extensible.
estensione, *n.f.* Extension, extent, stretch, surface; enlargement; (*Mus.*) compass, range. **Per —,** in a wider sense; **una vasta — di terreno,** a large area.
estensivo, *a.* Extensive.
estenso, *a.* Extended, full. **Per —,** in full.
estensore, *n.m.* Compiler, editor, drafter (of documents, etc.).
estensore, *a.* (*Anat.*) Extensor.
estenuamento, *n.m.* Extenuation.
estenuante, *a.* Extenuating, weakening, enervating, debilitating.
estenuare, *v.t.* To weaken, to extenuate, to debilitate, to exhaust.
estenuarsi, *v.r.* To become exhausted, to get tired.
estenuazione, *n.f.* Extenuation, exhaustion.
esteriore, *n.m.a.* Exterior, outside.
esteriorità [-à], *n.f.* Outward appearance.
esteriormente, *adv.* Exteriorly.
esterminare, *v.t.* To exterminate [cp. **sterminare**].
esterminio [estermInio], *n.m.* (*obs.*) Extermination, destruction [cp. **sterminio**].
esternamente, *adv.* Externally.
esternare, *v.t.* To disclose (one's feelings), to manifest, to demonstrate.
esternarsi, *v.r.* To open one's mind, to expose one's feelings.
esterno, *n.m.* Exterior. outside; day-school boy; (*Med.*) non-resident physician or surgeon. **Dall'—,** from without; **all'—,** outside.
esterno, *a.* External, outward, outside. **Scolaro —,** day-boy; **posto —,** outside seat (on tram or bus).
estero [Estero], *n.m.a.* Foreign countries; foreign. **Andare all'—,** to go abroad; **politica estera,** foreign policy; **affari esteri,** foreign affairs; **commercio estero,** foreign trade.
esterrefatto, *a.* Terrified, frightened.
estersivo, *a.* Cleansing.
estesamante, *adv.* Extensively.
esteso, *a.* Extensive, extended, large, wide; diffuse. **Narrare una cosa per —,** to tell something in detail.
esteta, *n.m.* Aesthete; fop.
estetica, *n.f.* (*Phil.*) Aesthetics.
esteticamente, *adv.* Aesthetically.
estetico [estEtico], *a.* Aesthetic, aesthetical.
estetismo, *n.m.* Aestheticism.
estimabile [estimAbile], *a.* Estimable.
estimare, *v.t.* To esteem, to value; to estimate [cp. **stimare**].
estimatore, *n.m.* Estimator.
estimazione, *n.f.* Estimation, esteem, regard.
estimo [Estimo], *n.m.* (*Law*) Rating, valuation.
estinguere [estInguere], *v.t.* To extinguish, to put out, to quench; to pay off (a debt). **— la sete,** to quench one's thirst; **— un debito,** to pay off a debt.
estinguersi [estInguersi], *v.r.* To go out (of a light); to pass away, to die out. **La famiglia si estingue con lui,** the family dies out with him.
estinguimento, *n.m.* Extinction.
estinto, *n.m.a.* Extinct, deceased, dead. **Gli estinti,** the dead.
estintore, *n.m.* Fire-extinguisher.
estinzione, *n.f.* Extinction; quenching; paying-off (of debt).
estirpare, *v.t.* To extirpate, to root out, to weed out, to eradicate. **— un dente,** to draw a tooth; **— un tumore,** to remove a tumour.
estirpazione, *n.f.* Eradication.
estivamente, *adv.* In a summerish style, as in summer.
estivo, *a.* Summery, summer. **I calori estivi,** summer heat; **indossare gli abiti estivi,** to put on summer clothes; **vacanze estive,** summer holidays; **ora estiva,** summer time; **stazione estiva,** summer (holiday) resort.
esto, *pron.* (*obs.*) This [cp. **questo**].
estollere [estOllere], *v.t.* To extol, to exalt.
estorcere [estOrcere], *v.t.* To extort, to wring from; (*Law*) to exact.
estorsione, *n.f.* Extortion.
estra, *n.m.* Extra.
estracorrente, *n.f.* (*Elec.*) Secondary current.
estradare, *v.t.* To extradite.
estradizione, *n.f.* Extradition.
estragiudiziale, *a.* (*Law*) Extra-judicial.
estraneo [estrAneo], *n.m.a.* Stranger; extraneous, foreign, alien.
estraordinario [cp. **straordinario**].
estrarre, *v.t.* To extract, to draw out; to draw, to select, to pick out; to quarry. **— a sorte.** to draw lots for.
estrattivo, *a.* Extractive.

estratto, *n.m.* Extract, excerpt, abstract, summary; essence. **— dell'atto di nascita, di morte,** birth, death certificate; **— di carne,** meat extract.
estravagante [cp. **stravagante**].
estrazione, *n.f.* Extraction, digging, quarrying; origin, descent; drawing (of a lottery, number, etc.). **Uomo di bassa —,** man of humble birth; **l'— d'un dente,** the drawing of a tooth; **— d'una lotteria,** drawing of a lottery.
estremamente, *adv.* Extremely.
estremista (*pl.* **estremisti**), *n.m.* Extremist.
estremità [-à], *n.f.* Extremity, end; extremes; verge, brink; tip, point. **Le —,** the extremities, the limbs; **— superiore,** upper end.
estremo, *n.m.* Extreme, utmost. **Fino all'—,** to the utmost; **esser ridotto all'—,** to be on the point of death, to be in a desperate plight; **andare agli estremi,** to go to extremes; **gli estremi si toccano,** extremes meet; **ricorrere agli estremi,** to resort to extremes, to take drastic measures.
estremo, *a.* Extreme; last, utmost. **L'estrema unzione,** extreme unction; **l'— Oriente,** the Far East.
estrinsecamente, *adv.* Extrinsically.
estrinsecare, *v.t.* To manifest, to evince.
estrinsecarsi, *v.r.* To make known one's thoughts; to reveal one's views.
estrinsecazione, *n.f.* Expression (of thoughts).
estrinseco [estrInseco], *a.* Extrinsic.
estro, *n.m.* Inspiration, fire, genius; whim, freak; (*Zool.*) gadfly. **— poetico,** poetic fire; **secondo l'—,** as the spirit moves; **se mi prende l'— di,** if I take a fancy to (do something).
estrosamente, *adv.* Whimsically, for a whim.
estrosità [-à], *n.f.* Freakishness.
estroso, *a.* Whimsical, capricious; freakish; fantastic.
estrudere [estrUdere], *v.t.* (*obs.*) To thrust forth, to extrude.
estuante, *a.* (*obs.*) Effervescent, ebullient.
estuario [estuArio], *n.m.* Estuary; gulf.
estumescenza, *n.f.* Swell (of the sea); high tide.
estuoso, *a.* Stormy.
esuberante, *a.* Exuberant, superabundant; effusive.
esuberantemente, *adv.* Exuberantly, effusively.
esuberanza, *n.f.* Exuberance, effusiveness; excess, plenty.
esulare, *v.i.* To go (voluntarily) into exile; to be extraneous. **Esula dalla mia competenza,** it is beyond my competence.
esulcerare, *v.t.* To exacerbate, to irritate; to grieve; to afflict.
esulcerazione, *n.f.* Exacerbation; worry.
esule [Esule], *n.m.* Exile, refugee.
esultante, *a.* Exultant, delighted.
esultanza, *n.f.* Exultation, rejoicing, rapture, delight.
esultare, *v.i.* To exult, to rejoice, to delight.
esultazione [cp. **esultanza**].
esumare, *v.t.* To exhume, to disinter; to unearth.
esumazione, *n.f.* Exhumation, disinterment.
esurire, *v.i.* (*obs.*) To be hungry.
età [-à], *n.f.* Age; epoch. **L'età dell'oro,** the golden age; **che — aveva?** how old was he? **di mezza —,** middle-aged; **d'—,** aged, old; **in tenera —,** of tender age; **minore —,** under age; **mostrare la propria —,** to look one's age.
etade, *n.f.* (*Poet.*) Age.
etane [Etane], *n.m.* (*Chem.*) Ethane.
etate, *n.f.* (*Poet.*) Age.
etera, *n.f.* Courtesan, hetaera.
etere [Etere], *n.m.* Ether (in all senses); (*Poet.*) sky, air.
etereo [etEreo], *a.* Ethereal.
eterico [etErico], *a.* Etheric.
eterizzare, *v.t.* To etherize.
eterizzazione, *n.f.* Etherization.
eternale, *a.* (*Lit.*) Eternal.
eternare, *v.t.* To render eternal, to make immortal, to immortalize, to perpetuate.
eternarsi, *v.r.* To become immortal, to be eternal.
eternità [-à], *n.f.* Eternity.
eterno, *a.* Eternal, everlasting, perpetual. **Il Padre Eterno,** God; **in eterno,** forever.
eteroclito [eterOclito], *a.* Heteroclite, anomalous.
eterodina, *n.f.* (*Radio*) Heterodyne.
eterodossia [eterodossIa], *n.f.* Heterodoxy.
eterodosso, *a.* Heterodox.
eterogeneità [-à], *n.f.* Heterogeneousness, heterogeneity.
eterogeneo [eterogEneo], *a.* Heterogeneous.
etesio [etEsio], *a.* Etesian (of Mediterranean winds).
etica [Etica], *n.f.* Ethics.
eticamente, *adv.* Ethically.
etichetta, *n.f.* Etiquette, ceremonial; label, docket, ticket. **— volante,** tie-on label.
etichettare, *v.t.* To label (in all senses).
etico (1) [Etico], *a.* Ethic, ethical; hectic.
etico (2) [Etico], *n.m.a.* (*Med.*) Consumptive.
etile, *n.m.* (*Chem.*) Ethyl.
etilene, *n.m.* (*Chem.*) Ethylene.
etimo [Etimo], *n.m.* (*Gram.*) Etymon.
etimologia [etimologIa], *n.f.* Etymology.
etimologicamente, *adv.* Etymologically.
etimologico [etimolOgico], *a.* Etymological.
etimologo [etimOlogo], *n.m.* Etymologist.
etiologia [etiologIa], *n.f.* Etiology.
etiope, etiopico [etIope, etiOpico], *n.m.a.* Ethiopian.
Etiopia [etiOpia], *n.f.* (*Geog.*) Ethiopia.
etisia [etisIa], *n.f.* (*Med.*) Phthisis, consumption.
etneo [etnEo], *a.* Pertaining to Mt. Etna.
etnico [Etnico], *a.* Ethnic.
etnografia [etnografIa], *n.f.* Ethnography.
etnografico [etnogrAfico], *a.* Ethnographic.
etnografo [etnOgrafo], *n.m.* Ethnographer.
etnologia [etnologIa], *n.f.* Ethnology.
etnologicamente, *adv.* Ethnologically.
etnologico, *a.* Ethnological.
etnologo [etnOlogo], *n.m.* Ethnologist.
etra, *n.f.* (*Poet.*) Air, sky, ether.
etrusco, *n.m.a.* Etruscan.
ettaedro, *n.m.* (*Geom.*) Solid body with seven faces, heptahedron.
ettagono [ettAgono], *n.m.* (*Geom.*) Heptagon.
ettaro [Ettaro], *n.m.* Hectare (2·471 acres).
ette, *n.m.* (*colloq.*) Trifle, mere nothing. **Non vale un —** worth nothing; **c'è mancato un — che cadesse,** he was within an ace of falling.

etto, ettogrammo, *n.m.* Hectogram (3·527 oz.).
ettolitro [ettOlitro], *n.m.* Hectolitre (22 gallons).
ettowatt, *n.m.* (*Elec.*) Hectowatt.
eucalipto, *n.m.* (*Bot.*) Eucalyptus.
eucaristia [eucaristIa], *n.f.* (*Eccles.*) Eucharist, Holy Communion.
eucaristico [eucarIstico], *a.* Eucharistic.
eufemismo, *n.m.* Euphemism.
eufemistico [eufemIstico], *a.* Euphemistic.
eufonia [eufonIa], *n.f.* Euphony.
eufonico [eufOnico], *a.* Euphonic, euphonious.
euforbia [eufOrbia], *n.f.* (*Bot.*) Euphorbia, spurge.
eufrasia [eufrAsia], *n.f.* (*Bot.*) Eye-bright.
eufuismo, *n.m.* (*Lit.*) Euphuism.
eufuistico [eufuIstico], *a.* Euphuistic.
eugenetica [eugenEtica], *n.f.* Eugenics.
eugenetico [eugenEtico], *a.* Eugenic.
eunuco, *n.m.a.* Eunuch; emasculated, castrated.
euripo, *n.m.* (*Geog.*) Arm of the sea with strong currents.
euritmia [euritmIa], *n.f.* Eurhythmy.
euritmica [eurItmica], *n.f.* Eurhythmics.
euritmico [eurItmico], *a.* Eurhythmic.
euro [Euro], *n.m.* (*Poet.*) East wind.
europeo [europEo], *n.m.a.* European.
eustachio [eustAchio], *n.m.* (*Anat.*) **Tromba d'Eustachio,** Eustachian tube.
eutanasia [eutanAsia], *n.f.* Euthanasia, painless death.
evacuare, *v.t.* To evacuate; to eject; to withdraw from.
evacuazione, *n.f.* Evacuation; withdrawal.
evadere [evAdere], *v.t.i.* To escape, to break loose, to get away; to despatch (business, etc.); to settle (affairs); to fill (orders, etc.).
evanescente, *a.* Evanescent.
evanescenza, *n.f.* Evanescence.
evangeliario [evangeliArio], *n.m.* (*Eccles.*) Service book containing Gospels, etc.
evangelicamente, *adv.* Evangelically.
evangelico [evangElico], *a.* Evangelical.
evangelista (*pl.* **evangelisti**), *n.m.* Evangelist.
evangelizzare, *v.t.* To evangelize.
evangelo, *n.m.* Gospel [cp. **vangelo**].
evaporabile [evaporAbile], *a.* Capable of evaporation.
evaporare, evaporarsi, *v.i.r.* To evaporate.
evaporazione, *n.f.* Evaporation.
evasione, *n.f.* Escape, flight; evasion; (*fig.*) escapism. (*Comm.*) **Dare —,** to answer to, to come up to; **in — a,** with reference to.
evasivamente, *adv.* Evasively.
evasivo, *a.* Evasive, vague.
evaso, *n.m.* Fugitive, escaper, runaway.
evenienza, *n.f.* Contingency, eventuality, occurrence.
evento, *n.m.* Event, occurrence, happening; result. **In ogni —,** at all events.
eventuale, *a.* Eventual, possible; probable.
eventualità [-à], *n.f.* Eventuality, possibility, contingency; event.
eventualmente, *adv.* Possibly; in any case.
eversione, *n.f.* (*Lit.*) Ruin, destruction.
evidente, *a.* Evident, plain, manifest, visible, obvious.
evidentemente, *adv.* Evidently.
evidenza, *n.f.* Clarity, obviousness, plainness. **Mettere in —,** to make evident; to make clear; to emphasize; **arrendersi all'—,** to be convinced.
evincere [evIncere], *v.t.* (*Law*) To evict, to turn out; (*obs.*) to regain.
evirare, *v.t.* To emasculate.
evirato, *n.m.* Eunuch, castrate.
evirato, *a.* Unmanly, effeminate; enfeebled.
evirazione, *n.f.* Castration.
evitabile [evitAbile], *a.* Avoidable.
evitare, *v.t.* To avoid, to shun, to evade; to keep away from. **— le spese,** to save expenses.
evizione, *n.f.* (*Law*) Eviction.
evo, *n.m.* Age, time, period. **L'— medio,** the Middle Ages; **— moderno,** modern times.
evocare, *v.t.* To evoke, to conjure up, to call up.
evocazione, *n.f.* Evocation; recollection.
evoluto, *a.* Up-to-date, progressive, developed.
evoluzione, *n.f.* Evolution.
evolversi, *v.r.* To evolve, to develop.
evulso, *a.* (*Lit.*) Uprooted, wrenched.
evviva! *inter.* Hurrah! Long live. **— il re!** Long live the King! **fare un —,** to give a cheer.
ex-, *prefix.* Ex- , former. **Ex-presidente,** ex-president.
extenso, *adv.* In full [cp. **esteso**].
extragiudiziale, *a.* By amicable settlement (out of court).
extraterritorialità [-à], *n.f.* Extraterritoriality.
eziandio [eziandIo], *adv.* Also, besides.

F

F, f, *n.m.f.* Sixth letter of the Italian alphabet.
fa, *n.m.* (*Mus.*) Fourth note of the diatonic scale of C major.
fa, *adv.* Ago, from now (of past). **Un' ora —,** an hour ago; **tre anni —,** three years ago.
fabbisogno, *n.m.* Requisites, what is necessary; estimate of expenditure or cost; (*Theat.*) property, properties.
fabbrica [fAbbrica], *n.f.* Building, construction, structure; workshop, works, mill, factory. **Marca di —,** trade-mark; **a prezzo di —,** at cost price.
fabbricabile [fabbricAbile], *a.* Manufacturable.
fabbricante, *n.m.* Manufacturer, maker; builder.
fabbricare, *v.t.* To build, to construct; to manufacture; to invent, to fabricate, to forge. **— vocaboli,** to coin new words.
fabbricato, *n.m.* Building, structure, premises.
fabbricatore, fabbricatrice, *n.m.f.* Manufacturer, maker; builder; inventor (of false news, etc.), fabricator.
fabbricazione, *n.f.* Manufacture; construction, make, making; (*fig.*) fabrication. **Di — estera,** of foreign make.
fabbriceria [fabbricerIa], *n.f.* (*Eccles.*) Vestry-board.
fabbriciere, *n.m.* (*Eccles.*) Vestryman; works overseer of a cathedral.
fabbro, *n.m.* Smith, artificer, maker; (*fig.*) inventor.

fabbroferraio [fabbroferrAio], *n.m.* Blacksmith.
faccenda, *n.f.* Affair, business, work, duty; matter, thing. **Le faccende di casa,** housework; **aver molte faccende,** to be very busy; **è una — seria!** it's a serious matter! it's a nasty business! **questa è un altra —,** this is a different matter; **troppe faccende da sbrigare,** too much work in hand, too many things to see to.
faccendaccia [faccendAccia], *n.f.* (*colloq.*) Nasty affair.
faccendiere, faccendiera, *n.m.f.* Busybody, meddler; factotum.
faccendone, *n.m.* Intriguer, busybody.
faccetta, *n.f.* (*Geom.*) Facet. (*Min.*) **A faccette,** cut into facets (of diamonds, etc.).
faccettare, *v.t.* To facet, to cut (a gem).
faccettatura, *n.f.* Faceting.
facchinaggio [facchinAggio], *n.m.* Porterage; drudgery.
facchinata, *n.f.* Coarse language, "Billingsgate"; drudgery, hard work.
facchineria [facchinerIa], *n.f.* Porter's hard work; coarse language.
facchinesco, *a.* Toilsome; mean.
facchino, *n.m.* Porter, carrier. **Fare il —,** to work like a slave; **— da carbone,** coal-heaver.
faccia [fAccia], *n.f.* Face, visage, cast of features, mien, appearance, expression; (*fig. colloq.*) impudence, cheek. **Di — a,** in front of; **di —,** opposite; **la casa di —,** the house opposite; **cambiare, mutare —,** to face about; **visto di —,** seen from the front; **— franca, — tosta, — di bronzo,** brazen-face, shamelessness; **ridere in —, ridere sulla — di qualcuno,** to laugh in someone's face; (*colloq.*) **viva la sua —!** Bless him! **voltar —,** to change one's opinion.
facciale, *a.* Facial.
facciata, *n.f.* (*Arch.*) Façade, front, frontage; page (of writing, printing, etc.).
facciola, facciuola, *n.f.* (*Law*) Lawyer's bands.
faccione, *n.m.* Large face. **Un bel —,** a jolly, good-humoured face.
face, *n.f.* Torch, lamp.
facella, *n.f.* (*Lit.*) Dim light, lamp.
facetamente, *adv.* Facetiously.
faceto, *a.* Facetious, jocular, waggish; witty.
facezia [facEzia], *n.f.* Facetiousness; jest, joke, pleasantry.
fachirismo, *n.m.* Fakirism.
fachiro, *n.m.* Fakir.
faciale, *a.* Facial. (*Anat.*) **Nervi faciali,** facial nerves [cp. **facciale**].
facicchiare, *v.t.* (*colloq.*) To work grudgingly; to bungle.
facidanno, *n.m.* (*obs.*) Thief, bad man (esp. one who damages crops, etc.).
faciente, *a.* Acting. **— funzione,** acting as deputy.
facile [fAcile], *a.* Easy, facile, simple; free; easy-going; inclined, prone. **È — all'ira,** he is prone to anger; **non è così —,** it's not so easy; **è — che arrivi domani,** he is likely to arrive tomorrow; **donna di facili costumi,** a woman of easy virtue.
facilità [-à], *n.f.* Facility, ease, easiness; readiness; fluency; aptitude.
facilitare, *v.t.* To facilitate, to make easy. (*Comm.*) **— nei prezzi,** to make low prices.
facilitazione, *n.f.* Facilitation; (*Comm.*) easy terms, accommodation. **Concedere delle facilitazioni,** to grant facilities.
facilmente, *adv.* Easily, probably.
facilone, *a.* Easy-going; superficial, amateurish.
facinoroso, *n.m.a.* Desperado; malefactor; violent, lawless, rascally.
facitore, *n.m.* Maker, doer, agent; steward
facocero, *n.m.* (*Zool.*) Wart-hog.
facoltà [-à], *n.f.* Faculty (in all senses); authority, power; (*pl.*) property, riches, wealth. **Non è in mia — di,** it is not in my power to; **— di Scienze,** Faculty of Science; **in possesso delle proprie —,** in full possession of his faculties; **uomo di molte —,** a wealthy man.
facoltativamente, *adv.* Optionally.
facoltativo, *a.* Optional.
facoltoso, *a.* Wealthy.
facondamente, *adv.* Fluently (of speech), eloquently.
facondia [facOndia], *n.f.* Fluency (of speech); loquacity.
facondo, *a.* Fluent, eloquent; talkative, garrulous.
facsimile [facsImile], *n.m.* Facsimile.
factotum, *n.m.* Handy-man, factotum.
faenza, *n.f.* Faience (pottery).
faggeto, *n.m.* Beech-wood; beech-grove.
faggina, *n.f.* Beech-nut.
faggio [fAggio], *n.m.* (*Bot.*) Beech (tree or wood). **Olio di —,** beech-nut oil.
faggiola, *n.f.* Beech-mast.
fagiana, *n.f.* Hen pheasant.
fagianaia [fagianAia], *n.f.* Pheasant preserve, pheasantry.
fagianella, *n.f.* (*Zool.*) Lesser bustard.
fagiano, *n.m.* Cock pheasant, pheasant.
fagiolaio [fagiolAio], *n.m.* (*colloq.*) Bean-eater, lover of beans.
fagiolata, *n.f.* A good bellyful of beans; (*fig.*) foolish remark.
fagiolino, *n.m.* French bean. **Fagiolini rampicanti,** runner beans.
fagiolo, fagiuolo, *n.m.* Bean. **Fagioli secchi,** haricot beans; (*colloq.*) **non mi va a —,** it doesn't please me; **è un gran —!** what a blockhead he is!
faglia [fAglia], *n.f.* (*Geol.*) Fault.
fagliare, *v.i.* To discard (at card games).
faglio [fAglio], *n.m.* Discard.
fagociti, *n.m.pl.* (*Biol.*) Phagocytes.
fagopiro [fagOpiro], *n.m.* (*Bot.*) Buckwheat.
fagottista, *n.m.* (*Mus.*) Bassoon-player.
fagotto, *n.m.* Bundle, parcel, packet; (*Mus.*) bassoon. **Far —,** to pack off, to be gone.
faida [fAida], *n.f.* Feud, vendetta; revenge, retaliation.
faina, *n.f.* (*Zool.*) Pole-cat.
falange, *n.f.* Phalanx; troop; (*Anat.*) phalange.
falangio [falAngio], *n.m.* (*Zool.*) Harvest-spider.
falangista, *n.f.* (*Zool.*) Phalanger; flying squirrel; (*Pol.*) member of Spanish Falange.
falarica [falArica], *n.f.* (*Hist.*) Fire-tipped arrow.
falasco, *n.m.* (*Bot.*) Bulrush, reed.
falbo, *a.* Tawny.

falcare, *v.t.* To bend (in the shape of a scythe); to curvet (of horses).
falcata, *n.f.* Curvet (of a horse).
falcato, *a.* Curved, hooked, horned. **Luna —,** crescent moon.
falce, *n.f.* Scythe, sickle. (*Pol.*) **— e martello,** hammer and sickle.
falcetto, *n.m.* Reaping-hook, bagging-hook.
falchetto, *n.m.* (*Zool.*) Hawk.
falciagione, *n.f.* (*Agric.*) Season for mowing.
falciare, *v.t.* To mow (with scythe), to scythe, to cut down.
falciata, *n.f.* Mowing (of a field); stroke with a scythe.
falciatore, *n.m.* Mower.
falciatrice, *n.f.* Mowing-machine; harvester.
falciatura, *n.f.* Mowing.
falcidia [falcIdia], *n.f.* Reduction, cutting down (of salaries, etc.).
falcidiare, *v.t.* To reduce, to cut down (salaries, etc.).
falciforme, *a.* Sickle-shaped.
falcinello, *n.m.* Bill-hook.
falcione, *n.m.* (*Agric.*) Hay-cutter.
falco, *n.m.* (*Zool.*) Hawk.
falcone, *n.m.* Falcon.
falconeria [falconerIa], *n.f.* Falconry.
falconetto, *n.m.* (*Hist.*) Falconet, small cannon.
falconiere, *n.m.* Falconer.
falda, *n.f.* Layer, flake, slice; flap, flounce; fold, plait, hem; brim (of hat); foot (of mountain). **— di neve,** snow-flake, **cappello a larghe falde,** broad-brimmed hat; **alle falde del monte,** at the foot of the mountain; **le falde di una giubba,** the hem of a coat.
faldato, *a.* Flaky; folded; flounced, pleated.
faldella, *n.f.* Lint.
faldistorio [faldistOrio], *n.m.* (*Eccles.*) Faldstool; episcopal seat.
faldoso, *a.* Pleated, in flakes.
falegname, *n.m.* Carpenter, joiner.
falegnameria [falegnamerIa], *n.f.* Carpentry, joinery.
falena, *n.f.* (*Zool.*) Moth, nocturnal moth; paper ash.
falerno, *n.m.* Falernian wine.
falla, *n.f.* Leak, leakage; fault in woven material. **Accecare una —,** to stop a leak; **aprirsi di una —,** to spring a leak; (*Radio*) **— di griglia,** grid leak.
fallace, *a.* Fallacious, deceitful; misleading, unsound, false.
fallacemente, *adv.* Fallaciously, deceitfully.
fallacia, fallacità [fallAcia, **-à**], *n.f.* Fallacy, fallaciousness; deceitfulness.
fallare, *v.i.t* To err, to mistake; to miss, to fail, to be mistaken. **Chi non fa non falla,** he who makes not mars not.
fallibile [fallIbile], *a.* Fallible, liable to err.
fallibilità [-à], *n.f.* Fallibility.
fallico [fAllico], *a.* Phallic.
fallimentare, *a.* Leading to bankruptcy; disastrous. **Massa —,** bankruptcy assets; **procedura —,** bankruptcy proceedings.
fallimento, *n.m.* (*Comm.*) Failure, insolvency, bankruptcy; breakdown. **Fare —,** to go bankrupt, to fail.
fallire, *v.t.i.* To fail, to miss, to fall short; to be unsuccessful; (*Comm.*) to fail, to go bankrupt; to default; to become insolvent. **— il colpo,** to miss the mark; **— in un'impresa,** to fail in an undertaking.
fallito, *p.p.a.* Failed, unsuccessful, unprofitable; insolvent, bankrupt. **Egli è —,** he has gone bankrupt; **dichiararsi —,** to declare oneself bankrupt.
fallo (1), *n.m.* Fault, blemish, defect; error, slip, mistake; failure. **Senza —,** without fail; **cogliere in —,** to catch out, to catch in a mistake; **mettere un piede in —,** to take a false step; (*Tennis*) **— di piede,** footfault.
fallo (2), *n.m.* Phallus.
fallofora [fallOfora], *n.f.* (*Lit.*) Whore, harlot.
falo, *n.m.* Bonfire. **Fare un —,** to make a bonfire.
faloppa, *n.f.* Defective silk-cocoon; (*fig.*) boaster.
falotico [falOtico], *a.* (*obs.*) Fantastic.
falpalà [-à], *n.f.* Flounce, furbelow.
falsa, *n.f.* Discord.
falsamente, *adv.* Falsely, untruthfully.
falsamento, *n.m.* Distortion.
falsamonete, *n.m.* Coiner, forger (of paper money) [cp. **falsario**].
falsaporta, *n.f.* Secret door, concealed door; blind door.
falsare, *v.t.* To misrepresent, to alter, to distort, to misconstrue; to forge.
falsariga, *n.f.* Guide-sheet of ruled paper in a writing pad; (*fig.*) example. **Seguire la —,** to imitate, to copy.
falsario [falsArio], *n.m.* Forger, coiner.
falsatura, *n.f.* Insertion in a dress.
falseggiare, *v.i.* To play false; (*Mus.*) to sing falsetto.
falsetto, *n.m.* (*Mus.*) Falsetto.
falsificabile [falsificAbile], *a.* Capable of being forged.
falsificamento, *n.m.* Falsification.
falsificare, *v.t.* To falsify, to forge, to debase, to adulterate. **— merci,** to adulterate, to imitate articles (for sale).
falsificatore, *n.m.* Falsifier, forger.
falsificazione, *n.f.* Falsification, forgery.
falsiloquio [falsilOquio], *n.m.* (*obs.*) Falsehood.
falsità [-à], *n.f.* Falsehood, falsity, lie; duplicity, insincerity.
falso, *n.m.* Falsehood; forgery; feint (in fencing). **Giurare il —,** to commit perjury; **commettere un —,** to commit a forgery; **essere nel —,** to be in error.
falso, *a.* False, feigned, untrue, wrong; counterfeit, adulterated; double-faced, double-dealing, tricky; disloyal; bogus. **Monete false,** debased coins; **prendere una strada falsa,** to deviate from the right path, to go astray; **fare un passo —,** to take a false step; **— allarme,** false alarm; **chiave falsa,** false key; **biglietto —,** forged bank note.
fama, *n.f.* Fame, repute, reputation, notoriety, renown; report. **Essere in — di,** to have the reputation of; **di — mondiale,** of world-wide reputation; **godere — di,** to enjoy repute; **è —,** it is said; **corre — che,** it is rumoured that; **una — usurpata,** an undeserved reputation.
famato, *a.* Famed. **Mal —,** of bad reputation, notorious [cp. **famoso**].
fame, *n.f.* Hunger, great appetite; starvation, dearth, famine. **Aver —,** to be hungry; **morir di —,** to starve; **una — da lupi,** a

ravenous hunger, the hunger of a hunter; **cavarsi la —**, to appease one's hunger; **lasciarsi morir di —**, to starve oneself to death.
famedio [famEdio], *n.m.* Temple of fame; site reserved for the bodies of famous men in a cemetery.
famelicamente, *adv.* Greedily, voraciously.
famelico [famElico], *a.* Famishing, starving, ravenously hungry.
famigerato, *a.* Ill-famed, notorious, of ill-repute.
famiglia [famIglia], *n.f.* Family, kindred, kin; home, parentage, race; attendants, entourage. **Sacra Famiglia,** Holy Family; **mettere su —**, to form a family; **capo di —**, head of the house; **far le cose in —**, to do things privately; **alla buona in —**, without ceremony, in a homely style; **esser di buona —**, to come of a good family.
familiare, famigliare, *n.m.a.* Familiar; intimate; homely.
familiarità, famigliarità [-à, -à], *n.f.* Familiarity, intimacy.
familiarizzare, *v.t.* To familiarize.
familiarizzarsi, *v.r.* To become familiar, to familiarize oneself, to grow accustomed.
familiarmente, *adv.* Familiarly.
famosamente, *adv.* Famously.
famoso, *a.* Famous, renowned, celebrated; notorious.
famulo [fAmulo], *n.m.* (*obs.*) Manservant, valet.
fanalaio [fanalAio], *n.m.* Lighthouse keeper; lamp-lighter.
fanale, *n.m.* Lamp, light; street lamp, lamp-post; lantern of a ship; headlight. **A fanali spenti,** with lights out; (*Motor*) **fanali anteriori, posteriori,** headlights, tail-lights.
fanalista (*pl.* **fanalisti**), *n.m.* Lighthouse keeper; lamp-lighter.
fanaticamente, *adv.* Fanatically.
fanatico [fanAtico], *n.m.a.* Fanatic, zealot; fanatic, fanatical.
fanatismo, *n.m.* Fanaticism, bigotry.
fanatizzare, *v.i.t.* To become fanatical; to become crazy; to make fanatical.
fanciulla, *n.f.* Girl, young girl; maid, lass.
fanciullaggine [fanciullAggine], *n.f.* Childishness, childish action or behaviour.
fanciullata, *n.f.* Childish trick, childish action.
fanciulleggiare, *v.i.* To act childishly (of grown-ups).
fanciullescamente, *adv.* Childishly, in a puerile way.
fanciullesco, *a.* Childish, boyish, puerile.
fanciullezza, *n.f.* Childhood; girlhood, boyhood.
fanciullo, *n.m.* Boy, child; lad, young fellow.
fanciullo, *a.* Young, youthful.
fanciullone, *n.m.* Simple-minded man.
fandonia [fandOnia], *n.f.* White lie, fib, yarn, fable; humbug.
fanello, *n.m.* (*Zool.*) Linnet.
fanfaluca, *n.f.* Flake; (*fig.*) tall story, yarn; whim, freak, fad; trifle.
fanfano [fAnfano], *n.m.* Chatterbox, scatter-brain.
fanfara, *n.f.* Fanfare; brass band, military band and its music.
fanfaronata, *n.f.* Bluster, bragging talk, boasting.
fanfarone, *n.m.* Braggart ,blusterer.
fanfera [fAnfera], *adv.* [cp. **vanvera**].
fanga, *n.f.* Deep mud, quagmire.
fangaia [fangAia], *n.f.* Muddy stretch of road.
fangatura, *n.f.* Course of mud baths, mud-bathing.
fanghiglia [fanghIglia], *n.f.* Mud, slime, mire.
fango, *n.m.* Mud, mire, slime; filth; (*pl.*) mud-baths. **Gettar — a qualcuno,** to throw mud at someone; **— di mare,** mud from the sea-bed.
fangosità [-à], *n.f.* Muddiness.
fangoso, *a.* Muddy, slimy, greasy.
fannullone, *n.m.* Lounger, idler, slacker; good-for-nothing.
fano, *n.m.* Fane, temple.
fanoni, *n.m.pl.* Whalebone; (*Eccles.*) papal maniples.
fantaccino, *n.m.* (*Mil.*) Infantryman, "foot-slogger", private.
fantasia [fantasIa], *n.f.* Fancy, imagination; whim, caprice; freak; fanciful object; (*Mus.*) fantasia. **Oggetti di —**, fancy articles; **opere di —**, works of fiction; **aver — d'una cosa,** to have a fancy for something; **a —**, at pleasure, at choice.
fantasima, fantasma, *n.f.* Spectre, phantasm, ghost.
fantasioso, *a.* Capricious, fanciful.
fantasmagoria [fantasmagorIa], *n.f.* Illusions, phantasmagoria.
fantasticaggine [fantasticAggine], *n.f.* Fancifulness, daydream.
fantasticamente, *adv.* Fantastically.
fantasticare, *v.i.* To fancy, to dream, to imagine, to muse, to day-dream.
fantasticheria [fantasticherIa], *n.f.* Fancifulness; day-dream, reverie, foolish fancies.
fantastico [fantAstico], *a.* Fanciful, fantastic, fabulous, imaginary; extravagant, whimsical, odd, queer.
fantasticone, *n.m.f.* Day-dreamer.
fante, *n.m.f.* Infantryman; (*Cards*) knave, jack; (*obs.*) servant, maidservant. **Scherza coi fanti e lascia stare i santi,** joke with men and not with saints, *i.e.*, be reverent; **il monumento al —**, the war memorial to fallen infantrymen.
fanteria [fanterIa], *n.f.* (*Mil.*) Infantry.
fantesca, *n.f.* Maidservant, maid.
fantino, *n.m.* Jockey.
fantocciata, *n.f.* Poorly performed puppet show.
fantoccio [fantOccio], *n.m.* Puppet, marionette, doll; (artist's) lay figure; (*fig.*) simpleton. **I fantocci,** puppet show.
fantoccione, *n.m.* Big puppet; baby.
fantolino, *n.m.* Baby, child.
farabolone, *n.m.* Gossiper, chatterer.
farabutto, *n.m.* Swindler, rascal, scoundrel, knave.
farad, *n.m.* (*Elec.*) Farad.
faraglioni, *n.m.pl.* Cliffs.
faraona, *n.f.* (*Zool.*) Guinea-fowl.
Faraone, *n.m.* (*Hist.*) Pharaoh; (*Cards*) faro.
farcino, *n.m.* (*Vet.*) Farcy.
farda, *n.f.* Dirty rag; sputum; (*colloq.*) bale (of goods).
fardaggio [fardAggio], *n.m.* (*Mil.*) Baggage.

fardello, *n.m.* Bundle, parcel, package; burden. **Far —,** to be off, to go.
fardo, *n.m.* Package; roll; bale.
fare (*pres.p.* **facendo;** *p.p.* **fatto),** *v.t.* To do, to make, to form, to create; to work, to effect, to perform; to practise; to compose, to write; to run; to have, to get, to keep; to give, to take, to obtain (provisions, etc.); to deal (cards); to cause, to think, to believe; to say, to charge; to call. **— ritorno,** to return; **— una parte,** to act a role; **— la barba,** to shave; **— sangue,** to bleed; **farla ad uno,** to take someone in; **te l'ho fatta!** I caught you! **far attenzione,** to pay attention; **— bel tempo,** to be fine weather; **— caldo, freddo,** (weather) to be warm, cold; **— presto,** to hurry up; **— il callo,** to become hardened; **— una passeggiata,** to take a walk; **— coda,** to queue (at a shop); **far fare,** to have something done, to get something done; **— male,** to hurt; **— silenzio,** to keep silence; **farla da gran signore,** to act the nobleman; **— da sè,** to shift for oneself; **fate voi, faccia Lei,** I leave it to you; **fate pure, faccia pure,** please yourself, do as you like; **— per proprio conto,** to look after oneself; **— di tutto, — il possibile,** to do one's utmost; **— una visita,** to pay a call; **— in modo che,** to see to it that; **farsi strada,** to go ahead, to make one's way; **— Quaresima,** to keep Lent; **— un brindisi,** to drink a toast; **— poco caso di,** to make light of; **il vino mi fa male,** wine does not agree with me; **si fa presto a dire,** it's easy to say; **farne da vendere,** to act foolishly; (*Naut.*) **— vela,** to set sail; **— a metà,** to go halves; **ciò non fa per me,** this does not suit me; **— a tempo,** to be in time; **— da cucina,** to cook; **— finta,** to feign; **— fronte,** to face; **— andare una macchina,** to start a machine; **— chiamare qualcuno,** to send for someone; **— vedere,** to show; **— sapere,** to tell, to inform [cp. **farsi**].
fare, *n.m.* Manner, air; behaviour, style; beginning; workmanship. **Egli ha un — antipatico,** he has unpleasant manners; **sul — del giorno,** at break of day.
faretra, *n.f.* Quiver.
faretrato, *a.* Bearing a quiver.
farfalla, *n.f.* (*Zool.*) Butterfly; (*Mech.*) throttle.
farfalleggiare, *v.i.* To flutter about.
farfallino, *n.m.* Small butterfly or moth; (*fig.*) empty-headed person.
farfallone, *n.m.* Large moth or butterfly; (*fig.*) blunder, howler.
farfanicchio [farfanIcchio], *n.m.* Little man who puts on airs.
farfaro [fArfaro], *n.m.* (*Bot.*) Colt's foot.
farfugliare, *v.i.* To stammer, to mumble.
farfuglione, *n.m.* Stammerer, mumbler.
farina, *n.f.* Flour, meal. **Fior di —,** fine flour; **— gialla,** maize meal; **— di frumento,** wheaten meal; **— di riso,** ground rice; **— d'avena,** oatmeal; **farine alimentari,** farinaceous foods; **non è — del suo sacco,** this is not his own work; **questo non fa —,** this doesn't cut any ice.
farinaccio [farinAccio], *n.m.* Flour-dust.
farinaceo [farinAceo], *a.* Farinaceous. **I farinacei,** farinaceous foods.
farinaio [farinAio], *n.m.* Meal-store.
farinaiolo, farinaiuolo, *n.m.* Meal merchant or dealer.
farinata, *n.f.* Meal porridge. **— d'avena,** oatmeal porridge.
faringe, *n.f.* (*Anat.*) Pharynx.
faringite, *n.f.* (*Med.*) Pharyngitis.
farinoso, *a.* Floury.
farisaicamente, *adv.* Pharisaically.
farisaico [farisAico], *a.* Pharisaical; hypocritical.
fariseismo, *n.m.* Pharisaism; self-righteousness.
fariseo [farisEo], *n.m.* Pharisee; hypocrite.
farmaceutica [farmacEutica], *n.f.* Pharmaceutics.
farmaceutico [farmacEutico], *a.* Pharmaceutical.
farmacia [farmacIa], *n.f.* Pharmacy, chemist's shop; drug store.
farmacista (*pl.* **farmacisti),** *n.m.* Pharmacist, dispensing chemist, apothecary.
farmaco [fArmaco], *n.m.* Medicine, drug.
farmacologia [farmacologIa], *n.f.* Pharmacology.
farmacopea [farmacopEa], *n.f.* Pharmacopoeia.
farneticamente, *adv.* Deliriously, ravingly.
farneticamento, *n.m.* Deliriousness.
farneticare, *v.i.* To rave, to wander (in mind); to be delirious; to talk nonsense.
farnetico [farnEtico], *n.m.a.* Madman; madness; raving, delirious.
farnia [fArnia], *n.f.* (*Bot.*) Broad-leaved oak.
faro, *n.m.* Lighthouse, beacon, light; (*Motor.*) headlight. (*Motor.*) **— anti-abbagliamento,** anti-dazzle headlight; (*Aviat.*) **— di atterraggio,** landing light; **nave —,** lightship.
farragine [farrAgine], *n.f.* Farrago, medley hotch-potch, mixture.
farraginoso, *a.* Muddled, confused; ill-assorted.
farro, *n.m.* (*Bot.*) Spelt.
farsa, *n.f.* Farce.
farsesco, *a.* Farcical.
farsetto, *n.m.* (*Hist.*) Doublet; (*Mil.*) thick waistcoat; pullover.
farsi, *v.r.* To make oneself, to become; to be done, to be made. **— capire,** to make oneself understood; **— amare,** to make oneself loved; **— bello,** to boast; **— male,** to hurt oneself, **— la barba,** to shave oneself, to shave; **— strada,** to make one's way; **— vedere,** to show oneself; **— avanti,** to come forward; **— pagare,** to enforce payment [cp. **fare**].
fascetta, *n.f.* Corset; band, strip; wrapper; ribbon (for medals). **— da giornale,** newspaper wrapper.
fascettaia [fascettAia], *n.f.* Corset-maker.
fascia [fAscia], *n.f.* Band, bandage, swaddling-band; wrapper, cover; (*Arch.*) fillet; (*Naut.*) planking. **Spedire sotto —,** to send under cover.
fasciame, *n.m.* (*Naut.*) Plating, sheathing.
fasciare, *v.t.* To bandage, to wrap; to swaddle; to surround; to bind up (a sore). **— una ferita,** to dress a wound.
fasciarsi, *v.r.* To wrap oneself up.
fasciatura, *n.f.* Bandage, bandaging; swaddling-clothes; dressing (of wounds).

fascicolato, *a.* Bound together, bunched together.
fascicoletto, *n.m.* Pamphlet.
fascicolo [fascIcolo], *n.m.* Single number of a periodical; booklet, pamphlet; dossier.
fascina, *n.f.* Faggot, bundle of sticks.
fascinaia [fascinAia], *n.f.* Wood-store; wood-shed.
fascinaio [fascinAio], *n.m.* Dealer in logs, wood-dealer.
fascinazione, *n.f.* Fascination.
fascino [fAscino], *n.m.* Fascination, charm. **Subire il — di,** to be under the spell of.
fascinotto, *n.m.* Bundle of firewood.
fascio [fAscio], *n.m.* Bundle; bunch; (*fig.*) burden; (*Anat.*) fascicle; (*Hist.*) fasces borne by lictors; union, coalition, league. **Riunire in —,** to gather in a bundle; **— di luce,** beam of light; **— di raggi,** pencil of rays; **far d'ogni erba —,** to collect indiscriminately, to make no distinction; **andare in —,** to go to ruin.
Fascismo, *n.m.* (*Pol.*) Fascism.
fascista, *n.m.f.* (*Pol.*) Fascist, member of the Fascist Party.
fascisticamente, *adv.* Fascistically.
fascistico [fascIstico], *a.* Fascist, pertaining to Fascism.
fascistizzare, *v.t.* To convert to Fascism.
fase, *n.f.* Phase, stage ; cycle, period. **Fasi della luna,** phases of the moon.
faselo, *n.m.* (*Naut.*) Yacht, cutter.
fasimetro [fasImetro], *n.m.* (*Elec.*) Phase meter.
fasservizi, *n.m.* Errand boy, odd man.
fassimile [fassImile], *n.m.* Facsimile.
fastello, *n.m.* Faggot, bundle (hay, wood, etc.).
fasti, *n.m.pl.* Records, annals.
fastidiare, *v.t.* To disturb, to trouble, to give trouble.
fastidio [fastIdio], *n.m.* Trouble, concern, care; disturbance, annoyance, disgust; tedium, ennui. **Pieno di fastidi,** full of cares; **dare —,** to give trouble, to be a nuisance.
fastidiosaggine [fastidiosAggine], *n.f.* Nuisance.
fastidiosamente, *adv.* Troublesomely.
fastidioso, *a.* Troublesome, annoying, vexing; tedious, wearisome.
fastidire, *v.t.* To trouble, to annoy; to weary [cp. **infastidire**].
fastigio [fastIgio], *n.m.* Summit, top; splendour; ridge; (*Arch.*) pediment.
fasto, *n.m.* Pomp, luxury, display; ostentation.
fastosamente, *adv.* Pompously ostentatiously.
fastosità [-à], *n.f.* Pomp, luxury.
fastoso, *a.* Pompous, ostentatious; luxurious; gorgeous.
fata, *n.f.* Fairy. **Regno delle fate,** fairyland; **racconto di fate,** fairy tale.
fatale, *a.* Fatal, fateful, destined, inevitable.
fatali, *n.m.pl.* (*Comm.*) Days of grace.
fatalismo, *n.m.* Fatalism.
fatalista, *n.m.f.* Fatalist.
fatalità [-à], *n.f.* Fatality; fate, destiny; accident, mischance.
fatalmente, *adv.* Fatally.
fatare, *v.t.* To charm, to bewitch.
fatatura, *n.f.* Enchantment.
fatebenefratelli, fatebenesorelle, *n.m.f.pl.* Members of a religious order having care of the sick.
fatica, *n.f.* Fatigue, weariness; lassitude; labour, toil, work; pain, trouble. **Non rispiarmiare —,** to spare no pains; **durar —,** to work laboriously; **a gran —,** with great labour; **è — sprecata,** it's labour lost; (*Mil.*) **berretto da —,** forage cap.
faticare, *v.i.* To toil, to drudge, to exert oneself. **— a,** to find difficult.
faticosamente, *adv.* Laboriously, with difficulty.
faticoso, *a.* Hard, fatiguing, wearisome, toilsome, exhausting, painful, difficult.
fatidicamente, *adv.* Prophetically.
fatidico [fatIdico], *a.* Prophetic.
fato, *n.m.* Fate, destiny, lot, fortune.
fatta, *n.f.* Sort, manner, kind; action; droppings (of wild animals). **Gente d'ogni —,** people of all sorts; **farne d'ogni —,** to do all sorts of foolish things; **di tal —,** of such a nature; **d'ogni —,** of every description.
fattaccio [fattAccio], *n.m.* Crime, ugly deed, wickedness.
fattamente, *adv.* **Sì —,** in such a manner.
fatterello, *n.m.* Unimportant happening, episode; trifling affair.
fattezze, *n.f.pl.* Features, countenance, lineaments.
fattibile [fattIbile], *a.* Feasible, practicable.
fatticcio [fattIccio], *a.* Robust, sturdy.
fattispecie [fattispEcie], *n.f.* (*Law*) Case in point, matter in hand.
fattivo, *a.* Useful, active, efficient; busy.
fattizio [fattIzio], *a.* Artificial, factitious.
fatto, *n.m.* Fact, action, deed, act; event, feat, achievement; matter, subject. **Sul —,** in the act; **in — di,** with regard to; **il — sta,** the fact remains; **badate ai fatti vostri,** mind you own business; **— d'arme,** feat of arms; **dire il — suo,** to speak one's mind; **per il solo — che,** by the simple fact that; **veniamo al —,** let's come to the point; **essere al —,** to be informed, to be aware of; **il — mio,** what suits me, just my cup of tea; **fatti diversi,** various news items.
fatto, *p.p.a.* Done, made, finished; complete. **Ecco —,** that's done; **è un uomo —,** he's a grown man; **abito —,** ready-made suit, reach-me-down; **— a mano,** hand-made; **a cose fatte,** too late; **a notte —,** late at night; **giorno —,** broad daylight.
fattora, *n.f.* Farmer's wife, housekeeper.
fattore, *n.m.* Land agent, farmer; factor; maker. **Il Supremo Fattore,** God; (*Math.*) **risoluzione in fattori,** resolution into factors.
fattoria [fattorIa], *n.f.* Farmhouse, farm buildings, dairy; steward's office.
fattorino, *n.m.* Messenger, delivery man, errand boy.
fattrice, *n.f.* Female animal kept for breeding purposes (brood mare, etc.).
fattucchiera, *n.f.* Witch, sorceress.
fattucchiere, *n.m.* Wizard, sorcerer; swindler, cheat.
fattucchieria [fattucchierIa], *n.f.* Witchcraft, sorcery.
fattura, *n.f.* Make, manufacture; workmanship; spell, charm; (*Comm.*) invoice, bill. **Gioiello di squisita —,** jewel of exquisite

workmanship; **quitanzare una —**, to receipt a bill; **— saldata**, receipted bill.
fatturagione, *n.f.* (*Comm.*) Despatch of invoice.
fatturare, *v.t.* To adulterate (wine); (*Comm.*) to invoice.
fatturista (*pl.* **fatturisti**), *n.m.* (*Comm.*) Invoice clerk.
fatuamente, *adv.* Fatuously, inanely.
fatuità [-à], *n.f.* Fatuity, silliness, conceit.
fatuo [fAtuo], *a.* Fatuous, inane, stupid, silly. **Fuochi fatui**, will-o'-the-wisp.
fatutto, *n.m.* Busybody.
fauci [fAuci], *n.f.pl.* (*Anat.*) Fauces; gullet, throat.
fauna [fAuna], *n.f.* (*Zool.*) Fauna.
fauno [fAuno], *n.m.* (*Myth.*) Faun.
faustamente, *adv.* Luckily; happily.
fausto [fAusto], *a.* Lucky, fortunate; happy. **— evento**, happy event.
fautore, fautrice, *n.m.f.* Protector, protectress; follower, supporter, partisan.
fava, *n.f.* Bean, broad bean. **Prendere due colombi a una —**, to kill two birds with one stone.
favagello, *n.m.* (*Bot.*) Celandine.
favarella, *n.f.* Bean soup.
favella, *n.f.* Speech, language, tongue. **Perder la —**, to lose one's tongue, to be silent; **la — toscana**, the Tuscan speech.
favellamento, *n.m.* Talking, speechifying.
favellare, *v.i.* To speak, to discourse.
favellatore, *n.m.* Talker.
faveto, *n.m.* (*Agric.*) Bean-field.
favetta, *n.f.* Small bean used in horse fodder.
favilla, *n.f.* Spark.
favo, *n.m.* Honeycomb; (*Med.*) carbuncle.
favola [fAvola], *n.f.* Fable, tale, story; untruth; laughing-stock. **Essere la — di tutti**, to be a by-word.
favoleggiare, *v.i.* To fable, to narrate, to tell.
favoleggiatore, *n.m.* Teller of fables.
favoloso, *a.* Fabulous, legendary; incredible; absurd.
favolosamente, *adv.* Fabulously.
favore, *n.m.* Favour, benefit; protection, regard, good-will; vogue, approval. **Per —**, please; **fare un —**, to do a favour; (*Comm.*) **giorni di —**, days of grace; **cambiale di —**, accommodation bill.
favoreggiamento, *n.m.* (*Law*) Backing, complicity.
favoreggiare, *v.t.* To favour, to back, to support.
favoreggiatore, *n.m.* (*Law*) Accomplice.
favorevole [favorEvole], *a.* Favourable, well-disposed, propitious. **Vento —**, propitious wind.
favorevolmente, *adv.* Favourably.
favorire, *v.t.* To favour, to protect, to promote, to foster; to support, to assist; to have the kindness to, to oblige, to consent, to agree. **Favorisca entrare**, please go in; **favorite dirmi**, kindly tell me; **favoriscano i biglietti!** tickets, please!
favorita, *n.f.* Favourite, king's mistress; (*Comm.*) letter. **Siamo in possesso della — vostra del 11 corr.**, Your favour of the 11th inst. to hand.
favoritismo, *n.m.* Favouritism.
favorito, *n.m.* Favourite, darling, pet. **I favoriti**, side-whiskers.
favorito, *a.* Favourite, favoured. (*Racing*) **Il cavallo —**, the favourite.
favule, *n.m.* (*Agric.*) Bean field.
fazio [fAzio], *n.m.* Simpleton. **Esser Fra Fazio**, to give away one's money.
fazione, *n.f.* Faction, party; (*obs.*) feat of arms. (*Mil.*) **Esser di —**, to be on duty.
faziosamente, *adv.* Factiously, seditiously.
faziosità [-à], *n.f.* Factiousness; sectarianism.
fazioso, *a.* Factious, sectarian, seditious; turbulent.
fazzoletto, *n.m.* Handkerchief.
fe, *n.f.* (*Poet.*) Faith [cp. **fede**].
febbraio [febbrAio], *n.m.* February.
febbre, *n.f.* Fever; (*colloq.*) temperature (of body); (*fig.*) excitement, heat. **Avere un po' di —**, to be feverish; **misurare la —**, to take the temperature.
febbricità [-à], *n.f.* Feverishness.
febbricitante, *a.* Feverish; restless.
febbrifugo [febbrIfugo], *n.m.* Febrifuge.
febbrile, *a.* Feverish, excited, restless; (*Med.*) febrile.
febbrilmente, *adv.* Feverishly, restlessly.
febbrone, *n.m.* Violent fever, high temperature.
febeo [febEo], *a.* (*Poet.*) Pertaining to Phoebus, the Sun.
Febo, *n.m.* (*Myth.*) Phoebus.
fecale, *a.* Faecal.
feccia [fEccia], *n.f.* Scum, sediment, dregs; (*fig.*) riff-raff, rabble.
fecciaia [fecciAia], *n.f.* Spigot-hole.
fecciaio [fecciAio], *a.* **Spina fecciaia**, spigot.
feccioso, *a.* Full of dregs.
fecciume, *n.m.* Quantity of sediment, dregs; (*fig.*) rabble, scum.
feci, *n.f.pl.* (*Med.*) Faeces, excreta, stools.
fecola [fEcola], *n.f.* Starch, fecula (from potatoes).
fecondabile [fecondAbile], *a.* Capable of fertilization.
fecondamente, *adv.* Fruitfully.
fecondare, *v.t.* To fecundate; to fertilize, to make fruitful.
fecondativo, *a.* Creative, fertilizing.
fecondatore, *n.m.* Fertilizer, one who fertilizes; stimulus.
fecondazione, *n.f.* Fecundation. **— artificiale**, artificial insemination.
fecondità [-à], *n.f.* Fecundity, fruitfulness, fertility.
fecondo, *a.* Fruitful, prolific, fertile, fecund, productive. **Terra feconda**, fertile soil.
feculento, *a.* Feculent, starchy.
fede, *n.f.* Faith, belief, creed; trust, confidence; credit; honesty; trust; certificate; (*colloq.*) wedding-ring. **Prestar — a**, to put faith in, to give credit to; **in mala —**, in bad faith; **far —**, to bear witness; **— di nascita**, birth certificate; **degno di —**, reliable; **romper —**, to break one's word.
fedecommesso, *n.m.* [cp. **fidecommesso**].
fedecommissario [fedecommissArio], *n.m.* (*Law*) Trustee.
fedele, *a.* Faithful; loyal, constant; trustworthy; exact.
fedeli, *n.m.pl.* **I fedeli**, the believers (members of a sect).

fedelmente, *adv.* Faithfully.
fedeltà [-à], *n.f.* Fidelity, faithfulness; loyalty, allegiance; (*Radio*) definition.
federa [fEdera], *n.f.* Pillow-case, pillow-slip.
federale, *a.* Federal.
federalismo, *n.m.* Federalism.
federalista (pl. **federalisti**), *n.m.* Federalist.
federalmente, *adv.* Federally.
federarsi, *v.r.* To confederate.
federativo, *a.* Federal.
federato, *n.m.* Confederate.
federazione, *n.f.* Federation.
fedifrago [fedIfrago], *a.* Faithless, treacherous, unfaithful.
fedina, *n.f.* (*Law*) Criminal record. **Le fedine,** side-whiskers (a relic of Austrian rule in Italy when officials wore such whiskers).
fegataccio [fegatAccio], *n.m.* Dare-devil.
fegatella, *n.f.* (*Bot.*) Liverwort, hepatica.
fegatelli, *n.m.pl.* Slices of pig's liver.
fegatino, *n.m.* Fowl's liver.
fegato [fEgato], *n.m.* Liver; (*fig.*) pluck, courage. **Aver disturbi di —,** to have liver trouble; (*fig.*) **aver del —,** to be plucky.
fegatoso, *a.* Bilious, acrimonious.
felce, *n.f.* (*Bot.*) Fern, bracken. **— maschio,** male fern.
felceto, *n.m.* Bed of ferns, fernery.
feldispato, *n.m.* (*Geol.*) Feldspar.
feldmaresciallo, *n.m.* (*Mil.*) Field-marshal.
felice, *a.* Happy, contented, glad; fortunate, lucky; joyful, exultant; felicitous, well-suited, apt. **Felice Lei!** you lucky fellow! **felice ritorno!** good to see you back! **Felice anno!** Happy New Year!
felicemente, *adv.* Happily, safely.
felicità [-à], *n.f.* Happiness; felicity, blissfulness, bliss. **— domestica,** domestic bliss.
felicitare, *v.t.* To congratulate; to make happy. **Dio vi feliciti!** God bless you!
felicitarsi, *v.r.* To congratulate; to rejoice. **— con un amico,** to congratulate a friend.
felicitazione, *n.f.* Felicitation, congratulation; greetings, good wishes.
felino, *a.* Feline, cattish; cruel, savage.
fellandrio [fellAndrio], *n.m.* (*Bot.*) Water-fennel.
fello, *a.* (*Poet.*) Wicked, fierce.
fellone, *n.m.a.* Felon, traitor; felonious; perfidious.
fellonescamente, *adv.* Feloniously.
fellonesco, *a.* Like a felon, felonious.
fellonia [fellonIa], *n.f.* Felony, perfidy; disloyalty.
felpa, *n.f.* Plush.
felpato, *a.* Covered with plush.
felsina [fElsina], *n.f.* **Acqua di —,** Toilet-water made at Bologna.
feltrare, *v.t.* To felt.
feltratura, *n.f.* Felting.
feltrazione, *n.f.* Filtration.
feltrificio [feltrifIcio], *n.m.* Felt factory.
feltro, *n.m.* Felt; felt hat; filter.
feluca, *n.f.* (*Naut.*) Felucca; cocked-hat.
felze, *n.f.* Cabin of a gondola; cover for this cabin.
femmina [fEmmina], *n.f.* Female; woman; hen. **Vite —,** female screw.
femmineo [femmIneo], *a.* Feminine, womanish; effeminate.
femminesco, *a.* Like a woman.
femminile, *n.m.* The feminine gender.
femminile, *a.* Feminine, womanly; female. (*Gram.*) **Genere —,** feminine gender; **scuola —,** girls' school.
femminilità [-à], *n.f.* Womanliness, femininity, feminity.
femminilmente, *adv.* Like a woman, in a womanish way.
femminino, *a.* Feminine.
femminismo, *n.m.* Feminism.
femminista, *n.m.f.* Feminist.
femorale, *a.* (*Anat.*) Femoral.
femore [fEmore], *n.m.* (*Anat.*) Femur, thigh-bone.
fenacetina, *n.f.* (*Med.*) Phenacetin.
fendente, *n.m.* Cleaving blow (with a sword); sabre-cut.
fendere [fEndere], *v.t.* To cleave to split, to chop, to cut open, to rend. **— la folla,** to squeeze through the crowd.
fendersi [fEndersi], *v.r.* To crack, to split, to burst asunder.
fendibile [fendIbile], *a.* Cleavable, possible to be split.
fendimento, *n.m.* Cleavage, splitting.
fenditoio [fenditOio], *n.m.* Blade (of a pruning or other knife).
fenditura, *n.f.* Cleavage, split, crack, cleft, fissure.
fenice, *n.f.* (*Myth.*) Phoenix.
fenicio [fenIcio], *a.* Phoenician.
fenico [fEnico], *a.* (*Chem.*) Carbolic. **Acido —,** carbolic acid.
fenicottero [fenicOttero], *n.m.* (*Zool.*) Flamingo.
fenolo, *n.m.* (*Chem.*) Phenol.
fenomenale, *a.* Phenomenal, prodigious.
fenomenico [fenomEnico], *a.* Concerning a phenomenon.
fenomeno [fenOmeno], *n.m.* Phenomenon.
fenomenologia [fenomenologIa], *n.f.* Phenomenology.
fera, *a.* (*Poet.*) Wild, savage [cp. **fiera**].
ferace, *a.* Fertile, productive, fruitful.
feracemente, *adv.* Fruitfully, productively.
feracità [-à], *n.f.* Fertility.
ferale, *a.* Fatal, deadly; funereal, dire; lugubrious.
feralmente, *adv.* Dolefully, direly; fatally.
fercolo [fErcolo], *n.m.* Dish, tray (esp. for bearing objects, etc., in a procession).
ferentari, *n.m.pl.* (*Hist. Mil.*) Light-armed troops.
feretro [fEretro], *n.m.* Bier, coffin; hearse; catafalque.
feria [fEria], *n.f.* Holiday (esp. public). (*Eccles.*) **Ferie,** week-days, ordinary days. **Prendersi le ferie,** to take one's holidays; **ferie estive,** summer holidays; **ferie natalizie,** Christmas holidays; **ferie spesate,** holidays with pay.
feriale, *a.* Ordinary; business, working. **Giorno —,** week-day, working day.
ferialmente, *adv.* Usually.
feribile [ferIbile], *a.* Vulnerable, susceptible of being wounded.
ferimento, *n.m.* Wounding, stabbing; affray.
ferinità [-à], *n.f.* Wildness, savageness, ferocity.
ferino, *a.* Wild, savage, untamed; bestial.
ferire, *v.t.* To wound, to strike, to stab; to

hit, to hurt, to injure; to offend. **— l'immaginazione,** to strike the imagination; **— l'onore,** to wound one's honour; **senza colpo —,** without resistance.
ferirsi, *v.r.* To wound oneself, to hurt oneself, to injure oneself.
ferita, *n.f.* Wound (*lit. and fig.*), injury, cut, hurt; (*Lit.*) cruelty, savagery, wildness. **Medicare una —,** to dress a wound.
ferito, *n.m.* Wounded man, injured person.
feritoia [feritOia], *n.f.* Loop-hole; (*Mech.*) vent.
feritore, feritrice, *n.m.f.* One who injures or wounds.
ferma, *n.f.* (*Mil.*) Term of (voluntary) service, service; (*Shooting*) pointing. **Cane da —,** pointer, setter.
ferma! *inter.* Stop!
fermabue, *n.m.* (*Bot.*) Rest-harrow.
fermacarte, *n.m.* Paper-weight.
fermacravatta, *n.f.* Tie-pin.
fermaglio [fermAglio], *n.m.* Clasp, buckle; brooch, clip.
fermamente, *adv.* Firmly, resolutely.
fermanello, *n.m.* Guard-ring.
fermapantalone, *n.m.* (*Cycling*) Trouser-clip.
fermapiede, *n.m.* (*Cycling*) Toe-clip.
fermare, *v.t.i.* To stop; to hold, to arrest; to fasten; to fix, to check; to keep steady; to point (of a dog). **— l'attenzione,** to fix the attention; **— la mente,** to fix one's mind upon; **far — il treno,** to stop the train.
fermarsi, *v.r.* To stop, to pause, to remain, to stay; (*Mech.*) to stall. **Fermiamoci,** let's stop; **quanto ti fermi?** how long are you staying? **— su,** to dwell upon; **— lungo la strada,** to stop on the way; **non si ferma mai** he never stops; **ci fermammo all'albergo,** we stayed at the hotel.
fermata, *n.f.* Stop, halt; stay, sojourn; call; (*Rail.*) station; (*Mus.*) pause. **— facoltativa,** request stop (for buses, etc.); **— di cinque minuti,** five minutes stop.
fermatura, *n.f.* Point of attachment; clasp.
fermentabile [fermentAbile], *a.* Capable of being fermented.
fermentare, *v.t.i.* To ferment, to effervesce.
fermentativo, *a.* Fermentative.
fermentazione, *n.f.* Fermentation.
fermento, *n.f.* Ferment, fermentation; leaven, (*fig.*) commotion, agitation, ferment.
fermezza, *n.f.* Firmness, steadiness, tenacity, consistency.
fermo, *n.m.* Stableness, stability; (*Law*) distraint, seizure; arrest. **Cane da —,** setter, pointer.
fermo, *a.* Firm, steady, stable; determined, resolute; motionless, still, stagnant, at a standstill. **Come torre ferma,** firm as a rock; **un treno —,** a standing train; **acqua ferma,** still water; **aspettare a piè —,** to wait motionless; **tener per —,** to believe firmly; **un proposito —,** a steady resolution; **punto —,** full stop; **tener —,** to stand fast; **— in posta,** poste restante.
fernambuco, *n.m.* (*Bot.*) Brazil wood, logwood.
fernette, *n.f.pl.* Wards of a key; tumblers of a lock.
feroce, *a.* Fierce, ferocious, cruel; wild, savage. **Bestie feroci,** wild beasts.
ferocemente, *adv.* Fiercely, savagely, ferociously.
ferocia, ferocità [ferOcia, -à], *n.f.* Fierceness, ferocity, cruelty, savagery.
ferraccio [ferrAccio] *n.m.* (*Metal.*) Pig-iron, cast-iron; scrap-iron,
ferraglio [ferrAglio], *n.m.* Scrap-iron, old iron.
ferragosto, *n.m.* Feast of the Assumption (August 15).
ferraio [ferrAio], *n.m.* Blacksmith.
ferraiuolo, *n.m.* Ample, heavy cloak.
ferrame, *n.m.* Iron ware, ironmongery, quantity of iron.
ferramenta, *n.f.pl.*, **ferramenti,** *n.m.pl*, Hardware, ironmongery, iron tools. **Negozio di —,** ironmonger's shop.
ferrana, *n.f.* (*Agric.*) Mixed crop for cattle, fodder.
ferrante, *a.* (Of a horse) grey.
ferrare, *v.t.* To shoe a horse; to bind with iron; to nail (of boots).
ferrareccia [ferrarEccia], *n.f.* Ironware, ironmongery, ironmonger's shop.
ferrata, *n.f.* Iron grating, railing.
ferrato, *a.* Shod (of a horse); iron; (*fig.*) well-protected, proof against. **Scarpe ferrate,** hob-nailed boots; **strada ferrata,** railroad.
ferratura, *n.f.* Shoeing (of horses); horse-shoes.
ferravecchio [ferravEcchio], *n.m.* Dealer in old iron; bric-a-brac.
ferrazzolo, *n.m.* Ironworker.
ferreo [fErreo], *a.* Strong, robust, hard, inflexible, unyielding; made of iron. **Corona ferrea,** iron crown.
ferretto, *n.m.* Small iron tool; iron gadget.
ferriata, *n.f.* Iron grating, railing.
ferriera, *n.f.* Ironworks, iron foundry; forge.
ferrifero [ferrIfero], *a.* Ferriferous.
ferrigno, *a.* Iron-grey; ferruginous.
ferro, *n.m.* Iron; irons (fetters); tool; horse-shoes; sword. **— da cavallo,** horse-shoe; **— da stirare,** flat-iron; **— da calza,** knitting-needle; **bistecca ai ferri,** grilled steak; **filo di —,** iron wire; **miniera di —,** iron mine; **mettere ai ferri,** to put in chains; **mettere a — e fuoco,** to lay waste; **— battuto,** wrought iron; **essere di —,** to be made of iron.
ferroso, *a.* Ferruginous, ferrous.
ferrovia [ferrovIa], *n.f.* Railway, railroad; (*colloq.*) railway station. **Ferrovie dello Stato,** State Railways; **per —,** by rail.
ferroviario [ferroviArio], *a.* Railway, rail. **Il traffico —,** railway traffic; **linea ferroviaria,** railway line; **rete ferroviaria,** railway system.
ferroviere, *n.m.* Railway man.
ferrugineo [ferrugIneo], **ferruginoso,** *a.* Ferruginous.
ferruminatore, *n.m.* Blow-pipe; blow-lamp.
fertile [fErtile], *a.* Fertile; fruitful, productive; prolific.
fertilità [-à], *n.f.* Fertility; fruitfulness, productivity.
fertilizzante, *n.f.* (*Agric.*) Fertilizer.
fertilizzare, *v.t.* To fertilize, to make productive.
fertilizzatore, *n.m.* Fertilizer; manure.

fertilmente, *adv.* Fruitfully, productively.
ferula [fErula], *n.f.* Rod, cane, ferule; wand.
fervente, *a.* Fervent, ardent, zealous, eager.
ferventemente, *adv.* Fervently.
fervenza, *n.f.* Fervour, ardour [cp. **fervore**].
fervere [fErvere], *v.i.* To be fervent, to be eager; to grow hot; to effervesce. **Il lavoro ferve,** work is very intense; **fervono i preparativi,** preparations are well advanced.
fervidamente, *adv.* Fervidly, ardently.
fervidezza, fervidità [-à], *n.f.* Fervour, ardour [cp. **fervore**].
fervido [fErvido], *a.* Fervid, ardent, impassioned.
fervore, *n.m.* Fervour, ardour, warmth, zeal; intense heat.
fervorino, *n.m.* Appeal, exhortation, admonition. **Fare un —,** to entreat, to make an appeal.
fervorosamente, *adv.* Fervidly, with great fervour.
fervoroso, *a.* Fervid, entreating, warm.
ferza, *n.f.* Scourge [cp. **sferza**].
ferzo, *n.m.* (*Naut.*) Strips of sail-cloth.
fescennino, *a.* (*Poet.*) Fescennine.
fessipedi [fessIpedi], *n.m.pl.* (*Zool.*) Cloven-hoofed animals.
fesso, *n.m.* Cleft, crack, fissure, chink; (*fig.*) blockhead.
fesso, *a.* Cracked; cloven, cleft; hoarse (of sound); (*fig.*) stupid, silly. **Dall'unghie fesse,** cloven-hoofed; **campana fessa,** cracked bell; **egli è un —,** he's a blockhead.
fessolino, *n.m.* Chink, crevice, small crack.
fessura, *n.f.* Fissure, cleft, crevice, slit, opening.
festa, *n.f.* Festival, festivity, feast; holiday; vacation; anniversary; rejoicing. **Far —,** to take a holiday, to make merry, to have a good time; **— nazionale,** national holiday; **mezza —,** half-holiday; **augurare le buone feste,** to wish someone a Merry Christmas, or Easter; **far — a qualcuno,** to welcome someone; **far la — a,** to bump off; **abiti da —,** one's Sunday best; **conciare uno pel dì delle feste,** to give someone a sound thrashing.
festaiolo, *n.m.* Reveller; master of the revels.
festante, *a.* Joyful, rejoicing, jubilant.
festeggiamento, *n.m.* Celebration, festivity.
festeggiare, *v.t.* To celebrate; to entertain, to welcome; to feast.
festevole [festEvole], *a.* Festive, joyful, merry, gay.
festevolezza, *n.f.* Rejoicing, joy, mirth.
festevolmente, *adv.* Festively, joyfully.
festicciola [festicciOla], *n.f.* Family party, family gathering.
festino, *n.m.* Feast, banquet, merry-making.
festività [-à], *n.f.* Festivity, rejoicing.
festivo, *a.* Festal, festive; merry. **Abiti festivi,** Sunday clothes; **riposo —,** Sunday rest; (*Rail*) **biglietto —,** week-end ticket.
festonare, *v.t.* To festoon.
festone, *n.m.* Festoon.
festosamente, *adv.* Joyfully, merrily.
festosità [-à], *n.f.* Festivity, mirth, joy; gaiety, joviality.
festoso, *a.* Festive, merry, joyful.
festuca, *n.f.* Straw, wisp of straw; mote.
fetale, *a.* (*Med.*) Foetal.
fetente, *a.* Fetid, stinking; filthy.
feticcio [fetIccio], *n.m.* Fetish.
feticismo, *n.m.* Fetishism.
feticista, *n.m.f.* Fetishist.
fetidamente, *adv.* Fetidly, stinkingly.
fetido [fEtido], *a.* Fetid, stinking, rank.
fetidume, *n.m.* Stench, rottenness, filth.
feto, *n.m.* (*Anat.*) Foetus.
fetore, *n.m.* Stink, fetidness, stench.
fetta, *n.f.* Slice, strip; part, share; (beef-) steak. **Una — di prosciutto,** a slice of ham; **pane a —,** sliced bread; **una — di pane tostato,** a piece of toast.
fettina, *n.f.* Small slice, sliver.
fettone, *n.m.* Large slice, hunk.
fettuccia [fettUccia], *n.f.* Tape, ribbon; small slice.
fettuccine, *n.f.pl.* Kind of ribbon-shaped spaghetti; noodles.
feudale, *a.* Feudal.
feudalismo, *n.f.* Feudalism.
feudalmente, *adv.* Feudally.
feudatario [feudatArio], *n.m.a.* Feudatory.
feudo, *n.m.* Fief, feud, domain, possession.
fez, *n.m.* Fez, tarboosh.
fia (*obs.*) [cp. **sia, essere**].
fiaba, *n.f.* Fable, fairy tale; (*fig.*) falsehood.
fiacca, *n.f.* Slackness, laziness; lassitude, weakness, indolence. (*Mil.*) **Battere la —,** to shirk work, to swing the lead.
fiaccacollo, *n.m.* Dangerous person or thing. **A —,** headlong.
fiaccamente, *adv.* Languidly.
fiaccamento, *n.m.* Breakdown.
fiaccare, *v.t.* To break down, to overcome; to exhaust; to wear out, to tire out, to prostrate.
fiaccarsi, *v.r.* **— il collo,** to break one's neck.
fiaccatura, *n.f.* Breaking up, splitting up.
fiaccheraio [fiaccherAio], *n.m.* Cabman, cabby.
fiacchere [fiAcchere], *n.m.* Cab.
fiacchezza, *n.f.* Slackness; weakness, lassitude, weariness, dullness; laziness.
fiacco, *a.* Slack; weak, tired, feeble; inefficient, unreliable; dull, sluggish.
fiaccola [fiAccola], *n.f.* Torch; blow-lamp.
fiaccolata, *n.f.* Torchlight procession.
fiaccona, *n.f.* Extreme lassitude, laziness.
fiaccone, *n.m.* Sluggard, slacker.
fiala, *n.f.* Phial.
fialetta, *n.f.* Small flask, bottle.
fiamma, *n.f.* Flame; blaze, fire; (*Naut.*) pennant; (*Mil.*) facings (on the collar); (*fig.*) lover, mistress. **Mettere a fuoco e —,** to lay waste; **la casa è in fiamme,** the house is in flames *or* ablaze; (*Motor.*) **ritorno di —,** back-fire; **— ossidrica,** oxyhydrogen flame.
fiammante, *a.* Blazing, flaming. **Nuovo —,** brand-new.
fiammare, *v.i.* To flame, to blaze, to shine.
fiammata, *n.f.* Blaze, sudden flame, flash. **Fare una —,** to make a good fire.
fiammeggiante, *a.* Flaming, blazing.
fiammeggiare, *v.i.* To flame, to blaze; to flash, to shine.
fiammella, *n.f.* Little flame, little light, flicker.
fiammetta, *n.f.* Flicker
fiammiferaio [fiammiferAio], *n.m.* Match vendor.

fiammifero [fiammIfero], *n.m.* Match. **Scatola di fiammiferi,** box of matches; **scatola per fiammiferi,** match-box.
fiammingo, *n.m.a.* Flemish.
fiammola [fiAmmola], *n.f.* (*Bot.*) Species of clematis.
fiancare, *v.t.* (*Arch.*) To strengthen the sides (of an arch, etc.); to flank.
fiancata, *n.f.* Blow on the side of the body; (*Naut.*) broadside.
fiancheggiamento, *n.m.* Flanking, propping; support; (*Mil.*) protecting the flank.
fiancheggiare, *v.t.* To flank, to border; to prop, to support; (*Mil.*) to flank.
fiancheggiatore, *n.m.* Flanker, supporter; skirmisher.
fianchetta, *n.f.* Side-piece (of a coat); waist-band (of trousers).
fianchetto, *n.m.* (*Arch.*) Lateral part of an arch.
fianco, *n.m.* Flank, side. **Al —,** by the side; **di —,** at the side, sideways; **a — di,** at the side of; **la porta di —,** the side door; **presentare il — alla critica,** to lay oneself open to criticism; (*Mil.*) **— destro! — sinistro!** right turn! left turn! (*Naut.*) **— destro, sinistro,** starboard, port side.
fiancuto, *a.* Broad in the beam; wide-flanked.
Fiandra, Fiandre, *n.f.s.pl.* (*Geog.*) Flanders.
fiasca, *n.f.* Flask, flagon; soldier's water-bottle.
fiascaio [fiascAio], *n.m.* Flask-maker.
fiascheggiare, *v.i.* (*colloq.*) To prove a fiasco, to fail.
fiaschetta, *n.f.* Small flask, flat bottle, hip-flask.
fiaschetteria [fiaschetterIa], *n.f.* Wine-shop; bar, refreshment room.
fiaschettone, *n.m.* (*Zool.*) Long-tailed tit.
fiasco, *n.m.* Flask (encased in straw, *e.g.* Chianti bottle), bottle; (*fig.*) utter failure, fiasco, ridiculous breakdown. **La commedia ha fatto —,** the comedy has been a complete failure.
fiat, *n.m.* Instant. **In un —,** in an instant.
fiata, *n.f.* (*obs.*) Time. **Molte fiate,** many times.
fiatare, *v.i.* To breathe; to whisper, to speak quietly. **Nessuno fiatava,** not a word was heard.
fiatata, *n.f.* Breathing.
fiato, *n.m.* Breath, breathing, respiration; slight breeze; strength. **Trattenere il —,** to hold one's breath; **prender —,** to take breath; **— sprecato,** wasted efforts; (*Mus.*) **strumenti a —,** wind instruments; **tutto d'un —,** all in one breath, without stopping.
fibbia [fIbbia], *n.f.* Buckle; clasp.
fibbione, *n.m.* Heavy buckle (on horses' harness).
fibra, *n.f.* Fibre; filament; nerve, strength, constitution, strength, stamina, backbone. **— vegetale,** vegetable fibre; **un uomo di —,** a man of strong character, of sound constitution.
fibrilla, *n.f.* Fibril.
fibrillare, *a.* Fibrillar.
fibrina, *n.f.* Fibrin.
fibrosità [-**à**], *n.f.* Fibrosity.
fibroso, *a.* Fibrous.
fibula [fIbula], *n.f.* Fibula (in all senses).
fibulare, *a.* Fibular.
ficaio [ficAio], *n.m.* Fig plantation. **Mese —,** September.
ficalbo, *n.m.* (*Bot.*) White fig.
ficcabile [ficcAbile], *a.* Capable of insertion.
ficcamento, *n.m.* Insertion, act of inserting.
ficcanaso, *n.m.* Meddler, intruder; Nosey Parker; busybody.
ficcare, *v.t.* To drive in, to thrust in, to poke into; to fix, to nail; to intrude. **— il naso in,** to poke one's nose into.
ficcarsi, *v.r.* To intrude into, to thrust into; to hide in. **Dove si è ficcato ?** Where is he hiding himself? **— in testa una cosa,** to get an idea into one's head.
ficchino, *n.m.* Meddler, Paul Pry.
fico, *n.m.* Fig; fig-tree. **Non vale un —,** it isn't worth a fig; **— secco,** dried fig; **fichi d'India,** prickly pears.
ficoso, *a.* (*colloq.*) Prim, affected.
fida, *n.f.* (*Agric.*) Land let for grazing.
fidalgo, *n.m.* Spanish hidalgo.
fidamente, *adv.* Faithfully.
fidanza, *n.f.* (*Lit*) Trust, confidence.
fidanzamento, *n.m.* Engagement, betrothal.
fidanzare, *v.t.* To affiance, to engage, to betroth.
fidanzarsi, *v.r.* To become engaged, to be betrothed.
fidanzato, fidanzata, *n.m.f.* Fiancé, fiancée; sweetheart.
fidare, *v.t.i.* To trust, to confide in, to rely upon; to entrust. **Egli fidava in lui,** he relied upon him.
fidarsi, *v.r.* To place trust in, to trust oneself to; to rely upon. **Si fidava di lui,** he trusted him; **— è bene, non — è meglio,** to trust is good, not to trust is better; **non mi fido,** I daren't.
fidatamente, *adv.* Faithfully, trustily.
fidatezza, *n.f.* Trustworthiness, fidelity.
fidato, *a.* Reliable, trustworthy, dependable, faithful. **Un impiegato —,** a trusted clerk.
fidecommesso, *n.m.* (*Law*) Deed of trust.
fideismo, *n.m.* (*Religion*) Fideism; justification by faith.
fideiussione, *n.f.* (*Law*) Suretyship.
fideiussore, *n.m.* (*Law*) Bailor, surety.
fidente, *a.* Confiding, trustful.
fidentemente, *adv.* Confidingly.
fidenziano, *a.* (*Lit.*) Macaronic, dog Latin (of style).
Fidia [fIdia], *n.m.* (*Hist.*) Phidias.
fidiaco [fidIaco], *a.* In the style of the sculptor Phidias; majestic in beauty.
fido, *n.m.* (*Comm.*) Credit. **A —,** on credit; **far —,** to give credit.
fido, *a.* Faithful, trusty, reliable; devoted.
fiducia [fidUcia], *n.f.* Confidence, faith, trust, reliance, assurance. **Nutro —,** I have confidence; **voto di —,** vote of confidence; (*Comm.*) **casa di —,** trustworthy house; **persona di —,** reliable person.
fiduciale, *a.* Trustworthy, fiducial. (*Geom.*) **Linea —,** base line.
fiduciariamente, *adv.* Trustingly; by means of a fiduciary.
fiduciario [fiduciArio], *a.* Fiduciary, trustee.
fiduciosamente, *adv.* Confidently, trustingly.
fiducioso, *a.* Confident, trustful, hopeful, relying on.

fiele, *n.m.* Gall, bile; (*fig.*) acrimony, rancour, bitterness.
fien, fieno [fIeno], *obs.* **saranno** [cp. **essere**].
fienaccio [fienAccio], *n.m.* Coarse hay.
fienagione, *n.f.* Hay-time; hay-harvest; hay-making.
fienaia [fienAia], *n.f.* Hay-loft, hay-barn.
fienaio [fienAio], *a.* Hay. **Falce fienaia,** scythe; **forca fienaia,** hay-fork.
fienile, *n.m.* Hay-loft.
fieno, *n.m.* Hay. **Far —,** to make hay; **febbre del —,** hay-fever.
fiera (1), *n.f.* Fair; exhibition; market; show. **— di beneficenza,** charity bazaar; **— campionaria,** sample fair; **roba di —,** trash; **— delle industrie inglesi,** British Industries Fair.
fiera (2), *n.f.* Wild beast.
fieramente, *adv.* Vehemently, fiercely; boldly; strongly.
fierezza, *n.f.* Pride (in a good sense), self-respect, dignity; fierceness, energy; vivacity; intrepidity.
fiero, *a.* Proud, high-spirited, self-respecting; disdainful; vehement, violent, fierce; severe. **Una fiera malattia,** a grave disease; **un carattere —,** a noble, proud character.
fievole [fiEvole], *a.* Feeble, weak, dim (of light or sound).
fievolezza, *n.f.* Feebleness, weakness.
fievolmente, *adv.* Feebly.
fifa, *n.f.* (*Zool.*) Plover; (*colloq.*) fear, cowardice, funk. **Aver —,** to be in a funk.
figaro [fIgaro], *n.m.* Barber; bolero.
figgere [fIggere], *v.t.* To fix, to fix in. **— lo sguardo,** to stare.
figlia [fIglia], *n.f.* Daughter; girl; (*Comm.*) counterfoil.
figliare, *v.t.* To bring forth (of animals); to farrow (pigs); to pup; to kitten; to calve, to foal, to lamb, etc.
figliastra, figliastro [figliAstra, figliAstro], *n.f.m.* Step-daughter, step-son.
figliata, *n.f.* Litter (of young).
figliatura, *n.f.* Bringing forth, giving birth.
figliazione, *n.f.* Parentage; issue, progeny, offspring. **Senza —,** without issue.
figlio [fIglio], *n.m.* Son; child; boy. **— maggiore,** eldest son; **— unico,** only child; **— naturale,** natural son, bastard; **aver cinque figli,** to have five children.
figlioccia, figlioccio [figliOccia, figliOccio], *n.f.m.* God-daughter, god-son.
figliuola, figliola, *n.f.* Daughter; girl.
figliuolanza, *n.f.* Offspring, progeny, children.
figliuolo, figliolo, *n.m.* Child; son; boy. **Un buon —,** a good fellow.
figmento, *n.m.* Figment.
fignolo [fIgnolo], *n.m.* (*Med.*) Boil.
fignoloso, *a.* Having boils.
figulina, *n.f.* Potter's craft.
figulo [fIgulo], *n.m.* Potter.
figura, *n.f.* Figure (in all senses), shape, form, appearance, image; picture, illustration; (*Cards*) court card. **Far una cattiva —,** to cut a poor figure; **far la — di,** to appear to be; **per —,** for show only; **un libro con belle figure,** a book with fine illustrations; (*Naut.*) **— di prua,** figure-head; **— rettorica,** figure of speech.
figurabile [figurAbile], *a.* Imaginable, figurable.
figuraccia [figurAccia], *n.f.* Bad figure. **Fare una —,** to cut a poor figure.
figuramento, *n.m.* Form, figure, configuration [cp. **configuramento**].
figurante, *n.m.* (*Theat.*) Ballet-dancer; super, walker-on.
figurare, *v.t.i.* To figure; to represent, to illustrate; to appear; to act, to play a part, to pretend; to dress well. **Egli figura tra i benefattori,** he figures as one of the patrons; (*Comm.*) **— nel conto,** to appear in the account.
figurarsi, *v.r.* To fancy, to imagine, to suppose. **Figurati! Si figuri!** just imagine! Fancy that! Not at all!
figuratamente, *adv.* Symbolically, figuratively (esp. in speech).
figurativamente, *adv.* Figuratively.
figurativo, *a.* Figurative, pictorial, plastic.
figurato, *a.* Figurative, metaphorical; figured, drawn, illustrated. (*Comm.*) **Conto —,** pro forma account.
figuratore, figuratrice, *n.m.f.* Designer, illustrator.
figurazione, *n.f.* Figuration, representation; fiction.
figuretta, figurina, *n.f.* Little figure; picture card; figurine, statuette.
figurinaio [figurinAio], *n.m.* Pedlar of statuettes.
figurino, *n.m.* Fashion-plate, model, pattern; book of fashions; fop, dandy.
figurista, *n.m.* Portrait-painter.
figuro, *n.m.* Blackguard, knave, scamp, cad, scoundrel.
fila, *n.f.* File, line, row, rank. **In prima —,** in the first row, in the first rank; **una — d'alberi,** a row of trees; **una — di carozze,** a line of carriages; **far —,** to form a queue; **di —,** one after the other; **tre giorni di —,** three days running; **— di stanze,** suite of rooms; (*Mil.*) **rompete le file!** dismiss! **per — destra!** right wheel! (*Theat.*) **palco di prima —,** box in the first tier.
filabile [filAbile], *a.* Suitable for spinning.
filaccia [filAccia], *n.f.* Bandage; thread. **— di cotone,** lint.
filaccione, *n.m.* Fishing-line; night-line.
filaccioso, filaccicoso, *a.* Fibrous; ragged, frayed.
filagrana, *n.f.* Filigree [cp. **filigrana**].
filaloro, *n.m.* Gold-wire drawer.
filamento, *n.m.* Filament, thread, fibre.
filamentoso, *a.* Filamentary.
filanda, *n.f.* Spinning-mill, silk-factory.
filandaia [filandAia], *n.f.* Silk-spinner.
filandiere, *n.m.* Silk-manufacturer.
filantropia [filantropIa], *n.f.* Philanthropy.
filantropicamente, *adv.* Philanthropically.
filantropico [filantrOpico], *a.* Philanthropic.
filantropo [filAntropo], *n.m.* Philanthropist.
filare, *v.t.i.* To spin; to pour out; to trickle, to run, to be off, to get clear; to rope (of a liquid); to smoke (of a lamp or candle); to flirt; (*Naut.*) to pay out (rope), to ease off (rope, etc.). **— via,** to march off; **— diritto,** to go straight; **far — una persona,** to make a person toe the line; **— a cento miglia,** to do a hundred miles an hour; **questo**

sciroppo fila, this syrup is ropy; **questo lume fila,** this lamp is smoking; **— all'inglese,** to take French leave; **fila!** be off with you!
filare, *n.m.* Line, row; range. **Filari delle vite,** rows of vines.
filarmonico [filarmOnico], *a.* Philharmonic.
filastrocca, *n.f.* Rigmarole, balderdash, yarn; children's nonsense rhyme.
filata, *n.f.* Long row, row.
filatelia [filatelIa], *n.f.* Philately, stamp-collecting.
filatelico [filatElico], *a.* Philatelic.
filatelista (*pl.* **filatelisti**), *n.m.* Philatelist, stamp-collector.
filaticcio [filatIccio], *n.m.* Coarse silk, floss-silk.
filato, *n.m.* Spun yarn. **I filati di cotone,** cotton yarns.
filato, *p.p.a.* Spun; run, hurried.
filatoio [filatOio], *n.m.* Spinning-jenny; spinning-mill.
filatore, filatrice, *n.m.f.* Spinner; cotton operative.
filatterio [filattErio], *n.m.* Phylactery.
filatura, *n.f.* Spinning; spinning-mill.
fileggiare, *v.i.* (*Naut.*) To flap (of sails).
filellenico [filellEnico], *a.* Philhellenic.
filelleno, *n.m.* Philhellene.
filettare, *v.t.* To border, to ornament with lines, to line; (*Mech.*) to thread (a screw).
filettatura, *n.f.* Edging, border; (*Mech.*) screw-thread.
filetto, *n.m.* Fillet, strip, band, (corporal's) stripe; thread (of screw); fillet (of beef), sirloin; frenum; snaffle-rein; fine penstroke.
filiale, *n.m.* Branch office or shop, branch establishment. **Una — della Banca d'Italia,** a branch of the Bank of Italy.
filiale, *a.* Filial. **Casa —,** branch office.
filialmente, *adv.* In a filial way.
filiazione, *n.f.* Filiation, descent; derivation.
filibustiere, *n.m.* Filibuster; adventurer.
filiera, *n.f.* (*Mech.*) Draw-plate; screw-plate; wire-gauge.
filiforme, *a.* Thread-like, filiform.
filiggine [filIggine], *n.f.* Soot [cp. **fuliggine**].
filigginoso, *a.* Sooty.
filigrana, *n.f.* Filigree; watermark (of paper).
filigranato, *a.* Filigreed. **Carta filigranata,** water-marked paper.
filipendula [filipEndula], *n.f.* (*Bot.*) Drop-wort.
filippica [filIppica], *n.f.* (*Lit.*) Philippic.
filippino, *n.m.* Native of the Philippines; (*Eccles.*) Oratorian.
filisteo [filistEo], *n.m.a.* Philistine.
fillossera [fillOssera], *n.f.* (*Agric.*) Phylloxera.
film, *n.m.* (*Cinema.*) Film. **Girare un —,** to shoot a film; **— di attualità,** newsreel [cp. **pellicola**].
filo, *n.m.* Thread (in all senses), yarn; wire; edge (of cutting instrument); blade (of grass); flow (of stream); clue, weak voice. **Aver del — da torcere,** to have work cut out for one; **dar del — da torcere,** to give no end of trouble; **— d'erba,** blade of grass; **il — d'un rasoio,** a razor-edge; **— spinato,** barbed wire; **— di refe,** sewing cotton; **— a piombo,** plumb-line; **— di ordito,** warp (weaving); **con un — di voce,** with a thin voice; **per — e per segno,** in detail, minutely; **passare a — di spada,** to put to the edge of the sword; **esser sospeso a un —,** to hang upon a thread; **un — (di qualcosa),** a bit (of something); (*Elect.*) **i fili,** the wiring; **un — telegrafico,** a telegraph wire; **senza fili,** wireless; **il — della corrente,** the stream (where the current is strongest); **esser ridotto un —,** to be worn to a shadow.
filobus [fIlobus], *n.m.* Trolley-bus.
filodrammatico [filodrammAtico], *n.m.* Amateur actor; lover of the drama.
filologia [filologIa], *n.f.* Philology.
filologicamente, *adv.* Philologically.
filologico [filolOgico], *a.* Philological.
filologo [filOlogo], *n.m.* Philologist.
Filomela, Filomena, *n.f.* (*Myth.*) Philomel; nightingale.
filoncino, *n.m.* Long, thin roll of bread; (*Geol.*) vein of mineral.
filondente, *n.m.* Kind of coarse canvas.
filone, *n.m.* (*Geol.*) Vein of mineral; stream of current; long roll of bread; (*colloq.*) cunning, crafty man. **— della corrente,** part of the stream where the current is strongest; (*colloq.*) **prendere un —,** to get an idea into one's head; **— di lava,** stream of lava; **— di marea,** tide-race.
filoso, *a.* Stringy, thready; filamentous.
filosofale, *a.* Philosophical. **Pietra —,** philosopher's stone.
filosofare, filosofeggiare, *v.t.* To philosophize; to muse, to ponder.
filosofema, *n.m.* Philosophical treatise, subject for philosophical disputation.
filosofia [filosofIa], *n.f.* Philosophy; (*colloq.*) serenity; resignation.
filosoficamente, *adv.* Philosophically.
filosofico [filosOfico], *a.* Philosophical.
filosofo [filOsofo], *n.m.* Philosopher.
filossera [cp. **fillossera**].
filovia [filovIa], *n.f.* Trolley-bus or telpher line.
filtrare, *v.t.i.* To filter, to filtrate, to strain, to percolate.
filtrazione, *n.f.* Filtration, filtering.
filtro, *n.m.* Filter, strainer; philtre, love-potion.
filugello, *n.m.* Silkworm.
filusello, *n.m.* Tissue made from floss silk.
filza, *n.f.* String; series, list; file (of papers); running stitch. **Una — di nomi,** an endless string of names; **una — di fandonie,** a tissue of lies; **una — di perle,** a string of pearls.
fimbria [fImbria], *n.f.* (*obs.*) Hem, fringe; (*Mus.*) finale.
fimo, *n.m.* Dung.
finale, *n.m.* End, close; (*Sport*) final; (*Mus.*) finale.
finale, *a.* Final, last, ultimate, definitive.
finalista (*pl.* **finalisti**), *n.m.* Finalist.
finalità [-à], *n.f.* Finality; purpose.
finalmente, *adv.* Finally, at last, in the end.
finamente, *adv.* Finely, with fineness.
finanche, financo, *adv.* Also, even.
finanza, *n.f.* Finance; Customs; (in *pl.*) finances, revenue, income. **Guardia di —,** customs official; **Ministro delle Finanze,** Finance Minister; **le mie finanze non me lo permettono,** my financial circumstances will not permit me.
finanziare, *v.t.* To finance, to provide with capital.

finanziariamente, *adv.* Financially.
finanziario [finanziArio], *a.* Financial. **Situazione —,** financial situation.
finanziatore, *n.m.* Financier, financer, financing party.
finanziere, *n.m.* Financier; Customs officer; (*Mil.*) frontier guard.
finca, *n.f.* Column (of writing, print, etc.), list.
finchè, *conj.* Till, until; as long as; while. **— non,** until; **— vivrà,** as long as he will live.
fine (1), *n.f.* End, close, termination; extremity, limit; conclusion, completion. **Essere in — di vita,** to be at the point of death; **condurre a —,** to complete; **dal principio alla —,** from beginning to end; **alla — dei conti,** all things considered; **alla —, in —,** after all; **volgere alla —,** to draw to a close; **mettere — a,** to put an end to; **alla — dell'anno,** at the end of the year; **non ne vedo la —,** I don't see where it will end.
fine (2), *n.m.* Aim, end, object, purpose. **A che — ?** to what end? **aver dei secondi fini,** to have an ulterior motive; **a fine di,** in order to; (*Comm.*) **salvo buon —,** reserving due payment, under the usual reserve.
fine, *a.* Slender, delicate, fine; thin, slim; refined; cunning.
finemente, *adv.* Finely; properly.
finestra, *n.f.* Window. **— sporgente,** bay-window; **— a due battenti,** french window; **— a ghigliottina, — a saliscendi,** sash-window; **guardare dalla —,** to look out of the window; **farsi alla —,** to come to the window.
finestrata, *n.f.* Slamming shut the window (in anger, etc.); row of windows.
finestrato, *a.* Fenestrated.
finestrino, *n.m.* Small window; guichet; (*Rail.*) carriage window, booking-office window.
finestrone, *n.m.* Large window; shop-window.
finetto, *n.m.* Thin, soft flannel.
finezza, *n.f.* Fineness, daintiness, exquisiteness; politeness, polish; shrewdness.
fingere [fIngere], *v.t.i.* To feign, to dissemble, to simulate; to pretend; to imagine, to suppose; to feature, to represent. **— una malattia,** to feign sickness; **finse di non vedermi,** he pretended not to see me.
fingersi [fIngersi], *v.r.* To feign, to pretend to be. **— pazzo,** to feign madness.
fingimento, *n.m.* Dissembling, feigning.
fingitore, fingitrice, *n.m.f.* Dissembler.
finimento, *n.m.* Completion, finishing touch; ornament, set (of jewelry, etc.). **Finimenti,** harness (of horse).
finimondo, *n.m.* End of the world; ruin, disaster, cataclysm.
finire, *v.t.i.* To finish, to end, to terminate, to conclude; to come to an end; to die. **È ora di finirla,** it is time to stop it; **— un discorso,** to conclude a speech; **Finitela!** Stop it! **questo non mi finisce,** this does not satisfy me; **andare a — male,** to come to grief; **tutto finisce,** everything comes to an end; **— bene,** to end well; **per —,** to sum up; **un per —,** a joke, a chestnut.
finitamente, *adv.* Finitely, completely; perfectly.
finitezza, *n.f.* Finish, perfection
finitimo [finItimo], *a.* Adjoining, neighbouring, contiguous.
finito, *p.p.a.* Finished, ended; skilful, consummate; perfect; exhausted, done for. **È bell'e finita,** it's all over; **farla finita,** to put an end to it; **un — musicista,** an accomplished musician; **un uomo —,** a man done for.
finitura, *n.f.* Completion, end, finish; finishing touch.
Finlandia [finlAndia], *n.f.* (*Geog.*) Finland.
finnico [fInnico], *a.* Finnish.
fino, *n.m.* (*Comm.*) Fineness, purity, quality; standard. **Ridurre il — di una moneta,** to lower the standard of a coin.
fino, *a.* Fine, thin, subtle; pure, dainty, excellent; keen, sharp; clever, cunning, shrewd. **Udito —,** a delicate ear; **persona fina,** refined person; **lineamenti fini,** delicate features.
fino, fin, *prep.adv.* Till, until, as long as; as far as; even. **— a Roma,** as far as Rome; **— a domani,** until tomorrow; **fin qui,** until now, hitherto, as far as here; **— ad ora,** up to now; **fin dove ?** how far? **fin quando ?** how long? **— là,** as far as there.
finocchio [finOcchio], *n.m.* (*Bot.*) Fennel.
finocchiona, *n.f.* Sausage flavoured with fennel.
finora, *adv.* Till now, as yet, hitherto.
finta, *n.f.* Simulation, feint, pretence; false pocket; (*Fencing*) feint; (*Football*) dribbling. **Far — di,** to pretend to, **lo fa solo per finta,** he's only pretending.
fintaggine [fintAggine], *n.f.* Insincerity; habit of pretending; pretence.
fintamente, *adv.* Insincerely, feignedly, falsely.
fintantochè, *adv.* Till, until.
finteria [finterIa], *n.f.* Insincerity.
finto, *n.m.* Hypocrite.
finto, *p.p.a.* Feigned; sham, artificial, false, counterfeit. **Denti finti,** false teeth; **capelli finti,** false hair; (*Mil.*) **finta battaglia,** sham fight.
finzione, *n.f.* Simulation, deceit, fiction, pretence; sham, imposture. **— giuridica,** legal fiction.
fio, *n.m.* Penalty. **Pagare il —,** to pay the penalty.
fiocaggine [fiocAggine], *n.f.* Hoarseness; loss of voice.
fiocamente, *adv.* Hoarsely.
fiocca, *n.f.* (*Anat.*) Instep.
fioccare, *v.i.* To snow, to fall in flakes; (*fig.*) to shower; to rain (of bullets). **I rimproveri fioccavano,** reproaches poured in; **le granate fioccavano,** it rained shells.
fiocchettare, *v.t.* To ornament with tassels.
fiocco, *n.m.* Flake, tuft, tassel; powder-puff; lock (of wool); (*Naut.*) jib; (*colloq.*) **Coi fiocchi,** first rate, capital; **un pianista coi fiocchi,** a first-rate pianist.
fiochezza, *n.f.* Hoarseness; debility.
fiocina [fiOcina], *n.f.* Harpoon; fishing-spear.
fiocinare, *v.t.* To harpoon.
fiocine [fiOcine], *n.m.* Grape-skin, grape-stone.
fiociniere, fiocinino, *n.m.* Harpooner.

fioco, *a.* Hoarse, weak, faint (esp. of sound); dim (of light).
fionco, *n.m.* (*Naut.*) Halyard.
fionda, *n.f.* Sling, catapult.
fioraia [fiorAia], *n.f.* Flower-girl.
fioraio [fiorAio], *n.m.* Florist.
fiorame, *n.m.* Floral design. **Una stoffa a fiorami,** flowered material.
fiorato, *a.* Flowered.
fiorcappuccio [fiorcappUccio], *n.m.* (*Bot.*) Larkspur.
fiordaligi, fiordaliso, *n.f.* Lily, fleur-de-lis.
fiordo, *n.m.* (*Geog.*) Fjord.
fiore, *n.m.* Flower; blossom, bloom; (*fig.*) prime, lustre; pick, choice; passages of verse or prose. (*Cards*) **Fiori,** clubs; **il fior —,** the best part; **una pianta in —,** a plant in bloom; **a fior d'acqua,** floating on the surface; **a fior di pelle,** superficially; **a fior di terra,** even with the ground; **in pieno —,** in full bloom; **fior di roba,** first-rate goods; **nel fior dell'età,** in the prime of life; (*colloq.*) **un fior di galantuomo,** one of the best, a very honest man.
fiorellino, fioretto, fiorettino, *n.m., dim.* Little flower.
fiorente, *a.* Flourishing, blooming.
fiorentemente, *adv.* Flourishingly, prosperously.
fiorentinamente, *adv.* In the Florentine manner.
fiorentineggiare, *v.i.* To use Florentine idioms, to affect the Florentine manner of speaking.
fiorentineria [fiorentinerIa], *n.f.* Affectation of Florentine speech.
fiorentinesco, *a.* Florentine.
fiorentinità [-à], *n.f.* Correctness of Florentine speech.
fiorentino, *n.m.* Native of Florence; Florentine speech.
fiorentino, *a.* Florentine.
fioretto, *n.m.* Little flower; (*Fencing*) foil; selection of choice literary passages; (*Mus.*) grace-note. **I Fioretti di San Francesco,** The Little Flowers of St. Francis; **tirare di —,** to practise foil fencing.
fiori, *n.m.pl.* (*Cards*) Clubs. **Il fante di —,** the knave of clubs.
floricultore, *n.m.* Floriculturist, nurseryman.
fiorifero [fiorIfero], *a.* Flowering.
fiorino, *n.m.* Florin.
fiorire, *v.t.i.* To blossom, to bloom, to flower; (*fig.*) to flourish, to thrive, to prosper; to strew with flowers. **Le arti fiorivano,** the arts flourished; **quando fioriscono le rose?** when do roses bloom?
fiorista, *n.m.f.* Maker or vendor of artificial flowers; flower-painter; nurseryman.
fiorita, *n.f.* Flowers or leaves strewn on the ground in front of a religious procession; collection of songs or poems; flowering.
fioritamente, *adv.* In a florid style.
fiorito, *a.* Flowery; in bloom; florid. **Un parlare —,** a florid style of speaking.
fioritura, *n.f.* Bloom, blossoming, efflorescence; (*fig.*) floridness; (*Mus.*) flourish. **In piena —,** in full bloom.
fiorrancino, *n.m.* (*Zool.*) Fire-crested wren.
fiorrancio [fiorrAncio], *n.m.* (*Bot.*) Marigold.
fiorume, *n.m.* (*Agric.*) Hay-dust.
flosso, *n.m.* Waist of a shoe-sole.
fiottare, *v.i.* To gurgle (of water); to murmur (of waves), to grumble; to surge.
fiotto, *n.m.* Movement of waves on the sea, surge, gush; jet. **Un — di sangue,** a gush of blood; **un — di parole,** a stream of words.
Firenze, *n.f.* (*Geog.*) Florence.
firma, *n.f.* Signature. **Mettere, apporre la —,** to append one's signature; **avere la —,** to be authorized.
firmamento, *n.m.* Firmament, sky.
firmano, *n.m.* (*Pol.*) Firman.
firmante, *n.m.* Signatory.
firmare, *v.t.i.* To sign.
firmarsi, *v.r.* To undersign, to subscribe.
firmatario [firmatArio], *n.m.* Signatory, signer.
fisamente, *adv.* Fixedly, attentively.
fisarmonica [fisarmOnica], *n.f.* (*Mus.*) Concertina, accordion.
fiscale, *a.* Fiscal, of the revenue; (*fig.*) inquisitorial. (*Law*) **Avvocato —,** public prosecutor.
fiscaleggiare, *v.i.* To search for faults; to investigate closely for evidence of a crime; to badger for taxes.
fiscalità [-à], *n.f.* Harassment, severity (in collection of taxes).
fiscalmente, *adv.* Fiscally.
fiscella, *n.f.* Wicker basket.
fischiamento, *n.m.* Hissing, whistling.
fischiare, *v.t.i.* To hiss, to whistle; to whizz, to whirr (of bullets). **— una commedia,** to boo a play; **gli orecchi mi fischiano,** my ears are singing; **mi fischiano le orecchie,** my ears burn, someone is talking of me; **il vento fischia** the wind is whistling.
fischiata, *n.f.* Hiss, whistle.
fischiatore, *n.m.* Whistler.
fischierella, *n.f.* Bird-whistle.
fischierellare, fischiettare, *v.t.i.* To whistle, to whistle softly.
fischiettio [fischiettIo], *n.m.* Whistling, hissing.
fischietto, *n.m.* (Child's) whistle; (*Naut.*) boatswain's pipe.
fischio [fIschio], *n.m.* Whistle (sound and instrument); hiss, hissing, buzz.
fischione, *n.m.* (*Zool.*) Curlew, widgeon.
fisco, *n.m.* Exchequer, public treasury; revenue, fisc.
fisetere, *n.m.* (*Zool.*) Sperm whale.
fisica [fIsica], *n.f.* Physics.
fisicamente, *adv.* Physically, materially.
fisico [fIsico], *n.m.a.* Physicist; physique; physical; natural; constitutional.
fisima [fIsima], *n.f.* Craze, crotchet, fad, whim, caprice. **Avere delle fisime,** to be a faddist.
fisiognomia [fisiognomIa], *n.f.* Physiognomy, character-reading by the features [cp. **fisonomia**].
fisiologia [fisiologIa], *n.f.* Physiology.
fisiologicamente, *adv.* Physiologically.
fisiologico [fisiolOgico], *a.* Physiological.
fisiologo [fisiOlogo], *n.m.* Physiologist.
fisioterapia [fisioterapIa], *n.f.* Physiotherapy.
fisioterapista, *n.m.* Physiotherapist.
fiso, *a.adv.* (*Lit.*) Intent, fixed; staringly, fixedly.

fisonomia [fisonomIa], *n.f.* Physiognomy, cast of features; face, aspect, look.
fisonomista, *n.m.f.* Physiognomist.
fissabile [fissAbile], *a.* Fixable.
fissaggio [fissAggio], *n.m.* (*Phot.*) Fixing; fixing-bath.
fissamente, *adv.* Fixedly, steadily; stably, steadfastly.
fissare, *v.t.* To fix, to fasten; to settle, to ascertain, to determine, to establish; to stare at, to gaze at; (*Phot.*) to fix; to engage (a servant, room at an hotel, etc.). — **un appuntamento,** to fix an appointment; — **un posto,** to secure a seat, to book a seat (at a theatre, etc.).
fissarsi, *v.r.* To settle down, to become fixed; to decide, to fix one's mind; to set one's heart on; to take up residence.
fissativo, *n.m.* Fixative.
fissato, *p.p.a.* Fixed, settled, established; obsessed.
fissazione, *n.f.* Fixation, obsession, fixed idea, monomania.
fissi! *v.i.* (*Mil.*) Eyes front!
fissità [-**à**], *n.f.* Fixity, fixedness; firmness, stability, stillness.
fisso, *a.* Fixed; still, fast, firm, unalterable; steady, regular. **Dimora fissa,** fixed abode; **prezzi fissi,** fixed prices.
fistola [fIstola], *n.f.* (*Med.*) Fistula; shepherd's pipe, pan-pipes; tube.
fitta, *n.f.* Sharp pain, stitch (in the side); pang; crowd; crevice; mark, bruise; spit (digging); quagmire; (*Naut.*) wedge. **Una — al cuore,** a pang at the heart.
fittabile, fittaiuolo, *n.m.* Tenant farmer.
fittamente, *adv.* Closely, densely; often.
fittanza, *n.f.* (*Agric.*) Lease; rent.
fittezza, *n.f.* Thickness, density.
fittile [fIttile], *a.* Fictile, moulded in clay.
fittizio [fittIzio], *a.* Fictitious, feigned, false, artificial, imaginary.
fitto, *n.m.* Rent; lease [cp. **affitto**].
fitto, *a.* Fixed, fastened, rooted; thick, dense, close; frequent. **Tenebra fitta,** pitch darkness; **nebbia fitta,** dense fog; **a capo —,** headlong; **egli si è — in mente,** he's got it into his head; **una fitta rete,** a close net; **parlare — —,** to talk nineteen to the dozen.
fittone, *n.m.* (*Bot.*) Main root, tap-root.
fittuario [fittuArio], *n.m.* Tenant.
fiumana, *n.f.* Swollen river, flood stream; (*fig.*) crowd.
fiume, *n.m.* River; stream, flow. **Il corso d'un —,** the course of a stream; **un — di parole,** a torrent of words.
fiumicello, fiumiciattolo, fiumicino, *n.m., dim.* Small river, brook.
fiutafatti, *n.m.* Eavesdropper, Paul Pry.
fiutare, *v.t.i.* To smell, to sniff, to scent; (*fig.*) to suspect, to trace, to hunt out, to detect. **— il pericolo,** to scent danger; **fiutar tabacco,** to take snuff, to snuff.
fiutasepolcri, *n.m.* Antiquarian.
fiutata, *n.f.* Smell, smelling; snuffing; intuition.
fiuto, *n.m.* (Sense of) smell, smell, scent; (*fig.*) flair, discernment.
flabello, *n.m.* (*Eccles.*) Flabellum, feather fan.
flaccidezza, flaccidità [-**à**], *n.f.* Flabbiness, flaccidity, limpness.
flaccido [flAccido], *a.* Flabby, flaccid, relaxed, weak, nerveless.
flacone, *n.m.* Phial, vial; small bottle.
flagellamento, *n.m.* Flagellation.
flagellante, *n.m.* Flagellant.
flagellare, *v.t.* To scourge, to flog, to thrash, to flagellate.
flagellarsi, *v.r.* To scourge oneself.
flagellatore, flagellatrice, *n.m.f.* Flagellator, castigator.
flagellazione, *n.f.* Scourging, thrashing, flagellation.
flagello, *n.m.* Scourge (in all senses); calamity, ruin; punishment.
flagrante, *a.* Flagrant; glaring. **Esser colto in —,** to be caught in the act.
flagrantemente, *adv.* Flagrantly.
flagranza, *n.f.* Flagrancy. **Sorpreso in —,** caught red-handed.
flamine [flAmine], *n.m.* (*Hist.*) Flamen.
flanella, *n.f.* Flannel. **Camicia di —,** flannel shirt.
flangia [flAngia], *n.f.* (*Mech.*) Flange.
flato, *n.m.* (*Med.*) Flatus, intestinal wind, flatulence.
flatulento, *a.* Flatulent.
flatulenza, *n.f.* (*Med*) Flatulence, flatulency.
flautato, *a.* (*Mus.*) Fluted, flute-like, clear, mellow.
flautello, *n.m.* (*Mus.*) Flageolet.
flautista, *n.m.f.* Flautist, flutist.
flauto [flAuto], *n.m.* (*Mus.*) Flute.
flavo, *a.* Tawny, yellow, fair.
flebile [flEbile], *a.* Feeble; plaintive; mournful.
flebilmente, *adv.* Feebly, plaintively.
flebite, *n.f.* (*Med.*) Phlebitis.
flebotomia [flebotomIa], *n.f.* Phlebotomy.
flebotomo [flebOtomo], *n.m.* Phlebotomist, blood-letter; barber-surgeon.
flemma, *n.f.* Phlegm; coolness, slowness.
flemmaticamente, *adv.* Phlegmatically.
flemmatico [flemmAtico], *a.* Phlegmatic.
flemmone, *n.m.* (*Med.*) Phlegmon.
flessibile [flessIbile], *a.* Flexible, pliable, supple.
flessibilità [-**à**], *n.f.* Flexibility, pliability, suppleness.
flessibilmente, *adv.* Flexibly.
flessione, *n.f.* Flexion, flexure; bend, bending, curve; (*Gram.*) inflexion.
flesso, *p.p.a.* Bent [cp. **flettere**].
flessore, *a.* (*Anat.*) Flexor.
flessuosità [-**à**], *n.f.* Pliability, suppleness.
flessuoso, *a.* Pliable, supple, flexuous; slender.
flettere [flEttere], *v.t.* To bend; (*Anat.*) to flex; (*Gram.*) to inflect.
flirtare, *v.i.* To flirt, to coquet.
fliscorno, *n.m.* (*Mus.*) Bugle, trumpet. (*fig.*) **Suonare il —,** to spy.
flocco, *n.m.* (*Naut.*) Jib.
flogistico [flogIstico], *a.* (*Med.*) Phlogistic.
flogosi, *n.f.* (*Med.*) Inflammation.
flora, *n.f.* (*Bot.*) Flora, vegetation.
floreale, *a.* Floral.
floricultore, *n.m.* Floriculturist, nurseryman.
floricultura, *n.f.* Floriculture.
floridamente, *adv.* Floridly, flourishingly.
floridezza, *n.f.* Floridity, prosperity.

florido [flOrido], *a.* Flourishing, prosperous, thriving; florid. **Aspetto —,** prosperous aspect.
florilegio [florilEgio], *n.m.* (*Lit.*) Anthology, florilegium.
floscezza, *n.f.* Flabbiness.
flosciamente, *adv.* Flabbily, limply.
floscio [flOscio], *a.* Flabby, flaccid, soft, nerveless, weak, limp. **Cappello, colletto —,** soft hat, soft collar.
flotta, *n.f.* Fleet, navy. **Flotta aerea,** air fleet.
flottante, *a.* Floating.
flottare, *v.i.* To float; (*Aviat.*) to taxi (of sea-plane).
flottazione, *n.f.* Floating [cp. **fluttuazione**].
flottiglia [flottIglia], *n.f.* Flotilla; fleet of small ships.
fluente, *a.* Fluent, copious; fluid, mobile, flowing.
fluidamente, *adv.* Fluidly, smoothly.
fluidezza, fluidità [-à], *n.f.* Fluidity; fluency.
fluido [flUido], *n.m.a.* Fluid; fluid, smooth, mobile.
fluire, *v.i.* To flow.
fluore, *n.m.* (*Chem.*) Fluor. **Spato —,** fluor-spar.
fluorescente, *a.* Fluorescent.
fluorescenza, *n.f.* Fluorescence.
fluoro, *n.m.* (*Chem.*) Fluorine.
flussione, *n.f.* (*Math.*) Fluxion; (*Med.*) morbid secretion, inflammation; catarrh.
flusso, *n.m.* (*Med.*) Flux, flowing; discharge, dysentery; (*Cards*) flush; flood-tide. **— e riflusso della marea,** ebb and flow of the tide.
flutto, *n.m.* Wave, surge; billow.
fluttuamento, *n.m.* Fluctuation, instability.
fluttuante, *a.* Fluctuating; floating. **Debito —,** floating debt.
fluttuare, *v.i.* To fluctuate; to rise and fall (as waves); to float.
fluttuazione, *n.f.* Fluctuation, wavering.
fluttuoso, *a.* Stormy, tempestuous (of the sea); irresolute.
fluviale, *a.* River, fluvial. **Navigazione —,** river-navigation.
fobia [fobIa], *n.f.* Dread, fear, morbid dislike; aversion; phobia.
foca, *n.f.* (*Zool.*) Seal.
focaccia [focAccia], *n.f.* Tart, bun, cake. **Render pan per —,** to give tit for tat.
focaccina, *n.f.* Tartlet.
focaia [focAia], *a.* **Pietra —,** flint (for striking a light).
focaiuolo, *n.m.* Flinty soil.
focale, *a.* Focal. **Distanza —,** focal length.
focatico [focAtico], *n.m.* (*Hist.*) Hearth-tax.
focato, *a.* Red-hot, reddish brown (of a horse).
foce, *n.f.* (*Geog.*) Mouth of a river; entrance to a valley; opening of a street into a city square.
focena, *n.f.* (*Zool.*) Porpoise.
focherello, *n.m.* Small fire.
fochista (*pl.* **fochisti**), *n.m.* (*Rail, etc.*) Stoker, fireman; firework-maker.
fociata, *n.f.* Opening of a valley.
focile, *n.m.* (*obs.*) Steel for a gun-flint.
foco [cp. **fuoco**].
focolaio [focolAio], *n.m.* Hot-bed (of infection); furnace bed.
focolare, *n.m.* Fireplace, hearth; fireside, home; furnace; (*fig.*) hotbed.
focone, *n.m.* (*Mil.*) Touch-hole (of a gun); (*Naut.*) ship's galley.
focosamente, *adv.* Ardently, vehemently.
focoso, *a.* Fiery, ardent, vehement. **Cavallo —,** high-spirited horse.
fodera [fOdera], *n.f.* Lining, sheathing; wain-scotting.
foderare, *v.t.* To line, to cover; to sheathe.
foderatura, *n.f.* Lining, sheathing.
fodero [fOdero], *n.m.* Scabbard, sheath (of a sword).
foga, *n.f.* Dash, transport, ardour.
foggia [fOggia], *n.f.* Fashion, manner, style, shape. **— di vestire,** manner of dressing; **alla — di,** after the style of; **a — di,** shaped like, in the shape of.
foggiare, *v.t.* To shape, to form, to mould, to fashion.
foglia [fOglia], *n.f.* Leaf, leaves; foil (of metal). **Tremare come una —,** to tremble like a leaf; **metter le foglie,** to bring forth leaves (of trees); (*fig.*) **mangiar la —,** to smell a rat, to see what is in the wind; (*Art*) **— d'acanto,** acanthus-leaf; **al cader delle foglie,** in the autumn, the fall; **foglie di rape,** turnip-tops.
fogliaccio [fogliAccio], *n.m.* Low-class news-paper, rag.
fogliaceo [fogliAceo], *a.* (*Bot.*) Foliaceous.
fogliame, *n.m.* Foliage, leafage, leaves. **Stoffa a —,** flowered material.
foglietta, *n.f.* Snuff; small leaf.
foglietto, *n.m.* Small sheet of paper. **— volante,** hand-bill.
foglio [fOglio], *n.m.* Sheet (of paper); leaf (of a book); newspaper; receipt. (*Mil.*) **— di via,** travelling pass; **voltiamo —,** let us change the subject; (*Comm.*) **— paga,** pay-roll; **— di via,** way-bill.
foglioso, *a.* Leafy.
fogna, *n.f.* Sewer; drain, sink; culvert.
fognare, *v.t.* To drain, to furnish with drains.
fognatura, *n.f.* Sewerage, drainage.
fognone, *n.m.* Main drain.
fogo, *n.m.* (*Tuscan*) Food going the wrong way. (*fig.*) **Far —,** (things) to go wrong.
foia [fOia], *n.f.* Lust, desire; rut (of animals).
fola, *n.f.* Fable; fib; silly tale.
folaga [fOlaga], *n.f.* (*Zool.*) Coot, moorhen.
folata, *n.f.* Gust, flurry (of wind); great number of anything at one time. **Una — di gente,** a sudden crowd.
folgorante, *a.* Shining, gleaming, flashing, dazzling.
folgorare, *v.t.i.* To lighten, to strike with lightning; to dazzle, to shine, to beam; to dart; to electrocute (by electric current).
folgore [fOlgore], *n.f.* Flash of lightning, thunderbolt, lightning, flash.
folgoreggiare, *v.i.* To flash, to dazzle, to dart.
folio [fOlio], *n.m.* Folio (book).
folklore, folclore, *n.m.* Folklore.
folla, *n.f.* Crowd; throng, multitude; mob. **In —,** in a crowd.
follare, *v.t.* To full (cloth); to press.
folle, *n.m.* Madman, lunatic.

folle, *a.* Mad, insane; foolish, senseless; (*Mech.*) free, loose. (*Mot.*) **In —,** in neutral gear.
folleggiamento, *n.m.* Madness; foolishness; merry-making.
folleggiare, *v.i.* To play the fool; to have a good time; to frolic.
follemente, *adv.* Madly.
folletto, *n.m.* Hobgoblin, elf, sprite, imp.
follia [follIa], *n.f.* Madness, insanity; foolishness, folly; extravagance. **Commettere delle follie,** to act foolishly.
follicolare, *a.* (*Anat.*) Follicular.
follicolo [follIcolo], *n.m.* Follicle.
foltamente, *adv.* Thickly, densely, closely.
foltezza, *n.f.* Thickness, density.
folto, *n.m.a.* Thick, midst, depth; thick, crowded. **Nel — della mischia,** in the thick of the fray; **nel — della notte,** at dead of night; **capelli folti,** luxuriant hair.
fomenta, *n.f.* (*Med.*) Fomentation.
fomentare, *v.t.* To foment (passions, etc.); to stir up, to excite, to foster.
fomentatore, fomentatrice, *n.m.f.* Fomentor, agitator.
fomentazione, *n.f.* (Act of) fomentation.
fomento, *n.m.* fomentation (in all senses).
fomite [fOmite], *n.m.* Tinder; incitement, cause, origin; incentive.
fonda, *n.f.* (*Mil.*) Holster; (*Naut.*) anchorage. **Nave alla —,** vessel at anchor.
fondaccio [fondAccio], *n.m.* Remnant, dregs, lees.
fondaco [fOndaco], *n.m.* Warehouse, magazine; draper's shop.
fondale, *n.m.* (*Naut.*) Anchorage; depth, bottom (of the sea); (*Theat.*) back-cloth.
fondamenta, *n.f.* (*Arch.*) Groundwork, footings.
fondamentale, *a.* Fundamental, primary; essential.
fondamentare, *v.t.* To lay foundations.
fondamento (*pl.* **fondamenti,** *m.*, **fondamenta,** *f.*), *n.m.f.* Foundation, basis; principle. **Porre le fondamenta d'un edificio,** to lay the foundations of a building; **i fondamenti della scienza,** the principles of science.
fondare, *v.t.* To found, to build, to ground, to establish; to endow. **— una cattedra,** to endow a (professorial) chair.
fondarsi, *v.r.* To be founded; to rely upon, to rest upon, to base oneself on.
fondata, *n.f.* [cp. **fondaccio**].
fondatamente, *adv.* Well-grounded; with good reason.
fondatezza, *n.f.* Base, ground, foundation; validity.
fondato, *p.p.a.* Founded, grounded; established; warranted. **Fondati sospetti,** well-founded suspicions.
fondatore, fondatrice, *n.m.f.* Founder, foundress.
fondazione, *n.f.* Foundation, founding; establishment; fund, endowment, donation; institution.
fondeggiare, *v.i.* (*Naut.*) To anchor, to come to anchor.
fondello, *n.m.* Shell-case, cartridge-case.
fondente, *n.m.* (*Metal.*) Flux for solder.
fondere [fOndere], *v.t.* To smelt (of metals); to melt, to fuse; to blend (colours, etc.); (*Comm.*) to merge.
fonderia [fonderIa], *n.f.* Foundry, smelting-works.
fondersi [fOndersi], *v.r.* To unite, to amalgamate; to merge, to melt.
fondezza, *n.f.* [cp. **profondità**].
fondi, *n.m.pl.* (*Comm.*) Funds.
fondiario [fondiArio], *a.* Of land or estate, landed. **Agente —,** estate agent; **proprietà fondiaria,** landed property; **tassa fondiaria,** land-tax.
fondibile [fondIbile], *a.* Fusible.
fondiglio [fondIglio], *n.m.* Sediment, dregs.
fondina, *n.f.* Pistol-case; (*colloq.*) soup-plate.
fonditore, *n.m.* Metal-founder, smith.
fonditura, *n.f.* Smelting, casting, fusing.
fondo, *n.m.* Bottom; background, end; ground floor, basement; (*Comm.*) fund; stock; residue; depth; estate, landed property. **Articolo di —,** leading article (in a newspaper); **— di magazzino,** stock-in-trade; **sapere una cosa a —,** to know something thoroughly; **mandare a — una nave,** to send a vessel to the bottom; **andare a —,** to founder, to sink; to get to the bottom of; (*Naut.*) **dar —,** to come to anchor; **— dei calzoni,** trouser-seat; **in — alla strada,** at the bottom of the street; **fondi di caffè,** coffee grounds; **a doppio —,** double-bottomed; (*Comm.*) **a — perduto,** permanently locked up; **— d'ammortamento,** sinking fund; **— di cassa,** cash on hand; **fondi residui,** surplus funds; (*Sport*) **corsa di —,** endurance test.
fondo, *a.* Deep, thick.
fondura, *n.f.* Deep place.
fonduta, *n.f.* (*Metal.*) Fusion of metal in a crucible; dish of melted cheese.
fonegenico, fonogenico [fonegEnico, fonogEnico], *a.* (*Radio, etc.*) Of a sound or voice suitable for broadcasting or recording.
fonetica [fonEtica], *n.f.* Phonetics.
foneticamente, *adv.* Phonetically.
fonetico [fonEtico], *a.* Phonetic.
fonica [fOnica], *n.f.* Phonics.
fonico [fOnico], *a.* Phonic.
fonografia [fonografIa], *n.f.* Phonography, shorthand.
fonografico [fonogrAfico], *a.* Phonographic. **Disco —,** gramophone record.
fonografo [fonOgrafo], *n.m.* Phonograph, gramophone.
fonogramma, *n.m.* Written telephone message.
fonologia [fonologIa], *n.f.* Phonology.
fonologo [fonOlogo], *n.m.* Phonologist.
fonotipia [fonotipIa], *n.f.* Making of gramophone records.
fontale, *a.* Originating, deriving. **Principio —,** originating principle.
fontana, *n.f.* Fountain.
fontanella, *n.f.* Small fountain; (*Anat.*) fontanelle.
fontaniere, *n.m.* Plumber.
fontanile, *n.m.* Conduit.
fonte, *n.m.f.* Source, spring, fountain; (*Eccles.*) font. **— battesimale,** font; **da — certa,** from a reliable source.
fontina, *n.f.* Kind of soft cheese.
fora (*obs.*) for **sarebbe** [cp. **essere**].

fora, *adv.* Outside [cp. **fuori**].
forabosco, *n.m.* (*Zool.*) Woodpecker.
foracchiare, *v.t.* To pierce, to riddle, to fill with holes.
foraggiamento, *n.m.* Foraging; (*colloq.*) bribing.
foraggiare, *v.t.* To forage, to supply.
foraggiera, *n.f.* Herbage suitable for fodder.
foraggiere, *n.m.* Forager.
foraggio [forAggio], *n.m.* Forage, fodder; (*colloq.*) bribe.
foramacchie [foramAcchie], *n.m.* (*Zool.*) Wren; woodpecker.
forame, *n.m.* (*Lit.*) Small hole, opening.
foramento, *n.m.* Boring, drilling.
foraneo [forAneo], *a.* (*Eccles.*) Rural, forane; from the country.
foraneve, *n.f.* (*Bot.*)Snowdrop [cp. **bucaneve**].
forapaglie [forapAglie], *n.m.* (*Zool.*) Sedge-warbler; wren.
forare, *v.t.* To bore, to pierce, to drill, to perforate, to riddle with holes; to puncture (a tyre); to punch (a ticket).
forasacco, *n.m.* (*Bot.*) Brome-grass.
forasiepe, *n.m.* (*Zool.*) Wren.
foratoio [foratOio], *n.m.* Gimlet, auger.
foratrice, *n.f.* Mechanical drill, boring machine.
foratura, *n.f.* Piercing, boring; puncture (of tyre).
forbici [fOrbici], *n.f.pl.* Scissors, shears; nippers, claws (of crab, scorpion, etc.).
forbiciata, *n.f.* Cut with scissors.
forbicina, *n.f.* (*Zool.*) Earwig.
forbire, *v.t.* To polish, to clean, to wipe; to furbish.
forbirsi, *v.r.* To clean oneself, to wipe. **— la bocca,** to wipe one's mouth.
forbitamente, *adv.* Cleanly, elegantly.
forbitezza, *n.f.* Polish, neatness, elegance; propriety (of speech).
forbito, *a.* Polished; faultless; elegant. **Parlar —,** elegant speech.
forbitore [forbitOre], *n.m.* Polisher, burnisher.
forca, *n.f.* (*Agric.*) Fork, pitch-fork, hay-fork; (*colloq.*) gibbet, gallows. **Avanzo di —,** gallows-bird; **far la — a qualcuno,** to play someone false, to do the dirty on someone; **far —,** to dodge school, to play truant.
forcaiuolo, forcaiòlo, *n.m.* Extreme reactionary.
forcata, *n.f.* (*Agric.*) Forkful of hay; blow with a pitch-fork.
forcatella, *n.f.* Fork-load
force, *n.f.pl.* (*Lit.*) Scissors, shears.
forcella, *n.f.* Forked implement; forked stick; fork of a tree, of a bicycle; merry-thought (of fowl), hairpin; narrow Alpine pass.
forchetta, *n.f.* Fork, table-fork. **— da frutta,** dessert-fork; **una buona —,** a hearty eater; **parlare in punta di —,** to talk affectedly; **colazione alla —,** knife-and-fork meal.
forchettata, *n.f.* Forkful, food taken up on a fork.
forchetto, *n.m.* Two-pronged fork; forked rod for taking things down from a rack, etc.
forchettone, *n.m.* Carving-fork.
forchino, *n.m.* (*Agric.*) Three-pronged pitch-fork, dung-fork.
forcina, *n.f.* Hairpin; small fork.
forcipe [fOrcipe], *n.m.* Forceps.
forcola [fOrcola], *n.f.* (*Naut.*) Rowlock.
forconata, *n.f.* (*Agric.*) Load of a pitchfork.
forcone, *n.m.* (*Agric.*) Pitchfork.
forcuto, *a.* Forked, forky, fork-like.
forellino, *n.m.* Little hole [cp. **foro**].
forense, *a.* Forensic. **I forensi,** the lawyers.
forese, *n.m.a.* Countryman, peasant; rustic, rural.
foresta, *n.f.* Forest.
forestale, *a.* Forest. **Guardia —,** ranger, forester; **leggi forestali,** forest laws.
foresteria [foresterIa], *n.f.* Guest rooms (in monastery).
forestiere, forestiero, *n.m.* Foreigner, visitor; stranger; guest.
forestiero, *a.* Foreign; outlandish, exotic.
forestierume, *n.m.* Crowd of foreigners; (undesirable) foreign ways.
forfait, *adv.* (*Comm.*) By the bulk, in bulk; by the job. **Trattare a —,** to contract by the bulk.
forfecchia [forfEcchia], *n.f.* (*Zool.*) Earwig.
forfora [fOrfora], *n.f.* Scurf, dandruff.
forgia [fOrgia], *n.f.* (*Mech.*) Forge, smithy.
forgiare, *v.t.* (*Mech.*) To forge, to shape [cp. **fucinare**].
foriero, *n.m.a.* Precursor, forerunner; portent, harbinger; precursory, premonitory, portending.
forma, *n.f.* Shape, form, conformation, figure; model, mould, cast; formality, manner. **— di cappello,** hat-block; **— di scarpe,** shoe-last; **è pura —,** it is pure formality; **sotto — di,** in the shape of; **— di formaggio,** shape of cheese; **prendere una —,** to assume a form, to take shape.
formabile [formAbile], *a.* Formable, shapeable.
formaggiaio [formaggiAio], *n.m.* Cheesemonger; cheese-maker.
formaggiera, *n.f.* Dish for grated cheese.
formaggino, *n.m.* Small cheese, *usu.* made from sheep's milk.
formaggio [formAggio], *n.m.* Cheese.
formaio [formAio], *n.m.* Maker of shoe-lasts.
formaldeide [formaldEide], *n.f.* (*Chem.*) Formaldehyde.
formale, *a.* Formal, clear, solemn; conventional, regular; explicit; outward, exterior.
formalina, *n.f.* (*Chem.*) Formalin.
formalismo, *n.m.* Formalism.
formalista (*pl.* **formalisti**), *n.m.* Formalist.
formalità [-à], *n.f.* Formality, form; rule; mere form. **È una pura —,** it is mere formality; **adempiere una —,** to comply with a formality.
formalizzare, *v.t.* To astonish, to shock, to scandalize.
formalizzarsi, *v.r.* To be attached to conventions; to be shocked, to be offended, to take offence, to take exception to.
formalmente, *adv.* Formally, plainly.
formante, *pres.p.a.* Forming, formative.
formare, *v.t.* To form, to shape, to mould, to model; to train, to instruct; to fashion, to constitute. (*Comm.*) **— una società,** to form a company.
formarsi, *v.r.* To be formed, to be constituted; to grow up, to develop, to take shape. (*Comm.*) **— una clientela,** to build up a connection.

formatamente, *adv.* Properly, perfectly; in good form, well-shaped.
formativo, *a.* Formative, plastic; creative.
formato, *n.m.* Shape, size; format (of a book).
formatore, formatrice, *n.m.f.* Modeller, maker, creator, educator.
formatura, *n.f.* The preparation of moulds.
formazione, *n.f.* Formation, shaping; creation, making; (*Mil.*) formation. (*Aviat.*) **Volare in —,** to fly in formation.
formella, *n.f.* Hole (in which to plant a tree); small paving-stone; briquette (of coal-dust, etc.); panel of a wooden ceiling.
formentone, *n.m.* Maize, Indian corn.
formica [formIca], *n.f.* (*Zool.*) Ant.
formicaio [formicAio], *n.m.* Ant-hill.
formicaleone, *n.m.* (*Zool.*) Antlion.
formichiere, *n.m.* Ant-eater.
formico [fOrmico], *a.* Formic.
formicolante, *a.* Swarming, teeming, thronged (with people); formicant.
formicolare, *v.i.* To swarm, to teem with people.
formicolarsi, *v.r.* To be numbed, to feel pins and needles. **La gamba mi formicola,** my leg has gone to sleep.
formicolio [formicolIo], *n.m.* Swarming; tingling. **Un — nella mano,** pins and needles in one's hand.
formicone, *n.m.* (*Zool.*) Large ant.
formidabile [formidAbile], *a.* Formidable, dreadful.
formidabilità [-à], *n.f.* Formidability.
formidabilmente, *adv.* Formidably.
formio [fOrmio], *n.m.* (*Bot.*) New Zealand flax.
formosità [-à],*n.f.*Beauty, shapeliness; plumpness.
formoso, *a.* Beautiful, shapely; plump, chubby.
formula, formola [fOrmula, fOrmola], *n.f.* Formula; wording, form of expression.
formulare, *v.t.* To formulate, to word, to express, to set forth, to state, to work out.
formulario [formulArio], *n.m.* Set of formulas, formulary.
fornace, *n.f.* Furnace, kiln; brickyard. (*fig.*) **Questa stanza è una —,** this room is a veritable furnace.
fornacella, *n.f.* Ash-pit.
fornaciaio [fornaciAio], *n.m.* Worker in a kiln; brick-maker.
fornaciata, *n.f.* Furnace-fuel; contents of a furnace.
fornaio, fornaia [fornAio, fornAia], *n.m.f.* Baker, baker's wife.
fornarina, *n.f.* Baker's daughter; baker's wife.
fornata, *n.f.* Batch of loaves [cp. **infornata**].
fornellata, *n.f.* Quantity of fuel for a stove.
fornello, *n.m.* Stove, kitchen range; (*Mech.*) blast-furnace; pipe-bowl. **— a gas, — elettrico,** gas, electric stove.
fornicare, *v.i.* To fornicate.
fornicatore, fornicatrice, *n.m.f.* Fornicator.
fornicazione, *n.f.* Fornication.
fornice [fOrnice], *n.m.* (*Arch.*) Fornix.
fornimento, *n.m.* Supply, provision; outfit, equipment, fittings; requisites.
fornire, *v.t.* To furnish, to supply with, to provide with.
fornirsi, *v.r.* To provide oneself with, to supply oneself with.
fornitore, fornitrice, *n.m.f.* Purveyor, tradesman, contractor.
fornitura, *n.f.* Supply; contract (esp. for outfits, etc.).
forno, *n.m.* Oven; furnace; baker's shop, bakehouse. **— crematorio,** crematorium; **alto —,** blast furnace.
foro (1) [fòro], *n.m.* Forum, tribunal, court of law; the Bar. **Il Foro italiano,** the Italian Bar; **il Foro romano,** the Roman Forum.
foro (2) [fóro], *n.m.* Hole, opening; orifice; perforation, bore. **Il — della serratura,** the keyhole.
forosetta, *n.f.* (*colloq.*) Country girl.
forra, *n.f.* Gorge, ravine.
forse, *n.m.* Doubt. **Essere in forse,** to be in doubt; **mettere in —,** to cast doubt upon; **lasciare in —,** to leave in doubt; **senza —,** undoubtedly.
forse, *adv.* Perhaps, probably. **Non è — vero ?** Can you say it's not true ?
forsechè, *adv.* It may be that, perhaps.
forseddio, forse Dio, *adv.* Emphatic assertion (when doubt has been cast).
forsennatamente, *adv.* Furiously, recklessly, frantically.
forsennatezza, *n.f.* Madness, frenzy; fury.
forsennato (1), *n.m.* Madman; desperado.
forsennato (2), *a.* Mad, frantic, desperate.
forte (1), *n.m.* Main part; strong point, forte; bulk, sourness; (*Mil.*) fortress, fort, stronghold. **La musica non è il suo —,** music is not his strong point.
forte (2), *a.* Strong, vigorous, powerful; sturdy, robust, hale, healthy; considerable, large, heavy, high; loud (of sound); pungent, acrid; (*Mus.*) forte. **Cassa —,** safe; **a più — ragione,** with better reason; **è troppo —,** it's too bad; **è più — di me,** I can't help it; **— perdita,** heavy loss.
forte (3), *adv.* Strongly; vehemently; loudly. **Parlar —,** to talk loudly; **correre forte,** to run fast; **giuocare —,** to play high.
fortemente, *adv.* Vigorously, sturdily; forcefully.
forteto, *n.m.* Thicket.
fortezza, *n.f.* Strength, fortitude, firmness; courage; (*Mil.*) fortress, fort.
forticcio [fortIccio], *a.* Sourish, acid, tart.
fortiera, *n.f.* (*Naut.*) Bank on the ocean bed.
fortificabile [fortificAbile], *a.* Defendable; adaptable for fortification.
fortificamento, *n.m.* Act of fortifying; corroboration.
fortificante, *n.m.* Fortifier, strengthener.
fortificare, *v.t.* To fortify (in all senses), to strengthen; to invigorate.
fortificarsi, *v.r.* To fortify oneself, to strengthen oneself.
fortificativo, fortificatore, *a.* Fortifying, invigorating.
fortificazione, *n.f.* (*Mil.*) Fortification.
fortigno, *a.* Sour, tart.
fortilizio [fortilIzio], *n.m.* (*Mil.*) Fort, castle.
fortino, *n.m.* (*Mil.*) Block-house, redoubt.
fortissimo, *a. super.* Very loud; very strong.
fortitudine [fortitUdine], *n.f.* (*Lit.*) Fortitude.
fortore, *n.m.* Sourness, tartness; acid smell or taste.
fortuitamente, *adv.* Casually, fortuitously.

fortuito [fortUito], *a.* Casual, accidental, fortuitous.
fortuna, *n.f.* Fortune, luck, chance; prosperity, happiness; riches, property, wealth; (*Myth.*) Fortune. **Buona, cattiva —,** good, bad luck; **Che —!** What luck! How lucky! **per —,** fortunately; **augurare —,** to wish success; **rovescio di —,** reversal of fortune; (*Aviat.*) **atterraggio di —,** forced landing; (*Comm.*) **— di mare,** damage and accidents at sea; (*Naut.*) **— di mare,** storm at sea; **vela di —,** storm-sail.
fortunale, *n.m.* Gale, storm at sea.
fortunatamente, *adv.* Fortunately.
fortunato, *a.* Fortunate, lucky, auspicious; prosperous. (*colloq.*) **Fortunatissimo!** Very glad to meet you!
fortunosamente, *adv.* Stormily.
fortunoso, *a.* Eventful, risky; agitated, stormy.
foruncolo [forUncolo], *n.m.* (*Med.*) Boil, carbuncle.
forviare, *v.t.* To lead astray, to mislead [cp. **fuorviare**].
forviarsi, *v.r.* To stray.
forza, *n.f.* Strength, force, might, power; fortitude (esp. of mind), firmness; violence, compulsion. **— motrice,** driving-power; **a — di,** by dint of; **— maggiore,** force majeure, an act of God; **è —,** it must be, it is necessary; **per —,** against one's will; **farsi —,** to muster one's courage; **con tutta —,** with all one's might; **è superiore alle mie forze,** it is beyond my power; (*Elec.*) **di cento cavalli di —,** of 100 h.p.; (*Mil.*) **attaccare in forze,** to attack in force; (*Law*) **in — d'un decreto,** by virtue of a decree.
forzamento, *n.m.* Forcing.
forzare, *v.t.* To force; to compel, to constrain, to strain; to break open. **— una cassaforte,** to force a safe; **— la mano,** to force one's hand; **— un blocco,** to run a blockade.
forzatamente, *adv.* Perforce, of necessity.
forzato, *n.m.* Convict; galley-slave.
forzato, *a.* Forced, compelled, compulsory. (*Mil.*) **Marce forzate,** forced marches; (*Law*) **lavori forzati,** penal servitude; (*Comm.*) **prestito —,** forced loan.
forzatore, *n.m.* Strong man (at a circus, etc.).
forziere, *n.m.* Strong-box, coffer, safe.
forzosamente, *adv.* Compulsorily.
forzoso, *a.* Forced, compulsory.
forzuto, *a.* Strong, muscular.
foscaggine [foscAggine], *n.f.* Obscurity, darkness, gloom [cp. **oscurità**].
foscamente, *adv.* Obscurely, gloomily.
foschia [foschIa], *n.f.* Fog, mist.
fosco, *a.* Dark, dull; foggy, misty; dismal, gloomy.
fosfato, *n.m.* (*Chem.*) Phosphate.
fosfina, *n.f.* (*Chem.*) Phosphine.
fosfito, *n.m.* (*Chem.*) Phosphite.
fosforeggiare, *v.i.* To exhibit phosphorescence.
fosforeo, fosforescente, *a.* Phosphorescent.
fosforescenza, *n.f.* Phosphorescence.
fosforico [fosfOrico], *a.* (*Chem.*) Phosphoric.
fosforo [fOsforo], *n.m.* (*Chem.*) Phosphorus.
fosforoso, *a.* Phosphorous.
fosfuro, *n.m.* (*Chem.*) Phosphide.
fossa, *n.f.* Ditch; trench; pit; tomb, grave. (*fig.*) **Scavarsi la —,** to bring about one's own ruin.
fossaiuolo, *n.m.* (*Agric.*) Hedger and ditcher.
fossato, *n.m.* Ditch, moat, stream.
fossetta, *n.f.* Dimple.
fossile [fOssile], *n.m.a.* Fossil. **Carbone —,** coal, pit coal.
fossilizzarsi, *v.r.* To become fossilized, to become antiquated.
fossilizzazione, *n.f.* Fossilization.
fosso, *n.m.* Ditch, moat, canal.
fotochimica [fotochImica], *n.f.* Photochemistry.
fotoelettrico [fotoelEttrico], *a.* Photoelectric.
fotogenico [fotogEnico], *a.* Photogenic.
fotografare, *v.t.* To photograph, to take a photo. **Farsi —,** to have one's photo taken.
fotografia [fotografIa], *n.f.* Photography; photograph. **— a colori,** colour photography; **— al lampo,** flashlight photo.
fotograficamente, *adv.* Photographically.
fotografico [fotogrAfico], *a.* Photographic. **Macchina fotografica,** camera.
fotografo [fotOgrafo], *n.m.* Photographer, camera-man.
fotoincisione, *n.f.* Photogravure.
fotolitografia [fotolitografIa], *n.f.* Photolithography.
fotometria [fotometrIa], *n.f.* Photometry.
fottuto, *a.* (*vulg.*) Damned, ruined, lost.
fra, *n.m.* Brother [cp. **frate**].
fra, *prep.* Between, among, within. **— due giorni,** within two days, in two days; **fra di noi,** between ourselves; **— poco,** shortly, in a moment; **— i monti,** among the mountains; **parlare — sè,** to talk to oneself [cp. **tra**].
frac, fracche, *n.m.* (*colloq.*) Frock-coat; evening clothes, tails.
fracassamento, *n.m.* Smashing up, shattering.
fracassare, *v.t.* To smash to pieces, to shatter, to crash.
fracassarsi, *v.r.* To break; to crash (to the ground); **— una gamba,** to break a leg.
fracasso, *n.m.* Din, noise, hubbub; bustle. **Far —,** to make a noise; (*fig.*) to make a fuss.
fracassone, *n.m.* (*colloq.*) Noisy fellow; blusterer.
fracco, *n.m.* (*colloq.*) **Un — di legnate,** a good thrashing.
fradicio, fracido [frAdicio, frAcido], *a.* Drenched, soaked to the skin; rotten, putrid, rotten (of fruits). **Ubriaco —,** blind drunk, beastly drunk; **bagnato —,** wet to the skin.
fradiciume, *n.m.* Wetness, rottenness; foulness, putridity.
fragile [frAgile], *a.* Fragile, frail, brittle; weak. (*Comm.*) **Merci fragili,** fragile with care.
fragilità [-à], *n.f.* Fragility, brittleness.
fragilmente, *adv.* Weakly, fragilely.
fragnere [cp. **frangere**].
fragola [frAgola], *n.f.* Strawberry.
fragolaia [fragolAia], *n.f.* Strawberry-bed.
fragolino, *n.m.* (*Zool.*) Red sea-bream.
fragore, *n.m.* Din, clang, roar, crash, great noise.
fragorio [fragorIo], *n.m.* Prolonged noise, continuous roaring.
fragoroso, *a.* Noisy; resounding, roaring.
fragrante, *a.* Fragrant, perfumed, sweet-smelling.
fragranza, *n.f.* Fragrance, perfume.
fraintendere [fraintEndere], *v.t.* To misunderstand.

frainteso, *a.* Misunderstood.
frale, *a.* (*Lit.*) Frail, feeble.
fralezza, *n.f.* Frailty.
frammassone, *n.m.* Freemason.
frammassoneria [frammassonerIa], *n.f.* Freemasonry.
frammassonico [frammassOnico], *a.* Masonic.
frammentario [frammentArio], *a.* Fragmentary, disconnected, incomplete.
frammentisti, *n.m.pl.* Authors of literary "fragments".
frammento, *n.m.* Fragment, piece, detached portion.
frammescolare, *v.t.* To mingle, to intermingle.
frammesso, *n.m.* Interlude; (*Cooking*) entremets.
frammesso, *a.* Inserted, interposed.
frammettente, *a.* Interfering; intruding, intrusive.
frammettere [frammEttere], *v.t.* To interpose, to insert.
frammettersi [frammEttersi], *v.r.* To interfere, to meddle; to intervene.
frammezzare, *v.t.* To divide; to place between, to interject, to intermingle.
frammezzo, *adv.prep.* Amidst, among, between. **Non porre tempo —,** not to lose any time.
frammischiamento, *n.m.* Mingling, mixture.
frammischiare, *v.t.* To mingle, to mix, to blend.
frammisto, *a.* Intermingled.
frana, *n.f.* Landslide, landslip; subsidence.
franamento, *n.m.* (Act of) landslide.
franare, *v.i.* To slide down, to subside; to crumble, to sink (of land).
francamente, *adv.* Freely, openly, frankly.
francare, *v.t.* To frank (a letter), to pre-pay; to release. **Non franca la spesa,** it doesn't pay, it isn't worth while [cp. **affrancare**].
francatura, *n.f.* Postage, pre-payment (of letter or parcel).
francescano, *n.m.a.* Franciscan.
Francesco, *n.m.* Francis.
francescone, *n.m.* Old Tuscan silver coin.
francese, *n.m.f.a.* Frenchman, Frenchwoman; French language; French. **I Francesi,** the French.
franceseggiare, *v.i.* To ape French ways and speech.
francesemente, *adv.* In the French way.
francesismo, *n.m.* Gallicism.
francheggiare, *v.t.* To reassure, to give confidence to.
francheggiarsi, *v.r.* To take courage, to feel reassured.
franchezza, *n.f.* Frankness, openness, sincerity; freedom.
franchigia [franchIgia], *n.f.* Exemption, immunity, privilege. **— diplomatica,** diplomatic privilege.
Francia [frAncia], *n.f.* (*Geog.*) France.
franco, *n.m.* Franc (currency).
franco, *a.* Frank, sincere, open, outspoken, candid, above-board; free, immune, exempted. **— di porto,** carriage free; **faccia franca,** bold face; **farla franca,** to escape scot-free.
franco, *adv.* Frankly.
francobollo, *n.m.* Postage stamp, stamp. **Raccolta di francobolli,** stamp-collection.
francofilo [francOfilo], *n.m.a.* Francophil.
francofobo [francOfobo], *n.m.a.* Francophobe.
francolino, *n.m.* (*Zool.*) Ptarmigan.
frangente, *n.m.* Difficulty, emergency, predicament, quandary; accident; (*Naut.*) breaker; rock; shallow. **Trovarsi in un —,** to be in a quandary, in a ticklish position.
frangere [frAngere], *v.t.* To break, to break to pieces, to crush [cp. **infrangere**].
frangersi [frAngersi], *v.r.* To break against. **Le onde si frangono sugli scogli,** the waves break on the rocks.
frangia [frAngia], *n.f.* Fringe, border, edging; (*fig.*) embellishment of a story.
frangiare, *v.t.* To fringe.
frangiatura, *n.f.* Fringe, edging.
frangibile [frangIbile], *a.* Breakable.
frangibilità [-à], *n.f.* Fragility, breakability.
frangiflutti, *n.m.* Breakwater.
frangimento, *n.m.* Breaking, smashing.
frangionda, *n.m.* Breakwater.
frangivento, *n.m.* (*Motor.*) Windscreen.
frangitura, *n.f.* Time and operation of olive-crushing.
franoso, *a.* Precipitous; crumbling, subsiding.
frantendere [cp. **fraintendere**].
franto, *a.* Broken, crushed.
frantoiano, *n.m.* (*Agric.*) Labourer on an olive-press.
frantoio [frantOio], *n.m.* (*Agric.*) Oil-press, olive-press.
frantumare, *v.t.* To smash, to shatter, to crumble.
frantumarsi, *v.r.* To break into pieces; to be shattered; to crash.
frantumi, *n.m.pl.* Splinters, fragments, broken bits. **Andare in —,** to go to pieces.
frappa, *n.f.* Flap, fringe; painted foliage.
frappe cocktail, *n.m.* Cocktail-shaker.
frappeggiare, *v.t.* To paint foliage.
frapponimento, *n.m.* Interposition, interposing.
frapporre, *v.t.* To interpose, to insert, to place between. **Non — indugi,** to waste no time.
frapporsi, *v.r.* To interfere, to intervene.
frapposizione, *n.f.* Interposition, intervention; interference.
frari, *n.m.pl.* Friars.
frasario [frasArio], *n.m.* Phrase-book; collection of phrases; phraseology; constant use of trite phrases.
frasca, *n.f.* Leafy bough, branch; bush (before an inn as sign-board); idle story; (*pl.*) trifles, gew-gaws. **Saltar di palo in —,** to talk at random; **al buon vino non occorre —,** good wine needs no bush.
frascame, *n.m.* Leafy boughs, branches.
frascato, *n.m.* Bower, arbour, shady place. (*Jewish*) **Festa dei Frascati,** Feast of Tabernacles.
frascheggiare, *v.i.* To flirt, to trifle, to toy, to dally; to rustle (of branches).
frascheggio [frascheggIo], *n.m.* Rustling.
frascheria [frascherIa], *n.f.* Trifle, rubbishy thing.
fraschetta, *n.f.* Twig, small bough; (*fig.*) saucy girl, flirt.

fraschetto, *n.m.* (*Naut.*) Boatswain's pipe or whistle.
frasconaia [frasconAia], *n.f.* Bird decoy (made of brushwood).
frascone, *n.m.* (*Agric.*) Bean-pole, pea-stick; (*fig.*) moping fowl; dejected person.
frascume, *n.m.* Leafy spot; quantity of leaves.
frase, *n.f.* Phrase, sentence. **Frasi fatte,** set phrases.
fraseggiamento, *n.m.* Phrasing.
fraseggiare, *v.i.* To phrase, to form phrases.
fraseggiatore, *n.m.* Phrase-monger.
fraseggio [frasEggio], *n.m.* Phrase-making; (*Mus.*) marking of phrases.
fraseologia [fraseologIa], *n.f.* Phraseology.
frassinella, *n.f.* (*Bot.*) Dittany.
frassineto, *n.m.* Ash plantation.
frassino [frAssino], *n.m.* (*Bot.*) Ash, ash-tree.
frastagliamento, *n.m.* Notching, denticulation.
frastagliare, *v.t.* To notch, to indent; to slash, to cut; (*Arch.*) to denticulate.
frastagliatura, *n.f.* Notching.
frastaglio [frastAglio], *n.m.* Notching, indentation; gash, cut; ornamentation.
frastornamento, *n.m.* Hindrance, disturbance.
frastornare, *v.i.* To divert from; to hinder, to disturb, to trouble.
frastornio [frastornIo], *n.m.* Hindrance, disturbance.
frastuono, *n.m.* Noise, din, uproar; hubbub; thunderous roar.
fratacchione, *n.m.* (*colloq.*) Great, fat friar.
fratacchiotto, *n.m.* (*colloq.*) Squat, tubby friar.
fratata, *n.f.* (*colloq.*) Action or speech of friars.
frate, *n.m.* Friar; monk; brother. **Farsi —,** to turn monk; **— laico,** lay brother [*dims.* **fratone, fratino, fraticello,** etc.].
fratellame, *n.m.* (*colloq.*) All the brothers and sisters of a family.
fratellanza, *n.f.* Brotherhood, fraternity.
fratellastro, *n.m.* Half-brother, step-brother.
fratellevole [fratellEvole], *a.* Brother-like, affectionate.
fratellino, *n.m.* Younger brother.
fratello, *n.m.* Brother; fellow-man; one of the same community; friar. **— di latte,** foster-brother, **— gemello,** twin-brother; **— d'armi,** brother in arms, comrade.
frateria [fraterIa], *n.f.* Friary, community of monks.
fraternamente, *adv.* Fraternally.
fraternità [-à], *n.f.* Fraternity, brotherhood; brotherliness.
fraternizzare, *v.i.* To fraternize.
fraterno, *a.* Fraternal, brotherly.
fratescamente, *adv.* Monkishly, like a friar.
fratesco, *a.* Monkish.
fraticello [cp. **frate**].
fratino, *n.m.* (*Eccles.*) Novice in certain orders.
fratricida, *n.m.a.* Fratricide (criminal); fratricidal.
fratricidio [fratricIdio], *n.m* Fratricide (crime).
fratta, *n.f.* Thicket of bramble, bush, brake.
frattaglie [frattAglie], *n.f.pl.* Giblets, lights (of animals), pluck.
frattanto, *adv.* Meanwhile, in the meantime.
frattempo, *n.m.* Interval, meanwhile. **Nel —,** in the meantime.
fratto, *a.* (*Lit.*) Broken.
frattura, *n.f.* Fracture (in all senses); breakage. **— composta,** compound fracture.
fratturare, *v.t.* To fracture, to break.
fratturarsi, *v.r.* To break. **— la gamba,** to break one's leg.
fraudare, *v.t.* [cp. **frodare** and **defraudare**].
fraudatore, *n.m.* Defrauder; smuggler.
fraude [cp. **frode**].
fraudolentemente, *adv.* Fraudulently.
fraudolento, *a.* Fraudulent.
fraudolenza, *n.f.* Fraudulence, fraud.
frazionare, *v.t.* To break into small pieces, to divide, to separate into fractions.
frazione, *n.f.* Fraction, portion, fragment; hamlet, cluster of houses; (*Eccles.*) fraction. **— commune,** vulgar fraction.
freatico [freAtico], *a.* Of an underground stream or water.
freccia [frEccia], *n.f.* Arrow, dart, shaft; (compass) needle.
frecciare, *v.t.* To shoot an arrow.
frecciata, *n.f.* Arrow-shot; (*fig.*) taunt, gibe.
freddamente, *adv.* Coldly.
freddare, *v.t.* To chill; to kill.
freddarsi, *v.r.* To grow cold; to kill oneself.
freddezza, *n.f.* Coldness, coolness, chilliness; indifference, reserve. **Trattare con —,** to treat with coldness, to give the cold shoulder to.
freddo, *n.m.* Cold, chilliness, cold weather. **Soffrire il —,** to feel the cold; **prender —,** to catch cold; (*colloq.*) **non mi fa nè caldo nè —,** I don't care a button.
freddo, *a.* Cold, cool, chilly; frigid, indifferent; lifeless, reserved. **Sangue —,** cold blood; **fa molto —,** it's very cold; **accoglienza fredda,** cool reception.
freddoloso, *a.* Chilly, sensitive to cold.
freddura, *n.f.* Wintry cold; (*Med.*) a cold; (*colloq.*) pun, joke.
freddurista (*pl.* **freddurist**i), *n.m.* Punster; chatterbox, bore.
frega, *n.f.* Unbridled desire; rut (of animals).
fregaccio [fregAccio], *n.m.* Scrawl (with pen or pencil).
fregagione, *n.f.* Friction, rubbing; (*Med.*) embrocation.
fregare, *v.t.* To rub, to chafe; to apply friction; to scrub; to scrape; (*colloq.*) to cheat, to take in.
fregarsene, *v.r.* (*colloq.*) To laugh at, to despise. **Io me ne frego,** I don't care a damn.
fregarsi, *v.r.* To rub oneself; (*colloq.*) to fawn. **— le mani,** to rub one's hands.
fregata (1), *n.f.* Rubbing; (*colloq.*) cheat, swindle.
fregata (2), *n.f.* (*Naut.*) Frigate; (*Zool.*) frigate-bird. **Capitano di —,** commander (naval rank).
fregatura, *n.f.* Rubbing, scrubbing; (*vulg.*) deception, fraud, swindle.
fregiamento, *n.m.* Ornamentation.
fregiare, *v.t.* To deck out, to adorn, to ornament, to decorate, to embellish.
fregiarsi, *v.r.* To adorn oneself. **— il petto di medaglie,** to deck one's chest with medals.

fregiatura, *n.f.* Ornament, bordering, decoration.
fregio [frEgio], *n.m.* Decoration; (*Arch.*) frieze.
frego, *n.m.* Scrawl, stroke, line. **Dar di —,** to cross out; (*Law*) to quash.
fregola [frEgola], *n.f.* Spawning (of fish); rutting (of deer); lust, violent desire.
freisa [frEisa], *n.m.* Kind of Piedmontese wine.
fremebondo, *a.* Quivering, trembling; passionate; fuming, furious.
fremente, *a.* Trembling, fuming, shuddering.
fremere [frEmere], *v.i.* To shudder, to tremble, to quiver; to vibrate, to rustle; to fume with rage; to fret. **Sentirsi —,** to be all in a flutter.
fremito, *n.m.* Tremble, trembling, quivering, vibration; thrill; shudder; roaring. **Un — d'orrore,** a thrill of horror; **i fremiti della tigre,** the roaring of a tiger; **il — del bosco,** the sighing of the trees.
frenabile [frenAbile], *a.* Brakeable.
frenare, *v.t.* To curb, to restrain, to repress, to check, to control; to bridle (a horse); (*Motor.*) to pull up, to brake, to apply the brake. **— la lingua,** to bridle one's tongue; (*Motor.*)**— bruscamente,** to pull up suddenly.
frenarsi, *v.r.* To restrain oneself.
frenastenia [frenastenIa], *n.m.* (*Med.*) Mental deficiency.
frenata, *n.f.* Braking, applying the brake.
frenatore, *n.m.* (*Rail.*) Brakesman.
frenello, *n.m.* (*Anat.*) Frenum; (*Naut.*) cable.
frenesia [frenesIa], *n.f.* Frenzy, fury, rage; delirium; folly.
freneticamente, *adv.* Frenziedly, furiously.
frenetico [frenEtico], *n.m.a.* Frenzied person; frenzied, frantic; phrenetic.
freniatra, *n.m.* (*Med.*) Alienist, psychiatrist.
freniatria [freniatrIa], *n.f.* Cure of mental diseases.
frenico [frEnico], *a.* (*Anat.*) Phrenic.
frenite, *n.f.* (*Med.*) Phrenitis.
freno, *n.m.* Bit, curb, bridle; check, restraint; brake. **— a nastro,** band-brake; **— sul mozzo,** hub-brake; **— sui cerchioni,** rim-brake; **— a mano,** hand brake; **— a pedale,** foot brake; **— di sicurezza,** emergency brake; **— a depressione,** vacuum brake; **ceppo di —,** brake-block; **tamburo di —,** brakedrum; **stringere il —** to apply the brake; **serrare il —,** to put on the brake; **mordere il —,** to champ the bit, to swallow one's wrath; **senza —,** unrestrained.
frenocomio [frenocOmio], *n.m.* Asylum, madhouse, mental institution.
frenologia [frenologIa], *n.f.* Phrenology.
frenologo [frenOlogo], *n.m.* Phrenologist.
frenulo [frEnulo], *n.m.* (*Anat.*) Frenum.
frequentare, *v.t.* To attend, to frequent, to haunt, to associate, to resort. **— la scuola,** to attend school; **— un porto,** to touch at a port, to call at a port.
frequentativo, *a.* Frequentative.
frequentato, *a.* Frequented, crowded, popular (of a resort, etc.).
frequentatore, frequentatrice, *n.m.f.* Frequenter, regular visitor, customer.
frequentazione, *n.f.* Repetition; frequenting.
frequente, *a.* Frequent, common, oft-repeated. **Di —** often; **polso —,** rapid pulse; **uso —,** frequent usage.
frequentemente, *adv.* Frequently.
frequenza, *n.f.* Frequency, frequence; attendance.
fresa, *n.f.*(*Mech.*) Fraise.
fresare, *v.t.* (*Mech.*) To countersink.
frescamente, *adv.* Freshly, recently.
frescante, *n.m.* (*Art.*) Painter in fresco.
frescare, *v.t.* (*Art*) To paint in fresco.
frescheggiare, *v.i.* To take fresh air, to enjoy the open air.
freschetto, *a.* Rather cool, fresh.
freschezza, *n.f.* Freshness (in all senses); coolness (of weather).
freschino, *a.* Coolish.
fresco, *n.m.* Coolness, freshness. **Al —,** in the open air; **tener al—,** to keep in a cool place; **prendere il —,** to take the air; **fa —,** it's quite cool.
fresco, *a.* Cool; fresh, new, green; recent; florid. **Burro —,** fresh butter; **uova fresche,** new-laid eggs; **pane —,** new bread; **di —,** quite recently; (*fig.*) **stare —,** to be in a fix; **Starete freschi!** Between you, you'll make a mess of it!
frescolino, *a.* Rather cool, fresh.
frescura, *n.f.* Cool air, freshness. **Prendere una —,** to take a chill.
fretta, *n.f.* Haste, hurry; speed, quickness. **In —,** in a hurry; **in — e furia,** in great haste; **aver —,** to be in a hurry; **far —,** to hurry; **non c'è —,** there's no hurry.
frettare, *v.t.* (*Naut.*) To scrape the bottom of a ship; to scrub.
frettolosamente, *adv.* Hastily.
frettolosità [-à], *n.f.* Hastiness, hurry.
frettoloso, *a.* Hasty, quick, hurried.
freudismo, *n.m.* Freudism.
friabile [friAbile], *a.* Friable.
friabilità [-à], *n.f.* Friability.
fricassea, *n.f.* Fricassee.
friganea [friganEa], *n.f.* (*Zool.*) Caddis-fly.
friggere [frIggere], *v.t.* To fry, to bake; to fizzle, to sputter. (*colloq.*) **Vai a farti —!** go to blazes!
friggio [friggIo], *n.m.* Sizzling.
friggitore, *n.m.* Fried-food seller; fried-fish shop.
frigidario [frigidArio], *n.m.* (*Hist.*) Frigidarium.
frigidezza, frigidità [-à], *n.f.* Frigidity, coldness.
frigido [frIgido], *a.* Frigid, cold.
frigio [frIgio], *a.* (*Hist.*) Phrygian. **Berretto frigio,** Phrygian cap.
frignare, *v.i.* To whimper (of children); to whine.
frignone, *n.m.* Whiner, whimperer; crying child.
frigorifero [frigorIfero], *n.m.* Refrigerator, "frig"; cold storage; ice-chamber.
frigorifico [frigorIfico], *a.* Freezing, causing freezing.
Frine, *n.f.* Phryne.
fringuello, *n.m.* (*Zool.*) Chaffinch.
frinire, *v.i.* To chirp (of insects), to stridulate.
frino, *n.m.* (*Zool.*) Species of large, poisonous spider.
frinzello, *n.m.* Badly-sewn seam; cicatrix of a wound.
frisare, *v.t.* (*Billiards*) To make a grazing stroke; to cause to kiss.

friscello, *n.m.* Flour sweepings; mill-dust.
Frisia [frIsia], *n.f.* (*Geog.*) Frisia. **Cavalli di —,** chevaux de frise.
friso, *n.m.* (*Billiards*) Kissing.
fritta, *n.f.* Frit (used in glass-making).
frittata, *n.f.* Omelette. (*colloq.*) **Fare una —,** to make a mess of a thing.
frittella, *n.f.* Fritter, pancake; grease mark on clothes.
frittelloso, *a.* Covered with grease-spots.
fritto, *n.m.* Fry, fried food. **— misto,** mixed fry.
fritto, *p.p.a.* Fried. **Sono —,** I'm worn out, I'm done for; **cose fritte e rifritte,** stale things, hackneyed stuff.
frittura, *n.f.* Fry, frying; fritter. **— di pesci,** dish of fried fish.
friulano, *n.m.a.* Of Friuli.
frivolamente, *adv.* Frivolously.
frivoleggiare, *v.i.* To trifle, to act or speak frivolously.
frivolezza, frivolità [-**à**], *n.f.* Frivolity, frivolousness; pettiness.
frivolo [frIvolo], *a.* Frivolous, trifling, trumpery; futile, petty.
frizione, *n.f.* Friction, massage; (*Mech.*) clutch; dry shampoo; (*fig.*) disagreement, conflict. (*Motor.*) **Innesto a —,** friction clutch.
frizionare, *v.t.* To massage.
frizzamento, *n.m.* Smarting; biting jest.
frizzante, *a.* Pungent, cutting, piquant; sparkling (wine); bracing (weather).
frizzare, *v.i.* To smart; to be pungent; to sting.
frizzo, *n.m.* Caustic remark, witticism; taunt, gibe. **Lanciare dei frizzi,** to gibe at, to sneer at.
frizzore, *n.m.* Smarting.
frodare, *v.t.i.* To defraud, to deceive; to smuggle.
frodatore, *n.m.* Defrauder, cheat, swindler.
frode, *n.f.* Fraud; deception, cheating, imposture. **Introdurre di —,** to smuggle in.
frodo, *n.m.* Smuggling. **Merce di —,** smuggled goods; **cacciatore di —,** poacher.
frodolentemente, *adv.* Fraudulently.
frodolento, *a.* Fraudulent. **Bancarotta frodolenta,** fraudulent bankruptcy.
frodolenza, *n.f.* Fraudulence, fraud.
froge, *n.f.pl.* Nostrils (of a horse).
frollamento, *n.m.* Hanging of meat.
frollare, *v.t.i.* To soften, to hang (of meat), to make tender; to hang until high.
frollatura, *n.f.* Softening (of meat).
frollo, *a.* Soft, tender; high (of game, etc.); slack, weak, tired. **Pasta —,** short pastry.
fromba, frombola [frOmbola], *n.f.* Sling.
frombolare, *v.t.* To sling, to throw with a sling.
fromboliere, *n.m.* (*Hist.*) Slinger; archer.
froncolo [frOncolo], *n.m.* (*Zool.*) Seagull.
fronda, *n.f.* Leafy branch, bush; (*Hist.*) Fronde. (*Pol.*) **Vento di —,** opposition.
frondeggiante, *a.* Leafy.
frondeggiare, *v.i.* To break into leaf, to bear leaves.
frondista (*pl.* **frondisti**), *n.m.* (*Pol.*) Political opposer, member of the opposition.
frondosità [-**à**], *n.f.* Leafiness; foliation; luxuriance.
frondoso, *a.* Leafy.
fronima [frOnima], *n.f.* (*Zool.*) Large crayfish.
frontale, *n.m.a.* Frontal; mantelpiece; frontal (in all senses).
fronte, *n.f.m.* (*Anat.*) Forehead, brow; front. **— alta,** high forehead; **a — alta,** with head held high; **di —,** in front, opposite; **far — a,** to cope with, to face; **tener — a,** to make headway against; **— diplomatico,** diplomatic front; (*Mil.*) **Dietro front!** About turn! **mettere a —,** to compare with; **far — indietro,** to turn back; **a — a —,** face to face; **chinar la —,** to bow to a decision.
fronteggiare, *v.t.* To face, to meet; to cope with; to oppose, to withstand.
frontespizio [frontespIzio], *n.m.* Frontispiece; title-page.
frontiera, *n.f.* Frontier, border.
frontino, *n.m.* Front (false hair).
frontista (*pl.* **frontisti**), *n.m.* Owner of frontage on lake, river, etc.
frontone, *n.m.* (*Arch.*) Pediment.
fronzolo [frOnzolo], *n.m.* Trinket, finery, gewgaw.
fronzuto, *a.* Leafy; green.
frosone, *n.m.* (*Zool.*) Hawfinch.
frotta, *n.f.* Troop, crowd, band, flock. **Arrivare a —,** to flock; **— di pesci,** shoal of fish.
frottola [frOttola], *n.f.* Fib, lie; silly story, idle yarn. **Frottole,** nonsense.
frottolone, *n.m.* Liar, fibber, story-teller.
frufrù [-**ù**], *n.m.* Rustling noise (of silken underwear).
frugacchiamento, *n.m.* Rummaging, searching.
frugacchiare, *v.t.* To rummage, to search for.
frugale, *a.* Frugal, thrifty, sparing.
frugalità [-**à**], *n.f.* Frugality, thrift.
frugalmente, *adv.* Frugally.
frugamento, *n.m.* Ransacking, rummaging about.
frugare, *v.t.* To search for, to rummage about for, to ransack; to poke (with a stick); to ferret out.
frugata, *n.f.* Rummage, search for.
frugifero [frugIfero], *a.* Fruitful.
frugivoro [frugIvoro], *a.* Frugivorous.
frugnolare, *v.t.* To hunt or fish by lantern-light.
frugo, *n.m.* (*Comm.*) **Uso e —,** wear and tear.
frugolo, frugolino [frUgolo], *n.m.* Restless child; lively youngster.
fruibile [fruIbile], *a.* (*Law*) Enjoyable.
fruire, *v.i.* To enjoy, to use; to possess; to avail oneself of.
fruitivo, *a.* Fruitive.
fruizione, *n.f.* Fruition; (*Law*) enjoyment, use of.
frulana, *n.f.* (*Agric.*) Scythe, bagging-hook, sickle; country dance [cp. **furlana**].
frullare, *v.t.i.* To spin round; to whip up, to beat up (eggs, etc.); to flutter. **Cosa ti frulla per capo?** What fancies are you getting into your head?
frullino, *n.m.* Egg-whisk, eggbeater.
frullio [frullIo], *n.m.* Whirring, fluttering.
frullo, *n.m.* Whirr, rustle, beating (of wings), flutter; beater (for eggs, making chocolate, etc.). **Prendere a —,** to accept without thinking.
frullone, *n.m.* Bolter, sifting machine.

frumentaceo [frumentAceo], *a.* Cereal.
frumentario [frumentArio], *a.* Pertaining to corn, wheat.
frumento, *n.m.* Wheat, corn, grain. **Farina di —,** wheaten flour; **campo di —,** wheat-field.
frumentone, *n.m.* Maize, Indian corn.
frusciare, *v.i.* To rustle.
fruscio [fruscIo], *n.m.* Rustling, rustle.
fruscolo [frUscolo], *n.m.* Twig; scrap of anything).
frusone, *n.m.* (*Zool.*) Hawfinch.
frusso, *n.m.* (*Cards*) Flush.
frusta, *n.f.* Whip, scourge, lash.
frustagno, *n.m.* Fustian cloth.
frustare, *v.t.* To whip; to flog, to scourge; (*fig.*) to wear out clothes.
frustata, *n.f.* Lash, cut (with a whip); lashing; (*fig.*) satire.
frustatore, frustatrice, *n.m.f.* Scourger; flagellator.
frustatura, *n.f.* Flogging, whipping, thrashing.
frustino, *n.m.* Riding-whip.
frusto, *n.m.* Bit, morsel, little piece. **A — a —,** bit by bit.
frusto, *a.* Worn out, decayed; tattered, threadbare.
frustone, *n.m.* Big stick, long whip; green twig without leaves.
frustrare, *v.t.* To frustrate, to defeat, to thwart, to render vain; to disappoint; to deceive.
frustratorio [frustratOrio], *a.* Fallacious, deceptive.
frustrazione, *n.f.* Frustration, defeat.
frutice [frUtice], *n.m.* Shrub.
fruticeto, *n.m.* Shrubbery.
frutta (*pl.* **frutta, frutte**), *n.f.* Fruit. **Alle —,** at dessert; **coltello da —,** fruit knife; **— e dolci,** dessert; **mi piace la —,** I'm fond of fruit; **— in scatola,** tinned fruit; **commercio della —,** fruit trade.
fruttaiolo, *n.m.* Fruiterer.
fruttame, *n.m.* Fruit of all kinds; fruitage.
fruttante, *a.* Fruit-bearing.
fruttare, *v.t.i.* To fructify, to bear fruit; to yield fruit; to pay; to bear interest. (*Comm.*) **Capitale che non frutta,** capital that does not yield interest; **— il 10%,** to bear interest at 10%; **un commercio che frutta,** a paying business.
fruttata, *n.f.* Tart of candied fruits.
fruttato, *n.m.* Yield of fruit.
frutteto, *n.m.* Orchard.
frutticultore, *n.m.* Fruit-grower.
frutticultura, *n.f.* Fruit-growing.
fruttiera, *n f.* Fruit-dish.
fruttifero [fruttIfero], *a.* Fruitful, fruit-bearing; (*Comm.*) profitable, bearing interest; paying, remunerative. **Deposito —,** deposit on interest; **buono —,** interest-bearing security.
fruttificare, *v.i.* To fructify.
fruttificazione, *n.f.* Fructification.
fruttifico [fruttIfico], *a.* Fruitful.
fruttivendolo [fruttivEndolo], *n.m.* Fruiterer; greengrocer.
fruttivoro [fruttIvoro], *a.* Fruitivorous.
frutto (*pl.* **frutti,** *m.*; **frutta,** *f.*), *n.m.* Fruit; profit; interest, income, yield. **Dare —,** to bear fruit; **frutti di mare,** shell-fish; **— proibito,** forbidden fruit; **A che —?** What for? **— acerbo,** unripe fruit; **con —,** advantageously, at a profit; **senza —,** fruitlessly, vainly; **metter a —,** to put to interest; **trarre —,** to profit, to take advantage.
fruttuosamente, *adv.* Fruitfully.
fruttuoso, *a.* Fruitful, useful, helpful.
fu, *past def.* **essere**. Late, deceased. **Il fu Antonio,** the late Anthony.
fuciacca [cp. **fusciacca**].
fucilare, *v.t.* To execute by shooting, to shoot.
fucilata, *n.f.* Shot, fusilade.
fucilazione, *n.f.* Execution (by shooting).
fucile, *n.m.* Gun, rifle. **Tiro di —,** gun-shot; **— da caccia,** shot-gun, sporting rifle; **— a due canne,** double-barrelled gun; **— ad aria,** air-gun; **— mitragliatore,** tommy-gun, sub-machine gun.
fucileria [fucilerIa], *n.f.* Musketry, rifle-fire, fusilade.
fuciliere, *n.m.* Rifleman, fusilier.
fucina, *n.f.* Forge, smithy.
fucinale, *n.m.* Puddling-furnace (in iron-works).
fucinare, *v.t.* To forge (metal); to mould, to shape.
fuco, *n.m.* (*Zool.*) Drone.
fucsia [fUcsia], *n.f.* (*Bot.*) Fuchsia.
fucsina, *n.f.* Aniline red dye.
fuffigno, *n.m.* Knot in a skein of wool, etc.
fuga, *n.f.* Flight, escape; (*Mus.*) fugue. **Mettere in —,** to put to flight; **darsi alla —,** to take to flight; **— di gas,** gas escape; **— di stanze,** suite of rooms.
fugace, *a.* Fleeting, transient, ephemeral.
fugacemente, *adv.* Fleetingly.
fugacità [-à], *n.f.* Fugacity.
fugare, *v.t.* To put to flight, to rout, to disperse.
fuggente, *a.* Fleeting, transient, vanishing.
fuggevole [fuggEvole], *a.* Fleeting, fugitive, transient.
fuggevolezza, *n.f.* Transience, transiency.
fuggevolmente, *adv.* Fleetingly.
fuggiascamente, *adv.* In a fugitive manner.
fuggiasco, *n.m.a.* Fugitive, runaway.
fuggifatica, *n.m.* Shirker, slacker, sluggard.
fuggifuggi, *n.m.* Stampede, panic flight. **Vi fu un — generale,** there was a general stampede.
fuggilozio [fuggilOzio], *n.m.* Pastime, hobby.
fuggimento, *n.m.* Flight, fleeing.
fuggire, *v.t.i.* To flee, to fly, to run away, to escape; to elope; to shun, to avoid. **— dal paese,** to fly the country; **— la folla,** to escape the crowd; **egli fuggì in tempo,** he made off just in time.
fuggitivamente, *adv.* In a fugitive way.
fuggitivo, *n.m.a.* Fugitive, runaway, refugee.
fulcro, *n.m.* Fulcrum, pivot.
fulgente, *a.* Shining, brilliant, refulgent.
fulgere [fUlgere], *v.i.* To shine.
fulgidezza, *n.f.* (*Poet.*) Shiningness; splendour, effulgence.
fulgido [fUlgido], *a.* Shining, dazzling, refulgent.
fulgore, *n.m.* Splendour, brightness, refulgence.
fuliggine [fulIggine], *n.f.* Soot, grime.
fuligginoso, *a.* Sooty; dusky.
fullone, *n.m.* (*Hist.*) Fuller, cleaner.

fulmicotone, *n.m.* Gun-cotton.
fulminante, *n.m.* Percussion cap; lucifer match.
fulminante, *a.* Fulminating.
fulminare, *v.t.* To fulminate; to strike by lightning; to hit, to batter; to dumbfound; to electrocute.
fulminato, *n.m.* (*Chem.*) Fulminate.
fulminato, *a.* Struck by lightning; thunderstruck; electrocuted; burnt out; dumbfounded.
fulminazione, *n.f.* Fulmination, electrocution.
fulmine [fUlmine], *n.m.* Thunderbolt, lightning; (*fig.*) invective; multitude. **Un — a ciel sereno,** a bolt from the blue; **colpito da —,** struck by lightning.
fulmineità [-à], *n.f.* Great speed, extraordinary rapidity.
fulmineo [fulmIneo], *a.* Flashing, vehement; extremely rapid.
fulminio [fulminIo], *n.m.* Incessant lightning.
fulvo, *a.* Tawny, fawn, yellow, reddish.
fumacchio [fumAcchio], *n.m.* Smoke-plume; fumarole (of a volcano); piece of smoking charcoal.
fumaiolo, *n.m.* Chimney-stack, smoke-stack; factory chimney stalk; funnel (of steamer).
fumante, *a.* Smoking, reeking; boiling.
fumare, *v.t.i.* To smoke (in all senses); to reek, to fume; to evaporate. **Fumate la pipa?** Do you smoke a pipe? **È vietato —,** No smoking.
fumaria [fumAria], *n.f.* (*Bot.*) Fumitory.
fumarola, *n.f.* (*Geol.*) Fumarole.
fumata, *n.f.* Smoke, pipe-smoke, puff of smoke; smoke signal. **Fare una —,** to have a smoke.
fumasigari [fumasIgari], *n.m.* Cigar-holder.
fumatoio [fumatOio], *n.m.* Smoking-room.
fumatore, fumatrice, *n.m.f.* Smoker. (*Rail.*) **Fumatori,** smoking-compartment.
fumetto, *n.m.* Anisette (liqueur); strip cartoon; comics (in papers).
fumicare, *v.i.* To smoke, to steam, to emit fumes.
fumicoso, *a.* Steamy.
fumido [fUmido], *a.* Smoky, reeking with smoke.
fumigazione, *n.f.* Fumigation.
fumista (*pl.* **fumisti**), *n.m.* Heating engineer.
fumivoro [fumIvoro], *a.* Smoke-consuming.
fumo, *n.m.* Smoke, fume; reek, exhalation; vapour; (*fig.*) conceit, vanity; humbug. **Andare in —,** to come to nothing; **far —,** to smoke; **i fumi del vino,** the fumes of wine; **molto — e poco arrosto,** much talking but nothing to show for it; **vender del —,** to humbug.
fumogeno [fumOgeno], *a.* Smoke-producing. **Bomba fumogena,** smoke-bomb; **cortina fumogena,** smoke-screen.
fumosità [-à], *n.f.* Smokiness.
fumoso, *a.* Smoky.
funaio [funAio], *n.m.* Rope-maker.
funambolo [funAmbolo], *n.m.* Rope-walker, rope-dancer.
funame, *n.m.* Cordage; rigging.
funata, *n.f.* Lash from a rope.
fune, *n.f.* Rope, cord, cable; (*Hist.*) rack, torture.
funebre [fUnebre], *a.* Funeral, funereal, gloomy, dismal, mournful. **Marcia —,** funeral march; **i funebri,** the funeral; **carro —,** hearse.
funebremente, *adv.* Funereally.
funerale, *n.m.* Funeral, interment, burial.
funereo [funEreo], *a.* Funereal; dismal, sad, gloomy.
funestamente, *adv.* Lamentably, fatally, dismally.
funestare, *v.t.* To sadden, to afflict, to distress, to cast a gloom over; to ruin.
funesto, *a.* Deadly, baleful, lamentable, dismal, sorrowful, distressing.
funga, *n.f.* Mouldiness, mould.
fungaia [fungAia], *n.f.* Mushroom-bed; (*fig.*) sudden crowd.
fungere [fUngere], *v.i.* To act as (deputy), to perform the functions of.
funghire, *v.i.* To grow mouldy, to become mouldy.
fungibile [fungIbile], *a.* (*Law*) Fungible.
fungo, *n.m.* Mushroom, fungus; mould. **Funghi mangerecci,** edible fungi; **raccogliere funghi,** to go mushrooming.
fungosità [-à], *n.f.* Mouldiness; dry-rot; (*Med.*) proud flesh.
fungoso, *a.* Fungous, mouldy.
funicella, *n.f.* Cord, thin rope, strong string.
funicolare, *n.m.a.* Funicular; funicular railway.
funicolo [funIcolo], *n.m.* (*Anat.*) Umbilical cord.
funivia [funivIa], *n.f.* Cable railway, telpher railway (for passengers).
funzionale, *a.* Functional.
funzionamento, *n.m.* Working, functioning, in operation. **Il — del motore è perfetto,** the working of the motor is perfect.
funzionante, *a.* Functioning, operating, working.
funzionare, *v.i.* To operate, to work, to function; to run, to act. **Il motore non funziona,** the motor doesn't work; **Come funzionano questi comitati?** How do these committees operate?
funzionario [funzionArio], *n.m.* Functionary, public servant, civil servant.
funzione, *n.f.* Function; operation, working; activity, office duty; ceremony. **Facente funzioni,** acting, deputy; **entrare in —,** to take up one's duties; **— religiosa,** religious service.
fuochista, *n.m.* Stoker [cp. **fochista**].
fuoco, foco, *n.m.* Fire, burning, combustion; flame, flames; heat; fireplace, hearth; (*Mil.*) firing; (*fig.*) ardour, passion; focus. **— artificiale,** firework; **metter troppa carne al —** to have too many irons in the fire; **farsi di —,** to blush; **— fatuo,** will o' the wisp; **— di paglia,** flash in the pan; **starsene presso al —,** to sit by the fire; **metter la mano sul —,** to stake one's reputation on; **accendere il —,** to light the fire; **a prova di —,** fire-proof; **far — e fiamme,** to do the utmost; **vigile del —,** fireman, fire-watcher; **colpo di —,** shot (from a gun); **arma da —,** firearm; **getta — dagli occhi,** his eyes flash fire; (*Phot. etc.*) **mettere a —,** to focus; **fuori —,** out of focus.
fuor, fuora [cp. **fuori**].

fuoravia! *inter.* Get out of the way! Get out!

fuorchè, *adv.conj.* Save, except, saving; unless.

fuori, *prep.adv.* Out, outside; without; except; abroad. **— di mano,** out of the way; **essere — di sè,** to be beside oneself; **— di casa,** out (to visitors), out of doors; **il di —,** the outside; **— di tempo,** ill-timed; **— d'uso,** obsolete, out-of-date; **dal di —,** from without; **— pericolo,** out of danger; **— pasto,** between meals; **— di posto,** out of place; **— servizio,** off-duty; out of action; **— di strada,** astray; mistaken; **— di vista,** out of sight; **— misura,** beyond measure; **mettere —,** to expose for sale. (*Theat.*) **Fuori!** Recall (for curtain).

fuoribordo, *n.m.* (*Naut.*) Outboard (motor).

fuormisura, *adv.* Out of all reason, excessively.

fuoruscito, *n.m.* Exile, refugee; outlaw; émigré.

fuorviare, *v.t.* To mislead, to send astray [cp. **forviare**].

fuorviarsi, *v.r.* To go astray, to stray, to lose one's way.

furbacchiolo, *n.m.* Cunning lad, "smart kid".

furbacchione, *n.m.* Cunning fellow, rascal.

furbacchiotto, *a.* Roguish.

furbaccio [furbAccio], *a.* Sly.

furbamente, *adv.* Cunningly.

furberia [furberIa], *n.f.* Cunning, slyness; finesse; astuteness.

furbescamente, *adv.* Astutely, cunningly.

furbesco, *a.* Cunning, artful. **Lingua furbesca,** thieves' slang.

furbizia [furbIzia], *n.f.* Cunning, wile.

furbo, *n.m.* Cunning fellow. **Fare il —,** to be subtle; **— matricolato,** a thorough-paced rogue.

furbo, *a.* Cunning, sly, artful, crafty, wily.

furbone, *n.m.* Rogue.

furente, *a.* Furious, mad, enraged, angry; frantic.

fureria [furerIa], *n.f.* (*Mil.*) Orderly room.

furetto, *n.m.* (*Zool.*) Ferret.

furfantaggine [furfantAggine], *n.f.* Rascality.

furfantaglia [furfantAglia], *n.f.* Collection of rogues.

furfante, *n.m.* Knave, rogue, rascal, scoundrel.

furfanteggiare, *v.i.* To live like a rogue, to act as a rogue.

furfanteria [furfanterIa], *n.f.* Roguery, rascally action.

furfantesco, *a.* Rascally.

furgoncino, *n.m.* Motor-wagon, light van.

furgone, *n.m.* Wagon, van; freight-car. **— postale,** mail van.

furia [fUria], *n.f.* Fury, rage, anger, frenzy; haste, hurry. **A — di,** by dint of; **la — del vento,** the violence of the wind; **in fretta e —,** in great haste; **di —,** in haste; **farsi venire le furie,** to fly into a rage; **aver —,** to be in a hurry.

furibondo, *a.* Furious, angry; raging, frantic, vehement.

furiere, *n.m.* (*Mil.*) Company orderly sergeant; quartermaster-sergeant.

furiosamente, *adv.* Furiously.

furiosetto, *n.m.a.* (*colloq.*) Spitfire.

furioso, *a.* Furious, violent, angry; frantic; mad.

furore, *n.m.* Fury, frenzy, rage; (*fig.*) enthusiasm, furore.

furoreggiare, *v.i.* To make a hit, to be a success.

furtivamente, *adv.* Stealthily, furtively, secretively.

furtivo, *a.* Stealthy, secret, furtive.

furto, *n.m.* Theft, larceny; burglary, robbery (with violence). **Piccolo —,** pilfering.

fusaggine [fusAggine], *n.f.* Spindle-wood.

fusaio [fusAio], *n.m.* Spindle-maker.

fusata, *n.f.* Spindleful.

fusato, *a.* Tapering [cp. **affusolato**].

fuscello, fuscellino, *n.m.* Twig, bit of straw; (*fig.*) thin man.

fusciacca, *n.f.* Sash.

fusciacco, *n.m.* (*Eccles.*) Embroidered velvet hangings on the crucifix when borne in procession.

fusciarra, *n.m.* Scamp, rogue.

fusella, *n.f.* Implement for winding ropes.

fusellato, *a.* Tapering.

fusello, *n.m.* (*Mech.*) Journal of an axle; axle-end; spindle.

fusibile [fusIbile], *n.m.a.* (*Elect.*) Fuse, fuse-wire; fusible. (*Elect.*) **Piombo —,** fuse wire, fuse.

fusibilità [-à], *n.f.* Fusibility.

fusiera, *n.f.* Spindle-holder; box for spindles.

fusiforme, *a.* Tapering, spindle-shaped.

fusione, *n.f.* Fusion, melting; liquefaction; (*Art*), casting (for sculpture); (*Comm.*) amalgamation (of firms). **Punto di —,** melting point.

fusionista (*pl.* **fusionisti**), *n.m.* (*Pol.*) Fusionist, advocate of political fusion.

fuso (*pl.* **fusi,** *m.*, **fusa,** *f.*), *n.m.* Spindle; distaff; (*Mech.*) end of axle; shaft; shank; (*Naut.*) shank of an anchor. **Diritto come un —,** as straight as a pole; **far le fusa,** to purr (of a cat).

fusoliera, *n.f.* (*Aviat.*) Fuselage.

fusone, *n.m.* (*Zool.*) Two-year-old stag.

fusorio [fusOrio], *a.* Melting, casting. **Forno —,** blast-furnace.

fusta, *n.f.* (*Hist. Naut.*) Pirate galley.

fustagno, *n.m.* Fustian cloth.

fustaio [fustAio], *n.m.* Saddle-maker, saddler.

fustigare, *v.t.* To flog, to whip, to thrash, to scourge.

fustigazione, *n.f.* Flogging, thrashing.

fusto, *n.m.* Stem, stalk (of plant), trunk (of tree or body); shaft (of column); cask, barrel (of wine). **— da letto,** bedstead; **— della chiave,** shank of a key; **quell'uomo ha un bel —,** that man has a fine figure.

futile [fUtile], *a.* Futile, trifling; vain, frivolous, petty.

futilità [-à], *n.f.* Futility; triviality; trifle.

futilmente, *adv.* Futilely.

futuramente, *adv.* In the future.

futurismo, *n.m.* Futurism.

futurista, *n.m.a.* Futurist.

futuristico [futurIstico], *a.* Futuristic.

futuro, *n.m.a.* The future, futurity; (*Gram.*) future tense; future, forthcoming, to come. **In —,** in the future.

fuzzicare, *v.t.* To search, to poke about.

G

G, g, *n.m.f.* Seventh letter of the Italian alphabet; pronounced hard before "a", "o" and "u" (as in **gamba, gola, gusto**); soft like "j" before "e" and "i" (as in **gente, gita**); hard when combined with "h" (as in **ghiaccio**); liquid when combined with "li" (as in **figlio, figlie**); nasal when combined with "n" (as in **ogni**).
gabarra, *n.f.* (*Naut.*) Barge, lighter.
gabarriere, *n.m.* Bargee.
gabbacristiani, gabbacompagno, gabbadeo, gabbamondo, *n.m.* Cheat, swindler, impostor; hypocrite.
gabbanella, *n.f.* (Hospital) white overall, tunic; gown.
gabbano, *n.m.* Gaberdine; overcoat; cloak.
gabbare, *v.t.i.* To deceive, to take in, to swindle; to impose upon.
gabbarsi, *v.r.* To make fun of, to jeer at.
gabbasanti, *n.m.* Hypocrite.
gabbatore, gabbatrice, *n.m.f.* Impostor.
gabbia [gAbbia], *n.f.* Cage; frame; crate; muzzle (for oxen); prison; (*Naut.*) crow's nest. — **dell'ascensore,** lift-cage.
gabbiaio [gabbiAio], *n.m.* Bird-cage maker.
gabbiano, *n.m.* (*Zool.*) Seagull.
gabbiata, *n.f.* Cageful of birds.
gabbiere, *n.m.* (*Naut.*) Look-out (at masthead).
gabbione, *n.m.* Large cage, crate.
gabbo, *n.m.* Jest; derision, mockery. **Pigliare a —,** to take as a joke; to make a joke of, to laugh at.
gabella, *n.f.* Tax, excise, custom duty.
gabellabile [gabellAbile], *a.* Dutiable, taxable.
gabellare, *v.t.i.* To tax; to charge; (*fig.*) to pass off as; to take in. — **uno per,** to pass one off as.
gabelliere, gabellotto, *n.m.* Exciseman, customs officer.
gabinetto, *n.m.* Closet, small room; study; consulting-room; (*Pol.*) cabinet; lavatory, toilet. — **da bagno,** bathroom; **andare al —,** to go to the lavatory; **una crisi di —,** a cabinet crisis.
gaelico [gaElico], *a.* Gaelic.
gaffa, *n.f.* Social mistake, gaffe; (*Naut.*) boat-hook.
gaggia [gaggIa], *n.f.* (*Bot.*) Acacia (tree and flower).
gagliarda, *n.f.* Galliard (dance).
gagliardamente, *adv.* Vigorously, strongly, bravely.
gagliardetto, *n.m.* Pennon, pennant.
gagliardia [gagliardIa], *n.f.* Vigour, energy, strength; bravery.
gagliardo, *a.* Vigorous, sturdy, energetic; valiant.
gaglioffaggine, gagliofferia [gaglioffAggine, gagliofferIa], *n.f.* Stupidity, clumsiness.
gaglioffo, *n.m.a.* Blockhead, lout; clumsy, stupid, loutish.
gagnolamento, *n.m.* Whimpering; yelping, howling.
gagnolare, *v.i.* To yelp, to howl, to whimper, to whine.
gagnolio [gagnolIo], *n.m.* Continual howling, whining.
gaiamente, *adv.* Gaily, merrily.
gaiezza, *n.f.* Gaiety, merriment, cheerfulness; brightness (of colours, clothes, etc.).
gaio [gAio], *a.* Gay, joyful; sprightly, merry, cheerful; vivacious.
gala, *n.f.* Gala, festivity; show, pomp; frill, **Vestito di —,** gala dress; **serata di —,** gala evening (at opera, etc.); **far —,** to make holiday; **mettersi in —,** to dress up.
galano, *n.m.* Tasselled ribbon.
galante, *a.* Amatory, erotic; attentive to women. **Avventura —,** love intrigue.
galanteggiare, *v.i.* To play the gallant, to flirt.
galantemente, *adv.* politely (to women).
galanteria [galanterIa], *n.f.* (Love) intrigue; politeness, gallantry, courtesy; delicacy.
galantina, *n.f.* Galantine.
galanto, *n.m.* (*Bot.*) Snowdrop.
galantomismo, *n.m.* Gentlemanly behaviour, courtesy.
galantomone, *n.m.* Real gentleman, courtly man.
galantuomo, *n.m.* Gentleman, man of integrity and honour; honest man.
galassia [galassIa], *n.f.* Galaxy; (*Astron.*) the Milky Way.
galateo [galatEo], *n.m.* Code of manners; good breeding; book of etiquette.
galattofago [galattOfago], *n.m.* One who subsists on a milk diet.
galattometro [galattOmetro], *n.m.* Instrument for gauging the density of milk.
galbano, *n.m.* (*Bot.*) Galbanum.
galea [galEa], *n.f.* (*Naut.*) Galley; helmet.
galeazza, *n.f.* (*Naut.*) Large galley.
galena, *n.f.* (*Min.*) Galena. (*Radio*) **Apparecchio a —,** crystal set.
galeotta, *n.f.* (*Naut.*) Galliot, small galley.
galeotto, *n.m.* Galley-slave; convict; (*colloq*). "artful dodger"; pimp, procurer.
galera, *n.f.* (*Naut.*) Galley; prison; convict. **Vita di —,** life of drudgery.
galero, *n.m.* (*Eccles.*) Skull-cap worn by a pope, bishop or prelate.
galestro, *n.m.* (*Geol.*) Marl.
Galilea, *n.f.* (*Geog.*) Galilee.
galileiano, *a.* Concerned with Galileo and his school.
Galileo [galilEo], *n.m.a.* Galileo (the philosopher); Galilean.
galla, *n.f.* (*Bot.*) Gall; oak-apple; blister, air-bubble; swelling; (*fig.*) unreliable person. **A —,** afloat, on the surface; **stare a —,** to float; **venire a —,** to rise to the surface; **tenersi a —,** to keep above water.
gallare, *v.t.* To fertilize (of a cock bird); (*obs.*) to boast.
gallastrone, *n.m.* Old fowl, old cock.
gallatura, *n.f.* Fertilization (by a cock, of eggs).
galleggiabilità [-à], *n.f.* Ability to float.
galleggiamento, *n.m.* Floating, buoyancy. **Linea di —,** water-line (of a vessel).
galleggiante, *n.m.a.* Buoy; float; vessel, barge, lighter; floating, afloat. **Bacino —,** floating dock.
galleggiare, *v.i.* To float, to be afloat, to keep afloat; to rest on the surface.
galleria [gallerIa], *n.f.* Gallery; arcade; (*Rail.*) tunnel. — **d'arte,** art gallery.
Galles, *n.m.* Wales.

gallese, *n.m.a.* Welshman; Welsh language; Welsh.
galletta, *n.f.* Ship's biscuit; army biscuit; kind of grape; kind of mushroom.
galletto, *n.m.* Cockerel; (*fig.*) lively person.
Gallia, *n.f.* (*Hist.*) Gaul.
gallicanismo, *n.m.* Gallicanism, doctrine of the French Church.
gallicano, *n.m.a.* Gallican (of the French Church).
gallicismo, *n.m.* Gallicism.
gallicizzare, *v.t.* To Gallicize, to adopt or ape French ways.
gallico [gAllico] (1), *a.* Gallic, French. **Morbo —,** syphilis.
gallico [gAllico] (2), *a.* (*Chem.*) Gallic. **Acido —,** gallic acid.
gallina, *n.f.* Hen. **— faraona,** guinea-hen; guinea-fowl; **— prataiola,** moor-hen; **latte di —,** egg-flip; **raspatura di —,** scrawl, bad writing; **chi di — nasce convien che razzoli,** he's a chip of the old block; **è meglio un uovo oggi che una — domani,** a bird in the hand is worth two in the bush.
gallinaccio [gallinAccio], *n.m.* Turkey-cock.
gallinaceo [gallinAceo], *a.* (*Zool.*) Gallinaceous; of the order of domestic fowls.
gallinaio [gallinAio], *n.m.* Vendor of cocks; stealer of fowls; owner of fighting cocks.
gallinella, *n.f.* Moor-hen; pullet. (*Astron.*) **Le sette Gallinelle,** the Pleiades.
gallo (1), *n.m.* Cock. **Al canto del —,** at cock-crow; **essere il — della Checca,** to be cock of the walk; to be a lady's man; **fare il —,** to look big. (*Boxing*) **peso —,** bantam-weight.
gallo (2), *n.m.* Gaul, man of Gaul.
galloccia [gallOccia], *n.f.* (*Naut.*) Belaying cleat.
gallonaio [gallonAio], *n.m.* Maker or vendor of lace.
gallonare, *v.t.* To trim with lace or braid; to decorate with stripes.
gallone (1), *n.m.* (*Mil.*) Chevron, stripe; silver or gold stripe for badge of rank. **Bagnare i galloni,** to drink on one's promotion.
gallone (2), *n.m.* Gallon (of liquid).
galloria [gallOria], *n.f.* Merriment, mirth; merry-making [cp. **baldoria**].
gallozza, gallozzola [gallOzzola], *n.f.* Bubble; blister; oak-gall.
galoppante, *a.* Galloping.
galoppare, *v.i.* To gallop; to hurry, to rush about.
galoppata, *n.f.* Gallop, galloping.
galoppatoio [galoppatOio], *n.m.* Riding ground, track.
galoppino, *n.m.* Errand-boy, messenger; (*fig.*) fag, drudge. **— elettorale,** canvasser.
galoppo, *n.m.* Gallop. **Di —,** at a gallop; **piccolo —,** canter.
galoscia [galOscia], *n.f.* Golosh. **Un paio di galoscie,** a pair of goloshes.
galvanicamente, *adv.* Galvanically.
galvanico [galvAnico], *a.* Galvanic.
galvanismo, *n.m.* Galvanism.
galvanizzare, *v.t.* To galvanize (in all senses).
galvanometro [galvanOmetro], *n.m.* Galvanometer.
galvanoplastica [galvanoplAstica], *n.f.* Galvanoplasty, electro-deposition.
galvanoscopio [galvanoscOpio], *n.m.* Galvanoscope.
gamba, *n.f.* Leg (in all senses). **Essere in —,** to be brisk, to feel lively; **stare in —,** to be careful; **prendere sotto —,** to take lightly; **mandare a gambe levate, mandare a gambe all'aria,** to send headlong, to overturn; **darsela a gambe,** to take to one's heels; **aver buona —,** to be a good walker; **rimettersi in gambe,** to recover one's strength; **incrociare le gambe,** to cross one's legs; **bisogna fare il passo secondo la —,** one must cut one's coat according to one's cloth.
gambale, *n.m.* Boot-tree; legging; (*Hist.*) greave; stem of a plant.
gambata, *n.f.* Kick. **Dar la — ad uno,** to supplant someone.
gamberettino, gamberetto, *n.m.* (*Zool.*) Shrimp.
gambero [gAmbero], *n.m.* (*Zool.*) Crayfish. **— di mare,** lobster.
gambetto, *n.m.* Trip (of the heels); kick. (*Chess*) gambit; stalk of a plant. **Fare, dare il —,** to trip up [cp. **dare lo sgambetto**].
gambiera, *n.f.* (*Hist.*) Greave, leg armour.
gambitto, *n.m.* (*Chess*) Gambit.
gambo, *n.m.* Stem; stalk; shaft (of a tool); handle.
gamella, *n.f.* (*Mil.*) Mess-tin.
gamma, *n.f.* Third letter of Greek alphabet; (*Mus.*) gamut; range; scale. **— d'onde,** range of waves in wireless.
ganascia [ganAscia], *n.f.* (*Anat.*) Jaw. (*colloq.*) **Mangiare a quattro ganascie,** to gobble, to eat greedily; (*Mech.*) **stecca a —,** fish-plate.
ganascino, *n.m.* Cheek (esp. of a child). **Pigliare per il —,** to pinch a child's cheek.
ganascione, *n.m.* Blow on the jaw.
gancetto, gancettino, *n.m.* Clasp, catch; paper-clip.
ganciata, *n.f.* Hooking, (act of) hooking.
gancio [gAncio], *n.m.* Hook; catch; fastening, clasp. **— della finestra,** window-catch; (*Naut.*) **— d'accosto,** boat-hook; (*fig.*) **quell'uomo è un —,** that fellow's a grasper.
ganga, *n.f.* (*Min.*) Matrix, gangue; ore.
gangamo [gAngamo], *n.f.* Drag-net, oyster-net.
gangherare, *v.t.* To set on hinges; to furnish with hinges; to hook, to clasp.
gangherella, *n.f.* Eye (for a hook).
ganghero [gAnghero], *n.m.* Hinge, pivot; hook, clasp. **Esser fuori dei gangheri,** to be beside oneself with rage; **uscire dai gangheri,** to become furious.
ganglio [gAnglio, both gs hard], *n.m.* (*Anat.*) Ganglion.
gangola [gAngola], *n.f.* Swollen neck-gland; swollen tonsil.
gangrena, *n.f.* Gangrene [cp. **cancrena**].
Ganimede, *n.m.* (*Myth.*) Ganimede; ladies' man; dandy.
ganza, *n.f.* Concubine, mistress.
ganzo, *n.m.* Paramour; pimp, pander.
gara, *n.f.* Competition, contest, match; rivalry, emulation; (*Comm.*) tender (for contract). **A —,** for a wager; **andare a —,** to compete, to vie with one another; **— di nuoto,** swimming-race; **— eliminatoria,** heat (in sport); **— libera,** open event; **—**

a vantaggi, handicap; **vincere la —,** to carry off the prize.
garante, *n.m.a.* Guarantor, surety, warrentor; guaranteeing, warranting, vouching. **Star —,** to be guarantee.
garantire, *v.t.* To guarantee, to warrant; to go bail for; to make sure.
garantito, *p.p.a.* Guaranteed, secured; warranted. **— che oggi non viene,** it's certain he won't come today; (*Comm.*) **titoli garantiti,** guaranteed stock.
garanzia [garanzIa], *n.f.* Guarantee, pledge, security. (*Comm.*) **— addizionale,** collateral security; **— solidale,** joint guarantee; **basato su — immobiliare,** based on real estate, mortgage.
garbaccio [garbAccio], *n.m.* Ill-mannered action; bad manners, rudeness.
garbare, *v.i.* To please, to suit; to appeal (to one). **Questo non mi garba,** this isn't to my liking.
garbatamente, *adv.* Politely; suitably; gracefully.
garbatezza, *n.f.* Politeness, good manners; courtesy; gracefulness.
garbato, *p.p.a.* Polite, pleasing; amiable, courteous, well-mannered.
garbino, *n.m.* South-west wind.
garbo, *n.m.* Courtesy, good manners; elegance; tact; good cut (of clothes); habit, custom. **Uomo di —,** courteous man; **con bel —,** with good grace; **cantare con —,** to sing pleasingly; **senza —,** awkwardly.
garbo, *a.* Sour, bitter (of wine, fruit, etc.).
garbuglio [garbUglio], *n.m.* Confusion, disorder, turmoil; entanglement.
garbuglione, *n.m.* Bungler; mischief-maker.
gardenia [gardEnia], *n.f.* (*Bot.*) Gardenia.
gareggiamento, *n.m.* Competition, emulation.
gareggiare, *v.i.* To compete, to vie, to emulate; to contend.
gareggiatore, *n.m.* Competitor.
garetta, *n.f.* (*Mil.*) Sentry-box; watchman's hut.
garetto, *n.m.* Back of the heel; fetlock (of horse), pastern. **Aver buoni garetti,** to be a good walker.
garganella, *n.f.* **Bere a —,** to gulp down, to swallow at a draught.
gargarismo, *n.m.* Gargling, gargle.
gargarizzare, *v.i.* To gargle.
gargarozzo, *n.m.* (*colloq.*) Throat, gullet. **Prendere per il —,** to take by the throat.
gargo, *a.* (*obs.*) Crafty.
gargotta, *n.f.* Cook-shop, third-rate eating house.
garibaldino, *n.m.* One of Garibaldi's men.
garitta, *n.f.* (*Mil.*) Sentry-box.
garofanare, *v.t.* To season with cloves.
garofano [garOfano], *n.m.* (*Bot.*) Pink, carnation; clove. **Chiodo di —,** clove.
garontolo [garOntolo], *n.m.* Blow in the arm-pit.
garrese, *n.m.* Withers (of a horse).
garrimento, *n.m.* Warbling, chirping.
garrire, *v.i.* To warble, to chirp; to flap (of a flag, etc.); to chide, to rebuke, to scold.
garrito, *n.m.* Chirping, twittering; screeching, scolding.
garrulamente, *adv.* Garrulously.
garrulità [-à], *n.f.* Garrulity, talkativeness.
garrulo [gArrulo], *a.* Garrulous, talkative, loquacious; chattering.
garza, *n.f.* Gauze; lint; (*Zool.*) heron; jaw of a horse.
garzaia [garzAia], *n.f.* Heronry.
garzare, *v.t.* To teasel cloth, to tease out.
garzatrice, *n.f.* Carding machine, carder.
garzatura, *n.f.* Carding.
garzella, *n.f.* Carder, carding comb.
garzetta, *n.f.* (*Zool.*) Heron.
garzo, *n.m.* (*Bot.*) Teasel; carding, teaseling.
garzolo, *n.m.* Carded hemp; purified candle-wax.
garzona, *n.f.* Dairy-maid, farm-girl, land-girl.
garzoncello, *n.m.* Lad, boy.
garzone, *n.m.* Youth, boy, lad; shop-boy, errand-boy; apprentice.
gas, *n.m.* (*pl.* **gas**) **Becco del —,** gas-burner; **cucina a —, fornello a —,** gas oven, gas cooker; **contatore del —,** gas-meter; **stufa a —,** gas fire, gas-stove; **lampada a —,** gas-lamp; **fuga di —,** gas escape; **chiudere il —,** to turn down the gas; **aprire il —,** to turn on the gas; **tubo del —,** gas-pipe; **luce del —,** gas-light; (*Mil.*) **— asfissianti,** poisonous gases; **attacco coi —,** gas-attack; **maschera anti-gas,** gas-mask; (*Motor.*) **— di scarico,** exhaust.
gasare, *v.t.* (*Mil.*) To gas.
gassista (*pl.* **gassisti**), *n.m.* Gas-fitter, gas-man.
gassogeno [gassOgeno], *n.m.* Gazogene.
gassometro [gassOmetro], *n.m.* Gasometer.
gassosa, *n.f.* Aerated water, fizzy lemonade.
gassosità [-à], *n.f.* Gassiness.
gassoso, *a.* Gaseous; aerated. **Acqua gassosa,** aerated water, soda-water.
gastaldo [cp. **castaldo**].
gasteropodi [gasterOpodi], *n.m.pl.* (*Zool.*) Gasteropoda.
gastigare [cp. **castigare**].
gastricismo, *n.m.* (*Med.*) Gastric complaints.
gastrico [gAstrico], *a.* (*Med.*) Gastric.
gastrite, *n.f.* (*Med.*) Gastritis.
gastroenterite, *n.f.* (*Med.*) Gastro-enteritis.
gastronomia [gastronomIa], *n.f.* Gastronomy.
gastronomico [gastronOmico], *a.* Gastronomic.
gastronomo [gastrOnomo], *n.m.* Gastronome.
gatta, *n.f.* Cat, tabby-cat, she-cat; pussy-cat. **— ci cova,** there's something in the wind; there's a snake in the grass; **far la — morta,** to act the simpleton; **avere una — da pelare,** to be in a fix.
gattaio [gattAio], *n.m.* Cat's-meat man.
gattabuia [gattabUia], *n.f.* (*colloq.*) Prison, "quod". **Andare in —,** to be run in.
gattamorta, *n.f.* (*colloq.*) Hypocrite; sly dog.
gattaiola, *n.f.* Hole cut (in door, etc.) for the cat to pass through.
gattesco, *a.* Cat-like, feline.
gattice [gAttice], *n.m.* (*Bot.*) White poplar.
gattino, *n.m.* Kitten. **Fare i gattini,** to be sea-sick.
gatto, *n.m.* Cat; (*colloq.*) pussy-cat, puss. **— selvatico,** wild cat; **Gatto cogli stivali,** Puss in Boots; (*Motor*) **occhi di —,** cat's eyes, reflectors; **essere in quattro gatti,** to be few people in number; **non c'era un —,** there wasn't a soul there.

gattomammone, *n.m.* Witch's cat; (*Zool.*) species of ape.
gattone, *n.m.* Tom-cat, big cat; (*fig.*) sly fellow.
gattoni, *adv.* Stealthily. **Andar —,** to go on all fours.
gattopardo, *n.m.* (*Zool.*) Leopard.
gattuccio [gattUccio], *n.m.* (*Zool.*) Dog-fish; (*Mech.*) key-hole saw.
gaudeamus, *n.m.* **Vivere in —,** to live a jolly life, to enjoy life.
gaudente, *n.m.a.* Epicurean, man of pleasure, gay dog; jolly, cheerful.
gaudentemente, *adv.* Jollily, cheerfully, merrily.
gaudio [gAudio], *n.m.* Mirth, joy, cheerfulness, merriment.
gaudiosamente, *adv.* Mirthfully, gaily.
gaudioso, *a.* Mirthful, gay, joyful, jolly.
gavazza, *n.f.* Revel, noisy pleasure.
gavazzare, *v.i.* To revel, to make merry, to have a good time.
gavetta, *n.f.* (*Mil.*) Mess-tin. **Venir dalla —,** to rise from the ranks.
gaviale, *n.m.* (*Zool.*) Indian crocodile, mugger.
gavigne, *n.f.pl.* (*obs.*) Armpits.
gavina, *n.f.* (*Zool.*) Seamew.
gavio [gAvio], *n.m.* (*Mech.*) Felloe.
gavitello, *n.m.* (*Naut.*) Buoy.
gavocciolo [gavOcciolo], *n.m.* Tumour.
gavotta, *n.f.* (*Mus.*) Gavotte.
gaz [cp. **gas**].
gazza, *n.f.* (*Zool.*) Magpie; (*fig.*) noisy woman, quean.
gazzarra, *n.f.* Uproar, squabble, din.
gazzella, *n.f.* (*Zool.*) Gazelle, antelope.
gazzetta, *n.f.* Newspaper, gazette; (*fig.*) gossip, busybody.
gazzettante, gazzettiere, *n.m.* Journalist, reporter, newspaper-man.
gazzettino, *n.m.* Gazette, news-sheet, newspaper; (*fig.*) gossip, chatterbox.
gazzo, *n.m.* (*Hist.*) Cap of the Doge of Genoa.
gazzo, *a.* Greenish blue.
geco, *n.m.* (*Zool.*) Gecko, kind of lizard.
geenna, *n.f.* Gehenna, hell.
gelamento, *n.m.* Freezing, congelation.
gelare, *v.i.* To freeze, to be frozen, to be cold. **— dalla paura,** to be frozen stiff (with fear); **sentirsi — il sangue,** to feel one's blood run cold.
gelarsi, *v.r.* To be chilled, to be frozen, to be congealed. **Qui si gela,** it's very cold here.
gelata, *n.f.* Frost, icy weather.
gelatamente, *adv.* Frostily, freezingly.
gelateria [gelaterIa], *n.f.* Ice-cream shop, stall.
gelatiera, *n.f.* Ice-cream freezer.
gelatiere, *n.m.* Ice-cream maker or vendor.
gelatina, *n.f.* Jelly, gelatine, isinglass. **— di frutta,** fruit jelly; **— esplosiva,** blasting gelatine; **— vegetale,** vegetable jelly.
gelatinoso, *a.* Gelatinous.
gelato, *n.m.* Ice-cream, ice. **— alle fragole,** strawberry ice.
gelidamente, *adv.* Icily.
gelidezza, gelidità [-**à**], *n.f.* Frigidity; stiffness (of manner).
gelido [gElido], *a.* Icy, gelid; (*fig.*) frigid, forbidding.
gelo, *n.m.* Frost, ice, cold; (*fig.*) coldness (of manner). **Mettere il — addosso,** to be a wet blanket, to be a kill-joy; **corroso dal —,** frost-bitten.
gelone, *n.m.* Chilblain.
gelosamente, *adv.* Jealously.
gelosia [gelosIa], *n.f.* Jealousy, envy, rivalry; Venetian shutter or blind.
geloso, *a.* Jealous; envious, suspicious; watchful, solicitous.
gelsato, *a.* Planted with mulberry trees.
gelseto, *n.m.* Mulberry orchard.
gelso, *n.m.* Mulberry (tree and fruit).
gelsomino, *n.m.* Jasmine, jessamine.
Geltrude, *n.f.* Gertrude.
gemebondo, *a.* Doleful, plaintive.
gemella, *n.f.* Twin sister.
gemellipara [gemellIpara], *n.f.* Woman who has borne twins.
gemello, *n.m.a.* Twin; twin brother; (*Astron.*) Gemini; twin; double; similar. **Gemelli siamesi,** Siamese twins; **bottoni gemelli,** cuff-links.
gemere [gEmere], *v.i.* To moan, to wail, to groan; to lament, to complain; to coo (of doves); to drip, to trickle (of liquids); (*colloq.*) **Far — i torchi,** to publish something of one's own.
gemicare, *v.i.* To trickle out.
geminare, *v.t.* To double, to collect in pairs; to repeat; to damascene.
geminazione, *n.f.* Doubling.
gemino [gEmino], *a.* Double.
gemitio [gemitIo], *n.m.* Trickling, continual dripping; wailing.
gemito [gEmito], *n.m.* Moan, wail, wailing, groan, weeping, lamentation; cooing (of doves).
gemma, *n.f.* Gem, jewel, precious stone; (*Bot.*) bud. **Mettere le gemme,** to bud.
gemmare, *v.i.* To bud, to gemmate.
gemmarsi, *v.r.* To bedeck oneself with jewels.
gemmazione, *n.f.* Budding, gemmation.
gemmifero [gemmIfero], *a.* Gemmiferous.
gendarme, *n.m.* Gendarme, policeman, Carabiniere.
gendarmeria [gendarmerIa], *n.f.* Police force.
genealogia [genealogIa], *n.f.* Genealogy.
genealogico [genealOgico], *a.* Genealogical. **Albero —,** family tree.
genealogista (*pl.* **genealogisti**), *n.m.* Genealogist.
generalato, *n.m.* Office and period of command of a general; generalship.
generale (1), *n.m.* General, chief. **Maggiore —,** major-general; **tenente —,** lieutenant-general.
generale (2), *n.f.* General matters; summons by drum. **Stare sulle generali,** to keep to general topics; (*Mil.*) **suonare la —,** to beat quarters.
generale, *a.* General, common, universal, public; generic; vague. **Assemblea —,** general assembly; **console —,** Consul-General; (*Mil.*) **quartier —,** headquarters; (*Law*) **procuratore —,** Attorney-General; (*Comm.*) **quietanza —,** receipt in full; (*Theat.*) **prova —,** dress rehearsal; **parlare in —,** to speak in a general way; **elezioni generali,** general elections.

generalissimo, *n.m.* (*Mil.*) Commander-in-chief [cp. **generale** (1)].
generalità [-à], *n.f.* Generality; main body; general principles; personal particulars (name, address, age, etc.).
generalizio [generalIzio], *a.* Pertaining to a general (also of a religious order).
generalizzare, *v.t.* To generalize.
generalizzazione, *n.f.* Generalization.
generalmente, *adv.* Generally, on the whole, in the main.
generamento, *n.m.* Generation, begetting.
generare, *v.t.* To generate, to beget, to breed, to procreate; to cause.
generativo, *a.* Generative.
generatore, *n.m.* Generator (in all senses).
generazione, *n.f.* Generation; reproduction, propagation; progeny, offspring; kind, species. **La nuova —,** the new generation; **— spontanea,** spontaneous generation.
genere [gEnere], *n.m.* Kind, species, sort, description, class; (*Gram.*) gender; (*Lit.*) genre, style, manner; (*Bot.Zool.*) genus. **Il — umano,** mankind; **in —,** in general; **— d'affari,** line of business; **unico del suo —,** unique of its kind; (*Art*) **pittura di —,** genre painting.
generi [gEneri], *n.m.pl.* Commodities, produce. **— alimentari,** foodstuffs, eatables; **— di lusso,** articles of luxury.
genericamente, *adv.* Generically.
genericità [-à], *n.f.* Generality, vagueness.
generico (1) [genErico], *n.m.* (*Theat.*) Utility-man.
generico (2) [genErico], *a.* Generic; vague, indefinite.
generino, *n.m.* Thing, creature; anything (in a general sense). **Un bel —!** That's a fine thing!
genero [gEnero], *n.m.* Son-in-law.
generosamente, *adv.* Generously, liberally.
generosità [-à], *n.f.* Generosity, liberality; high-mindedness.
generoso, *a.* Generous, liberal, open-handed; high-spirited, gallant, noble; fertile.
genesi [gEnesi], *n.f.* Genesis, beginning. **La Genesi,** the Book of Genesis.
genetica [genEtica], *n.f.* Genetics.
genetico [genEtico], *a.* Genetic.
genetliaco [genetlIaco], *n.m.a.* Birthday.
genga, *n.f.* Slut, sluttish girl.
gengiva, *n.f.* (*Anat.*) Gum.
genia [genIa], *n.f.* Low-down set, vulgar lot, rabble, scum.
geniale, *a.* Talented, clever; spirited, original; genial, kindly.
genialità [-à], *n.f.* Geniality; genius, talent, inventiveness, cleverness.
genialmente, *adv.* Genially.
genietto, *n.m.* Sprite, elf.
genio [gEnio], *n.m.* Genius, talent; master-mind; inclination; (*Mil.*) engineers. **Il — civile,** civil engineers; **fare a proprio —,** to do as one likes; **per questa cosa non ho —,** I don't like this; **non andare a —,** to dislike; **contro —,** against one's wish; **il — d'una lingua,** the genius of a language; **i geni italiani,** the master-minds of Italy; **— tutelare,** genus loci; (*Mil.*) **un militare del —,** a soldier of the Engineers.
genitale, *a.* Genital.
genitali, *n.m.pl.* (*Anat.*) The genitals.
genitivo, *n.m.a.* (*Gram.*) Genitive.
genito [gEnito], *a.* Born, begotten. **Primogenito,** first-born.
genitore, genitrice, *n.m.f.* Parent, father, mother. **I genitori,** the parents.
genitura, *n.f.* Procreation, nativity, birth.
gennaio [gennAio], *n.m.* January. (*fig.*) **Sudare di —,** to be in great trouble.
Genova [gEnova], *n.f.* Genoa.
genovese, *n.m.a.* Genoese.
gentaccia, gentaglia [gentAccia, gentAglia], *n.f.* Rabble, mob, riff-raff.
gente, *n.f.* People, folk, persons; race, nation; family, clan, house; men, crew. **— per bene,** respectable people; **— di mare,** sailors, seafaring people; **la dannata —,** the damned, sinners; **Quanta —!** What a crowd! **— di servizio,** servants; **— di chiesa,** church folk; **— di mondo,** fashionable people; **C'è — ?** Is there anyone there? **diritto delle genti,** the law of nations.
gentildonna, *n.f.* Gentlewoman, lady.
gentile, *n.m.a.* Gentile, pagan.
gentile, *a.* Kindly, kind, obliging courteous, polite; amiable, well-disposed; tender (in all senses). **Il sesso —,** the gentle sex.
gentilescamente, *adv.* Nobly.
gentilesco, *a.* Noble, of gentle birth; concerning Gentiles, pagan.
gentilesimo [gentilEsimo], *n.m.* Religion of pagans.
gentilezza, *n.f.* Kindness, amiability, courtesy, courteousness, politeness; gentleness, gracefulness. **Mi faccia la — di,** please be so kind as to; **ricambiare una —,** to return a kindness.
gentilità [-à], *n.f.* Paganism, pagandom.
gentilizio [gentilIzio], *a.* Noble, ancestral; heraldic. **Stemma —,** coat of arms.
gentilmente, *adv.* Politely.
gentiluomeria [gentiluomerIa], *n.f.* Gentlemanliness.
gentiluomo, *n.m.* Gentleman, nobleman; man of honour.
genuflessione, *n.f.* Genuflexion.
genuflesso, *a.* Kneeling (in worship).
genuflettersi [genuflEttersi], *v.r.* To genuflect, to kneel (in worship).
genuinamente, *adv.* Genuinely.
genuinità [-à], *n.f.* Genuineness, veracity, authenticity, frankness.
genuino, *a.* Genuine, real, true, natural, authentic.
genziana, *n.f.* (*Bot.*) Gentian.
geocentrico [geocEntrico], *a.* Geocentric.
geodesia [geodesIa], *n.f.* Geodesy.
geodetico [geodEtico], *a.* Geodetic.
geografia [geografIa], *n.f.* Geography.
geograficamente, *adv.* Geographically.
geografico [geogrAfico], *a.* Geographic, geographical.
geografo [geOgrafo], *n.m.* Geographer.
geologia [geologIa], *n.f.* Geology.
geologico [geolOgico], *a.* Geological.
geologo [geOlogo], *n.m.* Geologist.
geometra [geOmetra], *n.m.* Geometrician; land-surveyor.
geometria [geometrIa], *n.f.* Geometry.
geometricamente, *adv.* Geometrically.

geometrico [geomEtrico], *a.* Geometric, geometrical.
geopolitica [geopolItica], *n.f.* Geopolitics.
georgica [geOrgica], *n.f.* (*Poet.*) Georgic, poem on rural life, husbandry.
georgico [geOrgico], *a.* (*Poet.*) Georgic, rural.
georgofilo [georgOfilo], *n.m.* One versed in the science of agriculture.
Geova [gEova], *n.m.* Jehovah.
geranio [gerAnio], *n.m.* (*Bot.*) Geranium.
gerarca (*pl.* **gerarchi**), *n.m.* Hierarch, chief, leader; (*Pol.*) Fascist leader.
gerarchia [gerarchIa], *n.f.* Hierarchy; organization by rank; dignity, authority, precedence.
gerarchico [gerArchico], *a.* Hierarchical, according to rank and precedence. **Trasmettere una domanda per via —,** to send a request through the appropriate channels.
gerba, *n.f.* (*Bot.*) Sedge.
geremiade [geremIade], *n.f.* Jeremiad, lamentation.
Geremia [geremIa], *n.m.* Jeremiah.
gerente, *n.m.* Manager; confidential clerk; agent; editor (of newspaper). **Socio —,** managing partner.
gerenza, *n.f.* Management; direction (of a business); agency.
gergo, *n.m.* Jargon, slang; gibberish. **Parlare in —,** to talk slang.
Gerico [gErico], *n.f.* Jericho.
gerla, *n.f.* Basket (carried on the back).
gerlata, *n.f.* Basketful.
gerlo, *n.m.* Basket; (*Naut.*) sail-gasket.
Germania [germAnia], *n.f.* Germany.
germanicamente, *adv.* In the German style.
germanico [germAnico], *a.* Germanic, Teutonic.
germanismo, *n.m.* Teutonism; anything adopted from the Germans.
germanizzare, *v.t.* To Germanize, to make German.
germano, *n.m.* Brother; (*Zool.*) wild duck.
germano, *a.* Akin, germane, related, of the same blood. **Fratello —,** brother by same parents.
germanofilo, germanofobo [germanOfilo, germanOfobo], *n.m.a.* Germanophile, Germanophobe.
germe, *n.m.* Germ (in all senses), embryo; seed, origin.
germicida, *n.m.a.* Germicide.
germinale, *a.* Germinating, in germ.
germinare, *v.i.* To germinate [cp. **germogliare**].
germinativo, *a.* Germinative.
germinazione, *n.f.* Germination, growth, development.
germogliare, *v.i.* To bud, to sprout, to blossom.
germogliazione, *n.f.* Budding, blossoming.
germoglio [germOglio], *n.m.* Bud, shoot, sprout, offspring.
gerofante, *n.m.* Hierophant.
geroglifico [geroglIfico], *n.m.a.* Hieroglyphic.
Gerolamo [gerOlamo], *n.m.* Jerome.
gerontocomio [gerontocOmio], *n.m.* Home for the aged.
Gerosolimitani, *n.m.pl.* (*Hist.*) Knights Hospitaller of St. John of Jerusalem.
gerra, *n.f.* Cart-cover made of basket-work.
gerundio, *n.m.* (*Gram.*) Gerund.
gerundivo, *a.* (*Gram.*) Gerundive.
Gerusalemme, *n.f.* Jerusalem.
gessaia [gessAia], *n.f.* Chalk-pit.
gessaio [gessAio], *n.m.* Plasterer; maker of plaster casts.
gessare, *v.t.* To plaster; to adulterate wine (with lime).
gessatura, *n.f.* Plaster-work; liming of wine.
gessinaio [gessinAio], *n.m.* Plasterer; figure-maker.
gesso, *n.m.* Chalk; plaster; (*Art*) gesso-work. **— per scrivere,** chalk (for blackboards, etc.); **modello in —,** plaster cast.
gessoso, *a.* Chalky.
gesta, geste, *n.f.pl.* Deeds, feats, exploits, achievements. **Canzoni di —,** epic songs, *chansons de geste.*
gestante, *n.f.* Pregnant woman.
gestatoria [gestatOria], *a.* (*Eccles.*) Gestatorial. **Sedia —,** (Pope's) gestatorial chair.
gestazione, *n.f.* Gestation.
gesticolamento, *n.m.* Gesticulation.
gesticolare, *v.i.* To gesticulate, to make gestures.
gesticolazione, *n.f.* Gesticulation.
gestione, *n.f.* Management, administration (of public or private affairs). (*Rail.*) **Capo —,** manager of freight department.
gestire, *v.i.* To gesticulate; (*Comm.*) to administer, to manage, to conduct (business).
gesto, *n.m.* Gesture; action, act, movement. **Fare dei gesti,** to gesture; **un bel —,** a fine gesture; **— col capo,** significant nod.
gestore, *n.m.* Manager, director, administrator; (*Rail.*) traffic superintendent.
gestro, *n.m.* Affected grimace.
Gesù, *n.m.* Jesus. **Gesù Cristo,** Jesus Christ.
gesuita (*pl.* **gesuiti**), *n.m.* (*Eccles.*) Jesuit.
gesuiteria [gesuiterIa], *n.f.* Jesuitry.
gesuiticamente, *adv.* Jesuitically.
gesuitico [gesuItico], *a.* Jesuitical.
gesuitismo, *n.m.* Jesuitism, Jesuitry.
geto, *n.m.* Jess (in falconry).
gettaione, *n.m.* (*Bot.*) Corn-cockle.
gettamento, *n.m.* Throwing, hurling.
gettare, gittare, *v.t.* To throw, to fling, to hurl; to throw away, to cast off; to cast, to mould; to drop; to lay (foundations, etc.); to emit, to shoot forth. **— via,** to throw away, to cast away; **— gli occhi su,** to cast one's eyes on; **— in mare,** to throw overboard; **— l'ancora,** to cast anchor; **— il denaro,** to squander one's money; **— il fango su qualcuno,** to throw mud at someone; **— a terra,** to knock down; **— luce su,** to throw light on; **— giù,** to depreciate, to belittle.
gettarsi, *v.r.* To throw oneself, to rush, to pounce, to fall upon; to jump, to drop down, to fall. **— nelle braccia,** to throw oneself into someone's arms; **— nella mischia,** to throw oneself into a fight.
gettata, *n.f.* Cast, throw; jetty, pier; range (of a weapon); shoot (of plant).
gettatoio [gettatOio], *n.m.* Dump, refuse-heap.
gettatore, *n.m.* Metal-founder.
gettito [gEttito], *n.m.* Jetsam, jettison; jetty, breakwater; (*Fin.*) revenue, yield (of taxation). **Far — di,** to jettison.

getto, *n.m.* Throw, throwing; casting (metal); jet, spout; shoot, sprout; flash; draft (of a letter, etc.) **Un — d'acqua,** a water jet; **fare una cosa di —,** to do something at a single stroke; **a — continuo,** continuously, without stopping; **far — di,** to cast away; **di primo —,** the first draft (of a letter, etc.).
gettone, *n.m.* Counter, token.
gheiscia [ghEiscia], *n.f.* Geisha.
gheppio [ghEppio], *n.m.* (*Zool.*) Kestrel.
gheriglio [gherIglio], *n.m.* Kernel (of a nut).
gherlino, *n.m.* (*Naut.*) Small cable, rope; warp.
gherminella, *n.f.* Trick, trickery, hoax.
ghermire, *v.t.* To snatch, to seize; to clutch; to carry off.
ghermitore, *n.m.* Snatcher.
gherone, *n.m.* Gusset.
ghetta, *n.f.* Gaiter.
ghettina, *n.f.* Spat, short gaiter.
ghetto, *n.m.* Ghetto, Jewish quarter. (*colloq.*) **Fare un —,** to raise an uproar.
ghettume, *n.m.* Confusion, muddle; dirt.
ghezzo, *a.* Black, blackish.
ghia, *n.f.* Tackle block, whip, sling.
ghiacciaia [ghiacciAia], *n.f.* Ice-chest, refrigerator; deep-freeze; ice-house.
ghiacciaio [ghiacciAio], *n.m.* Glacier.
ghiacciare, *v.t.* To freeze, to ice, to congeal.
ghiacciarsi, *v.r.* To be frozen, to be congealed.
ghiacciata, *n.f.* Iced drink.
ghiaccio [ghiAccio], *n.m.* Ice; frost. **Freddo come il —,** as cold as ice; **campo di —,** ice-field; **lastrone di —, ghiaccio galleggiante,** ice floe; **rompere il —,** to break the ice.
ghiacciolo, ghiacciuolo, *n.m.* Icicle; hailstone.
ghiaia [ghiAia], *n.f.* Gravel.
ghiaiata, *n.f.* Sprinkling of gravel; gravel path.
ghiaieto, *n.m.* Shingly bed of a river; shingle.
ghiaione, *n.m.* Coarse gravel; debris.
ghiaioso, *a.* Shingly, gravelly.
ghianda, *n.f.* (*Bot.*) Acorn.
ghiandaia [ghiandAia], *n.f.* (*Zool.*) Jay.
ghiandola [ghiAndola], *n.f.* (*Anat.*) Gland [cp. **glandola**].
ghiareto, *n.m.* River-bed of shingle, shingle bank.
ghibellino, *n.m.a.* Ghibelline.
ghiera, *n.f.* Ferrule (of walking-stick); metal ring.
ghiglia, *n.f.* Braid on uniform, frog.
ghigliottina, *n.f.* Guillotine.
ghigliottinare, *v.t.* To guillotine, to behead.
ghigna, *n.f.* (*colloq.*) Grimace, ugly face; (*fig.*) cheek, impudence.
ghignare, *v.i.* To sneer, to grin evilly.
ghignata, *n.f.* Sneer, ugly grin.
ghignazzare, *v.i.* To sneer, to laugh at (unkindly) [cp. **sghignazzare**].
ghigno, *n.m.* Mocking smile, grin; sneer.
ghinda, *n.f.* (*Naut.*) Halyard.
ghindare, *v.t.* (*Naut.*) To hoist.
ghinea [ghinEa], *n.f.* Guinea (21 shillings).
ghingheri [ghIngheri], *n.m.pl.* **Essere, mettersi in —,** to dress up, to be smartly dressed.
ghiotta, *n.f.* Dripping-pan.
ghiottamente, *adv.* Gluttonously, piggishly.
ghiotto, *a.* Gluttonous, greedy; voracious; covetous; dainty, delicious (of food). **Un boccone —,** a dainty morsel; **una ghiotta notizia,** a choice piece of news.
ghiottone, *n.m.* Glutton, gourmand; gourmet, epicure.
ghiottoneggiare, *v.i.* To gourmandize.
ghiottoneria [ghiottonerIa], *n.f.* Gluttony; delicacy, dainty.
ghiozzo, *n.m.* (*Zool.*) Gudgeon; (*fig.*) blockhead.
ghirba, *n.f.* (*Mil.*) Water-skin; skin. **Salvar la —,** to save one's skin.
ghiribizzare, *v.i.* To be whimsical, to be faddy.
ghiribizzo, *n.m.* Whim, fancy, caprice; freak. **Mi salta il — di,** I have a fancy to.
ghiribizzosamente, *adv.* Fancifully.
ghiribizzoso, *a.* Whimsical, faddy, capricious.
ghirigoro, *n.m.* Scroll, flourish; scrawl. **A —,** zig-zag.
ghirlanda, *n.f.* Garland, wreath, festoon of flowers.
ghirlandaio [ghirlandAio], *n.m.* Wreath-maker.
ghiro, *n.m.* (*Zool.*) Dormouse. **Dormire come un —,** to sleep like a log.
ghironda, *n.f.* (*Mus.*) Hurdy-gurdy, barrel-organ.
ghisa, *n.f.* Cast-iron, pig-iron. **— di fonderia,** foundry pig-iron; **— lavorata,** wrought casting.
già, *adv.* Already; formerly, once, previously; indeed, really; yes, of course. **È — andato,** he has gone already; **non è — lo stesso,** indeed, it isn't the same; **Già!** Of course, yes! **il — deputato,** the former deputy; **abiti — fatti,** ready-made clothes.
giacca, *n.f.* Jacket, coat.
giacchè, *conj.* Since, as; now that; **— lo vuoi,** since you want it.
giacchetta, *n.f.* Coat, jacket. **In —,** in a lounge suit.
giacchettino, *n.m.* Jacket, cardigan.
giacchio [giAcchio], *n.m.* Sweep-net, seine.
giaccio [giAccio], *n.m.* (*Naut.*) Tiller.
giacente, *a.* Lying down; unclaimed; (*Law*) in abeyance. **Posta —,** unclaimed letters; **merci giacenti in stazione,** goods lying at the station.
giacenza, *n.f.* (*Comm.*) Demurrage, stoppage; in bond, in store; unsold goods. **— di cassa,** cash in hand.
giacere, *v.i.* To lie, to lie down, to rest; to lie dormant; to be situated, to be placed. **Qui giace,** here lies; **porsi a —,** to lie down.
giaciglio [giacIglio], *n.m.* Couch, pallet, truckle bed; bedding.
giacimento, *n.m.* (*Geol.*) Bed, layer. **— di minerali,** deposit of ores; **— di carbone,** coal-bed.
giacinto, *n.m.* (*Bot.*) Hyacinth.
giacitoio [giacitOio], *n.m.* Lair; bed, couch; sleeping-place.
giacitura, *n.f.* Lying down, recumbent position; way of lying.
giaco, *n.m.* (*Hist.*) Coat of mail.
Giacobbe, *n.m.* Jacob.
giacobinismo, *n.m.* Jacobinism.
giacobino, *n.m.a.* Jacobin.
giacobita, *n.m.a.* Jacobite.

Giacomo [giAcomo], *n.m.* James.
giaculatoria [giaculatOria], *n.f.* Brief prayer; exhortation; chiding; oath.
giaculatorio [giaculatOrio], *a.* Ejaculatory.
giada, *n.f.* (*Min.*) Jade.
Giaffa, *n.f.* Jaffa.
giaggiolo, *n.m.* (*Bot.*) Iris; gladiolus.
giaguaro, *n.m.* (*Zool.*) Jaguar.
giaietto, *n.m.* (*Min.*) Jet.
gialappa, *n.f.* (*Med.*) Jalap.
giallamina, *n.f.* (*Med.*) Calamine.
giallastro, *a.* Yellowish.
gialleggiare, *v.i.* To be yellow, to turn yellow.
gialletto, *a.* Slightly yellow.
giallezza, *n.f.* Yellowness.
gialliccio [gallIccio], *a.* Faintly yellow.
giallino, *a.* Pale yellow.
giallo, *n.m.a.* Yellow; (*Lit.*) thriller. **— d'uovo,** yolk of egg; **— di cromo,** chrome yellow.
giallognolo [giallOgnolo], *a.* Faded yellow, yellowish.
giallore, *n.m.* Yellowness.
giallume, *n.m.* Ugly yellow, excessive yellow.
Giamaica, *n.f.* Jamaica.
giambico [giAmbico], *a.* (*Poet.*) Iambic.
giambo, *n.m.* (*Poet.*) Iambus.
giammai, *adv.* Never. **Non lo farà —,** he'll never do it.
gianduiotto, *n.m.* Kind of chocolate sweet, chocolate-drop.
gianfrullo, gianfrullone, *n.m.* Stupid fellow, blockhead.
giannetta, *n.f.* Walking-stick.
giannettata, *n.f.* Blow with a walking-stick.
Gianni, *n.m.* John, Johnny.
giannizzero [giannIzzero], *n.m.* (*Hist.*) Janizary; (*fig.*) underling.
Giano, *n.m.* (*Myth.*) Janus; (*Arch.*) covered gallery. **Giano bifronte,** double-faced person.
giansenismo, *n.m.* (*Eccles.*) Jansenism.
Giappone, *n.m.* Japan.
giapponese, *n.m.a.* Japanese.
giapponeseria [giapponeserIa], *n.f.* Japanese fancy goods.
giara, *n.f.* Jar, bowl; cup.
giarda, *n.f.* (*Vet.*) Spavin.
giardinaggio [giardinAggio], *n.m.* Gardening. **Fare del —,** to garden.
giardinetto, *n.m.* Small garden.
giardiniera, *n.f.* Gardener's wife, woman gardener; flower-stand; basket-chaise (carriage); sort of salad. **Maestra —,** kindergarten mistress.
giardiniere, *n.m.* Gardener; nurseryman.
giardino, *n.m.* Garden. **Disegnare un —,** to lay out a garden; **— d'inverno,** winter garden; **— pensile,** roof garden; **— pubblico,** public garden; **— d'infanzia,** kindergarten; **— zoologico,** zoological gardens, zoo.
giarrettiera, *n.f.* Garter.
Giasone, *n.m.* (*Myth.*) Jason.
giaurro, *n.m.* Giaour, infidel.
Giava, *n.f.* (*Geog.*) Java.
giavazzo, *n.m.* (*Min.*) Jet.
giavellotto, *n.m.* Javelin.
gibbone, *n.m.* (*Zool.*) Gibbon monkey.
gibbosità [-à], *n.f.* Convexity, gibbosity.
gibboso, *a.* Humped, hunch-backed; gibbous; bumpy (of a road).
giberna, *n.f.* Cartridge-pouch, cartridge-box.
gibetto, *n.m.* Gibbet, gallows.
gibigiana, *n.f.* Reflected shaft of light (by mirror).
Gibilterra, *n.f.* Gibraltar.
gibus, *n.m.* Opera-hat, gibus.
gichero [gIchero], *n.m.* (*Bot.*) Arum; lords-and-ladies.
giga, *n.f.* (*Mus.*) Jig.
gigante, *n.m.a.* Giant, gigantic.
giganteggiare, *v.i.* To tower like a giant.
gigantescamente, *adv.* Gigantically.
gigantesco, *a.* Gigantic, colossal.
gigantessa, *n.f.* Giantess.
gigliaceo [gigliAceo], *a.* Liliaceous, lily-like.
gigliato, *a.* Strewn or planted with lilies; stamped with a lily (of coins).
giglio [gIglio], *n.m.* Lily; (*Hist.*) lily of Florence, fleur-de-lis of France.
gilda, *n.f.* Guild, gild.
gilè [-è], *n.m.* Waistcoat.
gin, *n.m.* Gin.
gineceo [ginecEo], *n.m.* (*Arch.Bot.*) Gynaeceum.
ginecologia [ginecologIa], *n.f.* Gynaecology.
ginecologo [ginecOlogo], *n.m.* Gynaecologist.
ginepraio [ginceprAio], *n.m.* Thicket of junipers. (*fig.*) **Trovarsi, cacciarsi in un —,** to be in a fix.
ginepro, *n.m.* (*Bot.*) Juniper.
ginestra, *n.f.* (*Bot.*) Broom; genista. **— spinosa,** gorse.
ginestrella, *n.f.* (*Bot.*) Dyer's broom
ginestrone, *n.m.* Gorse.
Ginevra, *n.f.* Geneva.
ginevrino, *n.m.a.* Genevese.
gingillare, gingillarsi, *v.i.r.* To trifle, to toy; to linger.
gingillino, *a.* Trifler, trifle.
gingillo, *n.m.* Trinket, toy, trifle; bibelot.
gingillone, *n.m.* Loiterer, lazybones.
gingiva [cp. **gengiva**].
ginnasiale, *a.* Pertaining to a grammar school. **Licenza —,** school-leaving certificate.
ginnasio [ginnAsio], *n.m.* Gymnasium (grammar school); gymnasium.
ginnasta, *n.m.* Gymnast, athlete.
ginnastica [ginnAstica], *n.f.* Gymnastics; physical training.
ginnastico [ginnAstico], *a.* Gymnastic, athletic. **Concorso —,** gymnastic display.
ginnetto, *n.m.* Jennet, small horse.
ginnico [gInnico], *a.* Gymnastic, athletic. **Giochi ginnici,** athletic games.
ginocchiata, *n.f.* Nudge with the knee.
ginocchiello, *n.m.* Knee-cap; knee-guard.
ginocchio, *n.m.* Knee. **In —,** on one's knees.
ginocchioni, *adv.* On one's knees. **Gettarsi —,** to fall on one's knees.
Giobbe, *n.m.* Job. **Pazienza di Giobbe,** the patience of Job.
giobertiano, *n.m.a.* Student of, or relating to Gioberti.
giocare, giuocare, *v.t.i.* To play; to sport, to frolic, to trifle; to deceive; to take part in a game; to game, to gamble; to make a fool of. **— a scacchi,** to play chess; **— a carte scoperte,** to act openly; **A che giuoco giochiamo ?** What are we playing at ? **— d'astuzia,** to play a cunning game; **— una partita,** to play a game.

giocarsi, *v.r.* To gamble away, to stake; to cheat, to deceive; to make sport of. **— la riputazione,** to stake one's reputation; **— della buona fede altrui,** to take advantage of another's good faith.
giocata, *n.f.* Game, play, stake, wager; turn (at playing).
giocatore, giocatrice, *n.m.f.* Player; gamester, gambler, speculator. **— di tennis,** tennis-player; **— di calcio,** football-player; **— di Borsa,** stock-jobber.
giocattolo [giocAttolo], *n.m.* Toy, plaything.
giocherellare, *v.i.* To play, to amuse oneself, to trifle.
giocherello, *n.m.* Toy, plaything; trifle.
giochetto, *n.m.* Pastime, game; trick, subterfuge. **Scoprire il —,** to find out the trick.
giochevole [giochEvole], *adv.* Playful.
gioco [cp. **giuoco**].
giocoforza, *n.f.* Necessity, *force majeure.* **È — partire,** we've got to go.
giocolare, *v.i.* To juggle; to act on the tight-rope.
giocoliere, *n.m.* Juggler, acrobat.
giocolo [giOcolo], *n.m.* Device, mechanism, gadget.
giocondamente, *adv.* Cheerfully, jollily.
giocondare, *v.t.* To gladden, to cheer.
giocondità [-à], *n.f.* Jocundity, mirth, joy, sprightliness, cheerfulness, gaiety.
giocondo, *a.* Jocund, gay, mirthful, cheery, joyous.
giocosamente, *adv.* Jocosely, jocularly.
giocosità [-à], *n.f.* Jocoseness; mirth; facetiousness.
giocoso, *a.* Jocose, jocular, humorous, facetious.
giogaia [giogAia], *n.f.* (*Geog.*) Ridge, chain of mountains; dewlap (of an ox).
giogatico [giogAtico], *n.m.* (*Agric.*) Money paid for hire of oxen for ploughing.
giogo, *n.m.* Yoke (in all senses); ridge, mountain pass; summit, peak. **Scuotere il —,** to shake off the yoke.
gioia (1) [giOia], *n.f.* Joy, delight; mirth, gaiety, gladness, exultation; happiness; (*Comm.*) consideration for goodwill. **Fuochi di —,** fireworks; **Gioia mia,** my darling.
gioia (2) [giOia], *n.f.* Gem, jewel. **Astuccio delle gioie,** jewel-case.
gioielleria [gioiellerIa], *n.f.* Jewelry, jewellery; jeweller's shop.
gioielliere, *n.m.* Jeweller.
gioiello, *n.m.* Jewel, gem.
gioiosamente, *adv.* Joyously.
gioioso, *a.* Joyous, gay, merry, cheerful.
gioire, *v.i.* To rejoice, to be glad, to delight. **— di una cosa,** to delight in something, to be glad of something.
giolito [giOlito], *n.m.* Rest, relaxation, enjoyment.
Giona, *n.m.* Jonah.
Gionata [giOnata], *n.m.* Jonathan.
Giordano, *n.m.* River Jordan.
Giorgio [giOrgio], *n.m.* George.
giorgina, *n.f.* (*Bot.*) Dahlia.
giornalaccio [gionalAccio], *n.m.* Scurrilous newspaper, rag.
giornalaio [giornalAio], *n.m.* Newsagent, newspaper boy.
giornale, *n.m.* Newspaper, journal; diary; (*Comm.*) journal, day-book. (*Naut.*) **— di bordo,** log-book.
giornaliere, giornaliero, *n.m.a.* Day-labourer; daily, day by day.
giornalino, *n.m.* Children's newspaper.
giornalismo, *n.m.* Journalism.
giornalista [*pl.* **giornalisti, -e**], *n.m.f.* Journalist.
giornalistico [giornalIstico], *a.* Journalistic.
giornalmente, *adv.* Daily; day by day.
giornante, *n.m.f.* Day-labourer; charwoman.
giornata, *n.f.* (Duration of) day, day-time; day's work; day's wages; day's journey, march; stage; (*Mil.*) battle. **In —,** before night; **lavorare a —,** to work by the day; **vivere alla —,** to live from hand to mouth; **a gran giornate,** by great strides, by forced marches; **— lavorativa,** working-day.
giornea [giornEa], *n.f.* (*Hist.*) Coat, gown.
giorno, *n.m.* Day, day-time, daylight. **Buon —,** good morning, good day, good afternoon; **in pieno —,** in broad daylight; **— di magro,** fast day; **— di consegna,** delivery day; **— di corriere,** mail-day; **giorni di grazia,** days of grace; **oggigiorno,** nowadays; **avanti —,** before daylight; **sul far del —,** at daybreak; **mettere a —,** to bring to one's notice; **essere a —,** to be up-to-date, to be well informed; **qualsiasi —,** any day; **— per —,** day by day; **di — in —,** day after day; **— feriale,** week-day; **ordine del —,** agenda (of a meeting), (*Mil.*) despatches; (*Mil.*) **mettere all'ordine del —,** to mention in despatches; **verrà a giorni,** he will come in a few days; **— del giudizio,** day of judgment; **il — innanzi,** the previous day; **il — dopo,** the next day; **in pieno —,** in broad daylight; **i prezzi del —,** the current prices.
Giosafat [giOsafat], *n.m.* Jehoshaphat.
Giosia [giosIa], *n.m.* Josiah.
giostra, *n.f.* Joust, tournament; merry-go-round.
giostrare, *v.i.* To joust, to tilt.
giostratore, *n.m.* Jouster; champion.
Giosuè, *n.m.* Joshua.
giottesco, *a.* (*Art*) After the manner of Giotto.
giovamento, *n.m.* Benefit, profit, relief, advantage.
giovanaccio [giovanAccio], *n.m.* Young scamp, young rascal.
giovanaglia [giovanAglia], *n.f.* Crowd of rowdy young people.
giovane, giovine [giOvane, giOvine], *n.m.f.a.* Young person (of either sex), youth, girl; young, youthful, tender; inexperienced. **— di negozio,** shop-assistant; **Giovine Italia,** Young Italy (Mazzini's movement).
giovanetta, giovinetta, *n.f.* Young girl, girl, lass.
giovanetto, giovinetto, *n.m.* Youth, youngster, boy, lad.
giovanezza, giovinezza, *n.f.* Youth, youthfulness; prime of life.
giovanilmente, *adv.* Youthfully.
giovanile, *a.* Young, youthful; juvenile. **Letteratura —,** children's books.
Giovanna, *n.f.* Jane, Joan.
Giovanni, *n.m.* John.
giovanotta, *n.f.* Young woman.
giovanotto, *n.m.* Young man; bachelor.

giovare, *v.t.i.* To be of use, to do good; to help, to benefit; to avail oneself. **Questo clima mi giova,** this climate suits me; **le parole non giovano,** words are of no avail; **giova sperare,** it is good to hope.
giovarsi, *v.r.* To make use of, to profit by, to benefit by. **Mi giovo dei tuoi consigli,** I avail myself of your advice; **— a vicenda,** to help one another.
Giove, *n.m.* Jove.
giovedì [-ì], *n.m.* Thursday. **— santo,** Maundy Thursday.
giovenca, *n.f.* Heifer.
giovenco, *n.m.* Steer, bullock.
giovenile, *a.* Juvenile.
gioventù [-ù], *n.f.* Youth, youthfulness; young people (in general).
giovereccio [gioverEccio], *a.* Pleasant, agreeable, helpful.
giovevole [giovEvole], *a.* Helpful; profitable, beneficial, useful, salutary.
giovevolmente, *adv.* Helpfully, profitably.
gioviale, *a.* Jovial, gay, jolly, cheerful.
giovialità [-à], *n.f.* Joviality, jollity, jolliness.
giovialmente, *adv.* Jovially.
giovialone, *n.m.* Cheery fellow.
giovinastro, *n.m.* Young ruffian.
giovine, giovinetto, giovinezza [cp. **giovane,** etc.].
gipsoteca, *n.f.* (*Art*) Gallery of casts.
girabile [girAbile], *a.* (*Comm.*) Negotiable (of a bill); turning, revolving.
giracapo, *n.m.* Dizziness.
giradisco, *n.m.* Record-player.
giradito, *n.m.* (*Med.*) Whitlow.
giraffa, *n.f.* (*Zool.*) Giraffe.
giramento, *n.m.* Turning round; circular motion; dizziness, giddiness. **— di capo, — di testa,** giddiness.
giramondo, *n.m.* Globe-trotter; wanderer, vagrant.
girandola [girAndola], *n.f.* Catherine-wheel; (*fig.*) turncoat; caprice; featherbrain.
girandolare, *v.i.* To stroll about, to wander about, to loiter.
girandolino, *n.m.* Weather-cock; talkative fellow.
girandolone, *n.m.* Lounger, loiterer.
girante, *n.m.* (*Comm.*) Endorser (of a bill).
girante, *a.* Turning, revolving.
girare, *v.t.i.* To turn, to rotate, to turn round, to spin round, to go about, to tour, to travel; to endorse; (*Cinema.*) to shoot a film; to circulate; to turn sour (of milk, etc.). **La terra gira,** the earth goes round; **— sul proprio asse,** to revolve on one's own axis; **— l'occhio intorno,** to cast one's eyes around; **— la manovella,** to turn the handle; (*Naut.*) **— di bordo,** to tack; (*Billiards*) **— la palla,** to screw; (*Comm.*) **— una cambiale,** to endorse a bill; **mi gira la testa,** I feel dizzy; **— un angolo,** to go round a corner; (*Cinema.*) **— una pellicola,** to shoot a film.
girarsi, *v.r.* To turn round.
girarrosto, *n.m.* Spit, roasting-jack; turnspit.
girasole, *n.m.* (*Bot.*) Sunflower.
girata, *n.f.* Turn, turning; stroll, walk. (*Cards*) deal, dealing; (*Comm.*) endorsement; (*Mil.*) reprimand.
giratario [giratArio], *n.m.* (*Comm.*) Endorsee.
giratina *n.f.* Stroll, short walk.
giratorio [giratOrio], *a.* Revolving, gyratory, rotatory.
giravolta, *n.f.* Turning round, quick turn, pirouette; (*fig.*) change of front.
gire, *v.i.* (*obs.*) To go.
girella, *n.f.* Pulley; small wooden disk, revolving disk; draughtsman (game); (*fig.*) turncoat, time-server.
girellare, *v.i.* To stroll about, to saunter, to lounge.
girello, *n.m.* Metal ring; bracelet; centre of an artichoke; steak cut from back of thigh.
girellonare, *v.i.* To stroll about, to lounge.
girellone, *n.m.* Loafer, loiterer, idler.
giretto, *n.m.* Stroll, short walk, constitutional.
girevole [girEvole], *a.* Revolving, turning, movable; capricious, fickle. **Ponte —,** revolving bridge, turn-bridge.
girfalco, girifalco, *n.m.* (*Zool.*) Gerfalcon.
girigogolo [girigOgolo], *n.m.* Scrawl, flourish (in writing); silly talk.
girino, *n.m.* (*Zool.*) Tadpole.
girio [girIo], *n.m.* Whirling, turning.
giro, *n.m.* Turn, turning; circulation, rotation, revolution (of wheel, etc.); walk, stroll; tour, excursion; circle, circuit; endorsement. (*Sport*) lap. **Andare in —,** to go round, to go about; **mettere in —,** to circulate, to spread; **fare un — di parole,** to use a circumlocution; **il — del mondo,** round-the-world tour; **prendere in —,** to tease, to pull one's leg; **andiamo a fare un —,** let's go for a walk; (*Comm.*) **— di fondi,** cash transfer; **a — di posta,** by return of post; **— d'affari,** turn-over.
girobussola [girobUssola], *n.f.* Gyrocompass.
Girolamo [girOlamo], *n.m.* Jerome.
girondino, *n.m.a.* Girondin.
gironzare, gironzolare, *v.i.* To stroll about, to lounge, to saunter; to hang about.
giropilota, *n.m.* (*Aviat.*) "George", automatic pilot.
giroscopio [giroscOpio], *n.m.* Gyroscope.
girotondo, *n.m.* Round dance.
girovagare, *v.i.* To stroll about, to rove, to wander, to roam, to hike.
girovago [girOvago], *n.m.a.* Tramp; rambler, hiker; wandering, errant. **Mercante —,** hawker, pedlar; **attori girovaghi,** strolling players.
gita, *n.f.* Excursion, trip; tour. **— di piacere,** pleasure trip.
gitana, *n.f.* Spanish Gypsy woman; Spanish dance.
gitano, *n.m.* Spanish Gypsy.
gitante, *n.m.* Tripper, tourist. **— a piedi,** hiker.
gittare, *v.t.* To throw [cp. **gettare**].
giù, *adv.* Down, below; downwards; downstairs. **Su e —,** up and down; **in —, all'ingiù,** downwards; **— il cappello!** Hats off! **e giù acqua,** always this rain; (*fig.*) **questo non mi va —,** I can't swallow this; **su per —,** approximately; (*colloq.*) **essere molto —,** to look poorly, to be run down; **andiamo —,** let's go down.
giubba (1), *n.f.* Mane (of a lion).
giubba (2), *n.f.* Jacket; dress coat, tails.
giubbettino, *n.m.* Jumper (dress).
giubbetto (1), *n.m.* Coatee; coat; bodice.

giubbetto (2), *n.m.* Gibbet.
giubbone, *n.m.* Thick coat, heavy coat.
giubilante, *a.* Jubilant, exultant, joyful.
giubilare (1), *v.i.* To exult, to rejoice, to be jubilant.
giubilare (2), *v.t.* To pension off.
giubilazione, *n.f.* Jubilation, exultation; superannuation.
giubileo [giubilEo], *n.m.* Jubilee.
giubilo [giUbilo], *n.m.* Jubilation, jubilance, rejoicing, mirth.
giuccheria [giuccherIa], *n.f.* Stupidity, foolishness.
giucco, *n.m.a.* Silly fellow, ass; stupid; foolish [cp. **ciuco**].
Giuda, *n.m.* Judah; Judas.
giudaico [giudAico], *a.* Jewish, Judaic.
giudaismo, *n.m.* Judaism.
Giudea [giudEa], *n.f.* Judea.
giudeo [giudEo], *n.m.a.* Jew; Jewish.
giudicabile [giudicAbile], *a.* Ready for judgment.
giudicante, *a.* Judging.
giudicare, *v.t.i.* To judge, to deem; to hear or try a cause; to examine, to consider, to decide; to criticize, to estimate. **— male una persona,** to form a bad opinion of someone; **— dalle apparenze,** to judge from appearances; **— opportuno,** to deem fitting, to think advisable; **lo giudico un galantuomo,** I consider him a man of integrity.
giudicato, *n.m.a.* (*Law*) Sentence, judgment; judged, deemed, thought.
giudicatore, *n.m.* Judge (in all senses).
giudicatura, *n.f.* Judicature.
giudice [giUdice], *n.m.* Judge, magistrate, justice; referee, arbiter. **— conciliatore,** justice of the peace; (*Sport*) **— di campo, — arbitro,** referee; **farsi —,** to set oneself up as a judge; **lasciar — alcuno,** to let someone else judge; **presentarsi al —,** to appear before the judge; **non sono buon — in materia,** I am not a good judge in this matter.
Giuditta, *n.f.* Judith.
giudiziale, *a.* Judicial.
giudizialmente, *adv.* Judicially.
giudiziario [giudiziArio], *a.* Judiciary, judicial. **Errore —,** judicial error; **procedimento —,** judicial proceedings; **cronaca giudiziaria,** law reports.
giudizio [giudIzio], *n.m.* Judgment, sentence; trial; decision; discernment, common sense; opinion, advice; prudence, wisdom. **Uomo di —,** man of sense; **senza —,** heedless, rash, scatter-brained; **a mio —,** in my opinion; **metter —,** to settle down, to become wise; **dente del —,** wisdom tooth; **chiamare in —,** to summon to court; **farsi un — di,** to form an opinion of; **il giorno del —,** judgment day; **il — finale,** the Last Judgment.
giudiziosamente, *adv.* Judiciously.
giudizioso, *a.* Judicious, wise, discerning, considerate.
giuggiola [giUggiola], *n.f.* Jujube; (*fig.*) trifle. **È una —,** it's a mere trifle; **andare in brodo di giuggiole,** to show the utmost delight.
giuggiolena, *n.f.* (*Bot.*) Sesame.
giuggiolino, *a.* Reddish yellow in colour.
giuggiolo [giUggiolo], *n.m.* (*Bot.*) Jujube-tree.
giugno, *n.m.* June.
giugulare, *v.t.* To oppress, to strangle.
giugulare, *a.* Jugular. **Vena —,** jugular vein.
giulebbare, *v.t.* To stew fruit, to sweeten; to render palatable.
giulebbarsi, *v.r.* (*colloq.*) To swallow, to put up with; to cherish; to sweeten.
giulebbe, *n.m.* Julep, syrup, treacle; anything too sweet. **Frutta in —,** stewed fruit.
Giulia [giUlia], *n.f.* Julia.
Giuliano, *n.m.* Julian.
Giulie [giUlie], *n.f.pl.* Julian Alps.
Giulietta, *n.f.* Juliet.
Giulio [giUlio], *n.m.* Julius. **Giulio Cesare,** Julius Caesar.
giulivo, *a.* Joyful, joyous, gay, cheerful.
giulività [-**à**], *n.f.* Jolliness, gaiety, joy.
giullare, *n.m.* Jester, buffoon; jongleur, minstrel; strolling player.
giullaresco, *a.* Like a jongleur.
giumella, *n.f.* Quantity contained in cupped hands. **Bere a —,** to drink from the cupped hands.
giumenta, *n.f.* Mare.
giumento, *n.m.* Pack-horse, beast of burden.
giunca, *n.f.* (*Naut.*) Junk, Chinese junk.
giuncaia [giuncAia], *n.f.* Place covered with reeds.
giuncata, *n.f.* Junket, curds.
giunchiglia [giunchIglia], *n.f.* (*Bot.*) Jonquil, daffodil.
giunco, *n.m.* (*Bot.*) Rush, reed.
giungere [giUngere], *v.t.i.* To arrive, to come, to reach, to attain; to join, to link, to connect. **Egli giunse troppo tardi,** he arrived too late; **ciò mi giunge nuovo,** that's news to me; **— in porto,** to reach harbour; **— a fare, a dire,** to go so far as to do, to say; **— le mani,** to join one's hands (in prayer); **— in cattive condizioni,** to arrive in bad condition.
giungimento, *n.m.* Joining; arrival.
giungla, *n.f.* Jungle.
Giunone, *n.f.* (*Myth.*) Juno.
giunonico [giunOnico], *a.* Junoesque; beautiful, queenly.
giunta, *n.f.* Surplus, make-weight; addition; appendix; extra; council, committee. **Per —,** in addition; **a prima —,** in the first instance.
giuntamente, *adv.* Jointly.
giuntare, *v.t.* To sew together, to join, to tack, to baste; to cheat.
giunteria [giunterIa], *n.f.* Trickery.
giunto, *n.m.* (*Mech.*) Joint, coupling; clutch. **— cardanico,** cardan joint.
giunto, *p.p.a.* Come to, arrived at; joined. **A mani giunte,** with clasped hands.
giuntura, *n.f.* Joint, articulation; juncture.
giunzione, *n.f.* (*Mech.*) Joint, junction, coupling.
giuocare [cp. **giocare**].
giuoco, gioco, *n.m.* Game, play; sport, pastime, recreation; fun, amusement; gambling, gaming; (*Tennis,* etc.) set; (*Mech.*) play. **— d'azzardo,** game of chance, gambling; **— di parole,** pun, play upon words; **aver buon —,** to have an easy task; **per —,** for fun, in sport; **questo non è —,** this isn't playing the game; **prendersi — di,** to pull one's leg, to laugh at; **— leale,** fair play, **— di mano,** sleight of hand; **portare in —,** to bring into play; **— di carte,** game of cards; pack of

cards; **— di borsa,** gambling in stocks; (*Football*) **fuori —,** off-side; **campo di —,** playing-field; (*Motor.*) **— inutile,** backlash.
Giura (*Geog.*), *n.f.* Jura.
giurabbacco! giuraddio! *inter.* By God! By Jove!
giuramento, *n.m.* Oath. **Prestar — a,** to swear in; **fare un —,** to take the oath, to swear; **deferire il —,** to administer an oath; **falso —,** perjury; **mancare al —,** to break an oath.
giurare, *v.t.* To swear, to take an oath; to promise. **— il falso,** to commit perjury.
giurato, *n.m.* Juryman, juror. **Il verdetto dei giurati,** the verdict of the jury.
giurato, *a.* Sworn. **Nemico —,** sworn enemy.
giuratorio [giuratOrio], *a.* On oath, sworn.
giure, *n.m.* Law, jurisprudence.
giureconsulto, *n.m.* Jurist.
giurì [-ì], *n.m.*, **giuria** [giurIa], *n.f.* Jury (in all senses).
giuridicamente, *adv.* Juridically.
giuridico [giurIdico], *a.* Juridical. **Andare per via giuridica,** to proceed by legal means.
giurisdizionale, *a.* Jurisdictional.
giurisdizione, *n.f.* Jurisdiction.
giurisperito, *n.m.* Jurist, able lawyer.
giurisprudenza, *n.f.* Jurisprudence, Law.
giurista, *n.m.* Jurist.
giuro, *n.m.* Oath [cp. **giuramento**].
giusdicente, *n.m.* Magistrate.
Giuseppe, *n.m.* Joseph.
giuspatronato, *n.m.* (*Eccles.*) Patronage of a living.
giusquiamo [giusquIamo], *n.m.* (*Bot.*) Henbane.
giusta, *prep.* According to, in conformity with. **— le norme stabilite,** according to established rule.
giustacuore, *n.m.* (*Hist.*) Jerkin.
giustamente, *adv.* Justly, rightly, properly; exactly.
giustaposizione, *n.f.* Juxtaposition.
giustezza, *n.f.* Justness, fairness, equity, rectitude; exactness, precision.
giustificabile [giustificAbile], *a.* Justifiable.
giustificabilmente, *adv.* Justifiably.
giustificare, *v.t.* To justify, to vindicate, to make good; to explain.
giustificarsi, *v.r.* To justify oneself, to defend oneself, to excuse oneself.
giustificatamente, *adv.* Justifiably.
giustificativo, *a.* Justificative.
giustificazione, *n.f.* Justification; excuse. **A titolo di —,** in order to justify.
giustizia [giustIzia], *n.f.* Justice; fairness, equity, uprightness; court, police. **Assicurare alla —,** to arrest, to capture, to bring to justice; **Ministro di Grazia e Giustizia,** Minister of Justice; **farsi — da sè,** to take the law into one's own hands.
giustiziare, *v.t.* To execute, to put to death.
giustiziere, *n.m.* Executioner.
giusto, *a.* Just, right, fair, upright, equitable; righteous; exact, accurate, precise; fit, proper, suitable; legitimate, lawful. **Il peso —,** correct weight; **un colpo —,** a good shot; **il — mezzo,** the happy medium; **per dirla giusta,** to speak the truth; **statura giusta,** medium height; **a giusta ragione,** with good reason; **Giusto Cielo!** Good Heavens!
giusto, giusto appunto, *adv.* Precisely, indeed.
glabro, *a.* Hairless, smooth; glabrous.
glaciale, *a.* Glacial, icy, frozen, frigid (on manner). **Epoca —,** ice age; **silenzio —,** frozen silence.
gladiatore, *n.m.* Gladiator.
gladiatorio [gladiatOrio], *a.* Gladiatorial.
gladio [glAdio], *n.m.* Short two-edged sword.
gladiolo [gladIolo], *n.m.* (*Bot.*) Gladiolus.
glandola [glAndola], *n.f.* (*Anat.*) Gland.
glandolare, *a.* Glandular.
glauco [glAuco], *a.* Sea-green, light blue; glaucous.
***gleba,** *n.f.* Glebe; sod, turf; land. **Servi della gleba,** serfs.
***glene,** *n.f.* (*Anat.*) Socket.
gli, *a.pl.* The [before impure "s" and "z" and vowels; cp. **il**].
gli, *pers.pron.* Him, to him. **Mandagli il libro,** send the book to him.
***glicerina,** *n.f.* Glycerine.
***glicine** [glIcine], *n.f.* (*Bot.*) Wistaria.
***gliconio,** *n.m.a.* (*Poet.*) Glyconic verse.
gliela, glielo, gliene, etc., *pron.* It to her, it to him, some to him, etc. **Gliela diede,** he gave it to her; **gliene porto,** I am bringing some to him.
***glifo,** *n.m.* (*Mech.*) Throttle.
***glittica** [glIttica], *n.f.* Art of cutting gems.
***glittoteca,** *n.f.* Collection of cut gems.
globale, *a.* Total, inclusive, global. **Somma —,** lump sum.
globalmente, *adv.* In the mass, globally.
globo, *n.m.* Globe, sphere, ball; the earth. **— dell'occhio,** eye-ball, **— del lume,** gas or other light globe.
globosità [-à], *n.f.* Globosity.
globoso, *a.* Globous, globose.
globulare, *a.* Globular.
globulo [glObulo], *n.m.* Globule.
gloria (1) [glOria], *n.f.* Glory; fame, renown; splendour, grandeur, brilliance; (*Art*) glory, halo. **Acquistar —,** to acquire glory; **farsi — di,** to glory in; **aspettare in —,** to wait in excitement; **lavorare per la —,** to work without recompense; **seta —,** rayon.
gloria (2) [glOria], *n.m.* Portion of the Mass beginning **Gloria in excelsis.**
gloriarsi, *v.r.* To boast, to feel pride, to glory in, to take a pride in.
glorificamento, *n.m.* Glorifying, glorification.
glorificare, *v.t.* To glorify, to exalt, to magnify, to extol, to laud.
glorificativo, *a.* Glorifying, laudatory.
glorificatore, glorificatrice, *n.m.f.* Glorifier, praise.
glorificazione, *n.f.* Glorification, laudation, praise.
gloriosamente, *adv.* Gloriously.
glorioso, *a.* Glorious, illustrious, celebrated; proud, vain.
glossa, *n.f.* Gloss, comment, explanation, annotation.
glossare, *v.t.* To annotate, to gloss.
glossario [glossArio], *n.m.* Glossary.
glossatore, *n.m.* Annotator, glossarist.
glossinia [glossInia], *n.f.* (*Zool.*) Tse-tse fly.

* In words marked with an asterisk the initial "g" is hard.

glossologia [glossologIa], *n.f.* Glossology, science of comparative philology.
glottide [glOttide], *n.f.* (*Anat.*) Glottis.
glottologia [glottologIa], *n.f.* Linguistics.
glottologo [glottOlogo], *n.m.* Glottologist.
glucinio [glucInio], *n.m.* (*Min.*) Glucinium.
glucosio [glucOsio], *n.m.* (*Chem.*) Glucose.
glu glu, *n.m.* Gurgle, gobble (of a turkey).
gluma, *n.f.* (*Bot.*) Glume.
glutinare, *v.t.* To glutinize.
glutine [glUtine], *n.m.* Gluten.
glutinoso, *a.* Glutinous, viscous.
glutinosità [-à], *n.f.* Viscosity.
gnacchera, *n.f.* (*Mus.*) Castanet [cp. **nacchera**].
gnaffe! *inter.* My word! Fiddlesticks!
gnagnera [gnAgnera], *n.f.* (*colloq.*) Caprice, fancy; indolence, off-colour feeling.
gnao, gnau, *n.m.* Mew, mewing (of a cat).
gnaulare, *v.i.* To mew; to whine (of a child).
gnaulata, *n.f.*, **gnaulio** [gnaulIo], *n.m.* Mewing, continuous mewing.
gneis, *n.m.* (*Geol.*) Gneiss.
gnocco, *n.m.* Dumpling (of flour or potato flour); (*fig.*) bump, lump; blockhead.
gnomico [gnOmico], *a.* (*Lit.*) Gnomic.
gnomo, *n.m.* Gnome, sprite, goblin.
gnomone, *n.m.* Gnomon (of a sundial).
gnorri, *n.m.* Ignorance. **Fare lo —,** to feign ignorance, to turn a deaf ear.
gnosi, *n.f.* Gnosis, knowledge.
gnosticismo, *n.m.* Gnosticism.
gnostico [gnOstico], *a.* Gnostic.
gobba, *n.f.* Hump, humpback; protuberance. **Aver la —,** to be humpbacked; **una —,** a hunchbacked woman.
gobbo, *n.m.a.* Hunchback (man), hump; hunchbacked, humped. **Andare —,** to go bent double.
gobboni, *adv.* Bent, **Andar —,** to go bent.
goccia [gOccia], *n.f.* Drop; dram; particle, small quantity. **Gocce,** drop earrings; **— a —,** drop by drop; **a gocce,** in drops; **rassomigliarsi come due gocce d'acqua,** to be as like as two peas; **bevine una —,** take a drop.
gocciare, gocciolare, *v.i.* To drip, to fall in drops; to trickle, to dribble. **Il sudore gli gocciolava dalla fronte,** the sweat was rolling from his forehead; **gli gocciola il naso,** his nose runs.
gocciola [cp. **goccia**].
gocciolamento, *n.m.* Dropping, dripping.
gocciolatoio [gocciolatOio], *n.m.* (*Arch.*) Drip-stone.
gocciolatura, *n.f.* Dropping, dripping.
gocciolio [gocciolIo], *n.m.* Continuous dripping (of a tap, etc.).
gocciolo [gOcciolo], *n.m.* Nip, drop, tot (of liquor).
gocciolone, *n.m.* Large drop; (*fig.*) tear.
godere, *v.t.i.* To enjoy, to take pleasure in, to rejoice; to possess; to be delighted with; to benefit from; to have a good time; to use, to utilize. **— buona salute,** to enjoy good health; **— credito,** to have credit; **chi si contenta gode,** a contented mind is a perpetual feast; **godo di sapervi bene,** I'm glad to know you're well.
godereccio [goderEccio], *a.* Enjoyable, delightful; pleasure-loving.
godersi, *v.r.* To enjoy; to enjoy oneself.
godersela, *v.r.* To enjoy oneself, to have a good time; to enjoy life.
godibile [godIbile], *a.* Enjoyable.
godimento, *n.m.* Enjoyment, pleasure; possession, use of.
godio [godIo], *n.m.* (*obs.*) Great and continued pleasure.
goditore, goditrice, *n.m.f.* One who takes pleasure in things; a jolly soul.
goduta, *n.f.* Happiness; enjoyment (of food, etc.) [cp. **godimento**].
goffaggine [goffAggine], *n.f.* Clumsiness; dullness; awkwardness; blunder, gaffe.
goffamente, *adv.* Awkwardly, clumsily.
goffo, *a.* Clumsy, awkward, dull; bashful.
Goffredo, *n.m.* Godfrey; Geoffrey.
gogna, *n.f.* Pillory. **Mettere alla —,** to pillory, to hold up (to execration).
gol, *n.m.* (*Football*) Goal.
gola, *n.f.* Throat, neck; gluttony, greed; gorge, narrow passage (in mountains); straits; (*Mech.*) groove. **Aver l'acqua alla —,** to be in great difficulties; **mal di —,** sore throat; **far —,** to make one's mouth water; **prender per la —,** to seize by the throat; **a piena —,** at the top of one's voice; **peccare di —,** to be sinfully gluttonous; **avere una — d'oro,** to have a golden voice.
goldoniano, *a.* In the manner of Goldoni.
golena, *n.f.* Dry portion of a river between the bank and the stream.
goletta, *n.f.* (*Naut.*) Schooner; collar of a woman's dress.
goletto, *n.m.* Collar [cp. **colletto**].
golf, *n.m.* (*Sport*) Golf; jersey, sweater.
golfare, *n.m.* (*Naut.*) Eye-bolt.
Golfiera, *n.f.* (*Geog.*) Gulf Stream.
golfo, *n.m.* Gulf, bay. **— di Biscaglia,** Bay of Biscay.
Golgota [gOlgota], *n.f.* Golgotha.
Golia [golIa], *n.m.* Goliath.
goliardico [goliArdico], *a.* (*Lit.*) Goliardic; pertaining to students. **Berretto —,** student's cap.
goliardo, *n.m.* Goliard, wandering student (in Middle Ages); university student; merry fellow.
golino, *n.m.* Grip of the throat (between finger and thumb).
golosamente, *adv.* Greedily.
golosità [-à], *n.f.* Gluttony, greed; tasty bit, tit-bit.
goloso, *n.m.a.* Glutton, epicure; greedy, gluttonous; covetous.
golpato, *a.* (*Agric.*) Blighted, mildewed.
golpe, *n.f.* (*Agric.*) Blight, mildew.
gombina, *n.f.* (*Agric.*) Thong of a flail.
gomena [gOmena], *n.f.* (*Naut.*) Cable, hawser. **— da rimorchio,** tow-rope.
gomitata, *n.f.* Thrust or shove with the elbow. **Farsi largo a gomitate,** to elbow one's way through.
gomito [gOmito] (*pl.* **gomiti,** *m.*, **gomite,** *f.*), *n.m.* Elbow; elbow bend (in road); (*Mech.*) crank. **Far —,** to bend an elbow; (*fig.*) **olio di —,** elbowgrease; (*colloq.*) **alzare il —**, to drink hard; **appoggiare il — su,** to rest one's elbows on; (*Mech.*) **— d'un asse,** crank of a shaft; **albero a —,** crank-shaft.
gomitolare, *v.t.* To wind into a ball.

gomitolo [gomItolo], *n.m.* Ball of thread, skein, clew.
gomma, *n.f.* Gum, resin, rubber, India rubber; (*Motor*, etc.) tire, tyre. **— elastica,** india-rubber; **— da cancellare,** rubber (for erasing); **tela di —,** rubber-cloth; **guanti di —,** rubber gloves; **— arabica,** gum arabic; (*Motor.*) **cambiare una —,** to change a tyre; **scoppio d'una —,** puncture, tyre-burst; **— piena,** solid tyre; **— da masticare,** chewing-gum.
gommato, *a.* Gummed. **Carta gommata,** gummed paper.
gommifero [gommIfero], *a.* (*Bot.*) Gummiferous.
gommoso, *a.* Gummy, viscous, sticky.
gondola [gOndola], *n.f.* Gondola, Venetian boat.
gondoliere, *n.m.* Gondolier.
gonfalone, *n.m.* Gonfalon, standard, banner.
gonfalonierato, *n.m.* (*Hist.*) Dignity and office of Gonfalonier.
gonfaloniere, *n.m.* Standard-bearer; (*Hist.*) gonfalonier.
gonfia [gOnfia], *n.m.* Glass-blower.
gonfiaggine [gonfiAggine], *n.f.* (Feeling of) repletion; (*fig.*) self-satisfaction.
gonfiagione, *n.f.,* **gonfiamento,** *n.m.* Swelling, inflation; (*fig.*) bombast.
gonfianuvoli, *n.m.* Boaster.
gonfiare, *v.t.* To fill with air, to blow up, to swell, to inflate; to pump up (tyre, etc.); to cram; to push, to boom, to boost, to exaggerate.
gonfiarsi, *v.r.* To swell, to be inflated, to be puffed up.
gonfiatoio [gonfiatOio], *n.m.* Tyre-pump.
gonfiatore, *n.m.* Inflater; (*fig.*) pushful man, booster; bore.
gonfiatura, *n.f.* Swelling; exaggeration, puffing up, boom; humbug.
gonfiezza, *n.f.* Swelling, inflation, distension; (*fig.*) bombast.
gonfio [gOnfio], *a.* Swollen, swelled, inflated, distended; proud, conceited, puffed up; bombastic, high-sounding (style). **A gonfie vele,** successfully, with flying colours; **— di sè,** conceited, puffed up with pride; **un fiume —,** a swollen river.
gonfione, *n.m.* Fat man; conceited fellow.
gonfiore, *n.m.* Swelling, inflation.
gonga, *n.f.* (*Med.*) Swollen gland (esp. in neck).
gongola [gOngola], *n.f.* (*Zool.*) Mussel, cockle.
gongolamento, *n.m.* Gloating.
gongolante, *a.* Elated, overjoyed, exultant, rejoicing.
gongolare, *v.i.* To be elated, to be overjoyed, to exult; to gloat.
goniometria [goniometrIa], *n.f.* Goniometry.
goniometro [goniOmetro], *n.m.* Goniometer, protractor.
gonna, gonnella, *n.f.* Skirt, petticoat, slip; gown; (*fig.*) the female sex. **Gonne corte,** short skirts; **star attaccato alla — della mamma,** to be tied to mother's apron strings.
gonnellona, *n.f.* Gad-about woman.
gonnellone, *n.m.* Voluminous skirt.
gonorrea [gonorrEa], *n.f.* (*Med.*) Gonorrhoea.
gonzo, *n.m.* Simpleton, ninny, blockhead **Fare il —,** to play the fool.
gora, *n.f.* Channel, conduit, mill-stream, mill-pond; stagnant water, pond.
gorata, *n.f.* Mill-race.
gorbia [gOrbia], *n.f.* Spike; gouge, chisel [cp. **sgorbia**].
gordiano, *a.* Gordian. **Nodo —,** gordian knot.
gorga, *n.f.* (*Anat.*) Gullet.
gorgata, *n.f.* Draught (of liquid), drink.
gorgheggiare, *v.i.* To warble; (*Mus.*) to trill, to quaver.
gorgheggio [gorghEggio], *n.m.* Warbling (of birds), trilling.
gorgia [gOrgia], *n.f.* (*Anat.*) Throat; guttural mode of speaking; burr.
gorgiare, *v.i.* To speak gutturally.
gorgiera, *n.f.* Ruff, frilled collar; (*Hist.*) gorget.
gorgo, *n.m.* Whirlpool, vortex, eddy; gulf, abyss.
gorgogliamento, *n.m.* Gurgling, bubbling purling.
gorgogliare, *v.i.* To gurgle, to bubble, to purl, to rumble (of water).
gorgoglio [gorgOglio], *n.m.* Gurgling, bubbling.
Gorgone, *n.f.* (*Myth.*) Gorgon.
gorgozzule [gorgozzUle], *n.m.* (*colloq.*) Gullet, throat.
gorilla, *n.m.* (*Zool.*) Gorilla.
gota, *n.f.* (*Anat.*) Cheek.
gotata, *n.f.* Blow on the cheek.
Goti, *n.m.pl.* Goths.
goticismo, *n.m.* Gothicism.
gotico [gOtico], *a.* Gothic.
gotta, *n.f.* (*Med.*) Gout.
gottazza, *n.f.* Long-handled scoop or ladle.
gotto, *n.m.* Goblet; contents of a goblet; drop, tot (of liquor). **Bere un —,** to have a dram.
gottoso, *a.* (*Med.*) Gouty.
governabile [governAbile], *a.* Manageable.
governale, *n.m.* (*Naut.*) Rudder, helm.
governamento, *n.m.* Act of governing, government.
governante, *n.f.* Governess, house-keeper.
governanti, *n.m.pl.* Rulers, statesmen.
governare, *v.t.* To govern, to direct, to control, to guide, to manage, to regulate; to steer, to be at the helm; to curry (a horse); (*Agric.*) to manure. **— male,** to misgovern.
governarsi, *v.r.* To control oneself; to act, to regulate.
governativo, *a.* Governmental, government. **Impiegato —,** government official; **scuola governativa,** state school; **palazzo —,** government house.
governatorato, *n.m.* Governorship.
governatore, governatrice, *n.m.f.* Governor; governor's wife.
governo, *n.m.* Government; management, direction, control; executive power; grooming (of horses); (*Agric.*) manuring, tilling; steering, guiding. **Parlar male del —,** to speak ill of the government; **il — della casa,** housekeeping, household management.
gozzaia [gozzAia], *n.f.* Contents of a bird's crop.
gozzata, *n.f.* Cropful; gulp.
gozzo, *n.m.* (Bird's) crop; (*Med.*) goitre; (*Naut.*) fishing-smack.

gozzoviglia [gozzovIglia], *n.f.* Debauch, debauchery, revelry, orgy; merrymaking.
gozzovigliare, *v.i.* To revel, to riot; to overeat; to behave licentiously.
gozzuto, *a.* (*Med.*) Goitrous.
gracchia [grAcchia], *n.f.* (*Zool.*) Jackdaw.
gracchiamento, *n.m.* Croaking, cawing.
gracchiare, *v.i.* To croak; to caw.
gracchiata, *n.f.* Croaking.
gracchio [grAcchio], *n.m.* (*Zool.*) Jackdaw; crow.
Gracco, *n.m.* Gracchus.
gracidamento, *n.m.* Croaking (of frogs).
gracidare, *v.i.* To croak.
gracidio [gracidIo], *n.m.* Croaking, croak.
gracile [grAcile], *a.* Frail, delicate; slender; feeble. **Complessione —,** delicate constitution.
gracilità [**-à**], *n.f.* Slenderness, frailness; weakness.
gracilmente, *adv.* Delicately, slenderly.
gracimolo [cp. **racimolo**].
gracola [grAcola], *n.f.* (*Zool.*) Myna, Indian starling.
gradare, *v.i.* To slope [cp. **graduare**].
gradassata, *n.f.* Blustering, bragging, bravado.
gradasso, *n.m.* Braggart, boaster, bully.
gradatamente, *adv.* Gradually, by degrees, step by step.
gradazione, *n.f.* Gradation, graduation, degree; (*Art*) shading. **— alcoolica,** degree of alcoholic strength.
gradevole [gradEvole], *a.* Pleasant, agreeable, acceptable, palatable.
gradevolezza, *n.f.* Pleasantness; palatableness, agreeableness.
gradiente, *n.m.* Gradient.
gradimento, *n.m.* Liking, taste; flavour; approval, consent, accord; approbation. **Ciò non è di mio —,** this is not to my liking; **con vostro —,** subject to your approval.
gradina, *n.f.* Sculptor's chisel.
gradinare, *v.t.* To cut steps (esp. in ice or snow); to chisel.
gradinata, *n.f.* Flight of steps, staircase; tier of seats; (*Theat.*) balcony.
gradinatura, *n.f.* Cutting of steps; chiselling.
gradino, *n.m.* Step (of staircase); tread (of step); (*fig.*) rank, degree. **È salito un altro —,** he's gone up one.
gradire, *v.t.* To receive with pleasure, to accept gratefully; to like, to appreciate, to welcome. **Voglia — i miei cordiali ringraziamenti,** please accept my hearty thanks.
gradito, *p.p.a.* Well-received, welcome; appreciated. (*Comm.*) **Ho ricevuto la vostra gradita (lettera) del 20 corrente,** your favour of the 20th inst. to hand.
grado (1), *n.m.* Wish; liking; pleasure. **Di buon —,** willingly; **a malgrado di,** in spite of; **a suo —,** at his pleasure; **saper —,** to be thankful; **ricevere di buon —,** to receive favourably; **prendere di buon —,** to take in good part; **vi saprò —,** I shall be obliged to you; **andare a —,** to be agreeable.
grado (2), *n.m.* Degree; dignity, rank, grade; gradation, progression; (*Mil.*) rank. **Dieci gradi sotto zero,** ten degrees below zero; **il — di capitano,** the rank of captain; **— — accademico,** academic degree; **a — a —,** by degrees; **al massimo —,** to the highest degree; **non essere in — di,** not to be in a position to; **— di parentela,** degree of relationship; **— di latitudine,** degree of latitude; **— di durezza,** degree of hardness.
graduabile [graduAbile], *a.* Capable of being graduated.
graduale, *a.* Gradual, progressive. (*Comm.*) **Bollo —,** proportional stamp duty.
gradualmente, *adv.* Gradually, by degrees.
gradualità [**-à**], *n.f.* Gradualness.
graduare, *v.t.* To graduate, to grade; to set, to adjust (an instrument, etc.).
graduato, *n.m.a.* (*Mil.*) Non-commissioned officer; graduated, graded. **Graduati e truppa,** rank and file.
graduatoria [graduatOria], *n.f.* List in order of merit, graduated list, scale; pass-list.
graduazione, *n.f.* Graduation, gradation, grading, scale; preferment, promotion.
graffiamento, *n.m.* Scratch, scratching.
graffiare, *v.t.i.* To scratch, to claw, to tear.
graffiarsi, *v.r.* To scratch one another. **I ragazzi si graffiarono,** the boys clawed at one another.
graffiasanti, *n.m.* Hypocrite, bigot.
graffiata, graffiatura, *n.f.* Scratch, scratching.
graffio [grAffio], *n.m.* Scratch; hook, grapnel.
graffito, *n.m.* Mural scribbling or drawing [cp. **sgraffito**].
grafia [grafIa], *n.f.* Handwriting; spelling.
grafica [grAfica], *n.f.* Graphic arts.
graficamente, *adv.* Graphically.
grafico [grAfico], *a.* Graphic.
grafio [grAfio], *n.m.* Stile (for writing on wax, etc.).
grafite, *n.f.* Blacklead, graphite.
grafologo [grafOlogo], *n.m.* Graphologist.
grafomania [grafomanIa], *n.f.* Mania for writing.
gragnola, gragnuola, *n.f.* Hail.
gragnolare, *v.i.* To hail, to rain hailstones.
gramaglia [gramAglia], *n.f.* Mourning, crape. **In gramaglie,** in mourning.
gramigna, *n.f.* Weed; couch-grass.
gramignoso, *a.* Weedy.
gramma [cp. **grammo**].
grammatica [grammAtica], *n.f.* Grammar.
grammaticale, *a.* Grammatical.
grammaticalmente, *adv.* Grammatically.
grammatico [grammAtico], *n.m.a.* Grammarian; grammatical.
grammo, *n.m.* Gramme, gram.
grammofono [grammOfono], *n.m.* Gramophone, phonograph.
gramo, *a.* Wretched, poor, miserable. **Vita grama,** miserable life.
gramola [grAmola], *n.f.* Kneading-trough; implement for bruising flax or hemp.
gramolare, *v.t.* To knead; to crush, to bruise (flax, etc.).
gramolata, *n.f.* Kind of iced drink.
gran [cp. **grande**].
grana, *n.f.* Grain (of wood, etc.); texture; cochineal dye. **Formaggio di —,** kind of Parmesan cheese; **a — fina,** fine-grained; (*Mil.*) **avere delle grane,** to have troubles.
granadiglia [granadIglia], *n.f.* (*Bot.*) Passion-flower; granadilla.
granaglia [granAglia], *n.f.* Gold or silver in granules; wheat; grain.

granaglie [granAglie], *n.f.pl.* Cereals, wheat, grain. **Negoziante in —,** grain dealer.
granaio [granAio], *n.m.* Granary; barn.
granaiolo [granaiOlo], *n.m.a.* Grain-dealer; (*Zool.*) granivorous.
granare, *v.t.* To grain, to ripen, to run to seed.
granario [granArio], *a.* Pertaining to grain.
granata, *n.f.* Broom, besom; (*Mil.*) grenade. **— a mano,** hand-grenade; **manico della —,** broomstick.
granataio [granatAio], *n.m.* Maker or seller of brooms.
granatiere, *n.m.* (*Mil.*) Grenadier; (*fig.*) very tall person.
granatina, *n.f.* Syrup of pomegranate.
granatino, *n.m.* Grenadine (fabric.)
granato, *n.m.a.* (*Min.*) Garnet; deep red colour.
grancancelleria [grancancellerIa], *n.f.* Chancellery.
grancane, *n.m.* (*Hist.*) The Grand Khan.
grancassa, *n.f.* (*Mus.*) Bass drum; big drum. **Battere la —,** to announce noisily.
grancella, *n.f.* (*Zool.*) Hen crab.
granchiesco, *a.* Crab-like.
granchio [grAnchio], *n.m.* (*Zool.*) Crab; (*Med.*) cramp; claw (of a hammer); (*fig.*) serious blunder. **Prendere un —,** to make a bad blunder; (*Naut.*) to catch a crab.
granchiolino, *n.m.* Small crab.
granciporro, *n.m.* Big crab; serious blunder.
grande, *n.m.* Adult, grown-up; magnate; grandee. **In —,** on a large scale; **grandi e piccoli,** old and young.
grande, gran, grand', *a.* Great, large, huge, big; wide, spacious; tall, high, lofty; full-grown, grown-up; grand, majestic, stately; heavy, strong. **Grand'uomo,** great man; **uomo —,** tall man; **farsi —,** to grow up; **a gran passi,** with great strides; **gran mondo,** smart set; **gran caldo,** great heat; **a — velocità,** at great speed; **un gran che,** something extraordinary.
grandeggiare, *v.i.* To stand above, to stand out, to tower, to dominate; to show off, to put on airs.
grandemente, *adv.* Greatly, to a great degree; deeply; highly.
grandezza, *n.f.* Greatness, largeness, bigness, magnitude; quantity, bulk; grandeur, loftiness; (*Math.*) quantity. **— naturale,** life-size; **— d'animo,** magnanimity; **Sua —,** His Highness.
grandezzata, *n.f.* Bragging, showing off, ostentation.
grandigia [grandIgia], *n.f.* Ostentation, pomp, haughtiness, arrogance.
grandiglione, *n.m.* Overgrown lad, hobbledehoy.
grandiloquente, *a.* Grandiloquent, bombastic, resounding.
grandiloquenza, *n.f.* Grandiloquence, pomposity, bombast.
grandinare, *v.i.* To hail; to pour down.
grandinata, *n.m.* Hail-storm.
grandine [grAndine], *n.f.* Hail. **Chicchi di —,** hail-stones; **— di colpi,** shower of blows.
grandinifugo [grandinIfugo], *n.m.* Large-mouthed gun fired to disperse hail-storms.
grandiosamente, *adv.* Grandiosely.
grandiosità [-à], *n.f.* Magnificence, grandeur.
grandioso, *a.* Grandiose, majestic, stately, imposing, magnificent.
grandisonante, *a.* High-sounding, eloquent; highfalutin.
granduca, *n.m.* Grand Duke.
granducale, *a.* Pertaining to a Grand Duke.
granducato, *n.m.* Grand Duchy.
granduchessa, *n.f.* Grand Duchess.
granello (*pl.* **granelli,** *m.,* **granella,** *f.*), *n.m.* Grain, particle, seed; stone, pip (of fruit); kernel (of nut). **Un — di buon senso,** a grain of common sense; **i granelli,** the testicles (of animals); **le granella,** cereals.
granelloso, *a.* Seedy, full of seeds.
granfatto, *adv.* Much, very, a great deal. **Non è —,** it is not long since; **non mi piace —,** I don't like it much.
granfia [grAnfia], *n.f.* Claw, talon. **Capitar nelle granfie di,** to fall into the clutches of.
granfiare, *v.t.* To clutch, to seize.
granifero [granIfero], *a.* Graniferous.
granigione, *n.m.* Formation of the grain (in wheat); seeding.
granire, *v.i.* To seed, to grow (of wheat); to granulate; to grain (a surface); (*Mus.*) to play distinctly. **— i denti,** to teethe.
granita, *n.f.* Variety of ice-cream.
granitico [granItico], *a.* Granite; solid, unshakeable.
granito, *n.m.* (*Min.*) Granite.
granito, *a.* Seeded, full of grain; robust (of a person).
granitura, *n.f.* Seeding (of wheat); milled edge (of a coin).
granivoro [granIvoro], *a.* (*Zool.*) Granivorous.
granmaestro, *n.m.* Grand Master (Masonry, chivalry, etc.).
granmercè, *inter.* Many thanks (*irony*); thanks for nothing.
grano, *n.m.* Grain, corn, wheat; pip; bead (of rosary); grain (measure). **Battere il —,** to thresh grain; **un — di buon senso,** a grain of common sense.
granocchia [granOcchia], *n.f.* (*Zool.*) Frog [cp. **ranocchia**].
granone, granturco, *n.m.* (*Agric.*) Maize, Indian corn.
granulare, *v.t.* To granulate, to form grains.
granulare, *a.* Granular.
granulatoio [granulatOio], *n.m.* Powder-mill; mill; sieve.
granulazione, *n.f.* Granulation.
granulo [grAnulo], *n.m.* Granule.
granuloso, *a.* Granulous, gritty.
grappa, *n.f.* (*Mech.*) Clamp, cramp-iron; (*Typ.*) brace; aqua vitae.
grappino, *n.m.* (*colloq.*) Pick-me-up, tot of brandy; hook; grapnel.
grappolo [grAppolo], *n.m.* Bunch (of grapes, etc.); cluster. **A grappoli,** in clusters.
grasceta, *n.f.* (*Agric.*) Fine pasture, lush meadows.
grascia [grAscia], *n.f.* Lard, fat. **Grascie,** victuals.
graspo, *n.m.* Grape-stalk.
grassaccio [grassAccio], *n.m.a.* Immensely fat (man).
grassamente, *adv.* Richly, plentifully; (*fig.*) largely.
grassatore, *n.m.* Highwayman.

grassazione, *n.f.* Highway robbery; aggression, robbery with violence.
grassello, *n.m.* Lump of fat, suet; slaked lime.
grassetto, *n.m.* (*Typ.*) Heavy type.
grassezza, *n.f.* Fatness, plumpness; (*Agric.*) richness of soil, fertility; plenty, abundance.
grasso, *n.m.* Fat, fatness; suet; grease; dirt. **Mangiar di —,** to eat meat; **macchia di —,** grease spot; **— di balena,** blubber; (*Chem.*) **i grassi,** the fats.
grasso, *a.* Fat, plump, stout; greasy; fleshy; fertile, productive; plentiful, abundant; lewd, immodest, smutty, licentious. **Giorni grassi,** days when meat may be eaten; **martedì —,** Shrove Tuesday; **tempo —,** cloudy weather; **terreno —,** fertile land; **piante grasse,** fleshy-leaved plants; **diventar —,** to grow fat; **parlar —,** to tell smutty stories.
grassoccio [grassOccio], *a.* Plump.
grassotto, *a.* Very fat, too fat; plump.
grassume, *n.m.* Grease, fattiness; dirt; manure.
grata, *n.f.* Grating, grate.
gratamente, *adv.* Gratefully.
gratella, *n.f.* Grill, gridiron. **Carne alla —,** grill.
graticciare, *v.t.* To trellis.
graticciata, *n.f.* Trellis, lattice; fence.
graticcio [gratIccio], *n.m.* Trellis work; basket-work; hurdles.
graticola [gratIcola], *n.f.* Grating, grating in confessional; grill, gridiron. **Cucinare alla —,** to grill.
graticolare, *v.t.* To close with a grating; to grill; to graticulate.
graticolato, *n.m.* Iron railing; grating; trellis-work.
gratificante, *a.* Gratifying.
gratificare, *v.t.* To reward, to recompense; to bestow a gratuity on; (*fig.*) to fob off with.
gratificarsi, *v.r.* To win one's favour.
gratificazione, *n.f.* Reward, gratuity; gratification.
gratis, *adv.* Free, gratis. **— a richiesta,** free on application.
gratitudine [gratitUdine], *n.f.* Gratitude, thankfulness.
grato, *a.* Agreeable, pleasant; acceptable; grateful, thankful; kind. **Una grata compagnia,** an agreeable company; **io vi sono —,** I am grateful to you; **mi è — il dirvi,** I'm glad to tell you.
grattacapo, *n.m.* Care, concern; uneasiness, annoyance, trouble; worry, preoccupation. **Aver dei grattacapi,** to have lots of troubles; **dare dei grattacapi a,** to make someone worry.
grattacielo, grattanuvole [grattanUvole], *n.m.* (*Arch.*) Skyscraper.
grattamento, *n.m.* Rubbing, scratching.
grattare, *v.t.* To rub, to scratch, to scrape; to grate (cheese, etc.); to rub out, to erase.
grattata, grattatura, *n.f.* Scratching.
grattaticcio [grattatIccio], *n.m.* (Mark left by) erasure.
grattino, *n.m.* Ink-eraser (liquid or knife).
grattugia [grattUgia], *n.f.* Grater.
grattugiare, *v.t.* To grate (cheese, etc.).
gratuitamente, *adv.* Gratuitously, free of charge.
gratuito [gratUito], *a.* Free of charge, gratuitous; uncalled for, unnecessary, unwarranted. **Prestito —,** loan without interest; **posto —,** scholarship (at a school, etc.); **asserzione gratuita,** unwarranted assertion; (*Law*) **a titolo —,** without consideration.
gratulante, *a.* Congratulatory, complimentary.
gratulatorio [gratulatOrio], *a.* Congratulatory.
gravabile [gravAbile], *a.* Taxable, subject to taxation or duty.
gravafogli, *n.m.* Letter-weight.
gravame, *n.m.* Burden, heavy taxation; gravamen.
gravamento, *n.m.* Burden; sequestration (by creditors).
gravante, *a.* (*Law*) Bearing, lying. **Ipoteca — sull'immobile,** mortgage bearing on real property.
gravare, *v.t.i.* To weight down, to oppress; to burden with, to load.
gravato, *p.p.a.* Burdened, weighted; oppressed; encumbered. **— di forti debiti,** burdened with heavy debts; **— di lavoro,** over-worked; **— d'assegno,** cash on delivery, C.O.D.
grave, *n.m.a.* Weight; heavy, grave, serious; solemn; momentous; dangerous; (*Mus. Gram.*) grave. **Ammalato —,** seriously ill; **non ti sia —,** don't worry about it; **— responsabilità,** grave responsibility; **è una cosa —,** it's a serious matter; **negligenza —** gross negligence.
gravemente, *adv.* Gravely, seriously; dangerously.
graveolente, *a.* Evil-smelling, stinking.
gravezza, *n.f.* Weight, heaviness; burden; excess; weariness, trouble; tax.
gravidanza, *n.f.* Pregnancy.
gravido [grAvido], *a.* Pregnant (in all senses). **Panino —,** roll with savoury filling.
gravina, *n.f.* Pick-axe, pick.
gravità [-à], *n.f.* Gravity (in all senses); seriousness; weight, burden; deepness (of sound); importance. **Centro di —,** centre of gravity.
gravitare, *v.i.* To gravitate, to tend towards.
gravitazione, *n.f.* Gravitation.
gravosamente, *adv.* Heavily; painfully.
gravosità [-à], *n.f.* Heaviness; irksomeness, onerousness.
gravoso, *a.* Heavy, burdensome, onerous, irksome; sad, painful. **Incarico —,** irksome task.
grazia [grAzia], *n.f.* Grace, gracefulness, charm; favour; good will; leave, pardon, mercy. **Di —,** please; **l'anno di —,** the year of Our Lord; **colpo di —,** finishing blow; **stato di —,** state of grace; **essere nelle grazie di,** to be in the good graces of; **mi faccia —,** please pardon me, kindly do me the favour; **in — di,** for the sake of; **con vostra buona —,** with your permission; **Alla grazia!** I say! **troppa —,** too much of a good thing; **la — di Dio,** the grace of God; (*Law*) **domanda di —,** petition for mercy, reprieve.
graziare, *v.t.* To pardon; to quash a sentence.
grazie, *inter.* Thank you! Thanks! **— mille, tante —,** thank you very much. **— alla vostra gentilezza,** thanks to your kindness.

graziosamente, *adv.* Gracefully; graciously, kindly.
graziosità [-**à**], *n.f.* Gracefulness, graciousness.
grazioso, *a.* Gentle, kind; charming; polite; graceful; gracious; pretty, comely; gratuitous. **Prestito —,** loan without interest; **invito —,** courteous invitation.
greca, *n.f.* (*Mil.*) Zig-zag braid on an Italian general's cap; (*Art*) key pattern; Greek-fret.
grecale, *n.m.a.* North-east wind; north-east.
grecamente, *adv.* In a Greek style.
Grecia [grEcia], *n.f.* Greece.
grecismo, *n.m.* Hellenism.
grecista (*pl.* **grecisti**), *n.m.* Hellenist; Greek scholar.
grecizzare, *v.t.* To Hellenize; to speak or write in the Greek style.
greco, *n.m.a.* Greek; north-east wind.
gregario [gregArio], *n.m.a.* Private soldier; political follower; gregarious.
gregge, *n.m.,* **greggia** [grEggia], *n.f.* (*pl.* **le greggi** and **gregge**). Flock, herd; (*fig.*) crowd, mob; (*Eccles.*) flock, congregation.
greggio, grezzo [grEggio], *a.* Raw, untrained; not dressed, unbleached. **Cuoio —,** raw hide; **materie gregge,** raw material; **zucchero —,** brown sugar.
gregoriano, *a.* (*Eccles.*) Gregorian. **Canto —,** plain chant.
Gregorio [gregOrio], *n.m.* Gregory.
grembialata, grembiulata, *n.f.* Apronful.
grembiale, grembiule, *n.m.* Apron; pinafore.
grembialino, *n.m.* Pinafore, child's apron.
grembo, *n.m.* Lap; bosom; womb. **— materno,** motherly bosom; womb; **seder in — a,** to sit on somebody's lap.
gremire, *v.t.* To crowd, to throng; to fill, to stuff full.
gremirsi, *v.r.* To stuff oneself, to eat to satiety.
greppia [grEppia], *n.f.* Manger, crib; rack; (*fig.*) living, livelihood. **Stare attaccato alla —,** to cling to one's wages; **mangiare a più d'una —,** to have more than one string to one's bow.
greppina, *n.f.* Lounge chair, chaise-longue.
greppo, *n.m.* Ravine, steep slope; cliff, rocky slope. **Fare il —,** to pout, to jib (of a child).
gres, *n.m.* (*Geol.*) Sandstone.
greto, *n.m.* Shingle bed of a river; shingle; beach (of the seashore).
gretola, *n.f.* Bar (of a cage); (*fig.*) cavil; pretext, excuse.
gretoso, *a.* Shingly.
grettamente, *adv.* Meanly, pettily.
gretteria, grettezza [gretterIa], *n.f.* Meanness, pettiness, narrow-mindedness.
gretto, *a.* Mean, petty, narrow-minded; stingy, niggardly.
greve, *a.* Heavy, oppressive; ponderous, burdensome; grievous, sorrowful. **Tempo —,** stuffy weather.
grevemente, *adv.* Heavily, ponderously.
grezzo [cp. **greggio**].
grida, *n.f.* Proclamation, ban, edict, decree.
gridacchiare, *v.i.* To cry constantly, to moan.
gridare, *v.i.* To cry aloud, to shout, to scream, to shriek, to bawl. **— una persona,** to reprove someone publicly; **lo gridarono re,** they made him king by acclamation.
gridata, *n.f.* Screaming, scolding.
gridatore, *n.m.* Town-crier.
gridio [gridIo], *n.m.* Crying, bawling, incessant yelling.
grido (*pl.* **gridi,** *m.,* **gride, grida,** *f.*), *n.m.* Cry, scream, shout, shriek, clamour, outcry; squeak; (*fig.*) fame, renown. **Di —,** celebrated, famous; **acquistar —,** to gain repute; **— di guerra,** war-cry, slogan; **gettare un —,** to utter a cry; **senza un —,** without a sound.
grifagno, *a.* Rapacious, ravenous; hawk-like. **Occhi grifagni,** eyes of a hawk.
grifarsi, *v.r.* To eat greedily, to guzzle.
grifo, *n.m.* Snout, muzzle; (*Myth*) griffin.
grifone, *n.m.* Griffin; vulture.
grigiastro, *a.* Greyish.
grigio [grIgio], *a.* Grey, dismal, dull. **Capelli grigi,** grey hair.
Grigioni, *n.m.pl.* (*Geog.*) Grisons.
grigiore, *n.m.* Greyness, dullness.
grigioverde, *a.* Greyish-green; (*Hist.*) colour of Italian army service uniform. **In —,** in service uniform.
griglia [grIglia], *n.f.* Venetian blind, grating, grille; grill, gridiron; (*Radio*) grid.
Grignolino, *n.m.* Type of Piedmontese wine.
grillaia [grillAia], *n.f.* Barren ground.
grillare, *v.i.* To simmer; to hiss; to ferment. **— il cervello,** to have whims.
grilletto, *n.m.* Trigger (of firearm).
grillo, *n.m.* (*Zool.*) Cricket; (*fig.*) whim, fancy, fad. **Il — del focolare,** the cricket on the hearth; **mi salta il —,** I have a whim; **avere grilli pel capo,** to be capricious, to indulge in fancies; (*colloq.*) **Indovinala grillo!** Guess, if you can!
grillotalpa, *n.m.* (*Zool.*) Mole-cricket.
grillotti, *n.m.pl.* Gold fringe to epaulets.
grimaldello, *n.m.* Instrument for picking locks; jemmy.
grinfia [grInfia], *n.f.* Claw, talon [cp. **granfia**].
grinta, *n.f.* Ugly face, sulky look.
grinza, *n.f.* Wrinkle, fold, crease; ripple (on water). **Non fa una —,** it is flawless, it is quite straight.
grinzoso, *a.* Wrinkled, full of creases.
gripo, *n.m.* Kind of fishing-net.
grippe, *n.m.* (*Med.*) Influenza.
grippia [grIppia], *n.f.* (*Naut.*) Rope of an anchor-buoy.
grippiale, *n.m.* (*Naut.*) Anchor buoy.
grisatoio [grisatOio], *n.m.* Glazier's hack-knife.
griselle, *n.f.pl.* (*Naut.*) Ratlines.
grissino, *n.m.* Long thin roll of bread.
Groenlandia [groenlAndia], *n.f.* Greenland.
groenlandese, *n.m.a.* Greenlander, of Greenland.
gromma, *n.f.* Tartar (of wine), crust; dregs, lees.
grommare, *v.i.* To form a crust.
grommoso, *a.* Encrusted, crusted.
gronda, *n.f.* Eaves (of roof), gutter. **Cappello a —,** sou'wester.
grondaia [grondAia], *n.f.* Gutter; stack-pipe.
grondare, *v.t.i.* To drip, to drop, to trickle; to stream; to pour out.
grondatoio [grondatOio], *n.m.* Eaves.
grondone, *n.m.* Gutter.
grondoni, *adv.* **Andar —,** to move slowly, gazing on the ground.

grongo, *n.m.* (*Zool.*) Conger eel.
groppa, *n.f.* Back, croup (of horse); rump; shoulder; mountain ridge. **In —,** on the back; **saltare in —,** to leap into the saddle.
groppiera, *n.f.* Crupper.
groppo, *n.m.* Knot, entanglement; squall (at sea). **Sentirsi un — alla gola,** to have a lump in one's throat.
groppone, *n.m.* Back, croup. **Aver tant'anni sul —,** to be weighed down with one's years; **piegare il —,** to put one's back into it; to humble oneself.
gropposo, *a.* Knotty.
grossa, *n.f.* Gross, 12 dozen [cp. **grosso**].
grossamente, *adv.* Largely, grossly, coarsely.
grosseria [grosserIa], *n.f.* Gold or silver work on a large scale, opposite of **minuteria.**
grossezza, *n.f.* Size, bigness, bulk; coarseness, grossness.
grossiere, *n.m.* goldsmith making large things.
grossista, *n.m.* (*Comm.*) Wholesale dealer.
grosso, *n.m.* Gross (in all senses); bulk, main part. **Il — dell'esercito,** the bulk of the army; **il — della gamba,** the calf of the leg.
grosso, *a.* Big, large; fat, wide, thick; heavy, deep; gross, coarse, clumsy; (*Comm.*) wholesale. **Mare —,** rough sea; **fiume —,** swollen river; **caccia grossa,** big-game shooting; **grande e —,** big fat man; **pezzo —,** big-wig, V.I.P.; **dito —,** thumb, big toe; **dirle grosse,** to talk tall; **farle grosse,** to act foolishly; **dormita grossa,** deep sleep; **dormire della grossa,** to sleep like a log; **Questa è grossa!** This is the limit! (*Comm.*) **casa grossa,** wholesale house.
grossolanamente, *adv.* Coarsely, grossly, roughly, rudely.
grossolanità [-à], *n.f.* Coarseness, grossness, roughness, vulgarity; clumsiness.
grossolano, *a.* Coarse, gross, unrefined, vulgar, clumsy, rough, rude; awkward.
grossularia [grossulAria], *n.f.* (*Bot.*) Gooseberry; green mineral.
grossume, *n.m.* Sediment.
grotta, *n.f.* Cave, den; grotto; rocky wall. **La Grotta Azzurra,** the Blue Grotto.
grottescamente, *adv.* Grotesquely.
grottescheria [grottescherIa], *n.f.* Grotesqueness.
grottesco, *n.m.a.* Grotesque; extravagant, ludicrous.
grottoso, *a.* Cavernous.
groviglio [grovIglio], *n.m.* Knot, tangle, entanglement; intricacy; confusion. **Trovarsi in un —,** to be in a tangle.
gru, grue, grua, *n.f.* (*Zool.Mech.*) Crane. **— mobile,** travelling crane; **— fissa,** stationary crane.
gruccia [grUccia], *n.f.* Crutch; latch. **Andar colle grucce,** to walk with crutches.
grucciata, *n.f.* Blow with a crutch.
gruccione, *n.m.* (*Zool.*) Bee-eater.
grue [cp. **gru**].
gruera, *n.f.* Gruyère cheese.
grufolare, *v.i.* To grub up, to poke about, to root (like a pig).
grufolarsi, *v.r.* To wallow in mire.
grugare, *v.i.* To coo.
grugnire, *v.i.* To grunt.
grugnito, *n.m.* Grunt.
grugno, *n.m.* Snout; (*colloq.*) face. **Fare il —,** to pout.
grullaggine, grulleria [grullAggine, grullerIa], *n.f.* Stupidity, nonsense, foolishness.
grullo, *n.m.a.* Stupid, silly.
gruma [cp. **gromma**].
grumereccio [grumerEccio], *n.m.* Late hay, second crop, aftermath.
grumo, *n.m.* Clot (of milk, blood, etc.).
grumolo [grUmolo], *n.m.* Core, heart (of vegetable).
grumoso, *a.* Clotted, thick.
gruppetto, *n.m.* Small group; (*Mus.*) roulade, run.
gruppo, *n.m.* Group, cluster, assemblage; society. **Disporre in gruppi,** to group; **in —,** in a group; (*Radio*) **— di lunghezze d'onda,** wave-band.
gruzzolo [grUzzolo *n.m.* Savings, hoard, money laid by.
guadabile [guadAbile], *a.* Fordable.
guadagnare, *v.t.i.* To gain, to earn; to obtain, to acquire; to win, to deserve; to make up for. **— terreno,** to gain ground; **— una scommessa,** to win a bet; **— tempo,** to gain time; **non c'è nulla da guadagnare,** there's nothing to be gained; **— tempo perduto,** to make up for lost time; **— un porto,** to reach a harbour.
guadagnarsi, *v.r.* To earn for oneself. **— da vivere,** to earn a livelihood.
guadagneria [guadagnerIa], *n.f.* (Illicit) profit.
guadagno, *n.m.* Gain, profit; benefit, advantage; earnings, winnings. **— netto,** net gain; **— lordo,** gross profit; **amore del —,** love of lucre; **fare gross guadagni,** to make large profits.
guadare, *v.t.* To ford, to wade across.
guado, *n.m.* Ford. **Passare a —,** to ford.
guadoso, *a.* Fordable.
guai! *inter.* Woe! Woe betide! **— ai vinti,** woe to the vanquished.
guaico, *n.m.* (*Bot.*) Guaiacum, lignum vitae.
guaime, *n.m.* (*Agric.*) After-grass.
guaina, *n.f.* Sheath, case; scabbard.
guaio [guAio], *n.m.* Woe, plight, trouble, misfortune, calamity; (*Mech.*) failure; lamentation, moaning. **Aver molti guai,** to have many troubles; **cacciarsi nei guai,** to drift into difficulties; **passare un brutto —,** to meet with serious difficulty, to be in a fix. **Che —!** What a fix!
guaire, *v.i.* To howl, to yelp, to whine (of dogs), to wail.
guaito [guAito], *n.m.* Howl, wail, whine, yelping.
gualcamento, *n.m.* Fulling (of cloth).
gualcare, *v.t.* To full cloth.
gualcheratore, *n.m.* Fuller.
gualchiera, *n.f.* Fulling-mill.
gualcire, *v.t.* To crumple [cp. **sgualcire**].
gualdana, *n.f.* (*Hist.*) Raid into enemy territory.
gualdrappa, *n.f.* Caparison, horse-cloth.
guancia [guAncia], *n.f.* (*Anat.*) Cheek.
guancialata, *n.f.* Blow with a pillow.
guanciale, *n.m.* Pillow; cushion. **Dormir tra due guanciali,** to be free of all anxiety.
guanciata, *n.f.* Slap.

guano, *n.m.* (*Agric.*) Guano, bird manure.
guantaio [guantAio], *n.m.* Glover, glove-maker.
guanteria [guanterIa], *n.f.* Glove-shop.
guantiera, *n.f.* Glove-box; tray.
guanto, *n.m.* Glove. **Un paio di guanti,** a pair of gloves; **trattar coi guanti,** to handle carefully; **gettare, raccogliere il —,** to challenge, to accept the challenge; **guanti di pelle lavabile,** wash-leather gloves; **guanti di pugilato,** boxing-gloves; **calzare come un —,** to fit like a glove.
guardabarriere, *n.m.* (*Rail.*) Keeper of gate at a level crossing.
guardaboschi, *n.m.* Forester; woodman.
guardacaccia [guardacAccia], *n.m.* Game-keeper.
guardacasa, *n.m.f.* Housekeeper; custodian.
guardacoste, *n.m.* Coastguard, coastguard vessel.
guardacucina, *n.m.* Scullery.
guardafreni, *n.m.* (*Rail.*) Brakesman.
guardalato, *n.m.* (*Naut.*) Fender.
guardalinee [guardalInee], *n.m.* (*Football*) Linesman.
guardamagazzino, *n.m.* Storekeeper.
guardamandrie [guardamAndrie], *n.m.* Herdsman.
guardamano, *n.m.* Basket-hilt, trigger-guard; handrail.
guardaporto, *n.m.* (*Naut.*) Guard-ship.
guardaportone, *n.m.* Door-keeper; door-porter.
guardare, *v.t.i.* To look at, to gaze at, to watch, to pay attention, to behold; to consider, to observe, to view, to heed; to guard, to keep, to protect; to beware; to face. **— di buon occhio,** to look upon favourably; **farsi —,** to make oneself noticed; **— intorno** to look around; **— fisso,** to stare at; **Guarda!** Look! Behold! **Dio me ne guardi!** May God preserve me! Heaven preserve us! **la casa guarda a nord,** the house faces north; **— pel sottile,** to be very particular.
guardaroba, *n.f.* Cloak-room, wardrobe; cupboard.
guardarobiera, *n.f.* Cloak-room attendant; (*Theat.*) wardrobe mistress.
guardarsi, *v.r.* To guard against, to beware, to take care; to look at each other. **Guardati dai pericoli,** beware of danger; **— negli occhi,** to look into one another's eyes; **— dai borsaiuoli,** beware of pick-pockets.
guardasala, *n.m.* (*Rail.*) Ticket-collector, inspector.
guardasigilli, *n.m.* Keeper of the Seals.
guardata, *n.f.* Gaze, stare, look, glance.
guardataccia [guardatAccia], *n.m.* Frown, scowl, black look.
guardatina, *n.f.* Glance.
guardatura, *n.f.* Look, appearance; manner of looking.
guardavivande, *n.m.* Meat-safe.
guardia [guArdia], *n.f.* Guard, watch; policeman; guardsman; (*Mil.*) sentry; escort, custody, protection, vigilance, defence, care, keeping. **Far la —,** to keep watch; **stare in —,** to be on one's guard; **— medica,** ambulance station; **— del corpo,** bodyguard; **corpo di —,** guard-room; (*Fencing*) **In —!** Parry! **foglio di —,** fly-leaf.
guardialinee [guardialInee], *n.m.* (*Football*) Linesman.
guardiamarina, *n.m.* (*Naut.*) Midshipman.
guardiana, *n.f.* Herdswoman.
guardianato, *n.m.* (*Law*) Guardianship.
guardiano, *n.m.* Guard, keeper, watch; guardian; warder (of a prison); (*Eccles.*) superior of a religious house, **Padre —,** father superior.
guardina, *n.f.* Lock-up, cell; (*Mil.*) guard-room.
guardinfante, *n.m.* Crinoline.
guardingamente, *adv.* Cautiously, warily.
guardingo, *a.* Wary, cautious, careful, circumspect.
guardiolo, *n.m.* (*Mil.*) Guard-room, guard-house.
guardo, *n.m.* (*Lit.*)Look, aspect [cp. **sguardo**].
guarentigia [guarentIgia], *n.f.* (*Law*) Guaranty; guarantee.
guarentire [cp. **garantire**].
guari, *adv.* (Used only in the negative). Much. **Non è —,** it is not long ago; **non — lontano,** not far off.
guaribile [guarIbile], *a.* Curable.
guarigione, *n.f.* Recovery, healing, cure. **In via di —,** on the way to recovery.
guarire, *v.t.i.* To heal, to cure; to recover, to mend, to heal up. **— una malattia,** to cure a disease; **sta guarendo,** he's getting better.
guarirsi, *v.r.* To recover.
guaritore, *n.m.* Healer.
guarnacca, *n.f.* Cloak, long robe; dressing-gown.
guarnello, *n.m.* (*obs.*) Petticoat.
guarnigione, *n.f.* Garrison. **Munire di —,** to garrison.
guarnimento, *n.m.* Trimming, dressing; fitting out; (*Naut.*) digging; (*Mil.*) fortification, guard, defence.
guarnire, *v.t.* To trim, to deck, to garnish; to furnish, to provide with, to equip, to supply; to dress (food), to season. **— un abito,** to trim a dress; **— una fortezza,** to garrison a fortress.
guarnirsi, *v.r.* To furnish oneself with, to provide oneself with.
guarnito, *p.p.a.* Furnished, equipped; seasoned, garnished. **Un piatto —,** a dish with vegetables.
guarnitura, guarnizione, *n.f.* Trimming; furnishing, equipment, facing; garnishing, seasoning; (*Mech.*) packing.
Guascogna, *n.f.* Gascony.
guasconata, *n.f.* Gasconade, bragging, bravado.
guascone, *n.m.a.* Gascon.
guastafeste, *n.m.* Spoil-sport, kill-joy, wet blanket; crashing bore.
guastamento, *n.m.* Wasting, spoiling.
guastamestieri, *n.m.* Bungler, botcher; scab (in a strike).
guastare, *v.t.* To damage, to spoil, to waste; to ruin, to destroy, to hurt; to mar, to impair. **— le uova nel paniere,** to upset one's plans; **— la festa,** to spoil the sport.
guastarsi, *v.r.* To decay, to go bad, to go wrong, to get spoiled, to change for the worse. **— il sangue,** to get worried; **— con qualcuno,** to fall out with someone; **il latte si è guastato,** the milk has turned sour.

guastastomaco [guastastOmaco], *n.m.* Indigestible food.
guastatore, *n.m.* Spoiler, destroyer; (*Mil.*) sapper; (*pl.*) demolition squad.
guasto, *n.m.* Damage, havoc; trouble; accident. **— alle macchine,** engine trouble; **— al motore,** breakdown of the motor, motor trouble.
guasto, guastato, *a.* Spoiled, spoilt; marred, tainted; corrupted; flat, sour. **Uova guaste,** rotten eggs; **gusto —,** vitiated taste.
guatare, *v.t.i.* To stare at, to gaze at, to eye, to look askance at.
guatarsi, *v.r.* To stare at each other.
guattero, guattera [guAttero], *n.m.f.* Scullion, kitchen-boy; scullery-maid.
guattire, *v.i.* To give tongue (of hounds), to bay.
guazza, *n.f.* Dew, moisture.
guazzabugliare, *v.t.* To make a muddle, to muddle along.
guazzabuglio [guazzabUglio], *n.m.* Hotch-potch, mixture, muddle, medley; confusion.
guazzare, *v.i.* To paddle, to dabble in water; to wallow (in mud, etc.); to ford.
guazzata, *n.f.* Dew fall.
guazzatoio [guazzatOio], *n.m.* Horse-pond, watering-place.
guazzetto, *n.m.* Stew, hash; ragout.
guazzo, *n.m.* Puddle, muddy pool, bog; slush; ford. **Pittura a —,** gouache painting.
guazzoso, *a.* Wet with dew; dewy, slushy.
gubbia [gUbbia], *n.f.* Three horses harnessed abreast.
guelfo, *n.m.a.* Guelph.
guercio [guErcio], *a.* One-eyed; squinting.
guernire [cp. **guarnire**].
guerra, *n.f.* War, warfare; struggle, strife, feud. **Lo scoppio della —,** the outbreak of war; **zona di —,** war zone; **— aerea,** air warfare; **in —,** at war; **in piede di —,** on a war footing; **aver fatto la —,** to have seen active service; **— di logoramento,** war of attrition; **— di trincea,** trench warfare.
guerrafondaio [guerrafondAio], *n.m.* War-monger.
guerreggiante, *a.* Belligerent.
guerreggiare, *v.i.* To wage war; to be in opposition.
guerrescamente, *adv.* Martially, in a war-like manner.
guerresco, *a.* Warlike, martial, bellicose.
guerriere, guerriero, *n.m.a.* Warrior; warlike.
guerriglia [guerrIglia], *n.f.* Guerilla, guerilla warfare.
guerrigliere, *n.m.* Bush-fighter, guerilla partisan.
gufare, *v.i.* To hoot (of an owl).
gufo, *n.m.* (*Zool.*) Owl; (*Eccles.*) amice.
guglia [gUglia], *n.f.* Spire; obelisk; pyramid. **Le guglie del duomo,** the cathedral spires.
gugliata, *n.f.* Needleful (of thread).
Guglielmo, *n.m.* William.
guida, *n.f.* Guide, leader; guide-book; directory; guidance; rail; steering, direction; rein (harness); (*Motor*) drive. **Far da —,** to act as guide; **— del telefono,** telephone directory; (*Motor*). **volante di —,** steering-wheel; **— a destra, sinistra,** right-, left-hand drive.
guidabile [guidAbile], *a.* Amenable, leadable.
guidaiolo, *n.m.* Bell-wether; animal wearing a bell.
guidalesco, *n.m.* (*Vet.*) Sore (on horses and donkeys).
guidamento, *n.m.* Guiding, driving.
guidare, *v.t.i.* To guide, to lead; to direct, to conduct; to manage; to drive (a vehicle), to ride; **— l'automobile,** to drive the car; **— una motocicletta,** to ride a motor-bike.
guidarsi, *v.r.* To guide oneself, to manage oneself.
guidatore, *n.m.* Guide, leader; driver (of car).
guiderdone, *n.m.* (*Lit.*) Reward, recompense, guerdon.
guidetto, *n.m.* Hand-saw, tenon saw.
Guido, *n.m.* Guy.
guidone, *n.m.* Pennon; marking flag.
guidoslitta, *n.f.* Bob-sleigh, sled.
guiggia [guIggia], *n.f.* Sandal-strap, lace for sandals, etc.
guindolo [guIndolo], *n.m.* Reel (in weaving).
guinzagliare, *v.t.* To put on the leash.
guinzaglio [guinzAglio], *n.m.* Leash. **Tenere al —,** to hold in leash.
guisa, *n.f.* Mode, way, guise, manner. **A — di,** like, as; **in ogni —,** in every form; **di — che,** so that; **in tal —,** in such a way.
guitteria [guitterIa], *n.f.* Poverty, meanness.
guitto, *n.m.* (*Theat.*) Poor strolling player.
guitto, *a.* Low, poor, beggarly.
guizzamento, *n.m.* Darting hither and thither.
guizzante, *a.* Quivering, darting; wriggling.
guizzare, *v.i.* To dart (of fish); to flicker; to vibrate; to frisk; to quiver, to wriggle; to flash.
guizzo, *n.m.* Darting, dart, wriggle; flash; flicker, vibration. **In un —,** in a flash.
guscio [gUscio], *n.m.* Shell (of eggs, nuts, etc.); cover; pod, hull; pan (of scales). **Non uscir dal —,** not to come out of one's shell.
gustabile [gustAbile], *a.* Enjoyable.
gustaccio [gustAccio], *n.m.* Bad taste, nasty flavour.
gustamento, *n.m.* Tasting, enjoying.
gustare, *v.t.i.* To taste, to relish, to savour, to enjoy; to take delight in. **— la musica,** to enjoy music; **non mi gusta questo vino,** I don't care for this wine.
gustazione, *n.f.* Tasting, gustation.
gustevole [gustEvole], *a.* Pleasantly flavoured, palatable, appetizing, enjoyable.
gusto, *n.m.* Taste; relish, savour; palate; inclination, liking, gusto; style, manner, refinement. **Prender —,** to find pleasure; **cattivo —,** bad taste, vulgar; **non è di mio —,** it isn't to my liking; **di —,** with zest; **uomo di buon —,** man of good taste.
gustosamente, *adv.* Tastefully, tastily.
gustosità [-à], *n.f.* Tastefulness; pleasantness.
gustoso, *a.* Tasteful, tasty, pleasant.
guttaperca, *n.f.* Guttapercha.
gutturale, *a.* Guttural.
gutturalmente, *adv.* Gutturally.

H

H, h, *n.f.* (called **acca**). Eighth letter of the Italian alphabet. It is a voiceless consonant, used as an initial only in four forms of the verb **avere (ho, hai, ha, hanno)** to prevent

confusion with other words of the same sound. It also appears in certain exclamations, *e.g.* **ah! ahimè! eh! oh! ohimè!** as well as in foreign words, some of which are given below. **h** is employed to harden the letters **c** and **g** before the vowels **e** and **i**, *e.g.* **che, chi**.
hamster, *n.m.*
handicap, *n.m.*
hangar, *n.m.*
harem, *n.m.*
harmonium, *n.m.*
hegeliano, *a.* Hegelian.
helium, *n.m.*
hertziano, *a.* Hertzian.
hidalgo, *n.m.*
hihon! *inter.* He-haw (ass's bray).
hinterland, *n.m.*
home rule, *n.m.*
hornpipe, *n.m.*
hotel, *n.m.*
humour, *n.m.*
humus, *n.m.*

I

I,i, *n.m.f.* Ninth letter of the Italian alphabet. The use of **j** for **i** in cases where it may be intended as a semi-vowel is becoming very rare. Whether a vowel or a semi-vowel, **i** is generally used to-day, as in **iattanza, paio, beccaio,** which in rare cases may be spelled **jattanza, pajo, beccajo.** The **j** is occasionally found as forming the plural of words ending in unaccented **io**, *e.g.* **ufficio, ufficj; principio, principj.** Such a spelling is to be discarded. The simplest solution of the question of these plurals in **io** would seem to be that of using one **i** only when no doubt may arise, and two in other cases; *e.g.* **ozio, ozi; ufficio, uffici;** but **principio, principii; arbitrio, arbitrii.**
i, *n.m.* (*fig.*) **Metter i puntini sugli i,** to dot one's i's.
i, *a.m.pl.* The [cp. **il**].
Iadi [Iadi], *n.f.pl.* (*Myth. Astron.*) Hyades.
Iafet, *n.m.* Japheth.
ialino, *a.* Translucent, hyaline.
ialite, *n.m.* (*Min.*) Hyalite.
iarda, *n.f.* (English measure) yard.
iatagano, *n.m.* (*Mil.*) Yataghan, Turkish sabre.
iato, *n.m.* (*Gram.*) Hiatus.
iattanza, *n.f.* Bragging, boastfulness, braggadoccio, arrogance.
iattura, *n.f.* Misfortune, calamity, loss.
Iberi, *n.m.pl.* Iberians.
iberico [ibErico], *a.* Iberian.
ibernante, *a.* (*Zool.*) Hibernating.
ibernazione, *n.f.* Hibernation.
ibi, ibis, *n.m.* (*Zool.*) Ibis.
ibisco, *n.m.* (*Bot.*) Hybiscus.
ibridare, *v.t.* To hybridize, to interbreed.
ibridismo, *n.m.* Hybridism.
ibrido [Ibrido], *n.m.a.* Hybrid, cross-bred, mongrel.
icastica [icAstica], *n.f.* The art of representing objects with reality.
icastico [icAstico], *a.* Graphic, pictorial, figurative.
iccasse [Iccasse], *n,f.* The letter X.
icneumone, *n.m.* (*Zool.*) Ichneumon.
icnografia [icnografIa], *n.f.* (*Arch.*) Ground-plan.
icona, icone, *n.f.* (*Eccles.*) Ikon, image.
iconoclasta, iconoclaste (*pl.* **iconoclasti**), *n.m.* Iconoclast.
iconoclastico [iconoclAstico], *a.* Iconoclastic.
iconografia [iconografIa], *n.f.* Iconography.
icore, *n.m.* (*Myth.*) Ichor; (*Med.*) pus.
icosaedro, *n.m.* (*Geom.*) Icosahedron.
idalgo, *n.m.* Hidalgo.
Iddio, *n.m.* God [cp. **Dio**].
idea, *n.f.* Idea, conception, thought; plan, design; notion, opinion, image. **Aver una mezza — di,** to have the intention of; **neanche per —,** not at all, not in the least; **farsi un'— di,** to form an idea of; **dar un'—,** to give an idea; **cambiar d'—,** to change one's mind ; **ho l'— che,** I rather think that; **Quale —!** What an idea! (*colloq.*) **solo un'—, un ideina,** just a bit, just a tiny bit.
ideabile [ideAbile], *a.* Imaginable.
ideale, *n.m.a.* Ideal.
idealismo, *n.m.* Idealism.
idealista (*pl.* **idealisti**), *n.m.* Idealist.
idealistico [ideallstico], *a.* Idealistic.
idealità, *n.f.* Ideality.
idealizzare, *v.t.* To idealize.
idealmente, *adv.* Ideally.
ideare, *v.t.* To imagine, to form the idea of, to conceive; to scheme, to plan, to project.
ideatore, ideatrice, *n.m.f.* Inventor, originator.
identicamente, *adv.* Identically.
identicità [-**à**], *n.f.* Similarity, likeness.
identico [idEntico], *a.* Identical; the same size.
identificabile [identificAbile], *a.* Identifiable.
identificare, *v.t.* To identify.
identificarsi, *v.r.* To identify oneself with something.
identificazione, *n.f.* Identification.
identità [-**à**], *n.f.* Identity. **Carte d'—,** papers of identity.
ideografia [ideografIa], *n.f.* Ideography, ideograph.
ideogramma, *n.m.* Ideogram.
ideologia [ideologIa], *n.f.* Ideology, theory, abstraction.
ideologo [ideOlogo], *n.m.* Ideologist, theorist.
idi, *n.m.pl.* (*Hist.*) Ides.
idilliaco, idillico [idillIaco, idIllico], *a.* Idyllic.
idillio [idIllio], *n.m.* Idyll.
idioma, *n.m.* Language, speech, idiom, vernacular.
idiomatico [idiomAtico], *a.* Idiomatic, peculiar to a language. **Espressioni idiomatiche,** idioms.
idiosincrasia [idiosincrasIa], *n.f.* Idiosyncrasy; aversion, repugnance.
idiota (*pl.* **idioti**), *n.m.a.* Idiot, imbecile, stupid.
idiotaggine [idiotAggine], *n.f.* Idiocy, imbecility, ignorance.
idioticamente, *adv.* Idiotically.
idiotico [idiOtico], *a.* Idiotic.
idiotismo, *n.m.* Idiom, vernacular expression, vulgar expression; idiocy.

idiotizzare, *v.t.* To use idioms.
idiozia [idiozIa], *n.f.* Idiocy.
idolatra (*pl.* **idolatri**), *n.m.a.* Idolater; idolatrous.
idolatrare, *v.t.* To worship idols; to adore; to idolize.
idolatria [idolatrIa], *n.f.* Idolatry; worship; love.
idolatricamente, *adv.* Idolatrously.
idolatrico [idolAtrico], *a.* Idolatrous.
idoleggiamento, *n.m.* Idolization.
idoleggiare, *v.t.* To idolize, to make an idol of.
idolo [Idolo], *n.m.* Idol; fetish.
idoneamente, *adv.* Usefully, suitably.
idoneità [-à], *n.f.* Aptitude, fitness.
idoneo [idOneo], *a.* Suitable, fit, qualified; capable, able.
idra, *n.f.* (*Myth.*) Hydra.
idracido [idrAcido], *n.m.* (*Chem.*) Hydracid.
idrante, *n.m.* Hydrant.
idrargirio [idrargIrio], *n.m.* (*Min.*) Mercury.
idratare, *v.t.* (*Chem.*) To hydrate.
idratazione, *n.f.* Hydration.
idrato, *n.m.* (*Chem.*) Hydrate.
idraulica [idrAulica], *n.f.* Hydraulics.
idraulicamente, *adv.* Hydraulically.
idraulico [idrAulico], *n.m.a.* Hydraulic engineer, plumber; hydraulic.
idria [Idria], *n.f.* (*Hist.*) Water-jar, pitcher.
idrico [Idrico], *a.* (*Chem.*) Hydric.
idro, *n.m.* (*Zool.*) Water-snake; (*Aviat.*) seaplane [cp. **idrovolante**].
idro-, *prefix.* Hydro-; water.
idrocefalo [idrocEfalo], *n.m.* (*Med.*) Person suffering from water on the brain.
idrofilo [idrOfilo], *a.* Absorbent. **Cotone —,** cotton-wool.
idrofobia [idrofobIa], *n.f.* (*Med.*) Hydrophobia.
idrofobo [idrOfobo], *a.* Mad, rabid. **Cane —,** mad dog.
idrofono [idrOfono], *n.m.* Hydrophone.
idrofugo [idrOfugo], *a.* Waterproof.
idrogeno [idrOgeno], *n.m.* (*Chem.*) Hydrogen.
idrografo [idrOgrafo], *n.m.* Hydrographer.
idrologio [idrolOgio], *n.m.* Clepsidra, water-clock.
idromante, *n.m.* Water-diviner, dowser.
idromanzia [idromanzIa], *n.f.* Hydromancy, divination by water.
idropatia [idropatIa], *n.f.* (*Med.*) Hydropathy.
idropico [idrOpico], *a.* (*Med.*) Dropsical.
idropisia [idropisIa], *n.f.* (*Med.*) Dropsy.
idroplano, *n.m.* (*Aviat.*) Hydroplane; seaplane.
idroscalo, *n.m.* (*Aviat.*) Seaplane air-port; seaplane station.
idroscopio [idroscOpio], *n.m.* Hydroscope.
idrosilurante, *n.m.* (*Aviat.*) Torpedo-carrying seaplane, torpedo bomber.
idrostatica [idrostAtica], *n.f.* Hydrostatics.
idrostatico [idrostAtico], *a.* Hydrostatic.
idroterapia [idroterapIa], *n.f.* (*Med.*) Hydrotherapy.
idrovolante, *n.m.* (*Aviat.*) Seaplane.
idruro, *n.m.* (*Chem.*) Hydrate.
Iefte, *n.m.* Jephtha.
iemale, *a.* Wintry.
iena, *n.f.* (*Zool.*) Hyena.
Ieova [iEova], *n.m.* Jehovah.
ieraticamente, *adv.* Hieratically.
ieratico [ierAtico], *a.* Hieratic.
ieri, *adv.* Yesterday. **— l'altro, l'altro —** the day before yesterday; **— sera, iersera,** last evening, last night; **otto giorni —,** yesterday week.
ierofante, *n.m.* Hierofant, high priest.
ieroglifico [ieroglIfico], *n.m.a.* Hieroglyphic.
iettatore, *n.m.* Possessor of the evil eye; bearer of bad luck.
iettatura, *n.f.* Evil eye; bad luck.
Ifigenia [ifigenIa], *n.f.* (*Myth.*) Iphigenia.
igiene, *n.f.* Hygiene, hygienics; sanitation.
igienicamente, *adv.* Hygienically.
igienico [igiEnico], *a.* Hygienic; (*colloq.*) safe, prudent. **Carta igienica,** toilet paper.
igienista, *n.m.* Hygienist.
ignaro, *a.* Ignorant (of), unaware (of), unacquainted (with). **Egli è — del fatto che,** he is unaware of the fact that.
ignavia [ignAvia], *n.f.* Laziness, indolence, sloth.
ignavo, *n.m.a.* Sluggard; coward; lazy, slothful, cowardly.
igneo [Igneo], *a.* Fiery; igneous.
ignescenza, *n.f.* Ignition.
ignicolo [ignIcolo], *n.m.* (*Hist.Chem.*) Portion of fire supposed to exist in every body.
ignifero [ignIfero], *a.* (*Chem.*) Igniferous.
ignito, *a.* Burning, fiery.
ignivomo [ignIvomo], *a.* (*Lit.*) Vomiting fire.
ignizione, *n.f.* Ignition.
ignobile [ignObile], *a.* Ignoble, vile, base.
ignobilmente, *adv.* Ignobly.
ignobilità [-à], *n.f.* Ignobility, baseness.
ignominia [ignomInia], *n.f.* Ignominy, disgrace, dishonour, infamy, shame.
ignominiosamente, *adv.* Ignominiously.
ignominioso, *a.* Ignominious, disgraceful, shameful.
ignorabile [ignorAbile], *a.* To be ignored.
ignorantaggine [ignorantAggine], *n.f.* State of ignorance, stupidity; ignorance of how to behave.
ignorante, *n.m.a.* Ignoramus, stupid fellow, blockhead; ignorant, illiterate, uninstructed.
ignorantello, *n.m.a.* Dunce; backward, rather dull.
ignorantemente, *adv.* Ignorantly, illiterately.
ignorantone, *n.m.* Absolute dunce, very ignorant person.
ignoranza, *n.f.* Ignorance; unconsciousness; error; backwardness; obscurantism.
ignorare, *v.t.* To be ignorant of, to be unaware of, not to know; to disregard, to ignore. **Egli ignora che,** he is unaware of the fact that.
ignorato, *p.p.a.* Unknown; ignored.
ignotamente, *adv.* Secretly, in an unknown way; incognito.
ignoto, *n.m.a.* Unknown (person); ignored, unknown, strange. **Figlio d'ignoti,** of unknown parentage; **il Milite —,** the Unknown Warrior.
ignudamente, *adv.* Nakedly, barely.
ignudare, *v.t.* To strip naked [cp. **spogliare**].
ignudarsi, *v.r.* To strip oneself, to undress.
ignudo, *a.* Naked, bare.
igrometria [igrometrIa], *n.f.* Hygrometry.
igrometro [igrOmetro], *n.m.* Hygrometer.

iguana, *n.f.* (*Zool.*) Iguana.
ih! *inter.* Fie! Shame! Tut-tut!
il, *def.art.m.* (*pl.* **i, gli**).
ilarante, *n.m.* (*Chem.*) Laughing-gas.
ilare [Ilare], *a.* Merry, cheerful, gay, hilarious.
ilarità [-à], *n.f.* Hilarity, gaiety.
Ildebrando, *n.m.* Hildebrand.
ileo [Ileo], *n.m.* (*Anat.*) Ileum.
iliaco, *a.* (*Anat.*) Iliac.
Iliade [ilIade], *n.f.* The Iliad. **Un — di guai,** a string of woes.
ilice [Ilice], *n.f.* (*Bot.*) Ilex; holm oak.
ilio [Ilio], *n.m.* (*Anat.*) Ileum; (*Myth.*) Ilium, Troy.
illacrimabile [illacrimAbile], *a.* Not to be wept for; unworthy of tears.
illacrimato, *a.* Unwept, unregretted, unmourned.
illaidire, *v.t.* To render ugly; to disfigure.
illanguidimento, *n.m.* Languor, lassitude; fading, falling of (interest, etc.).
illanguidire, *v.t.i.* To weaken, to enfeeble; to languish, to grow weary, to droop, to wither, to fade, to fall off.
illaqueare, *v.t.* (*Lit.*) To ensnare.
illativo, *a.* Inferential.
illaudabile [illaudAbile], *a.* (*Lit.*) Unpraiseworthy, blameworthy.
illazione, *n.f.* Illation, deduction, inference.
illecitamente, *adv.* Illicitly.
illecito [illEcito], *a.* Illicit, unlawful, forbidden.
illegale, *a.* Illegal, unlawful, contrary to Law.
illegalità [-à], *n.f.* Illegality, unlawfulness.
illegalmente, *adv.* Illegally, unlawfully.
illeggiadrire, *v.t.* To embellish, to adorn; to grow beautiful.
illeggibile [illeggIbile], *a.* Illegible, unreadable.
illegittimità [-à], *n.f.* Illegitimacy.
illegittimo [illegIttimo], *a.* Illegitimate, spurious; unlawful, illegal, unjust. **Figlio —,** illegitimate child.
illepidamente, *adv.* Ungracefully.
illepido [illEpido], *a.* Ungraceful.
illeso, *a.* Unharmed, unhurt, uninjured.
illetterato, *a.* Illiterate, unlearned, ignorant.
illibatamente, *adv.* Purely, chastely.
illibatezza, *n.f.* Purity, chastity.
illibato, *a.* Pure, spotless; chaste.
illiberale, *a.* Illiberal.
illiberalità [-à], *n.f.* Illiberality.
illimitatamente, *adv.* Unlimitedly, unreservedly; endlessly.
illimitato, *a.* Unlimited, unrestricted, boundless, endless.
illimitazione, *n.f.* Lack of all limits, unboundedness.
illinese, *n.m.a.* Native of, or from Illinois (U.S.A.).
illiquidire, *v.i.* To dissolve, to become liquid, to melt.
illirico [illIrico], *n.m.a.* Illyrian.
illividimento, *n.m.* Lividity, lividness.
illividire, *v.t.i.* To make livid; to turn livid.
illogicamente, *adv.* Illogically.
illogicità [-à], *n.f.* Illogicality.
illogico [illOgico], *a.* Illogical; absurd.
illucente, *a.* Resplendent.
illudente, *a.* Illusive, delusive, deceptive.
illudere [illUdere], *v.t.* To deceive, to delude; to beguile.
illudersi [illUdersi], *v.r.* To deceive oneself. **Non bisogna —,** we must not deceive ourselves.
illuminante, *a.* Illuminating, lighting up; illustrating.
illuminare, *v.t.* To lighten, to throw a light upon, to illumine; to brighten; to enlighten. **Il sole illumina la luna,** the sun illuminates the moon.
illuminarsi, *v.r.* To become enlightened; to become visible; to brighten. **Il suo viso s'illuminò,** his face brightened.
illuminato, *p.p.a.* Lit-up, illuminated; enlightened. **— a giorno,** flood-lit.
illuminazione, *n.f.* Illuminating, lighting. **— a giorno,** flood-lighting.
illune, *a.* (*Lit.*) Moonless.
illusione, *n.f.* Illusion, self-deception; dream. **— ottica,** optical illusion.
illusionista (*pl.* **illusionisti**), *n.m.* Conjuror, illusionist.
illuso, *n.m.a.* Day-dreamer; deluded, deceived.
illusoriamente, *adv.* Deceptively.
illusorio [illusOrio], *a.* Illusory, deceptive, delusive.
illustrare, *v.t.* To illustrate (in all senses); to elucidate; to make illustrious.
illustrativo, *a.* Illustrative.
illustratore, illustratrice, *n.m.f.* Illustrator.
illustrato, *a.* Illustrated. **Giornale —,** illustrated newspaper; **cartolina postale illustrata,** picture post-card.
illustrazione, *n.f.* Illustration, plate, picture; celebrity; ornament.
illustre, *a.* Illustrious, distinguished, famous, renowned.
illustrissimo, *a.* Most illustrious (used as a formal address). **— signore,** Dear sir.
illuvie [illUvie], *n.f.* Dirt.
illuvione, *n.f.* Inundation [cp. **alluvione**].
ilota, *n.m.* (*Hist.*) Helot.
imagine [imAgine] [cp. **immagine**].
imago, *n.f.* (*Poet.*) Image.
Imalaia [imalAia], *n.m.* (*Geog.*) Himalaya.
imamo, *n.m.* Imam (Mohammedan priest).
imbacchetonire, *v.i.* To become a bigot, to turn bigot.
imbacuccare, imbacuccarsi, *v.t.r.* To wrap up, to muffle up; to muffle oneself.
imbalconato, *n.m.a.* Bright red; rose-coloured.
imbaldanzire, imbaldanzirsi, *v.i.r.* To grow bold, to become defiant.
imballaggio [imballAggio], *n.m.* Packing; wrapping; cost of packing. **Carta da —,** packing paper, brown paper.
imballare, *v.t.* To pack, to wrap up. (*Motor.*) **— il motore,** to race the engine.
imballatore, imballatrice, *n.m.f.* Packer.
imballatura, *n.f.* Packing; cost of packing.
imballo, *n.m.* Packing.
imbalordire, *v.t.i.* To stun, to bewilder; to be bewildered.
imbalsamare, *v.t.* To embalm, to stuff (animals).
imbalsamatore, *n.m.* Embalmer.
imbalsamazione, *n.f.* Embalmment.
imbambagiare, *v.t.* To wrap in cotton-wool.
imbambolato, *a.* Stunned; dull; bewildered; sleepy.
imbambolire, *v i.* To grow childish.

imbandierare, *v.t.* To deck with flags, to beflag. **La città era imbandierata,** the town was decked with flags.
imbandigione, *n.f.* Preparation for a banquet; the meal itself.
imbandire, *v.t.* To lay the table for a banquet; to prepare. **Tavola imbandita,** well-furnished table.
imbando, *n.m.* (*Naut.*) Slack of a rope.
imbarazzamento, *n.m.* Embarrassment.
imbarazzante, *a.* Embarrassing, perplexing, awkward.
imbarazzare, *v.t.* To embarrass; to encumber, to entangle; to trouble, to perplex.
imbarazzarsi, *v.r.* To be perplexed, to become embarrassed; to meddle with.
imbarazzo, *n.m.* Embarrassment, difficulty, trouble, fix; encumbrance; obstruction; obstacle; bewilderment; quandary. **— di stomaco,** indigestion; **essere d'— a,** to be in one's way; **trovarsi negli imbarazzi,** to find oneself in difficulties.
imbarbarimento, *n.m.* Becoming barbarian.
imbarbarire, *v.t.i.* To make or become barbarian; to become uncivilized; to get corrupt (of a language).
imbarbogire, *v.i.* To pass into second childhood.
imbarcadero, *n.m.* Landing-stage; wharf; pier.
imbarcamento, *n.m.* Embarkation, embarking.
imbarcare, *v.t.* To ship, to take on board. **— carbone,** to coal.
imbarcarsi, *v.r.* To embark, to go on board; to sail; (*fig.*) to engage upon. **— in un'impresa arrischiata,** to embark upon a risky enterprise.
imbarcatoio [imbarcatOio], *n.m.* Landing-stage, wharf.
imbarcazione, *n.f.* Embarkation; boat, craft, skiff, barge; dinghy. **— di salvataggio,** life-boat; **— a vela,** sailing boat; **— di bordo,** pinnace.
imbarco, *n.m.* Embarkation, embarking; landing-stage, wharf. **Buono d'—,** shipping order; **porto d'—,** port of shipment.
imbarilare, *v.t.* To pack in a barrel, to barrel; to store wine in barrels.
imbarrare, *v.t.* To bar up, to close with bars.
imbasamento, *n.m.* Groundwork; (*Arch.*) footing.
imbasare, *v.t.* To base, to put on a base.
imbasatura, *n.f.* Base; (*Arch.*) footings.
imbastardimento, *n.m.* Debasement, degeneracy, corruption.
imbastardire, *v.t.i.* To debase, to bastardize; to degenerate; to bastardize.
imbastardirsi, *v.r.* To degenerate, to become degenerate.
imbastare, *v.t.* To put a pack-saddle on.
imbastimento, *n.m.* Tacking, basting, stitching together.
imbastire, *v.t.* To tack, to baste, to sew lightly; (*fig.*) to rough out, to sketch, to frame.
imbastitura, *n.f.* Stitching, tacking, basting; (*fig.*) outline, rough.
imbattersi [imbAttersi], *v.r.* To come across, to meet with, to fall in with, to run across. **Si era imbattuto in un amico,** he had come across a friend.
imbattibile [imbattIbile], *a.* Unbeatable, invincible, unconquerable.
imbattibilità [-à], *n.f.* Invincibility.
imbatto, *n.m.* Casual meeting.
imbattuto, *a.* Unbeaten.
imbaulare, *v.t.* To pack up, to put in a trunk.
imbavagliare, *v.t.* To gag; (*fig.*) to silence.
imbavare, *v.t.i.* To drivel, to slobber.
imbeccare, *v.t.* To feed young birds; (*fig.*) to prompt, to put words in one's mouth.
imbeccata, *n.f.* Hint, suggestion, prompting. **Prendere l'—,** to take the hint.
imbecillaggine [imbecillAggine], *n.f.* Imbecility, silliness; piece of foolishness.
imbecille, *n.m.a.* Imbecile.
imbecillemente, *adv.* Stupidly.
imbecillire, *v.t.i.* To bamboozle; to grow stupid.
imbecillità [-à], *n.f.* Imbecility, stupidness.
imbelle, *a.* Unwarlike; faint-hearted, cowardly.
imbellettamento, *n.m.* Making up, painting the face.
imbellettarsi, *v.r.* To make up, to rouge, to paint one's face; to masquerade.
imbellettatura, *n.f.* Making up, paint, rouge.
imbellire, *v.t.* To adorn, to embellish; to become prettier.
imbellirsi, *v.r.* To make oneself more attractive.
imberbe, *a.* Beardless; young, green.
imberciare, *v.t.* To hit the mark; to guess aright.
imberrettare, imberrettarsi, *v.i.r.* To put a cap on.
imbertescare, *v.t.* (*obs.*) To fortify, to build strong towers.
imbertonirsi, *v.r.* (*obs.*) To fall deeply in love.
imbestialire, *v.t.i.* To become brutish, to grow furious; to enrage, to brutalize.
imbevere [imbEvere], *v.t.* To absorb, to imbibe, to saturate.
imbeversi [imbEversi], *v.r.* To become imbued with; to be saturated.
imbevimento, *n.m.* Absorption, saturation.
imbevuta, *n.f.* Damp.
imbiaccamento, *n.m.* White-leading.
imbiaccare, *v.t.* To coat with white-lead.
imbiaccarsi, *v.r.* To paint one's face white.
imbiadare, *v.t.* (*Agric.*) To sow with oats.
imbiancamento, *n.m.* Whitening; white-washing.
imbiancare, *v.t.i.* To whitewash, to whiten; to bleach; to turn white (of hair); to dawn (of the sky). **Un sepolcro imbiancato,** a whited sepulchre.
imbiancarsi, *v.r.* To turn pale; to grow grey.
imbiancatoio [imbiancatOio], *n.m.* Bleaching works.
imbiancatora, *n.f.* Fine laundress.
imbiancatore, *n.m.* Laundryman; bleacher.
imbiancatura, *n.f.* Whitewashing; bleaching.
imbianchino, *n.m.* Whitewasher, house-painter; (*colloq.*) dauber.
imbianchire, *v.t.* To whiten; to grow pale; to grow grey.
imbibere [imbIbere], *v.i.* to imbibe [cp. **imbevere**].
imbibizione, *n.f.* Absorption; imbibing.
imbietolire, *v.i.* To become a dunce; to be enraptured about a trifle.

imbiettare, *v.t.* To wedge.
imbiettatura, *n.f.* Wedging.
imbigiarsi, *v.r.* To become grey.
imbiondire, *v.i.* To become fair (of hair); to ripen (of grain).
imbiondirsi, *v.r.* To tint one's hair.
imbirbonire, *v.i.* To become a rascal; to grow rascally.
imbitumare, *v.t.* To tar.
imbizzarrimento, *n.m.* Excitement, fit of rage.
imbizzarrire, *v.t.* To excite.
imbizzarrirsi, *v.r.* To get excited, to fly into a rage; (of a horse) to frisk, to grow restive or mettlesome.
imbizzire, imbizzirsi, *v.i.r.* To become angry, to fly into a rage.
imboccamento, *n.m.* Feeding.
imboccare, *v.t.* To feed, to spoon-feed; to enter (of a road, etc.); to suggest; to put a wind instrument to one's mouth; (*Mech.*) to fit (as cogs); to bit (a horse); to put words into one's mouth. **— una strada,** to enter a street (or a lane, etc.).
imboccatura, *n.f.* Mouth, entrance, outfall; (*Mus.*) mouthpiece; entrance (to a street, etc.); (*Mus.*) method of applying one's lips to a mouthpiece.
imbocciare, *v.i.* To come into bud; (*colloq.*) to hit the mark [cp. **imbroccare**].
imbocco, *n.m.* Mouth, entrance, opening. **L'— d'una galleria,** the entrance to a tunnel.
imbolsimento, *n.m.* Broken-windedness.
imbolsire, *v.i.* To become broken-winded; to grow pursy.
imbonimento, *n.m.* Advertising one's goods, advertisement; puff.
imbonire, *v.t.* To appease; to mollify.
imbonitore, *n.m.* Auctioneer; barker.
imborghesire, imborghesirsi, *v.i.r.* To become bourgeois, to adopt middle-class ways.
imborsare, *v.t.* To pocket; to put in one's purse; (*fig.*) to contain, to hold.
imboscare, *v.t.* To hide in a wood, to place in ambush.
imboscarsi, *v.r.* To hide; to lie in ambush; to shelter; (*fig.*) to get out of, to shirk; (*colloq.*) to find a "cushy" job in wartime.
imboscata, *n.f.* Ambuscade, ambush.
imboscato, *n.m.* (*Mil.*) Shirker, slacker.
imboschimento, *n.m.* Afforestation.
imboschire, *v.t.i.* To afforest.
imboschirsi, *v.r.* To run wild, to become covered with trees.
imbottare, *v.t.* To barrel, to put into casks.
imbottato, *n.m.* Wine in barrels; excise duty on wine in cask.
imbottatoia, imbottatoio [imbottatOia, -o], *n.f.m.* Funnel used for barrelling wine.
imbottatura, *n.f.* Barrelling; proper time for barrelling.
imbottavino, *n.m.* Funnel for barrelling [cp. **imbottatoia**].
imbottigliamento, *n.m.* Bottling.
imbottigliare, *v.t.* To bottle; to bottle up (in all senses).
imbottinare, *v.t.* (*Agric.*) To manure.
imbottire, *v.t.* To pad, to stuff, to fill; to quilt; to upholster. **Un portafoglio ben imbottito,** a well-filled purse.
imbottita, *n.f.* Quilt, eiderdown.
imbottitura, *n.f.* Stuffing, padding, quilting **— di cuoio,** leather upholstery.
imbovinare, *v.t.* To spread cowdung (to make floors, etc.).
imbozzacchire, *v.i.* To shrivel up; to wither away.
imbozzimare, *v.t.* To dress with size; to smear.
imbraca, *n.f.* Breeching-strap (of horses' harness); sling (for workmen).
imbracare, *n.f.* To strap up, to sling, to rope; to breech (a child).
imbracatura, *n.f.* (*Naut.*) Sling, slinging.
imbracciare, *v.t.* To pass the arm through the sling of a gun, etc.; to level (a gun).
imbracciatoie [imbracciatOie], *n.f.pl.* Goldsmith's tongs, pliers.
imbracciatura, *n.f.* Sling of a rifle.
imbrachettare, *v.t.* To mend a torn page by pasting on a slip of paper.
imbrancare, *v.t.* To put (an animal) in the herd.
imbrancarsi, *v.r.* To join the herd; to mix in bad company; to fall in with the crowd.
imbrattacarte, *n.m.* Scribbler.
imbrattamento, *n.m.* Soiling, tainting, smear.
imbrattamondo, *n.m.* Bungler, muddler.
imbrattamuri, *n.m.* Bad painter, dauber.
imbrattare, *v.t.* To soil, to dirty, to stain, to smear; to defile.
imbrattarsi, *v.r.* To soil oneself (*lit. & fig.*).
imbrattascene, *n.m.* Fifth-rate actor, ham actor, barn-stormer.
imbrattatele, *n.m.* Dauber.
imbrattatovaglie [imbrattatovAglie], *n.m.* Ill-cooked meal.
imbrattatura, *n.f.* Smear.
imbratto, *n.m.* Ill-done work; daub; badly-written article; revolting dish.
imbrecciare, *v.t.* To ballast a road, to metal, to macadamize.
imbrecciatura, *n.f.* Ballasting (a road).
imbrentina [imbrEntina], *n.f.* (*Bot.*) Rock-rose, cystus.
imbriacare [cp. **ubbriacare**].
imbriacatura, *n.f.* Getting drunk; (*fig.*) blind passion.
imbricconire, *v.i.* To turn rogue.
imbrigare, *v.t.* To make trouble, to disturb.
imbrigarsi, *v.r.* To interfere; to trouble oneself.
imbrigliamento, *n.m.* Bridling, curbing, harnessing (a waterfall, etc.).
imbrigliare, *v.t.* To bridle, to harness, to curb, to restrain. **— un fiume,** to harness a river.
imbroccare, *v.t.* To hit the mark, to guess aright, to hit upon.
imbroccata, *n.f.* (*Fencing*) Downward thrust.
imbroccatura, *n.f.* (*Mech.*) Cog.
imbrodare, imbrodolare, *v.t.* To strain, to soil; to make a mess of (a job).
imbrodolarsi, *v.r.* To stain oneself, to spill food down one's clothes; to bedaub oneself.
imbrodolio [imbrodolIo], *n.m.* Messiness.
imbrogliare, *v.t.* To tangle, to entangle; to confuse; to embroil; to be in the way; to cheat, to take in; (*Naut.*) to clew up sails.
imbrogliarsi, *v.r.* To get confused, to get mixed up (in mind); to become entangled,

to be embroiled. — **nel parlare,** to stutter, to get flustered.
imbrogliatamente, *adv.* Confusedly.
imbrogliato, *p.p.a.* Confused, entangled; intricate.
imbroglio [imbrOglio], *n.m.* Tangle entanglement, trouble, scrape; intrigue, swindle, cheat; imbroglio, predicament.
imbroglione, *n.m.* Swindler, cheat; intriguer, meddler.
imbroncare, *v.t.* (*Naut.*) To strike the flag, to lower to half-mast.
imbronciarsi, *v.r.* To frown, to look sulky, to pout, to take offence, to grow dark (sky); to be surly.
imbronciato, *a.* Sulky; surly; frowning.
imbrunali, *n.m.pl.* (*Naut.*) Scuppers.
imbrunare, *v.i.* To turn dark, to become overcast.
imbrunire, *v.t.i.* To turn dark, to make dark; to tan (of the sun); to grow dark. **Sull'—,** at dusk.
imbruschire, *v.i.* To become brusque.
imbruttimento, *n.m.* Disfigurement.
imbruttire, imbruttirsi, *v.t.i.r.* To disfigure, to mar, to make ugly; to grow ugly.
imbucare, *v.t.* To post a letter, to put a letter in the pillar-box; to put in a hole.
imbucarsi, *v.r.* To creep into a hole.
imbuggerarsi, *v.r.* Not to care a rap about, to be indifferent to.
imbuire, *v.i.* To become stupid.
imbullettare, *v.t.* To put hobnails in boots.
imburrare, *v.t.* To butter. **Crostino imburrato,** buttered toast.
imburreggiare, *v.t.* To flatter, to butter up.
imbuscherarsi, *v.r.* To be indifferent to [cp. **imbuggerarsi**].
imbusecchiare, *v.t.* To fill sausage skins; to eat too much, to stuff.
imbussolare, *v.t.* To put (a vote) in the ballot-box.
imbutiforme, *a.* Funnel-shaped.
imbuto, *n.m.* Funnel.
imbuzzare, *v.t.* To overfeed, to cram.
Imene, *n.m.* (*Myth.*) Hymen; (*Anat.*) hymen; wedlock, wedding, marriage.
imeneo, *a.* Nuptial.
imenei, *n.m.pl.* Nuptials, wedding.
imenotteri [imenOtteri], *n.m.pl.* (*Zool.*) Hymenoptera.
imitabile [imitAbile], *a.* Imitable.
imitare, *v.t.* To imitate, to copy, to mimic, to ape; to counterfeit.
imitativo, *a.* Imitative.
imitatore, imitatrice, *n.m.f.* Imitator.
imitazione, *n.f.* Imitation; copy, likeness; counterfeit, falsification.
immacchiarsi, *v.r.* To hide in the bushes.
immacolatamente, *adv.* Stainlessly, spotlessly.
immacolato, *a.* Immaculate, spotless, pure; (*Eccles.*) **L'Immacolata,** Our Lady.
immagazzinamento, *n.m.* Storage.
immagazzinare, *v.t.* To store up, to accumulate; to store, to warehouse.
immaginabile [immaginAbile], *a.* Imaginable, conceivable.
immaginabilmente, *adv.* Conceivably.
immaginamento, *n.m.* Imagining, imagination.
immaginare, immaginarsi, *v.i.r.* To imagine, to conceive, to suppose, to fancy; to contrive, to devise, to invent; to picture to oneself. **S'immagini,** just imagine.
immaginariamente, *adv.* In imagination.
immaginario [immaginArio], *a.* Imaginary.
immaginativa, *n.f.* Imaginative faculty imagination.
immaginazione, *n.f.* Imagination; fancy, fantasy.
immagine [immAgine], *n.f.* Image, effigy, likeness, figure; (*Eccles.*) ikon, sacred image; imagery, metaphor, simile.
immaginosamente, *adv.* Imaginatively, fantastically.
immaginoso, *a.* Imaginative, creative, with a fertile imagination; fantastic
immagrire, *v.i.* To grow thin [cp. **dimagrire**].
immalinconire, *v.i.* To become melancholy, to sadden.
immancabile [immancAbile], *a* Unfailing, infallible; inevitable, certain.
immancabilmente, *adv.* Unfailingly, without fail.
immane, *a.* Huge, monstrous, tremendous; cruel.
immaneggiabile [immaneggiAbile], *a.* Intractable, unwieldy.
immanente, *a.* Immanent.
immanenza, *n.f.* Immanence.
immangiabile [immangiAbile], *a.* Uneatable.
immanifesto, *a.* Obscure.
immanità [-à], *n.f.* Terribleness, cruelty, ferocity.
immansueto, *a.* Untamed, fierce.
immantinente, *adv.* At once, immediately.
immarcescibile [immarcescIbile], *a.* Incorruptible.
immarcescibilmente, *adv.* Incorruptibly.
immascherarsi, *v.r.* To mask, to put on a mask, to wear a mask.
immateriale, *a.* Incorporeal, immaterial.
immaterialità [-à], *n.f.* Immateriality.
immaterialmente, *adv.* Immaterially.
immatricolarsi, *v.r.* To matriculate; to register.
immatricolazione, *n.f.* Matriculation.
immaturamente, *adv.* Immaturely.
immaturità [-à], *n.f.* Immaturity.
immaturo, *a.* Unripe, immature; premature.
immedesimarsi, *v.r.* To identify oneself, to become one with.
immedesimazione, *n.f.* Absorption; identification with.
immediatamente, *adv.* At once, immediately.
immediatezza, *n.f.* Immediacy, directness.
immediato, *a.* Immediate, proximate, direct; without delay, instant.
immedicabile [immedicAbile], *a.* Incurable, irreparable.
immedicabilmente, *adv.* Incurably, irreparably.
immeditatamente, *adv.* Unpremeditatedly.
immeditato, *a.* Unpremeditated.
immelensire, *v.i.* To grow dull, to become stupid.
immellettare, *v.t.* To soil, to dirty, to begrime.
immelmarsi, *v.r.* To get muddy, to muddy one's clothes.

immemorabile [immemorAbile], *a.* Immemorial. **Da tempo —,** from time immemorial.
immemore [immEmore], *a.* Forgetful, unmindful; ungrateful. **— di sè,** forgetful of self.
immensamente, *adv.* Immensely.
immensità [-à], *n.f.* Immensity, hugeness, vastness.
immenso, *a.* Immense, huge, vast; immeasurable; (*colloq.*) big, great.
immensurabile [immensurAbile], *a.* Immeasurable.
immensurabilità [-à], *n.f.* Immensity.
immensurabilmente, *adv.* Immeasurably.
immensurato, *a.* Infinite, immense.
immergere [immErgere], *v.t.* To plunge, to immerse, to dip, to soak; to sink.
immergersi [immErgersi], *v.r.* To plunge into, to dive, to sink. **— nella lettura,** to immerse oneself in reading.
immeritamente, *adv.* Undeservedly, unjustly.
immeritato, *a.* Undeserved.
immeritevole [immeritEvole], *a.* Undeserving, unworthy.
immeritevolmente, *adv.* Undeservedly, unworthily.
immersione, *n.f.* Immersion; plunge, quick bath. (*Naut.*) **Linea d'—,** water-line; **fare un'—,** to make an immersion.
immerso, *p.p.a.* Immersed, plunged; concentrated, absorbed.
immettere [immEttere], *v.t.* To bring in, to usher in; (*fig.*) to infuse, to instil, to inspire. **— una nave in bacino,** to dock a ship.
immettersi [immEttersi], *v.r.* To penetrate, to insinuate oneself; to enter into.
immezzire, *v.i.* To become over-ripe, to go rotten (of fruit, etc.).
immigrante, immigrato, *n.m.a.* Immigrant.
immigrare, *v.i.* To immigrate.
immigrazione, *n.f.* Immigration.
imminente, *a.* Imminent, impending; at hand. **Pericolo —,** impending danger.
imminenza, *n.f.* Imminence.
immischiare, *v.t.* To implicate, to involve.
immischiarsi, *v.r.* To meddle, to interfere; to mix with; to be involved in. **— negli affari altrui,** to meddle in other folks' business.
immisericordiosamente, *adv.* Mercilessly.
immisericordioso, *a.* Merciless, hard-hearted.
immiserire, *v.t.i.* To impoverish, to make miserable; to become poor; to grow weak.
immissario [immissArio], *n.m.* (*Geog.*) Tributary, affluent.
immissione, *n.f.* Inflow; induction; breaking (in).
immistione, *n.f.* (*Law*) Interference.
immisurabile, *a.* Immeasurably.
immisurabilmente, *adv.* Immeasurably.
immite, *a.* (*Lit.*) Harsh, cruel, pitiless, severe (of climate).
immobile [immObile], *a.* Motionless, immobile, set; still; immovable, fixed, stationary. **Beni immobili,** real estate.
immobili, *n.m.pl.* Premises; real estate.
immobiliare, *a.* Real (of estate).
immobilità [-à], *n.f.* Immobility, stillness, immovableness.
immobilitare, immobilizzare, *v.t.* To immobilize, to render motionless; (*Comm.*) to lock up capital.
immobilizzazione, *n.f.* (*Comm.*) Locking up (of capital).
immobilmente, *adv.* Immovable.
immoderatamente, *adv.* Immoderately.
immoderatezza, *n.f.* Immoderation, immoderateness, excess.
immoderato, *a.* Immoderate, intemperate, unrestrained.
immodestamente, *adv.* Immodestly.
immodestia [immodEstia], *n.f.* Immodesty; impudence.
immodesto, *a.* Immodest, unblushing.
immolare, *v.t.* To immolate, to sacrifice.
immolarsi, *v.r.* To immolate oneself.
immolazione, *n.f.* Immolation, sacrifice.
immollare, *v.t.* To soak, to moisten, to drench.
immondamente, *adv.* Filthily, impurely.
immondezza, *n.f.* Uncleanliness, foulness, dirt.
immondizia [immondIzia], *n.f.* Dirtiness, filth. **Le immondizie,** rubbish, refuse, garbage.
immondo, *a.* Filthy, dirty; unclean, impure, foul.
immorale, *a.* Immoral, dishonest, unprincipled.
immoralità [-à], *n.f.* Immorality.
immoralmente, *adv.* Immorally.
immorbidire, immorbidirsi, *v.i.r.* To soften, to grow soft.
immorsare, *v.t.* To bit (a horse).
immortalare, *v.t.* To immortalize, to perpetuate.
immortalarsi, *v.r.* To be immortalized, to become immortal.
immortale, *n.m.a.* Immortal.
immortalità [-à], *n.f.* Immortality.
immortalmente, *adv.* Immortally.
immoto, *a.* Motionless, still, fixed; unmoved.
immucidire, *v.i.* To grow musty, to go bad.
immune, *a.* Immune, free, exempt; uninjured.
immunità [-à], *n.f.* Immunity; exemption; prerogative, privilege.
immunizzare, *v.t.* To immunize, to render or become immune; to free (from infection, etc.).
immunizzazione, *n.f.* Immunization.
immusire, *v.i.* To pout; to sulk, to look black.
immusonito, *a.* Gloomy, sulky, sullen.
immutabile [immutAbile], *a.* Unchangeable, immutable, invariable.
immutabilità [-à], *n.f.* Immutability.
immutato, *a.* Unchanged, unaltered.
imo, *n.m.a.* Deepest, lowest, bottommost; humblest.
imoscapo, *n.m.* (*Arch.*) Thickness of a column at the lowest part of the shaft.
impaccare, *v.t.* To pack, to wrap up, to make into a parcel.
impaccatore, *n.m.* Packer.
impaccatura, *n.f.* Packing, package, bundle.
impacchettare, *v.t.* To make into packages; to wrap up.
impacciare, *v.t.* To hinder, to embarrass; to tangle, to entangle; to encumber, to be in the way.

impacciarsi, *v.r.* To meddle with, to interfere. **Non — d'una cosa,** not to meddle with something.
impacciato, *a.* Embarrassed, ill at ease; awkward, clumsy; entangled. **Avere un'aria impacciata,** to look embarrassed; **sentirsi —,** to feel uneasy.
impaccio [impAccio], *n.m.* Trouble, tangle; encumbrance, impediment, obstacle; difficulty, embarrassment; nuisance, bother. **Trarsi d'—,** to get out of a scrape; **questa sedia è d'—,** this chair is in the way.
impaccioso, *a.* Tiresome.
impacco, *n.m.* (*Med.*) Compress, poultice.
impaciarsi, *v.r.* (*Cards*) To win an equal number of games, to draw.
impadronirsi, *v.r.* To take possession of, to appropriate; to master, to have command of. **— d'una lingua,** to master a language.
impagabile [impagAbile], *a.* Priceless, invaluable; (*colloq.*) very funny.
impaginare, *v.t.* (*Print.*) To page, to make into pages, to make up.
impaginatore, *n.m.* (*Print.*) Clicker.
impaginatura, impaginazione, *n.f.* Pagination, make-up.
impagliare, *v.t.* To pack with straw, to cover with straw; to stuff (animals).
impagliata, *n.f.* (*Agric.*) Chopped straw for fodder.
impagliatino, *n.m.* Seat of a straw-bottomed chair.
impagliatore, *n.m.* Taxidermist, stuffer (of animals); chair-mender.
impagliatura, *n.f.* Covering with straw; packing in straw; chair-mending.
impalancato, *n.m.* (*Mil.*) Palissade.
impalare, *v.t.* To impale; (*Agric.*) to stake vines, etc.
impalato, *a.* Impaled; stiff, rigid; bolt upright.
impalcare, *v.t.* To floor, to plank; to erect scaffolding.
impalcatura, *n.f.* Scaffolding, planking; ceiling; structure, frame; ramification of tree branches, stag's horns, etc.
impallare, *v.t.* (*Golf, Billiards,* etc.). To stymie.
impallidire, *v.i.* To turn pale; to become dim; to wane; to be overshadowed. **Egli impallidì,** he turned pale; **la sua stella impallidisce,** his star is on the wane.
impallinare, *v.t.* To fire small shot at.
impalmamento, *n.m.* Betrothal.
impalmare, *v.t.* To give one's hand (in marriage), to get engaged, to betroth; to marry.
impalpabile [impalpAbile], *a.* Impalpable.
impalpabilità [-à], *n.f.* Impalpability.
impalpabilmente, *adv.* Impalpably.
impaludarsi, *v.r.* To turn into a swamp; to stagnate.
impanare, *v.t.* To cover with breadcrumbs; (*Mech.*) to cut the thread of a screw. **Cotoletta impanata,** breaded cutlet.
impanatura, *n.f.* (*Mech.*) Threading of a screw.
impancarsi, *v.r.* To set oneself up (as a judge); to read someone a lecture.
impaniare, *v.t.* To set snares, to bird-lime; to entrap.
impaniarsi, *v.r.* To get entangled; to be deceived (with flattery, etc.).
impannare, *v.t.* To cover with cloth or paper; to cover a window with paper.
impannata, *n.f.* Paper window-covering.
impantanare, *v.t.* To bemire, to throw mud at.
impantanarsi, *v.r.* To get muddy, to be bemired; to stick in the mud; (*fig.*) to get entangled.
impaperarsi, *v.r.* To mispronounce (a word); to get flustered; to be made a fool of.
impappinarsi, *v.r.* To get confused (in speech); to get flustered; to falter, to stammer.
imparacchiare, *v.i.* To learn little, to learn imperfectly.
imparadisare, *v.t.* To make ecstatic.
imparagonabile [imparagonAbile], Incomparable.
imparare, *v.t.* To learn, to acquire knowledge, to understand, to realize. **— a mente, a memoria,** to learn by heart; **— a proprie spese,** to learn to one's cost; **— a vivere,** to learn manners.
imparaticcio [imparatIccio], *n.m.* First attempt, beginner's work; ill-assimilated knowledge.
impareggiabile [impareggiAbile], *a.* Unparalleled, unrivalled, incomparable, unsurpassable.
impareggiabilmente, *adv.* Uncomparably.
imparentarsi, *v.r.* To become related to (by marriage); to marry into. **Esser male imparentato,** to have undesirable connections.
impari [Impari], *a.* Unequal, odd (of numbers), uneven; unfit, inadequate. **Egli è — al compito affidatogli,** he is not up to his job.
imparità [-à], *n.f.* Inequality; imparity.
imparruccarsi, *v.r.* To put on a wig.
imparruccato, *a.* Bewigged.
impartibile [impartIbile], *a.* Indivisible.
impartire, *v.t.* To impart, to bestow, to grant; to communicate. (*Eccles.*) **— la benedizione,** to give the blessing; **— una lezione,** to give a lesson.
imparziale, *a.* Impartial, equitable, fair-minded.
imparzialità [-à], *n.f.* Impartiality.
imparzialmente, *adv.* Impartially.
impassibile [impassIbile], *a.* Impassible; impassive, unalterable, unmoved; stiff, rigid, stand-offish, reserved.
impassibilità [-à], *n.f.* Impassibility; stand-offishness, reserve.
impassibilmente, *adv.* Impassively.
impastare, *v.t.* To knead, to work into dough; to paste, to fasten with paste; to incorporate, to mingle; (*Art*) to mix colours on the palette.
impastatrice, *n.f.* Kneading-trough; mechanical mixer.
impastatura, *n.f.* Kneading; pasting.
impasticciare, *v.t.* To make a hash of, to bungle; to daub [cp. **pasticciare**].
impasticciarsi, *v.r.* To get into a mess, to get into trouble.
impasticcione, *n.m.* Bungler [cp. **pasticcione**].
impasto, *n.m.* Mixture, medley; thick colour; (*Art*) impasto.
impastocchiare, *v.t.* To tell lies, to mislead.

impastoiare, *v.t.* To shackle, to hobble, to tether; to hinder, to impede.
impastranarsi, *v.r.* To wrap oneself up in a cloak.
impataccare, impataccarsi, *v.t.r.* To soil with greasy stains.
impatriare, *v.t.* To repatriate.
impattare (1), *v.i.* To be quits, to make equal scores (in games).
impattare (2), *v.t.* To bed cattle.
impaurire, *v.t.* To frighten, to terrify; to intimidate.
impaurirsi, *v.r.* To get frightened; to be intimidated.
impaurito, *p.p.a.* Frightened; afraid.
impavidamente, *adv.* Fearlessly.
impavido [impAvido], *a.* Fearless, intrepid, undaunted.
impazientare, impazientire, *v.t.* To put out of patience.
impazientarsi, impazientirsi, *v.r.* To lose patience, to become impatient.
impaziente, *a.* Impatient; restless, fretful.
impazientemente, *adv.* Impatiently.
impazienza, *n.f.* Impatience; restlessness.
impazzamento, *n.m.* Going mad, derangement.
impazzare, impazzire, *v.i.* To go mad, to become insane; to be frantic. **Far —,** to drive mad; **— per qualcosa,** to be crazy for something.
impazzata, *n.f.* Insane manner. **Procedere all'—,** to proceed furiously.
impazzimento, *n.m.* Madness; insanity; nuisance, trouble.
impazzito, *a.* Mad, insane.
impeccabile [impeccAbile], *a.* Impeccable, blameless, faultless, irreproachable.
impeccabilità [-à], *n.f.* Impeccability.
impecettare, *v.t.* To stain, to smear, to mess.
impeciamento, *n.m.* Tarring.
impeciare, *v.t.* To tar, to smear with tar; (*fig.*) to entangle. **Impeciato di pregiudizi,** steeped in prejudice.
impeciarsi, *v.r.* To become entangled.
impeciatura, *n.f.* Tarring.
impecorire, *v.i.* To become as stupid as a sheep.
impecorito, *a.* Sheepish.
impedantirsi, *v.r.* To become pedantic, to become a pedant.
impedenza, *n.f.* (*Elect.*) Impedance.
impedibile [impedIbile], *a.* Liable to hindrance.
impediente, *n.m.* (*Eccles.*) Impediment (to marriage).
impedimenti, impedimenta, *n.m.pl.* Impedimenta; baggage.
impedimento, *n.m.* Impediment, obstacle, hindrance, drawback; (*Med.*) retention of urine.
impedire, *v.t.* To hinder, to obstruct, to impede; to prevent, to forbid; to preclude, to debar. **— il passo,** to bar the way; **ciò non gli impedì di partire,** this didn't prevent him from leaving.
impedirsi, *v.r.* To make an impediment; to hinder; to forbid.
impeditamente, *adv.* In an occupied manner; obstructively.
impeditivo, *a.* Obstructive.
impedito, *p.p.a.* Impeded, prevented; taken, occupied, engaged. **Rimasto — in una gamba,** lost the use of one of his legs.
impegnare, *v.t.i.* To pledge, to pawn; to engage, to bind (by promise or contract), to fix; to order, to hire; to book (a seat); (*Mil.*) to engage (in battle). **— la parola,** to pledge one's word; **— un auto,** to engage a taxi.
impegnarsi, *v.r.* To pledge oneself, to bind oneself, to enter into an engagement; (*Law*) to go bail; to embark in; to get involved.
impegnativo, *a.* Binding, compelling. (*Comm.*) **Offerta impegnativa,** firm offer.
impegnato, *a.* Engaged, pledged, pawned; entangled, involved; (*Naut.*) fouled (rope).
impegno, *n.m.* Pledge, engagement, obligation, promise; diligence, zeal, care, attention; (*Comm.*) liability. **Adempiere un —,** to fulfil an engagement; **avere un — precedente,** to have a previous engagement; **fare una cosa con —,** to do a thing with diligence; **pieno d'—,** full of good will, zealous.
impegnoso, *a.* Difficult, troublesome.
impegolare, *v.t.* To tar, to smear with tar, to cover with pitch.
impegolarsi, *v.r.* (*fig.*) To become involved.
impelagarsi, *v.r.* (*fig.*) To embroil oneself, to plunge into a sea (of trouble).
impelare, *v.t.* To scatter hair about. **Il cane impela le vesti,** the dog is covering the clothes with hairs.
impellente, *a.* Impellent, urgent; stringent; inoperative.
impellere [impEllere], *v.t.* To impel, to force, to constrain; to thrust aside.
impellicciare, impellicciarsi, *v.t.r.* To wrap in furs.
impenetrabile [impenetrAbile], *a.* Impenetrable; unfathomable; inscrutable. **— all'aria,** air-tight.
impenetrabilità [-à], *n.f.* Impenetrability.
impenetrabilmente, *adv.* Impenetrably.
impenitente, *a.* Impenitent, unrepenting, hardened, incorrigible.
impenitenza, *n.f.* Impenitence; obduracy.
impennacchiare, *v.t.* To adorn with plumes.
impennaggio [impennAggio], *n.m.* (*Aviat.*) Fins.
impennare, *v.t.* To cover with feathers; (*Naut.*) to hoist a flag; (*fig.*) to take up one's pen.
impennarsi, *v.r.* To rear, to prance (of a horse); (*Aviat.*) to climb; to become fledged; (*fig.*) to fire up (with anger), to take offence.
impennata, *n.f.* Rearing (of a horse); (*Aviat.*) tail down, climb.
impennonare, *v.t.* (*Naut.*) To hoist a pennon.
impensabile [impensAbile], *a.* Unthinkable.
impensata, *adv.* **All'—,** unexpectedly, unawares.
impensatamente, *adv.* Unexpectedly.
impensato, *a.* Unforeseen, unexpected.
impensierire, *v.t.* To preoccupy, to worry, to cause anxiety.
impensierirsi, *v.r.* To become thoughtful; to be concerned, to get uneasy, to feel uncomfortable.
impensierito, *p.p.a.* Uneasy, anxious.
impepare, *v.t.* To pepper.

imperante, *a.* Reigning (as an emperor, etc.). **Traiano —,** during the reign of Trajan.
imperare, *v.i.* To rule, to dominate, to prevail; to command, to dictate.
imperativamente, *adv.* Imperatively.
imperativo, *n.m.a.* Imperative.
imperatore, *n.m.* Emperor.
imperatorio [imperatOrio], *a.* Imperial.
imperatrice, *n.f.* Empress.
impercettibile [impercettIbile], *a.* Imperceptible.
impercettibilità [-à], *n.f.* Imperceptibility.
impercettibilmente, *adv.* Imperceptibly.
imperciocchè, *conj.* (*obs.*) Since, whereas, inasmuch as.
imperdibile [imperdIbile], *a.* Impossible to be lost.
imperdonabile [imperdonAbile], *a.* Unpardonable.
imperdonabilmente, *adv.* Unpardonably.
imperfettamente, *adv.* Imperfectly.
imperfetto, *n.m.a.* Imperfect; faulty, defective.
imperfezione, *n.f.* Imperfection, fault, defect; flaw.
imperforato, *a.* Imperforate.
imperiale, *n.m.* Top of a bus, upper deck (of bus or coach).
imperiale, *a.* Imperial.
imperialismo, *n.m.* Imperialism.
imperialista (*pl.* **imperialisti**), *n.m.a.* Imperial; imperialistic.
imperialmente, *adv.* Imperially.
imperio [impErio], *n.m.* Authority, command; imperiousness; empire.
imperiosamente, *adv.* Imperiously.
imperiosità [-à], *n.f.* Imperiousness.
imperioso, *a.* Imperious, overbearing, high-handed, domineering; urgent, pressing; authoritative.
imperitamente, *adv.* Unskilfully, inexpertly.
imperito, *a.* Unskilled, unskilful, inexpert.
imperituro, *a.* Imperishable, ever-lasting.
imperizia [imperIzia], *n.f.* Unskilfulness, inexperience.
imperlare, *v.t.* To adorn with pearls; to cover with drops.
imperlato, *p.p.a.* Adorned with pearls; (*fig.*) covered with sweat.
impermalimento, *n.m.* Taking a thing amiss; ill-temper.
impermalirsi, *v.r.* To take offence; to take it ill; to take a thing amiss. **— di una cosa,** to resent a thing.
impermeabile [impermeAbile], *n.m.a.* Waterproof; mackintosh, raincoat.
impermeabilità [-à], *n.f.* Impermeability.
impermutabile [impermutAbile], *a.* Unchangeable, that cannot be changed.
impermutabilità [-à], *n.f.* Unchangeableness, unchangingness.
impernare, imperniare, *v.t.* To hinge upon, to turn on a pivot; to base, to found.
imperniarsi, *v.r.* To be founded upon.
imperniatura, *n.f.* Pivot, hinge.
impero, *n.m.* Empire; dominion; rule. **Avere — su sè stesso,** to be self-controlled.
imperocchè, *conj.* (*obs.*) For, because.
imperscrutabile [imperscrutAbile], *a.* Inscrutable, unsearchable, unfathomable.
imperscrutabilità [-à], *n.f.* Inscrutability.
imperscrutabilmente, *adv.* Inscrutably.
impersonale, *a.* Impersonal.
impersonalmente, *adv.* Impersonally.
impersonare, impersonarsi, *v.t.r.* To impersonate, to personify.
impersuadibile [impersuadIbile], *a.* Unpersuadable.
impersuasibile [impersuasIbile], *a.* Unconvincible.
impersuaso, *a.* Unconvinced.
imperterrito [impertErrito], *a.* Dauntless, fearless, undaunted.
impertinente, *a.* Impertinent, insolent, offensive, impudent, cheeky.
impertinentemente, *adv.* Impertinently.
impertinenza, *n.f.* Impertinence, insolence; cheek.
imperturbabile [imperturbAbile], *a.* Imperturbable.
imperturbabilità [-à], *n.f.* Imperturbability.
imperturbabilmente, *adv.* Imperturbably.
imperturbato, *a.* Unperturbed.
imperversamento, *n.m.* Anger, rage.
imperversare, *v.i.* To rage (of weather); to inveigh against, to grow furious.
impervio [impErvio], *a.* Impervious; hard, difficult.
impestare, *v.t.* To infect.
impetecchito, *a.* Spotty, blotchy; miserly.
impetigine [impetIgine], *n.f.* (*Med.*) Impetigo.
impeto [Impeto], *n.m.* Impetus, impulse, driving force; impetuosity, dash, rush, onset; transport, rage. **Di primo —,** hasty, impulsive; **agire d'—,** to act impulsively; **pieno d'—,** full of go; **fare — su,** to launch an attack on.
impetrabile [impetrAbile], *a.* Obtainable by treaty.
impetrante, *a.* Suppliant.
impetrare, *v.t.* To entreat, to beseech, to implore; to obtain (by asking for).
impettito, *a.* Erect, upright, stiff; stand-offish, reserved. **Camminare —,** to strut.
impetuosamente, *adv.* Impetuously.
impetuosità [-à], *n.f.* Impetuosity, vehemence.
impetuoso, *a.* Impetuous, dashing, vehement, violent, precipitate.
impiacevolire, *v.t.* To render pleasant.
impiacevolirsi, *v.r.* To make oneself pleasant.
impiagamento, *n.m.* (*Med.*) Ulceration.
impiagare, impiagarsi, *v.i.r.* To be ulcerated, to ulcerate.
impiagatura, *n.f.* Ulceration.
impiallacciare, *v.t.* To veneer.
impiallacciatura, *n.f.* Veneer, veneering.
impianellare, *v.t.* To tile, to pave with tiles.
impiantamento, *n.m.* Installing; planting.
impiantare, *v.t.* To set up, to plant, to install, to fix firmly; to establish, to found; (*Comm.*) to open (an account). **— casa,** to set up house; **— un affare,** to start a business.
impiantire, *v.t.* To floor, to pave.
impiantito, *n.m.* Floor, wood floor; tiled pavement.
impianto, *n.m.* Setting up, installation, fitting; plant, installation; establishment. **Gl'impianti sanitari,** the sanitary arrangements; **un — elettrico,** an electric plant, a power-station; **l'— dell'acqua,** the water system; **spese d'—,** initial outlay; (*Naut.*) **— del timone,** steering-gear.

impiastracarte, impiastrafogli, *n.m.* Scribbler.
impiastramento, *n.m.* Daubing, smearing, soiling, plastering.
impiastrare, *v.t.* To plaster, to daub.
impiastrarsi, *v.r.* To dirty oneself, to smear oneself; to paint one's face.
impiastratore, impiastratrice, *n.m.f.* Dauber.
impiastricciare, *v.t.* To daub here and there.
impiastro, *n.m.* (*Med.*) Poultice, plaster; (*fig.*) bore; clumsy patch, botch.
impiccagione, *n.f.* Hanging (of a body).
impiccare, impiccarsi, *v.t.r.* To hang, to hang oneself.
impiccatore, *n.m.* Hangman.
impiccatura, *n.f.* Hanging.
impicciare, *v.t.* To embarrass, to embroil, to encumber.
impicciarsi, *v.r.* To meddle with, to interfere.
impicciativo, *a.* Embarrassing.
impiccinire, *v.t.i.* To make or grow smaller, to diminish, to lessen; to depreciate.
impiccio [impIccio], *n.m.* Embarrassment, trouble, scrape, mess. **È un bell'—!** What a nuisance! **trovarsi negli impicci,** to be in a quandary or predicament.
impicciolimento, *n.m.* Reduction (in size); belittling.
impicciolire, *v.t.i.* To make or grow smaller; to depreciate, to belittle.
impicciolirsi, *v.r.* To grow smaller, to humble oneself.
impiccione, *n.m.f.* Bore, meddler, mischief-maker.
impiccioso, *a.* Embarrassing, annoying.
impidocchiare, *v.t.* To make lousy.
impidocchiarsi, *v.r.* To become lousy.
impiegabile [impiegAbile], *a.* Employable; (money) possible to be invested.
impiegare, *v.t.* To employ, to engage; to use, to spend; to invest (money), to put to interest. **— male il proprio tempo,** to waste one's time; **ho impiegato due giorni,** it took me two days; **Quanto impiega?** How long does it take? **— un segretario,** to engage a secretary; **— un capitale,** to invest capital.
impiegarsi, *v.r.* To get employment, to find a job; to be employed.
impiegatizio [impiegatIzio], *a.* Clerical (of clerks).
impiegato, *n.m.* Employee, clerk.
impiegatume, *n.m.* (*contempt.*) Crowd of clerks.
impiego, *n.m.* Employment, employ, situation; occupation, business, post; use; (*Comm.*) investment. **Trovare —,** to find a job; **è un buon —,** it's a good investment.
impietosire, *v.t.* To fill with pity, to touch with pity.
impietosirsi, *v.r.* To be moved with compassion.
impietrimento, *n.m.* Petrifaction.
impietrire, impietrare, *v.t.i.* To petrify (in all senses), to turn to stone.
impigliare, *v.t.* To entangle.
impigliarsi, *v.r.* To become entangled; to be involved.
impiglio [impIglio], *n.m.* Entanglement; intrigue.
impigrire, *v.t.* To make lazy.
impigrirsi, *v.r.* To grow lazy.
impigro, *a.* (*obs.*) Active, diligent.
impillaccherare, *v.t.* To splash with mud.
impinguamento, *n.m.* Fattening.
impinguare, *v.t.* To fatten; to enrich (soil, etc.); to manure.
impinguarsi, *v.r.* To grow fat; to enrich oneself, to grow rich.
impinguativo, *a.* Fattening.
impinzare, *v.t.* To cram, to stuff. **— un libro con note,** to cram a book with footnotes.
impiolare, *v.i.* (*Agric.*) To sprout (of grain).
impiombare, *v.t.* To seal with lead; to roof or cover with lead; to stop (a tooth); (*Naut.*) to splice a rope.
impiombatura, *n.f.* Sealing; stopping (of a tooth); (*Naut.*) splice, splicing.
impiombato, *a.* Sealed with lead.
impiparsi, *v.r.* To be indifferent, not to care a rap. (*colloq.*) **Aver l'aria di me ne impipo,** to look as though one doesn't care a damn; **io me ne impipo,** I couldn't care less.
impippiare, *v.t.* To feed young birds by the beak.
impiumare, *v.t.* To feather, to line with feathers, to adorn with plumes.
impiumarsi, *v.r.* To be fledged; to wear feathers; (*colloq.*) to start a beard.
implacabile [implacAbile], *a.* Implacable, ruthless, inexorable.
implacabilità [-à], *n.f.* Ruthlessness, implacability.
implacabilmente, *adv.* Implacably.
implacato, *a.* Implacable, unrelenting, inveterate.
implacidire, *v.t.* To appease.
implicare, *v.t.* To implicate, to involve, to imply.
implicazione, *n.f.* Implication.
implicitamente, *adv.* Implicitly.
implicito [implIcito], *a.* Implicit, implied, understood.
implorabile [implorAbile], *a.* Possible to ask for.
implorare, *v.t.* To implore, to entreat, to beseech, to beg for.
implorazione, *n.f.* Supplication, entreaty, prayer.
implume, *a.* Featherless; unfledged.
impluvio [implUvio], *n.m.* (*Arch.*) Impluvium, gutter.
impoetico [impoEtico], *a.* (*Lit.*) Unpoetic.
impoliticamente, *adv.* Injudiciously, unwisely.
impolitico [impolItico], *a.* Impolitic, injudicious; imprudent.
impollinazione, *n.f.* (*Bot.*) Pollination.
impolluto, *a.* Unpolluted, clean.
impolpare, *v.t.i.* To fatten, to grow fat; (*fig.*) to stuff (with footnotes, etc.).
impoltronirsi, *v.r.* To become lazy.
impolverare, *v.t.* To cover with dust.
impolverarsi, *v.r.* To get dusty.
impomatare, impomatarsi, *v.t.r.* To apply pomade to the hair.
impomiciare, *v.t.* To rub with pumice-stone.
imponderabile [imponderAbile], *a.* Imponderable.
imponente, *a.* Imposing, grand, impressive, commanding, stately, majestic.

imponenza, *n.f.* Grandeur, impressiveness, imposingness, magnificence.
imponibile [imponIbile], *a.* Taxable, rateable. **L'—,** assessable income.
imponibilità [-à], *n.f.* Taxability.
impopolare, *a.* Unpopular.
impopolarità [-à], *n.f.* Unpopularity.
impopolarmente, *adv.* Unpopularly.
impoppato, *a.* (*Naut.*) Down by the stern.
imporporare, *v.t.* To make purple, to redden.
imporporarsi, *v.r.* To turn red, to blush.
imporre, *v.t.* To impose, to enjoin, to lay upon; to force; to inflict.
imporsi, *v.r.* To get the upper hand, to impress oneself upon; to have one's way, to be overbearing; (*Sport*) to win. **La sua autorità s'impone,** his authority is recognized; **le elezioni s'impongono,** elections are inevitable; **egli s'impose,** he got the upper hand.
importante, *a.* Important, weighty, serious, momentous.
importanza, *n.f.* Importance, consequence, moment, weight. **Aver grande —,** to be of importance, to carry weight.
importare (1), *v.t.* To import, to introduce (from abroad); to imply, to involve, to mean.
importare (2), *v.i.* To matter, to be of consequence, to be material, to be necessary. **Non importa,** it doesn't matter; never mind; **Cosa importa?** What does it matter? **importa molto,** it's of importance.
importatore, importatrice, *n.m.f.* (*Comm.*) Importer.
importazione, *n.f.* Importation, import. **Dazio d'—,** import duty.
importo, *n.m.* (*Comm.*) Total amount, sum; (*Arith.*) carrying forward.
importunamente, *adv.* Importunately.
importunare, *v.t.* To importune, to trouble, to annoy; to tease.
importunità [-à], *n.f.* Importunity.
importuno, *n.m.a.* Importunate; troublesome, annoying.
impositore, *n.m.* (*Print.*) Stone-hand.
imposizione, *n.f.* Imposition (in all senses), tax; injunction.
impossente, *a.* Impotent; powerless.
impossessarsi, *v.r.* To become master of, to take possession of, to master.
impossibile [impossIbile], *a.* Impossible, impracticable. (*colloq.*) **Far l'—,** to do one's utmost.
impossibilità [-à], *n.f.* Impossibility.
impossibilitare, *v.t.* To make impossible.
impossibilmente, *adv.* Impossibly.
imposta (1), *n.f.* Tax; duty, tribute. **Imposte dirette,** direct taxes; **— sul reddito,** income tax; **— sul patrimonio,** capital levy.
imposta (2), *n.f.* Shutter; leaf (of a folding door).
impostame, *n.m.* (All the) shutters.
impostare, *v.t.* To post a letter, to mail; to place, to define; to state (a problem); to lay foundations. **— un problema,** to formulate a problem; **— una nave,** to lay down a ship.
impostarsi, *v.r.* To take up one's position.
impostatura, *n.f.* Posting, setting, placing.
impostazione, *n.f.* Posting (of letters); bearing, attitude; foundation, base.
imposte, *n.f.pl.* Taxes [cp. **imposta**].
impostemire, *v.i.* (*Med.*) To form an abscess.
impostore, impostora, *n.m.f.* Impostor, swindler; liar.
impostura, *n.f.* Imposture, fraud, deceit.
imposturare, *v.t.* To carry out an imposture.
impotente, *a.* Impotent (in all senses).
impotenza, *n.f.* Impotence, impotency; powerlessness; inability.
impoverimento, *n.m.* Impoverishment, decay, exhaustion; pauperization.
impoverire, *v.t.* To impoverish, to make poor.
impoverirsi, *v.r.* To become poor.
impraticabile [impraticAbile], *a.* Impracticable, not feasible; impassable (of roads, etc.).
impraticabilità [-à], *n.f.* Impracticability.
impratichire, *v.t.* To exercise, to accustom, to train, to make familiar with.
impratichirsi, *v.r.* To practise, to make oneself familiar with, to drill.
imprecare, *v.i.* To curse, to imprecate.
imprecatorio [imprecatOrio], *a.* Imprecatory.
imprecazione, *n.f.* Imprecation, malediction.
imprecisione, *n.f.* Inaccuracy, inexactitude, imprecision.
impreciso, *a.* Inaccurate, inexact; vague.
impregiudicabile [impregiudicAbile], *a.* Incapable of being prejudiced.
impregiudicato, *a.* Unprejudiced.
impregnamento, *n.m.* Impregnating, impregnation.
impregnare, *v.t.* To impregnate, to fecundate; to saturate.
impregnarsi, *v.r.* To be imbued; to be soaked, to be saturated.
impregnazione, *n.f.* Impregnation, fecundation.
impremeditatamente, *adv.* Unpremeditatedly.
impremeditato, *a.* Unpremeditated.
imprendere [imprEndere], *v.t.* To undertake, to begin, to initiate; to set to.
imprendibile [imprendIbile], *a.* Impregnable, invincible, unassailable.
imprendimento, *n.m.* Undertaking.
imprenditore, *n.m.* Contractor, manager. **— di lavori,** building contractor.
impreparato, *a.* Unprepared, unready, inefficient.
impreparazione, *n.f.* Unpreparedness, inefficiency.
impresa, *n.f.* Undertaking, enterprise, deed; (*Comm.*) concern, firm, management; (*Her.*) device, motto; (*Theat.*) management. **— edilizia,** firm of builders; **una nobile —,** a noble deed; **iniziare una nuova —,** to engage in a new enterprise.
impresario [impresArio], *n.m.* Contractor, manager; (*Theat.*) manager, impresario. **— di pompe funebri,** funeral undertaker.
imprescienza, *n.f.* Lack of foresight.
imprescindibile [imprescindIbile], *a.* Inescapable, indispensable, necessary; urgent.
imprescrittibile [imprescrittIbile], *a.* Indefeasible, imprescriptible.
impressionabile [impressionAbile], *a.* Impressionable, sensitive, apprehensive, susceptible.

impressionabilità [-à], *n.f.* Impressionability, emotionalism.
impressionante, *a.* Striking, startling, impressive.
impressionare, *v.t.* To impress, to affect strongly, to make an impression; to alarm, to scare; (*Phot.*) to expose.
impressionarsi, *v.r.* To be impressed; to be alarmed, to worry; to be deeply affected.
impressione, *n.f.* Impression (in all senses). **Far buona —,** to impress favourably.
impressionismo, *n.m.* (*Art*) Impressionism.
impressionista (pl. **impressionisti**), *n.m.* (*Art*) Impressionist.
impresso, *p.p.a.* Impressed; stamped, printed, engraved.
impressore, *n.m.* (*Print.*) Taker-off, pressman.
imprestare, *v.t.* To lend.
imprestito, *n.m.* Loan, borrowing, lending.
impretarsi, *v.r.* (*colloq.*) To become a priest.
impreteribile [impreterIbile], *a.* Indispensable; absolute.
impreteribilmente, *adv.* Indispensably.
imprevedibile [imprevedIbile], *a.* Unforeseeable, unforeseen, unexpected.
imprevedutamente, *adv.* Unexpectedly.
impreveduto, *a.* Unexpected.
imprevidente, *a.* Improvident, without foresight.
imprevidentemente, *adv.* Improvidently.
imprevidenza, *n.f.* Improvidence.
imprevisto, *a.* Unforeseen, unexpected.
impreziosire, *v.t.* To make precious.
imprigionamento, *n.m.* Arrest, imprisonment.
imprigionare, *v.t.* To imprison, to lock up, to take into custody.
imprima, *adv.* Before all. **All'—,** at first
imprimamente, *adv.* First of all.
imprimere [imprImere], *v.t.* To impress, to imprint, to print; to stamp; to mark, to inculcate. **La forza che imprime il moto,** the force that sets in motion.
improbabile [improbAbile], *a.* Improbable, unlikely.
improbabilmente, *adv.* Improbably.
improbità [-à], *n.f.* Wickedness, malice, dishonesty.
improbo [Improbo], *a.* Wicked, dishonest; hard (of work), painful, toilsome; continual.
improduttività [-à], *n.f.* Barrenness, unproductiveness.
improduttivo, *a.* Unproductive.
impronta, *n.f.* Stamp, mark, impression, trace, imprint. **— digitale,** finger-print; **lasciare un'—,** to leave one's mark.
improntamente, *adv.* With effrontery, impudently; indiscreetly.
improntare, *v.t.* To impress, to mark; to characterize.
improntitudine [improntitUdine], *n.f.* Effrontery; indiscretion, rashness.
impronto, *n.m.* (*Print.*) Mark of print on other side of a page.
impronto, *a.* Importunate, rash. **All'—,** extempore, impromptu, at first sight.
impronunziabile [impronunziAbile], *a.* Unpronounceable.
improperio [impropErio], *n.m.* Abuse, insult, abusive language; reproach.
impropizio [impropIzio], *a.* Unfavourable, ill-timed.
impropriamente, *adv.* Improperly.
improprietà [-à], *n.f.* Impropriety; inaccuracy (of expression).
improprio [imprOprio], *a.* Improper, unbecoming; erroneous, inaccurate (of words), unappropriate.
improrogabile [improrogAbile], *a.* Admitting of no delay, undeferrable.
improsciuttire, *v.i.* To grow old and thin; to become withered.
improvvidamente, *adv.* Improvidently, imprudently.
improvvidenza, *n.f.* Improvidence.
improvvido [imprOvvido], *a.* Improvident, thoughtless, inconsiderate.
improvvisamente, *adv.* Unexpectedly suddenly.
improvvisamento, *n.m.* Improvisation.
improvvisare, *v.t.* To improvise, to extemporize, to do something off-hand; to deliver a speech extempore, to speak extempore.
improvvisata, *n.f.* Pleasant surprise; unexpected arrival.
improvvisatore, improvvisatrice, *n.m.f.* Improvisor.
improvvisazione, *n.f.* Improvisation.
improvviso, *a.* Sudden, unexpected, unforeseen. **All'—,** suddenly, all at once.
improvisto, *a.* Unexpected, unprepared.
imprudente, *a.* Imprudent, heedless, unwary, rash.
imprudentemente, *adv.* Imprudently.
imprudenza, *n.f.* Imprudence, rashness.
imprunare, *v.t.* To hedge with thorns.
impube, impubere [impUbere], *a.* Under the age of puberty.
impudente, *a.* Impudent, immodest, shameless, saucy.
impudenza, *n.f.* Impudence, shamelessness, effrontery.
impudicamente, *adv.* Immodestly.
impudicizia [impudicIzia], *n.f.* Immodesty, unchastity.
impudico, *a.* Immodest, lewd, wanton, shameless.
impugnabile [impugnAbile], *a.* (*Law*) Impugnable.
impugnare, *v.t.* To seize, to brandish, to grip; to take up arms; to call in question, to impugn, to dispute, to contest, to disclaim. **— un testamento,** to contest a will.
impugnatura, *n.f.* Handle, hilt, grip.
impugnazione, *n.f.* Refutation, denial, opposition.
impulciare, *v.t.* To give fleas to.
impulciarsi, *v.r.* To become infested with fleas.
impulitamente, *adv.* Rudely, discourteously.
impulitezza, *n.f.* Rudeness, lack of manners; dirtiness.
impulito, *a.* Rude, discourteous, rough; unpolished; dirty.
impulsione, *n.f.* Impulsion.
impulsività [-à], *n.f.* Impulsiveness, rashness.
impulsivo, *a.* Impulsive, rash, hasty.
impulso, *n.m.* Impulse, impulsion, impetus, stimulus. **Cedere a un —,** to yield to impulse; **dare — a,** to set going.
impune, *a.* Scatheless, unharmed; unpunished.

impunemente, *adv.* With impunity, scot-free.
impunità [-à], *n.f.* Impunity.
impunitamente, *adv.* Without punishment.
impunito, *a.* Unpunished.
impuntare, impuntarsi, *v.i.r.* To stumble, to halt, to stick fast; to stutter; to jib (of a horse); to stick to one's point; to be obstinate.
impuntato, *a.* Obstinate; still.
impuntatura, *n.f.* Stopping (of a clock).
impuntigliarsi, *v.r.* To stick to one's point, to be obstinate; to take it into one's head.
impuntire, *v.t.* To quilt, to sew, to stitch.
impuntitura, *n.f.* Quilting.
impuntuale, *a.* Unpunctual.
impuntualità [-à], *n.f.* Unpunctuality.
impuntura, *n.f.* Back-stitching.
impuramente, *adv.* Impurely.
impurità [-à], *n.f.* Impurity, foulness.
impuro, *a.* Impure, unclean, defiled.
imputabile [imputAbile], *a.* Imputable, accountable.
imputare, *v.t.* To impute, to ascribe, to attribute; (*Law*) to charge with, to accuse. **— di un delitto,** to charge with a crime.
imputato, *n.m.a.* Defendant, accused; charged.
imputazione, *n.f.* Imputation, charge.
imputrescibile [imputrescIbile], *a.* That cannot go bad, not liable to rot.
imputridimento, *n.m.* Putrefaction, rotting.
imputridire, *v.i.* To go bad, to rot, to decay, to become putrid.
imputridirsi, *v.r.* To putrefy.
impuzzire, *v.i.* To become stinking.
in, *prep.* (with an article it becomes **nel, nella,** etc.). In, into, within; at; on; of; by. **Andare in barca,** to go for a row; **salire in treno,** to go on the train; **essere in molti,** to be many; **andare in Francia,** to go to France; **in forse,** in doubt; **in quanto a ciò,** as for that; **essere in tre,** to be in three; **andare in città,** to go to town; **tradurre in inglese,** to translate into English; **in alto,** up, above; **in basso,** down, below; **essere in guerra,** to be at war; **in pace,** at peace; **in campagna,** in the country; **in casa,** at home; **se io fossi in voi,** if I were in your place; **in isbaglio,** by mistake.
inabile [inAbile], *a.* Unfit, unable, incapable; unqualified; unskilful; (*Mil.*) unfit.
inabilità [-à], *n.f.* Inability.
inabilitare, *v.t.* To disable; to disqualify.
inabilitato, *n.m.* Disabled person.
inabilitazione, *n.f.* Disability.
inabilmente, *adv.* Unskilfully, awkwardly.
inabissare, *v.t.* To engulf, to submerge.
inabissarsi, *v.r.* To sink, to be submerged, to be engulfed.
inabitabile [inabitAbile], *a.* Uninhabitable.
inabitato, *a.* Uninhabited.
inaccessibile [inaccessIbile], *a.* Inaccessible, out of reach.
inaccessibilità [-à], *n.f.* Inaccessibility.
inaccessabilmente, *adv.* Inaccessibly.
inaccesso, *a.* Inaccessible, out of reach.
inaccettabile [inaccettAbile], *a.* Unacceptable.
inaccordabile [inaccordAbile], *a.* Irreconcilable, impermissible; untunable.
inaccorto, *a.* Unskilful; unwary, incautious.
inaccusabile [inaccusAbile], *a.* Unimpeachable, not open to accusation.
inacerbire, *v.t.* To make bitter, to embitter.
inacerbirsi, *v.r.* To grow bitter.
inacetire, *v.i.* To turn sour, to turn into vinegar.
inacidire, *v.i.* To turn acid.
inacquare, *v.t.* To water.
inacutire, *v.t.* To sharpen, to make acute.
inacutirsi, *v.r.* To become sharp.
inadattabile [inadattAbile], *a.* Unadaptable.
inadattabilità [-à], *n.f.* Inadaptability.
inadatto, *a.* Unfit, unsuitable; unqualified; unbecoming.
inadeguatamente, *adv.* Inadequately.
inadeguatezza, *n.f.* Inadequacy.
inadeguato, *a.* Inadequate, insufficient.
inadempibile [inadempIbile], *a.* Impracticable, impossible to be fulfilled.
inadempimento, inadempiènza, *n.m.f.* Unfulfilment, non-execution; heedlessness, negligence.
inadempito, inadempiuto, *a.* Unfulfilled, unexecuted; unfinished.
inadoprabile [inadoprAbile], *a.* Unfit for use, unusable.
inafferrabile [inafferrAbile], *a.* Impossible to grasp or seize; out of reach.
inaffettato, *a.* Unaffected, without affectation.
inaffiatoio [inaffiatOio], *n.m.* Watering-can.
inaggregabile [inaggregAbile], *a.* Impossible to unite.
inagguagliabile [inagguagliAbile], *a.* Incomparable.
inaiare, *v.t.* (*Agric.*) To spread out for threshing.
inalare, *v.t.* To inhale, to inspire, to breathe in.
inalatore, *n.m.* (*Med.*) Inhaler.
inalazione, *n.f.* Inhalation.
inalbamento, *n.m.* Whitening, making white, turning white.
inalbare, *v.t.i.* To become white, to whiten.
inalberamento, *n.m.* Hoisting (of the flag); rearing (of a horse).
inalberare, *v.t.* To hoist (a flag); to plant trees on.
inalberarsi, *v.r.* To rear (of a horse); to lose one's temper; to take offence.
inalidire, *v.t.* To dry up; to dry (meat, etc.).
inalienabile [inalienAbile], *a.* Inalienable.
inalterabile [inalterAbile], *a.* Unalterable, unchangeable.
inalterabilità [-à], *n.f.* Unchangeableness.
inalterabilmente, *adv.* Unalterably.
inalveare, *v.t.* To canalize (a river).
inalveazione, *n.f.* Canalization.
inalzare, *v.t.* To raise [cp. **innalzare**].
inamabile [inamAbile], *a.* Unpleasant, unlovable.
inamarire, *v.i.* To become bitter, to be embittered.
inameno, *a.* Unattractive.
inamidare, *v.t.* To starch. **Colletto inamidato** starched collar.
inamidatura, *n.f.* Starching.
inammendabile [inammendAbile], *a.* Impossible to correct; incorrigible.
inammissibile [inammissIbile], *a.* Inadmissible, unacceptable.
inammissibilità [-à], *n.f.* Inadmissibility.
inamovibile [inamovIbile], *a.* Irremovable.
inane, *a.* Vain, futile, inane; empty.

inanellare, *v.t.* To curl, to form into rings; to offer marriage, to wed.
inanellato, *a.* Curly; be-ringed.
inanimare, inanimire, *v.t.* To encourage, to stir, to excite, to animate [cp. **animare**].
inanimato, *a.* Inanimate, lifeless, dispirited.
inanimirsi, *v.r.* To take courage, to take heart.
inanità [-**à**], *n.f.* Futility, emptiness, inanity.
inanizione, *n.f.* Inanition, exhaustion.
inappagabile [inappagAbile], *a.* Impossible to satisfy.
inappagato, *a.* Unsatisfied, unfulfilled.
inappellabile [inappellAbile], *a.* (*Law*) Admitting of no appeal; absolute, final.
inappetente, *a.* Without appetite.
inappetenza, *n.f.* Loss of appetite.
inapplicabile [inapplicAbile], *a.* Inapplicable.
inapplicato, *a.* Negligent, without application.
inapplicazione, *n.f.* Negligence, lack of diligence.
inapprensibile [inapprensIbile], *a.* Hard to understand, incomprehensible.
inapprezzabile [inapprezzAbile], *a.* Priceless, invaluable, inestimable; imperceptible; inappreciable.
inapprodabile [inapprodAbile], *a.* (*Naut.*) Unsuitable for landing; unapproachable for vessels.
inappuntabile [inappuntAbile], *a.* Irreproachable, unexceptionable.
inappuntabilmente, *adv.* Irreproachably.
inappurabile [inappurabile], *a.* Unascertainable, impossible to clear up.
inappurato, *a.* Unascertained, unverified, unsettled.
inarabile [inarAbile], *a.* (*Agric.*) Inarable, unploughable.
inarato, *a.* (*Agric.*) Unploughed.
inarcamento, *n.m.* Arching, curving, bending; cambering.
inarcare, *v.t.* To bend, to curve, to arch, to camber. — **le ciglia,** to raise one's eyebrows.
inarcarsi, *v.r.* To bend oneself.
inarcatura, *n.f.* Arching, cambering, camber; curve.
inargentare, *v.t.* To silver-plate, to plate.
inargentato, *a.* Silver-plated; white, silver (of the moon, of the hair).
inargentatura, *n.f.* Silvering, plating.
inarguto, *a.* Slow in thought, speech, etc.
inaridire, *v.t.* To dry up, to parch; to wither.
inaridirsi, *v.r.* To become arid. to become parched.
inarmonicamente, *adv.* Inharmoniously, discordantly.
inarmonico [inarmOnico], *a.* Inharmonious, inharmonic, discordant.
inarmonioso, *a.* Inharmonious.
inarrivabile [inarrivAbile], *a.* Unattainable, inaccessible; unbeatable; inimitable.
inarrivabilmente, *adv.* Inimitably, incomparably; unattainably.
inarticolatamente, *adv.* Inarticulately.
inarticolato, *a.* Inarticulate.
inascoltato, *a.* Unheeded, disregarded.
inasinire, *v.t.i.* To grow stupid, to become stupid, to get dull.
inaspettabile [inaspettAbile], *a.* Improbable.
inaspettatamente, *adv.* Unexpectedly.
inaspettato, *a.* Unexpected, unforeseen.
inasprimento, *n.m.* Hardening, stiffening, aggravation, embitterment, exacerbation. — **di tasse,** tightening up of taxation.
inasprire, *v.t.* To embitter, to irritate, to aggravate, to exacerbate, to exasperate.
inasprirsi, *v.r.* To become embittered; to become more wintry (weather).
inassegnabile [inassegnAbile], *a.* Not assignable.
inastare, *v.t.* To hoist (a flag); (*Mil.*) to raise (a standard), to fix (bayonets).
inattaccabile [inattaccAbile], *a.* Unassailable; unattackable.
inattaccabilità [-**à**], *n.f.* Unassailability.
inattendibile [inattendIbile], *a.* Unreliable, untrustworthy; unfounded, groundless.
inattendibilità [-**à**], *n.f.* Unreliability, untrustworthiness.
inattento, *a.* Unattentive, heedless, careless.
inattenzione, *n.f.* Inattention, carelessness.
inatteso, *a.* Unexpected, unlooked for, unforeseen; sudden.
inattingibile [inattingIbile], *a.* Unattainable.
inattitudine [inattitUdine], *n.f.* Inaptitude.
inattività [-**à**], *n.f.* Inactivity; inaction.
inattivo, *a.* Inactive, dormant; idle, slack.
inatto, *a.* Awkward, unapt; unsuited.
inattuabile [inattuAbile], *a.* Impracticable.
inattuabilità [-**à**], *n.f.* Impracticability.
inaudibile [inaudIbile], *a.* Inaudible.
inaudito, *a.* Unheard of, incredible, unprecedented; prohibitive.
inaugurale, *a.* Inaugural.
inaugurare, *v.t.* To inaugurate; to commence, to open (an exhibition, etc.), to unveil (a monument, etc.).
inaugurazione, *n.f.* Inauguration, opening. unveiling.
inauspicatamente, *adv.* Inauspiciously.
inauspicato, *a.* Inauspicious, unpropitious, ill-omened.
inavvedutamente, *adv.* Carelessly, inadvertently, without due consideration.
inavvedutezza, *n.f.* Inadvertence, carelessness; inattention.
inavveduto, *a.* Careless, unwary, inadvertent.
inavvertente, *a.* Incautious, inadvertent.
inavvertentemente, *adv.* Inadvertently, incautiously.
inavvertenza, *n.f.* Inadvertence.
inavvertitamente, *adv.* Unthinkingly, inadvertently.
inavvertito, *a.* Unobserved, unperceived; careless; inattentive; ill-informed.
inazione, *n.f.* Inaction, idleness, inertia.
inazzurrare, inazzurrarsi, *v.t.r.* To turn blue.
incaciare, *v.t.* To sprinkle grated cheese (on soup, etc.).
incaciatura, *n.f.* Grated cheese (as a condiment).
incadaverimento, *n.m.* Cadaverous appearance.
incadaverire, *v.i.* To become like a corpse.
incagliamento, *n.m.* (*Naut.*) Stranding, grounding; impediment.
incagliare, *v.t.i.* To strand; (*fig.*) to hamper; to bring to a standstill.

incagliarsi, *v.r.* (*Naut.*) To run aground; to be hampered.
incaglio [incAglio], *n.m.* (*Naut.*) Stranding; obstacle, hindrance, hitch.
incalappiare, *v.t.* To ensnare.
incalcare, *v.t.* To trample down, to stamp.
incalcatura, *n.f.* Trampling; pressing down of grapes.
incalcinare, *v.t.* (*Agric.*) To lime-wash, to dress with lime.
incalcolabile [incalcolAbile], *a.* Incalculable.
incalcolabilmente, *adv.* Incalculably.
incalescenza, *n.f.* (*Med.*) Increased feverishness.
incaliginare, *v.i.* To grow misty, to become clouded (of vision).
incallimento, *n.m.* Hardening; callousness; callosity.
incallire, *v.t.* To become horny; (*fig.*) to make callous, to injure, to harden.
incallirsi, *v.r.* To become hardened, to grow callous.
incalorimento, *n.m.* Heating, warming.
incalorire, *v.t.* To warm up, to heat.
incalorirsi, *v.r.* To become heated, to get excited.
incalvire, *v.i.* To become bald.
incalzamento, *n.m.* Chasing, following, pursuit.
incalzante, *a.* Pressing after, pursuing.
incalzare, *v.t.* To chase, to pursue, to follow up closely, to press hard. **Il tempo incalza,** time presses; **— il nemico,** to pursue the enemy.
incalzo, *n.m.* Support, stiffening, reinforcement.
incamerabile [incamerAbile], *a.* (*Law*) Liable to confiscation.
incameramento, *n.m.* (*Law*) Confiscation.
incamerare, *v.t.* To confiscate, to annex.
incamiciare, *v.t.* To whitewash, to plaster, to coat; to apply rough-cast.
incamiciata, *n.m.* (*Mil.*) Night assault (with troops wearing white shirts, etc., for identification).
incamiciatura, *n.f.* Plastering, liming; rough-cast.
incamminamento, *n.m.* Starting, giving a start to.
incamminare, *v.t.* To set going, to start; to put in the right path; to initiate.
incamminarsi, *v.r.* To set out, to make for, to start walking, to make one's way to; (*Comm.*) to start a business. **S'incamminarono verso casa,** they started home.
incanagliare, incanaglire, *v.i.* To become a rascal.
incanagliarsi, *v.r.* To keep bad company.
incanalamento, *n.m.* Canalization.
incanalare, *v.t.* To canalize; to direct, to convey.
incanalatura, *n.f.* Canalization; groove.
incancellabile [incancellAbile], *a.* Indelible, ineffaceable; unforgettable. **Ricordo —,** ineffaceable memory.
incancellabilmente, *adv.* Indelibly.
incancherire, *v.i.* (*Med.*) To become cancerous.
incancrenire, *v.i.* (*Med.*) To become gangrenous.
incandescente, *a.* Incandescent.
incandescenza, *n.f.* Incandescence.
incannaggio [incannAggio], *n.m.* Reeling, winding (silk, etc.).
incannare, *v.t.* To reel, to wind (silk, etc.).
incannata, *n.f.* Bobbinful.
incannatoio [incannatOio], *n.m.* Winder; spool.
incannatore, incannatrice, *n.m.f.* Bobbin-winder, reeler.
incannatura, *n.f.* Silk-winding, bobbin-winding.
incannucciare, *v.t.* To trellis; to make supports for plants; (*Med.*) to put into splints.
incannucciata, *n.f.* Trellis, lattice-work; (*Med.*) splint.
incannucciatura, *n.f.* Trellising.
incantabile [incantAbile], *a.* Unsingable.
incantagione, *n.f.*, **incantamento,** *n.m.* Enchantment, charm, spell, magic; incantation.
incantare, *v.t.* To enchant, to charm, to bewitch, to enrapture, to fascinate.
incantarsi, *v.r.* To become enchanted, to be astonished; to be bewitched; (*Mech.*) to jam, to stop working; to stand gaping (at something); to be woolgathering.
incantatore, incantatrice, *n.m.f.* Enchanter, enchantress, charmer.
incantesimo [incantEsimo], *n.m.* Magic, sorcery, spell, enchantment.
incantevole [incantEvole], *a.* Enchanting, delightful, exquisite.
incantevolmente, *adv.* Delightfully, enchantingly.
incanto, *n.m.* Enchantment, charm, fascination, spell; (*Comm.*) auction sale. **Vendere all'—,** to sell by auction; **le cose vanno d'—,** it's all going quite smoothly; **è un —,** it's a dream, it's a delight.
incantucciarsi, *v.r.* To hide oneself in a corner; to get into a corner.
incanutimento, *n.m.* Growing white-haired.
incanutire, *v.i.* To grow white-haired, to turn grey or white; to grow old.
incapacciatura, *n.f.* Slip-knot.
incapace, *a.* Incapable, unable; unqualified; disqualified.
incapacità [-à], *n.f.* Incapacity, inability.
incapacitato, *a.* Disabled.
incaparbire, incaparbirsi, *v.i.r.* To become obstinate.
incaparbito, *a.* Obstinate.
incapestrare, *v.t.* To halter.
incapestrarsi, *v.r.* To get entangled.
incapestrato, *a.* Haltered, tethered; entangled.
incaponirsi, *v.r.* To insist obstinately, to persist in, to be pig-headed.
incappare, *v.i.* To run into, to fall in with, to get into; to fall into (a snare).
incappellare, *v.t.* To put on a hat; (*Naut.*) to rig a mast-head.
incappottarsi, *v.r.* To wrap oneself in a cloak; to put on one's overcoat.
incappucciarsi, *v.r.* To put on a hood, to muffle oneself.
incapricciarsi, incapriccirsi, *v.r.* To take a fancy to; to fall in love, to become infatuated.
incarbonimento, *n.m.* Carbonization.
incarbonire, *v.t.* To carbonize.
incarbonirsi, *v.r.* To become carbonized.

incarceramento, *n.m.* Incarceration, imprisonment.
incarcerare, *v.t.* To imprison, to incarcerate.
incarcerazione, *n.f.* Imprisonment, incarceration.
incarco [cp. **incarico**].
incardinare, *v.t.* To hinge.
incardinarsi, *v.r.* To be hinged, to hinge upon; (*fig.*) to be based upon, to depend upon.
incaricare, *v.t.* To charge, to entrust, to give directions, to commission. **Lo incaricai di far le mie scuse,** I entrusted him with making my excuses.
incaricarsi, *v.r.* To take upon oneself; to take charge of. **Non incaricartene,** don't bother about that.
incaricato, *n.m.* Deputy, agent, proxy; commissioner. **— d'affari,** chargé d'affaires; **professore —,** lecturer head of department.
incaricato, *p.p.a.* Charged with, appointed.
incarico [incArico], *n.m.* Charge, commission, errand, task; appointment, assignment. **Per — di,** on the part of, on behalf of; **assumersi l'—,** to take it upon oneself; **dare un — di fiducia,** to entrust with a delicate mission.
incarnamento, *n.m.* Embodiment, incarnation.
incarnare, *v.t.* To embody, to incarnate; to represent, to impersonate; to wound, to pierce the flesh.
incarnatino, *a.* Flesh-coloured, pink.
incarnato, *a.* Incarnate; flesh-coloured, rose-pink.
incarnazione, *n.f.* Incarnation; embodiment.
incarnire, *v.i.* To grow in. **Unghia incarnita,** ingrowing nail.
incarognire, *v.i.* To rot, to become carrion; to grow lazy; to become a rascal.
incarrucolare, *v.t.* To put a rope on a pulley.
incartamento, *n.m.* (Sets of) papers, notes, documents, dossier.
incartapecorire, *v.i.* To become wrinkled like parchment.
incartare, *v.t.* To wrap in paper.
incartata, *n.f.* Paper packing, wrapping; paper spread over a window.
incarto, *n.m.* (Sets of) papers, etc. [cp. **incartamento**].
incartocciare, *v.t.* To wrap up in paper, to make a parcel of, to put in a paper bag.
incartocciarsi, *v.r.* To turn up, to curl, to become shrivelled.
incartonare, *v.t.* To place between pasteboards.
incasellare, *v.t.* To pigeon-hole, to file for reference.
incassamento, *n.m.* Packing, boxing, putting in boxes.
incassare, *v.t.* To pack (in a case), to encase, to put in a box; to collect cash, to receive money; (*Boxing*) to take punishment. **— un debito,** to collect a debt.
incassarsi, *v.r.* To be encased; to be cut through.
incassato, *p.p.a.* Packed, encased; cashed, taken (money), collected; hollow. **Una strada incassata,** a sunken road.
incassatura, *n.f.* Encasing, socket.
incasso, *n.m.* (Cash) takings, collection; profit. (*Comm.*) **Gl'incassi,** the proceeds (of a sale, etc.); **buono d'—,** money order; **presentare all'—,** to present for collection.
incastellare, *v.t.* To fortify; to raise fortifications.
incastonare, *v.t.* To mount (a gem), to set; to insert.
incastonatura, *n.f.* Setting, mounting.
incastramento, *n.m.* Embedding, fitting, mortising.
incastrare, *v.t.* To fit in, to embed, to enclose firmly, to mortise, to wedge.
incastratura, *n.f.* Mortising, embedding.
incastro, *n.m.* Mortise, groove, joint, recess. **Unire per —,** to mortise; **— a coda di rondine,** dove-tailing.
incatarrarsi, *v.r.* To catch cold.
incatarrato, *a.* Suffering from catarrh.
incatenacciare, *v.t.* To shoot a bolt, to lock.
incatenamento, *n.m.* Fastening, tying up.
incatenare, *v.t.* To chain up, to fasten, to shackle; to join; (*fig.*) to captivate.
incatenatura, *n.f.* Chaining, shackling, fastening up.
incatorzolire, *v.i.* To shrivel (of fruit).
incatramare, *v.t.* To tar, to smear with tar.
incatramatura, *n.f.* Tarring.
incattivire, *v.t.i.* To grow wicked; to make cross.
incattivirsi, *v.r.* To grow wicked, to get cross.
incautamente, *adv.* Unwarily, rashly, incautiously.
incauto [incAuto], *a.* Unwary, incautious, imprudent, rash, careless.
incavalcare, *v.t.* To place upon, to superimpose; to overlap; to place astride.
incavalcato, *a.* Astride.
incavalcatura, *n.f.* Superimposing, superimposition.
incavare, *v.t.* To hollow out, to excavate; to carve, to incise.
incavarsi, *v.r.* To become hollow.
incavato, *a.* Hollow; notch.
incavatura, *n.f.* Hollow, cavity; socket.
incavernare, *v.t.i.* To hollow out a cavern, to enter or place in a cavern.
incavezzare, *v.t.* To halter (a horse).
incavicchiare, *v.t.* To peg, to peg down.
incavigliare, *v.t.* To fasten with pegs.
incavo, *n.m.* Notch, socket, hollow.
incedere [incEdere], *v.i.* To step forward, to stride, to strut, to walk majestically.
incelare, *v.t.* (*Lit.*) To place in heaven.
incendiabile [incendiAbile], *a.* Inflammable.
incendiare, *v.t.* To set on fire, to set fire to.
incendiarsi, *v.r.* To catch fire.
incendiario [incendiArio], *n.m.a.* Incendiary.
incendio [incEndio], *n.m.* Fire, blaze; conflagration. **Assicurazione incendi,** fire insurance; **spegnere un —,** to put out a fire; **domare un —,** to get a fire under control; **— doloso,** arson; **pompa da —,** fire-engine; **un — scoppiò,** a fire broke out.
incenerare, *v.t.* To strew with ashes.
incenerimento, *n.m.* Incineration, cremation.
incenerire, *v.t.* To reduce to ashes to incinerate.
incenerirsi, *v.r.* To burn to ashes.
incensamento, *n.m.* Censing; flattery. **Mutuo —,** mutual flattery.
incensare, *v.t.* To cense, to offer incense to; to flatter, to cajole.

incensazione, *n.f.* (*Eccles.*) Censing.
incensiere, *n.m.* (*Eccles.*) Censer, thurible.
incenso, *n.m.* Incense; flattery, adulation.
incensurabile [incensurAbile], *a.* Irreproachable.
incensurato, *a.* Uncensured, blameless. (*Law*) **Essere —**, to be a first offender.
incentivo, *n.m.* Incentive, incitement, spur, stimulus.
incentramento, *n.m.* Centralization.
incentrare, *v.t.* To centralize, to concentrate.
inceppamento, *n.m.* Obstruction.
inceppare, *v.t.* To obstruct; to clog, to hinder; to fetter; to encumber; to embarrass; to entangle.
incepparsi, *v.r.* To get entangled, to become clogged; to jam; (*Aviat.*) to cut out.
inceppato, *a.* Clogged.
inceppatura, *n.f.* (*Naut.*) Fouling (of rope, anchor, etc.).
inceralaccare, *v.t.* To seal with wax.
incerare, *v.t.* To wax.
incerata, incerato, *n.f.m.* Oil-cloth, tarpaulin, oilskin. (*fig.*) **Essere vestito d'—**, to be indifferent to public opinion.
inceratura, *n.f.* Water-proofing.
incerchiare, *v.t.* To hoop, to encircle.
incerchiarsi, *v.r.* To get in the form of a hoop.
incerconire, *v.i.* To become sour (of wine).
incertamente, *adv.* Uncertainly.
incertezza, *n.f.* Uncertainty, indecision, doubt; irresolution.
incerto (1), *n.m.* Uncertainty. **Incerti**, casual earnings, occasional profit; perquisites.
incerto (2), *a.* Uncertain, doubtful; insecure; unsettled; undecided; irresolute, wavering. **Tempo —**, unsettled weather.
incespicare, *v.i.* To stumble, to trip; to falter; to stutter.
incessabile [incessAbile], *a.* Incessant, unceasing, continuous.
incessabilmente, *adv.* Unceasingly, inexorably.
incessante, *a.* Incessant, continuous, ceaseless.
incessantemente, *adv.* Incessantly.
incesso, *n.m.* Gait, carriage; stride.
incesto, *n.m.* Incest.
incestuoso, *a.* Incestuous.
incetta, *n.f.* Cornering (of a commodity), forestalling, buying up. **Fare — di**, to corner, to monopolize.
incettare, *v.t.* To buy up, to forestall, to monopolize, to corner.
incettatore, incettatrice, *n.m.f.* Forestaller, monopolizer.
inchiavacciare, inchiavadare, *v.t.* To lock the door, to bolt; to lock up.
inchiavare, *v.t.* To lock.
inchiavistellare, *v.t.* To padlock.
inchiesta, *n.f.* Inquiry, research; inquest; investigation. (*Law*) **Fare un'—**, to hold an inquest.
inchinamento, *n.m.* Inclining, bow.
inchinare, *v.t.i.* To bend, to bow the head, to stoop; to incline.
inchinarsi, *v.r.* To bow, to incline the head, to bend forward; to submit oneself, to yield to.
inchinevole [inchinEvole], *a.* Pliant, bending; willing; yielding.
inchinevolmente, *adv.* Pliably.
inchino, *n.m.* Bow, reverence, curtsy. **Fare un —**, to make one's bow.
inchiodamento, *n.m.* Nailing, fastening with nails.
inchiodare, *v.t.* To nail, to nail down; to rivet; (*Mil.*) to spike a gun.
inchiodarsi, *v.r.* (*colloq.*) To run into debt.
inchiodatura, *n.f.* Nailing down, fastening down; riveting.
inchiostrare, *v.t.* To ink, to spatter with ink.
inchiostro, *n.m.* Ink. **— copiativo**, copying ink; **— per marcare**, marking-ink; **— di china**, India ink; **— da stampa**, printing ink.
inchiostroso, *a.* Inky.
inchiudere [inchiUdere], *v.t.* To include; to enclose, to shut.
inchiuso, *p.p.a.* Included, enclosed [cp. **accluso**].
inchiusura, *n.f.* Imprisonment; enclosure.
inciampamento, *n.m.* Stumbling, tripping.
inciampare, *v.i.* To stumble, to trip, to make a false step, to meet unexpectedly. **— in uno**, to happen on someone.
inciampata, *n.f.* Stumble, stumbling.
inciampicone, *n.m.* Stumbler, person given to stumbling.
inciampo, *n.m.* Obstacle, hindrance, drawback, stumbling-block.
incicciare, *v.t.* To scratch, to make a slight cut.
incidentale, *a.* Incidental; secondary.
incidentalmente, *adv.* Incidentally.
incidente (1), *n.m.* Incident (in all senses), occurrence; accident. **— ferroviario**, railway accident; **— stradale**, road accident.
incidente (2), *a.* Incidental.
incidentemente, *adv.* Fortuitously, by chance.
incidenza, *n.f.* Incidence. **Per —**, by chance; **angolo d'—**, angle of incidence.
incidere [incIdere], *v.t.* To engrave, to carve, to cut into; (*Med.*) to lance; (*fig.*) to penetrate.
incielare, *v.t.* To place in heaven.
incignare, *v.t.* To wear (a dress, etc.) for the first time; to broach (a barrel).
incile, *n.m.* Drain, canal.
incimicito, *a.* Infested with bugs.
incimurrito, *a.* Having nasal catarrh.
incincignare, *v.t.* To crumple (clothes, etc.).
incinerazione, *n.f.* Incineration.
incinta, *a.* Pregnant, with child, in the family way.
incipiente, *a.* Incipient, beginning, in the first stages.
incipollire, *v.i.* To become sodden with damp (of wood); to lose leaves (of tree).
incipollatura, *n.f.* Softening.
incipriare, incipriarsi, *v.t.r.* To powder the face.
inciprignire, *v.t.* To fester, to inflame.
inciprignirsi, *v.r.* To fester, to gather.
incirca, *adv.* About. **All'—**, approximately.
incirconciso, *a.* Uncircumcised.
incircoscrittibile [incircoscrittIbile], *a.* Illimitable.
incircoscritto, *a* Uncircumscribed, without limits.
incisione, *n.f.* Incision, cut; engraving; notch. **— in legno**, wood-cut; **— ad acquaforte**, etching; **— a stampa**, print.
incisivo, *a.* Incisive, sharp, trenchant. (*Anat.*) **Denti incisivi**, incisors.

inciso, *a.* Incised, engraved.
incisore, *n.m.* Engraver.
incitamento, *n.m.* Incentive, incitement, stimulus, urge.
incitare, *v.t.* To incite, to stir, to urge; to prompt; to spur; to instigate.
incitatore, incitatrice, *n.m.f.* Inciter, instigator.
incitazione, *n.f.* Incitement, instigation.
incitrullire, *v.i.* To grow stupid, to become silly.
incittadinirsi, *v.r.* (Of a countryman) to become a city-dweller; to take up residence in a town.
inciuccarsi, *v.r.* (*colloq.*) To get drunk.
inciuchire, *v.i.* To become ignorant, to become stupid.
incivile, *a.* Uncivil, ill-mannered, rude; uncivilized.
incivilimento, *n.m.* Becoming civilized.
incivilire, *v.t.* To civilize, to refine.
incivilirsi, *v.r.* To become civilized.
incivilmente, *adv.* Barbarously.
inciviltà [-à], *n.f.* Incivility; want of manners, rudeness; barbarism.
inclemente, *a.* Inclement, severe, rough.
inclemenza, *n.f.* Inclemency, severity.
inclinabile [inclinAbile], *a.* Inclinable.
inclinamento, *n.m.* Leaning, inclination; (*Naut.*) list.
inclinante, *a.* Inclining.
inclinare, *v.t.i.* To incline, to bend, to lean.
inclinarsi, *v.r.* To be inclined, to lean down or forward; (*Naut.*) to list; to dip (of magnetic needle). (*Aviat.*) **— in curva,** to bank.
inclinato, *p.p.a.* Inclined (in all senses); slanting, sloping, bent.
inclinazione, *n.f.* Inclination (in all senses), slant; dip (of needle).
incline, *a.* Inclined, disposed; bent; prone.
inclinevole [inclinEvole], *a.* Inclined.
inclito [Inclito], *a.* (*Lit.*) Illustrious, famous.
includere [inclUdere], *v.t.* To include, to comprise; to enclose.
inclusione, *n.f.* Inclusion.
inclusivamente, *adv.* Inclusively.
inclusivo, *a.* Inclusive.
incluso, *a.* Included, enclosed; comprised.
incoare, *v.t.* (*Law*) To commence an action.
incoativo, *a.* Inchoative.
incoato, *a.* Inchoate, just begun.
incoazione, *n.f.* Commencement, beginning.
incoccare, *v.t.* To notch (an arrow), to fit an arrow to the string.
incocciare, *v.i.* To remain obstinate, to persist.
incocciarsi, *v.r.* To fly into a rage; to be obstinate.
incodardire, *v.i.* To become cowardly.
incoercibile [incoercIbile], *a.* Uncoercible, unrestrainable.
incoerente, *a.* Incoherent; inconsistent; discordant.
incoerenza, *n.f.* Incoherence, inconsistency.
incogliere [incOgliere], *v.i.* To befall, to happen. **Mal gliene incolse,** evil befell him.
incognita [incOgnita], *n.f.* Unknown quantity; obscure matter.
incognito [incOgnito], *n.m.a.* Unknown (person). **In —,** incognito.
incoiare, *v.i.t.* To become leathery; to strengthen with leather.
incollamento, *n.m.* Sticking, pasting up; (*Mech.*) jamming (of a valve).
incollare, *v.t.* To paste, to glue, to stick.
incollarsi, *v.r.* To put on the neck, to place on the shoulders.
incollatore, *n.m.* Bill-sticker, bill-poster.
incollatura, *n.f.* Pasting, sticking; (*Sport*) neck. **Vincere per un'—,** to win by a neck.
incollerire, incollerirsi, *v.i.r.* To get angry, to lose one's temper, to fly into a rage.
incolonnare, *v.t.* To form into columns (in all senses).
incolore, incoloro, *a.* Uncoloured, colourless, pale.
incolpabile [incolpAbile], *a.* Blameless; blameworthy.
incolpabilità [-à], *n.f.* Blamelessness.
incolpabilmente, *adv.* Blamelessly.
incolpamento, *n.m.* Accusation.
incolpare, *v.t.* To blame, to inculpate, to accuse, to put the blame on; to incriminate.
incolpatore, *n.m.* Accuser.
incolpevole [incolpEvole], *a.* Innocent, blameless.
incolpevolmente, *adv.* Innocently.
incoltamente, *adv.* Roughly, in an uncultured manner, boorishly.
incolto, *a.* Uncultivated, waste (of land); uncultured, rough, boorish; slovenly, untidy.
incolume [incOlume], *a.* Unharmed, unhurt, uninjured; safe and sound.
incolumità [-à], *n.f.* Safety, preservation.
incombente, *n.m.a.* Incumbence; incumbent, overhanging, impending; oppressive. **Documenti incombenti,** required documents.
incombenza, *n.f.* Errand, commission, task; duty. **Assumersi l'— di,** to take upon oneself to; **fare delle incombenze,** to go on errands; **le sue incombenze,** his task, his duty.
incombenzare, *v.t.* To charge (with a duty), to entrust, to commission.
incombere [incOmbere], *v.i.* To weigh upon; to overhang; (*fig.*) to be incumbent upon, to concern.
incombriccolarsi, *v.r.* To mix in bad company.
incombustibile [incombustIbile], *a.* Incombustible; fire-proof.
incombustibilità [-à], *n.f.* Incombustibility.
incominciamento, *n.m.* Beginning, commencement.
incominciare, *v.t.i.* To begin, to commence; to start. **Quando s'incomincia?** When do we start?
incomitato, *a.* Unaccompanied.
incommensurabile [incommensurAbile], *a.* Incommensurable.
incommensurabilità [-à], *n.f.* Incommensurability.
incommerciabile [incommerciAbile], *a.* Unsellable, unmarketable.
incommutabile [incommutAbile], *a.* Incommutable, unalterable.
incommutevole [incommutEvole], *a.* Immutable.
incomodamente, *adv.* Inconveniently, uncomfortably.
incomodare, *v.t.* To disturb, to trouble, to inconvenience.

incomodarsi, *v.r.* To trouble, to put oneself to trouble, to disturb oneself. **Non s'incomodi,** don't trouble.
incomodato, *a.* Disturbed; indisposed, unwell.
incomodità [-à], *n.f.* Inconvenience, discomfort; annoyance.
incomodo [incOmodo], *n.m.* Trouble, annoyance, inconvenience; indisposition, ailment. (*colloq.*) **Levare l'—,** to take one's leave; **fare da terzo —,** to be one too many.
incomodo [incOmodo], *a.* Uncomfortable, inconvenient, troublesome.
incomparabile [incomparAbile], *a.* Incomparable, unequalled, matchless.
incomparabilità [-à], *n.f.* Incomparableness.
incomparabilmente, *adv.* Incomparably.
incompartibile [incompartIbile], *a.* Indivisible.
incompatibile [incompatIbile], *a.* Incompatible, inconsistent with.
incompatibilità [-à], *n.f.* Incompatibility. **— di carattere,** incompatibility of temperament.
incompattamente, *adv.* Without firmness, without consistency.
incompatto, *a.* Not compact.
incompetente, *a.* Incompetent, unqualified; inefficient.
incompetentemente, *adv.* Incompetently.
incompetenza, *n.f.* Incompetence.
incompiutamente, *adv.* Incompletely.
incompiutezza, *n.f.* Incompleteness.
incompiuto, *a.* Unfinished, incomplete; unfulfilled.
incompletamente, *adv.* Incompletely, imperfectly.
incompletezza, *n.f.* Incompleteness.
incompleto, *a.* Incomplete, imperfect, unfinished; defective.
incomportabile [incomportAbile], *a.* Insufferable, intolerable.
incomportabilmente, *adv* Insufferably.
incompostamente, *adv.* In a disorderly manner, unsuitably; unbecomingly.
incompostezza, *n.f.* Disorder, discomposure, confusion.
incomposto, *a.* Discomposed, disorderly; unbecoming.
incomprensibile [incomprensIbile], *a.* Incomprehensible, unintelligible; inconceivable.
incomprensibilità [-à], *n.f.* Incomprehensibleness.
incomprensibilmente, *adv.* Incomprehensibly.
incomprensione, *n.f.* Incomprehension, lack of understanding.
incompreso, *a.* Misunderstood, unappreciated.
incompressibile [incompressIbile], *a.* Incompressible.
incomputabile [incomputAbile], *a.* Incomputable, incalculable.
incomputabilmente, *adv.* Incalculably.
incomunicabile [incomunicAbile], *a.* Incommunicable.
incomunicabilità [-à], *n.f.* Incommunicability.
incomunicabilmente, *adv.* Incommunicably
inconcare, *v.t.* To put in the wash-tub.
inconcatura, *n.f.* Washing in a tub.
inconcepibile [inconcepIbile], *a.* Inconceivable, incredible, surprising.
inconciliabile [inconciliAbile], *a.* Irreconcilable, incompatible.
inconciliabilità [-à], *n.f.* Incompatibility.
inconciliabilmente, *adv.* Incompatibly.
inconcludente, *a.* Inconclusive; irrelevant. **Un uomo —,** a man who never finishes anything off.
inconcludentemente, *adv.* Inconclusively.
inconcusso, *a.* Unshaken, firm, steady, stable.
incondizionatamente, *adv.* Unconditionally.
incondizionato, *a.* Unconditional, absolute.
inconfessabile [inconfessAbile], *a.* Not possible to be confessed, unavowable; unmentionable.
inconfesso, *n.m.* (*Eccles.*) One who has not made confession; not confessed, unrevealed.
inconfondibile [inconfondIbile], *a.* Not liable to confusion (with something else).
inconfortabile [inconfortAbile], *a.* Inconsolable.
inconfutabile [inconfutIbile], *a.* Irrefutable, undisputable.
inconfutabilmente, *adv.* Irrefutably.
incongiungibile [incongiungIbile], *a.* That cannot be connected; incompatible.
incongiunto, *a.* Not joined, disunited.
incongruente, *a.* Inconsistent, inconsequent.
incongruenza, *n.f.* Incongruity; inconsistency.
incongruo [inciOngruo], *a.* Incongruous.
inconoscibile [inconoscIbile], *a.* Unknowable.
inconosciuto, *a.* Unknown.
inconsapevole [inconsapEvole], *a.* Unaware, ignorant, unconscious; unacquainted with, uninformed.
inconsapevolezza, *n.f.* Unawareness, ignorance, want of information.
inconsciamente, *adv.* Unconsciously, unawares.
inconscio [incOnscio], *a.* Unaware, unconscious (in all senses).
inconseguente, *a.* Inconsequent, disconnected.
inconseguentemente, *adv.* Inconsequently.
inconseguenza, *n.f.* Inconsequence.
inconsiderabile [inconsiderAbile], *a.* Inconsiderable, imperceptible.
inconsideratamente, *adv.* Inconsiderately, rashly.
inconsideratezza, *n.f.* Inconsiderateness, lack of consideration; rashness.
inconsiderato, *a.* Inconsiderate.
inconsiderazione, *n.f.* Lack of consideration; want of prudence.
inconsistente, *a.* Inconsistent, inconsequent; futile; flimsy; foot-loose.
inconsistenza, *n.f.* Inconsistency; flimsiness.
inconsolabile [inconsolAbile], *a.* Inconsolable.
inconsolabilmente, *adv.* Inconsolably.
inconsolato, *a.* Disconsolate.
inconsueto, *a.* Unusual; unaccustomed.
inconsultamente, *adv.* Ill-advisedly; without due consideration.
inconsulto, *a.* Thoughtless, ill-advised, unreflecting.
inconsumabile [inconsumAbile], *a.* Inconsumable.
inconsumato, *a.* Unconsumed.

inconsutile [inconsUtile], *a.* Seamless, unsewn. **Tunica — di Cristo,** the seamless garment of Christ.
incontaminabile [incontaminAbile], *a.* Incontaminable.
incontaminezza, *n.f.* Purity.
incontaminato, *a.* Uncontaminated, undefiled, immaculate.
incontanente, *adv.* Suddenly, at once, immediately, forthwith.
incontemplabile [incontemplAbile], *a.* Impossible to contemplate.
incontentabile [incontentAbile], *a.* Difficult to please; insatiable, unappeasable; never satisfied; exacting.
incontentabilità [-à], *n.f.* Fastidiousness; insatiability; pretension.
incontestabile [incontestAbile], *a.* Incontestable, indisputable, unquestionable.
incontestabilmente, *adv.* Incontestably.
incontestato, *a.* Undisputed.
incontinente, *a.* Incontinent, unchaste, lewd; without restraint.
incontinentemente, *adv.* Incontinently.
incontinenza, *n.f.* Incontinence, licentiousness.
incontrare, *v.t.i.* To meet, to meet with, to come across, to fall in with; to prove popular, to succeed, to meet with favour. **— il gusto della gente,** to strike popular taste; **— bene,** to be lucky, to make a hit.
incontrarsi, *v.r.* To meet, to come across, to come in contact with; to come into collision; to agree; to coincide.
incontrastabile [incontrastAbile], *a.* Indisputable, incontestable.
incontrastabilmente, *adv.* Indisputably.
incontrastato, *a.* Undisputed; uncontested.
incontro, *n.m.* Meeting, meeting face to face, encounter; (*Sport*) match, game; favour. **Un brutto —,** an awkward meeting; **ciò ha avuto —,** this has been received with favour.
incontro, *adv.prep.* Towards; opposite. **All'—,** on the contrary; **andare — a qualcuno,** to go to meet someone.
incontroverso, *a.* Undisputed.
incontrovertibile [incontrovertIbile], *a.* Incontrovertible, incontestable, unimpeachable.
incontrovertibilmente, *adv.* Incontrovertibly.
inconturbabile [inconturbAbile], *a.* Imperturbable.
inconturbato, *a.* Unperturbed.
inconvenevole, *a.* Unbecoming, unsuitable.
inconveniente, *n.m.a.* Inconvenience, drawback, trouble; inconvenient. **È un serio —,** it is a serious drawback.
inconvenientemente, *adv.* Inconveniently.
inconvenienza, *n.f.* Inconvenience; impropriety.
inconversabile [inconversAbile], *a.* Unsociable, not talkative.
inconvertibile [inconvertIbile], *a.* Inconvertible.
inconvertibilità [-à], *n.f.* Inconvertibility.
inconvincibile [inconvincIbile], *a.* Inconvincible.
inconvinto, *a.* Unconvinced.
incoraggiamento, *n.m.* Encouragement, stimulus, inspiration, support, incentive. **A titolo d'—,** by way of encouragement.
incoraggiante, *a.* Encouraging.
incoraggiare, *v.t.* To encourage; to hearten, to inspirit; to stir up; to promote, to foster, to forward.
incoraggiarsi, *v.r.* To take courage.
incordamento, *n.m.* (*Mus.*) Stringing; (*Med.*) stiffening of muscles.
incordare, *v.t.* (*Mus.*) To string, to adjust the strings.
incordarsi, *v.r.* (*Med.*) To become stiff (of a muscle).
incordatura, *n.f.* (*Mus.*) Stringing (as a whole); (*Med.*) stiffening of the neck or other muscles.
incornarsi, *v.r.* To become obstinate.
incornatura, *n.f.* Obstinacy.
incorniciare, *v.t.* To frame, to put in a frame.
incorniciatura, *n.f.* Framing.
incoronamento, *n.m.* Crowning.
incoronare, *v.t.* To crown.
Incoronata, *n.f.* (*Eccles.*) Our Lady crowned.
incoronazione, *n.f.* Crowning, coronation.
incorporamento, *n.m.* (Act of) incorporation.
incorporare, *v.t.* To incorporate, to embody; to annex; to assimilate.
incorporarsi, *v.r.* To incorporate, to become incorporated.
incorporazione, *n.f.* Incorporation.
incorporeamente, *adv.* Incorporeally.
incorporeità [-à], *n.f.* Immateriality.
incorporeo [incorpOreo], *a.* Incorporeal, not material.
incorre [cp. **incogliere**].
incorreggibile [incorreggIbile], *a.* Incorrigible; hopeless. **Questo ragazzo è —,** this lad is hopeless.
incorreggibilità [-à], *n.f.* Incorrigibility.
incorreggibilmente, *adv.* Incorrigibly.
incorrentirsi, *v.r.* To become rigid.
incorrere [incOrrere], *v.i.* To incur, to fall into. **— in errore,** to fall into error; **— nel biasimo generale,** to incur universal censure; **— in una multa,** to incur a fine.
incorrettamente, *adv.* Incorrectly.
incorrettezza, *n.f.* Incorrectness, inaccuracy.
incorretto, *a.* Incorrect, faulty, inaccurate.
incorrezione, *n.f.* Lack of correction.
incorrottamente, *adv.* Uncorruptly, purely; with integrity.
incorrotto, *a.* Uncorrupted.
incorruttibile [incorruttIbile], *a.* Incorruptible, honest.
incorruttibilmente, *adv.* Honestly, incorruptibly.
incorruzione, *n.f.* Lack of corruption; preservation.
incorso, *p.p.a.* Fallen. **— in errore,** fallen into error [cp. **incorrere**].
incortinare, *v.t.* To curtain.
incosciente, *a.* Unconscious; unconscientious; rash, reckless; senseless, foolish.
incoscienza, *n.f.* Unconsciousness; lack of conscience; irresponsibility; rashness, foolishness.
incospicuo [incospIcuo], *a.* Inconspicuous.
incostante, *a.* Inconstant, unsteady, fickle, changeable.
incostantemente, *adv.* Inconstantly.
incostanza, *n.f.* Inconstancy, unsteadiness, fickleness.
incostituzionale, *a.* Unconstitutional.

incostituzionalmente, *adv.* Unconstitutionally.
increanza, *n.f.* Incivility, bad manners.
increato, *n.m.a.* Uncreated; the Godhead.
incredibile [incredIbile], *a.* Incredible, inconceivable, unbelievable.
incredibilità, *n.f.* Incredibility.
incredibilmente, *adv.* Incredibly.
incredulità, *n.f.* Incredulity, unbelief.
incredulo [incrEdulo], *n.m.a.* Unbeliever; incredulous, unbelieving; diffident.
incremento, *n.m.* Increment, increase, furtherance; growth. (*Comm.*) **Dare — a,** to favour, to push.
increscere [cp. **rincrescere**].
increscevolmente, *adv.* Regrettably, unfortunately.
increscioso, *a.* Lamentable, regrettable; wearisome, irksome.
increspamento, *n.m.* Wrinkling; curling, crisping.
increspare, incresparsi, *v.t.r.* To wrinkle, to curl (hair, etc.); to ripple (of water).
increspatura, *n.f.* Curling, wrinkling; ripple, ruffling; undulation.
incretinire, incretinirsi, *v.i.r.* To become an idiot.
incriminabile [incriminAbile], *a.* Liable to prosecution.
incriminare, *v.t.* To incriminate; to accuse.
incriminazione, *n.f.* Accusation, charge; impeachment.
incrinare, *v.t.* To crack, to split; to impair.
incrinarsi, *v.r.* To become cracked, to crack, to split.
incrinato, *a.* Cracked (of pottery, etc.).
incrinatura, *n.f.* Flaw, crack.
incriticabile [incriticAbile], *a.* Irreproachable; not admitting of criticism.
incrociamento, *n.m.* Crossing; cross-breeding.
incrociare, *v.t.i.* To cross, to fold (the arms); to cross-breed; (*Naut.*) to cruise.
incrociarsi, *v.r.* To cross each other, to interlace.
incrociato, *a.* Crossed. **Parole incrociate,** crossword (puzzle).
incrociatore, *n.m.* (*Naut.*) Cruiser.
incrociatura, *n.f.* Crossing, intersection.
incrocicchiamento, *n.m.* Interlacing, intertwining.
incrocicchiare, *v.t.* To interlace; to intersect.
incrocicchiatura, *n.f.* Interlacing.
incrocio [incrOcio], *n.m.* Crossing (of roads); cross-breeding, hybrid.
incrollabile [incrollAbile], *a.* Unshakeable, firm, steady.
incrostamento, *n.m.* Encrusting, concretion.
incrostare, *v.t.* To encrust; (*Art*) to inlay; (*Naut.*) to foul (ship's bottom); to foul (a gun).
incrostatura, incrostazione, *n.f.* Encrustation, coating.
incrudelire, *v.i.* To grow cruel, to rage; to use cruelty; to become wild.
incrudire, *v.i.* To become harsher, to grow severe, to aggravate.
incrudimento, *n.m.* Growing harsh, worsening; aggravation.
incrudito, *a.* Harsh, severe.
incruento, *a.* Bloodless (of a victory, etc.).
incrunare, *v.t.* To thread (a needle).
incruscare, *v.t.* To cover with bran, to place in bran.
incruscarsi, *v.r.* To use stilted language [cp. **crusca**].
incubare, *v.t.* To incubate; to brood, to mature.
incubatrice, *n.f.* Incubator.
incubazione, *n.f.* Incubation.
incubo [Incubo], *n.m.* Incubus, nightmare; obsession.
incudine [incUdine], *n.f.* Anvil. **Esser fra l'— e il martello,** to be between the devil and the deep sea.
inculcamento, *n.m.* Inculcation.
inculcare, *v.t.* To inculcate, to impress upon, to instil, to enforce.
inculcazione, *n.f.* Inculcation.
inculto, *a.* Rough, uncultivated, uneducated [cp. **incolto**].
incultura, *n.f.* Lack of culture.
incunabolo [incunAbolo], *n.m.* Incunabulum.
incuneare, *v.t.* To wedge in, to insert, to force in.
incuocere [incuOcere], *v.t.* To cook slightly, to half-cook; to submit to a slight heat.
incuorare, *v.t.* To hearten, to inspirit, to encourage.
incupire, *v.t.i.* To darken (in colour), to deepen; to grow darker, to become gloomy.
incurabile [incurAbile], *a.* Incurable.
incurabilità [-à], *n f.* Incurability.
incurabilmente, *adv.* Incurably.
incurante, *a.* Careless, heedless; indifferent; regardless.
incuranza, *n.f.* Carelessness, negligence, heedlessness.
incuria [incUria], *n.f.* Carelessness, indifference; negligence, neglect.
incuriosamente, *adv.* Incuriously, without curiosity.
incuriosire, *v.t.* To make curious, to arouse one's curiosity; to rouse interest.
incuriosirsi, *v.r.* To become curious or inquisitive.
incurioso, *a.* Incurious, indifferent, uninterested.
incursione, *n.f.* Incursion, raid, inroad. **— aerea,** air-raid.
incurvabile [incurvAbile], *a.* Unbendable; bendable.
incurvare, *v.t.* To bend, to curve, to arch.
incurvarsi, *v.r.* To warp.
incurvato, *a.* Bent, curved; stooping.
incurvatura, *n.f.* Bending, curvature.
incurvirsi, *v.r.* To become bent, to stoop.
incustodito, *a.* Unguarded.
incutere [incUtere], *v.t.* To inspire, to command, to strike with (awe, etc.). **— rispetto,** to command respect; **— terrore,** to strike with terror.
indaco [Indaco], *n.m.* (*Bot.*) Indigo; blue dye, deep blue colour.
indaffarato, *a.* Busy; fussy.
indagamento, *n.m.* Investigation.
indagare, *v.t.* To investigate, to inquire into, to trace out; to search into.
indagatore, *n.m.a.* Investigator; examining, searching, penetrating.
indagazione, *n.f.* Investigation.
indagine [indAgine], *n.f.* Inquiry, search, investigation; research.

indarno, *adv.* In vain, vainly.
indebitamente, *adv.* Unduly.
indebitamento, *n.m.* Indebtedness, running into debt.
indebitare, *v.t.* To cause to run into debt.
indebitarsi, *v.r.* To run into debt; to get into debt.
indebito [indEbito], *a.* Undue, unjust; unlawful; illegal; unbecoming. **Appropriazione indebita,** embezzlement.
indebolimento, *n.m.* Weakening, enfeeblement; decrease.
indebolire, *v.t.* To weaken, to enfeeble, to enervate; to diminish; (*Photo.*) to reduce.
indebolirsi, *v.r.* To weaken, to grow feeble; to decline, to flag; to become faint (of sounds, colours, etc.).
indecente, *a.* Indecent, improper, indelicate; obscene.
indecentemente, *adv.* Indecently.
indecenza, *n.f.* Indecency.
indecifrabile [indecifrAbile], *a.* Undecipherable, illegible; unintelligible.
indecisione, *n.f.* Indecision, irresolution, hesitation.
indeciso, *a.* Undecided, doubtful; unsettled; hesitant.
indeclinabile [indeclinAbile], *a.* Indeclinable, invariable; unavoidable.
indeclinabilità [-à], *n.f.* Impossibility of being declined.
indecomponibile [indecomponIbile], *a.* indecomposable.
indecorosamente, *adv.* Indecorously, unbecomingly.
indecoroso, *a.* Indecorous, unbecoming, unseemly.
indefessamente, *adv.* Indefatigably; incessantly.
indefesso, *a.* Indefatigable, untiring, unwearied.
indefettibile, *a.* Indefectible, unfailing.
indefettibilità [-à], *n.f.* Indefectibility.
indefettibilmente, *adv.* Indefectibly, unfailingly.
indeficiente, *a.* Constant, invariable; eternal.
indeficienza, *n.f.* Constancy, continuousness.
indefinibile [indefinIbile], *a.* Indefinable; inexplicable.
indefinibilmente, *adv.* Indefinably.
indefinitamente, *adv.* Indefinitely.
indefinitezza, *n.f.* Indefiniteness.
indefinito, *a.* Indefinite.
indegnamente, *adv.* Unworthily, contemptibly.
indegnità [-à], *n.f.* Unworthiness; indignity, insult.
indegno, *a.* Worthless, unworthy, undeserving, contemptible, base, vile.
indeiscente, *a.* (*Bot.*) Indehiscent.
indelebile [indelEbile], *a.* Indelible, ineffaceable.
indelebilmente, *adv.* Indelibly.
indeliberatamente, *adv.* Without deliberation, unthinkingly.
indeliberato, *a.* Without forethought, unprepared, hasty; impulsive.
indeliberazione, *n.f.* Lack of forethought.
indelicatamente, *adv.* Indelicately.
indelicatezza, *n.f.* Indelicacy; unscrupulousness.
indelicato, *a.* Indelicate, improper; unscrupulous.
indemaniare, *v.t.* To hand over land to the State.
indemoniare, *v.t.* To drive mad, to make wicked.
indemoniarsi, *v.r.* To behave like one possessed.
indemoniato, *n.m.a.* Demoniac, one possessed of a devil; demoniac, possessed, devilish; frantic; furious.
indenne, *a.* Safe, unharmed, undamaged.
indennità [-à], *n.f.* Indemnity, compensation; allowance (for expenses).
indennizzare, *v.t.* To indemnify, to reimburse, to compensate (for damage, etc.), to grant an (expense) allowance.
indennizzo, *n.m.* Indemnity, allowance.
indentare, *v.t.* To cut teeth; (*Mech.*) to cog, to engage, to put in gear.
indentatura, *n.f.* Teething (of children); (*Mech.*) toothing; indentation.
indentrarsi, *v.r.* To penetrate.
indentro, *adv.* Within, inside, inwards.
indeprecabile [indeprecAbile], *a.* Inevitable.
inderogabile [inderogAbile], *a.* To be strictly observed (of a condition).
indescrivibile [indescrivIbile], *a.* Indescribable.
indescrivibilmente, *adv.* Indescribably.
indeterminabile [indeterminAbile], *a.* Indeterminable, undefined.
indeterminatamente, *adv.* Indefinitely; illimitably.
indeterminatezza, *a.* Indeterminateness.
indeterminato, *a.* Indetermined, indefinite.
indeterminazione, *n.f.* Indetermination.
indettare, *v.t.* To coach someone on what he is to say.
indettarsi, *v.r.* To come to an agreement with others as to what is to be said.
indevoto, *a.* Irreligous, undevout.
indevozione, *n.f.* Lack of devotion; irreverence.
indi, *adv.* Thence; afterwards; there. **— a poco,** shortly afterwards.
India, *n.f.* India. **Le Indie Orientali, Occidentali,** the East, West Indies; **castagno d'—,** horse-chestnut; **canna d'—,** bamboo cane; **fico d'—,** prickly pear; **pollo** or **gallo d'—,** turkey; **porcellino d'—,** guinea-pig.
indiana, *n.f.* Indian woman; printed cotton material.
indianista, *n.m.* Student of Indian languages.
indiano, *n.m.a.* Indian. **In fila indiana,** in single file; **far l'—,** to feign ignorance.
indiarsi, *v.r.* To sink oneself in the Godhead.
indiavolamento, *n.m.* Devilment.
indiavolato, *a.* Devilish, possessed; furious; (*fig.*) stormy. **Un baccano —,** a terrific row.
indicabile [indicAbile], *a.* Indicable; capable of being indicated.
indicante, *a.* Indicative of.
indicare, *v.t.* To indicate, to point out; to name, to mention; to show; to state, to mean; to suggest.
indicativo, *n.m.a.* Indicative.
indicato, *a.* Indicated, hinted; stated, mentioned, quoted; suitable, advisable, fit, right, proper.

indicatore, *n.m.* Indicator, gauge, sign; guide-book; time-table; directory. **— stradale,** traffic sign; **— telefonico,** telephone directory; **— di pressione,** pressure gauge; **— della velocità,** speed indicator.
indicatore, *a.* Indicatory, indicating. **Cartello —,** sign-post.
indicazione, *n.f.* Indication, direction, sign, information.
indice [Indice], *n.m.* Index, table, list; fore-finger; hand (of clock, etc.).
indicibile [indicIbile], *a.* Inexpressible, unspeakable, indescribable.
indicibilmente, *adv.* Inexpressibly.
indietreggiamento, *n.m.* Withdrawal, falling back, retreat.
indietreggiare, *v.i.* To fall back, to withdraw; to lose ground; to recoil.
indietro, *adv.* Back, backwards, behind; slow (of timepiece); (*Naut.*) abaft. **All'—,** backwards; **volgersi —,** to turn back; **stare —,** to lag behind; **lasciare —,** to leave behind; **questo bambino è —,** this is a backward child.
indifendibile [indifendIbile], *a.* Indefensible.
indifendibilmente, *adv.* Indefensibly.
indifeso, *a.* Defenceless, undefended, unprotected; unarmed.
indifferente, *a.* Indifferent; apathetic; unbiased.
indifferentemente, *adv.* Indifferently; indiscriminately.
indifferentismo, *n.m.* Apathy, unconcern; indifferentism.
indifferenza, *n.f.* Indifference, unconcern.
indifferibile [indifferIbile], *a.* Undeferrable, that cannot be deferred or delayed.
indigeno [indIgeno], *n.m.a.* Indigenous, native; domestic.
indigente, *n.m.a.* Pauper; indigent, needy, in want, destitute.
indigenza, *n.f.* Indigence, poverty.
indigeribile [indigerIbile], *a.* Indigestible.
indigestione, *n.f.* Indigestion. **Fare un'—,** to get indigestion; to eat too much.
indigesto, *a.* Undigested; indigestible; (*fig.*) crude, boring.
indigeti [indIgeti], *n.m.pl.* Local or tutelary gods.
indignare, *v.t.* To rouse to anger, to excite to wrath.
indignarsi, *v.r.* To be indignant, to be roused, to be angry; to be shocked.
indignato, *a.* Indignant.
indignazione, *n.f.* Indignation, anger; disdain.
indiligente, *a.* Negligent.
indiligenza, *n.f.* Negligence.
indimenticabile [indimenticAbile], *a.* Unforgettable.
indimenticabilmente, *adv.* Unforgettably.
indimostrabile [indimostrAbile], *a.* Incapable of proof; indemonstrable.
indimostrato, *a.* Unproved.
indipendente, *a.* Independent; free; self-asserting.
indipendentemente, *adv.* Independently.
indipendenza, *n.f.* Independence; freedom.
indire, *v.t.* To notify, to announce, to intimate; to call, to convene; to arrange, to appoint.
indirettamente, *adv.* Indirectly.
indiretto, *a.* Indirect (in all senses).
indirizzamento, *n.m.* Address, direction.
indirizzare, *v.t.* To address (a letter, etc.), to direct, to show the way; to dedicate.
indirizzarsi, *v.r.* To address oneself to; to set out for; to direct one's steps towards.
indirizzo, *n.m.* Address (of letters, etc.); direction, guide; turn, start; dedication. **— al bisogno,** address in case of need.
indiscernibile [indiscernIbile], *a.* Indiscernible, invisible.
indisciplina, *n.f.* Indiscipline, unruliness.
indisciplinatamente, *adv.* Without discipline, in an unruly manner.
indisciplinatezza, *n.f.* Unruliness.
indisciplinato, *a.* Undisciplined, unruly.
indiscretamente, *adv.* Indiscreetly, impertinently, incautiously; foolishly.
indiscretezza, indiscrezione, *n.f.* Indiscretion; impertinence; news leakage.
indiscreto, *a.* Indiscreet; impertinent; incautious; foolish, rash; inquisitive.
indiscusso, *a.* Undisputed, indisputable.
indiscutibile [indiscutIbile], *a.* Indisputable, unquestionable.
indiscutibilmente, *adv.* Indisputably.
indispensabile [indispensAbile], *a.* Indispensable, requisite, necessary.
indispensabilità [-à], *n.f.* Indispensability.
indispensabilmente, *adv.* Indispensably.
indispettire, *v.t.* To vex, to irritate; to taunt, to tease.
indispettirsi, *v.r.* To get vexed, to get irritated; to be piqued.
indispettito, *a.* Vexed, annoyed.
indisporre, *v.t.* To trouble, to annoy, to disgust, to make disinclined.
indisposizione, *n.f.* Indisposition (in all senses).
indisposto, *a.* Indisposed, unwell, poorly.
indisputabile [indisputAbile], *a.* Indisputable.
indisputabilmente, *adv.* Indisputably.
indisputato, *a.* Undisputed.
indissipabile [indissipAbile], *a.* Uneffaceable, not possible to be dissipated.
indissolubile [indissolUbile], *a.* Indissoluble, stable; binding.
indissolubilità [-à], *n.f.* Indissolubility.
indissolubilmente, *adv.* Indissolubly.
indistaccabile [indistaccAbile], *a.* Undetachable.
indistinguibile [indistinguIbile], *a.* Indistinguishable.
indistinguibilmente, *adv.* Indistinguishably.
indistintamente, *adv.* Indistinctly, indiscriminately.
indistinto, *a.* Indistinct, confused; dim (of light), faint; vague (of sound).
indistinzione, *n.f.* Confusion, indistinctness.
indistruttibile [indistruttIbile], *a.* Indestructible.
indistruttibilità [-à], *n.f.* Indestructibility.
indistruttibilmente, *adv.* Indestructibly.
indivia [indIvia], *n.f.* (*Bot.*) Endive.
individuale, *a.* Individual, single, particular.
individualismo, *n.m.* Individualism.
individualista, *n.m.* Individualist.
individualistico, *a.* Individualistic.
individualità [-à], *n.f.* Individuality.
individualizzare, *v.t.* To individualize.

individualmente, *adv.* Individually.
individuare, *v.t.* To detect; to mark out, to single out; to identify; to individualize.
individuazione, *n.f.* Individualization.
individuo [indivIduo], *n.m.* Individual, single person; fellow. **Chi è quell' — ?** Who's that fellow?
indivisamente, *adv.* Without distinction, equally; jointly.
indivisibile [indivisIbile], *a.* Indivisible.
indivisibilità [-à], *n.f.* Indivisibility.
indivisibilmente, *adv.* Indivisably.
indiviso, *a.* Undivided, joint, whole.
indivotamente, *adv.* Impiously, irreligiously.
indiziare, *v.t.* To suspect, to point to, to throw suspicion on; to hint at.
indiziario [indiziArio], *a.* (*Law*) Circumstantial; based on suspicions. **Prova indiziaria,** circumstantial evidence.
indizio [indIzio], *n.m.* Sign, mark, indication, symptom; inkling; (*Law*) circumstantial evidence, suspicious circumstance.
indizione, *n.f.* (*Hist.*) Indiction.
indo, *n.m.a.* Indian.
Indo, *n.m.* (*Geog.*) River Indus.
indocile [indOcile], *a.* Indocile, untractable, unruly.
indocilire, *v.t.* To render docile, to tame.
indocilità [-à], *n.f.* Indocility, untameableness, unruliness.
indocilmente, *adv.* In an unruly manner.
indoeuropeo, *n.m.a.* Indo-european.
indoganamento, *n.m.* Declaring at custom house. **Porto di —,** port of entry.
indoganare, *v.t.* (*Comm.*) To report (a cargo) to the customs.
indogermanico, *a.* Indo-European.
indolcire, *v.t.* To sweeten, to soften.
indole [Indole], *n.f.* Character, nature, temperament, disposition. **Di buona —,** good-natured; **una questione d'— delicata,** a matter of a delicate nature.
indolente, *a.* Indolent (in all senses); slothful, lazy, listless.
indolentemente, *adv.* Indolently.
indolenza, *n.f.* Indolence, apathy, indifference.
indolenzimento, *n.m.* Benumbing, numbness; muscular pain, stiffness.
indolenzire, *v.t.* To make numb, to make stiff.
indolenzirsi, *v.r.* To get numb, to get stiff, to become sore.
indolenzito, *a.* Benumbed, numb; torpid; stiff, sore.
indolimento, *n.m.* Slight sensation of pain.
indolire, indolirsi, *v.i.r.* To feel pain.
indomabile [indomAbile], *a.* Indomitable; untameable; ungovernable.
indomabilmente, *adv.* Indomitably.
indomani, *n.m.* Morrow, following day. **L'indomani,** the next day.
indomato, indomito, *a.* Untamed; indomitable.
indomenicato, *a.* Dressed in Sunday best.
indomitamente, *adv.* Indomitably.
indomito [indOmito], *a.* Untamed, indomitable.
indonnire, *v.i.* To grow into womanhood.
indorare, *v.t.* To gild.
indoramento, *n.m.* Gilding.
indorare, *v.t.* To gild. **— la pillola,** to gild the pill, to sweeten the medicine.
indorato, *a.* Gilded, gilt; dipped in yolk of egg before frying.
indoratore, *n.m.* Gilder.
indoratura, *n.f.* Gilding.
indossare, *v.t.* To put on (clothes), to wear.
indossata, *n.f.* Trying on (clothes).
indossatrice, *n.f.* Mannequin, model.
indosso, *adv.* On one's back; about one, on one's person. **Avete danaro — ?** Have you got any money on you? [cp. **addosso**].
Indostan [indostAn], *n.m.* (*Geog.*) Hindustan.
indostanico, indostano [indostAnico], *n.m.a.* Hindustani.
indottamente, *adv.* Ignorantly.
indotto (1), *a.* Untaught, illiterate, ignorant, unlearned.
indotto (2), *n.m.* (*Elect.*) Armature.
indotto (3), *a.* Induced; (*Elect.*) inductive.
indovinabile [indovinAbile], *a.* Guessable, possible to foretell; foreseeable.
indovinamento, *n.m.* Guessing, foretelling.
indovinare, *v.t.* To guess; to conjecture, to suppose; to foretell; to hit the mark. **Tirare a —,** to judge by guesswork; (*colloq.*) **indovinala grillo,** see if you can guess it.
indovinato, *a.* Guessed; well-done, well-conceived; successful.
indovinazione, *n.f.* Divination.
indovinello, *n.m.* Riddle, conundrum, enigma, puzzle. **Sciogliere un —,** to solve a riddle.
indovino, *n.m.* Sooth-sayer, fortune-teller, diviner.
indovutamente, *adv.* Unduly.
indovuto, *a.* Inconvenient, undue; not due.
indozzamento, *n.m.* Moping (of animals).
indrappellare, *v.t.* (*Mil.*) To troop, to form into a squadron.
indrappellato, *a.* (*Mil.*) In close formation.
indubbiamente, *adv.* Without doubt, undoubtedly.
indubbio [indUbbio], *a.* Undoubted, certain.
indubitabile [indubitAbile], *a.* Indubitable, unquestionable.
indubitabilmente, *adv.* Indubitably.
indubitatamente, *adv.* Undoubtedly, unquestionably.
indubitato, *a.* Undoubted.
inducente, *a.* Inducing.
inducere [indUcere], *v.t.* [cp. **indurre**].
inducimento, *n.m.* Inducement.
indugiare, *v.i.* To delay, to be late; to be long, to lag, to tarry, to hesitate. **Non possiamo — più oltre,** we cannot delay any longer.
indugiarsi, *v.r.* To linger, to loiter. **— su,** to dwell upon, to linger over.
indugiatore, indugiatrice, *n.m.f.* Loiterer, dawdler.
indugio [indUgio], *n.m.* Delay; hesitation; postponement; procrastination.
indulgente, *a.* Indulgent, lenient, tolerant.
indulgentemente, *adv.* Leniently.
indulgenza, *n.f.* Indulgence (in all senses); leniency, forbearance. (*Eccles.*) **— plenaria,** plenary indulgence.
indulgere [indUlgere], *v.t.i.* To indulge, to yield to; to grant, to allow (as a favour).
indulto, *n.m.* (*Law*) Free pardon; amnesty; (*Eccles.*) indult.
indumento, *n.m.* Garment, article of clothing; vestment.
indurimento, *n.m.* Hardening.

indurire, *v.t.* To harden, to stiffen, to make hard.
indurirsi, *v.r.* To become hard; to grow callous; to get inured; to strengthen oneself.
indurre, *v.t.* To induce, to persuade, to lead, to entice; (*Elect.*) to induce. **— in errore,** to lead into error; **— in tentazione,** to lead into temptation.
indursi, *v.r.* To resolve, to decide; to be induced to.
industre, *a.* Industrious.
industremente, *adv.* Industriously.
industria [indUstria], *n.f.* Industry (in all senses); ingenuity, diligence; trade, manufacture. **— chiave,** key-industry.
industriale, *n.m.a.* Industrialist, manufacturer; employer; industrial, manufacturing.
industrialismo, *n.m.* Industrialism.
industrializzare, *v.t.* To industrialize.
industrializzazione, *n.f.* Industrialization.
industrialmente, *adv.* Industrially.
industriarsi, *v.r.* To strive hard, to exert oneself; to do one's best.
industriosamente, *adv.* Industriously.
industrioso, *a.* Industrious.
induttanza, *n.f.* (*Elect.*) Inductance.
induttivamente, *adv.* Inductively, by induction.
induttività [-à], *n.f.* Inductivity.
induttivo, *a.* Inductive.
induttore, *n.m.* (*Elect.*) Inductor.
induzione, *n.f.* (*Elect.*) Induction. **Rocchetto d'—,** induction coil.
inebbriamento, *n.m.* Inebriation, intoxication.
inebbriante, *a.* Inebriating, intoxicating.
inebbriare, *v.t.* To make drunk, to inebriate, to intoxicate, to elate.
inebbriarsi, *v.r.* To get drunk; to become elated, to be enraptured.
inebbrioso, *n.m.* Drunkard.
inebetito, *a.* Stupefied; imbecile, stupid, obtuse.
inebriare, *v.t.* [cp. **inebbriare**].
ineccepibile [ineccepIbile], *a.* Unexceptionable. **Informazioni ineccepibili,** reliable information; **onestà —,** proved honesty.
ineccitabile [ineccitAbile], *a.* Unexcitable.
inedia [inEdia], *n.f.* Fasting, starvation; boredom.
inedito [inEdito], *a.* Unpublished.
ineducabile [ineducAbile], *a.* Impossible to educate.
ineducatamente, *adv.* Impolitely, rudely.
ineducato, *a.* Impolite, ill-bred, unmannerly.
ineducazione, *n.f.* Impoliteness, lack of manners.
ineffabile [ineffAbile], *a.* Ineffable unspeakable, inexpressible.
ineffabilità [-à], *n.f.* Ineffability.
ineffabilmente, *adv.* Ineffably.
ineffettuabile [ineffettuAbile], *a.* Impracticable, unfeasible.
ineffettuabilità [-à], *n.f.* Impracticability.
ineffettuazione, *n.f.* Failure to carry out.
inefficace, *a.* Inefficacious, ineffective; ineffectual.
inefficacemente, *adv.* Ineffectively.
inefficacia [inefficAcia], *n.f.* Inefficacy.
inefficiente, *a.* Inefficient.
inefficienza, *n.f.* Inefficiency.
ineguaglianza, *n.f.* Inequality, disparity, unevenness, roughness.
ineguagliato, *a.* Unequalled, unparalleled.
ineguale, *a.* Unequal; uneven, irregular; rough.
inegualità [-à], *n.f.* Inequality.
inegualmente, *adv.* Unequally.
inelegante, *a.* Inelegant; ungraceful.
inelegantemente, *adv.* Inelegantly.
ineleganza, *n.f.* Inelegance.
ineliggibile [ineliggIbile], *a.* Ineligible.
ineliggibilità [-à], *n.f.* Ineligibility.
ineloquente, *a.* Ineloquent.
ineluttabile [ineluttAbile], *a.* Ineluctable, inevitable, inescapable.
ineluttabilmente, *adv.* Ineluctably.
inemendabile [inemendAbile], *a.* Impossible to amend, difficult to correct.
inemendabilmente, *adv.* Without possibility of correction.
inemendato, *a.* Unamended, uncorrected.
inenarrabile [inenarrAbile], *a.* Inexpressible, unspeakable.
inequabile [inequAbile], *a.* Inequable.
inequabilmente, *adv.* Inequably.
inequivalente, *a.* Not equivalent.
inequivocabile [inequivocAbile], *a.* Unambiguous, clear, unequivocal.
inerente, *a.* Inherent, belonging to; attending, concerning.
inerentemente, *adv.* Inherently.
inerenza, *n.f.* Inherence.
inerme, *a.* Unarmed, defenceless.
inerpicare, inerpicarsi, *v.i.r.* To clamber up, to climb, to scale.
inerte, *a.* Inert, lifeless, sluggish, inactive; (*Comm.*) dormant.
ineruditamente, *adv.* Unlearnedly.
inerudito, *a.* Unlearned, ignorant.
inerzia [inErzia], *n.f.* Inertia, inertness; sluggishness, laziness. **Forza d'—,** force of inertia.
inesattamente, *adv.* Inexactly, inaccurately; unpunctually.
inesattezza, *n.f.* Inexactitude, inaccuracy.
inesatto, *a.* Inexact, inaccurate, incorrect.
inesaudibile [inesaudIbile], *a.* That cannot be granted.
inesaudito, *a.* Ungranted.
inesauribile [inesaurIbile], *a.* Inexhaustible.
inesauribilmente, *adv.* Inexhaustibly.
inesausto, *a.* Unexhausted, inexhaustible.
inescare, *v.t.* To bait (a hook) [cp. **innescare**].
inescogitabile [inescogitAbile], *a.* Unthinkable, beyond the power of thought.
inescusabile [inescusAbile], *a.* Inexcusable, unpardonable.
inescusabilmente, *adv.* Inexcusably.
ineseguibile [ineseguIbile], *a.* Impracticable, unenforceable.
inesercitato, *a.* Inexperienced; out of practice.
inesigibile [inesigIbile], *a.* (*Comm.*) Uncollectable, worthless (cheque). **Crediti inesegibili,** bad debts.
inesistente, *a.* Non-existent.
inesistenza, *n.f.* Non-existence.
inesorabile [inesorAbile], *a.* Inexorable, inflexible, ruthless.
inesorabilità [-à], *n.f.* Inexorableness.
inesorabilmente, *adv.* Inexorably.
inesperienza, *n.f.* Inexperience.

inespertamente, *adv.* Inexpertly, unskilfully.
inesperto, *a.* Inexpert, unskilful; inexperienced.
inespiabile [inespiAbile], *a.* Inexpiable.
inespiato, *a.* Unexpiated.
inesplicabile [inesplicAbile], *a.* Inexplicable, unaccountable.
inesplicabilmente, *adv.* Unaccountably.
inesplodibile [inesplodIbile], *a.* Unexplodable, explosion-proof. **Recipiente —,** safety can (for petrol).
inesplorabile [inesplorAbile], *a.* Inscrutable, unexplorable.
inesplorato, *a.* Unexplored.
inesploso, *a.* Unexploded.
inesprimibile [inesprimIbile], *a.* Inexpressible, unspeakable.
inesprimibilmente, *adv.* Inexpressibly.
inespugnabile [inespugnAbile], *a.* Impregnable.
inespugnabilità [-à], *n.f.* Impregnability.
inespugnabilmente, *adv.* Impregnably.
inespurgato, *a.* Unexpurgated.
inessicabile [inessicAbile], *a.* Incapable of being dried.
inesteso, *a.* With neither length nor breadth.
inestimabile [inestimAbile], *a.* Inestimable, priceless.
inestimato, *a.* Unesteemed, unforeseen.
inestinguibile [inestinguIbile], *a.* Inextinguishable, unquenchable; everlasting.
inestinguibilmente, *adv.* Inextinguishably.
inestirpabile [inestirpAbile], *a.* Ineradicable.
inestricabile [inestricAbile], *a.* Inextricable.
inestricabilmente, *adv.* Inextricably.
inettamente, *adv.* Ineptly, unsuitably.
inettezza, *n.f.* Ineptness.
inettitudine [inettitUdine], *n.f.* Ineptitude, ineptness, unfitness, unsuitability.
inetto, *a.* Inept, unfit, unsuitable; incapable.
inevitabile [inevitAbile], *a.* Inevitable, unavoidable.
inevitabilmente, *adv.* Inevitably.
inezia [inEzia], *n.f.* Trifle, bagatelle, mere nothing.
infaceto, *a.* Insipid, wishy-washy.
infacondamente, *adv.* With lack of eloquence.
infacondia [infacOndia], *n.f.* Dullness of speech, lack of eloquence; unreadiness of speech.
infacondo, *a.* Ineloquent.
infagottare, *v.t.* To wrap up, to bundle up.
infagottarsi, *v.r.* To muffle oneself up, to wrap up; to dress unbecomingly.
infallantemente, *adv.* Without fail, certainly.
infallibile [infallIbile], *a.* Infallible, unfailing.
infallibilista, *n.m.* (*Eccles.*) Believer in the infallibility of the Pope.
infallibilità [-à], *n.f.* Infallibility.
infallibilmente, *adv.* Infallibly.
infamante, *a.* Causing infamy; giving occasion to slander.
infamare, *v.t.* To defame, to render infamous, to disgrace; to brand with infamy.
infamarsi, *v.r.* To render oneself infamous, to dishonour oneself.
infamatore, infamatrice, *n.m.f.* Defamer, slanderer.
infamatorio [infamatOrio], *a.* Defamatory, slanderous; disgraceful.
infame, *a.* Infamous, disgraceful, vile, detestable.
infamemente, *adv.* Infamously.
infamia [infAmia], *n.f.* Infamy, ignominy, disgrace, baseness, shame.
infamità [-à], *n.f.* Infamy.
infanatichirsi, *v.r.* To become a fanatic.
infangare, *v.t.* To bespatter with mud.
infangarsi, *v.r.* To get muddy, to be spattered with mud.
infantastichire, *v.t.i.* To fill the head with fancies; to become capricious.
infante, *n.m.* Infant, child, babe; infante (of Spain).
infanteria [infanterIa], *n.f.* [cp. **fanteria**].
infanticida, *n.m.* One guilty of infanticide.
infanticidio [infanticIdio], *n.m.* Infanticide.
infantile, *a.* Infantile, childish. **Asilo —,** kindergarten.
infanzia [infAnzia], *n.f.* Infancy, childhood; children (in general).
infarcimento, *n.m.* Stuffing, cramming.
infarcire, *v.t.* To stuff, to cram.
infarinare, *v.t.* To flour, to sprinkle with flour; to powder, to whiten; (*fig.*) to grow grey.
infarinarsi, *v.r.* To become floury; to powder oneself.
infarinato, *p.p.a.* Floured; (*fig.*) with a smattering of learning.
infarinatura, *n.f.* Flouring; (*fig.*) smattering, superficial knowledge. **Avere un' — d'una scienza,** to have a smattering of a science.
infastidimento, *n.m.* Annoyance, nuisance; inconvenience.
infastidire, *v.t.* To annoy, to vex, to bore; to inconvenience, to molest, to trouble.
infastidirsi, *v.r.* To be vexed; to get bored; to get annoyed.
infaticabile [infaticAbile], *a.* Indefatigable, tireless, untiring.
infaticabilmente, *adv.* Indefatigably.
infatti, *adv.* In fact, in effect, indeed, really.
infattibile [infattIbile], *a.* Impracticable.
infatuarsi, *v.r.* To become infatuated.
infatuazione, *n.f.* Infatuation.
infaustamente, *adv.* Inauspiciously.
infausto [infAusto], *a.* Inauspicious, unlucky, ill-omened, ill-starred.
infecondamente, *adv.* Unfruitfully, barrenly.
infecondità [-à], *n.f.* Barrenness, sterility, unfruitfulness.
infecondo, *a.* Unfruitful, barren, sterile.
infedele, *n.m.a.* Infidel; unfaithful person; unfaithful, faithless, false, disloyal; inaccurate.
infedeltà [-à], *n.f.* Infidelity; disloyalty, unfaithfulness; breach of trust.
infederare, *v.t.* To put (the pillow) into the pillow-case.
infelice, *a.* Unhappy, unfortunate, unlucky, wretched, miserable; unsuccessful; difficult, awkward. **Un amore —,** an unhappy love affair; **rendere —,** to make unhappy.
infelicemente, *adv.* Unhappily.
infelicità [-à], *n.f.* Unhappiness, misery; infelicity; adversity.
infelicitare, *v.t.* To make unhappy.
infellonirsi, *v.r.* To become cruel.
infemminire, *v.i.* To become effeminate.
inferenza, *n.f.* Inference.

inferigno, *a.* Brown (of bread).
inferimento, *n.m.* Inference, implication.
inferiore, *n.m.a.* Inferior, lower; subordinate. **Gli arti inferiori,** the legs.
inferiorità [-à], *n.f.* Inferiority.
inferiormente, *adv.* Below, in the lower part.
inferire, *v.i.* To infer, to deduce, to imply; to launch, to inflict (a blow).
inferitura, *n.f.* Inference; (*Naut.*) earing.
infermare, *v.t.* To weaken to nullify (a law, etc.) [cp. **infirmare**].
infermarsi, *v.r.* To fall sick, to be taken ill.
infermeria [infermerIa], *n.f.* Infirmary, hospital; (*Naut.*) sick-bay.
infermiccio [infermIccio], *a.* Sickly.
infermiera, *n.f.* Nurse, hospital nurse.
infermiere, *n.m.* Male nurse, hospital orderly.
infermità [-à], *n.f.* Sickness, infirmity, unsoundness. **— di mente,** unsoundness of mind, madness.
infermo, *n.m.a.* Invalid, patient, sick person; infirm, sick, ill.
infernale, *a.* Infernal, hellish.
infernalmente, *adv.* Infernally.
inferno, *n.m.* Hell; horror.
infero [Infero], *a.* Lower, inferior. **Gli inferi,** inhabitants of hell; hell.
inferocire, *v.t.i.* To make fierce; to become fierce.
inferocirsi, *v.r.* To become wild, to get fierce; to act cruelly.
inferraiolarsi, *v.r.* To wrap oneself in a cloak.
inferriata, *n.f.* Railing, grating; grille.
infertile [infErtile], *a.* Unfertile, unfruitful.
infertilire, *v.t.* To fertilize.
infertilità [-à], *n.f.* Infertility, unfruitfulness.
infervoramento, *n.m.* Fervour, becoming filled with fervour.
infervorare, *v.t.* To inspire with fervour.
infervorarsi, *v.r.* To be filled with fervour, to become excited; to be fervent, to plunge into, to enter upon (a discussion, etc.).
infestamente, *adv.* Noxiously.
infestamento, *n.m.* Infesting; importunity.
infestare, *v.t.* To infest, to harass, to plague; to overrun; to importune, to molest.
infestazione, *n.f.* Infestation.
infesto, *a.* Noxious, ruinous, inimical; hostile, tiresome.
infetidire, *v.t.i.* To make fetid; to become fetid.
infettamento, *n.m.* Infection; corruption.
infettare, *v.t.* To infect, to corrupt, to taint, to pollute.
infettivo, *a.* Infectious, contagious, catching.
infetto, *a.* Infected, corrupted, polluted.
infeudare, *v.t.* (*Law*) To enfeoff; (*fig.*) to take over, to absorb.
infezione, *n.f.* Infection, contagion; contamination.
infiacchimento, *n.m.* Enfeeblement.
infiacchire, *v.t.* To enfeeble, to weaken, to enervate.
infiacchirsi, *v.r.* To weaken, to grow feeble; to decline, to flag.
infiammabile [infiammAbile], *a.* Inflammable, combustible.
infiammabilità [-à], *n.f.* Inflammability. **Punto di —,** flash point.
infiammare, *v.t.* To enflame, to kindle, to ignite; to set on fire; (*fig.*) to stir up.
infiammarsi, *v.r.* To take fire, to catch fire, to be ignited; (*fig.*) to become excited, to be roused; (*Med.*) to become inflamed.
infiammato, *a.* Inflamed.
infiammatorio [infiammatOrio], *a.* Inflaming, (*Med.*) phlogistic.
infiammazione, *n.f.* Inflammation.
infiascare, *v.t.* To bottle, to put into flasks.
inficiare, *v.t.* to disclaim, to repudiate.
infidamente, *adv.* Falsely, treacherously.
infido, *a.* False, faithless, treacherous, untrustworthy.
infierire, *v.i.* To become wild, to grow furious; to rage (of an epidemic, etc.); to be pitiless.
infievolire, *v.i.* To weaken, to grow feeble.
infievolirsi, *v.r.* To grow weak, to become feeble.
infiggere [infIggere], *v.t.* To drive in, to knock in, to nail.
infiggersi, *v.r.* To penetrate, to get driven in; to become impressed (in the mind).
infilacappi, infilaguaine, infilanastri, *n.m.* Bodkin.
infilare, *v.t.* To thread (a needle); to string (beads); to introduce, to pierce, to transfix, to run through; to enter, to go through; to put on (trousers, etc.); (*Mil.*) to enfilade.
infilarsi, *v.r.* To slip into, to put on.
infilata, *n.f.* String, row, series; (*Mil.*) enfilade.
infiltramento, *n.m.* Filtering.
infiltrarsi, *v.r.* To penetrate, to infiltrate, to percolate, to seep; (*fig.*) to insinuate oneself.
infiltrazione, *n.f.* Infiltration.
infilzamento, *n.m.* Piercing, stringing.
infilzare, *v.t.* To pierce, to run through, to transfix; to string together; **— bugie,** to tell a lot of lies.
infilzata, *n.f.* Series, row, suite, string.
infilzato, *p.p.a.* Pierced through, transfixed; filed. (*fig.*) **Madonnina infilzata,** demure girl.
infilzatura, *n.f.* Stringing, piercing; things strung together; unclassified articles.
infimamente, *adv.* To the lowest degree.
infimo [Infimo], *a.* Lowest; basest, vilest; last. **D'— grado,** of the lowest grade.
infine, *adv.* At last, finally, in the end, after all.
infingardaggine [infingardAggine], *n.f.* Laziness, slackness, sloth.
infingardamente, *adv.* Lazily, slothfully.
infingardezza, *n.f.* Laziness.
infingardia [infingardIa], *n.f.* Disinclination to work, slackness.
infingardire, *v.i.* To grow lazy.
infingardo, *a.* Lazy, slack, slothful, sluggish.
infingersi [infIngersi], *v.r.* To simulate, to feign, to pretend [cp. **fingere**].
infingimento, *n.m.* Dissimulation, dissembling, feigning.
infinità [-à], *n.f.* Infinity, infinitude, infiniteness; vastness.
infinitamente, *adv.* Infinitely.
infinitesimale, *a.* Infinitesimal.
infinitesimo [infinitEsimo], *n.m.* Infinitesimal. || *a.* insignificant, negligible, infinitesimal.
infinitezza, *n.f.* Infiniteness.
infinito, *n.m.a.* Infinite; boundless, unlimited, endless; (*Gram.*) infinitive.
infinitudine [infinitUdine], *n.f.* Infinitude.
infino, *prep.* Until, till; as far as; up to.

infinocchiare, *v.t.* To make a fool of, to take in, to cheat, to dupe.
infinocchiatura, *n.f.* Hoax, fooling, dupery.
infinta, *n.f.* Deception, sham [cp. **finta**].
infintamente, *adv.* Feignedly [cp. **fintamente**].
infinto, *a.* Feigned, sham [cp. **finto**].
infioccare, *v.t.* To adorn with tassels.
infiochire, *v.i.* To become hoarse, to weaken.
infiorare, infiorarsi, *v.t.r.* To strew or adorn with flowers, to flower; to bedeck oneself with flowers.
infiorentinirsi, *v.r.* To become a Florentine; to adopt Florentine speech, etc.
infiorescenza, *n.f.* (*Bot.*) Inflorescence.
infirmare, *v.t.* To invalidate, to weaken, to impeach; to disaffirm. (*Law*) — **un atto,** to invalidate a deed.
infirmazione, *n.f.* Invalidation, weakening.
infischiarsi, *v.r.* (*colloq.*) To make light of, to be indifferent to, not to care a rap. **Io me ne infischio,** I couldn't care less.
infisso, *n.m.* Fixture in a structure, *e.g.* door, window-frame. **Infissi,** fixtures.
infistolire, *v.i.* To become fistulous.
infittire, *v.t.i.* To thicken, to grow thick; to become heavy (of rain, etc.).
inflazione, *n.f.* Inflation (of currency).
inflessibile [inflessIbile], *a.* Inflexible, unbending.
inflessibilità [-à], *n.f.* Inflexibility.
inflessione, *n.f.* Inflection (in all senses).
inflettere [inflEttere], *v.t.* (*Gram.*) To inflect.
infliggere [inflIggere], *v.t.* To inflict, to impose upon. — **una punizione,** to inflict a punishment.
inflizione, *n.f.* Infliction.
influente, *n.m.* [cp. **affluente**].
influente, *a.* Influential.
influenza, *n.f.* Influence, ascendancy, power, control, authority; bearing; (*Med.*) influenza.
influenzare, *v.t.* To influence, to affect, to exercise influence upon; to bias.
influenzato, *a.* Influenced, affected; (*Med.*) suffering from influenza.
influire, *v.t.* To influence, to bias, to sway, to affect. (*Comm.*) — **sui prezzi,** to affect prices.
influsso, *n.m.* Influx; influence, effect.
infocamento, *n.m.* Heating, making red hot.
infocare, *v.t.* To heat, to make red hot; to inflame, to excite.
infocarsi, *v.r.* To become heated; to become red hot (in all senses).
infocato, *a.* Burning, red hot, blazing; (*fig.*) ardent; flushed with anger.
infoderare, *v.t.* To sheathe.
infognarsi, *v.r.* To sink (in mire, etc.), to become bogged.
infoltire, *v.t.i.* To make or grow thick, to thicken.
infondatamente, *adv.* Groundlessly.
infondatezza, *n.f.* Unfoundedness, groundlessness.
infondato, *a.* Unfounded, baseless, groundless, unwarranted. **Un'accusa infondata,** a baseless charge.
infondere [infOndere], *v.t.* To infuse, to instil, to inculcate, to inspire with.
infondimento, *n.m.* Inculcation.
inforabile [inforAbile], *a.* Unpierceable.
inforcare, *v.t.* To take up on a pitch-fork; to bestride (a horse, cycle, etc.); to put on (spectacles).
inforcarsi, *v.r.* To fork (of a road, etc.).
inforcata, *n.f.* Forkful, load on a pitch-fork.
inforcatura, *n.f.* Forking (of a road, etc.); bestriding.
inforestierirsi, *v.r.* To make oneself like a foreigner, to talk as such.
informabile [informAbile], *a.* Capable of being informed.
informare, *v.t.* To inform, to instruct, to direct, to guide; to shape, to mould; to conform; to inspire, to imbue; to characterize.
informarsi, *v.r.* To inquire, to ask for information; to inform oneself; to conform with; to comply.
informativa, *n.f.* (*Law*) Information.
informativo, *a.* Informative.
informato, *p.p.a.* Acquainted, informed.
informatore, informatrice, *n.m.f.* Informer, spy; (*Mil.*) scout.
informazione, *n.f.* Information, inquiry, investigation. **Assumere informazioni,** to obtain information, to make inquiries; **ufficio informazioni,** information office; **servizio informazioni,** intelligence service.
informe, *a.* Shapeless.
informemente, *adv.* Shapelessly.
informicolamento, *n.m.* Tingling.
informicolare, informicolire, *v.t.* To cause to tingle; to give one pins and needles.
informicolarsi, *v.r.* To tingle, to have pins and needles. **Ho una gamba informicolata,** my leg has gone to sleep.
infornaciare, *v.t.* To put in the kiln.
infornapane, *n.m.* Baker's peel.
infornare, *v.t.* To put in the oven.
infornata, *n.f.* Batch (of bread in the oven); (*fig.*) batch, group, lot.
infortire, *v.i.* To turn sour (of wine).
infortuna, *n.f.* Ill fortune [cp. **sfortuna**].
infortunato, *n.m.* Unfortunate man; one who has suffered an accident, a casualty. || *a.* unfortunate [cp. **sfortunato**].
infortunio [infortUnio], *n.m.* Accident, mishap, mischance, misfortune, disaster. (*Law*) — **sul lavoro,** accident during employment.
inforzare, *v.t.i.* To reinforce, to strengthen; to aggravate; to turn sour (of wine).
infoscamento, *n.m.* Darkening; becoming gloomy.
infoscare, *v.t.* To darken; to confuse.
infoscarsi, *v.r.* To grow dark, to darken.
infossamento, *n.m.* Hollow, cavity, depression (in ground).
infossare, *v.t.* To bury, to dig; to lower (a road, etc.); to bury in the ground; to store in a pit.
infossarsi, *v.r.* To become hollow.
infossato, *a.* Sunken, fallen in. **Occhi infossati,** hollow eyes.
infra, *prep.* Between, among, what follows. **Autorizzato a fare quanto —,** authorized to perform the following.
infracidamento, *n.m.* Wetting, soaking.
infracidare, infradiciare, *v.t.i.* To wet, to soak, to drench.
infracidire, infradicire, *v.i.* To rot, to decay.

infradiciarsi, *v.r.* To get wet through, to be soaked; to become rotten.
infradiciata, *n.f.* Soaking, thorough wetting.
infralimento, *n.m.* Weakening, growing weak.
infralire, *v.i.* To grow frail.
inframettente, *a.* Meddlesome, interfering.
inframettenza, *n.f.* Interference, meddling; intervention.
inframettere [inframEttere], *v.t.* To interpose, to intervene.
inframettersi [inframEttersi], *v.r.* To interfere, to intervene, to meddle.
inframmischiarsi [cp. **frammischiarsi**].
infrancesare, infrancesarsi, *v.t. r.* To Frenchify; to become Frenchified.
infrangere [infrAngere], *v.t.* To break, to smash, to shatter; to crush; (*fig.*) to transgress, to violate; to infringe.
infrangersi [infrAngersi], *v.r.* To break up, to get smashed.
infrangibile [infranglbile], *a.* Unbreakable.
infrangibilmente, *adv.* Unbreakably.
infrangimento, *n.m.* Infraction.
infranto, *a.* Broken, smashed, crushed. **Col cuore —,** broken-hearted.
infrantoiata, *n.f.* Heap of olives in the press.
infrantoio [infrantOio], *n.m.* Olive-press, oil-press [cp. **frantoio**].
infrapporre, *v.t.i.* To interpose [cp. **frapporre**].
infrarosso, *a.* Infra-red (rays).
infrascare, *v.t.* To cover with branches; (*fig.*) to over-load with ornament.
infrascato, *n.m.* Tent of boughs.
infrascatura, *n.f.* Plaiting of boughs into a covering.
infrasconare, *v.t.* To layer (a plant or bough).
infrascritto, *a.* (*Law*) Undermentioned, undersigned; hereby named.
infratarsi, *v.r.* To become a monk.
infrattanto, *adv.* In the meantime, meanwhile [cp. **frattanto**].
infrazione, *n.f.* Infraction, breach, violation; infringement.
infreddagione, *n.f.* Chill, slight cold in the head [cp. **raffreddore**].
infreddamento, *n.m.* Cold, catching cold.
infreddarsi, *v.r.* To catch cold.
infreddato, *a.* Suffering from a cold.
infreddatura, *n.f.* Cold, chill. **Prendere un'—,** to catch cold.
infreddolirsi, *v.r.* To shiver with cold.
infrenabile [infrenAbile], *a.* Impossible to check or restrain.
infrenamento, *n.m.* Restraining, check, curb, brake.
infrenare, *v.t.* To restrain, to bridle, to curb.
infrenesire, *v.i.* To become frenzied, to have a frenzied wish for.
infrequente, *a.* Infrequent, uncommon.
infrequentemente, *adv.* Infrequently.
infrequenza, *n.f.* Infrequency, uncommonness.
infrigidire, *v.t.i.* To chill, to render frigid, to become chilled.
infrollire, *v.t.i.* To soften; to become tender (of meat, etc.); to get tainted (of meat); (*fig.*) to get slack, to weaken.
infrondire, *v.i.* (*Bot.*) To put forth leaves.
infronzolare, *v.t.* To deck out, to adorn gaudily.
infronzolarsi, *v.r.* To deck oneself out.
infruscare, *v.t.* (*obs.*) To tangle inextricably.
infruttifero [infruttIfero], *a.* Unfruitful, fruitless; sterile; (*Comm.*) not bearing interest
infruttuosità [-à], *n.f.* Fruitlessness.
infruttuoso, *a.* Unfruitful, fruitless; unprofitable.
infula [Infula], *n.f.* (*Eccles.*) Lappet of a mitre; mitre.
infunare, *v.t.* (*Naut.*) To rig, to fit the rigging.
infunata, infunatura, *n.f.* (*Naut.*) Rigging.
infuocare [cp. **infocare**].
infuori, *prep.adv.* Out, outwards. **— di, — da,** except.
infurbire, *v.i.* To grow cunning, to become shrewd.
infurfantire, *v.i.* To turn rogue.
infuriare, *v.t.i.* To enrage, to infuriate; to get angry, to rage.
infuriarsi, *v.r.* To become furious, to grow violent; to fly into a passion.
infusibile [infusIbile], *a.* Infusible.
infusibilità [-à], *n.f.* Infusibility.
infusione, *n.f.* Infusion.
infuso, *n.m.a.* Infusion, infused.
infusori, *n.m.pl.* (*Zool.*) Infusoria.
infuturarsi, *v.r.* To live into the future, to be immortal.
ingabbanarsi, *v.r.* To wrap oneself in a cloak.
ingabbiare, *v.t.* To put in a cage, to cage; to lock up; (*Naut.*) to erect the frame of a ship.
ingaggiamento, *n.m.* Enlistment.
ingaggiare, *v.t.* To enlist, to enrol; (*Mil.*) to engage in battle.
ingaggiatore, *n.m.* Recruiting sergeant.
ingaggio [ingAggio], *n.m.* Enlistment, enrolment.
ingagliardimento, *n.m.* Strengthening, growing strong.
ingagliardire, *v.t.* To invigorate, to strengthen.
ingagliardirsi, *v.r.* To grow strong; to get stronger.
ingalluzzirsi, *v.r.* To strut, to swagger, to give oneself airs, to show off [cp. **ringalluzzirsi**].
ingangherare, *v.t.* To hinge.
ingannabile [ingannAbile], *a.* Easily cheated, "green".
ingannamento, *n.m.* Deception, swindle.
ingannare, *v.t.* To deceive, to cheat, to beguile, to swindle; to betray. **— il tempo,** to while away the time.
ingannarsi, *v.r.* To be mistaken, to be wrong; to err; to deceive oneself.
ingannatore, ingannatrice, *n.m.f.* Deceiver, swindler.
ingannevole [ingannEvole], *a.* Deceiving, deceitful, misleading.
ingannevolmente, *adv.* Deceitfully.
inganno, *n.m.* Deceit, deception; fraud, cheat, trick, imposture; stratagem. **Cadere in —,** to be mistaken, to be misled.
ingarbugliamento, *n.m.* Entanglement.
ingarbugliare, *v.t.* To entangle; to confuse, to muddle; to perplex; to deceive.
ingarbugliarsi, *v.r.* To get muddled, to get entangled.
ingarbuglione, *n.m.* Bungler, muddler.
ingarzullire, *v.i.* [cp. **ingalluzzirsi**].
ingavonarsi, *v.r.* (*Naut.*) To heel over (of a ship), to list.

ingavonato, *a.* (*Naut.*) On her beam ends.
ingegnaccio [ingegnAccio], *n.m.* Uncultivated talent; misdirected ability.
ingegnamento, *n.m.* Use of one's wits.
ingegnarsi, *v.r.* To exert oneself, to strive, to endeavour; to manage, to do one's best. **Ingegnati!** Set your wits to work! Get on with it!
ingegnere, *n.m.* Civil engineer.
ingegneria [ingegnerIa], *n.f.* Civil engineering.
ingegno, *n.m.* Talent, genius; ability, skill, cleverness, brains; understanding; device, contrivance, tool, gadget; mechanism. **Un uomo d'—,** a man of talent; **un'alzata d'—,** a happy thought; **aguzzare l'—,** to contrive; to sharpen one's wits.
ingegnosamente, *adv.* Ingeniously.
ingegnosità [-à], *n.f.* Ingenuity, cleverness; industry.
ingegnoso, *a.* Ingenious, clever, brainy; able, industrious.
ingelosire, *v.t.i.* To make or become jealous.
ingelosirsi, *v.r.* To be jealous, to become jealous.
ingemmare, *v.t.* To adorn with jewels.
ingemmarsi, *v.r.* To bedeck oneself with jewellery.
ingeneramento, *n.m.* Engendering.
ingenerare, *v.t.* To engender; to produce, to cause.
ingenerosamente, *adv.* Ungenerously.
ingenerosità [-à], *n.f.* Lack of generosity.
ingeneroso, *a.* Ungenerous.
ingenitamente, *adv.* Congenitally.
ingenito [ingEnito], *a.* Congenital, inborn, innate.
ingente, *a.* Huge, very great; substantial, important.
ingentilimento, *n.m.* Refining, polishing.
ingentilire, *v.t.* To refine, to ennoble, to polish.
ingentilirsi, *v.r.* To become more refined, to improve in manners; to refine one's style; to become civilized.
ingenuamente, *adv.* Ingenuously, innocently, candidly.
ingenuità [-à], *n.f.* Ingenuousness, simplicity, candour, *naïveté*; simple-mindedness.
ingenuo [ingEnuo], *a.* Ingenuous, candid; simple-minded. **Che —!** How simple you are! **Povero —!** Poor fool!
ingerenza, *n.f.* Interference, interposition, meddling.
ingerire, *v.t.* To swallow, to ingest.
ingerirsi, *v.r.* To meddle with, to interfere in.
ingessare, *v.t.* To whitewash, to lime-wash; to plaster; (*Med.*) to put in plaster; (*Billiards*) to chalk a cue.
ingessatura, *n.f.* Plastering; plaster.
inghiaiare, *v.t.* To gravel, to strew with gravel, to ballast (a road, railway track, etc.).
inghiaiata, *n.f.* Ballast (for road, railway, etc.).
Inghilterra, *n.f.* England.
inghiottimento, *n.m.* Swallowing, gulp.
inghiottire, *v.t.* To swallow, to gulp down; to engulf; (*fig.*) to put up with, to swallow (a lie, an insult, etc.).
inghiottonire, *v.t.i.* To make or become a glutton.
inghirlandare, *v.t.* To adorn with garlands, to wreathe; to encircle.
ingiallimento, *n.m.* Yellowing, turning yellow, withering.
ingiallire, *v.i.* To turn yellow; to wither, to fade (of a flower).
ingiallito, *a.* Yellowed, yellowish.
ingigantire, *v.t.i.* To amplify, to magnify, to exaggerate; to grow enormously.
ingigantirsi, *v.r.* To become gigantic, to be exaggerated.
ingigliare, *v.t.* To adorn with lilies.
inginocchiamento, *n.m.* Kneeling, genuflexion.
inginocchiarsi, *v.r.* To kneel, to kneel down, to genuflect.
inginocchiatoio [inginocchiatOio], *n.m.* Kneeling-stool, prie-dieu; faldstool.
inginocchiatura, *n.f.* Kneeling, genuflexion.
inginocchioni, *adv.* On one's knees.
ingiocondo, *a.* Cheerless.
ingioiarsi, ingioiellarsi, *v.r.* To wear jewellery.
ingiù, *adv.* Downwards, down. **Col capo all'—,** head downwards.
ingiudicato, *a.* (*Law*) Undecided.
ingiungere [ingiUngere], *v.t.* To intimate, to enjoin, to impose, to command; to prescribe.
ingiunzione, *n.f.* Injunction, order, command.
ingiuria [ingiUria], *n.f.* Insult, affront, abuse, vituperation; wrong, outrage. **Scagliare ingiurie,** to hurl insults.
ingiuriare, *v.t.* To abuse, to revile, to insult; to call bad names; to wrong; to outrage; to offend, to scorn.
ingiuriatore, *n.m.* Abuser, insulter; wrongdoer.
ingiurioso, *a.* Abusive, insulting, offensive, outrageous.
ingiustamente, *adv.* Unjustly.
ingiustificabile [ingiustificAbile], *a.* Unjustifiable.
ingiustificabilmente, *adv.* Unjustifiably.
ingiustificato, *a.* Unjustified, unwarranted.
ingiustizia [ingiustIzia], *n.f.* Injustice, wrong; injury. **Riparare un'—,** to redress an injustice.
ingiusto, *a.* Unjust, unfair, wrong.
inglese, *n.m.f.a.* Englishman, Englishwoman; English. **Gli inglesi,** the English; **andarsene all'—,** to take French leave; **sabato —,** Saturday half-holiday; **sale —,** Epsom salts; **zuppa —,** trifle (confection).
ingloriosamente, *adv.* Ingloriously.
inglorioso, *a.* Inglorious.
ingobbire, *v.i.* To become hunch-backed; (*fig.*) to drudge [cp. **sgobbare**].
ingoffire, *v.t.* To make clumsy.
ingoffirsi, *v.r.* To become awkward or clumsy.
ingoiamento, *n.m.* Swallowing, engulfing.
ingoiare, *v.t.* To swallow; to engulf.
ingolfarsi, *v.r.* To plunge into, to be engulfed; to become entangled. **— nei debiti,** to run into debt.
ingollare, *v.t.* To gulp down, to swallow, to gobble up, to bolt (food).
ingolosire, *v.t.i.* To make or become greedy.
ingolosirsi, *v.r.* To become greedy.
ingombramento, *n.m.* Encumbrance, embarrassment.

ingombrante, *a.* Cumbersome, encumbering, cumbrous; bulky.
ingombrare, *v.t.* To encumber, to embarrass, to obstruct; to burden; to be in the way; to stop up; (*Rail.*) to block the line.
ingombro, *n.m.a.* Encumbrance, obstacle; blockage, obstruction; overcrowded, flooded (with goods, etc.).
ingommare, *v.t.* To gum, to paste. **Carta ingommata,** gummed paper.
ingordamente, *adv.* Gluttonously, greedily; eagerly.
ingordigia [ingordIgia], *n.f.* Greediness, greed, voracity.
ingordina, *n.f.* (*Tech.*) Coarse file, rasp.
ingordo, *n.m.a.* Glutton; greedy, gluttonous, voracious; covetous; eager.
ingorgamento, *n.m.* [cp. **ingorgo**].
ingorgare, *v.t.* To obstruct, to choke, to block.
ingorgarsi, *v.r.* To be choked up, to become blocked.
ingorgo, *n.m.* Obstruction, block; (*fig.*) bottleneck; **— nel traffico,** traffic jam.
ingovernabile [ingovernAbile], *a.* Ungovernable.
ingozzare, *v.t.* To swallow, to gulp down, to cram; (*fig.*) to swallow (an insult).
ingozzata, *n.f.* Blow to jam a hat down on one's head.
ingozzatura, *n.f.* Swallowing; jamming one's hat over one's eyes; (*Med.*) oesophagial obstruction by a foreign body.
ingracilire, *v.i.* To grow slim; to become thin, to become delicate.
ingranaggio [ingranAggio], *n.m.* (*Mech.*) Gear, gearing; cogs; system, working. **— differenziale,** differential gear; (*Motor.*) **scatola dell'—,** gear-box; **— dello sterzo,** steering-gear; **— della prima velocità,** low gear; **gl'ingranaggi d'un orologio,** the cogwheels of a clock.
ingranare, *v.t.i.* To throw into gear, to put into gear; to interlock; to be in gear.
ingranchire, *v.t.i.* To benumb, to grow stiff, to get cramp.
ingrande, *adv.* **All'—,** on a large scale.
ingrandimento, *n.m.* Enlargement (in all senses); growth, advancement; (*Cinema.*) close-up.
ingrandire, *v.t.i.* To enlarge, to amplify, to magnify, to extend; to increase, to exaggerate, to grow tall, to grow.
ingrandirsi, *v.r.* To become larger, to increase, to grow greater.
ingranditore, *n.m.* Amplifier; enlarger.
ingrassabue, *n.m.* (*Bot.*) Corn marigold.
ingrassaggio [ingrassAggio], *n.m.* Lubricating, greasing, oiling.
ingrassamento, *n.m.* Fattening; fatness; (*Agric.*) manuring; lubrication.
ingrassare, *v.t.i.* To fatten, to make or grow fat; (*Agric.*) to manure; to lubricate.
ingrassarsi, *v.r.* To grow fat, to get stout.
ingrassatore, *n.m.* Lubricator.
ingrasso, *n.m.* Fattening; (*Agric.*) manure. **Da —,** kept for fattening.
ingratamente, *adv.* Ungratefully.
ingraticciare, *v.t.* To hurdle, to fence with hurdles; to trellis.
ingraticciata, *n.f.* Trellis-work.
ingraticciatura, *n.f.* Trellising; hurdling.
ingraticolamento, *n.m.* Fenced with trellis.
ingraticolare, *v.t.* To close with grating, to fence with trellis.
ingraticolato, *n.m.* Grating.
ingratitudine [ingratitUdine], *n.f.* Ingratitude, ungratefulness.
ingrato, *a.* Ungrateful, thankless. **Un compito —,** a thankless task.
ingravidamento, *n.m.* Pregnancy.
ingravidare, *v.t.* To make pregnant.
ingravidarsi, *v.r.* To become pregnant.
ingraziarsi, *v.r.* To insinuate oneself, to ingratiate oneself (with).
ingrazionirsi, *v.r.* (*obs.*) To ingratiate oneself by underhand means.
ingrediente, *n.m.* Ingredient; component part; element.
ingresso, *n.m.* Entrance, way in; admittance. **Vietato l'—,** no admittance; (*Rail.*) **biglietto d'—,** platform ticket; **porta d'—,** entrance door.
ingrinzire, *v.t.i.* To wrinkle.
ingrinzirsi, *v.r.* To become wrinkled.
ingrossamento, *n.m.* Enlargement, swelling, growth.
ingrossare, *v.t.* To enlarge, to make big, to swell up, to increase; to blunt, to make dull.
ingrossarsi, *v.r.* To grow big, to get fat, to swell; to rise. **Il mare s'ingrossa,** the sea is getting rough.
ingrosso, *adv.* (*Comm.*) **All'—,** wholesale, in the lump; **vendere all'—,** to sell wholesale; **prezzo all'—,** wholesale price.
ingrugnare, ingrugnire, ingrugnirsi, *v.i.r.* To look sulky, to frown, to pout.
ingrugnito, *a.* Frowning, sulky, sullen, bad-tempered.
ingrugnitura, *n.f.* Scowl, frown.
ingrullire, *v.i.* To become silly.
inguadabile [inguadAbile], *a.* Unfordable.
inguainare, *v.t.* To sheathe (the sword).
ingualcibile [ingualcIbile], *a.* Uncrushable.
inguantarsi, *v.r.* To put on gloves.
inguaribile, *a.* Incurable.
inguaribilmente, *adv.* Incurably.
inguinale, *a.* (*Anat.*) Inguinal.
inguine [Inguine], *n.m.* (*Anat.*) Groin.
ingurgitamento, *n.m.* Ingurgitation, swallowing.
ingurgitare, *v.t.* To gulp down, to swallow.
ingusciare, *v.i.* To retire into the shell.
ingustabile [ingustAbile], *a.* Tasteless.
inibire, *v.t.* To inhibit, to forbid, to prevent, to restrain.
inibitorio [inibitOrio], *a.* Inhibitory.
inibizione, *n.f.* Inhibition.
inidoneità [-à], *n.f.* Unfitness (for).
iniettare, *v.t.* To inject, to introduce (as a liquid).
iniettore, *n.m.* Injector.
iniezione, *n.f.* Injection, inoculation; (*colloq.*) prick.
inimmaginabile [inimmaginAbile], *a.* Unimaginable.
inimmaginabilità [-à], *n.f.* Impossibility of being imagined.
inimmaginabilmente, *adv.* Unimaginably.
inimicare, *v.t.* To alienate, to estrange; to treat as an enemy.

inimicarsi, *v.r.* To become unfriendly; to become hostile, to be on bad terms (with).
inimicizia [inimicIzia], *n.f.* Enmity, hostility, animosity.
inimico [inimIco], *a.* Inimical, hostile.
inimitabile [inimitAbile], *a.* Inimitable.
inimitabilmente, *adv.* Inimitably.
ininfiammabile [ininfiammAbile], *a.* Fireproof. **Ininfiammabili,** fire-proofing materials.
inintelligente, *a.* Unintelligent.
inintelligibile [inintelligIbile], *a.* Unintelligible.
inintelligibilità [-à], *n.f.* Unintelligibility.
inintelligibilmente, *adv.* Unintelligibly.
ininterrottamente, *adv.* Uninterruptedly.
ininterrotto, *a.* Uninterrupted.
iniquamente, *adv.* Wickedly, wrongly.
iniquità [-à], *n.f.* Iniquity, wickedness.
iniquitosamente, *adv.* Iniquitously.
iniquitoso, *a.* Iniquitous [cp. **iniquo**].
iniquo [inIquo], *a.* Iniquitous, wicked, unjust; wretched.
iniziale, *n.f.a.* Initial; opening; original. **Le iniziali del mio nome,** my initials; **prezzo —,** starting price.
inizialmente, *adv.* Initially.
iniziamento, *n.m.* Beginning, opening.
iniziare, *v.t.* To initiate, to originate; to start, to begin; to instruct; to introduce.
iniziativa, *n.f.* Initiative. **Prender l'—,** to take the initiative.
iniziato, *n.m.a.* Initiate ; initiated.
iniziazione, *n.f.* Initiation.
inizio [inIzio], *n.m.* Beginning, start. (*Football*) **Calcio d'—,** kick-off.
innacquamento, *n.m.* Watering down (of wine, etc.).
innacquare, *v.t.* To water down (wine, etc.); to dilute.
innaffiamento, *n.m.* Sprinkling (with water).
innaffiare, *v.t.* To water, to sprinkle.
innaffiatoio [innaffiatOio], *n.m.* Watering-can.
innaffiatrice, *n.f.* Watering-cart.
innalzamento, *n.m.* Raising, elevation.
innalzare, *v.t.* To raise, to elevate, to lift; to exalt; to erect; to heighten; to extol, to ennoble. **— una casa,** to build a house.
innalzarsi, *v.r.* To exalt oneself, to extol oneself; to rise. **— a volo,** to rise in flight.
innamoracchiamento, *n.m.* Falling slightly in love; a passing love affair.
innamoracchiarsi, *v.r.* To have a slight love affair, to be a little in love.
innamoramento, *n.m.* Falling in love; fondness; courtship.
innamorare, *v.t.* To fill with love, to enamour, to inspire with love, to fascinate.
innamorarsi, *v.r.* To fall in love (with); to become fond (of).
innamorata, *n.f.* Lover; mistress; sweetheart.
innamoratamente, *adv.* Lovingly, like a lover.
innamorato, *n.m.a.* Lover, sweetheart; enamoured, in love. **Essere — di,** to be in love with, to be fond of.
innamorazzarsi, *v.r.* To fall passionately in love.
innanzi, *prep.adv.* Before, forward; in the presence of; toward, in front. **Tirare —,** to carry on, to muddle through; **— tutto,** first of all; **d'ora —,** from now on; **farsi —,** to come forward; **— tempo,** before the time, prematurely; **andare —,** to go on, to proceed; **— negli anni,** well on in years; **andare troppo —,** to go too far (in all senses).
innario [innArio], *n.m.* (*Eccles.*) Hymnary.
innato, *a.* Innate, inborn.
innaturale, *a.* Unnatural.
innavigabile [innavigAbile], *a.* Unnavigable; unseaworthy.
innegabile [innegAbile], *a.* Undeniable.
inneggiare, *v.t.i.* To sing the praises (of); to extol, to exalt; to eulogize, to sing hymns (to).
innervazione, *n.f.* (*Med.*) Innervation.
innescare, *v.t.* To prime (a charge, blasting, etc.), to fuse.
innesco, *n.m.* Priming; detonator.
innestamento, *n.m.* Grating, graft (*Agric.*).
innestare, *v.t.* (*Agric.*) To graft, to engraft; to cross-breed; (*Med.*) to inoculate, to vaccinate; (*Mech.*) to clutch, to throw into gear, to engage.
innestatura, *n.f.* Grafting.
innesto, *n.m.* (*Agric.*) Grafting, graft; (*Med.*) inoculation, vaccination; (*Mech.*) clutch, coupling. **— a frizione,** friction clutch; **sbarra d'—,** clutch-shaft.
inno, *n.m.* Hymn, anthem; song; canticle. **— nazionale,** national anthem; **inni sacri,** hymns, sacred songs.
innocente, *n.m.a.* Innocent; not guilty, guiltless; harmless, inoffensive; simple, silly. **Dichiararsi —,** to plead not guilty; **la strage degli innocenti,** the massacre of the innocents.
innocentemente, *adv.* Innocently.
innocentino, *n.m.* Demure person; sanctimonious fellow. **Fare l'—,** to look as though butter would not melt in one's mouth.
innocenza, *n.f.* Innocence; (*fig.*) childhood.
innocuamente, *adv.* Innocuously.
innocuità [-à], *n.f.* Innocuousness.
innocuo [innOcuo], *a.* Innocuous, harmless, inoffensive; innocent.
innodia [innodIa], *n.f.* Hymnody.
innologia [innologIa], *n.f.* Hymnology.
innominabile [innominAbile], *a.* Unspeakable, unmentionable; shameful.
innominatamente, *adv.* Namelessly.
innominato, *n.m.a.* Unnamed, nameless.
innondare, *v.t.* To inundate [cp. **inondare**].
innormale, *a.* [cp. **anormale**].
innormalità [-à], *n.f.* [cp. **anormalità**].
innormalmente, *adv.* [cp. **anormalmente**].
innovamento, *n.m.* Innovation.
innovare, *v.t.i.* To innovate, to change, to alter; to reform.
innovatore, innovatrice, *n.m.f.* Innovator.
innovazione, *n.f.* Innovation, novelty, alteration, new departure.
innumerabile [innumerAbile], *a.* Innumerable, numberless, countless.
innumerabilmente, *adv.* Countlessly.
innumerato, *a.* Unnumbered, countless.
innumerevole [innumerEvole], *a.* Innumerable.
inobbediente, *a.* Disobedient.
inobliabile [inobliAbile], *a.* Unforgettable.
inoccupato, *a.* Unoccupied, empty, vacant.

inoculare, *v.t.* To inoculate (in all senses).
inoculazione, *n.f.* Inoculation, vaccination.
inodorare, *v.t.* To give a smell to.
inodoro, *a.* Odourless, inodorous, scentless.
inoffensibile [inoffensIbile], *a.* Invulnerable.
inoffensivo, *a.* Inoffensive, harmless, innocuous.
inoffeso, *a.* Unharmed, unhurt.
inofficioso, *a* (*Law*) Invalid.
inoliare, *v.t.* (*Eccles.*) To administer unction; to add oil to (food).
inoltramento, *n.m.* Forwarding, transmitting.
inoltrare, *v.t.* To forward (letters, etc.), to send on; to proffer; to transmit, to ship; to tender.
inoltrarsi, *v.r.* To advance, to go forward, to proceed; to enter (upon). **— in una questione,** to go deeply into a matter.
inoltrato, *a.* Advanced, gone ahead; with the greater part gone. **A notte inoltrata,** far into the night, late in the night.
inoltre, *adv.* Besides, moreover, in addition to.
inoltro, *n.m.* Forwarding, transmission, shipping. **— delle lettere,** forwarding of letters.
inondamento *n.m.* Inundating, inundation.
inondante, *a.* Inundating. (*Eccles.*) **Grazia —,** inundating grace.
inondare, *v.t.* To inundate, to flood; to overflow; to submerge.
inondazione, *n.f.* Inundation, flood.
inonestamente, *adv.* Without honour, dishonourablv, dishonestly.
inonestà [-à], *n.f.* [cp. **disonestà**].
inonesto, *a.* [cp. **disonesto**].
inonoratamente, *adv.* Dishonourably, without honour.
inonorato, *a.* Without honour, without praise, unhonoured; dishonoured.
inoperante, *a.* Inoperative.
inoperosamente, *adv.* Idly, inactively.
inoperosità [-à], *n.f.* Inactivity, idleness.
inoperoso, *a.* Idle, inactive.
inopia [inOpia], *n.f.* Poverty, penury, indigence, destitution, want.
inopinabile [inopinAbile], *a.* Unthinkable, unimaginable; unforeseeable.
inopinabilmente, *adv.* Unthinkably; unforeseeably.
inopinatamente, *adv.* Unexpectedly.
inopinato, *a.* Unexpected, unforeseen.
inopportunamente, *adv.* Inopportunely.
inopportunità [-à], *n.f.* Untimeliness, unseasonableness.
inopportuno, *a.* Inopportune, untimely, unseasonable; awkward.
inoppugnabile [inoppugnAbile], *a.* Incontestable, indisputable.
inoppugnabilmente, *adv.* Incontestably.
inorare, *v.t.* To gild [cp. **dorare**].
inordinanza, *n.f.* Disorder, lack of order.
inordinatamente, *adv.* Confusedly.
inordinatezza, *n.f.* Disorder.
inordinato, *a.* Disordered, confused, without arrangement.
inorganicamente, *adv.* Inorganically.
inorganico [inorgAnico], *a.* (*Chem.*) Inorganic.
inorgoglire, inorgoglirsi, *v.i.r.* To become proud, to be puffed up; to become arrogant, to become elated.
inornatamente, *adv.* In an unadorned fashion.
inornato, *a.* Unadorned.
inorpellamento, *n.m.* Tinselling.
inorpellare, *v.t.* To tinsel.
inorpellatura, *n.f.* Tinsel-work.
inorridire, *v.t.i.* To frighten, to horrify, to strike with horror.
inorridirsi, *v.r.* To take fright, to be frightened, to be horrified, to be stricken with horror; to be aghast.
inortodossia [inortodossIa], *n.f.* Unorthodoxy.
inortodosso, *n.m.a.* Unorthodox, heretic.
inoscularsi, *v.r.* To join (of rivers, canals, etc.); to effect a junction.
inospitale, *a.* Inhospitable; desolate, barren.
inospitalità [-à], *n.f.* Inhospitality.
inospitalmente, *adv.* Inhospitably.
inospite [inOspite], *a.* Inhospitable, uninhabited, desolate.
inossare, *v.i.* To become bony; to cut teeth.
inosservabile [inosservAbile], *a.* Unobservable, imperceptible.
inosservabilmente, *adv.* Imperceptibly.
inosservante, *a.* Unobservant.
inosservanza, *n.f.* Inattention, failure to observe, non-observance, non-performance.
inosservato, *a.* Unobserved, unnoticed, unperceived.
inossidabile [inossidAbile], *a.* Rustless, stainless. **Acciaio —,** stainless steel.
inostrare, *v.t. r.* To adorn with purple; (*Eccles.*) to don the cardinal's hat.
in ottavo, *n.m.a.* (*Print.*) Octavo.
inottusire, *v.i.* To become blunt, to become dull; to be stupid.
inquadramento, *n.m.* Framing, fitting in, inserting; (*Mil.*) grouping.
inquadrare, *v.t.* To frame; to insert; to enclose; to distribute, to arrange; to embody; (*Mil.*) to group, to embody.
inquadrarsi, *v.r.* To be inserted, to fit in; to be incorporated.
inqualificabile [inqualificAbile], *a.* Unaccountable; unspeakable, beyond words. **Condotta —,** unaccountable behaviour.
inquartare, *v.t.* (*Herald.*) To quarter; (*Agric.*) to plough for the fourth time.
inquartazione, *n.f.* (*Agric.*) Fourth ploughing; (*Metal.*) quartation.
in quarto, *n.m.a.* (*Print.*) Quarto.
inquietamente, *adv.* Unquietly, uneasily.
inquietante, *a.* Disquieting.
inquietare, *v.t.* To disquiet, to make uneasy, to worry, to alarm.
inquietarsi, *v.r.* To be uneasy, to be worried, to get alarmed.
inquietezza, *n.f.* Disquietude, uneasiness.
inquieto, *a.* Restless, unquiet, uneasy, fidgetty; troubled, agitated.
inquietudine [inquietUdine], *n.f.* Restlessness; uneasiness; anxiety, gloom.
inquilino, *n.m.* Tenant (in a block of flats), lodger, boarder.
inquinamento, *n.m.* Pollution, fouling.
inquinare, *v.t.* To pollute, to make foul. **Acqua inquinata,** foul water.
inquinarsi, *v.r.* To be polluted, to be defiled; to become foul.
inquinazione, *n.f.* Pollution, fouling.
inquirente, *a.* (*Law*) Examining (judge); investigating.
inquisire, *v.t.* To investigate, to enquire (into); to search, to investigate.

inquisitivo, *a.* Enquiring, investigating.
inquisitore, *n.m.* (*Eccles.*) Inquisitor.
inquisitoriale, *a.* Inquisitorial.
inquisizione, *n.f.* (*Eccles.*) Inquisition.
insabbiamento, *n.m.* Silting up, sanding.
insabbiarsi, *v.r.* To silt up, to be choked with sand; (*fig.*) to get bogged.
insaccamento, *n.m.* Packing, sacking, bagging.
insaccare, *v.t.* To put in a sack, to sack, to bag; to pocket; to stuff up; to fill (sausage skins).
insaccarsi, *v.r.* To crowd (into); to pack oneself (into); to hide; to dress badly.
insaccato, *p.p.a.* Packed, bagged, sacked. **Carni insaccate,** sausages; **corsa degli insaccati,** sack-race.
insalare, *v.t.* To salt.
insalata, *n.f.* Salad; (*fig.*) muddle, jumble. **Condire l'—,** to dress the salad; **fare un'—,** to make a hash of it.
insalatiera, *n.f.* Salad-bowl.
insaldabile [insaldAbile], *a.* Unmendable.
insaldare, *v.t.* To starch (collars, etc.).
insaldatura, *n.f.* Starching.
insalivare, *v.t.* To moisten with saliva.
insalivazione, *n.f.* Insalivation.
insalubre, *a.* Unhealthy, insalubrious, unwholesome; insanitary.
insalubrità [-à], *n.f.* Unwholesomeness, insalubrity.
insalutato, *a.* Unsaluted. **Andarsene — ospite,** to go away without saying good-bye.
insalvatichire [cp. **inselvatichire**].
insanabile [insanAbile], *a.* Uncurable; irremediable.
insanabilmente, *adv.* Incurably.
insanamente, *adv.* Insanely, idiotically.
insanguinamento, *n.m.* Blood-stain.
insanguinare, *v.t.* To stain with blood; to cover with blood.
insanguinarsi, *v.r.* To be bloody, to become blood-stained.
insania [insAnia], *n.f.* Insanity; folly, madness.
insanire, *v.i.* To go mad, to become insane.
insano, *a.* Insane, mad, foolish; morbid.
insaponare, *v.t.* To soap, to lather; (*fig.*) to flatter.
insaponarsi, *v.r.* To lather oneself (for shaving).
insaponata, insaponatura, *n.f.* Soaping, lathering.
insaporire, *v.t.* To flavour.
insaporito, *a.* Tasty; flavoured.
insaporo, *a.* Tasteless.
insaputa, *n.f.* Without the knowledge of. **All'— di,** unknown to; **a mia —,** unknown to me, without my knowledge.
insaturabile [insaturAbile], *a.* Incapable of being saturated; insatiable.
insaziabile [insaziAbile], *a.* Insatiable, greedy, ravenous, voracious.
insaziabilità [-à], *n.f.* Insatiability.
insaziabilmente, *adv.* Insatiably.
insaziato, *a.* Insatiate, unappeased.
inscatolare, *v.t.* To can, to tin.
inscenare, *v.t.* (*Theat.*) To put on the stage; to stage. (*fig.*) **— una dimostrazione,** to stage a demonstration.
inscenatore, *n.m.* (*Theat.*) Producer; scene-painter.
inschiavire, *v.t.* (*obs.*) To enslave.
insciente, *a.* Ignorant; unaware of.
inscientemente, *adv.* Unknowingly, in ignorance.
inscienza, *n.f.* Ignorance (of a law, etc.); unawareness.
inscindibile [inscindIbile], *a.* Inseparable.
inscindibilità [-à], *n.f.* Inseparability.
inscritto, *p.p.a.* Inscribed, registered, entered, recorded [cp. **iscritto**].
inscrivere [inscrIvere], *v.t.* To inscribe, to register, to enter, to record [cp. **iscrivere**].
inscriversi, *v.r.* To join (a society, etc.), to enlist; to put one's name down for; to subscribe. **— a una società,** to join a society; **— a una scuola,** to enrol in a school [cp. **iscriversi**].
inscrizione, *n.f.* Inscription; registration; entry, subscription; record; booking. **Tassa d'—,** registration fee [cp. **iscrizione**].
inscrutabile [inscrutAbile], *a.* Inscrutable.
inscrutabilità [-à], *n.f.* Inscrutability.
inscrutabilmente, *adv.* Inscrutably.
inscurire, *v.t.* To obscure, to darken.
insecchire, *v.t.i.* To dry up, to shrivel.
insecchito, *p.p.a.* Dried up, shrivelled; lank.
insecutore, *n.m.* Persecutor; follower.
insediamento, *n.m.* Installation (in office), investiture.
insediare, *v.t.* To instal; to put in office; to place, to set up.
insediarsi, *v.r.* To be installed, to take office.
insegna, *n.f.* Flag, banner, standard, ensign; coat-of-arms; insignia; sign-board; characteristic.
insegnabile [insegnAbile], *a.* Teachable.
insegnamento, *n.m.* Teaching, instruction, tuition, lesson.
insegnante, *n.m.a.* Teacher; teaching.
insegnare, *v.t.* To teach, to instruct; to show, to explain. **— una lingua,** to teach a language.
insegnativo, *a.* Instructive, didactic.
inseguimento, *n.m.* Pursuit, chase, following-up.
inseguire, *v.t.* To pursue, to run after, to chase; to press, to follow up.
insellare, *v.t.* To saddle.
insellatura, *n.f.* Saddle-back.
inselvarsi, *v.r.* To hide oneself in a wood.
inselvatichire, *v.i.* To grow wild; to become rough in manners; to be unsociable.
inseminato, *a.* Unsown, uncultivated; barren.
insenatura, *n.f.* (*Geog.*) Inlet, creek, small bay; harbour.
insensataggine [insensatAggine], *n.f.* Lack of common sense; crazy act.
insensatamente, *adv.* Insensately, crazily.
insensatezza, *n.f.* Senselessness, folly; rashness.
insensato, *a.* Senseless, crazy; rash.
insensibile [insensIbile], *a.* Insensible, unfeeling, dull, hard-hearted; imperceptible.
insensibilità [-à], *n.f.* Insensibility.
insensibilmente, *adv.* Insensibly.
insensitività [-à], *n.f.* Insensitiveness.
insensitivo, *a.* Insensitive.
inseparabile [inseparAbile], *a.* Inseparable, indivisible.
inseparabilmente, *adv.* Inseparably.
insepolto, *a.* Unburied.
insequestrabile [insequestrAbile], *a.* Not liable to sequestration.

inserimento, *n.m.* Insertion, act of insertion; introduction; addition.
inserire, *v.t.* To insert, to introduce; to engraft; to interpolate; (*Elect.*) to connect, to plug in.
inserirsi, *v.r.* To be included (in); to become part of.
inserta, *n.f.* Enclosure (letter, papers, etc.).
inserto, *n.m.a.* Enclosed (papers, etc.); inserted.
inservibile [inservIbile], *a.* Unserviceable.
inserviente, *n.m.* Attendant, servant.
inserzione, *n.f.* Insertion; advertisement (in a newspaper).
inserzionista (*pl.* **inserzionisti**), *n.m.* Advertiser.
insetticida, *n.m.a.* Insecticide.
insettivoro [insettIvoro], *a.* Insectivorous.
insetto, *n.m.* Insect.
inseverire, *v.i.* To become severe.
insidia [insIdia], *n.f.* Snare, trap, ambush; deceit; plot; danger. **Tendere un'—,** to lay a snare.
insidiare, *v.t.* To ensnare, to entice, to trap, to tempt; to lie in wait (for).
insidiatore, insidiatrice, *n.m.f.* Plotter; tempter.
insidiosamente, *adv.* Insidiously.
insidioso, *a.* Insidious; treacherous, deceitful.
insieme, *n.m.* The whole; the total result; the general effect.
insieme, *adv.* Together, jointly; at the same time. **Mettere —,** to collect, to put together, to assemble (machinery); **Mettersi —,** to associate, to join together.
insieparsi, *v.r.* To hide behind a hedge.
insigne, *a.* Notable, signal, famous, renowned, illustrious; notorious.
insignificante, *a.* Insignificant, irrelevant, immaterial; meaningless.
insignire, *v.t.* To decorate (with an honour, etc.), to confer an order on; to bestow a title on.
insignorirsi, *v.r.* To become master (of), to become the ruler (of), to hold sway; to take possession (of).
insinattanto, *prep.* So far.
insincerità [-à], *n.f.* Insincerity.
insincero, *a.* Insincere, false, dissembling.
insinchè, *prep.* Until.
insino, *prep.* Until, till; as far as.
insinora, *adv.* Until now.
insinuabile [insinuAbile], *a.* Insinuable; capable of insinuation.
insinuante, *a.* Insinuating, sly; ingratiating.
insinuare, *v.t.* To insinuate, to hint, to suggest; to instil.
insinuarsi, *v.r.* To insinuate oneself, to steal in, to creep (into).
insinuativamente, *adv.* Insinuatingly.
insinuativo, *a.* Insinuative.
insinuazione, *n.f.* Insinuation, innuendo; suggestion.
insipidamente, *adv.* Insipidly.
insipidezza, insipidità [-à], *n.f.* Insipidness, insipidity.
insipido [insIpido], *a.* Insipid, tasteless; dull.
insipiente, *a.* Incapable, ignorant; foolish.
insipientemente, *adv.* Ignorantly; ineptly.
insipienza, *n.f.* Ignorance, silliness.
insistente, *a.* Insistent, persevering; obstinate.
insistenza, *n.f.* Insistence, insistency; obstinacy; perseverance.
insistere [insIstere], *v.i.* To insist, to persist, to urge, to press; to dwell upon (a subject, etc.).
insito [Insito], *a.* (*Lit.*) Inherent; inborn.
insoave, *a.* (*Lit.*) Rough, not suave, disagreeable.
insociabile [insociAbile], *a.* Unsociable
insociabilità [-à], *n.f.* Unsociability.
insociabilmente, *adv.* Unsociably.
insociale, *a.* Unsocial.
insocievole [insociEvole], *a.* Unsociable.
insoddisfatto, *a.* Unsatisfied; dissatisfied.
insoddisfazione, *n.f.* Dissatisfaction.
insofferente, *a.* Intolerant, impatient.
insofferentemente, *adv.* Intolerantly.
insofferenza, *n.f.* Intolerance, impatience.
insoffribile [insoffrIbile], *a.* Insufferable, intolerable.
insoffribilità [-à], *n.f.* Insufferability.
insoffribilmente, *adv.* Insufferably
insolazione, *n.f.* Sunstroke.
insolente, *a.* Insolent, overbearing, insulting; saucy.
insolentemente, *adv.* Insolently.
insolentire, *v.t.i.* To abuse, to insult, to offend; to use abusive language.
insolenza, *n.f.* Insolence, arrogance; sauciness.
insolfare, *v.t.* To fumigate with sulphur.
in solido, *a.* (*Comm.*) Jointly liable.
insolitamente, *adv.* Unusually, rarely.
insolito [insOlito], *a.* Unusual, uncommon; unwonted.
insollire, *v.t.* (*obs.*) To weaken, to soften.
insolubile [insolUbile], *a.* Insoluble, unsolvable.
insolubilità [-à], *n.f.* Insolubility.
insolubilmente, *adv.* Insolubly.
insoluto, *a.* Unsolved, unexplained; open (of cheques); unpaid; insolvent.
insolvente, *a.* Insolvent.
insolvenza, *n.f.* Insolvency.
insolvibile [insolvIbile], *a.* That cannot be paid (of a cheque).
insomma, *adv.* In short, briefly, in a word; after all; on the whole.
insommergibile [insommergIbile], *a.* Unsinkable.
insondabile [insondAbile], *a.* Unfathomable.
insonne, *a.* Sleepless, wakeful. **Notte —,** a sleepless night.
insonnia [insOnnia], *n.f.* Insomnia, sleeplessness.
insonnito, insonnolito, *a.* Drowsy, sleepy.
insopportabile [insopportAbile], *a.* Insupportable, insufferable, intolerable.
insopportabilità [-à], *n.f.* Insufferableness.
insopportabilmente, *adv.* Insupportably.
insordire, *v.i.* To become deaf.
insordito, *a.* Grown deaf.
insorgente, *a.* Insurgent.
insorgere [insOrgere], *v.i.* To arise, to rise, to rise up (in revolt), to rebel.
insorgimento, *n.m.* Uprising, revolt.
insormontabile [insormontAbile], *a.* Insurmountable.
insorto, *n.m.a.* Rebel, insurgent.
insospettato, *a.* Unsuspected.
insospettire, *v.t.* To arouse suspicions (in), to cause to be suspicious.

insospettirsi, *v.r.* To become suspicious; to begin to suspect.
insostenibile [insostenIbile], *a.* Unbearable, intolerable; untenable; indefensible.
insozzare, *v.t.* To defile, to soil, to stain, to tarnish.
insozzarsi, *v.r.* To soil oneself (esp. morally).
insperabile [insperAbile], *a.* Not to be hoped for, beyond all hope.
insperanzire, *v.t.* To comfort, to instil hope.
insperatamente, *adv.* Unexpectedly; in an unhoped-for manner.
insperato, *a.* Unexpected.
inspessire, *v.t.* To make dense.
inspettore [cp. **ispettore**].
inspiegabile [inspiegAbile], *a.* Inexplicable, unexplainable, unaccountable.
inspiegato, *a.* Unexplained.
inspirare [cp. **ispirare**].
instabile [instAbile], *a.* Unstable, unsettled, unsteady; insecure.
instabilità [-**à**], *n.f.* Instability.
instabilmente, *adv.* Unstably, unsteadily.
installare, *v.t.* To instal, to fit up.
installarsi, *v.r.* To settle down *or* in.
installazione, *n.f.* Installation, plant.
instancabile [instancAbile], *a.* Untiring, unwearied, indefatigable.
instancabilmente, *adv.* Indefatigably.
instantemente, *adv.* Insistantly.
instaurare, *v.t.* To set up, to establish.
instaurazione, *n.f.* Establishment, installation.
insterilire, *v.t.* To sterilize [cp. **isterilire**].
instillare, *v.t.* To instil, to inculcate, to inspire.
instillazione, *n.f.* (*Med.*) Dropping of liquid into the eye.
institore, *n.m.* Administrator, factor, agent.
instradare, *v.t.* To set on the right road [cp. **istradare**].
insù, *adv.* Upwards, up. **Naso all'—,** turned-up nose; **guardare all'—,** to look upwards.
insubordinatamente, *adv.* Insubordinately.
insubordinatezza, *n.f.* Insubordination.
insubordinato, *a.* Insubordinate.
insubordinazione, *n.f.* Insubordination.
insuccesso, *n.m.* Failure.
insudiciamento, *n.m.* Soiling, fouling; dirt.
insudiciare, *v.t.* To soil, to dirty; to defile, to stain; to tarnish.
insudiciarsi, *v.r.* To become soiled, to get dirty.
insueto, *a.* (*Lit.*) Unaccustomed.
insufficiente, *a.* Insufficient; inadequate, unfit.
insufficientemente, *adv.* Insufficiently.
insufficienza, *n.f.* Insufficiency, want, lack; unfitness, incapacity.
insufflare, *v.t.* (*Lit.*) To blow into, to inspire, to insufflate; (*fig.*) to suggest.
insufflazione, *n.f.* Inspiration, insufflation.
insulare, *a.* Insular.
insularità [-**à**], *n.f.* Insularity.
insulina, *n.f.* Insulin.
insulsaggine [insulsAggine], *n.f.* Fatuity, silliness; stupidity, dullness.
insulsamente, *adv.* Fatuously, foolishly.
insulso, *a.* Insipid, fatuous, silly.
insultante, *a.* Insulting, abusive, offensive.
insultare, *v.t.* To revile, to abuse, to insult, to offend.
insulto, *n.m.* Insult, abuse; affront, offence; (*Med.*) fit, stroke, attack.
insuperabile [insuperAbile], *a.* Insuperable, unsurpassable.
insuperabilità [-**à**], *n.f.* Insuperability.
insuperabilmente, *adv.* Insuperably.
insuperbirsi, *v.r.* To become proud, to grow arrogant, to boast, to swell with pride.
insurrezionale, *a.* Insurrectionary.
insurrezione, *n.f.* Insurrection, rising, revolt, rebellion.
insussistente, *a.* Non-existent, unreal, unsubstantial, unfounded.
insussistenza, *n.f.* Unreality, non-existence, insubstantiality.
intabaccarsi, *v.r.* To become tobacco-stained.
intabarrarsi, *v.r.* To wrap up in a mantle, to muffle oneself up.
intaccare, *v.t.i.* To cut into, to notch; to damage, to impair; to prejudice; to corrode; (*Naut.*) to rise (of wind); (*Comm.*) to draw (on one's capital); to hesitate in one's speech.
intaccatura, *n.f.* Notch, dent, incision; impediment.
intagliamento, *n.m.* Carving.
intagliare, *v.t.* To carve, to cut, to sculpture, to incise, to engrave.
intagliatore, *n.m.* Sculptor, engraver.
intaglio [intAglio], *n.m.* Intaglio, carving; engraving. **— in legno,** wood-cut.
intanarsi, *v.r.* To hide (oneself) [cp. **rintanarsi**].
intanfire, *v.i.* To become musty.
intangibile [intangIbile], *a.* Intangible; not to be touched.
intangibilità [-**à**], *n.f.* Intangibility.
intangibilmente, *adv.* Intangibly.
intanto, *adv.* Meanwhile, in the meantime; while, whilst. **— che,** while, until.
intarlare, *v.i.* To become worm-eaten.
intarsiamento, *n.m.* Inlay, veneering.
intarsiare, *v.t.* To inlay, to veneer.
intarsio [intArsio], *n.m.* Inlaid work, inlaying; veneer, veneering.
intasamento, *n.m.* Obstruction, stoppage.
intasare, *v.t.* To obstruct, to clog, to block, to stop up, to choke.
intasarsi, *v.r.* To be choked up, to be clogged to be stuffed up (with a cold in the nose).
intascare, *v.t.* To pocket.
intassellare, *v.t.* (*Arch.*) To dowel, to plug.
intatto, *n.m.* Intact, untouched; undamaged, unimpaired.
intavolare, *v.t.* To board up; to set on foot, to initiate, to start; to set (chessmen, etc.) on a board.
intavolato, *n.m.* Boarding, planking, wainscotting.
intavolatura, *n.f.* Boarding up; (*Mus.*) system of notation.
integerrimo [integErrimo], *a.* Upright, incorruptible.
integrabile [integrAbile], *a.* Capable of integration.
integrale, *a.* Integral, essential, whole; in full. **Pane —,** wholemeal bread; **rimborso —,** reimbursement in full.
integralmente, *adv.* Integrally, fully, in full.
integramente, *adv.* Uprightly, honestly, with integrity.
integramento, *n.m.* Integration.

integrante, *a.* Integrating, completing.
integrare, *v.t.* To integrate, to make whole, to make into a whole; to complete.
integrato, *a.* Completed; (*Comm.*) fully paid.
integrazione, *n.f.* Integration.
integrità [-**à**], *n.f.* Integrity, rectitude.
integro [Integro], *a.* Upright, honest; high-minded; entire.
integumento, *n.m.* Integument, skin.
intelaiare, *v.t.* To put on the loom, to set up the loom; to frame.
intelaiatura, *n.f.* Frame, frame-work; (bicycle) frame; (*Motor*) chassis.
intelletto, *n.m.* Intellect, understanding, mind, reason, sense.
intellettuale, *n.m.a.* Intellectual; learned; refined.
intellettualismo, *n.m.* Intellectualism.
intellettualità [-**à**], *n.f.* Intellectuality; the intellectuals, intelligenzia.
intellettualmente, *adv.* Intellectually.
intellezione, *n.f.* Intellection, understanding.
intelligente, *a.* Intelligent, clever, skilled, sensible.
intelligentemente, *adv.* Intelligently.
intelligenza, *n.f.* Intelligence; understanding, mind, reason; communication, information.
intelligibile [intelligIbile], *a.* Intelligible.
intelligibilità [-**à**], *n.f.* Intelligibility.
intelligibilmente, *adv.* Intelligibly.
intemerata, *n.f.* Rebuke, reprimand, scolding; long and boring speech.
intemerato, *a.* Upright, honest, high-minded; faultless, stainless.
intemperante, *a.* Intemperate, immoderate.
intemperantemente, *adv.* Intemperately, immoderately.
intemperanza, *n.f.* Intemperateness, intemperance.
intemperatamente, *adv.* Intemperately.
intemperato, *a.* Intemperate.
intemperie [intempErie], *n.f.* Foul weather, inclement weather.
intempestivamente, *adv.* Untimely, unseasonably, inopportunely, inappropriately.
intempestività [-**à**], *n.f.* Untimeliness.
intempestivo, *a.* Untimely, unseasonable, inopportune, ill-timed.
intendente, *n.m.* Connoisseur; superintendent, manager, surveyor, inspector.
intendenza, *n.f.* Superintendence; management; excise office; (*Mil.*) commissariat.
intendere [intEndere], *v.t.* To understand; to hear; to intend, to mean; to conceive (a notion). **Darla ad —,** to make one believe; **gli ho fatto —,** I made him understand; **cosa intendi fare?** What do you mean to do?
intendersi [intEndersi], *v.r.* To agree, to come to terms, to be agreed; to know about; to be a good judge (of), to be an expert; to have a knack; to understand. **Intendersene di,** to be well acquainted with, to be an expert in; **intendersela,** to get on well together; **S'intende!** Of course! Naturally!
intendimento, *n.m.* Understanding, mind; intention, plan.
intenditore, intenditrice, *n.m.f.* Connoisseur, expert; one quick to grasp (an idea).
intenebramento, *n.m.* Darkening, obscuring.
intenebrare, *v.t.* To darken, to obscure.
intenerimento, *n.m.* Emotion; tenderness, compassion.
intenerire, *v.t.* To soften, to move, to affect.
intenerirsi, *v.r.* To be moved, to be affected, to feel compassion.
intensamente, *adv.* Intensely.
intensificare, *v.t.* To intensify; to make more frequent, to increase.
intensificarsi, *v.r.* To strengthen, to increase.
intensificazione, *n.f.* Intensification.
intensità [-**à**], *n.f.* Intensity, ardour; concentration; severity.
intensivamente, *adv.* Intensively.
intensivo, *a.* Intensive.
intenso, *a.* Intense, vehement; severe; ardent, determined, concentrated; extreme, excessive.
intentamente, *adv.* Intently.
intentare, *v.t.* (*Law*) To bring an action. **— causa a,** to bring an action against.
intentato, *a.* Untried, unattempted.
intento (1), *n.m.* Intent, aim, design, purpose, intention, object.
intento (2), *a.* Intent, fixed, concentrated, earnest, busy.
intenzionale, *a.* Intentional, deliberate, studied.
intenzionalmente, *adv.* Intentionally, deliberately.
intenzionato, *a.* Disposed, inclined. **Bene —,** well-meaning.
intenzione, *n.f.* Intention, design, purpose, intent, aim, object; wish. **Che intenzioni ha?** What is your object? **ho l' intenzione di,** I have a mind to; **avere delle buone intenzioni,** to be well-meaning.
intepidire [cp. **intiepidire**].
interamente, *adv.* Wholly, entirely, quite.
interbinario [interbinArio], *n.m.* (*Rail.*) Space between up and down lines.
intercalare, *v.t.* To intercalate, to insert, to interpolate.
intercalare, *n.m.* Refrain, repeated expression, pet phrase.
intercalare, *a.* Intercalary. **Giorno —,** 29th February in Leap Years.
intercalazione, *n.f.* Interpolation.
intercapedine [intercapEdine], *n.f.* (*Arch.*) Interstice, interval, cavity (between walls).
intercedente, *a.* Interceding.
intercedenza, *n.f.* Mediation, intercedence.
intercedere [intercEdere], *v.i.* To intercede, to plead, to mediate; to intervene (in all senses), to stand between (distance, time, etc.).
intercessione, *n.f.* Intercession, intervention.
intercessore, *n.m.* Intercessor, mediator.
intercettamento, *n.m.* Intercepting, act of interception.
intercettare, *v.t.* To intercept; to seize, to stop; to preclude, to obstruct.
intercettato, intercetto, *p.p.a.* Intercepted.
intercezione, *n.f.* Interception.
interchiudere [interchiUdere], *v.t.* To block up, to close in, to enclose.
intercidere [intercIdere], *v.t.* To cut in two.
intercisamente, *adv.* Interruptedly.
intercisione, *n.f.* Cutting in two, halving.
intercolunnio [intercolUnnio], *n.m.* (*Arch.*) Intercolumniation.

intercomunicante, *a.* Intercommunicating.
intercomunicare, *v.t.* To intercommunicate.
intercorrere [intercOrrere], *v.i.* To intervene, to intercede, to elapse (of time, etc.).
intercostale, *a.* (*Anat.*) Intercostal.
intercutaneo [intercutAneo], *a.* (*Anat.*) Subcutaneous.
interdetto, *n.m.a.* (*Eccles.*) Interdict; prohibited, forbidden; perplexed, perturbed; confused; disqualified.
interdire, *v.t.* To interdict, to prohibit, to forbid; to disable, to disqualify.
interdizione, *n.f.* (*Law*) Interdiction, deprivation of civil rights. (*Mil.*) **Tiro d'—,** barrage, curtain-fire.
interessamento, *n.m.* Interest, concern, sympathy.
interessante, *a.* Interesting, appealing, attractive. (*colloq.*) **Essere in stato —,** to be pregnant.
interessanza, *n.f.* Interest (in a business).
interessare, *v.t.i.* To interest, to concern, to call upon; to affect, to matter; to apply to. **— una persona in un affare,** to associate with a person in a business; **a me non interessa,** it does not matter to me.
interessarsi, *v.r.* To take an interest in, to concern oneself with; to take in hand. **S'interessa troppo dei fatti miei,** he takes too much interest in my affairs.
interessatamente, *adv.* Interestedly, from interested motives.
interessatezza, *n.f.* Self-interest.
interessato, *n.m.* Person concerned; shareholder.
interessato, *a.* Interested, concerned; self-interested, selfish.
interesse, *n.m.* Interest (in all senses), concern; share; self-interest, selfishness. **— composto,** compound interest; **fare il proprio —,** to look after one's own interests; **nell' — di,** in the interests of; **interessi contrastanti,** conflicting interests; **gli interessi decorreranno dal,** interest will be payable from.
interessenza, *n.f.* (*Comm.*) Interest, commission; share; profit-sharing.
interezza, *n.f.* Entirety, entireness, completeness, totality.
interferenza, *n.f.* Interference (in all senses); intermeddling; intervention.
interferire, *v.i.* To interfere; to intervene, to meddle.
interfogliare, *v.t.* To interleave.
interiettivo, *a.* Interjectional.
interiezione, *n.f.* (*Gram.*) Interjection; ejaculation.
interinale, *a.* Temporary, provisional.
interinalmente, *adv.* Temporarily.
interinato, *n.m.* Interim, temporary tenure.
interino, *n.m.* One holding office temporarily.
interiora, *n.f.pl.* Entrails, bowels; butcher's offal.
interiore, *n.m.a.* Interior, internal, inner part.
interiorità [-à], *n.f.* Inner part, interior, inwardness.
interiormente, *adv.* Interiorly.
interito, *a.* Bolt upright; stiff; stock still.
interlinea [interlInea], *n.f.* (*Typ.*) Space between lines, lead.
interlineare, *v.t.* (*Typ.*) To interline, to lead.
interlocutore, *n.m.* Speaker, interlocutor; questioner.
interlocutorio [interlocutOrio], *a.* Interlocutory.
interlocuzione, *n.f.* Interlocution; question.
interloquire, *v.i.* To intervene (in a discussion, etc.), to join in, to chime in, to interject.
interludio [interlUdio], *n.m.* Interlude.
interlunio [interlUnio], *n.m.* Interlunar period; period when the moon is not visible.
intermediario [intermediArio], *n.m.* Medium, agent; go-between, middleman.
intermedio [intermEdio], *a.* Intermediary, middle.
intermettersi [intermEttersi], *v.r.* To intervene, to interfere.
intermezzare, *v.t.* To interpose, to interject.
intermezzo, *n.m.* (*Mus.*) Intermezzo, interlude; interval.
interminabile [interminAbile], *a.* Endless, interminable.
interminabilmente, *adv.* Interminably.
interminato, *a.* Endless, unfinished; (*Poet.*) boundless [cp. **sterminato**].
intermissione, *n.f.* Intermission.
intermittente, *a.* Intermittent, relaxing at intervals.
intermittenza, *n.f.* Intermittence.
internamente, *adv.* Internally.
internamento, *n.m.* Internment. **Campo d'—,** internment camp.
internare, *v.t.* To intern; to place (a lunatic) under restraint.
internarsi, *v.r.* To enter into, to throw oneself into, to identify oneself with; to penetrate, to go deeply into.
internato, *n.m.* Internee; boarder; boarding-school.
internazionale, *n.m.a.* International.
internazionalismo, *n.m.* Internationalism.
internazionalmente, *adv.* Internationally.
interno (1), *n.m.* Interior, inner part, inside. **Ministro dell'—,** Minister of the Interior; **l'— d'una chiesa,** the interior of a church; (*Football*) **gl'interni,** the inside players.
interno (2), *a.* Internal, interior, inner; resident. **Mercato —,** home market; **alunno —,** boarder (at school); **navigazione interna,** inland navigation.
intero, *n.m.a.* Whole, total, totality, entirety; entire, all, complete; (*Math.*) integral. **Per —,** wholly; **un — giorno,** a whole day; **il mondo —,** the whole world.
interpellante, *n.m.a.* Interpellant.
interpellanza, *n.f.* Interpellation, interrogation, question.
interpellare, *v.t.* To interpellate, to question, to summon, to call upon; to apply; (*Law*) to take objection to.
interpetrare [cp. **interpretare**].
interplanetario [interplanetArio], *a.* Interplanetary.
interpolamento, *n.m.* Interpolation.
interpolare, *v.t.* To interpolate, to insert.
interpolatamente, *adv.* At intervals.
interpolazione, *n.f.* Interpolation.
interponimento, *n.m.* Interposition.
interporre, *v.t.* To interpose, to intrude.
interporsi, *v.r.* To interpose, to intervene, to mediate.

interposizione, *n.f.* Interposition, intervention.
interposto, *a.* Interposed. **Per interposta persona,** through the medium of.
interpretabile [interpretAbile], *a.* Explainable, capable of interpretation.
interpretare, *v.t.* To interpret; to explain, to expound, to construe; to represent, to render; (*Theat.*) to act.
interpretativo, *a.* Explanatory.
interpretazione, *n.f.* Interpretation; rendering, version. **Dare una falsa —,** to give a false interpretation; to misunderstand.
interprete [intErprete], *n.m.* Interpreter; commentator. **Parlare a mezzo d'un —,** to speak through an interpreter.
interpunzione, *n.f.* (*Gram.*) Punctuation. **Segni d'—,** punctuation marks.
interramento, *n.m.* Interment, burial; filling up with earth; silting up.
interrare, *v.t.* To inter, to bury, to earth up; to fill up with earth; to silt up.
interrarsi, *v.r.* To silt up.
interregno, *n.m.* Interregnum.
interrimento, *n.m.* [cp. **interramento**].
interrire, *v.i.* [cp. **interrare**].
interrogare, *v.t.* To interrogate, to question; to ask; to consult.
interrogativa, *n.f.* [cp. **interrogatorio**].
interrogativamente, *adv.* Interrogatively.
interrogativo, *a.* Interrogative. **Punto —,** question mark.
interrogatore, *n.m.* Interrogator; questioner.
interrogatorio [interrogatOrio], *n.m.* Examination, cross-examination.
interrogazione, *n.f.* Interrogation, question, enquiry, query.
interrompere [interrOmpere], *v.t.* To interrupt, to break off; to discontinue, to stop; (*Elect.*) to switch off, to disconnect. **— le comunicazioni,** to cut the communications; **— il viaggio,** to break the journey; (*Elect.*) **— la corrente,** to cut off the current.
interrompersi [interrOmpersi], *v.r.* To interrupt oneself; to stop, to cease.
interrompimento, *n.m.* Interruption.
interrottamente, *adv.* Interruptedly.
interrotto, *a.* Interrupted, broken off; blocked (of a road); cut off. **Voce interrotta,** broken voice.
interruttore, *n.m.* Interrupter, heckler; (*Elect.*) switch. **Girare l'—,** switch on (off).
interruzione, *n.f.* Interruption; break; breakdown; interval, gap, stoppage. **Senza —,** uninterruptedly.
intersecare, *v.t.* To intersect, to cut across.
intersecazione, *n.f.* Intersection.
intersezione, *n.f.* Intersection, crossing (of lines, etc.).
interstatale, *a.* (*Pol.*) Inter-state.
interstiziale, *a.* Interstitial.
interstizio [interstIzio], *n.m.* Interstice; space, opening, crevice.
intervallare, *v.t.* To make an interval, to separate, to interspace.
intervallo, *n.m.* Interval; break, gap; space; (*Football*) half-time. **A intervalli,** at intervals.
interveniente, *a.* Intervening.
intervenire, *v.i.* To intervene, to join in, to take part, to attend; to happen, to come to pass. **— a una cerimonia,** to attend a ceremony; **— nella lotta,** to take part in the fight; **intervenne che,** it happened that.
interventista, *n.m.* (*Pol.*) Interventionist.
intervento, *n.m.* Intervention; participation, presence, attendance.
intervenuto, *n.m.* Person present. **Gli intervenuti,** those present, the public.
intervenzione, *n.f.* Intervention.
intervista, *n.f.* Interview.
intervistare, *v.t.* To interview.
interzare, *v.t.* To insert (as a third component).
interzato, *a.* (*Herald.*) **— per palo,** party per pale.
intesa, *n.f.* Agreement, understanding; (*Pol.*) entente. **Secondo l'—,** as agreed upon.
inteso, *p.p.a.* Understood, listened to, heard. **Non darsi per —,** to turn a deaf ear; **siamo intesi,** it is agreed.
intessere [intEssere], *v.t.* To interweave, to weave, to intertwine.
intessitura, *n.f.* Interweaving.
intestare, *v.t.* To head, to place at the head of; to enter (in an account); to register (under a name).
intestarsi, *v.r.* To be obstinate, to stick to one's point; to take it into one's head.
intestato, *a.* (*Comm.*) Registered; (*Law*) intestate; headed (paper).
intestazione, *n.f.* Heading, head-line, title.
intestinale, *a.* (*Anat.*) Intestinal.
intestino, *n.m.* (*Anat.*) Intestine, bowels, entrails.
intestino, *a.* Internal, intestine, domestic. **Lotte intestine,** domestic feuds.
intiepidire, *v.t.* To make lukewarm.
intiepidirsi, *v.r.* To grow lukewarm.
intignarsi, *v.r.* To become moth-eaten.
intimamente, *adv.* Intimately.
intimare, *v.t.* To intimate, to declare; to summon, to enjoin; to notify.
intimazione, *n.f.* Intimation, summons; instruction; notification.
intimidazione, *n.f.* Intimidation.
intimidire, *v.t.* To intimidate, to frighten, to cow.
intimidirsi, *v.r.* To become timid, to grow shy.
intimità [-à], *n.f.* Intimacy; inwardness; privacy; confidence.
intimo [Intimo], *a.* Intimate; internal, inward; close (in friendship, etc.); familiar. **Amico —,** intimate friend; **gli intimi,** the nearest relations.
intimorimento, *n.m.* Frightening, overawing
intimorire, *v.t.* To frighten, to intimidate.
intimorirsi, *v.r.* To be frightened, to be scared.
intingere [intIngere], *v.t.* To dip, to soak; to moisten.
intingolo [intIngolo], *n.m.* Sauce; gravy; ragout; tasty dish.
intinto, *n.m.* Sauce.
intinto, *p.p.a.* Dipped, soaked.
intirannire, *v.i.* To tyrannize.
intirizzire, *v.t.* To benumb with cold, to chill; to freeze.

intisichire, *v.t.i.* To weaken, to impoverish; to languish, to become consumptive.
intitolamento, *n.m.* Naming, entitling.
intitolare, *v.t.* To entitle, to name, to call; to dedicate.
intitolazione, *n.f.* Entitling, title, heading.
intollerabile [intollerAbile], *a.* Intolerable, unbearable.
intollerabilmente, *adv.* Intolerably.
intollerante, *a.* Intolerant.
intollerantemente, *adv.* Intolerantly.
intolleranza, *n.f.* Intolerance.
intombare, *v.t.* To entomb [cp. **seppellire**].
intonacare, *v.t.* To whitewash, to distemper, to plaster.
intonacatura, *n.f.* Whitewashing, distempering; plastering.
intonaco [intOnaco], *n.m.* Plaster. **Dare l'—,** to plaster.
intonare, *v.t.* To intone, to attune, to tune (instruments); (*fig.*) to harmonize, to bring together; to begin a song.
intonarsi, *v.r.* To be in tune (with); to harmonize (with).
intonazione, *n.f.* Intonation.
intonso, *a.* (*Print.*) Untrimmed (of sheets); (*Poet.*) unshorn, unshaven.
intontimento, *n.m.* Giddiness, stupor, shock.
intontire, *v.t.* To stun, to daze, to make giddy or dizzy.
intontirsi, *v.r.* To be stunned, to turn giddy; to be astounded.
intoppamento, *n.m.* Stumbling; obstruction.
intoppare, *v.i.* To stumble; to come across; to be in the way, to obstruct.
intoppo, *n.m.* Obstacle, hitch, hindrance, stumbling-block; obstruction.
intorbidamento, *n.m.* Disturbance (of waters), troubling; muddiness.
intorbidare, intorbidire, *v.t.* To make muddy, to make turbid; to foul; to darken; to confuse.
intorbidarsi, *v.r.* To get muddy, to grow turbid.
intormentimento, *n.m.* Stiffness, cramp.
intormentirsi, *v.r.* To get numbed, to become cramped, to get cramp.
intorniare, *v.t.* To surround.
intorno, *prep.adv.* About, around, round. **Guardarsi d'—,** to look around; **andare —,** to go around; **levati d'—,** go away, leave me alone; **intorno intorno,** on every side, all around; **darsi —,** to trouble oneself about; **— alla vita,** around one's waist.
intorpidimento, *n.m.* Torpidity, numbness; sleepiness.
intorpidire, *v.t.* To weaken, to enervate.
intorpidirsi, *v.r.* To become torpid, to grow torpid, to become benumbed; to grow weak or sleepy.
intortigliare, *v.t.* To twist, to tangle.
intoscanire, *v.t.i.* To make or become like a Tuscan (in speech, etc.).
intossicare, *v.t.* To poison; to intoxicate.
intossicazione, *n.f.* poisoning; intoxication.
intostire, *v.i.* To grow hard.
intozzare, *v.i.* To grow dumpy.
intra [cp. **tra, fra**].
intradosso, *n.m.* (*Arch.*) Intrados.
intraducible [intraducIbile], *a.* Untranslatable.
intrafinefatta, *adv.* (*obs.*) At once, immediately.
intralasciare, *v.t.* To leave off, to neglect, to interrupt [cp. **tralasciare**].
intralciamento, *n.m.* Hindering, hindrance, encumbrance.
intralciare, *v.t.* To entangle, to hinder, to encumber, to embarrass; to impede.
intralcio [intrAlcio], *n.m.* Obstacle, hitch, hindrance.
intramesso, *n.m.* Anything thrust in between; side-dish.
intramettere [intramEttere], *v.t.* To interpose, to put between.
intramettersi [intramEttersi], *v.r.* To interfere; to stand between.
intramezzare, *v.t.* To partition; to alternate; to intermingle; to interpose.
intransigente, *a.* Uncompromising, irreconcilable, intransigent.
intransigenza, *n.f.* Intransigence; uncompromisingness; severity.
intransitivamente, *adv.* Intransitively.
intransitivo, *a.* (*Gram.*) Intransitive.
intrappolare, *v.t.* To entrap, to ensnare; to take in, to deceive.
intrapporre, *v.t.* To interpose [cp. **frapporre**].
intraprendente, *a.* Enterprising; bold, energetic; resourceful.
intraprendenza, *n.f.* Enterprise, initiative, boldness.
intraprendere [intraprEndere], *v.t.* To undertake; to assume; to begin, to start; to set out.
intraprenditore, *n.m.* Contractor; organizer.
intrapresa, *n.f.* Enterprise, undertaking, exploit [cp. **impresa**].
intrasgredibile [intrasgredIbile], *a.* Inviolable.
intrattabile [intrattAbile], *a.* Intractable, unmanageable, refractory; hard, rude, forbidding.
intrattabilmente, *adv.* Intractably.
intrattenere, *v.t.* To entertain; to detain; to amuse; to harbour, to hold in mind; to carry on (a correspondence).
intrattenersi, *v.r.* To linger, to stop, to dwell (upon); to keep company.
intrattenimento, *n.m.* Entertainment, pastime, diversion.
intravedere, intravvedere, *v.t.* To have a glimpse of; to see dimly; to foresee, to anticipate.
intravenoso, *a.* (*Med.*) Intravenous.
intraversare, *v.t.* To cross; to put obstacles in the way of [cp. **traversare**].
intravvenire, *v.i.* To occur, to happen; to intervene.
intrecciare, *v.t.* To intertwine, to interlace, to interweave; to plait; to splice (ropes); to dance, to join hands(in country dancing).
intrecciarsi, *v.r.* To interlace.
intreccio [intrEccio], *n.m.* Intermingling, interlacing; plaiting; plot (of a story).
intregnare, *v.t.* (*Naut.*) To serve (a rope).
intrepidamente, *adv.* Intrepidly.
intrepidezza, intrepidità [-à], *n.f.* Intrepidity, courage, fearlessness, bravery.
intrepido [intrEpido], *a.* Fearless, brave, undaunted, intrepid.
intricamento, *n.m.* Intricacy, complication.

intricare, *v.t.* To entangle, to involve, to complicate, to embroil.
intricarsi, *v.r.* To get entangled, to get embroiled.
intricatamente, *adv.* Intricately.
intricatezza, *n.f.* Intricacy, complication.
intricato, *a.* Intricate, entangled.
intridere [intrIdere], *v.t.* To kneed, to mix, to temper.
intridimento, *n.m.* Kneading.
intrigante, *n.m.a.* Intriguer, meddler, busybody; intriguing.
intrigare, *v.i.* To intrigue, to plot; to meddle, to interfere.
intrigarsi, *v.r.* To meddle (with), to become mixed up (in).
intrigatamente, *adv.* Interferingly.
intrigo, *n.m.* Intrigue, plot, conspiracy. (*colloq.*) **Fiutare l'—,** to smell a rat.
intrigone, *n.m.* Meddler, busybody.
intrinsecamente, *adv.* Intrinsically.
intrinsecarsi, *v.r.* To be intimately connected with; to penetrate deeply (into).
intrinseco [intrInseco], *a.* Intrinsic, real; familiar, intimate.
intrinsichezza, *n.f.* Intimacy.
intriso, *n.m.* Paste, mixture.
intriso, *p.p.a.* Soaked, drenched, imbued (with blood, etc.) [cp. **intridere**].
intristimento, *n.m.* Growing sickly; fading away.
intristire, *v.i.* To grow sickly; to wither, to droop; to pine away; to grow melancholy.
introdotto, *p.p.a.* Introduced, shown in, admitted, let in.
introducimento, *n.m.* Introduction, entry.
introdurre, *v.t.* To introduce, to bring in; to let in; to show in; to import into; to insert. **Introducetelo,** show him in.
introdursi, *v.r.* To introduce oneself; to penetrate; to intrude; to creep in; to break in.
introduttivo, *a.* Introductory.
introduttore, *n.m.* Introducer.
introduttorio [introduttOrio], *a.* Introductory.
introduzione, *n.f.* Introduction (in all senses).
introgolamento, *n.m.* Spilling, messing.
introgolare, *v.t.* To spill (upon), to make a mess on.
introgolone, *n.m.* One who spills; careless eater.
introitare, *v.t.* To cash in, to receive cash, to collect (money).
introito [intrOito], *n.m.* Profit, return, yield, proceeds, takings; (*Eccles.*) introit.
intromessa, *n.f.* Intervention, intrusion.
intromettersi [intromEttersi], *v.r.* To meddle with, to interfere, to intervene; to mediate.
intromissione, *n.f.* Intromission, interference; intervention, mediation; intrusion.
intronamento, *n.m.* Deafening, stunning.
intronare, *v.t.* To deafen, to stun with noise.
intronata, *n.f.* Deafening noise; exorbitant demand.
intronataggine [intronatAggine], *n.f.* Daze, stupor.
intronato, *a.* Deafened, stunned; thunderstruck.
intronfiare, *v.i.* To grow haughty.
intronfiatura, *n.f.* Haughtiness.
intronizzare, *v.t.* To enthrone.
introrso, *a.* Turned inwards.
introspezione, *n.f.* Introspection.
introvabile [introvAbile], *a.* Not to be found, undiscoverable.
intrudere [intrUdere], *v.t.* To intrude, to thrust in.
intrudersi [intrUdersi], *v.r.* To intrude, to interfere.
intrufolarsi, *v.r.* To creep in, to poke about, to interlope, to intrude.
intrugliare, *v.t.* To mix, to concoct.
intruglio [intrUglio], *n.m.* Hotch-potch, bad mixture, mash, medley; jumble, mess.
intrupparsi, *v.r.* To join company with, to mix with; to assemble; to troop.
intrusione, *n.f.* Intrusion, interference.
intruso, *n.m.* Intruder, interloper.
intuffamento, *n.m.* Dipping.
intuffare, *v.t.* To dip, to steep, to soak.
intugliare, *v.t.* (*Naut.*) To bend hawsers to one another; to shackle (a chain).
intuire, *v.t.* To perceive by intuition; to guess, to sense.
intuitivamente, *adv.* Intuitively.
intuitivo, *a.* Intuitive, intuitional; clear, evident.
intuito [intUito], *n.m.* Intuition, intuitiveness.
intuizione, *n.f.* Intuition.
intumescente, *a.* Swelling.
intumescenza, *n.f.* Swelling, tumefaction.
intumidire, inturgidire, *v.i.* To swell, to inflate.
inuguale, *a.* Unequal [cp. **ineguale**].
inulto, *a.* (*Lit.*) Unavenged.
inumanamente, *adv.* Inhumanly.
inumanità [-à], *n.f.* Inhumanity.
inumano, *a.* Inhuman, barbarous, savage
inumare, *v.t.* Inhume, to bury, to inter.
inumazione, *n.f.* Inhumation, interment.
inumidimento, *n.m.* Moistening.
inumidire, *v.t.* To moisten, to wet, to damp.
inumidirsi, *v.r.* To get wet. **Gli s'inumidirono gli occhi,** his eyes filled.
inurbamento, *n.m.* Becoming a town-dweller.
inurbanamente, *adv.* Impolitely, rudely.
inurbano, *a.* Impolite, rude, ill-mannered.
inurbarsi, *v.r.* To become a town-dweller.
inusato, *a.* Obsolete, unusual.
inusitatamente, *adv.* Unusually.
inusitato, *a.* Obsolete, unusual.
inutile [inUtile], *a.* Useless; vain, fruitless, futile.
inutilità [-à], *n.f.* Uselessness, inutility.
inutilmente, *adv.* Uselessly, vainly.
inuzzolire, *v.t.* To excite one's desire, to make one's mouth water.
invadente, *a.* Encroaching, invading; pushing (of a person).
invadere [invAdere], *v.t.* To invade, to intrude, to break in; to violate; to trespass.
invaghimento, *n.m.* Falling in love.
invaghire, *v.t.* To attract, to charm.
invaghirsi, *v.r.* To fall in love (with); to become enamoured of; to grow to like.
invalere, *v.i.* To come into fashion, to become prevalent.
invalidabile [invalidAbile], *a.* Capable of being validated.
invalidamente, *adv.* Invalidly.

invalidare, *v.t.* To invalidate, to make void.
invalidazione, *n.f.* Invalidation.
invalidità [-à], *n.f.* Invalidity.
invalido [invAlido], *n.m.* Invalid, infirm person; (*Mil.*) disabled soldier.
invalido [invAlido], *a.* Invalid (in all senses); void.
invaligiare, *v.t.* To pack up *or* in.
invallarsi, *v.r.* (*Geog.*) To flow down into a valley.
invalso, *a.* Prevalent, current; established. **L'uso —,** current usage.
invanire, *v.t.* To make vain *or* useless.
invanirsi, *v.r.* To become vain, to grow conceited.
invano, *adv.* In vain, vainly, to no purpose.
invarcabile [invarcAbile], *a.* Impassable.
invarcabilmente, *adv.* Impassably.
invariabile [invariAbile], *a.* Invariable, unchangeable, inalterable.
invariabilità [-à], *n.f.* Invariableness.
invariabilmente, *adv.* Invariably.
invariatamente, *adv.* Unvariedly.
invariato, *a.* Unvaried.
invasamento, *n.m.* Infatuation; obsession.
invasare (1), *v.t.* To obsess, to possess.
invasare (2), *v.t.* To pot, to put in a vase; (*Naut.*) to put a ship upon the cradle.
invasatura, *n.f.* (*Naut.*) Launching-cradle.
invasazione, *n.f.* Obsession, possession; potting; (*Naut.*) putting on the cradle.
invasione, *n.f.* Invasion; inroad, irruption.
invasore, *n.m.* Invader.
invecchiamento, *n.m.* Growing old, ageing; ripening.
invecchiare, *v.t.* To make old; to age; to make one look old.
invecchiarsi, *v.r.* To make oneself look old; to grow old, to age.
invecchiato, *a.* Old, aged.
invece, *adv.prep.* Instead, instead of; on the contrary.
inveire, *v.i.* To inveigh (against), to rail at, to cast abuse at; to revile.
invelare, *v.t.* (*Naut.*) To put on a press of sail.
invelenimento, *n.m.* [cp. **avvelenamento**].
invelenire, *v.t.* To poison, to embitter, to envenom [cp. **avvelenare**].
invendibile, *a.* Unsaleable, unmarketable.
invendibilità [-à], *a.* Unsaleableness.
invendicato, *a.* Unpunished, unrevenged.
invenduto, *a.* Unsold.
inventamento, *n.m.* [cp. **invenzione**].
inventare, *v.t.* To invent; to contrive, to devise; to discover; to find out; to forge, to fabricate.
inventariare, *v.t.* To inventory, to catalogue.
inventario [inventArio], *n.m.* Inventory, stocktaking. (*fig.*) **Con beneficio d'—,** with reservations, for what it is worth.
inventatamente, *adv.* Without foundation, by means of fabrication.
inventato, *a.* Invented, false, fabricated; (*Lit.*) discovered, found.
inventiva, *n.f.* Inventiveness, inventive faculty.
inventivo, *a.* Inventive.
inventore, *n.m.* Inventor.
invenustà [-à], *n.f.* Inelegance; lack of space.
invenustamente, *adv.* Inelegantly.
invenusto, *a.* Inelegant, graceless.
invenzione, *n.f.* Invention. **Diritto d'—,** patent rights; **brevetto d'—,** patent.
inverdire, *v.i.* To become green, to turn green.
inverecondamente, *adv.* Immodestly.
inverecondia [inverecOndia], *n.f.* Immodesty.
inverecondo, *a.* Immodest, shameless.
inverisimigliante, *a.* Improbable, unlikely.
inverisimile [cp. **inverosimile**].
invermigliare, *v.t.i.* To redden, to grow red.
invermigliarsi, *v.r.* To blush, to go red.
inverminare, inverminire, *v.i.* To turn maggotty.
invernale, *a.* Wintry, winter.
invernata, *n.f.* Winter-time, winter (as a period); long winter.
inverniciamento, *n.m.* Varnishing.
inverniciare, *v.t.* To varnish.
inverniciatore, *n.m.* Varnisher.
inverniciatura, *n.f.* Varnishing, coat of varnish; (*fig.*) smattering.
inverno, *n.m.* Winter. **Nel cuore dell'—,** in the depth of winter; **d'—,** in winter-time; **passare l'—,** to winter.
invero, *adv.* Indeed, truly.
inverosimiglianza, *n.f.* Unlikeliness, improbability.
inverosimile [inverosImile], *a.* Unlikely, improbable, not true to life.
inverosimilmente, *adv.* Improbably.
inversamente, *adv.* Inversely.
inversione, *n.f.* Inversion; (*Mech.*) reversal.
inverso (1), *a.* Inverted, inverse, contrary. **In senso —,** in the opposite direction; **all'—,** backwards.
inverso (2), *adv.* (*obs.*) Towards [cp. **verso**].
invertebrato, *n.m.a.* Invertebrate.
invertibile [invertIbile], *a.* Reversible, invertible.
invertire, *v.t.* To invert, to reverse, to transpose.
invescare, *v.t.* To entrap, to ensnare.
invescarsi, *v.r.* (*Lit.*) To fall in love, to 'fall for'; to be drawn into.
investigabile [investigAbile], *a.* Open to investigation.
investigare, *v.t.* To investigate, to enquire (into); to search, to examine, to trace out.
investigativo, *a.* (*Law*). Investigating. **Agente —,** detective.
investigatore, investigatrice, *n.m.f.* Investigator, researcher.
investigazione, *n.f.* Investigation, research, inquiry.
investimento, *n.m.* Collision, crash, traffic accident; (*Comm.*) investment.
investire, *v.t.* To invest (in all senses); to empower; to knock down; to collide with; to run over or into; (*Naut.*) to foul; to ram.
investirsi, *v.r.* To enter into thoroughly; to collide with; (*Naut.*) to run aground.
investitore, investitrice, *n.m.f.* One who collides; (*Comm.*) investor.
investitura, *n.f.* Investiture, installation.
inveterato, *a.* Inveterate, obdurate.
invetriamento, *n.m.* Glazing.
invetriare, *v.t.* To glaze.
invetriata, *n.f.* Glass window, glass door; glazed frame; skylight.
invetriatura, *n.f.* Glaze, glazing.
invettiva, *n.f.* Invective.

invettivamente, *adv.* Abusively.
inviare, *v.t.* To send; to forward, to dispatch, to transmit; to ship.
inviato, *n.m.* Envoy, emissary. **— speciale,** special correspondent.
invidia [invIdia], *n.f.* Envy. **Per —,** out of envy.
invidiabile [invidiAbile], *a.* Enviable, to be envied.
invidiare, *v.t.* To envy, to be envious of.
invidiosamente, *adv.* Enviously.
invidioso, *a.* Envious.
invido [Invido], *a.* (*Lit.*) Envious.
invietire, *v.i.* To become rancid.
invigilare, *v.t.* To watch, to supervise, to invigilate.
invigliacchire, *v.i.* To turn coward.
invigorimento, *n.m.* Invigoration.
invigorire, *v.t.* To strengthen, to invigorate.
invigorirsi, *v.r.* To gain strength, to become stronger.
invilimento, *n.m.* Lowering, degradation; fall in prices.
invilire, *v.t.i.* To lower, to degrade; to depress, to dishearten; to become of no account, to lose heart; (*Comm.*) to fall (of prices).
invillanire, *v.i.* To become rude.
inviluppamento, *n.m.* Enveloping, wrapping.
inviluppare, *v.t.* To wrap up, to envelope, to hide; (*fig.*) to confuse.
inviluppo, *n.m.* Envelopment; tangle; parcel; covering, wrapper.
invincibile [invincIbile], *a.* Invincible, unconquerable.
invincibilità [-à], *n.f.* Invincibility.
invincibilmente, *adv.* Invincibly.
invio [invIo], *n.m.* Sending, forwarding; remittance (of money); consignment (of goods), shipment (by sea); the things sent, package, parcel.
inviolabile [inviolAbile], *a.* Inviolable.
inviolabilità [-à], *n.f.* Inviolability.
inviolabilmente, *adv.* Inviolably.
inviperire, *v.t.i.* To enrage, to grow bitter.
inviperirsi, *v.r.* To grow angry, to become embittered.
inviscerarsi, *v.r.* To plunge deeply into a subject.
invischiare [cp. **invescare**].
inviscidire, *v.i.* To become sticky.
invisibile [invisIbile], *a.* Invisible, imperceptible.
invisibilità [-à], *n.f.* Invisibility.
invisibilmente, *adv.* Invisibly.
inviso, *a.* Disliked, unpopular; hated.
invispire, *v.i.* To become brisk.
invitabile [invitAbile], *a.* Suitable for invitation.
invitante, *a.* Inviting, attractive.
invitare (1), *v.t.* To invite, to ask, to bid, to request; to call upon; to solicit, to beg.
invitare (2), *v.t.* To screw up [cp. **avvitare**].
invitato, *n.m.* Guest.
invito, *n.m.* Invitation; request; offer; attraction. **Ricusare un —,** to decline an invitation; **biglietto d'—,** invitation card.
invittamente, *adv.* Unconquerably.
invitto, *a.* Unconquered, unvanquished; unconquerable.
inviziarsi, *v.r.* To become vicious.
invocabile [invocAbile], *a.* Invocable.
invocare, *v.t.* To invoke, to implore, to appeal to; to solicit, to entreat.
invocativo, *a.* Invocatory.
invocatorio [invocatOrio], *a.* Invocatory, imploring.
invocazione, *n.f.* Invocation, entreaty, appeal.
invogliante, *a.* Appealing, attractive.
invogliare, *v.t.* To inspire with a wish, to make one wish; to tempt, to lead, to draw, to attract.
invoglio [invOglio], *n.m.* Wrapper; bundle.
involamento, *n.m.* Stealing, carrying off.
involare, *v.t.* To steal, to carry off.
involarsi, *v.r.* To steal away, to vanish, to disappear, to fly away.
involatore, involatrice, *n.m.f.* Thief.
involgere [invOlgere], *v.t.* To envelop, to wrap up; to involve, to comprise.
involgersi [invOlgersi], *v.r.* To wrap oneself up; to get involved.
involgimento, *n.m.* Wrapping up.
involontariamente, *adv.* Involuntarily.
involontario [involontArio], *a.* Involuntary, unintentional; excusable.
involpire, *v.i.* To become cunning, to get foxy.
involtare, *v.t.* To wrap up, to envelop, to enwrap.
involtata, *n.f.* Wrapping.
involto, *n.m.a.* Parcel, package, bundle; wrapped up; involved.
involtura, *n.f.* Wrapping, tying up.
involucro [invOlucro], *n.m.* Cover, covering, envelope, wrapper.
involuto, *a.* Involute, intricate, involved. **Uno stile —,** an involved style.
involuzione, *n.f.* Involution.
invulnerabile [invulnerAbile], *a.* Invulnerable.
invulnerabilità [-à], *n.f.* Invulnerability.
invulnerabilmente, *adv.* Invulnerably.
inzaccherare, *v.t.* To splash with mud, to bemire.
inzaccherarsi, *v.r.* To get muddy.
inzafardare, *v.t.* To smear.
inzaffare, *v.t.* To stuff.
inzavorrare, *v.t.* To load with ballast.
inzeppamento, *n.m.* Wedging; cramming.
inzeppare, *v.t.* To wedge; to fill, to cram.
inzeppatura, *n.f.* Wedge.
inzoccolato, *a.* Wearing clogs.
inzolfamento, *n.m.* Dressing with sulphur.
inzolfare, *v.t.* (*Agric.*) To dress with sulphur.
inzolfatura, *n.f.* Sulphuring.
inzotichire, *v.i.* To become boorish, to be clownish.
inzuccarsi, *v.r.* To get drunk; to fall madly in love; to be obstinate.
inzuccherare, *v.t.* To sugar, to sweeten; (*fig.*) to cajole.
inzuccheratura, *n.f.* Sprinkling with sugar; sweetening.
inzuppamento, *n.m.* Dipping, soaking.
inzuppare, *v.t.* To dip, to soak, to drench; to moisten, to steep.
inzupparsi, *v.r.* To get soaked, to get drenched (with rain, etc.), to get wet through.
inzuppato, *a.* Soaked, drenched; (*colloq.*) drunk.
io, *pron.* I. **Sono io,** it is I; **ve lo dico io,** I assure you; **io stesso,** I myself.

iodio [iOdio], *n.m.* (*Chem.*) Iodine.
iodoformio [iodofOrmio], *n.m.* Iodoform.
ioduro, *n.m.* (*Chem.*) Iodide.
Iokoama, *n.f.* Yokohama.
iole, *n.f.* (*Naut.*) Gig, jolly-boat, yawl.
ionico [iOnico], *a.* Ionic.
ionio [iOnio] (1), *n.m.a.* Ionian.
ionio [iOnio] (2), *n.m.* (*Chem.*) Ionium.
ionizzare, *v.t.* (*Chem.*) To ionize.
iono, ione, *n.m.* (*Elect.*) Ion.
iosa, *adv.* **A iosa,** in abundance, in great abundance, in plenty.
iosciamina, *n.f.* (*Chem.*) Hyoscin.
iota, *n.m.* Iota, jot. **Non saper un —,** to know less than nothing.
ipallage [ipAllage], *n.f.* (*Gram.*) Hypallage.
iperbole [ipErbole], *n.f.* (*Geom.*) Hyperbola; (*Gram.*) hyperbole.
iperboleggiare, *v.t.* To use hyperboles.
iperbolicamente, *adv.* Hyperbolically.
iperbolico [iperbOlico], *a.* Hyperbolic, bombastic, high-flown.
iperboreo [iperbOreo], *a.* (*Lit.*) Hyperborean, northern.
ipercritica [ipercrItica], *n.f.* Hypercriticism.
ipercritico [ipercrItico], *n.m.a.* Hypercritic, hypercritical; (*colloq.*) highbrow.
ipertrofia [ipertrofIa], *n.f.* (*Med.*) Hypertrophy.
ipnosi, *n.f.* Hypnosis.
ipnotico [ipnOtico], *a.* Hypnotic.
ipnotismo, *n.m.* Hypnotism.
ipnotista (*pl.* **ipnotisti**), *n.m.* Hypnotist.
ipnotizzare, *v.t.* To hypnotize.
ipoclorito, *n.m.* (*Chem.*) Hyperchloride.
ipocondria [ipocondrIa], *n.f.* (*Med.*) Hypochondria.
ipocondriaco [ipocondrIaco], *a.* Hypochondriac(al).
ipocrisia [ipocrisIa], *n.f.* Hypocrisy, dissembling, simulation.
ipocrita (*pl.* **ipocriti**) [ipOcrita], *n.m.* Hypocrite, dissembler.
ipocritamente, *adv.* Hypocritically.
ipocrito [ipOcrito], *a.* Hypocritical.
ipodermico [ipodErmico], *a.* (*Med.*) Hypodermic.
ipofosfito, *n.m.* (*Chem.*) Hypophosphite.
ipogastrico [ipogAstrico], *a.* (*Med.*) Hypogastric.
ipogeo [ipogEo], *n.m.* Hypogeum.
iposolfito, *n.m.* (*Chem.*) Hyposulphite.
ipostasi [ipOstasi], *n.f.* (*Eccles.*) Hypostasis.
ipoteca, *n.f.* Mortgage. **Gravato d'—,** mortgaged.
ipotecabile [ipotecAbile], *a.* Mortgageable.
ipotecare, *v.t.* To mortgage.
ipotecario [ipotecArio], *a.* Concerning mortgage. **Creditore —,** mortgagee; **debitore —,** mortgager.
ipotenusa, *n.f.* (*Geom.*) Hypotenuse.
ipotesi [ipOtesi], *n.f.* Hypothesis, conjecture. **nella migliore delle —,** at the best.
ipoteticamente, *adv.* Hypothetically.
ipotetico [ipotEtico], *a.* Hypothetical, conjectural.
ippica [Ippica], *n.f.* Horse-racing.
ippico [Ippico], *a.* Pertaining to horses. **Corse ippiche,** horse-races.
ippocampo, *n.m.* (*Zool.*) Sea-horse; (*Myth.*) hippocampus.
ippocastano, *n.m.* (*Bot.*) Horse-chestnut tree.
ippodromo [ippOdromo], *n.m.* Hippodrome, race-course.
ippofago [ippOfago], *n.m.* Eater of horseflesh.
ippopotamo [ippopOtamo], *n.m.* (*Zool.*) Hippopotamus.
iprite, *n.f.* (*Chem.Mil.*) Mustard gas.
ipsilon [Ipsilon], *n.m.* Letter Y.
ira, *n.f.* Anger, wrath, fury, ire. **L'— di Dio,** the wrath of God; (*colloq.*) **un'— di Dio,** pandemonium.
irace, *n.m.* (*Zool.*) Rock-rabbit.
iracondamente, *adv.* Wrathfully.
iracondia [iracOndia], *n.f.* Anger, wrath.
iracondo, *a.* Wrathful, wroth, irate, angry; hot-headed.
iranico [irAnico], *n.m.a.* Iranian.
irascibile [irascIbile], *a.* Irascible.
irascibilità [-à], *n.f.* Irascibility.
irascibilmente, *adv.* Irascibly.
iratamente, *adv.* Irately, angrily.
irato, *a.* Irate, angry.
irco, *n.m.* (*Zool.*) He-goat, billy-goat.
ire, *v.i.* (*Poet.*) To go, to depart.
iridare, *v.t.* To make iridescent
iride [Iride], *n.f.* Iris.
iridescente, *a.* Iridescent.
iridescentemente, *adv.* Iridescently.
iridescenza, *n.f.* Iridescence.
iridio [irIdio], *n.m.* (*Chem.*) Iridium.
Irlanda, *n.f.* Ireland.
irlandese, *n.m.a.* Irishman; Irish. **Gli irlandesi,** the Irish.
ironia [ironIa], *n.f.* Irony, sarcasm. **— della sorte,** irony of fate.
ironicamente, *adv.* Ironically.
ironico [irOnico], *a.* Ironical, ironic.
ironizzare, *v.t.* To use irony.
irosamente, *adv.* Wrathfully, irefully, angrily.
iroso, *a,* Wrathful, angry, enraged, irate.
irraccontabile [irraccontAbile], *a.* Not worth telling.
irradiamento, *n.m.* Irradiation, radiation.
irradiante, *a.* Radiant.
irradiare, *v.t.* To irradiate, to shed light upon; to radiate, to issue, to proceed (from a central point.)
irradiarsi, *v.r.* To shine, to brighten up, to irradiate.
irradiazione, *n.f.* Irradiation; radiation.
irraggiare, *v.t.* To irradiate.
irraggiungibile [irraggiungIbile], *a.* Out of reach, unattainable.
irragionevole [irragionEvole], *a.* Unreasonable, unreasoning, absurd.
irragionevolezza, *n.f.* Unreasonableness.
irragionevolmente, *adv.* Unreasonably.
irrancidire, *v.i.* To turn rancid *or* sour.
irrappresentabile [irrappresentAbile], *a.* Unactable, impossible to represent.
irrazionale, *a.* Irrational, illogical; **numeri irrazionali,** irrational numbers.
irrazionalità [-à], *n.f.* Irrationality.
irrazionalmente, *adv.* Irrationally.
irreale, *a.* Unreal.
irrealmente, *adv.* Unreally.
irrealtà [-à], *n.f.* Unreality.
irreclamabile [irreclamAbile], *a.* Unreclaimable.
irreconciliabile [irreconciliAbile], *a.* Irreconcilable.

irreconciliabilmente, *adv.* Irreconcilably.
irrecuperabile [irrecuperAbile], *a.* Unrecoverable; irrecoverable.
irrecuperabilmente, *adv.* Irrecoverably.
irrecusabile [irrecusAbile], *a.* Undeniable, impossible to refuse; irrefutable.
irrecusabilmente, *adv.* Undeniably.
irredentismo, *n.m.* (*Pol.*) Irredentism.
irredentista (*pl.* **irredentisti**), *n.m.* (*Pol.*) Irredentist.
irredento, *a.* (*Pol.*) Unredeemed (territory, population).
irrefragabile [irrefragAbile], *a.* Irrefragable; indisputable, unanswerable.
irrefrenabile [irrefrenAbile], *a.* Unrestrainable, impossible to curb.
irrefrenabilmente, *adv.* Unrestrainably.
irrefutabile [irrefutAbile], *a.* Irrefutable, undeniable.
irrefutabilità [-à], *n.f.* Irrefutability.
irrefutabilmente, *adv.* Irrefutably.
irreggimentare, *v.t.* To form into a regiment; to incorporate, to group.
irregolare, *a.* Irregular (in all senses).
irregolarità [-à], *n.f.* Irregularity.
irregolarmente, *adv.* Irregularly.
irregolatamente, *adv.* In an unregulated manner.
irregolato, *a.* Unregulated.
irreligione, *n.f.* Irreligion.
irreligiosamente, *adv.* Irreligiously.
irreligiosità [-à], *n.f.* Irreligiousness.
irreligioso, *a.* Irreligious.
irremediabile [irremediAbile], *a.* Irremediable.
irremissibile [irremissIbile], *a.* Irremissible; unpardonable.
irremovibile [irremovIbile], *a.* Immovable, relentless, obdurate.
irremovibilità [-à], *n.f.* Immovability, obduracy.
irremovibilmente, *adv.* Immovably, relentlessly.
irrendevole [irrendEvole], *a.* Unyielding, inflexible.
irrendevolezza, *n.f.* Unyieldingness.
irreparabile [irreparAbile], *a.* Irreparable.
irreperibile [irreperIbile], *a.* Undiscoverable, not to be found (again).
irreprensibile [irreprensIbile], *a.* Irreproachable.
irreprensibilmente, *adv.* Irreproachably.
irrepugnabile [irrepugnAbile], *a.* Unquestionable, irrefutable.
irrequietamente, *adv.* Restlessly, unquietly.
irrequietezza, *n.f.* Restlessness, inquietude.
irrequieto, *a.* Restless, unquiet, fidgety.
irrequietudine [irrequietUdine], *n.f.* Restlessness, inquietude.
irresistibile [irresistIbile], *a.* Irresistible.
irresistibilmente, *adv.* Irresistibly.
irresolutamente, *adv.* Irresolutely.
irresolutezza, *n.f.* Irresoluteness, hesitation.
irresoluto, *a.* Irresolute, hesitating, undecided.
irresolvibile [irresolvIbile], *a.* Unsolvable.
irresponsabile [irresponsAbile], *a.* Irresponsible, untrustworthy.
irresponsabilità [-à], *n.f.* Irresponsibility.
irresponsabilmente, *adv.* Irresponsibly.
irrestringibile [irrestringIbile], *a.* Unshrinkable.
irretire, *v.t.* To ensnare, to net, to entrap.
irrevocabile [irrevocAbile], *a.* Irrevocable, immutable, unalterable.
irrevocabilità [-à], *n.f.* Immutability, irrevocability.
irrevocabilmente, *adv.* Irrevocably.
irriconciliabile [irriconciliAbile], *a.* Irreconcilable.
irriconoscibile [irriconoscIbile], *a.* Unrecognizable.
irriconoscibilmente, *adv.* Unrecognizably.
irridere [irrIdere], *v.t.* To mock, to laugh at, to deride, to rail at, to scoff at.
irriducibile [irriducIbile], *a.* Irreducible, uncompromising, unbending.
irriducibilmente, *adv.* Irreducibly.
irriflessione, *n.f.* Thoughtlessness.
irriflessivamente, *adv.* Thoughtlessly.
irriflessivo, *a.* Thoughtless.
irrigabile [irrigAbile], *a.* Capable of irrigation.
irrigare, *v.t.* To irrigate, to water.
irrigatore, *n.m.* Irrigator.
irrigazione, *n.f.* Irrigation.
irrigidimento, *n.m.* Stiffening.
irrigidire, *v.t.* To stiffen.
irrigidirsi, *v.r.* To become stiff, to stiffen, to harden; (*fig.*) to resist, to stiffen (one's attitude).
irriguo [irrIguo], *a.* Well-watered.
irrilevante, *a.* Irrelevant.
irrimediabile [irrimediAbile], *a.* Irremediable; irretrievable.
irrimediabilmente, *adv.* Irremediably.
irrisione, *n.f.* Mockery, derision, railery.
irrisivo, *a.* Derisory, scornful.
irrisore, *n.m.* Mocker, scoffer.
irrisoriamente, *adv.* Derisively.
irrisorio [irrisOrio], *a.* Derisive, scornful; paltry. **Una somma irrisoria,** a paltry amount.
irrispettoso, *a.* Disrespectful.
irritabile [irritAbile], *a.* Irritable.
irritabilità [-à], *n.f.* Irritability.
irritabilmente, *adv.* Irritably.
irritante, *a.* Irritating, galling, aggravating.
irritare, *v.t.* To irritate, to provoke, to enrage, to excite; to fret, to annoy.
irritarsi, *v.r.* To become irritated, to grow angry; to worry.
irritazione, *n.f.* Irritation, anger; inflammation.
irrito [Irrito], *a.* (*Law*) Void, of no effect.
irritrattabile [irritrattAbile], *a.* Unretractable.
irritrosirsi, *v.r.* To become stubborn.
irriverente, *a.* Irreverent.
irriverentemente, *adv.* Irreverently.
irriverenza, *n.f.* Irreverence.
irrobustimento, *n.m.* Strengthening.
irrobustire, *v.t.* To strengthen, to invigorate, to fortify.
irrobustirsi, *v.r.* To grow stronger, to gain strength.
irrompere [irrOmpere], *v.i.* To rush in, to burst forth, to burst in; to break through, to overflow.
irrorare, *v.t.* To bedew; to irrigate.
irruente, *a.* Rushing, dashing, vehement impetuous.
irruenza, *n.f.* Vehemence; dash.
irruginirsi, *v.r.* To rust, to become rusty, to grow rusty.
irruvidire, *v.t.* To roughen, to make rough.

irruvidirsi, *v.r.* To become rough.
irruzione, *n.f.* Irruption, inroad, inrush.
irsuto, *a.* Hairy, bristly, shaggy, hirsute.
irto, *a.* Bristling, shaggy; erect, standing on end; full, crammed. **— di difficoltà,** bristling with difficuities; **— di citazioni,** bristling with quotations; **capelli irti,** hair standing on end.
isabella, *a.* **Color —,** light bay (of horses).
Isacco, *n.m.* Isaac.
isagoge [isAgoge], *n.f.* (*Lit.*) Introduction.
isagono [isAgono], *a.* (*Geom.*) Isogonic.
Isaia [isAia], *n.m.* Isaiah.
Iscariota, *n.m.* Iscariot.
ischeletrito, *a.* Reduced to a skeleton.
ischio [Ischio], *n.m.* (*Anat.*) Hip, hip-joint.
iscritto, *n.m.* Member, registered member.
iscritto, *a.* Registered, enlisted; inscribed. **In —,** in writing.
iscrivere [iscrIvere], *v.t.* To register; to subscribe, to inscribe.
iscriversi [iscrIversi], *v.r.* To register oneself; to join; to enlist.
iscrizione, *n.f.* Inscription, registration; enlistment; entry (for an examination, competition, etc.); **Modulo d'—,** entry form; **tassa d'—,** entrance fee.
Iside [Iside], *n.f.* Isis.
Islam, *n.m.* Islam.
islamismo, *n.m.* Islamism, Mohammedanism.
islamita (*pl.* **islamiti**), *n.m.* Mohammedan.
islamitico [islamItico], *a.* Mohammedan, Islamic.
Islanda, *n.f.* Iceland.
islandese, *n.m.a.* Icelander, Icelandic.
Ismaele, *n.m.* Ishmael.
isobara [isObara], *n.f.* Isobar.
isocrono [isOcrono], *a.* Isochronous.
isogono [isOgono], *a.* (*Geom.*) With equal angles.
isoipsa, *n.f.* (*Geog.*) Contour line.
isola [Isola], *n.f.* Island, isle; block of houses.
isolamento, *n.m.* Isolation, solitude, loneliness; (*Elect.*) insulation. **— acustico,** sound-proofing.
isolano, *n.m.a.* Islander; insular.
isolante, *a.* Isolating; (*Elect.*) insulating. **Nastro —,** insulating-tape.
isolare, *v.t.* To isolate, to cut off, to seclude; (*Elect.*) to insulate.
isolatamente, *adv.* Separately, apart.
isolato, *n.m.* Block of houses.
isolatore, *n.m.* (*Elect.*) Insulator.
isolazionista (*pl.* **isolazionisti**), *n.m.* (*Pol.*) Isolationist.
isoletta, isolotto, *n.f.m.* Islet.
isomerico [isomErico], *a.* (*Chem.*) Isomeric.
isoscele [isOscele], *a.* (*Geom.*) Isosceles.
isoterma, *n.f.* (*Geog.*) Isotherm.
isotopo [isOtopo], *n.m.* Isotope.
ispanico, *a.* Hispanic, Spanish.
ispettivo, *a.* Speculative; concerned with inspection.
ispettorato, *n.m.* Inspectorship; inspector's office.
ispettore, ispettrice, *n.m.f.* Inspector, surveyor, superintendent.
ispezionare, *v.t.* To inspect, to make an inspection.
ispezione, *n.f.* Inspection, supervision.
ispidamente, *adv.* Shaggily.
ispido [Ispido], *a.* Shaggy, bristling, hairy.
ispirare, *v.t.* To inspire, to infuse, to instil.
ispiratamente, *adv.* With inspiration, in an inspired manner.
ispirazione, *n.f.* Inspiration.
Israele, *n.m.* Israel.
israelita (*pl.* **israeliti**), *n.m.a.* Jewish, Israelite.
issare, *v.t.* To hoist (a flag, etc.); to heave up, to lift.
issopo, *n.m.* Hyssop.
istallare [cp. **installare**].
istantanea, *n f.* snapshot.
istantaneamente, *adv.* Instantaneously.
istantaneità [-à], *n.f.* Instantaneousness.
istantaneo [istantAneo], *a.* Instantaneous.
istante, *n.m.* Instant, moment; (*Law*) petitioner. **Sull'—,** immediately.
istante, *a.* Urgent, instant.
istantemente, *adv.* Instantly.
istanza, *n.f.* Petition, application; request, solicitation, entreaty; instance; (*Law*) question in a trial. **A — di,** at the instance of; **fare istanze,** to entreat.
isteria [isterIa], *n.f.* (*Med.*) Hysteria.
isterico [istErico], *a.* Hysterical.
isterilire, *v.t.* To sterilize; to make sterile.
isterilirsi, *v.r.* To be sterilized, to be made immune.
isterismo, *n.m.* Hysteria.
istesso, *a.* Same, like [cp. **stesso**].
istigare, *v.t.* To instigate, to incite.
istigazione, *n.f.* Instigation.
istillare [cp. **instillare**].
istintivamente, *adv.* Instinctively.
istintivo, *a.* Instinctive.
istinto, *n.m.* Instinct.
istituire, *v.t.* To institute, to found, to set up, to create, to establish.
istituto, *n.m.* Institute, college, school; foundation, institution, establishment.
istitutore, istitutrice, *n.m.f.* Tutor, preceptor; governess.
istituzione, *n.f.* Institution, foundation, institute, establishment.
istmo, *n.m.* Isthmus.
istologia [istologIa], *n.f.* Histology.
istologico [istolOgico], *a.* Histological.
istoria [istOria], *n.f.* History, story.
istoriare, *v.t.* To decorate, to paint with scenes from history or fiction.
istoriato, *a.* Storied; embellished.
istoriografo [istoriOgrafo], *n.m.* Historiographer.
istradamento, *n.m.* Directing, initiation, putting wise.
istradare, *v.t.* To direct; to put on the right path; to initiate.
istrice [Istrice], *n.m.* (*Zool.*) Porcupine.
istrione, *n.m.* Comedian; ham actor, histrion, clown.
istrionico [istriOnico], *a.* Histrionic.
istruire, *v.t.* To instruct, to teach, to educate; to inform, to advise. (*Law*) **— un processo,** to prepare a case.
istruito, *a.* Cultured, educated, accomplished.
istrumentale, *a.* Instrumental.
istrumentalmente, *adv.* Instrumentally.
istrumentare, *v.t.* (*Mus.*) To instrument; (*Law*) to draw up a contract [cp. **strumentare**].
istrumento, *n.m.* Tool, implement; (*Mus.*) instrument; (*Law*) deed, instrument.

istruttivamente, *adv.* Instructively, helpfully.
istruttivo, *a.* Instructive, illuminating, helpful.
istrutto, *a.* Instructed.
istruttore, *n.m.* Instructor, teacher. **Giudice —,** examining judge; **— militare,** drill sergeant.
istruttoria [istruttOria], *n.f.* (*Law*) Judicial enquiry.
istruttorio [istruttOrio], *a.* (*Law*) Preliminary.
istruzione, *n.f.* Instruction: knowledge, learning; education, teaching; direction, order.
istupidire, *v.t.* To make stupid; to bamboozle; to besot.
istupidirsi, *v.r.* To grow silly, to become foolish.
istupidito, *a.* Stupid, besotted.
Itaca [Itaca], *n.f.* Ithaca.
Italia [itAlia], *n.f.* Italy.
italianamente, *adv.* In the Italian way; like an Italian.
italianista (*pl.* **italianisti**), *n.m.* Italian scholar, one versed in Italian scholarship.
italianità [-à], *n.f.* Italian national character, spirit, or feelings.
italianizzare, *v.t.* To Italianize.
italiano, *n.m.a.* Italian.
italico [itAlico], *n.m.* (*Print.*) Italics.
italico [itAlico], *a.* Italian, Italic.
italo [Italo], *a.* Italian. **Italo-britannico,** Italo-British.
iterare, *v.t.* To iterate, to repeat.
iteratamente, *adv.* Repeatedly.
iterazione, *n.f.* Iteration, repetition.
itinerario [itinerArio], *n.m.* Itinerary, route. **Che — segui?** Which route do you take?
ito, *p.p.a.* Gone [cp. **ire**].
itterico [ittErico], *n.m.a.* Jaundiced (person or condition); affected with jaundice.
itterizia [itterIzia], *n.f.* (*Med.*) Jaundice.
ittiolo, *n.m.* (*Chem.*) Ichthyol.
ittiologia [ittiologIa], *n.f.* Ichthyology.
ittiologo [ittiOlogo], *n.m.* Ichthyologist.
ittiosauro [ittiosAuro], *n.m.* (*Zool.*) Ichthyosaurus.
iucca, *n.f.* (*Bot.*) Yucca.
iugero [iUgero], *n.m.* Land-measure (about ¼ acre).
Iugoslavia [iugoslAvia], *n.f.* Yugoslavia.
iugoslavo, *n.m.a.* Yugoslav.
iugulare, *a.* (*Anat.*) Jugular.
iugulo [iUgulo], *n.m.* (*Anat.*) Jugular.
iuniore, *n.m.a.* Junior.
iuta, *n.f.* (*Bot.*) Jute.
iutificio [iutifIcio], *n.m.* Jute factory.
Iutland, *n.m.* Jutland.
ivi, *adv.* There, in that place; then.
izza, *n.f.* (*Lit.*) Wrath, rancour.

J

J, j, *n.m.* Almost obsolete letter of the Italian alphabet, known as **i lungo**. Seldom employed in modern Italian, it was formerly used in diphthongs, *e.g.* **lavatojo**, and in the plural of words ending in "io", *e.g.* **lavatoj**. See introduction to letter I.

K

K, k, *n.m.f.* (kappa). This is not properly a letter of the Italian alphabet, in which its sound is represented by "c" or "ch". It occurs in certain foreign words and in the abbreviations **kg, km, kl** for Kilogramme, Kilometre, and Kilolitre.

L

L, l, *n.f.* Tenth letter of the Italian alphabet.
la (1), *def.art.* The (used before a feminine noun in the singular beginning with a consonant), *pl.* **le.**
la (2), *pron.* Her, it. **La vidi,** I saw her.
la (3), *n.m.* (*Mus.*) A, la. **Dare il la,** to set the fashion, to set the tone (of a conversation, etc.); to give the note.
là (4), *adv.* There, yonder. **Al di là di,** beyond, outside; **là oltre,** further on; **essere in là con gli anni,** to be getting on in years; **qua e là,** here and there.
labaro [lAbaro], *n.m.* Standard, banner; (*Hist.*) labarum.
labbrata, *n.f.* Smack on the lips with the back of the hand.
labbro, (*pl.* **labbri,** *m.,* **labbra,** *f.*), *n.m.* Lip; brim, border, edge. **— leporino,** hare-lip; **mordersi le labbra,** to bite one's lips.
labbrone, *n.m.* Thick-lipped person.
labdacismo, *n.m.* Lambdacism.
labe, *n.f.* (*Poet.*) Stain.
laberinto [cp. **labirinto**].
labiale, *n.m.a.* Labial.
labiata, *a.* (*Bot.*) Labiate.
labile [lAbile], *a.* Slippery, unsteady; fleeting, transitory; weak.
labilità [-à], *n.f.* Unsteadiness; weakness, feebleness.
labirinto, *n.m.* Labyrinth, maze.
laboratorio [laboratOrio], *n.m.* Laboratory; work-room, work-shop.
laboriosamente, *adv.* Laboriously.
laboriosità [-à], *n.f.* Laboriousness, industry.
laborioso, *a.* Laborious, industrious, assiduous, hard-working; toilsome, painful.
labrace, *n.m.* (*Zool.*) Bass.
laburismo, *n.m.* (*Pol.*) Labour.
laburista (pl. **laburisti**), *n.m.* (*Pol.*) Labour member, member of Labour Party.
lacca (1), *n.f.* Lacquer. **Cera —,** sealing-wax; **— in scaglia,** shellac.
lacca (2), *n.f.* (*Poet.*) Hollow, cavity; (*Anat.*) buttock.
laccare, *v.t.* To lacquer.
laccetto, *n.m.* String, lace, bootlace; (*colloq.*) sweetbread.
lacchè [-è], *n.m.* Valet, lackey, footman, man-servant, flunkey.
lacchezzo, *n.m.* Tit-bit.
lacciaia, *n.f.* Lasso.
laccio [lAccio], *n.m.* Lace, string; noose, snare; trap. **Tendere un —,** to lay a snare; **prendere al —,** to entrap, to catch in a trap; **lacci delle scarpe,** boot-laces.
lacciolo, *n.m.* Snare (for birds).
lacerabile [lacerAbile], *a.* Tearable.
laceramento, *n.m.* Tearing, laceration; wound.

lacerante, *a.* Tearing, rending. **Un grido —,** a rending cry.
lacerare, *v.t.* To tear, to rend, to lacerate; to harrow; to mangle. **— il cuore,** to rend one's heart.
laceratura, *n.f.* Laceration.
lacerazione, *n.f.* Tearing, rending, laceration; wound, cut.
lacero [lAcero], *a.* Worn-out, torn, in tatters, in rags.
lacerto, *n.m.* Sinew; muscular part of arm, biceps.
laconicamente, *adv.* Laconically.
laconicità [-à], *n.f.* Conciseness.
laconico [lacOnico], *a.* Laconic, concise, pithy.
laconismo, *n.m.* Laconic way of speaking.
lacrima, lagrima [lAcrima, lAgrima], *n.f.* Tear; (*fig.*) drop. **Piangere a calde lacrime,** to shed scalding tears; **scoppiare in lagrime,** to burst into tears; **colle lagrime agli occhi,** with tears in one's eyes.
lacrimabile, lacrimevole [lacrimAbile, lacrimEvole], *a.* Pitiful, lamentable.
lacrimale, lagrimale, *a.* Lachrymal.
lacrimare, lagrimare, *v.i.* To weep, to cry, to lament; (*fig.*) to trickle.
lacrimogeno [lacrimOgeno], *a.* Lachrymatory. **Gas —,** tear-gas; (*Mil.*) **bomba lacrimogena,** tear-shell.
lacrimosamente, *adv.* Tearfully, mournfully.
lacrimoso, lagrimoso, *a.* Tearful, mournful, lachrymose.
lacuale, *a.* Lacustral, pertaining to a lake.
lacuna, *n.f.* Gap, lacuna, interval; interruption. **Colmare una —,** to fill a gap.
lacunoso, *a.* Incomplete, deficient; full of blanks.
lacustre, *a.* Lacustrial; (*Geol.*) lacustrine.
ladano [lAdano], *n.m.* Kind of aromatic gum.
laddove, *adv.* Where, there; whereas, while, whilst.
ladino, *a.* Romansch, Ladin (spoken in the Engadine and Grisons); easy, smooth.
ladra, *n.f.* Woman thief.
ladreria [ladrerIa], *n.f.* Theft, robbery.
ladresco, *a.* Thievish.
ladro, *n.m.* Thief, robber; pickpocket. **Al ladro!** Stop thief!
ladro, *a.* Thievish; wretched; cruel, horrible; (*fig.*) bewitching, seductive. **Occhi ladri,** bewitching eyes; **una fame ladra,** a gnawing hunger.
ladrocinio [ladrocInio], *n.m.* Robbery on a big scale.
ladronaia [ladronAia], *n.f.* Nest of thieves.
ladronata, *n.f.* Robbery, piece of thievishness.
ladroncello, *n.m.* Petty thief, pilferer.
ladrone, *n.m.* Robber, highwayman.
ladroneccio [ladronEccio], *n.m.* Larceny, theft; unjust exaction.
ladroneria [ladronerIa], *n.f.* Theft, burglary, robbery.
ladronescamente, *adv.* Like a thief; burglariously.
ladronesco, *a.* Thievish.
ladruncolo [ladrUncolo], *n.m.* Petty thief, pilferer.
laggiù, *adv.* Down there, down below; yonder.
laghetto, *n.m.* Small lake; pond.
laghigiano, *n.m.* (*Hist.*) Lake-dweller.
lagna, *n.f.* (*Lit.*) Torment; complaint.
lagnanza, *n.f.* Complaint, censure, charge. **Sporgere delle lagnanze,** to lodge a complaint.
lagnarsi, *v.r.* To complain, to censure, to criticize, to object; to moan, to murmur.
lagno, *n.m.* Wailing, lamentation, groan.
lago, *n.m.* Lake, pool. (*Anat.*) **— del cuore,** ventricle.
lagrima [cp. **lacrima**]
laguna, *n.f.* Lagoon.
lagunare, *a.* Pertaining to lagoons.
lai, *n.m.pl.* Lamentations; (*Poet.*) lays.
laicale, *a.* Laic, lay.
laicato, *n.m.* Laity.
laicità [-à], *n.f.* Secularity, state of being laical.
laicizzare, *v.t.* To laicize.
laico [lAico], *n.m.a.* Lay, layman; secular, laic. **Frate —.** lay-brother; **i laici,** the laity.
laidamente, *adv.* In an ugly way, dishonestly.
laidezza, *n.f.* Foulness, filthiness, obscenity.
laido [lAido], *a.* Ugly, repellent; filthy, obscene, foul.
laidume, *n.m.* Filthiness; rubbish.
lama (1), *n.f.* Blade; knife, sword. **— di rasoio,** razor-blade.
lama (2), *n.f.* Sheet of water; morass; marsh; lowland.
lama (3), *n.m.* Lama, Buddhist priest.
lama (4), *n.m.* (*Zool.*) Llama.
lambente, *a.* Lapping (of water), skimming, touching lightly; lambent (of flame).
lambiccare, *v.t.* To distil.
lambiccarsi, *v.r.* **— il cervello,** to rack one's brains.
lambiccato, *a.* (*fig.*) Mannered, affected, overcoloured.
lambicco, *n.m.* (*Chem.*) Retort, alembic.
lambimento, *n.m.* Grazing, touching lightly.
lambire, *v.t.* To graze, to skim, to brush lightly; to lap (of water); to glide over.
lambrusca, lambrusco, *n.f.m.* Kind of vine; wine made from it.
lamella, *n.f.* Thin plate, lamella.
lamellare, *a.* Lamellar.
lamentabile [lamentAbile], *a.* Lamentable.
lamentare, *v.t.* To lament, to mourn; to complain, to deplore.
lamentarsi, *v.r.* To complain, to groan, to lament.
lamentazione, *n.f.* Lamentation, complaint, wailing.
lamentela, *n.f.* Complaint, lament.
lamentevole [lamentEvole], *a.* Lamentable, plaintive, doleful, mournful; regrettable.
lamentevolmente, *adv.* Lamentably, mournfully.
lamentio [lamentIo], *n.m.* Moaning, groaning, lamentation.
lamento, *n.m.* Lament, wailing; groan, moan; complaint; censure.
lamentosamente, *adv.* Mournfully, dolefully; complainingly.
lamentoso, *a.* Plaintive, mournful, doleful.
lamia [lAmia], *n.f.* Witch; (*Zool.*) variety of shark.
lamiera, *n.f.* Sheet-iron, metal plate. **— cilindrata,** rolled plate; **— ondulata,** corrugated sheet-iron.

lamina [lAmina], *n.f.* Lamina, thin plate, sheet (of metal).
laminare, *v.t.* To laminate, to beat or roll into thin plates.
laminatoio [laminatOio], *n.m.* Rolling-mill.
laminatura, *n.f.* Rolling (of metal).
lamio [lAmio], *n.m.* (*Bot.*) Dead-nettle.
lampa, *n.f.* (*Poet.*) Lamp.
lampada, *n.f.* Lamp, lantern, light; lamp-post. **— ad arco,** arc-lamp; **— di sicurezza,** safety-lamp; **— chiusa,** hurricane-lamp.
lampadario [lampadArio], *n.m.* Chandelier.
lampadina, *n.f.* Small lamp, electric-light bulb. **— tascabile,** pocket flashlight.
lampante, *a.* Clear, patent, manifest; shining.
lampeggiamento, *n.m.* Lightning, sheet lightning; flash.
lampeggiare, *v.i.* To lighten, to flash, to shine. **Lampeggia,** it is lightning
lampeggio [lampEggio], *n.m.* Lightning, sheet lightning; flash.
lampionaio [lampionAio], *n.m.* Lamplighter.
lampioncino, *n.m.* Small lamp; fairy lamp; paper-lantern.
lampione, *n.m.* Street-lamp, lamp-post; lamp, lantern.
lampista (pl. **lampisti**), *n.m.* Lamp-trimmer; lamp-lighter.
lampisteria [lampisterIa], *n.f.* Lamp room, lamp store.
lampo, *n.m.* Lightning, sheet lightning; flash. **In un —,** in a flash.
lampone, *n.m.* (*Bot.*) Raspberry.
lampreda, *n.f.* (*Zool.*) Lamprey.
lampredotto, *n.m.* (*Zool.*) Young lamprey; minced offal, tripe.
lana, *n.f.* Wool. **— pettinata,** worsted; **tessuto di —,** woollen material; (*fig.*) **una buona —,** a scamp, a rogue.
lanaiolo, *n.m.* Operative in a woollen mill.
lanceolato, *a.* Lanceolate.
lancetta, *n.f.* Lancet; hand of a clock or watch; (*Naut.*) launch.
lancia [lAncia], *n.f.* Spear, lance; (*Naut.*) launch, cutter, jolly-boat. **Spezzare una — per,** to take up the cudgels for; **una — spezzata,** a free-lance; **una buona —** a good fighter; **— d'un tubo,** nozzle of a hose; **— a benzina,** motor-boat; **— di salvataggio,** life-boat; **— a vapore,** steam-launch.
lanciabombe, *n.m.* (*Mil.*) Trench-mortar, bomber.
lanciaflamme, *n.m.* (*Mil.*) Flame-thrower.
lanciamento, *n.m.* Hurling, throwing; (*Comm.*) floating a company. (*Naut.*) launching.
lanciare, *v.t.* To hurl, to throw, to fling; to rush, to dash; to advertise, to launch (a company, etc.); to float (a loan; (*Sport*) to deliver (a ball); to fly (a kite); (*Aviat.*) to drop (bombs); (*Aviat.*) to catapult (a plane). **— una pietra,** to throw a stone; **— un'idea,** to make a suggestion, to throw out a hint; **— un attacco,** to launch an attack.
lanciarsi, *v.r.* To hurl oneself, to fling oneself, to dash, to rush; (*fig.*) to launch, to embark upon. (*Aviat.*) **— col paracadute,** to bale out.
lanciasiluri, *n.m.* (*Naut.*) Torpedo-tube.
lanciata, *n.f.* Blow with a lance; thrust.
lanciere, *n.m.* Lancer.
lanciero, *n.m.* Lancers (dance).

lancinante, *a.* Shooting (pain); stabbing, throbbing. **Dolore —,** shooting pain.
lancio [lAncio], *n.m.* Throwing, cast, throw (distance thrown); spring, bound; (*fig.*) launching, advertisement, puff; discharge (of torpedo, etc.). (*Aviat.*) **Pista di —,** runway.
landa, *n.f.* Moor, heath, barren land.
landò [-ò], *n.m.* Landau.
laneria [lanerIa], *n.f.* Woollen goods, woollens.
lanetta, *n.f.* Coarse or cheap wool; (*fig.*) sly fellow.
languente, *a.* Languishing, slack, drooping.
languidamente, *adv.* Languidly.
languidezza, *n.f.* Languidness, faintness.
languido [lAnguido], *a.* Languid, faint, weak, slack, drooping; lackadaisical.
languimento, *n.m.* Languor.
languire, *v.i.* To languish, to pine away; to decline, to fall off, to fade, to flag; to be stagnant. **La conversazione languiva,** the conversation flagged.
languore, *n.m.* Languor, languidness, lassitude, faintness.
laniere, *n.m.* Wool manufacturer.
lanificio [lanifIcio], *n.m.* Wool factory; wool manufacture.
lano, *a.* Woollen.
lanolina, *n.f.* Lanolin.
lanosità [-à], *n.f.* Woolliness.
lanoso, *a.* Woolly; hairy.
lanterna, *n.f.* Lantern, lamp; light-house; (*Arch.*) lantern, sky-light. **— cieca,** dark lantern; **— ad olio,** oil lamp; **— magica,** magic lantern; (*Tech.*) **— del cilindro,** control end of cylinder; (*fig.*) **mostrar lucciole per lanterne,** to gull, to make out geese as swans.
lanternino, *n.m.* Small lantern. (*fig.*) **Cercare col —,** to search carefully.
lanternone, *n.m.* Big lantern; (*fig.*) long, lank fellow.
lanugine [lanUgine], *n.f.* Soft hair, down.
lanuginoso, *a.* Downy.
lanuto, *a.* Woolly.
lanzichenecco, lanzo, *n.m.* (*Hist.*) Lansquenet; pikeman.
Laocoonte, *n.m.* (*Myth.*) Laocoon.
laonde, *adv.* (*obs*). Whence, therefore.
lapalissiano, *a.* Patent, obvious, superficial.
laparatomia [laparatomIa], *n.f.* (*Med.*) Laparatomy.
lapazio [lapAzio], *n.m.* (*Bot.*) Sorrel.
lapida [lApida], *n.f.* Stone slab (over a well, etc.).
lapidare, *v.t.* To stone; to persecute.
lapidaria [lapidAria], *n.f.* Science of reading inscriptions, epigraphy.
lapidario [lapidArio], *a.* Lapidary, monumental; sententious, pithy; terse.
lapidazione, *n.f.* Stoning.
lapide [lApide], *n.f.* Tablet, stone slab; tombstone, headstone. **— commemorativa,** memorial tablet.
lapidiscente, *a.* Petrifying.
lapidificare, *v.t.* To turn into stone.
lapillo, *n.m.* Small pebble; volcanic ash.
lapis, *n.m.* Lead pencil, pencil; crayon. **Temperare il —,** to sharpen a pencil.
lapislazzuli [lapislAzzuli], *n.m.* Lapislazuli.
lappe, *adv.* **Far —,** to smack one's lips greedily, to make one's mouth water.

lappola [lAppola], *n.f.* (*Bot.*) Burdock; (*fig.*) bore, nuisance.
lappone, *n.m.a.* Lapp, Laplander.
Lapponia [lappOnia], *n.f.* Lapland.
lardaiuolo, *n.m.* Pork butcher, bacon-seller.
lardellare, *v.t.* To lard, to stuff with bacon; (*fig.*) to interlard.
lardello, *n.m.* Slice of bacon; piece of fat.
lardite, *n.f.* French chalk; tailor's chalk.
lardo, *n.m.* Fat bacon, fat (esp. of pig), lard. **Fetta di —,** rasher of bacon.
lardone, *n.m.* Bacon, salt-pork.
lardoso, *a.* Fat (of meat).
larenzia [larEnzia], *n.f.* (*Zool.*) Carpet-moth.
largamente, *adv.* Widely, broadly, amply, abundantly.
largare, *v.t.* To widen; (*Naut.*) to spread (sail); to push off (from the shore), to get under way.
largheggiamento, *n.m.* Profuseness, liberality.
largheggiare, *v.t.i.* To abound; to give freely, to be bountiful; to give ample room, scope or permission; to be open-handed.
largheggiatore, largheggiatrice, *n.m.f.* Open-handed person.
larghezza, *n.f.* Breadth, broadness, width; bounty, liberality; largeness, scope, extent. **La — delle sue vedute,** his breadth of vision; **— di un fiume,** width of a river; **ventri metri di —,** twenty metres broad.
largire, *v.t.* To give liberally, to grant [cp. **elargire**].
largizione, *n.f.* Gift, donation, largesse.
largo, *n.m.* Breadth, width; open space; city square; (*Naut.*) offing. **Fare —,** to make room; **Fate largo!** Make way! Move on!; **farsi —,** to make one's way; **prendere il —,** to slink away; (*Naut.*) to stand for the offing, to stand out to sea; **dieci miglia al —,** 10 miles out to sea; **stare alla larga da,** to keep clear of; **Alla larga!** Keep away! Stand clear! || *a.* Broad, wide, large, extensive, ample; liberal, generous. **In lungo e in —,** on all sides, length and breadth, far and wide; **— dieci metri,** ten metres wide; **di manica larga,** easy-going; **— di spalle,** broad-shouldered; **larga differenza,** wide difference.
largura, *n.f.* Space, wide extent.
lari, *n.m.pl.* Lares, household goods; (*fig.*) family.
larice [lArice], *n.m.* (*Bot.*) Larch.
laringe, *n.f.* (*Anat.*) Larynx.
laringite, *n.f.* (*Med.*) Laryngitis.
laringoscopio [laringoscOpio], *n.m.* Laryngoscope.
laringotomia [laringotomIa], *n.f.* (*Med.*) Laryngotomy.
larva, *n.f.* Ghost, phantom; sham; (*Zool.*) Larva.
larvare, *v.t.* To disguise, to hide, to conceal.
larvatamente, *adv.* Disguisedly.
lasagne, *n.f.pl.* Variety of macaroni.
lasagnone, *n.m.* Blockhead, dunce.
lasca, *n.f.* (*Zool.*) Roach.
lascare, *v.t.* (*Naut.*) To slacken (a rope).
lasciapassare, *n.m.* Pass, permit.
lasciare, *v.t.* To leave, to quit, to abandon, to forsake; to allow, to let, to suffer, to permit; to bequeath; to omit, to leave off. **Lascialo parlare,** let him speak; **lascia fare a me,** leave it to me; **lasciò tutto all'ospedale,** he bequeathed everything to the hospital; **ha lasciato detto che,** he left word that; **lascialo stare,** leave him alone; **lasciare in asso,** to leave in the lurch; **— a desiderare,** to be unsatisfactory; **— fare,** to let things alone; **— in pace,** to let someone alone; **— andare,** to let things slide, to neglect; **— in libertà,** to set free; **— la porta aperta,** to leave the door open (in all senses); **— cadere,** to drop, to let fall; **— il paese,** to leave the country.
lasciarsi, *v.r.* To part; to allow oneself (to be seen, etc.). **Ci lasciammo,** we parted.
lascito, *n.m.* Legacy, bequest.
lascivamente, *adv.* Lasciviously, lustfully.
lascivia [lascIvia], *n.f.* Lasciviousness, lust, lewdness.
lascivo, *a.* Lascivious, lustful, wanton, lewd, unchaste.
lasco, *a.* (*Naut.*) Slack, slight. **Vento —,** slight wind.
lassativo, *n.m.a.* (*Med.*) Laxative.
lassezza, lassitudine, *n.f.* Lassitude, weariness, languor.
lasso, *n.m.* Lapse of time, period.
lasso, *a.* Weary, tired; miserable. **Ahi, lasso!** Alas!
lassù, *adv.* Up there, there above.
lastra, *n.f.* Slab, sheet, flag, flag-stone, plate (metal); glass, window-pane; (*Phot.*) glass negative. **Un pacchetto di lastre fotografiche,** a box of photographic plates; **una lastra di ghiaccio,** a slab of ice.
lastricamento, *n.m.* Paving with stones.
lastricare, *v.t.* To pave with stones, to flag.
lastrico, lastricato [lAstrico], *n.m.* Pavement, flag, flag-stone. **Trovarsi sul —,** to be reduced to beggary, to be in the gutter.
lastrone, *n.m.* Large plate; slab.
latamente, *adv.* Widely.
latebra, *n.f.* Recess, hiding-place.
latente, *a.* Latent; dormant; potential.
latentemente, *adv.* Latently.
laterale, *a.* Lateral, side. **Carrozzino —,** side-car.
lateralmente, *adv.* Laterally.
lateranense, *a.* Lateran.
laterano, *n.m.a.* Lateran (church and palace).
laterizio [laterIzio], *n.m.a.* Brick; building material. **Fabbrica di laterizi,** brick-kiln.
latezza, *n.f.* Wideness, width.
latice [lAtice], *n.f.* (*Bot.*) Latex.
latifondista, *n.m.* Great landowner, landed proprietor.
latifondo, *n.m.* Large landed property, large estate.
latinamente, *adv.* In the Latin style, in Latin.
latineggiante, *a.* Latinizing.
latinismo, *n.m.* Latinism.
latinista (*pl.* **latinisti**), *n.m.* Latinist, Latin scholar.
latinità [-à], *n.f.* Latinity.
latinizzare, *v.t.* To Latinize.
latino, *n.m.a.* Latin. **Capire il —,** to take a hint; **— maccheronico,** dog Latin; **— volgare,** Vulgar Latin, spoken Latin; **saper di —,** to have some Latin, to be accomplished; **vela latina,** lateen sail.
latitante, *n.m.a.* Absconder (from justice). absconding, fugitive. **Rendersi —,** to abscond.
latitanza, *n.f.* The state of being a fugitive (from justice).

latitudinario [latitudinArio], *a.* (*Eccles.*) Latitudinarian.
latitudine, *n.f.* Latitude; breadth, extension, comprehensiveness.
lato (1), *n.m.* Side (in all senses). **Sedere al—,** to sit beside; **dormire sul — destro,** to sleep on one's right side; **da un —, dal — l'altro,** on the one hand, on the other; **in ogni —,** everywhere; **dai due lati,** on both sides.
lato (2), *a.* Wide, broad, extensive. **In senso —,** in a broad sense.
latomia [latomIa, latOmia], *n.f.* (*Hist.*) Stone-quarry.
latore, *n.m.* Bearer (of a letter).
latramento, *n.m.* Barking; howling.
latrare, *v.i.* To bark, to howl.
latrato, *n.m.* Bark.
latria [latrIa], *n.f.* (*Eccles.*) Worship and reverence due to God alone.
latrina, *n.f.* Latrine, water-closet; public lavatory.
latrinaio [latrinAio], *n.m.* Public lavatory attendant.
latrocinio [latrocInio], *n.m.* Larceny, theft.
latta, *n.f.* Sheet-tin, tin plate, tinned iron; tin, can. **Scatola di —,** tin box; **articoli di —,** tin ware; **in latte,** in tins, in cans.
lattaia [lattAia], *n.f.* Milkmaid; good milker (cow).
lattaio [lattAio], *n.m.* Milkman.
lattaiolo, *n.m.* (Child's) milk-tooth.
lattante, *n.m.a.* Sucking, suckling, babe; unweaned.
lattare, *v.t.* To suckle [cp. **allattare**].
latte, *n.m.* Milk. **Fratello di —,** foster-brother; **— acido,** sour milk; **— condensato,** condensed milk; **— di pesce,** soft roe.
lattemiele, *n.m.* Whipped cream.
latteo [lAtteo], *a.* Milky. **Via Lattea,** Milky Way; **dieta lattea,** milk diet.
latteria [latterIa], *n.f.* Dairy (farm or shop).
lattescente, *a.* Lactescent.
latticini, *n.m.pl.* Dairy produce.
lattico [lAttico], *a.* (*Chem.*) Lactic.
lattiera, *n.f.* Milk-jug.
lattifero [lattIfero], *a.* Lactiferous.
lattiginoso, *a.* Milky, lacteous.
lattime, *n.m.* (*Med.*) Infantile eczema.
lattivendolo [lattivEndolo], *n.m.* Milkman.
lattoniere, *n.m.* Tinsmith.
lattonzolo [lattOnzolo], *n.m.* Sucking pig or calf.
lattuga, *n.f.* (*Bot.*) Lettuce; (*Hist.*) ruff, ruff collar.
lauda, laude [lAuda-e] (*pl.* **laudi**), *n.f.* Canticle, hymn of praise.
laudabile [laudAbile], *a.* Praiseworthy, laudable.
laudano [lAudano], *n.m.* Laudanum.
laudare, *v.t.* [cp. **lodare**].
laudativo, laudatorio [laudatOrio], *a.* Laudatory.
laudese, *n.m.* (*Hist.*) Singer of lauds, friar.
laurea [lAurea], *n.f.* Academical degree, doctorate; diploma; (*Poet.*) laurel. **Prendere la —,** to take one's degree.
laureando, *n.m.* Undergraduate (in final year), candidate for a degree.
laureare, *v.t.* To confer a degree (on).
laurearsi, *v.r.* To graduate, to take one's degree.
laureato, *n.m.a.* Graduate, laureate. **— in legge,** bachelor of law; **egli si è — in medicina,** he took a degree in medicine.
Laurenziana, *n.f.* Laurentian library in Florence.
lauretano, *a.* Of Loreto.
laureto, *n.m.* Laurel shrubbery.
lauro [lAuro], *n.m.* Laurel tree; bay.
lautamente, *adv.* Sumptuously, richly; abundantly.
lautezza, *n.f.* Abundance, plenty; generosity, sumptuousness.
lauto [lAuto], *a.* Sumptuous, bountiful, splendid, liberal; rich.
lava, *n.f.* (*Geol.*) Lava.
lavabile [lavAbile], *a.* Washable.
lavabo, *n.m.* Wash-stand, wash-hand-basin; lavatory; (*Eccles.*) lavabo, wash-basin.
lavacapo, *n.m.* Scolding.
lavacro, *n.m.* Bath; fountain; font; (*fig.*) purification, laving.
lavaggio [lavAggio], *n.m.* Washing, cleansing.
lavagna, *n.f.* Slate, blackboard. **Scrivere sulla —,** to write on the blackboard.
lavamano, *n.m.* Wash-hand-basin.
lavanda (1), *n.f.* Washing; (*Eccles.*) washing of the feet on Maundy Thursday.
lavanda (2), *n.f.* (*Bot.*) Lavender.
lavandaia [lavandAia], *n.f.* Washerwoman, laundress. **Mandare alla —,** to send to the wash; **il conto della —,** laundry bill.
lavanderia [lavanderIa], *n.f.* Laundry.
lavandino, *n.m.* Scullery sink; wash basin.
lavapiatti, *n.m.* Dish-washer, scullion.
lavare, *v.t.* To wash, to cleanse; to purify. (*fig.*) **— la testa,** to reprimand; **— i piatti,** to wash up; **una mano lava l'altra,** let's help one another.
lavarsi, *v.r.* To wash oneself. **— le mani,** to wash one's hands.
lavata, *n.f.* Washing. **— di testa, — di capo,** severe reprimand.
lavativo, *n.m.* (*Med.*) Enema, syringe, clyster; (*colloq.*) nuisance, bore.
lavatoio [lavatOio], *n.m.* Wash-house, wash-tub.
lavatrice, *n.f.* Washing machine.
lavatura, *n.f.* Washing; dish-water.
laveggio [lavEggio], *n.m.* Kind of saucepan.
lavina, *n.f.* Landslide.
lavorabile [lavorAbile], *a.* Workable.
lavoracchiare, *v.i.* To work carelessly or unwillingly.
lavoraccio [lavorAccio], *n.m.* Bad work.
lavorante, *n.m.f.* Worker, operative, "hand".
lavorare, *v.t.i.* To work, to labour; to drudge; to apply oneself; to be employed with; to study. **— a cottimo,** to do piece-work; **— a giornata,** to work by the day; **— la terra,** to till the soil; **— sott'acqua,** to work underhand.
lavorativo, *a.* Working; of work; (*Agric.*) tillable. **Giorno —,** working day; **ore lavorative,** working hours.
lavorato, *p.p.a.* Worked, wrought; ornate; cultivated. **Prodotti lavorati,** finished products.
lavoratore, lavoratrice, *n.m.f.* Workman, workwoman.
lavoratore, *a.* Working. **Le classi lavoratrici,** the working classes.

lavorazione, *n.f.* Workmanship, working; manufacture; (*Agric.*) cultivation.
lavorio [lavorIo], *n.m.* Continuous work, labouring, activity, action.
lavoro, *n.m.* Work, labour; toil, effort; job, occupation, employment; piece of work, task. **Senza —,** unemployed; **— gravoso,** drudgery, hard work; **— a cottimo,** piece-work; **— manuale,** manual labour; **eccesso di —,** overwork; **mettersi al —,** to set to work; **— d'ago,** needlework; **— in legno,** woodwork; **camera del —,** trade union; **lavori forzati,** hard labour.
lavorone, *n.m.* Important work.
lavoruccio [lavorUccio], *n.m.* Paltry job, useless task.
Lazio, *n.m.* (*Geog.*) Latium.
lazzaretto, *n.m.* Fever-hospital, lazaretto.
Lazzaro [lAzzaro], *n.m.* Lazarus.
lazzarone, *n.m.* (Neapolitan) beggar, loafer, vagabond.
lazzo, *n.m.* Buffoonery, drollery, jest, practical joke.
lazzo, *a.* Tart, sour, sharp.
le, *art.f.pl.* The. **Le case,** the houses.
le, *pron.* To her; them. **Le parlai,** I spoke to her; **le incontrai,** I met them.
leale, *a.* Loyal; fair, honest, trusty, true.
lealismo, *n.m.* Loyalism.
lealmente, *adv.* Loyally.
lealtà [-à], *n.f.* Loyalty, fidelity, honesty, trustiness.
leardo, *a.* Grey (of a horse).
lebbra, *n.f.* (*Med.*) Leprosy.
lebbroso, *n.m.a.* Leper; leprous.
leccamento, *n.m.* Licking.
leccapiatti, *n.m.* Guzzler, glutton; lick-spittle.
leccapiedi, *n.m.* Flatterer.
leccarda, *n.f.* Dripping-pan.
leccare, *v.t.* To lick, to lap; to skim; (*fig.*) to flatter; to finish off carefully, to polish (literary work, etc.).
leccata, *n.f.* Licking; skimming.
leccatamente, *adv.* Affectedly.
leccatore, leccatrice, leccazampe, *n.m.f.* Flatterer, lick-spittle.
leccese, *n.m.a.* Of or from Lecce.
lecceto, *n.m.* Grove of ilex trees.
leccio [lEccio], *n.m.* (*Bot.*) Ilex, holm-oak.
leccone, *n.m.* Glutton; parasite, sponger; lecher.
leccornia [leccornIa], *n.f.* Tit-bit, dainty morsel.
lecitamente, *adv.* Lawfully, with permission.
lecito [lEcito], *n.m.a.* Lawful, permissible, allowed, conceded, right. **Non è — far ciò,** it is not permitted to do that.
ledente, *a.* Hurtful.
ledere [lEdere], *v.t.* To hurt, to damage, to injure, to harm, to prejudice; to wound.
lega, *n.f.* League, union, confederation, society; quality, class; alloy (of metals); (*Geog.*) league (3 miles). **Di buona —,** of good class; **di bassa —,** low, vulgar, poor; **moneta di bassa —,** base coin.
legaccio, legacciolo [legAccio], *n.m.* String, garter, band; boot-lace; ribbon.
legale, *n.m.a.* Lawyer; legal, lawful; statutory. **Studio —,** lawyer's office; **ricorrere alle vie legali,** to have recourse to the law.
legalità [-à], *n.f.* Legality, lawfulness.
legalizzare, *v.t.* To legalize; to certify; to authenticate.
legalizzazione, *n.f.* Legalization; ratification.
legalmente, *adv.* Legally.
legame, *n.m.* Bond, tie; connection, union, link. **I legami d'amicizia,** the bonds of friendship.
legamento, *n.m.* Binding; (*Anat.*) ligament; (*Mus.*) ligature.
legare (1), *v.t.* To bind, to tie; to fasten, to join, to connect; to attach, to link, to tie up; to alloy; to set (jewels), to mount (a gem). **— un libro,** to bind a book; **— strettamente,** to bind fast; **— le mani,** to tie one's hands; **pazzo da —,** raving mad.
legare (2), *v.t.* To bequeath, to leave by will.
legarsi, *v.r.* To bind oneself. **— d'amicizia,** to form a friendship; (*fig.*) **legarsela al dito,** to bear a grudge, to have a grievance.
legatario [legatArio], *n.m.* Legatee.
legato, *n.m.* Bequest, legacy; legate, ambassador, envoy.
legato, *p.p.a.* Bound, tied, tied up; (*Mus.*) legato. **Un libro ben —,** a well-bound book.
legatore, *n.m.* Book-binder; (*Law*) testator.
legatoria [legatorIa], *n.f.* Book-bindery.
legatura, *n.f.* Bookbinding, binding; bond, tie; (*Anat.*) ligature; (*Mus.*) slur.
legazione, *n.f.* Legation (in all senses).
legge, *n.f.* Law; rule, ordinance, statute; constitution; act (of parliament). **Imporre la —,** to enforce the law; **la — è uguale per tutti,** the law is the same for all; **ricorrere alla —,** to have recourse to the law; **secondo la —,** according to the law; **a termini di —,** as by law enacted; **necessità non ha —,** necessity knows no law; **dettar —,** to lay down the law; **di —,** perforce; **proposta di —,** (parliamentary) bill.
leggenda, *n.f.* Legend, story, fable; reference note, explanatory note; symbols (on diagram, etc.), caption (to a picture).
leggendario [leggendArio], *a.* Legendary.
leggere [lEggere], *v.t.* To read; to peruse, to study. **— ad alta voce,** to read aloud; **nell'attesa di leggervi,** hoping to hear from you; (*colloq.*) **— la vita a qualcuno,** to speak ill of someone; **— fra le righe,** to read between the lines.
leggerezza, *n.f.* Lightness; levity; nimbleness; fickleness, frivolity, levity.
leggermente, *adv.* Lightly; thoughtlessly.
leggero, leggiero, *a.* Light, nimble, quick; slight; fickle, volatile, frivolous, flighty; thoughtless, inconsiderate. **Alla leggiera,** inconsiderately, rashly; **mano leggiera,** light hand; **in abiti leggieri,** lightly clad; **di leggieri,** easily.
leggiadramente, *adv.* Gracefully, prettily.
leggiadria [leggiadrIa], *n.f.* Prettiness, comeliness, grace, charm.
leggiadro, *a.* Pretty, graceful, comely, charming.
leggibile [leggIbile], *a.* Legible.
leggibilmente, *adv.* Legibly.
leggicchiare, *v.t.* To read cursorily, to skim.
leggiero [cp. leggero].
leggio [leggIo], *n.m.* Reading-desk, lectern; music-stand.
leggio [lEggio], *a.* (*Naut.*) Light in ballast.

leggitore, leggitrice, *n.m.f.* Reader.
legiferare, *v.i.* To enact laws, to dictate.
legionario [legionArio], *n.m.* Legionary.
legione, *n.f.* Legion; (*Mil.*) regiment (of carabinieri).
legislativo, *a.* Legislative.
legislatore, *n.m.* Legislator; jurist.
legislatura, *n.f.* Legislature.
legislazione, *n.f.* Legislation.
legista (*pl.* **legisti**), *n.m.* Lawyer, jurist.
legittima [legIttima], *n.f.* (*Law*) Legal share of property (irrespective of any bequest).
legittimamente, *adv.* Legitimately.
legittimare, *v.t.* To legitimize, to legitimate.
legittimazione, *n.f.* Legitimization.
legittimismo, *n.m.* (*Pol.*) Legitimism.
legittimista (*pl.* **legittimisti**), *n.m.* (*Pol.*) Legitimist; royalist.
legittimità, *n.f.* Legitimacy, lawfulness.
legittimo [legIttimo], *a.* Legitimate (in all senses).
legna, *n.f.* Firewood, fuel. **Metter legna al fuoco,** to add fuel to the fire; **— da ardere,** firewood.
legnaceo [legnAceo], *a.* Woody, ligneous.
legnaia [legnAia], *n.f.* Wood-store.
legnaiolo, *n.m.* Carpenter, joiner.
legname, *n.m.* Timber.
legnare, *v.t.* To cudgel, to thrash, to cane.
legnata, *n.f.* Thrashing; blow with a stick. **Dare un sacco di legnate,** to give a sound thrashing.
legnatico [legnAtico], *n.m.* Right to gather or cut firewood.
legnatura, *n.f.* Thrashing.
legno, *n.m.* Wood; timber; log; carriage; ship; club, cudgel; wood-block, wood-engraving. **— stagionato,** seasoned timber; **— compensato,** plywood; **testa di —,** blockhead; **pasta di —,** wood-pulp.
legnosità [-à], *n.f.* Woodiness, stiffness.
legnoso, *a.* Woody, ligneous; stiff.
leguleio [legulEio], *n.m.* Pettifogging lawyer.
legume, *n.m.* Vegetable; legume. **Un piatto di legumi,** a dish of vegetables.
leguminose, *n.f.pl.* Leguminous plants.
leguminoso, *a.* Leguminous.
lei, *pron.* Her, she; you. **Come sta Lei?** How are you? **vado da lei,** I am going to her.
Leida [lEida], *n.f.* Leyden.
Lemano, *n.m.* (*Geog.*) Leman. **Lago Lemano,** Lake Leman, Lake of Geneva.
lembo, *n.m.* Edge, border, margin, skirt; flap. **Un — di cielo,** a strip of blue sky.
lemma, *n.f.* (*Logic, Math.*) Lemma, assumption.
lemme, *adv.* **Lemme lemme,** very slowly, bit by bit; peacefully, gently.
Lemosì, *n.f.* Limoges.
lemure [lEmure], *n.m.* (*Zool.*) Lemur.
lemuri [lEmuri], *n.m.pl.* (*Hist.*) Lemures.
lena, *n.f.* Breath; vigour, energy, nerve. **Di —,** with zest; **un lavoro di lunga —,** a work requiring sustained effort; **con — affannata,** with panting breath; **perder la —,** to lose nerve.
lendine, *n.m.* (*Zool.*) Nit, egg of louse.
lene, *a.* (*Lit.*) Soft, faint, mellow, sweet.
lenemente, *adv.* Softly.
lenimento, *n.m.* Alleviation, soothing.
Leningrado, *n.m.* Leningrad.
lenire, *v.t.* To soothe, to assuage, to appease, to alleviate.
lenitivo, *a.* Soothing, lenitive, mitigating.
lenocinio [lenocInio], *n.m.* Procuration, pandering; (*fig.*) charm, allurement, artifice.
lenona, *n.f.* Procuress, bawd.
lenone, *n.m.* Procurer, pander, pimp
lentaggine [lentAggine], *n.f.* Slowness.
lentamente, *adv.* Slowly.
lentare, *v.i.* To slacken the pace, to go slower.
lente, *n.f.* Lens; eyeglass, monocle; (*Bot.*) lentil. **— d'ingrandimento,** magnifying glass; **— concava, convessa,** concave, convex lens; **portare le lenti,** to wear spectacles; **un piatto di lenti,** a dish of lentils.
lenteggiare, *v.i.* To grow loose, not to close properly.
lentezza, *n.f.* Slowness; slackness, tardiness, sluggishness.
lentia [lentIa], *n.f.* Brewer's sling for lowering barrels.
lenticchia [lentIcchia], *n.f.* (*Bot.*) Lentil.
lentiggine [lentIggine], *n.f.* Freckle.
lentigginoso, *a.* Freckled.
lentischio [lentIschio], *n.m.* (*Bot.*) Lentisk.
lento, *a.* Slow, tardy, slack; inactive, indolent, sluggish; loose. **Andare a passo —,** to walk slowly; **una vite lenta,** a loose screw; **una persona lenta,** a slow person.
lento, *adv.* Slowly. **Parlar —,** to speak slowly.
lenza, *n.f.* Fishing-line. **Pescare alla —,** to angle.
lenzuolo (*pl.* **lenzuoli,** *m.,* **lenzuola,** *f.*), *n.m.* Sheet (of a bed); (*fig.*) cover. **Tela da lenzuola,** sheeting; **— funebre,** winding-sheet, shroud.
leofante, *n.m.* (*obs.*) Elephant.
leonardesco, *a.* In the manner of Leonardo da Vinci.
leonato, *a.* Tawny.
leoncino, leoncello, *n.m.* Lion cub, young lion.
leone, *n.m.* (*Zool.*) Lion. **La parte del —,** the lion's share; **avere un coraggio da leone,** to be lion-hearted; **mostrar l'unghia del —,** to show one's mettle.
Leone, *n.m.* Leo.
leonessa, *n.f.* Lioness.
leonino, *a.* Leonine (in all senses). **Città leonina,** Vatican quarter of Rome (fortified by Pope Leo IV).
leopardo, *n.m.* (*Zool.*) Leopard.
lepidamente, *adv.* Facetiously, wittily.
lepidezza, *n.f.* Wit, humour; facetiousness; witticism.
lepido [lEpido], *a.* Facetious, jocular, witty, smart.
lepidotteri [lepidOtteri], *n.m.pl.* (*Zool.*) Lepidoptera.
lepore, *n.m.* (*Lit.*) Wit, humour.
leporino, *a.* **Labbro —,** hare-lip.
lepracchiotto, lepratto, *n.m.* Young hare, leveret.
lepre, *n.m.f.* (*Zool.*) Hare.
leprosario [leprosArio], *n.m.* Leper-house.
lercio [lErcio], *a.* Filthy, foul.
lerciume, *n.m.* Filthiness.
lesbico [lEsbico], *a.* Lesbian. **Amore —,** Lesbianism.
lesina [lEsina], *n.f.* Awl; (*fig.*) stinginess; economy, thrift.

lesinare, *v.i.* To be stingy, to haggle over prices; to be penny-wise.
lesineria [lesinerIa], *n.f.* Stinginess.
lesionare, *v.t.* To damage, to impair, to injure.
lesione, Lesion, hurt, injury; damage; offence; (*Law*) battery.
lesivo, *a.* Hurtful, injurious, offensive.
leso, *a.* Injured, hurt, offended. **La parte lesa,** the injured party.
lessare, *v.t.* To boil, to cook in water, to stew.
lessata, *n.f.* Boiling.
lessatura, *n.f.* Boiling.
lessico [lEssico], *n.m.* Lexicon, dictionary.
lessicografia [lessicografIa], *n.f.* Lexicography.
lessicografo [lessicOgrafo], *n.m.* Lexicographer.
lesso, *n.m.a.* Boiled meat, boiled.
lestamente, *adv.* Quickly, swiftly.
lestezza, *n.f.* Quickness; promptness, smartness; dexterity.
lesto, *a.* Quick, swift, nimble, agile; smart.
lestofante, *n.m.* Swindler, cheat.
letale, *a.* Lethal, deadly, mortal.
letalmente, *adv.* Lethally.
letamaio [letamAio], *n.m.* Dung-heap, heap of manure.
letamare, *v.t.* (*Agric.*) To manure.
letame, *n.m.* Manure, dung; litter; stable-manure.
letargia [letargIa], *n.f.* Lethargy.
letargicamente, *adv.* Lethargically.
letargico [letArgico], *a.* Lethargic.
letargo, *n.m.* Lethargy, torpor.
Lete, *n.m.* (*Myth.*) Lethe.
leticare [cp. **litigare**].
letichino, *n.m.* Wrangler, quarreller.
letificare, *v.t.* To give joy.
letizia [letIzia], *n.f.* Joy, mirth, merriness, gaiety, happiness.
letiziare, letiziarsi, *v.i.r.* To rejoice; to be happy.
letta, *n.f.* Glance, hasty perusal. **Dare una —,** to skim, to read cursorily.
lettera [lEttera], *n.f.* Letter, note; (*Typ.*) character, type. **Carta da —,** note paper; **— di presentazione,** letter of introduction; **— raccomandata,** registered letter; **— per via aerea,** air-letter; **laureato in lettere,** graduate in arts; **belle lettere,** belles lettres, literature; **un uomo di lettere,** a literary man; **— morta,** dead letter; **prendere alla —,** to take literally; **lettere e cifre,** words and figures; (*Comm.*) **— di credito,** letter of credit; **— d'avviso,** letter of advice; **— di vettura,** consignment note, way-bill; (*Typ.*) **— maiuscola,** capital letter; **— minuscola,** small (lower case) letter; **— di scatola,** block letter.
letterale, *a.* Literal.
letteralmente, *adv.* Literally.
letterariamente, *adv.* In a literary manner.
letterario [letterArio], *a.* Literary. **Proprietà letteraria,** copyright.
letterato, *n.m.* Man of letters, author; scholar.
letterato, *a.* Lettered, cultured.
letteratura, *n.f.* Literature.
lettico [lEttico], *n.m.a.* Latvian.
lettiera, *n.f.* Bedstead; (*Agric.*) litter (for beasts), straw, bedding.
lettiga, *n.f.* Litter, stretcher (wheeled).
lettighiere, *n.m.* Stretcher bearer.
lettino, *n.m.* Couch, bunk, berth.
letto (1), *n.m.* Bed (in all senses); couch; bedding for animals; bedstead. **Camera da —,** bedroom; **— matrimoniale,** double-bed; **— di fortuna,** shake-down; **— da campo,** camp-bed; **— pieghevole,** folding-bed; **andare a —,** to go to bed; **mettersi a —,** to take to one's bed; **stare fra — e lettuccio,** to be an invalid; **inchiodato a —,** bedridden; **— di morte,** death-bed; **dello stesso —,** of the same marriage; **— di fiume,** river-bed.
letto (2), *p.p.* Read [cp. **leggere**].
lettone, *n.m.a.* Latvian [cp. **lettico**].
lettorato, *n.m.* Lectureship.
lettore, lettrice, *n.m.f.* Lecturer.
lettura, *n.f.* Reading; lecture. **Sala di —,** reading-room; **libro di —,** reading-book, primer.
leucemia [leucemIa], *n.f.* (*Med.*) Leukæmia.
leucite, *n.f.* (*Min.*) Leucite.
leucoma, *n.m.* (*Med.*) Leucoma.
leucorrea, *n.f.* (*Med.*) Leucorrhoea; whites.
leva, *n.f.* Lever (in all senses); fulcrum; (*Mil.*) levy, conscription. **Far —,** to lever up; **— del freno,** brake-lever; **essere di —,** to be liable to conscription.
levabile [levAbile], *a.* Removable.
levante, *n.m.* The East. **Il Levante,** the Levant.
levantino, *n.m.a.* Levantine.
levare, *v.t.* To raise, to lift up; to take away, to remove; to quench, to appease; to deduct, to subtract; to extract; (*Cards*) to cut; (*Naut.*) to weigh (the anchor). **— il bollore,** to simmer; (*Mil.*) **— l'assedio,** to raise the siege; **— rumore,** to make a fuss; **— al cielo,** to extol to the skies; **— la seduta,** to adjourn the sitting; **— via,** to take away, to take off, to remove.
levarsi, *v.r.* To rise, to get up; to take off; to get off; to get out of the way. **— presto,** to get up early; **— il cappello,** to raise one's hat; **— in superbia,** to swell with pride, to get puffed up; **— il pan di bocca,** to make great sacrifices; **levati dalla testa questa idea,** put that idea out of your head; **levati di torno,** get out of my way; **levati la giacca,** take off your coat; **si leva il vento,** the wind is getting up; **si leva il sole,** the sun is rising.
levata, *n.f.* Rising, getting up, taking away; collection (of letters); wholesale purchase. **— del sole,** sunrise; **— di sangue,** letting of blood; **una — di scudi,** an outcry, a rising in arms.
levato, *p.p.a.* Raised, risen; taken away, removed; drawn; excepted. **Andare a gambe levate,** to go head over heels; **fuggire a gambe levate,** to take to one's heels; **a bandiere levate,** with flying colours.
levatoio [levatOio], *a.* **Ponte —,** drawbridge.
levatrice, *n.f.* Midwife.
levatura, *n.f.* Degree of intelligence, understanding, talent; standard, level. **Di alta —,** of lofty intellect.
levigare, *v.t.* To polish, to smooth, to gloss.
levigatezza, *n.f.* Polish, smoothness.
levigazione, *n.f.* Polishing, smoothing.
levita, *n.m.* Levite.

levità [-à], *n.f.* Levity, frivolity.
levitare, *v.i.* To levitate.
levitazione, *n.f.* Levitation.
levitico [levItico], *n.m.a.* Leviticus; levitical.
levriere, levriero, *n.m.* Greyhound.
lezio (*pl.* **lezi**) [lEzio], *n.m.* Affectation, mincing ways; coaxing.
lezione, *n.f.* Lesson, lecture; reprimand; (variant) reading. **Prendere lezioni da,** to take lessons from; **assistere ad una —,** to attend a lecture.
leziosaggine [leziosAggine], *n.f.* Affectation; mawkishness.
leziosamente, *adv.* Affectedly.
leziosità [-à], *n.f.* Affectation.
lezioso, *a.* Affected; high-flown; mawkish; lackadaisical.
lezzo, *n.m.* Stink, stench, bad smell.
lezzoso, *a.* Stinking, fetid.
lezzume, *n.m.* Stink, filth, foul mass, fetidness.
li (1), *pron. m.pl.* Them. **Li vidi,** I saw them; **per vederli,** in order to see them; **vedendoli,** seeing them; **al vederli,** on seeing them; **avendoli visti,** having seen them.
li (2), *art. m.pl.* (Archaic, poetic form, seldom used nowadays) The.
lì, *adv.* There, in that particular place; here, now. **State lì!** Stop where you are! **di lì a poco,** a few minutes afterwards; **lì per lì,** on the spur of the moment; **essere lì lì per,** to be on the point of; **di lì a un anno,** a year from then; **giù di lì,** thereabouts.
liana, *n.f.* (*Bot.*) Liana.
libagione, *n.f.* Libation, drink, drinking.
Libano [lIbano], *n.m.* (*Geog.*) Lebanon.
libano, *n.m.* (*Naut.*) Cable, rope (of esparto grass).
libare, *v.t.* To make a libation; to taste, to sip.
libazione, *n.f.* Libation.
libbra, *n.f.* Pound (weight).
libecciata, *n.f.* South-westerly gale.
libeccio [libEccio], *n.m.* South-west wind.
libellista (*pl.* **libellisti**), *n.m.* Libeller; pamphleteer.
libello, *n.m.* Libel, defamatory writing; pamphlet, written declaration.
libellula [libEllula], *n.m.* (*Zool.*) Dragon-fly.
libente, *a.* Willing, ready; desirous.
liberale, *n.m.a.* Liberal, generous, bountiful, open-handed. **Le arti liberali,** the liberal arts.
liberalismo, *n.m.* (*Pol.*) Liberalism.
liberalità [-à], *n.f.* Liberality, munificence.
liberalmente, *adv.* Liberally.
liberamente, *adv.* Freely.
liberamento, *n.m.* Liberation, liberating.
liberare, *v.t.* To deliver, to free, to liberate, to release, to set free; to relieve, to clear. **Liberarsi da un peso,** to free oneself from a burden.
liberarsi, *v.r.* To free oneself, to get rid of; to shake off.
liberatore, liberatrice, *n.m.f.* Deliverer, liberator.
liberazione, *n.f.* Liberation, deliverance; discharge, acquitance.
libercolo [libErcolo], *n.m.* Trashy or obscene book.
liberismo, *n.m.* (*Pol.*) Free trade.
liberista (*pl.* **liberisti**), *n.m.* (*Pol.*) Free-trader.
libero [lIbero], *a.* Free, independent, unrestrained; liberated, released; open, frank, outspoken; available, empty, vacant; clear, open; exempt; dissolute, licentious. **— arbitrio,** free will; **aria libera,** open air; **— scambio,** free trade; **— pensatore,** free-thinker; **disegno a mano libera,** free-hand drawing; (*Law*) **a piede —,** out on bail; **traduzione libera,** free translation.
libertà [-à], *n.f.* Liberty, freedom; independence. **Mi prendo la — di,** I take the liberty of; **mettere in —,** to set at liberty; **— di stampa,** freedom of the press; **— di parola,** freedom of speech.
libertario [libertArio], *n.m.a.* Libertarian.
liberticida, *n.m.a.* Liberticide; destroyer or destructive of liberty.
libertinaggio [libertinAggio], *n.m.* Licentiousness, debauchery.
libertino, *n.m.a.* Libertine, profligate, rake; rakish.
liberto, *n.m.* Freed slave.
Libia [lIbia], *n.f.* (*Geog.*) Libya.
libico [lIbico], *n.m.a.* Libyan.
libidine [libIdine], *n.f.* Lust, lechery.
libidinosamente, *adv.* Lustfully, wantonly.
libidinoso, *a.* Lustful, wanton, lascivious.
libito [lIbito], *n.m.* (*Lit.*) Will, desire; caprice. **A —,** at will, at pleasure.
libra, *n.f.* (*Lit.*) Balance, scales.
libraio [librAio], *n.m.* Bookseller.
libramento, *n.m.* Balancing, poising.
librare, *v.t.* To equipoise, to librate; to weigh.
librario [librArio], *a.* Pertaining to books. **Il commercio —,** the book trade.
librarsi, *v.r.* To balance, to hover, to flutter in the air. **— a volo,** to soar.
librazione, *n.f.* Balancing, poising; (*Astron.*) libration.
libreria [librerIa], *n.f.* Bookshop; library, book-case.
librettista (*pl.* **librettisti**), *n.m.* (*Mus.*) Librettist.
libretto, *n.m.* Booklet; notebook; (*Mus.*) libretto. **— di assegni,** cheque-book; **— della banca,** pass-book.
libro, *n.m.* Book (in all senses); volume. **— di lettura,** reading book, reader; **— esaurito,** book out of print; **— usato,** second-hand book; (*Comm.*) **— mastro,** ledger; **tenuta dei libri,** book-keeping; **mettere a —,** to enter (in ledger, etc.); (*Naut.*) **— di bordo,** log-book.
licantropia [licantropIa]; *n.f.* Lycanthropy.
licantropo [licAntropo], *n.m.* Were-wolf.
licaone, *n.m.* (*Zool.*) Species of African wild dog.
liccio [lIccio], *n.m.* Heddle (in weaving).
liceale, *a.* Pertaining to a **liceo** or high-school.
licealista (*pl.* **licealisti**), *n.m.* Scholar at a **liceo.**
licenza, *n.f.* Licence, permission, permit, leave of absence; dismissal; diploma; licentiousness, licence. **In —,** on leave; **con —,** with your permission; **dar —,** to grant permission; **— poetica,** poetic licence.
licenziamento, *n.m.* Dismissal, discharge.
licenziare, *v.t.* To dismiss, to discharge, to send away; to give the sack; to give notice; to grant a certificate; to license.
licenziarsi, *v.r.* To take leave, to say farewell; to give notice, to resign.

licenziato, *n.m.* Licentiate.
licenziosamente, *adv.* Licentiously.
licenziosità [-à], *n.f.* Licentiousness, debauchery; misrule.
licenzioso, *a.* Licentious, dissolute, loose (in manners), corrupt.
liceo [licEo], *n.m.* High school, grammar school.
lichene, *n.m.* (*Bot.*) Lichen.
lichenina, *n.f.* (*Chem.*) Lichenin.
licitare, *v.t.* To sell or bid at auction.
licitazione, *n.f.* Auction sale; bid at an auction.
lido, *n.m.* Seashore, shore, beach; (*fig.*) land, native shores. **Il Lido,** the Lido at Venice.
Liegi, *n.f.* (*Geog.*) Liège.
lieo [liEo], *n.m.* (*Poet.*) Wine, Bacchus.
lietamente, *adv.* Gladly, joyfully, cheerfully, merrily.
lietezza, *n.f.* Gladness, joy, merriness.
lieto, *a.* Glad, joyful, merry; pleased. **Sono — d'informarla,** I am pleased (*or* it gives me pleasure) to inform you; **— di conoscerla,** pleased to meet you!
lieve, *a.* Light, easy, slight, trifling; soft. **— come una piuma,** light as a feather.
lievemente, *adv.* Lightly, slightly.
lievezza, *n.f.* Lightness, easiness.
lievitare, *v.t.i.* To leaven, to ferment; to rise (of dough).
lievitatura, *n.f.* Leavening, fermenting.
lievito [liEvito], *n.m.* Leaven, yeast; baking-powder. **— di birra,** brewer's yeast; barm.
ligio [lIgio], *n.m.* Faithful, true, liege; servile, submissive; respectful.
lignaggio [lignAggio], *n.m.* Lineage, pedigree.
ligneo [lIgneo], *a.* Woody, ligneous.
lignite, *n.f.* (*Min.*) Lignite.
ligure [lIgure], *n.m.a.* Ligurian.
ligustico [ligUstico], *a.* Ligurian.
ligustro, *n.m.* (*Bot.*) Privet.
liliaceo [liliAceo], *a.* (*Bot.*) Liliaceous.
liliale, *a.* Lily-like, white as a lily.
Lilla, *n.f.* (*Geog.*) Lille.
lilla, *n.f.a.* Lilac.
lillipuziano, *n.m.a.* Lilliputian, dwarf.
lima, *n.f.* File, rasp; polish, finish.
limaccia [limAccia], *n.f.* (*Zool.*) Slug.
limaccio [limAccio], *n.m.* Deep mud, mire.
limaccioso, *a.* Muddy, turbid; slimy.
limare, *v.t.* To file; to file away; to polish.
limatura, *n.f.* Filings, dust of filing.
limbello, *n.m.* Cutting of leather or cloth; tenon (for mortise).
limbo, *n.m.* Limbo. **Va al Limbo!** go to Jericho!
limine [lImine], *n.m.* Threshold, border, limit.
limitabile [limitAbile], *a.* Limitable.
limitare, *v.t.* To limit, to bound, to confine, to circumscribe, to restrict.
limitare, *n.m.* Threshold; commencement, border.
limitarsi, *v.r.* To limit or confine oneself. **Devo limitarmi a,** I must confine myself to.
limitatamente, *adv.* In a limited fashion.
limitatezza, *n.f.* Limitation.
limitativamente, *adv.* In a limitative manner.
limitativo, *a.* Limitative.
limitazione, *n.f.* Limitation; limit, restraint.
limite [lImite], *n.m.* Limit, boundary; border; restraint, check. **— d'età,** age limit; **— di velocità,** speed limit; **limiti delle nevi perpetue,** snowline; **tenersi nei limiti,** to keep within bounds; **essere al — di,** to be on the verge of; **superare i limiti,** to exceed all bounds.
limitrofo [limItrofo], *a.* Bordering, adjacent, adjoining, neighbouring.
limo, *n.m.* Mud, slime, mire.
limonaio [limonAio], *n.m.* Lemon-seller.
limonata, *n.f.* Lemonade; lemon-squash.
limoncina, *n.f.* (*Bot.*) Lemon verbena.
limoncino, *n.m.* Small lemon.
limone, *n.m.* Lemon; lemon-tree. **Succo di —,** lemon juice.
limosinare, *v.i.* To beg for alms.
limosiniere, *n.m.* Almoner.
limosino, *n.m.* (*Motor.*) Limousine.
limosità [-à], *n.f.* Muddiness.
limoso, *a.* Muddy, slimy.
limpidamente, *adv.* Limpidly.
limpidezza, limpidità [-à], *n.f.* Limpidity, brightness, clearness, purity; terseness.
limpido [lImpido], *a.* Limpid, bright, clear, transparent; pure, terse.
linaiuolo, *n.m.* Flax-dresser.
lince, *n.f.* (*Zool.*) Lynx. **Avere occhi di —,** to be lynx-eyed.
linceo (1) [lInceo], *a.* Pertaining to a lynx.
linceo (2) [lincEo], *n.m.* Member of the scientific academy Dei Lincei.
linciaggio [linciAggio], *n.m.* Lynching, lawless execution.
linciare, *v.t.* To lynch.
lindamente, *adv.* Neatly.
lindezza, *n.f.* Neatness, spruceness, cleanness, tidiness.
lindo, *a.* Neat, clean, spruce, tidy. **È molto linda nel vestire,** she is very neatly dressed.
lindura, *n.f.* Neatness [cp. **lindezza**].
linea [lInea], *n.f.* Line (in all senses), row; delineation; lineage; direction. **In — retta,** in a direct line, in a straight line; **tirare una —,** to draw a line; **— ferroviaria,** railway line; **— aerea,** air line; **— di carico,** load-line; **— di montaggio,** assembly line; **— di partenza,** scratch line; (*Football*) **— di porta,** touch-line; **essere in prima —,** to be in the front line; **soldato di —,** soldier of the line; **leggere fra le linee,** to read between the lines; **— maschile,** male line.
linealmente, *adv.* Lineally, in the direct line.
lineamento, *n.m.* Lineament, feature, outline.
lineare, *v.t.* To delineate; to draw, to sketch.
lineare, *a.* Linear, straight.
lineetta, *n.f.* (*Typ.*) Hyphen, dash.
linfa, *n.f.* (*Anat.*) Lymph. (*fig.*) **Infondere nuova —,** to infuse new blood.
linfaticamente, *adv.* Languidly.
linfatico [linfAtico], *a.* Lymphatic, listless, weak, feeble.
linfatismo, *n.m.* Lymphatic constitution.
lingotto, *n.m.* (*Metal.*) Ingot.
lingua [lIngua], *n.f.* Tongue (in all senses); language, idiom. **— volgare,** vernacular; **— lunga,** slanderous tongue; **mala —,** evil tongue; **in — povera,** in plain words; **— materna,** mother tongue; (*Med.*) **— brutta, sporca,** coated tongue; **avere la — legata,** to be tongue-tied; **tenere la — a freno,** to hold one's tongue; **egli ha il dono delle lingue,** he has the gift of languages;

lingue straniere, foreign languages; **— di terra,** a tongue of land; **essere padrone di una —,** to master a language.
linguaccia [linguAccia], *n.f.* Slanderous tongue; spiteful person.
linguacciuto, *n.m.a.* Sharp-tongued person; talkative, gossipy.
linguaggio [linguAggio], *n.m.* Language, speech, idiom, diction.
linguaio, linguaiolo [linguAio], *n.m.* Purist, pedant.
linguale, *a.* Lingual.
linguella, linguetta, *n.f.* Leather strip; latchet for shoes, tongue (of shoe); paper filter; (*Mus.*) reed.
linguista (*pl.* **linguisti**), *n.m.* Linguist.
linguistica [linguIstica], *n.f.* Linguistics.
linguisticamente, *adv.* Linguistically.
linguistico [linguIstico], *a.* Linguistic.
linificio [linifIcio], *n.m.* Flax-mill.
linimento, *n.m.* (*Med.*) Liniment.
lino, *n.m.* Flax; linen. **Seme di —,** linseed; **olio di —,** linseed oil; **tela di —,** linen cloth.
linoleum [linOleum], *n.m.* Linoleum.
linone, *n.m.* Fine linen, lawn.
linotipia [linotipIa], *n.f.* (*Print.*) Linotyping.
linotipista (*pl.* **linotipisti**), *n.m.* (*Print.*) Linotype operator.
linotipo, *n.m.* (*Print.*) Linotype.
linseme, *n.m.* Linseed.
linteo, *n.m.* (*Eccles.*) Linen cloth, sudarium.
lintercolo [lintErcolo], *n.m.* (*Mus.*) Pocket violin, kit.
liocorno, *n.m.* Unicorn.
liofante, *n.m.* (*Poet.*) Elephant.
lionato, *a.* Tawny [cp. **leonato**].
Lione, *n.f.* (*Geog.*) Lyons.
lipemania [lipemanIa], *n.f.* (*Med.*) Melancholia.
lipoma, *n.f.* (*Med.*) Tumour.
lippa, *n.f.* Children's game of tip-cat.
lippo, *a.* (*obs.*) Blear-eyed.
Lipsia [lIpsia], *n.f.* (*Geog.*) Leipzig.
liquefacente, *a.* Melting.
liquefacimento, *n.m.* Liquefaction.
liquefare, liquefarsi, *v.i.r.* To liquefy, to melt.
liquefazione, *n.f.* Liquefaction.
liquidamente, *adv.* Liquidly.
liquidare, *v.t.* To liquidate (in all senses); to settle; to clear off; to wind up.
liquidato, *p.p.a.* Liquidated; paid off; wound up. **Uomo —,** a ruined man; **io l'ho —,** I got rid of him; **è —,** he's done for.
liquidatore, *n.m.* (*Comm.*) Liquidator.
liquidazione, *n.f.* Liquidation, sale, clearance sale. **— amichevole,** liquidation by arrangement; **— forzata,** compulsory liquidation; **— dei danni,** assessment of damages.
liquidità [-à], *n.f.* Liquidity.
liquido [lIquido], *n.m.* Liquid, fluid.
liquido [lIquido], *a.* Liquid, fluid, flowing; clear; (*Comm.*) due, payable. **Danaro —,** cash; **importo —,** balance due.
liquirizia [liquirIzia], *n.m.* Liquorice.
liquore, *n.m.* Liquor; liqueur; spirits, strong drink; juice.
liquoreria [liquorerIa], *n.f.* Bar, saloon; liquor shop.
liquorista (*pl.* **liquoristi**), *n.m.* Spirit-merchant, wine-merchant; publican.
lira (1), *n.f.* (Italian) lira. **— sterlina,** pound sterling.
lira (2), *n.f.* (*Mus.*) Lyre.
lirica [lIrica], *n.f.* Lyric poetry; operatic music.
liricamente, *adv.* Lyrically.
lirico [lIrico], *n.m.a.* Lyric poet; lyric, lyrical.
lirismo, *n.m.* (*Poet.*) Lyrical form.
lirista (*pl.* **liristi**), *n.m.* (*Mus.*) Player on the lyre.
Lisbona, *n.f.* (*Geog.*) Lisbon.
lisca, *n.f.* Fish-bone; stalk of hemp or flax; (*fig.*) morsel.
liscia [lIscia], *n.f.* Flat iron; polishing stone.
lisciamente, *adv.* Smoothly.
lisciamento, *n.m.* Smoothing, polishing; (*fig.*) flattering.
lisciare, *v.t.* To smooth, to gloss, to polish; to stroke; (*fig.*) to coax, to blandish, to flatter; to lick (of animals).
lisciarsi, *v.r.* To dress one's hair; to tidy oneself; to dress carefully; to preen (of birds).
lisciata, *n.f.* Smoothing; flattery.
lisciatoio [lisciatOio], *n.m.* Steel comb.
lisciatura, *n.f.* Smoothing, glossing; flattery.
liscio [lIscio], *a.* Smooth, even, glossy, polished; plain, simple. **Passarla liscia,** to get off lightly, to go unpunished; **messa liscia,** low mass.
lisciva, liscivia [liscIvia], *n.f.* Lye; washing-bath.
lisciviare, *v.t.* To wash with lye, to lixiviate.
lisciviatrice, *n.f.* Lixiviating-tub.
liscoso, *a.* Bony; stalky.
lisimachia [lisimAchia], *n.f.* (*Bot.*) Loosestrife.
liso, *a.* Worn-out, threadbare.
lista, *n.f.* List, schedule, roll; band, stripe, streak, line; menu, bill of fare. **— civile,** civil list; **— elettorale,** electoral roll, register of voters.
listare, *v.t.* To stripe, to edge, to border; to put on a list.
listello, *n.m.* (*Arch.*) Listel, fillet.
listino, *n.m.* List; time-table; price-list, quotation; specification.
litaniare, *v.t.* (*Eccles.*) To recite the litany; to sing the praises of.
litanie [litanIe], *n.f.pl.* (*Eccles.*) Litany
litantrace, *n.m.* Anthracite.
litargirio [litargIrio], *n.m.* (*Chem.*) Litharge.
lite, *n.f.* Litigation, dispute, quarrel, controversy, law-suit; contest; brawl, row. **Attaccar —,** to start a row; **intentare una — ad uno,** to bring an action against somebody; **vincere la —,** to win the action.
litiasi [litIasi], *n.f.* (*Med.*) Lithiasis, stone.
litigamento, *n.m.* Quarrelling, litigation.
litigante, *n.m.* Litigant; quarrelsome fellow.
litigare, *v.t.* To quarrel, to dispute, to wrangle, to have a row, to have words (with someone).
litigio [litIgio], *n.m.* Dispute, quarrel; contest; action at law.
litigiosamente, *adv.* Quarrelsomely.
litigioso, *a.* Quarrelsome, litigious.
litigone, *n.m.* Quarrelsome fellow.
litio [lItio], *n.m.* (*Chem.*) Lithium.
lito, *n.m.* (*Poet.*) Shore [cp. **lido**].
litocromia [litocromIa], *n.f.* Chromolithography.
litografare, *v.t.* To lithograph.

litografia [litografIa], *n.f.* Lithography.
litografico [litogrAfico], *a.* Lithographic.
litografo [litOgrafo], *n.m.* Lithograph.
litologia [litologIa], *n.f.* Lithology.
litorale, *n.m.* Coastline, seabord, littoral. || *a.* Littoral, coastal.
litote, *n.f.* (*Gram.*) Litotes.
litotomia [litotomIa], *n.f.* (*Med.*) Lithotomy.
litro, *n.m.* Litre.
littorale, *n.m.* Coast line, seaboard, littoral.
littore, *n.m.* (*Hist.*) Lictor.
littorina, *n.f.* (*Rail.*) Diesel car.
Lituania [lituAnia], *n.f.* (*Geog.*) Lithuania.
lituano, *n.m.a.* Lithuanian.
lituo [lItuo], *n.m.* (*Hist.*) Divining-rod.
liturgia [liturgIa], *n.f.* Liturgy.
liturgicamente, *adv.* Liturgically.
liturgico [litUrgico], *a.* Liturgical.
liturgista (*pl.* **liturgisti**), *n.m.* Liturgist.
liutaio [liutAio], *n.m.* Lute-maker, maker of stringed instruments.
liutista (*pl.* **liutisti**), *n.m.* Lutanist.
liuto, *n.m.* (*Mus.*) Lute.
livella, *n.f.* Mason's level; plummet. **— a bolla d'aria,** spirit-level; **— a cannocchiale,** surveyor's level.
livellamento, *n.m.* Levelling; standardization, equalization; adjustment.
livellare, *v.t.i.* To level, to make level; to standardize, to equalize (in all senses); to be on a level with.
livellario [livellArio], *n.m.* Leaseholder, tenant.
livellatore, *n.m.* Leveller.
livellazione, *n.f.* Levelling, standardization.
livello (1), *n.m.* Level, horizontal surface; plummet. **— delle acque,** water-line; (*Rail.*) **passaggio a —,** level-crossing; **a dieci metri sul — del mare,** 10 metres above sea-level.
livello (2), *n.m.* (*Law*) Lease, renting of land, land held on lease.
liviano, *a.* (*Lit.*) Pertaining to Livy.
lividamente, *adv.* Lividly.
lividezza, *n.f.* Lividness, leaden colour.
livido [lIvido], *n.m.* Bruise, contusion.
livido [lIvido], *a.* Livid, ashen, discoloured; envious.
lividore, *n.m.* Bruise, lividity; envy, spite.
lividura, *n.f.* Bruise, discoloured spot.
livore, *n.m.* Rancour, hatred, spite; acrimony; bitterness.
livornese, *n.m.a.* Of or from Leghorn.
Livorno, *n.m.* (*Geog.*) Leghorn.
livrea [livrEa], *n.f.* Livery.
lizza, *n.f.* (*Hist.*) (Tilting) lists. **Scendere in —,** to enter the lists, to take up the gauntlet.
lo, *art. m. s.* The (used before impure "s", "z" and "gn"). **Lo studio,** the studio.
lo, *pron.m.* Him, it. **Lo sgridai,** I scolded him; **lo vuole,** he wants it; **lo dicevo io,** I told you so; **non lo credo,** I don't think so; **lo so,** I know; **Carlo è molto obbediente, Giovanni lo è assai meno,** Charles is very obedient, John much less so.
lobato, *a.* Lobate, lobed.
lobbia [lObbia], *n.m.* Broad-brimmed hat.
lobo, lobulo [lObulo], *n.m.* (*Anat.*) Lobe, lobe of the ear.
locale, *n.m.* Place, house, premises, rooms; headquarters.
locale, *a.* Local.
località [-à], *n.f.* Locality, position, place.
localizzare, *v.t.* To localize, to circumscribe; to locate.
localizzazione, *n.f.* Localization.
localmente, *adv.* Locally.
locanda, *n.f.* Inn, hotel, lodging-house.
locandiere, locandiera, *n.m.f.* Landlord, innkeeper; landlady, hostess.
locare, *v.t.* To let, to lease; to rent.
locatario [locatArio], *n.m.* Lessee, tenant, lodger.
locativo, *a.* (*Gram.*) Locative; (*Law*) for letting. **Valore —,** letting value.
locatore, *n.m.* Lessor, landlord.
locazione, *n.f.* Tenancy, lease.
loco [cp. **luogo**].
locomobile [locomObile], *n.f.* Traction-engine, road-locomotive.
locomotiva, *n.f.* Locomotive, railway engine.
locomotivo, *a.* Locomotive.
locomotore, *n.m.* (*Rail.*) Electric locomotive.
locomotore, *a.* Locomotor.
locomotrice, *n.f.* Traction engine.
locomozione, *n.f.* Locomotion.
loculo [lOculo], *n.m.* Loculus, tomb, niche for ashes.
locusta, *n.f.* (*Zool.*) Locust.
locuzione, *n.f.* Locution, phrase, idiom, expression.
lodabile [lodAbile], *a.* Praiseworthy, laudable.
lodabilità [-à], *n.f.* Praiseworthiness.
lodamento, *n.m.* Praising, praise.
lodare, *v.t.* To praise, to commend, to laud; to celebrate, to extol. **Dio sia lodato,** God be praised; **il su lodato,** the above-mentioned; **— sino alle stelle,** to praise to the skies.
lodarsi, *v.r.* To praise oneself. **Chi si loda s'imbroda,** self-praise is no recommendation; **— di qualcuno,** to be pleased with someone; to be fond of someone.
lodativo, *a.* Laudatory.
lode, *n.f.* Praise, commendation; eulogy. **Tessere le lodi di,** to sing the praises of; **degno di —,** praiseworthy.
lodevole [lodEvole], *a.* Praiseworthy, commendable, laudable.
lodevolmente, *adv.* Commendably.
lodigiano, *n.m.a.* Pertaining to or native of the town of Lodi.
lodo, *n.m.* (*Law*) Arbitration, award; expert opinion.
lodola [lOdola], *n.f.* (*Zool.*) Lark, sky-lark [cp. **allodola**].
logaritmo, *n.m.* (*Math.*) Logarithm.
loggetta, *n.f.* Small arcade or open gallery.
loggia (*pl.* **logge**) [lOggia], *n.f.* Open gallery, balcony, loggia; Masonic lodge.
loggiato, *n.m.* Large loggia, open gallery; colonnade.
loggione, *n.m.* (*Theat.*) Upper gallery, "the gods".
logica [lOgica], *n.f.* Logic.
logicamente, *adv.* Logically.
logico [lOgico], *n m.a.* Logician; logical.
logistica [logIstica], *n.m.* (*Mil.*) Logistics.
logistico [logIstico], *a.* Logistic. (*colloq.*) **I servizi logistici,** board and lodging.
loglio [lOglio], *n.m.* (*Bot.*) Darnel, tare.
loglioso, *a.* Full of tares.
logogrifo [logOgrifo], *n.m.* Word puzzle, enigma.

logomachia [logomachIa], *n.f.* (*Lit.*) Logomachy.
logoramento, *n.m.* Wear, wear and tear, waste, attrition.
logorare, *v.t.* To wear out, to waste, to use up; to consume.
logorarsi, *v.r.* To wear oneself out; to worry. **Si logora la vita,** he's wearing himself out.
logorio [logorIo], *n.m.* Wear, waste, use; wear and tear.
logoro [lOgoro], *n.m.* Decoy (in shooting); decoy in falconry to recall the bird.
logoro [lOgoro], *a.* Worn out, consumed, used up, wasted, in tatters, in rags.
loia [lOia], *n.f.* Dirt or grease on the skin or clothes.
loiolesco, *a.* Jesuitical.
lolla, *n.f.* Chaff (of corn), husk.
lombaggine [lombAggine], *n.f.* (*Med.*) Lumbago.
lombale, *a.* (*Anat.*) Lumbar.
Lombardia [lombardIa], *n.f.* Lombardy.
lombardo, *n.m.a.* Lombard.
lombata, *n.f.* Loin (of meat).
lombatello, *n.m.* Fillet.
lombo, *n.m.* (*Anat.*) Loin; sirloin. **Aver buoni lombi,** to be robust.
lombrico, *n.m.* Earth-worm.
londinese, *n.m.a.* Londoner; of London.
Londra, *n.f.* (*Geog.*) London.
longanime [longAnime], *a.* Forbearing, long-suffering, patient, indulgent.
longanimità [-à], *n.f.* Long-suffering, forbearance, longanimity.
longarina, *n.f.* (*Arch.*) Iron girder.
longevità [-à], *n.f.* Longevity.
longevo, *a.* Long-lived.
longitudinale, *a.* Longitudinal.
longitudine [longitUdine], *n.f.* Longitude.
lontanamente, *adv.* From afar, distantly, remotely, vaguely.
lontananza, *n.f.* Distance; remoteness; absence. **Durante la sua —,** during his absence; **in —,** afar off.
lontano, *a.* Distant, remote, far; absent. **È un mio — parente,** he's a distant relative of mine; **in un — avvenire,** in the distant future; **son ben — dal crederlo,** I am far from believing it.
lontano, *adv.* Far away, far off, at a great distance. **Egli abita — da qui,** he lives far from here; **egli abita — dalla stazione,** he lives a long way from the station; **più —,** further on; **lo vidi da —,** I saw him in the distance; **egli vede —,** he is far-sighted; **chi va piano va sano e va —,** slow but sure; **tenersi —,** to stand aloof.
lontra, *n.f.* (*Zool.*) Otter.
lonza (1), *n.f.* (*Lit.*) Panther.
lonza (2), *n.f.* Loin (of meat).
loppa, *n.f.* Chaff (of corn).
loppio, loppo [lOppio], *n.m.* (*Bot.*) Maple tree.
loquace, *a.* Loquacious, talkative.
loquacemente, *adv.* Loquaciously.
loquacità [-à], *n.f.* Loquacity, talkativeness.
loquela, *n.f.* Speech, language; fluency of speech; gift of the gab.
lordaggine [lordAggine], *n.f.* Dirt.
lordamente, *adv.* Dirtily, filthily.
lordare, *v.t.* To soil, to dirty, to pollute, to defile.
lordarsi, *v.r.* To dirty oneself, to get dirty.
lordezza, *n.f.* Dirtiness.
lordo (1), *a.* Dirty, soiled; foul, impure.
lordo (2), *a.* Gross (not nett). **Peso —,** gross weight; **rendita lorda,** gross income.
lordume, lordura, *n.f.* Filth, filthiness; rubbish, refuse.
Lorena, *n.f.* (*Geog.*) Lorraine.
lorenese, *n.m.a.* Native of or pertaining to Lorraine.
loretano, *n.m.a.* Native of or pertaining to Loreto.
lori, *n.m.* (*Zool.*) Loris (lemur).
lorica, *n.f.* Breast-plate.
loro, *pron.a.* Their; they, them, to them. **Il — podere,** their farm; **il —, la —, i —, le —,** their, theirs; **— dicono che,** they say that; **dissi — che,** I told them that.
losanga, *n.f.* (*Heraldry*) Lozenge; (*Math.*) rhomb, lozenge.
Losanna, *n.f.* (*Geog.*) Lausanne.
losco, *a.* Squint-eyed; dim-sighted; one-eyed; (*fig.*) suspicious, equivocal. **Una figura losca,** a sinister figure; **affari loschi,** shady business, sharp practice.
loto (1), *n.m.* Mud, mire.
loto (2), *n.m.* (*Bot.*) Lotus.
lotofago [lotOfago], *n.m.* Lotus-eater.
lotta, *n.f.* Struggle, contest, strife; wrestling. **L'istinto della —,** the fighting instinct; **— di classe,** class warfare; **— americana,** all-in wrestling; **— libera,** catch-as-catch-can.
lottare, *v.i.* To wrestle; to struggle, to fight; to strive. **— contro l'avversità,** to struggle against adversity.
lottatore, *n.m.* Prize-fighter, wrestler, fighter.
lotteria [lotterIa], *n.f.* Lottery.
lotto, *n.m.* Government lottery; lot; parcel; apportionment; allotment (of ground). **Vincere un terno al —,** to have a great stroke of luck.
Lovanio, *n.m.* (*Geog.*) Louvain.
lozione, *n.f.* Lotion; cosmetic.
lubbione, *n.m.* [cp. **loggione**].
lubricamente, *adv.* Wantonly, lewdly.
lubricante, *n.m.a.* Lubricant.
lubricativo, *a.* Lubricative.
lubricità [-à], *n.f.* Lubricity, wantonness, lewdness; scurrility.
lubrico [lUbrico], *a.* Wanton, lewd, indecent; scurrilous.
lubrificare, *v.t.* To lubricate, to oil, to grease.
lubrificatore, *n.m.* Lubricator.
lubrificazione, *n.f.* Lubrication, greasing, oiling.
Luca, *n.m.* Luke.
lucanica [lucAnica], *n.f.* Variety of sausage.
lucarino, *n.m.* (*Zool.*) Goldfinch.
lucchese, *n.m.a.* Native of or pertaining to Lucca.
lucchetto, *n.m.* Padlock.
luccicante, *a.* Glittering, shining, gleaming; bright.
luccicare, *v.i.* To glitter, to shine, to glare; to twinkle, to sparkle; to gleam. **Gli luccicano gli occhi,** he has tears in his eyes; **non è tutt'oro quel che luccica,** all is not gold that glitters.
luccichio [luccichIo], *n.m.* Glitter.
luccicone, *n.m.* Large tear-drop.

luccio [lUccio], *n.m.* (*Zool.*) Pike.
lucciola [lUcciola], *n.f.* (*Zool.*) Fire-fly; glow-worm. **Prendere lucciole per lanterne,** to be under a misapprehension, to make a blunder.
lucco, *n.m.* (*Hist.*) Gown worn by Florentine citizens.
luce, *n.f.* Light; brightness; splendour; aperture, port-hole, opening; window; mirror; truth, understanding. **Le luci,** the eyes; **accender la —,** to put on the light; **spengere la —,** to put out the light; **alla prima —,** at daybreak; **è venuto in —,** it has come to light; **far — su,** to throw light upon; **mettere qualcuno in cattiva —,** to present someone in a bad light; **dare alla —,** to bring forth, to give birth; **alla — del sole,** openly, publicly; **— elettrica,** electric light; **— a gas,** gas-light; **— debole,** faint light.
lucente, *a.* Bright, shining, luminous; glittering.
lucentemente, *adv.* Brightly, glowingly.
lucentezza, *n.f.* Brightness, brilliancy; lustre.
lucere, *v.i.* To shine, to gleam.
Lucerna, *n.f.* (*Geog.*) Lucerne.
lucerna, *n.f.* Lamp, oil lamp; light; (*colloq.*) cocked hat.
lucernario [lucernArio], *n.m.* Skylight.
lucerniere, *n.f.* Lamp-stand.
lucertola [lucErtola], *n.f.* (*Zool.*) Lizard.
lucherino, *n.m.* (*Zool.*) Goldfinch.
Lucia [lucIa], *n.f.* Lucy.
lucidamente, *adv.* Lucidly, clearly.
lucidamento, *n.m.* Polishing, brightening; glazing.
lucidare, *v.t.* To polish, to gloss; to clean, to black (boots); to glaze; to trace (drawings).
lucidatore, lucidatrice, *n.m.f.* Polisher (man or woman). **— di vetri,** window cleaner.
lucidatrice, *n.f.* Polishing machine.
lucidatura, lucidazione, *n.f.* Polishing, cleaning, glazing.
lucidezza, *n.f.* Brightness, cleanness, lucidity.
lucidità [-à], *n.f.* Lucidity, clearness. **Ha gran — di mente,** he is very clear-minded; **intervallo di —,** lucid interval.
lucido [lUcido], *n.m.* Polish; brilliance, lustre; tracing (design). **— da scarpe,** shoe-polish; **dare il — alle scarpe,** to polish one's shoes.
lucido [lUcido], *a.* Bright, clear, brilliant; lucid; glossy; polished, smooth, terse.
Lucifero [lucIfero], *n.m.* Lucifer.
lucignolo [lucIgnolo], *n.m.* Wick.
lucore, *n.m.* (*Poet.*) Brightness, splendour.
lucrare, *v.i.* To gain; to earn; to profit (unduly); to speculate.
lucrativamente, *adv.* Lucratively.
lucrativo, *a.* Lucrative, profitable, paying, remunerative.
Lucrezio [lucrEzio], *n.m.* Lucretius.
lucro, *n.m.* Lucre; gain, profit; benefit.
lucrosamente, *adv.* Profitably, lucratively.
lucroso, *a.* Lucrative, profitable, remunerative, paying.
luculento, *a.* (*Poet.*) Bright, shining, gleaming.
luculliano, *a.* Sumptuous (of a feast); succulent, luxurious, Lucullian.
ludi, *n.m.pl.* Games, sports, festivals; (*fig.*) **— cartacei,** electioneering.
ludibrio [ludIbrio], *n.m.* Mocking, mockery, scorn, derision. **Essere il — di,** to be the laughing-stock of.
ludo, *n.m.* Game, recreation; public show.
lue, *n.f.* (*Med.*) Lues.
luffa, *n.f.* (*Bot.*) Loofah.
luglio [lUglio], *n.m.* July. **Farsi onore col sol di —,** to boast without warrant.
lugubre [lUgubre], *a.* Lugubrious, mournful, dismal, gloomy.
lugubremente, *adv.* Lugubriously.
lui, *pers.pron.m.* He, him. **Lui disse che,** he said that; **è lui,** it is he.
luì [luI], *n.m.* (*Zool.*) Wren.
Luigi, *n.m.* Louis, Lewis.
lumaca, *n.f.* (*Zool.*) Snail; slug; (*fig.*) slow-coach. **Scala a —,** spiral staircase; **a passo di —,** very slowly, at a snail's pace.
lumacone, *n.m.* Large snail; worm of a screw; (*fig.*) sluggard; tell-tale.
lumaio [lumAio], *n.m.* Lamplighter.
lume, *n.m.* Light; lamp, lighted candle; eye; star; visual faculty, sight; knowledge, understanding; enlightenment. **Tenere il —,** to play chaperon; **perdere il — degli occhi,** to be blinded by one's passions; **perdere il — della ragione,** to go mad; **spegnete i lumi!** Put out the lights! **spegnersi come un —,** to die peacefully, to flicker out; **i lumi,** the eyes.
lumeggiamento, *n.m.* Illumination, enlightenment.
lumeggiare, *v.t.* To light up, to illumine, to enlighten; to illustrate, to emphasize.
lumella, *n.f.* Vent-hole of a furnace.
lumen Christi, *n.m.* (*Eccles.*) Three candles lighted on Holy Saturday; blessed candle.
lumicino, *n.m.* Faint light; small lamp. (*fig.*) **Essere al —,** to be at the last extremity, to be near the end (death).
lumiera, *n.f.* Chandelier; bracket for lights.
luminara, luminaria [luminAria], *n.f.* Public illuminations.
luminare, *n.m.* Luminary (of learning).
luminello, *n.m.* Wick-holder (in an oil lamp), candle-socket; shadow light.
lumino, *n.m.* Night-light, small light.
luminosamente, *adv.* Luminously, clearly.
luminosità [-à], *n.f.* Luminosity, clearness, brilliance, terseness.
luminoso, *a.* Luminous, bright, brilliant, shining; terse.
luna, *n.f.* Moon. **— crescente,** crescent moon; **— calante,** waning moon; **— piena,** full moon; **chiaro di —,** moonlight, moonshine; **— nuova,** new moon; **primo quarto di —,** moon's first quarter; **avere la —,** to be in a bad mood; **essere nato sotto buona —,** to be lucky; **abbaiare alla —,** to exert oneself in vain; **— di miele,** honeymoon; **faccia di — piena,** full-faced person; **vivere nel mondo della —,** to live with one's head in the clouds.
lunare, *a.* Lunar.
lunario [lunArio], *n.m.* Almanac, calendar. (*fig.*) **Sbarcare il —,** to live from hand to mouth.
lunarista (*pl.* **lunaristi**), *n.m.* Almanac-maker; weather-prophet.
lunatico [lunAtico], *a.* Crazy, capricious; whimsical; moody.

lunato, *a.* Crescent-shaped.
lunazione, *n.f.* (*Astron.*) Lunation.
lunedì [**-ì**], *n.m.* Monday. **Fare il —,** to take the Monday off.
lunetta, *n.f.* (*Arch.*) Lunette; moon-shaped device.
lungaggine [lungAggine], *n.f.* Delay, lengthiness, slowness; wearisome business; tedious writing, speech, etc., rigmarole.
lungagnata, *n.f.* Tedious speech, rigmarole, tirade.
lungamente, *adv.* At great length.
lunge, lungi, *adv.* Far away, far off. **Da lungi,** from afar; **sia — da noi,** far be it from us; **— dal credere,** far from believing.
lungherone, *n.m.* (*Mech.*) Longitudinal bearing.
lunghesso, *prep.* Along. **— il fiume,** along the river.
lunghezza, *n.f.* Length; extent, extension; duration. (*Radio*) **— d'onda,** wave-length.
lungi [cp. **lunge**].
lungimirante, *a.* Far-seeing.
lungo, *a.* Long; slow, tedious; lasting, extensive; tall; thin, watered, diluted. **Uomo —,** tall man; **brodo —,** thin broth; **di gran lunga,** by far; **quanto è — ?** how long is it? **in — e in largo,** far and wide; **tirar di —,** to go one's way; **cadere — disteso,** to fall full-length; **saper la lunga,** to know one's own business; to know what's what; **tirare in — una cosa, tirare una cosa per le lunghe,** to keep putting something off; **a — andare,** in the long run; **aver le mani lunghe,** to pilfer.
lungo, *prep.* Along, by the side of. (*Naut.*) **— a bordo,** alongside.
luogo, *n.m.* Place, spot, site; room; position, region; abode; need, stead (lieu); passage (in a book); occasion, cause; (*Math.*) locus. **Fuor di —,** out of place; **aver —,** to take place; **far —,** to make room; **in qualche —,** somewhere; **in nessun —,** nowhere; **in — di,** instead of; **sul —,** on the spot; **in primo —,** in the first place; **un — comune,** a commonplace; (*Law*) **non — a procedere,** to dismiss a case.
luogotenente, *n.m.* Deputy, acting-, vice-; lieutenant.
luogotenenza, *n.f.* Lieutenancy.
lupa, *n.f.* She-wolf. **La —,** emblem of the city of Rome; **avere il mal di —,** to be ravenously hungry.
lupacchiotto, *n.m.* Wolf-cub.
lupaia [lupAia], *n.f.* Wolf's lair.
lupanare. *n.m.* Brothel.
lupesco, *a.* Wolfish.
lupetto, lupicino, *n.m.* Wolf-cub.
lupinaio [lupinAio], *n.m.* Field of lupins; seller of lupins.
lupinella, *n.f.* (*Bot.*) Sainfoin.
lupino, *n.m.* (*Bot.*) Lupin.
lupino, *a.* Lupine, wolfish.
lupo, *n.m.* (*Zool.*) Wolf. **— di mare,** (*Zool.*) sea-pike; (*colloq.*) old salt, sea-dog; **in bocca al —!** good luck! **cane —,** Alsatian dog; **freddo da lupi,** severe cold, bitter weather.
luppoliera, *n.f.* Hop-garden, hop-yard.
luppolo [lUppolo], *n.m.* (*Bot.*) Hop.
lurco, *a.* Gluttonous, greedy.
luridezza, luridità [**-à**], *n.f.* Filthiness.
lurido [lUrido], *a.* Foul, filthy, loathsome.
lusco, *n.m.* **Tra il — e il brusco,** at dusk [cp **losco**].
lusignolo [cp. **usignolo**].
lusinga, *n.f.* Allurement, enticement; flattery; attraction, charm.
lusingamento, *n.m.* Blandishment.
lusingare, *v.t.* To flatter, to blandish; to entice, to allure, to coax; to deceive.
lusingarsi, *v.r.* To flatter oneself, to deceive oneself; to dare to hope; to feel confident.
lusingatore, lusingatrice, *n.m.f.* Flatterer, deceiver, tempter, temptress.
lusingatore, lusinghevole [lusinghEvole], *a.* Flattering, tempting, alluring.
lusinghevolmente, *adv.* Temptingly.
lusinghiero, *a.* Flattering, alluring; promising; kind, sympathetic, favourable.
lusitano, *n.m.a.* Lusitanian ; Portuguese.
lussamento, *n.m.* Dislocation.
lussarsi, *v.r.* To dislocate, to put out of joint.
lussazione, *n.f.* (*Med.*) Dislocation.
Lussemburgo, *n.m.* (*Geog.*) Luxemburg.
lusso, *n.m.* Luxury, pomp, display, magnificence; extravagance. (*Rail.*) **Treno di —,** train de luxe; (*colloq.*) **fare del —,** to show off, to "swank"; **che lusso!** What a (vulgar) display!
lussuoso, *a.* Sumptuous, luxurious, rich; magnificent.
lussureggiante, *a.* Luxuriant; exuberant, fertile, prolific.
lussureggiare, *v.i.* To live in luxury; to grow luxuriantly.
lussuria [lussUria], *n.f.* Lust, concupiscence, wantonness, lechery.
lussuriosamente, *adv.* Lustfully, lecherously.
lussurioso, *a.* Lustful, lewd, concupiscent, wanton.
lustra, *n.f.* Deception, appearance, mere show; pretext; shift.
lustrale, *a.* Purifying, holy; sacrificial.
lustrare, *v.t.* To polish, to shine, to gloss; to brighten; (*fig.*) to flatter.
lustrascarpe, *n.m.* Shoe-black; boots (in a hotel).
lustratore, *n.m.* Polisher.
lustratura, *n.f.* Polishing.
lustrino, *n.m.* Sequin, tinsel, jet (trimming); shoe-black; (*fig.*) gaudy show.
lustro (1), *n.m.* Lustre, splendour; gloss, sheen; polish.
lustro (2), *n.m.* Lustrum (period of five years).
lustro, *a.* Shining, bright, lustrous; glossy; glittering; polished.
luteo [lUteo], *a.* Yellow, saffron.
luteranesimo, luteranismo [luteranEsimo], *n.m.* Lutheranism.
luterano, *n.m.a.* Lutheran, Protestant.
luto, *n.m.* Mud; clay [cp. **loto** (1)].
lutreola [lutrEola], *n.m.* (*Zool.*) Otter [cp. **lontra**].
lutto, *n.m.* Mourning, grief sorrow. **— pesante,** deep mourning; **portare il —, vestire a —,** to wear mourning; **carta da —,** black-edged note-paper.
luttuosamente, *adv.* Mournfully.
luttuoso, *a.* Mournful, doleful, sad, lamentable.
lutulento, *a.* Muddy, turbid, miry.

M

M, m, *n.m.f.* Eleventh letter of the Italian alphabet.
ma, *conj.* But; why; nay; however. **Ma!** expression of doubt or incredulity; **Ma che!** Not at all! **Ma si!** Yes, of course! **Ma come!** Most assuredly! Without doubt! **Coi se e coi ma non si fa nulla,** nothing is accomplished by ifs and buts.
macabro, *a.* Macabre, gruesome; weird; horrible. **Danza macabra,** dance of death.
macaco, macacco, *n.m.* (*Zool.*) Macaco (monkey).
macadam [macadAm], *n.m.* Macadam (paving).
macadamizzare, *v.t.* To macadamize.
macao, *n.m.* (*Cards*) Baccarat.
macaone, *n.m.* (*Zool.*) Swallow-tail butterfly.
macca, *n.f.* Abundance, plenty. **A —,** in abundance.
Maccabei [maccabEi], *n.m.pl.* (*Hist.*) Maccabees. **Giuda Maccabeo,** Judas Maccabeus.
maccarello, *n.m.* (*Zool.*) Mackerel.
maccheronata, *n.f.* Feast of macaroni.
maccherone (usu. in pl. **maccheroni**), *n.m.* Macaroni; spaghetti; (*fig.*) blockhead. **Cascare come il cacio sui maccheroni,** to happen at the right time, to be very welcome.
maccheronea [maccheronEa], *n.f.* (*Lit.*) Macaronic poem.
maccheronesco, maccheronico [maccherOnico], *a.* Macaronic; burlesque; dog Latin.
macchia [mAcchia] (1), *n.f.* Stain, mark, spot, speckle; blemish, blot. **Abito pieno di macchie,** suit covered with stains; **— solare,** sunspot.
macchia [mAcchia] (2), *n.f.* Sketch, rough drawing, draft; oddity, queer fellow.
macchia [mAcchia] (3), *n.f.* Thicket, wood, jungle. **Darsi alla —,** to take to the woods; to turn highwayman; **stampare alla —,** to print a pirated edition, to print clandestinely; **alla —,** secretly.
macchiaiuolo, *n.m.* (*Art*) Impressionist painter.
macchiamento, *n.m.* Stain.
macchiare, *v.t.* To stain, to blot, to mark, to speckle; to sully, to tarnish.
macchiarsi, *v.r.* To stain one's face or clothes, to dirty oneself, to get dirty; to disgrace oneself.
macchiatico [macchiAtico], *n.m.* Right to cut and collect undergrowth.
macchiato, *a.* Spotted, dirty; (of horses) dappled.
macchietta, *n.f.* Speck, spot; odd person, "character", eccentric.
macchiettare, *v.t.* To speckle, to dapple.
macchiettista (*pl.* **macchiettisti**), *n.m.* Sketcher; caricaturist; (*Theat.*) comedian.
macchina [mAcchina], *n.f.* Machine, engine; apparatus; (*Motor*) car; cycle; automaton; (*Phot.*) camera; (*Print.*) press, machine; machinery in general. **— a vapore,** steam engine; **— da scrivere,** typewriter; **— da cucire,** sewing-machine; **— fotografica,** camera; **— infernale,** bomb; **andare in —,** to go by (motor) car; **il giornale va in — alle due del mattino,** the paper goes to press at 2 a.m.; **mettere in moto una —,** to start an engine; **fare — in dietro,** to reverse the engine; to go back, retire.
macchinale, *a.* Mechanical.
macchinalmente, *adv.* Mechanically.
macchinamento, *n.m.* Machination, intrigue.
macchinare, *v.t.i.* To plot, to intrigue, to scheme.
macchinario [macchinArio], *n.m.* Machinery.
macchinazione, *n.f.* Machination, plot, intrigue.
macchinetta, *n.f.* (*Naut.*) Donkey-engine; small machine. **— del caffè,** coffee-maker.
macchinismo, *n.m.* Machinery.
macchinista (*pl.* **macchinisti**), *n.m.* Machinist, engine-driver; engineer.
macchinosamente, *adv.* In a complicated fashion.
macchinoso, *a.* Complicated, complex; involved, heavy.
macchiolina, *n.f.* Small spot, stain.
macco, *n.m.* Mash of beans. **A —,** in abundance.
macedone [macEdone], *n.m.a.* Macedonian.
Macedonia [macedOnia], *n.f.* (*Geog.*) Macedonia.
macedonia [macedOnia], *n.f.* Macedoine, fruit salad.
macellabile [macellAbile], *a.* Fit for the butcher.
macellaio [macellAio], *n.m.* Butcher.
macellamento, *n.m.* Slaughter (of beasts).
macellare, *v.t.* To butcher; to slaughter.
macellaro, *n.m.* Butcher.
macellatore, *n.m.* Slaughterer.
macellazione, *n.f.* Slaughter (of beasts).
macelleria [macellerIa], *n.f.* Butcher's shop.
macello, *n.m.* Slaughter-house, shambles; (*fig.*) massacre. **Carne da —,** cannon-fodder.
macerabile [macerAbile], *a.* Suitable for maceration.
maceramento, *n.m.* Maceration.
macerare, *v.t.* To macerate, to ret, to steep (flax, hemp, etc.).
macerarsi, *v.r.* To mortify oneself; to weaken.
maceratoio [maceratOio], *n.m.* Retting-tank; macerating-vat, rettery.
macerazione, *n.f.* Steeping, retting; (*fig.*) mortification.
macereto, *n.m.* Rubbish heap; debris, rubble.
maceria [macEria], *n.f.* Dry wall; (*pl.*) ruins; debris, wreckage.
macero [mAcero], *n.m.* Rettery, steeping-tank, retting-vat. **Mandare libri al macero,** to send books for pulping.
macerone, *n.m.* (*Bot.*) Alexanders (potherb resembling celery).
machera, *n.f.* Kind of short sword.
machia [mAchia], *n.f.* Cunning, dissimulation, feigning.
machiavellicamente, *adv.* Craftily.
machiavellico [machiavEllico], *a.* Machiavellian, crafty, cunning.
machiavellismo, *n.m.* Machiavellianism, political cunning.
macia [macIa], *n.f.* Heap of stones; debris [cp. **maceria**].
macie, *n.f.* (*Lit.*) Thinness.

macigno, *n.m.* Boulder, block of stone; hard stone.
macilento, macilente, *a.* Emaciated; lank.
macilenza, *n.f.* Emaciation.
macina [mAcina], *n.f.* Mill-stone.
macinabile [macinAbile], *a.* Capable of being ground.
macinacolori, *n.m.* Grinder of artists' colouring.
macinamento, *n.m.* Grinding, milling.
macinare, *v.t.* To grind, to mill; to pound, to crush.
macinata, *n.f.* Amount ground at a time; grinding, milling.
macinato, *n.m.* Flour, meal; (*Law*) **tassa sul —,** tax on flour.
macinatoio [macinatOio], *n.m.* Mill; olive-press; corn-mill.
macinatura, macinazione, *n.f.* Grinding, milling, pounding.
macinello, *n.m.* Tool for grinding artists' colours.
macinino, *n.m.* Coffee or pepper mill; (*colloq.*) ramshackle vehicle, bone-shaker.
macinio [macinIo], *n.m.* Continuous grinding.
macis, *n.m.* (*obs.*) Mace (spice).
maciulla, *n.f.* Brake (for flax).
maciullare, *v.t.* To break flax or hemp; (*fig.*) to chew, to crush.
macolare, *v.t.* To bruise (fruits, etc.); to stain.
macolazione, *n.f.* Bruising (fruit).
macolo [mAcolo], *a.* Bruised.
macrobiologia, *n.f.* macrobiology.
macrocefalia, *n.f.* macrocephaly.
macrocefalo [macrocEfalo], *a.* Macrocephalous.
macrocosmo, *n.m.* Macrocosm.
macroscopico, *a.* macroscopic, visible to the naked eye.
macula [mAcula], *n.f.* (*Lit.*) Stain, spot; blemish.
maculare, *v.t.* To stain; to tarnish.
madama, *n.f.* Madam; lady.
madamigella, *n.f.* Mademoiselle, miss; damsel.
madamina, *n.f.* Young shop-girl.
Maddalena, *n.f.* Magdalen, Madeleine.
maddaleone, *n.m.* (*Med.*) Roll of sticking-plaster.
Madera, *n.f.* (*Geog.*) Madeira; madeira wine.
madia [mAdia], *n.f.* Kneading-trough; bread-bin.
madido [mAdido], *a.* Wet, wet through, drenched, soaked; moist, damp. **— di sudore,** wet with sweat.
Madonna, *n.f.* Our Lady, the Blessed Virgin, The Virgin Mary; picture or statue of her; title of respect given to high-born woman (in Middle Ages and Renaissance); (*Art*) Madonna.
madonnina, *n.f.* Small picture or statue of Our Lady. **Una — infilzata,** a plaster saint, a prude.
madore, *n.m.* (*Lit.*) Moisture, dampness.
madornale, *a.* Big, gross, enormous, huge; **sproposito —,** gross error.
madornalità [-à], *n.f.* Grossness, hugeness.
madre, *n.f.* Mother (in all senses), parent; dam; womb; source; wine lees; (*fig.*) origin, cause; matrix; (*Comm.*) counterfoil. **Bolletta a — e figlia,** counterfoil printed form; **chiesa —,** mother church; **casa —,** mother house, head office; **lingua —,** mother-tongue; **è un mio parente per parte di —,** he is a relation of mine on my mother's side.
madreggiare, *v.i.* To take after one's mother; to be motherly, to mother.
madrepatria [madrepAtria], *n.f.* Mother-country, mother-land.
madreperla, *n.f.* Mother of pearl, nacre.
madreperlaceo [madreperlAceo], *a.* Made of mother of pearl, nacreous.
madrepora [madrEpora], *n.f.* (*Zool.*) Madrepore.
madreselva, *n.f.* (*Bot.*) Honeysuckle, woodbine.
madrevite, *n.f.* (*Mech.*) Female screw, nut.
madrigale, *n.m.* Madrigal.
madrigaleggiare, *v.t.* To compose or sing madrigals.
madrigna, *n.f.* Stepmother [cp. **matrigna**].
madrileno, *n.m.a.* Native of or concerning Madrid.
madrina, *n.f.* Godmother.
madroso, *a.* Porous (of a stone).
maestà [-à], *n.f.* Majesty; grandeur. **Sua Maestà,** His *or* Her Majesty.
maestosamente, *adv.* Majestically.
maestosità [-à], *n.f.* Majesty, stateliness, greatness, grandeur.
maestoso, *a.* Majestic, stately, grand; imposing.
maestra, *n.f.* Schoolmistress; teacher; (*Naut.*) mainsail. **Albero di —,** mainmast.
maestrale, *n.m.* North-west wind, mistral.
maestranza, *n.f.* Workmen, hands, operatives.
maestrevole [maestrEvole], *a.* Masterly, skilful; ingenious, excellent.
maestrevolmente, *adv.* Skilfully, in a masterly manner.
maestria [maestrIa], *n.f.* Skill, ability, cleverness; proficiency.
maestrina, *n.f.* Young schoolmistress.
maestro (1), *n.m.* Master; teacher, tutor, instructor; (*Geog.*) north-west. **— di scuola,** schoolmaster; **— di latino,** Latin master; **— di matematica,** maths. master; **di scherma,** fencing master; **— di ballo,** dancing-master; (*Naut.*) **— d'equipaggio,** boatswain; **— di cappella,** choir-master; **colpo da —,** master-stroke; **vento di —,** north-westerly wind.
maestro (2), *a.* Masterly, skilful, clever; main, chief. **Mano maestra,** chief hand; **albero —,** mainmast; **strada maestra,** main road; **muro —,** main wall.
mafia, maffia [mAfia, mAffia], *n.f.* Mafia (secret criminal society of Sicily).
mafioso, *n.m.a.* Member of or pertaining to the Mafia.
maga, *n.f.* Witch, sorceress, enchantress.
magagna, *n.f.* Taint; hidden fault or blemish; secret vice.
magagnare, *v.t.* To taint, to corrupt.
magari! *int. adv.* Would to God! I wish it were so! even, maybe, probably.
magazzinaggio [magazzinAggio], *n.m.* Warehouse dues; warehousing; storing, storage.
magazziniere, *n.m.* Warehouseman; store-keeper.

magazzino, *n.m.* Warehouse, storehouse, depot; shop; (*fig.*) heap, mass. **Fondi di —,** unsold stock; **merci in —,** goods on hand; **un — a prezzi popolari,** a low-price store; **magazzini a catena,** chain stores; **magazzini generali,** bonded warehouse.
magenta, *n.m.a.* Magenta colour.
maggesare, *v.t.* (*Agric.*) To let land lie fallow.
maggese, *n.m.* Fallow land.
maggiatico [maggiAtico], *a.* Fallow.
maggio [mAggio], *n.m.* Month of May; (*Lit.*) song of May; festival of May; **Primo —,** May Day.
maggiociondolo [maggiociOndolo], *n.m.* (*Bot.*) Laburnum.
maggiolata, *n.f.* May song.
maggiolino, *n.m.* (*Zool.*) May bug, cockchafer.
maggiorana, *n.f.* (*Bot.*) Marjoram.
maggioranza, *n.f.* Majority; pre-eminence. **A — di voti,** by a majority of votes; **in —,** for the most part.
maggiorare, *v.t.* (*Comm.*) To increase. **— il prezzo,** to raise the price.
maggiorasco, *n.m.* (*Hist.*) Entail; title and estate going to eldest son.
maggiorazione, *n.f.* (*Comm.*) Rise (in prices).
maggiordomo, *n.m.* Butler, steward.
maggiore, *n.m.* (*Mil.*) Major.
maggiore, *a.* Larger, bigger; greater; higher; older; major (in all senses). **Altare —,** high altar; **fratello —,** elder brother; **la — parte,** the majority, the largest part, most of; **forza —,** *force majeure;* **il — offerente,** highest bidder; (*Mil.*) **stato —,** staff; **egli è — di me di quattro anni,** he is 4 years older than I; **il figlio —,** the eldest son.
maggiorenne, *n.m.f.a.* Adult, of age.
maggiorente, *n.m.* Prominent man, notability.
maggiori, *n.m.pl.* Ancestors, forebears.
maggiorità [-à], *n.f.* Majority; (*Mil.*) staff.
maggiormente, *adv.* To a great degree, much more, all the more.
maggiostrina, *n.f.* (*obs.*) Straw hat.
magi, *n.m.pl.* The Magi.
magia [magIa], *n.f.* Magic; charm, enchantment. **— nera,** black magic.
magiaro, *n.m.a.* Magyar.
magicamente, *adv.* Magically.
magico [mAgico], *a.* Magic, magical. **Bacchetta magica,** magic wand; **lanterna magica,** magic lantern.
magione, *n.f.* (*Lit.*) Habitation, abode, dwelling.
magiostra, *n.f.* Variety of large strawberry.
magismo, *n.m.* (*Hist.*) Magism, Zoroastrianism.
magistero, *n.m.* Masterly skill, workmanship; teaching profession. **Scuola di —,** training-college.
magistrale, *a.* Masterly, magisterial; skilful. **Un lavoro —,** a masterly work; **con tono —,** in a magisterial voice; **scuola —,** training-college.
magistralità [-à], *n.f.* Magisterial tone and air.
magistralmente, *adv.* In a masterly manner.
magistrato, *n.m.* Magistrate, justice, judge.
magistratura, *n.f.* Magistracy, magistrature; the Bench.
maglia [mAglia], *n.f.* Stitch; mesh; knot, link; knitted garment, singlet, vest; network. **Lavorare a —,** to knit; **a —,** knitted, **è caduta una —,** I've dropped a stitch; **portare una — di lana,** to wear a woollen vest.
maglieria [maglierIa], *n.f.* Hosiery, knitted goods; hosier's shop.
maglietta, *n.f.* Split ring; light woollen vest.
maglio [mAglio], *n.m.* Mallet, sledgehammer.
magliuolo, *n.m.* (*Agric.*) Cutting from a vine; shoot.
magnanimamente, *adv.* Magnanimously.
magnanimo [magnAnimo], *a.* Magnanimous, noble-minded, high-souled; generous.
magnano, *n.m.* Locksmith, coppersmith.
magnare, *v.t.i.* (*colloq.*) To eat [cp. **mangiare**]
magnate, *n.m.* Magnate, grandee; notability; leading man.
magnatizio [magnatIzio], *a.* Appertaining to magnates; rich, noble.
magnesia [magnEsia], *n.f.* (*Chem.*) Magnesia.
magnesio [magnEsio], *n.m.* (*Chem.*) Magnesium.
magnete, *n.m.* Magnet; (*Motor.*) magneto.
magneticamente, *adv.* Magnetically.
magnetico [magnEtico], *a.* Magnetic; attractive.
magnetismo, *n.m.* Magnetism.
magnetite, *n.f.* Lode-stone, magnetite.
magnetizzare, *v.t.* To magnetize; to mesmerize.
magnetizzatore, magnetizzatrice, *n.m.f.* Magnetizer; charmer; mesmerizer.
magneto-elettrico, *a.* Magneto-electric.
magnetometro [magnetOmetro], *n.m.* Magnetometer.
magnificamente, *adv.* Magnificently.
magnificamento, *n.m.* Magnification.
magnificare, *v.t.* To magnify, to extol, to exalt; to exaggerate.
magnificenza, *n.f.* Magnificence, splendour, pomp. **Vostra —,** Your Excellency.
magnifico [magnIfico], *a.* Magnificent, splendid, admirable, wonderful.
magniloquente, *a.* Magniloquent, bombastic.
magniloquenza, *n.f.* Magniloquence.
magno, *a.* Great, illustrious, noble; lofty, solemn. **Aula magna,** great hall (of a university, etc.); **pompa magna,** high pomp and state.
magnolia [magnOlia], *n.f.* (*Bot.*) Magnolia.
mago, *n.m.* Wizard, magician, sorcerer.
magona, *n.f.* Iron-foundry; store of pig iron.
magoniere, *n.m.* Foreman in an iron-foundry.
Magonza, *n.f.* (*Geog.*) Mainz, Mayence.
magra, *n.f.* Low water. **Il fiume è in —,** the river is low; (*fig.*) **tempi di —,** hard times, lean times.
magramente, *adv.* Meagrely, thinly.
magrezza, *n.f.* Leanness, thinness, slenderness; scantiness.
magro, *n.m.* Lenten diet; lean (meat). **Giorno di —,** fast day.

magro, *a.* Lean, meagre; thin, slender; poor. **— come una sardella,** thin as a lath; **terreno —,** poor land; **pranzo —,** scanty dinner; **carne magra,** lean meat; **scusa magra,** lame excuse; **magra consolazione,** poor consolation; **diventar —,** to grow thin; **mangiar di —,** to abstain from eating meat.
mai, *adv.* Never; ever. **Mai più,** never again; **quanto mai,** very much indeed; **tante mai cose,** so many things; **come mai ?** how is that? **più che mai,** more than ever; **caso mai, se mai,** if ever, in case, if by chance; **meglio tardi che mai,** better late than never; **non si sa mai,** you never can tell.
maiala, *n.f.* (*Zool.*) Sow.
maiale, *n.m.* Pig, swine; hog. **Carne di —,** pork; **grasso di —,** lard; **pelle di —,** pigskin.
maialesco, *a.* Swinish, dirty, foul.
mainò, *adv.* Certainly not, by no means.
maio, *n.m.* Branch of may; mayflower.
maiolica [maiOlica], *n.f.* Majolica ware.
maionese, *n.f.* Mayonnaise sauce.
Maiorca, *n.f.* (*Geog.*) Majorca.
mais [mAis], *n.m.* (*Bot.*) Maize, Indian corn.
maiuscoletto, *n.m.* (*Typ.*) Small capital.
maiuscolo [maiUscolo], *a.* Capital letter (in writing or printing); (*fig.*) big, gross. **Errore —,** gross blunder.
mal [cp. **male**].
malacarne, *n.f.* Tainted meat; offal.
Malacca, *n.f.* (*Geog.*) Malacca. **Penisola di —,** Malaya, Malay Peninsula.
malaccetto, *a.* Unacceptable.
malaccio [malAccio], *n.m.* Serious evil; dangerous illness.
malaccio [malAccio], *adv.* Badly. **Non c'è —,** not so badly.
malaccolto, *a.* Unwelcome, unwanted, undesired.
malacconcio [malaccOncio], *a.* Unfit, unsuitable.
malaccortamente, *adv.* Ill-advisedly.
malaccortezza, *n.f.* Imprudence, ill-advisedness.
malaccorto, *a.* Ill-advised, imprudent, incautious, rash.
Malachia, *n.m.* Malachi.
malachite, *n.f.* (*Min.*) Malachite.
malacia [malacIa], *n.f.* Pregnant woman's longing (for special food).
malacreanza, *n.f.* Ill-breeding, bad manners, boorishness, rudeness.
malafede, *n.f.* Bad faith; **Essere in —,** to act in bad faith.
malaffare, *n.m.* Evil living; bad life. **Una donna di —,** a lady of easy virtue.
malaffetto, *a.* Ill-disposed.
malafitta, *n.f.* Quagmire.
malagevole [malagEvole], *a.* Hard, difficult, intricate, bad (road).
malagevolezza, *n.f.* Badness, difficulty; fatigue.
malagevolmente, *adv.* With difficulty, badly.
malagiato, *a.* Uncomfortable; poor, hard-up.
malagrazia [malagrAzia], *n.f.* Bad grace; incivility; uncouthness, rudeness.
malalingua [malalIngua], *n.f.* Back-biter, slanderer, evil tongue; gossip.
malamente, *adv.* Badly.
malandare, *v.i.* To go badly, to go to ruin; to take a turn for the worse.
malandato, *a.* In a bad way; in bad repair; reduced, worn-out; in poor health, run down.
malandrinaggio [malandrinAggio], *n.m.* Brigandage; robbery, highway robbery.
malandrinesco, *a.* Like a highwayman; rascally.
malandrino, *n.m.* Highwayman, footpad; rogue, rascal, scoundrel.
malanimo [malAnimo], *n.m.* Ill-will; rancour, grudge; malevolence.
malanno, *n.m.* Calamity, misfortune; illness. **Prendersi un —,** to fall ill.
malaparata, *n.f.* Impending danger or disaster. **Vista la —,** seeing that a storm is brewing.
malapena, *adv.* Barely, hardly, only just, with difficulty.
malaria [malAria], *n.f.* (*Med.*) Malaria.
malarico [malArico], *a.* Malarial.
malarnese, *n.m.* Bad state or condition; scamp, rogue, good-for-nothing.
malarrivato, *a.* Unwelcome, unfortunate, in a bad way; unlucky.
malaticcio [malatIccio], *a.* Sickly, unwell; delicate.
malato, *n.m.a.* Sick man, patient, invalid; ill, sick; sore. **Un piede —,** a sore foot; **cader —,** to fall ill.
malattia [malattIa], *n.f.* Illness, disease, sickness, malady, ailment, complaint. **— infettiva,** infectious disease; **una grave —,** a serious illness; **prendere una —,** to catch a complaint; **guarire da una —,** to recover from an illness.
malauguratamente, *adv.* Unluckily, inauspiciously.
malaugurato, *a.* Ill-omened, inauspicious, ill-fated; unlucky.
malaugurio [malaugUrio], *n.m.* Evil omen.
malaventura, *n.f.* Misadventure, misfortune.
malavita, *n.f.* Criminal underworld.
malavoglia [malavOglia], *n.f.* Disinclination; ill-will; unwillingness; sloth.
malavvedutamente, *adv.* Ill-advisedly, rashly.
malavveduto, *a.* Ill-advised, imprudent, rash.
malavventura, *n.f.* Mischance.
malavventuratamente, *adv.* By mischance.
malavventuroso, *a.* Ill-fated, unfortunate.
malavvezzo, *a.* Ill-bred, unmannerly.
malavviato, *a.* Vicious; unruly.
malavvisato, *a.* Ill-advised, unwise.
malazzato, *a.* Ailing, indisposed, sickly.
malcaduco, *n.m.* (*Med.*) Epilepsy.
malcapitato, *a.* Ill-fated, luckless, unfortunate.
malcautamente, *adv.* Incautiously.
malcauto, *a.* Incautious, rash.
malcerto, *a.* Uncertain, doubtful.
malcollocato, *a.* Misplaced.
malcominciato, *a.* Begun badly.
malcompostamente, *adv.* Confusedly.
malcomposto, *a.* Confused, badly composed; awkward.
malconcio [malcOncio], *a.* Battered, knocked about, bruised; (*fig.*) dilapidated, in a sorry plight.
malconsigliato, *a.* Ill-advised.

malcontento, *n.m.a.* Discontent, dissatisfaction, grievance; discontented, displeased; disappointed.
malcoperto, *a.* Insufficiently covered, half-naked.
malcorrisposto, *a.* Unrequited, ill-requited, not reciprocated. **Amore —,** unrequited love.
malcostumato, *a.* Ill-mannered; debauched.
malcostume, *n.m.* Debauchery; misconduct; bad habit, evil custom.
malcreato, *a.* Ill-bred, churlish.
malcurante, *a.* Careless; negligent.
malcurato, *a.* Not properly cared for; not well cured.
maldentato, *a.* With bad teeth; (*Zool.*) edentate.
maldestro, *a.* Awkward, clumsy, uncouth.
maldetto, *a.* Ill-said, badly expressed.
maldicente, *n.m.a.* Slanderer, back-biter; slanderous, calumnious.
maldicenza, *n.f.* Slander, calumny; gossip, scandal.
maldisposto, *a.* Ill-disposed, ill-intentioned, (**verso,** towards).
male, mal, *n.m.* Evil; ill; wrong; harm, damage; illness, disease, ache, pain; suffering, trouble; discomfort; misfortune. **Non fa —,** it does not hurt; **— di mare,** seasickness; **— di cuore,** heart disease; **— di ventre,** stomach-ache; **— di denti,** toothache; **— del paese,** homesickness; **avere —,** to have a pain; **voler —,** to bear ill-will; **niente di —,** no harm, no offence meant; **andare a —,** to go bad, to turn sour; **farsi —,** to hurt oneself; **metter —,** to cause trouble.
male, *adv.* Badly, ill, wrong, wrongly; uncomfortably; amiss; unwell. **Non c'è —,** pretty well, pretty good, all right; **star —,** to be ill; **andar —,** to go badly; **aversela a —,** to take it amiss; **di — in peggio,** from bad to worse; **manco —!** well and good, let it be so!; **sentirsi —,** to feel unwell; **pensar —,** to be in anxiety; **restar —,** to become annoyed; **cavarsela —,** to come off badly; **finir —,** to turn out badly; **meno — che sei venuto,** it is a good thing that you've come; **non farebbe — a una mosca,** he wouldn't hurt a fly.
maledettamente, *adv.* Cursedly.
maledetto! *inter.* Curse! Curse it!
maledetto, *a.* Cursed, damned; hateful, odious. **Alla maledetta,** furiously.
maledico [malEdico], *a.* Slanderous [cp. **maldicente**].
maledire, *v.t.* To curse; to detest.
maledizione, *n.f.* Malediction, curse, anathema, oath; plague, calamity, ill-luck.
maleducato, *a.* Uncivil, impolite, rude, ill-bred.
malefatta, *n.f.* Flaw (in making or manufacture); misdeed.
maleficamente, *adv.* Perniciously; harmfully; balefully.
maleficio, malefizio [malefIcio, malefIzio], *n.m.* Evil spell; crime; witchcraft.
malefico [malEfico], *a.* Pernicious, noxious, harmful.
malerba, *n.f.* Noxious weed.
malese, *n.m.a.* Malay.
Malesia [malEsia], *n.f.* (*Geog.*) Malaya.
malesperto, *a.* Inexpert.
malessere [malEssere], *n.m.* Indisposition, malaise; uneasiness; difficulty.
malestante, *a.* Poor, indigent.
malestrino, *n.m.* Mischievous child.
malestro, *n.m.* Damage, breakage (caused by children, etc.); piece of mischief.
malevolenza, *n.f.* Malevolence, spitefulness; ill-will, malice.
malevolo [malEvolo], *a.* Malevolent, ill-disposed, unfriendly, malicious.
malfare, *v.i.* To do evil, to do wrong.
malfatto, *n.m.* Misdeed.
malfatto, *a.* Badly made, ill-shapen.
malfattore, *n.m.* Evil-doer, criminal, malefactor.
malfermo, *a.* Unsteady, unstable, wavering; uncertain; sickly, delicate. **— in salute,** in indifferent health.
malfidato, *a.* Suspicious, distrustful.
malfido, *a.* Untrustworthy, treacherous, suspicious.
malfondato, *a.* Unsteady; ill-founded, baseless.
malformato, *a.* Malformed, badly formed.
malformazione, *n.f.* Malformation.
malfortunato, *a.* Unfortunate.
malfrancese, *n.m.* (*Med.*) Syphilis.
malgarbo, *n.m.* Bad grace, rudeness, impoliteness; clumsiness.
malgascio [malgAscio], *n.m.a.* Malagasy; of Madagascar.
malgiudicare, *v.t.* To misjudge (persons, etc.).
malgoverno, *n.m.* Misgovernment, misrule; mismanagement.
malgradito, *a.* Unwelcome, unwanted, disagreeable.
malgrado, *adv.* In spite of, notwithstanding. **— che,** although; **mio —,** against my will.
malgraziosamente, *adv.* Ungraciously.
malgrazioso, *a.* Ungracious, unattractive.
malguardato, *a.* Badly looked after; not kept in order; unguarded.
malgusto, *n.m.* Bad taste.
malia [malIa], *n.f.* Charm, spell, enchantment, witchcraft. **Rompere la —,** to break the spell.
maliarda, *n.f.* Enchantress, witch, sorceress.
maliardo, *n.m.* Wizard, sorcerer.
malibran, *n.f.* Kind of open carriage (named after the singer).
malico [mAlico], *a.* (*Chem.*) Malic. **Acido —,** malic acid.
malignamente, *adv.* Malignantly, spitefully.
malignare, *v.i.* To backbite, to slander, to malign.
malignità [-à], *n.f.* Malignity, malevolence; back-biting, slander, calumny.
maligno, *n.m.a.* Slanderer, spiteful person; backbiter; malignant, malign, spiteful, malicious, slanderous, malevolent, ill-disposed. **Tumore —,** malignant tumour; **spirito —,** evil spirit. **Il Maligno,** the devil.
malinconia [malinconIa], *n.f.* Melancholy, sadness, gloom, dejection; (*Med.*) melancholia.
malinconicamente, *adv.* Gloomily, in a melancholy manner.
malinconico [malincOnico], *a.* Melancholy, dejected, sad, depressed.

malinconioso, *a.* Melancholy, depressing, gloomy.
malincuore, *adv.* Unwillingly, reluctantly. **A —,** unwillingly.
malino, *adv.* Badly. **Non c'è —,** not so badly.
malintenzionato, *a.* Ill-intentioned, evil-minded.
malinteso, *n.m.* Misunderstanding, equivocation. **A scanso di malintesi,** to avoid misunderstandings.
malinteso, *a.* Misunderstood, mistaken.
malioso, *a.* Crafty, by enchantment.
malissimo, *adv.* Very badly.
malizia [malIzia], *n.f.* Malice; roguishness; shrewdness, cunning; archness.
malizietta, *n.f.* Artifice, trick.
maliziosamente, *adv.* Maliciously.
maliziosità [-à], *n.f.* Maliciousness.
malizioso, *a.* Malicious; shrewd, cunning; arch. **Sorriso —,** arch smile; **occhi maliziosi,** roguish eyes.
malleabile [malleAbile], *a.* Malleable, pliable.
malleabilità [-à], *n.f.* Malleability.
malleabilmente, *adv.* Pliably.
malleolo [mallEolo], *n.m.* (*Anat.*) Ankle-bone.
mallevadore, *n.m.* Surety, guarantor, bail. **Stare —,** to go bail; **restare —,** to stand surety.
mallevadoria [mallevadOria], *n.f.* Guarantee, bail, surety, security.
mallevare, *v.t.* To guarantee.
malleveria [malleverIa], *n.f.* Bail, security, suretyship.
mallo, *n.m.* Husk, shell (of a nut).
malmaritata, *n.f.* Unhappily-married woman.
malmaturo, *a.* Immature, unmatured.
malmenare, *v.t.* To illtreat, to mishandle; to beat, to ill-use.
malmenio [malmenIo], *n.m.* Constant ill-usage.
malmeritare, *v.i.* To deserve punishment.
malmesso, *a.* Badly arranged; shabbily dressed, badly dressed.
malnato, *a.* Ill-bred, rascally; ill-fated; misbegotten.
malnoto, *a.* Insufficiently known, little-known.
malo, *a.* Bad, ill, evil. **Mala sorte,** unhappy fate; **mala riuscita,** failure; **mala stagione,** bad season; **mala lingua,** slanderous tongue; **mala voglia,** ill-will; disinclination; **prendere in mala parte,** to take amiss; **cacciar qualcuno in — modo,** to send someone away with a flea in his ear.
malocchio [malOcchio], *n.m.* Evil eye. **Di —,** askance; unfavourably; **vedere qualcuno di —,** to look askance at someone.
malonesto, *a.* Dishonest.
malora, *n.f.* Ruin, perdition. **Andare in —,** to go to ruin; **mandare alla —,** to send to the devil, to send to blazes; **Alla —!** To hell with it!
malordinatamente, *adv.* In a disordered manner.
malordinato, *a.* Disordered.
malore, *n.m.* Sudden illness, indisposition; collapse, breakdown; misfortune. **Esser colto da —,** to be taken suddenly ill, to collapse.
malosservato, *a.* Unfulfilled.
malotico [malOtico], *a.* Malign, ill-disposed.
malpensante, *a.* Evil-thinking; ill-devised, badly thought out.
malpersuaso, *a.* Unpersuaded.
malpiglio [malpIglio], *n.m.* Angry look, frown, scowl; glance of disdain.
malpratico [malprAtico], *a.* Inexperienced, inexpert, unacquainted with.
malpreparato, *a.* Ill-prepared.
malprò [-ò], *n.m.* Harm, hurt (esp. from food).
malproprio [malprOprio], *a.* Unclean; improper.
malprovvisto, malprovveduto, *a.* Ill-provided.
malsania [malsanIa], *n.f.* Unhealthiness.
malsano, *a.* Unhealthy, unwholesome; morbid.
malsicuro, *a.* Insecure, unsafe, unsteady; uncertain.
malsincero, *a.* Insincere.
malsoddisfatto, *a.* Dissatisfied, discontented.
malsofferente, *a.* Intolerant, suffering unwillingly, impatient of.
malsonante, *a.* Evil-sounding; discordant.
malsussistente, *a.* Unsubstantial.
malta, *n.f.* (*Arch.*) Mortar.
maltagliati, *n.m.pl.* Kind of paste in mixed shapes for soups.
maltalento, *n.m.* Ill-will, evil mind; bad disposition.
maltempo, *n.m.* Foul weather.
maltenuto, *a.* Badly kept, unkept, unkempt.
maltese, *n.m.a.* Maltese.
malto, *n.m.* Malt.
maltolto, *n.m.a.* Extortion, exaction; ill-gotten gains; wrongly taken, extorted, ill-gotten.
maltrattamento, *n.m.* Ill-treatment, bullying, ill-usage.
maltrattare, *v.t.* To ill-treat; to abuse, to bully; to mob.
maltusiano, *a.* Malthusian.
maluccio [malUccio], *adv.* Badly. **Non c'è —,** not so badly.
malumore, *n.m.* Ill-humour, bad temper, crossness; discontent; discord. **Essere di —,** to be in a bad mood.
malusanza, *n.f.* Evil custom, bad habit.
malva, *n.f.* (*Bot.*) Mallow.
malvaccini, *n.m.pl.* (*Bot.*) Variety of geranium.
malvagiamente, *adv.* Wickedly, villainously.
malvagio [malvAgio], *a.* Wicked, villainous, rascally; noxious.
malvagità [-à], *n.f.* Wickedness, villainy, perfidy.
malvasia [malvasIa], *n.f.* Kind of grape; malmsey.
malvavischio [malvavIschio], *n.m.* (*Bot.*) Marsh mallow.
malvedere, *v.i.* To regard with ill favour; to look askance at.
malveduto, *a.* Disliked.
malvenuto, *a.* Unwelcome.
malversatore, *n.m.* Embezzler.
malversazione, *n.f.* Embezzlement, malversation.
malvestito, *a.* Badly dressed, shabby.
malvissuto, *a.* Dissolute, ill-living.
malvisto, *a.* Disliked, unpopular.
malvivente, *n.m.a.* Criminal, rogue; dissolute, ill-living.

malvivenza, *n.f.* Dissoluteness.
malvivo, *a.* Half-dead.
malvolentieri, *adv.* Unwillingly, reluctantly.
malvolere, *n.m.* Ill-will, rancour, malevolence.
malvoluto, *a.* Hated, detested, disliked.
malvone, *n.m.* (*Bot.*) Hollyhock.
mamma, *n.f.* Mother, mama; (*Poet.*) breast. **Mamma mia!** Dear me!
mammalucco, *n.m.* Mameluke; (*fig.*) blockhead, dolt.
mammario [mammArio], *n.* (*Anat.*) Mammary.
mammella, *n.f.* Breast; teat; udder (of cow, etc.).
mammellare, *a.* (*Anat.*) Mammary, mammillary.
mammifero [mammIfero], *n.m.* (*Zool.*) Mammal. **I mammiferi,** the mammalia.
mammifero [mammIfero], *a.* Mammiferous.
mammina, *n.f.* (*colloq.*) Mummy, mammy.
mammola [mAmmola], *n.f.* (*Bot.*) Sweet violet.
mammone, *n.m.* Mammon; (*Zool.*) mandril.
mammoso, *a.* Big-bosomed.
mammut, *n.m.* (*Zool.*) Mammoth.
manale, *n.m.* Saddler's and sailmaker's palm.
manata, *n.f.* Slap, pat, cuff; handful. **A manate,** by handfuls.
manca, *n.f.* Left hand, left side, left. **A —,** to the left, on the left.
mancamento, *n.m.* Deficiency; imperfection; faint, swoon.
mancante, *n.m.a.* Absentee; lacking, deficient, wanting, short. **— di danaro,** short of money; **gli oggetti mancanti,** the missing objects; **— di un braccio,** without an arm; **— di buon senso,** lacking common sense; **— di peso,** short in weight.
mancanza, *n.f.* Lack, want, deficiency; absence; fault, neglect; imperfection. **In — di,** in default of; **commettere una —,** to commit an offence; **per — di tempo,** for want of time; **sentire la — di una persona,** to miss a person.
mancare, *v.t.i.* To fall short, to fail, to miss; to lack, to want, to be wanting; to be in need of; to decrease, to decline; to cease, to come to an end; to stand in need of; to misfire; to be at fault; to turn faint. **— il colpo,** to miss one's aim; **— di parola,** to break one's word; **— ai vivi,** to die; **mancano tre volumi,** three volumes are missing; **mi manca l'aria nativa,** I miss my native air; **manca d'intelligenza,** he lacks intelligence; **non ci mancherebbe altro!** this would be the last straw! **non ci mancava altro,** that is the limit! **— poco,** to be very near; **io non mancherò di,** I will not fail to; **gli mancano i soldi,** he's hard up; **— di rispetto a,** to show disrespect to; **non — di venire,** don't fail to come; **— un'occasione,** to miss an opportunity; **manca mezz'ora,** there's still half an hour; **non mi manca nulla,** there is nothing I need; **quanto manca a partire?** how long do we wait before leaving? **manca l'acqua,** the water's turned off; **mancò poco che non accadesse una disgrazia,** there was almost an accident.
mancato, *p.p.a.* Unsuccessful, failed; missed.
mancatore, *n.m.* Defaulter; one who fails.
manchevole [manchEvole], *a.* Lacking, deficient, defective, faulty.
manchevolezza, *n.f.* Defectiveness, faultiness; defect.
manchevolmente, *adv.* Imperfectly.
mancia [mAncia], *n.f.* Tip, gratuity; gift, present. **Dare una —,** to tip; **dare uno scellino e mezzo di —,** to give a tip of 1/6.
manciata, *n.f.* Handful.
mancinismo, *n.m.* Left-handedness.
mancino, *n.m.a.* Left-handed man; left-handed; left (of hand or foot); intractable; dubious, dishonest. **Colpo —,** shady trick; **— manritto,** ambidextrous.
mancipio [mancIpio], *n.m.* (*Hist.*) Slave; servant.
manciù [-ù], *n.m.a.* Manchu.
Manciuria [manciUria], *n.f.* (*Geog.*) Manchuria.
manco, *a.* Left side. **Dal lato —, a mano manca,** on the left.
manco, *adv.* Not even; less. **— male,** so much the better; **— per sogno,** not in the least; **al —,** at least.
mandamentale, *a.* Departmental, divisional.
mandamento, *n.m.* District, division; area of (local) government.
mandante, *n.m.* (*Law*) Principal; abettor, instigator.
mandare, *v.t.* To send, to send on, to transmit; to forward, to dispatch; to emit, to utter, to put in circulation. **— ad effetto,** to carry out; **— a chiamare,** to send for; **— via,** to send away; **— a dire a,** to send word to; **— a male,** to spoil; **— a memoria,** to learn by heart; **— a prendere,** to send for; **— all'aria,** to waste, to ruin; **mandarla giù,** to accept with resignation; **— qualcuno al diavolo,** to tell someone to go to blazes; **— per posta, per ferrovia,** to send by post, by rail.
mandarinato, *n.m.* Office of mandarin.
mandarino (1), *n.m.* Mandarin.
mandarino (2), *n.m.* Mandarin (orange), tangerine.
mandata, *n.f.* Sending, dispatch; batch, lot, series; turn (of a key). **Chiudere a doppia —,** to double-lock.
mandatario [mandatArio], *n.m.* Mandatory, agent; (*Law*) abettor.
mandato, *n.m.* Warrant, mandate, commission, command; (*Comm.*) order (for payment); agency. **— di cattura,** warrant for arrest; **— di comparizione,** summons to appear; **— commerciale,** agency; **— di pagamento,** order for payment.
mandibola [mandIbola], *n.f.* (*Anat.*) Jaw, mandible.
mandola [mAndola], *n.f.* (*colloq.*) Almond.
mandola, *n.f.* (*Mus.*) Mandola.
mandolinista (*pl.* **mandolinisti**), *n.m.* Mandolin player.
mandolino, *n.m.* (*Mus.*) Mandolin.
mandorla [mAndorla], *n.f.* Almond; (*Arch.*) almond lozenge.
mandorlato, *n.m.* Almond paste, almond cake.
mandorlo [mAndorlo], *n.m.* (*Bot.*) Almond-tree.
mandra, mandria [mAndria], *n.f.* Herd, flock; drove; troop, host, crowd.

mandracchio [mandrAcchio], *n.m.* Inner part of a harbour.
mandragola, mandragora [mandrAgola, mandrAgora], *n.f.* (*Bot.*) Mandrake.
mandria [cp. **mandra**].
mandriano, *n.m* Herdsman, shepherd.
mandrillo, *n.m.* (*Zool.*) Mandrill ape.
mandrino, *n.m.* (*Tech.*) Chuck (for lathe); mandrel.
mandritta, *n.f.* Right hand. **A —,** to the right-hand side.
manducabile [manducAbile], *a.* Edible.
manducare, *v.t.* (*Lit.*) To eat.
mane, *n.f.* (*Lit.*) Morning, morn. **Da — a sera,** from morn to night.
maneggevole [maneggEvole] *a.* Easy to handle, manageable, handy.
maneggiabile [maneggiAbile], *a.* Manageable; handy.
maneggiamento, *n.m.* Handling, management.
maneggiare, *v.t.* To handle, to wield; to touch; to manage; to deal with; to conduct; to break in (horses). **Saper — la penna,** to wield a formidable pen.
maneggiarsi, *v.r.* To manage oneself, to control oneself.
maneggio [manEggio], *n.m.* Handling, treatment; management, administration; intrigue, machination; horsemanship, *manège*; riding-school. **— d'armi,** rifle drill.
maneggione, *n.m.* Meddler; intriguer; jack of all trades.
manente, *n.m.* (*obs.*) Wealthy land-owner.
manescalco, *n.m.* Farrier.
manescamente, *adv.* In a quarrelsome way.
manesco, *a.* Given to blows, truculent, quarrelsome; aggressive, brutal.
manette, *n.f.pl.* Handcuffs, manacles.
manevole [manEvole], *a.* Supple, pliable.
manforte, *n.f.* Aid, assistance, help. **Dare —,** to support, to back up; to lend a hand.
manga, *n.f.* Mango (fruit).
manganare, *v.t.* To mangle, to calender.
manganato, *n.m.* (*Chem.*) Manganate.
manganatura, *n.f.* Mangling, calendering.
manganello, *n.m.* Cudgel, club, stick.
manganese, *n.m.* (*Chem.*) Manganese.
mangano [mAngano], *n.m.* Calender, mangle; linen-press; (*Hist.*) ballista, mangonel.
mangereccio [mangerEccio], *a.* Edible, eatable, tasty.
mangeria [mangerIa], *n.f.* (*colloq.*) Defalcation; embezzlement; swindle; graft.
mangiabambini, *n.m.* Terrible-looking fellow.
mangiabile [mangiAbile], *a.* Eatable, edible.
mangiabilità [-à], *n.f.* Edibility.
mangiacaparra, *n.m.* Cheat, swindler.
mangiacarne, *n.m.* Glutton.
mangiacarte, *n.m.* Fussy lawyer.
mangiacristiani, *n.m.* Blusterer, terrible-looking fellow.
mangiaformiche, *n.m.* (*Zool.*) Ant-eater.
mangiaguadagno, *n.m.* Casual labourer.
mangiamento, *n.m.* Corrosion, gnawing, eating away.
mangiaminestre, *n.m.* Sponger.
mangiapagnotte, *n.m.* Useless official.
mangiapane, *n.m.* Loafer, idler.
mangiapreti, *n.m.* Rabid anticlerical.
mangiare, *v.t.i.* To eat, to feed; to consume; to corrode; to take, to appropriate; to squander; (*Chess and Cards*) to take. **Fare da —,** to prepare the food, to get the food ready; **— bene,** to have a good meal; **— a scrocco,** to eat at someone's expense, to eat on the cheap; **— troppo,** to overeat; **— un patrimonio,** to squander a patrimony; **— vivo uno,** to jump down someone's throat; **— uno cogli occhi,** to devour someone with one's eyes; **mangiarsi le unghie,** to bite one's nails; **mangiarsi il fegato,** to fume, to chafe with rage; **— le parole,** to clip one's words.
mangiata, *n.f.* Good meal, square meal; bellyful. **Fare una —,** to take one's fill.
mangiatoia [mangiatOia], *n.f.* Manger.
mangiatore, mangiatrice, *n.m.f.* Hearty eater.
mangiatura, *n.f.* Eating; insect-bite.
mangiatutto, *n.m.* Spendthrift, squanderer.
mangime, *n.m.* (*Agric.*) Fodder; chicken-feed.
mangione, *n.m.* Great eater, glutton.
mangiucchiare, *v.t.i.* To nibble, to eat without appetite, to toy with one's food.
mangosta, mangusta, *n.f.* (*Zool.*) Mongoose.
mani, *n.m.pl.* (*Myth.*) Manes , shades of the departed.
mania [manIa], *n.f.* Mania; crotchet, fad, fancy; hobby.
maniaco [manIaco], *n.m.a.* Maniac, maniacal; eccentric.
manica [mAnica], *n.f.* Sleeve; hose-pipe; channel; gang, band. **Un altro paio di maniche,** a different kettle of fish; **essere di — larga,** to be lenient, not too exacting; **aver qualcosa nella —,** to have something up one's sleeve; **una — di ladri,** a gang of thieves; **La Manica,** the English Channel.
manicaretto, *n.m.* Dainty dish, tit-bit, dainty.
manicato, *a.* Hafted, handled.
manicheismo, *n.m.* (*Eccles.*) Manicheism.
manicheo [manichEo], *n.m.a.* Manichaean.
manichino, *n.m.* Cuff, wrist-band; mannequin.
manico [mAnico], *n.m.* Handle, haft; (*Mus.*) neck of a stringed instrument. **— di scopa,** broomstick; (*colloq.*) **ciurlare nel —,** to play foul, to let down (the side); **avere il coltello dalla parte del —,** to rule the roost, to be boss.
manicomio [manicOmio], *n.m.* Lunatic asylum, mad-house, mental hospital.
manicotto, *n.m.* Muff; (*Mech.*) sleeve, coupling; tube, pipe.
maniera, *n.f.* Manner, mode, fashion, way; custom, usage; kind, species; style; affectation, mannerism. **Di — che, a — che,** so that; **in — da,** so as to; **alla — di,** after the manner of; **in nessuna —,** in no wise, not at all; **belle maniere,** fine manners; **in una — o l'altra,** by hook or by crook; **senza maniere,** ill-mannered; **con buone maniere,** kindly.
manieratamente, *adv.* Affectedly.
manierato, *a.* Affected, mincing, mannered.
manierismo, *n.m.* Mannerism.
maniero, *n.m.* (*Hist.*) Manor.
manierosamente, *adv.* Mincingly.
manieroso, *a.* Mincing; too polite.

manifattore, *n.m.* Manufacturer; workman, artisan.
manifattura, *n.f.* Manufacture; manufactory, factory; manufactured stuff or goods; cost of manufacturing; workmanship.
manifatturiere, *n.m.* Manufacturer; artisan.
manifatturiero, *a.* Manufacturing.
manifestamente, *adv.* Manifestly.
manifestare, *v.t.* To manifest, to reveal, to show, to display; to state, to declare, to express.
manifestarsi, *v.r.* To manifest oneself, to show oneself, to appear.
manifestazione, *n.f.* Manifestation; demonstration; exhibition.
manifesto, *n.m.* Manifesto, placard, bill, poster; (*Naut.*) manifest. **Pubblicare un —,** to issue a manifesto; **distribuire manifesti,** to distribute leaflets.
manifesto, *a.* Manifest, evident, clear, plain, apparent.
maniglia [manIglia], *n.f.* Handle (of door, drawer, etc.); bell-pull.
maniglione, *n.m.* (*Naut.*) Shackle of an anchor.
manigolda, *n.f.* Hussy, forward girl.
manigoldo, *n.m.* Rogue, rascal, scoundrel.
manilla, *n.f.* Hemp used for cordage, manilla rope.
maniluvio [manilUvio], *n.m.* Medicated bath for the hands.
manina, *n.f.* Little hand; (*Typ.*) fist.
manipolare, *v.t.* To manipulate, to handle; to adulterate; to falsify. **— con cura,** handle with care.
manipolatore, *n.m.* Manipulator.
manipolazione, *n.f.* Manipulation, handling; adulteration; falsification.
manipolo [manIpolo], *n.m.* Handful, small bunch; sheaf; (*Eccles.*) maniple; (*Mil.*) squad, detachment.
maniscalco, *n.m.* Farrier.
manna, *n.f.* (*Hist.*) Manna; (*fig.*) blessing; (*Agric.*) sheaf. (*colloq.*) **È stata una —** it's been a god-send.
mannaggia! [mannAggia], *inter.* (*vulgar*) Damn! Devil take it!
mannaia [mannAia], *n.f.* Axe, chopper; blade (of guillotine); (*fig.*) despotism. **Essere sotto la —,** to be in mortal danger.
mannaro, *n.m.* **Lupo —,** werwolf; bogey.
mannello, *n.m.* Sheaf, truss, bunch.
mannerino, *n.m.* Wether, castrated ram.
mano (*pl.* **mani**), *n.f.* Hand; skill, ability; handwriting; help, assistance; (*Cards*) lead, trick, deal, hand; touch; coat of paint; gang, band. **A — a —,** little by little; just as, as soon as; **a — salva,** without risk; **dar — a,** to give a hand to; **a mani vuote,** empty-handed; **a mani giunte,** with clasped hands; **a due mani,** with both hands; **aver le mani bucate,** to spend lavishly, to let money slip through one's fingers; **aver le mani in pasta,** to have a finger in the pie; **aver le mani lunghe,** to have far-reaching influence; **uomo alla —,** a tractable man; **fuori —,** out of the way; **ci si può dar la —,** we are in the same boat; **mettere le mani addosso a qualcuno,** to lay hands on someone; **stendere la —,** to beg; **stretta di —,** hand-shake; **a —,** by hand; **venire alle mani,** to come to blows; **far man bassa,** to steal, to rob; **a mani piene,** profusely; **aver la —,** to lead (at cards); **star con le mani in —,** to twiddle one's thumbs; **sotto —,** at hand, within reach; **tener — a,** to encourage (in wrong-doing); **di lunga —,** of old standing; **a — armata,** by main force; **chieder la — di,** to ask in marriage; **di prima, di seconda —,** first or second hand; **batter le mani,** to clap one's hands; **giuoco di —,** legerdemain, conjuring; **aver le mani legate,** to have one's hands tied.
manodopera [manodOpera], *n.f.* Manual work, labour.
manomessa, *n.f.* Wine from a newly-tapped cask.
manomesso, *a.* Opened (without authority, as a letter); violated; (illegally) searched.
manomettere [manomEttere], *v.t.* To lay hands upon, to tamper with; to lay waste; to impair, to damage; to open (letters, etc., illegally); (*Hist.*) to manumit, to set free.
manomissione, *n.f.* Damaging, tampering with, searching illegally; (*Hist.*) manumission.
manomorta, *n.f.* (*Law*) Mortmain.
manopola [manOpola], *n.f.* Gauntlet; arm-sling (in a carriage), elbow-rest; (*Radio*) knob (for tuning, etc.).
manoscritto, *n.m.a.* Manuscript.
manovale, *n.m.* Bricklayer's labourer, day-labourer.
manovella, *n.f.* Handle, crank, lever; hand-spike. (*Motor.*) **— d'avviamento,** starting-handle.
manovra, *n.f.* Manœuvre (in all senses); (*Naut.*) tacking; (*Rail.*) shunting.
manovrabile [manovrAbile], *a.* Manœuvrable.
manovramento, *n.m.* Manœuvring.
manovrare, *v.t.i.* To manœuvre; to handle a ship, to steer, to drive; to work (a machine); to behave. **Egli sa come — per sormontare la difficoltà,** he knows how to behave in order to surmount the difficulty.
manovratore, *n.m.* Driver (esp. of trams).
manovre, *n.f.pl.* (*Naut.*) Rigging. **— fisse,** standing rigging; **— correnti,** running rigging.
manritta, *n.f.* Right hand, to the right.
manritto, *a.* Right-handed.
manrovescio [manrovEscio], *n.m.* Blow, slap with the back of the hand; back-stroke.
mansalva, *adv.* **A —,** with impunity.
mansionario [mansionArio], *n.m.* (*Eccles.*) Beneficed priest.
mansione, *n.f.* Duty, office, function; permanent post.
manso, *a.* (*Poet.*) Gentle, mild.
mansuefare, *v.t.* To pacify, to quiet, to soothe, to appease.
mansuetamente, *adv.* Mildly, gently.
mansueto, *a.* Meek, gentle, peaceful; tame (of animals).
mansuetudine [mansuetUdine], *n.f.* Meekness, gentleness; tameness.
manteca, *n.f.* Grease, pomatum, pomade
mantecare, *v.t.* To beat into grease, to beat into a paste.
mantecato, *n.m.* Kind of ice-cream.

mantella, *n.f.* Woman's long cloak.
mantellare, *v.t.* To cover with a cloak, to cloak (in all senses).
mantelletta, *n.f.* Cape, cloak; (*Eccles.*) short mantle worn by higher clergy.
mantellina, *n.f.* Cape, small mantle, policeman's cape; (*Eccles.*) veil in front of an image.
mantellino, *n.m.* Short cloak; christening robe.
mantello, *n.m.* Mantle, cloak, cape; coat (of animals), hair.
mantenere, *v.t.* To maintain, to uphold; to keep; to preserve, to support. **— la propria parola,** to keep one's word; **— un segreto,** to keep a secret; **— la famiglia,** to keep one's family; **— il silenzio,** to hold one's peace; **— in vita,** to keep alive.
mantenersi, *v.r.* To maintain oneself, to last, to subsist. **— a galla,** to keep afloat; **— in buona salute,** to keep in good health.
mantenibile [mantenIbile], *a.* Maintainable.
mantenimento, *n.m.* Maintenance, sustenance, preservation, upkeep.
mantenitore, *n.m.* Preserver, maintainer.
mantenuta, *n.f.* Kept mistress, concubine.
mantica [mAntica], *n.f.* (*Lit.*) Divination.
mantice [mAntice], *n.m.* Bellows; carriage-hood.
mantide [mAntide], *n.f.* (*Zool.*) Mantis.
mantiglia [mantIglia], *n.f.* Mantilla.
mantiglio [mantIglio], *n.m.* (*Naut.*) Lift (for yards).
mantile, *n.f.* Kitchen cloth, drying cloth.
mantissa, *n.f.* (*Math.*) Mantissa.
manto, *n.m.* Royal or papal cloak. **— di neve,** mantle of snow.
Mantova [mAntova], *n.f.* (*Geog.*) Mantua.
mantovano, *n.m.a.* Mantuan. **Il Mantovano,** Virgil.
mantrugiare, *v.t.* To finger; to maul.
manuale, *n.m.a.* Manual; handbook, manual. **Lavoro —,** manual labour.
manualmente, *adv.* Manually.
manubrio [manUbrio], *n.m.* Handle, haft; dumb-bell, weight; handle-bar.
manufatto, *n.m.a.* Hand-made; manufactured.
manutengolo [manutEngolo], *n.m.* Receiver (of stolen goods); accomplice, abettor.
manutenzione, *n.f.* Upkeep, maintenance. **Spese di —,** expense of upkeep.
manza, *n.f.* Heifer.
manzina, *n.f.* (*Agric.*) Fallow land used as pasture.
manzo, *n.m.* Steer; bullock; beef. **— lesso,** boiled beef.
manzoniano, *a.* Of Manzoni.
maomettano, *n.m.a.* Mohammedan.
maomettismo, *n.m.* Islam, Mohammedanism.
Maometto, *n.m.* Mohammed.
maona, *n.f.* (*Naut.*) Type of Levantine craft; lighter.
mappa, *n.f.* Map, plan.
mappamondo, *n.m.* Map of the world showing the hemispheres; geographical globe.
marabù [-ù], *n.m.* (*Zool.*) Marabout.
marabutto, *n.m.* Marabout (Mohammedan holy man).
marachella, *n.f.* Trick, prank, peccadillo; fraud.
maramaglia [maramAglia], *n.f.* Rabble, mob, riff-raff.
marame, *n.m.* Waste, refuse, rubbish, garbage.
marameo! *inter.* You can't catch me with that! Try another! (and similar phrases). **Far —,** to thumb one's nose.
marangone, *n.m.* (*Naut.*) Diver; (*Zool.*) cormorant; joiner, carpenter.
marasca, *n.f.* (*Bot.*) Morello cherry.
maraschino, *n.m.* Maraschino liqueur.
marasma, *n.f.* (*Med.*) Marasmus, a wasting disease; (*fig.*) decay, atrophy.
marasso, *n.m.* (*Zool.*) Marsh viper.
marata, *n.f.* Force of the tide; action of the sea.
maratona, *n.f.* Marathon race.
maratoneta, *n.m.* Marathon competitor.
maraviglia [maravIglia], *n.f.* Wonder, wonderment, surprise, astonishment; marvel, wonder; (*Bot.*) kind of grape-vine. **Non mi fa —,** I'm not surprised; **essere una —,** to be a marvel; **compiere maraviglie,** to perform wonders; **a —,** wonderfully.
maravigliare, *v.t.* To surprise, to astonish, to amaze.
maravigliarsi, *v.r.* To wonder, to marvel, to be surprised, to be astonished, to be amazed. **Non c'è da maravigliarsene,** it is not surprising.
maravigliosamente, *adv.* Wonderfully.
maraviglioso, *a.* Wonderful, marvellous, astonishing, amazing.
marazzo, *n.m.* Swamp, marsh.
marazzoso, *a.* Swampy.
marca, *n.f.* Mark, token, sign; brand; border, march, district. **— di fabbrica,** trade-mark; **— da bollo,** revenue stamp (on documents, etc.); (*Naut.*) **— della linea di carico,** Plimsoll line; (*Geog.*) **Le Marche,** the Marches.
marcantonia [marcantOnia], *n.f.* (*colloq.*) Buxom lass, plump woman.
Marcantonio [marcantOnio], *n.m.* Mark Antony.
marcapunto, *n.m.* Cobbler's awl.
marcare, *v.t.* To mark, to brand, to stamp; to march (border between two countries). (*Sport*) **— i punti,** to keep the score; **— dei punti,** to score, to make points.
marcatamente, *adv.* In a marked manner.
marcato, *a.* Marked, pronounced.
marcatura, *n.f.* Marking.
marcescibile [marcescIbile], *a.* Corruptible, perishable.
marchesa, *n.f.* Marchioness.
marchesato, *n.m.* Marquisate.
marchese, *n.m.* Marquess, marquis.
Marchesi, *n.f.pl.* Marquesas Islands.
marchiano, *a.* Big, gross, enormous. **Spropositi marchiani,** gross blunders.
marchiare, *v.t.* To mark, to stamp, to brand; to stigmatize.
marchigiano, *n.m.a.* Person from, or relating to the Marche (Italian province).
marchio [mArchio], *n.m.* Brand; stigma; stain, blemish. **— di fabbrica,** trade-mark; **— d'infamia,** brand of infamy.
marchionale, *a.* Pertaining to a marquess.
marcia [mArcia] (1), *n.f.* (*Mil., Mus.*) March; (*Naut.*) way (of a ship); advance, course, progress; (*Motor.*) speed (gear). **— funebre,**

dead march; **in —,** on the march; **mettere in —,** to set going (a machine); **mettersi in —,** to start off; **essere in —,** to be on the march; (*Motor.*) **cambiare —,** to change gear; **macchina a tre marcie,** car with three speeds.
marcia [mArcia] (2), *n.f.* (*Med.*) Pus, purulent matter.
marciaia [marciAia], *n.f.* Cachexy (in sheep).
marciano, *a.* Relating to St. Mark. **Biblioteca Marciana,** St. Mark's Library, Venice.
marciapiede, *n.m.* Pavement, foot-path; (*Rail.*) station platform.
marciare, *v.i.* To march, to walk; to advance, to proceed; to travel; to work (of an engine). **Le cose non marciano bene,** things are not going well.
marciata, *n.f.* (*Mus.*) March; marching.
marcime, *n.m.* Stable manure.
marcimento, *n.m.* Suppuration.
marcino, *n.m.* Wine made from over-ripe grapes.
marcio [mArcio], *n.m.* Rot, rotten part; corruption.
marcio [mArcio], *a.* Rotten, decomposed, putrid; corrupt. **Uova marce,** rotten eggs; **avere torto —,** to be entirely in the wrong; **perderla marcia,** to lose a game without scoring a point; **a suo — dispetto,** in spite of him.
marciolino, *n.m.* Taste or smell of sourness.
marcioso, *a.* Rotten, putrid; filthy, foul.
marcire, *v.t.i.* To rot, to go bad, to decompose, to putrefy; to fester; to ret, to macerate; to become corrupt (morally). **— in prigione,** to rot in gaol; **lasciar — la frutta,** let the fruit go bad.
marcita, *n.f.* Flooded field, water-meadow.
marcitoio [marcitOio], *n.m.* Retting-vat.
marcitura, *n.f.* Rotting, retting.
marciume, *n.m.* Rottenness, putridity.
marco, *n.m.* Mark, sign; mark (money).
Marco, *n.m.* Mark, Marcus.
marconigrafia [marconigrafIa], *n.f.* Wireless telegraphy.
marconigramma, *n.m.* Marconigram.
marconista, *n.m.* Wireless operator.
mare, *n.m.* Sea; ocean; (*fig.*) great quantity; immensity. **Acqua di —,** sea water; **mal di —,** seasickness; **in —,** at sea; **gente di —,** seamen, seafaring folk; **portare acqua al —,** to carry coals to Newcastle; **cercare per terra e per —,** to seek everywhere; **prometter mari e monti,** to make wild promises; **in alto —,** on the high seas; **viaggiare per — e per terra,** to travel by land and sea; **sul livello del —,** above sea-level; **gettare in —,** to throw overboard; **il questione è ancora in alto —,** the matter is still undecided; **un — di gente,** a crowd of people; **— grosso,** rough sea; **verde —,** sea-green.
marea [marEa], *n.f.* Tide, ebb and flow. **Alta —, bassa —,** high, low tide.
mareggiamento, *n.m.* Seasickness.
mareggiare, *v.i.* To surge; to toss like the sea; to be seasick.
mareggiata, *n.f.* Wild, tempestuous sea; strong tide; gale.
maremma, *n.f.* Marsh, swampy coast.
maremmano, *a.* Pertaining to the Maremma (region of central Italy.)
maremoto, *n.m.* Submarine earthquake; tidal wave due to this.
marena, *n.f.* Morello cherry; drink made from this.
marengo, *n.m.* Twenty-franc gold piece.
marescalco, *n.m.* (*obs.*) Farrier.
maresciallo, *n.m.* (*Mil.*) Marshal; senior warrant officer; quartermaster. **— dei carabinieri,** police inspector.
maretta, *n.f.* Choppy sea; slight swell.
marezzare, *v.t.* To water (textiles); to marble (paper, etc.); to variegate.
marezzatura, *n.f.* Marbling, watering.
marezzo, *n.m.* Wavy lines (in wood grain, silk, etc.).
marga, *n.f.* (*Agric.*) Loam.
margarina, *n.f.* Margarine.
Margherita, *n.f.* Margaret.
margherita, *n.f.* Daisy, marguerite; pearl; (*Naut.*) sheepshanks tackle. **Dare le margherite ai porci,** to cast pearls before swine.
margheritina, *n.f.* Field daisy; glass bead.
marginale, *a.* Marginal.
marginare, *v.t.* To leave a margin; to border.
marginatura, *n.f.* Arrangement of the margin; edging, border.
margine [mArgine], *n.m.* Margin; border, edge. **— di guadagno,** margin of profit.
margottare, *v.t.* To propagate by layering; to plant an offshoot.
margotto, *n.m.* Layer (of strawberry, etc.); offshoot, offset.
margravio [margrAvio], *n.m.* (*Hist.*) Margrave.
Maria [marIa], *n.f.* Mary.
mariano, *a.* Of the Blessed Virgin Mary. **Mese —,** the month of May.
marina, *n.f.* Sea; sea-coast, sea-shore; navy, marine; Admiralty; (*Art*) sea-piece. **— mercantile,** merchant navy, merchant service; *ufficiale di —,* naval officer; **pittore di marine,** seascape painter.
marinaio [marinAio], *n.m.* Sailor, seaman, mariner; (*Mil.*) marine. **— di acqua dolce,** land-lubber; **— di coperta,** deck-hand; **— scelto,** A.B. (able seaman).
marinara, *n.f.* Child's sailor suit. **Colletta alla —,** sailor collar.
marinare, *v.t.* To pickle, to marinade. (*colloq.*) **— la scuola,** to play truant.
marinaro, *n.m.a.* Sailor; maritime.
marineria [marinerIa], *n.f.* Shipping; naval administration; navigation.
marinesca, *n.f.* Crew of a ship.
marinescamente, *adv.* In a sailorly style.
marinesco, *a.* Nautical, sailor-like, seamanlike.
marinismo, *n.m.* (*Lit.*) Marinism; literary affectation; euphuism.
marino, *a.* Of the sea, sea, marine, nautical. **Aria marina,** sea air; **sale —,** bay-salt; **ospizio —,** seaside hostel; **colonia marina,** seaside holiday camp.
mariolatria [mariolatrIa], *n.f.* (*Eccles.*) Mariolatry.
marioleria [driolerIa], *n.f.* Swindle, fraud; trick; prank.
mariolescamente, *adv.* Fraudulently.
mariolesco, *a.* Fraudulent, swindling.
mariolo, *n.m.* Swindler, cheat; rogue, rascal.

marionetta, *n.f.* Marionette, puppet.
marionettista (*pl.* **marionettisti**), *n.m.* Puppet-showman.
marionettistico [marionettIstico], *a.* Puppet. **Spettacolo —,** puppet show.
maritabile [maritAbile], *a.* Marriageable.
maritaggio [maritAggio], *n.m.* (*Lit.*) Marriage
maritale, *a.* Marital.
maritalmente, *adv.* Maritally. **Convivere —,** to live as husband and wife.
maritamento, *n.m.* Marrying, marriage.
maritare, *v.t.* To marry, to give in marriage, to unite.
maritarsi, *v.r.* (Of a woman) to marry, to get married; to wed; to join.
maritata, *n.f.* Married woman.
maritato, *a.* Married, coupled, united; mingled.
marito, *n.m.* Husband. **Figlia, ragazza da —,** marriageable daughter, girl; **— e moglie,** husband and wife; **tra moglie e — non mettere il dito,** don't interfere between husband and wife.
maritozzo, *n.m.* Lenten bun.
marittimo [marIttimo], *n.m.* Seaman.
marittimo [marIttimo], *a.* Maritime, marine, of the sea, sea.
mariuolo, *n.m.* Rogue, scoundrel.
marmaglia [marmAglia], *n.f.* Rabble.
marmare, *v.t.i.* To make or become cold as marble.
marmeggia [marmEggia], *n.f.* (*Zool.*) Maggot.
marmellata, *n.f.* Jam; marmalade.
marmiera, *n.f.* Marble quarry.
marmifero [marmIfero], *a.* (*Geol.*) Marble-bearing.
marmista (*pl.* **marmisti**), *n.m.* Worker in marble; monumental mason; marble polisher.
marmitta, *n.f.* Pot, stock-pot, saucepan; camp-kettle; (*Mil.*) large projectile.
marmittone, *n.m.* (*Mil.*) Coward; lead-swinger.
marmo, *n.m.* Marble. **Cava di —,** marble-quarry; **i marmi,** the marbles.
marmocchio [marmOcchio], *n.m.* Brat, urchin; infant.
marmoraio [marmorAio], *n.m.* Worker in marble; sculptor.
marmoreo [marmorEo], *a.* Marble-like, marmoreal.
marmorizzare, *v.t.* To marble.
marmotta, *n.f.* (*Zool.*) Marmot; (*fig.*) dunce, lazy-bones.
marna, *n.f.* (*Agric.*) Marl, loam.
marnare, *v.t.* To dress with marl.
marnatura, *n.f.* Marl dressing.
marniera, *n.f.* Marl pit.
marnoso, *a.* Loamy.
marocchino, *n.m.a.* Moroccan, morocco leather.
maronita, *n.m.* (*Eccles.*) Maronite.
maroso, *n.m.* Breaker, surge, billow, mountainous wave.
marra, *n.f.* (*Agric.*) Hoe, mattock; (*Naut.*) fluke of anchor.
marrano, *n.m a.* Rogue, scoundrel; rascally, vile.
marrascura, *n.f.* (*Agric.*) Long-handled bill-hook.
marrata, *n.f.* Stroke with a hoe.
marreggiare, *v.t.* To hoe.
marretta, *n.f.* Garden hoe.
marrobbio [marrObbio], *n.m.* (*Bot.*) Hore-hound.
marrone, *n.m.* Chestnut, chestnut colour; (*fig.*) gross blunder. **Marroni secchi,** dried chestnuts; **marroni canditi,** marrons glacés; **fare —,** to put one's foot in it.
marrone, *a.* Maroon, brown, chestnut.
marroneto, *n.m.* Chestnut plantation.
marruca, *n.f.* (*Bot.*) Jujube-tree; buckthorn.
marsala, *n.m.* Marsala wine.
marsigliese, *n.m.a.* Marseillese. **La Marsigliese,** the Marseillaise.
marsina, *n.f.* Tail-coat, evening dress. dress jacket.
marsovino, *n.m.* (*Zool.*) Porpoise.
marsupiale, *n.m.a.* (*Zool.*) Marsupial.
Marta, *n.f.* Martha.
Marte, *n.m.* (*Myth.*) Mars. **Campo di —,** drill-ground.
martedì [-ì], *n.m.* Tuesday. **— grasso.** Shrove Tuesday.
martellamento, *n.m.* Hammering, battering.
martellare, *v.t.* To hammer, to batter; to throb (of the pulse).
martellata, *n.f.* Blow with a hammer, blow stroke.
martellatura, *n.f.* Hammering, beating.
martelliano, *n.m.a.* (*Poet.*) **Verso —,** verse of 14 syllables.
martellina, *n.f.* Mason's hammer.
martellio [martellIo], *n.m.* Persistent hammering.
martello, *n.m.* Hammer; door-knocker; clapper. **Suonare a —,** to sound the alarm.
martinaccio [martinAccio], *n.m.* Kind of edible snail.
martinello, *n.m.* (*Motor.*) Jack; (*Naut.*) windlass, capstan.
martinetto, *n.m.* (*Naut.*) Windlass.
martingala, *n.f.* Martingale; strap at back of jacket.
Martinica, *n.f.* (*Geog.*) Martinique.
martinicca, *n.f.* Brake (for coaches, etc.).
Martino, *n.m.* Martin. **Estate di San —,** Indian summer; (*colloq.*) **fare San —,** to pack up, to move house; (*Zool.*) **martino pescatore,** kingfisher.
martire [mArtire], *n.m.f.* Martyr. **— del lavoro,** martyr to work.
martirio [martIrio], *n.m.* Martyrdom; torment, torture.
martirizzamento, *n.m.* Martyrization, martyrdom.
martirizzare, *v.t.* To martyr, to martyrize; to torment, to vex, to harass.
martirizzarsi, *v.r.* To make a martyr of oneself.
martirologio [matirolOgio], *n.m.* Martyrology.
martora [mArtora], *n.f.* (*Zool.*) Marten.
martoriamento, *n.m.* Torment, martyrdom.
martoriare, *v.t.* To martyr, to martyrize, to torment.
martoriarsi, *v.r.* To make a martyr of oneself; to worry, to torment oneself, to grieve. **È inutile —,** it is useless to worry.
martoriatore, *n.m.* Tormentor.
martorio, martoro [martOrio], *n.m.* (*Poet.*) Torture, torment.

marxismo, *n.m.* (*Pol.*) Marxism.
marxista (*pl.* **marxisti**), *n.m.* Marxist.
marza, *n.f.* (*Agric.*) Graft; scion.
marzaiolo, *a.* Of the month of March.
marzapane, *n.m.* Marzipan, marchpane.
marziale, *a.* Martial, warlike, military. **Aria —,** military bearing; **corte —,** court martial; **legge —,** martial law.
marzialità [-à], *n.f.* Soldierliness.
marziano, *n.m.* Martian, man from Mars.
marzio [mArzio], *a.* Martial, of Mars. **Campo —,** drill-ground.
marzo, *n.m.* Month of March.
marzocco, *n.m.* The heraldic lion emblem of Florence.
marzolino, marzuolo, *a.* Of the month of March.
mas, *n.m.* (*Naut.*) E-boat, fast armed motor-boat.
mascalcia [mascalcIa], *n.f.* Farriery.
mascalzonata, *n.f.* Piece of roguery.
mascalzone, *n.m.* Rascal, rogue, scoundrel, blackguard.
mascarpone, *n.m.* Kind of sweet fresh cheese.
mascella, *n.f.* (*Anat.*) Jaw, jaw-bone.
mascellare, *a.* Maxillary. **Dente —,** back-tooth, molar.
maschera [mAschera], *n.f.* Mask; masked figure (at a dance, etc.); masked man; disguise; masque; death-mask; (*Theat.*) attendant; (*Fencing*) face-guard. **— anti-gas,** gas-mask; **gettare la —,** to drop one's mask; **ballo in —,** masked ball, fancy-dress ball.
mascheramento, *n.m.* Concealment, disguise; (*Mil.*) camouflage.
mascherare, *v.t.* To mask, to disguise; to camouflage; to screen.
mascherarsi, *v.r.* To wear a mask, to masquerade.
mascherata, *n.f.* Masquerade.
mascheratura, *n.f.* Masking, disguising; camouflaging.
mascherina, *n.f.* Masked person, mask; mummer. (*colloq.*) **— ti conosco!** Try another! You can't kid me!
mascherone, *n.m.* (*Arch.*) Mask; grotesque; gargoyle; (*fig.*) ugly face.
maschiaccio [maschiAccio], *n.m.* Rough fellow; mannish woman; hoyden.
maschiamente, *adv.* In a virile way; stubbornly.
maschietta, *n.f.* Mannish girl; big girl; hoyden. **Cappelli alla —,** bobbed hair.
maschietto, *n.m.* Fine little boy.
maschiezza, *n.f.* Virility, manliness.
maschile, *a.* Male, masculine; manly, manful, virile. **Scuola —,** boys' school; **genere —,** masculine gender; **aspetto —,** manly looks.
maschio [mAschio], *n.m.* Male; boy; man; (*fig.*) tenon; shaft; keep (of a castle), fortress, main tower. **Ho tre maschi,** I have three boys.
maschio [mAschio], *a.* Male, manly, manful, vigorous, virile. **Un figlio —,** a boy, a male child, a son; **viso —,** a manly face; **vite maschia,** male screw.
maschiotta, *n.f.* Tomboy.
maschiotto, *n.m.* Strong lad, sturdy boy.
mascolinizzare, *v.t.* To make masculine, to render manly.
mascolinità [-à], *n.f.* Masculinity; manhood.
mascolino, *a.* Masculine.
masnada, *n.f.* Gang, armed set of ruffians; (*obs.*) group, company.
masnadiere, *n.m.* Highwayman, robber, bandit.
masochismo, *n.m.* Masochism.
massa, *n.f.* Mass, bulk; heap, lump, pile; majority. **Le masse,** the masses; **in —,** in a body, in bulk; **leva in —,** mass levy; **adunata in —,** mass meeting; **una — di gente,** a large crowd; **una — di lavoro,** a lot of work; (*Comm.*) **— fallimentare,** bankruptcy assets.
massacrare, *v.t.* To massacre, to slaughter, to butcher, to slay.
massacro, *n.m.* Massacre, slaughter, butchery; (*Heraldry*) deer's head.
massaggiare, *v.t.* To massage.
massaggiatore, massaggiatrice, *n.m.f.* Masseur, masseuse.
massaggio [massAggio], *n.m.* Massage.
massaia [massAia], *n.f.* Housewife.
massaio [massAio], *n.m.* Householder; husband; steward, farm superintendent.
massellare, *v.t.* To hammer, to beat out (hot iron).
massello, *n.m.* Lump of red-hot or beaten iron; lump, mass. **Oro in —,** gold ingot.
masseria [masserIa], *n.f.* Large farm; collection of farms under one management; stock of cattle; tenancy of farms.
masserizia [masserIzia], *n.f.* Furniture, household goods. **Far —,** to set aside, to save, to make economies.
masserizie [masserIzie], *n.f.pl.* Implements, utensils.
masseto, *n.m.* Rocky place; rough land.
massicciare, *v.t.* To ballast, to metal a road.
massicciata, massicciato, *n.f.m.* Metal (for a road), ballast; (*Rail.*) bed of track.
massiccio [massIccio], *n.m.* Massif, group of mountain peaks.
massiccio [massIccio], *a.* Massive, massy; bulky, solid. **Oro —,** solid gold.
massima [mAssima], *n.f.* Maxim, rule, principle. **In —,** as a rule, as a matter of principle; **un accordo di —,** an informal agreement; **aver per —,** to make it a rule, to make it a point.
massimale, *n.m.* (*Math.*) Maximum of a series.
massimalista (*pl.* **massimalisti**), *n.m.* (*Pol*). Maximalist, extreme Socialist.
massimamente, massime [mAssime], *adv.* Especially, chiefly, above all.
massimo [mAssimo], *n.m.* Maximum; utmost; highest. **Il — che posso darvi,** all that I can give you.
massimo [mAssimo], *a.* Greatest, highest, largest; best; utmost, supreme, maximum. **Con la massima stima,** Yours faithfully; **al —,** at the highest point, at the top, to the highest degree.
masso, *n.m.* Boulder, block (of stone); rock.
massone, *n.m.* Freemason; mason.
massoneria [massonerIa], *n.f.* Freemasonry.
massonicamente, *adv.* Masonically.
massonico [massOnico], *a.* (Free)masonic. **Loggia massonica,** Masonic lodge.

massoso, *a.* Rocky.
mastello, *n.m.* Tub, bucket (for carrying grapes, olives, etc.). **— per bucato,** wash-tub.
masticabile [masticAbile], *a.* Capable of being masticated.
masticamento, *n.m.* Mastication, chewing.
masticare, *v.t.* To chew, to masticate; (*fig.*) to mutter; to ponder over; to cogitate; to grumble. **— una lingua,** to know a little of a language; **gomma da —,** chewing-gum.
masticatorio [masticatOrio], *a.* Masticatory.
masticatura, *n.f.* Chewing.
masticazione, *n.f.* Mastication.
mastice [mAstice], *n.m.* Gum mastic; cement. **— di vetraio,** putty.
mastino, *n.m.* Mastiff.
mastio [mAstio], *n.m.* Male [cp. **maschio**].
mastite, *n.f.* (*Med.*) Mastitis.
mastodonte, *n.m.* (*Zool.*) Mastodon; (*fig.*) huge person.
mastodontico [mastodOntico], *a.* Enormous, huge; very bulky.
mastoide [mastOide], *n.f.* (*Anat.*) Mastoid.
mastoidite, *n.f.* (*Med.*) Mastoiditis.
mastra, *n.f.* Large kneading-trough.
mastro, *n.m.* Master; (*Comm.*) ledger. (*Naut.*) **— d'ascia,** master carpenter; (*Comm.*) **Libro —,** ledger; **registrare a —,** to post (a ledger); **— a fogli sciolti,** loose-leaf ledger.
masturbarsi, *v.r.* To masturbate.
masturbazione, *n.f.* Masturbation.
matassa, *n.f.* Skein; tangle. **Arruffare la —,** to create confusion.
mate, *n.f.* Matè, Paraguay tea.
matematica [matemAtica], *n.f.* Mathematics.
matematicamente, *adv.* Mathematically.
matematico [matemAtico], *n.m.a.* Mathematician; mathematical, mathematic.
matera, *n.f.* (*Naut.*) Part of the ship above the keel.
materassa, materasso, *n.f.m.* Mattress.
materassaio [materassAio], *n.m.* Mattress-maker.
materia [matEria], *n.f.* Matter (in all senses); subject; material; ground; occasion; (*Med.*) pus, stool evacuations. **Materie prime,** raw materials; (*Comm.*) **competente in —,** competent in the case; (*School*) **— facoltativa,** optional subject; **materie d'esame,** subjects of an examination.
materiale, *n.m.a.* Material. **— bellico,** war material; material, gross, coarse; actual, effectual.
materialismo, *n.m.* Materialism.
materialista (*pl.* **materialisti),** *n.m.* Materialist.
materialistico [materialIstico], *a.* Materialistic.
materialità [-à], *n.f.* Materiality.
materializzare, *v.t.* To materialize.
materializzazione, *n.f.* Materialization.
materialmente, *adv.* Materially.
materialone, *n.m.* (*colloq.*) Coarse, matter-of-fact person.
maternale, *a.* Maternal.
maternamente, *adv.* Maternally.
maternità [-à], *n.f.* Maternity, motherhood, **Casa di —,** maternity home.
materno, *a.* Maternal, motherly. **Lingua materna,** mother tongue.
matero [mAtero], *n.m.* (*Bot.*) Shoot from a pollarded tree.
materozzolo [materOzzolo], *n.m.* Wooden tab on a bunch of keys.
matita, *n.f.* Pencil, lead-pencil; crayon, chalk. **— a sfera,** ball-pointed pen.
matraccio [matrAccio], *n.m.* Glass bottle: retort.
matreselva, *n.f.* (*Bot.*) Honeysuckle.
matriarcato, *n.m.* Matriarchy.
matricale, *n.f.* (*Bot.*) Feverfew
matricaria [matricAria], *n.f.* (*Bot.*) Camomile; little centaury.
matrice [matrIce], *n.f.* Womb; matrix; mould; (*Comm.*) counterfoil.
matricida, *n.m.f. a.* Matricide (*person*); matricidal.
matricidio [matricIdio], *n.m.* Matricide (*crime*).
matricino, *n.m.* (*Bot.*) Shoots left to grow for underwood; (*Agric.*) beast left for breeding purposes.
matricola [matrIcola], *n.f.* Register fee or number; register, roll; university matriculation; freshman. **Festa delle matricole,** university rag.
matricolare, *v.t.* To register; to enter on a university roll.
matricolarsi, *v.r.* To matriculate.
matricolato, *a.* Matriculated, thorough. **Birbante —,** arrant knave, thorough-paced rascal.
matricolazione, *n.f.* Matriculation, registration.
matricolino, *n.m.* Freshman, first-year student.
matrigna, *n.f.* Step-mother; (*fig.*) cruel mother.
matrimoniale, *a.* Matrimonial, nuptial. **Letto —,** double bed.
matrimonialmente, *adv.* Matrimonially.
matrimonio [matrimOnio], *n.m.* Marriage, matrimony, wedlock; wedding. **— d'amore,** love-match; **chiedere in —,** to ask in marriage.
matrimonione, *n.m.* Wealthy marriage, good match.
matrizzare, *v.i.* To take after one's mother.
matrona, *n.f.* Matron; married woman.
matronale, *a.* Matronly.
matta, *n.f.* Mad woman, insane woman.
mattacchione, *n.m.* Jolly fellow, scatter-brain, wag.
mattaccino, *n.m.* Charlatan, jester, mimic; odd fellow; strolling player.
mattadore, *n.m.* Matador.
mattafione, *n.m.* (*Naut.*) Lashing.
mattaione, *n.m.* (*Geol.*) Kind of barren clay.
mattana, *n.f.* Mad freak, whim; fit of temper.
mattanza, *n.f.* Capture and slaughter of tunny fish.
mattare, *v.t.* To kill, to slaughter; (*Chess*) to checkmate.
mattata, *n.f.* Foolish action, mad freak, foolery.
mattatoio [mattatOio], *n.m.* Slaughter-house.
mattazione, *n.f.* Slaughter (of beasts).
matteggiare, *v.i.* To play the fool.
Matteo [mattEo], *n.m.* Matthew.
matterello (1), *n.m.* Rolling-pin, roller (of towel).
matterello (2), *a.* Foolish, crazy.

matteria, mattezza, mattia [matterIa, mattIa], *n.f.* Freak, craze, madness, piece of foolishness.
matticcio [mattIccio], *a.* Light-headed, thoughtless, feather-brained.
mattina, *n.f.* Morning, forenoon; dawn. **Domani —,** tomorrow morning.
mattinale, *a.* Matutinal, morning; early.
mattinata, *n.f.* Morning; morning-time, forenoon; (*Mus.*) morning song; (*Theat.*) matinée.
mattiniero, *a.* Early-rising. **Persona mattiniera,** early-riser.
mattino, *n.m.* Morning; dawn. **Di buon —,** early in the morning; **esposto al —,** facing east.
matto, *n.m.* Madman, lunatic; fool. **Fare il —,** to play the fool.
matto, *a.* Mad, insane, deranged; foolish; rash; excessive; dull, weak. **Diventar —,** to go mad; **gusto —,** frantic delight; **testa matta,** hot-headed fool; **scacco —, dare scacco —,** checkmate, to checkmate.
mattoide [mattOide], *n.m.a.* Half-crazy person; half-crazy, half-insane.
mattolina, *n.f.* (*Zool.*) Woodlark.
mattonaia [mattonAia], *n.f.* Brickyard.
mattonaio [mattonAio], *n.m.* Brickmaker.
mattoname, *n.m.* Quantity of bricks, brick-work.
mattonare, *v.t.* To pave with bricks.
mattonato, *n.m.a.* Brick floor; paved with bricks, or tiles.
mattone, *n.m.* Brick, tile; (*fig.*) bore, ponderous talker.
mattonella, *n.f.* Tile, small brick; (*Billiards*) cushion (on table).
mattutinante, *n.m.* (*Eccles.*) Priest who recites office of Matins.
mattutino, *n.m.a.* Matins; matutinal, early.
maturamente, *adv.* Ripely, maturely.
maturamento, *n.m.* Maturing, ripening.
maturanza, *n.f.* Ripening, maturation; ripeness.
maturare, *v.i.* To mature, to ripen; (*Med.*) to come to a head, to suppurate; (*Comm.*) to mature, to become payable, to become due.
maturatamente, *adv.* Ripely.
maturato, *a.* Ripened, matured; (*Comm.*) due, matured.
maturazione, *n.f.* Ripening, maturation; ripeness; (*Comm.*) maturity.
maturità [-à], *n.f.* Maturity, ripeness. **Esame di —,** examination before leaving school; matriculation exam.
maturo, *a.* Ripe, mature; fully developed; sound; weighty. **Età matura,** mature age.
Matusalemme, *n.m.* Methuselah.
mauriziano, *a.* Pertaining to the Order of St. Maurice and Lazarus.
Maurizio [maurIzio], *n.m.* Maurice.
mauro [mAuro], *n.m.a.* Moor; Moorish.
mausoleo [mausolEo], *n.m.* Mausoleum.
mazza, *n.f.* Club, loaded stick, hammer; mace, staff of office; walking-stick, cane; (*Sport*) mallet, bat; sledgehammer.
mazzacavallo, *n.m.* (*Agric.*) Balanced pole for drawing water from a well.
mazzachera [mazzAchera], *n.f.* Eel-pot.
mazzacorto, *n.m.* Coil of rope; string for a spinning-top.
mazzagatti, *n.m.* Pocket-pistol.
mazzapicchiare, *v.t.* To ram; to strike with a mallet.
mazzapicchio [mazzapIcchio], *n.m.* Beetle, mallet, rammer.
mazzata, *n.f.* Blow with a club; stunning blow.
mazzera [mAzzera], *n.f.* Bag of stones to weigh down a fishing-net.
mazzeranga, *n.f.* Beetle, rammer.
mazzerare, *v.t.* To drown by throwing into the water with a weight attached.
mazziere, *n.m.* Mace-bearer.
mazziniano, *n.m.a.* Follower of, or pertaining to Giuseppe Mazzini.
mazzo, *n.m.* Bunch (of flowers); pack (of cards); bundle, heap; packet; class, category. **Porre in un —,** to class in the same category; **mischiare il —,** to shuffle the cards.
mazzocchio [mazzOcchio], *n.m.* (*Hist.*) Ornamented Florentine hat; (*Bot.*) variety of endive.
mazzola, *n.f.* Mallet.
mazzolare, *v.t.* To strike with a mallet.
mazzolata, *n.f.* Blow with a mallet.
mazzolino, *n.m.* Nosegay.
mazzotto, *n.m.* Beetle used with wedges.
me, *pron.* Me, to me, for me. **Secondo me,** in my opinion; **tra me e me,** in my own mind; **faccio da me,** I do it by myself; **dimmelo,** tell me; **me ne ricordo,** I remember it.
me', *abbrev.* [cp. **mezzo, meglio**].
meandro, *n.m.* Meandering, wandering, winding; maze.
meato, *n.m.* (*Anat.*) Meatus; passage, channel, canal.
mecca, *n.f.* Silversmith's varnish; (*fig.*) an ideal place (after Mecca).
meccanica [meccAnica], *n.f.* Mechanics.
meccanicamente, *adv.* Mechanically.
meccanico [meccAnico], *n.m.a.* Mechanic, engineer, mechanician; chauffeur; mechanical; machinelike; automatic.
meccanismo, *n.m.* Mechanism, machinery gear.
meccanizare, *v.t.* To mechanize.
meccanizzazione, *n.f.* Mechanization.
mecenate, *n.m.* (*fig.*) Maecenas, patron (of art and literature); supporter.
meco, With me.
meconio [mecOnio], *n.m.* Meconium, first faeces of new-born child; opium.
medaglia [medAglia], *n.f.* Medal; ancient coin. **Il rovescio della —,** the reverse of the medal.
medagliere, *n.m.* Cabinet of coins, coin collection.
medaglietta, *n.f.* Small medal.
medaglione, *n.m.* Medallion; locket.
medaglista, *n.m.* Collector of medals or coins; maker of medals.
medesimamente, *adv.* In the same way.
medesimarsi, *v.r.* To identify oneself with.
medesimezza, *n.f.* Sameness, identicality.
medesimo [medEsimo], *a.pron.* Self, same, very same; himself, herself, itself. **Nel — tempo,** at the same time; **essere in tutto della medesima idea,** to be of the very same opinion.
media [mEdia], *n.f.* Average, mean. **In —** on an average.

medianico [mediAnico], *a.* Mediumistic, pertaining to phenomena produced by a spiritualistic medium.
mediano, *n.m.* (*Football*) Half-back.
mediano, *a.* Middle, average, medial; intermediate; (*Anat. Geol.*) median.
mediante, *prep.* By means of, through. **— l'aiuto di,** with the help of.
mediatamente, *adv.* Indirectly.
mediato, *a.* Mediate, indirect; interposed.
mediatore, mediatrice, *n.m.f.* Mediator, mediatrix; intermediary; (*Comm.*) broker, middleman; agent. **— di noleggi,** ship-broker; **— di assicurazione,** insurance broker; **far da —,** to act as intermediary.
mediazione, *n.f.* Mediation, intercession; (*Comm.*) commission, brokerage.
medicabile [medicAbile], *a.* Curable.
medicamento, *n.m.* Medicament, remedy; treatment.
medicamentoso, *a.* Medicinal.
medicare, *v.t.* To cure, to heal, to doctor, to treat; to dress (a wound).
medicarsi, *v.r.* To doctor oneself; to take medicine.
medicastro, *n.m.* Quack doctor.
medicatura, medicazione, *n.f.* Treatment; dressing (of wounds); medication. **Posto di medicazione,** first-aid post.
mediceo [medIceo], *a.* Medicean; pertaining to the Medici.
medicina, *n.f.* Medicine, physic; remedy. **Facoltà di —,** faculty of medicine; **studente in —,** medical student; **esercitare la —,** to practise medicine; **— legale,** forensic medicine.
medicinale, *n.m.a.* Medicine, drug, potion; medicinal.
medicinalmente, *adv.* Medicinally.
medico (*pl.* **medici**), *n.m.* Physician, doctor; medical officer. **— condotto,** municipal doctor; **— curante,** doctor attending; **— chirurgo,** surgeon; **— specialista,** specialist; **chiamare il —,** to call the doctor.
medievale, *a.* Medieval [cp. **medioevale**].
medio (1) [mEdio], *n.m.* Mean, medium; middle finger. (*Comm.*) **— circolante,** circulating medium.
medio (2) [mEdio], *a.* Middle, medium; intermediate; average. **Dito —,** middle finger; **velocità media,** average speed; **scuole medie,** secondary schools; **il Medio Evo,** the Middle Ages; **media età,** middle age; **prezzo —,** average price.
mediocre, *a.* Mediocre, middling; commonplace; indifferent, mean, poor; second rate.
mediocremente, *adv.* Poorly, moderately; meanly.
mediocrità [-à], *n.f.* Mediocrity; meanness, narrowness; narrow-mindedness.
medioevale, *a.* Medieval.
medioevalismo, *n.m.* Medievalism.
medioevalista (*pl.* **medioevalisti**), *n.m.* Medievalist.
medioevo, *n.m.* Middle Ages.
meditabile [meditAbile], *a.* Needing thought, requiring consideration.
meditabondo, *a.* Thoughtful, meditative; sunk in meditation, pensive.
meditamento. *n.m.* Thought, meditation.
meditare, *v.i.t.* To meditate, to ponder, to muse; to plan, to think over; to design; to plot.
meditatamente, *adv.* Designedly; advisedly, deliberately.
meditativo, *a.* Meditative, pondering, thoughtful.
meditazione, *n.f.* Meditation, musing, pondering.
Mediterraneo [mediterrAneo], *n.m.a.* Mediterranean.
medium [mEdium], *n.m.* Spiritualistic medium.
medusa, *n.f* (*Myth. Zool.*) Medusa; jelly-fish.
Mefistofele [mefistOfele], *n.m.* Mephistopheles.
mefistofelico [mefistofElico], *a.* Mephistophelean, sardonic.
mefite, *n.f.* Foetid air.
mefitico [mefItico], *a.* Mephitic, pestilential.
megafono [megAfono], *n.m.* Megaphone; loud-speaker.
megalomane [megalOmane], *n.m.a.* Megalomaniac.
megalomania [megalomanIa], *n.f.* Megalomania.
megaterio [megatErio], *n.m.* (*Zool.*) Magatherium.
megera, *n.f.* Hag, vixen; (*Myth.*) one of the Furies.
meglio (1) [mEglio], *n.m.* The best, the best thing. **Fare del proprio —,** to do one's best; **per il —,** for the best.
meglio (2) [mEglio], *adv.a.* Better. **Di bene in —,** better and better; **tanto —,** so much the better; **star —,** to feel better; **— di così non potrebbe andare,** it couldn't be better; **avere la —,** to have the upper hand; **— un uovo oggi che una gallina domani,** a bird in the hand is worth two in the bush.
mela, *n.f.* Apple. **Mele cotte,** stewed apples; **torta di mele,** apple tart.
melacotogna, *n.f.* Quince.
melagrana, *n.f.* Pomegranate.
melagrano, *n.m.* (*Bot.*) Pomegranate-tree.
melanconia [cp. **malinconia**].
melanzana, *n.f.* (*Bot.*) Egg-plant.
melarancia [melarAncia], *n.f.* Orange.
melassa, *n.f.* Molasses, treacle.
melata, *n.f.* Honey-dew.
melato, *a.* Honeyed, sugary; flavoured with honey; sweet.
mele [cp. **miele**].
melensaggine [melensAggine], *n.f.* Silliness, fatuity, stupidity.
melenso, *a.* Stupid, silly, fatuous.
meleto, *n.m.* Apple orchard.
meliaca [melIaca], *n.f.* Variety of apricot.
melica [mElica], *n.f.* (*Bot.*) Indian millet; maize.
melico [mElico], *a.* Lyrical.
meliloto, *n.m.* (*Bot.*) Mellilot.
melinite, *n.f.* (*Chem.*) Melinite.
melissa, *n.f.* (*Bot.*) Balm.
mellifero [mellIfero], *a.* Melliferous.
mellifluamente, *adv.* Mellifluously.
mellifluità [-à], *n.f.* Mellifluousness.
mellifluo [mellIfluo], *a.* Mellifluous, smooth and sweet; flattering; honeyed.

mellonaggine [mellonAggine], *n.f.* Stupidity.
mellonaia [mellonAia], *n.f.* Melon-bed.
mellone, melone, *n.m.* Melon.
melma, *n.f.* Mire, mud, slime.
melmoso, *a.* Muddy, slimy.
melo, *n.m.* (*Bot.*) Apple-tree.
melodia [melodIa], *n.f.* Melody, air, tune.
melodicamente, *adv.* In melody, melodiously.
melodico [melOdico], *a.* Melodious, tuneful, sweet (to the ear).
melodiosamente, *adv.* Melodiously.
melodioso, *a.* Melodious, tuneful.
melodista (*pl.* **melodisti**), *n.m.* Melodist, composer.
melodramma (*pl.* **melodrammi**), *n.m.* Melodrama; opera.
melodrammaticamente, *adv.* Melodramatically.
melodrammatico [melodrammAtico], *a.* Melodramatic; sentimental; operatic.
melodrammatista (*pl.* **melodrammatisti**), *n.m.* Writer of melodramas.
melograno, *n.m.* (*Bot.*) Pomegranate-tree.
melomania [melomanIa], *n.f.* Passion for music.
melomaniaco [melomanIaco], *n.m.* Music maniac.
melopea, *n.f.* (*Mus.*) Art of melody; accompaniment.
meluggine [melUggine], *n.f.* Crab apple.
membrana, *n.f.* (*Anat.*) Membrane; thin tissue, pellicle, film.
membranaceo [membranAceo], *a.* Membranaceous.
membranoso, *a.* (*Anat.*) Membranous.
membratura, *n.f.* Framework, limbs; structure.
membrettare, *v.t.* (*Arch.*) To ornament.
membretto, *n.m.* (*Arch.*) Ornament.
membro (*pl.* **membri,** *m.*, **membra,** *f.*), *n.m.* Limb, member (of the body), branch; member of a society, partner. **Le membra,** the limbs; **i membri del Consiglio,** the members of the Council.
membruto, *a.* Strong-limbed, squarely-built.
memento, *n.m.* Memento, souvenir; (*Eccles.*) prayer for the dead.
memorabile [memorAbile], *a.* Memorable, unforgettable.
memorabilmente, *adv.* Memorably.
memorando, *a.* Worth remembering.
memorare, *v.i.* To remember, to call to mind; to commemorate.
memore, *a.* Mindful; grateful.
memoria [memOria], *n.f.* Memory, remembrance, recollection; souvenir; memorial; memoir; communication. **Imparare, studiare, mandare a —,** to learn by heart; **richiamare alla —,** to remind; **smarrire la —,** to lose one's memory; **a — d'uomo,** from time immemorial; **le Memorie del Goldoni,** Goldoni's memoirs; **in — di,** in memory of.
memoriale, *n.m.* Memorial, written statement; record; petition.
memorialista (*pl.* **memorialisti**), *n.m.* Memorialist.
mena, *n.f.* Intrigue [cp. **mene**]
menadito, *adv* At one's finger-tips, perfectly, exactly. **Sapere una cosa a —,** to have a thing at one's finger-tips.
menamento, *n.m.* (Act of) being led.
menante, *n.m.* (*obs.*) Scribe.
menare, *v.t.* To lead, to conduct; to take; to bring; to draw; to strike; to wag. **— vanto,** to boast; **— la coda,** to wag the tail; **— pel naso,** to lead by the nose; **— il can per l'aia,** to put off day after day, to beat about the bush; **— le mani,** to come to blows; **— per le lunghe,** to put off, to procrastinate; **— un colpo,** to strike a blow; **— la lingua,** to talk scandal; **menarla buona,** to grant.
menarola, *n.f.* (*Mech.*) Borer, drill; carpenter's brace and bit.
menarrosto, *n.m.* Turnspit, jack.
menata, *n.f.* Blow; shake.
mencio [mEncio], *a.* Flabby, feeble.
menda, *n.f.* Fault, defect, error; blemish.
mendace, *a.* Mendacious, false, lying; deceitful.
mendacemente, *adv.* Mendaciously, falsely.
mendacio [mendAcio], *n.m.* Falsehood; false pretences.
mendare [cp. **emendare**].
mendicamente, *adv.* Like a beggar.
mendicante, *n.m.a.* Mendicant, beggar
mendicare, *v.i.* To beg, to ask alms; to implore.
mendicità [-à], *n.f.* Mendicity, beggary. **Ricovero di —,** workhouse.
mendico, *n.m.* Beggar, pauper.
mene, *n.f.pl.* Intrigues, underhand dealings, plots.
meneghino, *n.m.* Milanese dialect.
menestrello, *n.m.* Minstrel.
Menfi, *n.f.* (*Geog.*) Memphis.
meninge, *n.f.* (*Anat.*) Meninx.
meningite, *n.f.* (*Med.*) Meningitis.
menisco, *n.m.* Meniscus, concave lens.
menno, *a.* Beardless, eunuch, castrated.
meno, *n.m.* The least, the less. **Andare al —,** to be reduced to poverty; **il — che posso fare,** the least I can do.
meno, *adv.* Less, least; fewer; minus; except. **Per lo —,** at least; **fare a —,** to do without; **non posso fare a — di dire,** I can't help saying; **non essere da —,** to be up to the occasion; **a — che,** except that; **nè più nè —,** neither more nor less, just as much; **— male,** all the better; **venir —,** to faint, to fail; **tre — un quarto,** a quarter to three (o'clock); **venir — alla parola,** to break one's word; **niente —!** indeed! you don't say so! **in — che non si dica,** before you can say Jack Robinson; **tanto —,** still less; **assai —,** much less; **più o —,** more or less; **dieci — quattro,** ten minus four.
Meno, *n.m.* (*Geog.*) River Main.
menomamente, *adv.* By no means, in no wise, not in the least.
menomare, *v.t.* To diminish; to depreciate, to belittle; to detract; to impair; to prejudice.
menomazione, *n.f.* Depreciation, impairment.
menomo [mEnomo], *a.* Smallest, least [cp. **minimo**].
menopausa [menopAusa], *n.f.* (*Anat.*) Menopause.
mensa, *n.f.* Table, board; (*Mil.*) mess; (*Eccles.*) altar. **Levare le mense,** to rise from table.

mensile, *n.m.a.* Monthly wage or salary; monthly.
mensilità [-à], *n.f.* Monthly payment, monthly instalment.
mensilmente, *adv.* Once a month; by the month; monthly.
mensola [mEnsola], *n.m.* Bracket; (*Arch.*) corbel.
menta, *n.f.* (*Bot.*) Mint. **— romana,** penny-royal; **— peperina,** peppermint.
mentale, *a.* Mental, intellectual.
mentalità [-à], *n.f.* Mentality.
mentalmente, *adv.* Mentally.
mentastro, *n.m.* (*Bot.*) Horsemint.
mente, *n.f.* Mind, intellect, understanding, thought; memory, attention. **Sapere a —,** to know by heart; **imparare a —,** to learn by heart; **mi viene in —,** it occurs to me; **porger —,** to pay attention; (*Law*) **a — dell'articolo quarto,** according to the 4th paragraph; **passare per la —,** to cross one's mind; **tenere a —,** to keep in mind; **mi era uscito di —,** it had gone out of my mind.
mentecattaggine [mentecattAggine], *n.f.* Insanity.
mentecatto, *n.m.a.* Half-wit, idiot, fool; mad, insane, half-witted.
mentina, *n.f.* Peppermint lozenge.
mentire, *v.t.i.* To lie, to tell lies, to conceal the truth; to falsify, to misrepresent.
mentita, *n.f.* Flat denial.
mentitamente, *adv.* Falsely, lyingly.
mentito, *a.* False, feigned. **Sotto mentite spoglie,** in disguise.
mentitore, mentitrice, *n.m.f.* Liar.
mento, *n.m.* (*Anat.*) Chin. (*colloq.*) **L'onor del —,** the beard.
mentolo, *n.m.* (*Chem.*) Menthol.
mentore [mEntore], *n.m.* Mentor, adviser.
mentovare, *v.t.* To mention, to record.
mentre, *n.m.* Moment, while. **In quel —,** in that moment.
mentre, *conj.* While, whilst; whereas.
menzionare, *v.t.* To mention, to name; to call; to quote.
menzione, *n.f.* Mention. **Degno di —,** worth mentioning.
menzogna, *n.f.* Lie, falsehood, untruth, fib; misstatement. **Cumulo di menzogne,** pack of lies.
menzognero, *a.* False, lying, untrue, mendacious.
meramente, *adv.* Merely, purely.
meraviglia [cp. **maraviglia**].
mercante, *n.m.* Merchant; tradesman, trader, dealer; agent. **Fare orecchio di —,** turn a deaf ear; **— di buoi,** cattle dealer; **— di vino,** wine merchant.
mercanteggiare, *v.t.i.* To trade, to bargain, to deal in, to traffic.
mercantesco, mercantile, *a.* Mercantile.
mercantilismo, *n.m.* Mercantilism, commercialism.
mercantilmente, *adv.* Commercially.
mercanzia [mercanzIa], *n.f.* Trade; merchandise, wares, goods.
mercatino, *n.m.* Stall-holder (in a market).
mercato, *n.m.* Market; marketplace; dealing, traffic (in goods). **A buon —,** cheap, cheaply; **per sopra —,** into the bargain; **piazza del —,** market-square; **— del pesce,** fish-market; **far — di,** to prostitute; (*Comm.*) **— fermo,** steady market; **prezzo di —,** market-price; **— nero,** black market; **a Milano c'è — il mercoledì,** Wednesday is market-day in Milan.
mercatura, *n.f.* Trade, business, commerce.
merce, *n.f.* Goods, wares, merchandise. **Treno merci,** goods train; **— a condizione,** goods on sale or return.
mercè [-è], *n.f.* Grace, mercy; thanks to. **Chieder —,** to crave mercy; **la Dio —!** Thank God! **sono alla sua —,** I am at his mercy; **usare —,** to show mercy.
mercede, *n.f.* Reward, recompense; wage, salary.
mercenariamente, *adv.* In a mercenary way.
mercenario [mercenArio], *n.m.a.* Mercenary.
merceologia [merceologIa], *n.f.* Technology of commerce.
merceria [mercerIa], *n.f.* Haberdashery, drapery; draper's shop.
mercerizzato, *a.* Mercerized (cotton).
merciaio [merciAio], *n.m.* Haberdasher, draper.
merciaiolo, *n.m.* Peddler, hawker.
mercimonio [mercimOnio], *n.m.* Illicit trade, unscrupulous traffic.
mercoledì [-ì], *n.m.* Wednesday.
mercuriale, *n.m.* (*Comm.*) Market report, market statement.
mercuriale, *a.* Mercurial.
mercuriato, *n.m.* (*Chem.*) Mercuriate.
mercurico [mercUrico], *a.* (*Chem.*) Mercuric.
mercurio [mercUrio], *n.m.* Mercury (in all senses), quicksilver.
merda, *n.f.* Dung, (human) excrement; filth.
merdaio [merdAio], *n.m.* Dunghill.
merdosamente, *adv.* Filthily.
merdoso, *a.* Filthy, foul.
merenda, *n.f.* Light meal, snack; picnic. **È l'ora della —,** it is tea-time.
merendare, *v.i.* To have a snack, to go for a picnic; to have tea.
meretrice, *n.f.* Harlot, prostitute, whore.
meretricio [meretrIcio], *n.m.a.* Prostitution, meretriciousness; meretricious.
meria [mEria, merIa], *n.f.* Shady spot. **Stare alle merie,** to be in the open air.
meridiana, *n.f.* Sun-dial; (*Astron.*) meridian line.
meridiano, *n.m.a.* Meridian.
meridionale, *n.m.a.* Southerner, Southern.
meriggiare, *v.i.* To rest at noon, to lie in the shade; to take an afternoon nap.
meriggio [merIggio], *n.m.* Midday, noon.
meringa, *n.f.* Meringue.
merino, *n.m.* Merino; merino sheep.
meritamente, *adv.* Deservedly, justly.
meritare, *v.t.* To merit, to deserve; to require, to want. **Ben — di,** to deserve well of; **non merita la pena,** it isn't worth while; **— biasimo, lode,** to deserve blame, praise; **trattare una persona come merita,** to treat a person according to his deserts.
meritarsi, *v.r.* To be entitled to, to earn. **Se l'è meritato,** he has earned it; serve him right.
meritatamente, *adv.* Deservedly.
meritato, *a.* Deserved, merited.

meritevole [meritEvole], *a.* Deserving, meritorious; worthy.
meritevolmente, *adv.* Deservingly.
merito [mErito], *n.m.* Merit, worth, desert; reward. **Farsi — di una cosa,** to make a merit of something; **in ordine di —,** in order of merit; **render —,** to give due reward, to give credit; **in — a,** with reference to; **entrare nel — della questione,** to go into the matter fully; **parlare in — a,** to speak about; **io non ne ho nè colpa nè —,** it has nothing to do with me; **Dio ve ne renda —,** may God reward you.
meritoriamente, *adv.* Meritoriously.
meritorio [meritOrio], *a.* Meritorious, deserving.
merla, *n.f.* (*Zool.*) Hen blackbird.
merlango, merlano, *n.m.* (*Zool.*) Whiting.
merlato, *a.* Battlemented.
merlatura, *n.f.* Battlements.
merlettare, *v.t.* To trim with lace.
merletto, *n.m.* Lace; indentation. **Merletti di Venezia,** Venetian lace.
merli, *n.m.pl.* Battlements.
merlino, *n.m.* (*Naut.*) Twine for whipping a rope-end.
merlo, *n.m.* (*Zool.*) Blackbird; (*fig.*) simpleton.
merluzzo, *n.m.* (*Zool.*) Cod, codfish. **Olio di fegato di —,** cod-liver oil.
mero, *a.* Mere, simple, pure. **Per — caso,** by mere chance.
merovingio [merovIngio], *n.m.a.* Merovingian.
merto, *n.m.* (*Lit.*) Merit [cp. **merito**].
mesata, *n.f.* Month's wages; month (period of time).
mescere [mEscere], *v.t.* To pour out, to pour, to shed; to mix, to mingle.
meschinamente, *adv.* Meanly, poorly, wretchedly, shabbily.
meschinello, *a.* Poor, wretched, shabby, mean.
meschineria, meschinità [-à], *n.f.* Meanness, shabbiness, paltriness, stinginess; misery.
meschino, *n.m.a.* Wretched creature, miserable fellow; wretched, mean, paltry; shabby. **Fare una figura meschina,** to cut a poor figure.
meschita, *n.f.* (*obs.*) Mosque; castle, tower.
mesciroba, *n.f.* (*Eccles.*) Ewer.
mescita [mEscita], *n.f.* Bar, saloon, public-house, tap-room; wine-shop.
mescitore, mescitrice, *n.m.f.* Bar-tender, barmaid, barman.
mescolabile [mescolAbile], *a.* Mixable.
mescolamento, *n.m.* Mixing, mingling.
mescolanza, *n.f.* Mixture, blend; medley.
mescolare, *v.t.* To mix, to mingle, to blend; to stir, to whip; (*Cards*) to shuffle.
mescolarsi, *v.r.* To be associated, to mix with, to mingle with; to meddle with; to become involved in.
mescolata, *n.f.* (Action of) mixing, stirring; stir. **Dare una —,** to give a stir; **— delle carte,** shuffle of the cards.
mescolatamente, *adv.* Confusedly.
mescolio [mescolIo], *n.m.* Thorough mixing; mix-up; general muddle.
mese, *n.m.* Month; month's wages. **Fine del —,** end of the month; **quanti ne abbiamo del —,** what day of the month is it; (*Comm.*) **— scorso, — corrente, — prossimo,** ult., inst., prox.
mesenterio [mesentErio], *n.m.* (*Anat.*) Mesentery.
mesero, mesere [mEsero, mEsere], *n.m.* Woman's shawl (over head and shoulders).
mesmerico [mesmErico], *a.* Mesmeric.
mesmerismo, *n.m.* Mesmerism.
mesocarpo, *n.m.* (*Bot.*) Mesocarp.
mesozoico [mesozOico], *a.* (*Geol.*) Mesozoic.
messa (1), *n.f.* (*Eccles.*) Mass. **— alta, grande, cantata,** High Mass; **— bassa, piana,** Low Mass. **Andare a —,** to go to Mass; **libro da —,** missal.
messa (2), *n.f.* Placing, putting, setting up; putting forth (of buds); putting up (for sale); (*Cards, etc.*) stake played for; course (of a meal). (*Theat.*) **— in scena,** staging; (*Motor.*) **— in moto, in marcia,** starting; (*Comm.*) **— a bordo,** shipping; **— a magazzino,** warehousing; **— in vigore,** enforcement.
messaggeria [messaggerIa], *n.f.* Forwarding agency; goods department; stage coach; mail.
messaggero, *n.m.* Messenger; harbinger.
messaggio [messAggio], *n.m.* Message; news, communication.
messale, *n.m.* (*Eccles.*) Missal.
messe, *n.f.* Harvest, crop. **Le bionde messi,** the golden corn.
messere, *n.m.* (*Hist.*) Sir; gentleman.
Messia, *n.m.* Messiah.
messianico [messiAnico], *a.* Messianic.
messicano, *n.m.a.* Mexican.
Messico [mEssico], *n.m.* (*Geog.*) Mexico.
messinese, *n.m.a.* Person from, or relating to Messina.
messiticcio [messitIccio], *n.m.* (*Agric.*) Backward growth.
messo, *n.m.* Messenger, envoy; ambassador.
messo, *p.p.a.* Placed, put, set. **— insieme,** put together; **mal —,** badly dressed; badly arranged; **— in forse, in dubbio,** questioned, placed in doubt [cp. **mettere**].
mestamente, *adv.* Sadly.
mestamento, *n.m.* Stirring, mixing, mixture.
mestare, *v.t.* To stir with a ladle, to mix; to interfere, to meddle.
mestatore, mestatrice, *n.m.f.* Meddler, intriguer; agitator, ring-leader.
mestica [mEstica], *n.f.* Priming (for paint); paints on a palette.
mesticciare, *v.t.* To interfere, to meddle.
mesticheria [mesticherIa], *n.f.* Oil and colour shop.
mestierante, *n.m.* Worker, jobber; (*Lit.*) pot-boiler; opportunist.
mestiere, mestiero, *n.m.* Trade, craft, business, occupation, job; profession; employment. **Arti e mestieri,** arts and crafts; **essere del —,** to be in the trade; **di —,** by trade, by profession; **i ferri del —,** the tools of the trade.
mestieri, *adv.* Necessary. **È —, fa —,** it is necessary, it is required.
mestizia [mestIzia], *n.f.* Sadness, melancholy; affliction.
mesto, *a.* Sad, mournful, dejected, gloomy.
mestola [mEstola], *n.f.* Ladle; washerwoman's bat; bricklayer's trowel; bat.
mestolata, *n.f.* Ladleful; blow with a bat.

mestolo [mEstolo], *n.m.* Ladle, wooden spoon (for cooking). **Avere il — in mano,** to be boss, to rule the roost.
mestolone, *n.m.* Big spoon; lout, clumsy fellow; (*Zool.*) spoon-bill duck.
mestone, *n.m.* Wooden stick for stirring; clumsy busybody.
mestruale, *a.* (*Anat.*) Menstrual.
mestruare, *v.t.* To menstruate.
mestruazione, *n.f.* Menstruation.
mestruo [mEstruo], *n.m.* Menses, woman's period.
meta, *n.f.* Goal, aim; end, purpose, object; (*Agric.*) heap, pile (of hay, dung, etc.). **Arrivare alla —,** to reach the goal; **proporsi una —,** to set oneself a target.
metà [-à], *n.f.* Half; moiety. **Fare a —,** to go halves, to go fifty-fifty; **essere a —,** to be half way; **— prezzo,** half-price; **tagliare in —,** to cut in halves; **stare a — degli utili,** to go half-shares in profits; (*colloq.*) **la mia —,** my wife, my better half; **dividere per —,** to divide equally; **fermarsi a —,** to stop half-way (in all senses); **far le cose a —,** to do things by halves; **essere a — del mese,** to be halfway through the month.
metabolismo, *n.m.* Metabolism.
metacarpo, *n.m.* (*Anat.*) Metacarpus.
metacronismo, *n.m.* Metachronism, wrong-dating.
metafisica [metafIsica], *n.f.* Metaphysics.
metafisicamente, *adv.* Metaphysically.
metafisico [metafIsico], *n.m.a.* Metaphysician, metaphysical.
metafora [metAfora], *n.f.* Metaphor.
metaforeggiare, metaforizzare, *v.i.* To speak in metaphors, to speak metaphorically; to indulge in metaphors.
metaforicamente, *adv.* Metaphorically.
metaforico [metafOrico], *a.* Metaphorical.
metafrasi [metAfrasi], *n.f.* Translation word for word, metaphrase.
metallico [metAllico], *a.* Metallic. (*Comm.*) **Valuta metallica,** metallic currency.
metallifero [metallIfero], *a.* Metalliferous.
metallizzamento, metallizzazione, *n.m.f.* Metallization.
metallizzare, *v.t.* To metallize.
metallo, *n.m.* Metal, tone, timbre (of voice). (*colloq.*) **Il vil —,** money, filthy lucre.
metalloide [metallOide], *n.m.* Metalloid.
metallurgia [metallurgIa], *n.f.* Metallurgy.
metallurgico [metallUrgico], *a.* Metallurgical.
metallurgo [metAllurgo], *n.m.* Metallurgist.
metamorfico [metamOrfico], *a.* Metamorphic.
metamorfosare, *v.t.* To metamorphose.
metamorfosi [metamOrfosi], *n.m.* Metamorphosis, transformation.
metano, *n.m.* (*Chem.*) Fire-damp, methane.
metastasi [metAstasi], *n.f.* (*Med.*) Metastasis.
metastasiano, *a.* In the manner of Metastasio.
metatesi [metAtesi], *n.f.* Metathesis, transposition.
metempsicosi, *n.f.* Metempsycosis.
meteora [metEora], *n.f.* Meteor, shooting star.
meteoricamente, *adv.* Meteorically.
meteorico [meteOrico], *a.* Meteoric.
meteorite, *n.f.* Meteorite.
meteorologia [meteorologIa], *n.f.* Meteorology.
meteorologico [meteorolOgico], *a.* Meteorological. **Bollettino —,** weather forecast.
meteorologista, meteorologo [meteorOlogo], *n.m.* Meteorologist.
meticcio [metIccio], *n.m.a.* Mongrel; half-breed, half-caste, cross; half-bred.
meticolosamente, *adv.* Meticulously.
meticolosità [-à], **meticolosaggine** [meticolosAggine], *n.f.* Meticulousness, fastidiousness.
meticoloso, *a.* Meticulous; fastidious, finical, particular.
metile, *n.m.* (*Chem.*) Methyl.
metilico [metIlico], *a.* Methylic.
metodicamente, *adv.* Methodically.
metodicità [-à], *n.f.* Orderliness, method.
metodico [metOdico], *a.* Methodical.
metodismo, *n.m.* (*Eccles.*) Methodism.
metodista (*pl.* **metodisti**), *n.m.* Methodist.
metodo [mEtodo], *n.m.* Method; rule, system, order; custom. **È questione di —,** it is a matter of custom.
metodologia [metodologIa], *n.f.* Methodology.
metonimia [metonImia], *n.f.* Metonymy.
metonomasia [metonomAsia], *n.f.* Change of name.
metope [mEtope], *n.f.* (*Arch.*) Metope.
metraggio [metrAggio], *n.m.* Measurement in metres; length; (*Cinema.*) footage.
metricamente, *adv.* Metrically.
metrica [mEtrica], *n.f.* Metrics, prosody, metre, versification.
metrico [mEtrico], *a.* Metric, metrical. **Sistema — decimale,** metric or decimal system.
metro, *n.m.* Metre (in all senses). **Far le cose un tanto al —,** to work in a wholesale fashion. (A metre = 39·3701 ins.; **— quadrato,** square metre = 10·7639 sq. ft.; **— cubo,** cubic metre = 35·3148 cu. ft.).
metronomo [metrOnomo], *n.m.* (*Mus.*) Metronome.
metropoli [metrOpoli], *n.f.* Metropolis.
metropolita, *n.m.* (*Eccles.*) Metropolitan, archbishop.
Metropolitana, *n.f.* Underground railway, tube.
metropolitano, *n.m.a.* Metropolitan; constable, policeman.
mettere [mEttere], *v.t.i.* To put, to place, to lay, to set; to put on, to wear; to contribute; to suppose; to put forth (leaves, etc.) **— in ordine,** to set in order; **— in atto,** to accomplish; **— un abito,** to put on a coat; **— in Italiano,** to translate into Italian; **— i denti,** (of a baby) to cut teeth; **— conto di,** to be worth while; **— al corrente di,** to inform of; **— in dubbio una cosa,** to question something, to raise a doubt; **— in evidenza,** to bring into evidence, to put in evidence; **— insieme,** to put together; **— in libertà,** to set at liberty; **— male,** to set people at variance; **— paura,** to frighten; **— piede,** to set foot; **— a punto,** to get ready; **— a dormire,** to settle for the night, to settle for a nap; **— alla porta,** to show the door to, to turn out; **— all'ordine del giorno,** to put on the agenda; **— una pulce nell'orecchio,** to put ideas into someone's head; **mettiamo che sia così,** let us suppose that it is so; **il sentiero mette sullo stradone,** the path leads to the main road.

mettersi [mEttersi], *v.r.* To put on, to dress in, to get into; to enter into, to start; to set out. **— le scarpe,** to put one's shoes on; **— di buona volontà al lavoro,** to fall to work with a good will; **— in mezzo,** to interfere, to intervene; **— avanti,** to make oneself conspicuous; to step forward; **metterci troppo tempo,** to take too long; **quanto ci si mette ?** how long does it take? **— d'accordo,** to reach agreement; **— le mani nei capelli,** to tear one's hair (in desperation).
mettibocca, *n.m.* Meddler, mischief-maker.
mettiloro, *n.m.* Gilder.
mettimale, mettiscandali [mettiscAndali] *n.m.* Scandal-monger, mischief-maker.
mezza, *n.f.* Half-hour; one half; half share; (*Billiards*) short cue.
mezzadria [mezzadrIa], *n.f.* (*Agric.*) Metayage; crop-sharing system.
mezzadro, *n.m.* Metayer.
mezzafesta, *n.f.* Half-holiday; (*Eccles.*) feast day on which work is permitted.
mezzalana, *n.f.* Material half wool, half cotton; linsey-woolsey.
mezzaluna, *n.f.* Half-moon, crescent; (*fig.*) Turkey, the Crescent; curved blade for cooking-knife.
mezzana, *n.f.* Flat tile, flooring-tile; side of bacon; procuress, bawd; (*Naut.*) mizzen sail.
mezzanino, *n.m.* (*Arch.*) Mezzanine floor; entresol.
mezzano, *n.m.* Procurer, pimp, pander, go-between, intermediary.
mezzano, *a.* Middle, middle-sized, intermediate; middle class.
mezzanotte, *n.f.* Midnight.
mezzatinta, *n.f.* Half-tint; off-shade.
mezzeria [mezzerIa], *n.f.* Metayage; the middle part.
mezzetta, *n.f.* Half-litre jug.
mezzina, *n.f.* Jug.
mezzino, *n.m.* (*Football*) Half-back.
mezzo (1), *a.* Rotten (of fruit).
mezzo (2), *n.m.* Half; middle part, centre; mean; (*pl.*) means, riches. **Il giusto —,** the happy mean; **dare i mezzi per,** to provide means for; **un uomo di molti mezzi,** a man of ample means; **i mezzi di trasporto,** the means of transport; **il fine giustifica i mezzi,** the end justifies the means.
mezzo (3), *adv.a.* Half; medium, middle, mean. **A mezz'aria,** in the air; **mezzi termini,** half-measures, indefinite statement; **di mezza età,** of middle age, middle-aged; **a mezza voce,** timidly, in a low voice; **le mezze misure,** make-shifts, half measures; **nel bel —,** right in the middle; **a mezza strada,** half-way; **in — al mare,** in the open sea; **mezz'ora,** half-an-hour; **fare le cose a —,** to half-do things; **togliere, levare di —,** to get rid of; **a mezz'asta,** at half-mast; **andare di —,** to get involved, to get mixed; **per — di,** by means of; **una mezza verità,** a half-truth; **togliersi di —,** to clear out, to get away.
mezzobusto, *n.m.* Bust, head and shoulders.
mezzocerchio [mezzocErchio], *n.m.* Half-circle, semicircle.
mezzocolore, *n.m.* Neutral tint.
mezzodì [-ì], **mezzogiorno,** *n.m.* Mid-day, noon; south.
mezzolano, *a.* Mediocre.
mezzombra, *n.f.* (*Art*) Half-tone.
mezzomondo, *n.m.* Hemisphere.
mezzorilievo, *n.m.* (*Art*) Half-relief.
mezzotermine [mezzotErmine], *n.m.* Compromise, evasion, expediency, shift.
mezzuccio [mezzUccio], *n.m.* Subterfuge, mean device; make-shift.
mezzule, *n.m.* Movable stave of a barrel (for cleaning purposes).
mi, *n.m.* (*Mus.*) Mi, E.
mi, *pron.* Me, to me. **Dimmi,** tell me; **mi piace,** I like it; **non guardarmi,** don't look at me; **io mi son un,** I am one, as for me; **statemi bene,** keep well.
mia [cp. **mio**].
miagolamento, *n.m.* Mewing (of a cat).
miagolare, *v.t.* To mew; to whine (of bullets).
miagolio [miagolIo], *n.m.* Continual mewing.
miagolo [miAgolo], *n.m.* Mew (of a cat).
miaulare, *v.i.* To miaow.
miasma, *n.f.* Miasma, poisonous exhalation.
mica (1), *n.f.* Crumb, grain.
mica (2), *n.f.* (*Min.*) Mica.
mica, *adv.* Not at all, not in the least. **Non voglio — offendervi,** I do not in the least wish to offend you; **non costa — tanto,** it isn't really expensive.
micaceo [micacEo], *a.* Micaceous, containing mica.
micado, *n.m.* Mikado (of Japan).
micaschisto, *n.m.* (*Geol.*) Mica-schist, mica-slate.
miccia [mIccia], *n.f.* Fuse (for firing an explosive), slow-match.
miccino, *adv.* **A —,** sparingly.
micco, *n.m.* (*Zool.*) Ape; (*fig.*) debauchee.
micelio [micElio], *n.m.* (*Bot.*) Mycelium.
Micene, *n.f.* (*Geog.*) Mycenae.
michelaccio [michelAccio], *n.m.* Lazy fellow, loafer.
michelangiolesco, *a.* In the manner of Michelangelo; grand, grandiose.
Michele, *n.m.* Michael. **Giorno di San —,** Michaelmas; **fare San —,** to pack up.
micia [mIcia], *n.f.* Puss, pussy, pussy-cat.
micidiale, *a.* Deadly, murderous; homicidal.
micidialmente, *adv.* Murderously.
micino, *n.m.* Kitten.
micio [mIcio], *n.m.* Tom-cat, cat; tailor's chalk.
micologia [micologIa], *n.f.* Mycology.
micolina, *n.f.* Scrap, little bit.
micragna, *n.f.* (*colloq.*) Penury, hard-upness.
micragnoso, *a.* (*colloq.*) Sordid, wretched.
microbio, microbo [micrObio, mIcrobo], *n.m.* Microbe.
microcosmico [microcOsmico], *a.* Microcosmic.
microcosmo, *n.m.* Microcosm.
microfono [micrOfono], *n.m.* Microphone.
microfotografia [microfotografIa], *n.f.* Microphotography.
micrometro [micrOmetro], *n.m.* Micrometer.
microscopicamente, *adv.* Microscopically.
microscopico [microscOpico], *a.* Microscopical, microscopic.
microscopio [microscOpio], *n.m.* Microscope.

mida, *n.f.* (*Zool.*) Green turtle; species of monkey.
midolla, *n.f.* Pulp; (*Anat.*) medulla; crumb (of a loaf.) **Bagnato fino alla —,** wet through, soaked to the skin.
midollo, *n.m.* Marrow (of beasts), pith (of a plant); pulp, essence, pith, stamina. (*Anat.*) **Il — spinale,** the spinal cord.
midolloso, *a.* Pithy, full of marrow; crumbly.
miei, *pron.* My, mine. **I —,** my family, my own people [cp. **mio**].
miele, *n.m.* Honey. **Parole di —,** honeyed words; **luna di —,** honeymoon.
mielite, *n.f.* (*Med.*) Myelitis.
mietere [miEtere], *v.t.* To mow (grass); to cut (corn); to reap, to harvest. **— allori,** to win laurels.
mietitore, mietitrice, *n.m.f.* Mower, reaper; mowing-machine; reaping-machine, harvester.
mietitura, *n.f.* Mowing; harvest-time.
migale, *n.f.* (*Zool.*) Variety of poisonous spider.
migliaccio [migliAccio], *n.m.* Chestnut-flour cake; black-pudding.
migliaio (*pl.* **migliaia,** *f.*) [migliAio], *n.m.* Thousand. **Parecchie migliaia,** several thousand; **un — di lire,** about 1000 lire; **a migliaia,** by thousands.
migliarino, *n.m.* (*Zool.*) Chaffinch; (*fig.*) shower of shot.
miglio (1) [mIglio] (*pl.* **miglia,** *f.*), *n.m.* Mile. **— inglese,** English mile (1·524 km.); **esser lontano mille miglia dal,** never to dream of, never to imagine.
miglio (2) [mIglio] (*pl.* **migli**), *n.m.* Millet; bird-seed.
migliorabile [migliorAbile], *a.* Capable of improvement.
miglioramento, *n.m.* Improvement, recovery (of health), progress, amelioration, betterment.
migliorare, *v.t.i.* To improve, to ameliorate, to grow better, to recover, to mend. **Le cose migliorano,** things are improving; **migliora lentemente,** he is recovering slowly; **Come sta? Migliora.** How is he? He's improving.
migliorarsi, *v.r.* To improve oneself, to amend.
migliore, *a.* Better; higher; finer. **Il —,** the best; **con le migliori intenzioni,** with the best intentions; **nel — dei modi,** in the best possible way.
miglioria [migliorIa], *n.f.* Amelioration.
mignatta, *n.f.* (*Zool.*) Leech; (*fig.*) miser, usurer; importunate person; bore. **Attaccar mignatte,** to apply leeches.
mignattaio [mignattAio], *n.m.* Finder or vendor of leeches; (*Zool.*) species of curlew.
mignattino, *n.m.* (*Zool.*) Tern.
mignola [mIgnola], *n.f.* Olive blossom.
mignolare, *v.i.* To blossom (of the olive).
mignolatura, *n.f.* Flowering (of the olive).
mignolo [mIgnolo], *n.m.* Little finger, little toe; olive blossom.
mignone, *n.m.* Favourite; (*Print.*) minion.
mignotta, *n.f.* Harlot, whore.
migrare, *v.i.* To migrate.
migratore, *n.m.* Migrant.
migratorio [migratOrio], *a.* Migratory.
migrazione, *n.f.* Migration.
mila, *num.a.pl.* Two or more thousand. **Duemila, tremila,** etc. [cp. **mille**].
milanese, *n.m.a.* Milanese.
Milano, *n.m.* (*Geog.*) Milan.
miliardario [miliardArio], *n.m.* Multi-millionaire.
miliardo, *n.m.* Milliard; (*Am.*) billion.
miliare, *a.* **Pietra —,** milestone (in all senses); landmark.
milionario [milionArio], *n.m.* Millionaire; wealthy man.
milioncino, *n.m.* (*colloq.*) A cool million.
milione, *n.m.* Million.
milionesimo [milionEsimo], *n.m.* Millionth.
militante, *a.* Militant, combative, fighting. **Chiesa —,** Church militant.
militare, *v.i.* To militate; to serve; to stand for or against.
militare, *n.m.* Soldier, military man.
militarescamente, *adv.* Soldierly.
militaresco, *a.* Soldierlike; aggressive.
militarismo, *n.m.* Militarism.
militarista (*pl.* **militaristi**), *n.m.* Militarist.
militarizzare, *v.t.* To militarize.
militarmente, *adv.* By force of arms.
milite [mIlite], *n.m.* Militiaman; soldier. **Il — Ignoto,** the Unknown Warrior.
milizia [milIzia], *n.f.* Militia; warfare, art of war; army, legion.
millanta, *num.a.* Many thousand, a great number.
millantare, *v.t.* To boast of, to exaggerate. **Millantanto credito,** false pretences.
millantarsi, *v.r.* To brag, to swagger; to be proud of.
millantatore, millantatrice, *n.m.f.* Boaster, braggart.
millanteria [millanterIa], *n.f.* Bragging, swaggering.
mille (*pl.* **mila**), *num.a.* Thousand. (*Hist.*) **I Mille,** Garibaldi's Thousand; **— trecento,** thirteen hundred, one thousand three hundred; **Le Mille e una Notte,** the Arabian Nights.
millecuplo [millEcuplo], *a.* Thousandfold.
millefoglio [millefOglio], *n.m.* (*Bot.*) Milfoil, yarrow.
millenario [millenArio], *n.m.a.* Millenary, millennial; millenarian.
millennio [millEnnio], *n.m.* Millennium.
millepiedi, *n.m.* (*Zool.*) Centipede, millepede.
millesimo [millEsimo], *a.* Thousandth.
milligrammo, *n.m.* Milligramme (0·015 grain).
millilitro, *n.m.* Thousandth part of a litre.
millimetro [millImetro], *n.m.* Millimetre (0·039 in.).
milord, milorde, *n.m.* English lord, rich foreigner.
miluogo, *n.m.* Half-way house, half-way spot.
milza, *n.f.* (*Anat.*) Spleen; milt.
milzadella, *n.f.* (*Bot.*) Spotted nettle.
mima, *n.f.* Mime, pantomime dancer.
mimesi, *n.f.* Mimesis, voice imitation.
mimetico [mimEtico], *a.* Mimetic, imitative.
mimetismo, *n.m.* (*Zool.*) Protective mimicry.
mimica [mImica], *n.f.* Mimicry.
mimicamente, *adv* In mimicry.
mimico [mImico], *a.* Mimicking, comic, mimic.
mimmo, *n.m.* (*colloq.*) Baby, infant.

mimo, *n.m.* Mime, clown, mimic; dancer (in pantomime).
mimosa, *n.f.* (*Bot.*) Mimosa.
mina, *n.f.* Mine (to be exploded); bushel (measure); (*Hist.*) Greek coin. **— galleggiante,** floating mine; **— subacquea,** submerged mine; **— magnetica,** magnetic mine.
minabile [minAbile], *a.* Capable of being mined.
minaccevole [minaccEvole], *a.* Menacing.
minaccevolmente, *adv.* Menacingly.
minaccia [minAccia], *n.f.* Threat, menace. **Vane minaccie,** empty threats; **proferire minaccie,** to utter threats.
minacciare, *v.t.* To threaten, to menace.
minacciatore, *n.m.* Threatener.
minacciosamente, *adv.* Threateningly.
minaccioso, *a.* Threatening, menacing. **Tempo —,** threatening weather.
minare, *v.t.* To mine, to undermine, to sap; to injure. **Campo minato,** mine-field.
minareto, *n.m.* Minaret.
minatore, *n.m.* Miner, collier, pitman.
minatorio [minatOrio], *a.* Minatory, threatening. **Lettera minatoria,** threatening letter.
minchionare, *v.t.* (*Colloq.*) To mock, to laugh at; to make a fool of, to take in.
minchionatore, *n.m.* Jester, mocker, quiz.
minchionatura, *n.f.* Mockery, jest; foolery, leg-pulling.
minchione, *n.m.* Simpleton, ninny, dunce, fool.
minchioneria [minchionerIa], *n.f.* Foolish thing, folly, nonsense, piece of foolery, leg-pull.
minerale, *n.m.a.* Mineral.
mineralista (*pl.* **mineralisti**), *n.m.* Mineralogist.
mineralizzare, *v.t.* To mineralize.
mineralizzazione, *n.f.* Mineralization.
mineralogia [mineralogIa], *n.f.* Mineralogy.
mineralogista (*pl.* **mineralogisti**), *n.m.* Mineralogist.
minerario [minerArio], *a.* Relating to mines, mining. **Industria mineraria,** mining industry.
minestra, *n.f.* Soup (generally thick).
minestrina, *n.f.* Thin soup, clear soup.
minestrone, *n.m.* Thick soup with rice and vegetables; Scotch broth; (*fig.*) medley.
mingherlino, *a.* Slim, slender, frail.
miniare, *v.t.* To illuminate, to paint in miniature; to embellish; to describe in detail.
miniatore, miniatrice, *n.m.f.* Miniature-painter.
miniatura, *n.f.* Miniature.
miniaturista, *n.m.f.* Miniaturist.
miniera, *n.f.* Mine (in all senses); quarry. **— di carbone,** coal-mine; **— d'oro,** gold-mine.
minima [mInima], *n.f.* (*Mus.*) Minim.
minimamente, *adv.* In the least, not at all.
minimo [mInimo], *a.* Least, smallest, meanest, lowest; trifling, inconsiderable. **Senza la minima difficoltà,** without the slightest difficulty; **il prezzo —,** the lowest price.
minimo [mInimo], *n.m.* Minimum.
minio [mInio], *n.m.* Red lead.
ministeriale, *a.* Ministerial. **Crisi —,** ministerial crisis.
ministerialismo, *n.m.* (*Pol.*) Ardent support of a ministry.
ministerialmente, *adv.* Ministerially.
ministero, *n.m.* Ministry; office, function; minister's office; cabinet, administration. **— della Difesa, della Marina, degli Esteri, dell'Interno, delle Finanze,** War Office, Admiralty, Foreign Office, Home Office, Treasury; **il — si è dimesso,** the Cabinet has resigned; (*Law*) **pubblico —,** public prosecutor.
ministrare, *v.t.* To minister; to administer.
ministrativo, *a.* Administering; ministrative.
ministratore, *n.m.* (*Eccles.*) Administrator; deacon.
ministro, *n.m.* Minister (of state); priest; minister (diplomatic rank). **Primo —,** prime minister, premier; **— di Stato,** cabinet minister; **carta —,** foolscap paper.
minoranza, *n.f.* Minority (in all senses). **Essere in —,** to be in a minority.
minorare, *v.t.* To diminish, to lessen; to impair; to disable.
minorascato, *n.m.* Minority; condition of being a minor with estate in trust.
minorasco, *n.m.* (*Law*) Younger brother's estate in trust.
minorativo, *a.* Attenuating.
minorato, *a.* Diminished, lessened; impaired, disabled.
minorazione, *n.f.* Diminution, lessening; impairment; disablement.
minore, *a.* Less, minor, smaller; (*Law*) under age, minor; (*Mus.*) minor key. **Fratello —,** younger brother; **Asia Minore,** Asia Minor.
minorenne, *n.m.a.* (*Law*) Minor.
minorità [-à], *n.f.* Minority.
Minosse, *n.m.* (*Myth.*) Minos; (*fig.*) ruthless judge.
Minotauro, *n.m.* (*Myth.*) Minotaur.
minuendo, *n.m.* (*Math.*) Number from which another is subtracted, minuend.
minuetto, *n.m.* Minuet.
minugia [minUgia], *n.f.* (*Lit.*) Guts, bowels; (*Mus.*) cat-gut, string of an instrument.
minuire, *v.i.* To diminish.
minuscola [minUscola], *n.f.* (*Print.*) Lower-case letter; (*Palaeography*) minuscule.
minuscolo [minUscolo], *a.* Small, little, trifling; (*Print.*) lower-case.
minuta, *n.f.* Minute, draft, rough copy, note; bill of fare. **Fare la —,** to prepare a rough draft.
minutaglia [minutAglia], *n.f.* Minutiae; small rubbish; small fry.
minutamente, *adv.* Minutely, in detail, critically.
minutante, *n.m.* Taker of minutes (at a meeting); (*Comm.*) retailer.
minutare, *v.t.* To draw up minutes, to minute. **— una lettera,** to draft a letter.
minuteria [minuterIa], *n.f.* Trifles, knick-knacks, trinkets.
minutezza, *n.f.* Minuteness, smallness; minutiae.
minutiere, *n.m.* Dealer in small jewellery.
minuto, *n.m.* Minute (of time), instant. **Un — secondo!** (wait a) second! **in mezzo —,** in half-a-minute.

minuto, *a.* Minute, very small; petty, trifling; critical; particular; detailed, precise, exact; (*Comm.*) retail. **Vendere al —,** to sell retail; **pescheria minuta,** small fry (*also fig.*); **bestiame minuto,** smaller live-stock (such as pigs, sheep, goats); **gente minuta,** common people, man-in-the-street.
minuzia [minUzia], *n.f.* Minutia, trifle, minuteness; fastidiousness. **Perdersi in minuzie,** to be finicking, to be particular about trifles.
minuziosaggine [minuziosAggine], *n.f.* Minuteness; fastidiousness; accuracy.
minuziosamente, *adv.* Minutely, fastidiously.
minuziosità [-à], *n.f.* Minuteness, fastidiousness; accuracy.
minuzioso, *a.* Minute, detailed; fastidious; accurate.
minuzzaglia [minuzzAglia], *n.f.* Quantity of crumbs or morsels; (*fig.*) little people.
minuzzame, *n.f.* Quantity of broken pieces.
minuzzare, *v.t.* To break into small pieces.
minuzzolare, *v.t.* To break into crumbs, to crumble.
minuzzolo [minUzzolo], *n.m.* Bit, scrap, morsel, crumb; shrimp (of a child).
mio (*pl.* **miei, mie**), My, mine. **I miei,** my parents; **mio padre,** my father; **questo libro è mio,** this book is mine; **io vivo del mio,** I am of independent means.
miocardite, *n.f.* (*Med.*) Myocarditis.
miocele, *n.m.* (*Med.*) Muscular tumour.
miocene, *n.m.* (*Geol.*) Miocene period.
miope [mIope], *n.m.a.* Short-sighted person; short-sighted, myopic.
miopia [miopIa], *n.f.* Short-sightedness, myopia.
miosotide [miosOtide], *n.f.* (*Bot.*) Myosotis, forget-me-not [cp. **non-ti-scordar-di-me**].
mira, *n.f.* Aim (in all senses); direction; purpose, object; target. **Prender la —,** to take aim, to aim at; **aver buona —,** to be a good shot; **aver delle mire,** to have designs; **prender di — qualcuno,** to pester someone; **avere in — di,** to intend to; **non ebbe altra — che il bene,** he had only good intentions; **aver la — troppo alta, mirare troppo alto,** to aim too high.
mirabile [mirAbile], *a.* Admirable, wonderful, marvellous.
mirabilia [mirabIlia], *n.f.pl.* Wonders, marvellous things. **Dir — di,** to speak wonders of.
mirabilmente, *adv.* Wonderfully.
mirabolante, *a.* Amazing, stunning, astounding (*usu. ironically*).
miracolismo, *n.m.* Belief or faith in miracles.
miracolo [mirAcolo, *n.m.* Miracle; prodigy, wonder, marvel. **Per —,** by a miracle; **fare miracoli,** to work miracles.
miracolosamente, *adv.* Miraculously.
miracolosità [-à], *n.f.* Miraculousness.
miracoloso, *a.* Miraculous, prodigious, wonderful.
miraggio [mirAggio], *n.m.* Mirage; illusion.
mirando, *a.* Wonderful, admirable, marvellous.
mirare, *v.t.i.* To gaze at, to observe, to look at; to aim at, to tend to; to level (a gun). **— al bersaglio,** to aim at the target.
mirarsi, *v.r.* To look at oneself intently. **— nello specchio,** to look at oneself in the mirror; **— intorno,** to look around, to be on one's guard.
miratore, *n.m.* Good shot, marksman; gazer.
miriade [mirIade], *n.f.* Myriad, a very great number.
miriagrammo, *n.m.* Ten kilogrammes.
miriametro, *n.m.* Ten kilometres.
miriapodi [miriApodi], *n.m.pl.* (*Zool.*) Myriapoda.
mirica, mirice, *n.f.* (*Bot.*) Tamarisk, tamarisk-tree.
mirifico [mirIfico], *a.* Marvellous, wonderful, magnificent.
mirino, *n.m.* Foresight of gun or rifle; (*Phot.*) view-finder.
mirmica [mIrmica], *n.f.* (*Zool.*) Red ant.
mirmicoleone, *n.m.* (*Zool.*) Ant-lion.
mirmidoni [mirmIdoni], *n.m.pl.* (*Myth.*) Myrmidons.
miro, *a.* Wondrous; marvellous.
mirra, *n.f.* Myrrh.
mirride, *n.f.* (*Bot.*) Chervil.
mirrino, *n.m.* Extract of myrrh.
mirro, *n.m.* Measure for oil (about 10 kilos).
mirrolo, *n.m.* Oil of myrrh.
mirteo [mirtEo], *a.* Of myrtle.
mirteto, *n.m.* Myrtle grove.
mirtillo, *n.m.* (*Bot.*) Bilberry.
mirto, *n.m.* (*Bot.*) Myrtle.
misantropia [misantropIa], *n.f.* Misanthropy.
misantropicamente, *adv.* Misanthropically.
misantropico [misantrOpico], *n.m.a.* Misanthrope; misanthropic.
misantropo [misAntropo], *n.m.* Misanthrope.
misavventura, *n.f.* Misadventure.
miscea [miscEa], *n.f.* Trifle, bagatelle.
miscela, *n.f.* Mixture, medley; blend.
miscellanea [miscellAnea], *n.f.* Miscellany (literary, etc.).
miscellaneo [miscellAneo], *a.* Miscellaneous.
mischia [mIschia], *n.f.* Scuffle, affray, fight. **Gettarsi nella —,** to hurl oneself into the fray; **nel folto della —,** in the thick of the fight.
mischiamento, *n.m.* Mixing, mixture.
mischiare, *v.t.* To mix, to mingle, to blend; to jumble, to entangle.
mischiarsi, *v.r.* To intermingle, to meddle, to interfere, to mix.
mischiatamente, *adv.* In a confused manner, jumbled up.
mischiatura, *n.f.* Mixture, jumble.
misconoscere [misconOscere], *v.t.* To refuse recognition; to disregard; to repudiate, to disown.
misconosciuto, *a.* Disregarded, unappreciated.
miscredente, *n.m.a.* Unbeliever; unbelieving; miscreant.
miscredenza, *n.f.* Unbelief.
miscredere [miscrEdere], *v.i.* Not to believe (in a religious sense); to entertain a false belief.
miscuglio [miscUglio], *n.m.* Medley, mixture, blend.
miserabile [miserAbile], *a.* Wretched, unhappy; poor, needy; despicable, vile, miserable; mean, paltry. **Guadagno —,** very small profit.

miserabilità [-à], *n.f.* Indigence, destitution; vileness, lowness.
miserabilmente, *adv.* Miserably, meanly, poorly.
miseramente, *adv.* Unhappily.
miserando, *a.* Pitiable, miserable, wretched.
miserazione, *n.f.* Compassion, commiseration.
miserevole [miserEvole], *a.* Pitiable, miserable, lamentable, piteous.
miserevolmente, *adv.* Pitiably, miserably.
miseria [misEria], *n.f.* Distress, misery; indigence, destitution, penury, want; (*fig.*) trifle. **Costa una —,** it costs a mere nothing; **pianger —,** to plead poverty; **essere in —,** to be destitute; **perdersi in miserie,** to be particular about trifles; **raccontare le proprie miserie,** to relate one's misfortunes.
misericorde, *a.* Merciful, kind.
misericordia [misericOrdia], *n.f.* Mercy; pity, forgiveness, compassion. **La Misericordia,** lay association for giving aid in sickness, at funerals, etc.; **gridare —,** to cry for help, for assistance; **Misericordia!** Well, I never! Good gracious!
misericordiante, *n.m.* Member of La Misericordia.
misericordiosamente, *adv.* Mercifully, compassionately.
misericordioso, *a.* Merciful, kind.
misero [mIsero], *a.* Unhappy, miserable, wretched, pitiable; poor, needy, shabby; mean, vile; paltry; abject; stingy, niggardly. **Un compenso —,** a paltry reward; **un abito —,** a shabby coat, a bad fit.
miserrimo, *a.* Very wretched; appalling.
misfatto, *n.m.* Misdeed, crime.
misirizzi, *n.m.* (*colloq.*) Child's toy.
misogallo, *n.m.* Hater of all things French.
misogamia [misogamIa], *n.f.* Misogamy.
misoginia [misoginIa], *n.f.* Misogyny.
misogino [misOgino], *n.m.a.* Misogynist; misogynous.
misoneismo, *n.m.* Misoneism, hatred of anything new.
missionante, *n.m.* (*Eccles.*) Priest on mission.
missionario [missionArio], *n.m.a.* Missionary.
missione, *n.f.* Mission (in all senses).
missiva, *n.f.* Missive, letter, message.
mistagogo [mistAgogo], *n.m.* Mystagogue.
mistamente, *adv.* Promiscuously.
misteriosamente, *adv.* Mysteriously.
misteriosità [-à], *n.f.* Mysteriousness, secrecy, concealment.
misterioso, *a.* Mysterious, hidden, secret, enigmatical.
mistero, *n.m.* Mystery; secret, enigma, riddle; (*Theat.*) mystery-play. **Far — di una cosa,** to make a secret of something.
mistica [mIstica], *n.f.* Mystics, mystic theology.
misticamente, *adv.* Mystically.
misticismo, *n.m.* Mysticism.
misticità [-à], *n.f.* Mysticalness, mysticism.
mistico [mIstico], *n.m.a.* Mystic, mystical.
mistificare, *v.t.* To mystify, to hoax; to deceive, to cheat.
mistificatore, mistificatrice, *n.m.f.* Mystifier, hoaxer.
mistificazione, *n.f.* Mystification, hoax.
mistione, *n.f.* Mixture.
misto, *n.m.* Mixture.
misto, *a.* Mixed; compounded; variegated. **Scuola mista,** co-educational school; **fritto —,** mixed grill; **matrimonio —,** mixed marriage; **assicurazione mista,** comprehensive policy; (*Rail.*) **treno —,** train carrying passengers and goods.
mistrà [-à], *n.f.* Aniseed, aniseed cordial.
mistura, *n.f.* Mixture, blend; medley.
misturare, *v.t.* To mix, to mingle.
misura, *n.f.* Measure, measurement; extent, dimension, size; limit; moderation; rule, standard. **— di capacità,** measure of capacity; **pesi e misure,** weights and measures; **oltre —, fuor di —,** beyond measure, excessively; **passar la —,** to exceed the limits; **prender le misure d'un abito,** to take measurements for a suit; **mezze misure,** half-measures; **misure di polizia,** police measures; **a — che,** as; **farsi fare un abito su —,** to have a suit made to measure.
misurabile [misurAbile], *a.* Measurable.
misurabilmente, *adv.* Measurably.
misuramento, *n.m.* Measurement.
misurapioggia [misurapiOggia], *n.m.* Rain-gauge.
misurare, *v.t.* To measure; to estimate, to weigh; to gauge; to survey (land).
misurarsi, *v.r.* To put on, to try on; to compete with; to defy. **— con qualcuno,** to compete with someone.
misuratamente, *adv.* Measuredly, moderately.
misuratezza, *n.f.* Measure, moderation.
misurato, *a.* Measured; moderate; reserved (in manner), self-controlled.
misuratore, *n.m.* Measurer; gauge, meter. **— del gas,** gas-meter.
misurazione, *n.f.* Measurement, measuring; gauging; surveying.
misurino, *n.m.* Small measure; milk-can.
misuso, *n.m.* Misuse.
mite, *a.* Mild, gentle, meek; mellow; moderate, reasonable. **Prezzi miti,** moderate prices.
mitemente, *adv.* Mildly, meekly, gently.
mitera [mItera], *n.f.* Foolscap (placed on the head of a man in the pillory).
mitezza, *n.f.* Mildness, gentleness. (*Comm.*) **— di prezzi,** lowness of prices.
miticamente, *adv.* Mythically.
mitico [mItico], *a.* Mythical, legendary.
mitigamento, *n.m.* Mitigation.
mitigare, *v.t.* To mitigate, to alleviate; to appease, to allay, to assuage.
mitigarsi, *v.r.* To become humble; to placate.
mitigazione, *n.f.* Mitigation.
mitilo [mItilo], *n.m.* (*Zool.*) Mussel.
mito, *n.m.* Myth, legend; parable.
mitologia [mitologIa], *n.f.* Mythology.
mitologico [mitolOgico], *a.* Mythological.
mitologista (*pl.* **mitologisti**), **mitologo** [mitOlogo], *n.m.* Mythologist.
mitra (1), *n.f.* (*Eccles.*) Mitre.
mitra (2), *n.m.* Tommy-gun.
mitraglia [mitrAglia], *n.f.* Grape-shot.
mitragliare, *v.t.* To machine-gun; to pepper with shot.
mitragliata, *n.f.* Machine-gun fire.
mitragliatrice, *n.f.* Machine-gun.
mitragliere, *n.m.* Machine-gunner.
mitrale, *a.* (*Anat.*) Mitral.

mitrare, *v.t.* To crown (with mitre).
mitria [cp. **mitra** (1)].
mitriato, *a.* Mitred.
Mitridate, *n.m.* Mithridates.
mitridatico [mitridAtico], *n.m.* Antidote (to poison).
mitridatismo, *n.m.* Mithridatism.
mitridizzare, *v.t.* To render immune to poison; to be proof against poison.
mittente, *n.m.a.* Sender; sending, forwarding; despatching. **Rispedire al —,** return to sender.
mnemonica [mnemOnica], *n.f.* Mnemonics.
mnemonico [mnemOnico], *a.* Mnemonic.
mo', *abbrev.* of **modo,** *n.m.* Way. **A mo' d'esempio,** as an instance, by way of illustration.
mo', *adv.* Now, just now, a moment ago. **Guarda mo'!** Just look!
mobile (1) [mObile], *n.m.* Piece of furniture; (*Theol.*) heaven. **Il primo —,** the first of the nine heavens; **che bel —!** what a fool!
mobile (2) [mObile], *a.* Movable; mobile; changeable, fickie; **Le sabbie mobili,** the quicksands; **feste mobili,** movable feasts; **terreno —,** shifting soil.
mobili [mObili], *n.m.pl.* Furniture, movables, chattels, personal effects. **Beni —,** personal property.
mobilia [mobIlia], *n.f.* Furniture.
mobiliare, *v.t.* To furnish.
mobiliare, *a.* Movable, personal. **Proprietà —,** personal property.
mobiliato [cp. **ammobigliato**].
mobilio [mobIlio], *n.m.* Furniture.
mobilità [-à], *n.f.* Mobility; (*fig.*) fickleness.
mobilitare, mobilizzare, *v.t.* To mobilize (troops, capital, etc.).
mobilitazione, *n.f.* Mobilization.
mobilmente, *adv.* In a mobile manner; capriciously.
moca, *n.m.* Mocha coffee.
mocchetto, *n.m.* Moquette; carpet-wool.
moccicaglia [moccicAglia], *n.f.* Slime (of a snail), mucus (from the nose), snot.
moccicare, *v.i.* To run at the nose, to snivel.
moccichino, *n.m.* Handkerchief, nose-wipe.
moccio [mOccio], *n.m.* Nasal mucus, snot; glanders (of horses); slime.
moccioso, *a.* Snotty, slimy.
moccolaia [moccolAia], *n.f.* Candle-grease, candle-snuff.
moccoletto, *n.m.* Taper.
moccolino, *n.m.* Wax match; (*colloq.*) oath.
moccolo [mOccolo], *n.m.* Candle-end; wax taper; (*colloq.*) oath. **Portare il —,** to be one too many; **tirare moccoli,** to swear.
moccolone, *n.m.* Sniveller.
moco, *n.m.* (*Bot.*) Bitter vetch.
moda, *n.f.* Fashion; vogue, mode, pose. **Alla —,** in the latest fashion; **passato di —,** out of fashion, old-fashioned; **negozio di mode,** milliner's shop, costumier's; **vestirsi all'ultima —,** to dress in the latest style.
modale, *a.* Modal.
modalità [-à], *n.f.* Modality; way, method, manner; formalities.
modanatura, *n.f.* Moulding, shaping, modelling.
modano [mOdano], *n.m.* Mould, model; crochet-needle; netting-needle.
modella, *n.f.* Artist's model.
modellamento, *n.m.* Modelling.
modellare, *v.t.* To model, to mould, to shape; to design; to fashion.
modellarsi, *v.r.* To model oneself, to follow a pattern (of behaviour, etc.).
modellatore, modellatrice, *n.m.f.* Modeller, moulder.
modellatura, *n.f.* Modelling, moulding.
modello, *n.m.a.* Model (in all senses); pattern. **Un marito —,** a model husband; **dello stesso —,** of the same pattern.
modenese, *n.m.a.* Modenese, from Modena.
moderabile [moderAbile], *a.* Capable of being moderated.
moderamento, *n.m.* Moderation.
moderare, *v.t.* To moderate, to restrain, to control; to check, to curb.
moderarsi, *v.r.* To control oneself, to restrain oneself.
moderatamente, *adv.* Moderately.
moderatezza, *n.f.* Moderation, discretion, restraint; temperance.
moderativo, *a.* Moderative.
moderato, *n.m.* (*Pol.*) Progressive Conservative; moderate politician.
moderato, *a.* Moderate, restrained.
moderatore, *n.m.* Moderator.
moderazione, *n.f.* Moderation, discretion, restraint; temperance.
modernamente, *adv.* In a modern manner.
modernismo, *n.m.* Modernism.
modernista (*pl.* **modernisti**), *n.m.* Modernist.
modernità [-à], *n.f.* Modernity.
modernizzare, *v.t.* To modernize, to bring up to date.
moderno (1), *n.m.* Modern (man). **I moderni,** the Moderns.
moderno (2), *a.* Modern, new, contemporary, recent, up-to-date. **Storia moderna,** modern history.
modestamente, *adv.* Modestly; simply.
modestia [modEstia], *n.f.* Modesty; humility; simplicity; honesty; chastity.
modesto, *a.* Modest, unassuming, humble; moderate (of prices).
modicamente, *adv.* Moderately.
modicità [-à], *n.f.* Moderateness (of price), cheapness.
modico [mOdico], *a.* Moderate (esp. of prices), cheap, reasonable.
modifica [modIfica], *n.f.* Modification, alteration, change.
modificabile [modificAbile], *a.* Modifiable, liable to modification.
modificamento, *n.m.* Modification.
modificare, *v.t.* To modify, to alter, to change; to revise, to correct.
modificazione, *n.f.* Modification, alteration, change.
modista, *n.f.* Milliner, dressmaker.
modisteria [modisterIa], *n.f.* Milliner's, dressmaker's shop.
modo, *n.m.* Manner, way; mode, custom; means; (*Gram.*) mood; (*Mus.*) key. **A — mio,** in my own way; **in bel —,** with good manners; **trovar — di,** to manage to, to succeed in; **cattivi modi,** bad manners; **di — che,** in such a way as, so that; **non aver — di,** to have no means of, to find it impossible to; **oltre —,** extremely; **ad ogni —,** at

any rate; **persona a —,** honest person; **per — di dire,** so to speak, in a relative sense; **un — di dire,** an idiom, an idiomatic phrase, a colloquialism; **— di pensare,** way of thinking; **fare in — che,** to see that.
modula [mOdula], *n.f.* Rough draft.
modulare, *v.t.* To modulate, to inflect (voice, etc.), to tune; to harmonize.
modulatamente, *adv.* In a modulated manner.
modulazione, *n.f.* Modulation, inflection, variation.
modulo [mOdulo], *n.m.* Form (document with blanks to be filled in), printed form; rule, norm; pattern. **— da telegramma,** telegram-form; **riempire un —,** to fill in a form.
moerre, moerro, *n.m.* Moire silk; mohair.
mofeta, *n.f.* Place from which an acrid gas arises.
mofetico [mofEtico], *a.* Mephitic.
moffetta, *n.f.* (*Zool.*) Skunk.
mogano [mOgano], *n.m.* Mahogany.
moggio [mOggio], *n.m.* Corn-measure (about 5 bushels). **Una lucerna sotto il —,** a light under a bushel.
mogio [mOgio], *a.* Downcast, depressed, crestfallen. **Mogio mogio,** very subdued.
mogliazzo, *n.m.* (*colloq.*) Wedding.
moglie [mOglie], *n.f.* Wife. **Prender —,** to marry, to get married; **far passar per —,** to pass as one's wife (dims. **moglietta, moglina, mogliettina,** etc.).
moia [mOia], *n.f.* Salt-spring; volcanic tufa.
moina, *n.f.* Blandishment, fondling, coaxing ways; cajolery, wiles.
mola, *n.f.* Millstone, grindstone.
molare, *v.t.* To grind.
molare, *n.m.a.* Molar (tooth).
molcere [mOlcere], *v.t.* (*Poet.*) To assuage, to soothe, to allay.
mole, *n.f.* Mass, huge structure, massive building; bulk, burden. **Di gran —,** bulky; **la — del lavoro,** the mass of work.
molecola [molEcola], *n.f.* Molecule.
molecolare, *a.* Molecular.
molenda, *n.f.* Miller's charge for grinding.
molestamente, *adv.* Troublesomely.
molestamento, *n.m.* Molesting, molestation.
molestare, *v.t.* To molest, to importune, to annoy, to harass; to trouble, to disturb, to vex.
molestatore, molestatrice, *n.m.f.* One who molests, importuner.
molestia [molEstia], *n.f.* Molestation, annoyance, trouble, vexation, nuisance.
molesto, *a.* Troublesome, annoying, wearisome, tiring; irksome.
molibdeno, *n.m.* (*Min.*) Molybdenum.
molinismo, *n.m.* (*Eccles.*) Molinism.
molino [cp. **mulino**].
molla, *n.f.* Spring, mainspring. **Molle,** tongs; **serratura a —,** spring-lock; **da prendersi colle molle,** to be kept at arms-length, to be handled gingerly; **fare a tira e —,** to shilly-shally, to hesitate.
mollare, *v.t.* To let go; to slacken, to loose. **Non mollate!** Don't let go! Hang on!
molle (1), *n.m.* Soaking; softness. **Mettere in —,** to soak.
molle (2), *a.* Soft, delicate, tender; pliable, supple; loose; wet, soaked; slack, lax. **— di sudore,** soaked with perspiration.
molleggiamento, *n.m.* Elasticity; swaying.
molleggiare, *v.i.* To sway up and down, to be elastic, to work with elasticity.
mollemente, *adv.* Softly, pliably; slackly.
molletta, *n.f.* Small spring; clip, pincers; paper-clip; safety-pin; candle-snuffer.
mollettine, *n.f.pl.* Tweezers.
mollettiere, *n.f.pl.* Puttees.
mollettone, *n.m.* Thick flannel; swansdown.
mollezza, *n.f.* Softness, suppleness; pliability; slackness, effeminacy.
mollica, *n.f.* Crumb (of a loaf).
mollicchio [mollIcchio], *n.m.* Morass, swamp.
molliccio [mollIccio], *a.* Soft, flabby, flaccid.
mollificamento, *n.m.* Mollifying, mollification.
mollificare, *v.t.* To soften, to mollify, to ease.
mollificazione, *n.f.* Mollification.
mollume, *n.m.* Wetness after rain.
mollusco, *n.m.* (*Zool.*) Mollusc.
molo, *n.m.* Jetty, breakwater, mole; pier, quay, wharf.
molosso, *n.m.* Mastiff.
molteplice [moltEplice], *a.* Manifold, numerous, various, copious.
molteplicemente, *adv.* Numerously, variously.
molteplicità [-à], *n.f.* Multiplicity.
molticolore, *a.* Many-coloured.
moltiforme, *a.* Multi-form.
moltilatero [moltilAtero], *a.* Many-sided.
moltiloquio [moltilOquio], *n.m.* Chattering, talkativeness, gabbling.
moltiplica [moltIplica], *n.f.* (*Mech.*) Gear (of a cycle, etc.).
moltiplicabile [moltiplicAbile], *a.* Multipliable.
moltiplicamento, *n.m.* Multiplication.
moltiplicando, *n.m.* (*Math.*) Multiplicand.
moltiplicare, *v.t.* To multiply; to increase; to intensify.
moltiplicarsi, *v.r.* To augment, to increase.
moltiplicatore, moltiplicatrice, *n.m.f.* Multiplier.
moltiplicatrice, *n.f.* Multiplying machine.
moltiplicazione, *n.f.* Multiplication.
moltiplice [moltIplice], *n.f.* Multiple.
moltiplicemente, *adv.* By multiples.
moltiplicità [-à], *n.f.* Multiplicity.
moltisonante, *a.* High-sounding, loud; grandiose.
moltissimi [moltIssimi], *a.* Very many, a great number of.
moltissimo [moltIssimo], *a.* Very much, a great deal of, a lot of.
moltitudine [moltitUdine], *n.f.* Multitude, crowd; the many, the masses.
molto, *a.* Much; many; long (in time). **— rumore,** much noise; **molta gente,** many people; **molti colori,** many colours.
molto, *adv.* Very, much, greatly, largely; widely; well. **— lontano,** very far; **poter —,** to have much influence; **— bene,** very well; **star — meglio,** to be much better; **il — studio gli nuoce,** too much study does him harm; **a dir —,** at most; **fra non —,** presently, before long; **ci corre —,** there's a great difference.

Molucche, *n.f.pl.* (*Geog.*) Moluccas.
molva, *n.f.* (*Zool.*) Ling.
momentaneamente, *adv.* Momentarily, temporarily.
momentaneo [momentAneo], *a.* Momentary, temporary, transient, passing, fleeting.
momentino, *n.m.* Moment; (*colloq.*) half a moment.
momento, *n.m.* Moment (in all senses), second, instant; importance. **Un —!** Just a moment! **dal — che,** since, seeing that; **a momenti,** in a few moments; **cosa di lieve —,** a matter of no account; **al — buono,** at the right moment; **arrivare al — opportuno,** to arrive in the nick of time; **non vedere il — di,** to look forward very much to; **sino a questo —,** as yet; **all'ultimo —,** at the last moment; **per il —,** for the time being.
monaca [mOnaca], *n.f.* Nun. **Farsi —,** to take the veil, to become a nun.
monacale, *a.* Conventual; monastic; monkish.
monacalmente, *adv.* Monkishly.
monacanda, *n.f.* Novice (nun).
monacare, *v.t.* To make a nun.
monacarsi, *v.r.* To become a nun, or monk.
monacato, *n.m.* State of being a monk or nun.
monacazione, *n.f.* Taking the veil; entering a religious order.
monachina, *n.f.* (*Zool.*) Bull-finch.
monachismo, *n.m.* Monasticism.
monaco [mOnaco], *n.m.* Monk; friar. **L'abito non fa il —,** the cowl does not make the monk.
Monaco, *n.m.* (*Geog.*) Monaco (state of). **— di Baviera,** Munich.
monade [mOnade], *n.f.* Monad.
monadelfo, *a.* (*Bot.*) Monadelphous.
monadismo, *n.m.* Monadism.
monandro, *a.* (*Bot.*) Monandrous.
monarca (*pl.* **monarchi**), *n.m.* Monarch, sovereign, king, emperor; ruler.
monarcato, *n.m.* Sovereignty.
monarchia [monarchIa], *n.f.* Monarchy.
monarchicamente, *adv.* Monarchically.
monarchico [monArchico], *n.m.a.* Monarchist; monarchical.
monasteriale, *a.* Monasterial.
monastero, *n.m.* Convent, monastery.
monasticamente, *adv.* Monastically.
monastico [monAstico], *a.* Monastic, conventual; retired, contemplative.
monasticismo, *n.m.* Monasticism.
monatto, *n.m.* (*Hist.*) Bearer, attendant on a pest-cart.
Moncenisio [moncenIsio], *n.m.* (*Geog.*) Mt. Cenis.
moncherino, *n.m.* Stump (of arm).
monchezza, *n.f.* Lack of a hand.
monchino, *n.m.* Person with an amputated arm.
monco, *a.* Maimed, truncated, mutilated; one-armed; (*fig.*) incomplete, garbled.
moncone, *n.m.* Stump (esp. of leg).
monda, *n.f.* (*Agric.*) Weeding, cleaning of fields.
mondaccio [mondAccio], *n.m.* This miserable world.
mondamento, *n.m.* Cleansing, cleaning; peeling.
mondana, *n.f.* Prostitute.
mondanamente, *adv.* Mundanely, in a worldly way; as regards this world.
mondanità [-à], *n.f.* Worldliness, vanity.
mondano, *a.* Mundane, worldly; fond of society.
mondare, *v.t.* To clean; to peel; to weed, to winnow.
mondarisi, *n.f.pl.* Workers in rice fields.
mondarsi, *v.r.* To purge oneself (of faults, blame, etc.).
mondatura, *n.f.* Weeding, cleaning; winnowing; peeling.
mondezza, *n.f.* Purity, cleanliness; stainlessness.
mondezzaio [mondezzAio], *n.m.* Refuse heap; dust-bin.
mondiale, *a.* World-wide, universal. **Esposizione —,** world exhibition; **fama —,** world-wide fame; **guerra —,** world-war.
mondificazione, *n.f.* Cleansing.
mondiglia [mondIglia], *n.f.* Chaff; refuse, dross.
mondizia [mondIzia], *n.f.* Purity, cleanliness.
mondo, *n.m.* World; universe. **Il bel —,** high society; **venire al —,** to be born; **il migliore del —,** the best in the world; **uomo di —,** man of the world; (*colloq.*) **andare all'altro —,** to die; **cose dell'altro —,** amazing or absurd things; **un — di gente,** a mass of people; **dire un — di bene di,** to speak very highly of; **fare il giro del —,** to go round the world; **così va il —,** such is life; **da che — è —,** since the beginning of time.
mondo, *a.* Pure, spotless, clean, neat, free; cleansed, purified; peeled.
mondualdo, *n.m.* (*Law*) Guardian; order of the court.
monedula [monEdula], *n.f.* (*Zool.*) Crow; magpie.
monelleria [monellerIa], *n.f.* Prank, childish trick; monkey-trick, piece of mischief.
monellesco, *a.* Roguish; rascally.
monello, *n.m.* Little rogue, urchin; gamin.
moneta, *n.f.* Coin, money, piece of money. **Carta —,** paper money; **— spicciola,** small change; (*fig.*) plain words.
monetaggio [monetAggio], *n.m.* Outlay incurred in making money; mintage.
monetare, *v.t.* To mint.
monetario [monetArio], *a.* Monetary.
monetazione, *n.f.* Coinage; coining.
monetiere, *n.m.* Minter; coiner.
mongolo [mOngolo], *n.m.a.* Mongol, Mongolian.
mongolico [mongOlico], *a.* Mongolian.
monile, *n.m.* Jewel; necklace, bracelet.
monismo, *n.m.* (*Phil.*) Monism.
monista (*pl.* **monisti**), *n.m.* Monist.
monito [mOnito], *n.m.* Warning, intimation, monition.
monitore, *n.m.* Monitor (in all senses); teacher, preceptor, adviser.
monitorio [monitOrio], *n.m.* (*Eccles.*) Citation.
monizione, *n.f.* Admonition.
monna (1), *n.f.* (*Hist.*) Mistress, dame, lady.
monna (2), *n.f.* (*Zool.*) Ape.
monocero [monOcero], *n.m.* Unicorn; one-horned creature.
monocolo [monOcolo], *n.m.* Monocle, single eyeglass.

monocordo, *n.m.* Monochord, one-stringed instrument.
monocotiledone [monocotilEdone], *a.* (*Bot.*) Monocotiledonous.
monodia [monodIa], *n.f.* Monody.
monofase, *a.* (*Elect.*) Single-phase.
monogamia [monogamIa], *n.f.* Monogamy.
monogamico [monogAmico], *a.* Monogamous.
monogamo [monOgamo], *n.m.* Monogamist.
monogenesi [monogEnesi], *n.f.* Monogenesis.
monografia [monografIa], *n.f.* Monograph, dissertation.
monogramma (*pl.* **monogrammi**), *n.m.* Monogram.
monolitico, [monolItico], *a.* Monolithic.
monolito, *n.m.* Monolith.
monologo [monOlogo], *n.m.* Monologue.
monomania [monomanIa], *n.f.* Monomania.
monomaniaco [monomanIaco], *n.m.* Monomaniac.
monometallismo, *n.m.* Monometallism.
monoplano, *n.m.* (*Aviat.*) Monoplane.
monopolio [monopOlio], *n.m.* Monopoly, exclusive rights.
monopolista (*pl.* **monopolisti**), *n.m.* Monopolist.
monopolizzare, *v.t.* To monopolize, to engross.
monopolizzatore, *n.m.* Monopolizer.
monoposto, *n.m.* (*Aviat.*) Single-seater (plane).
monosillabicamente, *adv.* Monosyllabically.
monosillabico [monosillAbico], *a.* Monosyllabic.
monosillabo [monosIllabo], *n.m.a.* Monosyllable; monosyllabic.
monoteismo, *n.m.* Monotheism.
monoteista, *n.m.* Monotheist.
monotonia [monotonIa], *n.f.* Monotony, sameness; tediousness.
monotono [monOtono], *a.* Monotonous, tedious, wearisome.
monsignorato, *n.m.* Office and dignity of a monsignore.
monsignore, *n.m.* (*Eccles.*) Prelate; title of a prelate.
monsone, *n.m.* (*Meteor.*) Monsoon.
monstruoso [cp. **mostruoso**].
monta, *n.f.* Serving (of animals), covering; breeding season. **Da —,** for breeding; **stazione da —,** breeding stud, stud farm.
montacarico [montacArico], *n.m.* Goods lift; hoist.
montaggio [montAggio], *n.m.* Mounting, setting; assembly, erecting; (*Cinema.*) montage. **Officina di —,** assembling shop.
montagna, *n.f.* Mountain; hill. **Andare in —,** to go to the mountains.
montagnardo, *n.m.* (*Hist.*) Montagnard.
montagnola, *n.m.* Hillock, mound.
montagnolo, *a.* Concerning a mountain, mountain.
montagnoso, *a.* Mountainous, hilly.
montamento, *n.m.* Mounting, setting.
montanaro, *n.m.a.* Mountaineer; highlander, mountain-dweller; mountain, living in the mountains.
montanino, *a.* Mountain, of the hills.
montanista (*pl.* **montanisti**), *n.m.* Mining engineer.
montano, *a.* Mountain, mountainous. **Villaggio —,** mountain village.
montante, *n.f.* Step, support, stand; amount; (*Aviat.*) strut.
montare, *v.t.i.* To mount, to climb, to ascend; to mount (picture, guard, jewel, machine, etc.); to set up; to whip (cream); to wind (a watch); to stir, to rouse, to work up, to excite; to puff up, to boost; to furnish (a house); to cover (of cattle); to amount to. **— a cavallo,** to ride horseback; **— in furia, in collera, in bestia,** to fly into a passion; **non monta,** it doesn't matter; (*colloq.*) **— una cosa,** to boost a thing.
montarsi, *v.r.* To get excited, to make a fuss. **— la testa,** to get excited, to become swollen-headed.
montata, *n.f.* Mounting; ascent, hill.
montatoio [montatOio], *n.m.* Carriage-step; running-board.
montatore, *n.m.* Machine-fitter, setter, mounter.
montatura, *n.f* Mounting; puffing, boosting, (press) stunt; (*fig.*) got-up affair.
montavivande, *n.m.* Service-lift.
monte, *n.m.* Mountain, mount; hill; mass, pile; great deal. **— di pietà,** pawn-shop; **andare, mandare a —,** to come to nothing, to cause to fail, to frustrate; **a —,** up-stream; (*colloq.*) **un — di cose,** a heap of things; (*Comm.*) **in —,** in the bulk, in the lump; **calcolare in —,** to calculate on an average; **promettere mari e monti,** to promise the world; **salire in cima al —,** to climb to the top of a mountain.
Montecitorio [montecitOrio], *n.m.* Parliament-house in Rome.
monticello, *n.m.* Hillock, mound.
montone, *n.m.* Ram; mutton (meat). **Grasso di —,** mutton-tallow.
montuosità [-à], *n.f.* Hilliness, mountainousness.
montuoso, *a.* Mountainous, hilly.
montura, *n.f.* Uniform; livery.
monumentale, *a.* Monumental; stately, grand.
monumento, *n.m.* Monument, memorial; historic building. **Inalzare un —,** to raise a monument to.
mora (1), *n.f.* (*Bot.*) Mulberry; blackberry.
mora (2), *n.f.* Delay, respite; arrears (of wages); moratorium. **Esser in —,** to be in arrears.
mora (3), *n.f.* Cairn, heap of stones.
mora (4) [cp. **morra**].
mora (5), *n.f.* Negro; Moorish woman.
moraiolo, *n.m.* Black olive; morello cherry.
morale, *n.f.* Morals, ethics, moral philosophy; moral of a story, etc.; morality, morale (of troops, etc.).
morale, *a.* Moral (in all senses).
moraleggiare, *v.t.* To moralize.
moralista (*pl.* **moralisti**), *n.m.* Moralist, moralizer.
moralizzare, *v.t.* To moralize.
moralizzazione, *n.f.* Moralization; moral explanation of things and events.
moralmente, *adv.* Morally.
moratoria [moratOria], *n.f.* (*Comm.*) Moratorium.
moratorio [moratOrio], *a.* Dilatory.
moravo, *n.m.a.* Moravian.
morbidamente, *adv* Softly, tenderly; weakly.

morbidezza, *n.f.* Softness, smoothness; mellowness; delicacy; effeminacy.
morbido [mOrbido], *a.* Soft, tender; downy, smooth; delicate, mellow; effeminate.
morbidume, *n.m.* Over-soft stuff; thick mud.
morbifero [morbIfero], *a.* Morbiferous, disease-bringing.
morbiglione, *n.m.* (*Med.*) Chickenpox.
morbilità [-à], *n.f.* Morbid condition.
morbillo, *n.m.* (*Med.*) Measles.
morbo, *n.m.* Disease, malady; infection, contagion.
morbosamente, *adv.* Morbidly, unhealthily.
morbosità [-à], *n.f.* Morbidity, morbidness, unhealthiness.
morboso, *a.* Morbid, unhealthy, diseased, sickly; (*fig.*) morbid (in mind).
morchia [mOrchia], *n.f.* Dregs (of oil, etc.), oiliness.
morchioso, *a.* Thick (of oil).
mordacchia [mordAcchia], *n.f.* Twitch (for a horse); muzzle; gag.
mordace, *a.* Sharp, pungent, biting, satirical, caustic.
mordacemente, *adv.* Pungently, mordantly.
mordacità [-à], *n.f.* Sharpness, pungency.
mordente (1), *n.m.* (*Chem.*) Mordant; (*Mus.*) mordent; bite, grip, hold.
mordente (2), *a.* Biting, pungent.
mordere [mOrdere], *v.t.* To bite, to sting (of insects); to gnaw, to corrode. **— il freno,** to champ the bit.
mordersi, *v.r.* To bite oneself. **— le labbra,** to bite one's lips.
mordicare, *v.t.* To corrode.
mordicazione, *n.f.* Corrosion.
mordicchiare, *v.t.* To nibble, to gnaw.
morditore, morditrice, *n.m.f.* Biter, backbiter.
morditura, *n.f.* Bite, sting (of an insect).
moreccio [morEccio], *n.m.* (*Bot.*) Species of edible fungus.
morello, *a.* Blackish, nearly black.
morena, *n.f.* (*Geol.*) Moraine.
morente, *n.m.f.a.* Dying person; dying, fading.
moresca, *n.f.* Kind of folk dance; Moorish dance.
moresco, *a.* Moorish, moresque.
moretta, morettina, *n.f.* Brunette; Negro.
moretto, *n.m.* Dark-skinned boy; young Negro; Moorish lad.
moretto, *a.* Dark; black.
Morfeo [morfEo], *n.m.* (*Myth.*) Morpheus; sleep.
morfina, *n.f.* Morphia; morphine.
morfinomane [morfinOmane], *n.m.* Morphia fiend, morphia addict.
morfologia [morfologIa], *n.f.* Morphology.
morfologicamente, *adv.* Morphologically.
morfologico [morfolOgico], *a.* Morphological.
morgana, *n.f.* Mirage. **Fata —,** mirage.
morganaticamente, *adv.* Morganatically.
morganatico [morganAtico], *a.* Morganatic.
moria [morIa], *n.f.* Plague, pestilence; contagion; mortality. **In tempi di —,** in times of pestilence.
moribondo, *a.* Moribund, dying.
moriccia [morIccia], *n.f.* Ruin; dry-stone wall.
morigeratamente, *adv.* Decently, morally.
morigeratezza, *n.f.* Good behaviour, honesty of ways, good morals; sobriety.
morigerato, *a.* Well-bred, proper, decent, temperate, of good morals.
morigiana, *n.f.* (*Zool.*) Wigeon.
moriglione, *n.m.* (*Zool.*) Pochard duck.
morindina, *n.f.* Yellow colouring-matter.
morione, *n.m.* (*Hist.*) Morion, helmet.
morire, *v.i.* To die, to expire, to depart this life; to perish, to die out; to go out (of a fire). **— dalla voglia di,** to long for; **— di fame,** to starve; **far —,** to put to death, to kill; **sentirsi —,** to feel very ill or depressed, to feel like dying; **lasciar — un discorso,** to let a subject drop; **lasciar — il fuoco,** to let the fire go out.
morituro, *a.* About to die; doomed to death.
mormone, *n.m.a.* Mormon.
mormoracchiare, *v.t.* To grumble, to mutter under one's breath.
mormoramento, *n.m.* Murmuring, murmur, grumbling.
mormorare, *v.t.i.* To murmur, to whisper, to mutter; to grumble, to complain.
mormoratore, mormoratrice, *n.m.f.* Grumbler, murmurer.
mormorazione, *n.f.* Murmur, grumbling; complaint.
mormoreggiare, *v.i.* To murmur, to whisper; to rustle.
mormorio [mormorIo], *n.m.* Murmur, constant murmuring; whispering, grumbling.
moro (1), *n.m.* Moor, Negro; black animal.
moro (2), *n.m.* (*Bot.*) Mulberry-tree [cp. **gelso**].
moro (3), *a.* Dark brown; black-skinned; Moorish.
morosamente, *adv.* Tardily (in payment, etc.).
morosità [-à], *n.f.* Slowness, tardiness.
moroso, *n.m.* Sweetheart, lover [cp. **amoroso**]
moroso, *a.* In arrears. **Un socio —,** a member in arrears (with subscription).
morra, mora, *n.f.* Game for two played with extended fingers.
morsa, *n.f.* (*Mech.*) Vice, screw-vice; (*Arch.*) toothing.
morsaio [morsAio], *n.m.* Maker of horses' bits.
morsecchiare, *v.t.* To nibble.
morsello, *n.m.* Mouthful; morsel.
morsetto, *n.m.* Morsel, bit; (*Mech.*) small vice.
morsicare, *v.t.i.* To bite; to gnaw; to sting (of insects).
morsicatura, *n.f.* Bite, biting, sting, prick.
morsicchiare, *v.t.* To nibble.
morso, *n.m.* Mite; morsel; (horse's) bit; jaw of a vice; pinch, sting.
mortadella, *n.f.* Bologna sausage.
mortaio [mortAio], *n.m.* Mortar (for crushing); (*Mil.*) mortar.
mortale, *n.m.* Mortal, man.
mortale, *a.* Mortal, deadly, fatal. **Salto —,** somersault; **ferita —,** fatal wound; **i mortali,** the mortals; **peccato —,** mortal sin.
mortalità [-à], *n.f.* Mortality; loss of life; death-rate.
mortalmente, *adv.* Mortally.
mortamente, *adv.* Dully, without vivacity.
mortaretto, *n.m.* Squib (firework).
morte, *n.f.* Death. **Mettere a —,** to put to death; **darsi la —,** to commit suicide; **odiare a —,** to have a deadly hatred of;

in punto di —, at the point of death; **letto di —,** death-bed; **pena di —,** capital punishment; **averla a — con qualcuno,** to hate someone.
mortella, *n.f.* (*Bot.*) Myrtle.
morticino, morticina, *n.m.f.* Dead child.
mortifero [mortIfero], *a.* Deadly.
mortificamento, *n.m.* Mortifying, mortification.
mortificante, *a.* Mortifying.
mortificare, *v.t.* To mortify, to humiliate, to wound, to subdue, to repress; (*Med.*) to cauterize; to give a local anaesthetic.
mortificarsi, *v.r.* To mortify oneself.
mortificatamente, *adv.* By religious mortification.
mortificazione, *n.f.* Mortification (in all senses).
morto (1), *n.m.* Dead body, dead person, corpse; (*Cards*) dummy. **Giorno dei Morti,** All Souls' Day; **morti e feriti,** dead and wounded; **fare il —,** to swim on one's back.
morto (2), *p.p.a.* Dead, deceased; lifeless, inanimate; blunt; stagnant. **Acqua morta,** stagnant water; **mezzo —,** half-dead; **punto —,** deadlock; **nato —,** still-born; **morta stagione,** dead season; **— di fame,** starved to death; (*Comm.*) **capitale morto,** unemployed capital; (*Mil.*) **angolo —,** funk-hole; (*Rail.*) **binario —,** siding.
mortorio [mortOrio], *n.m.* Funeral, burial; funeral procession.
mortuario [mortuArio], *a.* Mortuary, funeral. **Carro —,** hearse; **fede mortuaria,** death certificate; **annunzio —,** announcement of death.
morva, *n.f.* Glanders.
morvidezza [cp. **morbidezza**].
Mosa, *n.f.* (*Geog.*) River Meuse.
mosaicista (*pl.* **mosaicisti**), *n.m.* Mosaic-worker.
mosaico [mosAico], *n.m.a.* Mosaic; (*Theol.*) Mosaic.
mosaismo, *n.m.* (*Theol.*) The Mosaic Law, Judaism.
mosca, *n.f.* (*Zool.*) Fly; (*fig.*) patch (on the face); beauty spot; imperial (beard); goatee. **Saltare la — al naso,** to get one's temper up; **— cieca,** blindman's buff; **con un pugno di mosche,** empty-handed; **una — bianca,** a rarity.
Mosca, *n.f.* (*Geog.*) Moscow.
moscaio [moscAio], *n.m.* Swarm of flies.
moscaiuola, *n.f.* Wire-gauze meat-cover; fly-trap.
moscaragno, *n.m.* (*Zool.*) Horse-fly; horse-tick.
moscardino, *n.m.* Young fop, "nut", dandy; (*Zool.*) species of dormouse.
moscardo, *n.m.* (*Zool.*) Sparrow-hawk.
moscatello, *n.m.* Muscatel grape; wine made from this, Muscatel.
moscato, *n.m.* Muscat wine.
moscato, *a.* With a musk flavour or smell. **Noce moscata,** nutmeg.
moscerino, *n.m.* (*Zool.*) Gnat, midge.
moschea [moschEa], *n.f.* Mosque.
moscherino, *n.m.* Midge.
moschettare, *v.t.* To shoot (with musket).
moschettata, *n.f.* Musket-shot.
moschettato, *a.* Speckled, streaked.
moschettatura, *n.f.* Speckle, streak.
moschetteria [moschetterIa], *n.m.* Musketry.
moschettiere, *n.m.* Musketeer.
moschetto, *n.m.* Musket, rifle.
moschettone, *n.m.* Blunderbuss; swivel or bar for a watch-chain; clip (for a sword).
moschicida, *n.f.* Killer of flies; **Carta —,** fly-paper.
mosciame, *n.m.* Salted and pressed tunny.
mosciezza, *n.f.* Flabbiness.
moscio [mOscio], *a.* Flabby, flaccid, soft; muffled (of sound); empty (of a pocket).
moscione, *n.m.* (*Zool.*) Fly abundant during vintage season; (*fig.*) drinker, boozer.
mosco, *n.m.* (*Zool.*) Musk-deer.
moscone, *n.m.* Blue-bottle fly, big fly; boy who hangs around the girls.
Mosè, *n.m.* Moses.
Mosella, *n.f.* (*Geog.*) Moselle.
mossa, *n.f.* Movement, gesture, motion; move (in game, war, etc.). **Una — falsa,** a false start; (*Games*) **la prima —,** the first move; **— di corpo,** motion of the bowels; **essere sulle mosse,** to be on the move; **prender le mosse da,** to start from.
mossiere, *n.m.* (*Sports*) Starter.
mosso, *p.p.a.* Moved; prompted; stirred, agitated; troubled; rough (of the sea).
mossolina, *n.f.* Muslin.
mostacchi, *n.m.pl.* Moustache.
mostacciata, *n.f.* Blow on the face.
mostaccio [mostAccio], *n.m.* Ugly face, mug.
mostacciolo, *n.m.* Spiced cake.
mostaio [mostAio], *a.* Juicy (of grapes).
mostarda, *n.f.* (French) Mustard. **— di Cremona,** pickles (containing fruits).
mostardiera, *n.f.* Mustard-pot.
mosto, *n.m.* Must, new wine, grape-juice, pear-juice.
mostoso, *a.* Musty.
mostra, *n.f.* Show, display, exhibition; semblance, appearance; parade; dial-plate; facings, lapel (on coat). **Sala di —,** show-room; **— di bottega,** show-case; **— campionaria,** sample fair; **mettere in —,** to show, to display; **far bella — di sè,** to look conspicuous, to stand out; **far — di,** to feign, to pretend.
mostrabile [mostrAbile], *a.* Possible to show.
mostramento, *n.m.* Showing, exhibiting.
mostrare, *v.t.i.* To show, to display, to exhibit, to manifest, to demonstrate; to seem. **— i denti,** to show one's teeth.
mostrarsi, *v.r.* To show oneself, to appear, to come out.
mostratempesta, *n.f.* Weather-glass, storm-glass.
mostravento, *n.m.* Weather-cock, vane.
mostreggiatura, *n.f.* Lapel, facings.
mostriciattolo [mostriciAttolo], *n.m.* Malformed person.
mostricino, *n.m.* Deformed child.
mostrina, *n.f.* Sample; (*Mil.*) facings on collar of uniform, tab.
mostrino, *n.m.* Second-dial on a watch.
mostro, *n.m.* Monster; prodigy.
mostruosamente, *adv.* Monstrously.
mostruosità [-à], *n.f.* Monstrosity.
mostruoso, *a.* Monstrous, unnatural, abnormal; huge; outrageous; atrocious.
mota, *n.f.* Mud, mire.
motacilla, *n.f.* (*Zool.*) Wagtail.

motaccio [motAccio], *n.m.* Deep mud.
moterello, *n.m.* Slight movement; (*Med.*) irregularity of the pulse.
moticchio [motIcchio], *n.m.* Deep mud in ruts.
motivare, *v.t* To motivate, to justify, to give reasons for; to allege; to assign as a motive.
motivazione, *n.f.* Motive, ground for, reason; statement.
motivo, *n.m.* Motive, cause, ground, incentive; (*Mus.*) theme, motif, tune. **Per gravi motivi,** for serious motives; **che bel —!** what a lovely tune!
moto, *n.m.* Movement, motion; emotion; commotion, riot, rising. **Mettere in —,** to start, to set in motion; **mettersi in —,** to set forth, to start; **far poco, molto —,** to take little or much exercise; **essere tutti in —,** to be all agog; **un — popolare,** a popular rising; **— perpetuo,** perpetual motion.
motoaratrice, *n.f.* Tractor-plough.
motobarca, *n.f.* Motor-boat.
motocarrozzetta, *n.f.* Motor-cycle and side-car.
motocicletta, *n.f.* Motor-cycle.
motociclista (*pl.* **motociclisti**), *n.m.* Motor-cyclist.
motociclistico [motociclIstico], *a.* Pertaining to motor-cycling.
motocultura, *n.f.* (*Agric.*) Farming with tractors.
motonave, *n.f.* Motor-vessel, motor-ship.
motopattino, *n.m.* Motor-scooter.
motopeschereccio [motopescherEccio], *n.m.* Motor fishing-boat, motor-trawler.
motore, *n.m.* Motor, engine. **— a benzina,** petrol engine; **— Diesel,** diesel motor; **mettere in moto il —,** to start the motor; **spegnere il —,** to shut off the engine; (*Naut.*) **— fuori bordo,** outboard motor.
motore, *a.* Propelling, driving; moving.
motorio [motOrio], *a.* Motory, driving; lively.
motorista (*pl.* **motoristi**), *n.m.* Motorist; motor-man; mechanic.
motoristico, *a.* Motor. **Gare motoristiche,** motor races.
motorizzare, *v.t.* To motorize.
motorizzazione, *n.f.* Motorization.
motoscafo, *n.m.* Motor-boat.
motoso, *a.* Muddy, miry.
motrice, *n.f.* Driving-car (on tramway, rail, etc.).
motrice, *a.* Moving, driving, propelling. **Forza —,** driving power.
motteggevole [motteggEvole], *a.* Jocular, facetious.
motteggevolmente, *adv.* Jestingly, banteringly.
motteggiamento, *n.m.* Pleasantry, witticism, joke.
motteggiare, *v.t.* To banter, to quiz, to make fun of.
motteggiatore, motteggiatrice, *n.m.f.* Jester, joker.
motteggio [mottEggio], *n.m.* Mockery, raillery, banter.
mottetto, *n.m.* (*Mus.*) Motet; (*Lit.*) motto.
motto, *n.m.* Word; witticism, joke; epigram; motto, maxim; device. **Senza far —,** without a word; **non far — di ciò,** not a word of this; **— arguto,** a witty saying; **il mio — è,** my motto is.
movente, *n.m.a.* Motive, cause, incentive; moving.
movenza, *n.f.* Movement, gesture; attitude.
movere [cp. **muovere**].
movibile [movIbile], *a.* Movable, pliable, flexible.
movimentato, *a.* Animated, excited, agitated; busy; eventful.
movimentista (*pl.* **movimentisti**), *n.m.* (*Rail.*) Traffic superintendent.
movimento, *n.m.* Movement, motion; change; activity; progress, move, advance; bustle, emotion, stir; disturbance; (*Rail.*) traffic. **Mettere in —,** to put in motion, to set working; **— d'affari,** turn-over.
Mozambico, *n.m.* (*Geog.*) Mozambique.
mozione, *n.f.* Motion (in a debate, etc.). **Presentare una —,** to move; **respingere una —,** to defeat a motion.
mozzamento, *n.m.* Mutilation; cutting off; docking.
mozzare, *v.t.* To cut off, to lop; to truncate, to mutilate; to dock (a tail); to take away (one's breath); to crop (ears).
mozzarella, *n.f.* Kind of sweet Neapolitan cheese.
mozzatore, *n.m.* Mutilator.
mozzatura, *n.f.* Cutting-off, lopping, docking; part cut off.
mozzetta, *n.f.* (*Eccles.*) Bishop's cape.
mozzetto, *n.m.* Ankle boot.
mozzicare, *v.t.* To lop off; to clip one's words.
mozzicoda, *a.* Stump-tailed.
mozzicone, *n.m.* Stump, fragment; cigar stub.
mozzo (1), *n.m.* Stable-boy; (*Naut.*) cabin-boy.
mozzo (2), *n.m.* Nave (of wheel), hub; boss (of piston).
mozzo (3), *a.* Cut short, docked, lopped; mutilated.
mozzone, *n.m.* Whip-lash.
mozzorecchi, *n.m.* Pettifogger; cropped horse or dog.
mucca, *n.f.* Cow, milch-cow.
muccaio [muccAio], *n.m.* Cow-keeper.
mucchio [mUcchio], *n.m.* Heap, pile, mass; (*colloq.*) a lot. **A mucchi,** in piles; in plenty.
mucciare, *v.i.* (*obs.*) To sneak off, to get away.
mucidità [-à], *n.f.* Mustiness.
mucido [mUcido], *a.* Mouldy, musty, dank.
mucillagine [mucillAgine], *n.f.* Mucilage.
mucillaginoso, *a.* Mucillaginous.
muco, mucco, *n.m.* (*Anat.*) Mucus.
mucosa, *n.f.* Mucous membrane.
mucosità [-à], *n.f.* Mucosity, sliminess.
mucoso, *a.* Mucous.
muda, *n.f.* Moulting, moulting season; mew, cage (for moulting birds).
muezzino, *n.m.* Muezzin.
muffa, *n.f.* Mould; mustiness. **Far la —,** to get musty; **trarre il cervel di —,** to clear the dust from one's brains.
muffare, muffire, *v.i.* To turn musty, to turn mouldy.
mufflone, *n.m.* (*Zool.*) Moufflon sheep.
muffola [mUffola], *n.f.* Kiln.
muffosità [-à], *n.f.* Mustiness, mouldiness; (*fig.*) haughtiness, pride.

muffoso, *a.* Mouldy; (*fig.*) haughty.
mugghiamento, *n.m.* Lowing, mooing.
mugghiare, *v.i.* To low, to moo; to bellow.
mugghio [mUgghio], *n.m.* Lowing, mooing, bellowing.
muggine [mUggine], *n.m.* (*Zool.*) Mullet.
muggire [cp. **mugghiare**].
muggito, *n.m.* Lowing, mooing, bellowing.
mugherino, *n.m.* (*Bot.*) Jessamine.
mughetto, *n.m.* (*Bot.*) Lily of the Valley.
mugliare [cp. **mugghiare**].
mugnaio [mugnAio], *n.m.* Miller.
mugolamento, *n.m.* Howl, yelp.
mugolare, *v.i.* To howl, to yelp; to bellow.
mugolio, mugolo [mugolIo, mUgolo], *n.m.* Constant howling, whining, yelping.
mugolone, *n.m.* Whiner, whimperer.
mula, *n.f.* She-mule. **Api mule,** worker-ants.
mulacchia [mulAcchia], *n.f.* (*Zool.*) Jackdaw.
mulaggine [mulAggine], *n.f.* Mulishness.
mulattiera, *n.f.* Mule-track.
mulattiere, *n.m.* Muleteer, mule-driver.
mulatto, *n.m.a.* Half-breed; half-bred.
mulesco, *a.* Mulish.
muletto, *n.m.* Young mule.
muliebre, *a.* Feminine, womanish.
muliebrità [**-à**], *n.f.* Womanliness, effeminacy.
mulinaia [mulinAia], *n.f.* Snow-blizzard.
mulinaio [mulinAio], *n.m.* Miller.
mulinare, *v.t.* To whirl round, to revolve (in one's mind), to muse.
mulinaro, *n.m.* Miller.
mulinello, *n.m.* Windlass, capstan; whirlwind; whirlpool; whirling round a stick, sword, etc.; ventilating-fan; fishing reel.
mulino, *n.m.* Mill. **— a vento,** windmill; **tirar l'acqua al proprio —,** to bring grist to one's own mill.
mulo, *n.m.* (*Zool.*) Mule; (*fig.*) bastard; stubborn fellow.
multa, *n.f.* Fine, penalty. **Prendere una —,** to be fined.
multare, *v.t.* To fine, to mulct, to impose a penalty.
multicolore, *a.* Many-coloured, multicoloured.
multiforme, *a.* Multiform.
multilaterale, *a.* Multi-lateral.
multiplo [mUltiplo], *n.m.a.* Multiple.
mummia [mUmmia], *n.f.* Mummy; (*fig.*) numskull.
mummificare, *v.t.* To mummify.
mummificazione, *n.f.* Mummification.
mungere [mUngere], *v.t.* To milk; (*fig.*) to squeeze, to exploit, to sponge on.
mungitoio [mungitOio], *n.m.* Milk-pail.
mungitore, *n.m.* Milker.
mungitura, *n.f.* Milking; (*fig.*) exploitation.
municipale, *a.* Municipal.
municipalità [**-à**], *n.f.* Municipality.
municipalizzare, *v.t.* To municipalize.
municipalmente, *adv.* Municipally.
municipio [municIpio], *n.m.* Municipality, corporation; town-hall.
munificamente, *adv.* Munificently.
munificente, *a.* Munificent, liberal, bountiful.
munificentemente, *adv.* Munificently.
munificenza, *n.f.* Munificence, liberality, generosity, bounty.
munifico [munIfico], *a.* Munificent, liberal, bountiful.
munire, *v.t.* To provide, to supply, to furnish; to secure, to strengthen, to fortify. **Ben munito,** well provided, secure, fortified.
munirsi, *v.r.* To fortify oneself against.
munizionamento, *n.m.* Ammunitioning.
munizionare, *v.t.* To munition.
munizione, *n.f.* Munition, ammunition. **Munizioni di bocca,** provisions, victuals.
munizioniere, *n.m.* (*Mil.*) Ammunition officer; munitions office; contractor.
munto, *p.p.a.* Exhausted [cp. **mungere**].
muovere [muOvere], *v.t.i.* To move, to stir, to excite; to toss, to agitate; to bring forward; to rouse, to induce; to provoke; to wage (war); to bring (a suit); to advance, to go. — **un dubbio,** to raise a doubt; **— una domanda,** to put a question; **— incontro, verso,** to advance towards; **— a riso,** to move to laughter.
muoversi [muOversi], *v.r.* To move, to budge, to stir. **Non ti muovere,** don't move; **eppur si muove,** and yet it moves; **nessuno si muova,** keep still everyone.
mura (1), *n.f.pl.* Walls (of a city). **San Paolo fuori le Mura,** St. Paul's without the city walls.
mura (2), *n.f.* (*Naut.*) Tack, rope for drawing the corner of a sail to its place.
muraglia [murAglia], *n.f.* Wall, high wall; rampart; bulwark; barrier.
muraglione, *n.m.* High wall, rampart.
murale, *a.* Mural, wall.
muramento, *n.m.* Walling; masonry.
murare, *v.t.* To wall, to wall up or in, to build a wall. **— una finestra,** to brick up a window.
murario [murArio], *a.* Mural.
murata, *n.f.* (*Naut.*) Bulwark.
muratore, *n.m.* Mason, bricklayer.
muratura, *n.f.* Walling, masonry.
murazzo, *n.m.* Sea-wall.
murena, *n.f.* (*Zool.*) Sea-eel, moray.
muria [mUria], *n.f.* (*obs.*) Brine.
muriatico [muriAtico], *a.* (*Chem.*) Muriatic (acid).
muricciolaio [muricciolAio], *n.m.* Keeper of an outdoor second-hand bookstall.
muricciolo [murIcciolo], *n.m.* Low wall, parapet wall.
murice [mUrice], *n.m.* (*Zool.*) Murex.
muriella, *n.f.* Game of hop-scotch; stone used in this game.
murmure [mUrmure], *n.m.* Murmur, babble.
muro (*pl.* **muri,** *m.*, **mura,** *f.*), *n.m.* Wall, barrier; obstacle. **— a secco,** dry wall; **metter colle spalle al —,** to put in an inescapable position; **— divisorio,** partition wall; **stare — a —,** to be next-door neighbours; **parlare al —,** to speak to deaf ears; **le mura domestiche,** the home.
murra, *n.f.* Stone used for making ancient Murrhine vases.
musa (1), *n.f.* (*Myth.*) Muse; poetical genius.
musa (2), *n.f.* (*Bot.*) Banana-palm.
musagete, *a.* Name applied to Apollo as leader of the Muses.
musaico [cp. **mosaico**].
musaragno, *n.m.* (*Zool.*) Shrew.
musare, *v.i.* To be on the alert; to stare; to sniff.
musata, *n.f.* Blow with the snout; cross look.

muscarina, *n.f.* Poisonous substance in fungi.
muschiato, *a.* Musky. **Bue —,** musk-ox.
muschio [mUschio] (1), *n.m.* Musk-deer.
muschio [mUschio] (2) [cp. **musco**].
muscicapa, *n.f.* (*Zool.*) Flycatcher.
musco, *n.m.* (*Bot.*) Moss.
muscolare, *a.* Muscular.
muscolatura, muscolazione, *n.f.* Musculature, the muscles, muscular system.
muscolo [mUscolo], *n.m.* Muscle.
muscolosità [-à], *n.f.* Muscularity, strength.
muscoloso, *a.* Muscular, brawny, strong.
muscoso, *a.* Mossy.
museo [musEo], *n.m.* Museum; (art) gallery.
museruola, *n.f.* Muzzle, nose-band. **Metter la —,** to muzzle; to gag.
musica [mUsica], *n.f.* Music; band. **— da camera,** chamber music; **far della —,** to have some music.
musicabile [musicAbile], *a.* Capable of being set to music.
musicale, *a.* Musical.
musicalità [-à], *n.f.* Taste or aptitude for music.
musicalmente, *adv.* Musically.
musicante, *n.m.* Professional musician, virtuoso.
musicare, *v.t.* To set to music; to play or sing.
musicista (*pl.* **musicisti**), *n.m.* Musician, composer.
musico [mUsico], *n.m.a.* Musician; musical.
musivo, *a.* Mosaic, tessellated.
muso, *n.m.* Muzzle, snout; face, mug. **Fare, tenere il —,** to look sulky, to pout; **— duro,** a sour face.
musoliera, *n.f.* Muzzle.
musone, *n.m.* Sulky fellow; pouter.
musoneria [musonerIa], *n.f.* Sulkiness; insolence.
musorno, *a.* (*Lit.*) Sulky, stupid; lowering (of the sky).
mussola, mussolina [mUssola], *n.f.* Muslin.
mussulmano, musulmano, *n.m.a.* Mussulman, Mohammedan, Moslem.
mustacchio, *n.m.* Moustache; whiskers.
mustango, *n.m.* (*Zool.*) Mustang.
mustela, *n.f.* (*Zool.*) Weasel.
muta, *n.f.* Change, turn; team; relay (of horses, etc.); pack (of hounds); set (of sails, jewels, etc.); moulting (of feathers). (*Mil.*) **Dare la —,** to relieve the guard; **a — a —,** by turns, turn and turn about.
mutabile [mutAbile], *a.* Mutable, changeable; fickle.
mutabilità [-à], *n.f.* Mutability.
mutabilmente, *adv.* Mutably, changeably.
mutacismo, *n.m.* Mytacism, wrong use of letter M.
mutamente, *adv.* Mutely.
mutamento, *n.m.* Change, alteration, mutation, variation. **— in meglio,** change for the better.
mutande, *n.f.pl.* Drawers, pants. **— da bagno,** bathing-drawers,-shorts.
mutare, *v.t.* To change, to alter, to modify, to vary; to shed (of animals); to moult.
mutarsi, *v.r.* To change.
mutazione, *n.f.* Change, mutation, alteration, variation.
mutevole [mutEvole], *a.* Changeable, unstable, unsettled.
mutevolezza, *n.f.* Mutability, changeableness, variation; inconstancy.
mutevolmente, *adv.* Unstably.
mutezza, *n.f.* Muteness, silence.
mutilamento, *n.m.* Mutilation.
mutilare, *v.t.* To maim, to mutilate; to curtail, to cut off.
mutilato, *n.m.* Cripple, disabled man; disabled soldier.
mutilato, mutilo [mUtilo], *a.* Mutilated, disabled; incomplete.
mutilazione, *n.f.* Mutilation.
mutismo, *n.m.* Dumbness; obstinate silence; taciturnity.
muto, *n.m.a.* Dumb person; dumb, mute, speechless; silent (of letters). **Sordo —,** deaf mute, deaf and dumb; (*Theat.*) **scena muta,** dumb show.
mutolo [mUtolo], *a.* Dumb.
mutria [mUtria], *n.f.* Haughty face, haughtiness; sour look; ugly face.
mutuale, *a.* Mutual.
mutualità [-à], *n.f.* Interchange, mutual help; reciprocity; mutual association (for charitable purposes).
mutuamente, *adv.* Mutually, reciprocally.
mutuante, *n.m.* Lender; mortgagee.
mutuante, *a.* Lending.
mutuare, *v.t.* To borrow; to lend money; to exchange, to mortgage.
mutuatario [mutuatArio], *n.m.* Borrower; mortgager.
mutuazione, *n.f.* Exchange.
mutuo [mUtuo], *n.m.* Loan (of money). **Capitale a —,** borrowed capital; **— ipotecario,** mortgage loan.
mutuo [mUtuo], *a.* Mutual, reciprocal. **Società di — soccorso,** mutual aid society.

N

N, n, *n.f.* Twelfth letter of the Italian alphabet.
nababbo, *n.m.* Nabob.
Nabucodonosor, *n.m.* Nebuchadnezzar.
nacchera [nAcchera], *n.f.* (*Mus.*) Castanet; (*Zool.*) sea-shell.
naccherino, *n.m.* Pretty little child.
nachero [nAchero], *n.m.a.* Dwarf; dwarfish.
nacqui [cp. **nascere**].
nadir, *n.m.* Nadir.
nafta, *n.f.* (*Chem.*) Naphtha, rock oil. **— greggia,** crude naphtha.
naftalina, *n.f.* (*Chem.*) Naphthaline.
naftolo, *n.m.* (*Chem.*) Naphthol.
naia [nAia], *n,f.* (*Zool.*) Cobra.
naiade [nAiade], *n.f.* (*Myth.*) Naiad, water nymph.
Nanchino, *n.m.* (*Geog.*) Nanking.
nanchino, *n.m.* Nankeen.
nanerottolo [nanerOttolo], *n.m.* Little man, dwarf.
nanfa, *n.f.* **Acqua —,** orange-flower water.
nanismo, *n.m.* Nanism.
nanna. *n.f.* (*colloq.*) Sleep (used when talking to little children). **Andare a —,** to go to bye-byes; **ninna-nanna,** hushaby. lullaby; **cantare la ninna-nanna,** to sing to sleep; **far la —,** to go to sleep.

nannodia [nannodIa], *n.f.* (*obs.*) Lullaby.
nano, *n.m.a.* Dwarf.
Nante, *n.f.* (*Geog.*) Nantes.
nanti, *adv.prep.* (*obs.*) Before. — **a me,** before me [cp. **innanzi**].
napea [napEa], *n.f.* Wood-nymph.
Napoleone, *n.m.* Napoleon.
napoleonico [napoleOnico], *a.* Napoleonic.
napoleonista (*pl.* **napoleonisti**), *n.f.* Napoleonist; Bonapartist.
napoletana, *n.f.* (*Cards*) Hand in the game of tressette; coffee pot.
napoletanamente, *adv.* In the Neapolitan manner.
napoletanismo, *n.m.* Neapolitan mode of speech.
napoletano, *n.m.a.* Neapolitan.
Napoli [nApoli], *n.f.* (*Geog.*) Naples.
nappa, *n.f.* Tassel, tuft; (*colloq.*) big nose.
nappina, *n.f.* Tuft; pom-pom; top-knot.
nappo, *n.m.* (*Lit.*) Goblet; drinking-cup.
narcisismo, *n.m.* Narcissism.
Narciso, *n.m.* (*Myth.*) Narcissus; (*Bot.*) narcissus.
narcosi, *n.f.* (*Med.*) Narcosis.
narcoticamente, *adv.* Soporifically.
narcotico [narcOtico], *n.m.a.* Narcotic, soporific.
narcotizzare, *v.t.* To narcotize.
nardo, *n.m.* (*Bot.*) Nard, spikenard.
nari, *n.f.pl.* Nostrils.
narice, *n.f.* (*Anat.*) Nostril.
narrabile [narrAbile], *a.* Possible to be narrated, tellable.
narrare, *v.t.* To relate, to narrate, to recount, to tell. — **una storia,** to tell a story.
narrativa, *n.f.* Narrative.
narrativamente, *adv.* In a narrative manner.
narrativo, *a.* Narrative.
narratore, narratrice, *n.m.f.* Narrator, story-teller.
narratorio [narratOrio], *a.* Narratory.
narrazione, *n.f.* Recital, narration, account; story.
nartece, *n.m.* (*Arch.*) Narthex; vestibule.
narvalo, *n.m.* (*Zool.*) Narwhal.
nasaggine [nasAggine], *n.f.* Speaking through the nose.
nasale, *a.* Nasal. **Suoni nasali,** nasal sounds.
nasalmente, *adv.* Nasally.
nasardo, *n.m.* (*Mus.*) Organ-stop with a nasal effect.
nasata, *n.f.* Blow on, or with, the nose.
nascente, *pres.p.a.* Rising, dawning, nascent; shooting (of plants) budding. **Il sole —,** the rising sun; **l'erba —,** the growing grass.
nascenza, *n.f.* Birth; growth.
nascere [nAscere], *v.i.* To be born, to come forth, to appear; to arise, to spring, to emanate; to proceed, to issue, to originate; to come up (of plants), to shoot forth; to dawn; to be hatched. — **vestito,** to be born under a lucky star; **far — difficoltà,** to cause difficulties; **è poeta nato,** he's a born poet; **egli nacque a Roma,** he was born at Rome; **questo fiume nasce da quel monte,** this river has its source on that mountain; **non sono nato oggi!** I wasn't born yesterday! I'm not such a fool as all that! **non sono nato per questo,** I'm not fit for this.
nascimento, *n.m.* Birth [cp. **nascita**].
nascita [nAscita], *n.f.* Birth; descent, extraction; origin. **Di —,** by birth; **di bassa —,** of humble origin; **cieco dalla —,** born blind; **giorno di—,** birthday; **fede di —,** birth certificate.
nascituro, *n.m.* Coming, about to be born; future.
nascondere [nascOndere], *v.t.* To hide, to conceal, to keep secret; to mask, to dissimulate, to dissemble; to disguise. **Io non nascondo nulla,** I have no secrets.
nascondersi [nascOndersi], *v.r.* To hide oneself; to be hidden from view; to keep out of sight. **Giuocare a —,** to play hide-and-seek.
nascondiglio [nascondIglio], *n.m.* Hiding-place; den, lair.
nascondimento, *n.m.* Hiding, concealing.
nasconditore, nasconditrice, *n.m.f.* Hider, concealer, dissembler.
nascosamente, nascostamente, *adv.* Secretly, stealthily.
nascoso, nascosto, *a.* Hidden, concealed, secret; underhand. **Di —,** secretly on the sly, by stealth.
naseggiare, *v.t.* To speak nasally.
nasello, *n.m.* (*Mech.*) Catch (on a door-latch); (*Zool.*) whiting.
nasiera, *n.f.* Nose-ring (for oxen, etc.); nose-band.
naso, *n.m.* Nose; face. **Soffiarsi il —,** to blow one's nose; **a lume di —,** at a glance, at first sight; at random; **menar per il —,** to lead by the nose; **naso a naso,** face to face; **sotto il — di,** before, under his very nose; **restare con un palmo di —,** to be taken in, to be left empty-handed, to be disappointed; **non cacciare il — nei miei affari,** don't poke your nose into my affairs; — **all'insù,** turned-up nose; **arricciare il —,** to turn up one's nose; **aver buon — per,** to have a flair for.
nasone, *n.m.* Big nose; big-nosed fellow.
naspo, *n.m.* Reel, winder.
nassa, *n.f.* Eel-pot, lobster-pot, bow-net.
nasso, *n.m.* (*Bot.*) Yew-tree [cp. **tasso**].
nastraio [nastrAio], *n.m.* Ribbon-seller or maker.
nastriforme, *a.* Ribbon-like.
nastrino, *n.m.* Little ribbon, tape; book-marker; tape (telegraph).
nastro, *n.m.* Ribbon, band, tape; strip; border. — **della macchina da scrivere,** type-writer ribbon; (*Elect.*) — **isolante,** insulating tape.
nasturzio [nastUrzio], *n.m.* (*Bot.*) Nasturtium; watercress.
nasuto, *a.* Big-nosed; alert.
Natale (1), *n.m.* Christmas, Christmas Day; the Nativity. **Vigilia di —,** Christmas Eve; **albero di —,** Christmas-tree; **auguri di —,** Christmas greetings; **Buon —!** Happy Christmas!
natale (2), *n.m.* Birth, birthday, birthplace, lineage. **Il — di Roma,** the day of Rome's founding; **ebbe i natali a Roma,** he was born in Rome; **di illustri natali,** high-born.
natale, *a.* Native, natal. **Città —,** birth-place.
natalizio [natalIzio], *n.m.a.* Birthday; natal, native. **Giorno —,** birthday.
natante, *n.m.a.* Boat, craft; floating, swimming.
natare [cp. **nuotare**].

natatoia [natatOia], *n.f.* Fin; web (of water-fowl); swimming-bladder.
natatorio [natatOrio], *a.* Swimming, natatory. **Vasca, piscina natatoria,** swimming-bath, swimming-pool.
natica [nAtica], *n.f.* (*Anat.*) Buttock.
natio [natIo], *a.* Native, natal. **Tetto —,** home; **aria natia,** native air.
nativamente, *adv.* By birth, from birth.
natività [-à], *n.f.* Nativity.
nativo, *n.m.a.* Native.
nato, *n.m.* Son, little one; young (of animals).
nato, *p.p.a.* Born; arisen; appeared. **— morto,** still-born; **— per soffrire,** born to suffer; **è un pittore —,** he is a born painter; **nata Silva,** née Silva.
natrice, *n.f.* (*Zool.*) Harmless water-snake.
natta, *n.f.* (*Med.*) Wen, tumour.
natura, *n.f.* Nature; temper, constitution; kind, sort, class. **Pagare in —,** to pay in kind; (*Art*) **— morta,** still life; **contro —,** unnatural; **timido per —,** shy by nature; **allo stato di —,** in a state of nature.
naturale, *n.m.* Temper, disposition, nature; constitution; (*Photo.*) life-size. **Figura al —,** life-size figure.
naturale, *a.* Natural, native, innate; easy, plain, unaffected; unadulterated; (*Mus.*) natural. **Grandezza —,** full-size; **storia —,** natural history; **figlio —,** illegitimate son; **la legge —,** the law of nature; **ordine —,** natural order; **Naturale!** Of course!
naturalezza, *n.f.* Naturalness; simplicity, easiness, sincerity. **Con —,** plainly, unaffectedly.
naturalismo, *n.m.* Naturalism.
naturalista (*pl.* **naturalisti**), *n.m.* Naturalist.
naturalistico [naturalIstico], *a.* Naturalistic.
naturalità [-à], *n.f.* Citizenship; political status; naturalization.
naturalizzare, *v.t.* To naturalize.
naturalizzarsi, *v.r.* To become naturalized, to obtain the rights of citizenship.
naturalizzazione, *n.f.* Naturalization. **Decreto di —,** decree of naturalization.
naturalmente, *adv.* Naturally, by nature.
naturare, *v.t.* To create, to form, to constitute.
naturarsi, *v.r.* To take the nature of.
naturato, *a.* Innate.
naturismo, *n.m.* Naturism.
naturista (*pl.* **naturisti**), *n.m.* Naturist.
naufragare, *v.i.* To be shipwrecked; (*fig.*) to be ruined, to fail; to fall through, to miscarry.
naufragio [naufrAgio], *n.m.* Shipwreck; (*fig.*) failure, utter ruin. **Far —,** to be shipwrecked.
naufrago [nAufrago], *n.m.* Shipwrecked person; (*fig.*) castaway, outcast; failure. **Un — della vita,** a castaway.
naumachia [naumachIa], *n.f.* (*Hist.*) Naumachy, sham sea-battle.
nausea [nAusea], *n.f.* Sickness, loathing, nausea; disgust, repulsion. **Sino alla —,** to the extent of loathing; **far —,** to disgust, to sicken.
nauseabondo, nauseante, *a.* Sickening, disgusting, repulsive; nauseous.
nauseare, *v.t.* To sicken, to nauseate; to disgust, to make sick.
nauseosamente, *adv.* Nauseatingly, disgustingly.
nauseoso, *a.* Sickening; nauseating, disgusting.
nauta, *n.f.* (*Lit.*) Navigator.
nautica [nAutica], *n.f.* Navigation; nautical science.
nautico [nAutico], *a.* Nautical, naval.
nautilo [nAutilo], *n.m.* (*Zool.*) Nautilus.
navale, *a.* Naval.
navalestro, *n.m.* Boatman, ferryman; bargee.
navarca, *n.m.* Ship's captain.
navata, *n.f.* (*Arch.*) Nave. **— laterale,** aisle.
nave, *n.f.* Ship; vessel, boat; liner. **— mercantile,** merchant vessel; **— a vapore,** steamship, steamer; **— a vela,** sailing-ship; **— cisterna, — petroliera,** tanker; **— da carico,** cargo boat; **— da guerra,** warship, man-o'-war; **— ammiraglia,** flag-ship; **— scuola,** training-ship.
navetta, *n.f.* Shuttle (of sewing-machine). **Far la —,** to go to and fro, to go up and down.
navicella, *n.f.* Small boat, barge; (*Aviat.*) nacelle (of a balloon); gondola (of airship).
navicellaio [navicellAio], *n.m.* Bargee, ferry-man; boatman.
navicellata, *n.f.* Barge-load, boat-load.
navicello, *n.m.* Bark, ship; barge.
navigabile [navigAbile], *a.* Navigable; sea-worthy; (of wines, etc.), fit to travel.
navigabilità [-à], *n.f.* Seaworthiness.
navigante, *n.m.* Seaman, sailor, navigator.
navigare, *v.t.i.* To navigate, to sail; to travel; to steer; (*fig.*) to behave, to act. **— contro vento,** to sail close to the wind; **— col vento in poppa,** to sail with a favourable wind; (*fig.*) **saper —,** to know how to live; **— ad ogni vento,** to be a turn-coat.
navigato, *a.* (*fig.*) Experienced; crafty, cunning.
navigatore, *n.m.* Navigator, seaman.
navigatorio [navigatOrio], *a.* Nautical, concerning navigation.
navigazione, *n.f.* Navigation, sailing. **— aerea,** aerial navigation; **— fluviale,** inland navigation; **— stimata,** dead-reckoning; **carta di —,** chart; **società di —,** steamship company.
naviglio [navIglio], *n.m.* Ship, boat; fleet, navy; canal, water-way. **Canale —,** ship-canal; **— ausiliare,** auxiliary craft; **— silurante,** torpedo-craft.
navone, *n.m.* (*Bot.*) Parsnip.
navonella, *n.f.* (*Zool.*) Cabbage butterfly.
Nazareno, Nazzareno, *n.m.a.* Nazarene.
Nazaret, Nazzaret, *n.f.* (*Geog.*) Nazareth.
nazionale, *a.* National; home. **Prodotti nazionali,** home products.
nazionalismo, *n.m.* Nationalism.
nazionalista (*pl.* **nazionalisti**), *n.m.* Nationalist.
nazionalità [-à], *n.f.* Nationality. **Prendere la — italiana,** to become a naturalized Italian.
nazionalizzare, *v.t.* To nationalize.
nazionalizzazione, *n.f.* Nationalization.
nazionalmente, *adv.* Nationally.
nazione, *n.f.* Nation; people, country; (*Hist.*) body of students from the same country.
nazismo, *n.m.* (*Hist.*) Nazism.
nazista, *n.m.* (*Hist.*) Nazi.
ne, *adv.pron.* Of it, of him, of her; some; from; (*obs.*) us, to us. **Prendine,** take some of it; **andiamocene,** let's go; **ne hai?** have you got some? **ne parlò con me,** he spoke of it to me; **aversene a male,** to take it ill.

ne', nei. In the. **Ne' miei panni,** in my shoes. [cp. **in**].
nè, *conj.* Neither, nor. **Nè questo nè quello,** neither this nor that; **nè bello nè brutto,** insignificant.
neanche, neanco, *adv.* Not even. **Neanche per sogno,** not at all; **neanche un soldo,** not a penny.
nebbia [nEbbia], *n.f.* Fog; mist, haze. — **spessa,** dense fog.
nebbiaccia [nebbiAccia], *n.f.* Dense fog; thick mist.
nebbiaio [nebbiAio], *n.m.* Foggy weather.
nebbietta, nebbiolina, *n.f.* Mist.
nebbiolo, *n.m.* Kind of Piedmontese red wine.
nebbione, *n.f.* Thick fog.
nebbiosità [-à], *n.f.* Fogginess, haziness, mistiness.
nebbioso, *a.* Foggy, misty, hazy.
nebulare, *a.* (*Astron.*) Nebular.
nebulosa, *n.f.* (*Astron.*) Nebula.
nebulosità [-à], *n.f.* Indistinctness, cloudiness, mistiness, nebulosity.
nebuloso, *a.* Foggy, misty, hazy; obscure; nebulous, cloudy, clouded.
neccio [nEccio], *n.m.* Chestnut cake.
necessariamente, *adv.* Necessarily.
necessario [necessArio], *n.m.a.* Necessary, needful, requisite; expedient, indispensable. **Ritenere —,** to deem necessary; **erede —,** heir at law.
necessità [-à], *n.f.* Necessity, need; indigence, penury, want. **Di assoluta —,** indispensable; **far di — virtù,** to make a virtue of necessity; **— non ha legge,** necessity knows no law; **che — c'è di gridare?** what need is there to shout? **per —,** from necessity.
necessitare, *v.t.i.* To necessitate, to be necessary, to need, to be in want of.
necessitoso, *a.* Necessitous.
necrofago [necrOfago], *n.m.* (*Zool.*) Burying-beetle.
necrofilia [necrofilIa], *n.f.* Necrophilism.
necroforo [necrOforo], *n.m.* Sexton.
necrologia [necrologIa], *n.f.* Obituary, obituary notice; funeral oration.
necrologico [necrolOgico], *a.* Necrological.
necrologio [necrolOgio], *n.m.* Obituary; necrology.
necromanzia [necromanzIa], *n.f.* Necromancy.
necropoli [necrOpoli], *n.f.* Necropolis.
necroscopia [necroscopIa], *n.f.* Autopsy.
necroscopico [necroscOpico], *a.* Post-mortem.
necrosi, *n.f.* (*Med.*) Necrosis, gangrene.
necrotizzare, *v.i.* (*Med.*) To mortify.
neerlandese, *n.m.a.* Dutchman, Dutch.
Neerlandia [neerlAndia], *n.f.* (*Geog.*) Netherlands.
nefandamente, *adv.* Nefariously, wickedly.
nefandezza, nefandità [-à], *n.f.* Nefariousness, wickedness, iniquity, infamy.
nefando, *a.* Nefarious, infamous, iniquitous, abominable.
nefariamente, *adv.* Nefariously, wickedly.
nefario [nefArio], *a.* Nefarious, wicked.
nefasto, *a.* Inauspicious, unlucky, unpropitious, ill-omened.
nefrite, *n.f.* (*Med.*) Nephritis.
nefritico [nefrItico], *a.* Nephritic.
negabile [negAbile], *a.* Deniable.
negabilità [-à], *n.f.* Possibility of denial.
negare, *v.t.* To deny, to refuse, to disavow, to disown, to contradict. **— l'accesso,** to refuse admittance.
negativa, *n.f.* Negative, denial, negation; (*Phot.*) negative.
negativamente, *adv.* Negatively.
negativismo, *n.m.* Negativism.
negativo, *a.* Negative; passive, inactive.
negato, *a.* Unsuited, unfit; refused.
negatore, negatrice, *n.m.f.* One who denies.
negatorio [negatOrio], *a.* Negatory.
negazione, *n.f.* Negation, denial; refusal; disavowal.
neghittosamente, *adv.* Lazily, indolently.
neghittoso, *a.* Lazy, indolent, slothful, listless; indifferent.
neglettamente, *adv.* Carelessly.
negletto, *a.* Careless, negligent, inaccurate; disregarded, ignored, neglected; untidy.
negli. [cp. **in**] In the.
***negligente,** *a.* Negligent, neglectful, careless; listless.
***negligentemente,** *adv.* Negligently.
***negligenza,** *n.f.* Negligence, carelessness; disregard, indifference; default.
***negligere** [neglIgere], *v.t.* To neglect, to disregard.
negoziabile [negoziAbile], *a.* Negotiable.
negoziabilità [-à], *n.f.* Negotiability.
negoziamento, *n.m.* Negotiation.
negoziante, *n.m.* Merchant, trader; dealer; shop-keeper. **— al minuto,** retailer.
negoziare, *v.t.i.* To negotiate; to trade, to traffic; to transact business.
negoziato, *n.m.* Negotiation, transaction, dealing. **Iniziare i negoziati,** to open negotiations.
negoziatore, negoziatrice, *n.m.f.* Negotiator.
negoziazione, *n.f.* Negotiation.
negozio [negOzio], *n.m.* Shop, store; business, affair; negotiation; commerce, trade. **Fare un buon —,** to make a good bargain; **giovane di —,** shop assistant; **— di droghiere,** grocer's shop; **aprire un —,** to open a shop.
negra, *n.f.* Negro (woman, girl).
negretto, *n.m.* Young Negro.
negrezza, *n.f.* Blackness.
negriere, negriero, *n.m.* Slave-dealer; (*Naut.*) slaver.
negriere, negriero, *a.* Slaver. **Nave negriera,** slave-ship.
negro, *n.m.* Negro.
negroide, *n.m.a.* Negroid.
negromante, *n.m.f.* Necromancer, sorcerer, sorceress.
negromantico [negromAntico], *a.* Necromantic.
negromanzia [negromanzIa], *n.f.* Necromancy, black magic, sorcery.
negus, *n.m.* Negus (of Abyssinia).
neh! *inter.* Look here! Indeed! I say! Isn't it!
nel, nella, nei, nelle, negli, nello. In the [cp. **in**].
nelumbo, *n.m.* (*Bot.*) Lotus.
nembifero [nembIfero], *a.* Cloudy, stormy.

* Words thus marked sound the first "g" hard.

nembo, *n.m.* Cloud, rain-cloud; shower of rain; squall. **Un — di polvere,** a cloud of dust.
nemboso, *a.* Cloudy, stormy.
Nembrotte, *n.m.* Nimrod.
Nemesi [nEmesi], *n.f.* (*Myth.*) Nemesis; (*fig.*) vengeance, retributive justice.
nemicamente, *adv.* Inimically, as an enemy.
nemicare [cp. **inimicare**].
nemico, *n.m.* Enemy; foe, adversary, antagonist. **Farsi un —,** to make an enemy; **mortale —,** mortal foe; **affrontare il —,** to face the enemy.
nemico, *a.* Hostile, inimical, contrary, adverse; unfriendly. **Nazioni nemiche,** enemy nations; **la sorte gli è stata nemica,** luck has been against him.
nemmanco, nemmeno, *conj.* Not even. (*colloq.*) **— per sogno,** I shouldn't dream of it.
nenia [nEnia], *n.f.* Dirge; lamentation; wailing; funeral dirge.
nenufar, nenufaro [nenufAr, nenUfaro], *n.m.* (*Bot.*) Nenuphar; water-lily.
neo, *n.m.* Mole, beauty-spot; (*fig.*) blemish, flaw.
neoclassicismo, *n.m.* Neo-classicism.
neofito [neOfito], *n.m.* Neophyte, new convert; novice, beginner, tyro.
neolatino, *a.* Neo-Latin, Romance. **Lingue neolatine,** Romance languages.
neolitico [neolItico], *a.* (*Geol.*) Neolithic.
neologia [neologIa], *n.f.* Neology, use of neologisms.
neologico [neolOgico], *a.* Concerning neologisms.
neologismo, *n.m.* Neologism.
neomaltusianismo, *n.m.* Birth-control.
neomaltusiano, *n.m.a.* Advocate of, advocating birth control.
neomenia [neomenIa], *n.f.* (*Lit.*) New moon.
neon, *n.m.* (*Elect.*) Neon. **Luce di —,** neon light.
neonato, *n.m.a.* New-born infant; new-born.
neoplasma (*pl.* **neoplasmi**), *n m.* Neoplasm, tumour.
neoplastico [neoplAstico], *a.* (*Med.*) Neoplastic.
neoplatonico [neoplatOnico], *a.* Neoplatonic.
neoplatonismo, *n.m.* Neoplatonism.
nepa, *n.f.* (*Zool.*) Water-scorpion.
nepente, *n.m.* (*Bot.*) Nepenthes.
nepitella, *n.f.* (*Bot.*) Cat-mint, calamint.
nepitello, *n.m.* (*Anat.*) Eyelid.
nepote [cp. **nipote**].
nepotismo, *n.m.* Nepotism; favouritism.
nepotista (*pl.* **nepotisti**), *n.m.* Nepotist.
neppure, *conj.* Not even.
nequità [-à], *n.f.* Iniquity [cp. **iniquità**].
nequitoso, *a.* (*obs.*) Wicked, iniquitous.
nequizia [nequIzia], *n.f.* Wickedness, iniquity; perfidy.
neracchiolo, *a.* Dark-complexioned.
nerastro, *a.* Blackish.
nerbare, *v.t.* To flog, to beat.
nerbata, *n.f.* Flogging; blow with a lash or whip; severe blow.
nerbatina, *n.f.* (*colloq.*) Good hiding.
nerbatura, *n.f.* Flogging, beating.
nerbo, *n.m.* Sinew, muscle; nerve, back-bone, stamina, force; whip. **Il — dell'esercito,** the back-bone of the army; **— di bue,** lash, thong.
nerboruto, nerbuto, *a.* Muscular, vigorous, sturdy, robust.
nereggiamento, *n.m.* Blackening.
nereggiare, *v.i.* To grow black, to turn black; to appear black.
nereide [nerEide], *n.f.* (*Myth.*) Nereid; sea-nymph.
neretto, *n.m.* (*Print.*) Heavy type, black type.
neretto, *a.* Blackish.
nerezza, *n.f.* Blackness; darkness.
nericcio [nerIccio], *a.* Blackish.
nero, *n.m.* Black; Negro; mourning. **Metter — sul bianco,** to put in writing; **vestirsi di —,** to dress in black, to wear mourning; **chiesa parata a —,** church draped in black.
nero, *a.* Black; dark, obscure; dirty, foul; bad, wicked; melancholy, low-spirited; brown (bread). **Il Mar Nero,** the Black Sea; **mani nere,** dirty hands; **avere pensieri neri,** to have black thoughts, to brood, to be in the dumps; **tavola nera,** black-board; **abito —,** evening dress; black suit; **aristocrazia nera,** Papal aristocracy.
nerofumo, *n.m.* Lamp-black.
nerognolo [nerOgnolo], *a.* Blackish.
Nerone, *n.m.* Nero.
neroniano, *a.* Neronian.
nerume, *n.m.* Quantity of black, black, smut; soot.
nervale, *a.* (*Anat.*) Nervine.
nervatura, *n.f.* Nervous system; (*Bot.*) nervation, ribbing.
nerveo [nervEo], *a.* (*Anat.*) Nervous, concerned with the nerves.
nervo, *n.m.* Nerve, sinew, stamina, pluck, courage; vein (of leaf); (*Arch.*) rib. **Far venire i nervi,** to get on one's nerves; **mancare di nervo,** to lack in energy; **avere i nervi,** to have a fit of nerves; **avere i nervi scoperti,** to be in a very excited state; **attacco di nervi,** a nervous attack.
nervosamente, *adv.* Nervously.
nervosismo, *n.m.* (*Med.*) Weakness or debility of the nerves; nervousness, agitation.
nervosità [-à], *n.f.* Nervousness; agitation, bad temper; irritability.
nervoso, *a.* Nervous; sinewy; irritable, highly-strung; restless; strong, pithy. **Sistema —,** nervous system; **un bambino —,** a highly-strung child; **malattia nervosa,** nervous disease; (*colloq.*) **mi fai venire il —,** you get on my nerves.
nesci, *n.m.* **Fare il —,** to pretend ignorance; to turn a deaf ear.
nesciente, *a.* Ignorant.
nescientemente, *adv.* Ignorantly, unwittingly.
nescienza, *n.f.* Ignorance.
nespola [nEspola], *n.f* (*Bot.*) Medlar; (*fig.*) blows, beating, thrashing. **Gli diede certe nespole,** he gave him a good hiding.
nespole! [nEspole], *inter.* (*colloq.*) By Jove! My word!
nespolo [nEspolo], *n.m.* (*Bot.*) Medlar-tree.
nesso, *n.m.* Connection, connexion; link; (*Mus.*) tie; nexus.
nessuno, *pron.a.* Nobody, no one, none; anybody; no. **In nessun modo,** not at all; in no case; **— dei presenti,** none of those present; **non c'è —,** there's no one; **è venuto**

— **a chiamarmi?** has anyone called for me? **nessuna cosa,** no thing, nothing at all, nothing; **nessunissimo,** not a single one.
nesto, *n.m.* (*Agric.*) Graft [cp. **innesto**].
Nestore [nEstore], *n.m.* (*Myth.*) Nestor; adviser; senior.
nettadenti, *n.m.* Tooth-brush, tooth-pick.
nettamente, *adv.* Squarely, clearly, frankly; cleanly, sharply, distinctly.
nettamento, *n.m.* Cleansing, cleaning.
nettapenne, *n.m.* Pen-wiper.
nettaporti, *n.m.* (*Naut.*) Dredger, dredge.
nettare, *v.t.* To clean, to cleanse; to polish.
nettare [nEttare], *n.m.* Nectar.
nettareo [nettAreo], *a.* Nectarean, nectareous.
nettario [nettArio], *n.m.* (*Bot.*) Nectary.
nettarsi, *v.r.* To clean oneself.
nettatoia [nettatOia], *n.f.* Builder's mortar-board.
nettatoio [nettatOio], *n.m.* Cleansing material.
nettatore, nettatrice, *n.m.f.* Cleaner.
nettatura, *n.f.* Cleaning, cleansing.
nettezza, *n.f.* Cleanliness; neatness; clearness, terseness. — **urbana,** city cleansing department.
netto, *a.* Clean, neat, tidy; terse, clear, limpid; distinct, sharp; (*Comm.*) net. **Un suono —,** a distinct sound; **prezzo —,** net price; **guadagno —,** net profit; **dire chiaro e —,** to speak frankly; **mani nette,** clean hands; **un taglio —,** a clean cut; **portar via di —,** to cut clean off; — **di spese,** free of charges; **contorni netti,** clear-cut edges.
nettunico [nettUnico], *a.* (*Geol.*) Neptunian. **Rocce nettuniche,** neptunian rocks.
nettunio [nettUnio], *n.m.* Neptunium (element).
neurastenia, nevrastenia [neurastenIa, nevrastenIa], *n.f.* (*Med.*) Neurasthenia.
neurastenico [neurastEnico], *a.* Neurasthenic.
neurologia [neurologIa], *n.f.* (*Med.*) Neurology,
neurologo [neurOlogo], *n.m.* Neurologist; nerve-specialist.
neuropatia [neuropatIa], *n.f.* (*Med.*) Neuropathy.
neuropatico, nevropatico [neuropAtico, nevropAtico], *a.* Neuropathic.
neurosi, *n.f.* (*Med.*) Neurosis.
neurotico [neurOtico], *n.m.a.* Neurotic.
neutrale, *a.* Neutral; indifferent.
neutralità [-à], *n.f.* Neutrality.
neutralizzare, *v.t.* To neutralize (in all senses) to counteract.
neutralizzazione, *n.f.* Neutralization.
neutralmente, *adv.* Neutrally.
neutro [nEutro], *n.m.* Neutral; (*Gram.*) neuter.
neutro [nEutro], *a.* Neutral; indifferent, impartial; indefinite; (*Gram.*) neuter. (*Mil.*) **Zona neutra,** neutral zone; **colore —,** neutral colour.
neutrone, *n.m.* (*Phys.*) Neutron.
nevaio [nevAio], *n.m.* Snow-field.
nevata, *n.f.* Snowfall, fall of snow.
nevato, *a.* Snow-white.
neve, *n.f.* Snow. **Coperto di —,** snow-capped (mountain); **valanga di —,** avalanche; **fiocco di —,** snow-flake; **bufera di —,** snow-storm; **spalare la —,** to shovel away the snow.
nevicare, *v.i.* To snow. **Nevica,** it is snowing.
nevicata, *n.f.* Snow-fall.
nevischio [nevIschio], *n.m.* Sleet, fine snow.
nevosità [-à], *n.f.* Snowiness.
nevoso, *a.* Snowy, snow-capped.
nevralgia [nevralgIa], *n.f.* (*Med.*) Neuralgia.
nevralgico [nevrAlgico], *a.* Neuralgic.
nevrastenia [cp. **neurastenia**].
nevrosi, *n.f.* (*Med.*) Neurosis [cp. **neurosi**].
nevvero, *inter.* Isn't it? Isn't it so? Isn't it true?
nibbio [nIbbio], *n.m.* (*Zool.*) Kite.
nicchia [nIcchia], *n.f.* Niche; nook, corner; safe job, sinecure.
nicchiamento, *n.m.* Hesitation.
nicchiare, *v.i.* To demur, to hesitate; to tarry; to shun.
nicchiarsi, *v.r.* To moan, to complain.
nicchio [nIcchio], *n.m.* Shell, conch-shell; priest's biretta.
nichel, nichelio [nichElio], *n.m.* (*Min.*) Nickel.
nichelare, *v.t.* To nickel.
nichelatura, *n.f.* Nickel-plating.
nichelino, *n.m.* (*colloq.*) Nickel coin.
nichelio [cp. **nichel**].
nichilismo, *n.m.* (*Pol.*) Nihilism.
nichilista (*pl.* **nichilisti**), *n.m.* Nihilist.
nicotina, *n.f.* Nicotine.
nicotinismo, *n.m.* Nicotinism.
nidata [cp. **nidiata**].
nidiace, *n.m.a.* Fledgling; unfledged.
nidiandolo [nidiAndolo], *n.f.* Nest-egg.
nidiata, *n.f.* Nestful, brood, covey. **Una — di bimbi,** a brood of children.
nidificare, *v.i.* To build a nest, to nest, to nidify.
nidificazione, *n.f.* Nesting, nest-building.
nido, *n.m.* Nest, roost; aerie, eyrie; (*fig.*) home
nidore, *n.f.* Bad smell, smell of rotten eggs.
nidoroso, *a.* Evil-smelling.
niego, *n.m.* Denial [cp. **diniego**].
niellare, *v.t.* To work in niello, to inlay with niello.
niellatore, *n.m.* Worker in niello.
niello, *n.m.* Niello, inlaid enamelwork, incised design on metal.
niente (1), *n.m.* Nothing, nothingness; trifle.
niente (2), *adv.a.* Nothing; not at all, in no way; no. **Far finta di —,** to pretend ignorance; — **affatto,** not at all; **far —,** to do nothing; — **paura,** no fear; **finire in —,** to come to nothing; **ci sono andato per —,** I went there for nothing; **ridursi al —,** to be reduced to poverty; **cose da —,** trifles, mere nothings.
nientedimeno, nientemeno, *adv.* Nothing less, not less; however.
nigella, *n.f.* (*Bot.*) Fennel-flower.
Nilo, *n.m.* (*Geog.*) Nile.
nimbo, *n.m.* Halo, nimbus, aureola; cloud, rain-cloud.
nimicare [cp. **inimicare**].
nimico [cp. **nemico**].
nimo, *pron.* (*obs.*) No one, nothing.
ninfa, *n.f.* Nymph; (*Zool.*) chrysalis, pupa.
ninfale, *n.m.* Poem or story of the nymphs.
ninfale, *a.* Nymphean.
ninfea [ninfEa], *n.f.* (*Bot.*) Water-lily.
ninfolo [nInfolo], *n.m.* Muzzle of an ox.
ninfomania [ninfomanIa], *n.f* (*Med.*) Nymphomania.

ninna-nanna, *n.f.* Lullaby.
ninnare, *v.t.* To lull, to dandle, to soothe to sleep, to sing to sleep.
ninnolare, *v.t.i.* To amuse a child, to play with a child; to trifle.
ninnolarsi, *v.r.* To waste time with trifles.
ninnolo [nInnolo], *n.m.* Knick-knack, trifle, toy.
ninnolone, *n.m.* Trifler.
nino, *n.m.* Pet, darling, child.
nipitella, *n.f.* (*Bot.*) Catmint.
nipote, *n.m.f.* Nephew, niece; grandchild, grandson, granddaughter. **I nipoti,** grandchildren, descendants.
nipotino, nipotina, *n.m.f.* Grandson, granddaughter.
nipotismo [cp. **nepotismo**].
nipponico [nippOnico], *a.* Japanese.
nirvana, *n.m.* Nirvana.
nissuno [cp. **nessuno**].
nitidamente, *adv.* Clearly, limpidly, distinctly.
nitidezza, *n.f.* Clearness, neatness; brightness; distinctness.
nitido [nItido], *a.* Clear, neat, terse; bright, shining.
nitore, *n.m.* Clear brilliance.
nitrato, *n.m.* (*Chem.*) Nitrate. **— d'argento,** silver nitrate.
nitrico [nItrico], *a.* (*Chem.*) Nitric. **Acido —,** nitric acid.
nitrificare, *v.t.* (*Chem.*) To nitrify.
nitrificazione, *n.f.* Nitrification.
nitrire, *v.i.* To neigh, to whinny.
nitrito, *n.m.* Neigh, neighing, whinnying.
nitro, *n.m.* (*Chem.*) Nitre. **Salnitro,** salt-petre.
nitrocellulosa, *n.f.* (*Chem.*) Nitrocellulose, guncotton.
nitrogeno [nitrOgeno], *n.m.* (*Chem.*) Nitrogen.
nitroglicerina (hard "g"), *n.f.* (*Chem.*) Nitro-glycerine.
nitroso, *a.* (*Chem.*) Nitrous.
nittalopia [nittalopIa], *n.f.* (*Med.*) Night-blindness.
niuno, *pron.* Nobody, no one.
nivale, *a.* Snowy.
niveo [nivEo], *a.* Snow-white, snowy.
Nizza, *n.f.* (*Geog.*) Nice.
nizzarda, *n.f.* Woman's large straw hat; old country dance.
nizzardo, *n.m.a.* Man of, or relating to Nice.
no, *adv.* No. **Io dico di no,** I say no; **credo di no,** I don't think so; **un no chiaro e tondo,** a flat refusal; **se no,** otherwise; **verrete, no?** you'll come, won't you?
nobile [nObile], *n.m.f.* Nobleman, noblewoman; person of rank.
nobile [nObile], *a.* Noble, great, lofty, eminent; magnanimous; illustrious; honourable, worthy. **Cuore —,** a noble soul; **primo piano —,** the first storey above the mezzanine; (*Theat.*) **padre —,** heavy father.
nobilesco, *a.* Of noble rank; upper-class.
nobiliare, *a.* Noble, aristocratic.
nobilitare, *v.t.* To ennoble; to elevate, to exalt.
nobilitarsi, *v.r.* To elevate oneself, to make oneself of higher rank.
nobilmente, *adv.* Nobly.
nobiltà [-à], *n.f.* Nobility, nobleness; loftiness, magnanimity; dignity.
nobilume, *n.m.* Petty nobility.
nocca, *n.f.* (*Anat.*) Knuckle.
nocchiere, nocchiero, *n.m.* (*Naut.*) Pilot steersman; (*fig.*) leader.
nocchieruto, *a.* Knotty, knobbly.
nocchino, *n.m.* Rap on the head with the knuckles.
nocchio [nOcchio], *n.m.* Knob, knot (in wood); (*Bot.*) node.
nocchioso, nocchiuto, *a.* Knotty; knobbly.
nocciola, *n.f.* Hazel-nut. **Color —,** hazel.
nocciolo (1), *n.m.* (*Bot.*) Hazel-tree.
nocciolo (2) [nOcciolo], *n.m.* Stone (of fruit); kernel; (*fig.*) gist, main point.
nocciuolo [cp. **nocciolo**].
noccoluto, *a.* With big knuckles.
noce, *n.m.f.* Walnut; nut; walnut-tree. **Legno di —,** walnut (wood); **guscio di —,** walnut-shell; **— del piede,** ankle-bone; **— moscata,** nutmeg; **— vomica,** nux vomica; **— del collo,** Adam's apple; **— di cocco,** coconut.
nocella, *n.f.* (*Anat.*) Ball and socket joint; wrist; joint of a pair of compasses.
nocemoscada, *n.f.* Nutmeg.
nocente, *a.* Noxious; harmful.
nocepesca, *n.f.* Nectarine.
nocepesco, *n.m.* Nectarine, -tree.
noceto, *n.m.* Walnut grove.
nocevole [nocEvole], *a.* Hurtful, harmful.
nocevolezza, *n.f.* Harmfulness.
nocevolmente, *adv.* Hurtingly, harmfully.
nocino, *n.m.* Children's game with nutshells.
nocivamente, *adv.* Noxiously, harmfully.
nocivo, *a.* Noxious, harmful, hurtful, injurious, pernicious.
nocumento, *n.m.* Damage, harm, injury, wrong.
nodale, *a.* Nodal.
nodatura, *n.f.* Knot (in wood).
nodello, *n.m.* Joint, wrist, ankle, etc.
noderoso [cp. **nodoso**].
nodo, *n.m.* Knot (in all senses), node; difficulty; bow (of tie, etc.); bond; plot; (*Anat.*) joint; (*Rail.*) junction. **— scorsoio,** slip-knot; **— gordiano,** Gordian knot; **— piano,** reef-knot; **— parlato,** clove hitch; **avere un — nella gola,** to have a lump in one's throat; **un — di tosse,** a fit of coughing; (*Naut.*) **dieci nodi,** ten knots (speed).
nodosamente, *adv.* Knottily; in a knotty form.
nodosità [-à], *n.f.* Knottiness.
nodoso, *a.* Knotty; knobby.
nodulo [nOdulo], *n.m.* Nodule.
Noè, *n.m.* Noah.
noetico [noEtico], *a.* Of Noah. **Era noetica,** antediluvian.
noi, *pron.pl.* We, us. **Vieni con noi,** come with us; **noi stessi,** ourselves; **noi andiamo,** we are going.
noia [nOia], *n.f.* Weariness, tedium, boredom, ennui, tediousness, tiresomeness; nuisance, annoyance. **Avere a —,** to dislike; **venire a — una cosa,** to be bored with something; **che —!** what a nuisance! **ho tante noie,** I have a lot of worries.
noialtri, *pron.* We; folk like us.
noiamento, *n.m.* Annoyance.
noiare, *v.t.* To annoy, to bother [cp. **annoiare**]
noiosamente, *adv.* Tiresomely.
noiosità [-à], *n.f.* Nuisance; boredom, tediousness.

noioso, *a.* Wearisome, tiresome; boring, tedious; annoying, irritating, vexing.
noleggiamento, *n.m.* Hire, hiring.
noleggiare, *v.t.* To hire; to charter, to freight; to let out on hire.
noleggiatore, noleggiatrice, *n.m.f.* Hirer; (*Naut.*) freighter, charterer.
noleggio [nolEggio], *n.m.* Hire; (*Naut.*) freight. **Vettura da —,** cab.
nolente, *a.* Unwilling. **Volente o —,** willy-nilly; **me —,** against my will.
nolo, *n.m.* Hire; (*Naut.*) freight, cargo. **Dare a —,** to let out on hire; **prendere a —,** to hire; **auto da —,** car for hire; **l'altezza dei noli,** the high freight charges.
nomade [nOmade], *n.m.a.* Nomad.
nomare [cp. **nominare**].
nome, *n.m.* Name; renown, reputation; denomination; family; (*Gram.*) noun, substantive. **Conoscere di — uno,** to know someone by name; **declinare il proprio —,** to give in one's name; **a mio —,** in my name; **— d'arte,** stage-name, pen-name; **a — di,** in the name of; **è noto sotto il — di,** he's known by the name of; **— di battesimo,** Christian name; **— e cognome,** name and surname; **— di fanciulla,** maiden name; **in — di Dio!** By God! **chiamare le cose col loro —,** to call a spade a spade; **avere un buon —,** to have a good reputation.
nomea [nomEa], *n.f.* Reputation; notoriety.
nomenclatura, *n.f.* Nomenclature.
nomignolo [nomIgnolo], *n.m.* Nickname.
nomina [nOmina], *n.f.* Nomination, election, appointment; repute, fame, reputation.
nominabile [nominAbile], *a.* Eligible, suitable for nomination.
nominale, *a.* Nominal. **Appello —,** roll call; **votazione per appello —,** poll by roll-call.
nominalmente, *adv.* Nominally.
nominanza, *n.f.* Renown, fame.
nominare, *v.t.* To name, to call; to nominate; to appoint, to elect; to speak of; to denominate. **È stato nominato professore,** he has been appointed professor; **è stato nominato presidente,** he was elected president.
nominarsi, *v.r.* To be named, to be called, to bear the name of; to nominate oneself.
nominatamente, *adv.* By name, particularly.
nominativamente, *adv.* Nominatively, by name.
nominativo, *n.m.a.* Nominative; (*Fin.*) inscribed, registered. **Titolo —,** inscribed bond; **azione nominativa,** registered share; **la lista dei nominativi,** the list of names.
nominato, *p.p.a.* Named, mentioned. **La persona sovra nominata,** the above-mentioned person.
nominatore, nominatrice, *n.m.f.* Nominator; patron, patroness.
nominazione, *n.f.* Nomination.
non, *adv.* Not, no. **Non vedi?** Don't you see? **non ho più nulla,** I have nothing left; **non ho casa,** I have no home; **non già che,** I don't mean that; **non sempre,** not always; **non solo,** not only; **non più,** no more; **non c'è di che,** don't mention it.
nona, *n.f.* (*Hist. Eccles.*) Nones.
nonagenario [nonagenArio], *n.m.a.* Nonagenarian.
nonagesimo [nonagEsimo], *a.* Ninetieth.
noncurante, *a.* Careless; listless, indifferent; unconcerned, heedless.
noncuranza, *n.f.* Carelessness, listlessness, indifference, unconcern; nonchalance, negligence.
nondimanco, nondimeno, *adv.* Nevertheless, yet, however; all the same, for all that.
non-intervento, *n.m.* Non-intervention.
nonno, nonna, *n.m.f.* Grandfather, grandmother. **I nonni,** grandparents; ancestors.
nonnulla, *n.m.* Trifle, mere nothing.
nono, *a.* Ninth.
nonostante, *adv.* Notwithstanding; in spite of. **— il freddo,** in spite of the cold.
nonpariglia [nonparIglia], *n.f.* (*Print.*) Nonpareil.
nonpertanto, *adv.* Nevertheless, however; still [cp. **nonostante**].
nonsenso, *n.m.* Nonsense, absurdity.
non-ti-scordar-di-me, *n.m.* (*Bot.*) Forget-me-not.
nonuplo [nOnuplo], *a.* Ninefold.
norcino, *n.m.* Pork-butcher; swine-gelder; (*colloq.*) clumsy surgeon.
nord, *n.m.* North; north country. **A — di,** north of; **verso —,** northwards; **Polo Nord,** North Pole; **America del Nord,** North America.
nord-est, *n.m.* North-east.
nordico [nOrdico], *n.m.a.* Northerly, northern; nordic. **I Nordici,** the Nordic races.
nord-ovest, *n.m.* North-west.
noria [nOria], *n.f.* Irrigation wheel; chain and bucket irrigation appliance.
Norimberga, *n.f.* (*Geog.*) Nuremberg.
norma, *n.f.* Rule, norm, principle; standard; direction, guidance; method, order. **Per tua —,** for your guidance; **secondo la —,** according to rule; **a — di legge,** according to law.
normale, *a.* Normal, regular, usual, customary, ordinary.
normalista, *n.m.f.* Pupil of a Normal School.
normalità [-à], *n.f.* Normality.
normalizzare, *v.t.* To normalize, to regularize.
normalizzazione, *n.f.* Normalization.
normalmente, *adv.* Normally.
Normandia [normandIa], *n.f.* (*Geog.*) Normandy.
normanno, *n.m.a.* Norman.
normativo, *a.* Guiding.
norvegese, *n.m.a.* Norwegian.
Norvegia [norvEgia], *n.f.* (*Geog.*) Norway.
nosocomio [nosocOmio], *n.m.* Hospital, infirmary.
nosogenesi [nosogEnesi], *n.f.* Origins of disease.
nosografia [nosografIa], *n.f.* Description of diseases.
nosologia [nosologIa], *n.f.* Nosology; science of diseases.
nossignora! nossignore! *adv.* No, Madam! No, Sir!
nostalgia [nostalgIa], *n.f.* Nostalgia, home-sickness.
nostalgico [nostAlgico], *a.* Nostalgic.
nostrale, nostrano, *a.* Domestic, home; home-grown; homely. **Produzione nostrana,** home product; **lana nostrana,** home-grown wool.
nostralmente, *adv.* In our own way, homely.

nostrano [cp. **nostrale**].
nostro (1), *n.m.* Our belongings, our people. **I nostri,** our people, our side.
nostro (2), *poss. pron., a.* Our, our own; ours. **Nostra madre,** our mother.
nostromo, *n.m.* (*Naut.*) Boatswain, bo's'un.
nota, *n.f.* Note, annotation; remark; list, memorandum; (*Mus.*) note; (*Comm.*) bill, account, invoice. **Prender —,** to take note; **prendere delle note,** to take notes, to jot down; **cosa degna di —,** a thing worthy of note; **edizione con note,** annotated edition; **— a piè di pagina,** footnote; (*Mus.*) **saltare una —,** to slur a note; **— del bucato,** washing-list.
notabile [notAbile], *n.m.a.* Notable, leading figure; person of distinction; notable, considerable, remarkable.
notabilità [-à], *n.f.* Notability, notable; man of mark; distinction.
notabilmente, *adv.* Notably.
notaio [notAio], *n.m.* Notary, solicitor; conveyancer.
notamento, *n.m.* Note, list.
notare, *v.t.* To note, to remark, to notice; to jot down, to take note; to consider, to take notice, to observe, to see. **Farsi —,** to attract notice; **gli ho fatto — che,** I remarked to him that, I brought to his notice that; **non ho notato nulla di male,** I didn't notice anything wrong; **— prezzi,** to quote prices.
notaresco, *a.* Like a pettifogging notary.
notariale, notarile, *a.* Notarial.
notariato, *n.m.* Profession of notary.
notaro [cp. **notaio**].
notata [cp. **nuotata**].
notazione, *n.f.* Notation.
noterella, *n.f.* Brief note.
notevole [notEvole], *a.* Remarkable, notable, considerable, important.
notevolmente, *adv.* Remarkably, notably.
notifica [notIfica], *n.f.* Notification, declaration; letter of advice; communication.
notificabile [notificAbile], *a.* Notifiable.
notificamento, *n.m.* Notification, manifest.
notificare, *v.t.* To notify; to make known, to inform; to intimate. (*Law*) **— una citazione,** to serve a summons.
notificazione, *n.f.* Notification, declaration; letter of advice.
notizia [notIzia], *n.f.* News, piece of news, tidings; report; information, notice, knowledge, notion. **Chiedere notizie di qualcuno,** to inquire about a person; **buone notizie,** good news; **aver — di,** to have news of, to have knowledge of; **avere notizie di qualcuno,** to hear from someone; **ultime notizie,** latest news; **quali notizie?** What's the news? **circola la — che,** there is a rumour that.
notiziario [notiziArio], *n.m.* Chronicle, miscellaneous news; tidings; news bulletin.
noto (1), *n.m.* Something known, a known thing.
noto (2), *n.m.* South wind.
noto (3), *a.* Known, well-known; obvious.
notomia, *n.f.* (*obs.*) Anatomy.
notoriamente, *adv.* Notoriously, notedly; publicly.
notorietà [-à], *n.f.* Notoriety.
notorio [notOrio], *a.* Well-known, noted; notorious (in bad sense); (*Law*) legal.
nottambulante, *n.m.f.* Night-nurse.
nottambulismo, *n.m.* Sleep-walking, somnambulism.
nottambulo [nottAmbulo], *n.m.* Sleep-walker, somnambulist.
nottante, *n.m.f.* Night-nurse.
nottata, *n.f.* Whole night, period of a night.
notte, *n.f.* Night; darkness, obscurity. **Di —,** by night; **questa —,** tonight; **sul far della —,** at night-fall; **— bianca,** sleepless night; **buona —!** Good night! **peggio che andar di —,** from bad to worse; **a — alta,** in the dead of night.
nottetempo, *adv.* **Di —,** at night-time.
nottivago [nottIvago], *n.m.* Night-prowler, night-wanderer.
nottola [nOttola], *n.f.* (*Zool.*) Species of owl or of bat; nightjar; wooden gate-latch. **— di sicurezza,** safety-catch.
nottolino, *n.m.* Door-latch.
nottolone, *n.m.* Great clumsy fellow; (*Zool.*) species of bat.
notturno, *n.m.* (*Mus.*) Nocturne.
notturno, *a.* Nocturnal, night; nightly. (*Aviat.*) **Volo —,** night-flight; **ritrovo —,** night-club.
nova, *a.* New [cp. **nuova**]; *n.f.* Kind of star.
novale, *n.f.* (*Agric.*) Newly-ploughed land.
novamente, *adv.* Afresh, again; lately, newly.
novanta, *num.a.* Ninety.
novantanove, *num.a.* Ninety-nine. **— probabilità su cento,** ninety-nine chances out of a hundred.
novantenne, *a.* Ninety years old.
novantesimo [novantEsimo], *num.a.* Ninetieth.
novantina, *n.f.* About ninety. **C'era una — di persone,** there were about ninety persons.
novantuno, *num.a.* Ninety-one.
novatore, novatrice, *n.m.f.* Innovator.
novazione, *n.f.* Innovation; renovation; renewal; (*Comm.*) conversion.
nove, *num.a.* Nine, ninth. **— volte su dieci,** nine times out of ten.
novecentesco, *a.* Twentieth-century.
novecentismo, *n.m.* Modernism; spirit and style of the 20th century.
novecento, *num.a.* Nine hundred. **Il Novecento,** the 20th century.
novella, *n.f.* Short story, story, tale; news, tidings; message. **Che novelle mi porti?** What news do you bring? **scrittore di novelle,** writer of short stories.
novellaio [novellAio], *n.m.* One greedy for news.
novellamente, *adv.* Anew, afresh, again; in a new way.
novellante, *n.m.* Teller of news, newsmonger.
novellare, *v.i.* To tell stories.
novellatore, novellatrice, *n.m.f.* Story-teller.
novelletta, *n.f.* Novelette.
novelliere, *n.m.* Story-writer, story-teller, novelist; gossip.
novellina, *n.f.* Short story for children.
novellino, *n.m.a.* Beginner, greenhorn, tender-foot; inexperienced, fresh; new; tender.
novellista (*pl.* **novellisti**), *n.m.* Novelist, story-writer; (*Pol.*) gossip-writer.

novellistica [novellIstica], *n.f.* Art of short-story writing; tales, stories.
novello, *a.* Fresh, new, novel, recent; newly-wed. **— fronda,** new leaf, tender leaf.
novembre, *n.m.* November.
novena, *n.f.* (*Eccles.*) Novena, nine days' devotion.
novenario [novenArio], *n.m.* (*Poet.*) Line of nine syllables.
novendiale, *a.* Nine days. (*Eccles.*) **Feste novendiali,** memorial ceremony nine days after a death.
novennale, *a.* Recurring every nine years; lasting nine years. (*Comm.*) **Buono —,** nine-year Treasury bond.
novenne, *a.* Nine years old.
novennio [novEnnio], *n.m.* Period of nine years.
noverare, *v.t.* To number, to count, to enumerate; to reckon.
noverca, *n.f.* (*Lit.*) Step-mother.
novero [nOvero], *n.m.* Number, list, class, category.
novilunio [novilUnio], *n.m.* New moon.
novissimo [novIssimo], *a.* Quite new, last, final, latest (thing). **I novissimi,** the four last things (death, judgment, heaven, hell).
novità [-à], *n.f.* Novelty, newness, innovation; news, tidings; originality. **Articoli di —,** fancy articles; **che —?** what news? **le — del giorno,** the news of the day.
novizia [novIzia], *n.f.* Novice; new convert; beginner, apprentice.
noviziato, *n.m.* Novitiate, noviceship; apprenticeship.
novizio [novIzio], *n.m.a.* Novice, beginner, apprentice; inexperienced.
novo [cp. **nuovo**].
novocaina, *n.f.* (*Med.*) Novocain (trade-name).
nozione, *n.f.* Notion, idea; knowledge, information, instruction.
nozze, *n.f.pl.* Wedding, nuptials, marriage, wedlock. **Il giorno delle —,** the wedding-day; **seconde —,** second marriage; **— d'argento, d'oro,** silver, golden wedding; **partecipazione di —,** wedding-card; **pare che vada a —,** he or she seems very happy.
nube, *n.f.* Cloud; haze, mist.
nubifragio [nubifrAgio], *n.m.* Cloud-burst, down-pour.
nubile [nUbile], *n.f.a.* Unmarried girl, marriageable girl; marriageable, unmarried.
nubilo [nUbilo], *a.* (*obs.*) Cloudy.
nuca, *n.f.* (*Anat.*) Nape (of the neck).
nucleare, *a.* Nuclear. **Scissione —,** nuclear fission.
nucleina, *n.f.* (*Chem.*) Nuclein.
nucleo [nUcleo], *n.m.* Nucleus; centre. **Il — della questione,** the gist of the question; **un — di uomini,** a group of men.
nudamente, *adv.* Nakedly, barely; bluntly, plainly.
nudare, *v.t.* To strip naked [cp. **denudare**].
nudarsi, *v.r.* To strip oneself naked, to take off one's clothes [cp. **denudarsi**].
nudezza, *n.f.* Nakedness, nudity [cp. **nudità**].
nudismo, *n.m.* Nudism.
nudista (*pl.* **nudisti**), *n.m.* Nudist.
nudità [-à], *n.f.* Nudity, nakedness; bareness, barrenness.
nudo, *n.m.* (*Art*) The nude.
nudo, *a.* Naked; bare, nude, uncovered; unadorned, simple, plain; barren. **A testa nuda,** bare-headed; **braccio —,** bare arm; **a piedi nudi,** bare-footed; **vedere ad occhio —,** to see with the naked eye; **— e crudo,** bluntly, without beating about the bush; **una camera nuda,** a bare room; **mezzo —,** half-naked; **mettere a —,** to lay bare, to strip; **sulla nuda terra,** on the bare ground.
nudrire, *v.t.* To nourish [cp. **nutrire**].
nughe, *n.f.pl.* Chatter, ineptitudes.
nugola, nugolo [cp. **nuvola, nuvolo**].
nulla, *n.m.* Nothingness, nothing. **Cose da —,** trifles; **cadere nel —,** to end in nothing.
nulla, *adv.* Nothing. **Non fa —,** it doesn't matter; **— di più bello,** nothing finer; **per —,** for nothing (in price).
nulladimeno, *adv.* Nonetheless, however, yet.
nullaggine [nullAggine], *n.f.* Nothingness.
nullamente, *adv.* In no way, by no means.
nullameno, *adv.* Nevertheless.
nullaosta, *n.m.* (*Law*) Permit.
nullatenente, *n.m.* One possessed of nothing.
nullatenenza, *n.f.* Non-possession of property.
nullismo, *n.m.* Nihilism.
nullità [-à], *n.f.* Nullity; nonentity, insignificance; (*Law*) nullity, invalidity. **Essere una —,** to be a nonentity.
nullo, *a.* Void, null, invalid, useless. **Questo documento è —,** this document is null and void; **rendere —,** to invalidate.
nume, *n.m.* Deity, divinity, god.
numeno [nUmeno], *n.m.* (*Phil.*) Noumenon.
numerabile [numerAbile], *a.* Numerable, possible to be counted.
numerale, *n.m.a.* Numeral.
numeralmente, *adv.* Numerically.
numerare, *v.t.* To enumerate, to count, to number.
numerario [numerArio], *n.m.* Ready cash, specie.
numeratamente, *adv.* In order of numbers, one by one.
numeratore, *n.m.* (*Math.*) Numerator.
numeratrice, *n.f.* Calculating machine.
numerazione, *n.f.* Numeration, notation, numbering. **— arabica,** Arabic numbers.
numericamente, *adv.* Numerically.
numerico [numErico], *a.* Numerical.
numerino, *n.m.* Number (in a lottery).
numerizzare, *v.t.* To enumerate, to number.
numero [nUmero], *n.m.* Number; figure; quantity; (*Lit.*) metre, rhythm; (*Theat.*) number, item (in a variety show). **Di —,** precisely; **— intero,** whole number; **numeri pari, dispari,** even, odd numbers; **— di cavalli vapore,** horse-power; **numeri indici,** index numbers; **passare nel — dei più,** to join the great majority, to die; **— legale,** quorum; **essere in — legale,** to form a quorum; **aver pochi numeri,** to be dull (of understanding).
numerosamente, *adv.* Numerously.
numerosità [-à], *n.f.* Numerousness.
numeroso, *a.* Numerous; (*Poet.*) rhythmical.
numida [nUmida], *n.f.* (*Zool.*) Guinea fowl.
numismatica [numismAtica], *n.f.* Numismatics.
numismatico [numismAtico], *n.m.a.* Numismatist; numismatical.

nummo, *n.m.* (*obs.*) Money, cash.
nummolario [nummolArio], *n.m.*(*obs.*) Banker, cashier.
nuncio [cp. **nunzio**].
nuncupativamente, *adv.* (*Law*) Nuncupatively.
nuncupativo, *a.* (*Law*) Nuncupative. **Testamento —,** nuncupative will, orally-made will.
nundine [nUndine], *n.f.pl.* Fair, market (originally held every nine days).
Nunziata, *n.f. abbrev.* of name of Annunziata.
nunziatura, *n.f.* Nunciature, office of nuncio.
nunzio [nUnzio], *n.m.* Nuncio (papal ambassador); messenger.
nuocere [nuOcere], *v.t.i.* To hurt, to harm, to injure; to prejudice, to wrong, to damage; to be harmful, to be injurious.
nuora, *n.f.* Daughter-in-law.
nuotare, *v.i.* To swim; to float; to wallow. **— nell'abbondanza,** to roll in wealth. **Sapete — ?** Can you swim? **— come un pesce,** to swim like a fish.
nuotata, *n.f.* Swimming, long swim; style of swimming.
nuotatoio [nuotatOio], *n.m.* Swimming-pool.
nuotatore, nuotatrice, *n.m.f.* Swimmer.
nuoto, *n.m.* Swimming.
nuova, *n.f.* News.
nuovamente, *adv.* Newly, recently, freshly.
nuovo, *n.m.* Something new.
nuovo, *a.* New; fresh; novel, recent; modern; unusual; inexperienced. **Di —,** again, once more; **— di zecca,** brand-new; **di bel —,** over again; **— agli affari,** inexperienced; **luna nuova,** new moon; **che c'è di — ?** What's the news? **— fiammante,** very new, brand-new; **rimesso a —,** restored, re-conditioned; **hai comperato una nuova villa?** Have you bought another house? (*Geog.*) **La Nuova Zelanda,** New Zealand.
nuraghe, *n.m.* Conical dolmen of Sardinia.
nutazione, *n.f.* (*Astron. Bot.*) Nutation; (*Med.*) St. Vitus's Dance.
nutricare, *v.t.* To nourish, to foster [cp. **nutrire**].
nutrice, *n.f.* Wet-nurse; foster-mother.
nutrimento, *n.m.* Nourishment, nutriment; food, aliment; feeding.
nutrire, *v.t.* To feed, to nourish, to suckle, to nurture; to foster, to cherish; to entertain. **— la speranza,** to cherish the hope.
nutrirsi, *v.r.* To feed on, to live on. **— di pane,** to live on bread.
nutritivo, *a.* Nourishing, nutritive, nutritious.
nutrito, *p.p.a.* Fed, nourished; sustained; strong; continuous.
nutritore, nutritrice, *n.m.f.a.* Nourisher, foster parent; nourishing.
nutrizione, *n.f.* Nutrition, nourishment.
nuvola [nUvola], *n.f.* Cloud. **Cielo senza nuvole,** cloudless sky; **— passeggera,** passing cloud; (*fig.*) **cader dalle nuvole,** to be startled, to be amazed; **aver la testa nelle nuvole,** to have one's head in the clouds to dream.
nuvolaccio [nuvolAccio], *n.m.* Storm-cloud, black cloud.
nuvolaglia [nuvolAglia], *n.f.* Mass of clouds.
nuvolame, *n.m.* Clouding (of a liquid).
nuvolata, *n.f* Cloudiness; shower; cloudburst.
nuvolato, *a.* Overcast.
nuvolo [nUvolo], *n.m.* Cloud; swarm, mass, a lot. **Un — di polvere,** a cloud of dust; **c'era un — di mosche,** there were swarms of flies.
nuvolo [nUvolo], *a.* Cloudy, overcast.
nuvolosità [-à], *n.f.* Cloudiness.
nuvoloso, *a.* Cloudy, overcast.
nuziale, *a.* Nuptial, bridal, wedding. **Marcia —,** wedding march.
nuzialmente, *adv.* Nuptially; fit for a wedding.

O

O, o, *n.m.f.* Thirteenth letter of the Italian alphabet. It has two sounds: open, as in **forte;** and closed, as in **forse.**
o, od, *conj.* Or, either. **O l'uno o l'altro,** either one or the other; **o vivo o morto,** dead or alive; **ieri od oggi,** yesterday or to-day.
O! Oh! *inter.* O! Oh!
ò [ò], *aux.v.* (*rare*) I have (instead of the more common **ho**).
oasi [Oasi], *n.f.* Oasis (in all senses).
obbediente, *a.* Obedient.
obbedientemente, *adv.* Obediently.
obbedienza, *n.f.* Obedience; compliance. **In — al disposto della legge,** in compliance with the provisions of the law.
obbedire, *v.i.* To obey; to submit; to comply with [cp. **ubbidire**].
obbiettare [cp. **obiettare**].
obbiettivo, *a.* Objective.
obbietto, *n.m.* Object, purpose, end.
obbligamento, *n.m.* Obliging; obligation.
obbligante, *a.* Obliging; binding.
obbligantemente, *adv.* Obligingly.
obbligare, *v.t.* To compel, to force, to bind, to constrain; to put in one's debt, to oblige. **Io fui obbligato a,** I was forced to; **vi sono molto obbligato,** I am much obliged to you.
obbligarsi, *v.r.* To bind oneself, to engage oneself.
obbligatamente, *adv.* Obligedly.
obbligato, *n.m.* (*Law*) One bound by an obligation.
obbligatoriamente, *adv.* Obligatorily.
obbligatorietà [-à], *n.f.* Compulsory character, bindingness.
obbligatorio (1) [obbligatOrio], *n.m.* (*Law*) Obligee.
obbligatorio (2) [obbligatOrio], *a.* Obligatory, compulsory, binding.
obbligazione, *n.f.* Obligation; (*Comm.*) bond, debenture; I.O.U.
obbligazionista, *n.f.* (*Comm.*) Bond-holder, debenture-holder.
obbligo [Obbligo], *n.m.* Obligation, compulsion; duty; indebtedness, engagement; (*Comm.*) bond. **Non ho l'— di andare,** I am not bound to go.
obblio [cp. **oblio**].
obbrobrio [obbrObrio], *n.m.* Opprobrium, infamy, disgrace.
obbrobriosamente, *adv.* Opprobriously.
obbrobriosità [-à], *n.f.* Opprobriousness.
obbrobrioso, *a.* Opprobrious, infamous, disgraceful.
obelisco, *n.m.* Obelisk.

oberato, *a.* Loaded, burdened (with debt, etc.).
obesità [-à], *n.f.* Obesity.
obeso, *a.* Obese, fleshy, corpulent.
obice [Obice], *n.m.* (*Mil.*) Howitzer.
obiettare, *v.i.* To object, to oppose, to allege; to remark.
obiettivamente, *adv.* Objectively.
obiettività [-à], *n.f.* Objectivity, detachment, impartiality, objectiveness.
obiettivo, *n.m.* Objective, aim, object; object-glass, lens.
obiettivo, *a.* Objective (in all senses), external, detached, impartial.
obiezione, *n.f.* Objection, opposition; disapproval; demurring. **Sollevare obiezioni,** to raise objections.
obitorio [obitOrio], *n.m.* Mortuary.
obituario [obituArio], *n.m.* Obituary; death-register.
obiurgazione, *n.f.* Objurgation.
oblato, oblata, *n.m.f.* Oblate; lay-brother, lay-sister; priest (in certain orders).
oblatore, oblatrice, *n.m.f.* Donor, founder.
oblazione, *n.f.* Oblation, gift, offering (*Eccles.*) presenting bread and wine (for consecration in the Mass).
obliabile [obliAbile], *a.* Forgettable.
obliare, *v.t.* To forget; to disregard, to neglect.
oblio [oblIo], *n.m.* Oblivion, forgetfulness; disregard.
oblioso, *a.* Oblivious, forgetful.
obliquamente, *adv.* Obliquely.
obliquare, *v.t.* To bend; (*Naut.*) to tack.
obliquità [-à], *n.f.* Obliquity; crookedness.
obliquo [oblIquo], *a.* Oblique, slanting, deviating; crooked, indirect; (*fig.*) false, underhand.
obliterare, *v.t.* To obliterate, to efface.
obliterazione, *n.f.* Obliteration.
oblivione, *n.f.* (*obs.*) Oblivion; forgetfulness.
oblivioso, *a.* Oblivious.
oblò [-ò], *n.m.* (*Naut.*) Port-hole.
oblungo, *a.* Oblong.
oboe [Oboe], *n.m.* (*Mus.*) Oboe, hautboy.
oboista, *n.m.f.* Oboist.
obolo [Obolo], *n.m.* Small coin, mite; obolus. **L'— di San Pietro,** Peter's Pence.
obsolèto, *a.* Obsolete.
obtrettatore, *n.m.* Detractor.
obtrettazione, *n.f.* Detraction, slander.
oc, *n.f.* **Lingua d'oc,** old Provençal speech.
oca, *n.f.* Goose; (*fig.*) silly person. **Far venir la pelle d'—,** to make one's flesh creep; **— maschio, ocone,** gander; **fare il becco all'—,** to give the finishing touch.
ocarina, *n.f.* (*Mus.*) Ocarina.
occasionale, *a.* Occasional, casual.
occasionalmente, *adv.* Occasionally.
occasionare, *v.t.* To occasion, to cause; to produce.
occasione, *n.f.* Occasion, opportunity, emergency; chance, bargain, job lot. **All'—,** on occasion; **alla prima —,** at the first opportunity; **coglier l'—,** to seize the opportunity; **discorso d'—,** appropriate speech; **comprare d'—,** to buy at sale price, to buy second-hand.
occaso, *n.m.* (*Lit.*) Sunset, setting; west; decline.
occhiaccio [occiAccio], *n.m.* Threatening glance; baleful look.
occhiaia [occhiAia], *n.f.* Eye-socket, orbit. **Aver le occhiaie,** to have black rings round the eyes.
occhialaio [occhialAio], *n.m.* Optician, spectacle-maker.
occhiale, *a.* Pertaining to the eye. **Denti occhiali,** eye-teeth.
occhialetto, occhialino, *n.m.* Monocle, single eyeglass.
occhiali, *n.m.pl.* Spectacles, eye-glasses. **Portare gli —,** to wear glasses.
occhialoni, *n.m.pl.* Goggles; large spectacles.
occhiare, *v.t.* (*obs.*) To eye, to sight.
occhiata, *n.f.* Glance, look, glimpse. **Dare un'— a,** to glance at, to have a look at; to wink; **gettare delle occhiate,** to cast glances.
occhiataccia [occhiatAccia], *n.f.* Nasty look, ugly scowl.
occhiatina, *n.f.* Rapid glance, glimpse, wink; tender look.
occhiato, *a.* Full of eyes.
occhiatura, *n.f.* Look, gaze.
occhiazzurro, *a.* Blue-eyed.
occhieggiare, *v.t.* To ogle, to glance, to cast glances at.
occhiellatura, *n.f.* Button-holing.
occhiello, *n.m.* Button-hole; eyelet; fly-leaf.
occhietto, *n.m.* Small eye. **Far l'— a,** to wink at.
occhino, *n.m.* Eye-bath.
occhio [Occhio], *n.m.* Eye; sight, view, look; port-hole. **A quattr'occhi,** face to face, privately, between ourselves; **a — e croce,** at a rough estimate; **veder di buon —,** to look on with favour; **dar nell'—,** to attract notice; (*Arch.*) **— di bue,** bull's eye; **costa un —,** it costs a lot; **a colpo d'—,** at a glance; **a vista d'—,** visibly, rapidly, apace; **sott'—,** under one's eyes; **aver male agli occhi,** to have sore eyes; **tener d'— qualcuno,** to keep watch on someone; **aver buon —,** to be sharpsighted; **far gli occhi dolci,** to give the glad eye; **in un batter d'—,** in a jiffy, in half a second; **un bel colpo d'—,** a fine view.
occhiolino, *n.m.* Wink. **Fare l'—,** to wink, to ogle.
occhione, *n.m.* (*Zool.*) Stone curlew.
occhiuto, *a.* Sharp-sighted, watchful, vigilant; rapacious.
occidentale, *n.m.a.* Westerner, western, occidental.
occidente, *n.m.* West, occident.
occiduo [occIduo], *a.* (*Lit.*) Setting, sinking (of the sun); western.
occipitale, *a.* (*Anat.*) Occipital.
occipite [occIpite], *n.m.* (*Anat.*) Occiput.
occitanico [occitAnico], *a.* Provençal.
occludere [occlUdere], *v.t.* To stop up, to shut.
occlusione, *n.f.* Occlusion; (*Med.*) stoppage.
occorrendo, *pres.p.a.* If necessary, in case of need.
occorrente, *n.m.a.* Requisite, necessary, needful; happening, occurring.
occorrenza, *n.f.* Occurrence, emergency, need **All'—,** in case of need.

occorrere [occOrrere], *v.i.* To be necessary, to be required; to want, to require; (*obs.*) to happen, to occur. **Ti occorre altro ?** Do you need anything else? **non occorre che tu venga,** there's no need for you to come.
occorso, *p.p.a.* Happened; (*Comm.*) met. **Le spese occorse,** expenses met.
occultabile [occultAbile], *a.* Possible to hide.
occultamente, *adv.* Occultly.
occultamento, *n.m.* Concealment, suppression.
occultare, *v.t.* To conceal, to hide, to keep secret.
occultazione, *n.f.* Concealment; (*Astron.*) occultation.
occultismo, *n.m.* Occultism.
occulto, *a.* Occult, secret, concealed; esoteric, mysterious; (*Astron.*) occulted; **Socio —,** sleeping partner.
occupabile [occupAbile], *a.* Occupiable.
occupamento, *n.m.* Incumbrance, impediment.
occupante, *n.m.a.* Occupant, occupier; occupying.
occupare, *v.t.* To occupy, to take possession of; to fill (a post, etc.); to engage, to employ; to inhabit. **— un alto posto,** to hold a high position.
occuparsi, *v.r.* To busy oneself, to apply oneself, to concern oneself; to work, to be employed. **Egli s'occupa di agricoltura,** he has taken up farming.
occupato, *a.* Occupied, engaged, taken (of a seat, etc.); employed, busy, taken up, absorbed.
occupatore, occupatrice, *n.m.f.* Occupier; invader.
occupazione, *n.f.* Occupation (in all senses); situation, post, job.
oceanico [oceAnico], *a.* Oceanic.
oceano [ocEano], *n.m.* Ocean; sea, main. **L'Oceano Atlantico, Artico,** the Atlantic, Arctic Ocean.
oceanografia [oceanografIa], *n.f.* Oceanography.
oceanografo [oceanOgrafo], *n.m.* Oceanographer.
ocone, *n.m.* (*colloq.*) Goose, idiot, silly chap.
ocra, *n.f.* Ochre.
ocraceo [ocrAceo], *a.* Ochrous.
oculare, *n.m.* Eye-piece (of telescope, etc.).
oculare, *a.* Ocular. **Testimonio —,** eye-witness.
oculario [oculArio], *n.m.* Oculist [cp. **oculista**].
ocularista (*pl.* **ocularisti**), *n.m.* Optician.
ocularmente, *adv.* Ocularly.
oculatamente, *adv.* Cautiously, with eyes open.
oculatezza, *n.f.* Caution, shrewdness; discernment.
oculato, *a.* Sharp-sighted, wary, cautious, shrewd, circumspect.
oculista (*pl.* **oculisti**), *n.m.* Oculist, eye-specialist.
oculistica [oculIstica], *n.f.* Ophthalmology.
oculistico [oculIstico], *a.* Oculistic.
od, *conj.* Or [cp. **o**].
oda, *n.f.* (*Poet.*) Ode.
odalisca, *n.f.* Odalisque.
ode, *n.f.* (*Poet.*) Ode, lyric.
odiabile [odiAbile], *a.* Worthy of hatred.
odiare, *v.t.* To hate, to abhor, to detest, to dislike. **Farsi odiare,** to make oneself hated.
odiatore, odiatrice, *n.m.f.* Hater, abhorrer.
odicina, *n.f.* Short ode.
odiernamente, *adv.* Nowadays, at present, at the present time.
odierno, *a.* Of to-day, present-day. **La vostra lettere odierna,** your letter of to-day.
odio [Odio], *n.m.* Hate, hatred; detestation, aversion, odium, loathing. **Avere in —,** to hate; **in — a,** against, out of spite for.
odiosamente, *adv.* Odiously, hatefully.
odiosità [-à], *n.f.* Hatefulness, odiousness, loathsomeness.
odioso, *a.* Hateful, odious, loathsome, repulsive.
Odissea [odissEa], *n.f.* Odyssey.
odometro [odOmetro], *n.m.* Pedometer, hodometer.
odontalgia [odontalgIa], *n.f.* Toothache.
odontoiatra, *n.m.f.* Odontologist.
odontoiatria [odontoiatrIa], *n.f.* Odontology, dentistry.
odorabile [odorAbile], *a.* Producing a smell.
odoraccio [odorAccio], *n.m.* Bad smell.
odoramento, *n.m.* Smelling, scenting.
odorante, *a.* Smelling, giving off a smell.
odorare, *v.t.i.* To smell, to scent. **— un fiore,** to smell a flower; **— di buono,** to smell nice.
odorato, *n.m.* Smell, scent, sense of smell.
odore, *n.m.* Smell; scent, odour; perfume, fragrance; (*fig.*) repute. **In — di santità,** in the odour of sanctity.
odorifero [odorIfero], *a.* Odoriferous.
odorosamente, *adv.* Odorously.
odoroso, *a.* Odorous, sweet-smelling, scented, fragrant, perfumed.
offa, *n.f.* Cake; biscuit; (*fig.*) reward, bribe, sop.
offella, *n.f.* Tart, cake.
offelleria [offellerIa], *n.f.* Pastrycook's shop.
offelliere, *n.m.* Pastrycook.
offendere [offEndere], *v.t.* To offend, to give offence; to hurt, to vex, to molest; to assail.
offendersi [offEndersi], *v.r.* To take offence, to be offended, to take exception to, to feel hurt. **— per nulla,** to be very touchy; **la luce offende la vista,** the light hurts one's eyes.
offendibile [offendIbile], *a.* Open to offence, liable to take offence.
offendimento, *n.m.* Offending, offence.
offenditore, *n.m.* Offender, transgressor, assailant.
offensiva, *n.f.* Offensive, attack. **Iniziar l'—,** to start an offensive.
offensivamente, *adv.* Offensively.
offensivo, *a.* Offensive, hurtful; damaging, insulting.
offensore, *n.m.* Offender, transgressor; assailant.
offerente, *n.m.* Bidder. **Al migliore —,** to the highest bidder.
offerire [cp. **offrire**].
offerta, *n.f.* Offer, offering, bid, proffer, tender; donation. **Declinare un'—,** to decline an offer; **si ricevono offerte,** donations are invited.
offertorio [offertOrio], *n.m.* (*Eccles.*) Offertory.
offesa, *n.f.* Offence, injury, affront; damage. **Recar —,** to give offence.
officiale [cp. **ufficiale**].
officiante, *a.* Officiating. **Sacerdote —,** officiating priest, celebrant.

officiare, *v.t.i.* To officiate; to act, to perform; to apply to, to address. — **una chiesa,** to have Mass celebrated in a church.
officina, *n.f.* Workshop, factory, works; laboratory. **Officine ferroviarie,** railway works; **capo —,** foreman.
officinale, *a.* (*Med.*) Officinal.
officio [cp. **ufficio**].
officiosamente, *adv.* Courteously, officiously.
officiosità [-à], *n.f.* Officiousness; courtesy, urbanity.
officioso, *a.* Obliging, helpful, urbane; semi-official, officious.
offrente, *n.m.* Bidder.
offrire, *v.t.* To offer, to tender, to propose; to proffer, to bid (a price); to present; to hold out. — **in dono,** to present as a gift; **offre molti pericoli,** it presents many dangers; **non offre interesse,** it does not offer any interest; — **i propri omaggi,** to offer one's respects.
offrirsi, *v.r.* To offer oneself; to present oneself.
offuscamento, *n.m.* Darkening, dimming; dimness (of sight, etc.).
offuscare, *v.t.* To darken, to dim; to eclipse.
offuscarsi, *v.r.* To grow dark, to grow dim; to be eclipsed.
offuscazione, *n.f.* Darkening, dimming, dimness.
ofite, *n.f.* (*Geol.*) Ophite.
oftalmia [oftalmIa], *n.f.* (*Med.*) Ophthalmia.
oftalmico [oftAlmico], *a.* Ophthalmic.
oftalmologia [oftalmologIa], *n.f.* Ophthalmology.
oggetti, *n.m.pl.* (*Comm.*) Articles, materials, requisites.
oggettivamente, *adv.* Objectively.
oggettivare, *v.t.* To objectify.
oggettivarsi, *v.r.* To assume concrete shape, to become concrete.
oggettività [-à], *n.f.* Objectivity, objectiveness.
oggettivo, *n.m.a.* Objective.
oggetto, *n.m.* Object (in all senses); theme, aim, purpose; subject; article. **A che — è venuto?** For what purpose has he come?
oggi, *adv.* To-day. — **a otto, a quindici,** this day week, fortnight; **a tutt'oggi,** up to the present; **da — innanzi,** from to-day on; **al giorno d'—,** nowadays.
oggidì, oggigiorno, *adv.* Nowadays, at the present time.
oggimai, *adv.* Now, this very day.
ogiva, *n.f.* (*Arch.*) Ogive, pointed arch.
ogivale, *a.* Ogival.
ogni, *a.* Every, each. **Ad — modo,** in any case; at any rate; — **volta,** every time; — **tanto,** now and again; — **giorno,** every day; **ad — costo,** at any cost; — **cinque settimane,** every five weeks; **sotto — rispetto,** in every respect.
ognintorno, *adv.* On every side.
Ognissanti, *n.m.* All Saints' Day.
ogniveggente, *a.* All-seeing.
ognora, *adv.* Always. — **che,** every time that.
ognuno, *pron.* Everyone, everybody, each one. — **per sè,** everyone for himself.
Oh! Ohè! Ohì! *inter.* Oh! Hallo! Ah! Oho!
Ohibò! Oibò! *inter.* For shame!
Ohimè! *inter.* Alas!
oidio [oIdio], *n.m.* (*Bot.*) Mildew (on vines).
oil, *n.f.* **Lingua d'oil,** *langue d'oil,* Old French.
Olà! *inter.* Hullo! Look out! Take care, there! Who's there?
Olanda, *n.f.* (*Geog.*) Holland.
olandese, *n.m.a.* Dutchman, Dutch.
oleaceo [oleAceo], *a.* Oily, oleaginous.
oleandro, *n.m.* (*Bot.*) Oleander.
oleario [oleArio], *a.* Oily, pertaining to oil.
oleastro, *n.m.* (*Bot.*) Wild olive.
oleato, *a.* Oiled. **Carta oleata,** oiled-paper.
olecrano, *n.m.* (*Anat.*) Point of the elbow, funny-bone.
oleico, *a.* (*Chem.*) Oleic.
oleifero [oleIfero], *a.* Oil. **Pianta oleifera,** oil-bearing plant.
oleificio [oleifIcio], *n.m.* Oil-mill; oil-works.
oleina, *n.f.* (*Chem.*) Oleine.
olente, *a.* (*Lit.*) Fragrant, scented.
oleodotto, *n.m.* Oil pipe-line.
oleografia [oleografIa], *n.f.* Oleograph.
oleosità [-à], *n.f.* Oiliness.
oleoso, *a.* Oily, greasy.
olezzante, *a.* Fragrant, sweet-smelling.
olezzare, *v.i.* To be fragrant, to give forth scent, to smell sweetly.
olezzo, *n.m.* Fragrance, scent, perfume.
olfattivo, *a.* Olfactory.
olfatto, *n.m.* Smell, sense of smell, olfaction.
olfattorio [olfattOrio], *a.* (*Anat.*) Olfactory.
oliandolo [oliAndolo], *n.m.* Oilman, oil-merchant.
oliare, *v.t.* To oil, to lubricate.
oliato, *a.* Oiled, oily.
oliatore, *n.m.* Oiler; oil-can.
olibano [olIbano], *n.m.* Frankincense.
oliena, *n.f.* Kind of Sardinian wine.
oliera, *n.f.* Cruet-stand.
oligarca, *n.m.* Oligarch.
oligarchia [oligarchIa], *n.f.* Oligarchy.
oligarchico [oligArchico], *a.* Oligarchic.
Olimpia [olImpia], *n.f.* (*Geog.*) Olympia.
olimpiaco [olimpIaco], *a.* Olympic. **Giuochi olimpiaci,** Olympic games.
olimpiade [olimpIade], *n.m.* Olympiad; the Olympic games.
olimpicamente, *adv.* With Olympian serenity.
olimpico [olImpico], *a.* Olympic; Olympian, lofty, superb, serene; detached.
olimpio [olImpio], *a.* Olympian.
olimpionico [olimpiOnico], *n.m.* Winner of an Olympic Games contest.
Olimpo, *n.m.* (*Myth.*) Olympus.
olio [Olio], *n.m.* Olive-oil; oil (in all senses). — **minerale,** mineral oil; oil, petrol; — **lubrificante,** lubricating oil; — **di paraffina,** medicinal paraffin oil; — **da tavola,** salad oil; — **di ricino,** castor oil; — **di merluzzo,** cod-liver oil; **sott'—,** in oil; **pittura ad —,** oil-painting; (*Eccles.*) **l'— santo,** Extreme Unction; **macchia d'—,** oil-stain; — **da ardere,** lamp oil; **bidone per —,** can for oil; **lampada ad —,** oil-lamp.
olioso, *a.* Oily [cp. **oleoso**].
oliva, *n.f.* Olive.
olivagno, *n.m.* (*Bot.*) Wild olive.
olivastro, *a.* Olive (colour), brown; tanned.
olivato, *a.* Planted with olive-trees.
oliveto, *n.m.* Olive grove.
olivetta, *n.f.* Cloth-covered button.

olivigno, *a.* Olive-coloured.
olivo, ulivo, *n.m.* Olive, olive-tree, olive wood [cp. **ulivo**].
olla, *n.f.* Pot, vase. — **cineraria,** cinerary urn.
olmaia [olmAia], *n.f.* Row of elm-trees.
olmeto, *n.m.* Elm grove.
olmetto, *n.m.* Young elm.
olmo, *n.m.* (*Bot.*) Elm, elm-tree.
olocausto [olocAusto], *n.m.* Holocaust, sacrifice.
Oloferne, *n.m.* Holophernes.
olografo [olOgrafo], *a.* Holograph.
olona, *n.f.* **Tela —,** sail-cloth.
oloturia [olotUria], *n. f.* (*Zool.*) Holothurian.
oltracciò, *adv.* Besides, moreover.
oltracotante, *a.* Arrogant, insolent, overbearing.
oltracotanza, *n.f.* Arrogance, insolence.
oltraggiabile [oltraggiAbile], *a.* Subject to outrage.
oltraggiamento, *n.m.* Insult, abuse.
oltraggiare, *v.t.* To abuse, to insult; to outrage; to violate.
oltraggiatore, *n.m.* Insulter, outrager.
oltraggio [oltrAggio], *n.m.* Insult, abuse, affront; injury; outrage; crime. — **al pudore,** outrage on common decency.
oltraggiosamente, *adv.* Outrageously, abusively.
oltraggioso, *a.* Outrageous; abusive, offensive, insulting.
oltralpe, *adv.* Beyond the Alps, north of the Alps; abroad.
oltramontano, *a.* Ultramontane, foreign, from beyond (north of) the Alps.
oltranza, *n.f.* Excess, extreme. **A —,** to the bitter end, to the last ditch; out and out.
Oltrarno, *n.m.* (*Geog.*) District of Florence across the Arno.
oltre, *adv.prep.* Beyond, further on, forward; besides, more than, together with. — **ogni credere,** beyond belief, past belief; **andar troppo —,** to go too far; **— a ciò,** besides this; **passare —,** to go on, to go beyond.
oltrechè, *adv.* Besides, apart from (the fact that).
oltremare, *a.* Overseas, from beyond the sea; transoceanic.
oltremarino, *n.m.* Ultramarine (colour).
oltremarino, *a.* Oversea.
oltremisura, oltremodo, *adv.* Beyond measure, exceedingly.
oltremondano, *a.* Of the other world.
oltremontanismo, *n.m.* Ultramontanism, clericalism.
oltrenaturale, *a.* Supernatural.
oltrepagato, *a.* Overpaid.
oltrepassare, *v.t.* To surpass, to go beyond; to overtake; to exceed, to overstep. — **i limiti,** to go too far, to overstep all bounds; **lasciarsi —,** to allow oneself to be overtaken.
oltretomba, *n.m.* The next world; the underworld.
omaccio [omAccio], *n.m.* Nasty fellow, ill-bred man [cp. **uomo**].
omaccione, *n.m.* Coarse fellow, big man (*lit.* and *fig.*).
omaggio [omAggio], *n.m.* Homage, respect, deference; submission. **In —,** as a compliment; — **dell'autore,** with the author's compliments; **rendere — a,** to do homage to, to pay one's respects to; **copia in —,** (of a book) presentation copy.
omai [cp. **ormai**].
omaro [Omaro], *n.m.* (*Zool.*) Crayfish, lobster.
ombelicale, *a.* (*Anat.*) Umbilical. **Cordone —,** umbilical cord.
ombelico, *n.m.* (*Anat.*) Navel, umbilicus.
ombra, *n.f.* Shade, shadow; darkness, obscurity; ghost, phantom; umbrage, offence. **Prender —,** to take umbrage; **non c'è — di dubbio,** there's not a shadow of doubt; **all'—,** in the shade; **è l'— di se stesso,** he's the mere shadow of himself; **aver paura della propria —,** to be afraid of one's own shadow.
ombracolo [ombrAcolo], *n.m.* (*obs.*) Shade (of trees); (*fig.*) defence, protection.
ombramento, *n.m.* Shadow, shading.
ombrare, *v.t.* To shade, to cast shade on; (*Art*) to shade.
ombrarsi, *v.r.* To take umbrage; to go into the shade, to withdraw oneself; to shy (of a horse).
ombratura, *n.f.* Shading.
ombreggiamento, *n.m.* Overshadowing; light shading.
ombreggiare, *v.t.* To shade, to cast shade on; to overshadow.
ombreggiatura, *n.f.* Shading.
ombrella, *n.f.* (*Bot.*) Umbel; (*colloq.*) umbrella.
ombrellaio [ombrellAio], *n.m.* Umbrella-maker.
ombrellata, *n.f.* Blow with an umbrella.
ombrellifere [ombrellIfere], *n.f.pl.* (*Bot.*) Umbelliferi.
ombrellino, *n.m.* Parasol, sunshade.
ombrello, *n.m.* Umbrella, sunshade.
ombrina, *n.f.* (*Zool.*) Sea-perch.
ombrometro [ombrOmetro], *n.m.* (*obs.*) Rain-gauge [cp. **pluviometro**].
ombrosamente, *adv.* Shadily; suspiciously.
ombrosità [-à], *n.f.* Irritability, shadiness, suspiciousness; touchiness.
ombroso, *a.* Shady; touchy, susceptible; restive (of a horse).
omega, *n.m.* Greek letter O.
omei [omEi], *n.m.pl.* Lamentation; cries of grief or woe.
omelia [omelIa], *n.f.* Homily.
omento, *n.m.* (*Anat.*) Omentum.
omeopaticamente, *adv.* Homeopathically.
omeopatia [omeopatIa], *n.f.* Homeopathy.
omeopatico [omeopAtico], *a.* Homeopathic.
omeopatista (*pl.* **omeopatisti**), *n.m.* Homeopathist.
omerale, *a.* (*Anat.*) Humeral.
omericamente, *adv.* Homerically.
omerico [omErico], *a.* Homeric; vast, huge.
Omero, *n.m.* Homer.
omero [Omero], *n.m.* (*Anat.*) Humerus; shoulder.
omertà [-à], *n.f.* (*Law*) Connivance.
omesso, *p.p.a.* Omitted, left out.
omettere [omEttere], *v.t.* To omit, to leave out, to pass over.
ometto, *n.m.* Little man [cp. **uomo**].
omiciattolo [omiciAttolo], *n.m.* Wretched little fellow.
omicida, *n.m.f. a.* Murderer, homicide; homicidal.

omicidio [omicIdio], *n.m.* Murder, homicide; manslaughter.
omino, *n.m.* Little man, manikin.
omissione, *n.f.* Omission, slip, error; gap. (*Comm.*) **Salvo errori ed omissioni,** E. & O.E.
omnibus [Omnibus], *n.m.* Omnibus, bus, motorbus; (*Rail.*) stopping train, slow train.
omo, *n.m.* (*colloq.*) Man [cp. **uomo**].
omofonia [omofonIa], *n.f.* Homophony, identity of sound.
omofono [omOfono], *a.* Homophonous.
omogeneamente, *adv.* Homogeneously.
omogeneità [-à], *n.f.* Homogeneity, homogeneousness.
omogeneo [omogEneo], *a.* Homogeneous; uniform.
omologamente, *adv.* Approvingly.
omologare, *v.t.* To approve, to confirm, to ratify.
omologazione, *n.f.* Approval, ratification.
omologia [omologIa], *n.f.* Approval.
omonimo [omOnimo], *n.m.a.* Homonym, namesake; homonymic.
omoplata, *n.m.* (*Anat.*) Shoulder-blade, scapula.
omosessuale, *n.m.a.* Homosexual.
omosessualismo, omosessualità [-à], *n.m.f.* Homosexuality.
omotetia [omotetIa], *n.f.* Like situation, a similar situation.
omotonia [omotonIa], *n.f.* Similarity of tone.
onagro, *n.m.* (*Zool.*) Onager.
onanismo, *n.m.* Onanism, masturbation.
onanista (*pl.* **onanisti**), *n.m.* Onanist, masturbator.
oncia [Oncia], *n.f.* Ounce. **A — a —,** little by little, gradually.
onciale, *a.* (*Hist.*) Uncial (writing).
oncino, *n.m.* Hook [cp. **uncino**].
oncologia [oncologIa], *n.f.* (*Med.*) Study of tumours.
oncoma, *n.f.* (*Med.*) Tumour.
oncotomia [oncotomIa], *n.f.* (*Med.*) Excision of a tumour.
onda, *n.f.* Wave (in all senses), billow, surge; undulation; (*Poet.*) sea, ocean. **Andare a onde,** to zigzag, to waver; **l'— della rivolta,** the tide of rebellion; **— luminosa,** light wave; **— sonora,** sound wave; (*Radio*) **lunghezza d'—,** wave-length; **onde lunghe, medie, corte,** long, medium, short wave-length.
ondante, *a.* Surging, brimming.
ondata, *n.f.* Surge, breaker; (*Mil.*) wave of storm troops. **— di caldo,** heat wave.
ondatra, *n.f.* (*Zool.*) Musk-rat.
onde, *adv.conj.pron.* Whence, wherefore; in order to; with which, by which, of which. **I mali — siamo afflitti,** the evils by which we are afflicted; **— io possa partire,** in order that I may go; **— vieni?** Where are you coming from?
ondechè, *adv.* Whence, therefore.
ondeggiamento, *n.m.* Waving, swinging; undulation, rolling.
ondeggiante, *a.* Tossing; wavering, hesitating.
ondeggiare, *v.i.* To roll, to wave, to toss, to undulate. **Le biade ondeggiavano al vento,** the ears of corn were waving in the wind.
ondisonante, *a.* Resounding with the waves.
ondosità [-à], *n.f.* Waviness.
ondoso, *a.* Wavy, billowy; rolling; stormy.
ondulamento, *n.m.* Undulation.
ondulare, *v.t.i.* To undulate, to toss, to roll. **— i capelli,** to wave the hair.
ondulato, *a.* Undulating, wavy.
ondulatorio [ondulatOrio], *a.* Undulatory.
ondulazione, *n.f.* Undulation, swell; waving. **— permanente,** permanent wave (hairdressing).
onerare, *v.t.* To burden; to load.
onerario [onerArio], *a.* Freight-carrying, bearing a load. **Nave oneraria,** cargo boat.
onere [Onere], *n.m.* Burden; responsibility, onus; (*Law*) charge.
oneroso, *a.* Burdensome, heavy, onerous.
onestà [-à], *n.f.* Honesty; honourableness, integrity; (*Poet.*) beauty, charm; modesty chastity. **Di provata —,** of tried integrity.
onestamente, *adv.* Honestly; fairly; virtuously.
onesto, *a.* Honest, upright, honourable; fair, equitable; decent, proper, virtuous; modest, chaste; courteous, polite; comely, fair. **Prezzi onesti,** reasonable prices; **accoglienze oneste e liete,** courteous and cheerful welcome; **giuoco —,** fair play.
onice [Onice], *n.m.* Onyx.
onisco, *n.m.* (*Zool.*) Wood-louse.
onninamente, *adv.* Altogether, utterly, entirely.
onnipossente, *n.m.a.* God, the Almighty; all-powerful.
onnipotente, *n.m.a.* God; omnipotent.
onnipotenza, *n.f.* Omnipotence.
onnipresente, *n.m.a.* Omnipresent.
onnisciente, *n.m.a.* Omniscient.
onniscienza, *n.f.* Omniscience.
onniveggente, *n.m.a.* All-seeing.
onnivoro [onnIvoro], *a.* Omnivorous.
onomastico [onomAstico], *n.m.* Patron saint's day; dictionary of names.
onomastico [onomAstico], *a.* Onomastic.
onomatopea [onomatopEa], *n.f.* Onomatopoeia.
onomatopeico [onomatopEico], *a.* Onomatopoeic.
ononide [onOnide], *n.f.* (*Bot.*) Rest-harrow.
onorabile, *a.* Honourable.
onorabilità, *n.f.* Honourableness.
onorabilmente, *adv.* Honourably.
onorando, *a.* Honourable.
onorantemente, *adv.* In an honouring way.
onoranza, *n.f.* Honour, tribute, celebration, homage, mark of esteem. **Le estreme onoranze,** the last honours.
onorare, *v.t.* To honour, to do honour to, to pay honour to; to celebrate; to confer honour upon.
onorario [onorArio], *n.m.a.* Honorarium, fee, stipend; honorary. **Socio —,** honorary member.
onorarsi, *v.r.* To pride oneself on, to deem it an honour; to have the honour to.
onoratamente, *adv.* Honourably.
onoratezza, *n.f.* Honourableness; respectability.
onorativo, *a.* Honouring, giving honour.
onorato, *a.* Honoured, honest, respected.
onore, *n.m.* Honour, distinction, rank, glory; integrity, rectitude, virtue; reputation, esteem, respect, credit; chastity. **Uscirne**

con —, to come off with credit; **parola d'—,** word of honour; **far —,** to do honour, to do justice; **con gli onori militari,** with military honours; **fare — alla firma,** to honour one's signature; **un punto d'—,** a point of honour; **ho l'— di informarvi,** I have the honour to inform you; **far gli onori di casa,** to receive guests; (*Theat.*) **serata d'—,** benefit performance.

onorevole [onorEvole], *a.* Honourable, respectable, respected. (*colloq.*) **È un —,** he's a (parliamentary) deputy.

onorevolezza, *n.f.* Honour, honourableness.

onorevolmente, *adv.* Honourably.

onorificamente, *adv.* Honorifically.

onorificenza, *n.f.* Honour, distinction, decoration. **Onorificenze di guerra,** war decorations.

onorifico [onorIfico], *a.* Carrying distinction, implying honour or respect.

onta, *n.f.* Shame, disgrace, affront, insult. **Ad — di,** in spite of.

ontaneto, *n.m.* Plantation of alders.

ontano, *n.m.* (*Bot.*) Alder.

ontogenesi [ontogEnesi], *n.f.* Ontogenesis.

ontologia [ontologIa], *n.f.* Ontology.

ontoso, *a.* Disgraceful, shame-making.

opacamente, *adv.* Opaquely; dully.

opaco, *a.* Opaque; impenetrable; dull.

opacità [-à], *n.f.* Opacity, opaqueness.

opale, *n.f.* Opal.

opalescente, *a.* Opalescent

opalino, *a.* Opaline.

opera [Opera], *n.f.* Work, action, performance, doing; institution; office of works; (*Theat.*) opera; (*Lit.*) work. **— pia,** charitable institution; **dare — a,** to see to, to attend to; **mettersi all'—,** to set to work; **opere complete di Boccaccio,** Boccaccio's complete works; **mano d'—,** labour; **mettere in —,** to set up, to bring into play; **all'—!** To work! (*Theat.*) **— comica, — buffa,** comic opera; **— lirica,** grand opera; **teatro dell'—,** opera-house.

operabile [operAbile], *a.* (*Med.*) Operable.

operaia [operAia], *n.f.* Workwoman, mill-girl.

operaio [operAio], *n.m.a.* Workman, labourer, worker; working. **Capo —,** foreman; **— a cottimo,** piece-worker; **casa operaia,** workman's dwelling.

operamento, *n.m.* Operation, operating.

operante, *a.* Operating, acting.

operare, *v.t.* To operate (in all senses); to work, to act, to perform.

operativamente, *adv.* Operatively, actively.

operativo, *a.* (*Med.*) Operative.

operato, *n.m.* Action, behaviour, conduct.

operato, *a.* (*Comm.*) Fancy. **Tela operata,** fancy material.

operatore, *n.m.* Operator (in all senses).

operatorio [operatOrio], *a.* (*Med.*) Operative.

operazione, *n.f.* Operation (in all senses); transaction. **Subire un'—,** to undergo an operation; (*Arith.*) **le quattro operazioni,** the four rules; (*Mil.*) **campo d'operazioni,** field of operations.

operculo [opErculo], *n.m.* (*Bot.Zool.*) Operculum.

operetta, *n.f.* (*Lit.*) Minor work; (*Mus.*) musical comedy, operetta.

operettista (*pl.* **operettisti**), *n.m.* Composer of musical comedies; comedian.

operosamente, *adv.* Actively, industriously.

operosità [-à], *n.f.* Industry, activity, laboriousness.

operoso, *a.* Active, industrious; requiring much labour.

opificio [opifIcio], *n.m.* Factory, mill, workshop; works.

opimo, *a.* Rich, fertile; bountiful, abundant. **Spoglie opime,** rich spoils.

opinabile [opinAbile], *a.* Questionable, doubtful; controversial.

opinabilmente, *adv.* Imaginably, conceivably; by way of opinion.

opinare, *v.i.* To think, to suppose, to opine, to deem; to be of the opinion.

opinione, *n.f.* Opinion (in all senses); judgment, conviction, belief, view. **— pubblica,** public opinion; **io sono d'— che,** I am of the opinion that; **condividere l'—,** to share the opinion.

opobalsamo [opobAlsamo], *n.m.* Balm of Gilead tree.

oppiaceo [oppiAceo], *n.m.* Opiate, narcotic.

oppiare, *v.t.* To mix opium; (*colloq.*) to drug.

oppiato, *n.m.* (*Med.*) Opiate.

oppilare, *v.t.* (*Med.*) To obstruct.

oppilativo, *a.* (*Med.*) Obstructive.

oppilazione, *n.f.* (*Med.*) Obstruction.

oppio [Oppio], *n.m.* Opium.

oppiofagia [oppiofagIa], *n.f.* Opium-eating.

oppiomane [oppiOmane], *n.m.* Opium addict, drug-fiend.

opponente, *n.m.a.* Opponent, antagonist; antagonistic, adverse.

opponimento, *n.m.* Opposition, opposing.

opporre, *v.t.* To oppose, to contrast, to set against; to refute, to resist, to refuse.

opporsi, *v.r.* To oppose, to be opposed, to withstand, to thwart; to set oneself against; to appeal against.

opportunamente, *adv.* Opportunely.

opportunismo, *n.m.* Opportunism.

opportunista (*pl.* **opportunisti**), *n.m.* Opportunist; time-server.

opportunità [-à], *n.f.* Opportunity, chance, occasion; expediency; appropriateness.

opportuno, *a.* Timely, well-timed, opportune; convenient, fit; advisable, proper, suitable. **Non mi pare —,** I don't think it advisable; **a tempo —,** at the right time, in due time.

oppositore, oppositrice, *n.m.f.* Opponent, opposer; adversary, antagonist.

opposizione, *n.f.* Opposition (in all senses); contrast; objection.

oppostamente, *adv.* Oppositely.

opposto, *n.m.a.* Opposite, contrary, reverse. **Tutto l'—,** quite the reverse, on the contrary; **la riva opposta,** the opposite bank; **in caso —,** in the contrary case.

oppressione, *n.f.* Oppression.

oppressivamente, *adv.* Oppressively, overbearingly.

oppressivo, *a.* Oppressive, crushing, overwhelming.

oppresso, *a.* Oppressed, overburdened, overwhelmed.

oppressore, *n.m.* Oppressor.

opprimente, *a.* Oppressing, heavy, crushing, grinding; close (of weather), suffocating

opprimere [opprImere], *v.t.* To oppress, to crush; to tyrannize; to overwhelm.
oppugnabile [oppugnAbile], *a.* Assailable, refutable.
oppugnabilità [-à], *n.f.* Assailability.
oppugnare, *v.t.* To assail; to oppugn, to oppose, to refute, to call in question.
oppugnatore, *n.m.* Assailer, refuter.
oppugnazione, *n.f.* Refutation; confutation.
oppure, *conj.* Or, or else.
opra, *n.f.* (*Poet.*) Day's work, payment for this, the worker himself.
oprante, *n.m.* (*Poet.*) Day labourer, journeyman.
oprare [cp. **operare**].
optare, *v.t.* To choose, to opt for.
opulento, *a.* Opulent, rich, wealthy; copious.
opulenza, *n.f.* Opulence, luxury.
opunzia [opUnzia], *n.f.* (*Bot.*) Cactus.
opuscolo [opUscolo], *n.m.* Booklet, pamphlet.
opzione, *n.f.* Option, choice.
or, *abbrev. for* **ora, orto. Or San Michele, orto San Michele.**
ora, *n.f.* Hour; time; present time. **Che — è?** What time is it? What is the time?; **di buon' —**, early (in the morning); **d'— in —**, from hour to hour, at any moment; **è — di finirla**, it's time to stop it; **l'— di accendere le luci**, lighting-up time; **— di chiusura**, closing time; **— ufficiale**, standard time; **— media di Greenwich**, Greenwich mean time; **— estiva, — legale**, summer time; **un' — fa**, an hour ago; **ore straordinarie**, over-time; **alla buon'—**, well and good; (*Radio*) **— per i piccoli**, children's hour; **non veder l'— di**, to be longing for.
ora, *adv.* Now, at present. **Or —**, just now; **per —**, for the present; **prima d'—**, before now; **proprio —**, just now; **fino ad —**, till now; **— dunque**, now then; **da — in avanti, in poi**, from henceforth; **— per sempre**, once for all.
oracoleggiare, *v.i.* To speak like an oracle, to give forth oracular remarks.
oracolo [orAcolo], *n.m.* Oracle, prophet, sage.
orafo [Orafo], *n.m.* Goldsmith.
orale, *a.* Oral; (*colloq.*) oral exam.
oralmente, *adv.* Orally, by word of mouth, verbally.
oramai, *adv.* Now, by this time, henceforward [cp. **ormai**].
orangutàn [-àn], *n.m.* (*Zool.*) Orang-utan.
orare, *v.i.* To pray [cp. **pregare**].
orario [orArio], *n.m.* Time-table, railway guide; roster, time-sheet. **In —**, punctual, in time; **— d'ufficio**, office hours.
orario [orArio], *a.* By the hour, per hour, horary. **Velocità oraria**, speed per hour; (*Radio*) **segnale —**, time-signal.
orata, *n.f.* (*Zool.*) Dorado, gilt-head.
oratore, *n.m.* Orator, speaker, public-speaker; master of rhetoric.
oratoria [oratOria], *n.f.* Oratory, eloquence.
oratoriamente, *adv.* Oratorically, in the manner of an orator.
oratoriano, *n.m.* (*Eccles.*) Oratorian.
oratorio (1) [oratOrio], *n.m.* (*Eccles.*) Oratory; (*Mus.*) oratorio.
oratorio (2) [oratOrio], *a.* Oratorical, oratorian.
oratrice, *n.f.* Woman speaker.
oratura, *n.f.* Gilding.
oraziano, *a.* Horatian, in the manner of Horace.
Orazio [orAzio], *n.m.* Horace.
orazione, *n.f.* Oration, speech, discourse, address; prayer. **Recitar le orazioni**, to say one's prayers.
orbaca, *n.f.* Berry of the laurel.
orbaco, *n.m.* (*Bot.*) Laurel.
orbare, *v.t.* To bereave, to deprive.
orbe, *n.m.* Orb, sphere; globe; world; orbit of a heavenly body.
orbene, *adv.* Well, now; well, then.
orbettino, *n.m.* (*Zool.*) Blind-worm.
orbetto, *n.m.* Little blind boy; (*Theat.*) the house, the audience.
orbezza, *n.f.* (*obs.*) Blindness.
orbicolare, *a.* Spherical, globular.
orbita [Orbita], *n.f.* Orbit (in all senses); limit. **Con gli occhi fuori dall'—**, with one's eyes starting out of one's head.
orbitale, *a.* Orbital.
orbo, *a.* Blind; deprived, bereft. (*colloq.*) **Botte da orbi**, a sound thrashing.
orca, *n.f.* (*Myth.*) Orc; (*Zool.*) grampus.
Orcadi [Orcadi], *n.f.pl.* (*Geog.*) The Orkney Islands.
orceolato, *a.* (*Bot.*) Pitcher-shaped.
orchessa, *n.f.* Ogress.
orchestra, *n.f.* Orchestra.
orchestrale, *a.* Orchestral.
orchestralmente, *adv.* Orchestrally.
orchestrare, *v.t.* To orchestrate.
orchestrazione, *n.f.* Orchestration.
orchestrina, *n.f.* Small orchestra.
orchidea [orchidEa], *n.f.* (*Bot.*) Orchid.
orchite, *n.f.* (*Med.*) Orchitis.
orciaia [orciAia], *n.f.* Room where jars are stored; cellar.
orciaio [orciAio], *n.m.* Maker or vendor of pitchers.
orcio [Orcio], *n.m.* Pitcher, jar, vase.
orciolaio [orciolAio], *n.m.* Potter.
orciolo, *n.m.* Pitcher, jug, jar.
orco, *n.m.* Ogre.
orda, *n.f.* Horde; mob, gang, crew.
ordigno, *n.m.* Tool, implement; mechanism, machine; contrivance.
ordinabile [ordinAbile], *a.* Capable of arrangement.
ordinale, *n.m.a.* (*Math.*) Ordinal.
ordinalmente, *adv.* Ordinally.
ordinamento, *n.m.* Order, disposition, arrangement; constitution; regulation, decree, ordinance.
ordinando, *n.m.* (*Eccles.*) Candidate for ordination.
ordinanza, *n.f.* Ordinance, regulation, decree; (*Mil.*) disposition; orderly, batman. **Ufficiale d'—**, orderly officer; **fuori —**, not in conformity with rules; **d'—**, according to rules; **l'—**, batman.
ordinare, *v.t.i.* To order, to command, to give orders, to direct; to dispose, to arrange, to set in order, to prepare; (*Eccles.*) to ordain. **— il pranzo**, to order dinner; **gli ordinai di andare**, I told him to go.
ordinariamente, *adv.* Ordinarily, usually.
ordinariato, *n.m.* Professorship; (*Eccles.*) bishopric.
ordinario [ordinArio], *n.m.* Bishop, ordinary, confessor; professor.

ordinario [ordinArio], *a.* Ordinary, normal, usual, accustomed; common, coarse, rough.
ordinarsi, *v.r.* To put oneself in order, to get ready.
ordinata, *n.f.* (*Geom.*) Ordinate.
ordinatamente, *adv.* In an ordered way, in orderly way, in order.
ordinatario [ordinatArio], *n.m.* (*Comm.*) Payee.
ordinativo, *a.* Regulating; (*Gram.*) ordinal.
ordinativo, *n.m.* Order. **— di consegna,** delivery order.
ordinato, *a.* Ordered, fixed, arranged; tidy, orderly, neat, trim; (*Eccles.*) ordained. **Una vita ordinata,** an orderly life; **una persona ordinata,** a tidy person.
ordinatore, ordinatrice, *n.m.f.* Organizer (of exhibitions, etc.); (*Eccles.*) ordainer.
ordinazione, *n.f.* Arrangement, disposition; prescription (for medicine, etc.). (*Comm.*) order; (*Eccles.*) ordination.
ordine [Ordine], *n.m.* Order, command; writ, decree, warrant; regulation, disposition, rule; class, category; (*Eccles.*) holy orders. **— del giorno,** agenda, order of the day; **dare gli ordini,** to give orders; **in buon —,** in good order; **parola d'—,** watch-word, password; **di prim'—,** first-rate, of the first order; **in — alfabetico,** in alphabetical order; **mettere in —,** to set in order; **— pubblico,** public order; **a nuovo —,** until further orders; **richiamare all'—,** to call to order; **— cavalleresco,** order of knighthood.
ordire, *v.t.* To lay the warp (of a loom); to plot, to intrigue, to scheme.
ordito, *n.m.* Warp; network; plotting (of maps, etc.). **Un — di menzogne,** a tissue of lies.
orditore, *n.m.* Warping-mill.
oreade [orEade], *n.f.* (*Myth.*) Oread, dryad, nymph.
orecchia, *n.f.* Ear, hearing [cp. **orecchio**].
orecchiabile [orecchiAbile], *a.* Catchy (of a tune); superficial, amateurish.
orecchiante, *n.m.* Person who plays or sings by ear; amateur; eavesdropper.
orecchiata, *n.f.* Blow on the ear; pull of the ear.
orecchietta, *n.f.* (*Anat.*) Auricle (of the heart).
orecchino, *n.m.* Ear-ring.
orecchio [orEcchio], *n.m.* Ear. **Esser tutto orecchi,** to be all ears; **duro d'orecchi,** hard of hearing; **aver — per la musica,** to have an ear for music; **prestar —,** to listen to; **far orecchie di mercante,** to turn a deaf ear; **con le orecchie basse,** crestfallen.
orecchione, *n.m.* Large ear; (*Mil.*) trunnion of a gun; (*Zool.*) species of bat.
orecchioni, *n.m.pl.* (*Med.*) Mumps.
orecchiuto, *a.* Long-eared.
orefice [orEfice], *n.m.* Goldsmith, jeweller.
oreficeria [oreficerIa], *n.f.* Goldsmith's or jeweller's shop; the wares sold there.
oreria [orerIa], *n.f.* Goldsmith's work.
oretta, *n.f.* Short hour, about an hour.
orezzo, *n.m.* Light breeze.
orfana, orfanella [Orfana], *n.f.* Orphan girl, female orphan.
orfano [Orfano], *n.m.a.* Orphan.
orfanello, *n.m.* Orphan boy.
orfanezza, *n.f.* Orphanhood.
orfanotrofio [orfanotrOfio], *n.m.* Orphanage.
Orfeo [orfEo], *n.m.* (*Myth.*) Orpheus.
orfico [Orfico], *a.* Orphic.
organaio [organAio], *n.m.* Organ-builder.
organamento, *n.m.* Organizing.
organare, *v.t.* To organize, to co-ordinate.
organdisse, *n.m.* Organdie (material).
organetto, *n.m.* Street-organ, barrel-organ. **Sonatore d'—,** organ-grinder.
organettista (*pl.* **organettisti**), *n.m.* Organ-grinder.
organicamente, *adv.* Organically; systematically.
organico [orgAnico], *a.* Organic, structural, fundamental. **Chimica organica,** organic chemistry.
organino, *n.m.* Accordion.
organismo, *n.m.* Organism, living structure.
organista (*pl.* **organisti**), *n.m.* Organist.
organizzamento, *n.m.* Organization.
organizzare, *v.t.* To organize, to set up, to arrange.
organizzarsi, *v.r.* To organize (into a party, etc.).
organizzatore, *n.m.* Organizer.
organizzazione, *n.f.* Organization; structure, arrangement.
organo [Organo], *n.m.* Organ (in all senses). **Gli organi vocali,** the vocal organs; **canne d'—,** organ-pipes; **— del partito liberale,** organ of the liberal party.
orgasmo, *n.m.* Orgasm; excitement.
orgia (*pl.* **orge**) [Orgia], *n.f.* Orgy, revel, drunken bout, debauch; profusion.
orgiastico [orgiAstico], *a.* Orgiastic, bacchanalian.
orgoglio [orgOglio], *n.m.* Pride; ostentation, boasting, haughtiness. **Nobile —,** noble pride.
orgogliosamente, *adv.* Proudly, haughtily.
orgoglioso, *a.* Proud, elated; haughty, boastful.
oricalco, *n.m.* (*Lit.*) Brass; trumpet.
orice [cp. **orige**].
orientale, *n.m.a.* Oriental.
orientalista (*pl.* **orientalisti**), *n.m.* Orientalist.
orientalmente, *adv.* Orientally.
orientamento, *n.m.* Orientation; direction, bearings.
orientarsi, *v.r.* To find one's bearings; to see what one is about.
orientazione, *n.f.* Orientation, direction, bearings.
oriente, *n.m.* East, orient. **L'estremo Oriente, il vicino Oriente,** the Far, Near East; **il Grande Oriente,** the Grand Orient (Masonic lodge).
orifiamma, *n.m.* Oriflamme; banner.
orifizio, orificio [orifIzio, orifIcio], *n.m.* Orifice; hole, aperture; mouth.
origano [orIgano], *n.m.* (*Bot.*) Marjoram.
orige, *n.m.* (*Zool.*) Oryx.
originale, *n.m.* Original, manuscript; queer person. **È un —,** he's an odd fellow.
originale, *a.* Original; first, primary; new, fresh, novel; odd, strange, queer, eccentric. **Peccato —,** original sin.
originalità [-à], *n.f.* Originality, novelty, freshness; inventiveness.

originalmente, *adv.* Originally.
originare, *v.t.i.* To originate, to derive, to proceed; to begin, to start.
originariamente, *adv.* In the beginning.
originario [originArio], *a.* Proceeding from, deriving from, originating; native. — **italiano,** of Italian extraction.
origine [orIgine], *n.f.* Origin; source, descent, derivation, extraction, birth. **Di alta —,** of high birth.
origliare, *v.i.* To eavesdrop; to spy.
origliere, *n.m.* Pillow.
orina, *n.f.* Urine.
orinale, *n.m.* Urinal, chamber-pot.
orinare, *v.i.* To urinate, to make water.
orinatoio [orinatOio], *n.m.* Public urinal, convenience.
orinatorio [orinatOrio], *a.* Urinary.
orinazione, *n.f.* Urination.
oriolaio [oriolAio], *n.m.* Watchmaker.
oriolo, *n.m.* (*obs.*) Watch [cp. **orologio**].
Orione, *n.m.* (*Myth. Astron.*) Orion.
oriundo, *a.* Originating, native. — **tedesco,** of German origin or extraction.
oriuolo [cp. **orologio**].
orizzontale, *a.* Horizontal, level, flat, plane.
orizzontalità [-à], *n.f.* Flatness, horizontalness.
orizzontalmente, *adv.* Horizontally.
orizzontare, *v.t.* To place horizontally.
orizzontarsi, *v.r.* To find one's bearings, to find the way; to grow accustomed.
orizzonte, *n.m.* Horizon. **All'—,** on the horizon.
Orlando, *n.m.* Roland.
orlare, *v.t.* To hem, to border, to edge.
orlatrice, *n.f.* Seamstress.
orlatura, *n.f.* Hemming, hem-stitching, edging, bordering.
orlo, *n.m.* Hem (of cloth, etc.); border, edge, brink. **Sull' — dell'abisso,** on the brink of the precipice; **sull'— della rovina,** on the verge of ruin; — **vivo,** sharp edge.
orma, *n.f.* Trace, footprint, footstep, track, mark. **Seguire le orme di,** to follow in the footsteps of.
ormai, *adv.* By now, by this time; at last; henceforth.
ormare, *v.t.* To follow the tracks of, to trail.
ormeggiamento, *n.m.* (*Naut.*) Dropping anchor; mooring.
ormeggiare, *v.t.* (*Naut.*) To moor, to cast anchor.
ormeggiarsi, *v.r.* To moor.
ormeggio [ormEggio], *n.m.* Mooring, moorings; hawser. (*Aviat.*) **Pilone d'—,** mooring-mast; (*Naut.*) — **di poppa,** stern-fast; — **di prua,** head-fast; — **di canapa,** hemp mooring hawser.
ormone, *n.m.* (*Physiol.*) Hormone.
ornamentale, *a.* Ornamental, decorative.
ornamentazione, *n.f.* Ornamentation.
ornamento, *n.m.* Ornament, decoration.
ornare, *v.t.* To adorn, to decorate, to deck, to embellish, to beautify.
ornatamente, *adv.* Ornately.
ornatezza, *n.f.* Ornateness.
ornato, *n.m.* Ornamental design, decoration; art of design.
ornatura, *n.f.* Ornamentation.
orneblenda, *n.f.* (*Min.*) Hornblende.
ornello, *n.m.* (*Bot.*) Flowering ash.
ornitologia [ornitologIa], *n.f.* Ornithology.
ornitologico [ornitolOgico], *a.* Ornithological.
ornitologo [ornitOlogo], *n.m.* Ornithologist.
ornitomanzia [ornitomanzIa], *n.f.* Ornithomancy, divination by watching birds' flight.
ornitorinco, *n.m.* (*Zool.*) Ornithorhynchus; duck-billed platypus.
orno [cp. **ornello**].
oro, *n.m.* Gold; money, wealth. — **puro,** pure gold; **vello d'—,** golden fleece; **età dell'—,** golden age; **moneta d'—,** gold coin; **miniera d'—,** gold-mine.
orobanche, *n.f.* (*Bot.*) Broom-rape.
orografia [orografIa], *n.f.* Orography, description of mountains.
orologeria [orologerIa], *n.f.* Watchmaking, watchmaker's shop.
orologiaio [orologiAio], *n.m.* Watch and clock maker.
orologio [orolOgio], *n.m.* Watch, clock, timepiece. — **da torre,** tower clock; — **a cariglione,** chiming clock; — **solare,** sundial; — **da polso,** wrist-watch; **il tuo — è indietro,** your watch is slow; **caricare l'—,** to wind up one's watch or clock.
oroscopo [orOscopo], *n.m.* Horoscope.
orpellamento, *n.m.* Tinselling.
orpellare, *v.t.* To tinsel.
orpellatura, *n.f.* Tinsel-work.
orpello, *n.m.* Tinsel.
orpimento, *n.m.* (*Min.*) Orpiment.
orrendamente, *adv.* Frightfully, horribly, hideously.
orrendo, *a.* Frightful, horrible, dreadful, hideous.
orrevole [orrEvole], *a.* (*obs.*) Honourable.
orribile [orrIbile], *a.* Horrible, dreadful, fearful, atrocious.
orribilità [-à], *n.f.* Dreadfulness.
orribilmente, *adv.* Horribly, dreadfully.
orridamente, *adv.* Horridly.
orridezza, *n.f.* Horror, atrocity.
orridità [-à], *n.f.* Horridness.
orrido [Orrido], *n.m.* Dreadful place, precipice, ravine.
orrido [Orrido], *a.* Horrid, dreadful, frightful, fearful.
orripilante, *a.* Hair-raising.
orripilazione, *n.f.* Gooseflesh.
orrore, *n.m.* Horror, dread, abomination, hideousness, atrocity. **Avere in —,** to detest, to loathe.
orsa, *n.f.* She-bear. (*Astron.*) — **maggiore, minore,** Great, Little Bear.
orsacchiotto, orsatto, *n.m.* Bear-cub.
orsino, *a.* Ursine, bearish.
orso, *n.m.* Bear. — **bruno,** brown bear; — **polare,** polar bear; — **grigio,** grizzly bear.
orsoio [orsOio], *n.m.* Twisted silk.
Orsola [Orsola], *n.f.* Ursula.
orsolina, *n.f.a.* Nun of or concerning the Ursuline Order.
orsù, *inter.* Well then! Come on!
ortaggi, *n.m.pl.* Pot-herbs, greens, vegetables.
ortaglia [ortAglia], *n.f.* Kitchen garden, vegetable garden; market-garden.
ortense, *a.* (*Lit.*) Pertaining to a garden.
ortensia [ortEnsia], *n.f.* (*Bot.*) Hydrangea.
ortica, *n.f.* (*Bot.*) Nettle; (*fig.*) stimulus.
orticaio [orticAio], *n.m.* Nettle-bed.

orticare, *v.t.* To sting.
orticaria [orticAria], *n.f.* (*Med.*) Nettle-rash.
orticarsi, *v.r.* To become nettled.
orticello, *n.m.* Small kitchen-garden, small garden.
orticheggiare, *v.t.* To sting with a nettle.
orticheto, *n.m.* Nettle-bed.
orticultore, *n.m.* Horticulturist.
orticultura, *n.f.* Horticulture; gardening.
ortivo, *a.* Garden, cultivated.
orto (1), *n.m.* Kitchen-garden; orchard. **— botanico,** botanical garden.
orto (2), *n.m.* (*obs.*) East, Levant; beginning; sunrise.
orto (3), *p.p.a.* (*obs.*) Risen.
ortodossamente, *adv.* In an orthodox way.
ortodossia [ortodossIa], *n.f.* Orthodoxy.
ortodosso. *a.* Orthodox.
ortogonale, *a.* (*Geom.*) Perpendicular.
ortogonalmente, *adv.* Perpendicularly.
ortogonio [ortogOnio], *n.m.* (*Geom.*) Rectangle.
ortografia [ortografIa], *n.f.* Orthography, spelling.
ortografico [ortogrAfico], *a.* Orthographic.
ortolano, *n.m* Greengrocer, market-gardener; (*Zool.*) ortolan.
ortopedia [ortopedIa], *n.f.* Orthopaedy.
ortopedico [ortopEdico], *n.m.a.* Orthopaedic surgeon; orthopaedic.
orvietano, *n.m.a.* Orvieto wine; of Orvieto.
orza, *n.f.* (*Naut.*) Weather halyard, luff-tackle; bowline. **A orza!** keep her close to the wind; **Orza!** Luff!
orzaiolo, *n.m.* (*Med.*) Sty in the eye.
orzare, *v.t.* (*Naut.*) To luff.
orzata (1), *n.f.* Barley-water.
orzata (2), *n.f.* (*Naut.*) Luff.
orzeggiare, *v.t.* (*Naut.*) To keep bearing to windward.
orzo, *n.m.* Barley. **— brillato,** hulled barley.
Osanna, *n.m.* Hosanna; shout of praise; acclamation.
osannare, *v.i.* To sing hosannas, to sing hymns of praise.
osare, *v.i.* To dare; to risk; to venture, to be bold enough. **Oso sperare che,** I venture to hope that; **egli non osava,** he didn't dare.
oscenamente, *adv.* Obscenely.
oscenità [-à], *n.f.* Obscenity, indecency.
osceno, *a.* Obscene, indecent.
oscillare, *v.i.* To oscillate, to swing, to vibrate; to fluctuate, to waver, to hesitate.
oscillatorio [oscillatOrio], *a.* Oscillatory.
oscillazione, *n.f.* Oscillation.
oscitante, *a.* Uncertain of purpose.
oscitanza, *n.f.* (*obs.*) Hesitation, negligence.
osco, *n.m.a.* Oscan.
osculazione, *n.f.* Osculation, kissing.
oscuramente, *adv.* Obscurely.
oscuramento, *n.m.* Darkening, obscuration; black-out (in wartime).
oscurantismo, *n.m.* Obscurantism.
oscurantista (*pl.* **oscurantisti**), *n.m.* Obscurantist.
oscurare, *v.t.* To darken, to dim, to obscure; to eclipse.
oscurarsi, *v.r.* To grow dark; to be overcast.
oscurazione, *n.f.* Darkening, obscuration.
oscurezza, *n.f.* Obscureness [cp. **oscurità**].
oscurità [-à], *n.f.* Darkness, obscurity, dimness.
oscuro, *a.* Dark, obscure; dim; mysterious; doubtful; unknown, humble (birth, etc.). **Essere all'—,** to be in the dark (*lit.* & *fig.*); (*Photo.*) **camera oscura,** dark-room; **senso —,** obscure meaning.
Osiride [osIride], *n.m.* Osiris.
osmano, *a.* Turkish.
osmio [Osmio], *n.m.* (*Min.*) Osmium.
osmosi, *n.f.* (*Med.*) Osmosis.
ospedale, *n.m.* Hospital, infirmary. **— da campo,** field dressing-station; **nave —,** hospital ship; **entrare all'—,** to go to hospital.
ospitale, *a.* Hospitable.
ospitaliere, *a.* Pertaining to a hospital.
Ospitalieri, *n.m.pl.* The Knights Hospitallers of Malta.
ospitalità [-à], *n.f.* Hospitality.
ospitalmente, *adv.* Hospitably.
ospitare, *v.t.* To give hospitality, to entertain; (*colloq.*) to put up for the night; to shelter.
ospite [Ospite], *n.m.* Host (who gives hospitality); guest (who receives it).
ospizio [ospIzio], *n.m.* Hostel, hospice; almshouse, home (institution). **— marino,** seaside holiday home (for children); **— di mendicità,** workhouse.
ossa, *n.f.pl.* Bones [cp. **osso**].
ossalato, *n.m.* (*Chem.*) Oxalate.
ossalico [ossAlico], *a.* (*Chem.*) Oxalic.
ossalite, *n.f.* (*Min.*) Oxalite.
ossame, *n.m.* Pile of bones, quantity of bones.
ossario [ossArio], *n.m.* Charnel-house, ossuary.
ossatura, *n.f.* Skeleton; rib-work (of a ship); frame, framework; hull (of a ship).
ossecrare, *v.t.* (*Lit.*) To implore, to beseech, to obsecrate.
osseina, *n.f.* (*Chem.*) Osseine.
osseo [Osseo], *a.* Osseous, bony.
ossequente, *a.* Obedient, submissive, yielding; obsequious. **— alle leggi,** law-abiding.
ossequiare, *v.t.* To pay homage to, to greet, to pay respects to.
ossequio [ossEquio], *n.m.* Homage, respect, regard. **I migliori ossequi,** kindest regards.
ossequiosamente, *adv.* Obsequiously.
ossequiosità [-à], *n.f.* Obsequiousness.
ossequioso, *a.* Obsequious, respectful.
osservabile [osservAbile], *a.* Observable.
osservabilmente, *adv.* Observably.
osservandissimo [osservandIssimo], *a.* (*obs.*) Title of respect, most worthy.
osservante, *n.m.a.* Observant; (*Eccles.*) **Minori Osservanti,** strict followers of the Franciscan Rule.
osservanza, *n.f.* Observance, compliance; fulfilment, performance; regard; the rule of the Minori Osservanti. **Con perfetta —,** I remain respectfully yours.
osservare, *v.t.* To observe, to note, to notice, to remark; to consider, to watch, to see. **Far —,** to draw one's attention; **— la domenica,** to observe Sunday.
osservatamente, *adv.* Attentively, observingly.
osservato, *p.p.a.* Observed, noted, considered.
osservatore, osservatrice, *n.m.f.* Observer; onlooker, spectator.

osservatorio [osservatOrio], *n.m.* Observatory; (*Mil.*) observation post.
osservazione, *n.f.* Observation; observance; remark, comment, note; reflection, censure, reproach. **Spirito d'—,** power of observation; **fare un'—,** to make a remark.
ossessionare, *v.t.* To obsess, to worry.
ossessionato, *n.m.* One obsessed, in a state of exaltation.
ossessione, *n.f.* Obsession.
ossesso, *n.m.* Victim of obsessions.
ossesso, *p.p.a.* Obsessed, possessed.
ossetto, *n.m.* (*Anat.*) Small bone (esp. of the ear).
ossia [ossIa], *conj.* Or, or rather; that is to say; in fact.
ossiacanta, *n.f.* (*Bot.*) Thorn bush.
ossianico [ossiAnico], *a.* Pertaining to the works of Ossian.
ossicino, *n.m.* Small bone.
ossidabile [ossidAbile], *a.* Oxidizable.
ossidare, *v.t.* To oxidize.
ossidarsi, *v.r.* To become oxidized.
ossidazione, *n.f.* Oxidization.
ossidiana, *n.f.* (*Min.*) Obsidian.
ossidionale, *a.* (*Hist.*) Obsidional, referring to the crown given by the Romans to one who relieved a besieged city.
ossido [Ossido], *n.m.* (*Chem.*) Oxide.
ossidrico [ossIdrico], *a.* (*Chem.*) Oxyhydrogen. **Cannello —,** oxyhydrogen blowlamp.
ossifero [ossIfero], *a.* (*Geol.*) Containing fossilized bones.
ossigenare, *v.t.* To oxygenate; to peroxide (hair).
ossigenazione, *n.f.* Oxygenization.
ossigeno [ossIgeno], *n.m.* (*Chem.*) Oxygen.
ossitono [ossItono], *a.* (*Poet.*) Oxytone.
osso (*pl.* **ossi,** *m.,* **ossa,** *f.*), *n.m.* Bone; fruit stone. **Fino all'—,** to the bone; **bagnato fino all'ossa,** wet through to the skin; **— sacro,** sacrum; **— buco,** marrow-bone: **— di balena,** whalebone; **rompersi l'— del collo,** to break one's neck; **in carne ed ossa,** flesh and blood, in person.
ossoso, *a.* Bony.
ossuario [ossuArio], *n.m.* Cinerary urn.
ossuto, *a.* Bony; lean; strong.
osta, *n.f.* (*Naut.*) Stay (of rigging). (*Law*) **Nulla osta,** permit, pass; consent.
ostacolare, *v.t.* To hinder, to oppose, to impede, to obstruct; to interfere with. **— il passaggio,** to obstruct the passage.
ostacolo [ostAcolo], *n.m.* Obstacle, impediment, hindrance, handicap. **Rimuovere un —,** to remove an obstacle; **corsa a ostacoli,** obstacle-race; steeple-chase.
ostaggio [ostAggio], *n.m.* Hostage. **In —,** as a hostage.
ostante, *adv.* **Ciò non —,** nonetheless.
ostare, *v.i.* To impede, to be in the way, to form an obstacle, to oppose.
oste (1), *n.m.* Innkeeper, landlord, host. **Fare i conti senza l'—,** to reckon without one's host.
oste (2), *n.f.* (*Lit.*) Army, host. **L'— nemica,** the enemy hosts.
osteggiare, *v.t.* To oppose, to be hostile to, to obstruct.
osteggiatore, osteggiatrice, *n.m.f.a.* Adversary, enemy; hostile, unfriendly.
osteite, *n.f.* (*Med.*) Osteitis.
ostello, *n.m.* (*Poet.*) Abode, dwelling, house; refuge. **— della gioventù,** youth hostel.
ostensibile [ostensIbile], *a.* Ostensible; professed.
ostensibilmente, *adv.* Ostensibly.
ostensivamente, *adv.* Demonstrably.
ostensivo, *a.* Demonstrable, ostensible.
ostensore, *n.m.* Exhibitor.
ostensorio [ostensOrio], *n.m.* (*Eccles.*) Monstrance.
ostentamento, *n.m.* Parade, showing-off.
ostentare, *v.t.* To show off, to parade, to exhibit; to boast.
ostentatore, ostentatrice, *n.m.f.a.* Boaster, ostentatious person; ostentatious, boastful.
ostentazione, *n.f.* Ostentation, boasting; affectation, pretence.
osteologia [osteologIa], *n.f.* (*Anat.*) Osteology.
osteria [osterIa], *n.f.* Inn, tavern; public-house.
ostessa, *n.f.* Hostess, landlady (of an inn).
ostetrica [ostEtrica], *n.f.* Midwife.
ostetricamente, *adv.* Obstetrically.
ostetricia [ostetrIcia], *n.f.* Obstetrics, midwifery.
ostetrico [ostEtrico], *n.m.a.* Obstetrician, gynaecologist; obstetrical.
ostia [Ostia], *n.f.* (*Eccles.*) The Host; consecrated wafer; wafer (for sealing letters, etc.); sacrificial victim.
ostiario [ostiArio], *n.m.* (*Eccles.*) Door-keeper.
ostichezza, *n.f.* Irksomeness.
ostico [Ostico], *a.* Irksome; repulsive, unpalatable; difficult; harsh.
ostile, *a.* Hostile, inimical, unfriendly, adverse.
ostilità [-à], *n.f.* Hostility, opposition; aversion.
ostilmente, *adv.* Inimically, in a hostile way.
ostinarsi, *v.r.* To grow obstinate, to be obstinate; to persist in, to insist on, to cling to. **Si ostina a rifiutare,** he persists in refusing.
ostinatamente, *adv.* Obstinately, persistently.
ostinatezza, ostinazione, *n.f.* Obstinacy, stubbornness, pig-headedness; persistence.
ostinato, *a.* Obstinate, stubborn, pig-headed.
ostolare, *v.i.* To hanker after.
ostracismo, *n.m.* Ostracism. **Dare l'— a,** to taboo.
ostracizzare, *v.t.* To ostracize, to exclude; to banish.
ostralega [ostrAlega], *n.f.* (*Zool.*) Oyster-catcher.
ostrica [Ostrica], *n.f.* (*Zool.*) Oyster.
ostricaio, ostricaro [ostricAio], *n.m.* Oyster-bed; oyster-seller.
ostricultura, *n.f.* Oyster-culture.
ostro, *n.m.* (*Lit.*) Purple; south wind; south.
ostrogoto, *n.m.a.* Ostrogoth; (*fig.*) Goth, vandal, barbarian.
ostruente, *a.* Obstructing, obstructive; (*Med.*) obstruent.
ostruimento, *n.m.* Obstruction.
ostruire, *v.t.* To obstruct, to block up; to hinder. **— il passaggio,** to obstruct the passage.
ostruttivo, *a.* Obstructive.
ostruzione, *n.f.* Obstruction, hindrance; impediment, stoppage.

ostruzionismo, *n.m.* (*Pol.*) Obstructionism.
ostruzionista (*pl.* **ostruzionisti**), *n.m.* Obstructionist.
otalgia [otalgIa], *n.f.* (*Med.*) Earache, otalgia.
otarda, *n.f.* (*Zool.*) Bustard.
otaria [otAria], *n.f.* (*Zool.*) Sea-lion.
Otello, *n.m.* Othello.
otite, *n.f.* (*Med.*) Otitis.
otoiatria [otoiatrIa], *n.f.* (*Med.*) Otology, study of the diseases of the ear.
otre, *n.m.* Goat-skin wine-bottle, wine-skin; (*fig.*) drunkard.
otta, *n.f.* (*obs.*) Hour.
ottacordo, *n.m.* (*Mus.*) Ancient 8-stringed instrument.
ottaedro, *n.m.* (*Geom.*) Octahedron.
ottagono [ottAgono], *n.m.* Octagon.
ottagonale, *a.* Octagonal.
ottangolare, *a.* Octangular.
ottano, *n.m.* (*Chem.*) Octane.
ottanta, *a.* Eighty.
ottantamila, *a.* Eighty thousand.
ottantenne, *a.* Eighty years old.
ottantesimo [ottantEsimo], *n.m.a.* Eightieth.
ottantina, *n.f.* Eighty, four-score. **Ha passato l'—,** he's over eighty.
ottarda, *n.f.* (*Zool.*) Great bustard.
ottare [cp. **optare**].
ottativamente, *adv.* Optatively.
ottativo, *a.* (*Gram.*) Optative (mood).
ottava, *n.f.* Octave; (*Poet.*) stanza of eight lines.
ottavino, *n.m.* (*Mus.*) Octave-flute, piccolo.
Ottavio [ottAvio], *n.m.* Octavius.
ottavo, *n.m.a.* Eighth; (*Print.*) octavo; (*Mus.*) octave.
ottemperanza, *n.f.* Obedience, compliance.
ottemperare, *v.i.* To obey, to comply with.
ottenebramento, *n.m.* Darkening, obscuration.
ottenebrare, *v.t.* To darken, to obscure.
ottenebrarsi, *v.r.* To become darkened, to cloud over, to get dim.
ottenebrazione, *n.f.* Darkening.
ottenere, *v.t.* To obtain, to gain, to acquire, to secure; to reach, to win. **— il proprio scopo,** to reach one's goal; **far —,** to procure (something).
ottenibile [ottenIbile], *a.* Obtainable.
ottenimento, *n.m.* Getting, acquisition.
ottenne, *a.* Eight years old.
ottennio [ottEnnio], *n.m.* Period of eight years.
Ottentotto, *n.m.* Hottentot.
ottetto, *n.m.* (*Mus.*) Octet.
ottica [Ottica], *n.f.* Optics.
ottico [Ottico], *n.m.a.* Optician; optical. **Effetto —,** light effect.
ottimamente, *adv.* Very well, very good, excellently, admirably.
ottimate, *n.m.* Dignitary, person of importance.
ottimismo, *n.m.* Optimism.
ottimista (*pl.* **ottimisti**), *n.m.* Optimist.
ottimistico [ottimIstico], *a.* Optimistic.
ottimo [Ottimo], *n.m.a.* Best; excellent, perfect; capital, first-rate.
otto, *a.* Eight; eighth. **Domani —,** tomorrow week.
ottobrata, *n.f.* October excursion.
ottobre, *n.m.* Month of October.
ottobrino, *a.* Of the month of October.
ottocentesimo [ottocentEsimo], *a.* Eight hundredth.
ottocentismo, *n.m.a.* Nineteenth century (in Art and Literature).
ottocento, *n.m.a.* Eight hundred; the Nineteenth Century.
ottomana, *n.f.* Ottoman, sofa, settee.
ottomano, *n.m.a.* Ottoman, Turk; Turkish.
ottomila, *a.* Eight thousand.
ottonaio [ottonAio], *n.m.* Brass-worker.
ottoname, *n.m.* Brass-ware.
ottonario [ottonArio], *n.m.a.* (*Poet.*) Verse of eight syllables.
ottone, *n.m.* Brass. (*Mus.*) **Gli ottoni,** the brass, brass instruments
ottopode [ottOpode], *n.m.* (*Zool.*) Octopod.
ottuagenario [ottuagenArio], *n.m.a.* Octogenarian.
ottundere [ottUndere], *v.t.* To blunt, to deaden, to dull, to numb; to enfeeble, to weaken.
ottuplo [Ottuplo], *a.* Eightfold.
otturamento, *n.m.* Blocking up.
otturare, *v.t.* To block up, to stop up, to plug, to bung; to obturate; to stop (a tooth).
otturatore, *n.m.* Obturator; (*Phot.*) shutter; (*Mil.*) breech-block.
otturazione, *n.f.* Obturation, plugging.
ottusamente, *adv.* Obtusely.
ottusangolo [ottusAngolo], *a.* Obtuse-angled.
ottusità [-à], *n.f.* Obtuseness, bluntness, dullness.
ottuso, *a.* Obtuse (in all senses); blunt, dull, slow-witted.
ovaia [ovAia], *n.f.* (*Anat.*) Ovary.
ovaio [ovAio], *n.m.* Egg-dealer.
ovaio [ovAio], *a.* Good layer (of eggs).
ovaiolo, *n.m.* Egg-cup.
ovale, *a.* Oval. (*Football*) **Palla —,** Rugby ball.
ovalità [-à], *n.f.* Ovalness.
ovario [ovArio], *n.m.* (*Bot. Anat.*) Ovary.
ovariotomia [ovariotomIa], *n.f.* (*Med.*) Ovariotomy.
ovarite, *n.f.* (*Bot.*) Ovaritis.
ovato, *a.* (*obs.*) Oval, ovate.
ovatta, *n.f.* Cotton-wool, wadding, padding.
ovattare, *v.t.* To wad, to stuff with wadding.
ovazione, *n.f.* Ovation.
ove, *adv.* Where; whilst; whereas. **Ove che sia,** anywhere.
ovest, *n.m.* West.
Ovidio [ovIdio], *n.m.* Ovid.
ovidotto, *n.m.* (*Anat.*) Oviduct.
oviforme, *a.* Egg-shaped, oviform.
ovile, *n.m.* Sheepfold, pen; fold.
ovino, *a.* Ovine, of sheep.
oviparo [ovIparo], *a.* Oviparous.
ovo [cp. **uovo**].
ovoidale, *a.* Ovoidal.
ovoide [ovOide], *n.m.* Ovoid.
ovolo [Ovolo], *n.m.* (*Arch.*) Ovolo; (*Bot.*) egg mushroom.
ovoviviparo [ovovivIparo], *a.* Ovoviviparous.
ovulare, *a.* Ovular.
ovulazione, *n.f.* (*Anat.*) Ovulation.
ovulo [Ovulo], *n.m.* (*Anat.*) Ovule, ovum.
ovunque, *adv.* Everywhere; anywhere; on all sides.
ovveramente, *adv.* Truly.
ovvero, *conj.* Or, or indeed, or else; otherwise.

ovvia! *inter.* Oh, come! [cp. **orsù**].
ovviamente, *adv.* Obviously.
ovviare, *v.t.* To obviate, to avoid, to prevent; to remove.
ovvio [Ovvio], *a.* Obvious, plain, clear, manifest.
oziare, ozieggiare, *v.i.* To idle, to trifle, to lounge, to loaf, to be lazy.
ozio [Ozio], *n.m.* Idleness, sluggishness, inaction; (*Lit.*) leisure.
oziosaggine [oziosAggine], *n.f.* Idleness, sluggishness.
oziosamente, *adv.* Idly.
oziosità [-à], *n.f.* Idleness; idle talk.
ozioso, *a.* Idle, inactive, unemployed; lazy; (*Comm.*) uninvested (capital).
ozonizzare, *v.t.* To ozonize.
ozonizzatore, *n.m.* Ozonizer.
ozono, *n.m.* (*Chem.*) Ozone.
ozonometro [ozonOmetro], *n.m.* Ozonometer.

P

P, p, *n.m.* Fourteenth letter of the Italian alphabet.
pabolo [pAbolo], *n.m.* (*Lit.*) Pabulum, food.
pacatamente, *adv.* Quietly, peaceably, staidly, calmly, placidly.
pacatezza, *n.f.* Staidness, calmness, quietness.
pacato, *a.* Staid, calm, sober, placid, demure.
pacca, *n.f.* Slap, blow (with the open hand).
paccheo [pacchEo], *n.m.* (*colloq.*) Silly fellow.
pacchetto, *n.m.* Packet, small parcel.
pacchia [pAcchia], *n.f.* Food; good eating and drinking.
pacchiamento, *n.m.* Guzzling.
pacchiano, *n.m.* A cad; *a.* caddish, vulgar.
pacchiare, *v.i.* To guzzle, to eat voraciously.
pacchierone, *n.m.* Big, stout fellow.
pacchina, *n.f.* Slap on the back of the head.
pacciame, *n.m.* Dead leaves, twigs, etc.
pacco, *n.m.* Parcel, packet; bundle; package. **Spedire per — postale,** to send by parcel post.
paccottiglia [paccottIglia], *n.f.* Trumpery wares, shoddy goods, trash.
pace, *n.f.* Peace, calm, tranquillity, stillness; silence. **Lasciare in —,** to leave alone; **non darsi —,** to give oneself no peace; **metter —,** to make peace; **con vostra buona —,** by your leave; **conferenza della —,** peace conference; (*Sport*) **siamo —,** we have drawn (the game).
pachiderma, *n.m.* (*Zool.*) Pachyderm.
paciere, *n.m.* Peacemaker.
pacificabile [pacificAbile], *a.* Reconcilable.
pacificamente, *adv.* Pacifically.
pacificamento, *n.m.* Pacification.
pacificare, *v.t.* To pacify; to reconcile, to appease.
pacificarsi, *v.r.* To be reconciled (with one another).
pacificatore, pacificatrice, *n.m.f.* Peacemaker, pacifier.
pacificazione, *n.f.* Pacification.
pacifico [pacIfico], *a.* Peaceful, pacific, conciliatory; calm, tranquil. **L'Oceano Pacifico,** the Pacific Ocean.
pacifismo, *n.m.* Pacifism.
pacifista (*pl.* **pacifisti**), *n.m.* Pacifist.
pacioccone, pacione, *n.m.* Good-natured fellow, jovial and fat man.
padella, *n.f.* Frying-pan, pan; bed-pan, warming-pan. **Cader dalla — nella brace,** to fall from the frying-pan into the fire.
padellata, *n.f.* Panful; blow with a frying-pan.
padellina, *n.f.* Small frying-pan; glass ring to catch candle-drips.
padiglione, *n.m.* Pavilion; tent; shelter; exhibition building. (*Anat.*) **— dell'orecchio,** ear-lap.
Padova [pAdova], *n.f.* (*Geog.*) Padua.
padovano, *n.m.a.* Paduan.
padre, *n.m.* Father; parent. **Il Santo Padre,** the Holy Father, the Pope; **Padre Eterno,** God; (*Theat.*) **— nobile,** heavy father; **i padri,** one's forefathers.
padreggiare, *v.i.* To take after one's father.
padrigno, *n.m.* Step-father.
padrino, *n.m.* God-father; second (in a duel).
padrona, *n.f.* Mistress, landlady; proprietress. **— di casa,** landlady.
padronale, *a.* Patronal, belonging to the master. **Carrozza —,** private carriage.
padronanza, *n.f.* Mastery, command; self-restraint, self-control.
padronato, *n.m.* Possession (of property, etc.).
padroncino, *n.m.* Young master; owner's son.
padrone, *n.m.* Master, owner; chief, principal, manager; employer, boss. **— di casa,** landlord; **esser — di sè,** to have self-control; **ognuno è — di pensare a modo suo,** everyone has the right to think as he likes.
padroneggiare, *v.t.* To domineer, to master; to control, to rule.
padroneggiarsi, *v.r.* To control oneself, to exercise self-control.
padronesco, *a.* Masterful.
padule, *n.m.* Marsh [cp. **palude**].
paesaggio [paesAggio], *n.m.* Landscape; scenery, view.
paesano, *n.m.a.* Peasant, rustic.
paese, *n.m.* Country, region, land; village, little town. **Tutto il mondo è —,** men are the same all the world over; **— nativo,** native place; **di che — siete ?** Which country are you from?; (*colloq.*) **mandare a quel —,** to send to the devil.
paesello, *n.m.* Village.
paesista (*pl.* **paesisti**), *n.m.* Landscape painter.
paesistico [paesIstico], *a.* Pertaining to scenery.
paesone, *n.m.* Large village.
paf! paffe! paffete [pAffete], *inter.* Bang!
paffutello, *a.* Bonny (of a child).
paffuto, *a.* Plump; fleshy; chubby.
paffutezza, *n.f.* Plumpness.
Pafo, *n.m.* (*Geog.*) Paphos.
paga, *n.f.* Pay, wages, salary. **Giorno di —,** pay-day; **mezza —,** half-pay; **busta —,** pay-packet; **foglio di —,** pay-roll.
pagabile [pagAbile], *a.* Payable.
pagaia [pagAia], *n.f.* Canoe paddle.
pagamento, *n.m.* Payment, pay. **— alla consegna,** payment on delivery, C.O.D.; **— rateale,** payment by instalments.

paganamente, *adv.* Heathenishly, in a pagan way.
paganeggiare, *v.i.* To act or think in a pagan way.
paganesimo [paganEsimo], *n.m.* Paganism, heathendom.
paganizzare, *v.t.* To make a pagan of, to paganize.
pagano, *n.m.a.* Pagan, heathen.
pagare, *v.t.* To pay; to settle, to liquidate; to reward; to stand (drinks). **— il fio,** to pay the penalty; **— un occhio,** to pay through the nose; **— in contanti,** to pay cash; **paga e porta via,** cash and carry; **farsi —,** to get paid, to get one's due; (*fig.*) **— di persona,** to make a personal sacrifice.
pagatore, pagatrice, *n.m.f.* Payer; paymaster.
pagella, *n.f.* School report.
paggetto, *n.m.* Page-boy, buttons.
paggio [pAggio], *n.m.* Page, valet.
pagherò [-ò], *n.m.* (*Comm.*) Promissory note, I.O.U.
pagina [pAgina], *n.f.* Page, leaf (of a book). **Voltar —,** to turn the page, to turn over a new leaf.
paginatura, *n.f.* Pagination, paging.
paglia [pAglia], *n.f.* Straw; chaff. **Uomo di —,** man of straw; **cappello di —,** straw-hat; **fuoco di —,** a nine days' wonder.
pagliaccesco, *a.* Clownish, foolish.
pagliacciata, *n.f.* Buffoonery.
pagliaccio [pagliAccio], *n.m.* Clown, buffoon; charlatan.
pagliaio [pagliAio], *n.m.* Pile of straw; haystack. **Cane da —,** watch-dog.
pagliardo, *n.m.* Libertine, dissolute fellow.
pagliato, *a.* Straw-coloured.
paglericcio [paglierIccio], *n.m.* Palliasse, straw mattress.
paglierino, *a.* Straw-coloured, yellowish.
paglieto, *n.m.* Reed-bed.
paglietta, *n.f.* Straw-hat; (*colloq.*) petty lawyer.
paglietto, *n.m.* Straw-mat; (*Naut.*) fender, collision-mat.
pagliuca, pagliuzza, *n.f.* Speck of straw, mote, particle of dust.
pagnotta, *n.f.* Loaf (of bread); (*fig.*) pay, wages; (*Mil.*) ration bread.
pagnottella, *n.f.* Little loaf.
pagnottista (*pl.* **pagnottisti**), *n.m.* (*colloq.*) Man who works for his wages only; potboiler; hireling.
pago, *n.m.* (*Hist.*) Village, rural district.
pago, *a.* Satisfied, pleased, contented.
pagoda, *n.f.* Pagoda.
paguro, *n.m.* (*Zool.*) Hermit-crab.
paio (*pl.* **paia** *f.*) [pAio], *n.m.* Pair, couple, brace. **Fare il —,** to be matched; **un — d'ore,** a couple of hours; **è un altro — di maniche,** that's quite another matter.
paiolata, *n.f.* Potful, boilerful.
paiolina, *n.f.* Urn (for tea, etc.).
paiolino, *n.m.* Small boiler; (*colloq.*) bowler hat.
paiolo, paiuolo, *n.m.* Boiler, copper, cauldron; kettle.
pala, *n.f.* Shovel; blade (of oar, propeller, etc.); altar-piece.
paladinesco, *a.* After the style of the paladins.
paladino, *n.m.* Paladin, knight-errant; champion.
palafitta, *n.f.* Pile-dwelling, pile-embankment.
palafittare, *v.t.* To drive piles, to strengthen with piles.
palafreniere, *n.m.* Groom; footman; (*Hist.*) squire.
palafreno, *n.m.* Palfrey, saddle-horse.
palagio [palAgio], *n.m.* (*Lit.*) Palace [cp. **palazzo**].
palamento, *n.m.* Oars of a boat.
palamidone, *n.m.* (*colloq.*) Frock-coat; (*fig.*) tall, pompous fellow.
palamite, *n.f.* (*Fishing*) Paternoster; long-line.
palanca, *n.f.* Stake; plank; girder; (*colloq.*) ha'penny; money.
palanchino, *n.m.* Palanquin.
palanco, *n.m.* Roller for moving heavy weights; tackle; gear for launching ships.
palancone, *n.m.* (*colloq.*) Penny.
palandra, *n.f.* (*Naut.*) Monitor; lateen-rigged vessel; (*colloq.*) long coat.
palandrana, *n.f.* Shabby, long coat.
palare, *v.t.* To stake (a plant, etc.); to drive in stakes.
palata, *n.f.* Stroke (with an oar); shovelful; blow with a shovel.
palatale, *a.* (*Anat.*) Palatal.
palatina, *n.f.* Fur tippet.
palatino, *n.m.a.* Palatine.
palatizzare, *v.t.* To palatalize.
palato, *n.m.* (*Anat.*) Palate; sense of taste, taste.
palatura, *n.f.* Staking, palissading.
palazzina, *n.f.* Small palace; villa; country mansion.
palazzo, *n.m.* Palace; mansion, palatial house; (*colloq.*) large tenement dwelling; big block of flats.
palazzotto, *n.m.* Country house; manor house, villa.
palchettista, palchista (*pl.* **palchettisti, palchisti**), *n.m.* (*Theat.*) Box-holder.
palchetto, *n.m.* (*Theat.*) Box; stand, shelf; scaffolding.
palco, *n.m.* Stand, stage, platform; scaffold; (*Theat.*) box, stall. **— di proscenio,** stage-box.
palcoscenico [palcoscEnico], *n.m.* (*Theat.*) Stage.
paleo [palEo], *n.m.* Top, whipping-top, peg-top; (*Bot.*) dog-grass.
paleografia [paleografIa], *n.m.* Palaeography.
paleografico [paleogrAfico], *a.* Palaeographic.
paleografo [paleOgrafo], *n.m.* Palaeographer.
paleolitico [paleolItico], *a.* Palaeolithic.
paleontologia [paleontologIa], *n.f.* Palaeontological.
paleontologo [paleontOlogo], *n.m.* Palaeontologist.
palesamento, *n.m.* Revelation, disclosure.
palesare, *v.t.* To reveal, to make known, to manifest, to make public.
palesarsi, *v.r.* To make oneself known; to reveal oneself as.
palese, *a.* Evident, manifest, clear, obvious.
palesemente, *adv.* Evidently, obviously clearly.
Palestina, *n.f.* (*Geog.*) Palestine.
palestra, *n.f.* Gymnasium; (*fig.*) physical exercise.

paletta, *n.f.* (Fire) shovel; paddle-board (of boat); blade (of oar, propeller, etc.); artist's palette.
palettare, *v.t.* (*Agric.*) To stake.
palettata, *n.f.* Shovelful.
palettina, *n.f.* Small shovel.
paletto, *n.m.* Stake, post, small pole; bolt (of door).
palina, *n.f.* Small pole, post, stake; measuring-rod.
palingenesi [palingEnesi], *n.f.* Palingenesis.
palinodia [palinodIa], *n.f.* Palinode; recantation, retraction.
palinsesto, *n.m.* Palimpsest.
palio [pAlio], *n.m.* Cloak; cloth (given as a prize at races); race; race-course; prize. **Correre il —,** to run the race; **— nel sacco,** sack-race.
paliotto (*Eccles.*) Altar frontal.
palischermo, *n.m.* Skiff, small boat, dinghy; pinnace.
palissandro, *n.m.* Rosewood.
palizzata, *n.f.* Palissade, stake fence; railing.
palla, *n.f.* Ball; bullet; shot. **— di neve,** snowball; **— di gomma,** rubber ball; **giuocare alla —,** to play ball; **prender la — al balzo,** to catch on the rebound, to seize the opportunity.
pallacanestro, *n.m.* (*Sport*) Net-ball; basket-ball.
pallacorda, *n.f.* Lawn-tennis, tennis; tennis-court.
Pallade [pAllade], *n.f.* (*Myth.*) Pallas.
palladio [pallAdio], *n.m.* Palladium; (*fig.*) shield, protection, safeguard.
pallaio [pallAio], *n.m.* Billiard-marker; bowling-green; maker or seller of balls.
pallamaglio [pallamAglio], *n.m.* Pall-mall, croquet.
pallata, *n.f.* Blow from a ball.
pallato, *a.* Marked with round spots.
palleggiamento, *n.m.* Bandying, tossing.
palleggiare, *v.t.* To toss about, to bandy; to shift; to play ball; (*Football*) to dribble.
palleggiarsi, *v.r.* **— le responsabilità,** to saddle each other with the responsability.
palleggio [pallEggio], *n.m.* Bandying, tossing; (*Tennis*) volleying; (*Football*) dribbling.
pallente, *a.* (*Lit.*) Palescent.
pallesco, *n.m.a.* (*Hist.*) Adherent of, or pertaining to the Medici.
palletta, *n.f.* (*Mil.*) Grape-shot.
palliamento, *n.m.* Palliation, excuse.
palliare, *v.t.* To palliate, to extenuate, to veil, to disguise.
palliatamente, *adv.* Extenuatingly.
palliativo, *n.m.a.* Palliative.
pallidamente, *adv.* Pallidly, wanly, palely.
pallidezza, *n.f.* Paleness, wanness, pallor; faintness.
pallidino, palliduccio, *a.* Rather pale, wan, somewhat pale.
pallido [pAllido], *a.* Pale, pallid, ashen, wan, faintly-coloured.
pallina, *n.f.* Small ball, (child's) marble.
pallino, *n.m.* Little ball; (*Bowls*) jack; (*Billiards*) red ball; pellet, small shot; knob; (*colloq.*) hobby, fixed idea.
pallio [pAllio], *n.m.* (*Eccles.*) Pallium.
pallonaio [pallonAio], *n.m.* Maker of balls.
pallonata, *n.f.* (*colloq.*) Bluff, bravado.
palloncino, *n.m.* (Child's) balloon; Chinese lantern.
pallone, *n.m.* Football; game of pallone; court where pallone is played; balloon. **— frenato, — drago,** captive balloon; **— di sbarramento,** barrage-balloon.
pallore, *n.m.* Pallor; paleness.
pallotta, pallottola [pallOttola], *n.f.* Shot, bullet; small ball, pellet; (*Bowls*) wood, bowl.
pallottolaia [pallottolAia], *n.f.* Bowling-green; skittle-alley.
pallottoliere, *n.m.* Abacus, counting-frame.
palma, *n.f.* Palm (in all senses). **— del martirio,** martyr's palm; **Domenica delle Palme,** Palm Sunday; **olio di —,** palm-oil; **portar la —,** to bear the palm; **in — di mano,** in the palm of the hand.
palmare, *a.* Palmary; evident, manifest; (*Anat.*) palmar.
palmata, *n.f.* Slap with the palm of the hand.
palmato, *a.* (*Zool.*) Palmate, webbed.
palmento, *n.m.* Hopper that receives the ground flour in a mill; mill-stone. **Mangiare a due palmenti,** to eat greedily.
palmeto, *n.m.* Grove of palm-trees, palm-grove.
palmetta, *n.f.* Palmetto.
palmipede [palmIpede], *n.m.* (*Zool.*) Web-footed.
palmizio [palmIzio], *n.m.* Palm-tree, palm-branch.
palmo, *n.m.* Palm (of the hand), hand's-breadth, span. **— a —,** little by little, inch by inch, thoroughly; **restare con un — di naso,** to be disappointed, to be beaten; **lungo un —,** a span long.
palmola [pAlmola], *n.f.* Wooden hay-fork.
palo, *n.m.* Pale, stake, post. **— di ferro,** crow-bar; **dritto come un —,** straight as a die; **— telegrafico,** telegraph-pole; **saltare di — in frasca,** to make a rambling speech; (*Sport*) **— della porta,** goal-post; **— di partenza, — di arrivo,** starting, winning post.
palombaro, *n.m.* Diver.
palombella, *n.f.* (*Zool.*) Wood-pigeon.
palombo, *n.m.* (*Zool.*) Ring-dove; dog-fish.
palpabile [palpAbile], *a.* Palpable, touchable; tangible, manifest, plain.
palpabilità [-à], *n.f.* Palpability, tangibility.
palpabilmente, *adv.* Palpably.
palpamento, *n.m.* Touching; (*Med.*) palpation.
palpare, *v.t.* To touch, to feel, to handle; (*Med.*) to palpate.
palpatina, *n.f.* Light touch.
palpebra [pAlpebra], *n.f.* (*Anat.*) Eyelid.
palpebrare, *v.i.* To blink.
palpeggiamento, *n.m.* Touching, feeling; palpation.
palpeggiare, *v.t.* To touch, to feel, to handle; (*Med.*) to palpate.
palpitamento, *n.m.* Palpitation.
palpitante, *a.* Palpitating, throbbing; (*fig.*) thrilling.
palpitare, *v.i.* To palpitate, to pant, to throb, to pulsate.
palpitazione, *n.f.* Palpitation, throbbing.
palpitio [palpitIo], *n.m.* Throbbing, fluttering.
palpito [pAlpito], *n.m.* Heart-beat, throb; (*Poet.*) passion, love.
paltò [-ò], *n.m.* Overcoat.

paltoncino, *n.m.* Woman's or boy's coat.
paltoniere, *n.m.* Beggar, vagabond; one who button-holes his victim.
paludamento, *n.m.* (*Hist.*) Roman cloak, military mantle.
palude, *n.f.* Marsh, swamp; quagmire; morass.
paludoso, *a.* Marshy, boggy. **Terreno —,** boggy land.
palustre, *a.* Marsh. **Uccelli palustri,** marsh birds, moor-fowl; **febbre —,** marsh fever.
pamela, *n.f.* Wide-brimmed straw hat.
pampa, *n.f.* (*Geog.*) Pampas.
pampano, pampino, [pAmpano, pAmpino], *n.m.* Vine-tendril, vine-leaf.
pampinoso, *a.* Covered with vine-leaves.
panacea [panacEa], *n.f.* Panacea, universal remedy.
panaio [panAio], *n.m.* Variety of apple.
panama [pAnama], *n.m.* Panama hat.
panare, *v.t.* To crumb, to cover with bread-crumbs.
panata, *n.f.* Panada, bread-soup.
panatica [panAtica], *n.f.* (*colloq.*) Store of bread, bread ration.
panato, *a.* Fried in bread-crumbs. **Acqua panata,** toast-water.
panattiera, *n.f.* Bread-basket.
panbollito, *n.m.* Pap.
panca, *n.f.* Bench, long seat, form. **Scaldar le panche,** to remain idle at school.
pancaccio [pancAccio], *n.m.* Plank-bed.
pancata, *n.f.* Benchful of people.
pancetta, *n.f.* Round belly, paunch; fat bacon.
panchetta, *n.f.* Small bench, low bench.
panchetto, *n.m.* Stool; desk; footstool.
panchina, *n.f.* Garden bench, garden seat; (*Rail.*) low platform.
pancia [pAncia], *n.f.* Belly, paunch. **A — all'aria,** flat on one's back; **far —,** to grow fat, to get stout.
panciata, *n.f.* Bellyful.
panciafichista (*pl.* **panciafichisti**), *n.m.* (*colloq.*) Opportunist; shirker.
panciera, *n.f.* (*Hist.*) Cuirass; woollen body-belt.
panciolle, *adv.* **Stare in —,** to lounge in a chair, to unbutton one's waistcoat and take it easy.
panciotto, *n.m.* Waistcoat.
panciuto, *a.* Corpulent, big-bellied.
pancone, *n.m.* Plank, board; large bench; carpenter's bench.
pancotto, *n.m.* Pap, boiled bread.
pancreas [pAncreas], *n.m.* (*Anat.*) Pancreas.
pancreatico [pancreAtico], *a.* Pancreatic.
pandemonio [pandemOnio], *n.m.* Pandemonium, confusion, uproar.
pandetta, *n.f.* Digest, alphabetical index. **Le Pandette,** Justinian's Pandects.
pandora, *n.f.* (*Mus.*) Ancient type of lute.
panduro, *n.m.* (*Mil. Hist.*) Pandour.
pane, *n.m.* Bread; loaf, roll; lump; pat (of butter). **— raffermo,** stale bread; **render — per focaccia,** to give tit for tat; **dire — al —,** to call a spade a spade; **avere tre pani per coppia,** to get a great advantage; **avrai il — che ti meriti,** you'll get what you deserve.
panegirico [panegIrico], *n.m.* Panegyric, eulogy.
panegirista (*pl.* **panegiristi**), *n.m.* Panegyrist.
panella, *n.f.* (Coal) briquette.
panello, *n.m.* Oil-cake; briquette.
panereccio [panerEccio], *n.m.* (*Med.*) Whitlow [cp. **patereccio**].
panetteria [panetterIa], *n.f.* Baker's shop, bakery.
panettiere, *n.m.* Baker.
panetto, *n.m.* Small loaf, roll.
panettone, *n.m.* Milanese sweet cake.
panfilo [pAnfilo] *n.m.* (*Naut.*) Yacht.
panforte, *n.m.* Ginger-bread (made at Siena).
pangrattato, *n.m.* Bread raspings, fried bread-crumbs; soup with bread-crumbs in it.
pania [pAnia], *n.f.* Bird-lime; snare, trap; entanglement.
paniccia [panIccia], *n.f.* Paste. **Farne —,** to pound into jelly.
panico [pAnico], *n.m.a.* Panic; [panIco], (*Bot.*) panic grass.
paniera, *n.f.* Open basket, panier.
panieraio [panierAio], *n.m.* Basket-maker or vendor.
panierata, *n.f.* Basketful.
paniere, *n.m.* Basket.
panierino, *n.m.* Small basket.
panificare, *v.t.* To make bread.
panificazione, *n.f.* Bread-making; baking.
panificio [panifIcio], *n.m.* Bakery, bakehouse.
panino, *n.m.* Roll, bun. **— gravido,** sandwich.
panione, *n.m.* Twig covered with bird-lime.
panioso, *a.* Sticky, gluey.
paniuzza, *n.f.* Limed twig.
panizzare, *v.t.* (*obs.*) To bake bread.
panna, *n.f.* Cream; (*Motor.*) breakdown, accident. **— montata,** whipped cream; (*Motor.*) **essere in —,** to have a breakdown; (*Naut.*) **in —,** lying to.
pannaiolo, *n.m.* (*obs.*) Draper.
pannare, *v.i.* To rise (of cream).
panneggiamento, *n.m.* Drapery.
panneggiare, *v.i.* To drape.
panneggio [pannEggio], *n.m.* Drapery, draping.
pannello, *n.m.* (*Arch.*) Panel; decorative picture.
pannicello, pannilino, *n.m.* Bit of cloth, nappy, rag. **Pannicelli caldi,** useless remedies.
panno, *n.m.* Cloth, woollen cloth; blanket. **Mettersi nei panni di qualcuno,** to put oneself in another person's shoes; **tagliare i panni addosso a uno,** to tear someone's reputation to rags.
pannocchia [pannOcchia], *n.f.* (*Bot.*) Spike; corn-cob.
pannocchietta, *n.f.* Small ear of maize.
pannolano (*pl.* **pannilani**), *n.m.* Woollen cloth.
pannolino (*pl.* **pannilini**), *n.m.* Linen cloth.
panoplia [panOplia], *n.f.* Panoply.
panorama, *n.m.* Panorama.
panoramicamente, *adv.* Panoramically.
panoramico [panorAmico], *a.* Panoramic.
panslavismo, *n.m.* Panslavism.
pantagruelico [pantagruElico], *a.* Pantagruelian.
Pantalone, *n.m.* (*Theat.*) Pantaloon; (*colloq.*) taxpayer.
pantaloni, *n.m.pl.* Pantaloons, trousers.
pantano, *n.m.* Bog, swamp, quagmire, puddle, slough.
pantanoso, *a.* Boggy, marshy.

panteismo, *n.m.* Pantheism.
panteista (*pl.* **panteisti**), *n.m.* Pantheist.
panteisticamente, *adv.* Pantheistically.
panteistico [panteIstico], *a.* Pantheistic.
Panteon [pAnteon], *n.m.* Pantheon.
pantera, *n.f.* (*Zool.*) Panther.
pantofola [pantOfola], *n.f.* Slipper.
pantografo [pantOgrafo], *n.m.* Pantograph.
pantomima, *n.f.* (*Theat.*) Pantomime.
pantomimico [pantomImico], *a.* Pantomimic.
panzana, *n.f.* Yarn, idle story, fable, nonsense.
Paolo [pAolo], *n.m.* Paul; (*Hist.*) a Tuscan coin.
paolotto, *n.m.a.* Devout; bigot; bigoted.
paonazzo, *a.* Violet, purple; peacock-blue.
paone [cp. **pavone**].
papà (*pl.* **papà**), *n.m.* Papa, daddy, dad, father.
Papa (*pl.* **papi**), *n.m.* Pope, pontiff.
papabile [papAbile], *a.* Eligible to be, or likely to be Pope.
papale, *a.* Papal.
papalina, *n.f.* Skull-cap.
papalino, *n.m.a.* Adherent to the papacy, papalist, one of the Pope's party; papal. **Soldato —,** papal soldier.
papalista (*pl.* **papalisti**), *n.m.* Papalist, adherent of the papal party.
papato, *n.m.* Papacy, pontificate.
papavero [papAvero], *n.m.* (*Bot.*) Poppy; (*fig.*) man of importance.
papera [pApera], *n.f.* Goose, young gosling; (*fig.*) foolish woman; (*Theat.*) blunder (over a word); Spoonerism.
papero [pApero], *n.m.* Gosling, gander.
paperottolo [paperOttolo], *n.m.* Little gosling; silly fellow.
papesco, *a.* Popish.
papilla, *n.f.* (*Anat.*) Papilla.
papillare, *a.* Papillary.
papiro, *n.m.* Papyrus.
papismo, *n.m.* (System of) papacy, popery.
papista (*pl.* **papisti**), *n.m.* Papist.
pappa, *n.f.* Pap, infant-food, soaked bread. **Aver la — fatta,** to have everything done and ready; **una — fredda,** milksop, mollycoddle.
pappafico, *n.m.* (*Naut.*) sky-sail; diver's helmet; (*colloq.*) small beard.
pappagallescamente, *adv.* In parrot-fashion.
pappagallesco, *a.* Parrot-like.
pappagallo, *n.m.* (*Zool.*) Parrot. **Fare il —,** to talk like a parrot.
pappagorgia [pappagOrgia], *n.a.* Double chin.
pappardelle, *n.f.pl.* Ribbon macaroni in gravy, esp. with jugged hare.
pappare, *v.t.* To gulp down, to swallow, to gorge.
pappata, *n.f.* Gorge, good blow-out.
pappataci, *n.m.* Complaisant husband; one who takes what he gets without questioning; (*Zool.*) gnat, mosquito.
pappatore, pappatrice, *n.m.f.* Guzzler.
pappatoria [pappatOria], *n.f.* Eating, feasting; bellyful.
pappina, *n.f.* Pap; poultice.
pappino, *n.m.* (*colloq.*) Hospital orderly.
pappo, *n.m.* (*colloq.*) Bread.
pappolata, *n.f.* Tasteless, insipid food; thin soup, swill; (*fig.*) tedious speech, tirade.
pappolone, *n.m.* Chatterer, great talker.
pappone, *n.m.* Glutton.
paprica [pAprica], *n.f.* Red pepper.
papula [pApula], *n.f.* (*Med.*) Pimple, papula.
parabola [parAbola], *n.f.* Parable, allegory; (*Geom.*) parabola.
parabolicamente, *adv.* Allegorically.
parabolico [parabOlico], *a.* Allegorical, in parable style; (*Geom.*) parabolic.
parabordo, *n.m.* (*Naut.*) Fender; skid.
parabrezza, *n.f.* (*Motor.*) Windshield.
paracadutato, *n.m.a.* Dropped by parachute, parachuted.
paracadute, *n.m.* (*Aviat.*) Parachute.
paracadutista (*pl.* **paracadutisti**), *n.m.* Parachutist. (*Mil.*) **Riparti di paracadutisti,** paratroops.
paracalli, *n.m.* (*Med.*) Corn-plaster.
paracamino, *n.m.* Fire-screen.
paracarro, *n.m.* Curbstone; roadside post.
paracenere [paracEnere], *n.m.* Fire-guard, fender.
paracielo, *n.m.* Canopy; awning; roof.
Paracleto, *n.m.* Paraclete, Holy Ghost.
paracolpi, *n.m.* Rubber buffer, fender.
paracqua [parAcqua], *n.m.* Umbrella.
paradigma, *n.m.* Paradigm.
paradisea [paradisEa], *n.f.* (*Zool.*) Bird of paradise.
paradisiaco [paradisIaco], *a.* Paradisiac.
paradiso, *n.m.* Paradise; heaven, perfect bliss.
paradossale, *a.* Paradoxical.
paradosso, *n.m.* Paradox.
parafango, *n.m.* Mud-guard, (*Am.*) fender.
paraferna, *n.f.* (*Law*) Jointure, married woman's property.
paraffina, *n.f.* Paraffin wax.
parafoco, *n.m.* Fire-guard.
parafrasare, *v.t.* To paraphrase.
parafrasi [parAfrasi], *n.f.* Paraphrase.
parafrastico [parafrAstico], *a.* Paraphrastic.
parafulmine [parafUlmine], *n.m.* Lightning-conductor, lightning-rod.
parafuoco, *n.m.* Fire-screen, fire-guard.
paraggio [parAggio], *n.m.* Coastal area. **Paraggi,** environs, neighbourhood.
paragonabile [paragonAbile], *a.* Comparable.
paragonare, *v.t.* To compare, to liken.
paragone, *n.m.* Comparison. **Pietra di —,** touch-stone; **far il —,** to compare; **in — di,** in comparison with.
paragrafare, *v.t.* To paragraph.
paragrafo [parAgrafo], *n.m.* Paragraph.
paraguai, *n.m.* (*colloq.*) Overalls; overcoat.
paralisi [parAlisi], *n.f.* (*Med.*) Paralysis.
paralitico [paralItico], *n.m.a.* Paralytic.
paralizzare, *v.t.* To paralyse.
paralizzarsi, *v.r.* To become paralysed.
paralizzato, *a.* Paralysed.
parallasse, *n.f.* (*Astron.*) Parallax.
parallela, *n.f.* Parallel. **Le parallele,** parallel-bars.
parallelamente, *adv.* In parallel lines.
parallelismo, *n.m.* Parallelism.
parallelo, *n.m.a.* Parallel.
parallelogrammo, *n.m.* Parallelogram.
paralogismo, *n.m.* Paralogism, fallacy.
paralume, *n.m.* Lamp-shade; eye-shade.
paramano, *n.m.* Wristband; (*Eccles.*) maniple.
paramecio, *n.m.* (*Zool.*) Paramecium.

paramento, *n.m.* (*Eccles.*) Vestment; (church) hangings.
paramezzale, *n.m.* (*Naut.*) Keelson.
paramosche, *n.m.* Gauze dish-cover; flytrap.
parancare, *v.t.* (*Naut.*) To hoist with tackle.
paranco, *n.m.* (*Naut.*) Tackle.
paraninfo, *n.m.* Matrimonial agent.
paranza, *n.f.* (*Naut.*) Sloop, trawler, fishing-boat.
paraocchi, *n.m.pl.* Goggles; horse-blinders.
parapetto, *n.m.* Parapet.
parapiglia [parapIglia], *n.m.* Confusion, hurly-burly, turmoil; bustle.
parapioggia [parapiOggia], *n.m.* Umbrella.
parare, *v.t.* To decorate, to adorn, to deck; to parry, to avert, to keep off, to ward off; to prepare, to protect. **— una chiesa**, to decorate a church; **la chiesa era parata a lutto**, the church was draped in black; **— un colpo**, to parry a blow; (*colloq.*) **non so dove vada a —**, I don't know what he's driving at.
pararsi, *v.r.* To dress up; to present oneself; to shelter; (*Eccles.*) to vest oneself.
parasceve, *n.f.* (*Eccles.*) Good Friday.
parasole, *n.m.* Parasol.
paraspruzzi, *n.m.* (*Motor.*) Mud-guard, (*Am.*) fender.
parassita, *n.m.a.* Parasite (in all senses).
parassitario, parassitico [parassitArio, parassItico], *a.* Parasitical.
parassitismo, *n.m.* Parasitism.
parastatale, *a.* Concerning an institution recognized by the State.
parata, *n.f.* Parade, display, show; guard; (*Fencing*) parry. **In abito di —**, in full dress, full uniform; **sfilamento in —**, march past; **vedere la mala —**, to perceive the danger.
paratasche, *n.m.* Pocket-flap.
paratia [paratIa], *n.f.* (*Naut.*) Bulkhead. **Paratie stagne**, water-tight compartments.
parato, *n.m.* Tapestry, hangings. **Carta da parati**, wall-paper.
paratore, *n.m.* Decorator.
paratura, *n.f.* Decoration.
paraurti, *n.m.* (*Motor.*) Bumper.
paravento, *n.m.* Screen; (*Motor.*) wind-shield.
paraveste, *n.m.* Dress-guard (on a cycle).
Parca, *n.f.* (*Myth.*) Fate.
parcamente, *adv.* Sparingly, economically.
parcare, parcheggiare, *v.t.* (*Motor. etc.*) To park.
parcella, *n.f.* Bill, note of expenses, account of lawyer's fees.
parcheggiare, *v.t.* (*Motor. etc.*) To park.
parcheggio [parchEggio], *n.m.* Parking, parking place. **Divieto di —**, No parking.
parco, *n.m.* Park (in all senses); enclosure, paddock; yard.
parco, *a.* Sparing, frugal, economical; sober. **— di lodi**, sparing of praise.
pardo, *n.m.* (*Zool.*) Leopard.
parecchio [parEcchio], *n.m.a.* A good deal, a good many, quite a lot; considerable time, etc.
parecchio [parEcchio], *adv.* Several; much, very much.
pareggiabile [pareggiAbile], *a.* Comparable, that may be made equal.
pareggiamento, *n.m.* Levelling; balancing; putting on an equality.
pareggiare, *v.t.i.* To equalise, to equal; to make level, to square up; (*Comm.*) to balance; (*Sport*) to draw; to be quits.
pareggiarsi, *v.r.* To compare oneself with.
pareggio [parEggio], *n.m.* (*Comm.*) Balancing, balance; (*Sport*) draw, tie; a drawn game.
paregorico [paregOrico], *n.m.* (*Med.*) Paregoric.
parelio [parElio], *n.m.* (*Astron.*) Parhelion.
parentado, *n.m.* Relationship; relations, relatives; marriage.
parentali, *n.m.pl.* Celebration (in honour of the dead).
parente, *n.m.a.* Relative, relation, kinsman; related to. **— stretto**, near relative; **parenti poveri**, poor relations.
parentela, *n.m.* Relationship, relations, relatives; affinity.
parentesi [parEntesi], *n.f.* Parenthesis. **Fra —**, in brackets; **tra —**, incidentally.
parentetico [parentEtico], *a.* Parenthetical.
parere, *v.i.* To seem, to look, to appear; to judge, to think. **Che ve ne pare?** What do you think of it? **Le pare?** Don't you think? **mi pare di sì**, I think so; **pare molto stanco**, he seems very tired; **pare di sognare**, it seems a dream.
parere, *n.m.* Opinion; mind; advice. **Cambiar —**, to change one's mind; **prendere un — da un avvocato**, to take counsel's opinion.
parergo, *n.m.* Addition; (*Arch.*) extension.
paretaio [paretAio], *n.m.* Wall where nets are spread to catch birds.
parete, *n.f.* (Inner) wall, partition; vertical cliff. **Pareti domestiche**, home, family.
pargoleggiare, *v.i.* To act or talk like a child, to become childish.
pargoletto, pargolo [pArgolo], *n.m.* (*Poet.*) Baby, little child.
pari, *n.m.a.* Equal; peer; alike, even, similar; even (number). **Essere —**, to be quits, to be all square; **un nostro —**, one of ours; **numero —**, an even number; **da par suo**, as it is to be expected from him; **senza —**, unequalled, without comparison; **saltare a piè —**, to leap with both feet together, to skip; **in — tempo**, at the same time; **essere — al compito**, to be up to the job; **Camera dei Pari**, House of Peers; (*Comm.*) **alla —**, at par; **sopra, sotto la —**, above, below par.
paria [pAria], *n.m.* Pariah.
parietale, *a.* (*Anat.*) Parietal.
parificamento, *n.m.* Making equal.
parificare [cp. **pareggiare**].
Parigi, *n.f.* (*Geog.*) Paris.
parigina, *n.f.* Kind of slow-combustion stove.
parigino, *n.m.a.* Parisian.
pariglia [parIglia], *n.f.* Pair, couple, match. **Render la —**, to give tit for tat.
parimente, parimenti, *adv.* Likewise, equally, also.
pario [pArio], *a.* Parian (marble).
parità [-à], *n.f.* Parity, likeness, equality.
paritetico [paritEtico], *a.* Joint (action or decision of a committee).
parlabile [parlAbile], *a.* Possible to be spoken.
parlachiaro, *n.m.* Plain speaker, one who speaks his mind.
parlamentare, *v.i.* To parley; to discuss.
parlamentare, *n.m.a.* Parliamentarian, parliamentary.

parlamentario [parlamentArio], *n.m.* Envoy; bearer of a flag of truce.
parlamento, *n.m.* (*Pol.*) Parliament; parley, conference, meeting.
parlante, *a.* Speaking, talking, expressible. **Ritratto —,** speaking likeness; **cinema —,** talkies; (*Radio.*) **alto —,** loud-speaker.
parlantina, *n.f.* Loquacity, garrulousness; (*colloq.*) gift of the gab.
parlare, *v.i.* To speak, to talk, to converse; to make a speech, to address. **— a torto e a traverso,** to talk foolishly; **— a cuore aperto,** to speak frankly; **— nel naso,** to speak through the nose; **— alla muta,** to talk by signs; **— al muro,** to speak to a blank wall; **— della pioggia e del bel tempo,** to talk of this and that; **— in punta di forchetta,** to drawl, to speak affectedly; **— fra i denti,** to mumble.
parlare, *n.m.* Speech, speaking, talk; dialect.
parlata, *n.f.* Speech, conversation; delivery.
parlatore, *n.m.* Speaker, orator.
parlatorio [parlatOrio], *n.m.* Parlour (in convents, etc.).
parlatura, *n.f.* Speech, delivery, mode of speaking.
parlottare, parlucchiare, *v.t.i.* To chat; to jabber; to mumble.
parmense, parmigiano, *n.m.a.* Parmesan; of Parma.
Parnaso, Parnasso, *n.m.* (*Myth.*) Parnassus; (*fig.*) poetry, poets.
parnassiano, *a.* Parnassian.
paro [cp. **paio, pari**].
parocchi, *n.m.pl.* (Horses') blinkers.
parodia [parodIa], *n.f.* Parody.
parodiare, *v.t.* To parody, to ridicule, to burlesque.
parodista (*pl.* **parodisti**), *n.m.* Parodist.
parola, *n.f.* Word, term; speech; oratory; maxim, proverb; parole. **Avere la —,** to have the right to speak, to have the word; **domandare la —,** to ask leave to speak; **mancare di —,** to break one's word; **— d'onore,** word of honour; **amico a parole,** friend in words only; **— per —,** verbatim, word for word; **venire a parole,** to come to words, to quarrel; **non far —,** to say nothing; **il libro in —,** the book in question; **giuoco di parole,** a pun, a play on words; **parole incrociate,** crossword puzzle.
parolaccia [parolAccia], *n.f.* Ugly word, bad language.
parolaio [parolAio], *n.m.* Long-winded speaker; gas-bag, wind-bag.
paroletta, parolina, *n.f.* Nice word, kind word.
parolona, parolone, *n.f.m.* Big word, long word; fine-sounding word.
parossismo, *n.m.* Paroxysm.
parossitono [parossItono], *n.m.a.* (*Gram.*) Paroxytone.
parotide [parOtide], *n.f.* (*Med.*) Parotid gland.
parrasio [parrAsio], *a.* Arcadian.
parricida(*pl.* **parricidi**) [cp.**patricida**].
parricidio [parricIdio] [cp. **patricidio**].
parrocchetto, *n.m.* (*Naut.*) Fore-topmast; (*Zool.*) parakeet.
parrocchia [parrOcchia], *n.f.* Parish; parish church.
parrocchiale, *a.* Parochial.
parrocchialmente, *adv.* Parochially.
parrocchiano, *n.m.* Parishioner.
parroco [pArroco], *n.m.* Parish priest.
parrucca, *n.f.* Wig; periwig, peruke; (*fig.*) wigging, scolding.
parrucchiere, *n.m.* Hair-dresser, barber.
parruccone, *n.m.* (*fig.*) Big-wig; reactionary.
parsimonia [parsimOnia], *n.f.* Parsimony, frugality; sobriety; thrift.
parsimonioso, *a.* Parsimonious, frugal, sparing.
parso [cp. **parere**].
partaccia [partAccia], *n.f.* Shameful action; sharp reproof.
parte, *n.f.* Share, part; portion; side, place; party; (*Theat.*) role. **Prendere una cosa in buona —,** to take a thing in good part; **in mala —,** amiss; **sapere da buona —,** to know on good authority; **un uomo di —,** a party man; **da — del mio amico,** on the part of my friend; **in nessun'altra —,** nowhere else; **da una — e dall'altra,** on both sides; **d'altra —,** on the other hand; **da tutte le parti,** on every side; **a —,** separately, apart; **da — mia,** on my behalf; **da — a —,** through; **metter da —,** to put aside; **sapere la —,** to know one's part; **tirare da —,** to take aside; **far — a qualcuno,** to share with someone; (*Mech.*) **parti di ricambio,** spare parts; (*Law*) **— civile,** plaintiff.
partecipante, *n.m.a.* Participant; privy to.
partecipanza, *n.f.* Participation.
partecipare, *v.t.i.* To participate, to take part; to attend (a meeting); to share, to partake in; to communicate, to inform, to acquaint; to bestow, to grant. **— al dolore di qualcuno,** to share in someone's grief.
partecipatore, partecipatrice, *n.m.f.* Participant; informant; sharer.
partecipazione, *n.f.* Participation; taking part. **— di matrimonio,** wedding-announcement.
partecipe [partEcipe], *a.* Sharing, taking part. **Esser — di,** to share.
parteggiamento, *n.m.* Siding with, backing, support.
parteggiare, *v.i.* To side with, to back; to take sides.
Partenone, *n.m.* Parthenon.
partenopeo [partenopEo], *a.* (*Hist. Poet.*) Neapolitan.
partente, *n.m.* Departing traveller; (*Racing*) starter.
partente, *a.* Departing.
partenza, *n.f.* Departure, leaving, setting out; sailing. **Punto di —,** starting-point; **ora di —,** time of departure; **dopo la sua —,** after his departure, after he left.
partibile [partIbile], *a.* Divisible.
particella, *n.f.* Particle.
participare [cp. **partecipare**].
participiale, *a.* Participial.
participio [particIpio], *n.m.* (*Gram.*) Participle.
particola [partIcola], *n.f.* Particle; (*Eccles.*) consecrated wafer, Host.
particolare, *n.m.a.* Particular; private, personal. **Dare particolari,** to give particulars; **udienza —,** private audience.

particolareggiare, *v.t.* To particularize, to give details.
particolarità [-à], *n.f.* Particularity, peculiarity.
particolarmente, *adv.* Particularly, peculiarly.
partigiana, *n.f.* Partisan, halberd.
partigianeria [partigianerIa], *n.f.* Partisanship.
partigiano, *n.m.a.* Partisan; party, sectarian.
partimento, *n.m.* Division, separating.
partire, *v.t.i.* To leave, to set out, to depart, to start, to sail; to go away, to move; to share, to part, to divide. **— per un viaggio,** to set out on a journey; **lasciar —,** to let go, to let off (a gun, etc.). **Quando parte il treno?** When does the train leave? **partirò domani,** I shall start tomorrow.
partirsi, partirsene, *v.r.* To go away, to part from, to depart from.
partita, *n.f.* (*Comm.*) Quantity, lot, stock; entry item; (*Sport*) game, round, match, rubber. (*Comm.*) **— doppia,** double entry; **una — di calcio,** a football match; **una — a scacchi,** a game of chess; **fare una —,** to make a four (at cards); **essere della —,** to be one of the party.
partitamente, *adv.* Separately, in detail.
partitivo, *n.m.a.* (*Gram.*) Partitive.
partito, *n.m.* Party (political, etc.); side, course of action; proposal, bargain; resolve; (matrimonial) match; benefit; purpose; odds (in a game). **Essere a mal —,** to be in a bad way; **prendere un —,** to come to a decision, to make up one's mind; **un buon —,** a good (matrimonial) match; **a — preso,** on purpose, of set purpose; **prendere — pro o contro,** to side with or against; **tirar — da tutto,** to turn everything to account.
partitura, *n.f.* (*Mus.*) Score; partition.
partizione, *n.f.* Division, partition.
parto, *n.m.* Child-birth, birth, delivery, confinement; (*fig.*) fruit (of industry, etc.). **Morire di —,** to die in childbirth; **dolori del —,** labour pains; **è un — della sua fantasia,** it is the fruit of his imagination.
partoriente, *n.f.a.* Woman in labour; parturient, in labour.
partorire, *v.t.i.* To give birth to, to be delivered of, to bring forth; (*fig.*) to produce.
parvente, *a.* Apparent, visible, seeming; manifest.
parvenza, *n.f.* Appearance, semblance; show, pretence.
parvo [cp. **piccolo**].
parziale, *a.* Partial, biased, one-sided; incomplete. **Elezione —,** by-election.
parzialità [-à], *n.f.* Partiality, bias.
parzialmente, *adv.* Partially; unfairly, with bias.
pascere [pAscere], *v.t.i.* To feed, to nourish; to pasture, to graze; to browse, to feed on.
pascersi [pAscersi], *v.r.* To feed oneself, to feed on. (*fig.*) **— di vane speranze,** to cherish vain hopes.
pascià [-à], *n.m.* Pasha. **Stare come un —,** to live like a lord.
pascimento, *n.m.* (*obs.*) Pasturing, grazing.
pasciona, *n.f.* Rich grazing land; (*fig.*) prosperity.
pascolare, *v.t.i.* To feed, to pasture, to graze; to browse.
pascolo [pAscolo], *n.m.* Meadow, pasturage, pasture; food.
Pasqua [pAsqua], *n.f.* Easter. **— di rose,** Whitsunday; **contento come una —,** as happy as the day is long; **vigilia di —,** Easter Eve.
pasquale, *a.* Paschal, Easter. **Uovo —,** Easter egg; **l'agnello —,** the Paschal lamb.
pasquinata, *n.f.* Lampoon, pasquinade.
passabile [passAbile], *a.* Passable, tolerable.
passabilmente, *adv.* Passably.
passacaglia [passacAglia], *n.m.* (*Mus.*) Passacaglia.
passacavallo, *n.m.* (*Naut.*) Transport vessel for horses.
passaggio [passAggio], *n.m.* Passage, transit; crossing, voyage; gangway, way; thoroughfare, traffic; (*Lit.*) passage, extract. **Di —,** in passing; **diritto di —,** right of way; **— vietato,** no thoroughfare; **— a livello,** level-crossing; **— sotterraneo,** sub-way; **— tracciato da chiodi,** studded pedestrian crossing; **— zebrato,** zebra crossing.
passaiola, *n.f.* Stepping-stone.
passamano, *n.m.* Lace trimming, lace, braid.
passamanteria [passamanterIa], *n.f.* Trimming, passementerie.
passante, *n.m.* Passer-by, pedestrian; slot (in a belt) for the thong.
passante, *a.* Passing; digestible.
passaporto, *n.m.* Passport.
passare, *v.t.i.* To pass, to pass along, to go through; to elapse; to transfer, to hand over; to disappear, to pass away; to be accepted, to be current; to call upon, to look in; (*Comm.*) to post (in ledger, etc.), to enter; to filter, to strain, to sift; to vanish; to spend (time); to undergo; to cross; to surpass. **— i limiti,** to go too far; **— la vita,** to spend one's life; **— gli esami,** to pass one's exams; **tutto passa,** nothing can last; **— a fil di spada,** to put to the edge of the sword; **— sotto silenzio,** to pass over in silence; **— oltre,** to go on, to proceed; **passa di qui,** come this way; **— per Parigi,** to pass through Paris; **il pericolo è passato,** the danger is over; **passarsi di,** to abstain from; **passarsela bene,** to get on well.
passata, *n.f.* Passage, passing; touch, glance (at a book, etc.); passing mood; vogue; shower (of rain); (*Agric.*) ridge; (*Cooking*) mash.
passatempo, *n.m.* Pastime, diversion; sport, game, hobby; amusement.
passatina, *n.f.* Light glance; slight shower of rain.
passatello, *a.* Elderly.
passatista (*pl.* **passatisti**), *n.m.* Traditionalist, lover of olden times.
passato, *n.m.* Past, past life, time past; (*Gram.*) past tense. **Nel —,** formerly, in the past.
passato, *p.p.a.* Past; faded; underdone (of food).
passatoia, *n.f.* Stair-carpet; strip of carpet (along a passage, etc.).
passatoio [passatOio], *n.m.* Stepping-stone.
passatore, *n.m.* Passer; ferryman.
passatura, *n.f.* Darn (in clothes, etc.).
passavanti, *n.m.* (*Theat.*) Free pass; (*Naut.*) companion-ladder; gangway.

passavivande, *n.m.* Service-hatch.
passavia, *n.m.* Flying-bridge.
passeggero, *n.m.* Passenger, traveller.
passeggero, *a.* Passing, fleeting, transient, transitory. **Nuvole passeggere,** passing clouds.
passeggiare, *v.t.i.* To walk, to take a walk, to stroll. **— a cavallo,** to go for a ride; **— in carrozza,** to go for a drive.
passeggiata, *n.f.* Walk, promenade; drive (in carriage or motor-car); ride (on horseback). **Fare una —,** to go for a walk.
passeggiatore, *n.m.* Person taking a walk.
passeggiero [cp. **passeggero**].
passeggio [passEggio], *n.m.* Public walk; walk, promenade; walking.
passera [pAssera], *n.f.* (*Zool.*) Hen-sparrow; flounder.
passeraio [passerAio], *n.m.* Twittering of sparrows; (*fig.*) chattering, chatter.
passerella, *n.f.* Footbridge; gangway.
passero [pAssero], *n.m.* (*Zool.*) Sparrow.
passerotto, *n.m.* Young sparrow.
passetto, *n.m.* Short step.
passibile [passIbile], *a.* Liable.
passibilità [-à], *n.f.* Liability.
passibilmente, *adv.* Liably.
passiccio [passIccio], *a.* Faded, withered.
passiflora, *n.f.* (*Bot.*) Passion-flower.
passino, *n.m.* Child's step, toddler's step.
passio [pAssio], *n.m.* (*Eccles.*) Gospel story of the Passion; (*fig.*) a long-winded story.
passionale, *n.m.* (*Eccles.*) Book of martyrs, martyrology.
passionale, *a.* Impassioned, vehement. **Delitto —,** crime committed in the heat of passion.
passionalità [-à], *n.f.* Passionateness; excitability; passion.
passionatamente, *adv.* Passionately.
passionato, *a.* Impassioned; excited, passionate [cp. **appassionato**].
passione, *n.f.* Passion, emotion, suffering; love; longing, ardour, vehemence; (*Eccles.*) the Passion. **Domenica di Passione,** Passion Sunday; **fior di —,** passion-flower.
passito, *n.m.* Variety of wine.
passivamente, *adv.* Passively.
passività [-à], *n.f.* Inactivity; (*Comm.*) liabilities, indebtedness.
passivo, *n.m.* (*Gram.*) Passive; (*Comm.*) outstanding debts, liabilities, debit side. **L'attivo e il —,** assets and liabilities; credit and debit side.
passivo, *a.* Passive, inactive; (*Gram.*) passive.
passo, *n.m.* Step, pace, march; passage (in a book); pass, narrow passage; channel; footprint, footfall; (*Geog.*) straits; (*Mech.*) pitch of a screw. **Andare al —,** to walk, to pace; **di buon —,** at a good pace; **cedere il —,** to give way (on a pavement); **— a —,** little by little, step by step; **uccelli di —,** migratory birds; **al —,** at a walking pace; **segnare il —,** to mark time; **— alpino,** an Alpine pass; **— accelerato,** quick march; **Passo di Calais,** Straits of Dover; **a — di lumaca,** at a snail's pace; (*Traffic sign*) **andare al —, al —,** drive dead slow.
passo, *a.* Dried, shrivelled. **Uva passa,** raisin.
passone, *n.m.* Stake, strong post.
pasta, *n.f.* Dough, paste; cake, piece of pastry; any kind of alimentary paste (spaghetti, etc.); sausage-meat; (*fig.*) temperament, nature. **— asciutta,** macaroni and cheese; **— sfoglia,** puff-paste; **— dentifricia,** tooth-paste; **avere le mani in —,** to have a finger in the pie; **una buona — di figliolo,** a good-natured sort of fellow.
pastaio [pastAio], *n.m.* Macaroni-maker or vendor.
pastecca, *n.f.* (*Naut.*) Snatch-block.
pasteggiabile [pasteggiAbile], *a.* Suitable for meals (of wine).
pasteggiare, *v.i.* To eat at table; to drink wine at a meal.
pastellista (*pl.* **pastellisti**), *n.m.* Artist in pastels.
pastello, *n.m.* (*Art*) Pastel, coloured crayon; a pastel.
pastetta, *n.f.* Batter; (*fig.*) political fraud, gerrymandering.
pasticca, *n.f.* Lozenge, tablet [cp. **pastiglia**].
pasticcere, *n.m.* Pastry-cook, confectioner.
pasticceria [pasticcerIa], *n.f.* Pastry, pastry-cook's shop.
pasticciare, *v.t.i.* To make a mess of, to bungle; to entangle, to mingle; to intrigue.
pasticciere [cp. **pasticcere**].
pasticcino, *n.m.* Tartlet, patty; sweetmeat.
pasticcio [pastIccio], *n.m.* Pie, pasty; cake; (*fig.*) mess, scrape, muddle; humbug; botch; (*Art*) daub, pot-boiler. **Bel —!** There's a nice mess! **trovarsi nei pasticci,** to be in a fix.
pasticcione, *n.m.* Busybody, meddler; bungler.
pastificio [pastifIcio], *n.m.* Macaroni factory.
pastiglia [pastIglia], *n.f.* Pastille, lozenge.
pastina, *n.f.* Fine spaghetti; soup alphabet.
pastinaca, *n.f.* (*Bot.*) Parsnip.
pasto, *n.m.* Repast, meal; food; feeding; lights (offal). **Fuori —,** between meals; **— delle belve,** feeding the beasts; **di buon —,** a hearty appetite; **vino da —,** table-wine; **a tutto —,** freely, copiously.
pastocchia [pastOcchia], *n.f.* Nonsense, humbug, fraud; idle tale.
pastoia [pastOia], *n.f.* Fetter, shackle; impediment, clog; (horse's) pastern.
pastone, *n.m.* Dough; animal food, chicken-feed.
pastora, *n.f.* Shepherdess.
pastorale, *n.f.a.* Pastoral (in all senses); *n.m.* pastoral staff, crozier.
pastoralmente, *adv.* Pastorally.
pastore, *n.m.* Shepherd; pastor, minister, parish priest.
pastorello, pastorella, *n.m.f.* Shepherd lad, shepherdess.
pastorizia [pastorIzia], *n.f.* Stock-breeding.
pastorizio [pastorIzio], *a.* Pastoral, rural.
pastorizzare, *v.t.* To pasteurize (milk), to sterilize.
pastosità [-à], *n.f.* Softness, mellowness; stickiness.
pastoso, *a.* Soft, doughy, pulpy; sticky; mellow.
pastranaio [pastranAio], *n.m.* Cloak-room attendant.
pastrano, *n.m.* Overcoat, heavy coat; cloak.
pastricciano, *n.m.* (*Bot.*) Parsnip; (*fig.*) good, simple-minded fellow.

pastura, *n.f.* Pasture, pasturage.
pasturale, *n.m.* (Horse's) pastern.
pasturare, *v.t.i.* To pasture; to graze.
patacca, *n.f.* (*colloq.*) Stain, dirty mark; dud coin. **Non vale una —,** it isn't worth anything.
pataccone, *n.m.* (*colloq.*) Fat, cowardly person; dirty fellow.
pataffiona, *n.f.* Fat clumsy person.
patano [pAtano], *a.* (*colloq.*) Big, coarse.
patapum! [patapUm] *inter.* Bang! Thud!
patassio [patassIo], *n.m.* Row, quarrel.
patata, *n.f.* Potato. **Patate tenere,** new potatoes; **patate lesse,** boiled potatoes.
patataio [patatAio], *n.m.* Potato-merchant.
patatrac! [patatrAc] *inter. n.m.* Crash! Crack! Bang! Crash, bang.
patatucco, *n.m.* (*colloq.*) Clumsy fellow, lout, strange fellow.
patavino, *a.* Paduan.
patella, *n.f.* (*Zool.*) Limpet.
patema (*pl.* **patemi**), *n.m.* Affliction, worry, chagrin, pain.
patena, *n.f.* (*Eccles.*) Paten.
patentare, *v.t.* To license, to give a diploma to.
patente, *n.f.* Licence, certificate, patent, diploma. **— di sanità,** clean bill of health; (*Motor.*) **— di circolazione,** car licence; **— di autista, — di abilitazione,** driving licence.
patente, *a.* Patent, manifest, obvious, evident.
patentemente, *adv.* Patently, obviously.
pateracchio [paterAcchio], *n.m.* (*colloq.*) Agreement between two persons; marriage.
patereccio [paterEccio], *n.m.* (*Med.*) Whitlow.
paternale, *n.f.* Scolding, rebuke.
paternale, *a.* Paternal.
paternamente, *adv.* Paternally.
paternità [-à], *n.f.* Paternity, fatherhood; authorship.
paterno, *a.* Fatherly, paternal.
paternostro, *n.m.* Lord's Prayer, Paternoster.
pateticamente, *adv.* Pathetically.
patetico [patEtico], *a.* Moving, touching, affecting; sentimental.
pateticume, *n.m.* False pathos, sickly sentimentality.
patibile [patIbile], *a.* Endurable, passable, passing.
patibolare, *a.* Ripe for the gallows. **Faccia —,** gallows look, hang-dog look.
patibolo [patIbolo], *n.m.* Gallows, scaffold.
patimento, *n.m.* Suffering, pain, torment, grief.
patina [pAtina], *n.f.* Patina, varnish, coating, incrustation.
patinare, *v.t.* To daub, to coat, to varnish; to put dubbing on leather.
patinatura, *n.f.* Varnishing.
patinoso, *a.* (*Med.*) Furred (tongue).
patire, *v.t.i.* To suffer, to be in pain; to bear, to endure; to tolerate. **— il mal di mare,** to be seasick; **— la fame,** to starve.
patito, *a.* Lean, meagre, pulled down, worn out, suffered.
patogenesi [patogEnesi], *n.f.* (*Med.*) Pathogenesis.
patologia [patologIa], *n.f.* Pathology.
patologico [patolOgico], *a.* Pathological.
patologo [patOlogo], *n.m.* Pathologist.
patos, *n.m.* Pathos; emotion, pity.
Patrasso, *n.f.* (*Geog.*) Patras. **Andare a —** to go to the devil.
patria [pAtria], *n.f.* Native country, fatherland, home land. **Madre —,** mother country.
patriarca (*pl.* **patriarchi**), *n.m.* Patriarch.
patriarcale, *a.* Patriarchal.
patriarcalmente, *adv.* Patriarchally.
patriarcato, *n.m.* Patriarchate.
patricida, *n.m.f. a.* Parricide (*person*); parricidal.
patricidio [patricIdio], *n.m.* Crime of parricide.
patrigno, *n.m.* Step-father.
patrimoniale, *a.* Patrimonial.
patrimonio [patrimOnio], *n.m.* Patrimony; hereditary estate, inheritance. **— immobiliare,** real estate; **— mobiliare,** personal property.
patrio [pAtrio], *a.* Native, of one's own country; paternal. **Amor —,** patriotism.
patriota, patriotta (*pl.* **patrioti, patriotti**), *n.m.* Patriot; fellow-countryman.
patriotticamente, *adv.* Patriotically.
patriottico [patriOttico], *a.* Patriotic.
patriottismo, *n.m.* Patriotism.
patriotto [cp. **patriotta**].
patristica [patrIstica], *n.f.* (*Eccles.*) Patristics.
patriziato, *n.m.* Status of a patrician, nobility.
patrizio [patrIzio], *n.m.a.* Patrician.
patrizzare, *v.i.* To take after one's father.
patrocinante, *n.m.* Pleader, protector; (*Law*) counsel for defence.
patrocinare, *v.t.* To plead; to protect, to defend, to champion.
patrocinato, *n.m.* Client.
patrocinatore, *n.m.* Protector; defender; (*Law*) defending counsel.
patrocinio [patrocInio], *n.m.* Protection; patronage; defence; support.
patrologia [cp. **patristica**].
patrona, *n.f.* Female protecting saint.
patronale, *a.* Patronal.
patronato, *n.m.* Patronage; charitable institution.
patronessa, *n.f.* Patroness.
patronimico [patronImico], *n.m.a.* Patronymic.
patrono, *n.m.* Patron, protector; patron saint; (*Naut.*) skipper, captain.
patta, *n.f.* Draw (at games). **Essere pari e —,** to be quits, to be all square; to be a drawn game.
patteggiabile [patteggiAbile], *a.* Open to bargaining.
patteggiamento, *n.m.* Bargaining, agreement; compromise.
patteggiare, *v.t.i.* To bargain, to come to terms, to negotiate; to agree.
patteggiatore, patteggiatrice, *n.m.f.a* Bargainer, negotiator; bargaining.
pattinaggio [pattinAggio], *n.m.* Skating.
pattinare, *v.t.* To skate.
pattinatore, pattinatrice, *n.m.f.* Skater.
pattino [pAttino, pattIno], *n.m.* Skate; (*Aviat.*) skid.
patto, *n.m.* Pact, convention, agreement; condition; terms, understanding. **Patti chiari, amicizia lunga,** short reckonings make long friends; **a nessun —,** in no case; **a — che,** provided that; **venire a patti,** to come to terms.
pattona, *n.f.* Sort of polenta.

pattuglia [pattUglia], *n.f.* (*Mil.*) Patrol.
pattugliare, *v.t.i.* (*Mil.*) To patrol, to reconnoitre.
pattuire, *v.t.i.* To bargain, to agree; to arrange, to fix, to settle.
pattuito, *a.* Agreed. **La somma pattuita,** the agreed amount.
pattume, *n.m.* Dirt, rubbish; litter for cattle.
pattumiera, *n.f.* Dust-bin, garbage can.
patturne, *n.f.pl.* The blues, low spirits, the dumps.
pauperismo, *n.m.* Pauperism.
paura [paUra], *n.f.* Fear, dread; terror, apprehension; fright, alarm. **Aver —,** to be afraid; **far —,** to frighten; **senza —,** fearless; **per — di,** for fear of; **una terribile —,** a terrible fright.
paurosamente, *adv.* Fearfully, timidly.
pauroso, *a.* Fearful, afraid; timorous, timid; apprehensive.
pausa [pAusa], *n.f.* Stop, pause; rest. **Fare una —,** to pause.
pausare, *v.i.* To pause; to be deliberate.
pavana, *n.f.* (*Mus.*) Pavane.
paventare, *v.t.* To fear, to be afraid.
pavento, *n.m.* Fear [cp. **spavento**].
paventoso, *a.* Frightened, fearful.
pavesare, *v.t.* To adorn, to decorate; (*Naut.*) to dress ship; to deck with flags.
pavesata, *n.f.* (*Naut.*) Dressing with flags.
pavese, *n.m.a.* Of Pavia; standard.
pavidamente, *adv.* In fear, fearfully.
pavido [pAvido], *a.* Fearful, timorous, timid, shy; cowardly.
paviglione [cp. **padiglione**].
pavimentare, *v.t.* To floor (a house); to pave (a street).
pavimentazione, *n.f.* Flooring; paving.
pavimento, *n.m.* Floor (of a house); (street) pavement.
pavona, *n.f.* (*Zool.*) Pea-hen.
pavonazzo, *n.m.a.* Peacock blue; violet.
pavoncella, *n.f.* (*Zool.*) Lapwing.
pavoncello, pavoncino, *n.m.* Young peacock.
pavone, *n.m.* (*Zool.*) Peacock.
pavoneggiarsi, *v.r.* To strut (like a peacock); to show off, to boast.
pazientare, *v.i.* To have patience, to be patient, to forbear.
paziente, *n.m.f.* Patient, sufferer, sick person.
paziente, *a.* Patient, enduring, persevering, constant; calm.
pazientemente, *adv.* Patiently.
pazienza, *n.f.* Patience, perseverance, endurance, forbearance; (*Eccles.*) scapular. (*Cards*) **Giuoco di —,** patience; **perder la —,** to lose all patience; (*colloq.*) **Pazienza!** Never mind!
pazzacchione, *n.m.* (*obs.*) Scatter-brained fellow.
pazzamente, *adv.* Madly, insanely; foolishly.
pazzarello [cp. **pazzerello**].
pazzeggiare, *v.t.* To play the fool, to do mad things.
pazzerello, *a.* Silly, rash, foolish.
pazzescamente, *adv.* Foolishly, wildly, rashly.
pazzesco, *a.* Foolish, wild, rash.
pazzia [pazzIa], *n.f.* Insanity, madness, lunacy; folly; extravagance; craziness. **Accesso di —,** fit of madness.
pazzo, *n.m.a.* Madman, lunatic; fool; mad, insane. **Far diventar —,** to drive mad; **spese pazze,** wild extravagance; **— dal dolore,** insane with grief; **andar — per,** to go mad about.
pe', *abbrev.* for **per i**.
peana(*pl.* **peani**), *n.m.* Paean.
pecari, *n.m.* (*Zool.*) Pecary.
pecca, *n.f.* Defect, blemish, flaw; error.
peccabile [peccAbile], *a.* Liable to sin, peccable.
peccabilità [-à], *n.f.* Peccability.
peccaminosamente, *adv.* Sinfully, guiltily.
peccaminoso, *a.* Sinful, guilty, culpable.
peccante, *a.* Sinning.
peccare, *v.i.* To sin; to offend, to transgress; to fail; to be defective.
peccato, *n.m.* Sin; fault, error; pity. **— mortale, originale,** mortal, original sin; **Che —!** What a pity! **è un gran —,** it's a great pity.
peccatore, peccatrice, *n.m.f.* Sinner.
peccatuccio [peccatUccio], *n.m.* Peccadillo; slip, slight fault.
pecchia [pEcchia], *n.f.* (*Zool.*) Bee.
pecchione, *n.m.* (*Zool.*) Drone.
pece, *n.f.* Pitch. **— greca,** resin; **— liquida,** tar.
pechinese, *n.m.a.* Pekinese.
Pechino, *n.m.* (*Geog.*) Pekin.
pecioso, *a.* Smeared with pitch, pitchy; tarry.
pecora [pEcora], *n.f.* (*Zool.*) Sheep, ewe; (*fig.*) subservient person. **— segnata,** black sheep; **un gregge di pecore,** a flock of sheep.
pecoraggine [pecorAggine], *n.f.* Sheepishness, stupidity, docility.
pecoraio [pecorAio], *n.m.* Shepherd.
pecorame, *n.m.* Flock of sheep.
pecoreccio [pecorEccio], *a.* Sheepish.
pecorella, *n.f.* Little sheep, sheep. **— smarrita,** stray sheep; **il curato e le sue pecorelle,** the priest and his flock; **cielo a pecorelle,** fleecy clouds.
pecorescamente, *adv.* Sheepishly.
pecoresco, *a.* Sheepish.
pecorile, *n.m.a.* Sheepfold; sheepish.
pecorino, *n.m.* Lambkin; sheep's dung.
pecorino, *a.* Sheep's, sheep-like. **Formaggio —,** sheep's-milk cheese.
pecoro [pEcoro], *n.m.* (*colloq.*) Ram.
pecorone, *n.m.* (*fig.*) Man with no spirit; blockhead, dolt.
pecorume, *n.m.* (*fig.*) The common herd; crowd of imitators, etc.
peculato, *n.m.* Embezzlement (of public funds).
peculiare, *a.* Special, particular, peculiar to.
peculiarità [-à], *n.f.* Particular attribute, etc.
peculiarmente, *adv.* Peculiarly, particularly.
peculio (*pl.* **peculi**) [pecUlio], *n.m.* Savings, hoard, nest-egg, earnings; (*Mil.*) gratuity.
pecunia [pecUnia], *n.f.* Money.
pecuniariamente, *adv.* Pecuniarily.
pecuniario [pecuniArio], *a.* Pecuniary.
pecunioso, *a.* Rich, wealthy; avaricious, miserly.
pedaggiere, *n.m.* Toll-taker, turnpike-keeper.
pedaggio [pedAggio], *n.m.* Toll.
pedagna, *n.f.* (*Naut.*) Stretcher (for rowing).
pedagogia [pedagogIa], *n.f.* Education, pedagogy.
pedagogico [pedagOgico], *a.* Pedagogical.
pedagogista (*pl.* **pedagogisti**), *n.m.* Educationist.

pedagogo, *n.m.* Pedagogue; pedant.
pedalare, pedaleggiare, *v.t.i.* To pedal (a cycle), to cycle.
pedalata, *n.f.* Thrust of foot on pedal or treadle.
pedale, *n.m.* Pedal; treadle; (*Bot.*) trunk of a tree. (*Motor.*) **— d'innesto,** clutch.
pedaleggiare, *v.t.* (*Mus.*) To pedal (of an organ).
pedaliera, *n.f.* (*Mus.*) Pedal-keys, pedal-board.
pedalista (*pl.* **pedalisti**), *n.m.* Cyclist.
pedana, *n.f.* Foot-rest; foot-board, platform; rug; (*Sport*) jumping-off board.
pedantaggine [pedantAggine], *n.f.* Pedantry.
pedante, *n.m.a.* Pedant; pedantic.
pedanteggiare, *v.i.* To be pedantic.
pedanteria [pedanterIa], *n.f.* Pedantry.
pedantescamente, *adv.* Pedantically.
pedantesco, *a.* Pedantic.
pedata, *n.f.* Footprint; kick; footfall. **Tirar pedate,** to kick; **allungare una —,** to lodge a kick.
pedemontano, *a.* (*Lit.*) Piedmontese.
pederasta, *n.m.* Sodomite, pederast, homosexual.
pederastia [pederastIa], *n.f.* Sodomy, homosexuality.
pedestre, *a.* Pedestrian, dull, uninspired; low, ill-mannered.
pediatria [pediatrIa], *n.f.* (*Med.*) Treatment of sick children, pediatrics.
pediatrico [pediAtrico], *a.* Pediatric, for sick children.
pedicello, *n.m.* (*Bot.*) Small foot-stalk; (*Zool.*) mite.
pedicolare, *a.* (*Med.*) Pedicular. **Morbo —,** the itch.
pedicure, *n.m.f.* Chiropodist.
pedignone, *n.m.* Chilblain (on foot) [cp. **gelone**].
pediluvio [pedilUvio], *n.m.* Foot-bath; paddle (in sea, etc.).
pedina, *n.f.* (*Chess*) pawn; (*Draughts*) man. **Avere una buona —,** to hold a trump card.
pedinamento, *n.m.* Dogging footsteps, shadowing.
pedinare, *v.t.* To dog (the steps), to shadow, to trail, to spy.
pedissequo [pedIssequo], *n.m.a.* Fawner, lick-spittle; servile, fawning; clumsy.
pedivella, *n.f.* Pedal-arm (of a bicycle).
pedometro [pedOmetro], *n.m.* Pedometer.
pedonale, *a.* For pedestrians.
pedone, *n.m.* Pedestrian, foot-passenger; walker; (*Chess*) pawn.
peduccio [pedUccio], *n.m.* Bracket; pedestal; (*Arch.*) corbel. **Peducci,** (animal's) trotters.
pedule, *n.m.* Foot of a stocking. **Peduli,** rope-soled shoes, climbing shoes.
peduncolo [pedUncolo], *n.m.* (*Bot.*) Stalk, peduncle
Pegaso [pEgaso], *n.m.* (*Myth.*) Pegasus.
peggio [pEggio], *adv.* Worse, worst. **Alla —,** at the very worst; somehow or other; **di male in —,** from bad to worse; **avere la —,** to get the worst, to be beaten; **il — è,** the worst of it is; **— che mai,** worse than ever.
peggioramento, *n.m.* Growing worse, getting worse, deteriorating.
peggiorare, *v.t.i.* To make worse; to become worse, to grow worse.
peggiorativamente, *adv.* Depreciatingly, in a depreciating fashion.
peggiorativo, *n.m.a.* Pejorative, depreciatory.
peggiore, *a.* Worse. **Il —, la —, i peggiori, le peggiori,** the worst.
pegno, *n.m.* Pledge, token; forfeit. **Dare in —,** to pledge (one's word); to pawn; **prestito su —,** loan on security; **polizza di —,** pawn-ticket; **giuoco dei pegni,** game of forfeits; **in — d'amicizia,** as a token of friendship.
pegola [pEgola], *n.f.* Melted pitch.
pelago [pElago], *n.m.* (*Poet.*) Sea, ocean; (*fig.*) **— di guai,** sea of troubles.
pelame, *n.m.* (Animal's) hair, coat; plumage.
pelamento, *n.m.* Peeling, skinning.
pelandrone, *n.m.* (*colloq.*) Slacker, idler.
pelare, *v.t.* To peel, to strip, to pare; to pluck (a fowl), to skin; to squeeze out; to shave. **— le patate,** to peel the potatoes.
pelarsi, *v.r.* To lose one's hair, to become bald; to moult (of birds); to fall (of leaves).
pelata, *n.f.* Plucking, stripping; (*colloq.*) baldness.
pelatura, *n.f.* Paring, peeling, skinning.
pellaccia [pellAccia], *n.f.* Worthless fellow, idler.
pellagra, *n.f.* (*Med.*) Pellagra.
pellaio [pellAio], *n.m.* Tanner, currier; leather-dresser; leather merchant.
pellame, *n.m.* Skins, hides.
pelle, *n.f.* Skin; hide, leather; peel, rind; (*fig.*) life. **Non star nella — dalla gioia,** to go mad with delight; **far la — a uno,** to kill someone; **amici per la —,** faithful friends; **levar la —,** to scold severely; **rimetterci la —,** to die; **rischiare la —,** to risk one's life; **una buona —,** a rogue, a rascal; **far venire la — d'oca,** to make one's flesh creep; **conciare pelli,** to tan hides.
pellegrina, *n.f.* Pelerine, tippet; woman pilgrim.
pellegrinaggio [pellegrinAggio], *n.m.* Pilgrimage.
pellegrinare, *v.i.* To travel, to roam, to wander; to go on pilgrimage.
pellegrino, *n.m.a.* Pilgrim; wanderer; wandering; rare, exotic, beautiful.
pelletteria, *n.f.* Leather goods; leather shop.
pellicano, *n.m.* (*Zool.*) Pelican.
pellicceria [pelliccerIa], *n.f.* Furs, furrier's shop.
pelliccia [pellIccia], *n.f.* Fur, fur-coat.
pellicciaio [pellicciAio], *n.m.* Furrier, dealer in furs.
pellicola [pellIcola], *n.f.* Film, membrane; (*Phot.*) film. **— cinematografica,** cinematograph film; **— su rocchetto,** roll-film.
pellirossa (*pl.* **pellirosse**), *n.m.* Redskin, Red Indian.
pellucido [pellUcido], *a.* Pellucid, transparent.
pelo, *n.m.* Hair; fur, coat (of animals); nap (of cloth), pile (of carpet); surface (of water); crack (in a surface). **Contro —,** against the grain; **essere a un — da,** to be on the point of; **per un —,** by a hair's breadth; **cercare il — nell'uovo,** to split hairs; **essere di primo —,** to be in one's prime; **non aver peli sulla lingua,** to be outspoken; **a —,** bare-backed (riding); **cane dal — raso,** smooth-haired dog; **avere il — sullo stomaco,** to be unscrupulous.

pelosità [-à], *n.f.* Hairiness, shagginess.
peloso, *a.* Hairy, hirsute, shaggy. **Carità pelosa,** interested kindness; **coscienza pelosa,** easy-going conscience.
pelota, *n.f.* Basque ball game.
pelta, *n.f.* (*Hist.*) Small buckler.
peltro, *n.m.* Pewter.
peluria [pelUria], *n.f.* Soft hair, down.
peluzzo, *n.m.* Down; fine cloth.
pelvi, *n.f.* (*Anat.*) Pelvis.
pelvico [pElvico], *a.* (*Anat.*) Pelvic.
pena, *n.f* Punishment; penalty; pain, suffering, anguish, distress; trouble, grief; difficulty. **Darsi la —,** to take the trouble; **far —,** to move to pity; **soffrirne la —,** to suffer for it; **non vale la —.** it isn't worth while; **a mala —,** scarcely, hardly; **sotto — di,** under pain of; **— di morte,** capital punishment; **vale la — d'andarci,** it's worth while to go there.
penale, *a.* Penal.
penalista (*pl.* **penalisti**), *n.m.* Criminologist; jurist.
penalità [-à], *n.f.* Penalty.
penalizzare, *v.t.* To penalize.
penalmente, *adv.* Penally.
penare, *v.i.* To suffer, to be in pain; to strive, to labour; to take pains.
penati, *n.m.pl.* (*Myth.*) Penates, household gods.
pencolare, *v.i.* To totter, to dangle, to hang down; to hesitate, to waver.
pendaglio [pendAglio], *n.m.* Pendant; sword-frog; tenter-hook; bed curtain. **— da forca,** gallows-bird.
pendente, *a.* Hanging, dangling; leaning; unsettled. **Torre —,** leaning tower.
pendente, *n.m.* Pendant, ear-drop.
pendenza, *n.f.* Slope, declivity, gradient; (*Comm.*) pending business. **Lite in —,** pending law suit; **— della strada,** the gradient of the road.
pendere [pEndere], *v.i.* To hang, to dangle, to overhang; to incline, to slope; to lean; to be pending. **— dalle labbra di,** to hang on one's lips.
pendice, *n.f.* Slope, declivity; hill-side.
pendio [pendIo], *n.m.* Slope, declivity; gradient; steepness, inclination.
pendola [pEndola], *n.f.* Clock, pendulum clock; time-piece.
pendolo [pEndolo], *n.m.* Pendulum.
pendone, *n.f.* Festoon.
pendulo [pEndulo], *a.* Hanging, pendulous.
pene, *n.m.* (*Anat.*) Penis.
penerata, *n.f.* Warp fringe.
penetrabile [penetrAbile], *a.* Penetrable.
penetrabilità [-à], *n.f.* Penetrability.
penetrale, *n.m.* Recess, innermost recess. **Penetrali,** the inner and most sacred chamber of a temple.
penetramento, *n.m.* Penetrating, penetration.
penetrante, *a.* Penetrating; penetrant; piercing.
penetrare, *v.t.* To penetrate; to pass through, to pierce; to enter into, to steal into; to pervade; to fathom; to see through; to convince. **Esser penetrato di una necessità,** to be alive to a necessity.
penetrazione, *n.f.* Penetration; sharpness; insight.
penicillina, *n.f.* (*Med.*) Penicillin.
peninsulare, *a.* Peninsular.
penisola [penIsola], *n.f.* Peninsula.
penitente, *n.m.a.* Penitent.
penitenza, *n.f.* Penance; repentance, penitence; forfeit (in games). **Far —,** to do penance.
penitenziale, *a.* Penitential.
penitenziario [penitenziArio], *n.m.* Penitentiary, prison, gaol, reformatory.
penitenziere, *n.m.* (*Eccles.*) Penitentiary.
penna, *n.f.* Feather; pen, quill; (*Poet.*) wing; (*fig.*) writer; head of a hammer; kind of macaroni; (*Naut.*) yard. **— d'oca,** quill pen; **lasciar nella —,** to omit; **una buona —,** a good writer; **— stilografica,** fountain pen; **scorso di —,** slip of the pen; **— a sfera,** ball-pointed pen.
pennacchiera, *n.f.* Plume on a helmet.
pennacchietto, *n.m.* Small plume.
pennacchio [pennAcchio], *n.m.* Plume, crest, panache; cloud of smoke.
pennacchiuto, *a.* Plumed; wearing feathers.
pennaio [pennAio], *n.m.* Worker in ornamental feathers.
pennaiolo, *n.m.* Pen-case; scribbler, penny-a-liner, pot-boiler.
pennata, *n.f.* Penful of ink; stroke of the pen.
pennatato, *n.m.* Stroke with a bill-hook.
pennato, *n.m.* Bill-hook.
pennato, *a.* Feathered.
pennecchio [pennEcchio], *n.m.* Flax or wool on the distaff.
pennella, *n.f.* White-wash brush.
pennellare, pennelleggiare, *v.t.i.* To paint.
pennellata, *n.f.* Brush-stroke, touch of the brush.
pennellatura, pennellazione, *n.f.* Brush-work, painting; (*Med.*) painting.
pennelleggiare [cp. **pennellare**].
pennello, *n.m.* Paint-brush, brush; (*fig.*) painter. **— per barba,** shaving-brush; **stare a —,** to fit like a glove; **l'arte del —,** painting (pictures); **fatto a —,** well finished.
pennino, *n.m.* Nib, pen-nib.
pennoncello, *n.m.* Small flag; streamer.
pennoncino, *n.m.* (*Naut.*) Light yard (for small craft).
pennone, *n.m.* Pennon, flag, banner; (*Naut.*) yard (of a ship).
pennoniere, *n.m.* Standard-bearer.
pennuto, *n.m.a.* Feathered creature, bird; feathered, fledged.
penombra, *n.f.* Twilight, dim light, half-shadow; (*Astron.*) penumbra. **Star nella —,** to keep in the background, to hold aloof.
penosamente, *adv.* Painfully, troublesomely.
penoso, *a.* Painful; trying, difficult, troublesome; toilsome.
pensabile [pensAbile], *a.* Thinkable.
pensamento, *n.m.* Thinking, thought.
pensante, *a.* Thinking. **Ben —,** right-minded.
pensare, *v.t.i.* To think, to ponder, to reflect; to believe, to imagine; to judge, to consider; to remember; to provide for. **Senza pensarci,** without thinking; **pensarci su,** to think it over; **dar da —,** to make one think, to cause uneasiness; **modo di —,** way of thinking; **— e ripensare,** to brood over; **ci penso io,** I'll see to it; **— al passato,** to ponder over the past; **— a,** to think (of person); **— di,** to think (of things); **pensa il male che avete fatto,** think of the harm you've done.

pensata, *n.f.* Thought, idea.
pensatamente, *adv.* On purpose, intentionally.
pensatoio [pensatOio], *n.m.* (*colloq.*) Thinking-place. **Entrare nel —,** to put on one's thinking-cap.
pensatore, pensatrice, *n.m.f.* Thinker. **Libero —,** free-thinker.
pensiero, *n.m.* Thought; idea; intention; mind, intellect; culture; opinion; reflexion; care, trouble; memory; meditation. **Darsi —,** to care about, to mind; **essere sopra —,** to be uneasy; to be absorbed in thought; **cambiar —,** to change one's mind; (*Bot.*) **viola del —,** pansy.
pensieroso, *a.* Thoughtful, pensive; serious, grave, sedate.
pensile [pEnsile], *a.* Hanging, suspended. **Giardino —,** hanging garden, garden on a terrace.
pensilina, *n.f.* Pent-house; lean-to; roof (over railway platforms, etc.).
Pensilvania [pensilvAnia], *n.f.* (*Geog.*) Pennsylvania.
pensionante, *n.m.* Boarder.
pensionare, *v.t.* To pension, to pension off.
pensionario [pensionArio], *n.m.* Pensioner.
pensionato, *n.m.* Pensioner, superannuated man; boarding-school.
pensione, *n.f.* Pension, allowance, annuity, superannuation; boarding-house, private hotel. **Tenere —,** to keep boarders; **andare in —,** to be pensioned off, to retire.
penso, *n.m.* Task, imposition.
pensosamente, *adv.* Thoughtfully, pensively.
pensoso, *a.* Thoughtful, pensive, serious, grave.
pentacolo [pentAcolo], *n.m.* Pentacle, five-pointed star.
pentagono [pentAgono], *n.m.* (*Geom.*) Pentagon.
pentametro [pentAmetro], *n.m.* (*Poet.*) Pentameter.
pentateuco [pentatEuco], *n.m.* Pentateuch.
Pentecoste, *n.f.* Pentecost, Whitsuntide. **Domenica di —,** Whitsunday.
pentimento, *n.m.* Repentance, regret.
pentirsi, *v.r.* To repent, to be sorry; to regret; to change one's mind. **Mi son pentito,** I have repented, I'm sorry.
pentola [pEntola], *n.f.* Earthenware pot, large pot, cauldron; kettle. **Sapere quel che bolle in —,** to know what's going on, to find out what's brewing.
pentolaio [pentolAio], *n.m.* Potter; vendor of earthenware pots.
pentolata, *n.f.* Potful.
pentolino, pentolo [pEntolo], *n.m.* Small pot, can, pannikin, pan.
penultimamente, *adv.* Penultimately.
penultimo [penUltimo], *a.* Penultimate, last but one.
penuria [penUria], *n.f.* Penury, need, want.
penzolare, *v.i.* To hang, to overhang; to swing; to dangle, to hang down.
penzolo [pEnzolo], *n.m.* Hanging cluster of grapes.
penzolone, penzoloni, *adv.* Hanging, dangling. **Stare —,** to hang down, to swing in the air.
peonia [peOnia], *n.f.* (*Bot.*) Peony.
peota, *n.f.* (*Naut.*) Type of Venetian boat.
pepaiola, *n.f.* Pepper-pot; pepper-mill.
pepato, *a.* Peppered, spiced; (*fig.*) pungent, peppery; exorbitant (of price). **Pan —,** gingerbread.
pepe, *n.m.* Pepper. **— di Caienna,** Cayenne pepper.
peperino, *n.m.* (*Geol.*) Stone composed of lava, tufa, etc.
peperone, *n.m.* (*Bot.*) Capsicum, chilli. **Peperoni sott'aceto,** pickled chillies.
pepita, *n.f.* Nugget (usu. gold).
peplo, *n.m.* (*Arch.*) Peplum.
pepolino, *n.m.* (*Bot.*) Thyme.
Peppe, *n.m.* (*colloq.*) Joe [GIUSEPPE].
peppola [pEppola], *n.f.* (*Zool.*) Mountain finch.
pepsina, *n.f.* Pepsin.
peptico [pEptico], *a.* Peptic.
peptone, *n.m.* Peptone.
per, *prep.* For, by, through, in, to, during, on account of, by means of, in order to. **Mandare per posta,** to send by post; **per mezzo di,** by means of; **essere per partire,** to be on the point of starting; **per lo meno,** at least; **per ora,** at present; **per tempo,** early; **per l'appunto,** precisely; **per altro,** on the other hand; **per lo più,** for the most part; **per modo che,** so that; **per così dire,** so to speak; **per uno, per due,** by ones and twos; **per quanto ricco,** however rich; **per l'addietro,** heretofore, formerly.
pera, *n.f.* (*Bot.*) Pear; (*colloq.*) head.
peranco, *adv.* Yet.
perbacco! *inter.* By Jove!
perbene, *a.* Respectable, well brought up.
perbene, *adv.* Nicely.
percalle, *n.m.* Cotton cambric.
percallina, *n.f.* Glazed cotton material.
percentuale, *n.f.* Percentage.
percepibile [percepIbile], *a.* Perceptible, noticeable.
percepire, *v.t.* To perceive, to conceive, to get, to collect, to cash, to receive.
percettibile [percettIbile], *a.* Perceptible.
percettibilità [-à], *n.f.* Perceptibility.
percettività [-à], *n.f.* Perceptiveness.
percettivo, *a.* Perceptive.
percettore, *n.m.* Tax-collector.
percezione, *n.f.* Perception, discernment; (*Law*) collection, receipt.
perchè [-è], *n.m.* The why, the reason why.
perchè, *conj.* Because, for, in order that, since. **Non so —,** I don't know why; **perchè mai?** Why, then? Why ever?
perchè, *inter.* Why?
perciò, *adv.* Therefore, for that reason.
perciocchè, *adv.* For, because; since.
percome, *n.m.* The why. **Il perchè e il —,** the how and the wherefore.
percorrenza, *n.f.* Time required to cover a certain distance; route; fare.
percorrere [percOrrere], *v.t.* To run through, to go through; to travel, to make, to cover (distance); to glance through. **— cento miglia all'ora,** to cover 100 miles an hour; **— il paese,** to travel all over the country.
percorso, *n.m.* Distance, stretch, run; route, way; voyage. **Il — più breve,** the shortest route.
percossa, *n.f.* Blow, stroke.
percotimento, *n.m.* Striking.

percotitore, *n.m.* One who strikes, striker.
percuotere, percotere [percuOtere, percOtere], *v.t.* To strike, to hit, to knock, to smite, to beat; to clash.
percussione, *n.f.* Percussion.
percussore, *n.m.* knocker, hammer.
perdente, *n.m.a.* Loser; losing.
perdere [pErdere], *v.t.i.* To lose, to be deprived of; to miss (a train, etc.); to waste, to ruin, to undo; to leak. **— di vista,** to lose sight of; **è tempo perso,** it's a waste of time; **— al giuoco,** to lose at gambling; (*colloq.*) **ho perso la corsa,** I lost the train.
perdersi [pErdersi], *v.r.* To be lost, to lose oneself, to get lost; to fall into disuse; to disappear; to ruin oneself. **— d'animo,** to lose heart; **— dietro una persona,** to be crazy about someone; **la lettera si è perduta,** the letter has been lost.
perdibile [perdIbile], *a.* Capable of being lost, easily lost.
perdifiato, *adv.* **A —,** at the top of one's voice.
perdigiorno, *n.m.* Idler, slacker; good-for-nothing.
perdimento, *n.m.* Losing, loss.
perdinci! *inter.* By Jove! Bother!
perdita, *n.f.* Loss, detriment, waste (of time). **Le perdite della guerra,** losses in the war; **le perdite,** war casualties; **— della memoria,** loss of memory; **essere in —,** to be a loser; to be out of pocket; **subire una —,** to incur a loss.
perditempo, *n.m.* Loss of time, waste of time, time lost.
perditore, perditrice, *n.m.f.* Loser.
perdizione, *n.f.* Perdition.
perdonabile [perdonAbile], *a.* Forgivable, pardonable.
perdonanza, *n.f.* Pardon; (*Eccles.*) indulgence.
perdonare, *v.t.* To forgive, to pardon; to excuse. **Perdoni!** Excuse me!
perdono, *n.m.* Forgiveness, pardon, remission. **Vi chiedo —,** I beg your pardon.
perdurabile [perdurAbile], *a.* Durable.
perdurabilità [-à], *n.f.* Durability.
perdurabilmente, *adv.* Durably.
perduranza, *n.f.* Lastingness, endurance.
perdurare, *v.t.* To last, to continue, to hold out; to persevere.
perdurevole [perdurEvole], *a.* Durable, lasting.
perdutamente, *adv.* Desperately; hopelessly. **Lo ama —,** she was madly in love with him.
perduto, *p.p.a.* Lost; wasted; ruined; forlorn; dishonoured. **Donna perduta,** an abandoned woman; **tempo —,** wasted time; **a corpo —,** whole-heartedly; desperately, rashly; **sono —,** I'm lost, I'm done for.
peregrinare, *v.i.* To wander about, to roam, to rove, to ramble.
peregrinazione, *n.f.* Peregrination.
peregrinità [-à], *n.f.* Peculiarity, oddity, strangeness.
peregrino, *a.* Rare; peculiar, queer, odd. **Idea peregrina,** strange idea.
perenne, *a.* Everlasting, perpetual, perennial; inexhaustible.
perennemente, *adv.* Everlastingly.
perennità [-à], *n.f.* Perpetuity.
perento, *a.* (*Law*) Lapsed, annulled, extinguished; out-of-date.
perentoriamente, *adv.* Peremptorily.
perentorio [perentOrio], *a.* Peremptory, imperious.
perenzione, *n.f.* (*Law*) Annulling; lapse of a right; extinction of a claim.
perequare, *v.t.* To equalize, to standardize.
perequazione, *n.f.* Equalization (of payments, etc.).
pereto, *n.m.* Pear orchard.
peretta, *n.f.* (*Sport*) Flying spur attached to a horse in a riderless race; (*Med.*) rubber syringe.
perfettamente, *adv.* Perfectly.
perfettibile [perfettIbile], *a.* Perfectible.
perfettibilità [-à], *n.f.* Perfectibility.
perfetto, *n.m.* (*Gram.*) Perfect tense.
perfetto, *a.* Perfect, thorough, complete; blameless; absolute; ripe.
perfezionabile [perfezionAbile], *a.* Capable of being perfected or improved.
perfezionamento, *n.m.* Perfecting, finishing, completion. **Studi di —,** post-graduate studies.
perfezionare, *v.t.* To perfect, to make perfect; to develop; to improve; to finish, to complete; to carry out.
perfezionarsi, *v.r.* To improve oneself, to get perfect; to learn thoroughly.
perfezione, *n.f.* Perfection, perfectness; accomplishment; finish. **Alla —,** to perfection, perfectly well.
perficere [perfIcere], *v.t.* (*obs.*) To perfect.
perfidamente, *adv.* Perfidiously.
perfidia [perfIdia], *n.f.* Perfidy, treachery, faithlessness; wickedness.
perfidioso, *a.* (*obs.*) Perfidious.
perfido [pErfido], *n.m.a.* Perfidious person; perfidious, treacherous; (*Med.*) malignant (of disease); (*colloq.*) **Albione perfida,** England, Britain (politically).
perfine, *adv.* **Alla —,** finally, at last, in short.
perfinire, *n.m.* Closing sentence or words, wind-up; chestnut, joke.
perfino, *adv.* Even, also.
perforabile [perforAbile], *a.* Perforable, liable to perforation.
perforamento, *n.m.* Perforation.
perforante, *a.* Piercing, perforating.
perforare, *v.t.* To pierce, to perforate, to bore through, to drill, to punch. **— un biglietto,** to punch a ticket.
perforatrice, *n.f.* (*Mech.*) Drill, borer; rock-drill.
perforazione, *n.f.* Perforation.
perfusione, *n.f.* Spraying.
pergamena, *n.f.* Parchment.
pergamenato, *a.* Parchment-like.
pergamo [pErgamo], *n.m.* (*Lit.*) Pulpit.
pergola [pErgola], *n.f.* Bower, arbour, vine-trellis; pergola.
pergolato, *n.m.* Trellis-work, bower, pergola.
pericardio [pericArdio], *n.m.* (*Anat.*) Pericardium.
pericardite, *n.f.* (*Med.*) Pericarditis.
pericolamento, *n.m.* Peril, imperilling.
pericolante, *a.* In danger, in jeopardy, tottering, unsafe.
pericolare, *v.i.* To be in danger, to be in a perilous position.

pericolo [perIcolo], *n.m.* Danger, peril; jeopardy; risk, hazard. **Mettere in —,** to endanger; **essere in —,** to be in danger; **correre un —,** to run a risk.
pericolosamente, *adv.* Dangerously, perilously.
pericoloso, *a.* Dangerous, perilous, risky, hazardous.
pericranio [pericrAnio], *n.m.* (*Anat.*) Pericranium.
peridoto, *n.m.* (*Min.*) Peridot.
perielio [periElio], *n.m.* (*Astron.*) Perihelion.
periferia [periferIa], *n.f.* Periphery; outskirts (of a city).
perifrasare, *v.t.* To express by circumlocution.
perifrasi [perIfrasi], *n.f.* Periphrasis.
perifrastico [perifrAstico], *a.* Periphrastic.
perigeo [perigEo], *n.m.* (*Astron.*) Perigee.
periglio [perIglio], *n.m.* (*Poet.*) Peril [cp. pericolo].
periglioso, *a.* Perilous.
perimetro [perImetro], *n.m.* Perimeter.
periodare, *v.t.* To break up into sentences.
periodicamente, *adv.* Periodically.
periodicità [-à], *n.f.* Periodicity.
periodico [periOdico], *n.m.a.* Periodical; recurring.
periodo [perIodo], *n.m.* Period (in all senses); sentence; stage, spell (of time).
periostio [periOstio], *n.m.* (*Anat.*) Periosteum.
periostite, *n.f.* (*Med.*) Periostitis.
peripateticamente, *adv.* Peripatetically.
peripatetico [peripatEtico], *n.m.a.* Peripatetic; itinerant.
peripezia [peripezIa], *n.f.* Vicissitude, accident, change of luck, ups and downs (of life).
periplo [pEriplo], *n.m.* Voyage round the world, circumnavigation.
perire, *v.i.* To perish, to die; to decay, to disappear, to be lost.
periscopio [periscOpio], *n.m.* Periscope.
peristaltico [peristAltico], *a.* (*Anat.*) Peristaltic.
peristilio [peristIlio], *n.m.* (*Arch.*) Peristyle.
peritamente, *adv.* Done by an expert, expertly.
peritanza, *n.f.* (*Poet.*) Bashfulness, shyness; shame.
peritarsi, *v.r.* To be shy; to hesitate, not to dare. **Egli non si perita,** he does not hesitate.
perito, *n.m.* Expert; surveyor. **— traduttore,** sworn translator; **— ragioniere,** chartered accountant.
perito, *a.* Expert, skilled; versed, learned.
peritoneo [peritonEo], *n.m.* (*Anat.*) Peritoneum.
peritonite, *n.f.* (*Med.*) Peritonitis.
peritosamente, *adv.* Timidly, hesitantly.
peritoso, *a.* Hesitant, timid, shy.
perituro, *a.* Perishable; subject to decay; mortal.
perizia [perIzia], *n.f.* Skill, ability, dexterity; (*Law*) expert opinion; valuation, survey, appraisement.
periziare, *v.i.* To make a survey, to appraise, to estimate, to value. (*Racing*) **Corsa periziata,** handicap.
perla, *n.f.* Pearl (in all senses); gem. **Pescatore di perle,** pearl-diver; **la — dei martiri,** the pearl among martyrs.
perlaceo, perlato [perlAceo], *a.* Pearly, pearled; nacreous.
perlagione, *n.f.* Play of colours in mother-of-pearl.
perlaio [perlAio], *n.m.* Worker in pearls; pearl-dealer.
perlettina, perletto, perlina, *n.f.m.f.* Small pearl; bead.
perlustrare, *v.t.* (*Mil.*) To scout, to reconnoitre; to search, to explore.
perlustratore, *n.m.* Scout.
perlustrazione, *n.f.* Scouting, reconnoitring; search.
permalosità [-à], *n.f.* Touchiness, irritability, peevishness.
permaloso, *a.* Touchy, irritable, peevish, cross.
permanente, *n.f.* Permanent wave (of the hair).
permanente, *a.* Permanent, standing; lasting, perpetual.
permanentemente, *adv.* Permanently.
permanenza, *n.f.* Permanence, stay, residence; duration.
permanere, *v.i.* To persist, to remain, to last, to stay.
permanganato, *n.m.* (*Chem.*) Permanganate.
permeabile [permeAbile], *a.* Permeable, penetrable.
permeabilità [-à], *n.f.* Permeability.
permeare, *v.t.* To permeate, to imbue, to saturate.
permesso, *n.m.* Permission, leave; licence, permit. **Essere in —,** to be on leave; **— di passaggio,** pass, permit; **con —,** allow me, by your leave; **Permesso?** May I come in?
permettere [permEttere], *v.t.* To permit, to allow, to authorize; to let, to admit; to tolerate, to suffer. **Non posso — che,** I cannot allow that.
permettersi [permEttersi], *v.r.* To take the liberty, to venture to.
permissibile [permissIbile], *a.* Permissible.
permissione, *n.f.*(*obs.*) Permission, concession.
permissivamente, *adv.* Permissively.
permissivo, *a.* Permissive.
permuta [pErmuta], *n.f.* Exchange, barter.
permutabile [permutAbile], *a.* Exchangeable.
permutabilità [-à], *n.f.* Changeableness.
permutamento, *n.m.* Exchange, change.
permutare, *v.t.* To exchange, to barter; to re-arrange.
permutazione, *n.f.* Change, transposition. **— atmosferica,** atmospherical change.
pernice, *n.f.* (*Zool.*) Partridge.
perniciosamente, *adv.* Perniciously, fatally.
pernicioso, *a.* Pernicious, malignant, ruinous fatal, destructive. (*Med.*) **Febbre perniciosa,** malignant fever.
pernio, perno [pErnio], *n.m.* Pivot, hinge; axis; support, basis; turning-point; stud.
pernottamento, *n.m.* Passing the night; a night's stay.
pernottare, *v.i.* To spend the night, to stay (for the night).
pero, *n.m.* (*Bot.*) Pear-tree.
però, *conj.* However, yet, but; therefore, thereupon; on that account.
perocchè, *conj.* Since, for; because.
perondino, *n.m.* (*colloq.*) Young fop, dude.
perone [pErone], *n.m.* (*Anat.*) Fibula.

peronospora [peronOspora], *n.f.* (*Agric.*) Mildew.
perorare, *v.t.i.* To plead (in a court), to defend; to harangue; to perorate.
perorazione, *n.f.* Peroration.
perossido [perOssido], *n.m.* (*Chem.*) Peroxide.
perpendicolare, *n.f.a.* Perpendicular.
perpendicolarmente, *adv.* Perpendicularly.
perpendicolo [perpendIcolo], *adv.* **A —,** perpendicularly, vertically.
perpetrare, *v.t.* To commit, to perpetrate (a crime, etc.).
perpetrazione, *n.f.* Perpetration.
perpetua [perpEtua], *n.f.* Priest's housekeeper (from character in "I Promessi Sposi").
perpetualmente, perpetuamente, *adv.* Perpetually.
perpetuare, *v.t.* To perpetuate, to make live a long time.
perpetuarsi, *v.r.* To become perpetual.
perpetuazione, *n.f.* Perpetuation.
perpetuità [-à], *n.f.* Perpetuity.
perpetuo [perpEtuo], *a.* Perpetual, constant, uninterrupted, everlasting. **In —,** perpetually, forever, in perpetuity; **moto —,** perpetual motion.
perplessamente, *adv.* Perplexedly.
perplessità [-à], *n.f.* Perplexity, irresolution, hesitation.
perplesso, *a.* Perplexed, puzzled, embarrassed, irresolute, undecided, hesitating.
perquisire, *v.t.* To search (by police, etc.).
perquisizione, *n.f.* (Police) search, investigation. **Fare una —,** to search (house, etc).
perrucca [cp. **parrucca**].
perscrutare [cp. **scrutare**].
persecutore, persecutrice, *n.m.f.* Persecutor, persecutrix; bore, importunate person.
persecuzione, *n.f.* Persecution. **Mania di —,** persecution mania; paranoia.
perseguire, *v.t.* To pursue, to follow up; to aim at; to seek.
perseguitare, *v.t.* To persecute, to molest, to harass, to worry; to importune.
Perseo [pErseo], *n.m.* (*Myth. Astron.*) Perseus.
perseverante, *a.* Persevering, perseverant.
perseverantemente, *adv.* Perseveringly.
perseveranza, *n.f.* Perseverance, steadiness, persistence.
perseverare, *v.i.* To persevere, to persist, to insist.
persiana, *n.f.* Venetian blind; shutter (with slats), persienne.
persiano, *n.m.a.* Persian.
persica [cp. **pesca**].
persicata, *n.f.* Peach conserve, peach jam.
persico [pErsico], *a.* Persian. (*Zool.*) **Pesce —,** perch; (*Geog.*) **Golfo Persico,** Persian Gulf.
persino, *adv.* Even, also.
persistente, *a.* Persistent, persevering.
persistenza, *n.f.* Persistence; perseverance.
persistere [persIstere], *v.i.* To persist, to insist, to continue, to persevere.
perso (1), *a.* Lost [cp. **perdere**].
perso (2), *a.* (*Lit.*) Purple, very dark brown; dark.
persona, *n.f.* Person, individual; body, shape, figure; self; (*Gram.*) person. **In —,** in person, personally; **è la bontà in —,** she's goodness itself; **venne in —,** he came himself; **pagar di —,** to make a personal sacrifice, to take a personal share; **per —,** per head, apiece; **Quante persone!** What a lot of people! What a crowd!
personaggio [personAggio], *n.m.* Personage, person of rank; personality; (*Theat.*) character (in a play); (*Theat.*) **personaggi,** dramatis personae.
personale, *n.m.* Staff, personnel; body, figure. **Il — insegnante,** the teaching staff.
personale, *a.* Personal, individual; single. **Biglietto —,** non-transferable ticket; **riservata —,** private and confidential (of a letter).
personalità [-à], *n.f.* Personality; personage, notability, man of mark; (*Law*) personality.
personalmente, *adv.* Personally.
personcina, *n.f.* Tiny person; slender figure.
personificare, *v.t.* To personify; to impersonate.
personificazione, *n.f.* Personification, impersonation. **È la — della bontà,** he's kindness personified.
perspicace, *a.* Sharp, discerning, sagacious, perspicacious, keen.
perspicacemente, *adv.* Shrewdly, sagaciously.
perspicacia [perspicAcia], *n.f.* Acuteness, perspicacity, penetration.
perspicacità [-à], *n.f.* Perspicacity.
perspicuamente, *adv.* Perspicuously.
perspicuità [-à], *n.f.* Perspicuity.
perspicuo [persplcuo], *a.* Perspicuous, clear, lucid.
persuadente, *a.* Persuading, persuasive.
persuadere, *v.t.* To persuade, to convince; to induce; to influence.
persuadersi, *v.r.* To convince oneself, to be convinced.
persuadibile, persuasibile [persuadIbile, persuasIbile], *a.* Persuasible.
persuasione, *n.f.* Persuasion; conviction; opinion, belief.
persuasiva, *n.f.* Persuasiveness.
persuasivamente, *adv.* Persuasively.
persuasivo, *a.* Persuasive, convincing.
persuaso, *p.p.a.* Convinced, persuaded.
persuasore, *n.m.* Persuader, inducer.
pertanto, *adv.* Therefore, still; consequently; nevertheless. **Non —,** notwithstanding, nevertheless.
pertica [pErtica], *n.f.* Perch, pole, rod; perch (measurement). **Essere una —,** to be tall and slender.
perticata, *n.f.* Blow with a pole.
perticatore, *n.m.* Measurer, surveyor.
perticazione, *n.f.* Measurement.
pertichino, *n.m.* Professional vocalist's understudy.
perticone, *n.m.* Tall thin person.
pertinace, *a.* Pertinacious, stubborn, persistent; obstinate.
pertinacemente, *adv.* Pertinaciously.
pertinacia [pertinAcia], *n.f.* Pertinacity, stubbornness, obstinacy, wilfulness.
pertinente, *a.* Pertinent, pertaining; appropriate, relevant.
pertinenza, *n.f.* Pertinence, competence.
pertosse, *n.f.* (*Med.*) Whooping-cough.
pertrattare [cp. **trattare**].
pertugiare, *v.t.* To bore, to drill; to open.

pertugio [pertUgio], *n.m.* Hole, opening, gap, aperture.
perturbamento, *n.m.* Perturbation, disorder; confusion.
perturbare, *v.t.* To perturb, to trouble, to disquiet, to disorder, to agitate.
perturbatamente, *adv.* In a perturbed manner; confusedly.
perturbatore, perturbatrice, *n.m.f.* Perturber, disturber; mischief-maker.
perturbazione, *n.f.* Perturbation, trouble, disorder, confusion, disturbance.
Perù, *n.m.* (*Geog.*) Peru. (*colloq.*) **Valere un —,** to be of great value.
peruginesco, *a.* (*Art*) After the style of Perugino.
perugino, *n.m.a.* Native of or pertaining to Perugia.
peruviano, *n.m.a.* Peruvian.
pervadere [pervAdere], *v.t.* To pervade, to permeate, to run through.
pervenire, *v.i.* To attain to, to arrive at, to reach. **Gli pervenne una lettera,** a letter reached him; **— alla meta,** to attain the goal; **— al trono,** to succeed to the throne.
perversamente, *adv.* Perversely, wickedly.
perversione, *n.f.* Perversion, depravity.
perversità [-à], *n.f.* Depravity, corruption, wickedness.
perverso, *a.* Depraved, wicked, corrupt; perfidious.
pervertimento, *n.m.* Perversion, depravity.
pervertire, *v.t.* To pervert, to corrupt, to lead astray.
pervertirsi, *v.r.* To become depraved, to be perverted.
pervertito, *n.m.* Pervert.
pervertitore, pervertitrice, *n.f.* Corrupter, perverter.
pervicace, *a.* Stubborn, obstinate, perverse.
pervicacemente, *adv.* Stubbornly.
pervicacia [pervicAcia], *n.f.* Stubbornness, obstinacy.
pervinca, *n.f.* (*Bot.*) Periwinkle.
pervio [pErvio], *a.* (*Lit.*) Pervious.
pesa, *n.f.* Weighing-machine; weigh-house.
pesabile [pesAbile], *a.* Weighable.
pesaggio [pesAggio], *n.m.* Weighing.
pesalettere [pesalEttere], *n.m.* Letter-scales.
pesamento, *n.m.* Weighing.
pesante, *a.* Heavy, weighty; lumpish; massive; ponderous, boring, wearisome. **Avere la testa —,** to feel drowsy; **lavoro —,** hard work; **aria —,** sultry weather.
pesantemente, *adv.* Heavily, weightily.
pesantezza, *n.f.* Weight, heaviness; dullness, oppressiveness; tiresomeness.
pesare, *v.t.i.* To weigh; to be heavy; to gravitate; (*fig.*) to consider, to examine; to influence. **Quanto pesi?** What do you weigh? **pesa dieci quintali,** it weighs ten quintals; **— le parole,** to weigh one's words; **quanto mi pesa il dire,** how hard it is for me to tell you; **— una persona,** to weigh someone, to size up a person.
pesarsi, *v.r.* To weigh oneself.
pesata, *n.f.* Weighing.
pesatamente, *adv.* Weightily.
pesatore, *n.m.* Weigher.
pesatura, *n.f.* Weighing.
pesca [pèsca] (1), *n.f.* (*Bot.*) Peach. **— duracina,** cling-stone peach.
pesca [pésca] (2), *n.f.* Fishing; catch; fishery. **Industria della —,** fishing industry; **barca da —,** fishing-boat; **— con la lenza,** angling; (*colloq.*) **— di beneficenza,** charity bazaar.
pescaggio [pescAggio], *n.m.* Draught (of a ship).
pescagione, *n.f.* Fishing; draught (of a ship); draught (of fish).
pescaia [pescAia], *n.f.* Dam, weir; sluice, flood-gate.
pescare, *v.t.i.* To fish; to fish out, to pick out; to draw out, to draw (of a ship); to pick up; to find out. **— all'amo,** to angle; (*fig.*) **— nel torbido,** to fish in troubled waters; (*Naut.*) **— due metri,** to draw two metres.
pescareccio [cp. **peschereccio**].
pescata, *n.f.* Fishing; netful, catch, draught of fish.
pescatore, pescatrice, *n.m.f.* Fisherman, fisher, angler. **— di perle,** pearl-diver; (*Zool.*) **martin —,** kingfisher.
pescatorio [pescatOrio], *a.* Fishing.
pesce, *n.m.* Fish. **— di mare,** sea-fish; salt-water fish; **spina di —,** fish-bone; **— d'aprile,** April fool; **non saper che pesci pigliare,** not to know which way to turn; **essere un — fuori d'acqua,** to be a fish out of water; **non essere nè carne nè —,** to be neither fish, flesh nor fowl; **essere muto come un —,** to be without a word, to be silent; **esser sano comeun —,** to be as sound as a bell.
pescecane, *n.m.* (*Zool.*) Shark; dog-fish; (*colloq.*) profiteer.
peschereccio [pescherEccio], *a.* Relating to fishing. **Barche pescherecce,** fishing-boats.
pescheria [pescherIa], *n.f.* Fish-market; fishmonger's shop; **— minuta,** whitebait.
peschiera, *n.f.* Fish-pond, fish-tank.
pesciaiola, *n.f.* Fish-kettle; (*Zool.*) merganser.
pesciaiolo, *n.m.* Fishmonger.
pescicoltura, *n.f.* Pisciculture, fish-breeding.
pescio [pEscio], *n.m.* (*obs.*) Fish [cp. **pesce**].
pesciolino, *n.m.* Little fish, small fry; white-bait.
pescivendolo [pescivEndolo], *n.m.* Fish-monger; fish-hawker.
pesco, *n.m.* (*Bot.*) Peach-tree.
pescoso, *a.* Full of fish. **Lago —,** lake abounding in fish.
pesezza, *n.f.* Weightiness; weight.
pesi, *n.m.pl.* Weights for scales.
peso (1), *n.m.* Weight (in all senses); gravity, burden, load; heaviness; importance, consequence. **— netto,** net weight; **— lordo,** gross weight; **vendere a —,** to sell by weight, **vendere a — d'oro,** to sell at a high figure; **il — degli anni,** the weight of years; **essere di —,** to be a burden; **aver due pesi e due misure,** to be unfair; **— morto,** dead weight; **levare di —,** to take away bodily; (*Sport*) **— piuma,** feather-weight; **—leggiero, medio, massimo,** light-, medium-, heavy-weight.
peso (2), *n.m.* Peso (Spanish and American coin).
peso, *a.* Heavy, weighty, massive.
pessario [pessArio], *n.m.* (*Med.*) Pessary.
pessimamente, *adv.* Very badly.

pessimismo, *n.m.* Pessimism.
pessimista (*pl.* **pessimisti**), *n.m.* Pessimist.
pessimistico [pessimIstico], *a.* Pessimistic.
pessimo [pEssimo], *a.* Very bad; worst; very wicked. — **soggetto,** a bad lot, a scoundrel.
pesta, *n.f.* Beaten track; footprint, footstep. **Sulle peste di,** on the track of; **lasciare nelle peste,** to leave in the lurch; **trovarsi nelle peste,** to find oneself in difficulties.
pestamento, *n.m.* Beating, pounding, thumping.
pestare, *v.t.* To pound, to beat soundly, to thrash; to stamp on, to trample on; to grind, to crush; to strum (on a piano). — **i piedi a,** to stamp on someone's feet; — **i piedi,** to stamp one's feet; — **l'acqua nel mortaio,** to labour to no effect.
pestata, *n.f.* Pounding.
pestatoio[pestatOio],*n.m.* Pestle [cp. **pestello**].
pestatore, *n.m.* Pounder, beater. — **di pianoforte,** piano-thumper.
pestatura, *n.f.* Beating; pounding, thumping.
peste, *n.f.* Plague, pestilence; pest (in all senses); calamity, nuisance.
pestello, *n.m.* Pestle.
pestifero [pestIfero], *a.* Pestiferous, pestilential; hurtful, noxious; pernicious.
pestilente, *a.* Pestilent, pestilential; noxious.
pestilenza, *n.f.* Pestilence, plague; (*fig.*) ruin.
pestilenziale, *a.* Pestilential, infectious, contagious; destructive.
pestilenzialmente, *adv.* Pestilentially; infectiously.
pestilenzioso, *a.* Objectionable, pestilential.
pestio [pestIo], *n.m.* Trampling, constant pounding, stamping of feet.
pesto, *p.p.a.* Pounded, battered, bruised, contused; trampled upon. **Carta pesta,** papier mâché; **essere di carta pesta,** to have no backbone; **occhi pesti,** eyes tired (from overwork or illness); **buio —,** pitch dark; **viso —,** face all black and blue.
pestone, *n.m.* Large pestle; rammer.
petalo [pEtalo], *n.m.* (*Bot.*) Petal.
petardo, *n.m.* Petard; firework cracker; (*Rail.*) fog-signal.
petaso [pEtaso], *n.m.* (*Hist.*) Petasus, wide-brimmed hat. — **alato,** winged hat of Hermes.
petente, *n.m.a.* Petitioner; petitioning.
petizione, *n.f.* Petition; entreaty, request. — **di principio,** begging the question.
peto, *n.m.* Breaking wind (from the anus).
petraia [petrAia], *n.f.* Heap of stones; stone quarry; stony ground.
Petrarca, *n.m.* Petrarch.
petrarcheggiare, *v.i.* To write in the style of Petrarch.
petrarchesco, *a.* Petrarchian.
petrarchista (*pl.* **petrarchisti**), *n.m.* Admirer or imitator of Petrarch.
petrificare, *v.t.* To petrify.
petrificazione, *n.f.* Petrifaction.
petroliera, *n.f.* (*Naut.*) Tanker, oil-tanker.
petroliere, *n.m.* Incendiary.
petrolifero [petrolIfero], *a.* Oil-bearing. **Campo —,** oil-field.
petrolio [petrOlio], *n.m.* Petroleum; oil; paraffin oil, kerosene.
petroso, *a.* Stony, rocky, flinty.
pettata, *n.f.* Blow on the chest; steep hill.
pettegola [pettEgola], *n.f.* Gossiping woman; gossip, busybody; (*Zool.*) redshank.
pettegolare, *v.i.* To gossip, to chatter.
pettegolata, *n.f.* Chatter, gossip.
pettegolezzo, *n.m.* Gossip, tittle-tattle, idle talk.
pettegolo [pettEgolo], *n.m.a.* Scandal-monger, talker, gossip; scandal-mongering.
pettina [pEttina], *n.f.* Pocket-comb, small comb.
pettinare, *v.t.* To comb, to card (wool); (*fig.*) to scold, to find fault.
pettinarsi, *v.r.* To comb one's hair.
pettinata, *n.f.* Combing; (*fig.*) scolding.
pettinatore, pettinatrice, *n.m.f.* Hair-dresser.
pettinatrice, *n.f.* Carding-machine (for wool).
pettinatura, *n.f.* Hair-dressing, hair-do; combing; head-dress; carding (wool).
pettine [pEttine], *n.m.* Comb; (*Zool.*) scallop. — **di tartaruga,** tortoise-shell comb; — **fitto,** close-toothed comb; **tutti i nodi vengono al —,** murder will out.
pettinella, *n.f.* Fine-toothed comb.
pettiniera, *n.f.* Case for combs; dressing-case.
pettirosso, *n.m.* (*Zool.*) Robin; redbreast.
petto, *n.m.* Chest, breast, bosom; heart, mind. **Mal di —,** consumption; **a — di,** in comparison with; — **a —,** face to face; **prendere di —,** to face squarely; **giacca a doppio —,** double-breasted jacket.
pettorale, *n.m.* Breast-band (harness); breast-plate; (*Eccles.*) pectoral.
pettorale, *a.* Pectoral.
pettorina, *n.f.* Stomacher; slip in front of Italian peasant's corset.
pettorutamente, *adv.* Pompously.
pettoruto, *a.* Full-breasted, strutting; pompous, conceited (in bearing).
petulante, *a.* Pert, cheeky; over-bearing, arrogant; petulant.
petulantemente, *adv.* Arrogantly.
petulanza, *n.f.* Pertness, sauciness; arrogance.
petunia [petUnia], *n.f.* (*Bot.*) Petunia.
pevera [pEvera], *n.f.* Wooden funnel for filling wine casks.
pezza, *n.f.* Piece (of cloth, etc.); towel; patch; wrapper; dressing (for wound); time. **Per lunga —,** for a long time; **metterci una —,** to patch it up (in all senses).
pezzalana, *n.f.* Baby's nappy, diaper.
pezzato, *a.* Speckled, spotted; patched.
pezzatura, *n.f.* Speckledness, spottedness; dappled effect.
pezzente, *n.m.a.* Beggar, wretch; beggarly.
pezzenteria [pezzenterIa], *n.f.* (*obs.*) Crowd of beggars.
pezzetta, *n.f.* Lint or rag for washing and binding up wounds.
pezzettino, *n.m.* Tiny scrap, very small piece.
pezzetto, *n.m.* Scrap, little bit.
pezzo, *n.m.* Piece, bit; part, fragment; gun; (*Chess, Draughts*) piece, man; period of time; newspaper article; (*Mus.*) composition. **Tutto di un —,** stiff, unbending, upright; **ho aspettato un —,** I've been waiting some time; **per un —,** for a long time; — **di terra,** patch of land; **un — di giovanotto,** a well-built youngster; **fare in pezzi,** to tear in pieces; **un — grosso,** a very important man,

V.I.P.; — **duro,** Neapolitan ice-cream; — **d'asino,** awful ass; (*Mech.*) **pezzi di ricambio,** spare parts; — **di artiglieria,** piece of ordnance.
pezzola, *n.f.* Handkerchief.
piaccichiccio [piaccichIccio], *n.m.* Sticky place or material.
piaccicone, *n.m.* Bungler, muddler.
piaccicoso, *a.* Sticky (esp. mouth).
piacente, *a.* Charming, pretty, pleasant, agreeable.
piacentemente, *adv.* Pleasingly.
piacere, *v.i.* To like, to please, to be pleasing, to be pleasant, to be agreeable; to care for, to be fond of. **Come vi piace,** as you like; **egli piace a tutti,** he is liked by everybody; **lo faccio per piacervi,** I do it just to please you; **il lavoro mi piace,** I like work.
piacere, *n.m.* Pleasure, favour, consent; delight, joy; amusement. **Per —,** if you please; **a — tuo,** at your pleasure; **fare un —,** to do a favour; **danaro pei minuti piaceri,** pocket-money, **apprendo con —,** I learn with pleasure; **Piacere!** How do you do? (said on being introduced).
piacevole [piacEvole], *a.* Pleasing, agreeable; charming, amusing, pleasant.
piacevoleggiare, *v.i.* To joke, to jest.
piacevolezza, *n.f.* Pleasantness, charm.
piacevolmente, *adv.* Pleasantly, charmingly.
piacimento, *n.m.* Pleasure; content; wish. **Non è di mio —,** it is not to my liking; **a —,** at pleasure.
piaga, *n.f.* Sore, wound; scar; (*fig.*) calamity. **Mettere il dito sulla —,** to hit the nail on the head; (*colloq.*) **che —!** What a bore!
piagare, *v.t.* To wound, to produce a sore.
piagarsi, *v.r.* To ulcerate.
piaggeria [piaggerIa], *n.f.* Flattery, adulation.
piaggia (*pl.* **piagge**) [piAggia], *n.f.* Seashore; slope, sloping hill [cp. **spiaggia**].
piaggiamento, *n.m.* Flattery.
piaggiare, *v.t.* To flatter, to coax, to blandish.
piaggiata, *n.f.* Sea-coast.
piaggiatore, *n.m.* Flatterer.
piagnere [cp. **piangere**].
piagnisteo [piagnistEo], *n.m.* Wailing, bewailing, whining; lamentation.
piagnoloso, *a.* Tearful, mournful, miserable.
piagnone, *n.m.* Querulous person, tearful person; mourner.
piagnucolamento, *n.m.* Wailing.
piagnucolare, *v.i.* To whimper, to cry, to whine (of a child).
piagnucolio [piagnucolIo], *n.m.* Wailing, weeping, crying, whining.
piagnucolone, *n.m.* Whimperer, wailer.
piagnucoloso, *a.* Weeping, whining, wailing, plaintive.
piagoso, *a.* Full of sores.
pialla, *n.f.* Carpenter's plane.
piallaccio [piallAccio], *n.m.* Veneer.
piallare, *v.t.* To plane.
piallata, *n.f.* Planing; stroke with a plane.
piallatore, *n.m.* Planer.
piallatura, *n.f.* Planing; shavings.
piallatrice, *n.m.* Planing machine.
pialletto, *n.m.* Plasterer's smoothing board.
piamente, *adv.* Piously.
piana, *n.f.* Plain, plateau, table-land; thick plank; squared stone, ashlar.
pianamente, *adv.* Smoothly, softly; plainly, simply.
pianare, *v.t.* To smooth, to plane.
pianeggiare, *v.i.* To be flat, to become nearly flat (of land); to be level.
pianella, *n.f.* Slipper; thin and flat tile.
pianerottolo [pianerOttolo], *n.m.* Staircase landing.
pianeta (*pl.* **pianeti**), *n.m.* (*Astron.*) Planet. **Esser nato sotto un dato —,** to be born under a certain planet.
pianeta (*pl.* **pianete**), *n.f.* (*Eccles.*) Chasuble.
pianezza, *n.f.* Flatness; simplicity; pleasantness.
pianforte [cp. **pianoforte**].
piangente, *a.* Weeping, crying; tearful. (*Bot.*) **Salice —,** weeping willow.
piangere [piAngere], *v.t.i.* To weep, to shed tears, to cry; to bewail, to lament, to mourn for; to deplore. — **la morte di un amico,** to mourn over a friend's death; — **a calde lagrime,** to weep scalding tears, to have one's cry out; **piango i miei peccati,** I bewail my sins.
piangevole [piangEvole], *a.* Lamentable.
piangevolmente, *adv.* Sadly, weepingly.
piangolare [cp. **piagnucolare**].
piangoloso, *a.* Whining, whimpering.
pianificare, *v.t.* To plan.
pianificazione, *n.f.* Planning.
pianigiano, *n.m.a.* Lowlander; lowlands.
pianino, *adv.* Gently, softly.
pianissimo [pianIssimo], *a.* Very softly, very slowly.
pianista, *n.m.f.* (*Mus.*) Pianist.
piano, *n.m.* Plain, flat country, level land; plan, delineation; project; plot, scheme; floor, storey; (*Geom.*) plane. — **terreno,** ground floor; **casa a cinque piani,** five-storeyed house; — **d'azione,** plan of action; **in —,** horizontally, flat, on a level; **fare dei piani,** to make plans; — **regolatore,** town-planning; (*Cinema.*) **primo —,** close-up.
piano, *a.* Plain, level, flat; smooth, even; plain, clear, intelligible; unassuming. **Figura piana,** plane figure; **corsa piana,** flat race.
piano, *adv.* Softly, gently; slowly; quietly. **Pian piano,** very gently, very quietly.
pianoforte, piano, *n.m.* Piano, pianoforte. **Piano a coda,** grand piano; **piano verticale,** upright, cottage piano.
pianoro, *n.m.* Plain, plateau, flat ground.
pianta, *n.f.* Plant, tree; plan, ground-plan; map; sole (of foot); lineage, race. **Rifare di sana —,** to do over again, to renew completely; **nominare in — stabile,** to put on the permanent staff; **la — d'una città,** the plan of a city; **la — d'un edificio,** the plan of a building; — **stradale,** road map.
piantaggine [piantAggine], *n.f.* (*Bot.*) Plantain.
piantagione, *n.f.* Plantation; planting.
piantamento, *n.m.* Planting.
piantare, *v.t.* To plant; to set up, to erect; to fix, to drive in; to place; to forsake, to quit, to abandon; to give the slip to; to jilt; (*Aviat.*) to stall. — **in asso,** to leave in the lurch; — **le tende,** to put up tents, to encamp; — **gli occhi addosso,** to stare at; **esser ben piantato,** to be well built, to be stout; (*colloq.*) — **carote,** to tell tall stories; to fib; — **chiodi,** to get into debt.

piantata, *n.f.* Row of plants; planting.
piantatore, *n.m.* Planter.
piantatura, *n.f.* Planting.
pianterreno, *n.m.* Ground floor.
pianticella, *n.f.* Small tree, plant.
pianto, *n.m.* Weeping, crying, tears. **Prorompere in —,** to burst into tears.
pianto, *p.p.a.* Wept, deplored, regretted, mourned [cp. **piangere**].
piantonaia [piantonAia], *n.f.* Nursery-garden.
piantonaio [piantonAio], *n.m.* Nurseryman.
piantonare, *v.t.* To guard over, to watch over.
piantone, *n.m.* (*Mil.*) Orderly, guard, sentinel. **Essere di —,** to be on duty.
pianura, *n.f.* Plain, flat country, lowland, tableland.
piare, *v.i.* To twitter, to chirp.
piastra, *n.f.* Plate, slab; sheet; piastre (coin). **— d'acciaio,** steel plate.
piastrella, *n.f.* Child's quoit; tile.
piastriccio [piastrIccio], *n.m.* Medley, hotchpotch, miscellany.
piastricciano, *n.m.* Dolt, blockhead.
piastrone, *n.m.* Metal plate; flagstone; (*Fencing*) plastron; (shirt) front.
piatire, *v.i.* To litigate.
piato, *n.m.* Lawsuit, dispute.
piatta, *n.f.* (*Mil., etc.*) Pontoon.
piattaforma, *n.f.* Platform.
piattaia [piattAia], *n.f.* Plate-rack, dresser.
piattaio [piattAio], *n.m.* Crockery dealer.
piatto, *n.m.* Dish, plate; course (at a meal); scale (of balance); flat side; (*Mus.*) cymbal. **Un — di minestra,** a plate of soup; **lavare i piatti,** to wash the dishes, to wash up; **— forte,** the main course (at dinner); (*colloq.*) **un — di buona ciera,** a hearty welcome.
piatto, *a.* Flat, even; plain; dull.
piattola [piAttola], *n.f.* (*Zool.*) Black-beetle, cockroach; crab-louse; (*colloq.*) bore, grouser.
piattoloso, *a.* Lousy.
piattonare, *v.t.* To strike with the flat of a sword.
piazza, *n.f.* Square, market-place, open space in a town; market; (*Naut.*) upper deck; (*fig.*) crowd, mob, rabble. **Vettura di —,** cab, taxi; (*Mil.*) **— forte,** fortress; **— d'armi,** parade ground; **fare la —,** to go round for orders; **letto a due piazze,** double-bed; **mettere in —,** to spread abroad, to expose; **far — pulita di,** to make a clean sweep; (*colloq.*) **essere in —,** to be bald; (*Golf*) **— d'arrivo,** putting-green, **prezzo di —,** market price.
piazzaiolata, *n.f.* Street row, shindy.
piazzaiolo, *n.m.* Loafer, street rowdy, cad.
piazzale, *n.m.* Open space, esplanade; square.
piazzare, *v.t.* To place.
piazzarsi, *v.r.* (*Sport*) To be placed; to place oneself.
piazzata, *n.f.* Street row, squabble.
piazzato, *p.p.a.* (*Sport*) Placed.
piazzetta, *n.f.* Small square.
piazzino, *n.m.* Lounger, market hanger-on.
piazzista (*pl.* **piazzisti**), *n.m.* Commercial traveller, canvasser.
piazzuola, *n.f.* Small square; (*Mil.*) gun platform; (*Golf*) **— di partenza,** tee.
pica, *n.f.* (*Zool.*) Magpie.
picaresco, *a.* (*Lit.*) Picaresque.
picca, *n.f.* Pike, spear, lance; pick, pick-axe; pique, tiff. (*Cards*) **Picche,** spades; **mettere a —,** to provoke; **risponder picche,** to give a flat refusal; **per —,** out of spite; **il fante di picche,** the knave of spades; a self-important fool.
piccante, *a.* Piquant, appetizing; sharp, spicy; stimulating.
piccare, *v.t.* To pique, to irritate, to sting.
piccarsi, *v.r.* To be offended; to pique oneself (on). **Si picca di saper cantare,** he piques himself on being able to sing.
piccata, *n.f.* Pike-thrust.
piccato, *a.* Piqued, annoyed; larded. **Frittura piccata,** grilled and larded veal.
picchè [-è], *n.m.* Piqué (cotton fabric).
piccheggiare, *v.t.* To tease, to taunt; to retort cheekily.
picchettamento, *n.m.* Embroidery of a hem.
picchettare, *v.t.* To stipple; to stake out; to picket; (*Mus.*) to bow in spiccato style.
picchetto, *n.m.* Picket; small stake; (*Cards*) piquet. **— d'onore,** guard of honour. **Essere di —,** to be ready for immediate use.
picchiamento, *n.m.* Knocking, striking.
picchiapetto, *n.m.* Hypocrite; bigot.
picchiare, *v.t.* To knock; to strike, to beat; to hit, to tap, to thump; (*Aviat.*) to nose-dive. **— di santa ragione,** to give a sound thrashing; **picchia e ripicchia,** by dint of persistence; **— all'uscio,** to knock at the door.
picchiarsi, *v.r.* To fight, to come to blows, to scuffle.
picchiata, *n.f.* Blow, beating; (*Aviat.*) nose-dive.
picchiere, *n.m.* (*Hist.*) Pikeman, halbardier.
picchierellare, *v.t.i.* To tap (with a hammer).
picchierello, *n.m.* Sculptor's hammer.
picchiettare, *v.t.* To speckle, to stipple, to dapple; to patter, to drum (on the floor, etc.).
picchiettato, *a.* Speckled.
picchiettatura, *n.f.* Speckling, stippling.
picchiettio [picchiettIo], *n.m.* Constant drumming or tapping.
picchio [pIcchio] (1), *n.m.* (*Zool.*) Woodpecker.
picchio [pIcchio] (2), *n.m.* Knocking, knock.
picchiottare, *v.t.* To tap on the door.
picchiotto, *n.m.* Door-knocker.
piccia [pIccia], *n.f.* Batch (of loaves); string (of onions, etc.).
piccineria [piccinerIa], *n.f.* Meanness, narrow-mindedness, pettiness.
piccino, *n.m.* Little child, young lad. **Povero —!** poor mite! **I piccini,** the little ones.
piccino, *a.* Very little, very small; tiny, mean, **Farsi — —,** to grow shy, to try to escape; **vino —,** light wine.
picciolo [pIcciolo] (1) [cp. **spicciolo**], *n.m.* Small coin; farthing. **Non avere un —,** not to have a farthing in the world.
picciolo [picciOlo] (2), *n.m.* (*Bot.*) Stalk (of pear, apple, etc.).
picciolo [pIcciolo], *a.* (*Lit.*) Little, small.
piccionaia [piccionAia], *n.f.* Dove-cote, pigeon-house, pigeon-loft; (*Theat.*) gallery, gods.
piccione, *n.m.* (*Zool.*) Pigeon, dove. **— viaggiatore,** carrier-pigeon; **prendere due piccioni con una fava,** to kill two birds with one stone; **tiro al —,** pigeon-shooting.

picciotto, *n.m.* (*colloq.*) Neapolitan or Sicilian lad.
picco, *n.m.* Peak, mountain peak; (*Naut.*) gaff. (*Naut.*) **La nave colò a —,** the vessel went to the bottom; **mandare a —,** to sink, to send to the bottom; **a —,** vertically, plumb, sheer.
piccolezza, *n.f.* Smallness, littleness, insignificance; pettiness, meanness; mean act, cattiness.
piccolino, *n.m.* Little lad.
piccolo [pIccolo], *n.m.* Little boy, little one; pageboy. **I piccoli,** the little children, the young (of animals); **da —,** as a child.
piccolo [pIccolo], *a.* Little, small, short; diminutive; trifling; narrow-minded; humble; low; slow. **In —,** in miniature; **— di testa,** mean, narrow-minded; **ore piccole,** small hours (of morning); **— borghese,** lower middle class; **piccole spese,** small expenses; (*Rail.*) **a piccola velocità,** by goods train; **in — tempo,** in a short while.
picconata, *n.f.* Blow with a pick-axe.
piccone, *n.m.* Pick-axe, pick; stone-mason's hammer.
picconiere, *n.m.* Labourer with a pick-axe.
piccosaggine, piccosità [piccosAggine, **-à**], *n.f.* Touchiness, irritability, peevishness.
piccoso, *a.* Touchy, peevish, irritable.
piccozza, *n.f.* Ice-axe; hatchet.
picea [pIcea], *n.f.* (*Bot.*) Pineaster.
piceo [pIceo], *a.* (*Lit.*) Pitchy, black.
picozzo, *n.m.* (*Anat.*) One of the incisors in a horse's jaw.
picrico [pIcrico], *a.* (*Chem.*) Picric.
pidocchieria [pidocchierIa], *n.f.* Stinginess, niggardliness, sordidness; mean action.
pidocchio [pidOcchio], *n.m.* (*Zool.*) Louse; (*colloq.*) stingy person.
pidocchioso, *a.* Lousy; niggardly, stingy.
piede, piè, *n.m.* Foot (in all senses), footing; trotter; leg (of table, etc.); bottom, base, support; condition, state; standard. **Stare in piedi, stare sui due piedi,** to stand, to stand up; **sui due piedi,** on the spot, at once, offhand; **da capo a piedi,** from head to foot; **alzarsi in piedi,** to rise, to stand up; **a piedi,** on foot; **corsa a piedi,** foot-race; **salto a piedi,** standing jump; **di piè fermo,** steadily, firmly; **ritratto in piedi,** full-length portrait; **mettere qualcuno sotto i piedi,** to treat someone badly; **camminare in punta di piedi,** to walk on tiptoe; **ai piedi della montagna,** at the foot of the mountain; **una cosa fatta coi piedi,** a clumsy bit of work; **tenere il — in due staffe,** to have a foot in both camps; **prender —,** to take root, to gain a footing; (*Theat.*) **posti in piedi,** standing-room; **avere il — marino,** to get one's sea-legs; **levarsi dai piedi,** to get rid of; **avere un — nella fossa,** to have one foot in the grave; **il collo del —,** the ankle; **battere i piedi,** to stamp; **il — di casa,** thrift, domestic economy; way of living; (*Law*) **a piede libero,** on bail; (*Mil.*) **pied'arm!** ground arms! **puntare i piedi,** to dig one's heels in.
piedistallo, *n.m.* Pedestal; base, support. (*fig.*) **Essere sul —,** to be extolled, to be put on a pedestal.
piega, *n.f.* Fold, tuck, crease, pleat; wrinkle; turn, bend. **Prendere una cattiva —,** to take a turn for the worse; **la — dei calzoni,** trouser-crease.
piegabile [piegAbile], *a.* Pliable, flexible.
piegamento, *n.m.* Bending, folding; flexion; retreat, falling back.
piegare, *v.t.* To fold, to fold up, to tuck, to pleat; to bend; to twist; to submit, to give way; (*Mil.*) to retreat, to fall back. **— le ginocchia,** to bend one's knees; **— il giornale,** to fold the paper.
piegarsi, *v.r.* To yield, to submit, to bend; to crease. **— ai voleri di qualcuno,** to yield to someone's wishes.
piegata, *n.f.* Bend, fold.
piegatore, piegatrice, *n.m.f.* Folder, creaser; plaiter.
piegatura, *n.f.* Folding, plaiting; curve, bend.
pieghеggiare, *v.t.* To drape (with folds).
pieghettare, *v.t.* To plait; to pleat, to kilt; to gather.
pieghettatura, *n.f.* Pleating, tuck (in dress).
pieghevole [pieghEvole], *a.* Pliable, supple, flexible; yielding, docile, submissive, amenable. **Sedia —,** folding-chair, deck-chair.
pieghevolezza, *n.f.* Pliability, suppleness, flexibility; submissiveness.
pieghevolmente, *adv.* Pliably.
piego, *n.m.* Packet (of papers), folder; small parcel; cover.
Piemonte, *n.m.* (*Geog.*) Piedmont.
piemontese, *n.m.a.* Piedmontese.
piena, *n.f.* Flood, overflow; crowd, throng; fullness. **C'era una —,** there was a big crowd; **il fiume è in —,** the river is in spate; **nella — dei suoi sentimenti,** in the fullness of his feelings.
pienamente, *adv.* Fully, completely.
pienezza, *n.f.* Fullness; ripeness, maturity; height. **Nella — delle sue forze,** at the height of his powers.
pieno, *n.m.* Full part; full space; fullness, perfection; height, depth. **Nel — della notte,** in the dead of night.
pieno, *a.* Full, filled; crowded, packed; replete; complete. **— zeppo,** chock-full; **a pieni voti,** unanimously; **— di sè,** self-centred; **in — giorno,** in broad daylight; **— di polvere,** covered in dust; **colpo in —,** home-thrust; **con pieni poteri,** with full powers; **luna piena,** full moon; (*colloq.*) **esserne —,** to be fed-up.
pienotto, *a.* Fat, plump, fleshy.
pietà [**-à**], *n.f.* Pity, compassion, mercy; piety; (*Art*) Pietà. **Monte di —,** pawnbroker's shop; **fare —,** to move to pity; **aver —,** to feel compassion; **per —!** For pity's sake! **per —,** out of pity; (*Relig.*) **pieno di —,** full of piety.
pietade, *n.f.* (*Lit.*) Pity.
pietanza, *n.f.* Dish of meat; dish of food, portion (of food).
pietismo, *n.m.* Pietism.
pietista (*pl.* **pietisti**), *n.m.* Pietist.
pietosamente, *adv.* Charitably, compassionately; piteously.
pietoso, *a.* Pitiful, lamentable, pitiable; charitable; pitiful, compassionate, merciful; pious. **Una scena pietosa,** a pitiful scene.

pietra, *n.f.* Stone; (*Med.*) calculus. — **tombale,** tomb-stone; — **preziosa,** precious stone; — **di paragone,** touchstone; — **filosofale,** philosopher's stone; **l'età della —,** the Stone Age; — **miliare,** milestone; — **dello scandalo,** rock of offence; — **per affilare,** whetstone; — **del focolare,** hearth-stone; — **focaia,** flint; **metterci sopra una —,** to bury the hatchet, to forget it all.
pietrame, *n.m.* Heap of stones.
pietrata, *n.f.* Blow with a stone.
pietrificare, *v.t.* To petrify; to harden into stone.
pietrificarsi, *v.r.* To become petrified.
pietrificazione, *n.f.* Petrifaction.
pietrino, *a.* Stone, (made of) stone.
pietrisco, *n.m.* Gravel; debris, rubble.
Pietro, *n.m.* Peter.
pietrosità [-à], *n.f.* Stoniness.
pietroso, *a.* Stony; flinty, rocky.
pievanale, *a.* Rustic, rural.
pievano, *n.m.* Parish priest.
pieve, *n.m.* Parish church; parish.
pifferaio, pifferaro [pifferAio], *n.m.* Piper, fife-player.
piffero [pIffero], *n.m.* (*Mus.*) Fife, pipe. **Fare come i pifferi di montagna,** to come back crestfallen, to be baulked, to go for wool and come home shorn.
pigiama, *n.m.* Pyjamas.
pigiamento, *n.m.* Pressing, crushing, squeezing.
pigiare, *v.t.* To press, to crush, to squash, to squeeze; to cram. — **l'uva,** to press the grapes; **un pigia pigia,** a dreadful squeeze, an awful crush.
pigiarsi, *v.r.* To crowd, to crush.
pigiata, *n.f.* Crushing, pressing.
pigiatore, pigiatrice, *n.m.f.* Presser, crusher, wine-presser; wine-press.
pigiatura, *n.f.* Pressing, crushing; pressing of grapes.
pigio [pigIo], *n.m.* Great squeezing, constant crushing.
pigionale, *n.m.* Lodger, tenant.
pigione, *n.f.* Rent. **Prendere a —,** to rent; **stare a —,** to live in rooms.
pigliabile [pigliAbile], *a.* Seizable.
pigliamento, *n.m.* Taking, seizure.
pigliamosche, *n.m.* (*Zool.*) Flycatcher; (*Bot.*) fly-trap.
pigliare, *v.t.* To take, to seize, to catch; to engage; to assume. — **uno per un altro,** to take one for another; — **un bagno,** to take a bath; — **fuoco,** to catch fire; — **la palla al balzo,** to seize the opportunity; — **a destra,** to turn to the right; — **appunti,** to take notes; — **le cose sul serio,** to take things seriously; (*colloq.*) **Che ti piglia?** What's the matter with you?
pigliarsi, *v.r.* To take, to catch (cold). — **un raffreddore,** to catch a cold; — **l'incarico,** to undertake a task; **pigliarsela con uno,** to fall out with someone; — **una sbornia,** to get drunk; **pigliarsela a male,** to take offence, to take it amiss.
piglio [pIglio], *n.m.* Taking hold, hold; look, bearing, aspect. **Dar di —,** to seize; **con — severo,** with a harsh look; **ha un — simpatico,** he has a way with him.
pigmento, *n.m.* Pigment.
pigmeo [pigmEo], *n.m.* Pigmy, dwarf.
pigna, *n.f.* Pine-cone; (*Arch.*) breakwater on the buttress of a bridge; top of a cupola.
pignatta, *n.f.* Pot, cauldron, cooking-pot, kitchen-pot.
pignolo *n.m.* Pine kernel; (*fig.*) pedant; martinet.
pignoramento, *n.m.* Distraint; pawning.
pignorare, *v.t.* (*Law*) To distrain; to pawn.
pignoratario [pignoratArio], *n.m.* Distrainer.
pignorazione, *n.f.* Distraint.
pigolamento, *n.m.* Chirping.
pigolare, *v.i.* To chirp, to cheep.
pigolio [pigolIo], *n.m.* Chirping.
pigramente, *adv.* Lazily, idly.
pigrezza, pigrizia [pigrizIa], *n.f.* Laziness, indolence, sloth.
pigro, *a.* Lazy, slack, slothful, indolent; slow, dull.
pila, *n.f.* Heap, pile; pier (of a bridge), buttress; basin; (*Elec.*) battery, cell, pile; (*Eccles.*) font, stoup. — **di Volta,** voltaic pile; — **di ricambio,** refill for electric torch.
pilastrata, *n.f.* Row of small pillars.
pilastro, *n.m.* Pillar, column, pilaster.
Pilato, *n.m.* Pilate. **Mandare da Erode a —,** to send from pillar to post.
pileo [pIleo], *n.m.* (*Hist.*) Pileus, falet cap.
piletta, *n.f.* (*Eccles.*) Stoup.
pillacchera [pillAcchera], *n.f.* Splash of mud.
pillaccheroso, *a.* Splashed with mud.
pillare, *v.t.* (*obs.*) To ram down, to tread down.
pillo, *n.m.* Rammer, beetle.
pillola [pIllola], *n.f.* Pill. **Indorare la —,** to gild the pill.
pillottare, *v.t.* To baste meat (on the jack).
pillotto, *n.m.* Dripping-pan.
pilo, *n.m.* (*Lit.*) Javelin.
pilone, *n.m.* Pillar, column; pylon, pier (of a bridge). (*Aviat.*) — **d'ormeggio,** mooring-mast.
piloro, *n.m.* (*Anat.*) Pylorus.
pilota, *n.m.* Pilot; airman; steersman; (*Motor.*) driver; guide. **Battello —,** pilot-boat.
pilotaggio [pilotAggio], *n.m.* Pilotage. (*Aviat.*) **Scuola di —,** flying-school.
pilotare, *v.t.* (*Aviat.*) To pilot; (*Motor.*) to drive; (*fig.*) to take around, to pilot around.
piloto [cp. **pilota**].
piluccare, *v.t.* To pluck off the grapes; to pick, to nibble; to pick up.
piluccarsi, *v.r.* To tear one's hair.
piluccone, *n.m.* Beggar, one who is always asking.
pimento, *n.m.* Allspice; red pepper.
pimpinella, *n.f.* (*Bot.*) Pimpernel.
pimpirimpi [-ì], *n.m.* **Polvere del —,** magic powder, miraculous remedy.
pina, *n.f.* Pine cone [cp. **pigna**].
pinaccia [pinAccia], *n.f.* (*Naut.*) Pinnace.
pinacoteca, *n.f.* Picture-gallery.
pinastro, *n.m.* (*Bot.*) Pinaster.
pindarico [pindArico], *a.* Pindaric. **Voli pindarici,** Pindaric flights.
Pindaro [pIndaro], *n.m.* Pindar.
pineale, *a.* (*Anat.*) Pineal. **Glandola —,** pineal gland.
pineta, pineto, *n.f.m.* Pine wood; pine forest.
pingere [pIngere], *v.t.* To paint; to push [cp. **spingere**].

pingue, *a.* Fat, plump, obese, corpulent; fertile, rich; lucrative. **Pingui guadagni,** large gains, handsome profit.
pinguedine [pinguEdine], *n.f.* Fatness, plumpness, obesity, corpulence.
pinguemente, *adv.* Obesely ; richly.
pinguezza, *n.f.* Obesity.
pinguino, *n.m.* (*Zool.*) Penguin.
pinifero [pinIfero], *a.* Pine-bearing.
pinna, *n.f.* (Fish's) fin; (*Zool.*) variety of mollusc. **Le pinne,** the outer walls of the nose.
pinnacolo [pinnAcolo], *n.m.* Pinnacle, peak, spire.
pinnipedi [pinnIpedi], *n.m.pl.* (*Zool.*) Pinnipeds; seals, fin-footed beasts.
pino, *n.m.* (*Bot.*) Pine-tree, pine (wood); (*Poet.*) ship. **— vulcanico,** cloud of smoke from a volcano resembling a pine-tree.
pinocchiata, *n.f.* Tartlet flavoured with pine-seeds.
pinocchio, pinolo [pinOcchio], *n.m.* Pine-seed; (*Lit.*) children's book by Collodi (Carlo Lorenzini). **Sembra un Pinocchio,** he looks like a marionette.
pinta, *n.f.* Pint (measure of capacity).
pintura [cp. **pittura**].
pinza, *n.f.* Pincers; pliers; forceps.
pinzare, *v.t.* To sting, to bite (of insects).
pinzata, *n.f.* Sting, puncture.
pinzette, *n.f.* Tweezers, small pliers.
pinzo, *n.m.* Sting (of an insect).
pinzochera [pinzOchera], *n.f.* Bigot; devotee.
pinzuto, *a.* Sharp-pointed.
Pio, *n.m.* Pius. **Pio Nono,** Pius IX.
pio, *a.* Pious, religious; godly, charitable; obedient. **Opera pia,** charitable institution; **luogo —,** religious institution; (*Anat.*) **pia madre,** pia mater.
pio [cp. **pio pio**].
pioggerella, *n.f.* Drizzle, fine rain.
pioggia [piOggia], *n.f.* Rain; shower. **— dirotta,** downpour; **Le piogge,** the Rains (in India, etc.).
piolo, piuolo, *n.m.* Peg, pin; small stake, pole; rung (of a ladder). **Scala a pioli,** ladder; **dritto come un —,** straight as a ram-rod.
piombaggine [piombAggine], *n.f.* Plumbago, blacklead.
piombare, *v.t.i.* To seal (with lead); to plumb, to solder; to stop (a tooth); to fall upon, to crash upon, to pounce on; to fall, to drop. **— addosso,** to rush upon, to pounce on; **— un dente,** to stop a tooth; **— nella miseria,** to be reduced to poverty; **— a terra,** to crash to the ground.
piombatura, *n.f.* Leading, sealing; stopping, filling (of a tooth).
piombifero [piombIfero], *a.* Lead-bearing.
piombinare, *v.t.* (*Naut.*) To sound, to plumb.
piombinazione, *n.f.* (*Naut.*) Sounding, casting the lead.
piombino, *n.m.* Plummet, plumb-line; lead seal.
piombo, *n.m.* Lead; plummet, plumb, plumb-line; bullet. **A —,** plumb, sheer, perpendicular; **andar coi piedi di —,** to proceed with caution, to go very cautiously; **mettere i piombi,** to seal; **sentirsi i piedi di —,** to feel very tired.
pioniere, *n.m.* Pioneer.
pio pio, *n.m.* Chirping, twittering of young birds. **Far — —,** to chirp.
pioppaia [pioppAia], *n.f.* Poplar wood, poplar grove.
pioppo, *n.m.* Poplar.
piota, *n.f.* Sole of the foot; sod, turf; soil round a root.
piotare, *v.t.* To turf.
piova [cp. **pioggia**].
piovano, *n.m.* Parish priest, curate [cp. **pievano**].
piovano, *a.* Pertaining to rain. **Acqua piovana,** rain-water.
piovasco, *n.m.* (*Lit.*) Heavy shower, squall.
piovente, *n.m.* Pitch of a roof.
piovere [piOvere], *v.i.* To rain; to shower, to pour; to fall; to drip; to slope (of a mountain, etc.). **— a dirotto,** to pour; **— a catinelle,** to rain cats and dogs; **sta per —,** it's going to rain; **le palle piovevano,** it rained bullets; (*fig.*) **— sul bagnato,** to add insult to injury.
piovigginare, *v.i.* To drizzle.
piovigginoso, *a.* Drizzling.
piovorno, piovoso, *a.* Rainy; threatening (of the clouds).
piovosità [-à], *n.f.* Raininess, rainfall.
piovra, *n.f.* (*Zool.*) Octopus; (*fig.*) blood-sucker, vampire.
piovuta, *n.f.* Rainfall.
pipa, *n.f.* Pipe (in all senses). **Caricare la —,** to fill one's pipe; **fumar la —,** to smoke a pipe; **la cannuccia della —,** the stem of the pipe.
pipare, *v.t.* To smoke a pipe.
pipata, *n.f.* Pipeful, a smoke.
piperino, piperno, *n.m.* (*Geol.*) Kind of lava used for paving-stones.
pipetta, *n.f.* Small pipe; pipette.
pipilare, *v.i.* To twitter.
pipistrello, *n.m.* (*Zool.*) Bat; (*obs.*) voluminous overcoat.
pipita, *n.f.* Hang-nail, agnail; pip (of fowls).
pippolo [pIppolo], *n.m.* Pimple.
pira, *n.f.* Pyre, funeral pile.
piramidale, *a.* Pyramidal; huge.
piramidalmente, *adv.* Like a pyramid.
piramide [pirAmide], *n.f.* Pyramid.
pirata (*pl.* **pirati**), *n.m.* Pirate.
pirateggiare, *v.i.* To go a-pirating, to practise piracy.
pirateria [piraterIa], *n.f.* Piracy, robbery.
piratesco, piratico [pirAtico], *a.* Piratical.
Pirenei, *n.m.pl.* (*Geog.*) Pyrenees.
Pireo [pirEo], *n.m.* (*Geog.*) Piraeus.
pirico [pIrico], *a.* **Polvere pirica,** gunpowder.
pirite, *n.f.* (*Min.*) Pyrites.
piroetta, *n.f.* Pirouette.
piroettare, *v.i.* To pirouette.
piroga, *n.f.* (*Naut.*) Pirogue, canoe.
pirografia [pirografIa], *n.f.* Pyrography, burning-in (designs), etc.
piromante, *n.m.* Diviner by fire.
piromanzia [piromanzIa], *n.f.* Pyromancy, divination by fire.
pirometro [pirOmetro], *n.m.* Pyrometer.
pirone, *n.m.* (*Mus.*) Peg, for tightening string.
piroscafo [pirOscafo], *n.m.* Steamer, steam-ship. **— da carico,** cargo-boat.
pirosi, *n.f.* (*Med.*) Heartburn.
pirotecnica, pirotecnia [pirotEcnica], *n.f.* Pyrotechnics, fireworks.

pirotecnico [pirotEcnico], *a* Pyrotechnic. **Spettacolo —,** fireworks.
pirrico [pIrrico], *a.* Pyrrhic. **Danza pirrica,** Pyrrhic dance.
pisano, *n.m.a.* Pisan, of Pisa.
piscatorio [piscatOrio], *a.* Piscatorial.
piscia [pIscia], *n.f.* Urine, piss; stale (of horses).
pisciare, *v.i.* To make water, to urinate; to stale (of horses).
pisciata, *n.f.* Urination.
pisciatoio [pisciatOio], *n.m.* Public urinal.
piscicoltura, *n.f.* Pisciculture, fish-breeding.
piscina, *n.f.* Bathing-pool, swimming-pool; fish-pond.
piscio [pIscio], *n.m.* Urine; stale (of horses).
pisellaio [pisellAio], *n.m.* Field of peas.
pisellata, *n.f.* Dish of peas.
pisello, *n.m.* (*Bot.*) Pea.
pisolare, *v.i.* To doze, to nap, to snooze.
pisolo, pisolino [pIsolo], *n.m.* Nap, snooze. **Fare un —,** to take a nap.
pispigliare [cp. **bisbigliare**].
pispola [pIspola], *n.f.* (*Zool.*) Meadow-lark; bird-whistle.
pissi, *n.m.* Chattering. **Si senti un gran — —,** One could hear a great chattering.
pisside [pIsside], *n.f.* (*Eccles.*) Pyx.
pista, *n.f.* (Racecourse) track, race-course, course, speedway; trace, footstep, trail; scent, clue; (*Aviat.*) runway. **Seguire la — di qualcuno,** to be on someone's tracks.
pistacchio [pistAcchio], *n.m.* (*Bot.*) Pistachio (tree and nut).
pistagna, *n.f.* Coat-collar, facings; flounce.
pistillo, *n.m.* (*Bot.*) Pistil.
pistola, *n.f.* Pistol. **— mitragliatrice,** sub-machine gun.
pistolese, *n.m.* Hunting-knife.
pistolettata, *n.f.* Pistol-shot.
pistolotto, *n.m.* (*colloq.*) Emphatic peroration; tirade; purple patch.
pistone, *n.m.* Piston; (*Mus.*) cornet-à-piston.
Pitagora [pitAgora], *n.m.* Pythagoras.
pitagorico [pitagOrico], *a.* Pythagorean. **Tavola pitagorica,** multiplication table.
pitale, *n.m.* Chamber-pot.
piteco, *n.m.* (*Lit.*) Monkey.
pitoccare, *v.i.* To go begging, to beg; to be a miser.
pitoccheria [pitoccherIa], *n.f.* Niggardliness, sordidness; beggarly action.
pitocco, *n.m.a.* Beggar; miser; beggarly, niggardly.
pitone, *n.m.* (*Zool.*) Python.
pitonessa, *n.f.* Witch, pythoness; fortune-teller.
pittima [pIttima], *n.f.* Plaster (for application); bore, man who splits hairs; (*Zool.*) species of diving bird.
pittore, *n.m.* Painter.
pittorello, *n.m.* Indifferent painter, dauber.
pittorescamente, *adv.* Picturesquely.
pittoresco, *a.* Picturesque.
pittorico [pittOrico], *a.* Pictorial
pittrice, *n.f.* Woman painter.
pittura, *n.f.* Picture, painting. **— a olio,** oil-painting; **— all'acquerello,** water-colour.
pitturaccia [pitturAccia], *n.f.* Daub.
pitturare, *v.t.* To paint, to depict.
pituita [pitUita], *n.f.* Phlegm, mucus (of the nasal cavity).
pituitario [pituitArio], *a.* (*Anat.*) Pituitary. **Glandola pituitaria,** pituitary gland.
più, *adv.* More. **A — non posso,** to the very utmost; **sempre —,** more and more; **ciò che mi piace di —,** what I like best; **— presto,** sooner, quicker; **— volte,** several times; **i —,** most people; **mai —,** never again; **per lo —,** for the most part; **— oltre,** further; **tutt'al —,** at the most; **il —,** the most; **— e — volte,** often and often; **un anno e —,** more than a year; **non ne voglio —,** I don't want any more of it; **cinque — due,** five plus two; **in —,** in addition; **nè — nè meno,** neither more nor less; **andare nel numero dei —,** to join the great majority.
piuma, *n.f.* Feather, plume; pen. **Letto di —,** feather-bed; **guanciale di —,** feather pillow; **— di struzzo,** ostrich-feather; (*Sport*) **peso —,** feather-weight.
piumaccio [piumAccio], *n.m.* Feather-pillow.
piumaggio [piumAggio], *n.m.* Plumage.
piumato, *a.* Feathered.
piumino, *n.m.* Eiderdown quilt; feather duster. **— per la cipria,** powder-puff.
piumoso, *a.* Feathery, downy.
piuolo [cp. **piolo**].
piuttosto, *adv.* Rather, somewhat; sooner. **Vorrei morire —,** I would sooner die; **è — ignorante,** he is rather ignorant.
piva, *n.f.* (*Mus.*) Bagpipe, pipe. **Ritornare colle pive nel sacco,** to fail in one's purpose.
pivello, *n.m.* (*colloq.*) Dandy, swell.
piviale, *n.m.* (*Eccles.*) Cope.
piviere, *n.m.* (*Zool.*) Plover; (*Eccles.*) parish.
pizza, *n.f.* Neapolitan savoury bun.
pizzaguerra, *n.m.* Mischief-maker.
pizzardone, *n.m.* (*colloq.*) Roman policeman.
pizzicagnolo [pizzicAgnolo], *n.m.* Pork-butcher, delicatessen dealer, cheese-monger; Italian warehouseman.
pizzicare, *v.t.* To pinch, to nip; to sting, to bite (of insects); to tingle, to prick; (*Mus.*) to pluck (strings), to play pizzicato. **Sentirsi — le mani,** to feel one's hands itch to slap someone.
pizzicata, *n.f.* Pinch, nip.
pizzicato, *a.* (*Mus.*) Pizzicato, plucked; pinched.
pizzicheria [pizzicherIa], *n.f.* Delicatessen shop, Italian warehouse, pork-butcher's shop, [cp. **salumeria**].
pizzichino, *n.m.* Kind of snuff.
pizzico [pIzzico], *n.m.* Pinch (of salt, etc.); nip, tingling. **Un — di sale,** a pinch of salt.
pizzicore, *n.m.* Itch, smart, tingling, sting.
pizzicottare, *v.t.* To pinch, to nip.
pizzicottata, *n.f.* Pinching.
pizzicotto, *n.m.* Pinch, nip. **Dare un — a uno,** to give someone a pinch.
pizzo, *n.m.* Pointed beard, imperial, goatee; mountain peak; lace. **Pizzo di Venezia,** Venetian lace.
placabile [placAbile], *a.* Appeasable, placable; mild, forgiving.
placabilità [-à], *n.f.* Placability.
placabilmente, *adv.* Mildly, placably.
placamento, *n.m.* Appeasement, pacification.

placare, *v.t.* To appease, to calm, to soothe, to placate, to quiet. — **l'ira,** to appease one's anger.
placarsi, *v.r.* To be appeased, to subside (of wrath).
placatore, placatrice, *n.m.f.* Appeaser.
placca, *n.f.* Plate; slab; badge. — **della porta,** door-plate.
placcare, *v.t.* To plate (silver, etc.).
placenta, *n.f.* (*Anat.*) Placenta.
placidamente, *adv.* Placidly, calmly, mildly.
placidezza, placidità [-à], *n.f.* Placidity, calmness, mildness, peacefulness, serenity.
placido [plAcido], *a.* Placid, calm, tranquil; mild, peaceful.
placito [plAcito], *n.m.* (*Hist.*) Decree; judgment; approval [cp. **beneplacito**].
plafone, *n.m.* (*colloq.*) Ceiling.
plaga, *n.f.* Country, region, district, extent of land, sea or sky.
plagiare, *v.i.* To plagiarize.
plagiario [plagiArio], *n.m.* Plagiarist.
plagio [plAgio], *n.m.* Plagiary, plagiarism.
planare, *v.i.* (*Aviat.*) To volplane, to glide; to plane.
planata, *n.f.* (*Aviat.*) Volplane.
plancia [plAncia], *n.f.* (*Naut.*) Ledge for charts, etc., on the bridge; bridge.
planetario [planetArio], *n.m.a.* (*Astron.*) Orrery, planetarium; planetary.
planimetria [planimetrIa], *n.f.* Plane geometry.
planimetro [planImetro], *n.m.* (*Geom.*) Planimeter.
planisfero, *n.m.* (*Astron.*) Planisphere, star-map.
plantigrado [plantIgrado], *n.m.* (*Zool.*) Plantigrade.
plasma, *n.m.* Plasma.
plasmabile [plasmAbile], *a.* Formable, mouldable.
plasmare, *v.t.* To form, to mould, to shape, to model, to form.
plasmatore, *n.m.* Moulder.
plasmodio [plasmOdio], *n.m.* (*Biol.*) Plasmodium.
plastica [plAstica], *n.f.* Plastic art, modelling. — **chirurgica,** plastic surgery.
plastici [plAstici], *n.m.pl.* Plastics, plastics materials.
plasticità [-à], *n.f.* Plasticity, suppleness.
plastico [plAstico], *a.* Plastic.
platano [plAtano], *n.m.* (*Bot.*) Plane-tree.
platea [platEa], *n.f.* (*Theat.*) Pit; orchestra stalls.
plateale, *a.* Common, vulgar, low.
platealmente, *adv.* Commonly, vulgarly.
platinare, *v.t.* To plate with platinum.
platino [plAtino], *n.m.* Platinum.
platinotipia [platinotipIa], *n.f.* Platinotype.
Platone, *n.m.* Plato.
platonicamente, *adv.* Platonically.
platonico [platOnico], *a.* Platonic.
platonismo, *n.m.* Platonism.
platonista (*pl.* **platonisti**), *n.m.* Platonist.
plaudente, *a.* Cheering, applauding. **Popolo —,** cheering crowds.
plaudire, *v.i.* To applaud [cp. **applaudire**].
plausibile [plausIbile], *a.* Plausible, probable, reasonable.
plausibilità [-à], *n.f.* Plausibility.
plausibilmente, *adv.* Plausibly.
plauso [plAuso], *n.m.* Applause, praise, approbation; distinction (in exams).
plaustro [plAustro], *n.m.* (*Lit.*) Large wagon, cart, ox-cart; (*Astron.*) Charles's Wain, the Great Bear.
plebaccia, plebaglia [plebAccia, plebAglia], *n.f.* Mob, crowd, canaille, riff-raff, rabble.
plebe, *n.f.* Common people, populace.
plebeamente, *adv.* Commonly, in a plebeian way.
plebeo [plebEo], *n.m.a.* Plebeian.
plebiscito, *n.m.* Plebiscite.
pleiade [plEiade], *n.f.* Pleiad; select number of persons (in art, poetry, etc.); (*Astron.*) **Le Pleiadi,** the Pleiades.
plenariamente, *adv.* Plenarily.
plenario [plenArio], *a.* Plenary, full, complete, absolute. **Indulgenza plenaria,** plenary indulgence; **seduta plenaria,** plenary session.
plenilunio [plenilUnio], *n.m.* Full moon.
plenipotenza, *n.f.* Full power, full authority.
plenipotenziario [plenipotenziArio], *n.m.a.* Plenipotentiary.
plenitudine [plenitUdine], *n.f.* Plenitude.
pleonasmo, *n.m.* (*Gram.*) Pleonasm.
pleonastico [pleonAstico], *a.* Pleonastic.
plesso, *n.m.* (*Anat.*) Plexus.
pletora [plEtora], *n.f.* Plethora; superabundance, excess.
pletorico [pletOrico], *a.* Plethoric; overfull, excessive.
plettro, *n.m.* (*Mus.*) Plectrum.
pleura [plEura], *n.f.* (*Anat.*) Pleura.
pleurite, pleurisia [pleurisIa], *n.f.* (*Med.*) Pleurisy.
plicata, *n.f.* (*Eccles.*) Chasuble worn in Lent.
plico, *n.m.* Packet (of letters), cover, envelope.
Plinio [plInio], *n.m.* Pliny.
plinto, *n.m.* (*Arch.*) Plinth.
pliocene, *n.m.* (*Geol.*) Pliocene period.
pliocenico [pliocEnico], *a.* (*Geol.*) Pliocene.
plorare, *v.i.* (*Lit.*) To weep.
plotone, *n.m.* (*Mil.*) Platoon, squad. — **d'esecuzione,** firing-squad.
plumbeo [plUmbeo], *a.* Leaden, lead, plumbeous; (*fig.*) dull, heavy.
plurale, *n.m.a.* Plural. **Al —,** in the plural.
pluralità [-à], *n.f.* Plurality, majority.
pluralizzare, *v.t.* To put in the plural.
plusvalore, *n.m.* (*Comm.*) Plus value.
pluteo [plUteo], *n.m.* Bookcase; book-shelves.
plutocrate [plutOcrate], *n.m.* Plutocrat.
plutocraticamente, *adv.* Plutocratically.
plutocratico [plutocrAtico], *a.* Plutocratic.
plutocrazia [plutocrazIa], *n.f.* Plutocracy.
plutonico [plutOnico], *a.* (*Geol.*) Plutonic.
plutonio [plutOnio], *n.m.* (*Min.*) Plutonium.
pluviale, *a.* Rainy, pertaining to rain. **Acqua —,** rain-water.
pluvio [plUvio], *a.* (*Lit.*) Of rain. **Giove —,** Jupiter Pluvius.
pluviometro [pluviOmetro], *n.m.* Rain-gauge.
pneumatica [pneumAtica], *n.f.* Pneumatics.
pneumatico [pneumAtico], *n.m.* Pneumatic tyre, tyre.
pneumatico [pneumAtico], *a.* Pneumatic. **Posta pneumatica,** pneumatic dispatch; **pompa pneumatica,** pneumatic pump.

pneumonia, pneumonite, *n.f.* (*Med.*) Pneumonia [cp. **polmonite**].
po' [cp. **poco**].
poccia [pOccia], *n.f.* (*colloq.*) Breast.
pochettino, pochetto, pochino, *adv.* Very little; little while.
pochezza, *n.f.* Scarcity, lack, insufficiency; littleness, smallness, narrowness.
pochissimo [pochIssimo], *a.* Very little, very few.
poco, *adv. a.* Little, small; scanty; few; in a small quantity; insufficient; shortly, short while, short time. **Fra —,** shortly; **da —,** not long ago; **per —,** for a short while; **— fa,** just now, a moment ago; **a — a —,** little by little; **— dopo,** soon after; **per — che,** however little; **a ogni —,** every now and then; **— manca che,** all but; **aspetta un —,** wait a moment; **un — di buono,** a good-for-nothing; **— su — giù,** thereabouts, approximately; **dammene ancora un po',** give me a little more of it.
pocolino, *a., adv.* Very little.
podagra, *n.f.* (*Med.*) Gout, podagra.
podagroso, *a.* Gouty.
podere, *n.m.* Farm, small holding; small landed property; (*obs.*) power.
poderosamente, *adv.* Powerfully.
poderoso, *a.* Powerful, mighty; sturdy, vigorous; solid.
podestà [-à] (1), *n.m.* Mayor, administrative head of a community.
podestà [-à] (2), *n.f.* Power [cp. **potestà**].
podestarile, *a.* Mayoral.
podesteria [podesterIa], *n.f.* Town-hall, offices of town government.
podice [pOdice], *n.m.* (*Anat.*) Anus.
podismo, *n.m.* (*Sport*) Foot-racing, foot-race, running-match, sprinting.
podista (*pl.* **podisti**), *n.m.* (Professional) runner, sprinter.
podistico [podIstico], *a.* (*Sport*) Sprinting, running. **Gara podistica,** running-match, foot-race.
poema (*pl.* **poemi**), *n.m.* Epic poem, narrative poem.
poemetto, *n.m.* Short narrative poem.
poero [pOero], *a.* (*Lit.*) Poor [cp. **povero**].
poesia [poesIa], *n.f.* Poetry; short poem.
poeta (*pl.* **poeti**), *n.m.* Poet.
poetare, *v.i.* To write poetry, to versify; to be a poet.
poetastro, *n.m.* Poetaster.
poeteggiare, *v.i.* To pose as a poet, to be poetical.
poetessa, *n.f.* Poetess.
poetica [poEtica], *n.f.* Art of poetry, poetics.
poeticamente, *adv.* Poetically.
poetico [poEtico], *a.* Poetical, poetic.
poetizzare, *v.t.* To make poetical, to versify.
poffare! poffarbacco! poffar il Cielo! *inter.* Good heavens! By Jove!
poggia [pOggia], *n.f.* (*Naut.*) Halyard; lee-side.
poggiacapo, *n.m.* Head-rest; antimacassar.
poggiaiolo, *n.m.* Hill man, man of the hill country.
poggiapiedi, *n.m.* Foot-rest, footstool.
poggiare, *v.t.i.* (*Naut.*) To sheer off, to put back to port; to bear to; to lean on; to rest on; to be based on. **— a destra,** to bear to the right; **poggia su solida base,** it rests on a solid base.
poggiarsi, *v.r.* To lean against.
poggiata, *n.f.* (*Naut.*) Sheering off; slope, declivity, hill-side.
poggio [pOggio], *n.m.* Hill, hillock, hill-top.
poggiolo, *n.m.* Balcony, parapet; hillock, knoll.
poggioso, *a.* Hilly.
poi, *adv.* Afterwards, then; after. **Da ora in —,** henceforth, in future; **prima o —,** sooner or later; **da allora in —,** from that time on, thenceforward; **da oggi in —,** from to-day; **e — ?** what next?
poiana, *n.f.* (*Zool.*) Kite, buzzard.
poichè, *conj.* Since, after; because.
polacca, *n.f.* Polonaise.
polacco, *n.m.a.* Pole, Polish. **I Polacchi,** the Poles.
polare, *a.* Polar. **Stella —,** the Pole Star.
polarità [-à], *n.f.* Polarity.
polarizzare, *v.t.* To polarize.
polarizzazione, *n.f.* Polarization.
polca, *n.f.* Polka.
poledro, *n.m.* Colt.
polemica [polEmica], *n.f.* Polemics; controversy, disputation.
polemicamente, *adv.* Polemically.
polemico [polEmico], *a.* Polemical.
polemista (*pl.* **polemisti**), *n.m.* Controversialist, writer on polemical subjects.
polemizzare, *v.i.* To argue.
polena, *n.f.* (*Naut.*) Figure-head.
polenta, *n.f.* Polenta, pudding made from maize or chestnut flour. (*fig.*) **Essere una —,** to be a sluggard.
polentaio [polentAio], *n.m.* Vendor of polenta.
polesine [polEsine], *n.m.* Delta at river mouth.
poliambulanza, *n.f.* Dispensary, out-patients department; first-aid post.
poliandria [poliandrIa], *n.f.* Polyandry.
poliarchia [poliarchIa], *n.f.* Polyarchy, government by the many.
policlinica, policlinico [policlInica, policlInico], *n.f.m.* Polyclinic, general hospital.
policromia [policromIa], *n.f.* Polychromy.
policromo [polIcromo], *n.m.* Polychrome.
poliedro [poliEdro], *n.m.* (*Geom.*) Polyhedron.
polifonia [polifonIa], *n.f.* Polyphony.
polifono [polIfono], *a.* Polyphonic.
poligamia [poligamIa], *n.f.* Polygamy.
poligamo [polIgamo], *n.m.a.* Polygamist; polygamous.
poliglotta, poliglotto, *n.m.a.* Polyglot.
poligonale, *a.* (*Geom.*) Polygonal.
poligono [polIgono], *n.m.* (*Geom.*) Polygon; (*Bot.*) poligonum; (*Mil.*) shooting range.
poligrafia [poligrafIa], *n.f.* Polygraphy.
poliomielite, *n.f.* (*Med.*) Poliomyelitis.
polipo [pOlipo], *n.m.* (*Zool.*) Polyp; (*Med.*) polypus.
polisarcia [polisarcIa], *n.f.* (*Med.*) Corpulence, obesity.
polisillabico [polisillAbico], *a.* Polysyllabic.
polisillabo [polisIllabo], *n.m.a.* Polysyllable, polysyllabic.
politeama (*pl.* **politeami**), *n.m.* Theatre, music-hall.
politecnico [politEcnico], *n.m.a.* Polytechnic; school of engineering.
politeismo, *n.m.* Polytheism.
politeista (*pl.* **politeisti**), *n.m.* Polytheist.

politeistico [politeIstico], *a.* Polytheistic.
politica [polItica], *n.f.* Politics; policy; statecraft, statesmanship; discretion, shrewdness. **Parlare di —,** to talk politics; **— estera,** foreign policy; **avere molta —,** to be crafty.
politicamente, *adv.* Politically.
politicante, *n.m.* Petty politician, dabbler in politics.
politico [polItico], *n.m.a.* Politician; statesman; tactful person, schemer; political.
politicone, *n.m.* Schemer.
polito, *a.* Clean, polished [cp. **pulito**].
polizia [polizIa], *n.f.* Police; police station; regulations for public order. **Chiamare la —,** to call the police; **— di circolazione,** traffic police, traffic cops; **— stradale,** traffic regulations.
poliziesco, *a.* Relating to the police. **Romanzo —,** detective story, thriller.
poliziotto, *n.m.* Policeman; detective.
polizza [pOlizza], *n.f.* (Insurance) policy; voucher; bill, cheque; lottery ticket. **— di assicurazione,** assurance policy; **— di carico,** bill of lading; **— del Monte di Pietà,** pawn-ticket.
polizzino, *n.m.* (*Eccles.*) Confession ticket.
polla, *n.f.* Spring, fountain, source.
pollaio [pollAio], *n.m.* Hen-coop, poultry-run, poultry-yard, hen-house.
pollaiolo, *n.m.* Poulterer.
pollame, *n.m.* Poultry, fowls.
pollanca, *n.f.* Young turkey; chick.
pollastra, *n.f.* Pullet, young hen; (*fig.*) young girl, simple girl.
pollastrella, *n.f.* Chick.
pollastro, *n.m.* Cockerel, young fowl; (*fig.*) youngster, stripling, lad.
polleria, *n.f.* Poultry market, poulterer's shop; poultry, fowls (for table).
pollice [pOllice], *n.m.* (*Anat.*) Thumb; inch. **— del piede,** big-toe.
pollicultore, *n.m.* Poultry farmer.
pollicultura, *n.f.* Poultry-farming.
pollina, *n.f.* Fowl-manure, fowl-droppings.
polline [pOlline], *n.m.* (*Bot.*) Pollen.
pollinifero [pollinIfero], *a.* Polliniferous.
pollino (1), *n.m.a.* Poultry. **Pidocchio —,** poultry louse.
pollino (2), *n.m.* Marsh, swamp.
pollo, *n.m.* Fowl, chicken. **Far ridere i polli,** to make a fool of oneself; **andare a letto all'ora dei polli,** to go to bed very early; **conoscere i propri polli,** to know one's customers, to know whom one has to do with; **essere come i polli di mercato,** to be one good and one bad; **— d'India,** turkey.
pollone, *n.m.* (*Bot.*) Shoot, sucker.
polluto, *a.* Polluted, defiled.
polluzione, *n.f.* Pollution.
polmonare, *a.* (*Anat.*) Pulmonary.
polmonaria [polmonAria], *n.f.* (*Bot.*) Lungwort.
polmone, *n.m.* (*Anat.*) Lung.
polmonite, *n.f.* (*Med.*) Pneumonia.
polo, *n.m.* (*Geog. Geom., etc.*) Pole; (*Sport*) polo. **Poli magnetici,** magnetic poles.
polodizia [polodIzia], *n.f.* Polarity.
polonese, *n.m.a.* (*obs.*) Polish.
Polonia [polOnia], *n.f.* (*Geog.*) Poland.
polonio [polOnio], *n.m.* (*Min.*) Polonium.
polpa, *n.f.* Pulp (of fruit); flesh (of animals).
polpaccio [polpAccio], *n.m.* Calf (of leg).
polpacciolo, *n.m.* Piece of flesh.
polpacciuto, *a.* Fleshy, plump.
polpastrello, *n.m.* Ball of finger or thumb.
polpetta, *n.f.* Rissole, croquette; (*colloq.*) reproof; poison (for dogs, etc.).
polpettone, *n.m.* Meat roll; hash. (*fig.*) **Quel libro è un gran —,** that book contains much more paper and words than sense.
polpo, *n.m.* (*Zool.*) Octopus.
polposo, polputo, *a.* Pulpy; fleshy, plump.
polsino, *n.m.* Cuff, wrist-band. **Bottoni da polsini,** cuff-links.
polso, *n.m.* (*Anat.*) Wrist; pulse, pulsation; (*fig.*) nerve, energy, strength, vigour. **Tastare il —,** to feel the pulse; **— frequente,** quick pulse; **un uomo di —,** a strong man; **orologio da —,** wrist-watch.
poltiglia [poltIglia], *n.f.* Slush, slime; mush; batter; pulp.
poltiglioso, *a.* Muddy, slimy.
poltrire, *v.i.* To idle, to idle away, to be lazy, to spend in idleness, to lie in bed.
poltrona, *n.f.* Arm-chair, easy chair; (*Theat.*) stall. **— a dondolo,** rocking-chair.
poltronaggine [poltronAggine], *n.f.* Laziness.
poltroncina, *n.f.* Small easy chair; (*Theat.*) pit stall.
poltrone, *n.m.* Lazy man, slacker, sluggard. lazybones; coward, poltroon.
poltroneggiare, *v.i.* To live without working, to be work-shy.
poltroneria [poltronerIa], *n.f.* Laziness, sloth; cowardice.
poltronescamente, *adv.* Cowardly, in a cowardly way.
poltronesco, *a.* Cowardly.
polve, *n.f.* (*Poet.*) Dust [cp. **polvere**].
polveraio [polverAio], *a.* Dusty, gusty. **Gennaio — empie il granaio,** a dry, gusty January makes a full granary.
polvere [pOlvere], *n.f.* Dust; powder; gunpowder; (*Med.*) powder. **Fare la —,** to dust (the house); **in —,** in powder. **caffè in —,** ground coffee; **ridurre in —,** to powder, to reduce to powder; **nuvola di —,** cloud of dust; **sollevar —,** to raise dust.
polveriera, *n.f.* Powder-magazine.
polverificio [polverifIcio], *n.m.* Powder-factory.
polverina, *n.f.* (Medicinal) powder.
polverino, *n.m.* (*obs.*) Sand-box.
polverio [polverIo], *n.m.* Cloud of dust.
polverizzamento, *n.m.* Pulverization.
polverizzare, *v.t.* To reduce to powder, to pulverize; to atomize; to smash.
polverizzatore, *n.m.* Atomizer.
polverizzazione, *n.f.* Pulverization.
polverone, *n.m.* Cloud of dust.
polveroso, *a.* Dusty.
polverume, *n.m.* Quantity of dust, heap of dust.
polviglio [polvIglio], *n.m.* Fine powder; (*Med.*) powder.
polviscolo [cp. **pulviscolo**].
pomario [pomArio], *n.m.* Orchard, fruit-garden.
pomata, *n.f.* Ointment, pomade; salve.
pomato, *a.* Concerning apples, or orchards.
pomellato, *a.* Dappled (of a horse).
pomello, *n.m.* (*colloq.*) Cheek-bone.

pomeridiano, *a.* Afternoon. **Alle due pomeridiane,** at two in the afternoon.
pomeriggio [pomerIggio], *n.m.* Afternoon.
pometo, *n.m.* Orchard, apple-orchard.
pomice [pOmice], *n.m.* Pumice-stone.
pomicultura, *n.f.* Fruit-growing, pomiculture.
pomidoro, pomodoro, *n.m.* Tomato. **Salsa di —,** tomato-sauce.
pomo, *n.m.* (*Bot.*) Apple-tree; apple; any apple-like fruit; pommel (of saddle); hilt (of sword); knob; rose (of watering-can). **— d'Adamo,** Adam's apple; **il — della discordia,** the apple of discord; (*Naut.*) **— d'albero,** masthead truck.
pomodoro [cp. **pomidoro**].
pomologia [pomologIa], *n.f.* Treatise, etc., on fruit-growing.
pompa (1), *n.f.* Pomp, ostentation, show, display, parade; splendour. **Pompe funebri,** funeral ceremonies; undertakers; **far — di,** to make a show of.
pompa (2), *n.f.* Pump. **— da incendio,** fire-engine; **— aspirante,** suction-pump. **— da bicicletta,** bicycle pump.
pompare, *v.t.i.* To pump; to suck up.
pompata, *n.f.* Pumpful, pumping.
pompeggiare, *v.i.* To make a display, to flaunt.
pompeggiarsi, *v.r.* To flaunt, to strut; to deck oneself out.
Pompei [pompEi], *n.f.* (*Geog.*) Pompei.
pompeiano, *n.m.a.* Pompeian.
pompiere, *n.m.* Fireman. **I pompieri,** the fire-brigade.
pompieristico [pompierIstico], *a.* Concerned with the fire-brigade. **Gara pompieristica,** firemen's display.
pomposamente, *adv.* Pompously.
pomposità [-à], *n.f.* Pomposity, pompousness; ostentation.
pomposo, *a.* Pompous, inflated, ostentatious; magnificent, grand.
ponce, poncino, *n.m.* Punch. **— al rum,** rum punch.
poncio [pOncio], *n.m.* Poncho (S. American cloak).
ponderabile [ponderAbile], *a.* Ponderable, weighable.
ponderabilità [-à], *n.f.* Ponderability.
ponderare, *v.t.i.* To ponder, to consider, to weigh, to reflect; to muse.
ponderatamente, *adv.* After reflection, after pondering.
ponderatezza, ponderazione, *n.f.* Consideration, deliberation, circumspection.
ponderosità [-à], *n.f.* Heaviness, weight.
ponderoso, *a.* Heavy, ponderous; stodgy.
pondo, *n.m.* Weight, burden.
ponente, *n.m.* (*Geog.*) West; west wind.
ponentino, *n.m.* Westerly breeze.
ponimento, *n.m.* Placing, setting.
pontaio [pontAio], *n.m.* Scaffold-builder.
ponte, *n.m.* Bridge; platform; scaffolding; (*Naut.*) deck. **— levatoio,** drawbridge; **— sospeso,** suspension-bridge; **— girevole,** swing-bridge; **— di barche,** pontoon-bridge; (*Mil.*) **fare una testa di —,** to make a bridge-head; (*Naut.*) **a due, a tre ponti,** two- three-decked; **— principale,** main deck; **— della passeggiata, delle scialuppe,** promenade, boat-deck.
pontefice [pontEfice], *n.m.* Pontiff, the Pope; **il Sommo —,** the Supreme Pontiff.
ponticello, *n.m.* Small bridge; (*Mus.*) bridge (of violin, etc.).
ponticino, *n.m.* (*Billiards*) Cue-rest.
pontiere, *n.m.* (*Mil.*) Sapper employed on pontoons.
pontificale, *n.m.a.* Pontifical.
pontificalmente, *adv.* Pontifically.
pontificare, *v.i.* To pontificate; to officiate (as Pope); to dictate; to lecture.
pontificato, *n.m.* Pontificate.
pontificio [pontifIcio], *a.* Pontifical, papal.
pontile, *n.m.* Landing-stage; gangway.
ponto, *n.m.* (*Poet.*) Sea.
pontone, *n.m.* Pontoon; ferry-boat, lighter.
pontoniere, *n.m.* [cp. **pontiere**].
ponzamento, *n.m.* Straining, labouring.
ponzare, *v.t.i.* To strain, to labour, to make an effort.
ponzatura, *n.f.* Effort, straining, tension.
Ponzio Pilato [pOnzio], *n.m.* Pontius Pilate.
poplite [pOplite], *n.m.* (*Anat.*) Back of the knee.
popolaccio [popolAccio], *n.m.* Rabble, mob, populace.
popolano, *n.m.a.* Man of the people; artisan, workman; (*Eccles.*) parishioner; of the people.
popolare, popolarsi, *v.t.r.* To people, to populate; to crowd.
popolare, *a.* Popular, common, prevalent; liked, admired; commonplace, ordinary. **Render —,** to popularize.
popolarescamente, *adv.* Popularly.
popolaresco, *a.* Popular; genuine; vulgar, common.
popolarità [-à], *n.f.* Popularity.
popolarizzare, *v.t.* To popularize.
popolarmente, *adv.* Popularly.
popolato, *a.* Populated.
popolazione, *n.f.* Population. **Eccesso di —,** over-population.
popolino, *n.m.* Common folk.
popolo [pOpolo] (1), *n.m.* People; nation; populace, multitude, crowd. **— minuto,** common people, workmen; **— grasso,** bourgeoisie.
popolo [pOpolo] (2), *n.m.* (*Bot.*) [cp. **pioppo**].
popoloso, *a.* Populous, crowded.
poponaia [poponAia], *n.f.* Melon-bed.
popone, *n.m.* (*Bot.*) Melon.
poppa (1), *n.f.* (Woman's) breast; nipple, teat; dug (of animals). **Dare la —,** to nurse, to suckle.
poppa (2), *n.f.* (*Naut.*) Stern, poop. **A —,** astern; **avere il vento in —,** to have a fair wind, to prosper, to thrive.
poppante, *n.m.* Suckling, sucking child, baby, infant.
poppare, *v.t.i.* To suck, to take the breast.
poppata, *n.f.* Sucking.
poppatoio [poppatOio], *n.m.* Feeding-bottle; pacifier.
poppiere, *n.m.* Stern rower in a gondola.
popputa, *a.* Full-breasted, big-breasted (woman).
porca (1), *n.f.* Sow.
porca (2), *n.f.* (*Agric.*) Ridge between two furrows.
porcaio, porcaro [porcAio], *n.m.* Swineherd; dirty place, pigsty; shady affair.

porcamente, *adv.* Swinishly, piggishly.
porcareccia [porcarEccia], *n.f.* Pig-farm.
porcaro, *n.m.* Swineherd.
porcellana, *n.f.* Porcelain; china, chinaware.
porcellino, *n.m.* Sucking-pig; dirty little child. **— d'India,** guinea-pig.
porcello, *n.m.* Young pig, piglet.
porcellone, *n.m.* (*fig.*) Dirty or ill-mannered person.
porcheria [porcherIa], *n.f.* Dirt, filth; dirty piece of work, dirty deed; rubbish, trash; scurrility, obscenity.
porcheriola, *n.f.* Dirt, obscenity, dirty action.
porchetta, *n.f.* Roast sucking-pig.
porcile, *n.m.* Pig-sty.
porcino, *a.* Porcine, pertaining to the pig. **Carne porcina,** pork; **fungo —,** boletus (edible fungus).
porco, *n.m.* Pig; swine; hog; pork (meat); (*fig.*) dirty man.
porcospino, *n.m.* (*Zool.*) Porcupine.
porcume, *n.m.* Heap of dirty things; dirtiness.
porfido [pOrfido], *n.m.* Porphyry.
porgere [pOrgere], *v.t.i.* To hand, to reach out; to offer, to present; to give; to deliver; to bear, to bring. **— la mano,** to hold out one's hand, to give a helping hand; **— aiuto,** to give assistance; **— fede,** to believe, to give credit to; **— orecchio,** to listen; **— bene,** to have a good delivery.
porgersi [pOrgersi], *v.r.* To present oneself, to offer oneself.
porgimento, *n.m.* Offer, presentation; delivery.
porgitore, porgitrice, *n.m.f.* Offerer, presenter (esp. of a letter, etc.).
pornografia [pornografIa], *n.f.* Pornography.
pornografico [pornogrAfico], *a.* Pornographic.
poro, *n.m.* Pore.
porosità [-à], *n.f.* Porosity, porousness.
poroso, *a.* Porous.
porpora [pOrpora], *n.f.* Purple; (*fig.*) cardinalate.
porporato, *n.m.a.* (*Eccles.*) Cardinal; clothed in purple.
porporeggiare, *v.t.* To dye purple.
porporina, *n.f.* (*Chem.*) Purpurin.
porporino, *a.* Purple.
porraccio [porrAccio], *n.m.* (*Bot.*) Asphodel.
porraceo [porrAceo], *a.* Leek-green.
porre, *v.t.* To put, to place, to set, to lay; to suppose, to imagine. **— da parte,** to put aside; **— un freno,** to check, to put a brake on; **— in opera,** to set up, to put in action; **— ai voti una mozione,** to put a motion to the vote; **— la prima pietra,** to lay the foundation stone; **por mente,** to take heed; **— cura,** to take care; **— in oblio,** to forget; **por mano a,** to begin; to set to work; **poniamo che,** let us suppose that [cp. **porsi**].
porrina, *n.f.* (*Bot.*) Bulb of leek; seedling oak.
porro, *n.m.* (*Bot.*) Leek ; (*Med.*) wart.
porroso, *a.* Warty.
porsi, *v.r.* To place oneself. **— all'opera,** to set to work; **— addosso,** to put on [cp. **porre**].
porta, *n.f.* Door, gate; doorway, gateway; threshold; exit; entrance; (*Football*) goal. **— di strada,** front door, street door; **— di servizio,** backdoor; **— di soccorso,** emergency exit; **mettere alla —,** to turn out of doors; **battere alla —,** to knock at the door; **essere — a —,** to be next-door to someone; **prender la —,** to go, to leave; **sfondare una — aperta,** to crack a nut with a sledge-hammer; **— a due battenti,** double-door; **le porte della città,** the city gates; **sbattere la — in faccia a qualcuno,** to slam the door in someone's face.
portabagaglio [portabagAglio], *n.m.* Carrier (on bicycle, etc.); porter.
portabandiera, *n.m.* Standard-bearer.
portabiglietti, *n.m.* Note-case, card-case.
portabile [portAbile], *a.* Portable.
portacappelli, *n.m.* Hat-box; hatstand.
portacarte, *n.m.* Folder (for papers, etc.).
portacatino, *n.m.* Washstand.
portacenere [portacEnere], *n.m.* Ashtray.
portaceste, *n.m.* (*Theat.*) Dresser.
portacoltelli, *n.m.* Knife-rest.
portaerei [portaErei], *n.m.* (*Naut.*) Aircraft carrier.
portaferiti, *n.m.* Stretcher-bearer.
portafiammiferi [portafiammIferi], *n.m.* Match-box.
portafiaschi, *n.m.* Bottle-rack.
portafiori, *n.m.* Flower-basket; flower-stand.
portafogli, portafoglio [portafOglio], *n.m.* Pocket-book, wallet; portfolio.
portafortuna, *n.m.* Mascot.
portagioie, portagioielli, *n.m.* Jewel-case, jewel-box.
portalapis, *n.m.* Pencil-holder.
portale, *n.m.* (*Arch.*) Portal, doorway.
portalettere [portalEttere], *n.m.* Postman.
portamantello, *n.m.* Portmanteau, valise.
portamento, *n.m.* Gait, carriage, bearing; behaviour; (*Mus.*) fingering.
portampolle, *n.m.* Cruet-stand.
portamusica [portamUsica], *n.m.* Music-stand.
portante, *n.m.* Carrying-chair, carrier.
portante, *a.* Bearing. **Ben —,** well-preserved.
portantina, *n.f.* Sedan-chair, litter.
portaombrelli, portombrelli, *n.m.* Umbrella-stand.
portaordini [portaOrdini], *n.m.* Messenger.
portaorologio [portaorolOgio], *n.m.* Watch-pocket.
portapacchi, *n.m.* Carrier (for bicycle, etc.); messenger boy.
portapenne, *n.m.* Pen-holder.
portapiatti, *n.m.* Plate-rack.
portapranzi, *n.m.* Tray; trolley.
portare, *v.t.* To bear, to carry, to bring; to fetch, to take; to wear; to lead, to induce, to incite; to cause; to produce, to bring forward, to allege; to set; (*Comm.*) to post (a ledger, etc.). **— a spasso,** to take round, to take for a walk; **— il lutto,** to wear mourning; **— in palma di mano,** to extol to the skies; **questa strada porta a,** this road leads to; **— profitto,** to be profitable; **— uno,** to favour one; **— un baule,** to carry a trunk; **— bene gli anni,** to carry one's years well; **— il lume,** to play gooseberry; **— i calzoni,** to wear the trousers (of a woman); **portate via quello!** take that away! **non porta la spesa,** it doesn't pay; **— vasi a Samo,** to carry coals to Newcastle; **portami con te,** take me with you; **ciò ti porterà fortuna,** this will bring you good luck; **mi porti un bicchiere di vino,**

bring me a glass of wine; **portatemi un cucchiaio,** bring me a spoon; **— un bambino in collo,** to carry a baby in one's arms; **— pazienza,** to be patient; **— rancore,** to bear a grudge; **esser portato ad esempio,** to be held up as an example; **— danno,** to cause damage; **— un abito scuro,** to wear a dark suit; **portatelo qui!** bring it here! [cp. **portarsi**].

portaritratti, *n.m.* Photograph-frame.

portarsi, *v.r.* To go, to move; to behave; to keep (well); to be worn. **Si portò a Roma,** he moved to Rome; **— da gentiluomo,** to behave like a gentleman.

portasapone, *n.m.* Soap-dish.

portasigari, portasigarette, *n.m.* Cigar-case; cigarette-case.

portaspazzature, *n.m.* Dustpan.

portaspilli, *n.m.* Pin-cushion.

portata, *n.f.* Reach, range; course (at a meal); span, capacity; (*Naut.*) tonnage; (*Mus.*) staff, stave. **A — di mano,** within easy reach; **essere a — di voce,** to be within call; **a — d'orecchio,** within hearing; **questo non è alla mia —,** this is beyond me, beyond my understanding; **di prima —,** of the utmost importance; **mettersi alla — di,** to come down to someone's level; **la — d'un cannone,** the range of a gun; **un pranzo di tre portate,** a three-course meal.

portatile [portAtile], *a.* Portable.

portato, *n.m.* Outcome, result; effect.

portato, *p.p.a.* Brought, carried; inclined, bent; given to, addicted to (in a bad sense).

portatore, portatrice, *n.m.f.* Bearer, carrier; (luggage) porter. **Pagabile al —,** payable to bearer.

portatura, *n.f.* Carriage, bearing.

portauovo, *n.m.* Egg-cup.

portavivande, *n.m.* Tray.

portavoce, *n.m.* Megaphone, speaking-trumpet; (*fig.*) mouthpiece. **Il — autorizzato,** the authorized mouthpiece, spokesman.

portello, *n.m.* Little door, opening; (*Naut.*) port-hole.

portento, *n.m.* Portent, prodigy; wonder.

portentosamente, *adv.* Portentously, prodigiously, wonderfully.

portentoso, *a.* Portentous, prodigious, wonderful.

porticato, *n.m.* Porch, arcade, colonnade.

portico [pOrtico], *n.m.* Porch, portico, arcade. **Passeggiare sotto i portici,** to stroll in the arcade.

portiera, *n.f.* Door-curtain; portress.

portiere, *n.m.* Door-keeper, hall-porter; janitor; (*Football*) goal-keeper.

portinaio [portinAio], *n.m.* Door-keeper, concierge.

portineria [portinerIa], *n.f.* Porter's lodge.

portinsegna, *n.m.* Standard-bearer.

porto (1), *n.m.* Harbour, port, sea-port, haven. **Entrare in un —,** to enter a harbour; (*fig.*) **condurre a buon —,** to bring to a successful issue; **essere a buon —,** to be well advanced (in a work); (*Comm.*) **diritti di —,** harbour dues.

porto (2), *n.m.* (*Comm.*) Carriage, postage. **— franco,** carriage-paid; **— assegnato,** cash on delivery; **— d'armi,** licence to carry weapons, gun licence; **— affrancato,** postage prepaid.

porto, *p.p.* [cp. **porgere**].

Portogallo, *n.m.* (*Geog.*) Portugal.

portoghese, *n.m.a.* Portuguese.

portolano, *n.m.* (*Naut.*) Sailing directions.

portombrelli, *n.m.* Umbrella-stand.

portone, *n.m.* Front gate, front-door; carriage entrance.

portuale, *n.m.* Docker, dock labourer.

portuale, portuario [portuArio], *a.* Of a port. **Diritti portuari,** harbour dues.

portulaca, *n.f.* (*Bot.*) Purslane.

portuoso, *a.* (*Naut.*) Affording harbourage.

porzioncella, porziocina, *n.f.* Very small portion.

porzione, *n.f.* Portion, part, lot, share; helping (of a dish).

posa, *n.f.* Rest, pause; attitude, pose, posture; sediment; setting, placing; (*Phot.*) exposure; (*Painting*) sitting (for a portrait). **Senza —,** incessantly; **una bella —,** a graceful attitude; **avere delle pose,** to give oneself airs; **— della prima pietra,** laying the foundation stone; (*Phot.*) **una — lunga,** a long exposure; **non trovar —,** to be restless.

posacenere [posacEnere], *n.m.* Ash-tray; ash-pan.

posamento, *n.m.* Placing, setting, laying.

posamine, *n.m.* (*Naut.*) Mine-layer.

posapiano, *n.m.* Sluggard; slow-coach; (label with words) "Handle with Care"; "Fragile."

posapiedi, *n.m.* Foot-stool.

posare, *v.t.i.* To lay, to lay down, to set down, to place, to put; to rest, to pause; to pose, to assume an attitude; to sit (for portrait or photo). **Posalo sul tavolo,** put it on the table; **— la prima pietra,** to lay a foundation stone; **— una questione,** to put a question.

posarsi, *v.r.* To alight, to perch; to settle, to place oneself.

posata, *n.f.* Cover (knife, fork, spoon, etc.); pose; rest (of birds of passage). **Posate d'argento,** silver service.

posatamente, *adv.* Unhurriedly, deliberately, sedately.

posateria [posaterIa], *n.f.* Cutlery, plate.

posatezza, *n.f.* Sedateness, calm, coolness, composure.

posato, *p.p.a.* Composed, sedate, tranquil, staid, quiet.

posatore, posatrice, *n.m.f.* Poser, poseur, affected man or woman.

posbellico [posbEllico], *a.* Post-war.

poscia [pOscia], *adv.* After, then, afterwards; **— che,** *conj.* since, after.

poscritta, poscritto, *n.f.m.* Postscript.

posdomani, *adv.* Day after tomorrow.

posdatare, *v.t.* To post-date (letter, cheque, etc.).

positiva, *n.f.* (*Phot.*) Positive.

positivamente, *adv.* Positively.

positivismo, *n.m.* Positivism.

positivista (*pl.* **positivisti**), *n.m.* Positivist.

positivo, *a.* Positive; real, certain, concrete, matter-of-fact. **Un uomo —,** a matter-of-fact man.

positura, *n.f.* Posture, position, place.

posizione, *n.f.* Position, situation; posture, attitude, place; condition, standing, status. **La casa è in una bella —,** the house is well situated; **prendere —,** to take a stand; **una**

brillante —, a high position (in politics, rank, etc.); **farsi una —**, to get on in the world.
posolino, *n.m.* Crupper (harness).
posponimento, *n.m.* Postponement, adjournment; delay.
posporre, *v.t.* To postpone, to put off, to defer; to adjourn; to procrastinate.
posposizione, *n.f.* Postponement, deferment; adjournment.
posposto, *p.p.a.* Postponed, deferred.
possa, *n.f.* Power, might, strength. **A tutta —**, with might and main.
possanza, *n.f.* Power, might, force.
possedere, *v.t.* To own, to possess; to master, to be versed in. **— bene una lingua,** to master a language; **possiedi un'automobile?** have you got a car?
possedimento, *n.m.* Possession, property; colony.
posseditore, posseditrice, *n.m.f.* Possessor.
possente, *a.* Powerful, mighty, potent; masterful.
possentemente, *adv.* Powerfully.
possessione, *n.f.* Property, estate, possession, ownership.
possessivamente, *adv.* Possessively.
possessivo, *a.* Possessive.
possesso, *n.m.* Possession, owning, ownership; property, estate; occupation, tenure. **Prender — di,** to take possession of.
possessore, *n.m.* Owner, possessor, proprietor.
possessorio [possessOrio], *a.* (*Law*) Possessory.
possibile [possIbile], *a.* Possible; practicable, feasible; probable. **Farò il —**, I'll do what I can, I'll do my best; **al più presto —**, as soon as possible.
possibilità [**-à**], *n.f.* Possibility; power; chance.
possibilmente, *adv.* If possible; possibly.
possidente, *n.m.* Proprietor, owner; landowner; man of means.
posta (1), *n.f.* Post, mail, post-office. **Fermo in —**, poste-restante; **— aerea,** air mail; **spedire per —**, to send by post; **andare alla —**, to go to the post-office; **Ministero delle Poste,** Postmaster-General; **mettere una lettera alla —**, to post a letter.
posta (2), *n.f.* Stake, bet (in games); item, entry; lying in wait; stage; stall (for beasts). **Raddoppiare la —**, to double the stake; **fare la — a uno,** to lie in wait for someone; **a bella —**, **a —**, **apposta,** on purpose, intentionally; **a sua —**, as he pleases; **di —**, quickly; **stare alla —**, to watch.
postale, *n.m.* (*Naut.*) Mail-boat, packet.
postale, *a.* Postal. **Ufficio —**, post-office; **vaglia —**, money order; **cartolina —**, post-card; **pacco —**, parcel post; **timbro —**, postmark; **furgone —**, mail-van.
postare, *v.t.* To place; to post.
postbellico [postbEllico], *a.* Post-war.
posteggiare, *v.i.* To lie in wait, to watch for; (*Motor.*) to park.
posteggiatore, *n.m.* Stall-holder (in street market, etc.).
posteggio [postEggio], *n.m.* Stand, cab-stand, cab-rank; (*Motor.*) parking-place.
postelegrafico [postelegrAfico], *a.* Postal (service, employees, etc.).
postelegrafonico [postelegrafOnico], *a.* Postal (telegraph, telephone, etc.).
postema, *n.f.* (*Med.*) Boil, abscess.
postergare, *v.t.* To throw over the shoulder, to toss away; to postpone, to defer.
posteri [pOsteri], *n.m.pl.* Posterity, remote descendants.
posteria [posterIa], *n.f.* Village all-sorts shop.
posteriore, *a.* Posterior; subsequent, following; hind. **In tempi posteriori,** in later times.
posteriormente, *adv.* Subsequently; from behind, from the back.
posterità [**-à**], *n.f.* Posterity, descendants.
posticciamente, *adv.* Artificially.
posticcio [postIccio], *a.* Artificial, false, sham. **Capelli posticci,** false hair.
posticino, *n.m.* Small place, small situation.
posticipare, *v.t.* To postpone, to defer, to put off. **Pagamento posticipato,** deferred payment.
posticipatamente, *adv.* After the proper time, after it is due.
posticipazione, *n.f.* Postponement, deferment; delay.
postiere, *n.m.* Post-horse keeper, master of a post-stage.
postiglione, *n.m.* Postillion.
postilla, *n.f.* Gloss, marginal note; comment; explanation.
postillare, *v.t.* To annotate, to make notes, to gloss, to comment.
postillatore, *n.m.* Annotator.
postillatura, *n.f.* Glossing, annotation.
postino, *n.m.* Postman.
posto, *n.m.* Place, room, post; spot, site, situation, position; appointment, job; room, vacancy. **Fare —**, to make room; (*Theat. etc.*) **posti riservati,** reserved seats; **non c'è —**, there's no room; **sul —**, on the spot; **se fossi al suo —**, if I were in his place; **fuori (di) —**, out of place; **prender —**, to take one's seat; **egli cerca un —**, he's looking for a job; (*Rail.*) **— d'angolo,** corner seat; **— in piedi,** standing-room; **— di pronto soccorso,** first-aid post.
posto, *p.p.* Placed, situated, put. **— che,** since, supposing that [cp. **porre**].
postremo, *a.* (*Lit.*) Last.
postribolo [postrIbolo], *n.m.* Brothel.
postulante, *n.m.* Applicant, petitioner; (*Eccles.*) postulant.
postulare, *v.t.* To claim, to apply for, to solicit, to postulate.
postumo [pOstumo], *n.m.* (*Med.*) Consequence, aftermath (of an illness).
postumo [pOstumo], *a.* Posthumous.
postura, *n.f.* Place, site, situation; posture.
postutto, *adv.* **Al —**, in the end, at most.
potabile [potAbile], *a.* Drinkable, potable. **Acqua —**, drinking-water.
potagione, *n.f.* [cp. **potatura**].
potaiolo, *n.m.* Pruning-knife.
potamento, *n.m.* Pruning, lopping.
potare, *v.t.* To prune, to lop; to cut back.
potassa, *n.f.* (*Chem.*) Potash.
potassico [potAssico], *a.* Potassic.
potassio [potAssio], *n.m.* (*Min.*) Potassium.
potatoio [potatOio], *n.m.* Pruning-knife, pruning-hook.
potatore, *n.m.* Pruner.

potatura, *n.f.* Pruning, lopping; pruning-time.
potentato, *n.m.* Potentate, chief, ruler.
potente, *a.* Potent, powerful, mighty; strong, vigorous; wealthy; forcible, cogent.
potentemente, *adv.* Powerfully, potently.
potenza, *n.f.* Power, potence, potency, might, force, sway, empire; influence. **Le grandi potenze,** the Great Powers; (*Math.*) **elevare alla terza —,** to raise to the third power; **elevare all'ennesima —,** to raise to the *n*th degree.
potenziale, *n.m.a.* Potential.
potenzialità [-**à**], *n.f.* Potentiality, power, force.
potenzialmente, *adv.* Potentially.
potenziare, *v.t.* To make potent, to give power, to strengthen.
potere, *v.i.* To be able; to be allowed, to have power, to be capable; may, can, could, might. **Non ne posso più,** I have had enough; I can't stand it any longer; **Si può?** May I come in? **a più non posso,** that's all I can do; one's utmost; **lavorare a più non posso,** to work oneself to death; **non posso,** I cannot; **può capitare che,** it may happen that; **può essere, può darsi,** it may be; **non posso venire,** I cannot come; **non posso farci nulla,** I can't do anything; **non può essere,** it can't be.
potere, *n.m.* Power, might, authority; ability; capacity; rule, sway, government; possession. **Non è in mio —,** it is not in my power; **pieni poteri,** full powers, full authority; **avere — su qualcuno,** to hold sway over someone; **— esecutivo,** executive power; **salire al —,** to take power, to rise to power.
potestà [-**à**], *n.f.* Authority, power [cp. **podestà**].
pottiniccio [pottinIccio], *n.m.* (*vulg.*) Mud; badly muddled work.
poveraccio [poverAccio], *n.m.* Poor fellow! poor devil!
poveraglia [poverAglia], *n.f.* Poor people; beggars.
poveramente, *adv.* Poorly, meanly.
poverello, poveretto, *n.m.* Poor man ; beggar. **Il poverello d'Assisi,** St. Francis.
poverino, *n.m.* Poor little chap.
povero [pOvero], *n.m.* Poor man, poor creature; pauper; mendicant, beggar.
povero [pOvero], *a.* Poor, indigent, needy; humble; unfortunate. **— in canna,** destitute; **— di spirito,** poor-spirited; **Povero me!** Alas, poor me! **in parole povere,** in plain language.
povertà [-**à**], *n.f.* Poverty, indigence, penury; meanness; scantiness.
pozione, *n.f.* Potion.
pozza, *n.f.* Pool, puddle.
pozzanghera [pozzAnghera], Puddle, pool.
pozzetta, *n.f.* Dimple (on the face); small pool.
pozzetto, *n.m.* Tank, reservoir; small well.
pozzo, *n.m.* Well; (mine) shaft; tank; fountain. **— artesiano,** artesian well; **— nero,** cesspool; **— petrolifero,** oil-well; **scavare un —,** to dig a well; **è un — di sapienza,** he's a mine of learning.
pozzolana, *n.f.* (*Min.*) Pozzolana; volcanic dust.
pracrito [prAcrito], *n.m.* Prakrit (languages).
Praga, *n.f.* (*Geog.*) Prague.
pragmatismo, *n.m.* Pragmatism.
pragmatista (*pl.* **pragmatisti**), *n.m.* Pragmatist.
prammatica [prammAtica], *n.f.* Prescribed way, customary form, formality, custom. **Di —,** usual, customary, formal, prescribed; **risposta di —,** regulation answer.
pranzare, *v.i.* To dine.
pranzatore, pranzatrice, *n.m.f.* Diner.
pranzetto, *n.m.* Light dinner, snack.
pranzo, *n.m.* Dinner; dinner-party.
prassi, *n.f.* Praxis, use, practice.
prataiolo, *a.* Field, meadow. (*Bot.*) **Fungo —,** meadow mushroom.
pratare, *v.t.* To sow grass.
pratello, *n.m.* Lawn.
pratense, *a.* Field, meadow.
prateria [praterIa], *n.f.* Meadow-lands; grass-land.
pratica [prAtica], *n.f.* Practice (in all senses); custom, routine, habit; dealing, proceeding; experience, training; business; papers, documents; affair, matter, dealing; (*Naut.*) pratique. **Mettere in —,** to put into practice; **acquistar — negli affari,** to acquire experience in business; **fare pratiche,** to make arrangements; **fare —,** to practise; **ammaestrato dalla —,** taught by experience; **avere — di,** to be skilled in; **pratiche religiose,** religious observances.
praticabile [praticAbile], *a.* Practicable, feasible, possible; passable (of roads).
praticabilità [-**à**], *n.f.* Practicability.
praticamente, *adv.* Practically.
praticante, *n.m.* Apprentice; church-goer.
praticare, *v.t.i.* To practise; to frequent, to have intercourse; to perform, to make, to execute; to contrive; to open. **È medico ma non pratica,** he's a doctor but he doesn't practise; **— una persona,** to be on familiar terms with someone.
praticato, *a.* Practised, experienced.
praticello, *n.m.* Lawn, paddock.
praticità [-**à**], *n.f.* Practicability; expediency, convenience; usefulness.
pratico [prAtico], *n.m.* Practitioner, expert.
pratico [prAtico], *a.* Practical, experienced, skilful; useful, convenient, expedient.
praticone, *n.m.* Quack; man who works by intuition.
prativo, *a.* Meadow, meadowy. **Terreno —,** meadow-land.
prato, *n.m.* Meadow, grass-land, pasture-land. (*Bot.*) **Regina dei prati,** meadow-sweet.
pratolina, *n.f.* (*Bot.*) Daisy; ox-eye daisy.
pratolino, *n.m.* Common edible mushroom.
pravamente, *adv.* Wickedly.
pravità [-**à**], *n.f.* Wickedness, depravity.
pravo, *a.* (*Lit.*) Wicked.
pre [cp. **prete**].
preaccennare, *v.t.* To indicate in advance; to hint.
preaccennato, *a.* Aforesaid.
preadamitico [preadamItico], *a.* Before Adam; (*colloq.*) very ancient.
prealpi, *n.f.pl.* Alpine foothills.
preambolo [preAmbolo], *n.m.* Preamble, introduction; preface.
preannunziare, *v.t.* To announce in advance; to foretell.

preannunzio [preannUnzio], *n.m.* Forewarning, notice.
preavvertire, *v.t.* To inform beforehand, to warn; to advise of.
preavvisare, *v.t.* To inform in advance, to forewarn; to notify, to give notice to.
preavviso, *n.m.* Forewarning, warning, advice, notice. **Dare un — di tre giorni,** to give three days' notice; **senza —,** without warning.
prebellico [prebEllico], *a.* Pre-war.
prebenda, *n.f.* (*Eccles.*) Prebend; (*colloq.*) soft job.
prebendario [prebendArio], *n.m.* (*Eccles.*) Prebendary.
precariamente, *adv.* Precariously.
precarietà [-à], *n.f.* Precariousness.
precario [precArio], *a.* Precarious, uncertain, doubtful, hazardous.
precauzionale, *a.* Precautionary.
precauzione, *n.f.* Precaution, caution, care; wariness, foresight. **Prender le precauzioni,** to take precautions.
prece, *n.f.* (*Lit.*) Prayer.
precedente, *n.m.* Precedent. **I precedenti,** the precedents; **senza precedenti,** without precedent, unequalled.
precedente, *a.* Foregoing, preceding, previous, former.
precedentemente, *adv.* Previously.
precedenza, *n.f.* Precedence, priority. **Aver la —,** to have precedence; **in —,** previously.
precedere [precEdere], *v.t.i.* To go before, to precede; to have precedence; to go ahead of, to distance, to outrun, to lead.
precessione, *n.f.* (*Astron.*) Precession.
precettare, *v.t.* (*Law*) To summon, to cite; (*Mil.*) to call to arms.
precettista (*pl.* **precettisti**), *n.m.* Author of literary precepts.
precettistica [precettIstica], *n.f.* Literary precepts.
precetto, *n.m.* Precept, maxim, order, rule, commandment; summons. **Festa di —,** religious holiday of obligation; **adempiere** or **osservare il — pasquale,** to fulfil one's Easter duties.
precettore, *n.m.* Tutor, preceptor, instructor, teacher.
precingere [precIngere], *v.t.* To girdle, to encircle.
precinto, *n.m.* Precinct, boundary.
precipitare, *v.t.i.* To precipitate, to rush, to hurl down, to dash to the ground; to hurry, to hasten; to crash, to fall headlong; to fall down, to tumble down; (*Chem.*) to precipitate; (*Aviat.*) to crash. **Non —!** Don't rush matters! **egli precipitò al suolo,** he crashed to the ground.
precipitarsi, *v.r.* To rush, to hurl oneself, to run, to dash.
precipitatamente, *adv.* Precipitately.
precipitato, *n.m.* (*Chem.*) Precipitate.
precipitato, *a.* Rash, hasty; sudden; rushed, dashed, crashed. **Una partenza precipitata,** a sudden departure.
precipitazione, *n.f.* Precipitation, precipitancy, over-haste, rashness; **Agire con —,** to act rashly.
precipite [precIpite], *a.* Steep, precipitous, headlong.
precipitevole [precipitEvole], *a.* Hasty, impetuous; steep.
precipitevolissimevolmente, *adv.* (*hum.*) Precipitately, violently.
precipitosamente, *adv.* Precipitously.
precipitoso, *a.* Precipitous, steep; headlong, precipitate; rash, hasty.
precipizio [precipIzio], *n.m.* Precipice, ravine, steep cliff, downfall. **L'orlo del —,** the brink of the precipice; **a —,** precipitately, hurriedly; headlong.
precipuamente, *adv.* Principally, chiefly, mainly.
precipuo [precIpuo], *a.* Principal, main, chief; special.
precisamente, *adv.* Precisely, particularly.
precisare, *v.t.* To specify, to define exactly, to determine; to make clear; to state precisely.
precisione, *n.f.* Precision, preciseness; exactitude, exactness.
preciso, *a.* Precise, exact, definite, accurate, sharp (of time); strict, formal; scrupulous; identical.
precitato, *a.* Above-mentioned; afore-mentioned, aforesaid.
preclaramente, *adv.* Illustriously.
preclaro, *a.* Illustrious, celebrated, eminent.
precludere [preclUdere], *v.t.* To preclude, to debar, to prevent; to shut out.
precluso, *p.p.a.* Shut out, debarred, precluded.
precoce, *a.* Precocious; premature, early.
precocemente, *adv.* Precociously.
precocità [-à], *n.f.* Precociousness, precocity.
precognizione, *n.f.* Foreknowledge, precognition.
preconcetto, *n.m.a.* Preconception; bias, prejudice; prejudiced, preconceived. **Idee preconcette,** preconceived ideas.
preconizzare, *v.t.* To foretell, to predict, to prophesy.
preconoscenza, *n.f.* Foreknowledge.
preconoscere [preconOscere], *v.t.* To know beforehand, to have foreknowledge.
preconoscimento, *n.m.* Foreknowledge.
precorrente, *a.* Anticipating.
precorrere [precOrrere], *v.t.i.* To anticipate, to forestall, to outrun.
precursore, *n.m.* Forerunner, precursor, harbinger.
precursore, *a.* Premonitory.
preda, *n.f.* Prey; booty, plunder, spoil; victim. **Uccello di —,** bird of prey; **in — a,** at the mercy of; overwhelmed by (an emotion).
predace, *a.* Predacious, predatory, rapacious.
predamento, *n.m.* Plundering, preying.
predare, *v.t.* To prey, to pillage, to plunder.
predatore, predatrice, *n.m.f.* Robber, pillager, plunderer.
predecessore, *n.m.* Predecessor.
predella, *n.f.* (*Eccles.*) Altar-step, predella; brake, bridle.
predellino, *n.m.* Foot-stool; foot-board (of carriage); child's high chair.
predestinare, *v.t.* To predestine, to predestinate; to pre-ordain.
predestinato, *n.m.a.* Predestinate; predestined.
predestinazione, *n.f.* Predestination.

predeterminare, *v.t.* To predetermine.
predeterminazione, *n.f.* Predetermination.
predetto, *a.* Aforesaid; foretold.
prediale, *a.* Agrarian. **Tassa —,** land tax.
predica [prEdica], *n.f.* Sermon, preaching; lecture, admonition. **Fare la — a uno,** to lecture someone.
predicamento, *n.m.* Preaching, sermonizing.
predicare, *v.t.i.* To preach, to deliver a sermon; to sermonize; to lecture, to reprimand. **— al deserto,** to preach to deaf ears.
predicato, *n.m.* (*Gram.*) Predicate.
predicatore, *n.m.* Preacher.
predicazione, *n.f.* Preaching, predication.
predicozzo, *n.m.* Reproof, scolding; admonition, rebuke; sermonizing. **Fare un —,** to sermonize, to lecture (someone).
prediletto, *n.m.a.* Dearest, favourite, pet.
predilezione, *n.f.* Predilection, partiality, preference.
prediligere [predilIgere], *v.t.* To prefer, to hold dearer.
predio [prEdio], *n.m.* (*Hist.*) Landed property.
predire, *v.t.* To predict, to foretell. **— l'avvenire,** to foretell the future.
predisporre, *v.t.* To predispose, to pre-arrange.
predisposizione, *n.f.* Predisposition, pre-arrangement.
predisposto, *p.p.a.* Predisposed; inclined, favourable.
predizione, *n.f.* Prediction, prophecy.
predominante, *a.* Predominant, prevalent, prevailing.
predominanza, *n.f.* Predominance, prevalence; ascendancy.
predominare, *v.i.* To predominate, to prevail; to emerge. **— sugli altri,** to prevail over the others.
predominio [predomInio], *n.m.* Predominance, pre-eminence, superiority; mastery, ascendancy, dominion.
predone, *n.m.* Plunderer, robber; highwayman.
preesistenza, *n.f.* Pre-existence.
prefabbricato, *a.* Prefabricated.
prefato, *a.* Above-mentioned, aforesaid.
prefazio [prefAzio], *n.m.* (*Eccles.*) Preface of the Mass.
prefazione, *n.f.* Preface, introduction, foreword.
preferenza, *n.f.* Preference, precedence, predilection, partiality.
preferenziale, *a.* Preferential. (*Comm.*) **Titoli preferenziali,** preference shares.
preferibile [preferIbile], *a.* Preferable.
preferibilmente, *adv.* Preferably.
preferire, *v.t.* To prefer, to choose, to like better, to give the preference to.
preferito, *a.* Favourite, preferred.
prefettizio [prefettIzio], *a.* Prefectorial, prefectural.
prefetto, *n.m.* Prefect, civil governor.
prefettura, *n.f.* Prefecture.
prefica [prEfica], *n.f.* (*Hist.*) Hired mourner.
prefiggere [prefIggere], *v.i.* To pre-establish, to fix beforehand, to pre-arrange, to determine; (*Gram.*) to prefix.
prefiggersi [prefIggersi], *v.r.* To determine, to propose to oneself; to resolve, to purpose.
prefiguramento, *n.m.* Prefiguring.
prefigurare, *v.t.* To prefigure.
prefisso, *n.m.* (*Gram.*) Prefix.
prefisso, *p.p.a.* Pre-arranged, predetermined; fixed, appointed.
pregare, *v.t.* To pray; to beg to ask, to implore, to entreat; to invite, to request, to beseech. **— Dio,** to pray to God; **sii buono, ti prego,** be good, please; **ti prego di scusarmi,** I beg your pardon; **farsi —,** to need pressing; **— per qualcuno,** to pray for someone; **si accomodi, prego!** do sit down!
pregevole [pregEvole], *a.* Worthy, valuable, precious.
pregevolezza, *n.f.* Worth, value, merit.
preghiera, *n.f.* Prayer; request, entreaty. **Viva —,** earnest request; **libro di preghiere,** prayer-book; **dir le preghiere,** to say one's prayers; **rivolgere una — a,** to make a request to.
pregiabile [pregiAbile], *a.* Worthy, estimable, valued.
pregiare, *v.t.* To appreciate, to value, to prize.
pregiarsi, *v.r.* To have the pleasure to, to beg to, to have the honour to. **Mi pregio annunciarle,** I beg to inform you.
pregiato, *p.p.a.* Appreciated, worthy, esteemed, valued, valuable. (*Comm.*) **Ho ricevuto la sua pregiata lettera,** I have received your esteemed letter; **pregiatissimo signore,** dear sir (*in a letter*).
pregio [prEgio], *n.m.* Worth, value; prize; reputation; appreciation, estimation; excellence. **Tenere in gran —,** to hold in great esteem.
pregiudicare, *v.t.* To prejudice; to jeopardize; to damage, to injure, to harm.
pregiudicarsi, *v.r.* To prejudice one's chance, to harm one's reputation.
pregiudicativo, *a.* Prejudicial, harmful.
pregiudicato, *n.m.* (*Law*) Person who has already been convicted and served a sentence; a ruffian.
pregiudicato, *a.* Suspected, suspect.
pregiudiziale, *n.f.* (*Law*) Prejudgement; point of order; previous question.
pregiudizievole [pregiudiziEvole], *a.* Prejudicial, harmful.
pregiudizievolmente, *adv.* Prejudicially.
pregiudizio [pregiudIzio], *n.m.* Prejudice, bias; detriment, inconvenience, damage. **Portare — a,** to prejudice, to jeopardize; **senza —,** unprejudiced, unbiased; **senza — di,** without prejudice to.
pregnante, *a.* Pregnant (in all senses), significant.
pregnanza, pregnezza, *n.f.* Pregnancy.
pregno, *a.* Full; pregnant, gravid; rich in, teeming with.
prego, *n.m.* (*Lit.*) Prayer, entreaty.
prego! *inter.* Please! Thank you! Excuse me! Not at all! All right!
pregustare, *v.t.* To enjoy beforehand, to foretaste; to anticipate. **— il piacere di,** I anticipate the pleasure of.
pregustazione, *n.f.* Foretaste; anticipation.
preindicato, *a.* Indicated beforehand.
preistoricamente, *adv.* Prehistorically.
preistorico [preistOrico], *a.* Prehistoric.
prelatesco, *a.* Prelatical.

prelatizio [prelatIzio], *a.* Concerning Church dignitaries.
prelato, *n.m.* Prelate, bishop; cardinal.
prelatura, *n.f.* Prelacy.
prelazione, *n.f.* (*Law*) Preference, pre-emption. **Diritto di —,** right of pre-emption.
prelevamento, *n.m.* Withdrawal (of money), drawing out; deduction; order, indent.
prelevare, *v.t.* To take away; to withdraw, to draw out (money), to indent upon.
prelevazione, *n.f.* Withdrawal (from a bank), drawing out; indent.
prelezione, *n.f.* Introductory lecture, opening address (to students).
prelibare, *v.t.* To have a foretaste of, to taste, to sample in advance.
prelibatamente, *adv.* Deliciously.
prelibato, *a.* Excellent, delicious, exquisite.
prelibazione, *n.f.* Foretaste.
preliminare, *n.m.a.* Preliminary. **I preliminari,** the preliminaries.
prelodato, *a.* Already mentioned with praise; aforesaid.
preludere, preludiare [prelUdere], *v.i.* To prelude, to foreshadow.
preludio [prelUdio], *n.m.* Prelude, beginning.
prematuramente, *adv.* Prematurely.
prematuro, *a.* Premature, untimely. **Parto —,** premature birth.
premeditare, *v.t.* To premeditate, to plan.
premeditatamente, *adv.* Deliberately, with premeditation.
premeditato, *a.* Premeditated, intended, intentional; (*Law*) wilful.
premeditazione, *n.f.* Premeditation; malice aforethought.
premente, *a.* Pressing, urgent. **Tromba —, pompa —,** force-pump.
premere [prEmere], *v.t.i.* To press, to compress, to squeeze; to crush, to weigh down; to urge, to be urgent, to pursue; to care, to matter, to concern, to mind. **È un affare che preme,** it is a pressing matter; **mi preme di vederlo,** I am longing to see him; **egli preme su di lui,** he urges him; **Preme** (on a letter), immediate.
premessa, *n.f.* Premise, premiss, antecedent proposition, previous statement.
premesso, *a.* Set before, advanced.
premettere [premEttere], *v.t.* To premise, to lay down (as a fact); to prefix; to state in advance; to give preference to.
premiabile [premiAbile], *a.* Qualified to receive a prize, deserving a prize.
premiando, *n.m.* Prize-winner.
premiare, *v.t.* To reward, to recompense, to award a prize to.
premiato, *n.m.* Prize-winner.
premiatore, premiatrice, *n.m.f.* Prize-giver.
premiazione, *n.f.* Reward, recompense; award; distribution of prizes, prize-giving.
preminente, *a.* Pre-eminent, eminent.
preminenza, *n.f.* Pre-eminence.
premio [prEmio], *n.m.* Prize, recompense, reward; (*Comm.*) premium. **— di assicurazione,** insurance premium; **dare un —,** to award a prize; **prendere il primo —,** to obtain the first prize.
premito [prEmito], *n.m.* (*Med.*) Contraction; straining.
premitura, *n.f.* Pressing, pressure.
premolare, *n.m.* (*Anat.*) Premolar.
premonitorio [premonitOrio], *a.* Premonitory.
premonizione, *n.f.* Premonition, forewarning.
premorienza, *n.f.* (*Law*) Prior death, predecease.
premorire, *v.i.* To die before another, to predecease.
premunire, *v.t.* To secure beforehand, to strengthen beforehand; to warn, to caution.
premunirsi, *v.r.* To provide against; to protect oneself. **— da, contro,** to arm oneself against.
premunizione, *n.f.* Precaution, protection, guarding.
premura, *n.f.* Haste, hurry, urgency; zeal, eagerness, solicitude, earnestness; care, kindness, attention. **Aver —,** to be in a hurry; **circondare di premure,** to overwhelm with kindness; **far —,** to press, to urge; **farsi — di,** to take care of, to hasten to.
premurosamente, *adv.* Eagerly; attentively, thoughtfully; politely.
premuroso, *a.* Eager, earnest; kind, attentive, polite; zealous, obliging.
prence, *n.m.* (*Poet.*) Prince [cp. **principe**].
prendere [prEndere], *v.t.i.* To take, to take up, to take away, to catch, to grasp, to seize, to take hold of; to capture, to apprehend; to get; to exact; to accept; to hit; to attain; to deal with; to observe (times); to turn; to go (right or left); to congeal, to curdle. **— a,** to begin, to start, to set about; **— terra,** to land; **— animo,** to take courage; **— fiato,** to take breath; **— di mira,** to aim at; to stare at; **— moglie,** to marry, to take a wife; **— fuoco,** to catch fire; **prendete a destra,** turn to the right; **— un raffreddore,** to catch a cold; **— la fuga,** to take to flight; **— a nolo,** to hire; **— parte a,** to take part in; **— il treno,** to catch the train; **prenderla male,** to take it amiss; **— cibo,** to take food; **— in giro,** to make fun of; (*Aviat.*) **— quota,** to gain height; **— posizione,** to take up a position; **prese a volergli bene,** she began to love him; **— commiato,** to take leave, to say good-bye; **— il coraggio a due mani,** to take one's courage in both hands; **vuol — un caffè con noi ?** will you have a cup of coffee with us ? **ho preso dei libri alla biblioteca,** I borrowed some books from the library.
prendersi [prEndersi], *v.r.* To catch; to lay hold of; to become entangled; to congeal. **— tanti fastidi,** to take too much trouble; **mi prendo la libertà di,** I take the liberty of; **— a schiaffi,** to come to blows; **prendersela,** to take it ill, to worry about; **prendersela comoda,** to take things easy.
prendibile [prendIbile], *a.* Seizable.
prendimento, *n.m.* Taking, seizing.
prendisole, *n.m.* Sun-suit.
prenditore, prenditrice, *n.m.f.* Receiver; payee; acceptor of a bill.
prenditoria, *n.f.* (*colloq.*) Lottery office.
prenome, *n.m.* Christian name.
prenominato, *n.m.a.* Above-mentioned (person), aforesaid.
prenotare, *v.t.* To book (seats, etc.), to engage.
prenotarsi, *v.r.* To book for oneself.
prenotazione, *n.f.* Booking.

prenozione, *n.f.* Foreknowledge.
prensile [prEnsile], *a.* Prehensile.
prenunziare, *v.t.* To announce in advance [cp. **preannunziare**].
prenunzio [prenUnzio], *n.m.* Advance notice.
preoccupare, *v.t.* To preoccupy; to worry; to trouble, to bother, to make anxious. **non si preoccupi,** don't worry.
preoccuparsi, *v.r.* To be preoccupied, to get worried; to take trouble.
preoccupazione, *n.f.* Preoccupation; anxiety, concern, worry, care.
preopinante, *n.m.* Previous speaker.
preordinare, *v.t.* To prearrange, to predispose.
preordinazione, *n.f.* Prearrangement.
preparante, *a.* Preparatory.
preparare, *v.t.* To prepare, to dispose, to make ready, to provide; to lay (a fire); to read for (an exam). **— la tavola,** to lay the table. **— il pranzo,** to prepare lunch, to get lunch ready.
prepararsi, *v.r.* To prepare oneself. **— agli esami,** to prepare for the exams.
preparativo, *n.m.a.* Preparation; preparatory.
preparato, *n.m.* (*Med.*) Preparation.
preparatore, *n.m.* Teacher, coach, tutor.
preparatorio [preparatOrio], *a.* Preparatory, preparative.
preparazione, *n.f.* Preparation.
preponderante, *a.* Preponderant, predominant, prevailing.
preponderanza, *n.f.* Preponderance.
preponderare, *v.t.* To outweigh, to preponderate, to prevail over.
preporre, *v.t.* To place before, to put first, to prefer; to place at the head. **Vedersi — un altro,** to see oneself superseded by another.
prepositivo, *a.* (*Gram.*) Prepositive.
prepositura, *n.f.* Office, or residence, of a provost.
preposizione, *n.f.* (*Gram.*) Preposition.
preposto, *n.m.* Provost; rector.
prepotente, *n.m.a.* Overbearing (fellow), insolent, oppressive, arrogant.
prepotenza, *n.f.* Arrogance, bullying; insolence; injustice.
prepuzio [prepUzio], *n.m.* (*Anat.*) Prepuce, foreskin.
preraffaellita, *n.m.a.* (*Art*) Pre-Raphaelite.
prerogativa, *n.f.* Prerogative, privilege, faculty.
presa, *n.f.* Seizure, taking, capture, conquest; catch, grasp, grip; influence, hold; handle, holder; pinch (of snuff); intake; joint; (*Elect.*) terminal. **— di corrente,** main switch; **— d'acqua,** spout, hydrant; **— d'una città,** capture of a city; **alle prese,** at grips; **far —,** to coagulate, to set; **cane da —,** setter; **— in giro,** hoax; persiflage; **essere alle prese,** to quarrel, to come to blows; **pigliare una — di tabacco,** to take a pinch of snuff; **— di contatto,** coming in touch; **dar —,** to give occasion; **— di possesso,** taking possession of; **egli non ha — su di lui,** he has no influence over him.
presagio [presAgio], *n.m.* Omen, presage; prognostic; foreboding; forecast.
presagire, *v.t.i.* To presage, to portend, to foresee, to predict.
presago, *a.* Foreseeing, foretelling; foreknowing; prescient.
presbite [prEsbite], *n.m.a.* Long-sighted (person), long-sighted.
presbiterato, *n.m.* (*Eccles.*) Presbyterate, priesthood.
presbiteriano, *n.m.a.* Presbyterian.
presbiterianismo, *n.m.* Presbyterianism.
presbiterio [presbitErio], *n.m.* Presbytery.
prescegliere [prescEgliere], *v.t.* To choose, to single out, to select.
presciente, *a.* Prescient, foreknowing.
prescienza, *n.f.* Prescience, foreknowledge.
prescindere [prescIndere], *v.i.* To leave out of consideration, to abstract from. **Prescindendo da, a — da,** leaving on one side, quite apart from.
presciutto [cp. **prosciutto**].
prescrittibile [prescrittIbile], *a.* Subject to prescription.
prescrittivo, *a.* Prescriptive.
prescritto, *p.p.a.* Prescribed, laid down, directed, ordered.
prescrivere [prescrIvere], *v.t.* To prescribe, to lay down, to order, to direct. **— una medicina,** to prescribe a medicine.
prescrizione, *n.f.* Prescription (in all senses).
presella, *n.f.* Carpenter's punch; piece of reclaimed land.
presentabile [presentAbile], *a.* Presentable.
presentabilità [-à], *n.f.* Presentability.
presentaneo [presentAneo], *a.* (*obs.*) Instant.
presentare, *v.t.* To present, to offer, to tender; to give; to introduce; to exhibit; to propose, to send in. **— un amico,** to introduce a friend; **— un progetto di legge,** to introduce a (parliamentary) bill; **Le presento i saluti di mio fratello,** my brother sends his regards; **— le proprie dimissioni,** to resign.
presentarsi, *v.r.* To present oneself, to appear, to come forth; to introduce oneself; to visit. **Quando si presenterà l'occasione,** when the opportunity offers; **— a qualcuno,** to introduce oneself to a person; **— bene,** to have a good appearance.
presentazione, *n.f.* Presentation; introduction. **Lettera di —,** letter of introduction.
presente (1), *n.m.a.* Present (in all senses), present time, present tense; gift. **Al —,** for the time being, for the present; **un bel —,** a fine gift; **tener —,** to keep in mind.
presente (2), *n.f.* (*Comm.*) Present letter.
presentemente, *adv.* At present, now.
presenti, *n.m.pl.* Those present; onlookers.
presentimento, *n.m.* Foreboding, presentiment, presage.
presentire, *v.t.* To forebode, to portend, to foreshadow; to anticipate.
presenza, *n.f.* Presence, aspect, look, mien, deportment; appearance, attendance. **— di spirito,** presence of mind; **avere una bella —,** to be good-looking; **di —,** personally; **in — di,** in the presence of; **fare atto di —,** to put in an appearance.
presenziale, *a.* Present, in person.
presenzialmente, *adv.* Personally.
presenziare, *v.t.i.* To be present, to attend, to take part.
presepio, presepe [presEpio], *n.m.* (*Eccles.*) Manger (of Christ), crib.
preservamento, *n.m.* Preserving, preservation.
preservante, *n.m.* (Food) preservative.

preservare, *v.t.* To preserve, to keep; to protect, to defend, to guard; to save.
preservarsi, *v.r.* To save oneself; to keep, to be preserved.
preservativo, *n.m.a.* Preservative.
preservatore, preservatrice, *n.m.f.* Preserver.
preservazione, *n.f.* Preservation.
preside [prEside], *n.m.* Headmaster (of a school); dean (of a faculty); principal; president.
presidente, *n.m.* President; chairman.
presidentessa, *n.f.* Lady president; president's wife.
presidenza, *n.f.* Presidency, chairmanship.
presidenziale, *a.* Presidential.
presidiare, *v.t.* (*Mil.*) To garrison; to guard, to protect.
presidiario [presidiArio], *a.* Of a garrison.
presidio [presIdio], *n.m.* Garrison; guard, defence.
presiedere, *v.i.* To preside, to take the chair; to act as chairman; to sway, to influence.
preso, *p.p.a.* Taken, seized, caught [cp. **prendere**].
pressa, *n.f.* Press (in all senses); crowd, throng; haste; pressure.
pressacarte, *n.m.* Paperweight.
pressante, *a.* Urgent, pressing.
pressantemente, *adv.* Urgently.
pressappoco, press'a poco, *adv.* Approximately, nearly, thereabout.
pressare, *v.t.* To press (in all senses).
pressatoio [pressatOio], *n.m.* (*Mech.*) Press.
pressatura, *n.f.* Pressing.
pressi, *n.m.pl.* Neighbourhood, environs. **Nei — di,** in the neighbourhood of.
pressione, *n.f.* Pressure (in all senses). **Far pressioni su uno,** to put pressure upon someone; **ad alta, bassa —,** at high, low pressure.
presso, *prep.adv.* Near, close to, by; at about; on the point of; in comparison with. **Qui —,** near here, close by; **— al mare,** near the sea; **a un di —,** very nearly, about; **ambasciatore — la corte di,** ambassador at the court of; **egli è — a morire,** he's on the point of death; **— di me,** at my house; near me.
pressochè, *adv.* Almost, nearly.
pressoio [pressOio], *n.m.* (*Mech.*) Press.
pressorizzato, *a.* Pressurized.
pressura, *n.f.* Pressure, oppression.
prestabilire, *v.t.* To pre-arrange, to fix beforehand.
prestamente, *adv.* Quickly, soon, readily.
prestamento, *n.m.* Loan, lending.
prestanome, *n.m.* (*colloq.*) Figurehead, man of straw, dummy.
prestante, *a.* Vigorous, strong, sturdy, well-built, well-formed; excellent.
prestantemente, *adv.* Vigorously; excellently.
prestanza, *n.f.* Excellence, handsomeness; fine presence, dignified bearing.
prestare, *v.t.* To lend; to give, to render, to ascribe, to attribute; to take (an oath). **— aiuto,** to help, to give assistance; **— attenzione,** to pay attention; **— giuramento,** to swear; **— fede,** to believe; **— orecchio,** to listen; **— un libro,** to lend a book; **— il fianco alla critica,** to expose oneself to criticism; **— danaro a,** to lend money to.
prestarsi, *v.r.* To lend oneself, to give a helping hand; to adapt oneself; to favour, to countenance; to give way to.
prestatore, prestatrice, *n.m.f.* Lender.
prestazione, *n.f.* Lending, loan; tax, impost. **Prestazioni,** services (rendered).
prestezza, *n.f.* Quickness, speed, rapidity, swiftness; alertness.
prestidigitazione, *n.f.* Conjuring, sleight of hand.
prestigiatore, prestidigitatore, *n.m.* Conjurer, juggler.
prestigio [prestIgio] (1), *n.m.* Prestige, influence; weight (of authority).
prestigio [prestIgio] (2), *n.m.* Trick, sleight of hand, conjuring. **Giuochi di —,** conjuring tricks.
prestigioso, *a.* (*Lit.*) Brilliant, magic (of style).
prestinaio [prestinAio], *n.m.* (Lombard) Baker.
prestino, *n.m.* (Lombard) Baker's shop; oven.
prestino, *adv.* Rather early, earlyish, fairly quickly.
prestissimo [prestIssimo], *adv.* Very quickly; very early.
prestito [prEstito], *n.m.* Loan; lending, borrowing. **Prendere in —,** to borrow; **dare in —,** to lend; **— pubblico,** public loan; **emettere un —,** to issue a loan; **contrarre un —,** to borrow money.
presto, *a.* Quick, swift, nimble; prompt.
presto, *adv.* Quickly; soon, early; immediately, at once. **Fa —!** Make haste! Hurry up! **alzarsi —,** to get up early; **tornerò —,** I shan't be long; I'll be back soon; **al più — possibile,** as soon as possible; **si fa — a dire,** it is easy to say.
presule [prEsule], *n.m.* (*Eccles.*) Prelate.
presumere [presUmere], *v.i.* To presume, to suppose, to conjecture; to be over-confident, to boast; to take for granted. **Presume troppo di sè,** he thinks too much of himself; **— di,** to rely on.
presumibile [presumIbile], *a.* Presumable.
presumibilità [-à], *n.f.* Presumability.
presumibilmente, *adv.* Presumably.
presuntivamente, *adv.* Presumptively.
presuntivo, *a.* Presumptive, apparent.
presunto, *p.p.a.* Presumed, supposed, likely; apparent.
presuntuosaggine [presuntuosAggine], *n.f.* Presumption; arrogance.
presuntuosamente, *adv.* Presumptuously.
presuntuosità [-à], *n.f.* Presumptuousness.
presuntuoso, *a.* Over-confident; presumptuous; arrogant, conceited; rash, forward.
presunzione, *n.f.* Presumption; conjecture; arrogance; assurance, over-confidence.
presupporre, *v.t.* To presuppose, to assume; to imply.
presuppositivo, *a.* Presupposing.
presupposizione, *n.f.* Presupposition, assumption, implication.
presupposto, *n.m.* Conjecture, presupposition, premise.
prete, *n.m.* Priest; clergyman, minister.
pretendente, *n.m.* Pretender (to the throne); aspirer; claimant; lover, wooer.
pretendere [pretEndere], *v.t.i.* To claim, to lay claim to, to aspire to, to pretend to; to affirm, to assert, to demand; to contend; to

ask for (in price). **Quanto pretendete di quest'oggetto?** How much are you asking for this?
pretensione, *n.f.* Claim; pretension; affectation.
pretenzioso, *a.* Pretentious, ostentatious; mannered, affected.
preterintenzionale, *a.* (*Law*) Unintentional (of a crime).
preterire, *v.t.i.* To omit, to neglect; to disobey (instructions); to break off (an engagement).
preterito [pretErito], *n.m.* (*Gram.*) Preterite, past tense; (*colloq.*) buttocks.
preterizione, *n.f.* Omission.
pretermettere [pretermEttere], *v.t.* To pretermit, to omit, to pass over.
preternaturale, *a.* Preternatural.
preternaturalmente, *adv.* Preternaturally.
pretesa, *n.f.* Pretence, pretension, claim, demand. **Persona senza pretese,** unaffected person; **avere delle pretese,** to be very exacting; to demand too much; (*colloq.*) **Belle pretese!** You expect too much!
pretesco, *a.* (*contempt.*) Priestly.
pretesto, *n.m.* Pretext, excuse; plea. **Col — di,** under the pretext of; **servir di —,** to be a pretext for; **allegare un —,** to make an excuse.
pretino, *n.m.a.* Young priest; priest-like.
pretore, *n.m.* Police magistrate, stipendiary; judge.
pretoriano, *n.m.a.* (*Hist.*) Pretorian.
prettamente, *adv.* Clearly, simply, frankly, openly; merely.
pretto, *a.* Clear; frank; good, pure, real; plain, mere. **Un — ignorante,** an ignoramus; **egli parla in — toscano,** he speaks pure Tuscan.
pretura, *n.f.* Police-court; district-court; court of first instance.
prevalente, *a.* Prevailing, prevalent, predominant, preponderant.
prevalentemente, *adv.* Prevalently.
prevalenza, *n.f.* Prevalence, preponderance; superiority.
prevalere, *v.i.* To prevail, to predominate, to be superior, to be predominant. **— su,** to prevail over.
prevalersi, *v.r.* To avail oneself; to take advantage of. **— d'una cosa,** to avail oneself of something.
prevaricamento, *n.m.* Prevarication.
prevaricare, *v.i.* To prevaricate; to act dishonourably, to betray a trust.
prevaricatore, prevaricatrice, *n.m.f.* Embezzler, defaulter; prevaricator.
prevaricazione, *n.f.* Breach of trust, embezzlement; default.
prevedere, *v.t.* To foresee; to expect, to anticipate; to foreknow, to foreshadow, to forecast. **Era da —,** it was to be expected; **— il rialzo dei prezzi,** to foresee a rise in prices.
prevedibile [prevedIbile], *a.* Foreseeable.
preveggente, *a.* Foreseeing, far-sighted; prescient.
preveggenza, *n.f.* Foresight, forethought.
preveniente, *a.* Anticipating.
prevenire, *v.t.* To anticipate, to forestall; to precede, to get the start of; to hinder, to prevent; to ward off; to warn, to forewarn. **— una malattia,** to ward off an illness; **— dell' arrivo,** to give advance notice of one's arrival.
preventivamente, *adv.* In anticipation, in advance.
preventivare, *v.t.* To estimate; to allocate (costs, etc.).
preventivo, *n.m.* Estimate. **Fare un —,** to make an estimate.
preventivo, *a.* Preventive; warding off; estimated, anticipated. (*Law*) **Carcere —,** prison while awaiting trial; (*Comm.*) **bilancio —,** estimated budget; (*Med.*) **cura preventiva,** preventive treatment.
prevenuto, *n.m.* (*Law*) Suspect, accused; defendant.
prevenuto, *a.* Warned; prejudiced, biased.
prevenzione, *n.f.* Anticipation; prepossession; prevention; prejudice, bias; (*Law*) charge; precautionary measures. **Avere delle prevenzioni contro qualcuno,** to be biased (or prejudiced) against someone.
previamente, *adv.* Previously.
previdente, *a.* Foreseeing, provident, far-sighted.
previdentemente, *adv.* With foresight.
previdenza, *n.f.* Foresight; prudence. **— sociale,** State insurance.
previo [prEvio], *a.* (*Law*) Prior, previous. **— avviso,** upon notice.
previsibile [previsIbile], *a.* Foreseeable.
previsione, *n.f.* Prevision, foresight; anticipation, forecast. **In — di,** in anticipation of; **previsioni meteorologiche,** weather forecast.
prevosto, *n.m.* (*Eccles.*) Rector [cp. **preposto**].
preziosamente, *adv.* Preciously.
preziosità [-à], *n.f.* Preciousness, preciosity, affectation.
prezioso, *n.m.* Precious object, jewel.
prezioso, *a.* Precious; valuable, costly, dear; excellent; affected, precious. **Pietra preziosa,** precious stone; **fare il —,** to be affected (in manners, etc.).
prezzemolo [prezzEmolo], *n.m.* (*Bot.*) Parsley.
prezzo, *n.m.* Price; value; reward, cost; terms; fare; rate. **— fisso,** fixed price; **— corrente,** market price; **a buon —,** cheap, cheaply; **vendere sotto —,** to under-sell, to sell below value; **listino dei prezzi,** price-list; **— di costo,** cost-price; **a qualunque —,** at any price; **a — della vita,** at the cost of one's life; **— esagerato,** fancy price; **— all'ingrosso,** wholesale price; **il — è aumentato, diminuito,** the price has gone up, come down.
prezzolare, *v.t.* To hire; to bribe.
prezzolato, *p.p.a.* Hired (to do something wrong), bribed.
pria, *adv.* (*Poet.*) Before.
priapismo, *n.m.* Priapism.
priapo [prIapo], *n.m.* Priapus.
prigione, *n.f.* Prison, gaol. **Mettere in —,** to send to gaol.
prigionia [prigionIa], *n.f.* Imprisonment; captivity.
prigioniero, *n.m* Prisoner. **Furono tutti fatti prigionieri,** they were all taken prisoners.
prillare, *v.t.* To whirl.
prillo, *n.m.* Whirl.
prima, *n.f.* First; (*Rail.*) first class; (*Theat.*) first performance, première; (*Comm.*) **— di cambio,** first of exchange.
prima, *adv.* Before, formerly, earlier, sooner; first, at first, firstly. **— di tutto,** first of all;

sulle prime, a tutta —, at first; **quanto — verrai, meglio sara,** the sooner you come the better; **ti prego di venire quanto —**, please come as soon as possible; **come —**, as before; **poco —**, not long before; **— o poi**, sooner or later; **vieni —**, come earlier; **— di pranzo,** before dinner.
primamente, *adv.* Firstly, in the first place.
primariamente, *adv.* Principally, primarily.
primario [primArio], *n.m.* (*Med.*) Head physician or surgeon in a hospital.
primario [primArio], *a.* Primary, first, original, primitive; principal, main.
primate, *n.m.* (*Eccles.*) Primate.
primaticcio [primatIccio], *a.* Early, new (of fruit, vegetables, etc.).
primatista (*pl.* **primatisti**), *n.m.f.* (*Sport*) Record-holder.
primato, *n.m.* Primacy, supremacy; pre-eminence, excellence, superiority; (*Sport*) record.
primavera, *n.f.* Spring, springtime; (*fig.*) prime.
primaverile, *a.* Spring, of spring, vernal.
primazia [primazIa], *n.f.* Primacy.
primeggiare, *v.i.* To excel, to be pre-eminent, to take the lead; to stand first.
primevo, *a.* Primeval.
primiera, *n.f.* (*Cards*) Primero.
primieramente, *adv.* Firstly, in the first place.
primiero, *a.* First, principal.
primigenio [primigEnio], *a.* Original, from the first.
primitivamente, *adv.* Primitively.
primitivo, *n.m.a.* Primitive; primal, early, original.
primizia [primIzia], *n.f.* Early fruit, etc.; fresh news, latest novelty. **Le primizie,** the first-fruits.
primo, *n.m.* First; first person; leader, chief; first day; principal (in duel).
primo, *a.* First, chief, foremost; principal; leading, opening; old, ancient; primitive, primary; (*Math.*) prime; (*Comm.*) raw. **— nato,** first-born; **dal — momento,** from the very first; **materie prime,** raw materials; **di prima mano,** first-hand; **in — luogo,** first of all, in the first instance; **di — pelo,** very young, inexperienced; **di — ordine,** first rate, first class; **numero —**, prime number; **essere il —**, to be the first; **— —**, the very first.
primogenitore, primogenitrice, *n.m.f.* Progenitor.
primogenito [primogEnito], *n.m.* First-born, eldest son.
primogenitura, *n.f.* Primogeniture.
primordiale, *a.* Primordial, primeval; primitive.
primordio [primOrdio], *n.m.* Beginning, origin, outset. **Nei primordi,** in the beginning, at the outset.
primula [prImula], *n.f.* (*Bot.*) Primrose.
principale, *n.m.a.* Principal, master, boss, employer, proprietor; principal, main, chief; essential, fundamental. **La questione —**, the main question.
principalmente, *adv.* Principally, essentially.
principato, *n.m.* Principality.
principe [prIncipe], *n.m.* Prince. **— ereditario,** crown prince; **vivere da —**, to live like a prince; **— consorte,** prince consort.
principescamente, *adv.* In a princely style.
principesco, *a.* Princely, prince-like.
principessa, *n.f.* Princess.
principiante, *n.m.f.* Beginner, novice, apprentice.
principiare, *v.t.i.* To begin, to commence, to start, to initiate.
principino, *n.m.* Young prince.
principio [princIpio], *n.m.* Beginning, commencement, start; principle, precept, maxim, rule. **Da —**, in the beginning, at first; anew; **uomo senza principii,** unprincipled man; **dal — alla fine,** from beginning to end.
princisbecco, *n.m.* Pinchbeck.
priora, *n.f.* (*Eccles.*) Prioress.
priorato, *n.m.* (*Eccles.*) Priory, office of prior.
priore, *n.m.* Prior.
prioria [priorIa], *n.f.* Priory.
priorità [-à], *n.f.* Priority.
prisco, *a.* (*Poet.*) Ancient, early.
prisma (*pl.* **prismi**), *n.m.* Prism.
prismatico [prismAtico], *a.* Prismatic.
pristinamente, *adv.* Formerly, in primitive times.
pristino, *a.* Pristine, primitive, primal, ancient, former.
privamento, *n.m.* Deprivation, privation.
privare, *v.t.* To deprive, to take away from, to strip; to bereave.
privarsi, *v.r.* To deprive oneself, to give up, to deny oneself, to renounce; to abstain from.
privatamente, *adv.* In private, privately.
privativa, *n.f.* Patent right, monopoly. **— dei tabacchi,** tobacco monopoly.
privativamente, *adv.* Exclusively.
privativo, *a.* Exclusive; privative.
privato, *n.m.* Private person, citizen.
privato, *a.* Private; particular, personal; deprived, bereft, stripped. **In —**, in private, privately; **carrozza privata,** private carriage; **lettera privata,** confidential letter.
privazione, *n.f.* Privation, need, want; deprivation.
privilegiare, *v.t.* To privilege, to grant a privilege to, to benefit.
privilegiato, *a.* Privileged; (*Comm.*) preferential.
privilegio [privilEgio], *n.m.* Privilege; benefit, advantage, right, immunity, favour. **Godere di un —**, to enjoy a privilege.
privo, *a.* Devoid, lacking, wanting; deprived, destitute. **— di amici,** friendless; **— di notizie,** without news; **— di tutto,** utterly destitute; **— di buon senso,** lacking in common sense.
pro, *n.m.* Advantage, utility, good, profit. **A che — ?** To what purpose? What for? **parlare a — di,** to speak in favour of; (*colloq.*) **buon — ti faccia,** much good may it do you.
proavo, proava, *n.m.f.* Great-grandfather, great-grandmother.
probabile [probAbile], *a.* Probable, likely; credible.
probabilità [-à], *n.f.* Probability.
probabilmente, *adv.* Probably.
probamente, *adv.* Uprightly.
probativo, probatorio [probatOrio], *a.* Probationary, probative.
probità [-à], *n.f.* Probity, uprightness, honesty, integrity.

probiviri, *n.m.pl.* (*Law*) Umpires, scrutineers, arbiters.
problema (*pl.* **problemi**), *n.m.* Problem; question; puzzle, riddle, enigma.
problematicamente, *adv.* Problematically.
problematicità [-à], *n.f.* Questionability.
problematico [problemAtico], *a.* Problematic, doubtful, questionable, equivocal.
probo, *a.* Upright, just, honest, straight.
proboscide [probOscide], *n.f.* Trunk (of elephants, etc.); proboscis (of insects).
procaccevole [procaccEvole], *a.* Industrious, hard-working.
procaccia [procAccia], *n.m.* Postman, odd-job man; messenger.
procacciante, *n.m.a.* Meddlesome person, go-ahead fellow; meddlesome; industrious.
procacciare, *v.t.* To get, to obtain, to procure; to earn; to acquire; to gain, to provide.
procacciarsi, *v.r.* To attain by one's own endeavours; to earn one's living.
procacciatore, procacciatrice, *n.m.f.* Profiteer, jobber.
procace, *a.* Pert, saucy, cheeky, forward; provoking.
procacemente, *adv.* Pertly, cheekily.
procacità [-à], *n.f.* Coquetry, cheekiness, impertinence.
procedente, *a.* Proceeding.
procedere [procEdere], *v.i.* To proceed, to advance; to continue, to act, to behave; to derive, to originate; (*Law*) to prosecute, to proceed against. **Il suo modo di — non mi piace,** I don't like the way he behaves.
procedere [procEdere], *n.m.* Conduct, behaviour.
procedimento, *n.m.* Proceeding, advancement, progress; procedure, course, method.
procedura, *n.f.* Procedure.
procedurale, *a.* Pertaining to procedure.
procella, *n.f.* Storm (at sea), tempest, hurricane, gale.
procellaria [procellAria], *n.f.* (*Zool.*) Stormy petrel.
procellosamente, *adv.* Stormily.
procelloso, *a.* Stormy, tempestuous.
proceri [prOceri], *n.m.pl.* Grandees, magnates.
processabile [processAbile], *a.* Indictable, liable to prosecution.
processare, *v.t.* To prosecute, to try.
processionale, *n.m.a.* Processional.
processionalmente, *adv.* In procession.
processionare, *v.i.* To go in procession.
processione, *n.f.* Procession.
processo, *n.m.* Process, course, development, progress; method, process; (*Law*) trial. **Sotto —**, under trial; **— verbale,** official record; **in — di tempo,** in process of time.
processuale, *a.* (*Law*) Concerned with a trial.
procidenza, *n.f.* (*Med.*) Prolapse.
procinto, *n.m.* **Essere in —**, to be on the point of, to be about to.
proclama, *n.m.* Proclamation, declaration, announcement.
proclamare, *v.t.* To proclaim, to announce, to declare; to promulgate, to issue.
proclamatore, proclamatrice, *n.m.f.* Proclaimer.
proclamazione, *n.f.* Proclamation.
proclive, *a.* Inclined, disposed, prone to.
proclività [-à], *n.f.* Proclivity, bent, inclination, propensity.
procombere [procOmbere], *v.i.* To fall forward dead; to fall forward.
proconsolare, *a.* Proconsular.
proconsolato, *n.m.* Proconsulate.
proconsole [procOnsole], *n.m.* Proconsul.
procrastinamento, *n.m.* Procrastination.
procrastinare, *v.i.* To procrastinate, to defer, to put off, to postpone.
procrastinatore, procrastinatrice, *n.m.f.* Procrastinator.
procrastinazione, *n.f.* Procrastination.
procreamento, *n.m.* Procreation, begetting.
procreare, *v.t.* To beget, to procreate, to generate.
procreatore, *n.m.* Procreator.
procreazione, *n.f.* Procreation.
procura, *n.f.* (*Law*) Proxy, procuration; power of attorney. **Sposarsi per —**, to marry by proxy.
procurare, *v.t.* To procure, to obtain, to acquire, to provide; to cause; to attempt, to endeavour.
procurarsi, *v.r.* To provide for oneself, to procure for oneself. **— un impiego,** to find employment, to get a job.
procuratore, *n.m.* (*Law*) Procurator, attorney. **— della Repubblica,** public prosecutor; **— fiscale,** procurator fiscal.
proda, *n.f.* Bank, shore, border, side; (*obs.*) prow (of ship).
prode, *n.m.* Hero, valiant man, brave man.
prode, *a.* Brave, gallant, courageous, valiant, bold.
prodeggiare, *v.i.* (*Naut.*) To hug the shore.
prodemente, *adv.* Bravely, gallantly, heroically.
prodezza, *n.f.* Bravery, prowess, valour, gallantry; gallant action; bravado.
prodiere, prodiero, *n.m.* (*Naut.*) Sailor in the bow; leading vessel of a squadron.
prodigalità [-à], *n.f.* Prodigality, lavishness.
prodigalmente, *adv.* Prodigally.
prodigalizzare, *v.t.* To spend prodigally, to lavish.
prodigamente, *adv.* Lavishly, prodigally.
prodigare, *v.t.* To lavish, to give liberally, to give away, to pour out (money, etc.).
prodigarsi, *v.r.* To devote oneself; to expose oneself.
prodigio [prodIgio], *n.m.* Prodigy, wonder, miracle, marvel. **Far prodigi,** to perform wonders.
prodigiosamente, *adv.* Prodigiously.
prodigiosità [-à], *n.f.* Prodigiousness.
prodigioso, *a.* Prodigious, wonderful, marvellous.
prodigo [prOdigo], *n.m.a.* Prodigal; lavish. **Il figliuol —,** the Prodigal Son.
proditoriamente, *adv.* Treacherously.
proditorio [proditOrio], *a.* Treacherous.
prodotto, *n.m.* Product, production, produce; output, result. **Prodotti del suolo,** products of the soil; **prodotti chimici,** chemical products.
prodotto, *p.p.a.* Produced; caused [cp. **produrre**].
prodromo [prOdromo], *n.m.* Symptom, premonitory indication, commencement.
producibile [producIbile], *a.* Producible.

produrre, *v.t.* To produce; to yield, to bear; to cause, to bring about; to give rise to; to manufacture. **— dei testimoni,** to bring forward witnesses; **— dei danni,** to cause damage; **incidenti che possono — la morte,** accidents that may cause death; **— sulla scena,** to produce on the stage.
prodursi, *v.r.* To occur, to happen; to put oneself forward; to show one's abilities. **— una ferita,** to injure oneself.
produttivita [-à], *n.f.* Productivity, productiveness.
produttivo, *a.* Productive, fruitful.
produttore, produttrice, *n.m.f.a.* Producer, manufacturer; manufacturing.
produzione, *n.f.* Production, output; (*Theat.*) play.
proemiale, *a.* Prefatory, introductory, proemial.
proemiare, *v.t.* (*Lit.*) To preface.
proemio [proEmio], *n.m.* Preface, foreword, introduction.
profanamente, *adv.* Profanely.
profanamento, *n.m.* Profaning, profanation.
profanare, *v.t.* To profane, to violate, to desecrate, to debase, to degrade, to pollute.
profanatore, profanatrice, *n.m.f.* Desecrator, violator.
profanazione, *n.f.* Profanation, desecration, defilement.
profano, *n.m.* Layman, unskilled person. **— dell'arte,** inexpert.
profano, *a.* Profane, unholy; irreverent, impious; ignorant, unskilled.
profenda, *n.f.* Provender, fodder; food.
proferibile [proferIbile], *a.* Utterable, expressible, pronounceable.
proferimento, *n.m.* Pronunciation, uttering, utterance.
proferire, *v.t.* To utter, to express, to pronounce (judgement, opinion, etc.). **— minacce,** to utter threats; **non — sillaba,** not to utter a word.
proferirsi, *v.r.* To offer one's services, to proffer oneself.
professare, *v.t.i.* To profess, to exercise, to practise; to declare; to acknowledge.
professarsi, *v.r.* To make a profession, to profess oneself.
professatamente, *adv* Professedly.
professionale, *a.* Professional. **Scuola —,** vocational school; **malattia —,** occupational disease.
professione, *n.f.* Profession (in all senses).
professionista (*pl.* **professionisti**), *n.m.* Professional man; (*Sport*) professional.
professo, *n.m.a.* (*Eccles.*) Professed (monk).
professorale, *a.* Professorial.
professorato, *n.m.* Professorship.
professore, *n.m.* Professor; teacher, lecturer; instructor.
professoressa, *n.f.* Woman professor, teacher.
profeta (pl. **profeti**), *n.m.* Prophet.
profetare, *v.t.i.* To prophesy, to predict, to foretell.
profetessa, *n.f.* Prophetess.
profeticamente, *adv.* Prophetically.
profetico [profEtico], *a.* Prophetic.
profetizzare, *v.t.* To predict, to prophesy, to foretell.
profezia [profezIa], *n.f.* Prophecy, prediction.
profferimento, *n.m.* Offer, proffer.
profferire, profferirsi, *v.t.r.* To proffer, to offer; to utter.
profferta, *n.f.* Offering, offer, tender.
proficiente, *n.m.a.* Proficient.
proficuamente, *adv.* Profitably.
proficuo [profIcuo], *a.* Profitable, advantageous, useful.
profilamento, *n.m.* Profile.
profilare, *v.t.* To outline, to represent in profile.
profilarsi, *v.r.* To show clearly; to hint at.
profilassi, *n.f.* (*Med.*) Prophylaxis; prevention.
profilato, *p.p.a.* Outlined, in profile. **Viso —,** sharply-cut features.
profilatticamente, *adv.* Prophylactically.
profilattico [profilAttico], *a.* (*Med.*) Prophylactic, preventive.
profilo, *n.m.* Profile, outline, contour; side-face, side-view, section. **Di —,** sideways, in profile.
profittare, *v.i.* To profit, to benefit, to gain, to take advantage.
profittevole [profittEvole], *a.* Profitable, advantageous, paying.
profittevolmente, *adv.* Profitably.
profitto, *n.m.* Profit, gain, advantage, benefit. **Trarre — da,** to take advantage of, to benefit from; **a — di,** for the benefit of, in aid of; (*Comm.*) **partecipazione ai profitti,** profit-sharing.
profluvio [proflUvio], *n.m.* Overflowing, flow, flood, super-abundance; (*Med.*) discharge.
profondamente, *adv.* Profoundly, deeply.
profondamento, *n.m.* Sinking, sounding.
profondare, *v.t.i.* To sink; to become deeper.
profondarsi, *v.r.* To sink; to become immersed.
profondere [profOndere], *v.t.* To lavish, to squander.
profondersi [profOndersi], *v.r.* To overwhelm (with kindness, etc.); to be lavish.
profondezza, *n.f.* Profundity, depth.
profondità [-à], *n.f.* Profundity, depth, penetration.
profondo, *n.m.* Depth, bottom, profundity.
profondo, *a.* Deep, profound; penetrating; abstruse, obscure; complete, intense; extreme. **Un — sospiro,** a deep sigh; **— silenzio,** profound silence; **sonno —,** deep sleep.
profugo [prOfugo], *n.m.a.* Refugee, fugitive.
profumamento, *n.m.* Perfuming.
profumare, *v.t.* To perfume, to scent.
profumarsi, *v.r.* To scent oneself, to put on scent.
profumatamente, *adv.* Very generously, handsomely; dearly. **Pagare —,** to pay a high price; **ricompensare —,** to reward generously.
profumato, *a.* Perfumed, scented, fragrant; dear, expensive.
profumeria [profumerIa], *n.f.* Perfumery; perfumery-shop.
profumiere, *n.m.* Perfumer.
profumo, *n.m.* Perfume, scent, sweet smell, fragrance. **Mandar —,** to smell sweet.
profusamente, *adv.* Profusely.
profusione, *n.f.* Profusion, lavishness, super-abundance, copiousness. **A —,** in plenty, profusely.

profuso, *a.* Profuse, lavish.
progenie [progEnie], *n.f.* Progeny, offspring, issue.
progenitore, progenitrice, *n.m.f.* Progenitor, ancestor, ancestress.
progettare, *v.t.* To scheme, to project, to plan; to devise.
progettista (*pl.* **progettisti**), *n.m.* Planner, designer, schemer.
progetto, *n.m.* Project, scheme, plan, design; intention. **— di massima,** outline plan; **— di legge,** (parliamentary) bill.
prognosi [prOgnosi], *n.f.* (*Med.*) Prognosis, forecast.
programma (*pl.* **programmi**), *n.m.* Programme; prospectus; line of action; (*Pol.*) platform. **Secondo il —,** according to programme; (*Sport*) **— delle corse,** race-card; **svolgere il —,** to carry out the programme.
progredire, *v.i.* To progress, to advance; to develop, to improve; to proceed.
progredito, *a.* Advanced, up-to-date, modern.
progressione, *n.f.* Progression, progress, advancement; course.
progressista (*pl.* **progressisti**), *n.m.* (*Pol.*) Progressist, progressionist.
progressivamente, *adv.* Progressively.
progressivo, *a.* Progressive.
progresso, *n.m.* Progress; advancement, advance; increase; improvement, development. **Fare molti progressi negli studi,** to make good progress in one's studies; **in — di tempo,** in the course of time.
proibire, *v.t.* To prohibit, to forbid; to prevent, to hinder, to debar. **Gli fu proibito di partire,** he was forbidden to leave; **gli proibì di partire,** he forbade him to leave.
proibitivo, *a.* Prohibitive (of price, etc.).
proibito, *p.p.a.* Forbidden. **È — fumare,** no smoking allowed; **— l'ingresso,** no admittance; **frutto —,** forbidden fruit.
proibizione, *n.f.* Prohibition.
proibizionismo, *n.m.* Prohibitionism.
proibizionista (*pl.* **proibizionisti**), *n.m.* Prohibitionist.
proiettare, *v.t.* To project, to shoot forward, to jut out. (*Cinema.*) **— una pellicola,** to show a film.
proiettile [proiEttile], *n.m.* Projectile, missile, bullet.
proiettore, *n.m.* Search-light, projector; head-lamp.
proiezione, *n.f.* Projection **Conferenza con proiezioni,** lecture with lantern-slides.
prolasso, *n.m.* (*Med.*) Prolapse, prolapsis.
prole, *n.f.* Offspring, progeny, children, issue. **Numerosa —,** large family; **senza —,** childless.
prolegomeni [prolegOmeni], *n.m.pl.* Prolegomena, introductory remarks.
proletariato, *n.m.* Proletariat; working classes.
proletario [proletArio], *n.m.a.* Proletarian.
proliferazione, *n.f.* Proliferation.
prolifero [prolIfero], *a.* Prolific.
prolificare, *v.t.* To beget, to breed, to generate; to proliferate.
prolifico [prolIfico], *a.* Prolific; fruitful, productive.
prolissamente, *adv.* Wordily, prolixly.
prolissità [-à], *n.f.* Prolixity, diffuseness, wordiness.
prolisso, *a.* Prolix, diffuse, wordy, long-winded.
prologo [prOlogo], *n.m.* Prologue; introduction.
prolungabile [prolungAbile], *a.* Extensible, prolongable.
prolungamento, *n.m.* Prolongation, extension, lengthening.
prolungare, *v.t.* To prolong, to extend; to lengthen, to protract; to delay. **— la moratoria,** to extend the moratorium.
prolungarsi, *v.r.* To extend, to continue; to get prosy.
prolungatamente, *adv.* At great length.
prolungazione, *n.f.* Prolongation, extension, protraction; delay.
prolusione, *n.f.* Introduction, inaugural lecture.
promemoria [promemOria], *n.m.* Memorandum, memo.
promessa, *n.f.* Promise. **Mantener la —,** to keep one's word, to keep a promise.
promesso, *p.p.a.* Promised. **La terra promessa,** the promised land; **promessi sposi,** betrothed (couple), engaged (couple).
Prometeo [promEteo], *n.m.* (*Myth.*) Prometheus.
promettente, *a.* Promising, hopeful, bidding fair.
promettere [promEttere], *v.t.* To promise, to give one's word; to determine, to resolve. (*colloq.*) **— mari e monti,** to make wild promises; **— bene,** to be promising, to bid fair.
promettersi [promEttersi], *v.r.* To promise each other; to get engaged.
promettitore, promettitrice, *n.m.f.* One who promises.
prominente, *a.* Prominent, jutting out, projecting; conspicuous, eminent.
prominentemente, *adv.* Prominently.
prominenza, *n.f.* Prominence.
promiscuamente, *adv.* Promiscuously.
promiscuità [-à], *n.f.* Promiscuity.
promiscuo [promIscuo], *a.* Promiscuous. **Scuola promiscua,** co-educational school.
promissivamente, *adv.* By way of a promise.
promissivo, *a.* Promissory.
promissorio [promissOrio], *a.* (*Law, Comm.*) Promissory.
promontorio [promontOrio], *n.m.* (*Geog.*) Promontory, headland.
promosso, *a.* Promoted; successful (applicant); passed (of an exam) [cp. **promuovere**].
promotore, *n.m.* Promoter; organizer.
promovere [cp. **promuovere**].
promovimento, *n.m.* Promoting, fostering, promotion.
promozione, *n.f.* Promotion, advancement, furtherance, fostering. **— per merito,** promotion for merit.
promulgamento, *n.m.* Promulgation.
promulgare, *v.t.* To promulgate, to proclaim, to issue.
promulgazione, *n.f.* Promulgation, publication.
promuovere [promuOvere], *v.t.* To promote; to further, to help on, to foster; to encourage; to advance; to raise, to elevate; to pass (an exam). **È stato promosso agli esami,** he passed the exams.

pronazione, *n.f.* (*Anat.*) Pronating, turning the hand palm downwards.
pronipote, *n.m.f.* Grand-nephew, grand-niece. **I pronipoti,** descendants.
prono, *a.* Prone, prostrate; bowed down; ready, inclined.
pronome, *n.m.* (*Gram.*) Pronoun.
pronominale, *a.* (*Gram.*) Pronominal.
pronosticamento, *n.m.* Prognostication, prophecy.
pronosticare, *v.t.i.* To prognosticate, to foretell, to predict.
pronosticazione, *n.f.* Prognostication.
pronostico [pronOstico], *n.m.* Prognostic, prediction, forecast; omen.
prontamente, *adv.* Promptly, readily.
prontezza, *n.f.* Readiness, promptness, quickness.
pronto, *inter.* (*Telephone*) Hello! Are you there!
pronto, *a.* Ready, prompt; quick, alert. **— all'ira,** quick-tempered; **stare pronti,** to be in readiness; **ingegno —,** quick intelligence; **sei — ?** are you ready? **avere la risposta pronta,** to have a ready answer; **pronta cassa, pronti contanti,** ready money, cash; (*Telephone*) **Pronto! Pronti!,** Hello!
prontuario [prontuArio], *n.m.* Ready-reckoner; hand-book; reference book.
pronubo [prOnubo], *n.m.* (*obs.*) Bridesman; best man.
pronunzia, pronuncia [pronUnzia], *n.f.* Pronunciation, delivery; utterance.
pronunziabile [pronunziAbile], *a.* Pronounceable.
pronunziamento, *n.m.* Utterance, declaration; (*Hist.*) pronunciamiento.
pronunziare, pronunciare, *v.t.* To pronounce, to articulate; to speak, to utter, to deliver (a judgement, etc.). **Non si è voluto — su ciò,** he did not wish to commit himself on this point.
pronunziarsi, *v.r.* To declare oneself, to express oneself; to decide.
pronunziato, *p.p.a.* Pronounced, marked, prominent; decided.
propagabile [propagAbile], *a.* Capable of being propagated.
propaganda, *n.f.* Propaganda, canvassing (at elections); advertising. **Far —,** to advertise.
propagandare, *v.t.* To propagandize, to advertise, to publicize.
propagandista (*pl.* **propagandisti**), *n.m.* Propagandist.
propagare, *v.t.* To propagate, to disseminate, to diffuse, to spread abroad, to broadcast.
propagarsi, *v.r.* To spread, to be diffused.
propagatore, propagatrice, *n.m.f.* Propagator, disseminator.
propagazione, *n.f.* Propagation, spreading; divulgation.
propagginamento, *n.m.* (*Agric.*) Layering.
propagginare, *v.t.* (*Agric.*) To layer; (*Hist.*) to bury head downwards.
propagginazione, *n.f.* (*Agric.*) Layering.
propaggine [propAggine], *n.f.* Layer; offspring, descent.
propalare, *v.t.* To divulge, to report, to spread (news), to broadcast (news).
propalatore, propalatrice, *n.m.f.* Spreader of news.
propalazione, *n.f.* Divulgation, spreading (of news, etc.).
propendere [propEndere], *v.i.* To incline, to lean; to be disposed, to be inclined; to be partial, to tend.
propensione, *n.f.* Propension, propensity, inclination, tendency; disposition.
propenso, *a.* Inclined, disposed; favourable.
Properzio [propErzio], *n.m.* Propertius.
propina, *n.f.* Examiner's fee.
propinare, *v.t.* To toast, to drink the health of; to pour out. **— il veleno,** to administer the poison.
propinquità [-à], *n.f.* Nearness, propinquity, proximity.
propinquo [propInquo], *a.* Near, neighbouring, close by; related.
propiziamente, *adv.* Propitiously, favourably.
propiziare, *v.t.* To propitiate, to conciliate; to make propitious.
propiziarsi, *v.r.* To propitiate, to gain (esteem, etc.).
propiziatore, propiziatrice, *n.m.f.* Propitiator.
propiziatorio [propiziatOrio], *a.* Propitiatory.
propiziazione, *n.f.* Propitiation.
propizio [propIzio], *a.* Propitious, favourable.
propoli [prOpoli], *n.f.* Propolis (of bees).
proponente, *n.m.a.* Proposer; proposing.
proponibile [proponIbile], *a.* Proposable.
proponimento, *n.m.* Resolve, purpose, resolution, intent. **Far — di,** to resolve to.
proporre, *v.t.* To propose, to offer, to put forward, to bid; to propound. **— ad esempio,** to hold up as an example.
proporsi, *v.r.* To intend, to purpose, to resolve; to offer oneself. **— un compito,** to set oneself a task.
proporzionale, *a.* Proportional; **rappresentanza —,** proportional representation.
proporzionalità [-à], *n.f.* Proportionality.
proporzionalmente, *adv.* Proportionally.
proporzionare, *v.t.* To proportion, to regulate, to adjust.
proporzionatamente, *adv.* Proportionately.
proporzionato, *a.* Proportionate.
proporzione, *n.f.* Proportion (in all senses). **Di grandi proporzioni,** on a big scale.
proposito [propOsito], *n.m.* Purpose, object, intention, design; determination, resolve; view, aim. **A —!** By the way! (*colloq.*) **capitare a —,** to come at the right time. **a — di,** with respect to, with regard to; in connexion with; **di —,** seriously, earnestly; purposely, on purpose; **mutar —,** to change one's mind; **male a —,** ill-timed, out-of-place; **senza —,** to no purpose; **a — di che?** For what reason? Why?
propositura, *n.f.* Presbytery, rectory.
proposizione, *n.f.* Proposition (in all senses).
proposta, *n.f.* Proposal, proposition; offer. (*Pol.*) **— di legge,** (parliamentary) bill; **fare una —,** to make a proposal, to suggest; **— di matrimonio,** proposal of marriage.
proposto, *n.m.* (*Eccles.*) Priest, curate [cp. **preposto**].
proposto, *p.p.a.* Proposed.
propriamente, *adv.* Properly, exactly, correctly; appropriately.
proprietà [-à], *n.f.* Propriety, correctness; ownership, property, possession; rights;

landed property, estate; peculiarity — **letteraria,** copyright; **avere delle — in Italia,** to have landed estates in Italy; **di mia —,** belonging to me; **parlare con —,** to speak correctly.
proprietario [proprietArio], *n.m.* Owner, proprietor; landlord.
proprio [prOprio], *n.m.* One's own. **Vivere del —,** to live on private means.
proprio [prOprio], *a.* Proper, actual, individual; original; exact, accurate, convenient; neat, clean; (*Gram.*) proper; **Amor —,** self-respect, proper pride; **nome —,** Christian name; **il — figlio,** one's own son; **un metodo tutto —,** a method all one's own.
proprio [prOprio], *adv.* Really, exactly, indeed, just. **Proprio!** Really! Indeed! — **così,** quite so; **è — mio,** it's really my own; **— all'ultimo momento,** at the very last moment; **è uscito — ora,** he's gone out this very minute.
propugnacolo [propugnAcolo], *n.m.* Bulwark; stronghold.
propugnare, *v.t.* To champion, to support, to back; to advocate; to plead for.
propugnatore, propugnatrice, *n.m.f.* Supporter, champion.
propugnazione, *n.f.* Support, backing.
propulsare, *v.t.* (*Lit.*) To propel.
propulsione, *n.f.* Propulsion, driving power: **— a reiazione,** jet-propulsion.
propulsivo, *a.* Propulsive, propellent.
propulsore, *n.m.* Propeller.
prora, *nf.* (*Naut.*) Bow, prow, head.
proroga [prOroga], *n.f.* Postponement, delay, respite, adjournment, prorogation.
prorogabile prorogAbile], *a.* Capable of deferment, deferable.
prorogare, *v.t.* To put off, to adjourn, to postpone; to prorogue. **— di cinque giorni,** to postpone for five days.
prorompente, *a.* Bursting forth, breaking out.
prorompere [prorOmpere], *v.i.* To burst out, to break out; to exclaim. **— in lacrime,** to burst into tears.
prosa, *n.f.* Prose. **Teatro di —,** theatre (as opposed to an opera house); drama.
prosaicamente, *adv.* Prosaically.
prosaicità [-à], *n.f.* Prosaicness.
prosaico [prosAico], *a.* Prosaic; dull, commonplace.
prosapia [prosApia], *n.f.* Progeny, stock, lineage, descent.
prosastico [prosAstico], *a.* Prose, in prose; prosaic.
prosatore, prosatrice, *n.m.f.* Prose-writer.
proscenio [proscEnio], *n.m.* (*Theat.*) Proscenium.
prosciogliere [prosciOgliere], *v.t.* To release, to acquit, to set free; (*Eccles.*) to absolve. (*Law*) **— in istruttoria,** to dismiss a case.
proscioglimento, *n.m.* Acquittal, deliverance, release; absolution.
prosciolto, *p.p.a.* Acquitted, released.
prosciugabile [prosciugAbile], *a.* Reclaimable (of land), capable of being drained.
prosciugamento, *n.m.* Draining (land); reclamation; drying up, drainage.
prosciugare, *v.t.* To drain land, to reclaim land.
prosciugarsi, *v.r.* To be drained or reclaimed.
prosciutto, *n.m.* Ham. **— cotto,** boiled ham.
proscrivere [proscrIvere], *v.t.* To proscribe, to banish, to exile, to outlaw; (*fig.*) to reject, to exclude.
proscritto, *n.m.a.* Exile, banished person; proscribed, banished.
proscrizione, *n.f.* Proscription, banishment.
prosecuzione, *n.f.* Continuation, prosecution (of studies, etc.).
proseggiare, *v.i.* To write prose.
proseguimento, *n.m.* Continuation; resumption.
proseguire, *v.t.* To pursue, to continue, to carry on, to follow up; to resume; to persist. **Deve — gli studi,** he has to continue his studies; **devo — il viaggio,** I have to resume my journey; (*on letters*) **far —,** please forward.
proselite, proselito [prosElite, prosElito], *n.m.* Proselyte; partisan, follower.
proselitismo, *n.m.* Proselytism.
prosieguo [prosiEguo], *n.m.* Course. **In — di tempo,** in course of time, in due time.
prosit! *inter.* Your health! (when drinking).
prosodia [prosodIa], *n.f.* Prosody.
prosodico [prosOdico], *a.* Prosodic.
prosopopea [prosopopEa], *n.f.* Affectation, affected gravity; ascription of speech to the dead or lifeless things.
prosperamente, *adv.* Prosperously.
prosperamento, *n.m.* Prospering, prosperity.
prosperare, *v.i.* To prosper, to thrive, to flourish; to get on, to succeed.
prosperevole [prosperEvole], *a.* (*Lit.*) Prosperous.
prosperità [-à], *n.f.* Prosperity; thriving, success, wealth.
prospero [prOspero], *a.* Prosperous, flourishing, thriving; happy.
prosperosamente, *adv.* Prosperously.
prosperoso, *a.* Prosperous, flourishing; healthy, vigorous.
prospettare, *v.i.* To show; to look out upon, to face (landscape); to show in perspective; to describe.
prospetticamente, *adv.* In perspective.
prospettico [prospEttico], *a.* Perspective.
prospettiva, *n.f.* Perspective; outlook, view, prospect; expectation. **Avere una —,** to look forward to, to expect; **— aerea,** aerial perspective.
prospettivamente, *adv.* According to the laws of perspective.
prospetto, *n.m.* Prospect, view; outlook; prospectus; table, summary, statement; (*Arch.*) façade. **Di —,** facing, in front, front view.
prospiciente, *a.* Overlooking, facing, opposite. **— il mare,** facing the sea.
prosseneta, *n.m.* Go-between, intermediary.
prossimamente, *adv.* Nearly, closely; very near (in time), very soon, shortly.
prossimità [-à], *n.f.* Proximity, nearness, closeness. **In — di,** near, close to, in the neighbourhood of.
prossimo [prOssimo], *n.m.* Neighbour, fellow-creature. **Amare il —,** to love one's neighbour.
prossimo [prOssimo], *a.* Next, near, nearest; neighbouring. **Parente —,** near relation; **il mese —,** next month; (*Gram.*) **passato —,**

present perfect; **— alla fine,** near the end; **nel — avvenire,** in the near future; **esser — alla partenza,** to be on the point of departure; **essere — alla cinquantina,** to be nearly fifty.
prostata [prOstata], *n.f.* (*Anat.*) Prostate gland.
prostatico [prostAtico], *a.* Prostatic.
prostendere [prostEndere], *v.t.* To stretch out, to extend.
prostendersi [prostEndersi], *v.r.* To spread, to stretch oneself; to lie down.
prosternare, *v.t.* To lay low, to cause to prostrate.
prosternarsi, *v.r.* To prostrate oneself, to cast oneself on the ground, to kneel; to bow low.
prosternazione, *n.f.* Prostration; kneeling down.
prostituire, *v.t.* To prostitute, to defile, to dishonour, to debase.
prostituirsi, *v.r.* To prostitute oneself; to debase oneself.
prostituta, *n.f.* Prostitute, harlot.
prostituzione, *n.f.* Prostitution.
prostramento, *n.m.* Prostration.
prostrare, *v.t.* To prostrate, to cast down; to fatigue, to weary, to dispirit.
prostrarsi, *v.r.* To prostrate oneself; to kneel down.
prostrazione, *n.f.* Prostration, dejection, exhaustion, weariness; depression.
protagonista, *n.m.f.* Protagonist; (*Theat.*) leading actor or actress.
proteggere [protEggere], *v.t.* To protect, to favour, to patronize; to support; to guard, to defend.
proteina, *n.f.* (*Chem.*) Protein.
protendere [protEndere], *v.t.* To stretch, to stretch out, to extend, to hold out, to spread. **— le braccia,** to stretch out one's arms.
protendersi [protEndersi], *v.r.* To stretch oneself, to spread out. **— dalla finestra,** to lean out of the window.
Proteo [prOteo], *n.m.* (*Myth.*) Proteus.
protervamente. *adv.* Arrogantly, insolently.
protervia [protErvia], *n.f.* Arrogance, insolence, impudence; obstinacy.
protervo, *a.* Arrogant, insolent, forward, haughty; rash, impetuous.
proteso, *p.p.a.* Stretched out, held out.
protesta, *n.f.* Protest, protestation; declaration; dissent, remonstrance. **Proteste di amore,** protestations of love.
protestante, *n.m.a.* Protestant.
protestantesimo [protestantEsimo], *n.m.* Protestantism.
protestare, *v.t.* To protest; to dissent; to declare. **— la propria innocenza,** to protest one's innocence; **— contro,** to protest against; (*Comm.*) **— una cambiale,** to protest a bill of exchange.
protestarsi, *v.r.* To declare oneself.
protestatore, protestatrice, *n.m.f.* Protestor.
protestazione, *n.f.* Protestation.
protesto, *n.m.* Protestation; *Comm.*) Protest (of bill of exchange).
protettivo, *a.* Protective.
protètto, *n.m.a.* Protégé; favourite. **Il mio —** my protégé; protected, defended.
protettorato, *n.m.* Protectorate.
protettore, protettrice, *n.m.f.* Protector, protectress.
protezione, *n.f* Protection; support, help; patronage. **Esser sotto la — di,** to be under the protection of; **misure di — antiaerea,** air-raid precautions.
protezionismo, *n.m.* (*Pol.*) Protectionism.
protezionista (*pl.* **protezionisti),** *n.m.* (*Pol.*) Protectionist.
proto, *n.m.* Printing overseer.
protocollare, *a.* relating to protocol. **Norme protocollari,** rules of protocol.
protocollare, *v.t.* To register.
protocollo, *n.m.* Protocol; register; ceremonial, political etiquette. **Carta —,** foolscap paper.
protomartire [protomArtire], *n.m.* Protomartyr.
protonotario [protonotArio], *n.m.* (*Eccles.*) Protonotary.
protoplasma, *n.m.* Protoplasm.
prototipo [protOtipo], *n.m.* Prototype.
protozoi [protozOi], *n.m.pl.* (*Zool.*) Protozoa.
protrarre, *v.t.* To protract, to prolong, to lengthen out; to defer.
protrazione, *n.f.* Protraction, prolonging.
protuberante, *a.* Protuberant.
protuberanza, *n.f.* Protuberance, prominence.
prova, *n.f.* Proof, trial, test; essay, experiment, examination; ordeal, experience; (*Theat.*) rehearsal; (*Law*) evidence; (*Print.*) proof. **Mettere a dura —,** to put to a severe test; **addurre prove,** to bringevidence; **prendere in —,** to take on trial; **— d'amicizia,** mark of friendship; **prove orali,** oral tests; **dar buona —,** to give good results; **— di velocità,** speed trial; **a —,** on trial; **a — di bomba,** bomb-proof; **un amico a tutta —,** a tried friend; **sostenere dure prove,** to undergo a severe test; **la — del fuoco,** ordeal by fire; (*Theat.*) **— generale,** dress rehearsal.
provabile [provAbile], *a.* Provable, open to testing.
provare, *v.t.i.* To try, to test, to prove; to experience, to feel (pain, etc.); to try on (clothes); (*Theat.*) to rehearse; (*Law*) to bring evidence, to prove. **— un abito,** to try on a dress; **— un rimedio,** to try a remedy; **— un fatto,** to prove a fact; **— disgusto,** to feel disgust; **essere provato dalla sventura,** to be tried by adversity.
provarsi, *v.r.* To attempt, to endeavour; to exercise oneself.
provatamente, *adv.* Surely, assuredly, certainly.
provatura, *n.f.* (rare) Cheese made from buffalo's milk.
provenda, *n.f.* (*Lit.*) Provender, food.
proveniente, *a.* Coming from, proceeding from, arising.
provenienza, *n.f.* Origin, provenance, derivation, source.
provenire, *v.i.* To come from; to proceed, to arise; to derive; to originate.
provento, *n.m.* Income; profit, proceeds, revenue.
Provenza, *n.f.* (*Geog.*) Provence
provenzale, *n.m.a.* Provençal.
provenzaleggiare, *v.i.* To imitate Provençal (literature, etc.).

proverbiale, *a.* Proverbial; notorious.
proverbialmente, *adv.* Proverbially.
proverbiare, *v.t.* To scold, to lecture; to jeer at.
proverbio [provErbio], *n.m.* Proverb, maxim, adage.
proverbioso, *a.* Full of proverbs.
provetta, *n.f.* Test-tube.
provetto, *a.* Experienced, skilful, expert, competent; mature (in age).
provincia [provIncia], *n.f.* Province; country; district. **In —,** in the provinces.
provinciale, *n.m.a.* Provincial, rustic; narrow-minded. (*Eccles.*) **Padre —,** provincial.
provincialismo, *n.m.* Provincialism.
provincialmente, *adv.* Provincially.
provino, *n.m.* Sample; (*Mech.*) gauge; (*Cinema*) try-out, rehearsal, audition; (*colloq.*) trailer (of a film).
provocabile [provocAbile], *a.* Provokable.
provocante, *a.* Provoking, irritating; provocative; alluring.
provocantemente, *adv.* Provokingly.
provocare, *v.t.* To provoke, to rouse, to challenge, to irritate, to instigate.
provocativamente, *adv.* Provocatively.
provocativo, *a.* Provocative.
provocatore, provocatrice, *n.m.f.* Provoker. **Agente —,** *agent provocateur.*
provocatorio [provocatOrio], *a.* Provocatory.
provocazione, *n.f.* Provocation, instigation, irritation, challenge.
provvedere, *v.t.i.* To provide, to supply, to purvey, to furnish; to take steps, to see to. **Provvederò,** I'll see to it.
provvedersi, *v.r.* To provide oneself, to get.
provvedimento, *n.m.* Provision, measure (to be taken), precaution, steps.
provveditore, *n.m.* Purveyor, provider; steward, manager; superintendant. **— agli studi,** director of education.
provvidamente, *adv.* Providently.
provvidente, *a.* Provident, foreseeing, careful.
provvidentemente, *adv.* Providently, frugally, carefully.
provvidenza, *n.f.* Providence.
provvidenziale, *a.* Providential.
provvidenzialmente, *adv.* Providentially.
provvido [prOvvido], *a.* Provident; beneficial, wise; thrifty.
provvigione, *n.f.* Provision, provisions, victuals; (*Comm.*) commission.
provvisionato, *a.* (*Mil.*) Provisioned.
provvisione, *n.f.* Provision; quantity, a good deal. **Ne ho una buona —,** I've a good stock of it.
provvisoriamente, *adv.* Provisorily, provisionally; temporarily.
provvisorio [provvisOrio], *a.* Provisory, provisional, temporary. **Governo —,** provisional government.
provvista, *n.f.* Provision, supply; purchase. **Ho fatto le mie provviste,** I have made my purchases; **le provviste sono esaurite,** the provisions are exhausted; **andare a far le provviste,** to go shopping.
prozio, prozia [prozIo, prozIa], *n.m.f.* Great-uncle, great-aunt.
prua, *n.f.* (*Naut.*) Bow, prow.
prudente, *a.* Prudent, cautious, discreet, wise, circumspect; wary.
prudentemente, *adv.* Prudently.
prudenza, *n.f.* Prudence, caution, discretion, wariness; wisdom.
prudenziale, *a.* Precautionary, prudential.
prudenzialmente, *adv.* In a precautionary manner.
prudere [prUdere], *v.i.* To itch; to smart. (*fig.*) **Mi prudono le mani,** I itch to give (him, her, etc.) a smack.
prudore [cp. **prurito**].
prueggiare, *v.t.* (*Naut.*) To keep the bow to; **— la marea,** to stem the tide.
prueggio [pruEggio], *n.m.* (*Naut.*) Keeping the bow to. **Stare a —,** anchored with the bow to; **a — del vento,** head to wind.
prugna, *n.f.* (*Bot.*) Plum. **— secca,** prune.
prugno, *n.m.* (*Bot.*) Plum-tree.
prugnolo [prUgnolo] (1), *n.m.* (*Bot.*) Wild plum.
prugnolo [prugnOlo] (2), *n.m.* Kind of edible fungus.
pruina, *n.f.* (*Poet.*) Hoar-frost; bloom on fruit.
prunaio, pruneto [prunAio], *n.m.* Thicket of thorn, thorn-brake.
pruno, *n.m.* (*Bot.*) Thorn-bush.
prurigine [prurIgine], *n.f.* Itching; (*Med.*) prurigo.
pruriginoso, *a.* Itching, itchy.
prurito, *n.m.* Itch, itching; smarting; (*Med.*) prurigo; (*fig.*) pruriency, desire.
Prussia [prUssia], *n.f.* (*Geog.*) Prussia. **Blu di —,** Prussian blue.
prussiano, *n.m.a.* Prussian.
prussico [prUssico], *a.* (*Chem.*) Prussic. **Acido —,** prussic acid.
pseudonimo [pseudOnimo], *n.m.* Pseudonym.
psicanalisi [psicanAlisi], *n.f.* Psycho-analysis.
Psiche, *n.f.* (*Myth.*) Psyche; (*fig.*) the soul.
psichiatra, psichiatro, *n.m.* Psychiatrist.
psichiatria [psichiatrIa], *n.f.* Psychiatry.
psichiatrico [psichiAtrico], *a.* Psychiatric.
psichico [psIchico], *a.* Psychic.
psicoanalisi [psichoanAlisi], *n.f.* Psycho-analysis.
psicologia [psicologIa], *n.f.* Psychology.
psicologicamente, *adv.* Psychologically.
psicologico [psicolOgico], *a.* Psychological.
psicopatia [psicopatIa], *n.f.* Psychopathy.
psicopatico [psicopAtico], *n.m.a.* Psychopath; psychopathic.
psicosi, *n.f.* Psychosis.
pubblicabile [pubblicAbile], *a.* Publishable.
pubblicamente, *adv.* Publicly.
pubblicano, *n.m.* (*Hist.*) Publican, tax-gatherer.
pubblicare, *v.t.* To publish; to give out, to issue, to advertise, to make known; to edit. **— un romanzo a puntate,** to publish a novel in instalments.
pubblicatore, pubblicatrice, *n.m.a.* One who makes things known, who issues information, etc.
pubblicazione, *n.f.* Publication (in all senses). **— di matrimonio,** banns of marriage.
pubblicista (*pl.* **pubblicisti**), *n.f.* Publicist.
pubblicità [-à], *n.f.* Publicity; advertisement, notice; (*colloq.*) bally-hoo. **Piccola —,** small advertisements.
pubblicitario [pubblicitArio], *a.* Advertising, publicity.

pubblico [pUbblico], *n.m.* Public; general public, people; audience. **In —,** in public, openly.
pubblico [pUbblico], *a.* Public; open, unrestricted; common. **Giardini pubblici,** public gardens or parks; **il bene —,** the public good; **la forza pubblica,** the police; **il debito —,** the national debt.
pube, *n.m.* (*Anat.*) Pubes.
pubere [pUbere], *n.m.a.* Adolescent.
pubertà [-à], *n.f.* Puberty.
pubescente, *n.m.a.* Adolescent, pubescent.
puddinga, *n.f.* (*Min.*) Pudding-stone.
pudenda, *n.f.pl.* Pudenda, genitals.
pudibondo, *a.* Shame-faced, bashful, shy; modest.
pudicamente, *adv.* Chastely; bashfully.
pudicizia [pudicIzia], *n.f.* Shame, modesty, bashfulness, reserve; chastity.
pudico, *a.* Chaste, modest, bashful; pure.
pudore, *n.m.* Shame, bashfulness, shyness, modesty, reserve.
puericultura, *n.f.* Early education; children's welfare.
puerile, *a.* Childish, puerile; futile.
puerilità [-à], *n.f.* Puerility, childishness; futility.
puerilmente, *adv.* In a puerile manner.
puerizia [puerIzia], *n.f.* Childhood.
puerpera [puErpera], *n.f.* Woman in travail, woman in labour.
puerperale, *a.* (*Med.*) Puerperal.
puerperio [puerpErio], *n.m.* Lying-in, childbirth, labour; confinement.
pugilato, *n.m.* Boxing, pugilism.
pugilatore, *n.m.* Boxer, pugilist.
pugilistico [pugilIstico], *a.* Pugilistic.
puglia [pUglia], *n.f.* Counter (in games, etc.).
pugliese, *n.m.a.* Native of or belonging to Apulia.
pugna, *n.f.* (*Lit.*) Fight, battle, combat.
pugnace, *a.* Pugnacious.
pugnacemente, *adv.* Pugnaciously.
pugnalare, *v.t.* To stab.
pugnalata, *n.f.* Stab, stabbing.
pugnale, *n.m.* Dagger.
pugnare, *v.i.* To fight.
pugnata, *n.f.* Fight; blow with the fist; handful.
pugnello, pugnetto, *n.m.* Handful.
pugnere [cp. **pungere**].
pugnitopo, *n.m.* (*Bot.*) Butcher's broom.
pugno (*pl.* **pugni,** *m.*, **pugna,** *f.*) *n.m.* Fist; handful; punch (blow); handwriting. **Fare a pugni,** to box, to fight; to contrast; **un — di farina,** a handful of flour; **— di ferro,** mailed fist; **prendere a pugni,** to beat, to thump; **di suo —,** in his own handwriting; **con un — di mosche,** empty-handed.
pula, *n.f.* Chaff.
pulce, *n.f.* (*Zool.*) Flea. (*fig.*) **Mettere una — nell'orecchio,** to put a doubt in someone's mind; **color —,** puce.
pulcella, *n.f.* (*Lit.*) Young girl, maid, virgin.
pulciaio [pulciAio], *n.m.* Nest of fleas, flea-bag.
Pulcinella, *n.m.* Punch, Mr. Punch; buffoon.
pulcino, *n.m.* Chick, chicken. **Un — nella stoppa,** a helpless creature.
pulcioso, *a.* Full of fleas.
puledra, *n.f.* Filly.
puledro, *n.m.* Colt, foal.
puleggia [pulEggia], *n.f.* Pulley.
pulica, puliga [pUlica, pUliga], *n.f.* Air-bubble (in glass, etc.).
pulimento, *n.m.* Cleaning, polishing, polish.
pulire, *v.t.* To clean, to cleanse, to polish; to brush, to sweep. **— le scarpe,** to clean one's shoes; **— una strada,** to sweep a road; **— il pavimento,** to scrub the floor.
pulirsi, *v.r.* To clean oneself. **— il naso,** to blow one's nose; **— i denti,** to clean the teeth.
puliscipenne, *n.m.* Pen-wiper.
puliscipiedi, pulisciscarpe, *n.m.* Door-mat; foot-scraper.
pulita, *n.f.* Clean, cleaning; brushing up; washing. **Dare una —,** to clean.
pulitamente, *adv.* Neatly, cleanly.
pulitezza, *n.f.* Cleanliness, cleanness; polish; tidiness, propriety.
pulito, *a.* Clean, neat; polished, well-kept; smooth; terse. **Coscienza pulita,** clear conscience; **far piazza pulita,** to make a clean sweep; **aver la tasca pulita,** to have an empty pocket.
pulitore, pulitrice, *n.m.f.* Cleaner, polisher.
pulitura, *n.f.* Cleansing, cleaning, polishing.
pulizia [pulizIa], *n.* . Cleanliness, tidiness, neatness; cleaning. **Gran —,** spring-cleaning; **far —,** to clean; (*fig.*) **fare una bella —,** to make a clean sweep.
pullulamento, *n.m.* Swarming, shooting forth.
pullulare, *v.i.* To spring up, to bud forth; to bubble; to swarm. **La piazza pullulava di gente,** the square was swarming with people.
pullulazione, *n.f.* Swarming, shooting forth.
pulpito [pUlpito], *n.m.* Pulpit. **Montare in —,** to hold forth at great length, to sermonize; (*colloq.*) **senti da che — viene la predica,** listen to who is talking.
pulsante, *n.m.a.* Push-button; pulsating, throbbing, vibrating.
pulsare, *v.i.* To pulsate, to beat, to throb; to vibrate, to quiver.
pulsazione, *n.f.* Pulsation, beating, throbbing, throb.
pulsimetro [pulsImetro], *n.m.* (*Med.*) Pulsimeter.
pulvinare, *n.m.* (*Hist.*) Imperial box in the circus; (*Theat.*) grand stand (in an amphitheatre).
pulviscolo [pulvIscolo], *n.m.* Fine dust, spray (of water).
pulzella, *n.f.* Maid, virgin.
pulzellona, *n.f.* Old maid.
pum! *inter.* Bang!
puma, *n.f.* (*Zool.*) Puma.
pungente, *a.* Pungent, stinging, sharp, piercing; caustic, biting. **Freddo —,** piercing cold; **parole pungenti,** sharp words.
pungere [pUngere], *v.t.* To prick, to sting; to goad (oxen); to excite, to stimulate; to offend, to irritate. **— sul vivo,** to cut to the quick; **esser punto da un'ape,** to be stung by a bee.
pungersi [pUngersi], *v.r.* To prick oneself. **— le mani,** to prick one's fingers.
pungiglione, *n.m.* Sting (of insect), prickle; stimulus.

pungitoio [pungitOio], *n.m.* Goad, prick.
pungitopo [cp. **pugnitopo**].
pungolare, *v.t.* To goad (in all senses).
pungolo [pUngolo], *n.m.* Goad; stimulus, spur.
punibile [punIbile], *a.* Punishable.
punibilità [-à], *n.f.* Liability to punishment.
punico [pUnico], *a.* (*Hist.*) Punic, Carthaginian.
punimento, *n.m.* Punishment, punishing.
punire, *v.t.* To punish, to chastise, to correct. **— di morte,** to punish with death.
punitivo, *a.* Punitive. **Spedizione punitiva,** punitive expedition.
punitore, punitrice, *n.m.f.* Chastiser, punisher.
punitore, *a.* Punitive, punishing.
punizione, *n.f.* Punishment, chastisement, correction. **Per —,** as punishment; **infliggere una —,** to inflict a punishment; **merita una — esemplare,** he deserves to be severely punished.
punta, *n.f.* Point, tip, end, extremity; top, summit; cape, point; nib (of pen); dash, run; stitch (in side), pain, discomfort. **La — di una spada,** sword-point; **la — del naso,** the tip of the nose; **avere sulla — della lingua,** to have on the tip of one's tongue; **avere sulla — delle dita,** to have at one's finger-tips; **cappello a tre punte,** three-cornered hat; **in — di piedi,** on tip-toe; **a —,** pointed; **far la — a,** to sharpen; **ore di —,** rush-hours (of traffic); **cane da —,** pointer (dog); **parlare in — di forchetta,** to speak affectedly; **— di diamante,** glass-cutter's diamond.
puntale, *n.m.* Ferrule, metal tip.
puntamento, *n.m.* Pointing; (*Mil.*) laying (a gun).
puntapiedi, *n.m.* (*Naut.*) Stretcher (of a row-boat).
puntare, *v.t.i.* To point (telescope, gun, etc.); to level, to fix (eyes, etc.); to stake, to bet, to wager; to pin. **— un fucile,** to point a gun; **— una somma,** to stake a sum; **— i piedi,** to take a stand.
puntata, *n.f.* Issue, number (of periodical, etc.), instalment (of serial), stake, bet; thrust; (*fig.*) gibe, taunt. **Uscire a puntate,** to appear in instalments.
puntatore, *n.m.* (*Mil.*) Gunner, gun-layer.
puntatura, *n.f.* Pointing; (*Mil.*) laying (of a gun).
punteggiamento, *n.m.* Dotting.
punteggiare, *v.t.* To dot; to punctuate.
punteggiatura, *n.f.* Punctuation; dotting.
punteggio [puntEggio], *n.m.* Dotting; marking, counting; (*Sport*) score; points.
puntellamento, *n.m.* Propping, staying, buttressing; supporting.
puntellare, *v.t.* To prop, to stay, to shore up; to back, to support.
puntellatura, *n.f.* Propping up, shoring up.
puntello, *n.m.* Prop, stay; support.
punteria [punterIa], *n.f.* (*Mil.*) Laying a gun.
punteruolo, *n.m.* Punch (tool), awl; bodkin; (*Zool.*) weevil.
puntiglio [puntIglio], *n.m.* Point of honour, punctilio; spite, pique.
puntigliosamente, *adv.* Punctiliously.
puntiglioso, *a.* Punctilious, particular. **Esser —,** to stand upon points, to be particular.
puntina, *n.f.* Drawing-pin, (*Am.*) thumbtack.
puntino, *n.m.* Dot, point. **A —,** nicely, fittingly; **cotto a —,** cooked to a turn; **mettere i puntini sugli i,** to dot one's i's.
puntiscritto, *n.m.* Laundry-mark.
punto, *n.m.* Point, dot, spot; instant, moment; place; stitch (in sewing); (*Gram.*) stop; mark (at school); particle. **— di vista,** point of view, standpoint; **in buon —,** at the right moment; **di — in bianco,** suddenly, all at once, point blank; **— d'onore,** point of honour; **— d'appoggio,** support, fulcrum; **— di partenza,** starting point; **di tutto —,** perfectly, smartly; **arrivare in buon —,** to arrive in the nick of time; **— fermo,** full stop; **— morto,** deadlock; **essere a mal —,** to be in a bad way; **buoni punti,** good marks (at lessons); **punto interrogativo,** question mark; **due punti,** colon; **— e a capo,** next paragraph; **— e virgola,** semicolon; **far —,** to put a stop to, to end; **qui sta il —!** here's the rub! **voglio sapere a che — siamo,** I want to know where we've got to; **essere sul — di,** to be on the point of; **— di ebollizione,** boiling-point; **— di congelamento,** freezing-point; **— per —,** in detail; **alle due in —,** at two o'clock sharp; **— a giorno, in croce,** open-work, cross-stitch; **a un tal —,** to such a degree; **mettere a —,** to overhaul; (*Sport*) **far —,** to score; (*Med.*) **dar due punti,** to give two stitches; **dar dei punti al diavolo,** to be cleverer than the devil.
punto, *p.p.a.* Pricked, stung [cp. **pungere**].
punto, *adv.* Not, no, not at all. **Non ha — giudizio,** he has no sense; **nè — nè poco,** nothing at all; **non mi piace —,** I don't like it at all.
puntone, *n.m.* Rafter; girder; strut; (*Mil.*) salient.
puntuale, *a.* Punctual; precise, exact.
puntualità [-à], *n.f.* Punctuality.
puntualmente, *adv.* Punctually.
puntuazione, *n.f.* Punctuation.
puntura, *n.f.* Puncture, sting, prick, (insect) bite. **La — d'una zanzara,** mosquito bite; (*Med.*) **fare delle punture,** to make (hypodermic) injections.
puntuto, *a.* Pointed; piercing, cutting, sharp.
punzecchiamento, *n.m.* Stinging, pricking; (*fig.*) teasing.
punzecchiare, *v.t.* To sting, to prick; to spur, to goad; to tease, to vex; to pin-prick.
punzecchiatura, *n.f.* Stinging, pricking; teasing, pin-pricking.
punzecchio [punzEcchio], *n.m.* Sting, prick.
punzonare, *v.t.* To punch, to punch out, to stamp, to mark.
punzonatrice, *n.f.* (*Mech.*) Punching machine.
punzone, *n.m.* Punch, die-stamp; punch (with the fist).
pupa, *n.f.* (*Zool.*) pupa; (*colloq.*) baby girl, little girl.
pupattola [pupAttola], *n.f.* Doll; little girl.
pupazzettare, *v.t.* To sketch, to caricature.
pupazzettista (*pl.* **pupazzettisti**), *n.m.* Caricaturist.
pupazzetto, *n.m.* Caricature, sketch.
pupazzo, *n.m.* Puppet; caricature.
pupazzola [pupAzzola], *n.f.* Doll, little girl.
pupilla, *n.f.* Female pupil, ward; (*Anat.*) pupil.

pupillare, *a.* Pupillary.
pupillo, *n.m.* Pupil, ward.
pupo, *n.m.* (*colloq.*) Baby boy, little fellow.
puramente, *adv.* Purely, simply, merely; candidly.
purchè, *conj.* Provided that, on condition that.
purchessia [purchessIa], *a.* Whatever, any, of any kind, whatsoever.
pure, *conj.* Yet, still, however; likewise, also, even; somehow; really. **Va —,** go if you wish, you may go; **pur dianzi,** just now; **fate —,** please do; **glielo dissi — io,** I too told him so; **lo dissi a lui —,** I told him too; **pur di riuscire,** just to succeed; **non —,** not only, not even; **senza —,** without even; **come —,** as well as.
purezza, *n.f.* Purity, pureness; chastity; clearness, transparence, neatness.
purga, *n.f.* Purge (of the system); purging.
purgagione, purgamento, *n.f.m.* Purging, purge.
purgante, *n.m.* Purgative, purge, aperient. **Prendere un —,** to take an aperient.
purgare, *v.t.* To purge (in all senses), to cleanse, to purify; (*fig.*) to atone for, to expiate; to expurgate.
purgarsi, *v.r.* To take an aperient, to purge oneself; to expiate; to clear oneself (of an accusation).
purgatezza, *n.f.* Purity of literary style.
purgativo, *a.* Purgative.
purgato, *p.p.a.* Purged; correct, pure; terse; expurgated.
purgatorio [purgatOrio], *n.m.* (*Eccles.*) Purgatory.
purgatura, purgazione, *n.f.* Purging, cleansing; expiation; acquittal.
purgo, *n.m.* Tank for rinsing washing.
purificare, *v.t.* To purify, to cleanse.
purificarsi, *v.r.* To purify oneself.
purificativo, *a.* Purificative.
purificatore, *n.m.* Purifier.
purificazione, *n.f.* Purification, purifying, cleaning.
purismo, *n.m.* (*Lit.*) Purism.
purista (*pl.* **puristi**), *n.m.* Purist.
purità [-à], *n.f.* Purity, pureness, innocence; chastity; clearness, neatness.
puritanismo, *n.m.* Puritanism.
puritano, *n.m.a.* Puritan.
puro, *a.* Pure, clear, clean, unmixed; neat; free, simple, mere; unadulterated; exempt; chaste, innocent, genuine, real, plain. **Pura perdita,** utter waste; **— sangue,** thoroughbred; **la pura verità,** the plain truth.
purpureo [purpUreo], *a.* Purple; crimson.
purtroppo! *inter.* Alas! unfortunately. **— è vero,** it's only too true; **— non lo conosco,** unfortunately I do not know him.
purulento, *a.* (*Med.*) Purulent, festered.
purulenza, *n.f.* (*Med.*) Purulence.
pus, *n.m.* (*Med.*) Pus, matter.
pusignare, *v.i.* (*obs.*) To take a late supper.
pusigno, *n.m.* (*obs.*) Late supper.
pusillanime [pusillAnime], *n.m.a.* Coward; pusillanimous, faint-hearted; mean-spirited; shy.
pusillanimità [-à], *n.f.* Pusillanimity, faint-heartedness.
pusillo, *a.* Mean, weak, small, pusillanimous; humble, of no account.
pustola [pUstola], *n.f.* (*Med.*) Pustule, pimple, boil.
pustoloso, *a.* Pimply.
putacaso, *adv.* (*colloq.*) For instance, let us suppose.
putativamente, *adv.* Putatively.
putativo, *a.* Putative, reputed, supposed. **Padre —,** putative father.
putido [pUtido], *a.* Stinking.
Putifarre, *n.m.* Potiphar.
putiferio [putifErio], *n.m.* Pandemonium, row, confusion, uproar; stench, stink.
putire, *v.i.* To stink.
putredine [putrEdine], *n.f.* Putrefaction, rottenness, decomposition.
putredinoso, *a.* Rotten, putrescent, decomposed.
putrefaciente, *a.* Putrescent, putrifying.
putrefare, *v.i.* To putrefy, to decompose, to rot.
putrefarsi, *v.r.* To putrefy, to become putrid.
putrefazione, *n.f.* Putrefaction, corruption.
putrescente, *a.* Putrescent, starting to putrefy.
putrescenza, *n.f.* Putrescence.
putridità [-à], *n.f.* Putridity, putridness.
putrido [pUtrido], *a.* Putrid, corrupt, rotten, decomposed.
putridume, *n.m.* Rottenness, putridity.
putta, *n.f.* (*Lit.*) Young girl.
puttana, *n.f.* Harlot, prostitute, whore, strumpet.
putteneggiare, *v.i.* To play the whore, to be a prostitute.
puttaneria [puttanerIa], *n.f.* Whoredom, harlotry.
puttaniere, *n.m.* Frequenter of harlots, whoremonger.
puttino, *n.m.* Little child, lovely child.
putto, *n.m.* Child (in painting or sculpture).
puzza, *n.f.* Stink, stench, offensive smell.
puzzacchiare, puzzicchiare, *v.i.* To smell rather nasty.
puzzare, *v.i.* To stink, to smell nasty. **— di,** to smell of.
puzzo, *n.m.* Stink, stench.
puzzola [pUzzola], *n.f.* (*Zool.*) Pole-cat; (*Bot.*) bad-smelling kind of fungus.
puzzolente, *a.* Stinking, fetid.
puzzolentemente, *adv.* Fetidly.
puzzone, *n.m.* Evil-smelling person; skunk; grouser.

Q

Q, q, *n.f.* Fifteenth letter of the Italian alphabet.
qua, *adv.* Here. **Qua e là,** here and there; **al di qua,** on this side; **fatti in qua,** come nearer; **da un mese in qua,** for the last month; **il mondo di qua,** the world we live in; **più qua,** later on.
quacquerismo, *n.m.* Quakerism.
quacquero, quacchero [quAcquero, quAcchero], *n.m.* Quaker, member of the Society of Friends.
quaderna, *n.f.* Set of four numbers played in a lottery.

quadernaccio [quadernAccio], *n.m.* Scrap-book, book for rough drafts.
quadernario [quadernArio], *n.m.* Set of four; (*Poet.*) strophe of four lines.
quaderno, *n.m.* Copy-book, exercise-book; quire (of sheets).
quadra, *n.f.* (*Naut.Astron.*) Quadrant; fourth part of the meridian; (*Naut.*) square sail. (*Naut.*) **Alla —,** square-rigged; (*fig.*) **dare la — a qualcuno,** to hold someone up to ridicule.
quadragesima [quadragEsima], *n.f.* (*Eccles.*) Lent; quadragesima.
quadragesimale, *a.* (*Eccles.*) Lenten.
quadragesimo [quadragEsimo], *a.* Fortieth.
quadraio [quadrAio], *n.m.* Picture-seller.
quadramento, *n.m.* Squaring.
quadrangolare, *a.* Quadrangular.
quadrangolo [quadrAngolo], *n.m.* Quadrangle.
quadrante, *n.m.* Quadrant; clock-face, dial; portable sun-dial; (*Hist.*) old Roman coin. **Pagare fin all'ultimo —,** to pay to the last farthing.
quadrare, *v.t.i.* To square; to fit, to suit, to agree; to adjust; (*Comm.*) to balance. **Ciò non gli quadrava,** that wasn't to his liking.
quadrato, *n.m.* Square; (*Naut.*) ward-room.
quadrato, *a.* Square; (*fig.*) shrewd, sensible; firm, determined. (*Math.*) **Radice quadrata,** square root; **una testa quadrata,** head screwed on the right way; **metro —,** square metre.
quadratura, *n.f.* Squaring; quadrature.
quadrella, *n.f.* Large, four-sided file.
quadrello (*pl.* **quadrelli,** *m.*, **quadrella,** *f.*), *n.m.* (*Hist.*) Arrow, quarrel; square tile; brick; flooring-tile.
quadreria [quadrerIa], *n.f.* Picture-gallery.
quadrettato, *a.* Chequered (of fabric), check.
quadretto, quadrettino, *n.m.* Small square, check. **Stoffa a quadretti,** check cloth.
quadri, *n.m.pl.* (*Cards*) Diamonds.
quadriennio [quadriEnnio], *n.m.* Term of four years.
quadrifogliato, *a.* Four-leaved.
quadrifoglio [quadrifOglio], *n.m.* (*Bot.*) Four-leaved clover, shamrock.
quadriforme, *a.* Square, four-sided.
quadriga, *n.f.* (*Hist.*) Quadriga, chariot.
quadriglia [quadrIglia], *n.f.* Quadrille; check square (in fabric).
quadrigliati, *n.m.pl.* (*Cards*) Italian card game.
quadrilatero [quadrilAtero], *n.m.a.* Quadrilateral.
quadrimestre, *n.m.* Term of four months.
quadrimotore, *n.m.* (*Aviat.*) Four-engined plane.
quadripartire, *v.t.* To divide into four parts.
quadrireme, *n.f.* (*Naut. Hist.*) Quadrireme galley.
quadrivio [quadrIvio], *n.m.* Cross-roads, four-cross-way.
quadro, *n.m.* Picture, painting; square, check; view, outline; framework; panel, list; (*Mil.*) cadre. **In —,** square; (*Mil.*) **completare i quadri,** to complete the staff; (*Elec.*) **— commutatore,** switch-board.
quadro, *a.* Square; (*fig.*) sensible. **Vela quadra,** square sail; **spalle quadre,** square shoulders.
quadrotto, *n.m.* Square-ruled paper.
quadrumane [quadrUmane], *n.m.* (*Zool.*) Quadrumane, primate.
quadrupede [quadrUpede], *n.m.* (*Zool.*) Quadruped.
quadruplicare, *v.t.* To multiply by four, to quadruplicate.
quadruplicatamente, *adv.* In quadruplicate.
quadruplo [quAdruplo], *n.m.* Quadruple.
quaggiù, *adv.* Down here, here below; in this world.
quaglia [quAglia], *n.f.* (*Zool.*) Quail.
quagliamento, *n.m.* Curdling.
quagliare, quagliarsi, *v.t.i.r.* To curdle.
quagliata, *n.f.* Junket.
quaglio [quAglio], *n.m.* Rennet.
qualche, *a.* Some, a few, any. **— libro,** some books, a few books; **in — luogo,** somewhere; **— volta,** sometimes; **in — modo,** somehow; **non lo vedo da — tempo,** I have not seen him for some time.
qualcosa, qualchecosa, *n.f.* Something, anything; more or less.
qualcuno, qualcheduno, *pron.* Somebody, anybody, someone, something. **Diventar —,** to become someone, to rise in the world.
quale, *pron.a.* Which, what; who; some; as, just as. **— vuoi?** Which do you want? **— visse tale morì,** as he lived so did he die; **l'amico del — parlai,** the friend of whom I spoke; **— rovina!** What a ruin! **colui il —,** he who; **il libro al — vi riferite,** the book to which you refer; **uomo che non è tanto per la —,** a man who behaves badly.
qualifica [qualIfica], *n.f.* Qualification, title, attribute.
qualificabile [qualificAbile], *a.* Qualifiable.
qualificare, *v.t.* To qualify; to describe, to designate.
qualificativo, *a.* Qualifying.
qualità [-à], *n.f.* Quality; nature, property, attribute; kind, sort. **Di prima —,** of the first quality; **belle —,** good qualities.
qualitativo, *a.* Qualitative.
qualmente, *adv.* How, as. **Come —,** in which way, how.
qualora, *adv.* In case, given that, if ever; whenever.
qualsiasi, qualsisia, qualsivoglia [qualsIasi], *pron.* Whichever, whatsoever, whatever; any.
qualunque, *pron.a.* Whatever, whichever; every, each, any, either. **A — costo,** at any cost; **una persona —,** an ordinary person; **uomo —,** (also **uomo della strada**), the man in the street.
qualvolta, *adv.* Whenever. **Ogni —,** whenever.
quando, *adv.* When, whenever. **Quand'ecco!** Lo and behold! **fin —?** until when? **a — a —, di — in —,** now and again; from time to time; **quand'anche,** even if; **da — in qua?** since when? **— a piedi — a cavallo,** sometimes on foot sometimes on horseback; **il — te lo dirò,** I'll tell you exactly when.
quantità [-à], *n.f.* Quantity; extent, size, measure. **In —,** in plenty; **una grande —,** a great lot, a great deal.
quantitativo, *n.m.* (*Comm.*) Amount, quantity. **Il — disponibile,** the available amount.

Q R

quanto, *n.m.* As much as, how much. **— ha sofferto,** all he has suffered; **tutti quanti, tutto —,** everybody, everything.
quanto, *a.* How much, as much as, as long as, as far as. **Quanta gente,** how many people; **avrà — danaro gli occorre,** he will have as much money as he needs; **— rumore!** What a noise.
quanto? *pron.* How much? **— costa?** how much is it? **Quanti siamo?** How many are we?
quanto, *adv.* How, how much; as. **In — a,** as for, with regard to; **per — sia forte,** for all his strength; **bella quant'altra mai,** beautiful as can be; **— a me,** as for me; **— agli altri,** as for the others; **in — che,** inasmuch as; **per — si dica,** whatever they may say; **per — strano sembri,** strange as it may seem.
quantunque [quantUnque], *conj.* Although, though.
quaranta, *n.m.a.* Forty.
quarantamila, *n.m.a.* Forty thousand.
quarantena, *n.f.* Quarantine. **Mettere in —,** to put in quarantine.
quarantenne, *a.* Forty years old.
quarantennio [quarantEnnio], *n.m.* Term of forty years.
quarantesimo [quarantEsimo], *a.* Fortieth.
quarantina, *n.f.* Set of forty, about forty; forty years of age; (*Med.*) quarantine.
quarantottata, *n.f.* Rash venture; noisy speeches.
quarantottesco, *a.* Of the year 1848; (*fig.*) warlike; noisy; swaggering.
quarantotto, *n.m.a.* Forty-eight; (*Hist.*) the revolutionary year 1848; (*colloq.*) confusion. **Fare il —,** to start a pandemonium.
quaresima [quarEsima], *n.f.* (*Eccles.*) Lent.
quaresimale, *n.m.a.* Lenten sermon; Lenten.
quaresimalista (*pl.* **quaresimalisti**), *n.m.* Lenten preacher.
quarta, *n.f.* Quadrant; quarter.
quartabono, *n.m.* Set-square; carpenter's square.
quartale, *n.m.* (*Theat.*) Fourth part of an actor's salary.
quartana, *a.* (*Med.*) Quartan. **Febbre —,** quartan ague.
quartato, *a.* Quartered; sturdy (in physique).
quartetto, *n.m.* (*Mus.*) Quartet.
quarticello, *n.m.* Small quarter; about a quarter of an hour.
quartiere, *n.m.* Quarter (of city, ship, etc.), district; quarters, lodgings, flat; (*Mil.*) quarter. **Non dar —,** to give no quarter; **— generale,** headquarters.
quartierino, *n.m.* Small apartment, small flat.
quartiermastro, *n.m.* Quarter-master.
quartina, *n.f.* (*Poet.*) Quatrain.
quartino, *n.m.* (*Mus.*) Flageolet; small clarinet; small wine-measure (about a pint).
quartirolo, *n.m.* Kind of cheese from Lombardy.
quarto, *n.m.a.* Quarter; fourth; quarter of an hour; (*Print.*) quarto. **Un brutto — d'ora,** a bad quarter of an hour; **edizione in —,** quarto edition.
quartodecimo [quartodEcimo], *n.m.a.* Fourteenth.
quartogenito [quartogEnito], *n.m.* Fourth child of a family.
quartuccio [quartUccio], *n.m.* Fourth part of a litre (of wine).
quartultimo [quartUltimo], *n.m.a.* Fourth from the end.
quarzifero [quarzIfero], *a.* (*Geol.*) Quartziferous.
quarzo, *n.m.* (*Geol.*) Quartz.
quarzoso, *a.* Quartzy.
quasi, *adv.* Almost, nearly, approximately; as if, about. **Vengono — tutti,** nearly all of them are coming; **— —,** very nearly; **— ci vado,** I've half a mind to go; **senza —,** without hesitation.
quasimente, *adv.* (*colloq.*) Almost.
quassia [quAssia], *n.f.* (*Bot.*) Quassia.
quassù, *adv.* Up here.
quaterna [cp. **quaderna**].
quaternario [quaternArio], *a.* (*Geol.*) Quaternary.
quatriduano, *a.* Four days old, of four days.
quattamente, *adv.* Squattingly, squatly.
quatto, *a.* Squat, crouched; cowering. **Andarsene — —,** to slip away on the sly.
quattordicenne, *n.m.a.* Fourteen years old.
quattordicesimo, *n.m.a.* Fourteenth.
quattordici [quattOrdici], *n.m.a.* Fourteen.
quattrinaio [quattrinAio], *n.m.* Rich man, stingy fellow, miser.
quattrino, *n.m.* Farthing. **Quattrini,** money; **far quattrini,** to make money; **non vale un —,** it is worthless.
quattro, *n.m.a.* Four. **A quattr'occhi,** in private, tête-à-tête; **farsi in —,** to do one's utmost; **far — passi,** to take a stroll; **fare il diavolo a —,** to make the devil's own row; **dirgliene —,** to give him a piece of one's mind; **in — e quattr'otto,** right away, at once, suddenly; **come due e due fanno —,** as sure as eggs is eggs; **tiro a —,** four in hand (coach).
quattrocentesco, *a.* Of the 15th century.
quattrocentista (*pl.* **quattrocentisti**), *n.m.* Artist or author of the 15th century.
quattrocento, *n.m.* Four hundred; the 15th century.
quattromila, *a.* Four thousand.
quegli, quei, *pron.* He. **— rispose,** he answered.
quello, *a.* (*pl.* **quei, quegli, quella, quelle,** following the same rules as the definite article; as a *pron. pl.m.* **quelli**) That; he, she; what. **Non è più quello,** he is no longer the same; **è quello che ci vuole,** it is what we want; **e quello disse,** and he said; **in quella che,** at the very moment when; **da quel che vedo,** from what I see; **in quel di Padova,** in the neighbourhood of Padua; **quelli di Firenze,** the people of Florence; **quello degli altri,** other people's things.
querceto, *n.m.* Oak wood, oak plantation.
quercia (*pl.* **querce**) [quErcia], *n.f.* (*Bot.*) Oak, oak-tree.
quercino, *a.* Oak, oaken.
querciola, *n.f.* Small oak. **Far —,** to stand on one's head.
querela, *n.f.* Complaint; (*Law*) action at law, lawsuit. **Dar —,** to summons, to bring into court.
querelante, *n.m.* (*Law*) Plaintiff.
querelare, *v.t.* (*Law*) To bring an action against, to summons, to prosecute.

querelarsi, *v.r.* To take legal proceedings.
querimonia [querimOnia], *n.f.* Lamentation, complaint, querulousness.
querulo [quErulo], *a.* Querulous, complaining, peevish.
quesito, *n.m.* Problem, query, question. **Proporre un —,** to pose a problem, to put a question.
questi, *pron.* He, this one, this person.
questionabile [questionAbile], *a.* Doubtful, questionable.
questionamento, *n.m.* Questioning, doubting, doubt.
questionare, *v.i.* To quarrel, to dispute, to wrangle.
questionario [questionArio], *n.m.* Set of questions, questionnaire; exam papers.
questione, *n.f.* Question, inquiry; proposition, subject, matter; dispute, controversy, contrast; law suit. **Fuor di —,** out of the question; **venire a —,** to quarrel, to start an argument; **la — capitale,** the main question.
questo, *a.pron.* This, this one; the latter. **Quest'oggi,** to-day, this very day; **questa è bella,** this is a nice thing; **— o quello,** this or that; (*colloq.*) **con — ti saluto,** with this I say good-bye; **— poi no!** That won't do!
questore, *n.m.* Chief constable (in large towns); (*Pol.*) parliamentary whip; (*Hist.*) quaestor.
questua [quEstua], *n.f.* Begging, request for alms; collection of alms.
questuante, *n.m.a.* Beggar; begging.
questuare, *v.i.* To beg; to seek for alms.
questura, *n.f.* Police office, police headquarters.
questurino, *n.m.* Police agent.
queto [cp. **quieto**].
qui, *adv.* Here. **Son qui,** I'm here; **nativo di qui,** native of this place; **di qui non si passa,** no thoroughfare, no admittance here; **da qui a qui,** from here to here; **qui presso,** close by, near here; **di qui a domani,** from now until tomorrow; **venite di qui,** come this way; **di qui a due giorni,** in two days, two days hence.
quia, *adv.* Because. **Stare al —,** to be reasonable; **venire al —,** to come to the point.
quiddità [-à], *n.f.* Quiddity.
quiescente, *a.* Quiescent.
quiescenza, *n.f.* Quiescence. **Trattamento di —,** retiring pension.
quietamente, *adv.* Quietly.
quietamento, *n.m.* Quietening, quieting.
quietanza, *n.f.* (*Comm.*) Receipt, quittance.
quietanzare, *v.t.* To give a receipt for, to receipt a bill, etc.
quietare, *v.t.* To quiet, to calm, to appease, to soothe.
quietarsi, *v.r.* To quiet down, to become quiet.
quiete, *n.f.* Quiet, quietness, calm, calmness, rest, tranquillity, peace.
quietismo, *n.m.* (*Relig.*) Quietism.
quieto, *a.* Quiet, calm, peaceful, placid; mild, retired.
quietudine [quietUdine], *n.f.* Quietude.
quinario [quinArio], *n.m.* (*Poet.*) line of five syllables.
quinci, *adv.* Hence, from here.
quindi, *adv.* Hence, therefore, then; afterwards. **Quind'innanzi,** from this time forward, henceforward; **— è inutile,** so it is useless.
quindicenne, *n.m.a.* Fifteen years old.
quindicesimo [quindicEsimo], *n.m.a.* Fifteenth.
quindici [quIndici], *a.* Fifteen.
quindicimila, *a.* Fifteen thousand.
quindicina, *n.f.* Fortnight.
quindicinale, *a.* Fortnightly.
quinquagenario [quinquagenArio], *n.m.a.* (Person) fifty years old.
quinquagesima [quinquagEsima], *n.f.* (*Eccles.*) Quinquagesima Sunday.
quinquennale, *a.* Quinquennial.
quinquennio [quinquEnnio], *n.m.* Quinquennium, period of five years.
quinta, *n.f.* (*Mus.*) Fifth; (*Theat.*) wings, flies. (*fig.*) **Dietro le quinte,** behind the scenes.
quintale, *n.m.* Quintal (hundred kilos).
quinterno, *n.m.* Five sheets of paper, quire; copy-book.
quintessenza, *n.f.* Quintessence.
quintetto, *n.m.* *Mus.*) Quintet; party of five persons.
quintina, *n.f.* Five winning numbers in the State lottery.
quintino, *n.m.* Wine measure, fifth of a litre.
quinto, *n.m.a.* Fifth. **Quinta colonna,** Fifth Column.
quintogenito [quintogEnito], *n.m.* Fifth child of a family.
quintultimo quintUltimo], *n.m.* Last but five.
quintuplicare, *v.t.* To multiply fivefold.
quintuplice, *a.* Fivefold.
quintuplo [quIntuplo], *n.m.* Fivefold amount.
quiritta, *adv.* (*obs.*) Precisely here, just here.
quisquiglia, quisquilia [quisquIglia, quisquIlia], *n.f.* Trifle, triviality.
quissimile [quissImile], *n.m.* Something similar, something of the sort.
quistione [cp. **questione**].
quitanza [cp. **quietanza**].
quivi, *adv.* There; then.
quondam, *adv.* Formerly, late (deceased). **Il — re,** the late king.
quota, *n.f.* Quota, part, share, contribution; (*Mil.*) Height, hill, elevation; (*Aviat.*) height. (*Mil.*) **— 188,** hill 188; (*Aviat.*) **prendere —,** to climb, to gain height; **volare a bassa —,** to fly low; **— di volo,** altitude.
quotare, *v.t.* To assess, to value; to quote (prices, etc.).
quotazione, *n.f.* (*Comm.*) Quotation (of prices).
quotidiano, *n.m.a.* Daily (newspaper); daily.
quotidianamente, *adv.* Daily, every day.
quotizzare, *v.t.* (*Comm.*) To assess.
quotizzazione, *n.f.* Assessment.
quoto, quoziente, *n.m.* (*Math.*) Quotient; ratio.

R

R, r, *n.f.* Sixteenth letter of the Italian alphabet. **Perdere l'R, perdere l'erre,** to go out of one's mind.
rabarbaro [rabArbaro], *n.m.* (*Bot.*) Rhubarb.
rabattino, *n.m.a.* Hard worker, toiler; hard-working.

rabballinare, *v.t.* To wrap up, to roll up, to pack inside.
rabbaruffare, *v.t.* To pull about, to discompose, to ruffle.
rabbaruffarsi, *v.r.* To scuffle together, to rumple one's dress; to become discomposed.
rabbassare, *v.t.* To lower again.
rabbattere [rabbAttere], *v.t.* To pull a door to, to leave on the jar, to half-close (window, etc.).
rabbatuffolare [cp. **abbatuffolare**].
rabbellire, *v.t.* To embellish, to furbish up once more.
rabbellirsi, *v.r.* To improve in looks; to adorn oneself.
rabberciamento, *n.m.* Botching, patching.
rabberciare, *v.t.* To botch, to patch, to patch up.
rabberciatore, rabberciatrice, *n.m.f.* Botcher, patcher, mender.
rabberciatura, *n.f.* Botching, patching up, mending.
rabbi, *n.m.* Rabbi.
rabbia [rAbbia], *n.f.* Rage, fury, passionate anger; rabies, hydrophobia. **Muovere a —,** to enrage someone; **la — del danaro,** the rage for wealth.
rabbinico [rabbInico], *a.* Rabbinic, rabbinical.
rabbino, *n.m.* Rabbi. **Il gran —,** the Chief Rabbi.
rabbiosamente, *adv.* Furiously, with extreme rage.
rabbioso, *a.* Furious, enraged, choleric; rabid.
rabbiuzza, *n.f.* Spite, grudge.
rabboccare, *v.t.* To fill to the brim; to refill; (*Tech.*) to grout (brickwork).
rabboccatura, *n.f.* Filling to the brim; grouting.
rabbonacciare, *v.i.* To grow quiet, to calm down (in temper).
rabbonacciarsi, *v.r.* To become friends again, to be reconciled.
rabbonire, *v.t.* To appease, to pacify, to calm.
rabbonirsi, *v.r.* To become pacified, to become quiet.
rabbriccicare, *v.t.* To patch up, to make the best of it.
rabbrividire, *v.i.* To shiver, to shudder (with fear).
rabbrunare, *v.t.* To make darker.
rabbruscamento, *n.m.* Darkening (of the sky), becoming overcast.
rabbruscare, *v.i.* To darken (of the sky), to become overcast, to be threatening (of the weather).
rabbruscarsi, *v.r.* To become morose, to get into a black mood.
rabbruscolare, *v.t.* To save, to save up.
rabbuffamento, *n.m.* Disorder; reprimand.
rabbuffare, *v.t.* To throw into disorder, to disorder, to ruffle, to discompose; to reprimand.
rabbuffarsi, *v.r.* To become ruffled; to be overcast (of the weather).
rabbuffo, *n.m.* Stern rebuke, reprimand.
rabbuiare, rabbuiarsi, *v.i.r.* To grow dark (of the sky). **Il tempo si rabbuia,** the weather is threatening.
rabdomante, *n.m.* Dowser, water-diviner.
rabdomanzia [rabdomanzIa], *n.f.* Water-divining, dowsing.
rabelesiano, *a.* Rabelaisian.
rabescare, *v.t.* To ornament with arabesques.
rabesco, *n.m.* Arabesque.
rabicano, *n.m.* Bay horse with coat flecked with white hairs.
rabido [rAbido], *a.* Rabid.
raccapezzare, *v.t.* To make out, to understand, to find out; to collect (facts); to gather one's thoughts.
raccapezzarsi, *v.r.* To understand, to make out; to find one's way. **Non mi ci raccapezzo,** I can't make it out.
raccapricciamento, *n.m.* Striking with horror.
raccapricciante, *a.* Ghastly; terrifying.
raccapricciare, *v.t.* To horrify, to frighten, to terrify.
raccapricciarsi, *v.r.* To be horrified, to be terrified; to shake with terror.
raccapriccio [raccaprIccio], *n.m.* Horror; fear, terror; disgust.
raccartocciare, *v.t.* To curl up.
raccartocciarsi, *v.r.* To curl, to curl up.
raccattacenere [raccattacEnere], *n.m.* Ash-pan; ash-tray.
raccattare, *v.t.* To pick up (from the ground), to collect.
raccattaticcio [raccattatIccio], *n.m.* Rubbish, valueless trifles.
raccattatore, raccattatrice, *n.m.f.* Gatherer, picker-up.
raccattatura, *n.f.* Rubbish, collections of worthless trifles.
raccenciare, *v.t.* To mend, to patch up.
raccenciarsi, *v.r.* To wear better clothes, to put on a better appearance; (*fig.*) to improve one's personal affairs.
raccertare, raccertarsi, *v.i.r.* To make quite sure; to confirm one's opinions.
racchetare, *v.t.* To quiet, to soothe, to comfort.
racchetta, *n.f.* Racquet, racket.
racchiocciolarsi, *v.r.* To curl up, to curl into a ball; to shrink into, to cower, to huddle up.
racchiudere [racchiUdere], *v.t.* To contain, to enclose, to hold; to shut up.
racciabattare, *v.t.* To patch, to patch up, to cobble, to botch.
raccoccare, *v.t.* To readjust, to adjust afresh.
raccogliere [raccOgliere], *v.t.* To gather, to collect together, to pick up; to pluck (flowers, etc.); to gather in, to reap. **— francobolli,** to collect stamps; **— pere,** to pick pears; **— allori,** to gather laurels; **— le forze,** to gather together one's strength; **— la sfida,** to take up the challenge; **chi semina vento raccoglie tempesta,** who sows the wind reaps the whirlwind.
raccogliersi [raccOgliersi], *v.r.* To assemble, to collect one's thoughts, to concentrate, to reflect; to pull oneself together.
raccoglimento, *n.m.* Gathering, collection; concentration (of mind), absorption; meditation, retirement.
raccogliticcio [raccoglitIccio], *n.m.a.* Gathering of odds and ends; assemblage of persons; picked up haphazardly, gathered here and there. **Truppe raccogliticce,** troops mustered at random.

raccoglitore, raccoglitrice, *n.m.f.* Collector, gatherer, compiler.
raccolta, *n.f.* Collection; harvest; assembly. **Una — di libri rari,** a collection of rare books; (*Mil.*) **chiamare a —,** to rally.
raccoltamente, *adv.* Meditatively, attentively, contemplatively.
raccolto, *n.m.* Harvest, crop.
raccolto, *p.p.a.* Gathered, collected; compact; quiet. **Un quartiere—,** a quiet quarter (of a town). **—in se stesso,** retired within himself.
raccomandabile [raccomandAbile], *a.* Suitable for recommendation; recommendable.
raccomandare, *v.t.* To recommend; to commit, to entrust; to register by post.
raccomandarsi, *v.r.* To recommend oneself; to implore, to entreat. **— a Dio,** to commend oneself to God; **mi raccomando,** please don't forget; please do this; **— alle gambe,** to run away.
raccomandata, *n.f.* Registered letter.
raccomandatario [raccomandatArio], *n.m.* Person who is recommended (by letter).
raccomandato, *p.p.a.* Recommended; registered (of a letter).
raccomandazione, *n.f.* Recommendation; registration (of a letter).
raccomodamento, *n.m.* Mending, repairing.
raccomodare, *v.t.* To mend, to repair, to put in order.
raccomodatore, raccomodatrice, *n.m.f.* Repairer.
raccomodatura, *n.f.* Repairing, mending, putting right.
racconciamento, *n.m.* Repairing.
racconciare, *v.t.* To mend, to repair; to amend.
racconciarsi, *v.r.* To be reconciled; to clear up (a difficulty); to settle (of the weather); to recover (one's health, looks, etc.).
racconciatura, *n.f.* Mending, repairing; clearing (of the weather).
racconcio [raccOncio], *a.* Repaired, mended, put to rights; improved.
raccontabile [raccontAbile], *a.* Worth the telling, fit to be told.
raccontafavole [raccontafAvole], *n.m.* Liar, story-teller.
raccontare, *v.t.* To tell, to relate, to recount, to narrate.
raccontatore, raccontatrice, *n.m.f.* Narrator.
racconto, *n.m.* Tale, story, narrative, narration, relation; report.
raccoppiare, *v.t.* To reunite.
raccorciamento, *n.m.* Shortening, contraction; retrenchment.
raccorciare, raccorcire, *v.t.* To shorten.
raccorciarsi, *v.r.* To grow shorter, to shrink.
raccorcio [raccOrcio], *n.m., a.* Shortening, shrinkage; shortened.
raccordamento, *n.m.* Connection, link up.
raccordare, *v.t.* To connect, to link together.
raccordo, *n.m.* Connection. (*Rail.*) **— ferroviario,** railway-junction; **— binario,** siding.
raccostamento, *n.m.* Bringing together, causing to approach, comparison.
raccostare, *v.t.* To bring near, to bring together, to bring close; to compare, to put side by side.
raccostarsi, *v.r.* To get close together, to become friends again.
raccozzare, *v.t.* To bring together.
raccozzarsi, *v.r.* To assemble, to get together; to meet.
racemo, *n.m.* (*Bot.*) Raceme; bunch of grapes.
Rachele, *n.f.* Rachel.
rachitico [rachItico], *a.* (*Med.*) Rickety; (*Bot.*) stunted.
rachitide [rachItide], *n.f.* (*Med.*) Rickets.
rachitismo, *n.m.* Rickets; stuntedness.
racimolare, *v.t.* To pick (grapes), to glean (grapes); (*fig.*) to pick up here and there, to scrape together.
racimolatore, racimolatrice, *n.m.f.* Gleaner, picker, collector.
racimolatura, *n.f.* Gleaning; what is gleaned (of grapes).
racimolo [racImolo], *n.m.* Small bunch of grapes, raceme.
racquietare, *v.t.* To quieten.
racquietarsi, *v.r.* To calm oneself.
racquistamento, *n.m.* Recovery (of an object).
racquistare, *v.t.* To recover, to regain, to get once more.
racquisto, *n.m.* Recovery, regaining.
rada, *n.f.* (*Naut.*) Roadstead, roads.
radamente, *adv.* Thinly, sparsely, rarely, seldom.
radancia [radAncia], *n.f.* (*Naut.*) Thimble.
radar, *n.m.* (*Radio*) Radar.
radatura, *n.f.* Bare place (in cloth); bald patch (on the head).
radazza, *n.f.* Mop, swab.
radazzare, *v.t.* (*Naut.*) To swab (the deck).
raddensabile [raddensAbile], *a.* Capable of being thickened.
raddensamento, *n.m.* Thickening, becoming thicker.
raddensare, *v.t.* To thicken, to make thicker, to condense further.
raddensarsi, *v.r.* To become thicker.
raddirizzamento, *n.m.* Putting straight.
raddirizzare, *v.t.* To correct, to put straight again; to send to the right.
raddirizzarsi, *v.r.* To turn to the right.
raddobbare, *v.t.* (*Naut.*) To refit, to repair.
raddobbo, *n.m.* Repair, repairing; refitting.
raddolcimento, *n.m.* Sweetening, softening, appeasing.
raddolcire, *v.t.* To sweeten, to soften; to soothe, to assuage.
raddolcirsi, *v.r.* To get sweet, to be soothed; to become mild (of weather).
raddoppiamento, *n.m.* Doubling, reduplication.
raddoppiare, *v.t.* To double, to redouble. **— gli sforzi,** to redouble one's efforts.
raddoppiatamente, *adv.* Doubly; in twice the quantity or extent.
raddoppio [raddOppio], *n.m.* Doubling, redoubling; (*Billiards*) double.
raddrizzamento, *n.m.* Straightening; redressing (an injustice, etc.).
raddrizzare, *v.t.* To straighten, to put right [cp. **raddirizzare**].
raddrizzatore, *n.m.* (*Elect.*) Rectifier.
raddurre [cp. **ridurre**].
radere [rAdere], *v.t.* To shave; to graze, to raze, to erase; to skip. **— al suolo,** to raze to the ground.
radersi, *v.r.* To shave oneself, to shave.

radezza, *n.f.* Sparseness, rarity, thinness (of distribution); infrequency.
radiale, *a.* Radial, radiating.
radiante, *a.* Radiant, beaming, shining.
radiare (1), *v.t.* To cancel, to erase, to strike off (from a list, etc.).
radiare (2), *v.i.* To radiate, to emit rays, to beam, to shine.
radiato, *p.p.a.* Erased, cancelled, struck off; radiated; surrounded by rays.
radiatore, *n.m.* Radiator (in all senses).
radiazione, *n.f.* Radiation; cancellation.
radica [rAdica], *n.f.* Root; brier-wood.
radicale, *n.m.a.* Radical (in all senses); *n.f.* (*Gram.*) root.
radicalismo, *n.m.* (*Pol.*) Radicalism.
radicalmente, *adv.* Radically.
radicamento, *n.m.* Taking root, striking root.
radicare, radicarsi, *v.t.r.* To root, to take root.
radicato, *p.p.a.* Rooted, deep-seated.
radicchia, radicchiella [radIcchia], *n.f.* (*Bot.*) Dandelion.
radicchio [radIcchio], *n.m.* Wild chicory.
radice, *n.f.* Root (in all senses); origin, source; (*Bot.*) radish. (*Math.*) **— quadrata,** square root; **prender —,** to take root; **liberarsi da una — guasta,** to have the decayed root (of a tooth) removed.
radio [rAdio] (1), *n.m.* (*Min.*) Radium.
radio [rAdio] (2), *n.f.* Radio, wireless, broadcasting-station. **Trasmettere per —,** to broadcast; **ascoltare la —,** to listen in.
radioattività [-à], *n.f.* Radioactivity.
radioattivo, *a.* Radioactive.
radiocomunicazione, *n.f.* Radio communication.
radiocronaca [radiocrOnaca], *n.f.* News broadcast.
radiocronista (*pl.* **radiocronisti**), *n.m.* Radio commentator; news broadcaster.
radiodiffusione, *n.f.* Broadcasting.
radiofaro, *n.m.* Radio beacon.
radiofonico [radiofOnico], *a.* Wireless, radio. **Apparecchio —,** wireless set; **stazione radiofonica,** wireless station, broadcasting station; **programma —,** broadcasting programme.
radiogenico [radiogEnico], *a.* Suitable for broadcasting, radiogenic. **Voce radiogenica,** good broadcasting voice.
radiogoniometro [radiogoniOmetro], *n.m.* Radio direction-finder.
radiografare, *v.t.* To X-ray, to take an X-ray photograph.
radiografia [radiografIa], *n.f.* Radiography.
radiogramma, *n.f.* Radiogram, Marconigram.
radiogrammofono, *n.m.* Radio-gramophone.
radiologia [radiologIa], *n.f.* Radiology.
radiologo [radiOlogo], *n.m.* Radiologist.
radioscopia [radioscopIa], *n.f.* Radioscopy.
radiosità [-à], *n.f.* Brightness, radiance.
radioso, *a.* Radiant, bright, beaming.
radiotelefono, *n.m.* Radio-telephone.
radiotelegrafare, *v.t.* To send a radio message.
radiotelegrafia [radiotelegrafIa], *n.f.* Radiotelegraphy.
radiotelegrafista (*pl.* **radiotelegrafisti**), *n.m.* Wireless operator.
radiotelegramma, *n.m.* Marconigram, wireless cable, radio-telegramme.
radioterapia [radioterapIa], *n.f.* Radiotherapy.
radiotrasmettere [radiotrasmEttere], *v.t.* To broadcast. **Stazione trasmittente,** broadcasting station.
radiotrasmissione, *n.f.* Broadcasting.
radissimamente, *adv.* Very thinly, very sparsely.
raditura, *n.f.* Erasing, scratching out; shaving.
rado, *a.* Sparse, rare, infrequent, thin, scattered; occasional; seldom. **Capelli radi,** thin hair; **di —,** seldom.
radunamento, *n.m.* Assemblage, meeting, assembly.
radunanza, *n.f.* Assembly, gathering.
radunare, radunarsi, *v.i.r.* To assemble, to gather, to collect, to muster.
radunata, *n.f.* Assembly, gathering, rally.
raduno, *n.m.* Rally, gathering.
radura, *n.f.* (Forest) glade; bare patch.
rafano [rAfano], *n.m.* (*Bot.*) Horse radish, radish.
Raffaele, *n.m.* Raphael.
raffaellesco, *a.* After the style of Raphael.
Raffaello, *n.m.* Raphael (the artist).
raffazzonamento, *n.m.* Patching up, mending, repairing; refashioning, recasting.
raffazzonare, *v.t.* To patch, to mend; to recast.
raffazzonatore, raffazzonatrice, *n.m.f.* Repairer, mender.
raffazzonatura, *n.f.* Patching, repairing, refashioning.
rafferma, *n.f.* Confirmation (of particulars); (*Mil.*) re-enlistment.
raffermare, *v.t.* To confirm, to strengthen, to solidify; to renew (a contract, etc.); to re-enlist, to re-engage.
raffermarsi, *v.r.* To become consolidated, to get harder; to re-engage oneself.
raffermo, *a.* Firm, hard; stale (of bread).
raffibbiare, *v.t.* To buckle again.
raffica [rAffica], *n.f.* Squall, violent gust of wind; hail shower. **— di proiettili,** shower of bullets.
raffidare, *v.t.* To reassure, to give confidence.
raffidarsi, *v.r.* To assure oneself, to reassure oneself. **Mi raffido a te,** I place my confidence in you.
raffigurabile [raffigurAbile], *a.* Recognizable.
raffiguramento, *n.m.* Representation, recognition.
raffigurare, *v.t.* To recognize; to represent, to resemble, to symbolize.
raffigurarsi, *v.r.* To imagine.
raffigurazione, *n.f.* Recognition.
raffilare, *v.t.* To sharpen, to whet, to grind, to set, to hone; to pare.
raffilatoio [raffilatOio], *n.m.* Sharpener, clipper, parer.
raffilatura, *n.f.* Sharpening, setting, whetting; paring.
raffinamento, *n.m.* Refining, thinning.
raffinare, *v.t.* To refine; to pare down, to make thinner.
raffinarsi, *v.r.* To become refined; to become thinner; (*fig.*) to become sly.
raffinatamente, *adv.* Refinedly.

raffinatezza, *n.f.* Refinement.
raffinato, *a.* Refined (in all senses); subtle, ingenious, polished.
raffinatoio [raffinatOio], *n.f.* Refiner's furnace.
raffinatore, *n.m.* Refiner.
raffinatura, *n.f.* Refinement.
raffineria [raffinerIa], *n.f.* Refinery; sugar refinery.
raffio [rAffio], *n.m.* Hook, grappling-iron; harpoon.
raffittire, raffittirsi, *v.i.r.* To thicken, to get thick.
rafforzamento, *n.m.* Reinforcement, strengthening.
rafforzare, *v.t.* To reinforce, to strengthen.
rafforzarsi, *v.r.* To be strengthened, to become stronger, to be fortified.
raffreddamento, *n.m.* Cooling; abatement, slackening off.
raffreddare, *v.t.* To cool.
raffreddarsi, *v.r.* To cool off, to cool down; to catch cold.
raffreddato, *p.p.a.* Cooled off, cold. **Essere —,** to have a cold.
raffreddore, *n.m.* Cold, chill. **— di petto,** cold on the chest; **prendere un —,** to catch a cold.
raffrenare, *v.t.* To restrain, to curb, to check, to repress.
raffrenarsi, *v.r.* To restrain oneself, to hold oneself in *or* back.
raffrescamento, *n.m.* Cooling.
raffrescare, *v.t.* To cool [cp. **rinfrescare**].
raffrescarsi, *v.r.* To grow cool, to become cool, to turn cooler.
raffrescata, *n.f.* Cooling; fall in the temperature.
raffrontamento, *n.m.* Comparison.
raffrontare, *v.t.* To compare, to confront with; to bring together; to collate.
raffrontarsi, *v.r.* To compare oneself with.
raffronto, *n.m.* Comparison.
rafia [rAfia], *n.f.* Rafia.
raganella, *n.f.* (*Zool.*) Tree-frog; rattle, clapper.
ragazza, *n.f.* Girl; maid, maiden; sweetheart.
ragazzaglia [ragazzAglia], *n.f.* Crowd of children; gang of noisy boys.
ragazzata, *n.f.* Childish action, boyish prank, trick.
ragazzetto, ragazzino, *n.m.* Little boy, young lad.
ragazzo, *n.m.* Boy, lad; shop-boy; young waiter.
ragazzotto, *n.m.* Sturdy youngster, big boy.
ragazzume, *n.m.* Crowd of youngsters.
raggentilire, *v.t.* To make refined, to educate, to teach good manners to.
raggentilirsi, *v.r.* To improve in manners.
raggiamento, *n.m.* Radiation, radiance; (*fig.*) extent, spread.
raggiante, *a.* Radiant; beaming, shining. **— di gioia,** radiant with delight.
raggiare, *v.i.* To radiate, to emit rays, to shine.
raggiera, *n.f.* Aureole, halo; (*Eccles.*) rays of a monstrance.
raggio [rAggio], *n.m.* Ray of light, beam; gleam; (*Geom.*) radius; spoke (of a wheel). **— di speranza,** ray of hope. **— d'affari,** business district or circuit.
raggiornare (1), *v.t.* To postpone to another day [cp. **aggionare**].
raggiornare (2), *v.i.* To dawn, to start another day.
raggiramento, *n.m.* Swindle, trick, deceit.
raggirare, *v.t.* To cheat, to swindle, to trick, to deceive.
raggirarsi, *v.r.* To turn about, to go around; to ramble. **— nel letto,** to turn in one's bed.
raggiratore, raggiratrice, *n.m.f.* Swindler, cheat, trickster.
raggiro, *n.m.* Trick, cheat, subterfuge.
raggiungere [raggiUngere], *v.t.* To overtake, to rejoin, to attain; to hit (a target); to achieve, to acquire; to reach. **— il limite,** to reach the limit.
raggiungersi [raggiUngersi], *v.r.* To reunite, to join again; to meet again.
raggiungimento, *n.m.* Attainment, achievement. **Al — dell'età maggiore,** on reaching one's majority; **— dello scopo,** attainment of one's ends.
raggiustamento, *n.m.* Readjustment, repairing; reconciliation.
raggiustare, *v.t.* To readjust, to repair; to reconcile.
raggiustarsi, *v.r.* To be reconciled, to become friends again.
raggomitolamento, *n.m.* Coiling, rolling up, winding into a ball.
raggomitolare, *v.t.* To roll up, to make into a ball, to coil.
raggomitolarsi, *v.r.* To curl up, to shrink; to roll oneself up.
raggranchito, *a.* Numbed, benumbed.
raggranellare, *v.t.* To scrape together, to glean; to gather.
raggravamento, *n.m.* Making worse again, becoming worse.
raggravarsi, *v.r.* To become worse.
raggrinzamento, *n.m.* Wrinkling, shrivelling; frowning.
raggrinzare, raggrinzire, *v.t.i.* To wrinkle, to shrivel, to become wrinkled.
raggrinzarsi, raggrinzirsi, *v.r.* To become wrinkled.
raggrovigliare, *v.t.* [cp. **aggrovigliare**].
raggrumamento, *n.m.* Clotting.
raggrumare, raggrumarsi, *v.t.r.* To clot, to become clotted.
raggruppamento, *n.m.* Grouping; cluster, group.
raggruppare, *v.t.* To group, to assemble; to tie up together.
raggrupparsi, *v.r.* To form a group, to cluster, to form into a knot.
raggruzzolare, *v.t.* To collect savings, to save up.
ragguagliabile [ragguagliAbile], *a.* Comparable, capable of being equalized.
ragguagliamento, *n.m.* Equalization, levelling; comparison.
ragguagliare, *v.t.* To compare, to balance, to equalize, to level; to report, to inform. **— le partite,** to balance accounts.
ragguaglio [ragguAglio], *n.m.* Balance, comparison, equalization; report, information. **Ulteriori ragguagli,** further details.
ragguardevole [ragguardEvole], *a.* Considerable, notable, extensive, remarkable.
ragguardevolezza, *n.f.* Importance.

ragguardevolmente, *adv.* Considerably, extensively; importantly.
ragia [rAgia], *n.f.* Rosin, resin; (*fig.*) fraud, deceit.
ragionamento, *n.m.* Reasoning, discussion, argument.
ragionare, *v.i.* To argue, to discuss, to chat, to talk things over.
ragionatamente, *adv.* Reasonably, rationally, sensibly, logically.
ragionato, *a.* Logical, reasoned; talked over, discussed.
ragionatore, *n.m.* Reasoner.
ragione, *n.f.* Reason, judgement; law, right; account; justice, ownership; ratio, rate; price; (*Comm.*) style (of a firm); (*Comm.*) **— sociale,** firm. **Aver —,** to be right; **farsi una —,** to set one's mind at rest; **dar la — di una cosa,** to explain a thing; **render di pubblica —,** to make generally known; **avere buone ragioni,** to have good grounds (for belief); **dare — a,** to decide in favour of, to agree with; **rendersi —,** to understand, to account for; **a più forte —,** with greater reason; **non intendere —,** not to understand reason; **in — di quattro miglia all'ora,** at the rate of four miles an hour.
ragioneria [ragionerIa], *n.f.* Accountancy, book-keeping.
ragionevole, *a.* Reasonable.
ragionevolezza, *n.f.* Reasonableness.
ragionevolmente, *adv.* Reasonably.
ragioniere, *n.m.* Accountant, book-keeper.
ragliamento, *n.m.* Braying, bray (of an ass).
ragliare, *v.i.* To bray.
ragliata, *n.f.* Braying.
raglio [rAglio], *n.m.* Bray.
ragna, *n.f.* Spider's web, cobweb; fowling-net; floss silk; worn patch (in cloth).
ragnare, *v.i.* To become threadbare; to get filmy; (of the sky) to be covered with fleecy clouds; (*fig.*) to chafe, to fret; to set a snare.
ragnatela, ragnatelo, *n.f.m.* Spider's web, cobweb.
ragnato, *a.* Threadbare.
ragnatura, *n.f.* Bare patch in a garment.
ragno, *n.m.* (*Zool.*) Spider.
ragù [-ù], *n.m.* Ragout, stew.
rai, *n.m.pl.* (*Lit.*) Rays(of the sun).
Raimondo, *n.m.* Raymond.
raion [rAion], *n.m.* Rayon.
ralla, *n.f.* Cart-grease; swivel.
rallacciare, *v.t.* To retie, to tie up again.
rallargare, *v.t.* To widen.
rallargarsi, *v.r.* (Of the weather) to clear up, to clear.
rallegramento, *n.m.* Rejoicing, joy, mirth. **Far i rallegramenti a qualcuno,** to congratulate someone; **vivi rallegramenti,** hearty congratulations.
rallegrare, *v.t.* To cheer, to gladden, to cause to rejoice.
rallegrarsi, *v.r.* To rejoice, to be glad; to cheer up; to be delighted. **— con una persona,** to congratulate a person.
rallegrata, *n.f.* Horse's gambol.
rallegrativo, *a.* Cheering, heartening.
rallegratore, rallegratrice, *n.m.f.* One who rejoices.
rallegratura, *n.f.* Air of rejoicing, joyful air.
rallentamento, *n.m.* Slowing up, slackening, relaxation, lessening.
rallentare, *v.t.i.* To slow down, to lessen, to slacken, to relax. **Un film rallentato,** a slow-motion picture; **rallenta nel Corso,** slow down in the Corso; **— le corde,** to slacken the ropes; (*fig.*) to loosen the reins.
rallentarsi, *v.r.* To slow down, to become slack, to relax.
rallentatore, *n.m.* Slow-motion apparatus.
rallevare, *v.t.* To bring up a child.
rallignare, *v.i.* To take root, to strike root again.
rallino, *n.m.* Bed for the pintle of a gate.
ralluminare, *v.t.* To illuminate, to restore light to.
rallungare, *v.t.* To draw out, to extend.
rama, *n.f.* Branch, twig, bough, sprig.
ramaglia [ramAglia], *n.f.* Loppings, etc., from a tree.
ramaio [ramAio], *n.m.* Copper-smith, tinker.
ramaiolata, *n.f.* Ladleful.
ramaiolo, *n.m.* Ladle, soup-ladle.
ramanzina, *n.f.* Scolding, reprimand.
ramare, *v.t.* To copper, to plate with copper; (*Agric.*) to apply sulphate of copper.
ramarro, *n.m.* (*Zool.*) Green lizard.
ramatura, *n.f.* Coppering.
ramazza, *n.f.* Besom, twig broom.
rame, *n.m.* (*Min.*) Copper. **Moneta di —,** copper coin, small change.
ramerino, *n.m.* (*Bot.*) Rosemary.
rametto, ramicello, *n.m.* Twig, small branch.
ramiere, *n.m.* Copper-smith.
ramifero [ramIfero], *a.* Copper-bearing; branch-bearing.
ramificare, ramificarsi, *v.i.r.* To branch, to branch out, to ramify.
ramificazione, *n.f.* Ramification; branch.
ramifico [ramIfico], *a.* Producing branches.
ramingare, *v.i.* (*Lit.*) To wander, to roam, to ramble.
ramingo, *n.m.* Wandering, roaming, roving; solitary, hermit.
ramino, *n.m.* Copper pot, copper kettle.
rammaricare, *v.t.* To chagrin, to grieve; to render gloomy; to sadden; to vex, to torment.
rammaricarsi, *v.r.* To grieve, to regret; to complain; to fret.
rammarichio [rammarichIo], *n.m.* Continual lamentation, constant moaning.
rammarico [rammArico], *n.m.* Grief, sorrow, regret; groan. **Con profondo —,** with profound regret.
rammassare, *v.t.* To amass again; to gather up, to collect.
rammemorare, *v.i.* To remember.
rammendare, *v.t.* To darn, to mend.
rammendatrice, *n.f.* Mender, darner.
rammendatura, *n.f.* Darning, mending.
rammendo, *n.m.* Darn, repair, mending.
rammentare, *v.t.* To call to mind, to recall, to remind.
rammentarsi, *v.r.* To remember, to recollect.
rammentatore, *n.m.* Prompter, one who reminds.
rammodernare, *v.t.* To modernize, to bring up to date.
rammollimento, *n.m.* Softening. **— cerebrale,** softening of the brain.

rammollire, *v.t.* To soften, to mollify.
rammollirsi, *v.r.* To soften, to grow soft, to become effeminate.
rammorbidire, *v.t.* To soften.
rammortare, *v.t.* To tan, to steep.
rammucchiare, *v.t.* To collect, to gather.
ramno, *n.m.* (*Bot.*) Buckthorn.
ramo, *n.m.* Branch (in all senses); bough; arm (of a river); antler. **Un — di pazzia,** a touch of insanity; **un — d'affari,** a line of business.
ramolaccio [ramolAccio], *n.m.* (*Bot.*) Horse-radish.
ramoscello, *n.m.* Twig.
ramoso, *a.* Branched, full of branches.
rampa, *n.f.* Claw, paw; flight of stairs; ramp; steep slope.
rampante, *a.* (*Her.*) Rampant.
rampata, *n.f.* Slope.
rampicante, *n.m.* (*Zool.*) Climber; (*Bot.*) creeper.
rampicante, *a.* (*Bot.*) Rambling, climbing.
rampicare, rampicarsi, *v.i.r.* To climb, to clamber.
rampichino, *n.m.* (*Zool.*) Tree-creeper (bird).
rampicone, *n.m.* Grappling-iron.
rampinata, *n.f.* Strike with a hook, hook.
rampino, *n.m.* Hook, prong, prong of a fork.
rampogna, *n.f.* Rebuke, reproof.
rampognare, *v.t.* To reprove, to rebuke severely.
rampollare, *v.i.* To spring, to gush out, to shoot forth, to shoot up (of a plant).
rampollo, *n.m.* Spring (of water); scion, off-spring; (*colloq.*) child.
ramponare, *v.t.* To harpoon.
rampone, *n.m.* Harpoon.
rana, *n.f.* (*Zool.*) Frog. **Nuoto a —,** breast-stroke.
rancare, *v.i.* [cp. **arrancare**].
ranciato, *a.* Orange-coloured.
rancico [rAncico], *n.m.* Bad taste in the mouth (after eating sour food).
rancidezza, *n.f.* Rancidity, rancidness.
rancidire, *v.i.* To turn rancid.
rancidità [-à], *n.f.* Rancidity.
rancido [rAncido], *a.* Rancid, rank. **Saper di —,** to smell rancid, to taste rancid.
rancidume, *n.m.* Rancid stuff; something stale.
ranciere, *n.m.* Mess-cook, army cook.
rancio [rAncio], *n.m.* (*Mil.*) Mess, ration.
rancio [rAncio], *a.* Orange-coloured, orange (in colour).
ranco, *a.* Limping.
rancore, *n.m.* Rancour, spite, grudge, bitterness. **Serbare — contro qualcuno,** to have a grudge against someone.
randa, *n.f.* Edge, extremity; (*Naut.*) spanker. **A — a —,** close by, near at hand.
randagio [randAgio], *n.m.a.* Wanderer; stray, wandering, rambling.
randellare, *v.t.* To cudgel, to cane, to beat.
randellata, *n.f.* Blow with a cudgel.
randello, *n.m.* Club, cudgel.
ranella, *n.f.* (*Mech.*) Washer (for bolt and nut).
rango, *n.m.* Rank, degree, condition, station (in life). **In —,** in a row.
rannicchiarsi, *v.r.* To crouch, to squat, to curl oneself up.
rannicchiato, *a.* Squat, squatting.
ranno, *n.m.* Lye.
rannobilire, *v.t.* To ennoble, to redeem.
rannodamento, *n.m.* Retying, reknotting, renewing.
rannodare, *v.t.* To retie; to renew (friendship, etc.), to make it up again.
rannodarsi, *v.r.* To reunite, to reassemble.
rannuvolamento, *n.m.* Clouding over.
rannuvolare, rannuvolarsi, *v.i.r.* To cloud over, to become cloudy, to grow dark and gloomy (in all senses).
ranocchia [ranOcchia], *n.f.* Frog.
ranocchiaia [ranocchiAia], *n.f.* Swampy place (frequented by frogs), marsh.
ranocchiaio [ranocchiAio], *n.m.* Seller of frogs; frog-eater.
ranocchio [ranOcchio], *n.m.* (*Zool.*) Frog; (*fig.*) squat person; (*colloq.*) little boy, little lad.
rantolare, *v.i.* To rattle (in one's throat), to have the death-rattle.
rantolio [rantolIo], *n.m.* Continuous rattling in the throat.
rantolo [rAntolo], *n.m.* Death-rattle; very heavy breathing.
rantoloso, *a.* Rattling.
ranuncolo [ranUncolo], *n.m.* (*Bot.*) Buttercup; ranunculus.
rapa, *n.f.* (*Bot.*) Turnip; (*fig.*) blockhead, silly fellow. **Non valere una —,** not worth a tinker's curse.
rapace, *a.* Rapacious. **Uccello —,** bird of prey.
rapacemente, *adv.* Rapaciously.
rapacità [-à], *n.f.* Rapacity.
rapaio [rapAio], *n.m.,* Turnip field; (*fig.*) confusion, muddle, mess. **È un certo —!** It's a regular mess!
rapare, *v.t.* To cut close; to crop one's hair.
rapata, *n.f.* Hair-crop.
rapida [rApida], *n.f.* Rapids (of a river).
rapidamente, *adv.* Rapidly.
rapidezza, rapidità [-à], *n.f.* Rapidity, swiftness, quickness. **Con —,** quickly.
rapido [rApido], *n.m.* (*Rail.*) Express, fast train.
rapido [rApido], *a.* Rapid, quick, swift.
rapimento, *n.m.* Ravishment, abduction, rape; ecstasy, rapture.
rapina, *n.f.* Robbery, rapine. **Animali di —,** beasts of prey.
rapinare, *v.t.* To rob.
rapinatore, rapinatrice, *n.m.f.* Robber, bandit.
rapineria [rapinerIa], *n.f.* Robbery.
rapire, *v.t.* To carry off, to steal by force; to ravish, to rape; to kidnap, to abduct; (*fig.*) to transport with delight, to enrapture.
rapitore, *n.m.* Ravisher; kidnapper.
rappacificamento, *n.m.* Reconciliation.
rappacificare, rappaciare, *v.t.* To reconcile; to pacify.
rappacificarsi, *v.r.* To become reconciled; to be pacified.
rappacificazione, *n.f.* Reconciliation.
rappattumarsi, *v.r.* To be friends once more, to make it up.
rappezzamento, *n.m.* Patching up, mending.
rappezzare, *v.t.* To patch up, to put together again, to mend.
rappezzatura, *n.f.* Patching up, putting together; patchwork.
rappezzo, *n.m.* Patch, patchwork, patched place; pretext, flimsy excuse.

rappiccare, *v.t.* To hang up again, to refasten; to start all over again; to renew.
rappiccarsi, *v.r.* To become rekindled, (of a fire) to break out afresh.
rappiccinire, *v.t.* To belittle, to make smaller.
rappicciolire, rappicciolirsi, *v.i.r.* To diminish, to become smaller.
rappigliamento, *n.m.* Coagulation, thickening.
rappigliare, rappigliarsi, *v.i.r.* To coagulate, to thicken, to curdle; to harden.
rapportare, *v.t.* To report, to relate, to tell, to inform; to reproduce.
rapportarsi, *v.r.* To have reference to, to relate to; to be advised by.
rapporto, *n.m.* Report, statement, relation; connection, intercourse, terms; reference, ratio. **In — a,** in reference to, in connexion with; **sotto ogni —,** in every respect; **sotto questo —, in** this respect; **rapporti internazionali,** international relations; **l'ho messo in — col mio socio,** I've put him in touch with my partner; **rapporti sessuali,** sexual intercourse; **rompere i rapporti,** to sever *or* weaken relations.
rapprendere [rapprEndere], *v.t.* To curdle.
rapprendersi [rapprEndersi], *v.r.* To curdle, to thicken, to set; to become numbed, to get cramp.
rappresaglia [rappresAglia], *n.f.* Reprisal, retaliation.
rappresentabile, *a.* Representable.
rappresentante, *n.m.* Representative, agent.
rappresentanza, *n.f.* Representation; (*Comm.* agency; (*Pol.*) deputation. (*Comm.*) — **esclusiva,** sole agency; (*Pol.*) — **proporzionale,** proportional representation.
rappresentare, *v.t.* To represent, to act as agent; (*Theat.*) to present, to perform, to put on, to play (a part); (*Cinema*) to show a film.
rappresentativo, *a.* Representative.
rappresentazione, *n.f.* Representation; description; (*Theat.*) performance. (*Lit.*) **Sacra —,** miracle play.
rapsodia [rapsodIa], *n.f.* Rhapsody.
rapsodista (*pl.* **rapsodisti), rapsodo,** *n.m.* Rhapsodist.
raramente, *adv.* Rarely, seldom.
rarefabile [rarefAbile], *a.* Rarefiable.
rarefacente, *a.* Rarefying.
rarefare, *v.t.* To rarefy.
rarefarsi, *v.r.* To become rarefied; to diminish.
rarefattibile [rarefattIbile], *a.* Rarefiable.
rarefazione, *n.f.* Rarefaction, diminution.
rarità [-à], *n.f.* Rarity, curiosity, rare example; scarcity.
raro, *a.* Rare, scarce; exceptional, uncommon.
rasare, *v.t.* To smooth; to shave (beard); to clip (a hedge).
raschiamento, *n.m.* Scraping, erasure, scratching, grating.
raschiare, *v.t.* To scrape; to erase; to grate; to scratch. **— via,** to scrape off.
raschiarsi, *v.r.* To clear one's throat, to hawk.
raschiata, *n.f.* Scraping, erasure.
raschiatoio [raschiatOio], *n.m.* Scraper.
raschiatura, *n.f.* Scraping, erasure, scrapings.
raschietto, raschino, *n.m.* Scraper, eraser.
raschio [rAschio], *n.m.* Scraper, scratching; roughness of the throat.
rasciugamento, *n.m.* Drying up.
rasciugare, *v.t.* To dry up, to dry; to exhaust.
rasentare, *v.t.* To graze, to shave past, to skim; to border upon; to brush, to touch lightly.
rasente, *prep.* Close to. (*Naut.*) **Veleggiare — terra,** to hug the coast.
rasiera, *n.f.* Grater, scraper.
raso, *n.m.* Satin.
raso, *a.* Shaved, cropped; cancelled; grazed, skimmed, cut close. **Campagna rasa,** open country; **a — di,** flush with; **pieno —,** full to the brim; **— al suolo,** razed to the ground; **far tavola rasa,** to make a clean sweep.
rasoiata, *n.f.* Razor-cut.
rasoio [rasOio], *n.m.* Razor. **— di sicurezza,** safety-razor; **— elettrico,** electric shaver.
raspa, *n.f.* Rasp, grater; heavy file.
raspamento, *n.m.* Rasping, grating.
raspante, *a.* Rasping; sour.
raspare, *v.t.* To rasp, to scrape; (of fowls) to scratch; (of horses) to paw, to stamp.
raspaticcio [raspatIccio], *n.m.* Bad workmanship, scamped work.
raspatura, *n.f.* Rasping, grating, filings.
raspino, *n.m.* File, smoothing file; small bunch of grapes.
raspo, *n.m.* Bunch of grapes, grape-stalk; (*Vet.*) mange.
rasposo, *a.* Rough.
rassegna, *n.f.* Review (in all senses); (*Mil.*) parade, muster; detailed description of events, etc.
rassegnare, *v.t.* To pass in review; to submit (documents); to resign. **Ha rassegnato le proprie dimissioni,** he has offered (*or* submitted) his resignation.
rassegnarsi, *v.r.* To resign oneself, to submit oneself.
rassegnato, *p.p.a.* Resigned, submitted, submissive.
rassegnazione, *n.f.* Resignation, submission.
rasserenamento, *n.m.* Clearing up; cheering up.
rasserenare, *v.t.* To clear up, to calm.
rasserenarsi, *v.r.* To clear up (of the weather), to brighten (of the sky); to regain one's serenity.
rassestare, *v.t.* To readjust. **— il bilancio,** to balance the budget.
rassettamento, *n.m.* Arrangement, rearrangement, settlement, adjustment.
rassettare, *v.t.* To set in order, to arrange, to rearrange, to adjust; to repair, to put right.
rassettatura, *n.f.* Adjustment, settlement, arrangement.
rassicurante, *a.* Reassuring, encouraging.
rassicurare, *v.t.* To reassure, to encourage.
rassicurarsi, *v.r.* To become assured, to be reassured; to make sure.
rassicurazione, *n.f.* Assurance, reassurance.
rassodamento, *n.m.* Consolidation, strengthening; drying up.
rassodare, *v.t.i.* To consolidate, to make firm, to strengthen.
rassodarsi, *v.r.* To become firm, to be strengthened, to consolidate.

rassomigliante, *a.* Like, resembling.
rassomiglianza, *n.f.* Resemblance, likeness.
rassomigliare, rassomigliarsi, *v.i.r.* To resemble, to look like, to be like.
rastrellamento, *n.m.* Raking, search, searching.
rastrellare, *v.t.* To rake, to search, to sweep; to round up ; (*Mil.*) to mop up.
rastrellata, *n.f.* Rakeful.
rastrellatura, *n.f.* Raking; (*Mil.*) mopping up.
rastrelliera, *n.f.* (*Agric.*) Hay-rack, crib; plate-rack; arms-rack, arms-stand; hat-stand.
rastrello, *n.m.* (*Agric.*) Rake; lattice.
rasura, *n.f.* Erasure; cut, scrape, graze.
rata, *n.f.* Rate; portion, share, instalment. **Comprare a rate,** to buy by instalments; **pro —,** in part.
ratafia [ratafIa], *n.m.* Ratafia; cherry-brandy.
rateale, *a.* By instalments; periodic, partial.
ratealmente, *adv.* By instalments, periodically.
ratifica, *n.f.* Ratification.
ratificare, *v.t.* To ratify, to confirm; to affirm.
ratificazione, *n.f.* Ratification.
ratizzare, *v.t.* To assess, to rate.
rato, *a.* (*Law*) Ratified, confirmed.
rattaccare, *v.t.* To refasten, to reunite.
rattacconamento, *n.m.* Patching, repairing (of shoes, etc.).
rattacconare, *v.t.* To repair (shoes, etc.), to cobble.
rattamente, *adv.* Quickly, swiftly.
rattemperarsi, *v.r.* To control oneself.
rattenere, *v.t.* To check, to keep back, to restrain, to hold in; to remember.
rattenersi, *v.r.* To restrain oneself, to hold oneself in.
rattenuta, *n.f.* Retention, restraint, detention; catch-pit (for stagnant water); deduction or retention of salary, wages, etc.
rattezza, *n.f.* Quickness, celerity.
rattizzare, *v.t.* To poke the fire; (*fig.*) to excite, to stir up, to kindle.
ratto (1), *n.m.* Rape, kidnapping, abduction. **Il — delle Sabine,** the rape of the Sabine women.
ratto (2), *n.m.* (*Zool.*) Rat. **— d'acqua,** water-rat.
ratto, *adv.a.* Quickly; quick, rapid, swift.
rattoppamento, *n.m.* Patching, mending.
rattoppare, *v.t.* To patch, to mend; to remedy.
rattoppatura, *n.f.* Patching, mending.
rattoppo, *n.m.* Patch, patchwork.
rattrappimento, *n.m.* Shrinking, contraction; numbing; (*fig.*) paralysis.
rattrappire, *v.t.i.* To shrink, to contract; to benumb.
rattrappirsi, *v.r.* To become paralysed; to contract.
rattrarre, rattrarsi, *v.i.r.* To contract.
rattristamento, *n.m.* Grief, sadness, gloom.
rattristante, *a.* Grieving; gloomy; sorrowful, sad.
rattristare, rattristarsi, *v.i.r.* To grieve; to become sad.
rattristire, *v.t.* To grieve, to make sad; to depress; to make feeble, to weaken; (of ground) to become sterile.
rattristirsi, *v.r.* To droop, to grow feeble.
raucamente, *adv.* Hoarsely, raucously.
raucedine [raucEdine], *n.f.* Hoarseness.
rauco [rAuco], *a.* Hoarse, raucous.
Raulo [rAulo], *n.m.* Ralph.
ravanello, *n.m.* (*Bot.*) Small radish.
ravennate, *n.m.a.* Of or pertaining to Ravenna.
ravioli, *n.m.pl.* Ravioli, pastry enclosing meat, etc.
ravizzone, *n.m.* Rape, colza. **Olio di —,** colza-oil.
ravvalorare, *v.t.* To strengthen.
ravvedersi, *v.r.* To repent, to see one's error, to acknowledge one's faults or mistakes, to amend one's ways, to reform.
ravvedimento, *n.m.* Repentance; amendment, reformation.
ravveduto, *p.p.a.* Repentant, amended.
ravviamento, *n.m.* Arrangement, setting in order; starting afresh.
ravviare, *v.t.* To put in order, to tidy, to adjust.
ravviarsi, *v.r.* To start again; to tidy one's hair, etc. **— verso casa,** to walk home again.
ravviata, *n.f.* Arrangement; combing (of the hair). **Darsi una — ai capelli,** to tidy one's hair.
ravviatamente, *adv.* In order, tidily.
ravviato, *p.p.a.* Arranged, set right; started afresh; combed, tidied.
ravvicinamento, *n.m.* Drawing near; (*fig.*) reconciliation ; rapprochement.
ravvicinare, *v.t.* To draw near again; to reconcile; to compare.
ravvicinarsi, *v.r.* To draw near; to become reconciled, to make it up again.
ravvicinato, *p.p.a.* Drawn near, brought close; reconciled. (*Cinema.*) **Una visuale ravvicinata,** a close-up.
ravvisabile [ravvisAbile], *a.* Recognizable.
ravvisare, *v.t.* To recognize, to perceive; to deem.
ravvivamento, *n.m.* Revivification, reanimation; rekindling (of a fire).
ravvivare, *v.t.* To revive, to re-vivify, to animate; to stir (the fire).
ravvolgere [ravvOlgere], *v.t.* To wrap up, to envelop, to roll up, to fold up, to muffle.
ravvolgersi [ravvOlgersi], *v.r.* To become enveloped; to get involved.
ravvolgimento, *n.m.* Winding, wrapping up, rolling up.
ravvoltolare, *v.t.* To wrap up completely. (*fig.*) **— nel fango,** to lead a dissolute life.
raziocinamento, *n.m.* Ratiocination.
raziocinante, *n.m.f.* Reasoner, one who thinks things out.
raziocinare, *v.i.* To reason.
raziocinativo, *a.* Reasoning.
raziocinio [raziocInio], *n.m.* Reason, reasoning, thinking, ratiocination.
razionale, *a.* Rational.
razionalismo, *n.m.* Rationalism.
razionalista (*pl.* **razionalisti**), *n.m.* Rationalist.
razionalità [-à], *n.f.* Rationalness, rationality.
razionalmente, *adv.* Rationally.
razionamento, *n.m.* Rationing.
razionare, *v.t.* To ration, to put on a fixed allowance.

razione, *n.f.* Ration, daily portion, fixed allowance; portion. — **ridotta,** short ration.
razza (1), *n.f.* Race; kind; breed, variety, sort. **Di — pura,** thoroughbred; **di — incrociata,** cross-bred; **che — di gente siete!** what a strange crowd you are! **che — d'impiccio,** what a dreadful muddle!
razza (2), *n.f.* Spoke of a wheel.
razza (3), *n.f.* (*Zool.*) Ray (fish), thornback.
razzamaglia [razzamAglia], *n.f.* Rabble, riff-raff.
razzia [razzIa] (1), *n.f.* Raid, foray.
razzia [razzIa] (2), *n.f.* Insect-powder.
razziale, *a.* Racial.
razziare, *v.t.* To raid, to make a foray, to plunder.
razziatore, *n.m.* Raider.
razzismo, *n.m.* Racialism.
razzo, *n.m.* Rocket; spoke (of a wheel). — **luminoso,** star-shell.
razzolare, *v.i.* To scrape, to scratch (as a fowl); to weed, to hoe; to rummage, to ransack.
razzolata, razzolatura, *n.f.* Scraping, scratching.
razzuffarsi, *v.r.* To start fighting again, to come to blows again.
re (1), *n.m.* King.
re (2), *n.m.* (*Mus.*) D.
reagente, *n.m.* Reagent.
reagire, *v.i.* To react, to respond.
reale, *a.* Real, true; royal.
realismo, *n.m.* Realism.
realista (*pl.* **realisti**), *n.m.* Realist; royalist.
realistico [realIstico], *a.* Realistic.
realizzabile [realizzAbile], *a.* Realisable.
realizzare, *v.t.* To realize, to effect, to obtain; to fetch (price); to carry out (a plan).
realizzarsi, *v.r.* To come true, to be realized, to happen. **Il mio sogno si è realizzato,** my dream has come true.
realizzazione, *n.f.* Realization. **Di difficile —,** difficult to achieve.
realmente, *adv.* Really, truly; royally.
realtà [-à], *n.f.* Reality. **In —,** really.
reame, *n.m.* Realm, kingdom.
reamente, *adv.* Guiltily.
reato, *n.m.* Crime, misdemeanour, punishable offence. **Corpo del —,** evidence; **sorprendere in flagrante —,** to take in the very act.
reattivo, *n.m.a.* Reagent; reactive.
reattore, *n.m.* (*Aviat.*) Jet plane.
reazionario [reazionArio], *n.m.a.* Reactionary.
reazione, *n.f.* Reaction (in all senses), counter-revolution. (*Aviat.*) **Propulsione a —,** jet-propulsion; **apparecchio a —,** jet-plane; — **chimica,** chemical reaction.
rebbiare, *v.t.* To prod with a fork.
rebbiata, *n.f.* Blow with a fork.
rebbio [rEbbio], *n.m.* Prong (of a fork); fork.
reboante, *a.* High-sounding, bombastic, highfalutin.
rebus, *n.m.* Rebus, picture-puzzle, riddle.
recalcitrante, *n.m.a.* Recalcitrant.
recanatese, *n.m.a.* Native of, or pertaining to Recanati. **Il grande —,** Giacomo Leopardi.
recapitare, *v.t.* To send, to deliver, to hand over. **Si prega di far —,** please forward.
recapito [recApito], *n.m.* Delivery; destination, address; place of call. — **a domicilio,** delivery to the house.
recare, *v.t.* To bring; to fetch; to carry, to take; to cause, to produce; to render, to translate; to ascribe. — **ad effetto,** to carry into effect; — **a fine,** to finish, to bring to an end; — **disturbo,** to cause trouble.
recarsi, *v.r.* To go, to betake oneself; to come. — **ad onore,** to take as an honour; — **a mente,** to recall, to bring to mind; — **a cuore,** to take to heart.
recato, *p.p.a.* Brought, fetched, carried. **Mi sono — a,** I have gone to.
recedere [recEdere], *v.i.* To withdraw, to recede; to give up. — **da un'impresa,** to give up an undertaking.
recedimento, *n.m.* Withdrawal, desisting.
recensione, *n.f.* Book-review.
recensire, *v.t.* To review (a book).
recensore, *n.m.* Reviewer.
recente, *a.* Recent, new; late. **Di —,** recently.
recentemente, *adv.* Recently.
recentissime, *n.f.pl.* Latest news.
recere [rEcere], *v.i.* To vomit, to retch.
recesso, *n.m.a.* Recess, recession, retiring renouncement, withdrawal; withdrawn, retired.
recettività [-à], *n.f.* Receptivity.
recettivo, *a.* Receptive.
recezione, *n.f.* Reception; admission (into office); receipt.
recidere [recIdere], *v.t.* To cut off, to excise, to retrench, to cut down (expenses); (*Agric.*) to plough over again.
recidersi [recIdersi], *v.r.* To split up, to tear in pieces.
recidiva, *n.f.* Relapse.
recidività [-à], *n.f.* Relapse, recidivity; (*Law*) fraud.
recidivo, *n.m.a.* Recidivist, old offender, old lag, habitual criminal; (*Law*) wilful; relapsing.
recingere [recIngere], *v.t.* To enclose, to surround; to encompass.
recinto, *n.m.* Enclosure, fenced-in place, pen; enclosing fence.
recipiente, *n.m.* Vessel, container.
reciproca [recIproca], *n.f.* (*Math.*) Reciprocal.
reciprocamente, *adv.* Reciprocally.
reciprocanza, *n.f.* Reciprocality.
reciprocare, *v.t.* To reciprocate.
reciprocazione, *n.f.* Reciprocation.
reciprocità [-à], *n.f.* Reciprocity.
reciproco [recIproco], *a.* Reciprocal; mutual; inverse.
recisa, *n.f.* Wound, cut.
recisamente, *adv.* Decidedly, sharply, definitely; cuttingly.
recisione, *n.f.* Cutting off; excision; retrenchment.
reciso, *a.* Curt, short, uncompromising, decided. **Rifiuto —,** flat refusal.
recita [rEcita], *n.f.* Recital; (*Theat.*) performance.
recitabile [recitAbile], *a.* Suitable for recitation or performance.
recitante, *n.m.* Reciter, performer.
recitare, *v.t.* To recite, to repeat; to say, to act (on the stage), to play, to perform. — **la lezione,** to repeat a lesson; (*Theat.*) — **una parte,** to play a part; — **a memoria,** to say by heart.
recitativo, *n.m.* (*Mus.*) Recitative.

recitatore, recitatrice, *n.m.f.* Reciter.
recitazione, *n.f.* Recitation, recital; (*Theat.*) performance, acting.
reclamante, *n.m.* Claimant; complainant.
reclamare, *v.t.i.* To claim; to complain, to protest, to lodge a complaint. **— il pagamento,** to claim the payment; **ho reclamato con energia,** I protested vigorously.
reclame, *n.f.* Advertisement.
reclamistico [reclamIstico], *a.* Advertising.
reclamo, *n.m.* Complaint; claim. **Appoggiare un —,** to endorse a claim; **sporgere un — contro qualcuno,** to lodge a complaint against someone.
reclinare, reclinarsi, *v.i.r.* To recline, to rest, to lean (upon); to slope.
reclusione, *n.f.* Seclusion; imprisonment, confinement.
recluso, *n.m.* Recluse; prisoner, convict.
reclusorio [reclusOrio], *n.m.* Prison, penitentiary, convict establishment.
recluta [rEcluta, reclUta], *n.m.* Recruit.
reclutamento, *n.m.* Recruitment, enlistment.
reclutare, *v.t.* To recruit, to enlist.
recondito [recOndito], *a.* Recondite, hidden, concealed, abstruse; innermost; solitary.
record, *n.m.* (*Sport*) Record. **— di distanza,** long-distance record; **— di velocità,** speed-record.
recriminare, *v.t.* To recriminate.
recriminatorio [recriminatOrio], *a.* Recriminatory.
recriminazione, *n.f.* Recrimination; complaint.
recrudescenza, *n.f.* Recrudescence.
recto, *n.m.* Face (of a document, etc.).
redarguibile [redarguIbile], *a.* Liable to reproach, questionable.
redarguire, *v.t.* To blame, to reproach; to query, to challenge a statement; to scold.
redarguizione, *n.f.* Blame, reproach.
redatto, *a.* Drawn up (of a deed, etc.). **Atto — da notaio,** deed under the authority of the notary public.
redattore, *n.m.* Newspaper editor; journalist, reporter.
redazione, *n.f.* Editing; drawing-up; wording, terms; editorial staff, editor's office.
redditivo, redditizio [redditIzio], *a.* Paying, profitable.
reddito [rEddito], *n.m.* Rent, revenue, income. **Vivere di —,** to live on one's income; **godere un largo —,** to enjoy a large income; **imposta sul —,** income-tax.
redento, *p.p.a.* Redeemed, ransomed.
redentore, *n.m.* Redeemer. **Il Redentore,** the Saviour.
redenzione, *n.f.* Redemption, ransom.
redigere [redIgere], *v.t.* To draw up, to draft, to compile; to compose, to write, to edit (a newspaper, etc.). **— un memoriale,** to draw up a memorial.
redimere [redImere], *v.t.* To redeem, to ransom, to liberate.
redimersi [redImersi], *v.r.* To redeem oneself, to free oneself.
redimibile [redimIbile], *a.* Redeemable.
redimibilità [-à], *n.f.* Redeemableness.
redina, redine [rEdina -e], *n.f.* Reins (in all senses); brake.
redivivo, *a.* Returned to life. **Un Garibaldi —,** a new Garibaldi.
reduce [rEduce], *n.m.* (*Mil.*) Ex-service man, veteran.
reduce [rEduce], *a.* Returned, come back.
reduplicare, *v.t.* To redouble, to duplicate.
refe, *n.m.* Thread, yarn.
referendario [referendArio], *n.m.* Papal official referee; referee; (*colloq.*) informer, spy.
referendum, *n.m.* Referendum.
referenza, *n.f.* Reference, testimonial; information.
referto, *n.m.* Report (on a matter), medical report.
refettorio [refettOrio], *n.m.* Refectory.
refezionare, *v.i.* To take refreshment.
refezione, *n.f.* Refection, refreshment, light meal; lunch.
refrattario [refrattArio], *n.m.* Refractory person; law-breaker.
refrattario [refrattArio], *a.* Refractory, stubborn, unmanageable; fire-proof. **Terra refrattaria,** fire-clay; **mattone —,** fire-brick.
refrigerante, *n.m.* Refrigerator.
refrigerare, *v.t.* To cool, to refresh; to refrigerate; to alleviate.
refrigeratore, *n.m.* Refrigerator.
refrigerazione, *n.f.* Refrigeration.
refrigerio [refrigErio], *n.m.* Refreshment, comfort, solace.
refurtiva, *n.f.* Stolen goods.
refuso, *n.m.* (*Print.*) Wrong letter, misprint.
refutare, *v.t.* (*obs.*) To refute.
regalare, *v.t.* To present, to make a present of, to bestow; to make a present to, to give away. **— un libro a qualcuno,** to present someone with a book.
regalato, *p.p.a.* Given away, presented, bestowed; (*fig.*) cheap.
regale, *a.* Royal, regal, kingly.
regalia [regalIa], *n.f.* Present, gift; tip; patronage.
regalità [-à], *n.f.* Royalty.
regalmente, *adv.* Royally.
regalo, *n.m.* Present, gift; donation. **Dare in —,** to make a present of; **mi fareste un — se,** you would greatly oblige me by.
regaluccio [regalUccio], *n.m.* Small gift.
regamo [rEgamo], *n.m.* (*Bot.*) Marjoram.
regata, *n.f.* Regatta.
rege, *n.m.* (*Poet.*) King.
regesto, *n.m.* Chronological list of documents.
reggente, *n.m.f.* Regent.
reggenza, *n.f.* Regency.
reggere [rEggere], *v.t.i.* To support, to bear, to hold up; to govern, to rule; to maintain; to bear (ice); to stand, to last, to hold out, to continue, to endure. **— un bimbo in collo,** to carry a child on one's arm; **— il moccolo,** to be one too many; **— al calore,** to stand heat; **— al confronto con,** to bear comparison with; **— alla prova,** to stand the trial; **— all'urto,** to stand the brunt.
reggersi [rEggersi], *v.r.* To stand, to stand firm, to last; to govern oneself. **Non poter — in piedi,** to be unable to stand.
reggia [rEggia], *n.f.* Royal palace.
reggiano, *n.m.a.* Native of or pertaining to Reggio.

reggicatinella, *n.m.* Washstand.
reggifiasco, *n.m.* Bottle-stand, bottle-rack.
reggilume, *n.m.* Lampstand.
reggimentale, *a.* Regimental.
reggimento, *n.m.* Regiment; government; regime.
reggipancia [reggipAncia], *n.m.* Body-belt.
reggipetto, *n.m.* Breast-band (harness); (woman's) brassière.
reggiposata, *n.m.* Knife-rest.
reggiseno, *n.m.* Brassière [cp. **reggipetto**].
reggitore, reggitrice, *n.m.f.* Ruler, administrator, governor; manager, manageress.
regia [regIa], *n.f.* State monopoly of tobacco, salt, etc.; (*Theat., Cinema*) staging, producing, work of the producer; stage direction.
regicida, *n.m.a.* Regicide (criminal); regicidal.
regicidio [regicIdio], *n.m.* Regicide (crime).
regime [regIme], *n.m.* Régime, government; regimen, diet.
regina, *n.f.* Queen.
regio [rEgio], *a.* Royal.
regionale, *a.* Regional.
regionalismo, *n.m.* Regionalism, provincialism.
regionalistico [regionalIstico], *a.* Provincial.
regione, *n.f.* Region, district.
regista (*pl.* **registi**), *n.m.* (*Cinema*) Director; (*Theat.*) producer.
registrabile [registrAbile], *a.* That may be booked or registered.
registrare, *v.t.* To register, to book, to enter up; to regulate (a watch).
registratore, *n.m.* Registrar; register. **— di cassa,** cash-register; **— di velocità,** speedometer.
registrazione, *n.f.* Registration; entry (bookkeeping), posting.
registro, *n.m.* Register (in all senses), record; (*Comm.*) books. **Ufficio del —,** registry-office; **tassa di —,** stamp-duty, registration fee; (*fig.*) **cambiar —,** to change one's tune, to alter one's behaviour.
regnante, *n.m.a.* Ruler, king; reigning; prevailing.
regnare, *v.i.* To reign, to rule, to govern; to prevail, to predominate; to be in vogue.
regnicolo [regnIcolo], *n.m.a.* Native (of a kingdom).
regno, *n.m.* Kingdom (in all senses); reign. **Il — animale,** the animal kingdom; **Il Regno Unito,** the United Kingdom; **durante il — di,** during the reign of.
regola [rEgola], *n.f.* Rule, order; regulation; moderation. **È di —,** it is customary; **di —,** as a rule, normally; **in —,** in order, regular; **per tua —,** for your guidance.
regolamentare, *a.* According to rule, regular, prescribed.
regolamento, *n.m.* Regulation, settlement. **— dei conti,** settlement of accounts.
regolare, *v.t.* To regulate, to control; to govern; to settle (accounts, etc.), **— un orologio,** to regulate a watch.
regolare, *a.* Regular; punctual.
regolarità [-à], *n.f.* Regularity.
regolarizzare, *v.t.* To regularize.
regolarmente, *adv.* Regularly.
regolarsi, *v.r.* To conduct oneself, to behave.
regolatamente, *adv.* In a regular manner.
regolatezza, *n.f.* Moderation, regularity, orderliness.
regolato, *a.* Regulated, governed, ruled; orderly, well-regulated; moderate.
regolatore, regolatrice, *n.m.f.* Regulator, governor (in all senses).
regolizia [regolIzia], *n.f.* Liquorice.
regolo [rEgolo], *n.m.* Ruler (for drawing lines). **— calcolatore,** slide-rule.
regredire, *v.i.* To regress, to go back, to lose ground.
regressione, *n.f.* Regression.
regressivo, *a.* Regressive.
regresso, *n.m.* Regression, decline; recourse. **Senza — a me,** without recourse to me.
reietto, *n.m.a.* Outcast.
reiezione, *n.f.* Rejection.
reimporre, *v.t.* To re-impose.
reimportare, *v.t.* To re-import.
reina, *n.f.* (*Poet.*) Queen.
reincarnazione, *n.f.* Reincarnation.
reintegramento, *n.m.* Reintegration.
reintegrare, *v.t.* To reintegrate, to reinstate; to compensate, to indemnify.
reintegrazione, *n.f.* Reintegration.
reità [-à], *n.f.* Guilt, wickedness, guiltiness.
reiteramento, *n.m.* Reiteration.
reiterare, *v.t.* To reiterate, to repeat.
reiteratamente, *adv.* Repeatedly.
reiterazione, *n.f.* Reiteration, repetition.
relativamente, *adv.* Relatively, comparatively.
relatività [-à], *n.f.* Relativity.
relativo, *a.* Relative, proportionate; contingent, regarding. **— a,** concerning; **in senso —,** in a relative sense.
relatore, relatrice, *n.m.f.* Reporter.
relazione, *n.f.* Report, relation, affinity, connection, acquaintanceship. **Compilare una —,** to draw up a report; **relazioni amichevoli,** friendly relations; **non ho relazioni con lui,** I have no connection with him; **ho molte relazioni,** I have many acquaintances; **rompere le relazioni,** to break off (*or* to sever) relations.
relegamento, *n.m.* Relegation.
relegare, *v.t.* To relegate, to banish; to confine.
relegazione, *n.f.* Relegation, banishment; confinement.
religione, *n.f.* Religion; (*Eccles.*) religious order.
religiosa, *n.f.* Nun.
religiosamente, *adv.* Religiously.
religiosità [-à], *n.f.* Religiousness, religiosity.
religioso, *n.m.* Monk, friar, member of a religious order.
religioso, *a.* Religious, devout, pious.
reliquia [relIquia], *n.f.* Relic; remnant.
reliquiario [reliquiArio], *n.m.* Reliquiary, shrine.
relitti, *n.m.pl.* Wreckage. **— del mare,** stranded goods, flotsam and jetsam.
relitto, *n.m.a.* Wreck (in all senses); flotsam; forlorn.
remare, *v.i.* To row. **— a piatto,** to feather one's oars.
remata, *n.f.* Rowing, row; stroke.
rematore, rematrice, *n.m.f.* Rower; oarsman, -woman.
remeggiare, *v.t.* To row; to flap (wings).
remeggio [remEggio], *n.m.* Rowing; flapping (of wings); oars.

remigamento, *n.m.* Rowing.
remigare, *v.i.* To row.
reminiscenza, *n.f.* Reminiscence, recollection.
remissibile [remissIbile], *a.* Pardonable, excusable.
remissibilmente, *adv.* Pardonably.
remissione, *n.f.* Remission, forgiveness (of a debt, etc.). **Senza —,** without mercy.
remissivamente, *adv.* Submissively, humbly; obediently.
remissivo, *a.* Submissive, humble, meek; yielding.
remo, *n m.* Oar. **Barca a remi,** rowing-boat; **pala del —,** blade of the oar.
remolino, remolo [rEmolo], *n.m.* Gust of wind, eddy; whirlwind.
remora [rEmora], *n.f.* Obstacle, impediment, delay; restraint; (*Zool.*) sucking-fish; (*Naut.*) deadwater in the wake of a ship.
remoto, *a.* Remote, distant, far-off; secluded. (*Gram.*) **Passato —,** past definite; **luoghi remoti,** lonely spots.
removibile [removIbile], *a.* Removable.
rena, *n.f.* Sand, sands.
renaio [renAio], *n.m.* Sand-bank, sands; sand-pit.
renaiolo, *n.m.* Sand-digger; sand-carrier.
renale, *a.* (*Anat.*) Renal.
renano, *a.* (*Geog.*) Of the Rhine; Rhenish.
Renato, *n.m.* René.
rendere [rEndere], *v.t.* To render, to give back, to surrender, to restore, to return; to pay, to repay; to give, to yield, to produce; to play, to act (a part); to translate. **— conto di un avvenimento,** to give an account of what's happened; **— l'anima,** to die; **— felice un bambino,** to make a child happy; **— testimonianza,** to testify; **— parola per parola,** to translate word for word.
rendersi [rEndersi], *v.r.* To make oneself (do something); to become, to turn; to yield. **— conto,** to understand; **— popolare,** to become popular.
rendiconto, *n.m.* Report, rendering of accounts, statement of assets, etc.
rendimento, *n.m.* Yield, product; efficiency. **— di grazie,** thanksgiving; **— di conti,** handing-in of accounts.
rendita [rEndita], *n.f.* Income, rent, revenue; stock. **— vitalizia,** life annuity; **— annua,** yearly income.
rene, *n.m.* (*Anat.*) Kidney [cp. **reni**].
renella, *n.f.* (*Med.*) Gravel.
renelloso, *a.* (*Med.*) Affected with gravel.
reni, *n.f.pl.* (*colloq.*) The loins, the reins, the back. (*fig.*) **Rompere le — a,** to break the back of; **voltare le —,** to turn one's back.
reniforme, *a.* Kidney-shaped.
renitente, *a.* Unwilling, disinclined, stubborn; recalcitrant. (*Mil.*) **— alla leva,** defaulter.
renitenza, *n.f.* Resistance, stubbornness, recalcitrance.
renna, *n.f.* (*Zool.*) Reindeer.
Reno, *n.m.* (*Geog.*) The Rhine; the Reno, a tributary of the Po.
renoso, *a.* Sandy.
reo, *n.m.a.* Convict, guilty person; accused; culprit; guilty; evil.
reometro [reOmetro], *n.m.* Rheometer.
reostato [reOstato], *n.m.* (*Elect.*) Rheostat.
reparto, *n.m.* Department; allotment, assessment; (*Mil.*) detachment. **Capo —,** head of a department (of a store, etc.); shop-walker.
repellente, *a.* Repellent.
repellere [repEllere], *v.t.* To repel.
repentaglio [repentAglio], *n.m.* Risk, danger, peril. **Mettere a —,** to risk.
repente, *a.* Sudden, unexpected; steep; rapid. **Di —,** suddenly.
repentemente, repentinamente, *adv.* Suddenly, unexpectedly, all of a sudden.
repentino, *a.* Sudden, unexpected.
reperibile [reperIbile], *a.* Easily found, to be found.
reperire, *v.t.* To find, to find again.
reperto, *n.m.* Evidence; medical report.
repertorio [repertOrio], *n.m.* Repertory; inventory; catalogue; collection.
repleto, *a.* (*Lit.*) Replete.
replica [rEplica], *n.f.* Answer, rejoinder, repartee; repetition; objection; (*Art*) replica; (*Theat.*) run of a play. **Argomento che non ammette —,** argument admitting of no reply; **la centesima — dell'opera,** the 100th performance of the opera.
replicare, *v.t.* To reply, to retort, to make a rejoinder; to repeat; to give another performance.
replicatamente, *adv.* Repeatedly.
reprensione, *n.f.* Rebuke, reprehending.
repressione, *n.f.* Repression.
repressivo, *a.* Repressive.
reprimenda, *n.f.* Reprimand.
reprimere [reprImere], *v.t.* To repress, to put down; to quell, to restrain.
reprimersi [reprImersi], *v.r.* To control oneself, to restrain oneself.
reprimibile [reprimIbile], *a.* Restrainable.
reprobo [rEprobo], *n.m.a.* Reprobate.
repubblica [repUbblica], *n.f.* Republic.
repubblicano, *n.m.a.* Republican.
repulisti, *n.m.* (*Colloq.*) **Fare —,** to make a clean sweep.
repulsione, *n.f.* Repulsion, aversion.
repulsivo, *a.* Repulsive.
repulsore, *n.m.* (*Rail.*) Buffer.
reputare, *v.t.i.* To repute, to deem, to consider, to think, to be of the opinion [cp. **riputare**].
reputarsi, *v.r.* To consider oneself, to think oneself. **Mi reputo felice di,** I consider myself happy to.
reputato, *a.* Reputed, esteemed. **Persona reputata,** person of repute.
reputazione, *n.f.* Reputation.
requiare, *v.i.* To rest.
requie [rEquie], *n.f.* Peace, quiet, rest; pause; requiem. **Senza —,** unceasingly; unremittingly; **non dar —,** not to leave a person in peace.
requisire, *v.t.* To requisition, to commandeer.
requisito, *n.m.* Requisite, qualification.
requisitoria [requisitOria], *n.f.* (*Law*) Charge, charge-sheet; address by the prosecutor; indictment.
requisizione, *n.f.* Requisition.
resa, *n.f.* Surrender; delivery; return, rendering (of accounts). **Intimare la —,** to summon to surrender.
rescindere [rescIndere], *v.t.* To rescind, to annul, to cancel.

rescindibile [rescindIbile], *a.* Capable of being cancelled *or* annulled.
rescissione, *n.f.* Rescission, abrogation.
rescritto, *n.m.* Rescript.
reseda, *n.f.* (*Bot.*) Mignonette.
resezione, *n.f.* (*Med.*) Resection.
residente, *n.m.a.* Resident.
residenza, *n.f.* Residence.
residenziale, *a.* Residential.
residuale, *a.* Residual.
residuare, *v.i.* To be left, to remain, to form the residue.
residuario [residuArio], *n.m.a.* Residuary.
residuo [resIduo], *n.m.* Residue, remainder, balance.
resina [rEsina], *n.f.* Resin, rosin.
resinoso, *a.* Resinous.
resipiscenza, *n.f.* Recognition of error, resipiscence.
resipola [resIpola], *n.f.* (*Med.*) Erysipelas [cp. **risipola**].
resistente, *a.* Resistant, strong, tough; enduring, firm, strong; fast (of colours). **— alla pioggia,** water-proof, rain-proof; **— al fuoco,** fire-proof.
resistenza, *n.f.* Resistance, endurance; opposition; strength, toughness; stamina. **Fare —,** to resist; **— dell'aria,** air-resistance.
resistere [resIstere], *v.i.* To resist, to endure, to hold out; to oppose; to stand (the test), to be proof against. **— alla fatica,** to endure fatigue.
reso, *p.p.a.* Made; rendered, given back; produced; expired; explained; delivered. (*Comm.*) **— franco a bordo,** delivered free on board [cp. **rendere**].
resocontista (*pl.* **resocontisti**), *n.m.* Reporter.
resoconto, *n.m.* Report, accounts [cp. **rendiconto**].
respingente, *n.m.* (*Rail.*) Buffer.
respingere [respIngere], *v.t.* To repel, to push back, to drive back, to repulse; to reject, to refuse; to pluck (at an exam). **— il nemico,** to repulse the enemy; **— l'assalto,** to repel the assault; **— al mittente,** to return to sender.
respingimento, *n.m.* Rejection.
respingitore, *n.m.* (*Rail.*) Buffer.
respinto, *p.p.a.* Driven back, thrust back, refused; dismissed, rejected; returned to sender.
respirabile [respirAbile], *a.* Breathable.
respirare, *v.t.i.* To breathe, to respire; to inhale; to take breath. **— l'aria fresca,** to breathe fresh air; **— a pieni polmoni,** to take a deep breath.
respiratorio [respiratOrio], *a.* Respiratory.
respirazione, *n.f.* Breathing, respiration. **Difficoltà di —,** shortness of breath.
respiro, *n.m.* Breath, breathing; pause, delay, respite; instalment. **Esalare l'ultimo —,** to die.
responsabile [responsAbile], *a.* Responsible, liable.
responsabilità [-à], *n.f.* Responsibility, liability. **Attribuire la — a,** to hold a person responsible; **assumersi la —,** to take upon oneself the responsibility.
responsivo, *a.* Responsive.
responso, *n.m.* Response, answer, reply.
ressa, *n.f.* Crowd, throng; pressure. **Far —** to crowd.
resta, *n.f.* Fish-bone; beard (of corn); string (of onions); pause, delay. **Senza —,** without stopping.
restante, *n.m.a.* Remainder; remaining.
restare, *v.i.* To remain, to stay; to be left. **— indietro,** to stay behind; **— d'accordo,** to be in agreement; **— in asso,** to be abandoned; **— a casa,** to stay at home.
restaurare, *v.t.* To restore; to repair. **— un dipinto,** to restore a painting.
restauratore, *n.m.* Restorer.
restaurazione, *n.f.* Restoration, re-establishment.
restauro [restAuro], *n.m.* Restoration, repair.
restiamente, *adv.* Restively.
restio [restIo], *n.m.* Restiveness.
restio [restIo], *a.* Restive, restless; stubborn; reluctant, unwilling.
restituibile [restituIbile], *a.* Repayable.
restituire, *v.t.* To return, to give back, to pay back; to restore.
restituirsi, *v.r.* To return to one's home. **— in famiglia,** to return to one's family.
restituzione, *n.f.* Restitution; restoration; return.
resto, *n.m.* Rest, remainder, residue; remnant; change (of money). **Dar il —,** to give the change; **i resti mortali,** the mortal remains; **resti del cibo,** scraps of food, left-overs; **del —,** however, besides.
restringere [restrIngere], *v.t.* To tighten, to squeeze; to restrict; to straiten; to shrink, to reduce; to limit.
restringersi [restrIngersi], *v.r.* To restrain oneself, to limit oneself; to contract, to get narrower. **— nelle spese,** to cut down one's expenses.
restringibile [restringIbile], *a.* Shrinkable.
restringimento, *n.m.* Restraining, limitation; tightening, contracting.
restrittivo, *a.* Restrictive.
restrizione, *n.f.* Restriction. **Senza —,** unreservedly.
resurrezione, *n.f.* Resurrection.
resuscitare, *v.t.* To resuscitate.
retaggio [retAggio], *n.m.* Inheritance, heritage; property.
retata, *n.f.* Netful, catch, haul; (police) raid.
rete, *n.f.* Net, network (in all senses); (*Football*) goal; snare. **— ferroviaria,** railway system; **quante reti hanno segnate?** how many goals have they scored? **tendere le reti,** to lay a snare.
reticella, *n.f.* Small net; gas-mantle; (*Rail.*) luggage-rack.
reticente, *a.* Reticent.
reticenza, *n.f.* Reticence.
reticola [retIcola], *n.f.* Reticule.
reticolare, *v.t.* To mark in squares, to reticulate.
reticolare, *a.* Reticular.
reticolato, *n.m.* Barbed-wire, wire entanglement.
retina [rEtina] (1), *n.f.* (*Anat.*) Retina.
retina [retIna] (2), *n.f.* (Woman's) hair-net.
retore [rEtore], *n.m.* Rhetorician.
retorica [retOrica], *n.f.* Rhetoric.
retorico [retOrico], *a.* Rhetorical.

retribuire, *v.t.* To reward, to repay, to pay.
retribuzione, *n.f.* Retribution; reward.
retrivo, *a.* Retrograde, backward; reactionary; out-of-date.
retro, *n.m.* Back, back-room; verso (of coin, etc.). **Sul —,** on the back.
retro, *adv.* Behind, after. **Vedi —,** see the other side, P.T.O.
retroattivo, *a.* Retro-active.
retrobottega, *n.m.* Back-shop.
retrocamera [retrocAmera], *n.f.* Back-room.
retrocarica [retrocArica], *a.* Breech-loading. **Fucile a —,** breech-loader.
retrocedere [retrocEdere], *v.t.i.* To go back, to recede, to draw back; to turn back; to degrade; to retreat.
retrocedimento, *n.m.* Turning back, giving back.
retrocessione, *n.f.* Retrocession, degradation.
retrocesso, *a.* Gone back, withdrawn; retreated.
retrocucina, *n.f.* Back-kitchen.
retrodatare, *v.t.* To post-date.
retrogradare, *v.i.* To go backward.
retrogradazione, *n.f.* (*Astron.*) Retrogradation.
retrogrado [retrOgrado], *n.m.a.* Reactionary; retrograde, backward, reactionary.
retroguardia [retroguArdia], *n.f.* (*Mil.*) Rear-guard.
retroscena, *n.m.* (*Theat.*) Back-stage; (*fig.*) intrigue, behind the scenes.
retroscritto, *a.* Written on the back.
retrospettivo, *a.* Retrospective.
retrostanza, *n.f.* Back-room; recess, closet.
retrovendita [retrovEndita], *n.f.* Resale.
retroversione, *n.f.* (*Med.*) Retroversion.
retrovie, *n.f.pl.* (*Mil.*) Lines of communication; back-areas.
retta, *n.f.* Straight line; attention; wear, resistance; charges, terms (for boarding, etc.). **Dar —,** to pay attention; **non dategli —,** don't mind him; (*Racing*) **— d'arrivo,** home stretch.
rettamente, *adv.* In a straight line; honestly, uprightly.
rettangolare, *a.* Rectangular.
rettangolo [rettAngolo], *n.m.* Rectangle.
rettifica [rettIfica], *n.f.* Rectification, correction.
rettificabile [rettificAbile], *a.* Rectifiable.
rettificare, *v.t.* To rectify, to correct, to amend; to mend; to make straight.
rettificazione, *n.f.* Rectification.
rettifilo, *n.m.* Straight line; straight road.
rettile [rEttile], *a.* Creeping.
rettile [rEttile], *n.m.* (*Zool.*) Reptile.
rettilineo [rettilIneo], *n.m.a.* Straight, straight line; rectilinear.
rettitudine [rettitUdine], *n.f.* Rectitude, uprightness, honesty.
retto, *n.m.* (*Anat.*) Rectum.
retto, *a.* Upright, straightforward; correct; right (angle, etc.). **Uomo —,** an upright man; **il — cammino,** the right path (morally).
rettorato, *n.m.* (*Univ.*) Vice-Chancellorship; rectorship.
rettore, *n.m.* Vice-Chancellor (of a University); (*Am.*) President; rector; principal (of a college, etc.); prior.
rettorica, *n.f.* Rhetoric.
rettoricamente, *adv.* Rhetorically.
rettorico [rettOrico], *a.* Rhetorical.
rettoricume, *n.m.* Verbiage, empty talk.
rettrice, *n.f.* Headmistress, principal (of girls' school, etc.).
reuccio [reUccio], *n.m.* Petty ruler, small king.
reuma [rEuma], *n.m.* (*Med.*) Rheumatism.
reumatico [reumAtico], *n.m.a.* Rheumatic.
reumatismo, *n.m.* Rheumatism.
reumatizzato, *a.* Rheumaticky, suffering from rheumatism.
revellente, *n.m.a.* (*Med.*) Counter-irritant.
reverendo, *n.m.a.* Priest, clergyman, minister of religion; reverend.
reverente, *a.* Reverent.
reverentemente, *adv.* Reverently.
reverenza, *n.f.* Reverence; bow, curtsy.
reverenziale, *a.* Reverential.
revisione, *n.f.* Revision. (*Comm.*) **— dei conti,** audit of accounts.
revisore, *n.m.* Auditor; reviser. **— di bozze,** proof-reader.
revoca [rEvoca], *n.f.* Revocation.
revocabile [revocAbile], *a.* Revocable.
revocabilità [-à], *n.f.* Revocability.
revocamento, *n.m.* Revocation.
revocare, *v.t.* To revoke, to repeal.
revocazione, *n.f.* Revocation, repeal.
revolver, *n.m.* Revolver.
revolverata, *n.f.* Revolver shot.
revulsione, *n.f.* Revulsion.
revulsivo, *a.* Revulsive.
rezzo, *n.m.* Shade; coolness; breeze.
ri-, *prefix.* Again (as English **re-**. The meaning of many of the compounds can be obtained from reference to the simple form.)
riabbassare, *v.t.* To lower again.
riabbattere [riabbAttere], *v.t.* To beat down again.
riabbellire, *v.t.* To embellish anew.
riabbottonarsi, *v.r.* To button up one's clothes again.
riabbracciare, riabbracciarsi, *v.t.r.* To embrace again; to make friends with one another.(*Colloq.*) **Non vedo l'ora di riabbracciarti,** I am looking forward to seeing you again.
riabilitare, *v.t.* To rehabilitate.
riabilitazione, *n.f.* Rehabilitation; discharge (from bankruptcy).
riabitare, *v.t.* To re-inhabit.
riabituare, riabituarsi, *v.t.r.* To accustom again, to get accustomed once more.
riaccendere [riaccEndere], *v.t.* To rekindle, to light again.
riaccomodare, *v.t.* To rearrange; to mend again.
riaccompagnare, *v.t.* To conduct back, to see home. **Egli la riaccompagnò a casa,** he saw her home.
riacquistare, *v.t.* To regain, to recover; to buy back.
riacquisto, *n.m.* Repurchase; recovery.
riaddormentarsi, *v.r.* To fall asleep again.
riaffermare, *v.t.* To reaffirm.
riaffittare, *v.t.* To re-let; to hire again.
riaggiustare, *v.t.* To readjust, to repair.
riallacciare, *v.t.* To fasten again; to renew (a friendship).
rialto, *n.m.* Knoll, rise in the ground; embankment; steps in front of a church, etc.; relief (in a surface).

rialzamento, *n.m.* Elevation, raising up.
rialzare, *v.t.* To raise, to elevate, to heighten. **— il prezzo,** to raise the price.
rialzarsi, *v.r.* To lift up again, to raise again; to rise, to get up again.
rialzista (*pl.* **rialzisti**), *n.m.* (*Comm.*) Bull (on stock exchange).
rialzo, *n.m.* Rise (in price); advance; lifting up, prominence. **— dell'interesse,** rise in the rate of interest.
riammalarsi, *v.r.* To fall sick again, to have a relapse.
riammettere [riammEttere], *v.t.* To readmit.
riammissione, *n.f.* Readmission.
riammogliarsi, *v.r.* To marry again.
riandare, *v.t.i.* To revise, to go over again; to recall; to return, to go back again. **— con la mente,** to muse, to ponder over.
rianimare, *v.t.* To reanimate, to cheer.
rianimarsi, *v.r.* To cheer up, to become cheered.
riapertura, *n.f.* Reopening.
riapparire, *v.i.* To reappear.
riapparizione, *n.f.* Reappearance.
riaprire, riaprirsi, *v.t.r.* To reopen. **— una vecchia ferita,** to reopen an old wound.
riarmare, *v.t.i.* To rearm.
riarmo, *n.m.* Rearmament.
riarso, *a.* Burned, scorched; dry, parched.
riassettare, *v.t.* To put in order again, to refit.
riassetto, *n.m.* Rearrangement; readjustment; repair, refit.
riassicurazione, *n.f.* Reinsurance.
riassumere [riassUmere], *v.t.* To resume, to sum up; to summarize; to re-employ.
riassunto, *n.m.* Summary, recapitulation.
riassunzione, *n.f.* Resumption.
riattaccare, *v.t.* To attack again; to hang up, to put back (receiver, etc.).
riattaccarsi, *v.r.* To adhere again.
riattamento, *n.m.* Restoration, repair.
riattare, *v.t.* To repair, to restore, to refit; to rearrange.
riattivare, *v.t.* To re-establish, to renew; to restore.
riavere, *v.t.* To have again, to get back, to recover.
riaversi, *v.r.* To get back, to revive, to pick up (in health). **— da una malattia,** to recover one's health.
riavuto, *p.p.a.* Recovered, got back.
riavvallare, *v.t.* To renew a bill of exchange.
riavvallo, *n.m.* Renewal (of a bill).
riavvicinamento, *n.m.* (*fig.*) Reconciliation; rapprochement.
riavvicinare, *v.t.* To bring near again; (*fig.*) to reconcile.
ribadire, *v.t.* To clinch, to rivet (in all senses), to nail down; to confirm.
ribadito, *p.p.a.* Riveted; fixed in the mind.
ribaditoio [ribaditOio], *n.m.* Riveting-hammer.
ribaditore, *n.m.a.* Riveter; riveting, clinching.
ribaditura, *n.f.* Riveting.
ribalderia [ribalderIa], *n.f.* Rascality, scoundrelism.
ribaldo, *n.m.* Scoundrel, rascal, ruffian.
ribalta, *n.f.* Hinged part or flap (of table, etc.); (*Theat.*) footlights. **Presentarsi alla —,** to appear before the footlights; (fig.) to be called to the limelight.
ribaltabile [ribaltAbile], *a.* Tipping; folding. **Seggiolino —,** folding chair.
ribaltamento, *n.m.* Capsizing, upsetting.
ribaltare, *v.t.i.* To capsize, to upset; to overturn.
ribaltatura, *n.f.* Capsizing, upsetting, overturning.
ribaltone, *n.m.* Upset, jolt.
ribalzare, *v.i.* To rebound.
ribassare, *v.t.i.* To lower, to reduce; to drop, to fall. **La temperatura è ribassata,** the temperature has fallen; **i prezzi sono ribassati del cinque per cento,** prices have dropped 5 per cent.
ribassista (*pl.* **ribassisti**), *n.m.* (*Comm.*) Bear (on stock exchange).
ribasso, *n.m.* Fall (in prices); abatement, discount, reduction. **È in —,** his reputation is on the decline.
ribattere [ribAttere], *v.t.i.* To hit back; to hammer; to knock again; to clinch, to repel; (*Sport*) to return (a ball); to retort; to iron (a seam).
ribattitore, *n.m.* Riveter; (*Tennis, etc.*) player who returns the ball.
ribattitura, *n.f.* Riveting.
ribattuta, *n.f.* (*Sport*) Return of the service.
ribattuto, *p.p.a.* Beaten back, repulsed; confuted; pressed, riveted.
ribellare, *v.t.* To incite to rebellion, to urge to rebel.
ribellarsi, *v.r.* To rebel, to revolt, to rise against.
ribelle, *n.m.a.* Rebel; rebellious.
ribellione, *n.f.* Rebellion, revolt, uprising.
ribes, *n.m.* (*Bot.*) Ribes, gooseberry; red, black currant.
riboccare, *v.i.* To overflow; to be full to the brim.
ribocco, *n.m.* Super-abundance. **A —,** in plenty.
ribollimento, *n.m.* Effervescence; ebullition; agitation.
ribollire, *v.t.i.* To boil up again, to be overheated; to be agitated.
ribollitura, *n.f.* Reboiling.
ribotta, *n.f.* Spree, beano, junketing, spread. **Far —,** to go on the spree.
ribrezzo, *n.m.* Loathing; horror; revulsion; disgust. **Far —,** to cause disgust, to disgust.
ributtante, *a.* Repulsive, loathsome; shocking; hideous.
ributtare, *v.t.i.* To repel, to repulse, to reject; to disgust; to make indignant.
ricacciare, *v.t.* To drive back, to drive out again, to drive back again, to repulse.
ricadere, *v.i.* To fall again, to relapse. **Far — il torto sopra l'impiegato,** to let the blame fall on the clerk.
ricaduta, *n.f.* Relapse.
ricalcare, *v.t.* To tread, to press down; to retrace; to trace (a drawing, etc.). **— i propri passi,** to retrace one's steps.
ricalcatura, *n.f.* Tracing.
ricalcitramento, *n.m.* Recalcitration.
ricalcitrare, *v.i.* To be refractory, to be restive, to be stubborn.
ricamare, *v.t.* To embroider.
ricamatrice, *n.f.* Embroiderer.
ricamatura, *n.f.* Embroidery.

ricambiare, *v.t.* To reciprocate, to return (a compliment, etc.); to requite. — **il saluto,** to return a bow; — **bene per male,** to return good for evil; — **una visita,** to return a visit.
ricambiarsi, *v.r.* To exchange (compliments, etc.).
ricambio [ricAmbio], *n.m.* Reciprocation; requital; exchange, return, replacement; (*Med.*) metabolism. **Pezzo di —,** spare part, spare; **in —,** in return; — **di saluti,** return of greetings.
ricamo, *n.m.* Embroidery (in all senses).
ricantare, *v.t.* To sing over again; (*fig.*) to declare openly; to recant.
ricapitolare, *v.t.* To recapitulate, to sum up.
ricapitolazione, *n.f.* Recapitulation.
ricaricamento, *n.m.* Reloading.
ricaricare, *v.t.* To reload, to reship. — **l'orologio,** to wind up one's watch; — **il fucile,** to reload the gun.
ricattare, *v.t.* To blackmail; to extort.
ricattatore, *n.m.* Blackmailer; extortioner.
ricatto, *n.m.* Blackmail, extortion.
ricavare, *v.t.* To extract, to draw out from; to deduce; to derive, to obtain. — **un largo reddito,** to derive a large income.
ricavato, ricavo, *n.m.* Profits, proceeds. — **lordo,** gross profit.
riccamente, *adv.* Richly.
Riccardo, *n.m.* Richard.
ricchezza, *n.f.* Riches, wealth; richness. **Imposta di — mobile,** income-tax.
riccio [rIccio] (1), *n.m.* Curl, lock (of hair). **Farsi i ricci,** to curl one's hair.
riccio [rIccio] (2), *n.m.* (*Zool.*) Hedgehog; (*Bot.*) prickly husk of the chestnut.
riccio [rIccio], *a.* Curly, curled.
ricciolo [rIcciolo], *n.m.* Curl, lock (of hair).
riccioluto, ricciuto, *a.* Curly-headed, curly.
ricco, *n.m.* Rich man. **I ricchi e i poveri,** the rich and the poor.
ricco, *a.* Rich, wealthy; costly. — **sfondato,** fabulously wealthy.
riccone, *n.m.a.* Very rich man; very rich.
ricerca, *n.f.* Research, inquiry, investigation; demand.
ricercare, *v.t.* To seek for, to seek out, to search for; to investigate. — **le parole,** to select the right words.
ricercatezza, *n.f.* Affectation, preciosity. **Senza —,** unaffectedly.
ricercato, *p.p.a.* Sought after, sought for, wished for; affected. **Il ladro è — dalla polizia,** the police are seeking for the thief; **stile —,** laboured style.
ricercatore, ricercatrice, *n.m.f.* Investigator, researcher.
ricetta, *n.f.* Recipe, prescription. — **medica,** medical prescription.
ricettacolo [ricettAcolo], *n.m.* Receptacle.
ricettamento, *n.m.* Reception, receiving (of stolen goods).
ricettare, *v.t.* To harbour, to shelter (a fugitive criminal); to receive (stolen goods).
ricettario [ricettArio], *n.m.* Recipe-book; book of prescriptions.
ricettatore, ricettatrice, *n.m.f.* Receiver, fence.
ricettazione, *n.f.* Receiving of stolen goods.
ricettività [-à], *n.f.* Receptivity.
ricettivo, *a.* Receptive.
ricetto, *n.m.* Shelter, retreat, refuge. **Dar —** to shelter.
ricevente, *n.m.* Recipient.
ricevere [ricEvere], *v.t.i.* To receive, to admit; to welcome; to harbour, to shelter; to lodge, to take in guests or boarders; to receive visitors; to cash, to collect.
ricevimento, *n.m.* Reception; welcome; receipt (of letter, etc.). **Dar un —,** to give a party.
ricevitore, *n.m.* Recipient, one who receives; (telephone) receiver. **Alzare il —,** to lift the receiver; **abbassare il —,** to replace the receiver.
ricevitoria [ricevitorIa], *n.f.* Receiving office; lottery office.
ricevuta, *n.f.* Receipt. — **a saldo,** receipt in full; **accusare — di,** to acknowledge receipt of.
ricezione, *n.f.* (*Radio*) Reception.
richiamare, *v.t.* To call back, to recall; (*Mil.*) to call up; to summon; to call again; to bring together; to attract attention; to rebuke. — **all'ordine,** to call to order; — **alla memoria,** to recall, to call to mind, to remind; — **in vita,** to restore to life; — **indietro,** to call back.
richiamarsi, *v.r.* To complain of; to refer to; to apply to.
richiamo, *n.m.* Recall, call, summons; admonition, reproof; bird-call, decoy; cross-reference; (sound) signal; (*Mil.*) call-up.
richiedente, *n.m.* Petitioner, applicant.
richiedere [richiEdere], *v.t.* To request, to require; to ask for again; to send for, to summon. — **il medico,** to send for the doctor; — **una spesa,** to entail expense; — **pazienza,** to require patience.
richiesta, *n.f.* Request; demand, application. **Una grande — di,** a great request for; **franco a —,** free on application.
richiesto, *a.* In request, sought after, in demand.
richiudere [richiUdere], *v.t.* To close again; to shut up, to close.
richiuso, *p.p.a.* Closed, shut up.
ricingere [cp. **recingere**].
ricino [rIcino], *n.m.* (*Bot.*) Ricinus, castor-oil palm. **Olio di —,** castor-oil.
ricogliere [ricOgliere], *v.t.* To re-gather, to reassemble; to collect again.
ricognizione, *n.f.* Recognition; acknowledgement; avowal; (*Mil.*) reconnaissance.
ricollegare, *v.t.* To reunite, to rebind, to link up again.
ricollegarsi, *v.r.* To join again, to be re-united.
ricollocamento, *n.m.* Replacement.
ricollocare, *v.t.* To replace.
ricolmare, *v.t.* To heap up, to fill to overflowing, to fill to the brim.
ricolmo, *a.* Full, brimful; heaped up.
ricolorare, *v.t.* To recolour.
ricominciamento, *n.m.* Recommencement.
ricominciare, *v.t.* To recommence, to begin again.
ricommettere [ricommEttere], *v.t.* To commit again. — **un fallo,** to relapse into a fault.
ricomparire, *v.i.* To reappear.
ricomparsa, *n.f.* Reappearance.
ricompensa, *n.f.* Recompense, compensation, reward. **In —,** as a return for, in recompense.

ricompensare, *v.t.* To recompense, to reward.
ricompera, *n.f.* Repurchase.
ricomporre, *v.t.* To reassemble (machinery, etc.); to recompose.
ricomporsi, *v.r.* To recover one's calm, to recover oneself; to become composed; to settle (of weather).
ricomprare, *v.t.* To buy back.
riconcentrarsi, *v.r.* To concentrate one's thoughts.
riconciliare, *v.t.* To reconcile.
riconciliarsi, *v.r.* To become reconciled.
riconciliazione, *n.f.* Reconciliation.
ricondizionare, *v.t.* To repair, to recondition.
ricondotto, *p.p.a.* Brought back, led back.
ricondurre, *v.t.* To bring back, to lead back, to reconduct. **— a casa,** to take home; **— al dovere,** to bring back to his duty; **— sano e salvo,** to bring back safe and sound.
riconferma, *n.m.* Confirmation (of news, etc.).
riconfermare, *v.t.* To confirm, to reconfirm.
ricongiungere [ricongiUngere], *v.t.* To rejoin, to reunite.
ricongiunzione, *n.f.* Joining together again; reunion.
riconoscente, *a.* Grateful, thankful.
riconoscenza, *n.f.* Gratitude, thankfulness.
riconoscere [riconOscere], *v.t.* To recognize, to acknowledge; to reward; to identify. **— una persona,** to recognize a person; **— un debito,** to acknowledge a debt.
riconoscersi [riconOscersi], *v.r.* To declare oneself, to acknowledge (one's indebtedness).
riconoscibile [riconoscIbile], *a.* Recognizable.
riconoscimento, *n.m.* Recognition, acknowledgement; identification. (*Motor.*) **Targa di —,** number-plate; **tessera di —,** pass, identity card.
riconquista, *n.f.* Reconquest.
riconquistare, *v.t.* To reconquer; to regain.
riconsacrare, *v.t.* To reconsecrate.
riconsegna, *n.f.* Redelivery, reconsignment.
riconsegnare, *v.t.* To reconsign, to redeliver.
ricontare, *v.t.* To count again, to re-count.
riconversione, *n.f.* Reconversion.
riconvertire, *v.t.* To reconvert.
riconvocare, *v.t.* To reassemble.
riconvocazione, *n.f.* Reassembly.
ricopertamente, *adv.* Covertly, stealthily.
ricoperto, *p.p.a.* Covered up, covered, hidden.
ricopia [ricOpia], *n.f.* Fresh copy, clean copy.
ricopiare, *v.t.* To copy, to copy again; to make a fair copy.
ricordabile [ricordAbile], *a.* Memorable, notable.
ricordanza, *n.f.* Remembrance, memory, recollection.
ricordare, *v.t.i.* To call to mind, to remember, to recollect; to mention. **Ricordatemi a lui,** remember me to him; **ricordo la mia gioventù,** I call to mind my youthful days; **per quanto io possa —,** to the best of my recollection.
ricordarsi, *v.r.* To recollect, to remember, to be reminded of. **Mi ricordo d'aver letto questo libro,** I recollect having read this book; **se me ne ricordo bene,** if I remember rightly.
ricordevole [ricordEvole], *a.* Memorable; mindful.
ricordo, *n.m.* Recollection, remembrance, memory; souvenir; record; memoir; memorandum, note, reminder; tradition. **I ricordi d'un re,** a king's memoirs; **conservare gradito — di,** to retain a happy memory of.
ricoricarsi, *v.r.* To lie down again.
ricorreggere [ricorrEggere], *v.r.* To revise, to correct again.
ricorrente, *n.m.* Petitioner.
ricorrente, *a.* Recurrent, recurring.
ricorrenza, *n.f.* Recurrence; anniversary.
ricorrere [ricOrrere], *v.i.* To recur, to appear again; to resort to, to have recourse to. **La Pasqua ricorre il 13 aprile,** Easter falls on 13 April; **— ai rimedi,** to have recourse to remedies; **— a misure legali,** to have recourse to the Law; **— in appello,** to appeal.
ricorso, *n.m.* Appeal, claim, petition; return, recurrence.
ricostituente, *n.m.* Reconstituent, restorative; (*Med.*) a tonic.
ricostituire, *v.t.* To reconstitute, to reconstruct, to rebuild.
ricostituzione, *n.f.* Reconstitution, re-establishment.
ricostruire, *v.t.* To reconstruct, to rebuild.
ricostruzione, *n.f.* Reconstruction, rebuilding.
ricotta, *n.f.* Butter-milk curd. (*fig.*) **Fatto di —,** a weakling, spineless.
ricoverare, *v.t.* To shelter, to give shelter to; to recover. **— all'ospedale,** to take into hospital.
ricoverarsi, *v.r.* To take refuge, to take shelter, to shelter.
ricoverato, *n.m.* Inmate (of hospital, etc.).
ricovero [ricOvero], *n.m.* Retreat, asylum, shelter; dug-out; (*Rail.*) cab (of an engine); **—, antiaereo,** air-raid shelter.
ricreamento, *n.m.* Recreation, amusement.
ricreare, *v.t.* To amuse, to give recreation, to divert; to re-create.
ricrearsi, *v.r.* To amuse oneself, to take recreation.
ricreativo, *a.* Recreative, amusing, pleasant, light (reading, etc.).
ricreatorio [recreatOrio], *n.m.* Recreation-room.
ricreazione, *n.f.* Recreation, amusement; sport, pastime; hobby. **Ore di —,** play-time; **alla —,** at play.
ricredersi [ricrEdersi], *v.r.* To change one's mind, to recant; to realize one's mistake; to become disillusioned.
ricrescere [ricrEscere], *v.t.* To grow again, to grow larger or taller; to multiply.
ricrescimento, *n.m.* Increase (in number, bulk, etc.); multiplication.
ricucire, *v.t.* To sew again.
ricucitura, *n.f.* Patching, sewing up.
ricuocere [ricuOcere], *v.t.* To recook, to cook again; to reheat.
ricuperabile [ricuperAbile], *a.* Recoverable.
ricuperare, *v.t.* To recover; to salve. **— la salute,** to recover one's health; **— il tempo perduto,** to make up for lost time; **— una nave,** to save a ship; **— un carico,** to salve a cargo.
ricuperazione, ricupero [ricUpero], *n.f.m.* Recovery, salvage; rescue.

ricurvo, *a.* Bent, curved.
ricusa, *n.f.* Refusal, denial; objection.
ricusabile [ricusAbile], *a.* Refusable.
ricusare, *v.t.* To refuse; to reject; to deny; (*Law*) to challenge a witness.
ricusazione, *n.f.* Refusal.
ridacchiare, *v.i.* To titter, to giggle; to laugh ironically.
ridanciano, *a.* Merry, cheerful, full of laughter.
ridare, *v.t.* To give back; to give again.
ridda, *n.f.* Round dance, reel; (*fig.*) whirl; mass (of news).
ridente, *a.* Laughing, smiling, cheerful, bright.
ridere [rIdere], *v.i.* To laugh, to smile. **— di,** to laugh at, to mock; **— sotto i baffi,** to laugh in one's sleeve; **scoppiare dal —,** to burst out laughing; **una cosa da —,** a laughing matter, something ridiculous; **per —,** for fun; **non potei trattenermi dal —,** I couldn't help laughing.
ridere [rIdere], *n.m.* Laugh, laughter.
ridersi [rIdersi], *v.r.* To laugh at; to make fun of; to make a fool of.
ridestare, *v.t.* To waken, to rouse again.
ridetto, *a.* Retold.
ridevole [ridEvole], *a.* Ridiculous, absurd.
ridicibile [ridicIbile], *a.* Repeatable.
ridicolaggine [ridicolAggine], *n.f.* Nonsense.
ridicolmente, *adv.* Ridiculously.
ridicolo [ridIcolo], *n.m.a.* Ridicule, ridiculousness; ridiculous, absurd; ludicrous, laughable.
ridire, *v.t.* To tell again, to repeat.
ridivenire, ridiventare, *v.i.* To become again.
ridomandare, *v.t.* To ask for again.
ridonare, *v.t.* To give again.
ridondante, *a.* Redundant.
ridondanza, *n.f.* Redundancy, redundance.
ridondare, *v.i.* To be superabundant.
ridosso, *n.m.* Sheltered place (from wind or sea); (*Naut.*) lee-side. **A —,** close by, very near, at the back of.
ridotta, *n.f.* (*Mil.*) Redoubt.
ridotto, *n.m.* Resort, retreat, haunt; shelter; (*Theat.*) foyer.
ridotto, *p.p.a.* Reduced, lessened. **Prezzi ridotti,** cut prices; **mal —,** in a bad way [cp. **ridurre**].
riducibile [riducIbile], *a.* Reducible.
riducibilità [-à], *n.f.* Possibility of reduction.
ridurre, *v.t.* To reduce, to lessen to lower; to blight; to compel, to oblige; (*Mus.*) to arrange. **— in polvere,** to reduce to powder; **— alla disperazione,** to reduce to despair; **— a nulla,** to bring to nothing.
ridursi, *v.r.* To be reduced to, to reduce oneself; to arrive at. **Le cose si ridussero a tal punto,** matters reached such a pitch.
riduzione, *n.f.* Reduction, abatement, discount; (*Mus.*) arrangement.
riecco, *inter.* Here (it is, they are) again; once more.
riecheggiare, *v.i.* To re-echo, to resound.
riedere [riEdere], *v.i.* (*Poet.*) To return.
riedificare, *v.t.* To rebuild.
riedificazione, *n.f.* Rebuilding.
rieleggere [rielEggere], *v.t.* To re-elect.
rielezione, *n.f.* Re-election; by-election.
riempibile [riempIbile], *a.* That may be filled.
riempimento, *n.m.* Filling, filling-up.
riempire, riempiere, *v.t.* To fill, to fill up; to fill in (forms, etc.); to stuff oneself (eating).
riempitivo, *n.m.* Stuffing (for geese, etc.); (*Gram.*) pleonasm.
riempitivo, *a.* Superfluous, pleonastic.
rientramento, *n.m.* Re-entrance.
rientrante, *a.* Re-entering; receding.
rientrare, *v.i.* To re-enter, to come in again; to return home; to recede, to withdraw; to be included. **Ciò non rientra nei miei doveri,** that is no part of my duties; **— in se stesso,** to retire into oneself, to introspect.
rientrata, *n.f.* Re-entry; reappearance.
rientro, *n.m.* Re-entry; contraction.
riepilogare, *v.t.* To recapitulate; to summarize.
riepilogo [riepIlogo], *n.m.* Recapitulation, summary, résumé.
riesaminare, *v.t.* To re-examine.
riesportare, *v.t.* To re-export.
riesportazione, *n.f.* Re-exportation.
rievocare, *v.t.* To evoke, to recall, to conjure up again.
rifabbricare, *v.t.* To rebuild.
rifacimento, *n.m.* Remaking, restoring, refashioning; (*Lit.*) rifacimento.
rifare, *v.t.* To remake, to do again, to repair, to rebuild, to restore; to make good; to imitate; to give back, to indemnify; to repeat. **— di sana pianta,** to do a thing all over again; **— la strada,** to retrace one's steps; **— il letto,** to make the bed; **— la camera,** to do the room.
rifarsi, *v.r.* To begin again, to become again; to recover (health, losses, etc.); to get even with, to be revenged; to clear up (weather). **— più bello,** to grow more handsome; **mi sono rifatto della perdita,** I have made up for my loss; **— da capo,** to begin all over again; **non sapere da che parte —,** not to know where to start.
rifascio [rifAscio], *adv.* **A rifascio,** in confusion, pell-mell. **Andare a —,** to go to rack and ruin.
rifatta, *n.f.* (*Comm.*) Compensation.
rifatto, *p.p.a.* Remade, done again. **Villano —,** upstart [cp. **rifare**].
riferibile [riferIbile], *a.* Referable.
riferimento, *n.m.* Reference.
riferire, *v.t.* To relate, to report; to refer; to attribute; to return (thanks).
riferirsi, *v.r.* To refer, to concern. **Le mie parole non si riferiscono a te,** what I say does not concern you.
rifermare, *v.i.* To stop again.
riffa, *n.f.* Lottery, raffle; violence. **Di — o di raffa,** by hook or by crook.
rifiatare, *v.i.* To take breath, to take a deep breath; to pause.
rifiatata, *n.f.* Breathing; rest. **Dare una —,** to give a breather.
rifilare, *v.t.* To spin again. **— un pugno,** to give a good punch.
rifinimento, *n.m.* Finish, finishing; weariness, exhaustion.

rifinire, *v.t.i.* To finish, to give the finishing touch; to exhaust, to wear down; to stop, to leave off, to cease.
rifinirsi, *v.r.* To wear oneself out, to get run down (in health).
rifinitezza, *n.f.* Exhaustion, weariness.
rifinitura, *n.f.* Finish, final touch.
rifiorimento, *n.m.* Flourishing; revival; flowering again.
rifiorire, *v.t.i.* To adorn, to retouch; (*Mus.*) to add flourishes; to flourish, to flourish again, to bloom again; to thrive.
rifiorita, *n.f.* Flourishing.
rifioritura, *n.f.* Reflorescence; embellishment; (*Mus.*) flourish.
rifischiare, *v.t.i.* To whisper (scandal, etc.); to whistle back.
rifischione, *n.m.* Informer.
rifiutabile [rifiutAbile], *a.* Refusable, capable of denial.
rifiutare, *v.t.i.* To refuse, to decline; to reject; to renounce, to deny.
rifiutarsi, *v.r.* To refuse. **— di fare,** to refuse to do.
rifiuto, *n.m.* Refusal; refuse, waste; scum; (*Cards*) revoke; escaped steam or liquid. **Rifiuti di carta,** waste paper; **i rifiuti della società,** the outcasts of society; **merce di —,** rubbish, litter.
riflessamente, *adv.* By reflexion, indirectly, as in a mirror.
riflessione, *n.f.* Reflection (in all senses), reflexion; deliberation, consideration. **Senza —,** without due thought.
riflessivamente, *adv.* After consideration.
riflessivo, *a.* Meditative; (*Gram.*) reflexive.
riflesso, *n.m.a.* Reflex; reflection, reflected.
riflessore, *n.m.* Reflector (in a telescope).
riflettere [riflEttere], *v.t.i.* To reflect (in all senses), to throw back; to consider. **Senza —,** without thinking.
riflettersi [riflEttersi], *v.r.* To be reflected, to reflect.
riflettore, *n.m.* Reflector, searchlight. **Raggio del —,** beam of a searchlight.
rifluire, *v.i.* To flow back, to ebb.
riflusso, *n.m.* Ebb, ebb-tide; reflux.
rifocillamento, *n.m.* Refreshment.
rifocillare, *v.t.* To refresh, to revive; to feed; to comfort.
rifocillarsi, *v.r.* To take refreshment, to have something to eat.
rifondere [rifOndere], *v.t.* To melt down again, to recast; to make good; to refund, to pay back.
rifondibile [rifondIbile], *a.* Reimbursable; capable of being recast.
riforbire, *v.t.* To refurbish.
riforbitura, *n.f.* Refurbishing.
riforma, *n.f.* Reform, reformation; (*Mil.*) unfitness for the service. **La Riforma,** the Reformation.
riformare, *v.t.* To reform, to improve; (*Mil.*) to invalid out.
riformatore, *n.m.* Reformer.
riformatorio [riformatOrio], *n.m.* Reformatory.
riformismo, *n.m.* (*Pol.*) Reformism.
rifornimento, *n.m.* Supply; refurnishing; filling. (*Motor.*) **Posto di —,** petrol station, (*Am.*) gas station.
rifornire, *v.t.* To refurnish; to supply with, to provide with.
rifornirsi, *v.r.* To furnish oneself with; (*Motor*) to fill up.
rifrangente, *a.* Refracting.
rifrangere [rifrAngere], *v.t.* To refract.
rifrangimento, *n.m.* Refraction.
rifrattore, *n.m.* Refractor.
rifrazione, *n.f.* Refraction.
rifreddo, *n.m.* Cold dish; side dish; hors d'œuvre.
rifriggere [rifrIggere], *v.t.* To fry again; to warm up; (*fig.*) to keep on repeating.
rifritto, *n.m.* Smell or taste of burning fat.
rifrittume, *n.m.* Hash-up of old stuff; re-hash.
rifrittura, *n.f.* Rigmarole, endless repetition.
rifuggire, *v.t.i.* To turn from, to flee from; to shun; to take refuge.
rifugiarsi, *v.r.* To take refuge, to shelter.
rifugiato, *n.m.* Refugee.
rifugio [rifUgio], *n.m.* Refuge, shelter, asylum. **Luogo di —,** place of safety; **dare — a,** to afford shelter to, to shelter; **— alpino,** alpine hut.
rifulgente, *a.* Refulgent, shining, glaring.
rifulgere [rifUlgere], *v.i.* To shine; to glare.
rifusibile [rifusIbile], *a.* That may be melted or cast again.
rifusione, *n.f.* (*Comm.*) Reimbursement; refunding, making good. **— dei danni,** indemnification.
riga, *n.f.* Line; streak, stripe; row; parting (of hair); (*Mus.*) staff. **Scrivere poche righe,** to scribble a few lines; **falsa riga,** lined guide-sheet under writing paper; **panno a righe,** striped material (*Mil.*) **in —!** Fall in! **rompete le righe!** Dismiss!
rigaglie, *n.f.pl.* Giblets.
rigagnolo [rigAgnolo], *n.m.* Streamlet, rivulet, brook; gutter.
rigare, *v.t.* To rule (lines); to furrow; to rifle (a gun). **— diritto,** to go straight, to act honestly, to behave correctly.
rigata, *n.f.* Blow with a ruler.
rigatino, *n.m.* Striped material.
rigato, *p.p.a.* Ruled, lined, striped; furrowed; rifled (of a gun). **Carta rigata,** ruled paper.
rigattiere, *n.m.* Old-clothes dealer. second-hand dealer.
rigatura, *n.f.* Ruling.
rigenerare, *v.t.* To regenerate.
rigenerazione, *n.f.* Regeneration.
rigettamento, *n.m.* Rejecting, rejection.
rigettare, *v.t.i.* To reject, to throw back; to vomit.
rigetto, *n.m.* Rejection.
rigidamente, *adv.* Rigidly, severely.
rigidezza, rigidità [-à], *n.f.* Rigidity, stiffness; strictness; austerity.
rigido [rIgido], *a.* Rigid, stiff; strict; austere, stern; severe (of cold). **Inverno —,** a hard winter.
rigiramento, *n.m.* Turning around; (*fig.*) swindling.
rigirare, *v.t.* To turn about, to go round; to surround; (*fig.*) to trick, to wheedle, to cajole; (*Comm.*) to re-endorse. **Saper come rigirarla,** to be smart, to know what's what.
rigirarsi, *v.r.* To turn round, to turn, to toss; (*fig.*) to get on well.

rigiro, *n.m.* Winding, turning, twisting; winding (of a river); (*fig.*) trick, subterfuge.
rigo, *n.m.* Line; (*Mus.*) staff.
rigoglio [rigOglio], *n.m.* (*Bot.*) Luxuriance, rankness of growth; exuberance.
rigogliosamente, *adv.* Luxuriantly.
rigoglioso, *a.* Luxuriant; rank.
rigogolo [rigOgolo], *n.m.* (*Zool.*) Golden oriole.
rigoletto, *n.m.* Circle of dancers hand in hand.
rigolino, *n.m.* Groove.
rigonfiamento, *n.m.* Swelling.
rigonfiare, *v.t.i.* To swell, to puff up, to reinflate.
rigonfio [rigOnfio], *a.* Swollen.
rigore, *n.m.* Rigour, severity; strictness; inclemency (of weather). **Di —,** strictly required; **a —,** rigorously; in point of fact.
rigorista (*pl.* **rigoristi**), *n.m.* Strict moralist, rigorist.
rigorosamente, *adv.* Rigorously.
rigoroso, *a.* Rigorous, severe, strict.
rigovernare, *v.t.* To wash up (dishes); to clean; to groom, to curry (a horse); to manure again; to re-govern.
rigovernatura, *n.f.* Washing-up, cleaning; dishwater.
riguadagnare, *v.t.* To regain; to get back, to recover.
riguardante, *n.m.f.* Looker-on.
riguardante, *a.* Regarding, concerning; looking at again; facing.
riguardare, *v.t.i.* To look at again, to examine closely; to revise; to take care of, to be concerned with; to look at, to look out; to face, to front. **Ciò non mi riguarda,** that doesn't concern me, is not my business; **non è cosa che ti riguardi,** that has nothing to do with you.
riguardarsi, *v.r.* To look out for oneself, to beware of, to take care.
riguardata, *n.f.* Look, glance, glimpse.
riguardato, *a.* Wary, prudent.
riguardo, *n.m.* Care, regard, respect; attention, consideration. **Senza nessun —,** regardless; **con — a,** with respect to; **sotto questo —,** from this point of view; **avuto — che,** taking into consideration that.
riguardosamente, *adv.* Carefully, attentively.
riguardoso, *a.* Careful; respectful, considerate; prudent.
rigurgitamento, *n.m.* Overflow, regurgitation.
rigurgitante, *a.* Overflowing, flooding.
rigurgitare, *v.i.* To overflow; to gush back; to regurgitate.
rigurgito [rigUrgito], *n.m.* Overflow; regurgitation.
rigustare, *v.t.* To taste again.
rilasciamento, *n.m.* Relaxation, slackening, weakening; release.
rilasciare, *v.t.* To leave, to quit; to release, to relinquish; to grant; to loosen; to set free; to issue. **— un certificato,** to issue a certificate; **— un documento,** to deliver a deed.
rilasciarsi, *v.r.* To relax, to slacken, to grow weak.
rilascio [rilAscio], *n.m.* Release; delivery; issue; deduction. (*Naut.*) **— forzato,** compulsory putting into port.
rilassamento, *n.m.* Relaxation, slackening; (*Comm.*) slackness (of business).
rilassante, *n.m.a.* (*Med.*) Sedative, relaxing.
rilassare, *v.t.i.* To release, to relax, to let go; to weaken.
rilassarsi, *v.r.* To relax; to rest.
rilassatamente, *adv.* Loosely, slackly.
rilassatezza, *n.f.* Laxity, looseness.
rilassato, *a.* Lax, loose.
rilegamento, *n.m.* Rebinding, refastening.
rilegare, *v.t.* To bind (a book); to rebandage; to refasten.
rilegatore, *n.m.* Book-binder.
rilegatura, *n.f.* Binding (of a book), bookbinding.
rileggere [rilEggere], *v.t.* To reread, to read over again.
rilento, *adv.* **A —,** Slowly, carefully, cautiously.
rilevamento, *n.m.* Surveying, map-making; drawing (a plan, etc.); reviving; bringing up; (*Naut.*) bearing. **— alla bussola,** compass-bearing.
rilevante, *a.* Important, considerable; prominent.
rilevare, *v.t.i.* To take up, to take away, to take over; to draw; to relieve (a sentry, etc.); to detect, to perceive, to jut out, to protrude; to amount. **— un negozio,** to take over a shop; **— un errore,** to point out a mistake; **fare — che,** to bring to notice that; **— dei difetti,** to find fault.
rilevarsi, *v.r.* To rise again, to stand up again, to get up again.
rilevatamente, *adv.* In relief; eminently, splendidly.
rilevatario [rilevatArio], *n.m.* Lessee, transferee; purchaser.
rilevato, *a.* Protruding, projecting, prominent.
rilievo, *n.m.* Relief, projection; remark. **Cosa di poco —,** matter of little importance; **mettere in —,** to give prominence to; **una cosa degna di —,** a matter worthy of remark.
rilucente, *a.* Shining, glittering.
rilucentezza, *n.f.* Brilliancy, shine; glitter.
rilucere [rilUcere], *v.i.* To shine, to glitter.
riluttante, *a.* Reluctant.
riluttanza, *n.f.* Reluctance.
rima, *n.f.* Rhyme; poetry; lyrical verse. **Terza —,** 3-line connected stanzas employed by Dante, etc.; **ottava —,** 8-line heroic stanzas of Ariosto, etc.; **rispondere per le rime,** to pay back someone in his own coin, to give tit for tat.
rimandare, *v.t.* To send back, to send again; to postpone; to put off, to defer; to refer; to reject. **— da Erode a Pilato,** to send from pillar to post; **— da oggi a domani,** to procrastinate; **— a pagina 50,** to refer (the reader) to page 50.
rimando, *n.m.* Sending back, return; postponement; reference.
rimaneggiamento, *n.m.* Rearrangement; doing over again; altering, alteration.
rimaneggiare, *v.t.* To do over again; to rehandle; to rearrange; to alter, to change; to reform.
rimanente, *n.m.a* Remainder; remaining.
rimanenza, *n.f.* Remainder, residue; stay. **— a saldo,** balance due.
rimanere, *v.t.i.* To remain, to stay, to stop; to live, to dwell; to leave off; to be situated. **— in carica,** to stay in office; **— al posto,**

to hold one's place; — **indietro,** to stay behind; — **a casa,** to keep indoors; — **d'accordo circa,** to be in agreement on; — **in forse,** to remain in suspense; — **debitore,** to be in debt; — **meravigliato,** to be astonished; — **morto sul colpo,** to be struck dead on the spot; — **di sasso,** to be dumbfounded; **dove siete rimasti ?** where did you leave off? **vuole — a cena da noi ?** won't you stay for dinner?
rimanersi, *v.r.* To remain, to stay.
rimangiare, rimangiarsi, *v.t.r.* To eat again; (*fig.*) to retract, to eat one's words; to break a promise.
rimarcare, *v.t.* To remark, to notice.
rimarchevole [rimarchEvole], *a.* Remarkable, noticeable.
rimarco, *n.m.* Remark.
rimare, *v.t.i.* To rhyme; to make verse.
rimarginare, *v.t.* To heal up; to cicatrize.
rimarginarsi, *v.r.* To become healed, to heal.
rimario [rimArio], *n.m.* Rhyming dictionary.
rimaritarsi, *v.r.* To marry again.
rimasuglio [rimasUglio], *n.m.* Remains, bits, crumbs; residue.
rimatore, rimatrice, *n.m.f.* Rhymester.
rimbacuccarsi, *v.r.* To muffle oneself up.
rimbaldanzire, rimbaldanzirsi, *v.i.r.* To grow bold.
rimbalzare, *v.i.* To rebound; to spring back.
rimbalzello, *n.m.* (Game of) ducks and drakes.
rimbalzo, *n.m.* Rebound. **Di —,** indirectly.
rimbambimento, *n.m.* Dotage, second childhood.
rimbambinire, rimbambire, *v.i.* To grow childish.
rimbambito, *n.m.a.* Dotard; childish; doting.
rimbarcare, rimbarcarsi, *v.t.r.* To re-embark.
rimbarco, *n.m.* Re-embarkation.
rimbeccare, *v.t.i.* To peck; to retort, to answer rudely, to cheek.
rimbeccarsi, *v.r.* To quarrel, to be at loggerheads.
rimbecco, *n.m.* Retort, repartee; curt reply.
rimbecillire, *v.i.* To grow silly; to become stupid.
rimboccamento, *n.m.* Tucking up.
rimboccare, *v.t.* To tuck up. **Rimboccarsi le maniche,** to tuck up one's sleeves.
rimboccatura, rimbocco, *n.f.m.* Tucking-up.
rimbombante, *a.* Resounding, booming.
rimbombare, *v.i.* To boom, to resound.
rimbombo, *n.m.* Loud noise, booming, roar, reverberation.
rimborsabile [rimborsAbile], *a.* Repayable.
rimborsare, *v.t.* To reimburse, to pay back, to repay.
rimborso, *n.m.* Reimbursement, repayment.
rimboscamento, *n.m.* Reafforestation.
rimboscare, rimboschire, *v.t.* To reafforest, to replant with trees.
rimboschimento, *n.m.* Reafforestation.
rimbottare, *v.t.* To re-barrel.
rimbrottare, *v.t.* To reproach, to rebuke severely.
rimbrotto, *n.m.* Harsh rebuke, severe reproach.
rimbucare, rimbucarsi, *v.t.* To put back into its hole, to return to its hole.
rimediabile [rimediAbile], *a.* Remediable.
rimediare, *v.t.i.* To remedy, to put right. — **ad un torto,** to right a wrong.
rimedio [rimEdio], *n.m.* Remedy, cure; medicine. **Senza —,** irremediable; **non c'è —,** there's no help for it.
rimembranza, *n.f.* Remembrance.
rimembrare, *v.t.* To remind, to call to mind; to remember.
rimenare, *v.t.* To bring back again; to shake, to jolt; to handle; to stir, to mix.
rimenata, *n.f.* Shaking, handling; scolding.
rimenio [rimenIo], *n.m.* Continual jolting, shaking up.
rimeritare, *v.t.* To requite, to recompense.
rimerito [rimErito], *n.m.* Recompense.
rimescolamento, *n.m.* Mingling, mixing; confusion; (*Cards*) shuffling; fright, shock.
rimescolare, *v.t.* To mix, to mix up, to blend; to confuse, to muddle; (*Cards*) to shuffle. **Sentirsi — il sangue,** to feel one's blood run cold.
rimescolarsi, *v.r.* To mix oneself up with; to mingle, to be blended with; to be scared, to be terrified; to receive a shock.
rimescolata, *n.f.* Mixing, mingling; (*Cards*) shuffle, shuffling.
rimescolio [rimescolIo], *n.m.* Continual changing; mixture; confusion; shock.
rimescolo [rimEscolo], *n.m.* Start, jump (from nerves).
rimessa, *n.f.* Coach-house, shed; replacement; (*Comm.*) remittance; (*Motor.*) garage; (*Aviat.*) hangar; (*Bot.*) sprout, growth, shoot.
rimessamente, *adv.* Submissively.
rimesso, *p.p.a.* Mild, submissive [cp. **rimettere**].
rimestare, *v.t.* To stir up, to shake, to agitate, to toss, to wave about.
rimettere [rimEttere], *v.t.* To replace, to put back; to put again; to defer, to put off; to submit; to pardon; to remit; to repay; to lose; to bring up, to vomit; to cut (teeth); to throw out shoots. — **pace fra certe persone,** to reconcile certain persons; — **in possesso,** to restore to possession; — **ad un'altra settimana,** to put off to next week; — **a nuovo,** to restore, to put in working order; — **i danni,** to remit the damages; — **una lettera,** to deliver a letter; — **fondi,** to remit money.
rimettersi [rimEttersi], *v.r.* To place oneself again; to compose oneself; to improve (of the weather). **Me ne rimetto a voi,** I leave the affair to you to settle; — **al lavoro,** to get back to work; — **a letto,** to go to bed again; — **in salute,** to regain one's health; — **al bello,** (the weather) to settle.
rimirare, *v.t.* To gaze at intently; to stare at.
rimodernamento, *n.m.* Modernization.
rimodernare, *v.t.* To modernize, to renew.
rimodernarsi, *v.r.* To become up-to-date, to bring oneself up-to-date.
rimonta, *n.f.* (*Mil.*) Remount; vamping (of a boot or shoe).
rimontare, *v.t.i.* To remount; to go back; to reascend; to assemble (machinery); to wind up (a clock, etc.); to vamp (shoe, etc.); to go upstream; to date from. — **il fiume,** to go up the river.
rimontatura, *n.f.* Assembling (machinery); putting together; remounting.

rimorchiare, *v.t.* To tow, to haul. (*Motor.*) **Carro rimorchiato,** trailer.
rimorchiatore, *n.m.* (*Naut.*) Tug; tow-boat.
rimorchiatura, *n.f.* Towing; hauling.
rimorchio [rimOrchio], *n.m.* Tow, towing, trailer. **Prendere a —,** to take in tow; (*Motor.*) **un —,** a trailer.
rimordere [rimOrdere], *v.t.* To prick (of conscience); to feel remorse.
rimorso, *n.m.* Remorse.
rimosso, *p.p.a.* Removed, dismissed [cp. **rimuovere**].
rimostranza, *n.f.* Remonstrance.
rimostrare, *v.i.* To remonstrate, to complain.
rimovibile [rimovIbile], *a.* Removable, liable to dismissal.
rimovimento, *n.m.* Removal, dismissal.
rimozione, *n.f.* Removal, displacement; dismissal.
rimpadronirsi, *v.r.* To take possession of again.
rimpallare, *v.t.* (*Billiards*) To kiss.
rimpallo, *n.m.* (*Billiards*) Kiss.
rimpannucciarsi, *v.r.* (*fig.*) To better oneself; to be better off.
rimpastare, *v.t.* To reknead; to rearrange, to re-form.
rimpasto, *n.m.* Re-mixing; shuffle. (*Pol.*) **— ministeriale,** cabinet shuffle.
rimpatriare, *v.t.i.* To repatriate; to return to one's country.
rimpatrio [rimpAtrio], *n.m.* Repatriation.
rimpettirsi, *v.r.* To swell with pride; to be cocky.
rimpetto, *prep.* Opposite, facing; face to face. **Di — al teatro,** opposite the theatre.
rimpiangere [rimpiAngere], *v.t.* To regret, to mourn over.
rimpianto, *n.m.a.* Regret; regretted.
rimpiattare, *v.t.* To hide, to conceal.
rimpiattarsi, *v.r.* To hide oneself; to lurk.
rimpiatterello, rimpiattino, *n.m.* Game of hide-and-seek.
rimpiazzare, *v.t.* To replace.
rimpicciolire, rimpiccolire, *v.t.i.* To make smaller; to grow smaller.
rimpiegare, *v.t.* To re-employ.
rimpiego, *n.m.* Re-employment.
rimpinzamento, *n.m.* Cramming, stuffing; overflowing.
rimpinzare, rimpinzarsi, *v.t.r.* To cram, to stuff; to overeat oneself.
rimpolpare, *v.t.i.* To fatten; to enrich.
rimproverare, *v.t.* To reproach; to reprove, to scold, to reprimand; to blame.
rimproverarsi, *v.r.* To reproach oneself with; to regret, to repent. **Non ho niente da rimproverarmi,** I have nothing to be ashamed of.
rimprovero [rimprOvero], *n.m.* Reproach, scolding; reprimand.
rimuginare, *v.t.* To search for, to rummage for; (*fig.*) to turn over (in one's mind).
rimunerare, *v.t.* To remunerate.
rimunerativo, *a.* Remunerative, rewarding.
rimunerazione, *n.f.* Remuneration.
rimuovere, rimovere, *v.t.* To remove, to displace; to dissuade; to dismiss; to deter. **— la terra,** to dig, to move soil; **— cielo e terra,** to move heaven and earth.
rimutamento, *n.m.* Further change.
rinascente, *a.* Reviving, coming back; reborn.
rinascenza, *n.f.* Revival [cp. **rinascimento**].
rinascere [rinAscere], *v.i.* To revive, to be born again; to spring up afresh; to reappear.
rinascimento, rinascita [rinAscita], *n.m.f.* Revival; rebirth; Renaissance.
rinato, *a.* Reborn.
rincagnarsi, *v.r.* To frown, to scowl.
rincagnato, *a.* **Naso —,** snub-nosed.
rincalzamento, *n.m.* Chase, pursuit; reinforcement; (*Agric.*) forcing, earthing up.
rincalzare, *v.t.* To chase, to pursue; to reinforce; (*Agric.*) to earth up, to force; to urge, to prop up; to tuck in (bedclothes).
rincalzata, *n.f.* Support, prop; earthing up, forcing.
rincalzo, *n.m.* Reinforcement, support, prop.
rincantucciare, *v.t.* To corner, to drive into a corner.
rincantucciarsi, *v.r.* To hide oneself.
rincarare, *v.t.i.* To raise the price of; to rise in price, to become dearer.
rincaro, *n.m.* Rise in price; rising cost.
rincasare, *v.i.* To return home, to go home.
rinchiudere [rinchiUdere], *v.t.* To shut up, to enclose, to shut in.
rinchiuso, *n.m.* Enclosure, enclosed place. **Sapere di —,** to have a close smell.
rincontrare, rincontrarsi, *v.i.r.* To meet again, to meet.
rincontro, *n.m.* Encounter, meeting; comparison. **Di —,** on the other hand.
rincoramento, *n.m.* Encouragement.
rincorare, *v.t.* To encourage, to cheer.
rincorarsi, *v.r.* To be encouraged, to be heartened.
rincorporare, *v.t.* To incorporate, to re-embody.
rincorrere [rincOrrere], *v.t.* To chase after, to pursue.
rincorsa, *n.f.* Short run, spring. **Prendere la —,** to dart away, to sprint.
rincrescere [rincrEscere], *v.i.* To be sorry for, to regret, to cause regret. **Mi rincresce che,** I'm sorry that; **mi rincresce che non sia qui,** I'm sorry he isn't here; **se non ti rincresce,** if you don't mind; **mi rincresce di non essere potuto venire,** I am sorry I couldn't come.
rincrescevole [rincrescEvole], *a.* Regrettable, annoying; unpleasant.
rincrescevolmente, *adv.* Regrettably.
rincrescimento, *n.m.* Regret.
rincrudimento, *n.m.* Worsening (esp. of weather conditions); aggravating.
rincrudire, rincrudirsi, *v.i.r.* To grow worse (of weather); to be exasperated, to grow embittered.
rinculare, *v.i.* To recoil, to draw back; to shrink.
rinculo, *n.m.* Recoil.
rindebitarsi, *v.r.* To run into debt again.
rindossare, *v.t.* To put on again (of clothes).
rinettare, *v.t.* To clean again.
rinfacciamento, *n.m.* Reproach, casting in one's teeth.
rinfacciare, *v.t.* To reproach with, to cast in one's teeth.
rinfagottare, *v.t.* To bundle up again; (*fig.*) to dress badly.
rinfiammare, *v.t.* To rekindle.

rinfiancare, *v.t.* To prop, to support.
rinfianco, *n.m.* Prop, support; flanking.
rinfocolamento, *n.m.* Rekindling.
rinfocolare, rinfocolarsi, *v.t.r.* To rekindle (in all senses).
rinfoderare, *v.t.* To sheathe (one's sword).
rinforzamento, *n.m.* Reinforcement, strengthening.
rinforzare, *v.t.* To reinforce, to strengthen; to support, to prop up.
rinforzarsi, *v.r.* To grow stronger, to strengthen oneself.
rinforzo, *n.m.* Reinforcement; support.
rinfrancare, *v.t.* To hearten, to encourage, to reinvigorate.
rinfrancarsi, *v.r.* To be oneself again.
rinfrescamento, *n.m.* Refreshment; refreshing, cooling.
rinfrescante, *n.m.a.* Cooling drink; refreshing.
rinfrescare, *v.t.* To cool, to refresh; (*Art*) to restore a painting. **— la memoria,** to recall to memory.
rinfrescarsi, *v.r.* To have a cooling drink, to refresh oneself; to cool down.
rinfrescata, *n.f.* Cooling; refreshing (drink or rain).
rinfresco, *n.m.* Refreshment, light refreshment; provisions.
rinfronzire, *v.i.* To put out fresh leaves.
rinfronzirsi, *v.r.* To make oneself smart.
rinfusa, *adv.* **Alla —,** In confusion, higgledy-piggledy; (*Comm.*) in bulk.
rinfusamente, *adv.* Confusedly, anyhow.
ringagliardimento, *n.m.* Reinforcing, strengthening.
ringagliardirsi, *v.r.* To get strengthened.
ringalluzzarsi, ringalluzzirsi, *v.r.* To become elated, to get cocky; to be as pleased as Punch.
ringentilirsi, *v.r.* To become gentle.
ringhiare, *v.i.* To snarl, to growl.
ringhiera, *n.f.* Banisters; railing; balcony.
ringhio [rInghio], *n.m.* Snarl, growl.
ringhioso, *a.* Snarling.
ringiovanimento, *n.m.* Rejuvenation.
ringiovanire, *v.t.i.* To rejuvenate, to make younger; to look younger, to recover vigour.
ringraziamento, *n.m.* Thanks, returning thanks, thanksgiving.
ringraziare, *v.t.* To thank, to give thanks (for); to refuse, to decline with thanks.
rinnalzarsi, *v.r.* To rise again.
rinnamorarsi, *v.r.* To fall in love again.
rinnegabile [rinnegAbile], *a.* That may be repudiated.
rinnegamento, *n.m.* Disclaimer, disownment, repudiation.
rinnegare, *v.t.* To deny, to disown, to repudiate; to abjure; to recant.
rinnegato, *n.m.a.* Renegade.
rinnestare, *v.t.* (*Agric.*) To re-graft; (*Med.*) to revaccinate. (*Mech.*) **— una marcia,** to re-engage a gear.
rinnesto, *n.m.* (*Med.*) Revaccination.
rinnovabile [rinnovAbile], *a.* Renewable.
rinnovamento, *n.m.* Renewal.
rinnovare, *v.t.* To renew, to renovate; to wear new clothes; to repeat.
rinnovazione, *n.f.* Renewal, renovation.
rinnovellamento, *n.m.* Renewing, renewal.
rinnovellare, *v.t.* To renew, to renovate.
rinnovo, rinnuovo, *n.m.* Renewal (of bill, etc.).
rinoceronte, *n.m.* (*Zool.*) Rhinoceros.
rinomanza, *n.f.* Renown, fame.
rinomare, *v.t.* To make famous, to make celebrated.
rinomato, *p.p.a.* Famous, renowned, celebrated.
rinominare, *v.t.* To reappoint.
rinsaccare, *v.t.* To pack again.
rinsaldamento, *n.m.* Consolidation; restarching.
rinsaldare, *v.t.* To starch again, to re-solder; (*fig.*) to strengthen, to consolidate.
rinsanguare, *v.t.* To reinvigorate; to give new life to.
rinsanguarsi, *v.r.* To become prosperous again, to be in funds.
rinsanire, *v.i.* To regain one's health, to recover.
rinsavire, *v.i.* To recover one's wits, to get sensible again.
rinserrare, *v.t.* To shut up again; to shut in; to tie tighter.
rinterzare, *v.t.* To repeat for the third time.
rintoccare, *v.i.* To toll, to strike (of a clock).
rintocco, *n.m.* Knell, toll, striking (of a clock). **Suonare a rintocchi,** to sound the alarm.
rintracciabile [rintracciAbile], *a.* Traceable.
rintracciamento, *n.m.* Investigation, searching out.
rintracciare, *v.t.* To trace out, to find out, to track.
rintrecciare, *v.t.* To intertwine, to interlace.
rintronamento, *n.m.* Deafening noise, booming.
rintronare, *v.t.i.* To resound, to deafen, to stun; to boom.
rintuzzamento, *n.m.* Rejection, rebuff, repulse; blunting, dulling.
rintuzzare, *v.t.* To repel, to rebuff, to rebut; to hit back; to blunt.
rintuzzarsi, *v.r.* To become blunt.
rinuncia, rinunzia [rinUncia, rinUnzia], *n.f.* Renunciation, renouncement.
rinunciare, rinunziare, *v.t.* To renounce, to give up, to relinquish; to resign, to refuse.
rinunciatario [renunciatArio], *n.m.* (*Law*) Renouncee; (*Polit.*) defeatist.
rinvalidare, *v.t.* To confirm.
rinvelenire, *v.t.i.* To embitter, to envenom yet more; to grow bitter.
rinvelinirsi, *v.r.* To become embittered.
rinvenimento, *n.m.* Finding, discovery; recovery; return to one's senses.
rinvenire, *v.t.i.* To find, to discover, to rediscover; to recover one's health or strength; to come to oneself; to soften; to swell.
rinvenirsi, *v.r.* To find a way out, to find out.
rinverdimento, *n.m.* Growing green again.
rinverdire, *v.t.i.* To revive, to make green again; to become green, to freshen; to revive.
rinvestimento, *n.m.* Reinvestment.
rinvestire, *v.t.* To reinvest, to re-employ (capital); to strengthen.
rinviare, *v.t.* To adjourn, to defer, to postpone; to send back.
rinvigorimento, *n.m.* Strengthening, reinvigorating.
rinvigorire, *v.t.* To strengthen, to invigorate.

rinvigorirsi, *v.r.* To become strong again, to regain strength.
rinvilio [rinvIlio], *n.m.* Depreciation (of value), abatement; fall (in prices).
rinvilire, *v.t.i.* To lower prices; to fall in price, to become cheaper.
rinvio [rinvIo], *n.m.* Dismissal; adjournment, postponement.
rio, *n.m.* Brook, rivulet, stream; canal.
rio, *a.* (*Poet.*) Wicked; cruel; guilty.
rioccupare, *v.t.* To reoccupy.
rioccupazione, *n.f.* Reoccupation.
rionale, *a.* Of a (suburban) district of a town.
rione, *n.m.* Ward (of a city), quarter, district.
riordinamento, *n.m.* Rearrangement; restoration of order; reorganization.
riordinare, *v.t.* To rearrange, to set in order, to reorganize; to order afresh.
riordinatore, riordinatrice, *n.m.f.* Reorganizer.
riorganizzare, *v.t.* To reorganize.
riorganizzazione, *n.f.* Reorganization.
riottoso, *a.* Quarrelsome; sulky, stubborn; riotous.
ripa, *n.f.* Steep place; (river) bank; seashore, beach.
ripagare, *v.t.* To repay, to recompense.
riparabile [riparAbile], *a.* Reparable.
riparare, *v.t.i.* To repair, to mend; to refit (a ship); to make amends; to parry, to ward off; to keep out; to remedy; to indemnify; to take shelter. **— ad un inconveniente,** to remedy an inconvenience; **— in campagna,** to repair to the country; **— il torto,** to redress the wrong.
ripararsi, *v.r.* To shelter oneself, to take shelter, to take refuge. **— dal sole,** to take shelter from the sun.
riparatore, riparatrice, *n.m.f.* Repairer, mender.
riparazione, *n.f.* Repair; recovery; amends. **In —,** under repair; **accordare — per una offesa,** to atone for an injury.
riparlare, *v.i.* To speak again.
riparlarsi, *v.r.* To become reconciled, to make up (after a quarrel). **Ne riparleremo,** we'll talk about this later.
riparo, *n.m.* Shelter; remedy; dam, dyke; screen. **Mettersi al —,** to get under cover, to take cover; **al —,** in safety; **senza —,** without remedy; **al — da ogni pericolo,** beyond all danger.
ripartibile [ripartIbile], *a.* Divisible, possible to be shared.
ripartimento, *n.m.* Division, distribution.
ripartire ,*v.t.i.* To divide, to allot, to share, to distribute; to go away again, to start again. **Il treno riparte tra dieci minuti,** the train leaves in 10 minutes.
ripartitamente, *adv.* In lots, separately, severally.
ripartizione, *n.f.* Distribution, division.
riparto, *n.m.* Distribution, division; department; (*Mil.*) body, squad.
ripassare, *v.t.i.* To look over again; to reread, to review; to revise; to overhaul; to strop (a razor); to grind (a tool); to go back, to come back; to call again. **Sono ripassato da voi tre volte,** I have called on you three times.
ripassata, *n.f.* Revision, re-examining; re-reading. **Dare una —,** to give the "once-over".
ripasso, *n.m.* Return; revision.
ripensamento, *n.m.* Afterthought, second thought.
ripensare, *v.t.i.* To think of, to recall to mind; to think over.
ripentimento, *n.m.* Repentance.
ripentirsi, *v.r.* To repent; to change one's mind.
ripercossa, *n.f.* Repercussion.
ripercosso, *p.p.a.* Beaten back, thrown back.
ripercotere, ripercuotere [ripercOtere, ripercuOtere], *v.t.i.* To beat again, to beat back; to send back again, to reflect back; to rebound, to echo.
ripercotimento, ripercussione, *n.m.f.* Repercussion.
riperdere [ripErdere], *v.t.* To lose again.
ripescare, *v.t.* To fish up, to find again, to get hold of.
ripetente, *n.m.* Pupil who has not been moved up, backward boy.
ripetente, *a.* Repeating, renewing.
ripetere [ripEtere], *v.t* . To repeat, to rehearse; to recommence; to claim. **— una richiesta,** to renew a request; **far — una lezione,** to hear a lesson; **ripete sempre la stessa storia,** he is always singing the same tune.
ripetitore, ripetitrice, *n.m.f.* Private teacher, coach.
ripetizione, *n.f.* Repetition, recurrence; rehearsal; private tuition, private lesson. **Orologio a —,** repeater (watch) ; **fucile a —,** repeating rifle.
ripetutamente, *adv.* Repeatedly.
ripetuto, *a.* Repeated, reiterated.
ripiano, *n.m.* Level ground, terrace; plateau; (staircase) landing.
ripiantare, *v.t.* To replant.
ripicco, *n.m.* Retaliation; pique, spite; tit for tat.
ripidezza, *n.f.* Steepness.
ripido [rIpido], *a.* Steep.
ripiegamento, *n.m.* Folding, bending back; falling back; (*Mil.*) withdrawal, retreat.
ripiegare, *v.t.i.* To refold, to fold again; to turn again, to turn (to right or left).
ripiegarsi, *v.r.* To turn; to fold up again; to bend down; to shift about, to swerve; (*Mil.*) to fall back, to retreat.
ripiegata, *n.f.* Bend (of a river); sudden turn.
ripiegatura, *n.f.* Folding, doubling up, fold.
ripiego, *n.m.* Expedient, substitute, make-shift.
ripienezza, *n.f.* Repletion, surfeit.
ripieno, *n.m.* Stuffing (for veal, etc.).
ripieno, *a.* Full, replete; stuffed with.
ripigliare, *v.t.* To retake, to begin again, to recommence; to resume; to reprimand. **— un racconto,** to resume a story; **— sonno,** to drop asleep again; **— animo,** to take courage again.
ripigliarsi, *v.r.* To recover, to regain one's strength.
ripiombare, *v.i.* To sink down again, to sink again. **— sul nemico,** to fall on the enemy once more.
riponimento, *n.m.* Replacement.
ripopolamento, *n.m.* Re-population.
ripopolare, *v.t.* To re-populate.
riporre, *v.t.* To replace, to put again, to put back; to hide, to conceal, to put away;

to reckon again. — **fiducia in,** to place confidence in; — **nel fodero,** to sheathe.
riporsi, *v.r.* To resume, to set about (doing) again.
riportare, *v.t.* To carry back, to bring back, to bring again; to relate, to report; to receive, to get; to carry over (*Book-keeping*), to carry forward, to bring forward. — **il premio,** to carry off the prize; — **un danno,** to suffer a loss; — **un libro,** to return a book.
riportarsi, *v.r.* To refer, to appeal. **Mi riporto alla mia lettera,** I refer you to my letter.
riportatore, riportatrice, *n.m.f.* Reporter; (*colloq.*) tell-tale, sneak.
riporto, *n.m.* Patchwork; (*Book-keeping*) amount to be carried forward.
riposante, *a.* Pleasant, soothing, restful.
riposare, *v.t.i.* To rest, to refresh by rest; to place again; to rest, to pause; to lie down; to sleep. — **in,** to rely upon; **ha riposato bene?** did you sleep well? — **durante il discorso;** to pause in the course of the speech; **qui riposa,** here lies.
riposarsi, *v.r.* To rest, to rest oneself, to lie down. — **dopo il lavoro,** to rest after working.
riposata, *n.f.* Pause, rest, halt.
riposatamente, *adv.* Calmly, quietly, peacefully.
riposatoio [riposatOio], *n.m.* (*obs.*) Landing (on a staircase).
riposo, *n.m.* Rest, repose, quiet, retirement; (*Theat.*) no performance. **Collocato a —,** pensioned off; **buon —,** goodnight, sleep well.
ripossedere, *v.t.* To repossess.
ripostamente, *adv.* Secretly; slyly, in an underhand manner.
ripostiglio [ripostIglio], *n.m.* Repository; locker; lumber-room; recess, nook; hiding-place.
riposto, *a.* Hidden, secret; replaced.
riprendere [riprEndere], *v.t.i.* To take back, to retake, to recover, to recapture; to take up again, to resume; to reprove; to pick up (a stitch); to start again; to reply, to retort.
riprendersi [riprEndersi], *v.r.* To recover (strength), to revive; to resume; to correct oneself (when speaking).
riprendevole, riprensibile [riprendEvole, riprensIbile], *a.* Reprehensible.
riprensione, *n.f.* Reprehension.
riprensivo, *a.* Reprehensive.
ripresa, *n.f.* Recapture; resumption, renewal, recommencement; revival; darn, darning; burden (of a song); recovery; (*Sport*) round, bout; (*Football, etc.*) return match; — **del viaggio,** resumption of the journey; **a più riprese,** at various times, at intervals.
ripresentare, *v.t.* To re-present; to show again.
ripresentarsi, *v.r.* To reappear, to present oneself again.
ripreso, *p.p.a.* Retaken, taken again; resumed [cp. **riprendere**].
ripristinamento, *n.m.* Reinstatement, restoration.
ripristinare, *v.t.* To restore, to re-establish; to renew.
ripristinazione, *n.f.* Restoration, renewal.
riproducibile [riproducIbile], *a.* Capable of reproduction.
riproducimento, *n.m.* Reproduction, reproducing.
riprodurre, *v.t.* To reproduce.
riprodursi, *v.r.* To be reproduced, to breed, to reproduce; to happen, to occur, to recur.
riproduttività [-à], *n.f.* Reproductivity.
riproduttivo, *a.* Reproductive.
riproduttore, *n.m.* One who reproduces; sire.
riproduzione, *n.f.* Reproduction.
ripromettere [ripromEttere], *v.t.* To promise again, to renew a promise.
ripromettersi [ripromEttersi], *v.r.* To hope (to do something), to intend, to have in mind; to hope for, to expect.
riprova, *n.f.* New evidence, fresh proof; confirmation. **A — di ciò,** in confirmation of this.
riprovare, *v.t.i.* To reprove; to censure, to blame; to find fault with; to disown; to reject; to try again; to go through again.
riprovarsi, *v.r.* To try again; to exert oneself again.
riprovato, *p.p.a.* Tried again; unsuccessful; rejected.
riprovazione, *n.f.* Reprobation; rejection.
riprovevole [riprovEvole], *a.* Blameable, blameworthy; shameful.
ripubblicazione, *n.f.* Republication.
repudiabile [ripudiAbile], *a.* Possible of being repudiated.
ripudiare, *v.t.* To repudiate.
ripudio [ripUdio], *n.m.* Repudiation.
ripugnante, *a.* Repugnant, disgusting.
ripugnanza, *n.f.* Repugnance, aversion, disgust, revulsion; reluctance.
ripugnare, *v.i.* To be repugnant; to disgust; to be contrary, to be inconsistent; to be reluctant.
ripulimento, *n.m.* Cleaning, cleaning up; retouching, touching up.
ripulire, *v.t.* To clean again, to clean up; to clear away, to sweep the board; to retouch, to perfect.
ripulirsi, *v.r.* To tidy oneself, to smarten oneself.
ripulisti [cp. **repulisti**].
ripulita, *n.f.* Cleaning, making fresh and new; retouching, touching up. **Darsi una —,** to brush oneself up, to have a tidy up.
ripulitura, *n.f.* Cleaning.
ripullulare, *v.i.* To swarm again, to spread far and wide.
ripulsa, *n.f.* Repulse; denial, refusal.
ripulsione, *n.f.* Repulsion, aversion.
ripulsivo, *a.* Repulsive, disgusting.
riputazione, *n.f.* Reputation.
riquadramento, *n.m.* Squaring; (house) redecoration.
riquadrare, *v.t.* To square; to redecorate the interior walls of a house; to measure (area).
riquadratore, *n.m.* (House) decorator.
riquadratura, *n.f.* Squaring; redecoration.
riquadro, *n.m.* Square, panel; redecoration.
risacca, *n.f.* Surf.
risaia [risAia], *n.f.* Rice-field.
risaldamento, *n.m.* Resoldering, rewelding.
risaldare, *v.t.* To resolder, to solder.
risaldatura, *n.f.* Resoldering.

risalire, *v.t.i.* To reascend, to go up again, to rise again; to remount; to rise (in price). — **un cavallo,** to remount; — **all'origine,** to trace back to its origin; — **la corrente,** to go up-stream.
risaltare, *v.t.i.* To jump again; to project, to jut out, to stand out; to catch the eye, to make conspicuous. **Far —,** to enhance, to make more noticeable.
risalto, *n.m.* Standing out; prominence, relief; rebound. **Dar — a,** to enhance, to give prominence to, to bring into evidence.
risanabile [risanAbile], *a.* Curable.
risanamento, *n.m.* Healing; recovery; (*fig.*) reformation; drainage of land, reclamation of marshland; slum clearance.
risanare, *v.t.* To heal; to restore to health; to cure; to reclaim (land).
risanatore, risanatrice, *n.m.f.a.* Healer; healing.
risapere, *v.t.* To know (by report), to learn (by hearsay); to hear of, to get to know.
risaputo, *p.p.a.* Well known, known (by report). **È — che,** it is well known that.
risarcibile [risarcIbile], *a.* Capable of being compensated; reparable.
risarcimento, *n.m.* Compensation, damages; reparation.
risarcire, *v.t.* To compensate, to indemnify; to restore, to repair.
risata, *n.f.* Laughter, laugh; burst of laughter, roar of laughter.
risataccia [risatAccia], *n.f.* Horse laugh.
risazio [risAzio], *a.* **Essere sazio e —,** to be thoroughly sick (of something); to be fed up.
riscaldamento, *n.m.* Heating, heat; (*fig.*) excitement, irritation, anger. — **centrale,** central heating.
riscaldare, *v.t.i.* To heat, to warm, to warm up; (*fig.*) to inflame, to excite. — **dell'acqua,** to warm water; — **troppo,** to over-heat.
riscaldarsi, *v.r.* To warm oneself, to get warm; to get excited, to become heated in temper.
riscaldata, *n.f.* Warming up, warm.
riscaldatore, *n.m.* Heating apparatus, stove, heater; stoker.
riscaldato, *p.p.a.* Heated, warmed up again.
riscaldo, *n.m.* (*Med.*) Inflammation, irritation; heat-spot, pimple; feverishness, rash.
riscattabile [riscattAbile], *a.* Redeemable.
riscattare, *v.t.* To ransom, to redeem.
riscattarsi, *v.r.* To recover one's losses; to redeem one's reputation.
riscatto, *n.m.* Ransom, redemption.
riscendere [riscEndere], *v.i.* To descend again, to sink again.
rischiaramento, *n.m.* Illumination, brightening; enlightening.
rischiarare, *v.t.i.* To light up, to illuminate; to enlighten; to clarify.
rischiararsi, *v.r.* To brighten up, to clear, to clear up.
rischiare, *v.t.i.* To risk, to venture, to expose to risk; to run the risk.
rischiarire, rischiarirsi, *v.i.r.* To brighten, to become clear.
rischio [rIschio], *n.m.* Risk; danger, peril. **A suo — e pericolo,** at his own risk; **correre — di,** to run the risk of.
rischioso, *a.* Risky, hazardous, perilous.
risciacquamento, *n.m.* Rinsing.
risciacquare, *v.t.* To rinse.
risciacquata, *n.f.* Rinsing; scolding.
risciacquatura, *n.f.* Rinsing, dish-water, slops.
riscontare, *v.t.* (*Comm.*) To re-discount.
riscontrabile [riscontrAbile], *a.* That may be found, provable.
riscontrare, *v.t.* To meet; to compare, to confront, to collate; to find.
riscontrarsi, *v.r.* To meet, to cross; to fall in with; to agree, to tally; to match.
riscontratore, *n.m.* (*Comm.*) Auditor.
riscontro, *n.m.* Meeting, encounter; comparison, checking, verification; audit; reply, acknowledgement; draught (of air). — **di cassa,** verification of cash; — **di una copia,** collation of a copy; — **dei conti,** audit of the accounts; **in — alla vostra del,** in answer to your letter of the.
riscoprire, *v.t.* To rediscover, to uncover again.
riscorrere [riscOrrere], *v.t.* To read over yet again.
riscossa, *n.f.* (*Mil.*) retaking of a lost position; recovery; rescue; insurrection, revolt.
riscossione, *n.f.* Collection (of debts, etc.).
riscosso, *n.m.* Cash collected.
riscotibile [riscotIbile], *a.* Recoverable.
riscotimento, *n.m.* Collection (of money).
riscuotere, riscotere [riscuOtere, riscOtere], *v.t.* To rouse again, to shake again, to startle; to collect, to draw (money); to earn (praise); to make good a loss. — **gli applausi,** to win applause; — **lo stipendio,** to collect one's salary.
riscuotersi [riscuOtersi], *v.r.* To rouse oneself; to come to (after fainting), to start into action.
risecamento, *n.m.* Resecting, cutting off.
risecare, *v.t.* To cut off, to pare away; to cut down (expenses).
risecazione, *n.f.* (*Med.*) Resection.
riseccare, riseccarsi, *v.i.r.* To dry up.
risecchire, *v.i.* To get dry, to wither.
risecco, *a.* Dried up, withered.
risedere, *v.i.* To sit down again, to be reseated; to reside.
risega, *n.f.* Dent on the skin caused by a tight bandage, etc.
riseminare, *v.t.* (*Agric.*) To re-sow.
risentimento, *n.m.* Resentment.
risentire, *v.t.i.* To feel again; to feel the effects of; to hear again; to experience; to show signs of.
risentirsi, *v.r.* To resent, to feel offended, to get angry; to recover one's senses. — **per un'offesa,** to resent an affront.
risentitamente, *adv.* Resentfully, angrily.
risentito, *a.* Resentful, angry; heard again; felt again.
riserbare, *v.t.* To reserve.
riserbatamente, *adv.* Reservedly.
riserbatezza [cp. **riservatezza**].
riserbo, *n.m.* Reserve; discretion; self-restraint.
riserramento, *n.m.* Reshutting; closing tighter.
riserrare, *v.t.* To shut again, to relock; to close tighter.

riserva, *n.f.* Reserve (in all senses); reservation, modesty. **Faccio delle riserve,** I make certain reservations; (*Comm.*) **fondi di —,** reserve funds; **senza —,** unreservedly.
riservare, *v.t.* To reserve; to save for, to keep for, to put aside.
riservarsi, *v.r.* To reserve oneself, to reserve to oneself, to claim.
riservatamente, *adv.* With reservations, confidentially.
riservatezza, *n.f.* Reservedness, reserve, circumspection, prudence.
riservato, *p.p.a.* Reserved; private; confidential; cautious. **Posto —,** reserved seat; **entrata riservata,** private entrance; **lettera riservata,** private and confidential letter.
riservire, *v.t.* To return (a favour); to serve again.
riservista (*pl.* **riservisti**), *n.m.* (*Mil.*) Reservist.
risibile [risIbile], *a.* Laughable, ridiculous, very amusing.
risibilità [-à], *n.f.* Risibility, laughableness.
risicare, *v.t.i.* To risk. **Chi non risica non rosica,** nothing venture nothing win [cp. **rischiare**].
risico [rIsico], *n.m.* Risk.
risicoso, *a.* Risky.
risicultura, *n.f.* Rice-growing.
risiedere [risiEdere], *v.i.* To reside, to be resident, to live at, to dwell.
risipola [risIpola], *n.f.* (*Med.*) Erysipelas.
risma, *n.f.* Ream (of paper); quality, sort, class. **Gente di quella —,** people of that sort; **sono tutti della stessa —,** they're all tarred with the same brush.
riso (1), *n.m.* Rice.
riso (2) (*pl.* **risa** *f.*), *n.m.* Laugh; laughter; smile. **— beffardo,** sneer; **— soffocato,** chuckle, guffaw; **scoppiare delle risa,** to burst out laughing.
risoffiare, *v.i.* To blow again; (*fig.*) to inform upon, to sneak.
risognare, risognarsi, *v.i.r.* To dream again; (*fig.*) to imagine.
risolare, *v.t.* To re-sole (footwear).
risolatura, *n.f.* Re-soling.
risolino, *n.f.* Smile, pretty little laugh.
risollevare, *v.t.* To lift up again, to raise again.
risolto, *p.p.a.* Settled, solved, resolved [cp. **risolvere**].
risolubile [risolUbile], *a.* Solvable, capable of solution.
risolutamente, *adv.* Resolutely.
risolutezza, *n.f.* Resoluteness, resolution.
risolutivo, *a.* (*Med.*) Resolvent; (*Leg.*) resolutive; conclusive.
risoluto, *p.p.a.* Resolute, determined; resolved, energetic.
risoluzione, *n.f.* Resolution, decision; solution (of mathematical or other problem).
risolvente, *n.m.a.* Resolvent, solvent.
risolvere [risOlvere], *v.t.i.* To resolve, to settle; to solve, to dissolve; to annul. **— un problema,** to solve a problem; **— un dubbio,** to resolve a doubt.
risolversi [risOlversi], *v.r.* To resolve, to make a resolution; to end, to finish; to be transformed. **— a partire,** to decide to start; **— in nulla,** to come to nothing, to end in nothing.
risolvibile [risolvIbile], *a.* Resolvable, solvable
risolvibilità [-à], *n.f.* Capability of being solved.
risolvimento, *n.m.* Resolution; solution.
risonante, *a.* Resonant, resounding.
risonanza, *n.f.* Resonance.
risonare, *v.t.i.* To ring again, to play (music) again; to echo; to resound.
risone, *n.m.* Unpolished rice.
risorgente, *a.* Resurgent, rising up.
risorgere [risOrgere], *v.i.* To rise again, to revive; to resurrect.
risorgimento, *n.m.* Revival, rebirth, awakening. **Il Risorgimento,** Italy's great national revival in the mid-19th century.
risorsa, *n.f.* Resource, expedient, shift.
risortire, *v.i.* To go out again.
risorto, *p.p.a.* Risen again, resuscitated, resurrected; revived [cp. **risorgere**].
risospingere [risospIngere], *v.t.* To push back again, to repel.
risotto, *n.m.* Savoury dish of rice and meat, etc.
risovvenimento, *n.m.* Remembrance, recollection.
risovvenirsi, *v.r.* To remember, to recollect.
risparmiare, *v.t.* To save up, to put by, to hoard, to spare. **Vorrei risparmiarvi il disturbo,** I should like to save you the trouble; **non — sacrifici,** spare no pains.
risparmiarsi, *v.r.* To spare oneself, to take care of oneself, to look after one's own health and comfort.
risparmiatore, risparmiatrice, *n.m.f.* Saver, thrifty person.
risparmio [rispArmio], *n.m.* Saving, savings. **Cassa di —,** savings bank; **praticare il —,** to practise saving; **a — di spese,** to avoid, prevent, further expense.
rispecchiare, *v.t.* To reflect.
rispedire, *v.t.* To send back, to send on, to forward (letters, etc.).
rispedizione, *n.f.* Sending back; forwarding, reshipping.
rispettabile [rispettAbile], *a.* Respectable; considerable.
rispettabilità [-à], *n.f.* Respectability.
rispettare, *v.t.* To respect; to comply with.
rispettivamente, *adv.* Respectively. **— a,** in respect to.
rispettivo, *a.* Respective.
rispetto, *n.m.* Respect, regard. **Col massimo —,** with the utmost respect; **ispirare —,** to inspire with awe; **mancare di —,** to be wanting in respect; **farsi portare —,** to make oneself respected; **— a,** compared with; (*Naut.*) **di —,** spare.
rispettosamente, *adv.* Respectfully.
rispettoso, *a.* Respectful.
rispingere [rispIngere], *v.t.* [cp. **respingere**].
risplendente, *a.* Resplendent, shining, glittering, sparkling; glaring.
risplendentemente, *adv.* Resplendently.
risplendere [risplEndere], *v.i.* To shine, to glare, to sparkle; to be famous.
rispogliarsi, *v.r.* To undress again.
rispondente, *a.* **— a,** answering to; in keeping with.
rispondenza, *n.f.* Correspondence to, conformity with; agreement; relation.

rispondere [rispOndere], *v.t.i.* To answer, to reply, to write back; to correspond to, to agree with; to lead (direction); (*Cards*) to follow suit. — **affermativamente,** to reply in the affirmative; — **ad una chiamata,** to answer a call; — **ad una domanda,** to reply to a question; — **al telefono,** to answer the telephone; **rispondo di voi,** I answer for you; — **per le rime,** to answer tit for tat; **rispondo di sì,** I say "yes".
risposare, *v.t.i.* To marry again.
risposta, *n.f.* Reply, answer, response. — **pagata,** reply paid; **in — alla vostra lettera,** in reply to yours; **per tutta — gli disse che,** he merely replied that.
rispostaccia [rispostAccia], *n.f.* Rude answer, dusty answer.
rissa, *n.f.* Fight, affray, brawl, quarrel.
rissante, *n.m.a.* Brawler; brawling, fighting.
rissare, *v.i.* To quarrel, to brawl, to fight.
rissoso, *a.* Quarrelsome.
ristabilimento, *n.m.* Re-establishment; restoration; reinstatement.
ristabilire, *v.t.* To re-establish; to restore, to reinstate.
ristabilirsi, *v.r.* To be re-established; to recover one's health.
ristagnamento, *n.m.* Stagnation; stanching (blood, etc.).
ristagnare, *v.t.i.* To re-solder, to re-tin; to stanch (flow of blood, etc.); to stagnate.
ristagnarsi, *v.r.* To stagnate.
ristagnatura, *n.f.* Stagnation, slackness.
ristagno, *n.m.* Stopping, stanching; slackness. (*Comm.*) — **degli affari,** slackness of business.
ristampa, *n.f.* (*Print.*) Reprint, reprinting.
ristampare, *v.t.* To reprint.
ristare, *v.i.* To stop, to leave off, to give over, to cease for a while.
ristarsi, *v.r.* To refrain.
ristaurare [cp. **restaurare**].
ristivare, *v.t.* (*Naut.*) To re-stow.
ristorabile [ristorAbile], *a.* Restorable.
ristoramento, *n.m.* Refreshment, comfort; restoration.
ristorante, *n.m.* Restaurant; (*Rail.*) refreshment room.
ristorare, *v.t.* To restore, to refresh; to relieve; to make up (for).
ristorarsi, *v.r.* To partake of refreshment, to refresh oneself; to take food; to be refreshed.
ristoratore, ristorativo, *a.* Restorative, refreshing.
ristorazione, *n.f.* Restoration; refreshment.
ristornare, *v.t.* (*Comm.*) To cancel, to annul.
ristorno, *n.m.* Cancellation; restitution.
ristoro, *n.m.* Refreshment; solace, comfort, relief.
ristrettamente, *adv.* Narrowly, sparely; in a limited degree.
ristrettezza, *n.f.* Narrowness, straitness. — **di mente,** narrow-mindedness; **vivere in ristrettezze,** to live in straitened circumstances.
ristretto, *n.m.* Summary; lowest price. **Ditemi il — di questo articolo,** tell me your very lowest price for this article.
ristretto, *p.p.a.* Restricted; narrow, limited; tight; shrunken; abridged; reduced. **Caffè —,** strong coffee; **in —,** in short.
ristringere [ristrIngere], *v.t.* To tighten again, to shrink.
ristuccare, *v.t.* To plaster again; (*fig.*) to weary, to nauseate, to cloy.
ristucchevole [ristucchEvole], *a.* Tiring, wearying; cloying; loathsome.
ristucco, *a.* Tired, sick of; tired out; satiated.
ristudiare, *v.t.* To study again, to con over.
risucchio, *n.m.* Whirlpool; eddy.
risultamento, *n.m.* Result.
risultante, *a.* Resulting, ensuing, resultant.
risultanza, *n.f.* Result, outcome, issue.
risultare, *v.i.* To result, to follow, to ensue; to arise from, to proceed from; to appear, to transpire, to emerge; to turn out (to be). — **da una lettera,** to transpire from a letter; **che ne risulta?** what follows from that? **Non mi risulta,** I am not in a position to say.
risultato, *n.m.* Result, issue.
risuonare [cp. **risonare**].
risurrezione, *n.f.* Resurrection.
risuscitamento, *n.m.* Resuscitation, revival.
risuscitare, *v.t.i.* To resuscitate; to give new life to; to rise again (from the dead), to revive.
risvegliamento, *n.m.* Awakening, rousing.
risvegliare, *v.t.* To wake up, to awaken, to rouse; to stir up, to revive; to excite.
risvegliarsi, *v.r.* To wake up, to wake again.
risvegliatore, risvegliatrice, *n.m.f.a.* Awakener, knocker-up; awakening.
risveglio [risvEglio], *n.m.* Awakening, revival.
risvolta, risvolto, *n.f.m.* Sharp turn; turn-up of cuff, lapel, trousers.
ritagliare, *v.t.* To cut again, to recut; to clip off. — **il margine,** to trim.
ritaglio [ritAglio], *n.m.* Clipping, cutting, snippet, sample pattern; — **di tempo,** spare moment, minute to spare; **ritagli di giornale,** newspaper cuttings.
ritardamento, *n.m.* Deferment, postponement, adjournment; delay.
ritardare, *v.t.i.* To delay, to postpone, to adjourn, to put off; to be late, to be slow, to be behind time. **Il mio orologio ritarda,** my watch is slow; **il treno ha ritardato di venti minuti,** the train was twenty minutes late.
ritardatario [ritardatArio], *n.m.* Late-comer; defaulter (in payments).
ritardo, *n.m.* Delay, lateness. **Essere in —,** to be late; **subire —,** to suffer delay; **il treno è in — di un'ora,** the train is an hour late; **causare —,** to cause delay.
ritegno, *n.m.* Reserve, restraint; reluctance, hesitation; self-control; support. **Muro di —,** retaining-wall.
ritemperare, *v.t.* To resharpen, to re-temper.
ritemprare, *v.t.* To reinvigorate, to give strength to.
ritemprarsi, *v.r.* To be strengthened.
ritenere, *v.t.i.* To detain, to hold back, to retain; to think, to deem; to consider; to remember.
ritenersi, *v.r.* To restrain oneself, to refrain from; to consider oneself.
ritenitiva, ritentiva, *n.f.* Retentiveness, long memory.
ritentare, *v.i.* To try again; to make a fresh attempt.

ritentiva [cp. **ritenitiva**].
ritentivo, *a.* Retentive.
ritenuta, *n.f.* Deduction; retention. — **sullo stipendio,** deduction from salary.
ritenutamente, *adv.* Moderately, with reserve.
ritenutezza, *n.f.* Reserve, moderation.
ritenuto, *p.p.a.* Reserved, self-possessed; retained, kept back. — **che,** considering that.
ritenzione, *n.f.* Retention; (*Law*) retainer; (*Med.*) retention of urine.
ritingere [ritIngere], *v.t.* To re-dye.
ritiramento, *n.m.* Withdrawal, withdrawing, retiring; contraction; corrugation.
ritirare, *v.t.* To withdraw, to retract, to retire, to take back; to draw (pay, salary, etc.); to cash (cheque, etc.). — **l'accusa,** to withdraw the charge; — **un ordine,** to revoke an order; — **una promessa,** to recall a promise; — **la posta,** to collect the mail.
ritirarsi, *v.r.* To retire, to retreat, to withdraw, to contract, to shrink. — **in campagna,** to retire to the country; — **dal commercio,** to retire from business; — **in buon ordine,** to retreat in good order.
ritirata, *n.f.* (*Mil.*) Retreat; lavatory, water-closet. **Suonare la —,** to beat the retreat, to sound the retreat.
ritiratamente, *adv.* In retirement; separately; lonely.
ritirato, *p.p.a.* Retired, secluded, withdrawn; lonely.
ritiro, *n.m.* Withdrawal, retirement; seclusion. **Funzionario in —,** retired official; **il sacro —,** the cloister, life of a monk; — **di merci,** removal of goods; — **dalla circolazione,** withdrawal from circulation.
ritmica [rItmica], *n.f.* Rhythmics.
ritmicamente, *adv.* Rhythmically.
ritmico [rItmico], *a.* Rhythmical.
ritmo, *n.m.* Rhythm; measure, cadence.
rito, *n.m.* Rite, ceremony; usage, custom.
ritoccamento, *n.m.* Retouching.
ritoccare, *v.t.* To retouch, to touch up, to revise, to give the finishing touch.
ritoccarsi, *v.r.* To touch oneself up, to smarten oneself.
ritoccata, *n.f.* Retouch.
ritoccatura, *n.f.* Retouching.
ritocchino, *n.m.* Snack; mouthful between meals.
ritocco, *n.m.* Retouching, final touch, revision; make-up.
ritogliere [ritOgliere], *v.t.* To take back to take again, to take away.
ritogliersi [ritOgliersi], *v.r.* To get away again, to make off again.
ritolto, *p.p.a.* Retaken, taken away.
ritorcimento, *n.m.* Twisting; (*fig.*) retorting.
ritorcere [ritOrcere], *v.t.* To twist, to twist back; (*fig.*) to retort.
ritorcersi [ritOrcersi], *v.r.* To retort; to turn against.
ritornare, *v.t.i.* To give back, to return, to send back; to come back, to reappear; to recur. — **a casa,** to go back home, to come home; — **sopra una decisione,** to reverse a decision, to change one's mind; — **in sè,** to recover one's senses, to come to oneself.
ritornata, *n.f.* Return.
ritornello, *n.m.* (*Mus.Poet.*) Refrain; (*colloq.*) wearisome repetition.
ritorno, *n.m.* Return, coming back. **È di —,** he has come back; (*Rail.*) **biglietto di andata e —,** return ticket; (*Sport*) **partita di —,** return match; (*Motor.*) — **di fiamma,** back-fire; **al mio — da Londra,** on my return from London; **a buon giuoco buon —,** one good turn deserves another.
ritorsione, *n.f.* Retort, retaliation; retortion.
ritorta, *n.f.* Withy; chain, bond.
ritorto, *a.* Twisted.
ritradurre, *v.t.* To retranslate.
ritraente, *a.* Representing; inferring, deducing.
ritrarre, *v.t.* To draw back, to draw out, to extract; to derive; to deduce; to withdraw; to pull again; to draw, to represent, to paint, to portray. — **da,** to take after (a parent), to resemble; — **l'attenzione,** to divert the attention.
ritrarsi, *v.r.* To draw back, to withdraw. — **da un'impresa,** to withdraw from an undertaking; — **indietro,** to start back.
ritrattabile [ritrattAbile], *a.* Retractable.
ritratta, *n.f.* (*Comm.*) Redraft.
ritrattare, *v.t.* To retract, to recant; to rehandle; to withdraw; to portray.
ritrattazione, *n.f.* Retractation, recantation; withdrawal; portrayal.
ritrattile [ritrAttile], *a.* Retractile. (*Aviat.*) **Carro —,** retractable undercarriage.
ritrattino, *n.m.* Small portrait; miniature.
ritrattista (*pl.* **ritrattisti**), *n.m.* Portrait-painter.
ritratto, *n.m.* Portrait. — **in piedi,** full-length portrait; **farsi fare il —,** to have one's portrait painted; **è tutto il — di,** he's the very image of.
ritratto, *p.p.a.* Drawn; extracted.
ritrecine [ritrEcine], *n.m.* Sweep-net; mill-race. **Andare a —,** to go headlong to ruin.
ritrosa, *n.f.* Hair-net; fowling-net.
ritrosaggine [ritrosAggine], *n.f.* Backwardness; shyness, bashfulness; aversion.
ritrosamente, *adv.* Reluctantly, shyly; with aversion.
ritrosia, ritrosità [-à], *n.f.* Bashfulness, shyness; prudery; reluctance; aversion.
ritroso, *n.m.* Eddy, whirlpool; mouth of a net.
ritroso, *a.* Bashful, shy, backward; reluctant. **A —,** backwards; **fare tutto a —,** to do everything against the grain; **a — della corrente,** against the stream.
ritrovabile [ritrovAbile], *a.* Recoverable, discoverable.
ritrovamento, *n.m.* Discovery; recovery.
ritrovare, *v.t.* To find again, to meet again; to recover; to call upon, to visit, to meet.
ritrovarsi, *v.r.* To meet one another again; to be oneself again. **Non mi ci ritrovo più,** I don't know where I am, I'm thoroughly bewildered.
ritrovato, *n.m.* Discovery, invention; expedient.
ritrovatore, *n.m.* Discoverer, inventor.
ritrovo, *n.m.* Assembly, club; meeting-place, rendezvous; gathering, party.
rittamente, *adv.* Straightly, straight on; upright.
ritto, *n.m.* Right side; upper side; upright, support.

ritto, *a.* Straight; upright, erect. **Tenere ritta la testa,** to hold one's head up; **tenersi —,** to stand upright.
ritto, *adv.* Directly, straightly, straight on.
rittorovescio [rittorovEscio], *adv.* Upside down; the wrong way; anti-clockwise.
rituale, *n.m.a.* Ritual; customary.
ritualismo, *n.m.* Ritualism.
ritualmente, *adv.* Ritually.
rituffare, *v.i.* To plunge again.
riudire, riudirsi, *v.t.r.* To hear again; to hear one another again.
riunimento, *n.m.* Reuniting, reassembling.
riunione, *n.f.* Meeting; reunion, gathering.
riunire, *v.t.* To assemble, to gather, to bring together, to collect; to reconcile, to reunite, to rejoin.
riunirsi, *v.r.* To meet, to come together again, to be reunited, to be reconciled.
riusare, *v.t.* To use again.
riusarsi, *v.r.* To become fashionable again.
riuscibile [riuscIbile], *a.* Likely to succeed.
riuscire, *v.i.* To succeed, to get on, to thrive; to result, to turn out to be, to end by being; to appear, to look; to lead to, to give access to; to arrive at; to go out again. **— bene,** to get on well; **— difficile,** to present difficulties; **— insufficiente,** to prove insufficient; **questa strada riesce al palazzo,** this road leads to the palace; **— all' esame,** to pass an exam.
riuscita, *n.f.* Success; issue; result. **Far buona —,** to turn out well.
riuscito, *a.* Successful.
riva, *n.f.* Bank, shore, seashore. **— destra,** right bank (of a river).
rivaccinare, *v.t.* (*Med.*) To revaccinate.
rivagheggiare, *v.t.* To long for again; (*fig.*) to pursue further.
rivale, *n.m.a.* Rival.
rivaleggiare, *v.i.* To rival, to vie, to compete.
rivalersi, *v.r.* To reimburse oneself, to make good one's losses.
rivalicare, *v.t.* To recross.
rivalità [-à], *n.f.* Rivalry.
rivalsa, *n.f.* Revenge; (*Leg.*) lien; reimbursement.
rivalutare, *v.t.* To revalue, to restore the value of.
rivangare, *v.t.* To dig up again.
rivarcare, *v.t.* To recross.
rivedere, *v.i.* To see again; to meet again; to revise, to touch up; to review. **Arrivederci! Arrivederla!** Good-bye, au revoir! **arrivederci a domani,** good-bye till to-morrow; **— le bozze,** to read proofs.
rivedibile [rivedIbile], *a.* Open to examination, subject to revision; (*Mil.*) temporarily unfit.
riveditore, riveditrice, *n.m.f.* Reviser; proof-reader.
riveduta, *n.f.* Revision.
rivelamento, *n.m.* Revelation.
rivelare, *v.t.* To reveal; to disclose (a secret, etc.).
rivelarsi, *v.r.* To reveal oneself.
rivelatore, *n.m.* Revealer; (*Radio*) detector.
rivelazione, *n.f.* Revelation, disclosure; (*colloq.*) eye-opener.
rivendere [rivEndere], *v.t.* To resell; to retail.
rivendibile [rivendIbile], *a.* Resaleable.
rivendicare, *v.t.* To vindicate; to claim. **— un diritto,** to vindicate a right.
rivendicatore, rivendicatrice, *n.m.f.* Vindicator; avenger.
rivendicazione, *n.f.* Vindication.
rivendita [rivEndita], *n.f.* Resale; retailing, retail selling. **— di sale e tabacchi,** shop licensed to retail salt and tobacco (government monopolies).
rivenditore, rivenditrice, *n.m.f.* Retailer; small shopkeeper.
rivendugliolo [rivendUgliolo], *n.m.* Huckster, hawker, costermonger; second-hand dealer.
rivenire, *v.i.* To come back again; to come to one's senses.
riverberamento, *n.m.* Reverberation.
riverberare, *v.t.* To reverberate; to reflect; to dazzle.
riverberarsi, *v.r.* To reverberate, to be reflected back.
riverberazione, *n.f.* Reverberating.
riverbero [rivErbero], *n.m.* Reverberation; reflection; dazzle. **Di —,** indirectly.
riverente, *a.* Reverent.
riverentemente, *adv.* Reverently.
riverenza, *n.f.* Reverence, respect; bow; curtsy.
riverenziale, *a.* Reverential.
riverire, *v.t.* To honour, to revere; to respect; to pay one's respects to. **La riverisco distintamente,** with kind regards (at end of a letter).
riverito, *a.* Revered; esteemed. **La sua riverita lettera,** your esteemed letter.
riversamento, *n.m.* Outpouring, outpour.
riversare, *v.t.* To pour out, to pour; to shift (liability, etc.).
riversarsi, *v.r.* To upset, to pour over; to flow.
riversato, *p.p.a.* Poured out; overturned.
riversibile [riversIbile], *a.* Reversible, revertible; (*Law*) subject to reversion.
riversibilità [-à], *n.f.* Reversibility.
riversione, *n.f.* (*Law*) Reversion.
riverso, *n.m.* Reverse, wrong side; set-back, misfortune.
riverso, *a.* Reversed, upset.
rivestimento, *n.m.* Casing, covering, lining; (*Mil.*) revetment.
rivestire, *v.t.* To reclothe, to cover; to line; to take up (a post). **— con tavole,** to board up; **— d'autorità,** to clothe with authority; **— di zinco,** to line with zinc.
rivestirsi, *v.r.* To dress oneself again; to put on new clothes.
rivestitura, *n.f.* Covering, lining (material).
riviera, *n.f.* Coast; seashore. **La Riviera di Ponente,** the Riviera west of Genoa.
rivierasco, *n.m.a.* Inhabitant of or pertaining to the Riviera; riverside resident.
rivincere [rivIncere], *v.t.i.* To win back, to have one's revenge (at a game).
rivincita [rivIncita], *n.f.* (*Sport, etc.*) Return match, revenge.
rivisita, *n.f.* Return visit.
rivisitare, *v.t.* To revisit.
rivista, *n.f.* Review, inspection; review, magazine; revue. **Passare in —,** to review.
rivisto, *p.p.a.* Revised, reviewed, examined; seen again.

rivivere [rivIvere], *v.i.* To revive, to come to life again.
rivivificare, *v.t.* To revivify.
rivivificazione, *n.f.* Revivification.
rivo, *n.m.* Stream; brook.
rivocare [cp. **revocare**].
rivolare, *v.i.* To fly again, to fly back.
rivolere, *v.t.* To wish again, to be willing again.
rivolgere [rivOlgere], *v.t.* To turn, to turn over; to direct, to address; to overturn; to turn over in one's mind; to dissuade. **— la parola,** to address one's words; **— l'attenzione a,** to turn one's attention to; **— una domanda,** to put a question; **— i passi verso,** to direct one's steps towards; **— le spalle a uno,** to turn one's back on someone; **— una preghiera,** to make an earnest request.
rivolgersi [rivOlgersi], *v.r.* To turn round; to apply to, to address oneself to; to change one's mind. **Si rivolga a me,** apply to me (for help, etc.).
rivolgimento, *n.m.* Revolution, change; disturbance, upheaval.
rivolo [rIvolo], *n.m.* Rivulet, brook.
rivolta, *n.f.* Revolt; mutiny, rebellion; sharp bend.
rivoltante, *a.* Revolting, disgusting.
rivoltare, *v.t.* To turn over, to overthrow; to turn inside out; to revolt, to disgust. **Ciò mi rivolta,** that disgusts me.
rivoltarsi, *v.r.* To rebel, to revolt; to turn over, to turn back. **Mi si rivolta lo stomaco,** it disgusts me.
rivoltatura, *n.f.* Turning (a coat) inside out.
rivoltella, *n.f.* Revolver. **— a sei colpi,** six-shooter; **colpo di —,** revolver-shot.
rivoltellata, *n.f.* Revolver-shot; report of this.
rivoltolare, *v.t.* To turn over, to roll over, to roll.
rivoltolarsi, *v.r.* To roll, to roll about in, to wallow. **— nel fango,** to wallow in the mire.
rivoltolio [rivoltolIo], *n.m.* Constant turning (as of a wheel).
rivoltolone, *n.m.* Somersault.
rivoltoloni, *adv.* **A —,** turning over and over.
rivoltoso, *n.m.a.* Revolutionary, rebel; rebellious.
rivoluzionare, *v.t.* To revolutionize; to incite to rebellion.
rivoluzionario [rivoluzionArio], *n.m.a.* Revolutionary.
rivoluzione, *n.f.* Revolution.
rivomitare, *v.t.* To vomit up again.
rivulsione, *n.f.* Revulsion.
rivulsivo, *a.* Revulsive.
rizzamento, *n.m.* Straightening, redressing; bristling (of the hair).
rizzare, *v.t.* To straighten, to make straight; to build, to erect; to bristle (of hair). **— la cresta,** to hold one's head high; **hanno rizzato una casa,** they built a house.
rizzarsi, *v.r.* To rise, to stand up; to bristle. **Gli si rizzarono i capelli in capo,** his hair stood on end.
roano, *n.m.a.* Roan (horse).
roba, *n.f.* Things; goods; stuff; wares; clothes. **Quanta —!** What a lot of stuff! **dir — da chiodi di qualcuno,** to speak badly of someone; **— da mangiare,** food, victuals; **Bella —!** That's a nice state of affairs! That's a fine thing, indeed! **un monte di —,** a heap of stuff; **non è — tua,** it isn't your stuff; **— d'altri,** other people's property.
robaccia [robAccia], *n.f.* Rubbish, trash.
robbia [rObbia], *n.f.* (*Bot.*) Madder.
robetta, *n.f.* Trifle, thing of no value.
robinetto, *n.m.* Tap; cock [cp. **rubinetto**].
robustamente, *adv.* Robustly.
robustezza, *n.f.* Robustness, strength, sturdiness.
robusto, *a.* Robust, sturdy, strong; vigorous.
rocaggine [rocAggine], *n.f.* Hoarseness.
rocamente, *adv.* Hoarsely.
rocca (1), *n.f.* Fortress, stronghold; rock; chimney-pot. **Cristallo di —,** rock-crystal.
rocca (2), *n.f.* Distaff.
roccetto, *n.m.* (*Eccles.*) Rochet; surplice.
rocchetto, *n.m.* Bobbin, reel, spool; (*Elect.*) coil. **— d'induzione,** induction coil.
rocchio [rOcchio], *n.m.* Billet of wood; sausage; string (of sausages, etc.).
roccia [rOccia], *n.f.* Rock, cliff, crag.
rocciatore, *n.m.* Rock-climber; cragsman.
roccioso, *a.* Rocky.
rocco, *n.m.* (*Chess*) Rook, castle; (*Eccles.*) crozier.
rochezza, *n.f.* Hoarseness.
roco, *a.* Hoarse [cp. **rauco**].
Rodano [rOdano], *n.m.* (*Geog.*) Rhône.
rodere [rOdere], *v.t.* To gnaw, to nibble; to eat into, to eat away; to consume, to corrode; (*fig.*) to undermine, to torture. **— il freno,** to champ the bit.
rodersi [rOdersi], *v.r.* To fret, to worry; to chafe with anger. **— le unghie,** to bite one's nails.
Rodesia [rodEsia], *n.f.* (*Geog.*) Rhodesia.
rodesiano, *n.m.a.* Rhodesian.
Rodi, *n.f.* (*Geog.*) Rhodes.
rodimento, *n.m.* Gnawing, worry, fretting, anxiety.
roditore, *n.m.* (*Zool.*) Rodent.
roditore, *a.* Gnawing, corroding.
rododendro, *n.m.* (*Bot.*) Rhododendron.
Rodolfo, *n.m.* Rudolph.
rodomontata, *n.f.* Rodomontade, boasting, bragging.
rodomonte, *n.m.* Braggart, boaster, swanker.
Rodrigo, *n.m.* Roderick.
rogare, *v.t.* (*Law*) To draw up (a deed, etc.).
rogatore, *n.m.* Drafter (of deeds, etc.).
rogazioni, *n.f.pl.* (*Eccles.*) Rogation days.
rogito [rOgito], *n.m.* (*Law*) Deed; attestation, instrument.
rogna, *n.f.* (*Med.*) Scab, itch; mange.
rognone, *n.m.* Kidney (butcher's offal).
rognoso, *a.* Itchy, scabby; mangy.
rogo (1), *n.m.* Funeral pyre.
rogo (2), *n.m.* (*Bot.*) Briar, bramble [cp. **rovo**].
Rolando, *n.m.* Roland.
rollare, *v.i.* To roll (of a ship).
rollio [rollIo], *n.m.* Continual rolling.
Roma, *n.f.* (*Geog.*) Rome.
romagnolo, *n.m.a.* Inhabitant of or pertaining to Romagna.
romaico [romAico], *n.m.a.* Romaic (modern Greek).
romaiolata, *n.f.* Ladleful.

romaiolo, *n.m.* Ladle.
romanamente, *adv.* In the Roman way, like the Romans.
romancio [romAncio], *n.m.a.* Romansch, Ladin (of the Grisons).
romanesco, *n.m.a.* Roman dialect; pertaining to it.
Romania [romanIa], *n.f.* (*Geog.*) Rumania.
romanico [romAnico], *a.* Romance (language); (*Arch.*) Romanesque.
romanismo, *n.m.* Idiom of Roman dialect.
romanista (*pl.* **romanisti**), *n.m.* Specialist in Roman Law.
romano, *n.m.a.* Roman. **Alla romana,** everyone paying his share.
romanticamente, *adv.* Romantically.
romanticheria [romanticherIa], *n.f.* Romantic nonsense; romantic sentimentality.
romanticismo, *n.m.* Romanticism.
romantico [romAntico], *a.* Romantic; fanciful, fantastic, sentimental.
romanza, *n.f.* (*Mus.*) Romance; song, ballad.
romanzeggiare, *v.i.* To romance.
romanzescamente, *adv.* Romantically.
romanzesco, *a.* Romantic; like a romance; adventurous.
romanziere, *n.m.* Novelist.
romanzo, *n.m.* Novel; romance.
romanzo, *a.* Romance (languages).
romba, *n.f.* Rumble; roar, din; (*fig.*) thunder.
rombare, *v.i.* To rumble; to roar; to peal, to toll.
rombo (1), *n.m.* Rumble, roar; din; (*fig.*) thunder.
rombo (2), *n.m.* (*Geom.*) Rhomb.
rombo (3), *n.m.* (*Zool.*) Turbot.
romboide [rombOide], *n.m.* (*Geom.*) Rhomboid.
romeno, *n.m.a.* Rumanian.
romeo [romEo], *n.m.* Pilgrim (going to Rome).
romita, *n.f.* Anchoress, woman hermit.
romitaggio [romitAggio], *n.m.* Hermitage.
romito, *n.m.a.* Hermit, solitary; lonely.
romitorio [romitOrio], *n.m.* Hermitage.
Romolo [rOmolo], *n.m.* (*Myth.*) Romulus.
rompere [rOmpere], *v.t.i.* To break, to smash, to break up; to break off, to snap; to interrupt; to cancel. **— il digiuno,** to break one's fast; **— il ghiaccio,** to break the ice; **— la testa,** to rack one's brains; to tease; **— il proponimento,** to change one's mind; **romperla con uno,** to fall out with somebody; **— gli stivali,** (*vulg.*) **le scatole,** to bore, to weary out; **— in pianto,** to burst into tears.
rompersi [rOmpersi], *v.r.* To break, to get broken. **— il collo,** to break one's neck; **— la testa,** to break one's head; **— sugli scogli,** to break up on the rocks (of a ship).
rompibile [romplbile], *a.* Breakable.
rompicapo, *n.m.* Annoyance, worry; puzzle, riddle.
rompicollo, *n.m.* Daredevil; dangerous spot, precipice. **A —,** headlong.
rompighiaccio [rompighiAccio], *n.m.* Ice-axe; ice-breaker.
rompimento, *n.m.* Breaking; (*fig.*) nuisance. **— di capo,** puzzling job; deafening noise.
rompinoci, *n.m.* Nutcracker.
rompionde, *n.m.* Breakwater.
rompiscatole, rompistivali [rompiscAtole], *n.m.* Bore, wearisome person.
rompitesta, *n.m.* Puzzle, riddle.
rompitore, rompitrice, *n.m.f. a.* Person who breaks things; breaking.
rompitutto, *n.m.* Clumsy person (always breaking things).
ronca, *n.f.* Billhook, bagging-hook.
ronchetto, *n.m.* Pruning-knife.
ronchione, *n.m.* Crag, high rock.
ronciglio [roncIglio], *n.m.* Hook; gaff.
ronco, *n.m.* Billhook, bagging-hook; (*fig.*) deadlock.
roncola [rOncola], *n.f.* Hedging billhook.
roncolata, *n.f.* Stroke with a billhook.
roncolo [rOncolo], *n.m.* Gardening-knife. **Gambe a —,** bow legs.
ronda, *n.f.* (*Mil.*) Rounds, round; patrol; watch. **Far la —,** to patrol.
rondine [rOndine], *n.f.* (*Zool.*) Swallow; martin. **Coda di —,** swallow-tail; **una — non fa primavera,** one swallow does not make a summer.
rondinella, *n.f.* (*Zool.*) Martin, swallow. **— di mare,** tern.
rondò [-ò], *n.m.* (*Poet.*) Rondeau.
rondone, *n.m.* (*Zool.*) Swift.
ronfare, *v.i.* To snore.
ronzamento, *n.m.* Buzzing, humming.
ronzare, *v.i.* To buzz, to hum; to whir; to tingle (of the ears); (*fig.*) to flirt, to hang around (a woman).
ronzino, *n.m.* Nag, pad, jade, worn-out horse.
ronzio [ronzIo], *n.m.* Continual humming or buzzing.
ronzone, *n.m.* Bluebottle fly; stallion; man who hangs around girls.
rorido [rOrido], *a.* Dewy.
rosa, *n.f.* (*Bot.*) Rose; rose, pink (colour). **— canina,** sweet-briar; **— tea,** tea-rose; **— muscosa,** moss-rose; **— dei venti,** compass-card; **— di diamanti,** rose-diamond; **Pasqua di rose,** Whitsunday, Pentecost; **fresco come una —,** fresh as a daisy.
rosaceo [rosAceo], *a.* Rosaceous.
rosaio [rosAio], *n.m.* Rose-bush, rose-tree.
rosario [rosArio], *n.m.* Rosary, chaplet. **Recitare il —,** to say the rosary.
rosato, *a.* Rosy. **Acqua rosata,** rose-water.
rosbiffe, rosbif, *n.m.* Roast beef.
rosellina, *n.f.* Damask rose.
roseo [rOseo], *a.* Rosy, rose-coloured, pink.
roseto, *n.m.* Rosery, rose-garden.
rosetta, *n.f.* Rosette.
rosicante, *n.m.a.* Rodent; gnawing.
rosicare, *v.t.* To gnaw, to nibble; (*fig.*) to get bit by bit.
rosicatura, rosicchiamento, *n.f.m.* Nibbling, gnawing.
rosicchiare, *v.t.* To nibble, to gnaw.
rosicchio [rosIcchio], *n.m.* Dry crust of bread.
rosignolo, rosignuolo, *n.m.* Nightingale.
rosmarino, *n.m.* (*Bot.*) Rosemary.
rosolaccio [rosolAccio], *n.m.* Poppy.
rosolare, *v.t.* To roast brown.
rosolia [rosolIa], *n.f.* (*Med.*) German measles.
rosolio [rosOlio], *n.m.* Rosolio.
rosone, *n.m.* Rose-window; rose ornament.
rospo, *n.m.* (*Zool.*) Toad; surly person.
rossastro, *a.* Reddish.

rosseggiare, *v.i.* To redden, to grow red.
rossetto, *n.m.* Rouge; lipstick.
rossetto, *a.* Reddish.
rossezza, *n.f.* Redness.
rossiccio, rossigno [rossIccio], *a.* Reddish.
rosso, *n.m.a.* Red. **— d'uovo,** yolk of an egg; **diventare —,** to blush, to turn red. **La Croce Rossa,** the Red Cross.
rossore, *n.m.* Redness, blush, flush; (*fig.*) shame. **Avere — di,** to be ashamed of.
rosta, *n.f.* Fanlight.
rosticcere, rosticciere, *n.m.* Proprietor of a rôtisserie *or* grill.
rosticceria [rosticcerIa], *n.f.* Rôtisserie, grill.
rostrato, *a.* Beaked.
rostro, *n.m.* Rostrum, platform; beak.
rota [cp. **ruota**].
rotabile [rotAbile], *a.* Passable for wheeled traffic.
rotaia, *n.f.* Wheel-rut, wheel-track; (*Rail.*) rail. **Uscir dalle rotaie,** to go off the rails (in all senses).
rotamento, *n.m.* Rotation, wheeling.
rotante, *a.* Wheeling, rotating.
rotare, *v.i.* To rotate, to wheel, to revolve.
rotativa, *n.f.* (*Print.*) Rotary machine.
rotatorio [rotatOrio], *a.* Rotatory, rotary.
rotazione, *n.f.* Rotation.
roteamento, *n.m.* Wheeling, rotating; rolling.
roteare, *v.i.* To rotate, to revolve, to wheel.
rotella, *n.f.* Small wheel, castor (of furniture); roller; (*Anat.*) knee-cap. **Pattino a rotelle,** roller-skate.
rotolamento, *n.m.* Rolling.
rotolare, *v.t.i.* To roll, to roll up. **— per le scale,** to tumble down stairs.
rotolarsi, *v.r.* To roll oneself, to roll; to wallow.
rotolo [rOtolo], *n.m.* Roll, bundle; scroll; coil (of rope). **Andare a rotoli,** to go to the dogs; to get ruined.
rotolone, *n.m.* Tumble, fall; (*fig.*) ruin, failure.
rotonda, *n.f.* Rotunda.
rotondamente, *adv.* Roundly.
rotondare, rotondeggiare, *v.t.* To round, to make round; to put in round figures.
rotondeggiante, *a.* Roundish.
rotondezza, rotondità [-à], *n.f.* Rotundity, roundness, plumpness.
rotondo, *a.* Round, plump.
rotta, *n.f.* Course, route; overthrow, rout, retreat. (*Naut.*) **— ortodromica,** great-circle sailing; **cambiare —,** to alter the course; **mettere in —,** to rout; **andare a — di collo,** to go headlong, to go to ruin.
rottame, *n.m.* Scrap; (*Naut.*) wreckage.
rottamente, *adv.* Jerkily, spasmodically.
rottami, *n.m.pl.* Rubbish, bits, scraps; wrecks.
rotti, *n.m.pl.* Small change (money). **Cento lire e rotti,** a hundred odd lire.
rotto, *n.m.* Break, fracture; fraction. **Uscirne pel — della cuffia,** to get out by the skin of one's teeth.
rotto, *p.p.a.* Broken, smashed; worn out; addicted to, given to. **— al vizio,** given up to vice; **— dalla stanchezza,** worn out.
rottura, *n.f.* Breaking, rupture, fracture, break; breakage. **— dei rapporti,** breaking off of relations.
rotula [rOtula], *n.f.* (*Anat.*) Knee-cap.
rovaio [rovAio], *n.m.* North wind.
rovano, *a.* Roan, reddish (of a horse).
rovello, *n.m.* Fury, rage.
roventare, *v.t.* To make red-hot.
rovente, *a.* Red-hot; scorching.
rovere [rOvere], *n.m.* (*Bot.*) Oak.
rovereto, *n.m.* Plantation of oaks.
rovescia [rovEscia], *n.f.* Lapel; facing (of a sleeve, etc.). **Alla —,** inside out, upside down, backside foremost; **il mondo va alla —,** the world is going to the dogs.
rovesciamento, *n.m.* Upsetting, overthrow, overturning, capsize; spilling.
rovesciare, *v.t.* To upset, to overturn, to overthrow; to pour; to spill. **— la colpa addosso a,** to shift the blame on to.
rovesciarsi, *v.r.* To overturn, to be upset, to capsize; to fall down; to have a spill (on a bicycle).
rovesciato, *p.p.a.* Upset, overthrown; fallen down; capsized.
rovescio [rovEscio], *n.m.* Wrong side, reverse side; reverse; disaster; shower (of rain, etc.); (*Tennis*) backhand stroke. **Mettersi i panni a —,** to put on one's clothes inside out; **—d'ingiurie,** shower of abuse; **ogni medaglia ha il suo —,** no rose without a thorn; **per diritto e per —,** by hook or by crook.
rovescione, *n.m.* Slap with the back of the hand, box on the ear; heavy shower of rain. **A —, a rovescioni,** backwards, on the back.
roveto, *n.m.* Bramble bush; clump of briars; brake. **— ardente,** burning-bush.
rovina, *n.f.* Ruin; violence. **Andare in —,** to go to ruin; **cadere in —,** to fall in ruins.
rovinare, *v.t.i.* To ruin, to spoil; to fall into ruin; to collapse, to crumble.
rovinarsi, *v.r.* To ruin oneself, to be ruined.
rovinatore, *n.m.* Waster, despoiler.
rovinio [rovinIo], *n.m.* Ruin, downfall.
rovinoso, *a.* Ruinous, violent; impetuous.
rovistare, *v.t.i.* To ransack, to search, to rummage.
rovistio [rovistIo], *n.m.* Rummaging.
rovo, *n.m.* (*Bot.*) Briar, bramble.
rozza, *n.f.* Jade (horse).
rozzamente, *adv.* Roughly, clumsily, rudely.
rozzezza, *n.f.* Coarseness, rawness, roughness.
rozzo, *a.* Coarse, rough, raw; uncouth. **Modi rozzi,** uncouth manners; **tela rozza,** coarse material.
ruba, *n.f.* Theft, plunder, robbery. **Andare a —,** to sell easily; **mettere a —,** to steal, to plunder.
rubacchiamento, *n.m.* Pilfering.
rubacchiare, *v.t.i.* To pilfer.
rubacori, rubacuori, *n.m.f.* Lady-killer; charmer, charming woman.
rubamento, *n.m.* Robbery, theft; burglary.
rubapaghe, *n.m.* Man not worth his wages.
rubare, *v.t.* To steal, to thieve, to rob.
rubatore, rubatrice, *n.m.f.* Thief, robber, burglar.
ruberia [ruberIa], *n.f.* Robbery, theft.
rubicante, *a.* (*obs.*) Reddish.
rubicondo, *a.* Rubicund, ruddy, chubby.
Rubicone, *n.m.* (*Geog.*) Rubicon.
rubidio [rubIdio], *n.m.* (*Min.*) Rubidium.
rubinetto, *n.m.* Tap, cock. **— per gas,** gas-tap; **— per l'acqua,** water-cock; (*Am.*) faucet.

rubino, *n.m.* Ruby.
rubizzo, *a.* Hale, hearty, healthy.
rublo, *n.m.* Rouble.
rubrica, *n.f.* Rubric; heading, title; column; address book; rules and regulations.
rubricare, *v.t.* To enter (in a book); to write (in a visitor's book, etc.).
rude, *a.* Coarse, rough, rude, unpolished; harsh. **Linguaggio —,** coarse language.
rudemente, *adv.* Coarsely, roughly.
ruderi [rUderi], *n.m.pl.* Ruins.
rudimentale, *a.* Rudimentary.
rudimento, *n.m.* Rudiment.
ruffa, *n.f.* Throng, crowd, jostling. **Fare a ruffa raffa,** to scramble to get what one can.
ruffiana, *n.f.* Procuress, bawd.
ruffianeggiare, *v.t.* To pander, to play the bawd, to procure (for immoral purposes).
ruffiano, *n.m.* Procurer, pimp, white-slave dealer.
ruga, *n.f.* Wrinkle.
rugghiare, *v.i.* To roar.
ruggine [rUggine], *n.f.* Rust, mildew, blight; (*fig.*) grudge, rancour, bad feeling. **C'è della — fra loro,** there's bad blood between them.
rugginire, *v.i.* To get rusty.
rugginoso, *a.* Rusty.
ruggire, *v.i.* To roar.
ruggito, *n.m.* Roar.
rugiada, *n.f.* Dew.
rugiadoso, *a.* Dewy.
rugosità [-à], *n.f.* Wrinkledness; roughness, unevenness.
rugoso, *a.* Wrinkled.
ruina [cp. **rovina**].
ruletta, *n.f.* Roulette.
rullaggio [rullAggio], *n.m.* (*Aviat.*) Taxi-ing.
rullamento, *n.m.* Rolling.
rullare, *v.t.i.* To roll (grass, etc.); to roll (of a ship); (*Aviat.*) to taxi.
rullio [rullIo], *n.m.* Rolling.
rullo, *n.m.* Roller, roll; drum, cylinder; roll (of drum). **Scrittoio a —,** roll-top desk.
rum, *n.m.* Rum.
Rumania [rumanIa], *n.f.* (*Geog.*) Rumania.
rumeno, *n.m.a.* Rumanian.
ruminante, *n.m.a.* Ruminant.
ruminare, *v.t.i.* To ruminate, to chew the cud; to muse, to ponder.
ruminazione, *n.f.* Rumination; chewing the cud.
rumore, *n.m.* Noise, din, clamour, outcry, uproar. **Far —,** to make a noise.
rumoreggiamento, *n.m.* Noise, outcry, clamour.
rumoreggiante, *a.* Noisy; restless; rumbling.
rumoreggiare, *v.i.* To make a noise, to raise an outcry; to rumble.
rumorio [rumorIo], *n.m.* Continual noise, rumbling.
rumorosamente, *adv.* Noisily.
rumoroso, *a.* Noisy, clamorous; talked-of.
ruolo, *n.m.* Roll, list; (regular) staff; (*Theat.*) character. **Passare in —,** to become an established member of staff.
ruota, rota, *n.f.* Wheel. **— dentata,** cog-wheel; **— d'ingranaggio,** gear-wheel; **— di ricambio,** spare wheel; **— motrice,** driving-wheel; **far la —,** to spread out the tail (of a peacock), to strut.
rupe, *n.f.* Cliff, rock.
rupestre, *a.* Rocky.
rupia [rupIa], *n.f.* Rupee.
rurale, *n.m.a.* Countryman; rural.
ruscelletto, *n.m.* Little brook, streamlet.
ruscello, *n.m.* Brook, stream.
ruspa, *n.f.* Scraping; roller (machine).
ruspare, *v.t.* To scratch about (as a hen); to pick up chestnuts.
russamento, *n.m.* Snoring,
russare, *v.i.* To snore.
Russia [rUssia], *n.f.* (*Geog.*) Russia.
russo, *n.m.a.* Russian.
russofilo [russOfilo], *n.m.a.* Russophile.
russofobo [russOfobo], *n.m.a.* Russophobe.
rusticaggine [rusticAggine], *n.f.* Rusticity.
rusticamente, *adv.* Rustically, rurally.
rusticano, *a.* Rustic; of the peasants. **Cavalleria rusticana,** rustic chivalry.
rustichezza, rusticità [-à], *n.f.* Rusticity.
rustico [rUstico], *n.m.a.* Rustic, peasant.
ruta, *n.f.* (*Bot.*) Rue.
ruteno, *n.m.a.* Ruthenian.
rutilante, *a.* (*Poet.*) Shining, sparkling.
rutilare, *v.i.* To sparkle.
ruttare, *v.i.* To belch.
rutto, *n.m.* Belch, belching.
ruvidamente, *adv.* Coarsely, harshly; ruggedly; roughly.
ruvidezza, ruvidità, *n.f.* Roughness, harshness, coarseness.
ruvido [rUvido], *a.* Rough, rude; harsh; coarse, unpolished (in manners). **Modi ruvidi,** bad manners.
ruzza, *n.f.* Quarrel, dispute, altercation.
ruzzare, *v.i.* To romp, to sport, to frolic; to prance.
ruzzo, *n.m.* Romping, frolicsomeness; prank, gambol.
ruzzola [rUzzola], *n.f.* Spinning-top.
ruzzolare, *v.t.i.* To roll, to trundle; to tumble down, to topple over. **— una botte,** to trundle a barrel.
ruzzolone, *n.m.* Tumble, fall.
ruzzoloni, *adv.* **Andare a —,** to fall headlong, to fall head over heels.

S

S, s, *n.f.* Seventeenth letter of the Italian alphabet.
Saba, *n.f.* (*Geog.*) Sheba.
sabatico [sabAtico], *a.* Sabbatical. **Anno —,** sabbatical year, seventh year.
sabato [sAbato], *n.m.* Saturday; sabbath.
sabaudo [sabAudo], *a.* Of Savoy; of the royal house of Savoy.
sabbia [sAbbia], *n.f.* Sand.
sabbiaia, sabbionaia [sabbiAia, sabbionAia], *n.f.* Sand-pit.
sabbiare, *v.t.* To sand, to scatter sand.
sabbione, *n.m.* Gravel; sandy soil.
sabbioso, *a.* Sandy.
sabotaggio [sabotAggio], *n.m.* Sabotage.
sabotare, *v.t.* To sabotage.
sabotatore, *n.m.* Saboteur.
sacca, *n.f.* Bag, wallet, satchel; (*Mil.*) pocket, sac. **— da viaggio,** travelling bag; kit-bag.
saccapane, *n.m.* Haversack.

S

saccarina, *n.f.* Saccharine.
saccarino, *a.* Saccharine.
saccarosio, *n.m.* Saccharose.
saccata, *n.f.* Sackful, bagful.
saccente, *n.m.* Wiseacre, pedant; dabbler in knowledge; (*f.*) bluestocking. **Fare il —,** to appear clever; to look knowing.
saccenteria [saccenterIa], *n.f.* Appearance of knowing; pretension to understanding; sciolism.
saccentone, *n.m.* Wiseacre, pedant.
saccheggiamento, *n.m.* Sacking, pillaging, looting.
saccheggiare, *v.t.* To sack, to pillage, to plunder.
saccheggiatore, *n.m.* Pillager.
saccheggio [sacchEggio], *n.m.* Sack, pillage.
sacchetto, *n.m.* Little sack; (paper) bag.
sacco, *n.m.* Sack, bag, pouch; sac; sackcloth; sack (of a town, etc.). **A sacchi,** in quantities; **avere un — di cose da fare,** to have a heap of things to do; **andarsene con le pive nel —,** to go off empty-handed; **mettere uno nel —,** to beat someone in an argument; **— postale,** mail-bag; **— a terra,** sandbag; **— a pelo,** sleeping-bag; **esser colto con le mani nel —,** to be caught red-handed.
saccoccia [saccOccia], *n.f.* Pocket.
saccone, *n.m.* Palliasse.
sacello, *n.m.* (*Lit.*) Chapel.
sacerdotale, *a.* Sacerdotal, priestly.
sacerdotalmente, *adv.* Sacerdotally.
sacerdote, *n.m.* Priest.
sacerdotessa, *n.f.* Priestess.
sacerdozio [sacerdOzio], *n.m.* Priesthood; ministry.
sacra, *n.f.* (*Eccles.*) Anniversary of the consecration of a church; village religious holiday and fair.
sacramentale, *a.* Sacramental; solemn.
sacramentalmente, *adv.* Sacramentally.
sacramentare, *v.t.i.* To administer the Sacraments; to take an oath, to swear.
sacramentarsi, *v.r.* To receive the Sacraments, to communicate.
sacramento, *n.m.* Sacrament, Eucharist; oath.
sacrare, *v.t.* To consecrate; to dedicate.
sacrario [sacrArio], *n.m.* Sanctuary, shrine.
sacrarsi, *v.r.* To consecrate oneself to, to devote oneself to.
sacrato, *n.m.* Square in front of a church.
sacrestano, sacrestia [cp. **sagrestano, sagrestia**].
sacrificare, *v.t.i.* To sacrifice, to offer up; to give up.
sacrificarsi, *v.r.* To sacrifice oneself.
sacrificatore, sacrificatrice, *n.m.f.* Sacrificer.
sacrificio [sacrifIcio], *n.m.* Sacrifice; offering; privation.
sacrilegamente, *adv.* Sacrilegiously.
sacrilegio [sacrilEgio], *n.m.* Sacrilege.
sacrilego [sacrIlego], *n.m.a.* Sacrilegious person; sacrilegious.
sacripante, *n.m.* Blusterer; hector, bully.
sacristia [cp. **sagrestia**].
sacro, *a.* Sacred, holy; consecrated. **Ordini sacri,** holy orders; (*Anat.*) **osso —,** sacrum.
sacrosanto, *a.* Sacrosanct, sacred.
sadismo, *n.m.* Sadism.
saetta, *n.f.* Arrow, dart; hand (of a watch); flash (of lightning), thunderbolt; restless child; (*Geom.*) sagitta, gnomon (of sundial). **Correre come una —,** to run like the wind.
saettamento, *n.m.* Shooting (arrows); archery.
saettare, *v.t.* To shoot (with bow); to throw a dart, to dart; to dart (rays of sunshine).
saettatore, saettatrice, *n.m.f.* Archer.
saettata, *n.f.* Bow-shot.
saettiere, *n.m.* Archer.
saettiforme, *a.* Arrow-shaped.
saffico, *a.* (*Poet.*) Sapphic.
Saffo, *n.f.* (*Myth.*) Sappho.
sagace, *a.* Sagacious, shrewd, clever, keen.
sagacemente, *adv.* Sagaciously, cleverly.
sagacia, sagacità [sagAcia, **-à**], *n.f.* Sagacity, shrewdness, cleverness.
saggezza, *n.f.* Wisdom, prudence, sageness.
saggiamente, *adv.* Sagely, wisely, judiciously.
saggiare, *v.t.* To test, to try; to sample; to taste [cp. **assaggiare**].
saggiatore, *n.m.* Assayer, tester.
saggiatura, *n.f.* Testing, assaying; sampling.
saggiavino, *n.m.* Pipkin used in wine-tasting; wine-taster.
saggina, *n.f.* (*Bot.*) Millet.
sagginale, *n.m.* Millet-stalk.
sagginare, *v.t.* To fatten (cattle).
saggio [sAggio] (1), *n.m.* Essay; test, trial; sample, specimen; (*Comm.*) rate (of interest). **— critico,** critical essay; **inviato in —,** specimen sent herewith.
saggio [sAggio] (2), *n.m.* Wise man, sage. **I sette saggi,** the seven sages.
saggio [sAggio], *a.* Wise, prudent, sage; sensible; well-behaved, good (of a child).
saggiolo, *n.m.* Sample taste; little bottle with wine sample.
saggista, *n.m.f.* Essayist.
sagittario [sagittArio], *n.m.* Archer; (*Astron.*) Sagittarius.
sagittato, *a.* Arrow-shaped.
sagoma [sAgoma], *n.f.* Moulding, mould; shape; (*Arch.*) mould; (*fig.*) queer person.
sagomare, *v.t.* To mould.
sagra, *n.f.* Consecration (of building); festival; patron saint's day.
sagrare, *v.i.* To swear, to curse.
sagrato (1), *n.m.* Curse, swearing; oath, expletive.
sagrato (2), *n.m.* Square in front of a church; consecrated ground, churchyard.
sagrestano, *n.m.* Sacristan, sexton.
sagrestia [sagrestIa], *n.f.* Sacristy, vestry.
sagri [-ì], **sagrino,** *n.m.* Shagreen.
sagrista (*pl.* **sagristi**), *n.m.* Sacristan, sexton.
sagù [-ù], *n.m.* (*Bot.*) Sago. **Palma del —,** sago-palm.
saia [sAia], *n.f.* Serge, twill.
saio [sAio], *n.m.* (Monk's) cowl, frock.
sala (1), *n.f.* Hall; room; (hospital) ward; auditorium, (*Theat.*) house. **— di ricevimento,** drawing-room; **— da pranzo,** dining-room; **— d'aspetto,** waiting-room; **— da ballo,** ball-room; **— da bagno,** bathroom; **— d'armi,** fencing-school.
sala (2), *n.f.* Axle-tree. **— anteriore, posteriore.** front axle, back axle.
salacca, *n.f.* (*Zool.*) Pilchard.
salace, *a.* Salacious, lascivious, lecherous; spicy, pungent.

salacità [-**à**], *n.f.* Lasciviousness, salacity; spiciness.
salagione, *n.f.* Salting, pickling, curing.
salamandra, *n.f.* Salamander.
salame, *n.m.* Spiced pork sausage; (*fig.*) lout, clumsy fellow, blockhead.
salamelecco, *n.m.* Salaam, bow, obeisance.
salamoia [salamOia], *n.f.* Brine, pickle.
salare, *v.t.* To salt, to corn (beef). **— la scuola,** to play truant.
salariare, *v.t.* To pay wages to; to hire.
salariato, *n.m.* Wage-earner, one in receipt of wages.
salario [salArio], *n.m.* Wage, pay; wage-system.
salassare, *v.t.* To bleed, to let blood; (*fig.*) to extort (money), to bleed.
salasso, *n.m.* Blood-letting, bleeding; (*fig.*) extortion.
salata, *n.f.* Salting, immersing in brine.
salatamente, *adv.* Very dearly (in price).
salato, *n.m.* Salt meat, salt pork; cold meat (ham, etc.).
salato, *p.p.a.* Salted, dried; (*fig.*) high-priced. **Pagare —,** to pay very dear; **costare —,** to cost a lot.
salatura, *n.f.* Salting, pickling.
salceto, *n.m.* Clump of willows.
salciccia [salcIccia], *n.f.* Sausage [cp. **salsiccia**].
salcigno, *a.* Knotty (of wood), tough.
salcio [sAlcio], *n.m.* Willow-tree.
salciolo, *n.m.* Withy.
salcrautte [salcrAutte], *n.m.* Sauerkraut.
salda, *n.f.* Starch-water. **Dare la — a,** to starch.
saldabile [saldAbile], *a.* Capable of being soldered.
saldamente, *adv.* Firmly, solidly.
saldamento, *n.m.* Soldering; (*Comm.*) settlement in full.
saldare, *v.t.* To solder, to weld; to strengthen; (*Comm.*) to settle in full. **— un conto,** to settle an account.
saldarsi, *v.r.* To heal (of a wound).
saldatoio [saldatOio], *n.m.* Soldering-iron.
saldatore, *n.m.* Solderer, welder.
saldatura, *n.f.* Soldering, welding; solder; healing (of a wound); (*Comm.*) receipt in full. **— ossidrica,** oxy-hydrogen welding; **— a ottone,** brazing.
saldezza, *n.f.* Firmness, steadiness; resolution; stability.
saldo, *n.m.* (*Comm.*) Balance of an account; settlement. **Ricevuta a —,** receipt in full; **pagare a —,** to pay in full.
saldo, *a.* Firm, steady, steadfast; massive, solid; strong. **Star —,** to stand firm; **salda amicizia,** firm friendship.
sale, *n.m.* Salt; (*fig.*) wit, judgement, common sense; pungency (of wit). **— marino,** sea-salt; **— di cucina,** kitchen salt; **— inglese,** Epsom salts; **aver — in testa,** to have one's head screwed on the right way; **dolce di —,** silly, simple; insipid; **rimaner di —,** to be dumbfounded.
salesiano, *n.m.a.* (*Eccles.*) Salesian (order founded by St. John Bosco and placed under the protection of St. Francis de Sales).
salgemma, *n.m.* Rock-salt.
salice [sAlice], *n.m.* Willow-tree [cp. **salcio**].
salicilato, *n.m.* (*Chem.*) Salicylate.
salicilico [salicIlico], *a.* (*Chem.*) Salicylic.
salico [sAlico], *a.* (*Hist.*) Salic. **Legge salica,** Salic law.
salicornia [salicOrnia], *n.f.* (*Bot.*) Glass-wort.
saliente, *n.m.a.* Salient; projecting, jutting; prominent.
saliera, *n.f.* Salt-cellar.
salifero [salIfero], *a.* Saliferous.
salificare, *v.t.* To salify.
salina, *n.f.* Salt-pit, salt-marsh; salt-works.
salino, *a.* Salty, saline.
salire, *v.t.i.* To mount, to go up, to ascend, to climb; to amount to. **— sopra un albero,** to climb a tree; **— le scale,** to go upstairs; **— in carrozza,** to get into a carriage; **— in pulpito,** to mount the pulpit; **— di prezzo,** to rise in price; **— in alto grado,** to reach a high rank; **i prezzi sono saliti alle stelle,** prices have risen sky-high.
saliscendi, *n.m.* Going up and down; door-latch. **Un — di scale,** going up and down the stairs.
salita, *n.f.* Ascent; ascension; slope, rising ground; increase.
saliva, *n.f.* Saliva, spittle.
salivale, salivare, *a.* Salivary.
salivare, *v.i.* To salivate.
salivazione, *n.f.* Salivation.
salma, *n.f.* Corpse; mortal remains; burden.
salmastro, *a.* Salty, brackish.
salmeggiamento, *n.m.* Psalm-singing.
salmeggiare, *v.i.* To sing psalms.
salmeggiatore, salmeggiatrice, *n.m.f.* Psalmodist, psalm-singer.
salmeria [salmerIa], *n.f.* (*Mil.*) Pack-train, mule-train.
salmì [-**ì**], *n.m.* Salmi, stew.
salmista, *n.m.* Psalmist.
salmo, *n.m.* Psalm.
salmodia [salmodIa], *n.f.* Psalmody.
salmodiare, *v.t.* To sing psalms.
salmone, *n.m.* (*Zool.*) Salmon.
salnitrare, *v.t.* To cover with saltpetre.
salnitro, *n.m.* Saltpetre, nitre.
salnitroso, *a.* Nitrous.
Salomone, *n.m.* Solomon.
salone, *n.m.* Hall (for assemblies, etc.), saloon; drawing-room.
salottino, *n.m.* Sitting-room; boudoir.
salotto, *n.m.* Drawing-room; parlour.
salpare, *v.i.* (*Naut.*) To weigh anchor; to set sail, to sail.
salsa, *n.f.* Sauce. **— di pomodoro,** tomato-sauce; **— bianca,** melted butter, white sauce; **— piccante,** sauce tartare; ketchup.
salsamentario [salsamentArio], *n.m.* Pork-butcher; dealer in salted foods.
salsapariglia, *n.f.* Sarsaparilla.
salsedine [salsEdine], *n.f.* Saltiness.
salsiccia [salsIccia], *n.f.* Sausage.
salsicciaio [salsicciAio], *n.m.* Sausage-maker.
salsiccione, salsicciotto, *n.m.* Thick sausage.
salsiera, *n.f.* Sauce-boat.
salso, *a.* Salt, briny, salty.
salsume, *n.m.* Saltiness; salt meat.
saltabecca, *n.f.* (*Zool.*) Grasshopper.
saltabeccare, *v.i.* To hop, to jump, to skip.
saltaleone, *n.m.* Spiral spring.
saltamartino, *n.m.*(*Zool.*) Grasshopper; jumping toy, jack-in-the-box; fidgety child.

saltare, *v.t.i.* To leap, to jump, to jump over; to spring, to skip. **— a cavallo,** to leap into the saddle; **— su,** to jump up; **— un fosso,** to jump a ditch; **— addosso a,** to fall upon; **— agli occhi,** to catch one's eye; **— di palo in frasca,** to ramble; **farsi — il cervello,** to blow one's brains out; **— in collera,** to fly into a passion; **— una pagina,** to skip a page (when reading); **— in testa,** to come into one's head (of an idea); **— la mosca al naso,** to become annoyed, to lose one's temper.
saltarello, *n.m.* Short jump, skip, hop; (*Ballet*) saltarella.
saltatoio [saltatOio], *n.m.* Perch (in bird-cage).
saltatore, saltatrice, *n.m.f.* Jumper, dancer; rope-dancer.
saltellamento, *n.m.* Skipping; hopping, frisking.
saltellare, *v.i.* To skip, to frisk about (like a child).
saltellone, saltelloni, *adv.* **A —,** by leaps and bounds.
salterellare, *v.i.* To skip about, to hop about.
salterello, *n.m.* Skip, little hop; firework cracker.
salterio [saltErio], *n.m.* Psalter, book of psalms; (*Mus.*) psaltery.
saltimbanco, *n.m.* Mountebank; tumbler, acrobat.
salto, *n.m.* Jump, leap, hop, skip; vault, spring. **D'un —,** at a leap; **a salti,** by leaps and bounds, by fits and starts; **— mortale,** somersault; **far quattro salti,** to have a dance; **i salti d'un fiume,** rapids of a river.
saltuariamente, *adv.* In a desultory way; by fits and starts.
saltuario [saltuArio], *a.* Desultory, irregular, at intervals.
saluberrimo [salubErrimo], *a.* Very salubrious, very healthy.
salubre, *a.* Healthy, salubrious.
salubremente, *adv.* Healthily.
salubrità [-à], *n.f.* Healthiness, salubrity; wholesomeness.
salumaio [salumAio], *n.m.* Pork-butcher; dealer in salted goods.
salume, *n.m.* Salt meat (ham, etc.).
salumeria [salumerIa], *n.f.* Pork-butcher's shop; delicatessen shop.
salumiere, *n.m.* Pork-butcher; keeper of a delicatessen shop.
salutare(1), *v.t.* To salute, to greet, to bow to; to welcome; to send regards to; to say good-bye to. **La saluto devotamente,** I remain yours truly; **mi saluti suo padre,** remember me to your father.
salutare(2), *a.* Salutary, wholesome, beneficial.
salutarmente, *adv.* Beneficially.
salutazione, *n.f.* Salutation, greeting.
salute, *n.f.* Health; well-being, safety; salvation. **— pubblica,** public welfare; **pieno di —,** in the best of health; **casa di —,** nursing-home; **bere alla — di,** to drink the health of.
salutista (*pl.* **salutisti**), *n.m.* Salvationist (Salvation Army member).
saluto, *n.m.* Salute, salutation, greeting; compliments, regards. **Gradisca i miei saluti,** Believe me, Yours truly; **ricambiare un —,** to return a salute, to return compliments.
salva, *n.f.* Salvo, volley, salute (of guns); round (of applause).
salvacondotto, *n.m.* Safe-conduct; permit.
salvadanaio [salvadanAio], *n.m.* Money-box.
salvagente, *n.m.* Life-belt; (traffic) island; safety zone.
salvaguardare, *v.t.* To safeguard; to protect.
salvaguardarsi, *v.r.* To guard against. **— il diritto,** to reserve to oneself the right.
salvaguardia [salvaguArdia], *n.f.* Safeguard.
salvamento, *n.m.* Safety, rescue; delivery; preservation. **Arrivare in —,** to arrive in safety; **trarre in —,** to save.
salvando, *prep.* Saving, but for.
salvare, *v.t.* To save, to deliver, to rescue, to preserve. **— la vita a qualcuno,** to save someone's life; **Dio ti salvi!** God bless you!
salvarsi, *v.r.* To save oneself, to take refuge; to arrive in safety. **Si salvi chi può,** each for himself, the Devil take the hindmost; **— l'anima,** to save one's soul.
salvataggio [salvatAggio], *n.m.* Rescue; (*Naut.*) salvage. **Cintura di —,** life-belt; **scala di —,** fire-escape; **battello di —,** lifeboat.
salvatichezza [cp. **selvatichezza**].
salvatore, *n.m.a.* Saviour; rescuer, deliverer; saving, redeeming.
salvazione, *n.f.* Salvation; rescue, safety.
salve! *inter.* Hail! **Salve Regina,** prayer to Our Lady beginning with those words.
salvezza, *n.f.* Safety, salvation. **Esercito della —,** Salvation Army.
salvia [sAlvia], *n.f.* (*Bot.*) Sage.
salvietta, *n.f.* Table-napkin.
salviettina, *n.f.* Small towel.
salvo, *n.m.* Safety; condition, reservation. **Essere in —,** to be in a place of safety.
salvo, *a.* Safe, secure. **Sano e —,** safe and sound.
salvo, *adv. prep.* Except, excepting; excepted; save, barring. **— errore od omissione,** errors and omissions excepted, E. & O.E.; **— contr'ordini,** contrary orders excepted; **arrivare sano e —,** to arrive safe and sound; **trarre qualcuno in —,** to save someone (from danger).
samaritano, *n.m.a.* Samaritan.
sambuco, *n.m.* (*Bot.*) Elder-tree.
Samuele, *n.m.* Samuel.
San, *abbrev.* **Santo.**
sanabile [sanAbile], *a.* Curable; capable of being healed.
sanabilità [-à], *n.f.* Curableness.
sanare, *v.t.* To heal, to cure; to put right, to rectify; to make (a place) healthy.
sanativo, *a.* Sanative, healing.
sanatore, sanatrice, *n.m.f.a.* Healer; healing.
sanatoria [sanatOria], *n.f.* Act of indemnity.
sanatorio [sanatOrio], *n.m.* Sanatorium.
sancire, *v.t.* To decree, to sanction; to ratify.
sandalo [sAndalo] (1), *n.m.* (*Bot.*) Sandalwood, sandal.
sandalo [sAndalo] (2), *n.m.* Sandal (shoe); (*Naut.*) punt, lighter.
sandolino, *n.m.* (*Naut.*) Sculler; scull; canoe.
sangue [sAngue], *n.m.* Blood; parentage, family, stock; race, origin, extraction. **Di puro —,** thorough-bred; **far — dal naso,** to bleed at the nose; **a — caldo,** in hot blood; **ciò non mi va a —,** I don't like it at all; **analisi del —,** blood-test; **trasfusione del —,** blood transfusion; **un principe del —,** a prince of the blood; **bistecca al —,** underdone steak.

sanguigno [sangulgno], *a.* Sanguine; full-blooded. **Temperamento —,** sanguine temperament; **vasi sanguigni,** blood-vessels.
sanguinaccio [sanguinAccio], *n.m.* Blood-pudding, black-pudding.
sanguinante, *a.* Bleeding.
sanguinare, *v.i.* To bleed. **mi sanguina il cuore,** it breaks my heart.
sanguinario, *a.* Sanguinary, bloody; blood-thirsty.
sanguine, sanguinello [sAnguine], *n.m.* (*Bot.*) Dogwood.
sanguineo [sangulneo], *a.* Blood-stained.
sanguinolente, sanguinolento, *a.* Bloody, blood-stained; dripping with blood.
sanguinosamente, *adv.* Bloodily, in a sanguinary way.
sanguinoso, *a.* Bloody, sanguinary; fierce, ferocious. **Una battaglia sanguinosa,** a bloody battle.
sanguisuga, *n.f.* (*Zool.*) Leech; (*fig.*) blood-sucker.
sanie [sAnie], *n.f.* (*Med.*) Pus.
sanità [-à], *n.f.* Health, soundness (of mind and body). **Patente di —,** bill of health.
sanitario [sanitArio], *a.* Sanitary. **Ufficio —,** health office; **ufficiale —,** health officer; **corpo —,** army medical corps.
sano, *a.* Healthy, sound; sane; salubrious; in good condition. **— e salvo,** safe and sound; **— come un pesce,** sound as a bell; **state —,** good-bye and take care of yourself; **di sana pianta,** entirely, afresh; **sono stato un anno — senza vederti ;** I have not seen you for a whole year.
sanscrito [sAnscrito], *n.m.a.* Sanskrit.
Sansone, *n.m.* Samson.
santabarbara [santabArbara], *n.f.* (*Naut.*) Powder-magazine.
santamaria, *n.m.* (*Zool.*) Kingfisher.
santamente, *adv.* Devoutly, in a holy manner.
santarello, santerello, *n.m.* Sanctimonious person; hypocrite.
santelmo, *n.m.* St. Elmo's fire.
santificamento, *n.m.* Sanctification.
santificante, *a.* Sanctifying.
santificare, *v.t.* To sanctify; to canonize; to keep religious holy days. **Sia santificato il Tuo nome,** hallowed be Thy name; **— la domenica,** to keep the Sabbath.
santificazione, *n.f.* Sanctification.
santimonia [santimOnia], *n.m.* Saintliness; sanctity; sanctimoniousness.
santino, *n.m.* Small image of a saint.
Santippe, *n.f.* Xantippe; (*fig.*) scold.
santissimo [santIssimo], *n.m.* The Blessed Sacrament.
santissimo [santIssimo], *a.* Most holy.
santità [-à], *n.f.* Holiness, saintliness, sanctity. **Sua Santità,** His Holiness the Pope.
santo, *n.m.* Saint; patron saint. **Non sapere a che — votarsi,** not to know where to turn.
santo, *a.* Holy; sainted; godly; hallowed, consecrated. **Santo Padre,** Holy Father (the Pope); **lo Spirito Santo,** the Holy Ghost; **la Santa Sede,** the Holy See; **Venerdì —,** Good Friday; **campo —,** churchyard, burial ground; **tutto il — giorno,** all day long, the livelong day.
santocchieria [santocchierIa], *n.f.* Sanctimoniousness; bigotry.
santocchio, *n.m.* Devotee; bigot.
santola [sAntola], *n.f.* Godmother.
santolina, *n.f.* (*Bot.*) Southern-wood.
santolo [sAntolo], *n.m.* Godfather.
santone, *n.m.* Hermit, saint; santon (Mohammedan religious); bigot.
santonina, *n.f.* (*Med.*) Santonin.
santuario [santuArio], *n.m.* Sanctuary, shrine.
sanzionare, *v.t.* To sanction; to approve, to ratify; to authorize.
sanzione, *n.f.* Sanction, ratification; approval; penalty.
sapere, *v.t.i.* To know, to have knowledge of, to be aware of; to understand, to learn of; to learn, to know how to, to be able to; to taste of, to smell of. **— a mente,** to know by heart; **— da buona fonte,** to know from a reliable source; **far —,** to inform; **saperla lunga,** to know a thing or two, to be cute; **— parlare l'inglese,** to be able to speak English; **— grato di,** to be grateful for; **la ragazza non sa scrivere,** the girl doesn't know how to write; **— di rinchiuso,** to smell stuffy; **— di vino,** to taste of wine; **mi sa male che,** I regret that; **ho saputo che,** I have learned that; **glielo farò sapere,** I'll let you know.
sapere, *n.m.* Knowledge, learning. **— è potere,** knowledge is power; **— fare,** know-how, wits.
sapidezza, sapidità [-à], *n.f.* Sapidness, flavour.
sapido [sApido], *a.* Savoury, well-flavoured.
sapiente, *n.m.f.a.* Scholar, learned person; learned, erudite, scholarly.
sapientemente, *adv.* Learnedly.
sapientone, *n.m.* Very learned person; (*fig.*) smatterer, sciolist.
sapienza, *n.f.* Wisdom, knowledge; learning.
saponaceo [saponAceo], *a.* Soapy; saponaceous.
saponaio [saponAio], *n.m.* Soap-maker.
saponaria [saponAria], *n.f.* (*Bot.*) Soap-wort.
saponata, *n.f.* Soap-suds, lather; soaping; (*fig.*) flattery.
sapone, *n.m.* Soap. **— da bagno, da toeletta,** bath-soap, toilet-soap; **— per la barba,** shaving-stick; **bolla di —,** soap-bubble.
saponeria [saponerIa], *n.f.* Soap-works.
saponetta, *n.f.* Cake of toilet-soap.
saponiera, *n.f.* Soap-dish.
saponificare, *v.t.* To saponify.
saponificazione, *n.f.* Saponification.
saponificio [saponifIcio], *n.m.* Soap-works.
saponoso, *a.* Soapy.
saporaccio [saporAccio], *n.m.* Bad taste.
sapore, *n.m.* Taste, flavour, savour. **Avere — di,** to taste of.
saporino, *n.m.* Delicate flavour.
saporire, *v.t.* To give a taste to, to flavour; to relish.
saporitamente, *adv.* With zest, with gusto; deliciously. **Ridere —,** to laugh heartily; **dormire —,** to sleep soundly.
saporito, *a.* Tasty, savoury; delicious; piquant; lively, witty; expensive.
saporoso, *a.* Tasty, well-flavourea.
saputa, *n.f.* Knowledge (of what has happened, etc.). **A — di,** to the knowledge of; **a mia —,** to my knowledge.
saputamente, *adv.* Consciously, with knowledge, knowingly, with design.

saputello, *n.m.* Wiseacre; sciolist; prig.
saputo, *p.p.a.* Known, acquainted with, learned, informed of. **Fare il —,** to pretend to knowledge.
saputona, *n.f.* Blue-stocking.
sarabanda, *n.f.* Saraband.
saracenico [saracEnico], *a.* Saracenic.
saraceno, *n.m.a.* Saracen. **Grano —** buckwheat.
saracinesca, *n.f.* Portcullis; sluice-gate; rolling shop-shutter; door-latch.
saracino, *n.m* Jousting dummy; (*fig.*) object of ridicule.
sarcasmo, *n.m.* Sarcasm.
sarcasticamente, *adv.* Sarcastically.
sarcastico [sarcAstico], *a.* Sarcastic.
sarchiamento, *n.m.* Weeding.
sarchiare, *v.t.* To weed.
sarchiatore, sarchiatrice, *n.m.f.* Weeder.
sarchiatrice, *n.f.* Mechanical weeder.
sarchiatura, *n.f.* Weeding.
sarchiellare, *v.t.* To take out weeds here and there.
sarchio [sArchio], *n.m.* Weeding-hook, hoe.
sarcofago [sarcOfago], *n.m.* Sarcophagus.
sarcoma, *n.f.* (*Med.*) Sarcoma.
Sardegna, *n.f.* (*Geog.*) Sardinia.
sardella, *n.f.* (*Zool.*) Pilchard.
sardina, *n.f.* (*Zool.*) Sardine.
sardo, *n.m.a.* Sardinian.
sardonicamente, *adv.* Sardonically.
sardonico [sardOnico], *a.* Sardonic, sneering.
sargia [sArgia], *n.f.* Serge; coverlet (for bed); flowered cretonne, etc., for curtains.
sarmento, *n.m.* (*Bot.*) Twig; vine-shoot; dried twig.
sarrochino, *n.m.* Pilgrim's cloak.
sarta, *n.f.* Dressmaker; tailoress.
sartie [sArtie], *n.f.pl.* (*Naut.*) Shrouds.
sartiame, *n.m.* (*Naut.*) Rigging, ropes, cordage.
sartina, *n.f.* Dressmaker's learner; grisette.
sarto, *n.m.* Tailor.
sartoria [sartorIa], *n.f.* Tailor's shop; tailoring; dressmaking.
sartorio [sartOrio], *n.m.* (*Anat.*) Sartorius (muscle).
sassaia [sassAia], *n.f.* Dam of stones (in a river); pile of stones; stony land.
sassaiola, *n.f.* Volley of stones (in a fight).
sassaiolo, *n.m.* (*Zool.*) Wood-pigeon.
sassata, *n.f.* Blow from a stone. **Prendere a sassate,** to throw stones at.
sassefrica [sassEfrica], *n.f.* (*Bot.*) Goat's beard, salsify.
sassello, *n.m.* (*Zool.*) Redwing.
sasseto, *n.m.* Patch of stony ground.
sassetto, *n.m.* Pebble, small stone.
sassifraga [sassIfraga], *n.f.* (*Bot.*) Saxifrage.
sasso, *n.m.* Stone; pebble; rock; tombstone. **Cuore di —,** stony-hearted; **restare di —,** to be petrified (with horror, surprise, etc.).
sassofono [sassOfono], *n.m.* (*Mus.*) Saxophone.
sassolino, *n.m.* Pebble.
sassone [sAssone], *n.m.a.* Saxon.
Sassonia [sassOnia], *n.f.* (*Geog.*) Saxony.
sassoso, *a.* Stony, full of stones.
Satana, Satanasso [sAtana], *n.m.* Satan.
satanico [satAnico], *a.* Satanic.
satellite [satEllite], *n.m.a.* Satellite.
satira [sAtira], *n.f.* Satire, lampoon.
satireggiare, *v.t.* Satirize.
satirescamente, *adv.* Like a satyr.
satiresco, *a.* Satyr-like.
satiricamente, *adv.* Satirically.
satirico [satIrico], *n.m.a.* Satirist; satirical.
satiro [sAtiro], *n.m.* Satyr.
satolla, *n.f.* Full meal, fill; bellyful.
satollamento, *n.m.* Satiety.
satollare, *v.t.* To fill, to satiate, to fill to repletion.
satollarsi, *v.r.* To satiate oneself.
satollo, *a.* Satiated, gorged; overfed.
satrapo [sAtrapo], *n.m.* Satrap.
saturare, *v.t.* To saturate.
saturazione, *n.f.* Saturation.
saturnali, *n.m.pl.* Saturnalia.
saturnino, *a.* Saturnine.
saturnio [satUrnio], *a.* Saturnian.
saturnismo, *n.m.* Lead-poisoning.
Saturno, *n.m.* (*Astron.*) Saturn.
saturo [sAturo], *a.* Saturated.
sauro [sAuro], *n.m.* Chestnut horse; saurian.
sauro [sAuro], *a.* Sorrel (horse).
Saverio [savErio], *n.m.* Xavier.
savio [sAvio], *n.m.a.* Sage; wise, good (of a child).
Savoia [savOia], *n.f.* (*Geog.*) Savoy.
savoiardo, *n.m.a.* Savoyard.
saziabile [saziAbile], *a.* Satiable.
saziabilità [-à], *n.f.* Satiability.
saziamento, *n.m.* Satiating, satiety.
saziare, *v.t.* To satiate, to glut; to satisfy fully.
saziarsi, *v.r.* To be satiated; to be tired of.
sazietà, *n.f.* Satiety, surfeit, glut. **A —,** to one's fill.
sazievole [saziEvole], *a.* Satiating, filling; sickening; cloying; tiresome.
sazievolmente, *adv.* Tiresomely, wearisomely.
sazio [sAzio], *a.* Satiated, full; annoyed, fed-up.
sbaccanare, *v.i.* To make a great noise, to make a din.
sbaccellare, *v.t.* To shell (peas, etc.).
sbacchettare, *v.t.* To dust, to beat (carpets, etc.).
sbacchiare, *v.t.* To bang.
sbacchio [sbacchIo], *n.m.* Constant banging.
sbaciucchiare, *v.t.* To keep on kissing, to cuddle.
sbadataggine [sbadatAggine], *n.f.* Carelessness, heedlessness; listlessness; oversight. **Per —,** through inadvertence.
sbadatamente, *adv.* Carelessly, through lack of attention.
sbadato, *a.* Careless, heedless, inattentive; inadvertent.
sbadigliamento, *n.m.* Yawning.
sbadigliare, *v.i.* To yawn, to gape.
sbadigliatore, sbadigliatrice, *n.m.f.* Person given to yawning.
sbadiglio [sbadIglio], *n.m.* Yawn, yawning.
sbafare, *v.t.* To scrounge (food); to eat too much, to eat greedily.
sbafo, *n.m.* Scrounging.
sbagliare, sbagliarsi, *v.i.r.* To mistake, to make a mistake, to err, to blunder.
sbagliare, *v.t.* To miss, to miscalculate. **— il bersaglio,** to miss the target; **— strada,** to take the wrong turning.

sbaglio [sbAglio], *n.m.* Mistake, error, blunder.
sbaldanzire, *v.t.i.* To dishearten; to be disheartened, to be cowed.
sbalestramento, *n.m.* Erratic movement, moving from side to side.
sbalestrare, *v.t.i.* To drive, to thrust; to fling, to hurl; to send from pillar to post; to miss the mark, to go wrong; to wander from one thing to another.
sbalestratamente, *adv.* Inconsiderately; vaguely.
sbalestrato, *a.* Unbalanced; rash; inconsiderate. **Uno spirito —,** an unbalanced mind.
sballare, *v.t.* To unpack, to unbale. (*colloq*). **Sballarle grosse,** to tell tall stories.
sballatura, *n.f.* Unpacking; enormous lie.
sballone, *n.m.* (*colloq.*) Boaster, braggart, teller of tall stories.
sballottamento, *n.m.* Tossing about.
sballottare, *v.t.* To toss about, to push around.
sbalordimento, *n.m.* Amazement, bewilderment; dismay.
sbalordire, *v.i.* To bewilder, to astound, to strike dumb (with amazement).
sbalordirsi, *v.r.* To be bewildered, to be astounded, to be dumbfounded.
sbalorditaggine [sbalorditAggine], *n.f.* Bewilderment, confusion; awkwardness.
sbalorditivo, *a.* Amazing, bewildering, incredible.
sbalzamento, *n.m.* Overthrow, hurling down; dismissal, "the sack"; removal.
sbalzare, *v.t.i.* To overthrow, to upset; to throw out; to fling down; to reverse; to remove; to dismiss; to spring up, to leap; to start (with fright, etc.); to fling oneself. **— da cavallo, di sella,** to unhorse, to throw from the saddle.
sbalzato, *p.p.a.* Overthrown, upset; reversed; dismissed; removed from one place to another.
sbalzellare, *v.t.i.* To jerk, to jolt; to bounce, to bump.
sbalzellio [sbalzellIo], *n.m.* Jostling, bouncing, bumping up and down.
sbalzelloni, *adv.* Only in the phrases **andare** *or* **correre a —,** to go by fits and starts.
sbalzo, *n.m.* Bound, spring, jerk, jolt; dash, rush. **A sbalzi,** by leaps and bounds; **dare uno —,** to startle, to give a start to; **di —,** suddenly; **lavoro a —,** work in relief (metal, etc.).
sbancare, *v.t.* To break the bank (at cards).
sbandamento, *n.m.* Disbanding; dispersal; (*Naut.*) list; (*Motor.*) skidding, swerve.
sbandare, *v.t.i.* To disband, to break up, to disperse; (*Naut.*) to list; (*Motor.*) to skid, to slip sideways, to swerve.
sbandarsi, *v.r.* (*Naut.*) To list; (*Motor.*) to skid, to swerve.
sbandatamente, *adv.* Helter-skelter.
sbandieramento, *n.m.* Display of flags.
sbandierare, *v.i.* To display or wave flags; to show off, to make a display.
sbandimento, *n.m.* Banishment.
sbandire, *v.t.* To banish.
sbaragliamento, *n.m.* Rout, dispersal, routing.
sbaragliare, *v.t.* To rout, to disperse, to throw into confusion.
sbaraglino, *n.m.* Backgammon.
sbaraglio [sbarAglio], *n.m.* Rout, dispersal; disorder, confusion; turmoil; risk, jeopardy. **Mettersi allo —,** to expose oneself to danger; **buttarsi allo —,** to run a risk, to venture, to take a chance.
sbarazzare, *v.t.* To free from obstructions; to clear, to rid of. **— la tavola,** to clear the table.
sbarazzarsi, *v.r.* To rid oneself of, to get rid of.
sbarazzinata, *n.f.* A boyish prank.
sbarazzino, *n.m.* A roguish boy, a little rogue; street urchin.
sbarbare, *v.t.* To shave; to uproot. **Farsi —,** to get shaved.
sbarbarsi, *v.r.* To shave, to have a shave.
sbarbatello, *n.m.* Youngster, lad, hobbledehoy; novice.
sbarbicamento, *n.m.* Uprooting.
sbarbicare, *v.t.* To uproot; to extirpate.
sbarbificarsi, *v.r.* (*facet.*) To shave oneself.
sbarcare, *v.t.i.* To disembark, to put ashore; to land, to discharge (cargo); **— il lunario,** to make both ends meet, to rub along.
sbarcatoio [sbarcatOio], *n.m.* Quay, wharf, landing-stage.
sbarco, *n.m.* Disembarkation, landing; unloading. **Luogo di —,** landing-place; **ponticello di —,** gangway, gang-plank.
sbardellatamente, *adv.* Immoderately.
sbarello, *n.m.* Tip-cart; tumbril.
sbarra, *n.f.* Bar, rail, barrier, barricade; (*Naut.*) tiller.
sbarramento, *n.m.* Obstruction; barricading; (*Mil.*) barrage; (*Comm.*) crossing (a cheque).
sbarrare, *v.t.* To bar, to stop up, to block up; to throw open, to open wide; (*Comm.*) to cross (a cheque). **— la strada,** to block the way; **— una parola,** to cross out a word; **— la porta,** to bolt the door; (*obs*). to throw open the door; **— gli occhi,** to stare, to open one's eyes (in surprise).
sbassare, *v.t.* To lower.
sbatacchiamento, *n.m.* Slamming, banging; knocking down.
sbatacchiare, *v.t.i.* To knock about, to bang, to slam, to knock down.
sbatacchio [sbatacchIo], *n.m.* Bang, banging, continual beating.
sbattere [sbAttere], *v.t.i.* To toss, to throw, to hurl, to fling; to bang, to slam (a door); to stamp one's feet; to whip (eggs); to flutter, to quiver. **— le ali,** to flap the wings; **— le porte,** to slam doors.
sbattersi [sbAttersi], *v.r.* To bang, to slam.
sbattezzarsi, *v.r.* To fret, to worry along; (*obs.*) to apostasize; to change one's name.
sbattimento, *n.m.* Beating, shaking, tossing. throwing about.
sbattuto, *p.p.a.* Beaten, tossed; depressed, harassed.
sbaulare, *v.t.* To unpack (a trunk).
sbavamento, *n.m.* Slobbering, slavering.
sbavare, *v.t.i.* To trim metal castings; to slobber, to slaver.
sbavatura, *n.f.* Slaver, dribbling; slime (of a snail); ragged edge of cast metal.
sbavone, *n.m.* Dribbler, slobberer.
sbellicarsi, *v.r.* **— dalle risa,** to split one's sides with laughing.

sbendare, *v.t.* To remove bandages; to unbind.
sberleffe, sberleffo, *n.m.* Grimace, mocking grin. **Fare gli sberleffi,** to make faces.
sberrettarsi, *v.t.* To take off one's cap, to salute.
sbevazzamento, *n.m.* Tippling, boozing.
sbevazzare, sbevucchiare, *v.i.* To tipple.
sbiadire, *v.i.* To fade, to lose its colour; to run (of a colour); to turn pale.
sbiancare, *v.t.i.* To whitewash, to bleach; to turn pale.
sbiancarsi, *v.r.* To grow pale, to turn white, to fade.
sbiancatura, *n.f.* Whitewashing; bleaching.
sbiasciare, *v.i.* To mumble, to mouth.
sbiecamente, *adv.* Obliquely, aslant, askew; awry, askance.
sbiecare, *v.t.i.* To look askance at; to put across, to put straight; to slant, to slope, to be awry.
sbieco, sbiescio [sbiEscio], *a.* Aslant, askew, awry; oblique. **Di —,** askew.
sbigottimento, *n.m.* Dismay, consternation; amazement; discouragement.
sbigottire, *v.t.* To frighten, to terrify; to dismay.
sbigottirsi, *v.r.* To be dismayed, to be terrified; to take fright.
sbigottito, *a.* Frightened; downcast, discouraged.
sbilanciamento, *n.m.* Loss of balance, loss of equilibrium; derangement.
sbilanciare, *v.t.i.* To unbalance, to unsettle; to throw out of balance; to cause or have a deficiency.
sbilanciarsi, *v.r.* To lose one's balance; to spend more than one can afford; to live beyond one's means.
sbilancio [sbilAncio], *n.m.* Want of balance; (*Comm.*) deficit; derangement.
sbilenco, *a.* Crooked; bandy-legged.
sbirciare, *v.t.i.* To eye, to look closely at; to ogle, to leer.
sbirciata, *n.f.* Ogle, leer, wink; close look at; side-glance.
sbirraglia [sbirrAglia], *n.f.* Police, constabulary; police spies.
sbirro, *n.m.* (Contemptuous term for a) policeman, constable; police spy, "copper's nark."
sbizzarrirsi, *v.r.* To indulge one's whims, to get one's own way.
sbloccare, *v.t.* (*Comm.*) To release, to disengage.
sblocco, *n.m.* (*Comm.*) Unfreezing (of prices).
sboccamento, *n.m.* Outfall, outflow, disemboguement; overflow; mouth (of river, etc.).
sboccare, *v.t.i.* To lead into; to flow into (of a river); to open into (of a street), to debouch.
sboccatamente, *adv.* Obscenely, indecently, without restraint.
sboccato, *a.* Foul-mouthed; hard-mouthed (of a horse).
sboccatura, *n.f.* Opening, mouth (of a river).
sbocciare, *v.i.* (*Bot.*) To open, to blossom, to blow, to bloom.
sboccio [sbOccio], *n.m.* Bloom, blossoming. **In pieno —,** in full bloom.
sbocco, *n.m.* Outlet; mouth of a river; opening; (*Comm.*) trade outlet, market. **— di sangue,** blood-spitting.
sbocconcellamento, *n.m.* Nibbling; mincing (of meat, etc.).
sbocconcellare, *v.t.* To nibble; to mince; to eat very slowly.
sbocconcellatura, *n.f.* Nibbling, mincing.
sbollire, *v.i.* To go off the boil, to stop boiling; to calm down (in one's passions).
sbornia [sbOrnia], *n.f.* Intoxication, drunkenness.
sborniarsi, *v.r.* To get drunk.
sbornione, *n.m.* Habitual drunkard, sot.
sborsamento, *n.m.* Disbursement.
sborsare, *v.t.* To disburse, to pay.
sborso, *n.m.* Disbursement, outlay.
sbottare, *v.i.* To burst out.
sbottonare, *v.t.* To unbutton.
sbottonarsi, *v.r.* To unbosom oneself, to lay bare one's feelings.
sbottonatura, *n.f.* Unbosoming oneself.
sbottoneggiare, *v.i.* To banter; to malign.
sbozzare, *v.t.* To sketch, to outline, to make a rough drawing.
sbozzatura, *n.f.* Sketch, outline.
sbozzino, *n.m.* Jack-plane.
sbozzo, *n.m.* Outline, rough draft, sketch.
sbozzolare, *v.t.i.* To take (silk-worm) cocoons from the branches; to emerge from the cocoon.
sbozzolarsi, *v.r.* To emerge from the cocoon.
sbozzolatura, *n.f.* Taking silk-worm cocoons from the branches.
sbracarsi, *v.r.* To take off one's trousers. — **— dalle rise,** to burst with laughter.
sbracatamente, *adv.* Excessively.
sbracato, *p.p.a.* Trouserless, unbreeched.
sbracciarsi, *v.r.* To turn up one's sleeves, to bare one's arms; to wave one's arms; (*fig.*) to get very busy; to use every effort.
sbraciare, *v.t.* To poke (the fire).
sbraciarsi, *v.r.* (*fig.*) to make a show (with one's money), to swagger, to talk big.
sbraciatoio [sbraciatOio], *n.m.* Poker.
sbracione, *n.m.* Boaster.
sbraitamento, *n.m.* Bawling, shouting, clamour.
sbraitare, *v.i.* To bawl, to shout, to clamour, to squall.
sbraitio [sbraitIo], *n.m.* Uproar, constant bawling and shouting.
sbraitone, *n.m.* Bawler.
sbramarsi, *v.r.* To satisfy one's longing
sbranare, *v.t.* To tear to pieces, to rend.
sbrancamento, *n.m.* Straying (from the flock); lopping, pruning.
sbrancare, *v.t.* To lop, to prune, to take away (from the flock).
sbrancarsi, *v.r.* To stray.
sbrandellare, *v.t.* To tear to pieces, to tear into shreds.
sbrandellarsi, *v.r.* To fall into tatters.
sbrano, *n.m.* Tear, rent.
sbrattare, *v.t.* To clean up, to clear, to put in order, to clear away.
sbratto, *n.m.* Clear up, cleaning.
sbravazzare, *v.i.* To brag, to boast; to bluster.
sbravazzata, *n.f.* Boast; bragging.
sbravazzone, *n.m.* Boaster, bragger, braggart.
sbrendolo [sbrEndolo], *n.m.* Rag, tatter, shred.
sbrendolone, *n.m.* Tatterdemalion.

sbriciolamento, *n.m.* Crumbling.
sbriciolare, *v.t.* To crumble, to break in small pieces; to mince.
sbriciolarsi, *v.r.* To crumble away.
sbriciolatura, *n.f.* Crumbling.
sbrigamento, *n.m.* Despatch, expedition, haste, hurrying up.
sbrigare, *v.t.* To despatch, to expedite; to finish off. **— la corrispondenza,** to answer letters.
sbrigarsi, *v.r.* To make haste, to hurry up. **Sbrigatevi,** make haste, hurry up, get a move on; **— di,** to get rid of.
sbrigativamente, *adv.* Expeditiously.
sbrigativo, *a.* Expeditious, quick, hasty.
sbrigliare, *v.t.* To unbridle; to loosen.
sbrigliata, *n.f.* Jerk of the reins.
sbrigliatamente, *adv.* Freely, openly, unrestrainedly.
sbrigliatezza, *n.f.* Unruliness; extravagance; sprightliness.
sbrigliato, *p.p.a.* Unbridled, unruly; dissolute; spirited, lively.
sbrindellare, *v.t.i.* To tear to pieces; to fall into rags.
sbrindello, *n.m.* Rag, tatter.
sbrindellone, *n.m.* Tatterdemalion.
sbrocco, *n.m.* Floss silk.
sbrogliamento, *n.m.* Disentanglement.
sbrogliare, *v.t.* To disentangle; to extricate; to disencumber.
sbrogliarsi, *v.r.* To extricate oneself from, to get clear of.
sbruffare, *v.t.* To squirt, to besprinkle; to spit upon.
sbruffata, *n.f.* Squirting, sprinkling; flush (of water).
sbruffo, *n.m.* Flush (of water), sprinkle; (*fig.*) bribe.
sbucare, *v.t.i.* To draw out (of a hole), to start (game, fox, etc.); to emerge, to come out, to issue forth.
sbucciamento, *n.m.* Peeling, skinning, husking.
sbucciare, *v.t.* To skin, to peel, to husk, to shell. **— una mela,** to peel an apple.
sbucciarsi, *v.r.* To scrape one's skin; to slough (of reptiles).
sbucciatura, *n.f.* Bruise, abrasion; shelling, husking.
sbudellare, *v.t.* To disembowel; to gut (fish); to stab in the stomach. **— un pollo,** to clean a chicken.
sbuffamento, *n.m.* Blowing, puffing, snorting, panting.
sbuffare, *v.i.* To puff, to pant, to snort; to fume (with anger); to blow a gust of wind.
sbuffata, sbuffo, *n.f.m.* Puff, snort; gust of wind.
sbugiardare, *v.t.* To give the lie to.
sburrare, *v.t.* To skim (milk).
sbuzzare, *v.t.* To disembowel, to rip up, to gut.
scabbia [scAbbia], *n.f.* Scab, itch; (*Med.*) scabies.
scabbiosa, *n.f.* (*Bot.*) Scabious.
scabbioso, *a.* Scabby.
scabro, *a.* Rugged, rough; knotty, gnarled.
scabrosamente, *adv.* Roughly; with difficulty.
scabrosità [-à], *n.f.* Ruggedness, roughness; hardness; knottiness; (*fig.*) difficulty.
scabroso, *a.* Rough, rugged; (*fig.*) difficult, intricate. **Un affare —,** a tricky business.
scaccato, *a.* Chequered, in squares.
scacchi, *n.m.pl.* Chess. **Giuocare a —,** to play chess; **una partita a —,** a game of chess.
scacchiera, *n.f.* Chess-board, draught-board.
scacchiere, *n.m.* Chess-board; Exchequer; zone.
scacchista (*pl.* **scacchisti**), *n.m.* Chess-player.
scacchistico [scacchIstico], *a.* Concerned with chess, chess.
scaccia [scAccia], *n.m.* Beater (at a shoot).
scacciamento, *n.m.* Driving out, expelling.
scacciamosche, *n.m.* Fly-flap, fly-whisk.
scacciapensieri, *n.m.* Pastime, diversion, hobby; (*Mus.*) jews-harp.
scacciare, *v.t.* To drive out, to expel, to drive away; to dispel.
scaccino, *n.m.* Verger, sexton.
scacco, *n.m.* Square (on chess-board); check (in all senses); failure, repulse. (*Chess*) **Scacco!** Check! **— matto!** Checkmate!; **dare — matto,** to checkmate; **subire uno —,** to meet a drawback, to suffer a defeat; **a scacchi,** chequered, in squares.
scadente, *a.* Inferior; falling, declining. **Di qualità —,** of poor quality; (*Comm.*) **un cambiale —,** a bill falling due.
scadenza, *n.f.* (*Comm.*) Maturity; expiration. **A breve, a lunga —,** short, long-dated; **una cambiale in —,** a bill falling due.
scadenzario [scadenzArio], *n.m.* (*Comm.*) Bill book, register of bills.
scadere, *v.i.* To fall off, to decline; to decrease; (*Comm.*) to fall due, to expire. **La cambiale scade il 1 ottobre,** the bill falls due on 1st October.
scadimento, *n.m.* Decay, decline.
scaduto, *p.p.a.* Due; expired; decayed.
scafandro, *n.m.* Diver's suit; diving apparatus.
scaffale, *n.m.* Book-case; book-shelves.
scafo, *n.m.* (*Naut.*) Hull; (*Aviat.*) body.
scagionare, *v.t.* To excuse, to acquit.
scagionarsi, *v.r.* To excuse oneself.
scaglia [scAglia], *n.f.* (Fish) scale; flake, shell (of tortoise, etc.); chip; spangle.
scagliare, *v.t.* To hurl, to fling, to toss, to throw.
scagliarsi, *v.r.* To rush at, to fall upon, to hurl oneself at; **— sul nemico,** to hurl oneself at the foe.
scagliola, *n.f.* Plaster of Paris; (*Bot.*) canary-grass.
scaglionare, *v.t.* (*Mil.*) To form in echelon.
scaglione, *n.m.* (*Mil.*) Echelon; (*Heraldry*) chevron; mountain terrace.
scaglioso, *a.* Scaly.
scagnozzo, *n.m.a.* Bungler; indigent priest; poor, miserable.
scala, *n.f.* Staircase, stairs; ladder; (*Music*) scale; extent. **— mobile,** escalator, moving-staircase; (*comm.*) cost-of-living index; **— di corda,** rope-ladder; **— a chiocciola,** spiral *or* winding staircase; **— metrica,** metric scale; **— a pioli,** ladder.
scalamento, *n.m.* Escalade.
scalandrone, *n.m.* (*Naut.*) Portable gangway.
scalappiare, *v.t.* To disentangle.
scalappiarsi, *v.r.* To disentangle oneself.
scalare, *v.t.* To scale down, to reduce; to graduate (payments, etc.), to shade (colours); to deduct; to climb, to ascend, to scale.

scalata, *n.f.* Scaling, climbing; escalade.
scalatore, scalatrice, *n.m.f.* Climber.
scalcagnare, *v.t.i.* To tread down at heels. **— qualcuno,** to tread on someone's heels.
scalcagnato, *a.* Down at heels.
scalcare, *v.t.* To carve (at table).
scalcatore, *n.m.* Carver.
scalciare, *v.i.* To kick.
scalcinare, *v.t.* To scrape off plaster.
scalcinato, *p.p.a.* Stripped of plaster; (*fig.*) shabby, seedy, down at heel.
scalcinatura, *n.f.* Stripping of plaster.
scalco, *n.m.* Steward; carver.
scaldabagno, *n.m.* Bathroom geyser.
scaldaletto, *n.m.* Warming-pan; hot-water-bottle.
scaldamani, scaldamano, *n.m.* Hand-warmer; children's game of hand on hand.
scaldamento, *n.m.* Heating; warming.
scaldapanche, *n.m.* Idle boy at school.
scaldapiatti, *n.m.* Plate-warmer.
scaldapiedi, *n.m.* Foot-warmer; hot-water bottle.
scaldare, *v.t.* To warm, to heat.
scaldarsi, *v.r.* To warm oneself; to become excited, to get heated.
scaldavivande, *n.m.* Chafing-dish; dish-warmer.
scaldino, *n.m.* Warming-pan.
scalea [scalEa], *n.f.* Flight of steps; (*Arch.*) perron.
scaleno, *a.* (*Geom.*) Scalene.
scaleo, *n.m.* Steps, double ladder.
scaletta, *n.f.* Stairway, short ladder, steps. (*Comm.*) **A —,** diminishing interest on amortization.
scalfire, *v.t.* To graze, to scratch.
scalfittura, *n.f.* Graze, scratch.
scalinata, *n.f.* Flight of steps; steps in front of a church, etc.
scalino, *n.m.* Step (of stairs, etc.), rung, round.
scalmana, *n.f.* (*Med.*) Chill, cold.
scalmanarsi, *v.r.* To catch cold; (*fig.*) to get bothered or flustered; to bustle. **Far le cose senza —,** to take things in one's stride.
scalmanato, *p.p.a.* Suffering with a cold; hurried, flustered, out of breath.
scalmo, *n.m.* (*Naut.*) Rowlock.
scalo, *n.m.* Wharf, quay; landing-place; port of call; land-fall; (*Rail.*) platform, goods-wharf; stocks (ship-building). **Porto di —,** port of call; **far —,** to put into port, to touch at; **— di alaggio,** slipway; **— ferroviario,** marshalling-yard; **bastimento sullo —,** vessel on the stocks; (*Aviat.*) **volo senza —,** non-stop flight.
scalogna, *n.f.* (*colloq.*) Bad luck.
scalogno, *n.m.* (*Bot.*) Shallot.
scalone, *n.m.* Grand or main staircase.
scaloppa, scaloppina, *n.m.* Scallop (of veal, etc.).
scalpellare, *v.t.* To chisel out, to carve.
scalpellatura, *n.f.* Chiselling.
scalpellino, *n.m.* Stone-mason; stone-cutter.
scalpello, *n.m.* Chisel; (*Med.*) scalpel. **— a freddo,** cold chisel.
scalpicciamento, *n.m.* Stamping of feet; tramp (of feet on a pavement).
scalpicciare, *v.i.* To tramp (on pavement, etc.); to scrape the feet.
scalpiccio [scalpiccIo], *n.m.* Continual tramping or shuffling of feet.
scalpitare, *v.i.* To paw the ground.
scalpitio [scalpitIo], *n.m.* Pawing the ground.
scalpore, *n.m.* Noise, bustle, fuss; complaint. **Menar —,** to make a fuss; to make a great noise (about a thing).
scaltramente, *adv.* Artfully, cunningly, slily.
scaltrezza, *n.f.* Cunning, craftiness, slyness; shrewdness, sharpness.
scaltrire, *v.t.* To smarten, to sharpen a person's wits, to wake up.
scaltrirsi, *v.r.* To sharpen one's wits, to grow wiser, to wake up (mentally).
scaltrito, *a.* Shrewd, experienced.
scaltro, *a.* Cunning, sly; smart, shrewd; crafty.
scalzacane, *n.m.* Ragamuffin, disreputable fellow.
scalzamento, *n.m.* Taking off one's shoes and stockings.
scalzare, *v.t.* To take off shoes and stockings; to undermine; (*Agric.*) to hoe.
scalzarsi, *v.r.* To take off one's shoes and stockings.
scalzato, *p.p.a.* Laid bare, undermined.
scalzo, *a.* Barefoot, barefooted. **Camminare —,** to go bare-footed.
scambiamento, *n.m.* Exchanging; mistaking (one person or thing for another).
scambiare, *v.t.* To exchange, to barter; to mistake (one person or thing for another).
scambietto, *n.m.* Quick movement of the feet (in ballet dancing).
scambievole [scambiEvole], *a.* Reciprocal, mutual.
scambievolezza, *n.f.* Reciprocity.
scambio [scAmbio], *n.m.* Exchange; substitution; mistake (in identification); (*Rail.*) switch-points. (*Pol.*) **Libero —,** free trade.
scambista (*pl.* **scambisti**), *n.m.* (*Rail.*) Pointsman, shunter. (*Pol.*) Free-trader.
scamiciarsi, *v.r.* To take off one's shirt, coat or waistcoat; to be in one's shirt-sleeves.
scamiciato, *p.p.a.* In shirt sleeves; shirtless; (*fig.*) rustic, countrified, plebeian.
scamosciare, *v.t.* To dress shammy-leather. **Pelle scamosciata,** shammy-leather.
scamosciatore, *n.m.* Man who dresses chamois skins.
scamoscio [scamOscio], *n.m.* Shammy-leather.
scampaforca, *n.m.* Hardened criminal; gallows-bird.
scampagnare, *v.i.* To go for a country excursion.
scampagnata, *n.f.* Trip in the country, picnic.
scampamento, *n.m.* Escape, safety.
scampanare, *v.i.* To ring (of bells), to chime, to peal.
scampanata, *n.f.* Peal, ringing, chiming.
scampanatore, *n.m.* Bell-ringer.
scampanellare, *v.i.* To ring (of a door-bell).
scampanellata, *n.f.* Ring (at the door), loud ring.
scampanellio [scampanellIo], *n.m.* Continual ringing.
scampanio [scampanIo], *n.m.* Pealing of bells, chime, chiming.

scampare, *v.t.i.* To save, to rescue, to deliver, to preserve; to escape, to get away, to reach safety. **Scamparla,** to save one's life, to get away in safety; **Dio ce ne scampi e liberi!** God preserve us! God forbid!
scampo, *n.m.* Safety; escape; flight; (*Zool.*) prawn. **Non c'è —,** there's no help for it.
scampolo [scAmpolo], *n.m.* Remnant, remainder, cutting.
scanagliare, *v.i.* To pour out vulgar abuse.
scanalare, *v.t.* To groove, to channel, to flute.
scanalatura, *n.f.* Channeling; fluting; (*Carp.*) rabbet.
scancio [scancIo], *n.m.* Oblique line. **Di —,** obliquely, slantingly, on the slant.
scandagliare, *v.t.* (*Naut.*) To sound, to take soundings. **— la situazione,** to probe the situation.
scandagliatore, *n.m.* (*Naut.*) Leadsman.
scandaglio [scandAglio], *n.m.* (*Naut.*) Sounding line, lead; sounding. **Lanciare lo —,** to heave the lead.
scandalizzare, *v.t.* To scandalize, to shock.
scandalizzarsi, *v.r.* To be scandalized, to be shocked.
scandalo [scAndalo], *n.m.* Scandal; shame. **Pietra dello —,** stumbling-block; (*Bible*) (*fig.*) scandal-monger; **soffocare uno —,** to hush up a scandal.
scandalosamente, *adv.* Scandalously.
scandalosità [-à], *n.f.* Scandalousness.
scandaloso, *a.* Scandalous, shocking.
scandere, scandire [scAndere], *v.t.* (*Poet.*) To scan.
Scandinavia [scandinAvia], *n.f.* (*Geog.*) Scandinavia.
scandinavo, *n.m.a.* Scandinavian.
scannamento, *n.m.* Butchery, slaughter, throat-cutting.
scannare (1), *v.t.* To cut the throat of; to slaughter, to butcher.
scannare (2), *v.i.* To unwind.
scannatoio [scannatOio], *n.m.* Slaughter-house, shambles.
scannatore, *n.m.* Cut-throat, slaughterer.
scannellamento, *n.m.* Channeling, grooving; fluting; unwinding.
scannellare, *v.t.* To groove, to flute; to channel; to unwind.
scannellatura, *n.f.* Grooving; fluting (in a column).
scannello, *n.m.* Small stool; portable writing-desk; rump-steak.
scanno, *n.m.* Bench, stool; seat; sand-bank (at river mouth).
scansafatiche, *n.m.* Loafer, idler; sluggard.
scansare, *v.t.* To avoid, to shun, to steer clear of; to move away; to parry. **— un colpo,** to ward off, to parry a blow.
scansarsi, *v.r.* To stand aside, to withdraw, to get out of the way; to dodge.
scansia [scansIa], *n.f.* Bookcase, book-shelves.
scansione, *n.f.* (*Poet.*) Scansion.
scanso, *n.m.* Avoidance. **A — di,** in order to avoid; **a — di equivoci,** to avoid misunderstandings.
scantinato, *n.m.* Basement (of house, etc.).
scantonamento, *n.m.* Turning over the corner.
scantonare, *v.t.i.* To round edges, to round off, to remove corners; to turn the corner (to avoid someone).
scantucciare, *v.t.* To cut off the crust of a loaf; to trim the edges of.
scanzonato, *a.* Free and easy, carefree; jolly.
scapaccionare, *v.t.* To rap on the head.
scapaccione, *n.m.* Rap on the head, slap, smack.
scapare, *v.t.* To cut off the head (of fish).
scaparsi, *v.r.* To lose one's head (with excitement, etc.); to rack one's brains.
scapata, *adv.* **Alla —,** thoughtlessly.
scapataggine [scapatAggine], *n.f.* Heedlessness, recklessness, thoughtlessness.
scapato, *a.* Reckless, thoughtless.
scapecchiare, *v.t.* To card flax.
scapecchiatoio [scapecchiatOio], *n.m.* Flax-comb.
scapestrarsi, *v.r.* To lead a dissolute life.
scapestrataggine [scapestratAggine], *n.f.* Libertinism.
scapestratamente, *adv.* Dissolutely.
scapestrato, *n.m.a.* Libertine, debauchee; scapegrace; dissolute, licentious; wild; debauched.
scapezzamento, *n.m.* Lopping, pollarding.
scapezzare, *v.t.* To lop, to pollard; to prune.
scapigliare, *v.t.* To rumple, to ruffle, to make dishevelled.
scapigliarsi, *v.r.* To rumple one's hair; to let one's hair down; (*fig.*) to lead a dissolute life.
scapigliato, *p.p.a.* Rumpled, ruffled; Bohemian; free-and-easy.
scapigliatura, *n.f.* Free and easy ways; bohemianism.
scapitare, *v.i.* To lose, to be a loser; (*fig.*) to sink.
scapito [scApito], *n.m.* Loss, damage; detriment. **Vendere a —,** to sell at a loss; **a — di qualcuno,** at the expense of someone else.
scapitozzare, *v.t.* To lop off, to cut off; to pollard.
scapola [scApola], *n.f.* (*Anat.*) Shoulder-blade; scapula.
scapolare, *n.m.* (*Eccles.*) Scapular.
scapolare, *v.t.i.* To rescue, to escape.
scapolarsi, *v.r.* To escape; to make off, to take French leave.
scapolo [scApolo], *n.m.* Bachelor, single man; single, unmarried.
scappamento, *n.m.* Escapement (of watch, etc.); escape (of gas, steam, etc.); (*Motor.*) exhaust.
scappare, *v.i.* To run away, to escape; to flee. **Lasciarsi — una parola,** to let drop a word; **lasciarsi — un errore,** to let slip a mistake; **— la pazienza,** to lose one's patience; **a scappa e fuggi,** in a tearing hurry; **chiudere la stalla quando sono scappati i bovi,** to close the stable-door when the horses have fled; **lasciarsi — un'occasione** to miss one's chance.
scapparsi, *v.r.* To take to flight, to make one's escape.
scappata, *n.f.* Escape, flight; short call (upon someone); excursion; outburst (of temper, etc.); escapade.
scappatella, *n.f.* Escapade, prank.
scappatoia [scappatOia], *n.f.* Way out; subterfuge, evasion; pretext.
scappellare, *v.t.* To knock a hat off.
scappellarsi, *v.r.* To raise one's hat, to take off one's hat (in greeting).

scappellata, *n.f.* Greeting (by raising the hat).
scappellottare, *v.t.* To give a rap on the head, to box the ears (of); to slap.
scappellotto, *n.m.* Rap on the head; box of the ears; slap. **Passare a scappellotti,** to scrape through an exam; **entrare a scappellotti,** to get in without paying.
scappucciarsi, *v.r.* To remove one's hood; (*fig.*) to blunder, to stumble, to trip; to go astray.
scappucciata, *n.f.* Stumble, false step.
scappuccio [scappUccio], *n.m.* Blunder.
scarabattola [scarabAttola], *n.f.* Show-case; glass cabinet; (*colloq.*) trash.
scarabeo [scarabEo], *n.m.* Scarab; (*Zool.*) dung-beetle, scarabæus.
scarabocchiare, *v.t.i.* To scrawl, to scribble.
scarabocchiatore, scarabocchiatrice, *n.m.f.* Scribbler.
scarabocchiatura, scarabocchio [scarabOcchio], *n.f.m.* Scrawl, scribble.
scaracchiare, *v.i.* To spit.
scaracchio [scarAcchio], *n.m.* Spittle, spit.
scarafaggio [scarafAggio], *n.m.* Cockroach, black-beetle.
scaramuccia [scaramUccia], *n.f.* Skirmish.
scaramucciare, *v.t.* To skirmish.
scaraventare, *v.t.* To hurl.
scaraventarsi, *v.r.* To throw oneself, to hurl oneself (into a fight, etc.).
scarceramento, *n.m.* Release from prison.
scarcerare, *v.t.* To release from prison, to set free.
scarcerazione, *n.f.* Release from prison, discharge; setting free.
scardare, *v.t.* To shell, to husk (chestnuts), to scale (fish).
scardassare, *v.t.* To card wool.
scardassatore, *n.m.* Wool-carder.
scardassatura, *n.f.* Wool-carding.
scardasso, *n.m.* Carder, wool-comb.
scardinare, *v.t.* To take off its hinges, to unhinge.
scarica [scArica], *n.f.* (*Mil.*) Volley; shower (of stones, etc.); discharge.
scaricabarili, *n.m.* **Fare a —,** to throw the blame upon each other; to pass the buck.
scaricalasino [scaricalAsino], *n.m.* Boys' game of riding on one another's shoulders.
scaricamento, *n.m.* Unloading, discharging.
scaricare, *v.t.i.* To discharge, to unload; to lighten; to empty. **— un fucile,** to discharge a gun; **— il vapore,** to blow off steam; **— la colpa addosso a un altro,** to put the blame on someone else.
scaricarsi, *v.r.* To relieve oneself (in all senses); to get rid of; to acquit oneself (of a duty, etc.); to discharge (of a river, etc.); to run down (of clock or watch).
scaricatoio [scaricatOio], *n.m.* Wharf, landing-stage; outfall, sewer; exhaust-pipe, drain-pipe.
scaricatore, *n.m.* Docker; waste-pipe.
scarico [scArico], *n.m.* Discharge, unloading; refuse-dump. (*Motor.*) **Tubo di —,** exhaust-pipe; (*Comm.*) **libro di —,** stock-book; **a — di coscienza,** for conscience's sake; **testimonio a —,** witness for the defence.
scarico [scArico], *a.* Unloaded, discharged; run down (of clock, etc.) **Capo —,** hare-brained person; **tempo —,** unclouded sky.
scarificare, *v.t.* To scarify.
scarificazione, *n.f.* Scarification.
scarlattina, *n.f.* (*Med.*) Scarlet-fever.
scarlatto, *n.m.a.* Scarlet.
scarmigliare, *v.t.* To ruffle, to rumple.
scarnamento, *n.m.* Loss of flesh.
scarnare, *v.t.* To remove superfluous flesh from; to flesh (skins).
scarnarsi, *v.r.* To grow thin.
scarnatoio [scarnatOio], *n.m.* Fleshing-knife.
scarnificare, *v.t.i.* To strip off the flesh, to tear flesh from; to lacerate; to grow thin.
scarnirsi, *v.r.* To grow thin, to become meagre.
scarnito, *a.* Thin, emaciated.
scarno, *a.* Thin, lean.
scarpa, *n.f.* Shoe, boot; skid (for a wheel); scarp, slope (of land).
scarpaccia [scarpAccia], *n.f.* Old, bad or worn-out shoe.
scarpata, *n.f.* Blow with a shoe; escarpment, slope (of land).
scarpetta, scarpina, *n.f.* Small shoe; pump; dancing-pump.
scarpone, *n.m.* Climbing-boot; large rustic shoe; (*colloq.*) a soldier of the Alpini corps.
scarrozzare, *v.t.i.* To take for a drive; to go for a drive.
scarrozzata, *n.f.* Carriage-drive, drive.
scarsamente, *adv.* Scarcely, barely, insufficiently, slightly.
scarseggiare, *v.i.* To get scarce, to get rare; to be lacking in; to run short.
scarsella, *n.f.* Purse; pocket.
scarsezza, scarsità [-à], *n.f.* Scarcity, scarceness; shortage, lack; want, penury; dearth. **— d'ingegno,** lack of intelligence.
scarso, *a.* Scarce, rare; insufficient, lacking; poor, indigent; short. **— di danaro,** short of money; **misura scarsa,** short measure.
scartabellare, *v.t.* To turn the leaves (of a book).
scartafaccio [scartafAccio], *n.m.* Scribbling-pad, waste-book.
scartamento, *n.m.* Rejection, rejecting; elimination; (*Rail.*) gauge. (*Rail.*) **Ferrovia a — ridotto,** narrow-gauge railway.
scartare, *v.t.i.* To reject; to discard; to lay aside; to unpack; (*Football*) to dribble.
scartata, *n.f.* Rejection; swerve (of a horse).
scartato, *p.p.a.* Rejected; (*Mil.*) invalided out.
scarto, *n.m.* Discard, refuse, scrap; defective or rejected articles; (*Football*) dribbling; (*Mil.*) man invalided out, rejected for service.
scartocciare, *v.t.* To unpack, to unwrap, to unfold.
scartoccio [scartOccio], *n.m.* Paper-bag; chimney (of oil-lamp).
scasare, *v.t.* To turn out (lodger, tenant, etc.).
scassare, *v.t.* To unpack, to remove from a case; to break open; (*Agric.*) to break up ground: to trench, to double-dig.
scassatore, *n.m.* Housebreaker.
scassinare, *v.t.* To break open; to pick (a lock).
scassinatore, *n.m.* Pick-lock, burglar, housebreaker.
scasso, *n.m.* House-breaking, burglary; (*Agric.*) trenching.
scatenamento, *n.m.* Unchaining, loosing; rousing.

scatenare, *v.t.* To unchain; (*fig.*) to rouse, to instigate.
scatenarsi, *v.r.* To break loose; (*fig.*) to burst into a rage, to break out.
scatola [scAtola], *n.f.* Box; tin, (*Am.*) can. — **di cartone,** cardboard box; **mettere in —,** to can (meat, etc.); **carne in —,** tinned meat; **rompere le scatole a,** to bore, to weary; **lettere di —,** block letters.
scatolaio [scatolAio], *n.m.* Box-maker.
scatolame, *n.m.* Tinned or canned foodstuffs; tinned food.
scatolone, *n.m.* Large box.
scattare, *v.i.* To spring up, to dash, to start; to go off (of a gun); to fly into a rage, to get excited. — **in piedi,** to spring to one's feet.
scatto, *n.m.* Spring, leap; outburst; sudden movement, jerk, click; spring-lock (of a door); detent (of clock, etc.).
scaturigine [scaturIgine], *n.f.* Source, origin.
scaturimento, *n.m.* Gushing out.
scaturire, *v.i.* To spring, to gush out; to spout; to arise (from), to issue (out of), to ensue.
scavalcare, *v.t.i.* To unhorse, to dismount; to oust, to displace; to skip (from one thing to another); to slip (a stitch). — **un muro,** to scale a wall; — **una siepe,** to jump over a fence.
scavallare, *v.i.* To frisk about.
scavamento, *n.m.* Excavation; digging out.
scavapozzi, *n.m.* Well-sinker
scavare, *v.t.* To dig out, to excavate; to hollow out; to sink (a well). **Da dove l'hai scavato?** Where on earth did you find that?
scavatore, *n.m.* Digger; miner.
scavatura, scavazione, *n.f.* Excavation, digging; hole, cavity.
scavezzacollo, *n.m.* Breakneck fall; scamp, dangerous fellow, rascal; daredevil. **A —,** rashly, precipitately.
scavezzare, *v.t.* To unbridle; to break. **Scavezzarsi il collo,** to break one's neck.
scavo, *n.m.* Excavation; material excavated. **Scavi,** archaeological excavations; — **di galleria,** piercing a tunnel.
scegliere [scEgliere], *v.t.* To choose, to select, to pick out; to prefer. **Non c'è da —,** there is no choice.
sceglitore, sceglitrice, *n.m.f.* Chooser, selector.
sceicco [sceIcco], *n.m.* Sheikh.
scelleraggine, scelleratаggine [scellerAggine, scelleratAggine], *n.f.* Villainy, wickedness.
scelleratamente, *adv.* Wickedly.
scelleratezza, *n.f.* Wickedness, villainy, rascality.
scellerato, *n.m.a.* Villain, scoundrel, wretch; wicked, villainous, evil.
scellino, *n.m.* Shilling.
scelta, *n.f.* Choice, pick, selection; quality.
sceltezza, *n.f.* Choiceness.
scelto, *p.p.a.* Chosen, selected; choice, exquisite [cp. **scegliere**].
scemamento, *n.m.* Diminution, reduction; abatement. — **delle acque,** abatement of the floods.
scemare, *v.t.i.* To diminish, to lessen; to reduce; to abate; to decrease, to decline, to fall; to wane (of the moon).
scemenza, *n.f.* Silliness, foolishness; idiocy; stupid thing.
scemo, *n.m.a.* Half-wit, imbecile; silly, foolish; half-empty, reduced (in quantity).
scempiaggine, scempiataggine [scempiAggine, scempiatAggine], *n.f.* Stupidity, foolishness.
scempio [scEmpio], *n.m.* Havoc, slaughter, massacre; torture; simpleton.
scempio [scEmpio], *a.* Silly, foolish; single (of flowers, etc.).
scena, *n.f.* Scene (in all senses); stage. (*Theat.*) **Messa in —,** scenery; **comparire in —,** to appear on the stage; **dietro le scene,** behind the scenes; — **muta,** dumb-show.
scenaccia [scenAccia], *n.f.* Scene (of temper), row.
scenario [scenArio], *n.m.* Scenery; scenario.
scenata, *n.f.* (Angry) scene, row; commotion. **Fare una —,** to make a row.
scendere [scEndere], *v.t.i.* To descend, to go down; to fall, to sink; to finish; to lower. — **a terra,** to land; — **da cavallo,** to alight from a horse; — **al Britannia,** to put up at the Britannia Hotel; — **le scale,** to go down stairs.
scendiletto, *n.m.* Bedside mat.
sceneggiamento, *n.m.* (*Theat.*) Staging; production; setting.
sceneggiare, *v.t.* (*Theat.*) To stage; to dramatize.
sceneggiatore, *n.m.* (*Theat.Cinema*) Scenario writer.
sceneggiatura, *n.f.* Staging; arrangement of scenes, production.
scenicamente, *adv.* Scenically.
scenico [scEnico], *a.* Scenic; theatrical. **Effetto —,** stage effect.
scenografia [scenografIa], *n.f.* Scene-painting.
scenografo [scenOgrafo], *n.m.* Scene-painter.
sceriffo, *n.m.* Sheriff.
scernere [scErnere], *v.t.* To discern, to distinguish; to select.
scernimento, *n.m.* Discernment, judgement.
scerpellone, *n.m.* Great blunder.
scervellarsi, *v.r.* To rack one's brains.
scervellato, *a.* Hare-brained; half-witted.
scesa, *n.f.* Downward slope, descent; declivity.
sceso, *p.p.a.* Descended [cp. **scendere**].
scetticamente, *adv.* Sceptically.
scetticismo, *n.m.* Scepticism.
scettico [scEttico], *n.m.a.* Sceptic; sceptical.
scettrato, *a.* Sceptred.
scettro, *n.m.* Sceptre. **Deporre lo —,** to abdicate, to lay down the crown.
sceveramento, *n.m.* Severance; dividing; parting.
sceverare, *v.t.* To sever, to set apart; to discriminate, to separate.
scevro, *a.* Destitute, deprived; exempt from, free from.
scheda, *n.f.* Card, slip of paper, form; application form. — **elettorale,** — **di voto,** ballot-paper.
schedario [schedArio], *n.m.* Card-index; filing-cabinet.
schedina, *n.f.* Football-pool coupon.
scheggia [schEggia], *n.f.* Splinter, chip; flake. **La — ritrae dal ceppo,** chip of the old block.

scheggiare, *v.t.* To splinter, to cut into chips.
scheggiarsi, *v.r.* To splinter.
scheletrico [schelEtrico], *a.* Skeleton-like.
scheletrirsi, *v.r.* To be reduced to a skeleton.
scheletrito, *a.* Reduced to a skeleton; like a skeleton.
scheletro [schEletro], *n.m.* Skeleton; frame, carcass.
schema (*pl.* **schemi**), *n.m.* Scheme, outline; project; plan.
schematicamente, *adv.* Schematically.
schematico [schemAtico], *a.* Schematic.
scherano, *n.m.* Cut-throat; brigand.
scherma, *n.f.* Fencing, swordsmanship. **Gara di —,** fencing competition, fencing bout; **maestro di —,** fencing-master; **tirare di —,** to fence.
schermaglia [schermAglia], *n.f.* Scuffle, scrimmage; skirmish; discussion.
schermidore, *n.m.* Fencer.
schermire, *v.t.i.* To parry, to defend; to fence.
schermirsi, *v.r.* To defend oneself. **— da,** to ward off, to shun.
schermitore, *n.m.* Fencer.
schermo, *n.m.* (*Cinema, Phot., Television, etc.*) Screen; defence.
schernevole [schernEvole], *a.* Contemptible, despicable; contemptuous, scornful, sneering.
schernevolmente, *adv.* Sneeringly, scoffingly, contemptuously.
schernire, *v.t.* To scoff at, to scorn, to mock, to jeer at; to despise. **— la religione,** to scoff at religion.
schernitivo, schernitore, *a.* Scoffing, sneering.
schernitore, schernitrice, *n.m.f.* Sneerer, scoffer.
scherno, *n.m.* Scorn; sneer, mockery, railing, derision; bantering. **Essere lo — di qualcuno,** to be the laughing-stock of someone.
scherzare, *v.i.* To joke, to jest; to make game of. **Non c'è da —,** it's no joking matter.
scherzevole [scherzEvole], *a.* Playful, joking; facetious; witty.
scherzevolmente, *adv.* Playfully; wittily.
scherzo, *n.m.* Joke, jest; trick; sport. **— di natura,** freak of nature; **per —,** in fun; **— di cattivo gusto,** joke in bad taste, practical joke; **scherzi a parte,** joking apart, seriously.
scherzosamente, *adv.* Playfully.
scherzoso, *a.* Playful.
schiaccia [schiAccia], *n.f.* Heavy trap; curling-tongs.
schiacciamento, *n.m.* Crushing, flattening, overwhelming; collapse.
schiaccianoci, *n.m.* Nut-cracker.
schiacciante, *a.* Crushing, overwhelming.
schiacciare, *v.t.* To crush, to squash, to bruise, to squeeze; to flatten; to overwhelm, to finish once and for all, to settle, to tread on, to stamp on. **— un sonnellino,** to take a nap; **— una noce,** to crack a nut.
schiacciarsi, *v.r.* To get crushed, to be squashed. **— un dito,** to crush one's finger.
schiacciata, *n.f.* Crushing; squashing, squeezing; a kind of flat cake.
schiaffare, *v.t.* To hurl, to throw.
schiaffeggiare, *v.t.* To slap (in the face), to box the ears.
schiaffo, *n.m.* Slap, smack; box on the ear; insult. **Pigliare a schiaffi,** to box the ears.
schiamazzare, *v.i.* To bawl, to make a noise, to shout; to cackle, to cluck, to squawk (of goose, hen, bird).
schiamazzatore, *n.m.* Brawler, noisy fellow.
schiamazzio [schiamazzIo], *n.m.* Continuous din, constant cackling, clucking.
schiamazzo, *n.m.* Noise, din, clatter, uproar; cackling, squawking, etc.
schiantare, *v.t.* To tear up, to break, to wrench off, to wrench away; to burst open.
schiantarsi, *v.r.* To crash, to split, to burst, to get smashed.
schiantatura, *n.f.* Tearing up.
schianto, *n.m.* Crash, smash, burst; noise of smashing; tearing; (*fig.*) pang, blow, affliction. **Di —,** suddenly, all of a sudden.
schiappa, *n.f.* Big chip of wood; rolling-pin; (*fig.*) duffer, rabbit (at games).
schiappino, *n.m.* Duffer (esp. at games).
schiare [cp. **sciare**].
schiarimento, *n.m.* Explanation, elucidation; clearing up.
schiarire, *v.t.i.* To make clear, to clarify, to elucidate; to explain, to throw light upon; to get clear, to brighten; to break (of day).
schiarirsi, *v.r.* To get clear, to brighten, to become bright; to grow thin (of hair); to be thinned out (of trees, etc.).
schiatta, *n.f.* Race, stock, family; generation; progeny; ancestors.
schiattare, *v.i.* To burst.
schiattire, *v.i.* To yelp, to squeak.
schiava, *n.f.* Female slave.
schiavitù [-ù], *n.f.* Slavery.
schiavo, *n.m.a.* Slave. **Fare —,** to enslave.
schiavone, *n.m.a.* (*Hist.*) Slav, Slavonic.
schiccheracarte, schiccherafogli, *n.m.* Scribbler.
schiccherare, *v.i.* To scribble; to blab.
schidionare, *v.t.* To put on the spit (for roasting).
schidionata, *n.f.* Birds on a spit.
schidione, *n.m.* Spit (for roasting).
schiena, *n.f.* Back, backbone; ridge (of hills). **Volgere la —,** to take to flight; **voltare la — a,** to turn one's back on.
schienale, *n.m.* (Chair) back; spine.
schiera, *n.f.* Rank, file, band, group, company. **A schiere,** in groups.
schieramento, *n.m.* Arraying, marshalling, drawing up.
schierare, *v.t.* To array, to marshal; to draw up.
schierarsi, *v.r.* To draw up, to marshal; (*fig.*) to take sides. **— in ordine di battaglia,** to draw up in fighting order.
schiettamente, *adv.* Frankly, openly; sincerely, plainly; flatly.
schiettezza, *n.f.* Frankness, sincerity.
schietto, *a.* Frank, open, sincere; open-hearted; genuine. **Vino —,** unadulterated wine; **a dirla schietta,** to speak openly, to make no bones about it.
schifamente, *adv.* Loathsomely.
schifare, *v.t.* To shun; to loathe.
schifarsi, *v.r.* To dislike intensely, to loathe; to feel reluctance (to do something).
schifezza, *n.f.* Nastiness, filth; disgust; nausea.

schifiltà [-à], *n.f.* Fastidiousness; coyness, assumed reluctance.
schifiltoso, *a.* Fastidious, hard to please; prudish.
schifo (1), *n.m.* Disgust, loathing. **Fare —,** to be disgusting; **prendere a —,** to take a dislike, to feel a loathing for.
schifo (2), *n.m.* (*Naut.*) Skiff.
schifosamente, *adv.* Loathsomely.
schifosità [-à], *n.f.* Loathsomeness; nastiness.
schifoso, *a.* Loathsome, disgusting, nauseating; filthy.
schimbescio [schimbEscio], *a.* [cp. **sghimbescio**].
schioccare, *v.t.i.* To crack (a whip), to snap (the fingers); to smack; to click. **— le mani,** to clap hands, to applaud.
schioccata, *n.f.* Crack of the whip.
schiocco, *n.m.* Crack, snap, smack.
schiodare, *v.t.* To unnail.
schiomare, *v.t.* To undo one's hair, to let one's hair down.
schioppettata, *n.f.* Gunshot, rifle-shot; report (of a gun).
schioppetto, *n.m.* Carbine.
schioppo, *n.m.* Gun, rifle; **tiro di —,** rifle-shot.
schiribizzo, *n.m.* Whim, fancy.
schisto, *n.m.* (*Geol.*) Schist.
schiudere, schiudersi [schiUdere, schiUdersi], *v.t.i.r.* To open; to blow (of flowers); to expand.
schiuma, *n.f.* Foam, froth; scum, dross. **— di mare,** meerschaum; **una — di birbante,** an arrant rogue.
schiumare, *v.t.i.* To skim, to cream; to froth, to foam.
schiumoso, *a.* Frothy, foaming.
schiuso, *p.p.a.* Opened [cp. **schiudere**].
schivabile [schivAbile], *a.* Avoidable.
schivafatiche, *n.m.* Shirker, work-dodger.
schivare, *v.t.* To avoid, to shun, to dodge.
schivo, *a.* Shy, bashful; averse from; contrary to.
schizofrenia [schizofrenIa], *n.f.* (*Med.*) Schizophrenia.
schizzamento, *n.m.* Gushing, squirting; splashing.
schizzare, *v.t.i.* To splash, to send out; to squirt; to sketch, to draw; to gush, to squirt. **— di fango,** to splash with mud.
schizzata, *n.f.* Splash, gush.
schizzatoio [schizzatOio], *n.m.* Syringe, squirt.
schizzettare, *v.t.* To syringe, to inject.
schizzettata, *n.f.* Syringing, injection.
schizzetto, *n.m.* Small syringe, hypodermic needle; scent-spray.
schizzinosamente, *adv.* Fastidiously, disdainfully; prudishly.
schizzinoso, *a.* Fastidious, squeamish; hard to please.
schizzo, *n.m.* Sketch; splash (of mud); squirt, jet, spurt.
sci, *n.m.* Ski.
scia, *n.f.* (*Naut.*) Wake, track.
scià [-à], *n.m.* Shah.
sciabola [sciAbola], *n.f.* Sabre.
sciabolare, *v.t.* To sabre.
sciabolata, *n.f.* Sabre-stroke.
sciabordare, *v.t.* To shake a liquid; to lap, to ripple.
sciacallo, *n.m.* (*Zool.*) Jackal.
sciacquare, *v.t.* To rinse, to wash out.
sciacquarsi, *v.r.* To rinse out one's mouth.
sciacquata, *n.f.* Rinsing.
sciacquatura, *n.f.* Rinsings, slops; dish-water.
sciaquio, *n.m.* Rippling; washing; splash.
sciagura, *n.f.* Misfortune, calamity, disaster; bad luck.
sciaguratamente, *adv.* Unluckily.
sciagurato, *n.m.* Unlucky fellow, poor devil; wretch.
sciagurato, *a.* Unfortunate, unlucky; wicked.
scialacquamento, *n.m.* Extravagance, squandering.
scialacquare, *v.t.* To squander, to dissipate (one's money); to waste.
scialacquatore, *n.m.* Wastrel, spendthrift.
scialacquio [scialacquIo], *n.m.* Squandering, wastefulness.
scialamento, *n.m.* Dissipation, squandering.
scialare, *v.t.i.* To dissipate, to squander.
scialarsi, *v.r.* To enjoy oneself; to indulge oneself.
scialbo, *a.* Pale, wan, faint, vague; dim; whitewashed.
scialle, *n.m.* Shawl.
scialo, *n.m.* Dissipation, squandering; show; lavishness; waste.
scialone, *n.m.* Wastrel, spendthrift.
scialuppa, *n.f.* (*Naut.*) Shallop; sloop; pinnace; launch.
sciamannarsi, *v.r.* To be careless (in dress, etc.).
sciamannato, *a.* Slovenly, careless, untidy.
sciamare, *v.i.* To swarm.
sciamatura, *n.f.* Swarming (of bees).
sciame, *n.m.* Swarm; crowd; host (of people). **A sciami,** in swarms.
sciampagna, *n.m.* Champagne.
sciancarsi, *v.r.* To dislocate one's hip; to lame oneself; to become lame.
sciancato, *n.m.a.* Cripple; crippled, lame.
sciarada, *n.f.* Charade.
sciare [sciAre], *v.i.* To ski; (*Naut.*) to go astern, to back water. **Andare a —,** to go ski-ing.
sciarpa, *n.f.* Scarf (round the neck); sash (over the shoulder or round the waist).
sciata [sciAta], *n.f.* Ski-run.
sciatica [sciAtica], *n.f.* (*Med.*) Sciatica.
sciatore, sciatrice, *n.m.f.* Skier.
sciattaggine [sciattAggine], *n.f.* Slovenliness; awkwardness.
sciattamente, *adv.* In a slovenly manner.
sciattare, *v.t.* To spill, to mar, to impair.
sciatteria, sciattezza [sciatterIa], *n.f.* Slovenliness, untidiness.
sciatto, *a.* Untidy, slovenly; clumsy.
sciattona, *n.f.* Slut, slattern.
sciattone, *n.m.* Sloven, untidy man.
scibile [scIbile], *n.m.a.* Knowledge; knowable.
scic, scicche, *a.* Stylish.
sciente, *a.* Knowing, aware of.
scientemente, *adv.* Knowingly, wittingly.
scientificamente, *adv.* Scientifically.
scientifico [scientIfico], *a.* Scientific.
scienza, *n.f.* Science; lore. **Di certa —,** of a certainty; **di propria —,** of one's own personal knowledge.
scienziato, *n.m.a.* Scientist; scholar.

scilinguagnolo [scilinguAgnolo], *n.m.* (*Anat.*) Fraenum, ligament of the tongue. **Aver sciolto lo —**, to have the gift of the gab; to have a ready tongue.
scilinguare, *v.i.* To stutter, to stammer.
scilinguatamente, *adv.* Stammeringly, stutteringly.
scilinguatura, *n.f.* Stuttering, stammering; tongue too big.
Scilla, *n.f.* (*Myth. Geog.*) Scylla.
scilla, *n.f.* (*Bot.*) Squill.
scimitarra, *n.f.* Scimitar.
scimmia [scImmia], *n.f.* (*Zool.*) Ape, monkey; (*fig.*) mimic.
scimmieggiare, *v.t.i.* To ape, to imitate, to mimic.
scimmiesco, *a.* Apish; simian.
scimmione, *n.m.* Barbary ape.
scimmiottare, *v.t.i.* To ape, to mimic.
scimmiotto, *n.m.* Young monkey; dressed-up monkey (on an organ). **Fare lo —**, to ape, to mimic.
scimpanzè [-**è**], *n.m.* Chimpanzee.
scimunitaggine [scimunitAggine], *n.f.* Silliness, foolishness; stupidity.
scimunitamente, *adv.* Stupidly.
scimunito, *n.m.* Dunce, blockhead, silly fellow.
scimunito, *a.* Silly, foolish, idiotic.
scindere [scIndere], *v.t.* To split, to part, to divide; to separate.
scindibile [scindIbile], *a.* Capable of being split or separated.
scintilla, *n.f.* Sparkle, spark.
scintillamento, *n.m.* Sparkling, scintillation.
scintillante, *a.* Sparkling, twinkling, glittering.
scintillare, *v.i.* To sparkle, to twinkle, to scintillate, to glitter.
scioccaggine [scioccAggine], *n.f.* Silliness, foolishness.
scioccamente, *adv.* Foolishly.
sciocchería, sciocchezza [sciocchería], *n.f.* Foolishness, stupidity; nonsense; foolish act. **Sciocchezze!** Rubbish! Don't talk nonsense!
sciocco, *n.m.* Fool, stupid fellow.
sciocco, *a.* Silly, stupid, foolish; insipid (in taste). **Non far lo —**, don't act (*or* play) the fool.
scioccone, *n.m.* Blockhead, fool, simpleton.
scioglibile [sciogllbile], *a.* Capable of being loosened.
sciogliere [sciOgliere], *v.t.* To untie, to loosen, to loose, to undo; to release, to set free; to annul; to clarify, to liquefy, to melt, to dissolve. **— il nodo,** to untie the knot; **— un matrimonio,** to dissolve a marriage; **— un voto,** to fulfil a vow; **— l'adunanza,** to close the meeting; **— un contratto,** to annul a contract; **— un inno,** to sing a hymn; **— un dubbio,** to resolve a doubt.
sciogliersi [sciOgliersi], *v.r.* To free oneself; to dissolve, to melt, to liquefy. **— in pianto,** to burst into tears.
scioglilingua [scioglilIngua], *n.m.* Tongue-twister.
scioglimento, *n.m.* Untying, loosening; dissolution; conclusion, breaking-up, termination.
scioltamente, *adv.* Freely, easily, fluently, unchecked.
scioltezza, *n.f.* Freedom, ease, fluency; agility.
sciolto, *p.p.a.* Loose, easy, free, nimble; unconstrained. **A briglia sciolta,** at full speed, headlong; **foglio —**, loose sheet (of paper); **avere la lingua sciolta,** to be talkative; **versi sciolti,** blank verse; **burro —**, melted butter; **la seduta è sciolta,** the meeting is closed.
scioperaggine [scioperAggine], *n.f.* Laziness, idleness.
scioperante, *n.m.a.* Striker; on strike.
scioperare, *v.i.* To go on strike, to strike, to walk out.
scioperataggine [scioperatAggine], *n.f.* [cp. **scioperaggine**].
scioperatamente, *adv.* Idly, being out of work.
scioperatezza, *n.f.* [cp. **scioperaggine**].
scioperato, *n.m.a.* Lazy, good for nothing.
sciopero [sciOpero], *n.m.* Strike. **— bianco,** sit-down strike; **— della fame,** hunger-strike; **diritto di —**, the right to strike.
scioperone, *n.m.* Lazy-bones.
sciorinamento, *n.m.* Airing (of clothes); spreading-out; display; disclosure.
sciorinare, *v.t.* To air clothes, to hang out (washing); to display; (*fig.*) to pour out (confidences, etc.), to display.
sciovinismo, *n.m.* (*Pol.*) Chauvinism.
sciovinista (*pl.* **sciovinisti**), *n.m.a.* Chauvinist.
Scipione, *n.m.* (*Hist.*) Scipio.
scipitaggine, scipitezza [scipitAggine], *n.f.* Insipidity, silliness; dullness.
scipitamente, *adv.* Sillily.
scipito, *a.* Insipid, tasteless; dull.
sciroccale, *a.* Sultry, southerly (of the wind).
scirocco, *n.m.* Sirocco, sultry south-east wind.
sciroppare, *v.t.* To preserve in syrup; to sweeten.
sciroppo, *n.m.* Syrup.
scisma (*pl.* **scismi**), *n.m.* Schism.
scismatico [scismAtico], *n.m.a.* Schismatic.
scissione, *n.f.* Scission, splitting, splitting-up.
scisso, *p.p.a.* Divided, split [cp. **scindere**].
scissura, *n.f.* Dissension, discord; cleft; furrow.
scita, *n.m.a.* Scythian.
sciupare, *v.t.* To spoil, to mar, to damage; to ruin; to waste, to squander. **— il tempo,** to waste one's time.
sciuparsi, *v.r.* To be spoiled, to spoil; to get rumpled. **— gli occhi,** to ruin one's eyes; **— una gamba,** to hurt one's leg.
sciupato, *p.p.a.* Wasted, spoiled; run down (in health).
sciupatore, *n.m.* Waster.
sciupinare, *v.t.* To destroy in haste or from spite.
sciupinio, sciupio [sciupinIo, sciupIo], *n.m.* Waste, wastage.
sciupone, *n.m.* Waster, one who squanders.
scivolamento, *n.m.* Slipping, sliding.
scivolare, *v.i.* To slip, to slide, to glide. **Mi scivolò di mano,** it slipped through my fingers.
scivolata, *n.f.* Slide, slip.
scivolo [scIvolo], *n.m.* Slide, glide; (*Aviat.*) runway, slip; (*Mus.*) trill.

scivolone, *n.m.* Slip (in walking).
sclerosi, *n.f.* (*Med.*) Sclerosis.
sclerotica [sclerOtica], *n.f.* (*Med.*) Sclerotic.
scocca, *n.f.* (*Motor.*) Body.
scoccamento, *n.m.* Flinging, hurling, darting.
scoccare, *v.t.i.* To shoot, to shoot off; to throw, to let fly; to fling; to dart off; to strike (the hours). **Scoccano le cinque,** it's striking five.
scoccato, *p.p.a.* Flung, shot, struck (of the hour). **Son appena scoccate le cinque,** it has just struck five.
scocciante, *a.* Boring, tiresome.
scocciare, *v.t.* To break (an egg-shell); (*fig.*) to bore; to harass.
scocciarsi, *v.r.* To get bored.
scocciatore, scocciatrice, *n.m.f.* Bore, wearisome person.
scocco, *n.m.* Shooting, letting fly; twang (of a bow); striking (of the hour).
scodare, *v.t.* To dock (a tail).
scodella, *n.f.* Bowl, soup-plate; porringer.
scodellare, *v.t.* To serve, to dish up; to pour out.
scodellata, *n.f.* Plateful, helping.
scodellino, *n.m.* Small plate; (*Motor. etc.*) sump.
scodinzolare, *v.i.* To wag the tail.
scoglia [scOglia], *n.f.* Sloughed skin (of a snake).
scogliera, *n.f.* Reef (of rocks), cliff.
scoglio [scOglio], *n.m.* Reef; rock; (*fig.*) difficulty. **Urtare contro uno —,** to run up against a difficulty, to meet a snag.
scoglioso, *a.* Rocky.
scoiare, *v.t.* To skin [cp. **scuoiare**].
scoiattolo [scoiAttolo], *n.m.* (*Zool.*) Squirrel.
scola, *n.f.* [cp. **scuola**].
scolamento, *n.m.* Flowing, running, dripping, straining.
scolara, *n.f.* School-girl.
scolare, *v.t.i.* To drain off, to drip; to flow, to run (of a liquid).
scolaresca, *n.f.* Students (in a body), pupils; school-children.
scolarescamente, *adv.* Like a school-child.
scolaresco, *a.* Pertaining to school or to school-children, school.
scolaro, *n.m.* Schoolboy.
scolastica [scolAstica], *n.f.* Scholasticism.
scolastico [scolAstico], *a.* Scholastic. **Anno —,** school year; **libri scolastici,** school-books.
scolasticamente, *adv.* Scholastically.
scolatoio [scolatOio], *n.m.* Drain, drain pipe; sink; strainer.
scolatura, *n.f.* Dregs, sediment; dripping; draining.
scollacciarsi, *v.r.* To bare one's neck or chest; to wear a low dress.
scollacciato, *a.* Low-necked (dress); woman so dressed; (*fig.*) immodest; licentious (of books, etc.).
scollare, *v.t.* To unglue, to unstick; to cut away the neck of a garment.
scollarsi, *v.r.* To become unglued; to come off, to get unstuck.
scollato, *p.p.a.* Low-necked (dress); unstuck, unglued.
scollatura, *n.f.* Baring one's neck; décolletage; lowness of neck (in a frock); unglueing.
scollegamento, *n.m.* Disconnection, uncoupling.
scollegare, *v.t.* To disjoin; to disconnect.
scollegarsi, *v.r.* To become undone, to get disconnected.
scolo, *n.m.* Drainage; leakage; drain.
scoloramento, *n.m.* Discoloration.
scolorare, *v.t.* To discolour.
scolorina, *n.f.* (*Chem.*) Chloride.
scolorire, *v.i.* To lose colour, to fade, to run (of colours).
scolorirsi, *v.r.* To lose colour, to grow pale.
scolorito, *a.* Colourless, discoloured.
scolpare, *v.t.* To exculpate; to excuse.
scolparsi, *v.r.* To defend oneself, to excuse oneself.
scolpimento, *n.m.* Sculpturing, carving.
scolpire, *v.t.* To sculpture, to carve (in stone, etc.), to chisel; to enunciate clearly.
scolpitamente, *adv.* Clearly, distinctly.
scolta, *n.f.* Sentry; night-watchman. **Essere di —,** to be on guard, to be on sentry duty.
scoltura, *n.f.* Sculpture.
scombiccherare, *v.t.* To scribble.
scombinare, *v.t.* To disarrange, to discompose, to separate; (*Print.*) to distribute type.
scombro, *n.m.* (*Zool.*) Mackerel.
scombuglio [scombUglio], *n.m.* Disorder, confusion.
scombuiare, *v.t.*, to turn upside down, to throw into disorder, to confuse.
scombussolamento, *n.m.* Upsetting, confusion.
scombussolare, *v.t.* To upset, to turn upside down; to disturb, to disarrange, to cause confusion.
scombussolio [scombussolIo], *n.m.* Disorder, continuous confusion.
scommessa, *n.f.* Bet, wager, stake. **Fare una —,** to make a bet.
scommettere [scommEttere], *v.t.* To wager, to stake, to bet; to disconnect, to disjoin.
scommettitore, scommettitrice, *n.m.f.* Better, one who wagers.
scommettitura, *n.f.* Disjunction.
scomodamento, *n.m.* Inconvenience, disturbance.
scomodare, *v.t.* To trouble, to inconvenience.
scomodarsi, *v.r.* To trouble oneself, to disturb oneself, to inconvenience oneself. **Non si scomodi!** Please don't trouble!
scomodo [scOmodo], *n.m.* Discomfort, inconvenience.
scomodo [scOmodo], *a.* Inconvenient, uncomfortable, troublesome.
scompaginamento, *n.m.* Throwing into disorder; (*Print.*) breaking up type.
scompaginare, *v.t.* To disarrange, to break up; (*Print.*) to break up type.
scompagnamento, *n.m.* Being odd, not matching.
scompagnato, *a.* Odd, not matching.
scomparire, *v.i.* To disappear, to fade away, to vanish; to cut a poor figure; **— dalla scena,** to disappear.
scomparsa, *n.f.* Disappearance; loss.
scompartimento, *n.m.* Division; (*Rail.*) compartment.
scompartire, *v.t.* To partition; to distribute; to allot.
scompiacente, *a.* Unaccommodating, unhelpful, disobliging.

scompiacenza, *n.f.* Lack of complaisance, unhelpfulness.
scompiacere, *v.t.* To disoblige.
scompigliamento, *n.m.* Disorder, disarrangement.
scompigliare, *v.t.* To throw into disorder, to ruffle, to upset; to embroil.
scompigliatamente, *adv.* Topsy-turvy; in a disordered fashion.
scompiglio [scompIglio], *n.m.* Disorder, confusion; fuss and bother.
scompleto, *a.* Incomplete.
scomponibile [scomponIbile], *a.* Decomposable.
scomponimento, *n.m.* Decomposition.
scomporre, *v.t.* To break up, to take to pieces; to analyse; to disarrange; to decompose; to discompose, to trouble, to agitate; (*Math.*) to resolve; (*Print.*) to distribute. **— una frase,** analyse a sentence; **— una macchina,** to take down machinery, to take a machine to pieces.
scomporsi, *v.r.* To decompose; to be troubled, to get agitated; to lose one's temper, to get upset. **Senza —,** without losing one's composure.
scomposizione, *n.f.* Decomposition; perturbation; (*Print.*) distribution of type; taking down machinery.
scompostamente, *adv.* In disorder.
scompostezza, *n.f.* Discomposure, disorder, confusion.
scomposto, *p.p.a.* Discomposed, in disorder; unseemly.
scomunica [scomUnica], *n.f.* Excommunication.
scomunicare, *v.t.* To excommunicate.
scomunicato, *n.m.a.* Excommunicate; excommunicated.
sconcatenamento, *n.m.* Lack of connection.
sconcatenare, *v.t.* To unchain, to disconnect.
sconcertamento, *n.m.* Disconcertedness.
sconcertante, *a.* Disconcerting, baffling.
sconcertare, *v.t.* To disconcert, to perturb; to baffle.
sconcerto, *n.m.* Perturbation; confusion, discord, disagreement; want of harmony.
sconcezza, *n.f.* Indecency, obscenity; unbecomingness.
sconciamente, *adv.* Unbecomingly, indecently.
sconciare, *v.t.* To spoil, to mar; to disarrange.
sconciarsi, *v.r.* To miscarry; to strain (a muscle, etc.), to sprain.
sconciatura, *n.f.* Miscarriage; thing done badly.
sconcio [scOncio], *n.m.a.* Indecency, disorder, damage; indecent, obscene, unbecoming, unseemly. **Parole sconcie,** indecent words, foul language.
sconcludere [sconclUdere], *v.t.* To undo; to break off (an engagement, etc.).
sconclusionato, *a.* Inconclusive; rambling, disconnected, inconsequent.
sconcluso, *a.* Undone, broken off.
sconcordanza, *n.f.* Discord, disagreement, disharmony.
scondito, *a.* Unseasoned.
sconfacente, sconfacevole [sconfacEvole], *a.* Unbecoming, unsuitable.
sconfessare, *v.t.* To disown, to disavow.
sconfessione, *n.f.* Disavowal, disowning.
sconficcare, *v.t.* To pull out (a nail), to unfasten; to take to bits.
sconfiggere [sconfIggere], *v.t.* To defeat, to discomfit, to rout.
sconfiggimento, *n.m.* Discomfiture, defeat.
sconfinamento, *n.m.* Crossing the frontier; overstepping, trespassing; breaking bounds.
sconfinare, *v.i.* To cross the frontier; to break bounds; to overstep; (*fig.*) to exceed the limits.
sconfinato, *a.* Boundless, unlimited, unbounded.
sconfitta, *n.f.* Rout, defeat; discomfiture.
sconfortante, *a.* Discouraging, disheartening.
sconfortare, *v.t.* To discourage, to dishearten.
sconfortarsi, *v.r.* To get discouraged; to be disheartened.
sconforto, *n.m.* Discouragement; distress, anguish; vexation.
scongiurare, *v.i.* To entreat, to conjure, to implore; to avert, to remove; to exorcise.
scongiurazione, scongiuro, *n.f.m.* Entreaty, supplication; exorcism.
sconnessamente, *adv.* Disconnectedly, in a desultory manner.
sconnessione, *n.f.* Disconnectedness, lack of connection; desultoriness.
sconnesso, *a.* Rambling, disconnected.
sconnettere [sconnEttere], *v.t.i.* To disconnect, to disjoin; to wander in mind or speech.
sconoscente, *a.* Ungrateful.
sconoscentemente, *adv.* Ungratefully, thanklessly.
sconoscenza, *n.f.* Ingratitude, thanklessness, ungratefulness.
sconoscere [sconOscere], *v.t.i.* To be ignorant of, not to know; to fail to recognize; to be ungrateful for; to disown.
sconosciuto, *n.m.* Stranger.
sconosciuto, *a.* Unknown, unrecognized; unappreciated.
sconquassamento, *n.m.* Crashing, smashing, shattering; destroying.
sconquassare, *v.t.* To smash, to shatter, to destroy, to ruin; to upset.
sconquasso, *n.m.* Crash, smash; destruction; ruin.
sconsacrare, *v.t.* To desecrate.
sconsideratamente, *adv.* Without consideration, rashly.
sconsideratezza, *n.f.* Thoughtlessness, lack of forethought; rashness.
sconsiderato, *a.* Rash, heedless.
sconsiderazione, *n.f.* Heedlessness.
sconsigliabile [sconsigliAbile], *a.* Inadvisable.
sconsigliare, *v.t.* To dissuade, to discourage, to advise against.
sconsigliatamente, *adv.* Rashly, unadvisedly.
sconsigliatezza, *n.f.* Rashness, heedlessness.
sconsigliato, *a.* Rash; indiscreet, ill-advised.
sconsiglio [sconsIglio], *n.m.* Dissuasion.
sconsolare, *v.t.* To discourage; to deprive of consolation.
sconsolatamente, *adv.* Disconsolately.
sconsolato, *a.* Disconsolate.
sconsolazione, *n.f.* Grief, disconsolateness, affliction.
scontabile [scontAbile], *a.* (*Comm.*) Discountable, payable.

scontare, *v.t.* (*Comm.*) To discount, to deduct; to take discount from; to pay for, to atone for, to expiate. **— la pena,** to take the punishment for; **— i peccati,** to do penance for one's sins.
scontatore, *n.m.* (*Comm.*) Discounter.
scontentamento, *n.m.* Discontent, discontenting, disappointment.
scontentare, *v.t.* To dissatisfy, to disappoint; to displease.
scontentezza, *n.f.* Discontent; disappointment; dissatisfaction.
scontento, *n.m.* Discontent, dissatisfaction; displeasure.
scontento, *a.* Discontented, dissatisfied (with); disappointed.
scontista (*pl.* **scontisti**), *n.m.* (*Comm.*) Bill discounter.
sconto, *n.m.* (*Comm.*) Discount, reduction, abatement, deduction; allowance.
scontorcere [scontOrcere], *v.t.* To contort; to writhe.
scontorcimento, *n.m.* Contortion.
scontrare, *v.t.* To encounter, to meet with.
scontrarsi, *v.r.* To encounter, to run up against; (*Rail.*) to collide.
scontrino, *n.m.* Check, ticket (of admission), voucher; receipt.
scontro, *n.m.* Collision, crash (of trains, etc.); (*Mil. Sport*) encounter, engagement; match.
scontrosaggine, scontrosità [scontrosAggine, **-à**], *n.f.* Peevishness, touchiness, crossness, cantankerousness.
scontroso, scontrosino, *a.* Cross, peevish, irritable, touchy, cantankerous, difficult (in temper).
sconturbare, *v.t.* To trouble, to perturb.
sconvenevole [sconvenEvole], *a.* Unseemly, indecorous, unbefitting, improper.
sconvenevolezza, *n.f.* Unseemliness, lack of good breeding, bad manners.
sconvenevolmente, *adv.* In an unseemly manner.
sconveniente, *a.* Unsuitable, unbecoming; indecent.
sconvenienza, *n.f.* Unsuitableness, unseemliness, impropriety, indecency.
sconvenire, *v.i.* To be unbecoming, to be unseemly, to be unsuitable.
sconvolgere [sconvOlgere], *v.t.* To upset, to overthrow, to overturn; to turn upside down; to derange. **— la mente,** to derange one's mind; **— lo stomaco,** to upset one's stomach.
sconvolgimento, *n.m.* Confusion, overturning, upsetting; derangement.
sconvolto, *p.p.a.* Overturned, upset; convulsed; perturbed.
scopa, *n.f.* (*Bot.*) Broom; broom (for sweeping); Italian card game.
scopare, *v.t.i.* To sweep.
scopata, *n.f.* Sweeping, sweep.
scopatura, *n.f.* Sweeping; sweepings, pieces.
scoperchiare, *v.t.* To uncover, to remove the lid of; to unroof.
scoperta, *n.f.* Discovery; disclosure, revelation; invention; (*Mil.*) reconnaissance. **— di un segreto,** finding out a secret; **— di un complotto,** unmasking of a plot; **alla —,** openly, publicly.
scopertamente, *adv.* Openly.
scoperto, *n.m.* Open air, open place. **Allo —,** in the open air; **dormire allo —,** to sleep out in the open; **mettere allo —,** to lay bare.
scoperto, *a.* Open, exposed, uncovered, bare; unprotected; clear, open, manifest. **A capo —,** bare-headed; **un conto —,** an overdrawn (banking) account.
scopeto, *n.m.* (*Bot.*) Heath.
scopetta, *n.f.* Brush, broom.
scopettare, *v.t.* To dust, to sweep lightly.
scopo, *n.m.* Aim, end, purpose, object; design. **— precipuo,** main object; **adatto allo —,** fit for the purpose; **raggiungere lo —,** to achieve one's purpose.
scopola [scOpola], *n.f.* (*colloq.*) Smack, cuff (on the ear).
scoppiamento, *n.m.* Uncoupling; bursting, explosion.
scoppiare (1), *v.i.* To burst, to explode; to break out; to blow up; to die. **— di rabbia,** to fume with rage; **— dalle risa,** to split one's sides with laughing; **— in pianto,** to burst into tears.
scoppiare (2), *v.t.* To uncouple.
scoppiettamento, *n.m.* Crackling (noise).
scoppiettare, *v.i.* To crackle.
scoppiettio [scoppettIo], *n.m.* Continual crackling.
scoppio [scOppio], *n.m.* Burst, bursting; explosion; outbreak; report (of explosion, etc.); **— della caldaia,** bursting of the boiler; **— della guerra,** outbreak of war; **— di risa,** roar of laughter; **motore a —,** internal combustion engine.
scopribile [scoprIbile], *a.* Discoverable.
scoprimento, *n.m.* Finding out, discovering, uncovering, disclosing.
scoprire, *v.t.* To find out, to discover; to detect; to descry, to disclose; to expose, to unveil. **— una stella,** to discover a star; **— terra,** to sight land; **— un complotto,** to detect a plot.
scoprirsi, *v.r.* To take off one's hat; to expose oneself; to make oneself known; to betray oneself, to unburden one's mind.
scopritore, scopritrice, *n.m.f.* Discoverer, inventor.
scoraggiamento, *n.m.* Discouragement.
scoraggiare, scoraggire, *v.t.* To discourage, to dishearten.
scoraggiarsi, scoraggirsi, *v.r.* To be discouraged, to get disheartened; to be daunted.
scoramento, *n.m.* Discouragement.
scorare, *v.t.* To dishearten.
scorbacchiare, *v.t.* To hold up to contempt.
scorbia [scOrbia], *n.f.* Gouge [cp. **sgorbia**].
scorbio [scOrbio], *n.m.* Blot [cp. **sgorbio**].
scorbutico [scorbUtico], *a.* (*Med.*) Scorbutic; (*colloq.*) cantankerous.
scorbuto, *n.m.* (*Med.*) Scurvy.
scorciamento, *n.m.* Shortening, foreshortening.
scorciare, *v.t.i.* To shorten, to foreshorten; to curtail.
scorciarsi, *v.r.* To get shorter.
scorciatoia [scorciatOia], *n.f.* Short cut, bypath.
scorcio [scOrcio], *n.m.* End, close; finale; (*Art.*) foreshortening. **Lo — del giorno,** the close of the day; **sullo — dell'anno,** towards the end of the year.

scordare, scordarsi (1), *v.t.r.* To put out of tune; to get out of tune; (*fig.*) to set at variance.
scordare, scordarsi (2), *v.t.r.* To forget. **Non-ti-scordar-di-me,** forget-me-not.
scordatamente, *adv.* Discordantly.
scordatura, *n.f.* (*Mus.*) Discordance.
scordevole [scordEvole], *a.* Forgetful.
scordone, *n.m.* Forgetful person.
scorgere [scOrgere], *v.t.* To perceive, to descry; to notice. **Senza farsi —,** stealthily, unperceived.
scoria [scOria], *n.f.* Dross, slag; scoria.
scornare, *v.t.* To dishorn; (*fig.*) to hold up to shame, to put to shame.
scorneggiare, *v.t.* To butt (of a goat).
scorniciare, *v.t.* To make picture frames; to unframe.
scorno, *n.m.* Shame, disgrace; ignominy. **Avere a —,** to hold in contempt.
scoronare, *v.t.* To uncrown; to lop (a tree).
scorpacciata, *n.f.* Bellyful. **Fare una —,** to have a good blow-out.
scorpione, *n.m.* (*Zool.*) Scorpion.
scorporare, *v.t.* To disembody; to disincorporate, to separate; to spend from capital.
scorporo [scOrporo], *n.m.* separation, disincorporation.
scorrazzamento, *n.m.* Roving, rambling; raiding.
scorrazzare, *v.i.* To rove, to wander hither and thither; to run about from place to place; (*Mil.*) to raid.
scorrere [scOrrere], *v.t.i.* To scour (the country), to run through; to raid; to glance at; to glide, to flow, to run; to elapse.
scorreria [scorrerIa], *n.f.* Raid, incursion, inroad.
scorrettamente, *adv.* Incorrectly; improperly.
scorrettezza, *n.f.* Incorrectness; misbehaviour, impropriety.
scorretto, *a.* Incorrect, improper.
scorrevole [scorrEvole], *a.* Gliding, flowing, fluent.
scorrevolezza, *n.f.* Fluency (of language).
scorrevolmente, *adv.* Fluently.
scorrezione, *n.f.* Incorrectness, error.
scorribanda, *n.f.* Incursion, inroad, raid.
scorsa, *n.f.* Glance. **Dare una — a un libro,** to glance at a book; **una — di penna,** a slip of the pen.
scorso, *n.m.* Slip, oversight; mistake (in speech, etc.).
scorso, *p.p.a.* Run, run out; elapsed, last, past. **L'anno —,** last year.
scorsoio [scorsOio], *a.* **Nodo —,** slip-knot.
scorta, *n.f.* Escort; guide; reserve, reserve money; stock, supply; provision; subvention.
scortamento, *n.m.* Shortening, foreshortening.
scortare (1), *v.t.* To escort, to accompany; to convoy.
scortare (2), *v.t.* To shorten, to foreshorten.
scortecciamento, *n.m.* Barking (of trees, etc.), peeling.
scortecciare, *v.t.* To bark, to take off the bark; to strip; to peel.
scortese, *a.* Unkind; rude, impolite, discourteous, uncivil.
scortesemente, *adv.* Rudely, impolitely.
scortesia [scortesIa], *n.f.* Rudeness, discourtesy; unkindness.
scorticamento, *n.m.* Skinning, flaying; (*fig.*) fleecing.
scorticare, *v.t.* To skin, to flay, to excoriate; (*fig.*) to fleece, to swindle.
scorticaria [scorticAria], *n.f.* Type of fishing-net.
scorticata, *n.f.* Flaying; scratch; (*fig.*) fleecing.
scorticatore, scorticatrice, *n.m.f.* Skinner.
scorticatura, *n.f.* Abrasion.
scortichino, *n.m.* Skinner's knife; (*fig.*) extortioner.
scorto, *p.p.a.* Perceived, descried [cp. **scorgere**].
scorza, *n.f.* Bark, rind; (*fig.*) outside, exterior, outward appearance.
scorzare, *v.t.* To bark, to peel, to rind; to strip.
scorzatura, *n.f.* Barked portion of a tree.
scorzone, *n.m.* (*Zool.*) Black adder; boor, uncouth fellow.
scorzonera, *n.f.* (*Bot.*) Scorzonera, black salsify.
scorzoneria [scorzonerIa], *n.f.* Boorishness, churlishness.
scosa, *n.f.* (*Naut.*) Bilge-keel.
scoscendere [scoscEndere], *v.t.i.* To split, to cleave; to slide down, to collapse.
scoscendersi, *v.r.* To crash down, to collapse.
scoscendimento, *n.m.* Precipice, ravine, steep descent, cliff.
scosceso, *a.* Steep, precipitous; rugged, craggy.
scosciare, *v.t.* To sever the leg (of a fowl).
scosciarsi, *v.r.* To spread the legs (in dancing, etc.).
scossa, *n.f.* Shake, shaking, jerk, shock; (*fig.*) misfortune, calamity. **A scosse,** by fits and starts; **— di terremoto,** earthquake shock; **— elettrica,** electric shock; **una perdita che è stata una bella —,** a loss that was a great shock to him.
scosso, *p.p.a.* Shaken, suffered a shock; weakened; excited.
scossone, *n.m.* Shake, jerk, shock. **Dare uno —,** to give a shake.
scostamento, *n.m.* Moving away, removal, putting aside, separation.
scostante, *a.* Uninviting, forbidding.
scostare, *v.t.* To remove, to move away, to put aside.
scostarsi, *v.r.* To go away, to get out of the way; to make way (for); to stand aloof; to wander (from the subject). **Scostati!** Get out of the way! Get out!; **— dall' argomento,** to wander from the point.
scostolare, *v.t.* To take out the ribs; to smooth out a fold.
scostumatamente, *adv.* Profligately, lewdly.
scostumatezza, *n.f.* Profligacy, licentiousness; coarse manners.
scostumato, *a.* Profligate, licentious, rude; dissolute, vulgar.
scotano [scOtano], *n.m.* (*Bot.*) Fustic.
scotennare, *v.t.* To skin, to flay; to scalp.
scotere [cp. **scuotere**].
Scoti, *n.m.pl.* (*Hist.*) (Picts and) Scots.

scotimento, *n.m.* Shaking, jolting; shock.
scotio [scotIo], *n.m.* Continual jolting. **Lo scotio della carrozza,** the jolting of the carriage.
scotitoio [scotitOio], *n.m.* Strainer; salad-basket.
scotitore, *n.m.* Shaker.
scotola [scOtola], *n.f.* Beetle for beating hemp.
scotolare, *v.t.* To beat hemp.
scotta, *n.f.* (*Naut.*) Sheet; whey.
scottamento, *n.m.* Burning, burn, scald.
scottante, *a.* Burning (in all senses); (*fig.*) stinging.
scottare, *v.t.i.* To scald, to burn, to scorch; (*fig.*) to sting. **Ne rimase scottato,** he was a loser by it.
scottarsi, *v.r.* To burn oneself, to get scalded.
scottata, *n.f.* Scalding, parboiling.
scottatura, *n.f.* Scald, burn, burning; sunburn.
scotto, *n.m.* Bill, account, reckoning; scot, share (of a bill). **Pagar lo —,** to pay one's share; (*fig.*) to pay (for a mistake).
scovamento, *n.m.* Discovery; ferreting out.
scovare, *v.t.* To drive out, to dislodge; to find out, to ferret out, to worm out, to discover.
scovolo, scovolino [scOvolo], *n.m.* (*Mil.*) Sponge (for a gun).
Scozia [scOzia], *n.f.* Scotland.
scozzare, *v.t.* (*Cards*) To shuffle.
scozzata, *n.f.* (*Cards*) Shuffle.
scozzese, *n.m.a.* Scot, Scotsman; Scots, Scottish; (of cloth) tartan, plaid.
scozzonare, *v.t.* To train, to break in (a horse); (*fig.*) to coach, to tutor.
scozzonatore, *n.m.* Horse-breaker, trainer.
scozzonatura, *n.f.* Horse-breaking.
scozzone, *n.m.* Trainer, horse-breaker.
scranna, *n.f.* High-backed chair; magistrates' chair of office.
screanzatamente, *adv.* Ill-manneredly, rudely.
screanzato, *a.* Ill-mannered, impolite, rude, coarse, uncouth, ill-bred.
screditare, *v.t.* To discredit; to bring into disrepute.
scredito [scrEdito], *n.m.* Discredit, disrepute.
scremare, *v.t.* To skim, to cream off; to take the best of. **Latte scremato,** skim-milk.
screpolare, screpolarsi, *v.i.r.* To crack, to split.
screpolato, *a.* Cracked; chapped (of hands).
screpolatura, *n.f.* Crack, chink, split, cleft.
screpolo [scrEpolo], *n.m.* Crack, fissure.
screziare, *v.t.* To speckle, to variegate.
screziatura, *n.f.* Speckling, marbling.
screzio [scrEzio], *n.m.* Speckling; (*fig.*) friction, dissension, difference, variance. **C'è uno — fra noi,** we are at variance, we don't see alike.
scriba (*pl.* **scribi**), *n.m.* Scribe; copyist.
scribacchiare, *v.t.* To scribble, to scrawl.
scribacchiatore, scribacchino, *n.m.* Scribbler, hack-journalist.
scricchiare, *v.i.* To creak.
scricchio [scrIcchio], *n.m.* Creaking (of shoes).
scricchiolamento, *n.m.* Creaking, creak; grating.
scricchiolare, *v.i.* To creak, to grate.
scricchiolio [scricchiolIo], *n.m.* Continual creaking or grating.
scricciolo [scrIcciolo], *n.m.* (*Zool.*) Wren.
scrigno, *n.m.* Coffer, safe; strong-box, money-box; jewel-case.
scriminatura, *n.f.* Parting (of the hair).
scrimolo [scrImolo], *n.m.* Brink, edge.
scrinare, *v.t.* To clip (mane or tail of a horse).
scrio [scrIo], *a.* (*Tuscan*) Pure; precise; downright. **Vino —,** unadulterated wine; **una bugia scria,** a downright lie.
scristianare, scristianeggiare, scristianizzare, *v.t.* To dechristianize, to make a Christian lose his Faith.
scritta, *n.f.* Inscription, written document, notice; (*Law*) contract, deed; sign-board.
scritto, *n.m.* Writing, written document; handwriting; written work, literary work. **In —,** in writing; **i miei scritti,** my writings, my literary works.
scritto, *p.p.a.* Written [cp. **scrivere**].
scrittoio [scrittOio], *n.m.* Bureau, writing-desk; office; study.
scrittore, scrittrice, *n.m.f.* Writer, author, authoress.
scrittorello, scrittoruccio [scrittorUccio], *n.m.* Hack-journalist, scribbler.
scrittura, *n.f.* Writing; handwriting; document; (*Comm.*) entry (in ledger, etc.); (*Theat.*) engagement; Scripture. **Doppia —,** double-entry book-keeping; **— a macchina,** typewriting; **la Sacra Scrittura,** the Holy Scriptures.
scritturale, *n.m.* Clerk, copyist; book-keeper; scribe.
scritturale, *a.* Scriptural.
scritturare, *v.t.* (*Comm.*) To enter (in ledger, etc.), to write-up (the books); (*Theat.*) to engage.
scritturazione, *n.f.* (*Theat.*) Engagement; (*Comm.*) posting (ledger, etc.).
scritturista, *n.m.* Expounder of the Scriptures.
scrivacchiare, *v.t.* To scribble, to scrawl.
scrivania [scrivanIa], *n.f.* Writing-desk.
scrivano, *n.m.* Clerk, copyist; (*Naut.*) mate, second in command.
scrivente, *n.m.* Writer.
scrivere [scrIvere], *v.t.* To write, to write down, to mark. **Macchina da —,** typewriter; **carta da —,** writing-paper; **come si scrive questa parola?** how do you spell this word? **occorrente per —,** writing-materials; **era scritto,** it was bound to happen.
scrivibile [scrivIbile], *a.* Capable of being written.
scroccare, *v.t.* To sponge (on someone), to scrounge; to extort. **— un pranzo,** to cadge a dinner.
scroccatore, *n.m.* Sponger, scrounger, cadger; hanger-on; swindler.
scrocchiare, *v.i.* To crackle; to creak.
scrocchio [scrOcchio], *n.m.* Crackling; creaking.
scrocco, *n.m.* Sponging, scrounging, cadging; sneaking.
scroccone, *n.m.* Sponger, cadger; swindler.
scrofa, *n.f.* (*Zool.*) Sow.
scrofola [scrOfola], *n.f.* (*Med.*) Scrofula.

scrofoloso, *a.* Scrofulous.
scrollamento, *n.m.* Shaking, tossing, jolting, shrugging (the shoulders).
scrollare, *v.t.* To shake, to jolt; to shrug (one's shoulders).
scrollata, scrollatina, *n.f.* Shaking, jolting; **— di spalle,** shrug of one's shoulders.
scrollo, *n.m.* Shake, shaking, toss; vibration.
scrosciante, *a.* Roaring, hissing (of falling water). **Pioggia —,** pelting rain.
scrosciare, *v.i.* To roar, to rumble; to clatter. **— di risa,** to burst with laughter.
scroscio [scrOscio], *n.m.* Roar, thunder; crack, crash. **Piovere a —,** to rain in torrents, to shower; **— di risa,** burst of laughter; **— di applauso,** round of applause, burst of applause.
scrostamento, *n.m.* Removing of the crust; peeling.
scrostare, *v.t.* To remove the crust from, to strip, to peel.
scrostatura, *n.f.* Peeling; bare patch.
scroto, *n.m.* (*Anat.*) Scrotum.
scrudimento, *n.m.* Warming, taking the chill off.
scrudire, *v.t.* To take off the rough, to take the chill off.
scrupolo [scrUpolo], *n.m.* Scruple, qualm; doubt; hesitation. **Farsi — di,** to be reluctant to, to scruple to; **non aver — di,** not to hesitate to; **uomo senza scrupoli,** unprincipled *or* unscrupulous person.
scrupolosamente, *adv.* Scrupulously.
scrupolosità, *n.f.* Scrupulousness, conscientiousness; caution.
scrupoloso, *a.* Scrupulous, conscientious; cautious, careful.
scrutabile [scrutAbile], *a.* Scrutable; searchable.
scrutamento, *n.m.* Scrutiny, scrutinizing, investigation.
scrutare, *v.t.* To search into, to scrutinize; to investigate; to enquire into; to penetrate; to stare; to pry into.
scrutatore, scrutatrice, *n.m.f.* Scrutineer; investigator; inquisitive.
scrutatore, *a.* Searching, inquisitive; penetrating.
scrutinamento, *n.m.* Scrutinizing, scrutiny.
scrutinare, *v.t.* To scrutinize.
scrutinatore, scrutinatrice, *n.m.* Scrutineer.
scrutinio [scrutInio], *n.m.* Scrutiny (of votes); ballot; voting, votes; averaging of marks (at school). **A — segreto,** by secret ballot.
scucire, *v.t.* To unstitch, to unpick, to take down (sewing).
scucitura, *n.f.* Unpicking.
scudaio [scudAio], *n.m.* Shield-maker.
scudato, *a.* Armed with a shield; shielded, protected.
scuderia [scuderIa], *n.f.* (Racing, palace, etc.) stable; private stable (on a large scale). **Garzone di —,** stable-boy.
scudetto, *n.m.* Small shield; keyhole guard; (*Herald.*) escutcheon.
scudiera, *adv.* **Alla —,** riding-style. **Calzoni alla —,** riding-breeches; **stivali alla —,** riding-boots.
scudiero, *n.m.* Equerry (to a royalty); (*Hist.*) squire (to a knight); esquire.
scudisciare, *v.t.* To whip, to horsewhip, to lash.
scudisciata, *n.f.* Whipping, lash with a whip.
scudiscio [scudIscio], *n.m.* Horsewhip, switch, riding-whip.
scudo, *n.m.* Shield, buckler; (*fig.*) defence, protection; defender; (*Herald.*) escutcheon; crown (coin). **Levata di scudi,** insurrection, rising in arms.
scuffia [scUffia], *n.f.* Cap; coif [cp. **cuffia**].
scuffina, *n.f.* Rasp (for wood); grater.
sculacciare, *v.t.* To spank a child on the buttocks.
sculacciata, *n.f.* Spanking, spank.
sculaccione, *n.m.* Sound spanking.
sculettare, *v.i.* (*colloq.*) To waddle, to walk with a waddle.
sculto, *p.p.a.* Sculptured, carved.
scultore, scultrice, *n.m.f.* Sculptor, sculptress.
scultorio [scultOrio], *a.* Sculptural; well-made, finely built.
scultura, *n.f.* Sculpture, carving.
scuoiare, *v.t.* To skin, to flay.
scuola, *n.f.* School, college; class-room; class; tendency, method, system. **— elementare** primary school; **— serale,** evening school; **far —,** to teach, to give a lesson; (*fig.*) to have a following; **maestro di —,** schoolmaster; **marinare la —, salare la —,** to play truant.
scuotere [scuOtere], *v.t.* To shake, to shake off; to stir, to move; to wake up; to disregard, to weaken. **— il capo,** to shake one's head; **— una cassetta,** to shake a box: **— le spalle,** to shrug one's shoulders; **— la polvere di dosso,** to give a good thrashing.
scuotersi [scuOtersi], *v.r.* To shake oneself; to be roused; to move restlessly, to fidget; to awake. **Bisogna — !** You must stir yourself!
scuotimento, *n.m.* Shaking.
scuramente, *adv.* Obscurely.
scure, *n.f.* Axe, hatchet; (*fig.*) **Tagliato con la —,** a rough-hewn character.
scuretto, *n.m.* Window-shutter; small axe.
scuretto, *a.* Rather dark, growing dusk.
scurezza, *n.f.* Obscureness, obscurity, darkness.
scuriada, scuriata, *n.f.* Horsewhip.
scuriosare, *v.i.* To pry, to look upon with curiosity, to peer into.
scurire, *v.t.i.* To darken, to obscure; to tone down (a colour); to grow dark.
scurirsi, *v.r.* To grow dark.
scurità [-à], *n.f.* Darkness, obscurity.
scuro, *n.m.* Darkness, dark; obscurity; shading (of a picture); window-shutter.
scuro, *a.* Dark, obscure; gloomy; deep (of colour). **Essere allo —,** to be in the dark (in all senses).
scurrile, *a.* Scurrilous; licentious, lewd.
scurrilità [-à], *n.f.* Scurrility; licentiousness.
scurrilmente, *adv.* Scurrilously.
scusa, *n.f.* Apology; excuse; pretext. **Chiedere —,** to apologize; to make excuses, to beg pardon; **lettera di —,** letter of apology; **— magra,** lame excuse.
scusabile [scusAbile], *a.* Excusable, pardonable.
scusabilità [-à], *n.f.* Possibility of excuse.
scusabilmente, *adv.* Excusably.

scusare, *v.t.* To excuse; to justify; to pardon, to forgive. **Scusi!** I beg your pardon; **mi voglia —,** please excuse me; please accept my apologies; **scusate se è poco!** Is that all!; **— un errore,** to forgive a mistake.
scusarsi, *v.r.* To apologize for, to excuse oneself; to justify oneself; to beg pardon. **Si è scusato con il suo amico,** he apologized to his friend; **mi son scusato,** I have declined the invitation (with apologies).
scusso, *a.* Plain, bare. **Mangiare pane —,** to eat dry bread.
sdamare, *v.i.* To move a back-row man at draughts.
sdarsi, *v.r.* To lose heart, to give up trying.
sdaziamento, *n.m.* Clearing (through the customs).
sdaziare, *v.t.* To clear (through the customs); to pay duty.
sdebitarsi, *v.r.* To pay off one's debts; to discharge one's obligations; to fulfil one's engagements.
sdegnamento, *n.m.* Disdain.
sdegnare, *v.t.* To disdain, to despise, to scorn; to dislike (food); to irritate.
sdegnarsi, *v.r.* To be irritated, to get angry, to be offended; to become indignant.
sdegnatamente, *adv.* Indignantly.
sdegno, *n.m.* Indignation, anger, wrath; disdain, contempt. **Muovere a —,** to rouse the indignation (of someone).
sdegnosamente, *adv.* Disdainfully, scornfully.
sdegnosità [**-à**], *n.f.* Scornfulness.
sdegnoso, *a.* Disdainful, scornful; indignant.
sdentare, *v.t.* To break the teeth (of).
sdentarsi, *v.r.* To break one's teeth, to loosen a tooth; to lose one's teeth.
sdentato, *a.* Toothless. (*Zool.*) **Gli sdentati,** the edentata.
sdentatura, *n.f.* Toothlessness.
sdiacciare, *v.t.i.* To thaw [cp. **sghiacciare**].
sdigiunare, *v.i.* To break one's fast, to breakfast.
sdilinquimento, *n.m.* Swoon, fainting fit; great emotion; sentimentality.
sdilinquire, *v.t.i.* To weaken; to be languid.
sdilinquirsi, *v.r.* To swoon, to faint; to become mawkishly sentimental.
sdimenticarsi, *v.r.* To forget.
sdimezzare, *v.t.* To halve.
sdiricciare, *v.t.* To husk (chestnuts).
sdoganare, *v.t.* To clear at the customs.
sdolcinatezza, *n.f.* Affectation; mawkishness, sentimentality.
sdolcinato, *a.* Affected, sugary, mawkish; mealy-mouthed.
sdolcinatura, *n.f.* Affectation, mawkishness.
sdoppiamento, *n.m.* Uncoupling, separating, doubling.
sdoppiare, *v.t.* To uncouple, to separate into two; to double.
sdoppiarsi, *v.r.* To become uncoupled; to be separated into two parts.
sdossarsi, *v.r.* To take off one's clothes, to undress.
sdottorare, sdottoreggiare, *v.i.* To pose as a learned person; to sermonize, to lecture.
sdraiare, *v.t.* To stretch out (at full length), to stretch.
sdraiarsi, *v.r.* To lie down, to stretch oneself out; to recline; to throw oneself down (on a bed).
sdraiato, *p.p.a.* Lying down, at full length, reclining.
sdraio [sdrAio], *a.* Lying down, reclining at full length, recumbence. **Sedia a —,** deck-chair, chaise longue.
sdraione, sdraioni, *adv.* In a prostrate position. **Starsene — sull'erba,** to lie at full length on the grass.
sdrucciolamento, *n.m.* Slipping, sliding, slither.
sdrucciolare, *v.i.* To slip, to slide, to slither.
sdrucciolevole [sdrucciolEvole], *a.* Slippery (in all senses); greasy, slimy.
sdrucciolevolmente, *adv.* Greasily, in a slippery way.
sdrucciolo [sdrUcciolo], *n.m.* Slide, slippery place, slip; steep slope.
sdrucciolo [sdrUcciolo], *a.* Slippery; fleeting, transient; (*Gram.*) proparoxytone. **Parola sdrucciola,** word accented on antepenultimate syllable.
sdrucciolone, *n.m.* Slip, slide. **Prendere uno —,** to slip.
sdruccioloni, *adv.* **A —,** slipping and sliding.
sdruccioloso, *a.* Slippery, greasy, slimy.
sdrucio [sdrUcio], *n.m.* Tear, rip, rent.
sdrucire, *v.t.* To tear, to rip, to rend; to unstitch.
sdrucirsi, *v.r.* To become unstitched.
sdrucito, *a.* Thread-bare, unstitched; rent; worn-out.
sdrucitura, *n.f.* Rent, rip; unstitching.
sdruscire [cp. **sdrucire**].
se, *conj.* If, whether; suppose. **Se vuoi,** if you like; **Se sapessi!** If only you knew! **se non altro,** if nothing else; **se mai,** if anything; **anche se,** even if; **se no,** otherwise, if not; **se non altro,** at least.
se, *pron.* (for **si** when accompanied by other conjunctive pronouns). **Se ne andò,** he went off; **se lo mise in tasca,** he put it in his pocket; **se ne ride,** he's laughing at it.
sè, *pron.* Himself herself, itself; oneself, themselves. **Essere fuori di sè,** to be beside oneself; **egli lo fece da sè,** he did it by himself; **fare da sè,** to shift for oneself; **parlava fra sè e sè,** he was talking to himself.
sebaceo [sebAceo], *a.* Sebaceous.
sebbene, *conj.* Although, though.
secante, *n.f.a.* (*Geom.*) Secant.
secare, *v.t.* To cut, to bisect, to cleave.
secca, *n.f.* Sand-bank, shoal; (*fig.*) embarrassment, difficulty. **Dare nelle secche,** to run aground.
seccaggine [seccAggine], *n.f.* Nuisance, bother; tedium; dryness.
seccamente, *adv.* Drily (in all senses), bluntly, gruffly.
seccamento, *n.m.* Drying up, drying; annoyance; nuisance.
seccante, *a.* Boring, tiresome, troublesome.
seccare, *v.t.i.* To dry, to dry up; to wither; to bore, to weary; to vex, to annoy. **Non seccatemi!** Don't bother me!
seccarsi, *v.r.* To become withered, to dry up; to be bored.
seccata, *n.f.* Drying; annoyance, bother.
seccativo, *a.* Drying, seccative.

seccatoio [seccatOio], *n.m.* Drying-room (for fruit, chestnuts, etc.).
seccatore, seccatrice, *n.m.f.* Bore, nuisance, tiresome person.
seccatura, *n.f.* Drying (of chestnuts, etc.); nuisance, bother.
secchereccio [seccherEccio], *a.* Half-dry.
secchezza, *n.f.* Dryness; stiffness; thinness.
secchia [sEcchia], *n.f.* Pail, bucket. **Piovere a secchie,** to rain cats and dogs; **La Secchia Rapita,** The Stolen Bucket (poem by Tassoni).
secchiata, *n.f.* Bucketful.
secchiello, secchiellino, *n.m.* Small pail, can.
secchio [sEcchio], *n.m.* Pail, bucket. **— da carbone,** coal-scuttle.
seccia [sEccia], *n.f.* (*Agric.*) Stubble.
secco, *n.m.* Dry weather, drought; dryness; dry land.
secco, *a.* Dry, arid; dried up, withered; barren, bare, meagre, lean; stiff, frigid, cold; harsh, curt, sharp; bald (in style). **Pane —,** stale bread; **tempo —,** dry weather; **avere la gola secca,** to be parched with thirst; **lasciare in —,** to leave in the lurch; **muro a —,** dry wall; **rimanere a —,** to be stranded (in all senses); **dare in —,** to run aground.
secco, *adv.* Drily, coldly (in response), sharply. **Bere —,** to drink hard; **essere a —,** to be short of money; **pulitura a —,** dry-cleaning (of suits).
seccore, *n.m.* Dryness.
seccume, *n.m.* Dryness; dried stuff (e.g. fruits).
secentesimo, *a.* Six hundredth.
secentismo, *n.m.* (*Lit.*) 17th-century affectation; mannerism, euphuism.
secentista (*pl.* **secentisti**), *n.m.* 17th-century author or artist.
secentistico [secentIstico], *a.* 17th-century; affected, high-flown.
secernere [secErnere], *v.t.* To secrete; to segregate, to separate.
secessione, *n.f.* Secession. (*Hist.*) **Guerra di —,** American Civil War.
secessionismo, *n.m.* Secessionism.
secessionista (*pl.* **secessionisti**), *n.m.* Secessionist.
seco, *pron.* With him, with her, with them, with oneself.
secolare, *n.m.* Layman. **I secolari,** the laity.
secolare, *a.* Secular; century-old; age-long, time-honoured.
secolarescamente, *adv.* Secularly.
secolaresco, *a.* Secular; worldly.
secolarità [-à], *n.f.* Secularity; secularism.
secolarizzare, *v.t.* To secularize.
secolo [sEcolo], *n.m.* Century; age, era; secular life; (*Eccles.*) the world. **— d'oro,** golden age; **mi pare un —,** it seems ages; **per tutti i secoli dei secoli,** for ever and ever.
seconda, *n.f.* (*Anat.*) After-birth, placenta; (*Mus.*) second; (*Rail.*) second class; **un biglietto di —,** a second-class ticket.
seconda, *adv.* Well. **Andare a —,** to take a favourable course, to go well; **a — del vostro desiderio,** according to your wishes.
secondamente, *adv.* Secondly, in the second place; accordingly.
secondare, *v.t.* To second, to support, to back; to comply with; to favour; to follow.
secondariamente, *adv.* Secondarily; secondly.
secondario [secondArio], *a.* Secondary; minor. (*Rail.*) **Linea secondaria,** branch line.
secondatore, secondatrice, *n.m.f.* Seconder.
secondino, *n.m.* Under-gaoler, warder.
secondo, *n.m.* Second (in all senses). **Fra un —,** in a second; (*Naut.*) **— di bordo,** first mate, second in command.
secondo, *a.* Second; next, secondary; favourable, propitious. **Di seconda mano,** second-hand; **non — a nessuno,** second to none; **senza secondi fini,** without any mental reservation; **il primo, il —,** the former, the latter; (*Motor.*) **seconda velocità,** second gear.
secondo, *prep.* According to. **— me,** in my opinion; **— le regole,** according to rules; **— il merito,** according to merit; **— i casi,** it depends.
secondochè, *conj.* As, according to, according as.
secondogenito [secondogEnito], *n.m.a.* Younger son; second son; second-born.
secondogenitura, *n.f.* Right of the second-born.
second'ordine [second'Ordine], *a.* Second-rate.
secreto (1) [cp. **segreto**].
secreto (2), *n.m.* (*Physiol.*) Secretion.
secreto (3), *p.p.a.* Secreted.
secretorio [secretOrio], *a.* Secretory.
secrezione, *n.f.* Secretion.
securo [cp. **sicuro**].
sedano [sEdano], *n.m.* (*Bot.*) Celery.
sedare, *v.t.* To appease, to quiet, to calm, to soothe, to assuage.
sedativo, *n.m.a.* Sedative.
sedatamente, *adv.* Sedately.
sedato, *a.* Calm, quieted; sedate.
sede, *n.f.* Seat (in all senses); residence; centre, locality; site, place. **La Santa Sede,** the Holy See; **— centrale,** head office; **cambiar —,** to change one's residence.
sedentario [sedentArio], *a.* Sedentary.
sedente, *a.* Sitting.
sedere, *v.i.* To sit, to sit down, to take a seat, to be seated, to be situated. **Siedi!** Take a seat! **alzarsi da —,** to rise from one's seat; **star a —,** to keep one's seat; **— a mensa,** to sit down to table [cp. **sedersi**].
sedere, *n.m.* Sitting down; backside, bottom, buttocks.
sederino, *n.m.* Folding seat (in a carriage, etc.); turn-up seat.
sedersi, *v.r.* To sit down, to take a seat [cp. **sedere**].
sedia [sEdia], *n.f.* Chair, seat. **— a bracciuoli,** arm-chair; **— a dondolo,** rocking-chair; **— a sdraio,** lounge, deck-chair; **— pieghevole,** camp-chair; **— gestatoria,** Pope's processional litter; **— elettrica,** electric chair.
sediario [sediArio], *n.m.* (*Eccles.*) Bearer of the pope's sedia gestatoria.
sedicenne, *n.m.a.* Sixteen years old.
sedicente, *a.* Self-styled, would-be. **Il — poeta,** the would-be poet.
sedicesimo [sedicEsimo], *a.* Sixteenth.
sedici [sEdici] (1), *n.m.a.* Sixteen.
sedici [sEdici] (2), *n.m.* (*colloq.*) Bottom, backside, buttocks.
sedile, *n.m.* Seat, bench.
sedimentario [sedimentArio], *a.* Sedimentary.

sedimentazione, *n.f.* Sedimentation.
sedimento, *n.m.* Sediment; lees, dregs; deposit.
sedimentoso, *a.* Sedimentary.
sediolino, *n.m.* Small seat; rumble seat.
sedizione, *n.f.* Sedition, insurrection, rebellion.
sediziosamente, *adv.* Seditiously.
sedizioso, *n.m.a.* Rebel; seditious, rebellious, unlawful.
sedo, *n.m.* (*Bot.*) Sedum, stone-crop, orpine.
sedotto, *p.p.a.* Seduced, betrayed, led astray, enticed, allured. **Una ragazza sedotta,** a ruined girl.
seducente, *a.* Seducing, attractive, alluring, inviting, seductive, tempting.
seducibile [seducIbile], *a.* Seducible, ripe for seduction.
sedulità [-à], *n.f.* Sedulousness.
sedurre, *v.t.* To seduce, to entice, to lead astray, to tempt; to corrupt; to charm.
seduta, *n.f.* Sitting, meeting, session. **Convocare la —,** to summon the meeting; **rinviare la —,** to adjourn the meeting; **levare la —,** to close the meeting.
seduttore, seduttrice, *n.m.f.* Seducer, tempter, temptress.
seduzione, *n.f.* Seduction, temptation, enticement, charm.
sega, *n.f.* Saw. **— circolare,** circular saw; **— a nastro,** band-saw; **— per metalli,** hack-saw; **— da traforo,** fretsaw.
segale, segala [sEgale, sEgala], *n.f.* (*Bot.*) Rye. **Pane di —,** rye bread.
segaligno, *a.* Thin, slender; weather-beaten, brown.
segamento, *n.m.* Sawing.
segantino, *n.m.* Sawyer.
segare, *v.t.* To saw, to saw off; to cut, to mow (grass); (*Med.*) to open (a vein). **— il grano,** to reap corn.
segatore, *n.m.* Mower, reaper; man who saws.
segatura, *n.f.* Mowing; sawing; sawdust.
seggio [sEggio], *n.m.* Seat, throne; chair, seat (in official or political body); (*Eccles.*) see, cathedral stall. **— presidenziale,** chair (of a committee, etc.); **il — di San Pietro,** the papacy.
seggiola [sEggiola], *n.f.* Chair; kitchen chair.
seggiolaio [seggiolAio], *n.m.* Chair-maker or mender.
seggiolina, seggiolino, *n.f.m.* Child's chair, high chair; (*Motor.*) dicky, tip-up seat.
seggiolone, *n.m.* Arm-chair, easy chair.
segheria [segherIa], *n.f.* Saw-mill.
seghetta, *n.f.* Hand-saw, small saw, fret-saw.
seghettare, *v.t.* To notch.
seghettato, *a.* Dentate, toothed, notched, serrated.
seghetto, *n.m.* Hack-saw.
segmentare, *v.t.* To cut into segments.
segmento, *n.m.* Segment.
segnacarte, *n.m.* Book-mark.
segnacaso, *n.m.* (*Gram.*) Preposition.
segnacolo [segnAcolo], *n.m.* Mark, sign, emblem, indication.
segnalare, *v.t.* To signal; to signalize, to bring to notice; to inform, to point out.
segnalarsi, *v.r.* To distinguish oneself.
segnalatamente, *adv.* Signally.
segnalato, *a.* Signal, noteworthy, conspicuous. **Un favore —,** a signal favour.
segnalatore, *n.m.* Signaller, signalman.
segnalazione, *n.f.* Signalling; signal. **Fare segnalazioni,** to signal; (*Rail.*) **cabina di —,** signal-box; **segnalazioni semaforiche,** semaphore signals.
segnale, *n.m.* Signal, sign, mark; token; omen. **— indicatore,** signpost; (*Radio.*) **— orario,** time-signal; **— di pioggia,** sign of rain.
segnalibro, *n.m.* Book-mark.
segnamento, *n.m.* Marking, mark, sign.
segnare, *v.t.* To mark, to sign; to leave a mark; to note, to indicate; to score (in a game). **— a dito,** to point at; (*Mil.*) **— il passo,** to mark time.
segnarsi, *v.r.* To cross oneself; to sign. **Mi segno Suo devotissimo,** I remain yours truly.
segnatamente, *adv.* Markedly; especially, particularly.
segnatario [segnatArio], *n.m.a.* Signatory.
segnatasse, *n.m.* Post-office mark on letter for postage due.
segnato, *a.* Marked; indicated, pointed out; (*colloq.*) ill-favoured, deformed. **Pecora segnata,** (*fig.*) black sheep.
segnatore, *n.m.* Marker, scorer.
segnatura, *n.f.* Marking; noting; pointing at; signing; (*Print.*) signature; (*Eccles.*) tribunal of the Holy See.
segno, *n.m.* Sign, beckon, nod; signal; mark; token; target; trace, vestige; standard, degree, measure. **Il — della croce,** the sign of the Cross; **colpire nel —,** to hit the bull's-eye; **per filo e per —,** in perfect order, in full detail; **metter la testa a —,** to reform, to settle down; **fare dei segni colla mano,** to make signs with one's hand; **in — d'amicizia,** as a token of friendship; **passare il —,** to overstep the limits, to be more than a joke; (*Print.*) **— ammirativo, interrogativo,** exclamation, question mark; **fare stare a —,** to hold in check, to keep in awe; **segni dello Zodiaco,** signs of the Zodiac.
sego, *n.m.* Tallow; suet.
segolo [sEgolo], *n.m.* Billhook, bagging-hook.
segone, *n.m.* Pit-saw; large cross-cut saw.
segoso, *a.* Fatty, suety.
segregamento, *n.m.* Segregation, isolating.
segregare, *v.t.* To segregate, to isolate.
segregarsi, *v.r.* To isolate oneself, to withdraw (from company); to live in retirement.
segregazione, *n.f.* Segregation, isolation, seclusion. **— cellulare,** solitary confinement.
segreta, *n.f.* Dungeon; secret place; (*Eccles.*) secret prayer (at Mass).
segretamente, *adv.* Secretly, in secret.
segretaria [segretAria], *n.f.* Woman secretary.
segretariale, *a.* Secretarial.
segretariato, *n.m.* Secretaryship; secretariat.
segretario [segretArio], *n.m.* Secretary; amanuensis. **— di stato,** secretary of state; **— particolare,** private secretary; **— d'università,** registrar.
segreteria [segreterIa], *n.f.* Secretary's office; secretarial staff.
segretezza, *n.f.* Secrecy.
segreto, *n.m.* Secret; privacy, secrecy; secret drawer. **In —,** in confidence; **— professionale,** professional reticence: **il — di Pulcinella,** an open secret.

segreto, *a.* Secret, hidden, private. **Tener —,** to keep secret.
seguace, *n.m.* Follower, partisan, adherent, supporter.
seguente, *a.* Following, next; successive, ensuing.
seguentemente, *adv.* Successively, next; consequently.
seguenza, *n.f.* Sequence; series.
segugio [segUgio], *n.m.* Bloodhound.
seguimento, *n.m.* (Act of) following.
seguire, *v.t.i.* To follow, to go after, to come after; to attend, to accompany; to pursue; to observe; to forward. **— la moda,** to follow the fashion; **far — una lettera,** to forward a letter; **— il consiglio di,** to take the advice of; **— un discorso,** to follow a speech; **ne segue che hanno ragione,** it follows (from that) that they are right; **segue a tergo,** please turn over, P.T.O.
seguitamente, *adv.* Successively, in succession, consecutively.
seguitare, *v.t.i.* To follow up, to pursue; to continue, to persist, to persevere. **— a leggere,** to go on reading.
seguito [sEguito], *n.m.* Following, train, retinue; sequel, consequence, continuation; succession, series. **Non aver molto —,** to have only a small following; **di —,** successively, continuously; **un — di disgrazie,** a succession of disasters; **in —,** following upon; **la cosa non ebbe —,** the matter was dropped; **il — del re,** the king's retinue; **e così di —,** and so on, and so forth; **in — a,** owing to, on account of; **il — al prossimo numero,** to be continued in our next issue.
sei, *n.m.* Six.
seicento, *a.* Six hundred. **Il Seicento,** the 17th century.
seimila, *a.* Six thousand.
selce, *n.f.* Flint.
selciare, *v.t.* To pave.
selciato, *n.m.* Pavement, paved roadway.
selciatore, *n.m.* Paviour.
selciatura, *n.f.* Paving.
selcioso, *a.* Flinty, full of flints.
selenite, *n.f.* (*Min.*) Selenite.
selenografia [selenografIa], *n.f.* (*Astron.*) Selenography.
selettività [-à], *n.f.* Selectivity.
selettivo, *a.* Selective. **Una radio molto selettiva,** a very selective wireless set.
seletto, *a.* Select.
selettore, *n.m.* Selector.
selezionare, *v.t.* To select, to pick out, to choose.
selezione, *n.f.* Selection, choice.
sella, *n.f.* Saddle. **Cavallo da —,** saddle-horse; **salire in —,** to mount (a horse).
sellaio [sellAio], *n.m.* Saddler.
sellare, *v.t.* To saddle.
sellatura, *n.f.* Saddling.
selleria [sellerIa], *n.f.* Saddlery; saddler's shop; harness-room.
sellino, *n.m.* Small saddle.
seltz, selz, *n.f.* Soda-water, selzer-water.
selva, *n.f.* Wood, forest; (*fig.*) mass, great quantity.
selvaggia [selvAggia], *n.f.* Savage woman, female savage.
selvaggiamente, *adv.* Savagely, rudely, furiously.
selvaggina, *n.f.* Game (birds, deer, etc.).
selvaggio [selvAggio], *n.m.* Savage, wild man; unsociable fellow.
selvaggio [selvAggio], *a.* Wild, savage, uncivilized; rough, unsociable; brutal.
selvaticamente, *adv.* Wildly, savagely.
selvatichezza, *n.f.* Wildness, untamableness; shyness, unsociableness.
selvatico [selvAtico], *a.* Wild, untamed; unsociable; rough, fierce.
selvaticume, *n.m.* Wildness (of animals).
selvereccio [selverEccio], *a.* Wild, untamed.
selvicoltura, selvicultura, *n.f.* Silviculture, forestry.
selvoso, *a.* Woody.
semaforista (*pl.* **semaforisti**), *n.m.* Signalman.
semaforo [semAforo], *n.m.* Semaphore, signal-post; traffic lights.
semantica, semasiologia [semAntica, semasiologIa], *n.f.* Semantics, semasiology.
semata, *n.f.* Barley-water.
sembiante, *n.m.* Semblance; countenance, appearance, look, features, mien. **Far — di,** to pretend, to feign; **far — di nulla,** to feign indifference.
sembianza, *n.f.* Look, countenance, aspect, features; resemblance.
sembrare, *v.t.i.* To seem, to appear, to look like, to appear to be, to resemble; to deem, to think, to be of the opinion. **Sembrava piovesse,** it looked like raining; **sembra di no,** it doesn't look like it; **Cosa te ne sembra ?** What do you think of it? **sembra strano,** it seems strange; **sembra un ladro,** he looks like a thief; **sembra sua madre,** he looks like his mother; **sembra seta,** it feels and looks like silk.
seme, *n.m.* Seed (in all senses); germ; breed, race; origin; (*Anat.*) semen; (*Cards*) suit. **— di bachi,** silkworms' eggs; **il — della discordia,** the seeds of discord.
sementa, *n.f.* Sowing; seed-time; seed sown.
sementare, *v.t.* To sow; to sow broadcast.
semente, *n.f.* Seed, sowing.
sementire, *v.i.* To run to seed.
semenza, *n.f.* Seed (in all senses); (*Anat.*) semen; (*fig.*) progeny, race; source, origin.
semenzaio [semenzAio], *n.m.* Seed-bed; seed-merchant.
semenzire, *v.i.* To run to seed.
semestrale, *a.* Half-yearly.
semestralmente, *adv.* Half-yearly, every six months.
semestre, *n.m.* Half-year.
semi-, *prefix,* Half. (These compounds are noted only when the second part of the compound needs explanation.)
semiaperto, *a.* Half-open, ajar.
semibiscroma, *n.f.* (*Mus.*) Demisemiquaver.
semibreve, *n.f.* (*Mus.*) Semibreve.
semicerchio, semicircolo [semicErchio, semicIrcolo], *n.m.* Semicircle.
semicroma, *n.f.* (*Mus.*) Semiquaver.
semicupio [semicUpio], *n.m.* Hip-bath.
semideo, semidio, *n.m.* Demigod.
semifinale, *n.m.* (*Sport*) Semi-final.
semifinalista (*pl.* **semifinalisti**), *n.m.* (*Sport*) Semi-finalist.

semiminima [semimInima], *n.f.* (*Mus.*) Crotchet.
semina [sEmina], **seminagione,** *n.f.* Seed-time; sowing; seed.
seminale, *a.* Seminal.
seminare, *v.t.* To sow (in all senses); to scatter, to strew, to spread; to disseminate. **— la discordia,** to sow discord; **— i danari,** to lavish one's money, to squander.
seminario [seminArio], *n.m.* Seminary.
seminarista (*pl.* **seminaristi**), *n.m.* Seminarist.
seminato, *n.m.* (*Agric.*) Ground that has been sown; seed-bed. (*fig.*) **Uscire dal —,** to digress, to wander from the subject.
seminatoio [seminatOio], *n.m.* Seed-drill.
seminatore, *n.m.* Sower.
seminatrice, *n.f.* (*Agric.*) Seeding-machine.
seminatura, seminazione, *n.f.* Seeding, semination, sowing; insemination.
seminfermità, *n.f.* (*Law*) Partial insanity.
seminudo, *a.* Half-naked.
semiologia [semiologIa], *n.f.* (*Med.*) Symptomatology.
semioscurità, *n.f.* Half-light, dusk, twilight.
semirigido [semirIgido], *a.* (*Aviat.*) Semi-rigid.
semiserio [semisErio], *a.* Half-serious.
semisfera, *n.f.* Hemisphere.
semispento, *a.* Half-burnt (of coal, etc.).
semita, *n.m.* Semite.
semitico [semItico], *a.* Semitic.
semitono, *n.m.* (*Mus.*) Semitone.
semivivo, *a.* Half-dead, lingering between life and death.
semivolo, *n.m.* (*Tennis*) Half-volley.
semola [sEmola], *n.f.* Bran; fine flour; (*fig.*) freckle.
semolino, *n.m.* Semolina.
semovente, *a.* Self-propelled; automatic.
Sempione, *n.m.* (*Geog.*) Simplon.
sempiternamente, *adv.* Everlastingly.
sempiterno, *a.* Everlasting.
semplice [sEmplice], *a.* Simple, unmixed; single; mere, bare; plain; uncomplicated; easy; common; unaffected, unpretentious. **Soldato —,** private soldier; **una — coincidenza,** a mere coincidence; **uomo —,** simple-minded man; **la — verità,** the unvarnished truth; (*Comm.*) **partita —,** single-entry (book-keeping).
semplicemente, *adv.* Simply, merely; plainly.
semplici, *n.m.pl.* Simples (herbs).
semplicione, *n.m.* Plain good-natured fellow.
sempliciotto, *n.m.a.* Simpleton; naïve, credulous.
semplicismo, *n.m.* Over-simplification.
semplicista (*pl.* **semplicisti**), *n.m.* Herbalist.
semplicistico [semplicIstico], *a.* Over-simplified.
semplicità, *n.f.* Simplicity; easiness, plainness; unpretentiousness; artlessness.
semplificare, *v.t.* To simplify.
semplificazione, *n.f.* Simplification.
sempre, *adv.* Always, ever. **Per —,** for ever; **— più,** always more. **È — vero che,** it is nevertheless true that; **è — a Parigi,** he's still in Paris.
sempreché, *conj.* On condition that, provided that.
sempreverde, *n.m.a.* Evergreen.
sempreviva, *n.f.* (*Bot.*) Everlasting (plant, shrub, etc.).
semprevivo, *n.m.* (*Bot.*) House-leek.
sena, senna, *n.f.* (*Bot.*) Senna.
senapa, senape [sEnapa, -e], *n.f.* Mustard.
senapiera, *n.f.* Mustard-pot.
senapismo, *n.m.* Mustard-plaster.
senario [senArio], *n.m.* (*Poet.*) Verse of six syllables.
senato, *n.m.* Senate; senate house.
senatorato, *n.m.* Senatorship.
senatore, *n.m.* Senator.
senatoriale, senatorio [senatOrio], *a.* Senatorial.
senese, *n.m.a.* Sienese; pertaining to Siena.
senile, *a.* Senile.
senilità [-à], *n.f.* Senility, old age.
senilmente, *adv.* In a senile way, agedly.
seniore, *n.m.a.* Senior; older, elder.
Senna, *n.f.* (*Geog.*) Seine.
senna, *n.f.* (*Bot.*) Senna.
sennino, *n.m.* Clever young fellow.
senno, *n.m.* Sense, wisdom, judgement, good sense. **Con —,** wisely; **uscir di —,** to go crazy, to become insane; **il — di poi,** wisdom after the event.
seno (1), *n.m.* Bosom, breast; (*fig.*) womb, depth; (*Geog.*) cove, inlet, bay. **Tornare in — famiglia,** to return to the bosom of the family; **nel — della Chiesa,** in the bosom of Mother Church.
seno (2), *n.m.* (*Math.*) Sine.
Senofonte, *n.m.* (*Hist.*) Xenophon.
senofobia [senofobIa], *n.f.* Xenophobia, hatred of foreigners.
senofobo [senOfobo], *n.m.* Xenophobe.
senonché, se no, *adv.conj.* Otherwise, else; except, save.
sensale, *n.m.* Broker, middleman. **— di cambiali,** bill-broker.
sensatamente, *adv.* Sensibly, judiciously; wisely.
sensatezza, *n.f.* Good sense, sense, judgement.
sensato, *a.* Sensible, judicious; with consideration, prudent.
sensazionale, *a.* Sensational, exciting.
sensazione, *n.f.* Sensation, feeling; sense.
senseria [senserIa], *n.f.* Brokerage, agency.
sensibile [sensIbile], *a.* Sensible, sensitive, susceptible, responsive; noticeable; tender, sore; (*Phot.*) sensitive. **— al freddo,** sensitive to cold; **— alle ingiurie.** sensitive to injuries, touchy.
sensibilità [-à], *n.f.* Sensitiveness, sensibility, susceptibility, sensitivity.
sensibilizzare, *v.t.* To sensitize.
sensibilmente, *adv.* Sensibly, considerably, appreciably.
sensitiva, *n.f.* Sensitiveness; (*Bot.*) sensitive plant.
sensitivamente, *adv.* Sensitively.
sensitività [-à], *n.f.* Sensitiveness.
sensitivo, *a.* Sensitive, sensible, impressible, excitable; sensory.
senso, *n.m.* Sense; perception, feeling, sentiment; meaning; direction; sensuality. **Buon —,** common sense, good sense; **— figurato,** figurative sense; **in tutti i sensi,** in all its meanings, in all directions; **In che — va?** Which way does it go? **strada a — unico,** one-way street; **circolazione in — unico,**

one-way traffic; **in — contrario,** in the opposite direction; **a mio —,** in my opinion; **fare —,** to make sense; **a — di legge,** according to law.
sensorio [sensOrio], *a.* Sensory.
sensuale, *a.* Sensual, carnal, voluptuous, lewd.
sensualismo, *n.m.* Sensualism.
sensualista (*pl.* **sensualisti**), *n.m.* Sensualist.
sensualistico [sensualIstico], *a.* Sensualistic.
sensualità [-à], *n.f.* Sensuality, voluptuousness; lewdness.
sensualmente, *adv.* Sensually.
sentenza, *n.f.* Saying, maxim, aphorism; (*Law*) sentence, verdict, judgement; award, decree. **Pronunziare una —, emanare una —,** to deliver a judgement, to pass a sentence.
sentenziale, *a.* Sententious.
sentenziare, *v.t.i.* (*Law*) To sentence; to decree; to pass judgement; to talk in a sententious way.
sentenziosamente, *adv.* Sententiously.
sentenziosità [-à], *n.f.* Sententiousness.
sentenzioso, *a.* Sententious; pithy.
sentiero, *n.m.* Path, track, pathway, footpath.
sentimentale, *n.m.f.a.* Sentimentalist; sentimental.
sentimentalismo, *n.m.* Sentimentalism.
sentimentalità [-à], *n.f.* Sentimentality.
sentimentalmente, *adv.* Sentimentally.
sentimento, *n.m.* Sentiment, feeling, sensibility; opinion.
sentina, *n.f.* (*Naut.*) Bilge; (*fig.*) sink (of vice).
sentinella, *n.f.* (*Mil.*) Sentry, sentinel. **Di —,** on sentry-go; **cambiar le sentinelle,** to change the guard.
sentire, *v.t.i.* To feel, to be sensible or conscious of, to perceive; to hear, to listen; to guess; to foresee; to smell, to taste; to taste of, to savour of. **Senti!** Listen! **— rumore,** to hear a noise; **l'ho sentito dire,** I have heard say; **Senti un po'!** Listen to me! Look here! **— il freddo,** to feel the cold; **— mal di capo,** to have a headache; **— fame,** to be hungry; **sento la vostra mancanza,** I miss you; **— di avere commesso un errore,** to be aware of having made a mistake; **— di buono,** to smell nice; **sentiamo di che si tratta,** let's see what it's all about; **— tutte e due le campane,** to hear both sides of an argument.
sentirsi, *v.r.* To feel, to feel oneself. **Si sente triste,** he feels sad; **non si sente bene,** he doesn't feel well; **si sentiva onorato,** he felt himself honoured; **non mi sento di farlo,** that's beyond me, I'm not up to doing that.
sentita, *n.f.* Hearsay. **Per —, per — dire,** by hearsay.
sentitamente, *adv.* Cordially, warmly, heartily, sincerely.
sentito, *p.p.a.* Strong; heartfelt, cordial. **I miei sentiti ringraziamenti,** my warmest thanks.
sentore, *n.m.* Sign, hint, inkling, premonition. **Aver — di,** to have an inkling of.
senza, *prep.* Without, free from. **Far —,** to do without; **senz'altro,** at once, without delay; certainly, of course; **— che lo sapessi,** quite unknown to me.
senzapatria [senzapAtria], *n.m.* (*Pol.*) Renegade, traitor; stateless person.
senzatetto, *n.m.a.* Homeless; vagabond.
senziente, *a.* Sentient.
sepaiola, *n.f.* (*Zool.*) Wren.
sepalo [sEpalo], *n.m.* (*Bot.*) Sepal.
separabile [separAbile], *a.* Separable, detachable.
separabilità [-à], *n.f.* Separability.
separamento, *n.m.* Separation, separating.
separare, *v.t.* To separate, to part, to divide, to detach, to sever.
separarsi, *v.r.* To part (company), to separate; to branch off.
separatamente, *adv.* Separately.
separatezza, *n.f.* Separateness.
separatismo, *n.m.* Separatism.
separatista (*pl.* **separatisti**), *n.m.* Separatist.
separativo, *a.* Separate.
separato, *p.p.a.* Separated, separate.
separazione, *n.f.* Separation; partition, division; leave-taking; severance.
sepolcrale, *a.* Sepulchral.
sepolcreto, *n.m.* Cemetery; vault; tomb.
sepolcro, *n.m.* Sepulchre, tomb, vault, grave. **— di famiglia,** family vault; (*fig.*) **sepolcri imbiancati,** whited sepulchres.
sepolto, *p.p.a.* Buried, interred, entombed. **— vivo,** buried alive.
sepoltura, *n.f.* Burial, interment; tomb, sepulchre.
seppellimento, *n.m.* Burial, interment.
seppellire, *v.t.* To bury, to inter; (*fig.*) to hide.
seppellirsi, *v.r.* To hide oneself, to bury oneself (in work, etc.).
seppellitore, *n.m.* Grave-digger, sexton.
seppia [sEppia], *n.f.* (*Zool.*) Cuttle-fish; (*Art*) sepia.
seppure, *conj.* If even, even when.
sepsi, *n.f.* (*Med.*) Sepsis.
sequela, *n.f.* Succession, sequence, sequel. **Una — di guai,** a succession of troubles, a chapter of accidents.
sequenza, *n.f.* Sequences (in all senses).
sequestrabile [sequestrAbile], *a.* Liable to sequestration.
sequestramento, *n.m.* Sequestering, sequestration.
sequestrare, *v.t.* (*Law*) To sequester, to distrain, to confiscate, to attach, to sequestrate; to shut up illegally; to censor (Press, etc.).
sequestratario [sequestratArio], *n.m.* (*Law*) Sequestrator, trustee of property distrained or seized.
sequestrazione, *n.f.* Sequestration.
sequestro, *n.m.* (*Law*) Sequestration, confiscation; distraint; embargo; (*Med.*) sequestrum (of bone).
ser, sere, *n.m.* (*obs.*) Sir, master.
sera, *n.f.* Evening. **Buona —,** good evening, good night; **di —,** at night; **fa —,** it's growing dark; **verso —,** at dusk; **ier l'altro —,** the night before last; **da mane a —,** from morning till night.
serafico [serAfico], *a.* Seraphic.
serafino, *n.m.* Seraph.
serale, *a.* Evening; nightly. **Scuola —,** evening school.
seralmente, *adv.* Every evening, nightly.

serata, *n.f.* Evening; evening party; (*Theat.*) evening performance. — **d'onore,** benefit night.
serataccia [seratAccia], *n.f.* Wet night; bad night.
seratante, *n.m.* (*Theat.*) Actor for whom benefit is held.
serbabile [serbAbile], *a.* Preservable, storable.
serbare, *v.t.* To keep, to preserve; to put by, to save up; to store. — **in vita,** to keep alive.
serbarsi, *v.r.* To keep oneself, to remain, to preserve oneself. — **la salute,** to take care of one's health.
serbatoio [serbatOio], *n.m.* Tank, reservoir. — **della benzina,** petrol-tank.
serbo (1), *n.m.* Custody, keeping; reserve. **Tenere in —,** to preserve, to keep in store; **mettere in —,** to put by, to save up, to store up.
serbo (2), *n.m.a.* Serb; Serbian. **Serbo-croato,** Serbo-Croatian.
serenamente, *adv.* Serenely, brightly, cloudlessly.
serenare, serenarsi, *v.t.r.* To clear up (of the sky).
serenata, *n.f.* Serenade; serenity. **Fare una —a,** to serenade.
serenella, *n.f.* (*Bot.*) Lilac.
serenissimo [serenIssimo], *n.m.a.* (Title of) Most Serene, Serene Highness. (*Hist.*) **La Serenissima,** the Republic of Venice.
serenità [-à], *n.f.* Serenity; calm, peace; brightness.
sereno, *n.m.* Clear sky, clear starlit sky. **Dormire al —,** to sleep in the open.
sereno, *a.* Serene, bright, cloudless, clear; calm, peaceful, tranquil.
sergente, *n.m.* Sergeant. — **maggiore,** sergeant-major.
seriamente, *adv.* Seriously; earnestly; gravely. — **malato,** seriously ill.
serici [sErici], *n.m.pl.* Silk manufacturers; silk operatives.
serico [sErico], *a.* Silken, silk; silky. **Industria serica,** silk industry.
sericultore, *n.m.* Sericulturist; silk manufacturer.
sericoltura, *n.f.* Sericulture, silk industry.
serie [sErie], *n.f.* Series; succession; sequel; set; range. — **di conferenze,** course of lectures; **produzione in —,** mass production.
serietà [-à], *n.f.* Seriousness, gravity, austerity; sincerity.
serio [sErio], *a.* Serious, grave, earnest, thoughtful, austere; genuine. **Sul —,** in earnest; **fare sul —,** to be in earnest; **prendere la cosa sul —,** to take the thing seriously.
seriocomico, seriogiocoso [seriocOmico], *a.* Serio-comic.
seriola, *n.f.* (*Zool.*) Species of Mediterranean mackerel.
serizzo, *n.m.* (*Min.*) Gneiss.
sermonare, *v.i.* To sermonize, to speak at great length.
sermoncino, *n.m.* Short sermon, exhortation; reprimand, lecture.
sermone, *n.m.* Sermon; admonition; lecture.
sermoneggiare, *v.i.* To sermonize, to preach; to give a lecture (to).
serotino [serOtino], *a.* Late, tardy, behind time (esp. of fruits ripening, etc.); of evening, at dusk.
serpa, *n.f.* Coachman's box-seat.
serpaio [serpAio], *n.m.* Place abounding in snakes.
serparo, *n.m.* Snake-charmer.
serpe, *n.m.* Serpent, snake.
serpeggiamento, *n.m.* Coiling, winding, tortuousness.
serpeggiante, *a.* Winding, sinuous, coiling, serpentine; circuitous.
serpeggiare, *v.i.* To wind, to be coiled, to be crooked; to meander; to creep; to lie concealed. **La strada serpeggiava,** the road wound round.
serpentario [serpentArio], *n.m.* (*Zool.*) Secretary bird.
serpente, *n.m.* Serpent, snake; — **a sonagli,** rattlesnake.
serpentiforme, *a.* Serpent-like in shape.
serpentina, *n.f.* (*Geol.*) Serpentine.
serpentino, *n.m.* Worm (of a still).
serpentino, *a.* Serpentine, sinuous; snake-like. **Una lingua serpentina,** a venomous tongue.
serpentone, *n.m.* Large snake; (*Mus.*) serpent.
serpigine [serpIgine], *n.f.* (*Med.*) Ringworm.
serqua [sErqua], *n.f.* Dozen (eggs, etc.); great quantity, lots of.
serra (1), *n.f.* Greenhouse, glass-house, hot-house, conservatory; crowd; **Un — —,** a crush, a disorderly mob; **fiori di —,** hothouse flowers; — **per palme,** palm-house.
serra (2), *n.f.* Mountain chain, sierra; mountain pass.
serrafila, *n.m.* (*Mil.*) Rear-rank man.
serrafreno, *n.m.* (*Rail.*) Brakesman.
serraglio [serrAglio], *n.m.* Menagerie, cage (for wild beasts); harem, seraglio.
serramanico [serramAnico], *adv.* **Coltello a —,** clasp-knife; spring-knife.
serrame, *n.m.* Lock, fastening.
serramento, *n.m.* Locking, lock, bolt.
serranda, *n.f.* Damper (of flues).
serraporta, *n.f.* Door-spring; door-closer.
serrare, *v.t.i.* To shut, to close, to lock (in, out, etc.); to press; to shake (by the hand); to squeeze; to hold tightly; (*Mil.*) to close up (ranks); (*Naut.*) to take in sails. — **i denti,** to clench the teeth; — **il pugno,** to clench one's fist; — **la porta,** to lock the door; **il pianto gli serrò la gola,** tears choked him; — **a chiave una porta,** to lock a door.
serrarsi, *v.r.* To close up, to stand closer. — **addosso a,** to press upon, to crowd upon.
serrata, *n.f.* Closing, shutting; enclosure; lock-out (of workers). **Gl'industriali dichiararono la —,** the employers declared a lock-out.
serratamente, *adv.* Tightly, closely, compactly.
serrato, *a.* Close, tight, compact, close-packed. **Galoppo —,** quick gallop; **in file serrate,** in serried ranks; **un discorso —,** a concise speech; **tempo —,** threatening sky.
serratura, *n.f.* Lock, door-lock. — **di sicurezza,** safety-lock; **buco della —,** keyhole.

serretta, *n.f.* (*Bot.*) Saw-wort; (*Naut.*) grating.
Serse, *n.m.* (*Hist.*) Xerxes.
serto, *n.m.* (*Lit.*) Garland, wreath.
serva, *n.f.* Maidservant, housemaid, servant-girl. **La — padrona,** The Maid Turned Mistress.
servaggio [servAggio], *n.m.* Servitude, bondage, slavery; serfdom.
servare [cp. **conservare**].
servente, *n.m.* Servant; (*Mil.*) gunner; (*Eccles.*) lay brother; (*Tennis*) server.
servente, *a.* Serving, in waiting. **Cavaliere —,** lover (to a married woman), cicisbeo.
servetta, *n.f.* Waiting-maid; (*Theat.*) soubrette.
servibile [servIbile], *a.* Usable, in good repair.
servidorame, *n.m.* Servants (as a body), flunkeys.
servigio [servIgio], *n.m.* Service, favour [cp. **servizio**].
servile, *a.* Servile, slavish; mean; menial, low.
servilità [-à], *n.f.* Servility, slavishness.
servilmente, *adv.* Slavishly, fawningly.
servire, *v.t.i.* To serve, to wait on; to be of use, to have the function of; to attend to; (*Football*) to pass. **— la messa,** to serve at Mass; **A che serve cio ?** What's the use of that? **per servirla,** at your service; **— di norma,** to serve as a rule; **non serve dirglielo,** it's no use to tell him; **in che cosa posso servirla ?** what can I do for you?
servirsi, *v.r.* To use, to make use of; to help oneself at table. **Si serva!** Help yourself! **— di,** to make use of, to employ.
servitorame, *n.m.* Servants (in a body).
servitore, *n.m.* Servant, manservant; waiter.
servitù [-ù], *n.f.* Servitude, slavery, bondage; subjection; "the servants"; (*Law*) easement, user. (*Law*) **— di passaggio,** right of way.
serviziale, *n.m.* (*Med.*) Enema.
servizievole [serviziEvole], *a.* Obliging, helpful, willing; useful, handy.
servizio [servIzio], *n.m.* Service (in all senses); purpose; favour; use, function; set; kindness, attention; attendance, waiting (at restaurant). **Donna di —,** domestic servant, maidservant; **mezzo —,** half-day help; **scala di —,** back-door, tradesmen's entrance; **— divino,** divine service; **prestar —,** to serve; **un — di porcellana,** a porcelain dinner or tea service; **— da tavola,** dinner-service; **un — da tè,** a tea-set; **buono a tutti i servizi,** jack-of-all-trades; (*Rail.*) **— diretto,** through service; **fare un viaggio e due servizi,** to kill two birds with one stone.
servo, *n.m.* Servant, manservant, valet; (*Hist.*) serf. **— suo,** (in letters) your obedient servant.
servo, *a.* Servile, slavish.
servomotore, *n.m.* (*Eng.*) Servomotor.
servotta, *n.f.* Strong servant-girl.
sesamo [sEsamo], *n.m.* (*Bot.*) Sesame. **Olio di —,** oil of sesame; **— apriti!** Open Sesame!
sesquipedale, *a.* Sesquipedalian, big sounding (of words, etc.).
sessagenario [sessagenArio], *n.m.a.* Sexagenarian.
sessagesima, *n.f.* (*Eccles.*) Sexagesima Sunday.
sessagesimo [sessagEsimo], *a.* Sixtieth [cp. **sessantesimo**].
sessanta, *a.* Sixty.
sessantenne, *n.m.a.* Sexagenarian; sixty years old.
sessantesimo [sessantEsimo], *a.* Sixtieth.
sessantina, *n.f.* Three score, about sixty. **Quell'uomo ha superato la —,** that man is in his sixties.
sessenale, *a.* Sexennial, every six years.
sessenne, *a.* Six-year-old.
sessennio [sessEnnio], *n.m.* Period of six years.
sessile [sEssile], *a.* (*Bot.*) Sessile.
sessione, *n.f.* Session, term, sitting.
sesso, *n.m.* Sex. **Il bel —,** the fair sex; **d'ambo i sessi,** of both sexes.
sessola [sEssola], *n.f.* (*Naut.*) Bail, bailing ladle; scoop.
sessuale, *a.* Sexual.
sessualità [-à], *n.f.* Sexuality.
sessualmente, *adv.* Sexually.
sesta, *n.f.* (*Eccles.*) Sext, sixth hour; (*Mus.*) sixth.
sestante, *n.m.* (*Naut.*) Sextant.
seste, *n.f.pl.* (Pair of) compasses; (*colloq.*) long legs.
sesterzio [sestErzio], *n.m.* (*Hist.*) Sesterce.
sestetto, *n.m.* (*Mus.*) Sextet.
sestina, *n.f.* (*Poet.*) Six-line stanza, sestina.
sesto, *n.m.* Order, measure; (*Arch.*) curve of an arch; (*Print.*) format. (*Arch.*) **— acuto,** pointed arch, ogive; **mettere in —,** to put in order, to tidy up.
sesto, *a.adv.* Sixth, sixthly.
sestodecimo [sestodEcimo], *a.* Sixteenth.
sestultimo [sestUltimo], *a.* Sixth before the last.
sestuplo [sEstuplo], *a.* Sextuple, sixfold.
seta, *n.f.* Silk. **Baco da —,** silk-worm; **— artificiale** artificial silk; **— greggia,** raw silk.
setaccio [setAccio], *n.m.* Sieve [cp. **staccio**].
setaceo [setAceo], *a.* Silky.
setaiolo, setaiuolo, *n.m.* Silk merchant; silk weaver.
sete, *n.f.* Thirst (in all senses); drought. **Aver —,** to be thirsty; **cavarsi la —,** to quench one's thirst.
seteria [seterIa], *n.f.* Silk, silk stuff; silk factory. **Seterie,** silk goods, silks.
seticoltura [cp. **sericultura**].
setificio [setifIcio], *n.m.* Silk-mill, silk-factory.
setola [sEtola], *n.f.* Bristle, coarse hair; chap (in the skin), crack.
setolino, *n.m.* Little brush, hat-brush; whisk.
setoloso, *a.* Bristly, hairy.
setoluto, *a.* Covered with bristles.
setone, *n.m.* (*Med.*) Seton.
setta, *n.f.* Sect, faction.
settagono [settAgono], *n.m.* (*Geom.*) Heptagon.
settangolare, *a.* (*Geom.*) Heptangular.
settanta, *n.m.a.* Seventy.
settantenne, *n.m.a.* Septuagenarian; seventy years old.
settantesimo [settantEsimo], *a.* Seventieth.
settantina, *n.f.* About seventy; seventy years old.
settario [settArio], *n.m.a.* Sectarian.
settatore, *n.m.* Follower, disciple; partisan.

sette, *n.m.a.* Seven; (*colloq.*) rent in the shape of a 7. **Un — nei calzoni,** a jagged tear in one's trousers.
settecentesco, *a.* Pertaining to the 18th century.
settecentesimo [settecentEsimo], *a.* Seven hundredth.
settecentista (*pl.* **settecentisti**), *n.m.* (*Lit.*) 18th-century writer.
settecento, *n.m.a.* Seven hundred. **Il Settecento,** the 18th century.
settembre, *n.m.* September.
settembrino, *a.* Of September, September.
settemila, *a.* Seven thousand.
settemplice [settEmplice], *a.* Sevenfold.
settenario [settenArio], *n.m.* Period of seven (days or years); (*Poet.*) line of 7 syllables.
settennale, *a.* Septennial.
settenne, *n.m.a.* Seven years old.
settennio [settEnnio], *n.m.* Period of seven years.
settentrionale, *n.m.a.* Northerner; northern, north, northerly.
settentrione, *n.m.* North.
setticemia [setticemIa], *n.f.* (*Med.*) Septicaemia, blood-poisoning.
setticlavio [setticlAvio], *n.m.* (*Mus.*) Seven keys.
settico [sEttico], *a.* (*Med.*) Septic.
settima [sEttima], *n.f.* (*Med.*) Period of seven (week, days, etc.); (*Eccles.*) 7-day office for the dead; (*Mus.*) seventh.
settimana, *n.f.* Week. **Settimana Santa,** Holy Week; **la — ventura,** next week; **la — scorsa,** last week.
settimanale, *n.m.* Weekly paper; weekly wages.
settimanale, *a.* Weekly.
settimanalmente, *adv.* Weekly, week by week, every week; by the week.
settimino, *n.m.* Seven-months' child; (*Mus.*) septet.
settimo [sEttimo], *a.* Seventh. **Essere al — cielo,** to be in the seventh heaven.
setto, *n.m.* (*Anat.*) Septum.
settore, *n.m.* Sector; area; zone, compartment.
settuagenario [settuagenArio], *n.m.a.* Septuagenarian.
settuagesima [settuagEsima], *n.m.* (*Eccles.*) Septuagesima Sunday.
settuplo [sEttuplo], *a.* Sevenfold.
severamente, *adv.* Severely, rigorously, austerely.
severità [-à], *n.f.* Severity, rigour, sternness, harshness, strictness.
severo, *a.* Severe, rigorous, austere; strict, harsh, stern. **Tono —,** a harsh voice.
sevizia [sevIzia], *n.f.* Cruelty, barbarity; torture, ill-treatment.
seviziare, *v.t.* To ill-treat, to maltreat; to torture.
sevo, *n.m.* Tallow [cp. **sego**].
sezionamento, *n.m.* Dissection, partition, division.
sezionare, *v.t.* To dissect; to section, to partition, to divide.
sezione, *n.f.* Section (in all senses); group; (*Anat.*) dissection.
sfaccendare, *v.i.* To be busy, to bustle, to hustle.
sfaccendato, *n.m.a.* Idler, loafer; unoccupied, idle.
sfaccettare, *v.t.* To facet, to cut facets on.
sfaccettatura, *n.f.* Facet, faceting.
sfacchinare, *v.i.* To drudge, to toil, "to work like a slave."
sfacchinata, *n.f.* Hard work, tough job.
sfacciataggine [sfacciatAggine], *n.f.* Effrontery, impudence, shamelessness. **Avere la — di,** to have the effrontery to.
sfacciatamente, *adv.* Impudently, with effrontery.
sfacciato, *a.* Saucy, pert, cheeky; impudent, brazen-faced; glaring (colour); dazzling (light).
sfacelo, *n.m.* Ruin, dissolution, decay; breakdown. **Andare in —,** to fall into ruin.
sfacimento, *n.m.* Undoing, decay, dissolution.
sfagliare, sfagliarsi, *v.t.r.* (*Cards*) To discard.
sfaglio [sfAglio], *n.m.* (*Cards*) Discard.
sfagno, *n.m.* Peat-moss.
sfalda, *n.f.* Flake, scale.
sfaldamento, *n.m.* Peeling, flaking.
sfaldare, *v.t.* To scale, to flake off.
sfaldarsi, *v.r.* To flake, to peel off, to scale off, to exfoliate.
sfaldatura, *n.f.* Flaking, peeling, scaling off.
sfalsare, *v.t.* To distort (facts, truth, etc.); to misrepresent; (*Fencing*) to parry.
sfamare, *v.t.* To satisfy (hunger), to feed.
sfamarsi, *v.r.* To appease one's hunger.
sfamato, *a.* Satiated; sated, glutted.
sfangare, sfangarsi, *v.t.i.r.* To clean off mud, to get out of the mire; to splash through mud; (*fig.*) to muddle through; to get out of difficulties. **Sfangarsela,** to get out of a scrape.
sfare, *v.t.* To undo; to melt, to dissolve [cp. **sfarsi**].
sfarfallamento, *n.m.* Fluttering.
sfarfallare, *v.i.* To flutter about, to flit from thing to thing; to emerge from the cocoon.
sfarfallone, *n.m.* Blunder.
sfarinare, *v.t.* To pulverize.
sfarinarsi, *v.r.* To crumble into powder.
sfarsi, *v.r.* To weaken, to decompose [cp. **sfare**].
sfarzo, *n.m.* Luxury, display, pomp, ostentation.
sfarzosamente, *adv.* Luxuriously, sumptuously.
sfarzosità [-à], *n.f.* Luxury, sumptuousness, pomp, magnificence, ostentation, showing-off.
sfarzoso, *a.* Sumptuous, luxurious, costly, magnificent.
sfasciamento, *n.m.* Unwrapping, unbinding; dismantling; crumbling, fall, ruin.
sfasciare, *v.t.* To unbind, to unbandage, to undo, to unwrap; to loose; to dismantle.
sfasciarsi, *v.r.* To fall to pieces, to collapse, to be wrecked (of a ship).
sfasciatura, *n.f.* Unwrapping; fall, ruin, crumbling.
sfascio [sfAscio], *n.m.* Ruin.
sfasciume, *n.m.* Ruin, wreck, debris; litter, rubbish.
sfatamento, *n.m.* Discredit, exposure, unmasking.
sfatare, *v.t.* To unmask, to expose, to discredit, to explode (a theory, etc.).
sfaticato, *a.* Lazy.

sfatto, *a.* Undone; exhausted, worn out, ruined; over-cooked.
sfavillamento, *n.m.* Sparkle, brilliancy, glitter, scintillation.
sfavillante, *a.* Sparkling, glittering.
sfavillantemente, *adv.* Sparklingly.
sfavillare, *v.i.* To sparkle, to shine, to scintillate.
sfavillio [sfavillIo], *n.m.* Scintillation, sparkle; brightness.
sfavore, *n.m.* Disfavour, disapproval; aversion.
sfavorevole [sfavorEvole], *a.* Unfavourable, contrary, adverse.
sfavorevolmente, *adv.* Unfavourably, adversely.
sfavorire, *v.t.* To treat unfairly; to disoblige; to prejudice; to wrong.
sfebbrare, *v.i.* To recover from a fever.
sfebbrato, *a.* Free from fever; with normal temperature.
sfegatarsi, *v.r.* To exert oneself to the utmost; to be frantic; to get excited; to bawl and shout, to work oneself into a passion.
sfegatatamente, *adv.* Excitedly, frantically.
sfegatato, *a.* Excited, frantic; fanatical.
sfendere [cp. **fendere**].
sfenoide [sfenOide], *n.m.* (*Anat.*) Sphenoid.
sfera, *n.f.* Sphere (in all senses); circle (of acquaintances); ball, globe; field, province. **Sfere celesti,** heavenly spheres; **— d'attività,** sphere of activity; (*Mech.*) **cuscinetto a sfere,** ball bearings; **— dell'orologio,** clock-hand.
sfericamente, *adv.* Spherically.
sfericità [-à], *n.f.* Sphericalness, sphericity.
sferico [sfErico], *a.* Spherical.
sferoidale, *a.* (*Geom.*) Spheroidal.
sferoide [sferOide], *n.m.* Spheroid.
sferra, *n.f.* Old horseshoe; old iron. **Sferre,** cast-off clothes.
sferraiolarsi, *v.r.* To cast off one's cloak.
sferrare, *v.t.i.* To let loose, to unchain, to free; to unshoe (a horse); to rush out impetuously. **— un calcio,** to launch a kick; (*Mil.*) **— un attacco,** to launch an attack.
sferrarsi, *v.r.* To cast a shoe (of a horse).
sferrato, *a.* Unshod (of a horse).
sferratura, *n.f.* Unshoeing a horse.
sferravecchiare, *v.t.* (*colloq.*) To rummage about, to poke about.
sfervorato, *a.* Cooled down (in feelings, etc.), indifferent.
sferza, *n.f.* Whip, lash; scourge. **La — del sole,** the blazing, scorching sun.
sferzare, *v.t.* To whip; to lash, to flog, to scourge; to blame.
sferzata, *n.f.* Cut with a whip; thrashing, lashing; stern reprimand.
sferzatore, sferzatrice, *n.m.f.* Flogger; flagellant.
sferzino, *n.m.* Whipcord, lash.
sfiaccolare, *v.i.* To flare, to glow.
sfiaccolato, *a.* Weak, worn-out, jaded.
sfiammare, *v.i.* To blaze up, to flare up.
sfiancamento, *n.m.* Break-down, collapse; (*Med.*) dilatation.
sfiancare, *v.t.i.* To exhaust, to wear out, to cave in.
sfiancarsi, *v.r.* To overwork oneself, to knock oneself up.
sfiancato, *a.* Worn out, broken-backed.
sfiatamento, *n.m.* Breathlessness; shortness of breath.
sfiatare, *v.i.* To breathe out, to exhale; to escape (gas, air, etc.).
sfiatarsi, *v.r.* To lose one's breath (shouting).
sfiatato, *p.p.a.* Breathless, out of breath. **Un cantante —,** a breathless singer.
sfiatatoio [sfiatatOio], *n.m.* Air-hole; air-funnel; vent.
sfiatatura, *n.f.* Breathlessness.
sfiato, *n.m.* Vent.
sfibbiare, *v.t.* To unbuckle, to unclasp, to unfasten, to undo.
sfibbiarsi, *v.r.* (*fig.*) To unbutton oneself, to cast aside restraint; to speak one's mind; to let fly (insults, etc.).
sfibbiatura, *n.f.* Unbuckling, unfastening.
sfibramento, *n.m.* Weakening, enervation.
sfibrante, *a.* Enervating.
sfibrare, *v.t.* To enervate, to weaken; to unnerve.
sfibrarsi, *v.r.* To become enervated, to be enfeebled.
sfida, *n.f.* Challenge, defiance; contest. **Con aria di —,** in a challenging manner.
sfidare, *v.t.* To challenge, to defy; to dare, to face. **— a duello,** to challenge to a duel; **— un pericolo,** to face a danger. **Sfido io!** Of course! Rather! No wonder!
sfidatore, *n.m.* Challenger.
sfiducia [sfidUcia], *n.f.* Distrust; lack of confidence. **Voto di —,** vote of no confidence.
sfiduciare, *v.t.* To discourage, to dishearten.
sfiduciarsi, *v.r.* To be disheartened, to get discouraged.
sfienare, *v.t.* (*Agric.*) To take in hay, to clear away grass.
sfigurare, *v.t.i.* To disfigure, to spoil; to cut a poor figure, to look shabby.
sfigurato, *a.* Disfigured, unrecognizable.
sfilaccia [sfilAccia], *n.f.* Threads.
sfilacciare, *v.t.* To fray out, to unravel.
sfilacciarsi, *v.r.* To become unravelled, to be frayed.
sfilacciatura, *n.f.* Fraying out; threads.
sfilamento, *n.m.* Unthreading, unstringing; becoming loose; (*Mil.*) march past, procession.
sfilare, *v.t.i.* To unthread, to unstring, to unravel; to turn the edge (of a razor); (*Mil.*) to march past, to file off.
sfilarsi, *v.r.* To become unthreaded, to chafe, to fray.
sfilata, *n.f.* March past, procession; string (of vehicles).
sfilatamente, *adv.* In file, one after the other; in a disorderly way.
sfilato, *a.* Out of order, out of line; unthreaded.
sfilatura, *n.f.* Unthreading, slipped stitch (in knitting). **Una — nelle calze,** a ladder in one's stocking.
sfinge, *n.f.* Sphinx.
sfinimento, *n.m.* Exhaustion, weakness, feebleness; swoon, faint; breakdown.
sfinire, *v.t.i.* To exhaust, to wear out; to faint.
sfinirsi, *v.r.* To become exhausted.
sfinitezza, *n.f.* Exhaustion.
sfintere, *n.m.* (*Anat.*) Sphincter.
sfioccamento, *n.m.* Unravelling, fraying out.
sfioccare, *v.t.* To unravel, to fray out.

sfiocinare, *v.t.* To remove grape-stones and skin; to harpoon.
sfioramento, *n.m.* Grazing, touching lightly, rubbing or brushing past.
sfiorare, *v.t.* To graze, to touch lightly, to touch upon, to rub or brush past; to caress; to skim over. **— un argomento,** to touch on a subject in passing; *(Tennis)* **— la rete,** to touch the net (of a ball); **— l'acqua col remo,** to feather one's oars.
sfiorire, *v.i.* To fade, to wither, to languish.
sfioritura, *n.f.* Fading, withering, fall of blossoms.
sfissare, *v.t.* To cancel an agreement, to cancel a contract.
sfittare, *v.t.* To leave (a house, etc.) unlet, to keep untenanted.
sfitto, *p.p.a.* Unlet, empty (of a house).
sfociamento, *n.m.* Inflow (of a river); inlet.
sfociare, *v.i.* To flow into, to open into (of a river, etc.).
sfoconare, *v.t.* To poke the fire, to stir up a blaze.
sfoderamento, *n.m.* Unsheathing.
sfoderare, *v.t.* To unsheathe, to draw (sword); (*fig.*) to show off, to display, to parade.
sfogamento, *n.m.* Venting, giving vent, pouring forth.
sfogare, *v.t.* To give vent to, to vent, to pour forth.
sfogarsi, *v.r.* To unbosom oneself, to give vent to one's feelings. **Ho bisogno di sfogarmi,** I must let off steam; **si sfogò in ingiurie,** he burst into a stream of abuse; **— la fame,** to appease one's hunger.
sfogatamente, *adv.* Unreservedly, openly.
sfogatoio [sfogatOio], *n.m.* Air-hole, vent.
sfoggiamento, *n.m.* Display, parade, flaunting.
sfoggiare, *v.t.i.* To display, to flaunt, to parade. **— richezza,** to make a display of wealth.
sfoggiatamente, *adv.* Flauntingly, ostentatiously.
sfoggio [sfOggio], *n.m.* Display, show, ostentation; pomp, luxury; abundance.
sfoglia [sfOglia], *n.f.* Flake, thin layer; foil (metal). **Pasta —,** puff-pastry.
sfogliamento, *n.m.* Stripping off of leaves.
sfogliare, *v.t.* To strip off leaves; to turn the pages (of a book), to draw (cards). **— un libro,** to browse, to go through a book.
sfogliarsi, *v.r.* To shed leaves, to flake off.
sfogliata, *n.f.* Glance (through a book); puff-paste, thin pastry.
sfogliatura, *n.f.* (*Agric.*) Exfoliation, stripping of leaves, shedding of leaves.
sfogliazione, *n.f.* Exfoliation; fall of leaves in autumn.
sfoglioso, *a.* Flaky.
sfogo, *n.m.* Vent, free play; outlet, relief; development; (*Med.*) eruption. **— di un arco,** height of an arch; **dar — a,** to give free play to. (*Comm.*) **merce che non trova —,** goods that do not sell.
sfolgorante, *a.* Flashing, dazzling; refulgent, radiant.
sfolgorare, sfolgoreggiare, *v.t.i.* To flash, to dazzle, to blaze forth.
sfolgoratamente, *adv.* Dazzlingly, flashingly.
sfolgorio [sfolgorIo], *n.m.* Refulgence, radiance, splendour, brightness, glitter.
sfollagente, *n.m.* Truncheon, life-preserver.
sfollamento, *n.m.* Dispersal, disbandment, scattering, break-up (of meeting, etc.); (*Mil.*) evacuation (of civilians).
sfollare, sfollarsi, *v.t.i.r.* To disperse (a crowd, etc.), to scatter; to evacuate (inhabitants, etc.).
sfollato, *n.m.* Evacuee; displaced person.
sfondamento, *n.m.* Breaking through, breaking open.
sfondare, *v.t.* To break through, to burst open, to stave in, to knock out the bottom.
sfondarsi, *v.r.* To burst at the bottom (of a cask, etc.).
sfondato, *p.p.a.* Broken through, shattered; bottomless; worn out. **Ricco —,** fabulously rich.
sfondo, *n.m.* (*Art*) Background.
sforacchiare, *v.t.* To pierce through; to pierce with holes, to bore holes in.
sforacchiatura, *n.f.* Boring holes, piercing.
sformare, *v.t.i.* To disfigure, to deform, to put out of shape; to remove from the mould.
sformarsi, *v.r.* To get out of shape; (*fig.*) to lose patience.
sformato, *n.m.* Food cooked in a mould.
sformato, *p.p.a.* Deformed, disfigured; shapeless; ugly.
sfornare, *v.t.* To take out of the oven; to put forth, to exhibit.
sfornata, *n.f.* Batch (in all senses).
sfornire, *v.t.* To deprive, to dispossess.
sfornito, *p.p.a.* Deprived, dispossessed; destitute, lacking.
sfortuna, *n.f.* Bad luck, misfortune.
sfortunatamente, *adv.* Unfortunately.
sfortunato, *a.* Unlucky, unfortunate, unhappy.
sforzamento, *n.m.* Forcing, compulsion.
sforzare, *v.t.* To force, to constrain, to compel; to urge.
sforzarsi, *v.r.* To endeavour, to exert oneself, to strive, to do one's utmost, to attempt.
sforzatamente, *adv.* Unnaturally, affectedly.
sforzato, *p.p.a.* Forced; affected, unnatural; rich (of wine).
sforzo, *n.m.* Effort, endeavour, exertion; stress. **Fare lo — di,** to make an effort to; **senza —,** without effort.
sfossare, *v.t.* To dig up, to dig out of.
sfottere [sfOttere], *v.t.* (*colloq.*) To vex, to pin-prick.
sfracassamento, *n.m.* Smashing, crushing, shattering.
sfracassare [cp. **sfracellare**].
sfracellamento, *n.m.* Smash, smashing.
sfracellare, *v.t.* To smash to atoms, to shatter, to crush.
sfracellarsi, *v.r.* To get smashed, to crash. **Si sfracellò al suolo,** it crashed to the ground.
sfracellio, sfracello [sfracellIo], *n.m.* Smash.
sfranare [cp. **franare**].
sfrancesarsi, *v.r.* To free oneself from French ways.
sfranchire, *v.t.* To give freedom to, to give confidence.
sfranchirsi, *v.r.* To gain confidence.
sfrangiare, *v.t.* To unravel, to fray out.
sfrascare, *v.t.* To strip of foliage.
sfratare, *v.t.* To unfrock (a priest).

sfratarsi, *v.r.* To renounce Holy Orders.
sfrattare, *v.t.* To dismiss, to turn out, to expel, to evict (tenants, etc.).
sfratto, *n.m.* Eviction, expulsion; dismissal. **Dare lo —,** to evict.
sfregamento, *n.m.* Rubbing, friction.
sfregare, *v.t.* To rub, to massage.
sfregata, *n.f.* Rubbing, friction, massage.
sfregiare, *v.t.* To deface, to disfigure; (*fig.*) to disgrace, to cast a slur (upon).
sfregiatore, sfregiatrice, *n.m.f.* Disfigurer; defamer, slanderer.
sfregio [sfrEgio], *n.m.* Disfigurement, gash, cut; scar; slur, affront.
sfrenare, *v.t.* To unbridle, to let loose, to give rein to; to unchain.
sfrenarsi, *v.r.* To rage; to throw off all restraint, to let oneself go.
sfrenataggine [sfrenatAggine], *n.f.* Licence, licentiousness.
sfrenatamente, *adv.* Unrestrainedly, loosely; licentiously.
sfrenatezza, *n.f.* Wildness, looseness, licentiousness, profligacy.
sfrenato, *a.* Unbridled, unchained, unrestrained; loose, licentious, dissolute.
sfriggere [sfrIggere], *v.i.* To hiss, to sputter, to sizzle.
sfriggolare, sfrigolare, *v.i.* To sputter (in a frying-pan).
sfringuellare, *v.i.* To chirp, to twitter; to chatter.
sfrittellarsi, *v.r.* To get spattered with grease.
sfrondamento, *n.m.f.* Stripping off leaves; divestment; spoliation.
sfrondare, *v.t.* To strip off leaves; to divest, to take off; to rid of; to curtail.
sfrondatura, *n.f.* Stripping off leaves; despoilment.
sfrontataggine, sfrontatezza, *n.f.* Impudence, effrontery, shamelessness.
sfrontatamente, *adv.* Impudently, with effrontery.
sfrontato, *a.* Impudent, shameless; cheeky; brazen-faced.
sfruconare, *v.i.* To poke about, to prod.
sfrusciare, *v.i.* To rustle.
sfruttamento, *n.m.* Exploitation, profiteering.
sfruttare, *v.t.i.* To exploit, to sweat (labour); to profiteer; to exhaust (mines etc.); to profit by, to abuse; to misuse; to sterilize. **— una miniera,** to exploit a mine.
sfruttarsi, *v.r.* To become exhausted, to be worked out.
sfruttatore, sfruttatrice, *n.m.f.* Exploiter, sweater; profiteer.
sfucinata, *n.f.* Output (of books, etc.), batch.
sfuggente, *a.* Fleeting; receding (forehead, chin).
sfuggevole [sfuggEvole], *a.* Fleeting, transitory, transient.
sfuggevolmente, *adv.* Fleetingly.
sfuggimento, *n.m.* Escape, flight.
sfuggire, *v.t.i.* To escape, to avoid, to shun; to miss; to get off, to get away; to pass unnoticed. **— dalle mani,** to slip from one's hands; **lasciarsi — un segreto,** to let a secret out; **lasciarsi — un' occasione,** to miss an opportunity.
sfuggita, *adv.* In passing. **Alla —, di —,** incidentally, in passing hastily, in a hurry.
sfumamento, *n.m.* Evaporation; disappearance.
sfumare, *v.t.i.* To tone down (in colour, etc.), to shade, to tint; (*Mus.*) to diminish; to evaporate, to vanish, to disappear; to come to nothing; to end in smoke.
sfumatamente, *adv.* Well-shaded; little by little, by degrees.
sfumatezza, *n.f.* Delicacy of shading.
sfumatura, *n.f.* Shade, shading, hue; gradation.
sfumino, *n.m.* (*Art*) Stump (for shading).
sfuriare, *v.i.* To rage, to fly into a passion.
sfuriata, *n.f.* Outburst of rage, fit of passion; tirade.
sgabbiare, *v.t.* To uncage.
sgabellare, *v.t.* To take out of bond.
sgabellarsi, *v.r.* To get rid of.
sgabello, *n.m.* Stool.
sgabuzzino, *n.m.* Poky little room; closet; lumber-room; (*Mil.*) dug-out.
sgagliardare, sgagliardire, *v.t.* To weaken, to enfeeble.
sgagliardarsi, *v.r.* To grow feeble.
sgallare, *v.t.i.* To blister.
sgallettare, *v.i.* To flirt.
sgallettio [sgallettIo], *n.m.* Flirting, coquetry.
sgambare, *v.t.i.* To break the stalk (of a flower); to stride, to walk fast.
sgambata, *n.f.* Long walk; run.
sgambettare, *v.i.* To walk with short paces, to mince; to trot along; to frisk, to trip; to toddle.
sgambettio [sgambettIo], *n.m.* Tripping, gambol, playing about.
sgambetto, *n.m.* Caper, trip, jump, frisk. **Dare lo — a,** to trip up; to get someone else's job, to supplant.
sganasciamento, *n.m.* Burst of laughter.
sganasciarsi, *v.r.* To dislocate one's jaw. **— dal ridere,** to split one's sides with laughing.
sganasciata, *n.f.* Roar of laughter.
sganciamento, *n.m.* Unhooking; release.
sganciare, *v.t.* To unhook, to release, to unfasten; (*Aviat.*) to drop (bombs, etc.); (*Rail.*) to unhook (cars, etc.).
sgangheramento, *n.m.* Unhinging, dislocating.
sgangherare, *v.t.* To unhinge, to dislocate; to disarrange.
sgangheratamente, *adv.* Immoderately, rudely, awkwardly, clumsily.
sgangherato, *a.* Unhinged, loose-jointed, awkward, gangling; disarranged; shattered; immoderate (of laughter). **Una macchina sgangherata,** an elderly, dilapidated car.
sgannare, *v.t.* (*Poet.*) To undeceive.
sgarbataggine [sgarbatAggine], *n.f.* Rudeness, incivility.
sgarbatamente, *adv.* Rudely, impolitely.
sgarbatezza, sgarberia [sgarberIa], *n.f.* Rudeness, incivility, uncouthness.
sgarbato, *a.* Rude, impolite, uncivil; uncouth, clumsy, awkward.
sgarbo, *n.m.* Piece of rudeness, bad grace, incivility.
sgargarizzare [cp. **gargarizzare**].
sgargiante, *a.* Showy, gaudy.
sgarrare, *v.i.* To be mistaken, to be wrong; to err, to make a slip.

sgattaiolare, *v.i.* To slip away, to slink off; to wriggle out (of a difficulty).
sgavazzare [cp. **gavazzare**].
sgelare, *v.t.i.* To thaw, to melt.
sgelo, *n.m.* Thaw.
sghembato, *a.* Crooked; cut on the slant.
sghembo, *a.* Crooked, oblique, slanting, awry; tortuous. **A —,** awry, on the slant, obliquely. **Colla cravatta a sghembo,** with his tie askew.
sgheronato, *a.* Cut on the skew.
sgherro, *n.m.* Constable; police-spy; bailiff; assassin, hired ruffian.
sghiacciare, *v.i.* To thaw.
sghignare, *v.i.* To grin.
sghignazzamento, *n.m.* Scornful laughter.
sghignazzare, *v.i.* To laugh scornfully, to grin; to sneer, to guffaw.
sghignazzata, *n.f.* Burst of derisive laughter; guffaw.
sghilembo, *a.* Bent, crooked, malformed.
sghimbescio [sghimbEscio], *a.* Crooked, tortuous, slanting. **A —,** awry, aslant.
sghiribizzo [cp. **ghiribizzo**].
sgobbare, *v.i.* To drudge, to fag; (*colloq.*) to swot.
sgobbo, *n.m.* Fag, drudge; drudgery.
sgobbone, *n.m.* (*colloq.*) Swotter; hard-worker; coach (of pupils).
sgocciolare, *v.t.i.* To pour out in drops; to drip, to trickle, to drop.
sgocciolatoio [sgocciolatOio], *n.m.* (*Arch.*) Drip-stone; gutter; eaves.
sgocciolatura, *n.f.* Dripping, drop.
sgocciolio [sgocciolIo], *n.m.* Continual dripping.
sgocciolo [sgOcciolo], *n.m.* Last drop; dripping. **Essere agli sgoccioli,** to be on the last lap, to be finishing.
sgolarsi, *v.r.* To shout oneself hoarse.
sgomberamento, sgombramento, *n.m.* Removal, clearing out, moving (from one's house); (street) cleaning.
sgomberare, sgombrare, *v.t.i.* To clear out, to remove, to sweep away; to go away, to remove (one's place of residence).
sgombero, sgombro (1), *n.m.* Removal, clearance (of land, etc.).
sgombro (2), *n.m.* (*Zool.*) Mackerel.
sgombro, sgombero, *a.* Empty, unoccupied, free.
sgomentare, *v.t.* To alarm, to frighten, to dismay.
sgomentarsi, *v.r.* To be daunted, to be dismayed, to get frightened.
sgomento, *n.m.a.* Alarm, dismay, fright; alarmed, frightened.
sgominare, *v.t.* To rout, to defeat, to put to flight, to scatter.
sgominio [sgominIo], *n.m.* Rout, dispersal; confusion.
sgomitolare, *v.t.* To unwind.
sgommare, *v.t.* To ungum.
sgonfiamento, *n.m.* Deflation, collapse.
sgonfiare, *v.t.i.* To deflate, to empty; to bring down; to go down (of a tyre, etc.); (*colloq.*) to debunk; to annoy, to vex, to bother.
sgonfiarsi, *v.r.* To become deflated; (*Med.*) to go down (of a swelling).
sgonfiatura, *n.f.* Deflation.
sgonfio [sgOnfio], *a.* Deflated, let down, gone down (of swelling).
sgonfiotto, *n.m.* Pastry puff; fritter.
sgonnellare, *v.i.* To fuss; to gad about (of women).
sgonnellona, *n.f.* Gad-about, busybody.
sgorbia [sgOrbia], *n.f.* Gouge (chisel).
sgorbiare, *v.t.* To scribble, to scrawl; to blot.
sgorbio [sgOrbio], *n.m.* Scribble, blot, smudge.
sgorgamento, *n.m.* Outflowing, outpouring; overflow.
sgorgare, *v.i.* To flow out, to gush out, to pour out; to spring, to well; to disgorge. **— dal cuore,** to spring from one's heart.
sgorgo, *n.m.* Outflow, discharge, outlet, gush, flow.
sgovernare, *v.i.* To misgovern.
sgoverno, *n.m.* Misgovernment, mismanagement.
sgozzare, *v.t.* To cut the throat of; to slaughter.
sgozzino, *n.m.* Usurer.
sgradevole [sgradEvole], *a.* Disagreeable, unpleasant.
sgradevolezza, *n.f.* Unpleasantness.
sgradevolmente, *adv.* Unpleasantly.
sgradire, *v.t.i.* To displease; to dislike.
sgradito, *a.* Unpleasant; undesirable, disliked.
sgraffa, *n.f.* (*Print.*) Brace.
sgraffiare, *v.t.* To scratch, to scrape (with the nails); to pilfer, to steal.
sgraffiatura, *n.f.* Scratch, abrasion.
sgraffignare, *v.t.* To scratch; to pilfer, "to pinch".
sgraffio [sgrAffio], *n.m.* Scratch, abrasion.
sgrammaticare, *v.i.* To make mistakes in grammar, to speak ungrammatically.
sgrammaticato, *a.* Ungrammatical.
sgrammaticatura, *n.f.* Grammatical error, bad grammar.
sgranamento, *n.m.* Husking, shelling.
sgranare, *v.t.* To husk, to shell. (*fig.*) **— gli occhi,** to open the eyes wide, to stare.
sgranarsi, *v.r.* To crumble, to fall to dust.
sgranatura, *n.f.* Husking, shelling.
sgranchire, *v.t.* To stretch.
sgranchirsi, *v.r.* To stretch oneself; to rouse oneself to action. **— le gambe,** to stretch one's legs.
sgrandire, *v.t.* To enlarge.
sgrandirsi, *v.r.* To grow bigger, to become larger.
sgranellare, *v.t.* To shell, to husk.
sgranellatura, *n.f.* Shelling, husking.
sgranocchiare, *v.t.* To crunch, to nibble.
sgrassare, *v.t.* To skim the grease from, to take the fat from. **— un abito,** to remove the grease-stains from a coat.
sgraticciare, *v.t.* To disentangle, to unravel, to undo.
sgravamento, *n.m.* Lightening, relieving; alleviation.
sgravare, *v.t.* To lighten, to unload, to unburden; to relieve.
sgravarsi, *v.r.* To lighten oneself, to unburden oneself; (*Med.*) to be delivered (of a child), to give birth to; to litter (of dogs, etc.); **— la coscienza,** to ease one's conscience.

sgravio [sgrAvio], *n.m.* Relief, alleviation. **A — di coscienza,** for conscience' sake; **sgravi fiscali,** tax reductions.
sgraziataggine [sgraziatAggine], *n.f.* Clumsiness, awkwardness.
sgraziatamente, *adv.* Unluckily, unfortunately; awkwardly.
sgraziato, *a.* Ungraceful, awkward, clumsy; unlucky, unfortunate.
sgretolamento, *n.m.* Crumbling away, shattering; breaking down, nibbling.
sgretolare, *v.t.i.* To break up, to shatter; to nibble (bread, etc.); to gnash (one's teeth).
sgretolarsi, *v.r.* To crumble, to fall to pieces, to break down.
sgridare, *v.t.* To scold, to rebuke, to chide, to rail at.
sgridata, *n.f.* Scolding, reprimand, reproof, rebuke.
sgrigliolo [sgrIgliolo], *n.m.* Creaking (of shoes).
sgrinfie [sgrInfie], *n.f.pl.* Claws, thievish hands.
sgrondare, *v.i.* To trickle [cp. **grondare**].
sgrossare [cp. **digrossare**].
sgrovigliare, *v.t.* To disentangle, to undo, to unknot.
sgrugnare, *v.t.* To strike in the face.
sgrugnata, *n.f.* Blow in the face.
sgrugno, sgrugnone, *n.m.* Blow in the face, cuff on the cheek, heavy slap.
sguaiataggine [sguaiatAggine], *n.f.* Grossness, vulgarity, coarseness; stupidity.
sguaiatamente, *adv.* Grossly, vulgarly.
sguaiato, *n.m.* Ill-mannered, coarse fellow.
sguaiato, *a.* Gross, unrefined, coarse; tasteless, vulgar; clumsy.
sguainare, *v.t.* To unsheathe, to draw (a sword).
sgualcire, *v.t.* To rumple, to crumple, to wrinkle.
sgualdrina, *n.f.* Whore, harlot, strumpet; slut, (*colloq.*) tart.
sguancia [sguAncia], *n.f.* Cheek-strap of a bridle.
sguardo, *n.m.* Look, glance; sight, view. **Al primo —,** at first glance; **ha uno — triste,** he has a wistful look; **gettare uno — sopra,** to have a look at, to take a glance at; **— tenero,** tender look.
sguarnire, sguernire, *v.t.* To strip off, to despoil; to dismantle.
sguattera, sguattero [sguAttera, -o], *n.f.m.* Scullery-maid; scullery-boy, scullion.
sguazzare, *v.t.i.* To paddle about (in water), to wallow. **— nella richezza,** to roll in wealth.
sguercire, *v.t.i.* To squint.
sguernire [cp. **sguarnire**].
sguinzagliare, *v.t.* To unleash, to let loose, to unchain; to launch.
sguisciare, sguizzare, *v.i.* To wriggle, to slip away; to slither, to slide.
sgusciare, *v.t.i.* To shell, to husk; to slip away, to make off.
si , *pron.* Oneself, one, himself, herself; we; each other. **Si dice,** they say, people say, it is said; **si salutarono,** they bowed to each other; **si crederebbe,** one would imagine; **Che cosa si dirà?** What will people think? **Dove si va?** Where are we going? **non si può vivere qui,** one cannot live here, it is impossible to live here; **mi si dice che,** I'm told that; **si amano,** they love one another; **egli si loda,** he praises himself.
si, *n.m.* (*Mus.*) Si, B.
sì, *adv.* Yes; thus, so. **Sì davvero,** yes, indeed; **essere fra il sì e il no,** to be in doubt; **dire di sì,** to say yes; **mi par di sì,** I think so; **un giorno sì e l'altro no,** every other day; **la lingua del sì,** Italian; **è sì bello,** it's so nice; **rispondere di —,** to answer in the affirmative.
sia, *conj.* Either, whether or. **Sia l'uno che l'altro,** both.
siamese, *n.m.a.* Siamese.
sibarita (*pl.* **sibariti**), *n.m.* Sybarite.
Siberia [sıbEria], *n.f.* (*Geog.*) Siberia.
siberiano, *n.m.a.* Siberian.
sibilante, *n.f.a.* Sibilant.
sibilare, *v.i.* To hiss, to whistle.
sibilio [sibilIo], *n.m.* Prolonged hissing, whistling.
sibilla, *n.f.* Sibyl, prophetess.
sibillino, *a.* Sibylline, oracular, cryptic.
sibilo [sIbilo], *n.m.* Hiss, whistle; wheezing.
sicano, *n.m.a.* (*obs.*) Sicilian.
sicario [sicArio], *n.m.* Cut-throat; hired assassin, ruffian.
sicchè, *conj.* So that, thus, therefore.
siccità [-à], *n.f.* Drought, dryness; dry weather.
siccome, *conj.adv.* As, for, since. **— lo desidero,** since I wish it.
Sicilia [sicIlia], *n.f.* (*Geog.*) Sicily.
siciliano, *n.m.a.* Sicilian.
sicofante, *n.m.* Spy, hired ruffian, informer; sycophant.
sicomoro [sicOmoro, sicomOro], *n.m.* (*Bot.*) Sycamore.
siculo [sIculo], *n.m.a.* (*Lit.*) Sicilian.
sicumera, *n.f.* Conceit, self-sufficiency, priggishness, ostentation, pomposity.
sicura, *n.f.* Safety-catch (in firearms).
sicuramente, *adv.* Assuredly, certainly; safely.
sicurezza, *n.f.* Safety, security; sureness, certainty; assurance, trust, confidence. **Valvola di —,** safety-valve; **aver la — di,** to have the certainty of, to be sure of; **la pubblica —,** the police; **misura di —,** precautionary measure; **rasoio di —,** safety-razor; **uscita di —,** emergency exit; **lampada di —,** safety lamp, Davy lamp.
sicuro, *n.m.* Safety. **Stare al —,** to stay in a safe place; **mettere al —,** to put in safety.
sicuro, *a.* Sure, certain; safe, secure; firm, steady, trustworthy. **Ne siete —?** Are you sure of it? **un amico —,** a trusty friend; **di —,** for certain; **— di sè,** self-confident; **a colpo —,** for certain; **in mani sicure,** in safe hands.
sicurtà [-à], *n.f.* Assurance, insurance guarantee, security.
siderale, *a.* Sidereal.
sidereo [sidEreo], *a.* Starry.
siderite, *n.f.* (*Min.*) Siderite, loadstone.
siderurgia [siderurgIa], *n.f.* Iron-working, iron-industry.
siderurgico [siderUrgico], *a.* Iron, iron-working. **Stabilimento —,** iron-works.
sidro, *n.m.* Cider.
sienese, *n.m.a.* Sienese.
siepaia [siepAia], *n.f.* Hedgerow.

siepare, *v.t.* To hedge (a field).
siepe, *n.f.* Hedge; barrier; (*Sport*) hurdle. **Corsa di siepi,** steeple-chase.
siero, *n.m.* Whey; (*Med.*) serum.
sieroso, *a.* Serous.
sieroterapia [sieroterapIa], *n.f.* (*Med.*) Serum-therapy.
siesta, *n.f.* Siesta, nap, "forty-winks". **Fare la —,** to rest after lunch.
siffattamente, *adv.* In such a manner.
siffatto, *a.* Such, such a.
sifilicomio [sifilicOmio], *n.m.* Hospital for venereal diseases.
sifilide [sifIlide], *n.f.* (*Med.*) Syphilis.
sifilitico [sifilItico], *n.m.a.* Syphilitic.
sifonare, *v.t.* To siphon.
sifone, *n.m.* Siphon.
sigaraia, sigaraio [sigarAia, -o], *n.f.m.* Cigar-maker.
sigaretta, *n.f.* Cigarette.
sigaro [sIgaro], *n.m.* Cigar. **— leggero,** mild cigar.
sigillare, *v.t.* To seal; to close, to stop up; to mark, to stamp.
sigillatura, *n.f.* Sealing, seal.
sigillo, *n.m.* Seal, signet; mark, impression.
sigla, *n.f.* Initials, monogram; abbreviation.
signifero [signIfero], *n.m.* (*Hist.*) Standard-bearer.
significamento, *n.m.* Signification, meaning.
significante, *a.* Significant, expressive.
significantemente, *adv.* Significantly.
significanza, *n.f.* significance.
significare, *v.t.i.* To mean, to signify, to denote; to indicate, to imply; to make known. **Cosa significa?** What does it mean? **non significa nulla,** it doesn't mean anything, it is immaterial.
significativo, *a.* Significant; noteworthy; expressive.
significativamente, *adv.* Significantly, expressively.
significato, *n.m.* Meaning; sense, significance; import, importance.
signora, *n.f.* Lady; woman; Madam, Mrs.; wife. **La — Rossi,** Mrs. Rossi; **si signora, sissignora,** yes, Madam; **è una vera —,** she is a true lady; **Nostra Signora,** Our Lady.
signore, *n.m.* Gentleman, Sir, Mr.; Our Lord, God. **Si signore, sissignore,** yes, Sir; **il — Rossi,** Mr. Rossi; **da gran —,** in lordly style; **fare il —,** to live on one's income, to live well; **passarsela da —,** to live like a lord; **pregare il Signore,** to pray God.
signoreggiamento, *n.m.* Domination.
signoreggiare, *v.t.i.* To rule over, to dominate (in all senses); to domineer, to command, to control.
signorescamente, *adv.* In a lordly style.
signoresco, *a.* Lordly, gentlemanly.
signoria [signorIa], *n.f.* Mastery, rule, sovereignty, dominion; (*Hist.*) governing council of a medieval city or republic; signoria, seignory. **Prego la Signoria Vostra** (abbrev. **V.S.**), I beg you, Sir (in correspondence).
signorile, *a.* Gentlemanly, refined, lordly, noble, stately, aristocratic.
signorilità [-à], *n.f.* Gentlemanliness, refinement of manners, courtliness; generosity, liberality.
signorilmente, *adv.* In a courtly way.
signorina, *n.f.* Young lady, unmarried woman; Miss.
signorino, *n.m.* Young man, Master.
signorona, *n.f.* Lady of rank; wealthy woman.
signorone, *n.m.* Man of birth, man of title; wealthy man.
signorotto, *n.m.* Country squire; petty lord, lordling.
silene, *n.f.* (*Bot.*) Campion.
silente, *a.* Silent, still.
silenziario [silenziArio], *n.m.* Trappist, Silentiary.
silenziatore, *n.m.* (*Motor., etc.*) Silencer; (*Am.*) muffler.
silenzio [silEnzio], *n.m.* Silence, stillness; taciturnity; (*Mil.*) last post. **Far —,** to keep silent; **passare sotto —,** to pass over in silence; **serbare il —,** to keep silent (about something); **Silenzio!** Silence! Hold your tongue!
silenziosamente, *adv.* Silently, noiselessly.
silenziosità [-à], *n.f.* Noiselessness, stillness; taciturnity.
silenzioso, *a.* Silent, quiet, noiseless; taciturn. **Una camera silenziosa,** a sound-proof room.
silfide [sIlfide], *n.f.* Sylph.
silicato, *n.m.* (*Chem.*) Silicate.
silice [sIlice], *n.f.* (*Geol.Min.*) Silica, flint.
siliceo [silIceo], *a.* Siliceous, flinty.
silicio [silIcio], *n.m.* (*Metal.*) Silicon, silicium.
sillaba [sIllaba], *n.f.* Syllable. **Non disse —,** he didn't say a word; **non sapere una — di,** to be completely ignorant of.
sillabare, *v.t.* To spell out; to articulate.
sillabario [sillabArio], *n.m.* Spelling-book, primer.
sillabazione, *n.f.* Syllabification.
sillabico [sillAbico], *a.* Syllabic.
sillabo [sIllabo], *n.m.* Syllabus (in all senses).
sillepsi, sillessi, *n. f.* (*Gram.*) Syllepsis.
silloge, *n.f.* (*Lit.*) Collection.
sillogismo, *n.m.* Syllogism.
sillogistica [sillogIstica], *n.f.* Syllogistics.
sillogistico [sillogIstico], *a.* Syllogistic.
sillogizzare, *v.i.* To syllogize.
silo, *n.m.* (*Agric.*) Silo. **Conservazione nel —,** ensilage.
silografia [silografIa], *n.f.* Wood-engraving.
silografo [silOgrafo], *n.m.* Wood-engraver.
siluetta, *n.f.* Silhouette.
siluramento, *n.m.* Torpedoing.
silurante, *n.f.* Torpedo-boat. **Aero —,** torpedo-carrying aircraft.
silurare, *v.t.* To torpedo; (*fig.*) to cashier, to sack, to dismiss.
siluro, *n.m.* Torpedo; (*Zool.*) silurus, cat-fish.
silvano, *a.* Sylvan.
silvestre, *a.* Wild, rustic, woody.
silvestrini, *n.m.pl.* (*Eccles.*) Sylvestrine monks (Benedictines).
silvia [sIlvia], *n.f.* (*Zool.*) Bird of the warbler family.
silvicoltore, *n.m.* Forester; forest-keeper.
silvicultura, *n.f.* Forestry.
simbiosi, *n.f.* (*Biol.*) Symbiosis.
simboleggiamento, *n.m.* Symbolization.
simboleggiare, simbolizzare, *v.t.* To symbolize, to typify, to represent.
simbolicamente, *adv.* Symbolically.

simbolico [simbOlico], *a.* Symbolic, symbolical.
simbolismo, *n.m.* Symbolism.
simbolizzare [cp. **simboleggiare**].
simbolo [sImbolo], *n.m.* Symbol, emblem, type; creed. **— degli apostoli,** the Apostles' Creed.
simetria [cp. **simmetria**].
similare, *a.* Similar, alike, homogeneous.
similarità [**-à**], *n.f.* Similarity, likeness, homogeneity.
simile [sImile], *n.m.* Fellow, equal, match; fellow creature. **I nostri simili,** our fellow men; **amate vostri —,** love your fellows.
simile [sImile], *a.* Similar, equal, alike; resembling. **Con gente —,** with such people; **in — circostanza,** in like circumstances; **— a lui,** like him; **in modo —,** in a similar manner; **molto — al padre,** very like his father.
similitudine [similitUdine], *n.f.* Likeness, similitude, similarity; simile.
similmente, *adv.* Likewise, equally, similarly, in the same way.
similoro, *n.m.* Pinchbeck, tinsel.
simmetria [simmetrIa], *n.f.* Symmetry, proportion.
simmetricamente, *adv.* Symmetrically.
simmetrico [simmEtrico], *a.* Symmetric, symmetrical.
simmetrizzare, *v.t.* To symmetrize, to make symmetrical.
simoneggiare, *v.i.* (*Eccles.*) To practise simony.
simonia [simonIa], *n.f.* Simony.
simoniacamente, *adv.* By means of simony.
simoniaco [simonIaco], *n.m.a.* Simoniac.
simpatia [simpatIa], *n.f.* Liking, inclination, attachment, affection; fellow-feeling, sympathy (in all senses). **Nutrire — per,** to sympathize with; **ho una grande — per,** I have a great liking for.
simpaticamente, *adv.* Kindly, sympathetically.
simpatico [simpAtico], *a.* Attractive, charming, genial, nice, agreeable, congenial. **È un uomo —,** he's a nice man; **inchiostro —,** sympathetic ink, invisible ink; (*Med.*) **sistema del gran —,** sympathetic nerve; **mi è molto —,** I like him very much.
simpatizzante, *n.m.a.* Sympathizer, supporter; sympathizing.
simpatizzare, *v.i.* To inspire sympathy, to sympathize, to get on with, to take a liking to.
simposiarco, *n.m.* (*Lit.*) Head of the banquet; toast-master.
simposio [simpOsio], *n.m.* Symposium, banquet.
simulacro, *n.m.* Image, semblance, simulacrum; shadow; sham.
simulamento, *n.m.* Simulation.
simulare, *v.t.i.* To simulate, to feign, to dissemble, to counterfeit.
simulatamente, *adv.* Dissemblingly.
simulatore, simulatrice, *n.m.f.* Dissembler.
simulazione, *n.f.* Simulation, dissembling, feigning, shamming.
simultaneamente, *adv.* Simultaneously.
simultaneità [**-à**], *n.f.* Simultaneousness.
simultaneo [simultAneo], *a.* Simultaneous.
sinagoga, *n.f.* Synagogue.
sinallagmatico [sinallagmAtico], *a.* Bilateral.
sinceramente, *adv.* Sincerely, truly; honestly; really. **— lieto,** truly happy.
sincerare, *v.t.* To convince; to assure; to acquit; to testify.
sincerarsi, *v.r.* To make oneself sure, to satisfy oneself, to be convinced.
sincerità [**-à**], *n.f.* Sincerity, frankness, honesty, candour. **— di linguaggio,** frankness, bluntness of speech.
sincero, *a.* Sincere, true, open, pure, genuine; downright; heartfelt. **La mia sincera opinione,** my honest opinion; **vino —,** pure, unadulterated wine.
sinchè [cp. **finchè**].
sincopare, *v.t.* To syncopate; to elide, to contract.
sincopato, *p.p.a.* Syncopated. **Musica sincopata,** rag-time, jazz.
sincopatura, *n.f.* Syncopation.
sincope [sIncope], *n.f.* Syncope (in all senses); syncopation, elision.
sincretismo, *n.m.* Syncretism.
sincronismo, *n.m.* Synchronism.
sincronizzare, *v.t.i.* To synchronize.
sincrono [sIncrono], *a.* Synchronous, simultaneous.
sindacabile [sindacAbile], *a.* Controllable, subject to supervision; verifiable.
sindacabilità [**-à**], *n.f.* Liability to control.
sindacale, *a.* Pertaining to a syndicate or corporation.
sindacalismo, *n.m.* Syndicalism.
sindacalista *pl.* **sindacalisti**), *n.m.* Syndicalist, trade-unionist.
sindacare, *v.t.* To control, to audit; to censure.
sindacato, *n.m.* (*Comm.*) Syndicate, trust; (*Pol.*) trade (union; guild; mayoralty.
sindacatore, sindacatrice, *n.m.f.* Controller, supervisor; censor; (*fig.*) fault-finder.
sindacazione, *n.f.* Control, supervision.
sindaco [sIndaco], *n.m.* Mayor (of city or borough); (*Comm.*) auditor.
sinderesi [sindEresi], *n.f.* Sting of conscience. (*colloq.*) **Perder la —,** to act foolishly.
sindone [sIndone], *n.f.* (*Eccles.*) Sindon; Christ's shroud.
sinecura, *n.f.* Sinecure.
sineddoche [sinEddoche], *n.f.* Synecdoche.
sinedrio [sinEdrio], *n.m.* (*Hist.*) Sanhedrin; (*fig.*) council, congress.
sineresi [sinEresi], *n.f.* (*Gram.*) Synaeresis.
sinfonia [sinfonIa], *n.f.* Symphony.
sinfonico [sinfOnico], *a.* Symphonic.
singhiozzare, *v.i.* To sob; to hiccup. **Parlava singhiozzando,** he spoke while sobbing.
singhiozzio [singhiozzIo], *n.m.* Sobbing; hiccuping.
singhiozzo, *n.m.* Sob; hiccup.
singolare, *n.m.* (*Gram.*) Singular; (*Tennis*) singles.
singolare, *a.* Singular (in all senses); remarkable; peculiar, odd; single.
singolarità [**-à**], *n.f.* Singularity; peculiarity, oddness.
singolareggiare, *v.i.* To be singular, to be odd (in appearance, etc.).

singolarizzare, *v.t.* To single out, to singularize.
singolarmente, *adv.* Singularly, singly.
singolo [sIngolo], *n.m.* Individual, person. **I singoli,** the individuals; (*Tennis*) singles; (*Rowing*) skiff.
singolo [sIngolo], *a.* Single, individual. **In ogni — caso,** in each case.
singulto, *n.m.* Sob; hiccup.
siniscalco, *n.m.* (*Hist.*) Seneschal.
sinistra, *n.f.* Left hand, left-hand side; (*Pol.*) the left. **Tenere la —,** keep to the left; **voltare a —,** to turn to the left.
sinistramente, *adv.* Grimly, inauspiciously, ominously; disastrously.
sinistrato, *a.* Damaged, hit; bombed out.
sinistro, *n.m.* Accident, mishap, disaster.
sinistro, *a.* Left, left-hand; sinister, ill-omened, ominous; grim.
sinistrorso, *a.* Turning from the observer's right to the left; sinistrorse.
sino, *prep.* Until, till, up to; as far as. **— quando,** till when; **— a Roma,** as far as Rome; **— domani,** until tomorrow; **sin dove ?** How far? **sino d'allora,** since then [cp. **fino**].
sinodale, *a.* (*Eccles.*) Synodal.
sinodo [sInodo], *n.m.* Synod.
sinologo [sinOlogo], *n.m.* Sinologue, scholar in Chinese.
sinonimamente, *adv.* Synonymously.
sinonimico [sinonImico], *a.* Synonymous.
sinonimo [sinOnimo], *n.m.a.* Synonym; synonymous.
sinora [cp. **finora**].
sinossi, *n.f.* Synopsis, summary.
sinottico [sinOttico], *a.* Synoptic, synoptical. **Vangeli sinottici,** synoptic gospels.
sinoviale, *a.* (*Anat.*) Synovial.
sinovite, *n.f.* (*Med.*) Synovitis.
sintassi, *n.f.* Syntax.
sintattico [sintAttico], *a.* Syntactic.
sintesi [sIntesi], *n.f.* Synthesis.
sinteticamente, *adv.* Synthetically.
sintetico [sintEtico], *a.* Synthetic.
sintetizzare, *v.t.* To synthetize.
sintomatico [sintomAtico], *a.* Symptomatic, indicative.
sintomatologia [sintomatologIa], *n.f.* Symptomatology.
sintomo [sIntomo], *n.m.* Symptom; sign, indication.
sintonia [sintonIa], *n.f.* (*Radio*) Syntony.
sintonizzare, *v.t.* (*Radio*) To syntonize, to tune-up.
sinuosamente, *adv.* Sinuously.
sinuosità [-à], *n.f.* Sinuosity, tortuousness, crookedness; bend. **Le — del fiume,** the windings of the river.
sinuoso, *a.* Sinuous, tortuous, crooked, winding.
sionismo, *n.m.* Zionism.
sionista, *n.m.* Zionist.
sipario [sipArio], *n.m.* (*Theat.*) Curtain. **Alzare, calare il —,** to raise, to lower the curtain.
Siracusa, *n.f.* (*Geog.*) Syracuse.
sire, *n.m.* Lord, Sire (when addressing the King).
sirena, *n.f.* (*Myth.*) Siren; (signal) siren, hooter.
Siria [sIria], *n.f.* (*Geog.*) Syria.
siriaco, siriano [sirIaco], *n.m.a.* Syrian.
siringa, *n.f.* Syringe; (*Bot.*) syringa, lilac.
siringare, *v.t.* To syringe; to inject; (*colloq.*) to cheat, to take in.
siringatura, *n.f.* Syringing, injection.
Sirio [sIrio], *n.m.* (*Astron.*) Sirius.
sirocchia [sirOcchia], *n.f.* (*obs.*) Sister.
sirocco [cp. **scirocco**].
siroppo, *n.m.* Syrup [cp. **sciroppo**].
sirti, *n.f.pl.* Quicksands.
Sisifo [sIsifo], *n.m.* (*Myth.*) Sisyphus. **Lavoro di —,** labour of Sisyphus.
sismico [sIsmico], *a.* Seismic, seismal.
sismografia [sismografIa], *n.f.* Seismography.
sismografo [sismOgrafo], *n.m.* Seismographer.
sismologia [sismologIa], *n.f.* Seismology.
sismologo [sismOlogo], *n.m.* Seismologist.
sissignora, sissignore, *adv.* Yes, Madam; Yes, Sir [cp. **sì**].
sistema (pl. **sistemi**), *n.m.* System; method, co-ordination, arrangement. **— metrico,** (*or* **decimale**), metric system; **cambiar —,** to change one's methods; (*Rail.*) **— di blocco,** block-system.
sistemare, *v.t.* To arrange, to regulate, to systematize; to reorganize.
sistemarsi, *v.r.* To settle down.
sistematicamente, *adv.* Systematically.
sistematico [sistemAtico], *a.* Systematic.
sistematore, *n.m.* Reorganizer; maker of systems.
sistemazione, *n.f.* Systemization; arrangement, regulation; reorganization; lay-out. **— di un affare,** settlement of a matter; (*Naut.*) **— della stiva,** trimming the hold.
sistino, *a.* Sistine (from Pope Sixtus IV). **Capella Sistina,** Sistine Chapel.
sistola [sIstola], *n.f.* Hose (for watering).
sistole [sIstole], *n.f.* (*Anat.*) Systole.
sistro, *n.m.* (*Mus.*) Sistrum.
sitibondo, *a.* Thirsty, parched with thirst; greedy, avid; eager.
sitiologia [sitiologIa], *n.f.* Sitiology, dietetics.
sito (1), *n.m.* Place, spot, position, site.
sito (2), *n.m.* Stench, stink, bad smell.
sito, *a.* Situated, sited, placed.
situare, *v.t.* To place, to site, to set. **Casa ben situata,** well-sited house.
situazione, *n.f.* Situation, position; condition, place, post.
Siviglia, *n.f.* (*Geog.*) Seville.
sizigia [sizIgia], *n.f.* (*Astron.*) Syzygy.
sizza, *n.f.* Bitterly cold north wind.
slabbrare, *v.t.i.* To cut off the lips; to break the top of a bottle; to chip, to break off; to overflow, to brim over.
slabbratura, *n.f.* Chipping, breaking off.
slacciare, *v.t.* To unlace, to unbind, to untie, to unfasten, to unbutton.
slacciarsi, *v.r.* To loosen one's dress; to unbutton oneself.
slanciamento, *n.m.* Hurling, flinging.
slanciare, *v.t.* To hurl, to fling, to throw; to urge, to impel.
slanciarsi, *v.r.* To rush on, to hurl oneself on; to dash forward.
slanciato, *p.p.a.* Dashed, hurled; slender, graceful, well-built, slim.
slancio [slAncio], *n.m.* Dash, bound, rush, onset; impetus; impulse. **Di primo —,** at the first impulse, at the onset, at once; **pieno di —,** full of go; **prender lo —,** to take a run.

slargamento, *n.f.* Enlargement.
slargare, *v.t.* To enlarge, to widen.
slargatura, *n.f.* Enlargement.
slattamento, *n.m.* Weaning.
slattare, *v.t.* To wean.
slavato, *a.* Pale, wan, colourless; insipid.
slavatura, *n.f.* Paleness, wanness.
slavo, *n.m.a.* Slav, Slavonic.
slavofilo [slavOfilo], *n.m.a.* Slavophil.
slavofobo [slavOfobo], *n.m.a.* Slavophobe.
sleale, *a.* Disloyal; unfair; treacherous.
slealmente, *adv.* Disloyally.
slealtà [-à], *n.f.* Disloyalty; perfidiousness; dishonesty; treachery.
slegamento, *n.m.* Unbinding, untying; loosening.
slegare, *v.t.* To untie, to undo, to unfasten, to disconnect.
slegarsi, *v.r.* To loosen oneself; to become untied, to get undone.
slegatamente, *adv.* Loosely, disconnectedly.
slegatura, *n.f.* Unfastening, disconnecting.
Slesia [slEsia], *n.f.* (*Geog.*) Silesia.
slitta, *n.f.* Sledge, sleigh; bob-sleigh. **Corsa in —,** sledge-ride.
slittamento, *n.m.* Sliding, gliding; (*Motor.*, etc.) skid, side-slip.
slittare, *v.i.* To slide, to glide; to ride in a sledge; (*Motor.*, etc.) to skid, to side-slip.
slittata, *n.f.* (*Motor.*) Skid.
slogamento, *n.m.* Dislocation.
slogare, *v.t.* To dislocate.
slogarsi, *v.r.* To dislocate; to get dislocated. **— il braccio,** to dislocate one's arm.
slogatura, *n.f.* Dislocation.
sloggiamento, *n.m.* Dislodgement; expulsion.
sloggiare, *v.t.i.* To dislodge, to drive out, to expel; to move, to leave one's house; to retire; to decamp.
slombare, *v.t.* To break the back of; to unnerve; to exhaust.
slombarsi, *v.r.* To knock oneself up, to get worn out.
slombato, *a.* Nerveless, flaccid, enervated.
slontanamento, *n.m.* Moving away.
slontanare, *v.t.* To remove, to move away.
slontanarsi, *v.r.* To withdraw to a distance.
Slovacchia, *n.f.* (*Geog.*) Slovakia.
slovacco, *n.m.a.* Slovak.
sloveno, *n.m.a.* Slovene.
slungare, *v.t.* To prolong.
smaccare, *v.t.* To put to shame.
smaccato, *a.* Sickening; excessive.
smacchiare, *v.t.* To clean, to remove stains from; to scour.
smacchiatore, smacchiatrice, *n.m.f.* Cleaner.
smacchiatura, *n.f.* Cleaning, scouring.
smacco, *n.m.* Shame, humiliation, mortification; affront, insult; failure.
smagarsi, *v.r.* To lose heart, to lose courage, to be dismayed.
smagliante, *a.* Shining, brilliant, dazzling; gaudy.
smagliare (1), *v.t.* To undo meshes (of a net, etc.); to unravel (knitting).
smagliare (2), *v.i.* To shine, to sparkle, to glitter, to glare.
smagliarsi, *v.r.* To ladder (of stockings).
smagliatura, *n.f.* Ladder (in stockings).
smagnetizzare, *v.t.* To demagnetize.
smagnetizzazione, *n.f.* Demagnetization.
smagrare, smagrire, *v.i.* To grow thin, to become lean.
smagrimento, *n.m.* Emaciation, leanness.
smaliziare, *v.t.* To sharpen the wits of; to make crafty.
smaliziato, *a.* Crafty, cunning.
smaltamento, *n.m.* Enamelling.
smaltare, *v.t.* To enamel; to glaze.
smaltato, *p.p.a.* Enamelled. **— di fiori,** smothered in flowers.
smaltatura, *n.f.* Enamel-work, enamelling.
smaltimento, *n.m.* Digesting, digestion; getting rid of.
smaltire, *v.t.* To get rid of; to sell off; to digest, to sleep off. **— la sbornia,** to sleep off drunkenness; **— un'ingiuria,** to swallow an insult.
smaltista (*pl.* **smaltisti**), *n.m.* Enameller.
smaltitoio [smaltitOio], *n.m.* Drain, sewer; public urinal.
smalto, *n.m.* Enamel, glaze; (*Anat.*) enamel (of teeth).
smammolarsi, *v.r.* To laugh heartily; to be very happy.
smanacciare, *v.i.* To clap (the hands) loudly.
smanacciata, *n.f.* Loud applause.
smanceria [smancerIa], *n.f.* Affectation, affectedness; simpering; mawkishness. **Fare delle smancerie,** to smirk.
smanceroso, *a.* Affected, mincing; mawkish, over-nice.
smangiare, *v.t.* To eat away, to corrode, to wear down.
smangiarsi, *v.r.* To consume oneself (with rage, despair, etc.).
smangiatura, *n.f.* Corrosion.
smania [smAnia], *n.f.* Craze, rage, desire, frenzy; restlessness.
smaniare, *v.i.* To rave, to be delirious; to talk wildly; to covet, to desire morbidly; to be restless.
smaniatamente, *adv.* Ravingly.
smanicarsi, *v.r.* To roll up one's sleeves.
smanierato, *a.* Ill-mannered.
smaniglio [smanIglio], *n.m.* Bracelet.
smaniosamente, *adv.* Longingly, desirously.
smanioso, *a.* Raving, desirous, craving, longing; covetous.
smantellamento, *n.m.* Dismantling.
smantellare, *v.t.* To dismantle.
smargiassare, *v.i.* To bully, to hector; to bluster; to brag, to boast.
smargiassata, smargiasseria [smargiasserIa], *n.f.* Bluster, swaggering; bragging; bullying.
smargiasso, *n.m.* Braggart; bully.
smarginare, *v.t.* To trim the margins.
smarra, *n.f.* (*Agric.*) Hoe.
smarratura, *n.f.* Hoeing.
smarrimento, *n.m.* Loss; bewilderment, perplexity; miscarriage (of justice).
smarrire, *v.t.* To lose (one's senses, etc.), to mislay; to miss (the way); to bewilder.
smarrirsi, *v.r.* To lose oneself, to go astray; to be bewildered.
smarritamente, *adv.* Wanderingly, confusedly.
smarrito, *a.* Bewildered, frightened; lost, gone astray, wandering. **Pecorella smarrita,** lost sheep; **sguardi smarriti,** wild looks;

ufficio di oggetti smarriti, lost-property office.
smascellamento, *n.m.* Dislocation of the jaw.
smascellarsi, *v.r.* To dislocate one's jaw; (*fig.*) to roar with laughter, to split one's sides laughing.
smascheramento, *n.m.* Unmasking, exposure.
smascherare, smascherarsi, *v.t.r.* To unmask.
smatassare, *v.i.* To undo a skein; to disentangle.
smattonare, *v.t.* To raise pavement.
smelare, *v.i.* To take honey from the comb.
smelatura, *n.f.* Taking honey.
smelensito, *a.* Very stupid.
smembramento, *n.m.* Dismemberment, partitioning.
smembrare, *v.t.* To dismember, to partition, to divide up.
smembrarsi, *v.t.* To be dismembered.
smembratura, *n.f.* Dismemberment.
smemorare, smemorarsi, *v.i.r.* To forget.
smemorataggine [smemoratAggine], *n.f.* Forgetfulness, absent-mindedness.
smemoratamente, *adv.* Forgetfully, absent-mindedly.
smemoratezza, *n.f.* Loss of memory.
smemorato, *a.* Forgetful; absent-minded; negligent; inadvertent.
smemoriato, *n.m.* One who has lost his memory.
smencire, *v.t.* To enervate.
smentire, *v.t.* To deny, to repudiate; to contradict, to give the lie to, to belie. **— una notizia,** to deny a report.
smentirsi, *v.r.* To contradict oneself; to break a promise.
smentita, *n.f.* Denial, contradiction, repudiation. **Dare una — a,** to give the lie to, to contradict flatly.
smeraldino, *a.* Emerald green.
smeraldo, *n.m.* (*Min.*) Emerald.
smerciare, *v.t.* To sell, to market, to dispose of.
smercio [smErcio], *n.m.* Sale; market, demand.
smergo, *n.m.* (*Zool.*) Cormorant, diver.
smerigliare, *v.t.* To polish with emery; to grind (glass).
smerigliato, *a.* Emery. **Carta smerigliata,** emery-paper; **vetri smerigliati,** ground-glass windows.
smeriglio [smerIglio] (1), *n.m.* Emery.
smeriglio [smerIglio] (2), *n.m.* (*Zool.*) Species of hawk; variety of dogfish.
smerlare, smerlettare, *v.r.* To border with scallops, to scallop.
smerlo, *n.m.* Scallop edging.
smesso, *a.* Disused, cast-off. **Abiti smessi,** cast-off clothing.
smettere [smEttere], *v.t.i.* To leave off, to cast off; to give up; to drop, to cease; **ho smesso di fumare,** I have given up smoking; **— il lavoro,** to leave off working; **Smettila!** Stop it! **È ora di smetterla,** it's time to stop it.
smezzamento, *n.m.* Halving.
smezzare, *v.t.* To cut in half, to halve; to interrupt.
smidollare, *v.t.* To take out the marrow; to unnerve, to enfeeble.
smidollarsi, *v.r.* To grow weak, to lose strength.
smidollato, *a.* Nerveless, feeble, flaccid.
smilace, *n.f.* (*Bot.*) Smilax.
smilzo, *a.* Thin, slender, lean; spare; empty.
sminuire, *v.t.* To lessen, to diminish.
sminuzzamento, *n.m.* Breaking into little pieces.
sminuzzare, *v.t.* To smash to bits, to break into little bits.
smirneo [smirnEo], *n.m.a.* Man of or belonging to Smyrna.
smistamento, *n.m.* Sorting; (*Rail.*) shunting; (*Mil.*) **Ospedale di —,** casualty clearing station; **posto di —,** clearing-station.
smistare, *v.t.* To sort; to distribute; to divert; (*Rail.*) to shunt.
smisurabile [smisurAbile], *a.* Immeasurable.
smisuratamente, *adv.* Immeasurably.
smisuratezza, *n.f.* Immensity, immeasurableness.
smisurato, *a.* Immeasurable, immense, huge, boundless.
smobiliare, *v.t.* To unfurnish, to move the furniture from.
smobiliato, *a.* Unfurnished.
smobilitare, *v.t.* To demobilize.
smobilitazione, *n.f.* Demobilization.
smobilizzo, *n.m.* (*Comm.*) Release of capital.
smoccolare, *v.t.i.* To snuff (a candle); (*colloq.*) to swear, to curse.
smoccolatoio [smoccolatOio], *n.m.* Snuffers.
smoccolatura, *n.f.* Snuffing (candle).
smodare, *v.i.* To exaggerate, to exceed (eating, etc.).
smodatamente, *adv.* Excessively.
smodato, smoderato, *a.* Excessive, exaggerated, immoderate; intemperate.
smoderare [cp. **smodare**].
smoderatezza, *n.f.* Excess, intemperance; extravagance.
smoderazione, *n.f.* Lack of moderation; excess; intemperance.
smogliato, *a.* Without a wife, bachelor.
smoking, *n.m.* Dinner-jacket.
smonacarsi, *v.r.* To leave the cloister (monk or nun).
smontaggio, smontamento [smontAggio], *n.m.* (*Mech.*) Dismounting, taking to pieces.
smontare, *v.t.i.* To dismount, to alight (from train, etc.); to undo, to dismantle, to take to pieces; to fade (of colours); (*Mil.*) to relieve (the guard). **— una macchina,** to take down an engine; **— dalla carrozza,** to alight from the carriage; **— da cavallo,** to dismount; (*fig.*) **— una calunnia,** to expose a slander.
smontatoio [smontatOio], *n.m.* Wharf.
smorfia [smOrfia], *n.f.* Grimace, wry face; coaxing smile. **Fare le smorfie,** to make faces.
smorfiosa, *n.f.* Flirt, coquette.
smorfiosamente, *adv.* Mincingly; skittishly.
smorfioso, *n.m.a.* Wheedler, coaxer; affected, mincing; skittish; wheedling.
smortezza, *n.f.* Pallor.
smorticcio [smortIccio], *a.* Wan, sallow.
smortire, *v.i.* To turn pale.
smorto, *a.* Pale, wan, ashen, pallid; dull (of metal); dead (of colour); bleak.
smorzamento, *n.m.* Toning down, appeasing, softening.

smorzare, *v.t.* To tone down (colours, etc.); to shade (a lamp, etc.); to extinguish (a light); to quench (thirst); to attenuate, to reduce; to depress. **— un suono,** to deaden a sound; **— un colore,** to tone down a colour.
smorzarsi, *v.r.* To be extinguished; to be softened down; to grow fainter; to go out (of a light); to die away (of a sound).
smorzatore, *n.m.* Damper; fire-extinguisher; (*Motor.*) **— di scosse,** shock-absorber.
smorzatura, *n.f.* Toning down, shading; attenuation.
smossa, *n.f.* Movement; motion.
smosso, *p.p.a.* Removed, displaced; stirred, shifted. **Terra smossa,** tilled soil [cp. **smuovere**].
smotta, *n.f.* Landslide.
smottamento, *n.m.* Crumbling away, falling in.
smottare, *v.i.* Caving in (of soil), crumbling away.
smottatura, *n.f.* Landslide.
smozzare, *v.t.* To cut off, to lop off, to chip; to curtail.
smozzicare, *v.t.* To cut to pieces, to break in pieces; to maim, to mutilate; to cut short. **— le parole,** to clip one's speech.
smozzicatura, *n.f.* Cutting short; lopping.
smungere [smUngere], *v.t.* To drain, to dry up, to suck; to exhaust; (*fig.*) to swindle, to fleece.
smungitura, *n.f.* Draining, sucking; (*fig.*) sponging.
smunire, *v.t.* To dismantle, to leave undefended.
smunto, *a.* Pale, emaciated, worn out; thin, lean.
smuovere [smuOvere], *v.t.* To move, to shift, to displace; to stir, to agitate; to dissuade. **Il vento smuove le foglie,** the wind flutters the leaves; **— la terra,** to dig, to hoe; **non si è lasciato — dalle mie preghiere,** he did not allow himself to be swayed by my entreaties.
smuoversi, *v.r.* To be moved (in all senses).
smurare, *v.t.* To level a wall.
smussamento, *n.m.* Blunting, bevelling; rounding the edge.
smussare, *v.t.* To blunt, to round off (angles, etc.); to bevel, to chamfer, (*fig.*) to reduce, to smooth; to soften; to deaden, to dull.
smussatura, *n.f.* Bevel edge.
smusso, *n.m.* Bevel (tool); chamfer.
smusso, *a.* Bevelled; blunted.
snaturamento, *n.m.* Perversion, distortion; change of nature.
snaturare, *v.t.* To alter the nature of; to distort, to misrepresent.
snaturatamente, *adv.* Unnaturally, pervertedly.
snaturatezza, *n.f.* Unnaturalness.
snaturato, *a.* Unnatural; wicked, cruel; monstrous; perverted.
snazionalizzarsi, *v.r.* To be denationalized.
snebbiare, *v.t.i.* To clear away (cloud, mist, etc.).
snebbiarsi, *v.r.* To clear up (of the sky).
snellamente, *adv.* Swiftly, lightly, nimbly.
snellezza, *n.f.* Nimbleness, gracefulness, slenderness.
snello, *a.* Nimble, slender, graceful, slim; brisk, active.
snervamento, *n.m.* Enervation.
snervante, *a.* Enervating, exhausting.
snervare, *v.t.* To enervate, to exhaust; to unnerve; to enfeeble.
snervatezza, *n.f.* Debility, enervation, weakness.
snidare, *v.t.* To dislodge, to drive out; (*fig.*) to find out, to discover.
snobismo, *n.m.* Snobbishness, snobbery.
snocciolare, *v.t.* To take out the kernel; (*fig.*) to rattle off (stories); to explain; to pay out readily.
snocciolatamente, *adv.* Openly, clearly, in the open, without reserve.
snodamento, *n.m.* Untying; disentangling.
snodare, *v.t.* To untie, to unfasten; to loosen, to unknot. **— le membra,** to limber the joints, to flex one's joints; **— la lingua,** to start talking.
snodarsi, *v.r.* To become unwound; to uncoil (of a snake); to wind (of a road).
snodatamente, *adv.* Flexibly; agilely.
snodato, *a.* Supple, flexible, agile; articulate; submissive, adaptable.
snodatura, *n.f.* Articulation (of the joints).
snodevole [snodEvole], *a.* Articulated, flexible.
snudare, *v.t.* To bare, to lay bare; to unsheathe (sword).
soave, *a.* Sweet, gentle, exquisite, delightful.
soavemente, *adv.* Sweetly, gently.
soavità [-à], *n.f.* Sweetness, gentleness, softness, delightfulness.
soavizzare, *v.t.* To sweeten, to soften.
sobbalzare, *v.i.* To start, to jump; to jerk; to start up.
sobbalzo, *n.m.* Start, jump, jerk. **Con un —,** with a jerk.
sobbarcarsi, *v.r.* To burden oneself with, to take upon oneself.
sobbollimento, *n.m.* Simmering.
sobbollire, *v.i.* To simmer.
sobborgo, *n.m.* Suburb.
sobbuglio [cp. **subbuglio**].
sobillamento, *n.m.* Instigation, incitement.
sobillare, *v.t.* To instigate, to incite.
sobillatore, sobillatrice, *n.m.f.* Instigator.
sobillazione, *n.f.* Instigation, incitement.
sobriamente, *adv.* Soberly; frugally.
sobrietà, *n.f.* Sobriety, temperance, moderation; frugality.
sobrio [sObrio], *a.* Sober, temperate, moderate; frugal.
socchiudere [socchiUdere], *v.t.* To half-shut, to leave (a door) ajar.
socchiuso, *a.* Ajar, half-shut, half-open.
soccida, soccio [sOccida, sOccio], *n.f.m.* (*Agric.*) Agistment (of cattle).
socco, *n.m.* (*Theat.*) Buskin; light comedy.
soccombente, *a.* Overcome, subjugated. **Rimanere —,** to be the loser.
soccombere [soccOmbere], *v.i.* To succumb; to be overcome; to yield; to die.
soccorrere [soccOrrere], *v.t.i.* To help, to aid, to succour; to occur, to come to mind.
soccorrersi [soccOrrersi], *v.r.* To help one another.
soccorrevole [soccorrEvole], *a.* Helpful, helping; charitable. **Mano —,** a helping hand.
soccorrevolmente, *adv.* Helpfully.
soccorrimento, *n.m.* Help, succour, aid.

soccorritore, soccorritrice, *n.m.f.* Helper, succourer.
soccorso, *n.m.* Help, succour, aid, relief, assistance. **Pronto —,** first aid; **società di mutuo —,** friendly society; **gridare al —,** to cry for help; **prestare —,** to render assistance; **uscita di —,** emergency exit; **porgere —,** to bring help.
soccoscio [soccOscio], *n.m.* Rump (of beef).
socera [cp. **suocera**].
socia [sOcia], *n.f.* (Female) partner.
sociabile [sociAbile], *a.* Sociable.
sociabilità [-à], *n.f.* Sociability.
sociabilmente, *adv.* Sociably.
sociale, *a.* Social; (*Comm.*) registered; company's. **Statuto —,** articles of association; **benessere —,** social welfare.
socialismo, *n.m.* Socialism.
socialista (*pl.* **socialisti**), *n.m.* Socialist.
socialistico [socialIstico], *a.* Socialistic.
socialità [-à], *n.f.* Sociability.
socializzare, *v.t.* To socialize.
socializzazione, *n.f.* Socialization.
socialmente, *adv.* Socially.
società, *n.f.* Society; association; community; club; companionship; (*Comm.*) firm, partnership, company. **Uomo di —,** society man; **abito da —,** evening dress; **far — con,** to associate oneself with; **alta —,** high society; (*Comm.*) **— anonima,** joint stock company; **— edilizia,** building society; **— di mutuo soccorso,** friendly society; **— d'assicurazione,** insurance company; **— in accomandita,** limited partnership; **— ferroviaria,** railway company.
socievole [sociEvole], *a.* Sociable, companionable.
socievolezza, *n.f.* Sociability.
socievolmente, *adv.* Sociably.
socio [sOcio], *n.m.* Associate; member (of a club, etc.); (*Comm.*) partner.
sociologia [sociologIa], *n.f.* Sociology.
sociologo [sociOlogo], *n.m.* Sociologist.
Socrate [sOcrate], *n.m.* Socrates.
socratico [socrAtico], *a.* Socratic.
soda, *n.f.* (*Chem.*) Soda.
sodaglia [sodAglia], *n.f.* (*Agric.*) Unploughed land.
sodale, *n.m.* (*Lit.*) Friend, companion; associate.
sodalizio [sodalIzio], *n.m.* Society, club, association; confraternity; guild.
sodamente, *adv.* Solidly, firmly.
sodare, *v.t.* To strengthen, to harden; to consolidate; to full (cloth); (*fig.*) to assure.
soddisfacente, *a.* Satisfactory; gratifying; adequate.
soddisfacentemente, *adv.* Satisfactorily.
soddisfacimento, *n.m.* Satisfaction; fulfilment; discharge (of a debt).
soddisfare, *v.t.* To satisfy, to fulfil; to please; to appease; to make good, to make amends; to answer; to discharge. **— un debito,** to pay a debt; **non dobbiamo — i suoi capricci,** we ought not to gratify his whims.
soddisfarsi, *v.r.* To be satisfied.
soddisfazione, *n.f.* Satisfaction. **Riuscire di piena —,** to be quite satisfactory; **con mia grande —,** to my entire satisfaction, much to my satisfaction.
sodezza, *n.f.* Firmness, consistency; solidity; compactness.
sodio [sOdio], *n.m.* (*Chem.*) Sodium.
sodisfare [cp. **soddisfare**].
sodo, *n.m.* Solidity, firm ground; foundation. **Posare sul —,** to be on firm ground.
sodo, *a.* Solid, firm, consistent, well-grounded, stable; compact; heavy; untilled (land). **Uovo —,** hard-boiled egg.
sodo, *adv.* Solidly, firmly. **Dormir —,** to sleep soundly; **picchiar —,** to strike hard; **lavorare —,** to work hard.
sodomia [sodomIa], *n.f.* Sodomy.
sodomita (*pl.* **sodomiti**), *n.m.* Sodomite.
sofà [-à], *n.f.* Sofa, settee.
sofferente, *n.m.a.* Sufferer; suffering.
sofferenza, *n.f.* Suffering, pain; endurance, patience. (*Comm.*) **Cambiale in —,** unmet bill.
sofferire [cp. **soffrire**].
soffermarsi, *v.r.* To stop a little, to pause; to hesitate; to dwell (on a subject).
soffermata, *n.f.* Pause, brief stay.
sofferto, Suffered, borne, undergone [cp. **soffrire**].
soffiamento, *n.m.* Blowing, puffing, panting.
soffiare, *v.t.i.* To blow, to puff; to blow out; to breathe, to pant; to prompt; to spit (of a cat); to huff (at draughts). **Il vento soffia,** the wind is blowing; **— come un mantice,** to puff like a grampus; **— sul fuoco,** to blow the fire; **— sulla candela,** to blow out the candle.
soffiarsi, *v.r.* **— il naso,** to blow one's nose; **— le dita,** to blow on one's fingers.
soffiata, *n.f.* Puff, breath (of wind), slight breeze.
soffiatore, *n.m.* (*Glass*) blower; prompter, inciter.
soffice [sOffice], *a.* Soft, light; tender. **Una poltrona —,** a well-padded easy-chair.
sofficemente, *adv.* Softly, lightly.
soffieria [soffierIa], *n.f.* (*Mech.*) Blast mechanism in a furnace.
soffietto, *n.m.* Bellows; (*fig.*) (publisher's) blurb; puff, favourable review.
soffio [sOffio], *n.m.* Puff, breath; blast of air; breathing, blowing; spitting (of a cat). **D'un —, in un —,** in an instant, in a flash; **come un —,** like a flash; **un — di vento,** a puff of wind, a gust; (*Med.*) **un — al cuore,** a murmur of the heart.
soffione, *n.m.* Bellows-pipe, forge-bellows; (*Geol.*) fumarole, jet of boiling vapour; (*Bot.*) dandelion.
soffitta, *n.f.* Garret, attic; lumber-room.
soffittare, *v.t.* To ceiling.
soffitto, *n.m.* Ceiling.
soffocamento, *n.m.* Choking, suffocation.
soffocante, *a.* Stifling, suffocating, choking; stuffy, close, oppressive (of weather).
soffocare, *v.t.i.* To suffocate, to stifle, to choke, to smother; to suppress. **Qui si soffoca,** it is very stuffy in here; **— una sommossa,** to suppress a rebellion.
soffocatamente, *adv.* Suffocatingly.
soffocatore, *n.m.a.* Smotherer; asphyxiating.
soffocazione, *n.f.* Suffocation, choking. **Morto per —,** suffocated, strangled.
soffondere [soffOndere], *v.t.* To spread over, to besprinkle.

soffreddare, *v.i.* To cool.
soffreddo, *a.* Cool.
soffregamento, *n.m.* Rubbing.
soffregare, *v.t.* To rub.
soffribile [soffrIbile], *a.* Endurable, supportable, bearable.
soffriggere [soffrIggere], *v.t.* To fry lightly.
soffrimento, *n.m.* Suffering.
soffrire, *v.t.i.* To suffer, to endure, to support, to bear; to put up with, to tolerate. **— un torto,** to suffer a wrong; **— il freddo,** to suffer from cold; **non posso — queste cose,** I cannot stand these things; **la sua salute ne soffre,** his health is affected by it; **quell'uomo non posso soffrirlo,** I can't bear that man.
soffritto, *n.m.* Sauce of onions fried in butter.
soffuso, *a.* Suffused, flushed; besprinkled; spread over.
sofisma, *n.m.* Sophism.
sofista (*pl.* **sofisti**), *n.m.* Sophist.
sofistica [sofIstica], *n.f.* Sophistry.
sofisticamente, *adv.* Sophistically.
sofisticamento, *n.m.* Sophistic method.
sofisticare, *v.t.i.* To quibble, to sophisticate; to adulterate; to tamper with.
sofisticato, *a.* Sophisticated; adulterated; artificial.
sofisticazione, *n.f.* Adulteration.
sofisticheria [sofisticherIa], *n.f.* Sophistry, quibble, cavilling.
sofistico [sofIstico], *a.* Sophistic(al), captious, quibbling; fallacious.
sofisticone, *n.m.* Quibbler; know-all.
sofo, *n.m.* (*Lit.*) Sage, wise man of old; (*fig.*) wiseacre.
Sofocle [sOfocle], *n.m.* Sophocles.
sofocleo [sofoclEo], *a.* Sophoclean.
soggettaccio, *n.m.* Rogue, bad subject.
soggettare, *v.t.* To subdue, to subject [cp. **assoggettare**].
soggettivamente, *adv.* Subjectively.
soggettivismo, *n.m.* Subjectivism.
soggettività [-à], *n.f.* Subjectivity.
soggettivo, *a.* Subjective (in all senses).
soggetto, *n.m.* Subject (in all senses); theme, argument; matter, topic; fellow, person. **Recitare a —,** to act extempore, off-hand; **commedia a —,** improvised comedy, unrehearsed play; **egli è un cattivo —,** he's a bad fellow; **cambiamo —,** let's change the subject.
soggetto, *a.* Subject, subjected; exposed; subdued; liable; amenable. **— a norme,** subject to rules; **— a modificazione,** subject to alteration.
soggezione, *n.f.* Subjection; awe, respect; timidity; uneasiness. **Tenere in —,** to hold in subjection; **aver — di,** to stand in awe of; **far —,** to inspire awe or respect; **sentirsi in —,** to feel uneasy.
sogghignare, *v.i.* To sneer, to smile or laugh derisively, to grin maliciously; to laugh up one's sleeve.
sogghigno, *n.m.* Sneer, grin; mocking laugh.
soggiacere, *v.i.* To succumb; to be subjected to, to go under; to be liable.
soggiacimento, *n.m.* Subjection; dependence.
soggiogamento, *n.m.* Subjugation, enthralment.
soggiogare, *v.t.* To subjugate, to subdue, to enslave.
soggiogazione, *n.f.* Subjugation, enslavement; conquest.
soggiornare, *v.i.* To sojourn, to make a stay; to live, to dwell, to reside.
soggiorno, *n.m.* Sojourn, stay; living-room. **Tassa di —,** residence tax; **permesso di —,** residence permit.
soggiungere [soggiUngere], *v.t.i.* To add; to append, to subjoin; to reply, to answer; to retort.
soggiuntivo, *n.m.a.* (*Gram.*) Subjunctive.
soggolo, *n.m.* Chin-strap; (*Eccles.*) nun's wimple.
sogguardare, *v.t.* To look askance at; to wink at, to eye slyly.
soglia [sOglia], *n.f.* Threshold, doorstep.
soglio [sOglio], *n.m.* Throne.
sogliola [sOgliola], *n.f.* (*Zool.*) Sole. **Una — fritta,** fried sole; **filetto di —,** filleted sole.
sognabile [sognAbile], *a.* Imaginable, conceivable.
sognare, *v.t.i.* To dream, to imagine, to conceive of, to long for; to fancy; to muse; to talk at random.
sognarsi, *v.r.* To fancy. **Tu ti sogni!** You're dreaming!
sognatore, sognatrice, *n.m.f.a.* Dreamer; dreaming.
sogno, *n.m.* Dream; reverie; vision. **Fare un —,** to have a dream; **— ad occhi aperti,** day-dream; **neppur per —,** on no account.
soia [sOia], *n.f.* (*Bot.*) Soya-bean.
sol, *n.m.* (*Mus.*) Sol, G.
sola, *n.f.* (*Comm.*) Sole. **— di cambio,** sole of exchange.
solaio [solAio], *n.m.* Attic, box-room; garret; ceiling.
solamente, *adv.* Only, exclusively, solely; merely.
solare, *a.* Solar; sun; sunlight (treatment, etc.) **Macchie solari,** sun-spots; **sistema —,** solar system.
solata, *n.f.* Sunstroke; long spell of sunshine.
solatio [solatIo], *n.m.a.* Sunny spot facing south; sunny.
solatura, *n.f.* Soling (shoe or boot).
solcabile [solcAbile], *a.* Ploughable.
solcare, *v.t.* To plough, to furrow (in all senses). **— l'oceano,** to plough the seas.
solcata, *n.f.* Furrow; wake, track.
solco, *n.m.* Furrow; track; wake (of a ship). **Uscire dal —,** to leave the straight and narrow path.
solcometro [solcOmetro], *n.m.* (*Naut.*) Log. **Gettare il —,** to heave the log.
soldanato, *n.m.* Sultanate.
soldanella, *n.f.* (*Bot.*) Blue moonwort.
soldano, *n.m.* Sultan.
soldataglia [soldatAglia], *n.f.* Mob of soldiers.
soldatesca, *n.f.* Soldiery; out-of-hand troops.
soldatescamente, *adv.* In a soldierly manner.
soldatesco, *a.* Soldierly, soldier-like.
soldatino, *n.m.* Soldier boy, little soldier; toy soldier.
soldato, *n.m.* Soldier. **Far il —,** to do military service; **— di ventura,** soldier of fortune; (*colloq.*) **— del papa,** harmless soldier.
soldino, *n.m.* Halfpenny, very small sum.

soldo, *n.m.* Soldo; penny; money; pay, wages. **Senza un —,** penniless; **non vale un —,** not worth a penny, worthless; **essere al — di,** to be in the pay of.
soldone, *n.m.* Penny.
sole, *n.m.* Sun; sunshine. **Raggio di —,** ray of sunlight; **al primo —,** at sunrise; **un occhio di —,** a gleam of sunshine; **aver qualcosa al —,** to own a bit of land; **ciò è chiaro come il —,** it's as clear as daylight; **un colpo di —,** a sunstroke; **riscaldarsi al —,** to bask in the sun.
solecchio [solEcchio], *n.m.* Canopy, shield from the sun. **Farsi —,** to shield one's eyes from the sun.
solecismo, *n.m.* Solecism.
soleggiamento, *n.m.* Sunning, exposing to the sun.
soleggiare, *v.t.i.* To spread in the sun, to sun; to bask in the sun.
soleggiato, *a.* Exposed to the sun, sunny, bright.
solenne, *a.* Solemn; grave, serious; formal; impressive; thorough; terrific. **Un — mentitore,** a downright liar; **un errore —,** a serious mistake.
solennemente, *adv.* Solemnly, gravely.
solennissimo [solennIssimo], *a.* **Un — ceffone,** a resounding smack.
solennità [-à], *n.f.* Solemnity; rite, ceremony; impressiveness.
solennizzamento, *n.m.* Solemnization.
solennizzare, *v.t.* To solemnize.
solere, *v.i.* (*pres.* **soglio, suoli, suole, sogliamo, solete, sogliono**). To be wont, to be accustomed, to be in the habit of. **Suole fare una passeggiata,** he's accustomed to taking a walk; **soleva andare a Roma ogni mese,** he used to go to Rome every month.
solerte, *a.* Diligent, conscientious, industrious; careful.
solertemente, *adv.* Diligently, carefully.
solerzia [solErzia], *n.f.* Diligence, attention, industriousness.
soletta, *n.f.* Sole (of stocking); sock (for boot or shoe). **— di cemento,** reinforced concrete ceiling.
soletto, *a.* Alone, all alone, lonely. **Solo —,** quite alone.
solfa, *n.f.* (*Mus.*) Sol-fa, gamut; scale. (*fig.*) **Battere la stessa —,** to harp on the same string.
solfanello, *n.m.* Sulphur match. **Accendersi come un —,** to flare up in anger [cp. **zolfanello**].
solfara, solfatara, *n.f.* Sulphur-mine.
solfato, *n.m.* (*Chem.*) Sulphate.
solfeggiare, *v.i.* (*Mus.*) To sol-fa.
solfeggio [solfEggio], *n.m.* (*Mus.*) Sol-fa, solmisation, solfeggio.
solferino, *n.m.a.* Dark red.
solfito, *n.m.* (*Chem.*) Sulphite.
solfo, *n.m.* Sulphur [cp. **zolfo**].
solforato, *a.* Sulphuretted ; sulphated.
solforico [solfOrico], *a.* (*Chem.*) Sulphuric. **Acido —,** sulphuric acid.
solforoso, *a.* Sulphurous ; sulphated.
solfureo [solfUreo], *a.* Sulphureous.
solfuro, *n.m.* (*Chem.*) Sulphide.
solicello, *n.m.* Misty sun, dim sun; wintry sun.
solidale, *a.* Supporting; loyal; sympathetic; united. **Essere pienamente — con,** to be in whole-hearted agreement with.
solidalmente, *adv.* Jointly.
solidamente, *adv.* Solidly, firmly.
solidare, *v.t.* To solidify; to consolidate.
solidariamente, *adv.* Jointly and severally. **— responsabile,** jointly and severally liable.
solidarietà [-à], *n.f.* Solidarity, support, fellowship; joint liability.
solidario [solidArio], *a.* Joint and several, joint.
solidezza, *n.f.* Solidity, soundness.
solidificabile [solidificAbile], *a.* Capable of being solidified.
solidificare, *v.t.* To solidify.
solidificazione, *n.f.* Solidification.
solidità [-à], *n.f.* Solidity.
solido [sOlido], *n.m.* Solid (in all senses). (*Law*) **In —,** jointly.
solido [sOlido], *a.* Solid, strong, firm, steady, stable; sound, substantial. **Una tinta solida,** a fast dye.
soliloquio [solilOquio], *n.m.* Soliloquy.
solingamente, *adv.* Solitarily.
solingo, *a.* Solitary, lonely.
solino, *n.m.* Collar, neck-band (of shirt); cuff.
solista, *n.m.f.* (*Mus.*) Soloist.
solitamente, *adv.* Usually, as a rule.
solitariamente, *adv.* Solitarily.
solitario [solitArio], *n.m.* Hermit, recluse; solitaire (diamond); (*Cards*) Patience. **Fare un —,** to play Patience.
solitario [solitArio], *a.* Lonely, solitary; secluded, desert. **Un luogo —,** a lonely spot; (*Zool.*) **verme —,** tape-worm.
solito [sOlito], *a.* Usual, habitual, customary, ordinary. **Di —, per —,** usually, as a rule; **al —,** as usual; **fuori del —,** unusual; **essere alle solite,** to be at one's usual; **essere — di, a,** to be used to, to be in the habit of; **come il —,** just as usual; **è la solita storia,** it's the same old story; **siamo alle solite!** here we are again!
solitudine [solitUdine], *n.f.* Solitude, loneliness; retreat, wilderness.
solivago [solIvago], *a.* Wandering alone.
sollazzamento, *n.m.* Solace, amusement.
sollazzare, *v.t.* To amuse, to entertain, to divert.
sollazzarsi, *v.r.* To enjoy oneself, to make merry; to amuse oneself; to sport; to have a good time.
sollazzevole [sollazzEvole], *a.* Amusing, pleasant, merry.
sollazzevolmente, *adv.* Amusingly.
sollazzo, *n.m.* Amusement, enjoyment, pleasure, sport, pastime.
sollecitamente, *adv.* Promptly, quickly, with despatch; eagerly.
sollecitamento, *n.m.* Hastening, urging.
sollecitare, *v.t.i.* To hasten, to urge; to solicit; to press, to entreat.
sollecitativo, *a.* Pressing, urgent.
sollecitatore, sollecitatrice, *n.m.f.* Petitioner, pleader.
sollecitatoria [sollecitatOria], *n.f.* (*Law*) Letter of reminder.
sollecitazione, *n.f.* Haste; entreaty, solicitation, pressure.

sollecito [sollEcito], *a.* Speedy, prompt, quick; eager; concerned, solicitous; diligent.
sollecitudine [sollecitUdine], *n.f.* Haste, promptness; solicitude, care.
solleone, *n.m.* Dog-days.
solleticamento, *n.m.* Tickling; exciting.
solleticare, *v.t.* To tickle; to stimulate; to flatter. **— la curiosità,** to excite curiosity; **— l'appetito,** to tempt, to whet the appetite.
solletico [sollEtico], *n.m.* Tickling, tickle; stimulus. **Soffrire il —,** to be ticklish; **fare il —,** to tickle.
sollevabile [sollevAbile], *a.* Capable of being raised.
sollevamento, *n.m.* Lifting, raising; rising, revolt; relief.
sollevare, *v.t.* To lift, to raise, to heave up; to comfort, to relieve. **— una pietra,** to lift a stone; **— una questione,** to raise a question; **— dubbi,** to raise doubts.
sollevarsi, *v.r.* To rise, to rebel, to revolt; to get up.
sollevato, *p.p.a.* Uplifted, raised. **Di spirito —,** uplifted in spirit.
sollevatore, sollevatrice, *n.m.f.* Agitator, sedition-monger.
sollevazione, *n.f.* Rising, revolt, rebellion; sedition.
sollievo, *n.m.* Relief, alleviation, ease, comfort. **Tirare un sospiro di —,** to heave a sigh of relief.
sollione, *n.m.* Dog-days [cp. **solleone**].
solluccherarsi, *v.r.* To be beside oneself with happiness.
sollucchero [sollUcchero], *n.m.* Rapture, thrill. **Andare in —,** to go into raptures, to rave (about a thing).
solo, *n.m.* (*Mus.*) Solo.
solo, *a.* Alone; single; lonely, solitary; only, unique. **Un — uomo,** one man only; **un — foglio di carta,** a single sheet of paper; **da —,** by oneself, alone; **le disgrazie non vengono mai sole,** troubles never come singly; **parlare da — a —,** to have a tête-à-tête.
solo, *adv.* Only, singly. **Non —,** not only.
solstiziale, *a.* (*Astron.*) Solstitial.
solstizio [solstIzio], *n.m.* (*Astron.*) Solstice.
soltanto, *adv.* Only.
solubile [solUbile], *a.* Soluble.
solubilità [-à], *n.f.* Solubility.
solutivo, *n.m.a.* Solvent, laxative.
soluzione, *n.f.* Solution; break in continuity; (*Law*) discharge.
solvente, *n.m.a.* Solvent.
solvenza, *n.f.* Solvency.
solvere [sOlvere], *v.t.* To dissolve; to liquefy; to settle (a debt).
solvibile [solvIbile], *a.* (*Comm.*) Solvent; reliable.
solvibilità [-à], *n.f.* Solvency.
soma, *n.f.* Load (for a pack-saddle), burden; weight.
Somalia [somAlia], *n.f.* (*Geog.*) Somalia.
somalo, *n.m.* Somali; monetary unit of Somalia.
somarello, *n.m.* Little donkey.
somaro, *n.m.* Ass, donkey; baggage-animal.
somatico [somAtico], *a.* (*Med.*) Bodily, physical.
someggiabile [someggiAbile], *a.* Portable (by baggage-animals).
someggiare, *v.t.* To carry by mules.
somiere, somiero, *n.m.* Pack-animal, beast of burden.
somigliante, *a.* Resembling, like, similar. **Ritratto —,** a good likeness.
somiglianza, *n.f.* Likeness, resemblance, image. **A — di,** like.
somigliare, *v.t.i.* To resemble, to be like. **I due fratelli non si somigliano,** the two brothers are not alike; **si somigliano come due gocce d'acqua,** they are as like as two peas.
somma, *n.f.* Sum, total; addition; sum (of money); (*Arith.*) addition. **Fare una —,** to add up a sum; **tirare le somme,** to sum up (in conclusion); **tirate le somme,** all things considered.
sommacco, *n.m.* (*Bot.*) Sumach.
sommamente, *adv.* Greatly, highly, in the highest degree.
sommare, *v.t i.* To sum up, to add up; to amount to. **Tutto sommato,** all things being taken into consideration.
sommariamente, *adv.* Summarily; briefly.
sommario [sommArio], *n.m.* Summary, epitome; abridgement; abstract.
sommario [sommArio], *a.* Summary, compendious, abridged, concise; without delay.
sommergere [sommErgere], *v.t.* To submerge, to flood, to swamp, to put under water, to sink; to overwhelm.
sommergersi, *v.r.* To sink; to be flooded; to dive (of a submarine).
sommergibile [sommergIbile], *n.m.a.* (*Naut.*) Submarine; submersible.
sommergimento, sommersione, *n.m.f.* Submersion, submergence.
sommessamente, *adv.* In a low voice; humbly; softly; submissively.
sommessivamente, *adv.* Submissively.
sommessivo, *a.* Submissive.
sommesso, *a.* Low (of voice); humble, meek, submissive.
sommetta, *n.f.* Small sum (of money). **Una bella —,** a pretty penny.
sommettere [cp. **sottomettere**].
somministramento, *n.m.* Administration, provision.
somministrare, *v.t.* To administer (medicine, etc.); to provide.
somministratore, *n.m.* Provider.
somministrazione, *n.f.* Administering, administration.
sommissione, *n.f.* Submission, compliance, obedience.
sommità [-à], *n.f.* Summit, top; vertex, apex.
sommo, *n.m.* Summit, top; the highest. **Il — della gloria,** the height of glory; **al —,** at the top; **i sommi,** great men; **per sommi capi,** briefly, in short.
sommo, *a.* Highest, lofty; supreme; uppermost; sublime. **In — grado,** in the highest degree.
sommossa, *n.f.* Sedition, rebellion, riot.
sommosso, *a.* Excited; troubled; moved [cp. **sommuovere**].
sommovimento, *n.m.* Stirring up, rising, revolt, movement, agitation.
sommovitore, sommovitrice, *n.m.f.* Agitator, instigator.
sommozzatore, *n.m.* Frogman.

sommuovere, sommovere [sommuOvere, sommOvere], *v.t.* To stir up, to agitate, to move, to incite, to instigate; to excite.
sonabile [sonAbile], *a.* (*Mus.*) Playable.
sonacchiare, sonicchiare, *v.t.* To strum.
sonagliera, *n.f.* Collar with bells attached.
sonaglio [sonAglio], *n.m.* Harness-bell, rattle. (*Zool.*) **Serpente a sonagli,** rattlesnake.
sonante, *a.* Sounding, resounding; ringing; resonant, sonorous. **Denaro —,** hard cash, ready money.
sonare, *v.t.* To sound, to ring [cp. **suonare**].
sonata, *n.f.* Loud ringing (of bell, etc.); (*Mus.*) sonata.
sonatore, sonatrice, *n.m.f.* (*Mus.*) Player, executant, performer. (*colloq.*) **Buona notte sonatori!** That's that! That's all there is to it!
sonda, *n.f.* (*Naut.*) Sounding-line, sounding-rod; (*Med.*) probe.
sondabile [sondAbile], *a.* Capable of being sounded.
sondaggio [sondAggio], *n.m.* Sounding; public-opinion poll; (*Mining*) boring.
sondare, *v.t.* (*Naut., Med.*) To sound; to probe, to examine; to fathom, to search. **— qualcuno,** to sound someone; **— una piaga,** to probe a wound.
soneria [sonerIa], *n.f.* Striking mechanism (of a clock); strike; alarm bell; chime.
sonettare, *v.t.* To write sonnets.
sonettista (*pl.* **sonettisti**), *n.m.* Sonneteer.
sonetto, *n.m.* Sonnet.
sonnacchiosamente, *adv.* Sleepily.
sonnacchioso, *a.* Sleepy, drowsy.
sonnambula [sonnAmbula], *n.f.* Fortune-teller; medium; sleep-walker.
sonnambulismo, *n.m.* Somnambulism, sleep-walking.
sonnambulo [sonnAmbulo], *n.m.* Somnambulist, sleep-walker.
sonnecchiare, *v.i.* To doze; to slumber.
sonnellino, *n.m.* Nap, short sleep, doze. **Schiacciare un —,** to take a nap.
sonnifero [sonnIfero], *n.m.a.* Narcotic, sleeping-draught; somniferous.
sonniloquio [sonnilOquio], *n.m.* Talking in one's sleep.
sonniloquo [sonnIloquo], *n.m.* One who talks in his sleep.
sonno, *n.m.* Sleep, slumber; rest. **Aver —,** to be sleepy; **cadere dal —,** to be overcome with sleep; **— profondo,** sound sleep; **aver il— leggero,** to be a light sleeper; **metter —,** to induce sleep; **prender —,** to go to sleep; **dormire d'un — solo,** to sleep through the night; (*Med.*) **malattia del —,** sleepy sickness.
sonnolento, *a.* Sleepy, drowsy, somnolent.
sonnolenza, *n.f.* Sleepiness, somnolence; drowsiness.
sonoramente, *adv.* Sonorously, soundly. **— battuto,** soundly thrashed.
sonorità [-à], *n.f.* Sonorousness, sonority.
sonoro, *a.* Sonorous, sounding, resonant. **Onda sonora,** sound-wave; (*Cinema.*) **film —,** sound-film; **colonna sonora,** sound-track.
sontuosamente, *adv.* Sumptuously.
sontuosità [-à], *n.f.* Sumptuousness, luxury; magnificence.
sontuoso, *a.* Sumptuous, luxurious, magnificent.
soperchiare [cp. **soverchiare**].
soperchieria [soperchierIa], *n.f.* Insolence, outrageous conduct; imposition; bullying.
sopimento, *n.m.* Soothing; alleviation.
sopire, *v.t.* To soothe, to allay, to lull.
sopore, *n.m.* Torpor, lethargy, drowsiness.
soporifero [soporIfero], *a.* Soporific.
soporosamente, *adv.* Soporifically.
soporoso, *a.* Soporific.
soppalco, *n.m.* Lumber-room, loft.
soppannare, *v.t.* To line.
soppanno, *n.m.* Lining.
soppedaneo [soppedAneo], *n.m.* Mat, door-mat.
soppelo, *n.m.* Joint of meat cut from the shoulder.
sopperire, *v.i.* To provide for, to cater for. **— alle spese,** to meet expenditure.
soppesare, *v.t.* To weigh in one's hand; (*fig.*) to consider, to judge.
soppeso, *n.m.* **Prender, alzar di —,** to raise in one's arms, to raise with both hands.
soppiano, *a.* Softly, sotto voce.
soppiantamento, *n.m.* Supplanting.
soppiantare, *v.t.* To supplant, to oust, to dispossess, to deprive.
soppiantatore, soppiantatrice, *n.m.f.* Supplanter.
soppiatto, *adv.* **Di —,** stealthily, secretly; slyly.
soppiattone, *n.m.* Close person, dissembler.
sopportabile [supportAbile], *a.* Endurable, bearable, supportable.
supportabilmente, *adv.* Bearably.
sopportamento, *n.m.* Support; endurance.
sopportare, *v.t.* To bear, to endure, to suffer; to support, to second, to substantiate, to corroborate; to prop. **Non posso sopportarlo,** I can't bear him; **— la fame e il freddo,** to endure hunger and cold.
sopportarsi, *v.r.* To be borne, to be endured. **È difficile a —,** it is hard to bear.
sopportazione, *n.f.* Tolerance, patience, forbearance; endurance.
sopportevole [sopportEvole], *a.* Bearable, endurable.
sopportevolmente, *adv.* Endurably.
sopporto, *n.m.* Support; endurance. (*Mech.*) **— a rulli,** roller-bearings.
soppressa, *n.f.* (*Mech.*) Press, calender.
soppressare, *v.t.* To press.
soppressione, *n.f.* Suppression; repression, stifling.
sopprimere [sopprImere], *v.t.* To suppress, to repress, to stifle; to eliminate, to destroy; to conceal.
sopra, sovra, *prep.* On, upon, above, over; (*as prefix*) super-, extra-, over-, sur-, (thus used, the following consonant is usually doubled). **Come —,** as above-mentioned; **di sopra, disopra,** upstairs; (*colloq.*) **dormirci —,** to sleep on it; to put it off; **pensarci —,** to think it over; **è sopra i sessant'anni,** he's upwards of sixty, he is in his sixties; **mettiamoci una pietra sopra,** let's forget it.
soprabbondanza, *n.f.* Superabundance.
soprabbusto, *n.m.* Bodice.
soprabito [soprAbito], *n.m.* Overcoat.
sopraccapo, *n.m.* Care, anxiety, trouble; preoccupation.
sopraccaricare, *v.t.* To overload.

sopraccarico [sopraccArico], *n.m.a.* Supercargo; excessive load; overloaded.
sopraccarta, *n.f.* Envelope, cover; address on envelope.
sopraccassa, *n.f.* Case (of a watch).
sopraccennato, *a.* Above-mentioned.
sopracciglio [sopraccIglio], *n.m.* Eyebrow.
sopraccitato, *a.* Above-mentioned.
sopraccoperta, sopracoperta, *n.f.* Quilt, counterpane; book-jacket; enclosing envelope; (*Naut.*) upper deck.
sopraddetto, *a.* Aforesaid.
sopraelevare, *v.t.* To raise, to heighten, to elevate.
sopraelevato, *a.* Raised, elevated; overhead (of a railway, etc.).
sopraffacimento, *n.m.* Overpowering.
sopraffare, *v.t.* To overpower, to overwhelm, to overcome, to conquer, to oppress. **Essere sopraffatto da,** to be overwhelmed by.
sopraffazione, *n.f.* Oppression, tyranny.
sopraffino, *a.* Superfine, very fine, of extra quality; very clever, cunning.
sopraggitto, *n.m.* Oversewing, whipping (needlework).
sopraggiungere [sopraggiUngere], *v.t.i.* To overtake, to come upon, to reach; to arrive, to come; to happen.
sopraggiunta, *n.f.* Unexpected arrival; unforeseen appearance. **Per —,** into the bargain.
sopraindicato, *a.* Aforementioned.
sopraintendente [cp. **soprintendente**].
sopraluogo, *n.m.adv.* (*Law*) Visit on the spot, investigation on the site; on the spot; (*Comm.*) delivery on the spot.
sopramaniche [sopramAniche], *n.f.pl.* Sleeve-guards.
soprammercato, *n.m.* Surplus; to boot, over and above. **Per —,** into the bargain.
soprammisura, *adv.* Beyond measure; excessively.
soprammobile [soprammObile], *n.m.* Knick-knack.
soprannaturale, *a.*Supernatural.
soprannaturalmente, *adv.* Supernaturally.
soprannome, *n.m.* Nickname; sobriquet, appellation.
soprannominare, *v.t.* To nickname; to name.
soprannominarsi, *v.r.* To be nicknamed.
soprannumerario [soprannumerArio], *n.m.a.* Supernumerary.
soprannumero [soprannUmero], *n.m.* Surplus, excess. **In —,** in addition, in excess.
soprano, *n.m.a.* (*Mus.*) Soprano.
sopranolo, *n.m.* (*Comm.*) Primage.
soprappagare, *v.t.* To overpay.
soprappensiero, *adv.* Thoughtfully; wistfully, absent-mindedly.
soprappiù [-ù], *n.m.* Surplus; extra, addition.
soprapporre, *v.t.* To superpose, to place over.
soprapremio [sopraprEmio], *n.m.* (*Comm.*) Additional premium.
soprapprezzo, *n.m.* Overprice, excess price.
sopraprofitto, *n.m.* Extra profit; excess profit.
soprascarpa, *n.f.* Overshoe, galosh.
soprascritta, *n.f.* Superscription; address (on envelope).
soprasensibile [soprasensIbile], *a.* Supersensible.
soprassalto, *n.m.* Start, jerk, jolt, sudden movement. **Di —,** suddenly, with a jerk; **svegliarsi di —,** to wake with a start.
soprassata, *n.f.* Sausage made from pig's head; brawn.
soprassedere, *v.i.* To defer, to postpone, to put off; to preside over.
soprassello, *n.m.* Additional burden. **Per —,** into the bargain.
soprassoldo, *n.m.* Extra pay.
soprasstalli, *n.m.pl.* (*Naut.*) Demurrage.
soprastamento, *n.m.* Superiority; standing over; delay.
soprastante, *n.m.* Overseer, supervisor.
soprastante, *a.* Overhanging, overlooking; impending; rising higher; at the head of. **Piano —,** the floor above; the top floor.
soprastare [cp. **sovrastare**].
soprastruttura, *n.f.* Superstructure.
soprattassa, *n.f.* Surtax; supertax.
sopratterra, *adv.* Above ground; alive.
soprattutto, *adv.* Above all, especially.
sopraumano, *a.* Superhuman.
sopravanzare, *v.t.i.* To out-do, to outshine; to overcome; to overhang, to jut out; to remain over. **Il vestito sopravanza due dita buone,** this dress is at least two inches too long.
sopravanzo, *n.m.* Surplus, remainder; residue; balance. **Di —,** more than enough.
sopravveniente, *a.* Overcoming; intervening.
sopravvenienza, *n.f.* Contingency; sudden coming, intervention.
sopravvenire, *v.i.* To befall, to happen; to come suddenly; to intervene; to crop up; to drop in (on a visit).
sopravvento, *n.m.* Upper hand, advantage. **Avere il — su,** to have the upper hand of.
sopravvento, *adv.* (*Naut.*) Windward. **Isole —,** Windward Islands.
sopravvenuta, *n.f.* Unexpected arrival.
sopravveste, *n.f.* Overall; overcoat.
sopravvissuto, sopravvivente, *n.m.a.* Survivor; surviving.
sopravvivenza, *n.f.* Survival.
sopravvivere, *v.i.* To survive, to outlive. **— ad un amico,** to outlive a friend.
sopreccedente, *a.* Far exceeding, superabounding.
sopredificare, *v.t.* To build upon.
soprintendente, *n.m.* Superintendent.
soprintendenza, *n.f.* Superintendence.
soprintendere [soprintEndere], *v.t.* To superintend, to direct, to control.
soprumano [cp. **sopraumano**].
sopruso, *n.m.* Overbearing act, abuse of powe", tyranny, imposition; insult; outrage.
soqquadrare, *v.t.* To turn topsy-turvy.
soqquadro, *n.m.* Confusion, disorder; commotion. **Mettere a —,** to throw into confusion, to turn upside down.
sor, sora, *n.m.f.* (*colloq.*) Mr.; Mrs.
sorba, *n.f.* (*Bot.*) Sorb-apple; service-tree.
sorbettare, *v.t.* To freeze (ice-cream, etc.).
sorbettarsi, *v.r.* (*fig.*) To listen to a rigmarole.
sorbettiera, *n.f.* Ice-box.
sorbettiere, *n.m.* Ice-cream seller.
sorbetto, *n.m.* Ice-cream; iced drink; sherbet.
sorbire, *v.t.* To sip; to swallow.

sorbirsi, *v.r.* To submit to, to be subject to. **— un affronto,** to swallow an insult.
sorbo, *n.m.* (*Bot.*) Service-tree, sorb-apple tree.
sorcio [sOrcio], *n.m.* (*Zool.*) Mouse; rat.
sordaggine [sordAggine], *n.f.* Hardness of hearing, slight deafness.
sordamente, *adv.* Dully, with a rumbling sound, hollowly, deeply.
sordastro, *a.* Hard of hearing.
sordezza, *n.f.* Deafness.
sordidamente, *adv.* Sordidly, dirtily.
sordidezza, *n.f.* Dirtiness, sordidness.
sordido [sOrdido], *a.* Dirty; sordid, mean, ignoble; niggardly.
sordina, sordino, *n.f.m.* (*Mus.*) Mute; sordine. **In sordina,** quietly, noiselessly; on the sly; **alla sordina,** stealthily.
sordità [-à], *n.f.* Deafness.
sordo, *n.m.* Deaf person. **I sordi,** deaf people; **parlare ai sordi,** to waste one's breath; **fare il —,** to turn a deaf ear.
sordo, *a.* Deaf; dull, insensible; muffled (of sound); hollow (voice); underhand. **Dolore —,** a dull ache; **sala sorda,** hall with bad acoustics; **— spaccato, — come una campana,** deaf as a post, deaf as a door-nail.
sordomuto, *n.m.a.* Deaf mute; deaf and dumb.
sorella, *n.f.* Sister. **— di latte,** foster-sister; **da —,** like a sister; **— maggiore,** elder sister.
sorellastra, *n.f.* Step-sister, half-sister.
sorellevole [sorellEvole], *a.* Sisterly.
sorgente, *n.f.* Source, spring, fountain; cause, origin, beginning. **Le sorgenti d'un fiume,** the sources of a river; **acqua di —,** spring water; **sorgenti termali,** hot springs; **le sorgenti della ricchezza,** the sources of wealth.
sorgente, *a.* Rising. **La luna —,** the rising moon.
sorgere [sOrgere], *v.i.* To rise, to get up, to arise; to issue, to spring, to flow from. **Il monte sorge,** the hill rises; **— a parlare,** to rise to speak; **il sole sorge,** the sun is rising.
sorgimento, *n.m.* Rise, source.
sorgiva, *n.f.* Spring (of water).
sorgivo, *a.* Springing, issuing. **Acqua sorgiva,** spring water.
sorgo, *n.m.* (*Bot.*) Sorghum.
soriano, *a.* Syrian. **Gatto —,** tabby cat.
sorite, *n.f.* Chain-syllogism.
sormontabile [sormontAbile], *a.* Surmountable.
sormontare, *v.t.* To surmount, to surpass, to overcome.
sornacchiare, *v.t.* To spit up, to cough up.
sornione, *a.* Artful, foxy, crafty, sly.
sororale, *a.* (*Lit.*) Sisterly.
sorpassare, To surpass, to overtake; to outdo, to excel.
sorpassato, *a.* Out-of-date, old-fashioned.
sorpasso, *n.m.* (*Motor.*) Overtaking, passing. **Divieto di —,** no overtaking, (*Am.*) no passing.
sorprendente, *a.* Surprising, astonishing, amazing.
sorprendentemente, *adv.* Surprisingly.
sorprendere [sorprEndere], *v.t.i.* To surprise, to astonish, to take unawares; to take advantage of. **— la buona fede altrui,** to deceive another person.
sorpresa, *n.f.* Surprise, wonder, astonishment. **Di —,** by surprise; **con mia grande —,** greatly to my surprise; **fare una —,** to spring a surprise.
sorreggere [sorrEggere , *v.t.* To ho'd up, to sustain, to prop up.
sorridente, *a.* Smiling.
sorridentemente, *adv.* Smilingly.
sorridere [sorrIdere], *v.i.* To smile. **Mi sorride l'idea,** the idea appeals to me; **— a,** to smile on; **— di,** to smile at.
sorrisino, sorrisetto, *n.m.* Half smile, slight smile.
sorriso, *n.m.* Smile. **— beffardo,** sneer; **— di pietà,** pitying smile.
sorsata, *n.f.* Gulp, draught; sip.
sorseggiare, sorsare, *v.t.i.* To sip; to gulp, to take a draught; to tipple.
sorsellino, sorsetto, *n.m.* Taste, sip, just a drop.
sorso, *n.m.* Sip; gulp, draught; drink, drop. **A sorsi,** in sips; **in un —,** at a gulp.
sorta, *n.f.* Sort, kind, quality. **Ogni — di gente,** all sorts of people; **farne di ogni —,** to make all kinds of mistakes; **senza guadagno di —,** without any gain whatsoever; **di — che,** so that; **di tal —,** in such a way.
sorte, *n.f.* Lot; luck, chance, fortune; destiny, fate; augury. **Toccare in —,** to be one's lot, to fall to one's lot; **aver la mala —,** to have bad luck; **tirare a —,** to draw lots; **la — delle armi,** the fortunes of war; **le sorti del mondo,** the future of mankind.
sorteggiare, *v.t.i.* To draw lots, to draw by lot.
sorteggio [sortEggio], *n.m.* Drawing of lots, draw.
sortilegio [sortilEgio], *n.m.* Sorcery, witchcraft.
sortilego [sortIlego], *n.m.* Sorcerer.
sortire (1), *v.t.* To draw or choose by lot, to obtain by lot; to be endowed with. **— buon esito,** to turn out well, to succeed.
sortire (2), *v.i.* To go out, to come out; to emerge, to issue, to spring.
sortita, *n.f.* (*Mil.*) Sally; (*colloq.*) exit, way out; (*Theat.*) actor's entrance; (*fig.*) wisecrack, smart reply, sally.
sorto [cp. **sorgere**].
sorvegliante, *n.m.* Caretaker, watchman, keeper; overseer, inspector.
sorveglianza, *n.f.* Supervision, surveillance, inspection, watching, care.
sorvegliare, *v.t.* To watch over, to watch, to inspect, to invigilate; to supervise, to keep an eye on.
sorvegliato, *p.p.a.* Watched, supervised; (*Law*) under police observation.
sorvolare, *v.t.i.* To fly over, to pass over; to rise above. **— il territorio nemico,** to fly over enemy territory.
sorvolata, *n.f.* (*Aviat.*) Flight (over).
soscritto [cp. **sottoscritto**].
sosia [sOsia], *n.m.* (One's) double, second self.
sospendere [sospEndere], *v.t.* To hang up, to suspend; to defer; to interrupt; to discontinue, to adjourn. **— i pagamenti,** to suspend payment; **— il lavoro,** to stop working; **— un alunno dalla scuola,** to send a pupil down, to suspend a pupil.

sospensione, *n.f.* Suspension, discontinuance, adjournment. **Molla di —,** suspension spring; **— dall'ufficio,** suspension from office; **conti in —,** outstanding accounts.
sospensiva, *n.f.* Delay; adjournment.
sospensivamente, *adv.* Doubtfully, dubiously.
sospensivo, *a.* Doubtful, uncertain; suspensive.
sospensorio [sospensOrio], *n.m.* (*Anat.*) Suspensorium; suspensory muscle or bandage; truss.
sospensorio [sospensOrio], *a.* Suspensory.
sospesamente, *adv.* Uncertainly.
sospeso, *a,* Hanging, suspended; uncertain. **In —,** in suspense, undecided; **ponte —,** suspension bridge; **tenere in —,** to keep in suspense.
sospettabile [sospettAbile], *a.* Liable to suspicion; open to suspicion.
sospettabilità [-à], *n.f.* Liability to suspicion.
sospettamente, *adv.* Suspectly.
sospettare, *v.t.i.* To suspect; to distrust, to doubt; to surmise, to imagine.
sospetto, *n.m.* Suspicion; doubt, distrust; diffidence, timidity; suspect (person).
sospetto, *a.* Suspicious.
sospettosamente, *adv.* Suspiciously, timidly.
sospettoso, *a.* Suspicious; diffident, distrustful, timid, cautious.
sospingere [sospIngere], *v.t.* To push, to impel; to stimulate, to goad.
sospingimento, *n.m.* Pushing, push, shove.
sospinto, *a.* Pushed, shoved. **Ad ogni piè —,** at every step, constantly.
sospirare, *v.t.i.* To sigh, to long for, to sigh for, to desire.
sospiro, *n.m.* Sigh; breath, gasp, long-drawn sigh.
sospirosamente, *adv.* Plaintively, sighingly.
sospiroso, *a.* Sighing, plaintive.
sossopra, *adv.* Topsy-turvy, upside down. **Mettere —,** to turn upside down.
sosta, *n.f.* Stop, pause, stay; suspension; respite; (*Comm.*) demurrage. **Diritti di —,** demurrage duty; **far — a,** to stop at; **senza —,** incessantly; (*Motor.*) **divieto di —, proibizione di —,** no parking.
sostantivamente, *adv.* Substantively.
sostantivare, *v.t.* To substantiate.
sostantivo, *n.m.a.* Substantive.
sostanza, *n.f.* Substance; essence, gist; solidity, firmness; wealth, property, riches; patrimony, estate. **— alimentare,** foodstuff.
sostanziale, *a.* Substantial.
sostanzialità [-à], *n.f.* Substantiality.
sostanzialmente, *adv.* Substantially.
sostanziare, *v.t.* To substantiate.
sostanzioso, *a.* Substantial; nutritious, nourishing; full-bodied (of wine).
sostare, sostarsi, *v.i.r.* To stop, to stay; to pause, to halt.
sostegno, *n.m.* Support, prop, stay; buttress; supporter, help. **— della vecchiaia,** support of old age; **muro di —,** supporting wall, retaining wall.
sostenere, *v.t.* To sustain, to bear, to uphold, to support; to maintain; to provide for, to feed. **— una parte,** to play a part; **— un principio,** to uphold a principle; **— un attacco,** to meet an attack; **— una perdita,** to sustain a loss.
sostenersi, *v.r.* To bear; to uphold; to support oneself.
sostenibile [sostenIbile], *a.* Sustainable, maintainable.
sostenimento, *n.m.* Support, maintenance.
sostenitore, sostenitrice, *n.m.f.* Supporter, maintainer.
sostentamento, *n.m.* Subsistence, maintenance, sustenance.
sostentare, *v.t.* To support (a family, etc.), to maintain; to sustain.
sostentazione *n. f.* Maintenance.
sostenutezza, *n.f.* Stiffness; reservedness, reserve; haughtiness.
sostenuto, *p.p.a.* Supported, sustained; reserved, haughty, distant. **Fare il —,** to be uppish, to give the cold shoulder.
sostituibile [sostituIbile], *a.* Replaceable.
sostituire, *v.t.* To replace, to substitute; to supersede; to deputize for.
sostituto, *n.m.* Substitute, deputy.
sostitutore, sostitutrice, *n.m.f.* Replacer, substitute.
sostituzione, *n.f.* Substitution, replacement. **In — di,** in place of.
sostrato, *n.m.* Substratum, subsoil.
sottaceti, *n.m.pl.* Pickles.
sottacqua, *adv.* Underwater.
sottana, *n.f.* Skirt; slip.
sottanina, *n.f.* Petticoat (under-skirt).
sottecchi, *adv.* Stealthily, by stealth. **Guardar —,** to look out of the corner of one's eye.
sottendere [sottEndere], *v.t.* (*Geom.*) To subtend.
sottentrare, *v.i.* To replace; to succeed, to take the place of; to slip in, to creep in.
sotterfugio [sotterfUgio], *n.m.* Subterfuge, expedient; evasion, shift.
sotterra, *adv.* Underground.
sotterramento, *n.m.* Burying, burial, interment.
sotterranea [sotterrAnea], *n.f.* Tube, underground (railway).
sotterraneo [sotterrAneo], *n.m.* Cave, vault, underground passage.
sotterraneo [sotterrAneo], *a.* Subterranean, underground.
sotterrare, *v.t.* To bury, to inter; to hide, to conceal; (*Agric.*) to earth up.
sottesa, *n.f.* (*Geom.*) Chord.
sotteso, *a.* (*Geom.*) Subtending.
sottigliezza, *n.f.* Thinness, fineness; (*fig.*) subtlety, finesse, ingenuity.
sottile, *a.* Thin, slender; tenuous, fine; subtle, acute, sharp, discerning; insidious. **Sottili distinzioni,** subtle distinctions; **guardare per il —,** to split hairs, to quibble; **voce —,** thin voice; (*Med.*) **mal —,** consumption.
sottilità [-à], *n.f.* Thinness, fineness.
sottilizzare, *v.i.* To draw fine distinctions, to split hairs, to chop logic.
sottilmente, *adv.* Slenderly; subtly.
sottinsù, *adv.* **Da —,** from below, upwards (*esp. ref. to* ceiling paintings).
sottintendente, *n.m.* Assistant manager.
sottintendenza, *n.f.* Assistant managership.
sottintendere [sottintEndere], *v.t.* To understand (by implication), to take as meant, to imply; to guess. **Si sottintende,** it's understood.

sottinteso, *n.m.* Implication, thing understood; double meaning. **Senza sottintesi,** without mental reservations.
sotto, *adv.prep.* Under, underneath, beneath; below, down; in, by. **Andar —,** to go under, to go underneath, **di —,** underneath, below, downstairs; **scendere di —,** to go downstairs, to go below; **— Natale,** towards Christmas; **— la tenda,** under canvas; **— le coperte,** in bed; **andar — il treno,** to be run over by a train; **— la pioggia,** in the rain; **— condizione,** on condition; **sott'olio,** in oil; (*Mil.*) **— le armi,** on active service.
sotto-, *prefix,* Under-, assistant-, sub-.
sottocapo, *n.m.* Second in command.
sottocchi, sottocchio [sottOcchio], *adv.* Under one's eyes, at hand.
sottoclausola [sottoclAusola], *n.f.* Sub-clause.
sottocoda, *n.m.* Crupper (of a horse).
sottocommissione, *n.f.* Sub-committee.
sottocoperta, *n.f.* Coverlet; (*Naut.*) lower deck.
sottocoppa, *n.f.* Saucer.
sottocorrente, *n.f.* Under-current.
sottocutaneo [sottocutAneo], *a.* Subcutaneous.
sottodiacono [sottodiAcono], *n.m.* (*Eccles.*) Sub-deacon.
sottofascia [sottofAscia], *n.m.* Printed matter (by post in open envelope).
sottogamba, *adv.* Carelessly, in one's stride, without the slightest effort.
sottogola, *n.m.* Chin-strap.
sottolineare, *v.t.* To underline; (*fig.*) to emphasize, to accentuate.
sottolineatura, *n.f.* Underlining.
sottolunare, *a.* Sublunary.
sottomano, *n.m.* Writing-pad, blotting-pad; tip, gratuity. **Di —,** underhand, secretly; **aver qualcosa —,** to have something ready *or* at hand.
sottomarino, *n.m.a.* Submarine.
sottomesso, *a.* Subdued, obedient, submissive, respectful.
sottomettere [sottomEttere], *v.t.* To subdue, to subject; to submit, to put forward; to vanquish.
sottomettersi [sottomEttersi], *v.r.* To yield, to acquiesce, to give in.
sottominare, *v.t.* To undermine.
sottoministro, *n.m.* (*Pol.*) Under-secretary.
sottomissione, *n.f.* Submission, subjection; submissiveness; humility. **Ridurre i rebelli in —,** to reduce the rebels to submission.
sottomurata, *n.f.* (*Arch.*) Substructure; footings.
sottonotato, *a.* Undermentioned.
sottopancia [sottopAncia], *n.m.* Belly-band (of a horse), girth-strap.
sottopassaggio [sottopassAggio], *n.m.* Subway, underground passage.
sottopiede, *n.m.* Foot-strap (for spurs); cork sole.
sottoporre, *v.t.* To submit; to subject, to subjugate.
sottoporsi, *v.r.* To undergo, to submit to. **— ad un'operazione,** to undergo an operation.
sottoportico [sottopOrtico], *n.m.* (*Arch.*) Porch.
sottoposizione, *n.f.* Subjection, submission, subordination.
sottoposto, *n.m.a.* Subordinate.
sottoprefetto, *n.m.* Sub-prefect.
sottoprefettura, *n.f.* Sub-prefecture.
sottopriore, *n.m.* (*Eccles.*) Sub-prior.
sottoprodotto, *n.m.* By-product.
sottordine [sottOrdine], *adv.* **In —,** subordinately; subject to orders.
sottoscala, *n.f.* Space beneath stairs.
sottoscritto, *n.m.a.* Undersigned.
sottoscrittore, *n.m.* Subscriber, signatory.
sottoscrivere [sottoscrIvere], *v.t.i.* To subscribe, to sign, to endorse; to assent, to agree; to adhere. **— a un prestito,** to subscribe to a loan.
sottoscriversi [sottoscrIversi], *v.r.* To sign oneself. **Mi sottoscrivo Suo devotissimo,** I remain yours faithfully (formal end of letter).
sottoscrizione, *n.f.* Subscription; fee; signature. **Fare una — per,** to raise a subscription for.
sottosegretario [sottosegretArio], *n.m.* Under-secretary.
sottosopra, *adv.* Upside down, topsy-turvy.
sottospecie [sottospEcie], *n.f.* Sub-species.
sottostante, *a.* Underneath, lying below, down below.
sottostare, *v.i.* To be under, to lie below, to be subordinate; to undergo, to experience. **— ad una perdita,** to suffer a loss.
sottosuolo, *n.m.* Subsoil.
sottotenente, *n.m.* (*Mil.*) Second-lieutenant; (*Naut.*) **— di vascello,** sub-lieutenant.
sottoterra, *adv.* Underground.
sottotitolo [sottotItolo], *n.m.* Sub-title.
sottovaso, *n.m.* Saucer for flowerpot.
sottovento, *n.adv.* Lee; leeward.
sottoveste, *n.m.* Waistcoat; under-garment.
sottovoce, *adv.* In an undertone, in a low voice.
sottraendo, *n.m.* (*Math.*) Subtrahend.
sottrarre, *v.t.* To take away, to subtract; to deduct; to steal from; to embezzle; to deliver from, to release; to rescue; to guard.
sottrarsi, *v.r.* To escape from, to get out of. **— a un pericolo,** to escape a danger.
sottrazione, *n.f.* Subtraction, removal; taking away; theft.
sottufficiale, *n.m.* (*Mil.Naut.*) Non-commissioned officer; warrant officer.
sovente, soventemente, *adv.* Often, frequently.
soverchiamente, *adv.* Excessively, immoderately.
soverchiante, *a.* Overwhelming, crushing; surpassing.
soverchiare, *v.t.i.* To overcome, to surpass, to surmount; to bully, to browbeat, to oppress; to be in excess.
soverchiatore, soverchiatrice, *n.m.f.a.* Overbearing person; overbearing.
soverchieria [soverchierIa], *n.f.* Bullying, browbeating, arrogance, imposition.
soverchio [sovErchio], *n.m.a.* Excess, surplus; excessive.
sovesciare, *v.t.* (*Agric.*) To plough in.
sovra [cp. **sopra**].
sovrabbondante, *a.* Superabundant, copious; emphatic; high-flown (of style).
sovrabbondantemente, *adv.* Superabundantly, copiously.

sovrabbondanza, *n.f.* Superabundance, plenty.
sovrabbondare, *v.i.* To superabound, to be in excess; to be plentiful.
sovrabbondevole [sovrabbondEvole], *a.* Superabundant, copious.
sovrana, *n.f.* Sovereign, queen.
sovranamente, *adv.* Royally, in royal style; superlatively.
sovraneggiare, *v.t.i.* To rule; to domineer.
sovranità [-à], *n.f.* Sovereignty.
sovrano, *n.m.a.* Sovereign; supreme.
sovrapporre, *v.t.* To lay upon, to place upon, to superimpose.
sovrapporsi, *v.r.* To place oneself above; to get the mastery of.
sovrapposizione, *n.f.* Superposition; overlapping.
sovraproduzione, *n.f.* Over-production.
sovrastante, *a.* Overhanging; (*fig.*) imminent, threatening.
sovrastare, *v.i.* To overtop, to overhang, to stand above; to excel, to be superior; to threaten, to be imminent.
sovreccellente, *a.* Super-excellent.
sovreccitare, *v.t.* To over-excite.
sovreccitato, *a.* Overstrung, over-excited, worked-up, agitated.
sovrimporre, *v.t.* To superimpose.
sovrimposta, *n.f.* Super-tax.
sovrumanamente, *adv.* Superhumanly.
sovrumano, *a.* Superhuman; supernatural.
sovvenibile [sovvenIbile], *a.* Capable of being helped; able to be remembered.
sovvenimento, *n.m.* Help, assistance; recollection.
sovvenire (1), *v.t.* To help, to assist, to aid.
sovvenire (2), **sovvenirsi,** *v.i.r.* To remember, to recollect, to call to mind.
sovvenire, *n.m.* (*Lit.*) Recollection, remembrance, souvenir.
sovventore, *n.m.* Provider, helper, supporter.
sovvenzionare, *v.t.* To subsidize, to aid financially, to finance.
sovvenzione, *n.f.* Subvention, subsidy.
sovversione, *n.f.* Subversion; overthrow.
sovversivo, *n.m.a.* Political agitator; subversive.
sovvertimento, *n.m.* Subversion, overturning, overthrow.
sovvertire, *v.t.* To subvert, to overthrow, to upset.
sovvertitore, sovvertitrice, *n.m.f.* Subverter.
sozzamente, *adv.* Filthily, nastily.
sozzare, *v.t.* To make foul [cp. **insozzare**].
sozzezza, *n.f.* Filthiness, nastiness.
sozzo, *a.* Filthy, nasty, foul; obscene.
sozzume, sozzura, *n.m.f.* Filth, dirt, beastliness; pollution.
spaccalegna, *n.m.* Wood-cutter.
spaccamento, *n.m.* Splitting, cleaving.
spaccamontagne, spaccamonti, *n.m.* Braggart.
spaccapietre, *n.m.* Stone-breaker.
spaccare, *v.t.* To cleave, to split. **— in due,** to cut in two.
spaccarsi, *v.r.* To split asunder, to break in two; to crack, to burst.
spaccatamente, *adv.* Decidedly.
spaccato, *n.m.* (*Arch.*) Section; cleft, split.
spaccatura, *n.f.* Cleavage, split, fissure; crevice, crack, cleft.
spacchettare, *v.t.* To undo (a parcel).
spacciabile [spacciAbile], *a.* Saleable.
spacciare, *v.t.* To sell; to sell out; to sell off; to circulate; to dispatch, to get rid of, to kill. **Spacciarle grosse,** to spin yarns, to tell tall stories; **— una faccenda,** to press forward a matter; **è spacciato !** He is finished, he is done for.
spacciarsi, *v.r.* To pass for, to pretend to be. **Si spaccia per avvocato,** he sets up for being a lawyer; **si spaccia per ricco,** he gives out that he's wealthy.
spacciato, *p.p.a.* Done for, lost; undone, given up (by doctors, etc.). **Siamo spacciati,** we're ruined; **è bello e —,** he's done for.
spacciatamente, *adv.* At once, hurriedly.
spacciatore, *n.m.* Seller; distributor; passer of false money.
spaccio [spAccio], *n.m.* Sale; shop; tobacco shop. **— di vino,** wine-shop.
spacco, *n.m.* Split, crack.
spacconata, *n.f.* Boast, bravado, brag.
spaccone, *n.m.* Braggart; blusterer; swaggerer, boaster.
spada, *n.f.* Sword; (*Cards*) spade. **Passare a fil di —,** to put to the sword; **a — tratta,** openly, utterly; (*Zool.*) **pesce —,** sword-fish.
spadaccino, *n.m.* Swordsman; a gallant; a bully.
spadaio, spadaro [spadAio], *n.m.* Swordmaker.
spadina, *n.f.* Sword-shaped hairpin.
spadino, *n.m.* Short sword; dirk.
spadone, *n.m.* Big sword, sabre; broadsword.
spadronare, spadroneggiare, *v.i.* To domineer, to boss.
spaesato, *n.m.* Out of one's element; disconcerted.
spaghetti, *n.m.pl.* Spaghetti, fine macaroni.
spaghetto, *n.m.* String, twine, pack-thread; (*colloq.*) fear.
spagliamento, *n.m.* Removal of straw.
spagliare, *v.t.* To remove straw (from bottle, etc.); to feed (animals) on straw.
spagliarsi, *v.r.* To spread over the fields (of floods).
spagliatura, *n.f.* Unpacking (of things in straw).
spaglio [spAglio], *n.m.* Flooding.
Spagna, *n.f.* (*Geog.*) Spain.
spagnolaggine, spagnolata [spagnolAggine], *n.f.* Bravado, boasting.
spagnoleggiare, *v.i.* To affect Spanish manners.
spagnolescamente, *adv.* Like a Spaniard.
spagnolesco, *a.* In Spanish style.
spagnoletta, *n.f.* Sash-bolt (of window); kind of cigarette.
spagnolismo, *n.m.* Spanish ways, words, etc.
spagnolo, spagnuolo, *n.m.a.* Spaniard; Spanish.
spago, *n.m.* String, cord; twine, pack-thread; (*colloq.*) fear, funk. **Un pezzo di —,** a bit of string.
spaiare, *v.t.* To separate a pair; to unmatch.
spaiato, *a.* Odd, unmatched.
spalancare, *v.t.* To throw wide open, to open wide. **— la porta,** to throw open the door; **— gli occhi,** to open one's eyes wide, to stare.

spalancatamente, *adv.* Too open, too wide.
spalare, *v.t.* To shovel, to shovel away (snow, etc.); to feather (oars).
spalata, spalatura, *n.f.* Shovelling.
spalcare, *v.t.* To remove scaffolding; to cut down boughs.
spalco, *n.m.* Distinction. **Attore di —,** distinguished actor.
spalla, *n.f.* Shoulder; back; aid, support. **Alzare le spalle,** to shrug one's shoulders; **volgere le spalle,** to turn one's back; **vivere alle spalle altrui,** to live at another's expense; **volgere le spalle,** to take to flight.
spallaccio [spallAccio], *n.m.* Shoulder-strap.
spallarsi, *v.r.* To dislocate one's shoulder.
spallata, *n.f.* Push with the shoulder; shrug of the shoulders.
spalleggiamento, *n.m.* Support, backing.
spalleggiare, *v.t.* To support, to back, to favour.
spalleggiatore, *n.m.* Supporter, backer.
spalletta, *n.f.* Parapet, embankment.
spalliera, *n.f.* Back (of chair, etc.); espalier (tree).
spallina, spallino, *n.f.m.* Epaulet; shoulder-strap. **Bagnare le spalline,** to toast a man on his promotion.
spallone, *n.m.* Smuggler.
spalluccia [spallUccia], *n.f.* Narrow shoulder. **Fare spallucce,** to shrug one's shoulders.
spalmare, *v.t.* To smear, to spread, to coat, to dab. **— il pane di burro,** to butter the bread.
spalmata, spalmatura, *n.f.* Smear, smearing, coat; dab (of butter, etc.).
spalto, *n.m.* (*Mil.*) Glacis, bastion, embankment.
spampanamento, *n.m.* Stripping (of leaves, etc.); (*fig.*) boasting, ostentation.
spampanare, *v.t.* To strip (a vine) of leaves.
spampanarsi, *v.r.* To shed leaves; to open (of a rose); (*fig.*) to boast, to show off.
spanare, *v.t.* (*Agric.*) To remove the earth from around a root; (*Mech.*) to break the thread of a screw.
spanciare, *v.i.* To bulge, to burst.
spanciarsi, *v.r.* **— dalle risa,** to split one's sides with laughing.
spanciata, *n.f.* Bellyful.
spandere [spAndere], *v.t.i.* To spill, to pour out, to slop; to scatter; to leak. **Questa bottiglia spande,** this bottle leaks; **spendere e —,** to squander.
spandimento, *n.m.* Spilling, pouring out; leakage.
spanna, *n.f.* Span; short distance. **Lungo una —,** a span wide; **avere la vista corta una —,** not to see beyond the end of one's nose.
spannare, *v.t.* To skim milk, to cream.
spannato, *a.* Skimmed (milk).
spannatura, *n.f.* Skimming.
spannocchiare, *v.t.* (*Agric.*) To strip maize stalks.
spantanarsi, *v.r.* To get oneself out of a morass.
spanto, *a.* Spread, poured forth, spilt.
spappagallare, *v.i.* To chatter like a parrot, to chatter.
spappolare, *v.t.* To pulp, to crush, to mash.
spappolarsi, *v.r.* To become mushy; to be dissolved.
sparadrappo, *n.m.* (*Med.*) Sticking-plaster.
sparagiaia [sparagiAia], *n.f.* Asparagus bed.
sparagio, sparago [spAragio, spArago], *n.m.* Asparagus.
sparagnare, *v.i.* To economize.
sparamento, *n.m.* Discharge (of firearm).
sparapane, *n.m.* Idler, loafer.
sparare, *v.t.i.* To shoot, to fire, to discharge (a gun, etc.); to rip open. **Tutte le batterie sparavano,** all the batteries were firing; **— le ultime cartucce,** to fight to the last ditch; **spararle grosse,** to tell tall stories.
spararsi, *v.r.* To shoot oneself. **— una revolverata,** to shoot oneself with a revolver.
sparata, *n.f.* Discharge (of firearms), volley. **Parlare alla —,** to talk openly, without interruptions.
sparato, *n.m.* Shirt-front; fly (in trousers).
sparato, *p.p.a.* Shot.
sparatore, sparatrice, *n.m.f.* Shooter, shot.
sparatoria [sparatOria], *n.f.* Indiscriminate shooting, exchange of shots, firing.
sparecchiamento, *n.m.* Clearing away.
sparecchiare, *v.t.* To clear away, to clear the table.
sparecchio [sparEcchio], *n.m.* Clearing the table.
spareggio [sparEggio], *n.m.* Deficit, difference, disparity, inequality; (*Sport*) replay.
spargere [spArgere], *v.t.* To spread, to strew, to scatter; to disseminate; to shed, to spill. **— lagrime,** to shed tears; **— la voce,** to spread the rumour; **— il proprio sangue,** to shed one's blood; **— fiori,** to strew flowers.
spargimento, *n.m.* Spreading, shedding, spilling. **Senza — di sangue,** without bloodshed.
spargitore, spargitrice, *n.m.f.* Spreader, disseminator. **— di notizie,** news-vendor; spreader of news.
sparigliare, *v.t.i.* To make odd, to unmatch.
sparire, *v.i.* To disappear, to vanish; to abscond.
sparizione, *n.f.* Disappearance.
sparlamento, *n.m.* Backbiting, malicious gossip.
sparlare, *v.i.* To speak ill of, to backbite, to slander; to talk scandal about.
sparlatore, sparlatrice, *n.m.f.* Backbiter, slanderer; scandal-monger.
sparnazzamento, *n.m.* Scattering, squandering.
sparnazzare, *v.i.* To scatter, to squander.
sparo, *n.m.* Shot, report, detonation, explosion. **Si udì uno —,** a shot was heard.
sparpagliamento, *n.m.* Spreading, diffusion; dispersal.
sparpagliare, *v.t.* To spread, to scatter; to disseminate; to disperse.
sparsamente, *adv.* Sparsely, here and there.
sparso, *a.* Scattered, spread, sprinkled, strewn. **Capelli sparsi,** dishevelled hair.
spartanamente, *adv.* Like a Spartan.
spartano, *n.m.a.* Spartan.
spartiacque [spartiAcque], *n.m.* (*Geog.*) Watershed.
spartibile [spartIbile], *a.* Divisible.
spartire, *v.t.* To divide up, to partition, to separate; to share, to distribute; (*Mus.*) to score. **Non aver nulla da — con,** to have nothing in common with.

spartitamente, *adv.* Separately, one by one, dividedly.
spartito, *n.m.* (*Mus.*) Score.
spartizione, *n.f.* Partition, division, distribution.
sparto, *n.m.* (*Bot.*) Esparto grass.
sparutezza, *n.f.* Thinness, emaciation; scantiness, meagreness.
sparuto, *a.* Thin, lean, emaciated; lank; scanty, scarce.
sparviere, sparviero, *n.m.* (*Zool.*) Hawk.
spasimante, *n.m.* Ardent wooer, lover; lovesick lad.
spasimare, *v.i.* To suffer agonies; to be in great pain; to long for, to desire ardently.
spasimatamente, *adv.* Ardently, intensely.
spasimo, spasmo [spAsimo], *n.m.* Agony, pain; spasm.
spasmodicamente, *adv.* Spasmodically.
spasmodico [spasmOdico], *a.* Spasmodic.
spassare, *v.t.* To amuse, to give amusement, to divert.
spassarsi, *v.r.* To amuse oneself, to enjoy oneself. **Spassarsela,** to have a good time.
spasseggiare [cp. **passeggiare**].
spassevole [spassEvole], *a.* Amusing, diverting.
spassionarsi, *v.r.* To calm oneself; to free oneself from passion.
spassionatamente, *adv.* Dispassionately, impartially.
spassionatezza, *n.f.* Impartiality, dispassionateness.
spassionato, *a.* Dispassionate, impartial.
spasso, *n.m.* Amusement, recreation, diversion; walk. **Andare a —,** to go for a walk; **essere a —,** to be out of work; **mandare a —,** to get rid of, to give the sack to; **prendersi — di,** to make fun of.
spassoso, *a.* Amusing, diverting, pleasant, entertaining.
spastare, *v.t.* To ungum, to unpaste.
spastoiare, *v.t.* To unshackle, to set free.
spastoiarsi, *v.r.* To rid oneself of.
spato, *n.m.* (*Min.*) Spar.
spatola [spAtola], *n.f.* Spatula; (*Theat.*) Harlequin's wooden sword.
spatriamento, *n.m.* Expatriation.
spatriare [cp. **espatriare**].
spauracchio [spaurAcchio], *n.m.* Bogey, bugbear; scarecrow.
spaurimento, *n.m.* Alarm, fright.
spaurire, *v.t.* To frighten, to alarm.
spaurirsi, *v.r.* To take fright, to be frightened.
spavaldamente, *adv.* Arrogantly; boldly, shamelessly.
spavalderia [spavalderIa], *n.f.* Arrogance, effrontery; boastfulness.
spavaldo, *a.* Arrogant, bold-faced; insolent; boisterous, unruly, aggressive.
spaventapasseri [spaventapAsseri], *n.m.* Scarecrow.
spaventare, *v.t.* To frighten, to terrify, to scare, to alarm.
spaventarsi, *v.r.* To take fright, to be frightened, to be scared or alarmed.
spaventatamente, *adv.* Fearfully, timorously.
spaventevole [spaventEvole], *a.* Frightful, dreadful, fearful, terrible; enormous.
spaventevolmente, *adv.* Frightfully.
spavento, *n.m.* Fright, fear, scare; terror. **Far —,** to frighten, to cause alarm, to scare.
spaventosamente, *adv.* Fearfully, terribly, terrifyingly.
spaventoso, *a.* Frightful, dreadful, terrible.
spaziale, *a.* Spatial.
spaziare, *v.i.* To wander at large; to dilate, to expatiate.
spazieggiare, *v.t.* To space out.
spazieggiatura, *n.f.* Spacing.
spazientirsi, *v.r.* To lose patience.
spazio [spAzio], *n.m.* Space; room, interval, extension; interval of time. **— libero,** open space; **— per trenta persone,** room for thirty persons. **Non c'è — sufficiente,** there's not enough room.
spaziosamente, *adv.* Spaciously.
spaziosità [-à], *n.f.* Spaciousness, roominess, wideness.
spazioso, *a.* Ample, wide; roomy, spacious, capacious, extensive.
spazzacamino, *n.m.* Chimney-sweep.
spazzamento, *n.m.* Sweeping, cleaning, cleansing.
spazzamine, *n.m.* (*Naut.*) Mine-sweeper.
spazzaneve, *n.f.* Snow-plough; (*Ski-ing*) snow-plough position.
spazzare, *v.t.* To sweep, to clear; to clean. **— via,** to sweep away; **— le scale,** to sweep the stairs.
spazzata, *n.f.* Sweeping, riddance.
spazzatina, *n.f.* Dusting.
spazzatura, *n.f.* Sweepings; refuse, dirt.
spazzaturaio [spazzaturAio], *n.m.* Dustman, garbage collector; scavenger.
spazzavento, *n.m.* Windswept spot.
spazzino, *n.m.* Dustman; scavenger.
spazzola [spAzzola], *n.f.* Brush. **— da capelli,** hairbrush; **— da panni,** clothes brush.
spazzolaio [spazzolAio], *n.m.* Brush-maker.
spazzolare, *v.t.* To brush, to brush up; to dust.
spazzolarsi, *v.r.* To brush oneself. **— capelli,** to brush one's hair.
spazzolata, *n.f.* Brushing, brush-up.
spazzolino, *n.m.* Small brush. **— da denti,** tooth-brush.
specchiaio [specchiAio], *n.m.* Looking-glass maker.
specchiamento, *n.m.* Reflection (in a mirror).
specchiarsi, *v.r.* To look at oneself in a mirror; to be reflected. **— in uno,** to take someone as a model.
specchiato, *a.* Mirrored; flawless; upright, honest.
specchiera, *n.f.* Looking-glass, cheval-glass, pier-glass.
specchietto, *n.m.* Hand-mirror; (*fig.*) statement of accounts, summary.
specchio [spEcchio], *n.m.* Mirror, looking-glass; example, pattern. **Guardarsi nello —,** to look at oneself in the glass; **uno — d'acqua,** a sheet of water; **armadio a —,** wardrobe with mirror; **— ustorio,** burning-glass; (*Motor.*) **— retrospettivo,** driving mirror.
speciale, *a.* Special; peculiar, particular.
specialista (*pl.* **specialisti**), *n.m.a.* Specialist. **Farsi visitare da uno —,** to visit a specialist.
specialità [-à], *n.f.* Specialty, speciality.
specializzare, specializzarsi, *v.t.r* To specialize.

specializzato, *a.* Skilled; qualified. **Mano d'opera specializzata,** skilled labour.
specialmente, *adv.* Especially.
specie [spEcie], *n.f.* Species; kind, sort, quality. **— d'affari,** line of business; **— umana,** mankind; **sotto — di,** under pretence of; (*colloq.*) **far —,** to surprise, to astonish.
specie [spEcie], *adv.* Especially.
specifica [specIfica], *n.f.* Note, memorandum; bill.
specificamente, *adv.* Specifically.
specificamento, *n.m.* Specification.
specificare, *v.t.* To specify.
specificazione, *n.f.* Specification, detailed account.
specifico [specIfico], *n.m.a.* Specific. **Peso —,** specific gravity.
specillo, *n.m.* (*Med.*) Probe.
speciosamente, *adv.* Speciously.
speciosità [-à], *n.f.* Speciousness, plausibility.
specioso, *a.* Specious, plausible.
speco, *n.m.* Cave, cavern; den.
specola [spEcola], *n.f.* (*Astron.*) Observatory.
specolo [spEcolo], *n.m.* (*Med.*) Speculum.
speculabile [speculAbile], *a.* Open to speculation.
speculare, *v.t.i.* To speculate (in all senses); to observe; to meditate.
speculatamente, *adv.* Intentionally.
speculativa, *n.f.* Speculative faculty.
speculativamente, *adv.* Speculatively.
speculativo, *a.* Speculative.
speculatore, speculatrice, *n.m.f.* Speculator (in all senses).
speculazione, *n.f.* Speculation. **— fortunata,** successful speculation.
spedale, *n.m.* Hospital [cp. **ospedale**].
spedaliere, *n.m.a.* (*Hist.*) Knight Hospitaller; male nurse.
spedalità [-à], *n.f.* Hospital treatment.
spedarsi, *v.r.* To get footsore.
spediente, *n.m.* Expedient, makeshift.
spedire, *v.t.* To send, to forward, to dispatch. **— per ferrovia,** to send by rail; **dare un malato per spedito,** to give up hope for one sick.
spedirsi, *v.r.* To make haste, to hurry up; to be quick.
speditamente, *adv.* Quickly, promptly; fluently.
speditezza, *n.f.* Quickness, promptitude; readiness.
speditivamente, *adv.* Expeditiously.
speditivo, *a.* Expeditious, prompt.
spedito, *a.adv.* Quick, prompt, fluent; easy; fluently, quickly.
speditore, speditrice, *n.m.f.* Sender.
spedizione, *n.f.* Sending, dispatch, consignment; expedition (in all senses).
spedizioniere, *n.m.* Forwarding agent; carrier, shipper.
speglio [spEglio], *n.m.* (*Poet.*) Mirror.
spegnare, *v.t.* To redeem (from pawn).
spegnere [spEgnere], *v.t.* To extinguish, to put out, to quench; to turn out (lights, etc.), to switch off. **Spegni la luce,** put out the light; **— la sete,** to quench one's thirst; **— un incendio,** to extinguish a fire; **— un debito,** to pay a debt; (*Motor.*) **— il motore,** to shut off the engine.
spegnersi [spEgnersi], *v.r.* To be extinguished, to go out; to die out; to die, pass away, to vanish. **Il fuoco si è spento,** the fire has gone out; **si spense dolcemente,** he passed away peacefully.
spegnimento, *n.m.* Extinction (of fire); putting out (of light).
spegnimoccolo [spegnimOccolo], *n.m.* Candle-extinguisher.
spegnitoio [spegnitOio], *n.m.* Fire-extinguisher.
spegnitura, *n.f.* Extinction.
spelacchiare, *v.t.* To strip (of hair), to shear; (*fig.*) to fleece.
spelacchiarsi, *v.r.* To lose one's hair, to become bald.
spelacchiato, *a.* Bald, bare, shorn; (*fig.*) fleeced.
spelagare, *v.t.* (*Lit.*) To rescue, to set free.
spelare, *v.t.* To strip (of hair); to shear, to skin.
spelatura, *n.f.* Shearing.
spelazzare, *v.t.* To clean and card wool.
speleologia [speleologIa], *n.f.* Speleology, study of caves.
spellamento, *n.m.* Skinning; abrasion, blister.
spellare, *v.t.* To skin, to flay, to excoriate; (*fig.*) to extort (money).
spellarsi, *v.r.* To abrade one's skin; to peel (after a fever).
spellatura, *n.f.* Abrasion.
spellicciare, *v.t.* To skin.
spelonca, *n.f.* Cave, den.
spelta, *n.f.* (*Agric.*) Spelt.
speme, *n.f.* (*Poet.*) Hope.
spendaccione, *n.m.* Spendthrift.
spendere [spEndere], *v.t.i.* To spend, to pay out; to lay out, to expend; to employ, to make use of. **— e spandere,** to squander; **— un patrimonio,** to squander a fortune; **— il proprio tempo,** to devote one's time to.
spendereccio [spenderEccio], *a.* Prodigal, lavish.
spendibile [spendIbile], *a.* Spendable.
spendibilità [-à], *n.f.* Currency (of a bill, etc.).
spendicchiare, *v.t.* To spend a little at a time.
spendita [spEndita], *n.f.* Spending; uttering. **— di biglietti falsi,** offering forged notes.
spenditore, spenditrice, *n.m.f.* Spender, spendthrift.
spennacchiare, spennare, *v.t.* To pluck feathers; to pluck (a bird); (*fig.*) to fleece.
spensierataggine [spensieratAggine], *n.f.* Thoughtlessness; rashness, carelessness.
spensieratamente, *adv.* Thoughtlessly.
spensieratezza, *n.f.* Thoughtlessness, fickleness; rashness.
spensierato, *a.* Thoughtless, giddy-brained, fickle; elated; rash; carefree.
spento, *a.* Extinguished, put out; dead; exhausted [cp. **spegnere**].
spenzolare, *v.i.* To hang down, to dangle.
spenzolone, spenzoloni, *adv.* Dangling, hanging down.
spera, *n.f.* Sphere, globe; mirror; beam, ray; (*Lit.*) sky.
sperabile [sperAbile], *a.* To be hoped for. **E —,** it is to be hoped.

speranza, *n.f.* Hope; trust, confidence; expectation. **Senza —,** hopelessly; **con la — di,** in the hope of; **finchè c'è vita c'è —,** while there's life there's hope.
speranzosamente, *adv.* Hopefully.
speranzoso, *a.* Hopeful, confident.
sperare, *v.t.i.* To hope, to hope for; to trust, to expect; to rely on. **Lo spero,** I hope so; **spero in Dio,** I put my trust in God.
sperdere [spErdere], *v.t.* To disperse, to scatter, to dispel; to lose.
sperdersi [spErdersi], *v.r.* To be dispersed, to be scattered, to scatter; to get lost, to go astray; to disappear, to vanish.
sperduto, *a.* Lost, dispersed; missing.
spereggiare, *v.i.* To shine.
sperequazione, *n.f.* Unequal distribution; inequality of salaries, etc.
spergiurare, *v.t.i.* To abjure; to perjure oneself.
spergiuratore, spergiuratrice, *n.m.f.* Perjurer.
spergiurazione, *n.f.* Perjury.
spergiuro, *n.m.a.* Perjurer, perjury; perjured, false.
spericolato, *n.m.a.* Daring person, daredevil; rash; foolhardy.
sperimentale, *a.* Experimental.
sperimentalmente, *adv.* Experimentally.
sperimentare, *v.t* To experiment, to try, to test.
sperimento, *n.m.* Experiment.
sperma, *n.m.* (*Anat.*) Sperm, semen.
spermaceti, *n.m.* Spermaceti.
spermatozoo [spermatozOo], *n.m.* Spermatozoon.
speronara, *n.f.* (*Naut.*) Small row-boat.
speronare, *v.t.* (*Naut.*) To ram (a ship), to come into collision.
speronata, *n.f.* Prick with a spur; (*Naut.*) ramming.
sperone, *n.m.* Spur; (*Naut.*) ram; (*Arch.*) spur, abutment, buttress, counterfort [cp. **sprone**].
sperperamento, *n.m.* Wasting, squandering, dissipation.
sperperare, *v.t.* To waste, to squander, to dissipate.
sperperatore, sperperatrice, *n.m.f.* Waster, squanderer.
sperperio, sperpero [sperperIo, spErpero], *n.m.* Waste, squandering, dissipation.
sperpetua [sperpEtua], *n.f.* Bad luck.
sperso, *a.* Lost, dispersed, scattered [cp. **sperdere**].
sperticatamente, *adv.* Excessively.
sperticato, *a.* Overdone, exaggerated; enormous; too tall (of a tree). **Elogio —,** too high praise.
spesa, *n.f.* Expense, cost, price; shopping; expenses; outlay. **A proprie spese,** at one's own expense; **pagare le spese,** to defray expenses; **andare a far la —,** to go shopping; **non vale la —,** it isn't worth while.
spesare, *v.t.i.* To pay someone's expenses; to employ.
spesato, *p.p.a.* Paid for; all expenses paid; treated. **Egli è — di tutto,** all his expenses are paid.
spessamente, *adv.* Frequently, often.
spesseggiamento, *n.m.* Frequency.
spesseggiare, *v.t.i.* To repeat, to reiterate; to be frequent, to become frequent.
spessezza, *n.f.* Thickness, density.
spessire, *v.t.* To make thick, to thicken.
spesso, *a.* Thick, dense; frequent. **Spesse volte,** very often; **bosco —,** a dense wood.
spesso, *adv.* Often, frequently.
spessore, *n.m.* Thickness; depth; ply (of wood).
spetrare, *v.t.* To soften; (*fig.*) to soften somebody's heart.
spettabile [spettAbile], *a.* Worthy of respect, honourable, distinguished. (*Comm.*) **Spett. ditta,** Messrs.
spettabilità [-à], *n.f.* Respectability; importance.
spettacolo [spettAcolo], *n.m.* Spectacle, sight, view, scene; (*Theat.*) show, performance. (*Cinema, Theatre*) **— continuato,** continuous performance.
spettacolosamente, *adv.* Spectacularly, in a spectacular way.
spettacoloso, *a.* Spectacular, sensational.
spettante, *a.* Concerning, belonging to.
spettanza, *n.f.* Concern; competence; ownership; due, fee. **Non è di sua —,** it is not his duty, it is not within his competence.
spettare, *v.i.* To belong to, to concern, to be one's duty; to be due. **Ciò mi spetta per diritto,** this is due to me by right; **spetta a voi decidere,** it is up to you to decide.
spettatore, spettatrice, *n.m.f.* Spectator; bystander. (*Theat.*) **gli spettatori,** the audience.
spettegolare, *v.i.* To gossip.
spettinare, *v.t.* To ruffle someone's hair.
spettinarsi, *v.r.* To ruffle one's hair, to become dishevelled; to take down one's hair.
spettinato, *a.* Dishevelled, ruffled.
spettorarsi, *v.r.* To bare one's chest.
spettrale, *a.* Spectral, ghostly (in all senses). **Analisi —,** spectral analysis.
spettro, *n.m.* Ghost, spectre, apparition, phantom; spectrum.
spettroscopia [spettroscopIa], *n.f.* Spectroscopy.
spettroscopico [spettroscOpico], *a.* Spectroscopic.
spettroscopio [spettroscOpio], *n.m.* Spectroscope.
speziale, *n.m.* Chemist, druggist; grocer.
spezie [spEzie], *n.f.pl.* Spices.
spezieria [spezierIa], *n.f.* Chemist's, druggist's or grocer's shop; grocery, spices.
spezzabile, *a.* Breakable, fragile.
spezzamento, *n.m.* Breaking, fracture.
spezzare, *v.t.* To break, to fracture, to shatter, to shiver.
spezzarsi, *v.r.* To break; to get broken. **— una gamba,** to break one's leg; **mi si spezza il cuore al pensiero che,** my heart grows sick at the thought of.
spezzatamente, *adv.* Brokenly, disjointedly, spasmodically.
spezzati, *n.m.pl.* Small change, currency.
spezzatino, *n.m.* Stew. **— di vitello,** stewed veal; meat cubes.
spezzatura, *n.f.* Break, breakage; odd volume from a set.
spezzettare, *v.t.* To cut up small; to shake to pieces; to mince.

spezzonare, *v.t.* (*Aviat.*) To drop bombs on; to release a bomb-stick.
spezzone, *n.m.* (*Aviat.*) Bomb-stick; incendiary bomb.
spia, *n.f.* Spy; informer; sneak, tell-tale. **Far la —,** to sneak.
spiacente, *a.* Sorry; unpleasant. **Sono — di,** I am sorry to (or for); **sono — di informarla,** I regret to inform you; **sono — di quanto è successo,** I am sorry for what has happened.
spiacere, *v.i.* To displease, to be sorry.
spiacevole [spiacEvole], *a.* Unpleasant, disagreeable.
spiacevolezza, *n.f.* Unpleasantness.
spiacevolmente, *adv.* Unpleasantly.
spiacimento, *n.m.* Displeasure; unpleasantness.
spiaggia [spiAggia], *n.f.* Seashore, beach. **Una — sabbiosa,** a sandy shore.
spiaggiata, *n.f.* Coastline.
spiamento, *n.m.* Spying; sneaking.
spianamento, *n.m.* Levelling.
spianare, *v.t.* To level, to make level; to raze, to demolish; to dismantle; to smooth; to plane (wood, etc.); (*fig.*) to elucidate, to make plain. **— al suolo,** to raze to the ground; **— il legno,** to plane wood; **— il fucile contro,** to level one's gun at.
spianata, *n.f.* Open space, flat space; esplanade.
spianatoio [spianatOio], *n.m.* Rolling-pin.
spiano, *n.m.* Levelling, open space, esplanade. **A tutto —,** to any amount, boundlessly, without limit; profusely, unremittingly.
spiantamento, *n.m.* Uprooting.
spiantare, *v.t.* To uproot; to dismantle, to break up, to demolish.
spiantato, *n.m.* Penniless fellow; homeless person.
spiantazione, spianto, *n.f.m.* Ruin, destruction.
spiare, *v.t.i.* To spy upon, to spy out; to watch; to inquire into; to eavesdrop.
spiarola, *n.f.* Peep-hole, spy-hole.
spiatore, *n.m.* Scout.
spiattellare, *v.t.* To reveal, to declare openly, to speak the truth about.
spiattellatamente, *adv.* Openly, without reserve, plainly.
spiazzo, *n.m.* Open ground, esplanade; clearing (in a forest).
spica, *n.f.* Ear of corn [cp. **spiga**].
spiccante, *a.* Conspicuous, striking; shining, bright.
spiccare, *v.t.i.* To detach, to pluck off, to cut off; to speak distinctly; to make clear (the meaning); to stand out, to emerge; to be conspicuous; to jut out; to excel. **— un salto,** to take a leap; **— il volo,** to fly upwards, to fly away; **— le parole,** to enunciate clearly; **— il bollore,** to come to the boil; **la sua figura spiccava in mezzo alle altre,** his figure stood out among the others; (*Comm.*) **— una tratta,** to draw a bill.
spiccarsi, *v.r.* To become detached, to sever.
spiccatamente, *adv.* Distinctly; conspicuously.
spiccato, *a.* Distinct, sharp, clear; remarkable. **Una spiccata inclinazione per,** a marked inclination for.
spicchio [spIcchio], *n.m.* Segment (of an orange, etc.); quarter (of apple, etc.); clove (of garlic).
spicchiare, *v.t.* To slice or quarter (fruit, etc.).
spicciare, *v.t.i.* To despatch (business, etc.); to gush out; to dash away.
spicciarsi, *v.r.* To make haste, to hurry. **Spicciati! Spicciatevi!** Make haste! Hurry up!
spicciativo, *a.* Quick, expeditious; businesslike.
spiccicare, *v.t.* To articulate clearly; to detach, to sever.
spiccio [spIccio], *a.* Quick, prompt, speedy; businesslike.
spicciolame. *n.f.* Collection of little things, quantity of small change.
spicciolare, *v.t.* To detach, to pluck, to pick to pieces, to pick off; to change for small money.
spicciolata, *adv.* **Alla —,** few at a time; gradually, little by little.
spicciolatamente, *adv.* Gradually.
spicciolo [spIcciolo], *a.* Small, minute. **Spiccioli,** small change; **non ho spiccioli,** I have no change.
spicco, *n.m.* Prominence, show; vividness; fine appearance. **Fare —,** to make a fine show, to show off.
spicilegio [spicilEgio], *n.m.* Scrap-book; common-place book; anthology.
spicinare, *v.t.* To break in small pieces; to eat away, to corrode.
spidocchiare, *v.t.* To delouse, to louse.
spiedo, *n.m.* Kitchen spit.
spiegabile [spiegAbile], *a.* Explicable.
spiegamento, *n.m.* Explanation, unfolding; display; (*Mil.*) deployment.
spiegare, *v.t.* To unfold; to unfurl; to spread out, to display; to explain, to expound; to account for; to interpret; to justify; (*Mil.*) to deploy. **— le ali,** to spread the wings; **— le vele,** to set sail; **— la bandiera,** to unfurl the flag; **— Dante,** to expound Dante.
spiegarsi, *v.r.* To explain oneself, to make oneself clear; to open; (*Mil.*) to deploy. **Mi spiego ?** Do I make myself clear ?
spiegatamente, *adv.* Openly, clearly.
spiegativo, *a.* Explanatory, declaratory.
spiegatore, *n.m.* Showman; expounder.
spiegatura, *n.f.* Unfolding (of linen, etc.).
spiegazione, *n.f.* Explanation; unfolding; spreading. **Chiedere spiegazioni,** to ask for explanations.
spiegazzamento, *n.m.* Crumpling, creasing.
spiegazzare, *v.t.* To crumple, to rumple, to crease.
spiegazzato, *a.* Crumpled, sagging (of a garment).
spietatamente, *adv.* Mercilessly, ruthlessly, cruelly.
spietatezza, *n.f.* Ruthlessness, cruelty.
spietato, *a.* Ruthless, implacable, pitiless, merciless.
spifferare, *v.t.i.* To speak out openly, to keep nothing back; to play the pipe, to blow out, to whistle (of the wind).
spifferata, *n.f.* Sound of bagpipes, piping.

spiffero [spIffero], *n.m.* Draught (of air).
spifferone, *n.m.* Tell-tale.
spiga, *n.f.* Ear of corn; (*Med.*) spica bandage. **Stoffa a —,** twilled cloth, twill; **mattonata a —,** herring-bone brickwork.
spiganardo, *n.m.* (*Bot.*) Spikenard.
spigare, *v.t.* To form ears (of corn); to twill (cloth). **Panno spigato,** twill.
spighetta, *n.f.* Braid, trimming.
spigionarsi, *v.r.* To remain unlet (of a house, etc.).
spigionato, *a.* Unlet.
spigliatamente, *adv.* Easily, freely.
spigliatezza, *n.f.* Ease, agility; composure, self-possession.
spigliato, *a.* Self-possessed, easy, free, frank.
spigo, *n.m.* (*Bot.*) Lavender.
spigolamento, *n.m.* Gleaning.
spigolare, *v.t.* To glean.
spigolatore, spigolatrice, *n.m.f.* Gleaner.
spigolatura, *n.f.* Gleaning, gleanings.
spigolo [spIgolo], *n.m.* Corner, angle, edge.
spigoso, *a.* Full of ears (of corn).
spigrirsi, *v.r.* To shake off one's sloth; to pull oneself together.
spilla, *n.f.* Scarf-pin, tie-pin; brooch. **— di diamanti,** diamond brooch; **— di balia,** safety-pin.
spillaccherare, *v.t.* To brush off mud, to brush oneself.
spillaio [spillAio], *n.m.* Pin-maker.
spillare, *v.t.* To broach (a cask, etc.), to tap. **— una botte,** to tap a barrel; (*fig.*) **— danaro a,** to worm money out of.
spillatico [spillAtico], *n.m.* Pin-money.
spillatura, *n.f.* Broaching, tapping.
spillo, *n.m.* Pin; hair-pin; gimlet. **— di sicurezza,** safety-pin; **punta di —,** pin-point; **puntura di —,** pin-prick; (*fig.*) **colpi di —,** pin-pricks.
spillone, *n.m.* Hat-pin.
spilluzzicare, *v.t.* To nibble, to peck at (food); to pilfer.
spilluzzico [spillUzzico], *adv.* **A —,** little by little, bit by bit.
spilorceria [spilorcerIa], *n.f.* Stinginess, niggardliness, avarice, meanness, sordidness.
spilorcia [spilOrcia], *n.f.* (*Naut.*) Line for drawing in nets.
spilorcio [spilOrcio], *n.m.a.* Miser; stingy, miserly, avaricious, sordid, niggardly.
spiluccare, *v.t.* To pluck off [cp. **piluccare**].
spilungone, *n.m.a.* Tall, thin man, lanky fellow; tall and thin.
spina, *n.f.* Thorn, prickle; sting (of insect); bone (of fish); plug (of barrel); (*Elect.*) plug; (*fig.*) sorrow, grief. **— dorsale,** spine, back-bone; **a —,** twilled; **essere sulle spine,** to be on tenter-hooks; **uva —,** gooseberry; **— al cuore,** a thorn in one's side; **non c'è rosa senza —,** no rose without a thorn.
spinace, spinacio [spinAcio], *n.m.* (*Bot.*) Spinach.
spinaio [spinAio], *n.m.* Thicket [cp. **spineto**].
spinale, *a.* (*Anat.*) Spinal.
spinapesce, *adv.* **A —,** herring-bone, indented.
spinare, *v.t.* To prick (with thorns), to pierce.
spinato, *a.* Thorny; barbed; twilled. **Filo —,** barbed wire.
spincione, *n.m.* (*Zool.*) Chaffinch.
spineto, *n.m.* (*Bot.*) Brier-bush, thorn-bush; thicket.
spinetta, *n.f.* (*Mus.*) Spinet.
spingarda, *n.f.* (*Hist.*) Swivel-gun.
spingere [spIngere], *v.t.* To push, to thrust, to shove. **— alla disperazione,** to drive to desperation; **— all'eccesso,** to carry to excess.
spingersi [spIngersi], *v.r.* To thrust oneself forward, to push forward; to make a way for oneself.
spingitore, *n.m.* Thruster.
spinite, *n.f.* (*Med.*) Spinal meningitis.
spino, *n.m.* (*Bot.*) Thorn-tree, thorn.
spinosità [-à], *n.f.* Thorniness; difficulty, thorny question, ticklishness.
spinoso, *n.m.* (*Zool.*) Hedgehog.
spinoso, *a.* Thorny (in all senses). **Una questione spinosa,** a delicate question.
spinta, *n.f.* Push, shove, thrust; impulse, stimulus. **Dare la —,** to give a push.
spinte o sponte, *adv.* Willy-nilly.
spinterogeno [spinterOgeno], *n.m.* (*Mech.*) Distributor.
spinto, *p.p.a.* Pushed; daring, high, excessive.
spintonare, *v.t.i.* To push, to jostle, to elbow.
spintone, *n.m.* Violent push, shove. **Dare uno — a qualcuno,** to give someone a push.
spiombare, *v.t.i.* To remove (leaden) seals; to weigh as heavy as lead.
spiombatore, *n.m.* Railway thief.
spionaggio [spionAggio], *n.m.* Espionage, spying.
spioncino, *n.m.* Spy-hole.
spione, *n.m.* Spy, master-spy.
spiovente, *n.m.* (*Arch.*) Eaves.
spiovente, *a.* Falling, drooping, sloping. **Spalle spioventi,** stooping shoulders.
spiovere [spiOvere], *v.i.* To stop raining; to run off (water); to flow. **Capelli spioventi sulle spalle,** hair falling over the shoulders.
spippolare, *v.i.* (*colloq.*) To sing; to rattle off, to pick off.
spira, *n.f.* Coil, spiral; spire. **Fatto a —,** forming a spiral; **le spire di un serpente,** a serpent's coils.
spirabile [spirAbile], *a.* Breathable, fit to be breathed.
spiraglio [spirAglio], *n.m.* Opening; air-hole, vent-hole; peep-hole; sky-light; (*fig.*) gleam. **Aprire uno —,** to offer a gleam of hope.
spirale, *n.m.a.* Spiral. **Molle a —,** spiral spring.
spiralmente, *adv.* Spirally.
spiramento, *n.m.* Breath, inspiration.
spirante, *a.* Blowing; (*Gram.*) aspirate.
spirare, *v.t.i.* To breathe out, to exhale; to inspire; to blow, to breathe; to expire, to die; (*Comm.*) to come to an end, to fall due.
spirare, *n.m.* Expiration. **Allo — della settimana,** at the end of the week.
spirazione, *n.f.* In-breathing, inspiration.
spiritale, *a.* (*Lit.*) Spiritual.
spiritare, *v.i.* To be possessed (by a devil); to shiver, to tremble (with terror).
spiritatamente, *adv.* Madly, insanely, like one possessed.
spiritato, *a.* Crazy, mad, possessed; terrified.
spiritello, *n.m.* Sprite.
spiritico [spirItico], *a.* Spiritualistic. **Una seduta spiritica,** a seance.

spiritismo, *n.m.* Spiritualism.
spiritista (*pl.* **spiritisti**), *n.m.* Spiritualist.
spiritistico [spiritIstico], *a.* Spiritualistic.
spirito [spIrito], *n.m.* Spirit (in all senses); soul, intellect, mind; ghost; wit, humour; alcohol; leader, moving spirit; (*Gram.*) breathing. **Lo Spirito Santo,** the Holy Ghost; **presenza di —,** presence of mind; **fare dello —,** to play the wit; **prontezza di —,** ready wit; **povero di —,** small-minded; **i grandi spiriti,** the master minds; **persona di —,** person of talent; **— folletto,** hobgoblin, imp; **— di corpo,** esprit de corps; **— denaturato,** methylated spirits; **credere agli spiriti,** to believe in ghosts; (*Gram.*) **— dolce, aspro,** smooth, rough breathing.
spiritosaggine [spiritosAggine], *n.f.* Would-be witticism; attempt at wit.
spiritosamente, *adv.* Wittily, vivaciously.
spiritosità [-à], *n.f.* Wittiness, witticism, joke, pun, sally; spiritous content.
spiritoso, *a.* Witty; jocular, humorous; spirituous, strong (of alcohol). **Bevande spiritose,** alcoholic drinks; **risposta spiritosa,** witty retort.
spirituale, *a.* Spiritual.
spiritualismo, *n.m.* (Philosophical) spiritualism.
spiritualità [-à], *n.f.* Spirituality.
spiritualizzare, spiritualizzarsi, *v.t.r.* To spiritualize.
spiritualizzazione, *n.f.* Spiritualization.
spiritualmente, *adv.* Spiritually.
spiro, *n.m.* (*Lit.*) Breath; soul, spirit.
spirocheta, *n.m.* (*Med.*) Spirillum.
spirto, *n.m.* (*Poet.*) Spirit [cp. **spirito**].
spiumacciare, *v.t.* To shake up a (feather) bed.
spiumare, *v.t.* To pluck, to pull out the feathers; (*fig.*) to fleece.
spiumarsi, *v.r.* To lose one's feathers.
spizzicare, *v.t.* To take a little of, to nibble, to peck at (food).
spizzicatura, *n.f.* Picking out; (*Print.*) faulty impression.
spizzico [spIzzico], *adv.* **A —,** by degrees, little by little.
splendente, *a.* Bright, shining, brilliant, glittering.
splendentemente, *adv.* Brightly, brilliantly.
splendere [splEndere], *v.i.* To shine, to glitter, to sparkle, to glisten, to scintillate.
splendidamente, *adv.* Magnificently, splendidly.
splendidezza, *n.f.* Magnificence [cp. **splendore**].
splendido [splEndido], *a.* Magnificent, splendid, sumptuous, rich, marvellous, gorgeous.
splendore, *n.m.* Brightness, magnificence, refulgence, brilliance; glory, gorgeousness. **Il sole nel suo —,** the sun in its splendour.
splene, *n.m.* (*Anat.*) Spleen [cp. **milza**].
splenetico [splenEtico], *a.* Splenetic, ill-tempered; suffering from spleen trouble.
splenio [splEnio], *n.m.* (*Anat.*) Splenius (neck muscle).
Spluga, *n.f.* (*Geog.*) Splügen. **Passo dello Spluga,** Splügen Pass.
spocchia [spOcchia], *n.f.* (*colloq.*) Bumptiousness, swagger, boast.
spodestare, *v.t.* To dispossess, to deprive of power.
spodestarsi, *v.r.* To divest oneself of power.
spoetizzare, *v.t.* To take away the romance of, to disenchant.
spoetizzarsi, *v.r.* To be disillusioned; to lose ideals.
spoglia [spOglia], *n.f.* Spoil, booty; mortal remains; slough (of snake); hide (of wild beast). **Sotto mentite spoglie,** in borrowed plumes; **dividersi le spoglie,** to divide the spoils; **la — mortale,** the mortal remains.
spogliamento, *n.m.* Spoliation; exploitation, dispossession, plundering; undressing.
spogliare, *v.t.* To undress, to divest; (*fig.*) to dispossess, to deprive; to plunder, to despoil; to examine carefully. **— la vecchia corrispondenza,** to go through old letters.
spogliarsi, *v.r.* To undress oneself, to take off one's clothes. **— nudo,** to strip to the skin; to undress.
spogliatoio [spogliatOio], *n.m.* Dressing-room.
spogliatore, spogliatrice, *n.m.f.* Plunderer, despoiler.
spogliatura, spogliazione, *n.f.* Spoliation, plundering, dispossessing.
spoglio [spOglio], *n.m.* Selection, sorting; stripping; examination; cast-off clothes. **Fare lo — della corrispondenza,** to go through one's correspondence.
spoglio [spOglio], *a.* Deprived, destitute; bare, unclothed, naked; barren, bleak.
spola, *n.f.* Shuttle. (*fig.*) **Fare la —,** to go up and down, to ply (like a steamer).
spoletta, *n.f.* (*Mil.*) Fuse (for a shell).
spoliazione, *n.f.* Spoliation; pillage, robbery.
spoliticare, *v.i.* To talk politics.
spollaiare, *v.t.* To knock off the perch; (*fig.*) to dislodge.
spollonare, *v.t.* (*Agric.*) To trim vines.
spolmonarsi, *v.r.* To lose one's breath (with talking); to shout oneself hoarse.
spolpare, *v.t.* To strip the flesh from the bone; (*fig.*) to fleece, to swindle, to drain of money.
spoltrirsi, *v.r.* To shake off sloth.
spolverare, *v.t.* To dust, to clean; (*fig.*) to make a clean sweep. (*colloq.*) **— le spalle,** to give a good drubbing to.
spolverata, *n.f.* Dusting, clean, brush-up.
spolveratore, spolveratrice, *n.m.f.* One who dusts, duster.
spolveratura, *n.f.* Dusting, whisking, flicking off dust.
spolverina, *n.f.* Dust-coat; overall.
spolverino, *n.m.* Feather-whisk; drying-sand; (*obs.*) pounce-box.
spolverio [spolverIo], *n.m.* Cloud of dust.
spolverizzare, *v.t.* To powder; to pulverize; (*Art*), to pounce.
spolvero [spOlvero], *n.m.* Dusting; fine flour; (*fig.*) smattering (of knowledge); (*Art*) pounce.
sponda, *n.f.* Bank, border, margin, edge; shore; parapet. **— d'un letto,** side of a bed; **— del mare,** shore; **— d'un fiume,** river-bank.
spondeo [spondEo], *n.m.* (*Poet.*) Spondee.
sponderola, *n.f.* (*Tech.*) Plough (plane).
spongiforme, *a.* (*Zool.*) Spongiform.
spongiosità [-à], *n.f.* Sponginess.
spongioso, *a.* Spongy [cp. **spugnoso**].

sponsali, *n.m.pl.* Nuptials, wedding, marriage.
spontaneamente, *adv.* Spontaneously.
spontaneità [-à], *n.f.* Spontaneity, spontaneousness.
spontaneo [spontAneo], *a.* Spontaneous, voluntary, natural. **Offerta spontanea,** free offer.
sponte o spinte, *adv.* Willy-nilly [cp. **spinte**].
spopolamento, *n.m.* Depopulation.
spopolare, *v.t.* To depopulate.
spoppare, *v.t.* To wean [cp. **slattare** or **svezzare**].
spora, *n.f.* (*Bot.*) Spore.
sporadicamente, *adv.* Sporadically.
sporadico [sporAdico], *a.* Sporadic.
sporcacciamento, *n.m.* Dirtying, dirtiness.
sporcacciare, *v.t.* To dirty, to make dirty.
sporcaccione, *n.m.* Filthy fellow.
sporcamente, *adv.* Dirtily, filthily.
sporcare, *v.t.* To soil, to foul, to dirty; to stain; to defile; to besmirch.
sporchezza, sporcheria, sporcizia [sporcherIa, sporcIzia], *n.f.* Dirt, dirtiness, filthiness, uncleanness, foulness.
sporco, *a.* Dirty, foul, unclean, filthy.
sporgente, *a.* Protruding, projecting, jutting out.
sporgenza, *n.f.* Projection, protrusion; prominence.
sporgere [spOrgere], *v.i.t.* To jut out, to project, to protrude; to lean out; to put out, to extend; to hand out; (*Law*) to tender. **— la mano,** to hold out one's hand; **sporgimi quella penna,** hand me that pen; **— querela,** to bring a law suit [cp. **porgere**].
sporgersi [spOrgersi], *v.r.* To lean out, to stretch out; to protrude. (*Rail.*) **È vietato —,** do not lean out of the window.
sporgimento, *n.m.* Projecting, holding out.
sport, *n.m.* Sport. **Il mondo dello —,** the sporting world.
sporta, *n.f.* Hamper, basket, shopping-basket.
sportata, *n.f.* Basketful.
sportello, *n.m.* (Shop) shutter; wicket; booking-office, ticket-window; small door. **La banca ha chiuso gli sportelli,** the bank has closed its doors; (*Rail.*) **gli sportelli dei vagoni,** the carriage doors.
sportivamente, *adv.* Sportingly, sportively.
sportivo, *n.m.a.* Sportsman; sporting, sportive. **Edizione sportiva,** sporting edition (of a newspaper).
sporto, *n.m.* Projection; stall (in front of a shop) [cp. **sporgenza**].
sportula [spOrtula], *n.f.* (*obs.*) Bribe (to a judge).
sposa, *n.f.* Bride, betrothed girl; spouse, wife. **Andar — a,** to be married to; **abito da —,** wedding-dress.
sposalizio [sposalIzio], *n.m.* Wedding, marriage, nuptials.
sposare, *v.t.* To give in marriage; to marry; (*fig.*) to adopt, to embrace (a cause, etc.).
sposarsi, *v.r.* To get married, to marry, to wed. **Si sposarono ieri,** they got married yesterday,
sposato, *a.* Married.
sposereccio [sposerEccio], *a.* Nuptial. **Abito —,** wedding dress.
sposetta, sposina, *n.f.* Young bride, young wife.
sposino, *n.m.* Young bridegroom, young husband.
sposo, *n.m.* Bridegroom, husband. **Gli sposi,** the married couple; **i promessi sposi,** the betrothed.
spossamento, *n.m.* Exhaustion, fatigue.
spossare, *v.t.* To exhaust.
spossatamente, *adv.* Wearily.
spossatezza, *n.f.* Fatigue, weariness, tiredness; lassitude, languor; exhaustion.
spossato, *a.* Wearied. **Mi sento —,** I feel worn out.
spossessare, *v.t.* To dispossess, to deprive of; to oust.
spostamento, *n.m.* Displacement, removal, change.
spostare, *v.t.* To displace, to remove; to misplace; to alter.
spostarsi, *v.r.* To change one's place, to move (one's residence); to travel.
spostato, *n.m.* A misfit; a déclassé.
spranga, *n.f.* Bar; bolt, cross-bar; rail.
sprangare, *v.t.* To bar, to bolt.
sprangatura, *n.f.* Bolting, barring.
spranghetta, *n.f.* Window-catch.
spratto, *n.m.* (*Zool.*) Sprat.
sprazzo, *n.m.* Ray, flash, spark; sprinkling, splash. **Uno — di luce,** a flash of light.
sprecamento [cp. **spreco**].
sprecare, *v.t.* To waste, to squander, to dissipate. **— il fiato,** to waste one's breath; **— il tempo,** to waste one's time.
spreco, sprecamento, *n.m.* Waste, wasting, squandering, dissipation.
sprecone, sprecatore, *n.m.* Squanderer, wastrel, spendthrift.
spregevole [spregEvole], *a.* Contemptible, despicable, vile, worthless; mean.
spregevolmente, *adv.* Contemptibly.
spregiare, *v.t.* To despise, to slight; to disdain.
spregiatamente, *adv.* Contemptuously.
spregiativo, *a.* Disdainful, disparaging.
spregiatore, *n.m.* Scorner.
spregio [sprEgio], *n.m.* Contempt, scorn, disdain. **Tenere in —,** to hold in contempt.
spregiudicare, *v.t.* To free from prejudice.
spregiudicarsi, *v.r.* To rid oneself of one's prejudices.
spregiudicatamente, *adv.* Impartially.
spregiudicatezza, *n.f.* Open-mindedness, lack of prejudice.
spregiudicato, *a.* Impartial, unbiased, open-minded.
spremere [sprEmere], *v.t.* To press, to squeeze, to compress, to wring. **— danari da,** to wring money from.
spremitoio [spremitOio], *n.m.* Fruit-squeezer.
spremitura, *n.f.* Squeezing, wringing.
spremuta, *n.f.* Squash. **— di limone,** lemon-squash.
spretarsi, *v.r.* To renounce holy orders; to unfrock.
sprezzabile [sprezzAbile], *a.* Contemptible, despicable.
sprezzamento, *n.m.* Contempt.
sprezzante, *a.* Disdainful, scornful, contemptuous.
sprezzantemente, *adv.* Disdainfully, scornfully.
sprezzare, *v.t.* To contemn, to disdain, to despise, to scorn.

sprezzatore, sprezzatrice, *n.m.f.a.* Scorner, despiser; contemptuous.
sprezzo, *n.m.* Scorn, disdain, contempt.
sprigionamento, *n.m.* Release; discharge.
sprigionare, *v.t.r.* To set free, to release; (*fig.*) to emit, to exhale; to rise.
sprillare, *v.i.* To spout forth.
sprillo, *n.m.* Jet; spout.
sprimacciare, *v.t.* To shake up (a mattress).
sprimacciata, *n.f.* Shaking.
springare, *v.i.* (*Lit.*) To leap, to jump about; to kick, to fling.
sprizzare, *v.t.i.* To sprinkle, to spout, to spurt; to burst forth, to gush out.
sprocco, *n.m.* Shoot (of plant); twig.
sprofondamento, *n.m.* Sinking, foundering; subsidence (of soil).
sprofondare, *v.t.i.* To sink, to send to the bottom, to submerge; to subside, to collapse, to sink, to founder. **Il terreno sprofondò sotto i piedi,** the ground gave way under his feet; **— nel sonno,** to sink into slumber.
sprofondarsi, *v.r.* To sink, to sink in. **— nel letto,** to sink right into bed; **— in meditazioni,** to be plunged in deep thought.
sproloquio [sprolOquio], *n.m.* Long-winded speech, speechifying.
spronaio [spronAio], *n.m.* Spurrier, spur-maker.
spronamento, *n.m.* Spurring; incitement.
spronare, *v.t.* To spur; to goad, to incite, to stimulate; (*Naut.*) to ram [cp. **speronare**].
spronata, *n.f.* Prick with spurs.
spronato, *a.* Spurred (of fowls, etc.); with dew-claws (of a dog).
sprone, *n.m.* Spur; cock's spur; (*Naut.*) ram (of battleship); (*Arch.*) buttress; stimulus, incentive. **Correre a — battuto,** to ride at full tilt; **dare di —,** to spur on.
spronella, *n.f.* Rowel (of a spur).
sproporzionale, *a.* Disproportionate.
sproporzionalità [-à], **sproporzione,** *n.f.* Disproportion.
sproporzionare, *v.t.* To proportion wrongly.
sproporzionatamente, *adv.* Disproportionately.
sproporzionato, *p.p.a.* Disproportionate.
spropositare, *v.i.* To blunder, "to drop a brick"; to talk nonsense.
spropositatamente, *adv.* Mistakenly.
sproposito [spropOsito], *n.m.* Mistake, blunder; folly; crime; absurdity. **Usare a —,** to misapply; **uno —,** an extravagance, a piece of folly; **a —,** unopportunely.
spropriare, *v.t.* To expropriate, to dispossess.
spropriarsi, *v.r.* To get rid of one's property.
spropriazione, *n.f.* Dispossession.
sproprio [sprOprio], *n.m.* Expropriation.
sprovvedere, *v.t.* To leave unprovided for.
sprovvedutamente, *adv.* Incautiously, without foresight, unthinkingly.
sprovveduto, sprovvisto, *a.* Unprovided for, destitute; wanting, lacking; out of (goods, etc.). **Alla sprovvista,** unexpectedly, unawares.
spruzzaglia [spruzzAglia], *n.f.* Spray, drizzle.
spruzzare, *v.t.* To spray, to sprinkle; to splash. **— di zucchero,** to sprinkle with sugar.
spruzzata, *n.f.* Sprinkling, sprinkle, spray; drizzle, shower.
spruzzatore, *n.m.* Sprayer.
spruzzo, *n.m.* Spray, sprinkle; drizzle, shower.
spudoratamente, *adv.* Impudently, brazenly.
spudoratezza, *n.f.* Impudence, shamelessness, immodesty.
spudorato, *a.* Impudent, unblushing, shameless, brazen.
spugna, *n.f.* Sponge. **Bere come una —,** to drink heavily, to be a drunkard.
spugnata, spugnatura, *n.f.* Sponge over, sponge down, sponging.
spugnosità [-à], *n.f.* Sponginess.
spugnoso, *a.* Spongy; porous, absorbent.
spulare, *v.t.* To winnow (grain).
spulatoio [spulatOio], *n.m.* Flail.
spulatura, *n.f.* Winnowing.
spulciare, spulciarsi, *v.t.r.* To get rid of fleas; (*fig.*) to examine very closely, to go over inch by inch.
spulciatura, *n.f.* Close scrutiny.
spulezzare, *v.i.* To run away, to flee, to make off.
spulire, *v.t.* To polish (glass).
spulizzire, *v.t.* To clean, to clean up.
spuma, *n.f.* Foam, froth (of beer, etc.); lather.
spumante, *a.* Foaming, frothing; sparkling (of wine).
spumare, *v.i.* To foam, to froth; to sparkle.
spumata, *n.f.* Foam, froth, spray.
spumeggiante, *a.* Foaming.
spumeggiare, *v.i.* To foam, to froth.
spumone, *n.m.* Iced sweet with whipped cream.
spumosità [-à], *n.f.* Foaming, spumescence, frothiness.
spumoso, *a.* Foamy, frothy, spumescent.
spuntare, *v.t.i.* To blunt, to break off the point of; to trim; to undo; to overcome, to prevail over; to delete, to erase; to verify, to check; to appear; to rise (of the sun, etc.); to peep out, to sprout forth; to begin to be visible; to well (of tears). **Spuntarla,** to succeed, to win one's way; **spunta la luna,** the moon is rising; **lo vidi — di lontano,** I saw him appear a long way off; **— i prezzi,** to control prices; **— come funghi,** to spring up like mushrooms; **— i capelli,** to trim one's hair; **— un conto,** to check an account.
spuntare, *n.m.* Rise. **Allo — del giorno,** at daybreak.
spuntarsi, *v.r.* To get blunt. **La mia matita si è spuntata,** my pencil has lost its point.
spuntatura, *n.f.* Blunting; cutting off the tip; tip, stump.
spuntellare, *v.t.* To remove the props.
spuntiera, *n.f.* (*Naut.*) Trawl-beam.
spuntino, *n.m.* Snack (meal); snack bar. **Fare uno —,** to have a snack.
spunto, *n.m.* A beginning, a cue, a hint; acidity (of urine). **Dare lo —,** to give the start-off; to give the cue.
spuntone, *n.m.* A pointed tool; a crag.
spunzecchiare, *v.t.* To prick.
spunzonare, *v.t.* To elbow; to prod.
spurgamento, *n.m.* Purging, purge.
spurgare, *v.t.* To purge, to clean.

spurgarsi, *v.r.* To spit, to expectorate, to clear one's throat.
spurgazione, *n.f.* Expectoration.
spurgo, *n.m.* Cleansing; expectoration; (*Med.*) discharge.
spurio [spUrio], *a.* Spurious.
sputacchiare, *v.i.* To keep on spitting.
sputacchiera, *n.f.* Spittoon.
sputacchio [sputAcchio], *n.m.* Spittle; mucus.
sputapepe, *n.m.* (*colloq.*) Petulant person, snarler.
sputare, *v.t.i.* To spit. **È vietato —,** spitting strictly prohibited; **— addosso a,** to spit on; **— in aria,** to be hoisted with one's own petard; **ingoiare amaro e — dolce,** to put a good face on it; **— tondo,** to show off.
sputasenno, sputasentenze, *n.m.* Wiseacre, sententious fellow.
sputato, *p.p.a.* Spat; (*colloq.*) resembling, like.
sputo, *n.m.* Spittle, spit.
squacqueratamente, *adv.* Without moderation, heedlessly.
squadernare, *v.t.* To turn over the pages, to examine; to show openly; to scatter about.
squadra (1), *n.f.* (*Mil.*) Squad; (*Naut.*) squadron; detachment; group; (*Sport*) team. **— calcistica,** football team; **lavorare a —,** to do team-work; **— di soccorso,** breakdown gang; **— volante,** flying squad.
squadra (2), *n.f.* (*Geom.*) Set square; square rule. **A —,** at right-angles; **fuori di —,** out of the square; **dar la — a uno,** to make someone believe; **uscire di —,** to overstep the mark; (*fig.*) **essere fuori di —,** to be unbalanced; to be wrong; to be deranged.
squadrare, *v.t.* To square; to adjust; to look one squarely in the face. **— da capo a piedi,** to look one up and down; (*colloq*). **quella cosa non mi squadra,** that thing does not go well with me; I do not like that.
squadratura, *n.f.* Squaring.
squadriglia [squadrIglia], *n.f.* Squad; (*Naut. Aviat.*) squadron. **— da bombardamento,** bombing squadron; **— di cacciatorpediniere,** destroyer flotilla.
squadrista (*pl.* **squadristi**), *n.m.* (*Hist.*) Member of Fascist squad.
squadristico [squadrIstico], *a.* Pertaining to sports teams.
squadro, *n.m.* Squaring; (carpenter's, etc.) square.
squadrone, *n.m.* Squadron.
squagliamento, *n.m.* Melting; (*fig.*) flight, escape.
squagliare, *v.t.* To melt down.
squagliarsi, *v.r.* To melt away; (*fig.*) to steal away, to make off; to make oneself scarce.
squalificare, *v.t.* To disqualify.
squalifica, *n.f.* Disqualification.
squallidezza, *n.f.* Dreariness, gloom; squalidness.
squallido [squAllido], *a.* Miserable, dreary, cheerless, bleak; squalid.
squallore, *n.m.* Dreariness, gloom; squallor.
squalo, *n.m.* (*Zool.*) Shark; dog-fish.
squama, *n.f.* Scale (of fish etc.); flake (of metal, etc.).
squamare, squamarsi, *v.t.r.* To scale, to flake off.
squamoso, *a.* Scaly, in flakes.
squarciagola, *adv.* **A —,** At the top of one's voice.
squarcimento, *n.m.* Rending, tearing, ripping.
squarciare, *v.t.* To rend, to tear; to lacerate, to mangle, to split.
squarciarsi, *v.r.* To be rent asunder, to be torn.
squarcio [squArcio], *n.m.* Rent, gash, tear, laceration; fragment; (*fig.*) extract from a book. **— poetico,** poetical extract.
squarcione, *n.m.* Braggart.
squarquoio [squarquOio], *a.* (*Lit.*) Decrepit, senile.
squartamento, *n.m.* Quartering.
squartare, *v.t.* To quarter, to chop, to split. **— lo zero,** to split hairs.
squartata, *n.f.* Gash, tear.
squartatoio [squartatOio], *n.m.* Chopper, butcher's cleaver.
squartatura, *n.f.* Quartering.
squassamento, *n.m.* Shaking, jolting; shock.
squassare, *v.t.* To shake, to jolt, to shock; to brandish; to toss.
squasso, *n.m.* Violent shock, jolt.
squattrinare, *v.t.i.* To render penniless; to count every penny; to consider minutely; to haggle over ha'pence.
squattrinarsi, *v.r.* To be left penniless, to be destitute.
squattrinato, *a.* Penniless, impecunious.
squilibrare, squilibrarsi, *v.t.r.* To put out of balance, to upset the balance of; to lose one's balance; to get into difficulties.
squilibrato, *a.* Unbalanced; crazy, insane, deranged.
squilibrio [squilIbrio], *n.m.* Lack of balance; inequality, difference. **— mentale,** mental derangement.
squilla (1), *n.f.* (*Bot. Zool.*) Squill.
squilla (2), *n.f.* Chime, bell, harness-bell, cow-bell; the sound of the evening Angelus bell.
squillante, *a.* Shrill, piercing, clanging; clear.
squillantemente, *adv.* Shrilly.
squillare, *v.i.* To ring, to peal; to shrill, to clang; to blare.
squillo, *n.m.* Blast (of trumpet); peal (of bell); sudden ring or sound.
squinternare, *v.t.* To turn over the leaves of a book; to disarrange; to upset.
squisitamente, *adv.* Exquisitely, intensely.
squisitezza, *n.f.* Excellence, exquisiteness, refinement.
squisito, *a.* Excellent, exquisite, delicious; intense, profound.
squittinare, *v.t.* To vote.
squittinio [squittInio], *n.m.* Balloting, scrutiny of votes [cp. **scrutinio**].
squittire, *v.i.* To yelp, to squeak, to hoot.
squoiare, *v.t.* To skin [cp. **scuoiare**].
sradicamento, *n.m.* Eradication, uprooting, extirpation.
sradicare, *v.t.* To eradicate, to uproot, to extirpate, to root out.
sragionamento, *n.m.* Nonsense, false reasoning.

sragionare, *v.i.* To talk nonsense, to ramble (in speech).
sragionevole [sragionEvole], *a.* Unreasonable, irrational.
sregolamento, *n.m.* Disorder, irregularity.
sregolatamente, *adv.* Dissolutely, in a disordered fashion.
sregolatezza, *n.f.* Dissipation, intemperance; disorder.
sregolato, *a.* Intemperate, immoderate, disorderly.
srugginire, *v.t.* To rub the rust off.
stabbiare, *v.i.* To be folded (sheep); to dung, to manure.
stabbiatura, *n.f.* Dunging, manuring.
stabbio [stAbbio], *n.m.* Dung, manure.
stabbiolo, *n.m.* Pigsty.
stabile [stAbile], *n.m.* Building, house, premises; real estate.
stabile [stAbile], *a.* Fixed, settled, stable, durable, permanent. **Beni stabili,** real estate; **un'offerta —,** a firm offer; **impiegato in pianta —,** employee on the staff.
stabilimento, *n.m.* Establishment; works, factory; settlement.
stabilire, *v.t.* To settle, to fix; to decide; to establish, to define, to determine; ascertain. **— una regola,** to lay down a rule.
stabilirsi, *v.r.* To establish oneself, to settle down. **Si stabilì a Roma,** he settled in Rome.
stabilità [-à], *n.f.* Stability, stableness, steadiness, firmness.
stabilizzazione, *n.f.* Stabilization.
stabilizzare, *v.t.* To stabilize.
stabilmente, *adv.* Stably, firmly; solidly.
stabulario [stabulArio], *n.m.* Pound (for stray cattle); stable.
staccabile [staccAbile], *a.* Detachable. **Foglio —,** loose-leaf.
staccamento, *n.m.* Detachment, separation [cp. **distacco**].
staccare, *v.t.i.* To take off, to detach, to pull off; to unhook; to articulate distinctly; to stand out clearly.(*Rail.*) **— un carro,** to drop off a car; **— dalla matrice,** to detach (a coupon) from its stub; **— un assegno,** to issue a cheque, to draw a cheque.
staccarsi, *v.r.* To part from, to separate, to become untied, to become loose; (*Art*) to stand out (from background); (*Aviat.*) to take off.
staccatamente, *adv.* In a detached way; interruptedly, brokenly.
staccatezza, *n.f.* Separation, detachment.
staccato, *a.* Detached; (*Mus.*) staccato.
stacciaio [stacciAio], *n.m.* Sieve-maker.
stacciare, *v.t.* To sieve, to bolt.
stacciata, *n.f.* Sieveful; sifting.
stacciatura, *n.f.* Sifting, sieving.
staccio [stAccio], *n.m.* Sieve.
staccionata, *n.f.* Wooden fence.
stacco, *n.m.* Separation, detachment; separate piece. **Fare —,** to be in contrast with; **— d'abito,** cutting of cloth (for a suit).
stadera, *n.f.* Steelyard.
stadio [stAdio], *n.m.* Stadium, sports ground; stage, phase, degree. **All'ultimo —,** at the last stage, hopeless; **lo — di una malattia,** the stage of an illness.
staffa, *n.f.* Stirrup; footboard (of a vehicle). **Il bicchiere della —,** the stirrup-cup; **perder le staffe,** to lose one's temper; **tenere il piede in due staffe,** to have two strings to one's bow.
staffare, *v.t.* To put one's foot in the stirrup; to mount.
staffetta, *n.f.* Messenger, courier, dispatch-rider; (*Rail.*) pilot-engine. (*Sport*) **Corsa a —,** relay-race.
staffiere, *n.m.* Groom; footman.
staffilamento, *n.m.* Whipping, flogging, thrashing.
staffilare, *v.t.* To whip, to flog, to thrash.
staffilata, *n.f.* Flogging, thrashing; stroke of a whip; (*fig.*) cruel taunt.
staffilatura, staffilazione, *n.f.* Flogging, whipping, thrashing.
staffile, *n.m.* Whip, lash; thong; stirrup-leather.
staggiare, *v.t.* To prop (trees).
staggimento, *n.m.* (*Law*) Distraint; sequestration.
staggio [stAggio], *n.m.* Prop, stay; shaft (of a ladder); chair-back; bar (of bird-cage).
staggire, *v.t.* (*Law*) To distrain upon, to sequester.
stagionamento, *n.m.* Seasoning, ripening, maturing.
stagionare, stagionarsi, *v.t.i.r.* To season, to mature, to ripen.
stagionato, *a.* Seasoned, ripe, mature; elderly.
stagionatura, *n.f.* Ripening.
stagione, *n.f.* Season, time. **La — morta,** the dead season; **fuor di —,** out of season; **il colmo della —,** the height of the season; **prezzi di —,** top-season charges.
stagliare, *v.t.i.* (*Lit.*) To hack, to hew; to stand out; to tally.
stagnaio [stagnAio], *n.m.* Tinsmith.
stagnamento, *n.m.* Tinning, soldering; stagnation.
stagnante, *a.* Stagnant, stagnating. **Acqua —,** stagnant water.
stagnare (1), *v.t.* To tin, to solder. **Ferro stagnato,** tin-plate.
stagnare (2), *v.t.i.* To stagnate; to dry up; to stanch (blood).
stagnata, *n.f.* Tin can, tin (receptacle); tinning; packet (wrapped in tin-foil).
stagnatura, *n.f.* Tinning.
stagnino, *n.m.* Tinsmith, tinker.
stagno (1), *n.m.a.* (*Min.*) Tin. **A —,** well sealed; water-tight; (*Aviat.*) **cabina stagna,** pressurized cabin.
stagno (2), *n.m.* Pond, pool.
stagnola, *n.f.* Silver-paper, tin-foil.
staio [stAio] (*pl.* **stai,** *m.,* **staia,** *f.*), *n.m.* Bushel (measure and quantity). **A staia,** in plenty, plentifully; **cappello a staio,** top-hat.
stalagmite, stalammite, *n.f.* (*Geol.*) Stalagmite.
stalattite, *n.f.* (*Geol.*) Stalactite.
stalla, *n.f.* Stable; cow-shed; sheep-fold; pigsty. **Mozzo di —,** stable-boy; **chiudere la — dopo fuggiti i buoi,** to lock the stable door when the horse has gone.
stallaggio [stallAggio], *n.m.* Stabling.
stallare, *v.t.* To stable.
stallata, *n.f.* Horses, cattle, etc., in stable.
stallatico [stallAtico], *n.m.* Stabling; stable manure, dung.

stalliere, *n.m.* Stable-man, stable-boy.
stallo, *n.m.* (Choir) stall, (bishop's) throne; (*Chess*) stalemate.
stallone, *n.m.* Stallion.
stamane, stamani, stamattina, *adv.* This morning.
stambecco, *n.m.* (*Zool.*) Wild goat.
stamberga, *n.f.* Hovel, garret.
stambugio [stambUgio], *n.m.* Dark stuffy room; den, garret.
stamburare, *v.t.i.* To beat a drum, to drum; to praise, to puff up.
stamburata, *n.f.* Roll of a drum, beat of drum, drumming; puffing up.
stame, *n.m.* (*Bot.*) Stamen; thread, fine wool. **— della vita,** thread of life.
stamigna, *n.f.* Cloth used for sieving.
stampa, *n.f.* Stamp, impression; press, printing; impress, mark; printed matter (for post); engraving, print. **A —,** in print; **in corso di —,** now printing; **mandare alla —,** to send to press; **dare alle stampe,** to publish; **errore di —,** misprint; **raccolta di stampe,** collection of engravings; **avere una buona —,** to have a good press; **spedire come stampe,** to send as printed matter; **riservato per la —,** reserved for the Press; **ritagli di —,** press cuttings.
stampabile [stampAbile], *a.* Printable; worth printing.
stampare, *v.t.* To print; to publish; to impress, to stamp; to mould; to strike (coins). **— un articolo,** to print an article; **— tessuti,** to print textiles; **— un bacio,** to imprint a kiss.
stampatello, *n.m.* Block capitals; (*Print.*) heavy type.
stampato, *n.m.* Printed matter (by post); printed form.
stampatore, *n.m.* Printer.
stampella, *n.f.* Crutch.
stamperia [stamperIa], *n.f.* Printing-house, printing-works.
stampiglia [stampIglia], *n.f.* Rubber stamp; board exhibiting numbers drawn in the lottery; form.
stampigliare, *v.t.* To rubber-stamp.
stampino, *n.m.* Stencil, stencil-plate.
stampo, *n.m.* Stamp, mould; shape, form; kind, sort, class. **Un uomo del vecchio —,** a man of the old school; **di ogni —,** of every kind; **essere dello stesso —,** to be tarred with the same brush.
stanare, *v.t.* To dislodge, to drive out.
stanca, *n.f.* (*Naut.*) Slack-water.
stancamente, *adv.* Wearily.
stancare, *v.t.* To tire, to weary, to fatigue, to overwork; to exhaust. **— la pazienza,** to exhaust one's patience.
stancarsi, *v.r.* To get tired, to grow weary, to get fatigued, to become exhausted.
stancheggiare, *v.t.* To bore to death, to weary, to irritate.
stanchevole [stanchEvole], *a.* Tiresome, tedious, wearing, fatiguing, wearisome.
stanchezza, *n.f.* Fatigue, tiredness, weariness; lassitude.
stanco, *a.* Tired, weary, exhausted, fatigued. **— morto,** tired out.
stanga, *n.f.* Bar, pole, shaft; cross-bar, swing-bar.
stangare, *v.t.* To bar, to bar up; (*colloq.*) to thrash.
stangata, *n.f.* Blow (with a bar).
stanghetta, *n.f.* Small bar; bolt (of lock), door-bolt; side (of spectacles). **Occhiali a stanghetta,** spectacles.
stangone, *n.m.* Pole, bar, shaft.
stanotte, *adv.* Tonight; last night.
stante, *a.* Standing, current; this present. **Seduta —,** on the spot; **il mese —,** the present month; **bene —,** well-to-do.
stante, *prep.* Since, for, owing to, on account of. **— la guerra,** owing to the war; **poco —,** shortly afterwards; **— che,** because of, seeing that.
stantio [stantIo], *a.* Stale; rancid; flat.
stantuffata, *n.f.* Piston-stroke.
stantuffo, *n.m.* (*Mech.*) Piston; plunger (of pump).
stanza, *n.f.* Room; abode, habitation, residence; (*Mil.*) garrison; (*Poet.*) stanza. **Prendere —,** to take up residence; **— da letto,** bedroom; (*Comm.*) **— di compensazione,** clearing-house.
stanziale, *a.* Permanent.
stanzialmente, *adv.* Permanently, fixedly.
stanziamento, *n.m.* Grant, assignment; settlement; appropriation; (*Mil.*) lodging.
stanziare, *v.t.i.* To allocate, to assign, to grant; to deliberate; to station, to lodge. **— una somma,** to allocate a sum; **— in bilancio,** to budget for.
stanzino, *n.m.* Small room.
stappare, *v.t.* To uncork.
stare, *v.i.* To stay; to be; to stop, to stand, to remain; to wait; to live; to reside; to fit, to suit. **— a sedere,** to be sitting; **sto a vedere,** I'm waiting to see; **— coricato,** to lie down; **— in campagna,** to live in the country; **questo cappello mi sta bene,** this hat suits me; **— in piedi,** to stand, to stand up; **Sta ritto!** Stand up! **Sta zitto!** Keep quiet! Shut up! **Come sta? Come state? Come stai?** How do you do? **— bene, — male,** to be well, to be ill; **sta per uscire,** he's just going out; **gli sta bene,** it serves him right; **tutto sta che voglia,** it all depends on him; **Dove stai di casa?** Where do you live? **star sulle spine,** to be on tenter-hooks; **è un uomo che sta bene,** he's a man of means; **— attento,** to pay attention; **— con le mani in mano,** to be idle; **sta bene!** all right! **stai allegro!** Cheer up! **è una cosa che mi sta a cuore,** it is a matter very near my heart; **— in forse,** to hesitate; **— in guardia,** to be on the look-out; (*Mil.*) **— sull'attenti,** to stand to attention.
starna, *n.f.* (*Zool.*) Gray partridge.
starnazzare, *v.i.* To flutter, to flap the wings; to dust (of birds).
starnutamento, *n.m.* Sneezing.
starnutare, starnutire, *v.i.* To sneeze.
starnuto, *n.m.* Sneeze, sneezing.
stasare, *v.t.* To unstop, to open.
stasera, *adv.* This evening, tonight.
stasi, *n.f.* (*Med.*) Stasis; lull; inactivity, standstill, stagnation.
statale, *n.m.a.* Civil servant; State employee; State, of the State.
statare, *v.i.* (*obs.*) To summer, to pass the summer; (*Agric.*) to leave fallow.

statario [statArio], *a.* Steady; (*Law*) summary. **Battaglia stataria,** pitched battle.

state, *n.f.* (*colloq.*) Summer [cp. **estate**].

staterello, *n.m.* Petty state.

statica [stAtica], *n.f.* Statics.

statico [stAtico], *a.* Static.

statista (*pl.* **statisti**), *n.m.* Statesman.

statistica [statIstica], *n.f.* Statistics.

statistico [statIstico], *a.* Statistical.

statizzare, *v.t.* To nationalize (property, etc.).

stato, *n.m.* State (in all senses); nation, government; condition, situation; rank, status; profession, occupation; account; return, list, statement; (*Mil.*) staff. **— di assedio,** state of siege, martial law; **uomo di —,** statesman; **— d'animo,** mood, state of mind; **colpo di —,** coup d'état; **in quale —!** in what a state! **— di salute,** state of health; **essere in — interessante,** to be pregnant; **in buono —,** in good repair; (*Mil.*) **Stato Maggiore,** General Staff; **Gli Stati Uniti,** the United States, U.S.A. ; **Stati della Chiesa,** the Papal States.

statolatria [statolatrIa], *n.f.* Exaggerated worship of the State.

statoscopio [statoscOpio], *n.m.* Statoscope.

statua [stAtua], *n.f.* Statue. **Inalzare una —,** to erect a statue.

statuaria [statuAria], *n.f.* Statuary, sculpture.

statuario [statuArio], *a.* Statuary; statuesque.

statuetta, *n.f.* Statuette.

statuire, *v.i.* To decree, to ordain; to resolve.

statura, *n.f.* Height, stature, size. **Di che — è?** How tall is he?

statutale, statutario [statutArio], *a.* Statutory.

statuto, *n.m.* Statute; constitution; articles of association; by-laws.

stavolta, *adv.* This time.

staza [cp. **stazza**].

stazionare, *v.i.* To stand, to stay, to stop.

stazionario [stazionArio], *a.* Stationary.

stazione, *n.f.* Station (in all senses). **— climatica,** health resort; **— balneare,** watering-place; **— di polizia,** police-station; **— di pompieri,** fire-station; (*Rail.*) **— capolinea,** terminus; (*Radio*) **— radiotelegrafica,** wireless station; **— radio di Roma,** Rome broadcasting station.

stazza, *n.f.* (*Naut.*) Tonnage. **— lorda,** gross tonnage.

stazzare, *v.i.* (*Naut.*) To have tonnage of (of a ship); to gauge, to measure. **Quanto stazza quel bastimento?** What is the tonnage of that vessel?

stazzatura, *n.f.* Tonnage.

stazzonamento, *n.m.* Rumpling, creasing, wrinkling.

stazzonare, *v.t.* To rumple, to crease, to wrinkle.

stazzone, *n.m.* Station; shop.

stearico [steArico], *a.* (*Chem.*) Stearic. **Candela stearica,** tallow candle.

stearina, *n.f.* (*Chem.*) Stearine.

steatite, *n.f.* (*Min.*) Steatite.

stecca, *n.f.* Slat; rib (of fan or umbrella); skewer; billiard-cue; paper-knife; splint; (*Rail.*) fish-plate; (*Mus.*) false note.

steccaia [steccAia], *n.f.* Mill-dam.

steccadenti, *n.m.* Tooth-pick.

steccare, *v.t.* To fence in; to rail off; (*Med.*) to put in splints; (*Mus.*) to be out of tune.

steccata, *n.f.* Blow with stick.

steccato, *n.m.* Palisade, paling, fence.

stecchetto, *n.m.* Small stick. **Tenere a —,** to keep on short rations; to skimp.

stecchino, *n.m.* Toothpick.

stecchirsi, *v.r.* To become stiff, to stiffen.

stecchito, *a.* Stiff, rigid; stark; dead. **— dal freddo,** stiff with cold; **magro —** lean, famished; **cadere morto —,** to fall stone dead.

stecco, *n.m.* Stick; twig; wooden pin; toothpick; (*fig.*) a thin person. **Sottile come uno —,** as thin as a lath.

stecconare, *v.t.* To fence in.

stecconata, stecconato, *n.f.m.* Palisade, stockade, fencing.

steccone, *n.m.* Stake, picket.

Stefano [stEfano], *n.m.* Stephen.

stegola [stEgola], *n.f.* (*Agric.*) Plough-handle.

stela, stele, *n.f.* (*Arch.*) Stele, pillar.

stella, *n.f.* Star (in all senses); rowel (of spur); asterisk; (*fig.*) fate. **— polare,** Pole Star; **— cadente,** shooting star; **— mattutina,** morning star; (*Zool.*) **— di mare,** star-fish; **portare alle stelle,** to extol to the skies; **essere nato sotto cattiva —,** to be born under an unlucky star; **seguire la propria —,** to follow one's star, to follow one's destiny; **veder le stelle,** to see stars (from a blow); (*Theat. etc.*) **— nascente,** rising star.

stellante, *a.* Sparkling, shining (of eyes).

stellare, *a.* Stellar, starry.

stellaria [stellAria], *n.f.* (*Bot.*) Star-wort.

stellato, *a.* Starry, covered with stars; starlit.

stelletta, *n.f.* Little star; asterisk; star rank-badge.

stellina, *n.f.* Little star; star-shaped paste (in soup); (*Cinema*) starlet.

stellionato, *n.m.* (*Law*) Stellionate.

stelloncino, *n.m.* Short paragraph, snappy paragraph in a newspaper; asterisk.

stellone, *n.m.* Large star; lucky star.

stelo, *n.m.* (*Bot.*) Stalk, stem.

stemma (*pl.* **stemmi**), *n.m.* (*Heraldry*) Escutcheon, coat of arms; crest.

stemmato, *a.* Blazoned, armorial.

stemperamento, *n.m.* Melting, dissolving.

stemperare, *v.t.* To dissolve, to melt, to mix.

stemperarsi, *v.r.* To melt. **— in lagrime,** to dissolve in tears.

stemperatamente, *adv.* Excessively, immoderately.

stemperato, *a.* Dissolved; immoderate.

stempiato, *a.* With bald temples; (*colloq.*) huge, immense.

stendardo, *n.m.* Flag, banner, standard, ensign.

stendere [stEndere], *v.t.* To spread, to spread out; to extend, to stretch out; to write down, to draw up (a document); to smooth out. **— i panni,** to hang out the clothes; **— le gambe,** to stretch one's legs; **— una domanda,** to draw up an application; **— un velo,** to draw a veil.

stendersi [stEndersi], *v.r.* To stretch oneself; to spread, to extend. **La città si stende più verso sud,** the town extends more towards the south.

stendimento, *n.m.* Stretching out, spreading out, extending.
stenditoio [stenditOio], *n.m.* Drying-place; tenter (for weaving).
stenebrare, *v.t.* To dispel darkness; to enlighten.
stenodattilografo [stenodattilOgrafo], *n.m.* Shorthand-typist.
stenografare, *v.t.* To write shorthand; to take down in shorthand.
stenografia [stenografIa], *n.f.* Shorthand, stenography.
stenografico [stenogrAfico], *a.* Shorthand.
stenografo, stenografa [stenOgrafo, -a], *n.m.f.* Shorthand-writer, stenographer.
stenosi, *n.f.* (*Med.*) Stenosis, constipation.
stenotipista, *n.m.f.* [cp. **stenodattilografo**].
stentare, *v.t.i.* To struggle for a living, to struggle through; to be in want; to have difficulty (in doing a thing). **Stento a riconoscerlo,** I can hardly recognize him; **— la vita,** to be hard up; **stenta a decidersi,** he can't make up his mind.
stentatamente, *adv.* Weakly, in a laboured way, with difficulty.
stentatezza, *n.f.* Awkwardness, gawkiness, stuntedness; difficulty.
stentato, *p.p.a.* Stunted; laboured; weak, delicate, lean; ill-grown; awkward; halting. **Un bambino —,** a stunted child; **un parlare —,** halting speech; **una vita stentata,** a life of drudgery, a dog's life.
stenterello, *n.m.* (*Theat.*) Mask character of the Florentine theatre; a poor wretch, lean fellow.
stento, *n.m.* Privation, want, need; toil, drudgery; effort, fatigue, difficulty. **Morir di stenti,** to die of want; **a —,** with difficulty; **egli parlava a —,** he could hardly speak.
stentoreo [stentOreo], *a.* Stentorian, loud.
stentucchiare, *v.i.* To labour under difficulties; to be in straitened circumstances.
steppa, *n.f.* (*Geog.*) Steppe.
sterco, *n.m.* Dung, excrement. **Lo — del demonio,** money, filthy lucre.
stercoraceo [stercorAceo], *a.* Stercoraceous, stercoral.
stereoscopia [stereoscopIa], *n.f.* Stereoscopy.
stereoscopio [stereoscOpio], *n.m.* Stereoscope.
stereometria [stereometrIa], *n.f.* Solid geometry.
stereotipare, *v.t.* To stereotype.
stereotipia [stereotipIa], *n.f.* Stereotyping, stereotype.
sterile [stErile], *a.* Sterile, barren; unfruitful, unproductive; useless.
sterilità [-à], *n.f.* Sterility, barrenness, unfruitfulness.
sterilizzare, *v.t.* To sterilize.
sterilizzatore, *n.m.* Sterilizer.
sterilmente, *adv.* Sterilely.
sterlina, *n.f.* Sterling, pound sterling.
sterminabile [sterminAbile], *a.* Exterminable, eradicable.
sterminamento, *n.m.* Extermination.
sterminare, *v.t.* To exterminate, to destroy; to root out, to extirpate; to demolish.
sterminatamente, *adv.* Endlessly, immensely, enormously.
sterminatezza, *n.f.* Immeasurable size, immensity, boundlessness.
sterminato, *a.* Endless, boundless, huge, enormous, immense; exterminated.
sterminatore, sterminatrice, *n.m.f.* Exterminator, destroyer.
sterminio [stermInio], *n.m.* Extermination, destruction, ruin, slaughter; a huge quantity an infinity.
sterno, *n.m.* (*Anat.*) Sternum, breast-bone.
sternutare, sternutire, *v.i.* To sneeze [cp. **starnutare**].
sternuto, *n.m.* Sneeze.
sterpaglia [sterpAglia], *n.f.* Brushwood, undergrowth, suckers.
sterpagnola, *n.f.* (*Zool.*) Hedge-sparrow.
sterpaio [sterpAio], *n.m.* Thicket.
sterpame, *n.m.* Heap of brushwood, undergrowth.
sterpare, *v.t.* To clear of undergrowth.
sterpo, *n.m.* Stump, stub; brushwood.
sterposo, *a.* Brushy; thorny.
sterramento, *n.m.* Digging; excavation.
sterrare, *v.t.* To dig up, to turn up the ground; to dig out, to excavate.
sterratore, *n.m.* Navvy, digger.
sterro, *n.m.* Digging up, excavation; spoil (dug up). **Lavori di —,** excavation work, earthworks.
stertore, *n.m.* Stertorous breathing.
sterzare (1), *v.t.* To divide into three; to divide into equal portions; to thin out (trees, etc.); to blend (tobacco, etc.).
sterzare (2), *v.t.i.* (*Motor.*, etc.) To swerve, to turn; to steer.
sterzarsi, *v.r.* To work in turns; to share out (work, etc.).
sterzata, *n.f.* (*Motor.*, etc.) Swerve, sudden turn.
sterzo, *n.m.* (*Motor.*) Steering gear; front wheels, axles, etc., of a carriage.
stesamente, *adv.* Spread out.
steso, *p.p.a.* Stretched, spread out; laid on; written out. **— per terra,** stretched on the ground [cp. **stendere**].
stessere, *v.t.* To unravel.
stesso, *a.pron.* Same; self, very. **È lo — uomo,** he is the same man; **io uscirò lo —,** I shall go out all the same; **oggi —,** this very day; **fa lo —, è lo —,** it's all the same, it doesn't matter; **nello — momento preciso,** at that very moment; **è lui —,** it's he himself; **la bontà stessa,** goodness itself; **fiducia in sè stesso,** confidence in himself; **i bambini stessi lo amano,** even children like it.
stesura, *n.f.* Drawing up (a document), drafting; draft.
stetoscopio [stetoscOpio], *n.m.* Stethoscope.
stia, *n.f.* Hen-coop.
stiacciata, *n.f.* Cake, bun, bannock.
stiancia [stiAncia], *n.f.* (*Bot.*) Reed.
stibio [stIbio], *n.m.* (*Min.*) Antimony.
stiffelius [stiffElius], *n.m.* Frock-coat.
Stige, *n.m.* (*Myth.*) Styx.
stigio [stIgio], *a.* Stygian.
stigliare, *v.t.* To heckle flax.
stigma, *n.m.* Stigma, mark, stamp, brand.
stigmate, *n.f.pl.* Signs of the wounds of Christ, stigmata.
stigmatizzare, *v.t.* To censure, to stigmatize.
stilare, *v.t.* To pen, to word. **— in conto,** to invoice; **— un conto,** to make out an account.

stile (1), *n.m.* Style, language; mode of expression. **In grande —,** on a grand scale; **lo — è l'uomo,** the style is the man; **— di vita,** way of life.
stile (2), *n.m.* Stylus; dagger, stiletto.
stilettare, *v.t.* To stab.
stilettata, *n.f.* Dagger-thrust, stab with a dagger.
stiletto, *n.m.* Stiletto; pointed dagger.
stiliforme, *a.* Styliform.
stilista (*pl.* **stilisti**), *n.m.* Stylist.
stilistica [stilIstica], *n.f.* Rhetoric; rules of literary work; stylistics.
stilistico [stilIstico], *a.* Stylistic.
stilizzare, *v.t.* (*Art*) To stylize, to form a style; to draw conventionally.
stilla, *n.f.* Drop, drip. **— a —,** drop by drop.
stillamento, *n.m.* Dripping, dropping.
stillare, *v.t.i.* To drip, to ooze, to exude; to distil. **Stillarsi il cervello,** to rack one's brains.
stillicidio [stillicIdio], *n.m.* Constant dripping; oozing, percolation.
stillo, *n.m.* Still (for distilling).
stilo, *n.m.* Stylus; (*Arch.*) shaft of a column; (*colloq.*) *n.f.* fountain pen, stylographic pen.
stilografico [stilogrAfico], *a.* Stylographic. **Penna stilografica,** stylographic pen; fountain-pen.
stima, *n.f.* Esteem, respect, regard; consideration; (*Comm.*) valuation, estimate. **Godere la — di,** to enjoy the esteem of; **tenere in —,** to hold in esteem; **con la massima —,** Yours faithfully (in letters); **fare la —,** to estimate, to value.
stimabile [stimAbile], *a.* Estimable, respectable.
stimabilità [-à], *n.f.* Worth, estimability, estimableness.
stimare, *v.t.* To esteem, to value, to think, to regard, to consider. **— sotto il valore,** to underestimate; **— un anello,** to value a ring.
stimarsi, *v.r.* To esteem oneself, to think oneself. **— fortunato,** to think oneself lucky.
stimatore, *n.m.* Estimator, valuer, appraiser.
stimazione, *n.f.* Esteem, estimation.
stimmate, stimate [stImmate, stImate], *n.f.pl.* [cp. **stigmate**].
stimolante, *a.* Stimulating.
stimolare, *v.t.* To excite, to stimulate; to spur, to incite, to instigate; to goad, to urge.
stimolativo, *n.m.a.* Stimulative.
stimolatore, stimolatrice, *n.m.f.* Stimulator, inciter.
stimolo [stImolo], *n.m.* Stimulus, incitement; goad, spur.
stimolazione, *n.f.* Stimulation.
stincata, *n.f.* Blow or kick on the shin.
stinco, *n.m.* (*Anat.*) Tibia, shin, shin-bone.
stingere [stIngere], *v.t.i.* To discolour, to fade; (*fig.*) to deface.
stingersi [stIngersi], *v.r.* To fade, to lose colour; to become obscured.
stinto, *a.* Faded, discoloured.
stipa, *n.f.* Brushwood; (*Bot.*) various kinds of grass.
stipare, *v.t.* To cut brushwood; to pile up; to crowd; to pack closely.
stiparsi, *v.r.* To crowd, to throng.
stipato, *a.* Crowded. **Sala stipata,** crowded room.
stipendiare, *v.t.* To engage (on payment), to pay a salary to; to hire; to employ.
stipendiato, *n.m.a.* Stipendiary; salaried.
stipendio [stipEndio], *n.m.* Stipend, salary **Essere agli stipendi di,** to be in the pay of.
stipettaio [stipettAio], *n.m.* Cabinet-maker.
stipetto, *n.m.* Small cabinet.
stipite [stIpite], *n.m.* Jamb, doorpost; family, stock; stalk (of plant. etc.).
stipo, *n.m.* Cabinet (for curios, etc.); chest of drawers; what-not.
stipulante, *n.m.* (*Law*) Stipulator, contractor.
stipulare, *v.t.* To stipulate, to lay down; to arrange, to settle terms. **— un contratto,** to draw up a contract.
stipulazione, *n.f.* Stipulation.
stiracalzoni, *n.m.* Trouser-press.
stiracchiamento, *n.m.* Pulling, tugging, straining; over-stretching; (*fig.*) distortion.
stiracchiare, *v.t.* To pull about, to strain; to quibble, to cavil; to haggle. **— sul prezzo,** to haggle over the price.
stiracchiarsi, *v.r.* To stretch oneself.
stiracchiato, *a.* Forced, distorted, over-strained.
stiramento, *n.m.* Stretching; contraction; extension, pulling out.
stirare, *v.t.* To stretch out, to draw out, to extend; to iron (linen, etc.). **— le braccia,** to stretch one's arms.
stirarsi, *v.r.* To stretch oneself; to stretch.
stiratoio [stiratOio], *n.m.* Ironing-blanket; ironing-board, drawing board.
stiratora, stiratrice, *n.f.* Laundress.
stiratoria [stiratorIa], *n.f.* Laundry.
stiratura, *n.f.* Ironing.
stireria [stirerIa], *n.f.* [cp. **stiratorìa**].
stiro, *n.m.* Ironing. **Ferro da —,** iron, flat-iron.
stirpe, *n.f.* Stock, race; descent, lineage, extraction.
stiticamente, *adv.* Costively; grudgingly, stingily.
stitichezza, *n.f.* Costiveness, constipation.
stitico [stItico], *a.* Costive, constipated; (*fig.*) close-fisted, stingy.
stiva, *n.f.* (*Naut.*) Hold; (*Agric.*) plough-handle.
stivaggio [stivAggio], *n.m.* (*Naut.*) Stowage.
stivalare, *v.t.* To put boots on.
stivale, *n.m.* Boot. **Mettersi gli stivali,** to put on one's boots; (*fig.*) **rompere gli stivali a qualcuno,** to bother someone, to plague someone; **Lo Stivale,** Italy; (*colloq.*) **dottore dei miei stivali,** a bad doctor; doctor 'my foot'.
stivaletto, *n.m.* Ankle-boot, half-boot.
stivalone, *n.m.* Jack-boot, top-boot; fishing-boot.
stivamento, *n.m.* Stowing, stowage.
stivare, *v.t.* (*Naut.*) To stow (cargo); to pack, to cram.
stivarsi, *v.r.* To crowd in, to pack oneself in.
stivatore, *n.m.* Stevedore.
stivatura, *n.f.* Stowage.
stizza, *n.f.* Irritation, vexation; anger, rage, wrath. **Sfogare la —,** to vent one's bad temper; **far venire la — a,** to vex.
stizzire, *v.t.* To anger, to irritate.
stizzirsi, *v.r.* To get angry, to be vexed; to fly into a rage.
stizzito, *a.* Angry; cross, in a pet.

stizzosamente, *adv.* Peevishly, irritably.
stizzoso, *a.* Peevish, irritable; angry; choleric; spiteful.
stoccafisso, *n.m.* Dried cod, stockfish.
Stoccarda, *n.f.* (*Geog.*) Stuttgart.
stoccata, *n.f.* Thrust (with rapier, etc.), stab; (*fig.*) demand for money. **Dare una —,** to give a thrust; (*colloq.*) to suddenly demand money.
stoccheggiare, *v.i.* To thrust, to parry.
stocco, *n.m.* Rapier. **Bastone a —,** sword-stick.
Stoccolma, *n.f.* (*Geog.*) Stockholm.
stoffa, *n.f.* Stuff, material, fabric, cloth; (*fig.*) sort; condition, worth; nature. **Aver la — di,** to have the makings of; (*colloq.*) **essere una buona —,** to be a bad lot.
stoia [stOia], *n.f.* Mat (of straw or rush); hassock; roller-blind, sun-blind.
stoicamente, *adv.* Stoically.
stoicismo, *n.m.* Stoicism.
stoico [stOico], *n.m.a.* Stoic; stoical.
stoino [stoIno], *n.m.* Door-mat.
stola, *n.f.* Stole.
stolidamente, *adv.* Stupidly.
stolidezza, stolidità [-à], *n.f.* Silliness, foolishness, stupidity, weakmindedness.
stolido [stOlido], *a.* Silly, stupid.
stollo, *n.m.* Pole around which a haystack is built.
stolone, *n.m.* (*Eccles.*) Embroidery on a cope or stole; (*Bot.*) stolon.
stoltamente, *adv.* Foolishly, stupidly, senselessly.
stoltezza, *n.f.* Foolishness, stupidity, silliness; weak-mindedness.
stolto, *n.m.a.* Fool, silly fellow; foolish, stupid, silly.
stomacaggine [stomacAggine], *n.f.* Loathing, nausea.
stomacare, *v.t.* To sicken, to nauseate, to disgust.
stomacarsi, *v.r.* To be nauseated by; to become sick of.
stomachevole [stomachEvole], *a.* Loathsome, disgusting, sickening, revolting.
stomachevolmente, *adv.* Loathsomely.
stomachico [stomAchico], *n.m.a.* Stomachic.
stomaco [stOmaco], *n.m.* Stomach. **Dare di —,** to retch, to vomit; **mal di —,** stomach-ache; **aver sullo —,** to have heavy on one's stomach; **andare a —,** to agree, to fit.
stomacosamente, *adv.* Disgustingly.
stomacoso, *a.* Disgusting.
stomacuccio [stomacUccio], *n.m.* (*colloq.*) Weak stomach, poor digestion.
stomatico [stomAtico], *n.m.a.* Stomachic; tonic.
stomatite, *n.f.* (*Med.*) Stomatitis.
stonamento, *n.m.* Discord, singing or playing out of tune.
stonare, *v.i.* To be out of tune, to sing or play wrong; to be dissonant; to jar, to clash; to disagree.
stonato, *a.* Out of tune; jarring, discordant; out of place.
stonatura, *n.f.* Discord, jarring note.
stoppa, *n.f.* Tow, oakum. **Uomo di —,** man of straw; **testa di —,** blockhead; **un pulcino nella —,** very confused, muddled.
stoppabuchi, *n.m.* Stop-gap.
stoppaccio [stoppAccio], *n.m.* Wad; wadding.
stoppare, *v.t.* To plug (with tow), to stop.
stoppia [stOppia], *n.f.* (*Agric.*) Stubble.
stoppiniera, *n.f.* Taper-holder.
stoppino, *n.m.* Wick, taper.
stopposo, *a.* Tow-like; woolly.
storcere [stOrcere], *v.t.* To twist; to dislocate, to distort, to wrench; to misrepresent, to alter. **— la bocca,** to make a wry face.
storcersi [stOrcersi], *v.r.* To twist, to writhe; to dislocate (a limb). **— un braccio,** to dislocate one's arm; **— un piede,** to sprain an ankle.
storcimento, *n.m.* Twisting; dislocation.
stordimento, *n.m.* Dizziness, stupor; stupefaction, bewilderment.
stordire, *v.t.* To stun, to daze, to bewilder; to deafen.
stordirsi, *v.r.* To distract oneself from unpleasant thoughts, to forget one's troubles.
storditaggine [storditAggine], *n.f.* Heedlessness, foolishness; flightiness, giddiness.
storditamente, *adv.* Rashly, thoughtlessly, heedlessly.
storditezza, *n.f.* Heedlessness, rashness; recklessness.
stordito, *a.* Stunned, bewildered; rash, heedless, reckless; giddy, scatter-brained.
storia [stOria], *n.f.* History; story, tale. **Quante storie per nulla!** What a to-do about nothing! **— antica,** ancient history; **non fate tante storie,** don't stand on ceremony; don't make such a fuss.
storicamente, *adv.* Historically.
storicità [-à], *n.f.* Historicity.
storico [stOrico], *n.m.a.* Historian; historical, historic.
storieggiare, *v.t.* [cp. **istoriare**].
storiella, *n.f.* Little story; fib, white lie.
storiografia [storiografIa], *n.f.* Historiography.
storiografo [storiOgrafo], *n.m.* Historian, historiographer.
storione, *n.m.* (*Zool.*) Sturgeon.
stormeggiare, *v.i.* To flock, to herd together; to ring the tocsin.
stormire, *v.i.* To rustle.
stormire, *n.m.* Rustle, rustling. **Lo — delle foglie,** the rustling of the leaves.
stormo, *n.m.* Flock (of birds), flight (of planes); host; swarm. **A stormi,** in swarms; **suonare a —,** to ring the tocsin, to give the alarm.
stornare, *v.t.* To avert, to turn aside, to parry, to ward off; to cancel; to dissuade; (*Law*) to misappropriate; (*Comm.*) to transfer (in book-keeping). **— il colpo,** to ward off the blow; **— i fondi,** to divert funds; **— un'ordinazione,** to cancel an order.
stornellare, *v.i.* To sing (folksongs, etc.).
stornello (1), *n.m.* (*Zool.*) Starling.
stornello (2), *n.m.* (*Poet.*) Verse of three lines.
stornello, *a.* Grey, grizzled [cp. **storno**].
storno (1), *n.m.* Starling; bay horse.
storno (2), *n.m.* Turning aside; (*Comm.*) book-keeping transfer; cancellation; (*Law*) misappropriation.
storno, *a.* Dappled, grey; bay.
storpiamento, *n.m.* Crippling, mutilation, maiming.
storpiare, *v.t.* To cripple, to maim; to spoil, to mangle; to bungle.

storpiarsi, *v.r.* To be crippled, to be maimed.
storpiatamente, *adv.* Distortedly.
storpiato, *a.* Crippled; distorted.
storpio [stOrpio], *n.m.a.* Cripple; crippled, maimed, distorted.
storta, *n.f.* (*Med.*) Sprain; wrench; bend (of a river); (*Chem.*) retort.
stortamente, *adv.* Crookedly; askew; the wrong way.
stortezza, *n.f.* Crookedness, distortion; falseness.
storto, *a.* Crooked, twisted; askew; deformed; wrenched; wrong, false, distorted. **Gambe storte,** bandy legs; **guardare —,** to squint, **idee storte,** wrong notions.
stortura, *n.f.* Distortion, deformity; mistaken notion, error.
stovaina, *n.f.* (*chem.*) stovaine.
stovigliaio [stovigliAio], *n.m.* Potter, maker or vendor of earthenware.
stoviglie, stoviglierie [stovIglie], *n.f.pl.* Crockery, crocks, household utensils.
stozzo, *n.m.* Punch (tool).
stra-, *prefix.* Very, extremely, super-, over-.
strabalzare, *v.i.* To jump about, to toss about, to shake, to toss; to jolt.
strabalzoni, *adv.* Joltingly, bumpily.
strabastare, *v.i.* To be more than enough, to abound.
strabello, *a.* (*colloq.*) Extremely beautiful.
strabene, *adv.* Very well, excellently.
strabere, *v.i.* To drink too much.
strabico [strAbico], *n.m.a.* Person with a squint; squinting.
strabiliante, *a.* Bewildering, dazzling, stunning, amazing.
strabiliare, strabiliarsi, *v.i.r.* To be amazed at, to wonder at; to be astonished. **Fare —,** to amaze, to bewilder.
strabismo, *n.m.* Squinting, squint.
straboccamento, *n.m.* Overflowing; excess.
straboccare, *v.i.* To overflow, to superabound.
straboccatamente, *adv.* Excessively.
straboccato, *a.* Excessive; impetuous.
strabocchevole [strabocchEvole], *a.* Overflowing, plentiful; excessive. **Una folla —,** an overwhelming crowd.
strabocchevolmente, *adv.* Plentifully, abundantly.
stracaricare, *v.t.* To overload, to overburden.
stracarico [stracArico], *a.* Overloaded; overburdened. **— di anni,** overburdened with years; **— di lavoro,** overworked.
stracaro, *a.* Very dear, prohibitive (in price).
stracca, *n.f.* Fatigue. **Alla —,** wearily; **prendere una —,** to overwork.
straccaggine [straccAggine], *n.f.* Weariness, fatigue.
straccale, *n.m.* Breeching-strap; braces.
straccare, *v.t.* To tire out, to weary.
stracceria [straccerIa], *n.f.* Rags, tatters.
stracchezza, *n.f.* Tiredness, weariness, fatigue.
stracchino, *n.m.* Variety of cheese.
stracciabile [stracciAbile], *a.* Tearable.
stracciafoglio [stracciafOglio], *n.m.* Rough note-book, rough draft.
stracciaio, stracciuolo [stracciAio], *n.m.* Rag-merchant, rag-picker, rag-and-bone man.
stracciamento, *n.m.* Tearing.
stracciare, *v.t.* To rend, to tear, to lacerate. **— una lettera,** to tear up a letter.
stracciato, *a.* In rags. **Uomo tutto —,** man in rags and tatters.
stracciatura, *n.f.* Tearing, tear.
straccio [strAccio], *n.m.a.* Rag, tatter, scrap; in rags. **Carta straccia,** waste paper.
straccione, *n.m.* Ragged fellow, tatterdemalion; ragamuffin.
stracco, *a.* Tired, worn out with fatigue; poor, weak.
stracollare, *v.i.* To fall over [cp **tracollare**].
stracollarsi, *v.r.* To sprain (a muscle, etc.).
stracontento, *a.* Extremely happy, overjoyed.
stracotto, *n.m.a.* Stew; overdone, overcooked.
stracuocere [stracuOcere], *v.t.* To overdo, to overcook.
strada, *n.f.* Road; way, street; route. **— maestra,** high road, main road; **— nazionale,** arterial road; **— carrozzabile,** carriage road; **— ferrata,** railway; **essere fuori di —,** to be astray; **aprirsi la —,** to make one's way; **mettere sulla buona —,** to put on the right road; **insegnar la — a qualcuno,** to show someone the way; **— battuta,** beaten track; **esser sulla —,** to be in dire want; **— facendo,** on the way; **tagliar la —,** to bar the way; **ladro di —,** footpad, highwayman; **non so quale — seguire,** I don't know what course to adopt.
stradale, *n.m.* Country road.
stradale, *a.* Road, pertaining to roads. **Codice —,** highway code; **incidenti stradali,** road accidents; **manutenzione —,** road up-keep; **pianta —,** road-map; **regolamento —,** rule of the road.
stradamento, *n.m.* Road-making; guiding.
stradario [stradArio], *n.m.* Road-book.
stradatamente, *adv.* Continually, uninterruptedly.
stradella, stradetta, stradicciuola, *n.f.* Lane, alley.
stradina, *n.f.* Narrow lane.
stradino, *n.m.* Road-worker, road-mender.
stradivario [stradivArio], *n.m.* (*Mus.*) Violin made by Stradivarius (1644-1737).
stradone, *n.m.* High road, main road.
stradoppio [stradOppio], *a.* More than double.
straduccia, straducola [stradUccia, stradUcola], *n.f.* Lane.
strafalciare, *v.i.* To act thoughtlessly.
strafalcione, *n.m.* Blunder, mistake, error, howler.
strafare, *v.i.* To overwork, to do too much, to do more than is needed.
strafatto, *a.* Overdone (cookery); over-ripe.
strafelarsi, *v.r.* To gasp for breath.
strafelato, *a.* Tired out, worn-out, breathless.
strafelice, *a.* Overjoyed, supremely happy.
straforo, *adv.* **Di —,** on the sly, stealthily.
strafottente, *a.* (*slang*) Indifferent (to others), unconcerned; careless (of what others think or feel); insolent, impudent.
strafottenza, *n.f.* (*vulgar*) Disregard of others; insolence, cheek.
strafottersi [strafOttersi], *v.r.* (*vulgar*) To be indifferent (to other's opinion); to be careless; not to care a tinker's cuss.

strage, *n.f.* Slaughter, massacre, carnage, destruction. **Fare —,** to destroy, to wreak havoc.
straglio [strAglio], *n.m.* (*Naut.*) Stay. **Vela di —,** stay-sail.
stragodere, *v.i.* To enjoy oneself to the utmost.
stragrande, *a.* Huge, immense, enormous.
stralciare, *v.t.* (*Agric.*) To prune, to lop; to settle a matter; (*Comm.*) to balance (accounts); to select, to pick out, to take out.
stralciatura, *n.f.* Pruning.
stralcio [strAlcio], *n.m.* (*Agric.*) Pruning, lopping; compromise; extract; (newspaper) cutting. (*Comm.*) winding-up, liquidation.
strale, *n.m.* Arrow, dart. **Gli strali d'amore,** Cupid's darts.
stralodare, *v.i.* To overpraise.
stralucente, *a.* Shiny, glossy.
stralunamento, *n.m.* Staring; rolling of the eyes.
stralunare, *v.i.* To open the eyes wide, to roll the eyes.
stralunato, *a.* Rolling, wild (of eyes); vacant (in appearance); upset, discomposed.
stramaglia [stramAglia], *n.f.* [cp. **strame**].
stramaledire, *v.t.* To curse heartily.
stramazzare, *v.i.t.* To tumble down, to fall, to collapse; to knock down.
stramazzata, *n.f.* Heavy fall, bump, thud; violent blow.
stramazzo, *n.m.* Coarse blanket used as mattress; fall.
stramazzone, *n.m.* Tumble, heavy fall, thud.
strambamente, *adv.* Oddly, extravagantly.
stramberia [stramberIa], *n.f.* Queerness, oddity, eccentricity, whim.
strambo, *a.* Queer, odd, eccentric, extravagant.
strambotto, *n.m.* (*Poet.*) Rustic love song, folk song.
strame, *n.m.* Straw, litter; forage.
strampalataggine, strampaleria [strampalatAggine, strampalerIa], *n.f.* Extravagance, oddness.
strampalato, *a.* Extravagant, foolish, odd, senseless. **Discorso —,** senseless speech; **errore —,** gross blunder.
stranamente, *adv.* Strangely, oddly, eccentrically.
stranezza, *n.f.* Strangeness, queerness, oddity; singularity, peculiarity; whim.
strangolamento, *n.m.* Strangling, choking.
strangolare, *v.t.* To strangle, to throttle, to choke; (*fig.*) to fleece.
strangolarsi, *v.r.* To choke, to suffocate.
strangolatore, strangolatrice, *n.m.f.* Strangler.
strangolazione, *n.f.* Strangulation, strangling.
stranguglione, *n.m.* (*Vet.*) Strangles; (*colloq.*) hiccup.
straniare, *v.t.* To estrange, to alienate.
straniarsi, *v.r.* To be estranged; to stand aloof; to drift apart.
straniero, *n.m.a.* Foreigner, alien; foreign.
stranio [strAnio], *a.* (*Lit.*) Foreign.
strano, *a.* Strange, queer, odd, curious; unusual; peculiar. **Mi par — che,** it seems strange to me that.
straordinariamente, *adv.* Extraordinarily, peculiarly; enormously, immensely.
straordinarietà [-à], *n.f.* Peculiarity, extraordinariness.
straordinario [straordinArio], *a.* Extraordinary, peculiar, exceptional, unusual, remarkable. **Lavoro —,** overtime.
strapagare, *v.t.* To over-pay.
straparlare, *v.i.* To talk too much; to talk nonsense, to ramble, to wander (in speech); to rave.
strapazzamento, *n.m.* Over-working, sweating (labour).
strapazzare, *v.t.* To over-work, to ill-treat; to reprimand, to rebuke, to scold; to bungle, to make a mess of.
strapazzarsi, *v.r.* To tire oneself out; to be careless of one's health.
strapazzata, *n.f.* Reprimand, rebuke, scolding; strain, fatigue, effort.
strapazzatamente, *adv.* Roughly, harshly.
strapazzato, *a.* Ill-used, over-worked. **Uova strapazzate,** scrambled eggs.
strapazzo, *n.m.* Fatigue; over-work, toil, strain; rough usage. **Abito da —,** working-clothes.
strapazzosamente, *adv.* Roughly, regardlessly; wearily.
strapazzoso, *a.* Wearisome.
straperdere [strapErdere], *v.i.* To lose heavily.
strapiantare, *v.t.* To transplant.
strapieno, *a.* Overfull, overfilled.
strapiombare, *v.i* To be out of plumb, to lean out, to overhang. **Rocche strapiombanti,** overhanging cliffs.
strapiombo, *adv.* **A —,** jutting out, overhanging.
strapontino, *n.m.* (*Motor.*) Tip-up seat.
strapotente, *a.* Overpowering, very powerful.
strapotenza, *n.f.* Very great power.
strappabile [strappAbile], *a.* Easily snatched.
strappamento, *n.m.* Wresting, snatching away; a muscular sprain.
strappare, *v.t.* To snatch, to tear away, to pull away; to extirpate, to root out; to wring, to extort. **— un dente,** to draw a tooth; **— una pianta,** to uproot a plant.
strapparsi, *v.r.* To tear oneself away, to break away. **— i capelli,** to tear one's hair; **— il vestito,** to tear one's clothes.
strappata, *n.f.* Pull, snatch, tug.
strappatura, strappo, *n.f.m.* Pull, snatch, tug, jerk; rent, tear; (*Law*) infraction, **fare uno — alle proprie abitudini,** to depart from one's usual habits; **a strappi,** by jerks; **uno strappo muscolare,** a sprain.
strapunto, *n.m.* Quilt.
strapuntino, *n.m.* (*Motor.*) Tip-up seat.
straricco, *a.* Very rich, immensely wealthy.
straripamento, *n.m.* Overflowing, overflow, flood, inundation.
straripare, *v.i.* To overflow, to flood, to inundate.
strascicamento, *n.m.* Trailing, dragging along; drawling (in speech).
strascicare, *v.t.* To trail, to drag; to drawl. **— i piedi,** to drag one's feet, to shamble.
strascicarsi, *v.r.* To crawl, to drag oneself along, to shuffle.
strascichio [strascichIo], *n.m.* Sound or action of dragging or shuffling; trailing along.

strascico [strAscico], *n.m.* Trailing, trail; train (of a dress); sequel, consequences.
strascicone, *n.m.* Shambler, shuffler.
strasciconi, *adv.* Draggingly, shufflingly, drawlingly.
strascinare, *v.t.* To drag along the ground [cp. **trascinare**].
strascino [strAscino], *n.m.* Drag-net; drawnet (for birds); harrow.
strasecolare, *v.i.* To be amazed, to wonder at.
strass, strasso, *n.m.* Artificial or synthetic diamond.
stratagemma, strattagemma (*pl.* **stratagemmi**), *n.m.* Stratagem, trick, artifice.
stratega (*pl.* **strateghi**), *n.m.* Strategist; (*Hist.*) strategus.
strategia [strategIa], *n.f.* Strategy.
strategicamente, *adv.* Strategically.
strategico [stratEgico], *a.* Strategic.
stratificare, stratificarsi, *v.t.r.* To stratify; to be stratified.
stratificazione, *n.f.* Stratification.
stratiforme, *a.* Stratiform.
strato, *n.m.* Bed, layer, stratum; coat (of paint, etc.). — **sociale,** class, rank.
stratosfera, *n.f.* Stratosphere.
stratta, *n.f.* Pull, jerk.
strattagemma [cp. **stratagemma**].
strattone, *n.m.* Wrench, violent pull or jerk. **A strattoni,** by fits and starts.
stravagante, *a.* Odd, queer, extravagant, strange, eccentric.
stravagantemente, *adv.* Oddly, extravagantly.
stravaganza, *n.f.* Oddity, oddness, peculiarity, extravagance (of behaviour), eccentricity.
stravasamento, *n.m.* (*Med.*) Extravasation.
stravecchio [stravEcchio], *a.* Very old; ripe, mellow (of wine).
stravedere, *v.t.i.* To make a mistake; to see not too clearly.
stravincere [stravIncere], *v.t.* To win all along the line; to abuse one's victory.
straviziare, *v.i.* To be intemperate; to be debauched, to indulge in.
stravizio [stravIzio], *n.m.* Debauch, debauchery, vice, dissoluteness, excess.
stravolgimento, *n.m.* Wrenching, overturning; distortion.
stravolgere [stravOlgere], *v.t.* To wriggle, to twist; to wrench; to distort.
stravoltamente, *adv.* Troublesomely; convulsively; topsy-turvy.
stravolto, *a.* Upset, troubled, disturbed; crooked, twisted, turned upside-down. **Una faccia stravolta,** a troubled expression.
straziamento, *n.m.* Distress; ill-treatment.
straziante, *a.* Distressing, heart-rending, torturing, agonizing; appalling, dire.
straziare, *v.t.* To tear, to rend, to lacerate; to torture; to distress, to torment, to rack; to defame, to slander. — **l'orecchio,** to grate on one's ear.
strazio [strAzio], *n.m.* Torture, torment, anguish, agony; destruction; slander. **Fare — di qualcuno,** to slander someone; **fecero — del suo corpo,** they tore him to pieces.
strega, *n.f.* Witch, sorceress.
stregamento, *n.m.* Spell, witchery.
stregare, *v.t.* To bewitch; to charm, to affect by magic.
stregone, *n.m.* Wizard, sorcerer.
stregoneria [stregonerIa], *n.f.* Sorcery, witchcraft; bewitchment.
stregua [strEgua], *n.f.* Rate, degree, measure, standard. **Alla stessa —,** by the same standard; **a questa —,** at this rate.
stremare, *v.t.* To exhaust, to tire out.
stremarsi, *v.r.* To get tired out, to be worn out.
stremenzire, *v.t.* [cp. **striminzire**].
stremo [cp. **estremo**].
strenna, *n.f.* Gift, present. — **di Natale,** Christmas gift.
strenuamente, *adv.* Strenuously.
strenuità [-**à**], *n.f.* Strenuousness.
strenuo [strEnuo], *a.* Strenuous, vigorous; brave; unrelaxing, persistent; ardent, eager.
strepente, *a.* (*Lit.*) Noisy, clamorous.
strepitamento, *n.m.* Noise; making a noise, shouting, blustering [cp. **strepito**].
strepitare, *v.i.* To make a noise; to clamour, to shout.
strepito [strEpito], *n.m.* Noise, uproar, din, tumult.
strepitosamente, *adv.* Noisily, uproariously.
strepitoso, *a.* Noisy, boisterous, uproarious, roistering; tumultuous. **Successo —,** striking success; **vittoria strepitosa,** resounding victory.
streptococco, *n.m.* (*Med.*) Streptococcus.
streptomicina, *n.f.* (*Med.*) Streptomycin.
stretta, *n.f.* Squeeze, pressure; grip, hold; clasp; (mountain) pass, narrow passage; distress, pang. — **di mano,** hand-shake; — **al cuore,** anguish of heart; **essere alle strette,** to be in dire straits; **mettere alle strette,** to corner, to press closely; — **di spalle,** shrug of the shoulders.
strettamente, *adv.* Narrowly, straitly. **È — necessario,** it is absolutely necessary; **è — proibito,** it is strictly forbidden.
strettezza, *n.f.* Narrowness; strictness; distress, hardship, need; straits, straitened means. **Strettezze finanziarie,** financial difficulties; — **di tempo,** want of time.
stretto, *n.m.* (*Geog.*) Straits, strait.
stretto, *adv.a.* Narrow, tight, strait; limited, confined; strict, rigorous; near, intimate, close. **Tieni —,** hold tightly; **stia — a me,** keep close to me; **nello — senso della parola,** in the strict meaning of the word; **vocale stretta,** close vowel; **abito —,** tight coat; **è un mio — parente,** he's a near relation of mine; — **puntualità,** strict punctuality; **questa camera è troppo stretta per me,** this room is too narrow for me.
strettoia [strettOia], *n.f.* Bandage; narrow passage. **Trovarsi nelle strettoie,** to be in difficulties.
strettoio [strettOio], *n.m.* Press; wine-press.
strettura, *n.f.* Pressure.
stria, *n.f.* Streak, stripe; furrow; fluting.
striare, *v.t.* To streak, to stripe; to groove.
striato, *a.* Striped.
striatura, *n.f.* Stripe, streak.
stricco, *n.m.* (*Naut.*) Runner, running tackle.
stricnina, *n.f.* (*Chem.*) Strychnine.
strida, *n.f.pl.* Shrieks, screams, cries [cp. **strido**].
stridente, *a.* Strident, shrill, grating; harsh; jarring, clashing (of colours). **Voce —,** strident voice; **contrasto —,** violent contrast.

stridere [strIdere], *v.i.* To creak, to squeak, to grate; to clash (colours, etc.), to be discordant, to jar.
stridio [stridIo], *n.m.* Continuous creaking; shrieking; jarring.
strido (*pl.* **strida**, *f.*), *n.m.* Shriek, shrill cry, screech.
stridore, *n.m.* Creaking, shrieking; gnashing (of teeth).
stridulanti, *n.m.pl.* (*Zool.*) Crickets, cicadas.
stridulo [strIdulo], *a.* Piercing, shrill, sharp, stridulous.
strigare, *v.t.* To disentangle, to unravel.
strige, *n.f.* (*Zool.*) Screech-owl.
striglia [strIglia], *n.f.* Curry-comb.
strigliare, *v.t.* To curry, to groom; to thrash, to give a dressing down to.
strigliata, *n.f.* Currying; thrashing, dressing down.
strillare, *v.i.* To shriek, to scream, to squall, to squeal.
strillata, *n.f.* Loud cry, squeal.
strillo, *n.m.* Shriek, scream, cry, squeal.
strillone, *n.m.* News-boy.
striminzire, *v.t.* To stint; to stunt (in growth).
striminzirsi, *v.r.* To grow thin, to become stunted.
striminzito, *a.* Emaciated, thin, lean; stunted.
strimpellamento, *n.m.* Strumming.
strimpellare, *v.t.i.* To strum (the piano), to scrape (the violin).
strimpellata, *n.f.* Strumming.
strinare, *v.t.* To singe (linen, etc.).
strinato, strinatura, *n.m.f.* Singe, singeing. **Puzzo di —,** smell of singeing.
stringa, *n.f.* Shoe- or boot-lace; lace.
stringare, *v.t.* To lace tightly, to fasten; to condense, to make concise.
stringatamente, *adv.* Concisely.
stringatezza, *n.f.* Tightness, conciseness.
stringato, *a.* Tight, close-fitting; concise.
stringente, *a.* Pressing, urgent, close, searching, cogent; compelling. **Interrogatorio —,** close cross-examination; **bisogno —,** urgent need.
stringenza, *n.f.* Urgency, stringency.
stringere [strIngere], *v.t.i.* To press, to tie; to squeeze, to constrain, to compress, to tighten; to bind together (in friendship, etc.); to stipulate; (*Naut.*) to keep close to the wind. **— la mano a uno,** to shake hands with someone; **— una vite,** to tighten a screw; **— i pugni,** to clench one's fists; **— alleanza,** to form an alliance; **— al cuore,** to hug; **— i nodi,** to tighten the knots; **il tempo stringe,** time presses; **stringi stringi,** when all is said and done.
stringersi [strIngersi], *v.r.* To draw close to; to squeeze oneself. **— nelle spalle,** to shrug one's shoulders; **mi si stringe il cuore,** my heart bleeds for you; **stringetevi un poco,** make room, please; **— in amicizia,** to make friends (with).
stringimento, stringitura, *n.m.f.* Pressing, squeezing, narrowing; (*fig.*) sorrow, pain.
strippare, *v.t.i.* To cram, to guzzle, to gorge.
strippapelle, *adv.* **Mangiare a —,** to guzzle, to eat till one is full.
strippata, *n.f.* Excessive eating.
striscia [strIscia], *n.f.* Streak, stripe, strip, strap; razor-strop. **La — della lumaca,** the track of a snail; (*Motor.*) **— di corrimento,** tread of a tyre; **a strisce,** in stripes.
strisciamento, *n.m.* Creeping, sliding; crawl; dragging, shuffling; skimming; (*fig.*) flattery.
strisciante, *a.* Creeping, crawling; cringing, fawning.
strisciare, *v.t.i.* To drag, to trail along; to graze, to skim; to stroke (cat, etc.); to flatter; to grovel; to creep, to crawl, to slink; to cringe.
strisciata, strisciatura, *n.f.* Rubbing; stroking; creeping, crawl; (*fig.*) flattering.
striscio [strIscio], *n.m.* Smear (for microscope work); grazing, skimming.
striscio [strIscio], *adv.* **Di —,** grazingly. **Ferita di —,** graze (of the skin); abrasion.
striscione, *n.m.* Placard, poster; (*rare*) flatterer.
striscioni, *adv.* Crawling, shuffling along.
stritolabile [stritolAbile], *a.* Capable of being crushed or ground.
stritolamento, *n.m.* Crushing, grinding, pounding.
stritolare, *v.t.* To crush, to grind, to pound; to smash, to break up, to destroy.
strizzalimoni, *n.m.* Lemon-squeezer.
strizzare, *v.t.* To squeeze, to press, to squash; to wring. **— l'occhio,** to wink.
strizzata, *n.f.* Squeezing; wink.
strofa, strofe, *n.f.* (*Poet.*) Strophe, stanza.
strofinaccio [strofinAccio], *n.m.* Duster.
strofinare, *v.t.* To rub, to scour; to polish, to clean, to scrape, to scrub.
strofinarsi, *v.r.* To rub oneself (against something). **Il gatto si strofino contro il muro,** the cat rubbed itself against the wall.
strofinata, *n.f.* Rubbing, polishing; cleaning.
strofinio [strofinIo], *n.m.* Constant rubbing, friction.
strologare, *v.t.i.* To study; to prophesy, to foretell, to predict.
strombazzare, *v.t.* To trumpet, to blare forth; to advertise, to broadcast; to brag.
strombazzata, *n.f.* Trumpeting; brag, boast, vaunt.
strombazzatore, *n.m.* Braggart.
strombettare, *v.i.* To trumpet.
strombo, *n.m.* (*Arch.*) Splay; (*Zool.*) whelk.
stroncare, *v.t.* To break, to cut off short; (*fig.*) to criticize sharply, to slate.
stroncatura, *n.f.* (*fig.*) Destructive criticism, sharp critique, savage review.
stronco, *n.m.a.* Cripple; maimed, broken, worn out.
stronfiare, *v.i.* To snort.
stronzio [strOnzio], *n.m.* (*Min.*) Strontium.
stronzo, *n.m.* (*colloq.*) Ball of dung; turd.
stropicciamento, *n.m.* Rubbing, shuffling.
stropicciare, *v.t.* To rub, to shuffle or scrape (one's feet).
stropicciarsi, *v.r.* To rub oneself. **— il naso,** to rub one's nose.
stropicciata, stropicciatura, *n.f.* Rubbing, shuffling.
stropiccio [stropiccIo], *n.m.* Stamping, noise of shuffling feet.
strozza, *n.f.* Throat, windpipe, gullet; throttle.
strozzamento, *n.m.* Strangling, throttling.

strozzare, strozzarsi, *v.t.r.* To strangle, to throttle, to choke, to suffocate.
strozzato, *a.* Strangled, throttled. (*Med.*) **Ernia strozzata,** strangulated hernia.
strozzatura, *n.f.* Choking; narrow neck (of a vessel); narrow passage.
strozzinaggio [strozzinAggio], *n.f.* Usury; profiteering.
strozzino, *n.m.* Usurer, money-lender; profiteer.
strubbiare, *v.t.* To waste, to spoil.
struggere [strUggere], *v.t.* To melt, to consume; to destroy.
struggersi [strUggersi], *v.r.* To long for, to worry, to fret, to pine for; to consume oneself (with desire), to languish; to be afflicted. **Si strugge dalla voglia di sapere,** he longs to know; **— in lagrime,** to dissolve in tears.
struggicuore, *n.m.* Heart-break.
struggimento, *n.m.* Longing, aching for; impatience, boredom; distress, sorrow, anguish; melting, liquefaction.
strulleria [strullerIa], *n.f.* Foolishness.
strullo, *n.m.a.* Booby, fool; foolish.
strumentale, *a.* Instrumental (in all senses).
strumentalmente, *adv.* Instrumentally.
strumentare, *v.t.* (*Mus.*) To instrument, to score; (*Law*) to draw up (deeds, etc.).
strumentatura, *n.f.* (*Mus.*) Instrumentation; instrumental score.
strumentazione, *n.f.* Instrumentation.
strumento, *n.m.* Instrument (in all senses); document, deed; tool, implement.
strusciamento, *n.m.* Wearing, wear, rubbing.
strusciare, *v.t.* To wear out, to rub, to chafe; to rumple.
strusciarsi, *v.r.* To fawn upon; to cringe, to crawl to.
strusciata, *n.f.* Rub. **Dare una —,** to give a rub.
strutto, *n.m.* Lard.
strutto, *p.p.a.* Destroyed, demolished [cp. **struggere**].
struttura, *n.f.* Structure.
struzzo, *n.m.* (*Zool.*) Ostrich. **Stomaco di —,** stomach of an ostrich; (*fig.*) cast-iron stomach.
Stuardo, *n.m.* Stuart, Stewart.
stuccamento, *n.m.* Plastering.
stuccare, *v.t.* To plaster, to stucco; to surfeit, to disgust, to bore.
stuccarsi, *v.r.* To be bored; to be bothered; to be surfeited with.
stuccatore, *n.m.* Plasterer.
stuccatura, *n.f.* Stucco-work, plastering.
stucchevole [stucchEvole], *a.* Tiresome, wearisome, tedious; disgusting.
stucchevolezza, *n.f.* Weariness, disgust, annoyance; insipidity, affectedness.
stucchevolmente, *adv.* Tiresomely, artificially.
stucchinaio [stucchinAio], *n.m.* Maker and vendor of plaster figures.
stucchino, *n.m.* Plaster figure, statuette.
stucco, *n.m.* Stucco, plaster; putty; plaster figure. **Restar di —,** to be taken aback, to be dumb-founded.
stucco, *p.p.a.* Bored, disgusted, offended.
stuccoso, *a.* Weary, tired.
studente, *n.m.* Student; scholar, pupil.
studentesca, *n.f.* Students (as a body).
studentesco, *a.* Student's, student.
studentessa, *n.f.* Woman student.
studiacchiare, *v.i.* To study fitfully; to study carelessly.
studiare, *v.t.i.* To study; to learn; to read; to watch; to examine. **Studia medicina,** he is studying medicine.
studiarsi, *v.r.* To try, to endeavour, to strive, to do one's utmost. **Egli si studiava di far bene,** he endeavoured to behave well.
studiatamente, *adv.* On purpose, deliberately; affectedly.
studiato, *p.p.a.* Affected, studied, deliberate; artificial.
studio [stUdio], *n.m.* Study; care, heed; preparation; attainments; office; studio, working-room; (*Art*) sketch, study; (*Lit.*) essay, study. **— d'avvocato,** lawyer's chambers; **mise ogni — a far ciò,** he did it with the utmost care; **allo —,** under consideration, under examination; **— dal vero,** study from nature; **ha fatto dei buoni studi,** he has had a good education; **ha finito i suoi studi,** he has finished his education; **a bello —,** on purpose.
studiolo, *n.m.* Little workroom, small office.
studiosamente, *adv.* Studiously.
studioso, *n.m.* Scholar; observer, student. **Gli studiosi di questi libri,** those who study these books.
studioso, *a.* Studious; diligent, eager, keen.
stuellare, *v.t.* (*Med.*) To plug.
stuello, *n.m.* (*Med.*) Plug, tampon.
stufa, *n.f.* Stove; oven, hot-house. **— a petrolio,** oil-stove; **— economica,** kitchen range.
stufaiola, *n.f.* Stewpan, casserole.
stufare, *v.t.* To stew, to warm up; (*fig.*) to bore, to annoy, to weary.
stufarsi, *v.r.* To get bored, to be wearied; to get sick of.
stufato, *n.m.a.* Stew, stewed meat; stewed, braised.
stufo, *a.* Weary, bored; vexed, annoyed, tired; fed up. **Sono —!** I'm fed up!
stuoia [stuOia], *n.f.* Mat, matting.
stuoino, *n.m.* Door-mat.
stuolo, *n.m.* Troop; throng, multitude, band, crowd.
stuonare [cp. **stonare**].
stupefacente, *n.m.* Narcotic, soporific; drug.
stupefacente, *a.* Stupefying, astounding.
stupefare, *v.t.* To stupefy, to surprise, to astound.
stupefatto, *a.* Astonished, amazed, bewildered.
stupefazione, *n.f.* Stupefaction, astonishment; insensibility.
stupendamente, *adv.* Wonderfully, marvellously.
stupendo, *a.* Wonderful, admirable, marvellous; surprising; splendid, magnificent.
stupidaggine [stupidAggine], *n.f.* Nonsense, stupidity, absurdity; foolishness.
stupidamente, *adv.* Stupidly, foolishly.
stupidezza, *n.f.* Dullness of mind, stupidity, obtuseness.
stupidire, *v.t.i.* To make stupid; to become or be stupid [cp. **istupidire**].
stupidità [-à], *n.f.* Silliness, stupidity, foolishness, obtuseness, dullness.

stupido [stUpido], *n.m.* Dullard, blockhead, dunce, dolt.
stupido [stUpido], *a.* Silly, daft, stupid, idiotic; dull, lumpish.
stupire, *v.t.i.* To surprise, to amaze, to astonish.
stupirsi, *v.r.* To wonder at, to be surprised.
stupito, *p.p.a.* Amazed, astonished, surprised.
stupore, *n.m.* Amazement, surprise, wonder, astonishment, stupefaction; stupor.
stuprare, *v.t.* To rape, to ravish, to violate.
stupratore, *n.m.* Ravisher.
stupro, *n.m.* Rape, violation (of a virgin).
stura, *n.f.* Opening (of a bottle), uncorking; (*fig.*) beginning. **Dar la —,** to give vent; to vent (one's feelings).
sturabottiglie [sturabottIglie], *n.m.* Cork-screw.
sturare, *v.t.* To uncork, to open (a bottle). **— gli orecchi a qualcuno,** to give someone a piece of one's mind.
sturbamento, *n.m.* Disturbance.
sturbare, *v.t.* To disturb [cp. **turbare**].
sturbo, *n.m.* [cp. **disturbo**].
stuzzicadenti, *n.m.* Toothpick.
stuzzicamento, *n.m.* Prodding, poking; teasing; irritation.
stuzzicante, *a.* Teasing, irritating; stimulating.
stuzzicare, *v.t.* To poke, to prod, to stir up (excitement); to vex, to tease, to irritate, to annoy; to allure, to stimulate, to whet. **— l'appetito,** to stimulate the appetite; **— la curiosità,** to excite curiosity.
stuzzichino, *n.m.* Tormentor; snack, relish.
su, *adv.prep.* On, upon, up, over, above; out, about. **Su per giù,** roughly; approximately; **tirar su,** to bring up; **parlare su un argomento,** to speak about a subject; **Su! coraggio!** Cheer up! **andar su,** to ascend, to go up; **su e giù,** up and down; **i su e giù,** the ups and downs; **sul serio,** in earnest, seriously; **sul punto di,** on the point of; **su larga (piccola) scala,** on a large (small) scale; **sul mare,** at sea, on the sea; **Sta su!** Stand up! **Vieni su!** Come upstairs! **Su, via!** Come on! **su pei monti,** up the mountains; **dieci su cento,** ten per cent; **sui cinquantanni,** about fifty years old, in his fifties; **metter su un negozio,** to set up shop; **sul fare del giorno,** at daybreak. (With definite article **su** becomes **sugli, sui, sul, sullo, sulla, sulle.**)
suaccennato, *a.* Above-mentioned.
suadente, suasivo, suasorio [suasOrio], *a.* Persuasive.
subacqueo [subAcqueo], *a.* Subaqueous.
subaffittare, *v.t.* To sub-let.
subaffitto, *n.m.* Sub-letting; sub-let.
subaffittuario [subaffittuArio], *n.m.* Sub-tenant.
subagente, *n.m.* Sub-agent.
subalpino, *a.* Sub-alpine; Piedmontese.
subalterno, *n.m.a.* Subaltern, subordinate. (*Mil.*) **Ufficiale —,** junior officer.
subappaltare, *v.t.* To sub-contract.
subappaltatore, *n.m.* Sub-contractor.
subasta, *n.f.* Auction [cp. **asta**].
subbia [sUbbia], *n.f.* Stone-mason's chisel.
subbiare, *v.t.* To chisel.
subbietto [cp. **soggetto**].
subbio [sUbbio], *n.m.* Weaver's beam, warp-beam.
subbuglio [subbUglio], *n.m.* Hubbub, uproar, confusion, turmoil. **Mettere in —,** to set in an uproar, to set by the ears.
subcosciente, *n.m.a.* Subconscious.
subcoscienza, *n.f.* Subconsciousness.
subcutaneo [subcutAneo], *a.* (*Med.*) Subcutaneous.
subdolamente, *adv.* Treacherously, craftily.
subdolo [sUbdolo], *a.* Treacherous, deceptive; crafty, deceitful; insidious.
subentrare, *v.i.* To succeed to, to take the place of; to replace.
subiettività [-à], *n.f.* Subjectivity, subjectiveness.
subiettivo [cp. **soggettivo**].
subire, *v.t.* To suffer, to endure, to undergo, to bear. **— un operazione,** to undergo an operation; **— un mutamento,** to suffer a change.
subissare, *v.t.* To overthrow, to ruin; to send to the bottom.
subisso, *n.m.* Confusion, ruin; (*fig.*) great quantity, infinity. **Un — di applausi,** a roar of applause; **un — di gente,** a great crowd.
subitamente, *adv.* Suddenly; unexpectedly.
subitaneamente, *adv.* Suddenly, unawares; abruptly, promptly.
subitaneità [-à], *n.f.* Suddenness, unexpectedness.
subitaneo [subitAneo], *a.* Sudden, abrupt, quick, prompt.
subitezza, *n.f.* Unexpectedness, suddenness.
subito [sUbito], *a.* Sudden; quick, unexpected. || *n.m.* Instant. **In un —,** in an instant.
subito [sUbito], *adv.* At once, immediately, quickly. **Vengo —,** I'm coming at once; **— dopo,** immediately after.
sublimare, *v.t.* To raise up, to exalt, to make sublime; to sublimate.
sublimato, *n.m.* (*Chem.*) Sublimate.
sublimazione, *n.f.* Sublimation; idealization, elevation.
sublime, *a.* Sublime, elevated, lofty; eminent.
sublimemente, *adv.* Sublimely.
sublimità [-à], *n.f.* Sublimity, elevation, loftiness; grandeur.
sublunare, *a.* Sublunar, sublunary.
subnormale, *a.* Subnormal.
suboceanico [suboceAnico], *a.* Sub-oceanic.
subodorare, *v.t.* To know by intuition, to smell out, to suspect, to get wind of. **— l'imbroglio,** to smell a rat.
subordinamento, *n.m.* Subordination.
subordinare, *v.t.* To subordinate.
subordinatamente, *adv.* Subordinately.
subordinato, *n.m.a.* Subordinate.
subordinazione, *n.f.* Subordination, dependency.
subornare, *v.t.* To suborn.
subornazione, *n.f.* Subornation, bribery.
substrato, *n.m.* Substratum, basis, foundation.
suburbano, *a.* Suburban.
suburbio [subUrbio], *n.m.* Suburb [cp. **sobborgo**].
succedaneo [succedAneo], *n.m.a.* Substitute, surrogate.
succedente, *a.* Subsequent, following.
succedere [succEdere], *v.i.* To succeed (in all senses), to follow, to happen, to follow (in time), to occur, to befall. **Cosa succede?** What's happening? What's going on?

successe che, it happened that; **— al trono**, to succeed to the throne.
succedere [succEdere], *n.m.* Succession.
succedersi [succEdersi], *v.r.* To follow one another. **Il — degli avvenimenti**, the course of events.
succedimento, *n.m.* Happening.
succeditore, succeditrice, *n.m.f.* Successor, heir, heiress.
successibile [successIbile], *a.* In line of succession.
successibilità [-à], *n.f.* Right of succession.
successione, *n.f.* Succession.
successivamente, *adv.* Consecutively, successively; then, thereupon.
successivo, *a.* Next, successive, following.
successo, *n.m.* Success; issue, result, outcome; succession. **Con —**, successfully; **in — di tempo**, in process of time.
successo, *p.p.a.* Happened, succeeded [cp. **succedere**].
successore, *n.m.* Successor.
successorio [successOrio], *a.* Relating to succession.
succhiamento, *n.m.* Suction, sucking.
succhiare, succhiarsi, *v.t.r.* To suck, to suck up; to sip. **Succhiarsi le dita**, to suck one's fingers; *(colloq.)* **succhiarsi un'offesa**, to pocket an insult.
succhiata, *n.f.* Suck.
succhiatoio [succhiatOio], *n.m.* *(Zool.)* Proboscis, sucker.
succhiellamento, *n.m.* Boring, drilling.
succhiellare, *v.t.* To bore, to pierce.
succhiello, *n.m.* Gimlet, auger.
succhio [sUcchio], *n.m.* Sap, juice; *(fig.)* pith.
succhione, *n.m.* *(Bot.)* Sucker, shoot; *(fig.)* blood-sucker, parasite.
succiare [cp. **succhiare**].
succidere [succIdere], *v.t.* To cut down to the root.
succino [sUccino], *n.m.* Yellow amber.
succintamente, *adv.* Succinctly, briefly.
succintezza, *n.f.* Brevity, conciseness; *(colloq.)* shortness (of skirt).
succinto, *a.* Short, succinct, brief, concise; *(cclloq.)* with skirts tucked up; scanty (of clothes). **In —**, in short, briefly; **vestito —**, short frock, simple dress; **discorso —**, short and pithy speech.
succio [sUccio], *n.m.* Suck, sucking.
succiola [sUcciola], *n.f.* Boiled chestnut.
succlavio [succlAvio], *a.* *(Anat.)* Sub-clavian.
succo, *n.m.* Juice, sap; *(fig.)* gist, substance, essence. **— gastrico**, gastric juice; **il — della questione**, the gist of the matter.
succosamente, *adv.* Pithily, concisely, compendiously.
succosità [-à], *n.f.* Juiciness; conciseness.
succoso, *a.* Juicy; *(fig.)* pithy.
succubo [sUccubo], *n.m.* Succubus.
succulento, *a.* Succulent, tasty; exquisite; savoury; juicy.
succursale, *n.m.a.* Branch; branch office; annexe.
succutaneo [succutAneo], *a.* Sub-cutaneous.
sucido [cp. **sudicio**].
sud, *n.m.a.* South. **Al —**, southward; **America del Sud**, South America; **sud-americano**, South American; **sud-est, sud-ovest**, south-east, south-west.
sudacchiare, *v.i.* To perspire slightly.
sudamini [sudAmini], *n.m.pl.* Heat-spots.
sudante, *a.* Sweating, perspiring.
sudare, *v.i.* To sweat, to perspire; to ooze, to exude; *(fig.)* to toil. **— freddo**, to be in a blue funk; to be on tenter-hooks.
sudario [sudArio], *n.m.* Shroud, winding-sheet; *(Eccles.)* sudarium.
sudata, *n.f.* Sweat, sweating, heavy sweat. **Fare una —**, to get into a sweat.
sudatamente, *adv.* Perspiringly; with effort.
sudaticcio [sudatIccio], *a.* Perspiring somewhat.
sudato, *a.* Sweaty, in a sweat. **Sono tutto —**, I am sweating heavily.
suddecano, *n.m.* *(Eccles.)* Sub-dean.
suddetto, *a.* Above-mentioned, aforesaid.
suddiacono [suddiAcono], *n.m.* *(Eccles.)* Subdeacon.
sudditanza, *n.f.* Subjection; citizenship.
suddito, *n.m.a.* Subject, citizen.
suddividere [suddivIdere], *v.t.* To subdivide, to split, to divide.
suddivisione, *n.f.* Subdivision, division.
suddiviso, *a.* Subdivided.
sud-est, *n.m.a.* South-east; south-eastern.
sudiceria, sudicezza [sudicerIa], *n.f.* Dirtiness, filth, nastiness; obscenity; foul language; dirty trick.
sudiciamente, *adv.* Dirtily, obscenely.
sudicio [sUdicio], *a.* Dirty, filthy, nasty, unclean; obscene.
sudiciume, *n.m.* Dirt, filth, nastiness; rubbish, refuse.
sudore, *n.m.* Sweat, perspiration. **Madido di —**, all of a sweat; **il — della fronte**, the sweat of one's brow.
sudorifero [sudorIfero], *n.m.a.* *(Med.)* Sudoriferous.
sudorifico [sudorIfico], *a.* Sudorific.
sud-ovest, *n.m.a.* South-west; south-western.
suesposto, *a.* Above-stated.
sufficente, sufficiente, *a.* Sufficient, adequate, enough. **— a sè stesso**, self-supporting.
sufficientemente, *adv.* Sufficiently.
sufficienza, sufficenza, *n.f.* Sufficiency, adequacy; *(fig.)* haughtiness, pride.
suffisso, *n.m.* Suffix.
suffraganeo [suffragAneo], *n.m.a.* *(Eccles.)* Suffragan.
suffragare, *v.t.* To support, to assist; *(Eccles.)* to intercede for, to pray for (the dead).
suffragetta, *n.f.* Suffragette.
suffragio [suffrAgio], *n.m.* *(Pol.)* Suffrage, vote; *(Eccles.)* suffrage, prayer. **— universale**, universal suffrage.
suffumicare, *v.t.* To fumigate.
suffumicazione, suffumigio [suffumIgio], *n.f.m.* Fumigation, disinfection.
suffusione, *n.f.* *(Med.)* Suffusion.
suffuso, *p.p.a.* Suffused, wet. **Occhi suffusi di lagrime**, eyes suffused with tears.
suga, sugante, *n.f.* **Carta —**, blotting-paper [cp. **asciugante**].
sugare, *v.t.* *(Agric.)* To manure, to dung; to absorb [cp. **asciugare**].
suggellamento, *n.m.* Sealing, affixing seals.
suggellare, *v.t.* To seal, to seal up; to stop up, to close, to shut; to stamp. **— il fato di**, to seal the fate of; **— col sangue**, to seal with one's blood.

suggello, *n.m.* Seal, stamp. **Mettere i suggelli,** to affix the seals; **sotto — del segreto,** under the seal of secrecy [cp. **sigillo**].
suggere [sUggere], *v.t.* To suck [cp. **succhiare**].
suggerimento, *n.m.* Suggestion, hint, prompting, advice.
suggerire, *v.t.* To suggest, to prompt; to propose, to advise.
suggeritore, *n.m.* (*Theat.*) Prompter.
suggestionabile [suggestionAbile], *a.* Suggestible, impressionable, easily influenced.
suggestionabilità [-à], *n.f.* Impressionability.
suggestionare, *v.t.* To hypnotize, to mesmerize; to influence.
suggestione, *n.f.* (Hypnotic) suggestion, undue influence.
suggestivamente, *adv.* Impressively.
suggestivo, *a.* Impressive, startling. **Domanda suggestiva,** an exciting question.
suggezione [cp. **soggezione**].
sughereto, *n.m.* Plantation of cork-trees.
sughero [sUghero], *n.m.* Cork; cork-tree; (*fig.*) **Testa di —,** giddy-pate.
sugheroso, *a.* Corky, cork-like.
sugli, sui. On the [cp. **su**].
sugna, *n.f.* Lard; cart-grease; dubbin.
sugo, *n.m.* Juice, sap; gravy; (*fig.*) gist, essence, matter. **Persona senza —,** a dull fellow; **senza —,** purposeless, empty; **— di carne,** gravy; **Con che — ?** To what end? **il — del discorso,** the gist of the speech.
sugosamente, *adv.* Succulently, juicily.
sugosità [-à], *n.f.* Juiciness; conciseness.
sugoso, *a.* Juicy; (*fig.*) significant, pregnant.
suicida, *n.m.f.a.* (Person committing) suicide; suicidal.
suicidarsi, *v.r.* To commit suicide.
suicidio [suicIdio], *n.m.* (Act of) suicide.
suindicato, *a.* Above-mentioned.
suino, *a.* Porcine; of swine, of pigs. **Carne suina,** pork.
suino, *n.m.* Swine, hog.
sul, sullo, sulla, sulle. On the [cp. **su**].
sulfureo [sulfUreo], *a.* Sulphureous.
sullodato, *a.* Above-praised, above-mentioned, afore-said.
sultana, *n.f.* Sultana. **Uva —,** sultana (fruit).
sultanina, *n.f.* Sultana raisin.
sultano, *n.m.* Sultan.
summentovato, sunnominato, *a.* Above-mentioned; above-named.
sunteggiare, *v.t.* To summarize; to put in a nutshell.
sunto, *n.m.* Summary, abridgement, compendium, epitome, abstract.
suntuario [suntuArio], *a.* Sumptuary (laws).
suntuoso, *a.* Sumptuous [cp. **sontuoso**].
suo, sua, *a.pron.* His, her, hers, its; their. **Vuol fare a suo modo,** he will have his own way; **egli ha sciupato tutto il suo,** he has squandered all his fortune; **egli ha del suo,** he's a man of means; **dir la sua,** to speak one's mind; **dalla sua,** on his side; **ha avuto la sua,** he's got his deserts; **egli ne ha fatta una delle sue,** he's been up to his tricks again; **ha i suoi quarant'anni,** he has turned forty; **un suo amico,** a friend of his (hers); **egli vive con i suoi,** he lives with his people; **stare sulle sue,** to be reserved.
suocera, suocero [suOcera, suOcero], *n.f.m.* Mother-in-law; father-in-law.
suola, *n.f.* Sole (of boot or shoe).
suolo, *n.m.* Ground, soil; floor, pavement; standing-room. **Radere al —,** to raze to the ground; **cadde al —,** he tumbled down; **— fertile,** fertile soil; **su — straniero,** on foreign soil.
suonare, *v.t.i.* To ring, to sound, to play (a musical instrument); to strike. **— il piano,** to play the piano; **— il campanello,** to ring the bell; **suona la tromba,** the trumpet sounds; **questa parola suona male,** this word sounds wrong; **— a orecchio,** to play by ear; **l'ora sta per —,** the hour is about to strike.
suonatore, *n.m.* Player [cp. **sonatore**].
suono, *n.m.* Sound; music; report, fame. **— delle campane,** the chiming of the bells; **— del tamburo,** beat of the drum.
suora, *n.f.* Nun, sister.
superabile [superAbile], *a.* Surmountable, superable.
superabilità [-à], *n.f.* Possibility of being surmounted.
superamento, *n.m.* Overcoming.
superare, *v.t.* To surpass; to overcome, to surmount; to outdo, to get the better of, to conquer. **— un ostacolo,** to surmount a difficulty; **— gli esami,** to pass exams; **— in numero,** to out-number.
superbamente, *adv.* Proudly, haughtily, splendidly.
superbia [supErbia], *n.f.* Pride; haughtiness; presumption; arrogance.
superbo, *a.* Proud, haughty, arrogant, conceited; grand, superb, splendid.
superficiale, *a.* Shallow, superficial, irrelevant; hasty.
superficialità [-à], *n.f.* Superficiality, shallowness; irrelevance.
superficialmente, *adv.* Superficially, on the surface.
superficie (*pl.* **superficie, superfici**), *n.f.* Surface, superficies; area, outside. (*Geom.*) **Misura di —,** square measure.
superfluamente, *adv.* Superfluously.
superfluità [-à], *n.f.* Superfluity, superfluousness.
superfluo [supErfluo], *n.m.* Surplus, superfluity; excess.
superfluo [supErfluo], *a.* Superfluous, unnecessary, needless.
superfortezza, *n.f.* (*Aviat.*) Superfortress.
superiora, *n.f.* (*Eccles.*) Superior in a convent. **Madre —,** Mother Superior.
superiore, *n.m.a.* Superior; above, higher; high-minded, lofty. **I suoi superiori,** his betters; **padre —,** Father Superior; **uomo —,** high-minded man; **al piano —,** on the upper floor; **labbro —,** upper lip.
superiorità [-à], *n.f.* Superiority; high-mindedness.
superiormente, *adv.* Above, on the upper side; in a higher degree, in a superior manner.
superlativamente, *adv.* Superlatively.
superlativo, *n.m.a.* Superlative.
supernamente, *adv.* Divinely, celestially.
superno, *a.* Supernal, celestial, heavenly. divine.

superstite [supErstite], *n.m.a.* Survivor; surviving; outliving.
superstizione, *n.f.* Superstition.
superstiziosamente, *adv.* Superstitiously.
superstizioso, *a.* Superstitious.
superuomo, *n.m.* Superman.
supinamente, *adv.* In a supine posture; carelessly, supinely, indifferently.
supino, *n.m.* (*Gram.*) Supine.
supino, *a.* Supine, on one's back; servile, fawning. **Cadde —,** he fell on his back.
suppellettile [suppellEttile], *n.f.* Furniture, furnishings; household goods; equipment.
suppergiù, *adv.* More or less, nearly, about, approximately.
supplementare, *a.* Supplementary, additional; subsidiary.
supplemento, *n.m.* Supplement; extra; additional part; (*Rail.*) excess fare.
supplente, *n.m.f.* Substitute, deputy; (*Med., etc.*) locum tenens. **Insegnante —,** temporary teacher.
supplenza, *n.f.* Substitution; temporary post.
suppletivo, suppletorio [suppletOrio], *a.* Supplementary.
supplì [-ì], *n.m.* Rissole, croquette.
supplica [sUpplica], *n.f.* Petition, supplication; request; demand.
supplicante, *n.m.f.a.* Suppliant; petitioner.
supplicantemente, *adv.* Supplicatingly, entreatingly.
supplicare, *v.t.i.* To supplicate, to beg, to implore, to entreat; to petition.
supplicatore, supplicatrice, *n.m.f.a.* Suppliant, supplicant.
supplicazione, *n.f.* Supplication, entreaty, request.
supplice, supplichevole [sUpplice, supplichEvole], *a.* Suppliant, entreating, imploring.
supplichevolmente, *adv.* Entreatingly.
supplire, *v.t.i.* To replace, to substitute; to make good; to provide; to meet (a necessity). **— il ministro,** to take the minister's place; **— alle spese,** to meet expenditure.
suppliziare, *v.t.* To torture; to put to death.
supplizio [supplIzio], *n.m.* Torture, torment; capital punishment; (*fig.*) anguish, pain.
supponibile [supponIbile], *a.* Supposable.
supporre, *v.t.i.* To suppose, to imagine, to guess; to presume, to believe, to think.
supporto, *n.m.* Prop, stay, support.
suppositivamente, *adv.* Conjecturally.
suppositivo, *a.* Conjectural.
suppositiziamente, *adv.* Supposititiously.
suppositizio [suppositIzio], *a.* Supposititious, substitute.
supposizione, *n.f.* Supposition, hypothesis, conjecture, surmise, guess.
supposta, *n.f.* (*Med.*) Suppository.
supposto, *n.m.a.* Supposition; supposed, presumed. **— che,** supposing that; **partendo dal — che,** taking for granted that.
suppurabile [suppurAbile], *a.* (*Med.*) Suppurative.
suppuramento, *n.m.* (*Med.*) Suppuration.
suppurare, *v.i.* To suppurate, to fester.
suppurativo, *n.m.a.* (*Med.*) Suppurative.
suppurazione, *n.f.* (*Med.*) Suppuration, gathering.
supremamente, *adv.* Supremely.
supremazia [supremazIa], *n.f.* Supremacy; hegemony; preponderance.
supremo, *a.* Supreme, highest, uttermost; extreme, last. **L'ora suprema,** one's last hour, the supreme hour; **L'Essere Supremo,** God; **— addio,** last farewell; **suprema felicità,** supreme bliss.
sur [cp. **su**].
surrealismo, *n.m.* (*Art*) Surrealism.
surrenale, *a.* (*Anat.*) Suprarenal.
surrettizio [surrettIzio], *a.* Surreptitious.
surriferito, *a.* Above-mentioned.
surriscaldamento, *n.m.* Superheating.
surriscaldare, *v.t.* To superheat; to overheat.
surrogabile [surrogAbile], *a.* Replaceable.
surrogamento, *n.m.* Substitution, replacing.
surrogante, *n.m.a.* Substitute; substituting.
surrogare, *v.t.* To replace, to take the place of, to substitute.
surrogato, *n.m.* Substitute.
suscettibile [suscettIbile], *a.* Susceptible, sensitive, liable; touchy, easily offended.
suscettibilità [-à], *n.f.* Susceptibility, sensitiveness, touchiness.
suscitamento, *n.m.* Excitement; stirring up; arousing.
suscitare, *v.t.* To rouse, to provoke, to stir, to excite; to promote, to cause. **— la collera,** to rouse to anger; **— un panico,** to start a panic; **— discordie,** to stir up discord.
susina, *n.f.* Plum. **— secca,** prune.
susino, *n.m.* (*Bot.*) Plum-tree.
suso, *adv.* (*Lit.*) Up, above.
suspicione, *n.f.* (*Law*) Suspicion.
susseguente, *a.* Subsequent, following.
susseguentemente, *adv.* Subsequently.
susseguenza, *n.f.* Succession, subsequence.
susseguire, *v.i.* To follow on, to succeed (another person, etc.).
sussidiare, *v.t.* To subsidize; to contribute; to protect; to help.
sussidiario [sussidiArio], *a.* Subsidiary, auxiliary, supplementary.
sussidio [sussIdio], *n.m.* Subsidy, help, assistance; dole.
sussiego, *n.m.* Gravity, stiffness (of demeanour), haughtiness; conceit, priggishness.
sussistente, *a.* Existent, subsisting.
sussistenza, *n.f.* Subsistence, livelihood; (*Mil.*) supply service. **Sussistenze,** victuals, rations, provisions.
sussistere [sussIstere], *v.i.* To subsist, to exist.
sussultare, *v.i.* To start, to give a start, to jump; to tremble; (heart) to beat violently, to palpitate.
sussulto, *n.m.* Start, jump, tremor.
sussultorio [sussultOrio], *a.* Jerky; (*Geol.*) moving vertically, upheaving.
sussurrare, *v.t.* To whisper; to murmur, to rustle; to grumble.
sussurratore, sussurratrice, *n.m.f.* Whisperer; grumbler.
sussurrio [sussurrIo], *n.m.* Continual whispering; constant grumbling.
sussurro, *n.m.* Whisper, whispering; murmur, rustle; grumble, grumbling.
susta, *n.f.* (*obs.*) Spring; side (of spectacles).
sutura, *n.f.* (*Anat. Med.*) Suture.
suturare, *v.t.* To suture; to stitch.
suzzare, *v.t.* (*colloq.*) To suck up, to absorb.
svagamento, *n.m.* Recreation, diversion.

svagare, *v.t.* To amuse, to divert, to distract.
svagarsi, *v.r.* To amuse oneself; to while away the time, to relax.
svagataggine [svagatAggine], *n.f.* Liking for amusement.
svagatezza, *n.f.* Distraction; amusement.
svagativo, *a.* Amusing, diverting, relaxing
svagato, *a.* Inattentive, absent-minded; heedless, thoughtless.
svago, *n.m.* Diversion, amusement, recreation. **Darsi un po' di —,** to take it easy.
svagolarsi, *v.r.* To while away the time.
svaligiamento, *n.m.* Plunder, wholesale robbery; housebreaking.
svaligiare, *v.t.* To plunder, to rifle; to rob, to burgle, to ransack a house, to rob of everything; to unpack one's valise.
svaligiatore, *n.m.* Burglar, thief.
svalorizzare, *v.i.* To depreciate (in value).
svalorizzazione, *n.f.* Depreciation.
svalutare, *v.t.* To depreciate, to devalue, to undervalue, to underestimate, to belittle.
svalutazione, *n.f.* Devaluation, depreciation; under-valuation.
svampare (1), *v.i.* To burst (into flame), to escape (of steam, etc.).
svampare (2), *v.i.* To quieten down (in mind); to evaporate.
svanimento, *n.m.* Disappearance, vanishing, fading away; growing feeble.
svanire, *v.i.* To vanish, to fade away, to disappear, to evaporate; to lose its essential quality.
svanito, *p.p.a.* Vanished, disappeared. **Testa —,** empty-headed.
svano, *n.m.* Recess (in a wall), gap [cp. **vano**].
svantaggio [svantAggio], *n.m.* Disadvantage; damage, detriment, handicap, drawback. **Mi trovo in condizione di —,** I labour under a disadvantage.
svantaggiosamente, *adv.* Unfavourably.
svantaggioso, *a.* Unfavourable, disadvantageous; detrimental, prejudicial.
svanzica [svAnzica], *n.f.* (*Hist.*) Austrian coin.
svaporabile [svaporAbile], *a.* Evaporable.
svaporamento, *n.m.* Evaporation.
svaporare, *v.i.* To evaporate; to vanish.
svaporazione, *n.f.* Evaporation.
svariamento, *n.m.* Variation.
svariare, *v.t.* To change, to divert, to cause to vary.
svariarsi, *v.r.* To wander, to err; to waver; to change (colour), to be different from.
svariatamente, *adv.* Differently, in varied style.
svariatezza, *n.f.* Variety.
svariato, *p.p.a.* Various, different, variegated; assorted; several.
svario [svArio], *n.m.* Variation; difference, mistake.
svarione, *n.m.* Blunder, mistake, oversight, (*colloq.*) howler.
svasare, *v.t.* To plant out (from flower-pot).
svasatura, *n.f.* Planting out; widening, enlarging.
svecchiamento, *n.m.* Renewal, rejuvenation; modernization; (*Agric.*) pruning.
svecchiare, *v.t.* To freshen up; to rejuvenate; to renew; to modernize; to prune.
svecchiatura, *n.f.* Renewal; replacement (of worn-out parts); pruning, lopping.
svedese, *n.m.a.* Swede; Swedish.
sveglia [svEglia], *n.f.* Alarm-clock, alarum, alarm-signal; (*Mil.*) reveille. **Caricare la — per le sei,** to set the alarm for six o'clock.
svegliamento, *n.m.* Awakening.
svegliare, *v.t.* To wake up, to arouse, to stir up, to quicken, to animate. **— l'attenzione,** to arouse the attention, to call the attention; **— la memoria,** to awaken one's memory [cp. **svegliarsi**].
svegliarino, *n.m.* Alarm-clock; reminder.
svegliarsi, *v.r.* To awake, to wake up; to be awakened; to be revived. **— da un lungo sonno,** to awake from a long sleep [cp. **svegliare**].
svegliata, *n.f.* Awakening
svegliatezza, *n.f.* Promptness, quickness, readiness; wakefulness.
svegliato, sveglio [svEglio], *a.* Wide-awake, knowing; "all there"; clever, quick. **Tenere —,** to keep awake.
svelamento, *n.m.* Display, revealing, disclosure.
svelare, *v.t.* To reveal, to disclose; to unveil.
svelarsi, *v.r.* To unveil, to reveal one's feelings, to betray oneself.
svelatamente, *adv.* Openly, manifestly.
svelenarsi, svelenirsi, *v.r.* To vent one's anger; to free from poison.
svellere [svEllere], *v.t.* To extirpate, to root out, to eradicate, to pull out, to pluck out.
sveltezza, *n.f.* Quickness, speed, promptness, swiftness; slimness; liveliness (of spirit).
sveltire, *v.t.* To quicken, to smarten, to smarten up; to make slender; to render supple.
sveltirsi, *v.r.* To become quick; to get slender; to free oneself (from embarrassment).
svelto, *a.* Quick, nimble, swift, prompt; slender, elegant; lively, brisk. **— d'ingegno,** quick-witted.
svenamento, *n.m.* Severing of the veins.
svenare, svenarsi, *v.t.r.* To open the veins, to bleed, to sever one's veins.
svendere [svEndere], *v.t.* To sell off; to undersell.
svendita, *n.f.* Sale, selling-off; underselling.
svenevolaggine [svenevolAggine], *n.f.* Mawkishness, sentimentality.
svenevole [svenEvole], *a.* Mawkish, maudlin, languid, lackadaisical.
svenevolezza, *n.f.* Mawkishness, affectation; airs and graces, simpering.
svenie [svEnie], *n.f.pl.* Simpering, smirking.
svenimento, *n.m.* Swoon, faint, fainting fit.
svenire, *v.i.* To faint, to swoon. **Sentirsi —,** to feel like fainting; to feel discomposed or vexed.
sventagliare, sventagliarsi, *v.t.r.* To fan; to fan oneself; (*fig.*) to hail (bullets, etc.).
sventare, *v.t.* To frustrate, to baffle, to thwart; to ward off, to counteract; to parry, to prevent; to avoid. **— una trama,** to foil a plot.
sventataggine [sventatAggine], **sventatezza,** *n.f.* Heedlessness, recklessness, rashness, thoughtlessness.
sventato, *p.p.a.* Thwarted, frustrated; heedless, reckless, rash, thoughtless.

sventola [svEntola], *n.f.* Fan (for blowing up charcoal); bellows; (*slang*) glancing blow.
sventolamento, *n.m.* Flapping, fluttering, waving (of flags, etc.).
sventolare, *v.t.i.* To flutter, to flap, to fan; to unfurl; to agitate, to shake; to wave (a flag, etc.).
sventolarsi, *v.r.* To fan oneself.
sventolio [sventolIo], *n.m.* Flapping, constant fluttering. **— di bandiere,** waving of flags.
sventramento, *n.m.* Disembowelling; demolition (of houses), slum-clearance.
sventrare, *v.t.* To disembowel, to gut; to empty; to demolish (slums, etc.).
sventura, *n.f.* Misfortune; accident, mishap; havoc; sorrow, grief; bad luck. **Per colmo di —,** as the last straw; **provato dalla —,** tried by misfortune.
sventuratamente, *adv.* Unluckily.
sventurato, *n.m.a.* Unlucky person; unfortunate.
svenuto, *a.* Fainted, swooned, unconscious, in a faint.
sverginamento, *n.m.* Rape, deflowering.
sverginare, *v.t.* To rape, to ravish.
svergognamento, *n.m.* Shame, ignominy, disgrace.
svergognare, *v.t.* To disgrace, to shame, to humiliate.
svergognatamente, *adv.* Shamelessly.
svergognatezza, *n.f.* Shamelessness.
svergognato, *a.* Shameless; disgraceful; impudent.
svernamento, *n.m.* Wintering.
svernare, *v.i.* To winter, to pass the winter; (*Zool.*) to hibernate.
sverza, *n.f.* Stick, splinter.
sverzino, *n.m.* Whip; whip-cord.
svesciare, *v.t.* To blurt out, to blab.
svescione, *n.m.* Tell-tale.
svestire, svestirsi, *v.t.r.* To undress; to undress oneself.
svettamento, *n.m.* Lopping, pruning.
svettare, *v.t.* (*Agric.*) To pollard, to lop.
svettatura, *n.f.* Pollarding, lopping.
svevo, *n.m.a.* Swabian. **Età sveva,** age of the Hohenstaufen emperors.
Svezia, *n.f.* (*Geog.*) Sweden.
svezzamento, *n.m.* Weaning.
svezzare, *v.t.* To wean.
sviamento, *n.m.* Deviation, going astray; following the wrong scent; error. **— di una merce,** miscarriage of goods.
sviare, *v.t.i.* To mislead, to lead astray; (*Rail.*) to switch.
sviarsi, *v.r.* To go astray, to lose one's way; to fall into error.
sviato, *a.* Misguided, misled; gone astray; derailed.
svicolare, *v.i.* To turn aside (to avoid meeting someone), to slink away.
svignare, svignarsela, *v.i.r.* To slip off, to sneak away, to make oneself scarce, to decamp.
svigorimento, *n.m.* Weakening, loss of vigour, enfeeblement.
svigorire, svigorirsi, *v.t.r.* To weaken, to enfeeble; to become feeble.
svilimento, *n.m.* Depreciation.
svilire, *v.i.* To depreciate.
svillaneggiamento, *n.m.* Insult, abuse, affront.
svillaneggiare, *v.t.* To insult, to affront, to offend, to abuse, to revile.
sviluppabile [sviluppAbile], *a.* Capable of development.
sviluppamento, *n.m.* Development.
sviluppare, *v.t.* To develop; to unfold, to display, to extend. **— una fotografia,** to develop a negative; **— un argomento,** to develop an argument.
svilupparsi, *v.r.* To grow, to grow up; to increase.
sviluppo, *n.m.* Development, growth, increase, progress; expansion, opening out. **Età dello —,** puberty.
svinare, *v.t.* To draw wine (from the vat).
svinatura, *n.f.* Tunning of wine.
svincolamento, *n.m.* Disengagement, release; clearance (at the Customs).
svincolare, *v.t.* To release, to disengage; to clear (at the Customs); to redeem (from pawn); to take delivery of; to collect one's luggage.
svincolarsi, *v.r.* To free oneself, to get free from; to escape, to get loose. **— da,** to wriggle away from, to get out of (doing something).
svincolo [svIncolo], *n.m.* Release; clearance (at Customs); liberation.
svisamento, *n.m.* Disfigurement; alteration, falsification; misrepresentation.
svisare, *v.t.* To misrepresent, to falsify, to distort (facts, etc.).
svisceramento, *n.m.* (*fig.*) Careful examination; research.
sviscerare, *v.t.* To eviscerate, to gut; (*fig.*) to exhaust, to get to the bottom of. **— un argomento,** to go deeply into a subject.
svisceratamente, *adv.* Fondly, ardently, passionately, with deep affection.
svisceratezza, *n.f.* Fondness, attachment; deep affection, ardent love.
sviscerato, *a.* Heartfelt, passionate, affectionate, loving; devoted, sincere. **Amore —,** passionate love; **amico —,** bosom friend.
svista, *n.f.* Oversight, mistake, slip. **Per —,** through an oversight.
svitare, *v.t.* To unscrew.
svitatura, *n.f.* Unscrewing.
sviticchiare, *v.t.* To disentangle, to untwine.
Svizzera [svIzzera], *n.f.* (*Geog.*) Switzerland.
svizzero [svIzzero], *n.m.a.* Swiss. **Guardia svizzera,** the Swiss Guard (Papal).
svociarsi, *v.r.* To shout oneself hoarse.
svogliamento, *n.m.* Disinclination.
svogliare, *v.t.* To make disinclined, to deter; to disgust.
svogliarsi, *v.r.* To be disinclined for; to take a dislike to.
svogliataggine, svogliatezza [svogliatAggine], *n.f.* Unwillingness, indifference, listlessness; carelessness, negligence, laziness.
svogliatamente, *adv.* Unwillingly.
svogliato, *a.* Unwilling, slack; languid, listless, lax.
svogliatone, *n.f.* Lazybones, slacker.
svolare, *v.i.* (*obs.*) To fly, to flutter.
svolazzamento, *n.m.* Fluttering, flying hither and thither.

svolazzare, *v.i.* To fly about, to flap, to flutter, to hover.
svolazzio [svolazzIo], *n.m.* Continual fluttering, hovering.
svolazzo, *n.m.* Flutter; flourish (in handwriting); ornamentation.
svolgere [svOlgere], *v.t.* To unroll, to unfold, to spread out, to display; to set forth; to explain. **— un soggetto,** to develop a subject.
svolgersi [svOlgersi], *v.r.* To develop; to occur, to happen; to unroll. **Mentre questi fatti si svolgevano,** while these things were happening.
svolgimento, *n.m.* Unfolding, unrolling; development; treatment; working out (of a problem, etc.).
svolta, *n.f.* Bend, turn, curve; winding; direction. **Una — stretta,** a sharp turn; **una — della fortuna,** a turn of fortune.
svoltamento, *n.m.* Bend, turning.
svoltare, *v.t.i.* To go round, to turn; to unroll. **— a destra,** to turn to the right.
svoltata, *n.f.* Bend, curve, turn, turning.
svolto, *n.m.* Turn.
svolto, *p.p.a.* Unrolled; (*fig.*) developed, evolved; treated.
svoltolamento, *n.m.* Rolling about, wallowing.
svoltolare, *v.t.* To roll.
svoltolarsi, *v.r.* To roll in, to wallow.
svotare, svuotare, *v.t.i.* To empty; to pour out, to discharge.
svotarsi, svuotarsi, *v.r.* To empty; (*Med.*) to go to stool.
svuotamento, *n.m.* Emptying; discharging.

T

T, t, *n.f.* Eighteenth letter of the Italian alphabet. **Fatto a T,** T-shaped.
tabaccaia, tabaccaio [tabaccAia, -o], *n.f.m.* Tobacconist.
tabaccare, *v.i.* To take snuff, to snuff.
tabacchiera, *n.f.* Snuff-box.
tabacco, *n.m.* Tobacco; snuff. **— da naso,** snuff; **una presa di —,** a pinch of snuff; **fiutar —,** to take snuff; **— da fumo,** pipe-tobacco.
tabaccone, *n.m.* Heavy snuff-taker.
tabaccoso, *a.* Snuffy; smelling of tobacco.
tabarro, *n.m.* Cloak, mantle.
tabe, *n.f.* (*Med.*) Tabes.
tabella, *n.f.* Table, list, schedule; prospectus; tablet. **— degli interessi,** interest table; **in forma di —,** in tabular form.
tabellare, *a.* Tabular.
tabellone, *n.m.* Poster (outside churches, etc.).
tabernacolo [tabernAcolo], *n.m.* Tabernacle; shrine; ciborium; niche, canopy.
tabetico [tabEtico], *n.m.a.* (*Med.*) Tabetic.
tabì [-ì], *n.m.* Tabby (material).
tablino, *n.m.* (*Arch.*) Tablinum.
tabù [-ù], *n.m.* Taboo.
tacca, *n.f.* Notch, nick, cut, indentation; (*fig.*) defect; quality, state. **Di mezza —,** middling quality.
taccagneria [taccagnerIa], *n.f.* Stinginess, niggardliness; greediness, avarice.
taccagno, *a.* Miserly, niggardly, avaricious, stingy, mean; sordid.
taccheggiatore, taccheggiatrice, *n.m.f.* Shop-lifter.
taccherella, *n.f.* Blemish, slight defect.
tacchino, tacchina, *n.m.f.* (*Zool.*) Turkey (cock or hen). **Fare il —,** to strut about, to boast.
taccia [tAccia], *n.f.* Blemish, fault; imputation, charge, reproach.
tacciabile [tacciAbile], *a.* Liable to, chargeable with.
tacciare, *v.t.* To impute to, to accuse of, to charge with. **— uno di disonestà,** to charge someone with dishonesty.
tacco, *n.m.* Heel (of shoe, etc.). **Tacchi alti,** high heels; **tacchi di gomma,** rubber heels; (*colloq.*) **alzare il —,** to take to one's heels.
taccola [tAccola], *n.f.* Blemish, defect; trifle, bagatelle; (*fig.*) chatterbox; (*Zool.*) jackdaw; (*Bot.*) kind of pea.
taccolare, *v.i.* To chatter, to talk incessantly.
taccolata, *n.f.* Gossip; nonsense.
taccolone, *n.m.* (*colloq.*) Chatterbox.
tacconare, *v.t.* To patch, to piece; to sew on a double sole.
taccone, *n.m.* (*colloq.*) Patch, tag; large heel.
taccuino, *n.m.* Memorandum-book, note-book; agenda; almanac.
tacere, *v.t.i.* To be silent, to hold one's tongue, to say nothing; to pass over in silence, to suppress, to keep silent about; to conceal. **Far —,** to silence; to hush; **Taci!** Hold your tongue! Shut up! **tutto tace,** all is still; **chi tace acconsente,** silence gives consent; **mettere in—,** to hush up.
tacheometro [tacheOmetro], *n.m.* Tachometer.
tachimetro [tachImetro], *n.m.* Speedometer.
tacitamente, *adv.* In silence, silently; tacitly.
tacitare, *v.t.* To silence, to appease, to satisfy (a creditor).
tacitarsi, *v.r.* To come to terms with.
tacito [tAcito], *a.* Silent; tacit, implied, understood. **Socio —,** sleeping partner.
Tacito [tAcito], *n.m.* Tacitus.
taciturnamente, *adv.* Taciturnly.
taciturnità [-à], *n.f.* Taciturnity.
taciturno, *a.* Taciturn, reserved, silent; sulky.
taciuto, *p.p.a.* Passed over in silence; kept silent.
tafanario [tafanArio], *n.m.* (*colloq.*) Backside, bottom.
tafano, *n.m.* (*Zool.*) Gadfly, horse-fly; (*fig.*) bore, importunate fellow.
tafferia [tafferIa], *n.f.* Shallow wooden bowl.
tafferuglio [tafferUglio], *n.m.* Scrimmage, scuffle, tussle; brawl, wrangle, altercation.
taffetà [-à], *n.m.* Taffeta; (*Med.*) court-plaster, sticking-plaster.
taffete! [tAffete], *inter.* Bang! Crash! (Exclamation on hearing a loud noise).
taffiare, *v.i.* (*colloq.*) To guzzle.
taglia [tAglia], *n.f.* Size, stature, height; waist, shape, figure; ransom, reward, price; tax, impost poll-tax; (*Agric.*) layer (of an olive tree). **Porre una — sulla testa di,** to set a price on the head of; **una ragazza di — sottile,** a slender-waisted girl; **un uomo di mezza —,** a middle-sized man.
tagliabile [tagliAbile], *a.* Able to be cut.
tagliaborse, *n.m.* Pick-pocket, cut-purse.

tagliaboschi, *n.m.* Wood-cutter.
tagliacarte, *n.m.* Paper-knife.
tagliaferro, *n.m.* Knife of the finest steel.
tagliafili, *n.m.* Wire-cutter.
taglialegna, *n.m.* Woodman, wood-cutter.
tagliamare, *n.m.* (*Naut.*) Cut-water.
tagliamento, *n.m.* Cutting.
tagliando, *n.m.* Coupon, ticket, counterfoil.
tagliapesce, *n.m.* Fish-slice.
tagliapietre, *n.m.* Stone-cutter, stone-mason.
tagliare, *v.t.* To cut; to cut down, to cut out, to cut off; to carve, to hew, to fell, to trim, to prune; to detach, to separate, to divide. **— la coda,** to dock the tail; **— in due,** to cut in two; **— corto,** to cut short; **— i viveri,** to cut off supplies; **— la strada,** to cross someone's path; **— una pianta,** to fell a tree; **— le curve,** to cut bends (in the road); **— a fette,** to slice; **— i panni addosso,** to slander; **— la testa al toro,** to take the bull by the horns; **— un vino,** to mix wine; (*colloq.*) **— la corda,** to clear out, to run away, to slip the painter.
tagliarsi, *v.r.* To cut oneself; to have (one's hair) cut. **Mi sono tagliato il dito,** I've cut my finger.
tagliata, *n.f.* Cutting, cut; mowing (of hay, etc.).
tagliatelle, *n.f.pl.* Ribbon macaroni.
tagliato, *p.p.a.* Cut, shaped, cut out; inclined. **Esser — per,** to be cut out for.
tagliatore, tagliatrice, *n.m.f.* Cutter, tailor.
tagliatura, *n.f.* Cutting, cut.
taglieggiare, *v.t.* To tax, to burden with taxes; to extort; to assess; to set a price on someone's head.
taglieggiato, *p.p.a.* Ransomed.
tagliente, *a.* Cutting (in all senses); sharp, keen bitter (cold); biting (in words), harsh. **Freddo —,** piercing cold; **parole taglienti,** sharp words; **profilo —,** sharp-cut features; **— come un rasoio,** as sharp as a razor; **strumento —,** edged tool.
taglientemente, *adv.* Keenly, sharply; harshly.
tagliere, *n.m.* Trencher, platter.
taglierini, *n.m.pl.* Ribbon-macaroni [cp. **tagliatelli**].
taglio [tAglio], *n.m.* Cut, cutting; length (of material); slash, slit; edge; (*fig.*) style, kind. **— di capelli,** hair-cut; **— d'abito,** cut of cloth; length; **biglietto di grosso —,** note of high denomination; (*colloq.*) **bisogna darcene un —,** it's time to stop it; **arma da —,** keen-edged weapon; **ferita di —,** a slash; (*Agric.*) **— del fieno,** hay-harvest; **per —,** edgewise; **— dorato,** gilt-edges (of a book).
tagliola, tagliuola, *n.f.* Trap, snare.
tagliolo, tagliuolo, *n.m.* Chisel; scrap of meat.
taglione, *n.m.* Talion; retaliation; eye for an eye.
tagliuzzamento, *n.m.* Hashing, mincing.
tagliuzzare, *v.t.* To hash, to mince, to cut up small.
Tago, *n.m.* (*Geog.*) Tagus.
tait [tAit], *n.m.* Morning-coat.
talamo [tAlamo], *n.m.* (*Lit.*) Nuptial bed; (*Anat. Bot.*) thalamus.
talare, *a.* Reaching the ankles. **Abito —,** cassock, soutane.
talassocrazia [talassocrazIa], *n.f.* Naval supremacy.
talchè, *conj.* So that; such that.
talco, *n.m.* (*Min.*) Talc.
tale, *a.* Such, so, like. **Tale quale,** exactly alike; **un tale,** a certain man, so-and-so; **La Signora Tale dei Tali,** Mrs. So-and-so; **a tal punto,** to such a degree; **ridursi a — che,** to be in such a state that; **in — occasione,** on such an occasion.
taleggio [talEggio], *n.m.* Variety of Lombard cheese.
talentare, *v.i.* To please, to be pleasing, to appeal; to be to one's taste. **Questo non mi talenta,** this doesn't appeal to me.
talento (1), *n.m.* Talent, genius; skill, ability; pleasure, will, liking. **Voglio fare a mio —,** I want to have my own way, I want to please myself; **mal —,** ill-will, grudge, spite.
talento (2), *n.m.* (*Hist.*) Talent.
Talete, *n.m.* (*Hist.*) Thales.
Talia [talIa], *n.f.* (*Myth.*) Thalia.
talismano, *n.m.* Talisman, charm, amulet.
tallero [tAllero], *n.m.* Thaler (coin).
tallio [tAllio], *n.m.* (*Min.*) Thallium.
tallire, *v.i.* To run to seed, to seed.
tallo, *n.m.* (*Bot.*) Thallus; sprout.
talloncino, *n.m.* Coupon, ticket, slip.
tallone, *n.m.* Heel; voucher, stub (of cheque, etc.). **— d'Achille,** the heel of Achilles, Achilles tendon.
talmente, *adv.* To such a degree, so much, to such an extent, in such a way.
talora, *adv.* Sometimes, at times, now and then.
talpa, *n.f.* (*Zool.*) Mole; (*fig.*) blockhead. **Sordo come una —,** deaf as a door-post.
taluno, *pron.* Somebody, someone, some people.
talvolta, *adv.* Sometimes.
tamarice, tamerice, *n.f.m.* (*Bot.*) Tamarisk.
tamarindo, *n.m.* (*Bot.*) Tamarind.
tamarisco, *n.m.* (*Bot.*) Tamarisk.
tambellone, *n.m.* Large brick.
tamburaio [tamburAio], *n.m.* Drum-maker.
tamburare, tambureggiare, tamburellare, *v.i.* To beat a drum, to drum, to beat, to tap.
tamburello, *n.m.* Tambourine, timbrel; small drum.
tamburinare, tamburinarsi, *v.i.r.* To drum (with the fingers), to thrum.
tamburino, *n.m.* Drummer; drummer-boy; small drum; tambourine.
tamburlano, *n.m.* Drum for drying and airing clothes; coffee-roaster.
tamburo, *n.m.* Drum; drummer; barrel (of clock); cylinder (of revolver); revolving drum. **A tambur battente,** at full speed, at once; **suonare il —,** to beat the drum; **capo—,** drum-major.
tamia [tamIa], *n.f.* (*Zool.*) Small ground squirrel.
Tamigi, *n.m.* (*Geog.*) Thames.
tamponamento, *n.m.* Plugging, stopping; striking against; (*Rail.*) collision.
tamponare, *v.t.* To plug to stop, to stanch, (*Med.*) to tampon; (*Rail.*) to collide; to telescope.
tampone, *n.m.* Plug, stopper; bung; pad, wad, (*Med.*) tampon.

tam-tam, *n.m.* (*Mus.*) Tom-tom, gong.
tana, *n.f.* Den, hole, lair; cave, cavern; (*Zool.*) species of squirrel.
tanaglie [tanAglie], *n.f.pl.* Pincers, nippers.
tanagliare, *v.t.* To pinch, to nip.
tanagliata, *n.f.* Nip, pinch.
Tancredi, *n.m.* Tancred.
tanè [-è], *n.m.a.* Tan (colour); tawny.
tanfata, *n.f.* Smell, odour.
tanfo, *n.m.* Stench, stink; musty smell, stuffiness; bad breath. **Sapere di —,** to have a musty smell or taste.
tangente, *n.f.a.* (*Geom.*) Tangent; share; tangential.
tangenza, *n.f.* Tangency.
tangere [tAngere], *v.t.* To touch; to concern. **La tua insolenza non mi tange,** your impertinence does not affect me.
Tangeri [tAngeri], *n.f.* (*Geog.*) Tangier.
tanghero [tAnghero], *n.m.* Blockhead, dolt, lout, boor; cad.
tangibile [tangIbile], *a.* Tangible; clear, manifest.
tangibilità [-à], *n.f.* Tangibility.
tango, *n.m.* Tango (dance).
tannico [tAnnico], *a.* (*Chem.*) Tannic.
tannino, *n.m.* Tannin.
tantafera, tantaferata, *n.f.* Long-winded story, yarn, rigmarole.
Tantalo [tAntalo], *n.m.* (*Myth.*) Tantalus; (*Zool.*) species of ibis; (*Min.*) tantalum. **Il supplizio di —,** the torments of Tantalus.
tantino, *adv.* Small bit, trifle; soupçon, suspicion. **È un — sordo,** he's just a little deaf.
tanto, *n.m.* Amount, certain sum. **Gli dà un — all'anno,** he gives him so much a year; **due tanti,** twice as much.
tanto, *adv.a.* So, much; so much, to such a degree, to such an extent; just; so long, so many, so great. **— che,** so that, **— più,** the more; **ogni —,** every now and then; **di — in —,** from time to time; **una volta —,** for this once only; **tre volte —,** three times as much; **— meglio,** all the better; **— quanto,** as much as; **— quanto basta,** just enough; **tanti quanti,** as many as; **per —,** notwithstanding; **tant'è,** at any rate; **— vale,** one may as well; **più che —,** not much, little; **tanti grandi tanti piccoli,** great and small; **io non sono da —,** I'm not up to it; **se — mi dà —,** at such a rate, if things go on like this; **— che vivrò,** so long as I live.
tantolino, *n.m.* Little bit, tiny scrap.
tantosto, *adv.* Immediately, at once, as soon as.
tapinamente, *adv.* Wretchedly, meanly.
tapinare, *v.i.* To live wretchedly, to lead a wretched life; to go begging.
tapino, *n.m.* Poor devil, poor wretch; poor little thing.
tapino, *a.* Miserable, wretched, poor.
tapioca, *n.f.* Tapioca.
tapiro, *n.m.* (*Zool.*) Tapir.
tappa, *n.f.* Halting-place, pause, stage, stop; (*Sport*) lap. **Fare il viaggio in due tappe,** to do the journey in two stages; **a tappe,** by stages.
tappabuchi, *n.m.* Stop-gap.
tappare, *v.t.* To stop up, to cork, to bung, to plug, to cork; to muffle up.
tapparella, *n.f.* Rolling shutter.
tapparsi, *v.r.* To shut oneself up; to muffle oneself up. **— in casa,** to shut oneself in, to keep to the house.
tappetare, *v.t.* To carpet.
tappetino, *n.m.* Small carpet, rug.
tappeto, *n.m.* Carpet, rug, hearth-rug, mat; table-cloth, cover; **— verde,** gaming-table; lawn; **— del letto,** bedside mat; **mettere sul —,** to put forward, to have a show-down; **essere sul —,** to be on the tapis, to be discussed.
tappezzare, *v.t.* To paper (a wall); to hang, to deck; to cover; to line; to carpet (with flowers); to upholster.
tappezzeria [tappezzerIa], *n.f.* Tapestry, hangings; wall-paper; upholstery. (*colloq.*) **Far —,** to be a wallflower (at a dance).
tappezziere, *n.m.* Upholsterer; paper-hanger, decorator.
tappo, *n.m.* Cork; plug, stopper, bung. (*Mech.*) **— di assale,** axle-cap; (*Motor, Cycle*) **— di valvola,** valve-cap of tyre.
tara, *n.f.* Tare, allowance; (*fig.*) blemish, shortcoming; weakness; fault. **Bisogna fare la — di quel che dice,** one must take what he says with a pinch of salt.
tarabuso, *n.m.* (*Zool.*) Bittern.
tarallo, *n.m.* Kind of ring-shaped biscuit.
tarantella, *n.f.* Tarantella (Neapolitan dance).
tarantola [tarAntola], *n.f.* (*Zool.*) Tarantula. **Aver la —,** to be restless.
tarantolismo, *n.m.* (*Med.*) Tarantism.
tarare, *v.t.* (*Comm.*) To tare, to allow for tare.
tarato, *a.* Tainted, rotten, corrupted; weak, sickly; defective, wanting.
tarchia [tArchia], *n.f.* (*Naut.*) Sprit-sail.
tarchiato, *a.* Sturdy, strongly-built, thick-set.
tardamente, *adv.* Slowly, tardily; late.
tardamento, *n.m.* Delay, slowness.
tardanza, *n.f.* Lateness, slowness; delay.
tardare, *v.t.i.* To delay, to retard; to linger, to defer, to be late; to loiter; to long for. **Mi tarda di rivederti,** I long to see you; **quanto tarda a ritornare!** how long he is returning!
tardezza, *n.f.* Lateness; slowness.
tardi, *adv.* Late; slowly. **È —,** it's late; **sul —,** late in the evening; **far —,** to sit up late; to be late; **al più —,** at the latest; **più —,** later on; **o presto o —,** sooner or later; **meglio — che mai,** better late than never.
tardigrado [tardIgrado], *n.m.a.* (*Zool.*) Tardigrade.
tardivamente, *adv.* Tardily.
tardivo, *a.* Late; behindhand, tardy, sluggish; backward.
tardo, *a.* Behindhand, sluggish, tardy, slow; late, distant (in time). **I tardi nipoti,** posterity; **ora tarda,** late hour; **ingegno —,** slow intellect.
targa, *n.f.* Name-plate; (*Motor.*) number-plate; tablet; shield; (*Hist.*) buckler, targe; (*colloq.*) lump (of meat, etc.).
targare, *v.t.* (*Motor.*) to fix a number-plate.
targhetta, *n.f.* Small plate, name-plate.
tarì, *n.m.* (*Hist.*) Medieval Sicilian coin.
tariffa, *n.f.* Tariff, rate, rates; price-list, bill of fare; fare scale (of charges). **Tariffe doganali,** custom tariffs; **tariffe ferroviarie,** railway rates.

tariffare, *v.t.* To fix a tariff, to rate.
tarlare, tarlarsi, *v.t.i.r.* To be worm-eaten, to eat away (of worms).
tarlato, *a.* Worm-eaten.
tarlatura, *n.f.* Worm-hole; dust from these.
tarlo, *n.m.* (*Zool.*) Wood-worm, boring-worm; rot, dry rot; moth (in clothes); (*fig.*) gnawing (of conscience); notion.
tarma, *n.f.* (*Zool.*) Clothes-moth, moth.
tarmare, tarmarsi, *v.i.r.* To be moth-eaten.
taroccare, *v.i.* To grumble; to play at tarot; to play a trump card.
tarocchi, *n.m.pl.* (*Cards*) Italian game of tarot; trump cards, trumps.
taroccone, *n.m.* Grumbler.
tarpare, *v.t.* To clip the wings (in all senses); to pare away, to curtail.
tarsia [tarsIa], *n.f.* Inlaid woodwork; marquetry.
tarsiare, *v.t.* To inlay.
tarso, *n.m.* (*Anat.*) Tarsus, instep.
tartagliamento, *n.m.* Stuttering, stammering.
tartagliare, *v.t.i.* To stammer, to stutter.
tartagliata, *n.f.* Stammering.
tartaglione, *n.m.* Stutterer, stammerer.
tartana, *n.f.* (*Naut.*) Tartan (single-masted lateen-sailed craft).
tartareo [tartAreo], *a.* Tartarean, infernal.
tartarico [tartArico], *a.* Tartaric.
tartarizzare, *v.t.* (*Chem.*) To tartarize.
Tartaro [tArtaro] (1), *n.m.* (*Myth.*) Tartarus.
tartaro [tArtaro] (2), *n.m.a.* (*Geog.*) Tartar, Tatar.
tartaro [tArtaro] (3), *n.m.* (*Chem.*) Tartar; tartar (of teeth). **Cremore di —,** cream of tartar.
tartaruga, *n.f.* (*Zool.*) Tortoise; turtle (marine reptile); tortoise-shell; (*fig.*) sluggard, slow-coach. **Lavoro in —,** tortoise-shell work.
tartassamento, *n.m.* Vexation, torment.
tartassare, *v.t.* To harass, to vex, to torment; to bully.
tartina, *n.f.* Slice of bread spread with butter, jam, paste, etc.
tartufo, *n.m.* (*Bot. Cooking*) Truffle; (*fig.*) hypocrite.
tasca, *n.f.* Pocket. **Metter le mani in —,** to put one's hands in one's pockets; **— della giacca,** breast-pocket; **— ladra,** inner pocket; (*colloq.*) **romper le tasche,** to annoy, to importune; **averne piene le tasche,** to be fed up; **avere uno in —,** to dislike someone.
tascabile [tascAbile], *a.* Portable, pocket. **Dizionario —,** pocket dictionary.
tascapane, *n.m.* Haversack, pouch.
tascata, *n.f.* Pocketful.
taschino, *n.m.* Waistcoat pocket, small pocket.
taso, *n.m.* Wine sediment; tartar.
tassa, *n.f.* Tax; rate; fee; tribute; impost, duty. **— sul reddito,** income-tax; **— di famiglia,** poor-rate; **— di soggiorno,** visitor's tax; **— d'esame,** examination fee; **— di iscrizione,** registration fee; **— di bollo,** stamp-duty; **soggetto a —,** liable to taxation; **— di successione,** death duties.
tassabile [tassAbile], *a.* Taxable.
tassametro [tassAmetro], *n.m.* Taximeter.
tassare, *v.t.* To tax, to assess, to rate; to charge (with duty).
tassativamente, *adv.* Explicitly.
tassativo, *a.* Explicit, unconditional; compulsory.
tassatore, *n.m.* Tax assessor.
tassazione, *n.f.* Taxation, tax.
tassellare, *v.t.* To plug; to fix dowels.
tassellatura, *n.f.* Plugging.
tassello, *n.m.* Plug; dowel; peg.
tassì, *n.m.* Taxi. **Andare in —,** to taxi; to take a taxi.
tassidermia [tassidermIa], *n.f.* Taxidermy.
tassista (*pl.* **tassisti**), *n.m.* Taxi-driver, taximan.
tasso (1), *n.m.* (*Zool.*) Badger; (*Bot.*) yew-tree, yew; (*Mech.*) anvil.
tasso (2), *n.m.* (*Comm.*) Rate. **— di sconto,** discount rate.
tassobarbasso, *n.m.* (*Bot.*) Mullein, Aaron's beard.
tastare, *v.t.* To touch, to feel carefully, to probe, to sound, to finger; (*Med.*) to tent. **— il terreno,** to feel one's way, to explore the situation; **— il polso,** to feel the pulse.
tastata, *n.f.* Feeling, touching; stroking; fingering.
tasteggiare, *v.t.* To touch the keys of a piano, to touch lightly.
tastiera, *n.f.* (*Mus.*) Keyboard.
tasto, *n.m.* (*Mus.*) Key; touch; (telegraph) tapper. **Toccare un brutto —,** to strike a discordant note, to touch on a delicate matter; **non toccate quel —,** don't keep on harping on that string.
tastone, tastoni, *adv.* Gropingly. **Andare a tastoni,** to grope one's way.
tata, *n.f.* Nurse, nanny.
tato, *n.m.* Daddy.
tattica [tAttica], *n.f.* Tactics; cunning, craft.
tatticamente, *adv.* Tactically.
tattico [tAttico], *n.m.a.* Tactician; tactical.
tatticone, *n.m.* Sly fellow.
tattile [tAttile], *a.* Tactile.
tattilità [-à], *n.f.* Tactility.
tatto, *n.m.* Touch; feeling; tact. **Persona senza —,** tactless person; **conoscere al —,** to know by feel; **andare a —,** to feel one's way; **avere molto —,** to be very tactful.
tatuaggio [tatuAggio], *n.m.* Tattooing, tattoo.
tatuare, tatuarsi, *v.t.r.* To tattoo.
taumaturgia [taumaturgIa], *n.f.* Thaumaturgy; conjuring.
taumaturgo, *n.m.* Conjuror, magician, wonder-worker.
taurino, *a.* Bovine, taurine. **Collo —,** bull-necked.
tauromachia [tauromachIa], *n.f.* Bull-fight; art of bull-fighting.
tautologia [tautologIa], *n.f.* Tautology.
tautologico [tautolOgico], *a.* Tautological.
taverna, *n.f.* Tavern, inn; public-house.
taverniere, *n.m.* Publican, inn-keeper, tavern-keeper.
tavola [tAvola], *n.f.* Table; board, plank, slab; plaque; list, index; plate (illustration). **Amar la —,** to like good living; **mettersi a —,** to sit at table; **biancheria da —,** table-linen; **— da giuoco,** gaming-table; **— pitagorica,** multiplication table; (*fig.*) **mettere le carte in —,** to put one's cards on the table; **— di salvezza,** safety-plank; **— nera,** blackboard; **— rotonda,** round table.

tavolaccio [tavolAccio], *n.m.* Plank bed.
tavolata, *n.f.* Table spread for dinner; dinner party. **Che bella — !** What a spread!
tavolato, *n.m.* Planking; wooden floor; wainscotting; hoarding.
tavoletta, *n.f.* Tablet; small table. **— di cioccolata,** slab of chocolate.
tavoliere, *n.m.* Chess or draught board, card-table; (*Geog.*) plateau, table-land.
tavolino, *n.m.* Little table; writing-table, desk. **— da notte,** bedside table; **stare a —,** to be busy working; **uomo di —,** clerical worker; scholar.
tavolo [tAvolo], *n.m.* Table. **— da giuoco,** gaming-table; **— da studio,** writing-table; **— da toletta,** dressing-table.
tavolozza, *n.f.* (*Art*) Palette.
tazza, *n.f.* Cup, mug, basin. **Una — di tè,** a cup of tea; **una — da tè,** a teacup; **— di fontana,** basin of a fountain.
te, *pron.* Thee; you. **Te lo diedi,** I gave it to you; **conosci te stesso,** know thyself.
tè [-è], *n.m.* Tea. **Servizio da tè,** tea-set; **invitare al tè,** to ask to tea; **prendere il —,** to have tea; **l'ora del —,** tea time.
tea, *a.* Tea. **Rosa tea,** tea rose.
teatino, *a.* Of Chieti; (*Eccles.*) religious order.
teatrale, *a.* Theatrical; affected, showy.
teatralità [-à], *n.f.* Theatricality.
teatralmente, *adv.* Theatrically.
teatro, *n.m.* Theatre; playhouse, stage; drama; scene. **Andare a —,** to go to the theatre; **questo luogo fu — di un delitto,** this place was the scene of a crime; **il — italiano,** the Italian theatre; (*colloq.*) **è un —,** it's a perfect farce.
Tebaide [tebAide], *n.f.* (*Geog.*) Thebaid; (*fig.*) hermitage, solitude.
tebano, *a.* Theban.
Tebe, *n.f.* (*Geog.*) Thebes.
teca, *n.f.* Case, sheath.
tecnica [tEnica], *n.f.* Technics; technique.
tecnicamente, *adv.* Technically.
tecnicismo, *n.m.* Technicality.
tecnico [tEcnico], *n.m.a.* Technician; technical. **Termini tecnici,** technical terms; **scuola tecnica,** technical school.
tecnologia [technologIa], *n.f.* Technology.
tecnologico [tecnolOgico], *a.* Technological.
teco, *pron.* With thee, with you.
teda, *n.f.* (*Bot.*) Species of resinous tree; bridal torch; nuptials.
tedescamente, *adv.* In a German manner.
tedescheggiare, *v.t.* To ape the Germans, to side with the Germans.
tedescheria [tedescherIa], *n.f.* German ways; Germans in a horde.
tedeschizzare, *v.t.* To Germanize.
tedesco, *n.m.a.* German.
tediare, *v.t.* To weary, to bore; to annoy, to vex.
tedio [tEdio], *n.m.* Tediousness, tedium, weariness, boredom.
tediosamente, *adv.* Tediously, tiresomely.
tediosità [-à], *n.f.* Tediousness.
tedioso, *a.* Tiresome, tedious, irksome, wearisome, boring.
tegamata, *n.f.* Panful.
tegame, *n.m.* Pan, frying pan. **Uova al —,** fried eggs.
tegamino, *n.m.* Shallow pan, small frying pan.
teglia, tegghia [tEglia, tEgghia], *n.f.* Pan, baking-pan; pie-dish.
tegola, tegolo [tEgola, -o], *n.f.m.* Tile, roofing-tile; tiled roof. (*fig.*) **Un tegolo sulla testa,** an unexpected blow.
tegolaia [tegolAia], *n.f.* Tile-works.
tegolato, *n.m.* Tiling, tile-work.
tegumento, *n.m.* Integument, cover, covering.
teiera, *n.f.* Tea-pot.
teismo, *n.m.* Theism.
teista (*pl.* **teisti**), *n.m.* Theist.
tela, *n.f.* Linen, cloth, canvas, calico; (*Art*) picture, painting; (*Cinema*) screen; (*Theat.*) curtain; plot, intrigue. **— greggia,** bleached linen; **— di camicie,** shirting; **— per lenzuola,** sheeting; **— da materassi,** ticking; **— cerata,** oil-cloth (for tables, etc.); **— di ragno,** cobweb; **— metallica,** wire-gauze; (*Theat.*) **cala la —,** curtain.
telaggio [telAggio], *n.m.* Texture and quality of linen.
telaino, *n.m.* Small embroidery frame.
telaio [telAio], *n.m.* Loom; frame, tambour (for embroidery); (*Motor.*) chassis; window-sash; (*Print.*) chase. **— della bicicletta,** bicycle-frame; **— meccanico,** power-loom.
teleferica [telefErica], *n.f.* Overhead cable-way, telfer-line; aerial railway.
telefonare, *v.t.* To telephone, to phone, to ring up.
telefonata, *n.f.* Telephone call. (*colloq.*) **Ti farò una — domani,** I will ring you up tomorrow.
telefonia [telefonIa], *n.f.* Telephony.
telefonico [telefOnico], *a.* Telephonic, telephone. **Apparecchio —,** telephone set, telephone; **cabina telefonica,** call-box.
telefonista, *n.m.f.* Telephone operator, telephonist.
telefono [telEfono], *n.m.* Telephone. **Numero del —,** telephone number; **guida del —,** telephone directory.
telefotografia [telefotografIa], *n.f.* Telephotography.
telegiornale, *n.m.* Television news.
telegrafare, *v.t.* To telegraph, to wire.
telegrafia [telegrafIa], *n.f.* Telegraphy. **— senza fili,** wireless telegraphy.
telegraficamente, *adv.* Telegraphically.
telegrafico [telegrAfico], *a.* Telegraphic, telegraph.
telegrafista, *n.m.f.* Telegraphist, telegraph operator.
telegrafo [telEgrafo], *n.m.* Telegraph; telegraph office. **Palo del —,** telegraph pole.
telegramma (*pl.* **telegrammi**), *n.m.* Telegram, wire. **Mandare un —,** to send a wire, to telegraph; **— con risposta pagata,** reply-paid telegram.
telemetro [telEmetro], *n.m.* Range-finder; telemeter.
telepatia [telepatIa], *n.f.* Telepathy, thought-reading.
telepaticamente, *adv.* Telepathically.
telepatico [telepAtico], *a.* Telepathic.
telepatista, *n.m.f.* Telepathist.
teleria [telerIa], *n.f.* Linen, soft goods; linen-draper's shop.
teleschermo, *n.m.* Television screen.
telescopico [telescOpico], *a.* Telescopic.
telescopio [telescOpio], *n.m.* Telescope.

telescrivente, *n.m.* Teleprinter.
teletta, *n.f.* Light cloth, cotton.
televisione, *n.f.* Television. **Trasmettere per —,** to televise.
televisivo, *a.* Television, relating to television.
tellina, *n.f.* (*Zool.*) Cockle; cockle-shell.
tellurico [tellUrico], *a.* Telluric.
tellurio, telluro [tellUrio], *n.m.* (*Min.*) Tellurium.
telo (1), *n.m.* Breadth of cloth, width; **— a tenda,** tent-cloth.
telo (2), *n.m.* Javelin, dart.
telone, *n.m.* Coarse cloth; (*Theat.*) curtain.
tema (1), *n.m.* Theme, subject; exercise, composition; (*Gram.*) stem. **Uscir di —,** to wander from the subject; **ritornare sullo stesso —,** to harp on the same theme.
tema (2), *n.f.* Fear, dread; scare. **Per — che,** for fear lest.
tematico [temAtico], *a.* Thematic.
temenza, *n.f.* Dread, awe.
temerariamente, *adv.* Recklessly, rashly.
temerario [temerArio], *a.* Reckless, rash, foolhardy.
temere, *v.t.i.* To fear, to be afraid; to dread; to shrink from; to be unable to bear; to hesitate. **— Dio,** to fear God; **farsi —,** to make oneself feared; **teme d'essere scoperto,** he's afraid of being found out; **teme la luce,** it cannot stand the light.
temerità [-à], *n.f.* Temerity, rashness; foolhardiness.
Temi, Temide [tEmide], *n.f.* (*Myth.*) Themis.
temibile [temIbile], *a.* To be feared; fearful, dreadful; inspiring awe.
temolo [tEmolo], *n.m.* (*Zool.*) Grayling.
tempaccio [tempAccio], *n.m.* Bad weather.
tempera [tEmpera], *n.f.* Temper (of metals); (*Art*) distemper, tempera; (*Mus.*) tone, timbre. **Una lama di buona —,** a fine-tempered blade; **dipingere a —,** to paint in distemper.
temperalapis, temperamatite, *n.m.* Pencil-sharpener.
temperamento, *n.m.* Temperament, temper, disposition; mitigation; compromise, expedient. **Trovare un —,** to find a compromise.
temperante, *a.* Sober, moderate, temperate; mitigating; (*Med.*) sedative.
temperanza, *n.f.* Temperance, sobriety; self-restraint, moderation.
temperare, temperarsi, *v.t.r.* To alleviate to mitigate, to moderate; to sharpen (a pencil), to temper (a metal); to mix colours; to distemper.
temperato, *a.* Temperate, self-restrained; moderate. **Zona temperata,** temperate zone.
temperatamente, *adv.* Temperately, moderately.
temperatura, *n.f.* Temperature; tempering, hardening (of metals). (*Med.*) **Prendere la —,** to take one's temperature.
temperie [tempErie], *n.f.* Climate, temperature; atmosphere; mild weather.
temperinata, *n.f.* Cut with a penknife.
temperino, *n.m.* Penknife, pocket-knife.
tempesta, *n.f.* Storm, tempest, gale; hurricane, hail, hail-storm. **— di neve,** snow-storm; **mare in —,** stormy sea; **segnale di —,** storm-signal.
tempestare, *v.t.i.* To beset, to harass, to vex, to annoy; to hail, to storm, to rage; to get into a fury; to bombard; to enamel, to adorn. **Lo tempestò di pugni,** he rained blows upon him; **— di lettere,** to bombard with letters; **— di domande,** to overwhelm with questions; **tempestato di diamanti,** set with diamonds.
tempestio [tempestIo], *n.m.* Flood, outburst; torrent (of questions, etc.).
tempestivamente, *adv.* Timely, opportunely.
tempestivo, *a.* Opportune, timely, seasonable.
tempestosamente, *adv.* Stormily, tempestuously.
tempestoso, *a.* Stormy, tempestuous, raging; boisterous, tumultuous, agitated. **Una discussione tempestosa,** a stormy debate.
tempia [tEmpia], *n.f.* (*Anat.*) Temple.
tempiale, *n.m.* Frame of a loom.
tempio [tEmpio], *n.m.* Temple, church.
tempissimo [tempIssimo], *adv.* **Per —,** very early.
tempista, *n.m.f.* (*Mus.*) Executant who keeps time well; (*fig.*) person who does the right thing at the right time.
templare, *n.m.* (*Hist.*) Templar.
templo [cp. **tempio**].
tempo, *n.m.* Time; epoch, period; weather, season, climate; (*Gram.*) tense; (*Mus.*) tempo, beat, measure. **Di notte —,** at night, during the night; **per —,** betimes, early; **non aver —,** to have no time; **guadagnar —,** to gain time; **ha fatto il suo —,** he's had his day; **Come passa il —!** How time flies! **al — stesso,** at the same time; **prima del —,** before time; **a suo —, a — debito,** at the right time, at the right moment; **al —,** in the time of; **già da —,** long since; **con l'andar del —,** in the long run, in the course of time; **Da quanto — ?** How long ago? **un —,** once, formerly, **di — in —,** from time to time; **a un —,** simultaneously; **— fa,** long ago; **cattivo —,** bad weather; **prevedere il —,** to forecast the weather; **— permettendo,** weather permitting; **con ogni —,** in all weathers; (*Mus.*) **tenere il —,** to keep time; **aver buon —,** to be always joking; (*Gram.*) **il — futuro,** the future tense; (*Football*) **— primo, secondo,** first, second half.
tempora [tEmpora], *n.f.pl.* (*Eccles.*) Ember days.
temporale, *n.m.* Storm, rain storm, thunderstorm, gale.
temporale, *a.* Secular, temporal; (*Anat.*) temporal. **Potere —,** temporal power.
temporalesco, *a.* Stormy.
temporalità [-à], *n.f.* Temporality.
temporalmente, *adv.* Temporally, from a worldly standpoint.
temporaneamente, *adv.* Temporarily.
temporaneità [-à], *n.f.* Temporariness, temporary nature.
temporaneo [temporAneo], *a.* Temporary, transient, transitory.
temporeggiamento, *n.m.* Temporization, delay, procrastination.
temporeggiare, *v.i.* To temporize, to gain time; to put off, to procrastinate.
temporeggiatore, temporeggiatrice, *n.m.f.* Temporizer, procrastinator.

tempra, *n.f.* Temper; disposition; vigour, moral fibre, stamina.
temprare, temprarsi, *v.t.r.* To temper, to harden; to inure; to accustom. **— alle fatiche,** to inure oneself to fatigue.
tenace, *a.* Sticky, adhesive, viscous; tenacious, stubborn, unyielding.
tenacemente, *adv.* Tenaciously, stickily.
tenacia, tenacità [tenAcia, -à], *n.f.* Tenacity, tenaciousness; perseverance; stickiness; toughness, stiffness.
tenaglia [tenAglia], *n.f.* Pincers, pliers.
tenda, *n.f.* Tent, curtain, awning, hangings. **— da campo,** marquee; **levare le tende,** to strike tents; **mettere la —,** to pitch the tent; **vivere sotto la —,** to live under canvas, to camp out.
tendale, *n.m.* Large awning.
tendenza, *n.f.* Tendency, inclination, propensity.
tendenziosamente, *adv.* Tendentiously.
tendenziosità [-à], *n.f.* Tendentiousness, bias.
tendenzioso, *a.* Tendentious, insinuating, suggestive.
tender, *n.m.* (*Rail.*) Tender.
tendere [tEndere], *v.t.i.* To stretch forth, to stretch out, to hold out, to spread; to strain; to tend to, to show a tendency to; to bend (a bow). **— gli orecchi,** to strain one's ears; **— il braccio,** to stretch out one's arm; **— un'insidia,** to set a trap, to lay a snare; **— la mano,** to hold out one's hand; to give a helping hand; **— l'arco,** to bend the bow; **— le reti,** to spread nets; **— i nervi,** to strain one's nerves.
tendina, *n.f.* Curtain, blind. **Abbassare le tendine,** to lower the blinds.
tendine [tEndine], *n.m.* (*Anat.*) Tendon, sinew.
tendineo, tendinoso [tendIneo], *a.* Sinewy.
tenditoio [tenditOio], *n.m.* Clothes-post, clothes-horse.
tendone, *n.m.* Awning, large curtain; marquee.
tendopoli [tendOpoli], *n.f.* Camp, student's camp; camping.
tenebre [tEnebre], *n.f.pl.* Darkness, obscurity, gloom; (*Eccles.*) tenebrae, matins.
tenebria, tenebrore [tenebrIa], *n.f.m.* (*Lit.*) Darkness, obscurity.
tenebrosamente, *adv.* Darkly, obscurely.
tenebrosità [-à], *n.f.* Darkness, gloom.
tenebroso, *a.* Obscure, dark; sombre, gloomy.
tenente, *n.m.* Lieutenant. **— colonnello,** lieutenant-colonel; **— di vascello,** naval lieutenant.
tenenza, *n.f.* Lieutenancy.
teneramente, *adv.* Tenderly, fondly; delicately, gently.
tenere, *v.t.i.* To keep, to hold; to adhere, to stick; to deem, to think; to contain; to care about; to side with; to be like, to resemble; to gain, to win; to occupy (space); to be anxious. **— a bada,** to keep at bay; **— a una cosa,** to care about something; **— duro,** to hold on to, to hold fast; **— dietro,** to follow, to keep in touch with; **— a distanza,** to keep at a distance, to keep aloof; **— a mente,** to keep in mind; **— per uno, — dalla parte di uno,** to side with someone; **— conto di,** to take into account; **— per mano,** to hold by the hand; **— mano a,** to favour, to abet; **— la sinistra,** to keep to the left; **tengo per certo,** I'm sure; **— a stecchetto,** to keep short (of money, etc.); **— a battesimo,** to stand godfather to; **quella bottiglia tiene un litro,** that bottle holds a litre; **— i piedi in due staffe,** to have two strings to one's bow; **— il fiato,** to hold one's breath; **— indietro,** to keep back; **— a dozzina,** to take in boarders; **— l'amministrazione,** to keep accounts; **— d'occhio qualcuno,** to keep an eye on someone; **— la parola,** to keep one's word; (*Theat.*) **— il cartello,** to hold the stage, to have a long run; **egli tiene da sua madre,** he takes after his mother; **Che strada ho da — ?** Which road must I take? **tiene molto alla sua salute,** he takes great care of his health; **non c'è scusa che tenga,** there's no excuse for it [cp. **tenersi**].
tenerezza, *n.f.* Tenderness, affection, fondness, love. **Tenerezze,** caresses.
tenero [tEnero], *a.* Tender, delicate; loving, fond; soft, fragile; immature, young. **Aver del — per,** to be fond of; **egli è in tenera età,** he is of tender age; **carne tenera,** tender meat.
tenero [tEnero], *n.m.* Weak point; blind side; tender part.
tenersi, *v.r.* To keep oneself, to keep; to refrain; to regard oneself. **— al corrente,** to keep oneself up-to-date, to keep oneself informed; **— pronto,** to keep oneself ready, to be ready; **non posso tenermi in piedi,** I can't stand on my legs; **tenetevi a sinistra,** keep to the left; **da — al fresco,** to be kept cool [cp. **tenere**].
tenerume, *n.m.* Tender parts; soft things; mincing manners; gristle, cartilage.
tenia [tEnia], *n.f.* Tape-worm.
tenibile [tenIbile], *a.* Tenable.
tenimento, *n.m.* Holding; support; estate.
tenitore, *n.m.* Holder, keeper.
tennis, *n.m.* Lawn-tennis. **Campo di —,** tennis court; **— doppio,** doubles.
tennista, *n.m.f.* Tennis player.
tenore (1), *n.m.* Tenor, purport; way, mode; bearing; contents (of letter, etc.); terms; grade. **— di vita,** standard of living; **a — di,** conformably to.
tenore (2), *n.m.* (*Mus.*) Tenor; tenor voice.
tenoreggiare, *v.i.* (*Mus.*) To sing tenor.
tensile, *a.* Tensile.
tensione, *n.f.* Tension, strain (of nerves, etc.); pressure. (*Elect.*) **Alta, bassa —,** high, low tension.
tensore, *n.m.* (*Anat.*) Tensor.
tenta, *n.f.* (*Med.*) Probe, tent.
tentabile [tentAbile], *a.* Possible to attempt; open to temptation.
tentacolare, *a.* Tentacular.
tentacolo [tentAcolo], *n.m.* Tentacle.
tentare, *v.t.* To try, to attempt; to test, to feel; (*Med.*) to sound, to probe; to allure, to entice, to tempt, to seduce. **— un'impresa,** to attempt an undertaking; **— di resistere,** to try to resist; **— al peccato,** to tempt someone to sin.
tentativamente, *adv.* Tentatively.
tentativo, *n.m.* Endeavour, attempt, trial, experiment. **Fare un —,** to make an attempt.
tentatore, tentatrice, *n.m.f.* Tempter, temptress.

tentazione, *n.f.* Temptation; attraction.
tentenna, *n.m.* Waverer, irresolute person.
tentennamento, *n.m.* Vacillation, hesitation; oscillation.
tentennare, *v.t.i.* To shake, to waggle; to stagger, to waver, to vacillate; to oscillate; to be irresolute, to hesitate, to shilly-shally, to falter. **— il capo,** to shake one's head.
tentennio [tentennIo], *n.m.* Continual shaking.
tentennone, *n.m.* Irresolute person, waverer.
tentone, tentoni, *adv.* Gropingly, hesitatingly. **Cercare a tentoni,** to grope for.
tenue [tEnue], *a.* Thin, slender, tenuous, slight; watery; subtle; scanty. (*Anat.*) **Intestino —,** small intestine; **prezzo —,** moderate price.
tenuemente, *adv.* Tenuously, thinly, scantily.
tenuità [-à], *n.f.* Tenuity, thinness; smallness, slenderness; scantiness.
tenuta, *n.f.* Estate, property; tenure, possession; holding, landed property; farm; uniform, dress, clothes. **Essere in alta —,** to be in full uniform; **bassa —,** undress uniform; **— dei libri,** book-keeping; **a — d'acqua,** water-tight.
tenutario [tenutArio], *n.m.* Keeper, holder, possessor; landed proprietor.
tenuto, *p.p.a.* Held, bound, compelled; obliged. **Io non sono — a darti una,** I am not compelled to give you an explanation; **vi sarò molto — se,** I shall be greatly obliged if; **egli è — in gran conto,** he is held in great esteem [cp. **tenere**].
tenzonare, *v.i.* To dispute, to combat, to contend.
tenzone, *n.f.* (*Lit.*) Combat; competition; (troubadours') tenzon. **A singolar —,** in single combat, in a duel.
teocraticamente, *adv.* Theocratically.
teocratico [teocrAtico], *a.* Theocratic.
teocrazia [teocrazIa], *n.f.* Theocracy.
Teocrito [teOcrito], *n.m.* Theocritus.
teodolite, *n.m.* Theodolite.
teogonia [teogonIa], *n.f.* Theogony.
teologale, *a.* Theological.
teologare, *v.i.* To talk theologically, to discuss theology.
teologia [teologIa], *n.f.* Theology.
teologicamente, *adv.* Theologically.
teologico [teolOgico], *a.* Theological.
teologo [teOlogo], *n.m.* Theologian.
teorema (*pl.* **teoremi**), *n.m.* Theorem.
teoreticamente, *adv.* Theoretically.
teoretico [teorEtico], *a.* Theoretical.
teoria [teorIa], *n.f.* Theory; hypothesis; speculation, supposition; procession, string (of carriages, etc.).
teorica [teOrica], *n.f.* Theory.
teoricamente, *adv.* Theoretically.
teorico [teOrico], *n.m.a.* Theorist; theoretical, theoretic.
teorizzare, *v.i.* To theorize.
teosofia [teosofIa], *n.f.* Theosophy.
teosofo [teOsofo], *n.m.* Theosophist.
teosofista, *n.m.f.* Theosophist.
tepidario [tepidArio], *n.m.* (*Arch.*) Tepidarium.
tepidezza, *a.* Tepidness [cp. **tiepidezza**].
tepido [cp. **tiepido**].
tepore, *n.m.* Pleasant warmth; lukewarmness, tepidity (of climate).
teppa, teppaglia, *n.f.* Mob, rabble; gang of roughs; underworld.
teppismo, *n.m.* Hooliganism.
teppista (pl. **teppisti**), *n.m.* Hooligan, rough.
ter, *adv.* Thrice, three times.
terapeutica [terapEutica], *n.f.* Therapeutics.
terapeutico [terapEutico], *n.m.a.* Therapeutist; therapeutic.
terapia [terapIa], *n.f.* Therapy; treatment, cure.
teratologia [teratologIa], *n.f.* Teratology.
terbio [tErbio], *n.m.* (*Min.*) Terbium.
terebentina, *n.f.* Turpentine.
terebinto, *n.m.* (*Bot.*) Terebinth.
teredine [terEdine], *n.f.* (*Zool.*) Teredo.
Terenzio [terEnzio], *n.m.* Terence.
tergere [tErgere], *v.t.* To wipe, to scour, to clean. **— il pianto,** to dry one's tears; **tergersi la fronte,** to mop one's brow.
tergicristallo, *n.m.* (*Motor.*) Windscreen-wiper.
tergiversare, *v.i.* To evade, to hesitate, to beat about the bush, to shuffle.
tergiversatore, tergiversatrice, *n.m.f.* Dodger, shuffler.
tergiversazione, *n.f.* Evasion (of the point), hesitation; tergiversation, prevarication, beating about the bush.
tergo, *n.m.* Back, rear, hinder part. **A —,** behind, on the back; overleaf; in the rear; **da —,** from behind; **mostrare il —,** to show one's back.
termale, *a.* Thermal. **Acque termali,** hot springs.
terme, *n.f.pl.* Baths, thermal baths, hot baths; hot springs; public baths.
termico [tErmico], *a.* Thermic.
terminabile [terminAbile], *a.* Terminable.
terminale, *a.* Terminal, boundary, final.
terminare, *v.t.i.* To terminate, to limit, to bound; to settle, to finish, to put an end to, to end; to come to an end, to be over, to expire.
terminatamente, *adv.* Precisely.
terminativo, *a.* Terminating, terminative.
terminazione, *n.f.* End, termination; close; boundary.
termine [tErmine], *n.m.* Term, boundary, limit; termination, finish, close, end; (*Math.*) term; expression, word; terms, conditions. **Mezzi termini,** half measures, expedients; **passare i termini,** to go beyond the limits; **essere in buoni termini con uno,** to be on good terms with someone; **a — di legge,** according to the Law; **por — a,** to put an end to; **a rigor di termini,** strictly speaking; **contraddizione in termini,** contradiction in terms; **termini legali,** legal terms; **nel più breve —,** in the shortest time.
terminologia [terminologIa], *n.f.* Terminology.
termite [tErmite] (1), *n.f.* (*Zool.*) Termite, white ant.
termite [termIte] (2), *n.f.* (*Chem.*) Thermite.
termodinamica [termodinAmica], *n.f.* Thermodynamics.
termoelettrico [termoelEttrico], *a.* Thermoelectric.
termogeno [termOgeno], *a.* Thermogenic.
termomagnetico [termomagnEtico], *a.* Thermomagnetic.

termometro [termOmetro], *n.m.* Thermometer. — **a scala centigrada,** centigrade thermometer; — **clinico,** clinical thermometer.
Termopili [termOpili], *n.f.pl.* (*Geog.*) Thermopylae.
termos, *n.m.* Thermos flask, thermos.
termosifone, *n.m.* Heating-installation; radiator. **Riscaldamento a —,** central heating.
termostabile [termostAbile], *a.* Insulated (for heat).
termostato [termOstato], *n.m.* Thermostat.
terna, *n.f.* Group of three.
ternario [ternArio], *a.* Ternary.
terno, *n.m.* Draw of three numbers in a lottery; (*fig.*) piece of good luck.
terra, *n.f.* Earth, ground, land, soil; estate, property; world; country; (*Naut.*) shore. **Prender —,** to land, — **ferma,** dry land; **essere a —,** to be dispirited, to be run down; **essere — —,** to be small-minded, to be mean; **lavorare la —,** to till the soil; **per via di —,** by land; **scendere a —,** to land; **cader per —,** to fall to the ground, to fall down.
terracotta, *n.f.* Terracotta, earthenware.
terracqueo [terrAcqueo], *a.* Terraqueous.
terraglia [terrAglia], *n.f.* Pottery, earthenware, crockery.
terragnolo, terraiolo [terrAgnolo], *n.m.* Rock-dove.
Terranova, *n.f.m.* (*Geog.*) Newfoundland. **Un —,** a Newfoundland dog.
terrapieno, *n.m.* Embankment, platform, terrace, earthwork, rampart; (*Mil.*) terreplein.
terratico [terrAtico], *n.m.* (*Law.*) Rent paid by a farmer.
terrazza, *n.f.* Terraced roof; terrace.
terrazzano, *n.m.* Peasant, villager; native of a hill town.
terrazziere, *n.m.* Navvy.
terrazzino, *n.m.* Balcony; long window.
terrazzo, *n.m.* Terraced roof, balcony, belvedere; terrace; mosaic floor.
terremotati, *n.m.pl.* Victims of an earthquake.
terremoto, *n.m.* Earthquake. **Scossa di —,** earthquake shock.
terrenamente, *adv.* In a worldly manner.
terreno, *n.m.* Ground, soil, land; field; site. **Pian —,** ground-floor; — **piano,** level ground; **mancare il — sotto i piedi,** to be quite at a loss; **guadagnar —,** to gain ground; **scender sul —,** to fight a duel; **disputare il —,** to stand one's ground; (*Mil.*) **riconoscere il —,** to reconnoitre; **essere sul proprio —,** to be in one's element.
terreno, *a.* Worldly, mundane; terrestrial. **Piaceri terreni,** earthly pleasures.
terreo [tErreo], *a.* Earthy, earth-coloured; ashen, wan, pale; yellowish.
terrestre, *a.* Terrestrial; earthly.
terrestreità, terrestrità [-à], *n.f.* Earthliness.
terribile [terrIbile], *a.* Terrible, fearful, dreadful, awful, formidable; shocking.
terribilità [-à], *n.f.* Dreadfulness, fearfulness; awesomeness.
terribilmente, *adv.* Terribly.
terriccio [terrIccio], *n.m.* Soil, mould; loam.
terricciola, terricciuola, *n.f.* Small village.
terriere, *a.* Landed, land-owning. **Proprietà terriera,** landed property.
terrificante, *a.* Dreadful, terrible, awful, frightful, horrible, terrifying.
terrificare, *v.t.* To terrify, to frighten.
terrifico [terrIfico], *a.* Terrific, dreadful.
terrigeno [terrIgeno], *a.* Native to the soil.
terrigno, *a.* Earthy; wan, pale, yellowish; underground.
terrina, *n.f.* Earthenware pot or pan, jar; tureen.
territoriale, *n.m.a.* Territorial (in all senses).
territorialità [-à], *n.f.* Territoriality.
territorialmente, *adv.* Territorially.
territorio [territOrio], *n.m.* Territory, district; jurisdiction.
terrore, *n.m.* Terror, dread, awe; fright, fear. **Aver — di,** to have a terror of; **incutere — a,** to strike terror into.
terrorismo, *n.m.* Terrorism.
terrorista (*pl.* **terroristi**), *n.m.* Terrorist.
terrorizzare, *v.t.* To terrorize.
terroso, *a.* Earthy, grimy, muddy.
terrucola [terrUcola], *n.f.* Sterile land; hamlet, small village.
tersamente, *adv.* Tersely; neatly.
tersezza, *n.f.* Neatness, cleanness; terseness, clearness.
Tersicore [tersIcore], *n.f.* (*Myth.*) Terpsichore.
terso, *a.* Terse; neat, clear, bright.
terza, *n.f.* (*Eccles. Fencing*) Tierce; (*Rail.*) third class.
terzamente, *adv.* Thirdly.
terzana, *n.f.* (*Med.*) Tertian ague, tertian fever.
terzavolo, terzavola [terzAvolo, -a], *n.m.f.* Great-great-grandfather, great-great-grandmother.
terzeruolo, *n.m.* (*Naut.*) Reef. **Fare —,** to reef (a sail).
terzetto, *n.m.* Triplet, set of three; (*Mus.*) trio.
terziario [terziArio], *n.m.a.* Tertiary; member of the third order (Franciscans).
terzina, *n.f.* (*Poet.*) Triplet, tercet.
terzino, *n.m.* Bottle holding a third of a fiasco; (*Football*) full back.
terzo, *n.m.* Third, third part; third party. (*colloq.*) **Fare il — incomodo,** to be the extra; **in presenza di terzi,** in the presence of strangers.
terzo, *a.* Third. **Napoleone —,** Napoleon the Third; **in — luogo,** in the third place; (*Motor.*) **terza velocità,** third gear.
terzo, *adv.* Thirdly, in the third place.
terzogenito [terzogEnito], *n.m.a.* Third-born.
terzone, *n.m.* Packing-cloth.
terzultimo [terzUltimo], *a.* Antepenultimate.
terzuolo, *n.m.* (*Zool.*) Goshawk.
tesa, *n.f.* Brim, hat-brim; visor (of cap); tension; net (for catching birds); measure of length. **Cappello a larghe tese,** broad-brimmed hat.
tesaurizzare [cp. **tesoreggiare**].
teschio [tEschio], *n.m.* Skull, cranium.
tesi (*pl.* **tesi**), *n.f.* Thesis, dissertation, proposition. — **di laurea,** degree thesis; **in — generale,** as a general rule.
teso, *p.p.a.* Stretched, strained; taut, tight; highly strung (of nerves). **Rapporti tesi,** strained relations [cp. **tendere**].
tesoreggiare, *v.t.i.* To hoard, to treasure up, to store up.

tesoreria [tesorerIa], *n.f.* Treasury.
tesoriere, *n.m.* Treasurer.
tesoro, *n.m.* Treasure; treasury; (*fig.*) pet, darling. **Far —,** to treasure up; **buoni del —,** treasury bonds; **Tesoro mio!** My Darling!
Tespi, *n.f.* (*Myth.*) Thespis.
Tessalia [tessAlia], *n.f.* (*Geog.*) Thessaly.
tessalo [tEssalo], *n.m.a.* Thessalian.
tessera [tEssera], *n.f.* Ticket, card; ration card; pass. **— annonaria,** ration card; **— di riconoscimento,** identity card; membership card.
tesseramento, *n.m.* Enrolment; rationing.
tesserare, *v.t.* To enroll, to ration, to issue ration cards.
tesserato, *n.m.* Enrolled member (of a party).
tessere [tEssere], *v.t.* To weave (in all senses). **— le lodi di qualcuno,** to sing someone's praises.
tessile [tEssile], *a.* Textile. **Industria —,** textile industry.
tessilsacco, *n.m.* Moth-proof bag.
tessitore, tessitrice, *n.m.f.* Weaver; (*Zool.*) weaver-bird.
tessitura, *n.f.* Weaving, tissue; texture.
tessuto, *n.m.* Tissue; texture, cloth, fabric. **Un — di menzogne,** a tissue of lies; **negoziante di tessuti,** draper; **tessuti di lana,** woollen fabrics.
tessuto, *a.* Woven, knitted.
testa, *n.f.* Head; mind, wisdom, judgement, sense, brains; chief, head person; terminus; top. **— matta, — balzana,** crack-brained person; **— calda,** hot-head; **avere in —,** to have in mind; **tener —,** to stand up to; **mettersi in —,** to put into one's head; **a —,** per head; **una mela a —,** an apple each; **in —,** in front; **alla — del reggimento,** at the head of the regiment; **mal di —,** headache; **far di sua —,** to have one's own way; **un colpo di —,** a rash action; **— e croce,** heads or tails; **— di legno,** blockhead; **dalla — ai piedi,** from head to foot; **non saper dove batter la —,** not to know which way to turn; **tenere la — alta,** to carry one's head high, to have nothing to fear; (*Rail.*) **stazione di —,** terminus; **in — alla pagina,** at the top of the page; **ficcarsi in —,** to take it into one's head; **lo fece di sua —,** it was all his own idea; (*Mil.*) **— di ponte,** bridgehead; **— di sbarco,** beach-head; **— carica,** war-head (torpedo).
testabile [testAbile], *a.* Bequeathable.
testaccio [testAccio], *n.m.* Potsherd.
testaceo [testAceo], *n.m.a.* (*Zool.*) Testacean.
testamentario [testamentArio], *a.* Testamentary. **Esecutore —,** executor.
testamento, *n.m.* Will, testament. **Fare —,** to make one's will; **Vecchio, Nuovo Testamento,** Old, New Testament.
testardaggine [testardAggine], *n.f.* Obstinacy, stubbornness, headstrongness.
testardo, *a.* Obstinate, stubborn, self-willed, headstrong.
testare, *v.t.i.* To bequeath; to make one's will.
testata, *n.f.* Head; top; heading; butt-end; butt with the head. (*Naut.*) **— del baglio,** beam-end.
testatico [testAtico], *n.m.* Capitation tax.
testatore, testatrice, *n.m.f.* Testator, testatrix.
teste, *n.m.f.* (*Law*) Witness.
testè, *adv.* Just now, recently; a short while ago.
testereccio [testerEccio], *a.* Obstinate, stubborn.
testicciola, *n.f.* Lamb's or kid's head (for cooking).
testicolare, *a.* Testicular.
testicolo [testIcolo], *n.m.* (*Anat.*) Testicle.
testiera, *n.f.* Head-strap (of horse's harness); block (for hats and wigs).
testina, *n.f.* Small head; calf's head (for cooking).
testificare, *v.t.* To testify, to certify, to give evidence; to declare.
testificazione, *n.f.* Testifying, testimony.
testimone, *n.m.f.* Witness. **— d'accusa, di difesa,** witness for the prosecution, for the defence; **— oculare,** eye-witness.
testimoniale, *a.* Given in evidence, by the witness.
testimonianza, *n.f.* Witness, evidence, testimony. **Rendere —,** to bear witness.
testimoniare, *v.t.* To give evidence, to testify, to bear witness.
testimonio [testimOnio], *n.m.* Witness [cp. **testimone**]; best man.
testino, *n.m.* (*Print.*) 8-point type.
testo (1), *n.m.* Text; contents; (*Print.*) 16-point type. **Critica del —,** textual criticism; **libri di —,** text-books; **far —,** to be authoritative.
testo (2), *n.m.* Flower-pot; earthenware pot.
testolina, *n.f.* Little head; pretty little head; giddy-pate; (*fig.*) young girl.
testone, *n.m.* (*fig.*) Obstinate fellow, headstrong man.
testuale, *a.* Textual; exact, precise.
testualmente, *adv.* Textually, verbatim, word-for-word.
testuggine [testUggine], *n.m.* (*Zool.*) Tortoise, turtle; (*Hist.*) testudo.
testura, *n.f.* Texture.
tetanico [tetAnico], *a.* (*Med.*) Tetanic.
tetano [tEtano], *n.m.* (*Med.*) Tetanus.
tetracordo, *n.m.* (*Mus.*) Tetrachord.
tetraedro, *n.m.* (*Geom.*) Tetrahedron.
tetraggine [tetrAggine], *n.f.* Sombreness, gloom, sadness; dullness.
tetragonale, *a.* (*Geom.*) Tetragonal.
tetragono [tetrAgono], *n.m.a.* (*Geom.*) Tetragon; tetragonal; four-square; firm, well-grounded; steadfast, unflinching.
tetralogia [tetralogIa], *n.f.* Tetralogy.
tetramente, *adv.* Darkly, gloomily.
tetrametro [tetrAmetro], *n.m.* (*Poet.*) Tetrametre.
tetraone, *n.m.* (*Zool.*) Capercailzie.
tetrarca, *n.m.* (*Hist.*) Tetrarch.
tetro, *a.* Dark, sombre, sad, gloomy, dismal.
tetta, *n.f.* (*Anat.*) Nipple, teat; breast [cp. **mammella**].
tettare, *v.i.* To suck (at the breast).
tetto, *n.m.* Roof; house, home. **Senza —,** homeless; **essere a —,** to be under shelter; **gridare ai tetti,** to proclaim to the housetops; **star sotto i tetti,** to live in a garret; (*Motor.*) **— mobile,** sliding roof, sunshine roof.
tettoia [tettOia], *n.f.* Shed, lean-to; shelter (*Rail.*) glass roof (to station); penthouse.
tettonico [tettOnico], *a.* (*Geol.*) Tectonic.

Teutone [tEutone], *n.m.f.* Teuton.
teutonico [teutOnico], *a.* Teutonic.
Tevere [tEvere], *n.m.* (*Geog.*) Tiber.
thè [cp. **tè**].
ti, *pron.* Thee; you, to you.
tiara, *n.f.* Tiara.
tiberino, *a.* Of the Tiber.
tibia [tIbia], *n.f.* (*Anat.*) Tibia, shin-bone; (*Mus.*) tibia, pipe.
Tibullo, *n.m.* Tibullus.
tiburtino, *a.* Of Tivoli.
tic, *n.m.* (*Med.*) tic; habit, mannerism. **tic-tac,** tick (of clock).
ticchettare, *v.i.* To tick, to click.
ticchettio [ticchettIo], *n.m.* Ticking, clicking.
ticchio [tIcchio], *n.m.* Fancy, whim, caprice; hobby. **Gli saltò il — di,** he took it into his head to.
tiepidamente, *adv.* Tepidly.
tiepidezza, tiepidità [-à], *n.f.* Tepidity, tepidness, lukewarmness.
tiepido [tiEpido], *a.* Tepid, lukewarm; indifferent.
tifico [tIfico], *a.* Typhous.
tifo, *n.m.* (*Med.*) Typhus. (*Sport*) **Fare il — per,** to be a fan for.
tifoide, tifoidea [tifOide, tifoidEa], *n.f.* (*Med.*) Typhoid fever.
tifone, *n.m.* Typhoon, hurricane.
tifoso, *n.m.* Typhus patient; (*Sport*) fan, enthusiast. **— del calcio,** football fan, follower of football.
tifoso, *a.* Typhous.
tiglio [tIglio], *n.m.* (*Bot.*) Lime-tree, linden; bast; fibre. **Decotto di —,** infusion of lime-tree flowers.
tiglioso, *a.* Tough (of meat), fibrous.
tigna, *n.f.* (*Med.*) Porrigo, ring-worm, mange.
tignola, *n.f.* Moth, clothes-moth; book-worm; weevil.
tignoso, *n.m.a.* Person with ring-worm; scabby, niggardly.
tigrato, *a.* Striped, streaked, brindled; tabby.
tigre, *n.m.f.* (*Zool.*) Tiger, tigress.
tigresco, *a.* Tigerish.
tigrotto, *n.m.* Tiger cub.
timballista, *n.m.* (*Mus.*) Kettle-drummer.
timballo, *n.m.* Kettle-drum; (*Cooking*) timbale.
timbrare, *v.t.* To stamp, to post-mark.
timbratura, *n.f.* Stamping, post-marking.
timbro, *n.m.* Stamp, rubber-stamp; punch; post-mark; (*Mus.*) tone, timbre, tonality. **Data del — postale,** date of post-mark.
timidamente, *adv.* Timidly, shyly.
timidezza, timidità [-à], *n.f.* Timidity, timidness, shyness, bashfulness; diffidence.
timido [tImido], *a.* Timid, shy, bashful; nervous.
timo, *n.m.* (*Bot.*) Thyme; (*Anat.*) thymus.
timolo, *n.m.* (*Chem.*) Thymol.
timonare, *v.i.* (*Naut.*) To steer.
timone, *n.m.* (*Naut.*) Rudder, helm; (*fig.*) guidance, government; handle-bar (of bicycle); pole, shaft; **Tenere il —,** to steer, to be at the helm; **barra del —,** tiller; (*Aviat.*) **— di profondità,** elevator.
timoneggiare, *v.i.* To steer.
timonella, *n.f.* Four-wheeled gig, buggy.
timoniera, *n.f.* Wheel-house.
timoniere, *n.m.* Helmsman, steersman, pilot.
timorato, *a.* Timorous; respectful, devout; scrupulous. **— di Dio,** God-fearing.
timore, *n.m.* Fear, dread; apprehension, anxiety; awe. **— di Dio,** fear of God; **— panico,** panic fear; **per — di,** for fear of, lest.
timorosamente, *adv.* Timorously, with fear.
timoroso, *a.* Timorous, fearful; shy, timid; awe-struck.
timpanista, *n.m.* (*Mus.*) Kettle-drummer.
timpanite, *n.f.* (*Med.*) Tympanitis.
timpano [tImpano], *n.m.* Tympanum (in all senses); ear-drum; (*Mus.*) kettledrum. **Rompere i timpani,** to deafen one, to bother one.
tinaia [tinAia], *n.f.* Cellar, vat-room.
tina, *n.f.* Tub, small vat.
tinca, *n.f.* (*Zool.*) Tench.
tinello, *n.m.* Small vat; morning-room, breakfast-room, private dining-room; servants' hall.
tingere [tIngere], *v.t.* To dye; to tinge, to colour; to stain.
tingersi [tIngersi], *v.r.* To dye. **— i capelli,** to dye one's hair; **— col rossetto,** to put on lipstick, to put on rouge.
tingitura, *n.f.* Dyeing, colouring.
tinnire, *v.i.* To tinkle, to jingle.
tinnulo [tInnulo], *a.* Tinkling, jingling.
tino, *n.m.* Vat, large vat, tub.
tinozza, *n.f.* Wash-tub, tub.
tinta, *n.f.* Dye, colour, tincture; tint, hue; tinge; (*fig.*) touch, strain. **Una — chiara,** a light hue; **dipingere a fosche tinte,** to draw a gloomy picture.
tinteggiare, *v.t.* To tint; to tincture.
tinteggiatura, *n.f.* Tint, tincture.
tintinnabulo [tintinnAbulo], *n.m.* Hand-bell.
tintinnare, tintinnire, *v.i.* To tinkle, to clink, to jingle; to tingle. **Mi tintinnano gli orecchi,** my ears are ringing.
tintinnio [tintinnIo], *n.m.* Continuous tinkling or tingling.
tinto, *p.p.a.* Dyed, tinged, stained, soiled; (*fig.*) with a smattering of [cp. **tingere**].
tintoria [tintorIa], *n.f.* Dye-works; dry-cleaner's shop.
tintura, *n.f.* Dye, tint; tincture; (*fig.*) smattering. **— di iodio,** tincture of iodine; **— da capelli,** hair-dye.
tiorba, *n.f.* (*Mus.*) Theorbo.
tipicamente, *adv.* Typically.
tipico [tIpico], *a.* Typical.
tipo, *n.m.* Type, species, sort; example, pattern, model, specimen. **Che bel —!** What a queer chap! **— monetario,** monetary standard.
tipografia [tipografIa], *n.f.* Typography; printing-works.
tipograficamente, *adv.* Typographically.
tipografico [tipogrAfico], *a.* Typographical.
tipografo [tipOgrafo], *n.m.* Typographer.
tiptologia [tiptologIa], *n.f.* Spirit-rapping.
tira, *n.f.* Competition, wrangling, strife. **Fare a tira tira,** to scramble for.
tirabaci, *n.m.* Flirt.
tiraggio [tirAggio], *n.m.* Draught, drawing.
tiragliatore, *n.m.* Sharp-shooter.
tiralinee [tiralInee], *n.m.* Ruler; drawing-pen.

tiramantici [tiramAntici], *n.m.* Organ-blower.
tiramento, *n.m.* Pulling, tugging.
tirammolla, tiremmolla, *n.m.* (*Naut.*) Tow-rope, rope that is now taut now slack; (*fig.*) waverer, one who shilly-shallies.
tiranneggiamento, *n.m.* Tyrannizing.
tiranneggiare, *v.t.* To tyrannize; to hector, to dragoon.
tirannello, *n.m.* Petty tyrant.
tirannescamente, *adv.* Like a tyrant, tyrannously.
tirannesco, *a.* Tyrannous, despotic.
tirannia [tirannIa], *n.f.* Tyranny, despotism, oppression.
tirannicida, *n.m.* Tyrannicide (the doer).
tirannicidio [tirannicIdio], *n.m.* Tyrannicide (the act).
tirannico [tirAnnico], *a.* Tyrannical, despotic.
tiranno, *n.m.a.* Tyrant, despot, oppressor; tyrannical.
tirannide [tirAnnide], *n.f.* Tyranny, despotism.
tirante, *n.m.* Connecting-rod, tie-beam, tie-rod; brake-rod. **Tiranti dei calzoni,** braces; under-straps.
tirapiedi, *n.m.* Hangman's assistant; (*fig.*) henchman, understrapper.
tirapugni, *n.m.* Knuckle-duster.
tirare, *v.t.i.* To pull, to draw, to drag, to haul, to tug; to pluck, to shoot at, to fire at; to attract; to incline, to tend; to fence; to blow (of wind); to print, to print off; to extract, to deliver (a blow). **— una conclusione,** to draw a conclusion; **— la somma,** to sum up; **— dritto, — via,** to go along, to go straight ahead; **— giù,** to pull down, to botch a piece of work; **— calci,** to kick; **— un pugno,** to launch a blow; **— gli orecchi,** to pull a person's ears, to reprimand; **tirarla con i denti,** to live from hand to mouth, to endure hardships; **— a sorte,** to draw lots, to choose by lot; **— il collo,** to wring the neck; **— sul prezzo,** to bargain, to haggle; **— l'acqua al suo mulino,** to bring grist to one's mill; **— bene,** to be a good shot; **questo camino non tira,** this chimney doesn't draw; **— in lungo,** to protract matters; **tira vento,** the wind is blowing.
tirarsi, *v.r.* To bring to oneself, to draw aside, to draw back; to get out of. **— da parte,** to stand aloft; **— su,** to stand upright; to sit up; **— indietro,** to draw aside, to stand aloof; **— addosso,** to draw on oneself; **— avanti,** to muddle through, to get along somehow.
tirasassi, *n.m.* Catapult.
tirastivali, *n.m.* Boot-jack.
tirata, *n.f.* Pull; draw; long walk; tirade. **— d'orecchi,** reprimand, rebuke.
tiratappi, *n.m.* Corkscrew.
tiratezza, *n.f.* Tension.
tirato, *p.p.a.* Drawn, dragged, hauled; attracted; (*fig.*) stingy, miserly, mean, close-fisted.
tiratore, *n.m.* Marksman, shot. **— scelto,** sharpshooter; **— franco,** sniper; **— di scherma,** fencer.
tiratura, *n.f.* Printing, impression; circulation (of a journal, etc.); pull, drawing. **Libri a grande —,** best-sellers.
tiraturaccioli [tiraturAccioli], *n.m.* Corkscrew.
tirchieria [tirchierIa], *n.f.* Stinginess, niggardliness, avarice.
tirchio [tIrchio], *n.m.a.* Miser; miserly, mean, niggardlv, avaricious.
tirella, *n.f.* Trace (of harness).
tiremmolla, *n.m.* (*colloq.*) Demur, waveringness; shilly-shallying.
tiretto, *n.m.* Drawer.
tiritera, *n.f.* Long-winded yarn, silly story; rigmarole; endless speech.
tiro, *n.m.* Shooting, shot; range (of fire); reach; team (of horses); (*fig.*) trick, practical joke; (*Billiards*) stroke. **Essere a —,** to be at hand, to be within reach; **cavallo da —,** draught horse; **— a quattro,** four-in-hand; **gara di —,** shooting-match; **— a segno,** target-practice, shooting-range; **a — di fucile,** within rifle-shot; **— rapido,** rapid fire; **giuocare un brutto —,** to play a dirty trick; (*Mil.*) **— di sbarramento,** barrage-fire.
tirocinante, *n.m.f.* Apprentice; novice, tyro, beginner.
tirocinio [tirocInio], *n.m.* Apprenticeship; novitiate.
tiroide [tirOide], *n.f.a.* (*Anat.*) Thyroid.
tiroideo [tiroidEo], *a.* Thyroid, thyroidal.
tirolese, *n.m.a.* Tyrolese.
Tirolo, *n.m.* (*Geog.*) Tyrol.
tirreno, *a.* Tyrrhene, Tyrrhenian.
tirso, *n.m.* (*Hist.*) Thyrsus.
tisana, *n.f.* Infusion (of herbs). **— d'orzo,** barley-water.
tisi, tisichezza, *n.f.* (*Med.*) Phthisis, consumption, tuberculosis.
tisico [tIsico], *n.m.a.* Consumptive.
titanico [titAnico], *a.* Titanic.
titanio [titAnio], *n.m.* (*Min.*) Titanium.
Titano, *n.m.* (*Myth.*) Titan.
titillamento, *n.m.* Titillation, tickling.
titillare, *v.t.* To titillate, to tickle.
titillazione, *n.f.* Tickling.
titolare, *n.m.* Incumbent, occupier, office-holder; head of a firm.
titolare, *a.* Titular, regular, appointed; rightful.
titolato, *n.m.a.* Titled person; titled.
titolo [tItolo], *n.m.* Title, claim, right; deed, document; proof; qualification, status; title-page, heading; (*Comm.*) stocks, shares, securities. **A giusto —,** rightly; **A che —?** By what right? **a — d'incoraggiamento,** by way of encouragement; **dare dei titoli ad una persona,** to call someone names; **avere i titoli necessari,** to have the necessary qualifications; **— di credito,** letter of credit; (*Comm.*) **titoli industriali,** industrial securities; **a — di favore,** as a favour; **a — gratuito,** free; **a — privato,** private.
Titone, *n.m.* (*Myth*) Tithonus.
titubante, *a.* Hesitant, irresolute, hesitating, undecided, faltering; perplexed.
titubantemente, *adv.* Hesitatingly.
titubanza, *n.f.* Hesitation, demur, indecision, irresoluteness; perplexity.
titubare, *v.i.* To hesitate, to falter, to waver, to be undecided; to demur.
titubazione, *n.f.* Hesitation, perplexity.
Tiziano, *n.m.* Titian.
tizio, tizia [tIzio, -a], *n.m.f.* Some fellow, some woman; a certain person; (*colloq.*) what's-his-name.

tizzo, tizzone, *n.m.* Fire-brand, brand; smoking coal. **— d'inferno,** a scoundrel.
to'! *inter.* Look here! I say! Hallo! (in surprise).
toboga, *n.m.* (*Sport*) Toboggan.
tocca, *n.f.* Crape; (*colloq.*) hole in the road, gap in pavement.
toccabile [toccAbile], *a.* Touchable.
toccaferro, *n.m.* Children's game of touching iron instead of wood.
toccamano, *n.m.* Handshake (as a pledge).
toccamento, *n.m.* Contact, touch, touching, feeling.
toccante, *a.* Touching, affecting, concerning.
toccare, *v.t.i.* To touch, to handle, to feel, to finger; to hit, to tap, to strike; to taste; to play (the piano); to affect, to concern; to touch on, to convey, to mention; to reach, to attain; to draw (wages, etc.); to be the turn of, to fall to the lot of. **— con mano,** to ascertain, to find out; **— nel segno,** to hit the mark; **Bazza a chi tocca!** Here goes! Now for it! **— il cuore,** to touch the heart; **— sul vivo,** to sting to the quick; **— in sorte,** to befall; **— il cielo col dito,** to be in the seventh heaven; **— il polso,** to feel the pulse; (*Naut.*) **— un porto,** to call at a port; **Tocca a me?** Is it my turn? **tocca a lui partire,** it's his turn to leave, it's up to him to go; (*colloq.*) **tocca ferro,** touch wood.
toccarsi, *v.r.* To meet. **Gli estremi si toccano,** extremes meet.
toccasana, *n.m.* Cure-all, panacea, universal remedy.
toccata, *n.f.* Touch, touching; (*Mus.*) toccata.
toccatina, *n.f.* Gentle touch, touching; fingering; tap.
toccatutto, *n.m.* Meddler.
toccheggiare, *v.t.* To toll a bell.
toccheggio [tocchEggio], *n.m.* Tolling.
tocchetto, *n.m.* Little bit, morsel.
tocco (1), *n.m.* Touch, touching, feeling; beat, stroke, toll. **È il —,** it's one o'clock; **dare l'ultimo —,** to give the finishing touch; (*Mus.*) **avere un bel —,** to have a good touch.
tocco (2), *n.m.* (Judge's) cap; piece; figure. **Un bel — di giovane,** a strapping young fellow.
tocco, *p.p.a.* Touched; rather stupid, slightly mad.
toco, *n.m.* (*Zool.*) Toucan.
toeletta, toletta, *n.f.* Toilet, toilet-table, dressing-table; toilet-glass. **Far —,** to dress, to have a wash, to tidy oneself. **Gran —,** full dress; **gabinetto da —,** dressing-room.
toga, *n.f.* Official robe, gown; (*Hist.*) toga.
togato, *a.* Gowned, wearing a gown.
togliere [tOgliere], *v.t.* To take away, to take off, to clear away, to remove; to deprive, to rob; to prevent. **— a fare,** to undertake; **ciò non toglie che,** that does not prevent; **Tolga Iddio!** God forbid! **— il blocco,** to raise the blockade.
togliersi [tOgliersi], *v.r.* To get away, to free oneself, to get free. **— il cappello,** to take off one's hat; **— il vestito,** to take off one's dress; **toglietemelo dai piedi,** send him away, get rid of him; **— la fame,** to stay one's hunger; **— la vita,** to commit suicide; **— la voglia,** to gratify one's wishes; **— il pane di bocca,** to deny oneself for the sake of others.
toglimento, *n.m.* Taking, theft; subtraction.
toh! [cp.**to'!**].
tolda, *n.f.* (*Naut.*) Deck.
tolemaico [tolemAico], *a.* Ptolemaic.
toletta [cp. **toeletta**].
tollerabile [tollerAbile], *a.* Tolerable, endurable, bearable.
tollerabilità [-à], *n.f.* Bearableness.
tollerabilmente, *adv.* Tolerably, bearably.
tollerante, *a.* Tolerant; enduring, forbearing.
tolleranza, *n.f.* Tolerance, forbearance, toleration; endurance; (*Comm.*) allowance. **— sul peso,** allowance on weight.
tollerare, *v.t.* To suffer, to bear, to endure, to tolerate.
tollerato, *a.* Tolerated, suffered (unwillingly).
tolomea [tolomEa], *n.f.* (*Lit.*) Place for traitors in Dante's "Inferno".
Tolomeo [tolomEo], *n.m.* (*Hist.*) Ptolemy.
Tolone, *n.f.* (*Geog.*) Toulon.
Tolosa, *n.f.* (*Geog.*) Toulouse.
tolto, *p.p.a.* Taken off, removed. **Il mal —,** the ill-gotten gain [cp. **togliere**].
toma, *n.f.* **Promettere Roma e —,** to make boundless promises; **capire Roma per —,** to misunderstand.
tomaia [tomAia], *n.f.* Upper (of shoe), vamp.
tomba, *n.f.* Grave, tomb; death.
tombola [tOmbola] (1), *n.f.* Lottery, raffle.
tombola [tOmbola] (2), *n.f.* Fall, tumble.
tombolare, *v.i.* To tumble, to fall headlong.
tombolata, *n.f.* Fall, tumble.
tombolo [tOmbolo], *n.m.* Pillow for lace-making.
tomismo, *n.m.* (*Eccles.*) Thomism.
tomista (*pl.* **tomisti**), *n.m.* Thomist.
tomistico [tomIstico], *a.* Thomistic.
tomo, *n.m.* Tome, volume. (*colloq.*) **Un bel —,** a queer fish, an odd fellow.
tonaca [tOnaca], *n.f.* (*Eccles.*) Cowl, cassock; tunic. **Gettar la — alle ortiche,** to throw off the cowl.
tonale, *a.* (*Mus.*) Tonal.
tonalità [-à], *n.f.* Tonality.
tonante, *a.* Thundering.
tonare, tuonare, *v.i.* To thunder, to boom, to roar.
tonchio [tOnchio], *n.m.* (*Zool.*) Weevil.
tondare, *v.t.* To round, to round off, to trim [cp. **arrotondare**].
tondeggiamento, *n.m.* Rotundity.
tondeggiante, *a.* Roundish, plump, fat.
tondeggiare, *v.t.i.* To round; to be round.
tondello, *n.m.* Stopper (of a bottle); round (of beef).
tondere [tOndere], *v.t.* To shear (sheep), to clip.
tondino, *n.m.* Small plate, dish, saucer; (*Arch.*) astragal.
tonditura, *n.f.* Clipping, shearing.
tondo, *n.m.* Plate, saucer; globe; circle; (*Art*) round picture, tondo.
tondo, *adv.a.* Round, circular; simple, clear. **Cifre tonde,** round figures; **parlar chiaro e —,** to speak one's mind.
tonfano [tOnfano], *n.m.* Depth; deep (of a river).
tonfare, *v.i.* To plop, to splash.
tonfete! [tOnfete], *inter.* Slap! Bang!
tonfo, *n.m.* Fall, splash, thump, bang, plop.
tonica [tOnica], *n.f.* (*Mus.*) Key-note; tonic.

tonicità [-à], *n.f.* Tonicity.
tonico [tOnico], *n.m.a.* Tonic (in all senses).
tonificare, *v.t.* To invigorate, to brace.
tonnara, *n.f.* Fishing-net for tunny; fishing-grounds for tunny.
tonnarotto, *n.m.* Tunny-fisher.
tonnato, *a.* (Cooked with) tunny sauce.
tonneggiare, *v.t.* (*Naut.*) To warp.
tonnellaggio [tonnellAggio], *n.m.* Tonnage, burden (of ship).
tonnellata, *n.f.* Ton (weight). (*Naut.*) **— di stazza,** ton register.
tonnina, *n.f.* Pickled tunny.
tonno, *n.m.* (*Zool.*) Tunny, tunny-fish.
tono, *n.m.* Tone; accent, stress; lead; style, manner; (*Mus.*) tone, key. **In — acre,** in a harsh manner; **rispondere a —,** to give the right answer, to answer to the point; **cambiar —,** to sing another tune, to change one's manner; **dare il — a,** to give the keynote; **è il — che fa la musica,** it's the manner that counts; (*Mus.*) **— maggiore, — minore,** major, minor key.
tonsilla, *n.f.* (*Anat.*) Tonsil.
tonsillite, *n.f.* (*Med.*) Tonsilitis.
tonsura, *n.f.* (*Eccles.*) Tonsure. **Prender la —,** to take Holy Orders.
tonsurare, *v.t.* To tonsure.
tonsurato, *n.m.* Priest, monk, ecclesiastic.
tonto, *a.* Dull, silly, stupid.
topaia [topAia], *n.f.* Rat's nest; (*fig.*) hovel, slum.
topazio [topAzio], *n.m.* Topaz.
topica [tOpica], *n.f.* Dialectic argument. (*colloq.*) **Fare una —,** to make a faux pas, "to drop a brick".
topico [tOpico], *a.* Topical, local, to the point; (*colloq.*) risky; (*Med.*) external.
topinambur, *n.m.* (*Bot.*) Jerusalem artichoke.
topinara, *n.f.* (*Zool.*) Mole.
topo, *n.m.* (*Zool.*) Rat; mouse. **— acquaiolo,** water-rat; **— campagnuolo,** field-mouse; (*fig.*) **— d'albergo,** hotel thief.
topografia [topografIa], *n.f.* Topography.
topografico [topogrAfico], *a.* Topographical.
topografo [topOgrafo], *n.m.* Topographer.
topolino, *n.m.* Small mouse, mousie; (*colloq.*) baby motor car. **Topolino,** Mickey Mouse.
toporagno, *n.m.* (*Zool.*) Shrew.
toppa, *n.f.* Door-lock; patch, piece (let in). **Mettere una — a,** to mend, to patch up.
toppato, *a.* Dappled (of a horse).
toppo, *n.m.* Block, log; stump (of tree).
torace, *n.m.* (*Anat.*) Thorax.
toracico [torAcico], *a.* Thoracic.
torba, *n.f.* Peat.
torbida [tOrbida], *n.f.* Muddy stream, muddy water.
torbidamente, torbamente, *adv.* Muddily, turbidly.
torbidezza, torbezza, *n.f.* Muddiness; haziness, dimness (of sight); obscurity, darkness.
torbidiccio [torbidIccio], *a.* Rather muddy, turbid, not clear.
torbido [tOrbido], *n.m.* Trouble, agitation, disorder; disturbance. **Pescare nel —,** to fish in muddy waters.
torbido [tOrbido], *a.* Turbid, troubled, muddy; hazy, dim; disturbed; obscure. **Acque torbide,** troubled waters.
torbiera, *n.f.* Peat-bog, peat-moss.
torboso, *a.* Peaty.
torcere [tOrcere], *v.t.* To twist, to wring, to squeeze; to distort; to wrench. **— il collo a un pollo,** to wring a fowl's neck; **— la bocca,** to twist one's mouth; **— gli occhi,** to look askance; **— il naso,** to turn up one's nose; **— i panni,** to wring clothes; **— lo sguardo,** to avert one's eyes from.
torcersi, *v.r.* To writhe, to wriggle. **— dal ridere,** to roll with laughter; **— dal dolore,** to writhe in agony.
torchiare, *v.t.* To press.
torchiata, *n.f.* Pressure, squeeze.
torchiatura, *n.f.* Pressing.
torchio [tOrchio], *n.m.* Press; oil-press; wine-press; printing press. **Essere sotto i torchi,** to be in the press; (*slang*) **far gemere i torchi,** to send to press, to publish.
torcia [tOrcia], *n.f.* Torch.
torcicollo, *n.m.* (*Med.*) Stiff neck; wry neck; (*Zool.*) wryneck. **Buscarsi un —,** (*slang*) to get a crick in one's neck.
torciere, *n.m.* Torch-bearer; standard-lamp.
torcigliare, *v.t.* To twist.
torcilabbro, *n.m.* Twitch of the lips.
torcimento, *n.m.* Twisting, twist.
torcitoio [torcitOio], *n.m.* Silk-throwing machine.
torcitura, *n.f.* Twisting, twist.
torcoliere, *n.m.* Presser; machine-minder.
tordo, *n.m.* (*Zool.*) Thrush; (*fig.*) simpleton, fool.
toreadore, torero, *n.m.* Bull-fighter.
torinese, *n.m.a.* Native of, or pertaining to, Turin.
Torino, *n.f.* (*Geog.*) Turin.
torlo, *n.m.* Yolk of an egg [cp. **tuorlo**].
torma, *n.f.* Throng, crowd, multitude, band; herd; troop.
tormalina, *n.f.* (*Min.*) Tourmaline.
tormenta, *n.f.* (Alpine) snow-storm, blizzard; hurricane.
tormentare, *v.t.* To torment; to vex, to irritate, to harass, to worry.
tormentarsi, *v.r.* To worry, to torture oneself, to fret; to be restless.
tormentatore, tormentatrice, *n.m.f.* Tormentor.
tormento, *n.m.* Worry; torment; pain, grief, anguish; torture.
tormentosamente, *adv.* Tormentingly; painfully.
tormentoso, *a.* Tormenting, vexing, harassing, worrying.
tornaconto, *n.m.* Profit, gain, advantage; utility; benefit. **Non c'è —,** it isn't worth while; **fare il proprio —,** to seek one's own profit.
tornagusto, *n.m.* Appetizer.
tornante, *n.m.* Winding (of a road).
tornare, *v.i.* To come back, to return, to go back; to turn, to become again, to start again; to be worth while; to prove to be, to be right. **Questo vestito torna di moda,** this dress has come into fashion again; **non torna conto,** it's hardly worth while; **— in sè,** to come to oneself, to recover; **i miei conti non tornano,** my accounts do not balance; **— indietro,** to turn back; **non gli torna a onore,** it does not redound to his credit; **egli tornò a lavorare,** he went back

to work; **ciò torna a proposito,** this comes *à propos.*
tornasole, *n.m.* (*Bot.*) Sunflower; (*Chem.*) litmus.
tornata, *n.f.* Return; meeting, sitting (of an assembly); (*Poet.*) envoie.
torneamento [cp. **torneo**].
torneare, *v.i.* To joust, to tilt, to tourney.
torneatore, *n.m.* Jouster.
torneo, torneamento [tornEo], *n.m.* Tourney, joust, tournament.
torniaio [torniAio], *n.m.* Turner.
tornichetto, *n.m.* Turnstile.
tornio [tOrnio], *n.m.* Lathe, turning-lathe. **— a pedale,** foot-lathe.
tornire, *v.t.* To turn (in a lathe); to mould, to shape, to fashion.
tornito, *p.p.a.* Turned; well-shaped, rounded.
tornitore, *n.m.* Turner.
tornitura, *n.f.* Turning, turnery; shavings, chips.
torno, *n.m.* Turn; period. **In quel — di tempo,** about that time; **torno torno,** all round.
toro, *n.m.* (*Zool.*) Bull. **Tagliare la testa al —,** to remove a difficulty by drastic means.
torpedinare, *v.t.* To torpedo.
torpedine [torpEdine], *n.m.* Torpedo; (*Zool.*) torpedo-fish; (*Motor.*) racing-car.
torpediniera, *n.f.* Torpedo-boat.
torpedo, *n.m.* (*Motor.*) Touring car, open car.
torpedone, *n.m.* Motor-bus, motor-coach.
torpere [tOrpere], *v.i.* To remain torpid.
torpidamente, *adv.* Torpidly.
torpidezza, torpidità [-à], *n.f.* Torpidity [cp. **torpore**].
torpido [tOrpido], *a.* Torpid, sluggish, numbed; inactive.
torpore, *n.m.* Torpor, numbness, sluggishness, dullness.
torracchione, *n.m.* Ruined tower.
torraiuolo, *n.m.* (*Zool.*) Rock-pigeon.
torrazzo, *n.m.* Large, massive tower.
torre, *n.f.* Tower; (*Naut.*) turret; (*Chess*) rook, castle.
torre [cp. **togliere**].
torrefare, *v.t.* To roast, to scorch.
torrefazione, *n.f.* Roasting, scorching. **— del caffè,** coffee-roasting.
torreggiante, *a.* Towering.
torreggiare, *v.i.* To tower above, to overlook, to dominate.
torrente, *n.m.* Stream, torrent; flood. **Un — di lagrime,** a flood of tears.
torrentizio, torrenziale [torrentIzio], *a.* Torrential; impetuous.
torrenzialmente, *adv.* Torrentially.
torretta, torricella, *n.f.* Turret; conning-tower (of submarine).
torrido [tOrrido], *a.* Torrid; burning, scorching. (*Geog.*) **Zona torrida,** Torrid Zone.
torriere, torrigiano, *n.m.* Keeper of a tower.
torrione, *n.m.* Large tower, castle keep.
torrone, *n.m.* Nougat.
torsello, *n.m.* Pin-cushion; pad.
torsione, *n.f.* Torsion, twisting.
torso, *n.m.* (*Anat.*) Trunk; (*Art*) torso; core (of fruit); cabbage-stalk.
torsolo [tOrsolo], *n.m.* Stalk (of cabbage, etc.), stump; core (of fruit).
torta (1), *n.f.* Tart, pie, cake, pudding, pastry. **— di mele,** apple-tart.
torta (2), *n.f.* Twist, twisting. (*slang*) **Far la —,** to do some wire-pulling; to form a clique.
tortamente, *adv.* Tortuously.
tortellaio [tortellAio], *n.m.* Maker or vendor of tortelli.
tortellini, *n.m.pl.* Macaroni stuffed with meat, etc.
tortello, *n.m.* Fritter.
tortezza, *n.f.* Obliqueness, twist.
tortiera, *n.f.* Baking-tin, pie-dish.
tortiglione, *adv.* **A —,** spirally.
tortina, *n.f.* Tartlet.
torto, *n.m.* Wrong; fault; blame; injustice, injury; offence; damage. **A —,** unjustly, wrongly; **fare un — a uno,** to do someone a wrong; **dar — a uno,** to lay the blame on someone; **tu hai —,** you are wrong.
torto, *p.p.a.* Twisted, bent; tortuous; crooked.
tortora [tOrtora], *n.f.* (*Zool.*) Turtle-dove.
tortoreggiare, *v.i.* To coo.
tortorella, *n.f.* Young dove.
tortuosamente, *adv.* Tortuously.
tortuosità [-à], *n.f.* Tortuosity, tortuousness; crookedness.
tortuoso, *a.* Tortuous, crooked, twisted, winding; underhand; disingenuous.
tortura, *n.f.* Torture, torment; pain. **Mettere alla —,** to put to the rack.
torturare, *v.t.* To torture, to torment, to rack.
torturarsi, *v.r.* To torment oneself, to worry. **— il cervello,** to rack one's brain.
torvamente, *adv.* Grimly, threateningly.
torvo, *a.* Grim, sullen; ghastly, hideous.
torzone, *n.m.* (*colloq.*) Lay friar; boor.
tosa, *n.f.* (*colloq.*) Girl, lass.
tosamento, *n.m.* Shearing.
tosare, *v.t.* To shear, to clip; to shave.
tosatore, *n.m.* Shearer.
tosatura, *n.f.* Shearing, clipping. **— delle pecore,** sheep-shearing.
Toscana, *n.f.* (*Geog.*) Tuscany.
toscanamente, *adv.* In the Tuscan manner.
toscaneggiare, *v.i.* To affect Tuscan pronunciation and style.
toscaneria [toscanerIa], *n.f.* Tuscan ways.
toscano, tosco, *n.m.a.* Tuscan; variety of cigar.
tosco, *n.m.* Poison.
toso, *n.m.* (*colloq.*) Lad, boy.
tosone, *n.m.* Fleece. **— d'oro,** Golden Fleece.
tosse, *n.f.* Cough. **— asinina, — canina,** whooping-cough.
tossicchiare, *v.i.* To keep on coughing, to have a tickling cough.
tossico [tOssico], *n.m.* Poison.
tossico [tOssico], *a.* Toxic, poisonous. **Gas tossico,** poison gas.
tossicologia [tossicologIa], *n.f.* Toxicology.
tossicologico [tossicolOgico], *a.* Toxicological.
tossina, *n.f.* (*Med.*) Toxin.
tossire, *v.i.* To cough.
tostamente, *adv.* Speedily, quickly, soon.
tostare, *v.t.* To toast (bread), to roast (coffee); to scorch.
tostatura, *n.f.* Toasting, roasting.
tosticchiare, *v.t.* To toast slightly, to brown.
tostino, *n.m.* Coffee-roaster; bread-toaster.
tosto, *p.p.a.* Toasted, roasted. **Pane —,** toast; (*fig.*) **faccia tosta,** cheek, brazenness, impudence.

tosto, *adv.* Soon, quickly, promptly, at once, **— che,** as soon as.
totale, *n.m.* Total, total amount.
totale, *a.* Entire, whole; absolute; total.
totalità [-à], *n.f.* Totality, whole.
totalitario [totalitArio], *a.* Totalitarian.
totalizzatore, *n.m.* (*Racing*) Totalizator.
totalmente, *adv.* Totally, wholly, utterly.
totano [tOtano], *n.m.* (*Zool.*) Cuttlefish.
totocalcio [totocAlcio], *n.m.* Football pool.
tovaglia [tovAglia], *n.f.* (White) tablecloth.
tovagliolino, *n.m.* Bib, small napkin; baby's bib.
tovagliolo, *n.m.* Napkin, table-napkin; tray-cloth.
tozzo, *n.m.* Bit, morsel (of bread, etc.), small piece.
tozzo, *a.* Short, squat, thick-set, stumpy.
tozzolare, *v.t.* To beg for bread.
tra, *prep.* Between, among, amongst. **— noi,** between ourselves, amongst friends; **— me,** to myself; **— tutto,** all things considered [cp. **fra**].
trabaccolo [trabAccolo], *n.m.* (*Naut.*) Trawler, lugger; rickety vehicle, ramshackle contraption.
traballare, *v.i.* To reel, to stagger about, to sway, to rock; to jolt.
traballio [traballIo], *n.m.* Reeling, staggering, rocking, swaying; jolting.
traballone, *n.m.* Jolt, shake.
trabalzamento, *n.m.* Jolting, tossing.
trabalzare, *v.t.i.* To jolt; to swing, to toss; to shift, to move.
trabiccolo [trabIccolo], *n.m.* Warming-pan; airer (for linen); ramshackle vehicle.
traboccamento, *n.m.* Overflowing; weighing down.
traboccante, *a.* Overflowing, full to overflowing (with joy, etc.).
traboccare, *v.i.* To overflow, to run over; to weigh down. **Fare — la bilancia,** to turn the scales.
trabocchetto, *n.m.* Pitfall, snare; man-trap.
trabocchevole [trabocchEvole], *a.* Excessive, overflowing, superabundant.
trabocchevolmente, *adv.* Excessively.
trabocco, *n.m.* Overflow.
tracannare, *v.t.* To gulp down, to swallow, to drink at a draught.
traccagnotto, *a.* Squat, dumpy, short; sturdy, stocky.
traccheggiare, *v.t.* To dally, to temporize; to molest.
traccheggio [traccheggIo], *n.m.* Lingering, dallying; molestation.
traccia [trAccia], *n.f.* Footstep, footprint; trace; track, trail; sign, mark; outline, plan, groundwork. **Dare la —,** to give the outline; **seguire le tracce di,** to follow the traces of; **essere in — di,** to be on the track of.
tracciamento, *n.m.* Tracing, outlining, sketching.
tracciare, *v.t.* To delineate, to sketch, to lay down, to outline; to trace, to track.
tracciato, *n.m.* Sketch, outline; plan, scheme; trace. **Il — d'una strada,** layout of a street.
trace, *n.m.a.* Thracian.
trachea [trachEa], *n.f.* (*Anat.*) Trachea, windpipe.
tracheotomia [tracheotomIa], *n.f.* (*Med.*) Tracheotomy.
Tracia [trAcia], *n.f.* (*Geog.*) Thrace.
tracolla, *n.f.* Shoulder-belt; cross-belt. **A —,** across the shoulders, over the shoulder.
tracollamento, *n.m.* Collapse, downfall.
tracollare, *v.i.* To fall, to collapse; to overbalance, to stagger. **Fare — la bilancia,** to turn the scales.
tracollo, *n.m.* Downfall; break-down; (*Comm.*) slump. **Dare il —,** to give the finishing stroke.
tracoma, *n.m.* (*Med.*) Trachoma.
tracorrere [tracOrrere], *v.i.* To run swiftly.
tracotante, *a.* Arrogant, haughty, overbearing, over-weening.
tracotanza, *n.f.* Arrogance, haughtiness.
tradimento, *n.m.* Betrayal, treachery; treason. **Alto —,** high treason; (*colloq.*) **questo è un —,** this is foul play, this is a dirty trick.
tradire, *v.t.* To betray; to reveal, to give away (a secret); to deceive, to be unfaithful to.
tradirsi, *v.r.* To betray oneself, to give oneself away; to be false.
traditamente, *adv.* Treacherously.
traditore, traditrice, *n.m.f.a.* Traitor, traitress, betrayer; treacherous.
tradizionale, *a.* Traditional.
tradizionalismo, *n.m.* Traditionalism.
tradizione, *n.f.* Tradition; (*Law*) delivery.
tradotta, *n.f.* (*Mil.*) Leave-train; troop-train.
traducibile [traducIbile], *a.* Translatable.
tradurre, *v.t.* To translate; to turn, to render; to interpret; to express; to represent. **— in, — da,** to translate into, to translate from; **— alle carceri,** to take to prison; **— in atto,** to carry out.
traduttore, traduttrice, *n.m.f.* Translator. **— giurato,** sworn translator.
traduzione, *n.f.* Translation; (*Law*) transfer.
traente, *n.m.* (*Comm.*) Drawer.
trafelamento, *n.m.* Panting; fatigue.
trafelare, *v.i.* To pant; to labour, to exert oneself; to be tired out. **Essere trafelato,** to be out of breath.
trafficante, *n.m.* Trader, dealer; trafficker (in bad sense), intriguer.
trafficare, *v.i.* To deal, to trade; to traffic; to intrigue; to bustle; to carry on business.
traffico [trAffico], *n.m.* Traffic (in all senses); trade, commerce. **— stradale,** road traffic.
trafficone, *n.m.* Busybody, meddler.
trafiggere [trafIggere], *v.t.* To transfix, to pierce, to run through.
trafiggimento, *n.m.* Transfixion.
trafila, *n.f.* Draw-plate, wire-gauge; (*fig.*) string, series; regular course, routine; channel. **Bisogna seguire tutta la —,** the usual course must be followed.
trafilare, *v.t.* To draw wire.
trafilatura, *n.f.* Wire-drawing.
trafiletto, *n.m.* Snappy paragraph (in a newspaper); satirical criticism.
trafitta, trafittura, *n.f.* Piercing, sting; pang, stab (of pain).
traforamento, *n.m.* Perforation; boring (of tunnel, etc.).
traforare, *v.t.* To perforate, to pierce, to bore; to tunnel; to fretwork, to do open work in embroidery.
traforatore, *n.m.* Fretworker.

traforatrice, *n.f.* Piercing-machine.
traforo, *n.m.* Perforation; tunnel; fretwork, open-work (embroidery). **Il — del Sempione,** the Simplon Tunnel.
trafugamento, *n.m.* Stealing, purloining.
trafugare, *v.t.* To steal, to purloin, to take away, to carry off.
trafugatamente, *adv.* Stealthily, by stealth.
trafugo, *adv.* **Di —,** by stealth.
tragedia [tragEdia], *n.f.* Tragedy.
tragediografo [tragediOgrafo], *n.m.* Writer of tragedies, dramatist.
traghettare, *v.i.* To ferry across.
traghettatore, *n.m.* Ferry-man.
traghetto, *n.m.* Ferry. **Nave —,** ferry-boat.
tragica [trAgica], *n.f.* Tragedienne.
tragicamente, *adv.* Tragically.
tragicità [-à], *n.f.* Tragicality.
tragico [trAgico], *n.m.a.* Tragedian; tragic, tragical.
tragicomico [tragicOmico], *a.* Tragicomic.
tragicommedia [tragicommEdia], *n.f.* Tragicomedy.
tragittare, *v.i.* To pass through, to pass, to travel through.
tragitto, *n.m.* Trip, journey, voyage, crossing (by sea); way, distance. **Durante il —,** during the journey, voyage, etc.
traguardo, *n.m.* Back-sight (of gun); (*Sport*) winning-post; level. **Tagliare il —,** to pass the winning-post.
Traiano, *n.m.* (*Hist.*) Trajan.
traiettoria [traiettOria], *n.f.* Trajectory.
trainare, *v.t.* To drag, to haul.
traino [trAino], *n.m.* Sledge (for loads on ground); haulage; truck; waggon-load.
tralasciamento, *n.m.* Omission; interruption.
tralasciare, *v.t.* To omit, to leave out; to cease, to give up, to desist.
tralcio [trAlcio], *n.m.* Vine-shoot, vine-branch; shoot (of climbing plant); (*Anat.*) stump of umbilical cord.
traliccio [tralIccio], *n.m.* Sacking, buckram; trellis-work, lattice-work; grating.
tralice, *adv.* **In —,** obliquely; askance.
tralignamento, *n.m.* Degeneration.
tralignare, *v.i.* To degenerate, to fall off.
tralucere [tralUcere], *v.i.* To shine through, to glisten; to be transparent.
tram, tramvai, *n.m.* Tram, tram-car [cp. **tranvai**].
trama, *n.f.* Weft, woof; (*fig.*) plot, conspiracy. **Ordire una —,** to lay a plot.
tramaglio [tramAglio], *n.m.* Drag-net.
tramagnino, *n.m.* (*Theat.*) Pupil dancer, figurant.
tramandare, *v.t.* To transmit, to hand down, to convey. **— ai posteri,** to hand down to posterity; **memorie tramandate di padre in figlio,** traditions passed down from father to son.
tramare, *v.t.i.* To weave; to plot, to intrigue.
trambustare, *v.i.* To bustle, to fuss.
trambustio, trambusto [trambustIo], *n.m.* Bustle, fuss, disorder, confusion.
tramenare, *v.t.* To turn upside down, to rummage about.
tramenio [tramenIo], *n.m.* Bustling, bustle, fuss.
tramescolare, *v.t.* To mix up, to blend.
tramestare, *v.i.* To jumble up.
tramestio [tramestIo], *n.m.* Jumbling up, things topsy-turvy, muddle.
tramezza, *n.f.* Division; partition wall; second sole (of shoe).
tramezzabile [tramezzAbile], *a.* Divisible.
tramezzamento, *n.m.* Insertion; division. **Senza —,** uninterruptedly.
tramezzare, *v.t.* To insert, to partition, to divide, to separate.
tramezzatamente, *adv.* In a mixed way.
tramezzato, *a.* Interrupted.
tramezzo, *n.m.* Partition wall, bulkhead; interval.
tramezzo, *prep.* Amongst; between, among.
tramischiare, *v.t.* To mix, to mingle [cp. **mischiare**].
tramite [trAmite], *n.m.* Way, path; agency, medium, channel. **Per il — regolare,** through the proper channel; **per vostro —,** by your help.
tramoggia [tramOggia], *n.f.* Hopper, mill-hopper.
tramontana, *n.f.* North wind; north. **Perdere la —,** to lose one's bearings, to be put out of countenance.
tramontano, *a.* Northerly, from the north.
tramontare, *v.i.* To set, to go down, to decline, to fade, to disappear, to wane.
tramonto, *n.m.* Setting, sunset; decline, wane. **Il — della luna,** the setting of the moon; **un bel —,** a fine sunset; **essere sul —,** to be on the wane.
tramortimento, *n.m.* Swoon, fainting-fit.
tramortire, *v.t.i.* To stun; to faint, to fall senseless.
tramortito, *p.p.a.* Senseless, inanimate.
trampoli [trAmpoli], *n.m.pl.* Stilts. **Sui —,** on stilts.
trampolieri, *n.m.pl.* (*Zool.*) Waders (birds).
trampolino, *n.m.* Spring-board, diving-board.
tramutabile [tramutAbile], *a.* Transmutable.
tramutabilità [-à], *n.f.* Transmutability.
tramutamento, *n.m.* Transmutation, change.
tramutare, *v.t.* To change, to alter, to transmute; to decant (wine).
tramutarsi, *v.r.* To be transmuted, to become modified.
tramutatore, *n.m.* Transmuter.
tramutazione, tramuta, *n.f.* Transmutation, change; displacement, removal; decanting.
tramvai, tramvia, *n.f.* Tramway [cp. **tranvia**].
trancia [trAncia], *n.f.* Slice, rasher (of bacon); shears.
tranciare, *v.t.* To cut, to slice.
tranello, *n.m.* Snare, trap; pitfall; plot. **Tendere un —,** to set a trap; **cadere in un —,** to fall into a snare.
trangugiamento, *n.m.* Swallowing, gulping.
trangugiare, *v.t.* To swallow, to gulp down; to gobble up.
trangugiatore, trangugiatrice, *n.m.f.* Guzzler, glutton.
tranne, *adv.* Save, except, excepting, but.
tranquillamente, *adv.* Tranquilly.
tranquillante, *n.m.* (*Med.*) Tranquillizer, sedative.
tranquillare, tranquillizzare, *v.t.* To tranquillize, to quieten, to calm, to soothe.
tranquillità [-à], *n.f.* Tranquillity, peacefulness, serenity, calmness, quiet.

tranquillizzarsi, *v.r.* To become quiet, to quiet down.
tranquillo, *a.* Peaceful, calm, tranquil, still, serene. **Lasciami —,** let me alone; **mare —,** calm sea.
transalpino, *a.* Transalpine.
transatlantico [transatlAntico], *n.m.a.* (*Naut.*) Liner; transatlantic.
transatto [cp. **transigere**].
transazione, *n.f.* Transaction; (*Law*) agreement, compromise, concession; composition (debtor's).
transetto, *n.m.* (*Arch.*) Transept.
transeunte, *a.* (*Lit.*) Transient.
transfuga, *n.m.* (*Lit.*) Deserter, fugitive.
transiberiana, *n.f.* Trans-Siberian railway.
transigere [transIgere], *v.i.* To come to terms, to compromise; to transact. (*Comm.*) **Transatto e estinto,** finally settled.
transitante, *n.m.* Passer-by.
transitare, *v.i.* To pass through, to go by. **Merci transitanti,** goods in transit.
transitivamente, *adv.* Transitively.
transitivo, *n.m.a.* (*Gram.*) Transitive.
transito [trAnsito], *n.m.* Transit; passage; route. **Vietato il —,** no thoroughfare.
transitoriamente, *adv.* Transiently.
transitorio [transitOrio], *a.* Transitory, temporary, transient, momentary.
transizione, *n.f.* Transition. **Periodo di —,** period of transition.
translucido [translUcido], *a.* Translucent.
transpadano, *a.* (*Geog.*) Beyond the Po, on the left bank of the Po.
transunto, *n.m.* Summary, précis, extract; certified copy [cp. **sunto**].
transustanziazione, *n.f.* (*Eccles.*) Transubstantiation.
trantran, tran tran, *n.m.* (*colloq.*) Routine, hum-drum happening. **Il solito —,** the same old thing.
tranvai, *n.m.* Tram, tram-car.
tranvia, *n.m.* Tramway, tram-line; tram service.
tranviario [tranviArio], *a.* Tram, of trams.
tranviere, *n.m.* Tram-driver or conductor.
trapanamento, *n.m.* Drilling, boring, piercing; (*Med.*) trepanning.
trapanare, *v.t.* To bore, to drill, to perforate, to pierce; (*Med.*) to trepan.
trapanatura, trapanazione, *n.f.* Perforation, boring; (*Med.*) trepanning. **— del cranio,** trepanning of the skull.
trapano [trApano], *n.m.* Drill, borer, auger; (*Med.*) trepanning saw.
trapassabile [trapassAbile], *a.* Penetrable, pierceable.
trapassamento, *n.m.* Transfixing, piercing, boring.
trapassare, *v.t.i.* To transfix, to run through; to bore; to cross; to pass beyond; to trespass; to die, to pass away.
trapassato, *n.m.* (*Gram.*) Past-perfect, pluperfect tense.
trapassato, *a.* Dead, deceased.
trapasso, *n.m.* Death; transit, passage; transition; (*Law*) transfer, conveyance, assignment.
trapelamento, *n.m.* Leakage.
trapelare, *v.i.* To leak (in all senses), to leak out, to transpire; to ooze out. **Non trapelava nulla,** nothing leaked out.
trapelo, *n.m.* Additional draught-horse; (*Naut.*) tug-rope, hawser.
trapestio [trapestIo], *n.m.* Stamping (of the feet).
trapezio [trapEzio], *n.m.* (*Geom.*) Trapezium; trapeze.
trapiantamento, *n.m.* (*Med.*) Transplantation, graft; removal, transfer.
trapiantare, *v.t.* To transplant, to graft, to transfer.
trapiantarsi, *v.r.* To emigrate, to settle (abroad).
trapianto, *n.m.* (*Med.*) Graft. **— di ossa,** bone-grafting.
trappista (*pl.* **trappisti**), *n.m.a.* (*Eccles.*) Trappist.
trappoco, *adv.* Shortly, soon.
trappola [trAppola], *n.f.* Trap, pitfall, snare. **— da topi,** mouse-trap; **cadere in —,** to be caught in a trap; **tendere una —,** to set a trap.
trappolare, *v.t.* To entrap.
trappoleria [trappolerIa], *n.f.* Deceit, trick, swindle, deception.
trappolino, *n.m.* [cp. **trampolino**].
trappolone, *n.m.* Trickster, shady fellow.
trapunta, *n.f.* Quilt, counterpane.
trapuntare, *v.t.* To quilt, to embroider.
trapunto, *n.m.* Embroidery, quilting.
trarre, *v.t.i.* To draw, to pull, to drag, to haul; to lead; to fling; to heave (a sigh); to go, to approach. **Lo trasse in disparte,** he took him aside; **— in inganno,** to deceive, to trick; **ad un — di sasso,** at a stone's throw; (*Comm.*) **— a vista,** to draw at sight; **— la sete,** to quench one's thirst; **— vendetta,** to take vengeance.
trarsi, *v.r.* To draw. **— d'impaccio,** to get out of a scrape [cp. **tirarsi**].
trasalire, *v.i.* To start, to jump, to spring. **Far —,** to startle.
trasandamento, *n.m.* Negligence.
trasandare, *v.t.* To neglect.
trasandato, *a.* Uncared for, neglected, neglectful; slovenly, shabby; shambling.
trasbordare, *v.t.* To tranship; to transfer.
trasbordatura, *n.f.* Transhipping.
trasbordo, *n.m.* Transhipment; transference.
trascegliere [trascEgliere], *v.t.* To choose, to select, to single out, to sort.
trascendentale, *a.* Transcendental.
trascendentalmente, *adv.* Transcendentally.
trascendente, *a.* Transcendent.
trascendenza, *n.f.* Transcendence.
trascendentalismo, *n.m.* Transcendentalism.
trascendere [trascEndere], *v.i.* To transcend, to surpass, to rise above, to exceed; to exaggerate; to let oneself go (in excess, etc.). **— alle mani,** to come to blows.
trascendimento, *n.m.* Transcendence; excess.
trasceso, *p.p.a.* Transcended; gone too far.
trascinamento, *n.m.* Dragging, drawing.
trascinare, *v.t.* To drag, to draw, to trail; to carry; to go heavily; to urge on, to stir; to carry away. **— l'esistenza,** to drag out one's existence; **— i piedi,** to drag one's feet, to shamble, to shuffle one's feet; **— nel fango,** to drag through the mud.
trascinarsi, *v.r.* To drag oneself along, to crawl; to lag behind.
trascoloramento, *n.m.* Paling, changing colour; discoloration.

trascolorare, *v.t.i.* To discolour, to change the colour of.
trascolorarsi, *v.r.* To turn pale; to blush, to change colour.
trascorrere [trascOrrere], *v.t.i.* To pass, to spend (time); to elapse; to pass over; to travel, to go through, to roam; to omit (to mention). **— le vacanze in campagna,** to pass one's holidays in the country.
trascorrevole [trascorrEvole], *a.* Transient.
trascorrevolmente, *adv.* Transiently, in passing.
trascorrimento, *n.m.* Lapse (of time), passage, passing.
trascorso, *n.m.* Lapse of time; fault, lapse, error.
trascorso, *p.p.a.* Past, elapsed; travelled.
trascrittore, trascrittrice, *n.m.f.* Transcriber, copyist.
trascrivere [trascrIvere], *v.t.* To transcribe, to copy out.
trascrizione, *n.f.* Transcription; transfer; fair copy.
trascurabile [trascurAbile], *a.* Negligible.
trascuraggine, trascuranza [trascurAggine], *n.f.* Carelessness, negligence; heedlessness, neglect, disregard, indifference.
trascurare, *v.t.* To neglect, to disregard; to ignore, to overlook; to slight; to omit. **— un consiglio,** to disregard advice.
trascurataggine, trascuratezza [cp. **trascuraggine**].
trascurato, *a.* Careless, slovenly, negligent.
trasecolamento, *n.m.* Amazement.
trasecolare, *v.i.* To be astonished, to be taken aback; to be set wondering; to be amazed, to be bewildered.
trasferibile [trasferIbile], *a.* Transferable.
trasferimento, *n.m.* Transfer, removal; assignment.
trasferire, *v.t.* To transfer, to remove, to convey; to transport; to postpone; to assign.
trasferirsi, *v.r.* To change one's place, to remove (one's home); to leave one's seat; to go, to come.
trasferta, *n.f.* Transfer; travelling allowance, expenses.
trasfiguramento, *n.m.* Transfiguration.
trasfigurare, trasfigurarsi, *v.t.r.* To transfigure, to transform; to be transfigured, to be transformed.
trasfigurazione, *n.f.* Transfiguration, transformation.
trasfondere [trasfOndere], *v.t.* To transfuse, to inspire.
trasformabile [trasformAbile], *a.* Transformable.
trasformamento, *n.m.* Transformation.
trasformare, *v.t.* To transform, to turn into, to convert, to alter.
trasformativo, *a.* Transformative.
trasformatore, *n.m.* (*Elect.*) Transformer.
trasformazione, *n.f.* Transformation, conversion, change.
trasformismo, *n.m.* Transformism.
trasformista (*pl.* **trasformisti**), *n.m.* Transformist; quick-change artist.
trasfusione, *n.f.* Transfusion. **— del sangue,** transfusion of blood.
trasgredire, *v.t.i.* To transgress, to trespass; to violate, to infringe; to disobey.
trasgredimento, trasgressione, *n.m.f.* Transgression; infringement.
trasgressore, *n.m.* Transgressor.
traslatamente, *adv.* Metaphorically, figuratively.
traslatare, *v.t.* (*obs.*) To transfer, to remove.
traslato, *n.m.a.* Metaphor; metaphorical.
traslazione, *n.f.* Transfer, conveyance, removal; (*Eccles.*) translation.
traslocare, *v.t.i.* To remove; to displace, to transfer; to change address.
trasloco, traslocamento, *n.m.* Removal; transfer, displacement. **Far —,** to remove; **furgone da —,** furniture-van, pantechnicon.
traslucente, traslucido [traslUcido], *a.* Translucent.
trasmettere [trasmEttere], *v.t.* To transmit, to forward, to send; to communicate, to convey; to hand on; (*Radio*) to broadcast. **— una comunicazione,** to forward a communication.
trasmettitore, *n.m.* Transmitter.
trasmigramento, *n.m.* Transmigration.
trasmigrare, *v.i.* To transmigrate.
trasmigrazione, *n.f.* Transmigration. **— delle anime,** transmigration of souls.
trasmissibile [trasmissIbile], *a.* Transmittable, negotiable.
trasmissione, *n.f.* Transmission; conveyance, transfer; (*Radio*) broadcast; (*Mech.*) shafting. **Cinghia di —,** conveyor-belt.
trasmissore, *n.m.* Transmitter
trasmittente, *n.m.* (*Radio*) transmitter, transmitting set (or station).
trasmodamento, *n.m.* Excess.
trasmodare, *v.i.* To exceed, to be immoderate, to go to excess.
trasmodatamente, *adv.* Excessively, immoderately.
trasmodato, *a.* Excessive, immoderate.
trasmutare, *v.t.* To transmute [cp. **tramutare**].
trasognamento, *n.m.* Abstraction, dream-like mood; astonishment.
trasognare, *v.i.* To dream, to day-dream.
trasognato, *a.* Dreamy, absent-minded, abstracted; lost in reverie, day-dreaming.
traspadano, *a.* Across the Po [cp. **transpadano**].
trasparente, *a.* Transparent; pellucid, clear; manifest, evident.
trasparenza, *n.f.* Transparency, transparence; clearness.
trasparire, *v.i.* To be transparent; to transpire; to appear, to be disclosed; to be obvious. **Dal suo viso traspariva l'emozione,** his face betrayed his emotion.
traspirare, *v.i.* To perspire, to sweat; to transpire, to appear.
traspirazione, *n.f.* Sweat, perspiration; transpiration.
trasporre, *v.t.* To transpose [cp. **trasportare**].
trasportabile [trasportAbile], *a.* Transferable, conveyable, removable.
trasportare, *v.t.* To transport, to convey, to transfer, to carry, to remove; (*Mus.*) to transpose. **Sentirsi trasportato verso una persona,** to feel drawn to a person.
trasportarsi, *v.r.* To betake oneself.
trasportatore, *n.m.* Carrier.

trasportazione, *n.f.* Transportation.
trasporto, *n.m.* Transportation, transport, conveyance, removal; carriage, porterage, haulage; rapture; (*Naut.*) transport ship, troopship. **— di gioia,** transport of joy; **mezzo di —,** means of transport; **spese di —,** cost of carriage; **— funebre,** funeral procession.
trasposizione, *n.f.* Transposition.
trassato, *n.m.* (*Comm.*) Drawee; payee.
trassinare, *v.t.* To misuse.
trasteverino, *n.m.a.* Of or from Trastevere (Rome).
trastulla, *a.* **Dar l'erba — a,** to feed with vain hopes.
trastullamento, *n.m.* Entertainment, amusement.
trastullare, *v.t.* To amuse, to entertain.
trastullarsi, *v.r.* To amuse oneself, to play, to trifle.
trastullo, *n.m.* Toy, plaything, amusement; pastime; laughing-stock.
trasudamento, *n.m.* Perspiring, perspiration.
trasudare, *v.t.i.* To perspire; to ooze through.
trasumanare, *v.t.* To spiritualize.
trasversale, *n.f.a.* Transverse, transversal; side-street, transverse line.
trasverso, *a.* Transverse.
trasvolare, *v.t.* To fly across; to pass over.
trasvolata, *n.f.* Flight across; Atlantic flight.
tratta, *n.f.* Tug, pull; (*Rail., etc.*) stretch, distance; (*Comm.*) draft; draw (of lots, etc.); period; throng; seine-net. **La — degli schiavi,** the slave-trade; **— a vista,** sight draft; **— dei bianchi,** sweating-system.
trattabile [trattAbile], *a.* Tractable, easily handled, manageable, pliant, docile.
trattabilità [-à], *n.f.* Tractability, docility.
trattabilmente, *adv.* Tractably.
trattamento, *n.m.* Treatment; treat; reception, entertainment; use, usage; dealing; salary, emolument; allowance (of food, etc.); catering (at an hotel, etc.). **Cattivo —,** ill treatment.
trattare, *v.t.i.* To treat, to use, to handle, to employ, to deal with; to treat of, to speak or write of; to discuss; to frequent. **— una materia,** to handle a subject; **— male,** to ill-treat; **— da amico,** to treat as a friend; **— molti affari,** to transact much business; **— chimicamente,** to treat chemically; **— onestamente,** to deal honestly [cp. **trattarsi**].
trattario [trattArio], *n.m.* (*Comm.*) Drawee.
trattarsi, *v.r.* To treat oneself; to be a question of. **Si tratta del mio onore,** my honour is at stake; **si tratta di pochi giorni,** it's a matter of a few days ; **non si tratta di questo,** that is not the point; **— male,** to fare badly; **— bene,** to live well, to regale oneself.
trattatista (*pl.* **trattatisti**), *n.m.* Essayist, writer of treatises.
trattativa, *n.f.* Negotiation, dealing. **Essere in trattative con uno,** to be in negotiations with someone; **trattative in corso,** pending negotiations.
trattato, *n.m.* Treaty; treatise. **— segreto,** secret treaty; **— di pace,** peace treaty; **— di aritmetica,** arithmetical treatise.
trattazione, *n.f.* Treatment (of a subject, etc.); management (of a business).
tratteggiare, *v.t.* (*Art*) To hatch; to outline; to sketch, to delineate.
tratteggio [trattEggio], *n.m.* Outline, sketching, delineating; cross-hatching.
trattenere, *v.t.* To keep back, to hold back; to detain; to deduct, to retain; to entertain, to amuse; to keep waiting. **— il riso,** to suppress one's laughter.
trattenersi, *v.r.* To stay, to remain; to refrain from.
trattenimento, *n.m.* Entertainment; reception, social, conversazione; detention, delay; stay, sojourn.
trattenitore, trattenitrice, *n.m.f.* Entertainer.
trattenuta, *n.f.* (*Comm.*) Deduction, amount deducted.
trattino, *n.m.* (*Print.*) Hyphen, dash.
tratto, *n.m.* Extent, period (of time); way, distance, tract, space; pull, tug, drag; stroke; act, deed; ways, manners, behaviour; features; passage (in a book, etc.). **— d'unione,** hyphen; **— di bontà,** good deed; **tutto a un —, a un —,** all of a sudden, suddenly; **di — in —, — —,** from time to time; **camminare per un lungo —,** to walk a long way; **un — di strada,** a stretch of road; **ci corre un buon —,** it's a good way off; **ha un — signorile,** he has refined manners; **i tratti del viso,** the features; **un — di spirito,** a flash of wit; **un — di terra,** a tract of land.
tratto, *p.p.a.* Drawn, dragged, led, pulled [cp. **trarre**].
trattone, *prep.* Except, save, excluding [cp. **tranne**].
trattore, *n.m.* Innkeeper, landlord, restaurant-keeper; (*Agric.*) tractor.
trattoria [trattorIa], *n.f.* Restaurant, inn, eating-house.
trattrice, *n.f.* (*Agric.*) Tractor; traction-engine.
trattura, *n.f.* Reeling, drawing (of silk).
tratturo, *n.m.* Cattle-track.
trauma [trAuma], *n.m.* (*Med.*) Trauma ; shock.
travagliare, *v.t.* To afflict, to distress, to torment; to overwork; to digest with difficulty. **Un'esistenza travagliata,** a wretched life.
travagliarsi, *v.r.* To worry oneself; to toil.
travaglio [travAglio], *n.m.* Pain, torment; labour, toil. **— di stomaco,** sickness, vomiting.
travagliosamente, *adv.* Toilsomely.
travaglioso, *a.* Toilsome, tiring.
travalicare, *v.t.* To cross over, to pass over; to go beyond; to overstep.
travamento, *n.m.* (*Arch.*) Framework of joists and beams.
travasare, *v.t.* To decant, to pour off; to re-pot.
travaso, *n.m.* Decanting, pouring off. (*Med.*) **— di sangue,** extravasation of blood.
travata, *n.f.* (*Arch.*) Truss.
travatura, *n.f.* (*Arch.*) Roof-timbers; rafter; girder.
trave, *n.f.* Beam; rafter; girder. **— armata,** reinforced girder.
travedere, *v.i.* To see imperfectly, to perceive dimly; to catch a glimpse of; to be very fond of.
travedimento, *n.m.* Distorted vision.

traveggole [travEggole], *n.f.pl.* Dimness of sight, distorted vision. **Avere le —,** to see double, to mistake one thing for another; to delude oneself.
traversa, *n.f.* Cross-bar, cross-piece; cross-road; (*Rail.*) sleeper; side-turning.
traversale, *a.* Transversal.
traversamente, *adv.* Transversely, slantwise.
traversamento, *n.m.* Slant.
traversare, *v.t.* To cross, to traverse.
traversata, *n.f.* (*Naut.*) Crossing, passage.
traversia [traversIa], *n.f.* Misfortune, mishap, *pl.* hardships.
traversiere, *n.m.* (*Naut.*) Ferry-boat.
traversina, *n.f.* (*Rail.*) Sleeper.
traversino, *n.m.* Bolster; (*Naut.*) brace.
traverso, *n.m.* Breadth; (*Naut.*) beam.
traverso, *a.* Cross, transverse, aslant, oblique; underhand, wrong, shady; adverse. **Mare —,** rough sea; **di —,** sideways, askance; **vie traverse,** shady methods; **tutto va a —,** everything goes wrong; **guardar di —,** to look askance.
traversone, *n.m.* Girder; cross-piece; (*Naut.*) north-easterly gale.
travertino, *n.m.* (*Geol.*) Travertine.
travestimento, *n.m.* Disguise; make-up.
travestire, *v.t.* To disguise; to travesty; to burlesque; to misrepresent.
travestirsi, *v.r.* To disguise oneself.
travetto, *n.m.* (*Arch.*) Joist, small beam; (*colloq.*) clerk, quill-driver.
traviamento, *n.m.* Perversion, corruption; deviation.
traviare, *v.t.* To mislead, to lead astray, to pervert.
traviarsi, *v.r.* To go astray, to lose one's way, to lose the right path.
traviata, *n.f.* Fallen woman.
travicello, *n.m.* Joist, small beam.
travisamento, *n.m.* Travesty, distortion, misrepresentation.
travisare, *v.t.* To distort (truth, etc.), to misrepresent; to disguise; to conceal.
travisarsi, *v.r.* To disguise oneself; to put on a mask.
travolgente, *a.* Sweeping, overwhelming.
travolgere [travOlgere], *v.t.* To overturn, to overthrow, to upset; to sweep before it, to carry away. **— gli occhi,** to roll the eyes.
travolgimento, *n.m.* Overthrow, overturning.
travolto, *p.p.a.* Upset, knocked down; overturned; upside down.
trazione, *n.f.* Traction, haulage. **— animale,** horse-traction; **— elettrica,** electric traction.
tre, *n.m.a.* Three. **A — a —,** three by three; **la regola del —,** the rule of three; **— volte tanto,** three times as much.
trealberi [treAlberi], *n.m.* (*Naut.*) Three-masted vessel, three-master.
trebbia [trEbbia], *n.f.* Threshing; flail.
Trebbiano, *n.m.* Variety of white wine
trebbiare, *v.t.i.* (*Agric.*) To thresh.
trebbiatore, *n.m.* Thresher.
trebbiatrice, *n.f.* Threshing-machine.
trebbiatura, *n.f.* Threshing.
trecca, *n.f.* Market-woman.
treccia [trEccia], *n.f.* Tress (of hair), plait, pigtail; straw plait.
trecciaio, trecciaiolo [trecciAio], *n.m.* Straw-plaiter.
trecentesimo [trecentEsimo], *a.* Three-hundredth.
trecentista, *n.m.f.* Writer or artist of the 14th century.
trecento, *n.m.a.* Three hundred; the 14th century.
tredicenne, *a.* Thirteen years old.
tredicesimo [tredicEsimo], *a.* Thirteenth.
tredici [trEdici], *n.m.a.* Thirteen, thirteenth.
tredicimila, *a.* Thirteen thousand.
tredicina, *n.f.* About thirteen.
trefolo [trEfolo], *n.m.* Strand (of a rope).
tregenda, *n.f.* Witches' sabbath, pandemonium.
treggia [trEggia], *n.f.* Sledge.
treggiata, *n.f.* Sledge-load.
treggiatore, *n.m.* Sledge-driver.
tregua, *n.f.* Truce, respite, rest, armistice. **Non dar —,** to give no rest.
tremacuore, tremacore, *n.m.* Palpitation; anxiety.
tremante, *a.* Shuddering, trembling, quivering.
tremare, *v.i.* To tremble, to shudder, to quiver; to quake; to shiver; to flicker. **— dal freddo,** to shiver with cold; **— di paura,** to tremble with fright; **la mano mi trema,** my hand shakes.
tremarella, *n.f.* Nerviness, anxiety; (*colloq.*) funk. **Aver la —,** to be in a funk, to be in a stew.
tremebondo, *a.* Trembling, shuddering.
tremendamente, *adv.* Terribly, dreadfully.
tremendo, *a.* Terrible, dreadful, awful, fearful; tremendous.
trementina, *n.f.* Turpentine.
tremila, *a.* Three thousand.
tremillesimo [tremillEsimo], *a.* Three-thousandth.
tremito [trEmito], *n.m.* Trembling, shaking, quivering; flickering.
tremolamento, *n.m.* Trembling; twinkling, glittering.
tremolante, *a.* Trembling, quivering; flickering, twinkling.
tremolare, *v.i.* To shake, to tremble; to vibrate; to quake; to flicker; to shimmer; to falter (in speech).
tremolante, *a.* Shivering (with cold).
tremolio [tremolIo], *n.m.* Continual trembling, quivering; flickering.
tremolo [trEmolo], *n.m.a.* (*Mus.*) Tremolo; trembling, tremulous.
tremore, *n.m.* Tremor.
tremoto, *n.m.* Earthquake; (*colloq.*) fidgety child [cp. **terremoto**].
treno (1), *n.m.* Train (in all senses); retinue; pace, rate; style (of life). **— merci,** goods train; **— diretto,** through train; **— direttissimo,** express train; **— omnibus,** slow train; **perdere il —,** to miss the train; **— blindato,** armoured train; **— di lusso,** train de luxe; **un — di vita,** a way of life; **tenere un gran —,** to live in style.
treno (2), *n.m.* (*Poet.*) Threnody, lament.
trenodia [trenodIa], *n.f.* Threnody.
trenta, *n.m.a.* Thirty, thirtieth.
trentamila, *a.* Thirty thousand.
trentenne, *a.* Thirty year old.

trentennio [trentEnnio], *n.m.* Space of thirty years.
trentesimo [trentEsimo], *a.* Thirtieth.
trentina, *n.f.* About thirty. **Uomo sulla —,** a man of about thirty; **c'era una — di persone,** there were about thirty people.
Trentino, *n.m.* (*Geog.*) The Trentino.
Trento, *n.m.* (*Geog.*) Trent (Italy), Trento.
trentunesimo [trentunEsimo], *a.* Thirty-first.
trentuno, *a.* Thirty-one.
trepidamente, *adv.* Timorously.
trepidante, *a.* Anxious, apprehensive; trembling; timorous.
trepidantemente, *adv.* Anxiously, tremblingly.
trepidanza [cp. **trepidazione**].
trepidare, *v.i.* To tremble with fear; to be alarmed; to be anxious, to be agitated.
trepidazione, trepidanza, *n.f.* Alarm, flurry, trepidation, fear.
trepido [trEpido], *a.* Timorous, trembling; anxious.
treppiede, treppiedi, *n.m.* Tripod; trivet; three-legged stool.
tresca, *n.f.* (Love) intrigue, affair, liaison; country dance.
trescare, *v.i.* To have an intrigue with; to caper about.
trescone, *n.m.* Noisy country dance.
tresette, *n.m.* An Italian card-game.
trespolo [trEspolo], *n.m.* Trestle, support; rickety vehicle.
trevigiano, trevisano, *n.m.a.* Of Treviso.
Treviri [trEviri], *n.f.* (*Geog.*) Trèves, Trier.
triaca, *n.f.* (*Hist. Med.*) Theriac.
triade [trIade], *n.f.* Triad.
triangolare, *v.t.* To triangulate.
triangolare, *a.* Triangular.
triangolarmente, *adv.* Triangularly.
triangolazione, *n.f.* Triangulation.
triangolo [triAngolo], *n.m.* Triangle.
tribolamento, *n.m.* Harassing; tribulation.
tribolare, *v.t.i.* To vex, to afflict, to torment, to harass; to endure; to worry, to be distressed.
tribolato, *p.p.a.* Oppressed, vexed; worried.
tribolazione, *n.f.* Tribulation, affliction; distress, suffering.
tribolo [trIbolo], *n.m.* Tribulation; affliction; (*Bot.*) bramble, thorn, briar.
tribordo, *n.m.* (*Naut.*) Starboard.
tribù [-ù], *n.f.* Tribe, clan.
tribuna, *n.f.* Tribune, platform, pulpit, rostrum; (*Racing, Sports, etc.*) stand, grandstand; (*Mus.*) organ-loft. **— della stampa,** reporters' gallery.
tribunale, *n.m.* Tribunal, court of justice; bench.
tribunalmente, *adv.* As a judge, from the tribunal.
tribunesco, tribunizio [tribunIzio], *a.* Of a tribune, demagogic.
tribuno, *n.m.* (*Hist.*) Tribune; magistrate; demagogue.
tributare, *v.t.* To pay tribute to, to offer, to pay, to bestow (homage, etc.).
tributario [tributArio], *n.m.a.* Tributary. **Il — di un fiume,** a river's tributary.
tributo, *n.m.* Tribute (in all senses); debt.
tricheco, *n.m.* (*Zool.*) Walrus.
triciclo, *n.m.* Tricycle.
tricipite [tricIpite], *a.* Three-headed; (*Anat.*) triceps.
tricolore, *n.m.a.* Tricolour (flag); three-coloured.
tricorne, *a.* Three-horned.
tricorno, *n.m.* Three-cornered hat.
tricromia [tricromIa], *n.f.* Three-colour printing.
tric trac, *n.m.* (Game of) backgammon.
tricuspide, tricuspidale [tricUspide], *a.* Tricuspid.
tridentato, *a.* Tridentate.
tridente, *n.m.* Trident; hay-fork, pitch-fork.
tridentino, *a.* Of Trent. **Concilio —,** Council of Trent.
triduo [trIduo], *n.m.* (*Eccles.*) Triduo, triduum.
triennale, *a.* Triennial.
triennalmente, *adv.* Triennially.
trienne, *a.* Three years old, lasting three years.
triennio [triEnnio], *n.m.* Period of three years.
triestino, *a.* Of Trieste.
trifase, *a.* (*Elect.*) Three-phase.
trifogliato, *a.* (*Bot.*) Trifoliate, three-leaved.
trifoglio [trifOglio], *n.m.* (*Bot.*) Trefoil, clover, shamrock.
trifora [trIfora], *n.f.* (*Arch.*) Window divided into three by mullions.
triforcato, triforcuto, *a.* Trifurcate, three-pronged.
triforio [trifOrio], *n.m.* (*Arch.*) Triforium.
triforme, *a.* Triform.
trigemino [trigEmino], *n.m.a.* Triplet; (*Anat.*) trigeminus. **Fratelli trigemini,** boy triplets.
trigesimo [trigEsimo], *a.* Thirtieth.
triglia [trIglia], *n.f.* (*Zool.*) Mullet, red mullet. **Fare gli occhi di —,** to cast sheep's eyes at.
triglifo [trIglifo], *n.m.* (*Arch.*) Triglyph.
trigonometria [trigonometrIa], *n.f.* Trigonometry.
trigonometrico [trigonomEtrico], *a.* Trigonometric.
trilaterale, trilatero [trilAtero], *a.* Trilateral.
trilingue [trilIngue], *a.* Trilingual.
trillare, *v.i.* To trill; to ring, to sound; to warble (of birds).
trillo, *n.m.* Trill, trilling; shrill sound; (*Mus.*) shake.
trilobato, *a.* Trilobate.
trilogia [trilogIa], *n.f.* Trilogy.
trilustre, *a.* Fifteen-year, fifteen years old.
trimestrale, *a.* Quarterly, every three months.
trimestralmente, *adv.* Quarterly.
trimestre, *n.m.* Quarter (of a year), three months; quarter's rent, salary, etc.
trimotore, *n.m.* (*Aviat.*) Three-engined plane.
trimpellare, *v.i.* To stagger, to reel [cp. **strimpellare**].
trimpellio [trimpellIo], *n.m.* Staggering, reeling about.
trina, *n.f.* Lace, point-lace; fringe.
Trinacria, *n.f.* (*Geog. Hist.*) Sicily.
trinaia [trinAia], *n.f.* Lace-maker, lace-seller.
trinare, *v.t.* To deck with lace, to trim with lace.
trincare (1), *v.t.* (*Naut.*) To whip, to frap, to lash.
trincare (2), *v.t.i.* To drink; to tipple, to toss off (a drink); to clink glasses, to hob-nob.
trincata, *n.f.* Draught, deep drink; tippling.

trincatore, *n.m.* Tippler.
trincea, trincera [trincEa], *n.f.* (*Mil.*) Trench.
trinceramento, *n.m.* Entrenchment.
trincerare, *v.t.* To entrench.
trincerarsi, *v.r.* To entrench oneself; to dig in.
trincerista (*pl.* **trinceristi**), *n.m.* (*colloq.*) Soldier who served in the trenches.
trincetto, *n.m.* Shoemaker's knife; paring-knife.
trinchetta, *n.f.* (*Naut.*) Storm-sail.
trinchetto, *n.m.* (*Naut.*) Foremast; foresail.
trinciante, *n.m.* Carving-knife, carver.
trinciapaglia [trinciapAglia], *n.m.* (*Agric.*) Hay-cutter.
trinciaradici, *n.m.* Turnip-cutter, slicer.
trinciare, *v.t.i.* To carve, to cut up; (*fig.*) to talk wildly. **— sentenze,** to make sweeping assertions; **— i panni addosso a,** to slander.
trinciarsi, *v.r.* To split; to tear in the folds.
trinciato, *n.m.* Cut tobacco.
trinciatura, *n.f.* Carving.
trincone, *n.m.* Heavy drinker.
trinità [-à], *n.f.* Trinity. (*Geog.*) **La Trinità,** Trinidad.
trinitario [trinitArio], *n.m.a.* Trinitarian.
trino, *a.* (*Astron.*) Trine.
trinomio [trinOmio], *n.m.* (*Math.*) Trinomial.
trio, *n.m.* Trio, set of three.
trionfale, *a.* Triumphal.
trionfalmente, *adv.* Triumphally.
trionfante, *a.* Triumphant, victorious.
trionfantemente, *adv.* Triumphantly.
trionfare, *v.i.* To triumph; to conquer, to prevail; to exult. **— di,** to triumph over.
trionfatore, *n.m.* Victor, conqueror.
trionfo, *n.m.* Triumph; success, victory; (*Cards*) trump; epergne. **Portare in —,** to carry shoulder-high, to bear in triumph; **— da tavola,** centrepiece for a table, epergne.
Trioni, *n.m.pl.* (*Astron.*) Great and Little Bear.
trionice [triOnice], *n.f.* (*Zool.*) Snapping turtle.
tripartire, *v.t.* To divide in three.
tripartito, *p.p.a.* Tripartite.
tripartizione, *n.f.* Tripartition.
tripetalo [tripEtalo], *a.* Tripetalous.
tripla, *n.f.* (*Mus.*) Triple time.
triplano, *n.m.* (*Aviat.*) Triplane.
triplicare, *v.t.* To triple, to treble, to triplicate.
triplicato, *p.p.a.* Triplicated. **In —,** in a set of three.
triplicazione, *n.f.* Triplication.
triplice [trIplice], *a.* Triple, treble, threefold. **La — alleanza,** the Triple Alliance.
triplicemente, *adv.* Triply.
triplicità [-à], *n.f.* Tripleness; triad.
triplo, *n.m.a.* Treble, three; threefold, three times as much.
tripode [trIpode], *n.m.* Tripod.
Tripoli [trIpoli], *n.f.* (*Geog.*) Tripoli.
tripoli [trIpoli], *n.m.* (*Min.*) Rotten-stone.
tripolino, tripolitano, *n.m.a.* Tripolitan, of Tripoli.
trippa, *n.f.* Tripe; (*colloq.*) belly, paunch.
trippaio [trippAio], *n.m.* Tripe-seller.
tripperia [tripperIa], *n.f.* Tripe-shop.
trippone, *n.m.a.* Pot-bellied (fellow).
tripudiamento, *n.m.* Rejoicing.
tripudiare, *v.i.* To rejoice; to revel, to carouse, to feast.
tripudio [tripUdio], *n.m.* Rejoicing, jubilation, exultation.
triregno, *n.m.* (*Eccles.*) Papal tiara, triple crown.
trireme, *n.f.* (*Hist.*) Trireme.
trisavolo, trisavola [trisAvolo, -a], *n.m.f.* Great-great-grandfather, great-great-grandmother.
trisezione, *n.f.* (*Geom.*) Trisection.
trisillabico [trisillAbico], *a.* Trisyllabic.
trisillabo [trisIllabo], *n.m.a.* Trisyllable.
trisma, *n.m.* (*Med.*) Trismus, lockjaw.
tristaccio [tristAccio], *n.m.* Rogue, scoundrel, evil-doer.
tristamente, *adv.* Sadly; wickedly.
Tristano, *n.m.* Tristram.
triste, *a.* Sad, mournful, sorrowful; gloomy, melancholy; sullen. **Un aspetto —,** a mournful countenance; **tristi pensieri,** gloomy thoughts.
tristezza, *n.f.* Sadness; melancholy, depression; sorrow.
tristizia [tristIzia], *n.f.* Sadness; wickedness; wretchedness.
tristo, *n.m.* Scoundrel, rascal, villain.
tristo, *a.* Wicked; wretched; malicious, perverse; deplorable, miserable.
trisulco, *a.* Three-forked, three-pronged. **Folgore —,** forked lightning.
tritacarne, *n.m.* Mincing-knife, mincing-machine, mincer.
tritamente, *adv.* Tritely; distinctly, in detail; minutely.
tritamento, *n.m.* Mincing; cutting up small.
tritare, *v.t.* To mince, to hash, to pound; to crumble, to triturate.
tritatura, *n.f.* Hashing, mincing; pounding.
tritello, *n.m.* Bran, pollard.
trito, *p.p.a.* Minced, hashed; pounded; (*fig.*) trite, commonplace; worn-out, hackneyed. **Argomento — e ritrito,** a platitude.
tritolare, *v.t.* To crush, to pound.
tritolo [tritOlo], *n.m.* T.N.T.
Tritone, *n.m.* (*Myth.*) Triton; (*Zool.*) triton.
tritono, *a.* (*Mus.*) Tritone.
trittico [trIttico], *n.m.* (*Art*) Triptych.
trittongo, *n.m.* (*Gram.*) Triphthong.
tritume, *n.m.* Bits, crumbs, scraps.
triturabile [triturAbile], *a.* Triturable, capable of being ground.
triturare, *v.t.* To grind, to triturate; to rub down.
triturazione, *n.f.* Grinding, pounding, trituration.
triumvirato, *n.m.* Triumvirate.
triumviro [triUmviro], *n.m.* (*Hist.*) Triumvir.
trivella, *n.f.* [cp. **trivello**].
trivellare, *v.t.* To drill, to bore.
trivellatura, *n.f.* Drilling, piercing.
trivello, *n.m.* Brace (and bit); borer.
triviale, *a.* Vulgar, low, coarse.
trivialità [-à], *n.f.* Coarseness, vulgarity.
trivio [trIvio], *n.m.* Cross-roads; poor quarter, slum. **Modi da —,** foul language, coarse manners.
trocaico [trocAico], *a.* (*Poet.*) Trochaic.
trocantere, *n.m.* (*Anat.*) Trochanter.
trocheo [trochEo], *n.m.* (*Poet.*) Trochee.

trofeo [trofEo], *n.m.* Trophy.
trogloditi, *n.m.pl.* Troglodytes, cave-dwellers.
trogolo [trOgolo], *n.m.* Trough.
Troia [trOia], *n.f.* (*Hist.*) Troy.
troia [trOia], *n.f.* (*Zool.*) Sow; (*colloq.*) harlot, strumpet.
troiaio [troiAio], *n.m.* Pigstye; heap of muck.
troiano, *n.m.a.* Trojan.
troiata, *n.f.* (*colloq.*) Filthy act or thing.
Troilo [trOilo], *n.m.* (*Lit.*) Troilus.
trolle, *n.m.* Trolley.
tromba (1), *n.f.* Trumpet, bugle; motor-horn; pump, siphon; (elephant's) trunk; well (of staircase); public auction. **Suonare la —,** to sound the trumpet; **a suon di —,** by trumpet-call; **a —,** trumpet-shaped; **— acustica,** ear trumpet; **— d'aria,** whirlwind; **— marina,** water-spout; **— d'acqua,** whirlpool; **— idraulica,** hydraulic pump; (*Anat.*) **— d'Eustachio,** Eustachian tube.
tromba (2), *n.m.* Trumpeter.
trombaio [trombAio], *n.m.* Plumber.
trombare, *v.t.* To trumpet; (*colloq.*) to take in, to cheat; to reject, to defeat (at an election).
trombata, *n.f.* Trumpet call.
trombetta (1), *n.m.* Bugler, trumpeter; herald.
trombetta (2), *n.f.* Child's bugle.
trombettiere, *n.m.* Trumpeter, bugler.
trombonata, *n.f.* Trombone-playing.
trombone (1), *n.m.* Trombone; (*Mil.*) blunder buss.
trombone (2), **tromboncino,** *n.m.* (*Bot.*) Daffodil.
trombosi, *n.f.* (*Med.*) Thrombosis.
troncabile [troncAbile], *a.* Capable of curtailment.
troncamente, *adv.* Imperfectly, falteringly.
troncamento, *n.m.* Truncation; amputation; interruption, suppression.
troncare, *v.t.* To cut off, to break off, to cut short, to truncate; to interrupt, to curtail, to discontinue; to break in two. **— i rapporti,** to break off communications; **— una discussione,** to cut short a discussion; **— il capo,** to behead.
troncatamente, *adv.* Interruptedly.
troncativo, *a.* Brittle.
troncatura, *n.f.* Breaking-off.
tronchesino, tronchetto, *n.m.* Wire-cutters.
tronco, *n.m.* Tree-trunk; (*Rail.*) trunk-line.
tronco, *p.p.a.* Cut off, mutilated; imperfect, unfinished; interrupted. **Parola tronca,** truncated word; **lasciare in —,** to leave unfinished to leave off abruptly.
troncone, *n.m.* Stump; (*fig.*) lineage, stock.
troneggiare, *v.i.* To sit on a throne; to be supreme; to tower.
tronfiare, *v.i.* To strut; to show off, to puff, to pout; to spread its feathers (peacock etc.).
tronfiezza, *n.f.* Vain glory, boastfulness.
tronfio [trOnfio], *a.* Vainglorious, boastful, haughty, puffed up, conceited.
trono, *n.m.* Throne. **Salire al —,** to mount the throne.
tropicale, *a.* Tropical.
tropico [trOpico], *n.m.* (*Geog.*) Tropic. **— del Capricorno, del Cancro,** Tropic of Capricorn, of Cancer.
tropo, *n.m.* Trope, metaphor, figure of speech.
tropologia [tropologIa], *n.f.* Tropology.
troppo, *n.m.* Excess, superfluity. **Il — stroppia,** enough is as good as a feast.
troppo, *a.adv.* Too much, too. **— lontano,** too far, **— presto,** too fast; **un po' —,** rather too much; **pur —,** unfortunately; only too well; **— presto,** too early; **è di —,** it is not wanted, it is superfluous; **egli mangia —,** he eats too much; **— poco,** too little; **— pochi,** too few; **troppe parole,** too much said about it.
trota, *n.f.* (*Zool.*) Trout.
trottapiano, *n.m.* Slowcoach, dawdler.
trottare, *v.i.* To trot; (*fig.*) to walk fast, to bustle about.
trottata, *n.f.* Drive, ride; trot; run.
trottatoio [trottatOio], *n.m.* Riding-field.
trottatore, *n.m.* Trotter.
trotterellare, *v.i.* To trot along, to toddle (of a child).
trotterello, *n.m.* Jog-trot.
trotto, *n.m.* Trot. **Andare al —,** to trot.
trottola [trOttola], *n.f.* Top, peg-top, spinning-top.
trottolare, *v.i.* To spin round, to whirl.
trottolino, *n.m.* Toddler, little boy; restless child.
trovabile [trovAbile], *a.* Capable of being found.
trovadore [cp. **trovatore**].
trovamento, *n.m.* Finding, discovery.
trovare, *v.t.* To find, to find out, to hit upon, to detect, to discover; to meet, to come across; to deem, to think; to contrive. **— una scusa,** to find an excuse; **— a ridire,** to find fault; **andare a — uno,** to call on someone; **— cattivo, buono,** to dislike, to like; **— modo di,** to find a way to; **lasciare il tempo che trova,** to leave things unchanged [cp. **trovarsi**].
trovarobe, *n.m.* (*Theat.*) Theatrical costumier; property man.
trovarsi, *v.r.* To find oneself, to happen to be; to be situated; to meet one another; to feel. **— male,** to feel unhappy; to be uncomfortable; **non si trova,** it can't be found; **— agli estremi,** to be at death's door; **ci troveremo domani,** we shall meet tomorrow [cp. **trovare**].
trovata, *n.f.* Device, contrivance, invention; lucky hit; trick, expedient.
trovatello, *n.m.* Foundling.
trovato, *n.m.* Discovery, invention; contrivance.
trovato, *p.p.a.* Found, devised; thought; deemed.
trovatore, trovadore, *n.m.* (*Hist.*) Troubadour; finder.
trovero, troviero, *n.m.* (*Poet.*) Trouvère.
trozze, *n.f.pl.* (*Naut.*) Parrels.
truccare, *v.t.* To make up (one's face), to rouge; to disguise, to cheat. **Quella ragazza è troppo truccata,** that girl has too much make-up.
truccarsi, *v.r.* To make oneself up, to disguise oneself; to make up (face).
truccatore, *n.m.* (*Theat.*) Dresser.
truccatura, *n.f.* Make-up; making up; disguise.
trucco, *n.m.* Trick, cheat, swindle; make-up.
truccone, *n.m.* Trickster, swindler.

truce, *a.* Grim, stern, fierce, sinister, ghastly; cruel, atrocious, wicked.
trucemente, *adv.* Fiercely, cruelly, savagely, threateningly.
trucidare, *v.t.* To slaughter, to murder, to kill, to massacre.
truciolare, *v.t.* To chip.
truciolo [trUciolo], *n.m.* Chip, (wood) shaving.
trucolento, *a.* Truculent.
trucolenza, *n.f.* Truculence.
truffa, *n.f.* Theft; swindle, fraud, trick; deceit. **— all'americana,** confidence trick.
truffaldino, *n.m.a.* Rogue, trickster; rascal. **Tiro —,** rascally trick.
truffare, *v.t.* To swindle, to steal, to defraud, to trick, to take in. **Egli è stato truffato d'una forte somma,** he has been swindled out of a large sum.
truffatore, truffatrice, *n.m.f.* Swindler, cheat, thief.
trufferia [truffeIa], *n.f.* Theft, swindling [cp. **truffa**].
trufolare, *v.i.* To rummage.
trullaggine, trulleria [trullAggine, trullerIa], *n.f.* Stupidness, stupidity.
trullo, *n.m.a.* Silly, stupid.
truogolo [truOgolo], *n.m.* Trough [cp. **trogolo**].
truppa, *n.f.* Troop, troops, band, company, soldiers; (*Theat.*) troupe. **Truppe d'assalto,** shock troops; **militare di —,** private (soldier).
trust, *n.m.* (*Comm.*) Trust.
tu, *pron.* Thou; you. **Dare del tu,** to thee and thou; **a tu per tu,** face to face.
tuba, *n.f.* Trumpet; (*Anat.*) tube; (*colloq.*) top-hat.
tubare, *v.i.* To coo (as a dove); to bill and coo.
tubatura, tubazione, *n.f.* Pipes, system of pipes, plumbing system.
tubercolare, *a.* Tubercular.
tubercolo [tubErcolo], *n.m.* Tubercle.
tubercolosario [tubercolosArio], *n.m.* Sanatorium.
tubercolosi, *n.f.* (*Med.*) Tuberculosis, phthisis, consumption.
tubercoloso, tubercolotico [tubercolOtico], Consumptive; tuberculous.
tubercoluto, *a.* Tuberculate, tuberculated.
tuberiforme, *a.* Tuberiform.
tubero [tUbero], *n.m.* (*Bot.*) Tuber.
tuberosa, *n.f.* (*Bot.*) Tuberose.
tubetto, *n.m.* Small tube; (*Art*) tube paint.
tubino, *n.m.* (*colloq.*) Bowler hat.
tubo, *n.m.* Tube, pipe. **— di gomma,** rubber tube; **— di scarico,** exhaust pipe; **— dell'acqua,** hose-pipe, water-pipe; **— lanciasiluri,** torpedo-tube; **caldaia a tubi,** tubular boiler.
tubolare, *a.* Tubular.
tucano, *n.m.* (*Zool.*) Toucan.
Tucidide [tucIdide], *n.m.* Thucydides.
tuello, *n.m.* Quick of horse's hoof.
tufaceo [tufAceo], *a.* (*Geol.*) Tufaceous.
tuffamento, *n.m.* Diving, dive.
tuffare, *v.t.* To plunge, to dip, to immerse.
tuffarsi, *v.r.* To dive; to take a plunge. **— negli affari,** to plunge into business.
tuffata, *n.f.* Plunge, dive, dip.
tuffatore, *n.m.* Diver (when swimming).
tuffo, *n.m.* Dive, plunge, header; (*fig.*) sudden flush of blood; throb; fall of rain. **Fare un —,** to dive, to take a plunge; **— di remi,** dip of the oars; **avere un — al cuore,** to feel one's heart swell (with emotion).
tuffolino, *n.m.* (*Zool.*) Dabchick.
tuffolo [tUffolo], *n.m.* (*Zool.*) Diver (bird).
tufo, *n.m.* (*Geol.*) Tufa.
tugurio [tugUrio], *n.m.* Hovel, hut, dog-kennel; slum.
tulipano, *n.m.* (*Bot.*) Tulip.
tulle, *n.m.* Tulle.
tulliano, *a.* (*Lit.*) Ciceronian.
tumefare, *v.t.i.* To swell, to tumify.
tumefarsi, *v.r.* To swell, to become swollen.
tumefazione, *n.f.* Swelling, tumefaction.
tumidamente, *adv.* Tumidly, swollenly.
tumidezza, tumidità, *n.f.* Tumidity, inflation, swollen state.
tumido [tUmido], *a.* Swollen, inflated, tumid.
tumore, *n.m.* (*Med.*) Tumour.
tumulare, *v.t.* To bury, to inter.
tumulazione, *n.f.* Burial, interment.
tumulo [tUmulo], *n.m.* Tumulus, barrow; tomb, grave.
tumulto, *n.m.* Uproar, tumult, riot, disorder; confusion, turmoil.
tumultuante, *n.m.a.* Rioter; riotous; uproarious.
tumultuare, *v.i.* To riot, to be in an uproar, to create a disturbance.
tumultuariamente, *adv.* Tumultuously.
tumultuario [tumultuArio], *a.* Tumultuous, wild, tumultuary.
tumultuoso, *a.* Tumultuous, riotous, violent.
tungsteno, *n.m.* (*Chem.*) Tungsten
tunica [tUnica], *n.f.* Tunic.
tunichetta, *n.f.* Tunicle, little tunic.
Tunisi [tUnisi], *n.f.* (City of) Tunis.
Tunisia [tunisIa], *n.f.* (State of) Tunis; Tunisia.
tunisino, *n.m.a.* Tunisian.
tunnel, *n.m.* Tunnel.
tuo, *pron.a.* Thy, thine; your, yours. **Dalla tua,** in your favour; **il tuo e il mio,** your own and my own; **i tuoi,** your family, your people.
tuonare, *v.i.* To thunder, to roar.
tuono, *n.m.* Thunder; roar, roaring.
tuorlata, *n.f.* Beaten egg; egg-flip.
tuorlo, *n.m.* Yolk (of egg).
tura, *n.f.* Dam, dike.
turabuchi, *n.m.* Stop-gap.
turacciolo [turAcciolo], *n.m.* Cork, bung, stopper.
turamento, *n.m.* Stopping up, bunging, plugging.
turare, *v.t.* To stop, to plug, to cork, to bung; to stuff up. **— la bocca a uno,** to stop someone's mouth; **— un buco,** to stop up a hole; **— un dente,** to stop a tooth.
turarsi, *v.r.* To be stopped, to become obstructed. **— gli orecchi,** to stop one's ears; **— il naso,** to hold one's nose (for a bad smell).
turba, *n.f.* Multitude, turbulent crowd; rabble, mob.
turbabile [turbAbile], *a.* Easily disturbed, soon troubled.
turbamento, *n.m.* Uneasiness, anxiety; agitation, perturbation; commotion.

turbante, *n.m.* Turban.
turbare, *v.t.* To trouble, to upset, to disturb, to agitate; to worry, to perturb, to ruffle.
turbarsi, *v.r.* To become uneasy, to get agitated, to be worried; to grow murky, to become overcast.
turbatamente, *adv.* In a troubled manner.
turbativo, *a.* Disturbing, agitating.
turbato, *a.* Troubled, worried, disturbed, perturbed.
turbina, *n.f.* Turbine. **— a vapore,** steam turbine.
turbinare, *v.i.* To whirl, to eddy.
turbine [tUrbine], *n.m.* Whirlwind; gale, hurricane.
turbinio [turbinIo], *n.m.* Whirl, whirling; turmoil, storm; jostling crowd.
turbinosamente, *adv.* Stormily.
turbinoso, *a.* Stormy; whirling, eddying; tumultuous.
turbo, *n.m.* Turbine.
turbogeneratore, *n.m.* Turbo-generator.
turbolento, *a.* Turbulent, rowdy, disorderly, riotous; restless, troubled.
turbolenza, *n.f.* Turbulence.
turcasso, *n.m.* Quiver (for arrows).
turchescamente, *adv.* Like a Turk; roughly, cruelly.
turchesco, *a.* Turkish, Saracen.
turchese, *n.f.* Turquoise.
turchetto, *n.m.* (*Zool.*) Pouter pigeon.
Turchia [turchIa], *n.f.* (*Geog.*) Turkey.
turchinetto, *n.m.* Washerwoman's blue.
turchiniccio [turchinIccio], *a.* Bluish.
turchino, *n.m.a.* Blue, dark blue, deep blue.
turcimanno, *n.m.* Dragoman, interpreter.
turco, *n.m.a.* Turk, Turkish. **Bere, fumare come un —,** to drink like a fish, to smoke like a chimney.
turcofilo [turcOfilo], *n.m.a.* Turkophil.
turcomanno, *n.m.a.* Turkoman.
Turena, *n.f.* (*Geog.*) Touraine.
turgescente, *a.* Turgescent, swollen, turgid.
turgidamente, *adv.* Turgidly.
turgidezza, turgidità, *n.f.* Turgidity, turgidness; pompousness.
turgido [tUrgido], *a.* Turgid swollen; pompous, bombastic.
turibolo [turIbolo], *n.m.* (*Eccles.*) Thurible, censer.
turiferario [turiferArio], *n.m.* Thurifer, acolyte.
turificazione, *n.f.* Censing.
turismo, *n.m.* Touring, tourist business.
turista, *n.m.f.* Tourist.
turistico [turIstico], *a.* Tourist, touring.
turlupinare, *v.t.* To cheat, to deceive, to trick; to fool, to dupe, to take in, to gull.
turlupinatore, *n.m.* Swindler.
turlupinatura, *n.f.* Cheat, trick, swindle.
turno, *n.m.* Turn, rotation, succession; duty, service. **A —, per —,** by turns, in succession; **darsi il —,** to take turns; **— di servizio,** turn of duty; **medico di —,** doctor on duty.
turpe, *a.* Abject, mean, low, base, vile, shameful, despicable; depraved; indecent.
turpemente, *adv.* Abjectly, vilely.
turpiloquio [turpilOquio]. *n.m.* Obscene language, foul language, filthy talk, obloquy.
turpitudine [turpitUdine], *n.f.* Turpitude, baseness, depravity.
turrito, *a.* Turreted, battlemented.
tuta, *n.f.* (Workman's) overalls; boiler-suit.
tutela, *n.f.* Guardianship, tutelage, protection, care.
tutelare, *v.t.* To protect, to defend, to safeguard; to act as guardian.
tutelare, *a.* Tutelary, guardian.
tutore, tutrice, *n.m.f.* Guardian. **Fare da —,** to act as guardian.
tutorio [tutOrio], *a.* Tutelary. **Autorità tutoria,** superior authority.
tuttavia [tuttavIa], *adv.conj.* Yet, however, still, nevertheless; all the same.
tutto, *n.m.* All, whole, everything.
tutto, *a.adv.* All; whole; every; entire. **Ella era tutta pensosa,** she was very thoughtful; **ho fatto di — per persuaderlo,** I did all I could to convince him; **tutti i giorni,** every day; **— il giorno,** the whole day, all day long; **in — e per —,** entirely; **del —,** totally; **a tutta prima,** at first, at the first moment; **— di un pezzo,** all of a piece; **tutti i miei libri,** all my books; **tutta la famiglia,** the whole family; **— nudo,** stark naked; **per — il mondo,** the world over; **ecco — !** that's all! **è tutt'uno,** it's all the same; **— quanto,** all, everything; **tutti quanti,** everyone; **tutt'altro,** on the contrary; **tutti dicono,** they say, people say; **tutt'e tre,** all three, **da per —,** everywhere; **— a un tratto,** all of a sudden.
tuttochè, *conj.* Though, although.
tuttodì, *adv.* Always, continually.
tuttora, *adv.* Still, again, always.
tuzia [tUzia], *n.f.* (*Chem.*) Tutty.
tzigano, *n.m.a.* Tzigane, gipsy.

U

U, u, *n.f.m.* Nineteenth letter of the Italian alphabet.
uadi, *n.m.* Wadi, wady (African river or stream).
ubbia [ubbIa], *n.f.* Crotchet, fad, whim; superstition, delusion; prejudice. **Ha delle ubbie,** he's full of fads.
ubbidiente, *a.* Obedient, dutiful, submissive, docile.
ubbidientemente, *adv.* Obediently, submissively.
ubbidienza, *n,f.* Obedience, submission, docility; compliance. **— passiva,** passive obedience.
ubbidire, *v.t.i.* To obey [cp. **obbedire**].
ubbioso, *a.* Superstitious; faddy.
ubbriaco [cp. **ubriaco**].
ubertà [-à], *n.f.* Fertility, fruitfulness.
ubertosità [-à], *n.f.* Fertileness.
ubertoso, *a.* Fertile, fruitful.
ubi, *adv.* (*Lit.*) Where. **Trovare l'ubi consistam,** to find solid ground.
ubicato, *a.* Located, situated.
ubicazione, *n.f.* Location, position; whereabouts.
ubiquità [-à], *n.f.* Ubiquity, omnipresence.
ubriacare, *v.t.* To intoxicate, to make drunk.
ubriacarsi, *v.r.* To get drunk; to booze, to tipple.
ubriacato, *p.p.a.* Drunk, drunken, inebriated.
ubriacatura, *n.f.* Intoxication.
ubriachezza, *n.f.* Drunkenness, intoxication

ubriaco, *n.m.* Drunken man, drunk, drunkard.
ubriaco, *a.* Drunk, drunken, intoxicated, tipsy.
ubriacone, *n.m.* Drunkard.
uccella, *n.f.* Hen-bird.
uccellaccio [uccellAccio], *n.m.* Large bird; bird of prey.
uccellagione, *n.f.* Shooting (of birds); shooting season (for birds); feathered game.
uccellaia [uccellAia], *n.f.* Quantity of birds, flock.
uccellame, *n.m.* Feathered game, birds (at a shoot).
uccellamento, *n.m.* Bird-catching; joke, horseplay.
uccellare, *v.t.i.* To snare (birds), to go fowling; (*fig.*) to dupe, to cheat, to deceive.
uccellatore, uccellatrice, *n.m.f.* Fowler; swindler, cheat, trickster.
uccellatura, *n.f.* Deception, deceit, trickery.
uccelliera, *n.f.* Aviary.
uccello, *n.m.* Bird, fowl; (*fig.*) simpleton. **— rapace,** bird of prey; **— migratorio,** migrant; **— di mal augurio,** bird of ill omen; **veduta a volo d'uccello,** bird's eye view; **— da gabbia,** cage-bird; **— di bosco,** fugitive from justice; **— di passo,** bird of passage.
uccidere [uccIdere], *v.t.* To kill; to slay, to slaughter; to shoot (with firearms).
uccidersi [uccIdersi], *v.r.* To commit suicide, to kill oneself.
uccisione, *n.f.* Killing, slaughter; murder.
ucciso, *p.p.a.* Killed (in battle), dead.
uccisore, *n.m.* Slayer, killer; murderer.
Ucraina, *n.f.* (*Geog.*) Ukraine.
udibile [udIbile], *a.* Audible.
udienza, *n.f.* Audience; (court) hearing; sitting; interview; (*Law*) session. **Dare —,** to grant an interview; **sala delle udienze,** court room; **l'— è rinviata,** the hearing is adjourned.
udire, *v.t.* (**Io odo,** etc.) To hear, to listen to. **— un romore,** to hear a noise; **— la messa,** to go to Mass; **Udite ?** Can you hear? **Udite !** Listen! **per udito dire,** by hearsay.
udita, *n.f.* Hearsay.
udito, *n.m.* Hearing, sense of hearing. **— fino, sottile,** a quick ear.
uditore, uditrice, *n.m.f.* Hearer, listener; auditor.
uditorio [uditOrio], *n.m.a.* Audience, listeners, hearers; auditory.
udizione, *n.f.* Audition [cp. **audizione**].
udometro [udOmetro], *n.m.* Rain-gauge, udometer.
uff ! *inter.* Oh, what a bore! What a nuisance! Phew!
ufficiale, *n.m.* Officer. **— dell'esercito, della marina,** army, naval officer; **— giudiziario,** tipstaff, bailiff.
ufficiale, *a.* Official; formal.
ufficialetto, *n.m.* Young officer, subaltern.
ufficialità [-à], *n.f.* Officers (as a body); official body.
ufficialmente, *adv.* Officially, formally.
ufficiante, *a.* Officiating. **Sacerdote —,** officiating priest.
ufficiare, *v.i.* To officiate; to act for.
ufficiatore, *n.m.* (*Eccles.*) Officiating priest.
ufficiatura, *n.f.* Exercise of an office; (*Eccles.*) divine office, celebration.
ufficio [uffIcio], *n.m.* Office; appointment, position; agency, intervention, mediation; service, duty. **Ore d'—,** office hours; **capo —,** head of a department; **— postale,** post-office; **— di collocamento,** employment agency; **— d'informazioni,** inquiry office; **scrivere d'—,** to write formally, to write an official letter; (*Law*) **nominato d'—,** appointed by the Court; **vi ringrazio dei vostri buoni uffici,** I thank you for your good offices; (*Eccles.*) **— divino,** divine office; **— funebre,** funeral service; **Santo Ufficio,** Holy Office, Inquisition.
ufficiosamente, *adv.* Diplomatically, officiously, informally.
ufficiosità [-à], *n.f.* (Diplomatic) officiousness.
ufficioso, *a.* Officious; semi-official, informal; obliging.
uffizio [cp. **ufficio**].
ufo, *adv.* **A ufo,** gratis, gratuitously, for nothing; scot-free; uselessly. **Mangiare a ufo,** to cadge a meal.
uggia [Uggia], *n.f.* Ennui, boredom, tedium; aversion, dislike; shade. **Avere in —,** to have a dislike for.
uggiolamento, *n.m.* Whining, howling.
uggiolare, *v.i.* To whine, to howl (of dogs).
uggiolio [uggiolIo], *n.m.* Continual howling.
uggiosamente, *adv.* Wearisomely, irksomely.
uggioso, *a.* Wearisome, irksome; gloomy; boring, dull. **Tempo —,** dull weather.
ugna [cp. **unghia**].
ugnare, *v.t.* To cut obliquely, to rabbet.
ugnata, *n.f.* Scratch (with the nail).
ugnatura, *n.f.* Oblique cut or scratch.
ugnone, *n.m.* Talon, claw.
ugola [Ugola], *n.f.* (*Anat.*) Uvula; voice.
Ugonotto, *n.m.* (*Hist.*) Huguenot.
uguagliamento, *n.m.* Equalization, levelling down.
uguaglianza, *n.f.* Equality, similarity.
uguagliare, *v.t.* To equalize [cp. **eguagliare**].
uguagliarsi, *v.r.* To make oneself equal to.
uguale, *a.* Equal; same, uniform; level. **I nostri uguali,** our equals; **— al campione,** up to sample.
ugualità [-à], *n.f.* Equality.
ugualmente, *adv.* Equally; all the same, nevertheless.
uh! *inter.* Oh!
uhi! *inter.* Alas! Oh dear!
uhm! *inter.* Hum! Indeed!
uistiti [uIstiti], *n.m.* (*Zool.*) Marmoset.
ulano, *n.m.* (*Mil.*) Uhlan.
ulcera [Ulcera], *n.f.* (*Med.*) Ulcer.
ulceramento, *n.m.* Ulcerating, ulceration.
ulcerare, *v.t.* To ulcerate.
ulcerarsi, *v.r.* To become ulcerated.
ulcerazione, *n.f.* Ulceration.
ulceroso, *a.* Ulcerous.
uligine [ulIgine], *n.f.* Dampness.
uliginoso, *a.* Damp, moist.
uliva, *n.f.* Olive [cp. **oliva**].
ulna, *n.f.* (*Anat.*) Ulna.
ulteriore, *a.* Ulterior, further; subsequent. **Fare ulteriori ricerche,** to make further inquiries.
ulteriormente, *adv.* Further, besides; afterwards, later on, subsequently. **Esaminare — la questione,** to go further into the question.

ultima, *n.f.* (*colloq.*) Last word, parting shot.
ultimamente, *adv.* Lately, recently, in recent times, of late; at last.
ultimare, *v.t.* To finish, to bring to an end, to complete, to close.
ultimatum, *n.m.* Ultimatum. **Dare un —,** to send an ultimatum.
ultimazione, *n.f.* Completion, termination, finishing.
ultimissimo [ultimIssimo], *a.* The very latest, last; hindmost.
ultimo [Ultimo], *a.* Last, latest; (*Comm.*) last (month). **L'ultima volta,** the last time; **ultima moda,** latest fashion; **ultime notizie,** latest news; **da —,** lastly, finally; **dare l'— tocco,** to give the finishing touch; **fino all'—,** to the very last; **per —,** in the end, eventually; **arrivare —,** to arrive last.
ultimogenito [ultimogEnito], *n.m.a.* Last born (son), youngest.
ulto, *a.* (*Poet.*) Avenged.
ultore, ultrice, *n.m.f.* Avenger.
ultra-, *prefix.* Ultra-; beyond, in the highest degree. **Il non plus —,** the height, the extreme point, the highest pitch.
ultramontano, *a.* Ultramontane.
ultravioletto, *a.* Ultra-violet. **Raggi ultravioletti,** ultra-violet rays.
ululare, *v.i.* To howl, to wail, to hoot.
ululato, ululo [Ululo], *n.m.* Howl, howling, wailing, hooting (of a siren).
ulva, *n.f.* (*Bot.*) Kind of edible seaweed.
umanamente, *adv.* Humanly, as a man; kindly, humanely. **È — impossibile,** it's humanly impossible; **trattare —,** to treat humanely.
umanare, *v.t.* To humanize, to make human.
umanarsi, *v.r.* To become compassionate; (*Eccles.*) to become man.
umanazione, *n.f.* (*Eccles.*) Incarnation.
umanesimo, umanismo [umanEsimo], *n.m.* Humanism.
umanista (*pl.* **umanisti**), *n.m.* Humanist.
umanità [-à], *n.f.* Humanity; mankind, human race; kindness, humaneness. **Religione dell'—,** religion of humanity.
umanitario [umanitArio], *n.m.a.* Humanitarian.
umanitarismo, *n.m.* Humanitarianism.
umanizzare, *v.t.* To humanize, to make human; to uplift, to improve.
umano, *a.* Human; humane; compassionate, kind; elevating. **Il genere —,** the human race, mankind; **un atto —,** a humane deed; **egli è molto —,** he is very human; **le umane lettere,** the humanities, belles-lettres, literature.
umbellifere [umbellIfere], *n.f.pl.* (*Bot.*) Umbelliferous plants.
umbilicale, *a.* (*Anat.*) Umbilical.
umbilico, *n.m.* Umbelicus, navel.
umbratile [umbrAtile], *a.* (*Lit.*) Dim, shady; imaginary.
umbro, *n.m.a.* Umbrian.
umerale, *n.m.* (*Eccles.*) Humeral.
umettamento, *n.m.* Moistening, damping, wetting.
umettare, *v.t.* To moisten, to damp.
umettativo, *a.* Moistening.
umettazione, *n.f.* Dampening, moistening.
umidaccio [umidAccio], *n.m.* Damp weather.
umidamente, *adv.* Damply.
umidetto, *a.* Rather damp.
umidezza, *n.f.* Damp, dampness, humidity, moisture.
umidiccio [umidIccio], *a.* Dampish.
umidire, *v.t.* To dampen, to moisten.
umidità [-à], *n.f.* Humidity, dampness, moisture.
umido [Umido], *n.m.* Dampness, damp; stew. **Macchia d'—,** damp spot; **manzo in —,** stew, beef stew.
umido [Umido], *a.* Damp, wet, humid, moist. **Vento —,** damp wind; **occhi umidi di pianto,** eyes wet with tears; **tempo —,** damp weather.
umidore [cp. **umidità**].
umile [Umile], *a.* Humble, modest, lowly, simple, unpretentious; submissive; low. **Di umili natali,** of humble birth; **servizi umili,** menial tasks.
umilemente, *adv.* (*Poet.*) Humbly.
umiliamento, *n.m.* Humiliation, humbling, abasement, lowering.
umiliante, *a.* Humiliating, mortifying; lowering.
umiliare, *v.t.* To humiliate, to humble, to mortify; to offer humbly.
umiliarsi, *v.r.* To humiliate oneself, to stoop to, to truckle to; to give way.
umiliazione, *n.f.* Humiliation, humbling, abasement.
umilmente, *adv.* Humbly, modestly, unpretentiously; meekly.
umiltà [-à], *n.f.* Humility, modesty, meekness, lowliness, self-abasement.
umo, *n.m.* Humus, soil.
umoraccio [umorAccio], *n.m.* Bad humour, bad temper, black mood.
umore, *n.m.* Humour; disposition, mood, temper. **Essere di cattivo —,** to be in a bad temper; **essere di buon —,** to be in a happy mood, to be good-tempered; **un bell'—,** a wit, a wag; **senza —,** humourless.
umorismo, *n.m.* Humour, humorousness. **Manca di —,** he has no sense of humour.
umorista, *n.m.f.* Humorist.
umoristico [umorIstico], *a.* Humorous, comic; facetious. **Giornale —,** comic paper.
umoroso, *a.* Juicy, humid.
un, una [cp. **uno**].
unanime [unAnime], *a.* Unanimous, all of one mind. **Per voto —,** by unanimous consent.
unanimemente, *adv.* Unanimously.
unanimità [-à], *n.f.* Unanimity. **All'—,** unanimously.
unciale, *n.m.a.* Uncial.
uncinare, *v.t.* To hook, to grapple.
uncinato, *p.p.a.* Hooked. **Croce uncinata,** swastika, crooked cross.
uncinetto, *n.m.* Crochet-hook. **Lavorare all'—,** to crochet.
uncino, *n.m.* Hook; pretext. **A —,** hooked.
undecimo [undEcimo], *a.* Eleventh.
undicenne, *a.* Eleven years old.
undicesimo [undicEsimo], *a.* Eleventh.
undici [Undici], *a.* Eleven. **Sono le —,** it's eleven o'clock.
ungaro [Ungaro], *n.m.a.* Hungarian.
ungere [Ungere], *v.t.* To grease, to smear, to oil, to lubricate; to anoint; (*fig.*) to bribe, to flatter.

ungherese, *n.m.a.* Hungarian.
Ungheria [ungherIa], *n.f.* (*Geog.*) Hungary.
unghia [Unghia], *n.f.* Nail, claw; hoof, talon (of birds). **Cadere nelle unghie di,** to fall into the clutches of; **— incarnita,** ingrown nail; **tagliarsi le unghie,** to cut one's nails.
unghiata, *n.f.* Scratch (with fingernail).
unghiato, *a.* Furnished with claws, clawed.
unghiello, unghiolo, *n.m.* Sharp claw, claw (of bird or cat).
unghione, *n.m.* Large finger-nail; talon, claw.
unghiuto, *a.* Clawed; rapacious, predatory, grasping.
ungimento, *n.m.* Greasing; anointing.
ungitore, *n.m.* Greaser, lubricator; anointer.
ungitura, *n.f.* Greasing.
unguentare, *v.t.* To anoint, to smear (with ointment, etc.).
unguentario [unguentArio], *a.* Unguentary.
unguentiere, *n.m.* Perfumer.
unguento, *n.m.* Ointment, unguent; remedy, medicine; cure. **— refrigerante,** soothing ointment.
ungulati, *n.m.pl.* (*Zool.*) Ungulates.
unibile [unIbile], *a.* Easily united.
unicamente, *adv.* Uniquely, solely, only.
unicità [-à], *n.f.* Uniqueness; singleness, unity.
unico [Unico], *a.* Unique, one, only, sole, single. **È l'— mezzo,** it's the only means; **figlio —,** only son; **— nel suo genere,** the only thing of its kind; unique in its kind.
unicolore, *a.* Of one colour.
unicorno, *n.m.* Unicorn.
unificabile [unificAbile], *a.* That can be unified.
unificare, *v.t.* To unify; to unite, to amalgamate, to combine, to consolidate.
unificarsi, *v.r.* To amalgamate, to combine.
unificativo, *a.* Unifying.
unificato, *p.p.a.* (*Comm.*) Consolidated. **Fondo di ammortamento —,** consolidated funds.
unificazione, *n.f.* Unification, amalgamation; union; (*Comm.*) combine, consolidation.
uniformare, *v.t.* To standardize, to equalize, to bring into line.
uniformarsi, *v.r.* To comply with; to adapt oneself, to conform to.
uniformazione, *n.f.* Standardization, equalization.
uniforme, *n.f.* Uniform, regimentals, official dress. **Portare un'—,** to wear a uniform; **in grande —,** in full dress.
uniforme, *a.* Uniform, even, regular, equal, **— di dimensioni,** of uniform size.
uniformemente, *adv.* Uniformly.
uniformità [-à], *n.f.* Uniformity; conformity; monotony, sameness.
unigenito [unigEnito], *n.m.a.* Only begotten (son).
unilaterale, *a.* One-sided, unilateral; partial, unfair.
unilateralità [-à], *n.f.* One-sidedness, partiality, unfairness.
unimento, *n.m.* Union, fusion.
unione, *n.f.* Union; unity, concord, agreement; league, association. **L'— fa la forza,** union is strength; **— postale,** postal union; **Unione delle Repubbliche Socialiste Sovietiche,** U.S.S.R.; **un'— felice,** a happy match.
unionismo, *n.m.* Unionism.
unionista, *n.m.* Unionist.
uniparo [unIparo], *a.* (*Zool.*) Uniparous.
unipolare, *a.* (*Elect.*) Unipolar.
unire, *v.t.* To unite, to join, to connect; to add; to blend, to fuse; to enclose (in a letter). **Qui unito,** enclosed herewith.
unirsi, *v.r.* To unite, to join (forces), to join together. **— in matrimonio,** to be joined in matrimony; **molti si unirono ad essi,** many joined them.
unisessuale, *a.* Unisexual.
unisillabico [unisillAbico], *a.* Monosyllabic.
unisillabo [unisIllabo], *n.m.* Monosyllable.
unisono [unIsono], *n.m.a.* Unison, concord, agreement, harmony; unisonant. **Essere all'—,** to be in full accord.
unità [-à], *n.f.* Unity; unit. **— di misura,** unity of measurement; (*Math.*) **— dello stesso ordine,** units of the same denomination; (*Mil.*) **una grande —,** a large unit; (*Elect.*) **— elettrica,** electric unit.
unitamente, *adv.* Jointly, unitedly; together with. **— a,** in company with.
unitario, *n.m.a.* Unitarian. **Prezzo —,** one price only.
unitarismo, *n.m.* (*Eccles. Pol.*) Unitarianism.
unitezza, *n.f.* Oneness; unity; compactness; smoothness; uniformity.
unitivo, *a.* Serving to unite.
unito, *a.* United; equal, unvaried, uniform; (*Comm.*) enclosed. **La lettere unita,** the enclosed letter; **tinta unita,** even colour.
unitura, *n.f.* Oneness; point of union.
universale, *a.* Universal, world-wide; general. **Giudizio —,** Last Judgement; **suffragio —.** universal suffrage; (*Law*) **erede —,** sole heir.
universaleggiare, *v.t.* To universalize.
universalità [-à], *n.f.* Universality.
universalizzare [cp. **universaleggiare**].
universalmente, *adv.* Universally, commonly, generally.
universamente, *adv.* Throughout the universe; universally.
università [-à], *n.f.* University. **Andare all'—,** to go to the university.
universitario [universitArio], *n.m.a.* University man; university, college. **Berretto —,** college cap; **laurea universitaria,** university degree.
universo, *n.m.a.* Universe, whole world, creation, cosmos; universal.
univocazione, *n.f.* Agreement of name and meaning.
univoco [unIvoco], *a.* Univocal; unambiguous, unequivocal.
Unni, *n.m.pl.* (*Hist.*) Huns.
unnico, *a.* Hunnish.
uno, un, una, un', *indef. art.* A, an. **Un uomo,** a man; **uno straniero,** a foreigner; **una donna,** a woman, **un'ora,** an hour.
uno, una, *n.m.f.a.* One. **uno per uno,** one by one; **uno solo,** one only; **l'uno per cento,** one per cent; **uno di noi,** one of us; **nemmeno uno,** not a single one; **senza dire nè uno nè due,** without warning; **numero uno,** first rate; **un asino numero uno,** an egregious ass; **ad uno ad uno,** one by one; **in uno,** together, jointly; **è tutt'uno,** it's all one; **l'uno e l'altro,** the one and the other; **dall'uno all'altro,** from one to the other;

una delle solite, one of his usual tricks; **farne una grossa,** to do something very foolish; **un giorno o l'altro,** some day or other; **una volta per tutte,** once for all; **costano mille lire l'uno,** they cost a thousand lire each; **c'era una volta,** once upon a time.
unquanche, unquanco, *adv.* (*obs.*) Never.
untare, *v.t.* To grease, to oil, to smear; (*fig.*) to flatter.
untata, untatura, *n.f.* Anointing, greasing; flattery.
unto, *n.m.* Grease, oil; fat; flattery; (*Eccles.*) anointed one. **Macchie d'—,** grease spots; **l'— della carne,** fat (of meat).
unto, *a.* Greasy, oily; dirty, filthy; (*Eccles.*) anointed. **— e bisunto,** all greasy.
untore, *n.m.* Anointer; (*Hist.*) poisoner.
untume, *n.m.* Fat, grease; dirt, filth.
untuosità [-à], *n.f.* Greasiness; sanctimoniousness.
untuoso, *a.* Greasy; unctuous, sanctimonious.
unzione, *n.f.* Unction, ointment. **Estrema —,** extreme unction.
uomo (*pl.* **uomini**), *n.m.* Man; husband. **— d'affari,** business man; **— di mare,** seaman; **— qualunque,** man in the street, any man; **— di cuore,** kind-hearted man; **— di mezzi,** well-to-do man; **— d'ingegno,** clever man; **— da nulla,** mere cipher; **un pover'—,** a nonentity, poor fellow; **un — povero,** a poor man; **— fatto,** grown-up man; **farsi —,** to grow up; **da — a —,** as man to man; **lavorare a tutt'—,** to work hard, to do one's utmost.
uopo, *n.m.* Need, necessity. **È d'—,** it is necessary; **all'—,** to this end, for this purpose; in case of necessity.
uose, *n.f.pl.* Gaiters, leggings.
uovo (*pl.* **uova,** *f.*) *n.m.* Egg. **— crudo,** raw egg; **— affogato,** poached egg, **— fresco,** new-laid egg; **— guasto,** stale egg; **— sbattuto,** beaten-up egg; **uova strapazzate,** scrambled eggs; **uova sode,** hard-boiled eggs; **— bollito,** boiled egg; **uova al burro,** fried eggs; (*fig.*) **rompere le uova nel paniere,** to upset one's plans; **cercare il pelo nell'—,** to split hairs; **è meglio un — oggi che una gallina domani,** a bird in the hand is worth two in the bush; **camminare sulle uova,** to tread lightly; **acconciare le uova nel paniere,** to feather one's nest.
uovolo [uOvolo], *a.* Egg-shaped [cp. **ovolo**].
upupa [Upupa], *n.f.* (*Zool.*) Hoopoe; (*incorrectly*) owl.
uragano, *n.m.* Hurricane, gale, storm. **Un — d'applausi,** a storm of applause.
Urali, *n.m.pl.* (*Geog.*) Ural Mountains.
urango, *n.m.* (*Zool.*) Orang-utang.
uranio [urAnio], *n.m.* (*Min.*) Uranium.
uranismo, *n.m.* Homosexuality.
Urano, *n.m.* (*Astron.*) Uranus.
urbanamente, *adv.* Urbanely, civilly.
urbanesimo [urbanEsimo], *n.m.* Urbanism, movement into cities.
urbanistica [urbanIstica], *n.f.* Town-planning.
urbanità [-à], *n.f.* Urbanity, civility, politeness, courtesy.
urbano, *a.* Urban; urbane, civil, polite, courteous. **Vigile —,** city policeman; **distretti urbani,** urban districts; **nettezza urbana,** refuse collection.
Urbe, *n.f.* The City, Rome.
urea [urEa], *n.f.* (*Chem.*) Urea.
uremia [uremIa], *n.f.* (*Med.*) Uraemia.
urente, *a.* (*Lit.*) Burning.
uretere, *n.m.* (*Anat.*) Ureter.
uretra [Uretra], *n.f.* (*Anat.*) Urethra.
urgente, *a.* Urgent, pressing, immediate. **Caso —,** urgent case.
urgentemente, *adv.* Urgently.
urgenza, *n.f.* Urgency, promptness, speed. **Con la massima —,** with the utmost haste; **d'—,** urgently.
urgere [Urgere], *v.t.i.* To urge, to press; to be urgent. **Urge che tu vada,** it is most urgent that you should go; **urgono aiuti,** help urgently needed.
urì [-ì], *n.f.* Houri.
urico [Urico], *a.* (*Med.*) Uric.
urina, *n.f.* Urine [cp. **orina**].
urinario [urinArio], *a.* Urinary.
urlamento, *n.m.* Howling.
urlare, *v.t.i.* To shout, to howl, to yell; to hoot, to scream, to shriek, to bawl. **— a qualcuno,** to shout someone down; to set up a hue and cry.
urlata, *n.f.* Howling, yelling, shouting.
urlatore, urlatrice, *n.m.f.* Shrieker, shouter.
urlio [urlIo], *n.m.* Howling, yelling, shouting.
urlo (pl. **urli,** *m.*, **urla,** *f.*) Howl, yell, shout, shriek, hoot.
urlone, *n.m.* Noisy fellow, shouter.
urna, *n.f.* Urn; ballot-box; (*Lit.*) tomb. **— cineraria,** cinerary urn; **recarsi alle urne,** to vote, to go to the polls; **il responso delle urne,** the result of an election.
uro, *n.m.* (*Zool.*) Wild bull, aurochs.
urogallo, *n.m.* (*Zool.*) Black cock; capercailzie.
uroscopia [uroscopIa], *n.f.* (*Med.*) Uroscopy.
urrà! *inter.* Hurrah!
urta, *n.f.* Rancour, aversion.
urtacchiare, *v.t.* To keep on knocking.
urtamento, *n.m.* Knock.
urtante, *a.* Irritating, vexing, teasing; disappointing.
urtare, *v.t.i.* To knock, to hit, to strike; to dash against, to stumble upon; (*Naut.*) to collide with, to run foul of.
urtarsi, *v.r.* To collide, to come into collision; to jostle one another; to clash.
urtata, *n.f.* Push, shove, knock.
urto, *n.m.* Knock, shock; impact, collision, bump; rush; attack, onset. **Essere in — con qualcuno,** to be on bad terms with someone; **mettere in —,** to fall out with; **sostenere l'— dell'attacco,** to bear the brunt of the attack; **l'— fu terribile,** the impact was terrible; **— ferroviario,** railway crash.
urtone, *n.m.* Shove, knock, push. **Mi diede un —,** he gave me a shove.
usabile [usAbile], *a.* Usable.
usanza, *n.f.* Usage, custom, habit. **Secondo l'—,** according to custom; **è una cattiva —,** it's a bad habit; **una vecchia —,** an old custom.
usante, *n.m.* User.

usare, *v.t.i.* To use, to make use of; to employ, to exercise; to be customary, to be wont, to be accustomed, to be used, to be in the habit; to be fashionable, to be the thing. — **la massima cura,** to exercise the utmost care; — **pietà,** to show mercy; — **la cortesia di,** to be so kind as to; **questo non usa più,** this is out of fashion.
usarsi, *v.r.* To be in use, to be used; to be fashionable. **Si usa ancora,** it is still in use, it is still the fashion; **come s'usa,** as the custom is.
usata, *n.f.* [cp. **usanza**].
usatamente, *adv.* Commonly, customarily, usually.
usato, *p.p.a.* Used, employed; worn out; second-hand; customary, usual. **Libri usati,** second-hand books; **secondo l'—,** as usual; **più dell'—,** more than usual.
usatto, *n.m.* High boot, thigh-boot.
usbergo, *n.m.* Breastplate, cuirass; (*fig.*) protection, shield.
uscente, *a.* Going out, coming out; ending, finishing; retiring (from office); (*Comm.*) vacating, closing, expiring.
uscetto, *n.m.* Wicket-gate.
usciale, *n.m.* Glass door.
usciata, *n.f.* Bang (of door).
usciere, *n.m.* Usher, beadle; bailiff (sheriff's officer); doorkeeper. **Mandare gli uscieri,** to put in the bailiffs.
uscimento, *n.m.* Exit.
uscio [Uscio], *n.m.* Door, opening. **Prender l'—,** to go away; **chiudere l'—,** to close or shut the door; **sbattere l'—,** to bang the door; **star sull'—,** to stand at the door; **l'— di strada,** the front door, the street door.
usciolino, usciolo, *n.m.* Small door, wicket.
uscire, escire, *v.i.* To go out; to come out, to get out; to leave; to result, to emerge from, to issue; to be published; to end in. **Il libro è uscito,** the book has come out; — **dal seminato,** to digress; — **dalla memoria,** to escape one's memory; **uscirne bene, male,** to get the best, worst of it; — **in vocale,** to end in a vowel; **far —,** to let out; **Uscite!** Get out! Go out! — **di sè,** to go mad; to lose one's temper; — **alla luce,** to come into the open; to be published; — **dalle rotaie,** to go off the rails, to leave the metals; **egli sta per —,** he's just going out; **usciamo un po',** let's go for a walk.
uscita, *n.f.* Exit, way out; going out, coming out; outlet, outcome; retort, joke; (*Comm.*) expense, outlay. **All'— di,** at the end of, on leaving; **pagare una buon'—,** to pay an indemnity; **è il suo giorno di —,** this is her day out; (*Comm.*) **entrate e uscite,** assets and liabilities, credit and debit; **dazio d'—,** export duty.
usciuolo, *n.m.* Small door.
uscocchi, *n.m.pl.* (*Hist.*) Adriatic pirates.
usignuolo, usignolo, *n.m.* Nightingale.
usitatamente, *adv.* Commonly used.
usitato, *p.p.a.* Used, employed, in common use.
uso, *n.m.* Use; usage, custom, habit; wear and tear. **Far — di,** to make use of; **ad — di,** for the use of; **è una cosa molto in —,** it is a customary thing; **all'— romano,** after the Roman fashion; **oggetti fuori —,** worn-out articles, old clothes, etc.; **per mio — e consumo,** for my own use, on my own account; **secondo l'—,** according to custom; — **e consumo,** wear and tear.
usofrutto [cp. **usufrutto**].
usolare, *v.i.* To pry, to peep.
ussero, ussaro [Ussero, Ussaro], *n.m.* Hussar.
Ussiti, *n.m.pl.* (*Hist.*) Hussites.
ussoricida, *n.m.* Wife-killer, uxoricide.
ussoricidio [ussoricIdio], *n.m.* Uxoricide (crime) [cp. **uxoricidio**].
usta, *n.f.* (Dogs' sense of) scent.
ustionare, *v.t.* To burn, to scald; to scorch.
ustione, *n.f.* Burning, scorching.
usto, *n.m.* (*Naut.*) Main cable.
usto, *p.p.a.* (*Poet.*) Burnt.
ustolare, *v.i.* To whine for food, to beg (of animals).
ustolone, *n.m.* Whining beggar.
ustorio [ustOrio], *a.* Burning. **Specchio —,** burning glass.
usuale, *a.* Usual, customary, common, ordinary. **Nel modo —,** in the usual way; **alle condizioni usuali,** on the usual conditions.
usualità [-à], *n.f.* Usualness, commonness.
usualmente, *adv.* Usually, commonly, as a rule, generally.
usucapione, *n.f.* (*Law*) Usucaption, usucapio, possession by long custom.
usufruire, *v.t.* To avail oneself of, to take advantage of. — **d'un ribasso ferroviario,** to take advantage of a reduction in fares.
usufruttare, *v.t.* (*Law*) To enjoy usufruct, to occupy as a tenant.
usufrutto, *n.m.* Usufruct.
usufruttuario [usufruttuArio], *n.m.* Usufructuary, tenant.
usura, *n.f.* Usury; (*colloq.*) wear and tear, attrition. **Ad —,** with interest, in excess, too much; **l'— del macchinario,** the wear and tear of machinery; **guerra d'—,** war of attrition.
usuraio [usurAio], *n.m.* Usurer, money-lender.
usureggiare, *v.i.* To practise usury.
usuriere, *n.m.* Usurer.
usurpamento, *n.m.* Usurping, usurpation; encroachment.
usurpare, *v.t.* To usurp; to encroach upon.
usurpatore, usurpatrice, *n.m.f.* Usurper.
usurpatorio [usurpatOrio], *a.* Usurpatory.
usurpazione, *n.f.* Usurpation.
ut, *n.m.* (*Mus.*) The note "do."
utello, *n.m.* Small oil cruet.
utensile [utEnsile], *n.m.* Tool, implement, utensil. **Macchina —,** machine-tool.
utente, *n.m.a.* User, consumer (of gas, etc.); using.
utenza, *n.f.* Use, users (of gas, etc.); right of use.
uterino, *a.* Uterine. **Fratello —,** half-brother (by the same mother).
utero [Utero], *n.m.* (*Anat.*) Uterus, womb.
utile [Utile], *n.m.* Profit, gain; (*Comm.*) dividend. **L'— netto,** the net profit; **dividere gli utili,** to share the profits.
utile [Utile], *a.* Useful, serviceable, helpful, practical; effective. **Tornar —,** to prove useful; **rendersi — a,** to be of help to; **arrivare in tempo —,** to arrive in good time; **il termine — per iscriversi,** the last day for registration; **ritener —,** to deem useful.

utilità [-à], *n.f.* Usefulness, utility, serviceableness, use. **Essere di grande —**, to be of great use; **riuscire d'—**, to prove useful.
utilitario [utilitArio], *a.* Utilitarian.
utilitarismo, *n.m.* Utilitarianism.
utilitarista, *n.m.* Utilitarian.
utilizzabile [utilizzAbile], *a.* Usable, available.
utilizzare, *v.t.* To utilize, to employ, to make use of, to turn to account.
utilizzazione, *n.f.* Utilization, use.
utilmente, *adv.* Usefully, profitably.
utopia [utopIa], *n.f.* Utopia.
utopista, *n.m.* Utopian.
utopistico [utopIstico], *a.* Utopian; impracticable.
uva, *n.f.* Grape, grapes (collectively). **— secca, — passa,** raisin; **— spina,** gooseberry; **coglier l'—**, to gather grapes; **un grappolo d'—**, a bunch of grapes; **pigiar l'—**, to tread grapes; **— acerba,** sour grapes.
uvaceo [uvAceo], *a.* Grape-coloured.
uvaggio [uvAggio], *n.m.* Grapes of different kinds; wine made from these.
uvea [Uvea], *n.f.* (*Anat.*) Uvea (of the eye).
uvifero [uvIfero], *a.* Grape-bearing.
uxoricida, *n.m.* Wife-murderer.
uxoricidio [uxoricIdio], *n.m.* Wife-murder.
uzza, *n.f.* Sharpness in the air; breeze.
uzzo, *n.m.* Bulge, convexity, bulging side (of a cask).
uzzolo [Uzzolo], *n.m.* Longing, desire; caprice; passion for.

V

V, v, *n.m.f.* Twentieth letter of the Italian alphabet.
Va! vah! *inter.* Look! Look here!
vacabile [vacAbile], *a.* That may be vacant, likely to be vacant.
vacante, *a.* Vacant; free, empty, unoccupied. **Un posto —**, a vacancy, a vacant situation.
vacanza, *n.f.* Holiday, vacation, recess; vacancy. **Durante le vacanze,** during the holidays; **un giorno di —**, a day off; **le vacanze estive,** the summer holidays; **coprire una —**, to fill a vacancy.
vacare, *v.i.* To be vacant.
vacato, *p.p.a.* Vacant, empty.
vacca, *n.f.* Cow. **— da latte,** dairy cow, milch cow; **latte di —**, cow's milk.
vaccaio, vaccaro [vaccAio], *n.m.* Cow-herd, cow-keeper.
vaccherella, *n.f.* Small cow; heifer.
vaccheria [vaccherIa], *n.f.* Cow-house, byre; dairy farm.
vacchetta, *n.f.* Heifer; cow-hide.
vaccina, *n.f.* Cow.
vaccinabile [vaccinAbile], *a.* Ready for vaccination.
vaccinare, *v.t.* To vaccinate. **Bisogna farsi —**, one must be vaccinated
vaccinatore, *n.m.* Vaccinator.
vaccinazione, *n.f.* Vaccination.
vaccino, *n.m.* Vaccine, lymph.
vacillamento, *n.m.* Vacillation, hesitation; tottering, staggering, reeling, wobbling.
vacillante, *a.* Vacillating, tottering; flickering.
vacillanza, *n.f.* Hesitation.
vacillare, *v.i.* To totter, to vacillate; to reel, to stagger; to hesitate, to waver, to shilly-shally; to flicker.
vacillazione, *n.f.* Vacillation.
vacuità [-à], *n.f.* Vacuity; blankness, emptiness; futility.
vacuo [vAcuo], *n.m.a.* Vacuum; empty, void; vacuous; dull, vain; futile.
vademecum, *n.m.* Memorandum-book, vademecum.
va-e-vieni, *n.m.* Going-and-coming; see-saw motion.
vagabondaggine [vagabondAggine], *n.f.* Vagabondage.
vagabondaggio [vagabondAggio], *n.m.* Wandering, rambling; vagabondage, vagrancy.
vagabondare, vagabondeggiare, *v.i.* To wander, to stroll, to rove, to roam, to ramble; to tramp (the roads).
vagabondo, *n.m.a.* Vagrant, tramp, vagabond; errant, wandering, tramping.
vagamente, *adv.* Vaguely; charmingly, gracefully.
vagamento, *n.m.* Wandering.
vagante, *a.* Wandering, rambling, errant.
vagare, *v.i.* To wander, to ramble, to rove, to roam. **— col pensiero,** to muse; to wander.
vagazione, *n.f.* Wandering.
vagello, *n.m.* Dyer's vat; blue dye.
vagheggiamento, *n.m.* Longing, yearning, cherishing (a hope, etc.).
vagheggiare, *v.t.* To long for, to yearn for; to look lovingly at; to woo, to court; to cherish (a hope, etc.).
vagheggiatore, *n.m.* Man in love; courting swain.
vagheggino, *n.m.* Dandy, fop; lady-killer.
vaghezza, *n.f.* Desire, longing; charm, beauty; vagueness.
vagina, *n.f.* (*Anat.*) Vagina; sheath, envelope; (*obs.*) skin.
vaginale, *a.* Vaginal.
vagire, *v.i.* To cry feebly, to whimper, to wail (of infants).
vagito, *n.m.* (Infant's) wail or cry; whimper.
vaglia [vAglia] (1), *n.f.* Worth, merit; ability. **Pittore di —**, renowned artist; **uomo di —**, man of mark.
vaglia [vAglia] (2), *n.m.* Money order, postal order; cheque. **Spedire un —**, to send a postal order; **— internazionale,** money order; **— bancario,** banker's order.
vagliaio [vagliAio], *n.m.* Sieve-maker.
vagliare, *v.t.* To sift, to sieve, to winnow; to select, to pick out, to examine.
vagliata, *n.f.* Sifting.
vagliatura, *n.f.* Sifting; winnowing; siftings.
vaglio [vAglio], *n.m.* Sieve. **Passare al —**, to sift, to sieve.
vago, *a.* Pretty, lovely, charming, attractive, pleasing; longing for, desirous of; vague, ill-defined, indistinct, ambiguous; erratic, erring.
vagolare [cp. **vagare**].
vagonata, *n.f.* Waggon-load, truck-load, lorry-load.
vagoncino, *n.m.* Small waggon, truck.
vagone, *n.m.* (*Rail.*) Car, waggon, carriage, truck. **— letto,** sleeping-car; **— merci,**

(open) goods truck; — **ristorante,** dining-car; — **di terza classe,** third-class coach.
vaiano, *n.m.* Dark variety of grape.
vaiare, *v.i.* To turn dark (of grapes).
vaieggiare, *v.i.* To turn dark or blackish.
vainiglia [cp. **vaniglia**].
vaio [vAio], *n.m.a.* Blackish; brownish; spotted.
vaiolare, *v.i.* To turn black (of grapes).
vaiolo, vaiuolo, *n.m.* (*Med.*) Smallpox. — **spurio,** chickenpox.
vaioloso, *n.m.a.* Smallpox patient; suffering from smallpox, pock-marked; variolar, variolous.
valanga, *n.f.* Avalanche, snow-slip; (*fig.*) crowd, lot.
valdese, *n.m.a.* (*Eccles.*) Waldensian.
vale, *n.m.inter.* Farewell.
valente, *a.* Skilful, capable, clever, talented, expert.
valentemente, *adv.* Ably, skilfully.
valentia [valentIa], *n.f.* Skill, skilfulness, cleverness, ability, bravery; worth.
valentuomo, *n.m.* Worthy man, honest man.
valenza, *n.f.* Valour, worth; (*Chem.*) valency.
Valenza, *n.f.* (*Geog.*) Valencia (Spain).
valere, *v.i.* To be worth; to be valuable, to be of value; to cost; to be equal; to be valid; (*Comm.*) to have currency, to be current. **Vale la pena,** it's worth while; **a che vale?** what's the use of it? **vale a dire,** that is to say; **tanto vale,** one might as well; it's all the same; **farsi —,** to make oneself respected; **meglio varrebbe,** it would be better; **questo anello non vale niente,** this ring is worthless; **i suoi consigli non valsero a nulla,** his advice was of no avail; **Quanto vale questa collana?** What is the price of this necklace? **ciò varrà a renderlo migliore,** this will make him better; **questo biglietto vale fino a domani,** this ticket is valid until tomorrow; **non vale negarlo,** it's no use denying it; (*Sport*) **non vale,** it doesn't count, no score.
valeriana, *n.f.* (*Bot.*) Valerian.
valersi, *v.r.* To avail oneself of, to make use of, to profit by; to employ. **Si è valso della sua posizione per aiutarmi,** he took advantage of his position to help me.
valetudinario [valetudinArio], *n.m.a.* Valetudinarian.
valevole [valEvole], *a.* Efficacious, helpful; valid; available; valuable, useful. — **fino a domani,** valid until tomorrow.
valevolmente, *adv.* Helpfully, valuably.
valicabile [valicAbile], *a.* Fordable, possible to cross.
valicare, *v.t.* To pass, to cross, to surmount; to ford.
valico [vAlico], *n.m.* Passage, pass, mountain pass; gap; ford.
validamente, *adv.* Validly, effectively.
validare, *v.t.* [cp. **convalidare**].
validazione, *n.f.* Validation [cp. **convalidazione**].
validità [-à], *n.f.* Validity; worth; legality; strength, force. **La — d'un biglietto,** the validity of a ticket.
valido [vAlido], *a.* Valid; legal, binding; sound, well-grounded; sturdy, vigorous, able-bodied; effective.
valigeria [valigerIa], *n.f.* Trunk shop; sadler's shop, shop for leather goods.
valigetta, *n.f.* Suit-case, attaché-case, bag.
valigia [valIgia], *n.f.* Suit-case, portmanteau, travelling-bag. **Fare le valigie,** to pack; — **diplomatica,** diplomatic bag.
valigiaio [valigiAio], *n.m.* Trunk-maker.
vallare, *v.t.* (*Mil.*) To surround with ramparts.
valle, vallata, *n.f.* Valley, vale; dale. **A —,** downstream, **per monti e per valli,** o'er hill and dale.
Vallesia [vallEsia], *n.f.* (*Geog.*) Vaud (Switzerland).
valletta, *n.f.* Little valley, dale, vale, dell.
valletto, *n.m.* Valet; page, footman.
valligiano, *n.m.* Dalesman, dweller in a valley.
vallo, *n.m.* Rampart, vallum.
valloncello, *n.m.* Narrow valley, gorge, glen.
vallone (1), *n.m.* Narrow, deep valley, canyon.
vallone (2), *n.m.a.* Walloon.
valore, *n.m.* Value, price, worth, cost, amount; gallantry, valour, courage, bravery, prowess; (*Comm.*) security, stock share; investment, holding, money. **Aver —,** to be of value; **mettere in —,** to give value; — **intrinseco,** intrinsic value; — **nominale,** nominal value; **un uomo di —,** a man of distinction; **un atto di —,** an act of bravery; (*Comm.*) — **assegnato,** declared value; **valori mobili,** stocks and shares, securities.
valorizzare, *v.t.* To give full value to, to increase in value; to employ to advantage; to turn to account; to make known.
valorizzazione, *n.f.* Full appreciation, full value; improvement.
valorosamente, *adv.* Bravely, valorously.
valoroso, *n.m.* Brave man, gallant fellow.
valoroso, *a.* Brave, courageous, valiant.
Valpolicella, *n.f.* Variety of red wine from Verona.
valsente, *n.m.* (*Comm.*) Cash value; price.
valso, *p.p.a.* Valued [cp. **valere**].
valuta, *n.f.* (*Comm.*) Currency, money; value, market value, price. — **metallica,** specie, hard cash; — **cartacea,** paper money; — **in conto,** value on account; — **in contanti,** cash payment; — **intesa,** agreed value; — **estera,** foreign currency.
valutabile [valutAbile], *a.* Calculable, computable, capable of being valued.
valutare, *v.t.* To estimate, to appraise, to value; to rate; to consider, to weigh.
valutazione, *n.f.* Valuation, appreciation, estimation; estimate. **Fare una — di,** to give an appreciation of; to make an estimate of.
valva, *n.f.* (*Bot. Zool.*) Valve (of a shell, etc.).
valvola [vAlvola], *n.f.* (*Mech. Radio*) Valve, tube; (*Anat.*) valve. — **di sicurezza,** safety-valve; — **di scappamento,** exhaust valve; — **d'aspirazione,** inlet valve; — **a vapore,** steam-valve; (*Radio*) **apparecchio a sei valvole,** 6- tube set; — **schermata,** screen-grid tube.
valvolare, *a.* (*Anat.*) Valvular.
valzer, *n.m.* Waltz. **Ballare il —,** to waltz.
vampa, *n.f.* Blaze, flame; flash; heat (of flame); blush. **La — del sole,** the glare of the sun; **le vampe gli salirono al viso,** he turned crimson.
vampata, *n.f.* Blaze flame, burst of flame; rush (of hot air).

vampeggiamento, *n.m.* A flashing, a blazing.
vampeggiare, *v.i.* To flame, to blaze, to flash.
vampirismo, *n.m.* Vampirism, blood-sucking (in all senses).
vampiro, *n.m.* Vampire, blood-sucker.
vampo, *n.m.* Burst of flame [cp. **vampa**].
vanadio [vanAdio], *n.m.* (*Min.*) Vanadium.
vanagloria [vanaglOria], *n.f.* Vainglory, boastfulness, conceit, vanity, pride.
vanagloriarsi, *v.r.* To boast, to brag, to vaunt.
vanagloriosamente, *adv.* Vaingloriously, boastfully.
vanaglorioso, *a.* Vainglorious, boastful, conceited; arrogant.
vanamente, *adv.* Vainly, uselessly; conceitedly.
vandalico [vandAlico], *a.* Like a Vandal (in all senses).
vandalismo, *n.m.* Vandalism. **Commettere un —,** to commit a vandalism.
vandalo [vAndalo], *n.m.a.* Vandal (in all senses).
vaneggiamento, *n.m.* Raving; dotage; nonsense, wild talk.
vaneggiare, *v.i.* To rave, to be delirious; to talk wildly; to wander (in speech or thought).
vaneggiatore, vaneggiatrice, *n.m.f.* Day-dreamer; foolish talker, dotard.
vanello, *n.m.* (*Zool.*) Peewit.
vanerello, *n.m.a.* Fop, conceited fellow; conceited.
vanesata, *n.f.* Conceited action, piece of foppishness.
vanescente, *a.* Vanishing.
vanesio [vanEsio], *n.m.a.* Fop, conceited ass; foppish, vain, fatuous.
vanessa, *n.f.* (*Zool.*) Red admiral butterfly, vanessa.
vanga, *n.f.* Spade, mattock.
vangare, *v.t.* To dig, to delve; to turn up, to excavate.
vangata, *n.f.* Spadeful; stroke with a spade.
vangatore, *n.m.* Digger.
vangatura, *n.f.* Digging, delving.
vangelico [vangElico], *a.* Evangelical.
vangelista (pl. **vangelisti**), *n.m.* Evangelist.
vangelizzare, *v.t.* To evangelize, to preach the Gospel.
vangelo, *n.m.* Gospel. **I quattro vangeli,** the Four Gospels; (*fig.*) **questo è —,** this is the gospel truth.
vangheggia [vanghEggia], *n.f.* (*Agric.*) Ploughshare.
vanghettare, *v.t.* To trowel lightly.
vanghetto, *n.m.* (Garden) trowel.
vangile, *n.m.* Foot-piece of a spade.
vaniglia [vanIglia], *n.f.* Vanilla.
vanigliare, *v.t.* To flavour with vanilla.
vaniloquio [vanilOquio], *n.m.* Vain talk, chatter, nonsense. talking at random.
vanire [cp. **svanire**].
vanità [-à], *n.f.* Vanity; vainglory, conceit; emptiness, futility.
vanitosamente, *adv.* Vainly, conceitedly.
vanitoso, *a.* Vain, conceited, vainglorious, boastful; fatuous.
vanni, *n.m.pl.* (*Lit.*) Wings, pinions.
vano, *n.m.* Empty space; room; window or door embrasure; niche. **Stare nel — della finestra,** to stand in the window; **una casa di venti vani,** a house with twenty rooms.
vano, *a.* Vain, empty, inane, futile; fatuous; frivolous; vainglorious. **Sforzi vani,** vain efforts, **un nome —,** an empty name; **è — gridare,** it is useless to shout.
vantaggiare, *v.t.* To benefit [cp. **avvantaggiare**].
vantaggiatamente, *adv.* In a superior way excessively.
vantaggiato, *a.* Over and above. **Un metro —,** something over a metre.
vantaggino, *n.m.* Little bit extra, something thrown in.
vantaggio [vantAggio], *n.m.* Advantage, gain, benefit, profit; superiority, precedence; (*Sport*) start; (*Print.*) galley. **Prendere il — su,** to get the advantage over; **riuscire di sommo —,** to turn out very profitable; **A — di chi?** On whose behalf? **arrivai con un'ora di —,** I arrived with an hour to spare, an hour before time.
vantaggiosamente, *adv.* Advantageously.
vantaggioso, *a.* Advantageous, profitable, useful; favourable; beneficial; lucrative.
vantamento [cp. **vanteria**].
vantare, *v.t.* To praise, to glorify, to exalt, to extol; to boast, to vaunt; (*Comm.*) to set up (a claim).
vantarsi, *v.r.* To boast, to brag, to swagger.
vantatore, vantatrice, *n.m.f.* Boaster.
vanteria [vanterIa], *n.f.* Boasting, bragging, swaggering.
vanto, *n.m.* Vaunt, brag, boast; pride; honour, glory; ornament. **Menar —,** to brag; **è un — della nostra città,** he is one of the ornaments of our city; **avere il — sopra,** to carry the palm over.
vanume, *n.f.* Grain drying on the stalk; frivolous thing, vanity, bauble.
vanvera [vAnvera], *adv.* **A —,** at random, heedlessly, rashly. **Parlare a —,** to talk nonsense, to talk at random.
vaporabile [vaporAbile], *a.* Evaporable [cp. **evaporabile**].
vaporaio [vaporAio], *n.m.* (*colloq.*) Engine-driver, mechanic.
vapore, *n.m.* Vapour, fume, haze; steam; steamer, steamship; locomotive (of train); **— acqueo,** watery vapour; **— mercantile,** cargo-vessel; **macchina a —,** steam-engine; **a tutto —,** at full speed; **bagno a —,** vapour-bath; **caldaia a —,** boiler; **i vapori del vino,** the fumes of wine.
vaporetto, *n.m.* (*Naut.*) Steam-launch, steam-boat, steam ferry.
vaporiera, *n.f.* (*Lit.*) (Railway) locomotive.
vaporino, *n.m.* (*Naut.*) Steamer, steamboat.
vaporizzare, *v.t.* To vaporize; to spray.
vaporizzatore, *n.m.* Vaporizer, spray, atomizer.
vaporizzazione, *n.f.* Vaporization, evaporation.
vaporosità [-à], *n.f.* Vaporousness; haziness, vagueness.
vaporoso, *a.* Vaporous, hazy, misty, vague; light, transparent; filmy, gauzy.
varamento, *n.m.* Launching, launch.
varare, *v.t.* To launch (in all senses); (*Pol.*) to pass a Bill. **— un affare,** to float a business.

varcabile [varcAbile], *a.* Passable, possible to cross.
varcare, *v.t.* To cross, to pass, to go over, to surmount. **Egli ha varcato la quarantina,** he is over forty.
varco, *n.m.* Pass, passage, opening, outlet; gap. **Attendere al —,** to lie in wait for; **aprirsi un —,** to make one's way through, to break through.
variabile [variAbile], *a.* Variable, changeable; inconstant; irregular; unsettled (of weather). **È una ragazza —,** she's a fickle girl.
variabilità [-à], *n.f.* Changeableness, changeability, variability, inconstancy, fickleness.
variamente, *adv.* Variously.
variante, *n.f.* Variant; alteration, change, modification.
variante, *a.* Variable, changing, different.
variantemente, *adv.* Variably, variedly.
variare, *v.t.i.* To change, to alter, to vary, to modify, to diversify; to be different, to differ; to shift (of the wind).
variatamente, *adv.* Variedly, in a varied fashion.
variazione, *n.f.* Variation, alteration, difference, change, modification.
varice, *n.f.* (*Med.*) Varix.
varicella, *n.f.* (*Med.*) Chicken-pox.
varicoso, *a.* (*Med.*) Varicose. **Vene varicose,** varicose veins.
variegato, *a.* Variegated, dappled.
varieggiare, *v.i.* To vary, to differ constantly, to change frequently.
varietà [-à], *n.f.* Variety, variation, change, diversity; species, kind, sort; miscellany, odds and ends (of news). **Teatro di —,** music-hall; **spettacolo di —,** variety show; **vi era ogni — di fiori,** there was every sort of flower there.
variforme, *a.* Variform, multiform.
vario [vArio], *a.* Various; different, diverse; varied; heterogeneous; changeable, variable. **C'erano varie signore,** there were several ladies; **tempo —,** changeable weather.
variometro [variOmetro], *n.m.* Variometer.
variopinto, *a.* Many-coloured, variegated; speckled.
varo, *n.m.* Launch (of a ship), launching.
vasaio [vasAio], *n.m.* Potter.
vasame, *n.m.* Pottery.
vasca, *n.f.* Basin; bath, tub; tank; pool; reservoir. **— da bagno,** bath-tub.
vascello, *n.f.* (*Naut.*) Vessel, ship (esp. naval).
vaschetta, *n.f.* Small vase; basin; bulb (of thermometer).
vascolare, *a.* (*Anat.*) Vascular.
vascolo [vAscolo], *n.m.* (*Bot.*) Vasculum.
vasellame, *n.m.* China, crockery; plate (of metal). **— d'argento,** silver-plate.
vasello, *n.m.* Vase; receptacle, vessel.
vasetto, *n.m.* Small vase, jar. **— di marmellata,** pot of jam.
vasiforme, *a.* Vasiform.
vaso, *n.m.* Pot, vessel; vase; jar; (*Anat.*) vessel. **— di bronzo,** bronze vase; **— da fiori,** flower-pot; **— da notte,** chamber-pot; **mettere in —,** to pot; **— sanguigno,** blood-vessel; **portare vasi a Samo,** to carry coals to Newcastle.
vasomotore, *a.* (*Anat.*) Vasomotor.
vassallaggio [vassallAggio], *n.m.* Vassalage, servitude, dependence.
vassallo, *n.m.* Vassal, slave, dependent.
vassoio [vassOio], *n.m.* Tray. **— da tè,** tea-tray.
vastamente, *adv.* Vastly, hugely.
vastezza, vastità [-à], *n.f.* Hugeness, vastness, wide expanse, immensity.
vasto, *a.* Vast, huge, wide, large, broad. **Fronte vasta,** broad forehead; **— impero,** great empire.
vate, *n.m.* (*Lit.*) Bard, poet; prophet.
Vaticano, *n.m.* (*Geog. Pol.*) Vatican.
vaticinare, *v.t.i.* To prophesy, to foretell, to predict.
vaticinatore, vaticinatrice, *n.m.f.* Foreteller, prophet.
vaticinazione, *n.f.* Vaticination, prophecy.
vaticinio [vaticInio], *n.m.* Prophecy, prediction, foretelling.
vattelapesca! *inter.* Goodness knows! Who knows!
ve, *pron.* You, to you (used for **vi** before **lo, la, li, le, ne**). **Ve lo scrissi,** I wrote it to you; **ve lo porterò io,** I will bring it to you; **Quante ve ne mandano?** How many of them do they send to you? **ve ne pentirete,** you will repent of it; **Ve ne andate?** Are you going? **Ve ne state là tutte sole?** Are you girls stopping there all alone?
ve, *adv.* There (used for **vi** before *lo, la, li, le, ne*). **Ve n'era una quantità,** there was a lot of it; **ve ne sono molti,** there are many.
ve'! *inter.* Look! See!
vecchia [vEcchia], *n.f.* Old woman.
vecchiaccia [vecchiAccia], *n.f.* Hag, old witch.
vecchiaia [vecchiAia], *n.f.* Old age, age.
vecchiardo, *n.m.* Old man, bad old man. **Susanna e i vecchiardi,** Susannah and the elders.
vecchiata, *n.f.* Old usage, old customs.
vecchierella, vecchietta, *n.f.* Nice old woman, granny; poor old creature.
vecchierello, vecchietto, *n.m.* Good old man; poor old fellow.
vecchiezza, *n.f.* Old age, age.
vecchino, *n.m.* Dear old fellow, nice old boy.
vecchio [vEcchio], *n.m.* Old man; old (as opposed to new). **I miei vecchi,** my parents.
vecchio [vEcchio], *a.* Old, aged, elderly, advanced in years; ancient (of things), old-fashioned. **I vecchi,** old people; **essere — nel mestiere,** to be an old hand at the game.
vecchione, vecchiona, *n.m.f.* Very old man or woman. **Ospizio dei vecchioni,** home for the aged, almshouse.
vecchiotto, *n.m.a.* Elderly man; rather old, getting old, elderly.
vecchiume, *n.m.* Old-fashioned notions, old stuff.
veccia [vEccia], *n.f.* (*Bot.*) Vetch, tare.
vecciato, *a.* Vetchy, weedy, full of tares.
veccione, *n.m.* Wood vetch.
veccioni, *n.m.pl.* Buck-shot.
vece, *n.f.* Stead, place; succession; change. **Far le veci di,** to take the place of, to act as substitute for; **in mia —,** in my place; (*Lit.*) **con — assidua,** in alternate succession.
vedere, *v.t.i.* To see; to notice, to observe, to perceive; to look at; to consider, to note, to remark; to meet, to visit. **— chiaro in,** to see clearly (in a matter); **— per credere.**

seeing is believing; — **doppio**, to see double, to see the wrong thing; — **lontano**, to be long sighted, to be far-sighted; — **giusto**, to see right; **a mio modo di —**, in my view, to my way of thinking; **non — l'ora di partire**, to be longing to leave; **vedrò di accontentarti**, I shall do my best to please you; **vedi di venir presto**, see that you come soon; **fatti —**, come to see me, let's have a glimpse of you; **Vedremo!** We shall see! **vieni a —**, come and see; — **la luce**, to be born, to appear (of a book, etc.); — **di buon occhio**, to look at favourably; **non ci vedo**, I cannot see; — **avanti**, to see ahead; **stare a —**, to be on the look-out, to wait and see; **vedrò io**, I'll see to it; — **le stelle**, to see stars (in all senses); **chi s'è visto s'è visto**, there is nothing more to be said.
vedere, *n.m.* Sight, appearance. **Fa un bel —**, it makes a fine sight.
vedersi, *v.r.* To see oneself; to see each other, to meet. **Si vedevano molto spesso.** they met very often.
vedetta, *n.f.* Look-out, outpost, watch, sentinel, sentry; look-out man. **Stare in —**, to be on the look-out; to do sentry-go; **stare alle vedette**, to be on the look-out.
veditore, veditrice, *n.m.f.* Onlooker.
vedova [vEdova], *n.f.* Widow. **Restar —** to be left a widow.
vedovanza, *n.f.* Widowhood.
vedovare, *v.t.* To widow, to bereave.
vedovella, *n.f.* Young widow.
vedovile, *n.m.* (*Law*) Widow's dower.
vedovile, *a.* Widower's, widow's, of a widower or widow.
vedovo [vEdovo], *n.m.a.* Widower; widowed.
vedretta, *n.f.* Small glacier.
veduta, *n.f.* View; sight; panorama. **Avere grandi vedute**, to have large views, to be far-sighted.
veduto, *p.p.a.* Seen; noticed, observed. **A ragion veduta**, all things considered; — **di buon occhio**, well-liked, well-received.
veemente, *a.* Vehement, impetuous, violent; passionate, dashing
veementemente *adv.* Vehemently.
veemenza, *n.f.* Vehemence, impetuosity, impetuousness; ardour.
vegetabile [vegetAbile], *a.* Vegetable.
vegetale, *n.m.a.* Vegetable; plant life. **Regno —**, vegetable kingdom.
vegetare, *v.i.* To vegetate; merely to exist; to grow.
vegetarianismo, *n.m.* Vegetarianism.
vegetariano, *n.m.a.* Vegetarian.
vegetativo, *a.* Vegetative.
vegetazione, *n.f.* Vegetation.
vegeto [vEgeto], *a.* Hale, vigorous, robust, flourishing; thriving; luxuriant. **Vecchio —**, hale old man.
vegeto-minerale, *a.* Vegeto-mineral.
veggente, *n.m.a.* Seer, prophet; far-seeing, clear-sighted.
veggenza, *n.f.* Sight, insight, clear-sightedness.
veggio [vEggio], *n.m.* Warming-pan for the hands.
veglia [vEglia], *n.f.* Vigil, watch; sitting-up, staying up; evening party. **Essere tra il sonno e la —**, to be half-awake.
vegliamento, *n.m.* Watching, keeping watch.
vegliardo, *n.m.* Very old man.
vegliare, *v.t.i.* To watch (by a sick-bed); to attend; to sit up, to keep awake, to wake; to be on the watch, to be on guard. — **un ammalato**, to sit up with a sick person; — **su**, to keep an eye on.
vegliatore, *n.m.* Watchman, watcher.
vegliatrice, *n.f.* Night-nurse.
veglio [cp. **vegliardo**].
veglione, *n.m.* Masked ball (in a theatre).
vegnente, *a.* (*Lit.*) Coming, forthcoming.
veicolo [veIcolo], *n.m.* Vehicle (in all senses); conveyance. — **d'infezione**, carrier (of infection).
vela, *n.f.* Sail, canvas. **A gonfie vele**, with full sails set; successfully; — **maestra**, mainsail; **barca a —**, sailing-boat; **bastimento a —**, sailing-ship; **ammainare le vele**, to lower the sails, to strike the sails; **spiegare le vele**, to set sail.
velaio [velAio], *n.m.* Sail-maker.
velame, *n.m.* Sails (collectively); covering, veil. **Sotto il —**, under the veil (of allegory).
velamento, *n.m.* Covering, veiling.
velare, *v.t.* To veil, to cover; to hide, to conceal; to disguise; to glaze.
velario [velArio], *n.m.* Curtain; awning; disguise; (*Hist.*) velarium.
velarsi, *v.r.* To veil oneself, to put on a veil; to grow dim. **Gli occhi le si velarono di pianto**, her eyes grew dim with tears.
velatamente, *adv.* Covertly.
velato, *p.p.a.* Veiled, covered, clouded; dim, hazy. **Voce velata**, muffled voice.
velatura, *n.f.* Veiling, covering; glaze; (*Naut.*) set of sails.
veleggiamento, *n.m.* Sailing.
veleggiare, *v.i.* To sail.
veleggiata, *n.f.* Sail, sailing.
veleggiato, *a.* Furnished with sails.
velenifero [velenIfero], *a.* Poisonous, venomous.
veleno, *n.m.* Poison, venom. (*fig.*) **Mandar —**, to spit venom, to slander.
velenosamente, *adv.* Poisonously, venomously.
velenosità [-à], *n.f.* Venomousness; wickedness, malice.
velenoso, *a.* Poisonous, venomous; spiteful, malicious.
veleria [velerIa], *n.f.* Sail-loft, sail-room.
veletta, *n.f.* (Woman's) veil; (*Naut.*) look-out.
velettiere, *n.m.* Look-out, man on the look-out.
velia [vElia], *n.f.* (*Zool.*) Shrike.
veliere, veliero, *n.m.* Sailing-vessel, sailing-ship.
velina, *a.* **Carta —**, tissue-paper.
velino, *n.m.* Vellum.
velivolo [velIvolo], *n.m.* Aeroplane, plane, glider.
velleità [-à], *n.f.* Impulse, whim; inkling, notion, fancy. **Avere delle — letterarie**, to have an itch for writing.
vellicamento, *n.m.* Tickling, titillation.
vellicare, *v.t.* To tickle, to titillate.
vellicazione, *n.m.* Tickling.
vello, *n.m.* Fleece. — **d'oro**, Golden Fleece.
vellosità [-à], *n.f.* Hairiness, shagginess.
velloso, *a.* Shaggy, hairy, woolly.
vellutato, *a.* Velvety, velveted; soft.

vellutino, *n.m.* Fine velvet; velvet ribbon; velveteen.
velluto, *n.m.* Velvet. **Cappello di —,** velvet hat; **— di cotone,** velveteen.
velo, *n.m.* Veil; gauze, crape; film, cover; mist, fog. **Tessuto di —,** gauze; **prendere il —,** to take the veil, to become a nun; **far — a,** to blind, to obscure; **stendere un — su,** to draw a veil over; **cadere il — dagli occhi,** to be disillusioned.
veloce, *a.* Quick, swift, rapid, fleet; nimble. (*Sport*) **Corsa —,** sprinting.
velocemente, veloce, *adv.* Quickly, swiftly.
velocipedastro, *n.m.* Reckless cyclist, scorcher.
velocipede [veloclpede], *n.m.* (*obs.*) Bicycle.
velocista (*pl.* **velocisti**), *n.m.* (*Sport*) Sprinter.
velocità [-à], *n.f.* Speed, rapidity, quickness, velocity; swiftness. **A grande —,** at great speed; **— media,** average speed; **prova di —,** speed trial; (*Comm.*) **spedire a grande, a piccola —,** to forward by fast, slow train.
velocitazione, *n.f.* (*obs.*) Acceleration.
velodromo [velOdromo], *n.m.* (*Sport*) Cycle-track.
veltro, *n.m.* Greyhound.
vena, *n.f.* Vein (in all senses); seam (in soil); humour, mood; luck. **— d'acqua,** spring of water; **essere in —,** to be in the mood; **non sono in —,** I'm not in good form; **avere una — poetica,** to have a turn for poetry; **non avere sangue nelle vene,** to be lifeless, to be flabby and weak; **una — d'oro,** a vein of gold.
venagione, *n.f.* (*obs.*) Game, venison.
venale, *a.* Venal, hireling, mercenary, open to bribes; saleable. **Prezzo —,** sale price; **valore —,** selling value.
venalità [-à], *n.f.* Venality, sordidness.
venalmente, *adv.* Venally.
venamento, *n.m.* Streak, streaking.
venare, *v.t.* To vein, to streak, to marble.
venatore, venatrice, *n.m.f.* Hunter [cp. **cacciatore**].
venatorio [venatOrio], *a.* Hunting.
venatura, *n.f.* Veining, veinage; (*Bot.*) venation.
vendemmia [vendEmmia], *n.f.* Vintage, grape gathering; vintage time.
vendemmiabile [vendemmiAbile], *a.* Ripe for gathering.
vendemmiale, *a.* Of vintage.
vendemmiare, *v.t.i.* To gather grapes, to harvest grapes.
vendemmiatore, vendemmiatrice, *n.m.f.* Vintager, grape-gatherer.
vendere [vEndere], *v.t.* To sell, to vend; to sell at. **— all'ingrosso,** to sell wholesale; **— al minuto,** to sell retail; **— a peso,** to sell by weight; **— a contanti,** to sell for ready cash; **— a buon prezzo,** to sell cheaply; **— a rate,** to sell by instalments; **— all'asta,** to sell by auction; **— a resa,** to sell on approval; **ho ragioni da —,** I have reasons and to spare; (*fig.*) **— fumo,** to humbug, to bluff.
vendereccio [venderEccio], *a.* Saleable, marketable.
vendersi, *v.r.* To be sold; to find a purchaser. **Libri che si vendono subito,** books that have a quick sale.
vendetta, *n.f.* Revenge, vengeance. **Per —,** out of revenge; **gridare —,** to cry aloud for vengeance.
vendibile [vendIbile], *a.* Saleable, marketable.
vendicamento, *n.m.* (*obs.*) Revenge, vengeance.
vendicare, *v.t.* To avenge, to revenge, to vindicate.
vendicarsi, *v.r.* To avenge oneself, to take revenge.
vendicativamente, *adv.* Vindictively.
vendicativo, *a.* Vindictive, revengeful.
vendicatore, vendicatrice, *n.m.f.* Avenger; vindicator.
vendicchiare, *v.t.* To sell by retail; to sell in a small way.
vendita [vEndita], *n.f.* Sale; shop; (*Hist.*) lodge of secret society. **— all'ingrosso, al minuto,** wholesale, retail sale; **mettere in —,** to offer for sale; **— di giornali,** newsagent's stall; **casa in —,** house for sale; **— all'asta,** auction sale.
venditore, venditrice, *n.m.f.* Seller, vendor. **— ambulante,** pedlar; (*fig.*) **— di fumo,** bluffer.
venduto, *p.p.a.* Sold; bribed, corrupted.
veneficio [venefIcio], *n.m.* Poisoning.
venefico [venEfico], *a.* Venomous, poisonous.
venerabile [venerAbile], **venerando,** *a.* Venerable, reverend.
venerabilità [-à], *n.f.* Venerableness, venerability.
venerabilmente, *adv.* Venerably.
venerando [cp. **venerabile**].
venerare, *v.t.* To venerate, to revere; to worship.
venerazione, *n.f.* Veneration, reverence; esteem; respect.
venerdì [-ì], *n.m.* Friday. **— Santo,** Good Friday; (*colloq.*) **mancare di un —,** to be cracked, to have a screw loose.
Venere [vEnere], *n.f.* Venus; (*fig.*) beauty, charm; lust.
venereo [venEreo], *a.* (*Med.*) Venereal.
Veneto [vEneto], *n.m.* (*Geog.*) Venetia.
Venezia [venEzia], *n.f.* (*Geog.*) Venice.
veneziano, *n.m.a.* Venetian.
venia [vEnia], *n.f.* Pardon, forgiveness. **Chiedere —,** to beg pardon.
veniale, *a.* Venial, pardonable, excusable. **Peccato —,** venial sin.
venialmente, *adv.* Venially.
veniente, *a.* Coming, forthcoming. **Il mese —,** next month.
venimento, *n.m.* (*obs.*) Arrival; happening.
venire, *v.i.* To come, to be coming; to come to, to arrive; to reach; to proceed; to arise; to happen. **— alle mani,** to come to blows; **— a patti,** to come to terms; **— ad intesa,** to come to an understanding; **— meno,** to swoon, to faint away; **— giù,** to come down; **— incontro a,** to come towards; (*fig.*) to favour, to approve; **— alla luce,** to come to light; to be born; **Venite avanti!** Come forward! Come in! **Venite presto!** Come quickly! Hurry up! **— a galla,** to float, to come to the top; **— a noia,** to bore, to tire; **mi venne fatto di,** I managed to; **vengo da lontano,** I come from afar; **vieni dietro di me,** follow me; **vieni a trovarmi,** call on me, come and see me; **egli veniva dicendo,** he was saying; **vieni proprio a proposito,**

you have come at just the right moment; **mi vien detto,** I'm told; **mi viene un' idea,** I've got an idea; **andare e —,** to go up and down; **Cosa ti viene in mente?** What's the matter with you? **mi vien voglia di piangere,** I feel like crying; **— al nocciolo della questione,** to come to the point; **venir su bene,** to grow well (of a child); **mi venne il destro di,** I took the opportunity to; **— meno alla parola data,** to fail to keep one's word; **— ad un transazione,** to come to an agreement; **— in fama,** to become famous; **— a morte,** to die; **se n'è andato com'è venuto,** he has had his labour for his pains.

venoso, *a.* Venous.

ventaggine [ventAggine], *n.f.* (*obs.*) Whirlwind, hurricane, tornado.

ventagliaio [ventagliAio], *n.m.* Fan-maker.

ventagliare, ventagliarsi, *v.t.r.* To fan, to fan oneself.

ventaglio [ventAglio], *n.m.* Fan. **A —,** fanlike; **coda a —,** fan-tail.

ventare, *v.i.* To blow hard (of wind).

ventarola, ventaruola, *n.f.* Vane, weathercock; ventilator; fan (for blowing up charcoal fire).

ventata, *n.f.* Gust (of wind).

ventenne, *a.* Twenty year old.

ventennio [ventEnnio], *n.m.* Period of twenty years.

ventesimo [ventEsimo], *a.* Twentieth.

venti, *n.m.a.* Twenty, twentieth. **Il venti settembre,** the 20th September.

venticello, *n.m.* Breeze, gentle wind.

venticinque [venticInque], *a.* Twenty-five.

venticinquenne, *a.* Twenty-five year old.

venticinquesimo [venticinquEsimo], *a.* Twenty-fifth.

venticinquina, *n.f.* Person about twenty-five years of age.

ventilabro, *n.m.* Winnowing-fan; (*Mus.*) organ valve.

ventilare, *v.t.* To ventilate, to air; to fan; (*fig.*) to discuss, to express one's views.

ventilato, *p.p.a.* Ventilated; discussed; aired. **Una camera ventilata,** an airy room.

ventilatore, *n.m.* Ventilator; air-hole, air-shaft; fan. **— elettrico,** electric fan.

ventilazione, *n.f.* Ventilation, airing.

ventina, *n.f.* About twenty, score. **C'era una — di bambini,** there were a score of children.

ventino, *n.m.* (*Hist.*) Coin of twenty centesimi.

ventiquattro, *a.* Twenty-four; midnight. **Portare il cappello sulle —, sulle ventitrè,** to wear one's hat tilted to one side.

vento, *n.m.* Wind. **— di prua,** head-wind; **avere il — in poppa,** to sail before the wind; (*fig.*) to prosper; **farsi —,** to fan oneself; **mulino a —,** windmill; **tira —,** it's windy, the wind is getting up; **andare contro —,** to sail close to the wind; **Qual buon — ti porta?** What good fortune brings you here? **parlare al —,** to speak in vain; **— di tramontana,** north wind; **in balia del —,** at the mercy of the wind; **un colpo di —,** a gust of wind; **pascersi di —,** to feed on vain hopes.

ventola [vEntola], *n.f.* Fan; lamp-shade, wall candle sconce; fire-screen. **Muro a —,** partition wall.

ventolare, *v.t.i.* To fan, to winnow; to flutter, to waver.

ventosa, *n.f.* Sucker; (*Med.*) Cupping-glass. **Applicar delle ventose,** to cup.

ventosamente, *adv.* Windily, breezily, gustily.

ventosità [-à], *n.f.* Windiness; flatulence.

ventoso, *a.* Windy, breezy; (*fig.*) conceited; (*Med.*) flatulent.

ventraia [ventrAia], *n.f.* Belly, paunch.

ventrale, *a.* Ventral.

ventrata, *n.f.* Bellyful; litter of young.

ventre, *n.m.* Belly, abdomen, paunch; stomach, womb. **Dolor di —,** stomach-ache; **correre — a terra,** (of animals) to run at full speed; **tenersi il — dal ridere,** to burst with laughter; **far —,** to bulge, to swell out; **metter —,** to grow fat.

ventresca, *n.f.* Paunch (of pork, etc.) when cooked.

ventricolo [ventrIcolo], *n.m.* (*Anat.*) Ventricle.

ventriera, *n.f.* Belly-band, abdominal belt, body-belt.

ventriglio [ventrIglio], *n.m.* Gizzard, stomach (of birds).

ventriloquio [ventrilOquio], *n.m.* Ventriloquism.

ventriloquo [ventrIloquo], *n.m.* Ventriloquist.

ventrina, *n.f.* Tympanites, wind-dropsy (of animals).

ventrone, *n.m.* Big belly; fat person.

ventunesimo [ventunEsimo], *a.* Twenty-first.

ventuno, *a.* Twenty-one.

ventura, *n.f.* Fortune, luck, chance; destiny, fate. **Andare alla —,** to set out to seek one's fortune; **alla —,** at one's risk, at a venture, at random; **soldato di —,** mercenary soldier; **farsi dire la buona —,** to have one's fortune told; **per —,** by chance; **buona, mala —,** good, bad luck; **aver la — di,** to have the chance to, to have the good fortune to.

venturiere, venturiero, *n.m.* Adventurer, soldier of fortune [cp. **avventuriero**].

venturo, *a.* Next, forthcoming, coming, future. **L'anno —,** next year; **cose venture,** things to come; **i venturi,** posterity.

venturone, *n.m.* (*Zool.*) Variety of finch.

venturosamente, *adv.* Luckily; happily.

venturoso, *a.* Lucky, fortunate; venturesome.

venustà, *n.f.* (*Lit.*) Beauty, charm, comeliness, loveliness.

venusto, *a.* Beautiful, handsome, charming, comely.

venuta, *n.f.* Coming, arrival. **Alla mia —,** on my arrival, on coming.

venuto, *p.p.a.* Come, arrived. **Siate il ben —,** you are welcome; **l'ultimo —,** the last comer [cp. **venire**].

vepraio [veprAio], *n.m.* Bramble bush, brake.

vepre, *n.m.* Bramble, briar [cp. **rovo**].

ver', *prep.* (*Poet.*) Toward [cp. **verso**].

vera, *n.f.* (*colloq.*) Wedding-ring.

verace, *a.* True, veracious, truthful.

veracemente, *adv.* Truthfully.

veracità [-à], *n.f.* Veracity, truthfulness.

veramente, *adv.* Truly, really, indeed; as a fact.

veranda, *n.f.* Veranda, verandah.

veratro, *n.m.* (*Bot.*) Veratrum, hellebore.

verbale, *n.m.* Minutes (of meeting, etc.), record; statement. **Mettere a —,** to put in the

minutes; (*Law*) **fare un —,** to draw up a statement; **il — della seduta,** the minutes of the meeting.
verbale, *a.* Verbal, by word of mouth, oral.
verbalizzare, *v.t.* To minute; to place on record.
verbalmente, *adv.* Verbally, orally, by word of mouth.
verbasco, *n.m.* (*Bot.*) Mullein.
verbena, *n.f.* (*Bot.*) Vervain, verbena.
verbigrazia [verbigrAzia], *adv.* For instance, for example, *e.g.*
verbo, *n.m.* (*Gram.*) Verb; (*Eccles.*) the Word. **— irregolare,** irregular verb.
verbosamente, *adv.* Verbosely, wordily.
verbosità [-à], *n.f.* Wordiness, verbosity, verbiage, prolixity.
verboso, *a.* Wordy, verbose, prolix, prosy.
verdastro, *a.* Greenish.
verdazzurro, *a.* Sea-green.
verde, *n.m.a.* Green; vegetation; verdant; unripe; young. **Essere al —,** to be penniless; **nel — dell'età,** in the flower of youth; **in — età,** at a tender age.
verdea [verdEa], *n.f.* Kind of white grape.
verdebruno, verdecupo, *a.* Dark green.
verdechiaro, *a.* Light green.
verdeggiamento, *n.m.* Turning green.
verdeggiante, *a.* Verdant, green.
verdeggiare, *v.i.* To be verdant, to grow green.
verdegiallo, *a.* Apple-green.
verdemare, *a.* Sea-green.
verderame, *n.m.* Verdigris.
verdescuro, *a.* Dark green.
verdetto, *n.m.* Verdict; judgement, decision.
verdetto, *a.* Greenish.
verdezza, *n.f.* Greenness.
verdiccio, verdigno, verdognolo, verdolino [verdIccio, verdOgnolo], *a.* Greenish.
verdone, *n.m.* (*Zool.*) Greenfinch.
verdone, *a.* Dark green.
verdume, *n.m.* Greenness; green fodder.
verdura, *n.f.* Greens (vegetables); vegetation, verdure. **Minestra di —,** vegetable soup.
verecondamente, *adv.* Modestly, bashfully.
verecondia [verecOndia], *n.f.* Modesty, bashfulness; shyness.
verecondo, *a.* Modest, coy, bashful, shy.
verga, *n.f.* Twig; bar, rod, switch; wand; staff (of office); bar (of gold, etc.); **— pastorale,** crozier; **tremar come una —,** to shake like a leaf; **— d'oro, di ferro,** gold, iron bar; **— magica,** magician's wand.
vergare, *v.t.* To flog; to stripe, to streak, to rule (lines); to write, to pen. **— poche righe,** to jot down a few lines.
vergaro, *n.m.* Herdsman, shepherd.
vergata, *n.f.* Stroke with a switch; flogging.
vergatino, *n.m.* Striped material.
vergato, *a.* Striped, streaked; written. **Carta vergata,** ruled paper.
vergatura, *n.f.* Flogging; jotting down.
vergere [vErgere], *v.i.* To turn towards, to tend to.
vergenza, *n.f.* Tendency, propensity.
vergheggiare, *v.t.* To flog.
verghetta, *n.f.* Rod, switch.
verginale, *a.* Virginal, maidenly.
verginalmente, *adv.* Virginally.
vergine [vErgine], *n.f.a.* Virgin, maiden; girl; chaste, pure, undefiled, virginal. **La Beata Vergine,** the Blessed Virgin; **foresta —,** virgin forest.
verginella, *n.f.* Young girl, maid, lass.
verginità [-à], *n.f.* Virginity, maidenhood.
vergogna, *n.f.* Shame, modesty, shyness, bashfulness; disgrace, infamy, dishonour. **Senza —,** shameless, impudent; **sentire —,** to be ashamed; **uscirne con —,** to come out of it badly; **rosso di —,** blushing with shame; **è la — della famiglia,** he's the black sheep of the family; **—!** Shame!
vergognarsi, *v.r.* To be ashamed, to feel shame; to be shy.
vergognosamente, *adv.* Disgracefully.
vergognoso, *a.* Bashful, shy, timid; shameful, disgraceful; dishonourable.
vergola [vErgola], *n.f.* Double silk twist; small twig or rod.
veridicamente, *adv.* Truthfully, veraciously.
veridicità [-à], *n.f.* Truthfulness, veracity.
veridico [verIdico], *a.* True, veracious, truthful.
verifica [verIfica], *n.f.* Examination, ascertainment, checking, verification. **— dei conti,** audit of the accounts; **— di cassa,** count (of cash).
verificabile [verificAbile], *a.* Verifiable.
verificare, *v.t.* To verify, to check, to examine, to ascertain.
verificarsi, *v.r.* To happen, to occur, to take place; to come true.
verificato, *p.p.a.* Verified, checked.
verificatore, verificatrice, *n.m.f.* Verifier, examiner, controller.
verificazione, *n.f.* Verification; fulfilment.
verisimiglianza [cp. **verosimiglianza**].
verismo, *n.m.* (*Lit. Art*) Realism.
verista, *n.m.a.* Realist; realistic.
verità [-à], *n.f.* Truth, verity, truthfulness; fact. **Egli è la bocca della —,** he's truth itself; **la pura —,** the plain truth; **in —,** in truth, indeed; **dire la —,** to speak the truth; **scoprire la —,** to find out the truth.
veritiero, *a.* True, truthful, veracious; sincere.
verme, *n.m.* Worm; grub, maggot, chrysalis; cheese-mite. **— solitario,** tapeworm; **— d'una vite,** worm of a screw.
vermena, *n.f.* Twig.
vermicciolo, vermicciuolo, *n.m.* Small worm, grub, maggot.
vermicelli, *n.m.pl.* Vermicelli.
vermiciattolo [vermiciAttolo], *n.m.* Small worm, grub.
vermicolare, *a.* Vermicular; thready (of pulse).
vermicolaria [vermicolAria], *n.f.* (*Bot.*) Knotgrass.
vermiforme, *a.* Vermiform.
vermifugo [vermIfugo], *n.m.a.* Vermifuge, worm-powder; vermifugal.
vermigliezza, *n.f.* Redness.
vermiglio [vermIglio], *n.m.a.* Vermilion; ruby, ruddy, brilliant red, scarlet.
vermiglione, *n.m.* Vermilion (paint).
vermine [cp. **verme**].
verminoso, *a.* Verminous.
vermocane, *n.m.* Staggers (in a horse); (*obs.*) (*colloq.*) Zounds! Damn it!
vermut, vermutte, *n.m.* Vermouth.

vernaccia [vernAccia], *n.f.* Sardinian white wine.
vernacolo [vernAcolo], *n.m.a.* Patois, dialect, local speech.
vernale, *a.* Wintry; spring-like, vernal.
vernereccio [vernerEccio], *a.* Wintry.
vernare, *v.i.* To winter [cp. **svernare**].
vernice, *n.f.* Varnish; polish; paint; veneer, smattering, appearance. **Dare una mano di —,** to give a coat of varnish; **scarpe di —,** patent-leather shoes; **— per mobili,** French polish; **— antiruggine,** rust-resisting varnish.
verniciare, *v.t.* To varnish; to glaze, to polish.
verniciato, *a.* Polished, varnished.
verniciatore, *n.m.* House-painter, decorator.
verniciatura, *n.f.* Varnishing, glazing; gloss, veneer.
vernino, *a.* Wintry, of winter.
verno, *n.m.* Winter [cp. **inverno**].
vero, *n.m.* Truth; (*Art*) life, nature. **A dire il —,** to tell you the truth; **dipingere dal —,** to paint from Nature.
vero, *a.* True, real, veritable; natural, genuine, regular; right, proper; downright, thorough. **Non è —? Nevvero? Vero?** Is it not? Isn't it? **un — amico,** a true friend; **non mi par —,** it does not seem real, it can't be true; **il — colpevole,** the real culprit; **è un — sciocco,** he's a perfect fool.
verone, *n.m.* Balcony.
veronese, *n.m.a.* Of Verona.
veronica [verOnica], *n.f.* (*Bot.*) Veronica.
verosimigliante, *a.* Likely.
verosimiglianza, *n.f.* Likelihood, verisimilitude, probability.
verosimile [verosImile], *a.* Likely, probable, credible, life-like.
verosimilitudine [verosimilitUdine], *n.f.* Verosimilitude.
verosimilmente, *adv.* Probably.
verre [cp. **verro**].
verricello, *n.m.* Windlass, winch.
verrina, *n.f.* Auger.
verro, *n.m.* Boar.
verrocchio [verrOcchio], *n.m.* Olive-press.
verruca, *n.f.* (*Med.*) Wart; verruca.
verrucoso, *a.* Warty, verrucose.
versaccio [versAccio], *n.m.* Bad verse, bad poetry; scream, shriek; disdainful gesture.
versaiolo, *n.m.* Poetaster; would-be poet.
versamento, *n.m.* Payment; paying in (at bank); pouring out, shedding; discharge. **Fare un —,** to pay in; **distinta di —,** paying-in slip.
versante, *n.m.* (*Geog.*) Slope, side (of a mountain, etc.); watershed, draining area; (*Comm.*) depositor, payer.
versare, *v.t.i.* To pour out, to shed, to spill; (*Comm.*) to pay in (money); to overflow. **— lagrime,** to shed tears; **— per terra,** to spill on the ground; **versami da bere,** pour me out a drink; **egli versa in cattivissime acque,** he is in a bad way; **— una somma,** to pay out a sum (of money); **— la colpa sopra uno,** to lay the blame on someone; **— il proprio sangue per,** to shed one's blood for; **— in pericolo di vita,** to be in danger of one's life.
versatile [versAtile], *a.* Versatile, many-sided, quick-minded.
versatilità [-à], *n.f.* Versatility.
versato, *p.p.a.* Out-poured, spilled; paid in; versed, skilled, learned, well-read; experienced, able.
verseggiare, *v.i.* To versify.
verseggiatore, verseggiatrice, *n.m.f.* Versifier, rhymster.
verseggiatura, *n.f.* Versification.
versetto, *n.m.* Verse, passage; versicle. **— della Bibbia,** verse of the Bible.
versiera, *n.f.* She-devil; witch.
versificare [cp. **verseggiare**].
versificazione, *n.f.* Versification.
versilliberista, *n.m.* Writer of free verse.
versione, *n.f.* Version; translation. **Dare una diversa — di,** to give a different version of.
versipelle, *n.m.a.* Turn-coat; double-faced, two-faced.
verso, *n.m.* Verse, line (of verse), poetry; cry, shriek; song (of birds), noise (of animals); respect, manner, way; side, standpoint; mimicry. **— libero,** free verse; **— sciolto** blank verse; **scrivere versi,** to write verse; **strofa di tre versi,** stanza of three lines; **prendere uno per il suo —,** to know how to handle someone; **andare a — a uno,** to appeal to someone; **fare il — a uno,** to mimic someone; **non c'è — di persuaderlo,** there is no way to persuade him; **bisogna far le cose per il loro —,** one has to do things properly; **per un certo — egli ha ragione,** from a certain standpoint he is right; **il — del cane,** the noise of the dog.
verso, *prep.* Towards, to; about; against. **— mezzogiorno,** about noon; **— casa,** towards home; **— pagamento,** against payment; **— di,** in comparison with.
versta, *n.f.* (Russian) verst.
vertebra [vErtebra], *n.f.* (*Anat.*) Vertebra.
vertebrale, *a.* Vertebral.
vertebrato, *n.m.a.* Vertebrate.
vertente, *a.* Regarding, bearing upon, concerning; (*Law*) pending.
vertenza, *n.f.* (*Law*) Dispute, difference, controversy, question.
vertere [vErtere], *v.i.* To bear upon, to regard; to deal with.
verticale, *a.* Vertical.
verticalità [-à], *n.f.* Verticality.
verticalmente, *adv.* Vertically.
vertice [vErtice], *n.m.* (*Geom.*) Vertex; top, apex, summit. **Essere al — della gloria,** to be at the summit of glory.
verticillo, *n.m.* (*Bot.*) Verticil, whorl.
vertigine [vertIgine], *n.f.* Giddiness, dizziness, vertigo. **Avere le vertigini,** to feel giddy; **soffrire di vertigini,** to suffer from dizziness.
vertiginosamente, *adv.* Giddily, dizzily.
vertiginoso, *a.* Giddy, dizzy, vertiginous. **A velocità vertiginosa,** at breakneck speed.
veruno, *pron.* (*Lit.*) Not one, none, nobody; any, anyone.
verza, *n.f.* Cabbage, Savoy cabbage.
verzicare, *v.i.* To turn green [cp. **verdeggiare**].
verzicola [verzIcola], *n.f.* (*Cards*) Sequence of a sort.
verziere, *n.m.* Garden, kitchen garden; orchard; fruit and vegetable market.
verzino, *n.m.* (*Bot.*) Brazil wood.

verzura, *n.f.* Greenery, greens, verdure.
vescia [vEscia], *n.f.* (*Bot.*) Puff-ball; (*colloq.*) nonsense, empty chatter.
vescica, *n.f.* (*Anat.*) Bladder, vesica; blister. **— del fiele,** gall-bladder; **— natatoria,** swimming-bladder; (*fig.*) **— gonfiata,** conceited ass.
vescicale, *a.* (*Med.*) Vesical.
vescicante, *n.m.* (*Med.*) Vesicant, blistering ointment.
vescichetta, vescicola [vescIcola], *n.f.* Water-blister, vesicle.
vescovado, vescovato, *n.m.* Episcopate; bishopric; bishop's palace.
vescovile, *a.* Episcopal.
vescovo [vEscovo], *n.m.* Bishop.
vespa, *n.f.* (*Zool.*) Wasp.
vespaio [vespAio], *n.m.* Wasps' nest; (*fig.*) hornets' nest. **Stuzzicare un —,** to stir up a hornets' nest.
vespasiano, *n.m.* (*colloq.*) Street urinal.
vespero [vEspero], *n.m.* (*Lit.*) Evening; (planet) Venus, evening star.
vespertino, *a.* Evening.
vespro, *n.m.* Vespers; evening. **Vespri Siciliani,** Sicilian Vespers.
vessare, *v.t.* To harass, to bully, to vex, to persecute. **Una nave vessata dalla tempesta,** a storm-tossed vessel.
vessatorio [vessatOrio], *a.* Harassing, vexing, vexatious, oppressive.
vessazione, *n.f.* Vexation, oppression, imposition.
vessillario, vessillifero [vessillArio, vessillIfero], *n.m.* (*Hist.*) Standard-bearer.
vessillo, *n.m.* Banner, flag, ensign, standard.
vestaglia [vestAglia], *n.f.* Dressing-gown.
vestale, *n.f.* (*Hist.*) Vestal. **Le Vestali,** the Vestal Virgins.
veste, *n.f.* Dress; gown, frock; garment; suit of clothes; straw case for flask; (*fig.*) quality, capacity; authority, pretext; appearance. **In — ufficiale,** in an official capacity; **— da camera,** dressing-gown; **— da nozze,** wedding-dress; **aver — per intervenire,** to have authority to take action.
vestiario [vestiArio], *n.m.* Clothing, outfitting; clothes, costumes; (*Theat.*) wardrobe. **Capo di —,** wearing-apparel; garment, article of dress.
vestiarista, *n.m.* (*Theat.*) Costumier.
vestibolo [vestIbolo], *n.m.* Entrance hall, lobby, vestibule.
vesticciola, *n.f.* Child's frock; plain frock.
vestigio [vestIgio] (*pl.* **vestigi,** *m.*, **vestigia,** *f.*), *n.m.* Vestige; footprint, track, trace; remains. **Seguire le vestigia,** to follow the tracks.
vestimenta, *n.f.pl.* (*Lit.*) Clothes, clothing.
vestimento, *n.m.* Clothing; clothes, garments.
vestina, *n.f.* Child's frock.
vestire, *v.t.i.* To dress, to attire, to clothe; to put on, to wear. **— gli ignudi,** to clothe the naked; **— bene,** to dress well; **— da festa,** to wear one's Sunday clothes; **— di nero,** to dress in black, to put on mourning [cp. **vestirsi**].
vestire, *n.m.* Clothing, dress.
vestirsi, *v.r.* To dress, to dress oneself. **Vestiti in fretta!** Dress quickly! **gli alberi si vestono di foglie,** the trees are putting forth leaves.
vestitino, *n.m.* Little frock.
vestito, *n.m.* Dress; (man's) suit; frock. **Provarsi un —,** to try on a suit or frock; **farsi un — nuovo,** to make oneself a new frock or suit.
vestito, *p.p.a.* Dressed, clothed; covered. **Ben —,** well dressed; **morir —,** to die in comfortable circumstances.
vestitura, *n.f.* Dressing, robing.
vestizione, *n.f.* (*Eccles.*) Taking the veil; investiture.
vestone, *n.m.* Robe, vestment.
Vesuvio [vesUvio], *n.m.* (*Geog.*) Vesuvius.
veterano, *n.m.a.* Veteran; pioneer; experienced man; (*Mil.*) ex-service man.
veterinaria [veterinAria], *n.f.* Veterinary science.
veterinario [veterinArio], *n.m.a.* Veterinary surgeon, veterinary.
veto, *n.m.* Veto; prohibition. **Diritto di —,** right of veto; **mettere un —,** to put a ban on.
vetraio [vetrAio], *n.m.* Glass-blower; glazier.
vetrame, *n.m.* Glass ware.
vetrario [vetrArio], *a.* Pertaining to glass-making.
vetrata, *n.f.* Glass door, large window; stained-glass window.
vetrato, *a.* Glazed, of glass. **Carta vetrata,** glass-paper, sand-paper.
vetrato, *n.m.* (*Mountaineering*) Thin coating of ice on rock.
vetreria [vetrerIa], *n.f.* Glass-works; glass ware.
vetrice [vEtrice], *n.f.* (*Bot.*) Osier, willow.
vetriera, *n.f.* Glass door.
vetrificare, *v.t.* To vitrify.
vetrificarsi, *v.r.* To become vitrified.
vetrificazione, *n.f.* Vitrification.
vetrigno, *a.* Glassy.
vetrina, *n.f.* Shop-window; glass case, show-case (in museums, etc.).
vetrino, *n.m.* Microscope slide.
vetrino, *a.* Glassy; fragile, brittle.
vetrioleggiare, *v.t.* To throw vitriol at.
vetriolico [vetriOlico], *a.* Vitriolic.
vetriolo, *n.m.* (*Chem.*) Vitriol.
vetro, *n.m.* Glass, pane of glass; window. **Lastra di —,** pane of glass; **rimettere i vetri alla finestra,** to replace the window-panes.
vetrocromia [vetrocromIa], *n.f.* Painting on glass.
vetroso, *a.* Glassy, vitreous.
vetta, *n.f.* Top, summit; apex; (*Naut.*) end (of a rope). **Sulla — d'un monte,** on a mountain-top.
vettone, *n.m.* (*Bot.*) Sucker, shoot.
vettore, *n.m.* (*Geom.*) Vector; carrier (of goods, etc.).
vettovagliamento, *n.m.* Victualling, provisioning, supply. **Il — d'un esercito,** the victualling of an army.
vettovagliare, *v.t.* To provision, to supply.
vettovaglie [vettovAglie], *n.f.pl.* Victuals, provisions, food supplies.
vettura, *n.f.* Conveyance; carriage; cab; railway carriage; motor-car. **— di piazza,** cab; **— ristorante,** railway dining-car; **In —!** Take your seats! (*Motor.*) **— da corsa,** racing-car; **— a due posti,** two-seater; **— da turismo,** touring-car.

vetturetta, *n.f.* (*Motor.*) Small car, runabout car.
vetturino, vetturale, *n.m.* Driver, coachman, cabman, cabby.
vetustà [-à], *n.f.* Antiquity; decay; old age.
vetusto, *a.* Old, ancient, antique.
vezzeggiamento, *n.m.* Fondling, caressing; coaxing.
vezzeggiare, *v.t.* To caress, to fondle, to pet; to coax.
vezzeggiativo, *n.m.a.* Pet name; (*Gram.*) diminutive; coaxing, caressing.
vezzo, *n.m.* Habit, custom, way; knack; necklace, ornament. **— di perle,** pearl necklace; **avere il — di,** to be in the habit of, to have the knack of; **vezzi,** charms, attraction; **schiavo son dei vezzi tuoi,** I am a slave to your charms.
vezzosamente, *adv.* Prettily, charmingly.
vezzoso, *a.* Pretty, charming, comely, graceful.
vi, *pron.* To you, you. **Temo di importunarvi,** I am afraid to trouble you; **io vi do questo libro,** I give you this book.
vi, *adv.* There. **Vi andai,** I went there; **vi sono stato,** I've been there.
via, [vIa], *n.f.* Way, route, road, street; means, course, measure. **— lattea,** Milky Way; **Via Dante,** Dante Street; **vie di mezzo,** half-measures; **venire a vie di fatto,** to come to blows; **non c'è — di scampo,** there's no getting out of it; **andare per — legale,** to take legal steps; **mettersi la — tra le gambe,** to take to one's heels; **per la — più breve,** by the shortest route; (*Sport*) **dare il "Via",** to give the start; **per — di terra, di mare,** by land, by sea; **lungo la —,** by the wayside; **perdere la —,** to lose one's way; **aprire la — a,** to pave the way for; (*Mil.*) **foglio di —,** pass, travel warrant; **per — di Roma,** by way of Rome.
via, *adv.* Away; (*Rail., etc.*) via. **Mandar —,** to send away; **portar —,** to carry away; **andar —,** to go away; **gettar —,** to throw away; **essa è —,** she is away; **e — discorrendo,** and so forth.
via! *inter.* Go away! Come now! **Obbedisca, via!** Now then, do what you're told!
viabilità [-à], *n.f.* State of the roads, road conditions, viability.
viadotto, *n.m.* Viaduct.
viaggetto, *n.m.* Short trip, jaunt.
viaggiante, *a.* Travelling, on the way. **Merci viaggianti,** goods in transit; (*Rail.*) **personale —,** travelling staff, train crew.
viaggiare, *v.i.* To travel; to journey; to voyage (by sea). **— in aeroplano,** to travel by air; **— per diporto, per affari,** to travel for pleasure, for business; **— in prima classe,** to travel first class; **mi piace —,** I like to travel.
viaggiatore, viaggiatrice, *n.m.f.* Traveller; passenger. **— di commercio,** commercial traveller; **piccione —,** carrier-pigeon; **treno viaggiatori,** passenger train.
viaggio [viAggio], *n.m.* Journey, travel; tour; voyage. **Buon —!** Pleasant journey! **— di nozze,** honeymoon trip; **spese di —,** travelling expenses; **mettersi in —,** to set out, to go on one's travels; **fare un — e due servizi,** to kill two birds with one stone; **— circolare,** circular tour; **agenzia di —,** travel agency.
viale, *n.m.* Avenue.
viandante, *n.m.* Pedestrian, passer-by, wayfarer; tramp.
viatico [viAtico], *n.m.* Viaticum; (*obs.*) provisions for a journey.
viatore, viatrice, *n.m.f.* Wayfarer, traveller.
viatorio [viatOrio], *a.* Travelling.
viavai [viavAi], *n.m.* Coming and going; traffic, bustle, rush.
vibice [vIbice], *n.m.* (*Med.*) Livid weal.
vibramento, *n.m.* Vibrating, vibration.
vibrante, *a.* Vibrant, pulsating, throbbing; thrilling.
vibrare, *v.t.i.* To shake, to strike, to hit, to brandish, to hurl; to vibrate, to shake, to swing, to quiver; to thrill with. **— un colpo,** to strike a blow; **— la coda,** to lash the tail.
vibratamente, *adv.* Energetically.
vibratezza, *n.f.* Energy, force, power.
vibrato, *a.* Vigorous, sharp, energetic; concise, trenchant; bracing (of climate); (*Mus.*) vibrato.
vibratorio [vibratOrio], *a.* Vibratory.
vibrazione, *n.f.* Vibration, oscillation; quivering.
viburno, *n.m.* (*Bot.*) Guelder-rose.
vicaria, vicariato [vicarIa], *n.m.* Vicariate; vicarage.
vicario [vicArio], *n.m.* (*Eccles.*) Vicar.
vice-, *prefix.* Vice-, assistant, deputy.
vice-ammiraglio [vice-ammirAglio], *n.m.* Vice-admiral.
vicecancelliere, *n.m.* Vice-chancellor.
viceconsole [vicecOnsole], *n.m.* Vice-consul.
vice-direttore, *n.m.* Assistant manager.
vicegerente, *n.m.* Vicegerent.
vicemadre, *n.f.* Guardian; matron (of a boarding-school).
vicenda, *n.f.* Event, vicissitude; change, turn. **Le vicende della politica,** the political developments; **a —,** in turn, in rotation; **le vicende della guerra,** the fortunes of war.
vicendevole [vicendEvole], *a.* Mutual, reciprocal.
vicendevolezza, *n.f.* Mutuality, reciprocity, interchange.
vicendevolmente, *adv.* Mutually, reciprocally.
viceprefetto, *n.m.* Sub-prefect.
vicepresidente, *n.m.* Vice-president.
vicepresidenza, *n.f.* Vice-presidency.
vicerè [-è], *n.m.* Viceroy.
vicereale, *a.* Viceregal.
viceregina, *n.f.* Vicereine, wife of a viceroy.
vice-segretario [vice-segretArio], *n.m.* Assistant secretary.
viceversa, *adv.* Vice versa; on the contrary.
vicinale, *a.* Local, neighbouring, parish. **Strada —,** country road; (*Rail.*) **tariffa —,** short-distance tariff.
viciname, *n.m.* People of the neighbourhood.
vicinamente, *adv.* Closely, nearly.
vicinanza, *n.f.* Nearness, proximity; neighbourhood, surroundings. **Nelle vicinanze di,** in the neighbourhood of.
vicinante, *n.m.a.* Neighbour; neighbouring.
vicinato, *n.m.* Neighbourhood; neighbours (collectively). **Un buon —,** a good neighbourhood.
viciniore, *a.* (*Law*) Nearest (in succession).
vicinità [cp. **vicinanza**].

vicino, *n.m.* Neighbour. **I nostri vicini,** our neighbours.
vicino, *a.adv.* Near, close by, close to, neighbouring; near by, at hand, **Da —,** from nearby; **andiamo —,** let us go near; **la pioggia è vicina,** rain is near; **abita qui —,** he lives close by; **— alla follia,** near to madness; **è proprio qui —,** it is quite near.
vicissitudine [vicissitUdine], *n.f.* Vicissitude. **Vicissitudini,** events, changes, circumstances.
vico, *n.m.* Narrow street, lane, alley, passage; village, hamlet.
vicolo [vIcolo], *n.m.* Alley, passage. **— cieco,** blind-alley.
vidimare, *v.t.* To legalize; to visa (a passport), to endorse as correct.
vidimazione, *n.f.* (Passport) visa; stamping.
vie,[vIe], *adv.* Much by far. **— maggiormente,** much more so.
vie più, vieppiù, *adv.* More and more, very much more.
vietabile [vietAbile], *a.* Liable to be forbidden.
vietare, *v.t.i.* To prohibit, to forbid; to prevent, to impede, to obstruct, to hinder. **— l'ingresso,** to refuse admittance; **ciò non vieta di credere che,** this does not prevent one from thinking that.
vietato, *p.p.a.* Prohibited, forbidden. **— fumare,** smoking prohibited; **vietata l'affissione,** stick no bills; **— il posteggio,** no parking.
vieto, *a.* Trite, stale, musty, old, antiquated, obsolete.
vietume, *n.m.* Stale matter, old stuff.
vigente, *a.* (*Law*) In force, existing. **Le leggi vigenti,** existing laws.
vigere [vIgere], *v.i.* To be in force (of a law).
vigesimo [vigEsimo], *a.* Twentieth. **— primo,** twenty-first.
vigilante, *a.* Vigilant, watchful, attentive; wary.
vigilantemente, *adv.* Vigilantly.
vigilanza, *n.f.* Attention, care, vigilance, watchfulness. **Squadre di —,** (strike) pickets; **sotto la — della polizia,** under police supervision.
vigilare, *v.t.i.* To watch over, to keep a watch; to be vigilant, to be on the look-out; to superintend, to supervise.
vigile [vIgile], *n.m.* Watchman, policeman. **— urbano,** civic guard, civic police; **vigili del fuoco,** firemen, fire brigade; fire-watchers.
vigile [vIgile], *a.* Vigilant, watchful, alert; circumspect, wary.
vigilia [vigIlia], *n.f.* Vigil, wake, watch; eve (preceding the morrow). **— di Natale,** Christmas Eve; **— di Pasqua,** Easter Eve; **far —,** to keep vigil; **le lunghe vigilie della notte,** the long vigils of the night.
vigliaccamente, *adv.* In a cowardly, dastardly way.
vigliaccheria [vigliaccherIa], *n.f.* Cowardice, poltroonery; dastardliness.
vigliacco, *n.m.a.* Coward, poltroon; cowardly, dastardly; faint-heartedly.
vigliare, *v.t.* (*Agric.*) To sift corn.
viglietto [cp. **biglietto**].
vigna, *n.f.* Vineyard; vine. (*Eccles.*) **La — del Signore,** the Church.
vignaiolo, *n.m.* Vine-dresser.
vigneto, *n.m.* Vineyard.
vignetta, *n.f.* Drawing, vignette, sketch, cartoon.
vignettista, *n.m.f.* Cartoonist; illustrator.
vigogna, *n.f.* (*Zool.*) Vicugna, vicuna.
vigore, *n.m.* Vigour, force, strength, energy. **Questa legge entra in — oggi,** this law comes into force today; **egli è nel pieno —,** he's in full vigour.
vigoreggiare, *v.i.* To acquire vigour, to prosper, to thrive, to flourish.
vigoria [vigorIa], *n.f.* Vigorousness, vigour, energy, strength.
vigorosamente, *adv.* Vigorously.
vigorosità [-à], *n.f.* Vigorousness, energy, strength.
vigoroso, *a.* Sturdy, vigorous, robust, hardy, strong. **Un discorso —,** a vigorous speech.
vile, *n.m.* Poltroon, coward, dastard.
vile, *a.* Cowardly, low, vile, abject, degraded, despicable; paltry, worthless. **Vendere a vil prezzo,** to sell at a low price; **una — somma,** a paltry sum; **il vil metallo,** filthy lucre; **avere a —,** to think nothing of, to despise.
vilezza, *n.f.* Cowardliness [cp. **viltà**].
vilificare, *v.t.* To vilify.
vilipendere [vilipEndere], *v.t.* To vilify, to disparage, to revile, to defame, to abuse; to despise, to contemn.
vilipendio [vilipendIo], *n.m.* Abuse, insult, affront, contempt; offence.
vilipeso, *p.p.a.* Abused, insulted; despised, scorned.
villa, *n.f.* Country-house, villa, country residence; the country, countryside. **Andare in —,** to go into the country.
villaggio [villAggio], *n.m.* Village.
villanaccio [villanAccio], *n.m.* Boor, ill-bred man.
villanamente, *adv.* Rudely, incivilly, boorishly.
villanata, *n.f.* Piece of incivility, boorish action; rude words.
villanello, *n.m.* Country lad, peasant boy.
villanescamente, *adv.* Boorishly, ill-manneredly.
villanesco, *a.* Rustic, boorish.
villania [villanIa], *n.f.* Act of rudeness, incivility, discourtesy; insult, abuse. **Dir — a,** to be insulting to.
villano, *n.m.* Peasant, rustic; boor. **— rifatto,** cad, upstart, parvenu.
villano, *a.* Rude, discourteous; vulgar, boorish, impolite.
villanzone, *n.m.* Blackguard, rascal; clodhopper, bumpkin.
villeggiante, *n.m.* Holiday-maker, summer visitor.
villeggiare, *v.i.* To go to the country for the summer, to stay in the country for holidays, to visit a holiday resort.
villeggiatura, *n.f.* Country holidays, summering in the country; country residence. **Paese di —,** summer resort.
villereccio [villerEccio], *a.* Rustic, rural.
villetta, *n.f.* Country cottage.
villico [vIllico], *n.m.* Countryman, peasant, villager.
villino, *n.m.* Cottage, small country house.
villo, *n.m.* (*Bot.*) Hair, villi; (*Anat.*) villus.
villoso, *a.* Hairy, shaggy, woolly.
vilmente, *adv.* Vilely, basely.

viltà [-à], *n.f.* Cowardice, faint-heartedness; vileness, baseness, unworthiness, meanness.
vilucchio [vilUcchio], *n.m.* (*Bot.*) Bind-weed.
viluppo, *n.m.* Tangle, entanglement; confusion, mix-up.
viminata, *n.f.* Wicker-work.
vimine [vImine], *n.m.* (*Bot.*) Osier, withy; twig. **Cesto di vimini,** wicker basket.
vinaccia [vinAccia], *n.f.* Dregs of pressed grapes.
vinaccio [vinAccio], *n.m.* Bad wine.
vinacciolo, vinacciuolo, *n.m.* Grape-stone.
vinaio [vinAio], *n.m.* Wine-merchant; vintner.
vinario [vinArio], *a.* Of wine, wine, vinous.
vinattiere, *n.m.* Wine-seller.
vinca, vincapervinca, *n.f.* (*Bot.*) Periwinkle.
vincastro, *n.m.* Shepherd's crook; staff.
vincente, *n.m.a.* Winner; winning.
vincere [vIncere], *v.t.i.* To win, to conquer, to vanquish, to beat, to overcome, to defeat; to gain. **Darsi per vinto,** to give up the fight, to give in; **o — o morire,** to conquer or to die; **— una scommessa,** to win a bet; **— una concorrenza,** to win a competition; **essere vinto dalla stanchezza,** to be overcome by fatigue; **— una difficoltà,** to overcome a difficulty; **— al giuoco,** to win at play; **— le passioni,** to subdue one's passions; **— la mano,** to bolt (of a horse).
vincersi [vIncersi], *v.r.* To control oneself, to restrain oneself. **Bisogna —,** you must control yourself.
vincheto, *n.m.* Osier-bed.
vinciano, *a.* Concerning Leonardo da Vinci.
vincibile [vincIbile], *a.* Conquerable.
vincibosco, *n.m.* (*Bot.*) Honeysuckle.
vincido [vIncido], *a.* (*obs.*) Flexible; flabby.
vinciglio [vincIglio], *n.m.* Osier twig, withy.
vincita [vIncita], *n.f.* Winning, winnings; gain, prize; victory.
vincitore, vincitrice, *n.m.f.a.* Winner; victor, conqueror; winning.
vinco, *n.m.* (*Bot.*) Osier.
vinco, *a.* Not seasoned (of wood), soft.
vincolare, *v.t.* To bind, to tie; to engage; (*Comm.*) to place money in deposit account. **In conto vincolato,** on deposit.
vincolarsi, *v.r.* To bind oneself, to engage oneself.
vincolo [vIncolo], *n.m.* Bond, tie; chain, fetters. **I vincoli dell'amicizia,** the ties of friendship; **il — contrattuale,** the contractual tie; **libero da ogni —,** free from any encumbrance.
vindice [vIndice], *n.m.a.* Avenger; avenging.
vinello, *n.m.* Light wine.
vinicolo [vinIcolo], *a.* Pertaining to wine, wine-growing, wine-producing.
vinicoltura, *n.f.* Wine-growing, viniculture.
vinifero [vinIfero], *a.* Wine-producing.
vinificazione, *n.f.* Wine-making.
vino, *n.m.* Wine. **— da pasto,** table-wine, claret; **— nostrano,** local wine; **— da bottiglia,** choice wine, wine in bottle; **— bianco, rosso,** white, red wine.
vinolento, *n.m.* (*Lit.*) Drunkard, winebibber.
vinolenza, *n.f.* (*Lit.*) Drunkenness.
vinometro [vinOmetro], *n.m.* Vinometer.
vinosità [-à], *n.f.* Vinosity.
vinoso, *a.* Vinous.
vinto, *n.m.a.* Conquered, vanquished. **Guai ai vinti,** woe to the conquered.
vinucolo [vinUcolo], *n.m.* Weak wine.
viola, *n.f.* (*Bot.*) Viola, violet; (*Mus.*) viola. **— del pensiero,** pansy; **— mammola,** sweet violet; **— mariana,** Canterbury bell.
violabile [violAbile], *a.* Violable, infringeable.
violacciocca, *n.f.* (*Bot.*) Wallflower. **— rossa dei giardini,** stock, gilly-flower.
violaceo [violAceo], *a.* Violet (in colour).
violamento, *n.m.* Violating.
violare, *v.t.* To violate, to infringe; to transgress; to profane; to do violence to. **— un trattato,** to break a treaty; **— la legge,** to break the law.
violatore, violatrice, *n.m.f.* Transgressor, violator.
violazione, *n.f.* Violation, breach, infringement, transgression, rape. **— di domicilio,** house-breaking, illegal entrance.
violentamento, *n.m.* Forcing, doing violence.
violentare, *v.t.* To do violence to, to force; to outrage, to ravish, to rape.
violentemente, *adv.* Violently, furiously.
violento, *n.m.a.* Violent person; violent, furious, impetuous; raging, wild, fierce; rash, reckless; outrageous. **Morte violenta,** violent death; **atti violenti,** outrages, acts of violence.
violenza, *n.f.* Violence, fury, force; outrage, injury; duress. **Far — su,** to do violence to; **ricorrere alla —,** to resort to violence.
violetta, *n.f.* (*Bot.*) Sweet violet.
violetto, *n.m.a.* Violet (colour).
violinaio [violinAio], *n.m.* Violin-maker.
violinata, *n.f.* Violin solo; (*fig.*) flattery.
violinista, *n.m.f.* Violinist, fiddler.
violino, *n.m.* Violin, fiddle. **Primo —,** first violin. **Suoni il —?** Do you play the violin?
violo [cp. **viola**].
violoncellista, *n.m.f.* 'Cellist, violoncellist.
violoncello, *n.m.* Violoncello, 'cello.
violone, *n.m.* Bass violin, viola.
viottola [viOttola], *n.f.* Foot-path, field-path.
viottolo [viOttolo], *n.m.* Foot-path, narrow lane, alley.
vipera [vIpera], *n.f.* (*Zool.*) Viper, adder; (*fig.*) malignant person.
viperaio [viperAio], *n.m.* Viper's nest.
vipereo, viperino, *a.* Viperine, viperish, viperous; venomous, malignant.
vipistrello [cp. **pipistrello**].
viraggio [virAggio], *n.m.* (*Naut.Motor.*) Steering, turning; tacking; (*Phot.*) toning.
virago, *n.f.* Virago, amazon, termagant.
viramento, *n.m.* Turning, tacking [cp. **viraggio**].
virare, *v.t.i.* (*Naut.Motor.*) To turn, to veer, to steer; (*Aviat.*) to bank; (*Phot.*) to tone. **— di bordo,** to tack, to change course.
virata, *n.f.* (*Naut.*) Tacking, steering, putting about.
virgiliano, *a.* Virgilian.
Virgilio [virgIlio], *n.m.* Virgil.
virginale, virgineo [virgIneo], *a.* Virginal, virgin [cp. **verginale**].
virginia [virgInia], *n.m.* Kind of cigar.
virginità [-à], *n.f.* Virginity.
virgola [vIrgola], *n.f.* (*Gram.*) Comma. **Punto e —,** semicolon; **bacillo —,** comma bacillus.

virgolare, *v.t.* To mark with commas; to insert inverted commas.
virgolette, *n.f.pl.* Inverted commas, quotation marks. **Fra —,** in inverted commas, in quotes.
virgulto, *n.m.* Shoot, sapling; shrub.
virile, *a.* Manly, virile; masculine; vigorous; fearless; steady. **Età —,** full maturity.
virilità [-à], *n.f.* Manliness, virility, manhood; manfulness; energy, vigour; steadiness.
virilmente, *adv.* In a manly way, manfully.
viro, *n.m.* Man [cp. **uomo**].
virtù [-ù], *n.f.* Virtue, rectitude, uprightness; power; merit, valour; property, strength. **In — di,** by virtue of; **far di necessità —,** to make a virtue of necessity; **— cardinali,** cardinal virtues; **— magnetiche,** magnetic powers.
virtuale, *a.* Virtual.
virtualità [-à], *n.f.* Virtuality, potentiality.
virtualmente, *adv.* Virtually.
virtuosamente, *adv.* Virtuously.
virtuosità [-à], *n.f.* Virtuousness; (*Mus.*, etc.) virtuosity.
virtuoso, *n.m.* Virtuous man; (*Mus.*, etc.) virtuoso.
virtuoso, *a.* Virtuous, good, honest, straight, upright.
virulento, *a.* Virulent; poisonous; malignant; sharp, acrimonious.
virulenza, *n.f.* Virulence; animosity, enmity.
virus, *n.m.* Virus (in all senses).
visaccio [visAccio], *n.m.* Ugly face.
visaggio [visAggio], *n.m.* Visage, face.
viscerale, *a.* (*Med.*) Visceral. **Dolori viscerali,** gripes, colic.
viscere [vIscere] (*pl.* **visceri,** *m.*, **viscere,** *f.*), *n.m.* Internal organ (of the body); entrails, bowels, viscera; (*fig.*) inmost feelings, heart. **Non avere viscere,** to have no feelings (of pity); **senza viscere,** cruel, heartless; **avere viscere materne,** to have motherly feelings; **nelle — della terra,** in the bowels of the earth.
vischio [vIschio], *n.m.* (*Bot.*) Mistletoe; birdlime; (*fig.*) snare.
vischiosità [-à], *n.f.* Viscosity, stickiness.
vischioso, *a.* Viscous, sticky, glutinous.
viscidezza, viscidità, *n.f.* Viscidity, stickiness, sliminess.
viscido [vIscido], *a.* Sticky, slimy; viscid, clammy.
viscidume, *n.m.* Sticky stuff; nastiness, messiness.
visciola [vIsciola], *n.f.* (*Bot.*) Wild cherry.
visciolo [vIsciolo], *n.f.* Wild cherry tree.
visco [cp. **vischio**].
visconte, *n.m.* Viscount.
viscontessa, *n.f.* Viscountess.
viscosa, *n.f.* (*Chem.*) Viscose.
viscosità [-à], *n.f.* Viscosity, glutinousness, sliminess; clamminess.
viscoso, *a.* Viscous, slimy, sticky.
visetto, *n.m.* Pretty face.
visibile [visIbile], *a.* Visible, perceptible, evident, manifest.
visibilio [visibIlio], *n.m.* Profusion, great quantity. **Vi era un — di uccelli,** there were flocks and flocks of birds; **andare in —,** to go into raptures.
visibilità [-à], *n.f.* Visibility.
visibilmente, *adv.* Visibly.
visiera, *n.f.* Visor, peak (of cap); fencing-mask.
visigoto, *n.m.a.* Visigoth, Visigothic.
visino, *n.m.* Pretty little face.
visionario [visionArio], *n.m.a.* Visionary, dreamer; fanciful, imaginary, Utopian; unpractical.
visione, *n.f.* Sight; vision, apparition, phantom, hallucination. **Prender — di,** to take notice of, to have a sight of, to have a look at (documents, etc.); **avere una —,** to see as in a vision; **avere chiara — delle cose,** to have a clear vision of things.
visir, visire, *n.m.* Vizier.
visirato, *n.m.* Viziership.
visita [vIsita], *n.f.* Visit, call; inspection; visitation; supervision, examination. **Biglietto di —,** visiting-card; **fare una — a,** to call on; **— doganale,** customs inspection; **salvo —,** subject to inspection; **subire una — medica,** to be medically examined.
visitamento, *n.m.* Visitation.
visitare, *v.t.* To visit; to pay a visit, to call on; to examine. **— una città,** to visit a city; **— un parente,** to visit a relative; **dovete farvi — la vista,** you must have your eyes tested.
visitatore, visitatrice, *n.m.f.* Visitor; inspector.
visitazione, *n.f.* (*Eccles.*) Visitation.
visitina, *n.f.* Short call, looking-in (on a friend).
visivo, *a.* Visual, optic. **Organo —,** visual organ; **il campo —,** the visual field, field of vision.
viso, *n.m.* Face, visage; countenance; look. **— a —,** face to face; **a — aperto,** frankly, openly; **far buon —,** to look on favourably, to welcome; **far buon — a cattiva sorte,** to make the best of things; **— patito,** lean or haggard face; **sul —,** to one's face; **— accigliato,** sullen face, sullen look.
visone, *n.m.* (*Zool.*) American mink.
visorio [visOrio], *a.* Visual [cp. **visivo**].
vispezza, *n.f.* Liveliness, briskness.
vispo, *a.* Lively, vivacious, gay; sprightly, brisk; quick, nimble.
vissuto, *p.p.* Lived [cp. **vivere**].
vista, *n.f.* Sight; view, prospect, scenery; look; show; appearance. **Perdere la —,** to lose one's sight; **perdere di — qualcuno,** to lose sight of someone; **un difetto di —,** a defect of sight; **pagare a —,** to pay at sight; (*Mus.*) **leggere a prima —,** to play at sight; **seconda —,** second sight; **in —,** in sight; **persona in —,** well-known person; **far le viste di,** to pretend to; **alla — di quello spettacolo,** at the sight of that; **conoscere di —,** to know by sight; **Che bella —!** What a lovely view! **avere in —,** to have in view; **a — d'occhio,** visibly, to the sight; **punto di —,** point of view; **— corta,** short sight.
vistare, *v.t.* To visa (passport, etc.).
visto, *n.m.* Visa.
visto, *p.p.a.* Seen. **Essere mal —,** to be unpopular; **— che,** seeing that, considering that [cp. **vedere**].
vistosamente, *adv.* Showily.
vistosità [-à], *n.f.* Showiness, tawdriness, gaudiness.

vistoso, *a.* Showy, tawdry, gaudy; considerable, very large. **Una somma vistosa,** a very large sum of money.
visuale, *n.f.a.* Sight, view; visual.
vita, *n.f.* Life; existence; spirit, animation, liveliness, vitality; livelihood, living; body, waist. **Essere in —,** to be alive; **essere in fin di —,** to be at the point of death; **passare a miglior —,** to die; **stentar la —,** to struggle for a living; **tenor di —,** standard of living, manner of life; **la mala —,** the underworld; **donna di mala —,** prostitute; **a —,** lifelong, for life; **galera a —,** life imprisonment; **assicurazione sulla —,** life assurance; **ne va della —,** life is at stake; **vender cara la —,** to sell one's life dearly; **tornare in —,** to recover, to come round, to come to life; **godersi la —,** to enjoy oneself; **la — elegante,** high life, Society; **— campestre,** country life; **guadagnarsi la —,** to earn one's living; **prendere per la —,** to put one's arm round someone's waist; **una — sottile,** a slender waist; **ritto sulla —,** bolt upright.
vitaccia [vitAccia], *n.f.* Wretched life, miserable existence.
vitalba, *n.f.* (*Bot.*) Traveller's joy, clematis.
vitale, *a.* Vital, affecting life; essential, indispensable. **Forza —,** vital force; **una questione —,** a vital question.
vitalità [-à], *n.f.* Vitality, life, force, liveliness, vigour.
vitaliziare, *v.t.* To turn into an annuity.
vitalizio [vitalIzio], *n.m.a.* Life annuity; lifelong. **Fare un —,** to take out an annuity; **socio —,** life-member.
vitalmente, *adv.* Vitally.
vitame, *n.m.* Vines (collectively).
vitamina, *n.f.* Vitamin.
vite (1), *n.f.* Screw. **Girare la —,** to screw, to screw up; **a —,** screw-like; **verme d'una —,** thread of a screw; **— perpetua,** endless screw.
vite (2), *n.f.* (*Bot.*) Vine. **Tralci della —,** vine-branches; **— maritata,** vine trained on a tree; **piangere come una — tagliata,** to dissolve in tears.
vitella, *n.f.* Heifer.
vitello, *n.m.* Calf; veal. **Carne di —,** veal; **— arrosto,** roast veal; (*Zool.*) **— marino,** sea calf, seal.
viticchio [vitIcchio], *n.m.* (*Bot.*) Convolvulus.
viticcio [vitIccio], *n.m.* (*Bot.*) Tendril.
viticolo [vitIcolo], *a.* Suitable for vine-growing.
viticoltore, viticultore, *n.m.* Viticulturist, vine-grower.
viticultura, *n.f.* Viticulture, wine-growing.
vitifero [vitIfero], *a.* Vine-bearing.
vitigno, *n.m.* Vine stock, vine plant.
vitina, vitino, *n.f.m.* Slim waist; slender body; small screw.
vitreo [vItreo], *a.* Vitreous, glassy. **Occhio —,** glassy eye.
vittima [vIttima], *n.f.* Victim; prey; dupe. **Egli fu — di un imbroglione,** he was the dupe of a swindler; **— del dovere,** martyr to duty.
vitto, *n.m.* Food, nourishment; diet; board. **— e alloggio,** board and lodging; **— abbondante,** plentiful food; **— scarso,** insufficient food; **— sano,** wholesome fare.
vittoria [vittOria], *n.f.* Victory; success, triumph; (*Sport*) win; victoria (carriage). **Cantar —,** to boast of victory; **riportare una —,** to gain a victory.
vittoriale, *a.* Triumphal.
vittoriano, *n.m.a.* Victorian.
Vittorio [vittOrio], *n.m.* Victor.
vittoriosamente, *adv.* Victoriously.
vittorioso, *a.* Victorious, triumphant, conquering.
vittrice, *n.f.* Conquering [cp. **vincitrice**].
vituperando, *a.* Contemptible.
vituperare, *v.t.* To vituperate, to abuse, to revile, to insult; to disgrace.
vituperativo, *a.* Vituperative, abusive, defamatory.
vituperatore, vituperatrice, *n.m.f.* Reviler, vituperator, traducer.
vituperazione, *n.f.* Vituperation.
vituperevole, *a.* Vile, blameworthy; contemptible, shameful.
vituperevolmente, *adv.* Vilely, shamefully.
vituperio [vitupErio], *n.m.* Shame, dishonour, disgrace; insult, offensiveness, abuse; affront, outrage. **Coprire di vituperi,** to cover with abuse.
vituperosamente, *adv.* Vituperatively.
vituperoso, *a.* Vituperative, defamatory, abusive. **Parole vituperose,** abusive language.
viuzza, *n.f.* Lane, alley, narrow street.
viva! *inter.* Hurrah! Long live! **— la regina!** Long live the Queen!
vivacchiare, *v.i.* To be hard up, to get a bare living, to live from hand to mouth, to struggle along.
vivace, *a.* Brisk, lively, sprightly, vivacious; gay.
vivacemente, *adv.* Vivaciously.
vivacità [-à], *n.f.* Liveliness, briskness, vivacity, animation, sprightliness.
vivaddio! *inter.* Good heavens! By Jove! Rather!
vivagno, *n.m.* Selvage, selvedge; edge, margin, border.
vivaio [vivAio], *n.m.* (Plant) nursery, hot-bed; fish-pond.
vivamente, *adv.* Lively, vivaciously; warmly, ardently.
vivanda, *n.f.* Food, meat, dish (of food); viands.
vivandiera, *n.f.* (*Mil.*) Vivandière.
vivandiere, *n.m.* (*Mil.*) Sutler; canteen-keeper.
vivente, *a.* Living, alive. **Esseri viventi,** living beings; **quadro —,** living image; **— il padre,** during one's father's lifetime.
vivere [vIvere], *v.i.* To live, to exist, to be alive; to subsist; to dwell; to behave; to endure, to last. **— giorno per giorno,** to live from hand to mouth; **— bene,** to be well off; **— miseramente,** to have a hard life; **— del suo,** to live on one's income; **— alle spalle di,** to sponge (on someone); **modo di —,** way of living; **— a lungo,** to live long; **egli vive a Parigi,** he lives in Paris; **lascia —,** live and let live; **trovar da —,** to find a living; **— di frutta,** to live on fruit; **dar da —,** to get a living out of; **vivendo s'impara,** live and learn.
vivere [vIvere], *n.m.* Life, living. **Conoscere il — del mondo,** to know the way of the world, to be up to things, to know one's way about.

viveri [vIveri], *n.m.pl.* Provisions, foodstuff, victuals. **Caro —**, high cost of living; **tagliare i —**, to cut off supplies.
viverra, *n.f.* (*Zool.*) Civet cat.
vivezza, *n.f.* Liveliness, vivacity, brightness; splendour.
vividamente, *adv.* Vividly.
vivido [vIvido], *a.* Bright, vivid, glaring; vivacious, lively, vigorous.
vivificante, *a.* Vivifying, animating, enlivening; life-giving.
vivificare, *v.t.* To vivify, to enliven, to animate, to inspirit.
vivificativo, vivificatore, *a.* Vivifying [cp. **vivificante**].
vivificazione, *n.f.* Vivification, quickening, enlivening.
viviparo [vivIparo], *a.* (*Zool.*) Viviparous.
vivisettore, *n.m.* Vivisector.
vivisezione, *n.f.* Vivisection. **Fare la —**, to vivisect.
vivo, *n.m.* Living person, one alive; sensitive part, living flesh, quick. **I vivi,** the living; **mancare ai vivi,** to die; **pungere, toccare sul —**, to sting or touch to the quick; **taglia nel —**, to cut to the quick; **essere colto al —**, to be very lifelike (of a portrait, etc.).
vivo, *a.* Alive, living; brisk, alert, eager, keen; quick, lively; fiery; passionate, ardent. **Non c'era anima viva,** there wasn't a soul there; **colore —**, bright colour; **calce viva,** quicklime; **argento —**, quicksilver; **avere l'argento — addosso,** to be restless, to fidget; **pietra viva,** living rock; **a viva forza,** by main force; **a viva voce,** by word of mouth; **carne viva,** quick; **freddo —**, piercing cold; **acqua viva,** spring water; **egli ne provò un — dolore,** he felt a sharp pain; **farsi —**, to come forward, to be sociable.
vivole [vIvole], *n.f.pl.* Vives (horse disease).
viziare, *v.t.* To spoil; to impair, to mar; to vitiate; to render invalid. **Un bimbo viziato,** a spoilt child.
viziatamente, *adv.* Faultily, defectively, imperfectly.
vizio [vIzio], *n.m.* Vice; depravity, corruption; blemish, defect; bad habit; trick. (*Law*) **— di forma,** defect of form; technical error; **avere il — di ridere,** to have a trick of giggling; **il — del fumare,** the habit of smoking; (*Med.*) **— di cuore,** heart trouble.
viziosaggine [viziosAggine], *n.f.* Depravity, viciousness.
viziosamente, *adv.* Viciously.
viziosità [-à], *n.f.* Depravity, viciousness.
vizioso, *a.* Corrupted, depraved, vicious, wicked, immoral, dissipated.
vizzo, *a.* Dried up, withered, shrivelled; faded; flabby.
vocabolarietto, *n.m.* Pocket dictionary.
vocabolario [vocabolArio], *n.m.* Dictionary, vocabulary, lexicon.
vocabolo [vocAbolo], *n.m.* Term, word, expression.
vocale, *n.m.a.* Vowel; vocal.
vocalico [vocAlico], *a.* Vowel. **Suoni vocalici,** vowel sounds.
vocalizzare, *v.i.* To vocalize; (*Mus.*) to sing (in vowels).
vocalizzazione, *n.f.* (*Mus.*) Vocalization.
vocalizzo, *n.m.* Vocalization, vocalism.
vocalmente, *adv.* Vocally.
vocativo, *n.m.* (*Gram.*) Vocative (case).
vocazione, *n.f.* Vocation; call, calling; bent; talent. **Seguir la propria —**, to follow one's calling.
voce, *n.f.* Voice; speech; term, word; rumour; vote. **Non aver — in capitolo,** to have no voice in the matter; **abbassare la —**, to lower or drop one's voice; **dar sulla —**, to scold; **dar la — a,** to call someone; **— pubblica,** public opinion; **corre — che,** rumour has it that; **rifiutarono a una sol —**, they refused with one voice; **parlare ad alta —**, to talk loudly; **a viva —**, by word of mouth; **con un fil di —**, in a faint voice; **con — alterata,** in a shaking voice; **"sono" è — del verbo "essere"**, "sono" is part of the verb "essere"; (*Mus.*) **voci bianche,** boys' or girls' voices; **non essere in —**, not to be in good voice.
vociaccia [vociAccia], *n.f.* Hoarse, raucous voice; croak.
vociare, *v.i.* To shout, to bawl.
vociferare, *v.i.* To shout; to speak aloud; to report. **Si vocifera che,** it is rumoured that, report has it.
vociferazione, *n.f.* Vociferation, shouting; rumour, report.
vocina, *n.f.* Low voice, sweet tones.
vocio [vocIo], *n.m.* Shouting, vociferation, noise; bawling.
vocione, *n.m.* Loud voice; loud-voiced person.
vodca, *n.f.* Vodka.
voga (1), *n.f.* Fashion, vogue. **Canzone in —**, song of the day; **essere in —**. to be in fashion; **non è più in —**, it is out of fashion.
voga (2), *n.f.* Rowing, stroke. **— lunga,** long stroke. **Voga!** Give way!
vogare, *v.i.* To row; to glide over the water.
vogata, *n.f.* Rowing, stroke.
vogatore, vogatrice, *n.m.f.* Rower, oarsman.
vogavanti, *n.m.* Bow oar of a galley.
voglia [vOglia], *n.f.* Will, desire, wish; craving, longing; inclination; fancy; birthmark. **Avere buona —**, to be willing; **far le cose di mala —**, to do things unwillingly; **non ne ho —**, I don't feel like doing it; **levarsi la —**, to have one's way; **ne muore dalla —**, he is longing for it; **mi fa — di ridere,** you make me laugh; **ho — di piangere,** I feel like crying; **contro —**, against one's will; **ha una — sul viso,** he has a birthmark on his face.
vogliosamente, *adv.* Wishfully.
voglioso, *a.* Desirous, wishful; eager, willing; capricious.
vogliuzza, *n.f.* Whim, fancy, caprice.
voi, *pron.* You, yourself. **Voi stesso,** you yourself; **ora a voi,** it's your turn now; **dare del voi,** to address someone as "voi" (instead of the usual "Lei").
voialtri, *pron.* You folk, you others.
volamento, *n.m.* (*obs.*) Flying.
volanda, *n.f.* Dust (from a mill); fly-wheel.
volano, *n.m.* Shuttlecock; fly-wheel. **Giuoco del —**, battledore and shuttlecock.
volante, *n.m.* Fly-wheel; (*Motor.*) steering-wheel; shuttlecock; flounce (of dress). **Saper stare al —**, to know how to drive (a car).

volante, *a.* Flying. **Ponte —,** flying bridge; **colonna —,** flying column; **foglio —,** fly-sheet; **cervo —,** (child's) kite; **squadra —,** flying squad; **pesce —,** flying-fish.
volantino, *n.m.* Fly-wheel, wheel; leaflet.
volare, *v.i.* To fly, to take wing; to soar; to rush away. **Il tempo vola,** time flies; **— a Dio,** to die; **— in pezzi,** to fly in pieces; (*Aviat.*) **— su Roma,** to fly over Rome.
volare, *n.m.* Flying.
volata, *n.f.* Flight; run, sprint; (*Sport*) last lap; (*Mus.*) rapid succession of notes; (*Mil.*) chase (of gun). **In —,** at full speed; **di —,** hurriedly, at great speed; (*Sport*) **— finale,** final sprint, last lap.
volatica [volAtica], *n.f.* (*Med.*) Rash, eruption.
volatile [volAtile], *n.m.* Bird, winged creature.
volatile [volAtile], *a.* Volatile, evaporating; winged.
volatilità [-à], *n.f.* (*Chem.*) Volatility, evaporation.
volatizzare, volatilizzarsi, *v.i.r.* To volatilize, to evaporate.
volatilizzazione, *n.f.* Volatilization.
volatore, volatrice, *n.m.f.a.* Flier; flying.
volente, *a.* Willing. **— o nolente,** willy-nilly.
volenterosamente, *adv.* Willingly, complacently.
volenteroso, *a.* Willing, eager, keen; ready.
volentieri, *adv.* Willingly, gladly, with pleasure. **Ben —,** with great pleasure; **mal —,** unwillingly; with a bad grace.
volere, *v.t.i.* To will; to wish, to want, to desire; to choose, to determine; to try, to endeavour; to be willing; to need, to require. **Non voglio!** I won't! **Dio lo voglia!** God grant it! **Dio non voglia!** God forbid! **voler bene,** to love; **io gli voglio bene,** I love him; **— male,** to hate, to dislike; **— dire,** to mean (to say); **Che vuol dire questa parola?** What does this word mean? **vorrei sapere il perchè,** I should like to know why; **si vuole ch'egli sia l'autore di quella commedia,** they say he is the author of that comedy; **Ci vuol pazienza!** One must be patient! **— o no,** whether you like it or not; **l'ho fatto senza —,** I did it unintentionally; **vorrei parlargli,** I should like to speak to him; **fa come vuoi,** do as you like; **Chi mi vuole?** Who wants me? **per far ciò ci vogliono molti denari,** it takes a lot of money to do that; **vuol piovere,** it's going to rain; **bisogna saper —,** one must have a will of one's own; **Volete tacere o no!** Hold your tongue, will you! **Che cosa volete ancora?** What more do you want? **Quanto ci vuole fino alla stazione?** How long does it take to get to the station?
volere, *n.m.* Will. **Il buon —,** good will; **di suo —,** of his own accord.
volgare, *n.m.* Vernacular, vulgar tongue.
volgare, *a.* Common, vulgar, coarse, low; vernacular. **Era —,** Christian era; **linguaggio —,** vulgar tongue, vernacular.
volgarismo, *n.m.* Vulgarism.
volgarità [-à], *n.f.* Vulgarity, coarseness.
volgarizzare, *v.t.* To popularize, to vulgarize; to divulge.
volgarizzazione, *n.f.* Vulgarization.
volgarmente, *adv.* Vulgarly.
Volgata, *n.f.* (*Eccles.*) Vulgate.
volgere [vOlgere], *v.t.i.* To turn; to direct; to address; to translate. **— a destra,** to turn to the right; **— gli occhi,** to turn one's eyes; **— la mente a,** to turn one's thought to; **— le spalle,** to turn one's back; **lo spettacolo volgeva alla fine,** the show was drawing to a close; **— l'attenzione a,** to turn one's attention to; **— i passi,** to turn one's steps; **il tempo volge al bello,** the weather is changing to fair; **colore che volge al rosso,** colour tending towards red; **— in italiano,** to translate into Italian.
volgersi [vOlgersi], *v.r.* To turn round, to revolve; to be changed; to be translated, **— indietro,** to turn backwards.
volgibile [volgIbile], *a.* Turning, that may be turned.
volgimento, *n.m.* Change; event.
volgo, *n.m.* Populace, mob; common herd.
volgolo [vOlgolo], *n.m.* Bundle.
volicchiare, volitare, *v.i.* To flutter.
volitivo, *a.* Self-willed, headstrong, energetic, imperious.
volizione, *n.f.* Volition.
volo, *n.m.* Flight; flying, fly. **Prendere il —,** to take flight; to disappear; **a —,** by air, by flight; **in un —,** rapidly; **di —,** hurriedly, at once; **veduta a — d'uccello,** bird's-eye view; **a — d'uccello,** as the crow flies; **capire a —,** to grasp a thing at once; (*Aviat.*) **— di prova,** test flight; **alzarsi al —,** to take off; **in un sol —,** in a single flight, in one hop; **— transoceanico,** Transatlantic flight.
volontà [-à], *n.f.* Will, volition; purpose, determination; energy; desire, wish. **Le ultime —,** the last will; **di sua spontanea —,** of his own free will; **forza di —,** will-power; **a —,** at pleasure, at will, at option; **buona —,** good will; **senza —,** weak, spineless; **contro la mia —,** against my will; **— di ferro,** strong will.
volontariamente, *adv.* Voluntarily, of one's own will.
volontariato, *n.m.* (*Mil.*) Voluntary service.
volontario [volontArio], *n.m.a.* Volunteer; voluntary, free, spontaneous.
volpacchiotto, *n.m.* Fox-cub.
volpaia [volpAia], *n.f.* Fox's den, fox-hole, earth.
volpare, *v.i.* (*Agric.*) To get blighted (of corn) to get smut.
volpe, *n.f.* Fox; cunning fellow; (*Agric.*) blight, smut. **Caccia alla —,** fox-hunting, fox-hunt; **vecchia —,** crafty fellow.
volpetta, volpicella, volpicina, *n.f.* Fox-cub.
volpinamente, *adv.* Craftily.
volpino, *a.* Foxy, crafty, artful, sly. **Cane —,** small Roman dog.
volpone, *n.m.* Crafty person, cunning fellow.
volt, volta, *n.m.* (*Elect.*) Volt. (From Alessandro Volta, 1745-1827).
volta (1), *n.f.* Turn, time; turning, direction. **Alla — di,** in the direction of; **una —, due volte,** once, twice; **dar —,** to turn over (in bed, etc.); **c'era una —,** once upon a time there was; **partire alla — di,** to start for; **marciare alla — di Roma,** to march towards Rome; **alle volte, talvolta,** sometimes; **alla —,** one at a time; **dar di — al cervello,** to go off one's head; **— a —,** each time, **di**

— **in —,** from time to time; **tutto in una —,** all at once; **altre volte,** formerly, on other occasions; **poche volte,** seldom; **il più delle volte,** mostly, generally; **è la tua —,** it's your turn.
volta (2), *n.f.* Dome, vault, arch, canopy. **Una — a cupola,** a dome-shaped vault; **stanza a —,** vaulted room; **la — del cielo,** the vault of heaven; **chiave di —,** key-stone.
voltabile [voltAbile], *a.* That can be turned.
voltafaccia [voltafAccia], *n.m.* Change of sides, volte-face, sudden turn round.
voltaggio [voltAggio], *n.m.* (*Elect.*) Voltage.
voltaico [voltAico], *a.* (*Elect.*) Voltaic.
voltametro [voltAmetro], *n.m.* Voltameter.
voltare, *v.t.i.* To turn, to turn round, to swerve; to change round; to change front; to translate. **— a sinistra,** to turn to the left; **— le spalle,** to turn one's back; **— la pagina,** to turn the page; (*colloq.*) **— la frittata,** to change one's tune; **— casacca,** to change sides, to be a turncoat.
voltarsi, *v.r.* To turn oneself. **Egli si voltò,** he turned round; **— in meglio,** to take a turn for the better.
voltata, *n.f.* Turn, turning; curve, bend. **Alla prima —,** at the first turning.
volteggiamento [cp. **volteggio**].
volteggiare, *v.i.* To whirl, to twirl; to fly about, to flutter, to hover; to vault (on horseback); to shuffle, to wriggle.
volteggiatore, *n.m.* Vaulter, tumbler.
volteggio, volteggiamento [voltEggio], *n.m.* Vaulting, tumbling, leaping; trick-riding.
volterriano, *n.m.a.* Voltairean.
voltimetro [voltImetro], *n.m.* (*Elect.*) Voltmeter.
volto, *n.m.* Face, visage, countenance; aspect.
volto, *p.p.a.* Turned. **Naso — all'insù,** turned-up nose [cp. **volgere**].
voltolamento, *n.m.* Rolling, wallowing.
voltolare, voltolarsi, *v.i.r.* To roll, to wallow.
voltoloni, *adv.* By rolling, tumbling down.
voltone, *n.m.* Large vault, big arch.
voltura, *n.f.* (*Law*) Transfer, assignment.
volubile [volUbile], *a.* Inconstant, flighty, fickle, changeable; voluble; (*Bot.*) climbing.
volubilità [-à], *n.f.* Inconstancy, fickleness; volubility.
volubilmente, *adv.* Volubly; fickly.
volume, *n.m.* Volume (in all senses), book, bulk, size, mass.
voluminosamente, *adv.* Voluminously.
voluminosità, *n.f.* Bulkiness, volume.
voluminoso, *a.* Voluminous, bulky; roomy; ponderous.
voluta, *n.f.* (*Arch.*) Volute, scroll.
voluttà [-à], *n.f.* Voluptuousness, sensuality; lust, sensual pleasure.
voluttuario [voluttuArio], *a.* Luxury. **Spese voluttuarie,** luxury expenses.
voluttuosamente, *adv.* Voluptuously.
voluttuoso, *a.* Voluptuous, sensual.
volvere [cp. **volgere**].
volvolo [vOlvolo], *n.m.* (*Med.*) Volvulus.
vomero, vomere [vOmero, vOmere], *n.m.* Ploughshare.
vomico [vOmico], *a.* Emetic. **Noce vomica,** nux vomica.
vomitare, *v.i.* To vomit, to retch; to belch out; to eject, to discharge. **Aver voglia di —,** to feel squeamish; **— ingiurie,** to pour out abuse.
vomitativo, vomitatorio [vomitatOrio], *a.* Emetic, vomitory.
vomito [vOmito], *n.m.* Vomit, spew. **Eccitare il —,** to induce vomiting.
vomitorio [vomitOrio], *n.m.* Emetic; (*Hist.*) vomitory.
vongola [vOngola], *n.f.* (*colloq.*) Mussel.
vorace, *a.* Voracious, ravenous, famished, hungry.
voracemente, *adv.* Voraciously.
voracità [-à], *n.f.* Ravenousness, voracity, voraciousness, greediness.
voragine [vorAgine], *n.f.* Abyss, chasm, gulf; whirlpool.
voraginoso, *a.* Abysmal, bottomless.
vortice [vOrtice], *n.m.* Whirlpool, whirl; vortex; eddy.
vorticoso, *a.* Whirling, eddying.
vosco, *pron.* (*Lit.*) With you.
Vosgi, *n.m.pl.* (*Geog.*) Vosges.
vossignoria [vossignorIa], *n.f.* Your lordship, your ladyship.
vostro, *pron.a.* Your; yours. **I vostri,** your parents, your people; **il —,** your estate, **questo libro è —,** this book is yours.
votacessi, *n.m.* Emptier of cesspools.
votame, *n.m.* Emptiness, empty things.
votante, *n.m.f.* Voter.
votapozzi, *n.m.* Well-cleaner.
votare (1), *v.t.i.* To vote; to pass, to carry (a division); to go to the polls, to give one's vote; to consecrate. **— in massa,** to vote in a body; **— un ordine del giorno,** to pass a resolution.
votare (2) [cp. **vuotare**].
votarsi, *v.r.* To consecrate oneself, to devote oneself. **Non sapere a che santo —,** not to know which way to turn.
votato, *p.p.a.* Devoted; doomed.
votazione, *n.f.* Voting, polling, ballot. **Venire alla —,** to put to the vote.
votazza, *n.f.* Scoop, ladle, baler.
votivo, *a.* Votive, votary. **Offerta votiva,** votive offering.
voto, *n.m.* Vow; wish; vote; prayer; mark (for lessons). **— monastico,** monastic vow; **dare il — a,** to give one's vote to; **— decisivo,** casting vote; **mettere ai voti,** to put to the vote; **è — generale,** it is the general wish.
vui [cp. **voi**].
vulcanico [vulcAnico], *a.* Volcanic.
vulcanite, *n.f.* Vulcanite.
vulcanizzare, *v.t.* To vulcanize.
vulcanizzazione, *n.f.* Vulcanization.
vulcano, *n.m.* Volcano; (*Myth.*) Vulcan.
vulgata [cp. **volgata**].
vulgo [cp. **volgo**].
vulnerabile [vulnerAbile], *a.* Vulnerable.
vulnerabilità [-à], *n.f.* Vulnerability.
vulnerabilmente, *adv.* Vulnerably.
vulnerare, *v.t.* To wound [cp. **ferire**].
vulnerario [vulnerArio], *a.* Vulnerary, vulnerable [cp. **vulnerabile**].
vulva, *n.f.* (*Anat.*) Vulva.
vulvario [vulvArio], *a.* (*Anat.*) Vulvar.
vuotaggine [vuotAggine], *n.f.* Emptiness.
vuotamento, *n.m.* Emptying.
vuotare, *v.t.* To empty; to make vacant, to remove the contents from. **— il sacco,** to

have one's say out, to make a clean breast of it.
vuotarsi, *v.r.* To become empty; to empty oneself. **Il teatro s'è vuotato,** the theatre emptied.
vuotatura, *n.f.* Emptying.
vuoti, *n.m.pl.* Empties.
vuoto, *n.m.* Emptiness, empty space, vacuum, void. **Fare il —,** to make a vacuum, to cold-shoulder; **sentire il — intorno a sè,** to feel lonely, to feel neglected; **restare sospeso nel —,** to be suspended in a vacuum; **a —,** without effect, to no purpose; **un assegno a —,** a worthless cheque, a dud; **un — di cassa,** cash deficit; **colmare un —,** to fill a gap; **colmare un — di cassa,** to make good a deficit of cash.
vuoto, *a.* Empty, void; vacuous; vacant; vain, foolish; futile, meaningless, inane. **Rimanere a mani vuote,** to be left empty-handed; **essere a stomaco —,** to have an empty stomach; **— di senso,** meaningless; **una testa vuota,** an empty head; **aver le tasche vuote,** to be penniless; **— di,** devoid of.

W

W, w, *n.f.* This letter does not belong to the Italian alphabet and is found only in a few foreign words, mostly of English origin. Some of these are given here for the purpose of indicating their gender.
walkover, *n.m.*
warrant, *n.m.*
water-closet, *n.m.*
waterproof, *n.m.*
watt, *n.m.* (*Elect.*).
west, *n.m.a.*
whisky, *n.m.*
whist, *n.m.*
wolframio [wolfrAmio], *n.m.* Wolfram.

X

X, x, *n.f.* This letter is used only at the beginning of certain foreign words and in modern usage is commonly replaced by initial **s.**
X raggi, *n.m.pl.* X-rays.
xenofobia [xenofobIa], *n.f.* Xenophobia, hatred of foreigners.
xenofobo [xenOfobo], *n.m.* Xenophobe.
xeres, *n.m.* Sherry.
xilofonista, *n.m.* (*Mus.*) Xylophone player.
xilofono [xilOfono], *n.m.* (*Mus.*) Xylophone.
xilografia [xilografIa], *n.f.* Wood engraving.
xilografo [xilOgrafo], *n.m.* Wood engraver.
xilologia [xilologIa], *n.f.* Xylology, study of wood.

Y

Y, y, *n.f.* Found only in foreign words and mathematical symbols.
yacht, *n.m.*
yak, *n.m.*
Yankee, *n.m.f.a.*
yard, *n.f.* (English measure).

Z

Z, z, *n.f.* Twenty-first and last letter of the Italian alphabet.
zabaione, zabaglione, zabalone, *n.m.* Egg-flip with wine; custard mixed with Marsala.
zacchera [zAcchera], *n.f.* Splash of mud.
zaccherona, *n.f.* Slut.
zaccherone, *n.m.* Slovenly man, one careless of his looks.
zaccheroso, *a.* Mud-bespattered, muddy.
zaffare, *v.t.* To stop up, to plug, to bung.
zaffata, *n.f.* Spurt (of liquid); whiff (of foul air), stink, stench.
zafferano, *n.m.* Saffron. **Color di —,** saffron (colour).
zaffiro, *n.m.* Sapphire.
zaffo, *n.m.* Stopper, plug, bung.
zagaglia [zagAglia], *n.f.* Assegai, (native) spear.
zagagliata, *n.f.* Thrust with a spear, spear stroke.
zagara [zAgara], *n.f.* Orange-blossom.
zaino [zAino], *n.m.* Knapsack, rucksack, pack, haversack. **Fare — a terra,** to down packs; **fare lo —,** to pack one's rucksack.
zampa, *n.f.* Paw; claw, talon (of bird of prey); foot, leg. **Le zampe del gatto,** the cat's claws; **zampe di gallina,** crow's feet; **— di maiale.** pig's trotters; **— di vitello,** leg of veal.
zampare, *v.t.i.* To paw (the ground).
zampata, *n.f.* Blow with a paw.
zampetta, *n.f.* Little paw.
zampettare, *v.i.* To toddle (of a child); to totter.
zampillante, *a.* Streaming, gushing, spurting. (*fig.*) **Un riso —,** a peal of laughter.
zampillare, *v.i.* To gush, to spurt out, to stream; to spring (of water).
zampillio [zampillIo], *n.m.* Continuous streaming, gushing.
zampillo, *n.m.* Jet, spout, spurt.
zampino, *n.m.* Little paw; finger. (*fig.*) **Metterci lo —,** to put in one's word (for or against).
zampogna, *n.f.* (*Mus.*) Reed pipe; bag-pipe.
zampognaro, *n.m.* Piper.
zampone, *n.m.* Large paw; trotter; stuffed leg of pork.
zana, *n.f.* Basket; cradle; (*Arch.*) niche, recess; (road) gutter.
zanaio [zanAio], *n.m.* Basket-maker.
zanca, *n.f.* Leg, shank; claw.
zanella, *n.f.* Gutter, ditch.
zanfone, *n.m.* Basin for water in alum mine.
zangola [zAngola], *n.f.* Churn.
zangolare, *v.t.* To churn.
zangolatura, *n.f.* Churning.
zanna, *n.f.* Tusk (of elephant, etc.); fang (of dog, etc.). **Le zanne del cinghiale,** the boar's tusks.
zannare, *v.t.* To burnish (with a tusk, etc.).
zannata (1), *n.f.* Thrust with a tusk; bite.
zannata (2), *n.f.* Clown's trick, piece of buffoonery.
zanni, *n.m.* Buffoon, clown, zany.
zanneggiare, *v.i.* To play the fool, to act the clown.
zannuto, *a.* Tusked, fanged.
zanzara, *n.f.* Mosquito.
zanzariera, *n.f.* Mosquito-net.

zappa, *n.f.* (*Agric.*) Hoe, mattock. (*fig.*) **Darsi la — sui piedi,** to defeat one's own ends, to rap one's own knuckles.
zappare, *v.t.* To hoe; to till (the soil).
zappatore, *n.m.* Digger; (*Mil.*) sapper. **Genio zappatori,** corps of sappers.
zappatura, *n.f.* Hoeing.
zappetta, zappettina, *n.f.* Hoe, pick; (*Mil.*) trench-tool.
zappettare, *v.t.* To hoe.
zappetto, *n.m.* Small hoe.
zapponare, *v.t.* To dig with a mattock.
zappone, *n.m.* Mattock.
zar, *n.m.* Tsar.
zarina, *n.f.* Tsarina.
zatta, *n.f.* (*Naut.*) Lighter; (*Bot.*) variety of melon.
zattera [zAttera], *n.f.* (*Naut.*) Raft; lighter. **Ponte di zattere,** pontoon bridge.
zatteriere, *n.m.* Lighterman.
zavorra, *n.f.* Ballast; (*fig.*) worthless thing or person, rubbish, trash. **Nave in —,** ship in ballast.
zavorrare, *v.t.* To ballast.
zazzera [zAzzera], *n.f.* Long hair, head of hair; shock of hair.
zazzeruto, *a.* Long-haired, wearing one's hair long.
zeba, *n.f.* (*obs.*) Sheep, goat.
zebedei [zebedEi], *n.m.pl.* (*colloq.*) **Rompere gli —,** to bother, to annoy.
zebra, *n.f.* (*Zool.*) Zebra.
zebrato, *a.* Striped, streaky.
zecca (1), *n.f.* Mint (for coinage). **Nuovo di —,** brand new.
zecca (2), *n.f.* (*Zool.*) Tick.
zecchinetta, *n.f.* Kind of card-game.
zecchino, *n.m.* Sequin; (*Hist.*) old Italian coin.
zeffiro [zEffiro], *n.m.* Zephir; gentle breeze.
Zelanda, Zeelandia [zeelAndia], *n.f.* (*Geog.*) Zealand. **Nuova Zelanda,** New Zealand.
zelante, *n.m.a.* Zealous person, zealot; zealous, eager, conscientious.
zelantemente, *adv.* Zealously.
zelanteria [zelanterIa], *n.f.* Excessive zeal.
zelare, *v.i.* To show zeal, to make a show of zeal; to solicit.
zelatore, zelatrice, *n.m.f.* Zealous person; supporter (of a cause); zealot.
zelo, *n.m.* Zeal; keenness, eagerness. **Troppo —,** too much zeal, excessive zeal.
zendado, *n.m.* Sendal (silk fabric; silk shawl).
zenit [zEnit, zenIt], *n.m.* Zenith.
zenzero [zEnzero], *n.m.* Ginger.
zeppa, *n.f.* Wedge.
zeppare, *v.t.* To wedge; to fill, to cram in.
zeppo, *a.* Full, chock-full, crammed; packed, crowded, overcrowded. **Pieno —,** absolutely full, chock-a-block.
zerbino, *n.m.* Door-mat.
zerbinotto, *n.m.* Dandy, fop; lady-killer.
zero, *n.m.* Zero, cipher, naught, nothing. **Dieci gradi sotto —,** ten degrees below zero; **non conta uno —,** he is a mere cipher; **una cifra con due zeri,** a figure with two naughts; (in telephoning pronounced as *o*).
zeta, *n.f.* (Letter) z. **Dall'A alla —,** from beginning to end.
zeugma, zeuma [zEugma, zEuma], *n.m.* (*Gram.*) Zeugma.
zia, *n.f.* Aunt.
zibaldone, *n.m.* Medley, confusion; (literary) miscellany.
zibellino, *n.m.* (*Zool.*) Sable.
zibetto, *n.m.* (*Zool.*) Civet.
zibibbo, *n.m.* Raisin.
zietta, *n.f.* (*colloq.*) Auntie.
zigodattilo [zigodAttilo], *a.* (*Zool.*) Zygodactyl.
zigolo [zIgolo], *n.m.* (*Zool.*) Bunting.
zigomo [zIgomo], *n.m.* (*Anat.*) Cheek-bone.
zigrinare, *v.t.* To shagreen; to knurl.
zigrinato, *a.* Shagreen, shagreened.
zigrino, *n.m.* Shagreen.
zigzag, *n.m.* Zigzag; sharp turn. **Strada a —,** zigzag road; **camminare a —,** to go reeling, to stagger along.
zimarra, *n.f.* Gown, long coat; robe, (priest's) cassock.
zimbellare, *v.t.* To decoy.
zimbello, *n.m.* Decoy-bird; laughing-stock. **Egli divenne lo — di tutti,** he became the general laughing-stock.
zimologia [zimologIa], *n.f.* Zymology.
zimometro [zimOmetro], *n.m.* Zymometer.
zimosi, *n.f.* Zymosis.
zinale, *n.m.* Apron.
zincare, *v.t.* To galvanize (with zinc).
zinco, *n.m.* Zinc. **Ossido di —,** zinc-white; **fiori di —,** flowers of zinc.
zincografia [zincografIa], *n.f.* Zincography.
zincografo [zincOgrafo], *n.m.* (*Typ.*) Block-maker; process-engraver.
zincotipia [zincotipIa], *n.f.* Zincotype, zincotyping.
zingana, *n.f.* Gipsy music, gypsy song.
zingara [zIngara], *n.f.* Gipsy woman.
zingaresca, *n.f.* Gipsy music.
zingaresco, *a.* Gipsy, gipsyish; bohemian.
zingaro [zIngaro], *n.m.* Gipsy.
zingone, *n.m.* (*Bot.*) Shoot; stump (of branch).
zinnia [zInnia], *n.f.* (*Bot.*) Zinnia.
zio, *n.m.* Uncle.
zipolo [zIpolo], *n.m.* Spigot (of cask); peg, wedge.
zircone, *n.m.* (*Min.*) Zircon.
zirconio [zircOnio], *n.m.* Zirconium.
zirlare, *v.i.* To whistle or sing (like a thrush).
zirlio, zirlo [zirlIo], *n.m.* Whistling (of a thrush).
zita, zitella, *n.f.* Spinster, maid, unmarried woman.
zitellona, *n.f.* Old maid; spinster.
zitellone, *n.m.* Old bachelor, old-maidish bachelor.
zittire, *v.t.i.* To silence, to hush up, to quieten. **La commedia venne zittita,** the comedy was hissed.
zitto, *a.* Silent, quiet, noiseless. **Sta —!** Keep quiet! Shut up! **Zitto!** Hush! Hold your tongue!
zizzania [zizzAnia], *n.f.* (*Bot.*) Darnel; (*fig.*) discord, ill-feeling, dissension. **Mettere, seminare la —,** to sow dissension.
zoccolaio [zoccolAio], *n.m.* Clog-maker, maker of wooden shoes.
zoccolante, *n.m.* Franciscan friar.
zoccolare, *v.i.* To tramp about in clogs; to make a noise with one's shoes.
zoccolata, *n.f.* Blow with a clog.
zoccoletto, *n.m.* Small sabot or clog.

zoccolo [zOccolo], *n.m.* Wooden shoe, clog, sabot; patten; (horse's hoof); (*Arch.*) patten (of plinth); dado, skirting-board (around wall); (carriage) shoe.
zoccolone, *n.m.* Clog; (*fig.*) boor, churlish fellow.
zodiacale, *a.* Zodiacal.
zodiaco [zodIaco], *n.m.* Zodiac.
zolfaia [cp. **zolfara**].
zolfaio [zolfAio], *n.m.* Worker in a sulphur mine.
zolfanello, *n.m.* Sulphur match; match.
zolfara, zolfaia, zolfatara, *n.f.* Sulphur mine.
zolfare, *v.t.* To sulphur.
zolfatura, *n.f.* Sulphuration.
zolfino, *n.m.* Sulphur match; (*fig.*) spit-fire (person).
zolfo, *n.m.* Sulphur. **Fiori di —,** sulphur flowers.
zolforato, *a.* Sulphurated.
zolla, *n.f.* Clod, sod, turf. **— di zucchero,** lump of sugar.
zolletta, zollettina, *n.f.* Lump (of sugar).
zolloso, *a.* Lumpy.
zombare, *v.t.i.* (*colloq.*) To thump.
zombata, *n.f.* (*colloq.*) Thump, thumping.
zompare, *v.i.* (*colloq.*) To jump, to leap.
zompo, *n.m.* (*colloq.*) Jump.
zona, *n.f.* Zone; girdle, belt; area; (*Med.*) shingles. **— torrida,** Torrid Zone; **— di guerra,** war zone; **— di sicurezza,** safety zone; **dividere in zone,** to divide into zones.
zonzo, *adv.* **Andare a —,** to saunter, to wander about; to loaf.
zoofilia [zoofilIa], *n.f.* Zoophily.
zooiatria [zooiatrIa], *n.f.* Veterinary science.
zoologia [zoologIa], *n.f.* Zoology.
zoologico [zoolOgico], *a.* Zoological. **Giardino —,** zoological gardens, zoo.
zoologista (*pl.* **zoologisti**), *n.m.* Dealer in animals.
zoologo [zoOlogo], *n.m.* Zoologist.
zootecnica [zootEcnica], *n.f.* Zootechnics.
zoppaggine [zoppAggine], *n.f.* Limping, lameness, limp.
zoppicamento, *n.m.* Limp.
zoppicante, *a.* Limping, hobbling, lame. **Un ragionamento —,** a lame argument.
zoppicare, *v.i.* To limp, to be lame, to hobble; to run lamely, to halt. **Questo tavolo zoppica,** this table is rickety; **chi va con lo zoppo impara a —,** bad company corrupts good morals.
zoppicone, zoppiconi, *adv.* Lamely.
zoppo, *n.m.a.* Lame person; lame, limping, hobbling, halting. **Camminare —,** to hobble along; **una sedia zoppa,** a rickety chair.
zoticaggine, zotichezza [zotticAggine], *n.f.* Boorishness, roughness.
zotico [zOtico], *n.m.a.* Churlish fellow, boor; blockhead, dunce; boorish; clownish, stupid; clumsy, uncouth.
zoticone, *n.m.* Intolerable boor.
zozza, *n.f.* Grog.
zuavo, *n.m.* Zouave.
zucca, *n.f.* Pumpkin, gourd; (*colloq.*) head, pate, nut. **Una — vuota,** a blockhead; **non aver sale in —,** to be giddy-pated; **grattarsi la —,** to scratch one's head.
zuccaio [zuccAio], *n.m.* Field of pumpkins.
zuccata, *n.f.* Knock on the head, bump.
zuccherare, *v.t.* To sugar.
zuccheriera, *n.f.* Sugar bowl.
zuccherificio [zuccherifIcio], *n.m.* Sugar refinery.
zuccherino, *n.m.a.* Sweetmeat, toffee; sugary.
zucchero [zUcchero], *n.m.* Sugar. **— greggio, grasso,** brown sugar; **— in polvere,** white sugar (fine); **— in pezzi, a zollette,** lump-sugar; **— a velo,** powdered sugar; **— d'orzo,** barley-sugar; **pane di —,** sugar-loaf; **raffineria di —,** sugar refinery.
zuccherosità [-à], *n.f.* Sugariness.
zuccheroso, *a.* Sugary.
zucchetta, *n.f.* Small pumpkin, vegetable marrow, squash.
zucchetto, *n.m.* Skull-cap.
zucchino, *n.m.* Small marrow, Italian squash.
zuccone, *n.m.* Pumpkin; (*fig.*) blockhead.
zuccotto [cp. **zucchetto**].
zuffa, *n.f.* Fray, scrimmage, scuffle, scramble; row, altercation; quarrel.
zufolamento, *n.m.* Hissing, whistling; buzzing, singing (in the ears).
zufolare, *v.i.* To hiss, to whistle. **Mi zufolano le orecchie,** my ears are tingling, there's singing in my ears.
zufolatore, *n.m.* Whistler.
zufolio [zufolIo], *n.m.* Whistling, hissing, constant buzzing.
zufolo [zUfolo], *n.m.* Whistle, pipe; flageolet.
Zulù [-ù], *n.m.a.* Zulu.
zuppa, *n.f.* Soup; (*fig.*) tangle, mess, confusion; bore, long-winded speech. **— di verdura,** vegetable soup; **— inglese,** trifle; **se non è — è pan bagnato,** it is all the same thing; it is much of a muchness.
zuppare, *v.t.* To make soup; to moisten.
zuppatore, zuppatrice, *n.m.f.* (*colloq.*) Bore, wind-bag.
zuppiera, *n.f.* Soup tureen.
zuppo, *a.* Wet, soaked, drenched.
Zurigo, *n.m.* (*Geog.*) Zurich.
zurlare, *v.i.* To romp, to frolic; to be skittish.
zuzzerellone, zuzzurullona, *n.m.f.a.* Rollicking fellow or girl, tomboy; skittish.

ENGLISH–ITALIAN DICTIONARY

A

A, a [ei]. Prima lettera dell'alfabeto inglese; (*Mus.*) la, *m.* **A.1.**, di prim'ordine; **from A to Z,** dall'a alla zeta.

a [ə, ei], *indef. art.* Un, *m.*, una, *f.* **Twice a day,** due volte al giorno; **so much a week,** tanto per settimana.

aback [əˈbæk], *adv.* Dietro, indietro, a tergo; (*Naut.*) sull'albero. **Taken —,** sconcertato, preso all'improvviso.

abacus [ˈæbəkəs], *n.* Abbaco, *m.*; (*Arch.*) abaco, *m.*

abaft [əˈbɑːft], *adv.prep.* All'indietro, dietro di; (*Naut.*) di poppavia, a poppa.

abalienate [æbˈeiliəneit], *v.t.* (*Law*) Abalienare.

abandon [əˈbændən], *v.t.* Abbandonare, lasciare. || *n.* Abbandono, trasporto, brio, *m.*, disinvoltura, *f.* **To — oneself to,** abbandonarsi a, darsi a; **to — a claim,** rinunziare a un reclamo.

abandoned, *a.* Abbandonato, dissoluto, scellerato. **An — woman,** una donna perduta; **an — wretch,** uno sciagurato, un miserabile, *m.*

abandonment, *n.* Abbandono, *m.*

abase [əˈbeis], *v.t.* Abbassare, avvilire, umiliare.

abasement, *n.* Abbassamento, avvilimento, *m.*, umiliazione, *f.*

abash [əˈbæʃ], *v.t.* Sconcertare, confondere, svergognare.

abate [əˈbeit], *v.t.* Diminuire, ridurre, scemare; *v.t.i.* abbassare, abbattersi, indebolirsi; calmare, calmarsi, abbonacciarsi. **The wind is abating,** il vento diminuisce.

abatement, *n.* Diminuzione, *f.*, ribasso (*of price*), *m.*; riduzione, bonificazione, *f.*, sconto, *m.*

abatis [əˈbætiː], *n.* (*Mil.*) Abbattuta, *f.*

abattoir [əˈbætwɑːɹ], *n.* Macello, ammazzatoio, *m.*

abbacy [ˈæbəsi], *n.* L'ufficio d'abate in un convento; abbazia, *f.*

abbé [ˈæbei], *n.* Abate, *m.*

abbess, *n.* Badessa, abbadessa, *f.*

abbey, *n.* Badia, *f.*

abbot, *m.* Abate, *m.*

abbreviate [əˈbriːvieit], *v.t.* Abbreviare, compendiare; ridurre.

abbreviation, *n.* Abbreviazione, abbreviatura, *f.*, abbreviamento, *m.*

abbreviator, *n.* Abbreviatore, *m.*

abbreviatory, *a.* Abbreviativo.

ABC [eiˈbiːˈsiː], *n.* Abbicci, alfabeto, *m.*

abdicate [ˈæbdikeit], *v.t.i.* Abdicare, rinunziare. **To — one's rights,** abdicare ai propri diritti.

abdication [æbdiˈkeiʃən], *n.* Abdicazione, rinunzia, *f.*

abdomen [æbˈdoumen], *n.* Addome, *m.*

abdominal [æbˈdɔminəl], *a.* Addominale. **— belt,** ventriera, *f.*

abduce [æbˈdjuːs], *v.t.* Togliere, ritrarre, asportare, rapire.

abduct [æbˈdʌkt], *v.t.* Rapire, portar via (per forza).

abduction [æbˈdʌkʃən], *n.* Ratto, rapimento, *m.*, abduzione, *f.*

abductor, *n.* Rapitore, (*Anat.*) abduttore, *m.*

abeam [əˈbiːm], *adv.* (*Naut.*) Di traverso, a traverso. **— of,** pel traverso di.

abecedarian [eibisiˈdeəriən], *n.* Abecedario, *m.*

abed [əˈbed], *adv.* A letto, nel letto, coricato.

aberrance, aberrancy [æˈberəns, æˈberənsi], *n.* Aberrazione, *f.*

aberrant, *a.* Traviato, aberrante.

aberration [æbəˈreiʃən], *n.* Aberrazione, *f.*, traviamento, *m.* **— of the intellect,** aberrazione della mente.

abet [əˈbet], *v.t.* Aiutare, sostenere, incoraggiare, favorire, aver parte in, rendersi complice di. **To aid and —,** favoreggiare.

abetter, abettor, *n.* Incoraggiatore, favoreggiatore, *m.*

abeyance [əˈbeiəns], *n.* Giacenza, sospensione, *f.*; disuso, *m.* **In —,** giacente, in prescrizione, non più in vigore; **to fall into —,** cadere in disuso.

abhor [əbˈhɔːɹ], *v.t.* Aborrire, detestare, odiare, avere in orrore.

abhorrence [æbˈhɔrens], *n.* Aborrimento, orrore, *m.*, ripugnanza, avversione, *f.*

abhorrent, *a.* Odioso, ripugnante, abborrevole.

abhorrently, *adv.* Odiosamente, con ripugnanza.

abhorrer, *n.* Odiatore, aborritore, *m.*

abidance [əˈbaidəns], *n.* Perseveranza.

abide [əˈbaid], *v.i.* Dimorare, restare, stare, durare; soffrire, sopportare, tollerare. **To — by,** tenersi a, mantenere (una promessa, ecc.); (*colloq.*) **I can't — her,** non posso soffrirla.

abiding, *a.* Costante, immutabile, durevole, permanente.

abidingly, *adv.* Durevolmente, costantemente.

abigail [ˈæbigeil], *n.* (*Lit.*) Cameriera, serva, *f.*

ability [əˈbiliti], *n.* Abilità, facoltà, capacità, destrezza, *f.*, forze, *f.pl.*, talento, *m.* **To the best of our —,** nel miglior modo possibile; del nostro meglio.

abiogenesis [æbaioˈdʒenəsis], *n.* Abiogenesi, *f.*

abject [ˈæbdʒekt], *a.* Abietto, basso, vile, spregevole.

abjection, abjectness, *n.* Abiezione, *f.*, abbassamento, avvilimento, *m.*

abjectly, *adv.* Abbiettamente, bassamente.

abjuration [æbdʒu'reiʃən], *n.* Abiura, rinunzia, *f.*
abjure [æb'dʒuəɹ], *v.t.* Abiurare, rinunziare, ritrattare.
abjuring, *n.* Abiura, *f.*
ablactate [æb'lækteit], *v.t.* Slattare, spoppare, svezzare.
ablation [əb'leiʃən], *n.* Ablazione, *f.*
ablative ['æblətiv], *n.a.* (*Gram.*) Ablativo, *m.*
ablaze [ə'bleiz], *a.* In fiamme, in fuoco; (*fig.*) irato, eccitato.
able ['eibl], *a.* Abile, capace, destro, versato in. **To be — to,** essere capace di, essere in grado di, potere; **able-bodied,** aitante, robusto, forte, sano; **able-bodied seaman** (A.B.), marinaio scelto.
abloom [ə'blu:m], *adv.* Fiorito.
abluent ['æblu:ənt], *a.* (*Med.*) Abluente, detersivo, *m.*
ablush [ə'blʌʃ], *adv.* Arrossito, in fiamme. **Her face was —,** il suo viso era in fiamme.
ablution [ə'blu:ʃən], *n.* Abluzione, *f.*, lavamento, *m.* **He performed his ablutions,** si lavò.
abnegate ['æbnigeit], *v.t.* Rinunciare.
abnegation [æbni'geiʃən], *n.* Abnegazione, rinunzia, *f.*
abnormal [æb'nɔ:ɹməl], *a.* Anormale, irregolare; deforme.
abnormality [æbnɔ:ɹ'mæliti], *n.* Anormalità, deviazione, irregolarità, *f.*
abnormally, *adv.* Anormalmente, eccezionalmente.
aboard [ə'bɔ:ɹd], *adv.* (*Naut.*) A bordo; a bordo di. **To go —,** imbarcarsi; **to fall — of,** abbordare, assalire; **All —!** Partenza! Tutti a bordo!
abode [ə'boud], *n.* Casa, dimora, stanza, abitazione, *f.*, domicilio, soggiorno, *m.* **To take up one's —,** stabilirsi.
abode [*p.p.* **abide**].
abolish [ə'bɔliʃ], *v.t.* Abolire, sopprimere; annientare, distruggere; annullare, abrogare.
abolition [æbo'liʃən], *n.* Abolizione; distruzione, *f.*, annullamento, *m.*
abolitionist, *n.* Antischiavista, abolizionista, *m.*
abominable [ə'bɔminəbl], *a.* Abominabile, abominevole, orribile; infame.
abominableness, *n.* Abominio *m.*, abominatezza, *f.*
abominably, *adv.* Abominevolmente.
abominate [ə'bɔmineit], *v.t.* Abominare, detestare, aborrire.
abomination, *n.* Abominazione, infamia, *f.*
aboriginal [æbɔ'ridʒinəl], *n.a.* Aborigeno, primitivo, *m.*
aborigines [æbɔ'ridʒini:z], *n.pl.* Aborigeni.
abort [ə'bɔ:ɹt], *v.t.* Abortire.
abortion [ə'bɔ:ɹʃən], *n.* Aborto, *m.*, sconciatura, *f.*
abortive, *a.* Abortivo; mancato, fallito, vano.
abortively, *adv.* Prematuramente; senza resultato.
abortiveness, *n.* Insuccesso, *m.*
abound [ə'baund], *v.i.* Abbondare. **This district abounds in trees,** questo paese abbonda di alberi.
abounding, *a.* Abbondante.
about (1) [ə'baut], *prep.* Circa, intorno a, presso, verso, sopra, su, di, vicino a; al soggetto di, in riguardo a. **I know nothing — this affair,** non so nulla di quest'affare; **to talk —,** parlare di; **What is it all — ?** Di che si tratta? **to be busy — something,** occuparsi di una cosa; **there was a garden — the house,** c'era un giardino intorno alla casa; **— three years,** circa tre anni; **tell me all — it,** dimmi tutto; **she kept the girl — her,** essa teneva la fanciulla presso di sè; **I have no money — me,** non ho denaro addosso; **a book — animals,** un libro su gli animali; **I am thinking — my work,** penso al mio lavoro.
about (2) [ə'baut], *adv.* Intorno, attorno, verso, vicino; circa, all'incirca, presso a poco. **All —,** dappertutto; **— three o'clock,** verso le tre; **somewhere — here,** in qualche parte vicino; **to bring —,** cagionare; **to be — to,** stare sul punto di; **to send — his business,** mandare a spasso; **to beat — the bush,** andare fuori di strada; **turn and turn —,** a vicenda; **to hang —,** gironzare, bighellonare; **What are you — ?** Che cosa fate? **I was much put —,** ero molto seccato; (*Mil.*) **About turn!** Dietro front! (*Naut.*) **to go —,** virar di bordo.
above [ə'bʌv], *prep.adv.* Sopra, al di sopra, su, più di, superiore a. **— all,** sopratutto; **above-mentioned,** suddetto; **up —,** lassù in alto; **over and —,** oltre, inoltre; **as —,** come sopra.
abrade [ə'breid], *v.t.* Scorticare, raspare, grattare, logorare.
Abraham ['eibrəhæm], *n.* Abramo, *m.*
abrasion [ə'breiʒən], *n.* Abrasione, raschiatura, raspatura, *f.*; graffiatura, *f.*; attrito, logorio, *m.*
abreast [ə'brest], *adv.* Di fronte; in fila, di fianco. **Five —,** in fila per cinque; **— of,** all'altezza di; **to keep — of the times,** tenersi aggiornato, al corrente.
abridge [ə'bridʒ], *v.t.* Abbreviare, accorciare; riassumere, compendiare; restringere. **Abridged edition,** edizione ridotta.
abridgement, *n.* Abbreviazione, *f.*; compendio, sommario, sunto, *m.*
abridger, *n.* Abbreviatore, *m.*
abroach [ə'broutʃ], *adv.a.* Stappato; aperto, sturato, spillato.
abroad [ə'brɔ:d], *adv.* Fuori, al di fuori, all'estero. **To go —,** andare all'estero; **there is a rumour —,** corre voce; **to be all —,** essere confuso; **I was — late last night,** ero fuori tardi la notte passata; **to spread —** (*news, etc.*), diffondersi.
abrogate ['æbrogeit], *v.t.* Abrogare; abolire, revocare, annullare.
abrogation, *n.* Abrogazione, revoca, *f.*
abrupt [ə'brʌpt], *a.* Brusco, impulsivo; scosceso, ripido; precipitoso. **His manner is very —,** i suoi modi sono molto bruschi; **an — descent,** un pendio molto scosceso.
abruptly, *adv.* Bruscamente, di botto; precipitatamente. **To treat —,** trattare con sgarbo.
abruptness, *n.* Bruschezza, asprezza, *f.*; precipitazione, *f.*; durezza, scortesia, *f.*
abscess ['æbses], *n.* Ascesso, *m.*, postema, *f.*
abscissa [æb'sisə], *n.* (*Geom.*) Ascissa, *f.*
abscond [əb'skɔnd], *v.i.* Scappare, sparire, evadere; fuggire la giustizia; nascondersi, rendersi contumace.

absconder, *n.* Fuggitivo, contumace, *m.*
absence [ˈæbsəns], *n.* Assenza, lontananza, mancanza, omissione, *f.* **— of mind,** distrazione, disattenzione, *f.*; **leave of —,** congedo, *m.*
absent (1) [æbˈsent], *v.t.i.* Allontanare; assentarsi. **To — oneself,** assentarsi, andarsene.
absent (2) [ˈæbsənt], *a.* Assente, lontano. **Absent-minded,** distratto, preoccupato.
absentee [æbsənˈtiː], *n.* Assente, assenteista, *m.*; (*Mil.*) disertore, *m.*
absenteeism [æbsənˈtiːizm], *n.* Assenteismo, *m.*
absently, *adv.* Distrattamente, disattentamente.
absinthe [ˈæbsinθ], *n.* Assenzio, *m.*
absolute [ˈæbsəluːt], *a.* Assoluto, compiuto, illimitato; perfetto, vero.
absolutely, *adv.* Assolutamente, affatto.
absoluteness, *n.* Assolutezza, *f.*
absolution [æbsəˈluːʃən], *n.* Assoluzione, remissione, *f.*
absolutism, *n.* Assolutismo, *m.*
absolutist, *n.* Assolutista, *m.*
absolve [æbˈzɔlv], *v.t.* Assolvere, affrancare, liberare, svincolare, rilasciare. **He is absolved from all blame,** egli è assolto da ogni colpa.
absorb [əbˈsɔːɹb], *v.t.* Assorbire. **Absorbed in his work,** concentrato nel suo lavoro.
absorbability [əbsɔːɹbəˈbiliti], *n.* Assorbibilità, *f.*
absorbable, *a.* Assorbibile.
absorbent [əbˈsɔːɹbənt], *n.a.* Assorbente, *m.*
absorbing, *a.* Assorbente; molto interessante.
absorption [əbˈsɔːɹpʃən], *n.* Assorbimento, *m.*
abstain [əbˈstein], *v.i.* Astenersi da, privarsi di, trattenersi. **I — from interfering,** io mi trattengo dall'intervenire.
abstainer, *n.* Astinente, astemio, *m.*; antialcoolista, *m.*
abstaining, *n.* Astensione, *f.*
abstemious [əbˈstiːmiəs], *a.* Astemio; discreto, moderato, parco.
abstemiously, *adv.* Parcamente, discretamente.
abstemiousness, *n.* Temperanza, moderazione, *f.*
abstention [əbˈstenʃən], *n.* Astensione, *f.*
abstinence [ˈæbstinəns], *n.* Astinenza, *f.*; digiuno, *m.*
abstinent, *a.* Astinente.
abstract (1) [æbˈstrækt], *v.t.* Astrarre, separare, rimuovere; ridurre in sunto; rapire, appropriarsi.
abstract (2) [ˈæbstrækt], *n.* Compendio, sommario, sunto, riassunto, *m.* **In the —,** in astratto. || *a.* Astratto.
abstracted, *a.* Astratto, distratto.
abstractedly, *adv.* Distrattamente, astrattamente.
abstractedness, *n.* Astrattaggine, astrazione, distrazione, *f.*
abstraction [æbˈstrækʃən], *n.* Astrazione, astrattaggine, distrazione, *f.*
abstractly, *adv.* Astrattamente.
abstractness, *n.* Astrattezza, *f.*
abstruse [əbˈstruːs], *a.* Astruso, nascosto, oscuro, recondito.
abstrusely, *adv.* Astrusamente.
abstruseness, *n.* Astrusaggine, astruseria, astrusità, *f.*
absurd [æbˈsəːɹd], *a.* Assurdo.
absurdity, *n.* Assurdità, *f.*
absurdly, *adv.* Assurdamente.
abundance [əˈbʌndəns], *n.* Abbondanza, copia, ricchezza, *f.*; prosperità, *f.* **An — of people,** una folla.
abundant, *a.* Abbondante, copioso; ampio; fertile.
abundantly, *adv.* Abbondantemente, ampiamente, profusamente, in copia.
abuse (1) [əˈbjuːz], *v.t.* Abusare, fare abuso; ingiuriare, oltraggiare, svillaneggiare; maltrattare, malmenare; ingannare; usare immoderatamente (*of food, etc.*).
abuse (2) [əˈbjuːs], *n.* Abuso, *m.*, ingiuria, *f.*; eccesso, *m.*; insulto, oltraggio, *m.*, contumelia, *f.* **— of authority,** abuso d'autorità; **— of confidence,** abuso di fiducia.
abuser, *n.* Offensore, insultatore, *m.*
abusive [əˈbjuːziv], *a.* Ingiurioso, insultante, offensivo; abusivo.
abusively, *adv.* Ingiuriosamente, oltraggiosamente.
abusiveness, *n.* Ingiuria, insolenza, *f.*, oltraggio, *m.*
abut [əˈbʌt], *v.i.* Confinare, essere contiguo.
abutment, *n.* (*Arch.*) Rinfianco, pilastro, *m.*; confine, limite, *m.*
abuttal, *n.* Limite, *m.*; sporgenza, *f.*
abysmal [əˈbizməl], *a.* Abissale, profondo.
abyss [əˈbis], *n.* Abisso, baratro, *m.*; profondità, *f.*
Abyssinian [æbiˈsinjən], *n.a.* Abissino.
acacia [əˈkeiʃə], *n.* (*Bot.*) Acacia, *f.*
academic, academical [ækəˈdemik, ækəˈdemikəl], *a.* Accademico; teorico, senza senso pratico.
academically, *adv.* Accademicamente.
academicals, *n.pl.* Veste accademica, *f.*, costume universitario, *m.*
academician [əkædəˈmiʃən], *n.* Accademico, *m.*; membro di un'accademia.
academism [əˈkædəmizm], *n.* Filosofia accademica, *f.*; platonismo, *m.*
academist, *n.* Accademico, *m.*
academy [əˈkædəmi], *n.* Accademia, *f.*
acanthus [əˈkænθəs], *n.* (*Bot.*) Acanto, *m.*
accede [ækˈsiːd], *v.i.* Accedere, acconsentire, aderire.
accelerate [ækˈseləreit], *v.t.* Accelerare, affrettare.
acceleration [ækseləˈreiʃən], *n.* Accelerazione, *f.*, aumento di velocità, acceleramento, *m.*
accelerator [ækˈseləreitəɹ], *n.* Acceleratore, *m.*
accent (1) [ækˈsent], *v.t.* Accentare, accentuare.
accent (2) [ˈæksənt], *n.* Accento, tono, *m.* **Acute —,** accento acuto.
accentuate [ækˈsentjuːeit], *v.t.* Accentuare, parlare con enfasi.
accentuation [æksentjuːˈeiʃən], *n.* Accentuazione, enfasi, *f.*
accept [ækˈsept], *v.t.* Accettare; approvare, ammettere; gradire; riconoscere valido. **To — the consequences,** accettare le conseguenze; (*Comm.*) **to — a bill,** accettare una cambiale.
acceptable [ækˈseptəbl], *a.* Accettabile, gradevole.
acceptableness, *n.* Accettabilità, *f.*
acceptably, *adv.* Accettabilmente.

acceptance [æk'septəns], *n.* Accettazione, accoglienza, approvazione, *f.* (*Comm.*) **To cancel an —,** protestare una cambiale.
acceptation [æksep'teiʃən], *n.* Approvazione, *f.*; accezione, *f.*; significato, senso, *m.* **In the fullest — of the term,** nel pieno senso della parola.
accepter, acceptor, *n.* Accettante, *m.*
access ['ækses], *n.* Accesso, adito, *m.*, entrata, ammissione, *f.*; avvicinamento, *m.* **Difficult of —,** di difficile accesso; **— of a disease,** accesso di una malattia.
accessary [cp. **accessory**].
accessible [æk'sesibl], *a.* Accessibile.
accessibility [æksesi'biliti], *n.* Accessibilità, *f.*
accession [æk'seʃən], *n.* Accessione, venuta, adesione, *f.*, avvenimento, *m.*; aumento, acquisto, *m.* **— to the throne,** venuta al trono; **accessions to the library,** nuovi acquisti nella biblioteca, aggiunte alla biblioteca.
accessory [æk'sesəri], *n.a.* Accessorio, *m.*; (*Law*) complice, *m.f.*
accidence ['æksidəns], *n.* (*Gram.*) Morfologia, *f.*, accidente, *m.*
accident ['æksidənt], *n.* Accidente, incidente, caso, evento, *m.*; sfortuna, disgrazia, *f.* **By —,** per caso; **there's been an —,** c'è stata una disgrazia; **street —,** incidente stradale; **railway —,** disastro ferroviario; **— insurance,** assicurazione contro gli infortuni.
accidental [æksi'dentəl], *a.* Accidentale, incidentale; fortuito, casuale.
accidentally, *adv.* Fortuitamente, per caso, per sorte.
accidentalness, *n.* accidentalità, *f.*
acclaim [ə'kleim], *v.t.* Acclamare; applaudire, lodare. **He was acclaimed king,** lo acclamarono re. || *n.* Acclamazione, *f.*
acclamation [æklə'meiʃən], *n.* Acclamazione, *f.*; applauso, *m.*
acclamatory [ə'klæmətəri], *a.* Acclamativo, acclamatorio, lodativo.
acclimatization [əklaimətai'zeiʃən], *n.* Acclimatazione, acclimazione, *f.*
acclimatize [ə'klaimətaiz], *v.t.* Acclimatare, acclimare.
acclivity [ə'kliviti], *n.* Salita, erta, acclività, *f.*
accolade [æko'leid], *n.* Abbraccio, *m.*, abbracciata, *f.*
accommodate [ə'kəmədeit], *v.t.* Accomodare, adattare, aggiustare; sistemare; ospitare, alloggiare; provvedere di; ricevere; venire in aiuto a. **To — oneself to,** accomodarsi a; **they have accommodated their differences,** hanno composto le loro differenze; **How many can she — in her house?** Quante persone può ricevere in casa sua?
accommodating, *a.* Compiacente, servizievole, soccorrevole, accomodante.
accommodation [əkəmə'deiʃən], *n.* Accomodamento, adattamento, aggiustamento, *m.*, sistemazione, *f.*; alloggio, *m.*; prestito, *m.* **— bill,** cambiale di favore, cambiale di comodo.
accompaniment [ə'kʌmpənimənt], *n.* Accompagnamento, accoppiamento, *m.*
accompanist, *n.* Accompagnatore, *m.*, accompagnatrice, *f.*
accompany [ə'kʌmpəni], *v.t.* Accompagnare, tenere compagnia; associarsi.
accomplice [ə'kəmplis], *n.* Complice, *m.f.*, correo, *m.*
accomplish [ə'kəmpliʃ], *v.t.* Adempiere, effettuare, eseguire, mandare ad effetto; realizzare.
accomplished, *a.* Compito, perfetto; distinto; colto, bene educato. **An — woman,** una signora compita.
accomplishment, *n.* Adempimento, *m.*, effettuazione, esecuzione, *f.*; talento, compimento, *m.*, dote, cognizione, *f.*; realizzazione, *f.* **He has many accomplishments,** ha molte qualità.
accord [ə'kɔːɹd], *v.t.i.* Accordare, mettere d'accordo, accordarsi, confarsi; concedere. || *n.* Accordamento, accordo, *m.* **With one —,** d'accordo, di comun consenso, unanimamente; **of one's own —,** di sua propria volontà, spontaneamente, da sè.
accordance, *n.* Conformità, *f.*, accordo, *m.* **In — with the rules,** in conformità colle regole.
accordant, *a.* Conforme, consentaneo.
according, *adv.* Conforme, secondo. **— to him,** secondo lui; **— as I deserve,** secondo il mio merito.
accordingly, *adv.* In conseguenza, perciò, quindi.
accordion [ə'kɔːɹdiən], *n.* (*Mus.*) Fisarmonica, *f.*, organetto, *m.*
accost [ə'kəst], *v.t.* Avvicinare, abbordare; accostare; rivolgere.
accostable, *a.* Abbordabile.
accouchement [ə'kuːʃmɑ̃], *n.* Parto, sgravo, *m.*
accoucheur [ə'kuːʃəːɹ], *n.* Ostetrico, *m.*
accoucheuse [ə'kuːʃəːz], *n.* Levatrice, *f.*
account [ə'kaunt], *v.t.* Stimare, contare, tenere di (*or* a) conto, reputare. **To — for,** rendere ragione di; spiegare. || *n.* Conto, calcolo; racconto, ragguaglio, pregio, *m.*, relazione, storia, esposizione, ragione, notizia, *f.* **By all accounts,** secondo ciò che si dice; **on no —,** per niente, non affatto, punto; **on — of,** per causa di; **on that —,** perciò; **on his —,** per riguardo suo; **to call to —,** chiamare a ragione; **to give an — of,** render ragione di; **people of no —,** gente da poco; **to take into —,** tenere conto di; **to turn to —,** trarre profitto da, mettere a profitto; (*Comm.*) **as per — rendered,** come da conto accluso; **to keep accounts,** tenere i libri; **current —,** conto corrente; **in — with,** in conto con; **to open an —,** aprire un conto a; **to settle an —,** saldare un conto; **cash —,** conto di cassa; **account-book,** libro di conti.
accountable, *a.* Responsabile; attribuibile a.
accountancy [ə'kauntənsi], *n.* Ragioneria, contabilità, *f.*
accountant, *n.* Ragioniere, contabile, *m.*
accounting, *n.* Contabilità, *f.* **— machine,** macchina calcolatrice, *f.*
accouplement [ə'kʌplmənt], *n.* Accoppiamento, appaiamento, *m.*
accoutre [ə'kuːtəɹ], *v.t.* Corredare, fornire, guarnire; vestire; equipaggiare.
accoutrement [ə'kuːtəɹmənt], *n.* Corredo, apparecchio, fornimento, guarnimento, *m.*
accredit [ə'kredit], *v.t.* Accreditare, autorizzare.

accredited, *p.p.a.* Accreditato, approvato, autorizzato.
accretion [ə'kriːʃən], *n* Accrescimento, aumento, incremento, *m.*
accrue [ə'kruː], *v.i.* Accrescere, aumentare, accumulare, provenire, derivare; (*Comm.*) maturare (*of interest*).
accumbent [ə'kʌmbənt], *a.* Appoggiato sul gomito.
accumulate [ə'kjuːmjuːleit], *v.t.i.* Accumulare, ammassare, ammucchiare; accumularsi. **Much rubbish had accumulated,** molta robaccia si era ammucchiata.
accumulation, *n.* Accumulazione, massa, quantità, *f.*, mucchio, *m.*
accumulative, *a.* Accumulativo.
accumulator, *n.* Accumulatore, *m.*
accuracy ['ækjurəsi], *n.* Accuratezza, esattezza, precisione, *f.*
accurate ['ækjurət], *a.* Esatto, accurato, preciso, giusto.
accurately, *adv.* Esattamente, accuratamente.
accurateness, *n.* Accuratezza, correttezza, *f.*
accursed [ə'kəːɹsid], *a.* Maledetto; esecrabile.
accusable [ə'kjuːzəbl], *a.* Accusabile.
accusation [ækjuː'zeiʃən], *n.* Accusa, imputazione, incolpazione, *f.*
accusative [ə'kjuːzətiv], *n.a.* (*Gram.*) Accusativo, *m.*
accusatory [ækjuː'zeitəri], *a.* .*ccusatorio.
accuse [ə'kjuːz], *v.t.* Accusaıe, imputare, incolpare.
accused, *n.* Accusato, incolpato, *m.*
accuser, *n.* Accusatore, *m.*
accustom [ə'kʌstəm], *v.t.* Abituare, avvezzare, assuefare. **To — oneself to,** abituarsi a.
accustomed, *p.p.a.* Abituato, assuefatto; avvezzo; ordinario. **To be —,** solere, essere solito.
ace [eis], *n.* Asso, *m.*; (*Aviat.*) asso d'aviazione, *m.* **To be within an — of,** essere a un dito di, mancare pochissimo che; **— of spades,** asso di picche.
acephalous [ə'sefələs], *a.* Acefalo.
acerb [ə'səːɹb], *a.* Acerbo, agro.
acerbity [ə'səːɹbiti], *n.* Acerbità, *f.*; asprezza, durezza, *f.*
acescence [ə'sesəns], *n.* (*Chem.*) Acescenza, *f.*
acetate ['æsəteit], *n.* (*Chem.*) Acetato, *m.*
acetic [ə'siːtik], *a.* (*Chem.*) Acetico.
acetify [æ'setifai], *v.t.* Acetare.
acetone ['æsetoun], *n.* (*Chem.*) Acetone, *m.*
acetylene [ə'setiliːn], *n.* Acetilene, *m.* **— burner,** becco da acetilene; **— lamp,** lampada ad acetilene.
ache [eik], *v.i.* Dolere, far male. || *n.* Dolore, male, *m.* **My head aches,** mi duole la testa; **headache,** mal di testa; **toothache,** mal di denti, *m.*; **heartache,** crepacuore, *m.*
achieve [ə'tʃiːv], *v.t.* Effettuare; adempiere, eseguire, pervenire a; mandare ad effetto; raggiungere. **To — a reputation,** farsi una riputazione; **to — success,** riportare un successo; **to — one's end** raggiungere il proprio scopo.
achievement, *n.* Adempimento, compımento, *m.*; esecuzione, impresa, *f.*; risultato, successo, *m.*; **An heroic —,** un'eroica impresa; **achievements,** i successi, *m.pl.*
aching ['eikiŋ], *a.* Doloroso, palpitante.
achromatic [ækro'mætik], *a.* Acromatico.
achromatism [ə'kromətizm], *n.* Acromasia, *f.*, acromatismo, *m.*
achy ['eiki], *a.* Doloroso.
acicular [ə'sikjuləɹ], *a.* (*Bot.*) Acicolare.
acid ['æsid], *n.a.* Acido, *m.*; agro, *m.*; aspro, *m.*
acidify [ə'sidifai], *v.t.* Acidificare.
acidification [əsidifi'keiʃən], *n.* Acidificazione, *f.*
acidity [ə'siditi], *n.* Acidità, agrezza, *f.*
acidulate [ə'sidjuːleit], *v.t.* Acidulare.
acidulous [ə'sidjuːləs] *a.* Acidulo.
acierage ['æsiərid3], *n.* Acciaiatura, *f.*
acierate, *v.t.* Acciaiare.
aciniform [ə'sinifɔːɹm], *a.* (*Bot.*) Aciniforme.
acknowledge [æk'nɔlid3], *v.t.* Ammettere, riconoscere; confessare, accettare; accusare (*receipt of a letter*). **He acknowledged the boy as his son,** riconobbe il ragazzo come suo figlio; **he acknowledged his sin,** confessò il suo fallo; **I have acknowledged the letter,** ho accusato ricevuta della lettera.
acknowledgment, *n.* Ammissione, *f.*; riconoscimento, *m.*; nota di ricevuta, *f.*, ringraziamento, *m.*
acme ['ækmi], *n.* Colmo, apogeo, *m.*; cima, acme, *f.*
acne ['ækni], *n.* (*Med.*) Acne, *f.*
acock [ə'kɔk], *adv.* A tesa.
acolyte ['ækolait], *n.* Accolito, *m.*
aconite ['ækonait], *n.* (*Bot.*) Aconito, *m.*
acorn ['eikɔːɹn], *n.* Ghianda, *f.*
acotyledon [əkɔti'liːdən], *n.* (*Bot.*) Acotiledone, *m.*
acoustic [ə'kaustik], *a.* Acustico.
acoustics, *n.pl.* Acustica, *f.*
acquaint [ə'kweint], *v.t.* Avvertire, avvisare, far sapere. **To — oneself with,** ragguagliarsi su, mettersi al corrente di, prender conoscenza di; **to be acquainted with,** conoscere, intendersi di.
acquaintance, *n.* Conoscente, *m.f.*; conoscenza, *f.* **Friends and acquaintances,** amici e conoscenti; **to make the — of,** far la conoscenza di, **close —,** dimestichezza, *f.*; **to have a thorough — with,** conoscere a fondo.
acquaintanceship, *n.* Conoscenza, *f.*
acquest [ə'kwest], *n.* (*Law*) Acquisito, guadagno, *m.*
acquiesce [ækwi'es], *v.i.* Consentire; contentarsi; sottomettersi a; (*Law*) acquiescere.
acquiescence, *n.* Acquiescenza, *f.*, consentimento, *m.*
acquiescent, *a.* Acquiescente, rassegnato.
acquirable [ə'kwaiərəbl], *a.* Acquistabile.
acquire [ə'kwaiəɹ], *v.t.* Acquistare, ottenere, conseguire, guadagnare; imparare.
acquirement, *n.* Acquisto, *m.*; **acquirements,** talenti, *m.pl.*
acquirer, *n.* Acquistatore, *m.*
acquisition [ækwi'ziʃən), *n.* Acquisto, *m.*, acquisizione, *f.*
acquisitive [ə'kwizitiv], *a.* Acquisitivo, desideroso di guadagno.
acquisitiveness, *n.* Acquisitività, *f.*
acquit [ə'kwit], *v.t.* Assolvere, discolpare, liberare. **To — oneself well,** comportarsi bene.
acquittal, *n.* Assoluzione, liberazione, discolpa, *f.*; proscioglimento dall'accusa, *f.*
acquittance, *n.* Quietanza, *f.*
acre ['eikəɹ], *n.* Acro, iugero, *m.*

acreage [ˈeikəridʒ], *n.* Superficie di terreno, estensione, *f.*
acrid [ˈækrid], *a.* Acre, pungente, aspro, mordace.
acridity [əˈkriditi], *n.* Acredine, agrezza, *f.*
acridness, *n.* Acrità, *f.*
acrimonious [ækriˈmouniəs], *a.* Acrimonioso.
acrimoniously, *adv.* Ostilmente.
acrimony [ˈækriməni], *n.* Acrimonia, asprezza, *f.*
acrobat [ˈækrobæt], *n.* Acrobata, funambolo, *m.*
acrobatic [ækroˈbætik], *a.* Acrobatico.
acrobatics, *n.pl.* Acrobatismo, funambolismo, *m.*
acronycal [əˈkrɔnikəl], *a.* (*Astron.*) Acronico.
acropolis [əˈkrɔpolis], *n.* Acropoli, *f.*
across [əˈkrɔ:s], *prep.adv.* Attraverso, a traverso, di traverso; obliquamente; (*Crosswords*) orizzontalmente; a croce; dall'altra parte di. **— the road,** dall'altra parte della strada; **to go —,** traversare; **to reach —,** passare davanti con la mano; **to come —,** incontrare per caso.
acrostic [əˈkrɔstik], *n.* Acrostico, *m.*
act [ækt], *v.t.i.* Fare; dare, rappresentare, recitare; funzionare, operare, agire. ‖ *n.* Atto, fatto, *m.*; esercizio, *m.*, azione, *f.* **To — a part,** recitare una parte; **to — the part of a father,** fare da padre; **— as you think best,** fate come vi pare meglio; **he acted very well at that critical moment,** si condusse molto bene in quel frangente; **to — up to one's principles,** agire secondo i propri principii; **to — for,** agire per conto di; **to — up to,** conformarsi a; **to — from a sense of duty,** agire per sentimento di dovere; **in the —,** nell'atto; **caught in the very —,** colto in flagrante; **— of parliament,** atto, decreto del parlamento, *m.*; **— of God,** caso di forza maggiore, *m.*
acting, *n.* Recitazione, rappresentazione, *f.*; finta, *f.*
acting, *a.* Facente funzione, vice; (*Mech.*) **Double —,** a doppio effetto.
actinic [ækˈtinik], *a.* Attinico. **— rays,** raggi attinici.
action [ˈækʃən], *n.* Azione, *f.*, atto, fatto, *m.*; operazione, *f.*; efficacia, *f.*; (*Mil.*) battaglia, *f.*; (*Law*) processo, *m.* (*Mech.*) funzionamento, meccanismo, *m.* **Out of —,** fuori uso; **direct —,** azione diretta; (*Law*) **to bring an —,** muovere lite; **to put into —,** fare funzionare; (*Mil.*) **to go into —,** attaccare.
actionable, *a.* (*Law*) Processabile.
actionably, *adv.* (*Law*) Illegalmente.
active [ˈæktiv], *a.* Attivo, agile, svelto, energico. **An — mind,** una mente sveglia; **on — service,** in servizio attivo; (*Gram.*) **— voice,** voce attiva.
actively, *adv.* Attivamente, effettivamente; agilmente.
activity [ækˈtiviti], *n.* Attività, *f.*; agilità, *f.*; operosità, *f.*, movimento, *m.*
actor [ˈæktəɹ], *n.* Attore, *m.* **Leading —,** primo attore, *m.*
actress [ˈæktrəs], *n.* Attrice, *f.*
actual [ˈæktjuəl], *a.* Effettivo, presente, reale, vero, esistente.
actuality [æktuˈæliti], *n.* Realtà, verità, attualità, *f.*
actually, *adv.* Effettivamente, veramente, di fatto.
actualness, *n.* Realtà, verità, *f.*
actuary [ˈæktjuəri], *n.* Attuario, contabile, ragioniere, *m.*
actuate [ˈæktjueit], *v.t.* Attuare, attivare, animare, muovere, spingere.
acuity [əˈkju:iti], *n.* Acuità, acutezza, *f.*
aculeate [əˈkkju:lieit], *a.* (*Bot.Zool.*) Aculeato.
acumen [əˈkju:mən], *n.* Acume, *m.*, acutezza, *f.*
acuminate [əˈkju:mineit], *a.* (*Bot.Zool.*) Acuminato.
acute [əˈkju:t], *a.* Acuto, aguzzo; penetrante, perspicace, sottile. **— hearing,** udito fino; **acute-angled,** acutangolo.
acutely, *adv.* Sottilmente, acutamente, con acume.
acuteness, *n.* Acutezza, sagacità, sottilità, *f.*
adage [ˈædidʒ], *n.* Proverbio, adagio, *m.*
adagio [əˈdɑ:dʒiou], *n.adv.* (*Mus.*) Adagio, *m.*
Adam [ˈædəm], *n.* Adamo, *m.* **Adam's ale,** acqua, *f.*; **Adam's apple,** pomo d'Adamo, *m.*
adamant [ˈædəmənt], *a.* Duro, insensibile. **To be —,** essere duro, inflessibile.
adamantine [ædəˈmæntain], *a.* Adamantino.
adapt [əˈdæpt], *v.t.* Adattare, accomodare, aggiustare, arrangiare.
adaptability [ədæptəˈbiliti], *n.* Adattabilità, *f.*
adaptable [əˈdæptəbl], *a.* Adattabile, adattevole.
adaptation [ædæpˈteiʃən], *n.* Adattamento, *m.*
adapted, *a.* Adatto, atto, acconcio.
adapter, *n.* Ordinatore, riduttore, montatore, *m.*
add [æd], *v.t.* Aggiungere, attaccare, unire; addizionare, sommare; soggiungere. **To — to,** aumentare; **to — up,** sommare.
addendum [əˈdendəm], *n.* Addendo (*pl.* **addenda**); aggiunta, appendice, *f.*
adder [ˈædəɹ], *n.* (*Zool.*) Vipera, *f.* (*Bot.*) **Adder's tongue,** lingua di cane, *f.*; **adderwort,** viperina, *f.*
addict (1) [əˈdikt], *v.t.* Darsi in preda a, abbandonarsi a.
addict (2) [ˈædikt], *n.* Persona dedita a un vizio, *f.*
addicted, *a.* Dato, dedito. **— to drink,** dedito al bere.
addictedness, addiction, *n.* Inclinazione, propensione, *f.*
addition [əˈdiʃən], *n.* Addizione, aggiunta, somma, *f.*, aumento, supplemento, *m.* **In —,** in aggiunta, in più; **in — to this,** oltre a questo.
additional, *a.* Addizionale, supplementare; aggregato.
additionally, *adv.* Per giunta, per di più, inoltre.
addle [ˈædl], *v.t.* Render sterile. **To — one's brains,** stillarsi il cervello.
addled, *a.* Vuoto, putrido; sterile. **An — egg,** un uovo vuoto; **addle-pated, addle-headed,** scervellato.
address [əˈdres], *v.t.* Indirizzare, dirigere, rivolgere. ‖ *n.* Indirizzo, recapito, *m.*; discorso, *m.*; petizione, supplica, *f.*; (*fig.*) destrezza, prontezza, *f.* **To — oneself to one's work,** mettersi al lavoro; **to — letters,** indirizzare le lettere; **to pay one's addresses to,** corteggiare; **style of —,** titolo; **a man of good —,** un uomo garbato, di belle maniere; **an — from the pulpit,** un discorso dal pulpito.

addressee [ædre'si:], *n.* Destinatario, *m.*
addresser, *n.* Indirizzatore, mittente, *m.*
adduce [ə'dju:s], *v.t.* Addurre, allegare, citare, fornire, recare in appoggio.
adducible, *a.* Adducibile, citabile.
adduction [ə'dʌkʃən], *n.* Allegazione, citazione, *f.*
adductor, *n.* (*Anat.*) Adduttore, *m.*
ademption [ə'demʃən], *n.* (*Law*) Revoca, revocazione, adenzione, *f.*
adenitis [ædə'naitis], *n.* (*Med.*) Adenite, *f.*
adenoid ['ædenɔid], *a.* Adenoso. **Adenoids,** adenoidi, *n.f.pl.*
adept ['ædept], *n.* Adepto, esperto, perito, *m.*
adept [ə'dept], *a.* Esperto, pratico, abile, perito.
adequacy ['ædikwəsi], *n.* Sufficienza, adeguatezza, *f.*
adequate ['ædikwət], *a.* Adeguato, bastante, sufficiente; efficace; congruo.
adequately, *adv.* Adeguatamente, bastantemente, bastevolmente, a sufficienza.
adhere [æd'hiəɹ], *v.i.* Aderire, unirsi, attaccarsi; appiccicarsi. **To — to one's intention,** persistere nell'intenzione.
adherence, *n.* Adesione, aderenza, *f.*
adherent, *n.* Fautore, partigiano, seguace, *m.*
adhesion [əd'hi:ʒən], *n.* Adesione, *f.*, consenso, *m.*
adhesive, *a.* Adesivo, tenace, viscoso, appiccicaticcio. **— plaster,** cerotto adesivo, *m.*; **— tape,** tela gommata, *f.*; **— paper, stamp paper,** carta gommata, *f.*
adhesiveness, *n.* Adesività, tenacità, viscosità, *f.*
adhibit [æd'hibit], *v.t.* Applicare, adibire.
adiantum [ædi'æntəm], *n.* (*Bot.*) Adianto, capelvenere, *m.*
adieu [ə'dju:], *inter.n.* Addio, *m.*
adipose ['ædipous], *a.* Adiposo, grasso.
adit ['ædit], *n.* Adito, accesso, *m.*, entrata, *f.*
adjacency [ə'dʒeisənsi], *n.* Adiacenza, attiguità, contiguità, vicinanza, *f.*
adjacent [ə'dʒeisənt], *a.* Adiacente, attiguo, contiguo, vicino, limitrofo.
adjacently, *adv.* Contiguamente.
adjectival [ædʒək'taivəl], *a.* Aggettivale.
adjectivally [ædʒek'taivəli], *adv.* Aggettivalmente.
adjective ['ædʒektiv], *n.* Aggettivo, *m.*
adjoin [ə'dʒɔin], *v.i.* Confinare con, essere contiguo a.
adjoining, *a.* Attiguo, vicino, adiacente.
adjourn [ə'dʒə:ɹn], *v.t.i.* Aggiornare, rimandare, rimettere, rinviare, differire; aggiornarsi.
adjournment, *n.* Rinvio, aggiornamento, *m.*
adjudge [ə'dʒʌdʒ], *v.t.* Aggiudicare.
adjudgement, *n.* Giudizio, *m.*; condanna, *f.*
adjudicate [ə'dʒu:dikeit], *v.t.* Aggiudicare; dichiarare; condannare.
adjudication, *n.* Aggiudicazione, *f.*
adjudicator, *n.* Aggiudicante, *m.*
adjunct ['ædʒʌnkt], *n.* Aggiunta, appendice, *f.*, accessorio, complemento, *m.*
adjunction, *n.* Aggiunzione, *f.*
adjunctive, *a.* Aggiuntivo, addizionale.
adjunctively, *adv.* Di supplemento.
adjuration [ædʒu:'reiʃən], *n.* Scongiuro, *m.*
adjure [ə'dʒu:r], *v.t.* Scongiurare; pregare, supplicare.
adjust [ə'dʒʌst], *v.t.* Aggiustare, adattare; ordinare, sistemare (dei conti); bilanciare. **To — accounts,** pareggiare i conti; **to — one's differences with,** conciliarsi con.
adjustable, *a.* Regolabile, aggiustabile, riparabile. **— wrench,** chiave inglese.
adjuster, *n.* Aggiustatore, pacificatore, *m.*
adjustment, *n.* Aggiustamento, assestamento, *m.*
adjutancy ['ædʒutənsi], *n.* Ufficio d'aiutante, *m.*
adjutant ['ædʒutənt], *n.* (*Mil.*) Aiutante, aiutante maggiore, *m.* (*Zool.*) **— bird,** marabù, *m.*
adjuvant [ædʒ'u:vənt], *a.* Adiutorio.
admeasurement [əd'meʒərmənt], *n.* Misurazione, misura, *f.*
administer [əd'ministəɹ], *v.t.* Amministrare, governare; somministrare; dare. **To — an oath,** far prestare un giuramento; **to — the sacraments,** amministrare i sacramenti.
administrate [əd'ministreit], *v.t.* Governare.
administration, *n.* Amministrazione, *f.*, governo, *m.*; (*Comm.*) gestione, *f.*
administrative, *a.* Amministrativo.
administrator, *n.* Amministratore, curatore, *m.*; gerente, *m.*
administratorship, *n.* Ufficio d'amministratore, *m.*
admirable ['ædmərəbl], *a.* Ammirabile, stupendo.
admirably, *adv.* Ammirabilmente, a meraviglia.
admiral ['ædmərəl], *n.* Ammiraglio, *m.* **— of the Fleet,** Grande Ammiraglio; **vice-—,** vice-ammiraglio; **rear-—,** contrammiraglio.
Admiralty, *n.* Ammiragliato, *m.* **First Lord of the —,** ministro della marina, *m.*
admiration [ædmə'reiʃən], *n.* Ammirazione, *f.*; meraviglia, *f.*
admire [əd'maiəɹ], *v.t.i.* Ammirare; meravigliarsi.
admirer, *n.* Ammiratore, *m.*, ammiratrice, *f.*
admiring, *a.* Ammirativo, pieno d'ammirazione.
admiringly, *adv.* Con meraviglia.
admissibility [ədmisi'biliti], *n.* Ammissibilità, *f.*
admissible [əd'misəbl], *a.* Ammissibile, accettabile.
admissibly, *adv.* Accettabilmente.
admission [əd'miʃən], *n.* Ammissione, *f.*, ingresso, accesso, *m.*; confessione, *f.* **— free,** entrata libera, *f.*; **ticket of —,** biglietto d'ingresso, *m.*
admit [əd'mit], *v.t.* Ammettere, introdurre, ricevere; concedere; riconoscere, confessare.
admittance, *n.* Entrata, *f.*, ingresso, *m.* **No —,** vietato l'ingresso; **free —,** libero ingresso, *m.*, entrata libera, *f.*
admix [əd'miks], *v.t.* Mescolare, mischiare.
admixture [əd'mikstʃəɹ], *n.* Mescolanza, miscela, *f.*, mescolamento, *m.*
admonish [əd'moniʃ], *v.t.* Ammonire, esortare; riprendere.
admonisher, *n.* Ammonitore, *m.*, ammonitrice, *f.*
admonishment, admonition, *n.* Ammonizione, *f.*, avvertimento, consiglio, *m.*; esortazione, riprensione, *f.*
admonitive, admonitory, *a.* Ammonitorio; esortatorio.

adnate ['ædneit], *a.* (*Bot.*) Adnato.
ado [ə'du:], *n.* Pena, *f.*; rumore, baccano, fracasso, scalpore, imbroglio, *m.* **Much — about nothing,** molto rumore per nulla; **without more —,** senz'altro scalpore; **to make no more — about it,** non farci più rumore intorno.
adolescence [ædo'lesəns], *n.* Adolescenza, *f.*
adolescent, *n.a.* Adolescente, *m.f.*
Adonis [ə'dounis], *n.* Adone, *m.*
adopt [ə'dɔpt], *v.t.* Adottare; accettare. **To — a career,** seguire una carriera.
adoptable, *a.* Adottabile.
adopted, adoptive, *a.* Adottato, adottivo.
adopter, *n.* Adottatore, *m.*, adottatrice, *f.*
adoption [əd'ɔpʃən], *n.* Adozione, adottazione, scelta, *f.*
adorable [ə'dɔ:rəbl], *a.* Adorabile.
adorableness, *n.* Adorabilità, *f.*
adorably, *adv.* Adorabilmente.
adoration [ædo'reiʃən], *n.* Adorazione, *f.*
adore [ə'dɔ:ɹ], *v.t.* Adorare.
adorer, *n.* Adoratore, *m.*, adoratrice, *f.*
adoringly, *adv.* Con adorazione.
adorn [ədɔ:ɹn], *v.t.* Adornare, abbellire, fregiare, ornare, parare. **To — oneself,** adornarsi, ornarsi.
adornment, *n.* Adornamento, fregio, ornamento, abbellimento, paramento, *m.*
adown [ə'daun], *prep.adv.* In giù, all'ingiù, in basso [cp. **down**].
adrenalin [æ'dri:nəlin], *n.* Adrenalina, *f.*
Adriatic [eidri'ætik], *n.a.* Adriatico, *m.*
adrift [ə'drift], *a.adv.* Alla deriva, in deriva. **To go —,** andare alla deriva; abbandonarsi; **to turn —,** fare andare alla deriva; abbandonare.
adroit [ə'drɔit], *a.* Abile, destro, pronto; accorto, astuto.
adroitly, *adv.* Destramente.
adroitness, *n.* Destrezza, prontezza, scaltrezza, *f.*
adscititious [ædsi'tiʃəs], *a.* Ascitizio, accessorio.
adulate ['ædjuleit], *v.t.* Adulare, lusingare.
adulation, *n.* Adulazione, *f.*
adulator, *n.* Adulatore, *m.*
adulatory, *a.* Adulatorio, lusinghiero.
adult [ə'dʌlt], *n.a.* Adulto, *m.*, maturo.
adulterate [ə'dʌltəreit], *v.t.* Adulterare, contaminare; falsificare.
adulterate, adulterated, *a.* Adulterato, contaminato.
adulteration, *n.* Adulterazione, contaminazione, *f.*
adulterer, adulteress, *n.* Adultero, *m.*, adultera, *f.*
adulterine [ə'dʌltərain], *a.* Adulterino.
adulterous, *a.* Adultero.
adultery [ə'dʌltəri], *n.* Adulterio, *m.*
adumbrate [ə'dʌmbreit], *v.t.* Adombrare, accennare, abbozzare.
adumbration [ædʌm'breiʃən], *n.* Adombrazione, *f.*
adust [ə'dʌst], *a.* Adusto, abbronzato, scottato.
advance [əd'vɑ:ns], *v.t.* Avanzare, metter avanti; promuovere; presentare; anticipare (*payment*), prestare; *v.i.* avanzarsi, farsi innanzi, spingersi, crescere. || *n.* Avanzamento, progresso, avvicinamento, *m.*; (*Mil.*) avanzata, *f.*; rialzo, aumento (*of prices*), *m.*; (*Comm.*) anticipazione, *f.*; aumento (*of wages*). **To — an opinion,** esprimere un'opinione; **to — money,** prestare; **to — to a dignity,** elevare ad una dignità; **to make advances,** tentar di amicarsi, fare degli approcci; **in —,** anticipatamente; **to pay in —,** anticipare; **payment in —,** contro pagamento anticipato; **in — of,** avanti, davanti; **advance-guard,** avanguardia, *f.*
advancement, *n.* Avanzamento, *m.*, promozione, *f.*
advancer, *n.* (*Comm.*) Prestatore, *m.*
advantage [əd'vɑ:ntədʒ], *v.t.* Avvantaggiare, migliorare. || *n.* Vantaggio, beneficio, profitto, *m.*; superiorità, utilità, *f.* **To have the —,** avere il vantaggio; **to his —,** a suo pro, a suo vantaggio; **to show off to —,** far bella figura con; **to take — of,** avvantaggiarsi, profittare di; **to take unfair — of,** fare abuso di; **to get the —,** pigliar il vantaggio; (*Tennis*) **— in,** vantaggio alla battuta; **— out,** vantaggio alla rimessa.
advantageous [ædvən'teidʒəs], *a.* Vantaggioso, profittevole.
advantageously, *adv.* Vantaggiosamente.
advantageousness, *n.* Utilità, *f.*, vantaggio, *m.*
advent ['ædvənt], *n.* Venuta, *f.*, arrivo, *m.*; (*Eccles.*) Avvento, *m.*
adventitious [ædvəntiʃəs], *a.* Avventizio, accidentale, fortuito.
adventitiously, *adv.* Fortuitamente.
adventure [əd'ventjuɹ], *v.t.i.* Avventurare, arrischiare; avventurarsi, arrischiarsi, mettersi in pericolo. || *n.* Avventura, *f.*; avvenimento, caso, *m.*
adventurer, *n.* Avventuriere, *m.*; truffatore, imbroglione, *m.*
adventuresome, *a.* Avventuroso.
adventuress, *n.* Avventuriera, imbrogliona, *f.*
adventurous, *a.* Avventuroso; ardito, arrischievole, audace.
adventurousness, *n.* Audacia, temerità, *f.*
adverb ['ædvə:ɹb], *n.* Avverbio, *m.*
adverbial, *a.* Avverbiale.
adverbially, *adv.* Avverbialmente.
adversary ['ædvəɹsəri], *n.* Avversario, nemico, *m.*
adversative [əd'və:ɹsətiv], *a.* Avversativo.
adverse ['ædvə:ɹs], *a.* Avverso, contrario; sfortunato, infelice; sbilanciato.
adversely, *adv.* Avversamente, contrariamente.
adverseness, *n.* Opposizione, ostilità, *f.*
adversity, *n.* Avversità, miseria, sventura, *f.*, disastri, *m.pl.*, disgrazie, *f.pl.*
advert [əd'və:ɹt], *v.i.* Accennare, indicare; alludere, fare attenzione a.
advertise ['ædvəɹtaiz], *v.t.* Avvisare, dare notizia, pubblicare, propalare; fare pubblicità. **To — a product,** fare pubblicità per un prodotto; **to — for a clerk,** inserire un annunzio per un impiegato.
advertisement [əd'və:ɹtizmənt], *n.* Avviso, annunzio, *m.*; affisso, *m.*; inserzione, *f.*; pubblicità, reclame, *f.*
advertiser, *n.* Inserzionista, chi mette avviso in un giornale, *m.*
advertising, *n.* Pubblicità, *f.* **— agent, — practitioner,** agente di pubblicità, *m.*
advice [əd'vais], *n.* Avviso, consiglio, *m.*; informazioni, *f.pl.* **To take, to follow —,**

prendere, seguire un consiglio; **piece of —,** consiglio, suggerimento, *m.*; (*Comm.*) **letter of —,** lettera d'avviso, *f.*; **— -boat,** (*Naut.*) avviso, *m.*
advisable [əd'vaizəbl], *a.* Consigliabile, preferibile, prudente, utile.
advisableness, advisability, *n.* Prudenza, saggezza, *f.*; utilità, opportunità, *f.*
advise [əd'vaiz], *v.t.* Consigliare; avvisare, avvertire, prevenire; persuadere. **Ill-advised,** sconsigliato, imprudente; **to keep advised of,** tenere al corrente di; **to — with,** consultare.
advisedly, *adv.* Di proposito, seriamente.
adviser, *n.* Consigliere, *m.*
advisory, *a.* Consultativo, consultivo.
advocacy ['ædvəkəsi], *n.* Intervento, *m.*, intercessione, difesa, *f.*
advocate ['ædvoukeit], *v.t.* Propugnare, proporre; difendere, sostenere. || *n.* Avvocato; fautore, apologista, *m.*
advowee [ædvau'i:], *n.* (*Eccles.*) Conferitore, *m.*
advowson [əd'vauzən], *n.* (*Eccles.*) Patronaggio, *m.*, collazione, *f.*
adynamia [ædi'næmiə], *n.* (*Med.*) Adinamia, *f.*
adze ['ædz], *n.* Ascia, scure, *f.*
Aegean [i:'dʒi:ən], *n.* (*Geog.*) Egeo, l'Egeo, *m.*
aegis ['i:dʒis], *n.* Egida, *f.*
aeolian [i:'ouliən], *a.* Eolio.
aerate ['ɛəreit], *v.t.* Aerare, aerificare. **Aerated water,** acqua gassosa, *f.*
aeration, *n.* Aerazione, aerificazione, *f.*
aerial (1) ['ɛəriəl], *n.* (*Radio*) Antenna, *f.*
aerial (2) [ei'iəriəl], *a.* Aereo, eccelso.
aerie, aery, eyrie, eyry ['ɛəri, 'iəri], *n.* Nido, *m.*
aeriform ['eiərifɔ:ɹm], *a.* Aeriforme.
aerify, *v.t.* Empire d'aria.
aerobatics [ɛəro'bætiks], *n.* Aerobatica, *f.*
aerobus ['ɛərobʌs], *n.* Aerobus, *m.*
aerodrome [ɛəro'droum], *n.* Aerodromo, campo d'aviazione, *m.*
aerodynamics [ɛərodai'næmiks], *n.* Aerodinamica, *f.*
aerolite ['eiərolait], *n.* Aerolito, *m.*; meteorite, *f.*
aeronaut ['ɛərənɔ:t], *n.* Aeronauta, *m.*
aeronautical, *a.* Aeronautico.
aeronautics, *n.pl.* Aeronautica, *f.*
aeroplane, airplane ['ɛəroplein, 'ɛəɹplein], *n.* Aeroplano, velivolo, aereo, *m.*
aerostat ['ɛərostæt], *n.* Aerostato, *m.*
aerostatics, *n.pl.* Aerostatica, *f.*
aerostation, *n.* Aerostazione, *f.*
Aesop ['i:sop], *n.* Esopo, *m.*
aesthete ['i:sθi:t], *n.* Esteta, *m.*
aesthetic, aesthetical [i:s'θetik, i:s'θetəkəl], *a.* Estetico.
aesthetically, *adv.* Esteticamente.
aesthetics, *n.pl.* Estetica, *f.*
aestheticism [i:s'θetisizm], *n.* Estetismo, *m.*
aestival [i:s'taivəl], *a.* Estivo.
afar [ə'fɑ:ɹ], *adv.* Lontano, lungi, distante, lontanamente. **— off,** a distanza di; **from —,** da lontano.
affability [æfə'biliti], *n.* Affabilità, *f.*
affable ['æfəbl], *a.* Affabile, manieroso. **— manners,** modi affabili.
affably, *adv.* Affabilmente.
affair [ə'fɛəɹ], *n.* Affare, *m.*, faccenda, *f.*; amoretto, *m.*
affect [ə'fekt], *v.t.* Affettare, fingere, ostentare; commuovere, impressionare; turbare; influire su; danneggiare, nuocere. **He affected surprise,** egli finse di essere sorpreso; **the scene affected her deeply,** la scena la commosse molto; **this affects my interests,** ciò tocca i miei interessi.
affectation [æfək'teiʃən], *n.* Affettazione, *f.*
affected, *a.* Affettato, lezioso, manierato, artifizioso; commosso; ammalato di.
affectedly, *adv.* Affettatamente.
affecting, *a.* Commovente, emozionante; patetico.
affectingly, *adv.* Pateticamente.
affection [ə'fekʃən], *n.* Affezione, *f.*, affetto, amore, *m.*; malattia, *f.*
affectionate, *a.* Affettuoso, affezionato, amorevole.
affectionately, *adv.* Affezionatamente, con affezione.
affective, *a.* Affettivo.
affiance [ə'faiəns], *v.t.* Fidanzare; scambiarsi promessa di matrimonio. || *n.* Fidanzamento, *m.*; confidenza, fede, fiducia, *f.*
affianced, *a.* Fidanzato, promesso.
affidavit [æfi'deivit], *n.* (*Law*) Affidavit, *m.*, dichiarazione giurata, *f.*; testimonianza sotto giuramento, *f.*
affiliate [ə'filieit], *v.t.* Affiliare, associare, aggregare.
affiliation, *n.* Affiliazione, *f.*; adozione, *f.*
affinity [ə'finiti], *n.* Affinità, parentela, *f.*; attinenza, relazione, *f.*
affirm [ə'fə:ɹm], *v.t.* Affermare, confermare, dichiarare, asserire, attestare.
affirmable, *a.* Affermabile.
affirmation [æfə'meiʃən], *n.* Affermazione, *f.*; ratifica, *f.*
affirmative, *n.a.* Affermativa, *f.*; affermativo, *m.* **He answered in the —,** egli rispose di sì.
affirmatively, *adv.* Affermativamente.
affirmer, *n.* Affermatore, *m.*
affix (1) [ə'fiks], *v.t.* Affiggere, attaccare, apporre. **To — a seal,** apporre un sigillo; **to — a stamp,** attaccare un francobollo.
affix (2) ['æfiks], *n.* (*Gram.*) Affisso, *m.*
afflation [ə'fleiʃən], *n.* Afflazione, *f.*, soffio, *m.*; ispirazione, *f.*
afflatus [ə'fleitəs], *n.* Afflato, *m.*
afflict [ə'flikt], *v.t.* Affliggere, contristare, travagliare.
afflicting, afflictive, *a.* Affliggente, afflittivo.
affliction, *n.* Afflizione, tribolazione, *f.*; dolore, *m.*
afflictively, *adv.* Afflitivamente.
affluence ['æfluəns], *n.* Affluenza, abbondanza, ricchezza, *f.*
affluent, *a.* Ricco, opulento.
affluent, *n.* (*Geog.*) Affluente, tributario, *m.*
afflux ['æflʌks], *n.* (*Med.*) Afflusso, *m.*
afford [ə'fɔ:ɹd], *v.t.* Permettere, trovare il modo di, concedere, procurare, fornire, provvedere. **I cannot — the time,** non ne ho il tempo; **I cannot — it,** i miei mezzi non me lo permettono; **I cannot — to throw away my money,** non ho denaro da sprecare; **to — facilities,** offrire facilitazioni.
afforest [ə'fɔrəst], *v.t.* Rimboschire, imboschire.
afforestation, *n.* Rimboschimento, *m.*
affranchise [ə'fræntʃaiz], *v.t.* Affrancare, liberare da servitù.

affranchisement, *n.* Affrancamento, *m.*, liberazione, *f.*
affray [əˈfrei], *n.* Mischia, rissa, zuffa, baruffa, avvisaglia, *f.*
affreightment [əˈfreitmənt], *n.* Noleggio, *m.*
affright [əˈfrait], *v.t.* Impaurire, sbigottire, spaventare. || *n.* Spavento, terrore, *m.*
affrightedly, *adv.* Paurosamente.
affront [əˈfrʌnt], *v.t.* Insultare, oltraggiare, offendere. || *n.* Affronto, *m.*, ingiuria, offesa, *f.*; oltraggio, insulto, *m.*
affusion [əˈfjuːʒən], *n.* (*Chem.*) Affusione, *f.*
Afghan [ˈæfgæn], *n.a.* Afgano, *m.*
afield [əˈfiːld], *adv.* In campo. **To go far —,** andare lontano.
afire [əˈfaiəɹ], *adv.* In fuoco, ardente.
aflame [əˈfleim], *adv.* In fiamme.
afloat [əˈflout], *adv.* A galla, galleggiante. **A rumour is —,** corre voce; **to set a vessel —,** varare una nave.
afoot [əˈfut], *adv.* A piedi. **To set —,** cominciare.
afore [əˈfɔːɹ], *adv.prep.* Avanti, davanti; primo; (*Naut.*) a prua, di prua. **Afore-mentioned,** sopraccennato; **aforesaid,** suddetto, predetto, come sopra; **aforethought,** premeditato; **malice aforethought,** delitto premeditato.
aforetime, *adv.* Precedentemente.
afraid [əˈfreid], *a.* Impaurito, pauroso, sgomentato, sbigottito. **To be — of,** aver paura di, temere; **I'm — not,** ho paura di no.
afreet, afrit, afrite [ˈæfriːt], *n.* Demonio, *m.*
afresh [əˈfreʃ], *adv.* Di nuovo, daccapo, da capo.
African [ˈæfrikən], *n.a.* Africano, *m.*
aft, after [ɑːft, ɑːftəɹ], *adv.* (*Naut.*) A poppa; all'indietro. **Fore and —,** da poppa a prua.
after (1) [ɑːftəɹ], *prep.adv.conj.* Dopo, dopo che, dietro, appresso, in capo a, in seguito a; alla moda di; di poi. **— all,** dopo tutto, insomma; **one — the other,** uno dopo l'altro; **— the event,** a cose fatte, a fatto avvenuto; **day — day,** di giorno in giorno; **— having eaten,** dopo mangiato; **to look — a person,** occuparsi di una persona; **to ask — an invalid,** domandare di un malato.
after (2), *a.* Seguente, susseguente, futuro. **After-ages,** posterità, *f.*; **after-birth,** placenta, *f.*; **after-crop,** secondo raccolto, *m.*; **after-game,** rivincita, *f.*; **after-grass, aftermath,** guaime, fieno serotino, fieno settembrino, *m.*; (*fig.*) le conseguenze, *f. pl.*; il seguito, *m.*; i postumi, *m.pl.*; **after-pains,** dolori dopo il parto, *m.pl.*; **aftermost,** *a.* Ultimo; **afterthought,** secondo pensiero, ripensamento, *m.*
afternoon [ɑːftəɹnuːn], *n.* Dopopranzo, pomeriggio, *m.*
afterwards [ˈɑːftəɹwədz], *adv.* Dopo, in seguito, poi, più tardi.
again [əˈgein], *adv.* Ancora, ancora una volta, di nuovo; altresì, pure; d'altra parte, d'altronde. **— and —, time and —,** ripetutamente; **as large —,** grosso il doppio; **as much —,** altrettanto ancora; **never —,** mai più.
against [əˈgeinst], *prep.* Contro, avverso a, contrario a, di fronte a, rimpetto, di faccia. **— me,** contro di me; **— the wall,** contro il muro; **— my return,** per il mio ritorno; **— the grain,** a malincuore; **it goes — the grain with me,** non mi va a genio; **— payment,** contro pagamento; **to lean —,** appoggiarsi a; **for and —,** pro e contro; **over —,** in faccia a.
agami [ˈægəmi], *n.* (*Zool.*) Agami, *m.*
agamous [ˈægəməs], *a.* (*Bot.*) Agamo.
agape [əˈgeip], *adv.* A bocca aperta.
agaric [ˈægərik], *n.* (*Bot.*) Agarico, *m.*
agate [ˈægət], *n.* Agata, *f.*
agave [əˈgeivi], *n.* (*Bot.*) Agave, *f.*
age [eidʒ], *v.i.* Invecchiare. || *n.* Età, *f.*; secolo, evo, *m.*, epoca, *f.*; vecchiezza, *f.* **Golden —,** età dell'oro, *f.*; **he is not of age,** è minorenne; **to be of —,** essere maggiorenne; **to be twenty years of —,** avere venti anni; **it's ages since I saw you,** è un secolo che no ti ho visto; **Middle Ages,** Medio Evo, *m.*; **he has aged,** è invecchiato.
aged [ˈeidʒəd], *n.* I vecchi, *m.pl.* || *a.* Attempato, vecchio vecchio.
agedness, *n.* Età, *f.*
ageless, *a.* Senza età, eterno.
agency [ˈeidʒənsi], *n.* Azione, mediazione, *f.*; agenzia, impresa, *f.* **By his —,** per opera sua; **employment —,** agenzia di collocamento, *f.*; **travel —,** agenzia di viaggio, *f.*; **news —,** agenzia d'informazioni, *f.*; **sole —,** rappresentanza esclusiva, *f.*
agenda [əˈdʒendə], *n.* Ordine del giorno, *m.*
agent [ˈeidʒənt], *n.* Agente, rappresentante, fattore, mandatario, *m.*; (*Chem.*) sostanza, *f.* **Consular —,** agente consolare, *m.*; **commission —,** commissionario, *m.*; **to act as —,** agire in qualità di intermediario.
agglomerate [əˈglomərеit], *v.t.i.* Agglomerare, mettere insieme; agglomerarsi, unirsi. || *n.* (*Geol.*) Agglomerati, *m.pl.* || *a.* Agglomerato, ammassato.
agglomeration, *n.* Agglomerazione, *f.*; agglomeramento, *f.*
agglutinate [əˈgluːtineit], *v.t.i.* Agglutinare; agglutinarsi, attaccarsi.
agglutination, *n.* Agglutinazione, *f.*
agglutinative, *a.* Agglutinativo.
aggrandize [ˈægrəndaiz], *v.t.* Aggrandire, ingrandire, ampliare.
aggrandizement, *n.* Aggrandimento, ingrandimento, *m.*
aggravate [ˈægrəveit], *v.t.* Aggravare, accrescere; peggiorare, inacerbire; irritare, stuzzicare, esasperare.
aggravating, *a.* Irritante.
aggravation, *n.* Aggravazione, *f.*; irritazione, provocazione, *f.*
aggregate (1) [ˈægrəgət], *n.* Aggregamento, complesso, totale, *m.*; totalità, *f.* || *a.* Aggregato. **In the —,** in complesso, in blocco.
aggregate (2) [ˈægrəgeit], *v.t.* Aggregare.
aggregately, *adv.* Complessivamente.
aggregation, *n.* Aggregazione, *f.*
aggression [əˈgreʃən], *n.* Aggressione, *f.*
aggressive, *a.* Aggressivo, offensivo.
aggressiveness, *n.* Aggressività, *f.*
aggressor, *n.* Aggressore, assalitore, *m.*
aggrieve [əˈgriːv], *v.t.* Affligere, angustiare, offendere. **He felt himself aggrieved,** si sentiva offeso; **the aggrieved party,** la parte lesa, *f.*
aghast [əˈgɑːst], *a.* Spaventato, sbigottito, costernato, stupefatto.
agile [ˈædʒail], *a.* Agile, leggiero, snello, svelto, destro.

agileness, agility, *n.* Agilità, prestezza, *f.*
agio ['ædʒio], *n.* (*Comm.*) Aggio, agio, *m.*
agitate ['ædʒiteit], *v.t.* Agitare, dimenare; commuovere, turbare.
agitation, *n.* Agitazione, inquietudine, *f.*, turbamento, *m.*
agitator, *n.* Agitatore, *m.*
aglet, aiglet ['æglət], *n.* Puntalino, aghetto, *m.*
aglow [ə'glou], *a.adv.* Cocente, fervente; in fiamme, incandescente.
agnail ['ægneil], *n.* Pipita, *f.*, patereccio, *m.*
agnate ['ægneit], *n.a.* (*Law*) Agnato, *m.*
agnation, *n.* Agnazione, *f.*
agnomen [æg'noumən], *n.* Soprannome, *m.*
agnostic [əg'nɔstik], *n.a.* Agnostico, *m.*
agnosticism [əg'nɔstisizm], *n.* Agnosticismo, *m.*
ago [ə'gou], *adv.* Fa, passato, tempo fa. **Long —,** lungo tempo fa; **a year — yesterday,** ieri fa un anno; **that was five months —,** or sono cinque mesi; **a short time —,** poco tempo fa.
agog [ə'gɔg], *adv.* All'erta, in attesa; impaziente, eccitato. **To be all —,** essere in subbuglio, emozionato.
agoing [ə'gouiŋ], *adv.* In moto, in azione.
agonize ['ægənaiz], *v.i.* Soffrire, agonizzare; *v.t.* torturare, tormentare, angariare, straziare.
agonizing, *a.* Straziante.
agonizingly, *adv.* Angosciosamente.
agony ['ægəni], *n.* Angoscia, *f.*, tormento, strazio, *m.* **Death —,** agonia, *f.*; **to suffer agonies,** patire tormenti; **— column,** avvisi personali in un giornale, *m.pl.*
agouti [ə'gu:ti], *n.* (*Zool.*) Aguti, *m.*
agrarian [ə'grɛəriən], *a.* Agrario.
agree [ə'gri:], *v.i.* Essere d'accordo con, accordarsi, convenire, consentire, concedere; *v.t.* accordare, pareggiare, bilanciare, stabilire. **He agreed to go away,** consentì ad andar via; **I — with you,** son d'accordo con voi; **wine does not — with me,** il vino non mi confa; **that is agreed by all,** tutti sono d'accordo su ciò; **to — upon the price,** accordarsi sul prezzo.
agreeable [ə'gri:əbl], *a.* Gradevole, piacevole; amabile, simpatico. **An — man,** un uomo simpatico, *m.*; **to be — to,** essere disposto a.
agreeableness, *n.* Amabilità, piacevolezza, *f.*
agreeably, *adv.* Piacevolmente, cortesemente; conforme a, conformemente.
agreed [ə'gri:d], *a.* Convenuto, d'accordo, inteso. **— price,** prezzo convenuto, *m.*
agreement, *n.* Accordo, consenso, *m.*; patto, contratto, *m.*; intesa, convenzione, *f.* **To come to an —,** venire ad un accordo.
agricultural [ægri'kʌltjurəl], *a.* Agrario, agricolo. **— implements,** macchine agrarie; **— engine, traction engine,** locomobile; trattore.
agriculture ['ægrikʌltjəɹ], *n.* Agricoltura, *f.*
agriculturist, *n.* Agricoltore, coltivatore, *m.*
agrimony ['ægriməni], *n.* (*Bot.*) Agrimonia, argemone, *f.*
agrimotor ['ægrimoutəɹ], *n.* Trattrice, *f.*
agronomist [ə'grɔnəmist], *n.* Agronomo, *m.*
agronomy, agronomics [ə'grɔnəmi, ægrə'nɔmiks], *n.* Agronomia, *f.*
aground [ə'graund], *adv.a.* Arenato, incagliato; a secco. **To run —,** arenarsi, incagliarsi, dare in secco.
ague ['eigju:], *n.* Febbre intermittente, *f.* **— fit,** accesso di febbre, brivido.
aguish, *a.* Febbricitante.
ah! aha! [ə'hɑ:], *inter.* Ah!, Ah! Ah!
ahead [ə'hed], *adv.* Avanti, in avanti; in testa. **To get — of,** oltrepassare, superare; **Go —!** Avanti!
ahem! [ə'hem], *inter.* Ehm!, Ah!, Oh!
ahoy [ə'hɔi], *inter.* Ohè!, Olà! **Ship —!** Ohè della nave!
ahull [ə'hʌl], *adv.* (*Naut.*) A secco, senza vele.
ai ['ɑ:i:], *n.* (*Zool.*) Ai, bradipo, *m.*
aid [eid], *v.t.* Aiutare, assistere, soccorrere, sovvenire. || *n.* Aiuto, soccorso, sussidio, *m.* **Mutual —,** mutuo soccorso, *m.*; **with the — of,** coll'aiuto di; **lend me your —,** aiutatemi.
aide-de-camp ['eiddə'kã], *n.* (*Mil.*) Aiutante di campo, *m.*
aider, *n.* Aiutante, assistente, *m.*
aigrette ['eigret], *n.* Egretta, *f.*, pennacchio, *m.*
aiguille ['eigwi:l], *n.* Ago, *m.*, guglia, *f.*
ail [eil], *v.t.i.* Far male a; soffrire, avere. **What ails him?** Che cosa ha? **What ails you?** Che cosa ti duole? Che hai?
ailing, *a.* Malaticcio, sofferente.
ailment, *n.* Indisposizione, malattia, *f.*; incomodo, *m.*; acciacchi, *m.pl.*
aim [eim], *v.t.* Appuntare, puntare; mirare, tendere a, aspirare a. || *n.* Mira, *f.*, scopo, intento, oggetto, *m.*; (*of a weapon*) puntamento, *m.* **With this — in view,** a tale scopo; **to — a blow,** vibrare un colpo; **to take —,** prender la mira; puntare.
aimless, *a.* Senza scopo, inutile.
aimlessness, *n.* Mancanza di scopo, futilità, *f.*
ain't [eint], (*vulg.*) Non è, non sono; non ha, non hanno.
air (1) [ɛəɹ], *v.t.* Ventilare, arieggiare, stendere all'aria, sciorinare. **To — a room,** arieggiare una camera; **to — clothes,** asolare vestiti.
air (2), *n.* Aria, *f.*; aspetto, *m.*; cera, *f.*; brezza, *f.*, venticello, *m.*; maniera, *f.*, contegno, *m.*; (*Mus.*) aria, *f.* **A breath of —,** un soffio di vento, *m.*; **in the open —,** all'aria aperta; **to give oneself airs,** darsi delle arie, pavoneggiarsi; **to take the —,** prendere il fresco; **—-balloon,** pallone, aerostato, *m.*; **air-bladder,** vescica natatoria, *f.*; **airborne,** aerotrasportato; **aircraft,** apparecchio aereo, *m.*, aerei, velivoli, *m.pl.*; **air-current,** corrente d'aria, *f.*; **air-cushion,** cuscino di gomma, cuscino pneumatico, *m.*; **air-cylinder,** cilindro ad aria, *m.*; **air defence,** difesa antiaerea, *f.*; **airfield,** aerodromo, campo d'aviazione, *m.*; **air-gun,** fucile ad aria compressa, *m.*; **air-hole,** spiraglio, *m.*; **air lighthouse,** faro aereo, *m.*; **air line,** linea aerea, *f.*; **airmail,** posta aerea, *f.*; **airmail letter,** lettera per via aerea, *f.*; **airman,** aviatore, *m.*; **air mechanic,** motorista, *m.*; **airplane** [cp. **aeroplane**]; **fighter airplane,** apparecchio da caccia, *m.*; **air pocket,** buco d'aria, *m.*; **air-pump,** macchina pneumatica, *f.*; **air raid,** incursione aerea, *f.*; **airshaft,** pozzo di ventilazione, areatore, *m.*; **airship,** dirigibile, *m.*; **airport,** aeroporto, *m.*; **airtight,** a chiusa ermetica; **airway,** rotta aerea, *f.*, ventilatore, *m.*, **airwoman,** aviatrice, *f.*; **airworthy,** atto alla navigazione aerea.

airily, *adv.* Leggermente, allegramente.
airiness, *n.* Ariosità, *f.*; frivolezza, leggerezza, *f.*
airing, *n.* Ventilazione, *f.*, aeraggio, *m.*; passeggiata, boccata d'aria, *f.*
airy, *a.* Arioso, leggiero; frivolo.
airless, *a.* Senz'aria.
aisle [ail], *n.* Navata, *f.*
ait [eit], *n.* Isoletta, *f.*
aitchbone [eitʃboun], *n.* Osso della culatta (del bue), *m.*
ajar [əˈdʒɑːɹ], *a.* Socchiuso, mezz'aperto. **The door is —,** la porta è socchiusa.
akimbo [əˈkimbou], *adv.* **With arms —,** colle mani alle anche.
akin [əˈkin], *a.* Parente, affine, consanguineo; simile.
alabaster [ˈæləbɑːstəɹ], *n.* Alabastro, *m.* || *a.* Alabastrino.
alack!, alack-a-day! [əˈlæk, ɑˈlækədei], *inter.* Ahimè! ohimè!
alacrity [əˈlækriti], *n.* Alacrità, vivacità, *f.*
alarm [əˈlɑːɹm], *v.t.* Allarmare, inquietare, turbare, impaurire. || *n.* Allarme, avvertimento, *m.*; spavento, *m.* **Don't be alarmed,** non s'inquieti; **to give the —,** dare l'allarme; **— bell,** campana a martello, *f.* **— clock,** sveglia, *f.*
alarming, *a.* Allarmante, inquietante.
alarmingly, *adv.* In modo inquietante.
alarmist, *n.* Allarmista, *m.*
alarum [əˈlɑːrəm], *n.* Sveglia, *f.*
alas! [əˈlɑːs], *inter.* Ohimè!
alb [ælb], *n.* Camice, *m.*
albatros [ˈælbətrɔs], *n.* (*Zool.*) Albatro, *m.*
albeit [ɔːlˈbiːit], *adv.* Benchè, sebbene, quantunque, ancorchè.
albescent [ælˈbesənt], *a.* Biancheggiante.
albinism [ˈælbinizm], *n.* Albinismo, *m.*
albino [ælˈbiːnou], *n.a.* Albino, *m.*
album [ˈælbəm], *n.* Album, *m.*
albumen [ælˈbjuːmen], *n.* Albume, *f.*
albumin [ælˈbjuːmin], *n.* Albumina, *f.*
albuminoids [ælˈbjuːminɔidz], *n.pl.* Albuminoidi, *m.pl.*
albuminous, *a.* Albuminoso.
alburnum [ælˈbəːɹnəm], *n.* (*Bot.*) Alburno, *m.*
alcaic [ælˈkeiik], *n.a.* (*Poet.*) Alcaico, *m.*
alchemic, alchemical [ælˈkemik, ælˈkemikəl], *a.* Alchimistico, alchimiato.
alchemically, *adv.* Per alchimia.
alchemist [ˈælkəmist], *n.* Alchimista, *m.*
alchemy [ˈælkəmi], *n.* Alchimia, *f.*
alcohol [ˈælkəhɔl], *n.* Alcool, *m.*
alcoholic, *n.* Alcoolizzato, *m.* || *a.* Alcoolico.
alcoholism, *n.* Alcoolismo.
alcoholization [ælkəhɔlaiˈzeiʃən], *n.* Alcoolizzazione, *f.*
alcoholize, *v.t.* Alcoolizzare.
alcoholometer [ælkəhɔlˈɔmətəɹ], *n.* Alcoolometro, *m.*
alcoran [ˈælkɔrɑːn], *n.* Corano, *m.*
alcove [ˈælkouv], *n.* Alcova, *f.*
alder [ˈɔːldəɹ], *n.* (*Bot.*) Ontano, *m.*
alderman [ˈɔːldəɹmən], *n.* Assessore comunale, *m.*
ale [eil], *n.* Birra, *f.* **Alehouse,** birreria, taverna, *f.*; **ale-wife,** taverniera, ostessa, *f.*
alembic [əˈlembik], *n.* Lambicco, *m.*
alert [əˈləːɹt], *n.* Allarme, *m.*, vigilanza, *f.* || *a.* Vigilante, attento; svelto. **On the —,** all'erta.
alertness, *n.* Celerità, prontezza, *f.*; sollecitudine, *f.*
Alexandria [ælekˈzɑːndriə], *n.* (*Geog.*) Alessandria d'Egitto, *f.*
Alexandrian, Alexandrine [ælekˈzɑːndriən], *a.* Alessandrino.
alfa, alfa grass [ˈælfə], *n.* (*Bot.*). Sparto di Spagna, *m.*
alfresco [ælˈfrescou], *adv.a.* Al fresco, arioso, all'aria aperta.
alga (*pl.* **algae**) [ˈælgə], *n.* (*Bot.*) Alga, aliga, *f.*
algebra [ˈældʒebrə], *n.* (*Math.*) Algebra, *f.*
algebraic, algebraical [ældʒəbˈreik, ældʒəbˈreikəl], *a.* Algebrico.
algebraically, *adv.* Algebricamente.
algebrist [ˈældjəbrist], *n.* Algebrista, *m.*
Algerian [ælˈdʒiəriən], *n.a.* Algerino, *m.* **Algiers,** Algeri, *m.*
alguazil [ælˈgwɑːzil], *n.* Alguazile, *m.*
alias [ˈeiliæs], *n.* Nome assunto, nome falso, pseudonimo, *m.* || *adv.* Detto, altrimenti.
alibi [ˈælibai], *n.* (*Law*) Alibi, *m.*; (*colloq.*) scusa, *f.*, pretesto, *m.*
alidad [ˈælidæd], *n.* Alidada, *f.*
alien [ˈeiliən], *n.* Straniero, forestiere, *m.* || *a.* straniero; contrario; estraneo.
alienability, *n.* Alienabilità, *f.*
alienable, *a.* Alienabile.
alienate, *v.t.* Alienare.
alienation, *n.* Alienazione, *f.*; avversione, *f.*
alienator, *n.* Alienatore, *m.*
alienee [eiliəˈniː], *n.* Alienatario, *m.*
alienism, *n.* Alienismo, *m.*, psichiatria, *f.*
alienist, *n.* Alienista, *m.*
aliform [ˈeilifɔːɹm], *a.* Aliforme.
alight (1) [əˈlait], *a.* Illuminato, in fiamme, acceso.
alight (2), *v.i.* Scendere, smontare, posarsi; (*Aviat.*) atterrare (sul terreno), ammarare (sul mare). **The bird alighted on the ground,** l'uccello si posò sul terreno.
align [cp. **aline**].
alike [əˈlaik], *adv.a.* Egualmente, a un modo; imparzialmente; simile, somigliante. **To be —,** rassomigliarsi.
aliment [ˈælimənt], *n.* Alimento, *m.*
alimental, *a.* Alimentare.
alimentally, *adv.* In modo nutritivo.
alimentary, *a.* Alimentare. (*Anat.*) **— canal,** condotto alimentario, *m.*
alimentation, *n.* Alimentazione, nutrizione, *f.*
alimony [ˈæliməni], *n.* (*Law*) Pensione alimentare, alimonia, *f.*
aline, align [əˈlain], *v.t.* Allineare.
alinement, alignment, *n.* Allineamento, *m.*
aliquot [ˈælikwɔt], *n.a.* Aliquota, *f.*
alive [əˈlaiv], *a.* Vivo, vivente, in vita; sensibile. **Look —!** Spicciatevi! **no man —,** nessuno al mondo; **to be — with,** formicolare di; **to be quite — to,** comprendere bene; **to bury —,** sotterrare vivo; **to keep —,** mantenere in vita; **— to his own interests,** attento ai propri interessi.
alkalescence [ælkəˈlesənt], *n.* Alcalescenza, *f.*
alkalescent, *a.* Alcalescente.
alkali [ˈælkəlai], *n.* Alcali, *m.*
alkalify, *v.t.* Alcalizzare.

alkalimetry, *n.* Alcalimetria, *f.*
alkaline [ˈælkəˈlain], *a.* Alcalino.
alkalization, *n.* Alcalizzazione, *f.*
alkalize, *v.t.* Alcalizzare.
alkaloid [ˈælkəˈlɔid], *n.* Alcaloide, *m.*
alkanet [ˈælkənet], *n.* (*Bot.*) Alcanna, *f.*
all [ɑːl], *a.* Tutto, intero. || *adv.* Tutto, totalmente, in tutto, interamente. || *n.* Tutto, *m.* **— together,** tutti insieme; **— the way,** lungo tutto il cammino; **for — that,** nondimeno, malgrado ciò; **it's — nonsense,** è proprio una sciocchezza; **it's — the same to me,** per me è tutt'uno; **to go on — fours,** andare carponi; **with — speed,** a tutta velocità; **with — my heart,** di tutto cuore; **— at once,** tutt'a un tratto; **All right!** Va bene! **— the better,** tanto meglio; **I don't know at —,** non ne so niente; **not at —,** punto, niente affatto; **above —,** soprattutto; **all's well,** tutto va bene; **if that be —,** se si tratta soltanto di questo; **that's —,** ecco tutto; **all-important,** importantissimo; **all-round,** perfetto, compiuto; **to be on — fours with,** andare del pari; (*Mil.*) **— clear!** Cessato l'allarme! (*Sport*) **three —,** tre per parte; **All Saints,** Ognissanti. **All Fools' Day,** giorno dei pesci d'aprile.
allay [əˈlei], *v.t.* Calmare, mitigare, diminuire; scemare.
allayment, *n.* Mitigazione, *f.*
allegation [æliˈgeiʃən], *n.* Dichiarazione, allegazione, *f.*
allege [əˈledʒ], *v.t.* Dichiarare, allegare, addurre, citare.
allegiance, [əˈliːdʒəns], *n.* Fedeltà, lealtà, *f.* **Oath of —,** giuramento di fedeltà, *m.*
allegorical [æləˈgɔrikəl], *a.* Allegorico.
allegorically, *adv.* Allegoricamente.
allegorist, *n.* Allegorista, *m.*
allegory [ˈæləgɔri], *n.* Allegoria, *f.*
allelujah [æləˈluːjə], *inter.n.* Alleluia, *m.*
alleviate [əˈliːvieit], *v.t.* Alleviare, sollevare, lenire.
alleviation, *n.* Alleviazione, *f.*, alleviamento, sollievo, conforto, *m.*
alley [ˈæli], *n.* Vicolo, chiassuolo, *m.* **Blind —,** vicolo cieco, angiporto, *m.*
alliaceous [æliˈeiʃəs], *a.* (*Bot.*) Agliaceo.
alliance [əˈlaiəns], *n.* Alleanza, lega, *f.* **Triple —,** Triplice Alleanza, *f.*
allied [ˈælaid], *a.* Alleato.
alligator [ˈæligeitəɹ], *n.* (*Zool.*) Alligatore, *m.*
alliteration [əlitərˈeɪʃən], *n.* Allitterazione, *f.*
alliterative, *a.* Allitterativo.
allocate [ˈælokeit], *v.t.* Allogare, assegnare, accantonare (*money*).
allocation, *n.* Assegnazione, *f.*; accontonamento, *m.*
allocution [æləˈkjuʃən], *n.* Allocuzione, *f.*
allodial [əˈloudiəl], *a.* (*Law*) Allodiale.
allodium [əˈloudiəm], *n.* (*Law*) Allodio, *m.*
allopathic [æloˈpæθik], *a.* (*Med.*) Allopatico.
allopathist [əˈlɔpəθist], *n.* Allopatico, *m.*
allopathy [ˈælopæθi], *n.* Allopatia, *f.*
allot [əˈlɔt], *v.t.* Assegnare, distribuire, ripartire, accontonare.
allotment, *n.* Divisione, porzione, *f.*; appezzamento, podere, *m.*
allotropic [æloˈtrɔpik], *a.* (*Min.*) Allotropo.
allow [əˈlau], *v.t.* Concedere, permettere, accordare; tenere conto di. **— me,** permettemi; **to — oneself,** permettersi; **to — oneself to be mistaken,** riconoscere d'essersi sbagliato; **to — a discount,** concedere uno sconto; **to — of,** approvare.
allowable, *a.* Permissibile, convenevole.
allowance, *n.* Indulgenza, tolleranza, scusa, *f.*; pensione, *f.*; assegno, *m.*; concessione, *f.*; sconto, compenso, *m.* **To make — for,** essere indulgente verso; **to put on short —,** razionare; **trade —,** concessione speciale, riduzione, *f.*; **lodging —,** indennità d'alloggio, *f.*
allowed, *a.* Permesso, concesso.
alloy (1) [əˈlɔi], *v.t.* Amalgamare; diminuire.
alloy (2) [ˈælɔi], *n.* Lega (*of metals*), *f.*
all-spice [ˈɑːlspais], *n.* Pimento, *m.*
allude [əˈljuːd], *v.i.* Alludere (a), accennare (a), riferirsi (a).
allure [əˈljuəɹ], *v.t.* Attrarre, allettare, lusingare; cattivarsi.
allurement, *n.* Attrattiva, *f.*, allettamento, fascino, *m.*; seduzione, *f.*
alluring, *a.* Affascinante, seducente.
alluringly, *adv.* Lusinghevolmente.
allusion [əˈljuːʒən], *n.* Allusione, *f.*, accenno, *m.*
allusive, *a.* Allusivo.
allusively, *adv.* In modo allusivo.
alluvial [əˈljuːviəl], *a.* Alluvionale, alluviale.
alluvion, alluvium [əˈljuːviən, əˈljuːviəm], *n.* (*Geol.*) Alluvione, *f.*
ally (1) [əˈlai], *v.t.* Unire, combinare, alleare; *v.i.* Allearsi, unirsi, collegarsi, imparentarsi.
ally (2) [ˈæ lai], *n.* Alleato, *m.*
almagest [ˈælmədʒest], *n.* (*Lit.*) Almagesto, *m.*
almanac [ˈɔːlmənæk], *n.* Almanacco, calendario, *m.*
almightiness [ɔːlˈmaitinəs], *n.* Onnipotenza, *f.*
almighty, *a.* Onnipotente. **The Almighty,** Dio, Dio Onnipotente, *m.*
almond [ˈɑːmənd], *n.* Mandorla, *f.* **Burnt —,** mandorla tosta; **— tree,** mandorlo, *m.*
almoner [ˈɑːmənəɹ], *n.* Elemosiniere, *m.*
almost [ˈɔːlmoust], *adv.* Quasi, presso che, press'a poco, circa.
alms [ˈɑːmz], *n.* Elemosina, limosina, *f.*; carità, *f.* **Alms-giving,** elemosina, *f.*; **almshouse,** ospizio di carità, *m.*; **almsman,** chi vive di carità, *m.*; **alms-box,** cassetta per le elemosine, *f.*
aloe [ˈælou], *n.* (*Bot.*) Aloe, *m.*
aloetic [æloˈetik], *a.* (*Med.*) Aloetico.
aloft [əˈlɔft], *adv.* In alto, su, sopra; a riva.
alone [əˈloun], *a.* Solo, solitario, isolato; unico. || *adv.* Soltanto, solo, solamente. **All —,** tutto solo; **leave me alone, let me alone,** lasciatemi tranquillo; **let the child —,** lasciate stare il bambino.
along [əˈlɔŋ], *adv.* Lungo, accanto; rasente. **All —,** tutto il tempo, sempre; **all — the road,** lungo tutta la strada; **— with,** con; **Come —!** Andiamo! **Get — with you!** Andatevene!
alongside [əlɔŋˈsaid], *adv.* Vicino a, di fianco a, accanto a.
aloof [əˈluːf], *adv.* Lontano, lungi, discosto; da banda, da parte. **To stand —,** starsene da parte; **to hold —,** appartarsi, isolarsi, tenersi a distanza.
aloofness, *n.* Freddezza, indifferenza, *f.*
aloud [əˈlaud], *adv.* Ad alta voce.

alp [ælp], *n.* Alpe, alta montagna, *f.* **The Alps,** le Alpi, *f.pl.*
alpaca [ælˈpækə], *n.* (*Zool.*) Alpaca, *f.*; (*material*) alpaga, *f.*
alpenstock [ælpənˈstɔk], *a.* Alpenstoc, bastone ferrato, *m.*
alpha [ˈælfə], *n.* Alfa, *m.*
alphabet [ˈælfəbət], *n.* Alfabeto, abbicci, *m.*
alphabetic, alphabetical, *a.* Alfabetico.
alphabetically, *adv.* Alfabeticamente.
alpine [ˈælpain], *a.* Alpino, alpestre, montuoso. **— climbing,** alpinismo, *m.*
alpinist, *n.* Alpinista, *m.*
already [ɔːlˈredi], *adv.* Già, di già, in passato, altre volte.
Alsatian [ælˈseiʃən], *n.m.a.* Alsaziano, *m.* **— dog,** cane-lupo, *m.*
also [ˈɔːlsou], *adv.* Anche, inoltre, altresì, pure, del pari.
altar [ˈɔːltəɹ], *n.* Altare, *m.*, ara, *f.* **High —,** altar maggiore, *m.*; **— cloth,** paliotto, *m.*, tovaglia d'altare, *f.*; **—-piece,** pala d'altare, *f.*; **—-screen,** ancona, *f.*
alter [ˈɔːltəɹ], *v.t.* Cambiare, alterare, mutare, cangiare, trasformare; *v.i.* alterarsi, cambiare, mutarsi. **To — one's mind,** mutar proposito; **she has altered the date of her wedding,** ha cambiato il giorno dello sposalizio.
alterable, *a.* Variabile, mutabile.
alteration, *n.* Cambiamento, mutamento, *m.*, alterazione, trasformazione, *f.*
alterative, *n.a.* Alterativo, *m.*
altercate [ˈɔːltəɹkeit], *v.i.* Altercare, litigare.
altercation, *n.* Alterco, diverbio, *m.*, altercazione, disputa, *f.*
alternate [ˈɔːltəɹneit], *v.i.* Alternare; avvicendarsi.
alternate [ɔːlˈtəːɹnət], *a.* Alternato, alternativo.
alternately, *adv.* Alternatamente.
alternating, *a.* Alternante; (*Elec.*) alternato.
alternation, *n.* Alternazione, *f.*; avvicendamento, *m.*
alternative, *n.* Alternativa, *f.* ‖ *a.* Alternativo.
alternatively, *adv.* Alternativamente.
although [ɔːlˈðou], *conj.* Benchè, sebbene, quantunque, malgrado che.
altitude [ˈæltitjuːd], *n.* Altitudine, altezza, *f.*
altogether [ɔːltəˈgeðəɹ], *adv.* Affatto, tutt'affatto, interamente, in tutto e per tutto.
altruism [ˈæltruːizm], *n.* Altruismo, *m.*
altruist, *n.* Altruista, *m.*
altruistic, *a.* Altruistico.
altruistically, *adv.* Altruisticamente.
alum [ˈæləm], *n.* Allume, *m.*
alumina [əˈljuːminə], *n.* (*Chem.*) Allumina, *f.*
aluminium [æljuːˈminiəm], *n.* Alluminio, *m.*
alluminous, *a.* Alluminoso.
alveolar [ˈælvioləɹ], *a.* Alveolato.
always [ˈɔːlweiz], *adv.* Sempre.
am [æm], 1*st sing. pres. ind.* (io) sono [cp. **be**].
amain [əˈmein], *adv.* Di forza, a tutta forza, violentemente.
amalgam [əˈmælgəm], *n.* Amalgama, *m.*
amalgamate [əˈmælgəmeit], *v.t.* Amalgamare; *v.i.* combinare, amalgamarsi.
amalgamation, *n.* Amalgamazione, fusione, *f.*; combinazione, *f.*
amanuensis [əmænjuːˈensis], *n.* Amanuense, copista, segretario, *m.*
amaranth [ˈæmərænθ], *n.* Amaranto, *m.*
amaranthine, *a.* D'amaranto.
amass [əˈmæs], *v.t.* Ammassare, adunare.
amateur [ˈæməˈtəːɹ], *n.* Dilettante, amatore, *m.*
amateurish, *a.* Da dilettante, dilettantesco.
amativeness [ˈæmətivnəs], *n.* Amorosità, *f.*
amatory [ˈæmətəri], *a.* Amatorio, erotico.
amaurosis [æmɔːˈrousis], *n.* (*Med.*) Amaurosi, *f.*
amaze [əˈmeiz], *v.t.* Stupefare, stupire, stordire, sbalordire; sorprendere; meravigliare. **To be amazed,** rimanere stupefatto.
amazedly, *adv.* Attonitamente.
amazement, *n.* Stupefazione, meraviglia, sorpresa, *f.*
amazing, *a.* Meraviglioso, stupefacente.
amazingly, *adv.* Meravigliosamente.
amazon [ˈæməzən], *n.* Amazzone, *f.*; (*Geog.*) Le Amazzoni, *f.pl.*
amazonian, *a.* Amazzonio, da amazzone.
ambages [æmˈbeidʒiːz], *n.pl.* Ambagi, *f.pl.*
ambassador [æmˈbæsədəɹ], *n.* Ambasciatore, *m.*
ambassadorial, *a.* Ambasciatorio.
ambassadress, *n.* Ambasciatrice, *f.*
amber [ˈæmbəɹ], *n.* Ambra, *f.* **—-coloured,** ambrato, colore d'ambra.
ambergris [ˈæmbəɹgriːs], *n.* Ambra grigia, *f.*
ambidexter [æmbiˈdekstəɹ], *n.* Ambidestro, *m.*
ambidextrous, *a.* Ambidestro.
ambient [ˈæmbiənt], *n.m.a.* Ambiente.
ambiguity [æmbiˈgjuiti], *n.* Ambiguità, *f.*, equivoco, *m.*
ambiguous [æmˈbigjuəs], *a.* Ambiguo, dubbioso, equivoco.
ambiguously, *adv.* Ambiguamente.
ambit [ˈæmbit], *n.* Contorno, *m.*
ambition [æmˈbiʃən], *n.* Ambizione, *f.*
ambitious, *a.* Ambizioso. **To be — of,** ambire.
ambitiously, *adv.* Ambiziosamente.
ambivalence [æmˈbivələns], *n.* Ambivalenza, *f.*
amble [ˈæmbl], *v.i.* Ambiare, andare all'ambio. ‖ *n.* Ambio, *m.*; ambiatura, *f.*
amblyopia [æmbliˈoupiə], *n.* (*Med.*) Ambliopia, *f.*
ambrosia [æmˈbrouziə], *n.* Ambrosia, *f.*
ambrosial, *a.* Ambrosio.
ambs-ace [ˈæmzeis], *n.* (*Dice*) Duino, *m.*
ambulance [ˈæmbjuləns], *n.* Ambulanza, *f.*
ambulant, *a.* Ambulante.
ambulatory, *n.a.* Ambulatorio, *m.*
ambuscade [æmbəsˈkeid], *n.* Imboscata, *f.*, agguato, *m.*
ambush [ˈæmbuʃ], *v.t.* Mettersi in agguato. ‖ *n.* Imboscata, *f.* **To lie in —,** stare all'agguato.
ameer, amir [əˈmiəɹ], *n.* Emiro, *m.*
ameliorate [əˈmiːliəreit], *v.t.* Migliorare; *v.i.* avantaggiarsi.
amelioration, *n.* Miglioramento, *m.*, miglioria, *f.*
ameliorative, *a.* Migliorativo.
amen [ɑːmen, eiˈmen], *inter.n.* Amen, *m.*
amenability [əmiːnəˈbiliti], *n.* Remissività, sommissione, *f.*
amenable [əˈmiːnəbl], *a.* Sottomesso, consenziente, remissivo, arrendevole; (*Law*) attendibile.
amenableness, *n.* Sottomissione, *f.*; responsabilità, *f.*

amend [ə'mend], *v.t.* Emendare, correggere, rettificare; migliorare; *v.i.* emendarsi, correggersi, riformarsi.
amendable, *a.* Emendabile.
amendment, *n.* Emendamento, ritocco, *m.*
amends, *n.pl.* Ammenda, compensa, *f.* **To make —,** far ammenda.
amenity [ə'mi:niti], *n.* Amenità, *f.* **Amenities,** comodità, *f.pl.*
amerce [ə'mə:ɹs], *v.t.* Multare.
amercement, *n.* Multa, *f.*
American [ə'merikən], *n.a.* Americano, *m.* **— cloth** (oil-cloth), tela cerata.
Americanism, *n.* Americanismo, *m.*
americanize, *v.t.* Americanizzare.
amethyst ['æməθist], *n.* Ametista, *f.* || *a.* Ametistino.
amethystine [æmə'θistain], *a.* D'ametista, ametistino.
amiability [eimjə'biliti], *n.* Amabilità, gentilezza, *f.*
amiable ['eimiəbl], *a.* Amabile, simpatico, caro, gentile.
amiably, *adv.* Amabilmente, caramente.
amianthus [æmi'ænθəs], *n.* (*Min.*) Amianto, *m.*
amicability [æmikə'biliti], *n.* Amichevolezza, *f.*
amicable ['æmikəbl], *a.* Amichevole.
amicably, *adv.* Amichevolmente.
amice ['æmis], *n.* (*Eccles.*) Amitto, ammitto, *m.*
amid, amidst [ə'mid, ə'midst], *prep.* Fra, tra, in mezzo di, in mezzo a. (*Naut.*) **Amidships,** al centro della nave, a mezza nave; **— the tempest,** in mezzo alla tempesta.
amiss [ə'mis], *adv.a.* Impropriamente, male a proposito, male, improprio. **To do —,** far male; **to take —,** pigliare in mala parte; **there's something —,** c'è qualche cosa di male, qualcosa che non va.
amity ['æmiti], *n.* Amicizia, amistà, *f.*
ammeter ['æmi:təɹ], *n.* (*Elec.*) Amperometro, *m.*
ammonia [ə'mouniə], *n.* (*Chem.*) Ammoniaca, *f.*
ammoniac, ammoniacal, *a.* Ammoniacale, ammoniaco.
ammonite ['æmənait], *n.* (*Geol.*) Ammoniti, *m.pl.*
ammonium [ə'mouniəm], *n.* (*Chem.*) Ammonio, *m.*
ammunition [æmju'niʃən], *n.* Munizioni, *f.pl.* (*Mil.*) **— wagon,** vettura cassone, *f.*
amnesia [æm'ni:siə], *n.* (*Med.*) Amnesia, *f.*
amnesty ['æmnəsti], *n.* Amnistia, *f.* || *v.t.* Amnistiare.
amnion ['æmniən], *n.* (*Anat.*) Amnio, *m.*
amomum [ə'moumən], *n.* (*Bot.*) Amomo, *m.*
among, amongst [ə'mʌŋ, ə'mʌŋst], *prep.* Tra, fra, in mezzo a; nel numero di, presso, da. **— the French,** presso i Francesi; **from —,** tra, fra; **— ourselves,** tra noi; **one — many,** uno fra tanti; **to be — the number,** essere del numero.
amorous ['æmərəs], *a.* Amoroso, innamorato.
amorously, *adv.* Amorosamente.
amorousness, *n.* Amorosità, *f.*
amorphism, amorphousness [ə'mɔ:ɹfizm, ə'mɔ:ɹfəsnəs], *n.* Amorfia, *f.*
amorphous, *a.* Amorfo.
amortization, amortisement [əmɔ:ɹti'zeiʃən, ə'mɔ:ɹtizmənt], *n.* Ammortizzazione, *f.*
amortize, *v.t.* Ammortizzare.
amount [ə'maunt], *v.i.* Ammontare, sommare; ridursi a, avere importanza. || *n.* Somma, quantità, *f.*, montante, *m.* **His argument amounts to this,** il suo argomento si riduce a questo; **it all amounts to the same thing,** ammonta alla stessa cosa; **What is the — of the bill?** Quanto è l'ammontare del conto? **to the — of,** fino alla somma di.
amour ['æmuər], *n.* Amorazzo, intrigo, *m.*
ampere ['æmpεəɹ], *n.* (*Elect.*) Ampère, *m.*
ampersand ['æmpəɹsænd], *n.* (*Print.*) Il segno &, *m.*
amphibian [æm'fibiən], *n.* Anfibio, *m.*
amphibious [æm'fibiəs], *a.* Anfibio.
amphibiousness, *n.* Natura anfibia, *f.*
amphibological [æmfibə'lɔdʒikəl], *a.* Anfibologico.
amphibology [æmfi'bɔlədʒi], *n.* Anfibologia, *f.*
amphioscus [æmfi'ɔskəs], *n.* (*Zool.*) Anfiosso, *m.*
amphitheatre [æmfi'θi:ətəɹ], *n.* Anfiteatro, *m.*
amphitryon [æm'fitriən], *n.* Anfitrione, *m.*
amphora ['æmfərə], *n.* Anfora, *f.*
ample ['æmpl], *a.* Ampio, largo, copioso, abbondante.
ampleness, *n.* Ampiezza, estensione, *f.*
amplification [æmplifi'keiʃən], *n.* Estensione, amplificazione, *f.*
amplifier ['æmplifaiəɹ], *n.* (*Radio*) Amplificatore, *m.*
amplify, *v.t.* Amplificare, dilatare, aumentare, allargare.
amplitude ['æmplitju:d], *n.* Ampiezza, larghezza, estensione, *f.*; (*Astron.*) amplitudine, *f.*
amply, *adv.* Ampiamente.
ampulla [æm'pulə], *n.* Ampolla, *f.*
amputate ['æmpjuteit], *v.t.* Amputare, recidere.
amputation, *n.* Amputazione, *f.*, troncamento, *m.*
amuck, amok [ə'mʌk], *adv.* **To run —,** scatenarsi, correre all'impazzata.
amulet ['æmjulet], *n.* Amuleto, *m.*
amuse [ə'mju:z], *v.t.* Divertire, distrarre, ricreare. **To — oneself,** divertirsi, spassarsi.
amusement, *n.* Divertimento, passatempo, piacere, spasso, *m.*, distrazione, *f.*
amusing, *a.* Divertente, spassoso.
amusingly, *adv.* Lietamente.
amygdalin [ə'migdəlin], *n.* (*Chem.*) Amigdalina, *f.*
amyl ['æmil], *n.* (*Chem.*) Amilico, *m.*
an [æn], *indef.art.* Uno, una.
an [æn], *conj.* (*obs.*) Se.
Anabaptist ['ænəbæptist], *n.* Anabattista, *m.*
anachronism [ə'nækrənism], *n.* Anacronismo, *m.*
anachronistic [ə'nækrənistik], *a.* Anacronistico.
anacoluthon [ænəkə'lju:θən], *n.* Anacoluto, *m.*
anaconda [ænə'kɔndə], *n.* (*Zool.*) Anaconda, *f.*
Anacreon [ə'nækriən], *n.* Anacreonte, *m.*
anacreontic [ənækri'ɔntik], *a.* Anacreontico.
anaemia [ə'ni:miə], *n.* (*Med.*) Anemia, *f.*
anaemic, *a.* Anemico.
anaesthesia [ænes'θi:ziə], *n.* Anestesia, *f.*
anaesthetic [ænis'θetik], *n.a.* Anestetico, *m.*
anaesthetize [ə'ni:sθətaiz], *v.t.* Anestetizzare.
anaglyph ['ænəglif], *n.* Anaglifo, *m.*

anaglyphic, anaglyptic, *a.* Anagliptico.
anagoge, anagogy [ænə'goudʒi], *n.* Anagogia, *f.*
anagram ['ænəgræm], *n.* Anagramma, *m.*
anagrammatical, *a.* Anagrammatico.
anagrammatist, *n.* Anagrammatista, *m.*
anal ['einəl], *a.* (*Anat.*) Anale.
analects, analecta ['ænəlekts, ænə'lektə], *n.pl.* Frammenti scelti, *m.pl.*; spigolature, *f.pl.*
analeptic [ænə'leptik], *n.* (*Anat.*) Analettica, *f.*
analogical [ænə'lɔdʒikəl], *a.* Analogico.
analogically, *adv.* Analogicamente.
analogist, *n.* Analogista, *m.*
analogize, *v.t.* Argomentare per analogia.
analogous [ə'næləgəs], *a.* Analogo.
analogously, *adv.* Analogamente.
analogy [ə'nælədʒi], *n.* Analogia, *f.*
analysable [ænə'laizəbl], *a.* Analizzabile.
analyse ['ænəlaiz], *v.t.* Analizzare; (*Comm.*) fare lo spoglio di.
analysis [ə'nælisis], *n.* Analisi, *f.*
analyst ['ænəlist], *n.* (*Chem.*) Analizzatore, *f.*; (*Math.*) analista, *m.*
analytic, analytical [ænə'litik, ænə'litikəl], *a.* Analitico.
analytically, *adv.* Analiticamente.
analytics, *n.* Analitica, *f.*
anana, ananas [ə'neinəs, ə'nɑ:nəs], *n.* (*Bot.*) Ananasso, *m.*
anandrous [ə'nændrəs], *a.* (*Bot.*) Anandro.
anapaest ['ænəpəst], *n.* (*Poet.*) Anapesto, *m.*
anarchic, anarchical [ə'nɑ:ɹkik, ə'nɑ:ɹkikəl], *a.* Anarchico.
anarchically, *adv.* In modo anarchico.
anarchist, *n.* Anarchico, anarchista, *m.*
anarchy, *n.* Anarchia, *f.*
anastomosis [ənæstə'mousis], *n.* (*Anat.*) Anastomosi, *f.*
anathema [ə'næθəmə], *n.* Anatema, *m.*
anathematize, *v.t.* Anatematizzare.
anatomical [ænə'tomikəl], *a.* Anatomico.
anatomically, *adv.* Anatomicamente.
anatomist, *n.* Anatomista, *m.*
anatomize, *v.t.* Anatomizzare.
anatomy, *n.* Anatomia, *f.*
ancestor ['ænsestəɹ], *n.* Antenato, avo, progenitore, *m.*
ancestral [æn'sestrəl], *a.* Ereditario, avito, degli avi.
ancestry, *n.* Razza, stirpe, prosapia, famiglia, *f.*, lignaggio, *m.*
anchor ['æŋkəɹ], *v.t.i.* Ancorare, ormeggiare, ancorarsi. || *n.* Ancora, *f.* **Kedge —,** ancorotto, *f.*; **sheet —,** ancora di speranza, *f.*; **to weigh the —,** levar l'ancora; **to ride at —,** stare all'ancora; **to drop the —,** gettare l'ancora.
anchorage ['æŋkərədʒ], *n.* Ancoraggio, *m.*
anchoret, anchorite ['æŋkərət, 'æŋkərait], *n.* Anacoreta, eremita, *m.*
anchovy [æn'tʃouvi, 'æntʃouvi], *n.* Acciuga, alice, *f.* **— sauce,** salsa di acciughe, *f.*; **— paste,** acciugata, *f.*
anchylosis [æŋki'lousis], *n.* (*Med.*) Anchilosi, *f.*
ancient ['eintʃənt], *a.* Antico, vecchio. || *n.* Anziano, *m.*
anciently, *adv.* Anticamente.
ancientness, *n.* Antichità, *f.*
ancon (*pl.* **ancones**) ['æŋkən], *n.* (*Anat.*) Ancone, *m.*
and [ænd], *conj.* E, ed. **And so on,** e così via; **better and better,** di bene in meglio; **worse and worse,** di male in peggio; **and even, and yet,** anzi, eppure; **go and see,** andate a vedere; **they went in two by two,** entrarono a due a due; **a coach and four,** una carrozza a quattro cavalli.
andiron ['ændaiəɹn], *n.* Alare, *m.*
androgynous [æn'drɔdʒinəs], *a.* (*Bot.*) Androgino; (*Zool.*) ermafrodito.
androgyne ['ændrɔdʒin], *n.* Androgino, *m.*
anecdote ['ænəkdout], *n.* Aneddoto, *m.*, storiella, *f.*
anecdotal, *a.* Aneddotico.
anemograph [ə'nemogræf], *n.* Anemografo, *m.*
anemometer [æne'mɔmətəɹ], *n.* Anemometro, *m.*
anemone [ə'nemouni], *n.* (*Bot.*) Anemone, anemolo, *m.* **Sea —,** attinia, *f.*
anemoscope [ə'nemoskoup], *n.* Anemoscopio, *m.*
anent [ə'nent], *prep.* Circa, a proposito di.
aneroid ['ænərɔid], *a.* Aneroide. **— barometer,** barometro aneroide, *m.*
aneurism ['ænjurizm], *n.* (*Med.*) Aneurisma, *m.*
aneurismal, *a.* Aneurismatico.
anew [ə'nju:], *adv.* Di nuovo, da capo.
anfractuose [æn'fræktjuous], *a.* Anfrattuoso.
angel ['eindʒəl], *n.* Angelo, angiolo, *m.* **Guardian —,** angelo custode, *m.*; **— fish,** pesce angelo, *m.*
angelic, angelical [æn'dʒelik, æn'dʒelikəl], *a.* Angelico.
angelica, *n.* (*Bot.*) Angelica, *f.*
angelically, *adv.* Angelicamente.
angelus ['ændʒələs], *n.* Avemmaria, *f.*
anger ['æŋgəɹ], *n.* Collera, ira, stizza, rabbia, *f.*, furore, *m.* || *v.t.* Irritare, fare andare in collera, fare arrabbiare.
angina [æn'dʒainə], *n.* (*Med.*) Angina, *f.*
angiosperm ['ændʒiospəɹm], *a.* (*Bot.*) Angiosperme.
angle (1) ['æŋgl], *v.i.* Pescare (coll'amo).
angle (2) *n.* Angolo, canto, *m.*; cantonata, *f.* **Right angle,** angolo retto, *m.*
angled, *a.* **Right-angled,** ad angolo retto; **acute-angled,** ad angolo acuto; **rectangular,** rettangolare.
angler, *n.* Pescatore, *m.*
Anglican ['æŋglikən], *n.a.* Anglicano, *m.*
Anglice['æŋglisi], *adv.* In inglese.
Anglicism ['æŋglicizm], *n.* Anglicismo, *m.*
Anglicize, *v.t.*Anglicizzare.
angling ['æŋgliŋ], *n.* Pesca coll'amo, *f.*
Anglomania [æŋglou'meiniə], *n.* Anglomania, *f.*
Anglophobia [æŋglou'foubiə], *n.* Anglofobia, *f.*
Anglo-Saxon [æŋglousæksən], *n.a.* Anglosassone, *m.*
angola, angora [æŋ'goulə, æŋ'gɔ:rə], *n.* Capra d'angora, *f.*
angrily ['æŋgrili], *adv.* Con ira, adiratamente, stizzosamente.
angry, *a.* In collera, arrabbiato, incollerito, adirato, irato. **To get —,** montare in collera; **to be — with,** essere in collera con; **don't get —,** non arrabbiatevi.
anguine ['æŋgwain], *a.* In forma di serpente.

anguish ['æŋgwiʃ], *n.* Angoscia, *f.*, travaglio, *m.*
angular ['æŋgu:ləɹ], *a.* Angolare, angolato.
angularity, *n.* Forma angolare, *f.*
anhydrous [æn'haidrəs], *a.* Anidro.
anil ['ænil], *n.* (*Bot.*) Anil, anile, *m.*
anile ['ænail], *a.* Imbecille, di mente debole.
anility, *n.* Decrepitezza, *f.*
aniline ['ænilin], *n.* Anilina, *f.* — **dye,** tinta d'anilina, *f.*
animadversion [ænimədˈvəɹʃən], *n.* Animadversione, riprensione, *f.*
animal ['æniməl], *n.* Animale, bruto, *m.*, bestia, *f.* || *a.* Animale. — **kingdom,** regno animale; **draught —,** animale da tiro.
animalcular [æniˈmælkuləɹ], *a.* Microbico.
animalcule, *n.* Batterio, microbo, *m.*
animalism, *n.* Sensualità, bestialità, *f.*
animality, *n.* Animalità, *f.*
animalize, *v.t.* Imbestiare, abbrutire.
animate (1) ['ænimeit], *v.t.* Animare.
animate (2) ['ænimət], *a.* Vivo, vivente.
animated, *a.* Animato, vivo, gaio.
animating, *a.* Stimolativo, animante.
animation, *n.* Animazione, vivacità, *f.*
animism ['ænimizm], *n.* Animismo, *m.*
animist, *n.* Animista, *m.*
animosity [æniˈmɔsiti], *n.* Animosità, ostilità, *f.*
animus ['æniməs], *n.* Animo, *m.*, animosità, *f.*, mal talento, *m.*
anise ['ænis], *n.* (*Bot.*) Anace, anice, *m.* **Aniseed,** seme d'anice, *m.*; **anisette,** anisetta, *f.*
ankle ['æŋkl], *n.* Caviglia, *f.*, malleolo, noce del piede, *m.* **—-bone,** astragalo, *m.*; **—-deep,** sino alle caviglie; **— -joint,** collo del piede; **— sock,** calzino, *m.*
anklet, *n.* Ornamento per la caviglia, *m.*
annalist ['ænəlist], *n.* Annalista, *m.*
annals, *n.pl.* Annali, *m.pl.*
annates ['æneits], *n.pl.* Annualità, *f.pl.*
anneal [əˈni:l], *v.t.* Temprare, ricuocere, addolcire.
annealing, *n.* Ricuocitura, ricottura, tempera, *f.*
annelid ['ænəlid], *n.* (*Zool.*) Anellide, *f.*
annex (1) [əˈneks], *v.t.* Annettere, unire, aggiungere, allegare, attaccare, accludere.
annex (2) ['æneks], *n.* Annesso, *m.*, dipendenza, *f.*
annexation, *n.* Annessione, *f.*
annexed, *a.* Annesso, unito, congiunto, accluso.
annihilate [əˈnaihəleit], *v.t.* Annichilire, annientare, distruggere.
annihilation, *n.* Annichilimento, annientamento, *m.*
anniversary [æniˈvə:ɹsəri], *n.a.* Anniversario, *m.*
annotate ['ænouteit], *v.t.* Annotare, postillare.
annotation, *n.* Annotazione, chiosa, postilla, *f.*
annotator, *n.* Annotatore, chiosatore, *m.*
announce [əˈnauns], *v.t.* Annunziare, annunciare, far sapere.
announcement, *n.* Annunzio, avviso, invito, *m.*; comunicazione, *f.*
announcer, *n.* (*Radio*) Annunciatore, *m.*
annoy [əˈnɔi], *v.t.* Annoiare, dar fastidio, seccare, incomodare. **It's very annoying,** è una grande seccatura; **this man annoys me very much,** questo'uomo mi dà molto fastidio; **to be annoyed with,** avere a noia.
annoyance, *n.* Noia, molestia, seccatura, *f.*, fastidio, disturbo, *m.*
annoying, *a.* Seccante, noioso.
annoyingly, *adv.* In modo noioso, noiosamente.
annual ['ænjuəl], *a.* Annuale, annuo. || *n.* Annuario, *m.*; (*Bot.*) pianta annuale, *f.*
annually, *adv.* Annualmente, d'anno in anno, ogni anno.
annuitant [əˈnju:itənt], *n.* Redditùario, *m.*, chi vive d'un assegno annuale.
annuity, *n.* Annualità, *f.*, assegno annuale, pensione annuale, *m.* **Life —,** rendita vitalizia, *f.*, vitalizio, *m.*; **to buy an —,** fare un vitalizio.
annul [əˈnʌl], *v.t.* Annullare.
annular ['ænjuləɹ], *a.* Anulare.
annulate, annulated, *a.* (*Zool, etc.*) Anellato, anuloso.
annulet ['ænjulet], *n.* Anelletto, anellino, *m.*
annulment [əˈnʌlmənt], *n.* Annullamento, *m.*
annunciate [əˈnʌnsieit], *v.t.* Annunziare.
annunciation, *n.* Annunziazione, *f.*, annunzio, *m.* (*Eccles.*) **Feast of the Annunciation,** giorno dell'Annunziata, *m.*
annunciator, *n.* Annunziatore, *m.*
anode ['ænoud], *n.* (*Elect.*) Anodo, *m.*
anodyne ['ænodain], *n.a.* Anodino, *m.*
anoint [əˈnɔint], *v.t.* Ungere, unguentare; dare il crisma, dare l'olio santo.
anointed, *a.* Unto. **The Lord's —,** l'unto del Signore, *m.*
anomalistic [ənɔməˈlistik], *a.* (*Astron.*) Anomalistico.
anomalous [əˈnɔmələs], *a.* Anomalo, irregolare.
anomalously, *adv.* Irregolarmente.
anomaly, *n.* Anomalia, *f.*
anon [əˈnɔn], *adv.* Subito, presto, senza indugio, lì per lì, fra poco. **Ever and —,** di tempo in tempo, ogni tanto.
anonymous [əˈnɔniməs], *a.* Anonimo.
anonymously, *adv.* Anonimamente.
anonymity [ænoˈnimiti], *n.* Anonimità, *f.*; anonimo, *m.* **To keep one's —,** conservare l'anonimo.
anosmia [əˈnɔzmiə], *n.* (*Med.*) Anosmia, *f.*
another [əˈnʌðəɹ], *pron.a.* Altro, un altro; nuovo; secondo. **One after —,** l'uno dopo l'altro; **one —,** l'un l'altro; **that's quite — thing,** quella è ben'altra cosa; **to take one with —,** prendere uno coll'altro.
anserine ['ænsərain], *a.* (*Zool.*) Anserino.
answer ['ɑ:nsəɹ], *v.t.* Rispondere a, replicare; confutare; *v.i.* rispondere; riuscire; essere conforme a, corrispondere. || *n.* Risposta, replica, *f.* **This answers my purpose,** questo è adatto al mio scopo; **this scheme will never —,** questo progetto non riuscirà mai; **to — for,** essere responsabile di; **awaiting an —,** in attesa della vostra risposta; **in — to his letter,** in risposta alla sua lettera; **here's an — to the riddle,** ecco una soluzione dell'enigma.
answerable ['ɑ:nsərəbl], *a.* Responsabile; confutabile.
ant [ænt], *n.* (*Zool.*) Formica, *f.* **—-eater,** formichiere, *m.*; **—-hill,** formicaio, *m.*; **—-lion,** formicaleone, *m.*
antagonism [ænˈtægənizm], *n.* Antagonismo, *m.*, ostilità, *f.*

antagonist, *n.* Antagonista, avversario, *m.*
antagonize, *v.t.* Rendere ostile, contrastare a, metter l'uno contro l'altro.
Antarctic [æn'tɑːɹktik], *n.a.* Antartico, *m.*
antecedence [ænti'siːdəns], *n.* Antecedenza, priorità, *f.*
antecedent, *n.a.* Antecedente, *f.*
antecedently, *adv.* Antecedentemente.
antechamber ['æntitʃeimbəɹ], *n.* Anticamera, *f.*
antedate [ænti'deit], *v.t.* Antidatare.
antediluvian [æntidi'ljuːviən], *n.a.* Antidiluviano, *m.*
antelope ['æntiloup], *n.* Antilope, *f.*
antemeridian [æntimər'idiən], *a.* Antimeridiano.
antemundane [ænti'mʌndein], *a.* Anteriore alla creazione.
antenna (*pl.* **antennae**) [æn'tenə], *n.* Antenna, *f.*
antenuptial [ænti'nʌpʃəl], *a.* Antinuziale.
antepenult, antepenultimate [æntipən'ʌlt, æntipen'ʌltimeit], *n.a.* Terzultimo; sdrucciolo (*of verse, etc.*)
anterior [æn'tiəriəɹ], *a.* Anteriore, precedente.
anteriorly, *adv.* Anteriormente, prima.
anteroom ['æntirum], *n.* Anticamera, *f.*
anthelion [æn'θiːliən], *n.* (*Meteor.*) Antelio, *m.*
anthelmintic [ænθəl'mintik], *n.a.* (*Med.*) Antelmintico, *m.*
anthem ['ænθəm], *n.* Antifona, *f.*, inno, *m.* **National —,** inno nazionale, *m.*
anther ['ænθəɹ], *n.* (*Bot.*) Antera, *f.*
anthology [æn'θɔlədʒi], *n.* Antologia, *f.*, florilegio, *m.*; crestomazia, *f.*
Anthony's fire ['æntəniz faiəɹ], *n.* Erisipela, erpete, fuoco di Sant'Antonio.
anthracite ['ænθrəsait], *n.* Antracite, *f.* — **stove,** stufa ad antracite, *f.*
anthrax ['ænθræks], *n.* (*Med.*) Antrace, *m.*
anthropoid [ænθropɔid], *n.a.* (*Zool.*) Antropoide, *m.*
anthropological [ænθrəpo'lɔdʒikəl], *a.* Antropologico.
anthropologist, *n.* Antropologo, *m.*
anthropology, *n.* Antropologia, *f.*
anthropometry, *n.* Antropometria, *f.*
anthropomorphism [ænθrəpo'mɔːɹfizm], *n.* Antropomorfismo, *m.*
anthropomorphist, *n.* Antropomorfista, *m.*
anthropomorphous, *a.* Antropomorfo.
anthropophagous, *a.* Antropofago.
anti- ['ænti], *prefix.* Ante-, anti-, contro.
anti-aircraft [æntiɛəɹkrɑːft], *a.* Antiaereo.
antic ['æntik], *n.* Burla, buffoneria, *f.* **To play antics,** fare il buffone.
antichrist ['æntikraist], *n.* Anticristo, *m.*
anticipate [æn'tisipeit], *v.t.* Anticipare, prevedere, aspettare. **I do not — any difficulty,** non prevedo nessuna difficoltà; **he always anticipates his income,** spende sempre in anticipo.
anticipation, *a.* Anticipazione, aspettazione, previsione, *f.* **Thanking you in —,** ringraziandovi anticipatamente.
anticipatory, *a.* Preventivo, in anticipo.
anti-climax [ænti'klaimæks], *n.* Calata di tono, discesa, *f.*
anticlinal [ænti'klainəl], *a.* (*Geol.*) Anticlinale.
anti-constitutional [æntikɔnsti'tjuʃiənəl], *a.* Anticostituzionale.
anti-dazzle [ænti'dæzl], *a.* (*Motor.*) Anti, abbagliante. — **light,** faro anti-abbagliante, *m.*
antidote ['æntidout], *n.* Antidoto, *m.*
antilogy [æn'tilədʒi], *n.* Antilogia, *f.*
antimacassar [æntimə'kæsəɹ], *n.* Poggiacapo, *m.*
antimonial [ænti'mouniəl], *a.* (*Chem.*) Antimoniale.
antimony ['æntiməni], *n.* Antimonio, *m.*
antinomy [æn'tinəmi], *n.* Antinomia, *f.*
antipathetic [æntipə'θetik], *a.* Avverso.
antipathetically, *adv.* Avversamente.
antiphlogistic [æntiflo'dʒistik], *n.a.* (*Med.*) Antiflogistico, *m.*
antipathy [æn'tipəθi], *n.* Antipatia, avversione, *f.*
antiphony [æn'tifəni], *n.* (*Mus.*) Antifonia, *f.*
antipodal [æn'tipədəl], *a.* Antipodico.
Antipodes [æn'tipədiːz], *n.pl.* Antipodi, *m.pl.*
anti-pope [æntipoup], *n.* Antipapa, *m.*
antipyretic [æntipai'retik], *n.* Antipirina, *f.*
antiquarian, antiquary [ænti'kwɛəriən, 'æntikwəri], *n.a.* Antiquario, *m.*
antiquated ['æntikweitəd], *a.* Antiquato, vieto, antico.
antique [æn'tiːk], *a.* Vecchio, antico. ‖ *n.* Cosa antica, anticaglia, *f.*
antiquity [æn'tikwiti], *n.* Antichità, *f.*
antirrhinum [ænti'rainəm], *n.* (*Bot.*) Antirrino, *m.*, bocca di leone, *f.*
antiseptic [ænti'septik], *n.a.* Antisettico, *m.*
antisocial [ænti'souʃəl], *a.* Antisociale.
antistrophe [æn'tistrəfi], *n.* Antistrofe, antistrofa, *f.*
anti-tank ['ænti-tæŋk], *a.* Anticarro.
antithesis [æn'tiθəsis], *n.* Antitesi, *f.*
antithetic, antithetical [ænti'θetik, ænti'θetikəl], *a.* Antitetico.
anti-toxin [ænti'tɔksin], *n.* (*Med.*) Antitossina, *f.*
antitype ['æntitaip], *n.* Antitipo, *m.*
antler ['æntləɹ], *n.* Corno, *m.* **Antlers,** corna ramose del cervo, *f.pl.*
Antwerp ['æntwəɹp], *n.* (*Geog.*) Anversa, *f.*
anus ['einəs], *n.* (*Anat.*) Ano, *m.*
anvil ['ænvil], *n.* Incudine, *f.*
anxiety [æŋ'zaiəti], *n.* Ansia, inquietudine, preoccupazione, apprensione, *f.*, affanno, *m.*
anxious ['æŋkʃəs], *a.* Ansioso, inquieto, preoccupato, turbato, desideroso, premuroso. **To be — about,** essere ansioso di; **to be — to,** desiderare di; **an — state,** uno stato d'ansietà.
anxiously, *adv.* Ansiosamente, con affanno.
any ['eni], *a.adv.pron.* Alcuno, qualche, qualunque; di; più, tutto. **Any better,** meglio, **any further,** più lontano; — **more,** di più; ancora; — **of them,** qualcuno di essi; — **others,** ancora altri; **at — rate,** in ogni caso; **Have you — wine ?** Avete del vino ? **I have not —.** non ne ho niente; **not on — account,** per niente al mondo; **scarcely —,** quasi niente.
anybody, anyone, *pron.* Alcuno, ognuno, qualcuno, chiunque, qualcheduno, tutti, tutto il mondo. — **can understand that,** tutti possono capire quello; **like — else,** come tutti gli altri.
anyhow, *adv.* In ogni modo, nondimeno.

anything, *n.pron.* Qualche cosa, qualcosa, qualunque cosa, *f.* — **but,** tutt'altro che.
anywhere, *adv.* Dovunque, in qualche luogo; dappertutto. **Have you seen my book anywhere?** Ha visto in qualche luogo il mio libro? — **else,** in qualche altro luogo.
aorist ['eiərist], *n.* (*Gram.*) Aoristo, *m.*
aorta [ei'ɔːɹtə], *n.* (*Anat.*) Aorta, *f.*
apace [ə'peis], *adv.* Presto, a gran passi.
apanage [ə'pænədʒ], *n.* Appannaggio, *m.*
apart [ə'pɑːɹt], *adv.* A parte, in disparte, separatamente. **To come —,** sfarsi, disfarsi; — **from,** eccezione fatta di.
apartment [ə'pɑːɹtmənt], *n.* Stanza, camera, *f.* **Apartments,** alloggio, appartamento, *m.*
apathetic [æpə'θetik], *a.* Apatico.
apathetically, *adv.* Apaticamente.
apathy ['æpəθi], *n.* Apatia, *f.*
ape [eip], *v.t.* Scimmiottare. || *n.* (*Zool.*) Scimmia, *f.*; scimmiotto, *m.*
apeak [ə'piːk], *adv.* (*Naut.*) A picco.
aperient [ə'piəriənt], *n.a.* Lassativo, purgante, *m.*
aperitive, aperitif [ə'perətiv], *n.a.* Aperitivo, *m.*
aperture ['æpəɹtjəɹ], *n.* Apertura, *f.*, forame, buco, *m.*
apetalous [ə'petələs], *a.* (*Bot.*) Apetalo.
apex ['eipeks], *n.* Apice, *m.*, cima, punta, sommità, *f.*; apogeo, *m.*
aphaeresis [æfə'riːsis], *n.* (*Gram.*) Aferesi, *f.*
aphelion [ə'fiːliən], *n.* (*Astron.*) Afelio, *m.*
aphis ['eifis], *n.* (*Zool.*) Afide, *m.*
aphonia [ə'founiə], *n.* Afonia, *f.*
aphorism ['æfərizm], *n.* Aforismo, *m.*
aphoristic, *a.* Aforistico.
aphoristically, *adv.* Aforisticamente.
aphrodisiac [æfro'diziək], *n.a.* Afrodisiaco, *m.*
aphthae ['æfθiː], *n.pl.* (*Med.*) Afte, *f.pl.*
aphyllous [ə'filəs], *a.* (*Bot.*) Afillo.
apiary ['eipiəri], *n.* Alveare, apiario, *m.*
apiarist, *n.* Apicultore, *m.*
apiculture ['eipikʌltjəɹ], *n.* Apicultura, apiaria, *f.*
apiece [ə'piːs], *adv.* A testa, per uno, per ciascuno. **How much —?** Quanto costa l'uno?
apish ['eipiʃ], *a.* Scimmiesco. — **imitation,** scimmiottatura, *f.*
apishly, *adv.* Come una scimmia.
apishness, *n.* Scimmieggiatura, *f.*
aplomb [ə'plɔ̃], *n.* Sangue freddo, *m.*, freddezza, *f.*
apnœa ['æpniːə], *n.* (*Med.*) Apnea, *f.*
apocalypse [ə'pɔkəlips], *n.* Apocalissi, apocalisse, *f.*
apocalyptic, *a.* Apocalittico.
apocalyptically, *adv.* In modo apocalittico.
apocope [ə'pɔkəpi], *n.* (*Gram.*) Apocope, *f.*
apocrypha [ə'pɔkrifə], *n.* Gli apocrifi; testi spuri, *m.pl.*
apocryphal, *a.* Apocrifo; spurio.
apod ['æpɔd], *n.* (*Zool.*) Apode, *m.*
apodictic [æpə'diktic], *a.* Apodittico.
apodosis [æpə'dousis], *n.* (*Gram.*) Apodosi, *f.*
apogee ['æpədʒiː], *n.* Apogeo, *m.*
apologetic [əpɔlə'dʒetik], *a.* Apologetico; giustificativo, scusevole.
apologetically, *adv.* In modo giustificativo.
apologetics, *n.pl.* Apologetica, *f.*
apologist, *n.* Apologista, *m.*
apologize, *v.i.* Scusarsi, chieder scusa. **I apologized to him,** gli ho chiesto scusa; **to — for someone,** scusare qualcheduno.
apologue ['æpəlɔg], *n.* Apologo, *m.*
apology [ə'pɔlədʒi], *n.* Apologia, scusa, difesa, *f.*; perdono, *m.*
apophthegm [ə'pɔfθəm], *n.* Apoftegma, *m.*
apoplectic [æpo'plektik], *a.* Apoplettico, apopletico. — **fit,** colpo, tocco apoplettico.
apoplexy ['æpopleksi], *n.* Apoplessia, apoplesia, *f.*
apostasy [ə'pɔstəsi], *n.* Apostasia, *f.*
apostate, *n.* Apostata, *m.* || *a.* Apostatico.
apostatize, *v.i.* Apostatare.
apostle [ə'pɔsl], *n.* Apostolo, *m.* **Acts of the Apostles,** Gli Atti degli Apostoli, *m.pl.*
apostolate, apostleship, *n.* Apostolato, *m.*
apostolic, apostolical, *a.* Apostolico.
apostrophe [əpɔstrəfi], *n.* Apostrofe, *f.*
apostrophize, *v.t.* Apostrofare.
apothecary [ə'pɔθəkəri], *n.* Farmacista, *m.*
apotheosis [əpɔθi'ousis], *n.* Apoteosi, *f.*
appal [ə'pɔːl], *v.t.* Spaventare, sbigottire, impaurire, atterrire.
appalling, *a.* Spaventoso, terribile, spaventevole.
appanage [cp. **apanage**].
apparatus [æpə'reitəs], *n.* Apparato, apparecchio, congegno, *m.*
apparel [ə'pærəl], *v.t.* Vestire, ornare. || *n.* Vestiti, vestimenti, *m.pl.*, veste, *f.* **Wearing —,** articoli di vestiario, *m.pl.*
apparent [ə'pærənt], *a.* Apparente, visibile, evidente. **Heir —,** erede presunto, *m.*
apparently, *adv.* Apparentemente, per ciò che pare, a quanto pare.
apparition [æpə'riʃən], *n.* Apparizione, *f.*, fantasma, spettro, *m.*
apparitor [əpæritəɹ], *n.* Apparitore, *m.*
appeal [ə'piːl], *v.i.* Appellarsi, fare appello, richiamarsi; ricorrere a; attrarre, andare a genio. || *n.* Appello, ricorso, richiamo, *m.* **I — to you,** mi appello a voi; — **to arms,** chiamata alle armi, *f.*; **Court of Appeal,** Corte di Appello, *f.*
appealing, *a.* Supplichevole, attraente.
appealingly, *adv.* Supplichevolmente.
appear [ə'piəɹ], *v.i.* Apparire, comparire, parere; mostrarsi. **It appears that,** pare che, sembra che; **it would —,** parebbe, a quanto pare; **to — upon the scene,** comparire sulla scena.
appearance, *n.* Apparenza, sembianza, comparsa; venuta, *f.*; aspetto, *m.*; (*Law*) comparizione, *f.* **At first —,** a prima vista, a primo aspetto; **for the sake of appearances,** per salvar l'apparenze; **to all appearances,** all'apparenza; **to make one's first —,** debuttare, esordire; **to put in an —,** fare una comparsa, fare atto di presenza.
appeasable [ə'piːzəbl], *a.* Calmabile, placabile, contentabile.
appease [ə'piːz], *v.t.* Calmare, soddisfare, pacificare, placare, tranquillizzare. **To — one's appetite,** soddisfare l'appetito.
appeasement, *n.* Appagamento, *m.*; soddisfazione, *f.*

appellant [əˈpelənt], *n.a.* (*Law*) Appellante, *m.*
appellate, *a.* (*Law*) Appellato. **— court,** corte di appello, *m.*
appellation [æpəlˈeiʃən], *n.* Appellativo, nome, titolo, *m.*, denominazione, *f.*
appellative, *a.* Appellativo.
append [əˈpend], *v.t.* Appendere, aggiungere, attaccare.
appendage, *n.* Aggiunta, *f.*, accessorio, *m.*; appendice, *f.*
appendicitis [əpendiˈsaitis], *n.* (*Med.*) Appendicite, *f.*
appendix (*pl.* **appendixes, appendices**) [əˈpendiks], *n.* Appendice, aggiunta, *f.*, annesso, *m.*
apperception [æpəɹˈsepʃən], *n.* Percezione, *f.*
appertain [æpəɹˈtein], *v.i.* Appartenere, spettare, essere proprio di.
appetence [ˈæpətəns], *n.* Appetenza, *f.*
appetite [ˈæpətait], *n.* Appetito, gusto, *m.*; inclinazione, *f.* **To give an —,** fare appetire; **he has a keen —,** ha un buon appetito.
appetizer, *n.* Aperitivo, *m.*
appetizing, *a.* Appetitivo, appetitoso, gustoso.
applaud [əˈplɔːd], *v.t.* Applaudire, approvare.
applause [əˈplɔːz], *n.* Applauso, plauso, applaudimento, *m.*
apple [ˈæpl], *n.* Pomo, *m.*, mela, *f.* **— of the eye,** pupilla dell'occhio, *f.*; **Adam's —,** pomo d'Adamo, *m.*; **— orchard,** pomaio, meleto, *m.*; **— -tree,** melo, *m.*; **— -pie, — -tart,** torta di mele, *f.*; **— -pie bed,** letto a sacco, *m.*; **— -pie order,** ordine perfetto, *m.*; **— of discord,** pomo della discordia, *m.*
appliance [əˈplaiəns], *n.* Strumento, apparecchio, *m.*, macchina, applicazione, *f.*
applicability [æplikəˈbiliti], *n.* Applicabilità, adattabilità, *f.*
applicable [ˈæplikəbl], *a.* Applicabile, adattabile.
applicant, *n.* Aspirante, candidato, *m.*; petente, richiedente, *m.*
application, *n.* Applicazione, richiesta, domanda, *f.*; diligenza, cura, *f.* **— for a job,** domanda d'impiego; **to make an — to,** rivolgere un'istanza a; **— of the brake,** frenata, *f.*
apply [əˈplai], *v.t.* Applicare, adattare, apporre; applicarsi, dedicarsi; indirizzarsi; richiedere. **To — for a post,** richiedere un posto; **to — the brake,** mettere il freno, frenare; **applied sciences,** scienze applicate.
appoint [əˈpɔint], *v.t.* Nominare, fissare, assegnare, stabilire, decidere; guarnire. **To — a professor,** nominare un professore; **to — a time,** fissare un'ora.
appointee [əpɔinˈtiː], *n.* Persona nominata ad un impiego, *f.*
appointment, *n.* Nomina, *f.*; appuntamento, impiego, *m.* **To make an — with,** dare un appuntamento a.
apportion [əˈpɔːɹʃən], *v.t.* Distribuire, ripartire, suddividere.
apportionment, *n.* Distribuzione, suddivisione, *f.*, ripartimento, *m.*
apposite [ˈæpəzit], *a.* Apposito, adatto, acconcio.
appositely, *adv.* Appositamente, a proposito.
appositeness, *n.* Proprietà, *f.*
apposition, *n.* Apposizione, *f.*
appraisable [əˈpreizəbl], *a.* Valutabile.
appraise, *v.t.* Apprezzare, stimare, valutare.
appraisement, *n.* Apprezzamento, *m.*, stima, valutazione, *f.*; perizia, *f.*
appraiser, *n.* Stimatore, esperto, *m.*
appreciable [əˈpriːʃəbl], *a.* Apprezzabile; sensibile, percettibile, considerevole.
appreciably, *adv.* Sensibilmente.
appreciate [əˈpriːʃieit], *v.t.* Apprezzare, pregiare, stimare; *v.i.* rincarare, aumentare di valore. **I don't — this wine,** questo vino non mi va a genio; **these shares have appreciated in value,** queste azioni sono salite.
appreciation, *n.* Apprezzamento, pregio, *m.*, stima, *f.*; giudizio, *m.*; rincaro, *m.*
appreciative, *a.* Apprezzativo, sensibile. **He is very — of your kindness,** è molto sensibile alla vostra gentilezza.
apprehend [æpriˈhend], *v.t.* Apprendere, comprendere, capire, intendere; credere, supporre; temere; arrestare, prendere. **To be apprehended for theft,** essere arrestato per furto.
apprehensible, *a.* Comprensibile.
apprehension, *n.* Apprendimento, *m.*; timore, *m.*; arresto, *m.*, apprensione, *f.* **To be dull of —,** avere una mente tarda; **grounds for —,** motivo di timore; **to allay apprehensions,** calmare le apprensioni.
apprehensive, *a.* Inquieto, timoroso, apprensivo; intelligente, ricettivo. **To be — of,** temere.
apprehensively, *adv.* Apprensivamente.
apprehensiveness, *n.* Timore, *m.*, inquietudine, *f.*
apprentice [əˈprentis], *v.t.* Collocare. || *n.* Apprendista, allievo, *m.*; (*Naut.*) mozzo, *m.*
apprenticeship, *n.* Tirocinio, noviziato, *m.*
apprise [əˈpraiz], *v.t.* Informare, avvertire.
approach [əˈproutʃ], *v.t.i.* Avvicinarsi, appressarsi, accostarsi. || *n.* Avvicinamento, accostamento, accesso, *m.* **To be easy of —,** essere di facile accesso.
approachable, *a.* Accessibile, di facile accesso.
approbation [æprəˈbeiʃən], *n.* Approvazione, *f.*; consenso, *m.* **On —,** in prova.
approbatory, *a.* Probatorio, approvativo.
appropriate [əˈproupricit], *v.t.* Appropriarsi, impadronirsi; (*Comm.*) destinare, accantonare.
appropriate [əˈproupriət], *a.* Convenevole, proprio, adatto, atto.
appropriately, *adv.* Appropriatamente, in modo convenevole.
appropriateness, *n.* Proprietà, convenienza, *f.*
appropriation, *n.* Appropriazione, assegnazione, *f.*; (*Comm.*) destinazione, *f.*
approvable [əˈpruːvəbl], *a.* Approvabile, lodevole.
approval [əˈpruːvəl], *n.* Approvazione, sanzione, *f.* **On —,** in esame, in prova.
approve, *v.t.* Approvare, assentire a, sanzionare, convalidare; lodare.
approved, *a.* Stimato; approvato. **— (reform) school,** casa di correzione, *f.*
approver, *n.* (*Law*) Denunziatore dei suoi complici, *m.*
approving, *a.* Approvativo.
approvingly, *adv.* In modo approvativo.
approximate [əˈprɔksimeit], *v.t.* Approssimare; approssimarsi, appressarsi. || [əˈprɔksimət], *a.* Approssimativo.

approximately, *adv.* Approssimativamente, a un dipresso; circa, quasi.
approximation, *n.* Approssimazione, *f.*, avvicinamento, *m.*
appulse [ə'pʌls], *n.* (*Astron.*) Appulso, *m.*
appurtenance [ə'pəːɹtənəns], *n.* Appartenenza, pertinenza, *f.*
appurtenant, *a.* Appartenente.
apricot ['eiprikɔt], *n.* Albicocca, *f.* **—-tree,** albicocco, *m.*
April ['eipril], *n.* Aprile, *m.* **An — shower,** un acquazzone d'aprile, *m.*; **— fool,** pesce d'aprile, *m.*
apron ['eiprən], *n.* Grembiale, grembiule, *m.* **Tied to his mother's —-strings,** attaccato alle gonne della mamma; **an apronful of nuts,** una grembialata di noci, *f.*
apropos ['ɑːproupou], *adv.* A proposito.
apse [æps], *n.* (*Arch.*, *Astron.*) Abside, *f.*
apt [æpt], *a.* Atto, adatto, capace; pronto, intelligente.
apterous ['æptərəs], *a.* (*Zool.*) Attero.
apteryx ['æptəriks], *n.* (*Zool.*) Atterice, *f.*
aptitude, aptness ['æptitjuːd, 'æptnəs], *n.* Attitudine, disposizione, capacità, *f.*
aptly, *adv.* A proposito, giustamente.
aqua-fortis [ækwə'fɔːɹtis], *n.* Acquaforte, *f.*
aquamarine ['ækwəməriːn], *n.* Acquamarina, *f.*
aquarium [ə'kwɛəriəm], *n.* Acquario, *m.*
Aquarius [ə'kwɛəriəs], *n.* (*Astron.*) Aquario, *m.*
aquatic [ə'kwætik], *a.* Acquatico.
aqueduct ['ækwidʌkt], *n.* Acquedotto, *m.*
aqueous ['eikwiəs], *a.* (*Geol.*) Acqueo.
aquiline ['ækwilain], *a.* Aquilino.
Arab ['ærəb], *n.a.* Arabo, *m.* **Street —,** birichino di strada, *m.*
arabesque [ærəbesk], *n.a.* Arabesco, rabesco, *m.*
Arabian [ə'reibiən], *n.a.* Arabo, *m.*
Arabic, *a.* Arabo. **Arabic language,** la lingua araba, *f.*
arable ['ærəbl], *a.* Arabile, coltivabile.
arachnid [ə'ræknid], *n.* (*Zool.*) Aracnide, *m.*
Aramaean [ærə'miːən], *a.* Aramaico.
araucaria [ærau'kɛəriə], *n.* (*Bot.*) Araucaria, *f*
arbalest ['ɑːɹbəlest], *n.* Balestra, *f.*
arbiter ['ɑːɹbitəɹ], *n.* Arbitro, *m.*
arbitrage, arbitrament, *n.* Arbitrato, *m.*, sentenza arbitrale, *f.*
arbitrarily ['ɑːɹbitrərili], *adv.* Arbitrariamente.
arbitrariness, *n.* Arbitrarietà, *f.*
arbitrary, *a.* Arbitrario.
arbitrate, *v.t.i.* Arbitrare, giudicare.
arbitration, *n.* Arbitrato, *m.*; (*Comm.*) arbitraggio, *m.*
arbitrator, *n.* Arbitratore, arbitro, *m.*
arbor ['ɑːɹbəɹ], *n.* (*Mech.*) Albero, *m.*; coppaia, *f.*, asse, *m.*
arboreal, *a.* Arboreo.
arboriculture ['ɑːrbərikʌltjər], *n.* Arboricoltura, *f.*
arboriform, *a.* Arboreo.
arbour ['ɑːɹbəɹ], *n.* Pergola, *f.*, pergolato, *m.*
arbutus [ɑːɹ'bjutəs], *n.* (*Bot.*) Corbezzolo, *m.*
arc ['ɑːɹk], *n.* Arco, *m.* **— lamp,** lampada ad arco, *f.*
arcade, *n.* Galleria, *f.*; colonnato, *m.*, arcata, *f.*
Arcadian [ɑːɹ'keidiən], *a.* Arcade.
arcanum (*pl.* **arcana**), *n.* Arcano, mistero, *m.*
arch- [ɑːɹtʃ], *prefix,* Grande, capo-, arci-.
arch (1) [ɑːɹtʃ], *v.t.* Arcare, inarcare, curvare, piegare in arco; *v.i.* incurvarsi, piegarsi. || *n.* Arco, *m.*, volta, *f.* **Triumphal —,** arco trionfale, *m.*
arch (2), *a.* Furbo, malizioso.
archaeological [ɑːɹkiə'lɔdʒikəl], *a.* Archeologico.
archaeologist [ɑːɹki'ɔlədʒist], *n.* Archeologo, *m.*
archaeology, *n.* Archeologia, *f.*
archaic [ɑːɹ'keiik], *a.* Arcaico.
archaism ['ɑːɹkeiizm], *n.* Arcaismo, *m.*
archangel ['ɑːɹkeindʒəl], *n.* Arcangelo, *m.*
archbishop [ɑːɹtʃ'biʃəp], *n.* Arcivescovo, *m.*
archbishopric, *n.* Arcivescovado, *m.*
archdeacon [ɑːɹtʃ'diːkən], *n.* Arcidiacono, *m.*
archdeaconry, *n.* Arcidiaconato, *m.*
archducal [ɑːɹtʃ'djuːkəl], *a.* Arciducale.
archduchess [ɑːɹtʃ'dʌtʃəs], *n.* Arciduchessa, *f.*
archduchy, *n.* Arciducato, *m.*
archduke [ɑːɹtʃ'djuːk], *n.* Arciduca, *m.*
arched [ɑːɹtʃd], *a.* Arcato, curvo, piegato.
archer, *n.* Arciere, arciero, *m.*
archery, *n.* Tiro all'arco, *m.*
archetype ['ɑːɹkitaip], *n.* Archetipo, *m.*
arch-fiend [ɑːɹtʃ'fiːnd], *n.* Arcidiavolo, Satana, *m.*
arch-foe [ɑːɹtʃ'fou], *n.* Nemico mortale, *m.*
arch-heretic [ɑːɹtʃ'heretik], *n.* Eresiarca, *m.*
archidiaconal [ɑːɹkidai'ækənəl], *a.* Di arcidiacono.
archiepiscopal [ɑːɹkiə'piskəpəl], *a.* Arcivescovile.
archimandrite [ɑːɹki'mændrait], *n.* Archimandrita, *m.*
archipelago [ɑːɹki'peləgou], *n.* Arcipelago, *m.*
architect ['ɑːɹkitekt], *n.* Architetto, *m.*
architectonics [ɑːɹkitek'tɔniks], *n.pl.* Architettonica, *f.*
architectural [ɑːɹki'tektjurəl], *a.* Architettonico.
architecture ['ɑːɹkitektjueɹ], *n.* Architettura, *f.*
architrave ['ɑɹkitreiv], *n.* (*Arch.*) Architrave, *m.*
archives ['ɑːɹkaivz], *n.pl.* Archivio, *m.*
archivist, *n.* Archivista, *m.*
archly ['ɑːɹtʃli], *adv.* Maliziosamente, furbamente, con occhio furbo.
archness, *n.* Malizia, birichineria, astuzia, *f.*
archon ['ɑːɹkən], *n.* (*Hist.*) Arconte, *m.*
arch-priest [ɑːɹtʃ'priːst], *n.* Arciprete, *m.*
archway ['ɑːɹtʃwei], *n.* Volta, arcata, *f.*, arcale, arco, *m.*
arctic ['ɑːɹktik], *a.* Artico.
arcuate ['ɑːɹkjuːeit], *a.* Arcuato.
ardency, ardour ['ɑːɹdənsi, 'ɑːɹdəɹ], *n.* Ardore, fervore, *m.*
ardent ['ɑːɹdənt], *a.* Ardente, focoso, impaziente, animoso.
ardently, *adv.* Ardentemente, con ardore.
ardour ['ɑːɹdəɹ], *n.* Ardore, fervore, *m.*
arduous ['ɑːɹdjuːəs], *a.* Arduo, difficile; erto, ripido.
arduously, *adv.* Arduamente, con difficoltà.
arduousness, *n.* Arduità, difficoltà, *f.*
are [ɑːɹ], *pl.indic.* [**be**]. (*Telephone*) **Are you there ?** Pronto?, Chi parla ?
area ['ɛəriə], *n.* Area, *f.*, spazio, *m.*; superficie, *f.*; cortile davanti a una casa *m.*

areca [ə'ri:kə], *n.* (*Bot.*) Areca, *f.* — **nut,** noce di betel, *f.*
arefaction [ærə'fækʃən], *n.* Seccatura, *f.*
arena [ə'ri:nə], *n.* Arena, *f.*; circo, *m.*
arenose [ərə'nouz], *a.* Arenoso, arido.
aren't [ɑ:ɹnt], (*colloq.* **are not**). Non sono.
argent ['ɑ:ɹdʒənt], *a.* Argenteo; (*Heraldry*) bianco.
argentiferous [ɑ:ɹdʒən'tifərəs], *a.* Argentifero.
Argentine ['ɑ:ɹdʒəntain], *n.a.* Argentino, *m.* **The Argentine,** L'Argentina, *f.*
argil ['ɑ:dʒil], *n.* Argilla plastica, *f.*
argon ['ɑ:ɹgɔn], *n.* (*Chem.*) Argon, *m.*
argonaut ['ɑ:ɹgənɔ:t], *n.* Argonauta, *m.*
argosy ['ɑ:ɹgosi], *n.* Galeone, *m.*
argot ['ɑ:rgou], *n.* Gergo, *m.*
argue ['ɑ:ɹgju:], *v.t.* Provare, mostrare, indicare, sostenere; *v.i.* argomentare, ragionare, discutere. **That argues well for him,** ciò è di vantaggio a lui; **she argued me into this,** mi ha persuaso a fare questo.
argument, *n.* Argomento, ragionamento, *m.*, discussione, tesi, *f.*
argumentation, *n.* Argomentazione, *f.*
argumentative, *a.* Argomentativo, disputativo.
argumentatively, *adv.* Per argomento.
Argus [ɑ:ɹgəs], *n.* (*Myth.*) Argo, *m.*
argute [ɑ:ɹgju:t], *a.* Arguto, acuto, pronto.
Arian ['ɛəriən], *n.a.* Ariano, *m.*
Arianism, *n.* Arianismo, *m.*
arid ['ærid], *a.* Arido, secco, asciutto, sterile.
aridity, aridness, *n.* Aridità, siccità, *f.*
Aries ['ɛərii:z], *n.* (*Astron.*) Ariete, *m.*
aright [ə'rait], *adv.* Bene, con esattezza, correttamente, giustamente.
arise [ə'raiz], *v.i.* Levarsi, alzarsi; elevarsi (*of mountains, etc.*); risultare, provenire. **A prophet has arisen,** è sorto un profeta; **should the opportunity —,** si presentasse l'occasione favorevole.
aristocracy [æris'tɔkrəsi], *n.* Aristocrazia, *f.*
aristocrat ['æristəkræt], *n.* Aristocratico, *m.*
aristocratic, aristocratical, *a.* Aristocratico.
aristocratically, *adv.* In modo aristocratico.
Aristotelian [æristɔ'ti:liən], *n.a.* Aristotelico, *m.*
arithmetic [ə'riθmetik], *n.* Aritmetica, *f.*
arithmetical, *a.* Aritmetico.
arithmetically, *adv.* Aritmeticamente.
arithmetician [əriθmə'tiʃən], *n.* Aritmetico, *m.*
ark [ɑ:ɹk], *n.* Arca, *f.* **Noah's —,** l'arca di Noè, *f.*
arm (1) [ɑ:ɹm], *n.* Braccio, *m.*; arma, arme, *f.* **Arms** (*of offence, etc.*) armi, *f.pl.*; (*Heraldry*) **coat of arms,** stemma, *f.*, scudo, *m.*; **at arm's length,** a distanza; **man-at-arms,** uomo d'armi, *m.*; **with arms folded,** con le braccia incrociate; **within arm's reach,** a portata di mano; **with open arms,** a braccia aperte; **arm-in-arm,** a braccetto; **to be up in arms,** incollerirsi; **—-chair,** poltrona, *f.*, seggiolone, *m.*, **—-hole,** giro, *m.*; **—-pit,** ascella, *f.*
arm (2), *v.t.* Armare, munire; *v.i.* armarsi, prendere le armi.
armada [ɑ:ɹ'meidə], *n.* Armata, *f.*
armadillo [ɑ:ɹmə'dilou], *n.* (*Zool.*) Armadillo, *m.*
armament, *n.* Armamento, *m.*, armatura, *f.* **The burden of armaments,** il gravame degli armamenti, *m.*
armature, *n.* Armatura, *f.*; (*Elect.*) indotto, *m.*
armful, *n.* Bracciata, *f.*
armillary ['ɑ:ɹmiləri], *a.* Armillare. **— sphere,** sfera armillare, *f.*
armistice ['ɑ:ɹmistis], *n.* Armistizio, *m.*
armless, *a.* Senza braccia.
armlet, *n.* Armilla, *f.*, cerchietto, braccialetto, *m.*
armorial [ɑ:ɹ'mɔ:riəl], *a.* Araldico. **— bearings,** blasone, *m.*, stemma, *m.*
armour [ɑ:ɹməɹ], *n.* Armatura, *f.*, blindaggio, *m.* **— plate,** corazza, *f.*
armoured, *a.* Corazzato, blindato. **— car,** autoblinda, *f.*, carro blindato, *m.*; **— train,** treno blindato, *m.*; **— cruiser,** corazzata, *f.*
armourer, *n.* Armaiuolo, *m.*
armoury, *n.* Armeria, galleria d'armi, *f.*
armpit, *n.* Ascella, *f.*
army [ɑ:ɹmi], *n.* Esercito, *m.* **— corps,** corpo d'armata, *m.*; **— list,** annuario militare, *m.*; **standing —,** esercito permanente, *m.*, **to join the —,** andare soldato.
arnica ['ɑ:ɹnikə], *n.* (*Med.*) Arnica, *f.*
aroma [ə'roumə], *n.* Aroma, profumo, *m.*, fragranza, *f.*
aromatic [ærə'mætik], *a.* Aromatico.
around [ə'raund], *prep.adv.* Intorno, circa, attorno. **All —,** tutto intorno.
arouse [ə'rauz], *v.t.* Svegliare, destare, eccitare, provocare.
arow [ə'rou], *adv.* Di fila, in fila.
arpeggio [ɑ:r'pedʒiou], *n.* (*Mus.*) Arpeggio, *m.* **To play arpeggios,** arpeggiare.
arquebus [cp. **harquebus**].
arrack ['ærək], *n.* Arak, *m.*
arraign [ə'rein], *v.t.* Accusare, citare in giudizio.
arraignment, *n.* Accusa, imputazione, *f.*
arrange [ə'reindʒ], *v.t.* Arrangiare, aggiustare, accomodare, acconciare, assestare, combinare.
arrangement, *n.* Disposizione, *f.*, ordinamento, assestamento, *m.*; (*Mus.*) riduzione, *f.* **To make arrangements with,** combinare con; **to make arrangements for,** prender accordi per.
arrant ['ærənt], *a.* Notorio, insigne, matricolato. **An — rogue,** un birbante matricolato, un arcibriccone, *m.*
arrantly, *adv.* Notoriamente, sfacciatamente.
arras ['ærəs], *n.* Arazzo, *m.*
array [ə'rei], *v.t.* Parare, adornare; disporre, costituire; abbigliare (*of dress*). || *n.* Apparato, addobbo, adornamento, abbigliamento, *m.*; ordine, *f.* **In battle —,** in ordine di battaglia.
arrears [ə'riəɹz], *n.pl.* Arretrati, *m.pl.* **In —,** in arretrato.
arrest [ə'rest], *v.t.* Arrestare, mettere in arresto; fare cessare; (*the attention*) fissare; (*judgement*) sospendere. || *n.* Arresto, *m.*; fermata, *f.*; indugio, ritardo, *m.* **Under —,** in stato d'arresto.
arrester, *n.* (*Elect.*) Scaricatore, *m.*
arris ['æris], *n.* Comignolo, spigolo, *m.*
arrival [ə'raivəl], *n.* Arrivo, *m.*, venuta, *f.* (*Rail.*) **— platform,** marciapede d'arrivo, *m.*; **on the — of,** all'arrivo di.
arrive, *v.i.* Arrivare a, giungere. **To — at a decision,** decidersi, giungere ad una decisione; **to — at a conclusion,** concludere; **to — unexpectedly,** giungere inatteso.

arrogance [ˈærogəns], *n.* Arroganza, burbanza, *f.*
arrogant, *a.* Arrogante, burbanzoso.
arrogantly, *adv.* Arrogantemente.
arrogate [ˈærogeit], *v.t.* Arrogarsi.
arrogation, *n.* Presunzione, *f.*
arrow [ˈærou], *n.* Saetta, freccia, *f.*; (*Poet.*) strale, *m.* **—-head,** punta di freccia, *f.*
arrow-root, *n.* Maranta, *f.*; tubero edule, *m.*
arsenal [ˈɑːɹsənəl], *n.* Arsenale, *m.*
arsenic [ˈɑːɹsnik], *n.* Arsenico, *m.*
arsenical, *a.* Arsenicale.
arsenious, *a.* Arsenioso.
arson [ˈɑːɹsən], *n.* Incendio doloso, *m.*
art, *n.* Arte, *f.*; abilità, *f.*; tecnica, *f.*; accorgimento, *m.* **Fine arts,** belle arti, *f.pl.*; **— school,** scuola d'arte, *f.*; **the black —,** magia, *f.*
arterial [ɑːɹˈtiːriəl], *a.* (*Anat.*) Arteriale, arterioso; **— road,** strada nazionale, *f.*
artery [ˈɑːɹtəri], *n.* (*Anat.*) Arteria, *f.*
artesian [ɑːɹˈtiːʒən], *a.* Artesiano. **— well,** pozzo artesiano, *m.*
artful [ˈɑːɹtful], *a.* Astuto, furbo, accorto, sagace; ingegnoso, scaltro.
artfully, *adv.* Astutamente, artatamente.
artfulness, *n.* Astuzia, accortezza, scaltrezza, *f.*
arthritic [ɑːɹˈθritik], *a.* (*Med.*) Artritico.
arthritis [ɑːɹˈθraitis], *n.* (*Med.*) Artrite, *f.*
artichoke [ˈɑːɹtitʃouk], *n.* Carciofo, *m.* **Jerusalem —,** carciofo di Giudea, *m.*
article [ˈɑːɹtikl], *v.t.* Collocare come commesso di studio. || *n.* Articolo, oggetto, *m.*; merce, *f.*; clausola, *f.*; statuto, *m.* **Leading —,** articolo di fondo, *m.*; **writer of articles,** articolista, *m.*; **articles of war,** codice militare, *m.*; **articles of faith,** articoli di fede, *m.pl.*; **ship's articles,** regole d'equipaggio, *f.pl.*; **articles of association,** statuto di società anonima, *m.*; **definite —,** articolo determinato, *m.*; **articled clerk,** commesso di studio, *m.*
articular [ɑːɹˈtikjuləɹ], *a.* Articolare.
articulate, *v.t.i.* Articolare, pronunziare distintamente; articolarsi, esprimersi. || *a.* Distinto.
articulately, *adv.* Articolatamente, parte a parte.
artifice [ˈɑːɹtifis], *n.* Artificio, artifizio, inganno, stratagemma, *m.*
artificer [ɑːɹˈtifisəɹ], *n.* Artigiano, *m.*
artificial [ɑːɹtiˈfiʃəl], *a.* Artificiale, artifiziale; finto, posticcio. **— hair,** capelli posticci, *m.pl.*
artificiality, *n.* Natura artificiale, *f.*
artificially, *adv.* Artificialmente, in modo posticcio.
artillery [ɑːɹˈtiləri], *n.* Artiglieria, *f.* **Field —,** artiglieria di campagna, *f.*
artilleryman, *n.* Artigliere, *m.*
artisan [ˈɑːɹtizən], *n.* Artigiano, *m.*
artist, artiste [ˈɑːɹtist], *n.* Artista, *m.f.*
artistic, *a.* Artistico.
artistically, *adv.* Artisticamente.
artless [ˈɑːɹtləs], *a.* Ingenuo, naturale, schietto, semplice, innocente.
artlessly, *adv.* Ingenuamente, francamente.
artlessness, *n.* Ingenuità, schiettezza, *f.*
arum [ˈɛərʌm], *n.* (*Bot.*) Aro, *m.*
Aryan [ˈɛəriən], *n.a.* Ariano, *m.*
as [æz], *conj.adv.* Come, siccome, mentre; così . . . come; secondo, da. **As big as,** grande come; **as for,** quanto a; **admirable as he is,** per quanto sia ammirevole; **as she drew near,** mentre essa s'avanzava; **as if,** come se; **as it were,** per così dire; **as much as,** tanto quanto; **as yet,** finora; **be it as it may,** sia come si sia; **as soon as,** tosto che, appena che; **as far as,** fino a, sino a; **as well as possible,** il meglio possibile.
asafoetida [æsəˈfiːtidə], *n.* (*Chem.*) Assafetida, *f.*
asbestos [æsˈbestəs], *n.* Amianto, asbesto, *m.*
ascend [əˈsend], *v.t.i.* Ascendere, salire; innalzarsi. **To — the throne,** ascendere al trono; **to — the scaffold,** salire sul patibolo.
ascendant, *n.* Ascendente, *m.*, superiorità, autorità, *f.*
ascendancy, *n.* Autorità, influenza, superiorità, *f.*; ascendente, *m.*
ascension [əˈsenʃən], *n.* Ascensione, ascesa, salita, *f.* **— Day,** l'Ascensione, *f.*
ascent, *n.* Ascensione, ascesa, salita, *f.*; pendio, *m.*
ascertain [æsəɹˈtein], *v.t.* Accertarsi, assicurarsi, informarsi, appurare.
ascertainment, *n.* Accertamento, *m.*
ascetic [əˈsetik], *n.* Asceta, *m.* || *a.* Ascetico.
asceticism [əˈsetisizm], *n.* Ascetismo.
ascidium (*pl.* **ascidia**), *n.* (*Zool.*) Ascidia, *f.*
ascribable [əˈskraibəbl], *a.* Imputabile, attribuibile.
ascribe, *v.t.* Attribuire, assegnare, ascrivere; imputare.
ascription [əˈskripʃən], *n.* Attribuzione; imputazione, *f.*
aseptic [æˈseptik], *a.* Asettico.
asexual [æˈseksjuəl], *a.* Asessuale.
ash (1) [æʃ], *n.* (*Bot.*) Frassino, *m.* **—-grove,** frassineto, *m.*
ash (2), *n.* Cenere, *f.* **Ashes,** ceneri; **—-bin, —-pit,** bidone, *m.*; **—-tray,** portacenere, *m.*; **—-coloured,** cenerognolo; **Ash Wednesday,** Le Ceneri, *f.pl.*
ashamed [əˈʃeimd], *a.* Vergognoso, confuso. **To be — of,** vergognarsi di.
ashen, ashy, *a.* Colore di cenere, cenerino, cenerognolo.
ashlar [ˈæʃləɹ], *n.* (*Arch.*) Concio, *m.*, pietra di taglio, *f.*
ashore [əˈʃɔːɹ], *adv.* A terra, a secco; arenato. **To run —,** andare a secco, incagliarsi, arenarsi.
ashy [cp. **ashen**].
Asiatic, Asian [eiʃiˈætik, ˈeiʃən], *n.a.* Asiatico, *m.*
aside [əˈsaid], *adv.* A parte, in disparte, da banda. **To set —,** mettere da parte, (*Law*) annullare; **setting that —,** lasciando da parte quello; **to turn —,** *v.t.* stornare, distrarre; *v.i.* deviare; **to step —,** farsi da parte.
asinine [ˈæsinain], *a.* sinino, sciocco.
ask [ɑːsk], *v.t.* Domandare, interrogare; chiedere, pregare, richiedere; invitare. **To — a question,** domandare, fare una domanda; **to — to dine,** invitare a pranzo; **to — in,** pregare di entrare; **to — about,** domandare notizie di.
askance [əˈskæns], *adv.* Obliquamente, di sbieco. **To look — at,** guardare di sbieco, guardare di traverso.

askew [ə'skju:], *adv.* A sghembo, stortamente.
aslant [ə'slɑ:nt], *adv.* Obliquamente.
asleep [ə'sli:p], *a.* Addormentato. **To fall —,** addormentarsi.
aslope [ə'sloup], *adv.* In pendio, in declivio.
asp (1) [æsp], *n.* (*Zool.*) Aspide, aspido, *m.*
asp (2), **aspen,** *n.* (*Bot.*) Gattice, pioppino, *m.*
asparagus [ə'spærəgəs], *n.* Asparago, sparagio, *m.* **— bed,** asparageto, *m.*; sparagiaia, *f.*; **bundle of —,** mazzo di asparagi, *m.*
aspect ['æspekt], *n.* Aspetto, *m.*, vista, faccia, figura, *f.* **To have a northern —,** essere esposto a nord; **to bear the — of,** avere l'aria di.
aspen ['æspən], *n.a.* Tremula, alberella, *f.*; come foglia di tremula.
asperge [ə'spə:ɹdʒ], *v.t.* Aspergere.
asperity [ə'speriti], *n.* Asprezza, asperità, rigidezza, *f.*
asperse [ə'spə:ɹs], *v.t.* Aspergere; calunniare, diffamare. **To — someone's character,** diffamare qualcuno.
aspersion, *n.* Calunnia, *f.*
aspersorium [æspə:ɹ'sɔ:riəm], *n.* (*Eccles.*) Aspersorio, *m.*
asphalt ['æsfælt], *v.t.* Asfaltare. || *n.* Asfalto, *m.* || *a.* Di asfalto, asfaltico.
asphodel ['æsfədəl], *n.* (*Bot.*) Asfodelo, *m.*
asphyxia, asphyxy [æs'fiksiə, æs'fikzi], *n.* Asfissia, *f.*
asphyxiate, *v.t.* Asfissiare.
aspic (1) ['æspik], *n.* Aspic (*jelly*), *m.*
aspic (2), (*Zool.*) Vipera, *f.* [cp. **asp**].
aspirant [ə'spairənt], *n.* Aspirante, *m.f.*, candidato, *m.*
aspirate ['æspəreit], *v.t.* Aspirare. || ['æspərət], *n.a.* Aspirato, *m.*
aspiration, *n.* Aspirazione, *f.*
aspirator, *n.* Aspiratore, *m.*
aspire [ə'spaiɹ], *v.i.* Aspirare a, ambire.
aspiring, *a.* Ambizioso.
asquint [ə'skwint], *adv.* Di sbieco, di traverso.
ass [æs, ɑ:s], *n.* Asino, ciuco, somaro, *m.* **She- —,** asina, *f.*; **— foal,** asinello, *m.*; **to make an — of oneself,** fare delle sciocchezze.
assagai, assegai ['æsəgai], *n.* Zagaglia, *f.*
assail [ə'seil], *v.t.* Assalire, attaccare.
assailable, *a.* Attaccabile.
assailant, *n.* Assalitore, *m.*, assalitrice, *f.*
assassin [ə'sæsin], *n.* Assassino, *m.*
assassinate, *v.t.* Assassinare, ammazzare, uccidere.
assassination, *n.* Assassinio, *m.*
assassinator, *n.* Assassinatore, *m.*
assault [ə'sɔ:lt], *v.t.* Assalire, dare assalto, attaccare. || *n.* Assalto, attacco, *m.*; investimento, *m.*, aggressione, *f.*
assay [ə'sei], *v.t.* Saggiare, assaggiare; tentare. || *n.* Saggio (*of metals*), *m.*; tentativo, *m.*, prova, *f.*
assayer, *n.* Saggiatore, assaggiatore, *m.*
assemblage [ə'sembləd3], *n.* Assemblea, adunanza, *f.*, assembramento, *m.*
assemble [ə'sembl], *v.t.* Radunare, riunire; *v.i.* raccogliersi, radunarsi, riunirsi.
assembly, *n.* Adunanza, assemblea, riunione, *f.* **— room,** sala di riunione, *f.*
assent [ə'sent], *v.i.* Assentire, consentire, dare l'assenso; approvare. || *n.* Assenso, consenso, *m.*, approvazione, *f.*
assert [ə'sə:ɹt], *v.t.* Asserire, dichiarare, sostenere. **To — a right,** rivendicare un diritto.
assertion, *n.* Asserzione, *f.*; rivendicazione, *f.*
assertive, *a.* Assertivo.
assertively, *adv.* Assertivamente.
assertor, *n.* Assertore, *m.*
assess [ə'ses], *v.t.* Tassare, accertare; fissare.
assessable, *a.* Tassabile, valutabile, imponibile.
assessed, *a.* Tassato, valutato.
assessment, *n.* Imposta, tassazione, *f.*
assessor, *n.* Agente delle tasse, *m.*
assets ['æsets], *n.pl.* Attivo, *m.*, attività, *f.pl.*, fondi, *m.pl.* **— and liabilities,** attivo e passivo.
asseverate [ə'sevəreit], *v.t.* Asseverare.
asseveration, *n.* Asseverazione, *f.*
assiduity [æsi'dju:iti], *n.* Assiduità, diligenza, *f.*
assiduous [ə'sidju:əs], *a.* Assiduo.
assiduously, *adv.* Assiduamente.
assign [ə'sain], *v.t.* Assegnare, designare, fissare. || *n.* (*Law*) Erede, *m.*
assignable, *a.* Assegnabile.
assignation, *n.* Assegnazione, attribuzione, *f.*; determinazione, *f.*; appuntamento, *m.*
assignee [æsai'ni:], *n.* Agente, *m.* **Assignees in bankruptcy,** curatori di fallimento, *m.pl.*
assignment, *n.* Assegnazione, *f.* assegno, *m.*, cessione, *f.*
assignor, *n.* Assegnatore, *m.*, assegnatrice, *f.*
assimilable [ə'siməlabl], *a.* Assimilabile, assorbibile.
assimilate [ə'simileit], *v.t.* Assimilare, appropriarsi; *v.i.* assimilarsi, impadronirsi di.
assimilation, *n.* Assimilazione, *f.*
assimilative, *a.* Assimilativo.
assist [ə'sist], *v.t.* Assistere, aiutare, soccorrere.
assistance, *n.* Assistenza, *f.*, aiuto, soccorso, *m.* **To come to someone's —,** venire in soccorso a qualcheduno.
assistant, *n.* Aiuto, assistente, *m.* **Shop —,** commesso di negozio, *m.*; **— master,** assistente, *m.*
assize [ə'saiz], *n.* Assisa, *f.* **Assizes,** corte di assise, *f.*
associable [ə'souʃiəbl], *a.* Associabile.
associate [ə'souʃieit], *v.t.* Associarsi. || *n.* Socio, compagno, *m.* **To — with,** frequentare.
association, *n.* Associazione, *f.*; unione, *f.*; società, *f.*, comizio, consorzio, *m.* **— of ideas,** associazione d'idee, *f.*; **the associations of childhood,** i ricordi della fanciullezza, *m.pl.*; **Association Football,** giuoco del calcio, *m.*
assonance ['æsonəns], *n.* Assonanza, *f.*
assonant, *a.* Assonante.
assort [ə'sɔ:ɹt], *v.t.* Assortire, classificare, scegliere, convenire.
assorted, *a.* Assortito, scelto; misto.
assortment, *n.* Assortimento, *m.*, scelta, *f.*; miscuglio, *m.*
assuage [ə'sweid3], *v.t.* Mitigare, calmare, placare; lenire, addolcire.
assuagement, *n.* Mitigazione, *f.*, addolcimento, sollievo, *m.*
assuasive, *a.* Lenitivo, calmante.
assume [ə'sju:m], *v.t.* Assumere, arrogarsi, impegnarsi. **To — the responsibility,** assumere la responsabilità.

assumable, *a.* Supponibile, assumibile.
assumably, *adv.* Presumibilmente.
assumed, *a.* Assunto. **The author's — name,** il nome di battaglia dell'autore, *m.*; **under an — name,** sotto un nome assunto.
assuming, *a.* Presuntuoso, arrogante.
assumption [ə'sʌmʃən], *n.* Supposizione, congettura, presunzione, *f.*; (*Eccles.*) assunzione, *f.*
assumptive, *a.* Assuntivo.
assurance [ə'ʃuərəns], *n.* Assicurazione, certezza, *f.*; sicurezza, *f.*; impudenza, *f.* **Life —,** assicurazione sulla vita, *f.*
assure [ə'ʃuəɹ], *v.t.* Assicurare, accertare, stabilire. **To rest assured,** essere persuaso.
assuredly, *adv.* Sicuramente.
assuredness, *n.* Certezza, sicurezza, *f.*
assurer, *n.* Assicuratore, *m.*; persuasore, *m.*
Assyrian [ə'siriən], *n.a.* Assiro, *m.*
Assyriologist [æsiri'ɔlədʒist], *n.* Assiriologo, *m.*
astatic [ə'stætik], *a.* Astatico.
aster ['æstəɹ], *n.* (*Bot.*) Astro, *m.*
asterisk ['æstərisk], *n.* Asterisco, *m.*
astern [ə'stəːɹn], *adv.* (*Naut.*) A poppa, indietro. **To go —,** indietreggiare.
asteroid ['æstərɔid], *n.* (*Astron.*) Asteroide, *m.*
asthenia [æs'θiːniə], *n.* (*Med.*) Astenia, *f.*
asthenic, *a.* Debole.
asthma ['æsmə], *n.* (*Med.*) Asma, *f.*
asthmatic, *a.* Asmatico.
astigmatic [æstig'mætik], *a.* Astigmatico.
astigmatism, *n.* Astigmatismo, *m.*
astir [ə'stəːɹ], *adv.* Agitato, in moto, in piedi.
astonish [ə'stɔniʃ], *v.t.* Sorprendere, colpire di meraviglia, sbalordire. **To be astonished at,** meravigliarsi di.
astonished, *a.* Attonito, stupito, sorpreso.
astonishing, *a.* Sorprendente, meraviglioso.
astonishingly, *adv.* Sorprendentemente, straordinariamente.
astonishment, *n.* Sorpresa, meraviglia, *f.* **To strike with —,** colpire di meraviglia.
astound [ə'staund], *v.t.* Sbalordire, stupefare.
astounded, *a.* Attonito, stupefatto.
astounding, *a.* Incredibile, straordinario.
astraddle, astride [ə'strædl, ə'straid], *adv.* Cavalcione, cavalcioni, a cavalcione.
astragal ['æstrəgəl], *n.* Astragalo, *m.*
astrakhan [æstrə'kæn], *n.* Astracan, *m.*
astral ['æstrəl], *a.* Astrale.
astray [ə'strei], *adv.* Fuori di strada, fuori via; traviato. **To go —,** perdersi, andar smarrito, smarrirsi; **to lead —,** sviare, traviare.
astriction [ə'strikʃən], *n.* Costrizione, *f.*
astride [cp. **astraddle**].
astringency [ə'strindʒənsi], *n.* Severità, austerità, *f.*; qualità astringente, *f.*
astringent, *n.a.* Astringente, *m.*
astrolabe ['æstrouleib], *n.* Astrolabio, *m.*
astrologer [ə'strɔlədʒəɹ], *n.* Astrologo, *m.*
astrologic, astrological [æstrə'lɔdʒik, æstrə'lɔdʒikəl], *a.* Astrologico.
astrologically, *adv.* Astrologicamente.
astrology, *n.* Astrologia, *f.*
astronaut ['æstrənɔːt], *n.* Astronauta, *m.*
astronautics [æstrə'nɔːtiks], *n.pl.* Astronautica, *f.*
astronomer [ə'strɔnəməɹ], *n.* Astronomo, *m.*
astronomic, astronomical, *a.* Astronomico.
astronomically, *adv.* Astronomicamente.
astronomy, *n.* Astronomia, *f.*
astrophysics [æstrə'fiziks], *n.pl.* Astrofisica, *f.*
astute [ə'stjuːt], *a.* Astuto, furbo, sagace.
astutely, *adv.* Astutamente, con astuzia.
astuteness, *n.* Astutezza, astuzia, *f.*
asunder [ə'sʌndəɹ], *adv.* Disgiunto, separato. **To tear —,** squarciare.
asylum [ə'sailəm], *n.* Asilo, rifugio, ricovero, *m.* **Right of —,** diritto d'asilo, *m.*; **lunatic —,** manicomio, *m.*; **orphan —,** orfanotrofio, *m.*
asymmetrical [æsi'metrikəl], *a.* Asimmetrico.
asymptote ['æsimtout], *n.* (*Geom.*) Asintote, *f.*, asintoto, *m.*
at [æt], *prep.* A, in, presso, da, contro, in casa di, su. **At midday,** a mezzodì; **at least,** almeno; **at the same time,** allo stesso tempo; **at Milan,** a Milano; **at home,** a casa; **at church,** in chiesa; **at peace,** in pace; **at last,** in fine; **at the top,** in alto; **at Mrs.X's,** presso la Signora X; **at my brother's,** da mio fratello; **at first,** dapprima; **at hand,** a portata di mano; **at once,** subito; **to be hard at it,** lavorare accanitamente; **What are you at ?** Che cosa fate ? **not at all,** niente affatto; **at length,** finalmente; **at sea,** sul mare, in mare.
atavism ['ætəvizm], *n.* Atavismo, *m.*
atavistic, *a.* Atavistico.
ataxy [ə'tæksi], *n.* (*Med.*) Atassia, *f.* **Locomotor —,** atassia locomotrice, *f.*
ate [et], *past indic.* of **eat.**
atheism ['eiθiizm], *n.* Ateismo, *m.*
atheist, *n.* Ateo, *m.*
atheistic, atheistical, *a.* Ateistico.
atheistically, *adv.* Come un ateo.
Athenaeum [æθə'niːəm], *n.* Ateneo, *m.*
Athens ['æθənz], *n.* (*Geog.*) Atene, *f.*
athirst [ə'θəːɹst], *adv.* Assetato, sitibondo; avido.
athlete ['æθliːt], *n.* Atleta, *m.*
athletic, *a.* Atletico. **— sports,** riunione sportiva, *f.*
athletics, *n.pl.* Atletica, *f.*
at home [ət 'houm], *adv.* A casa. **— — day,** giorno di ricevimento, *m.*
athwart [ə'θwɔːɹt], *adv.* Obliquamente, di traverso.
a-tilt [ə'tilt], *adv.* In resta. **To run — at,** correre colla lancia in resta.
Atlantic [æt'læntik], *a.* (*Geog.*) Atlantico. **— Ocean,** l'oceano Atlantico, l'Atlantico, *m.*; **— liner,** transatlantico, *m.*
atlas ['ætləs], *n.* Atlante, *m.* (*in all senses*).
atmosphere ['ætməsfiəɹ], *n.* Atmosfera, *f.*
atmospheric, atmospherical, *a.* Atmosferico.
atmospherics, *n.* (*Radio*) Disturbi atmosferici, *m.pl.*
atoll ['ætɔl], *n.* Atollo, *m.*
atom ['ætəm], *n.* Atomo, *m.* **— bomb,** bomba atomica, *f.*; **to split the —,** disintegrare l'atomo.
atomic, atomical, *a.* Atomico.
atomicity, *n.* Atomicità, *f.*
atomizer, *n.* Vaporizzatore, polverizzatore, *m.*
atone [ə'toun], *v.t.i.* Espiare, fare ammenda. **To — for one's sins,** espiare i propri peccati.
atonement, *n.* Espiazione, *f.*
atonic [ə'tɔnik], *a.* (*Gram.*) Atono.
atop [ə'tɔp], *adv.* In cima.
atrabiliar, atrabilious [ætrə'biliəɹ, ætrə'biliəs], *a.* Atrabiliare, atrabiliario.

atrip [ə'trip], *adv.* Saltellante; (*Naut.*) ancora spedata.
atrium ['ætriəm], *n.* Atrio, *m.*
atrocious [ə'trouʃəs], *a.* Atroce.
atrociously, *adv.* Atrocemente.
atrociousness, atrocity, *n.* Atrocità, *f.*
atrophy ['ætrəfi], *v.t.i.* Atrofizzare, atrofizzarsi. || *n.* Atrofia, *f.*
atropine ['ætrəpin], *n.* (*Chem.*) Atropina, *f.*
attach [ə'tætʃ], *v.t.* Attaccare, legare, stringere, congiungere; affezionare; (*Law*) sequestrare. **He is very attached to his mother,** ama moltissimo la mamma; **to — importance to,** dare importanza a.
attachable, *a.* Attaccabile; sequestrabile.
attaché (ə'tæʃei], *n.* Addetto, *m.* **— case,** valigetta, *f.*
attachment, *n.* Attaccamento, *m.*, unione; affezione, *f.*; (*Law*) sequestro, *m.*
attack [ə'tæk], *v.t.* Attaccare, assalire, investire; (*Med.*) comunicarsi, attaccarsi. || *n.* Assalto, attacco, *m.*; (*of illness*) accesso, *m.*
attackable, *a.* Attaccabile.
attain [ə'tein], *v.t.* Pervenire a, raggiungere, conseguire, ottenere. **To — one's ends,** ottenere l'intento; **he has attained to the age of eighty,** ha compito gli ottant'anni.
attainable, *a.* Raggiungibile, conseguibile.
attainder, *n.* Proscrizione, confisca di beni, *f.*
attainment, *n.* Raggiungimento, acquisto, *m.*, acquisizione, *f.* **Attainments,** cognizioni, doti, *f.pl.*, talenti, *m.pl.*
attaint [ə'teint], *v.t.* Condannare, proscrivere, privare dei diritti civili.
attar ['ætɑːɹ], *n.* Essenza, *f.* **— of roses,** essenza di rose, *f.*
attemper [ə'tempəɹ], *v.t.* Temprare, moderare.
attempt [ə'tempt], *v.t.* Tentare di, cercare di, provare a, attentare a. || *n.* Tentativo, *m.*, prova, *f.*; attentato, attacco, *m.* **To — impossibilities,** tentare l'impossibile; **to — someone's life,** attentare alla vita di qualcuno; **to make an —,** tentare di fare; **to make every possible —,** tentare il tentabile.
attemptable, *a.* Tentabile.
attend [ə'tend], *v.t.* Accompagnare; assistere (*an invalid*), frequentare (*lectures, etc.*); *v.i.* attendere, occuparsi di, assistere a, partecipare a, ascoltare, prestare attenzione. **To — on,** servire; **Please —!** Favorisca ascoltare! **to — to one's business,** occuparsi dei propri affari.
attendance, *n.* Servizio, assistenza. **— included,** compreso il servizio; **to dance —,** far anticamera.
attendant, *n.* Servo, compagno, satellite, *m.* **Attendants,** seguito personale, *m.*, seguaci, *m. pl.*; **medical —,** medico di servizio, *m.*
attention [ə'tenʃən], *n.* Attenzione, cura, diligenza, *f.*, servizio, *m.* **All —,** tutto orecchi; **to call —,** mostrare, fare notare; **to pay —,** ascoltare, stare attento, badare; (*Mil.*) **Attention !, 'Shun !** Attenti!
attentive, *a.* Attento, intento; gentile, assiduo.
attentively, *adv.* Attentamente.
attentiveness, *n.* Attenzione, gentilezza, *f.*
attenuate [ə'tenjuːeit], *v.t.* Attenuare, assottigliare, scemare, dimagrare.
attenuated, *a.* Attenuato, magro; rarefatto (*of vapours*).
attenuation, *n.* Attenuamento, assottigliamento, *m.*
attest [ə'test], *v.t.* Attestare, certificare, affermare.
attestation, *n.* Attestazione, testimonianza, *f.*
attestor, *n.* Attestatore, *m.*
attic ['ætik], *n.* Soffitta, *f.*, solaio, abbaino, *m.*
attire [ə'taiɹ], *v.t.* Vestire, parare, abbigliare. || *n.* Vestito, vestimento, *m.*, abiti, *m.pl.*
attitude ['ætɪtjuːd], *n.* Atteggiamento, *m.*; posa, *f.*; posizione, *f.*
attitudinize [æti'tjuːdinaiz], *v.i.* Atteggiarsi, posare.
attorney [ə'təːɹni], *n.* Procuratore, avvocato, *m.* **Power of —,** mandato di procura, *m.*
attract [ə'trækt], *v.t.* Attrarre, attirare; cattivarsi.
attractable, *a.* Attirabile.
attractingly, *adv.* Attrattivamente.
attraction, *n.* Attrazione, attrattiva, seduzione, *f.*, fascino, *m.*
attractive, *a.* Attraente, seducente.
attractively, *adv.* Attraentemente.
attractiveness, *n.* Attrattiva, *f.*, fascino, *m.*
attributable [ə'tribjutəbl], *a.* Attribuibile, imputabile.
attribute, *v.t.* Attribuire, imputare, ascrivere, assegnare. || *n.* Attributo, *m.*; qualità, *f.*
attribution, *n.* Attribuzione, *f.*
attributive, *a.* Attributivo.
attributively, *adv.* (*Gram.*) Aggettivamente.
attrite [ə'trait], *a.* (*Eccles.*) Contrito.
attrition [ə'triʃən], *n.* Attrizione, *f.*, tritamento, logoramento, *m.*
attune [ə'tjuːn], *v.t.* Accordare, mettere d'accordo, intonare.
auburn ['ɔːbəɹn], *a.* Color castagno, castagno chiaro.
auction ['ɔːkʃən], *v.t.* Vendere all'incanto, vendere all'asta pubblica. || *n.* Incanto, *m.*, asta, vendita all'asta, *f.* **— room,** sala di vendite all'asta, *f.*
auctioneer [ɔːkʃə'niəɹ], *n.* Venditore all'asta, banditore, *m.*
audacious [ɔː'deiʃəs], *a.* Audace; arrischiato.
audaciously, *adv.* Audacemente.
audacity, audaciousness, *n.* Audacia, *f.*
audibility, audibleness, *n.* Intelligibilità, *f.*
audible ['ɔːdəbl], *a.* Udibile, intelligibile. **He was scarcely —,** appena si poteva udirlo.
audibly, *adv.* Ad alta voce, intelligibilmente.
audience ['ɔːdiəns], *n.* Udienza, *f.*; uditorio (*persons*), *m.*
audiometer [ɔːdi'ɔmətəɹ], *n.* Audiometro, *m.*
audit ['ɔːdit], *v.t.* Controllare, verificare, rivedere i conti. || *n.* Revisione dei conti, *f.*, riscontro, *m.*, verifica, *f.*
auditing, *n.* Verifica, revisione, *f.*, riscontro, *m.*
audition, *n.* Audizione, udienza, udizione, *f.*
auditor, *n.* Ascoltatore, *m.*; (*Comm.*) revisore, *m.*
auditorium, *n.* Auditorio, *m.*, sala dei concerti, *f.*
Augean [ɔː'dʒiːən], *a.* Di Augia. **The — stables,** le stalle d'Augia, *f.pl.*
auger ['ɔːgəɹ], *n.* Succhiello, *m.*, trivella, *f.*
aught [ɔːt], *n.* Qualche cosa. **For — I know,** per quanto io sappia.
augment [ɔːg'ment], *v.t.* Aumentare ingrandire; *v.i.* aumentarsi, crescere.
augmentation, *n.* Aumento, *m.*

augmentative, *a.* Aumentativo.
augur [ˈɔ:gəɹ], *v.t.i.* Augurare, predire, presagire, pronosticare. || *n.* Augure, *m.*
augury [ˈɔ:gju:ri], *n.* Augurio, *m.*, **Of good —,** di buono augurio.
August [ˈɔ:gəst], *n.* Agosto, *m.*
august [ɔ:ˈgʌst], *a.* Augusto.
Augustan, *a.* Augusteo. **The — age,** l'età augustea, *f.*
Augustine [ɔ:ˈgʌstin], *n.* Agostino, *m.*
auk [ɔ:k], *n.* (*Zool.*) Alca, *f.*
Aulic [ˈɔ:lik], *a.* Aulico.
aunt [ɑ:nt], *n.* Zia, *f.* **Great-aunt,** prozia, *f.*; **Aunt Sally** (a game), testa di Turco, *f.*
aura [ˈɔ:rə], *n.* Aura, *f.*
aural, *a.* Dell'orecchio. **— surgeon,** otoiatra, *m.*
aureate [ˈɔ:rieit], *a.* Aureo, d'oro.
aureole [ˈɔ:rioul], *n.* Aureola, *f.*
aureomycin [ɔ:roˈmaisin], *n.* (*Med.*) Aureomicina, *f.*
auricle [ˈɔ:rikl], *n.* (*Anat.*) Padiglione dell'orecchio, *m.*; orecchietta (*of heart*), *f.*
auricula [ɔ:ˈrikju:ləɹ], *n.* (*Bot.*) Orecchio d'orso, *m.*
auricular, *a.* Auricolare; verbale.
auriferous [ɔ:ˈrifərəs], *a.* Aurifero.
aurist [ˈɔ:rist], *n.* Otoiatra, *m.*
aurora [ɔ:ˈrɔ:rə], *n.* Aurora, *f.* **— borealis,** aurora boreale, *f.*
auroral, *a.* Aurorale.
auscultation [ɔ:skʌlˈteiʃən], (*Med.*) *n.* Ascoltazione, *f.*
auspice [ˈɔ:spis], *n.* Auspicio, auspice, *m.* **Under the auspices of,** sotto gli auspici di.
auspicious, *a.* Auspicale, di buon augurio.
auspiciously, *adv.* Auspicatamente.
auspiciousness, *n.* Buon augurio, *m.*
austere [ɔ:sˈtiəɹ], *a.* Austero, rigido.
austerely, *adv.* Austeramente.
austereness, austerity, *n.* Austerità, severità, *f.*; rigore, *m.*
austral [ˈɔ:strəl], *a.* Australe.
Australian [ɔ:sˈtreiliən], *n.a.* Australiano, *m.*
Austrian [ˈɔ:striən], *n.a.* Austriaco, *m.*
authentic [ɔ:ˈθentik], *a.* Autentico.
authentically, *adv.* Autenticamente.
authenticate, *v.t.* Autenticare, convalidare, constatare.
authentication, *n.* Autenticazione, *f.*
authenticity [ɔ:θenˈtisiti], *n.* Autenticità, *f.*
author [ˈɔ:θəɹ], *n.* Autore, *m.* **Authoress,** autrice, *f.*
authoritative [ɔ:ˈθɔritətiv], *a.* Autorevole.
authoritatively, *adv.* Autorevolmente.
authoritativeness, *n.* Autorità, autorevolezza. *f.*
authority, *n.* Autorità, *f.* **On good —,** da buona fonte; **on his own —,** di propria autorità; **the authorities,** le autorità, *f.pl.*; il governo, *m.*
authorization [ɔ:θəraiˈzeiʃən], *n.* Autorizzazione, *f.*
authorize, *v.t.* Autorizzare.
authorship [ˈɔ:θəɹʃip], *n.* Professione d'autore, *f.*, paternità (*of a book*), *f.* **The — of this book is unknown,** l'autore di questo libro è sconosciuto.
autobiographic, autobiographical [ɔ:tobaiəˈgræfik], *a.* Autobiografico.
autobiography, *n.* Autobiografia, *f.*
autocar [ˈɔ:toukɑ:ɹ], *n.* Automobile, auto, *m.f.*
autochthon (*pl.* **autochthones**) [ɔ:ˈtɔkθən], *n.* Autoctono, *m.*
autocracy [ɔ:ˈtɔkrəsi], *n.* Autocrazia, *f.*
autocrat, *n.* Autocrata, autocrate, *m.*
autocratic, *a.* Autocratico.
autocratically, *adv.* Autocraticamente.
autograph [ˈɔ:togræf], *v.t.* Autografare. || *n.* Autografo, *m.*
autographic, autographical, *a.* Autografico.
autography, *n.* Autografia, *f.*
autogyro [ɔ:toˈdʒairou], *n.* (*Aviat.*) Autogiro, *m.*
automatic, automatical [ɔ:toˈmætik, ɔ:toˈmætikəl], *a.* Automatico. **— machine,** distributore automatico, *m.*
automatically, *adv.* Automaticamente.
automation [ɔ:toˈmeiʃən], *n.* Automazione, *f.*
automaton (*pl.* **automata**) [ɔ:ˈtɔmətən, ɔ:ˈtɔmətə], *n.* Automa, *m.*
automobile [ɔ:təmoˈbi:l], *n.* Automobile, auto, *m.f.*
automobilist, *n.* Automobilista, *m.*
autonomous [ɔ:ˈtɔnəməs], *a.* Autonomo.
autonomy, *n.* Autonomia, *f.*
autopsy [ˈɔ:tɔpsi], *n.* Autopsia, *f.*
autumn [ˈɔ:təm], *n.* Autunno, *m.*
autumnal [ɔ:ˈtʌmnəl], *a.* Autunnale, di autunno.
auxiliary [ɔ:kˈziliəri], *n.a.* Ausiliare, ausiliario, *m.*
avail [əˈveil], *v.i.* Valersi, servirsi, giovare; *v.t.* avvantaggiare, servire. || *n.* Vantaggio, profitto, effetto, *m.*, efficacia, *f.* **To — oneself of,** avvantaggiarsi di; **of no —,** inutile, vano; **without —,** senza risultato; **to little —,** senza molto risultato, con scarso effetto.
available, *a.* Disponibile, utile, efficace.
availableness, availability, *n.* Disponibilità, accessibilità, *f.*
availably, *adv.* Utilmente, efficacemente.
avalanche [ˈævəlɑ:nʃ], *n.* Valanga, *f.*
avarice [ˈævərəs], *n.* Avarizia, taccagneria, *f.*
avaricious, *a.* Avaro, avido, taccagno, tirchio.
avariciously, *adv.* Avaramente, avidamente.
avast! [əˈvɑ:st], *inter.* (*Naut.*) Basta!
avatar [ˈævətəɹ], *n.* Incarnazione; fase, *f.*
avaunt! [əˈvɔ:nt], (*obs.*) Andatevene! Vattene!
avenaceous [ævəˈneiʃəs], *a.* (*Bot.*) Di avena, simile ad avena.
avenge [əˈvendʒ], *v.t.* Vendicare.
avenger, *n.* Vendicatore, *m.*, vendicatrice, *f.*
avenging, *a.* Vendicatore.
avenue [ˈævənju:], *n.* Viale; (*fig.*) accesso.
aver [əˈvə:ɹ], *v.t.* Affermare, sostenere.
average [ˈævərədʒ], *v.t.* Calcolare in media, prendere il mezzo termine. || *n.* Media, *f.*; (*Naut.*) avaria, *f.* || *a.* Medio, comune. **Above the —,** sopra la media; **on an —,** in media; **— value,** valore medio, *m.*; **— velocity,** velocità media, *f.*
averment [əˈvə:ɹmənt], *n.* Affermazione, *f.*
averse [əˈvə:ɹs], *a.* Avverso, contrario, nemico. **To be — to,** essere avverso a; **I am not averse to it,** non ho nulla in contrario.
aversely, *adv.* Avversamente.
averseness, aversion, *n.* Avversione, antipatia, *f.* **My pet aversion,** la mia antipatia, *f.*; **to take an aversion to,** prendere in avversione.
avert [əˈvə:ɹt], *v.t.* Sviare, stornare, allontanare, rimuovere.

aviary [ˈeiviəri], *n.* Uccelliera, *f.*
aviation [eiviˈeiʃən], *n.* Aviazione, *f.* — **ground,** campo d'aviazione, *m.*
aviator, *n.* Aviatore, *m.*, aviatrice, *f.*
avid [ˈævid], *a.* Avido.
avidity, *n.* Avidità, brama, *f.*
avocation [ævoˈkeiʃən], *n.* Avocazione, occupazione, *f.*, mestiere, *m.*
avoid [əˈvɔid], *v.t.* Evitare, schivare, scansare.
avoidable, *a.* Evitabile.
avoidance, *n.* L'evitare, lo scansare, *m.*; (*Law*) annullamento, *m.*
avoirdupois [ævəɹdjuːˈpɔiz], *n.* Peso inglese, *m.*
avouch [əˈvautʃ], *v.t.* Affermare, dichiarare.
avow [əˈvau], *v.t.* Confessare, dichiarare.
avowal, *n.* Dichiarazione, confessione, *f.*
avowedly, *adv.* Apertamente.
avulsion [əˈvʌlʃən], *n.* Strappamento, *m.*, avulsione, *f.*
await [əˈweit], *v.t.* Aspettare, attendere.
awake [əˈweik], *v.t.* Destare, svegliare; *v.i.* destarsi, svegliarsi. || *a.* Desto.
awaken, *v.t.* Destare, svegliare.
awakening, *n.* Sveglia, *f.*, risveglio, *m.* **A rude —,** un risveglio di soprassalto, *m.*
award [əˈwɔːɹd], *v.t.* Assegnare, aggiudicare. || *n.* Sentenza, *f.*; giudizio, *m.*; premio, *m.* **— a medal,** assegnare una medaglia; **to — a prize to,** premiare con.
aware [əˈwɛəɹ], *a.* Conscio, consapevole. **To be — of,** sapere, essere conscio di; **not to be aware of,** ignorare.
away [əˈwei], *adv.* Via, fuori; assente; lontano. **He has gone —,** è andato via; **to send —,** mandar via; **to take —,** portar via; **Away with you !** Via ! Va via ! **Right — !** Partenza !
awe [ɔː], *n.* Rispetto, *m.*, riverenza, *f.*; timore, *m.* **To strike with —,** intimorire, imporre rispetto; **to stand in — of,** avere timore di.
awestruck, *a.* Intimorito.
aweather [əˈweðəɹ], *adv.* (*Naut.*) Sopravvento.
aweigh [əˈwei], *adv.* (*Naut.*) A piombo (*of an anchor*).
awful [ˈɔːfəl], *a.* Terribile, impressionante, solenne.
awfully, *adv.* Terribilmente, orribilmente; (*colloq.*) molto.
awhile [əˈwail], *adv.* Qualche tempo, un pezzo. **Wait — !,** Aspettate un momento !
awkward [ˈɔːkwəɹd], *a.* Goffo, impacciato, balordo; difficile. **An — question,** una domanda imbarazzante; **the — age,** l'età ingrata.
awkwardly, *adv.* Goffamente, male a proposito.
awkwardness, *n.* Goffaggine, balordaggine, *f.*; difficoltà, *f.*, imbarazzo, *m.*
awl [ɔːl], *n.* Lesina, *f.*
awn [ɔːn], *n.* (*Bot.*) Arista, *f.*
awning, *n.* Tenda, *f.*
awry [əˈrai], *adv.a.* Obliquamente, di sbieco, storto.
axe [æks], *n.* Ascia, scure, accetta, *f.*
axil [ˈæksil], *n.* (*Bot.*) Ascella, *f.*
axiom [ˈækziəm], *n.* Assioma, *m.*
axiomatic, *a.* Assiomatico.
axis (*pl.* **axes**) [ˈæksis, ˈæksiːz], *n.* Asse, *m.*
axle [æksl], *n.* Asse, perno, albero, *m.* **— tree,** asse della ruota, *m.*
ay, aye [ai], *inter.* Sì, sì sì; sì bene, certo, certamente.
aye, *adv.* Sempre. **For ever and —,** per sempre.
azalea [əˈzeiliə], *n.* (*Bot.*) Azalea, *f.*
azimuth [ˈæziməθ], *n.* (*Astron.*) Azimut, *m.*
Azores [əˈzɔːɹz], *n.pl.* (*Geog.*) Le Azzorre, *f.pl.*
azotic [əˈzɔtik], *a.* (*Chem.*) Azotico.
azure [ˈæʒəɹ], *n.a.* Azzurro, *m.*
azyme [ˈæzim], *n.* (*Eccles.*) Azzimella, *f.*; azzimo, *m.*

B

B, b [biː]. Seconda lettera dell'alfabeto inglese; (*Mus.*) si, *m.*
baa [bɑː], *v.i.* Belare. || *n.* Belamento, *m.*
babble [bæbl], *v.i.* Balbettare, chiacchierare; mormorare (*of water*). || *n.* Balbettamento, *m.*, ciarla, *f.*; mormorio, *m.*
babbler, *n.* Ciarlone, *m.*, ciarlona, *f.*; chiacchierone, *m.*
babbling, *a.* Balbettante.
babe [beib], *n.* Bambino, *m.*, bambina, *f.*
Babel [ˈbeibəl], *n.* Babele, frastuono, *m.*; confusione, *f.*
baboon [bəˈbuːn], *n.* Babbuino, *m.*
baby [ˈbeibi], *n.* Bambino, fanciullo, neonato, piccino, *m.* **Baby brother,** fratellino, *m.*; **— carriage,** carrozzino, *m.*; **— clothes,** fasce, *f.pl.*; **— linen,** pannolini, *m.pl.*; **baby's nappy,** pannicello, *m.*; (*Motor.*) **— car,** topolino, *m.*; **— grand** (*piano*), pianoforte a mezzacoda, *m.*
babyhood, *n.* Infanzia, infantilità, *f.*
babyish, *a.* Infantile, bambinesco.
Babylon [ˈbæbilən], *n.* Babilonia, *f.*
Babylonian, *a.* Babilonese.
baccalaureate [bækəˈlɔːriət], *n.* Diploma, *m.*, laurea, *f.*
baccarat [ˈbækərɑː], *n.* Baccarà, *m.*
bachanal [ˈbækənəl], *a.* Bacchico.
bachanalia [bækəˈneiliə], *n.* Baccanali, *m.pl.*
bachanalian. bacchic, *a.* Bacchico.
bachelor [ˈbætʃələɹ], *n.* Celibe, scapolo, *m.*; baccelliere (*of Arts, etc.*), *m.*
bachelorhood, *n.* Celibato, *m.*
bacillus (*pl.* **bacilli**) [bəˈsiləs], *n.* Bacillo, *m.*
back [bæk], *n.* Dorso, dosso, *m.*, schiena, *f.*, reni, *f.pl.*; tergo, *m.*; (*Football*) terzino, *m.* || *adv.* Dietro, indietro, addietro; di ritorno. || *v.t.* Appoggiare, secondare, sostenere; controfirmare; (*betting*) scommettere; *v.i.* andare indietro, rinculare. **Behind one's —,** dietro le spalle; **to break the — of,** rompere la schiena di; **to fall on one's —,** cadere all'indietro; **to turn one's — on,** volgere il dorso a; **there and —,** andata e ritorno; **to call a person —,** richiamare una persona; **to expect a person —,** aspettare il ritorno di una persona; **seat with — to the engine,** posto di spalle alla macchina; **— -bone,** spina dorsale, *f.*; (*fig.*) forza, energia, *f.*; fermezza, decisione, *f.*; **— -chat,** impertinenza, *m.*; **— -door,** porta di servizio, porta posteriore, *f.*; porta riservata, *f.*; **— -fire,** ritorno di fiamma, *m.*; **— -hand,** scrittura rovesciata, *f.* (*Tennis*) **— -hander,** colpo di rovescio, *m.*, **— -number,** numero arretrato, *m.*, (*fig.*) di moda passata, antiquato; **— -pedal,** contropedalare; **— -room,** retro-

camera, retrostanza, *f.*; — **-sight,** alzo, *m.*, tacca di mira, *f.*; (*Naut.*) — **-stays,** paterazzi, paterassi, *m.pl.*; — **-stitch,** *n.* punto indietro, *m.*; — **-stroke,** colpo all'indietro, *m.*; — **-water,** riserva d'acqua, acqua fuori della corrente, *f.*

backbite, *v.t.i.* Sparlare di, diffamare.

backbiting, *n.* Diffamazione, denigrazione, *f.*

backer, *n.* Partigiano, protettore, *m.*; (*betting*) scommettitore, *m.*

backgammon, *n.* Tavola reale, *f.*; trictrac, *m.*

background, *n.* Sfondo, *m.*; (*fig.*) ambiente, retroscena, fondo, *m.*

backing, *n.* Sostegno, rinforzo, *m.*; (*going backwards*) ritirata, *f.*

backlash, *n.* Contraccolpo, rinculo, *m.*

backside, *n.* Parte posteriore, *f.*, deretano, *m.*

backslide, *v.i.* Apostatare, ricadere.

backslider, *n.* Recidivo, apostata, *m.*

backsliding, *n.* Ricaduta, recidiva, *f.*

backstairs, *n.pl.* Scala di servizio, scala privata, *f.*

backward, *a.* Tardivo, retrogrado, arretrato.

backwards, *adv.* Indietro, addietro, a ritroso, al rovescio. — **and forwards,** avanti e indietro.

backwardness, *n.* Tardezza, lentezza, *f.*, stato arretrato, *m.*; arretratezza, *f.*

backwash, *n.* Risacca, *f.*

backwater, *n.* Scia, *f.*; risucchio, *m.*

backwoods, *n.pl.* Foreste vergini, *f.pl.*

backwoodsman, *n.* Uomo delle foreste, *m.*

bacon [beikən], *n.* Lardo, *m.* **To save one's —,** (*vulg.*) salvare la pelle.

bacteria [bæk'tiəriə], *n.pl.* Batteri, *m.pl.*

bacterial, *a.* Batterico.

bacteriologist [bæktiəri'ɔlədʒist], *n.* Batteriologo, *m.*

bacteriology, *n.* Batteriologia, *f.*

bacterium, *n.* Batterio, *m.*

bad [bæd], *a.* Cattivo, malo, reo; guasto; scorretto; nocivo; brutto, grosso. || *n.* Male, *m.* **A — cold,** un brutto raffreddore; **a — egg,** un uovo guasto; — **for the health,** nocivo alla salute; **a — job,** un brutto affare, *m.*; **this meat has gone —,** questa carne è guasta; — **debt,** credito inesigibile, *m.*; — **language,** parole grossolane, *f.pl.*; **to feel —,** sentirsi male; **It's too —!** È insopportabile! **to go from — to worse,** andare di male in peggio; **to go to the —,** andare in rovina.

baddish, *a.* Piuttosto cattivo.

bade, *past indic.* of **bid.**

badge [bædʒ], *n.* Distintivo, *m.*, insegna, *f.*; emblema, *m.*, livrea, *f.* || *v.t.* Apporre un distintivo.

badger ['bædʒəɹ], *n.* (*Zool.*) Tasso, *m.* || *v.t.* Annoiare, tormentare, stuzzicare.

badinage [bædi'nɑːdʒ], *n.* Scherzo, *m.*, facezia, *f.*

badly, *adv.* Male, gravemente, malamente, nocivamente. **To behave —,** comportarsi male; **to turn out —,** volgere a male; **to need something —,** avere urgente bisogno di qualche cosa; **to be — off,** essere povero, star male a quattrini.

badness, *n.* Cattiveria. *f.*; cattiva qualità, imperfezione, *f.*; malvagità, *f.*; debolezza, *f.*

baffle ['bæfəl], *v.t.* Sconcertare, frustrare; ingannare. || *n.* Parafiamme, *m.*; (*Radio*) schermo acustico, *m.*

baffling, *a.* Sconcertante, frustrante; variabile (*of wind*).

bag [bæg], *v.t.* Insaccare, imborsare; (*colloq.*) sgraffignare, prendere; *v.i.* gonfiarsi. || *n.* Sacco, sacchetto, *m.*, borsa, saccoccia, tasca, *f.*; (*of game*) selvaggina. — **and baggage,** con armi e bagagli; (*colloq.*) **bags,** calzoni, *m.pl.*; **travelling- —,** sacco da viaggio, *m.*; valigia, *f.*; (*colloq.*) **the whole — of tricks,** tutta la batteria.

bagatelle [bægə'tel], *n.* Inezia, *f.*; (*game*) bagattella, *f.*

bagful, *n.* Saccata, *f.*

baggage ['bægədʒ], *n.* Bagaglio, *m.*; (*fig.*) briccona, impertinente, *f.* **A saucy —,** una ragazzaccia, *f.*

bagginess, *n.* Gonfiezza, *f.*

baggy, *a.* Gonfio.

bagpipes, *n.pl.* (*Mus.*) Cornamusa, piva, zampogna, *f.*

bail (1) [beil], *v.t.* Prestare cauzione. || *n.* Cauzione, garanzia, sicurtà, *f.* **To release on —,** rilasciare sotto cauzione; **to go —,** versare cauzione; **bailsman,** garante, mallevadore.

bail (2), *v.t.* Vuotare; aggottare, sgottare; (*Aviat.*) lanciarsi col paracadute.

bailer, *n.* Sessola, gottazza, votazza, *f.*

bailiff, *n.* Usciere addetto ad un tribunale, *m.*, ufficiale giudiziario, *m.*; agente, fattore, *m.*

bailment, *n.* Consegna, libertà, *f.*

bain-marie [bɛ̃ mariː], *n.* Bagnomaria, *m.*

bairn [bɛəɹn], *n.* Bambino, *m.*, bambina, *f.*

bait [beit], *v.t.* Inescare, adescare; tormentare, irritare; rinfrescare (*horses, etc.*) || *n.* Esca, *f.*; ristoro, *m.*, sosta, *f.*

baize [beiz], *n.* Saia, sargia, baietta, *f.* — **door,** porta foderata, *f.*

bake [beik], *v.t.i.* Cuocere al forno, infornare; cuocersi.

bakehouse, *n.* Forno, *m.*; panificio, *m.*

baker, *n.* Fornaio, panettiere, *m.*

bakery, *n.* Forno, panificio, *m.*

baking, *n.* Cottura, *f.*; infornata, *f.* — **-powder,** lievito, *m.*; — **-tin,** teglia, *f.*

balance ['bæləns], *v.t.* Bilanciare, pesare; saldare, pareggiare; *v.i.* bilanciarsi, pareggiarsi, oscillare. || *n.* Bilancia, *f.*; bilanciere (*of watch*), *m.*; (*Comm.*) bilancio, saldo, *m.*; equilibrio, *m.* **To keep one's —,** tenere l'equilibrio; **to turn the —,** dare il tracollo alla bilancia; — **of trade,** bilancia del commercio, *f.*; (*Pol.*) — **of power,** equilibrio politico, *m.*; (*Comm.*) **to strike a —,** fare il bilancio; — **sheet,** bilancio, *m.*

balancing, *n.* Bilanciamento, *m.*

balcony ['bælkəni], *n.* Balcone, *m.*, loggia, balconata, *f.*

bald [bɔːld], *a.* Calvo, pelato; nudo, disadorno.

baldachin ['bɔːldəkin], *n.* Baldacchino, *m.*

balderdash ['bɔːldəɹdæʃ], *n.* Ciance, frottole, *f.pl.*, cicalata, pappolata, *f.*

baldness, *n.* Calvizie, *f.*; nudità, povertà, *f.*

bale (1) [beil], *v.t.* Imballare. || *n.* Balla, *f.*; calamità, *f.*

bale (2) [cp. **bail**].

Balearic Islands [bæli'ærik 'ailəndz], *n.pl.* (*Geog.*) Le Baleari, *f.pl.*

baleful, *a.* Funesto, maligno, nocivo, calamitoso.

baling, *n.* Imballaggio, *m.*
balistite [ˈbælistait], *n.* Balistite, *f.*
balk, baulk [bɔːk], *v.t.* Frustrare, impedire, ostacolare; render vano; *v.i.* impuntarsi. || *n.* Trave, *f.* (*of timber*); inciampo, *m.*
Balkan [bɔːlkən], *a.* Balcanico.
Balkans, *n.pl.* (*Geog.*) Balcani, *m.pl.*, Balcania, *f.*
ball (1) [bɔːl], *n.* Palla, *f.*, pallone, *m.*, pallina, sfera, *f.*; globo, *m.* **— of the thumb**, polpastrello, *m.*; **— of string**, *etc.*, gomitolo, *m.*; **— and socket**, articolazione sferica, *f.*; **— bearings**, cuscinetti a sfere, *m.pl.*; **— cartridge**, cartuccia a pallottole, *f.*; **— cock**, chiave a galleggiante, *f.*
ball (2), *n.* Ballo, *m.* **— -room**, sala da ballo; **to open the —**, aprire le danze.
ballad [ˈbæləd], *n.* Ballata, *f.*; canzone, romanza, *f.*
ballade, *n.* (*Lit.*) Ballata, *f.*
ballast [ˈbæləst], *v.t.* Zavorrare; consolidare. || *n.* Zavorra, *f.*; (*fig.*) fermezza, saldezza, *f.* **Vessel in —**, bastimento in zavorra, *m.*
ballerina [bæləˈriːnə], *n.* Ballerina, *f.*
ballet [ˈbælei], *n.* Balletto, *m.* **— dancer**, ballerino, *m.*, ballerina, *f.*; **— skirt**, gonnellino, *m.*
ballistics [bəˈlistiks], *n.pl.* Balistica, *f.*
balloon [bəˈluːn], *n.* Pallone, aerostato, *m.* **Captive —**, pallone frenato, *m.*
ballooning, *n.* Aerostazione, *f.*
balloonist, *n.* Aeronauta, *m.*
ballot [ˈbælət], *v.i.* Votare a scrutinio segreto; eleggere a sorte. || *n.* Scrutinio, *m.*, votazione, *f.* **— box**, urna, *f.*; **— paper**, scheda di votazione, *f.*
balm [bɑːm], *n.* Balsamo, *m.*; conforto, *m.*
balmy, *a.* Balsamico, odoroso.
balsam [ˈbɔːlsəm], *n.* Balsamo, *m.*; balsamina, *f.*
baluster [ˈbæləstəɹ], *n.* Balaustro, *m.*
balustrade [bæləsˈtreid], *n.* Balaustrata, *f.*
bamboo [bæmˈbuː], *n.* Bambù, *m.*
bamboozle [bæmˈbuːzl], *v.t.* Corbellare, canzonare, mistificare.
bamboozlement, *n.* Inganno, *m.*
ban [bæn], *v.t.* Bandire, proscrivere, interdire. || *n.* Bando, *m.*, interdizione, scomunica, *f.*
banal [beinəl], *a.* Vieto, trito, banale.
banality, *n.* Banalità, *f.*
banana [bəˈnɑːnə], *n.* Banana, *f.* **— -tree**, banano, *m.*
band (1) [bænd], *v.t.* Fasciare, legare; collegare; *v.i.* collegarsi, unirsi. || *n.* Benda, striscia, *f.*; fascia, *f.*, nastro, *m.* **— -box**, cappelliera, *f.*; **— -saw**, sega a nastro, *f.*
band (2), *n.* Banda, musica, *f.*; compagnia, *f.* **— -master**, capobanda, *m.* **— -stand**, palco per banda, *m.*; **bandsman**, musico, bandista, *m.*; **— of robbers**, banda di ladroni, *f.*
bandage [ˈbændədʒ], *v.t.* Fasciare. || *n.* Benda, fascia, fasciatura, *f.*
bandit [ˈbændit], *n.* Bandito, brigante, *m.*
bandoleer, bandolier [bændəˈliəɹ], *n.* Bandoliera, *f.*
bandy [ˈbændi], *v.t.* Rimandare, ribattere. || *a.* Storto, dalle gambe storte. **To — words with**, scambiare parole con, disputare.
bane [bein], *n.* Veleno; flagello, *m.*, sventura, *f.*
baneful, *a.* Velenoso, dannoso.
bang [bæŋ], *v.t.i.* Sbattere, sbattacchiare, rimbombare. || *n.* Colpo, scoppio, rimbombo, *m.* || *inter.* Pum! Paf!
banging, *n.* Fracasso, *m.*, detonazione, *f.* **— of the door**, sbattimento della porta, *m.*
bangle [bæŋgl], *n.* Anello da polso, braccialetto, *m.*
banish [ˈbæniʃ], *v.t.* Bandire, esiliare.
banishment, *n.* Bando, esilio, *m.*
banister [ˈbænəstəɹ], *n.* Balaustra, *f.*
banjo [ˈbændʒou], *n.* (*Mus.*) Bangio, *m.*
bank (1) [bæŋk], *v.t.* Arginare. || *n.* Riva, sponda, *f.*, argine, *m.*
bank (2), *v.t.* Mettere in banca. || *n.* Banca, cassa, *f.*, banco, *m.* || *a.* Bancario. **— -note**, biglietto di banca, *m.*; **— -draft**, vaglia bancario, *m.*; **savings- —**, cassa di risparmio, *f.*; **— -rate**, tasso di sconto, *m.*
bank (3), *v.i.* (*Aviat.*) Inclinarsi in curva, virare.
banker, *n.* Banchiere, *m.*
banking, *n.* Professione bancaria, *f.*
bankrupt, *n.a.* Fallito, *m.* **To go —**, far bancarotta.
bankruptcy, *n.* Bancarotta, *f.*, fallimento, *m.*
banner [ˈbænəɹ], *n.* Bandiera, *f.*, gonfalone, vessillo, stendardo, *m.*
banns [bænz], *n.pl.* Bandi di matrimonio, *m.pl.*
banquet [ˈbæŋkwət], *n.* Banchetto, convito, *m.* **Banqueting hall**, sala da banchetto, *f.*
bantam [ˈbæntəm], *n.* Gallina giavanese, *f.* **— weight**, peso gallo, *m.*
banter [ˈbæntəɹ], *v.t.* Motteggiare, canzonare, beffeggiare, burlare. || *n.* Motteggio, *m.*, beffa, burla, *f.*
bantling, *n.* Fanciullino, marmocchio, *m.*
baptism [ˈbæptizm], *n.* Battesimo, *m.*
baptismal, *a.* Battesimale.
baptistery, *n.* Battistero, *m.*
baptize, *v.t.* Battezzare.
bar [bɑːɹ], *v.t.* Sbarrare, impedire; escludere; eccettuare. || *n.* Barra, sbarra, verga, stanga, barriera, *f.*; mescita, *f.*; bottiglieria, *f.*; bar, *m.*; (*Mus.*) battuta, *f.*; (*Law*) foro, *m.*; avvocatura, *f.*
barb [bɑːɹb], *n.* Punta, spina, *f.*; (*horse*), berbero, *m.* **Barbed wire**, ferro spinato, *m.*
barbarian [bɑːɹˈbɛəriən], *n.a.* Barbaro, *m.*
barbaric, barbarous [bɑːɹˈbærik, ˈbɑːɹbərəs], *a.* Barbaro.
barbarism, *n.* Barbarie, *f.*; (*Gram.*) barbarismo, *m.*
barbarity, *n.* Barbarie, *f.*
barbarous, *a.* Barbaro.
barbarousness, *n.* Barbarie, *f.*
barbate, *a.* (*Bot.*) Barbuto.
barbecue [ˈbɑːɹbekjuː], *v.t.* Cuocere intero. || *n.* Animale arrostito intero, *m.*
barber [ˈbɑːɹbəɹ], *n.* Barbiere, parrucchiere, *m.*
barberry [ˈbɑːɹbəri], *n.* (*Bot.*) Berbero, crespino, *m.*
Barcelona [bɑːɹsəˈlounə], *n.* (*Geog.*) Barcellona, *f.*
bard [bɑːɹd], *n.* Bardo, poeta, cantore, *m.*
bare [bɛəɹ], *v.t.* Mettere a nudo, nudare; denudare, sfoderare, sguainare. || *a.* Nudo, spogliato, svestito; semplice, solo, schietto; magro, povero; mero; esiguo. **To lay —**, smascherare, scoprire; **— -footed**, a piedi scalzi; **— -headed**, a capo scoperto; **— -faced**, sfacciato; **— -backed** (*riding*), a nudo, paelo.

barely, *adv.* Appena, scarsamente; poveramente.
bareness, *n.* Nudità, *f.*; povertà, scarsezza, *f.*
bargain [ˈbɑːɹgin], *v.i.* Contrattare, negoziare, mercanteggiare, pattuire; stiracchiare. || *n.* Affare, accordo, patto, mercato, cambio, *m.* **Into the —,** Di soprappiù, per soprammercato, per giunta.
bargainer, *n.* Mercante, affarista, *m.*
bargaining, *n.* Mercanteggiamento, *m.*, contrattazione, *f.*
barge (1) [bɑːɹdʒ], *n.* Chiatta, barca, *f.*
barge (2), *v.i.* (*colloq.*) **To — in,** intrudere, insinuarsi.
bargee, bargeman, *n.* Chiattaiuolo, barcaiuolo, *m.*
baritone [ˈbæritoun], *n.a.* (*Mus.*) Baritono, *m.*
bark (1) [bɑːɹk], *v.t.* Scortecciare, scorzare. || *n.* (*Bot.*) Scorza, corteccia, *f.*
bark (2), *v.i.* Abbaiare. || *n.* Abbaiare, abbaiamento, abbaio, *m.* **His — is worse than his bite,** abbaia ma non morde.
bark (3), *n.* (*Naut.*) Brigantino a palo, *m.*; nave, barca, *f.*
barking, *n.* Abbaiamento, *m.*
barker, *n.* Imbonitore, strillone, *m.*; cane che abbaia, *m.*
barley [bɑːɹli], *n.* Orzo, *m.* **— -sugar,** zucchero d'orzo, *m.*; **— -water,** tisana d'orzo, *f.*
barm [bɑːɹm], *n.* Lievito di birra, *m.*
barman, *n.* Barista, *m.*
barmy, *a.* Pieno di lievito; (*colloq.*) stupido, matto.
barn [bɑːɹn], *n.* Granaio, *m.* **— -yard,** corte del pollame, *f.*; (*Zool.*) **— owl,** barbagianni, *m.*
barnacle [ˈbɑːɹnəkl], *n.* (*Zool.*) Bernacla, *f.*, dattero di mare, *m.* **— goose,** oca selvatica, *f.*; (*colloq.*) **barnacles,** occhiali, *m.pl.*
barograph [ˈbærougræf], *n.* Barografo, *m.*
barometer, *n.* Barometro, *m.*
barometrical, barometric, *a.* Barometrico.
baron [ˈbærən], *n.* Barone, *m.*
baronage, *n.* Baronia, *f.*; dignità di barone, *f.*
baroness, *n.* Baronessa, *f.*
baronet, *n.* Baronetto, *m.*
baronial, *a.* Baronale.
barony, *n.* Baronia, *f.*
baroque [bəˈrɔk], *n.a.* Barocco, *m.*
baroscope [ˈbærəˈskoup], *n.* Baroscopo, *m.*
barque [bɑːɹk], *n.* (*Naut.*) Brigantino a palo, *m.*
barrack [ˈbærək], *v.t.* Alloggiare in caserma, accasermare; (*colloq.*) fischiare, applaudire ironicamente. || *n.* Baracca, *f.* (*usu. pl.*), caserma, *f.*
barrage [ˈbærɑːʒ], *n.* (*Mil.*) Sbarramento, *m.* **— balloon,** pallone di sbarramento, *m.*
barrator [ˈbærətəɹ], *n.* Marinaio colpevole di baratteria, *m.*
barratry, *n.* Baratteria, *f.*
barrel [ˈbærəl], *v.t.* Imbarilare, imbottare, metter nei barili. || *n.* Barile, *m.*, botte, *f.*; (*of gun, etc.*) canna, *f.*; (*of pipe, etc.*), cannuccia, *f.*; (*of clock*) tamburo, *m.* **— organ,** organetto a cilindro, *m.*; **double-barrelled gun,** fucile a due canne, *m.*
barren [ˈbærən], *a.* Sterile; arido.
barrenness, *n.* Sterilità, *f.*
barricade [bærəˈkeid], *v.t.* Barricare, ostruire. || *n.* Barricata, *f.*
barrier [ˈbæriəɹ], *n.* Barriera, *f.*, cancello, steccato, *m.*
barring [ˈbɑːriŋ], *prep.* Eccetto, eccettuando, eccettuato, salvo, fuorchè, tranne.
barrister [ˈbæristəɹ], *n.* Avvocato, *m.*; avvocato patrocinante, *m.*; penalista, *m.*
barrow [ˈbærou], *n.* Cariola, barella, *f.* **— boy,** rivendugliolo, fruttivendolo, *m.*
barter [ˈbɑːɹtəɹ], *v.t.* Barattare, cambiare, scambiare. || *n.* Baratto, cambio, *m.*, permuta, *f.*
Bartholomew [bɑːɹˈθɔləmjuː], *n.* Bartolomeo, *m.*
baryta [bəˈraitə], *n.* Barite, *f.*
basal [ˈbeisəl], *a.* Basico, fondamentale.
basalt [bəˈsɔːlt], *n.* Basalto, *m.*
basaltic, *a.* Basaltico.
bascule [ˈbæskjul], *n.* Basculla, *f.* **— bridge,** ponte a basculla, *m.*
base (1) [beis], *v.t.* Basare, fondare, imbasare. || *n.* Base, *f.*, fondamento, sostegno, *m.*; principio, *m.*; (*Tennis*) **— -line,** barra, *f.*
base (2), *a.* Vile, basso, ignobile, sordido, abbietto. **— -born,** illegittimo, di bassa origine; **— metal,** basso metallo, *m.*; **— coin,** moneta falsa, *f.*
baseless, *a.* Infondato, senza base.
basely, *adv.* In modo infame, vilmente, spregevolmente.
basement, *n.* Fondo, sotterraneo, *m.*, sottoscala, *m.*
baseness, *n.* Bassezza, viltà, *f.*
bash [bæʃ], *v.t.* (*colloq.*) Colpire violentemente, fracassare. || *n.* Colpo violento, *m.*
bashful, *a.* Vergognoso, timido, modesto.
bashfulness, *n.* Vergogna, modestia, timidezza, *f.*
bashfully, *adv.* Vergognosamente, timidamente.
basic [ˈbeisik], *a.* Fondamentale; (*Chem. etc.*) basico. **— English,** vocabolario di 850 parole essenziali.
basil [ˈbæzil], *n.* (*Bot*) Basilico, *m.*; (*hide*) bazzana, *f.*
basilica [bəˈzilikə], *n.* Basilica, *f.*
basilisk [ˈbæzilisk], *n.* Basilisco, *m.*
basin [ˈbeisən], *n.* Bacino, catino, *m.*, vasca, catinella, bacinella, scodella, *f.*; lavabo, lavamani, *m.*
basis (*pl.* **bases**) [ˈbeisis, ˈbeisiːz], *n.* Base, *f.*; fondamento, *m.*
bask [bɑːsk], *v.i.* Scaldarsi, sdraiarsi (*in the sun*).
basket [ˈbɑːskət], *n.* Paniere, panierino, *m.*, cesta, cestina, *f.*; **— -ball,** pallacanestro, *m.*; **— -maker,** panieraio, cestaio, canestraio, *m.*
basketful, *n.* Panierata, *f.*
Basque [bæsk], *n.a.* Basco, *m.*
bas-relief [ˈbɑːrəliːf], *n.* Bassorilievo, *m.*
bass (1) [beis], *n.a.* (*Mus.*) Basso, *m.* **— clef,** chiave di basso, *f.*; **— drum,** grancassa, *f.*
bass (2) [bæs], *n.* (*Zool.*) Branzino, pesce persico, *m.*
bass (3), **bast,** *n.* Corteccia del tiglio, *m.*
basset [ˈbæsət], *n.* (*Zool.*) Bassotto, *m.*; (*Game*) bassetta, *f.*
bassinet [ˈbæsənət], *n.* Culla di vimini, *f.*
bassoon [bəˈsuːn], *n.* (*Mus.*) Fagotto, *m.*
bast [bæst], *n.* Tiglio, *m.*
bastard [ˈbæstəɹd], *n.* Bastardo, *m.*, bastarda, *f.* || *a.* Spurio.

bastardy, *n.* Bastardaggine, *f.*
baste [beist], *v.t.* (*cooking*) Spruzzare (l'arrosto), bagnare con sugo; (*sewing*) imbastire; (*thrashing*) bastonare.
bastinado [bæsti'neidou], *n.* Bastonatura, *f.*
bastion ['bæstiən], *n.* Bastione, *m.*
bat (1) [bæt], *n.* Maglio, *m.*, mazza, racchetta, *f.* **Cricket-—,** mestola, *f.* || *v.t.* Colpire colla mazza.
bat (2), *n.* (*Zool.*) Pipistrello, *m.*
batch [bætʃ], *n.* Gruppo, *m.*; (*of loaves*) fornata, infornata, *f.*
bate [beit], *v.t.* Abbattere, ridurre, far ribassare. **With bated breath,** a voce bassa.
bath [bɑːθ], *v.t.* Lavare. || *n.* Bagno, *m.*; vasca da bagno, *f.* **—-tub,** tinozza, *f.*; **baths,** stabilimento di bagni, *m.*; **shower-—,** doccia, *f.*; **—-attendant,** bagnino, *m.*; **foot-—,** pediluvio, *m.*; **—-mat,** stuoia da bagno, *f.*; **—-chair,** poltrona a ruote, *f.*; **—-salts,** sali per bagno, *m.pl.*; **—-wrap,** accappatoio, *m.*
bathe [beið], *v.t.* Bagnare; *v.i.* bagnarsi, prendere un bagno. || *n.* Bagnata, *f.*
bather, *n.* Bagnante, *m.f.*
bathing, *n.* Bagnare, bagno, *m.*, bagni, *m.pl.* **—-cap,** cuffia da bagno, *f.*; **—-suit,** costume da bagno, *m.*; **— trunks,** mutandine da bagno, *f.pl.*; **—-resort,** stazione balneare, *f.*; **—-tent,** tenda da spiaggia, *f.*
bathometer [bə'θɔmətəɹ], *n.* Batometro, *m.*
bathos ['beiðɔs], *n.* Goffa calata di tono. *f.*
bathymetry [bæ'θimətri], *n.* Batometria, *f.*
bathysphere ['bæθisfiəɹ], *n.* Batiscafo, *m.*
bating ['beitiŋ], *prep.* Salvo, eccetto.
batman ['bætmən], *n.* (*Mil.*) Ordinanza, *f.*
baton ['bætɔn], *n.* Bastone, *m.*; bacchetta, *f.*; (*of bread*) bastoncello, *m.*
batrachia [bə'treikiə], *n.pl.* (*Zool.*) Batraci, *m.pl.*
batsman ['bætsmən], *n.* Giocatore di cricket, *m.*
battalion [bə'tæliən], *n.* Battaglione, *m.*
battels, *n.pl.* Rette per l'Università (a Oxford), *f.pl.*
batten ['bætən], *v.t.* **To — on,** ingrassarsi di; (*Naut.*) **to — down,** chiudere i boccaporti. || *n.* Asse, tavoletta, *f.*
batter (1) ['bætəɹ], *v.t.* Battere, spaccare, sfondare, bombardare.
batter (2), *n.* Pasta, farinata, *f.*
battering, *a.* Battente. **—-ram,** ariete, *m.*
battery, *n.* Batteria, *f.* (*Mil.*) **Horse-—,** batteria a cavallo, *f.*; (*Elec.*) **auxiliary —,** batteria ausiliare, *f.*; **to charge a —,** caricare una batteria.
battle [bætl], *v.i.* Combattere, battersi, lottare. || *n.* Battaglia, *f.*, combattimento, *m.* **—-axe,** azza, *f.*; **—-cry,** grido di guerra, *m.*; **—-cruiser,** incrociatore corazzato, *m.*; **—-field,** campo di battaglia, *m.*; **— array,** ordine di combattimento, *m.*; **that's half the —,** ecco un immenso vantaggio.
battledore ['bætldɔːɹ], *n.* Racchetta, *f.* **— and shuttlecock,** giuoco del volano, *m.*
battlement, *n.* Merlo, bastione, *m.*
battlemented, *a.* Merlato.
battler, *n.* Combattente, *m.*
battleship ['bætlʃip], *n.* Nave da battaglia, *f.*
battue [bæ'tuː], *n.* Battuta, *f.*
bauble [bɔːbl], *n.* Bagatella, bazzecola, *f.*
baulk [cp. **balk**].
bauxite ['bɔːksait], *n.* (*Min.*) Bauxite, *f.*
Bavaria [bə'vɛəriə], *n.* (*Geog.*) Baviera, *f.*
Bavarian, *n.a.* Bavarese, *m.f.*
bawbee [bɔː'biː], *n.* Monetina, *f.*, soldo, *m.*
bawd [bɔːd], *n.* Mezzana, *f.*
bawdiness, *n.* Oscenità, *f.*
bawdy, *a.* Osceno, sporco.
bawl [bɔːl], *v.i.* Gridare, vociare, urlare. || *n.* Grido, urlo, *m.*
bay (1) [bei], *n.* (*Geog.*) Baia, *f.*, seno, golfo, *m.*
bay (2), *n.* (*Bot.*) Lauro, *m.* **— rum,** lozione per i capelli, *f.*
bay (3), *v.i.* Abbaiare.
bay (4), *a.* Baio. || *n.* Cavallo baio, *m.*
bay (5), *n.* Bada, *f.* **To hold at —,** tenere a bada.
bay (6), *n.* (*Arch.*) Argine, vano, *m.* **—-window,** finestra sporgente, *f.*; **sick-—,** infermeria, *f.*
bayadere [bɑːjə'dɛəɹ], *n.* Baiadera, *f.*
bayonet ['beiənət], *n.* Baionetta, *f.* **— charge,** carica alla baionetta, *f.*
bazaar [bə'zɑːɹ], *n.* Bazar, *m.*
B.C. [biː'siː], *abbrev.* **Before Christ,** a.C., avanti Cristo.
bdellium ['deliəm], *n.* (*Bot.*) Bdellio, *m.*
be [biː], *v.i.&aux.* Essere; esistere; stare, trovarsi; avere, fare. **Be that as it may,** comunque sia; **as it were,** per dir così; **be it so,** così sia; **had it not been for him there would have been an accident,** se non fosse stato per lui ci sarebbe stata una disgrazia; **it may be so,** può darsi; **it might be so,** potrebbe darsi; **How is it that ?** Come accadde che?; **if it were not for,** se non fosse per; **if I were you,** se fossi in voi; **Is it to be wondered at if ?** c'è da meravigliarsi se? **it is cold,** fa freddo; **it is ten o'clock,** sone le dieci; **it is to be hoped,** è da sperare; **I am leaving,** me ne vado; **he was to go away yesterday,** doveva andar via ieri; **my hands are cold,** ho freddo alle mani; **nobody is to speak a word,** bisogna che nessuno dica una parola; **that is nothing to me,** non m'importa niente; **there is nothing to be seen here,** non c'è nulla da vedere qui; **there is,** c'è; **there are,** ci sono; **here is, here are,** ecco; **to be better,** stare meglio; **How are you ?** Come state? **to be mistaken,** sbagliarsi; **to be right,** avere ragione; **she is ten years old,** ella ha dieci anni; **to be wrong,** aver torto; **What's the matter ?** Cos'è successo? **let it be,** lasciate stare; **don't be long,** tornate presto; **Be off!** Via!; **What are you at ?** Che cosa fate? **Woe is me!** Guai a me!; **twice two is four,** due e due fanno quattro; **you would take her to be twenty,** le dareste vent'anni; **the winter is over,** l'inverno è finito; **for the time being,** per il momento.
beach [biːtʃ], *n.* Spiaggia, riva, marina, *f.*, lido, litorale, *m.* || *v.t.* Arenare, arenarsi. (*Mil.*) **—-head,** testa di ponte, *f.*
beach-comber ['biːtʃkouməɹ], *n.* Girellone di spiaggia, *m.*
beacon ['biːkən], *n.* Faro, fanale, *m.*, lanterna, *f.* || *v.t.i.* Illuminare, guidare.
bead [biːd], *n.* Grano, *m.*, perla, perlina, pallottola, *f.* **String of beads,** filo di perline,

m.; **to tell one's beads,** recitare il rosario; **to thread beads,** infilare perline.

beading, *n.* Ricamo in perle, *m.*

beadle [biːdl], *n.* Bidello, *m.*

beadsman, *n.* Uomo pio, *m.*; intercessore, *m.*

beady, *a.* Rotondo, luccicante. **— eyes,** occhi piccoli e scintillanti, *m.pl.*

beagle [biːgl], *n.* (*Zool.*) Cagnetto; (*obs.*) cane da caccia, *m.*

beak [biːk], *n.* Becco, rostro, *m.*; (*Naut.*) sperone, *m.*; (*colloq.*) magistrato, *m.*

beaked, *a.* Beccuto; adunco. **A — nose,** un naso adunco, *m.*

beaker, *n.* Coppa, *f.*, bicchiere, *m.*; (*Chem.*) storta, *f.*

beam [biːm], *n.* Trave, *f.*; timone (*of carriage, etc.*), *m.*; raggio (*of light*), *m.*; (*Mech.*) biella, bilanciere, *f.*; giogo (*of scales*), *m.*; (*Naut.*) larghezza, *f.* || *v.i.* Raggiare, splendere, irradiarsi; sorridere. **To kick the —,** far traboccare la bilancia; (*Naut.*) **on her —-ends,** ingavonata, sbandata; (*Radio*) **—-system,** onde a fasci, *f.pl.*

beaming, *a.* Raggiante, sfavillante; sorridente.

beamless, *a.* Oscuro, senza raggi.

bean [biːn], *n.* Fava, *f.*, fagiuolo, fagiolino, *m.* **Broad —,** fava grande, *f.*; **French —,** fagiolino, *m.*; **runner —,** fagiuolo rampicante, *m.*; **coffee —,** chicco, *m.*; bacca di caffè, *f.* (*colloq.*) **Full of beans,** pieno di energia; **—-feast,** festa, *f.*; (*colloq.*) **to spill the beans,** prendere una cantonata, divulgare un segreto; (*colloq.*) **to give him beans,** punirlo.

bear (1) [bɛəɹ], *n.* (*Zool.*) Orso, *m.*, orsa, *f.*; (*Stock Exchange*) ribassista, *m.* (*Astron.*) **Great Bear,** Orsa maggiore, *f.*; **polar —,** orso polare, *m.*; **grizzly —,** orso grigio, *m.*; **—-garden,** (*fig.*) baraonda, *f.*; **—-baiting,** lotta d'orsi, *f.*; **bear's grease,** pomata, *f.*; **—-leader,** domatore d'orsi, (*fig.*) tutore, *m.*; (*Bot.*) **bear's ear,** orecchio d'orso, *m.*

bear (2), *v.t.* Portare, sostenere, reggere; soffrire, sopportare, subire, tollerare; produrre, generare; fruttare; partorire, dare alla luce, procreare. **To — away,** riportare; **to — off,** portar via; **to — down on,** gettarsi addosso; **to — down,** abbattere; **to — oneself,** comportarsi, condursi; **to — out,** sostenere, confermare; **to — sway,** regnare, aver potere, dominare; **to — the expenses,** pagare le spese; **to — witness,** testimoniare; **to bring to — upon,** dirigere verso; **to bring pressure to —,** esercitare influenza; **to — a hand,** aiutare; **to — a grudge,** voler male; **to — in mind,** ricordarsi di; **to be borne away by** (*impulse, etc.*), lasciarsi trasportare da; **— with me,** pazienza; **to — towards,** dirigersi verso; **to — to the right, left,** inclinarsi a destra, a sinistra; **to — up,** avere coraggio, farsi animo; **to — with,** tollerare; **to — upon,** toccare; **she has borne her husband a son,** ha dato un figlio a suo marito.

bearable, *a.* Sopportabile, tollerabile.

bearably, *adv.* Sopportabilmente.

beard [biəɹd], *n.* Barba, *f.*; (*Bot.*) resta. || *v.t.* Bravare, sfidare.

bearded, *a.* Barbuto, barbato.

beardless, *a.* Imberbe; sbarbato. **A — boy,** un giovinetto ancora imberbe, *m.*

bearer [ˈbɛərəɹ], *n.* Portatore, latore, *m.*; (*Arch.*) mensola, *f.* (*Comm.*) **Payable to —,** pagabile al portatore; **he was the — of a letter,** era il latore d'una lettera; **— cheque,** assegno al portatore, *m.*; **stretcher- —,** portabarelle, *m.*; **coffin- —,** necroforo, *m.*; **— of a flag of truce,** parlamentario, *m.*

bearing, *n.* Portamento, contegno, piglio, aspetto, *m.*; (*Naut.*) rilevamento, *m.*; (*Heraldry*) stemma gentilizio, *m.*; (*Mech.*) cuscinetto, *m.*; **— rein,** imbrigliatura, *f.*; **to lose one's bearings,** smarrirsi, perdere la bussola; **to take one's bearings,** orientarsi; **beyond all —,** affatto insopportabile. || *prep.* **— on,** relativo.

bearish, *a.* Burbero, brutale.

bearskin [ˈbɛəɹskin], *n.* Pelle d'orso, *f.*

beast [biːst], *n.* Bestia, *f.*, animale, *m.* **— of burden,** somiero, *m.*; **to make a — of oneself,** imbestialirsi, abbrutirsi; **a wild —,** una fiera, una belva, *f.*

beastliness, *n.* Bestialità, brutalità, *f.*

beastly, *a.* Bestiale, disgustante; (*colloq.*) cattivo, brutto, schifoso.

beat [biːt], *v.t.* Battere; vincere, superare; pestare, stritolare; schiacciare; percuotere; *v.i.* palpitare, battere. || *n.* Colpo, battimento, *m.*, battuta, *f.*; palpitazione, *f.*; ronda (*of policeman*), *f.*; corso, giro, *m.* **To — one's breast,** battersi il petto; **to — about the bush,** tergiversare, prenderla larga; **the rain beats on the window,** la pioggia sferza contro la finestra; **that beats all,** quello è il colmo; **to — back,** respingere; **to — a retreat,** battere in ritirata; **to — black and blue,** dare un carico di legnate; **to — down** (*price*), fare diminuire; **to — the alarm,** suonare l'allarme; **to — time,** segnare il tempo; **to — up game,** fare la battuta; **to — eggs,** sbattere delle uova; **to — up someone's quarters,** andare a trovare qualcheduno; (*Naut.*) **to — about,** incrociare; **to — out to sea,** salpare; **at — of drum,** al rullo di tamburo.

beaten, *a.* Battuto, vinto; esausto.

beater, *n.* Battitore, *m.*; esploratore, *m.*; (*of game*), scaccia, *m.* **Carpet- —,** battipanni, *m.*

beatific [biːəˈtifik], *a.* Beatifico.

beatification, *n.* Beatificazione, *f.*

beatify, *v.t.* Beatificare.

beating, *n.* Battitura, percossa, bussa, *f.*; battimento, castigo, *m.*, punizione, *f.*; battito (*of pulse*), *m.*; rullo (*of drums*), *m.*

beatitude [biːˈætitjuːd], *n.* Beatitudine, felicità, *f.*

beau [bou], *n.* Bellimbusto, damerino, zerbino, *m.*

beauteous [ˈbjuːtiəs], *a.* Bello.

beauteously, *adv.* Bellamente.

beauteousness, *n.* Bellezza, venustà, beltà, *f.*

beautiful, *a.* Bello, vago, grazioso. || *n.* Bello, *m.*

beautifully, *adv.* Bellamente.

beautify, *v.t.* Abbellire, adornare; adornarsi.

beauty, *n.* Bellezza, beltà, vaghezza, *f.* **—-sleep,** primo sonno, *m.*; **—-spot,** luogo pittoresco, *m.*, (*mole*) neo, *m.*; **that's the — of it,** questo è il bello; (*colloq.*) **He's a —!** È una bella figura!

beaver [ˈbiːvəɹ], *n.* (*Zool.*) Castoro, castorino, *m.* **— hat,** cappello di castoro, *m.*

becalmed [bəˈkɑ:md], *a.* (*Naut.*) Abbonacciato. **The vessel was —,** la nave restò in bonaccia.
because [biˈkɔ:z], *conj.* Perchè, perciocchè; a causa che. **— of,** per causa di, a cagione di.
bechance [bəˈtʃɑ:ns], *v.t.i.* Accadere, arrivare. || *adv.* Per caso.
beck (1) [bek], *n.* Cenno, *m.* **To be at the — and call of,** essere agli ordini di.
beck (2), *n.* Ruscello, *m.*
becket, *n.* (*Naut.*) Attacco, gancio, *m.*
beckon [ˈbekən], *v.t.i.* Far cenno, accennare.
becloud [biˈklaud], *v.i.* Annuvolarsi.
become [biˈkʌm], *v.i.* Diventare, divenire; farsi, riuscire; *v.t.* andare bene, convenire, addirsi a. **To — accustomed to,** abituarsi a; **to — interested in,** darsi cura di; **to — known,** farsi conoscere; **What will — of him?** Che cosa sarà di lui? **it ill becomes her,** non le conviene, non le sta bene.
becoming, *a.* Conveniente, adatto. **Your hat is very —,** il vostro cappello vi sta bene.
becomingly, *adv.* Convenevolmente, garbatamente, con grazia.
bed [bed], *n.* Letto, giaciglio, *m.*; (*of sea*) fondo, *m.*; (*of river*) letto, alveo, *m.*; (*Geol.*) strato, giacimento, *m.*; (*garden*) aiuola, *f.* || *v.t.* Mettere a letto; piantare. **Flower —,** aiuola, *f.*; **camp- —,** letto da campo; *m.*; **— and board,** vitto e alloggio; **a double-bedded room,** una camera a due letti; **in —,** a letto; **to be brought to —,** partorire; **to keep one's —,** tenere il letto, essere ammalato; **to go to —,** andare a letto; **to put to —,** mettere a letto; **to — out plants,** trapiantare; **bedchamber, bedroom,** camera da letto, *f.*; **bedclothes,** coperte, *f.pl.*; **bedfellow,** compagno di letto, *m.*; **—-pan,** padella da letto, *f.*; orinale, *m.*; **—-post,** colonna del letto, *f.*; **bedside,** sponda del letto, *f.*; **bedstead,** lettiera, *f.*; **bedtime,** ora di coricarsi, *f.*; **bedroom slippers,** pantofole, ciabatte, *f.pl.*
bedabble [biˈdæbl], *v.t.* Bagnare, inumidire, schizzare.
bedaub [biˈdɔ:b], *v.t.* Imbrattare, dipingere male.
bedazzle [biˈdæzl], *v.t.* Abbagliare.
bedeck [biˈdek], *v.t.* Ornare, parare, abbellire.
bedding, *n.* Biancheria da letto, *f.*; giacitura, *f.*
bedevil [biˈdevəl], *v.t.* Ammaliare.
bedew [bi ˈdju:], *v.t.* Annaffiare, irrorare.
bedight [biˈdait], *a.* (*Poet.*) Ornato.
bedizen [biˈdaizn], *v.t.* Attillare, ornare, azzimare.
bedlam [ˈbedləm], *n.* Manicomio, *m.*
Bedouin [ˈbedowin], *n.a.* Beduino, *m.*
bedraggle [biˈdrægl], *v.t.* Infangare, inzaccherare.
bedwarf [biˈdwɔ:f], *v.t.* Impicciolire.
bee [bi:], *n.* Ape, pecchia, *f.* **In a — -line,** in linea retta, direttamente; **to have a — in one's bonnet,** avere un'idea fissa, avere una smania; **—-hive,** alveare, bugno, *m.*; arnia, *f.*; **—-keeping,** apicultura, *f.*; **—-keeper,** apicultore, *m.*; **queen- —,** ape regina, *f.*; **worker- —,** ape operaia, *f.*; **swarm of bees,** sciame d'api, *m.*
beech [bi:tʃ], *n.* Faggio, *m.* **— -marten,** faina, *f.*; **— -mast,** faggina, faggiuola, *f.*; **— -nut,** faggiuola, *f.*; **a — wood,** un faggeto, *m.*
beef [bi:f], *n.* Manzo, *m.*, carne di bove, carne di bue, *f.* **Boiled —,** manzo lesso, *m.*; **roast —,** rosbif, *m.*; **— -steak,** bistecca, *f.*; **—-tea,** brodo, *m.*
beef-eater, *n.* Guardia reale inglese, *f.*
beefy, *a.* Robusto, gagliardo.
Beelzebub [biˈelzəbʌb], *n.* Belzebù, diavolo, *m.*
beer [biəɹ], *n.* Birra, *f.* **To think no small — of oneself,** aver una grande opinione di sè.
beerhouse, beershop, *n.* Birreria, *f.*; **—-keeper,** birraio, *m.*
beery, *a.* Come birra; ubbriaco.
beestings [ˈbi:stiŋz], *n.pl.* Colostro, *m.*
beeswax [ˈbi:zwæks], *n.* Cera d'api, *f.*
beet, beetroot [bi:t, ˈbi:tru:t], *n.* (*Bot.*) Barbabietola, bietola, *f.*; **— -sugar,** zucchero di barbabietola, *m.*
beetle (1) [bi:tl], *n.* (*Zool.*) Scarafaggio, coleottero, *m.* **Black- —,** blatta, *f.*
beetle (2), *n.* Mazzuolo, maglio, battipalo, pillo, *m.*
beetle (3), *v.i.* Sporgersi, avanzarsi. **Beetling crags,** roccie sporgenti, *f.pl.*; **— -browed,** dalle folte ciglia.
beetroot [cp. **beet**].
befall [biˈfɔ:l], *v.t.i.* Accadere, succedere, avvenire.
befit [biˈfit], *v.t.* Convenire a, addirsi a.
befitting, *a.* Conveniente a, convenevole.
befog [biˈfɔg], *v.t.* Annebbiare; oscurare, confondere.
befool [biˈfu:l], *v.t.* Ingannare, frodare.
before [biˈfɔ:ɹ], *adv.* Prima, innanzi, avanti, anteriormente, per l'addietro, dapprima, già. || *prep.* Avanti di, innanzi a, prima di; davanti, dirimpetto a, di contro a. || *conj.* Avanti che, prima che, innanzi che, anzi che. **As —,** come prima; **— long,** fra non molto; **— leaving,** prima di partire; **to carry all — one,** avere sempre buona fortuna; **— you could say Jack Robinson,** in men che non si dica; **— God,** innanzi a Dio, al cospetto di Dio.
beforehand, *adv.* Anticipatamente, in precedenza. **To be —,** essere in anticipo.
beforetime, *adv.* Già, altre volte.
befoul [biˈfaul], *v.t.* Sporcare, imbrattare, lordare.
befriend [biˈfrend], *v.t.* Favorire, proteggere, aiutare, trattare da amico.
beg [beg], *v.t.i.* Mendicare, chieder l'elemosina; chiedere, pregiarsi di, pregare di. **To — the question,** fare una petizione di principio; **to — someone off,** fare che si perdoni qualcuno; **to — pardon,** domandare scusa; (*Comm.*) **I — to acknowledge receipt of your favour,** mi pregio accusare ricevuta della vostra pregiata.
begad! [biˈgæd], *inter.* (*slang.*) Per Dio!
beget [biˈget], *v.t.* Generare, procreare; cagionare, produrre.
begetter, *n.* Padre, autore, *m.*
beggar [ˈbegəɹ], *n.* Mendicante, *m.f.*, pitocco, accattone, mendico, *m.* || *v.t.* Impoverire, rovinare, ridurre alla miseria. **It beggars description,** è impossibile descriverlo; **beggars cannot be choosers,** chi mendica non può scegliere; **beggar-my-neighbour** (*game*), rubamazzetto, *m.*; (*colloq.*) **Poor —!** Poverino! Povero diavolo! *m.*

beggarly, *a.* Povero, misero, meschino.
beggary, *n.* Mendicità, miseria, *f.* **Reduced to —,** ridotto alla miseria.
begging, *n.* Accattonaggio, il chieder l'elemosina, *m.*
begin [bi'gin], *v.t.i.* Cominciare, incominciare, imprendere, iniziare, principiare, mettersi a. **To — afresh,** ricominciare; **to — at the beginning,** cominciare dal principio; **to — with,** in primo luogo; **to — upon,** mettersi a; **to — business,** esordire negli affari.
beginner, *n.* Esordiente, principiante, novizio, *m.*
beginning, *n.* Principio, inizio, cominciamento, *m.*, origine, *f.*
begird [bi'gəːɹd], *v.t.* Cingere, attorniare, circondare.
begone! [bi'gɔn], *inter.* Vattene!, Andatevene! **Let us —!** Andiamocene!
begonia [bi'gouniə], *n.* (*Bot.*) Begonia, *f.*
begotten [bi'gotən], *p.p.* **First —,** primogenito, *m.* [cp. **beget**].
begrime [bi'graim], *v.t.* Annerare, annerire, sporcare.
begrudge [bi'grʌdʒ], *v.t.* Ricusare, dare di mala volontà; mostrare invidia per.
beguile [bi'gail], *v.t.* Deludere, ingannare; incantare, divertire. **To — the time,** ingannare il tempo.
beguilement, *n.* Inganno, *m.*; divertimento, *m.*
beguiler, *n.* Ingannatore, *m.*, ingannatrice, *f.*; incantatore, *m.*, incantatrice, *f.*
Beguine [bə'giːn], *n.* Beghino, *m.*, beghina, *f.*
begum ['biːgəm], *n.* Principessa indiana, *f.*
behalf [bə'hɑːf], *n.* Favore, interesse, *m.*; difesa, parte, *f.* **On — of,** da parte di, per conto di, a nome di; **on your —,** in vostro favore.
behave [bi'heiv], *v.i.* Comportarsi, condursi, agire. **— yourself!** Comportati bene!, Sta buono! **well-behaved,** ben educato.
behaviour [bi'heivjəɹ], *n.* Condotta, *f.*, comportamento, contegno, *m.*; maniere, *f.pl.*
behead [bi'hed], *v.t.* Decapitare, decollare, mozzare il capo.
beheading, *n.* Decapitazione, decollazione, *f.*
behest [bi'hest], *n.* Comando, ordine, *m.*
behind [bi'haind], *prep.* Dietro di; dopo. || *adv.* Indietro, in ritardo. || *n.* Deretano, *m.*, parti posteriori, *f.pl.* **— the scenes,** dietro le quinte; **to put — one,** rifiutare di considerare; **— one's back,** all'insaputa di qualcuno, dietro le spalle di; **— time,** in ritardo; **— the times,** antiquato.
behindhand, *adv.* In ritardo, indietro.
behold [bi'hould], *v.t.i.* Vedere, guardare, mirare. || *inter.* Ecco! Guardate!
beholden, *a.* Obbligato. **— to,** grato a, obbligato a.
beholder, *n.* Spettatore, osservatore, *m.*
behoof [bi'huːf], *n.* Profitto, vantaggio, *m.* **On his —,** a suo vantaggio.
behove [bi'houv], *v.t.imp.* Convenire a. **It behoves him to go,** conviene che egli vada.
beige [beiʒ], *n.a.* Bigello, *m.*
being ['biːiŋ], *n.* Essere, *m.*, essenza, esistenza, *f.*; condizione, *f.*; stato, *m.* **The Supreme Being,** l'Ente supremo, *m.*; **for the time —,** per il momento, per il presente; **in —,** vigente, in esistenza.
belabour [bi'leibəɹ], *v.t.* Battere, bastonare. **There is no need to — the point,** non c'è bisogno di batter sul punto.
belated [bi'leitəd], *a.* Tardivo, tardo, in ritardo.
belaud [bi'lɔːd], *v.t.* Lodare soverchiamente.
belay [bi'lei], *v.t.* (*Naut.*) Attaccare, assicurare, ormeggiare. || *inter.* Basta! **Belaying-pin,** caviglia, *f.*
belch [beltʃ], *v.t.i.* Ruttare, eruttare; rigettare. || *n.* Rutto, *m.* **To — forth flames,** eruttare fiamme.
belching, *n.* Rutto, *m.*, eruttazione, *f.*
beldam, beldame ['beldəm], *n.* Vecchia donna, vecchiaccia, *f.*; strega, *f.*
beleaguer [bə'liːgəɹ], *v.t.* Assediare, investire, bloccare.
beleaguerment, *n.* Assedio, *m.*
belee [bə'liː], *v.t.* (*Naut.*) Mettersi sotto vento in posizione sicura.
belfry ['belfri], *n.* Campanile, *m.*, torre campanaria, *f.*
Belgian ['beldʒən], *n.* Belga, *m.f.* || *a.* Belgico, belga. **Belgium,** il Belgio, *m.*
Belial ['biːliəl], *n.* Diavolo, *m.* **Man of —,** reprobo, *m.*
belie [bə'lai], *v.t.* Smentire, mentire, contraffare; (*a promise*) mancare a; (*a hope*) ingannare.
belief [bi'liːf], *n.* Fede, credenza, opinione, *f.*; credo, *m.* **To the best of my —,** per quanto io sappia, per quanto a me consta; **past —,** incredibile.
believable, *a.* Credibile.
believe [bi'liːv], *v.t.i.* Credere, aver fede in, prestar fede a; opinare, aver opinione. **I — not,** credo di no; **I — so,** credo di sì; **I — you,** ti credo; **to make —,** dare ad intendere, fingere.
believer, *n.* Credente, *m.f.*
belike [bə'laik], *adv.* Probabilmente, forse.
belittle [bi'litl], *v.t.* Detrarre, rimpicciolire, diminuire.
bell (1) [bel], *n.* Campana, campanella, *f.*; (*Poet.*) squilla, *f.*; (*door*) campanello, *m.*; (*horse, cattle, etc.*) sonaglio, *m.* **Ring of bells,** scampanio, *m.*; **electric —,** campanello elettrico, *m.*; **hand- —,** campanello a mano, *m.*; **to ring the —,** suonare; **as sound as a —,** sanissimo; **to — the cat,** attaccare il sonaglio al gatto; **— -flower,** campanula, *f.*; **— -founder,** campanaio, *m.*; **— -glass,** campana di vetro, *f.*; **— -metal,** metallo di campana, *m.*; **— -pull,** cordone di campanello, *m.*; **— -push,** bottone di suoneria, *m.*; **— -ringer,** campanaro, *m.*; **— -tent,** tenda conica, tenda da campo, *f.*; **— -tower,** campanile, *m.*; **— -wether,** montone del campanaccio, *m.*; (*fig.*) guida, *f.*
bell (2), *v.i.* (*of deer*) Bramire, muggire, gridare.
belladonna [belə'dɔnə], *n.* (*Bot.*) Belladonna, *f.*
belle [bel], *n.* Bella, *f.*
belles-lettres [bel letr], *n.pl.* Belle lettere, *f.pl.*
bellicose ['belikouz], *a.* Bellico, guerresco.
bellicosity [beli'kɔsiti], *n.* Bellicosità, *f.*
bellied ['belid], *a.* Panciuto.
belligerent [bə'lidʒərənt], *n.a.* Belligerante, *m.*
belligerency, *n.* Ostilità, belligeranza, *f.*
bellow ['belou], *v.i.* Muggire, mugghiare, vociare, rombare. || *n.* Mugghio, muggito, *m.*

bellows, *n.pl.* Soffietto, mantice, *m.* **A pair of —,** un soffietto, *m.*
belly [ˈbeli], *n.* Pancia, *f.*, ventre, *m.* || *v.i.* Gonfiarsi. **— -ache,** male di pancia, *m.*; **— -band,** ventriera, *f.*
bellyful, *n.* Scorpacciata, *f.* **To get a — of,** fare una scorpacciata di.
belong [biˈlɔŋ], *v.i.* Appartenere (a), spettare (a), essere (di), provenire da. **That belongs to me,** quello appartiene a me.
belongings, *n.pl.* Beni, effetti personali, annessi e connessi, *m.pl.*, roba, *f.*; parentela, *f.*, congiunti, *m.pl.*
beloved [biˈlʌvd, biˈlʌved], *n.a.* Caro, amato, diletto, pregiato, prediletto, *m.*
below [biˈlou], *prep.* Sotto, al di sotto di, più in basso di. || *adv.* Abbasso, giù, laggiù. **Here —,** quaggiù; **— -stairs,** giù delle scale.
belt [belt], *n.* Cintura, cintola, correggia, *f.*; (*Geog.*) zona, *f.*; (*Mech.*) cinghia, *f.* || *v.t.* Cingere, attorniare; (*colloq.*) battere. **Shoulder- —,** bandoliera, *f.*; **to hit below the —,** dare un colpo proibito.
belting, *n.* Cintura, *f.*
belvedere [belvəˈdiəɹ], *n.* Belvedere, *m.*
bemire [biˈmaiɹ], *v.t.* Infangare, inzaccherare.
bemoan [biˈmoun], *v.t.* Rimpiangere, lamentare.
bemock [biˈmɔk], *v.t.* Canzonare, farsi burla di.
bemuse [biˈmju:z], *v.t.* Stordire, fare (*or* diventare) stupido.
bench [bentʃ], *n.* Banco, *m.*, panca, *f.*; sedile, *m.* **The Bench,** banco del giudice, *m.*, magistratura, *f.*; **workman's —,** banco, pancone, *m.*; **— of bishops,** concilio di vescovi, *m.*; **King's (Queen's) —,** la corte suprema, *f.*
bencher, *n.* Avvocato anziano, giurista, *m.*
bend [bend], *v.t.* Piegare, flettere, curvare, inchinare, inarcare; tendere; (*Naut.*) orzare; *v.i.* inchinare, piegare, cedere; applicarsi, dedicarsi. || *n.* Piega, curva, volta, *f.*; giro, *m.*; nodo, *m.* **On bended knees,** ginocchioni; **to — all one's endeavours,** dirigere i propri sforzi; **to — down,** inchinarsi; **to — one's brows,** aggrottare le ciglia; **to — back,** piegarsi all'indietro; **to — forward,** inchinarsi innanzi; **a — in the road,** una svolta della strada.
beneath [biˈni:θ], *prep.* Sotto, giù, al disotto di. || *adv.* Abbasso, sotto, di sotto, giù. **— contempt,** ignobile, vergognoso; **that action is — him,** quell'atto è indegno di lui.
benedick, benedict [ˈbenədik, ˈbenədikt], *n.* Uomo appena ammogliato, *m.* **To turn —,** ammogliarsi.
Benedictine [benəˈdiktin], *n.a.* Benedettino, *m.*, Benedettina, *f.*
benediction [benəˈdikʃən], *n.* Benedizione, *f.*
benedictory, *a.* Benedicente.
benefaction [benəˈfækʃən], *n.* Beneficio, benefizio, *m.*
benefactor, benefactress, *n.* Benefattore, *m.*, benefattrice, *f.*
benefice [ˈbenəfis], *n.* Benefizio, *m.*
beneficed, *a.* Beneficiato. **— clergyman,** beneficiato, *m.*
beneficence [beˈnefisəns], *n.* Beneficenza, *f.*
beneficent, *a.* Benefico.
beneficently, *adv.* Beneficamente.
beneficial, *a.* Vantaggioso, salutare.
beneficially, *adv.* Vantaggiosamente.
beneficiary, *n.* Beneficiario, beneficiato, *m.*
benefit [ˈbenəfit], *n.* Vantaggio, profitto, bene, *m.*; (*Theat.*) beneficiata, serata d'onore, *f.* || *v.t.* Far bene a, beneficare; *v.i.* profittare, avvantaggiarsi, guadagnare. **For the — of,** a vantaggio di; **to give the — of the doubt,** assolvere per non provata reità; **— society,** società di mutuo soccorso, *f.*
benevolence [beˈnevələns], *n.* Benevolenza, bontà, gentilezza, *f.*
benevolent, *a.* Benevolo; affettuoso.
benevolently, *adv.* Benevolmente.
benighted [biˈnaitəd], *a.* Sorpreso dalla notte; (*fig.*) nelle tenebre dell'ignoranza.
benign, benignant [biˈnain, beˈnignənt], *a.* Benigno, amorevole, benefico, buono, gentile.
benignity, *n.* Benignità, cortesia, bontà, *f.*
benignly, benignantly, *adv.* Benignamente.
benison [ˈbenizən], *n.* Benedizione, *f.*
Benjamin (1) [ˈbendʒəmən], *n.* Beniamino, *m.*; figlio prediletto, *m.*
benjamin (2), *n.* Benzoino, *m.*
bennet [ˈbenet], *n.* (*Bot.*) Erba benedetta, *f.*
bent (1) [bent], *n.* Attitudine, disposizione, tendenza, propensione, *f.* **To follow one's own —,** seguire la propria inclinazione.
bent (2), *a.* Curvato, curvo, piegato, inchinato; torto. **To be — on,** essere deciso a, essere fissato sopra.
bent (3), *past and p.p.* of **bend.**
bent, bentgrass (4), *n.* (*Bot.*) Agrostide, *f.*
benumb [biˈnʌm], *v.t.* Intorpidire, assiderare, agghiacciarsi, paralizzare.
benzine, benzene [ˈbenzi:n], *n.* Benzina, *f.*
benzoic, *a.* (*Chem.*) Benzoico.
benzoin, *n.* Benzoino, *m.*
benzoline, *n.* Benzolina, *f.*
beplaster [biˈplɑ:stəɹ], *v.t.* Intonacare, ingessare.
bequeath [biˈkwi:ð], *v.t.* Testare, legare, lasciare; trasmettere.
bequest [biˈkwest], *n.* Legato, lascito, *m.*, disposizione, testamentaria, *f.*
berate [biˈreit], *v.t.* Sgridare, riprendere.
Berber [bə:ɹbəɹ], *n.a.* Berbero, *m.*
berberry, berbery [ˈbə:ɹbəri], *n.* (*Bot.*) Berbero, crespino, *m.*
bereave [biˈri:v], *v.t.* Privare, orbare, spogliare. **To be bereft of hope,** essere senza speranza.
bereavement, *n.* Perdita, *f.*; lutto, *m.*
beret [ˈberi], *n.* Berretto, *m.*
bergamot (1) [bə:ɹgəmot], *n.* Pera bergamotta, *f.*
bergamot (2), *n.* Bergamotto, *m.* **— oil,** olio di bergamotto, *m.*
berry [ˈberi], *n.* Bacca, *f.*, granello, chicco, *m.* **Coffee in the —,** caffè in grani, *m.*
berth [bə:ɹθ], *n.* Posto, *m.*; (*Naut.*) ancoraggio, *m.*; letto, *m.*; cuccetta, *f.* || *v.t.* Ammarrare, ancorare. **To give a wide — to,** evitare, schivare, scansare.
beryl [ˈbə:rəl], *n.* (*Min.*) Berillo, *m.*
beseech [biˈsi:tʃ], *v.t.* Supplicare, implorare, scongiurare.
beseeching, *a.* Supplicante.
beseechingly, *adv.* Supplichevolmente, supplicantemente.

beseem [bi'si:m], *v.i.* Convenire a.
beset [bi'set], *v.t.* Assediare, assalire, assillare, imbarazzare. **— with,** in preda a.
besetting, *a.* Abituale. **— sin,** vizio inveterato, *m.*
beshrew [bi'ʃru:], *v.t.* Maledire.
beside [bi'said], *prep.* Vicino a, presso a, fuori di. **— the mark,** fuori centro, fuori di proposito; **— the question,** estraneo alla questione; **to be — oneself,** essere fuori di sè.
besides, *prep.* Oltre, oltre che. || *adv.* Inoltre, del resto, ancora di più, d'altronde.
besiege [bi'si:dʒ], *v.t.* Assediare.
besieger, *n.* Assediante, *m.*
beslaver [bi'sleivəɹ], *v.t.* Imbavare; (*fig.*) adulare.
besmear [bi'smiəɹ], *v.t.* Imbrattare, sporcare.
besmirch [bi'smə:ɹtʃ], *v.t.* Sporcare, macchiare.
besom ['bi:zəm], *n.* Scopa, *f.*
besot [bi'sɔt], *v.t.* Stupefare, abbrutire.
besotted, *a.* Istupidito, infatuato.
besottedly, *adv.* Scioccamente.
bespangle [bi'spæŋgl], *v.t.* Ornare di pagliuole. **Bespangled with,** scintillante di.
bespatter [bi'spætəɹ], *v.t.* Infangare, bruttare di fango, inzaccherare.
bespeak [bi'spi:k], *v.t.* Ordinare, comandare, prenotare; suggerire. **To — a pair of boots,** ordinare un paio di scarpe; **to — a place,** prenotare un posto; **his bearing bespeaks him a gentleman,** il suo contegno mostra che è gentiluomo.
bespoke, *a.* Confezionato su misura.
besprinkle [bi'spriŋkl], *v.t.* Spruzzare, aspergere.
best [best], *a.* Il migliore, ottimo. || *adv.* Meglio. || *n.* Il meglio, *m.* **At —,** alla meglio; **for the —,** per il meglio; **— man** (*at weddings*) paggio d'onore, testimonio, *m.*; **the — of everything,** il meglio di tutto; **the — of it is that,** il bello è che; **to act for the —,** agire con buone intenzioni; **to do one's —,** fare del proprio meglio; **to have the — of it,** avere il vantaggio; **to look one's —,** essere nel suo bello; **to make the — of it,** trarre il miglior partito; **to the — of my belief,** per quanto io sappia; **to put one's — foot foremost,** camminare molto presto; **in one's Sunday —,** con gli abiti migliori.
bested [bi'sted], *a.* **Sorely —,** in brutti frangenti.
bestial ['bestiəl], *a.* Bestiale, crudele, brutale.
bestiality, *n.* Bestialità, *f.*
bestially, *adv.* Bestialmente.
bestir [bi'stə:ɹ], *v.t.* **To — oneself,** muoversi, agitarsi, spicciarsi.
bestow [bi'stou], *v.t.* Donare, regalare; collocare, accordare; dare alloggio. **To — in marriage,** dare in matrimonio; **to — a kindness,** fare una gentilezza; **to — oneself,** collocarsi.
bestowal, *n.* Dono, *m.*, donazione, *f.*; conferimento, *m.*
bestrew [bi'stru:], *v.t.* Spargere di.
bestride [bi'straid], *v.t.* Inforcare, cavalcare, essere a cavalcioni.
bet [bet], *v.t.i.* Scommettere. || *n.* Scommessa, *f.* (*colloq.*) **You — !** Per certo!, Altro che!
betake [bi'teik], *v.r.* **To — oneself,** recarsi a, ricorrere a.
betel ['bi:təl], *n.* Noce di betel, *f.*
bethink [bi'θiŋk], *v.r.* **To — oneself,** rammentarsi di, ricordarsi di; **I bethought myself of a good idea,** mi è venuta in mente una buona idea.
Bethlehem ['beθlihem], *n.* (*Geog.*) Betlemme, *f.*
betide [bi'taid], *v.t.i.* Accadere, arrivare a. **Woe — you!** Guai a voi! **whate'er —,** qualunque cosa avvenga.
betimes [bi'taimz], *adv.* Di buon'ora, presto, a tempo.
betoken [bi'toukən], *v.t.* Significare, esser segno di, presagire, preannunziare.
betony ['betəni], *n.* (*Bot.*) Bettonica, *f.*
betray [bi'trei], *v.t.* Tradire, ingannare; rivelare, denunciare; lasciar trasparire. **To — oneself,** tradirsi; **to — one's trust,** abusare della fiducia di qualcuno.
betrayal, *n.* Tradimento, *m.*, perfidia, *f.*
betrayer, *n.* Traditore, *m.*, traditrice, *f.*
betroth [bi'trouð], *v.t.* Fidanzare, dar promessa di matrimonio.
betrothal, *n.* Fidanzamento, *m.*
betrothed, *n.a.* Fidanzato, *m.*, fidanzata, *f.*, promessi sposi, *m.pl.*
better (1) ['betəɹ], *a.* Migliore, superiore; preferibile. || *adv.* Meglio. || *n.* Superiore, *m.f.* || *v.t.* Migliorare, avvantaggiare. **My — half,** mia moglie, la mia metà; **I feel the — for that,** quella cosa mi ha fatto bene; **I am —, I feel —,** sto meglio; **— late than never,** meglio tardi che mai; **— and —,** di bene in meglio; **for — or for worse,** per il bene o per il male; **for the —,** per il meglio; **I had —,** farei meglio; **nothing could be —,** nulla potrebbe esser meglio; **so much the —,** tanto meglio; **to think — of,** cambiare proposito; **to — oneself,** migliorare le proprie condizioni.
better (2), *n.* Scommettitore, *m.*, scommettitrice, *f.*
betting, *n.* Lo scommettere, *m.*
betterment, *n.* Miglioramento, *m.*
between [bi'twi:n], *prep.* Fra, tra, in mezzo a. **— this and tomorrow,** fra oggi e domani; **— us,** fra noi; **— whiles,** intanto, **— wind and water,** a fior d'acqua; **— the devil and the deep sea,** fra due fuochi.
betwixt [bi'twikst], *prep.* Fra. **— and between,** nè tutto questo nè tutto quello.
bevel ['bevəl], *n.* Squadra, trasversale, *f.* || *a.* Obliquo, di sbieco. || *v.t.* Tagliare a sghembo. **A bevelled looking-glass,** uno specchio molato, *m.*; **— -edged,** coll'angolo a sghembo; **— -wheel,** ruota ad angolo, *f.*
bevelling, *n.* Smussatura, *f.*
beverage ['bevəridʒ], *n.* Bevanda, bibita, *f.*
bevy [bevi], *n.* Brigata, compagnia, comitiva, *f.*; (*of animals*) branco, *m.*, (*of birds*) stormo, *m.*
bewail [bi'weil], *v.t.* Lamentare, piangere, deplorare. **To — one's lot,** lamentarsi della propria sorte.
bewailing, *n.* Lamentazione, *f.*, pianto, *m.*
beware [bi'wɛəɹ], *v.i.* Guardarsi, badare; fare attenzione. **Beware of the dog,** Guardatevi dal cane; **— of pickpockets!** Attenti ai borsaiuoli! **— of the trains!** Attenti ai treni!
bewet [bi'wet], *v.t.* Umettare, bagnare.
bewhiskered [bi'wiskəɹəd], *a.* Baffuto.

bewilder [bi'wildəɹ], *v.t.* Confondere, disorientare, sviare; sconcertare, strabiliare.
bewilderment, *n.* Smarrimento, *m.*, stupefazione, *f.*
bewitch [bi'witʃ], *v.t.* Ammaliare, incantare; affascinare.
bewitching, *a.* Seducente, incantevole, affascinante.
bewitchingly, *adv.* Incantevolmente.
bewitchment, *n.* Incanto, *m.*, malìa, *f.*; fascino, *m.*
bewray [bi'rei], *v.t.* Tradire, scoprire, manifestare.
bey [bei], *n.* Bei, *m.*
beyond [bi'jɔnd], *prep.* Al di là di, oltre, fuori di. || *adv.* Lungi, da lungi, lontano. || *n.* Al di là. **Beautiful — description,** superiore ad ogni descrizione; **— measure,** fuor di misura; **this is — me,** non posso capire questo; **to go —,** andare più lontano di; **the back of —,** la parte più remota del mondo; **the life beyond,** l'al di là.
bezel ['bezl], *n.* Castone, taglio, *m.*
bezique [bi'zi:k], *n.* (*Cards*) Bazzica, *f.*
bezoar [be'zɔ:ɹ], *n.* Antidoto, calcolo, *m.*
biangular [bai'æŋgju:ləɹ], *a.* Con due angoli.
biannual [bai'ænju:əl], *a.* Biennale.
bias ['baiəs], *n.* Tendenza, inclinazione, attitudine, *f.*, pregiudizio, *m.*; parzialità, obliquità, *f.*; prevenzione, *f.* || *v.t.* Influenzare, propendere. **On the —,** obliquamente, di traverso; **free from —,** imparziale.
bib [bib], *n.* Bavaglio, bavaglino, *m.*
Bible [baibl], *n.* Bibbia, *f.*
biblical, *a.* Biblico.
bibliographer [bibli'ɔgrəfəɹ], *n.* Bibliografo, *m.*
bibliographical, *a.* Bibliografico.
bibliography, *n.* Bibliografia, *f.*
bibliomania, *n.* Bibliomania, *f.*
bibliomaniac, *n.* Bibliomane, *m.*
bibliophile, *n.* Bibliofilo, *m.*
bibulous ['bibju:ləs], *a.* Bibulo, ubriaco; assorbente.
bicarbonate [bai'kɑ:ɹbəneit], *n.* (*Chem.*) Bicarbonato, *m.*
bicentenary [baisen'ti:nəri], *n.a.* Bicentenario, *m.*
biceps ['baiseps], *n.* (*Anat.*) Bicipite, *m.*
bicker [bikəɹ], *v.i.* Litigare, altercare, disputare.
bickering, *n.* Litigio, *m.*
biconcave [bai'kɔnkeiv], *a.* Biconcavo.
biconvex [bai'kɔnveks], *a.* Biconvesso.
bicycle ['baisikl], *n.* Bicicletta, *f.* **— ride,** giro in bicicletta, *m.*
bicyclist, *n.* Ciclista, *m.f.*
bid [bid], *v.t.i.* Comandare, ordinare; invitare. || *n.* Offerta, *f.* **To — farewell,** dire addio; **to — a high price,** offrire un buon prezzo; **to make a — for,** fare un'offerta; **to — fair to do,** promettere di fare; **to — defiance,** sfidare.
biddable, *a.* Ubbidiente, docile.
bidder, *n.* Offerente, concorrente. **To the highest —,** al maggior offerente.
bidding, *n.* Comando, ordine, *m.*; invito, *m.*; offerta, *f.*
bide [baid], *v.t.i.* Aspettare; dimorare, abitare. **To — one's time,** aspettare l'opportunità.
bidental, bidentate [bai'dentəl, bai'denteit], *a.* (*Anat.*) Bidentato.
biennial [bai'eniəl], *a.* Biennale.
biennially, *adv.* Ogni due anni.
bier [biəɹ], *n.* Bara, *f.*
biffin ['bifin], *n.* Specie di mela, *f.*; mela cotta, *f.*
bifid [bai'fid], *a.* (*Bot.*) Bifido.
bifurcated ['baifəɹkeitid], *a.* Biforcato, biforcuto.
bifurcation, *n.* Biforcazione, *f.*
big [big], *a.* Grosso, grande, vasto, enorme; alto; incinta, gravida; orgoglioso, fiero. **To look —,** darsi delle arie; **to talk —,** far la voce grossa; **that cow is — with calf,** quella vacca è pregna; (*Motor*) **— end,** cuscinetto maggiore, *m.*
bigamist ['bigəmist], *n.* Bigamo, *m.*
bigamy, *n.* Bigamia, *f.*
bight [bait], *n.* (*Geog.*) Seno, golfo, *m.*, cala, baia, *f.*; (*of rope*) doppino, *m.*
bigness, *n.* Grossezza, grandezza, *f.*
bigot ['bigət], *n.* Bigotto, bacchettone, *m.*; fanatico, *m.*
bigoted, *a.* Bigotto, fanatico.
bigotry, *n.* Bigotteria, *f.*, bigottismo, *m.*
bigwig ['bigwig], *n.* Pezzo grosso, *m.* **He's a real —,** è un vero pezzo grosso.
bike [baik], *n.* (*colloq.*) Bicicletta, *f.* || *v.i.* Andare in bicicletta.
bilateral [bai'lætərəl], *a.* Bilaterale.
bilberry ['bilbəri], *n.* (*Bot.*) mirtillo, *m.*
bile [bail], *n.* (*Anat.*) Bile, *f.*; (*fig.*) bile, stizza, *f.*
bilge ['bildʒ], *n.* (*Naut.*) Sentina, *f.*; (*colloq.*) stupidaggine, *f.*; **— -water,** acqua della sentina, acqua di cala, *f.*; (*colloq.*) **to talk —,** dire stupidaggini.
biliary, *a.* Biliary.
bilious, *a.* Bilioso, collerico.
biliousness, *n.* Accesso di bile, *m.*; temperamento collerico, *m.*
bilingual [bai'liŋguəl], *a.* Bilingue.
bilk [bilk], *v.t.* Ingannare, frodare, evadere, scroccare.
bill (1) [bil], *n.* Becco. || *v.i.* beccarsi. **To — and coo,** carezzarsi l'un l'altro; **— -hook,** ascia, *f.*
bill (2), *v.t.* Affiggere, annunziare per mezzo di affissi. || *n.* Affisso, programma, cartellone, manifesto, *m.* **Parliamentary —,** progetto di legge, *m.* **Stick no Bills!** Divieto d'affissione! **— -sticker,** attacchino, *m.*
bill (3), *n.* Conto, *m.*, fattura, *f.*; (*Comm.*) biglietto, *m.*, cambiale, *f.* **— at sight,** biglietto pagabile a vista, *m.*; **— of exchange,** cambiale, *m.*; **— of fare,** lista, *f.*; **— of health,** patente di sanità, *m.*; **— of lading,** polizza di carico, *f.*; **— of parcels,** fattura, *f.*; **— of sale,** denunzia di vendita, *f.*; **— on demand,** cambiale a vista; **to discount a —,** scontare una cambiale; **tradesman's —,** conto, *m.*; **— -book,** scadenziere, *m.*; **— -broker,** sensale, *m.*; **— -case,** portamonete, *m.*; **— -file,** filza di conti, *f.*; **— -head,** fattura, *f.* **I wish to pay the —,** vorrei pagare il conto.
billet (1), *n.* Biglietto, *m.*, lettera, *f.* **— -doux,** lettera amorosa, *f.*
billet (2), *n.* Alloggio, accantonamento, *m.* || *v.t.* Alloggiare, accantonare. **Billeting officer,** ufficiale d'alloggiamento, *m.*

billet (3), *n.* Ceppo, *m.*; (*Heraldry*) plinto, *m.*
billiard [ˈbiljəɹd], *a.* Di bigliardo. **—-ball,** palla da bigliardo, *f.*; **—-cue,** stecca da bigliardo, *f.*; **—-table,** bigliardo, *m.*; **—-room,** sala da bigliardo, bigliardo; **—-marker,** segnapunti, *m.*
billiards, *n.pl.* Bigliardo, *m.* **To play a game of —,** fare una partita al bigliardo.
Billingsgate [ˈbiliŋzgət], *n.* (*fig.*) Parole ingiuriose, *f.pl.*, invettiva, *f.*
billion [ˈbiljən], *n.* Bilione (*English,* 1,000,000,000,000; *Amer.*, 1,000,000,000), *m.*
billow [ˈbilou], *n.* Onda, *f.*, flutto, *m.*, ondata, *f.* || *v.i.* Ondeggiare, fluttuare, spumare.
billowy, *a.* Ondoso.
billycock [ˈbilikɔk], *n.* Cappello basso di feltro, *m.*
billy goat [ˈbiligout], *n.* Caprone, *m.*
bimetallism [baiˈmetəlizm], *n.* Bimetallismo, *m.*
bimonthly [baiˈmʌnθli], *a.adv.* Ogni due mesi, bimestrale; (*twice a month*) bimensile.
bin [bin], *n.* Madia, *f.* **Wine- —,** ripostiglio pel vino, *m.*; **corn- —,** arca del grano, *f.*
binary [ˈbainəri], *a.* Binario.
bind [baind], *v.t.* Legare, attaccare; obbligare; costringere; impegnare; (*books*) rilegare; (*Med.*) costipare, rendere stitico; (*a wound*) bendare. **To — oneself,** impegnarsi; **I'll be bound,** io scommetto; **it was bound to happen,** doveva accadere; **to be bound over,** essere obbligato sotto pena d'ammenda; **to — apprentice,** mettere a novizio; **to — up,** fasciare, avvolgere; **this boat is bound for Naples,** questo bastimento è diretto a Napoli.
binder, *n.* Legatore, *m.*; (*Agric.*) macchina per legare i covoni, *f.*
bindery, *n.* Legatoria, *f.*
binding, *n.* Rilegatura, legatura, *f.* || *a.* Obbligatorio, impegnativo, valido; (*Med.*) astringente. **It is — upon me,** sono obbligato a.
bindweed [ˈbaindwiːd], *n.* (*Bot.*) Vilucchio, convolvolo, *m.*
binnacle [ˈbinəkl], *n.* (*Naut.*) Abitacolo, *m.*, chiesola, *f.*
binocular, binoculars [binˈɔkuləɹ], *n.n.pl.* Binocolo, *m.*
binomial [baiˈnoumiəl], *a.* (*Math.*) Binomio.
biogenesis [baiouˈdʒenəsis], *n.* Biogenesi, *f.*
biographer [baiˈɔgrəfəɹ], *n.* Biografo, *m.*
biographical, *a.* Biografico.
biography, *n.* Biografia, *f.*
biological [baiouˈlɔdʒikəl], *a.* Biologico.
biologist, *n.* Biologo, *m.*
biology, *n.* Biologia, *f.*
bipartite [baiˈpɑːɹtait], *a.* Bipartito.
biped [ˈbaiped], *n.* Bipede, *m.*
biplane [ˈbaiplein], *n.* (*Aviat.*) Biplano, *m.*
birch [bəːɹtʃ], *n.* (*Bot.*) Betulla, *f.* || *v.t.* Battere con una verga, sferzare. **—-rod,** verga, *f.*
birchen, *a.* Di betulla.
birching, *n.* Frustata, vergata, *f.*
bird [bəːɹd], *n.* Uccello, uccellino, (*Poet.*) augello, *m.* **—-cage,** gabbia di uccello, uccelliera, *f.*; **—-call,** richiamo, *m.*; **—-catcher,** uccellatore, *m.*; **—-fancier,** amatore d'uccelli, *m.*; **—-lime,** vischio, *m.*; **bird's-eye view,** veduta a volo d'uccello, *f.*; **—'s-nest,** nido di uccello, *m.*; **to go —nesting,** andare a snidare gli uccelli; **a — in the hand is worth two in the bush,** meglio un uovo oggi che una gallina domani; **to kill two birds with one stone,** pigliar due piccioni ad una fava; **birds of a feather flock together,** Dio li fa e poi li appaia.
biretta [biˈretə], *n.* Berretta, *f.*
birth [bəːɹθ], *n.* Nascita, *f.*, nascimento, *m.*; parto, *m.*; (*fig.*) origine, stirpe, *f.* **By —,** di nascita; **to give — to,** dare alla luce, partorire, (*fig.*) produrre; **of good —,** di buona razza; **—-control,** limitazione delle nascite, *f.*; **—-mark,** voglia, *f.*
birthday, *n.* Compleanno, giorno natalizio, *m.*
birthplace, *n.* Luogo natio, *m.*
birthright, *n.* Diritto di primogenitura, *m.*
Biscay [ˈbiskei], *n.* (*Geog.*) Biscaglia, *f.*
biscuit [ˈbiskit], *n.* Biscotto, biscottino, *m.*
bisect [baiˈsekt], *v.t.* Bisecare, dividere in due parti eguali.
bisection, *n.* Bisezione, *f.*
bisexual [baiˈseksjuəl], *a.* Bisesso, bisessuale.
bishop [ˈbiʃəp], *n.* Vescovo, prelato, *m.*; (*Chess*) alfiere, *m.*
bishopric, *n.* Vescovado, vescovato, episcopato, *m.*, diocesi, *f.*
bismuth [ˈbizməθ], *n.* (*Chem.*) Bismuto, *m.*
bison [ˈbaisən], *n.* (*Zool.*) Bisonte, *m.*
bissextile [biˈsekstail], *a.* Bisestile.
bistoury [ˈbisturi], *n.* (*Med.*) Bistorì, bisturi, bisturino, *m.*
bistre [ˈbistəɹ], *n.* Bistro, *m.*
bit (1) [bit], *n.* Pezzo, pezzettino, pezzetto, *m.*; (*of bread*) tozzo, *m.*; (*of food*) boccone, bocconcello, *m.*; brano, frammento, *m.* **A — older,** un poco più vecchio; **a good — older,** molto più vecchio; **— by —,** gradualmente, di grado in grado; **every — of it,** tutto quanto; **Not a — of it!** Neanche per idea! **I don't care a —!** Non mi fa niente! **to give a — — of one's mind,** parlare francamente; **a — of a coward,** piuttosto vile; **every — as,** tanto quanto; **wait a —,** aspettate un po'.
bit (2), *n.* Morso, *m.* || *v.t.* Mettere il morso ad un cavallo. **To champ the —,** mordere il freno.
bitch [bitʃ], *n.* Cagna, *f.*
bite [bait], *n.* Morso, *m.*, morsicatura, puntura, *f.*; boccone, *m.* || *v.t.* Mordere, morsicare; pungere, rodere, addentare; (*of wind*) tagliare; *v.i.* abboccare. **To — off,** morsicar via; **to — off more than one can chew,** fare il passo più lungo della gamba; **to — one's lips,** mordersi le labbra; **to — one's nails,** mangiare le unghie; **to — the dust,** morder la polvere; **Do the fish — ?** I pesci abboccano?
biter, *n.* Morditore, morsicatore, *m.* **The — bit,** il truffatore truffato.
biting, *a.* Mordente, pungente, mordace; tagliente; sarcastico.
bitingly, *adv.* Mordacemente, in modo pungente.
bitt [bit], *n.* (*Naut.*) Bitta, *f.*
bitter, *a.* Amaro, acre, agro, aspro; piccante, acido, pungente. || *n.* Amaro, *m.*; amarezza, *f.*; agrodolce, *m*; (*fig.*) **a — pill,** un boccone amaro, *m.*; **to the — end,** a oltranza.
bitterly, *adv.* Amaramente, con grande cordoglio. **It's — cold,** fa un freddo cane; **to weep —,** piangere dirottamente.

bittern, *n.* (*Zool.*) Tarabuso, *m.*
bitterness, *n.* Amarezza, asprezza, *f.*, rancore, *m.*
bitters, *n.pl.* Amaro, asperitivo, *m.*
bittersweet, *n.a.* Agrodolce, *m.*; *n.* (*Bot.*) Dulcamara, *f.*
bitumen ['bitju:mən], *n.* Bitume, *m*
bituminous, *a.* Bituminoso.
bivalve ['baivælv], *n.a.* Bivalve, *m.*
bivouac ['bivuæk], *v.i.* Bivaccare. || *n.* Bivacco, *m.*
bizarre [bi'zɑ:ɹ], *a.* Bizzarro, stravagante.
blab [blæb], *v.t.* Rivelare, diffondere; *v.i.* chiacchierare, cicalare. || *n.* Cicalone, *m.*
black [blæk], *a.* Nero, negro; oscuro; triste, lugubre; atroce, malvagio; sporco; (*Print.*) neretto. || *n.* Nero, negro, *m.* || *v.t.* Annerire; (*of boots, etc.*) lustrare, lucidare; nereggiare. **To beat — and blue,** ammaccare; **to look — at,** guardare di traverso; **a — eye,** un occhio pesto; **— market,** mercato nero; **in one's — books,** in grandissimo sfavore; **dressed in —,** vestito di nero; **to put in — and white,** mettere per iscritto; **— -ball,** palla nera, *f.*, voto contrario, *m.*; **— -beetle,** scarafaggio, *m.*; **— -board,** lavagna, *f.*; **— -currant,** ribes nero, *m.*; **— -lead,** piombaggine, grafite, *f.*; **— letter,** carattere gotico, *m.*; **— magic,** negromanzia, *f.*; **— pudding,** sanguinaccio, *m.*; **— sheep,** (*fig.*) pecora segnata, pecora nera, *f.*
blackamoor, *n.* (*off.*) Negro, *m.*
blackberry, *n.* Mora selvatica, *f.*; **— bush,** rovo, *m.*
blackbird, *n.* (*Zool.*) Merlo, *m.*
blackcap, *n.* (*Zool.*) Capinera, *f.*
blacken, *v.t.i.* Oscurarsi, diventar nero; diffamare, parlar male di.
blackguard ['blægɑ:ɹd], *n.* Briccone, furfante, birbante, *m.*; canaglia, *f.* || *a.* Disonesto, malvagio, tristo.
blacking, *n.* Lucido, lustro, *m.*
blackish, *a.* Nerastro, nerognolo.
blackleg, *n.* Scroccone, *m.*; (*strike-breaker*) crumiro, *m.*
blackly, *adv.* Tristamente, malignamente.
blackmail, *n.* Estorsione, *f.*, ricatto, *m.* || *v.t.* Ricattare, fare estorsioni.
blackmailer, *n.* Ricattatore, *m.*, ricattatrice, *f.*
blackness, *n.* Nerezza, *f.*
blackout, *n.* Oscuramento, *m.*; amnesia, *f.* || *v.t.* Oscurare, obliterare.
blacksmith, *n.* Fabbro, maniscalco, *m.* **Blacksmith's shop, smithy,** fucina, *f.*
bladder ['blædəɹ], *n.* Vescica, *f.*
bladderwort, *n.* (*Bot.*) Otricolaria, *f.*
blade [bleid], *n.* (*of knife, etc.*) Lama, *f*; (*of grass*) filo, *m.*; (*of corn*), spiga, *f.*; (*of an oar*) paletta, *f.*; (*of a propeller*) pala, *f.*; (*fig.*) gagliardo, giovinastro, *m.* **— -bone,** (*Anat.*) scapola, *f.*
blamable ['bleiməbl], *a.* Biasimabile, biasimevole.
blame [bleim], *n.* Biasimo, rimprovero, *m.*, responsabilità, colpa, *f.* || *v.t.* Biasimare, censurare, rimproverare, riprendere. **To lay the — on,** addossare la colpa a, far cadere la responsabilità su; **one can't — him,** non si può fargliene una colpa; **to bear the —,** sopportare il biasimo; **she is not to be blamed,** essa non merita biasimo.
blameless, *a.* Innocente, irreprensibile, senza colpa.
blamelessly, *adv.* Innocentemente.
blamelessness, *n.* Innocenza, irreprensibilità, *f.*
blameworthy, *a.* Meritevole di biasimo, biasimevole.
blanch [blɑ:ntʃ], *v.t.i.* Imbiancare; impallidire, scolorarsi.
blancmange [blə'mɔnʒ], *n.* Biancomangiare, *m.*
bland [blænd], *a.* Blando, dolce, mite, placido.
blandishment, *n.* Blandizia, persuasione, *f.*
blandly, *adv.* Blandamente, placidamente.
blandness, *n.* Dolcezza, soavità, *f.*
blank [blæŋk], *a.* Bianco, in bianco; vuoto; confuso, sconcertato. || *n.* Bianco, vuoto, *m.*, lacuna, *f.*; (*Comm.*) modulo, *m.*; **— -cartridge,** cartuccia a salve, *f.*; **— cheque,** assegno in bianco, *m.*; **— verse,** versi sciolti, *m.pl.*; **to draw —,** fare cilecca; **point- —,** chiaro e tondo, a bruciapelo; **to leave —,** lasciare in bianco.
blanket, *n.* Coperta di lana, *f.* || *v.t.* Avvolgere, coprire. **A wet —,** un guastafeste, *m.*
blankly, *adv.* Confusamente, turbatamente.
blankness, *n.* Vacuità, confusione, *f.*; turbamento, *m.*
blare [blɛəɹ], *v.i.* Squillare, ruggire. || *n.* Squillo, *m.*
blarney ['blɑ:ɹni], *n.* Adulazione, *f.*; moine, *f.pl.* || *v.t.i.* Lusingare, adulare, lisciare.
blaspheme, *v.t.i.* Bestemmiare.
blasphemer, *n.* Bestemmiatore, *m.*
blasphemous, *a.* Blasfemo, empio.
blasphemously, *adv.* Con bestemmie.
blasphemy, *n.* Bestemmia, *f.*
blast [blɑ:st], *n.* Colpo di vento; squillo, suono, *m.*; esplosione, *f.* || *v.t.* Fare scoppiare, fare esplodere; fulminare, minare; appassire; sfiorire; rovinare. **— -furnace,** alto forno, *m.*; **— -pipe,** tubo di soffiamento, *m.*
blasting, *a.* Distruttivo, rovinoso. || *n.* Esplosione, *f.*, scoppio, *m.*
blatant ['bleitənt], *a.* Schiamazzante, reboante; clamoroso, forte.
blatantly, *adv.* Con schiamazzo.
blaze [bleiz], *n.* Fiamma, *f.*, fuoco, *m.*; vampa, *f.*, ardore, splendore, *m.*; luce, *f.*; segno, *m.* || *v.i.* Ardere, brillare, risplendere, avvampare; *v.t.* segnare. **A — of temper,** una vampa di passione; **a — of colour,** uno splendore di colori; **a — of light,** un bagliore di luce; **to — up,** divampare; **to — away,** sparare continuamente; **to — abroad,** pubblicare, diffondere notizie su; **to — a trail,** segnare una pista.
blazer, *n.* Giacca di flanella, *f.*
blazing, *a.* Ardente, brillante, fiammeggiante, risplendente.
blazon ['bleizən], *v.t.i.* Illustrare, dar lustro, pubblicare. || *n.* Blasone, *m.*
blazonry, *n.* Araldica, *f.*
bleach [bli:tʃ], *v.t.i.* Imbiancare, diventar bianco.
bleacher, *n.* Imbiancatore, *m.*, imbiancatrice, *f.*; imbianchino *m.*
bleaching, *n.* Imbiancamento, *m.*; **— liquid,** lisciva, *f.*; **— -ground,** imbiancatoio, *m.*

bleak [bliːk], *a.* Nudo, freddo; squallido, ventoso, deserto; pallido; brullo.
bleakly, *adv.* Freddamente, squallidamente.
bleakness, *n.* Squallore, *m.*, nudità, *f.*; freddezza, rigidezza, *f.*
blear [bliəɹ], *a.* Cisposo. **— -eyed,** cisposo.
bleat [bliːt], *v.i.* Belare. || *n.* Belato, *m.*
bleating, *n.* Belato, *m.*
bleb [bleb], *n.* (*Med.*) Vescichetta, bolla, *f.*
bleed [bliːd], *v.i.* Sanguinare, versare sangue, perder sangue; *v.t.* salassare, cavar sangue; (*fig.*) cavare denari. **My heart bleeds for her,** mi scoppia il cuore per lei; **his nose is bleeding,** gli cola sangue dal naso.
bleeding, *n.* Salasso, *m.*, flebotomia, *f.*; flusso di sangue, *m.*, emoraggia, *f.*
blemish [ˈblemiʃ], *v.t.* Guastare, macchiare, sfigurare. || *n.* Difetto, *m.*, macchia, *f.*
blench [blenʃ], *v.i.* Indietreggiare, impallidire, esitare; chiudere gli occhi di fronte a.
blend [blend], *v.t.* Mischiare, mescolare, fondere; *v.i.* mescolarsi, immischiarsi. || *n.* Mescolamento, miscuglio, *m.*
blende [blend], *n.* (*Min.*) Blenda, *f.*
blending, *n.* Mescolamento, *m.*
blennorrhoea [blenɔˈriːə], *n.* (*Med.*) Gonorrea, blenorragia, *f.*
bless [bles], *v.t.* Benedire, santificare, consacrare; render felice, rallegrare. **God — you!** Dio vi benedica! **— my soul!** Dio mio!
blessed, blest [ˈblesid, blest], *a.* Benedetto, santo, beato; felice; consacrato. **The Blessed Virgin Mary,** La Santissima Vergine; **to be — with,** essere dotato di, godere di.
blessedness, *n.* Beatitudine, *f.*; felicità, *f.*; santità, *f.* **Single —,** celibato, *m.*
blessing, *n.* Benedizione, *f.*; felicità, grazia, *f.*, benefizio, *m.* **To ask a —** (*before meals*), dire la preghiera, dire il benedicite.
blether [ˈbleðəɹ], *v.i.* (*colloq.*) Blaterare; parlare scioccamente.
blight [blait], *v.t.* Appassire, sfiorire, indebolire svigorire; (*fig.*) frustrare, ingannare. || *n.* Golpe, *f.*; nebbia (*of corn*), *f.*; (*fig.*) peste, *f.*, influsso malefico, *m.* **The flowers are blighted,** i fiori sono appassiti; **all my hopes are blighted,** tutte le mie speranze sono svanite.
blighter, *n.* (*colloq.*) Pellaccia, *f.*
blind (1) [blaind], *a.* Cieco, orbo; oscuro; nascosto; (*fig.*) sconsigliato, ignaro. || *v.t.* Accecare, oscurare; abbagliare. || *n.* (*fig.*) Finta, *f.*, pretesto, *m.* **— alley,** vicolo cieco, *m.*; **— in one eye,** cieco da un occhio; **born —,** cieco nato; **to be — to,** essere incapace ad apprezzare; **— side,** lato debole; **— spot,** punto cieco; **stone- —,** completamente cieco; **struck —,** colpito da cecità; **blind man, woman,** cieco, *m.*, cieca, *f.*; **blindman's buff,** mosca cieca, *f.*; **— -drunk,** ubriaco fradicio.
blind (2), *n.* Tenda, cortina. **Venetian —,** persiana, gelosia, *f.*
blindfold, *a.* Con gli occhi bendati. || *v.t.* Bendare gli occhi.
blindly, *adv.* Ciecamente; inconsideratamente.
blindness, *n.* Cecità, *f.*; (*fig.*) ignoranza, *f.* **Colour- —,** daltonismo, *m.*
blink [bliŋk], *v.i.* Batter le palpebre; (*of light*) vacillare; *v.t.* ignorare, rifiutare di considerare. || *n.* Occhiata, *f.*; (*of light*) barlume, *m.* **We cannot — the fact,** non si può ignorare il fatto.
blinkers, *n.pl.* Paraocchi, *m.pl.*
blinking, *n.* Lo sbattere gli occhi, il batter gli occhi.
bliss [blis], *n.* Felicità, beatitudine, *f.*
blissful, *a.* Felice, beato. **In — ignorance,** in beata ignoranza.
blissfully, *adv.* Felicemente.
blissfulness, *n.* Felicità, *f.*
blister [ˈblistəɹ], *n.* Vescica, ampolla, bolla, *f.*; (*Med.*) vescicante, *m.* || *v.t.* Far venire vesciche; applicare un vescicante.
blithe, blithesome [blaið, ˈblaiðsəm], *a.* Gaio, allegro, giocondo, leggiadro.
blithely, *adv.* Gaiamente, allegramente.
blizzard [ˈblizəɹd], *n.* Burrasca di neve, *f.*; uragano, *m.*, tormenta, *f.*
bloat [blout], *v.t.i.* Gonfiare, enfiare; stragonfiare.
bloated, *a.* Gonfio, stragonfio.
bloater, *n.* Aringa affumicata, *f.*
blob [blɔb], *n.* Goccia. **Blobber-lipped,** colle labbra grosse.
block [blɔk], *n.* Blocco, ceppo, *m.*, massa, *f.*; (*Naut.*) girella, carrucola, *f.*; (*Print.*) matrice, *f.*; (*for hat*) forma, *f.*; (*stoppage*), ingombro, ostacolo, *m.* || *v.t.* Chiudere, bloccare, impedire, ostacolare. **— of houses,** isolato di case; **barber's —,** testa da parrucche, *f.*; **stumbling- —,** inciampo, intoppo, *m.*; **in — letters,** in stampatello; (*Print.*) **— -making,** stereotipia, *f.*; **— -tin,** stagno puro; **to — up,** bloccare, sbarrare; **he is a chip of the old —,** è proprio figlio di suo padre.
blockade, *n.* Blocco, assedio, *m.* || *v.t.* Bloccare, assediare. **To raise the —,** levare l'assedio.
blockhead, *n.* Sciocco, balordo, zuccone, *m.*
blockhouse, *n.* Fortino, *m.*
blockmaker, *n.* (*Print.*) Zincografo, *m.*
bloke [blouk], *n.* (*colloq.*) Un tipo, *m.*
blond, blonde, *a.* Biondo. || *n.* Biondo, *m.*; bionda, *f.*
blood [blʌd], *n.* Sangue, *m.*; (*fig.*) razza, stirpe, *f.*; (*dandy*) zerbinotto, bellimbusto, *m.* || *v.t.* Salassare; (*fig.*) spronare, incitare. **— -coloured,** colore di sangue; **— -feud,** faida, *f.*; **— -heat,** calore del sangue; **— -horse,** cavallo di razza, purosangue, *m.*; **— -letting,** flebotomia, *f.*; **— -money,** premio di delazione, *m.*; **— -poisoning,** setticemia, *f.*; **— -red,** rosso sanguigno; **— -relation,** parente, *m.f.*; **— -stained,** imbrattato di sangue; **— -sucker,** sanguisuga, *f.*; **— -vessel** vaso sanguigno, *m.*, vena, arteria, *f.*; **— -transfusion,** trasfusione di sangue; **his — is up,** gli s'è acceso il sangue; **in cold —,** a sangue freddo; **you can't get — out of a stone,** non si può cavare sangue da una rapa; **— is thicker than water,** il sangue non è acqua; **it makes one's — run cold,** ciò fa agghiacciare il sangue nelle vene; **to cause bad — between,** metter cattivo sangue tra.
bloodhound, *n.* Bracco, *m.*
bloodily, *adv.* Crudelmente, in modo sanguinario.
bloodless, *a.* Esangue, anemico; incruento.
bloodshed, *n.* Spargimento di sangue, *m.*, strage, *f.*

bloodshot, *a.* Iniettato di sangue.
bloodthirsty, *a.* Assetato di sangue.
bloody, *a.* Sanguinario, sanguinoso, insanguinato; (*colloq. vulg.*) maledetto.
bloom [blu:m], *n.* Fiore, *m.*; freschezza, *f.* (*on fruit*). || *v.i.* Fiorire, far fiori. **In the — of youth,** nel fiore degli anni; **in —,** in fiore.
bloomer, *n.* (*colloq.*) Errore, *m.*
bloomers, *n.pl.* Calzoni per donna, *m.pl.*
blooming, *a.* Fiorente; (*fig.*) rigoglioso, prosperoso; (*colloq.*) maledetto. || *n.* Fioritura, *f.*
bloomingly, *adv.* Fiorentemente.
blossom ['blɔsəm], *n.* Fiore, *m.* || *v.i.* Fiorire, essere in fiore.
blot [blɔt], *n.* Macchia, *f.*, sgorbio, scarabocchio, *m.* || *v.t.* Macchiare, scarabocchiare; (*with blotting-paper*) asciugare. **To — out,** cancellare; **blotting-case, blotting-book, blotting-pad,** cartella di carta assorbente, *f.*; **blotting-paper,** carta assorbente, carta suga, *f.*
blotch [blɔtʃ], *n.* Pustola, bolla, *f.*; macchia, *f.* || *v.t.* Coprire di pustole.
blotchy, *a.* Pustoloso.
blouse [blauz], *n.* Blusa; camicetta, *f.*
blow (1) [blou], *n.* Colpo, *m.*; botta, *f.*, urto, *m.* **A — with a stick,** una bastonata, *f.*; **at a single —,** d'un sol colpo; **to come to blows,** venire alle mani; **without striking a —,** senza colpo ferire; **to strike a — for,** aiutare.
blow (2), *v.i.* Soffiare, tirar vento; anelare, ansare; (*of flowers*) sbocciare; *v.t.* suonare (*a wind instrument*). **It is blowing,** tira vento; **to — over,** passare; **to — up,** far scoppiare; saltare in aria; **to — away,** dissipare; **to — hot and cold,** vacillare; **to — one's nose,** soffiarsi il naso; **to — out** (*a light*), spegnere; **to — out one's brains,** farsi saltar le cervella; **to — one's own trumpet,** lodarsi, cantar le proprie lodi; **— -fly,** mosca vomitoria, *f.*; (*colloq.*) **a good — -out,** una buona scorpacciata, *f.*; **— -pipe,** canna da soffiare, *f.*
blower, *n.* Soffiatore, *m.*; valvola, *f.*
blowy, *a.* Ventoso.
blowzy ['blauzi], *a.* Scarmigliato.
blubber (1) ['blʌbəɹ], *n.* Sugna, *f.*, grasso di balena, *m.*
blubber (2), *v.i.* Singhiozzare.
bludgeon ['blʌdʒən], *n.* Randello, *m.* mazza, *f.*, bastone, *m.* || *v.t.* Bastonare, randellare.
blue [blu:], *n.a.* Turchino, azzurro, blu, *m.* || *v.t.* Tingere in azzurro. (*Naut.*) **Blue Peter,** segnale di partenza, *f.*; **to look —,** essere nervoso *or* depresso; **the blues,** tristezza, *f.*; **in the blues,** triste; (*colloq.*) **a — funk,** uno spavento terribile; **Prussian —,** blu di Prussia; **sky- —,** celeste; **washing- —,** l'azzurro, *m.*; **— -bell,** giacinto selvatico, *m.*, campanula, *f.*; **— -bottle,** mosca vomitoria, *f.*; **— -book,** libro azzurro *m.*; **— -devils,** umor tetro, *m.*; **— -eyed,** dagli occhi azzurri; **— -jacket,** marinaio, *m.*; **— -print,** disegno di officina, *m.*; **— -mould** (*of cheese*), verdognolo, *m.*; **once in a — moon,** ad ogni morte di papa; **to turn the air —,** bestemmiare.
blueness, *n.* Colore turchino, colore blu, *m.*
bluestocking, *n.* Letterata, saccentona, *f.*
bluff (1) [blʌf], *a.* Brusco, franco, ardito, animoso.
bluff (2), *n.* (*Geog.*) Promontorio a picco, *m.*
bluff (3), *v.t.* Bluffare, fare un bluff. || *n.* Vanteria, iattanza, *f.*, inganno, pretesto, *m.*
bluffer, *n.* Millantatore, *m.*
bluffness, *n.* Franchezza, *f.*
bluish ['blu:iʃ], *a.* Bluastro, azzurrognolo.
blunder ['blʌndəɹ], *n.* Sbaglio, fallo, sproposito, errore, *m.*, svista, *f.* || *v.t.i.* Sbagliare, errare, inciampare. **To — upon,** trovare per caso; **to — out,** lasciarsi scappare parole.
blunderbuss ['blʌndəɹbʌs], *n.* Spingarda, *f.*
blunderer, *n.* Stupido, cretino, imbecille, imbroglione, *m.*
blunderingly, *adv.* Goffamente, stupidamente.
blunt [blʌnt], *a.* Spuntato, ottuso; (*fig.*) brusco, aspro. || *v.t.* Rintuzzare, spuntare; attutire.
bluntly, *adv.* Bruscamente, senza complimenti.
bluntness, *n.* Ottusità, *f.*; (*fig.*) bruschezza, schiettezza, *f.*
blur [bləːɹ], *n.* Macchia, imbrattatura, *f.*; oscurità, *f.* || *v.t.* Macchiare; oscurare.
blurred, *a.* Macchiato, oscuro, poco chiaro, indistinto.
blurb [bləːɹb], *n.* Soffietto editoriale, *m.*
blurt [bləːɹt], *v.t.* **To — out,** lasciar scappare; parlare bruscamente.
blush [blʌʃ], *v.i.* Arrossire, accendersi in viso. || *n.* Rossore, arrossimento, *m.* **At the first —,** a prima vista.
blushing, *a.* Rosso; vergognoso, timido.
blushingly, *adv.* Vergognosamente, modestamente.
bluster ['blʌstəɹ], *v.i.* Tempestare, agitarsi, infuriare. || *n.* Millanteria, spavalderia, fanfaronata, *f.*, furore, *m.*
blusterer, *n.* Fanfarone, spaccone, sfrontato, schiamazzatore, *m.*
blustering, *a.* (*of wind*) Burrascoso; spavaldo. **A — fellow,** bravaccione, spaccone, *m.*
blusteringly, *adv.* In modo spavaldo, sfrontatamente.
blustery, *a.* Tempestoso, burrascoso.
boa [bouə], *n.* (*Zool.*) Boa, *m.* **Feather —,** boa, *f.*
boar [bɔːɹ], *n.* Verro, *m.* **Wild —,** cinghiale, *m.*
board (1) [bɔːrd], *n.* Asse, *m.*, tavola, *f.*; pancone, *m.* || *v.t.* Impalcare, intavolare. **Notice- —,** cartello, *m.*, insegna, *f.*; (*Theat.*) **the boards,** il palcoscenico, *m.*; **chess- —,** scacchiere, *m.*; **draughts- —,** dama, *f.*; **above- —,** carte in tavola.
board (2), (*Naut.*) **On —,** a bordo; **to go on —,** imbarcarsi, andare a bordo; **to go by the —,** andare perduto, andare negletto; **to — a tram,** salire in tram.
board (3), *n.* Vitto, *m.*, dozzina, pensione, *f.* || *v.t.i.* Prendere in pensione, essere in pensione, prendere a dozzina. **— and lodging,** vitto e alloggio; **full —,** pensione completa, *f.*; **to put out to —,** mettere in pensione.
board (4), *n.* (*Comm., etc.*) Consiglio, *m.* **— of directors,** consiglio di amministrazione, *m.*; **Board of Trade,** Ministero del Commercio, *m.*; **Board of Inland Revenue,** Ministero delle Finanze, *m.*; **— of examiners,** commissione d'esami, *f.*
boarder, *n.* Pensionante, *m.f.*; pensionario, convittore, *m.*

boarding, *a.* Assito, tavolato. || *n.* Vitto, *m.*, pensione, *f.*; (*Naut.*) abbordaggio, *m.* **—-house,** pensione, *f.*; **—-school,** convitto, collegio, *m.*
boast [boust], *v.i.* Vantarsi, gloriarsi, millantare; *v.t.* possedere, vantare. || *n.* Vanto, orgoglio, *m.* **This house does not — a drawing-room,** questa casa non possiede un salotto da ricevimento.
boaster, *n.* Vantatore, *m.*, fanfarone, *m.*, millantatore, *m.*
boastful, *a.* Vanitoso, vanaglorioso.
boasting, *n.* Vanteria, millanteria, *f.*
boat [bout], *n.* Battello, *m.*, barca, lancia, *f.*; imbarcazione, *f.* || *v.t.i.* Andare in barca, trasportare per acqua. **Life- —,** battello di salvataggio, *m.*; **long- —,** scialuppa, *f.*; **steam- —,** piroscafo, *m.*; **fishing- —,** battello da pesca, peschereccio, *m.*; **—-house,** tettoia per imbarcazioni; darsena, *f.* **—-hook,** gancio, gancio d'accosto, *m.*; **—-load,** barcata, *f.*; **—-race,** regata, *f.*, gara di canottaggio, *f.*; **—-train,** treno speciale per imbarcarsi, *m.*; **to be in the same —,** trovarsi nello stesso caso; **we are in the same —,** possiamo darci la mano, siamo negli stessi guai.
boatman, *n.* Barcaiuolo, *m.*
boater, *n.* Specie di cappello di paglia, *f.*
boating, *n.* Canottaggio, *m.*
boatswain ['bousn], *n.* Nostromo, *m.*
bob [bɔb], *n.* Pendente, peso, pendaglio, *m.*; inchino (*curtsy*), *m.*; (*colloq.*) scellino, *m.* || *v.i.* Dondolare; fare un inchino. **Bobbed hair,** capelli corti, *m.pl.*; **to — up,** tornare a galla; **—-wig,** parrucca con riccioli, *f.*
bobbin, *n.* Rocchetto, *m.*, bobina, *f.*
bobby, *n.* (*colloq.*) Agente di polizia, poliziotto, *m.* **—-soxer,** ragazza adolescente, *f.*
bobsleigh ['bɔbslei], *n.* Guidoslitta, *f.*
bobstay ['bɔbstei], *n.* (*Naut.*) Fune di bompresso, *f.*
bobtail ['bɔbteil], *n.* Coda mozza, *f.* **Tag-rag and —,** plebaglia, marmaglia, *f.*
bobtailed, *a.* Mozzo di coda.
bode [boud], *v.t.i.* Presagire, pronosticare, prevedere. **To — well,** essere di buon augurio, promettere bene; **to — ill,** essere di cattivo augurio, non promettere niente di buono.
bodice ['bɔdis], *n.* Busto, *m.*; camicetta, *f.*
bodied ['bɔdid], *a.* Fornito di corpo. **Able- —,** robusto.
bodiless, *a.* Senza corpo, incorporeo.
bodily, *a.* Corporale, corporeo. || *adv.* Corporalmente, di persona; in massa, in blocco, intieramente. **— fear,** paura fisica; **to be in — fear,** temere per la vita.
bodkin ['bɔdkin], *n.* Punteruolo, spillone, *m.*
body ['bɔdi], *n.* Corpo, *m.*; sostanza, *f.*; gruppo, *m.*, classe, *f.*; collegio, *m.*; brigata, *f.*; grosso, *m.* **The — politic,** lo Stato, *m.*; **heavenly —,** stella, *f.*, pianeta, *m.*; **dead —,** cadavere, *m.*; **the — of a car,** la carrozzeria, *f.*; **—-belt,** ventriera, *f.*; **—-guard,** guardia del corpo, *f.*; **— of an aeroplane,** fusoliera, *f.*; **wine which has good —** vino generoso; **in a —,** tutti insieme.
bog [bɔg], *n.* Palude, *f.*, pantano, acquitrino, *m.*; (*colloq.*) latrina, *f.* || *v.t.i.* Impantanare, impantanarsi. **—-trotter,** contadino irlandese, *m.*
bogey (1) [bougi], *n.* (*Golf*) Norma, *f.*
bogey (2), **bogey man,** *n.* Orco, diavolo, *m.*
boggle [bɔgl], *v.i.* Esitare, indietreggiare, trasalire.
boggler, *n.* Pauroso, uomo esitante, *m.*
boggy, *a.* Paludoso, pantanoso.
bogie ['bougi], *n.* (*Rail.*) Carrello, *m.*
bogus ['bougəs], *a.* Falso, simulato, finto. **A — concern,** un affare losco, *m.*
Bohemian [bou'hi:miən], *n.a.* Boemo, *m.*; (*fig.*) zingaresco.
boil (1) [bɔil], *n.* (*Med.*) Foruncolo, fignolo, *m.*
boil (2), *v.t.* Fare bollire, lessare; *v.i.* bollire. **To — away,** evaporare; **to — over,** traboccare; (*fig.*) andare in furia; **to — up,** ribollire; **to — down,** condensare, ridurre; **to make the blood —,** far ribollire il sangue; **to keep the pot boiling,** guadagnarsi la vita; tirare la carretta.
boiled, *a.* Bollito, lesso. **A lightly — egg,** un uovo al latte, un uovo da bere, *m.*; **a hard- — egg,** un uovo sodo, *m.*; **— beef,** lesso di manzo, *m.*; **— potatoes,** patate lesse, *f.pl.*
boiler, *n.* Caldaia, *f.*; bollitore, *m.*; marmitta, casseruola, *f.* **—-maker,** calderaio, *m.*; **—-plate,** piastra, lamiera di caldaie, *f.*; **—-room,** sala delle caldaie, *f.*
boiling, *n.* Bollimento, bollore, *m.*, ebollizione, *f.* || *a.* Bollente, caldissimo. **— hot,** caldo bollente; **—-point,** punto d'ebollizione, *m.*
boisterous ['bɔistrəs], *a.* Violento, impetuoso, furioso, turbolento.
boisterously, *adv.* Impetuosamente, violentemente.
boisterousness, *n.* Impetuosità, violenza, *f.*
bold [bould], *a.* Ardito, audace, temerario; impudente, sfacciato; (*Print.*) neretto; chiaro. **To make — to,** prendersi la libertà di; **with a — front,** a viso aperto; **as — as brass,** sfacciato; **a — headland,** un promontorio dirupato; **—-faced,** sfrontato, sfacciato; (*Print.*) grassetto.
boldly, *adv.* Arditamente, temerariamente; sfacciatamente.
boldness, *n.* Arditezza, *f.*, coraggio, *m.*; sfacciataggine, *f.*
bole [boul], *n.* Tronco, *m.*; (*Min.*) bolo, *m.*
Bolivian [bɔ'liviən], *n.a.* Boliviano, *m.*
boll [bɔl], *n.* (*Bot.*) Baccello, *m.*
bollard ['bɔləɹd], *n.* (*Naut.*) Palo d'ormeggio, *m.*
Bolshevism ['bɔlʃevizm], *n.* Bolscevismo, *m.*
Bolshevist, *n.a.* Bolscevico, *m.*
bolster ['boulstəɹ], *n.* Capezzale, traversino, guanciale, *m.* || *v.t.* **To — up,** appoggiare, sostenere.
bolt (1) [boult], *n.* Paletto (*of door*), *m.*; dardo, *m.*, freccia, *f.*; strale, *m.*, saetta, *f.*; (*Mech.*) chiavarda, *f.* || *v.t.* Chiudere con catenaccio, mettere il chiavistello. **Thunder- —,** fulmine, *m.*; (*Naut.*) **—-rope,** ralinga, *f.*; **— upright,** diritto come un fuso; **to draw the —,** stangare l'uscio; **to shoot a —,** scagliare una saetta; **a — from the blue,** una grande sorpresa, fulmine a ciel sereno.
bolt (2), *v.i.* Scappare, fuggire, scampare, prendere la mano, partire come una freccia; *v.t.* inghiottire senza masticare, ingollare. || *n.* Fuga, *f.* **At one —,** ad un tratto.
bolting, *n.* Chiusura colla stanga, *f.*
bolus ['bouləs], *n.* (*Med.*) Bolo, *m.*
bomb [bɔm], *n.* Bomba, *f.* || *v.t.* (*Mil.*) Bombardare; (*Aviat.*) gettare bombe, lanciare bombe.

— **-proof,** a prova di bomba; — **-shell,** bomba, *f.*; (*fig.*) colpo di sorpresa, *m.*; **atomic —,** bomba atomica, *f.*; **hydrogen —,** bomba all'idrogeno, *f.*; **delayed-action- —,** bomba a scoppio ritardato, *f.*

bombard [bɔmˈbɑːɹd], *v.t.* Bombardare; assalire.

bombardier [bɔmbəˈdiəɹ], *n.* Bombardiere, *m.*

bombardment, *n.* Bombardamento, *m.*

bombardon, *n.* (*Mus.*) Bombardone, *m.*

bombasine, bombazine [ˈbɔmbəziːn], *n.* Bambagina, *f.*

bombast [ˈbɔmbæst], *n.* Ampollosità, *f.*; turgidezza, *f.*

bombastic [bɔmˈbæstik], *a.* Ampolloso; turgido.

bomber, *n.* (*Aviat.*) Apparecchio da bombardamento, bombardiere, *m.*

bona fide [ˈbounə ˈfaidi], *adv.* In buona fede; sinceramente, onestamente, || *a.* sincero, onesto.

bon-bon [ˈbɔ̃bɔ̃], *n.* Dolce, confetto, *m.*; caramella, *f.*

bond [bɔnd], *n.* Legame, vincolo, *m.*; obbligazione, *f.*; unione, *f.*; (*Comm.*) titolo, buono, *m.*; cauzione, *f.* || *v.t.* Mettere in deposito doganale; ipotecare; (*Arch.*) connettere. **In bonds,** in ferri, in prigione, in catene; **in —,** nel deposito doganale; **matrimonial —,** vincolo matrimoniale; **to take out of —,** svincolare; **bonded goods,** merce in dogana; **bonded warehouse,** magazzino doganale, deposito franco; **bonded storekeeper,** magazziniere, *m.*

bondage, *n.* Schiavitù, servitù della gleba, *f.*; confino, *m.*

bondholder, *n.* (*Comm.*) Azionista, *m.*

bondsman, *n.* Schiavo, servo della gleba, *m.*

bone [boun], *n.* Osso, *m.*; (*of fish*) lisca, spina, *f.* || *v.t.* Disossare; (*colloq.*) (*to steal*), rubare; chiappare. **Bones** (*remains*) ossa, *f.pl.*; **whale-bone,** osso di balena, *m.*; **— of contention,** pomo della discordia, *m.*; **he makes no bones about it,** non esita punto, non se ne fa scrupoli; **not to make old bones,** morire giovane; **to have a — to pick with someone,** aver un motivo di lite con qualcheduno; **what's bred in the — will out in the flesh,** la botte dà il vino che ha; — **-shaker,** velocipede, *m.*; — **-setter,** ortopedico, *m.*

boneless, *a.* Senz'ossa; disossato.

bonfire [ˈbɔnfaiəɹ], *n.* Falò, fuoco d'allegrezza, *m.*

bonnet [ˈbɔnət], *n.* (*woman's*) cappello, *m.*; (*man's*) berretto, *m.*; (*Motor.*) cofano, *m.* — **-box,** scatola per cappelli, *f.*; — **-maker,** modista, *f.*

bonny [ˈbɔni], *a.* Bellino, vezzoso, grazioso; gentile.

bonus [ˈbounəs], *n.* Premio, *m.*; mancia, gratifica, *f.*; avanzo, buono, soprassoldo, *m.* (*Comm.*) **— shares,** azioni di godimento, *f.pl.*

bony [ˈbouni], *a.* Ossuto, osseo; (*of fish*) pieno di lische.

bonze [bɔnz], *n.* Bonzo, *m.*

boo [buː], *v.t.i.* Fischiare. || *n.* Fischio, *m.*

booby, *n.* Scioccone, sempliciotto, goffo, *m.*; — **-trap,** acchiappatoio, tranello, *m.*; — **-prize,** premio di consolazione, *m.*

boobyish, *a.* Sciocco, goffo.

book [buk], *n.* Libro, libretto; registro, *m.* || *v.t.* Inscrivere, registrare, prenotare; *v.i.* prendere un biglietto per. **Log- —,** giornale di bordo, *m.*; **by — -post,** sotto fascia; **to take a leaf out of someone's —,** imitare qualcheduno; **on the books,** nella lista dei membri; **in someone's good books,** in favore presso qualcheduno; **to bring someone to —,** chiamare qualcuno alla resa dei conti; **to keep books,** tenere i conti, tenere la contabilità; — **-debt,** articolo dell'attivo, *m.*; **-ends,** — serralibri, *m.*; **—-keeper,** contabile, computista, *m.*; — **-keeping,** contabilità, *f.*; — **-maker,** (*Racing*) allibratore, *m.*; — **-marker,** segnalibro, *m*; — **-muslin,** organdis, *m.*; **— value,** valore contabile, *m.*

bookcase, *n.* Scaffale, *m.*, libreria, *f.*

booking, *n.* Registrazione, prenotazione, *f.* — **-clerk,** bigliettaio, *m.*; — **-office,** ufficio biglietti, *m.*, biglietteria, *f.*

bookish, *a.* Studioso; libresco; pedante.

booklet, *n.* Libretto, opuscolo, *m.*

bookseller, *n.* Libraio, *m.* **Bookseller's shop,** libreria, *f.*

bookshelf, *n.* Scaffale, *m.*

bookstall, *n.* Banco, chiosco, *m.*, edicola, *f.*

booktrade, *n.* Commercio librario, *m.*

bookworm, *n.* (*fig.*) Topo di biblioteca, *m.*; (*Zool.*) tignola, *f.*

boom (1) [buːm], *n.* (*Naut.*) Boma, asta, *f.*; (*of harbour*) ostruzione *f.*, catena di porto, *f.*

boom (2), *n.* Rimbombo, *m.* || *v.i.* Rimbombare, tuonare.

boom (3), *n.* (*Comm.*) Attività negli affari, *f.*; commercio vivace, *m.*; sviluppo straordinario, aumento rapido di valore, *m.* || *v.i.* Prosperare, aumentare rapidamente.

boomerang [ˈbuːməræŋ], *n.* Bomerang, *m.*

boon [buːn], *n.* Dono, beneficio, favore, vantaggio, *m.* || *a.* Gaio, gioioso; benigno, allegro. **It will be a great — to us,** ci sarà di gran vantaggio; **a — companion,** un compagnone.

boor [buːɹ], *n.* Contadino, rustico; rozzo, zotico, *m.*

boorish, *a.* Rozzo, zotico, incolto.

boorishness, *n.* Rozzezza, *f.*

boost [buːst], *v.t.* Batter la gran cassa per qualcuno o qualcosa. || *n.* Pubblicità chiassosa, *f.*

boot (1) [buːt], *n.* Stivale, *m.*, scarpa, *f.*; (*Motor.*) portabagagli, *m.* **Top-boots,** stivaloni, *m.pl.*; **boots** (*at an hotel*) garzone d'albergo, *m.*; — **-maker,** calzolaio, *m.*; — **-shop,** calzoleria, *f.*; — **-trees,** forme per stivali, *f. pl.*; (*colloq.*) **like old boots,** vigorosamente; **my heart sank into my boots,** avevo perduto tutto il coraggio; **I shouldn't like to be in your boots,** non vorrei essere al vostro posto.

boot (2), *n.* Profitto, vantaggio, *m.* **To —,** per giunta. || *v.t.* **What boots it?** A che serve?

bootee [buːˈtiː], *n.* Scarpetta per bambini, *f.*; calzatura di media altezza, *f.*

booth [buːð], *n.* Baracca, tenda, *f.* **Polling- —,** cabina elettorale, *f.*

bootjack [ˈbuːtdʒæk], *n.* Cavastivali, *m.*

bootlace, *n.* Stringa, *f.*

bootlegger [ˈbuːtlegəɹ], *n.* Contrabbandiere (di alcool), *m.*

bootless (1), *a.* Inutile, vano.

bootless (2), *a.* Senza scarpe.

bootlessly, *adv.* Inutilmente, invano.

bootlessness, *n.* Inutilità, *f.*
booty [ˈbuːti], *n.* Preda di guerra, *f.*; bottino, *m.*
booze [buːz], *v.i.* Ubriacarsi, inebbriarsi. || *n.* Gozzoviglia, *f.*
boozer, *n.* Ubriacone, beone, *m.*
boozy, *a.* Ubriaco, ebbro.
bo-peep [bouˈpiːp], *n.* **To play at —,** far capolino, far cucù.
boracic [bəˈræsik], *a.* (*Chem.*) Borico. **— acid,** acido borico, *m.*
borage [ˈbɔrədʒ], *n.* (*Bot.*) Borragine, borrana, *f.*
borax [ˈbɔːræks], *n.* (*Chem.*) Borace, *m.*
border [ˈbɔːɹdəɹ], *n.* Orlo, margine, confine, *m.*; frontiera, *f.*; (*garden*) aiuola, *f.* || *v.t.* Orlare; rasentare. **— town,** città di confine, *f.*; **that borders upon insolence,** ciò confina colla sfacciataggine; **he's bordering on fifty,** ha quasi cinquant'anni.
borderer, *n.* Abitante della frontiera, *f.*
bordering, *a.* Vicino, limitrofo, confinante.
borderland, *n.* Paese confinante, *m.*
borderline, *a.* **— case,** caso limite, *m.*
bore (1) [bɔːɹ], *v.t.* Forare, bucare, perforare; alesare, sondare. || *n.* Buco, foro, *m.*; alesaggio, *m.*; (*of a firearm*) calibro, *m.*; (*Min.*) sondaggio, *m.*; (*for water*) trivella, *f.*
bore (2), *v.t.* Annoiare, seccare, infastidire. || *n.* Seccatore, *m.*; seccatura, molestia, noia, *f.*
bore (3), *n.* (*tidal wave*) Riflusso, *m.*
boreal, *a.* Boreale. **Boreas,** Borea, *m.*
boredom, *n.* Noia, *f.*
borer, *n.* Foratore (*person*), *m.*; perforatrice (*tool*), *f.*
boric [ˈbɔrik], *a.* Borico.
boring, *n.* Foratura, *f.*; (*for water*) trivellamento, *m.*
born [bɔːɹn], *a.* Nato; partorito; di nascita. **To be —,** nascere, **— of poor parents,** nato da genitori poveri; **— again,** rigenerato; **— with a silver spoon in one's mouth,** nato vestito; **— under a lucky star,** nato sotto una buona stella; **first- —,** primogenito; **— blind,** cieco nato.
borne [bɔːɹn], *p.p.* **bear. — down,** accasciato, abbattuto.
boron [ˈbɔːrɔn], *n.* (*Chem.*) Boro, *m.*
borough [ˈbʌrə], *n.* Città, *f.*, comune, *f.*; borgo, *m.*; borgata, *f.*; municipio, *m.*
borrow [ˈbɔrou], *v.t.* Prendere in prestito, farsi prestare; adottare, derivare. **He borrowed a book from me,** mi ha preso un libro in prestito; **he has borrowed an idea of mine,** ha adottato una mia idea.
borrower, *n.* Chi prende in prestito; accattatore, *m.*
borrowing, *n.* Il prendere in prestito, *m.*; adozione, *f.*
boscage [ˈbɔskədʒ], *n.* Boscaglia, *f.*
bosh [bɔʃ], *n.* Sciocchezze, *f.pl.* || *inter.* Chiacchiere!
bosky [ˈbɔski], *a.* Alberato, cespuglioso.
bosom [ˈbuzəm], *n.* Seno, petto, *m.*; grembo, *m.* **— friend,** amico intimo, *m.*; **in the — of one's family,** in seno alla propria famiglia.
Bosphorus, Bosporus [ˈbɔsfərəs, ˈbɔspərəs], *n.* (*Geog.*) Il Bosforo, *m.*
boss (1) [bɔs], *n.* Bugna, protuberanza, *f.*; mozzo, *m.* **Propeller —,** mozzo dell'elica, *m.*
boss (2), *n.* Padrone, capo, *m.* || *v.t.* Comandare, dirigere.
botanic, botanical [bəˈtænik, bəˈtænikl], *a.* Botanico. **Botanic gardens,** orto botanico, *m.*
botanist, *n.* Botanico, *m.*; botanista, *m.f.*
botanize, *v.i.* Studiare botanica.
botany, *n.* Botanica, *f.*
botch [bɔtʃ], *n.* Abborracciamento, rattoppo, *m.* || *v.t.i.* Rattoppare, rammendare, abborracciare.
botcher, *n.* Pasticcione, abborracciatore, *m.*
both [bouθ], *a.pron.* Tutt'e due, l'uno e l'altro, ambedue, ambo. || *conj.* tanto . . . quanto; **— of us,** noi due; **on — sides,** dalle due parti; **she is — kind and good,** essa è tanto gentile quanto buona; **— you and I,** voi e io.
bother [ˈbɔðəɹ], *v.t.* Annoiare, seccare; importunare. || *n.* Noia, seccatura, *f.*; imbroglio, *m.* || *inter.* Che seccatura!, Al diavolo!
botheration, *inter.* Caspita!, Diamine!
bothersome, *a.* Fastidioso, tedioso.
bothie [ˈbɔθi], *n.* Casetta rustica, *f.*
bottle [bɔtl], *n.* Bottiglia, *f.*, fiasco, *m.*; || *v.t.* Imbottigliare, infiascare, mettere in bottiglie. **Hot-water —,** borsa d'acqua calda, *f.*; **to bring up on the —,** allattare artificialmente; **to — up,** restringere, imbottigliare; **— -green,** verde bottiglia.
bottled, *a.* Imbottigliato. **— up,** chiuso, impedito, ristretto.
bottling, *n.* Infiascatura, *f.*
bottom [ˈbɔtəm], *n.* Fondo, *m.*, base, *f.*; fondamento, piede, *m.*; deretano; (*of chair*) sedile, *m.*; (*of ship*) carena, *f.* || *a.* Inferiore, del fondo; il più basso. || *v.t.* Mettere il fondo a; *v.i.* toccare il fondo. **At —,** in fondo; **from top to —,** da cima a fondo; **to be at the — of an intrigue,** essere l'anima di una congiura; **to probe to the —,** esaminare a fondo; **to sink to the —,** andare a fondo; **— fishing,** pesca di fondo.
bottomless, *a.* Senza fondo. **The — pit,** l'inferno, *m.*
bottomry, *n.* (*Comm.*) Cambio marittimo, *m.*
boudoir [ˈbuːdwɑːɹ], *n.* Salottino, *m.*
bough [bau], *n.* Ramo, ramoscello, *m.*
bought [bɔːt], *p.p.* of **buy.** (*Comm.*) **— book,** libro degli acquisti, *m.*
bougie [ˈbuːdʒiː], *n.* (*Med.*) Tenta, *f.*
boulder [ˈbouldəɹ], *n.* Roccia, *f.*, masso, sasso, *m.*
bounce [bauns], *v.i.* Saltare, balzare, rimbalzare. || *n.* Salto, balzo, *m.*; (*fig.*) millanteria, bravata, *f.* **To — someone into doing something,** forzare qualcuno a fare una cosa contro sua voglia.
bouncer, *n.* Millantatore, *m.*; menzogna sfacciata, *f.*
bouncing, *a.* Grosso, gagliardo. **A — girl,** una ragazza prosperosa.
bound (1) [baund], *v.i.* Balzare, rimbalzare, lanciarsi. || *n.* Balzo, salto, *m.* **At a —,** in un balzo; **to advance by leaps and bounds,** andare avanti molto rapidamente, far progressi sorprendenti.
bound (2), *n.* Limite, termine, confine, *m.* || *v.t.* Limitare, confinare. **Beyond all bounds,** sconfinato; **to set bounds,** limitare.

bound (3), *a.* In viaggio a, avviato a, diretto a. **Homeward —,** di ritorno; **outward —,** in partenza; **Whither are you —?** Dove andate? **the vessel is — for Genoa,** la nave è diretta a Genova.

bound (4), *a.* Tenuto, obbligato, certo. **I was — to answer,** dovevo rispondere; **he's — to win,** è certo di vincere.

boundary ['baundəri], *n.* Limite, confine, *m.*, frontiera, *f.* **— line,** linea di demarcazione, linea di frontiera, *f.*

bounden, *a.* Obbligatorio, imperativo. **— duty,** dovere sacro, *m.*

bounding, *a.* Balzante.

boundless, *a.* Illimitato, senza termine, sconfinato.

boundlessness, *n.* Immensità, infinità, *f.*

bounteous ['bauntiəs], *a.* Benefico, generoso, liberale.

bounteously, *adv.* Beneficamente, liberalmente.

bounteousness, *n.* Beneficenza, *f.*

bountiful, *a.* Benefico, generoso.

bountifully, *adv.* Liberalmente, generosamente, largamente.

bounty, *n.* Bontà, generosità, beneficenza, liberalità, *f.*; premio, *m.*

bouquet [bu'kei], *n.* Mazzo, mazzetto di fiori, *m.*; (*of wine*) profumo, *m.*

Bourbon ['buːɹbən], *n.a.* Borbone, *m.*

bourgeon ['bəːɹdʒən], *v.i.* Germogliare.

bourgeois ['buːɹʒwɑː], *n.a.* Borghese, *m.*

bourn (1), **bourne** [bɔːɹn], *n.* Termine, *m.*, fine, meta, *f.*

bourn (2), *n.* Ruscello, *m.*

bourse [boəɹs], *n.* (*Comm.*) Borsa, *f.*

bout [baut], *n.* Colpo, attacco (*of illness*), *m.*; turno (*of work*), *m.*; lotta, partita (*of wrestling, etc.*), *f.* **A drinking —,** un'orgia, *f.*; **a — with the gloves,** una lotta a pugni, *f.*

bovine, *a.* Bovino.

bow (1) [bau], *v.t.* Piegare, inchinare, curvare; *v.i.* piegarsi, inchinarsi; salutare, sottomettersi a. ‖ *n.* Inchino, saluto, *m.* **To — down,** abbattere, accasciare, **to — out,** congedare coninchini; **I — to your decision,** mi rimetto alla vostra decisione; **to — down in adoration,** prosternarsi in adorazione; **to — the knee,** sottomettersi.

bow (2) [bau], *n.* (*Naut.*) Prora, prua, *f.*

bow (3) [bou], *n.* Arco, *m.*; archetto (*of violin*), *m.*; arcione (*of saddle*), *m.*; nodo (*of ribbon*), *m.*; (*neck-tie*) cravatta, *f.* **Bow-window,** finestra ad arco, finestra sporgente, *f.*; **to have two strings to one's —,** avere due corde al proprio arco; **to draw the long —,** esagerare assai; **— -compasses,** compasso a balaustro, *m.*; **— -shot,** tiro d'arco, *m.*; **— -legged,** sbilenco.

bowdlerize ['baudləraiz], *v.t.* Espurgare.

bowel ['bauəl], *n.* Budello, intestino, *m.* **Bowels,** budella, *f.pl.*, intestini, *m.pl.*; (*fig.*) pietà, compassione, *f.* **In the bowels of the earth,** nelle viscere della terra; **a motion of the bowels,** andar di corpo, *m.*

bower (1) ['bauəɹ], *n.* Pergola, *f.*, frascato, boschetto, *m.*

bower (2), *a.* (*Naut.*) **— anchor,** ancora di posta, *f.*

bowery, *a.* Verde, ombroso.

bowie-knife ['buːinaif], *n.* Coltellaccio, *m.*

bowl [boul], *n.* Tazza, scodella, ciotola, *f.*, vaso, *m.*; scodellino, *m.*; fornello (*of pipe*), *m.*; (*game*) boccia, *f.* ‖ *v.t.* Far rotolare, lanciare; *v.i.* (*cricket*) servire la palla. **To play bowls,** giuocare alle bocce; **to — out,** vincere; **to — over,** far cadere, (*fig.*) sconcertare.

bowler, *n.* Lanciatore di palla, *m.* **— -hat,** cappello duro, *m.*, bombetta, *f.*

bowline ['boulin], *n.* (*Naut.*) Bolina, orza, *f.*

bowling, *a.* **— -alley,** piano per giuocare alle bocce, *m.*: pallottolaio, *m.*; **— -green,** praticello per il giuoco delle bocce, *m.*

bowman, *n.* Arciere, *m.*

bowsprit ['bousprit], *n.* (*Naut.*) Bompresso, *m.*

bowyer ['bouəɹ], *n.* Arciere, *m.*, chi fabbrica archi.

box (1) [bɔks], *n.* Scatola, cassa, cassetta, *f.*; bossolo, bossoletto, *m.*; (*chest*) cofano, *m.*; (*driver's*) cassetta, *f.*; (*trunk*) baule, *m.*; (*for horses*) stalla, *f.*; (*Theat.*) palco, *m.* ‖ *v.t.* Incassare, mettere in una scatola. **Ballot- —,** urna, *f.*; **Christmas —,** strenna, *f.*; **hunting- —,** casino da caccia, *m.*; **sentry- —,** garitta, *f.*; **snuff- —,** tabacchiera, *f.*; **letter- —,** buca delle lettere, *f.*; (*Theat.*) **— -office,** biglietteria, *f.*; **strong- —,** cassa forte, *f.*; **money- —,** salvadanaro, *m.*; **— spanner,** chiave per dadi, *f.*; **— -spring mattress,** letto a molle, *m.*; **to put someone in the witness- —,** far venire uno al banco dei testimoni; (*Naut.*) **to — the compass,** fare il giro della bussola; **to — up,** confinare.

box (2), *v.i.* Lottare a pugni, fare a pugni, battersi; pugilare. **To — someone's ears,** schiaffeggiare, dare uno scappellotto a qualcheduno.

box (3), *n.* (*Bot.*) Bosso, *m.*

boxer, *n.* Pugilatore, *m.*; (*Zool.*) specie di cane.

boxing, *n.* Pugilato, *m.*; la boxe, *f.* **— -match,** partita di pugilato, *f.*; **— -glove,** guanto da pugilato, *m.*

boxwood, *n.* Legno di bosso, *m.*

boy [bɔi], *n.* Ragazzo, fanciullo, giovanetto, *m.* **— Scout,** Giovane Esploratore, *m.*; **cabin- —,** mozzo, *m.*; **choir- —,** corista, *m.*; **a naughty —,** un birichino, *m.*; **schoolboy,** scolaro, scolare, *m.* **My dear old —!** Caro mio!

boycott ['bɔikɔt], *v.t.* Boicottare. ‖ *n.* Boicottaggio, *m.*

boyhood, *n.* Puerizia, fanciullezza, *f.*

boyish, boylike, *a.* Puerile, fanciullesco.

boyishly, *adv.* Fanciullescamente.

boyishness, *n.* Fanciullaggine, puerilità, *f.*

brace [breis], *n.* Paio, *m.*; coppia, *f.*; (*Print.*) grappa, *f.*; (*carpenter's*) trapano, *m.*, menarola, *f.*; (*Arch.*) attacco, sostegno, rampone, *m.*; (*Naut.*) braccio di antenna, *m.* ‖ *v.t.* Attaccare, legare; serrare; rinvigorire, fortificare; (*Naut.*) bracciare. **A pair of braces,** bretelle, *f.pl.*, straccali, *m.pl.*

bracelet, *n.* Braccialetto, *m.*

bracer, *n.* Tonico, fortificante, *m.*

brach [brætʃ], *n.* Cagna, *f.*

brachial ['breikiəl], *a.* (*Anat.*) Brachiale.

brachycephalic [bræki'sefælik], *a.* Brachicefalo.

bracing, *a.* Fortificante, salubre.

bracken ['brækən], *n.* (*Bot.*) Felce, *f.*

bracket ['brækit], *n.* Mensola, *f.*, braccio, *m.*; (*Arch.*) modiglione, beccatello, *m.*; (*Print.*) parentesi, *f.* || *v.t.* Accoppiare; pareggiare; mettere fra parentesi. **To be bracketed** (*in exams., etc.*), essere classificato alla pari.
brackish ['brækiʃ], *a.* Salmastro.
bract [brækt], *n.a.* (*Bot.*) Brattea, *f.*
brad [bræd], *n.* Puntina, *f.*, chiodo, *m.*
bradawl ['brædɔːl], *n.* Punterolo, *m.*
bradshaw ['brædʃɔː], *n.* Orario delle ferrovie, *m.*
brae [brei], *n.* Costa della collina, *f.*
brag [bræg], *v.i.* Vantarsi. || *n.* Millanteria, *f.*
braggadocio [brægə'douʃiou], *n.* Millanteria, rodomontata, *f.*
braggart, *n.* Millantatore, fanfarone, spaccamonti, gradasso, *m.*
braggingly, *adv.* Con boria.
Brahmin ['brɑːmin], *n.a.* Bramano, bramino, *m.*
Brahminical, *a.* Bramanico.
braid [breid], *n.* Gallone, *m.*; (*of hair*) treccia, *f.* || *v.t.* Intrecciare; gallonare; ornare con galloni.
brails [breilz], *n.pl.* (*Naut.*) Corde per imbrigliar le vele, *f.pl.* **To — up**, imbrigliar le vele.
brain, brains [brein, breinz], *n.* Cervello, *m.*; testa, *f.*; senno, intelletto, giudizio, *m.* **To blow out one's brains**, bruciarsi le cervella; **to rack one's brains**, struggersi il cervello, scervellarsi; **to have something on the —**, andare matto per qualchecosa; **to have one's — turned**, divenire vanitoso; **to pick someone's —**, usare le idee di qualcheduno; **— -fag**, esaurimento nervoso, *m.*; **— -fever**, meningite, *f.*; **— -wave**, idea spontanea, *f.*; ispirazione, *f.*; **— -work**, lavoro mentale, *m.*
brain, *v.t.* Bruciare le cervella a.
brainless, *a.* Scervellato, stupido, stordito.
brainy, *a.* Abile, destro.
braise [breiz], *v.t.* Cuocere una cosa con fuoco sotto e sopra.
brake (1) [breik], *n.* (*Bot.*) Felce, *f.*; boscaglia, macchia, *f.*
brake (2), *n.* Freno, *m.* || *v.t.* Frenare. **Vacuum- —**, freno a depressione, *m.*; **emergency —**, freno di sicurezza, *m.*; (*Rail.*) **— -van**, furgone, *m.*; **to apply the —**, mettere il freno; **— block**, ceppo di freno, *m.*; **— cable**, fune di freno, *f.*; **— drum**, tamburo di freno, *m.*; **— lever**, leva del freno, *f.*; **— rod**, tirante del freno, *m.*
brake (3), *n.* Carrozzetta, *f.*
brakesman, *n.* Frenatore, *m.*
bramble ['bræmbəl], *n.* (*Bot.*) (*bush*) Rovo, *m.*; (*berry*) mora, *f.*
brambling, *n.* (*Zool.*) Fringuello alpino, *m.*
bran [bræn], *n.* Crusca, *f.* **— mash**, crusca bagnata.
branch [brɑːntʃ], *n.* Ramo, ramoscello, *m.*; (*shop, etc.*) succursale, *f.*; (*Rail.*) biforcazione, *f.* || *v.t.* Spandere rami, ramificare. (*Rail.*) **— line**, ferrovia secondaria, diramazione, *f.*; **to destroy root and —**, estirpare; **to — off**, biforcarsi, diramarsi; **to — out**, espandersi.
brand (1) [brænd], *n.* Tizzo, tizzone, *m.*; (*Poet.*) torcia, *f.*; stigma, *m.*; (*hot iron*) marchio, *m.*; (*Comm.*) marca di fabbrica, *f.* || *v.t.* Marchiare, segnare con un marchio; stigmatizzare. **— of infamy**, marchio d'infamia, *m.*; **— new**, nuovo di zecca; **branding-iron**, ferro da bollare, *m.*
brand (2), *n.* (*Poet.*) Spada, *f.*
brandish, *v.t.* Brandire; vibrare.
brandy, *n.* Acquavite, *f.*, cognac, *m.* **— and soda**, cognac con Seltz; **— -snap**, biscotto con zenzero, *m.*
brash [bræʃ], *a.* Sfacciato e presuntuoso, borioso. **— singer**, urlatore, *m.*
brass [brɑːs], *n.* Ottone, *m.*; bronzo, *m.*; (*colloq.*) (*money*), denaro, *m.*; (*cheek*) sfacciataggine, *f.*; (*Mus.*) gli ottoni, *m.pl.* **— band**, fanfara, *f.*; **— farthing**, quattrino, *m.*; **as bold as —**, senza vergogna; **I don't care a — farthing**, non me ne importa proprio nulla.
brassard ['bræsɑːɹd], *n.* Bracciale, *m.*; distintivo, *m.*
brasserie ['bræsəriː], *n.* Birreria, *f.*
brassiere ['bræsiəɹ], *n.* Reggipetto, *m.*
brassy ['brɑːsi], *a.* D'ottone, che somiglia ottone.
brat [bræt], *n.* Marmocchio, bambino, birichino, monello, *m.*; monella, *f.*
bravado [brə'vɑːdou], *n.* Bravata, rodomontata, *f.*
brave [breiv], *a.* Coraggioso, bravo, prode, animoso; onesto; bello, ammirevole, grande. || *n.* Bravo, *m.*; Pellirossa, *m.* || *v.t.* Sfidare, affrontare, resistere.
bravely, *adv.* Coraggiosamente; ammirevolmente.
bravery, *n.* Coraggio, *m.*, prodezza, bravura, *f.*
bravo, *n.* Bravo, sicario, *m.* || *inter.* Bravo! Bene!
brawl [brɔːl], *n.* Rissa, zuffa, *f.* || *v.i.* Rissare, azzuffarsi, questionare; (*of streams*) mormorare, gorgogliare.
brawler, *n.* Rissante, rissatore, accattabrighe, *m.*
brawn [brɔːn], *n.* Salame di porco sminuzzato, *m.*; coppa, soppressata, *f.*; (*fig.*) forza muscolare, *f.*
brawny, *a.* Muscoloso.
bray (1) [brei], *v.i.* Ragliare. || *n.* Raglio, *m.*, ragliata, *f.* (*fig.*) squillo (*of trumpets*), *m.*
bray (2), *v.t.* Pestare, tritare.
braze [breiz], *v.t.* Saldare, indurare con ottone.
brazen, *a.* D'ottone; (*fig.*) sfrontato, sfacciato. **— -faced**, senza vergogna, colla faccia tosta; **to — out a matter**, far lo sfacciato, aver la faccia tosta.
brazier (1) ['breiʒəɹ], *n.* Ottonaio, *m.*
brazier (2), *n.* (*for heat*) Braciere, *m.*
Brazil [brə'zil], *n.* (*Geog.*) Il Brasile, *m.* **— wood**, brasile, *m.*; **— -nut**, noce del Brasile, *m.*
Brazilian, *n.a.* Brasiliano, *m.*
brazing, *n.* Saldatura, *f.*
breach [briːtʃ], *n.* Breccia, *f.*; rottura, *f.*; interruzione, *f.*; infrazione, violazione, *f.* || *v.t.* Battere in breccia. **— of contract**, rottura di contratto, *f.*; **— of the peace**, tumulto, *m.*; **— of promise**, mancanza alla promessa di matrimonio, *f.*; **— of trust**, abuso di fiducia, *m.*; **to stand in the —**, sostenere l'assalto.
bread [bred], *n.* Pane, *m.* **Brown —**, pane scuro, *m.*; **new —**, pane fresco, *m.*; **home-made —**, pane casalingo, *m.*; **stale —**

pane raffermo, *m.*; **our daily —,** il pane quotidiano, *m.*; **a slice of — and butter,** fetta di pane e burro, *f.*; **to be in want of —,** mancare del pane; **to get one's —,** guadagnarsi il pane; **to know which side one's — is buttered,** sapere barcarmenarsi; **to eat the — of idleness,** mangiare il pane a tradimento; **— -crumbs,** briciole di pane, *m.pl.*; **— -shop,** panetteria, *f.*; **— -knife,** coltello per pane, *m.*; **— -winner,** sostegno della famiglia, *f.*; (*Bot.*) **— -fruit tree,** albero del pane, *f.*

breadless, *a.* Senza pane.

breadth [bredθ], *n.* Larghezza, *f.*; ampiezza, *f.*; (*of cloth*) altezza, *f.*

break [breik], *v.t.* Rompere, spezzare, frangere; violare, infrangere; domare, soggiogare, scoraggiare; correggere; (*of news*) comunicare; (*of a shock*) mitigare, attutire; *v.i.* rompersi, spezzarsi; prorompere, scoppiare; (*of day*) spuntare; crepare, spaccarsi, fendersi: (*Comm.*) fallire; (*of health*) affievolirsi, indebolirsi; (*of weather*) cambiare. || *n.* Rottura, frattura, *f.*; spacco, *m.*; fenditura, *f.*; interruzione, *f.*; (*of weather*) cambiamento, *m.* **To — in a horse,** domare un cavallo; **to — into,** invadere; **to — in upon,** irrompere su; **to — off,** staccare; **to — off relations with,** rompere le relazioni con; **to — one's journey,** interrompere il viaggio; **to — one's word,** mancare alla promessa; **to — someone's heart,** spezzare il cuore a qualcuno; **to — through,** farsi strada attraverso; **to — up for the holidays,** andare in vacanza; **to — up,** distruggere, disciogliere, dissolversi; **to — away,** strapparsi; **to — down in health,** ammalarsi; (*Motor., etc.*) **to — down,** avere una panna; **to — into tears,** scoppiare in lagrime; **to — loose,** scappare. liberarsi; **to — out** (*fire, epidemic, etc.*) scoppiare; **— of continuity,** soluzione di continuità, *f.*; **— of day,** alba, *f.*; **without a —,** senza interruzione; **— -down,** collasso, esaurimento, indebolimento, *m.*; (*of motor., etc.*) panna, *f.*; (*of train*) guasto, *m.*; **to — a vow,** rompere un voto. **— -down gang,** squadra di soccorso, *f.*

breakable, *a.* Fragile.

breakage, *n.* Rottura, frattura, *f.* **To charge for breakages,** far pagare i guasti.

breakaway, *n.* Evasione, fuga, *f.*

breaker, *n.* Rompitore, *m.*; trasgressore, *m.*; (*of animals*) domatore, *m.*; (*wave*) frangente, cavallone, *m.*

breakfast [ˈbrekfəst], *n.* Prima colazione. || *v.i.* Far colazione. **— -set,** servizio da colazione, *m.* ;**— -time,** ora della colazione, *f.*

breaking, *n.* Rottura, infrazione, *f.*; (*of voice*) cambiamento, *m.*

breakneck, *a.* Rompicollo. **At — speed,** a rompicollo.

breakwater, *n.* Diga, *f.*; frangiflutti, *m.*; frangionda, *m.*

bream (1), *n.* (*Zool.*) Scarda, *f.*

bream (2), *v.t.* (*Naut.*) Bruscare.

breast [brest], *n.* Seno, petto, *m.*; (*fig.*) cuore, *m.*, anima *f.*; (*of woman*) mammella, *f.* **At the —,** alle mammelle; **to make a clean — of,** confessare tutto; **— -deep,** fino al petto; **— -high,** ad altezza di petto; **— -pin,** spillo per la cravatta; **— -pocket,** taschino, *m.*; (*Swimming*) **— -stroke,** nuotata a rana, *f.*

breastbone, *n.* (*Anat.*) Sterno, *m.*

breastplate, *n.* Corazza, *f.*, pettorale, *m.*

breastsummer, bressummer [ˈbresəməɹ], *n.* (*Arch.*) Trave grossa per sostenere la fronte di una casa, *f.*; architrave, *m.*

breastwork, *n.* Parapetto, *m.*

breath [breθ], *n.* Respiro, fiato, alito, *m.*; respirazione, lena, *f.*; (*fig.*) vita, esistenza, *f.* **Last —,** ultimo respiro; **shortness of —,** respirazione difficile, *f.*; **a — of fresh air,** una boccata d'aria fresca, *f.*; **there isn't a — of wind,** non c'è un alito di vento; **beneath one's —,** sottovoce; **to be out of —,** essere senza fiato; **to gasp for —,** ansare; **to hold one's —,** trattenere il fiato; **to take —,** prendere fiato; **to take one's — away,** togliere il fiato sconcertare.

breathe [briːð], *v.t.i.* Respirare, alitare, fiatare, spirare. (*fig.*) **To — again,** tornare a respirare; **to — upon,** macchiare; **to — one's last,** esalare l'ultimo respiro.

breathing, *a.* Vivo, vivente. || *n.* Respirazione, aspirazione, *f.* **— -hole,** spiraglio, spiracolo, *m.*; **— -space,** tempo di respiro, *m.*

breathless, *a.* Sfiatato, senza fiato; morto.

breathlessness, *n.* Mancanza di respiro, *f.*, sfiatamento, *m.*

breech [briːtʃ], *n.* Deretano, *m.*; (*of firearms*) culatta, *f.* **— -block,** otturatore, *m.*; **— -loader,** arma a retrocarica, *f.*

breeches, *n.pl.* Calzoni, *m.pl.*, brache, *f.pl.* **Knee- —,** calzoncini, *m.pl.*; **— -buoy,** salvagente a brache, *m.*

breeching, *n.* (*Naut.*) Braca, *f.*; (*of horse*) straccale, *m.*

breed [briːd], *v.t.* Generare, procreare; (*fig.*) dare origine a, cagionare; (*of animals*) allevare; *v.i.* moltiplicare, nascere. || *n.* Razza, famiglia, stirpe, progenie, *f.* **Ill-bred,** screanzato, maleducato; **well-bred,** ben educato.

breeder, *n.* Allevatore, *m.*, allevatrice, *f.*

breeding, *n.* Educazione, creanza, *f.*; (*of cattle*) allevamento, *m.* **Good —,** buona creanza, *f.*; **in- —,** accoppiamento consanguineo, *m.*

breeze [briːz], *n.* Brezza, *f.*, venticello, *m.* **A gentle —,** una brezzolina, *f.*; (*Arch.*) **— -block,** un mattone di rifiuti di coke, *m.*

breezy, *a.* Arioso, fresco; vivace.

Bremen [ˈbremən], *n.* (*Geog.*) Brema, *f.*

bressummer [cp. **breastsummer**].

brethren [ˈbreðren], *n.pl.* Fratelli, confratelli, *m.pl.*

Breton [ˈbretən], *n.a.* Bretone, brettone, *m.*

breve [briːv], *n.* (*Mus.*) Breve, *m.*

brevet [ˈbrevet], *n.* (*Mil.*) Brevetto, *m.* **— rank,** grado onorario, *m.*

breviary [ˈbriːviəɹi], *n.* Breviario, *m.*

brevier [breˈviəɹ], *n.* (*Print.*) Garamoncino, *m.*

brevity [ˈbreviti], *n.* Brevità, concisione, *f.*

brew [bruː], *v.t.i.* Fare la birra, mescolare; essere in fermentazione; (*of a storm*) levarsi; (*fig.*) macchinare, ordire, tramare. || *n.* Mescolanza, *f.* **A storm is brewing,** si leva un temporale; **a good —,** una bella mescolanza, *f.*

brewer, *n.* Birraio, fabbricante di birra, *m.*

brewery, *n.* Birreria, fabbrica di birra, *f.*
brewing, *n.* Infusione; fermentazione di birra, *f.*
briar [cp. **brier**].
bribe [braib], *v.t.* Corrompere, sedurre, ungere la mano a. || *n.* Dono, donativo per corrompere, *m.*; (*fig.*) esca, offa, *f.*
bribery, *n.* Corruzione, *f.*, corrompimento, *m.*
bric-a-brac [ˈbrikəbræk], *n.* Anticaglie, *f.pl.*, ferravecchi, *m.pl.*
brick [brik], *n.* Mattone, *m.*; (*colloq.*) brav'uomo, *m.* || *a.* Di mattoni. || *v.t.* Ammattonare. **To — up,** murare con mattoni; (*children's*) **bricks,** le costruzioni, *f.pl.*; **— -bat,** pezzetto di mattone, *m.*; **— -dust,** polvere di mattoni, *f.*; **— -field,** mattonaia, *f.*; **— -kiln,** fornace per mattoni, *f.*
bricklayer, *n.* Muratore, *m.*
brickmaker, *n.* Mattonaio, fornaciaio, *m.*
brickwork, *n.* Costruzione in mattoni, *f.*
bridal [ˈbraidəl], *a.* Nuziale, di nozze, di sposa.
bride, *n.* Sposa, sposa novella, *f.*
bridecake, *n.* Torta di nozze, *f.*
bridegroom, *n.* Sposo, *m.*
bridesmaid, *n.* Damigella d'onore, *f.*
bridesman, *n.* Testimonio, paggio d'onore, *m.*
Bridewell, *n.* Casa di correzione, *f.*
bridge [bridʒ], *n.* Ponte, *m.*; (*foot*) passerella, *f.*; (*of violin, etc.*) ponticello, *m.*; (*of steamer*) ponte di commando, *m.*; (*of nose*) dorso, *m.*; (*Cards*) brigge, giuoco del ponte, *m.* || *v.t.* Costruire un ponte sopra, gettare un ponte su; colmare; **to — a gap,** colmare una lacuna; **— of boats,** ponte di barche, *m.*; **suspension- —,** ponte sospeso, *m.*; **swing- —,** ponte girevole, *m.*
bridgehead, *n.* Testa di ponte, *f.*
bridle [ˈbraidl], *n.* Briglia, *f.*, freno, *m.*; (*Naut.*) gomena, *f.*; (*Med.*) frenello, *m.* || *v.t.* Mettere la briglia a, imbrigliare, raffrenare; *v.i.* ringalluzzirsi, insuperbirsi, stizzirsi. **— -path,** strada mulattiera, *f.*
brief (1) [bri:f], *a.* Breve, corto, conciso.
brief (2), *n.* (*Law*) Conclusionale, sommario, sunto, incartamento, *m.* || *v.t.* Affidare una causa a, costituire; dare istruzioni precise.
briefless, *a.* (*Law*) Senza clienti.
briefly, *adv.* Brevemente, in modo conciso.
briefness, *n.* Brevità, concisione, *f.*
brier, briar [ˈbraiəɹ], *n.* (*Bot.*) Rovo, *m.*; pruno, *m.* **Sweet —,** rosa salvatica, *f.*; **— -rose,** rosa di macchia, *f.*; **— pipe,** pipa di radica, *f.*
brig [brig], *n.* (*Naut.*) Bric, brigantino, *m.*
brigade [briˈgeid], *n.* Brigata, *f.* || *v.t.* Far brigata, costituire in brigata.
brigadier [brigəˈdiəɹ], *n.* Comandante di brigata, *m.*
brigand [ˈbrigənd], *n.* Brigante, bandito, *m.*
brigandage, *n.* Brigantaggio, *m.*
brigantine [ˈbrigənti:n], *n.* (*Naut.*) Brigantino, *m.*, goletta, *f.*
bright [brait], *a.* Brillante, fulgente, lucente, chiaro; gaio, allegro; intelligente. **To see the — side,** vedere tutto colore di rosa; **a — boy,** un ragazzo intelligente, *m.*
brighten, *v.t.* Fare brillare, lustrare; lucidare; (*fig.*) rallegrare, animare; (*of weather*) rischiarare.
brightly, *adv.* Brillantemente, allegramente, gaiamente.
brightness, *n.* Splendore, lustro, *m.*, chiarezza, allegrezza, *f.*; vivacità, *f.*
Bright's disease, *n.* (*Med.*) Malattia di Bright, nefrite cronica, *f.*
brill [bril], *n.* (*Zool.*) Rombo liscio, *m.*
brilliance, brilliancy [ˈbriliəns, ˈbriliənsi], *n.* Lustro, splendore, *m.*, lucidezza, *f.*; (*fig.*) abilità, intelligenza, *f.*
brilliant, *n.* Lucente, splendido, brillante. || *n.* Brillante, *m.* **A — career,** una carriera brillante, *f.*
brilliantine, *n.* Brillantina, *f.*
brilliantly, *adv.* Splendidamente, brillantemente.
brim [brim], *n.* Orlo, bordo, *m.*; margine, *m.*; (*of hat*) tesa, *f.* || *v.i.* Essere pieno fino all'orlo. **To — over,** traboccare; **— -full,** tutto pieno, ricolmo.
brimless, *a.* Senz'orlo.
brimmed, *a.* Orlato. **Broad- —,** a tesa larga.
brimmer, *n.* Bicchiere pieno, *m.*
brimstone, *n.* Zolfo, *m.*
brindled [ˈbrindld], *a.* Brizzolato, chiazzato, tigrato.
brine, *n.* Salamoia, *f.*; acqua salata, *f.*
bring [briŋ], *v.t.* Portare, recare; menare, condurre, ricondurre; trasportare; ridurre; mettere. **To — about,** cagionare, produrre; **to — away,** menare, portare via; **to — back,** riportare; **to — down,** far scendere, abbattere, atterrare; **to — forth,** produrre, dare nascita a; **to — forward,** avanzare, mettere avanti; (*Comm.*) riportare; **to — in,** introdurre; **to — home to,** convincere di, far cadere la colpa su; **to — into fashion,** render di moda; **to — to pass,** cagionare; **— into question,** mettere in questione, porre sul tappeto; **to — nearer,** avvicinare; **to — on,** cagionare; **to — out,** fare uscire, pubblicare; **to — over,** menare, portare, convertire; (*Naut.*) **to — to,** mettere in panna; **to — to justice,** far processare; **to — to poverty,** ridurre in miseria; **to — to,** far tornare in sè; **to be brought to bed,** partorire; **to — together,** adunare, raccogliere, riconciliare; **to — to perfection,** portare alla perfezione, perfezionare; **to — under,** sottomettere, assoggettare; **to — up,** educare, allevare, tirar su; **to — up the rear,** essere l'ultimo, comandare la retroguardia; **to — word to,** fare sapere, prevenire; (*Comm.*) **brought forward,** riportato.
brink [briŋk], *n.* Argine, margine, orlo, *m.* **On the — of the grave,** con un piede nella fossa; **on the — of ruin,** sull'orlo della rovina.
briny [braini], *a.* Salmastro, salino. **The — deep,** il mare, *m.*
briony [cp. **bryony**].
briquette [briˈket], *n.* Mattonella, formella di carbone, *f.*
brisk [brisk], *a.* Vivace, pronto, agile, lesto, sveglio.
briskly, *adv.* Presto, lestamente, agilmente.
briskness, *n.* Vivacità, prontezza, agilità, *f.*
brisket [ˈbriskit], *n.* Petto di bue, *m.*
bristle [brisl], *n.* Setola, *f.*, pelo, *m.* || *v.i.* Rizzarsi, (*of hair*) arricciarsi. **To — up** (*with temper*), arrabbiarsi, offendersi.
bristling, *a.* Setolato, spinoso. **— with difficulties,** spinosissimo.

bristly, *a.* Setoloso, irsuto, ispido.
Britain [ˈbritən], *n.* (*Geog.*) La Gran Bretagna, *f.*
Britannia metal, *n.* Metallo inglese, *m.*
Britannic, *a.* Britannico.
British [ˈbritiʃ], *a.* Britannico, inglese. — **consul,** console britannico, *f.*; — **Isles,** Isole Britanniche, *f.pl.*
Briton, *n.* Inglese, *m.;* (*Hist.*) Britanno, *m.*
Brittany, *n.* (*Geog.*) La Bretagna, *f.*
brittle [britl], *a.* Fragile.
brittleness, *n.* Fragilità, *f.*
broach (1) [broutʃ], *n.* (*Cookery*) Spiedo, *m.*
broach (2), *v.t.* Spillare; (*fig.*) intavolare. ‖ *n.* Spillone, *m.* **To — a subject,** portare un argomento in discussione.
broach (3), *v.t.* (*Naut.*) **To — to,** girare contro vento.
broad [brɔːd], *a.* Largo, ampio, vasto; (*fig.*) libero, grosso, grossolano; marcato (*of accent*). **To give a — hint,** dare a divedere, far capire; **a — story,** un racconto salace, *m.*; — **daylight,** pieno giorno; **a — grin,** un sogghigno, *m.*; **a — distinction,** una vaga distinzione, *f.* — **awake,** svegliatissimo; **as — as it is long,** tutt'uno; — **-brimmed hat,** cappello a larghe tese, *m.*; — **-minded,** tollerante.
broadcast [ˈbrɔːdkɑːst], *v.t.* Disseminare, divulgare; (*Radio*) trasmettere per radio, radiodiffondere. ‖ *adv.* A volo, a caso. ‖ *n.* Programma radiofonico, *m.*
broadcaster, *n.* Diffusore; annunziatore; conferenziere alla radio, *m.*
broadcasting, *n.* Radiodiffusione, *f.* — **-station,** stazione radio, *m.*
broadcloth, *n.* Panno fino, *m.*
broaden, *v.i.* Allargarsi; *v.t.* allargare, estendere.
broadly, *adv.* Largamente; generalmente.
broadness, *n.* Larghezza, *f.*; salacitá, *f.*
broadside (1), *n.* (*Naut.*) Fiancata, bordata, *f.* **To fire a —,** tirare una bordata.
broadside (2), **broadsheet,** *n.* Manifesto, *m.*
broadsword *n.* Spadone, *m.*, sciabola, *f.*
brocade [broˈkeid], *n.* Broccato, *m.*
broccoli [ˈbrɔkoli], *n.* (*Bot.*) Broccoli, *m.pl.*
brochure [ˈbrɔʃjuːɹ], *n.* Opuscolo, *m.*
brocket [ˈbrkət], *n.* (*Zool.*) Cerbiatto, *m.*
brogue [broug], *n.* Accento dialettale d'Irlanda, *m.*; **brogues,** scarpe forti di cuoio, *f.pl.*
broil [brɔil], *v.t.* Arrostire sulla graticola. ‖ *n.* Rissa, zuffa, *f.*, tumulto, *m.*
broiling, *a.* Caldissimo, bruciante.
broke, *adv.* (*colloq.*) Al verde. alle strette.
broken [ˈbroukən], *a.* Rotto, spezzato, infranto, interrotto; (*of the voice*) fioco, fesso; (*of health*) acciaccato, deperito: — **sleep,** sonno interrotto, *m.*; **a — voice,** una voce fessa, *f.*; — **health,** salute malferma, *f.*; **to speak — English,** parlare un inglese imperfetto; — **weather,** tempo incerto, *m.*; — **-hearted,** col cuore spezzato; — **-winded,** bolso.
broker, *n.* Sensale, agente, *m.*; commissionario, *m.* **Ship- —,** sensale marittimo, *m.*; **stock- —,** agente di cambio, *m.*
brokerage, *n.* Senseria, *f.*
bromide [ˈbroumaid], *n.* (*Chem.*) Bromuro, *m.*
bromine, *n.* (*Chem.*) Bromo, *m.*
bronchia [ˈbrɔŋkiə], *n.pl.* (*Anat.*) Bronchi, *m.pl.*
bronchial, *a.* Bronchiale.
bronchitis [brɔŋˈkaitis], *n.* (*Med.*) Bronchite, *f.*
bronze [brɔnz], *n.* Bronzo, *m.* ‖ *v.t.* Abbronzare. ‖ *a.* Bronzeo.
brooch [broutʃ], *n.* Spilla, *f.*, fermaglio, *m.*
brood [bruːd], *n.* Covata, nidiata, *f.*; famiglia, *f.* ‖ *v.i.* Covare, ruminare. **To — over,** meditare; — **mare,** cavalla di razza, *f.*
broody, *a.* Che cova, covante. — **hen,** chioccia, *f.*
brook (1) [bruk], *n.* Ruscello, *m.*
brook (2), *v.t.* Soffrire, sopportare, tollerare.
brooklet, *n.* Ruscelletto, *m.*
broom [brum], *n.* Scopa, granata, *f.*; (*Bot.*) scopa, erica, ginestra, *f.* **New brooms sweep clean,** scopa nuova scopa bene.
broomstick, *n.* Manico di scopa, *m.*
broth [brɔθ], *n.* Brodo, *m.*; zuppa, *f.* (*fig.*) **A — of a boy,** un ragazzo per bene, *m.*
brothel [ˈbrɔθəl], *n.* Bordello, lupanare, postribolo, *m.*
brother [ˈbrʌðəɹ], *n.* Fratello, *m.*; collega, *m.*; (*Eccles.*) frate, *m.* — **-in-law,** cognato, *m.*; — **officer,** collega ufficiale, *m.*; **elder —,** fratello maggiore, *m.*; **younger —,** fratello minore, *m.*; **foster —,** fratello di latte, *m.*; **half- —,** fratellastro, *m.*
brotherhood, *n.* Fraternità, confraternita, *f.*
brotherless, *a.* Senza fratelli.
brotherly, *a.* Fraterno. — **love,** carità fraterna, *f.*
brougham [bruːm], *n.* Brum, *m.*, carrozza, *f.*, cupè, *m.*
brow [brau], *n.* Ciglio, *m.*; fronte, *f.*; (*of hill*) cima, *f.* **To knit one's brows,** aggrottare le ciglia; **to raise one's brows,** alzare le ciglia; **to smooth one's —,** spianare la fronte.
browbeat, *v.t.* Intímidire, minacciare.
brown [braun], *a.* Bruno, marrone; (*of skin*) abbronzato; scuro, (*of hair*) castagno. ‖ *n.* Bruno, color bruno, *m.*; brunezza, *f.* ‖ *v.t.* abbrunire; abbronzare; rosolare. — **bread,** pane scuro, *m.*; — **paper,** carta da pacchi, *f.*; — **boots,** scarpe gialle, *f.pl.*; — **sugar,** zucchero greggio, *m.*; **in a — study,** impensierito, soprappensiero.
brownie, *n.* Folletto, *m.*; (*Girl Guide*) Giovine Esploratrice, *f.*
brownish, *a.* Brunetto.
brownness, *n.* Colore bruno *or* marrone, *m.*
browse [brauz], *v.i.* Pascere, pascolare, brucare. ‖ *n.* Verdura, *f.*
bruin [ˈbruːin], *n.* Orso, *m.*
bruise [bruːz], *v.t.* Ammaccare, acciaccare, pestare. ‖ *n.* Ammaccatura, contusione, *f.*
bruised, *a.* Ammaccato, contuso.
bruiser, *n.* Pugilatore, *m.*
bruit [bruːt], *v.t.* Far correre voce, divulgare. ‖ *n.* (*obs.*) Rumore, *m.*, diceria, *f.*
brummagem [ˈbrʌmədʒəm], *a.* Posticcio, finto, di poco valore.
brunette [bruːˈnet], *n.* Brunetta, *f.*
brunt [brʌnt], *n.* Violenza, *f.*, impeto, *m.*; attacco, urto, *m.* **To bear the —,** sostenere l'impeto.
brush [brʌʃ], *n.* Spazzola, scopa, *f.*; pennello, setolino, *m.*; (*of fox*) coda, *f.*; (*affray*) schermaglia, *f.* ‖ *v.t.* Spazzolare, scopare. **To — away,** spazzare via; **to — past,** sfiorare; **to — up,** dare una spazzolata, (*fig.*) ripassare; **to — one's hair,** spazzolarsi i capelli.

brushing, *n.* Spazzolatura, *f.*
brushwood, *n.* Macchia, *f.*, frasche, *f.pl.*
brusque [brusk], *a.* Brusco, aspro.
brusqueness, brusquerie, *n.* Bruschezza, *f.*
Brussels ['brʌsəlz], *n.* (*Geog.*) Brusselle, *f.* **— carpet**, tappeto di Brusselle, *m.*; **— sprouts**, cavoli di Brusselle, *m.pl.*
brutal ['bru:təl], *a.* Brutale, bestiale; crudele, inumano.
brutality [bru:'tæliti], *n.* Brutalità, crudeltà, *f.*
brutalize, *v.t.* Abbrutire.
brutally, *adv.* Brutalmente.
brute, *n.* Bruto, animale, *m.*, bestia, fiera, belva, *f.* || *a.* Bruto, animale, selvaggio. **— force**, forza bruta, *f.*; **— beast**, bestia feroce, *f.*; **the — creation**, il regno animale, *f.*
brutish, *a.* Abbrutito, bestiale, brutale.
brutishly, *adv.* Bestialmente, brutalmente.
brutishness, *n.* Brutalità, *f.*
bryony ['braiəni], *n.* (*Bot.*) Brionia, *f.*
bubble [bʌbl], *n.* Bolla, bollicina, *f.*; (*fig.*) chimera, *f.*; progetto vano, *m.* || *v.i.* Far bolle; bollire, sibilare. **To — over**, traboccare; **to — -up**, gorgogliare, scaturire.
bubbling, *a.* Bollente.
bubonic, *a.* bubbonico; **— plague**, peste bubbonica.
buccaneer [bʌkə'niəɹ], *n.* Pirata, bucaniere, *m.* || *v.i.* Pirateggiare.
buck (1) [bʌk], *n.* (*Zool.*) Daino, caprone, *m.*; (*fig.*) damerino, *m.* **— -shot**, pallinacci, *m.pl.*; **— -rabbit**, coniglio, *m.*; **— -hare**, lepre, *m.*; **old —**, vecchio galante, *m.*
buck (2), *v.i.* Far capriole, inarcarsi, fare il bucato || *inter.* (*colloq.*) **— up!** Coraggio! Spicciatevi!
bucket, *n.* Secchia, *f.*, secchione, *m.*; (*Naut.*) bugliolo, *m.* (*colloq.*) **To kick the —**, morire; (*Comm.*) **— -shop**, agenzia di cambio irregolare, *f.*
buckle [bʌkl], *n.* Fibbia, *f.* || *v.t.* Affibbiare, piegare; *v.i.* piegarsi, torcersi. **To — to**, applicarsi a, cominciare a; **to — on armour**, indossare le armi.
buckler, *n.* Scudo, *m.*
buckram ['bʌkrəm], *n.* sorta di tela dura, *f.*
buckskin, *n.* Pelle di daino, *f.*
buckthorn, *n.* (*Bot.*) Spino cervino, *m.*
buckwheat, *n.* (*Bot.*) Grano saraceno, *m.*
bucolic [bju:'kɔlik], *a.* Bucolico. || *n.* Bucolica, *f.*
bud [bʌd], *n.* Bocciuolo, germoglio, bottone, *m.*, boccia, gemma, *f.*; (*fig.*) germe, *m.* || *v.i.* Spuntare, germogliare, mettere le gemme; *v.t.* innestare a occhio. **In —**, sbocciante, in bocciolo; **to nip in the —**, tagliar corto, soffocare sul bel principio; **a budding poet**, un poeta in erba, *m.*
Buddhism ['bʌdizm], *n.* Buddismo, *m.*
Buddhist, *n.* Buddista, *m.*
buddy, *n.* (*colloq.*) Amico intimo, *m.*
budge [bʌdʒ], *v.t.* Muovere; *v.i.* muoversi.
budget, *n.* Fascio, sacco, *m.*; (*Pol.Comm.*) bilancio pubblico, bilancio preventivo, *m.* || *v.t.* **To — for**, mettere in bilancio. **A — of news**, un fascio di notizie, *m.*
buff [bʌf], *n.a.* Fulvo, color camoscio, *m.* || *v.t.* Lucidare con pelle, rendere liscio. **— -leather**, pelle di bufalo, *f.*; **blind man's —**, mosca cieca, *f.*
buffalo ['bʌfəlou], *n.* (*Zool.*) Bufalo, *m.*
buffer, *n.* Tampone, respingente, paracolpi, reggiscosse, *m.* (*Pol.*) **— state**, stato cuscinetto, *m.*; (*colloq.*) **old —**, buon diavolo, *m.*
buffet (1) ['bʌfit], *n.* Schiaffo, *m.* || *v.t.* Dare uno schiaffo, schiaffeggiare; *v.i.* lottare contro. **Buffeted by the waves**, sbattuto dalle onde; **buffeted by fate**, tormentato dal fato.
buffet (2) ['bufei], *n.* Buffè, *m.*; credenza (*sideboard*), *f.*; **— car**, vagone ristorante, *m.*
buffoon [bə'fu:n], *n.* Buffone, *m.*
buffoonery, *n.* Buffoneria, *f.*
bug [bʌg], *n.* (*Zool.*) Cimice, *f.*; (*colloq.*) microbio, *m.* (*colloq.*) **A big —**, un pezzo grosso, *m.*
bugbear, *n.* Spauracchio, spaventacchio, *m.*
bugger ['bʌgəɹ], *v.t.* (*Law*) Sodomitare. || *n.* Sodomita, *m.*
buggy ['bʌgi], *n.* Baroccino, *m.*
bugle (1) ['bju:gl], (*Mus.*) Tromba, cornetta, *f.*, corno da caccia, *m.*
bugle (2), *n.* (*Bot.*) Bugola, *f.*
bugle (3), *n.* (*Dress*) Perlina di vetro, *f.*
bugler, *n.* Trombetta, trombettiere, *m.*
bugloss ['bju:glɔs], *n.* (*Bot.*) Buglossa, *f.*
build [bild], *v.t.* Edificare, fabbricare, costruire; (*fig.*) fondare, stabilire. || *n.* Forma, figura, fattezza, *f.*; costruzione, *f.* **To — on**, fondare su; (*fig.*) fidare in; **to — up**, edificare, murare; **a well-built man**, un uomo ben piantato, *m.*
builder, *n.* Costruttore, edificatore, fabbricatore, *m.*; (*workman*) muratore, *m.*
building, *n.* Edificio, edifizio, fabbricato, *m.*; costruzione, *f.* **— line**, allineamento, *m.*; **— materials**, materiale da costruzione, *m.*; **— society**, società edilizia, società immobiliare, *f.*; **— site**, terreno da costruzione, *m.*; area fabbricabile, *f.*
bulb [bʌlb], *n.* (*In all senses*) Bulbo, *m.*
bulbous, *a.* Bulboso.
Bulgarian [bʌl'gɛəriən], *n.a.* Bulgaro, *m.*
bulge [bʌldʒ], *n.* Gonfio, gonfiamento, *m.*, protuberanza, convessità, *f.* || *v.i.* Gonfiarsi.
bulging, *a.* Rigonfio.
bulk [bʌlk], *n.* Volume, *m.*, massa, grossezza, estensione, *f.*; (*Naut.*) carico, *m.* || *v.i.* Parere. **In —**, alla rinfusa, all'ingrosso; **to sell in —**, vendere all'ingrosso; **to — large**, parere importante.
bulkhead, *n.* Tramezzo, *m.*
bulkiness, *n.* Grossezza, massa, *f.*
bulky, *a.* Grosso, grande, voluminoso, ingombrante.
bull (1) [bul], *n.* (*Zool.*) Toro, *m.*; (*Irish*) sbaglio, svarione, *m.*; (*Stock Exchange*) rialzista, *m.* **Bull's-eye**, (*target*) barilozzo, *m.*; (*Arch.*) occhio di bue, *m.*; (*sweet*) confetto di menta, *m.*; **— -baiting**, il tormentare un toro con i cani, *m.*; **— -calf**, torello, *m.*; **— elephant**, elefante maschio, *m.*
bull (2), *n.* (*Eccles.*) Bolla, *f.*
bullace ['buləs], *n.* (*Bot.*) Prugnola di Marsilia, *m.*
bulldog, *n.* Molosso, bulldog, *m.*
bullet ['bulət], *n.* Palla, pallottola, *f.* **— -proof**, a prova di pallottole, blindato.
bulletin ['bulətin], *n.* Bollettino, *m.*
bulldozer, *n.* Apripista, *m.*; apparecchio per scassare il terreno, *m.*
bullfight, *n.* Corrida di tori, *f.*

bullfighter, *n.* Torero, *m.*
bullfinch, *n.* (*Zool.*) Ciuffolotto, *m.*
bullion ['buliən], *n.* Oro o argento in verghe, *m.*; (*fringe*) frangia d'oro o d'argento, *f.*
bullock ['bulək], *n.* (*Zool.*) Bue, *m.*
bully (1) ['buli], *n.* Bravaccio, provocatore, ammazzasette, smargiasso, prepotente, *m.* || *v.t.* Tormentare, intimidire, malmenare, bistrattare.
bully (2), *inter.* Bravo! **— for him!** Bravo lui!
bully (3), *n.* Manzo lesso in scatola, *m.*
bullyrag, *v.t.* (*colloq.*) Svillaneggiare.
bulrush ['bulrʌʃ], *n.* (*Bot.*) Giunco, *m.*
bulwark ['bulwəɹk], *n.* Baluardo, bastione, *m.*; (*Naut.*) murata, *f.*
bum [bʌm], *n.* Deretano, culo, *m.*; (*colloq. esp. American*) fannullone, *m.* **— -bailiff,** usciere, *m.*; **— -boat,** battello d'approvvigionamento, *m.*
bumble, *v.i.* Ronzare, sussurrare.
bumble-bee ['bʌmblbiː], *n.* (*Zool.*) Calabrone, *m.*
bump [bʌmp], *n.* Urto, colpo, *m.*, percossa, *f.*; enfiagione. *f.*; protuberanza, *f.* || *v.t.i.* Urtare, urtarsi contro, scontrarsi con. **To — against a wall,** urtare contro un muro; (*colloq.*) **to — off,** uccidere.
bumper, *n.* Bicchiere ricolmo, *m.*; (*Motor.*) reggiscosse, paraurti, *m.* **A — harvest,** una messe magnifica, *f.*; **a — crop,** una raccolta eccezionale, *f.*
bumpkin ['bʌmpkin], *n.* Villano, contadino, zotico, *m.*
bumptious ['bʌmpʃiəs], *a.* Presuntuoso, arrogante.
bumptiousness, *n.* Presunzione, prepotenza, *f.*
bumpy, *a.* Irregolare, poco piano. **A — road,** una strada accidentata, *f.*
bun [bʌn], *n.* Ciambella, focaccia, *f.*, panino, *m.*; (*of hair*) crocchia, *f.*
bunch [bʌntʃ], *n.* Mazzo, *m.*; fascetto (*of flowers*), *m.*; grappolo (*of grapes*), *m.*; nodo, *m.*; ciocca, *f.* || *v.t.* Mettere insieme, fare mazzo, affastellare; *v.i.* annodarsi, avvolgersi a nodo. **To — up,** raggomitolarsi.
bundle ['bʌndl], *n.* Involto, fagotto, fascio, fardello, pacco, *m.* || *v.t.* Affardellare, affastellare, mettere in filza; far fagotto. **A — of asparagus,** un mazzo di sparagi, *m.*; **a — of sticks,** una fascina di legna, *f.*; **a — of letters,** un fascio di lettere, *m.*; **to — out,** mandar via senza cerimonie.
bung (1) [bʌŋ], *n.* Turacciolo, zaffo, *m.* || *v.t.* Turare. **To have one's eyes bunged up,** avere gli occhi tutti gonfi; **— -hole,** buco, *m.*
bung (2), *v.t.* (*colloq.*) Gettare.
bungalow ['buŋgəlou], *n.* Casetta ad un solo piano, *f.*
bungle ['bʌŋgəl], *v.t.* Acciarpare, guastare, abborracciare; lavorare male. || *n.* Abborracciamento, guazzabuglio, *m.*; lavoro mal fatto, *m.*
bungler, *n.* Guastamestiere, acciarpatore, *m.*
bungling, *a.* Impacciato, goffo, malaccorto.
bunion ['bʌniən], *n.* Callo ai piedi, *m.*; callosità, *f.*; soprosso al pollice del piede, *m.*
bunk (1) [bʌŋk], *n.* Cuccetta, *f.*
bunk (2), *v.t.* (*colloq.*) Fuggire, fuggirsene; scappare.
bunk (3) [cp. **bunkum**].
bunker (1), *n.* Carbonaia, *f.*, cassone, carbonile, *m.*; **— -coal,** carbone per la macchina, *m.*
bunker (2), *n.* (*Golf*) Ostacolo, *m.*
bunkum, *n.* Ciarlatanata, *f.*, ciarle, *f.pl.*, paroloni, *m.pl.*, sciocchezze, *f.pl.*
bunny, *n.* (*colloq.*) Coniglio, *m.*
Bunsen burner, *n.* (*Chem.*) Becco di Bunsen, *m.*
bunt [bʌnt], *n.* (*Naut.*) Fondo di vela, *m.*
bunting (1), *n.* Stamigna, *f.*; (*flags*) bandiere, *f.pl.*
bunting (2), *n.* (*Zool.*) Verdone, crociere, *m.*
buoy [bɔi], *n.* Gavitello, *m.*; boa, *f.* || *v.t.* Indicare con boe. **Life- —,** gavitello di salvamento, salvagente, *m.*; **mooring- —,** boa, *f.*; gavitello d'ormeggio, *m.*; **to — up,** sostenere, tenere a galla.
buoyancy, *n.* Leggerezza, elasticità, vivacità, *f.*, brio, *m.*
buoyant, *a.* Galleggiante; vivace, leggiero, elastico; animato. **— disposition,** carattere vivace, *m.*
burble ['bəːɹbl], *v.i.* Ridacchiare, gorgogliare.
bur [cp. **burr**].
burden ['bəːɹdən], *n.* Fardello, carico, onere, peso, *m.*, soma, *f.*; (*of song*) ritornello, *m.*; (*Naut.*) portata, *f.*; tonnellaggio, *m.* || *v.t.* Caricare; premere, opprimere. **Beast of —,** bestia da soma, *f.*, somaro, *m.*; **the — of proof,** l'onere della prova, *m.*; **the — of years,** il peso degli anni, *m.*; **to be a — to,** essere di carico a.
burdensome, *a.* Oneroso, pesante, molesto.
burdock ['bəːɹdək], *n.* (*Bot.*) Bardana, *f.*
bureau ['bjuːrou], *n.* Scrivania, *f.*; ufficio, studio, *m.*
bureaucracy [bjuː'rɔkrəsi], *n.* Burocrazia, *f.*
bureaucrat, *n.* Burocrate, *m.*
bureaucratic, *a.* Burocratico.
burgeon ['bəːɹdʒən], *v.i.* Metter fuori boccioli, germogliare.
burgess ['bəːɹdʒes], *n.* Borghese, cittadino, elettore, *m.*
burgh [cp. **borough**].
burgher ['bəːɹgəɹ], *n.* Borghese, *m.*
burglar ['bəːɹgləɹ], *n.* Ladro con scasso, scassinatore, *m.* **— -alarm,** apparecchio di allarme contro il furto, *m.*
burglariously, *adv.* Con scasso.
burglary, *n.* Furto con scasso, *m.* **— insurance,** assicurazione contro i furti, *f.*
burgle, *v.t.* Rubare, commettere furto.
burgomaster ['bəːɹgomɑːstəɹ], *n.* Borgomastro, *m.*
Burgundy ['bəːɹgəndi], *n.* (*Geog.*) Borgogna, *f.*
burial ['beriəl], *n.* Sepoltura, *f.*, interramento, *m.*; esequie, *f.pl.*; funerale, *m.* **— -ground,** cimitero, camposanto, *m.*; **— -service,** ufficio funebre, *m.*
burin ['bjurin], *n.* Bulino, *m.*
burke [bəːɹk], *v.t.* Affogare, strangolare; (*fig.*) sopprimere, nascondere.
burlesque [bəːɹ'lesk], *n.* Farsa, burletta, *f.* || *a.* Burlesco. || *v.t.* Burlare, burlarsi di, travestire.
burliness ['bəːɹlinəs], *n.* Grossezza, corpulenza, *f.*
burly, *a.* Grosso, corpulento.

Burma [ˈbəːɹmə], *n.* (*Geog.*) Birmania, *f.*
Burmese, *n.a.* Birmano, *m.*
burn (1) [bəːɹn], *v.t.i.* Bruciare, ardere, incendiare, scottare; cuocere. || *n.* Bruciatura, scottatura, ustione, *f.* **To — one's boats,** bruciare le proprie navi, fare qualcosa di irrevocabile; **to — the candle at both ends,** spendere e spandere; **to — down,** distruggere a fuoco; **to — to ashes,** ridurre in cenere; **to — up,** consumare intieramente; **to make the fire —,** attizzare il fuoco; (*fig.*) **to — one's fingers,** rimanere scottato.
burn (2), *n.* Ruscello, *m.*
burner, *n.* Becco del gas, *m.*; bruciatore, *m.*
burning, *n.* Bruciatura, *f.*; combustione, *f.*, incendio, *m.*; (*of throat*) arsura, *f.*; (*of bricks*) cottura, *f.*, il cuocere, *m.* || *a.* Scottante, ardente, cocente. **To smell —,** sentire odore di bruciato; **a — question,** una questione scottante, *f.*; **— -glass,** specchio ustorio, *m.*
burnish [ˈbəːɹniʃ], *v.t.* Brunire.
burnisher, *n.* Brunitore, *m.*; (*tool*) brunitoio, *m.*
burnishing, *a.* Brunitura, *f.*
burnous [bəɹˈnuːz], *n.* Burnus, *m.*
burnt [bəɹnt], *a.* Bruciato. **— offering,** olocausto, *m.*; **— almond,** mandorla tostata, *f.*; **— Sienna,** terra di Siena, *f.*
burr, bur (1) [bəːɹ], *n.* (*Bot.*) Zeccola, lappola, bardana, *f.*; (*of metal*) superficie rozza, *f.*; (*Astron.*) anello nebuloso, *m.*
burr (2), *n.* Pronuncia forte dell'erre, *f.*; ronzio, *m.*
burrow [ˈbʌrou], *n.* Tana, *f.*, covile, *m.* || *v.i.* Farsi un buco, rintanarsi, scavare una tana. **Rabbit- —,** conigliera, *f.*
bursar [ˈbəːɹsəɹ], *n.* Tesoriere, economo, *m.*
bursarship, *n.* Borsa di studio, *f.*; economato, *m.*
burst [bəːɹst], *v.t.* Fare scoppiare, fare esplodere, rompere, spezzare; *v.i.* scoppiare, esplodere; (*of a bud*) sbocciare. || *n.* Scoppio, *m.*; esplosione, rottura, *f.*; (*of speed*) impeto, slancio, *m.*; parossismo, *m.* **To — open a door,** sfondare un uscio; **to — into tears,** scoppiare in lagrime; **to — out laughing,** sbottare a ridere; **to — in,** entrare subito, interrompere; **to — out,** esclamare; **to — with pride,** essere pieno d'orgoglio; **to — into flame,** scoppiare in fiamme, **to — upon the view,** comparire improvvisamente; **a — of applause,** uno scoppio d'applausi, *m.*; **a — of passion,** uno scoppio d'ira, *m.*
burthen [ˈbəːɹðən], *n.* (*Naut.*) Portata, *f.*, tonnellaggio, *m.*
burton [ˈbəːɹtən], *n.* Paranco, *m.*, taglia, *f.* (*colloq.*) **Gone for a —,** morto.
bury [ˈberi], *v.t.* Sotterrare, seppellire, interrare; fare l'ufficio funebre. **Buried in thought,** assorto in meditazione; **to have buried many relatives,** averne sotterrati parecchi.
bus, 'bus [bʌs], *n.* (*abbrev.* **omnibus**) Autobus, *m.* **— station,** autostazione, *f.*
busby [ˈbʌzbi], *n.* (*Mil.*) Colbac, *m.*
bush [buʃ], *n.* Cespuglio, arboscello, *m.*; macchia, *f.*; frascato, *m.*; (*Mech.*) bronzina, fodera di bronzo, *f.*; (*Australian*) terreno incolto, *m.*, oresta, *f.* **To beat about the —,** menare il can per l'aia; **good wine needs no —,** il buon vino non ha bisogno di frasca; **— -fighting,** guerriglia, *f.*
bushel [buʃəl], *n.* Staio, *m.* **To hide one's light under a —,** essere troppo modesto.
bushman, *n.* Abitatore delle foreste australiane, *m.*; indigeno dell'Africa del Sud, *m.*
bushranger, *n.* Galeotto evaso, *m.*
bushy, *a.* Folto, spesso, fitto.
busily [ˈbizili], *adv.* Attivamente, energicamente, con premura.
business [ˈbiznis], *n.* Affare, negozio, *m.*; faccenda, impresa, *f.*; mestiere, *m.*; commercio, *m.*; ordine del giorno, *m.* **Go about your —,** andatevene per i fatti vostri; **mind your own —,** badate ai fatti vostri; **in —,** negli affari; **to devote oneself to —,** darsi agli affari; **line of —,** genere di commercio, *f.*; **on —,** per affari; **to do a great deal of —,** avere molti affari; **to do — with,** negoziare con; **to give up —,** ritirarsi dagli affari; **to make it one's —,** incaricarsi di; **to settle a —,** concludere un affare; **to set up in —,** entrare nel commercio; **that's none of your —,** quello non vi riguarda; **— -card,** biglietto da visita, *m.*; **— -hours,** ore d'ufficio, *f.pl.*; **— premises,** locali commerciali, *m.pl.*; **— world,** mondo degli affari, *m.*
businesslike, *a.* Pratico, positivo, corretto, metodico.
buskin [ˈbʌskin], *n.* Stivale di cuoio, *m.*; (*fig.*) coturno, *m.*
buss [bʌs], *v.t.* (*obs.*) Baciare, abbracciare. || *n.* Bacio, *m.*
bust (1) [bʌst], *n.* Busto, petto, *m.*; **— bodice,** reggipetto, *m.*; sottovita, *f.*
bust (2) (*colloq.*), *p.p.a.* Rotto [cp. **burst**].
bustard [ˈbʌstəɹd], *n.* (*Zool.*) Ottarda, *f.*
bustle [ˈbʌsl], *n.* Movimento, moto, andirivieni, *m.*, agitazione, *f.*; (*of dress*) puf, *m.* || *v.i.* Agitarsi, dimenarsi, muoversi, affrettarsi, affaccendarsi.
bustling, *a.* Attivo, affaccendato, rumoroso.
busy [ˈbizi], *a.* Affaccendato, occupato, laborioso, diligente; (*of streets*) movimentato. || *v.i.* **To — oneself with,** occuparsi di.
busybody, *n.* Faccendiere, ficcanaso, imbroglione, pasticcione, *m.*
but [bʌt], *conj.* Ma; che; però; se non che; fuorchè, senza che. || *adv.* Eccetto, non . . . che; soltanto. || *prep.* Senza. || *n.* Ma, *m.* **— for,** se non fosse, senza; **— yesterday,** soltanto ieri; **it cannot — be considered strange,** non si può fare altro che considerarlo strano; **there is not one of them — has read it,** non c'è nessuno che non l'abbia letto; **to do nothing —,** non fare altro che; **nobody — he,** nessun altro che lui; **anything —,** tutt'altro che; **all —,** quasi; **— that,** se non fosse che; **he would have died — for her,** senza lei sarebbe morto; **the last — one,** il penultimo; **had he — known it,** se egli l'avesse saputo; **— for her prayers,** senza le sue preghiere.
butcher [ˈbutʃəɹ], *n.* Beccaio, macellaio, *m.* || *v.t.* Macellare; massacrare, ammazzare; far strage di. **Butcher's meat,** carne macellata, *f.*; **butcher's shop,** macelleria, beccheria, *f.*; (*Zool.*) **— -bird,** averla, *f.*
butchery, *n.* Massacro, *m.*; strage, *f.*
butler [ˈbʌtləɹ], *n.* Maggiordomo, *m.*

butment, *n.* (*Arch.*) Contrafforte, *m.*
butt (1) [bʌt], *n.* (*cask*) Botte, *f.*; (*of rifle*) calcio, *m.*; (*of cue*) manico, *m.*; (*of person*) zimbello, *m.*; (*of target*) terrapieno, *m.* **—-end,** estremità, *f.*; calcio, *m.*; **to make a — of someone,** far zimbello di qualcuno.
butt (2), *v.t.* Dar di testa contro, cozzare. || *n.* **The — of a goat,** il cozzo d'un capro, *m.*
butter [ˈbʌtəɹ], *n.* Burro, *m.* || *v.t.* Imburrare, spalmare di burro, condire col burro. **A pat of —,** un pane di burro, *m.*; **melted —,** burro fuso, *f.*; **bread and —,** pane e burro, *m.*; **—-dish,** piatto pel burro, *m.*; **—-scotch,** caramella di burro, *f.*; (*colloq.*) **to — up,** lusingare.
buttercup, *n.*(*Bot.*) Bottone d'oro, ranuncolo, *m.*
butterfly, *n.* (*Zool.*) Farfalla, *f.*
buttermilk, *n.* Siero di latte, *m.*
butterwort, *n.* (*Bot.*) Pinguicola, *f.*
buttery, *n.* Dispensa, *f.* || *a.* Coperto di burro, grasso, burroso.
buttock [ˈbʌtək], *n.* Natica, *f.*; (*of meat*) lombata, coscia, *f.*
button [ˈbʌtən], *n.* Bottone, *m.* || *v.t.* Abbottonare. (*hotel*) **Buttons,** paggio, *m.*; **—-hook,** allacciabottoni, *m.*; **to — oneself up,** abbottonarsi.
buttonhole, *n.* Occhiello, *m.*, asola, *f.*; (*of flowers*) mazzettino di fiori, *m.* || *v.t.* (*fig.*) Attaccare un bottone **—-stitch,** punto a occhiello, *m.*
buttress [ˈbʌtrəs], *n.* Contrafforte, *m.*; sostegno, appoggio, *m.* || *v.t.* Rinforzare, appoggiare, puntellare. **Flying- —,** arco rampante, arco a sprone, *m.*
buxom [ˈbʌksəm], *a.* Grassoccio; giocondo, paffuto, ben messo, formoso. **A — woman,** una donna formosa, *f.*
buxomness, *n.* Formosità, *f.*
buy [bai], *v.t.* Comprare, procurare, guadagnare, acquistare; (*to bribe*) corrompere. **To — off, to — out,** ricomprare, riscattare; **to — in,** fare le spese, approvvisionarsi di; **to — a pig in a poke,** comprare la gatta nel sacco; **to — up,** monopolizzare.
buyer, *n.* Compratore, *m.*, compratrice, *f.*
buying, *n.* Compra, *f.* **— in,** approvvigionamento, *m.*; **— up,** monopolio, *m.*
buzz [bʌz], *v.i.* Ronzare. || *n.* Ronzio, *m.*
buzzard, *n.* (*Zool.*) Bozzagro, *m.*
buzzer, *n.* Ronzatore, *m.*
by [bai], *prep.* Da, di, per; presso a, vicino a. || *adv.* Vicino, da parte, passato. **By all means,** ad ogni costo; **by day,** di giorno; **by no means,** in nessun modo; **by doing that,** ciò facendo; **by far,** di molto; **by measure,** a misura; **the time by my watch is ten o'clock,** secondo il mio orologio sono le dieci; **by oneself,** tutto solo; **by seven o'clock,** prima delle sette; **by sight,** di vista; **by this means,** per questo mezzo; **by turns,** a vicenda; **he works for me by the day,** lavora per me a giornata; **by the end of the day,** alla fine del giorno; **he was by me at the theatre,** stava accanto a me al teatro; **by the end of the month,** entro la fine del mese; **wider by three metres,** di tre metri più largo; **loved by all,** amato da tutti; **one by one,** ad uno ad uno; **he came by train,** venne col treno; **by land and sea,** per terra e per mare; **we came by Paris,** siamo venuti via Parigi; **known by the name of John,** conosciuto sotto il nome di Giovanni; **it missed him by an inch,** lo mancò per un pollice; **take warning by me,** prendi esperienza da me; **to stand by,** stare vicino, essere pronto; **to put by,** mettere da parte; **that is all gone by,** tutto quello è passato; **by and by,** fra poco, col tempo; **by the by,** a proposito; **close by,** vicinissimo; **by-blow** colpo traverso, *m.*; **by-election,** elezione locale, *f.*; **by-law,** regolamento, *m.*; **by-pass,** strada di collegamento, *f.*; (*gas*) tubetto regolatore del gas, *m.*; **by-path,** sentiero; **by-road, by-way,** via traversa, *f.*; (*Theat.*) **by-play,** controscena, *f.*; **by-product,** prodotto secondario, *m.*; **by-street,** strada secondaria, *f.*
bye-bye [ˈbaibai], *n.* (*colloq.*) Addio! *m*; || *inter.* Addio, arrivederci.
bygone [ˈbaigɔn], *a.* Passato. **Let bygones be bygones,** dimentichiamo il passato.
byname, *n.* Nomignolo, *m.*
bystander, *n.* Astante, *m.*; spettatore, *m.*, spettatrice, *f.*
byword, *n.* Proverbio, detto, *m.*; zimbello, *m.* **To become a —,** passare in proverbio, divenire lo zimbello.
Byzantian, Byzantine [biˈzæntiən, biˈzæntain], *a.* Bizantino.

C

C, c [siː], Terza lettera dell'alfabeto inglese; (*Mus.*) do, *m.*; **C-springs,** molle ad arco, *f.pl.*
cab [kæb], *n.* Vettura, carrozza, *f.*; (*of locomotive*) cabina, *f.*, ricovero, *m.* **—-driver,** vetturino, cocchiere, *m.*; **—-horse,** cavallo da vettura, *m.*; **—-rank, —-stand,** stazione di vetture, *f.*
cabal [kəˈbæl], *n.* Cabala, trama, *f.*; intrigo, *m.*; fazione, *f.* || *v.i.* Ordire una trama, congiurare, intrigare.
cabaret [ˈkæbərei], *n.* Caffè concerto, *m.* **—-show,** spettacolo di varietà, *m.*
cabbage [ˈkæbidʒ], *n.* Cavolo, *m.* **—-butterfly,** cavolaia, *f.*; **—-lettuce,** lattuga, *f.*; **—-palm,** palmizio, *m.*; **Savoy —,** verza, *f.*
cabbala [kəˈbælə], *n.* Cabala, *f.*
cabbalistic, *a.* Cabalistico.
cabby, *n.* (*colloq.*) Vetturino, *m.*
cabin [ˈkæbin], *n.* Cabina, camera, *f.*; capanna, casuccia, *f.* **—-passenger,** viaggiatore di prima classe, *m.*; (*Naut.*) passeggero di cabina, *m.*; **—-trunk,** baule da cabina, *m.*; **—-boy,** mozzo, camerotto, *m.*
cabinet, *n.* Gabinetto (*room*), *m.*; stipo, armadio (*furniture*), *m.* **—-Council,** consiglio dei ministri, *m.*; **—-minister,** ministro di stato, *m.*; **—-maker,** ebanista, stipettaio, *m.*; **—-making,** ebanisteria, *f.*; **—-gramophone,** fonografo a stipo, *m.*
cable [ˈkeibl], *n.* Cavo, *m.*; (*Naut.*) gomena, *f.* || *v.t.* Telegrafare, mandare un cablogramma; (*Naut.*) ormeggiare. **—-length,** lunghezza di una gomena, *f.*; **—-railway,** funicolare, *f.*; **submarine —,** cavo sottomarino, *m.*

cablegram, *n.* Cablogramma, *m.*
cabman (*pl.* **cabmen**), *n.* Vetturino, *m.*
caboose [kəˈbuːs], *n.* (*Naut.*) Cucina di bordo, *f.*; (*American*) furgone, *m.*
cabotage, *n.* Cabotaggio, *m.*
ca'canny [kɑːˈkæni], *inter.* Adagio! **— strike,** sciopero bianco, *m.*
cacao [kəˈkɑou], *n.* (*Bot.*) Cacao, *m.*
cachalot [ˈkæʃəlot], *n.* (*Zool.*) Capidoglio, *m.*
cache [kæʃ], *n.* Nascondiglio, *m.*; provviste nascoste, *f.pl.* || *v.t.* Nascondere.
cachectic [kəˈketik], *a.* (*Med.*) Cachettico.
cachexy, *n.* (*Med.*) Cachessia, *f.*
cachinnation [kækəˈneiʃən], *n.* Cachinno, riso smoderato, *m.*
cachou [ˈkæʃuː], *n.* Cacciù, *m.*; confetto di cacciù, *m.*; caramella, *f.*
cacique [kəˈsiːk], *n.* Cacico, caicco, *m.*
cackle [ˈkækl], *v.i.* Chiocciare (*of hens*), gracidare (*of geese*); (*fig.*) chiacchierare. || *n.* Grido delle galline, *m.*; chiacchiericcio, *m.*
cackler, *n.* Gallina che chioccia, *f.*; chiacchierone, *m.*, chiacchierona, *f.*
cackling, *n.* Grido delle galline, *m.*
cacoethes [kækoˈiːθiːz], *n.* Prurito, *m.*
cacophonous [kəˈkɔfənəs], *a.* Cacofonico.
cacophony, *n.* Cacofonia, *f.*
cactus [ˈkæktəs], *n.* (*Bot.*) Cacto, *m.*
cad [kæd], *n.* Cialtrone, omaccio, *m.*, canaglia, *f.*
cadastral [kəˈdæstrəl], *a.* (*Law*) Catastale.
cadastre [kəˈdæstəɹ], *n.* (*Law*) Catasto, *m.*
cadaverous [kəˈdævərəs], *a.* Cadaverico, di cadavere.
caddie [ˈkædi], *n.* (*Golf*) Ragazzo, portabastoni, *m.*
caddis [ˈkædis], *n.* (*Zool.*) Larva della frigànea, *f.*
caddish, *a.* Triviale, basso, volgare.
caddy, *n.* Scatola da tè, *f.*
cadence [ˈkeidəns], *n.* Cadenza, *f.*
cadet [kəˈdet], *n.* Cadetto, *m.*; figlio minore, *m.*
cadge [kædʒ], *v.t.* Mendicare, pitoccare.
cadger, *n.* Mendicante, pitocco, rigattiere, *m.*
cadi [ˈkeidi], *n.* Cadì, *m.*
Cadiz [kəˈdiz], *n.* (*Geog.*) Cadice, *f.*
cadmium [ˈkædmiəm], *n.* (*Min.*) Cadmio, *m.*
cadre [keidəɹ], *n.* (*Mil.*) Quadro, *m.*
caducity [kəˈdjuːsiti], *n.* Caducità, *f.*
caecal [ˈsiːkəl], *a.* (*Anat.*) Del cieco.
caecum, *n.* (*Anat.*) Cieco, *m.*
Caesarian [siːˈzɛəriən], *a.* Cesareo. (*Med.*) **— birth,** parto cesareo, *m.*
caesium [ˈsiːziəm], *n.* (*Min.*) Cesio, *m.*
caesura [siːˈzjuːrə], *n.* (*Poet.*) Cesura, *f.*
café [ˈkæfei], *n.* Caffè, *m.*
cafeteria [kæfiˈtɛəriə], *n.* Ristorante dove uno si serve da sè, *m.*
caffeine [ˈkæfiːn], *n.* (*Chem.*) Caffeina, *f.*
cage [keidʒ], *n.* Gabbia, *f.* || *v.t.* Mettere in gabbia, ingabbiare. **—-bird,** uccello di gabbia, *m.*
cagey [ˈkeidʒi], *a.* (*colloq.*) Cauto; astuto.
cairn [kɛəɹn], *n.* Tumulo, mucchio di pietre, *m.*
caiman [ˈkeimæn], *n.* (*Zool.*) Caimano, *m.*
caisson [ˈkeisən], *n.* Cassone, *m.*
caitiff [ˈkeitif], *n.* Furfante, codardo, *m.*; traditore, *m.*
cajole [kəˈdʒoul], *v.t.* Blandire, lusingare, piaggiare.
cajolery, *n.* Blandizie, moine, lusinghe, *f.pl.*
cake [keik], *n.* Dolce, *m.*, focaccia, torta, pasta, *f.* || *v.i.* Indurirsi, incrostarsi. **A — of soap,** un pezzo di sapone, *m.*; **cakes and ale,** le cose buone della vita, *f.pl.*; **you can't eat your — and have it,** quello che va nelle maniche non può andare nei calzoni; (*colloq.*) **they go like hot cakes,** vanno a ruba; **that takes the —,** questo è il colmo.
caked, *a.* Incrostato.
calabash [ˈkæləbæʃ], *n.* (*Bot.*) Zucca da fiaschi, *f.*, zucca vuota, *f.*
calamine [ˈkæləmain], *n.* (*Min.*) Calamina, *f.*
calamitous [kəˈlæmitəs], *a.* Calamitoso, disastroso, doloroso.
calamitously, *adv.* Disastrosamente.
calamity, *n.* Calamità, sfortuna, sventura, *f.*, disastro, *m.*
calash [kəˈlæʃ], *n.* Calesse, *m.*
calcareous [kælˈkɛəriəs], *a.* (*Min.*) Calcareo.
calceolaria [kælsioˈlɛəriə], *n.* (*Bot.*) Calceolaria, *f.*
calcine [ˈkælsiːn], *v.t.* (*Chem.*) Calcinare; *v.i.* calcinarsi.
calcination, *n.* Calcinazione, *f.*
calcium [ˈkælsiəm], *n.* Calcio, *m.*
calculable [ˈkælkuləbl], *a.* Calcolabile.
calculate, *v.t.* Calcolare.
calculated, *a.* Premeditato. **A — insult,** un affronto premeditato, *m.*; **— to,** adattato, atto a, capace di.
calculating-machine, *n.* Calcolatrice meccanica, *f.*
calculation, *n.* Calcolo, *m.*; (*fig.*) conclusione, *f.*
calculator, *n.* Calcolatore, *m.*, calcolatrice, *f.*
calculous, *a.* (*Med.*) Calcoloso.
calculus, *n.* (*Med.*) Calcoli, *m.pl.*; (*Math.*) calcolo, *m.*
caldron [cp. **cauldron**].
Caledonia, *n.* (*Hist.*) Scozia, *f.*
Caledonian [kæliˈdouniən], *a.* Caledone, Scozzese.
calefacient [kæliˈfæʃənt], *a.* (*Med.*) Calefacente.
calefaction, *n.* Calefazione, *f.*
calefactory, *a.* Che riscalda.
calendar [ˈkæləndəɹ], *n.* Calendario, almanacco, *m.*, lista, *f.*; elenco, *m.* **— month,** un mese secondo il calendario, *m.*; **a — year,** un anno di dodici mesi, *m.*
calender [ˈkæləndəɹ], *n.* Cilindro, *m.* || *v.t.* Cilindrare.
calendering, *n.* Cilindratura, *f.*
calends [ˈkæləndz], *n.pl.* (*Hist.*) Calende, *f.pl.* **Greek —,** calende greche.
calenture [ˈkælentʃuːɹ], *n.* (*Med.*) Febbre violenta, *f.*
calf (*pl.* **calves**) [kɑːf, kɑːvz], *n.* Vitello *m.*; (*of leg*) polpaccio, *m.* **Bound in —,** rilegato in pelle; **— love,** primo amore, *m.*; **calves-foot jelly,** gelatina di vitello, *f.*
calibrate [ˈkælibreit], *v.t.* Calibrare.
calibre [ˈkælibəɹ, kəˈliːbəɹ], *n.* Calibro (*in all senses*), *m.*
calico [ˈkælikou], *n.* Calicò, *m.* **Printed —,** indiana, *f.*; tessuto stampato, *m.*
calif, caliph [ˈkeilif], *n.* Califfo, *m.*
califate, *n.* Califfato, *m.*
calipash, calipee [ˈkælipæʃ, ˈkælipiː], *n.* Grasso della tartaruga, *m.*
calk (1) [cp. **caulk**].

calk (2) [kɔːk], *v.t.* Ferrare (*a horse*).
calkin, *n.* Chiodo di ferro da cavallo, *m.*
call [kɔːl], *n.* Grido, *m.*, chiamata, voce, *f.*; vocazione (*religious*), *f.*; visita, *f.*; telefonata, *f.*; (*at a port*) fermata, *f.*, scalo, rilascio, *m.*; (*Comm.*) domanda, chiamata, richiesta, *f.*; (*Cards*) invito, accenno, *m.*; obbligazione, *f.*; dovere, *m.*; (*of trumpet*) squillo, *m.* ‖ *v.i.* Chiamare, gridare; visitare; *v.t.* chiamare, nominare; convocare; svegliare; fare scalo. **Bugle-—,** squillo, *m.*; **bird-—,** grido d'uccello, *m.*; **roll-—,** appello, *m.*; **at —,** sull' istante; **at anybody's —,** agli ordini di chiunque; **to pay a —,** visitare; **you have no — to laugh,** non avete motivo di ridere; **within —,** a portata di voce; **to be called,** chiamarsi; **to — again,** visitare di nuovo; **to — at,** passare da; (*of trains, etc.*) fermarsi a; **to — out,** gridare; **to — a cab,** chiamare una vettura; **to — aside,** prendere a parte; **to — back,** richiamare; **to — down,** fare scendere; **to — for,** domandare, andare a prendere; **to — forth,** fare uscire; **to — in a doctor,** fare venire un dottore; **to — in money,** incassare danaro; **to — in question,** mettere in dubbio; **to — into action,** fare operare; **to — names,** insultare, vituperare; **to — off,** distrarre; **to — off a meeting,** rimandare un'adunanza; **to — out** (*for a duel*), sfidare a duello; **to — to the colours,** chiamare sotto le armi; **to — over the coals,** sgridare; **to — the roll,** fare l'appello; **to — together,** riunire, chiamare insieme; **to — to mind,** ricordarsi; **to — to order,** richiamare all'ordine; **to — to witness,** chiamare in testimonio; **to — up,** evocare, (*to waken*) svegliare, (*on telephone*) telefonare; **—-box,** cabina telefonica, *f.*; (*Theat.*) **—-boy,** buttafuori, *m.*
caller, *n.* Visitatore, *m.*, visitatrice, *f.*
calling, *n.* Mestiere, *m.*; professione, *f.*
calligraphic [kæli'græfik], *a.* Calligrafico.
calligraphy, *n.* Calligrafia, *f.*
callipers ['kælipəɹz], *n.pl.* Compasso a grossezze, calibro, *m.*
callisthenics [kælis'θeniks], *n.pl.* Ginnastica, *f.*
callosity [kə'lɔsiti], *n.* Callosità, *f.*
callous, *a.* Calloso, duro; (*fig.*) insensibile, crudele.
callously, *adv.* Crudelmente.
callousness, *n.* Insensibilità, crudeltà, *f.*
callow ['kælou], *a.* Implume; (*fig.*) giovane, senza esperienza, inesperto.
callus ['kæləs], *n.* Callo, *m.*
calm [kɑːm], *a.* Calmo, placido, tranquillo, quieto. ‖ *n.* Calma, bonaccia, *f.* ‖ *v.t.* Calmare, tranquillizzare. **To grow —,** calmarsi.
calmly, *adv.* Tranquillamente, con calma.
calmness, *n.* Calma, tranquillità, *f.*; (*colloq.*) sfrontatezza, *f.*
calomel ['kæləmel], *n.* (*Med.*) Calomelano, *m.*
caloric [kə'lɔrik], *n.* Calore, *m.*
calorie ['kæləri], *n.* Caloria, *f.*
calorific, *a.* Calorifico.
calorimeter, *n.* Calorimetro, *m.*
calumet ['kæləmet], *n.* Pipa degli indiani dell'America del Nord, *f.*
calumniate [kə'lʌmnieit], *v.t.* Calunniare.
calumniator, *n.* Calunniatore, *m.*
calumnious, *a.* Calunnioso.
calumny, *n.* Calunnia, *f.*
Calvary ['kælvəri], *n.* Calvario, *m.*
calve [kɑːv], *v.i.* Figliare, partorire.
calves [cp. **calf**].
Calvinism ['kælvinizm], *n.* Calvinismo, *m.*
Calvinist, *n.* Calvinista, *m.*
Calvinistic, *a.* Calvinistico.
calypso [kə'lipsou], *n.* Canto improvvisato delle Indie Occidentali, *m.*
calyx ['keiliks], *n.* (*Bot.*) Calice, *m.*
cam [kæm], *n.* (*Mech.*) Camma, *m.* **—-shaft,** albero a eccentrico, *m.*
camarilla [kæmə'rilə], *n.* Camarilla, *f.*
camber ['kæmbəɹ], *n.* Curvatura, convessità, *f.*, inarcamento, rialzo, *m.* ‖ *v.t.* Curvare, inarcare; *v.i.* inarcarsi.
cambist ['kæmbist], *n.* (*Comm.*) Cambiavalute, cambista, *m.*
cambric ['keimbrik], *n.* Tela battista, *f.*; cambrì, *m.*
came (1), *past* of **come.**
came (2), *n.* Verga di piombi per vetri, *f.*
camel ['kæməl], *n.* Cammello, *m.* **—-driver,** cammelliere, *m.*; **camel's hair,** pelo di cammello, *m.*; **camel's-hair brush,** pennello, *m.*
camellia [kə'miːliə], *n.* (*Bot.*) Camelia, *f.*
camelopard [kə'melopɑːɹd], *n.* (*Zool.*) Giraffa, *f.*, camelopardo, *m.*
cameo ['kæmiou], *n.* Cammeo, *m.*
camera ['kæmərə], *n.* Macchina fotografica, *f.* **Hand-—,** macchina a mano, *f.*; **cinecamera,** macchina da presa, *f.* **—-man,** fotografo, *m.*; **— obscura,** camera oscura, *f.*; **in —,** in sessione segreta.
camisole ['kæmisoul], *n.* Camiciuola, *f.*; giubbetto, copribusto, *m.*
camlet ['kæmlət], *n.* Cammellotto, *m.*
camomile ['kæmomail], *n.* Camomilla, *f.*
camouflage ['kæmoflɑːdʒ], *n.* Mascheramento, *m.* ‖ *v.t.* Mascherare; ingannare, mimetizzare.
camp [kæmp], *n.* Campo, *m.* ‖ *v.i.* Accamparsi; *v.t.* accampare. **To break —,** levare il campo; **to pitch a —,** accamparsi, porre il campo; **to — out,** accamparsi all'aperto; **—-bed,** letto da campo, *m.*; **—-stool,** sedia pieghevole, *f.*; **— followers,** gente al seguito d'un esercito, *m.pl.*
campaign [kæm'pein], *n.* (*Mil.*) Campagna, *f.* ‖ *v.i.* Fare una campagna.
campaigner, *n.* Soldato, *m.* **An old —,** un veterano, *m.*
campanula [kæm'pænjuːlə], *n.* (*Bot.*) Campanula, *f.*
camper, *n.* Campeggiatore, *m.*
camphor ['kæmfəɹ], *n.* Canfora, *f.*
camphorated, *a.* Canforato.
camping, *n.* Campeggio, accampamento, *m.*
can (1) [kæn], *n.* Scatola di latta, brocca di latta, *f.*, vaso, secchiello, *m.* ‖ *v.t.* Mettere in iscatola, conservare in iscatola. **Hot-water —,** brocca per l'acqua calda, *f.*; **milk-—,** pentolino del latte, *m.*; **a — of pears,** una latta di pere, *f.*
can (2), *v.aux.* Potere, essere capace; sapere (*to know how to*). **I have done all I —,** ho fatto tutto il possibile; **he — do everything necessary,** è capace di fare tutto il necessario; **Can the child read?** Sa leggere il fanciullo? **Can I go now?** Posso andare adesso? **Can it be possible that?** È possible che? **that cannot be,** è impossibile; **as soon as you can,** appena puoi.

Canada [ˈkænədə], *n.* (*Geog.*) Il Canadà, *m.*
Canadian, *n.a.* Canadese, *m.*
canaille [kəˈnai], *n.* Canaglia, *f.*
canal [kəˈnæl], *n.* Canale, *m.*
canalization [kænəlaiˈzeiʃən], *n.* Canalizzazione, *f.*
canalize, *v.t.* Canalizzare.
canary [kəˈnɛəri], *n.* (*Zool.*) Canarino, *m.*; (*wine*) vino delle Canarie, *m.* || *a.* Canarino. (*Geog.*) **Canary Islands,** Le Canarie, *f.pl.*; — **seed,** miglio, *m.*, canaria, *f.*
cancel [ˈkænsəl], *v.t.* Cancellare, annullare, revocare; (*Math.*) elidere. || *n.* (*Print.*) Pagina cassata, *f.*, foglio rifatto, *m.*
cancellated, *a.* (*Bot.Zool.*) Reticolato.
cancellation, *n.* Annullamento, *m.*
cancer [ˈkænsəɹ], *n.* (*Med.*) Cancro, *m.*
cancerous, *a.* Canceroso.
candelabrum (*pl.* **candelabra**) [kændiˈlæbrəm], *n.* Candelabro, *m.*
candid [ˈkændid], *a.* Franco, ingenuo, candido, schietto, puro. (*iron.*) **A — friend,** un amico schietto, *m.*
candidate [ˈkændideit], *n.* Candidato, aspirante, *m.*
candidature, *n.* Candidatura, *f.*
candidly, *adv.* Candidamente, schiettamente.
candidness, *n.* Schiettezza, ingenuità, sincerità, *f.*
candied [ˈkændid], *a.* Candito. — **peel,** cedri canditi, *m.pl.*
candle [ˈkændl], *n.* Candela, *f.* **Of 100 —-power,** da 100 candele; **the game isn't worth the —,** non vale la pena; **to burn the — at both ends,** strapazzarsi; **not fit to hold a — to,** non degno di essere paragonato a; **—-end,** moccolo, moccoletto, *m.*; **—-grease,** sego, grasso della candela, *m.*; **—-light,** luce di candela, *f.*; **by —-light,** al lume della candela.
Candlemas, *n.* (*Eccles.*) Candelora, *f.*
candlestick, *n.* Candeliere, *m.*; bugia, *f.*
candour [ˈkændəɹ], *n.* Sincerità, franchezza, *f.*
candy [ˈkændi], *n.* Zucchero candito, *m.*; confetto, *m.* || *v.t.* Candire; *v.i.* divenire candito.
candytuft [ˈkænditʌft], *n.* (*Bot.*) Iberide, *f.*
cane [kein], *n.* Canna, *f.*, giunco, *m.*; (*walking-stick*) mazza, *f.*; (*for naughty boys*) verga, bacchetta, *f.* || *v.t.* Bacchettare; (*chair-mending*) impagliare. — **sugar,** zucchero di canna, *m.*; **—-chair,** seggiola di vimini, *f.*
canicular [kəˈnikjuːləɹ], *a.* (*Astron.*) Canicolare.
canine [ˈkeinain], *a.* Canino.
caning, *n.* Vergata, bacchettata, *f.*
canister [ˈkænistəɹ], *n.* Scatola di latta, *f.* **Tea-—,** scatola per tè, *f.*; **—-shot,** mitraglia, *f.*
canker [ˈkæŋkəɹ], *n.* Cancro, *m.* || *v.t.* Rodere; corrompere; *v.i.* ulcerarsi. **—-worm** bruco, *m.*
cankered, *a.* Rosicchiato, roso; (*fig.*) corrotto.
cankerous, *a.* Ulcerato.
canned [ˈkænd], *a.* In iscatola. — **goods,** conserve in iscatole, *f.pl.*; scatolame, *m.*
cannibal [ˈkænəbəl], *n.* Cannibale, antropofago, *m.*
cannibalism, *n.* Cannibalismo, *m.*, antropofagia, *f.*
cannibalistic, *a.* Cannibalistico.
cannon [ˈkænən], *n.* Cannone, *m.*; (*Billiards*) carambola, *f.* || *v.t.* Cannoneggiare; (*Billiards*) carambolare. **—-ball,** palla di cannone, *f.*; **—-shot,** colpo di cannone, *m.*, cannonata, *f.*; (*Anat.*) **—-bone,** osso del metacarpo, *m.*
cannonade, *n.* Cannonata, *f.* || *v.t.* Cannonare, bombardare, cannoneggiare.
cannot [cp. **can** (2)].
cannular [ˈkænjuːləɹ], *a.* (*Med.*) Tubolare.
canny [ˈkæni], *a.* Scaltro, furbo, astuto, prudente.
canoe [kəˈnuː], *n.* Canoa, *f.*, (*Indian*) piroga, *f.*, canotto, *m.*; sandolino, *m.*
canoeing, *n.* Canottaggio, *m.*
canon [ˈkænən], *n.* (*Eccles.*) Canonico, *m.*; (*Mus.*) canone, *m.*; (*of taste*), criterio, *m.*; norma, *f.*; (*rule, law*) canone, *m.* — **law,** diritto canonico, *m.*; — **of criticism,** canone di critica, *m.*
canoness, *n.* Canonichessa, *f.*
canonical, *a.* Canonicale. **Canonicals,** vestiti sacerdotali, *m.pl.*
canonically, *adv.* Canonicamente.
canonist, *n.* Canonista, *m.*
canonization, *n.* Canonizzazione, *f.*
canonize, *v.t.* Canonizzare.
canonry, *n.* Canonicato, *m.*
canopy [ˈkænəpi], *n.* Padiglione, baldacchino, *m.*, tenda, *f.*; (*Arch.*) sporgenza, pensilina, *f.*; (*of heaven*) volta, *f.* || *v.t.* Coprire con un baldacchino.
canorous [kænˈɔrəs], *a.* Canoro.
cant (1) [kænt], *n.* Gergo, *m.*; affettazione, ipocrisia, *f.* || *v.i.* Parlare con affettazione *or* con ricercatezza; parlare senza sincerità. **A canting phrase,** una frase di moda, *f.*; **a canting hypocrite,** un bacchettone, un collotorto, *m.*
cant (2), *v.t.* Fare inclinare, far pendere; *v.i.* inclinarsi; (*Naut.*) sbandare. || *n.* Pendenza, inclinazione, *f.*
can't [kɑːnt], *abbrev.* **cannot** [cp. **can**].
Cantab [ˈkæntæb], *n.* (*colloq.*) Studente dell'università di Cambridge, *m.*
cantaloup [ˈkæntəluːp], *n.* Mellone, popone, *m.*
cantankerous [kænˈtæŋkərəs], *a.* Stizzoso, collerico, irritabile, bisbetico.
cantata [kænˈtɑːtə], *n.* (*Mus.*) Cantata, *f.*
canteen [kænˈtiːn], *n.* Cantina, *f.*, bettolino, *m.*; (*bottle*) tazza di latta, *f.*, bidone, *m.*
canter [ˈkæntəɹ], *v.i.* Andare a piccolo galoppo; *v.t.* fare andare a piccolo galoppo. || *n.* Piccolo galoppo, galoppo sciolto, *m.* **To win at a —,** vincere facilmente una corsa.
Canterbury bell [ˈkæntəɹbəri ˈbel], *n.* (*Bot.*) Campanula, *f.*
cantharis (*pl.* **cantharides**) [ˈkænθəris, kænˈθæridiːz], *n.* (*Zool.*) Cantaride, *f.*
canticle [ˈkæntikl], *n.* Cantico, *m.*
cantilever [ˈkæntiliːvəɹ], *n.* Modiglione, *m.*, mensola, *f.* **—-bridge,** ponte a sbalzo, *m.*
cantle [ˈkæntl], *n.* Fetta, *f.*, pezzettino, frammento, *m.*; (*of saddle*) arcione posteriore, *m.*
canto [ˈkæntou], *n.* Canto, *m.*
canton [ˈkæntɔn], *n.* Cantone (*in Switzerland*), *m.* || [kænˈtɔn], *v.t.* (*Mil.*) accantonare.
cantonal, *a.* Cantonale.
cantonment, *n.* (*Mil.*) Quartiere alloggiamento, *m.*
canvas [ˈkænvəs], *n.* Canovaccio, *m.* tela, *f.*; (*Naut.*) vela, *f.*; (*fig.*) quadro, *m.* (*Mil.*) **Under —,** in tenda, accampato; (*Naut.*) sotto vela.

canvass ['kænvəs], *v.t.* Discutere, dibattere, sollecitare. || *n.* Sollecitazione di voti, *f.* **To — a subject,** vagliare una questione; **to — for votes,** sollecitare i voti; **to — for orders,** sollecitare ordini.
canvasser, *n.* Sollecitatore, galoppino elettorale, *m.*
canyon ['kænjən], *n.* (*Geog.*) Anfratto, vallone, burrone, *m.*
caoutchouc ['kautʃu:k], *n.* Caucciù, *m.*; gomma elastica, *f.*
cap [kæp], *n.* Berretto, *m.*, cuffia, *f.*; copertura, *f.*; (*of cardinal*) berretta, *f.*; (*of firearms, etc.*) capsula, *f.*; (*Naut.*) cappelletto, *m.* || *v.t.* Mettere il berretto a, coprire; (*fig.*) sorpassare, vincere, coronare. **— and bells,** cappello a sonagliera, *m.*; **— in hand,** umilmente; **night- —,** berretta da notte, *f.*; (*drink*) bevanda calda, bevanda finale, *f.*; **skull- —,** papalina, *f.*; **to set one's — at,** cercare di cattivarsi le simpatie di; **the — fits,** torna a proposito; **to raise one's —,** far di berretto; **to — anecdotes,** parlare a botta e risposta; **to — verses,** prendere l'addentellato; **to — it all,** per rendere la cosa completa.
capability [keipə'biliti], *n.* Capacità, *f.*
capable, *a.* Capace, abile, atto.
capacious [kə'peiʃəs], *a.* Capace, ampio, vasto, esteso, spazioso.
capaciousness, *n.* Capacità, ampiezza, larghezza, *f.*
capacitate [kə'pæsiteit], *v.t.* Rendere capace, abilitare.
capacity, *n.* Capacità, abilità, facoltà, *f.* **Measure of —,** misura di capacità; **in an administrative —,** con una mansione amministrativa.
caparison [kə'pærisən], *n.* Gualdrappa, *f.* || *v.t.* Ingualdrappare; drappeggiare.
cape (1) [keip], *n.* (*Geog.*) Capo, *m.* **The Cape,** Il Capo di Buona Speranza.
cape (2), *n.* Mantello, *m.*, mantellina, *f.*
caper (1) ['keipəɹ], *n.* (*Bot.*) Cappero, *m.* **— sauce,** salsa piccante, *f.*
caper (2), *n.* Capriola, *f.*, salto, *m.* || *v.i.* Far capriole, saltare. **To cut capers,** far capriole.
capercailzie [keipəɹ'keilzi], *n.* (*Zool.*) Gallo alpestre, *m.*
capful, *n.* Cappellata, *f.* **A — of wind,** una breve raffica di vento, una folata, *f.*
capias ['keipiəs], *n.* (*Law*) Mandato di comparizione, *m.*
capillarity [kæpi'læriti], *n.* Capillarità, *f.*
capillary, *a.* Capillare.
capital (1) ['kæpitəl], *n.* Capitale, *f.* **Rome is the — of Italy,** Roma è la capitale d'Italia.
capital (2), *n.* (*Comm.*) Capitale, *m.*; (*Arch.*) capitello, *m.*; (*Print.*) maiuscola, *f.* || *a.* Capitale, eccellente, essenziale. **To make — of,** utilizzare, mettere a profitto; **fixed —,** beni immobili, *m.pl.*; **floating —,** ricchezza mobile, *f.*; **a — fellow,** un uomo eccellente, *m.*; **a — offence,** un delitto capitale, *m.*; **— punishment,** pena capitale, *f.*
capitalism, *n.* Capitalismo, *m.*
capitalist, *n.* Capitalista, *m.*
capitalization, *n.* Capitalizzazione, *f.*
capitalize, *v.t.* Capitalizzare.
capitally, *adv.* Benissimo, a meraviglia.
capitation, *n.* (*Law*) Testatico, *m.*
capitol, *n.* Campidoglio, *m.*
capitoline, *a.* Capitolino.
capitular, *a.* (*Eccles.*) Capitolare.
capitulary, *n.* Corpo di leggi, *m.*
capitulate, *v.i.* Capitolare.
capitulation, *n.* Capitolazione, *f.*; convenzione, *f.*
capon ['keipən], *n.* Cappone, *m.*
caponize, *v.t.* Capponare.
capped, *a.* Incappucciato.
caprice [kə'pri:s], *n.* Capriccio, ghiribizzo, *m.*
capricious, *a.* Capriccioso.
capriciously, *adv.* Capricciosamente, a capriccio.
capriciousness, *n.* Capricciosità, *f.*; umore fantastico, *m.*
Capricorn ['kæprikɔ:ɹn], *a.* (*Astron.*) Capricorno. || *m.* **Tropic of —,** tropico del Capricorno, *m.*
caprification [kæprifi'keiʃən], *n.* (*Agric.*) Caprificazione, *f.*
capsicum ['kæpsikəm], *n.* (*Bot.*) Peperone, *m.*
capsize [kæp'saiz], *v.i.* Capovolgersi, ribaltarsi; *v.t.* capovolgere. **The boat capsized,** la barca si capovolse.
capstan ['kæpstən], *n.* Argano, *m.*
capsular ['kæpsu:ləɹ], *a.* Capsulare, simile ad una capsula.
capsulate, capsulated, *a.* Con capsula, incapsulato.
capsule, *n.* Capsula, *f.*; (*Bot.*) pericarpo, *m.*
captain ['kæptin], *n.* Capitano, *m.*; (*Naut.*) (*naval*) capitano di vascello, *m.*, (*merchant service*) capitano marittimo, *m.* || *v.t.* Capitanare, guidare.
captaincy, captainship, *n.* Capitanato, grado di capitano, *m.*
caption, *n.* (*of illustration, chapter, etc.*) Intestazione, leggenda, *f.*; (*Law*) arresto, mandato d'arresto, *m.*
captious ['kæpʃəs], *a.* Capzioso, insidioso, ipercritico, sofistico.
captiously, *adv.* Capziosamente.
captiousness, *n.* Cavillosità, *f.*
captivate ['kæptiveit], *v.t.* Cattivare, affascinare, incantare.
captivating, *a.* Affascinante, seducente.
captivation, *n.* Seduzione, *f.*, fascino, incanto, *m.*
captive ['kæptiv], *n.a.* Prigioniero, schiavo, *m.*, prigioniera, schiava, *f.* **To lead —,** condurre prigioniero; **to take —,** far prigioniero; **to hold —,** tenere in prigionia.
captivity, *n.* Cattività, schiavitù, prigionia, *f.*
captor, *n.* Catturatore, *m.*
capture, *n.* Cattura, presa, *f.* || *v.t.* Catturare, far prigioniero, arrestare.
Capuchin ['kæpu:tʃin], *n.* (*Eccles.*) Cappuccino, *m.*, cappuccina, *f.* (*Zool.*) **— monkey,** scimmia cappuccina, *f.*
capybara [kæpi'bɑ:rə], *n.* (*Zool.*) Capibara, *m.*
car [kɑ:ɹ], *n.* Carro, *m.*, (*colloq.*) auto, *m.f.*; tram, *m.*; (*of balloon*) navicella, gondola, *f.* **Motor- —,** automobile, *m.f.*; macchina, *f.*; **tram- —,** tram, tranvai, *m.*; **dining- —,** vagone-ristorante, *m.*; **sleeping- —,** vagone-letto, *m.*; **— park,** parco automobilistico, *m.*
carabine [cp. **carbine**].
caracol, caracole ['kærəkoul], *n.* Caracollo, *m.* || *v.i.* Caracollare.
carafe [kə'ræf], *n.* Caraffa, *f.*
caramel ['kærəməl], *n.* Caramella, *f.*

carapace [ˈkærəpeis], *n.* Carapace, corazza di testuggine, *f.*
carat [ˈkærət], *n.* Carato, *m.*
caravan [ˈkærəvæn], *n.* Carovana, *f.*; (*horse- or car-drawn*) carro-carovana, *m.*
caravansary, caravanserai [kærəˈvænsəri], *n.* Caravanserraglio, *m.*
caravel, carvel [ˈkærəvəl, ˈkɑːɹvəl], *n.* (*Naut.*) Caravella, *f.*
caraway [ˈkærəwei], *n.* (*Bot.*) Carvi, comino, caro, *m.* **— seeds,** grani di carvi, *m.pl.*
carbide [ˈkɑːɹbaid], *n.* Carburo, *m.*
carbine, carabine [ˈkɑːɹbain], *n.* Carabina, *f.*
carbineer, *n.* Carabiniere, *m.*
carbo-hydrate [kɑːɹbouˈhaidreit], *n.* (*Chem.*) Idrato di carbonio, *m.*
carbolic [kɑːɹˈbɔlik], *a.* (*Chem.*) Fenico. **— acid,** acido fenico, *m.*
carbon [ˈkɑːɹbən], *n.* (*Chem.*) Carbonio, *m.*; (*Elect.*) carbone, *m.* **—-paper,** carta copiativa, *f.*; **— monoxide,** monossido di carbonio, *m.*
carbonate, *n.* Carbonato, *m.* **— of soda,** bicarbonato di soda, bicarbonato, *m.*
carbonic, *a.* Carbonico.
carboniferous, *a.* Carbonifero.
carbonization, *n.* Carbonizzazione, *f.*
carbonize, *v.t.* Carbonizzare; *v.i.* carbonizzarsi.
carboy [ˈkɑːɹbɔi], *n.* Damigiana, *f.*, fiascone, *m.*
carbuncle [ˈkɑːɹbʌŋkl], *n.* (*Med.*) Foruncolo, *m.*; (*Min.*) carbonchio, *m.*
carburate, carburet, *v.t.* (*Chem.*) Carburare.
carburetted, *a.* Carburato.
carburettor, *n.* (*Motor.Mech.*) Carburatore, *m.*
carcajou [ˈkɑːɹkəʒuː], *n.* (*Zool.*) Ghiottone, *m.*
carcanet [ˈkɑːɹkənət], *n.* (*obs.*) Collana, *f.*, monile, *m.*
carcase, carcass [ˈkɑːɹkəs], *n.* Carcame, *m.*, carcassa, *f.*
carcinoma [kɑːɹsiˈnoumə], *n.* (*Med.*) Carcinoma, *f.*
card (1) [kɑːɹd], *n.* Carta, *f.*, biglietto, *m.*; (*of card index*) scheda, *f.*; (*Golf*) scheda dei punti, *f.* **Invitation —,** biglietto d'invito, *m.*; **visiting- —,** biglietto da visita, *m.*; **— index,** schedario, *m.*; **post-card,** cartolina postale, *f.*; **playing-cards,** carte da giuoco, *f.pl.*; **a house of cards,** un progetto dubbio, *m.*; **a queer —,** una persona strana, *f.*; **it's on the cards,** è molto probabile; **to throw up the cards,** disperare; **a sure —,** una carta sicura; **to have a — up one's sleeve,** saper cavarsela; **to put one's cards on the table,** metter le carte in tavola; **compass —,** rosa dei venti, *f.*; **collecting- —,** sottoscrizione, *f.*; **—-player,** giocatore di carte, *m.*; **—-sharper,** baro, *m.*; **—-trick,** giuoco di prestigio colle carte, *m.*
card (2), *v.t.* (*Mech.*) Cardare, scardassare. **To — wool,** cardare lana.
cardamom [ˈkɑːɹdəməm], *n.* (*Bot.*) Cardamomo, cardamone, *m.*
cardboard, *n.* Cartone, cartoncino, *m.*
cardiac [ˈkɑːɹdiæk], *n.a.* (*Med.*) Cardiaco, *m.*
cardigan [ˈkɑːɹdigən], *n.* Panciotto a maglia, golf, *m.*; giacchettina di lana, *f.*
cardinal [ˈkɑːɹdinəl], *n.* (*Eccles.*) Cardinale, *m.* || *a.* Cardinale, principale, fondamentale. **— points,** punti cardinali, *m.pl.*; (*Zool.*) **— bird,** cardinale, *m.*
cardinalate, *n.* Cardinalato, *m.*
carding, *n.* Cardatura, *f.*, il cardeggiare, *m.* **—-machine,** macchina cardatrice, *f.*
cardoon [kɑːɹˈduːn], *n.* (*Bot.*) Cardone, *m.*
care [kɛəɹ], *n.* Cura, sollecitudine, premura, attenzione, *f.*; accuratezza, *f.*; precauzione, *f.*; ansietà, *f.*; custodia, *f.* || *v.i.* Curarsi, badare, farsi scrupolo. **— of (c/o) Mrs A.,** presso Signora A.; **in the — of a doctor,** in cura di un dottore; **take — he doesn't touch you,** badate che egli non vi tocchi; **Take — of yourself!** Abbiatevi cura! **Take (good) — in crossing the road!** State attento nel traversare la strada! **to put under the — of,** confidare alle cure di; **to take — not to,** guardare di non fare; **to take — of,** curare, prender cura di; **with —,** con cura; **to — for,** amare; curare; stimare, tenere in conto, tenerci; **I don't —,** non m'importa; **I don't — for it,** non mi piace; non mi interessa; **not to — for anyone,** non curarsi di nessuno; **I shouldn't — to go there,** non mi piacerebbe andarci; **I don't — a rap,** non me ne importa un corno; **I couldn't — less,** non me ne importa nulla; **—-worn,** logorato dal dolore.
careen [kəˈriːn], *v.t.* (*Naut.*) Carenare.
careening, *n.* Carenaggio, *m.*
career [kəˈriəɹ], *n.* Carriera, *f.*; corsa, *f.* || *v.i.* Andare di carriera, galoppare. **In full —,** a tutta carriera; **to — about,** correre su e giù, percorrere.
careerist, *n.* Arrivista, *m.*
careful [ˈkɛəɹful], *a.* Attento, sollecito; prudente, cauto; diligente. **Be —!** State attenti!
carefully, *adv.* Con cura, sollecitamente, cautamente, prudentemente.
carefulness, *n.* Cura, cautela, attenzione, *f.*
careless, *a.* Imprudente, incauto, negligente; trascurato; spensierato. **A — piece of work,** un lavoro trascurato.
carelessly, *adv.* Imprudentemente, incautamente.
carelessness, *n.* Negligenza, trascuratezza, noncuranza, *f.*
caress [kəˈres], *n.* Carezza, *f.* || *v.t.* Accarezzare.
caret [ˈkærət], *n.* Segno di omissione, *m.*
caretaker [ˈkɛəɹteikəɹ], *n.* Custode, guardiano, *m.*
cargo [ˈkɑːɹgou], *n.* Carico, *m.* **—-boat,** nave da carico, battello da carico, *m.*
Caribbean [kæriˈbiːən], *n.a.* **— Sea,** Mare dei Caraibi, *m.*
caribou [ˈkæribuː], *n.* (*Zool.*) Renna del Nord America, *f.*
caricature [kærikəˈtʃuːəɹ], *n.* Caricatura, *f.* || *v.t.* Disegnare caricature, mettere in caricatura.
caricaturist, *n.* Caricaturista, *m.*
caries [ˈkɛəriːz], *n.* (*Med.*) Carie, *f.*
carillon [kəˈriljən], *n.* Scampanio, carillon, *m.*
carking [ˈkɑːɹkiŋ], *a.* Pesante, penoso, inquietante. **— care,** dolore penoso, *m.*
carline [ˈkɑːɹlin], *n.* (*Bot.*) Carlina, *f.*
Carlovingian [kɑːɹlouˈviŋgiən], *a.* (*Hist.*) Carolingio.
carman (*pl.* **carmen**) [ˈkɑːɹmən, ˈkɑːɹmen], *n.* Carrettiere, barrocciaio, *m.*
Carmelite [ˈkɑːɹməlait], *n.* Carmelita, *m.f.*
carminative [ˈkɑːɹminətiv], *a.* (*Med.*) Carminativo.

carmine [ˈkɑːɹmain], *n.* Carminio, *m.* || *a.* Carminiato.
carnage [ˈkɑːɹnidʒ], *n.* Strage, carneficina, *f.*
carnal [ˈkɑːɹnəl], *a.* Carnale. **— -minded,** sensuale; mondano; **— -mindedness,** sensualità, *f.*; mondanità, *f.*
carnally, *adv.* Carnalmente.
carnation [kɑːɹˈneiʃən], *n.* (*Bot.*) Garofano, *m.*
carnelian [kɑːɹˈniːliən], *n.* Corniola, *f.*
carnival [ˈkɑːɹnivəl], *n.* Carnevale, carnovale, *m.*
carnivora [kɑːɹˈnivɔrə], *n.pl.* (*Zool.*) Carnivori, *m.pl.*
carnivorous, *a.* Carnivoro.
carny [ˈkɑːɹni], *v.t.* Persuadere con moine.
carob [ˈkærɔb], *n.* Carruba, *f.* **— -tree,** carrubo, *m.*
carol [ˈkærɔl], *n.* Cantico, canto, *m.*, canzone, *f.* || *v.i.* Cantare; (*of a lark*) gorgheggiare, trillare. **Christmas —,** canzone di Natale.
carotid [kəˈrɔtid], *n.* (*Anat.*) Carotide, *f.*
carousal, carouse, *n.* Gozzoviglia, orgia, *f.* bagordo, *m.*
carouse, *v.i.* Gozzovigliare, bagordare.
carouser, *n.* Beone, *m.*
carp (1) [kɑːɹp], *n.* (*Zool.*) Carpio, *m*
carp (2), *v.i.* Criticare, censurare, riprendere, biasimare, cavillare. **To — at,** riprendere.
carpel [ˈkɑːɹpəl], *n.* (*Bot.*) Carpello, *m.*
carpenter [ˈkɑːɹpəntəɹ], *n.* Falegname, legnaiuolo, carpentiere, *m.* || *v.i.* Fare il legnaiuolo.
carpentry, *n.* Carpenteria, *f.*
carpet [ˈkɑːɹpit], *n.* Tappeto, *m.* || *v.t.* Tappetare, guarnire di tappeto, coprire con un tappeto. **— -brush,** spazzola da tappeti, *f.*; **— -beater,** battipanni, *m.*; **— -sweeper,** scopa automatica, *f.*; (*fig.*) **on the —,** sul tappeto; **— -knight,** cavaliere di salotto, *m.*; **— -bag,** sacco da viaggio, *m.*
carping, *a.* Capzioso, sottile, mordace. **— criticism,** critica mordace, *f.*
carpingly, *adv.* Mordacemente.
carrack [ˈkærək], *n.* (*Naut.*) Galeone, *m.*
carriage [ˈkæridʒ], *n.* Carrozza, vettura, *f.*; (*Rail.*) vagone, *m.*, vettura, *f.*; trasporto, *m.*; (*fig.*) condotta, *f.*, contegno, portamento, *m.*; (*gun*) affusto, *m.*; (*Comm.*) spesa di trasporto, *f.*; carreggio, porto, *m.* **— and pair,** tiro a due, *m.*; **— entrance,** entrata per carrozze, *f.*; **— road,** strada carrozzabile, *f.*; (*Comm.*) **— forward,** porto assegnato; **— free,** porto franco; **— paid,** porto pagato.
carrier [ˈkæriəɹ], *n.* Carrettiere, barocciaio, *m.*; portatore, messaggero, *m.*; (*bicycle*) portabagagli, *m.* **— pigeon,** piccione viaggiatore, *m.*
carrion [ˈkæriən], *n.* Carogna, *f.* **— crow,** corvo, *m.*
carronade [kærəˈneid], *n.* Carronata, *f.*
carrot [ˈkærət], *n.* Carota, *f.*
carroty, *a.* Colore di carota. **— hair,** capelli colore carota, *m.pl.*
carry [ˈkæri], *v.t.* Portare, trasportare; menare; spedire; (*Arith.*) riportare; sostenere, sopportare. (*Arith.*) **Carried forward,** riportato; **to — into effect,** effettuare; **to — to excess,** esagerare, portare all'estremo; **he carries everything before him,** conduce tutto a buon fine; **to — about,** portarsi dietro; **to — away,** portar via; trasportare; **to — back,** riportare; **to — the day,** riportare vittoria, guadagnar la giornata; **to — it off,** riuscire; **to — off,** rapire; **to — on,** continuare, seguitare; (*fig.*) fare una tragedia; **to — on with a girl,** amoreggiare con una ragazza; **to — oneself well,** avere un bel portamento; **to — out,** effettuare, realizzare; **to — to and fro,** portare su e giù; **to — weight,** avere molta autorità; **to — one's years well,** portare bene i propri anni; **to — a jest too far,** spingere uno scherzo troppo innanzi; **to — coals to Newcastle,** portar vasi a Samo, fare un lavoro inutile; **the resolution was carried,** la proposta fu adottata.
carrying, *n.* Trasporto, porto, *m.* **— out,** esecuzione, *f.*
cart [kɑːɹt], *n.* Carro, *m.*; carretta, *f.*; furgone, *m.* || *v.t.* Trasportare col carro, carreggiare. **To — away,** caricare su carro; **— -horse,** cavallo da tiro, *m.*; **— -load,** carrettata, barocciata, *f.*; **— -road,** strada carreggiabile, *f.*; **— -shed,** rimessa di carri, *f.*; **— -wheel,** ruota di carro, *f.*; **to turn cart-wheels,** far la ruota; **— -wright,** carradore, *m.*
cartage, *n.* Carreggio, trasporto, *m.*
carte [kɑːɹt], *n.* Biglietto da visita, *m.*; lista, *f.* **— -blanche,** carta bianca, *f.*
cartel [ˈkɑːɹtel], *n.* (*Comm.*) Cartello, *m.*; scambio di prigionieri di guerra, *m.*
carter, *n.* Carrettiere, *m.*
Cartesian [kɑːɹˈtiːʒiən], *n.a.* Cartesiano, *m.*
Carthaginian [kɑːɹθəˈdʒiniən], *n.a.* Cartaginese, *m.f.*
Carthusian [kɑːɹˈθuːsiən], *n.a.* Certosino, *m.* **— monastery,** certosa, *f.*
cartilage [ˈkɑːɹtilidʒ], *n.* (*Anat.*) Cartilagine, *f.*
cartilaginous, *a.* Cartilaginoso.
cartographer, *n.* Cartografo, *m.*
cartography [kɑːɹˈtɔgrəfi], *n.* Cartografia, *f.*
carton [ˈkɑːɹtɔn], *n.* Scatola di cartone, *f.*
cartoon [kɑːɹˈtuːn], *n.* Vignetta, *f.*; disegno, *m.*; caricatura, *f.* **Strip —,** fumetto, *m.*
cartoonist, *n.* Caricaturista, *m.*
cartouche [kɑːɹˈtuːʃ], *n.* Cartoccio, *m.*
cartridge [ˈkɑːɹtridʒ], *n.* Cartuccia, *f.* **Blank —,** cartuccia a salve, *f.*; **ball- —,** cartuccia a palla, *f.*; **— -belt,** cartucciera, *f.*; **— -paper,** carta da disegno, *f.*; **— -pouch,** giberna, *f.*
caruncle [kəˈrʌŋkl], *n.* (*Med.*) Caruncola, *f.*
carve [kɑːɹv], *v.t.* (*meat, etc.*) Tagliare, trinciare; (*stone, etc.*) scolpire; (*wood*) intagliare; incidere.
carver, *n.* Scultore, intagliatore, *m.*; (*knife*) trinciante, *m.*
carving, *n.* Scultura, *f.*; intaglio, *m.*; incisione, *f.*; (*of meat*) il trinciare, *m.* **— in marble,** scultura in marmo, *f.*; **— -knife,** trinciante, *m.*; **— chisel,** scalpello, *m.*
caryatide [kæriˈætid], *n.* (*Arch. Myth.*) Cariatide, *f.*
cascade [kæsˈkeid], *n.* Cascata, *f.*
case (1) [keis], *n.* Astuccio, *m.*, cassa da imballaggio, *f.*; (*of watch*) scatola, *f.*; (*for jewels*) scrigno, *m.*; (*show*) vetrina, *f.*; (*Print.*) cassa, *f.* || *v.t.* Rinchiudere, rivestire, mettere in astuccio; imballare. (*Print*) **Upper — letters,** maiuscole, *f.pl.*; **lower — letters,** minuscole, *f.pl.*
case (2), *n* Caso, stato, *m.*; condizione, *f.*; (*Gram., Med., etc.*) caso, *m.*; (*Law*) causa, *f.*, processo, *m.* **As the — may be,** secondo le condizioni; **a — in point,** un esempio a pro-

posito; **if that be the —,** se la cosa è così; **in any —,** in tutti i casi; **in — he should come,** nel caso che egli venga; **in such a —,** in tal caso; **in that —,** in quel caso; **it is a very hard —,** è un caso pietosissimo; **that alters the —,** la cosa cambia aspetto; **the — is this,** si tratta di questo; **if ever it were the — that,** se si desse il caso che; **let's put the — that,** facciamo il caso che; **a — of conscience,** un caso di coscienza; (*Law*) **to state a —** giudicare una causa.

cased, *a.* Imballato, rinchiuso; coperto; blindato.

caseharden, *v.t.* Acciaiare; indurire, temprare.

casemate, *n.* (*Mil.*) Casamatta, *f.*

casement, *n.* (*window*) Finestra (a battenti), *f.*

cash [kæʃ], *n.* Danaro, *m.*, moneta, *f.*, contanti, *m.pl.*; valuta, *f.*; fondi, *m.pl.* ‖ *v.t.* Scontare, cambiare; incassare, pagare. **To be in —,** avere danaro, essere in fondi; **to be out of —,** essere senza danaro, essere al verde; **to pay —,** pagare in contanti; **to sell for —,** vendere a contanti; **— balance,** residuo di cassa, *m.*; **— down,** a contanti; **petty- —,** spese varie, *f.pl.*; **— in hand,** pronti contanti; **— on delivery,** pagamento alla consegna, *m.*; **to — a cheque,** incassare un assegno; **— -register,** registratore di cassa, *m.*; **— -book,** libro di cassa, *m.*; **— -account,** acconto di cassa, acconto in danaro, *m.*; **— -box,** scrigno, forziere, *m.*; **— -desk,** (*in shop*) cassa, *f.*

cashew, cashew nut [ˈkæʃuː], *n.* (*Bot.*) Noce d'anacardo, *f.*

cashier (1) [kæˈʃiəɹ], *n.* Cassiere, *m.*

cashier (2), *v.t.* (*Mil.*) Destituire, degradare.

cashmere [ˈkæʃmiəɹ], *n.* Casimirra, *f.* **— shawl,** scialle di casimirra, *m.*

casing, *n.* Copertura, coperta, *f.*, rivestimento, *m.*; telaio, *m.* **Door- —,** telaio di porta, *m.*

casino [kəˈsiːnou], *n.* Casinò, *m.*; sala da ballo, *f.*; casa da giuoco, *f.*

cask [kɑːsk], *n.* Botte, *f.*, barile, barilotto, *m.* ‖ *v.t.* Imbarilare, imbottare. **To taste of the —,** sapere di botte.

casket, *n.* Scrigno, cofano, *m.*; (*coffin*) cassa, *f.*

casque [kɑːsk], *n.* (*Hist.Lit.*) Casco, elmo, *m.*

cassation [kæsˈeiʃən], *n.* (*Law*) Cassazione, *f.*

casserole [ˈkæsəroul], *n.* Casseruola, teglia, *f.*

cassia [ˈkæsiə], *n.* (*Bot.*) Cassia, *f.*

cassock [ˈkæsək], *n.* Tonaca , *f.*

cassowary [ˈkæsəwəri], *n.* (*Zool.*) Casuario, *m.*

cast [kɑːst], *v.t.* Gettare, lanciare, buttare; fondere (*of metals*); (*of animals, trees*) spogliarsi di, lasciar cadere; (*Arith.*) calcolare, sommare, addizionare; (*statues, etc.*) gettare; (*Theat.*) distribuire le parti; *v.i.* (*fishing*) gettare la lenza; computare; considerare. ‖ *n.* Getto, lancio, *m.*; (*throw*) tiro, *m.*; (*metal*) forma, *f.*; (*plaster*) calco, *m.*; (*Theat.*) il complesso, la lista degli attori; (*Arith.*) somma, addizione, *f.* **To be — away,** naufragare, far naufragio; **to — about one,** considerare, cercare; **to — anchor,** gettar l'ancora; **to be — in a law-suit,** perdere una causa; **to — a shoe** (*of horses*) perdere un ferro; **to — aside,** mettere da parte, cessare di usare; **to — away,** gettare, rigettare; **to — down,** gettare in basso; **to — down the eyes,** abbassare gli occhi; **to be — down,** essere abbattuto; **to — lots,** tirare a sorte; **to — off,** rigettare, abbandonare, liberarsi di; (*Naut.*) levare l'ancora, disormeggiare; **to — on,** (*knitting*) metter su i punti, incrociare i punti; **to — out,** cacciare, metter fuori, scacciare; **to — up,** calcolare, computare; vomitare; **to — in someone's teeth that,** rinfacciare a qualcuno che; **to — the blame on,** incolpare, dare la colpa a; **to — a horoscope,** trarre un oroscopo; **to — one's eyes over,** gettare un colpo d'occhio su; **to — their young** (*of animals*), abortire; **— of mind,** carattere, *m.*; **— of features,** aspetto, *m.*; **to have a — in the eye,** essere guercio; **at one —,** d'un colpo; **a — of the net,** una retata, una gettata di rete, *f.*; **a — of the dice,** un tiro di dadi, *m.*; **— -off clothing,** vestiti vecchi, *m.pl.*; **— -iron,** ferro fuso, *m.*, ghisa, *f.*; **to — one's vote,** dare il proprio voto.

castanets [ˈkæstənets], *n.pl.* (*Mus.*) Nacchere, castagnette, *f.p* .

castaway [ˈkɑːstəwei], *n.* Naufrago, *m.*; (*fig.*) reprobo, *m.*

caste [kɑːst], *n.* Casta, *f.* **To lose —,** scendere dal rango sociale.

castellan [ˈkæstələn], *n.* (*Hist.*) Castellano, *m.*

castellated [ˈkæstəleitəd], *a.* Merlato.

caster, *n.* Fonditore, *m.*

castigate [ˈkæstigeit], *v.t.* Castigare, punire.

castigation, *n.* Castigo, *m.*, punizione, *f.*

castigator, *n.* Castigatore, *m.*

casting, *n.* Getto, il gettare, *m.*, (*fishing*) pesca a getto, *f.* (*Print.*) **— off,** valutazione, *f.*; **— on,** avviamento, *m.*; **— vote,** voto decisivo, *m.*

castle [ˈkɑːsl], *n.* Castello, *m.*; (*Chess*) torre, rocca, *f.* ‖ *v.t.* (*Chess*) Arroccare.

castled, *a.* Munito di castelli.

castor (1) [kɑːstəɹ], *n.* **— -oil,** olio di ricino, *m.*; **— -oil plant,** ricino, *m.*

castor (2), *n.* (*wheel*) Rotella, *f.*

castor (3), **caster,** *n.* (*for pepper*) Pepaiuola, *f.* **— -sugar,** polvere di zucchero, zucchero al velo, *m.*

castor (4), *n.* (*obs.*) (*beaver hat*) Castoro, *m.*

castrate [kæsˈtreit], *v.t.* Castrare.

castration, *n.* Castrazione, *f.*

casual [ˈkæʒjuːəl], *a.* Casuale, fortuito, incerto, accidentale; negligente, disattento. ‖ *n.* Vagabondo, *m.* **— labourer,** avventizio, lavorante giornaliero, *m.*; **— ward,** asilo notturno, *m.*

casually, *adv.* Fortuitamente, accidentalmente; in modo negligente, in modo irregolare.

casualness, *n.* Irregolarità, mancanza di cura, mancanza di metodo, *f.*

casualty, *n.* Accidente disgrazia, *f.*; vittima, *f.* **Casualties,** perdite, *f.pl.*; **— list,** elenco dei morti e feriti, *f.*

casuist, *n.* Casista, *m.*

casuistic, casuistical, *a.* Da casista, casistico.

casuistically, *adv.* In modo da casista.

casuistry, *n.* Casistica, *f.*

cat [kæt], *n.* Gatto, *m.*, gatta, *f.*; (*whip*) frusta, *f.* ‖ *v.t.*(*Naut.*) capponare l'ancora; (*colloq.*) vomitare. (*Naut.*) **— -head,** gru di capone, *f.*; **to live a — and dog life,** andar d'accordo come cane e gatto; **when the — is away the mice will play,** quando il gatto manca i topi ballano; **to rain cats and dogs,** piovere a catinelle;

cat's cradle, ripiglino, *m.*; **cat's eyes**, (*Motor.*) occhio di gatto; catarifrangente, *m.*; **—-fish**, (*Zool.*) lupo marino, *m.*; **cat's foot**, (*Bot.*) piede di gatto, *m.*, edera terrestre, *f.*; **cat's-paw**, venticello, *m.*; (*fig.*) zimbello di un furbo, *m.*; **to use someone as a cat's-paw**, cavar la castagna con la zampa del gatto; **cat-o'-nine-tails**, staffile a nove correggie, *m.*; **cat-o'mountain**, (*Zool.*) puma, *f.*

catachresis [kætə'kri:sis], *n.* (*Gram.*) Catacresi, *f.*

cataclysm ['kætəklizm], *n.* Cataclisma, sconvolgimento, disastro, *m.*

catacomb ['kætəkoum], *n.* Catacomba, *f.*

catafalque ['kætəfælk], *n.* Catafalco, *m.*

catalepsy ['kætəlepsi], *n.* (*Med.*) Catalessia, catalessi, *f.*

cataleptic, *a.* Catalessico.

catalogue ['kætələg], *n.* Catalogo, *m.* || *v.t.* Catalogare.

catamite ['kætəmait], *n.* Cinedo, *m.*

catapult ['kætəpʌlt], *n.* (*Mil.*) Catapulta, *f.*; (*boy's*) frombola, fionda, *f.* || *v.t.* Scagliare, frombolare; (*Aviat.*) lanciare, catapultare.

cataract ['kætərækt], *n.* Cateratta, cascata, *f.*; (*Med.*) cateratta, *f.*

catarrh [kə'tɑ:ɹ], *n.* (*Med.*) Catarro, *m.*

catarrhal, *a.* Catarrale.

catastrophe [kə'tæstrəfi], *n.* Catastrofe, *f.*

catastrophic, *a.* Catastrofico.

catcall ['kætkɔ:l], *n.* Fischio, *m.*

catch [kætʃ], *v.t.* Cogliere, pigliare, prendere, afferrare, acchiappare; raggiungere; sorprendere; *v.i.* attaccarsi, appiccarsi, sopraggiungere. || *n.* Presa, *f.*; guadagno, vantaggio, *m.*; (*fish*) pescata, retata, *f.*; (*trick*) trappola, *f.*, inganno, *m.*; (*door*) anello di porta, *m.*; (*window*) gancio, *m.*; (*Mus.*) canzone a ripresa, *f.* **To — the eye**, colpire l'occhio; **to — a train**, prendere un treno; **to — cold**, prendere un raffreddore; **to — up with**, raggiungere; **— to someone's eye**, incontrarsi cogli occhi; **to — one's breath**, trattenere il respiro; **if I — him at it**, se io l'acchiappo in flagrante; **You'll — it!** Avrete una sgridata! **I shall soon — him up**, lo raggiungerò tosto; **to —fire**, prendere fuoco; **to — hold of**, afferrare, **to — out**, scoprire sul fatto; **there's a — in it**, c'è qui un inganno; **there's no great — in that**, non c'è molto guadagno in quell'affare; **the meat has caught**, l'arrosto si è abbruciato; **he had a good — of fish**, ha fatto una bella pesca; **—-penny**, fatto solo per vendere; **—-word**, richiamo, *m.*

catching, *n.* Presa, *f.* || *a.* (*Med.*) Contagioso, attaccaticcio, infettivo.

catchy, *a.* Orecchiabile. **A — tune**, un motivo orecchiabile, *m.*

catechism ['kætikizm], *n.* Catechismo, *m.*

catechist, *n.* Catechista, *m.*

catechize, *v.t.* Catechizzare.

catechumen [kætə'kju:men], *n.* Catecumeno, *m.*

categorical [kæti'gɔrikəl], *a.* Categorico.

categorically, *adv.* Categoricamente.

category, *n.* Categoria, *f.*

catenary [kə'ti:nəri], *a.* Catenario.

cater ['keitəɹ], *v.i.* Provvedere, procacciare cibo.

caterer, *n.* Provveditore, fornitore, negoziante, *m.*

cater-cousin, *n.* Cugino in quarto grado, *m.*

caterpillar ['kætəpiləɹ], *n.* Bruco, *m.* **— tractor** (*reg. trade name*), trattore a cingoli, *m.*

caterwaul ['kætəɹwɔ:l], *v.i.* Miagolare.

caterwauling, *n.* Miagolio, *m.*, miagolata *f.*

catgut ['kætgʌt], *n.* Corda di budello, *f.*, corda di minugia, *f.*

catharsis [kə'θɑ:ɹsis], *n.* Catarsi, *f.*

cathedral [kə'θi:drəl], *n.* Cattedrale, *f.*, duomo, *m.* **— city**, città episcopale, *f.*

Catherine ['kæθəɹin], *n.* Caterina, *f.* **— wheel**, girandola, *f.*

catheter ['kæθitəɹ], *n.* (*Med.*) Catetere, *m.*

cathode ['kæθoud], *n.* (*Elec.*) Catodo, *m.*

catholic ['kæθəlik], *n.a.* Universale, generale, liberale. **Roman —**, cattolico.

Catholicism [kə'θɔlisizm], *n.* Cattolicismo, *m.*

catholicity, *n.* Cattolicità, *f.* (*in all senses*). **— of taste**, gusto eclettico, *m.*

catkin ['kætkin], *n.* (*Bot.*) Amento, *m.*

catlike, *a.* Felino.

cat-mint ['kætmint], *n.* (*Bot.*) Erba dei gatti, *f.*

catoptric [kə'tɔptrik], *a.* Catottrico.

catsup [cp. **ketchup**].

cattle [kætl], *n.* Bestiame, *m.*; bestie, *f.pl.* **—-bell**, campanaccio, *m.*; **—-market**, mercato del bestiame, *m.*; **—-plague**, peste bovina, *f.*; **—-shed**, stalla, *f.*; **—-show**, mostra bovina, *f.*; **—-truck**, vagone per bestiame, *m.*

catty, *a.* (*fig.*) Dispettoso.

Caucasian [kɔ:'keiʃiən], *n.a.* Caucasico, *m.* **The Caucasus**, Il Caucaso, *m.*

caucus ['kɔ:kəs], *n.* Comitato elettorale, *m.*; riunione di partito, *f.*; cabala, *f.*

caudal ['kɔ:dəl], *a.* Caudale.

caught, *past & p.p.* of **catch**.

caul [kɔ:l], *n.* (*Anat.*) Amnio, *m.*; cuffia, *f.*

cauldron ['kɔ:ldrən], *n.* Caldaia, *f.*; paiuolo, *m.*

cauliflower ['kɔliflauəɹ], *n.* Cavolfiore, *m.*

cauline ['kɔ:lain], *a.* (*Bot.*) Caulinario.

caulk, calk [kɔ:k], *v.t.* Calafatare.

caulker, calker, *n.* Calafatore, calafato, *m.*

caulking, calking, *n.* Calafataggio, *m.*

causal ['kɔ:zəl], *a.* Causale.

causality, *n.* Causalità, *f.*

causation, *n.* Causa, causalità, *f.*

causative, *a.* Causativo.

cause [kɔ:z], *n.* Causa, cagione, ragione, origine, *f.*, motivo, *m.*; (*Law*) causa, lite, *f.*, processo, *m.* || *v.t.* Causare, cagionare, produrre; fare. **There is — to believe**, c'è motivo di credere; **to show —**, spiegare le ragioni; **to plead a —**, difendere una causa; **to make common — with**, fare causa comune con; **to — a thing to be done**, far fare; **to — sorrow**, dar dolore; **to — to be punished**, far punire; **to — much comment**, dar luogo a molte dicerie.

causeless, *a.* Senza causa, senza motivo.

causelessly, *adv.* Senza causa, senza ragione.

causeway, *n.* Marciapiede, *m.*; strada selciata, *f.*, terrapieno, *m.*, diga, *f.*

caustic ['kɔ:stik], *a.* Caustico, aspro, acerbo. || *n.* (*Med.*) Caustico, *m.*

caustically, *adv.* Aspramente, acerbamente.

causticity, *n.* Causticità, *f.*

cauterization [kɔ:tərai'zeiʃən], *n.* (*Med.*) Cauterizzazione, *f.*

cauterize, *v.t.* Cauterizzare.

cautery, *n.* Cauterio, *m.*

caution [ˈkɔːʃən], *n.* Cautela, accortezza, prudenza, *f.*; avviso, *m.*; (*colloq.*) originale, *m.*, cosa strana, *f.* || *v.t.* Ammonire, avvertire, prevenire. **Dismissed with a —,** assolto con diffida; **— -money,** pegno, *m.*, garanzia, cauzione, *f.*; **he's a —,** è un vero originale.
cautionary, *a.* Ammonitorio, esortatorio.
cautious, *a.* Prudente, cauto, guardingo, accorto.
cautiously, *adv.* Cautamente, con cautela, prudentemente.
cautiousness, *n.* Prudenza, cautela, *f.*
cavalcade [kævəlˈkeid], *n.* Cavalcata, *f.*
cavalier [kævəˈliəɹ], *n.* Cavaliere, *m.* || *a.* Brusco; disinvolto; superbo, presuntuoso.
cavalierly, *adv.* Disinvoltamente, alteramente, in modo presuntuoso.
cavalry [ˈkævəlri], *n.* Cavalleria, *f.*
cavalryman, *n.* Soldato di cavalleria, *m.*
cave [keiv], *n.* Caverna, cava, grotta, *f.*, antro, *m.*; spelonca, *f.* || *v.t.* Cavare, scavare. **To — in,** scassare, (*fig.*) cedere; abbandonare la lotta; **— -dweller,** troglodita, *m.*
caveat [ˈkeiviət], *n.* (*Law*) Opposizione legale, *f.* **To enter a —,** chiedere una sospensiva.
cavern [ˈkævəɹn], *n.* Caverna, spelonca, *f.*, antro, *m.*
cavernous, *a.* Cavernoso.
caviar, caviare [ˈkæviɑːɹ], *n.* Caviale, *m.* **— to the general,** d'un gusto troppo fino per la folla.
cavil [ˈkævəl], *v.i.* Cavillare, sottilizzare. || *n.* Cavillo, arzigogolo, *m.*
caviller, *n.* Cavillatore, *m.*
cavilling, *n.* Cavillatore, *m.*
cavity [ˈkæviti], *n.* Cavità, *f.*, buco, vuoto, *m.*
cavy [ˈkeivi], *n.* (*Zool.*) Cavia, *f.*
caw [kɔː], *v.i.* Gracchiare.
cawing, caw, *n.* Il gracchiare, gracchiamento, *m.*
cayenne, cayenne pepper [keiˈen], *n.* Pepe di Caienna, *m.*
cayman, caiman [ˈkeimæn], *n.* (*Zool.*) Caimano, *m.*
cease [siːs], *v.i.* Cessare, desistere, smettere; *v.t.* cessare, sospendere, finire. || *n.* Cessazione, tregua, *f.* **To — working,** smettere di lavorare; **without —,** senza tregua; **Cease!** La smetta! La finisca!
ceaseless, *a.* Incessante, continuo.
ceaselessly, *adv.* Incessantemente, continuamente.
ceaselessness, *n.* Continuità, *f.*
ceasing, *n.* Cessazione, interruzione, fine, *f.* **Without —,** senza interruzione.
cecity [ˈsesiti], *n.* Cecità, *f.*
cedar [ˈsiːdəɹ], *n.* (*Bot.*) Cedro, *m.* **— -wood,** legno di cedro, *m.*
cede [siːd], *v.t.* Cedere, rinunciare. **He has ceded all his rights,** ha rinunciato a tutti i suoi diritti.
cedilla [səˈdilə], *n.* (*Gram.*) Cediglia, *f.*
ceil [ciːl], *v.t.* Soffittare, fare il soffitto.
ceiling, *n.* Soffitto, *m.*, volta, *f.*; massima altezza o livello.
celandine [ˈseləndain], *n.* (*Bot.*) Celidonia, *f.*
celebrant, *n.* (*Eccles.*) Celebrante, *m.*
celebrate [ˈselibreit], *v.t.i.* Celebrare, solennizzare.
celebrated, *a.* Celebre, famoso, illustre.
celebration, *n.* Celebrazione, *f.*
celebrity [səˈlebriti], *n.* Celebrità, *f.*
celerity [səˈleriti], *n.* Celerità, prestezza, velocità, *f.*
celery [ˈseləri], *n.* (*Bot.*) Sedano, apio, *m.* **A head of —,** un piede di sedano, *m.*
celestial [səˈlestiəl], *a.* Celeste, divino, angelico. **The — empire,** l'impero celeste, l'antica Cina; **a — globe,** un globo celeste, *m.*; **the Celestials,** i Cinesi, *m.pl.*
celestially, *adv.* Celestialmente.
celibacy [ˈselibəsi], *n.* Celibato, *m.*
celibate, *n.a.* Celibe, *m.*
cell [sel], *n.* Cella, cellula, *f.*; (*in bee-hive*) alveo, *m.*; (*Mil.*) prigione, cella di rigore, *f.*; (*Elect., etc.*) elemento, *m.* **Dry —,** pila a secco, *f.*
cellar, *n.* Cantina, *f.* || *v.t.* Mettere in cantina.
cellarage, *n.* Cantine, *f.pl.*, magazzinaggio, *m.*
cellarer, *n.* Cantiniere, *m.*
cellaret, *n.* Stipo da liquori, *m.*
'cellist [ˈtʃelist], *n.* Violoncellista, *m.f.*
'cello [ˈtʃelou], *n.* (*Mus.*) Violoncello, *m.*
cellular [ˈseluːləɹ], *a.* Cellulare.
celluloid, *n.* Celluloide, *f.*
cellulose, *n.* (*Chem.*) Cellulosa, *f.*
Celt [kelt, selt], *n.* Celto, *m.*
Celtic, *a.* Celtico.
cement [seˈment], *n.* Cemento; smalto, *m.* || *v.t.* Cementare; (*fig.*) unire, rinsaldare.
cementing, *n.* (*fig.*) L'unire, il rinsaldare, *m.*
cemetery [ˈsemetəri], *n.* Cimitero, camposanto, *m.*
cenotaph [ˈsenətɑːf], *n.* Cenotafio, *m.*
cense [sens], *v.t.* (*Eccles.*) Incensare.
censer, *n.* Incensiere, turibolo, *m.*
censor [ˈsensəɹ], *n.* Censore, *m.* || *v.t.* Censurare.
censorious, *a.* Critico, severo, caustico, censorio.
censoriously, *adv.* In modo severo, con biasimo.
censoriousness, *n.* Umore critico, *m.*, asprezza nel giudicare, *f.*
censorship, *n.* Censura, *f.*
censure [ˈsenʃəɹ], *n.* Censura, riprensione, *f.*, rimprovero, *m.* || *v.t.* Censurare, riprendere, biasimare.
censurer, *n.* Censore, critico, *m.*
census [ˈsensəs], *n.* Censimento, *m.* **To take the —,** censire, fare il censimento.
cent [sent], *n.* Cento, centesimo, *m.* **Ten per —,** dieci per cento; **ninety-nine per — of the people,** il novantanove per cento delle persone.
centaur [ˈsentɔːɹ], *n.* (*Myth.*) Centauro, *m.*
centaury, *n.* (*Bot.*) Centaurea, *f.*
centenarian [sentəˈnεəriən], *n.a.* Centenario, *m.*
centenary [senˈtiːnəri], *n.* Centenario, *m.*
centennial, *a.* Secolare.
centering, *n.* (*Arch.*) Armatura, *f.*
centesimal, *a.* Centesimale.
centigrade [ˈsentigreid], *a.* Centigrado.
centigram, *n.* Centigrammo, *m.*
centilitre, *n.* Centilitro, *m.*
centimetre, *n.* Centimetro, *m.*
centipede, *n.* (*Zool.*) Millepiedi, *m.*
cento, *n.* (*Lit.*) Centone, *m.*
central [ˈsentrəl], *a.* Centrale, principale. **— -heating,** termosifone, *m.*
centrality, *n.* Centralità, *f.*
centralization, *n.* Centralizzazione, *f.*
centralize, *v.t.* Centralizzare.

centrally, *adv.* Centralmente, nel mezzo.
centre [ˈsentəɹ], *n.* Centro, punto, *m.* ‖ *v.t.* Centrare; concentrare; trovare il centro; *v.i.* concentrarsi. **— of gravity,** centro di gravità, baricentro, *m.*; **—-bit,** trapano, *m.*; **—-piece,** trionfo da tavola, *m.*; (*Naut.*) **—-board,** chiglia di deriva, *f.*; (*Football*) **— forward,** centro attacco, *m.*; **— half,** centro mediano, *m.*
centric, *a.* Centrico.
centricity, *n.* Posizione centrale, *f.*
centrifugal [sentˈrifu:gəl], *a.* Centrifugo.
centripetal [sentˈripetəl], *a.* Centripeto.
centuple [sənˈtu:pl], *n.a.* Centuplo, *m.* ‖ *v.t.* Centuplicare.
centurion [senˈtu:riən], *n.* (*Hist.*) Centurione, *m.*
century [ˈsentju:ri], *n.* Secolo, *m.*
cephalic [seˈfeilik], *a.* Cefalico.
cephalopod [seˈfæləpɔd], *n.* (*Zool.*) Cefalopodo, *m.*
ceramic [səˈræmik, kəˈræmik], *a.* Ceramico.
ceramics, *n.pl.* Ceramica, *f.*
cereal [ˈsiəriəl], *n.a.* Cereale, *m.*
cerebellum [seriˈbeləm], *n.* (*Anat.*) Cervelletto, *m.*
cerebral [seˈribrəl], *a.* Cerebrale.
cerebration, *n.* Azione inconscia del cervello, *f.*
cerebritis [seriˈbraitis], *n.* (*Med.*) Cerebrite, *f.*
cerebrum, *n.* Cerebro, cervello, *m.*
cerecloth [ˈsiəɹklɔθ], *n.* Tela per imbalsamare, *f.*
cerement, *n.* Lenzuolo funebre, *m.*
ceremonial [seriˈmouniəl], *n.a.* Cerimoniale, rituale, *m.*
ceremonially, *adv.* Cerimonialmente.
ceremonious, *a.* Cerimonioso.
ceremoniously, *adv.* Cerimoniosamente.
ceremoniousness, *n.* Cerimoniosità, *f.*
ceremony, *n.* Cerimonia, *f.*; rito, *m.* **To stand on —,** far complimenti; **without —,** senza complimenti; **master of the ceremonies,** cerimoniere, *m.*
cerise [səˈri:z], *a.* Color ciliegia.
certain [ˈsə:ɹtin], *a.* Certo, sicuro, vero, indubitabile; qualche, alquanto, certo. **To make —,** far certo; **to know for —,** sapere per certo; **a — man,** un tale, *m.*; **a — thing** (*something*), una certa cosa, *f.*; **a — thing** (*a positive thing*), una cosa certa, *f.*; **one thing is —,** una cosa è certa.
certainly, *adv.* Certo, certamente, senza dubbio.
certainty, *n.* Certezza, sicurezza, *f.*; cosa certa, *f.* **To a —,** certamente, per certo.
certes [ˈsə:ɹti:z], *adv.* (*obs.*) Certamente.
certificate [səɹˈtifikit], *n.* Certificato, attestato, diploma, *m.* ‖ *v.t.* Certificare. **Birth —,** atto di nascita.
certificated, *a.* Autorizzato, diplomato.
certify, *v.t.* Attestare, affermare; vidimare; dichiarare; legalizzare (una firma).
certitude, *n.* Certezza, sicurezza, *f.*
cerulean [seˈru:liən], *a.* Cerulo, azzurro.
cerumen [səˈru:mən], *n.* Cerume, *m.*
ceruminous, *a.* Ceruminoso.
cervical [ˈsə:ɹvikəl], *a.* (*Anat.*) Cervicale.
cessation [seˈseiʃən], *n.* Cessazione, *f.*
cession [ˈseʃən], *n.* (*Law*) Cessione, *f.*
cesspit [ˈsespit], *n.* Cesso, *m.*, latrina, *f.*
cesspool, *n.* Fogna, *f.*, pozzo nero, *m.*
cetacean [seˈteiʃən], *n.* (*Zool.*) Cetaceo, *m.*
Ceylon [siˈlɔn], *n.* (*Geog.*) Ceylon, *m.*
chafe [tʃeif], *v.t.* Fregare, strofinare, stropicciare; irritare; rendere di cattivo umore; *v.i.* irritarsi, infiammarsi; (*of cable*) logorarsi. ‖ *n.* Malumore, *m.*, stizza, *f.* **To — under restraint,** mordere il freno.
chaff [tʃɑ:f], *n.* Pagliuzza, pagliuola, loppa, *f.*; (*fig.*) burle, beffe, *f.pl.*, motteggio, *m.* ‖ *v.t.* Burlare, beffare, canzonare. **Not to be caught with —,** non pronto a prendere lucciole per lanterne; **he's only chaffing you,** non parla che per scherzo; (*Agric.*) **—-cutter,** trinciapaglia, *m.*
chaffer [ˈtʃæfəɹ], *v.i.* Mercanteggiare, stiracchiare sul prezzo.
chaffering, *n.* Il mercanteggiare, *m.*
chaffinch [ˈtʃæfintʃ], *n.* (*Zool.*) Fringuello, *m.*
chafing, *n.* Irritazione, infiammazione, *f.*; fregamento, *m.* **—-dish,** scaldavivande, *m.*
chagrin [ʃəˈgri:n], *n.* Malumore, dispetto, fastidio, *m.*, stizza, *f.* ‖ *v.t.* Dar fastidio, indispettire.
chain [tʃein], *n.* Catena, catenella, *f.*; (*fig.*) concatenamento, *m.*; misura di lunghezza inglese, *f.* ‖ *v.t.* Incatenare, legare con una catena. **— of ideas,** serie di idee, *f.*; **in chains,** in catene; **— store,** succursale, *f.*; **—-armour,** armatura a maglia, *f.*; **— -gang,** i forzati, *m.pl.*; **—-pump,** pompa a catena, *f.*; **—-shot,** (*Mil.*) bombe incatenate, *f.pl.*; **—-stitch,** punto a catenella, *m.*
chair [tʃɛəɹ], *n.* Sedia, seggiola, *f.*; (*of university*) cattedra, *f.*; (*of chairman, etc.*) seggio, *m.*, presidenza, *f.*; (*Rail.*) cuscinetto, *m.* ‖ *v.t.* Portare in trionfo. **Chair!** All'ordine! **deck- —,** sdraio, *m.*, sedia a sdraio, *f.*; **armchair,** poltrona, *f.*; **folding- —,** sedia pieghevole, *f.*; **rocking- —,** dondola, *f.*; **sedan- —,** portantina, *f.*; **to be in the —,** tenere la presidenza; **to leave the —,** sciogliere la seduta; **with X in the —,** sotto la presidenza di X.; **—-maker,** fabbricante di sedie, *m.*
chairman, *n.* Presidente, *m.*
chairmanship, *n.* Presidenza, *f.*
chaise [ʃeiz], *n.* Calesse, *m.* **Post- —,** calesse di posta, *m.*
chalcedony [kælˈsedəni], *n.* Calcedonia, *f.*
chalcography [kælˈkɔgrəfi], *n.* Calcografia, *f.*
chaldron [ˈtʃɔ:ldrən], *n.* Misura inglese per il carbone, *f.*
chalice [ˈtʃælis], *n.* Calice, *m.*; coppa, *f.*
chalk [tʃɔ:k], *n.* Gesso, *m.*; calcare, *m.*; creta, *f.*; (*for blackboard*) gessetto, *m.* ‖ *v.t.* Scrivere col gesso; coprire di gesso. **To — out,** segnare, tracciare; (*colloq.*) **by a long —,** molto, vieppiù; **he doesn't know — from cheese,** non sa niente di niente; prende lucciole per lanterne. **—-pit,** cava di creta, *f.*; **—-stone,** (*Med.*) calcolo artritico, *m.*
chalkiness, *n.* Natura gessosa, *f.*
chalky, *a.* Gessoso, cretaceo, cretoso.
challenge [ˈtʃæləndʒ], *n.* Sfida, disfida, *f.*; (*fig.*) provocazione, domanda, *f.*; (*Law*) rifiuto di accettare un giurato, *m.*; (*Mil.*) il chi-va-la, *m.* ‖ *v.t.* Sfidare; provocare, domandare; (*Mil.*) fermare col chi-va-la. (*Sport*) **—-match,** campionato, *m.*; **to — to a duel,** sfidare a duello.

challenger, *n.* Provocatore, sfidatore, *m.*
chalybeate [kə'libieit], *a.* Ferruginoso. || *n.* Acqua ferruginosa, *f.*
chamber ['tʃeimbəɹ], *n.* Camera, stanza, sala, *f.*; gabinetto, *m.* || *v.t.* (*obs.*) Fare il libertino; rinchiudere in una camera. **— of Commerce,** Camera di Commercio, *f.*; (*Law*) **— -counsel,** avvocato consulente, *m.*; (*Law*) **in chambers,** (*of judges*), in camera; (*Law, Art, etc.*) **chambers,** studio, ufficio; **— -music,** musica da camera, *f.*; **— -pot,** orinale, *m.*, vaso da notte, *m.*
chambered, *a.* Diviso in scompartimenti. **Six- — revolver,** revolver a sei colpi, *m.*
chamberlain ['tʃeimbəɹlin], *n.* Ciambellano, *m.*; camerlengo, *m.*
chambermaid, *n.* Cameriera, *f.*
chameleon [kə'mi:liən], *n.* (*Zool.*) Camaleonte, *m.*
chamfer ['tʃæmfəɹ], *n.* Modanatura, sagoma, *f.*, smusso, *m.* || *v.t.* Scanalare, smussare, far la modanatura.
chamois [ʃæmwɑ:], *n.* (*Zool.*) Camoscio, *m.* **— -leather** [ʃæmi'leðəɹ] pelle di camoscio, *f.*
champ [tʃæmp], *v.t.* Mordere, masticare. **To — the bit,** mordere il freno.
champagne [ʃæm'pein], *n.* Vino di Sciampagna, sciampagna, *m.*
champaign [ʃæm'pein], *n.* Campagna aperta, *f.*
champion ['tʃæmpiən], *n.* Campione, difensore, propugnatore, *m.* || *v.t.* Difendere, sostenere, propugnare. **To — a cause,** propugnare *or* perorare una causa.
championship, *n.* Difesa, *f.*, campionato, *m.*
chance [tʃɑ:ns], *n.* Caso, azzardo, *m.*; sorte, ventura, occasione, *f.* || *a.* Fortuito, casuale, accidentale. || *v.i.* Accadere per caso, avvenire, succedere. **By —,** per caso, fortuitamente; **the main —,** interesse personale, *m.*; **the chances are against it,** è molto improbabile; **to take one's — of,** correr il rischio di; **to stand a good —,** aver molta probabilità; **games of —,** giuochi d'azzardo, *m.pl.*; **I'll — it,** correrò il rischio; **to — to meet,** incontrare per caso; **a — meeting,** un incontro fortuito, *m.*; **a — shot,** un colpo a caso, *m.*; **I am taking no chances,** non rischio niente; non mi arrischio.
chancel ['tʃɑ:nsəl], *n.* Coro, *m.*
chancellery, *n.* Cancelleria, *f.*
chancellor, *n.* Cancelliere, *m.* **Chancellor of the Exchequer,** Cancelliere dello Scacchiere, *m.*; **Lord Chancellor,** Gran Cancelliere, *m.*
chancellorship, *m.* Cancellierato, *m.*
chancery, *n.* Cancelleria, *f.* **To get into Chancery,** incappar nella legge; **a ward in Chancery,** un minorenne sotto tutela legale, *m.*
chancre ['ʃæŋkəɹ], *n.* (*Med.*) Ulcera venerea, *f.*
chancy, *a.* Incerto; rischioso.
chandelier [ʃændə'liəɹ], *n.* Candelabro, lampadario, *m.*
chandler ['tʃɑ:ndləɹ], *n.* Candelaio, droghiere, *m.* **Corn- —,** rivenditore di grano, *m.*; **ship- —,** fornitore marittimo, *m.*
chandlery, *n.* Spezieria, *f.*
change [tʃeindʒ], *n.* Cambiamento, cambio, mutamento, *m.*, vicenda, alterazione, *f.*; mutazione, variazione, *f.*; (*money*) spiccioli, *m.pl.*; (*of moon*) fase, *f.* || *v.t.* Cambiare, mutare, scambiare; dare il resto di; *v.i.* cambiarsi, variare, cambiare. **A — of linen,** una muta di biancheria, *f.*; **a — of front,** un cambiamento d'opinione, *m.*; **— of horses,** cambio di cavalli, *m.*; **— of heart,** conversione, *f.*; **to go away for a —,** andare in campagna, cambiare aria; **I have no —,** non ho spiccioli; **to gain by the —,** guadagnare sul cambio; **to — hands,** cambiare di padrone; **to — for the better, for the worse,** cambiare in meglio, in peggio; **to — places,** cambiare di posto; **to — colour,** cambiare di colore; **to — one's mind,** cambiare idea, cambiare proposito; **to — one's tune,** cambiar tattica; (*Motor.*) **to — gear,** cambiare velocità.
changeable, *a.* Variabile, mutabile, incostante.
changeableness, *n.* Variabilità, mutabilità, *f.*
changeably, *adv.* In maniera incostante, in maniera variabile.
changeless, *a.* Immutabile, costante.
changeling, *n.* Bambino sostituito, *m.*
changer, *n.* Cambiatore, *m.*
changing, *a.* Cangiante.
channel ['tʃænəl], *n.* Canale, stretto, *m.*; (*of rivers*) letto, *m.*; (*fig.*) via, *f.*, mezzo, *m.*; (*Geog.*) braccio di mare, *m.*; (*Arch.*) scanalatura, *f.* || *v.t.* Scavare un canale; (*Arch.*) scanalare. **The English Channel,** La Manica, *f.*; **the Channel Islands,** le Isole Normanne, *f.pl.*; **St George's Channel,** il Canale di San Giorgio, *m.*
chanson [ʃɑ̃:sɔ̃], *n.* Canzone, *f.*
chant [tʃɑ:nt], *n.* Canto fermo, *m.* || *v.t.i.* Cantare, salmeggiare.
chanter, *n.* Cantatore, *m.*
chanticleer [tʃænti'kliəɹ], *n.* Gallo, *m.*
chantry, *n.* Cappella, *f.*
chanty ['ʃænti], *n.* Canzone di marinaio, *f.*, cantilena, *f.*
chaos ['keiɔs], *n.* Caos, *m.*
chaotic, *a.* Caotico.
chap (1) [tʃæp], *v.t.* Screpolare; *v.i.* screpolarsi. || *n.* Screpolatura, *f.*
chap (2), *n.* (*colloq.*) Ragazzo, giovanotto, compagno, bravo, *m.* **My dear old —!** Mio caro!
chap (3), **chop,** *n.* Mascella, ganascia, *f.*
chaparral ['tʃæpəræl], *n.* Pruneto, *m.*, macchia, *f.*
chapel ['tʃæpəl], *n.* Cappella, *f.*; (*Print.*) associazione di operai in una stamperia, *f.* **— -of ease,** chiesetta succursale, *f.*
chaperon ['ʃæpərən], *n.* Accompagnatrice, chaperon, *f.* || *v.t.* Accompagnare.
chaplain ['tʃæplin], *n.* Cappellano, *m.*
chaplaincy, *n.* Cappellanato, *m.*
chaplet ['tʃæplit], *n.* Corona, ghirlanda, *f.*, rosario, *m.*
chapman (*pl.* **chapmen**) *n.* Mercante ambulante, *m.*
chapped, *a.* Screpolato.
chapter ['tʃæptəɹ], *n.* (*in all senses*) Capitolo. **To give — and verse,** mettere i punti sugl'i; **to the end of the —,** fino in fondo; **a — of accidents,** una serie di disgrazie, *f.* **— -house,** capitolo, *m.*
char (1) [tʃɑ:ɹ], *v.t.i.* Carbonizzare, ridurre in carbone.
char (2), *n.* (*Zool.*) Ombrina, *f.*
char (3), **chare,** *v.i.* Lavorare a giornata. || *n.* (*colloq.*) Donna di servizio a giornata, *f.*

char-a-banc ['ʃærəbæŋ], *n.* giardiniera, *f.*; autobus, *m.*
character ['kærəktəɹ], *n.* Carattere, *m.*, indole, *f.*, temperamento, *m.*; natura, specie, *f.*; tipo, segno, *m.*; scrittura, *f.*; (*of employee*) certificato di buona condotta, *m.*; (*in play, book, etc.*) personaggio, *m.* (*Theat.*) **— actor,** caratterista, *m.*; **a public —,** un pezzo grosso; **a man of bad —,** un uomo di dubbia fama, *m.*; **he's quite a —,** è un tipo curioso; **I don't like books of that —,** libri di quel genere non mi piacciono; **in —,** caratteristico, vero.
characteristic, *a.* Caratteristico. || *n.* Caratteristica, *f.*
characteristically, *adv.* In modo caratteristico, caratteristicamente.
characterize, *v.t.* Caratterizzare.
characterization, *n.* Il caratterizzare, *m.*; descrizione, rappresentazione, caratterizzazione, *f.*
characterless, *a.* Senza carattere.
charade [ʃə'rɑːd], *n.* Sciarada, *f.*
charcoal ['tʃɑːɹkoul], *n.* Carbone, carbone di legna, *m.* **—-burner,** carbonaio, *m.*; **— drawing,** disegno al carboncino, *m.*; **— pencil,** carboncino, *m.*
chare [cp. **char** (3)].
charge (1) [tʃɑːɹdʒ], *n.* Carica, *f.*, carico, *m.*; prezzo, *m.*; obbligo, impegno, *m.*; custodia, guardia, *f.*; (*Law*) atto d'accusa, *m.*, accusa, *f.*; (*judge's, bishop's*) esortazione, *f.*; dovere, ufficio. || *v.t.* Caricare; accusare, imputare; domandare, far pagare; (*a glass*) riempire; comandare. **At my —,** a mio carico, a mie spese; **free of —,** gratuito; **in — of,** in custodia di; **list of charges,** tariffa, *f.*; **the officer in —,** l'ufficiale comandante, *m.*; **to bring a — against,** accusare; **to give in —,** fare arrestare; **to take — of,** prendere cura di; **— sheet,** foglio di polizia, *m.*; **to — oneself with,** incaricarsi di; **to — with a liability,** dare la responsibilità; **to — to someone's account,** mettere sul conto di qualcuno; **to return to the —,** tornare alla carica.
charge (2), *n.* (*Mil.*) Carica, *f.* || *v.i.* Caricare. **To — the enemy,** caricare il nemico.
chargeable, *a.* A carico di; (*Law*) accusabile, imponibile, imputabile.
charger (1), *n.* Cavallo di battaglia, *m.*; destriero, *m.*
charger (2), *n.* Piatto, vassoio, *m.*
charily ['tʃɛərili], *adv.* Cautamente.
chariness, *n.* Cautela, prudenza, *f.*
chariot ['tʃæriət], *n.* Carro, *m.* **—-race,** corsa dei carri, *f.*
charioteer [tʃæriə'tiəɹ], *n.* Carrista, guidatore del carro, *m.*
charitable ['tʃæritəbl], *a.* Caritatevole, pietoso, benevolo.
charitably, *adv.* Caritatevolmente, benevolmente.
charity, *n.* Carità, pietà, benevolenza, *f.*; opera di beneficenza, elemosina, *f.* **— begins at home,** la carità comincia in famiglia; **—-school,** scuola gratuita, *f.*; **we helped her out of —,** la aiutammo per pura carità; **to ask for —,** chiedere l'elemosina; **Sister of Charity,** Suora di Carità, *f.*
charlatan ['tʃɑːɹlətən], *n.* Ciarlatano, *m.*
charlatanism, charlatanry, *n.* Ciarlatanismo, *m.*; ciarlataneria, *f.*
Charles's Wain ['tʃɑːɹlziz wein], *n.* (*Astron.*) L'Orsa maggiore, *f.*
charlock ['tʃɑːɹlɔk], *n.* (*Bot.*) Senape, *f.*
Charlotte ['ʃɑːɹlɔt], *n.* Carlotta, *f.* **— russe,** zuppa inglese, *f.*
charm [tʃɑːɹm], *n.* Incanto, fascino, allettamento, *m.*; (*trinket*) talismano, amuleto, portafortuna, *m.* || *v.t.* Incantare, affascinare, allettare, ammaliare. **Charms,** vezzi, *m.pl.*; **to — away,** scongiurare.
charmed, *a.* Incantato.
charmer, *n.* Incantatore, *m.*, incantatrice, *f.*
charming, *a.* Incantevole, dilettevole, delizioso.
charmingly, *adv.* Incantevolmente, d'incanto.
charnel-house ['tʃɑːɹnəlhaus], *n.* Ossario, *m.*
chart [tʃɑːɹt], *n.* Carta nautica, *f.*; diagramma, *m.* || *v.t.* Fare la carta di, tracciare.
charter, *n.* Carta, *f.*, statuto, *m.*; patente, *f.*; privilegio, *m.* || *v.t.* Stabilire, garantire con patenti; (*Naut.*) noleggiare. **—-party,** (*Comm.*) Contratto di noleggio di una nave, *m.*; **chartered accountant,** ragioniere, *m.*
charterer, *n.* Noleggiatore, *m.*
chartering, *n.* Noleggio, *m.*
Chartism, *n.* (*Hist.*) Cartismo, *m.*
Chartist, *n.* (*Hist.*) Cartista, *m.*
charwoman (*pl.* **charwomen**) ['tʃɑːɹwumən, 'tʃɑːɹwimin], *n.* Donna di grosso, faticante, *f.*
chary ['tʃɛəri], *a.* Prudente, cauto, circospetto. **— of doing,** poco disposto a fare.
chase [tʃeis], *n.* Caccia, *f.*; inseguimento, *m.*; (*Print.*) telaio, *m.* || *v.t.* Cacciare, inseguire, incalzare; (*metal, etc.*) cesellare. **To — away,** cacciar via; **to give — to,** dare la caccia a.
chaser, *n.* (*Naut.*) Cacciatore, *m.*; (*Aviat.*) aeroplano di caccia, *m.*
chasing, *n.* Cesellatura, *f.*
chasm [kæzm], *n.* Baratro, abisso, *m.*, voragine, fessura, *f.*, vuoto, *m.*
chassis ['ʃæsi], *n.* (*Motor.*) Telaio, *m.*
chaste [tʃeist], *a.* Casto, puro, continente, pudico; (*fig.*) di buon gusto.
chastely, *adv.* Castamente, pudicamente.
chasteness, *n.* Castità, pudicizia, purezza, *f.*
chasten ['tʃeisən], *v.t.* Castigare, punire, correggere, purificare.
chastening, *n.* Castigo, *m.*; punizione, purificazione, *f.*
chastise [tʃæs'taiz], *v.t.* Castigare.
chastisement ['tʃæstizmənt], *n.* Castigo, *m.*
chastity, *n.* Castità, purezza, *f.*
chasuble ['tʃæsjubl], *n.* (*Eccles.*) Pianeta, *f.*
chat [tʃæt], *n.* Chiacchierata, ciarla, *f.* || *v.i.* Conversare, chiacchierare. **To have a —,** far quattro chiacchiere.
chattel ['tʃætəl], *n.* Mobile, *m.* **Chattels,** effetti, beni mobili, *m.pl.*; **goods and chattels,** armi e bagagli.
chatter ['tʃætəɹ], *n.* Ciarla, chiacchiera, diceria, *f.* || *v.i.* Ciarlare, chiacchierare, cicalare; battere i denti.
chatterbox, *n.* Chiacchierone, *m.*; (*of a child*) chiacchierino, *m.*
chatterer, *n.* Ciancione, ciarlone, *m.*, ciancìona, *f.*
chattering, *n.* Chiacchierata, ciarla, *f.*; **— of the teeth,** il battere dei denti, *m.*
chatty, *a.* Ciarliero, loquace, garrulo.
chauffeur ['ʃoufəɹ], *n.* Conduttore, meccanico, *m.*; autista, *m.*

chaw [tʃɔ:], *v.t.* (*dial.*) Masticare.
cheap [tʃi:p], *a.* A buon mercato, a buon prezzo; di poco valore. **Dirt —,** a vil prezzo; **to hold —,** far poco caso di, tener in poco conto; (*colloq.*) **on the —,** a buon mercato; senza pagare; **— ticket,** biglietto a prezzo ridotto, *m.*; **— -jack,** mercante ambulante, *m.*
cheapen, *v.t.* Scemare il valore di; stiracchiare sul prezzo di.
cheaper, *a.* A miglior mercato, a miglior prezzo, meno costoso.
cheaply, *adv.* A buon mercato, economicamente.
cheapness, *n.* Buon mercato, vil prezzo, *m.*
cheat [tʃi:t], *n.* Inganno, *m.*, frode, truffa, furberia, *f.*; (*person*) furbo, furfante, scroccone, truffatore, *m.*; (*at cards*) baro, *m.* || *v.t.* Ingannare, truffare, scroccare; (*at cards*) barare.
cheating, *n.* Frode, furberia, *f.*
check (1) [tʃek], *v.t.* Reprimere, costringere, raffrenare; arrestare, far contenere, far moderare; (*Comm.*) verificare, controllare, riscontrare; (*Chess*) dare scacco a; (*luggage at station, etc.*) depositare. || *n.* Ostacolo, impedimento, inciampo, *m.*; freno, controllo, *m.*; (*Chess*) scacco, *m.*; (*Comm.*) contromarca, *f.*, scontrino, *m.* || *inter.* (*Chess*) Scacco! **To hold oneself in —,** dominarsi; **— -rail,** controrotaia, *f.*; **— -rein,** freno da cavallo, *m.*; **— -taker,** controllore, *m.*
check (2), *n.* (*pattern*) Disegno quadrettato, *m.*; (*material*) tela quadrettata, *f.* || *a.* A quadretti, a scacchi.
checking, *n.* Controllo, riscontro, *m.*; il reprimere, il restringere, *m.*
checkmate, *n.* Scacco matto, *m.* || *v.t.* Dare scacco matto; (*fig.*) impedire, ostacolare.
cheek [tʃi:k], *n.* Guancia, gota, *f.*; (*fig.*) sfrontatezza, impudenza, sfacciataggine, *f.* || *v.i.* (*colloq.*) Insolentire. **— by jowl,** stretti stretti; **to have the — to,** avere la sfrontatezza di; **to have plenty of —,** avere la faccia tosta; **— -bone,** zigomo, pomello, *m.*, **with high — -bones,** con zigomi sporgenti.
cheeky, *a.* Sfrontato, sfacciato, impudente.
cheep, *v.i.* Cinguettare, pigolare. || *n.* Pigolio, *m.*
cheer [tʃiəɹ], *n.* (*food, etc.*) Cibo, trattamento, *m.*, tavola, *f.*; (*joy*) allegrezza, gioia, *f.*; (*encouragement*) applauso, plauso, *m.*, acclamazione, *f.*; evviva, *m.* || *v.t.* Rallegrare, incoraggiare, animare, consolare; *v.i.* applaudire, rallegrarsi. **To be of good —,** avere coraggio; **plenty of good —,** tavola bene imbandita; **Cheer up!** Coraggio! **Three cheers!** Evviva! **To give a —,** gridare evviva.
cheerful, *a.* Allegro, lieto, gaio, ridente.
cheerfully, *adv.* Allegramente, di buona grazia, volentieri.
cheerfulness, *n.* Lietezza, gaiezza, contentezza, *f.*, buon umore, *m.*
cheerily, *adv.* Lietamente.
cheering, *n.* Applauso, *m.*, applausi, *m.pl.*; gli evviva, *m.pl.* || *a.* Consolante, incoraggiante.
cheerless, *a.* Triste, malinconico, oscuro.
cheery, *a.* Gaio, gioioso, contento, lieto.
cheese [tʃi:z], *n.* Formaggio, cacio, *m.* **Cream- —,** crema di formaggio, *f.*; **— -knife,** coltello per formaggio, *m.*; **— -mite,** acaro del formaggio, *m.*; **— -paring,** *n.* parsimonia, spilorceria, *f.* || *a.* Spilorcio.
cheesemonger, *n.* Formaggiaio, *m.*
cheesy, *a.* Che sa di formaggio.
cheetah [ˈtʃi:tə], *n.* (*Zool.*) Gattopardo, *m.*
chef [ʃef], *n.* Capo cuoco, *m.*
chef d'œuvre [ʃeiˈdə:vr], *n.* Capolavoro, *m.*
chemical [ˈkemikəl], *a.* Chimico.
chemically, *adv.* Chimicamente.
chemicals, *n.pl.* Prodotti chimici, *m.pl.*
chemise [ʃəˈmi:z], *n.* Camicia, *f.*
chemist [ˈkemist], *n.* (*scientist*) Chimico, *m.*; (*druggist*) farmacista, *m.* **Chemist's shop,** farmacia, *f.*
chemistry, *n.* Chimica, *f.*
chenille [ʃəˈni:l], *n.* Ciniglia, *f.*
cheque [tʃek], *n.* Assegno bancario, mandato, chèque, *m.* **— -book,** libretto degli assegni, *m.*; **counterfoil of —,** scontrino, *m.*; **crossed —,** assegno sbarrato, *m.*; **blank —,** assegno firmato in bianco, *m.*; **to cash a —,** incassare un assegno.
chequer, *v.t.* Disegnare a scacchi. **— -board,** scacchiera, dama, *f.*
chequered, *a.* A scacchi, a quadretti; (*fig.*) variato; equivoco.
chequers, *n.pl.* Scacchi, *m.pl.*; dame, *f.pl.*
cherish [ˈtʃeriʃ], *v.t.* Nutrire; amare, curare, aver caro; accarezzare. **To — an affection for,** nutrire affetto per; **to — the memory of,** tener cara la memoria di.
cheroot [ʃəˈru:t], *n.* Sigaro spuntato, *m.*
cherry [ˈtʃeri], *n.* Ciliegia, *f.* || *a.* Rosso ciliegia. **To take two bites at a —,** tentennare; **— -brandy,** acquavite di ciliege, *f.*; **— -orchard,** ciliegeto, *m.*; **— -pie,** torta di ciliege, *f.*; **— -stone,** nocciolo di ciliegia, *m.*; **— -tree,** ciliegio, *m.*; **wild —,** visciolo, *m.*
cherub (*pl.* **cherubs, cherubim**) [ˈtʃerəb, ˈtʃerubim], *n.* Cherubino, cherubo, *m.*
cherubic, *a.* Cherubico.
chervil [ˈtʃə:ɹvil], *n.* (*Bot.*) Cerfoglio, *m.*
chess [tʃes], *n.* Scacchi, *m.pl.* **— -board,** scacchiera, *f.*; **— -player,** scacchista, *m.*, giuocatore di scacchi, *m.*; **a game of —,** una partita a scacchi, *f.*; **to play —,** giuocare a scacchi.
chessman, *n.* Pezzo degli scacchi, *m.* **A set of chessmen,** un giuoco di scacchi, *m.*
chest (1) [tʃest], *n.* Cassa, *f.*, cofano, forziere, *m.*; cassone, *m.*, arca, madia, *f.* **Medicine- —,** cassetta di medicinali, *f.*; **— of drawers,** cassettone, comò, *m.*
chest (2), *n.* (*Anat.*) Petto, torace, *m.* **— -complaint,** malattia di petto, *f.*; **— -protector,** pettorina, *f.*; (*Mus.*) **— -note,** nota profonda, *f.*; **— -measurement,** misura del torace, *f.*; **broad-chested,** largo di petto.
chesterfield [ˈtʃestəɹfi:ld], *n.* (*couch*) Canapè, *m.*; (*garment*) soprabito chesterfield, *m.*
chestnut [ˈtʃesnʌt], *n.* Castagna, *f.*, marrone, *m.*; (*fig.*) storiella vecchia, *f.* || *a.* (*of horse*) sauro; (*of hair*) castagno. **— -tree,** castagno, marrone, *m.*; **horse —,** ippocastano, *m.*
cheval-glass [ʃəˈvæl glɑ:s], *n.* Psiche, *f.*
chevalier [ʃevəˈliəɹ], *n.* Cavaliere, *m.*
chevaux-de-frise [ʃəˈvou də ˈfri:z], *n.* Cavalli di Frisia, *m.pl.*
cheverel [ˈtʃevərəl], *n.* Pelle di capretto, *f.*
chevron [ˈʃevrən], *n.* (*Mil.*) Gallone, *m.*

chevy, chivy [tʃevi, tʃivi], *v.t.* Cacciare, scacciare.
chew [tʃu:], *v.t.i.* Masticare. || *n.* Cicca di tabacco, *f.* **To — the cud,** ruminare; **to — tobacco,** ciccare; (*colloq.*) **to — over,** meditare sopra.
chewing, *n.* Masticazione, *f.* **—-gum,** gomma dolce, gomma da masticare, *f.*
chicane [ʃi'kein], *n.* Cavillo, rigiro, *m.* || *v.i.* Cavillare, rigirare.
chicanery, *n.* Sofisticheria, *f.*, intrigo, sotterfugio, *m.*
chick [tʃik], *n.* Pulcino, pollastro, *m.*; (*fig.*) cocco, mimmo, pupo, *m.* **—-pea,** (*Bot.*) cece, *f.*
chicken, *n.* Pollo, pollastro, pulcino, *m.* **Don't count your chickens before they're hatched,** non dir quattro se non l'hai nel sacco; **she's no —,** non è più una bambina; **—-coop, —-run,** pollaio, *m.*; **—-hearted,** timido, pauroso, codardo; **to be —-hearted,** avere coraggio quanto una gallina; **—-pox** (*Med.*) varicella, *f.*, morbiglione, *m.*
chickweed, *n.* (*Bot.*) Anagallide, *f.*
chicory ['tʃikəri], *n.* (*Bot.*) Cicoria, *f.*
chide [tʃaid], *v.t.* Sgridare, rimproverare; *v.i.* brontolare, mormorare.
chiding, *n.* Sgridata, *f.*, rimprovero, biasimo, *m.*
chidingly, *adv.* Con rimprovero.
chief [tʃi:f], *n.* Capo, principale, superiore, *m.* || *a.* Capo, principale, primo, sommo. **The — thing is,** la cosa più importante è; **the — point,** il punto principale, *m.*; **— rabbi,** rabbino maggiore, *m.*; **the — town,** il capoluogo, *m.*; **commander-in- —,** comandante in capo, *m.*
chiefly, *adv.* Principalmente, soprattutto.
chieftain, *n.* Capo, caporione, capitano, *m.*
chiff-chaff ['tʃiftʃæf], *n.* (*Zool.*) Luì, *m.*
chiffon ['ʃifɔn], *n.* Chiffon, *m.*
chiffonier [ʃifə'niəɹ], *n.* Stipo, *m.*
chilblain ['tʃilblein], *n.* Gelone, *m.*
child (*pl.* **children**) [tʃaild, 'tʃildrən], *n.* Bambino, fanciullo, ragazzo, figlio, infante, *m.* **From a —,** sino dall'infanzia; **a — of nature,** un figlio della Natura, *m.*; **with —,** incinta, gravida; **—-birth,** parto, *m.*; **—-bearing,** gravidanza, *f.*; **— welfare,** puericoltura, *f.*; **child's-play,** giuoco da bambini, compito facile, *m.*
childhood, *n.* Infanzia, fanciullezza, *f.* **Second —,** rimbambimento senile, *m.*
childish, *a.* Bambinesco, puerile, infantile, fanciullesco. **To grow —,** rimbambire.
childishly, *adv.* Puerilmente.
childishness, *n.* Puerilità, fanciullaggine, *f.*
childless, *a.* Senza figli, senza prole.
childlike, *a.* Semplice, innocente.
children, *n.pl.* Figli, *m.pl.*; figliuolanza, prole, *f.* (*Radio*) **Children's hour,** ora dei bambini, *f.*
Chile ['tʃili], *n.* (*Geog.*) Il Cile, *m.*
chill [tʃil], *n.* Brivido, *m.*, infreddatura, *f.*; freddo, *m.*, febbretta, *f.* || *a.* Freddo, gelato, glaciale. || *v.t.* Raffreddare, gelare; (*fig.*) scoraggiare. **To catch a —,** prendere una febbretta; **to take the — off,** riscaldare un po'; **he has cast a — over the proceedings,** egli ha raffreddato l'ambiente; **a — reception,** un'accoglienza fredda, *f.*; **to be chilled** (*with horror, etc.*) rabbrividire.
chilliness, *n.* Freddo, *m.*, freddezza, *f.*
chilly, *a.* Freddino, freddoloso (*of persons*).
chilli ['tʃili], *n.* (*Bot.*) Peperone, *m.*
chime [tʃaim], *n.* Scampanio, cariglione, *m.*, scampanata, *f.* || *v.t.* Scampanare, far suonare; *v.i.* accordarsi con. **Chiming clock,** orologio a cariglione, *m.*
chimera [kai'miərə], *n.* Chimera, *f.*
chimerical, *a.* Chimerico.
chimerically, *adv.* Chimericamente.
chimney ['tʃimni], *n.* Camino, fumaiuolo, *m.*; (*lamp*) tubo, *m.* **—-corner,** canto del camino, *m.*; **—-flue,** gola del camino, *f.*; **—-piece,** caminiera, *f.*; **—-pot,** fumignolo, rocca di camino, *f.*; **—-pot hat,** cappello a cilindro, *m.*; **—-stack,** gruppo di camini, *m.*; **—-sweep,** spazzacamino, *m.*
chimpanzee [tʃimpæn'zi:], *n.* (*Zool.*) Scimpanzè, *m.*
chin [tʃin], *n.* Mento, *m.* **—-strap,** sottogola, *m.*; **—-deep,** fino al mento.
China (1) ['tʃainə], *n.* (*Geog.*) La Cina, *f.*
china (2), *n.* Porcellana, ceramica, *f.* || *a.* Di porcellana, della Cina. **—-clay,** caolino, *m.*, argilla da porcellana, *m.*; **— shop,** negozio di porcellane, *m.*; **—-cabinet,** vetrina, scansia, *f.*
Chinaman, *n.* Cinese, *m.*
Chinatown, *n.* Quartiere cinese, *m.*
chinchilla [tʃin'tʃillə], *n.* (*Zool.*) Cinciglia, *f.*
chine [tʃain], *n.* Schiena, *f.*; (*of pork*) coppa, *f.*
Chinese [tʃai'ni:z], *n.* Cinese, *m.f.* || *a.* Cinese. **— lantern,** lanterna cinese, *f.*; **—-white,** bianco di Cina, *m.*
chink [tʃiŋk], *n.* Fessura, crepatura, *f.*; tintinnio, suono, *m.* || *v.t.* Far tintinnare; *v.i.* tintinnare.
chintz [tʃints], *n.* Indiana, *f.*
chip [tʃip], *n.* Scheggia, *f.*; frammento, truciolo, *m.*; (*of wood*) fuscello, *m.* || *v.t.* Scheggiare, fender in schegge, truciolare. **To be a — of the old block,** essere proprio figlio di suo padre; **a bundle of chips,** una fascinetta, *f.*; **to have a — on one's shoulder,** sentirsi offeso; **chipped potatoes,** patate fritte, *f.pl.*
chirograph ['kairougræf], *n.* Chirografo, *m.*
chiropody [ʃi'rɔpədi], *n.* Chiropodia, *f.*
chiropodist, *n.* Chiropodista, pedicure, *m.*
chirp [tʃə:ɹp], *n.* Cinguettio, pigolio; (*of insects*) cicalio, canto, *m.* || *v.i.* Cinguettare, garrire; cantare. **The crickets are chirping,** i grilli cantano.
chirpy, *a.* (*colloq.*) Gaio, allegro.
chisel ['tʃizəl], *n.* Cesello, scalpello, *m.*; (*stonemason's*) subbia, *f.* || *v.t.* Cesellare, scalpellare, intagliare; (*colloq.*) truffare.
chit (1) [tʃit], *n.* Bambino, *m.*; (*slightingly*) ragazza, *f.*
chit (2), *n.* Biglietto, *m.*, nota, *f.*
chitchat ['tʃittʃæt], *n.* Chiacchiera, *f.*, cicaleccio, *m.*
chitterlings ['tʃitəɹliŋz], *n.pl.* Trippa, *f.*; budella, *f.pl.*
chivalrous ['ʃivəlrəs], *a.* Cavalleresco.
chivalry, *n.* Cavalleria, cortesia, *f.*
chive [tʃaiv], *n.* (*Bot.*) Cipollina, *f.*
chivy [cp. **chevy**].
chlamys ['klæmis], *n.* (*Hist.*) Clamide, *m.*
chloral ['klɔ:rəl], *n.* (*Chem.*) Cloralio, clorale, *m.*

chlorate, *n.* (*Chem.*) Clorato, *m.*
chloric, *a.* Clorico.
chloride, *n.* Cloruro, *m.* **— of lime,** cloruro di calce, *m.*
chlorine, *n.* Cloro, *m.*
chloroform, *n.* Cloroformio, *m.* || *v.t.* Cloroformizzare.
chlorophyll, *n.* (*Bot.*) Clorofilla, *f.*
chlorosis, *n.* (*Med.*) Clorosi, *f.*
chlorous, *a.* Cloroso.
chock [tʃɔk], *n.* Cuneo, *m.*, bietta, *f.* || *a.* **Chock-full,** ripieno, pieno zeppo.
chocolate [ˈtʃɔkəlit], *n.* Cioccolata, *f.*, cioccolatte, *m.* **Chocolates,** cioccolatini, *m.pl.*, chicche, *f.pl.* **A box of chocolates,** una scatola di cioccolatini, *f.*; **— cream,** cioccolatino alla crema, *m.*
choice [tʃɔis], *n.* Scelta, *f.*; elezione, *f.*, assortimento, *m.* || *a.* Scelto, squisito, ricercato; eletto. **Take your —,** fate la vostra scelta; **Hobson's —,** scelta forzata, *f.*; **a good — of books,** un buon assortimento di libri; **a — wine,** un vino scelto.
choiceness, *n.* Squisitezza, sceltezza, *f.*
choir [kwaiɹ], *n.* Coro, *m.* **— -boy,** corista, *m.*; **— -master,** maestro di cappella, *m.*
choke [tʃouk], *v.t.* Soffocare, strangolare, strozzare; (*fig.*) ingombrare; *v.i.* soffocarsi. **To — up,** ingorgare; **— -damp,** vapore asfissiante, ossido di carbonio, *m.*
choking, *n.* Soffocazione, strangolazione, *f.*, ingorgo, *m.*
choker, *n.* (*colloq.*) Cravatta, *f.*
choler [ˈkɔləɹ], *n.* Collera, bile, *f.*
cholera, *n.* (*Med.*) Colera, *m.* **— -morbus,** colera asiatico, *m.*
choleric, *a.* Collerico, bilioso.
choose [tʃuːz], *v.t.i.* Scegliere, eleggere, preferire, volere. **As you —,** come volete; **to pick and —,** sofisticare nella scelta.
chooser, *n.* Sceglitore, *m.*
choosing, *n.* Scelta, *f.*
chop [tʃɔp], *v.t.* Tagliare, tagliuzzare; (*meat*) sminuzzare; *v.i.* (*Naut.*) (*of wind*) cambiare. || *n.* Taglio, colpo, *m.*; (*of meat*) costoletta, fetta, *f.*; (*pork*) braciola di maiale, *f.*; (*of jaw*) mascella, *f.* **To — up** (*meat*), sminuzzare; **to — down a tree,** abbattere un albero; **to — sticks,** spaccare legna; **to — off,** troncare; **to — and change,** mutare sempre di proposito; **to — logic,** sofisticare, sottilizzare; **to lick one's chops,** leccarsi le labbra; **— -house,** trattoria, *f.*, ristorante, *m.*; **— -fallen,** [cp. **chap-fallen**].
chopper, *n.* Ascia, *f.*, coltellaccio, *m.*, mannaia, scure *f.*
chopping, *n.* Il tagliare, l'abbattere, *m.* **— -block,** tagliere, ceppo, *m.*
choppy, *a.* (*Naut.*) Ondeggiante, increspato. **There's a — sea,** c'è un po' di maretta.
chop-stick, *n.* Bacchetta per mangiare alla cinese, *f.*
choral [ˈkɔːrəl], *a.* Corale. **— society,** società corale, *f.*
chord [kɔːɹd], *n.* Corda, *f*; (*Mus.*) accordo, *m.*
chorea [ˈkɔːriə], *n.* (*Med.*) Ballo di San Vito, *m.*
choreographer [kɔriˈɔgrəfəɹ], *n.* Coreografo, *m.*
choreography, *n.* Coreografia, *f.*
chorister [ˈkɔristəɹ], *n.* Corista, *m.*
chortle [ˈtjɔːɹtl], *v.i.* (*colloq.*) Ridacchiare.
chorus [ˈkɔːrəs], *n.* Coro, ritornello, *m.*; ripresa, *f.* **In —,** in coro.
chough [tʃʌf], *n.* (*Zool.*) Gracchia, *f.*
chrestomathy [kresˈtɔməθi], *n.* Crestomazia, *f.*
chrism [krizm], *n.* (*Eccles.*) Olio consacrato, crisma, *m.*
Christ [kraist], *n.* Il Cristo, *m.*
christen [ˈkrisən], *v.t.* Battezzare.
Christendom [ˈkrisəndəm], *n.* Cristianità, *f.*
christening, *n.* Battesimo, *m.*
Christian [ˈkristiən], *n.a.* Cristiano, *m.*, cristiana, *f.* **— name,** nome di battesimo, *m.*; **— Science,** il culto degli Scientisti Cristiani, *m.*; **— era,** era cristiana, *f.*
Christianity, *n.* Cristianesimo, *m.*
christianize, *v.t.* Cristianizzare.
Christianlike, *a.* Cristiano.
Christianly, *adv.* Come un cristiano.
Christmas [ˈkrisməs], *n.* Il Natale, *m.* **— carol,** cantico di Natale, *m.*; **— Eve,** la vigilia di Natale, *f.*; **— present, — box,** strenna di Natale, *f.*; **— pudding,** budino natalizio, *m.*; **— tree,** albero di Natale, *m.*; **— -tide,** tempo di Natale, *m.*
chromate [ˈkroumeit], *n.* Cromato, *m.*
chromatic, *a.* Cromatico.
chrome [kroum], *n.* Cromato, *m.* **— yellow,** giallocromo, *m.*
chromium, *n.* Cromo, *m.* **— -plated,** al cromo.
chromolithography [kroumouliθˈɔgrəfi], *n.* Cromolitografia, *f.*
chronic [ˈkrɔnik], *a.* Cronico.
chronicle [ˈkrɔnikl], *n.* Cronaca, *f.* || *v.t.* Registrare; raccontare. **Book of Chronicles** (*Bible*), Paralipomeni, *m.pl.*
chronicler, *n.* Cronista, *m.*
chronographer [krɔnˈɔgrəfəɹ], *n.* Cronografo, *m.*
chronography, *n.* Cronografia, *f.*
chronologer, chronologist [krɔnˈɔlədʒəɹ], *n.* Cronologo, *m.*
chronological, *a.* Cronologico.
chronologically, *adv.* Cronologicamente.
chronology, *n.* Cronologia, *f.*
chronometer [krəˈnɔmitəɹ], *n.* Cronometro, *m.*
chrysalis [ˈkrisilis], *n.* (*Zool.*) Crisalide, *f.*
chrysanthemum [kriˈsænθiməm], *n.* (*Bot.*) Crisantemo, *m.*
chrysolite [ˈkrisəlait], *n.* Crisolito, *m.*
chrysophrase [ˈkrisoufreiz], *n.* Crisofrasso, *m.*
chub [tʃʌb], *n.* (*Zool.*) Ghiozzo, *m.*
chubby, *a.* Paffuto, grassotto.
chuck (1) [tʃʌk], *v.t.* Gettare, buttare, lanciare. || *n.* Lancio, *m.* **To — out,** buttar fuori; **to — away,** buttar via; **to — up the sponge,** abbandonare la gara; **to — under the chin,** accarezzare sotto il mento; **— -farthing,** giuoco di testa e croce.
chuck (2), *n.* (*Mech.*) Mandrino, *m.*
chuckle [ˈtʃʌkl], *v.i* Ridacchiare, gongolare. || *n.* Il ridacchiare; riso represso, *m.* **— -headed,** stupido.
chum [tʃʌm], *n.* (*colloq.*) Amico intimo, compagno di camera, camerata, *m.* **To — up,** farsi amici.
chummy, *a.* Amichevole, socievole.
chump [tʃʌmp], *n.* Ciocco, ceppo, tronco, *m.*; (*fig.*) imbecille, *m.* **— -chop,** costoletta, *f.*; (*colloq.*) **off his —,** matto, fuori di senno.

chunk [tʃʌŋk], *n.* Pezzo (di legno, formaggio, etc.); ceppo, *m.*
church [tʃəːɹtʃ], *n.* Chiesa, *f.* ‖ *v.t.* Benedire una donna dopo il parto. **To go to —,** andare in chiesa; **Church of England,** Chiesa Anglicana, *f.*; **— -service,** ufficio divino, *m.*; **— -goer,** devoto, *m.*
churching, *n.* Purificazione dopo il parto, *f.*
churchman, *n.* Ecclesiastico, *m.*; Anglicano, *m.*
churchyard, *n.* Camposanto, cimitero, *m.* **A — cough,** una tosse sepolcrale, *f.*
churl [tʃəːɹl], *n.* Villanzone, villano, zotico, *m.*
churlish, *a.* Rozzo, incolto, zotico, grossolano, maleducato.
churlishness, *n.* Rozzezza, *f.*
churn [tʃəːɹn], *n.* Zangola, *f.* ‖ *v.t.i.* Fare il burro, zangolare; agitare.
churning, *n.* Il fare il burro, *m.*
chyle [kail], *n.* Chilo, *m.*
chylify, *v.t.* Chilificare.
chyme [kaim], *n.* Chimo, *m.*
chymify, *v.t.* Chimificare.
ciborium [si'bɔːriəm], *n.* (*Eccles.*) Ciborio, *m.*
cicada [si'kɑːdə], *n.* (*Zool.*) Cicala, *f.*
cicatrice, cicatrix (*pl.* **cicatrices**) ['sikətris, 'sikətriks], *n.* Cicatrice, *f.*
cicatrization, *n.* Cicatrizzazione, *f.*
cicatrize, *v.t.i.* Cicatrizzare, cicatrizzarsi.
cider ['saidəɹ], *n.* Sidro, *m.* **— -apple,** mela da sidro, *f.*; **— -press,** strettoio da sidro, *m.*
cigar [si'gɑːɹ], *n.* Sigaro, *m.* **— -case,** portasigari, *m.*; **— -cutter,** tagliasigari, *m.*; **— -holder,** bocchino per sigaro, *m.*
cigarette, *n.* Sigaretta, *f.* **— -case,** portasigarette, *m.*; **— -holder,** bocchino, *m.*; **— -lighter,** accendi-sigaro, *m.*; **— -paper,** carta da sigarette, *f.*; **— -end,** mozzicone, *m.*
ciliary ['siliəri], *a.* (*Anat.*) Ciliare.
Cimmerian [si'miəriən], *a.* (*Lit.*) Cimmerio.
cinch [sintʃ], *n.* Sottopancia (*harness*), *f.*; (*colloq.*) una cosa certa, certezza, *f.*
cinchona [sin'tʃounə], *n.* (*Bot.*) Cincona, *f.*
cincture ['siŋktjəɹ], *n.* Cintura, *f.*
cinder ['sindəɹ], *n.* Cenere, brace, *m.*; scoria, *f.* **Cinders,** tizzoni spenti, *m.pl.* (*Sport*) **— -track,** pista di cenerumi, *f.*
Cinderella [sində'relə], *n.* Cenerentola, *f.*
cinecamera [sini'kæmərə], *n.* Macchina da presa, *f.*
cinema, cinematograph ['sinimə, sini'mætəgræf], *n.* Cinema, cinematografo, *m.* **— star,** divo, diva dei film, *m.f.*
cineraria [sinə'rɛəriə], *n.* (*Bot.*) Cineraria, *f.*
cinerary ['sinərəri], *a.* Cinerario.
cinnabar ['sinəbɑːɹ], *n.* Cinabro, *m.*
cinnamon ['sinəmən], *n.* Cannella, *f.*
cinquefoil ['siŋkfɔil], *n.* (*Bot.*) Cinquefoglie, *m.*
cipher ['saifəɹ], *n.* Cifra, *f.*; zero, *m.* ‖ *v.t.* Cifrare, scrivere in cifra; *v.i.* calcolare, conteggiare. **Written in —,** scritto in cifra; **he's a mere —,** è un uomo da nulla, una nullità, uno zero; **— -key,** chiave del cifrario, *f.*
ciphering, *n.* Calcolo, *m.*, aritmetica, *f.*
Circean [səɹ'siːən], *a.* (*Lit.*) Di Circe, magico.
circle [səːɹkl], *n.* Cerchio, circolo, *m.*; (*fig.*) ambiente, gruppo, cenacolo, *m.*; serie, *f.* ‖ *v.t.* Circondare di, accerchiare, circuire; *v.i.* girare attorno, volgersi intorno. **In a —,** in cerchio; **a vicious —,** un circolo vizioso, *m.*; **he moves in the highest circles,** frequenta l'alta società; **all your —,** tutti i vostri amici; (*Theat.*) **dress- —,** balconata, *f.*; (*Naut.*) **great —,** circolo massimo, *m.*
circled, *a.* Circondato.
circlet, *n.* Cerchietto, *m.*; corona, *f.*; anello, *m.*
circling, *a.* Accerchiante, circolare.
circuit ['səːɹkit], *n.* Circuito, giro, *m.*, circonferenza, *f.*; ambito, recinto, *m.* **A judge's —,** sfera d'azione d'un giudice, *f.*; (*Elect.*) **short —,** corto circuito, *m.*; **to make a wide —,** fare un largo giro.
circuitous [səːɹ'kjuitəs], *a.* Tortuoso, indiretto.
circuitously, *adv.* Indirettamente, per giri e rigiri.
circular ['səːɹkjuləɹ], *n.a.* Circolare, *f.* **A — letter,** una lettera circolare, *f.*; **— note,** lettera di credito, *f.*
circularly, *adv.* In circolo, a tondo, circolarmente.
circulate, *v.t.* Far circolare, spandere, diffondere; *v.i.* circolare, girare attorno.
circulating, *a.* Circolatorio, circolante. **— library,** biblioteca circolante, *f.*; **— medium,** moneta corrente, *f.*; **— decimal,** frazione periodica, *f.*
circulation, *n.* Circolazione, diffusione, *f.*; (*of newspapers, etc.*) tiratura, *f.*
circulatory, *a.* Circolatorio.
circumambient [səːɹkəm'æmbiənt], *a.* Circondante, vicino.
circumambulate, *v.t.i.* Andare attorno.
circumcise ['səːɹkəmsaiz], *v.t.* Circoncidere.
circumcision, *n.* Circoncisione, *f.*
circumference [səɹ'kʌmfərəns], *n.* Circonferenza, *f.*
circumferential, *a.* Di circonferenza, sferico.
circumflex ['səːɹkəmfleks], *n.a.* Circonflesso, *m.*
circumjacent [səːɹkəm'dʒeisənt], *a.* Circonvicino.
circumlocution [səːɹkəmlo'kjuʃən], *n.* Circonlocuzione, *f.*
circumnavigate [səːɹkəm'nævigeit], *v.t.* Circumnavigare.
circumnavigation, *n.* Circumnavigazione, *f.*
circumnavigator, *n.* Circumnavigatore, *m.*
circumscribe [səːɹkəm'skraib], *v.t.* Circoscrivere.
circumscription, *n.* Circoscrizione, *f.*
circumscriptive, *a.* Che circoscrive, restrittivo.
circumspect ['səːɹkəmspekt], *a.* Circospetto.
circumspection, *n.* Circospezione, *f.*
circumspectly, *adv.* Circospettamente.
circumstance ['səːɹkəmstæns], *n.* Circostanza, *f.*; stato, *m.* **Circumstances,** condizioni, *f.pl.*; mezzi, *m.pl.* **Extenuating circumstances,** circostanze attenuanti, *f.pl.*; **in straitened circumstances,** in condizioni difficili; **to be in easy circumstances,** essere agiato, in agiatezza; **under any circumstances,** in ogni caso; **to be circumstanced,** trovarsi.
circumstantial [səːɹkəm'stænʃəl], *a.* Circostanziato, circostanziale, dettagliato. (*Law*) **— evidence,** prove indiziarie, *f.pl.*; **— account,** relazione particolareggiata, *f.*
circumstantially, *adv.* Circostanziatamente.
circumstantiate, *v.t.* Circostanziare, confermare, stabilire.
circumvent [səːɹkəm'vent], *v.t.* Circonvenire, impedire.
circumvention, *n.* Circonvenzione, *f.*

circumvolution [səːɹkəmvəˈljuʃən], *n.* Circonvoluzione, *f.*
circus [ˈsəːɹkəs], *n.* Circo, *m.*; arena, *f.*; ippodromo, *m.*; piazza, *f.*
cirrhosis [siˈrousis], *n.* (*Med.*) Cirrosi, *f.*
cirrus [ˈsirəs], *n.* Cirro, *m.* — **clouds**, cirri, *m.pl.*
Cisalpine [sisˈælpain], *a.* Cisalpino.
cissy [ˈsisi], *a.* (*colloq.*) Effeminato.
cist [sist], *a.* (*Archaeol.*) Cista, *f.*
Cistercian [sisˈtəːɹʃən], *n.a.* Cistercense, *m.*
cistern [ˈsistəɹn], *n.* Cisterna, *f.*, serbatoio, *m.*; (*fig.*) stagno, *m.*
cistus [ˈsistəs], *n.* (*Bot.*) Cistio ,*m.*
citadel [ˈsitədəl], *n.* Cittadella, rocca, *f.*
citation [saiˈteiʃən], *n.* Citazione, *f.*
cite [sait], *v.t.* Citare; addurre; ingiungere.
citizen [ˈsitizən], *n.* Cittadino, borghese, abitante, *m.* **Fellow-** —, concittadino, compatriotta, *m.*; **the citizens**, la cittadinanza, *f.*
citizenship, *n.* Cittadinanza, *f.*
citrate [ˈsitreit], *n.* Citrato, *m.*
citric, *a.* Citrico.
citron [ˈsitrən], *n.* (*Bot.*) Cedro, *m.* — **-tree**, cedro, *m.*
city [ˈsiti], *n.* Città, *f.*, municipio, *m.* (*newspaper*) — **article**, bollettino finanziario, *m.*
civet [ˈsivit], *n.* (*Zool.*) Zibetto muschiato, *m.*; (*perfume*) zibetto, *m.*
civic [ˈsivik], *a.* Civico. **Civics**, le cose civiche, *f.pl.*, istruzione nelle cose civiche e politiche, *f.*
civil [ˈsivil], *a.* Civile, cortese; municipale. — **service**, amministrazione statale, *f.*; — **-servant**, funzionario statale, *m.*; — **-engineering**, ingegneria civile, *f.*
civilian, *n.* Borghese, *m.* || *a.* Borghese, civile. — **clothes**, **civvies**, abito borghese, *m.*
civility, *n.* Civiltà, gentilezza, cortesia, *f.*
civilization, *n.* Civiltà, *f.*
civilize, *v.t.* Civilizzare, incivilire.
civilly, *adv.* Garbatamente, cortesemente.
clack [klæk], *v.i.* Scricchiare, scricchiolare; ciarlare; *v.t.* far scricchiare. || *n.* Scricchio, *m.*; ciarla, *f.* — **-valve**, valvola a cerniera, *f.*
clad, *past* of **clothe**.
claim [kleim], *v.t.* Domandare, reclamare, richiedere; pretendere; asserire; (*Law*) rivendicare. || *n.* Domanda, pretensione, *f.*; titolo, diritto, reclamo, *m.*; (*mining*) concessione, *f.* **To lay** — **to**, pretendere al; **to put in a** —, avanzare un reclamo.
claimable, *a.* Esigibile.
claimant, *n.* Pretendente, reclamante, *m.*; **rightful** —, avente diritto, *m.*
clairvoyance [klɛəɹˈvɔiəns], *n.* Chiaroveggenza, *f.*
clairvoyant, *n.a.* Chiaroveggente, *m.f.*
clam [klæm], *n.* (*Zool.*) Pettine, *m.*, ostrica americana, *f.*
clamant [ˈkleimənt], *a.* Insistènte, urgente.
clamber [ˈklæmbəɹ], *v.i.* Arrampicarsi su.
clamminess [ˈklæminis], *n.* Umidità, viscidità, *f.*; viscosità, *f.*
clammy, *a.* Molliccio, umidiccio, viscido.
clamorous, *a.* Clamoroso, rumoroso, chiassoso. **To be** — **for**, domandare rumorosamente.
clamorously, *adv.* Con clamore, rumorosamente.
clamour, *n.* Clamore, rumore, *m.*; chiasso, *m.* || *v.i.* Gridare, vociferare. **To** — **against**, gridare contro, inveire contro; **to** — **for**, strepitare per avere.
clamp [klæmp], *n.* Rampone, uncino, strettoio, *m.*; grappa, *f.*; (*Agric.*) mucchio di patate *or* frutta ricoperto di paglia e terra. || *v.t.* Assicurare con rampone, fermare con grappe.
clan [klæn], *n.* Clan, *m.*, tribù, famiglia, *f.*
clandestine [klænˈdestin], *a.* Clandestino.
clandestinely, *adv.* Clandestinamente.
clang [klæŋ], *n.* Suono squillante, tintinnio, suono metallico, *m.* || *v.i.* Risuonare, squillare; *v.t.* far risuonare.
clangorous, *a.* Risonante.
clank [klæŋk], *n.* Sferragliamento, frastuono, rombo, *m.* || *v.i.* Sferragliare, strepitare.
clannish, *a.* Strettamente unito alla famiglia, particolaristico.
clanship, *n.* Associazione sotto un capo, *f.*; solidarietà, *f.*
clansman, *n.* Membro di un clan, *m.*
clap (1) [klæp], *n.* Colpo, *m.*; battimano, *m.* || *v.t.* Applaudire, batter le mani. **A** — **of thunder**, un tuono, *m.*; **to** — **one's hands**, batter le mani; **to** — **into prison**, gettare in prigione; **to** — **on the back**, battere sulla spalla; **I have never clapped eyes on him**, non l'ho mai visto.
clap (2), *n.* (*Med.*) Gonorrea, *f.*
clapper, *n.* Battaglio, batacchio (*of bell*), *m.*; (*rattle*) raganella, *f.*; applauditore, *m.*
clapping, *n.* Battimano, *m.*, applausi, *m.pl.*
claptrap, *n.* Sciocchezze, *f.pl.*, discorso stupido, *m.* || *a.* Bugiardo, sciocco.
claque [ˈklæk], *n.* Gente pagata per applaudire, *f.*
claret [ˈklærət], *n.* Chiaretto, bordò, *m.* || *a.* Granato.
clarification [klærifiˈkeiʃən], *n.* Chiarificazione, *f.*
clarify, *v.t.* Chiarificare; *v.i.* chiarificarsi.
clarinet, clarionet [ˈklærinet, klæriəˈnet], *n.* (*Mus.*) Clarinetto, *m.*
clarion [ˈklæriən], *n.* (*Mus.*) Cornetta, tromba, chiarina, *f.*
clarity [ˈklæriti], *n.* Chiarezza, limpidezza, *f.*
clash [klæʃ], *v.i.* Urtarsi, contrastare; (*of colours*) stonare. *v.t.* Far risuonare. || *n.* Urto, cozzo, scontro, *m.*; fracasso, *m.*; opposizione, *f.* **Their interests** —, i loro interessi sono opposti *or* si urtano.
clashing, *n.* Opposizione, *f.*; contrasto, urto, *m.*
clasp [klɑːsp], *n.* (*buckle*) Fibbia, *f.*, fermaglio, *m.*; abbraccio, amplesso, *m.* || *v.t.* Affibbiare; stringere, serrare; giungere insieme. **To** — **round the neck**, gettarsi al collo; **with clasped hands**, colle mani giunte; — **-knife**, coltello a serramanico, *m.*
class [klɑːs], *n.* Classe, *f.*; categoria, specie, qualità, *f.*; ceto, *m.* || *v.t.* Classificare, qualificare. **First-** —, di prima classe; — **-war**, lotta di classe, *f.*; **the middle** —, il ceto medio, *m.*; — **-consciousness**, coscienza di classe, *f.*; — **-book**, libro scolastico, *m.*; — **-list**, registro, *m.*; — **-room**, aula, *f.*
classic [ˈklæsik], *n.* Classico, *m.* **The Classics**, I Classici, *m.pl.*
classic, classical, *a.* Classico.
classically, *adv.* Classicamente.

classicism, *n.* Classicismo, *m.*
classicist, *n.* Classicista, *m.*
classification [klæsifi'keiʃən], *n.* Classificazione, *f.*
classify, *v.t.* Classificare.
classing, *n.* Classificazione, *f.*
classy, *a.* (*colloq.*) Di prim'ordine.
clatter ['klætəɹ], *n.* Rumore, fracasso, chiasso, strepito, cigolio, *m.* || *v.i.* Strepitare, cigolare, far chiasso.
clause [klɔ:z], *n.* Clausola, *f.*; articolo, *m.*; (*Gram.*) proposizione, *f.*
claustral ['klɔ:strəl], *a.* Claustrale.
claustrophobia [klɔ:stro'foubiə], *n.* (*Med.*) Claustrofobia, *f.*
clavate [klæ'veit], *a.* (*Bot.*) Claviforme.
clavichord ['klævikɔ:ɹd], *n.* (*Mus.*) Clavicordio, *m.*
clavicle ['klævikl], *n.* (*Anat.*) Clavicola, *f.*
claw [klɔ:], *n.* Artiglio, *m.*, unghia, *f.*; graffio, *m.* || *v.t.* Graffiare, dilaniare, uncinare. **Claws** (*of crab, etc.*) chele, pinze, branche, *f.pl.*; **—-hammer,** martello a penna fessa, *m.*; **to cut the claws of,** disarmare.
clawed, *a.* Fornito di artigli.
clay [klei], *n.* Argilla, creta, terra, *f.* **— pipe,** pipa di gesso, *f.*; **—-pit,** cava di argilla, cava di marga, *f.*; **— soil,** terra argillosa, *f.*; **—-pigeon,** piccione artificiale, *m.*
clayey, *a.* Argilloso.
claymore ['kleimɔ:ɹ], *n.* Spadone, *m.*
clean [cli:n], *a.* Pulito, netto, puro, mondo; (*of shoes*) lucido; (*of jump*) schietto. || *adv.* Interamente, affatto. || *v.t.* Pulire, nettare, lucidare; purificare, depurare. **to make a — breast of it,** confessare tutto; **to show a — pair of heels,** darsela a gambe, svignarsela; **— hands,** mani nette, *f.pl.*; **he has — hands,** egli ha la coscienza pura; **—-limbed,** ben proporzionato; **— linen,** biancheria di bucato, *f.*; **— -shaven,** sbarbato; **to make a — sweep,** fare piazza pulita; **to — vegetables,** mondare erbaggi; **to — out,** vuotare; **to — up,** fare pulizia; **to — down,** pulire da cima a fondo; (*colloq.*) **to come —,** confessare.
cleaner, *n.* Ripulitore, lustratore, *m.*; (*woman*) giornante, *f*; smacchiatore, *m.*
cleaning, *n.* Pulitura, pulizia, ripulitura, *f.* **Spring- —,** la gran pulizia annuale, *f.*
cleanliness, cleanness, *n.* Pulizia, nettezza, purezza, *f.*
cleanly, *a.* Netto, pulito; puro. || *adv.* Nettamente, pulitamente.
cleanse [klenz], *v.t.* Purgare, purificare, detergere. **To — of sin,** purgare dal peccato.
cleanser, *n.* Detersivo, *m.*
cleansing, *n.* Purificazione, *f.*
clear [kliəɹ], *a.* Chiaro; netto; lucido, limpido; trasparente; manifesto, evidente; libero. || *adv.* Chiaro, chiaramente. || *v.t.* Chiarificare; schiarire; (*a room*) sgombrare; (*rubbish*) spazzare; (*profit*) guadagnare; (*from blame*) esonerare; (*a table after a meal*) sparecchiare; (*through the Customs*) passare; (*a cheque*) compensare; (*a letter-box*) fare la levata; *v.i.* rischiarare, rasserenarsi (*of the weather*). **— of blame,** esente da biasimo; **to keep — of,** evitare, tenersi a distanza da; **the coast is —,** la via è libera; **to make —,** render chiaro, spiegare; **to — oneself,** discolparsi, riabilitarsi; **to — one's throat,** raschiarsi la gola; **the streets were cleared by rifle-fire,** le strade erano spazzate dalla moschetteria; (*Naut.*) **to — land,** sgomberare il terreno; **to — the decks for action,** prepararsi per un lavoro *or* una lotta; **to — a hedge** (*by jumping*) saltare una siepe; **to — from,** sbarazzare, liberare; (*colloq.*) **to — off,** andarsene, scappare, darsi alla fuga; **to — out,** ritirarsi, allontanarsi; **it's clearing up,** il tempo si rischiara; **—-cut,** cesellato, netto, stagliato; **— -headed,** acuto, sagace; **—-sighted,** chiaroveggente; **to — -starch,** inamidare; **three — days,** tre giorni interi.
clearance, *n.* Sgombero, sgombro, *m.*; (*Naut.*) congedo, *m.*, partenza *f.*; (*Comm.*) liquidazione, *f.*; (*Mech.*) spazio libero, *m.*; (*through customs*) sdoganamento, *m.* **— sale,** vendita di liquidazione, *f.*; **— papers,** patente doganale, *f.*
clearing, *n.* Schiarimento, *m.*; pagamento, regolamento, *m.*, difesa, giustificazione, *f.*; (*of a letter-box*) levata, *f.*; (*of woods*) radura, *f.*; (*of land*) dissodamento, *m.*; (*of rubbish*) spazzamento, *m.* (*Comm.*) **—-house,** stanza di compensazione, *f.*; (*fig.*) **—-up,** spiegazione, *f.*
clearly, *adv.* Chiaramente, chiaro, evidentemente.
clearness, *n.* Chiarezza, limpidezza, nettezza, trasparenza, *f.*
cleat [kli:t], *n.* Gattello, uncino, *m.*
cleavage ['kli:vidʒ], *n.* Fenditura, spaccatura, crepatura, *f.*; disaccordo, *m.*
cleave (1) [kli:v], *v.t.* Fendere, spaccare, dividere.
cleave (2), *v.i.* Attaccarsi, aderire.
cleaver, *n.* Mannaia, *f.*, coltellaccio, *m.*
clef [klef], *n.* (*Mus.*) Chiave, *f.*
cleft, *n.* Fessura, fenditura, *f.*, spacco, *m.* **To be in a — stick,** non trovar modo di togliersi da un impaccio. || *P.p.* of **cleave.**
clematis ['klemətis], *n.* (*Bot.*) Clematide, vitalba, *f.*
clemency ['klemənsi], *n.* Clemenza, dolcezza, mitezza, *f.* **The — of the weather,** la mitezza del tempo, *f.*
clement, *a.* Clemente, dolce, mite, indulgente.
clench [klentʃ], *v.t.* Ribadire; confermare. **To — the fists,** serrare i pugni; **to — the teeth,** stringere i denti; **to — a bargain,** concludere un affare.
clepsydra ['klepsidrə], *n.* Clessidra, *f.*
clerestory ['kliəɹstɔ:ri], *n.* (*Arch.*) Navata superiore, *f.*
clergy ['klə:ɹdʒi], *n.* Clero, *m.*
clergyman (*pl.* **clergymen**), *n.* Prete, chierico, sacerdote, *m.*
cleric ['klerik], *n.* Ecclesiastico, *m.*
clerical, *a.* Clericale; da impiegato, da scrivano. **A — error,** uno sbaglio della penna, un errore di trascrizione, *m.*
clericalism, *n.* Clericalismo, *m.*
clerically, *adv.* Clericalmente.
clerk [klɑ:ɹk], *n.* Impiegato, contabile, commesso, *m.*; scrivano, copista, *m.* **— of works,** capomastro, capoccia, *m.*
clerkship, *n.* Impiego di commesso, posto di commesso, *m.*

clever ['klevəɹ], *a.* Abile, intelligente, bravo, destro, capace; ben eseguito; ingegnoso. **To be — at school,** essere bravo a scuola; **to be — at painting,** saper dipingere bene.
cleverly, *adv.* Abilmente, bravamente, destramente.
cleverness, *n.* Abilità, destrezza, capacità, astuzia, *f.*
clew [klu:], *n.* Gomitolo, *m.*
click [klik], *v.i.* Cricchiare; (*colloq.*) accordarsi. ‖ *n.* Schiocco, ticchettio, *m.*
clicker, *n.* (*Print.*) Impaginatore, *m.*
clicking, *n.* Ticchettio, cricchio, tic-tac, *m.*
client ['klaiənt], *n.* Cliente, *m.*
clientele, *n.* Clientela, *f.*
cliff [klif], *n.* Scogliera, roccia, balza, costa dirupata, *f.*, precipizio, *m.*
climacteric [klai'mæktərik], *n.a.* Climaterico, *m.*
climate ['klaimit], *n.* Clima, *m.*
climatic, *a.* Climatico.
climatology, *n.* Climatologia, *f.*
climax ['klaimæks], *n.* Gradazione, *f.*; colmo, culmine, apogeo, *m.*
climb [klaim], *v.i.* Salire, montare, andare n alto, ascendere; scalare, arrampicarsi; *v.t.* salire. ‖ *n.* Salita, ascesa, scalata, arrampicata, *f.* **A stiff —,** una salita difficile, *f.*; (*fig.*) **to — down,** abbassare le proprie pretese, cedere; **to — a mountain,** scalare una montagna, arrampicarsi su per una montagna.
climber, *n.* Alpinista, *m.*; arrampicatore, scalatore, *m.*; (*Bot.*) rampicante, *m.*; (*fig.*) **social —,** arrivista, *m.*
clime [klaim], *n.* Clima, paese, *m.*
clinch [klintʃ], *v.t.* Ribadire; stringere; (*Naut.*) magliettare. ‖ *n.* (*Boxing*) Strette, *f.pl.*; (*Naut.*) maglia, *f.* **To — a bargain,** concludere un affare.
clincher, *n.* (*fig.*) Prova irrefragabile, *f.*
cling [kliŋ], *v.i.* Attaccarsi, aggrapparsi, stringersi, aderire. **To — together,** stringersi l'uno all'altro.
clinging, *a.* Aderente, tenace.
clinic ['klinik], *n.* Clinica, *f.*
clinical, *a.* Clinico. **— surgery,** clinica chirurgica, *f.*
clinically, *adv.* Clinicamente.
clink [kliŋk], *n.* Tintinnio, *m.*; (*colloq.*) carcere, *m.* ‖ *v.t.* (*glasses*) Toccare; *v.i.* tintinnare.
clinker, *n.* Scoria, *f.* (*Naut.*) **—-built,** costruito a lamine sovrapposte.
clip, *v.t.* Tagliare, ritagliare; (*ticket*) bucare; (*words*) mangiare; (*animals*) tosare; (*wings*) tarpare; (*shrubs*) potare. ‖ *n.* Tosatura, *f.* **Paper- —,** pinzetta da carte, *f.*
clipper, *n.* Tagliatore, *m.*; (*Naut.*) clipper, *m.*
clippers, *n.pl.* Forbici, *m.pl.*
clippie, *n.* (*colloq.*) Bigliettaia, *f.*
clippings, *n.pl.* Ritagli, *m.pl.*
clique [kli:k], *n.* Combriccola, *f.*
cloak [klouk], *n.* Mantello, *m.*; (*Mil.*) cappotto, *m.*; (*fig.*) velo, *m.*, maschera, *f.*; pretesto, *m.* ‖ *v.t.* Ammantare, velare, mascherare. **—-room,** guardaroba; vestiario, *m.*; (*Rail.*) deposito bagagli, *m.*
clock [klɔk], *n.* Orologio, *m.*, pendola, *f.*; (*of taxi*) tassimetro, *m.* **Alarm —,** sveglia, *f.*; **—-maker,** orologiaio, *m.*; **—-tower,** torre dell'orologio, *m.*
clockwise, *a.* Secondo il senso delle lancette dell'orologio.
clockwork, *n.* Meccanismo dell'orologio, *m.* **It goes like —,** va come un orologio; **— train,** trenino meccanico, *m.*
clod [klɔd], *n.* Zolla, *f.*
clodhopper, *n.* Contadino, villano, *m.*
clog (1) [klɔg], *n.* Zoccolo, *m.*; (*fig.*) intoppo, *m.*; (*for an animal*) pastoia, *f.* **—-dance,** ballo con gli zoccoli, *m.*
clog (2), *v.i.* Impacciarsi; *v.t.* impedire, ostruire.
cloister ['klɔistəɹ], *n.* Chiostro, *m.* ‖ *v.t.* Rinchiudere in convento.
cloistered, *a.* Rinchiuso.
cloistral, *a.* Claustrale, monastico.
close (1) [klouz], *v.t.* Chiudere, serrare; terminare, concludere; *v.i.* chiudersi, concludersi, finire, terminare; (*Mil.*) corpo a corpo. ‖ *n.* Termine, fine, conclusione, *f.*; chiuso, recinto, *m.*; chiusura, *f.*; (*Mus.*) cadenza, *f.* **To — a bargain,** concludere un affare; **to — one's days,** morire; **to — the ranks,** serrare le file; **to — in,** rinchiudere; **to — with an offer,** accettare una proposta; **to — up,** bloccare; **to — with** (*an arrangement*), accordarsi con, (*to grapple with*) battersi corpo a corpo; **to bring to a —,** terminare; **to draw to a —,** avvicinarsi alla fine; **closing-time,** ora di chiusura; **at — of day,** sull'imbrunire.
close (2) [klous], *a.* Chiuso; stretto, ristretto, denso, compatto; (*of weather*) afoso; (*of words*) discreto. ‖ *adv.* Presso, vicino, dappresso, strettamente. **To lie —,** celarsi; **— at hand,** vicinissimo; **— to,** vicino a; **in — confinement,** in stretto isolamento; **to have a — shave from,** andare a un pelo di, scamparla bella; **a — resemblance,** una forte somiglianza, *f.*; **—-fisted,** avaro, meschino; (*Naut.*) **—-hauled,** stretto al vento; (*Cinema*) **—-up,** visuale ravvicinata, *f.*; (*Cinema*) primo piano, *m.*
closely, *adv.* Vicino, dappresso, strettamente; attentamente. **To observe —,** osservare attentamente; **to guard —,** sorvegliare strettamente; **we are — related,** siamo stretti parenti; **to question —,** incalzare con domande.
closeness, *n.* Strettezza, densità, *f.*; discrezione, *f.*; avarizia, parsimonia, *f.*; esattezza *f.*; (*of air*) afa, *f.*
closet, *n.* Gabinetto, *m.*; armadio, *m.*; guardaroba, *m.* ‖ *v.t.* Rinchiudere in un gabinetto. **To be closeted with,** conferire a quattr'occhi; **water —,** gabinetto, *m.*, ritirata, *f.*
clot, *n.* Grumo, coagulo, *m.*; (*colloq.*) zuccone, imbecille, *m.* ‖ *v.i.* Coagulare, aggrumarsi.
cloth [klɔθ], *n.* Tela, stoffa, *f.*, panno, *m.*; tovaglia, coperta, *f.*; (*the clergy*), abito, *m.* **Linen —,** pannilino, *m.*; **table —,** tovaglia, *f.*; **to lay the —,** mettere la tovaglia, apparecchiare; **to remove the —,** sparecchiare; **American —,** tela incerata, *f.*; **—-merchant,** mercante di stoffe, *m.*
clothe [klouð], *v.t.* Vestire, coprire, rivestire. **To — oneself,** vestirsi.
clothes, *n.pl.* Vestiti, panni, vestimenti, vesti, *m.pl.* **In plain —,** in borghese; **old —,** vestiti vecchi, *m.pl.*; **old- — man,** rigattiere, *m.*; **—-basket,** cesta dei panni sudici, *f.*; **—-brush,** spazzola da panni, *f.*; **—-hook.**

attaccapanni, *m.*; **—-horse,** cavalletto, *m.*; **—-line,** corda per stendere la biancheria, *f.*; **—-peg,** pinza, *f.*, attaccapanni, *m.*; **—-prop,** pertica da tenditoio, *f.*

clothier, *n.* Pannaiuolo, *m.*; sarto, *m.*

clothing, *n.* Vestiti, panni, *m.pl.*

clotted, *a.* Grumoso, coagulato.

cloud [klaud], *n.* Nuvola, *f.*; nuvolo, *m.*; nube, ombra, *f.* || *v.t.* Coprir di nubi, oscurare, annuvolare, rannuvolare; *v.i.* annuvolarsi; adombrarsi. **To be under a —,** essere mal visto da tutti; **to fall from the clouds,** cascare dalle nuvole; **his face clouded,** il suo viso si rannuvolò; **—-burst,** nubifragio, acquazzone, *m.*; **a — of locusts,** uno sciame di locuste, *m.*

cloudily, *adv.* Oscuramente.

cloudiness, *n.* Oscurità, nuvolosità, *f.*

cloudless, *a.* Senza nuvole, sereno.

cloudy, *a.* Nuvoloso, coperto di nuvole, fosco, turbato; oscuro. **— weather,** tempo coperto, cielo coperto, *m.*; **it's getting —,** il cielo si annuvola.

clough [klʌf], *n.* Burrone, *m.*

clout (1) [klaut], *n.* Schiaffo, colpo, pugno, *m.* || *v.t.* Schiaffeggiare, battere.

clout (2), *n.* Pezza, toppa, *f.*, cencio, *m.*

clove [klouv], *n.* Chiodo di garofano, *m.* **— of garlic,** spicchio d'aglio, *m.*; **—-pink,** garofano, *m.*

cloven, *a.* Fesso, forcuto. **—-hoofed,** a piede fesso, bisulco.

clover ['klouvəɹ], *n.* (*Bot.*) Trifoglio, *m.* **To be in —,** essere nell'abbondanza; stare come un papa.

clown [klaun], *n.* Buffone, pagliaccio, zanni, *m.*; rustico, zoticone, *m.* || *v.i.* Far il pagliaccio.

clownish, *a.* Zotico, goffo; rustico.

clownishly, *adv.* Rozzamente, grossolanamente, in maniera sgarbata.

clownishness, *n.* Rusticità; grossolanità, sgarbatezza, *f.*

cloy [klɔi], *v.t.* Saziare, satollare.

cloying, *a.* Che sazia, sdolcinato.

club [klʌb], *n.* Bastone, randello, *m.*, mazza, *f.*; club, circolo, gruppo, *m.*, associazione, *f.*; (*golf*) bastone, *m.*; (*Cards*) fiore, *m.* || *v.t.* Battere, bastonare; *v.i.* unirsi in un circolo. **To — together,** pagare la propria quota; **—-foot,** piede deforme, *m.*; **—-law,** la legge del più forte, *f.*; **—-man,** membro di un circolo, *m.*; **—-house,** casino, *m.*

clubbable, *a.* Socievole.

cluck [klʌk], *v.i.* Chiocciare. || *n.* Chioccio, *m.*

clucking, *n.* Il chiocciare, *m.*

clue [klu:], *n.* Filo, *m.*; indicazione, chiave, *f.*, indizio, *m.*, traccia, *f.* **To give a — to,** mettere sulla buona via.

clump (1) [klʌmp], *n.* Gruppo, cespo, *m.*, massa, zolla, *f.* **A — of trees,** un boschetto di alberi, *m.*; **a — of wallflowers,** un cespo di violacciocche, *m.*

clump (2), *v.i.* Camminare pesantemente.

clumsily ['klʌmzili], *adv.* Goffamente, sgarbatamente.

clumsiness, *n.* Goffaggine, sgarbatezza, *f.*

clumsy, *a.* Goffo, sgarbato; grossolano, rozzo.

clung, *past* of **cling.**

cluster [klʌstəɹ], *n.* Ciuffo, grappolo, mazzetto, cespo, *m.*; sciame, *m.* || *v.i.* Crescere in grappoli, raggrupparsi. **A — of grapes,** un grappolo d'uva, *m.*; **— of bees,** sciame di api, *m.*

clutch (1) [klʌtʃ], *v.t.* Afferrare, impugnare, stringere fra le dita; (*Motor.*) innestare. || *n.* Presa, stretta, *f.*; (*Mech.*) indentatura, *f.*; (*Motor.*) innesto, *m.* **A drowning man clutches at straws,** un annegato s'aggrappa ai fuscelli; (*Motor.*) **to let in the —,** innestare.

clutch (2), *n.* Covata (*of eggs*), *f.*

clutter ['klʌtəɹ], *n.* Massa confusa, *f.*, fracasso, schiamazzo, *m.* || *v.t.* Riempire. **To — up,** ingombrare.

coach [koutʃ], *n.* Cocchio, *m.*, carrozza, vettura, diligenza, *f.*; (*of pupils*) maestro, insegnante, ripetitore, *m.*; (*Rail.*) vagone, *m.*; (*Sport*) allenatore, istruttore, *m.* || *v.t.* Preparare agli esami; *v.i.* andare in carrozza. **— and four,** tiro a quattro, *m.*; **mail —,** vettura da posta, *f.*; (*fig.*) **slow-—,** trottapiano, *m.*; **stage-—,** diligenza, *f.*; **—-box,** cassetta, *f.*; **—-house,** rimessa, *f.*; **—-builder,** carrozziere, *m.*; **—-horse,** cavallo da tiro, *m.*; **—-stand,** posteggio di carrozze, *m.*; **—-wrench,** chiave inglese, *f.*

coachman (*pl.* **coachmen**), *n.* Cocchiere, vetturino, *m.*

coadjutant [kou'ædʒu:tənt], *n.* Collaboratore, *m.*

coadjutor [kou'ædʒu:təɹ], *n.* Assistente, aiuto, coadiutore, *m.*

co-agent, *n.* Associato, socio, *m.*

coagulate [kou'ægu:leit], *v.t.i.* Coagulare, coagularsi.

coagulation, *n.* Coagulazione, *f.*

coagulative, *a.* Coagulativo.

coal [koul], *n.* Carbone, *m.* || *v.t.* Provvedere carbone; *v.i.* (*of steamers*) far carbone. **Live coals,** braci, *f.pl.*; **to call over the coals,** rimproverare; **to carry coals to Newcastle,** portare acqua al mare; **to heap coals of fire,** ricambiare il male col bene; **—-barge,** chiatta da carbone, *f.*; **—-bed,** strato carbonifero, *m.*; **—-black,** nero come il carbone; **—-box,** secchio per il carbone, *m.*; **—-bunker,** carbonile, *m.*; **—-cellar,** carbonaia, *f.*; **—-dust,** polvere di carbone, carbonigia, *f.*; **—-heaver,** carbonaio, *m.*; **—-hole,** carbonaia, carboniera, *f.*; **—-measure,** giacimento carbonifero, *m.*; **—-merchant,** mercante di carbone, *m.*; **—-mine,** miniera di carbone, *f.*; **—-miner,** minatore di carbone, *m.*; **—-scuttle,** secchio da carbone, *m.*; **—-seam,** strato carbonifero, *m.*; **—-station, coaling-station,** base per far carbone, *f.*; **—-tar,** catrame, *m.*; **—-wharf,** deposito di carbone, *m.*

coalesce [kouə'les], *v.i.* Unirsi, fondersi, congiungersi.

coalescence, *n.* Coesione, unione, *f.*

coalescent, *a.* Coalescente.

coalfield, *n.* Regione carbonifera, *f.*

coalition, *n.* Coalizione, lega, *f.*

coalitionist, *n.* Fautore di una coalizione, *m.*

coalman, *n.* Carbonaio, *m.*

coamings ['koumiŋz], *n.pl.* (*Naut.*) Orli dei boccoporti, *m.pl.*

coarse [kɔ:ɹs], *a.* Grossolano, rozzo, volgare; sgarbato, indelicato, osceno. **—-grained,** a grani grossi; poco raffinato.

coarsely, *adv.* Grossolanamente, rudemente.
coarsen, *v.t.* Irruvidire.
coarseness, *n.* Grossolanità, rozzezza, *f.*
coast [koust], *n.* Costa, costiera, *f.*, lido, litorale, *m.* || *v.i.* Navigare vicino; accostarsi, avvicinarsi; (*Cycling*) scendere a ruota libera. **—-guard,** guardiacoste, *m.*; **—-line,** litorale, *m.*, costiera, *f.*
coaster, coasting vessel, *n.* Battello di cabotaggio, *m.*
coasting, *n.* Cabotaggio, *m.*, navigazione costiera, *f.*
coastwise, *adv.* Lungo la costa. || *a.* Litoraneo.
coat [kout], *n.* Abito, soprabito, *m.*; giacca, giubba, giacchetta, *f.*; (*Mil.*) tunica, *f.*; (*of animals*) pelame, *m.*; (*of paint*) intonaco, *m.*; (*Anat.*) tunica, parete, *f.* || *v.t.* Coprire, vestire, rivestire; spalmare, intonacare. **Woman's —,** cappotta, *f.*; **— of mail,** corazza a maglia; **—-tail,** falda, *f.*; **dress- —, tail- —,** abito a coda, *m.*, marsina, *f.*; **frock- —,** redingote, *f.*, frac, *m.*: **morning- —,** abito a falde, dorsè, *m.*; **rain- —,** impermeabile, *m.*; **to cut one's — according to one's cloth,** vivere secondo i propri mezzi; (*fig.*) **to turn one's —,** cambiar partito, voltar casacca; **—-hanger, —-peg,** attaccapanni, *m.*
coatee, *n.* Giacca a falde corte, *f.*
coating, *n.* Panno per abiti, *m.*; intonaco, *m.*
coax [kouks], *v.t.* Blandire, accarezzare, lusingare, persuadere con moine.
coaxer, *n.* Lusingatore, *m.*
coaxing, *n.* Moine, blandizie, *f.pl.*
coaxingly, *adv.* Con moine, con blandizie.
cob [kɔb], *n.* (*horse*) Ronzino, *m.*; (*swan*), cigno, *m.*; (*maize*) spiga, pannocchia, *f.* **Corn on the —,** granturco, mais, *m.*
cobalt [ko'bɔlt], *n.* Cobalto, *m.*
cobble (1) ['kɔbl], *v.t.* Rammendare, rattoppare, raccomodare scarpe.
cobble (2), **cobble-stone,** *n.* Ciottolo. || *v.t.* Acciottolare.
cobbler, *n.* Calzolaio, ciabattino, *m.*
cobbling, *n.* Rammendatura, rattoppatura, *f.*
coble [koubl], *n.* (*Naut.*) Barcone, peschereccio, *m.*
cobnut, *n.* Avellana, *f.*
cobra ['kɔbrə], *n.* (*Zool.*) Cobra, *f.*
cobweb ['kɔbweb], *n.* Ragnatela, *f.*
coca ['koukə], *n.* (*Bot.*) Coca, *f.*
cocaine [ko'kein], *n.* Cocaina, *f.*
cocainism, *n.* Cocainomania, *f.*
coccyx ['kɔksiks], *n.* (*Anat.*) Coccige, *m.*
Cochin-China [kɔtʃin'tʃainə], *n.* (*Geog.*) Cocincina, *f.*
cochineal ['kɔtʃini:l], *n.* Cocciniglia, *f.*
cochlea ['kɔkliə], *n.* (*Anat.*) Coclea, *f.*
cock [kɔk], *n.* (*Zool.*) Gallo, *m.*; maschio degli uccelli, *m.*; (*tap*) rubinetto, *m.*, chiavetta, *f.*; (*of hay*) mucchio, *m.*, bica, *f.*; (*of a gun*) cane, *m.* || *v.t.* Elevare, alzare, drizzare; (*gun*) armare; (*hay*) ammucchiare. **—-and-bull story,** fandonia, fiaba, *f.*; **— of the walk,** il gallo della Checca; **—-a-hoop,** superbo come un gallo, trionfante; **to live like a fighting —,** vivere nell'abbondanza; (*colloq.*) **Old —!** Caro mio! **to — an eye,** ammiccare; **cocked-hat,** cappello a due punte, *m.*; **to knock into a cocked-hat,** sconfiggere completamente; **—-a-doodle-do,** chicchirichì, *m.*; **—-boat,** scialuppa, *f.*; **—-crow,** canto del gallo, *m.*, alba, *f.*; **—-fight,** combattimento di galli, *m.*; **—-horse,** cavalluccio di legno, *m.*; **to ride a —-horse,** montare a cavalcioni; **—-loft,** solaio, *m.*; **—-eyed,** a sghembo; **to — the ears,** tendere l'orecchio.
cockade, *n.* Coccarda, *f.*
Cockaigne [ko'kein], *n.* Cuccagna, *f.*, il paese di Cuccagna, *m.*
cockatoo [kɔkə'tu:], *n.* (*Zool.*) Cacatua, *m.*
cockatrice ['kɔkətris], *n.* Basilisco, *m.*
cockchafer ['kɔktʃeifəɹ], *n.* (*Zool.*) Maggiolino, *m.*
cocker, *v.t.* Accarezzare, viziare.
cockerel, *n.* Galletto, *m.*
cockle (1) ['kɔkl], *n.* (*Zool.*) Tellina, *f.*, cardio, *m.*; (*Bot.*) loglio, *m.* **It warms the cockles of my heart,** mi rallegra il cuore.
cockle (2), *v.t.* Increspare, raggrinzare; *v.i.* incresparsi.
Cockney ['kɔkni], *n.a.* Londinese; dialetto Londinese, *m.*
cockpit, *n.* Arena, *f.*; (*Naut.*) infermeria, *f.*; (*Aviat.*) carlinga, *f.*
cockroach, *n.* (*Zool.*) Blatta, *f.*
cockscomb, *n.* Cresta di gallo, *f.*; (*Bot.*) celosia, *f.*; (*fig.*) cicisbeo, bellimbusto, *m.*
cockshy, *n.* Bersaglio, *m.*; mira, *f.*
cocksure, *a.* Sicurissimo.
cocktail, *n.* Cocktail, bicchierino, *m.* **—-bar,** bar-cocktail, *m.*; **—-shaker,** shaker, *m.*
cocky, *a.* Vanitoso, impudente.
coco ['koukou], *n.* (*Bot.*) Cocco, *m.*
cocoa ['koukou], *n.* Cacao, *m.*; (*drink*) cioccolata, *f.*
coconut, cokernut ['koukənʌt], *n.* Cocco, *m.*; noce di cocco, *f.* **— palm,** cocco, *m.*; **— matting,** stuoia in fiore di cocco, *f.*
cocoon [kə'ku:n], *n.* Bozzolo, *m.*
cod, codfish [kɔd, kɔdfiʃ], *n.* (*Zool.*) Merluzzo, *m.*; (*dried*) baccalà, *f.* || *v.t.* (*colloq.*) **To cod,** turlupinare. **—-liver oil,** olio di fegato di merluzzo, *m.*
coddle ['kɔdl], *v.t.* Accarezzare, viziare. **To — oneself,** crogiolarsi.
code [koud], *n.* Codice, *m.*; cifrario, *m.*; cifra, *f.* || *v.t.* Cifrare, tradurre in cifra. **—-word,** parola in cifra, *f.*
codex, *n.* Codice, *m.*; manuscritto antico, *m.*
codger ['kɔdʒəɹ], *n.* (*colloq.*) Bonomo, originale, *m.*
codicil ['kɔdisil], *n.* Codicillo, *m.*
codification [kodifi'keiʃən], *n.* Codificazione, *f.*
codify, *v.t.* Codificare.
codling ['kɔdliŋ], *n.* (*Zool.*) Piccolo merluzzo, *m.*; (*Bot.*) specie di mela, *f.*
coeducation [kouedju:'keiʃən], *n.* Coeducazione, *f.*
coefficient [koue'fiʃənt], *n.* (*Math.*) Coefficiente, *m.*
coeliac ['si:liək], *a.* (*Anat.*) Celiaco.
coenobite ['senobait], *n.* Cenobita, *m.*
coequal [kou'i:kwəl], *a.* Eguale.
coequality, *n.* Eguaglianza, *f.*
coerce [kou'ə:ɹs], *v.t.* Forzare, costringere. coartare.
coercible, *a.* Coercibile.
coercion, *n.* Coartazione, coercizione, *f.*
coercive, *a.* Coercitivo.
coercively, *adv.* Forzatamente.
co-eternal [koui:'tə:ɹnəl], *a.* Coeterno.

coeval [kou'i:vəl], *a.* Coetaneo, coevo.
co-exist, *v.i.* Coesistere.
co-existence, *n.* Coesistenza, *f.*
co-existent, *a.* Coesistente.
coffee ['kɔfi], *n.* Caffè, *m.* **—-roaster,** tostino da caffè, *m.*; **—-bean, —-berry,** chicco di caffè, *m.*; **—-cup,** tazza da caffè, *f.*; **—-grounds,** feccia di caffè, *f.*; **—-house,** caffè; **—-mill,** macinino da caffè, *m.*; **—-pot,** caffettiera, *f.*; **— with milk,** caffè e latte, *m.*; **black —,** caffè nero, *m.*
coffer ['kɔfəɹ], *n.* Cofano, *m.*, cassaforte, *f.* **—-dam,** cassone, *m.*
coffin ['kɔfin], *n.* Cassa da morto, bara, *f.*, feretro, cataletto, *m.*
cog (1) [kɔg], *n.* (*Mech.*) Dente, *m.* **—-wheel,** ruota d'ingranaggio, ruota dentata, *f.*
cog (2), *v.i.* Truffare al giuoco dei dadi, barare.
cogency ['koudʒənsi], *n.* Forza, *f.*, potere, *m.*
cogent, *a.* Forte, convincente, calzante.
cogently, *adv.* Con forza.
cogitate ['kɔdʒiteit], *v.i.* Meditare, riflettere.
cogitation, *n.* Meditazione, riflessione, *f.*
cogitative, *a.* Cogitabondo.
cognac ['kɔniæk], *n.* Cognac, *m.*
cognate ['kɔgneit], *a.* Affine, analogo, congiunto.
cognation, *n.* Parentela, *f.*
cognisance, cognizance, *n.* Conoscenza, cognizione, notizia, *f.*; (*Law*) giurisdizione, *f.*
cognition, *n.* Cognizione, conoscenza, *f.*
cognitive, *a.* Conoscitivo.
cognizable, *a.* Conoscibile.
cognizant, *a.* (*Law*) Competente, conoscente.
cognomen [kɔg'noumən], *n.* Cognome, soprannome, nomignolo, *m.*
cohabit [kou'hæbit], *v.i.* Coabitare.
cohabitation, *n.* Coabitazione, *f.*
coheir [kou'ɛəɹ], *n.* Coerede, *m.*
coheiress, *n.* Coereditiera, *f.*
cohere [kou'hiəɹ], *v.i.* Aderire insieme, attaccarsi.
coherence, coherency, *n.* Coesione, coerenza, *f.*
coherent, *a.* Coerente, adesivo; consistente.
coherently, *adv.* Coerentemente.
cohesion [kou'hi:ʃən], *n.* Coesione, connessione, *f.*
cohesive, *a.* Coerente, aderente.
cohesiveness, *n.* Coesione, *f.*
cohort ['kouhɔːt], *n.* (*Hist.*) Coorte, *f.*
coif [kɔif], *n.* Cuffia, benda, *f.* ‖ *v.t.* Coprire di una cuffia. **Nun's —,** sacra benda, *f.*
coign [kɔin], *n.* **— of vantage,** posto dominante, *m.*
coil [kɔil], *n.* Rotolo, *m.*; rumore, trambusto, *m.*; (*of serpents*) spira, *f.*; (*of hair*) treccia, *f.*; (*Elect.*) bobina, *f.* ‖ *v.t.* Piegare, avvolgere, avvoltolare; *v.i.* ripiegarsi, avvolgersi. (*Lit.*) **This mortal —,** questo viluppo mortale; (*Elect.*) **induction —,** bobina d'induzione, *f.*
coin [kɔin], *n.* Moneta; (*collectively*) contanti, *m.pl.*, danaro, *m.*, valuta, *f.* ‖ *v.t.* Batter moneta, coniare; inventare, fabbricare. **Base —,** moneta falsa, *f.*; **coined money,** danaro monetato, *m.*; (*fig.*) **to — money,** arricchirsi; **to — words,** coniare parole; **to pay someone back in his own —,** ripagare qualcuno colla stessa moneta.
coinage, *n.* Coniazione, *f.*; conio *m.*
coincide [kouin'said], *v.i.* Coincidere; combinarsi.
coincidence [kou'insidəns], *n.* Combinazione, coincidenza, *f.*
coincident, *a.* Coincidente. **— with,** d'accordo con, conforme a.
coiner, *n.* Falsario, falso monetario, *m.*
coition [kou'iʃən], *n.* Coito, accoppiamento, *m.*
coir [kwaiɹ], *n.* Borra di cocco, *f.*
coke [kouk], *n.* Coke, *m.*
colander, cullender ['kʌləndəɹ], *n.* Colatoio, *m.*
colchicum ['kɔltʃikəm], *n.* (*Bot.*) Colchico, *m.*
cold [kould], *a.* Freddo. ‖ *n.* Freddo, *m.*, freddura, *f.*; (*Med.*) raffreddore, *m.* **I am —,** ho freddo; **it is —,** fa freddo; **to throw — water on,** dare una doccia fredda a; **the idea leaves me —,** l'idea non mi commuove; **to blow hot and —,** vacillare; **to give the — shoulder,** accogliere freddamente; **in — blood,** a sangue freddo; **— chisel,** scalpello, *m.*; **—-cream,** colcrem, *m.*; **a — snap,** colpo di freddo, *m.*; **—-drawn,** tirato a freddo; **—-hearted,** insensibile, di cuore freddo; **— steel,** arma bianca, *f.*; **— storage,** conservazione a freddo, *f.*; **to catch —,** raffreddarsi; **to have a —,** avere una raffreddore; **to catch one's death of —,** prendere un forte raffreddore; **— feet,** paura.
coldish, *a.* Freddino, fresco.
coldly, *adv.* Freddamente.
coldness, *n.* Freddezza, *f.*
coleoptera [kɔli'ɔptərə], *n.* (*Zool.*) Coleottera, *f.*
co-lessee [koule'si:], *n.* (*Law*) Coaffittuario, *m.*
colic ['kɔlik], *n.* (*Med.*) Colica, *f.*
collaborate [kɔ'læbəreit], *v.i.* Collaborare.
collaboration, *n.* Collaborazione, *f.*
collaborator, *n.* Collaboratore, *m.*
collapse [kə'læps], *v.i.* Cadere, crollare; accasciarsi, infiacchirsi; sgonfiarsi. ‖ *n.* Rovina, *f.*; avvilimento, crollo, *m.*; (*Med.*) collasso, *m.*, prostrazione, *f.*
collapsible, *a.* Pieghevole.
collar ['kɔləɹ], *n.* Collare, *m.*; (*of shirt*) colletto, *m.*; (*of coat*) bavero, *m.* ‖ *v.t.* Mettere un collare a, prendere per il collo; (*colloq.*) prendere, rubare. **Against the —,** contro cuore, di mala voglia; **to seize by the —,** afferrare per il bavero; **to slip the —,** scappare; (*Anat.*) **—-bone,** clavicola, *f.*; **—-stud,** bottoncino da colletto, *m.*
collate [kɔ'leit], *v.t.* Collazionare, riscontrare, confrontare.
collateral [kə'lætərəl], *a.* Collaterale, indiretto, sussidario, parallelo.
collaterally, *adv.* Collateralmente.
collation [kɔ'leiʃən], *n.* (*comparison*) Collazione, *f.*; collazionamento, riscontro, confronto, *m.*; (*meal*) colazione, merenda, *f.*; *Eccles.*) dono, conferimento di un beneficio, *m.*
colleague ['kɔli:g], *n.* Collega, consocio, *m.*
collect (1) [kə'lekt], *v.t.* Raccogliere, adunare, ammassare; (*debts*) riscuotere, percepire, ricuperare; (*letters*) fare la levata; *v.i.* adunarsi, ammassarsi. **To — for charity,** fare una colletta; **to — oneself,** comporsi, raccogliersi.
collect (2) ['kɔləkt], *n.* (*Eccles.*) Colletta, *f.*

collected, *a.* Raccolto; tranquillo, calmo.
collectedly, *adv.* Tranquillamente, con calma.
collectedness, *n.* Calma, *f.*; sangue freddo, *m.*
collection, *n.* Raccolta, collezione, *f.*; (*for charity*) colletta, *f.*; (*of extracts*) scelta, *f.*; (*of letters*) levata, *f.*; (*of taxes*) riscossione, *f.*; (*of literary works*) collana, collezione, *f.*
collective, *a.* Collettivo.
collectively, *adv.* Collettivamente.
collectivism, *n.* Collettivismo, *m.*
collectivist, *n.* Collettivista, *m.*
collector, *n.* Raccoglitore, collettore, *m.*; (*of taxes*) esattore, *m.*; (*of curios, etc.*) collezionista, *m.*; (*of customs*) ricevitore, *m.*
collectorship, *n.* Ricevitoria, *f.*
college ['kɔlidʒ], *n.* Collegio, convitto universitario, *m.*, università, *f.*; seminario, conservatorio, *m.*
collegian, *n.* Collegiale, membro di un collegio universitario, *m.*
collegiate, *a.* Collegiato.
collet ['kɔlət], *n.* Castone di un anello, *m.*
collide [kə'laid], *v.i.* Urtarsi, cozzare, venire in collisione.
collie ['kɔli], *n.* Cane da pastore, *m.*
collier, *n.* Minatore di carbone, *m.*; (*Naut.*) nave carboniera, *f.*
colliery, *n.* Miniera di carbone, *f.*
colligate ['kɔligeit], *v.t.* Collegare.
collimate, *v.t.* Collimare.
collision [kə'liʒən], *n.* Collisione, *f.*, urto, scontro, *m.*; (*of trains, etc.*) investimento, scontro, *m.* **To come into — with,** scontrarsi, venire in collisione.
collocate ['kɔlɔkeit], *v.t.* Collocare, allogare.
collocation, *n.* Collocamento, *m.*
collodion [kə'loudiən], *n.* (*Chem.*) Collodio, *m.*
colloid ['kɔlɔid], *n.a.* Colloide, *m.*
collop ['kɔləp], *n.* Fetta di carne, *f.*
colloquial [kɔ'loukwiəl], *a.* Familiare, colloquiale, conversativo.
colloquialism, *n.* Espressione familiare, *f.*
colloquially, *adv.* Familiarmente.
colloquy ['kɔləkwi], *n.* Colloquio, abboccamento, *m.*
collotype ['kɔloutaip], *n.* Collotipia, *f.*
collusion [kə'lu:ʒən], *n.* Collusione, *f.*
collusive, *a.* Collusivo.
collyrium [kə'liriəm], *n.* (*Med.*) Collirio, *m.*
colocynth ['kɔlousinθ], *n.* (*Bot.*) Colloquintide, *f.*
colon ['koulən], *n.* (*Anat.*) Colon, *m.*; (*Gram.*) due punti, *m.pl.*
colonel ['kə:ɹnəl], *n.* Colonnello, *m.*
colonial [kə'louniəl], *a.* Coloniale. ‖ *n.* Abitante di una colonia, *m.*
colonist, *n.* Colono, colonizzatore, *m.*
colonization, *n.* Colonizzazione, *f.*
colonize, *v.t.* Colonizzare.
colonnade [kɔlɔ'neid], *n.* Colonnato, *m.*
colony, *n.* Colonia, *f.*
colophon ['kɔlɔfən], *n.* (*Print.*) Foglio di chiusa, *m.*; sottoscrizione, *f.*
Colorado beetle [kolo'rɑ:dou bi:tl], *n.* (*Zool.*) Dorifora, *f.*
coloration [kʌlə'reiʃən], *n.* Colorazione, *f.*
colossal [kə'lɔsəl], *a.* Colossale.
Colosseum, *n.* Colosseo, *m.*
Colossus, *n.* Colosso, *m.*
colour ['kʌləɹ], *n.* Colore, colorito, *m.*; (*of complexion*) carnagione, *f.*; (*fig.*) pretesto, *m.*, apparenza, *f.*; (*pl. mil.*) bandiera, *f.* ‖ *v.t.* Colorire, dipingere, tingere; *v.i.* arrossire. **Is this a fast — ?** È questo un colore solido? **to change —,** cambiare colore; **under — of,** sotto colore di; **to hoist the colours,** inalberare la bandiera; **to strike one's colours,** ammainare la bandiera; **to see in its true colours,** vedere nella giusta luce; **to put a false — upon,** dare un'apparenza fittizia a; **to come off with flying colours,** vincerla splendidamente; **with the colours,** sotto le bandiere, sotto le armi; **to feel off- —,** sentirsi poco bene; **he coloured up to the eyes,** arrossì sino al bianco degli occhi; **—-blind,** affetto da daltonismo; **—-blindness,** daltonismo, *m.*
colourable, *a.* Specioso, plausibile, colorabile.
colourably, *adv.* Speciosamente.
coloured, *a.* Colorito, colorato. **Highly- —,** esagerato; **a — man,** un uomo di colore, *m.*
colouring, *n.* Colorito, *m.*; (*of complexion*) carnagione, *f.*
colourist, *n.* Colorista, *m.*
colourless, *a.* Senza colore, pallido; (*fig.*) insulso, insipido.
colporteur ['koulpɔːɹtəɹ], *n.* Agente, commesso, *m.*
colt [koult], *n.* Puledro, *m.*; (*fig.*) novizio, *m.* **Colt's-foot,** (*Bot.*) farfaro, *m.*
colubrine ['kɔlu:brain], *a.* Simile ad un serpente.
columbarium (*pl.* **columbaria**) [kɔləm'bɛəriəm], *n.* Colombario, *m.*
columbine ['kɔləmbain], *n.* (*Bot.*) Aquilegia, *f.*
column ['kɔləm], *n.* Colonna, *f.* **Newspaper —,** colonna di giornale, *f.*
columnar [kɔl'ʌmnəɹ], *a.* Colonnare, da colonna.
columned ['kɔləmd], *a.* A colonne, colonnato, fornito di colonne.
columnist ['kɔləmnist], *n.* Giornalista, articolista, *m.*
colure [kɔ'lju:ɹ], *n.* (*Astron.*) Coluro, *m.*
colza ['kɔlzə], *n.* Colza, *f.*
coma ['koumə], *n.* (*Med.*) Coma, *f.*, assopimento, *m.*; (*Astron., etc.*) chioma, *f.*
comatose ['kɔmətouz], *a.* Comatoso.
comb [koum], *n.* Pettine, *m.*; (*of cock*) cresta, *f.*; (*of honey*) favo, *m.* ‖ *v.t.* Pettinare; (*a horse*) strigliare. **Large-tooth —,** pettine rado, *m.*; **curry- —,** striglia, *f.*; **to — one's hair,** pettinarsi; (*fig.*) **to — out,** rastrellare.
combat ['kɔmbæt], *n.* Lotta, contesa, *f.*, combattimento, *m.*; battaglia, *f.* ‖ *v.t.i.* Combattere, lottare. **Single —,** duello, *m.*
combatant, *n.* Combattente, *m.*
combative, *a.* Combattivo, battagliero.
combativeness, *n.* Combattività, *f.*
comber, *n.* Pettinatore, *m.*; (*of wool*) cardatore, *m.*; (*wave*) cavallone, *m.*
combination [kɔmbi'neiʃən], *n.* Combinazione, *f.*; unione, associazione, *f.*; (*Law*) lega, *f.* **Combinations,** combinazione, *f.* (*mutande e corpetto uniti*).
combine (1) [kəm'bain], *v.t.* Combinare, unire; *v.i.* combinarsi, unirsi, accordarsi, convenire. **Combined movement,** moto simultaneo, *m.*

combine (2) ['kɔmbain], *n.* (*Comm.*) Trust, cartello, sindacato, *m.*
combing ['koumiŋ], *n.* Il pettinare, *m.*, pettinata, *f.*; (*of wool*) cardatura, *f.*
combustible [kəm'bʌstəbl], *a.* Combustibile.
combustibility, *n.* Combustibilità, *f.*
combustion, *n.* Combustione, *f.* (*Motor.*) **—-chamber,** camera di scoppio, *f.*
come [kʌm], *v.i.* Venire, pervenire, arrivare; accadere; risultare. **Can you — here?** Potete venire qua? **Come in!** Avanti! **Come on!** Andiamo! **Come what may,** qualunque cosa avvenga; **How comes it that...?** Come accade che ...? **I shall — and see you tomorrow,** verrò a trovarvi domani; **in time to —,** in avvenire; **to — about,** accadere, succedere; **to — after,** seguire, venire a cercare; **to — against,** urtar contro; **to — asunder,** rompersi, spezzarsi; **to — at,** raggiungere, ottenere; **to — away,** ritirarsi, venire via; **to — between,** intervenire, intromettersi; **to — by,** passare; ottenere, acquistare; **to — down,** scendere, abbassarsi (*of prices*); **to — for,** venire a cercare, venire per; **to — forward,** avanzarsi; **to — home,** tornare a casa; **it came home to him,** ne fu punto sul vivo; **to — in,** entrare, montare (*of the tide*), divenire di moda (*of fashion*); **to — in and out,** entrare e uscire; **to — into one's head,** venire in mente a uno; **to — near,** avvicinarsi; **to — next,** seguire, venire dopo; **to — of a good family,** appartenere ad una buona famiglia; **to — off,** staccarsi, (*fig.*) riuscire; **to — off victorious,** vincere, riuscir vincitore; **to — on,** avanzarsi, crescere; **to — out,** uscire, venir fuori, cadere (*of hair*), mostrarsi (*of stars*), scomparire (*of stains*); entrare in società (*of young women*); **to — out with,** lasciar scappare; **to — round,** tornare in sè; riprendere i sensi; (*fig.*) consentire; **to — to,** venire a, ridursi a; riaversi, riprendere coscienza; ammontare a (*of sums*); **to — together,** riunirsi; **to — to terms,** mettersi d'accordo; **to — under,** venire compreso sotto, venire a subire; **to — under notice,** venire notato; **to — undone,** sfarsi; **to — up,** venire su, crescere; **to — up with,** raggiungere; **to — to blows,** venire alle mani; **— off it!** piantala!
come-at-able [kʌm'ætəbl], *a.* Di facile accesso.
comedian [kə'mi:diən], *n.* Commediante, attore comico, *m.*
comedy, *n.* Commedia, *f.* **Musical —,** operetta, *f.*
comeliness ['kʌmlines], *n.* Bellezza; avvenenza, *f.*
comely, *a.* Bello, avvenente; (*fig.*) convenevole.
comer, *n.* Veniente, arrivante, *m.* **First —,** primo venuto, *m.*; **to challenge all comers,** sfidare chiunque.
comestible [kə'mestibl], *n.* Commestibile, *m.*, vivanda, *f.* || *a.* Commestibile, mangereccio.
comet ['kɔmit], *n.* Cometa, *f.*
comfit ['kʌmfit], *n.* Confetto, *m.*
comfort ['kʌmfəɹt], *n.* Conforto, *m.*, consolazione, comodità, *f.*; sollievo, benessere, comodo, agio, *m.* || *v.t.* Confortare, consolare, sollevare, incoraggiare. **To be of good —,** avere coraggio; **to like one's comforts,** amare i propri comodi; **to take —,** consolarsi.
comfortable, *a.* Comodo, confortevole, piacevole. **We are very — here,** ci troviamo molto bene qui; **to make oneself —,** mettersi a proprio agio.
comfortably, *adv.* Bene, comodamente, agevolmente. **— off,** benestante.
comforter, *n.* Confortatore, *m.*, confortatrice, *f.*; (*shawl*) sciarpa di lana, *f.*
comfortless, *a.* Senza comodi, scomodo.
comfortlessness, *n.* Incomodo, scomodo, sconforto, *m.*
comfrey ['kʌmfri], *n.* (*Bot.*) Consolida, *f.*
comfy ['kʌmfi], *a.* (*colloq.*) Confortevole.
comic, comical ['kɔmik, 'kɔmikl], *a.* Comico, umoristico, ridicolo, buffo. || *n.* Giornale umoristico. **Comic opera,** opera buffa, *f.*; **comic song,** canzone umoristica, *f.*
comicality, *n.* Comicità, *f.*
comically, *adv.* Comicamente.
coming ['kʌmiŋ], *n.* Venuta, *f.*, arrivo, *m.*; (*of Christ*) avvento, *m.* || *a.* Da venire, futuro, entrante, prossimo. **— and going,** andirivieni, *m.*; **the — week,** la settimana entrante, *f.*
comity ['kɔmiti], *n.* Cortesia, gentilezza, *f.* **The — of nations,** l'accordo fra le nazioni, *m.*
comma ['kɔmə], *n.* Virgola, *f.*; (*Mus.*) comma, *f.* **Inverted commas,** virgolette, *f.pl.*
command [kə'mɑ:nd], *n.* Comando, ordine, *m.*; potere, *m.*, autorità, *f.*; impero, *m.* || *v.t.* Comandare; possedere, poter disporre di; ispirare (*respect*), dominare (*a view of*). **At —,** a disposizione; **— of the sea,** il dominio dei mari, *m.*; **to be at someone's —,** stare agli ordini di qualcuno; **to give the word of —,** dare il comando; **to have a great — of words,** avere una grande facilità di parola; **yours to —,** ai vostri ordini.
commandant ['kɔməndænt], *n.* Comandante, *m.*
commandeer [kɔmən'diəɹ], *v.t.* Requisire.
commander, *n.* Comandante, *m.*; commendatore, *m.*; (*Naut.*) capitano di fregata, *m.* **—-in-chief,** comandante in capo, generalissimo, *m.*
commanding, *a.* Comandante; imponente, dominante (*overlooking*), autoritario. **A — presence,** un aspetto imponente, *m.*; **a — manner,** una maniera autoritaria, *f.*; **— officer,** comandante, *m.*
commandingly, *adv.* Autoritariamente, imperiosamente.
commandment, *n.* Comandamento, *m.*
commando [kə'mɑ:ndou], *n.* (*Mil.*) Reparto di truppe d'assalto; un soldato di questo, *m.*
commemorable [kə'memərəbl], *a.* Commemorabile, memorabile.
commemorate, *v.t.* Commemorare, celebrare.
commemoration, *n.* Commemorazione, *f.*
commemorative, *a.* Commemorativo.
commence [kə'mens], *v.t.* Cominciare, incominciare, iniziare, principiare; *v.i.* cominciare, mettersi a. **To — one's duties,** iniziare il proprio servizio.
commencement, *n.* Cominciamento, principio, inizio, *m.*
commend [kə'mend], *v.t.* Commendare, lodare; raccomandare, (*to entrust*) affidare.
commendable, *a.* Lodevole, raccomandabile.
commendably, *adv.* Lodevolmente.
commendam [kə'mendæm], *n.* (*Eccles.*) Commenda, *f.*

commendation, *n.* Lode, *f.*, elogio, *m.*; raccomandazione, *f.*
commendatory, *a.* Laudatorio.
commensal [kəˈmensəl], *n.* Commensale, *m.*
commensurability [kəmenʃərəˈbiliti], *n.* (*Math.*) Commensurabilità, *f.*
commensurable, *a.* Commensurabile, commisurabile.
commensurate, *a.* Proporzionato.
commensurately, *adv.* Proporzionatamente.
commensuration, *n.* Commisurazione, *f.*
comment [ˈkɔment], *n.* Commento, *m.*, nota, *f.* || *v.i.* Commentare; criticare. **To pass comments on,** criticare, fare osservazioni.
commentary, *n.* Commento, commentario, *m.*, annotazioni, *f.pl.*
commentator, *n.* Commentatore, chiosatore, *m.*; (*Radio*) cronista radiofonico, *m.*
commerce [ˈkɔməːs], *n.* Commercio, *m.*; traffico, *m.*; affari, *m.pl.*
commercial, *a.* Commerciale. **— law,** diritto commerciale, *m.*; **— treaty,** trattato di commercio, *m.*; **— traveller,** commesso viaggiatore, *m.*
commercialism, *n.* Commercialismo, *m.*
commercialize, *v.t.* Mettere in commercio, commerciare.
commercially, *adv.* Commercialmente.
commination [kɔmiˈneiʃən], *n.* Comminazione, *f.*
commingle [kəˈmiŋgl], *v.t.* Mischiare, mescolare, confondere; *v.i.* mescolarsi, mischiarsi.
comminute [ˈkɔminuːt], *v.t.* Ridurre in frantumi. (*Med.*) **Comminuted fracture,** frattura comminuta, *f.*
commiserate [kəˈmizəreit], *v.t.* Commiserare, compassionare, compiangere.
commiseration, *n.* Commiserazione, *f.*
commissariat [kɔmiˈsɛəriət], *n.* Commissariato, *m.*
commissary, *n.* Commissario, *m.*
commission [kəˈmiʃən], *n.* Commissione, *f.*, incarico, *m.*; perpetrazione (*of an act*), *f.*; (*Mil.*) brevetto, *m.*; (*Law*) mandato, *m.* || *v.t.* Incaricare, autorizzare, commissionare. **— agent,** commissionario, *m.*; (*Naut.*) **in —,** armato e fornito d'equipaggio; **on —,** su commissione; **commissioned officer,** ufficiale effettivo, *m.*
commissionaire, *n.* Portiere, *m.*
commissioner, *n.* Commissario, *m.* (*Law*) **— in bankruptcy,** curatore di fallimento, *m.*
commissure [ˈkɔmiʃuːə], *n.* (*Anat.*) Commessura, *f.*
commit [kəˈmit], *v.t.* Commettere, perpetrare; affidare, consegnare; mandare (*to prison*). **To — oneself,** impegnarsi; compromettersi; **to — for trial,** rinviare alle assise; **to — to memory,** imparare a memoria; **to — to writing,** mettere in iscritto.
committal, commitment [kəˈmitəl, kəˈmitmənt], *n.* Consegna, *f.*; impegno, *m.*; rinvio ad una commissione, *f.* **My commitments don't allow me to,** i miei impegni non mi permettono di.
committee [kəˈmiti], *n.* Comitato, *m.*; commissione, *f.* **— meeting,** adunanza di comitato, *f.*; **— room,** sala di commissione, *f.*; **select —,** comitato speciale, *m.*
commode [kəˈmoud], *n.* Comò, cassettone, *m.*, seggietta, *f.*, comodino, *m.*
commodious, *a.* Comodo, conveniente.
commodiously, *adv.* Comodamente.
commodiousness, *n.* Comodità, *f.*
commodity [kəˈmɔditi], *n.* Merce, derrata, *f.*, prodotto, *m.*
commodore [ˈkɔmədɔːə], *n.* Commodoro, *m.*
common [ˈkɔmən], *a.* Comune; ordinario, volgare; pubblico; inferiore; semplice, tipico. || *n.* Terreno pubblico, *m.*; brughiera, *f.* **— people,** il basso popolo, *m.*, la plebe, *f.*; **Book of Common Prayer,** libro di liturgia anglicana, *m.*; **— sense,** senso comune, *m.*; (*Mus.*) **— time,** tempo ordinario, *m.*; **in —,** in comune; **out of the —,** straordinario, insolito, fuori del comune; **to have nothing in — with,** non avere niente in comune con; **to live in —,** vivere in comune; **to make — cause with,** far causa comune con.
commonalty, *n.* Comunanza, *f.*; popolo, *m.*
commoner, *n.* (*Pol.*) Membro dei Comuni; (*Univ.*) studente non borsista; borghese, *m.*
commonly, *adv.* Generalmente, comunemente, in comune; ordinariamente; meschinamente.
commonplace [ˈkɔmənpleis], *a.* Comune, banale, triviale. || *n.* Banalità. **— book,** raccolta di poesie scelte, *f.*
commons, *n.pl.* Razione di cibo, *f.*; (*Pol.*) la Camera dei Comuni, *f.* **Short —,** una scarsa razione, *f.*
commonweal [ˈkɔmənwiːl], *n.* Bene pubblico, *m.*
commonwealth [ˈkɔmənwelθ], *n.* Stato, *m.*, comunità, *f.*
commotion [kəˈmouʃən], *n.* Disturbo, tumulto, movimento, *m.*
communal [ˈkɔmuːnəl], *a.* Comunale.
commune (1) [kəˈmjuːn], *v.i.* Conversare, intrattenersi con, conferire. **To — with one's thoughts,** meditare.
commune (2) [ˈkɔmjuːn], *n.* (*Hist.*) Comune, *m.*
communicable [kəˈmjuːnikəbl], *a.* Comunicabile.
communicant, *n.* Comunicante, *m.*; (*Eccles.*) comunicando, *m.*
communicate, *v.t.* Comunicare, far conoscere; partecipare; *v.i.* comunicare, comunicarsi; (*Eccles.*) comunicarsi.
communication, *n.* Comunicazione, *f.*, rapporto, *m.*; notizia, *f.*, comunicato, *m.* **— cord,** segnale d'allarme, *m.*
communicative, *a.* Comunicativo, espansivo.
communicator, *n.* Comunicatore, *m.*; (*Mech.*) avvisatore, *m.*
communion, *n.* Comunione, *f.*; (*Eccles.*) santa comunione, *f.* **—-cup,** calice, *m.*; **—-table,** altare, *m.*
Communism [ˈkɔmjuːnizm], *n.* Comunismo, *m.*
Communist, *n.* Comunista, *m.*
community, *n.* Comunità, società, *f.*, comune, *m.*
commutable [kəˈmjuːtəbl], *a.* Commutabile.
commutation, *n.* Commutazione, *f.*
commutator, *n.* (*Elect.*) Commutatore, *m.*
commute, *v.t.* Commutare.
compact (1) [kəmˈpækt], *a.* Compatto, denso, spesso, serrato, conciso.
compact (2) [ˈkɔmpækt], *n.* Patto, accordo, *m.*, alleanza, *f.*; (*for face powder*) cipria compatta, *f.*

compactly, *adv.* In modo compatto, concisamente.
compactness, *n.* Compattezza, concisione, *f.*; densità, *f.*
companion [kəmˈpænjən], *n.* Compagno, *m.*, compagna, *f.*, socio, camerata, *m.*; (*lady's*) dama di compagnia, *f.*; (*Naut.*) caposcala, *m.*, scala di cabina, *f.*
companionable, *a.* Socievole, compagnevole.
companionably, *adv.* Socievolmente.
companionship, *n.* Compagnia, società, *f.*, cameratismo, *m.*
company [ˈkʌmpəni], *n.* Compagnia, società, *f.*; comitiva, brigata, *f.*; (*Mil.*) compagnia, *f.*; (*Naut.*) equipaggio, *m.*; (*Comm.*) società anonima, *f.* **To request someone's —,** invitare qualcuno a; **to keep —,** tenere compagnia a; (*colloq.*) **to keep — with,** corteggiare; **to keep bad —,** essere male accompagnato, frequentare cattive compagnie; **to part —,** allontanarsi l'uno dall'altro; **we parted —,** ci separammo; **to make one of the —,** essere della partita.
comparable, *a.* Comparabile, paragonabile.
comparative, *n.a.* Comparativo, *m.*
comparatively, *adv.* Comparativamente, relativamente.
compare [kəmˈpɛəɹ], *v.t.* Comparare, paragonare, confrontare; *v.i.* competere, rivaleggiare. **Compared with,** in confronto a, a paragone di; **beyond —,** senza confronto, senza paragone; **not to be compared to,** da non paragonarsi con; **to — notes,** far uno scambio d'idee.
comparison, *n.* Confronto, paragone, *m.*, comparazione, *f.* **Beyond —,** senza confronto; **in — with,** in confronto a; **there's no —,** non c'è confronto.
compartment [kəmˈpɑːɹtmənt], *n.* Compartimento, scompartimento, *m.*, suddivisione, *f.* **Water-tight —,** paratia stagna, *f.*
compass [ˈkʌmpəs], *n.* Circonferenza, cinta, estensione, *f.*; circolo, *m.*, limiti, *m.pl.*; (*Naut.*) bussola, *f.*; (*of voice*) registro, *m.* || *v.t.* Circondare, andare attorno; inventare, complottare. **A pair of compasses,** un compasso, *m.*; **to keep within —,** moderarsi, tenersi nei limiti del dovere; **within —,** con misura; **to — someone's death,** complottare la morte di qualcuno; **to — about,** assediare; **compassed about with perils,** circondato da pericoli; **—-card,** rosa dei venti, *f.*; **—-needle,** ago della bussola, *m.*
compassion [kəmˈpæʃən], *n.* Compassione, pietà, *f.*
compassionate, *a.* Pieno di compassione. || *v.t.* Compassionare, compatire con, aver pietà di.
compassionately, *adv.* Con compassione, con pietà.
compatibility [kəmpætiˈbiliti], *n.* Compatibilità, *f.*
compatible, *a.* Compatibile.
compatibly, *adv.* Compatibilmente.
compatriot [kəmˈpætriət], *n.* Compatriota, *m.f.*
compeer [kɔmˈpiəɹ], *n.* Uguale, pari, compagno, camerata, *m.*
compel [kəmˈpel], *v.t.* Costringere, sforzare, obbligare.
compellable, *a.* Coercibile.
compendious [kəmˈpendiəs], *a.* Compendioso, breve, succinto, conciso.
compendiousness, *n.* Brevità, concisione, *f.*
compendium [kəmˈpendiəm], *n.* Compendio, sunto, sommario, *m.*
compensate [ˈkɔmpenseit], *v.t.* Compensare, rimunerare; *v.i.* compensarsi.
compensation, *n.* Compensazione, ricompensa, *f.*
compensatory, compensating, *a.* Compensativo.
compete [kəmˈpiːt], *v.i.* Competere, gareggiare, venire in gara con, far concorrenza. **To — for a prize,** concorrere a un premio.
competence, competency, *n.* Capacità, abilità, *f.*; competenza, *f.*; (*fig.*) agiatezza, *f.*, agio, *m.* **To have a —,** avere una rendita sufficiente, avere di che vivere.
competent, *a.* Capace, abile; competente. **To be — to do,** essere capace a fare.
competently, *adv.* Abilmente, in modo conveniente.
competition [kɔmpiˈtiʃən], *n.* Competizione, gara, concorrenza, *f.*, concorso, *m.* **To come into — with,** gareggiare con; **to offer for —,** bandire un concorso per.
competitive, *a.* Competitivo. **A — examination,** un esame di concorso, *m.*; **the — system,** la concorrenza, *f.*
competitor, *n.* Competitore, concorrente, *m.*
compilation, *n.* Compilazione, raccolta, *f.*
compile [kəmˈpail], *v.t.* Compilare.
compiler, *n.* Compilatore, *m.*
complacence, complacency [kəmˈpleisəns, kəmˈpleisənsi], *n.* Compiacenza, soddisfazione, *f.*
complacent, *a.* Compiacente, soddisfatto.
complacently, *adv.* Compiacentemente.
complain [kəmˈplein], *v.i.* Lagnarsi, lamentarsi, dolersi; (*fig.*) piangere; (*Law*) sporgere querela, dar querela.
complainant, *n.* (*Law*) Querelante, accusatore, *m.*
complaint, *n.* Lamento, *m.*, lagnanza, *f.*; (*illness*) malattia, *f.*, disturbo, *m.*; (*Law*) richiamo, *m.* **Cause of —,** motivo di lagnanza, *m.*; **to lodge a —,** sporgere querela, dar querela.
complaisance [kəmˈpleisəns], *n.* Compiacenza, *f.*
complaisant, *a.* Compiacente.
complaisantly, *adv.* Compiacentemente.
complement [ˈkɔmpləmənt], *n.* Complemento, *m.*
complementary, *a.* Complementare.
complete [kəmˈpliːt], *a.* Completo, compiuto; terminato, finito; assoluto, intiero. || *v.t.* Completare, compire, terminare, finire.
completely, *adv.* Completamente, assolutamente.
completeness, *n.* Perfezione, pienezza, *f.*
completion, *n.* Completamento, compimento, *m.*
complex [ˈkɔmpleks], *a.* Complesso; complicato, imbrogliato. || *n.* Complesso, aggregato, *m.* **To have a —,** avere un'idea fissa; **to have an inferiority —,** avere un complesso di inferiorità.
complexion, *n.* Carnagione, *f.*; (*fig.*) carattere, aspetto, *m.* **To put a different — on,** mostrare sotto un diverso aspetto.
complexity, *n.* Complessità, *f.*

compliance [kəm'plaiəns], *n.* Consentimento, consenso, *m.*, conformità, *f.* **In — with,** in conformità con.
compliant, *a.* Remissivo, docile, ubbidiente; accomodante.
complicate ['kɔmplikeit], *v.t.* Complicare, imbrogliare. **To — matters,** imbrogliare le cose.
complicated, *a.* Complicato.
complication, *n.* Complicazione, *f.*
complicity [kɔm'plisiti], *n.* Complicità, *f.*
compliment ['kɔmplimənt], *n.* Complimento, *m.*, lode, *f.*; ossequio, *m.* || *v.t.* Congratularsi con, felicitare, lodare. **Compliments of the season,** auguri (di Natale, ecc.), *m.pl.*; **to pay a —,** fare un complimento; **with the author's compliments,** omaggio dell'autore, *m.*
complimentary, *a.* Di felicitazione; di favore; di lode. **A — ticket,** un biglietto di favore, *m.*
compline, complin ['kɔmplin], *n.* (*Eccles.*) Compieta, *f.*
comply [kɔm'plai], *v.i.* Piegarsi, ubbidire, acconsentire. **To — with a request,** soddisfare una domanda.
component [kəm'pounənt], *a.* Componente, costitutivo. || *n.* (*Chem.*) Componente, corpo costitutivo, *m.* **— parts,** parti componenti, pezzi staccati, *m.pl.*
comport [kəm'pɔːɹt], *v.i.* Accordarsi con, convenire a. **To — oneself,** comportarsi.
comportment, *n.* Comportamento, *m.*, condotta, *f.*
compose [kəm'pouz], *v.t.* Comporre, inventare, formare. **To — oneself,** comporsi, calmarsi, rimettersi, raccogliersi.
composed, *a.* Composto; calmo, tranquillo; pacifico, sereno.
composedly, *adv.* Tranquillamente.
composedness, *n.* Compostezza, calma, serietà, *f.*
composer, *n.* (*Mus.*) Compositore, *m.*; autore, *m.*; (*of differences*) conciliatore, *m.*
composing, *a.* (*Med.*) Calmante. **— draught,** un calmante, *m.*; (*Print.*) **— -room,** stanza dei compositori, *f.*; **— -stick,** compositoio, *m.*
composite ['kɔmpəsit], *a.* Composto, composito.
composition, *n.* Composizione, *f.*, componimento, *m.*; saggio, *m.*; natura, *f.*; (*Comm.*) concordato, accomodamento, *m.*
compositor, *n.* (*Print.*) Compositore, *m.*
compost ['kɔmpɔst], *n.* (*Agric.*) Concime, *m.*
composure [kəm'pouʒuːɹ], *n.* Calma, tranquillità, compostezza, *f.*, sangue freddo, *m.*
compotation [kɔmpɔ'teiʃən], *n.* Libazione, *f.*
compound (1) ['kɔmpaund], *n.* Composto, *m.*, mescolanza, composizione, *f.*; recinto, campo di concentramento, *m.* || *a.* Composto, composito. **— interest,** interesse composto, *m.*
compound (2) [kəm'paund], *v.t.* Comporre, mescolare, combinare; *v.i.* accordarsi, transigere. **To — a felony,** farsi complice d'un delitto grave; **to — with one's conscience,** transigere colla propria coscienza.
compounder, *n.* Compositore, conciliatore, *m.*
comprehend [kɔmpri'hend], *v.t.* Comprendere, capire.
comprehensible, *a.* Comprensibile, intelligibile.
comprehension, *n.* Comprensione, *f.* **Beyond our —,** al di là della nostra comprensione.
comprehensive, *a.* Comprensivo, esteso.
comprehensively, *adv.* Comprensivamente, estesamente.
comprehensiveness, *n.* Comprensione, estensione, portata, *f.*
compress (1) ['kɔmpres], *n.* (*Med.*) Compressa, *f.*
compress (2) [kəm'pres], *v.t.* Comprimere, premere, condensare. **Compressed air,** aria compressa, *f.*
compressible, *a.* Comprimibile.
compression, *n.* Compressione, *f.*
compressor, *n.* (*Mech.*) Compressore, *m.*
comprise [kəm'praiz], *v.t.* Comprendere, contenere, abbracciare.
compromise ['kɔmprɔmaiz], *n.* Compromesso, accordo, *m.*, convenzione, *f.* || *v.t.* Accomodare; *v.i.* transigere. **To — oneself,** compromettersi.
compromising, *a.* Compromettente; dubbio. **A — situation,** una situazione molto imbarazzante, *f.*
comptometer [kɔm'tɔmətəɹ], *n.* Calcolatrice, *f.*
comptroller [kɔn'troulәɹ], *n.* Controllore, *m.* [cp. **controller**].
compulsion [kəm'pʌlʃən], *n.* Costrizione, *f.*, obbligo, *m.*
compulsive, *a.* Coercitivo.
compulsorily [kəm'pʌlsərili], *adv.* Per forza, forzatamente.
compulsory, *a.* Obbligatorio.
compunction [kəm'pʌŋkʃən], *n.* Compunzione, *f.*, rimorso, *m.*
computable [kəm'pjuːtəbl], *a.* Computabile, calcolabile.
computation, *n.* Computazione, *f.*, computo, *m.*
compute, *v.t.* Computare, calcolare, contare.
comrade ['kɔmrəd], *n.* Camerata, compagno, *m.*
comradeship, *n.* Cameratismo, *m.*, amicizia, *f.*
con (1) [kɔn], *n.* Il contro, *m.* **Pros and cons,** il pro e il contro.
con (2), *v.t.* Studiare, leggere, ripassare; (*Naut.*) governare.
concatenate [kɔn'kætineit], *v.t.* Concatenare, collegare, congiungere.
concatenation, *n.* Concatenamento, *m.*
concave ['kɔnkeiv], *a.* Concavo, cavo.
concavity [kən'kæviti], *n.* Concavità, *f.*
conceal [kən'siːl], *v.t.* Celare, nascondere, occultare; tener segreto; dissimulare, sopprimere.
concealable, *a.* Che si può nascondere.
concealment, *n.* Occultazione, *f.*, nascondimento, *m.*; (*hiding-place*) nascondiglio, *m.* **In —,** in segreto.
concede [kən'siːd], *v.t.* Concedere, accordare, ammettere. **To — the point,** ammettere una cosa; **to — a right,** concedere un diritto.
conceit [kən'siːt], *n.* Vanità, *f.*; amor proprio, *m.*, boria, albagia, *f.*; idea, fantasia, *f.*, pensiero, *m.* **To be out of — with oneself,** essere stufo di se stesso; **without —,** senza vanità; **a quaint —,** un pensiero grazioso, *m.*
conceited, *a.* Vanitoso, borioso, affettato. **To be —,** esser pieno di sè.
conceitedly, *adv.* Boriosamente, presuntuosamente.

conceitedness, *n.* Vanità, presunzione, *f.*
conceivable, *a.* Concepibile, intelligibile.
conceivably, *adv.* In modo concepibile. **You cannot — mean that,** non è possibile che voi vogliate dire quello.
conceive [kən'si:v], *v.t.i.* Concepire; comprendere, immaginare, pensare; esprimere.
concentrate ['kɔnsentreit], *v.t.* Concentrare; *v.i.* concentrarsi, raccogliersi.
concentration, *n.* Concentrazione, *f.* **— camp,** campo di concentramento, *m.*
concentric [kən'sentrik], *a.* Concentrico.
concept ['kɔnsept], *n.* Concetto, *m.*
conception [kən'sepʃən], *n.* Concezione, *f.*; idea, *f.*; concetto, *m.*
conceptive, *a.* Concettivo.
conceptual [kən'septu:əl], *a.* Concettuale.
concern [kən'sə:ɹn], *n.* Interesse, *m.*; ansietà, sollecitudine, *f.*; affare, *m.*; (*Comm.*) impresa, azienda, *f.*; (*colloq.*) cosa, *f.* || *v.t.* Riguardare, interessare, concernere; toccare. **That is my —,** questo è affare mio; **that's no — of yours,** ciò non vi riguarda; **he has a — in the business,** ha un interesse nell'azienda; **with great —,** con grande ansietà; **it concerns me to know,** m'importa di sapere; **to all whom it may —,** a tutti gl'interessati; **to be concerned about,** preoccuparsi di *or* per; **I am concerned about my mother's health,** la salute di mia madre mi preoccupa.
concernedly, *adv.* Ansiosamente, con interesse, con sollecitudine.
concerning, *prep.* Riguardo a, riguardante, relativo a.
concernment, *n.* Interesse, affare, *m.*, importanza, sollecitudine, *f.*
concert (1) [kən'sə:ɹt], *v.t.* Concertare; *v.i.* accordarsi, intendersi.
concert (2) ['kɔnsəɹt], *n.* Concerto, *m.* **In —,** di concerto; (*Mus.*) **—-pitch,** diapason da concerto, *m.*; **—-room,** sala da concerto, *f.*
concerted, *a.* (*Mus.*) Concertato.
concertina [kɔnsəɹ'ti:nə], *n.* Fisarmonica, *f.*
concerto [kɔn'tʃəɹtou], *n.* (*Mus.*) Concerto, *m.*
concession [kən'seʃən], *n.* Concessione, *f.*
concessionary, concessionaire, *n.* Concessionario, *m.*
conch [kɔŋk], *n.* (*Zool.*) Conchiglia, *f.*
concha ['kɔŋkə], *n.* (*Anat.*) Conca, *f.*
conchiferous [kɔŋ'kifərəs], *a.* (*Geol.*) Conchifero.
conchoid, *n.* Concoide, *f.*
conchologist, *n.* Conchigliologista, *m.*
conchology, *n.* Conchigliologia, *f.*
conciliate [kən'silieit], *v.t.* Conciliare.
conciliation, *n.* Conciliazione, *f.*
conciliator, *n.* Conciliatore, *m.*
conciliatory, *a.* Conciliativo.
concise [kən'sais], *a.* Conciso.
concisely, *adv.* Concisamente.
concision [kən'siʒən], *n.* Concisione, *f.*
conclave ['kɔnkleiv], *n.* Conclave, *m.*; (*fig.*) adunanza segreta, *f.*
conclavist, *n.* (*Eccles.*) Conclavista, *m.*
conclude [kɔn'klju:d], *v.t.* Concludere, conchiudere, terminare, finire; dedurre, inferire; *v.i.* terminare.
concluding, *a.* Finale, ultimo.
conclusion, *n.* Conclusione, fine, *f.*; deduzione, *f.*, argomento, *m.*; decisione, *f.* **In —,** in conclusione, insomma; **to try conclusions with,** dibattere una questione con, misurarsi con.
conclusive, *a.* Conclusivo, finale.
conclusively, *adv.* Conclusivamente.
conclusiveness, *n.* Carattere conclusivo, *m.*
concoct [kɔn'kɔkt], *v.t.* Preparare, macchinare, complottare.
concoction, *n.* Mistura, mescolanza, *f.*; preparato, intruglio, *m.*
concomitance [kɔn'kɔmitəns], *n.* Concomitanza, *f.*
concomitant, *n.* Accompagnamento, *m.* || *a.* Concomitante.
concomitantly, *adv.* Congiuntamente.
concord (1) ['kɔnkɔ:ɹd], *n.* Accordo, *m.*, armonia, *f.*; (*Gram.*) concordanza, *f.*
concord (2) [kən'kɔ:ɹd], *v.i.* Accordarsi, concordare.
concordance, *n.* Concordanza, *f.*, concordanze, *f.pl.*
concordant, *a.* Concorde, consenziente.
concordat, *n.* (*Hist.*) Concordato, *m.*
concourse ['kɔnkɔ:ɹs], *n.* Concorso, *m.*, folla, *f.*; affluenza, *f.*
concrescence [kən'kresəns], *n.* (*Biol.*) Concrescenza, *f.*
concrete ['kɔnkri:t], *n.* Cemento, calcestruzzo, *m.*; (*opposed to abstract*) il concreto, *m.* || *a.* Concreto. || *v.t.* Rendere concreto, concretare, cementare. **Reinforced —,** cemento armato, *m.*
concretely, *adv.* In concreto.
concreteness, *n.* Concretezza, *f.*
concretion, *n.* Concrezione, *f.*
concubinage [kən'kju:binədʒ], *n.* Concubinato, *m.*
concubine ['kɔnkju:bain], *n.* Concubina, *f.*
concupiscence [kən'kju:pisens], *n.* Concupiscenza, *f.*
concupiscent, *a.* Concupiscente.
concur [kən'kə:ɹ], *v.i.* Accordarsi, convenire con, concordare con.
concurrence, *n.* Accordo, assentimento, *m.*, adesione, coincidenza, *f.*
concurrent, *a.* Concorrente, d'accordo.
concurrently, *adv.* Insieme, di pari passo.
concussion [kən'kʌʃən], *n.* Scossa, *f.*, urto, *m.*; concussione, *f.* **— of the brain,** commozione cerebrale, *f.*
concussive, *a.* Che agita, che scuote.
condemn [kən'dem], *v.t.* Condannare; biasimare.
condemnable [kən'demnəbl], *a.* Condannabile.
condemnation, *n.* Condanna, *f.*, biasimo, *m.*
condemnatory, *a.* Condannatorio.
condemner [kən'deməɹ], *n.* Condannatore, biasimatore, *m.*
condensable [kən'densəbl], *a.* Condensabile.
condensation [kɔnden'seiʃən], *n.* Condensazione, *f.*
condense [kən'dens], *v.t.* Condensare, concentrare; (*fig.*) abbreviare, compendiare; *v.i.* condensarsi. **Condensed milk,** latte condensato, *m.*
condenser, *n.* Condensatore, *m.*
condescend [kɔndi'send], *v.i.* Accondiscendere, abbassarsi; degnare di.
condescending, *a.* Condiscendente, arrendevole, compiacente.
condescendingly, *adv.* Compiacentemente.

condescension, *n.* Condiscendenza, compiacenza, *f.*
condign [kən'dain], *a.* Condegno; adeguato, giusto.
condignly, *adv.* Giustamente.
condiment ['kɔndimənt], *n.* Condimento, *m.*
condition [kən'diʃən], *n.* Condizione, *f.*, stato, *m.* ‖ *v.t.* Condizionare. **In a — to,** in istato di; **in good —,** in buono stato; **on — that,** a condizione che.
conditional, *a.* Condizionale. ‖ *n.* (*Gram.*) Condizionale, *m.*
conditionally, *adv.* Condizionalmente, condizionatamente, sotto condizione.
conditioned, *a.* Condizionato, sistemato. **Well- —,** ben condizionato.
condole [kən'doul], *v.i.* Fare le proprie condoglianze, rammaricarsi, dolersi, condolersi con. **To — with someone on,** fare a qualcuno le proprie condoglianze per.
condolence, *n.* Condoglianza, *f.*
condonation [kɔndə'neiʃən], *n.* Condonazione, *f.*
condone, *v.t.* Condonare, perdonare.
condor ['kɔndəɹ], *n.* (*Zool.*) Condore, *m.*
conduce [kən'dju:s], *v.i.* Contribuire, tendere.
conducive, *a.* Che contribuisce, favorevole. **To be — to,** essere tale da promuovere.
conduciveness, *n.* Utilità, *f.*, vantaggio, *m.*; efficacia, *f.*
conduct (1) ['kɔndʌkt], *n.* Condotta, *f.*, contegno, *m.*; amministrazione, (*of affairs*), *f.*, maneggio, *m.* **Safe- —,** salvacondotto, *m.*
conduct (2) [kən'dʌkt], *v.t.* Condurre, menare, guidare; (*Mus.*) dirigere. **To — an affair,** trattare un affare; **to — a business,** dirigere un'impresa; **to — oneself well, badly,** comportarsi correttamente, scorrettamente.
conducting, *a.* Conducente.
conductor, *n.* Conduttore, *m.*; (*of business or orchestra*) direttore, *m.*; guida, *m.*; (*of bus, tram, etc.*) fattorino, bigliettaio, *m.* **Lightning- —,** parafulmine, *m.*; (*Elect., etc.*) **non- —,** cattivo conduttore, coibente, *m.*
conductress, *n.* Conduttrice, *f.*; (*of bus*) bigliettaia, *f.*
conduit ['kʌndit], *n.* Condotto, canale, tubo, *m.*
condyle ['kɔndil], *n.* (*Anat.*) Condilo, *m.*
cone [koun], *n.* (*Geom.Zool.*) Cono, *m.*; (*Bot.*) pina, pigna, *f.*; (*ice-cream*) cialdone, *m.* **—-shaped,** conico.
coney [cp. **cony**].
confab ['kɔnfæb], *n.* (*colloq.*) Colloquio a quattr'occhi, *m.*
confabulate [kən'fæbju:leit], *v.i.* Confabulare, chiacchierare in disparte.
confabulation, *n.* Confabulazione, *f.*
confection [kən'fekʃən], *n.* Confetto, *m.*; (*garment*) confezione, *f.*
confectioner, *n.* Confettiere, pasticciere, *m.* **Confectioner's shop,** pasticceria, *f.*
confectionery, *n.* Pasticceria, *f.*; pasticci, dolci, *m.pl.*
confederacy [kən'fedərəsi], *n.* (*Pol.*) Confederazione *f.*; cospirazione, congiura, *f.*
confederate [kən'fedəreit], *v.t.* Confederare; *v.i.* confederarsi. ‖ *a.* Confederato, alleato. ‖ *n.* Confederato, alleato; complice, correo, *m.*
confederation, *n.* Confederazione, *f.*
confer [kən'fə:ɹ], *v.t.* Conferire, accordare, donare; *v.i.* conferire, discorrere, abboccarsi con. **To — an honour on,** conferire un onore a.
conference, *n.* Conferenza, *f.*, abboccamento, *m.*; adunanza, *f.*
conferva [kən'fə:ɹvə], *n.* (*Bot.*) Conferva, *f.*
confess [kən'fes], *v.t.* Confessare, ammettere, riconoscere; (*Eccles.*) (*to hear a confession*) confessare; *v.i.* confessarsi. **To — one's faith,** professare la propria fede.
confessedly, *adv.* Apertamente.
confession, *n.* Confessione, *f.*; dichiarazione, *f.* **To go to —,** andare a confessarsi; **under seal of —,** sotto il sigillo della confessione.
confessional, *n.* (*Eccles.*) Confessionale, *m.*
confessor, *n.* Confessore, *m.* **Father —,** direttore spirituale, *m.*
confidant ['kɔnfidənt], *n.* Confidente, *m.f.*
confide [kən'faid], *v.t.* Confidare, affidare; *v.i.* confidarsi, affidarsi. **To — one's secrets,** confidarsi.
confidence, *n.* Confidenza, fiducia, sicurezza, baldanza, *f.* **In —,** in confidenza; **to have — in,** avere fiducia in; **— trick,** truffa all'americana, *f.*
confident, *a.* Confidente, sicuro.
confidential [kɔnfi'denʃəl], *a.* Confidenziale, intimo.
confidentially, *adv.* Confidenzialmente, in confidenza.
confidently, *adv.* Con sicurezza, confidentemente.
confiding, *a.* Fiducioso.
configuration [kənfigu:reiʃən], *n.* Configurazione, *f.*
confine [kən'fain], *v.t.* Confinare, rinchiudere, relegare; imprigionare; limitare. **To — oneself,** limitarsi; **to be confined to one's room,** star ritirato perchè indisposto; **to be confined** (*in childbirth*), partorire.
confinement, *n.* Imprigionamento, *m.*, detenzione, *f.*; parto, *m.* **In close —,** recluso; **solitary —,** segregazione cellulare, *f.*
confines ['kɔnfainz], *n.pl.* Confini, *m.pl.*
confirm [kən'fə:ɹm], *v.t.* Confermare; corroborare, convalidare; ratificare; (*Eccles.*) cresimare.
confirmation, *n.* Conferma, *f.*; (*Eccles.*) cresima, *f.*; affermazione, prova, *f.*
confirmatory, *a.* Confermativo, confermatorio, di conferma.
confirmed, *a.* Inveterato. **A — liar,** un bugiardo matricolato; **a — invalid,** un infermo da molti anni, un incurabile.
confiscate ['kɔnfiskeit], *v.t.* Confiscare.
confiscation, *n.* Confisca, *f.*
confiscatory, *a.* Confiscatorio.
conflagration [kɔnflə'greiʃən], *n.* Conflagrazione, *f.*, incendio, *m.*
conflict (1) ['kɔnflikt], *n.* Conflitto, combattimento, contrasto, *m.*, lotta, *f.* **— of opinion,** conflitto di opinioni, *m.*
conflict (2) [kən'flikt], *v.i.* Combattere, venire a conflitto.
conflicting, *a.* Opposto, contrario, contraddittorio.
confluence ['kɔnflu:əns], *n.* Confluenza *f.*, concorso, *m.*
confluent, *a.* Confluente. ‖ *n.* Affluente, *m.*

conform [kən'fɔːm], *v.t.* Conformare; *v.i.* conformarsi.
conformable, *a.* Conformabile, conforme.
conformably, *adv.* Conformemente, in conformità.
conformation, *n.* Conformazione, forma, *f.*
conformity, *n.* Conformità, *f.*
confound [kən'faund], *v.t.* Confondere, mischiare; turbare, sconcertare. **— him!** Che il diavolo se lo porti! **— it!** Diamine!
confounded, *a.* Maledetto, malaugurato.
confoundedly, *adv.* Terribilmente.
confraternity [kɔnfrə'təːɹniti], *n.* Confraternita, congregazione, *f.*
confrere ['kɔnfrɛəɹ], *n.* Confratello, collega, *m.*
confront [kən'frʌnt], *v.t.* Confrontare, riscontrare; affrontare, tener testa a; (*Law*) mettere a confronto.
confrontation, *n.* Confronto, riscontro, *m.*
confuse [kən'fjuːz], *v.t.* Confondere, mescolare, imbrogliare; turbare, sconcertare.
confused, *a.* Confuso, turbato, perplesso.
confusedly, *adv.* Confusamente, in confuso, alla rinfusa.
confusedness, *n.* Confusione, disordine, *f.*
confusion, *n.* Confusione, *f.*; perplessità, *f.*, imbarazzo, *m.*; tumulto, *m.* **In —,** alla rinfusa; **— worse confounded,** imbroglio sopra imbroglio.
confutation [kɔnfjuː'teiʃən], *n.* Confutazione, *f.*
confute, *v.t.* Confutare.
congeal [kən'dʒiːl], *v.i.* Congelarsi, rappigliarsi, gelarsi; *v.t.* congelare, gelare, agghiacciare.
congealment, congelation, *n.* Congelamento, *m.*, congelazione, *f.*
congenial [kən'dʒiːniəl], *a.* Simpatico, congeniale; confacente. **A — task,** un lavoro congeniale, *m.*
congeniality, *n.* Congenialità, simpatia, *f.*
congenital [kən'dʒenitəl], *a.* Congenito.
conger, conger eel ['kɔŋgəɹ, kɔŋgəɹ'iːl], *n.* (*Zool.*) Grongo, *m.*
congeries [kən'dʒeriiːz], *n.* Congerie, *f.*, mucchio, *m.*
congest [kən'dʒest], *v.t.* Accumulare, addensare; (*Med.*) congestionare.
congested, *a.* Addensato. **The traffic is very —,** il traffico è molto congestionato.
congestion, *n.* Massa, *f.*; congestione, *f.* (*Med.*) **— of the lungs,** congestione polmonare, *f.*
congestive, *a.* Che produce congestione.
conglobate, *a.* Conglobato.
conglomerate [kən'glɔməreit], *a.* Conglomerato. || *n.* (*Geol.*) Conglomerati, *m.pl.* || *v.t.* Conglomerare.
conglomeration, *n.* Conglomerazione, *f.*
conglutinate [kən'gluːtineit], *v.t.* Conglutinare.
congratulate [kən'grætjuːleit], *v.t.* Congratularsi con, felicitarsi, rallegrarsi. **I — you,** mi rallegro con voi, vi faccio le mie congratulazioni; **to — oneself,** rallegrarsi con se stesso.
congratulation, *n.* Congratulazione, felicitazione, *f.*, rallegramento, *m.*
congratulatory, *a.* Congratulatorio di felicitazione.
congregate ['kɔŋgrigeit], *v.t.* Congregare, radunare; *v.i.* adunarsi, riunirsi.
congregation, *n.* Congregazione, adunanza, *f.*
congregational, *a.* Di congregazione.
Congregationalism, *n.* (*Eccles.*) Sistema di una chiesa protestante indipendente.
congress ['kɔŋgres], *n.* Congresso, *m.* **—-man,** congressista, *m.*
congressional, *a.* Congressistico.
congruence ['kɔŋgruːəns], *n.* Congruenza, *f.*; convenienza, *f.*
congruent, *a.* Congruente.
congruity, *n.* Congruità, *f.*
congruous, *a.* Congruo, conveniente.
congruously, *adv.* Congruamente, in modo conveniente.
conic, conical, *a.* Conico.
conically, *adv.* Conicamente.
conics, *n.pl.* (*Math.*) Sezioni coniche, *f.pl.*
conifer ['kɔnifəɹ], *n.* (*Bot.*) Conifera, *f.*
conjectural [kən'dʒektjuːrəl], *a.* Congetturale, ipotetico.
conjecturally, *adv.* Congetturalmente.
conjecture [kən'dʒektʃəɹ], *v.t.i.* Congetturare, supporre. || *n.* Congettura, *f.*
conjoin [kən'dʒɔin], *v.t.* Congiungere, unire; *v.i.* congiungersi, unirsi, legarsi.
conjoint, *a.* Congiunto, unito, legato.
conjointly, *adv.* Congiuntamente, unitamente, d'accordo.
conjugal ['kɔndʒuːgəl], *a.* Coniugale.
conjugally, *adv.* Coniugalmente.
conjugate ['kɔndʒjuːgeit], *v.t.* Coniugare. || *a.* Coniugato.
conjugation, *n.* (*Gram.*) Coniugazione, *f.*
conjunct [kɔn'dʒʌŋkt], *a.* Congiunto, unito.
conjunction, *n.* (*Gram.*) Congiunzione, *f.*; unione, *f.* **In — with,** unitamente a.
conjunctiva [kɔndʒʌŋk'taivə], *n.* (*Anat.*) Congiuntiva, *f.*
conjuncture, *a.* Congiuntura, occasione, *f.*
conjuration, *n.* Preghiera, esortazione, *f.*; scongiuro, *m.*
conjure (1) [kən'dʒjuːɹ], *v.t.* Invocare, implorare, scongiurare.
conjure (2) ['kʌndʒəɹ], *v.t.* Stregare; esorcizzare; *v.i.* fare il prestigiatore. **To — up,** evocare.
conjurer, conjuror, *n.* Prestigiatore, illusionista, *m.*
conjuring, *n.* Illusionismo, *m.* **— trick,** giuoco di prestigio, *m.*
conk [kɔŋk], *v.i.* (*colloq.*) **To — out,** fermarsi, arrestarsi, incepparsi.
conker, *n.* Castagno, *m.*
connate [kɔ'neit], *a.* Connato. (*Bot.*) **— leaves,** foglie connate, *f.pl.*
connatural [kə'nætjuːrəl], *a.* Connaturale, connaturato.
connect [kə'nekt], *v.t.* Connettere, congiungere, attaccare, unire; (*in the mind*) associare; *v.i.* legarsi, unirsi.
connected, *a.* Connesso, congiunto, unito; continuo. **— by telephone,** connesso telefonicamente; **to be — with,** esser parente di, essere in rapporto con; **well-—,** di buona famiglia.
connecting-link, *n.* (*Mech.*) Anello di congiunzione, legame, *m.*
connecting-rod, *n.* (*Mech.*) Biella, *f.*
connection, connexion [kə'nekʃən], *n.*

Connessione, relazione, *f.*; nesso, *m.*; rapporto, *m.*; parentela; (*Comm.*) clientela, *f.*; setta; (*of trains, etc.*) coincidenza, *f.* **In this —,** a questo proposito.
connective, *a.* Connettivo.
connectively, *adv.* Congiuntamente.
conning-tower [ˈkɔnɪŋtauəɹ], *n.* (*Naut.*) Torretta di comando, *f.*, cassero, *m.*
connivance [kəˈnaivəns], *n.* Connivenza, *f.*
connive [kəˈnaiv], *v.i.* Chiudere un occhio su. **To — at,** tener mano a.
connoisseur [ˈkɔnəsəːɹ], *n.* Conoscitore, esperto, *m.*
connote [kəˈnout], *v.t.* Implicare, significare.
connotation, *n.* Significato, *m.*
connotative, *a.* Che implica, che significa.
connubial [kəˈnjuːbiəl], *a.* Coniugale, matrimoniale.
conoid [ˈkɔnɔid], *n.* (*Math.*) Conoide, *m.*
conoidal, *a.* Conoidale.
conquer [ˈkɔŋkəɹ], *v.t.* Vincere, conquistare, domare; *v.i.* riportare la vittoria, vincere.
conquerable, *a.* Vincibile, superabile.
conqueror, *n.* Vincitore, conquistatore, *m.*
conquest, *n.* Conquista, *f.*, acquisto, *m.* **To make a — of,** conquistare il cuore di.
consanguine, consanguineous, *a.* Consanguineo.
consanguinity, *n.* Consanguineità, *f.*
conscience [ˈkɔnʃəns], *n.* Coscienza, *f.* **A clear —,** una coscienza pulita; **a guilty —,** una coscienza sporca, *f.*; **in all —,** in tutta coscienza; **—-money,** denaro restituito anonimamente; **to be —-stricken,** sentirsi rimorder la coscienza.
conscienceless, *a.* Senza coscienza.
conscientious [kɔnʃiˈenʃəs], *a.* Coscienzioso, scrupoloso.
conscientiously, *adv.* Coscienziosamente.
conscientiousness, *n.* Coscienziosità, *f.*
conscionable, *a.* Giusto, ragionevole.
conscious [ˈkɔnʃəs], *a.* Conscio, cosciente; consapevole. **To be —,** essere conscio; **to be — of,** essere conscio di.
consciously, *adv.* Coscientemente, consapevolmente.
consciousness, *n.* Consapevolezza , percezione, conoscenza *f.* **To lose —,** perder conoscenza; **to regain —,** riprendere conoscenza.
conscript [ˈkɔnskript], *n.* Coscritto, *m.*
conscription, *n.* Coscrizione, *f.*
consecrate [ˈkɔnsikreit], *v.t.* Consacrare, santificare, benedire. **Consecrated bread,** pane consacrato, *m.*; **consecrated ground,** terra consacrata, *f.*
consecration, *n.* Consacrazione, *f.*
consecrator, *n.* Consacratore, consacrante, *m.*
consecratory, *a.* Sacramentale, consacratorio.
consecutive [kənˈsekjuːtiv], *a.* Consecutivo, seguente.
consecutively, *adv.* Consecutivamente, di seguito.
consensus [kənˈsensəs], *n.* Consenso, *m.*
consent [kənˈsent], *v.i.* Consentire, acconsentire. || *n.* Consenso, consentimento, accordo, *m.* **With one —,** di comune accordo.
consentaneous, *a.* Consentaneo, conforme.
consentient, *a.* (*Law*) Consenziente.
consequence [ˈkɔnsikwəns], *n.* Conseguenza, *f.*, effetto, *m.*; importanza, *f.* **In —,** per conseguenza; **in — of,** a causa di; **it is of no —,** non ha importanza; **Of what — is it to you ?** Che cosa importa a voi? **a man of —,** un uomo importante.
consequent, *a.* Conseguente. **— upon,** risultante da, per effetto di.
consequential, *a.* Conseguenziale, logico; (*fig.*) sufficiente, importante. **He is very —,** egli si da delle arie.
consequentially, *adv.* Conseguentemente, con un'aria d'importanza.
consequently, *adv.* Conseguentemente, quindi, perciò.
conservancy [kənˈsəːɹvənsi], *n.* Commissione delle acque, *f.*
conservation, *n.* Conservazione, *f.*
conservatism, *n.* Conservatorismo, *m.*
conservative, *a.* Conservativo, conservatore. || *n.* Conservatore, *m.*
conservator, *n.* Conservatore, *m.*
conservatory, *n.* (*for music*) Conservatorio, *m.*; (*hot-house*) serra, *f.*
conserve, *v.t.* Conservare, preservare. || *n.* Conserva, *f.*
consider [kənˈsidəɹ], *v.t.* Considerare, osservare, esaminare; stimare, reputare, giudicare; *v.i.* riflettere, deliberare.
considerable, *a.* Considerabile, considerevole, rilevante, notevole.
considerably, *adv.* Considerabilmente, notevolmente.
considerate [kənˈsidərit], *a.* Gentile, riguardoso, cortese, delicato. **It is very — of you,** è molto gentile da parte vostra.
considerately, *adv.* Riguardosamente.
considerateness, *n.* Gentilezza, cortesia, *f.*, riguardo, *m.*
consideration, *n.* Considerazione, *f.*, riguardo, giudizio, *m.*; compenso, *m.*, importanza, *f.* **In — of,** tenendo conto di, in vista di; **on further —,** tutto considerato; **out of — for him,** per riguardo suo; **to be under —,** venir dibattuto; **to take into —,** prendere in considerazione; **on no —,** per nessuna ragione.
considering, *prep.* Visto, considerato che. **That's not so bad, —,** non c'è male, tutto considerato.
consign [kənˈsain], *v.t.* Consegnare, affidare, mandare; (*Comm.*) consegnare, spedire. **To — to the grave,** deporre nella tomba.
consignee [kɔnsaiˈniː], *n.* Destinatario, *m.*
consignment, *n.* Consegna, spedizione, *f.* **— of goods,** mercanzie in consegna, *f.pl.*; **to send a —,** fare una spedizione.
consignor, *n.* Mittente, *m.*
consist [kənˈsist], *v.i.* Consistere, essere composto di; accordarsi, essere compatibile.
consistence, consistency, *n.* Consistenza, *f.*, accordo, *m.*; armonia, congruenza, *f.*
consistent, *a.* Consistente, tenace; compatibile, coerente, consequente.
consistently, *adv.* D'accordo, compatibilmente, conformemente.
consistorial, *a.* (*Eccles.*) Concistoriale.
consistory, *n.* Concistorio, *m.*
consolable [kənˈsouləbl], *a.* Consolabile.
consolation, *n.* Consolazione, *f.*
consolatory, *a.* Consolante, consolatorio.

console (1) [kən'soul], *v.t.* Consolare.
console (2) ['kɔnsoul], *n.* (*table*) Mensola, *f.*, tavolino, *m.*
consolidate [kən'sɔlideit], *v.t.* Consolidare; *v.i.* consolidarsi.
consolidation, *n.* Consolidamento, *m.*
consols [kɔn'sɔlz], *n.pl.* Consolidato, *m.*; rendita consolidata, *f.*
consonance ['kɔnsənəns], *n.* Consonanza, *f.*, accordo, *m.*, armonia, conformità, *f.* **In — with,** in conformità con.
consonant, *a.* Consonante; consono, conforme. || *n.* (*Gram.*) Consonante, *f.*
consonantal, *a.* Consonantico.
consort (1) ['kɔnsɔːt], *n.* Sposo, *m.*, sposa, *f.*; compagno, *m.*; (*Naut.*) conserva, *f.* **Prince Consort,** principe consorte, *m.*
consort (2) [kən'sɔːt], *v.t.* Associarsi, tener compagnia; armonizzare, essere compatibile con.
conspectus [kən'spektəs], *n.* (*Lit.*) Sguardo generale, *m.*, sinossi, *f.*, sommario, *m.*
conspicuous [kən'spikjuːəs], *a.* Cospicuo, notevole, considerevole, evidente. **To make oneself —,** farsi notare; **he was — by his absence,** egli brillò per la sua assenza.
conspicuously, *adv.* Cospicuamente.
conspicuousness, conspicuity, *n.* Notabilità, celebrità, distinzione, *f.*, splendore, *m.*
conspiracy [kən'spirəsi], *n.* Cospirazione, congiura, *f.*
conspirator, *n.* Cospiratore, congiurato, *m.*
conspire, *v.i.* Cospirare, congiurare, complottare; (*fig.*) concorrere, cooperare.
constable ['kʌnstəbl], *n.* (*Hist.*) Conestabile, *m.*; agente di polizia, *m.* **Chief —,** questore, capo della polizia, *m.*
constabulary, *n.* Polizia, *f.*
constancy ['kɔnstənsi], *n.* Costanza, fermezza, stabilità, *f.*; fedeltà, *f.*
constant, *a.* Costante, stabile, fermo, fedele; durevole, certo, continuo. || *n.* (*Math.*) Costante, *f.*
constantly, *adv.* Costantemente, continuamente; fedelmente; spesso.
constellation [kɔnstə'leiʃən], *n.* Costellazione, *f.*
consternation [kɔnstəɹ'neiʃən], *n.* Costernazione, *f.*, sbigottimento, *m.*
constipate ['kɔnstipeit], *v.t.* (*Med.*) Render stitico, costipare.
constipating, *a.* Astringente.
constipation, *n.* Stitichezza, costipazione, *f.*
constituency [kən'stitjuːənci], *n.* Collegio elettorale, *m.*; elettori, *m.pl.* **My —,** i miei elettori, *m.pl.*; il mio collegio, *m.*
constituent, *a.* Costituente; essenziale, elementare. || *n.* Parte costituente, *f.*; elettore, *m.*
constitute ['kɔnstitjuːt], *v.t.* Costituire, stabilire.
constitution, *n.* Costituzione, *f.*; (*physical*) complessione, *f.*; (*Pol.*) statuto, *m.*
constitutional, *a.* Costituzionale. || *n.* Passeggiata, *f.* **To take a —,** fare una passeggiata.
constitutionalism, *n.* Costituzionalismo, *m.*
constitutionalist, *n.* Costituzionale, *m.*
constitutionally, *adv.* Costituzionalmente.
constitutive, *a.* Costitutivo.
constrain [kən'strein], *v.t.* Costringere, sforzare; reprimere, racchiudere, serrare, stringere, obbligare.
constrained, *a.* Costretto. **A — voice,** una voce imbarazzata, *f.*; **a — manner,** una maniera compassata, *f.*
constrainedly, *adv.* Per forza, in modo imbarazzato, stentatamente.
constraint, *n.* Costrizione, *f.*; forza, *f.*; obbligazione, *f.*; imbarazzo, *m.* **Under —,** sorvegliato, sotto buona guardia.
constrict [kən'strikt], *v.t.* Stringere, comprimere, serrare.
constriction, *n.* Costrizione, *f.*
constrictive, *a.* (*Med.*) Costrittivo.
constrictor, *n.* (*Anat.*) Costrittore, *m.*; (*Zool.*) boa, *m.*
constringent, *a.* Restringente.
construct [kən'strʌkt], *v.t.* Costruire, formare, edificare, fabbricare; (*fig.*) comporre.
construction, *n.* Costruzione, *f.*; interpretazione, *f.*; senso, *m.* **To put a wrong — on,** interpretare in senso cattivo; **to put t , best — on,** dare l'interpretazione più favorevole a.
constructive, *a.* Costruttivo, formativo; dedotto, implicato. **— criticism,** critica costruttiva.
constructively, *adv.* Per induzione.
constructor, *n.* Costruttore, *m.*
construe [kən'struː], *v.t.* Tradurre, interpretare, spiegare; (*Gram.*) costruire.
consubstantial [kɔnsʌb'stænʃəl], *a.* (*Eccles.*) Consostanziale.
consubstantiate, *v.t.* Unire in una natura comune.
consubstantiation, *n.* Consustanziazione, *f.*
consul ['kɔnsəl], *n.* Console, *m.*
consular, *a.* Consolare.
consulate, *n.* Consolato, *m.*
consult [kən'sʌlt], *v.t.i.* Consultare; deliberare. **To — one's own interests,** seguire il proprio interesse.
consultant, *n.* Consulente, *m.*
consultation, *n.* Consultazione, consulta, *f.*; (*Med.*) consulto, *m.*
consulting, *a.* Consulente. **— -room,** gabinetto medico, ambulatorio, *m.*
consumable [kən'sjuːməbl], *a.* Consumabile.
consume, *v.t.* Consumare, mangiare; disfare, sperdere, distruggere; *v.i.* consumarsi, struggersi.
consumer, *n.* Consumatore, utente, *m.*
consuming, *a.* Consumante, che strugge. **— fire,** fuoco distruggitore, *m.*
consummate (1) ['kɔnsəmeit], *v.t.* Compire, finire, perfezionare, consumare.
consummate (2) [kən'sʌmət], *a.* Compiuto, perfetto, consumato; egregio, esimio. **He's a — ass,** è un asino calzato e vestito; **with — ease,** senza la minima difficoltà.
consummately, *adv.* Perfettamente, egregiamente.
consummation, *n.* Consumazione, *f.*, compimento, *m.*; (*fig.*) colmo, *m.* **This is the — of all my efforts,** questo è il coronamento di tutti i miei sforzi.
consumption [kən'sʌmʃən], *n.* Consumazione, distruzione, *f.*; (*Med.*) tisi, *f.*
consumptive, *a.* Consuntivo; (*Med.*) tisico, tubercolotico.
consumptiveness, *n.* Tisichezza, tendenza alla tisi, *f.*
contact ['kɔntækt], *n.* Contatto, rapporto, *m.*; (*Math.*) tangenza *f.* || *v.t.* Mettere a

contatto. **To bring into —,** mettere in rapporto; **to come into — with,** venire a contatto con.
contagion [kən'teidʒən], *n.* Contagio, *m.*
contagious, *a.* Contagioso, attaccaticcio.
contagiousness, *n.* Contagiosità, *f.*
contain [kən'tein], *v.t.* Contenere, accogliere, comprendere; reprimere, trattenere. **To — oneself,** contenersi, padroneggiarsi; **to — one's anger,** reprimere l'ira.
container, *n.* Recipiente, *m.*
contaminate [kən'tæmineit], *v.t.* Contaminare, macchiare, corrompere.
contamination, *n.* Contaminazione, corruzione, *f.*
contango [kən'tæŋgou], *n.* (*Comm.*) Riporto, *m.*
contemn [kən'tem], *v.t.* Sprezzare, disprezzare, tenere a vile.
contemplate ['kɔntempleit], *v.t.* Contemplare, considerare, riguardare, progettare; *v.i.* meditare, contemplare.
contemplation, *n.* Contemplazione, meditazione, *f.*; intenzione, *f.*; proposito, *m.*
contemplative [kən'templətiv], *a.* Contemplativo.
contemporaneity [kəntempərə'ni:iti], *n.* Contemporaneità, *f.*
contemporaneous, *a.* Contemporaneo.
contemporary, *n.a.* Contemporaneo, coevo, *m.*
contempt [kən'temt], *n.* Disprezzo, dispregio, sprezzo, disdegno, *m.* **— of court,** offesa alla corte, *f.*; **in —,** in dispregio; **to fall into —,** cadere in dispregio; **to feel — for,** sentir disprezzo per.
contemptible, *a.* Spregevole, vile.
contemptibleness, *n.* Viltà, bassezza, *f.*
contemptibly, *adv.* Spregevolmente, vilmente.
contemptuous [kən'temtju:əs], *a.* Sdegnoso, sprezzante.
contemptuously, *adv.* Sprezzantemente.
contemptuousness, *n.* Sdegnosità, alterigia, insolenza, *f.*
contend [kən'tend], *v.i.* Contendere, gareggiare, lottare, contrastare; dichiarare, affermare. **To — for a prize,** fare a gara per un premio; **to — for power,** disputarsi il potere; **to — that,** pretendere che.
contender, *n.* Contendente, concorrente, combattente, *m.*
contending, *a.* Contendente, lottante, combattente.
content [kən'tent], *n.* Contentezza, gioia, *f.* || *a.* Contento, soddisfatto, lieto. || *v.t.* Accontentare, appagare, soddisfare. **To be — with,** contentarsi di. **I will — myself with saying,** mi limiterò a dire.
content ['kɔntent], *n.* volume, *m.*; capacità, contenenza *f.*; (*pl.*) contenuto, *m.*; (*in books*) indice, sommario delle materie, *m.*
contented, *a.* Contento, soddisfatto, lieto. **Easily —,** di facile contentamento.
contentedly, *adv.* Con animo contento, tranquillamente.
contentedness, contentment, *n.* Contentezza, *f.*
contention [kən'tenʃən], *n.* Contenzione, contesa, disputa, *f.*; contrasto, *m.*
contentious, *a.* Contenzioso, litigioso.
contentiousness, *n.* Contenziosità, disposizione litigiosa, *f.*
contentment, *n.* Contentezza, *f.*
conterminal, conterminous [kɔn'tə:ɹminəl, kɔn'tə:ɹminəs], *a.* Conterminale, contiguo, limitrofo, attiguo.
conterminously, *adv.* Contiguamente.
contest (1) ['kɔntest], *n.* Lotta, contesa, *f.*; contrasto, combattimento, *m.*; gara, *f.*; concorso, *m.*
contest (2) [kən'test], *v.t.i.* Contestare, contrastare, disputare.
contestant, *n.* Contestatore, *m.*
context ['kɔntekst], *n.* Contesto, *m.*
contextual, *a.* Contestuale.
contiguity [kɔnti'gju:iti], *n.* Contiguità, vicinanza, *f.*
contiguous, *a.* Contiguo, vicino.
contiguously, *adv.* Contiguamente.
continence ['kɔntinəns], *n.* Continenza, castità, *f.*; moderazione, temperanza, *f.*
continent (1), *a.* Continente, casto; moderato, temperato.
continent (2), *n.* (*Geog.*) Continente, *m.*
continental, *a.* Continentale.
continently, *adv.* Continentemente, moderatamente.
contingence, contingency kən'tindʒəns, kən'tindʒənsi], *n.* Contingenza, congiuntura, *f.*; caso fortuito, *m.*
contingent, *a.* Contingente; casuale, accidentale, fortuito.
contingently, *adv.* Contingentemente.
continual [kən'tinju:əl], *a.* Continuo, incessante.
continually, *adv.* Continuamente, sempre.
continuance, *n.* Durata, *f.*; soggiorno (*in a place*), *m.*
continuation, *n.* Continuazione, *f.*, seguito, proseguimento, *m.*
continue [kən'tinju:], *v.t.* Continuare, seguitare, proseguire; aggiornare, prorogare; *v.i.* continuare, durare, restare. **To — some-one in office,** mantenere in carica qualcuno; **to — one's way,** riprendere il cammino.
continued, *a.* Continuo, ininterrotto. **To be — in our next,** continua, il seguito nel prossimo numero.
continuously, *adv.* Continuamente.
continuity [kɔnti'nju:iti], *n.* Continuità, *f.*
continuous, *a.* Continuo. (*Cinema.*) **— performance,** spettacolo permanente, *m.*
contort [kən'tɔ:ɹt], *v.t.* Contorcere, torcere.
contorted, *a.* Contorto, storto, stravolto.
contortion, *n.* Contorsione, *f.*; (*Med.*) distorsione, *f.*
contortionist, *n.* Contorsionista, *m.f.*
contour ['kɔntu:ɹ], *n.* Contorno, *m.* **— -lines,** linee di livello, *f.pl.*
contra ['kɔntrə], *prep.* Contro. || *n.* (*Comm.*) Contropartita.
contraband ['kɔntrəbænd], *n.* Contrabbando, *m.* || *a.* Proibito. **— of war,** contrabbando di guerra, *m.*; **— goods,** merci di contrabbando, *f.pl.*
contrabandist, *n.* Contrabbandiere, *m.*
contrabasso, *n.* (*Mus.*) Contrabbasso.
contract (1) [kən'trækt], *v.t.* Contrarre, restringere, raccorciare; accogliere, prendere (*a habit*); *v.i.* contrarsi, accorciarsi; (*Comm.*)

contrattare, fare contratto, impegnarsi. **To — the brows,** corrugare la fronte; **to — for,** contrattare per; **to — out of,** rescindere un contratto con pagamento di una penale.
contract (2) [ˈkɔntrækt], *n.* Contratto, accordo, patto, *m.*; convenzione, *f.* **By —,** per contratto; **sale by private —,** vendita privata, *f.*; **to put up to —,** dare in appalto; **—-note,** distinta, *f.*
contractedness, *n.* Contrazione, *f.*, accorciamento, *m.*
contractibility, *n.* Contrattibilità, *f.*
contractible, *a.* Contrattile.
contracting, *a.* (*Comm.*) **— party,** contraente, *m.*
contraction, *n.* Contrazione, *f.*, accorciamento, *m.*; abbreviazione, *f.*
contractor, *n.* Appaltatore, fornitore, impresario, imprenditore, *m.*
contractual, *a.* Contrattuale.
contradict [kɔntrəˈdikt], *v.t.* Contraddire, negare, smentire. **To — oneself,** smentirsi, contraddirsi.
contradiction, *n.* Contraddizione, smentita (*denial*), *f.*
contradictorily, *adv.* Contraddittoriamente.
contradictoriness, *n.* Natura contraddittoria, *f.*
contradictory, *a.* Contraddittorio, opposto.
contradistinction [kɔntrədisˈtiŋkʃən], *n.* Contrasto, *m.*, opposizione, *f.*
contradistinguish [kɔntrədisˈtiŋgwiʃ], *v.t.* Contraddistinguere, differenziare.
contralto [kənˈtrɑːltou], *n.a.* (*Mus.*) Contralto, *m.*
contrapuntal [kɔntrəˈpʌntl], *a.* (*Mus.*) Contrappuntistico.
contrapuntist, *n.* (*Mus.*) Contrappuntista, *m.*
contrariety [kɔntrəˈraiiti], *n.* Contrarietà, opposizione, avversità, antipatia, *f.*
contrarily, *adv.* Contrariamente, a rovescio.
contrariness, *n.* Contrarietà, opposizione, *f.*
contrariwise, *adv.* Contrariamente, al contario, in senso opposto.
contrary, *a.* Contrario, avverso. || *n.* Contrario, *m.* **On the —,** al contrario, all'opposto; **quite the —,** tutto al contrario; **to go by contraries,** procedere per contrari.
contrast (1) [ˈkɔntrɑːst], *n.* Contrasto, *m.* **To stand in —,** fare contrasto.
contrast (2) [kənˈtrɑːst], *v.t.i.* Contrastare, mettere in contrasto.
contrasting, *a.* In contrasto con.
contravene [kɔntrəˈviːn], *v.t.* Contravvenire a, trasgredire.
contravener, *n.* Contravventore, *m.*
contravention, *n.* Contravvenzione, trasgressione, *f.*
contribute [kənˈtribjuːt], *v.t.* Contribuire, pagare; *v.i.* contribuire a, concorrere, collaborare a.
contribution, *n.* Contributo, *m.*, contribuzione *f.*; articolo (*in newspaper, etc.*), *m.* **To lay under —,** mettere a contributo.
contributor, *n.* Contribuente, contributore, *m.*; collaboratore, *m.*
contributory, *a.* Tributario, che contribuisce.
contrite [ˈkɔntrait], *a.* Contrito, pentito.
contritely, *adv.* Contritamente.
contrition, *n.* Contrizione, *f.*, pentimento, *m.*
contrivable [kənˈtraivəbl], *a.* Che si può combinare.
contrivance, *n.* Invenzione, combinazione, *f.*, congegno, dispositivo, espediente, ritrovato, *m.*
contrive, *v.t.* Inventare, combinare, congegnare; *v.i.* ingegnarsi, industriarsi, riuscire. **You will only — to make matters worse,** riuscirà soltanto a far peggiorare le cose; **she contrives very well,** è una buona massaia.
contriving, *a.* Inventivo, fertile d'espedienti, ingegnoso, industre, diligente.
control [kənˈtroul], *n.* Comando, freno, *m.*; controllo, *m.*; autorità, padronanza, *f.*; potere, *m.* || *v.t.* Comandare, frenare, controllare, reprimere, raffrenare. **To — one's anger,** raffrenare l'ira; **free of all —,** libero di ogni freno.
controllable, *a.* Docile, ubbidiente, pieghevole.
controller, *n.* Governatore, direttore, *m.*; controllore, *m.*
controllership, *n.* Funzioni di direttore, *f.pl.*
controversial [kɔntrəˈvəːɹʃəl], *a.* Controverso, polemico.
controversialist, *n.* Controversista, polemista, *m.*
controversy [ˈkɔntrovəɹsi], *n.* Controversia, disputa, questione, discussione, *f.* **Beyond —,** fuori discussione.
controvert [kɔntroˈvəːɹt], *v.t.* Discutere, controvertere.
controvertible, *a.* Controvertibile.
contumacious [kɔntjuːˈmeiʃəs], *a.* Contumace; disubbidiente, ribelle, ricalcitrante.
contumaciously, *adv.* Ostinatamente.
contumaciousness, contumacy [kɔntjuːˈmeiʃəsnes, ˈkɔntjuːməsi], *n.* Contumacia, ostinatezza, disubbidienza, *f.*
contumelious [kɔntjuːˈmiːliəs], *a.* Contumelioso, ingiurioso, oltraggioso.
contumely [ˈkɔntjuːmili], *n.* Contumelia, villania, ingiuria, *f.*, vituperio, *m.*
contuse [kənˈtjuːz], *v.t.* Ammaccare, pestare, schiacciare, percuotere.
contusion, *n.* Contusione, percossa, ammaccatura, *f.*
conundrum [kəˈnʌndrəm], *n.* Indovinello, enigma, *m.*
convalesce [kɔnvəˈles], *v.i.* Rimettere in salute.
convalescence, *n.* Convalescenza, *f.*
convalescent, *n.a.* Convalescente. **— home,** convalescenziario, *m.*
convection [kənˈvekʃən], *n.* (*Elec.*) Trasporto, *m.*, convezione, *f.*
convenable [kənˈviːnəbl], *a.* Convocabile.
convene, *v.t.* Convocare, chiamare a raccolta; (*Law*) citare; *v.i.* convenire, riunirsi, adunarsi.
convener, *n.* Convocatore, presidente, *m.*
convenience [kənˈviːniəns], *n.* Comodità, *f.*, agio, comodo, *m.*; opportunità, convenienza, *f.*; luogo comodo (w.c.), *m.* **A marriage of —,** un matrimonio di convenienza, *m.*; **at your —,** a vostro agio; **at your earliest —,** alla prima opportunità.
convenient, *a.* Comodo, utile, adatto; conveniente. **If it is — to you,** se vi è comodo; **if you could make it —,** se voi poteste combinare.
conveniently, *adv.* Comodamente, senza sforzo.
convent [ˈkɔnvənt], *n.* Convento, *m.*

conventicle [kən'ventikl], *n.* Conventicola, *f.*
convention, *n.* Convenzione, *f.*, patto, accordo, *m.*; (*Pol.*) assemblea, convenzione, *f.*
conventional, *a.* Convenzionale.
conventionalism, *n.* Convenzionalismo, *m.*
conventionalist, *n.* Convenzionalista, *m.*
conventionality, *n.* Convenzionalità, *f.*
conventionally, *adv.* Convenzionalmente.
converge [kən'vəːɹdʒ], *v.i.* Convergere.
convergence, *n.* Convergenza, *f.*
convergent, *a.* Convergente.
conversable [kən'vəːɹsəbl], *a.* Conversevole, socievole.
conversance, *n.* Esperienza, pratica, *f.*
conversant, *a.* Versato, pratico, esperto. **— with,** versato in, pratico di.
conversation, *n.* Conversazione, *f.*, discorso, *m.*; (*Law*) commercio, *m.* **In earnest —,** in stretto colloquio; **private —,** discorso a quattr'occhi, *m.*; **to carry on a —,** avviare una conversazione.
conversational, *a.* Di conversazione, conversevole.
conversationalist, *n.* Parlatore, conversatore, *m.*
converse (1) [kən'vəːɹs], *v.i.* Conversare, trattenersi a discorrere, chiacchierare.
converse (2) ['kɔnvəɹs], *a.* Opposto, contrario. || *n.* Proposizione inversa, *f.*; (*Math.*) reciproca, *f.*, inverso, *m.*
conversely, *adv.* Reciprocamente.
conversion, *n.* Conversione, *f.*, cambiamento, *m.*; trasposizione, *f.*
convert (1) [kən'vəːɹt], *v.t.* Convertire, tramutare, trasformare; trasporre. **To be converted,** convertirsi.
convert (2) ['kɔnvəɹt], *n.* Convertito, *m.*, convertita, *f.*
converter, *n.* Convertitore, *m.*
convertibility, *n.* Convertibilità, *f.*
convertible, *a.* Convertibile, trasformabile.
convertibly, *adv.* Reciprocamente.
convex ['kɔnveks], *a.* Convesso.
convexity, *n.* Convessità, *f.*
convey [kən'vei], *v.t.* Trasportare (*goods, etc.*) portare, condurre, menare; esprimere, comunicare (*ideas, etc.*); (*Law*) fare il trapasso di. **To — a meaning,** dare un'idea; esprimere il senso d'una cosa.
conveyable, *a.* Trasmissibile; esprimibile.
conveyance, *n.* Trasporto, veicolo, *m.*, trasmissione, comunicazione, *f.*; (*Law*) trasferimento, *m.*, cessione, *f.*
conveyancer, *n.* (*Law*) Notaio, *m.*
conveyancing, *n.* Notariato, *m.*
conveyor, *n.* Portatore, latore, trasmettitore, *m.*; (*Mech.*) convogliatore, *m* **— -belt,** convogliatore a cinghia, *m.*
convict (1) [kən'vikt], *v.t.* Condannare, dichiarare colpevole; convincere.
convict (2) ['kɔnvikt], *n.* Condannato, forzato, galeotto, *m.* **— prison,** bagno penale, ergastolo, *m.*
conviction, *n.* Condanna, *f.*; convinzione, opinione, *f.* **Open to —,** pronto a ricredersi.
convince [kən'vins], *v.t.* Convincere, persuadere.
convincing, *a.* Convincente, conclusivo.
convincingly, *adv.* Convincentemente.
convivial [kən'viviəl], *a.* Conviviale, gioviale, festevole, allegro.
conviviality, *n.* Convivialità, socievolezza, giovialità, *f.*
convocation [kɔnvou'keiʃən], *n.* Convocazione, assemblea, *f.*
convoke, *v.t.* Convocare, adunare.
convolute, convoluted ['kɔnvəljuːt, kənvə'ljuːtid], *a.* (*Bot.*) Convoluto.
convolution, *n.* Accartocciamento, *m.*; (*Anat.*) circonvoluzione, *f.*
convolvulus (*pl.* **convolvuli**) [kən'vɔlvjuːləs, kən'vɔlvjuːlai], *n.* (*Bot.*) Convolvolo, vilucchio, *m.*
convoy (1) [kən'vɔi], *v.t.* Accompagnare, guidare, scortare.
convoy (2) ['kɔnvɔi], *n.* Convoglio, *m.*; scorta (*escort*), *f.*
convulse [kən'vʌls], *v.t.* Agitare, scuotere, fare spasimare, dare le convulsioni a. **To be convulsed with laughter,** torcersi dalle risa.
convulsed, *a.* Convulso, agitato, scosso.
convulsion, *n.* Convulsione, *f.*, spasimo, *m.* **Fit of convulsions,** accesso di convulsioni, *m.*; **to be seized with convulsions,** cadere in convulsioni.
convulsive, *a.* Convulsivo.
convulsively, *adv.* Convulsivamente.
cony, coney ['kouni], *n.* (*Zool.*) Coniglio, *m.*
coo [kuː], *v.t.i.* Tubare, mormorare. **To bill and —,** tubare.
cooee ['kuːiː], *n.* Grido, *m.* || *inter.* Ohè!
cooing, *n.* Il tubare, *m.*
cook [kuk], *n.* Cuoco, cuciniere, *m.*, cuoca, cuciniera, *f.* || *v.t.i.* Cuocere, cucinare, far la cucina; (*colloq.*) falsificare (*accounts*). **— -house,** cucina all'aperta, *f.*; **— -shop,** rosticceria, trattoria, *f.*; **head —,** capo cuoco, *m.*; (*fig.*) **to — up,** arrangiare, combinare; (*colloq.*) **his goose is cooked,** egli è spacciato; (*colloq.*) **What's cooking ?** Cosa c'è di nuovo ? Cosa facciamo ?
cooker, *n.* Fornello, forno a gas, forno elettrico, *m.*; cucina economica, *f.*
cookery, *n.* Culinaria, cucina, *f.* **— book,** libro di cucina, *m.*
cookie, *n.* Focaccina, *f.*
cool [kuːl], *a.* Fresco, freddino; calmo; indifferente. || *n.* Fresco, *m.*, freschezza, *f.* || *v.t.* Rinfrescare, raffreddare, intiepidire; calmare; *v.i.* divenir freddo, raffreddarsi. **As — as a cucumber,** con un sangue freddo inarrivabile; **How — he is !** Com'è indifferente! **it cost him a — thousand,** gli è costato la bellezza di mille sterline; **to keep —,** stare calmo; **he's a — hand,** è un disinvolto; **to — one's heels,** annoiarsi ad aspettare; **to — down,** calmarsi, ristorarsi.
cooler, *n.* Refrigerante, *m.*; (*Motor.*) radiatore, *m.*
coolie, *n.* Operaio indiano, *m.*
cooling, *a.* Rinfrescante. **A — drink,** una bibita rinfrescante, *f.*
coolish, *a.* Freschino, freschetto.
coolly, *adv.* Frescamente; a sangue freddo, freddamente.
coolness, *n.* Freschezza, *f.*, fresco, *m.*; indifferenza, *f.*, sangue freddo, *m.*
coomb, combe [kuːm], *n.* Vallone, valletta, *f.*
coon [kuːn], *n.* (*Zool.*) Tasso americano, *m.*; (*off.*) negro, *m.*, negra, *f.*
coop [kuːp], *n.* Stia, *f.*, pollaio, *m.* || *v.t.* Confinare, imprigionare. **To — up,** rinchiudere.

cooper, *n.* Bottaio, *m.*
cooperage, *n.* Mestiere di bottaio, *m.*
co-operate [kou'ɔpəreit], *v.i.* Cooperare, collaborare.
co-operation, *n.* Cooperazione, *f.*
co-operative, *a.* Cooperativo. **— stores,** magazzini cooperativi, *m.pl.*; **— society,** società cooperativa, *f.*
co-opt [kou'ɔpt], *v.t.* Eleggere membro d'un comitato coi suffragi dei membri esistenti.
co-ordinate [kou'ɔ:ɹdineit], *v.t.* Coordinare. || *a.* Coordinato. || *n.* (*Math.*) coordinata, *f.*
coot [ku:t], *n.* (*Zool.*) Folaga, *f.*
cop [kɔp], *n.* (*colloq.*) Poliziotto, *m.* || *v.t.* Afferrare.
copaiba, copayva [ko'peibə, ko'peivə], *n.* (*Bot.*) Coppaibe, copaive, *f.*
copal ['koupəl], *n.* Coppale, *m.*
coparcenary [kou'pɑ:ɹsenəri], *n.* (*Law*) Coeredità, *f.*
coparcener, *n.* Coerede, *m.*
copartner [kou'pɑ:ɹtnəɹ], *n.* Associato, socio, *m.*
copartnership, *n.* Associazione, *f.*
cope (1) [koup], *n.* (*Eccles.*) Piviale, *m.* || *v.t.* Coprire di un piviale.
cope (2), *v.i.* Lottare. **To — with,** lottare contro, tenere testa a, far fronte a.
Copenhagen [koupən'heigən], *n.* (*Geog.*) Copenaghen, *f.*
Copernican [kə'pə:ɹnikən], *a.* Copernicano.
copier, copyist ['kɔpiəɹ, 'kɔpiist], *n.* Copista, amanuense, *m.*; imitatore, *m.*
coping, *n.* Comignolo, *m.* **—-stone,** tegolo, *m.*
copious ['koupiəs], *a.* Copioso, abbondante.
copiously, *adv.* Copiosamente.
copiousness, *n.* Copiosità, abbondanza, *f.*
copper ['kɔpəɹ], *n.* Rame, *m.*; (*vessel*) caldaia, *f.*; (*colloq.*) poliziotto, *m.*; (*coin*) soldo, *m.* || *a.* Di rame. || *v.t.* Coprire di rame. **Coppers** (*money*), spiccioli, *m.pl.*, moneta, *f.* **—-bottomed,** foderato di rame; **—-coloured,** colore di rame; **— beech,** faggio rosso, *m.*
copperhead, *n.* (*Zool.*) Specie di serpente a sonagli.
copperplate, *n.* Incisione in rame, *f.* **— engraving,** incisione su rame, *f.*; **— writing,** calligrafia bellissima, *f.*
copperas ['kɔpərəs], *n.* (*Chem.*) Vetriolo verde, *m.*, copparosa, *f.*
coppice, copse ['kɔpis, kɔps], *n.* Bosco ceduo, boschetto, *m.*
Coptic ['kɔptik], *a.* Copto.
copula ['kɔpu:lə], *n.* (*Gram.*) Copula, *f.*
copulate, *v.t.* Copulare.
copulation, *n.* Copulazione, *f.*
copulative, *a.* (*Gram.*) Copulativo, congiuntivo.
copy ['kɔpi], *n.* Copia, *f.*; (*for writing*) esempio; (*of a printed book*) esemplare, *m.*; (*Print.*) manoscritto, *m.*; (*fig.*) imitazione, *f.* || *v.t.* Copiare, imitare. **Rough —,** minuta, bozza, mala copia, *f.*; **fair —,** copia in netto, bella copia, *f.*; **true —,** copia conforme; **—-book,** quaderno di calligrafia, *m.*
copyhold, *n.* (*Law*) Proprietà soggetta a diritto speciale, *f.*
copying, *n.* Trascrizione, *f.* **—-book,** copialettere, *m.*; **—-clerk,** copista, *m.*; **—-ink,** inchiostro copiativo, *m.*; **—-press,** copialettere, *m.*
copyright, *n.* Proprietà letteraria, *f.*, diritti d'autore, *m.pl.*
coquet (1) [kə'ket], *v.i.* Civettare, flirtare, frascheggiare.
coquet (2), **coquette,** *n.* Civetta, *f.*
coquetry, *n.* Civetteria, *f.*
coquettish, *a.* Civettuolo.
coracle ['kɔrəkl], *n.* Specie di battello da pesca.
coral ['kɔrəl], *n.* Corallo, *m.* || *a.* Di corallo, corallino. **A — necklace,** una collana di corallo, *f.*; **—-fisher,** pescatore di coralli, *m.*; **—-reef,** banco corallifero, *m.*
coralline, *n.a.* (*Bot.*) Corallina, *f.*
corbel ['kɔ:ɹbəl], *n.* (*Arch.*) Modiglione, *m.*, mensola, *f.*
cord [kɔ:ɹd], *n.* Corda, *f.*, cordoncino, spago, *m.*; (*fig.*) vincolo, legame, *m.* || *v.t.* Cordonare, legare con una corda. **—-wood,** legna, *f.*
cordage, *n.* (*Naut.*) Cordame, *m.*
cordate, *a.* (*Bot.*) Cordato.
corded, *a.* Legato con corde.
cordelier [kɔ:ɹdə'liəɹ], *n.* (*Eccles.*) Frate francescano, cordigliero, *m.*
cordial ['kɔ:ɹdiəl], *a.* Cordiale. || *n.* Cordiale, liquore, *m.*; (*Med.*) ricostituente, *m.*
cordiality, *n.* Cordialità, *f.*
cordially, *adv.* Cordialmente.
cordon ['kɔ:ɹdən], *n.* Cordone, *m.*
corduroy [kɔ:ɹdju:'rɔi, kɔ:ɹdə'rɔi], *n.* Fustagno, *m.* **Corduroys,** pantaloni di fustagno, *m.pl.*; **— road,** massicciata di tronchi d'albero, *m.*
cordwainer ['kɔ:ɹdweinəɹ], *n.* (*obs.*) Calzolaio, *m.*
core [kɔ:ɹ], *n.* (*of fruit*) Torso, torsolo, *m.*; (*of cables, etc.*) anima, *f.*; cuore, centro, *m.* || *v.t.* Togliere il torso. **Rotten to the —,** marcio fino al midollo.
co-religionist [kouri'lidʒənist], *n.* Correligionario, *m.*
co-respondent [koures'pɔndənt], *n.* (*Law*) Coimputato, *m.*; complice in adulterio, *m.f.*
coriaceous, *a.* Coriaceo.
coriander [kɔri'ændəɹ], *n.* (*Bot.*) Coriandolo, *m.*
Corinthian [kə'rinθiən], *n.a.* Corinzio, corintio, *m.*
cork [kɔ:ɹk], *n.* Sughero; (*for bottles*) tappo, turacciolo, *m.* || *v.t.* Turare, tappare. **—-tipped cigarette,** sigaretta con bocchino di sughero, *f.*; **—-tree,** sughero, *m.*
corkscrew, *n.* Cavatappi, cavaturaccioli, *m.* **— curl,** riccio, *m.*; **— staircase,** scala a chiocciola, *f.*
corky, *a.* Di sughero; che sa di sughero.
cormorant ['kɔ:ɹmərənt], *n.* (*Zool.*) Cormorano, marangone, *m.*; (*fig.*) ghiottone, *m.*
corn [kɔ:ɹn], *n.* Grano, frumento, *m.*; cereali, *m.pl.*; granturco, frumentone, mais, *m.*; (*on foot*) callo, *m.* **Ear of —,** spiga di grano, *f.*; **to tread on corns,** pestare i calli; **—-chandler,** granaiuolo, *m.*; **—-cob,** pannocchia di granturco, *f.*; **—-cockle,** gettaione, *m.*; **—-cure,** callifugo, *m.*; **—-cutter,** callista, *m.*; **—-flour,** farina di granturco, *f.*; **—-merchant,** mercante di grano, *m.*
corncrake, *n.* (*Zool.*) Re di quaglie, *m.*
cornea ['kɔ:ɹniə], *n.* (*Anat.*) Cornea, *f.*
corned-beef, *n.* Carne di bue salata, *f.*
cornel ['kɔ:ɹnəl], *n.* (*Bot.*) Corniola, *f.*
cornelian [kəɹ'ni:liən], *n.* Cornalina, *f.*

corner [ˈkɔːɹnəɹ], *n.* Angolo, canto (*interior*), *m.*; cantonata (*exterior*), *f.* spigolo (*sharp corner*), *m.*; (*fig.*) incetta, *f.*; accaparramento, *m.* || *v.t.* Incettare, accaparrare; mettere nell'imbarazzo. **To cut off a —,** prendere una scorciatoia; **to put a child in the —,** mettere un bimbo nel cantuccio; **—-stone,** pietra angolare, *f.*; (*Football*) **—-kick,** calcio d'angolo, *m.*

cornered, *a.* Ad angoli; (*fig.*) imbarazzato.

cornerwise, *a.* Diagonalmente.

cornet [ˈkɔːɹnit], *n.* (*Mus.*) Cornetta, *f.*; (*ice-cream*) cono, cialdone, *m.*

cornfield, *n.* Campo di grano, *m.*

cornflower, *n.* Fiordaliso, *m.*

cornice [ˈkɔːɹnis], *n.* (*Arch.*) Cornice, *f.*

Cornish [ˈkɔːɹniʃ], *a.* Di Cornovaglia.

cornucopia [kɔːɹnjuːˈkoupiə], *n.* Cornucopia, *f.*

Cornwall [ˈkɔːɹnwəl], *n.* (*Geog.*) Cornovaglia, *f.*

corny, *a.* (*colloq.*) Banale, trito.

corolla [kəˈrɔlə], *n.* (*Bot.*) Corolla, *f.*

corollary [kəˈrɔləri], *n.* Corollario, *m.*

corona [kəˈrounə], *n.* (*Astron.Bot.*) Corona, *f.*; (*Arch.*) grondaia, *f.*

coronach [ˈkɔrənɑːx], *n.* (*Scottish*) Nenia, *f.*

coronal [ˈkɔrənəl], *n.* Corona, ghirlanda, *f.*; (*Anat.*) coronale, *m.*

coronation, *n.* Incoronazione, *f.*

coroner, *n.* Giudice istruttore che inquisisce sulle morti violente, pretore.

coronet, *n.* Coroncina, corona, *f.*

corporal (1) [ˈkɔːɹpərəl], *n.* (*Mil.*) Caporale, *m.*

corporal (2), *a.* Corporeo, corporeale. || *n.* (*Eccles.*) Corporale, *m.* **— punishment,** pena corporale, *f.*

corporality, *n.* Corporalità, *f.*

corporally, *adv.* Corporalmente.

corporate, *a.* Incorporato, corporato. **A — body,** una corporazione, *f.*; **a — town,** un municipio, *m.*

corporation, *n.* Corporazione, *f.*, municipio, *m.*, consiglio municipale, *m.*; (*colloq.*) pancione, *m.*

corporative, *a.* Corporativo, collettivo.

corporeal [kɔːɹˈpɔːriəl], *a.* Corporeo, corporale; (*Law*) immobile.

corporeally, *adv.* Corporalmente, materialmente.

corposant, *n.* Fuoco di S. Elmo, *m.*

corps (*pl.* **corps**) [kɔːɹ], *n.* Corpo, *m.* **Army —,** corpo d'armata, *m.*

corpse [kɔːɹps], *n.* Cadavere, *m.*, salma, *f.* **— candle,** fuoco fatuo, *m.*

corpulence, corpulency, *n.* Corpulenza, pinguedine, *f.*

corpulent, *a.* Corpulento, panciuto, grasso.

corpus [ˈkɔːɹpəs], *n.* (*Lit.*) Corpo, *m.*, raccolta, *f.*

Corpus Christi, *n.* (*Eccles.*) Corpusdomini, *m.*

corpuscle [ˈkɔːɹpəsl], *n.* Corpuscolo, *m.*

corpuscular, *a.* Corpuscolare.

corral [kəˈrɑːl], *n.* Luogo chiuso per bestiame, *m.*

correct [kəˈɹekt], *a.* Corretto, esatto, giusto; convenevole, garbato, regolare; di buon gusto. || *v.t.* Correggere, rettificare, emendare; regolare; ammonire, punire. **That's the — thing to do,** quella è la cosa giusta da farsi; **to — oneself,** ravvedersi, emendarsi; **I stand corrected,** faccio atto di contrizione.

correction, *n.* Correzione, rettificazione, *f.*, ritocco, *m.*; punizione, *f.*, castigo, *m.* **I speak under —,** parlo salvo correzioni.

correctional, *a.* Correzionale.

correctitude, *n.* Correttezza, irreprensibilità, *f.*

corrective, *n.a.* Correttivo, *m.*

correctly, *adv.* Correttamente, esattamente, giustamente, convenevolmente.

correctness, *n.* Correttezza, esattezza, giustezza, *f.* **— of language,** purezza di lingua, *f.*; **— of a translation,** esattezza di una traduzione, *f.*

corrector, *n.* Correttore, *m.*

correlate [ˈkɔrileit], *v.i.* Essere correlativo, avere correlazione.

correlation, *n.* Correlazione, *f.*

correlative, *a.* Correlativo. || *n.* Parola correlativa, *f.*

correspond [kɔriˈspɔnd], *v.i.* Corrispondere, accordarsi, armonizzare; essere conforme.

correspondence, *n.* Corrispondenza, conformità, *f.*; accordo, *m.*; (*collection of letters*) carteggio, *m.* **Foreign —,** corrispondenza estera, *f.*

correspondent, *n.a.* Corrispondente, *m.f.* **War —,** corrispondente di guerra, *m.*

correspondently, *adv.* Corrispondentemente.

corresponding, *a.* Corrispondente, conforme, d'accordo.

correspondingly, *adv.* Nello stesso modo, proporzionatamente.

corridor [ˈkɔridəɹ], *n.* Corridoio, andito, *m.* **— carriage,** vagone a corridoio, *m.*

corrigible [ˈkɔridʒəbl], *a.* Correggibile.

corrival [kɔˈraivəl], *n.* Rivale, competitore, *m.*

corroborant [kəˈrɔbərənt], *n.a.* Corroborante, *m.*

corroborate, *v.t.* Corroborare, confermare, convalidare.

corroboration, *n.* Corroborazione, confermazione, *f.* **In — of,** in conferma di.

corroborative, *a.* Corroborativo.

corrode [kəˈroud], *v.t.* Corrodere, rodere; *v.i.* consumarsi, perire.

corroding, *a.* Corrosivo.

corrosion, *n.* Corrosione, *f.*

corrosive, *n.a.* Corrosivo, *m.* **— sublimate,** sublimato corrosivo, *m.*

corrosively, *adv.* Per corrosione.

corrosiveness, *n.* Natura corrosiva, azione corrosiva, *f.*

corrugate [ˈkɔrugeit], *v.t.i.* Corrugare, aggrinzare; ondulare. **Corrugated iron,** lamiera ondulata, *f.*

corrugation, *n.* Corrugazione, grinza, ruga, *f.*

corrupt [kəˈrʌpt], *v.t.* Corrompere, guastare, viziare; subornare, sedurre. || *a.* Corrotto, guasto, vizioso. **To become —,** corrompersi, guastarsi; **— practices,** broglio, *m.*

corrupter, *n.* Corruttore, *m.*, corruttrice, *f.*

corruptibility, *n.* Corruttibilità, *f.*

corruptible, *a.* Corruttibile.

corruptibly, *adv.* Corrottamente.

corrupting, corruptive, *a.* Corruttivo.

corruption, *n.* (*of style, language, etc.*) Corruzione, alterazione, *f.*; (*depravity*) corruttela, *f.*

corruptly, *adv.* Corrottamente.

corruptness, *n.* Corruttela, *f.*

corsage [kɔːɹˈsɑːʒ], *n.* Busto, giubbetto, *m.*

corsair ['kɔːɹsɛəɹ], *n.* Corsaro, *m.*
corse [kɔːɹs], *n.* (*Poet.*) Cadavere, *m.*
corset, *n.* Busto, *m.*
Corsican ['kɔːɹsikən], *n.a.* Corso, *m.*
corslet, *n.* Corsaletto, *m.*
cortex ['kɔːɹteks], *n.* (*Bot.*) Corteccia, *f.*
cortical, *a.* Corticale.
corundum [kə'rʌndəm], *n.* (*Min.*) Corindone, *m.*
coruscate ['kɔrəskeit], *v.i.* Corruscare, scintillare.
corruscation, *n.* Corruscazione, *f.*, bagliore, *m.*
corvette [kɔːɹ'vet], *n.* (*Naut.*) Corvetta, *f.*
corvine, *a.* Corvino.
coryza [kə'raizə], *n.* (*Med.*) Corizza, coriza, *f.*
cos, cos-lettuce [kɔs], *n.* Lattuga romana, *f.*
cosecant [kou'sekənt], *n.* (*Math.*) Cosecante, *f.*
cosignatory [kou'signətəri], *n.* Cofirmatario, *m.*
cosine ['kousain], *n.* (*Math.*) Coseno, *m.*
cosily ['kouzili], *adv.* Comodamente, comodo comodo.
cosmetic [kəz'metik], *n.* Cosmetica, *f.* || *a.* Cosmetico.
cosmic, cosmical ['kɔzmik, 'kɔzmikəl], *a.* Cosmico.
cosmically, *adv.* Cosmicamente.
cosmogony, *n.* Cosmogonia, *f.*
cosmographer, *n.* Cosmografo, *m.*
cosmographic, *a.* Cosmografico.
cosmography, *n.* Cosmografia, *f.*
cosmological [kɔzmə'lɔdʒikəl], *a.* Cosmologico.
cosmology, *n.* Cosmologia, *f.*
cosmopolitan [kɔzmə'pɔlitən], *n.a.* Cosmopolitico, *m.*
cosmopolite [kɔz'mɔpəlait], *n.* Cosmopolita, *m.*
cosmos ['kɔzmɔs], *n.* Cosmo, cosmos, *m.*
Cossack ['kɔsæk], *n.* Cosacco, *m.*
cosset ['kɔsət], *v.t.* Viziare. || *n.* Favorito, *m.*
cost [kɔst], *n.* Costo, prezzo, valore, *m.*, spesa, *f.* || *v.i.* Costare. **At any —**, a qualunque prezzo; **at the — of**, a costo di; **to sell at — price**, vendere a prezzo di costo; **net —**, prezzo netto; **— what it may**, costi quel che costi.
costal ['kɔstəl], *a.* (*Anat.*) Costale.
coster, costermonger ['kɔstəɹmʌngəɹ], *n.* Venditore ambulante di frutta o simili, fruttivendolo, *m.*
costing, *n.* (*Comm.*) Costo, *m.*
costive, *a.* Stitico.
costiveness, *n.* Stitichezza, *f.*
costliness, *n.* Prezzo alto, *m.*; lusso, sfarzo, *m.*, suntuosità, *f.*
costly, *a.* Di molto costo, caro; di gran lusso, lussuoso, sfarzoso, prezioso.
costmary ['kɔstməri], *n.* (*Bot.*) Balsamite, erba Santa Maria, *f.*
costume ['kɔstjuːm], *n.* Vestito, *m.*; costume, *m.*; (*lady's*) abito tailleur, *m.* (*Theat.*) **— -piece**, commedia in costume, dramma storico, *f.*
costumier, *n.* Sarto, *m.*, sarta, *f.*; (*Theat.*) vestiarista, *m.*
cosy ['kouzi], *a.* Comodo, gradevole, comodo e caldo. || *n.* Copri-teiera, *m.* **— corner**, cantuccio comodo, *m.*; **to make oneself —**, crogiolarsi.
cot (1) [kɔt], *n.* Capanna, casupola; casetta, *f.*
cot (2), *n.* Culla, *f.*, lettino, *m.*; (*Naut.*) amaca, *f.*
cotangent [kou'tændʒənt], *n.* (*Math.*) Cotangente, *f.*
cote [kout], *n.* Ricovero per gli animali, *m.* **Sheep- —**, ovile, *m.*; **dove- —**, colombaia, *f.*
co-tenant [kou'tenənt], *n.* Coinquilino, *m.*
coterie ['koutəriː], *n.* Circolo, *m.*; cricca, combriccola, *f.*
cothurnus [kə'θəːɹnəs], *n.* Coturno, *m.*
cotillion, cotillon [kə'tiliən], *n.* Cotillon, *m.*
cottage ['kɔtədʒ], *n.* Capanna, casupola, *f.*; casetta, *f.*; villino, *m.* **— -hospital**, piccolo ospedale, *m.*; **— piano**, piano verticale, *m.*
cottager, *n.* Contadino, *m.*, contadina, *f.*
cottar, cotter, *n.* Contadino, *m.*
cotter, *n.* (*Mech.*) Chiavetta, *f.*
cotton ['kɔtən], *n.* Cotone, *m.*, tela di cotone, *f.* || *v.i.* Essere d'accordo. **— cloth**, tela di cotone, *f.*; **— -gin**, macchina per sgranellare il cotone, *f.*; **— -goods**, cotonerie, cotonate, *f.pl.*; **— -mill**, cotonificio, *m.*; **— -plant**, cotone, *m.*, pianta del cotone, *f.*; **— -spinning**, filatura del cotone, *f.*; **— -waste**, cascame di cotone, *m.*; **— -wool**, ovatta, bambagia, *f.*; **— -yarn**, filo di cotone, *m.*; **to — to**, fare amicizia con; **to — on**, capire.
cotyledon [kɔti'liːdən], *n.* (*Bot.*) Cotiledone, *m.*
couch (1) [kautʃ], *n.* Canapè, divano, sofà, *m.*; (*fig.*) letto, *m.* || *v.i.* Coricarsi; *v.t.* disporre, stendere; esprimere, mettere in iscritto; (*a lance*) tenere in resta. **Couched in these terms**, redatto così.
couch (2) [kuːtʃ], *n.* (*Bot.*) Gramigna, *f.*
cougar ['kuːgəɹ], *n.* (*Zool.*) Coguaro, *m.*
cough [kɔːf; kɔf], *n.* Tosse, *f.* || *v.i.* Tossire. **To — up**, espettorare; **— -drop, lozenge**, pastiglia per la tosse, *f.*; **— -mixture**, decotto per la tosse, *m.*
coughing, *n.* Il tossire, colpo di tosse, *m.* **Fit of —**, insulto di tosse, *m.*
could, *past* of **can.**
coulisse [ku'liːs], *n.* (*Theat.*) Quinta, *f.*
coulter ['koultəɹ], *n.* Coltro, *m.*
council ['kaunsəl], *n.* Consiglio, *m.*; (*Eccles.*) concilio, *m.* **— -board**, tavola del consiglio, *f.*; **— -chamber**, camera del consiglio, *f.*
councillor, *n.* Consigliere, *m.*
counsel ['kaunsəl], *n.* Consiglio, avviso, *m.*, opinione, *f.*; (*Law*) avvocato, *m.* || *v.t.* Consigliare. **To take —**, consultare; **to keep one's own —**, tenere il segreto; **to take counsel's opinion**, consultare un avvocato.
counsellor, *n.* Consigliere, *m.*
count (1) [kaunt], *n.* Conte (*title*), *m.*
count (2), *n.* Calcolo, conto, *m.*, somma, *m.*; (*Law*) capo d'accusa, *m.* || *v.t.* Contare, numerare, annoverare; considerare, riguardare, stimare; attribuire; *v.i.* aver valore. **That was counted to him for righteousness**, quello gli fu attribuito a lode; **to — upon**, contare su; **that does not —**, quello non importa, non conta niente.
countenance ['kauntənəns], *n.* Viso, volto, *m.*; sembianza, fisionomia, *f.*; favore, aiuto, sostegno, *m.* || *v.t.* Secondare, appoggiare, aiutare, sostenere, difendere. **To be out of —**, essere confuso; **to change —**, alterarsi,

commuoversi; **to give — to,** secondare, appoggiare; **to keep one's —,** dare un contegno; **to put out of —,** sconcertare, turbare.
counter ['kauntəɹ], *n.* Contatore, calcolatore, *m.*; (*games*) gettone, *m.*; (*shop*) banco, *m.* || *adv.* Contro, al contrario, contrariamente. || *v.i.* Rispondere, dare un contraccolpo. **To run — to,** andar contro a; (*colloq.*) **— -jumper,** commesso di negozio, *m.*; (*Phys.*) **Geiger- —,** contatore Geiger, *m.*
counter- ['kauntəɹ], *prefix.* **contro-.**
counteract, *v.t.* Opporsi, ostacolare, contrariare; neutralizzare.
counteraction, *n.* Opposizione, *f.*, antagonismo, *m.*; resistenza, *f.*
counter-attraction, *n.* Attrazione opposta, *f.*
counter-balance, *n.* Contrappeso, *m.* || *v.t.* Contrappesare.
counter-bass, *n.* (*Mus.*) Contrabbasso, *m.*
counterblast, *n.* Contraccolpo, *m.*
counter-brace, *n.* (*Naut.*) Contraccinta, *f.*
counterchange, *v.t.* Contraccambiare; *v.i.* cambiare le parti.
countercharge, *n.* Contraccusa. || *v.t.* Contraccusare.
countercheck, *n.* Ostacolo, rimprovero, *m.* || *v.t.* Contrariare, tenere in iscacco.
counter-claim, *n.* Controrichiesta, *f.*
counter-current, *n.* Controcorrente, *f.*
counterfeit, *v.t.* Contraffare, imitare, simulare, falsare. || *n.* Falsificazione, contraffazione, *f.* || *a.* Contraffatto, simulato, falso.
counterfeiter, *n.* Contraffattore, *m.*
counterfoil, *n.* Matrice, madre, *f.*
counter-instructions, *n.pl.* Contrordine, *m.*
counter-irritant, *n.* Revulsivo, *m.*
countermand, *v.t.* Contrordinare. || *n.* Contrordine, *m.*
countermarch, *n.* Contromarcia, *f.* || *v.i.* Eseguire una contromarcia.
countermark, *n.* Contromarca, *f.* || *v.t.* Contromarcare.
countermine, *n.* (*Mil.*) Contromina, *f.* || *v.t.* Controminare; opporre, sventare, combattere.
counter-movement, *n.* Movimento contrario, *m.*
counterpane, *n.* Coltre, coperta da letto, *f.*
counterpart, *n.* Copia, *f.*; (*Law*) controparte, *f.*
counter-petition, *n.* Contropetizione, *f.*
counterplot, *n.* Artifizio opposto ad artifizio, *m.*
counterpoint, *n.* (*Mus.*) Contrappunto, *m.*
counterpoise, *n.* Contrappeso, *m.* || *v.t.* Contrappesare, bilanciare.
counter-poison, *n.* Contravveleno, *m.*
counter-pressure, *n.* Contropressione, *f.*
counter-project, *n.* Controprogetto, *m.*
counter-revolution, *n.* Controrivoluzione, *f.*
counter-revolutionary, *n.a.* Controrivoluzionario, *m.*
counter-seal, *v.t.* Contrassegnare. || *n.* Controsigillo, *m.*
countersign, *v.t.* Contrassegnare. || *n.* (*Mil.*) Contrassegno, *m.*, parola d'ordine, *f.*
countersignature, *n.* Controfirma, *f.*
countersink, *v.t.* Trapanare, fresare, accecare. || *n.* Fresatura, *f.*
counterstroke, *n.* Contraccolpo, *m.*
counter-tenor, *n.* (*Mus.*) Contraltino, *m.*
countervail, *v.t.i.* Contravvalere, eguagliare, essere equivalente.
counter-weight, *n.* Contrappeso, *m.*
countess, *n.* Contessa, *f.*
counting, *n.* Il contare, il calcolare, conto, computo, *m.* **— -house,** banco, *m.*, cassa, *f.*, ufficio, *m.*
countless, *a.* Innumerabile, innumerevole.
countrified ['kʌntrifaid], *a.* Provinciale, rustico, campagnuolo.
country, *n.* Paese, *m.*, regione, *f.*; (*opposed to town*) campagna, *f.*; (*opposed to capital*) provincia, *f.*; (*fatherland*) patria, *f.*; **Across —,** attraverso i campi; **— club,** circolo sportivo, *m.*; **— gentleman,** signore di provincia, *m.*; **— girl,** contadinella, *f.*; **— cottage,** villina, *f.*; **— dance,** danza villereccia, *f.*; **— house,** villa, casa di campagna, *f.*; **— life,** vita campestre, *f.*; **— town,** città di provincia, *f.*, borgo, paese, *m.*; **to live in the —,** vivere in campagna; **wine of the —,** vino del paese, vino nostrano, *m.*
countryman, *n.* Contadino, campagnuolo, rustico, *m.* **Fellow- —,** compatriotta, *m.*, compaesano, *m.*
countryside, *n.* Paese, contado, *m.*
countrywoman, *n.* Contadina, campagnuola, *f.* **Fellow- —,** compatriotta, *f.*
county ['kaunti], *n.* Contea, *f.*; provincia, *f.* **— town,** capoluogo di provincia, *m.*; **— court,** tribunale civile, *m.*
couple ['kʌpl], *n.* Coppia, *f.*, paio, *m.* || *v.t.* Accoppiare, appaiare; unire, giungere; associare; *v.i.* accoppiarsi. **Married —,** coniugi, *n.pl.*; **to go in couples,** andare due a due; **newly-married —,** sposini, *m.pl.*
couplet, *n.* (*Poet.*) Distico, *m.*
coupling, *n.* Accoppiamento, *m.*; (*Med.*) giuntura, *f.*; (*Mech.*) raccordo, giunto, *m.* **— -box,** manicotto, *m.*; **— -pin,** caviglia, *f.*
coupon ['ku:pɔn], *n.* Cedola, *f.*, tagliando, *m.*
courage ['kʌridʒ], *n.* Coraggio, animo, *m.*
courageous, *a.* Coraggioso, animoso.
courageously, *adv.* Coraggiosamente.
courageousness, *n.* Coraggio, *m.*, bravura, intrepidezza, *f.*
courier ['ku:riəɹ], *n.* Corriere, *m.*
course [kɔ:ɹs], *n.* Corso, corrente, *m.*; carriera, via, *f.*; procedimento, andamento, *m.*; (*of a meal*) portata, *f.*; (*Naut.*) rotta, *f.*; (*way of living*) condotta, *f.*; (*Arch.*) strato, *m.*; (*ground*) campo, terreno, *m.*; (*mining*) filone, *m.*; (*Med.*) mestrui, *m.pl.* || *v.t.* Cacciare; (*a horse*) far correre; *v.i.* (*of the blood*) correre, circolare. **To change one's —,** cambiar rotta; **that is a dangerous — to take,** quel modo di procedere è pieno di pericoli; **in the natural — of things,** nell'ordine naturale delle cose; **to take to evil courses,** darsi ad una vita disordinata; **in — of formation,** in via di formazione; **in — of time,** col tempo; **in due —,** a tempo debito; **in the — of a year,** nel corso di un anno; **of —,** naturalmente, è cosa intesa; **Why, of —!** Si figuri! **the illness must take its —,** la malattia deve fare il suo corso.
courser, *n.* Corsiere, destriero, *m.*
coursing, *n.* Caccia alla lepre, *f.*
court [kɔ:ɹt], *n.* Corte, *f.*, cortile, *m.*; commissione, *f.*; tribunale, *m.*; vicolo, *m.* || *v.t.* Corteggiare, far la corte a; cercare, invitare,

sollecitare. **Tennis- —,** campo di tennis, *m.*; **— of appeal,** corte d'appello, *f.*; **in open —,** in tribunale; **to go to —,** andare a corte; **to have a friend at —,** avere un buon amico a corte; **to pay — to,** corteggiare; **out of —,** che non merita considerazione; **to — death,** andare in cerca della morte; **to — inquiries,** offrirsi per dare informazioni; **— -card,** figura, *f.*; **— -dress,** abito di corte, *m.*; **— -hand,** scrittura curiale, *f.*; **— -martial,** corte marziale, *f.*; **— -plaster,** taffeta inglese, drappo inglese, *m.*; **— -shoes,** scarpe scollate, *f.pl.*

courteous [ˈkəːɹtiəs], *a.* Cortese, garbato, gentile.

courteously, *adv.* Cortesemente, gentilmente.

courteousness, *n.* Cortesia, gentilezza, *f.*

courtesan [kɔːɹtiˈzæn], *n.* Meretrice, cortigiana, *f.*

courtesy, *n.* Cortesia, gentilezza, *f.*

courtier, *n.* Cortigiano, *m.*

courtliness, *n.* Gentilezza, urbanità, eleganza, *f.*

courtly, *a.* Urbano, elegante.

courtship, *n.* Corteggiamento, *m.*

courtyard, *n.* Cortile, *m.*

cousin [ˈkʌzən], *n.* Cugino, *m.*, cugina, *f.* **Second —,** cugino in secondo grado, *m.*

cove (1) [kouv], *n.* Seno, *m.*, cala, insenatura, *f.*

cove (2), *n.* (*colloq.*) Uomo, compagno, *m.*

coven, covin [ˈkʌvən], *n.* Adunanza di streghe, *f.*

covenant [ˈkʌvənənt], *n.* Convenzione, *f.*, patto, contratto, accordo, *m.* ‖ *v.t.* Stipulare; *v.i.* convenire. **To enter into a —,** fare un patto.

Covenanter, *n.* (*Hist.*) Aderente ad un patto religioso nella Scozia, *m.*

Coventry [ˈkɔvəntri], *n.* **To send to —,** boicottare, scansare.

cover [ˈkʌvəɹ], *v.t.* Coprire, rivestire; nascondere, celare; provvedere a; (*of animals*) montare. ‖ *n.* Coperchio, *m.*; nascondiglio, *m*; (*of dishes, etc.*) coperta, *f.*; (*fig.*) pretesto, *n.*; (*of a book*) copertina, *f.*; (*Sport*) macchia, *f.*; (*at table*) coperto, *m.* **To — a distance of two miles,** percorrere due miglia; **that building covers much ground,** quell'edificio occupa una grande area; **to take —,** nascondersi; **under —,** al coperto; **under — of,** sotto pretesto di; **from — to —,** dal principio alla fine.

covering, *n.* Coperta, copertura, *f.*; intonaco; involucro, *m.*; vestiti, *m.pl.*; (*of animals*) monta, *f.*, accoppiamento, *m.* **A — letter,** una lettera d'accompagnamento, *f.*

coverlet, *n.* Coperta da letto, *f.*, copripiedi, *m.*

covert [ˈkʌvəɹt], *n.* Boscaglia, macchia, *f.* ‖ *a.* Coperto, segreto, nascosto, insidioso. **A — threat,** una vaga minaccia, *f.*; **a — glance,** un'occhiata di sottecchi, *f.*; **— -way,** cammino coperto, *m.*

covertly, *adv.* Segretamente.

coverture, *n.* Coperta, *f.*; (*Law*) condizione di donna sotto protezione del marito, *f.*

covet [ˈkʌvət], *v.t.* Bramare, agognare, aspirare, desiderare.

covetous, *a.* Bramoso, avido, avaro.

covetously, *adv.* Avidamente, avaramente.

covetousness, *n.* Bramosità, avarizia, *f.*

covey [ˈkʌvi], *n.* Covata, *f.*, stormo, *m.*

cow (1) [kau], *n.* Vacca, mucca, *f.*; (*of elephants, etc.*) femmina, *f.* **Milch —,** mucca, vacca lattifera, *f.*; **— -bane,** (*Bot.*) cicuta acquatica, *f.*; **— -catcher,** cacciapietre, *m.*; **— -dung,** sterco di vacca, *m.*; **— -keeper,** vaccaro, lattaio, *m.*

cow (2), *v.t.* Intimidire, domare.

coward, *n.* Codardo, vile, vigliacco, *m.*

cowardice, cowardliness, *n.* Codardia, viltà, vigliaccheria, pusillanimità, poltroneria, *f.*

cowardly, *a.* Codardo, vile, vigliacco, pauroso.

cowboy, *n.* Vaccaro, bovaro, *m.*; cowboy, *m.*

cower, *v.i.* Accoccolarsi, rannicchiarsi. **To — with fear,** accovacciarsi per timore.

cowherd, *n.* Vaccaro, buttero, *m.*

cowhide, *n.* Cuoio di vacca, *m.*, vacchetta, *f.*

cowhouse, cowshed, *n.* Vaccheria, stalla, *f.*

cowl, *n.* Cappuccio, *m.*, saio, *m.* **Chimney- —,** fumaiuolo, *m.*

cowpox, *n.* (*Med.*) Varicella, *f.*

cowry, *n.* (*Zool.*) Cauris, *m.*

cowshed, *n.* Vaccheria, stalla, *f.*

cowslip, *n.* (*Bot.*) Primaverina, *f.*

coxcomb [ˈkɔkskoum], *n.* Bellimbusto, vagheggino, zerbinotto, *m.*; (*Bot.*) celosia, cresta di gallo, *f.*

coxswain [ˈkɔksən], *n.* Timoniere, *m.*

coy [kɔi], *a.* Timido, riservato, ritroso.

coyly, *adv.* Timidamente.

coyness, *n.* Timidità, timidezza, *f.*

cozen [ˈkʌzən], *v.t.* Ingannare, truffare, frodare.

cozenage, *n.* Frode, truffa, *f.*

cozener, *n.* Ingannatore, truffatore, *m.*

cozy [cp. **cosy**].

crab [kræb], *n.* (*Zool.*) Granchio, *m.*; (*Astron.*) cancro, *m.*; (*Mech.*) verricello, argano, *m.*; piattola (*louse*), *f.* (*colloq.*) **To catch a —,** dare una palata a vuoto; **— -apple,** mela selvatica, *f.*; **— -tree,** melo selvatico, *m.*

crab, *v.t.* Avvilire, screditare.

crabbed, *a.* Bisbetico, stizzoso, aspro, rozzo; (*of writing*) illegibile; (*of a cudgel*) nodoso.

crabbedness, *n.* Asprezza, severità, *f.*; cattivo umore, *m.*

crack [kræk], *v.t.* Spaccare, fendere; schioccare (*a whip*); (*crockery*) incrinare; (*nuts*) rompere; (*a joke*) fare; (*a bottle of wine*) sturare; *v.i.* spaccarsi, fendersi, rompersi; (*of the skin*) screpolarsi; (*the voice*) cambiare. ‖ *n.* Rottura, fessura, *f.*; crepaccio, *m.*, crepa, *f.*; scoppio, *m.*, esplosione, *f.*; (*of a whip*) schiocco, *m.* ‖ *a.* Famoso, esperto, scelto, ottimo. **— of doom,** giudizio finale, *m.*; **in a —,** in un momento; **a — shot,** un tiratore scelto, *m.*; (*colloq.*) **to — up,** lodare; **— -brained,** pazzo, scervellato, stravagante.

cracked, *a.* Rotto, fesso; pazzo, strambo. **He's a little —,** è un po' tocco al cervello.

cracker, *n.* (*firework*) Petardo; biscotto, *m.*; galletta, *f.*; (*colloq.*) **Crackers,** matto.

cracking, *n.* Fenditura, screpolatura, *f.*, schiocco, *m.*

crackle, *v.i.* Crepitare, scoppiettare.

crackling, *n.* Crepitio, scoppiettio, *m.*; pelle di porco arrostito, *f.*

cracknel, *n.* Specie di biscotto duro, *m.*

cracksman, *n.* Ladro, scassinatore, *m.*

Cracow [ˈkrɑːkau], *n.* (*Geog.*) Cracovia, *f.*

cradle [ˈkreidl], *n.* Culla, *f.* ‖ *v.t.* Cullare. **From the —** dalla culla.

craft (1) [krɑːft], *n.* Arte, *f.*; artificio, *m.*; (*trade*) mestiere, *m.*; (*cunning*) astuzia, *f.* **The Craft,** Massoneria, *f.*
craft (2), *n.* Battello, *m.*, barca, *f.* **Small —,** piccole barche, *f.pl.*
craftily, *adv.* Astutamente, con inganno.
craftsman, *n.* Artefice, *m.*; artista, *m.*
crafty, *a.* Astuto, furbo, accorto.
crag [kræg], *n.* Rupe, roccia, *f.*; ghiaia, *f.*
cragged, craggy, *a.* Roccioso, erto, rupestre, dirupato.
cragginess, *n.* Rocciosità, *f.*
cragsman, *n.* Alpinista, rocciatore, *m.*
cram [kræm], *v.t.* Riempire; (*with food*) rimpinzare, insaccare, infarcire; preparare agli esami; *v.i.* rimpinzarsi. || *n.* (*colloq.*) Bugia, *f.* **To — poultry,** ingrassar pollame; **I shall — it down his throat,** glielo farò inghiottire per forza.
crammer, *n.* Ripetitore, *m.*
cramming, *n.* Il rimpinzamento, *m.*; ripetizioni, *m.pl.*
cramp [kræmp], *n.* (*Med.*) Crampo, *m.*; (*Mech.*) rampone, morsa, *f.* || *v.t.* Stringere, comprimere, serrare; intralciare, impacciare. **To be seized with —,** essere preso da un crampo; **—-iron,** rampone, *m.*
cramped, *a.* Difficile, impacciato, stentato. **A — style,** uno stile involuto, *m.*; **— writing,** scrittura stentata, *f.*
cranberry [ˈkrænbəri], *n.* (*Bot.*) Mortella di palude, *f.*
crane [krein], *n.* (*in all senses*) Gru, *m.* || *v.t.* Allungare il collo; *v.i.* spingersi avanti. **Steam —,** gru a vapore, *m.*; **travelling- —,** gru movibile, *m.*; **crane's-bill,** (*Bot.*) geranio selvatico, *m.*
craniological [kreinioˈlɔdʒikəl], *a.* Craniologico.
craniology, *n.* Craniologia, *f.*
craniometry, *n.* Craniometria, *f.*
cranium, *n.* Cranio, *m.*
crank [kræŋk], *n.* (*Mech.*) Manovella, *f.*; manubrio, gomito, *m.*; bisticcio *m.*; (*person*) originale, strambo, *m.* || *v.t.* Girare la manovella. || *a.* Debole, (*Naut.*) pronto a capovolgere. (*Motor.*) **To — up,** mettere in azione il motore; **quips and cranks,** giuochi di parole; **he's a regular —,** è una testa balzana; **—-arm,** manovella, *f.*; **—-pin,** perno di manovella, *m.*; **—-shaft,** albero a manovella, *m.*
cranky, *a.* Capriccioso, irragionevole, pazzerello.
cranny [ˈkræni], *n.* Crepa, fessura, *f.*, buco, *m.*
crape [kreip], *n.* Crespo, *m.* || *v.t.* Guarnire di crespo.
crapulent, crapulous [ˈkræpjuːlənt, ˈkræpjuːləs], *a.* Dato alla crapula, vizioso.
crapulence, *n.* Crapula, *f.*
crash (1) [kræʃ], *v.i.* Fracassarsi, rompersi, crollare; (*Aviat.*) precipitare; *v.t.* spaccare, fracassare. || *n.* Fracasso, schianto, *m.*; (*fig.*) rovina, distruzione, *f.*; (*Comm.*) fallimento, *m.*
crash (2), *n.* Canovaccio, *m.*
crass [kræs], *a.* Rozzo, grossolano, crasso; spesso. **— stupidity,** stupidità crassa, *f.*
crassness, *n.* Grossolanità, *f.*
crate [kreit], *n.* Cesta, gabbia, *f.*
crater, *n.* Cratere, *m.*
cravat [krəˈvæt], *n.* Cravatta, *f.*
crave [kreiv], *v.t.* Domandare, sollecitare, supplicare, implorare, bramare.
craven, *a.* Vile, pusillanime. || *n.* Vigliacco, codardo, *m.*
craw [krɔː], *n.* Gozzo, *m.*
crawfish, crayfish [ˈkrɔːfiʃ, ˈkreifiʃ], *n.* (*Zool.*) Gambero, *m.*
crawl [krɔːl], *v.i.* Strisciare, trascinarsi; andar carponi; insinuarsi. || *n.* Moto lento, strisciamento, *m.* **To — up,** arrampicarsi su; **to — with,** formicolare di.
crawling, *a.* Che va carponi, che si trascina, strisciante.
crayon [ˈkreiɔn], *n.* Matita, *f.*, pastello, *m.* || *v.t.* Dipingere a pastello, abbozzare.
craze [kreiz], *n.* Mania, smania, *f.* || *v.t.* Fare impazzire.
crazed, *a.* Folle, matto, pazzo.
crazily, *adv.* Pazzamente, insensatamente.
craziness, *n.* Pazzia, follia, *f.*; fragilità, *f.*
crazy, *a.* Folle, matto, pazzo, pazzerello, guasto, logorato.
creak [kriːk], *v.i.* Cigolare, scricchiare, stridere. || *n.* Cigolio, scricchiolio, stridio, *m.*
creaky, *a.* Cigolante, scricchiolante.
cream [kriːm], *n.* Panna, *f.*; (*artificial*) crema, *f.*; (*of a story*) bello, *m.*; (*fig.*) la migliore parte, *f.* || *v.t.* Scremare, aggiungere panna a; *v.i.* rappigliarsi. **Whipped —,** panna montata, *f.*; **—-cheese,** crema di formaggio, *f.*, formaggio alla crema, *m.*; **—-jug,** vasetto da panna, *m.*; (*paper*) **—-laid,** liscia, lucida.
creamery, *n.* Latteria, *f.*
crease [kriːs], *n.* Piega, crespa, ruga, grinza, *f.* || *v.t.* Increspare, aggrinzare, corrugare.
create [kriˈeit], *v.t.* Creare, originare, suscitare, causare, produrre, fare; (*colloq.*) menar scalpore.
creation, *n.* Creazione, *f.*; natura, *f.*; universo, *m.*
creative, *a.* Creativo.
creativeness, *n.* Virtù creatrice, *f.*
creator, *n.* Creatore, autore, *m.*; Iddio, *m.*
creature [ˈkriːtʃəɹ], *n.* Creatura, *f.*; bestia, *f.*, animale, *m.*; strumento, dipendente, *m.* **— comforts,** benessere materiale, *m.*
crèche [kreiʃ], *n.* (*day-nursery*) Nido, *m.*; asilo infantile, *m.*
credence [ˈkriːdəns], *n.* Credenza, fede, *f.*; credito, *m.*; (*Eccles.*) credenza, *f.* **To give — to,** credere; **to gain —,** acquistare credito.
credentials [kriˈdenʃəlz], *n.pl.* Credenziali, *f.pl.*
credibility, *n.* Credibilità, *f.*
credible, *a.* Credibile, degno di fede.
credibly, *adv.* Credibilmente. **To be — informed,** sapere da buona fonte.
credit [ˈkredit], *n.* Credito, *m.*; credenza, fede, stima, fiducia, *f.*; (*Comm.*) credito, *m.* || *v.t.* Credere, prestar fede a; (*Comm.*) accreditare. **I gave you — for more sense,** ti credevo più giudizioso; **on —,** a credito; **to give —,** vendere a credito; **to give — to,** prestar fede a; **letter of —,** lettera di credito, *f*,; **I — him with common sense,** credo che egli abbia buon senso.
creditable, *a.* Meritevole, stimabile, pregevole.
creditably, *adv.* Con onore, onorevolmente.
creditor, *n.* Creditore, *m.* **— side of an account,** l'attivo di un conto, *m.*

credo [ˈkriːdou], *n.* Credo, *m.*, professione di fede, *f.*
credulity, credulousness [kreˈdjuːliti, ˈkredjuːləsnis], *n.* Credulità, *f.*
credulous, *a.* Credulo.
credulously, *adv.* Con credulità.
creed [kriːd], *n.* Credo, *m.*; credenza, fede, religione, opinione, *f.* **The Apostles' Creed,** il credo degli apostoli, *m.*
creek [kriːk], *n.* Cala, *f.*, seno di mare, *m.*; fiumicello, *m.*
creel [kriːl], *n.* Paniere per riporre il pesce, *m.*
creep [kriːp], *v.i.* Strisciare, trascinarsi, andare carponi; insinuarsi. **To — in,** insinuarsi in; **to — on,** avanzarsi lento lento; **to — out,** andarsene inosservato; **to — over,** strisciare sopra; **to — up,** arrampicarsi su; **to feel one's flesh —,** sentirsi accapponare la pelle, sentirsi venire la pelle d'oca.
creeper, *n.* (*Bot.*) Rampicante, *m.*; (*Zool.*) rettile, *m.*; (*Mech.*) graffo, *m.*
creeping, *n.* Formicolio, *m.* || *a.* (*Bot.*) Rampicante.
creepy, *a.* Che dà la pelle d'oca, che fa rabbrividire.
creese, kris [kriːs], *n.* Pugnale dei malesi, *m.*
cremate [kriˈmeit], *v.t.* Cremare.
cremation, *n.* Cremazione, *f.*
crematorium [kreməˈtɔːriəm], *n.* Crematorio, *m.*
crematory, *a.* Crematorio.
cremona [kriˈmounə], *n.* (*Mus.*) Violino di Cremona, *m.*
crenate, crenated [ˈkreneit, krəˈneitəd], *a.* (*Bot.*) Dentellato.
crenellate [ˈkrenəleit], *v.t.* Guarnire di merli.
crenellation, *n.* Merlata, *f.*
Creole [ˈkriːoul], *n.* Creolo, *m.*
creosote [ˈkriosout], *n.* Creosoto, *m.*
crepitate [ˈkrepiteit], *v.i.* Crepitare.
crepitant, *a.* Crepitante.
crepitation, *n.* Crepitazione, *f.*
crept *past, p.p.* of **creep.**
crepuscular [kreˈpʌskjuːləɹ], *a.* Crepuscolare.
crescendo [kreˈʃendou], *adv.* (*Mus.*) Crescendo.
crescent [ˈkresənt], *n.* Mezzaluna, *f.* || *a.* Crescente.
cress [kres], *n.* (*Bot.*) Crescione, *m.* **Water- —,** crescione di fonte, *m.*
cresset [ˈkresit], *n.* Fanale, *m.*, fiaccola, torcia, *f.*
crest [krest], *n.* Cresta, *f.*; (*of helmet*), cimiero, pennacchio, *m.*; (*Heraldry*) stemma gentilizio, *m.*; (*of birds*) ciuffo, ciuffetto, *m.*; (*of a hill*) cima, *f.*
crested, *a.* Crestato; impennacchiato.
crest-fallen, *a.* Scoraggiato, abbattuto; vergognoso, umiliato.
cretaceous [krəˈteiʃəs], *a.* (*Geol.*) Cretaceo.
cretin [ˈkriːtin], *n.* Cretino, *m.*
cretinism, *n.* Cretinismo, *m.*
cretinous, *a.* Ebete, imbecille.
cretonne [kreˈtɔn], *n.* Cretonne, cotonina, *f.*
crevasse [krəˈvæs], *n.* Crepaccio, *m.*
crevice [ˈkrevis], *n.* Crepaccio, *m.*, fessura, spaccatura, *f.*
crew [kruː], *n.* Compagnia, *f.*; ciurma, cricca, *f.*; equipaggio, *m.*
crewel, *n.* Filo di lana da ricamo, *m.* **— work,** ricamo, *m.*
crib (1) [krib], *n.* Presepio, *m.*; mangiatoia, *f.*; (*hut*) capanna, *f.*; (*for child*) lettino, *m.*, culla, *f.*; (*job*) posto, *m.*
crib (2), *n.* (*colloq.*) Plagio, *m.*, traduzione, *f.* || *v.t.* Appropriarsi, rubare; plagiare, copiare.
cribbage, *n.* Specie di giuoco alle carte.
crick [krik], *n.* Crampo, spasimo, *m.* **A — in the neck,** torcicollo, *m.*
cricket (1) [ˈkrikit], *n.* (*Zool.*) Grillo, *m.*, cavalletta, *f.*
cricket (2), *n.* Il cricket, *m.* **It's not —,** non è giuoco leale; **— -ball,** palla di cricket, *f.*; **— -bat,** mazza di cricket, *f.*; **— -field,** campo di cricket, *m.*; **— match,** partita a cricket, *f.*
cricketer, *n.* Giuocatore di cricket, *m.*
crier [ˈkraiəɹ], *n.* Usciere, *m.* **Town- —,** banditore, *m.*
crime [kraim], *n.* Delitto, reato, misfatto, *m.* **To charge with a —,** incolpare di un delitto.
criminal [ˈkriminəl], *n.a.* Criminale, *m.*
criminality, *n.* Criminalità, *f.*
criminally, *adv.* Criminalmente.
criminate, *v.t.* Accusare, incolpare, incriminare, imputare.
criminology, *n.* Criminologia, *f.*
criminous, *a.* Criminoso, delittuoso.
crimp (1) [krimp], *v.t.* (*the hair*) Increspare, arricciare; (*material*) pieghettare.
crimp (2), *v.t.* Arruolare per frode o forza. || *n.* Arruolatore in questa maniera, *m.*
crimping, *n.* Arricciatura, increspatura, pieghettatura, *f.* **— -iron,** ferro da arricciare, *m.*
crimson [ˈkrimzən], *a.* Cremisino. || *n.* Cremisi, *m.* || *v.t.* Tingere di cremisi; *v.i.* arrossire.
cringe [krindʒ], *v.i.* Inchinarsi, strisciare, abbassarsi servilmente. **To — to,** adulare bassamente.
cringing, *n.* Adulazione, umiliazione, *f.*, avvilimento, *m.*
cringle [ˈkriŋgl], *n.* (*Naut.*) Gancio, brancarello, *m.*
crinkle [ˈkriŋkl], *v.t.* Increspare, aggrinzare, corrugare; *v.i.* incresparsi, aggrinzarsi. || *n.* Grinza, ruga, crespa, *f.*
crinoid, *n.* (*Zool.*) Crinoide, *m.*
crinoline [ˈkrinəlin], *n.* Crinolina, *f.*; (*material*) crinolino, *m.*
cripple [ˈkripəl], *n.* Storpio, sciancato, deforme, *m.*; zoppo, *m.* || *v.t.* Storpiare, rendere infermo; (*fig.*) impedire, guastare, paralizzare; (*Naut.*) avariare.
crippled, *a.* Storpio; avariato; (*fig.*) impedito, paralizzato.
crisis (*pl.* **crises**) [ˈkraisis, ˈkraisiːz], *n.* Crisi, *f.*
crisp [krisp], *a.* (*of pastry, etc.*) Croccante; (*of hair*) ricciuto, crespo; (*of air*) fresco, frizzante; friabile. || *v.t.* Arricciare, increspare; *v.i.* incresparsi. **Crisping-iron,** ferro pei capelli, *m.*
crispness, *n.* Spiccatezza; friabilità, *f.*; nettezza, *f.*
crisps, *n.pl.* Patatine fritte, *f.pl.*
criss-cross [ˈkriskrɔs], *v.i.* Incrociare.
criterion (*pl.* **criteria**) kraiˈtiəriən], *n.* Criterio, *m.*, norma, *f.*
critic [ˈkritik], *n.* Critico, *m.*
critical, *a.* Critico; (*fig.*) difficile, pericoloso. **A — affair,** un affare difficile, *m.*

critically, *adv.* Criticamente, scrupolosamente, da critico.
criticism ['kritisizm], *n.* Critica, censura, *f.*, biasimo, *m.* **Literary —,** critica letteraria, *f.*
criticizable [kriti'saizəbl], *a.* Criticabile.
criticize, *v.t.* Criticare, esaminare; biasimare, censurare; *v.i.* fare il critico, esercitar la critica.
critique [kri'ti:k], *n.* Saggio critico, *m.*
croak [krouk], *v.i.* (*of frogs*) Gracidare; (*of crows, etc.*) gracchiare; (*fig.*) brontolare, borbottare; lamentare; (*colloq.*) morire. || *n.* Gracchiamento, *m.*
croaker, *n.* Brontolone, *m.*; uccello di malaugurio, *m.*
croaking, *n.* Gracidio, gracchiamento, *m.*; brontolio, lamento, *m.*
Croat [krout], *n.* Croato, *m.*
crochet ['krouʃi], *n.* Lavoro a croscé, uncinetto, *m.* **— -hook,** uncinetto, *m.*
crock [krɔk], *n.* Vaso, *m.*, brocca, *f.*; coccio, *m.*; (*fig.*) infermo, *m.* (*colloq.*) **To — up,** ammalarsi.
crockery, *n.* Stoviglie, terraglie, *f.pl.*, vasellame, *m.*
crocodile ['krɔkodail], *n.* (*Zool.*) Coccodrillo, *m.* **— tears,** lagrime di coccodrillo, *f.pl.*
crocus ['kroukəs], *n.* (*Bot.*) Croco, *m.*
Croesus ['kri:səs], *n.* (*Myth.*) Creso, *m.*
croft [krɔft], *n.* Campicello, praticello, poderetto, *m.*
crofter, *n.* Coltivatore di un poderetto, *m.*
cromlech ['krɔmlek], *n.* Cromlech, *m.*
crone [kroun], *n.* Vecchiaccia, *f.*; strega, *f.*
crony, *n.* Compare, *m.*, comare, *f.*; compagno, amico, *m.*
crook [kruk], *n.* Uncino, *m.*; bordone, *m.*; (*of shepherd*) bastone, *m.*; (*Eccles.*) pastorale, *m.*; curva, *f.*; (*person*) ladro, truffatore, *m.* || *v.t.* Piegare, curvare, arcuare; *v.i.* curvarsi. **By hook or by —,** a diritto o a rovescio, di riffa o di raffa; **— -backed,** gobbo; **— -kneed,** sbilenco, sciancato.
crooked ['krukid], *a.* Obliquo, adunco, storto, tortuoso, di traverso; (*fig.*) disonesto, perverso, cattivo.
crookedly, *adv.* Obliquamente, di sghembo; malvagiamente.
crookedness, *n.* Curvatura, piegatura, *f.*; difformità, *f.*; cattiveria, *f.*
croon [kru:n], *v.i.* Canticchiare, canterellare.
crooner, *n.* Canticchiatore, *m.*
crop [krɔp], *n.* Raccolta, *f.*, raccolto, *m.*, messe, *f.*; mietitura, *f.*; (*of bird*), gozzo, *m.* || *v.t.* Tagliare, tosare, mozzare; (*to reap*) falciare, mietere; (*grass*) pascolare; *v.i.* produrre grano, portare frutta. **To — up,** capitare, accadere, sopprayenire; **hunting-—,** frustino da caccia, *m.*; **neck and —,** completamente; **second —,** guaime, secondo fieno, *m.*; **— -eared,** colle orecchie mozze (*of a horse*); **— -headed,** coi capelli corti, tosato, rapato.
cropper, *n.* (*colloq.*) Caduta, *f.* **To come a —,** stramazzare.
cropping-out, *n.* (*Geol.*) Affioramento, *m.*
croquet ['krouki], *n.* (*Sport*) Croquet, *m.*
croquette [kro'ket], *n.* Polpetta, *f.*
crosier, crozier ['krouʒəɹ], *n.* Croce episcopale, *f.*
cross [krɔs], *n.* Croce, *f.*, incrociamento, *m.*; (*fig.*) dolore, pena, *f.*; (*of breeds*) incrocio, *m.*; (*on letter "t"*) taglio, *m.*; mescolanza, *f.* || *a.* Obliquo, laterale, traverso; di mal umore, bisbetico, capriccioso, imbronciato, brusco. || *v.t.* Incrociare; (*a cheque*) sbarrare; passare, attraversare; (*fig.*) tormentare, impedire, contrariare; *v.i.* incrociare, fare una traversata (*voyage*). **Criss- —,** in croce; **sign of the —,** segno della croce, *m.*; **to bear one's —,** portare la propria croce; **— -word puzzle,** enigma a parole incrociate, *m.*; **— answer,** risposta brusca, *f.*; **a — woman,** una bisbetica, *f.*; **a — baby,** un bambino piagnucoloso, *m.*; **as — as two sticks,** di pessimo umore; **to — each other,** incrociarsi; **to — out,** cancellare; **to — one's mind,** venire in mente; **to — oneself,** segnarsi, farsi la croce; **to — over,** traversare, passare; **to — someone's path,** sbarrare il passo a qualcuno; **to — swords,** incrociare i ferri; disputare; **to — a fortune-teller's hand,** dare denaro ad un'indovina; **our letters crossed,** le nostre lettere s'incrociarono; **— -action,** azione impugnativa, *f.*; (*Eccles.*) **— -bearer,** crocifero, *m.*; **— -breed,** incrocio, *m.*; **— -examination,** interrogatorio, *m.*; **— -examine,** interrogare a fondo; **— -eyed,** strabico, guercio; **— -grained,** a fibre incrociate; aspro, bisbetico; **— -hatch,** tratteggiare; **— -legged,** colle gambe incrociate; **— -patch,** brontolone, *m.*; **— -piece,** traversa, *f.*, traversino, *m.*; **— -purpose,** contrasto, *m.*, contraddizione, *f.*; malinteso, *m.*; **— -question,** interrogare; **— -reference,** richiamo, *m.*; **— -road,** traversa, *f.*; **— -roads,** crocicchio, bivio, crocevia, *m.*; **— -stitch,** punto in croce; **— -summons,** riconvenzione, *f.*; **— -trees,** (*Naut.*) crocette, *f.pl.*
crossbar, *n.* Sbarra, *f.*
crossbeam, *n.* Chiave di volta, *f.*; (*Mech.*) bilanciere di macchina a vapore, *f.*
crossbill, *n.* (*Zool.*) Crociere, *m.*
crossbones, *n.pl.* Due ossa in croce, *f.pl.*
crossbow, *n.* Balestra, *f.*
crosscut, *v.t.* Tagliare a traverso. **— saw,** sega a due mani, *f.*
crossing, *n.* (*over a street*) Passaggio, *m.*; (*by sea*) traversata, *f.*; (*of breeds*) incrocio, *m.* (*Rail.*) **Level —,** passaggio a livello, *m.*
crossly, *adv.* Di cattivo umore, aspramente.
crossness, *n.* Cattivo umore, *m.*; sgarbatezza, malagrazia, *f.*
crossways, crosswise, *adv.* In croce, di traverso.
crotchet ['krɔtʃit], *n.* (*Mus.*) Semiminima, *f.*; (*fig.*) capriccio, *m.*
crotchety, *a.* Capriccioso, fantastico; bisbetico.
croton ['kroutən], *n.* (*Bot.*) Crotone, *m.*
crouch [krautʃ], *v.i.* Abbassarsi, accovacciarsi; rannicchiarsi. **The dog crouched at his master's feet,** il cane si accovacciò ai piedi del padrone.
croup (1) [kru:p], *n.* Groppa, *f.*, groppone, *m.*
croup (2), *n.* (*Med.*) Crup, *m.*
croupier ['kru:piəɹ], *n.* Biscazziere, *m.*
crow (1) [krou], *n.* (*Zool.*) Corvo, *m.*, cornacchia, *f.* **As the — flies,** a volo d'uccello; **to have a — to pluck with,** avere una gatta

da pelare con; avere una questione di lana caprina con; **—-bar,** leva di ferro, *f.*, raffio, *m.*; **crow's-foot,** (*Mil.*) tribolo, *m.*; **crow's-feet,** zampe di gallina, *f.pl.*; **crow's-nest,** (*Naut.*) coffa, *f.*
crow (2), *v.i.* (*of cocks*) Cantare. **To — over,** cantare vittoria, trionfare su.
crowd [kraud], *n.* Folla, turba, moltitudine, *f.*, affollamento, *m.* || *v.t.* Spingere, serrare, stringere; riempire, affollare; *v.i.* affollarsi, accalcarsi, affluire. **To — out,** escludere, lasciar fuori; (*Naut.*) **to — sail,** spiegar tutte le vele; **to — with,** riempire di; **to — in,** entrare in folla; **to — round,** affollarsi intorno.
crowded, *a.* Pieno, affollato, riempito di gente.
crowfoot, *n.* (*Bot.*) Ranuncolo, *m.*
crown [kraun], *n.* Corona; (*of hill*) cima, *f.*; (*of money*) corona, *f.*, scudo, *m.*; (*of hat or head*) cocuzzolo, *m.*; (*of tooth*) corona, *f.* || *v.t.* Coronare, incoronare; premiare, colmare; (*Draughts*) damare, far dama. **— prince,** principe ereditario, *m.*; **The Crown,** la Corona, *f.*; **to — all,** per colmo di sventura; **they crowned him king,** lo incoronarono re; **—-land,** beni della corona, *m.pl.*
crowning, *n.* Incoronazione, *f.* || *a.* Ultimo, supremo, finale. **A — mercy,** una grazia suprema, *f.*
crucial [ˈkruːʃiəl], *a.* Cruciale, decisivo, definitivo. **— test,** prova cruciale.
crucible [ˈkruːsibəl], *n.* Crogiuolo, *m.*
cruciferous [kruːˈsifərəs], *a.* (*Bot.*) Crocifero.
crucifix [ˈkruːsifiks], *n.* Crocifisso, *m.*
crucifixion, *n.* Crocifissione, *f.*
cruciform, *a.* Crociforme.
crucify, *v.t.* Crocifiggere.
crude [kruːd], *a.* Crudo, immaturo; rozzo, grossolano, zotico.
crudely, *adv.* Crudamente, rozzamente.
crudeness, crudity, *n.* Crudezza, rozzezza, *f.*
cruel [ˈkruəl], *a.* Crudele, aspro, atroce.
cruelly, *adv.* Crudelmente.
cruelty, *n.* Crudeltà, atrocità, inumanità, *f.*; (*Law*) sevizie, *f.pl.*
cruet [ˈkruːit], *n.* Ampollina, oliera, *f.*, portampolle, *m.*
cruise [kruːz], *n.* Crociera, *f.* || *v.i.* Incrociare. **On a —,** in crociera.
cruiser, *n.* Incrociatore, *m.* (*Naut.*) **Battle —,** incrociatore di battaglia, *m.*
cruising, *n.* Incrociamento, *m.* || *a.* Di crociera.
crumb [krʌm], *n.* Briciola, *f.*, minuzzolo, *m.*; midolla, mollica (*of loaf*), *f.* || *v.t.* Panare, sbriciolare. **—-brush,** spazzola per briciole, *f.*; **—-scoop,** mesta da briciole, *f.*
crumby, *a.* Pieno di briciole.
crumble [ˈkrʌmbl], *v.t.* Sbriciolare, sminuzzare; polverizzare, distruggere; *v.i.* sbriciolarsi, sgretolarsi; crollare, cadere in rovina.
crumbling, *a.* Crollante.
crumbly, *a.* Atto a sbriciolarsi, friabile, sgretoloso.
crumpet [ˈkrʌmpit], *n.* Focaccina, *f.*
crumple [ˈkrʌmpl], *v.t.* Sgualcire, spiegazzare, raggrinzare; *v.i.* raggrinzarsi, sgualcirsi. **To — up,** schiacciarsi.
crunch [ˈkrʌntʃ], *v.t.* Sgretolare, schiacciare.
crupper [ˈkrʌpəɹ], *n.* (*of horse*) Groppa, *f.*; (*harness*) groppiera, *f.*
crural [ˈkruːrəl], *a.* (*Anat.*) Crurale.
crusade [kruːˈseid], *n.* Crociata, *f.*
crusader, *n.* Crociato, *m.*
cruse [kruːz], *n.* Ampollina, *f.*
crush [krʌʃ], *n.* Calca, folla, serra, *f.* || *v.t.* Schiacciare, frantumare, stritolare, ammaccare, pestare; (*clothes*) sgualcire; sopprimere; accasciare, abbattere; rovinare. **To — in,** cacciare dentro; **to — out,** spremere; **to — a rebellion,** soffocare una rivolta; **—-hat,** gibus, *m.*
crusher, *n.* Torchio, *m.*; (*for olives, etc.*) frantoio, *m.*
crushing, *a.* Schiacciante; rovinoso, rovinante. || *n.* Schiacciamento, pestamento, *m.* **A — defeat,** una sconfitta schiacciante, *f.*; **—-machine,** sminuzzatrice, *f.*
crust [krʌst], *n.* Crosta, scorza, *f.* || *v.t.* Incrostare; *v.i.* incrostarsi, produrre una crosta.
crustacea [krʌsˈteiʃə], *n.* (*Zool.*) Crostacei, *m.pl.*
crustaceous, *a.* Crostaceo.
crusted, *a.* Incrostato.
crustily, *adv.* Aspramente, scontrosamente.
crustiness, *n.* Durezza, *f.*; malumore, *m.*, musoneria, *f.*
crusty, *a.* (*of bread*) Che ha molta crosta, crostoso; duro, aspro, arcigno.
crutch [krʌtʃ], *n.* Gruccia, stampella, *f.* **To walk on crutches,** camminare colle grucce.
crux [krʌks], *n.* Punto cruciale, busillis, *m.*
cry [krai], *n.* Grido. || *v.i.* Piangere, lamentarsi; (*to shout*) gridare; *v.t.* gridare, invocare; chiamare. **To — aloud,** gridare; **to — bitterly,** piangere a calde lagrime; **to — off,** rescindere; **to — out,** gridare, esclamare, chiamare; **to — out against,** lagnarsi di, inveire contro; **to — down,** condannare, criticare; **to — up,** lodare, vantare.
crying, *n.* Pianto, lamento, *m.*, grida, *f.pl.*; lagrime, *f.pl.*; (*of babies*) piagnucolio, *m.* || *a.* Piangente, lamentoso; piagnucoloso. **A — shame,** una grande vergogna, *f.*
crypt [kript], *n.* Cripta, *f.*
cryptic, *a.* Segreto, occulto.
cryptically, *adv.* Segretamente.
cryptogam [ˈkriptogæm], *n.* (*Bot.*) Crittogama, *f.*
cryptogamous, *a.* Crittogamo.
cryptogram, *n.* Cifra, *f.*
cryptography, *n.* Crittografia, *f.*
crystal [ˈkristəl], *n.* Cristallo, *m.* || *a.* Di cristallo, cristallino; **—-gazing,** leggere il futuro in un vetro.
crystalline, *a.* Cristallino.
crystallization, *n.* Cristallizzazione, *f.*
crystallize, *v.t.* Cristallizzare; *v.i.* cristallizzarsi. **Crystallized fruits,** frutta candita, *f.*
crystallography [kristəˈlɔgrəfi], *n.* Cristallografia, *f.*
crystalloid, *n.a.* Cristalloide, *f.*
crystallometry, *n.* Cristallometria, *f.*
cub [kʌb], *n.* Cucciolo, piccolo, *m.*; (*of lion*) leoncello, *m.*; (*of wolf*) lupacchiotto, *m.*; (*of bear*) orsacchiotto, *m.*; (*of fox*) volpicino, *m.*; (*Scout*) Giovane Esploratore, *m.* || *v.t.* Figliare; cacciare ai volpicini. (*fig.*) **An unlicked —,** un ragazzaccio, *m.*; **—-hunting,** caccia ai volpicini, *f.*
cubage, cubature [ˈkjuːbədʒ, ˈkjuːbətʃəɹ], *n.* Cubatura, *f.*

cubby hole ['kʌbi houl], *n.* (*colloq.*) Stanzuccia, *f.*
cube [kju:b], *n.* Cubo, dado, *m.* || *v.t.* Cubare. **— root,** radice cubica, *f.*; **— -sugar,** zucchero in quadretti, *m.*
cubeb ['kju:bəb], *n.* (*Bot.*) Cubebe, *m.*
cubic, cubical, *a.* Cubico.
cubicle, *n.* Cubicolo, *m.*, cameretta, *f.*
cubiform, *a.* Cubiforme.
cubist, *n.* (*Art*) Cubista, *m.*
cubism, *n.* (*Art*) Cubismo, *m.*
cuboid, *n.a.* Cuboide, *m.*
cubit, *n.* Cubito, *m.*
cuckold ['kʌkold], *n.* Becco, cornuto, *m.* || *v.t.* Far becco, far le corna.
cuckoo ['kuku], *n.* (*Zool.*) Cuculo, *m.* || *a.* (*colloq.*) Matto. **— -clock,** oriuolo col cuculo; **— -flower,** (*Bot.*) cardamina, *f.*; **— -pint,** (*Bot.*) gichero, gigaro, *m.*
cucullate ['kju:kəleit], *a.* (*Bot.Zool.*) Incappucciato.
cucumber ['kju:kʌmbəɹ], *n.* (*Bot.*) Cetriolo, *m.* **As cool as a —,** con sangue freddo.
cucurbit [kju:'kəɹbit], *n.* (*Bot.*) Zucca, cucurbita, *f.*
cud [kʌd], *n.* Ruminatura, *f.* **To chew the —,** ruminare.
cuddle ['kʌdl], *v.t.* Abbracciare, accarezzare; *v.i.* accoccolarsi. || *n.* Abbraccio, *m.* **To — up,** crogiolarsi, raggomitolarsi.
cuddy, *n.* (*Naut.*) Piccola cabina, *f.*
cudgel ['kʌdʒəl], *n.* Bastone, randello, *m.*; mazza, *f.* || *v.t.* Bastonare. **To — one's brains,** stillarsi il cervello; **to take up the cudgels for,** difendere.
cudgelling, *n.* Bastonatura, *f.*
cue [kju:], *n.* (*Theat.*) Parola, *f.*; suggerimento, *m.*; (*Billiards*) stecca, *f.* **To give the —,** dare lo spunto; **— -rack,** portastecche, *m.*
cuff (1) [kʌf], *n.* (*of shirt*) Polsino, *m.*; (*of coat*) paramano, *m.* **— -links,** bottoncini gemelli, *m.pl.*
cuff (2), *v.t.* Schiaffeggiare, scapaccionare, scappellottare. || *n.* Schiaffo, scapaccione, scappellotto, *m.*
cuirass [kwi'ræs], *n.* Corazza, *f.*
cuirassier, *n.* Corazziere, *m.*
culinary ['kju:linəri], *a.* Culinario.
cull [kʌl], *v.t.* Cogliere, raccogliere; scegliere.
cullender, colander ['kʌləndəɹ], *n.* Colatoio, *m.*; colabrodo, colapasta, *m.*
culm [kʌlm], *n.* (*Bot.*) Culmo, stelo, *m.*; (*Min.*) polvere di carbone antracite, *f.*
culminate ['kʌlmineit], *v.i.* Terminare, culminare; (*Astron.*) culminare.
culmination, *n.* Culmine, *m.*, fine, *f.*; (*Astron.*) culminazione, *f.*
culpability [kʌlpə'biliti], *n.* Colpabilità, colpevolezza, *f.*
culpable, *a.* Colpabile, colpevole.
culpably, *adv.* Colpevolmente.
culprit, *n.* Colpevole, *m.f.*; (*Law*) reo, *m.*
cult [kʌlt], *n.* Culto, *m.*, religione, *f.*
cultivable ['kʌltivəbl], *a.* Coltivabile.
cultivate, *v.t.* Coltivare.
cultivation, *n.* Coltivazione, coltura, *f.* **Under —,** messo a coltivazione.
cultivator, *n.* Coltivatore, cultore, *m.*
cultural, *a.* Culturale.
culture ['kʌltʃəɹ], *n.* Coltura, cultura, *f.*
cultured, *a.* Colto.
cultureless, *a.* Incolto, rozzo.
culverin ['kʌlvərin], *n.* (*Mil.*) Colubrina, *f.*
culvert ['kʌlvəɹt], *n.* Condotto, canale, *m.*
cumber ['kʌmbəɹ], *v.t.* Ingombrare, intralciare, imbarazzare. || *n.* Ingombro, impaccio, *m.*
cumbersome, cumbrous, *a.* Ingombrante, pesante, imbarazzante.
cumbersomeness, cumbrousness, *n.* Pesantezza, gravezza, molestia, *f.*
cumbrance, *n.* Ingombro, impaccio, *m.*; (*fig.*) noia, *f.*
cumin ['kʌmin], *n.* (*Bot.*) Cumino, *m.*
cumulate ['kju:mju:leit], *v.t.* Cumulare, accumulare.
cumulation, *n.* Ammasso, *m.*, accumulazione, *f.*
cumulative, *a.* Cumulativo.
cumulatively, *adv.* Cumulativamente.
cumulus, *n.* Cumulo, *m.* **— clouds,** cumuli, *m.pl.*
cuneate, cuneated ['kju:nieit], *a.* Cuneale.
cuneiform ['kju:nifɔɹm], *a.* Cuneiforme. **— writing,** caratteri cuneiformi, *m.pl.*
cunning ['kʌniŋ], *n.* Astuzia, accortezza, scaltrezza, *f.*; artificio, *m.*, destrezza, *f.* || *a.* Astuto, accorto, scaltro, furbo; abile.
cunningly, *adv.* Furbamente; abilmente.
cup [kʌp], *n.* Tazza, coppa, *f.*, chicchera; (*of flower*) calice, *m.* || *v.t.* (*Med.*) Salassare, applicar ventose. **— of bitterness,** l'amaro calice, *m.*; **his — of happiness was full,** la sua felicità era al colmo; **to be in one's cups,** essere ubbriaco; **a stirrup —,** bicchiere della staffa, *m.*
cupboard ['kʌbəɹd], *n.* (*for clothes, etc.*) Armadio, *m.*; (*sideboard*) credenza, *f.*; (*cabinet*) stipo, *m.* **Corner- —,** cantonale, *m.*; **— love,** amore interessato, *m.*
cupel ['kju:pəl], *n.* (*Min.*) Coppella, *f.* || *v.t.* Coppellare.
cupful, *n.* Tazza, *f.*
Cupid [kju:pid], *n.* (*Myth.*) Cupido, *m.*
cupidity, *n.* Cupidigia, cupidità, avidità, avarizia, *f.*
cupola ['kju:pələ], *n.* (*Arch.*) Cupola, *f.*
cupping-glass, *n.* Coppetta, *f.*, ventosa, *f.*
cupreous ['kju:priəs], *a.* (*Min.*) Cupreo.
cur [kə:ɹ], *n.* Botolo, cagnaccio, *m.*; (*fig.*) mascalzone, *m.*
curable ['kju:rəbl], *a.* Guaribile, curabile, sanabile.
curacao [kjurə'sou], *n.* Curasso, *m.*
curacy ['kju:rəsi], *n.* Vicariato, *m.*, cura, *f.*
curare [kju:'rɑ:ri], *n.* (*Chem.*) Curaro, curare, *m.*
curate ['kju:rət], *n.* Curato, *m.*
curative, *a.* Curativo.
curator [kju'reitəɹ], *n.* Direttore, conservatore, *m.*
curatorship, *n.* Cura, custodia, *f.*
curb (1) [kə:ɹb], *n.* Barbazzale, morso, *m.*; (*fig.*) freno, *m.* || *v.t.* Frenare, trattenere, moderare, reprimere. **— -bit,** morso, *m.*
curb (2) [cp. **kerb**].
curculio [kə:ɹ'ku:liou], *n.* (*Zool.*) Curculione, *m.*
curcuma ['kə:ɹ'kju:mə], *n.* (*Bot.*) Curcuma, *f.*
curd [kə:ɹd], *n.* Latte rappreso, *m.*, giuncata, *f.*
curdle, *v.t.* Coagulare, rappigliare, raggrumare; *v.i.* coagularsi; (*fig.*) ghiacciare. **To — someone's blood,** far agghiacciare il sangue a qualcuno.

curdy, *a.* Rappreso, coagulato, grumoso.
cure [kjuːəɹ], *n.* Guarigione, cura, *f.*; rimedio, *m.*; (*colloq.*) eccentrico, *m.* ‖ *v.t.* Guarire, sanare; rimediare, correggere; (*meat, etc.*) salare. **— of souls,** cura d'anime, *f.*; **to — herrings,** marinare le aringhe.
curer, *n.* (*healer*) Guaritore, *m.*; (*of meat, etc.*) salatore, *m.*
curfew [ˈkəːɹfjuː], *n.* Coprifuoco, *m.*
curio [ˈkjuːriou], *n.* Rarità, anticaglia, *f.*
curiosity [kjuriˈɔsiti], *n.* Curiosità, *f.* **Out of —,** per curiosità; **dealer in curiosities,** antiquario, *m.*
curious, *a.* Curioso, strano, singolare.
curiously, *adv.* Curiosamente, stranamente. **— enough,** davvero strano.
curl [kəːɹl], *n.* (*of hair*) Riccio, ricciolo; anello, *m.*; (*of smoke*) spirale, *f.* ‖ *v.t.* Arricciare, increspare; *v.i.* incresparsi, torcersi; (*of snakes*) snodarsi; (*of plants*) intrecciarsi; (*of waves*) ondulare. **To — up,** aggrovigliarsi; **to — up one's nose,** arricciare il naso; **to — one's lips,** torcer la bocca.
curled, *a.* Arricciato, ricciuto, crespo, inanellato.
curling, *n.* Arricciamento, *m.*, ondulazione, *f.*; (*Sport*) piastra su ghiaccio, *f.* **— -irons, — -tongs,** ferro pei capelli, *m.*
curly, *a.* Riccio, crespo, ricciuto. **— -headed,** ricciuto, riccioluto.
curlew [kəːɹˈljuː], *n.* (*Zool.*) Chiurlo, *m.*
curmudgeon [kəɹˈmʌdʒən], *n.* Uomo burbero; spilorcio, uomo tirchio, *m.*
curmudgeonly, *a.* Burbero; avaro.
currant [ˈkʌrənt], (*Bot.*) *n.* Ribes, *m.* **Black, red, white —,** ribes nero, rosso, bianco, *m.*; **dried —,** uva secca, uva passa, *f.*; **— bush,** ribes, *m.*
currency [ˈkʌrənsi], *n.* Circolazione, moneta, *f.*, corso, *m.* **Paper —,** circolazione cartacea, *f.*; **foreign —,** valuta straniera, *f.*; **legal —,** moneta legale, *f.*; **to give — to a word,** dar corso ad una parola.
current (1), *a.* Corrente, comune, odierno, in uso. **— price,** prezzo corrente, *m.*; **— events,** attualità, *f.pl.*; **the — issue of a paper,** il corrente numero di un giornale; **to pass —,** essere generalmente ammesso.
current (2), *n.* Corrente, *f.*, fiume, *m.*
currently, *adv.* Comunemente, generalmente. **It is — reported that,** corre voce che.
curricle [ˈkʌrikl], *n.* Biroccio, *m.*
curriculum [kʌˈrikjuːləm], *n.* Corso di studi, curricolo, *m.*
currier, *n.* Conciatore, *m.*
currish [ˈkəːriʃ], *a.* Ringhioso; avaro, vile.
currishly, *adv.* Vilmente.
curry [ˈkʌri], *v.t.* (*leather*) Conciare; (*a horse*) strigliare; (*food*) condire all'indiana. ‖ *n.* Riso all'indiana, *m.* **To — favour with,** cattivarsi il favore di; **— -comb,** striglia, *f.*
currying, [ˈkʌriiŋ], *n.* Conciatura, *f.*, strigliare, *m.*
curse [kəːɹs], *n.* Maledizione, imprecazione, esecrazione, bestemmia, *f.*; (*fig.*) flagello, danno, *m.*; (*Eccles.*) scomunica, *f.*, anatema, *m.* ‖ *v.t.* Maledire, dannare; scomunicare; *v.i.* bestemmiare, imprecare. **To be cursed with,** essere tormentato da.
cursed [ˈkəːɹsid], *a.* Maledetto, esecrabile.
cursedly, *adv.* Esecrabilmente, terribilmente.
cursing, *n.* Maledizione, *f.*
cursive, *a.* Corsivo.
cursorily, *adv.* Rapidamente, leggermente, di fretta.
cursoriness, *n.* Rapidità, leggerezza, *f.*
cursory, *a.* Rapido, leggiero, superficiale. **To give a — glance,** dare una rapida scorsa.
curt, *a.* Brusco, aspro, rigido, secco. **A — answer,** una risposta secca, *f.*
curtail [kəːɹˈteil], *v.t.* Accorciare, raccorciare, abbreviare; restringere, ridurre, diminuire; limitare. **To — expenses,** ridurre le spese; **to — privileges,** limitare i privilegi.
curtailment, *n.* Accorciamento, *m.*, abbreviazione, limitazione, *f.*
curtain [ˈkəːɹtin], *n.* Cortina, tenda, *f.*; (*Theat.*) sipario, *m.* ‖ *v.t.* Cortinare; coprire, velare. **A — lecture,** ammonizione coniugale, *f.*; (*Theat.*) **— -raiser,** commedietta, *f.*; **fire-proof —,** sipario di sicurezza, *m.*; **to drop the —,** calare il sipario; **— -rod,** portatende, *m.*
curtly, *adv.* Bruscamente.
curtsy, curtsey, *n.* Riverenza, *f.* ‖ *v.i.* Fare una riverenza.
curvature [ˈkəːɹvətʃəɹ], *n.* Curvatura, *f.* **— of the spine,** deviazione della colonna vertebrale, *f.*
curve [kəːɹv], *n.* Curvo, *m.*, curva, piega, *f.* ‖ *v.i.* Curvarsi, piegarsi.
curvet [kəːɹˈvet], *v.i.* Corvettare, salterellare, balzare. ‖ *n.* Corvetta, *f.*
curvilinear [kəːɹviˈliniəɹ], *a.* (*Geom.*) Curvilineo.
cushat [ˈkʌʃət], *n.* (*Zool.*) Colombo selvatico, *m.*
cushion [ˈkuʃən], *n.* Cuscino, guanciale, *m.*; cuscinetto, *m.*; (*Billiards*) sponda, mattonella, *f.* ‖ *v.t.* Fornire di cuscini; (*Billiards*) fare sponda; (*fig.*) sopprimere.
cushioned, *a.* Imbottito.
cushy [ˈkuʃi], *a.* (*colloq.*) Al sicuro. **A — job,** un posticino al sicuro, *m.*, un'imboscatura, *f.*
cusp [kʌsp], *n.* Vertice, *m.*, punta, *f.*; (*Arch.*) cuspide, *f.*; (*Geom.*) cuspidale, *m.*
cuspidate, cuspidated, *a.* (*Bot.*) Cuspidato.
cuspidal, *a.* Cuspidale.
cuss [kʌs], *n.* (*colloq.*) Maledizione, *f.*; furfante, mascalzone, *m.*
cussedness [ˈkʌsidnis], *n.* (*colloq.*) Perversità, *f.*; furfanteria, *f.*
custard [ˈkʌstəɹd], *n.* Crema, *f.*
custodian [kəsˈtoudiən], *n.* Custode, guardiano, *m.*
custody [ˈkʌstədi], *n.* Custodia, cura, guardia, *f.*; imprigionamento, arresto, *m.*, detenzione, *f.* **In close —,** sotto stretta sorveglianza; **in —,** in prigione; **to take into —,** arrestare; **to commit to someone's —,** affidare alla custodia di qualcuno.
custom [ˈkʌstəm], *n.* Uso, costume, *m.*; consuetudine, abitudine, usanza, *f.*; clientela, *f.* [cp. **customs**].
customarily, *adv.* Abitualmente, per uso, al solito.
customariness, *n.* Abitudine, *f.*
customary, *a.* Abituale, usuale, solito; consuetudinario.
customer, *n.* Cliente, avventore, *m.*; (*colloq.*) tipo, *m.* **A queer —,** un tipo curioso, *m.*; **an ugly —,** un tipo di furfante, *m.*; **— at a bank,** depositante, *m.*

customs, *n.pl.* Dogana, *f.* **Custom-house,** dogana, *f.*; **custom-house officer,** doganiere, *m.*; **— duty,** tariffa doganale, *f.*

cut [kʌt], *n.* (*cut, blow, stroke, etc.*) Colpo; taglio, *m.*; (*wound*) incisione, *f.*; (*clothes*) taglio, *m.*; (*of play, story, etc.*) omissione, *f.*; (*of meat*) taglio, *m.*; (*fig.*) affronto, insulto, *m.*; (*picture*) vignetta, *f.* || *v.t.* Tagliare, mozzare, dividere; (*to cleave*) fendere; (*to wound*) ferire; (*the throat*) scannare; (*fig.*) rifiutare di salutare; (*Cards*) alzare. || *a.* Tagliato. **A short —,** una scorciatoia, *f.*; **to — and thrust,** colpire di punta e di taglio; **to be a — above,** essere superiore a; **to — across,** tagliare di traverso; **to — a poor figure,** fare una magra figura; **to — along,** filare, scappare; **to — the cards,** alzare le carte; **to — down expenses,** ridurre le spese; **to — off,** tagliare, recidere, amputare, troncare, mozzare; **to — off someone's retreat,** tagliare la ritirata a qualcuno; **to — off with a shilling,** diseredare; **he's cutting his teeth,** gli spuntano i denti; **to — one's way,** farsi strada; **he has his work — out for him,** ha un lavoro difficile da fare; **to — short,** tagliare corto, tagliare a mezzo; interrompere; **to — small,** sminuzzare; **to — and run,** battersela; **to — to the heart,** ferire al cuore; **to — up rough,** mostrare sdegno; **— and dried,** bell'e fatto; **to — in** (*on road*), tagliare; (*Mech.*) **—-off,** otturatore, *m.*; (*Mech.*) **—-out,** valvola di sicurezza fusibile, *f.*; **—-throat,** assassino, (*usurer*) strozzino, scannatore, *m.*

cutaneous [kju:ˈteiniəs], *a.* Cutaneo.

cute [kju:t], *a.* Sagace, destro, fino.

cuteness, *n.* Sagacità, *f.*

cuticle [ˈkju:tikl], *n.* Cuticola, pellicola, epidermide, *f.*

cutlass [ˈkʌtləs], *n.* Daga, *f.*; scimitarra usata da marinai, *f.*

cutler, *n.* Coltellinaio, *m.*

cutlery, *n.* Coltellame, *m.*

cutlet, *n.* Costoletta, *f.*

cutpurse, *n.* Borsaiuolo, *m.*

cutter, *n.* (*person*) Tagliatore, *m.*; (*tool*) tagliatoio, *m.*; (*Naut.*) cutter, cottro, *m.*

cutting, *n.* Taglio, *m.*, incisione, *f.*; (*from newspaper*) ritaglio, *m.*; (*of plant*) rampollo, *m.*; (*Rail.*) trincea ferroviaria, *f.*; (*of teeth*) spuntare, *m.* || *a.* Tagliente; incisivo, aspro, mordente, sarcastico. **—-knife,** tagliatoio, *m.*, trancia, *f.*; **—-out,** taglio, il tagliar fuori, *m.*; **—-up,** tagliuzzamento, *m.*

cuttle-fish [ˈkʌtlfiʃ], *n.* (*Zool.*) Seppia, *f.* **—-bone,** osso di seppia, *m.*

cutty [ˈkʌti], *a.* Corto, mozzo. **— pipe,** pipa corta di gesso, *f.*

cutwater [ˈkʌtwɔ:təɹ], *n.* (*Naut.*) Tagliamare, *m.*; (*Arch.*) becco, *m.*

cyanide [ˈsaiənaid], *n.* (*Chem.*) Cianuro, *m.*

Cyclades [ˈsiklədi:s], *n.pl.* (*Geog.*) Le Cicladi, *f.pl.*

cycle [ˈsaikl], *n.* Ciclo, *m.*; (*bicycle*) bicicletta, *f.* || *v.i.* Andare in bicicletta, pedalare. **— of the moon,** ciclo lunare, *m.*; **—-racing,** corse di biciclette, *f.pl.*; **—-racing track,** velodromo, *m.*; **motor- —,** motocicletta, *f.*, moto-ciclo, *m.*; **—-car,** motocarrozzino, *m.*; vetturetta a motore, *f.*; **to ride a motor- —,** guidare una motocicletta.

cyclic, *a.* Ciclico.

cycling, *n.* Ciclismo, *m.* || *a.* Di ciclista.

cyclist, *n.* Ciclista, *m.f.*

cyclograph, *n.* Ciclografo, *m.*

cycloid, *n.* Cicloide, *f.*

cycloidal, *a.* Cicloidale.

cyclometer, *n.* Odometro, contagiri, *m.*

cyclone [ˈsaikloun], *n.* Ciclone, *m.*

cyclonic, *a.* Ciclonico.

Cyclopean [saiˈkloupiən], *a.* Ciclopico.

cyclopedia [saiklouˈpi:diə], *n.* Enciclopedia, *f.*

cyclostome [ˈsaikləstoum], *n.* (*Zool.*) Ciclostoma, *m.*, lampreda, *f.*

cyclostyle [ˈsaikləstail], *n.* Ciclostile, *m.*

cygnet [ˈsignit], *n.* (*Zool.*) Cignetto, piccolo cigno, *m.*

cylinder [ˈsilindəɹ], *n.* Cilindro, rullo, *m.*

cylindrical, *a.* Cilindrico.

cyma [ˈsaimə], *n.* (*Arch.*) Cimasa, *f.*

cymbal [ˈsimbəl], *n.* (*Mus.*) Piatti, *m. pl.*

cymbalist, *n.* Piattista, *m.f.*

cyme [saim], *n.* (*Bot.*) Cima, *f.*

Cymric [ˈsimrik, ˈkimrik], *a.* Gallese.

cynic [ˈsinik], *n.* Cinico, *m.*

cynical, *a.* Cinico.

cynically, *adv.* Cinicamente.

cynicism, *n.* Cinismo, *m.*

cynocephalous [sainouˈsefələs], *a.* (*Zool.*) Cinocefalo.

cynosure [ˈsainəʃəɹ], *n.* (*Astron.*) Cinosura, *f.*; (*fig.*) centro d'attrazione, punto di mira, *m.*

Cynthia [ˈsinθiə], *n.* Cinzia, *f.*

cypher [cp. **cipher**].

cypress [ˈsaiprəs], *n.* (*Bot.*) Cipresso, *m.* **—-grove,** cipresseto, *m.*; **—-wood,** legno di cipresso, *m.*

Cypriot [ˈsipriət], *n.* Cipriota, *m.f.*

Cyprus [ˈsaiprʌs], *n.* (*Geog.*) Cipro, *m.*

Cyrenaic [sirəˈneiik], *a.* Cirenaico.

Cyrillic [siˈrilik, kiˈrilik], *a.* Cirilliano.

cyst [sist], *n.* (*Med.*) Ciste, cisti, *f.*

cystic, *a.* Cistico.

cystitis [sisˈtaitis], *n.* (*Med.*) Cistite, *f.*

czar [cp. **tsar**].

Czech [tʃek], *n.a.* Ceco, *m.*

Czechoslovakia [tʃekouslouˈvɑ:kiə], *n.* (*Geog.*) Cecoslovacchia, *f.*

D

D, d [di:]. Quarta lettera dell'alfabeto inglese, *f.*; (*Mus.*) re, *m.*; **'d,** abbreviazione di *had* o *would.*

dab [dæb], *n.* Colpettino, *m*; macchia, *f.*; (*mud*) zacchera, *f.*; (*paint*) schizzo, *m.*; (*Zool.*) pianuzza, lima, *f.*; (*colloq.*) esperto, *m.* || *v.t.* Battere leggermente, picchiettare. **To — on,** applicare a colpi leggieri.

dabble, *v.t.* Tuffare, bagnare; imbrattare; umettare; *v.i.* bagnarsi, imbrattarsi. **To — in,** occuparsi, dilettarsi di. **To — on the Stock Exchange,** speculare, giocare in Borsa.

dabbler, *n.* Superficiale, dilettante, *m.*; guastamestieri, *m.*

dabchick [ˈdæbtʃik], *n.* (*Zool.*) Tuffetto, *m.*

dabster, *n.* (*colloq.*) Conoscitore, praticone, esperto, *m.*

dace [deis], *n.* (*Zool.*) Lasca, *f.*

dachshund [ˈdækshund], *n.* (*Zool.*) Bassotto, *m.*

dacoit [də'kɔit], *n.* Brigante nelle Indie, *m.*
dactyl ['dæktil], *n.* Dattilo, *m.*
dactylic, *a.* Dattilico.
dad, daddy [dæd, 'dædi], *n.* Papà, babbo, *m.*
daddy-longlegs [dædi'lɔŋlegz], *n.* (*Zool.*) Tipula, *f.*, zanzarone, *m.*
dado ['deidou], *n.* (*Arch.*) Zoccolo, dado, *m.*
daemon ['di:mən], *n.* Demone, *m.*
daffodil ['dæfodil], *n.* (*Bot.*) Giunchiglia, *f.*; tromboncino, *m.*
daft [dɑ:ft], *a.* Pazzo, matto, scervellato, sciocco.
dagger ['dægəɹ], *n.* Pugnale, stiletto, *m.*, daga, *f.*; (*Print.*) croce, *f.* **At daggers drawn,** ad armi corte, a coltello; **to look daggers at,** fare il viso dell'armi, fare gli occhiacci.
daguerrotype [də'geroutaip], *n.* Dagherrotipia, *f.*
dahlia ['deiliə], *n.* (*Bot.*) Dalia, *f.*
daily ['deili], *a.* Quotidiano, giornaliero, diurno. || *n.* Giornale (*newspaper*), *m.*; (*help*) giornante, *f.* || *adv.* Ogni giorno, giornalmente, giorno per giorno.
dainties ['deintiz], *n.pl.* Delicatezze, *f.pl.*, bocconcini, *m.pl.*
daintily, *adv.* Delicatamente, squisitamente.
daintiness, *n.* Delicatezza, squisitezza, *f.*; gusto delicato, *m.*
dainty, *a.* Delicato, squisito, grazioso. || *n.* Ghiottoneria, *f.*
dairy ['dɛəri], *n.* Latteria, *f.* **—-farm,** latteria, vaccheria, cascina, *f.*; **—-farmer,** casaro, *m.*
dairymaid, *n.* Lattaia, lattivendola, *f.*
dairyman, *n.* Lattivendolo, lattaio, *m.*
dais [deis], *n.* Palco, *m.*, impalcatura, *f.*
daisy ['deizi], *n.* (*Bot.*) Margheritina, *f.* **—-chain** ghirlanda di margheritine, *f.*
dale [deil], *n.* Valle, vallata, *f.* **Up hill and down —,** da monte a valle.
dalesman, *n.* Valligiano, *m.*
dalliance ['dæliəns], *n.* Ritardo, indugio, *m.*; carezze, *f.pl.*, vezzi, *m.pl.*
dally ['dæli], *v.i.* Indugiare, tardare; divertirsi; amoreggiare. **To — away the time,** sprecare il tempo.
Dalmatia [dæl'meiʃə], *n.* (*Geog.*) Dalmazia, *f.*
Dalmatian, *n.a.* Dalmata, *m.f.*; **— dog,** cane dalmata.
dalmatic [dæl'mætik], *n.* (*Eccles.*) Dalmatica, *f.*
Daltonism ['dɔ:ltənizm], *n.* Daltonismo, *m.*
dam (1) [dæm], *n.* Madre (*of animals*), *f.*
dam (2), *n.* Diga, barriera, *f.*; argine, sbarramento, *m.* || *v.t.* Sbarrare, arginare, porre una diga; arrestare, impedire.
damage ['dæmidʒ], *n.* Danno, guasto, *m.*; detrimento, *m.*; (*Naut.*) avaria, *f.*; (*Law*) risarcimento, indennizzo, *m.*; danni, *m.pl.* || *v.t.* Danneggiare, sciupare, guastare; avariare. **To — wilfully,** sabotare.
damageable, *a.* Danneggiabile.
damaged, *a.* Guasto; avariato.
damaging, *a.* Dannoso, pregiudizievole.
damascene ['dæməsi:n], *v.t.* Damaschinare.
damascening, *n.* Damaschineria, *f.*
damask, *n.* Damasco, *m.* **— rose,** rosa damaschina, *f.*
dame [deim], *n.* Donna, dama, *f.*
damn [dæm], *v.t.* Dannare, condannare; mandare al diavolo; (*fig.*) disapprovare; (*Theat.*) fischiare. || *inter.* Maledizione! || *n.* Bestemmia, *f.*
damnable ['dæmnəbl], *a.* Dannabile, esecrabile, odioso, maledetto.
damnably, *adv.* Dannabilmente.
damnation, *n.* Dannazione, *f.* || *inter.* Maledizione!
damnatory, *a.* Condannatorio.
damned [dæmd], *a.* Dannato, maledetto; (*Theat.*) fischiato.
damning, *a.* Conclusivo, schiacciante (*of evidence*); condannatorio.
damp [dæmp], *n.* Umido, *m.*, umidità, *f.* || *a.* Umido, molle, bagnato, madido. || *v.t.* Rendere umido, inumidire, bagnare; (*fig.*) scoraggiare; ammortire (*shock*). **Choke- —,** gas irrespirabile; **to — one's ardour,** smorzare l'ardore; **—-proof,** impermeabile.
damper, *n.* (*of chimney*) Serranda, *f.*, registro, *m.*; (*Mus.Radio*) sordina, *f.*; (*fig.*) guastafeste, *m.*; (*stamps, etc.*) spugna francobolli, *f.* **To put a — on a festivity,** fare il guastafeste.
dampish, *a.* Umidiccio.
dampness, *n.* Umidità, *f.*, vapore, *m.*
damsel ['dæmzl], *n.* Damigella, donzella, zitella, *f.*
damson ['dæmzən], *n.* Susina di Damasco, prugna damaschina, *f.* **—-tree,** prugno di Damasco, *m.*
dance [dɑ:ns], *n.* Ballo, *m.*, danza, *f.* || *v.t.* Ballare, danzare; far ballare. **—-music,** musica da ballo, *f.*; **— of death,** danza macabra, *f.*; **to lead someone a —,** menare qualcuno pel naso; **to lead the —,** guidare il ballo; **to — attendance,** fare anticamera; **—-frock,** veste da ballo; **—-partner,** cavaliere, *m.*, dama, *f.*
dancer, *n.* Danzatore, *m.*, danzatrice, *f.*; (*professional*) ballerino, *m.*, ballerina, *f.*
dancing, *n.* Il ballo, *m.*, la danza, *f.* **—-master,** maestro di ballo, *m.*; **—-school,** scuola di ballo, *f.*
dandelion ['dændilaiən], *n.* (*Bot.*) Dente di leone, *m.*; radicchiella, *f.*
dandified, *a.* Attillato.
dandify ['dændifai], *v.t.* Attillarsi.
dandle ['dændl], *v.t.* Dondolare, cullare, accarezzare.
dandruff ['dændrʌf], *n.* Forfora, *f.*
dandy ['dændi], *n.* Damerino, zerbinotto, *m.*; cicisbeo, *m.* || *a.* Elegante, galante.
dandyism, *n.* Affettazione, *f.*; modo da damerino, *m.*
Dane [dein], *n.* Danese, *m.f.*
danger ['deindʒəɹ], *n.* Rischio, pericolo, *m.* **To be in —,** pericolare, correr rischio; **—-signal,** segnale d'allarme, *m.*
dangerous, *a.* Pericoloso, rischioso.
dangerously, *adv.* Pericolosamente.
dangle ['dæŋgl], *v.i.* Ciondolare, penzolare; *v.t.* spenzolare, far penzolare. **He's always dangling after her,** le fa sempre il cascamorto.
dangler, *n.* Ciondolone, cicisbeo, *m.*
dangling, *adv.* Penzoloni, ciondoloni.
Danish, *a.* Danese.
dank [dæŋk], *a.* Umido, molle; umidiccio, molliccio. **— air,** aria umidiccia, *f.*
Dantean, Dantesque ['dæntiən, dæn'tesk], *a.* Dantesco.
Daphne ['dæfni], *n.* (*Myth.Bot.*) Dafne, *f.*
dapper ['dæpəɹ], *a.* Lindo, elegante; svelto, lesto. **A — little man,** un omettino, *m.*

dapple [dæpl], *v.t.* Screziare, variegare, macchiare.

dappled, *a.* Variegato, screziato, macchiato; pomellato (*of horses*).

darbies [ˈdɑːɹbiz], *n.pl.* (*colloq.*) Manette, *f.pl.*

dare [dɛəɹ], *v.i.* Osare, ardire; arrischiarsi, avventurarsi; *v.t.* sfidare, provocare. **I — say,** suppongo, credo bene; **I — not do it,** non oso farlo; **How — you?** Non so come abbia l'ardire! **—-devil,** temerario, ardito, audace.

daring, *a.* Ardito, audace, coraggioso. ‖ *n.* Coraggio, ardire, *m.*, audacia, *f.*

daringly, *adv.* Arditamente.

dark [dɑːɹk], *n.* Oscurità, *f.*, buio, *m.* ‖ *a.* Oscuro, buio, fosco; bruno (*of complexion*); (*fig.*) cupo, triste, sinistro. **After —,** a notte calata; **in the —,** al buio, all'oscuro; **—-lantern,** lanterna cieca, *f.*; **the Dark Ages,** il Medioevo, *m.*; **to grow —,** farsi scuro, annottare; **to keep in the —,** tenere all'oscuro; **a — saying,** un detto oscuro; **a — horse,** un'acqua cheta, *f.*; **— blue,** blù carico; (*Phot.*) **—-room,** camera oscura, *f.*

darken, *v.t.* Oscurare, offuscare, abbuiare; *v.i.* farsi scuro, annuvolarsi. **I will never — his door again,** non verrò mai più a trovarlo.

darkening, *n.* Oscuramento, *m.*

darkish, *a.* Scuretto, alquanto buio, nerastro.

darkling, *adv.* Nelle tenebre.

darkly, *adv.* Oscuramente.

darkness, *n.* Buio, *m.*, oscurità, *f.*, tenebre, *f.pl.*; (*of colours*) tinta caricata. **— of complexion,** colorito bruno, *m.*

darky, *n.* (*off.colloq.*) Negro, *m.*, negra, *f.*

darling [ˈdɑːɹliŋ], *n.* Favorito, prediletto, carino, *m.* ‖ *a.* Favorito, prediletto, carino. **My —,** tesoro mio.

darn [dɑːɹn], *v.t.* Rammendare. ‖ *n.* Rammendo, *m.*

darnel [ˈdɑːɹnəl], *n.* (*Bot.*) Loglio, *m.*

darning, *n.* Rammendatura, *f.* **—-needle,** ago da rammendare, *m.*; **—-wool,** lana da rammendare, *f.*

dart [dɑːɹt], *n.* Dardo (*weapon*), *m.*; (*movement*) guizzo, *m.* ‖ *v.t.* Lanciare, scagliare, dardeggiare; *v.i.* lanciarsi, scagliarsi. **To — off,** guizzar via; **game of darts,** giuoco dei dardi, *m.*

Darwinian [dɑːɹˈwiniən], *a.* Darviniano.

dash [dæʃ], *n.* Impeto, *m.*, foga, *f.*; guizzo, slancio, *m.*; (*Print.*) lineetta, *f.*; (*Teleg.*) linea, *f.*; (*small quantity*) tantino, *m.*, goccia, *f.* ‖ *v.t.* Gettare, lanciare; distruggere, abbattere; *v.i.* lanciarsi, precipitarsi. **A — of vinegar,** un tantino d'aceto; **to cut a —,** far una gran figura; **to make a — at,** precipitarsi su, lanciarsi su; **to — to pieces,** spezzare, frantumare; **all my hopes are dashed,** tutte le mie speranze sono frustrate; **to — off a poem,** improvvisare dei versi; **to — out,** lanciarsi fuori; **to — away,** scappar via; (*Motor.*) **—-board,** parafango, paraspruzzi, *m.*; (*Am.*) cruscotto, *m.*

dashing, *a.* Ardito, vivace, elegante.

dastard [ˈdæstəd], *n.* Codardo, vigliacco, *m.*

dastardliness, *n.* Codardia, vigliaccheria, *f.*

dastardly, *a.* Vile, codardo.

data [ˈdeitə], *n.pl.* Dati, *m.pl.*

date (1) [deit], *n.* (*Bot.*) Dattero, *m.* **—-palm,** palma da datteri, *f.*

date (2), *n.* Data, *f.*; (*colloq.*) appuntamento, *m.* ‖ *v.t.i.* Datare. (*Comm.*) **At long —,** a lunga scadenza; **at short —,** a breve scadenza; **under — of,** in data di; **out of —,** non più in uso, fuor d'uso, antiquato; **up to —,** moderno, d'attualità, aggiornato; **—-stamp,** timbro mobile, *m.*; **a church dating from the 14th century,** una chiesa che data dal Trecento; (*colloq.*) **to have a —,** avere un appuntamento.

dative [ˈdeitiv], *n.a.* (*Gram.*) Dativo, *m.*

datum [ˈdeitəm], *n.* Dato, *m.*

daub [dɔːb], *v.t.* Imbrattare, impiastrare. ‖ *n.* Imbratto, sgorbio, *m.*; pitturaccia, *f.*; (*for walls*) intonaco, *m.*

dauber, *n.* Imbrattatele, *m.*

daughter [ˈdɔːtəɹ], *n.* Figlia, figliuola, *f.* **—-in-law,** nuora, *f.*; **step- —,** figliastra, *f.*; **god- —,** figlioccia, *f.*; **grand—,** nipote, nipotina, *f.*; **great-grand—,** pronipote, *f.*

daughterly, *a.* Filiale.

daunt [dɔːnt], *v.t.* Intimidire, scoraggiare. **Nothing daunted,** per nulla intimidito.

dauntless, *a.* Impavido, intrepido.

dauntlessness, *n.* Intrepidezza, *f.*

dauphin [ˈdɔːfin], *n.* (*Hist.*) Delfino, *m.*

davenport [ˈdævənpɔːɹt], *n.* Divano (letto), *m.*

davit [ˈdeivit], *n.* (*Naut.*) Gru, *f.*

davy-lamp [ˈdeivilæmp], *n.* Lampada di sicurezza, *f.*

daw [dɔː], *n.* (*Zool.*) Cornacchia, *f.*

dawdle [dɔːdl], *v.i.* Gingillarsi, oziare, ciondolare. **To — over,** menar per le lunghe; **Don't —!** Sbrigatevi!

dawdler, *n.* Perditempo, fannullone, ciondolone, *m.*

dawn [dɔːn], *n.* Alba, *f.*; spuntar del giorno, *m.* ‖ *v.i.* Spuntare, albeggiare, far giorno. **Early —,** i primi albori, *m.pl.*; **it suddenly dawned on me,** mi venne subito in mente.

dawning, *a.* Albeggiante; nascente.

day [dei], *n.* Giorno, *m.*, giornata, *f.*; (*fig.*) battaglia, vittoria, *f.* **All —,** tutto il giorno; **at the present —,** in questi giorni; **broad —,** pieno giorno; **by —,** di giorno; **a fine —,** una bella giornata, *f.*; **— by —,** giorno per giorno; **from — to —,** di giorno in giorno; **from this — on,** d'ora innanzi; **Good —!** Buon giorno! **to this —,** fino ad oggi; **in the days of our fathers,** al tempo dei nostri padri; **the — after, the next —,** l'indomani, il giorno dopo; **the — before yesterday,** l'altrieri, avantieri; **the — after tomorrow,** posdomani, dopo domani; **this — week,** oggi a otto; **one of these fine days,** un giorno o l'altro; **What is the — of the month?** Quanti ne abbiamo del mese? **a hundred lire a —,** cento lire al giorno; **to carry the —,** guadagnar la battaglia; **to have had its —,** avere fatto il suo tempo; **—-boarder,** allievo esterno, *m.*; **—-book,** giornale, *m.*; **—-labourer,** giornaliere, operaio a giornata; **—-school,** scuola diurna, *f.*; **day's work,** giornata, *f.*; (*colloq.*) **to call it a —,** desistere da lavorare.

daybreak, *n.* Lo spuntar del giorno, *m.*, l'alba, l'aurora, *f.*

daydream, *n.* Sogno ad occhi aperti, vaneggiamento, *m.*

daylight, *n.* Giorno chiaro, *m.*, luce di giorno, *f.* **— saving,** ora estiva, *f.*

dayspring, *n.* Alba, *f.*
daytime, *n.* Giorno, *m.*
daze [deiz], *v.t.* Stordire, sbalordire, stupefare.
dazed, *a.* Stordito, stupefatto.
dazzle ['dæzl], *v.t.* Abbagliare, abbacinare; *v.i.* brillare. || *n.* Abbagliamento, *m.* (*Motor.*) **— -light,** faro abbagliante, *m.*
dazzling, *n.* Abbaglio. || *a.* Abbagliante.
deacon ['diːkən], *n.* Diacono, *m.*
deaconess, *n.* Diaconessa, *f.*
deaconry, deaconship, *n.* Diaconato, *m.*
dead [ded], *a.* Morto, estinto, spento, inanimato; (*of sleep*) profondo; (*of colour*) morto. || *n.* (*of night*) Silenzio, *m.* **The —,** i morti, *m.pl.* **— calm,** gran calma, *f.*; **— coal,** carbone estinto, *m.*; **— drunk,** ubbriaco fradicio; **— letter,** lettera morta, *f.*; **— -letter office,** ufficio lettere in giacenza, *m.*; **— loss,** perdita totale, *f.*; **— march,** marcia funebre, *f.*; **— reckoning,** calcolo della rotta, *m.*; **— sleep,** sonno profondo, *m.*; **— shot,** tiratore scelto, *m.*; **— stop,** brusca fermata, *f.*; **— season,** stagione morta, *f.*; **— wall,** muro cieco, *m.*; **— water,** acqua stagnante, *f.*; **— weight,** peso morto, *m.*; **to a — certainty,** con sicurezza assoluta, *f.*; **to drop down —,** cascar morto; **on a — level,** al pari perfetto, allo stesso livello; **in the — of winter,** nel cuor dell' inverno; (*Naut.*) **— -eye,** bigotta, carrucola, *f.*; **— -head,** chi ha biglietto gratuito; (*Naut.*) **— -light,** controsportello di cabina, *m.*; **— -nettle,** ortica morta, *f.*; (*traffic sign*) **Dead Slow,** Al passo; (*Elect.*) **— wire,** filo tagliato.
deaden, *v.t.* Ammortire, smorzare, attutire.
deadliness, *n.* Micidialità, velenosità, *f.*
deadlock, *n.* Incaglio, *m.*; punto morto, *m.*
deadly, *a.* Mortale, fatale; mortifero, velenoso; (*aim*) senza fallo. **— dull,** mortalmente noioso; (*Bot.*) **— nightshade,** belladonna, *f.*
deaf [def], Sordo; (*fig.*) insensibile. **— and dumb, — mute,** sordomuto; **— as a post,** sordo come una campana; **to turn a — ear,** fare il sordo, fare orecchio da mercante.
deafen, *v.t.* Assordare, intronare.
deafening, *a.* Intronante, assordante.
deafness, *n.* Sordità, *f.*
deal (1) [diːl], *n.* Abete, *m.*
deal (2), *n.* Quantità, *f.* **A good —,** molto; **by a good —,** di molto.
deal (3), *n.* (*Cards*) Dare, *m.*, mano, *f.*; (*Comm.*) affare, partito, patto, scambio, *m.* || *v.t.* (*Cards*) Distribuire, dare, fare; (*blow*) vibrare, dare; *v.i.* trafficare, commerciare. (*Cards*) **It's your—,** tocca a voi a fare il mazzo; **to — in,** commerciare in; **to — with,** trattare di; **to have a — with,** aver da fare con.
dealer, *n.* Negoziante, mercante, *m.*; (*Cards*) chi tiene il mazzo, *m.* **Wholesale —,** commerciante all'ingrosso, *m.*; **double- —,** furfante, imbroglione, *m.*
dealing, *n.* Modo d'agire, *m.*; condotta, *f.* **Dealings,** affari, rapporti, *m.pl.*; **double- —,** duplicità, *f.*
dean [diːn], *n.* (*Eccles.*) Decano, *m.*; (*of university, etc.*) preside di facoltà, *m.*
deanery, *n.* Decanato, *m.*; residenza d'un decano, *f.*
dear [diəɹ], *a.* Caro, costoso, prezioso; carino, gentile. || *adv.* Caro, caramente; molto. || *n.* Caro, diletto, *m.* **Dear me!** Povero me! **it will cost you —,** vi costerà caro; **Oh, dear!** Dio mio! **Oh dear no!** Mainò! Niente affatto! **My — fellow!** Caro mio!
dearly, *adv.* Caramente. **— -bought,** pagato a caro prezzo.
dearness, *n.* Carezza, *f.*
deary, *n.* (*colloq.*) Carino, *m.* **— me!** Dio mio!
dearth [dəːɹθ], *n.* Mancanza, scarsità, carestia, *f.*
death [deθ], *n.* Morte, *f.*; decesso, trapasso, *m.* **At the point of —,** in punto di morte, moribondo; **to be frozen to —,** morire di freddo; **sick unto —,** malato a morte; **to catch one's — of cold,** prendere un brutto raffreddore; **to die a natural —,** morire di morte naturale; **to frighten to —,** far morire di paura; **to put to —,** metter a morte; **that child will be the — of me,** quel fanciullo mi farà morire; **tired to —,** stanco morto; **— -bed,** letto di morte, *m.*; **— -blow,** colpo mortale, *m.*; **— -dealing,** fatale, mortale, mortifero, letale; **death's-head,** teschio, *m.*, testa da morto, *f.*; **— -rate,** indice di mortalità, *f.*; **— -rattle,** rantolo, *m.*; **— -roll,** lista dei morti, *f.*; **— -throes,** agonia, *f.*; **— -trap,** luogo pericoloso, tranello, *m.*; **— -warrant,** condanna a morte, *f.*; **— -watch beetle,** anobio, *m.*
deathless, *a.* Immortale, eterno.
deathlike, deathly, *a.* Cadaverico, mortale.
deave [diːv], *v.t.* Stordire.
debacle ['deibɑːkl], *n.* Rovina, *f.*
debar [di'bɑːɹ], *v.t.* Escludere, interdire, impedire. **To be debarred from one's rights,** essere privato dei propri diritti.
debark [diː'bɑːɹk], *v.t.i.* Sbarcare.
debarkation, *n.* Sbarco, *m.*
debase [di'beis], *v.t.* Degradare, avvilire; alterare, abbassare; (*of coins*) falsificare.
debasement, *n.* Degradazione, *f.*; alterazione, *f.*, avvilimento, *m.*
debasing, *a.* Degradante, avvilente.
debatable [di'beitəbl], *a.* Discutibile, contestabile.
debate [di'beit], *n.* Dibattimento, dibattito, *m.*; discussione, *f.* || *v.t.i.* Discutere, dibattere. **Debating society,** circolo di conferenza, *m.*
debater, *n.* Disputatore, argomentatore, *m.*
debauch [di'bɔːtʃ], *n.* Bagordo, *m.*, deboscia, orgia, gozzoviglia, *f.* || *v.t.* Corrompere, traviare, pervertire.
debauchee [dibɔː'ʃiː], *n.* Libertino, discolo, ubbriacone, *m.*
debaucher, *n.* Corruttore, seduttore, *m.*
debauchery, *n.* Crapula, dissolutezza, *f.*, libertinaggio, *m.*
debenture [di'bentʃəɹ], *n.* (*Comm.*) Obbligazione, *f.* **— -holder,** portatore di obbligazioni, *m.*; **— -stock,** capitale in obbligazioni, *m.*
debilitate [de'biliteit], *v.t.* Indebolire, debilitare.
debilitation, *n.* Indebolimento, *m.*
debilitated, *a.* Debilitato.
debility, *n.* Debolezza, debilità, *f.*
debit ['debit], *n.* Debito, *m.* || *v.t.* Addebitare.
debonair [debə'nɛəɹ], *a.* Bonario.
debouch [di'bautʃ], *v.i.* Sboccare.
debouchment, debouchure, *n.* Sbocco, sboccamento, *m.*

debt [det], *n.* Debito, *m.*; (*fig.*) obbligo, *m.*; (*owed by a person*) debito passivo, *m.*; (*owed to a person*) debito attivo, *m.* **Bad —**, credito inesigibile, *m.*; **deeply in —**, pieno di debiti; **I am greatly in your —**, vi devo molto; **in —**, indebitato (*in all senses*); **to discharge a —**, saldare un debito; **to run into —**, indebitarsi, contrarre debiti; **to get out of —**, sdebitarsi.
debtor, *n.* Debitore, *m.* **— -side**, lato del debito, *m.*
debunk [diː'bʌŋk], *v.t.* (*colloq.*) Sgonfiare.
debut [de'buː], *n.* (*Theat.*) Debutto, esordio, *m.* **To make one's —**, esordire.
debutant, debutante ['debjuːtənt], *n.* Esordiente, debuttante, *m.f.*
decade ['dekeid], *n.* Decade, *f.*
decadence, decadency ['dekədəns, 'dekədənsi], *n.* Decadenza, *f.*
decadent, *a.* Decadente.
decagon ['dekəgən], *n.* Decagono, *m.*
decahedron [dekə'hiːdrən], *n.* Decaedro, *m.*
decalogue ['dekəlɔg], *n.* Decalogo, *m.*
decamp [di'kæmp], *v.i.* Scappare, svignarsela.
decanal [di'keinəl], *a.* (*Eccles.*) Decanale, capitolare.
decant [di'kænt], *v.t.* Versare, travasare.
decanter, *n.* Caraffa, boccia, *f.*
decapitate [di'kæpiteit], *v.t.* Decapitare, decollare.
decapitation, *n.* Decapitazione, decollazione, *f.*
decapod ['dekəpɔd], *n.* (*Zool.*) Decapodo, *m.*
decarbonize [diː'kɑːɹbənaiz], *v.t.* Decarburare.
decasyllabic [dekəsi'læbik], *a.* Decasillabo.
decay [di'kei], *n.* Decadimento, deperimento, sfacelo, *m.*, dissoluzione, rovina, *f.*; (*of teeth*) carie, *f.*; marciume, *m.* ‖ *v.i.* Decadere, deperire, guastarsi; (*of teeth*) cariarsi; marcire, imputridire.
decease [di'siːs], *n.* Decesso, *m.*, morte, *f.* ‖ *v.i.* Morire.
deceased, *a.* Defunto, morto, estinto, deceduto.
deceit [di'siːt], *n.* Inganno, artifizio, *m.*, truffa, frode, *f.*; soperchieria, *f.*
deceitful, *a.* Fallace, ingannevole, perfido, menzognero.
deceitfully, *adv.* Perfidamente.
deceitfulness, *n.* Duplicità, perfidia, falsità, *f.*
deceivable [di'siːvəbl], *a.* Ingannabile.
deceive, *v.t.* Ingannare; abbindolare, illudere. **To — oneself**, illudersi.
deceiver, *n.* Ingannatore, *m.*, ingannatrice, *f.*
December [di'sembəɹ], *n.* Dicembre, *m.*
decemvir [di'semvəɹ], *n.* (*Hist.*) Decemviro, *m.*
decency ['diːsənsi], *n.* Decenza, convenienza, *f.*, decoro, *m.*; modestia, *f.*
decennial, *a.* Decennale.
decent, *a.* Decente, onesto, convenevole, decoroso; (*colloq.*) discreto, moderato.
decently, *adv.* Decentemente; (*colloq.*) discretamente.
decentralization [diːsentrəlai'zeiʃən], *n.* Dicentramento, *m.*
decentralize, *v.t.* Dicentrare.
deception [di'sepʃən], *n.* Inganno, *m.*; illusione, frode, *f.*
deceptive, *a.* Ingannevole, illusorio; fallace.
decibel ['desibel], *n.* (*Elect.*) Decibel, *m.*
decide [di'said], *v.t.* Decidere; *v.i.* decidersi, risolversi.
decided, *a.* Deciso, risoluto; chiaro, positivo.
decidedly, *adv.* Decisamente, risolutamente; senza dubbio.
deciduous [di'sidjuːəs], *a.* (*Bot.*) Deciduo.
decigram ['desigræm], *n.* Decigramma, *f.*
decimal, *n.a.* Decimale.
decimate, *v.t.* Decimare.
decimation, *n.* Decimazione, *f.*
decipher [di'saifəɹ], *v.t.* Decifrare.
decipherable, *a.* Decifrabile.
decipherer, *n.* Decifratore, *m.*
decipherment, *n.* Decifamento, *m.*
decision [di'siʃən], *n.* Decisione; (*fig.*) fermezza, risolutezza, *f.* **To come to a —**, decidersi, prendere una risoluzione.
decisive, *a.* Decisivo.
decisively, *adv.* Decisivamente.
decisiveness, *n.* Fermezza, risolutezza, *f.*
decivilize [diː'sivilaiz], *v.t.* Imbarbarire.
deck (1) [dek], *n.* (*Naut.*) Ponte, *m.*; coperta, tolda, *f.* **Fore- —**, castello di prua, *m.*; **lower —**, primo ponte, *m.*; **main —**, ponte di coperta, *m.*; **— -cabin**, cabina di coperta, *f.*; **— -chair**, sedia a sdraio, *f.*; **— -hand**, marinaio di ponte.
deck (2), *v.t.* Ornare, addobbare, guarnire, parare. **To — with flags**, pavesare; **to — with flowers**, decorare, infiorare.
deck (3), *n.* (*Cards*) Mazzo, *m.*
decking, *n.* Ornamento, abbellimento, *m.*
declaim [di'kleim], *v.t.* Declamare. **To — against**, inveire contro.
declaimer, *n.* Declamatore, *m.*
declamation, *n.* Declamazione, *f.*
declamatory, *a.* Declamatorio.
declaration [deklə'reiʃən], *n.* Dichiarazione, *f.*, proclama, *m.*
declarative, *a.* Dichiarativo, esplicativo.
declaratory, *a.* Dichiaratorio.
declare [di'kleəɹ], *v.t.* Dichiarare, proclamare, annunziare. **To — oneself**, dichiararsi; **to — oneself for**, dichiararsi favorevole a; **to — oneself against**, dichiararsi contrario a; **I —!** Impossibile! Veramente!
declaredly, *adv.* Dichiaratamente, apertamente.
declension [di'klenʃən], *n.* Decadenza, *f.*; (*Gram.*) declinazione, *f.*
declinable [di'klainəbl], *a.* Declinabile.
declination, *n.* (*Astron.*) Declinazione, *f.*
decline [di'klain], *v.t.i.* Declinare, chinare, pendere; abbassare; ricusare, rifiutare; (*Gram.*) declinare. ‖ *n.* Decadenza, *f.*, declino, abbassamento, *m.*; (*Med.*) consunzione, tisi, *f.*; (*Comm.*) (*in price*) ribasso. **To fall into a —**, essere tisico; deperire.
declinometer [dekli'nɔmitəɹ], *n.* Declinometro, *m.*
declivity [dek'liviti], *n.* Declivio, pendio, *m.*
decoction [di'kɔkʃən], *n.* Decozione, *f.*, decotto, *m.*
decode [diː'koud], *v.t.* Decifrare.
decollate [di'kɔleit], *v.t.* Decapitare.
decolorization [diːkʌlərai'zeiʃən], *n.* Decolorazione, *f.*
decolorize, *v.t.* Decolorare.
decomposable [diːkəm'pouzəbl], *a.* Decomponibile.
decompose, *v.t.* Decomporre, scomporre; *v.i.* decomporsi, scomporsi.
decomposite, *a.* Doppiamente composto, composto di composti.

decomposition, *n.* Decomposizione, *f.*
decorate [ˈdekəreit], *v.t.* Ornare, abbellire, guarnire, adornare, decorare.
decoration, *n.* Decorazione, *f.*; ornamento, abbellimento, *m.*
decorative, *a.* Decorativo.
decorator, *n.* Decoratore, *m.*
decorous, *a.* Decoroso, dignitoso, acconcio, decente.
decorously, *adv.* Decorosamente.
decorticate [diːˈkɔːɹtikeit], *v.t.* Scorticare.
decorum [diˈkɔːrəm], *n.* Decoro, *m.*
decoy [diˈkɔi], *v.t.* Adescare, allettare; sedurre. || *n.* (*bait*) Esca, *f.*; (*trap*) trappola, *f.*; (*place*) capannuccia, *f.*; (*person*) allettatore, lusingatore, *m.*, lusingatrice, *f.* **—-bird,** uccello di richiamo, *m.*
decrease [diːˈkriːs], *n.* Diminuzione, *f.*, ribasso, calo, *m.*; decrescenza, *f.* || *v.i.* Decrescere, diminuire, scemare; *v.t.* diminuire, scemare, ridurre.
decree [diˈkriː], *n.* Decreto, editto, *m.*, ordinanza, sentenza, *f.* || *v.t.* Decretare, ordinare. (*Law*) **— absolute,** sentenza definitiva, *f.*; **— nisi,** sentenza interlocutoria, *f.*
decrement [ˈdekrimənt], *n.* Diminuzione, decrescenza, *f.*
decrepit [diˈkrepit], *a.* Decrepito, caduco, debole.
decrepitude, *n.* Decrepitezza, vecchiezza, *f.*
decrepitate [diˈkrepiteit], *v.t.* Decrepitare; *v.i.* crepitare.
decretal [diˈkriːtəl], *n.* (*Hist.*) Decretale, *f.*
decrier [diˈkraiəɹ], *n.* Sparlatore, denigratore, *m.*
decry [diˈkrai], *v.t.* Screditare, sparlare di, denigrare.
decumbent [diˈkʌmbənt], *a.* (*Bot.Zool.*) Decombente; pendente.
decuple [ˈdekjuːpl], *a.* Decuplo. *v.t.* Decuplicare.
decussate, decussated [diˈkʌseit, diˈkʌsətəd], *a.* (*Bot.*) Decussato.
decussation, *n.* Decussazione, *f.*
dedicate [ˈdedikeit], *v.t.* Dedicare, consacrare, offrire.
dedication, *n.* Dedicazione, *f.*; (*of book*) dedica, *f.*
dedicated, [illegible]nsacrato, dedicato.
dedicatory [illegible]Dedicatorio.
deduce [diˈdjuːs], *v.t.* Dedurre, argomentare, inferire, desu[illegible]re.
deducible, *a.* Deducibile.
deduct [diˈdʌkt], *v.t.* Dedurre, detrarre, sottrarre.
deduction, *n.* Deduzione, d[illegible]razione, *f.*; (*Comm.*) ribasso, *m.*
deductive, *a.* Deduttivo. **— reasoning,** procedimento deduttivo, *m.*
deductively, *adv.* Deduttivamente.
deed [diːd], *n.* Atto, fatto, *m.*, azione, *f.*; gesto, *m.*; documento, certificato, titolo, *m.* **— of gift,** atto di donazione, *m.*; **marriage —,** atto di matrimonio, *m.*; **to draw a —,** redigere un atto; **to sign a —,** sottoscrivere un atto.
deem [diːm], *v.t.* Credere, giudicare, ritenere, considerare, stimare. **He is deemed worthy of great honour,** è ritenuto degno di molta stima; **I should — it a favour if you would come,** riterrei un favore se voi voleste venire; **he deemed it right to go,** pensava che fosse giusto andare.
deemster, *n.* Giudice nell'isola di Man, *m.*
deep [diːp], *a.* Profondo, basso, cupo; (*of colour*) carico; (*of sound*) sonoro, grave, profondo. || *n.* Mare, oceano, *m.*; abisso, *m.* **— mourning,** lutto pesante, *m.*; **this well is thirty feet —,** questo pozzo ha trenta piedi di profondità; **to drink —,** bere copiosamente; **he's a — one,** è molto astuto; **—-sea fishing,** pesca al largo; **—-laid,** segreto, profondo; **—-read,** erudito; **—-rooted,** profondamente radicato, inveterato; **—-seated,** profondo, intimo, riposto; **—-toned,** sonoro, cupo.
deepen, *v.t.* Approfondire, scavare; caricare (*of colour*); (*of sound*) abbassare; *v.i.* divenire più profondo. **Her colour deepened,** essa arrossì.
deepening, *n.* Profondamento, *m.*
deeply, *adv.* Profondamente, molto; cupamente; scaltramente.
deepness [cp. **depth**].
deer (*pl.* **deer**) [diəɹ], *n.* Cervo, daino, *m.* **—-stalking, —-hunting,** caccia al cervo, *f.*; **—-hound,** segugio, *m.*
deface [diˈfeis], *v.t.* Deturpare, abbruttire, guastare, sciupare; cancellare.
defaced, *a.* Sfigurato, guastato.
defacement, *n.* Deturpazione, *f.*, abbruttimento, *m.*
defalcate [ˈdiːfəlkeit], *v.i.* Truffare, malversare; sottrarre.
defalcation, *n.* Truffa, malversazione, *f.*
defalcator, *n.* Truffatore, *m.*
defamation [defəˈmeiʃən], *n.* Diffamazione, *f.*
defamatory, *a.* Diffamatorio.
defame, *v.t.* Diffamare, calunniare.
defamer, *n.* Diffamatore, *m.*
default [diˈfɔːlt], *n.* Mancanza, *f.*; difetto, *m.*; omissione, *f.*; mancanza, contumacia, *f.* || *v.i.* Mancare, venir meno a, violare un impegno. **Judgment by —,** condanna in contumacia, *f.*; **in — of,** in difetto di, in mancanza di.
defaulter, *n.* (*Law*) Contumace, *m.*; (*Comm.*) moroso, debitore, *m.*; (*Mil.*) renitente, *m.*
defeasance [diˈfiːzəns], *n.* (*Law*) Abrogazione, revocazione, *f.*
defeasible, *a.* Revocabile.
defeat [diˈfiːt], *n.* Disfatta, rotta, sconfitta, *f.* || *v.t.* Vincere, sconfiggere, abbattere; (*fig.*) frustrare. **To — the law,** eludere la legge; **to — one's own ends,** tirarsi la zappa sui piedi.
defecate [ˈdefəkeit], *v.t.i.* Defecare.
defecation, *n.* Defecazione, *f.*
defect [diˈfekt], *n.* Difetto, *m.*; mancanza, *f.*; macchia, imperfezione, *f.*
defection, *n.* Defezione, apostasia, *f.*, rinnegamento, *m.*
defective, *a.* Difettoso, imperfetto, deficiente; (*Gram.*) difettivo.
defectively, *adv.* Difettosamente.
defectiveness, *n.* Imperfezione, manchevolezza, *f.*
defence [diˈfens], *n.* Difesa, *f.* **In — of,** a difesa di.
defenceless, *a.* Senza difesa.
defencelessness, *n.* Mancanza di difesa, *f.*
defend [diˈfend], *v.t.* Difendere, proteggere.
defendable, *a.* Difendibile.

defendant, *n.* (*Law*) Imputato, convenuto, citato, *m.*
defender, *n.* Difenditore, difensore, *m.*
defensible, *a.* Difendibile; giustificabile, sostenibile.
defensive, *n.* Difensiva, *f.* || *a.* Difensivo. **On the —,** sulla difensiva.
defensively, *adv.* Difensivamente.
defer [di'fəːɹ], *v.t.* Differire, rimandare, rimettere; *v.i.* deferire, rimettersi, sottomettersi. **To — to someone's judgment,** deferire al giudizio di qualcuno.
deference ['defərəns], *n.* Deferenza, *f.*, rispetto, *m.* **Out of — to,** per riguardo a.
deferent, *a.* (*Anat.*) Deferente.
deferential [defə'renʃəl], *a.* Deferente, rispettoso.
deferentially, *adv.* Rispettosamente.
defiance [di'faiəns], *n.* Sfida, disfida, *f.*; disprezzo, *m.* **In — of,** a dispetto di; **to set at —,** sfidare; **to hurl —,** lanciare una sfida.
defiant, *a.* Provocante, temerario, spavaldo.
defiantly, *adv.* Spavaldamente.
deficiency [di'fiʃənsi], *n.* Deficienza, mancanza, scarsezza, *f.*, difetto, *m.*
deficient, *a.* Deficiente, mancante, insufficiente. **Mentally —,** deficiente; **to be — in,** mancare di.
deficit ['defisit], *n.* (*Comm.*) Deficit, *m.*; ammanco, *m.* **Cash —,** ammanco di cassa, *m.*; **to make good a —,** colmare un deficit.
defile (1) [di'fail], *n.* Gola, stretta, *f.* || *v.i.* Sfilare.
defile (2), *v.t.* Macchiare, lordare; violare, disonorare, contaminare.
defilement, *n.* Macchia, contaminazione, *f.*
defiler, *n.* Contaminatore, violatore, *m.*
definable [di'fainəbl], *a.* Definibile.
define, *v.t.* Definire, determinare.
definite ['definit], *a.* Definito, determinato.
definitely, *adv.* Definitamente.
definiteness, *n.* Determinatezza, precisione, *f.*
definition, *n.* Definizione, *f.*
definitive [di'finitiv], *a.* Definitivo, ultimo.
definitively, *adv.* Definitivamente.
deflagrate ['defləgreit], *v.t.* (*Chem.*) Deflagrare.
deflate [di'fleit], *v.t.* Sgonfiare; (*Comm.*) deflazionare.
deflation, *n.* Sgonfiamento, *m.*; (*Comm.*) deflazione, *f.*
deflect [di'flekt], *v.t.* Deflettere, sviare, stornare; sviarsi.
deflection, *n.* Deviazione; (*Elect.*) declinazione, *f.*
defloration [diːflɔ'reiʃən], *n.* Deflorazione, *f.*
deflower [di'flauəɹ], *v.t.* Deflorare, disfiorare; (*ravish*) violare.
defluent ['diːfluənt], *n.a.* (*Geol.*) Defluente, *m.*
defluxion [di'flʌkʃən], *n.* (*Med.*) Flussione, *f.*
deforest [diː'fɔrist], *v.t.* Sboscare, diboscare.
deforestation, *n.* Disboscamento, *m.*
deform [di'fɔːɹm], *v.t.* Deformare, sformare, deturpare.
deformation, *n.* Deformazione, *f.*
deformed, *a.* Deforme.
deformity, *n.* Deformità; bruttezza, *f.*
defraud [di'frɔːd], *v.t.* Defraudare, frodare, ingannare.
defrauder, *n.* Defraudatore, frodatore, truffatore, *m.*
defray [di'frei], *v.t.* Pagare. **To — the expenses,** pagare le spese.
deft [deft], *a.* Destro, svelto, lesto, abile.
deftly, *adv.* Destramente.
deftness, *n.* Destrezza, sveltezza, *f.*
defunct [di'fʌŋkt], *n.a.* Defunto, morto, *m.*
defy [de'fai], *v.t.* Sfidare, provocare, affrontare.
degeneracy [di'dʒenərəsi], *n.* Degenerazione, *f.*, tralignamento, *m.*
degenerate (1) [di'dʒenərət], *a.* Degenerato, tralignato, degenere.
degenerate (2) [di'dʒenəreit], *v.i.* Degenerare, tralignare.
degenerately, *adv.* Degeneratamente.
degeneration, *n.* Degenerazione, *f.*
deglutition [diːgluː'tiʃən], *n.* Deglutizione, *f.*
degradation [degrə'deiʃən], *n.* Degradazione, *f.*; avvilimento, *m.*
degrade [di'greid], *v.t.* Degradare, abbassare, avvilire.
degraded, *a.* Degradato, basso, vile, abbietto.
degrading, *a.* Umiliante, vergognoso, avvilente.
degradingly, *adv.* Vergognosamente.
degree [di'griː], *n.* Grado, *m.*; punto, stato, rango, *m.*; condizione, *f.*; ordine, *m.*; (*University*) laurea, *f.* **By degrees,** poco a poco, a gradi; **to a certain —,** fino a un certo punto; **to such a —,** a tal punto; **to take one's —,** laurearsi, prender la laurea; **honorary —,** titolo onorifico, *m.*, laurea ad honorem, *f.*; **of high —,** di alto lignaggio, di alta condizione.
degustation, *n.* Degustazione, *f.*
dehisce [diː'his], *v.i.* (*Bot.*) Aprirsi.
dehiscence, *n.* Deiscenza, *f.*
dehiscent, *a.* Deiscente.
dehumanize [diː'hjuːmənaiz], *v.t.* Disumanare.
de-icer [diː'aisəɹ], *n.* (*Aviat.*) Sostanza per prevenire la formazione dei ghiaccioli sulle ali.
deification [diːifi'keiʃən], *n.* Deificazione, *f.*
deify, *v.t.* Deificare.
deign [dein], *v.i.* Degnarsi; *v.t.* degnare, accordare, concedere. **He did not — to reply,** non si degnò di rispondere.
deism ['diːizm], *n.* Deismo, *m.*
deist, *n.* Deista, *m.*
deistic, deistical, *a.* Deistico.
deity, *n.* Deità, divinità, *f.*
deject [di'dʒekt], *v.t.* Abbattere, scoraggiare, demoralizzare.
dejected, *a.* Abbattuto, scoraggiato; triste, mesto.
dejectedly, *adv.* Mestamente.
dejectedness, dejection, *n.* Abbattimento, scoraggiamento, *m.*; (*Med.*) deiezione, *f.*
de jure [diː 'dʒjuːri], *adv.* Di diritto.
delate [di'leit], *v.t.* Denunziare.
delation, *n.* Delazione, *f.*
delator, *n.* Delatore, *m.*
delay [di'lei], *n.* Ritardo, indugio, *m.* || *v.t.* Rinviare, ritardare, differire, rimettere; *v.i.* indugiare, tardare, esitare, fermarsi.
delectable [di'lektəbl], *a.* Dilettevole, delittoso, piacevole.
delectability, *n.* Dilettevolezza, *f.*
delectably, *adv.* Dilettevolmente.
delectation, *n.* Diletto, piacere, *m.* **He read the poem for my —,** lesse la poesia per dilettarmi.

delegate [ˈdeligeit], *n.a.* Delegato, *m.* ‖ *v.t.* Delegare, deputare.
delete [diˈliːt], *v.t.* Cancellare.
deletion, *n.* Cancellatura, *f.*
deleterious [deliˈtiəriəs], *a.* Deleterio.
delft [delft], *n.* Maiolica di Delft, *f.*
deliberate (1) [diˈlibəreit], *v.t.i.* Deliberare, considerare, ponderare, esaminare; risolversi, discutere.
deliberate (2) [diˈlibərit], *a.* Intenzionale, voluto, premeditato; lento, cauto, prudente.
deliberately, *adv.* Deliberatamente, apposta, di proposito.
deliberateness, *n.* Prudenza, cautela, lentezza, *f.*
deliberation, *n.* Deliberazione, *f.*
deliberative, *a.* Deliberativo.
delicacy [ˈdelikəsi], *n.* Delicatezza, squisitezza, *f.*; ghiottoneria, *f.*; manicaretto, *m.*
delicate, *a.* Delicato, esile, tenero. **— feeling,** sentimento squisito, *m.*
delicately, *adv.* Delicatamente; (*fig.*) discretamente.
delicateness, *n.* Delicatezza, *f.*
delicious [diˈliʃəs], *a.* Delizioso, gustoso, squisito.
deliciously, *adv.* Deliziosamente.
deliciousness, *n.* Delizia, squisitezza, *f.*
delight [diˈlait], *n.* Delizia, *f.*, diletto, piacere, *m.* ‖ *v.t.* Piacere a, dilettare, incantare, rallegrare; *v.i.* compiacersi, dilettarsi, rallegrarsi. **To — in,** dilettarsi di.
delightful, *a.* Dilettevole, incantevole, delizioso.
delightfully, *adv.* Dilettevolmente.
delightfulness, *n.* Incanto, diletto, *m.*
delimit [diːˈlimit], *v.t.* Delimitare.
delimitation, *n.* Delimitazione, *f.*
delineate [diˈlinieit], *v.t.* Delineare, disegnare, tracciare; descrivere.
delineation, *n.* Schizzo, abbozzo, *m.*; descrizione, *f.*
delineator, *n.* Delineatore, descrittore, *m.*
delinquency [diˈliŋkwənsi], *n.* Delitto, misfatto, reato, *m.*
delinquent, *n.* Delinquente, malfattore, *m.*
deliquesce [deliˈkwes], *v.i.* Sciogliersi, fondersi.
deliquescence, *n.* Deliquescenza, *f.*
deliquescent, *a.* Deliquescente.
deliquium [deˈlikwiəm], *n.* (*Med.*) Deliquio, *m.*
delirious [diˈliriəs], *a.* Delirante, in delirio. **To become —,** cadere in delirio; **to be —,** delirare.
deliriously, *adv.* Pazzamente.
delirium, *n.* Delirio, vaneggiamento, *m.*; (*fig.*) entusiasmo, *m.* **— tremens,** delirium tremens, *m.*
deliver [diˈlivəɹ], *v.t.* Liberare, salvare, scampare; (*letters*) distribuire; consegnare, affidare, recare; esprimere, esporre; (*a speech, etc.*) pronunciare; (*a blow*) lanciare; (*Med.*) far sgravare; (*Tennis, etc.*) lanciare. **To — a message,** recare un messaggio; **to — from,** liberare da; **to — oneself up to,** abbandonarsi a; **to — up,** consegnare; **to be delivered of** (*a child*), partorire.
deliverable, *a.* (*Comm.*) Consegnabile.
deliverance, *n.* Liberazione, *f.*; discorso, *m.*
deliverer, *n.* Liberatore, salvatore, *m.*
delivery, *n.* Consegna, *f.*; (*of letters*) distribuzione, *f.*; (*surrender*) resa, *f.*; (*of a speech*) dizione, *f.*; (*of a child*) parto, *m.* **To take —,** prendere la consegna; **payment on —,** pagamento alla consegna; **— -van,** furgone, *m.*
dell [del], *n.* Valletta, *f.*
Delphic [ˈdelfik], *a.* Delfico.
delta [ˈdeltə], *n.* (*Geog.*) Delta, *m.*
deltoid, *a.* (*Anat.*) Deltoide.
delude [diˈljuːd], *v.t.* Deludere, ingannare, frustrare. **To — oneself,** ingannarsi, sbagliarsi.
deluding, *a.* Ingannevole, illusorio.
deluge [ˈdeljuːdʒ], *n.* Diluvio, *m.*; inondazione, *f.* ‖ *v.t.* Inondare, diluviare.
delusion [diˈljuːʒən], *n.* Illusione, *f.*, vaneggiamento, *m.*; inganno, *m.*
delusive, delusory, *a.* Illusorio, fallace, ingannevole, falso.
delusiveness, *n.* Illusorietà, fallacia, *f.*
delve [delv], *v.t.* Zappare, scavare, vangare. **To — into,** penetrare, sondare, investigare.
demagnetize [diːˈmægnitaiz], *v.t.* Smagnetizzare.
demagnetization, *n.* Smagnetizzazione, *f.*
demagogic [deməˈgɔgik], *a.* Demagogico.
demagogue [ˈdeməgɔg], *n.* Demagogo, *m.*
demagogy, *n.* Demagogia, *f.*
demand [deˈmɑːnd], *n.* Domanda, richiesta, *f.*; pretesa, esigenza, *f.* ‖ *v.t.* Domandare, richiedere, esigere. **In great —,** molto ricercato; **payable on —,** pagabile su domanda **— note** (*for taxes, etc.*) intimazione, *f.*
demandant, *n.* (*Law*) Querelante, *m.*
demander, *n.* Richiedente, *m.*
demarcation [diːmɑːɹˈkeiʃən], *n.* Demarcazione, *f.*
dematerialize [diːməˈtiəriəlaiz], *v.t.i.* Smaterializzare.
demean [diˈmiːn], *v.r.* To **— oneself,** condursi, comportarsi; degradarsi, abbassarsi.
demeanour, *n.* Condotta, *f.*; contegno, portamento, *m.*
demented, *a.* Pazzo, matto, impazzito, demente.
dementia [diˈmenʃə], *n.* (*Med.*) Demenza, *f.*
demerit [diːˈmerit], *n.* Demerito, fallo, *m.*; colpa, *f.*
demeritorious, *a.* Demeritorio.
demesne [diˈmein], *n.* Proprietà fondiaria, *f.*
demi- [ˈdemi], *prefix.* Semi, a mezzo.
demigod, *n.* Semidio, *m.*
demijohn, *n.* Damigiana, *f.*
demisable [diˈmaizəbl], *a.* (*Law*) Cedibile, trasferibile.
demise, *n.* Decesso, *m.*, morte, *f.*; (*Law*) cessione, *f.* ‖ *v.t.* Legare per testamento, lasciare, trasmettere.
demisemiquaver [demisemiˈkweivəɹ], *n.* (*Mus.*) Semibiscroma, *f.*
demission [diˈmiʃən], *n.* Dimissione, rinunzia, *f.*
demit, *v.t.* Dare le dimissioni, dimettersi.
demitone [ˈdemitoun], *n.* (*Mus.*) Semitono, *m.*
demiurge, *n.* Demiurgo, *m.*
demobilization [diːmobilaiˈzeiʃən], *n.* Smobilitazione, *f.*
demobilize, *v.t.* Smobilitare.
democracy [deˈmɔkrəsi], *n.* Democrazia, *f.*
democrat, *n.* Democratico, *m.*
democratic, democratical, *a.* Democratico.
democratically, *adv.* Democraticamente.

democratization, *n.* Democratizzazione, *f.*
democratize, *v.t.* Democratizzare.
demoded [diːˈmoudid], *a.* Fuori di moda, antiquato.
demolish [diˈmɔliʃ], *v.t.* Demolire.
demolition, *n.* Demolizione, *f.*
demon [ˈdiːmən], *n.* Demone, demonio, *m.*
demonetize [diːˈmʌnətaiz], *v.t.* (*Comm.*) Demonetizzare, smonetizzare.
demoniac, demoniacal, *a.* Demoniaco.
demonology, *n.* Demonologia, *f.*
demonstrable [diˈmɔnstrəbl], *a.* Dimostrabile.
demonstrably, *adv.* Dimostrativamente.
demonstrate, *v.t.* Dimostrare, mostrare.
demonstration, *n.* Dimostrazione, *f.*
demonstrative, *a.* Dimostrativo. **She is very —,** essa è molto espansiva.
demonstrator, *n.* Dimostratore; assistente insegnante, *m.*
demoralization [dimɔrəlaiˈzeiʃən], *n.* Demoralizzazione, *f.*; scoraggiamento, *m.*
demoralize, *v.t.* Demoralizzare, scoraggiare.
demoralizing, *a.* Demoralizzante, avvilente.
demos [ˈdiːmɔs], *n.* Il popolo, *m.*
Demosthenes [deˈmɔsθəniːz], *n.* (*Hist.*) Demostene, *m.*
demotic [deˈmɔtik], *a.* Demotico.
demulcent [diˈmʌlsənt], *a.* (*Med.*) Demulcente, lenitivo.
demur [diˈməːɹ], *n.* Esitazione, *f.*; scrupolo, *m.*; obbiezione, *f.* || *v.i.* Esitare, temporeggiare; eccepire, far difficoltà. **Without —,** senza fare obbiezioni; **to make a —,** far sorgere una difficoltà.
demure [diˈmjuːəɹ], *a.* Modesto, discreto, contegnoso, posato. **To look very —,** darsi un contegno, fare il sostenuto.
demurely, *adv.* Posatamente.
demureness, *n.* Contegnosità, compostezza, *f.*
demurrage [diˈmʌridʒ], *n.* (*Comm.*) Sosta, *f.*; magazzinaggio, *m.*; spese di magazzinaggio, *f.pl.*
demurrer, *n.* (*Law*) Eccezione pregiudiziale, *f.*
demy [deˈmai], *n.* (*Of paper*) Quadrato, *m.*; (*at Oxford University*) allievo borsista, *m.*
den [den], *n.* Tana, *f.*; (*of thieves*) spelonca, *f.*; nascondiglio, *m.*; (*colloq.*) gabinetto, *m.*
denationalization [diːnæʃənəlaiˈzeiʃən], *n.* Snazionalizzazione, *f.*
denationalize, *v.t.* Snazionalizzare.
denaturalization [diːnætjurəlaiˈzeiʃən], *n.* Snaturamento, *m.*
denaturalize, *v.t.* Snaturare.
denature [diˈneitʃəɹ], *v.t.* (*Chem.*) Denaturare.
dendrite [ˈdendrait], *n.* (*Geol.*) Dendrite, *f.*
deniable [deˈnaiəbl], *a.* Negabile.
denial [deˈnaiəl], *n.* Negazione, *f.*; rifiuto, rinnegamento, *m.*; smentita (*disclaimer*), *f.* **A flat —,** un rifiuto netto, *m.*; **self- —,** abnegazione, *f.*
denigrate [ˈdiːnigreit], *v.t.* Denigrare, spregiare, screditare.
denigration, *n.* Denigrazione, *f.*
denigrator, *n.* Denigratore, *m.*
denitrate, denitrify [diːˈnaitreit, diːˈnaitrifai], *v.t.* (*Chem.*) Privare d'acido nitrico.
denizen [ˈdenizən], *n.* Abitante, cittadino, *m.*
Denmark [ˈdenmɑːɹk], *n.* (*Geog.*) Danimarca, *f.*
denominate [diˈnɔmineit], *v.t.* Denominare, nominare, chiamare.
denomination, *n.* Denominazione; classe; setta, *f.*; (*unit*) taglio, valore, *m.*
denominational, *a.* Confessionale, settario.
denominative, *a.* Denominativo.
denominator, *n.* (*Math.*) Denominatore, *m.*
denotation [diːnouˈteiʃən], *n.* Denotazione, *f.*
denotative, *a.* Denotativo, denotante.
denote, *v.t.* Denotare, dinotare, mostrare, indicare.
denounce [diˈnauns], *v.t.* Denunziare, denunciare.
denouncement, *n.* Denunzia, notificazione, *f.*
denouncer, *n.* Denunziatore, *m.*, denunziatrice *f.*
dense [dens], *a.* Denso, spesso, fitto, folto; (*fig.*) stupido, sciocco, ottuso.
densely, *adv.* Densamente; scioccamente.
denseness, *n.* Sciocchezza, stupidità, *f.*
density, *n.* Densità, spessezza, *f.*
dent [dent], *n.* Incavo, *m.*, tacca, *f.* || *v.t.* Incavare, intaccare.
dental [ˈdentəl], *a.* Dentario; (*Gram.*) dentale. **— surgeon,** chirurgo dentista, *m.*
dentate, dentated, *a.* (*Bot.Zool.*) Dentellato.
denticle, *n.* (*Arch.*) Dentello, *m.*
denticulate, denticulated, *a.* Dentellato.
denticulation, *n.* Frastagliatura, *f.*
dentiform, *a.* Dentiforme.
dentifrice, *n.* Dentrifricio, *m.*
dentine, *n.* Dentina, *f.*
dentist, *n.* Dentista, *m.*
dentistry, *n.* Dentisteria, odontoiatria, *f.*
dentition, *n.* Dentizione, *f.*
denture, *n.* Dentiera, *f.*
denudate, denude [ˈdiːnjuːdeit, diˈnjuːd], *v.t.* Denudare, spogliare.
denudation, *n.* (*Geol.*) Denudazione, *f.*, spogliamento, *m.*
denunciation [dinʌnsiˈeiʃən], *n.* Denunzia, *f.*
deny [deˈnai], *v.t.* Negare, smentire, disdire; rifiutare, respingere. **To — oneself,** privarsi, rifiutarsi; **he is not to be denied,** non si può respingere la sua domanda; **it is not to be denied,** non si può negarlo; **to — oneself to someone,** rifiutare di ricevere qualcuno.
deobstruent [diːˈɔbstruːənt], *n.a.* (*Med.*) Deostruente, *m.*
deodar [ˈdiːoudɑːɹ], *n.* (*Bot.*) Deodara, *f.*
deodorant [diːˈoudərənt], *n.* Deodorante, *m.*
deodorization, *n.* Deodoramento, *m.*
deodorize, *v.t.* Deodorare.
deodorizer, *n.* Deodorante, *m.*
deoxidization [diːɔksidaiˈzeiʃən], *n.* (*Chem.*) Disossidazione, *f.*
deoxidize, deoxidate, *v.t.* Disossidare.
deoxygenate [diːˈɔksidʒəneit], *v.t.* Disossigenare.
deoxygenation, *n.* Disossigenazione, *f.*
depart [deˈpɑːɹt], *v.i.* Partire, andarsene; scostarsi, allontanarsi; (*fig.*) morire, decedere. **To — from,** partire da, allontanarsi da.
departed, *a.* Morto, defunto, trapassato, estinto. **The —,** i defunti, *m.pl.* **— joys,** gioie passate, *f.pl.*
department, *n.* Dipartimento, *m.*; (*Pol.*) dicastero, ufficio, *m.*; (*in shop*) riparto, *m.*; (*of studies*) ramo, *m.* **— store,** grande magazzino, *m.*; **intelligence —,** ufficio d'informazioni, *m.*; **sales —,** riparto vendite, *m.*; **it is hardly my —,** non è di mia competenza.
departmental, *a.* Dipartimentale.

departure [di'pɑːɹtʃəɹ], *n.* Partenza, dipartita, *f.*; distacco, allontanamento, *m.*; deviazione, *f.*; (*fig.*) morte, *f.* **A — from the truth,** uno strappo alla verità; **a — from duty,** un'infrazione al proprio dovere; **this is quite a new —,** questo è un'innovazione; (*Rail.*) **— platform,** marciapiede delle partenze, *f.*

depauperize [diː'pɔːpəraiz], *v.t.* Depauperare.

depend [di'pend], *v.i.* Dipendere da; contare su, fidarsi di, fare assegnamento su. **— upon it!** Siatene certo!; **that depends on circumstances,** ciò dipende dalle circostanze; **he depends on her for everything,** dipende da lei per tutto.

dependable, *a.* Leale, sicuro, fido, fidato.

dependant, dependent, *n.* Dipendente, *m.f.*

dependence, *n.* Confidenza, fede, *f.*, fiducia, *f.* **Don't place any — on what he says,** non fate assegnamento sulle sue parole.

dependency, *n.* Dipendenza, *f.*

dependent, *a.* Dipendente. **To be — on,** dipendere da.

dependently, *adv.* Dipendentemente.

depict [di'pikt], *v.t.* Dipingere, ritrarre, descrivere.

depilate ['depileit], *v.t.* Depilare.

depilation, *n.* Depilazione, *f.*

depilatory, *a.* Depilatorio.

deplete [di'pliːt], *v.t.* Diminuire, esaurire, vuotare.

depletion, *n.* Diminuzione, *f.*, esaurimento, *m.*

deplorable [di'plɔːrəbl], *a.* Deplorabile, deplorevole. **— behaviour,** contegno deplorevole, *m.*

deplorableness, *n.* Deplorevolezza, *f.*

deplorably, *adv.* Deplorevolmente.

deplore, *v.t.* Deplorare, lamentare; disapprovare.

deploy [di'plɔi], *v.t.* (*Mil.*) Spiegare, distendere; *v.i.* spiegarsi, stendersi.

deployment, *n.* Spiegamento, *m.*

deplume [diː'pluːm], *v.t.* Spennare, spiumare.

depolarization [diːpoulərai'zeiʃən], *n.* Depolarizzazione, *f.*

depolarize, *v.t.* Depolarizzare.

depone [di'poun], *v.t.* (*Law*) Deporre, testimoniare.

deponent, *n.a.* Deponente, *m.*

depopulate [diː'pɔpjuleit], *v.t.* Spopolare, depopolare.

depopulation, *n.* Spopolamento, *m.*, depopolazione, *f.*

deport [di'pɔːɹt], *v.t.* Espellere, esiliare, bandire. **To — oneself,** comportarsi, condursi, diportarsi.

deportation, *n.* Deportazione, relegazione, *f.*

deportment, *n.* Condotta, *f.*, diportamento, contegno, *m.*

depose [di'pouz], *v.t.* Deporre, detronizzare; attestare, testimoniare, testificare. **The king was deposed,** il re fu detronizzato; **the witness deposed to these facts,** il testimonio testificò di questi fatti.

deposit [de'pɔzit], *n.* Deposito, pegno, *m.*; sedimento, giacimento, *m.*; (*on account*) caparra, *f.*, versamento, *m.* || *v.t.* Depositare, consegnare. **To hold in —,** tenere in deposito; **to pay the —,** dare la caparra; **— account,** deposito vincolato, *m.*; **— receipt,** ricevuta di deposito, *f.*

depositary, *n.* Depositario, *m.*

deposition, *n.* Deposizione, testimonianza, *f.*

depositor, *n.* Depositante, *m.f.*

depository, *n.* Deposito, magazzino, *m.*

depot ['depou], *n.* Deposito, *m.*; (*American*) stazione ferroviaria, *f.*

depravation [deprə'veiʃən], *n.* Depravazione, *f.*

deprave, *v.t.* Depravare, viziare, corrompere.

depraved, *a.* Depravato, viziato, corrotto, malvagio. **A — taste,** un gusto depravato.

depravity [di'præviti], *n.* Depravazione, corruzione, *f.*, pervertimento, *m.*

deprecate ['deprikeit], *v.t.* Scongiurare, deprecare; disapprovare, biasimare. **We strongly — hasty action,** deprechiamo qualsiasi azione intempestiva.

deprecatingly, *adv.* Supplichevolmente; con biasimo.

deprecation, *n.* Deprecazione, supplica, *f.*

deprecative, deprecatory, *a.* Deprecativo, deprecatorio.

depreciate [di'priːʃieit], *v.t.* Deprezzare, svalutare; avvilire; *v.i.* diminuire di valore, subire un deprezzamento.

depreciation, *n.* Deprezzamento, *m.*, svalutazione, *f.* **— in the value of money,** deprezzamento della moneta, *m.*; **— account,** conto deperimento, *m.*

depreciatory, *a.* Deprezzativo.

depredate ['deprideit], *v.t.* Depredare, saccheggiare.

depredation, *n.* Depredazione, scorreria, *f.*, saccheggio, *m.*

depredator, *n.* Depredatore, saccheggiatore, *m.*

depress [di'pres], *v.t.* Abbassare, deprimere; umiliare, conculcare; (*fig.*) scoraggiare, abbattere, accasciare.

depressed, *a.* Scoraggiato, depresso.

depression, *n.* Depressione, *f.*; abbattimento, *m.*, tristezza, *f.*; (*Geol.Meteor.*) depressione, *f.*

depressor, *n.* (*Anat.*) Depressore, *m.*

deprivation [depri'veiʃən], *n.* Privazione, perdita, *f.*

deprive, *v.t.* Privare, spogliare.

depth [depθ], *n.* Profondità, *f.*; abisso, *m.*; (*fig.*) astrusità, densità, *f.* **The — of winter,** il cuore dell'inverno, *m.*; **in the depths of the sea,** al fondo del mare; **to go beyond one's —, to go out of one's —,** non toccare più fondo; **— of colour,** intensità di colore, *f.*; **— charge,** bomba di profondità, *f.*

depurate ['depjuːreit], *v.t.* Depurare.

deputation [depjuː'teiʃən], *n.* Deputazione, delegazione, *f.*

depute, *v.t.* Deputare, delegare.

deputy, *n.* Deputato, *m.*; sostituto, aggiunto, gerente, *m.* **—-chairman,** vice-presidente, *m.*; **—-judge,** giudice aggiunto, *m.*; **—-manager,** faciente funzione di direttore, vicedirettore, *m.*; **—-mayor,** vicesindaco, *m.*

deracinate [diː'ræsineit], *v.t.* Sradicare.

derail [diː'reil], *v.t.* Deragliare, sviare; *v.i.* uscire dalle rotaie.

derailment, *n.* Deragliamento, *m.*

derange [di'reindʒ], *v.t.* Disordinare, scomporre; fare impazzire, squilibrare. **To be deranged,** essere pazzo.

derangement, *n.* Confusione, *f.*; disordine, *m.*; alienazione mentale, *f.*

derelict ['derilikt], *a.* Derelitto, abbandonato. || *n.* (*Naut.*) Nave derelitta, *f.*; relitto, *m.*
dereliction, *n.* Abbandono, *m.*; mancanza, *f.* **— of duty,** mancanza al dovere, *f.*
deride [di'raid], *v.t.* Deridere, schernire, beffare.
deridingly, *adv.* Beffardamente.
derision [di'riʒən], *n.* Derisione, beffa, *f.*, scherno, *m.*
derisive, *a.* Derisivo, sarcastico, beffardo.
derisively, *adv.* Derisivamente.
derisory, *a.* Derisorio.
derivable [di'raivəbl], *a.* Deducibile, derivabile.
derivation, *n.* Derivazione, deduzione; etimologia, origine, *f.*
derivative [di'rivətiv], *n.* Derivato, *m.*; (*Med.*) derivativo, *m.*
derive, *v.t.i.* Derivare; nascere, procedere.
derm [dəːɹm], *n.* (*Anat.*) Derma, *m.*
dermatologist, *n.* Dermatologista, *m.*
dermatology [dəːɹmə'tɔlədʒi], *n.* Dermatologia, *f.*
derogate ['derəgeit], *v.t.i.* Derogare, togliere, detrarre, sminuire. **To — from,** derogare da.
derogation, *n.* Derogazione, *f.*
derogative, *a.* Derogativo.
derogatory, *a.* Derogatorio, disprezzante.
derrick ['derik], *n.* Gru, *f.*; (*Naut.*) albero di carico, *m.*
derring-do [deriŋ'duː], *n.* Audacia, *f.*
dervish ['dəːɹviʃ], *n.* Dervis, derviscio, *m.*
descant [des'kænt], *v.i.* Dissertare, commentare, discorrere. || *n.* ['deskænt] Aria, *f.*; canto, *m.*
descend [di'send], *v.i.* Scendere, smontare, discendere; (*fig.*) piegarsi, abbassarsi. **To be descended from,** discendere da; **he descended from his horse,** smontò dal cavallo; **the property descended to him,** l'eredità scese a lui.
descendant, *n.* Discendente, *m.f.*
descent, *n.* Scesa, discesa, *f.*, pendio, *m.*; china, *f.*; discendenza, derivazione, stirpe, *f.*; lignaggio, *m.* **The Descent from the Cross,** La Deposizione dalla Croce, *f.*
describable [di'skraibəbl], *a.* Descrivibile.
describe, *v.t.* Descrivere; raccontare.
description, *n.* Descrizione, *f.*; genere, sorta, qualità, *f.*
descriptive, *a.* Descrittivo.
descry [dis'krai], *v.t.* Scorgere, discernere, riuscire a vedere.
desecrate ['desikreit], *v.t.* Profanare.
desecration, *n.* Profanazione, *f.*
desert (1) [de'zəːɹt], *n.* Merito, *m.*
desert (2) ['dezəɹt], *n.* Deserto, *m.*; (*fig.*) solitudine, *f.* || *a.* Deserto, solitario, disabitato.
desert (3) [de'zəːɹt], *v.t.* Disertare, abbandonare.
deserted, *a.* Diserto; disertato, abbandonato.
deserter, *n.* Disertore, *m.*
desertion, *n.* Diserzione, *f.*, abbandono, *m.*
deserve [di'zəːɹv], *v.t.* Meritare, essere degno di.
deservedly, *adv.* Meritamente, a buon diritto, a giusta ragione.
deserving, *a.* Meritevole, degno, meritorio. **— of blame,** biasimevole.
desiccant ['desikənt], *a.* Disseccante.
desiccate, *v.t.* Disseccare; *v.i.* disseccarsi.
desiccation, *n.* Disseccazione, *f.*
desiccative, *a.* Disseccativo.
desideratum (*pl.* **desiderata**) [disidə 'reitəm], *n.* Desiderato, *m.*
design [di'zain], *n.* Disegno, *m.*; progetto, scopo, piano, *m.*; intenzione, mira, *f.*; (*fashion*) figurino, modello, *m.* || *v.t.* Disegnare; progettare, avere l'intenzione di; destinare. **By —,** apposta, di proposito; **to have designs upon,** aver dei disegni su; **he was designed for the medical profession,** egli fu destinato alla professione di medico.
designate ['dezigneit], *v.t.* Designare, indicare. || *a.* Designato.
designation, *n.* Designazione, *f.*
designedly, *adv.* Apposta, a bella posta, intenzionalmente.
designer, *n.* Disegnatore, *m.* disegnatrice *f.*; inventore, progettista, *m.*
designing, *a.* Astuto, intrigante.
desirable [di'zairəbl], *a.* Desiderabile; consigliabile; gradito, gradevole.
desirably, *adv.* In modo desirabile.
desire [di'zaiəɹ], *n.* Desiderio, *m.*, voglia, brama, *f.*; domanda, preghiera, *f.*; richiesta, *f.*; passione, *f.* || *v.t.* Desiderare, volere; pregare, richiedere. **By —,** a richiesta.
desirous, *a.* Desideroso, voglioso, bramoso.
desist [di'zist], *v.i.* Desistere, cessare, smettere.
desk [desk], *n.* Scrittoio, *m.*, scrivania, *f.* **Reading- —,** leggio, *m.*; **roll-top —,** scrivania a chiusura scorrevole, *f.*; **cashier's —,** cassa, *f.*
desolate (1) ['desəlit], *a.* Desolato; negletto, sconfortato, solitario; disabitato.
desolate (2) ['desouleit], *v.t.* Desolare, devastare, spopolare.
desolately, *adv.* Desolatamente.
desolation, *n.* Desolazione, devastazione, *f.*; afflizione, *f.*; spopolazione, *f.*
despair [dis'pɛəɹ], *n.* Disperazione, *f.* || *v.i.* Disperare, disperarsi, scorarsi. **In —,** in disperazione; **his life is despaired of,** si dispera della sua vita.
despairingly, *adv.* Disperatamente.
despatch [cp. **dispatch**].
desperado [despə'rɑːdou], *n.* Furfante, bandito, sgherro, *m.*
desperate ['despərit], *a.* Disperato, furibondo; terribile, accanito, furioso. **A — fight,** un combattimento furioso, *m.*; **a — illness,** una malattia inguaribile, *f.*
desperately, *adv.* Disperatamente, pericolosamente; terribilmente.
desperateness, *n.* Disperatezza, *f.*
desperation, *n.* Disperazione, furia, smania, *f.*, accanimento, *m.*
despicable ['despikəbl], *a.* Spregevole, vile, ignobile.
despicableness, *n.* Bassezza, viltà, spregevolezza, *f.*
despicably, *adv.* Vilmente, spregevolmente.
despise [dis'paiz], *v.t.* Disprezzare, sprezzare, spregiare, sdegnare.
despite [dis'pait], *n.* Dispetto, disprezzo, dispregio, disdegno, *m.*, stizza, *f.* **In — of,** a dispetto di, malgrado.
despiteful, *a.* Dispettoso, stizzoso.
despitefully, *adv.* Dispettosamente.
despoil [di'spɔil], *v.t.* Spogliare.
despoliation, *n.* Spogliazione, *f.*

despond [di'spɔnd], *v.i.* Disperare, scoraggiarsi, sconfortarsi.
despondency, *n.* Disperazione, *f.*, abbattimento, scoraggiamento, *m.*
despondent, *a.* Scoraggiato, abbattuto, sconsolato.
despondently, despondingly, *adv.* Sconsolatamente.
despot ['despɔt], *n.* Despota, *m.*
despotic, *a.* Dispotico.
despotically, *adv.* Dispoticamente.
despotism, *n.* Dispotismo, *m.*, tirannide, *f.*
desquamate ['deskwæmeit], *v.t.i.* (*Med.*) Squamare, squamarsi.
dessert [di'zəːɹt], *n.* Frutta, *f.*, dolce, *m.* **— -spoon,** cucchiaio da dolci; **at —,** alle frutta.
destination [desti'neiʃən], *n.* Destinazione, *f.*
destine, *v.t.* Destinare, dedicare, consacrare. **Destined to be happy,** destinato alla felicità.
destiny, *n.* Destino, fato, *m.*, sorte, *f.* **Man of —,** uomo fatale, *m.*
destitute ['destitjuːt], *a.* Indigente, privo, abbandonato, **— of,** privo di.
destitution, *n.* Miseria, indigenza, povertà, *f.*
destroy [di'strɔi], *v.t.* Distruggere, disfare, sterminare, rovinare, abbattere.
destroyer, *n.* Distruttore, devastatore, *m.*; (*Naut.*) cacciatorpediniere, *m.*
destroying, *a.* Distruttore.
destructible, *a.* Distruttibile.
destruction, *n.* Distruzione, rovina, *f.*, sterminio, annientamento, *m.*, strage, *f.*; (*fig.*) dannazione, *f.*
destructive, *a.* Distruttivo, distruttore; fatale, funesto.
destructively, *adv.* Distruttivamente.
destructiveness, *n.* Mania di distruzione, distruttività, rovinosità, *f.*
destructor, *n.* Fornace per bruciare i rifiuti, *m.*
desuetude ['dezwitjuːd], *n.* Dissuetudine, *f.*
desulphurize [diː'sʌlfəraiz], *v.t.* Dissolforare.
desultorily ['desəltərili], *adv.* Saltuariamente, senza ordine, senza metodo, sconnessamente.
desultoriness, *n.* Mancanza di metodo, *f.*
desultory, *a.* Caotico, saltuario, senza metodo.
detach [di'tætʃ], *v.t.* Staccare, distaccare, separare, disgiungere, isolare. **To become detached,** staccarsi.
detachable, *a.* Staccabile.
detached, *a.* Staccato, distaccato, separato; (*of houses*) isolato.
detachment, *n.* Distacco, *m.*; (*Mil.*) distaccamento, *m.*; isolamento, *m.*
detail (1) [di'teil], *v.t.* Dettagliare, esporre in dettaglio, particoleggiare; (*Mil.*) distaccare.
detail (2) ['diːteil], *n.* Dettaglio, particolare, *m.*, minuzia, *f.* **In —,** minuziosamente, dettagliatamente.
detailed ['diːteild], *a.* Minuto, particolareggiato.
detain [de'tein], *v.t.* Ritenere, trattenere; (*Law*) arrestare.
detainer, *n.* (*Law*) Detentore, *m.* **Writ of —,** sequestro di persona, *m.*
detect [di'tekt], *v.t.* Scoprire, scorgere, individuare.
detection, *n.* Scoperta, *f.*
detective, *n.* Agente investigativo, *m.* **— story,** romanzo poliziesco, *m.*
detector, *n.* (*Radio.*) Rivelatore, *m.*
detent [di'tent], *n.* (*Mech.*) Dente d'arresto, *m.*; grilletto, *m.*
detention, *n.* Detenzione, *f.*; arresto, imprigionamento, *m.*; (*at school*) punizione, *f.*
deter [di'təːɹ], *v.t.* Impedire, dissuadere, stornare, trattenere, scoraggiare. **To be deterred from,** essere distolto da.
detergent [di'təːɹdʒənt], *n.a.* Detersivo, *m.*
deteriorate [di'tiəriəreit], *v.t.i.* Deteriorare, logorare, logorarsi, guastare, guastarsi.
deterioration, *n.* Deterioramento, peggioramento, logorio, *m.*
determinable [di'təːɹminəble], *a.* Determinabile.
determinant, *n.* (*Math.*) Determinante, *m.*
determinate, *a.* Determinato, stabilito, fissato.
determinately, *adv.* Determinatamente.
determination, *n.* Determinazione, decisione, risoluzione, *f.*; (*Law*) sentenza, *f.*
determinative, *a.* Determinativo.
determine, *v.t.* Determinare, indicare, stabilire, limitare; *v.i.* risolversi, determinarsi, decidersi.
determined, *a.* Risoluto, deciso, determinato, fissato.
determinism, *n.* Determinismo, *m.*
detersive [di'təːɹziv], *a.* Detersivo.
detest [di'test], *v.t.* Detestare, odiare.
detestable, *a.* Detestabile, abominevole, odioso.
detestably, *adv.* Detestabilmente.
detestation, *n.* Detestazione, *f.* **To hold in —,** avere in orrore.
dethrone [di'θroun], Detronizzare.
dethronement, *n.* Detronizzazione, *f.*
detonate ['detəneit], *v.i.* Detonare; *v.t.* far detonare.
detonating, *a.* Esplosivo, detonante. **— powder,** polvere fulminante, *m.*
detonation, *n.* Detonazione, *f.*
detonator, *n.* Detonatore, *m.*
detour ['deituːɹ], *n.* Rigirata, *f.*; giro lungo, *m.*
detract [di'trækt], *v.t.i.* Detrarre, scemare, diminuire; sparlare, denigrare, calunniare. **To — from,** sparlare di, detrarre da.
detraction, *n.* Detrazione, maldicenza, diffamazione, calunnia, *f.*
detractor, *n.* Detrattore, *m.*, detrattrice, *f.*
detrain [diː'trein], *v.t.i.* Scendere dal treno, far scendere dal treno.
detriment ['detrimənt], *n.* Detrimento, pregiudizio, danno, *m.*
detrimental, *a.* Nocivo, pregiudizievole, dannoso.
detrimentally, *adv.* Nocivamente.
detrition [di'triʃən], *n.* (*Geol.*) Detrito, logorio, *m.*
detritus ['detritəs], *n.* (*Geol.*) Detriti, *m.pl.*
deuce [djuːs], *n.* Diavolo, *m.*; (*Tennis*) 40 pari, *m.*; (*Cards, Dice*) due, *m.* **What the —!** Diamine! **to play the — with,** rovinare.
Deuteronomy [djuːtər'ɔnəmi], *n.* Deuteronomio, *m.*
devaluation ['diːvæljuːeiʃən], *n.* Deprezzamento, svalutamento, *m.*
devastate ['devəsteit], *v.t.* Devastare, rovinare.
devastating, *a.* Devastante, rovinoso.
devastation, *n.* Devastazione, *f.*
devastator, *n.* Devastatore, *m.*
develop [di'veləp], *v.t.i.* Sviluppare, svolgere, svilupparsi.

developer, *n.* (*Phot.*) Sviluppatore, *m.*
development, *n.* Sviluppo, svolgimento, *m.*
deviate ['di:vieit], *v.i.* Deviare, traviare.
deviation, *n.* Deviazione, *f.*; (*fig.*) traviamento, *m.*
device [di'vais], *n.* Spediente, espediente; dispositivo, ritrovato, *m.*; invenzione, *f.*; (*Heraldry*) impresa, *f.*, motto, *m.*, emblema, stemma, *m.*
devil ['devəl], *n.* Diavolo, demonio. || *v.t.* Arrostire con pepe e spezie; *v.i.* sfacchinare per un altro. **The —!** Che diavolo! **the — is in him,** ha il diavolo in corpo; **Devil take it!** Che il diavolo lo porti! **there's the — to pay,** è un bel pasticcio; **give the — his due,** non fate il diavolo più nero che non è; **to play the very —,** fare il diavolo a quattro; **she- —,** diavolessa, *f.*; **dare- —,** temerario, *m.*; **printer's —,** apprendista stampatore, *m.*; (*Zool.*) **— -fish,** polipo, *m.*, piovra, *f.*; **— -worship,** culto del diavolo, *m.*; **— -may-care,** trascurato; spensierato.
devilish, *a.* Diabolico, maledetto, infernale.
devilishly, *adv.* Diabolicamente.
devilishness, *n.* Diabolicità, *f.*
devilment, *n.* Cattiveria, diavoleria, *f.*
devilry, deviltry, *n.* Diavoleria, malizia, *f.*; stregoneria, *f.*
devious ['di:viəs], *a.* Sviato, stornato, indiretto, remoto, fuori di mano, errante.
deviously, *adv.* Indirettamente.
devisable [di'vaizəbl], *a.* Immaginabile, concepibile; (*Law*) trasmissibile per testamento.
devise [di'vaiz], *v.t.* Inventare, immaginare, ideare, tramare; (*Law*) legare, disporre per testamento.
devisee [divai'zi:], *n.* (*Law*) Erede, legatario, *m.*
deviser, *n.* Ideatore, progettista, *m.*
devisor, *n.* (*Law*) Testatore, *m.*, testatrice, *f.*
devitalize [di:'vaitəlaiz], *v.t.* Privare di vitalità.
devoid [de'vɔid], *a.* Privo, spoglio, destituito, vuoto. **— of,** privo di, senza.
devolution [devə'lju:ʃən], *n.* Devoluzione, *f.*
devolve [di'vɔlv], *v.t.* Devolvere, trasferire; *v.i.* devolversi, ricadere, passare. **It devolves upon me,** tocca a me, ricade su di me.
devote [di'vout], *v.t.* Votare, consacrare, dedicare; consegnare, abbandonare.
devoted, *a.* Devoto, votato, consacrato; maledetto. **All her reproaches fell on his — head,** i rimproveri di lei caddero sul suo capo maledetto.
devotedly, *adv.* Devotamente, fedelmente.
devotedness, *n.* Devozione, *f.*
devotee [devə'ti:], *n.* Devoto, fedele, *m.*
devotion, *n.* Devozione, *f.*; devozioni, preghiere, *f.pl.* **To be at one's devotions,** star facendo le proprie devozioni.
devotional, *a.* Devoto, religioso, pio.
devour [di'vauɹ], *v.t.* Divorare; (*fig.*) distruggere.
devouring, *a.* Divorante, divoratore; distruttore.
devouringly, *adv.* Voracemente.
devout [di'vaut], *a.* Devoto, pio, religioso.
devoutly, *adv.* Devotamente.
devoutness, *n.* Devozione, pietà, *f.*
dew [dju:], *n.* Rugiada, *f.* **— -drop,** goccia di rugiada, *f.*
dewfall, *n.* Il cadere della rugiada, *m.*
dewlap, *n.* Giogaia, *f.*
dewy, *a.* Rugiadoso, fresco.
dexter ['dekstəɹ], *a.* Destro.
dexterity [deks'teriti], *n.* Destrezza, abilità, *f.*
dexterous, *a.* Destro, attivo, lesto, pronto, abile.
dexterously, *adv.* Abilmente.
dexterousness, *n.* Destrezza, *f.*
dextrin, *n.* (*Chem.*) Destrina, *f.*
dextrous [cp. **dexterous**].
diabetes [daiə'bi:ti:z], *n.* (*Med*) Diabete, *m.*
diabetic [daiə'betik], *a.* Diabetico.
diabolic, diabolical [daiə'bɔlik, daiə'bɔlikəl], *a.* Diabolico.
diabolically, *adv.* Diabolicamente.
diabolism [dai'æbəlizm], *n.* Stregoneria, *f.*, culto del diavolo, *m.*
diabolo [dai'æboulou], *n.* Diabolo (*game*), *m.*
diaconal [dai'ækənəl], *a.* Diaconale.
diaconate, *n.* Diaconato, *m.*
diacoustics [daiə'kaustiks], *n.pl.* Diacustica, *f.*
diacritical [daiə'kritikəl], *a.* Diacritico. **— marks,** segni diacritici, *m.pl.*
diadem ['daiədem], *n.* Diadema, *m.*
diaeresis (*pl.* **diaereses**) [dai'iərəsis, dai'iərəsi:z], *n.* (*Gram.*) Dieresi, *f.*
diagnose [daiəg'nouz], *v.t.* Diagnosticare.
diagnosis, *n.* Diagnosi, *f.*
diagnostic, *a.* Diagnostico.
diagonal [dai'ægənəl], *n.a.* Diagonale, *m.*
diagonally, *adv.* Diagonalmente.
diagram ['daiəgræm], *n.* Diagramma, grafico, *m.*
diagrammatic, *a.* Diagrammatico.
dial ['daiəl], *n.* (*of clock, etc.*) Quadrante, *m.*; (*of telephone*) disco, *m.*; (*of compass*) bussola, *f.* || *v.t.* (*Telephone*) Comporre il numero sul disco. **Sun- —,** meridiana, *f.*
dialect ['daiəlekt], *n.* Dialetto, *m.*
dialectal, *a.* Dialettale.
dialectic, dialectical, *a.* Dialettico.
dialectically, *adv.* Dialetticamente.
dialectician, *n.* Dialettico, *m.*
dialectics, *n.pl.* Dialettica, *f.*
dialogue ['daiəlɔg], *n.* Dialogo, *m.*
dialysis [dai'ælisis], *n.* (*Chem.*) Dialisi, *f.*
diameter [dai'æmitəɹ], *n.* Diametro, *m.*
diametric, diametrical, *a.* Diametrale.
diametrically, *adv.* Diametralmente.
diamond ['daiəmənd], *n.* Diamante, *m.*; losanga, *f.*, rombo, *m.*; (*Cards*) quadri, denari, *m.pl.* **A cut —,** un diamante tagliato, *m.*; **— cut —,** gli eguali s'incontrano; **a — of the first water,** un diamante della più bell'acqua; **a — ring,** un anello di brillanti, *m.*; **— -wedding,** nozze di diamante, *f.pl.*; **— -cutter,** lapidario, *m.*; **— -shaped,** romboidale, faccettato.
diapason [daiə'peizən], *n.* (*Mus.*) Diapason, *m.*
diaper ['daiəpəɹ], *n.* Biancheria damascata, tela operata, *f.*; (*Arch.*) decorazione a rombi, *f.*; fascia per bambino, *f.* || *v.t.* Damascare.
diaphanous [dai'æfənəs], *a.* Diafono, trasparente.
diaphragm ['daiəfræm], *n.* Diaframma, *m.*
diarist ['daiərist], *n.* Scrittore di diario, diarista, *m.*
diarrhoea [daiə'ri:ə], *n.* (*Med.*) Diarrea, *f.*
diary ['daiəri], *n.* Diario, *m.*
diastase ['daiəsteiz], *n.* (*Chem.*) Diastasia, *f.*

diastole, *n.* (*Anat.*) Diastole, *m.*
diathermal, diathermic [daiəˈθəːɹməl], *a.* Diatermico.
diathermy, *n.* Diatermia, *f.*
diatonic [daiəˈtɔnik], *a.* (*Mus.*) Diatonico.
diatonically, *adv.* Diatonicalmente.
diatribe [ˈdaiətraib], *n.* Diatriba, *f.*
dibble [dibl], *n.* Piuolo, piantatoio, *m.* || *v.t.* Piantare con un piuolo.
dibs [dibz], *n.pl.* (*colloq.*) Denaro, *m.*; (*game*) ossetti, *m.pl.*
dice [dais], *n.pl.* Dadi, *m.pl.* || *v.t.* Giuocare ai dadi. **—-box,** bossolo dei dadi, *m.*
dicer, *n.* Giuocatore ai dadi, *m.*
dichotomous [diˈkɔtəməs], *a.* (*Bot.*) Dicotomo.
dichotomy, *n.* Dicotomia, *f.*
dichromatic [daikrouˈmætik], *a.* Dicromatico.
dickens [ˈdikinz], *inter.* **What the —!** Che diamine!
dicker [ˈdikəɹ], *v.t.i.* (*colloq.*) Scambiare.
dicky [ˈdiki], *n.* Sedile posteriore di una vettura, *m.*; (*colloq.*) falso davanti di camicia, *m.*
dicky-bird [ˈdikibəːɹd], *n.* (*colloq.*) Uccellino, *m.*
dicotyledon [daikɔtiˈliːdən], *n.* (*Bot.*) Dicotiledone, *f.*
dicotyledonous, *a.* Dicotiledone.
dictate [dikˈteit], *v.t.* Dettare; *v.i.* ordinare, comandare. || *n.* Precetto, dettame, *m.*, norma, *f.*; consiglio, *m.*
dictation, *n.* Dettato, *m.*, dettatura, *f.*; (*fig.*) ordini, *m.pl.* **From his —,** sotto la sua dettatura.
dictator, *n.* Dittatore, *m.*
dictatorial, dictatory [diktəˈtɔriəl, dikˈteitəri], *a.* Dittatoriale, dittatorio; imperioso, autoritario.
dictatorially, *adv.* Dittatorialmente.
dictatorship, *n.* Dittatura, *f.*
diction [ˈdikʃən], *n.* Dizione, *f.*
dictionary [ˈdikʃənəri], *n.* Dizionario, vocabolario, lessico, *m.*
dictum (*pl.* **dicta**) [ˈdiktəm], *n.* Detto, *m.*
did [did], *past* of **do.**
didactic, didactical [diˈdæktik, diˈdæktikəl], Didattico.
didactically, *adv.* Didatticamente.
didactyl [daiˈdæktil], *n.* (*Zool.*) Didattilo, *m.*
diddle [didl], *v.t.* Gabbare, ingannare.
didymous [ˈdidiməs], *a.* (*Bot.*) Didimo.
die (1) [dai], *n.* (*for stamping*) Conio, timbro, *m.* **Die-sinker,** incisore di medaglie, *m.*
die (2) (*pl.* **dice**), *n.* Dado, *m.* **A cast of the —,** un tiro dei dadi, *m.*; **the — is cast,** il dado è gettato (*o* tratto).
die (3) *v.i.* Morire, trapassare; spegnersi, cessar di vivere, spirare. **He died yesterday,** egli morì ieri; **to — in one's bed,** morire nel proprio letto; **to — away,** spegnersi a poco a poco; **to — broken-hearted,** morire di crepacuore; **to — out,** estinguersi, spegnersi; **to — with laughing,** crepar dalle risa; **I'm dying to go away,** muoio di voglia d'andar via; **—-hard,** intransigente, *m.*
dielectric [daiəˈlektrik], *a.* Dielettrico.
diet (1) [ˈdaiət], *n.* Dieta, *f.*, regime, vitto, *m.* || *v.t.* Tenere a dieta; *v.i.* stare a dieta.
diet (2), *n.* (*Hist.*) Dieta, assemblea, *f.*
dietary, *n.* Regime dietetico, *m.* || *a.* Dietetico.
dietetic, *a.* Dietetico.
dietetics, *n.pl.* Dietetica, *f.*
differ [ˈdifəɹ], *v.i.* Differire da; discordare, disputare, litigare.
difference, *n.* Differenza, diversità, *f.*; dissensione, controversia, lite, *f.*; (*remainder*) resto, *m.* **It makes no —,** ciò non fa niente, ciò non importa; **to pay the —,** pagare la differenza; **to split the —,** fare a mezzo.
different, *a.* Differente, diverso, dissimile.
differential, *a.* Differenziale.
differentiate, *v.t.* Differenziare.
differentiation, *n.* Differenziazione, *f.*
differently, *adv.* Diversamente, differentemente.
difficult [ˈdifikəlt], *a.* Difficile, malagevole, faticoso. **— to please,** di difficile contentatura.
difficulty, *n.* Difficoltà, *f.*, imbarazzo, ostacolo, impedimento, *m.* **To be in a —,** trovarsi imbarazzato; **that is the —,** qui sta il busillis; **with —,** difficilmente, a fatica; **without —,** facilmente; **to make difficulties,** trovar sempre da dire, far delle difficoltà; **financial difficulties,** strettezze, *f.pl.*
diffidence [ˈdifidəns], *n.* Diffidenza, *f.*; timidità, *f.*
diffident, *a.* Diffidente, timido. **To be — of oneself,** non aver fiducia in sè stesso.
diffidently, *adv.* Diffidentemente.
diffluence [ˈdifluːəns], *n.* Fluidità, *f.*
diffract [diˈfrækt], *v.t.* Diffrangere.
diffraction, *n.* Diffrazione, *f.*
diffuse (1) [diˈfjuːz], *v.t.* Diffondere, spargere, emanare.
diffuse (2) [diˈfjuːs], *a.* Diffuso, sparso; esteso, prolisso. **A — style,** uno stile prolisso, *m.*
diffused, *a.* Diffuso.
diffuseness, *n.* Prolissità, verbosità, *f.*
diffusion, *n.* Diffusione, divulgazione, propagazione, *f.*
diffusive, *a.* Diffusivo.
dig [dig], *v.t.i.* Scavare; vangare, zappare. || *n.* Vangata, *f.*; (*fig.*) puntata, spinta, *f.* **To — open,** scavare; **to — out,** sterrare; **to — through,** penetrare; **to — up,** cavare dalla terra, sradicare; **a — in the ribs,** una puntata nelle costole; (*fig.*) **a nasty —,** un colpo mancino.
digamy [ˈdigəmi], *n.* Digamia, *f.*
digest (1) [diˈdʒest], *v.t.* Digerire, smaltire; disporre, ordinare; *v.i.* essere digerito.
digest (2) [ˈdaidʒest], *n.* Digesto, *m.*; raccolta, *f.*
digester, *n.* Digestore, *m.*
digestible, *a.* Digestibile, digeribile.
digestion, *n.* Digestione, *f.*
digestive, *n.a.* Digestivo, *m.*
digger [ˈdigəɹ], *n.* Zappatore, sterratore, scavatore, *m.*; minatore d'oro, *m.*
digging, *n.* Scavo, sterro, *m.*, zappatura, vangatura, *f.* **The diggings,** le miniere d'oro, *f.pl.*; **diggings** (*colloq.*) alloggio, *m.*
dight [dait], *a.* (*obs.*) Ornato, guarnito, adorno.
digit [ˈdidʒit], *n.* Dito, *m.*; (*Arith.*) cifra, *f.*
digital, *a.* Digitale.
digitalis [didʒiˈteilis], *n.* (*Bot.*) Digitale, *f.*
digitate, digitated, *a.* (*Bot.Zool.*) Digitato.
digitigrade [ˈdidʒitigreid], *n.a.* (*Zool.*) Digitigrade, *m.*
dignified [ˈdignifaid], *a.* Dignitoso, degno, nobile, solenne, augusto; distinto, decoroso. **— with the name of,** fregiato del nome di.

dignify, *v.t.* Onorare, esaltare, render degno; investire, fregiare.
dignitary, *n.* Dignitario, *m.*
dignity, *n.* Dignità, *f.*
digraph ['daigræf], *n.* Digramma, *m.*
digress [daigres], *v.i.* Digredire, divagare, perdersi in digressioni; sviarsi. **To — from,** allontanarsi da.
digression, *n.* Digressione, *f.*
digressive, *a.* Digressivo.
digressively, *adv.* Digressivamente, per digressione.
dike, dyke [daik], *n.* Diga, *f.*, argine, *m.*; fossa, *f.*; (*Geol.*) vena, *f.*, filone, *m.* || *v.t.* Arginare, digare, circondare di fossa.
dilapidate [di'læpideit], *v.t.* Dilapidare, sciupare; rovinare, logorare; *v.i.* rovinarsi, guastarsi.
dilapidated, *a.* Rovinato, dilapidato, sciupato.
dilapidation, *n.* Rovina, dilapidazione, *f.*
dilatable [dai'leitəbl], *a.* Dilatabile.
dilatation, dilation, *n.* Dilatazione, *f.*
dilate, *v.t.* Dilatare, ingrandire, espandere; *v.i.* dilatarsi, espandersi; (*fig.*) diffondersi, dilungarsi. **To — upon a subject,** diffondersi su un soggetto.
dilator, *n.* (*Anat.*) Muscolo dilatorio, *m.*
dilatoriness ['dilətərinis], *n.* Lentezza, trascuratezza, *f.*, ritardo, *m.*
dilatory, *a.* Dilatorio, tardo, lento.
dilemma [di'lemə], *n.* Dilemma, *m.*; imbarazzo, *m.*; alternativa, *f.* **The horns of a —,** i corni di un dilemma, *m.pl.*; **to be on the horns of a —,** essere al bivio.
dilettante (*pl.* **dilettanti**) [dili'tænti], *n.* Dilettante, *m.*
dilettantism, *n.* Dilettantismo, *m.*
diligence ['dilidʒəns], *n.* Diligenza, assiduità, cura, *f.*; (*coach*) diligenza, *f.*
diligent, *a.* Diligente, assiduo, zelante, accurato.
diligently, *adv.* Diligentemente.
dill [dil], *n.* (*Bot.*) Aneto, *m.* **—-water,** essenza d'aneto, *f.*
dilly-dally ['dilidæli], *v.i.* Tentennare, vacillare, gingillarsi.
dilly-dallying, *n.* Tentennamento, *m.*; vacillazione, *f.*
diluent [di'lju:ənt], *a.* Diluente.
dilute [dai'lju:t], *v.t.* Diluire, allungare, stemperare, annacquare.
dilution, *n.* Diluzione, *f.*; stemperamento, annacquamento, *m.*
diluvial, diluvian [di'lju:viəl], *a.* Diluviale, diluviano.
diluvium, *n.* Diluvio, *m.*
dim [dim], *a.* Appannato, offuscato, pallido; debole, fioco. || *v.t.* Oscurare, offuscare; appannare; (*Motor.*) abbassare. **To be —-sighted,** avere la vista torbida; **to grow —,** oscurarsi, appannarsi.
dime [daim], *n.* Moneta americana (10 cents).
dimension [di'menʃən], *n.* Dimensione, estensione, *f.*; grandezza, misura, *f.*; grado, *m.*
dimensional, *a.* Relativo alle dimensioni.
diminish [di'miniʃ], *v.t.i.* Diminuire, scemare, rimpicciolire, abbassare.
diminishing, *a.* Diminuente, calante.
diminishingly, *adv.* (*fig.*) Sfavorevolmente
diminution [dimi'nju:ʃən], *n.* Diminuzione, *f.*
diminutive [di'minju:tiv], *a.* Piccolo, piccino, minuto. || *n.* (*Gram.*) Diminutivo, *m.*
diminutively, *adv.* Diminutivamente.
diminutiveness, *n.* Piccolezza, *f.*
dimissory [di'misəri], *a.* (*Eccles.*) Dimissorio.
dimity ['dimiti], *n.* Basino, *m.*
dimly, *adv.* Oscuramente, foscamente; fiocamente. **—-lighted,** debolmente rischiarato, con luce fioca.
dimness, *n.* Penombra, *f.*; (*of sight*) offuscamento, *m.*; (*of glass, etc.*) appannamento, *m.*
dimorphic, dimorphous [dai'mɔ:ɹfik, dai'mɔ:ɹfəs], *a.* Biforme.
dimple [dimpl], *n.* Fossetta, pozzetta, *f.* || *v.t.* (*of water*) Increspare; *v.i.* formare fossette. **Her face dimpled,** le sue guance formarono due fossette.
dimpled, *a.* Con fossette, increspato.
din [din], *n.* Fracasso, frastuono, chiasso, fragore, strepito, *m.* || *v.t.* Ripetere, reiterare; stordire. **He's always dinning his warnings into me,** mi stordisce sempre colle sue ammonizioni.
dine [dain], *v.i.* Desinare, pranzare. **To — out,** pranzare fuori; **to — with Duke Humphrey,** rimanere senza pranzo.
diner, *n.* Desinatore, pranzatore, commensale, *m.*; ristorante stradale, *m.*
ding-dong ['diŋdɔŋ], *n.* Dindon, *m.* || *adv.* Precipitatamente, con furia.
dinghy ['diŋgi], *n.* (*Naut.*) Piccolo battello a remi, *m.*
dinginess ['dindʒinis], *n.* Scurezza, tinta nerastra, *f.*; sbiaditezza, *f.*; sudicio, *m.*
dingle [diŋgl], *n.* Valletta, *f.*
dingy ['dindʒi], *a.* Sudicio, scuro, nerastro; sbiadito, scolorito, stinto.
dining, *n.* Il pranzare, *m.* **—-hall,** refettorio, *m.*; **—-room,** sala da pranzo, *f.*; **—-rooms,** trattoria, *f.*, ristorante, *m.*; **—-table,** tavola da pranzo, *f.*; **—-car,** vagone ristorante, *m.*
dinner ['dinəɹ], *n.* Pranzo, desinare, *m.* **To be at —,** stare a pranzo; **—-jacket,** smoking, *m.*; **—-service,** servizio da tavola, *m.*; **—-time,** ora di pranzo, *f.*; **—-wagon,** portavivande, *m.*; **—-plate,** piatto, *m.*; **to give a — party,** offrire un pranzo.
dinosaur ['dainəsɔ:ɹ], *n.* (*Zool.*) Dinosauro, *m.*
dint (1) [dint], *n.* Forza, *f.* **By — of,** a forza di.
dint (2), *n.* Tacca, ammaccatura, impressione, *f.*
diocesan [dai'ɔsisən], *n.a.* Diocesano, *m.*
diocese ['daiousi:s], *n.* Diocesi, *f.*
dioptric [dai'ɔptrik], *a.* Diottrico. || *n.* Diottria, *f.*
dioptrics, *n.pl.* Diottrica, *f.*
diorama [daiərɑ:mə], *n.* Diorama, *m.*
dip [dip], *v.t.* Tuffare; immergere, bagnare; (*to lower*) abbassare; *v.i.* immergersi, abbassarsi; scendere. || *n.* Tuffo, *m.*; immersione, *f.*; (*colloq.*) bagno di mare, *m.*; (*of magnetic needle*) inclinazione, *f.*; (*of horizon*) depressione, *f.*; (*candle*) candela di sego, *f.* **To — into a book,** scorrere le pagine di un libro; **to — up water,** attingere acqua; (*Motor.*) **to — the headlights,** abbassare i fari; **the scale dips,** la bilancia trabocca.
diphtheria [dif'θiəriə], *n.* (*Med.*) Difterite, *f.*
diphtheric, diphtheritic, *a.* Difterico.
diphthong ['difθɔŋ], *n.* Dittongo, *m.*
diploma, *n.* Diploma, *m.*

diplomacy [di'plouməsi], *n.* Diplomazia, *f.*
diplomat, diplomatist ['diplomæt, di'ploumətist], *n.* Diplomatico, *m.*
diplomatic, *a.* Diplomatico.
diplomatically, *adv.* Diplomaticamente.
diplomatics, *n.pl.* Diplomatica, *f.*
diplomatist, *n.* Diplomatico, *m.*
dipper ['dipəɹ], *n.* (*Zool.*) Merlo d'acqua, *m.*; mestolo, *m.*; cucchiaione, *m.*; (*colloq.Astron.*) Orsa Maggiore.
dipping, *n.* Tuffo, *m.*; immersione, *f.*; inclinazione, *f.* **— -needle,** ago d'inclinazione, *m.*
dipsomania [dipsou'meiniə], *n.* (*Med.*) Dipsomania, *f.*
dipsomaniac, *n.* Alcoolizzato, *m.*
diptera ['diptərə], *n.pl.* (*Zool.*) Ditteri, dipteri, *m.pl.*
diptych ['diptik], *n.* Dittico, *m.*
dire [daiəɹ], *a.* Terribile, orrendo; atroce, tormentoso. **— necessity,** necessità crudele, *f.*
direct [di'rekt], *a.* Diretto, diritto, immediato; (*fig.*) chiaro, aperto, positivo. ‖ *v.t.* Dirigere; avviare, indirizzare; ordinare, comandare; indicare, additare. **To — a letter,** indirizzare una lettera; **to — attention to,** rivolgere l'attenzione a; **to — an appeal,** fare appello; **Can you — me to the nearest chemist?** Può indicarmi una farmacia qui vicina? (*Elect.*) **— current (D.C.),** corrente continua, *f.*
direction, *n.* Direzione, via, *f.*; parte, *f.*; istruzione, norma, *f.*; ordine, scopo, *m.*; meta, *f.*; indirizzo, *m.* **In all directions,** in tutte le direzioni; **In which — are you going?** Da che parte andate? **directions for use,** istruzioni per l'uso, *f.pl.*
directive, *n.a.* Direttivo, *m.*
directly, *adv.* Direttamente; addirittura; subito; tosto.
directness, *n.* Prontezza, immediatezza, *f.*; franchezza, *f.*
director, *n.* Direttore, dirigente, capo, *m.*; guida, *f.*; (*of a company*) amministratore, *m.* **Managing —,** amministratore delegato, *m.*
directorate, *n.* Direttorio, *m.*; consiglio d'amministrazione, *m.*
directorial, *a.* Direttoriale.
directory, *n.* Indicatore, annuario, *m.*, guida, *f.*; (*Hist.*) Direttorio, *m.* **Post Office —,** indicatore postale, *m.*; **telephone —,** guida del telefono, *f.*
directress, *n.* Direttrice, *f.*
direful ['daiəɹful], *a.* Terribile, orrendo, spaventevole.
direfully, *adv.* Spaventevolmente.
dirge [dəːɹdʒ], *n.* Nenia, *f.*; canto funebre, *m.*
dirigible ['diridʒəbl], *n.* Dirigibile, *m.*; aeronave, *f.* ‖ *a.* Dirigibile.
dirk [dəːɹk], *n.* Daga, *f.*, pugnale, *m.*
dirt [dəːɹt], *n.* Immondizia, *f.*; sudiciume, *m.*; spazzatura, lordura, *f.*; (*mud*) fango, *m.*; (*fig.*) sozzura, bruttura, *f.* **— -cheap,** a prezzo vile; **to eat —,** umiliarsi; **to fling — at,** parlare male di.
dirtily, *adv.* Sporcamente; (*fig.*) vilmente.
dirtiness, *n.* Sporcizia, sudiceria, *f.*; (*fig.*) viltà, bassezza, *f.*
dirty, *a.* Sporco, sudicio, sozzo, immondo, lordo, lurido, schifoso; (*fig.*) osceno, vile, basso; (*of weather*) orribile. ‖ *v.t.* Sporcare, lordare, macchiare infangare. **A — action,** un'azione disonesta, *f.*; **a — fellow,** un sudicione, *m.*; **— work,** un'azionaccia, una faccenda sporca, *f.*; **a — trick,** un brutto scherzo, un colpo mancino, *m.*
disability [disə'biliti], *n.* Inabilità, insufficienza, incapacità, *f.*
disable [dis'eibl], *v.t.* Inabilitare, invalidare, rendere incapace; rendere invalido; infermare; (*Mil.*) mutilare.
disabled, *a.* Inabilitato, incapacitato, invalido, infermo; (*Mil.*) mutilato; (*Naut.*) fuori uso. **— soldier,** mutilato, invalido di guerra, *m.*
disablement, *n.* Incapacità, impotenza, invalidità, *f.*
disabuse [disə'bjuːz], *v.t.* Disingannare. **— your mind of that idea,** disingannatevi.
disaccord [disə'kɔːɹd], *n.* Disaccordo, dissenso, *m.*
disaccustom [disə'kʌstəm], *v.t.* Disabituare, disavvezzare, disassuefare.
disadvantage [disəd'vɑːntidʒ], *n.* Svantaggio, incomodo, *m.*; perdita, *f.* **At a —,** con svantaggio, in perdita; **to be under a —,** essere in uno stato d'inferiorità.
disadvantageous, *a.* Svantaggioso, incomodo, sfavorevole.
disadvantageously, *adv.* Svantatggiosamente
disaffect [disə'fekt], *v.t.* Scontenare, alienare, disamorare, disaffezionare.
disaffected, *a.* Scontento; sleale.
disaffection, *n.* Disaffezione, infedeltà, *f.*
disaffirm [disə'fəːɹm], *v.t.* (*Law*) Infirmare.
disafforestation [disəfɔris'teiʃən], *n.* Diboscamento, *m.*
disaggregate [dis'ægregət], *v.t.* Disaggregare.
disaggregation, *n.* Disaggregazione, *f.*
disagree [dis'əgriː], *v.i.* Dissentire, discordare, non essere d'accordo con; litigare; far male a, non confarsi a. **This climate disagrees with my health,** questo clima mi fa male; **I — with you,** non sono d'accordo con voi.
disagreeable, *a.* Spiacevole, seccante, antipatico.
disagreeableness, *n.* Contrarietà, sconvenienza, *f.*; disagio, *m.*
disagreeably, *adv.* Spiacevolmente.
disagreement, *n.* Dissensione, *f.*; dissapore, disaccordo, *m.*; (*of figures*) discordanza, differenza, *f.*
disallow [disə'lau], *v.t.* Rifiutare, vietare, proibire; non ammettere.
disallowable, *a.* Non ammissibile.
disappear [disə'piəɹ], *v.i.* Sparire, scomparire, svanire.
disappearance, *n.* Sparizione, scomparsa, *f.*
disappoint [disə'pɔint], *v.t.* Deludere, frustrare, ingannare; sconcertare, mancare a. **To be disappointed,** rimaner deluso; **he was disappointed in love,** ha avuto un disinganno d'amore; **I was very disappointed in her,** essa ha ingannato le mie speranze; **don't — me,** non mancatemi di parola.
disappointment, *n.* Disappunto, *m.*; contrarietà, *f.*; disinganno, *m.*; seccatura, noia, *f.*
disapprobation, disapproval [disæprou'beiʃən, disə'pruːvəl], *n.* Disapprovazione, riprovazione, *f.*, biasimo, *m.*
disapprobatory, disapproving, *a.* Riprensivo, disapprovante.
disapprove, *v.t.i.* Disapprovare, riprovare, biasimare.

disarm [dis'ɑːɹm], *v.t.i.* Disarmare; (*fig.*) calmare, rabbonire.
disarmament, *n.* Disarmo, disarmamento, *m.*
disarrange [disə'reindʒ], *v.t.* Scompigliare, disordinare, confondere, arruffare. **Her hair was disarranged,** era scapigliata.
disarrangement, *n.* Scompiglio, disordine, *m.*
disarray [disə'rei], *v.t.* Disordinare; (*Mil.*) mettere in fuga. || *n.* Disordine, *m.*; (*fig.*) rotta, fuga, confusione, *f.*
disarticulate [disɑːɹ'tikjuːleit], *v.t.* (*Anat.*) Disarticolare.
disassociate [disə'souʃieit], *v.t.* Disassociare.
disaster [di'zɑːstəɹ], *n.* Disastro, *m.*, calamità, *f.*
disastrous, *a.* Disastroso, calamitoso.
disastrously, *adv.* Disastrosamente.
disavow [disə'vau], *v.t.* Ripudiare, disconoscere, sconfessare.
disavowal, *n.* Ripudio, *m.*, sconoscenza, sconfessione, *f.*
disband [dis'bænd], *v.t.* Licenziare, accomiatare, sbandare, congedare; *v.i.* licenziarsi, congedarsi.
disbanding, *n.* Licenziamento, congedo, *m.*
disbar [dis'bɑːɹ], *v.t.* (*Law*) Radiare dall'avvocatura.
disbelief [disbi'liːf], *n.* Incredulità, *f.*, scetticismo, *m.*
disbelieve [disbi'liːv], *v.t.* Non credere, diffidare. **To — every word,** non credere ad una sola parola.
disbeliever, *n.* Incredulo, scettico, miscredente, *m.*
disbranch [dis'brɑːntʃ], *v.t.* Potare, scapezzare.
disbud [dis'bʌd], *v.t.* Spollonare, mondare.
disburden [dis'bəːɹdən], *v.t.* Sgravare, scaricare, liberare, alleviare. **To — one's mind,** sfogarsi.
disburse [dis'bəːɹs], *v.t.i.* Sborsare.
disbursement, *n.* Sborso, *m.*, spese, *f.pl.*
disc [cp. **disk**].
discard [dis'kɑːɹd], *v.t.* Scartare, respingere, ricusare, gettare via; (*Cards*) scartare. || *n.* Scarto, rifiuto, *m.*
discern [di'ʒəːɹn], *v.t.* Scernere, discernere, vedere, percepire.
discernible, *a.* Visibile, discernibile, percepibile.
discernibly, *adv.* Visibilmente.
discerning, *a.* Acuto, perspicace, intelligente, sagace.
discerningly, *adv.* Sagacemente.
discernment, *n.* Discernimento, giudizio, *m.*, sagacità, *f.*
discharge [dis'tʃɑːɹdʒ], *n.* Scaricamento, scarico, sparo, *m.*; (*of a gun*) scarica, *f.*; (*of a duty*) adempimento, *m.*; (*of a debt*) rimborso, *m.*; (*acquittal*) assoluzione, liberazione, *f.*; (*Med.*) spurgo, *m.*, suppurazione, *f.*; (*Comm.*) pagamento, *m.*, quietanza, *f.*; (*of bankrupt*) riabilitazione, *f.*; (*Mil.*) congedo *m.* || *v.t.* Scaricare; sparare; liberare, scolpare; congedare, licenziare; pagare, soddisfare, adempire; *v.i.* suppurare.
discharger, *n.* (*Elec.*) Scaricatore, *m.*
disciple [di'saipl], *n.* Discepolo, *m.*
discipleship, *n.* Discepolato, *m.*
disciplinable [disi'plinəbl], *a.* Disciplinabile.
disciplinarian [disiplin'ɛəriən], *n.* Disciplinatore, *m.*
disciplinary, *a.* Disciplinare.
discipline ['disiplin], *n.* Disciplina, *f.* || *v.t.* Disciplinare, regolare, ammaestrare; punire, castigare.
disclaim [dis'kleim], *v.t.* Sconfessare, rinnegare, negare, ripudiare.
disclaimer, *n.* (*Comm.Law*) Denunzia, impugnazione, *f.*; smentita, *f.*
disclose [dis'klouz], *v.t.* Dischiudere, scoprire, svelare, manifestare; divulgare, pubblicare.
disclosure [dis'klouʒəɹ], *n.* Rivelazione, divulgazione, pubblicazione, *f.*
discoid ['diskɔid], *a.* Discoideo.
discoloration [diskʌlə'reiʃən], *n.* Scolorimento, *m.*
discolour, *v.t.i.* Scolorare, scolorire.
discomfit [dis'kʌmfit], *v.t.* Sconfiggere, vincere; frustrare, sconcertare.
discomfiture, *n.* Sconfitta, disfatta, *f.*; sconcerto, *m.*
discomfort [dis'kʌmfəɹt], *n.* Sconforto, incomodo, disagio, *m.*; dolore, *m.*, afflizione, *f.* || *v.t.* Rattristare, affliggere.
discommode [diskə'moud], *v.t.* Incomodare; annoiare, seccare.
discommodious, *a.* Incomodo.
discompose [diskəm'pouz], *v.t.* Scomporre, turbare, agitare, sconcertare, perturbare. **He was greatly discomposed,** era molto turbato.
discomposure, *n.* Turbamento, *m.*; agitazione *f.*
disconcert [diskən'səːɹt], *v.t.* Sconcertare, turbare.
disconnect [diskə'nekt], *v.t.* Sconnettere, disgiungere, disunire, staccare; (*Mech.*) disinnestare; (*Elec.*) interrompere, disinserire.
disconnected, *a.* Sconnesso, staccato.
disconnectedly, *adv.* Sconnessamente.
disconnectedness, *n.* Sconnessione, *f.*
disconsolate [dis'kɔnsolət], *a.* Sconsolato, afflitto, addolorato.
disconsolately, *adv.* Sconsolatamente.
disconsolateness, *n.* Sconsolatezza, *f.*
discontent, discontented, *n.a.* Scontento, malcontento, *m.*; insoddisfatto.
discontentedly, *adv.* Di mala voglia, contro genio.
discontentedness, discontentment, *n.* Scontentezza, *f.*
discontinuance [diskən'tinjuːəns], *n.* Interruzione, cessazione, *f.*
discontinue [diskən'tinjuː], *v.t.i.* Discontinuare, cessare, interrompere; tralasciare.
discontinuous, *a.* Discontinuo, intermittente, disgiunto.
discord ['diskɔːɹd], *n.* Discordia, *f.*; (*Mus.*) dissonanza, *f.*
discordance, *n.* Discordanza, *f.*
discordant, *a.* Discordante; discorde, dissimile. **— views,** opinioni divergenti.
discordantly, *adv.* Discordemente; (*Mus.*) dissonantemente.
discount ['diskaunt], *n.* Sconto, ribasso, *m.* || [dis'kaunt], *v.t.* Scontare; (*fig.*) non tenere in conto, detrarre da; *v.i.* fare uno sconto. **At a —,** con ribasso; **to grant a —,** concedere un ribasso; **—-rate,** saggio di sconto, *m.*; **to be at a —,** essere sotto la pari; (*fig.*) essere poco stimato.
discountable, *a.* Scontabile.

discounter, *n.* Scontista, *m.*
discounting, *n.* Sconto, *m.*
discountenance [disˈkauntənəns], *v.t.* Scoraggiare, disapprovare, biasimare.
discourage [disˈkʌridʒ], *v.t.* Scoraggiare.
discouragement, *n.* Scoraggiamento, *m.*
discouraging, *a.* Scoraggiante.
discourse (1) [ˈdiskɔːɹs], *n.* Discorso, *m.*, orazione, dissertazione, parlata, favella, *f.*; linguaggio, *m.*
discourse (2) [disˈkɔːɹs], *v.i.* Discorrere, parlare; (*Mus.*) suonare.
discourteous [disˈkəːɹtiəs], *a.* Scortese, incivile, villano.
discourteously, *adv.* Scortesemente.
discourtesy, *n.* Scortesia, villania, *f.*
discover [disˈkʌvəɹ], *v.t.* Scoprire, trovare; mostrare, far vedere, rivelare, palesare.
discoverable, *a.* Trovabile, scopribile.
discoverer, *n.* Scopritore, *m.*, scopritrice, *f.*
discovery, *n.* Scoperta, *f.*; scoprimento, *m.* **A voyage of —**, un viaggio di scoperta, *m.*
discredit [disˈkredit], *n.* Discredito, *m.*, disistima, vergogna, *f.* ‖ *v.t.* Discredere, non credere; discreditare, screditare. **To fall into —**, cadere in discredito; **to throw — on a person**, discreditare una persona.
discreditable, *a.* Screditabile, disonorevole.
discreditably, *adv.* Disonorevolmente.
discreet [disˈkriːt], *a.* Discreto, prudente, savio, circospetto.
discreetly, *adv.* Discretamente.
discreetness, *n.* Discrezione, prudenza, *f.*
discrepancy [disˈkrepənsi], *n.* Discrepanza, divergenza, *f.*, disaccordo, *m.*
discrepant, *a.* Discrepante, dissimile, contrario, divergente.
discrete [disˈkriːt], *a.* Separato, distinto.
discretion [disˈkreʃən], *n.* Discrezione, prudenza, *f.*, discernimento, giudizio, *m.* **To surrender at —**, arrendersi a discrezione; **to use one's own —**, fare secondo il proprio criterio; **years of —**, età della discrezione, *f.*
discretionary, *a.* Discrezionale. (*Law*) **— powers**, poteri discrezionali, *m.pl.*
discriminate [disˈkrimineit], *v.t.i.* Discriminare, distinguere, discernere.
discriminately, *adv.* Con discernimento.
discriminating, *a.* Acuto, sottile, perspicace, fine. **A — taste**, un gusto fino, *m.*
discrimination, *n.* Distinzione, *f.*, discernimento, giudizio, *m.*
discriminative, *a.* Giudizioso, acuto, perspicace.
discriminatory, *a.* Discriminante.
discrown [disˈkraun], *v.t.* Detronizzare, scoronare.
disculpate [disˈkʌlpeit], *v.t.* Scolpare, discolpare, giustificare.
discursive [disˈkəːɹsiv], *a.* Sconnesso, saltuario, incoerente.
discursively, *adv.* Sconnessamente.
discus [ˈdiskəs], *n.* Disco, *m.*
discuss [disˈkʌs], *v.t.* Discutere, dibattere.
discussion, *n.* Discussione, *f.*, dibattimento, *m.*; disamina, *f.*
discutient [disˈkjuːʃənt], *a.* (*Med.*) Risolvente.
disdain [disˈdein], *n.* Sdegno, disdegno, disprezzo, *m.* ‖ *v.t.* Sdegnare, disdegnare, disprezzare.
disdainful, *a.* Sdegnoso, sprezzante.
disdainfully, *adv.* Sdegnosamente.
disdainfulness, *n.* Sdegno, *m.*, sdegnosità, *f.*
disease [diˈziːz], *n.* Malattia, *f.*, male, morbo, *m.* **Foot-and-mouth —**, afta epizootica, *f.*
diseased, *a.* Malato; (*fig.*) turbato, sconvolto. **A — imagination**, una mente sconvolta, *f.*
disembark [disemˈbɑːɹk], *v.t.* Sbarcare; scaricare; *v.i.* sbarcare.
disembarkation, *n.* Sbarco, sbarcamento, *m.*
disembarrass [disemˈbærəs], *v.t.* Sbarazzare, liberare, sgombrare.
disembodied [disemˈbɔdid], *a.* Senza corpo. **— spirits**, spettri, *m.pl.*
disembodiment, *n.* Spiritualizzamento, *m.*; (*Mil.*) scioglimento, congedo, *m.*
disembody, *v.t.* Spogliare del corpo; (*Mil.*) sciogliere, congedare.
disembogue [disemˈboug], *v.i.* (*of a river*) Sboccare.
disembowel [disemˈbauəl], *v.t.* Sbudellare, sventrare.
disenchant [disenˈtʃɑːnt], *v.t.* Disincantare; rompere l'illusione.
disenchantment, *n.* Disincanto, *m.*; disillusione, *f.*
disencumber [disenˈkʌmbəɹ], *v.t.* Sgombrare, sbarazzare, svincolare; sgravare.
disencumbrance, *n.* Liberazione, *f.*, sgombro, *m.*
disendow [disenˈdau], *v.t.* Espropriare, diseredare.
disendowment, *n.* Espropriazione, *f.*
disengage [disenˈgeidʒ], *v.t.* Disimpegnare, sciogliere, sbarazzare, svincolare.
disengaged, *a.* Disimpegnato, disponibile.
disengagement, *n.* Disponibilità, *f.*, disimpegno, *m.*
disentangle [disenˈtæŋgl], *v.t.* Districare, disimpigliare, disimpacciare, sbrogliare, sbarazzare; (*fig.*) chiarire.
disentanglement, *n.* Districamento, *m.*; liberazione, *f.*
disenthral [disenˈθrɔːl], *v.t.* Emancipare, affrancare, svincolare.
disentitle [disenˈtaitl], *v.t.* Privare di un titolo *o* diritto.
disentomb [disenˈtuːm], *v.t.* Dissotterrare, esumare.
disestablish [disisˈtæbliʃ], *v.t.* Privare del carattere di istuzione pubblica.
disestablishment, *n.* Separazione della Chiesa dallo Stato, *f.*
disfavour [disˈfeivəɹ], *n.* Disfavore, *m.* ‖ *v.t.* Sfavorire, disapprovare, contrariare. **To be in great — with**, essere molto mal visto da.
disfiguration [disfigjuːˈreiʃən], *n.* Disfigurazione, *f.*, sfiguramento, *m.*
disfigure, *v.t.* Disfigurare, sfigurare, deturpare.
disfigurement, *n.* Sfregio, sfiguramento, *m.*, deturpazione, *f.*
disfranchise [disˈfræntʃaiz], *v.t.* Privare dei diritti politici.
disfranchisement, *n.* Privazione dei diritti politici, *f.*
disgorge [disˈgɔːɹdʒ], *v.t.* Vomitare; (*fig.*) emettere, rendere, restituire.
disgrace [disˈgreis], *n.* Vergogna, onta, *f.*, disonore, obbrobrio, *m.* ‖ *v.t.* Disonorare, avvilire, svergognare; (*dismiss*) destituire. **To be in —**, essere in disgrazia; **to be the —**

of, essere l'obbrobrio di; **to the — of,** recando onta a; **the boy is in —,** il ragazzo è in penitenza.
disgraceful, *a.* Vergognoso, obbrobrioso, ignominioso.
disgracefully, *adv.* Vergognosamente.
disgruntled [dis'grʌntld], *a.* Malcontento, di malumore.
disguise [dis'gaiz], *n.* Travestimento, *m.*, maschera, finzione, *f.* || *v.t.* Travestire, contraffare, mascherare, nascondere. **In —,** travestito.
disguised, *a.* Travestito, mascherato, contraffatto.
disgust [dis'gʌst], *n.* Disgusto, schifo, *m.*; nausea, ripugnanza, *f.* || *v.t.* Disgustare, nauseare, spiacere, offendere.
disgusting, *a.* Disgustoso, ripugnante, schifoso.
disgustingly, *adv.* Disgustosamente.
dish [diʃ], *n.* Piatto, *m.*, scodella, *f.*; (*food*) vivanda, pietanza, *f.*; (*Phot.*) bacinella, *f.* || *v.t.* Servire, scodellare. **Dishes,** vasellame, *m.*; **to wash the dishes,** lavare i piatti; **to — up,** servire, allestire; **—-cloth,** strofinaccio, *m.*; **—-cover,** coperchio, copripiatto, *m.*; **—-water,** risciacquatura, *f.*
dishabille [disæ'bi:l], *n.* Semivestito, *m.*, veste da camera, *f.pl.*
dishabituate [dishə'bitju:eit], *v.t.* Disabituare, disavvezzare.
disharmonize [dis'hɑ:ɹmənaiz], *v.t.* Disarmonizzare.
dishearten [dis'hɑ:ɹtən], *v.t.* Scoraggiare, abbattere, sconfortare.
disheartening, *a.* Scoraggiante.
dishevel [di'ʃevəl], *v.t.* Scarmigliare, arruffare.
dishevelled, *a.* Scapigliato, scarmigliato, arruffato.
dishonest [dis'ɔnist], *a.* Disonesto.
dishonestly, *adv.* Disonestamente.
dishonesty, *n.* Disonestà, *f.*
dishonour, *n.* Disonore, *m.*, infamia, vergogna, *f.* || *v.t.* Disonorare, far disonore a; (*Comm.*) mancare a un pagamento, lasciar protestare una cambiale.
dishonourable, *a.* Disonorevole, vergognoso.
dishonourably, *adv.* Disonorevolmente.
dishonoured, *a.* (*Comm.*) Protestato. **A — bill,** una cambiale protestata, *f.*; **a — cheque,** un assegno a vuoto, *m.*
dishorn [dis'hɔ:ɹn], *v.t.* Privare delle corna.
disillusion [disi'lju:ʒən], *v.t.* Disincantare, disingannare. || *n.* Disillusione, *f.*
disillusionment, *n.* Disinganno, *m.*
disinclination [disinkli'neiʃən], *n.* Avversione, antipatia, ripugnanza, *f.*
disincline [disin'klain], *v.t.* Svogliare, distogliere.
disincorporate [disin'kɔ:ɹpəreit], *v.t.* Privare dei diritti di corporazione.
disincorporation, *n.* Privazione di questi diritti, *f.*
disinfect [disin'fekt], *v.t.* Disinfettare.
disinfectant, *n.* Disinfettante, *m.*
disinfection, *n.* Disinfezione, *f.*
disinfector, *n.* Disinfettatore, *m.*
disingenuous [disin'dʒenju:əs], *a.* Insincero, in mala fede.
disingenuously, *adv.* Senza sincerità.
disingenuousness, *n.* Mancanza di sincerità, *f.*
disinherit [disin'herit], *v.t.* Diseredare.
disinheritance, *n.* Diseredazione, *f.*
disintegrate [dis'intigreit], *v.t.* Disgregare, disintegrare, disunire; *v.i.* disintegrarsi.
disintegration, *n.* Disintegrazione, *f.*
disinter [disin'tə:ɹ], *v.t.* Dissotterrare, esumare.
disinterested [dis'intərestid], *a.* Disinteressato, imparziale.
disinterestedly, *adv.* Disinteressatamente.
disinterestedness, *n.* Disinteresse, *m.*
disinterment, *n.* Esumazione, *f.*
disjoin [dis'dʒɔin], *v.t.* Disgiungere, separare, staccare.
disjoint [dis'dʒɔint], *v.t.* Disgiungere, smontare; (*Med.*) slogare.
disjointed, *a.* Disgiunto; (*fig.*) incoreente, sconnesso, scucito.
disjointedly, *adv.* Incoerentemente.
disjunctive [dis'dʒʌŋktiv], *a.* (*Gram.*) Disgiuntivo.
disk, disc [disk], *n.* Disco, m.
dislike [dis'laik], *v.t.* Non amare, sentire antipatia per; avere in uggia, avversare. || *n.* Avversione, antipatia, *f.* **To be disliked,** essere mal visto; **to take a — to,** prendere in antipatia, prendere in uggia.
dislocate ['disloukeit], *v.t.* Slogare, dislocare.
dislocation, *n.* Slogamento, *m.*, dislocazione, *f.*
dislodge [dis'lɔdʒ], *v.t.* Sloggiare, cacciare; rimuovere.
disloyal [dis'lɔiəl], *a.* Sleale, perfido, infedele.
disloyally, *adv.* Slealmente.
disloyalty, *n.* Slealtà, infedeltà, perfidia, *f.*
dismal ['dizməl], *a.* Lugubre, tetro, cupo; triste, funesto, melanconico.
dismally, *adv.* Tristemente, malinconicamente.
dismalness, *n.* Tristezza, *f.*
dismantle [dis'mæntl], *v.t.* Smantellare; (*Naut.*) disarmare; sfornire, spogliare.
dismast [dis'mɑ:st], *v.t.* (*Naut.*) Disalberare.
dismay [dis'mei], *n* Sgomento, spavento, *m.*; costernazione, *f.*; sconforto, avvilimento, scoraggiamento, *m.* || *v.t.* Sgomentare, spaventare, atterrire.
dismember [dis'membəɹ], *v.t.* Smembrare.
dismembering, dismemberment, *n.* Smembramento, *m.*
dismiss [dis'mis], *v.t.* Rinviare, mandar via; congedare, licenziare, destituire; respingere, rigettare; cacciare. **Let us — the subject,** non ne parliamo più; **to — from one's mind,** cacciar dalla mente; (*Mil.*) **Dismiss!** Rompete le righe!
dismissal, *n.* Licenziamento, congedo, *m.*; destituzione, *f.*; rinvio, *m.*
dismount [dis'maunt], *v.t.i.* Smontare; scendere da cavallo.
disobedience [diso'bi:diəns], *n.* Disubbidienza, disobbedienza, *f.*
disobedient, *a.* Disobbediente.
disobediently, *adv.* Disobbedientemente.
disobey [diso'bei], *v.t.i.* Disobbedire.
disoblige [diso'blaidʒ], *v.t.* Scompiacere a, fare uno sgarbo a.
disobliging, *a.* Scompiacente, sgarbato.
disobligingly, *adv.* Sgarbatamente.
disobligingness, *n.* Scortesia, sgarbatezza, *f.*
disorder [dis'ɔ:ɹdəɹ], *n.* Disordine, scompiglio, *m.*; confusione, *f.*; malattia, indisposizione, *f.*; tumulto, dissesto, *m.* || *v.t.* Disordinare, confondere, imbrogliare; turbare, scomodare.

disordered, *a.* In disordine, confuso, imbrogliato.
disorderly, *a.* Disordinato, sregolato, confuso; immorale, scostumato; tumultuoso, turbolento.
disorganization, *n.* Disorganizzazione, *f.*
disorganize, *v.t.* Disorganizzare.
disorientate [dis'ɔrienteit], *v.t.* Disorientare.
disown [dis'oun], *v.t.* Disconoscere, negare, ripudiare, sconfessare.
disparage [dis'pærədʒ], *v.t.* Disprezzare, sprezzare, dispregiare; screditare, menomare.
disparagement, *n.* Disprezzo, discredito, *m.*; scorno, *m.* **Without — to you,** senza voler menomare il vostro merito, senza volervi far torto.
disparaging, *a.* Ingiurioso, sprezzante.
disparagingly, *adv.* Sprezzantemente.
disparate ['dispærət], *a.* Disparato, disuguale, diverso.
disparity, *n.* Disparità, *f.*
dispart [dis'pɑːɹt], *v.t.i.* Dividere, separare, spartire.
dispassionate [dis'pæʃənit], *a.* Spassionato, calmo, imparziale.
dispassionately, *adv.* Spassionatamente.
dispatch [dis'pætʃ], *v.t.* Spacciare, mandare, inviare, spedire; uccidere. || *n.* Spedizione, *f.*, invio, *m.*; (*in writing*) dispaccio, *m.*; (*haste*) diligenza, prontezza, *f.* **—-rider,** staffetta, *f.*; **—-box,** cassetta per le comunicazioni ufficiali, *f.*; **—-case,** cartella da viaggio, *f.*; **use all —,** sbrigatevi; **mentioned in despatches,** citato all'ordine del giorno.
dispel [dis'pel], *v.t.* Disperdere, dissipare, cacciar via.
dispensable [dis'pensəbl], *a.* Dispensabile.
dispensary [dis'pensəri], *n.* Dispensario, *m.*, farmacia, *f.*
dispensation, *n.* Dispensazione, dispensa, *f.*; (*fig.*) legge, *f.*, ordine, *m.* **The Christian —,** la legge cristiana, *f.*; **the dispensations of Providence,** i decreti della Provvidenza, *m.pl.*
dispensatory, *a.* Dispensatorio.
dispense [dis'pens], *v.t.* Dispensare, distribuire, amministrare; (*Med.*) preparare medicamenti. **To — with,** fare senza di.
dispenser, *n.* (*Med.*) Farmacista, *m.*
dispeople [dis'piːpl], *v.t.* Spopolare.
dispersal [cp. **dispersion**].
disperse [dis'pəːɹs], *v.t.* Disperdere, sperdere, sparpagliare, disseminare; *v.i.* disperdersi.
dispersion, dispersal, *n.* Dispersione, *f.*
dispirit [dis'pirit], *v.t.* Scoraggiare, abbattere, disanimare.
dispirited, *a.* Abbattuto.
displace [dis'pleis], *v.t.* Spostare; (*from office*) destituire.
displacement, *n.* Spostamento, *m.*; destituzione, *f.*; (*Naut.*) dislocamento, *m.*
display [dis'plei], *n.* Mostra, esposizione, *f.*; pompa, *f.*; spettacolo, spiegamento, *m.* || *v.t.* Mostrare, ostentare, esporre, spiegare, manifestare. **To make a — of,** far mostra di; **a great — of troops,** un grande spiegamento di truppe, *m.*; **a fine — of fireworks,** bei fuochi d'artifizio, *m.pl.*; **— advertisement,** annunzio, *m.*; **—-model,** manichino, *m.*
displease [dis'pliːz], *v.t.* Dispiacere a, spiacere a, riuscire sgradito a, scontentare, annoiare, seccare.
displeased, *a.* Dispiacente, spiacente, scontento, seccato. **I am very — with you,** sono molto scontento di te.
displeasing, *a.* Spiacevole, antipatico.
displeasure [dis'pleʒəɹ], *n.* Dispiacere, *m.*, noia, molestia, *f.*; collera, stizza, *f.*, corruccio, *m.* **To incur —,** attirarsi ira.
displume [dis'pluːm], *v.t.* (*Poet.*) Spennare.
disport [dis'pɔːɹt], *v.r.* Divertirsi, spassarsi.
disposable [dis'pouzəbl], *a.* Disponibile.
disposal, *n.* Disposizione, collocazione, *f.*; vendita, *f.* **To have at one's —,** avere a propria disposizione; **— of goods,** vendita dei beni, *f.*
dispose [dis'pouz], *v.t.* Disporre, collocare; indurre; inclinare. **I am disposed to think,** sono disposto a credere; **evilly —,** male intenzionato; **to — of,** disfarsi di; vendere; (*of food*) mangiare; **to be disposed of,** da vendere; **to be disposed of by private contract,** da vendersi senza intermediari.
disposition, *n.* Disposizione, attitudine, inclinazione, *f.*, carattere, *m.*
dispossess [dispo'zes], *v.t.* Spossessare, spogliare.
dispossession, *n.* Spogliazione, *f.*
dispraise [dis'preiz], *v.t.* Criticare, biasimare. || *n.* Biasimo, *m.*
disproof [dis'pruːf], *n.* Confutazione, *f.*
disproportion [dispro'pɔːɹʃən], *n.* Sproporzione, *f.*
disproportionately, *adv.* Sproporzionatamente.
disproportioned, disproportionate, *a.* Sproporzionato.
disprove [dis'pruːv], *v.t.* Confutare, smentire, contraddire.
disputable [dis'pjuːtəbl], *a.* Discutibile, dubbio.
disputant, disputer, *n.* Disputante, disputatore, *m.*
disputation, *n.* Disputa, discussione, *f.*
disputatious, *a.* Disputativo, contenzioso, cavilloso.
dispute, *n.* Disputa, discussione, contesa, questione, *f.*, litigio, *m.* || *v.t.* Disputare, contestare, discutere, altercare, litigare; *v.i.* disputare, ragionare, argomentare. **Beyond —,** fuori discussione; **to — every inch of the ground,** contestare ogni pollice di terreno.
disqualification [diskwɔlifi'keiʃən], *n.* Squalifica, *f.*; incapacità, inabilità, *f.*; (*Law*) interdizione, *f.*
disqualified, *a.* (*Law*) Interdetto.
disqualify, *v.t.* Incapacitare, inabilitare; (*Sport*) squalificare.
disquiet [dis'kwaiət], *n.* Inquietudine, ansietà, *f.* || *v.t.* Inquietare.
disquieting, *a.* Inquietante, allarmante.
disquietness, disquietude, *n.* Inquietudine, *f.*
disquisition [diskwi'ziʃən], *n.* Disquisizione, dissertazione, *f.*
disregard [disri'gɑːɹd], *n.* Noncuranza, indifferenza, *f.*, sprezzo, *m.* || *v.t.* Ignorare, trascurare, mancare d'attenzione. **In — of,** a dispetto di, senza riguardo a; **to — instructions,** non far caso d'istruzioni.
disregardful, *a.* Noncurante, indifferente.
disrelish [dis'reliʃ], *n.* Disgusto, *m.*, avversione, *f.* || *v.t.* Avere in uggia, infastidirsi di.

disrepair [disri'pɛəɹ], *n.* Sfacelo, cattivo stato, *m.*; rovina, *f.* **To fall into —**, cadere in rovina, essere diroccato.
disreputable [dis'repju:təbl], *a.* Di cattiva fama; sconvenevole, disdicevole, indegno, screditato.
disreputably, *adv.* Sconvenevolmente, vergognosamente.
disrepute [disri'pju:t], *n.* Discredito, *m.*, disistima, *f.* **To bring into —**, screditare; **to fall into —**, discreditarsi, cadere in discredito.
disrespect [disri'spekt], *n.* Mancanza di rispetto, *f.*
disrespectful, *a.* Scortese, incivile, irriverente. **To be — to,** mancare di rispetto a.
disrespectfully, *adv.* Irriverentemente, senza rispetto.
disrobe [dis'roub], *v.t.* Svestire, spogliare; *v.i.* svestirsi, spogliarsi.
disroot [dis'ru:t], *v.t.* Sradicare.
disrupt [dis'rʌpt], *v.t.* Spezzare, rompere.
disruption, *n.* Rottura, *f.*
dissatisfaction [disætis'fækʃən], *n.* Malcontento, malumore, *m.*, scontentezza, *f.*
dissatisfied, *a.* Insoddisfatto, scontento.
dissatisfy, *v.t.* Scontentare.
dissect [di'sekt], *v.t.* Anatomizzare, dissezionare, sezionare.
dissection, *n.* Dissezione, *f.*
dissector, *n.* Dissettore, *m.*
disseize [di'si:z], *v.t.* (*Law*) Spossessare.
dissemble [di'sembl], *v.t.i.* Dissimulare, fingere, nascondere.
dissembler, *n.* Dissimulatore, ipocrita, *m.*
dissembling, *n.* Dissimulazione, ipocrisia, *f.*
disseminate [di'semineit], *v.t.* Disseminare, spargere, diffondere.
dissemination, *n.* Disseminazione, diffusione, *f.*
disseminator, *n.* Disseminatore, *m.*
dissension [di'senʃən], *n.* Dissensione, *f.* **To sow —**, seminare la discordia.
dissent [di'sent], *n.* Dissenso, *m.*; dissidio, *m.*; (*Eccles.*) scisma, *m.*, dissidenza, *f.* || *v.t.* Dissentire, discordare, opporsi. **To — from,** dissentire da.
dissenter, *n.* (*Eccles.*) Dissidente, scismatico.
dissenting, dissentient, *a.* Dissenziente, discorde. || *n.* Dissenziente, *m.* **Without a — voice,** all'unanimità.
dissepiment [di'sepimənt], *n.* (*Bot.Zool.*) Setto, diaframma, *m.*
dissert, dissertate [di'sə:ɹt, 'disəɹteit], *v.t.* Dissertare, disquisire.
dissertation, *n.* Dissertazione, *f.*
disserve [di'sə:ɹv], *v.t.* Disservire, rendere un cattivo servizio a.
disservice, *n.* Disservizio, danno, *m.*
dissever [di'sevəɹ], *v.t.* Separare, dividere.
disseverance, *n.* Separazione, divisione, *f.*
dissidence ['disidəns], *n.* Dissidenza, *f.*
dissident, *n.a.* Dissidente, *m.*
dissimilar [di'similəɹ], *a.* Dissimile, vario, diverso.
dissimilarity, *n.* Dissomiglianza, *f.*
dissimilate [di'simileit], *v.t.* Dissimilare,
dissimulate [di'simju:leit], *v.t.* Dissimulare.
dissimulation, *n.* Dissimulazione, *f.*
dissipate ['disipeit], *v.t.* Dissipare, dissolvere; *v.i.* disperdersi; menare una vita sregolata.
dissipated, *a.* Dissoluto.
dissipation, *n.* Dissipazione, vita sregolata, *f.*; divertimento, *m.*; dispersione, *f.*
dissociate [di'souʃieit], *v.t.* Dissociare, distaccare, disunire.
dissociation, *n.* Dissociazione, *f.*
dissociative, *a.* (*Chem.*) Dissociativo.
dissolubility [disəlju:'biliti], *n.* Dissolubilità, *f.*
dissoluble, *a.* Dissolubile.
dissolute ['disəlju:t], *a.* Dissoluto.
dissolutely, *adv.* Dissolutamente.
dissoluteness, *n.* Dissolutezza, *f.*
dissolution, *n.* Dissoluzione, *f.*; (*of Parliament, etc.*) scioglimento, *m.*; morte, *f.*
dissolve [di'zolv], *v.t.* Dissolvere, disunire, disfare, sciogliere; *v.i.* dissolversi, scomporsi, disfarsi. **To — into tears,** fondersi in lagrime; **to — partnership,** scogliere la società.
dissolvent, *n.a.* Dissolvente, *m.*
dissolver, *n.* Dissolvitore, *m.*
dissonance ['disənəns], *n.* Dissonanza, discordanza, *f.*
dissonant, *a.* Dissonante, discordante, discorde.
dissuade [di'sweid], *v.t.* Dissuadere, sconsigliare.
dissuasion, *n.* Dissuasione, *f.*
dissuasive, *a.* Dissuasivo.
distaff ['distɑ:f], *n.* Conocchia, rocca, *f.* **On the — side,** per parte di madre.
distance ['distəns], *n.* Distanza, lontananza, *f.*; spazio, intervallo, *m.* || *v.t.* Distanziare, oltrepassare. **At a —**, lontano; **in the —**, in lontananza, da lontano; **to keep at a —**, tenere a debita distanza; **to keep one's —**, mantenere le distanze; **within striking —**, a portata di mano; **at this — of time,** dopo tanti anni; **What is the — to ?** Quanto c'è di qui a?
distant, *a.* Distante, lontano, discosto; (*fig.*) riservato, freddo; assente. **A — likeness,** una vaga rassomiglianza; **he is very —**, è molto riservato; (*Rail.*) **— signal,** segnale a distanza, *m.*
distantly, *adv.* Distantemente, lontanamente; (*fig.*) freddamente.
distaste [dis'teist], *n.* Disgusto, *m.*, ripugnanza, avversione, antipatia, *f.*
distasteful, *a.* Antipatico, noioso.
distastefulness, *n.* Spiacevolezza, *f.*
distemper (1) [dis'tempəɹ], *n.* (*Art.*) Tempera, *f.*, intonaco, *m.* || *v.t.* Dipingere a tempera, intonacare.
distemper (2), *n.* (*in dogs*) Cimurro, *m.*; indisposizione, *f.*
distempered, *a.* Turbato, agitato.
distempering, *n.* Intonacatura, *f.*; pittura a tempera, *f.*
distend [dis'tend], *v.t.* Gonfiare, dilatare, allargare; *v.i.* gonfiarsi, dilatarsi.
distensible, *a.* Dilatabile.
distension, *n.* Gonfiezza, dilatazione, *f.*
distich ['distik], *n.* (*Poet.*) Distico, *m.*
distil [dis'til], *v.t.i.* Distillare; stillare, estrarre; gocciolare.
distillate, distillation, *n.* Distillazione, *f.*
distillatory, *a.* Distillatorio.
distiller, *n.* Distillatore, *m.*
distillery, *n.* Distilleria, *f.*
distilling, *n.* Distillazione, *f.*

distinct [dis'tiŋkt], *a.* Distinto, chiaro, accurato; differente, separato, diviso, spiccato.
distinction, *n.* Distinzione, *f.*
distinctive, *a.* Distintivo.
distinctively, *adv.* Distintivamente.
distinctiveness, *n.* Carattere distintivo, *m.*
distinctly, *adv.* Distintamente, chiaramente.
distinctness, *n.* Chiarezza, precisione, esattezza, *f.*
distinguish [dis'tiŋgwiʃ], *v.t.* Distinguere; *v.i.* differenziare.
distinguishable, *a.* Distinguibile.
distinguished, *a.* Distinto, insigne, famoso, esimio, eminente. **A — foreigner,** uno straniero di riguardo, *m.*; **a — man,** un uomo eminente, *m.*; **a — writer,** uno scrittore insigne, *m.*
distort [dis'tɔːɹt], *v.t.* Storcere, stortare, distorcere; (*one's features*) scomporre; (*fig.*) falsificare, falsare, alterare, travisare.
distorted, *a.* Storto, scomposto; (*fig.*) falsato, travisato, alterato.
distortion, *n.* Distorsione, *f.*; (*of the face*) smorfia, *f.*
distract [dis'trækt], *v.t.* Distrarre, sviare, distogliere; tormentare, turbare, sbalordire, impazzire.
distracted, *a.* Turbato; impazzito, fuori di sè.
distractedly, *adv.* Pazzamente.
distractedness, *n.* Confusione, pazzia, *f.*
distraction, *n.* Distrazione, *f.*; pazzia, disperazione, frenesia, *f.* **To drive to —,** fare impazzire; **to love to —,** amare alla follia.
distrain [dis'trein], *v.i.* (*Law*) Espropriare, sequestrare.
distraint, *n.* Espropriazione, *f.*, sfratto, *m.*
distraught [dis'trɔːɹt], *a.* Pazzo.
distress [dis'tres], *n.* Afflizione, *f.*, dolore, *m.*; ansietà, *f.*; miseria, indigenza, *f.*; (*Law*) espropriazione, *f.*; pericolo, accasciamento, *m.* || *v.t.* Affliggere, inquietare; accasciare, stremare. **Signal of —,** segnale di pericolo, *m.*; **to be in —,** essere in difficoltà; **a ship in —,** una nave in pericolo, *f.*
distressed, *a.* Afflitto, ansioso; stremato, in pericolo; indigente.
distressful, *a.* Infelice, disgraziato, sfortunato.
distressing, *a.* Affliggente, straziante, penoso.
distributable [dis'tribjuːtəbl], *a.* Ripartibile, distribuibile.
distribute, *v.t.* Distribuire, dispensare, ripartire.
distribution, *n.* Distribuzione, ripartizione, *f.*
distributive [dis'tribjuːtiv], *a.* Distributivo.
district ['distrikt], *n.* Distretto, *m.*, regione, *f.*; contado, *m.*; quartiere, circondario, *m.* **Postal —,** distretto postale, *m.*; **— visitor,** dama di carità, *f.*
distrust [dis'trʌst], *n.* Diffidenza, sfiducia, *f.*, sospetto, dubbio, *m.* || *v.t.* Diffidare di, non fidarsi di, non avere fiducia in, sospettare di.
distrustful, *a.* Diffidente, sospettoso, sfiduciato.
distrustfully, *adv.* Sospettosamente.
distrustfulness, *n.* Diffidenza, *f.*, sospetto, *m.*
disturb [dis'təːɹb], *v.t.* Turbare, agitare, disturbare, incomodare.
disturbance, *n.* Disturbo; tumulto, scompiglio, *m.*; confusione, commozione, *f.*
disturber, *n.* Disturbatore, *m.* **— of the peace,** disturbatore della quiete pubblica, *m.*
disunion [dis'juːniən], *n.* Disunione, *f.*
disunite, *v.t.* Disunire; *v.i.* disgiungersi, staccarsi.
disunity, *n.* Disunione, *f.*
disuse [dis'juːz], *n.* Disuso, *m.* **To fall into —,** cadere in disuso.
disused, *a.* Disusato, fuori uso.
disyllabic [disi'læbik], *a.* Disillabico.
ditch [ditʃ], *n.* Fossa, *f.*, fosso, fossato, *m.* || *v.t.* Circondare d'una fossa; (*colloq.*) lasciare nelle difficoltà; *v.i.* scavare una fossa. **To the last —,** sino all'ultimo; **—-water,** acqua di fosso, *f*; **as dull as ditch-water,** noioso da morire.
dither ['diðəɹ], *v.i.* Tremare, essere incerto.
dithyramb [diθi'ræm], *n.* (*Poet.*) Ditirambo, *m.*
dittany ['ditəni], *n.* (*Bot.*) Dittamo, *m.*
ditto ['ditou], *adv.* Idem, detto.
ditty ['diti], *n.* Canzonetta, *f.*
diuretic [daijuː'retik], *a.* (*Med.*) Diuretico.
diurnal [dai'əːɹnəl], *a.* Diurno, quotidiano.
diurnally, *adv.* Diurnamente.
divagate ['divəgeit], *v.i.* Divagare, digredire.
divagation, *n.* Divagazione, *f.*
divan [di'væn], *n.* Divano, *m.*; sala da fumare, *f.*
divaricate [di'værikeit], *v.i.* Divaricare, allargare.
dive [daiv], *v.i.* Tuffarsi, immergersi; (*Aviat.*) piombare. || *n.* Tuffo, sbalzo, *m.*, tuffata, *f.*; affondamento, *m.*; (*colloq.*) taverna sotterranea, *f.* (*Aviat.*) **Nose- —,** discesa in picchiata; **—-bombing,** bombardamento in picchiata, *m.*
diver, *n.* (*swimmer*) Tuffatore, *m.*; (*in helmet, etc.*) palombaro, *m.*; (*Zool.*) marangone, *m.*
diverge [di'vəːɹdʒ], *v.i.* Divergere; distaccarsi.
divergence, divergency, *n.* Divergenza, *f.*
divergent, *a.* Divergente.
divers ['daivəɹz], *a.* Diversi; parecchi, certi.
diverse [dai'vəːɹs], *a.* Diverso, vario, differente.
diversely, *adv.* Diversamente.
diversification, *n.* Diversificazione, *f.*
diversify, *v.t.* Diversificare, variare.
diversion, *n.* Diversione, *f.*; passatempo, *m.*; divagazione, *f.*
diversity, *n.* Diversità, varietà, *f.*
divert [di'vəːɹt], *v.t.* Deviare, distogliere; svagare, rallegrare. **To — oneself,** divertirsi.
diverting, *a.* Divertente.
divertingly, *adv.* Divertentemente.
Dives ['daiviːz], *n.* (*fig.*) Ricco, *m.*; (*Bible*) il ricco epulone, *m.*
divest [di'vest], *v.t.* Spogliare, svestire. **To — oneself of,** spogliarsi di.
dividable [di'vaidəbl], *a.* Divisibile.
divide, *v.t.* Dividere, spartire, separare, disunire; distribuire, ripartire; (*Pol.*) votare, mettere ai voti; *v.i.* dividersi, distribuirsi; votare. **To — up,** distribuire; **opinion was divided,** non erano d'accordo; **Divide!** Ai voti!
divided, *a.* Diviso. **—-skirt,** gonna-pantaloni, *f.*
dividend ['dividend], *n.* (*Comm.*) Dividendo, *m.*
divider, *n.* Divisore, *m.* **Dividers** (*of compasses*), compasso a molla, *m.*
divination, *n.* Divinazione, predizione, *f.*
divinatory, *a.* Divinatorio.
divine [di'vain], *a.* Divino. || *n.* Teologo, ecclesiastico, *m.* || *v.t.* Indovinare, predire, presagire.

divinely, *adv.* Divinamente.
diviner, *n.* Indovino, mago, *m.*
divining-rod, *n.* Bacchetta di rabdomante, *f.*
diving ['daiviŋ], *n.* Tuffo, *m.* **—-bell,** campana da palombaro, *f.*; **—-dress, —-suit,** scafandro, *m.*
divinity [di'viniti], *n.* Divinità, teologia; (*fig.*) dio, *m.*, dea, *f.*
divisibility [divizi'biliti], *n.* Divisibilità, *f.*
divisible, *a.* Divisibile.
division, *n.* Divisione, *f.*, spartimento, *m.*; (*fig.*) discordia, disunione, *f.*; (*electoral*) collegio, *m.* (*Math.*) **Compound —,** divisione composta, *f.*; **simple —,** divisione semplice, *f.*
divisional, *a.* Divisionale.
divisor, *n.* (*Math.*) Divisore, *m.*
divorce [di'vɔːɹs], *n.* Divorzio, *m.*; separazione, *f.* || *v.t.* Divorziare. **To sue for a —,** chiedere un divorzio.
divorcee, *n.* Divorziato, *m.*, divorziata, *f.*
divorcement, *n.* Divorzio, *m.*
divot ['divət], *n.* (*Golf*) Piota, *f.*
divulgation, *n.* Divulgazione, *f.*
divulge [dai'vʌldʒ], *v.t.* Divulgare, rivelare, pubblicare, palesare.
dizziness ['dizinis], *n.* Vertigine, *f.*, capogiro, *m.*
dizzy, *a.* Preso da vertigine; vertiginoso. **To make —,** far venire le vertigini; **to feel —,** patire di vertigini, avere il capogiro; **a — height,** un'altezza vertiginosa, *f.*
do [duː], *v.t.i.* Fare, compiere, commettere; bastare; (*cooking*) cuocere, far cuocere; agire, stare; andare; convenire; finire; ingannare, truffare. || *n.* Inganno, *m.*; affare, *m.* **To do up,** rifare, riparare; imballare, involtare; abbottonare; **done for,** perduto, rovinato; **it can't be done,** non si può farlo; **it's as good as done,** la cosa è quasi fatta; **overdone,** esagerato; troppo cotto; **please do your utmost,** favorite fare tutto il possibile; **such things aren't done,** non si fanno tali cose; **done up,** stanco stanco, sfinito; **to do away with,** sopprimere, distruggere; **to do evil,** far male; **to do good,** far bene; **to have nothing to do with,** non avere nulla da fare con; **Well done!** Bravo!, Benissimo! **what's done can't be undone,** cosa fatta capo ha; **What's to be done?** Cosa c'è da fare? **What would you have me do?** Che cosa volete che io faccia? **to do to death,** uccidere; **Have done!** Finitela! **to do one's worst,** fare del proprio peggio: **How do you do?** Come sta? **that will do,** basta così; **Has he done?** Ha finito? **that will never do,** ciò non andrà mai bene; **to do into English,** tradurre in inglese; **to do without,** fare senza; **I've done with him,** l'ho finita con lui; **Do be quiet!** State zitti! **What do you think of it?** Chc ve ne pare?
docile ['dousail], *a.* Docile.
docility, *n.* Docilità, *f.*
dock (1) [dɔk], *v.t.* Troncare, mozzare; limitare, diminuire; **To — expenses,** limitare le spese; **to — a tail,** troncare una coda, scodare.
dock (2), *n.* Bacino, dock, *m.*; darsena, *f.*; (*Law*) banco degli accusati, *m.*, sbarra, *f.* || *v.t.* Fare entrare in bacino, attraccare. **Dry-—,** bacino di carenaggio, *m.*; **floating-—,** bacino galleggiante, *m.*; **—-dues,** diritti di banchina, *m.pl.*; **—-gate,** chiusa del dock, *f.*
dock (3), *n.* (*Bot.*) Bardana, *f.*, lapazio, romice, *m.*
docker, dock-labourer, *n.* Scaricatore, stivatore, *m.*
docket, *n.* Registro, *m.*; (*Law*) attergato, *m.* *v.t.* Attergare.
dockyard, *n.* Arsenale, cantiere, *m.*
doctor ['dɔktəɹ], *n.* Dottore; medico, *m.* || *v.t.* Medicare, curare; (*fig.*) manipolare, cambiare, alterare; (*wine, etc.*) fatturare. **— of laws,** dottore in legge, *m.*; **— of medicine,** dottore in medicina, *m.*
doctoral, doctorial, *a.* Dottorale.
doctorate, *n.* Dottorato, *m.*
doctrinaire ['dɔktrinɛəɹ], *a.* Dottrinario.
doctrinal, *a.* Dottrinale.
doctrinally, *adv.* Dottrinalmente.
doctrine ['dɔktrin], *n.* Dottrina, *f.*
document ['dɔkjuːmənt], *n.* Documento, *m.*; certificato, attestato, *m.*, carta, *f.* || *v.t.* Documentare, confermare.
documentary [dɔkjuː'mentəri], *a.* Documentario. (*Cinema.*) **— film,** un documentario, *m.*; (*Law*) **— evidence,** prova scritta, *f.*
documentation, *n.* Documentazione, prova, *f.*
dodder (1) ['dɔdəɹ], *v.i.* Barcollare, vacillare, tremare.
dodder (2), *n.* (*Bot.*) Cuscuta, *f.*
doddering, *a.* Tremante, tremolante.
dodecagon [dou'dekəgən], *n.* (*Geom.*) Dodecagono, *m.*
dodecahedron, *n.* Dodecaedro, *m.*
dodge [dɔdʒ], *v.t.* Schivare, scansare; sfuggire; *v.i.* saltellare, spostarsi rapidamente; agire con sotterfugi, raggirare, ingannare, abbindolare. || *n.* Balzo, giro, rigiro, *m.*; (*fig.*) trucco, *m.*, gherminella, *f.* **To — about,** saltellare; **to — behind,** rimpiattarsi dietro; **to — aside,** balzar di fianco.
doe [dou], *n.* (*Zool.*) (*deer*) Daina, *f.*; (*rabbit*) coniglia, *f.* **—-skin,** pelle di daina, *f.*
doer ['duːəɹ], *n.* Fattore, autore, operatore, *m.*
does (1) [dʌz] [cp. **do**].
does (2) [douz] [cp. **doe**].
doff [dɔf], *v.t.* Levare, togliere. **To — one's hat,** levarsi il cappello; **to — one's coat,** togliersi l'abito.
dog [dɔg], *n.* Cane, *m.*, cagna, *f.*; (*colloq.*) furbo, scaltro, *m.* || *v.t.* Pedinare, seguire le orme di, spiare. **A sly —,** un furbacchione, *m.*; **fire-—,** alare, *m.*; **house-—,** cane da guardia, *m.*; **lap-—,** cagnolino, *m.*, cagnetta *f.*; **give a — a bad name,** dare addosso a; **let sleeping dogs lie,** lasciate stare il cane che dorme; **love me love my —,** rispettate il cane per il padrone; **to go to the dogs,** andare in malora; **to lead a dog's life,** vivere come un cane; **to — someone's footsteps,** pedinare qualcuno; **—-biscuit,** biscotto per i cani, *m.*; **—-fight,** combattimento di cani, (*fig.*) scaramuccia, *f.*; **—-kennel,** canile, *m.*; **— Latin,** latino barbaro, *m.*; **dog's-ear,** (*of page*) orecchia, *f.*; *v.t.* fare l'orecchia a; **—-show,** mostra di cani, *f.*; **—-violet,** viola senza odore, *f.*; **—-racing,** corse di levrieri, *f.pl.*
dogberry, *n.* (*Bot.*) Corniola, *f.*; (*fig.*) un uomo pomposo.
dogcart, *n.* Biroccino, *m.*
dogdays, *n.pl.* Giorni canicolari, *m.pl.*
doge ['douʒ], *n.* (*Hist.*) Doge, *m.*

dogfish, *n.* (*Zool.*) Palombo, *m.*
dogged [ˈdɔgid], *a.* Ostinato, risoluto, tenace; caparbio, accanito.
doggedly, *adv.* Ostinatamente; accanitamente.
doggedness, *n.* Ostinazione, ostinatezza, caparbietà, *f.*
doggerel [ˈdɔgəɹəl], *n.* Poesia burlesca, poesiaccia, *f.*
doggish, *a.* Cagnesco, brutale.
doggy, doggie [ˈdɔgi], *n.* Cagnolino, canino, *m.*
dogma [ˈdɔgmə], *n.* Dogma, domma, *m.*
dogmatic, dogmatical, *a.* Dommatico.
dogmatically, *adv.* Dommaticamente.
dogmatics, *n.pl.* Dommatica, *f.*
dogmatism, *n.* Dommatismo, *m.*
dogmatist, *n.* Dommatista, *m.*
dogmatize, *v.i.* Dommatizzare.
dogrose, *n.* (*Bot.*) Rosa di macchia, rosa canina, *f.*
dogstar, *n.* (*Astron.*) Sirio, *m.*
dogwood, *n.* (*Bot.*) Corniolo, *m.*
doily [ˈdɔili], *n.* Sottocoppa, *m.*, salviettina, *f.*
doing [ˈduːiŋ], *n.* Fatti, *m.pl.*, opere, imprese, *f.pl.* **That needs some —,** qui ci vuole molta abilità; **underhand doings,** raggiri, intrighi, *m.pl.*; **that's your —,** è colpa vostra.
doldrums [ˈdɔldrəmz], *n.pl.* (*Naut.*) Calme equatoriali, *f.pl.* (*fig.*) **To be in the —,** essere malinconico.
dole (1) [doul], *n.* Elemosina, carità, *f.*; parte, *f.*, dono, *m.*; sussidio di disoccupazione, *m.* ‖ *v.t.* Dare in elemosina. **To — out,** distribuire, ripartire.
dole (2), *n.* (*Poet.*) Dolore, *m.*, tristezza, *f.*; lamento, *m.*
doleful, *a.* Doloroso, triste, infelice, malinconico.
dolefully, *adv.* Dolorosamente.
dolefulness, *n.* Tristezza, infelicità, *f.*
dolicocephalic [dɔlikouseˈfælik], *a.* Dolicocefalo.
doll, dolly [dɔl, ˈdɔli], *n.* Bambola, pupattola, *f.*; fantoccio, *m.* **Doll's house,** casa di bambola, *f.*; **to play with dolls,** giocare alle bambole; **dolly-tub,** tinozza, *f.*
dollar [ˈdɔləɹ], *n.* Dollaro, *m.*
dolomite [ˈdɔlomait], *n.* (*Geol.*) Dolomite, dolomia, *f.* **The Dolomites,** Le Dolomiti, *f.pl.*
dolorous [ˈdɔlərəs], *a.* (*Poet.*) Doloroso, triste.
dolorously, *adv.* Dolorosamente.
dolour, *n.* Dolore, *m.*
dolphin [ˈdɔlfin], *n.* (*Zool.*) Delfino, *m.*
dolt [doult], *n.* Scimunito, sciocone, imbecille, stupido, *m.*
doltish, *a.* Scimunito, sciocco, stupido.
doltishly, *adv.* Scimunitamente.
doltishness, *n.* Scimunitaggine, scemenza, *f.*
domain [doˈmein], *n.* Dominio; demanio, *m.*
dome [doum], *n.* Duomo, *m.*, cupola, *f.*; (*fig.*) tempio, edifizio, *m.*
domed, *a.* Fatto a volta; fornito di cupola.
Domesday Book [ˈduːmzdei buk], *n.* (*Hist.*) Libro del Catasto d'Inghilterra, *m.*
domestic [doˈmestik], *a.* Domestico, casalingo; (*of animals*) addomesticato; (*trade, etc.*) interno. ‖ *n.* Domestico, *m.*; domestica, *f.*; servo, *m.*, serva, *f.*, servitore, *m.f.*
domestically, *adv.* Domesticamente.
domesticate, *v.t.* Addomesticare, domesticare, assuefare.
domesticated, *a.* (*of animals*) Addomesticato; (*of persons*) familiare, casalingo. **To become —,** addomesticarsi.
domestication, *n.* Addomesticazione, *f.*
domesticity [domesˈtisiti], *n.* Domestichezza, domesticità, *f.*
domicile [ˈdɔmisail], *n.* Domicilio, *m.* ‖ *v.t.* Domiciliare, stabilire.
domiciled, *a.* Stabilito, domiciliato, residente. **To become —,** domiciliarsi.
domiciliary, *a.* Domiciliare.
domiciliation, *n.* Residenza, *f.*
dominance [ˈdɔminəns], *n.* Dominio, *m.*
dominant, *a.* Dominante. ‖ *n.* (*Mus.*) Nota dominante, *f.*
dominate, *v.i.* Dominare, prevalere; *v.t.* dominare, governare, reggere.
domination, *n.* Dominazione, *f.*
domineer [dɔmiˈniəɹ], *v.i.* Tiranneggiare, signoreggiare.
domineering, *a.* Tirannico, imperioso, arrogante.
dominical [doˈminikəl], *a.* (*Eccles.*) Domenicale.
Dominican, *n.a.* (*Eccles.*) Domenicano, *m.*
dominion [doˈminiən], *n.* Dominio, potere, *m.*; dominazione, potestà, *f.*
domino [ˈdɔminou], *n.* Domino, *m.* **In a —,** in domino; **to play at dominoes,** giuocare a domino.
don (1) [dɔn], *n.* (*title*) Don, *m.*; (*fig.*) gran signore, *m.*; professore universitario, *m.*
don (2), *v.t.* Mettere, vestire, indossare.
donation [doˈneiʃən], *n.* Dono, *m.*, donazione, elargizione, *f.*; carità, elemosina, *f.*
Donatism, *n.* (*Eccles.*) Donatismo, *m.*
Donatist, *n.* Donatista, *m.*
donative [ˈdounətiv], *n.* Donativo, regalo, *m.*; mancia, *f.*
donatory, *a.* Donatario.
done, *a.* Fatto, finito; cotto, [cp. **do**].
donee [douˈniː], *n.* Donatario, *m.*
donkey [ˈdɔŋki], *n.* Asino, ciuco, somaro, *m.* **— -ride,** cavalcata sull'asino, *f.*; **— -boy,** asinaio, *m.*; **— -engine,** cavallino; **— -race,** corsa agli asini, *f.*
donnish, *a.* Pedantesco.
donor [ˈdounəɹ], *n.* Donatore, *m.*, donatrice, *f.*
do-nothing [ˈduːnʌθiŋ], *n.* Perdigiorno, fannullone, *m.*
don't, *abbrev.* **do not.**
doodle [ˈduːdl], *v.i.* Scrivere o disegnare spensieratamente, scarabocchiare.
doom [ˈduːm], *v.t.* Condannare; predestinare fatalmente. ‖ *n.* Condanna, sentenza, *f.*; (*fig.*) sorte, *f.*, destino, *m.* **The crack of —,** il giudizio finale, *m.*
doomsday, *n.* Il giorno del giudizio finale, il finimondo, *m.*
door [dɔːɹ], *n.* Porta, *f.*, uscio, *m.*; (*of car, railway carriage, etc.*) sportello, *m.* **Front- —,** porta principale, *f.*; **folding —,** porta a due battenti, *f.*; **house- —,** porta di casa, *f.*; **swing- —,** porta volante, *f.*; **revolving- —,** porta girevole, *f.*; **— -mat,** stuoia, *f.*; **— -step,** soglia, *f.*; **— -bell,** campanello, *m.*; **— -handle,** maniglia, *f.*; **— -keeper,** portinaio, portiere, *m.*; **— -post,** stipite, *m.*; **he lives next —,** abita nella casa vicina; **indoors,** in casa; **out of doors,** fuori, all'aria aperta; **the fault lies at his —,** la colpa è la

sua; **to close the — against,** proibire l'ingresso a; **to turn out of doors,** mettere alla porta; **with closed doors,** a porte chiuse; **three doors off,** la terza casa da qui.

doornail, *n.* Borchia del battente, *f.* **As dead as a —,** morto stramorto.

doorway, *n.* Entrata, *f.*, ingresso, *m.*

dope [doup], *n.* Narcotico, *m.*; (*Aviat.*) vernice, *f.*; grasso, *m.*; (*fig.*) informazione, *f.* || *v.t.* Somministrare un narcotico. **— -fiend,** morfinomane, cocainomane, *m.f.*

dor [dɔːɹ], *n.* (*Zool.*) Melolonta, *f.*

dorado [də'rɑːdou], *n.* (*Zool.*) Dorata, *f.*

Dorian ['dɔːɹiən], *n.a.* Doriano, *m.*

Doric, *n.a.* Dorico, *m.*

dormancy ['dɔːɹmənsi], *n.* Riposo, sonno, *m.*

dormant, *a.* Dormiente, addormentato, torpido; caduto in disuso. **To lie —,** dormire; (*Comm.*) stare inattivo.

dormer, dormer window ['dɔːɹməɹ], *n.* Abbaino, *m.*

dormitory ['dɔːɹmitəri], *n.* Dormitorio, *m.*

dormouse (*pl.* **dormice**) ['dɔːɹmaus], *n.* (*Zool.*) Ghiro, *m.*

dorsal ['dɔːrsəl], *a.* (*Anat.*) Dorsale.

dory ['dɔːri], *n.* (*Zool.*) Pesce dorato, pesce S. Pietro, *m.*

dosage ['dousidʒ], *n.* Dosatura, *f.*

dose [dous], *n.* Dose, *f.* || *v.t.* Dosare, somministrare dosi. **To strengthen the —,** rincarare la dose.

doss [dɔs], *v.i.* (*colloq.*) Dormire, coricarsi. **— -house,** dormitorio pubblico, *m.*

dossal, *n.* (*Eccles.*) Dossale, *m.*

dossier ['dɔsiəɹ], *n.* Incartamento, *m.*

dot [dɔt], *n.* Punto, puntino, *m.*; (*child*) piccolino, piccino, *m.* || *v.t.* Punteggiare; puntare. **To — one's i's,** mettere i punti sugli i, essere molto preciso.

dotage ['doutidʒ], *n.* Rimbambimento, *m.*, imbecillità, *f.*

dotard, *n.* Vecchio rimbambito, *m.*

dote, *v.i.* Rimbambire; vaneggiare. **To — on,** amare pazzamente, essere infatuato di.

dotingly, *adv.* Follemente.

dotted, *a.* Punteggiato; (*Mus.*) con punto. **— line,** linea punteggiata, *f.*; **the sea was — with ships,** il mare era punteggiato di navi.

dotterel ['dɔtərəl], *n.* (*Zool.*) Tortolino, piviere minore, *m.*

dotty ['dɔti], *a.* (*colloq.*) Stupido, un po' matto.

double [dʌbl], *a.* Doppio, duplice; (*fig.*) falso; (*bent*) curvo. || *n.* Doppio, duplicato, *m.*; (*Mil.*) passo doppio, *m.* || *adv.* Doppio, doppiamente. || *v.t.* Raddoppiare; piegare in doppio; (*fists*) stringere; moltiplicare per due; *v.i.* ripiegare, ritornare sui propri passi; (*to dodge*) fare una giravolta. **Bent —,** piegato in due; **— chin,** mento doppio, *m.*, pappagorgia, *f.*; **— Dutch,** gergo incomprensibile; **— entry** (*book-keeping*), partita doppia, *f.*; **at the —,** a passo di corsa; **— or quits,** lascia o raddoppia; **— -jointed,** slogato; **in — quick time,** a passo di corsa; (*spelling*) **double c,** doppia c; (*Telephone*) **3006,** tre doppio zero sei; **— barrelled,** a due canne; (*Mus.*) **— bass,** contrabasso, *m.*; **— -breasted** a doppio petto; **— dyed,** (*fig.*) matricolato; **— entendre,** doppio senso, *m.*; **— -faced,** doppio, furbo; **to — -lock,** serrare a doppia chiave; **— -dealing,** doppiezza, malafede, *f.*; **— -edged,** a due tagli; ambiguo; (*Tennis*) **doubles,** partita doppia, *f.*; **to — -cross,** fare il doppiogioco.

doubleness, *n.* Doppiezza, duplicità, *f.*

doublet ['dʌblit], *n.* (*Hist.*) Farsetto, *m.* giubba, *f.*

doubloon [dʌb'luːn], *n.* (*Hist.*) Doblone, *m.*

doubly, *adv.* Doppiamente.

doubt [daut], *n.* Dubbio, *m.*, incertezza, esitazione, *f.* || *v.i.* Dubitare, stare in dubbio, esitare, essere incerto; *v.t.* dubitare di, diffidare di. **Beyond a —,** senza dubbio; **beyond all —,** fuor di dubbio; **there is no — that,** non c'è dubbio che; **I make no — that,** non dubito che.

doubter, *n.* Chi dubita, scettico, incredulo, *m.*

doubtful, *a.* Dubbioso, ambiguo, incerto. **To be — of,** dubitare di.

doubtfully, *adv.* Dubbiosamente, incertamente.

doubtfulness, *n.* Dubbiezza, incertezza, ambiguità, *f.*

doubtless, *adv.* Senza dubbio, certamente.

douceur ['duːsəɹ], *n.* Regalino, *m.*, mancia, *f.*

douche [duːʃ], *n.* Doccia, *f.* || *v.t.i.* Docciare.

dough [dou], *n.* Pasta, *f.*

doughy, *a.* Pastoso, molle, molliccio.

doughtily ['dautili], *adv.* Prodemente.

doughtiness, *n.* Prodezza, *f.*

doughty ['dauti], *a.* Prode, gagliardo, valoroso.

dour [duəɹ], *a.* Severo, ostinato.

douse [daus], *v.t.* Immergere, tuffare; abbassare, spegnere, estinguere; (*Naut.*) calare.

dove [dʌv], *n.* (*Zool.*) Colomba, *f.* **Ring- —,** palombo, *m.*; **rock- —,** piccione selvatico, *m.*; **— -cote,** colombaia, *f.*

dovetail, *n.* Coda di rondine, *f.* || *v.t.* Congiungere a coda di rondine. || *v.i.* Combaciare.

dowager ['dauədʒəɹ], *n.* Vedova nobile; madre, *f.* **The — duchess,** la duchessa madre, *f.*

dowdy ['daudi], *a.* Male in arnese, goffo, infagottato, negletto. || *n.* Sciattona, *f.*

dowdiness, *n.* Goffaggine, *f.*

dowel ['dauəl], *n.* Caviglia, *f.*, perno, *m.* || *v.t.* Incavigliare, unire con caviglie.

dower ['dauəɹ], *n.* Dote, *f.*, doario, *m.* || *v.t.* Dotare.

dowered, *a.* Dotato; (*fig.*) adornato.

dowlas ['dauləs], *n.* Tela rozza, *f.*

down (1) [daun], *n.* Piumino, *m.*, (*on cheeks, flowers, etc.*) lanugine, peluria, *f.*; **— quilt,** piumino, *m.*

down (2), *n.* Collina erbosa, *f.*

down (3), *adv.* Giù, abbasso, a basso, di sotto; (*of prices*) ribassato; (*of the sun*) tramontato; (*downstream*) a valle; (*crossword clue*) verticalmente. **— in the mouth,** scoraggiato; **— with an illness,** ammalato; **to be — on one's luck,** essere disgraziato; **up and —,** su e giù; **— to here,** fino qui; **the blinds were —,** le tende erano calate; **he isn't — yet,** non è ancora sceso; **— the garden,** giù nel giardino; **I am going — town,** vado in città; **— the Thames,** giù per il Tamigi; **Down with . . .!** Abbasso . . .!

down (4), *a.* Abbattuto, abbassato, basso; caduto; tramontato. **The — train,** il treno discendente, il treno dalla città, *m.*; **on the — grade,** in ribasso.

down (5), *n.* Basso, *m.* **He has had many ups and downs,** ha avuto molti alti e bassi; (*colloq.*) **to have a — on,** odiare, prendere in antipatia.
down (6), *v.t.* Deporre, abbassare, abbattere. **To — tools,** scioperare.
downcast, *a.* Abbattuto.
downfall, *n.* Caduta, rovina, *f.*
downfallen, *a.* Caduto.
downhearted, *a.* Scoraggiato.
downhill, *a.* In discesa, in pendio. || *adv.* In discesa.
downpour, *n.* Acquazzone, *m.*
downright, *a.* Schietto, sincero, diretto, franco. || *adv.* Schiettamente, affatto, molto.
downstairs, *adv.* Giù. || *a.* Di sotto, dabbasso.
downtrodden, *a.* Calpestato, oppresso.
downward, *a.* In discesa, a pendio. || *adv.* Giù, in giù.
downy, *a.* Lanuginoso, soffice.
dowry, *n.* Dote, *f.*
dowse [cp. **douse**].
dowsing ['dausiŋ], *n.* Rabdomanzia, *f.* **— rod,** bacchetta divinatoria, *f.*
dowser ['dausəɹ], *n.* Rabdomante, *m.*
doxology [dɔk'sɔlədʒi], *n.* (*Eccles.*) Dossologia, *f.*
doyen ['dɔiən], *n.* Decano, *m.*
doyly, *n.* Salviettina, *f.*
doze [douz], *v.i.* Sonnecchiare, dormicchiare, assopirsi. || *n.* Sonnellino, pisolo, pisolino, *m.*, dormitura, *f.* **He was just dozing off,** egli stava appunto appisolandosi.
dozen ['dʌzən], *n.* Dozzina, *f.* **In dozens,** a dozzine; **a baker's —,** tredici; **to talk nineteen to the —,** cicalare.
drab [dræb], *a.* Grigiastro; (*fig.*) grigio, fosco. || *n.* Sgualdrina, prostituta, *f.*
drabbet, *n.* Tela grossolana, *f.*
drabble ['dræbl], *v.i.* Diguazzare; *v.t.* imbrattare.
drachm ['dræm], *n.* Dracma, dramma, *f.*
Draconian [drə'kouniən], *a.* Draconiano.
draff [dræf], *n.* Feccia, *f.*, rifiuto, *m.*
draft [drɑ:ft], *v.t.* Redigere, abbozzare; (*Mil.*) arruolare, distaccare. || *n.* Abbozzo, schizzo, *m.*; minuta, brutta copia, *f.*; (*Comm.*) tratta, *f.*, assegno, *m.*; vaglia, *m.* (*Mil.*) distaccamento, *m.*
draftsman [cp. **draughtsman**].
drag (1) [dræg], *v.t.* Trarre, trascinare, strascinare; (*a pond, etc.*) dragare. || *n.* Ostacolo, impedimento, impaccio, *m.* **To — about,** strascinare; **to — away from,** strappare da; (*fig.*) **to — in,** introdurre per forza; **to — out,** strappare fuori, protrarre; (*Naut.*) **to — the anchor,** strascinare l'ancora.
drag (2), *n.* (*carriage*) Carrozzone, *m.*; (*net*) rete a strascico, *m.*; (*dredger*) draga, *f.*; freno, *m.*, martinicca, *f.*; (*fig.*) ostacolo. **To be a — upon,** essere un ostacolo a; **to put on the —,** mettere la martinicca.
draggle [drægl], *v.t.* Infangare, bagnare, strascinare nel fango. **—-tailed,** sporco, bagnato.
dragoman (*pl.* **dragomans**) ['drægəmæn], *n.* Dragomanno, *m.*
dragon ['drægən], *n.* Drago, *m.* **Dragon's blood,** (*Chem.*) sangue di drago, *m.*; (*Zool.*) **—-fly,** libellula, *f.*
dragoon [drə'gu:n], *n.* (*Mil.*) Dragone, *m.* || *v.t.* Perseguitare, soggiogare; intimidire.
drain [drein], *v.t.* Fare scolare; sorbire; vuotare; prosciugare, disseccare; (*fig.*) esaurire; *v.i.* scolare; prosciugarsi. || *n.* Condotto, *m.*; scolo, *m.*; chiavica, *f.*; (*sewer*) fogna, *f.*; (*fig.*) esaurimento, *m.* **—-pipe,** tubo di drenaggio, *m.*
drainage, *n.* Drenaggio, *m.*, fognatura, *f.*: (*Agric.*) bonifica, *f.*; prosciugamento, *m.*
drainer, *n.* Scolatoio, canale di scolo, *m.*
drake [dreik], *n.* (*Zool.*) Anitrone, *m.* **To play ducks and drakes,** fare a rimbalzello; **to play ducks and drakes with one's money,** sperperare il proprio denaro.
dram [dræm], *n.* Bicchierino, *m.*; (*colloq.*) cicchetto, grappino, *m.*; (*weight*) dramma, *m.*; (*draught*) goccia, *f.* **—-drinker,** ubbriaco, *m.*; **—-shop,** bettola, *f.*
drama ['drɑ:mə], *n.* Dramma, *m.*; teatro, *m.*
dramatic [drə'mætik], *a.* Drammatico.
dramatist ['dræmətist], *n.* Drammaturgo, *m.*; autore drammatico, *m.*
dramatize, *v.t.* Drammatizzare.
drape [dreip], *v.t.* Drappeggiare; panneggiare.
draper, *n.* Pannaiuolo, drappiere, negoziante di stoffe, *m.*
drapery, *n.* Drapperia, *f.*; (*method of draping*) drappeggio, *m.* **Linen —,** teleria, *f.*; **woollen —,** stoffe di lana, *f.pl.*
drastic ['dræstik], *a.* Forte, energico; (*Med.*) drastico.
draught [drɑ:ft], *n.* Tiro, *m.*, tirata, *f.*; (*of air*) corrente d'aria, *f.*, spiffero, *m.*; (*drink*) sorso, *m.*, sorsata, bibita, bevanda, *f.*; (*medicine*) pozione, *f.*; (*of fish*) retata, *f.*; (*Naut.*) pescaggio, *m.*; (*chimney*) tiraggio, *m.*; (*writing*) brutta copia, *f.* || *v.t.* [cp. **draft**]. **Draughts** (*game*), giuoco della dama, *f.*; **at a single —,** ad un sorso; **in long draughts,** a gran sorsi; (*beer*) **on —,** di botte, spillata fresca; **—-horse,** cavallo da tiro, *m.*; **—-board,** scacchiere, tavoliere, *m.*
draughtsman, *n.* Disegnatore, *m.*; pezzo nel giuoco della dama, *m.*
draughty, *a.* Esposto a correnti d'aria.
draw [drɔ:], *v.t.* Tirare, trarre, attirare; (*a picture*) disegnare, tracciare; (*money*) riscuotere; (*teeth*) estrarre, cavare; (*water*) attingere; (*metal*) trafilare; *v.i.* tirare, trarsi; (*tea*) stare in infusione; (*sword*) sguainare. || *n.* Attrazione, *f.*; lotteria, *f.*; parte indecisa, *f.* **To — a bow,** tendere un arco; **to — aside,** trarre in disparte; **to — a sigh,** trarre un sospiro; **to — away,** ritirare, stornare, tirar via; **to — back,** tirare indietro; **to — down,** tirar giù; **to — forth,** fare uscire, suscitare, far venir fuori; **to — lots for,** trarre a sorte, sorteggiare; **to — out,** estrarre; (*fig.*) **to — in one's horns,** abbassar la cresta; **to — the long bow,** esagerare, dirle grosse; **to — up** (*a document*) redigere, compilare; **to — up** (*in line*), allineare, schierare; **to — the line at,** far punto fermo, non andar oltre; **to — in** (*of the day*), accorciarsi; **to — near,** avvicinarsi, avanzarsi; **to — oneself up,** raddirizzarsi; **to — together,** unirsi, adunarsi; **to — level with,** portarsi al livello di; (*Naut.*) **to — water,** pescare; **to — a game,** fare partita nulla.

drawback, *n.* Svantaggio, inconveniente, ostacolo, *m.*; (*Comm.*) rimborso d'esportazione, *m.* **It's a great —,** è un grave inconveniente.
drawbridge, *n.* Ponte levatoio, *m.*
drawee [drɔ:'i:], *n.* (*Comm.*) Trattario, *m.*
drawer, *n.* (*Comm.*) Traente, *m.*; (*in furniture*) cassetto, *m.* **Chest of drawers,** cassettone, *m.*
drawers, *n.pl.* Mutande, *f.pl.*
drawing, *n.* (*sketch*) Disegno, *m.*; (*lottery*) estrazione, *f.*; (*lots*) sorteggio, *m.* **Freehand —,** disegno a mano libera, *m.*; **— -board,** tavola da disegno, *f.*; **— -book,** quaderno da disegno, *m.*; **— -pen,** tiralinee, *m.*; **— -pin,** punta da disegno, *f.*; **— -room,** salotto, *m.*, (*at Court*) ricevimento, *m.*
drawl [drɔ:l], *v.i.* Strascicare le parole. ‖ *n.* Voce affettata, *f.* **To — out,** proferire con voce strascicata.
drawling, *a.* Strascicante.
drawn [drɔ:n], *a.* Indeciso; (*of a sword*) sguainato; (*of a face*) tirato, emaciato. **With — swords,** a spade sguainate; **a — game,** una partita nulla, *f.*; **— -work,** sfilatura, *f.*
dray [drei], *n.* Carro, carrettone, furgone, *m.* **— -horse,** cavallo da tiro, *m.*; **— -man,** carrettiere, *m.*
dread [dred], *v.i.* Temere, aver paura. ‖ *n.* Terrore, spavento, *m.*; tema, paura, *f.* ‖ *a.* Terribile, spaventoso; augusto, venerabile. **In — of,** per tema di; **to be in — of,** aver paura di, temere.
dreadful, *a.* Terribile, spaventoso, formidabile.
dreadfully, *adv.* Terribilmente.
dreadnought, *n.* (*Naut.*) Nave da battaglia, super-corazzata, *f.*
dream [dri:m], *n.* Sogno, *m.* ‖ *v.t.i.* Sognare; immaginare, fantasticare. **To — of someone,** sognare di uno; **I saw in a —,** vidi in sogno; **I never dreamt of such a thing,** non me lo sognavo nemmeno; **to — away one's time,** perdere il tempo in fantasticherie.
dreamer, *n.* Sognatore, *m.*, sognatrice, *f.*
dreamland, *n.* Paese di sogni, *m.*
dreamless, *a.* Senza sogni.
dreamlessly, *adv.* Senza sognare.
dreamlike, *a.* Visionario, fantast ico; vago mistico.
dreamy, *a.* Sognante, fantastico, visionario.
drear, dreary [driəɹ, 'driəri], *a.* Triste, lugubre, cupo, tetro.
drearily, *adv.* Tristemente, tetramente.
dreariness, *n.* Tetraggine, tristezza, *f.*, aspetto, cupo, *m.*
dredge (1) [dredʒ], *n.* Draga, *f.* ‖ *v.t.i.* Dragare.
dredge (2), *v.t.* Spargere. **To — with flour,** infarinare.
dredger (1), *n.* Draga, *f.*
dredger (2), *n.* Utensile per infarinare, *m.*
dredging, *n.* Dragatura, *f.*, dragaggio, *m.*
dree [dri:], *v.i.* **To — one's weird,** subire il proprio destino.
dreggy ['dregi], *a.* Feccioso, impuro.
dregs [dregz], *n.pl.* Feccia, *f.* **To the —,** sino alla feccia.
drench [drentʃ], *v.t.* Bagnare, inzuppare, inaffiare. ‖ *n.* Beverone, *m.*
drenching, *n.* Bagnata, *f.* ‖ *a.* **— rain,** pioggia penetrante, *f.*
Dresden ['dresdən], *n.* (*Geog.*) Dresda, *f.* **— china,** porcellana di Sassonia, *f.*
dress [dres], *v.t.* Vestire, abbigliare; ornare, addobbare; (*a wound*) medicare, fasciare; (*leather, cloth, etc.*) conciare; (*food*) preparare; (*with flags*) pavesare; (*Mil.*) allineare; (*Agric.*) concimare; (*stone*) tagliare; *v.i.* vestirsi, acconciarsi. ‖ *n.* Veste, *f.*, vestito, *m.*; (*fig.*) foggia, moda, *f.* **Badly dressed,** male in arnese, mal vestito; **to — oneself,** vestirsi; **to — out,** ornare; **to — down,** sgridare; **to — in mourning,** vestirsi a lutto; **to — for dinner,** vestirsi pel pranzo; **to — up,** abbigliarsi, mettersi in eleganza; **— clothes, evening —,** abito da sera, *m.*; **morning —,** dorsè, *m.*; **full —,** alta tenuta, *f.*; **— coat,** marsina, *f.*, frac, *m.*; (*Theat.*) **— rehearsal,** prova generale, *f.*; **— -circle,** prima galleria, *f.*
dresser, *n.* (*kitchen*) Credenza, *f.*; (*Theat.*) vestiarista, *m.f.*; (*Med.*) allievo chirurgo, *m.*
dressing, *n.* Acconciamento, *m.*; (*Med.*) medicazione, *f.*; (*food*) condimento, *m.*; (*Agric.*) concime, *m.* **— -down,** sgridata, ramanzina, *f.*; **— -case,** valigia necessaire, *f.*; astuccio da toeletta, *m.*; **— -gown,** veste da camera, vestaglia, *m.*; **— -room,** gabinetto da toeletta, *m.*, (*Theat.*) camerino, *m.*; **— -table,** toletta, toeletta.
dressmaker, *n.* Sarta, *f.*
dressmaking, *n.* Confezioni, *f.pl.*, sartoria, *f.*
drew, *past* of **draw.**
dribble ['dribəl], *v.i.* Gocciolare, sgocciolare; sbavare, colar bava; *v.t.* (*Football*) palleggiare. ‖ *n.* Goccia, bava, saliva, *f.*
dribbling, *n.* (*Football*) Palleggio, *m.*
driblet, *n.* Goccia, *f.*; (*fig.*) piccola somma, *f.* **In driblets,** a poco a poco.
dried [draid], *a.* Secco, seccato; prosciugato, asciugato. **— fruits,** frutta secca, *f.*
drier, *n.* Essiccatoio, stenditoio, *m.*; asciugatrice, *f.*
drift [drift], *n.* Direzione, mira, tendenza, *f.*; (*Naut.*) de iva, *f.*; (*of discourse*) piega, *f.*; (*of snow*) mucchio, turbine, *m.*; (*Geol.*) terreno alluvionale, *m.* ‖ *v.i.* Andare alla deriva, flottare, galleggiare, stare a galla, ammucchiarsi, accumularsi; *v.t.* spingere, mandare. **— ice,** ghiacci galleggianti, *m.pl.*
drifter, *n.* (*Naut.*) Motopeschereccio, *m.*
drill [dril], *n.* (*Mech.*) Trivello, succhiello, trapano, *m.*; (*Agric.*) solco, seminatoio, *m.*, seminatrice, *f.*; (*Mil.*) esercitazione, *f.*; (*material*) canevaccio, traliccio, *m.* ‖ *v.t.* Forare, perforare; addestrare, esercitare; seminare a solchi; *v.i.* esercitarsi, addestrarsi. **— -ground,** piazza d'armi, *f.*; **— -sergeant,** sergente istruttore, *m.*; **— -bow,** archetto, *m.*
drilling, *n.* (*Mil.*) Esercizi militari, *m.pl.*; perforazione, *f.* **— -machine,** perforatrice, *f.*
drily ['draili], *adv.* Seccamente, freddamente; causticamente.
drink [driŋk], *n.* Bevanda, bibita, *f.*; beveraggio, *m.*; bevuta, sorsata, *f.* ‖ *v.t.* Bere. **To have a —,** bere qualchecosa; **to take to —,** darsi al bere; **strong- —,** bevande alcooliche, *f.pl.*; **in —,** ubbriaco; **to — in,** assorbire; **to — off,** bere tutto d'un fiato; **to — to,** bere alla salute di; **to — like a fish,** bere come una spugna; **to — deep,** bere molto, tracannare; **to — oneself to death,** uccidersi col bere; **— -money,** mancia, *f.*; **— -offering,** libazione, *f.*

drinkable, *a.* Potabile, bevibile.
drinker, *n.* Bevitore, *m.*, bevitrice, *f.*; ubbriacone, *m.f.* **A hard —,** un ubbriacone, un beone, *m.*
drinking, *n.* Il bere, *m.*; ubbriachezza, *f.*, alcoolismo, *m.* || *a.* Potabile, da bere. **—-bout** orgia, *f.*; **—-fountain,** fontana pubblica, *f.*; **—-song,** canzone bacchica, *f.*; **—-trough** abbeveratoio, *m.*; **—-water,** acqua potabile, *f.*
drip [drip], *v.t.* Gocciolare, sgocciolare, colare; *v.i.* stillare, trapelare. || *n.* Goccia, *f.*, gocciolamento, *m.*; (*Arch.*) **— stone,** grondaia, *f.*
dripping, *n.* Gocciolamento, *m.*; (*fat*) grasso d'arrosto, *m.* **—-pan,** leccarda, *f.*
drive [draiv], *v.t.* Spingere, sospingere, cacciare; (*vehicle*) condurre, guidare; (*tunnel*) scavare; (*nail*) conficcare, piantare; (*screw*) girare, avvitare; (*Golf*) tirare il colpo; (*a machine*) azionare, pilotare; *v.i.* andare in carrozza, scarrozzare; (*Naut.*) andare in deriva. || *n.* Scarrozzata, passeggiata in carrozza, *f.*; strada carrozzabile, *f.*; energia, forza, *f.*; (*Golf*) colpo, *m.*; (*Tennis*) volata diritta, *f.* **To — away,** scacciare; **to — back,** respingere, ribattere; **to — in,** fare entrare, ficcar dentro; **to — mad,** render pazzo; **to — on,** spinger innanzi; **to — out,** fare uscire; **to — at,** tendere a, mirare a; **What is he driving at?** Dove vuol andar a parare? **to — by,** passare in carrozza; **to — faster,** affrettarsi; **Drive on!** Avanti! (*Naut.*) **to — ashore,** essere gettato sulla costa, arenarsi; (*road sign*) **Drive slowly,** Al passo, Adagio; (*Motor.*) **left-hand —, right-hand —,** guida a sinistra, a destra.
drivel ['drivəl], *n.* Bava, *f.*; stupidaggine, *f.* || *v.i.* Sbavare, fare bava; (*fig.*) dire sciocchezze, cianciare. **This is mere —,** queste sono sciocchezze.
driveller, *n.* Imbecille, *m.*
driver, *n.* Conduttore, *m.*; cocchiere, *m.*; (*of taxi*) autista, *m.*; (*Rail.*) macchinista, *m.*; (*Motor.*) guidatore, chauffeur, autista, *m.*; (*Golf*) mazza, *f.*, bastone, *m.*
driving, *n.* guida, condotta, *f.*; (*Mech.*) azionamento, *m.*, trasmissione, *f.*; (*nails*) conficcamento, *m.* || *a.* Movente, sospingente. **—-band, —-belt,** cinghia, *f.*; **—-shaft,** albero motore, *m.*; **—-mirror,** specchio retrospettivo, *m.*; **—-wheel,** ruota motrice, *f.*; **— rain,** pioggia sferzante, *f.*
drizzle ['drizl], *v.i.* Piovigginare. || *n.* Pioggerella, *f.* **Drizzling rain,** acquerugiola, *f.*
drizzly, *a.* Piovigginoso.
droll [droul], *a.* Comico, buffo, divertente, faceto. **A — fellow,** un capoameno, un buontempone, *m.*; **a — thing,** una cosa buffa, *f.*
drollery, *n.* Facezia, buffoneria, *f.*
drolly ['drouli], *adv.* Burlescamente, in modo scherzevole.
dromedary ['drɔmidəri], *n.* (*Zool.*) Dromedario, *m.*
drone (1) [droun], *n.* (*Zool.*) Fuco, pecchione, *m.*; (*fig.*) fannullone, *m.*
drone (2), *n.* Ronzio, *m.*; (*Mus.*) bordone, *m.* || *v.i.* Ronzare.
droning, *n.* Ronzio, *m.*
droop [dru:p], *v.i.* Languire, struggersi, piegarsi, pendere; (*of flowers*) appassirsi.
drooping, *a.* Languido, languente, debole; appassito. || *n.* Languore, *m.* **— spirits,** spirito abbattuto.
drop [drɔp], *n.* (*of liquid*) Goccia, gocciola, *f.*; (*fall*) caduta, *f.*; (*of gallows*) trabocchetto, *m.*; (*ear-ring*) orecchino, *m.*; (*sweets*) caramella, pastiglia, *f.*; (*drink*) sorso, gocciolino, *m.* || *v.t.* Lasciar cadere; abbandonare; (*the anchor*) gettare; (*stitch*) saltare, lasciar cadere; (*to desist*) cessare; *v.i.* gocciolare; cadere; (*of prices*) ribassare. **To — an acquaintance,** interrompere una relazione; **to — anchor,** gettare l'ancora; **— me a line,** fatemi avere una riga; **to — astern,** restare indietro; **to — down,** cadere a terra; **to — in on someone,** fare una visita a qualcuno; **to — off to sleep,** cominciare a dormire; **to — with fatigue,** essere affranto dalla fatica; **the correspondence dropped,** la corrispondenza cessò; (*Theat*) **—-curtain, —-scene,** sipario, *m.*; (*Football*) **—-kick,** calcio di rimbalzo, *m.*; **to — a tear,** versare una lagrima.
dropper, *n.* Contagocce, *m.*
droppings, *n.pl.* Sterco, *m.*
dropsical ['drɔpsikəl], *a.* (*Med.*) Idropico.
dropsy, *n.* Idropisia, *f.*
droshky ['drɔʃki], *n.* Carrozza russa, *f.*
dross [drɔs], *n.* Scoria, *f.*; (*fig.*) rifiuto, *m.*
drought [draut], *n.* Siccità, *f.*; (*fig.*) sete, *f.*
drove (1) [drouv], *n.* Gregge, branco, *m.*, mandra, *f.*; (*fig.*) folla, truppa, *f.*
drove (2), *past* of **drive.**
drover, *n.* Bovaro, boario, mandriano, *m.*
drown [draun], *v.t.* Annegare, affogare; (*sounds*) soffocare; (*fig.*) sommergere, affondare; *v.i.* annegare, affogare. **To be drowned,** essere annegato; **to — oneself,** annegarsi, affogarsi.
drowning, *n.* Sommersione, *f.*; annegamento, affogamento, *m.*
drowsily ['drauzili], *adv.* Sonnacchiosamente.
drowsiness, *n.* Sonnolenza, *f.*
drowsy, *a.* Sonnolento, sonnacchioso, assopito; soporifico.
drub [drʌb], *v.t.* Battere, percuotere, bastonare.
drubbing, *n.* Bastonatura, *f.*
drudge [drʌdʒ], *n.* Uomo di fatica, sgobbone, *m.*, sgobbona, *f.* || *v.i.* Sgobbare, faticare, tirar la carretta.
drudgery, *n.* Faticaccia, facchinata, *f.*; lavoro ingrato, *m.*
drug [drʌg], *n.* Farmaco, medicinale, *m.*, droga, *f.*; narcotico, *m.* || *v.t.* Narcotizzare; medicamentare. **—-store,** farmacia, *f.*; **— traffic,** commercio dei narcotici, *m.*
drugget ['drʌgit], *n.* Droghetto, bigello, *m.*
druggist ['drʌgist], *n.* Farmacista, *m.*
druid ['dru:id], *n.* (*Hist.*) Druido, *m.*
druidical, *a.* Druidico.
drum [drʌm], *n.* Tamburo, *m.*; (*of ear*) timpano, *m.*; cilindro, *m.* || *v.i.* Tamburellare, tamburеggiare, battere il tamburo; (*fig.*) tintinnare; *v.t.* cacciare a suon di tamburo. **Big —,** grancassa, *f.*; **kettle- —,** timpano, *m.*; **the beat of drums,** il rullo del tamburo, *m.*; **— major,** tamburo maggiore, *m.*; **—-stick,** bacchetta da tamburo, *f.*; gamba di pollo, *f.*
drummer, *n.* Tamburino, *m.*
drumming, *n.* Rullo del tamburo, *m.*

drunk [drʌŋk], *a.* Ubriaco, briaco; (*fig.*) ebbro. **Dead —,** ubriaco fradicio; **— with joy,** ebbro di gioia; **to get —,** ubriacarsi.
drunkard, *n.* Ubriacone, beone, *m.*, ubriacona, *f.*
drunken, *a.* Ubriaco, ebbro.
drunkenly, *adv.* Da ubriaco.
drunkenness, *n.* Ubriachezza, ebbrezza, *f.*
dry [drai], *a.* Secco, arido, asciutto; (*thirsty*) assetato; (*fig.*) mordace, caustico, pungente; noioso, seccante. || *v.t.* Asciugare, seccare, disseccare; *v.i.* seccarsi, asciugarsi. **— bread,** pane asciutto, *m.*; **a — cough,** una tosse secca, *f.*; **— humour,** spirito caustico, *m.*; **— goods,** mercerie, *f.pl.*; **— dock,** bacino di carenaggio, *m.*; **— land,** terraferma, *f.*; **— -nurse,** balia asciutta, *f.*; **— -rot,** fungo nel legno, tarlo del legno, *m.*; **— wall,** muro in pietra secca, *m.*; **— -shod,** a piedi asciutti; **— clean,** pulire a secco; **to — one's eyes,** asciugarsi gli occhi; **to — up,** inaridirsi, seccarsi.
dryad [ˈdraiəd], *n.* Driade, *f.*
dryer, drier [ˈdraiəɹ], *n.* Essiccante, seccativo, *m.*
drying, *n.* Riseccamento, *m.*, asciugatura, essiccazione, *f.* || *a.* Essiccante. **— -room,** essiccatoio, *m.*
dryly, drily, *a.* Seccamente, aridamente.
dryness, *n.* Siccità (*of season*), secchezza, aridità, *f.*
dual [ˈdju:əl], *a.* Doppio, duplice; (*Gram.*) duale. **— number,** numero duale, *m.*
dualist, *n.* Dualista, *m.*
duality, *n.* Dualità, *f.*
dub [dʌb], *v.t.* Creare cavaliere; (*colloq.*) nominare, chiamare; (*Cinema*) doppiare.
dubbin, dubbing (1), *n.* Grasso da stivali, *m.*
dubbing (2), *n.* (*Cinema*) Doppiaggio, *m.*
dubiety, dubiousness [ˈdju:biəti, ˈdju:biəsnəs], *n.* Dubbio, *m.*, dubbiezza, dubbiosità, *f.*
dubious, *a.* Dubbio, incerto, indeciso, dubbioso.
dubiously, *adv.* Dubbiamente.
dubitative [ˈdju:bitətiv], *a.* Dubitativo.
ducal [ˈdju:kəl], *a.* Ducale.
ducat [ˈdʌkət], *n.* (*Hist.*) Ducato, *m.*
duchess [ˈdʌtʃis], *n.* Duchessa, *f.*
duchy, *n.* Ducato, *m.*
duck [dʌk], *n.* (*Zool.*) Anitra, *f.*; (*of the head*) inchino, *m.*; (*material*) tela da vela, *f.*; (*dip*) tuffo, *m.*; (*colloq.*) caro, carino, *m.* || *v.t.* Tuffare, immergere; (*the head*) chinare; *v.i.* tuffarsi, immergersi; inchinarsi. **Wild —,** anitra selvatica, *f.*; (*fig.*) **a lame —,** uno mal ridotto, un minorato, *m.*; **to play ducks and drakes** [cp. **drake**]; (*Sport*) **duck's egg,** zero, *m.*; **— -weed,** lenticchia palustre, *m.*
duckbill, *n.* (*Zool.*) Ornitorinco, *m.*
ducking, *n.* Tuffo, *m.*, immersione, *f.*
duckling, *n.* Anitrino, anitroccolo, *m.*
ducky, *n.* (*colloq.*) Gioia mia, *f.*, tesoro mio, *m.*, carino, *m.*
duct [dʌkt], *n.* Condotto, tubo, *m.*; (*Anat.*) condotto, *m.*
ductile, *a.* Duttile; (*fig.*) docile, arrendevole.
ductility, *n.* Duttilità, *f.*; docilità, *f.*
dud [dʌd], *n.* Cosa che fa cilecca, *f.* *a.* Inutile. **— cheque,** assegno a vuoto, *m.*
dude [dju:d], *n.* Zerbinotto, bellimbusto, *m.*
dudgeon [ˈdʌdʒən], *n.* Risentimento, sdegno, *m.* **In high —,** sdegnatissimo; **to take in —,** prendere in mala parte.
duds [dʌdz], *n.pl.* Vestiti, *m.pl.*
due [dju:], *a.* Dovuto, debito, convenevole; (*Comm.*) dovuto, esigibile, pagabile. || *n.* Debito, *m.*; diritti, *m.pl.* || *adv.* Esattamente, direttamente. **In — form,** nella debita forma; **with — care,** con la debita cura; **in — time,** a tempo debito; **to fall —,** scadere; **it's — to him to say,** sta a lui a dire; **without — cause,** senza giusta causa; **the train is — at eight o'clock,** il treno deve arrivare alle otto; **this is — to a mistake,** ciò è dovuto ad un errore; **to give a man his —,** dare ad un uomo ciò che gli spetta; **to give the Devil his —,** essere giusto anche col diavolo; **town dues,** dazio, *m.*; **harbour dues,** diritti di porto, *m.pl.*
duel [ˈdju:əl], *n.* Duello, *m.*; (*fig.*) lotta contesa, *f.* **A — with swords,** un duello alla spada, *m.*; **to fight a —,** battersi in duello; **to challenge to a —,** sfidare a duello.
duelling, *n.* Il duellare, *m.*
duellist, *n.* Duellante, *m.*
duenna [dju:ˈenə], *n.* Governante, *f.*
duet [dju:ˈet], *n.* (*Mus.*) Duetto, *m.*
duffer [ˈdʌfəɹ], *n.* Scioccone, cretino, *m.*; (*at a game*) schiappa, *f.*, schiappino, *m.*
dug (1) [dʌg], *n.* Capezzolo, *m.*, mammella, *f.*
dug (2) *past* of **dig.** **— -out,** ricovero, *m.*, trincea coperta, *f.*
duke [dju:k], *n.* Duca, *m.*
dukedom, *n.* Ducato, *m.*
dulcet [ˈdʌlsit], *a.* Dolce, armonioso.
dulcify [ˈdʌlsifai], *v.t.* (*Chem.*) Dolcificare.
dull [dʌl], *a.* (*of persons*) Ottuso, insensibile; (*of the mind*) tardo, inerte, torpido; (*of weather*) grigio, nebbioso, fosco; (*of pain*) sordo; (*of sound*) sordo, cupo; (*blunt*) smussato; (*of colour*) oscuro, poco brillante; (*of hearing*) duro d'orecchi; (*of sight*) miope; (*Comm.*) stagnante, inattivo. || *v.t.* (*to blunt*) Smussare; (*to tarnish*) offuscare, appannare; (*to numb*) attutire, intorpidire. **A — fire,** un focherello, *m.*; **a — man,** un uomo noioso, *m.*; **to feel —,** annoiarsi; **a — thud,** un tonfo sordo, *m.*; **— -brained,** balordo, stupido, ottuso; **— -eyed,** dallo sguardo scialbo; **— -witted,** tardo di mente.
dullard, *n.* Stupido, tonto, imbecille, *m.*
dullish, *a.* Stupidino, noiosetto.
dullness, *n.* Stupidità, lentezza, *f.*; noia, *f.*; ottusità, *f.*; mancanza di colore, *f.*; (*of glass*) appannamento, offuscamento, *m.*
dully [ˈdʌli], *adv.* Stupidamente, noiosamente.
duly [ˈdju:li], *adv.* Debitamente, regolarmente; convenientemente. (*Comm.*) **— to hand,** debitamente pervenuto.
dumb [dʌm], *a.* Muto, silenzioso, tacito; (*fig.*) taciturno; (*colloq.*) uggioso. **— -bells,** manubrii ginnastici, *m.pl.*; **— -show,** pantomima, *f.*; **in — -show,** in scena muta; **— -waiter,** servitore inglese, *m.*
dumbfound [ˈdʌmfaund], *v.t.* Confondere, ridurre al silenzio, far tacere.
dumbfounded, *a.* Ammutolito, stordito.
dumbly [ˈdʌmli], *adv.* Mutamente, tacitamente.
dumbness, *n.* Mutezza, *f.*; mutismo, *m.*; (*fig.*) silenzio, *m.*

dummy ['dʌmi], *n.* Manichino, *m.*; muto, *m.*; uomo di paglia, *m.*; fantoccio, *m.*; imbecille, *m.*; (*Cards*) morto, *m.*; (*baby's*) poppatoio, *m.* || *a.* Finto, falso. (*Cards*) **To play —,** fare il morto.
dump [dʌmp], *v.t.* Deporre, lasciar cadere, gettare, buttare giù; (*Comm.*) vendere sottoprezzo. || *n.* Deposito, mucchio, *m.*, catasta, *f.* **Ammunition —,** deposito di munizioni.
dumping, *n.* (*Comm.*) Vendita sotto costo, *f.*
dumpling ['dʌmpliŋ], *n.* Gnocco, *m.* **Apple-—,** bodino di mele, *m.*
dumps [dʌmps], *n.pl.* Melanconia, tristezza, *f.* **To be in the —,** essere triste, aver la melanconia.
dumpy, *a.* Tozzo, basso e grasso.
dun (1) [dʌn], *a.* Bruno, nerastro; (*of horses*) sauro.
dun (2), *n.* Creditore insistente, *m.* || *v.t.* Importunare.
dunce [dʌns], *n.* Stupido, balordo, asino, ignorante, *m.*
dunderhead ['dʌndəɹhed], *n.* Testa di cavolo, *f.*, cretino, *m.*
dune [dju:n], *n.* Duna, *f.*
dung [dʌŋ], *n.* Sterco, letame, *m.*, escrementi, *m.pl.* || *v.t.* Concimare con letame. **—-cart,** carretta pel letame, *f.*; **—-hill,** letamaio, *m.*; (*Zool.*) **—-beetle,** scarabeo stercorario, *m.*
dungeon ['dʌndʒən], *n.* Prigione sotterranea, *f.*
dunnage ['dʌnidʒ], *n.* (*Naut.*) Contrapagliuolo, *m.*; zavorra, *f.*
duodecimal [dju:ou'desiməl], *a.* Duodecimo.
duodecimo, *n.* (*Print.*) In-dodicesimo, *m.*
duodenal [dju:ou'di:nəl], *a.* (*Anat.*) Duodenale.
duodenum [dju:ou'di:nəɹn], *n.* (*Anat.*) Duodeno, *m.*
duologue ['dju:əlog], *n.* Dialogo, *m.*
dupe [dju:p], *n.* Baggiano, gonzo, *m.*, vittima di un inganno, *f.* || *v.t.* Ingannare, truffare, gabbare.
dupery, *n.* Inganno, *m.*
duple ['dju:pl], *a.* Doppio.
duplex ['dju:pleks], *a.* Duplice, doppio.
duplicate (1) ['dju:plikeit], *v.t.* Copiare, duplicare, fare un duplicato.
duplicate (2) ['dju:plikit], *a.* Duplicato. || *n.* Duplicato, doppio, *m.* **In —,** in duplicato.
duplication, *n.* Duplicazione, *f.*
duplicator, *n.* Duplicatore, *m.*
duplicity [dju:'plisiti], *n.* Duplicità, doppiezza, dissimulazione, *f.*
durability [dju:rə'biliti], *n.* Durabilità, *f.*
durable ['dju:rəbəl], *a.* Durabile, durevole, resistente.
durably, *adv.* Durevolmente.
durance ['dju:rəns], *n.* Prigionia, *f.* **In — vile,** in prigione.
duration [dju:'reiʃən], *n.* Durata, *f.*
duress [dju:'res], *n.* Costrizione, prigionia, *f.* **Under —,** per forza, sotto costrizione.
during ['djuriŋ], *prep.* Durante.
durst, *past* of **dare.**
dusk [dʌsk], *n.* Crepuscolo, l'imbrunire, *m.*; (*fig.*) oscurità, *f.* **Towards —,** sull'imbrunire.
duskily, *adv.* Oscuramente.
duskiness, *n.* Oscurità, *f.*
dusky, *a.* Oscuro, fosco, nerastro; (*of complexion*) bruno.
dust [dʌst], *n.* Polvere, *f.*; spazzatura, *f.*; (*colloq.*) confusione, *f.*, strepito, *m.*; (*of the dead*) ceneri, *m.pl.* || *v.t.* Spolverare; (*sprinkle*) impolverare, cospargere. **Coal-—,** polvere di carbone, *f.*; **—-bin,** cassetta della spazzatura, bidone per spazzatura, *f.*; **—-coat,** spolverino, *m.*; **—-man,** spazzaturaio, *m.*; **—-pan,** paletta per le spazzature, *f.*; **—-sheet,** fodera, *f.*
duster, *n.* Strofinaccio, *m.*
dustiness, *n.* Polverosità, *f.*
dusty, *a.* Polveroso, polverulento.
Dutch [dʌtʃ], *a.* Olandese. || *n.* (*language*) Olandese, *m.* **— auction,** incanto, *m.*; **—-oven,** forno portatile, *m.*; **— courage,** finto coraggio, coraggio dato da stimolanti, *m.*
Dutchman, Dutchwoman, *n.* Olandese, *m.f.*
duteous ['dju:tiəs], *a.* Sottomesso, ubbidiente, docile.
dutiable ['dju:tiəbl], *a.* Doganabile, daziabile.
dutiful, *a.* Ubbidiente, rispettoso, sottomesso, ossequioso.
dutifully, *adv.* Ubbidientemente.
dutifulness, *n.* Ubbidienza, sommissione, *f.*
duty ['dju:ti], *n.* Dovere, *m.*; funzione, *f.*; (*customs*) imposta, tassa, *f.*, dazio, *m.*, diritti, *m.pl.*; (*Mil.*) servizio, *m.* **On —,** di servizio; **off —,** fuori servizio; **to do — for,** servire da; **to do one's —,** fare il proprio dovere; **to enter upon one's duties,** entrare in funzione; (*Comm.*) **— free,** franco di dazio; **— paid,** sdoganato.
duumvir [du:'ʌmvəɹ], *n.* (*Hist.*) Duumviro, *m.*
dwarf [dwɔ:ɹf], *n.* Nano, *m.*, nana, *f.* || *v.t.* Rimpicciolire.
dwarfish, *a.* Nano, piccolo.
dwarfishness, *n.* Nanismo, *m.*, piccolezza, *f.*
dwell [dwel], *v.i.* Abitare, dimorare, soggiornare, risiedere. **To — on,** insistere su, soffermarsi su, pensare sempre a.
dweller, *n.* Abitante, residente, *m.f.*
dwelling, *n.* Dimora, residenza, abitazione, casa, *f.* **—-house,** casa d'abitazione, *f.*; **—-place,** domicilio, *m.*
dwindle ['dwindl], *v.i.* Diminuire, scemare, decrescere; affievolirsi, consumarsi.
dwindling, *n.* Deperimento, *m.*, diminuzione, *f.*
dyad ['daiəd], *n.* (*Chem.*) Coppia, *f.*, paio, *m.*
dye [dai], *v.t.* Tingere, colorire; *v.i.* tingersi. || *n.* Tintura, tinta, *f.*; colore, *m.*; (*fig.*) carattere, *m.*, natura, *f.* **To — black,** tingere di nero; **a villain of the deepest —,** un furfante di tre cotte; **— works,** tintoria, *f.*; **—-stuffs,** sostanze coloranti, *f.pl.*
dyeing, *n.* Tintura, *f.*
dyer, *n.* Tintore, *m.* **Dyers and cleaners,** tintori e smacchiatori, *m.pl.*; (*Bot.*) **dyer's broom,** ginestra dei tintori, *f.*
dying ['daiiŋ], *a.* Moribondo, morente; estremo, ultimo. **A — man,** morente, moribondo, *m.*; **the —,** i moribondi, *m.pl.*; **to be —,** essere moribondo, essere in agonia; **— wishes,** ultimi desideri, *m.pl.*; **— words,** ultime parole, *f.pl.*
dyke [cp. **dike**].
dynamic [dai'næmik], *a.* Dinamico.
dynamically, *adv.* Dinamicamente.
dynamics, *n.pl.* Dinamica, *f.*
dynamism, *n.* Dinamismo, *m.*
dynamite ['dainəmait], *n.* Dinamite, *f.*

dynamiter, *n.* Dinamitardo, *m.*
dynamo [ˈdainəmou], *n.* Dinamo, *f.* **Electric —,** dinamo elettrica, *f.*
dynamometer [dainəˈmɔmitəɹ], *n.* Dinamometro, *m.*
dynast [ˈdainəst], *n.* Dinasta, *m.*
dynastic, *a.* Dinastico.
dynasty, *n.* Dinastia, *f.*
dysenteric [disenˈterik], *a.* (*Med.*) Dissenterico.
dysentery, *n.* Dissenteria, *f.*
dyspepsia, dyspepsy, *n.* (*Med.*) Dispepsia, *f.*
dyspeptic, *a.* Dispeptico.
dyspnoea [dispˈniːə], *n.* (*Med.*) Dispnea, *f.*
dysuria, dysury [disˈjuːriə, ˈdisjuːri], *n.* (*Med.*) Dissuria, *f.*

E

E, e [iː]. Quinta lettera dell'alfabeto inglese; (*Mus.*) mi, *m.*; *e.g.*, per esempio.
each [iːtʃ], *a.* Ciascuno, ognuno, ogni. || *pron.* Ciascuno, ognuno, ciascheduno, *m.*, ciascuna, ognuna, ciascheduna, *f.* **— other,** l'uno l'altro, gli uni gli altri; **for — other,** l'uno per l'altro, gli uni per gli altri; **they hate — other,** si odiano l'un l'altro; **give us a book each,** dateci un libro a testa.
eager [ˈiːgəɹ], *a.* Desideroso, bramoso, avido; vivo, ardente; impaziente, impetuoso; sollecito, premuroso.
eagerly, *adv.* Ardentemente, avidamente.
eagerness, *n.* Ardore, zelo, impeto, *m.*, brama, avidità, *f.*; vivacità, impazienza, *f.*
eagle [ˈiːgl], *n.* (*Zool.*) Aquila, *f.*; (*standard*) aquila, *f.*
eaglet, *n.* Aquilotto, *m.*
eagre [ˈiːgəɹ], *n.* Maroso, flutto della marea, *m.*
ear [iəɹ], *n.* (*Anat.*) Orecchio, *m.*; (*of corn*) spiga, *f.*; (*of jug, etc.*) ansa, *f.* **All ears,** tutt'orecchi; **over head and ears,** fin sopra i capelli; **an — for music,** un orecchio musicale, *m.*; **to prick up one's ears,** drizzare gli orecchi, tender l'orecchio; **to set by the ears,** aizzare; **to turn a deaf —,** far orecchio da mercante; **up to the ears,** fino agli orecchi; **to have someone's —,** avere entratura presso; **to give —,** dare orecchio; **to play by —,** suonare a orecchio; **—-ache,** mal d'orecchio, *m.*; **—-drop,** orecchino, *m.*; **—-drum,** (*Anat.*) timpano, *m.*; **to —-mark,** marcare all'angolo, contrassegnare; **—-phones,** cuffia, *f.*; **—-piece,** telefono, *m.*; **—-ring,** orecchino, *m.*; **within —-shot,** a portata d'orecchio; **—-trumpet,** cornetto acustico, *m.*; **—-wax,** cerume, *m.*
eared, *a.* Con orecchi, auricolato. (*of corn*) **Full- —,** con spighe grosse.
earl [əːɹl], *n.* Conte, *m.* **—-marshal,** conte maresciallo, *m.*
earldom, *n.* Contea, *f.*
earliest [ˈəːɹliəst], *a.* Il più antico, il più remoto; primissimo, prestissimo. **At your — convenience,** con cortese sollecitudine.
earliness, *n.* Prestezza, mattutinità, *f.*; ora poco avanzata, *f.*; (*of fruits, etc.*) precocità, *f.*
early, *a.* Mattutino; mattiniero, sollecito; primo, antico; precoce; (*of fruit, etc.*) primaticcio; presto, di buon'ora. *adv.* Presto, di buon'ora, di buon mattino, per tempo. **— morning tea,** il tè del mattino; **not earlier than,** non prima di; **— age,** tenera età, *f.*; **— ages,** tempi antichi, *m.pl.*; **the Early Church,** la Chiesa primitiva, *f.*; **an — visit,** una visita di buon'ora, *f.*; **to keep — hours,** andare presto a letto; **to be an — riser,** essere mattiniero, levarsi di buon mattino.
earn [əːɹn], *v.t.* Guadagnare, meritare, ottenere.
earnest [ˈəːɹnest], *a.* Zelante, serio, sincero, sollecito; ardente, caloroso. || *n.* Pegno, *m.*, caparra, garanzia, *f.* **— money,** caparra, *f.*; **Are you in —?** Parlate sinceramente? **in good —,** in buon fede, sul serio; **to be in —,** essere serio, fare sul serio.
earnestly, *adv.* Vivamente, seriamente, sinceramente; ardentemente.
earnestness, *n.* Fervore, zelo, *m.*, serietà, *f.*; attenzione, sollecitudine, diligenza, *f.*; premure, *f.pl.*
earnings, *n.pl.* Guadagno, *m.*, guadagni, *m.pl.*; salario, stipendio, *m.*; (*Comm.*) entrata, *f.*, profitto, *m.*
earth [əːɹθ], *n.* Terra, *f.*; terreno, suolo, *m.*; (*fox's*) tana, *f.*; (*the globe*) il mondo, *m.* || *v.t.* (*Agric.*) Interrare, coprire di terra, rincalzare; (*Elect.*) mettere a terra. **Mother —,** la madre terra, *f.*; **nothing on —,** niente al mondo; **Why on — did you do that?** Perchè mai avete fatto ciò? (*Elect.*) **— connection,** presa di terra, *f.*
earthborn, *a.* Mortale.
earthbound, *a.* Attaccato alle cose terrene.
earthen, *a.* Terreo; di terra, di argilla.
earthenware, *n.* Terraglie, stoviglie, *f.pl.*
earthiness, *n.* Terreità, *f.*
earthliness, *n.* Mondanità, terrestrità, *f.*
earthly, *a.* Terrestre, terreno, mondano. **—-minded,** mondano; **— mindedness,** mondanità, *f.*
earthquake, *n.* Terremoto, *m.*
earthwork, *n.* Terrapieno, *m.*
earthworm, *n.* Verme di terra, lombrico, *m.*
earthy, *a.* Terroso, di terra, coperto di terra; (*fig.*) grossolano.
earwig [ˈiəɹwig], *n.* (*Zool.*) Forfecchia, *f.*
ease [iːz], *n.* Agio, comodo, *m.*; quiete, riposo, *m.*; tranquillità, agiatezza, *f.*; disinvoltura, *f.*; facilità, *f.*; (*of pain*) sollievo, *m.* || *v.t.* Sollevare, alleviare; addolcire, lenire; sgravare; (*Naut.*) allentare. **At —,** ad agio; **ill at —,** inquieto; **to be at —,** star comodo; **Stand at —!** Riposo! **to take one's —,** mettersi a proprio agio; **with —,** facilmente, comodamente; **to — someone's mind,** calmare qualcuno; (*Naut.*) **— her!** Rallentate; **to — off,** mollare, allentare; **to — off** (*from doing something*), diminuire, alleggerire.
easel [iːzl], *n.* Cavalletto, *m.*
easement, *n.* Sollievo, *m.*; (*Law*) servitù, *f.*
easily [ˈiːzili], *adv.* Facilmente, agevolmente, senza pena. **He takes things —,** prende il mondo come viene.
easiness, *n.* Facilità, agevolezza, *f.*; bontà, dolcezza, *f.*
easing, *n.* Sollievo, alleviamento, *m.*
east [iːst], *n.* Est, oriente, levante, *m.* || *a.* D'est, d'oriente, di levante, orientale. **The Far East,** L'Estremo Oriente, *m.*; **— wind,**

vento d'est, vento di levante, *m.*; **the East Indies,** le Indie orientali, *f.pl.*

Easter ['i:stəɹ], *n.* Pasqua, *f.* — **day,** il giorno di Pasqua, *m.*; — **Eve,** il sabato santo, *m.*; — **-tide,** il tempo pasquale, *m.*; — **-egg,** uovo pasquale, *m.*

easterly, *a.* D'est, dell'est. || *adv.* Verso l'est, verso l'oriente, ad est.

eastern, *a.* Orientale, dell'est, situato ad est. **The Eastern Question,** la questione orientale, *f.*

eastward, *adv.* All'est, verso oriente, verso levante.

easy ['i:zi], *a.* Facile, agevole; tranquillo, calmo; gentile, compiacente; a suo agio; (*Comm.*) modico, moderato. || *adv.* Piano, con calma. **By — stages,** a piccole tappe; — **of belief,** credulo; — **manners,** maniere urbane, *f.pl.*; **I'm quite — on that score,** sono tranquillo a tal riguardo; **it's as — as possible,** è facilissimo; **to make oneself — about,** tranquillarsi su; **to take it —,** prendersela comodamente; **in — circumstances,** agiato, benestante; — **to get on with,** simpatico; — **-chair,** poltrona, *f.*; — **-going,** compiacente; indolente, incurante; facilone.

eat [i:t], *v.t.i.* Mangiare; rodere, smangiare; corrodere. **To — a good dinner,** mangiare bene; **to — away,** consumare, rodere; **to — up,** divorare; **to — one's words,** rimangiarsi le proprie parole, disdirsi; **to — one's heart out,** rodersi il cuore; **rust eats into iron,** la ruggine smangia il ferro; **eaten up by pride,** roso dall'orgoglio.

eatable, *a.* Mangiabile, mangereccio, commestibile. || *n.* Commestibile, *m.* **Eatables,** vivande, *f.pl.*, viveri, *m.pl.*

eater, *n.* Mangiatore, divoratore, *m.*, mangiatrice, divoratrice, *f.* **A great —,** una buona bocca, una buona forchetta, *f.*

eating, *n.* Il mangiare, *m.* — **and drinking,** il bere ed il mangiare; — **-house,** ristorante, *m.*, trattoria, *f.*; — **apples,** mele da tavola, *f.pl.*

eaves [i:vz], *n.pl.* Grondaia, *f.*

eavesdrop, *v.i.* Origliare, ascoltare segretamente.

eavesdropper, *n.* Spione, *m.*; che origlia alla porta. **Eavesdroppers hear no good of themselves,** chi sta in ascolteria sente cose che non vorria.

ebb [eb], *v.i.* Rifluire; (*fig.*) abbassarsi, declinare. || *n.* Riflusso, *m.*; (*fig.*) decadenza, *f.* **To — and flow,** fluire e rifluire; **at a low —,** molto basso; — **tide,** bassa marea, *f.*; **the — and flow,** il flusso e il riflusso, *m.*

ebbing, *a.* Rifluente; (*fig.*) in declino, in ribasso.

ebonite, *n.* Ebanite, *f.*

ebonize, *v.t.* Rendere nero come ebano.

ebony, *n.* Ebano, *m.* || *a.* D'ebano.

ebriety, *n.* Ebbrezza, ubbriachezza, *f.*

ebullience, *n.* Ebollizione, *f.*

ebullient, *a.* Bollente.

ebullition, *n.* Ebollizione, *f.*; (*fig.*) trasporto, accesso, *m.*

eccentric [ek'sentrik], *a.* Eccentrico; (*fig.*) stravagante, cervellotico. || *n.* Eccentrico, originale, *m.*; (*Mech.*) ingranaggio eccentrico, *m.*

eccentricity, *n.* Eccentricità, *f.*

Ecclesiastes [ekli:zi'æsti:z], *n.* L'Ecclesiaste, *m.*

ecclesiastic, *a.* Ecclesiastico. || *n.* Ecclesiastico, prete, sacerdote, *m.*

ecclesiastical, *a.* Ecclesiastico.

ecclesiastically, *adv.* Ecclesiasticamente.

echelon ['eʃəlɔn], *n.* (*Mil.*) Scaglione, *m.*

echinus [e'kainəs], *n.* (*Zool.*) Echino, riccio, *m.*

echo ['ekou], *n.* Eco, *m.f.* || *v.i.* Echeggiare, fare eco, risuonare; *v.t.* ripetere.

eclat [ek'lɑ:], *n.* Splendore, *m.*, pompa, *f.*

eclectic [ek'lektik], *n.a.* Eclettico, *m.*

eclecticism, *n.* Eclettismo, *m.*

eclipse [e'klips], *n.* Eclisse, *m.* || *v.t.* Eclissare; (*fig.*) sorpassare; *v.i.* eclissarsi.

ecliptic [e'kliptik], *n.* (*Astron.*) Eclittica, *f.* || *a.* Eclittico.

eclogue ['eklɔg], *n.* (*Poet.*) Egloga, *f.*

economic, economical [i:kə'nɔmik, i:kə'nɔmikəl], *a.* (*of things*) Economico; (*of persons*) economo, frugale.

economically, *adv.* Economicamente.

economics, *n.pl.* Economia, *f.* **Professor of —,** professore d'economia, *m.*

economist [e'kɔnəmist], *n.* Economista, *m.* **Political —,** scrittore di economia politica, *m.*

economize, *v.t.* Economizzare, risparmiare; *v.i.* fare economia.

economy [e'kɔnəmi], *n.* Economia, *f.* — **of Nature,** sistema delle leggi naturali, *f.*

ecstasy ['ekstəsi], *n.* Estasi, *f.*; rapimento, trasporto, *m.* **To go into ecstasies,** estasiarsi, andare in estasi.

ecstatic, ecstatical, *a.* Estatico.

ecumenical [i:kju:'menikəl], *a.* Ecumenico.

eczema ['ekzəmə], *n.* (*Med.*) Eczema, *m.*

edacious [e'deiʃəs], *a.* Edace.

edacity [e'dæsiti], *n.* Edacità, *f.*

eddy ['edi], *n.* Risucchio, vortice, turbine, *m.* || *v.i.* Turbinare, risucchiare, mulinare.

edelweiss ['eidəlvais], *n.* (*Bot.*) Stella alpina, *f.*

Eden ['i:dən], *n.* Eden, *m.* **The Garden of —,** l'Eden, il paradiso terrestre, *m.*

edentate [e'denteit], *n.a.* (*Zool.*) Sdentato, *m.*

edge [edʒ], *n.* Orlo, margine, limite, *m.*; sponda, estremità, *f.* (*of blade*) filo, taglio, *m.*; acutezza, acrimonia, *f.* || *v.t.* Orlare; arrotare, affilare; *v.i.* avanzare obliquamente, muoversi obliquamente. **To put to the — of the sword,** mettere a fil di spada; **to set one's teeth on —,** allegare i denti; **to take off the —,** smussare, rintuzzare; **to take the — off one's appetite,** calmare l'appetito; **to set on —,** irritare; **with gilt edges,** con taglio dorato; (*Naut.*) **to — away,** allontanarsi, filar via; **to — in,** infilarsi in; **to — one's way,** farsi luogo; — **-tool,** strumento tagliente, *m.*, arma a doppio taglio, *f.*; **to play with edged tools,** giuocare col fuoco.

edged, *a.* Orlato; arrotato, affilato.

edgeways, edgewise, *adv.* Di sbieco, di traverso, di costa, di lato, da canto.

edging, *n.* Orlo, bordo, *m.*, guarnizione, frangia, bordatura, *f.*

edible ['edibl], *a.* Mangiabile, mangereccio, commestibile.

edict ['i:dikt], *n.* Editto, proclama, *m.*

edification [edifi'keiʃən], *n.* Edificazione, *f.*, conforto, *m.*

edifice ['edifis], *n.* Edificio, edifizio, *m.*

edify ['edifai], *v.t.* Edificare.

edifying, *a.* Edificante.
edit ['edit], *v.t.* (*a newspaper*) Dirigere; redigere, pubblicare, curare. **Edited by,** a cura di; **to — a book,** curare l'edizione di un libro.
edition, *n.* Edizione, *f.* **School —,** edizione scolastica, *f.*
editor, *n.* (*of a journal*) Direttore, *m.*; (*of book, magazine, etc.*) redattore, *m.*
editorial, *a.* Editoriale, del direttore. || *n.* Articolo di fondo, articolo editoriale, **— staff,** redazione, *f.*
editorship, *n.* Direzione, *f.*
editress, *n.* Direttrice, redattrice, *f.*
educate ['edju:keit], *v.t.* Educare; affinare, ingentilire; istruire.
educated, *a.* Istruito, educato.
education, *n.* Educazione, cultura, istruzione, *f.*, insegnamento, *m.*
educational, *a.* Educativo, scolastico.
educator, *n.* Educatore, maestro, *m.*, educatrice, *f.*; pedagogo, *m.*
educe [e'dju:s], *v.t.* Condurre fuori, estrarre.
eduction, *n.* Estrazione, *f.*
edulcorate [e'dʌlkəreit], *v.t.* (*Chem.*) Dolcificare.
eel [i:l], *n.* (*Zool.*) Anguilla, *f.* **— -pot,** nassa, *f.*; **— -fishing,** pesca dell'anguilla, *f.*
eerie, eery ['iəri], *a.* Misterioso; lugubre, fantastico.
eeriness, *n.* Stranezza, *f.*
efface [e'feis], *v.t.* Cancellare, far scomparire; obliterare.
effaceable, *a.* Cancellabile.
effacement, *n.* Cancellatura, obliterazione, *f.*
effect [e'fekt], *n.* Effetto, risultato, scopo, *m.*; efficacia, *f.* || *v.t.* Effettuare, compiere, eseguire. **For —,** per fare effetto; **in —,** in realtà; **of no —,** inefficace, inutile; **to carry into —,** mandare ad effetto, eseguire; **to give — to,** dare esecuzione a; **to no —,** senza effetto, senza risultato; **to take —,** avere effetto, avere efficacia giuridica; **effects,** effetti, beni, mobili, *m.pl.*, roba, *f.*
effective, *a.* Efficente, efficace.
effectively, *adv.* Efficacemente.
effectless, *a.* Inutile, inefficace.
effectual, *a.* Efficace.
effectually, *adv.* Effettualmente.
effectuate [e'fektju:eit], *v.t.* Effettuare.
effectuation, *n.* Effettuazione, *f.*
effeminacy, effeminateness, *n.* Effeminatezza, *f.*
effeminate, *a.* Effeminato.
effeminately, *adv.* Effeminatamente.
effeminize, *v.t.* Effeminare.
effervesce [efəɹ'ves], *v.i.* Fermentare, spumare, bollire; (*fig.*) sfogarsi.
effervescence, *n.* Effervescenza, *f.*
effervescent, effervescing, *a.* Effervescente, gassoso.
effete [e'fi:t], *a.* Logoro, sterile, indebolito, stracco; usato, vecchio.
efficacious [efi'keiʃəs], *a.* Efficace.
efficaciously, *adv.* Efficacemente.
efficacy ['efikəsi], *n.* Efficacia, *f.*
efficiency [e'fiʃənsi], *n.* Efficenza, *f.*; (*Mech.*) rendimento, *m.*
efficient, *a.* Efficiente; (*of remedies*) efficace; (*of persons*) abile.
efficiently, *adv.* Efficientemente, abilmente.
effigy ['efidʒi], *n.* Effigie, *f.*
effloresce [eflɔ'res], *v.i.* Fiorire, schiudersi.
efflorescence, *n.* (*Chem.*) Efflorescenza, *f.*; (*Bot.*) fioritura, *f.*
efflorescent, *a.* Fiorente; (*Chem.Bot.*) efflorescente.
effluence ['eflu:əns], *n.* Emanazione, *f.*, efflusso, *m.*
effluent, *a.* Defluente.
effluvium (*pl.* **effluvia**) [e'flu:viəm], *n.* Effluvio, *m.*
efflux [ef'lʌks], *n.* Efflusso, flusso, *m.*, effusione, *f.*
effort ['efəɹt], *n.* Sforzo, *m.* **It is a great — for me,** mi costa molta fatica; **to use every —,** fare tutti gli sforzi; **to make a great —,** durare fatica.
effortless, *a.* Facile, senza sforzo.
effrontery [e'frʌntəri], *n.* Sfrontatezza, audacia, *f.*
effulgence [e'fʌldʒens], *n.* Lustro, splendere, *m.*
effulgent, *a.* Risplendente, lucente.
effulgently, *adv.* Lucentemente.
effuse [e'fju:z], *v.t.* Spargere, versare, effondere.
effusion, *n.* Effusione, *f.*; versamento, *m.*
effusive, *a.* Espansivo, effusivo.
effusiveness, *n.* Effusione, *f.*; espansività, *f.*
eft [eft], *n.* (*Zool.*) Ramarro d'acqua, *m.*, salamandra acquatica, *f.*; tritone, *m.*
egad! [i'gæd], *inter.* Perbacco! In fede mia!
egg (1) [eg], *n.* Uovo, *m.* **Hard-boiled —,** uovo sodo, *m.*; **new-laid —,** uovo fresco, *m.*; **poached eggs,** uova in camicia, *f.pl.*; **scrambled eggs,** uova strapazzate, *f.pl.*; **to lay eggs,** fare uova; **— -cup,** portauovo, *m.*; **— -flip,** zabaione, *m.*; **— -plant,** melanzana, *f.*; **— -shaped,** ovale; **— -shell,** guscio d'uovo, *m.*
egg (2), *v.t.* **To — on,** incitare, stimolare, istigare.
eglantine ['egləntain], *n.* (*Bot.*) Rosa canina, *f.*
ego ['egou], *n.* Io, *m.*
egoism, *n.* Egoismo, *m.*
egoist, *n.* Egoista, *m.*
egoistic, egoistical, *a.* Egoistico.
egotism, *n.* Egotismo, *m.*; autoesaltazione, *f.*
egotist, *n.* Egotista, vanitoso, *m.*
egotistic, egotistical, *a.* Egotistico, presuntuoso.
egregious [i'gri:dʒəs], *a.* (*facet.*) Enorme, solenne; egregio, distinto, insigne.
egregiously, *adv.* Egregiamente.
egregiousness, *n.* Eccellenza, elevatezza, *f.*; enormità, *f.*
egress ['i:gres], *n.* Uscita, *f.*, egresso, *m.*
egret ['i:gret], *n.* (*Zool.*) Airone, *m.*; (*tuft*) piumino, pennacchio, ciuffo, *m.*
Egypt ['i:dʒipt], *n.* (*Geog.*) L'Egitto, *m.*
Egyptian [i'dʒipʃən], *n.a.* Egiziano, *m.*
Egyptologist [i:dʒip'tɔlɔdʒist], *n.* Egittologo, *m.*
Egyptology, *n.* Egittologia, *f.*
eh, *inter.* Eh, che, dunque.
eider, eider duck ['aidəɹ, 'aidəɹdʌk], *n.* (*Zool.*) Anitra edredone, *f.* **— down,** piumino, *m.*, peluria, *f.*
eight [eit], *n.a.* Otto, *m.*
eighteen, *n.a.* Diciotto, *m.*
eighteenth, *n.a.* Diciottesimo, *m.*
eightfold, *a.* Ottuplo. || *adv.* Otto volte.
eighth ['eitθ], *n.a.* Ottavo, *m.*

eighthly, *adv.* In ottavo luogo.
eightieth, *n.a.* Ottantesimo, *m.*
eighty, *n.a.* Ottanta, *m.*
either [ˈaiðəɹ], *pron.* L'uno o l'altro, *m.*, l'una o l'altra, *f.*; ciascuno, *m.*, ciascuna, *f.*; tutti e due, *m.pl.* || *adv.* Anche; neanche, nemmeno, neppure. || *conj.* O, ovvero. **I don't expect — of them,** non aspetto nè l'uno nè l'altro; **on — side,** da tutte e due le parti; **nor I —,** neanche io; **he doesn't know it —,** non lo sa neppure lui; **he — knows it or he doesn't,** o egli lo sa o non lo sa; **— way,** in ogni modo.
ejaculate [eˈdʒækju:leit], *v.t.* Esclamare, gridare; (*fluid*) emettere.
ejaculation, *n.* Esclamazione, *f.*; (*fluid*) emissione, *f.*
ejaculatory, *a.* Giaculatorio.
eject [eˈdʒekt], *v.t.* Espellere, cacciar fuori, scacciare; (*Mech.*) eiettare; (*Law*) sfrattare.
ejection, ejectment, *n.* Espulsione, cacciata, *f.*; (*Law*) sfratto, *m.*; (*Med.*) eiezione, *f.*
ejector, *n.* Espulsore, estrattore, *m.*; (*Law*) usciere, *m.*
eke (1) [i:k], *v.t.* **To — out,** aumentare, supplire, compiere. **To — out a living,** riuscire a buscarsi il pane; sbarcare il lunario.
eke (2), *adv.* Anche.
elaborate [eˈlæbərit], *a.* Elaborato; accurato, minuzioso. || *v.t.* Elaborare, affinare; evolvere.
elaborately, *adv.* Laboriosamente, con tutta cura.
elaborateness, *n.* Elaboratezza, finezza, *f.*
elaboration, *n.* Elaborazione, *f.*
eland [ˈelənd], *n.* (*Zool.*) Alce del Capo, *m.*
elapse [eˈlæps], *v.i.* Passare, scorrere, decorrere.
elastic [eˈlæstik], *a.* Elastico. || *n.* Elastico, *m.*, gomma, *f.* **— band,** elastico, *m.*, fascia elastica, *f.*
elasticity [elæsˈtisiti], *n.* Elasticità, *f.*
elate [eˈleit], *v.t.* Esaltare, entusiasmare, rallegrare, animare.
elated, *a.* Esaltato, allegro, esultante, imbaldanzito, giubilante.
elatedly, *adv.* Con gioia, con giubilo.
elation, *n.* Esultanza, *f.*, trasporto, *m.*, allegria, *f.*
Elba [ˈelbə], *n.* (*Geog.*) Elba, *f.*
Elbe [ˈelbə], *n.* (*Geog.*) Elba, *f.*
elbow [ˈelbou], *n.* Gomito, *m.*; (*of chair*) bracciuolo, *m.* || *v.t.* Dare gomitate a. **At one's —,** a portata di mano, vicino; **out at elbow,** logoro; **to lean one's — on,** appoggiare il gomito su, **to push with the —,** urtare col gomito; **up to the elbows,** fino ai gomiti; **to — one's way,** farsi strada a furia di gomitate; **—-room,** agio, spazio, *m.*; **—-grease,** (*fig.*) olio di gomito, *m.*
eld [eld], *n.* (*obs. Lit.*) Vecchiaia, *f.*; passato, *m.*
elder (1) [ˈeldəɹ], *n.* (*Bot.*) Sambuco, *m.* **—-berry,** grana di sambuco, bacca di sambuco, *f.*; **—-flower,** fiore di sambuco, *m.*
elder (2), *a.* Più vecchio, maggiore; anziano. || *n.* Anziano, *m.* **Our elders,** i nostri maggiori, *m.pl.*
elderly, *adv.* Attempato, d'una certa età.
eldership, *n.* Anzianità, *f.*
eldest, *n.a.* Il più vecchio, il maggiore, il primogenito, *m.*
elecampane [ˈelikəmpein], *n.* (*Bot.*) Enula campana, *f.*
elect [eˈlekt], *v.t.* Eleggere, scegliere, nominare; *v.i.* decidersi di. || *a.* Eletto, scelto, nominato, || *n.pl.* Gli eletti, *m.pl.*
election, *n.* Elezione, scelta, *f.* **General —,** elezioni generali, *f.pl.*; **— agent,** galoppino elettorale, agente elettorale, *m.*
electioneer [elekʃəˈniəɹ], *v.i.* Sollecitare voti.
electioneering, *n.* Manovre elettorali, *f.pl.*
elective, *a.* Elettivo ; (*Am.*) facoltativo.
elector, *n.* Elettore, *m.*, elettrice, *f.*
electoral, *a.* Elettorale.
electorate, *n.* Elettorato, *m.*, gli elettori, *m.pl.*
electress, *n.* (*Hist.*) Elettrice, *f.*
electric [eˈlektrik], *a.* Elettrico. **— bell,** campanello elettrico, *m.*; **— radiator,** radiatore elettrico, *m.*; **— eel,** ginnoto, *m.*; **— shock,** scossa elettrica, *f.*; **— sign,** insegna luminosa, *f.*; **— torch,** lampada tascabile, *f.*
electrical, *a.* Elettrico. **— engineer,** ingegnere elettrotecnico, *m.*
electrically, *adv.* Elettricamente.
electrician [elekˈtriʃən], *n.* Elettricista, *m.*
electricity [elekˈtrisiti], *n.* Elettricità, *f.*
electrification [elektrifiˈkeiʃən], *n.* Elettrificazione, *f.*
electrify, *v.t.* Elettrificare; elettrizzare.
electro [cp. **electrotype**].
electrochemistry, *n.* Elettrochimica, *f.*
electrocute [eˈlektrokju:t], *v.t.* Fulminare; (*Law*) giustiziare con la sedia elettrica.
electrocution, *n.* Elettroesecuzione, *f.*, la sedia elettrica, *f.*
electrode [eˈlektroud], *n.* Elettrodo, *m.*
electro-dynamic, *a.* Elettrodinamico.
electro-dynamics, *n.* Elettrodinamica, *f.*
electrograph, *n.* Elettrografo, *m.*
electrolier [elektrəˈliəɹ], *n.* Lampadario a luce elettrica, *m.*
electrolysis [elekˈtrɔlisis], *n.* Elettrolisi, *f.*
electromagnet [elektrouˈmægnit], *n.* Elettromagnete, *m.*
electromagnetic, *a.* Elettromagnetico.
electron [eˈlektrɔn], *n.* Elettrone, *m.*
electroplate, *n.* Placcato, *m.* || *v.t.* Placcare.
electroscope, *n.* Elettroscopio, *m.*
electrostatics, *n.* Elettrostatica, *f.*
electrotherapy, *n.* (*Med.*) Elettroterapia, *f.*
electrotype, *n.* Elettrotipia, *f.*
electuary [eˈlektju:əɹi], *n.* (*Med.*) Elettuario, *m.*
eleemosinary [eləi:ˈmɔzinəri], *a.* Di elemosina, caritatevole.
elegance [ˈeligəns], *n.* Eleganza, *f.*
elegant, *a.* Elegante, fino. || *n.* Zerbinotto, bellimbusto, *m.*
elegantly, *adv.* Elegantemente.
elegiac [eliˈdʒaiək], *a.* (*Poet.*) Elegiaco. || *n.* Verso elegiaco, *m.*
elegist, *n.* Poeta elegiaco, *m.*
elegy, *n.* Elegia, *f.*
element [ˈelimənt], *n.* Elemento, fattore, *m.*; (*Chem.*) elemento, corpo semplice, *m.* **Elements,** rudimenti, *m.pl.*
elemental, *a.* Fondamentale.
elementary, *a.* Elementare; (*school*) primario.
elephant [ˈelifənt], *n.* (*Zool.*) Elefante, *m.* **A white —,** una cosa che dà più imbarazzo che non valga.

elephantiasis [elifən'taiəsis], *n.* (*Med.*) Elefantiasi, *f.*
elephantine [ele'fæntain], *a.* Elefantino; mastodontico.
elevate ['eliveit], *v.t.* Elevare, innalzare; (*fig.*) esaltare, ecitare.
elevated, *a.* Elevato.
elevation, *n.* Elevazione, *f.*; altezza, altitudine, altura, *f.*
elevator, *n.* Elevatore, montacarico, *m.*; (*lift*) ascensore, *m.*; (*Anat.*) elevatorio, *m.*
eleven [e'levən], *n.a.* Undici, *m.*
eleventh, *n.a.* Undecimo, undicesimo, decimo primo, *m.*
elf (pl. **elves**) [elf, elvz], *n.* Elfo, folletto, *m.*, fata, *f.* **—-child,** bambino sostituito dalle fate, *m.*; **—-lock,** riccio a nodo, *m.*
elfin, *a.* D'elfo, di folletto, incantato.
elfish, elvish, *a.* Di folletto, di fata.
elicit [e'lisit], *v.t.* Trarre fuori, far uscire, evocare, fare confessare. **To — an answer,** ottenere una risposta.
elide [e'laid], *v.t.* (*Gram.*) Elidere, sopprimere.
eligibility [elidʒə'biliti], *n.* Eleggibilità, *f.*
eligible ['elidʒəbl], *a.* Eleggibile; conveniente, vantaggioso. **An — match,** un partito vantaggioso, *m.*
eligibly, *adv.* Vantaggiosamente.
eliminate [e'limineit], *v.t.* Eliminare, togliere, scartare.
eliminating, *a.* Eliminatore.
elimination, *n.* Eliminazione, *f.*
elision [e'liʒən], *n.* (*Gram.*) Elisione, *f.*
elixir [e'likzəɹ], *n.* Elisir, *m.*
Elizabeth [e'lizəbeθ], *n.* Elisabetta, *f.*
Elizabethan [elizə'bi:θən], *a.* Elisabettiano.
elk [elk], *n.* (*Zool.*) Alce, *m.*
ellipse [e'lips], *n.* (*Geom.*) Elisse, *f.*
ellipsis (*pl.* **ellipses**), *n.* (*Gram.*) Elissi, ellissi, *f.*
ellipsoid [e'lipsɔid], *n.* Elissoide, *m.*
elliptic, elliptical, *a.* Elittico, ellittico.
elliptically, *adv.* Elitticamente, ellitticamente.
elm [elm], *n.* (*Bot.*) Olmo, *m.* **—-grove,** olmeto, *m.*; **row of elms,** olmaia, *f.*
elocution [elo'kju:ʃən], *n.* Elocuzione, *f.*
elocutionist, *n.* Professore di recitazione, *m.*; declamatore, dicitore, *m.*
elongate ['elɔŋgeit], *v.t.* Allungare, prolungare.
elongated, *a.* Allungato.
elongation, *n.* Allungamento, prolungamento, *m.*; (*Astron.*) elongazione, *f.*
elope [e'loup], *v.i.* Fuggire. **To — with,** fuggire con, farsi rapire da.
elopement, *n.* Fuga, *f.*
eloquence ['elokwəns], *n.* Eloquenza, *f.*
eloquent, *a.* Eloquente.
eloquently, *adv.* Eloquentemente.
else [els], *adv.* Altrimenti, oppure, altro, di più; se non. **Everybody —,** tutti gli altri; **everything —,** ogni altra cosa; **everywhere —,** in ogni altro luogo; **nobody —,** nessun altro; **nothing —,** niente di più. nient'altro; **nowhere —,** in nessun altro luogo; **something —,** qualchecos'altro; **What — ?** Che altro? **Where — ?** Dove altro? **Who — ?** Chi ancora?, Chi altro?
elsewhere, *adv.* Altrove, in altro luogo, in altra parte.
elucidate [e'lu:sideit], *v.t.* Elucidare, spiegare, chiarire.
elucidation, *n.* Spiegazione, *f.*; schiarimento, *m.*
elude [e'lju:d], *v.t.* Eludere, schivare, sfuggire a.
elusion, *n.* Elusione, *f.*
elusive, *a.* Elusivo, sfuggente, fuggevole; ingannevole.
elusiveness, *n.* Ingannevolezza, *f.*
Elysian [e'liziən], *a.* Elisio. **The — Fields,** I Campi Elisi, *m.pl.*
Elysium, *n.* Elisio, *m.*
emaciate [e'meiʃieit], *v.i.* Dimagrare.
emaciated, *a.* Emaciato, dimagrato, emunto. **To grow —,** emaciarsi, deperire.
emaciation, *n.* Emaciazione, *f.*, deperimento, *m.*
emanate ['eməneit], *v.i.* Emanare, provenire.
emanation, *n.* Emanazione, *f.*
emancipate [i'mænsipeit], *v.t.* Emancipare, liberare.
emancipated, *a.* Emancipato.
emancipation, *n.* Emancipazione, *f.*
emasculate [i'mæskjuleit], *v.t.* Evirare, castrare; (*fig.*) infiacchire, effeminare. || *a.* Castrato; (*fig.*) effeminato.
emasculation, *n.* Castrazione, *f.*; (*fig.*) effeminatezza, debolezza, *f.*
embalm [em'bɑ:m], *v.t.* Imbalsamare.
embalmer, *n.* Imbalsamatore, *m.*
embalming, *n.* Imbalsamazione, *f.*
embank [em'bæŋk], *v.t.* Incanalare, arginare, digare.
embankment, *n.* Diga, *f.*, argine, *m.*; banchina, *f.*, terrapieno, *m.* **The Thames Embankment,** il Lungo Tamigi, *m.*
embargo [em'bɑ:ɹgou], *n.* Embargo, *m.* **To impose an — on,** metter l'embargo su.
embark [em'bɑ:ɹk], *v.t.* Imbarcare; *v.i.* imbarcarsi; (*fig.*) impegnarsi.
embarkation, *n.* Imbarco, *m.*
embarrass [em'bærəs], *v.t.* Imbarazzare, impacciare, impedire.
embarrassing, *a.* Imbarazzante.
embarrassingly, *adv.* In modo imbarazzante.
embarrassment, *n.* Imbarazzo, impiccio, *m.*; difficoltà, perplessità, *f.*
embassy ['embəsi], *n.* Ambasciata, *f.*; ambasceria, *f.*
embattle, *v.t.* (*Mil.*) Schierare in ordine di battaglia; (*Arch.*) merlare, munire di parapetti merlati.
embattled, *a.* (*Arch.*) Merlato.
embattlement [cp. **battlement**].
embed, imbed [em'bed], *v.t.* Incastonare, ficcare, piantare.
embellish [em'beliʃ], *v.t.* Abbellire, ornare, decorare.
embellishment, *n.* Abbellimento, ornamento, *m.*; (*Mus.*) fiore, *m.*
ember ['embəɹ], *n.* Tizzone, *m.* **Embers,** ceneri calde, braci, *f.pl.*
ember-goose, *n.* (*Zool.*) Smergo maggiore, *m.*
Ember days, *n.pl.* (*Eccles.*) Quattro Tempora, *f.pl.*
embezzle [em'bezl], *v.t.* Malversare, truffare, appropriarsi frodolentemente.
embezzlement, *n.* Malversazione, truffa, appropriazione indebita, *f.*
embezzler, *n.* Malversatore, truffatore, *m.*
embitter [em'bitəɹ], *v.t.* Esacerbare, amareggiare, inasprire, esasperare.

embitterment, *n.* Inasprimento, *m.*
emblazon [em'bleizən], *v.t.* Blasonare; (*fig.*) pubblicare, proclamare.
emblem ['embləm], *n.* Emblema, *m.*
emblematic, emblematical, *a.* Emblematico.
emblematically, *adv.* Emblematicamente.
emblements, *n.pl.* (*Law*) Frutti sull'albero, *m.pl.*
embodiment [em'bɔdimənt], *n.* Personificazione, *f.*, incorporamento, *m.*
embody, *v.t.* Incorporare. **To — a clause,** incorporare una clausola.
embolden [em'bouldən], *v.t.* Incoraggiare, dare animo a.
embolism ['embolizm], *n.* (*Med.*) Embolia, *f.*; (*Astron.*) embolismo, *m.*
embosom [em'buzm], *v.t.* Abbracciare, avvolgere, cingere. **Embosomed in trees,** cinto di alberi.
emboss [em'bɔs], *v.t.* (*metal*) Incidere; intagliare; stampare.
embossed, *a.* A sbalzo, in rilievo. **— paper,** carta impressa, *f.*; **— postage stamp,** francobollo ad impressione, *m.*
embower [em'bauəɹ], *v.t.* Pergolare, coprir di fronde.
embrace [em'breis], *n.* Abbraccio, amplesso, *m.*, stretta, *f.* || *v.t.* Abbracciare, stringere, cingere; (*fig.*) afferrare, adottare; contenere. **To — the opportunity,** afferrare l'occasione.
embrocation [embrou'keiʃən], *n.* (*Med.*) Embrocazione, *f.*
embroider [em'brɔidəɹ], *v.t.* Ricamare; (*fig.*) esagerare.
embroiderer, *n.* Ricamatore, *m.*
embroideress, *n.* Ricamatrice, *f.*
embroidery, *n.* Ricamo, *m.* **—-frame,** telaio da ricamo, *m.*
embroil [em'brɔil], *v.t.* Imbrogliare, confondere, pasticciare.
embroilment, *n.* Imbroglio, *m.*, confusione, *f.*; pasticcio, *m.*
embryo ['embriou], *n.* Embrione, *m.* **In —,** in embrione; in erba.
embryo, embryonic, *a.* Embrionico.
embryologist, *n.* Embriologo, *m.*
embryology, *n.* Embriologia, *f.*
emend [e'mend], *v.t.* Emendare, correggere.
emendation, *n.* Emendazione, correzione, *f.*
emendator, *n.* Emendatore, correttore, *m.*
emerald ['emərəld], *n.* Smeraldo, *m.*
emerge [e'mə:ɹdʒ], *v.i.* Emergere, sorgere, apparire.
emergence, *n.* L'emergere, l'apparire, *m.*; emersione, *f.*
emergency, *n.* Emergenza, circostanza impreveduta, eventualità, crisi, *f.* **In an —,** in caso d'urgenza; **— brake,** freno di soccorso.
emergent, *a.* Emergente.
emeritus [e'meritəs], *a.* Emerito.
emersion, *n.* Emersione, *f.*
emery ['eməri], *n.* Smeriglio, *m.* **— paper,** carta smeriglio, *f.*; **— cloth,** tela smerigliata, *f.*
emetic [e'metik], *n.a.* (*Med.*) Emetico, *m.*
emigrant ['emigrənt], *n.* Emigrante, *m.f.*; emigrato, *m.*
emigrate, *v.i.* Emigrare.
emigration, *n.* Emigrazione, *f.* **— officer,** agente d'emigrazione, *m.*
eminence, eminency ['eminəns, 'eminənsi], *n.* Eminenza, collina, altura, *f.*; (*fig.*) celebrità, distinzione, *f.* **His Eminence,** Sua Eminenza, *f.*
eminent, *a.* Eminente, prominente, segnalato, celebre.
eminently, *adv.* Eminentemente, in alto grado.
emir ['emi:ɹ], *n.* Emiro, *m.*
emissary ['emisəri], *n.* Emissario, *m.*; spia, *f.*
emission [e'miʃən], *n.* Emissione, *f.*
emissive, *a.* Emissivo.
emit [e'mit], *v.t.* Emettere, esalare, emanare, lanciare.
emmet [cp. **ant**].
emollient [e'mɔliənt], *n.a.* (*Med.*) Emolliente, *m.*
emolument [e'mɔlju:mənt], *n.* Emolumento, salario, stipendio, *m.*; (*fig.*) profitto, guadagno, vantaggio, *m.*
emotion [e'mouʃən], *n.* Emozione, *f.*
emotional, *a.* Impressionabile, sensibile, emotivo.
emotionalism, *n.* Impressionabilità, *f.*
emotive [e'moutiv], *a.* Emotivo.
empale [cp. **impale**].
empanel [em'pænəl], *v.t.* (*Law*) Iscrivere nei giurati. **To — a jury,** formare la lista dei giurati.
emperor ['empərəɹ], *n.* Imperatore, *m.*
emphasis (*pl.* **emphases**) ['emfəsis, emfəsi:z], *n.* Enfasi, energia, efficacia, *f.* **To lay — upon,** Dare enfasi a.
emphasize ['emfəsaiz], *v.t.* Pronunciare con enfasi, dar rilievo a, accentuare, sottolineare.
emphatic [em'fætik], *a.* Enfatico, energico, vivo; (*fig.*) deciso, definito, risoluto.
emphatically, *adv.* Energicamente, nettamente.
emphysema [emfai'zi:mə], *n.* (*Med.*) Enfisema, *m.*
empire ['empaiɹ], *n.* Impero, *m.*; imperio, *m.*
empiric, empirical [em'pirik, em'pirikəl], *n.a.* Empirico, *m.*
empirically, *adv.* Empiricamente.
empiricism, *n.* Empirismo, *m.*
empiricist, *n.* Empirico, *m.*
emplacement [em'pleismənt], *n.* Appostamento, *m.*, postazione, *f.* **Machine-gun —,** postazione di mitragliatrice, *f.*
employ (1) [im'plɔi], *v.t.* Impiegare; adoperare, usare, utilizzare, valersi di. **To — a person,** impiegare una persona; **to — oneself in,** impiegarsi in, applicarsi a.
employ (2), **employment,** *n.* Impiego, lavoro, *m.*; occupazione, funzione, carica, *f.* **Out of —,** disoccupato, senza impiego; **to be in search of —,** cercare un impiego; **in my —,** al mio servizio; **employment agency,** ufficio di collocamento, *m.*
employable, *a.* Impiegabile.
employee [im'plɔii:], *n.* Impiegato, *m.*
employer, *n.* Padrone, principale, proprietario, datore di lavoro, *m.*
employment [cp. **employ** (2)].
emporium [em'pɔ:riəm], *n.* Emporio, *m.*
empower [im'pauəɹ], *v.t.* Autorizzare, conferire poteri a. **To be empowered,** essere autorizzato.
empress ['empres], *n.* Imperatrice, *f.*
emptiness ['emtinis], *n.* Vuoto, *m.*; (*fig.*) vacuità, inanità, leggerezza, *f.*

emption, *n.* (*Law*) Compra, *f.*
empty, *a.* Vuoto, vacuo; (*of streets*) deserto; (*fig.*) vano, sterile; (*of a post, chair, etc.*) vacante. || *n.* Vuoto, *m.* || *v.t.* Vuotare, evacuare, sgombrare; *v.i.* vuotarsi, scaricarsi. **To return the empties,** restituire i vuoti; **this river empties into the sea,** questo fiume si scarica nel mare; **—-handed,** a mani vuote; **on an — stomach,** a stomaco vuoto; **—-headed,** senza cervello.
empurple [im'pəːɹpl], *v.t.* Imporporare.
empyema, *n.* (*Med.*) Empiema, *m.*
empyrean [empi'riːən], *n.a.* Empireo, *m.*
emu ['iːmjuː], *n.* (*Zool.*) Emù, *m.*
emulate ['emjuːleit], *v.t.* Emulare, imitare, gareggiare con. **To — a hero's deeds,** emulare le gesta d'un eroe.
emulation, *n.* Emulazione, *f.* **Prompted by —,** spinto dall'emulazione; **in — of each other,** a gara l'uno con l'altro.
emulative, *a.* Emulo.
emulator, *n.* Emulatore, emulo, *m.*
emulous, *a.* Emulo, rivale; desideroso, bramoso.
emulously, *adv.* A gara, con emulazione.
emulsification [emʌlsifi'keiʃən], *n.* (*Chem.*) L'emulsionare, *m.*
emulsify, *v.t.* Emulsionare.
emulsion, *n.* (*Med.*) Emulsione, *f.*
emulsive, *a.* Emulsivo.
emunctory [e'mʌŋktəri], *n.* (*Anat.*) Emuntorio, *m.*
enable [e'neibl], *v.t.* Abilitare, rendere capace, metter in grado, mettere in condizione.
enact [e'nækt], *v.t.* Decretare, promulgare; compiere, eseguire. **As by law enacted,** a termini di legge; **a terrible tragedy was enacted,** una tragedia terribile ebbe luogo.
enactment, *n.* Promulgazione, *f.*, decreto, *m.*
enactor, *n.* Promulgatore, autore, *m.*
enallage [e'næləd3i], *n.* (*Gram.*) Enallage, *f.*
enamel [e'næməl], *n.* Smalto, *m.* || *v.t.* Smaltare. **— ware,** smalto, *m.* **—-work,** smaltatura, *f.*
enameller, enamellist, *n.* Smaltatore, *m.*
enamelling, *n.* Smaltatura, *f.*; smalto, *m.*
enamour [e'næməɹ], *v.t.* Innamorare. **To be enamoured of,** essere innamorato di.
encage [en'keid3], *v.t.* Ingabbiare, rinchiudere.
encamp [en'kæmp], *v.t.i.* Accampare, accamparsi.
encampment, *n.* Accampamento, *m.*
encase [en'keis], *v.t.* Incassare, rinchiudere, coprire, rivestire.
encash [en'kæʃ], *v.t.* Incassare.
encaustic [en'kɔːstik], *a.* Encaustico. || *n.* Encaustica, *f.*
enceinte, *a.* Incinta, gravida. || *n.* (*Mil.*) Cinta, *f.*
encephalic [ense'feilik], *a.* (*Anat.*) Encefalico.
encephalitis, *n.* (*Med.*) Encefalite, *f.*
enchain [en'tʃein], *v.t.* Incatenare.
enchant [in'tʃɑːnt], *v.t.* Incantare, ammaliare, affascinare.
enchanter, *n.* Incantatore, *m.*; stregone, *m.*
enchanting, *a.* Incantevole, affascinante.
enchantingly, *adv.* Incantevolmente.
enchantment, *n.* Incanto, *m.*, malia, magia, *f.*
enchantress, *n.* Incantatrice, *f.*; strega, *f.*
enchase, *v.t.* Incastonare.
encircle [en'səːɹkl], *v.t.* Cingere, circondare, attorniare.
enclasp, *v.t.* Abbracciare.
enclave ['enkleiv], *n.* (*Pol.*) Recinto, *m.*, oasi territoriale, *f.*
enclitic [en'klitik], *n.a.* (*Gram.*) Enclitico, *m.*
enclose [en'klouz], *v.t.* Circondare, attorniare, cingere, rinchiudere; (*in an envelope, etc.*) accludere, includere, allegare, unire. **We beg to —,** ci permettiamo di accludere.
enclosed, *a.* Circondato, cinto, rinchiuso; accluso, allegato, annesso. **— by walls,** cinto da mura; **— in a box,** rinchiuso in una scatola.
enclosure, *n.* Chiusura, *f.*; (*space enclosed*) chiuso, recinto, *m.*; (*in a letter*) allegato, *m.* **The enclosures were missing,** gli allegati mancavano.
encomiast [en'koumiæst], *n.* Encomiaste, lodatore, *m.*
encomiastic, *a.* Encomiastico.
encomium, *n.* Encomio, *m.*
encompass [en'kʌmpəs], *v.t.* Circondare, attorniare, racchiudere.
encore ['ɔŋkɔːɹ], *inter.* Bis! || *n.* Bis, *m.* || *v.t.* Domandare un bis. **To give an —,** bissare, ripetere.
encounter [en'kauntəɹ], *v.t.* Incontrare; combattere, lottare. || *n.* Incontro, scontro, *m.*; combattimento, *m.*; battaglia, *f.*; zuffa, *f.*
encourage [en'kʌrid3], *v.t.* Incoraggiare, promuovere, stimolare.
encouragement, *n.* Incoraggiamento, *m.*
encouraging, *a.* Incoraggiante.
encouragingly, *adv.* In modo incoraggiante.
encrimson [en'krimsən], *v.t.* Arrossare.
encroach [en'kroutʃ], *v.i.* Usurpare, abusare di, intrudersi, invadere. **They encroached on his territory,** invasero il suo territorio; **they encroached on his rights,** usurparono i suoi diritti; **they encroached on his hospitality,** abusarono della sua ospitalità.
encroachment, *n.* Abuso, *m.*; invadenza, usurpazione, *f.*
encrust [en'krʌst], *v.t.* Incrostare, rivestire.
encumber [en'kʌmbəɹ], *v.t.* Ingombrare, imbarazzare, gravare; ostruire. **An encumbered estate,** un possedimento gravato d'ipoteche, *m.*
encumbrance, *n.* Ingombro, imbarazzo, carico, *m.*; ipoteca, *f.* (*fig.*) **Without encumbrances,** senza figli.
encyclical [en'siklikəl], *a.* Enciclico. || *n.* (*Eccles.*) Enciclica, *f.*
encyclopedia [ensaiklə'piːdiə], *n.* Enciclopedia, *f.*
encyclopedic, *a.* Enciclopedico.
encyclopedist, *n.* Enciclopedista, *m.*
end [end], *n.* Fine, estremità, conclusione, *f.*, termine, *m.*; scopo, intento, *m.*; mira, *f.*; meta, *f.*; morte, *f.* || *v.t.* Finire, terminare, concludere; distrurre; mettere a morte; *v.i.* finire, venire al fine, esaurirsi; morire. **At an —,** finito, terminato; **at one's wits' —,** all'ultimo espediente; **by the — of next week,** alla fine della settimana prossima; **from — to —,** dal principio alla fine; **in the —,** alla fine, alla lunga; (*colloq.*) **no — of,** molti; **odds and ends,** cianfrusaglie, *f.pl.*; **on —,** ritto, dritto; **the ends of the earth,** le parti più remote della terra, *f.pl.*; **there's**

an — **of it,** ecco tutto; **there's no — to it,** non c'è limite ai nostri guai; **to attain one's ends,** giungere all'intento; **to come to a bad —,** finir male; **to draw to an —,** venire meno, volgere al termine; **to make an — of it,** farla finita; **to make both ends meet,** coprir le spese; **to make one's hair stand on —,** fare rizzare i capelli; **to serve one's own ends,** per i propri fini; **to the — that,** affinchè; **To what —?** A che scopo? **to no —,** senza scopo; **to place — to —,** mettere in fila; **— on,** con la punta; **at a loose —,** sfaccendato; **to be at the — of one's tether,** non poterne più; **approaching his latter —,** vicino alla morte; **to — in smoke,** andare in fumo; (*Print.*) **— papers,** fogli di guardia, *m.pl.*; (*colloq.*) **the —,** il colmo.

endanger [en'deindʒəɹ], *v.t.* Arrischiare, mettere in pericolo, avventurare; compromettere.

endear [en'diəɹ], *v.t.* Affezionare, render caro.

endearing, *a.* Affettuoso, caro, gentile.

endearment, *n.* Affezione, tenerezza, *f.*, vezzo, *m.*; carezza, *f.* **Term of —,** nome vezzeggiativo, *m.*

endeavour [en'devəɹ], *n.* Sforzo, tentativo, *m.* || *v.i.* Tentare di, sforzarsi di, cercare di, far di tutto per. **To redouble one's endeavours,** raddoppiare i propri sforzi.

endemic [en'demik], *a.* Endemico. **— disease,** endemia, *f.*

endemically, *adv.* Endemicamente.

ending, *n.* Fine, conclusione, *f.*, termine, *m.*; (*Gram.*) desinenza, *f.*

endive ['endiv], *n.* (*Bot.*) Indivia, *f.*

endless, *a.* Senza fine, infinito, eterno, perpetuo, interminabile. (*Mech.*) **— band,** cinghia continua, *f.*

endlessly, *adv.* Senza fine, perpetuamente.

endlessness, *n.* Perpetuità, infinità, *f.*

endocarditis [endoukɑːɹ'daitis], *n.* (*Med.*) Endocardite, *f.*

endocardium, *n.* Endocardio, *m.*

endocarp, *n.* (*Bot.*) Endocarpo, *m.*

endogamy [en'dɔgəmi], *n.* Endogamia, *f.*

endorse [en'dɔːɹs], *v.t.* Vistare, scrivere sul rovescio; (*a cheque*) attergare; (*to make payable to another*) girare; (*a passport*) vistare; (*fig.*) appoggiare, approvare; (*Law*) sanzionare. **To — a claim,** appoggiare un reclamo.

endorsee [endɔːɹ'siː], *n.* Giratario, *m.*

endorsement, *n.* Attergato, *m.*; girata, *f.*; visto, *m.*; appoggio, *m.*, approvazione, *f.*

endorser, *n.* Girante, *m.*; firmatario, *m.*

endosmose, endosmosis [en'dɔzmous, endɔs'mousis], *n.* Endosmosi, *f.*

endosperm ['endospəːɹm], *n.* (*Bot.*) Endosperma, *m.*

endow [en'dau], *v.t.* Dotare di, provvedere di, fornire di, sussidiare.

endowment, *n.* Dotazione, *f.*; sussidio, *m.*; (*fig.*) dote, *f.*, dono, *m.*; talento, *m.*

endue [endjuː], *v.t.* Dotare, investire.

endurable [en'djuːrəbl], *a.* Sopportabile, tollerabile.

endurance, *n.* Tolleranza, pazienza, resistenza, *f.* **Power of —,** resistenza, *f.*; **beyond —,** insopportabile; **— test,** prova di resistenza, *f.*

endure, *v.t.* Sopportare, soffrire, tollerare, reggere, resistere a; *v.i.* durare, continuare; sopportare. **I cannot — her,** non posso sopportarla.

enduring, *a.* Paziente; resistente, durabile, durevole, duraturo; permanente. **— fame,** fama duratura, *f.*

enduringly, *adv.* Pazientemente; permanentemente.

endways, endwise ['endweiz, 'endwaiz], *adv.* (*end to end*) Capo a capo; diritto, perpendicolarmente.

enema ['enəmə], *n.* Clistere, serviziale, *m.*, lavatura, *f.*

enemy ['enəmi], *n.* Nemico, avversario, antagonista, *m.* || *a.* nemico.

energetic, *a.* Energico, energetico.

energetically, *adv.* Energicamente.

energetics, *n.pl.* Energetica, *f.*

energize, *v.t.* Infondere energia a; (*Elec.*) caricare.

energumen [enəɹ'gjuːmən], *n.* Energumeno, *m.*

energy ['enəɹdʒi], *n.* Energia, *f.*

enervate ['enəɹveit], *v.t.* Snervare, infiacchire.

enervation, *n.* Snervamento, infiacchimento, *m.*

enfeeble [en'fiːbl], *v.t.* Indebolire, debilitare.

enfeeblement, *n.* Indebolimento, *m.*

enfeoff [en'fef], *v.t.* (*Hist.Law*) Infeudare.

enfeoffment, *n.* Infeudazione, *f.*

enfilade [enfi'leid], *n.* (*Mil.*) Infilata, *f.* || *v.t.* Infilare, battere d'infilata.

enfold [en'fould], *v.t.* Avviluppare, avvolgere; serrare.

enforce [en'fɔːɹs], *v.t.* Imporre, rafforzare; (*a law*) applicare; (*a demand, argument, etc.*) appoggiare; (*a right*) far valere. **To — obedience,** imporre ubbidienza.

enforceable, *a.* Eseguibile, che si può imporre.

enforced, *a.* Forzato, imposto.

enforcement, *n.* Costringimento, *m.*; esecuzione, applicazione, *f.*

enfranchise [en'fræntʃaiz], *v.t.* Affrancare, emancipare, concedere privilegi a; dare il voto a.

enfranchisement, *n.* Affrancamento, *m.*, emancipazione, *f.*

engage [en'geidʒ], *v.t.* Impegnare, occupare; (*lodgings, etc.*) ritenere; (*to hire*) noleggiare; (*attention*) attrarre; (*for a dance*) invitare; (*Mech.*) ingranare; *v.i.* impegnarsi, obbligarsi; combattere. **To — in battle,** attaccare battaglia; **to become engaged,** fidanzarsi; **to — a maidservant,** fissare una serva; **to — in an enterprise,** avventurarsi in un'impresa.

engaged, *a.* (*to marry*) Fidanzato; (*not at leisure*) occupato; (*Telephone*) linea occupata.

engagement, *n.* Impegno, obbligo, *m.*; appuntamento, *m.*; fidanzamento, *m.*; (*Mil.*) battaglia, *f.* **Not to keep an —,** mancare ad un appuntamento; **to be under an — to,** avere l'obbligo di; **to undertake an —,** assumere un impegno; **— ring,** anello di fidanzamento, *m.*

engaging, *a.* Attraente, seducente.

engagingly, *adv.* Attraentemente.

engender [in'dʒendəɹ], *v.t.* Generare, far nascere; (*fig.*) causare, produrre.

engine ['endʒin], *n.* Macchina, *f.*, motore, *m.*; (*Rail.*) locomotiva, *f.*; strumento, mezzo, *m.* **— of 10 h.p.,** macchina da dieci cavalli,

f.; **high-pressure —,** macchina ad alta pressione, *f.*; **steam- —,** macchina a vapore, *f.*; **to stop the —,** fermare la macchina; **fire- —,** pompa d'incendio, *f.*; **— -driver,** macchinista, *m.*; **— -house,** sala delle macchine, *f.*; **— -shed,** rimessa per locomotive, *f.*; **— -trouble,** panna di motore, *f.*; **— -turning,** rabescamento, *m.*
engineer, *n.* (*civil*) Ingegnere, *m.*; (*driver*) meccanico, macchinista, *m.*; (*Mil.*) ufficiale *or* soldato del Genio. || *v.t.* Combinare, macchinare; *v.i.* esercitare l'ingegneria. **Mining —,** ingegnere minerario, *m.*
engineering, *n.* Ingegneria, *f.*, genio, *m.* **Civil —,** genio civile, *m.*
England ['iŋglənd], *n.* (*Geog.*) Inghilterra, *f.*
English ['iŋgliʃ], *a.* Inglese; anglo. || *n.* Inglese, *m.*; lingua inglese, *f.* **An — girl,** una giovane inglese, *f.*; **in the — manner,** all'inglese; **the — Channel,** La Manica, *f.*; **in plain —,** molto chiaro; **to speak the Queen's —,** parlare correttamente.
Englishman, Englishwoman, *n.* Inglese, *m.f.*
engorge [en'gɔːɹdʒ], *v.t.* Divorare, ingoiare, inghiottire.
engraft [en'grɑːft], *v.t.* Innestare.
engrail [en'greil], *v.t.* (*Heraldry*) Dentellare.
engrain [en'grein], *v.t.* Tingere a forte tinta.
engrave [en'greiv], *v.t.* Incidere, intagliare.
engraver, *n.* Incisore, *m.*
engraving, *n.* Incisione, stampa, *f.* **Copper-plate —,** incisione in rame, *f.*; **line- —,** incisione a contorno, *f.*; **wood- —,** incisione in legno, *f.*
engross [en'grous], *v.t.* Scrivere in grossi caratteri; (*Comm.*) accaparrare, incettare, monopolizzare; assorbire, occupare. **Engrossed in,** completamente occupato da.
engrosser, *n.* Amanuense, *m.*; (*Comm.*) incettatore, accaparratore, *m.*
engrossment, *n.* Accaparramento, monopolio, *m.*; incetta, *f.*; copiatura di documenti, *f.*
engulf [en'gʌlf], *v.t.* Inghiottire, ingoiare, divorare.
enhance [en'hɑːns], *v.t.* Aumentare, intensificare; (*of price*) rincarare; (*fig.*) migliorare.
enhancement, *n.* Aumento, *m.*, intensificazione, *f.* **— of prices,** rincaro, *m.*
enharmonic [enhɑːɹ'mɔnik], *a.* (*Mus.*) Enarmonico.
enigma [e'nigmə], *n.* Enigma, *m.*
enigmatic, enigmatical, *a.* Enigmatico.
enigmatically, *adv.* Enigmaticamente.
enjoin [en'dʒɔin], *v.t.* Ingiungere, imporre, intimare.
enjoy [en'dʒɔi], *v.t.* Godere; possedere; amare; gustare, assaporare. **To — oneself,** divertirsi; **I enjoyed that dinner very much,** ho proprio goduto quel pranzo; **I — staying in bed,** mi piace stare a letto; **to — a little peace,** godere un po' di pace.
enjoyable, *a.* Divertente, simpatico, dilettevole, piacevole.
enjoyment, *n.* Godimento, piacere, diletto, *m.*
enkindle [en'kindl], *v.t.* Accendere, applicare fuoco a; (*fig.*) eccitare, istigare.
enlarge [en'lɑːɹdʒ], *v.t.* Allargare, amplificare, ingrandire; (*to set free*) liberare; *v.i.* ingrandirsi, accrescersi, sviluppare.
enlargement, *n.* Ingrandimento, aumento, *m.*; amplificazione, estensione, *f.*; (*from prison*) liberazione, *f.*; (*Med.*) dilatazione, ipertrofia, *f.*; (*Phot.*) ingrandimento, *m.*
enlarger, *n.* (*Phot.*) Ingranditore, *m.*
enlighten [en'laitən], *v.t.* Rischiarare, illuminare; (*fig.*) chiarire.
enlightenment, *n.* Schiarimento, *m.*, illuminazione, *f.*
enlist [en'list], *v.t.* Iscrivere; (*Mil.*) arruolare; *v.i.* arruolarsi.
enlistment, *n.* Arruolamento, *m.*, iscrizione, *f.*
enliven [en'laivən], *v.t.* Avvivare, ravvivare, animare.
enmity ['enmiti], *n.* Inimicizia, ostilità, *f.*; odio, *m.* **At — with,** ostile a, nemico di.
ennoble [en'noubl], *v.t.* Nobilitare; (*fig.*) elevare, esaltare.
ennoblement, *n.* Nobilitazione, *f.*; (*fig.*) esaltazione, *f.*
ennui [ɔn'wiː], *n.* Noia, *f.*, tedio, *m.*
enormity [e'nɔːɹmiti], *n.* Enormità, atrocità, scelleratezza, *f.*
enormous [e'nɔːɹməs], *a.* Enorme, smisurato.
enormously, *adv.* Enormemente.
enormousness, *n.* Enormità, grandezza, smisuratezza, *f.*
enough [i'nʌf], *adv.* Abbastanza, a sufficienza. || *a.* Sufficiente, bastante. || *n.* Abbastanza, *f.*; il necessario, *m.*, sufficienza, *f.* **That's —!** Basta! **it's — that,** basta che; **large —,** abbastanza grande; **more than —,** più che a sufficienza; **to be —,** bastare, essere bastante; **to have — and to spare,** avere più che abbastanza.
enquire [cp. **inquire**]
enrage [en'reidʒ], *v.t.* Arrabbiare, irritare, esasperare, fare andare in collera.
enrapture, *v.t.* Incantare, estasiare, rapire.
enrich [en'ritʃ], *v.t.* Arricchire.
enrichment, *n.* Arricchimento, *m.*
enrobe [en'roub], *v.t.* Vestire.
enrol [en'roul], *v.t.* Arruolare, iscrivere, registrare.
enrolment, *n.* Arruolamento, *m.*, iscrizione, *f.*
ensconce [en'skɔns], *v.t.* Nascondere, rimpiattare. **To — oneself in a corner,** nascondersi in un angolo; **to — oneself in an armchair,** sprofondarsi in una poltrona.
ensemble [ɔn'sɔmbl], *n.* Complesso, insieme, *m.*
enshrine [en'ʃrain], *v.t.* Deporre in un luogo santo; (*fig.*) conservare come reliquia.
enshroud [en'ʃraud], *v.t.* Avvolgere in un lenzuolo; velare.
ensign ['ensain, 'ensin], *n.* Insegna, *f.*; stendardo, *m.*, bandiera, *f.*; (*Mil.*) portabandiera, alfiere, *m.*; (*Naut.*) bandiera di poppa, *f.*
enslave [en'sleiv], *v.t.* Asservire, assoggettare, rendere schiavo.
enslavement, *n.* Schiavitù, *f.*; assoggettamento, *m.*
ensnare, *v.t.* Prendere in trappola; (*fig.*) sedurre, allettare.
ensue [en'sjuː], *v.i.* Seguire; derivare, succedere, risultare.
ensuing, *a.* Seguente, prossimo, successivo.
ensure [en'ʃjuːɹ], *v.t.* Assicurare.
entablature [en'tæblətʃəɹ], *n.* (*Arch.*) Trabeazione, *f.*, cornicione, *m.*

entail (1) [en'teil], *v.t.* Assegnare; (*fig.*) imporre, implicare, richiedere, cagionare. **It entails much work,** implica molto lavoro; **an entailed estate,** un possedimento soggetto a limitazioni circa la successione, *m.*
entail (2), **entailment,** *n.* Sostituzione, *f.*
entangle [en'tæŋgl], *v.t.* Imbrogliare, intralciare; (*fig.*) confondere, imbarazzare.
entanglement, *n.* Imbroglio, *m.*; confusione, *f.*; viluppo, intralcio, *m.* **Barbed-wire —,** reticolato di ferro spinato, *m.*
enter ['entəɹ], *v.t.* Entrare in, penetrare; (*names, etc.*) iscrivere; (*items*) registrare; (*Law*) spedire; (*book-keeping*) portare; *v.i.* entrare. **To — a profession,** darsi ad una professione; **to — one's name,** iscriversi; **to — the army,** farsi soldato, entrar nell'esercito; **to — the Church,** farsi prete; **to — for,** iscriversi a; **to — into,** prendere parte a; **to — upon,** cominciare, intraprendere; **to — upon an office,** assumere una carica; **to — into a partnership with,** entrare in società con; **to — more deeply into a subject,** approfondire una questione; **to — into possession,** prendere possesso.
entering, *n.* Entrata, *f.* **On —,** all'entrata.
enteric [en'terik], *a.* (*Med.*) Enterico. **— fever,** febbre tifoide, *f.*
enteritis [entə'raitis], *n.* (*Med.*) Enterite, *f.*
enterprise ['entəɹpraiz], *n.* Intrapresa, impresa, opera, *f.*; (*fig.*) iniziativa, *f.*
enterprising, *a.* Intraprendente, pieno d'iniziativa. **An — business man,** un uomo d'affari intraprendente.
entertain [entəɹ'tein], *v.t.* (*correspondence, discourse, etc.*) Tenere, mantenere; (*to receive*) ricevere; (*to amuse*) divertire, intrattenere; (*an idea*) avere, nutrire; (*hopes, etc.*) nutrire; (*proposal*) accettare, prendere in considerazione. **Do you — much ?** Ricevete molta gente in casa vostra ? **to — at dinner,** invitare a pranzo; **to — friendly intercourse,** mantenere rapporti d'amicizia.
entertainer, *n.* Canzonettista, *m.f.*; comico, dilettante, *m.*; ospite, *m.*
entertaining, *a.* Divertente, piacevole.
entertainingly, *adv.* Piacevolmente.
entertainment, *n.* Ricevimento, il ricevere, *m.*; divertimento, trattenimento, passatempo, *m.*, festa, *f.*
enthral [en'θɹɔ:l], *v.t.* Asservire, assoggettare; (*fig.*) incantare, cattivare.
enthrone [en'θroun], *v.t.* Incoronare; (*Eccles.*) investire, intronizare.
enthronement, *n.* Incoronazione, *f.*; insediamento, *m.*
enthuse [en'θju:z], *v.i.* (*colloq.*) Entusiasmarsi.
enthusiasm [en'θju:ziæzm], *n.* Entusiasmo, *m.* **Full of —,** pieno d'entusiasmo.
enthusiast, *n.* Entusiasta, *m.*
enthusiastic, *a.* Entusiastico.
enthusiastically, *adv.* Entusiasticamente.
enthymeme ['enθaimi:m], *n.* (*Logic*) Entimema, *m.*
entice [en'tais], *v.t.* Allettare, adescare; istigare, incitare; sedurre, attrarre. **To — away,** allettare; **to — to evil conduct,** istigare a far male.
enticement, *n.* Incanto, fascino, stimolo, *m.*, istigazione, *f.*; seduzione, tentazione, *f.*
enticer, *n.* Tentatore, seduttore, *m.*
enticing, *a.* Seducente, attraente, tentatore.
enticingly, *adv.* Seducentemente.
entire [en'taiəɹ], *a.* Intero, completo; perfetto, puro; tutto. || *n.* Specie di birra, *f.*; stallone, *m.* **His — affections,** tutti i suoi affetti.
entirely, *adv.* Interamente, in tutto e per tutto.
entirety [en'taiɹti], *n.* Intero, tutto, *m.*; totalità, *f.* **In its —,** nel suo complesso, nella sua interezza.
entitle [en'taitl], *v.t.* Intitolare, nominare; conferire un diritto a. **To be entitled to,** avere diritto a; **I am entitled to,** mi spetta, ne ho diritto.
entity ['entiti], *n.* Entità, *f.*; essere, *m.*
entoil [en'tɔil], *v.t.* Prendere in trappola.
entomb [en'tu:m], *v.t.* Seppellire, sotterrare.
entombment, *n.* Sepoltura, *f.*; seppellimento, *m.*; inumazione, *f.*
entomological [entəmə'lɔdʒikəl], *a.* Entomologico.
entomologist, *n.* Entomologo, *m.*
entomology, *n.* Entomologia, *f.*
entozoa [entɔ'zouə], *n.pl.* (*Zool.*) Entozoi, *m.pl.*
entr'acte ['ɔntrækt], *n.* (*Theat.*) Intervallo, *m.*; (*Mus.*) musica eseguita tra un atto e l'altro, *f.*
entrails ['entreilz], *n.pl.* Intestini, *m.pl.*, viscere, interiora, *f.pl.*
entrain [en'trein], *v.t.* Spedire in treno; *v.i.* mettersi in treno.
entrance (1) ['entrəns], *n.* Entrata, *f.*, ingresso, *m.*; (*fig.*) ammissione, iniziazione, *f.* **— -examination,** esame d'ammissione, *m.*; **— free,** entrata libera; **— -hall,** vestibolo, atrio d'ingresso, *m.*
entrance (2) [en'trɑ:ns], *v.t.* Estasiare, incantare; rapire.
entrancement, *n.* Estasi, *f.*, rapimento, *m.*
entrant ['entrənt], *n.* Concorrente, *m.*; (*for a race, etc.*) competitore, *m.*; participante, *m.*
entrap [en'træp], *v.t.* Prendere in trappola; (*fig.*) truffare, ingannare.
entreat [en'tri:t], *v.t.* Pregare, supplicare, implorare, sollecitare; importunare.
entreaty [en'tri:ti], *n.* Preghiera, supplica, petizione, *f.*
entrench [in'trentʃ], *v.t.* Trincerare, fortificare. **To — oneself behind,** trincerarsi dietro; **to — upon,** usurpare.
entrenching-tool, *n.* Attrezzi di trincera, *m.pl.*
entrenchment, *n.* Trinceramento, *m.*; trincea, *f.*
entrust [en'trʌst], *v.t.* Affidare, commettere, consegnare.
entry ['entri], *n.* Entrata, *f.*; iscrizione, *f.*; registrazione, *f.*; (*item*) articolo, *m.*; (*customs*) dichiarazione d'entrata, *f.*; (*Law*) presa di possesso, *f.* (*Comm.*) **Single- — bookkeeping,** contabilità in partita semplice, *f.*; **double- — bookkeeping,** contabilità in partita doppia, *f.*; **to make an — against,** portare a debito di; (*one-way street*) **— only,** senso unico, *m.*
entwine [en'twain], *v.t.* Intrecciare, intessere; stringere. **She entwined her arms about him,** essa lo strinse nelle braccia.
enumerate [i'nju:məreit], *v.t.* Enumerare, contare.
enumeration, *n.* Enumerazione, *f.*

enunciate [i'nʌnsieit], *v.t.* Enunciare, pronunziare.
enunciation, *n.* Enunciazione, *f.*; pronuncia, *f.*; (*Geom.*) enunciato, *m.*
enunciative, *a.* Enunciativo.
envelop [in'veləp], *v.t.* Avviluppare, avvolgere; (*Mil.*) accerchiare.
envelope ['enviloup, 'ɔnvəloup], *n.* Busta, *f.*; plico; (*Bot.*) involucro, *m.* **In an —**, in busta; **in the same —**, nello stesso plico; **stamped —**, busta affrancata, *f.*
envelopment, *n.* Copertura, *f.*; involucro, *m.*
envenom [en'venəm], *v.t.* Avvelenare; amareggiare.
enviable ['enviəbl], *a.* Invidiabile.
envious ['enviəs], *a.* Invidioso. **To look with — eyes at**, guardare con invidia.
enviously, *adv.* Invidiosamente.
environ [en'vairən], *v.t.* Accerchiare, attorniare, circondare.
environment, *n.* Accerchiamento, *m.*; condizioni, *f.pl.*; ambiente, *m.*
environs, *n.pl.* Dintorni, *m.pl.*
envisage [in'vizidʒ], *v.t.* Fronteggiare, contemplare, considerare.
envoy ['envɔi], *n.* Inviato, legato, *m.*
envy ['envi], *n.* Invidia, *f.* ‖ *v.t.* Invidiare.
enwrap [en'ræp], *v.t.* Avvolgere, avvoltolare.
Eocene ['i:ousi:n], *a.* (*Geol.*) Eocenico.
epact ['i:pækt], *n.* (*Astron.*) Epatta, *f.*
epaulet ['epɔ:let], *n.* Spallina, *f.*
epergne [e'pə:ɹn], *n.* Trionfo da tavola, *m.*, alzata da tavola, *f.*
ephemera (*pl.* **ephemerae**) [e'femərə, efeməri:], *n.* (*Zool.*) Effimera, *f.*
ephemeral, *a.* Effimero.
ephemeris (*pl.* **ephemerides**), *n.* (*Astron.*) Effemeride, *f.*
ephod ['efɔd], *n.* (*Eccles.*) Efod, *m.*
epic ['epik], *a.* Epico. ‖ *n.* Epopea, *f.*, poema epico, *m.*
epicedium [epi'si:diəm], *n.* (*Poet.*) Epicedio, *m.*
epicene [epi'si:n], *a.* (*Gram.*) Epiceno.
epicentrum [epi'sentrəm], *n.* (*Geol.*) Epicentro, *m.*
epicure ['epikju:ɹ], *n.* Epicureo, *m.*
epicurean, *n.a.* Epicureo, *m.*
epicureanism, *n.* Epicureismo, *m.*
epicycle ['episaikl], *n.* (*Astron.*) Epiciclo, *m.*
epidemic (1) [epi'demik], *n.* Epidemia, *f.*
epidemic (2), **epidemical**, *a.* Epidemico.
epidemiology, *n.* Epidemiologia, *f.*
epidermal, epidermic, *a.* Epidermico.
epidermis [epi'də:ɹmis], *n.* (*Anat.*) Epidermide, *f.*
epigastric, *a.* Epigastrico.
epigastrium [epi'gæstriəm], *n.* (*Anat.*) Epigastro, *m.*
epigenesis [epi'dʒenisis], *n.* Epigenesi, *f.*
epiglottis [epi'glɔtis], *n.* (*Anat.*) Epiglotta, *f.*
epigram ['epigræm], *n.* Epigramma, *m.*
epigrammatic, epigrammatical, *a.* Epigrammatico.
epigrammatically, *adv.* Epigrammaticamente.
epigrammatist, *n.* Epigrammatista, *m.*
epigraph ['epigræf], *n.* Epigrafe, *f.*; iscrizione, *f.*
epigraphic, *a.* Epigrafico.
epilepsy ['epilepsi], *n.* (*Med.*) Epilessia, *f.*, mal caduco, *m.*
epileptic, *n.a.* Epilettico. — **fit**, accesso epilettico, attacco epilettico, *m.*
epilogue ['epilɔg], *n.* Epilogo, *m.*
Epiphany [e'pifəni], *n.* (*Eccles.*) Epifania, Befana, *f.*
episcopacy [e'piskəpəsi], *n.* Episcopato, *m.*
episcopal, *a.* Episcopale, vescovile.
episcopalian, *n.a.* Chi favoreggia il governo episcopale della Chiesa, *m.*
episcopate, *n.* Episcopato, vescovato, *m.*
episode ['episoud], *n.* Episodio, *m.*
episodic, episodical, *a.* Episodico.
episodically, *adv.* Episodicamente.
epistle [e'pisl], *n.* Epistola, *f.*
epistolary, *a.* Epistolare.
epistolography [epistə'lɔgrəfi], *n.* Epistolografia, *f.*
epitaph ['epitæf], *n.* Epitaffio, *m.*
epithet ['epiθet], *n.* Epiteto, *m.*
epitome [e'pitəmi], *n.* Epitome, sunto, compendio, *m.*
epitomize, *v.t.* Riassumere, sunteggiare, compendiare.
epizootic [epizou'ɔtik], *a.* Epizootico.
epoch ['i:pɔk], *n.* Epoca, *f.* **— -making**, che fa epoca, storico.
epode ['epoud], *n.* (*Poet.*) Epodo, *m.*
eponym ['epənim], *n.* Eponimo, *m.*
epopee ['epopi:], *n.* (*Poet.*) Epopea, *f.*
Epsom salts ['epsəm 'sɔ:lts], *n.* Sale inglese, *m.*, sal d'Inghilterra, *m.*
equability [ekwə'biliti], *n.* Uniformità, uguaglianza, *f.*; (*fig.*) equanimità, *f.*
equable ['ekwəbl], *a.* Sereno, uguale, equanime; uniforme.
equably, *adv.* Serenamente, con equanimità.
equal ['i:kwəl], *a.* Uguale, eguale, pari; (*fig.*) equo, giusto, imparziale. ‖ *n.* Pari, uguale, *m.* ‖ *v.t.* Uguagliare, essere pari a, agguagliare. **He was — to the occasion**, egli era pari alla necessità; **to treat as an —**, trattare da pari a pari; **other things being —**, a parità di condizioni; **on — terms**, sopra un piede di uguaglianza.
equality [i:'kwɔliti], *n.* Uguaglianza, *f.*
equalization, *n.* Pareggiamento, *m.*; (*Law*) perequazione, *f.*; (*Pol.*) livellamento, *m.*
equalize, *v.t.* Pareggiare, equiparare.
equally, *adv.* Ugualmente.
equanimity [ekwə'nimiti], *n.* Equanimità, *f.*
equate [e'kweit], *v.t.* Rendere uguale.
equation [e'kweiʒən], *n.* (*Math.*) Equazione, *f.*
equator [e'kweitəɹ], *n.* Equatore, *m.*
equatorial, *a.* Equatoriale. ‖ *n.* (*telescope*) Equatoriale, *m.*
equerry ['ekweri], *n.* Cavallerizzo, scudiere, *m.*
equestrian [e'kwestriən], *a.* Equestre. ‖ *n.* (*horseman*) Cavaliere, *m.*; (*circus*) cavallerizzo, *m.*
equiangular [ekwi'æŋgju:ləɹ], *a.* (*Geom.*) Equiangolo.
equidistant, *a.* Equidistante.
equilateral, *a.* (*Geom.*) Equilaterale. ‖ *n.* Equilatero, *m.*
equilibration [ekwili'breiʃən], *n.* Equilibrazione, *f.*; equilabramento, *m.*
equilibrist, *n.* Equilibrista, *m.*
equilibrium, *n.* Equilibrio, *m.* **To keep one's —**, tenersi in equilibrio; **stable —**, equilibrio stabile, *m.*

equine [ˈekwain], *a.* Equino.
equinoctial [ekwiˈnɔkʃəl], *n.a.* Equinoziale, *m.*
equinox [ˈekwinɔks], *n.* Equinozio, *m.* (*Astron.*) **Precession of the equinoxes,** precessione degli equinozi, *f.*
equip [eˈkwip], *v.t.* Fornire, provvedere, equipaggiare, corredare, allestire.
equipage [ˈekwipədʒ], *n.* Equipaggio, *m.*
equipment, *n.* Equipaggiamento, corredo, fornimento, *m.*
equipoise [ˈekwipɔiz], *n.* Equilibrio, *m.*
equipollence, equipollency [iːkwiˈpɔləns, iːkwiˈpɔlənsi], *n.* Equipollenza, *f.*
equipollent, *a.* Equipollente.
equitable [ˈekwitəbl], *a.* Giusto, imparziale, equo.
equitably, *adv.* Giustamente.
equitation [ekwiˈteiʃən], *n.* Equitazione, *f.*
equity [ˈekwiti], *n.* Equità, *f.*
equivalence [ekˈwivələns], *n.* Equivalenza, *f.*, valore uguale, *m.*
equivalent, *n.a.* Equivalente, *m.* **To be — to,** equivalere a.
equivalently, *adv.* Ugualmente.
equivocal [eˈkwivəkəl], *a.* Equivoco, ambiguo.
equivocality, *n.* Equivocità, ambiguità, *f.*
equivocally, *adv.* Ambiguamente.
equivocate, *v.i.* Equivocare, cavillare.
equivocation, *n.* Equivoco, *m.*
equivocator, *n.* Equivocatore, *m.*
era [ˈiːrə], *n.* Era, *f.* **Christian —,** era cristiana, *f.*
eradiation [eˈreidieiʃən], *n.* Irradiamento, *m.*
eradicable [eˈrædikəbl], *a.* Estirpabile.
eradicate, *v.t.* Sradicare, estirpare.
eradication, *n.* Sradicamento, *m.*; estirpazione, *f.*
erasable [eˈreizəbl], *a.* Cancellabile.
erase, *v.t.* Cancellare, cassare, raschiare.
eraser, *n.* (*knife*) Raschino, *m.*; (*rubber*) gomma da cancellare, *f.*
erasure, *n.* Cancellatura, *f.*
ere [ɛəɹ], *adv. conj. prep.* Prima che, prima di, prima, più presto che; piuttosto che, fra più presto che; (*rather than*) piuttosto che. **— long,** fra poco; **— now,** già.
erect [eˈrekt], *a.* Eretto, ritto, diritto, dritto. || *adv.* In piedi. || *v.t.* Erigere, innalzare; (*a machine*) montare; costruire, edificare, stabilire.
erectile, *a.* (*Anat.*) Erettile.
erection, *n.* Erezione, costruzione, *f.*; (*of a machine*) montaggio, *m.*; edifizio, *m.*
erectness, *n.* Portamento eretto, *m.*, dirittezza, *f.*
erector, *n.* Costruttore, *m.*; (*of machine*) montatore, *m.*; (*Anat.*) erettore, *m.*
eremite [ˈerimait], *n.* (*obs.*) Eremita, *m.*
erg, ergon [əːɹg, ˈəːɹgən], *n.* Ergon, *m.*
ergo [ˈəːɹgou], *adv.* Dunque, ergo.
ergot [ˈəːɹgət], *n.* (*Bot.*) Granosprone, *m.*
ergotism, *n.* (*Med.*) Ergotismo, *m.*
ermine [ˈəːɹmin], *n.* (*Zool.*) Ermellino, *m.* || *a.* D'ermellino.
erne [ˈəːɹn], *n.* (*Zool.*) Aquila di mare, *f.*
erode [eˈroud], *v.t.* Rodere, corrodere; consumare.
erosion, *n.* Erosione, *f.*
erosive, *a.* Erosivo, corrosivo.
erotic [eˈrɔtik], *a.* Erotico.
erotomania [erɔtəˈmeiniə], *n.* Erotomania, *f.*
err [əːɹ], *v.i.* Errare, sviarsi; sbagliare.
errancy, *n.* Incertezza, *f.*
errand [ˈerənd], *n.* Commissione, *f.*, incarico, messaggio, *m.* **To go an —,** fare una commissione; **What is your — ?** Che cosa volete? **—-boy,** fattorino, galoppino, commesso, *m.*
errant [ˈerənt], *a.* Errante, randagio, ramingo, girovago. **Knight —,** cavaliere errante, *m.*
erratic [eˈrætik], *a.* Erratico, incerto, eccentrico, irregolare.
erratically, *adv.* Senza regola.
erratum (*pl.* **errata**), *n.* Erratum, *m.*
erroneous [eˈrouniəs], *a.* Erroneo, falso.
erroneously, *adv.* Erroneamente.
erroneousness, *n.* Erroneità, falsità, *f.*
error [ˈerəɹ], *n.* Errore, sbaglio, *m.*, colpa, *f.* **A slight —,** un errore di poco conto, *m.*; **printer's —,** errore di stampa, *m.*; **errors excepted,** salvo errore; **in —,** per errore.
Erse [əːɹs], *n.a.* Gaelico, *m.*
erstwhile [ˈəːɹstwail], *adv.* Fin'allora, di già.
erubescence [erjuːˈbesəns], *n.* Erubescenza, *f.*
erubescent, *a.* Rosso, arrossito.
eructation [erʌkˈteiʃən], *n.* Eruttazione, *f.*
erudite [ˈeruːdait], *a.* Erudito, dotto.
erudition, *n.* Erudizione, dottrina, *f.*
erupt [iˈrʌpt], *v.t.i.* Eruttare.
eruption [eˈrʌpʃən], *n.* (*in all senses*) Eruzione, *f.*
erysipelas [eriˈsipiləs], *n.* (*Med.*) Risipola, *f.*
erythema [eriˈθiːmə], *n.* (*Med.*) Eritema, *m.*
escalade [eskəˈleid], *n.* (*Mil.*) Scalata, *f.* || *v.t.* Dar la scalata, scalare.
escalator [ˈeskəleitəɹ], *n.* Scala mobile, *f.*
escallop, scallop [esˈkæləp, skæləp], *n.* (*Zool.*) Petonchio, *m.*
escapade [eskəˈpeid], *n.* Scappata, *f.*
escape [esˈkeip], *n.* Fuga, *f.*, scampo, *m.*; evasione, *f.*; (*of gas, steam, etc.*) scappamento, *m.* || *v.t.* Sfuggire, evitare, scansare, schivare; *v.i.* fuggire, evadere, scappare. **— of gas,** scappamento di gas; **—-valve,** valvola di sicurezza, *f.*; **fire- —,** apparecchio di salvataggio per incendio, *m.*, porta di sicurezza, *f.*; **there's no — from it,** non si può evitarlo; **to have a narrow —,** scamparla per miracolo; **it has escaped my memory,** mi è sfuggito dalla memoria; **to — from prison,** scappare dalla prigione; **an escaped prisoner,** un evaso, un fuggiasco, *m.*
escapement, *n.* (*Mech.*) Scappamento, *m.*
escarpment [eˈskɑːɹpmənt], *n.* Scarpa, scarpata, *f.*
eschatological [eskətəˈlɔdʒikəl], *a.* Escatologico.
eschatology, *n.* Escatologia, *f.*
escheat [isˈtʃiːt], *n.* (*Law*) Incameramento, *m.* || *v.t.* Incamerare, confiscare, toccare; *v.i.* decadere, essere devoluto allo Stato.
eschew [isˈtʃjuː], *v.t.* Evitare, astenersi da, rifuggire da.
escort (1) [esˈkɔːɹt], *v.t.* Scortare, accompagnare.
escort (2) [ˈeskɔːɹt], *n.* Scorta, *f.*
escritoire [ˈeskritwɑːɹ], *n.* Scrittoio, *m.*
esculent [ˈeskjuːlənt], *a.* Mangereccio, commestibile.
escutcheon [esˈkʌtʃən], *n.* Stemma, *f.*, scudo, *m.*
Eskimo [ˈeskimou], *n.a.* Esquimese, *m.f.*
esoteric, esoterical [esoˈterik], *a.* Esoterico.
esoterism, *n.* Esoterismo, *m.*

espalier [es'pæliəɹ], *n.* Spalliera, *f.*
esparto, esparto grass [es'pɑːɹtou, es'pɑːɹtou grɑːs], *n.* (*Bot.*) Sparto, *m.*
especial [es'peʃəl], *a.* Speciale, particolare.
especially, *adv.* Specialmente, soprattutto. **— as,** tanto più che.
espial [es'paiəl], *n.* L'atto di spiare, *m.*
espionage ['espiənɑːdʒ], *n.* Spionaggio, *m.*
esplanade [esplə'neid], *n.* Spianata, *f.*; passeggiata, *f.*
espousal [es'pauzəl], *n.* Sposalizio, *m.*; (*of a cause*) adesione, adozione, *f.*
espouse [es'pauz], *v.t.* Sposare; (*fig.*) adottare, abbracciare.
espy [es'pai], *v.t.* Scorgere, spiare, osservare.
esquire [es'kwaiɹ], *n.* Scudiero, *m.*; titolo usato nell'indirizzare lettere.
essay ['esei], *n.* (*written*) Saggio, *m.*; (*attempt*) tentativo, esperimento, *m.*; prova, *f.* || [e'sei] *v.t.* Tentare, far prova.
essayist ['eseiist], *n.* Autore di saggi, *m.*; saggista, *m.*
essence ['esəns], *n.* Essenza, *f.*
essential [e'senʃəl], *n.a.* Essenziale, *m.*
essentiality, essentialness, *n.* Essenzialità, *f.*
essentially, *adv.* Essenzialmente.
establish [es'tæbliʃ], *v.t.* Stabilire, istituire, fondare; confermare. **To — oneself,** stabilirsi; **to — a business,** metter su negozio, mettersi negli affari.
established, *a.* Stabilito, fondato, convenuto, confermato.
establishment, *n.* Stabilimento, *m.*, istituzione, *f.*; fondazione, *f.*; casa, *f.*; (*Eccles.*) la chiesa anglicana, *f.* **Branch —,** succursale, *m.*; (*Mil.*) **peace —,** piede di pace, *m.*
estafette [estə'fet], *n.* (*Mil.*) Staffetta, *f.*
estate [es'teit], *n.* Stato, *m.*; condizione, *f.*; proprietà, *f.*; ceto, *m.* **Real —,** beni immobili, *m.pl.*; **personal —,** beni mobili, *m.pl.*; **man's —** l'età virile, *f.*; **bankrupt's —,** attivo di un fallimento, *m.*; **— duty,** imposta sul patrimonio, *f.*; **of low —,** di basso stato; **— agent** (*steward*) fattore, intendente, *m.*; (*for sales, etc.*) agente immobiliare, *m.*; **— -office,** agenzia immobiliare, *f.*
esteem [es'tiːm], *n.* Stima, considerazione, *f.*, conto, *m.* || *v.t.* Stimare, apprezzare. **To — highly,** tenere in grande stima.
estimable, *a.* Stimabile, pregevole.
estimate ['estimət], *n.* Stima, valutazione, *f.*; preventivo, *m.*; bilancio, *m.*; (*fig.*) opinione, *f.*, giudizio, *m.* || ['estimeit] *v.t.* Preventivare, valutare, calcolare; (*fig.*) giudicare, apprezzare. **— of damages,** stima dei danni, *f.*; **a rough —,** una valutazione approssimativa, *f.*; **army estimates,** preventivo per l'esercito, *m.*
estimated, *a.* Stimato, valutato, periziato.
estimation, *n.* Stima, *f.*, giudizio, *m.*
estimator, *n.* Stimatore, *m.*
estival ['estivəl], *a.* Estivo.
estop [es'tɔp], *v.t.* (*Law*) Eccepire, sospendere.
estoppage, estoppel [es'tɔpədʒ, es'tɔpəl], *n.* Eccezione, sospensiva, *f.*
estrange [es'treindʒ], *v.t.* Alienare, allontanare.
estrangement, *n.* Alienazione, *f.*, allontanamento, *m.*
estreat [es'triːt], *v.t.* (*Law*) Estrarre, copiare. || *n.* Estratto autentico, *m.*
estuary ['estjuːəri], *n.* (*Geog.*) Estuario, *m.*
et cetera (*abbrev.* **etc., &c.**) [et'setərə], *n.* Eccetera, *m.*, (*abbrev.* ecc.).
etch [etʃ], *v.t.i.* Incidere all'acquaforte, bulinare; (*fig.*) disegnare.
etcher, *n.* Acquafortista, incisore, *m.*
etching, *n.* Incisione all'acquaforte, *f.*; acquaforte, *f.* **— needle,** bulino, *m.*
eternal [iːtəːɹnəl], *n.a.* Eterno, *m.*
eternally, *adv.* Eternamente.
eternity, *n.* Eternità, *f.*
eternize, eternalize, *v.t.* Eternare.
Etesian [e'tiːziən], *a.* Etesio.
ether ['iːθəɹ], *n.* Etere, *m.*
ethereal [e'θiəriəl], *a.* Etereo.
etherealize, *v.i.* Rendere etereo; (*fig.*) raffinare.
etheric, *a.* Eterico.
etherify, *v.t.* Eterificare.
etherize, *v.t.* Eterizzare.
ethic, ethical ['eθik, 'eθikəl], *a.* Etico.
ethically, *adv.* Eticamente.
ethics, *n.pl.* Etica, *f.*
Ethiopia [iːθi'oupiə], *n.* (*Geog.*) L'Etiopia, *f.*
Ethiopian, *n.a.* Etiope, *m.*
Ethiopic, *a.* Etiopico.
ethmoid ['eθmɔid], *n.a.* (*Anat.*) Etmoide, *f.*
ethnic, ethnical ['eθnik, 'eθnikəl], *a.* Etnico.
ethnographer [eθ'nɔgrəfəɹ], *n.* Etnografo, *m.*
ethnographic, *a.* Etnografico.
ethnography, *n.* Etnografia, *f.*
ethnological [eθnə'lɔdʒikəl], *a.* Etnologico.
ethnologist, *n.* Etnologo, *m.*
ethnology, *n.* Etnologia, *f.*
ethos ['iːθɔs], *n.* Carattere, *m.*; disposizione, *f.*
ethyl ['eθil], *n.* (*Chem.*) Etile, *m.*
etiolate ['iːtiouleit], *v.t.* Fare sbiadire, scolorire; fare intristire.
etiolation, *n.* Scolorimento, *m.*
etiquette ['etiket], *n.* Etichetta, *f.*, cerimoniale, *m.*
Etruscan [i'trʌskən], *n.a.* Etrusco, *m.*
etymological [etimə'lɔdʒikəl], *a.* Etimologico.
etymologically, *adv.* Etimologicamente.
etymologist, *n.* Etimologista, *m.*
etymology, *n.* Etimologia, *f.*
eucalyptus [juːkə'liptəs], *n.* (*Bot.*) Eucalipto, *m.*
Eucharist ['juːkərist], *n.* (*Eccles.*) Eucaristia, *f.*
eucharistic, *a.* Eucaristico.
eudiometer [juːdi'ɔmitəɹ], *n.* Eudiometro, *m.*
eudiometry, *n.* Eudiometria, *f.*
eugenic [juː'dʒenik], *a.* Eugenico.
eugenics, *n.pl.* Eugenica, eugenetica, *f.*
eulogist ['juːlədʒist], *n.* Panegirista, *m.*
eulogistic, *a.* Elogiativo.
eulogium, *n.* Elogio, *m.*
eulogize, *v.t.* Elogiare.
eulogy ['juːlədʒi], *n.* Elogio, *m.*
eunuch ['juːnək], *n.* Eunuco, *m.*
eupeptic [juː'peptik], *a.* Eupeptico.
euphemism ['juːfəmizm], *n.* Eufemismo, *m.*
euphemistic, *a.* Eufemistico.
euphemistically, *adv.* Eufemisticamente.
euphonic, euphonious [juː'fɔnik, juː'founiəs], *a.* Eufonico.
euphoniously, *adv.* Eufonicamente.
euphony ['juːfəni], *n.* Eufonia, *f.* **For the sake of —,** per eufonia.
Euphrates [juː'freitiːz], *n.* (*Geog.*) Eufrate, *m.*
euphuism ['juːfjuːizm], *n.* Preziosità, *f.*

euphuistic, *a.* Ampolloso.
Eurasian [juː'reiʒən], *n.a.* Eurasiano, *m.*
Europe ['juːrəp], *n.* (*Geog.*) Europa, *f.*
European [juːrə'piən], *n.a.* Europeo, *m.*
Europeanize, *v.t.* Europeizzare.
Eustachian tube [juː'steikiən tjuːb], *n.* (*Anat.*) Tromba d'Eustachio, *f.*
euthanasia [juːθə'neiʒə], *n.* Eutanasia, *f.*
evacuant [i'vækjuːənt], *n.a.* Evacuante, *m.*
evacuate [i'vækjuːeit], *v.t.i.* Evacuare.
evacuation, *n.* Evacuazione, *f.*; sfollamento, *m.*
evacuee [i'vækjuːiː], *n.* Sfollato, *m.*
evade [i'veid], *v.t.* Evitare, schivare, eludere, sottrarsi a. **To — the law,** eludere la legge.
evaluate [i'væljuːeit], *v.t.* Valutare.
evaluation, *n.* Valutazione, *f.*
evanesce [evə'nes], *v.i.* Svanire.
evanescence, *n.* Evanescenza, *f.*
evanescent, *a.* Evanescente, sfumato, fugace.
evangelical [evæn'dʒelikəl], *a.* Evangelico.
evangelist, *n.* Evangelista, *m.*
evangelize, *v.t.* Evangelizzare.
evaporable [e'væpərəbl], *a.* Evaporabile.
evaporate, *v.i.* Evaporare; *v.t.* fare evaporare.
evaporation, *n.* Evaporazione, *f.*
evasion [e'veiʒən], *n.* Evasione, *f.*; sotterfugio, pretesto, *m.*
evasive, *a.* Evasivo.
evasively, *adv.* Evasivamente.
evasiveness, *n.* Carattere evasivo, *m.*, ambiguità, incertezza, *f.*
eve [iːv], *n.* Vigilia, *f.*; sera, *f.* **At —,** a sera; **on the — of,** la vigilia di.
even (1) ['iːvən], *n.* (*Poet.*) Sera, *f.*
even (2), *a.* Eguale, uguale; piano, piatto, liscio, uniforme; (*of numbers*) pari. || *v.t.* Eguagliare, pareggiare, livellare. **— with,** a livello di, pari a; **to be — with,** rendere la pariglia a; **— reckoning makes lasting friends,** patti chiari, amici cari; **—-handed,** imparziale; **—-tempered,** calmo, placido, tranquillo; **an — number,** un numero pari.
even (3), *adv.* Anche, anzi, perfino, persino, parimente. **— as,** così come; **— now,** perfino ora, anche ora; **— so,** esattamente; **— though,** benchè; **— if,** anche se; **not —,** neanche, neppure.
evening ['iːvniŋ], *n.* Sera, serata, *f.*; (*fig.*) tramonto, *m.*, fine, *f.* || *a.* Serale, di sera. **A pleasant —,** una serata piacevole, *f.*; **— star,** stella della sera, *f.*, vespero, *m.*; **Good — !** Buona sera! **last —,** ieri sera, *f.*; **the — before,** la sera prima, *f.*; **tomorrow —,** domani sera, *f.*; (*man's*) **— dress,** abito da sera, *m.*, marsina, *f.*, abito a coda, *m.*; (*woman's*) **— dress,** toletta da sera, *f.*; **— gown,** veste da sera, *f.*; **in the — of his days,** sul declinare della vita; **to spend the —,** passare la serata.
evenly, *adv.* Egualmente, parimente; imparzialmente.
evenness, *n.* Uguaglianza, uniformità, *f.*; imparzialità, *f.* **— of temper,** indole eguale, indole serena, *f.*
evensong, *n.* (*Eccles.*) Inno della sera, *m.*
event [e'vent], *n.* Evento, caso, avvenimento, *m.*; (*Sport*) prova, *f.* **At all events,** in ogni caso; **in the — of,** in caso di.
eventful, *a.* Avventuroso, pieno di avvenimenti; importante, decisivo.
eventide ['iːvəntaid], *n.* Cadere del giorno, *m.*
eventual [e'ventʃuːəl], *a.* Finale, definitivo, conclusivo.
eventuality [eventʃjuː'æliti], *n.* Eventualità, *f.*
eventually, *adv.* Finalmente, alla fine.
eventuate, *v.i.* Accadere, succedere, riuscire.
ever ['evəɹ], *adv.* Sempre, mai. **As soon as —,** tosto che, appena che; **be it — so little,** per quanto poco; **— and anon,** di tempo in tempo; **— after,** d'allora in poi; **— so little,** un pochino, un tantino, *m.*; **for —,** per sempre; **for — and —,** eternamente; **if I have —,** se mai ho; **scarcely —,** quasi mai.
evergreen, *n.a.* Sempreverde, *m.*
everlasting, *a.* Eterno, immortale; continuo, incessante; perenne. || *n.* Eternità, *f.*; Iddio, *m.*
everlastingly, *adv.* Eternamente; incessantemente.
evermore, *adv.* Eternamente, sempre. **For —,** per sempre.
eversion [i'vəɹʃən], *n.* Eversione, *f.*
every ['evəri], *a.* Ogni, ognuno, ciascuno; tutti i, tutte le. **— day,** ogni giorno, tutti i giorni; **— little helps,** tutto aiuta; **— man for himself,** si salvi chi può; **— now and then,** di quando in quando; **— one,** ciascuno, *m.*, ciascuna, *f.*, tutti, *m.pl.*; **— other day,** ogni due giorni; **— fourth man,** un uomo su quattro; **— bit as much,** proprio tanto quanto.
everyone, everybody, *n.* Tutti, *m.pl.*, ognuno, *m.*, ognuna, *f.* **— for himself and God for all,** ognun per sè e Dio per tutti.
everything, *n.* Tutto, *m.* **— else,** ogni altra cosa.
everywhere, *adv.* Dappertutto, in qualsivoglia luogo, in tutti i luoghi, per ogni dove, dovunque.
evict [e'vikt], *v.t.* Spossessare, espellere, sfrattare.
eviction, *n.* Sfratto, *m.*, evizione, *f.*
evidence ['evidəns], *n.* Evidenza, testimonianza, *f.*, testimonio, *m.*; prova, *f.*; (*witness*) testimone, *m.*; rilievo, *m.* || *v.t.* Mostrare, provare, comprovare. **— for the accused,** prova a discarico, *f.*; **— for the prosecution,** prova a carico, *f.*; **to give —,** testimoniare; **to bring —,** addurre prove; **to bring into —,** mettere in rilievo; **to turn Queen's —,** denunziare i propri complici.
evident, *a.* Evidente, manifesto.
evidential, *a.* Probativo.
evidently, *adv.* Evidentemente.
evil ['iːvəl], *a.* Cattivo, reo, malvagio, tristo, maligno, perverso. || *n.* Male, torto, danno, *m.*; ingiuria, violenza, *f.*; oltraggio, *m.* **The — eye,** il malocchio, *m.*, la iettatura, *f.*; **the Evil One,** il diavolo, *m.*; **of — repute,** di cattiva fama; **an — tongue,** una mala lingua, *f.*; **— days,** avversità; **—-doer,** malfattore, *m.*; **—-minded,** malevolo, perverso; **—-speaking,** maldicenza, *f.*
evilly, *adv.* Male.
evilness, *n.* Malignità, perversità, cattiveria, *f.*
evince [e'vins], *v.t.* Mostrare, manifestare, dimostrare, indicare.
eviscerate [e'visəreit], *v.t.* Sventrare, sviscerare.
evisceration, *n.* Svisceramento, *m.*
evocation [evou'keiʃən], *n.* Evocazione, *f.*
evoke, *v.t.* Evocare.

evolution [evəˈlu:ʃən], *n.* Evoluzione, *f.*; sviluppo, svolgimento, *m.*; (*Math.*) estrazione, *f.*; (*Chem.*) esalazione, *f.*; (*fig.*) movimento, *m.*
evolve [eˈvɔlv], *v.t.* Svolgere, sviluppare; *v.i.* svilupparsi.
evulsion [eˈvʌlʃən], *n.* Strappamento, *m.*
ewe [ju:], *n.* (*Zool.*) Pecora, *f.* **— lamb,** agnella, *f.*
ewer [ˈju:əɹ], *n.* Brocca, *f.*
ex- (1) [eks], *prep.* Già, d'un tempo. **Ex-service man,** ex-combattente, *m.*
ex- (2), *prep.* Da, fuori. **Ex-warehouse,** fuori magazzino.
exacerbate [eksˈæsəɹbeit], *v.t.* Esacerbare, aggravare, esasperare.
exact [egˈzækt], *v.t.* Esigere, estorcere. || *a.* Esatto, preciso, rigoroso.
exacting, *a.* Esigente.
exaction, *n.* Estorsione, concussione, esazione, *f.*
exactitude, exactness, *n.* Esattezza, precisione, *f.*
exactly, *adv.* Esattamente, precisamente.
exactor, *n.* Esattore, *m.*
exaggerate [egˈzædʒəreit], *v.t.* Esagerare.
exaggeration, *n.* Esagerazione, *f.*
exaggerative, *a.* Esagerativo.
exalt [egˈzɔ:lt], *v.t.* Esaltare, sollevare, innalzare; vantare, lodare.
exaltation, *n.* Esaltazione, *f.*; innalzamento, *m.*
exaltedness, *n.* Altezza, elevatezza, *f.*
examination [egzæminˈeiʃən], *n.* Esame, *m.*, prova, *f.*; considerazione, investigazione, verifica, *f.*; (*Law*) interrogatorio, *m.*; ispezione, visita, *f.*; scrutinio, *m.* **Competitive —,** concorso, *m.*; **— paper,** foglio d'esame, *m.*; **viva voce —,** esame orale, *m.*; (*Comm.*) **— in bankruptcy,** verifica di fallimento; **to pass an —,** passare un esame; **to fail in an —,** essere bocciato all'esame; **entrance —,** esame d'ammissione, *m.*
examine [egˈzæmin], *v.t.* Esaminare, provare; (*Law*) interrogare; considerare, investigare; visitare, perquisire.
examinee [egzæmiˈni:], *n.* Esaminando, candidato, *m.*
examiner, *n.* Esaminatore, *m.*, esaminatrice, *f.*; (*of plays*) censore teatrale, *m.*; **Board of Examiners,** commissione d'esame, *f.*
example [ekˈzɑ:mpl], *n.* Esempio, esemplare, modello, *m.* **For —,** per esempio; **to set an —,** dar l'esempio; **to make an — of,** punir esemplarmente; **to take — by,** imitare l'esempio di; **without —,** senza precedenti.
exanimate [eksˈænimət], *a.* Esanime; abbattuto.
exarch [ˈeksɑ:ɹk], *n.* Esarca, *m.*
exasperate [egˈzæspəreit], *v.t.* Esasperare, irritare, inasprire.
exasperation, *n.* Esasperazione, irritazione, *f.*
excavate [ˈekskəveit], *v.t.* Scavare.
excavation, *n.* Scavo, *m.*
excavator, *n.* Scavatore, sterratore, *m.*; (*Mech.*) scavatrice, *f.*, macchina scavatrice, *f.*
exceed [ekˈsi:d], *v.t.* Eccedere, superare, oltrepassare, andare oltre.
exceeding, *a.* Eccedente.
exceedingly, *adv.* Estremamente, eccessivamente; (*as prefix*) stra-.

excel [ekˈsel], *v.t.i.* Eccellere, soprastare, sorpassare, vincere. **To — in,** eccellere in.
excellence, excellency, *n.* Eccellenza, superiorità, perfezione, *f.*; merito, *m.* **His Excellency,** Sua Eccellenza, *f.*
excellent, *a.* Eccellente. **Most —,** eccellentissimo.
excellently, *adv.* Eccellentemente, perfettamente.
except [ekˈsept], *v.t.* Eccettuare, escludere, omettere; *v.i.* eccepire, obiettare. || *prep.* Eccetto, eccettuato, all'infuori, salvo. || *conj.* Eccetto che, salvo che, fuorchè, senonchè.
excepting, *prep.* Eccetto, salvo.
exception [ekˈsepʃən], *n.* Eccezione, *f.*; obiezione, *f.* **By way of —,** in via eccezionale; **to take — to,** trovar a ridire, aversi a male, eccepire a; criticare, censurare; **to be an —,** costituire un'eccezione.
exceptionable, *a.* Criticabile, biasimevole.
exceptional, *a.* Eccezionale.
exceptionally, *adv.* Eccezionalmente.
excerpt [ˈeksə:ɹpt], *n.* Estratto, *m.*
excess [ekˈses], *n.* Eccesso, *m.*, dismisura, intemperanza, *f.*; (*of weight*) soprappeso, *m.* **To do to —,** fare all'eccesso; **— fare,** supplemento, *m.*; **— profits,** sopraprofitto, *m.*
excessive, *a.* Eccessivo, estremo.
excessively, *adv.* Eccessivamente.
exchange [eksˈtʃeindʒ], *n.* Scambio, ricambio, baratto, *m.*; (*Comm.*) cambio, *m.*; (*edifice*) borsa, *f.* || *v.t.* Scambiare, cambiare, barattare; *v.i.* formare oggetto di scambio. **Telephone —,** centralino, *m.*; **— -office,** cambiavalute, *m.*; **— business,** aggiotaggio, *m.*; **bill of —,** cambiale, *f.*; **rate of —,** corso del cambio, *m.*
exchequer [eksˈtʃekəɹ], *n.* Tesoro, erario, *m.*, tesoreria, *f.*; risorse, *f.pl.* **Chancellor of the Exchequer,** Cancelliere dello Scacchiere, *m.*
excisable [ekˈsaizəbl], *a.* Imponibile, soggetto a dazio.
excise, *n.* Imposta, *f.*, dazio, *m.*; tributi indiretti, *m.pl.*; regia, *f.* || *v.t.* Tassare, gravare d'imposta, daziare; tagliare.
exciseman, *n.* Daziere, *m.*
excision [ekˈsiʃən], *n.* Taglio, *m.*; omissione, *f.*
excitability [eksaitəˈbiliti], *n.* Eccitabilità, *f.*
excitable, *a.* Eccitabile, irritabile, impressionabile.
excite [ekˈsait], *v.t.* Eccitare, concitare, suscitare; destare, provocare; stimolare. **To — suspicion,** suscitare il sospetto.
excited, *a.* Fremente, turbato, eccitato.
excitedly, *adv.* Concitatamente.
excitement, *n.* Eccitazione, emozione, *f.*; eccitamento, stimolo, *m.*; febbre, esaltazione, *f.*; orgasmo, *m.*
exciter, *n.* (*Med, etc.*) Eccitatore, *m.*
exciting, *a.* Commovente, emozionante.
exclaim [eksˈkleim], *v.i.* Esclamare, gridare. **To — against,** inveire contro.
exclamation [eksklәˈmeiʃən], *n.* Esclamazione, *f.*; grido, *m.* **Note of —,** punto esclamativo, *m.*
exclamatory, *a.* Esclamativo.
exclude [eksˈklu:d], *v.t.* Escludere, eccettuare
excluding, *prep.* Senza contare, escluso.
exclusion, *n.* Esclusione, *f.*
exclusive, *a.* Esclusivo; unico, solo. **— of,** non compreso, escluso.

exclusively, *adv.* Esclusivamente.
exclusiveness, *n.* Esclusività, *f.*
exclusivism, *n.* Esclusivismo, *m.*
excogitate [eks'kɔdʒiteit], *v.t.* Escogitare; ritrovare, inventare.
excommunicate [ekskə'mju:nikeit], *v.t.* Scomunicare.
excommunication, *n.* Scomunica, *f.*
excoriate [eks'kɔrieit], *v.t.* Scorticare; escoriare.
excoriation, *n.* Scorticatura, *f.*; escoriazione, *f.*
excrement ['ekskrimənt], *n.* Escremento, *m.*
excrescence, excrescency [eks'kresəns, eks'kresənsi], *n.* Escrescenza, *f.*
excrescent, *a.* Escrescente.
excretion [eks'kri:ʃən], *n.* Escrezione, *f.*
excretive, excretory, *a.* Escretivo, escretorio.
excruciate [eks'kru:ʃieit], *v.t.* Tormentare, straziare.
excruciating, *a.* Atroce, straziante. **— pains,** dolori atroci, *m.pl.*
exculpate ['ekskʌlpeit], *v.t.* Discolpare, scolpare, assolvere.
exculpation, *n.* Discolpa, giustificazione, *f.*
exculpatory, *a.* Giustificativo.
excursion [eks'kə:ɹʃən], *n.* Escursione, corsa, gita, *f.*, viaggio, *m.*; (*fig.*) digressione, *f.* (*Rail.*) **— ticket,** biglietto ridotto, *m.*; **— train,** treno speciale, treno festivo, *m.*; **to go on an —,** fare una gita.
excursionist, *n.* Escursionista, gitante, *m.*
excursive, *a.* Digressivo, errante.
excursively, *adv.* Sconnessamente
excursiveness, *n.* Sconnessione, *f.*
excursus, *n.* Excursus, *m.*; dissertazione, *f.*
excusable [eks'kju:səbl], *a.* Scusabile, perdonabile.
excuse (1) [eks'kju:s], *n.* Scusa, giustificazione, *f.*, pretesto, *m.* **To find an —,** trovare un pretesto; **to admit of no —,** non ammettere scuse; **to serve as an —,** servire di scusa.
excuse (2) [eks'kju:z], *v.t.* Scusare, perdonare, scolpare, esonerare. **To — from,** dispensare da; **Excuse me!** Scusi!, Scusate!, Scusa! **please — me from lessons,** voglir dispensarmi dalle lezioni; **to — oneself for,** scusarsi di; **to — one's action,** giustificarsi.
exeat ['eksiət], *n.* Permesso di assentarsi, *m.*
execrable, ['eksikrəbl], *a.* Esecrabile.
execrably, *adv.* Esecrabilmente.
execrate, *v.t.* Esecrare, maledire.
execration, *n.* Esecrazione, *f.*
executable [ek'sekju:təbl], *a.* Eseguibile, fattibile.
executant, *n.* Esecutore, *m.*
execute ['eksikju:t], *v.t.* Eseguire, adempiere, mandare ad effetto; (*a document*) firmare, rendere esecutivo; giustiziare.
execution, *n.* Esecuzione, *f.*, adempimento, *m.*; compimento, *m.*; sequestro, *m.*; **In the — of one's duty,** nell'adempimento del proprio dovere; **to put into —,** dare esecuzione a, tradurre in atto.
executioner, *n.* Boia, carnefice, *m.*
executive, *a.* Esecutivo.
executor, *n.* Esecutore testamentario, *m.*
executorship, *n.* Esecuzione testamentaria, *f.*
executrix, *n.* Esecutrice testamentaria, *f.*
exegesis [eksi'dʒi:sis], *n.* Esegesi, *f.*
exegetical, *a.* Esegetico.
exemplar [ek'zemplәɹ], *n.* Esemplare, modello, tipo, *m.*
exemplariness, *n.* Esemplarità, *f.*
exemplary, *a.* Esemplare.
exemplification [ekzemplifi'keiʃən], *n.* Esemplificazione, *f.*
exemplify, *v.t.* Esemplificare, fare copia conforme.
exempt [eg'zemt], *v.t.* Esentare, dispensare. ‖ *a.* Esente. **— from military service,** esente dal servizio militare.
exemption, *n.* Esenzione, *f.*
exequies ['eksikwiz], *n.pl.* Esequie, *f.pl.*
exercise [eksəɹ'saiz], *n.* Esercizio, *m.*, pratica, *f.*; (*lesson*) tema, *f.*, compito, *m.* ‖ *v.t.* Esercitare, adoperare, usare; *v.i.* esercitarsi, addestrarsi, impratichirsi. **—-book,** quaderno, *m.*
exergue [ek'zə:ɹg], *n.* Esergo, *m.*
exert [eg'zə:ɹt], *v.t.* Esercitare, adoperare, fare uso di. **To — oneself,** fare sforzi, darsi da fare; **to — oneself to the utmost,** fare tutto il possibile.
exertion, *n.* Sforzo, *m.* **It is an — to him to speak,** deve fare uno sforzo per parlare.
exfoliation [eksfouli'eiʃən], *n.* (*Bot., Med.*) Esfogliazione, *f.*
exhalation [eksə'leiʃən], *n.* Esalazione, *f.*, respiro, *m.*
exhale, *v.t.i.* Esalare, emanare, spirare.
exhaust [eg'zɔ:st], *v.t.* Esaurire, consumare, distruggere, spossare. ‖ *n.* (*Motor.*) Scappamento, *m.* **To — someone's patience,** esaurire la pazienza di qualcuno; (*Motor.*) **—-box,** camera di scarico, *f.*; **—-pipe,** tubo di scappamento, *m.*; **—-valve,** valvola di scappamento, *f.*
exhausted, *a.* Esausto, esaurito.
exhaustible, *a.* Esauribile.
exhausting, *a.* Spossante, stancante.
exhaustive, *a.* Esauriente.
exhaustively, *adv.* Pienamente, a fondo.
exhaustless, *a.* Inesauribile.
exhibit [eg'zibit], *v.t.* Mostrare, esporre; (*Law*) esibire. ‖ *n.* Oggetto esposto, *m.*; (*Law*) documento, *m.*, pezza d'appoggio, *f.*
exhibition, *n.* Esposizione, mostra, *f.*; salone, *m.*; esibizione, *f.*; (*scholarship*) borsa di studio, *f.*; (*Law*) produzione di documenti, *f.*; (*fig.*) spettacolo, *m.* **Industrial —,** mostra dell'industria, *f.*; **to make an — of oneself,** dare spettacolo di sè.
exhibitioner, *n.* Detentore di borsa di studio, *m.*; borsista, *m.*
exhibitor, *n.* Espositore, *m.*
exhilarate [eg'ziləreit], *v.t.* Esilarare, rallegrare.
exhilarating, *a.* Esilarante.
exhilaration, *n.* Allegrezza, ilarità, *f.*
exhort [eg'zɔ:ɹt], *v.t.* Esortare.
exhortation, *n.* Esortazione, *f.*
exhortative, *a.* Esortativo.
exhortatory, *a.* Esortatorio.
exhumation [eks'ju:meiʃən], *n.* Esumazione, *f.* disseppellimento, *m.*
exhume, *v.t.* Esumare.
exigence, exigency, *n.* Esigenza, necessità, *f.*; bisogno, *m.*; emergenza, *f.*
exigent, *a.* Esigente, urgente, premuroso.
exigible, *a.* Esigibile.
exiguity [eksi'gju:iti], *n.* Esiguità, piccolezza, *f.*

exiguous [ek'zigju:əs], *a.* Esiguo.
exile [ek'zail], *n.* Esilio, bando, *m.*; (*person*) esule, proscritto, fuoruscito, profugo, *m.* || *v.t.* Esiliare, condannare all'esilio, proscrivere. **To drive into —,** esiliare; **to go into — voluntarily,** esulare.
exility [eg'ziliti], *n.* Esilità, tenuità, scarsezza, *f.*
exist [eg'zist], *v.i.* Esistere, vivere.
existence, *n.* Esistenza, vita, *f.* **To be in —,** esistere; **the struggle for —,** la lotta per l'esistenza, *f.*; **to call into —,** dare vita a.
existing, *a.* Esistente.
exit [eg'zit], *n.* Uscita, *f.*; (*fig.*) fine, morte, *f.* **To make one's —,** uscire, morire; (*Theat.*) — (*go off the stage*) esce.
exodus [ek'sədəs], *n.* Esodo, *m.*
exogenous [ek'zɔdʒənəs], *a.* (*Bot.*) Esogeno.
exonerate [eg'zɔnəreit], *v.t.* Esonerare, dispensare, liberare; discolpare, giustificare.
exoneration, *n.* Esonero, *m.*, destituzione, discolpa, *f.*
exophthalmia [eksɔf'θælmiə], *n.* (*Med.*) Esoftalmia, *f.*
exorbitance [eg'zɔ:ɹbitəns], *n.* Esorbitanza, *f.*; eccesso, *m.*
exorbitant, *a.* Esorbitante, eccessivo.
exorbitantly, *adv.* Eccessivamente; fuor di misura; enormemente.
exorcise ['eksɔɹsaiz], *v.t.* Esorcizzare.
exorciser, *n.* Esorcizzatore, *m.*
exorcism, *n.* Esorcismo, *m.*
exorcist, *n.* Esorcista, *m.*
exordial [eg'zɔ:ɹdiəl], *a.* Proemiale.
exordium, *n.* Esordio, *m.*
exosmosis [eksɔs'mousis], *n.* Esosmosi, *f.*
exoteric [eksə'terik], *a.* Essoterico.
exotic [eg'zɔtik], *a.* Esotico. || *n.* Pianta esotica, *f.*
expand [ek'spænd], *v.t.* Espandere, spandere, spiegare, allargare; *v.i.* spandersi, dilatarsi, allargarsi, gonfiarsi.
expanse, *n.* Distesa, estensione, *f.*; apertura, larghezza, *f.*
expansible, *a.* Espansibile.
expansion, *n.* Espansione, estensione, *f.*, distendimento, allargamento, *m.*; (*area*) distesa, *f.*
expansive, *a.* Espansivo.
expansiveness, *n.* Espansività, effusione, *f.*
expatiate [eks'peiʃieit], *v.i.* Diffondersi, dilungarsi, soffermarsi. **To — upon a subject,** soffermarsi su un argomento.
expatiation, *n.* Lungo discorso, *m.*
expatriate [eks'pætrieit], *v.t.* Espatriare.
expatriation, *n.* Espatrio, *m.*
expect [ek'spekt], *v.t.* Aspettare, contare su, presumere; sperare, anticipare, attendere, prevedere. **He is expected to make a speech,** si prevede che farà un discorso; **he is not expected to live,** non si crede che vivrà; **it was to be expected,** era d'aspettarsi; **I do not know what to —,** non so che cosa mi attende; **you are expected,** si conta su voi, vi aspettiamo; **the cost of living is higher than I expected,** il costo della vita è più alto di quanto mi sarei espettato; **to be expecting a baby,** attendere un bambino.
expectance, expectancy, *n.* Aspettativa, attesa, *f.*
expectant, *a.* Aspettante.
expectantly, *adv.* In attesa.
expectation, *n.* Aspettativa, attesa, *f.*; speranza, previsione, *f.*; (*of employ, etc.*) aspettativa, prospettiva, *f.* **Beyond one's expectations,** oltre le previsioni; **to live in —,** aspettare sempre; **in — of your reply,** in attesa della vostra risposta; **to answer one's expectations,** rispondere all'aspettativa; **— of success,** prospettiva di successo, *f.*; **to disappoint one's —,** diludere le speranze.
expectorant [ek'spektərənt], *n.* (*Med.*) Espettorante, *m.*
expectorate, *v.t.i.* Espettorare.
expectoration, *n.* Espettorazione, *f.*
expedience, expediency [ek'spi:diəns, ek'spi:diənsi], *n.* Vantaggio, *m.*, convenienza, praticità, utilità, *f.*
expedient, *a.* Pratico, utile, vantaggioso. || *n.* Espediente, mezzo, ripiego, ritrovato, *m.* **To have recourse to expedients,** ricorrere ad espedienti.
expediently, *adv.* A proposito, convenientemente.
expedite [ekspi'dait], *v.t.* Spedire, affrettare, sbrigare, facilitare.
expedition [ekspi'diʃən], *n.* Spedizione, impresa, *f.*; celerità, prestezza, speditezza, *f.* **To go on an —,** fare una spedizione.
expeditionary, *a.* Di spedizione. **— force,** corpo di spedizione, *m.*
expeditious [ekspi'diʃəs], *a.* Speditivo, sbrigativo, pronto, sollecito.
expeditiously, *adv.* Prontamente.
expeditiousness, *n.* Celerità, sollecitudine, *f*
expel [ek'spel], *v.t.* Espellere, scacciare.
expellent, *a.* Espulsivo.
expend [ek'spend], *v.t.* Spendere; (*fig.*) consumare, esaurire.
expenditure [ek'spenditʃəɹ], *n.* Spese, *f.pl.*; consumo, *m*, sacrificio, *m.*; sborso, *m.*
expense [eks'pens], *n.* Spesa, *f.*, spese, *f.pl.*, costo, carico, sborso, *m.* **At a great —,** con grande spesa; **at any —,** a qualunque costo; **at my —,** a spese mie; **free of —,** senza spesa; **incidental expenses,** spese casuali, *f.pl.*; **to clear one's expenses,** rifarsi delle spese; **to go to —,** spendere molto; **travelling expenses,** indennità di viaggio; **at the — of,** alle spese di; **at one's own —,** a proprie spese.
expensive, *a.* Caro, costoso, dispendioso.
expensively, *adv.* Con spesa enorme; costosamente.
expensiveness, *n.* Carezza, costosità, *f.*
experience [ek'spiəriəns], *n.* Esperienza, pratica, *f.* || *v.t.* Provare, subire, aver esperienza, conoscere per prova.
experienced, *a.* Esperto, pratico, versato.
experiment [eks'perimənt], *n.* Esperimento, *m.*; esperienza, *f.* || *v.t.* Esperimentare, sperimentare; *v.i.* fare esperimenti. **To — on,** fare esperimenti su.
experimental, *a.* Sperimentale.
expert (1) [eks'pəːɹt], *a.* Esperto, pratico, abile.
expert (2) ['ekspəɹt], *n.* Esperto, perito, *m.* **To submit a thing to an —,** sottomettere una cosa ad un perito.
expertly, *adv.* Abilmente.
expertness, *n.* Abilità, destrezza, *f.*
expiable ['ekspiəbl], *a.* Espiabile.
expiate ['ekspieit], *v.t.* Espiare.
expiation, *n.* Espiazione, *f.*
expiatory [ekspi'eitəri], *a.* Espiatorio.

expiration [ekspai'reiʃən], *n.* Fine, scadenza, *f.*; (*Med.Bot.*) espirazione, *f.*
expire [eks'paiɹ], (*to die*) Spirare; (*to come to an end*) terminare, finire, scadere. **His lease expires at the end of the year,** il suo fitto scade alla fine dell'anno
expiring, *a.* Cessante, che spira, che scade.
expiry, *n.* Fine, termine, scadenza, *f.* **At the — of our agreement,** alla scadenza del nostro accordo.
explain [ek'splein], *v.t.* Spiegare, manifestare.
explainable, *a.* Spiegabile.
explanation [eksplə'neiʃən], *n.* Spiegazione, *f.*; interpretazione, *f.*; schiarimento, *m.*
explanatory, *a.* Esplicativo, espositivo.
expletive ['eksplitiv], *a.* Pleonastico, espletivo. || *n.* Parola espletiva, *f.*; (*oath*) bestemmia, *f.*
explicable [eks'plikəbl], *a.* Spiegabile.
explicative, explicatory ['eksplikətiv, ekspli'keitəri], *a.* Esplicativo.
explicit [eks'plisit], *a.* Esplicito.
explicitly, *adv.* Esplicitamente.
explicitness, *n.* Chiarezza, *f.*
explode [eks'ploud], *v.t.* Far scoppiare, far saltare; *v.i.* scoppiare, esplodere. **To — with laughter,** scoppiare dalle risa; **an exploded theory,** una teoria screditata, *f.*
exploit ['eksplɔit], *n.* Fatto eroico, *m.*, prodezza, *f.* || *v.t.* Utilizzare; sfruttare. **Exploits,** gesta, *f.pl.*
exploitation, *n.* Utilizzazione, *f.*, sfruttamento, *m.*
exploiter, *n.* Sfruttatore, *m.*
explorable [eks'plɔ:rəbl], *a.* Esplorabile.
exploration [eksplɔ'reiʃən], *n.* Esplorazione, *f.*
exploratory, *a.* Esploratorio.
explore [eks'plɔ:ɹ], *v.t.* Esplorare.
explorer, *n.* Esploratore, *m.*, esploratrice, *f.*
explosion [eks'plouʒən], *n.* Esplosione, *f.*, scoppio, *m.*
explosive, *n.a.* Esplosivo, *m.* **High —,** alto esplosivo, *m.*
explosiveness, *n.* Esplosività, *f.*
exponent [eks'pounənt], *n.* Rappresentante, esponente, interprete, *m.*; (*Math.*) esponente, *m.*
export (1) ['ekspɔɹt], *n.* Esportazione, *f.*; prodotto d'esportazione, *m.* **— duty,** dazio di esportazione, *m.*; **— trade,** commercio d'esportazione, *m.*
export (2) [eks'pɔ:ɹt], *v.t.* Esportare.
exportation, *n.* Esportazione, *f.*
exporter, *n.* Esportatore, *m.*
expose [eks'pouz], *v.t.* Esporre, mostrare; (*fig.*) svelare, palesare, smascherare; (*Phot.*) esporre; (*a child*) abbandonare. **To — for sale,** esporre alla vendita; **to — a fraud,** smascherare un'impostura; **to — oneself,** esporsi; **to — oneself to ridicule,** esporsi al ridicolo.
exposition, *n.* Esposizione, interpretazione, *f.*
expositor [eks'pɔzitəɹ], *n.* Espositore, chiosatore, commentatore, *m.*
expostulate [eks'pɔstju:leit], *v.i.* Far rimostranze.
expostulation, *n.* Rimostranza, *f.*, rimprovero, *m.*
expostulatory, *a.* Ammonitorio.
exposure [eks'pouʒəɹ], *n.* Esposizione, *f.*; (*fig.*) scandalo, *m.*; (*Phot.*) l'esporre una lastra fotografica, *m.*, posa, *f.* **To die of —,** morire per assideramento.
expound [eks'paund], *v.t.* Spiegare, esporre, interpretare.
expounder, *n.* Interprete, *m.*
express [eks'pres], *a.* Espresso; esplicito. || *n.* Espresso, *m.*; treno direttissimo, *m.* || *v.t.* Esprimere; spedire; (*squeeze out*) spremere. **By — delivery,** per espresso. || *adv.* In fretta; speditamente.
expressible, *a.* Esprimibile.
expression, *n.* Espressione, *f.*
expressive, *a.* Espressivo.
expressively, *adv.* Espressivamente.
expressiveness, *n.* Forza di espressione, energia, *f.*
expressly, *adv.* Espressamente, a bella posta, apposta, appunto.
expropriate [eks'prouprieit], *v.t.* Espropriare.
expropriation, *n.* Espropriazione, *f.*
expulsion [eks'pʌlʃen], *n.* Espulsione, *f.*
expulsive, *a.* Espulsivo.
expunge [eks'pʌndʒ], *v.t.* Espungere.
expurgate ['ekspəɹgeit], *v.t.* Espurgare.
expurgation, *n.* Espurgazione, *f.*
expurgatory, *a.* Espurgatorio; purificatorio.
exquisite ['ekskwizit], *a.* Squisito, ricercato; (*of pain*) acutissimo. || *n.* Elegante, bellimbusto, *m.*
exquisitely, *adv.* Squisitamente, perfettamente.
exquisiteness, *n.* Squisitezza, ricercatezza, *f.*; (*of grief, pain, etc.*) violenza, *f.*
extant [ek'stænt], *a.* Esistente, attuale.
extemporaneous [ekstempə'reiniəs], *a.* Estemporaneo, improvviso.
extemporaneously, *adv.* Estemporaneamente, su due piedi.
extempore [eks'tempəri], *a.* Improvviso. || *adv.* Senza preparazione, su due piedi. **To speak —,** fare un discorso estemporaneo.
extemporize, *v.t.i.* Improvvisare.
extend [eks'tend], *v.t.* Estendere, stendere, allargare, allungare; prolungare, continuare; *v.i.* stendersi; prolungarsi; (*to spread*) propagarsi. **To — a railway line,** prolungare una linea ferroviaria; (*Mil.*) **extended order,** ordine sparso, *m.*
extendible, extensible [eks'tendəbl, eks'tensəbl], *a.* Estendibile.
extension, *n.* Estensione, *f.*; allargamento, *m.*; prolungamento, *m.* **To get an — of time,** ottenere una proroga.
extensive, *a.* Esteso, vasto, ampio, spazioso.
extensively, *adv.* Estesamente, ampiamente.
extensor, *n.* (*Anat.*) Estensore, *m.*
extent [eks'tent], *n.* Estensione, *f.*, grado, limite, punto, *m.* **To a certain —,** fino ad un certo punto; **to a great —,** ad un alto grado; **to the — of,** fino a, fino al punto di; **To what —?** Fin dove? Fino a qual punto?
extenuate [eks'tenju:eit], *v.t.* Estenuare, attenuare, diminuire.
extenuating, *a.* (*Law*) Attenuante. **— circumstances,** circostanze attenuanti, *f.pl.*
extenuation, *n.* Attenuazione, *f.*
exterior [eks'tiəriəɹ], *a.* Esteriore, esterno. || *n.* Esterno, *m.*
exteriorly, *adv.* Esteriormente, all'esterno.
exterminate [eks'tə:ɹmineit], *v.t.* Distruggere, sterminare, estirpare.
extermination, *n.* Distruzione, *f.*, sterminio, *m.*

external [eks'tə:ɹnəl], *a.* Esteriore, esterno.
externally, *adv.* Esternamente, dal di fuori.
externals, *n.pl.* Le esteriorità, le apparenze, *f.pl.*
exterritoriality [eksteritɔri'æliti], *n.* Extraterritorialità, *f.*
extinct [eks'tiŋkt], *a.* Estinto, spento, morto; disusato, vieto.
extinction, *n.* Estinzione, *f.*; (*of a debt*) ammortamento, *m.*
extinguish [eks'tiŋgwiʃ], *v.t.* Spegnere, estinguere; (*fig.*) ecclissare, oscurare.
extinguishable, *a.* Spegnibile.
extinguisher, *n.* (*for fire*) Estintore, *m.*; (*for candle*) spegnitoio, *m.*
extirpate ['ekstəɹpeit], *v.t.* Estirpare, distruggere.
extirpation, *n.* Estirpazione, *f.*, sradicamento, *m.*
extirpator, *n.* Distruttore, *m.*; estirpatore, *m.*
extol [eks'tɔl], *v.t.* Esaltare, lodare, innalzare, celebrare.
extort [eks'tɔ:ɹt], *v.t.* Estorcere, togliere a forza, strappare. **To — a promise,** strappare una promessa.
extortion, *n.* Estorsione, *f.*
extortionate, *a.* Oppressivo, esorbitante. **An — price,** un prezzo esorbitante, *m.*
extortioner, *n.* Chi estorce, *m.*; strozzino, *m.*
extra ['ekstrə], *a.* In più, addizionale, straordinario, supplementare, aggiunto, extra. || *adv.* Di più. || *n.* Supplemento, *m.*, aggiunta, *f.*; il di più, *m.*; **— charge,** spesa supplementare, *f.*
extract (1) ['ekstrækt], *n.* Estratto, brano, *m.*
extract (2) [ek'strækt], *v.t.* Estrarre, trarre fuori; scegliere. **To have a tooth extracted,** farsi cavare un dente.
extraction, *n.* Estrazione, *f.*; origine, *f.*; lignaggio, *m.* **Of French —,** d'origine francese.
extractive, *a.* Estrattivo.
extractor, *n.* Estrattore, *m.*
extradite ['ekstrədait], *v.t.* Estradare.
extradition, *n.* Estradizione, *f.*
extramundane [ekstrəmʌn'dein], *a.* Ultraterreno.
extramural [ekstrə'mju:rəl], *a.* Estramurale, fuori le mura.
extraneous [ek'streiniəs], *a.* Estraneo, straniero, non essenziale.
extraordinarily [eks'trɔ:ɹdinərili], *adv.* Straordinariamente.
extraordinary [eks'trɔ:ɹdinəri], *a.* Straordinario, raro.
extra-parochial [ekstrəpə'roukiəl], *a.* Fuori della parrocchia.
extraterritoriality [cp. **exterritoriality**].
extravagance [eks'trævəgəns], *n.* Stravaganza, *f.*; (*money*) spese stravaganti, *f.pl.*, prodigalità, *f.*, sperpero, *m.*
extravagant, *a.* Stravagante, prodigo; (*of price*) esorbitante.
extravagantly, *adv.* Prodigalmente, profusamente; eccessivamente.
extravasation [ekstrævə'seiʃən], *n.* (*Med.*) Estravasazione. *f.*
extreme [ek'stri:m], *a.* Estremo, ultimo. || *n.* Estremo, fine, termine, *m.*, estremità, *f.* **Extremes meet,** gli estremi si toccano; **to carry to extremes,** spingere agli estremi; **to go to extremes,** andare agli estremi; **— penalty,** pena di morte, *f.*; **— unction,** estrema unzione, *f.*
extremely, *adv.* Estremamente, in sommo grado.
extremity, *n.* Estremità, *f.*; eccesso, colmo, *m.*; imbarazzo, *m.* **To drive to extremities,** spingere agli estremi.
extricable ['ekstrikəbl], *a.* Districabile.
extricate ['ekstrikeit], *v.t.* Liberare, trarre d'impaccio, distrigare. **To — oneself,** liberarsi, cavarsela.
extrication, *n.* Liberazione, *f.*
extrinsic [eks'trinsik], *a.* Estrinseco.
extrude [eks'tru:d], *v.t.* Espellere.
extrusion, *n.* Espulsione, *f.*
exuberance [ek'zju:bərəns], *n.* Esuberanza, sovrabbondanza, *f.*
exuberant, *a.* Esuberante, sovrabbondante.
exuberantly, *adv.* Esuberantemente.
exudation [egzju:'deiʃən], *n.* Trasudazione, *f.*, trasudamento, *m.*
exude, *v.t.i.* Trasudare.
exulcerate [eg'zʌlsəreit], *v.t.* (*Med.*) Esulcerare.
exulceration, *n.* Esulcerazione, *f.*
exult [eg'zʌlt], *v.i.* Esultare, trionfare, gioire. **To — at,** rallegrarsi di.
exultant, *a.* Esultante, trionfante.
exultation, *n.* Esultazione, *f.*; giubilo, trionfo, *m.*
exultingly, *adv.* In trionfo, esultando.
eyas ['aiəs], *n.* (*Zool.*) Falconcello, *m.*
eye [ai], *n.* Occhio, *m.*; (*of needle*) cruna, *f.*; (*of hook and eye*) maglietta, *f.*; (*Naut.*) occhiello, *m.*; (*fig.*) vista, *f.*, sguardo, *m.*; (*Bot.*) gemma, *f.*, bottone, *m.* || *v.t.* Guardare, osservare, squadrare. **Before my very eyes,** proprio davanti ai miei occhi; **blind in one —,** guercio, cieco da un occhio; **farther than the — can reach,** a perdita d'occhio; **in the twinkling of an —,** in un batter d'occhio; **a practised —,** un occhio esperto; **with tears in his eyes,** con le lagrime agli occhi; **to cast one's eyes over,** dare un'occhiata a; **to cry one's eyes out,** struggersi in lagrime; **to have an — to,** aver riguardo a; **to see — to —,** esser della stessa idea; **to keep an — on,** sorvegliare, tener d'occhio; **to please the —,** piacere agli occhi; **to strike the —,** dar nell'occhio; **in the wind's —,** contro vento; **to set eyes on,** mettere gli occhi su; **to the naked —,** a occhio nudo; **to make eyes at,** guardare amorosamente; **— -opener,** rivelatore, *m.*; **— -piece,** oculare, *m.*; **— -tooth,** dente canino, *m.*
eyeball, *n.* Globo dell'occhio, *m.*
eyebright, *n.* (*Bot.*) Eufrasia, *f.*
eyebrow, *n.* Sopracciglio, *m.*
eyed, *a.* Occhiuto, dagli occhi. **Blue —,** dagli occhi azzurri; **one-—,** monocolo, guercio.
eyeglass, *n.* Monocolo, *m.* **Eyeglasses,** occhiali, *m.pl.*
eyehole, *n.* Occhiaia, orbita, *f.*
eyelash, *n.* Ciglia, *f.*
eyeless, *a.* Cieco.
eyelet, *n.* Occhiello, *m.*
eyelid, *n.* Palpebra, *f.*
eyeshot, *n.* Portata d'occhio, *f.*
eyesight, *n.* Vista, visione, *f.*
eyesore, *n.* (*fig.*) Pugno nell'occhio, *m.*

eyewitness, *n.* Testimone oculare, *m.*
eyot [cp. **ait**].
eyre [ɛəɹ], *n.* (*Law, Hist.*) Corte ambulante, *f.* **Justice in —,** giudice ambulante, *m.*
eyrie [ˈɛəri], *n.* Nido d'uccello da preda, *m.*

F

F, f, [ef]. Sesta lettera dell'alfabeto inglese; (*Mus.*) fa, *m.*
Fabian [ˈfeibiən], *n.a.* Fabiano, *m.*; (*fig.*) temporeggiatore, *m.*
fable [ˈfeibəl], *n.* Favola, *f.* || *v.t.i.* Favoleggiare, raccontar favole.
fabled, *a.* Favoloso, mitico.
fabric [ˈfæbric], *n.* (*material*) Stoffa, *f.*; tessuto, *m.*; (*edifice*) fabbrica, *f.*, edificio, *m.*; costruzione, *f.* **Dress fabrics,** stoffe per abiti, *f.pl.*; **furnishing fabrics,** tappezzerie, *f.pl.*
fabricate, *v.t.* Fabbricare, inventare.
fabrication, *n.* Invenzione, menzogna, *f.*
fabricator, *n.* Fabbricatore, costruttore, *m.*
fabulist [ˈfæbju:list], *n.* Favolatore, *m.*
fabulous, *a.* Favoloso.
fabulously, *adv.* Favolosamente.
fabulousness, *n.* Favolosità, *f.*
façade [fəˈsɑ:d], *n.* Facciata, *f.*
face [feis], *n.* Faccia, *f.*, volto, viso, *m.*; figura, fisonomia, *f.*; (*of animals*) muso, *m.*; (*of things*) superficie, *f.*; (*of clock, etc.*) quadrante, *m.*; (*impudence*) sfrontatezza, *f.*; (*grimace*) smorfia, boccacia, *f.* || *v.t.* Affrontare, far fronte a, opporre, fronteggiare. **Before my —,** in faccia; **— to —,** faccia a faccia; **in — of,** di fronte a; **he had the — to say,** ebbe la faccia tosta di dire; **to laugh in someone's —,** ridere in faccia a qualcuno; **to make faces at,** far boccace a; **to fly in the — of,** sfidare apertamente; **to pull a long —,** fare la faccia lunga; **to put a good — on something,** fare buon viso a; **to set one's — against,** opporsi a; **to shut the door in someone's —,** chiudere la porta in faccia a qualcuno; **to slap someone's —,** dare uno schiaffo a qualcuno; **to wash one's —,** lavarsi la faccia; **to save one's —,** giustificarsi, salvare la faccia; **to put a new — on,** cambiare l'aspetto di; (*fig.*) **to — the music,** affrontare una sfuriata; **— -powder,** cipria, *f.*; **— -cream,** crema per la pelle, *f.* **— -lifting,** chirurgia estetica del viso, *f.*; **— value,** valore nominale, *m.*
faced, *a.* Dalla faccia, dal viso; ricoperto, rivestito. **Double- —,** furbo, doppio; **full- —,** dalla faccia tonda, paffuto; **bold- —,** dalla faccia tosta.
facer, *n.* Difficoltà inattesa, *f.*; schiaffo, *m.*
facet [ˈfæset], *n.* Faccetta, *f.*
faceted, *a.* Sfaccettato.
facetiae [fəˈsi:ʃii:], *n.pl.* Facezie, *f.pl.*
faceting, *n.* Sfaccettatura, *f.*
facetious [fəˈsi:ʃəs], *a.* Faceto.
facetiously, *adv.* Facetamente.
facetiousness, *n.* Piacevolezza, *f.*
facia [ˈfæʃə], *n.* Insegna di negozio, *f.*
facial [ˈfeiʃəl], *a.* Facciale.
facile [ˈfæsail], *a.* Facile; affabile, pieghevole, condiscendente, remissivo.
facileness, *n.* Pieghevolezza, remissività, *f.*
facilitate [fəˈsiliteit], *v.t.* Facilitare.
facilitation, *n.* Facilitazione, *f.*
facility, *n.* Facilità, *f.*
facing [ˈfeisiŋ], *n.* Risvolto, *m.*; (*of dress*) guarnizione, *f.*; (*of stone*) rivestimento, *m.* || *adv.* Di fronte a, in faccia a, dirimpetto a. (*Rail.*) **— the engine,** nel senso del treno.
facsimile [fækˈsimili], *n.* Facsimile, *m.*
fact [fækt], *n.* Fatto, *m.*; verità, *f.* **In —,** infatti, difatti; **in point of —,** in verità; **matter-of-fact,** positivo, normale; **the — of the matter is,** il fatto sta, il fatto è.
faction [ˈfækʃən], *n.* Fazione, *f.*; (*fig.*) discordia, dissensione, *f.*
factious, *a.* Fazioso, partigiano.
factiously, *adv.* Faziosamente.
factiousness, *n.* Spirito fazioso, *m.*, faziosità, *f.*
factitious [fækˈtiʃəs], *a.* Artificiale; falso.
factitiously, *adv.* Artificialmente.
factitiousness, *n.* Falsità, *f.*; artificialità, *f.*
factitive [ˈfæktitiv], *a.* (*Gram.*) Efficiente, causativo.
factor [ˈfæktəɹ], *n.* Fattore, agente, *m.*; (*Math.*) fattore, *m.*
factory, *n.* Fabbrica, *f.*, opificio, stabilimento, *m.* **— -hand,** operaio di fabbrica, *m.*; **— inspector,** ispettore delle fabbriche, *m.*
factotum [fækˈtoutəm], *n.* Factotum, *m.*
factual [ˈfæktju:əl], *a.* Fattivo, effetivo.
faculty [ˈfækəlti], *n.* Facoltà, potenza, *f.*; talento, potere, *m.* **To lose the use of one's faculties,** perdere l'uso delle proprie facoltà.
fad [fæd], *n.* Capriccio, ghiribizzo, *m.*, ubbia, *f.*; (*fashion*) moda, *f.*
faddist, *n.* Persona capricciosa, *f.*, persona piena di ubbie, *f.*
faddy, *a.* Capriccioso.
fade [feid], *v.i.* Svanire, sbiadire, scolorire, stingersi; appassire, sfiorire; deperire; *v.t.* far sbiadire, far appassire. **To — out,** perire, svanire; **to — away,** appassire.
faded, *a.* Sbiadito, scolorito.
fadeless, *a.* Durevole.
faeces [ˈfi:si:s], *n.pl.* Feci, *m.pl.*
faecal [ˈfi:kəl], *a.* Fecale.
fag [fæg], *v.t.i.* (*at work*) Sgobbare; affaticare, strapazzarsi. || *n.* Strapazzo, *m.*, sgobbata, *f.*; (*colloq.*) sigaretta, *f.* **Fagged out,** stanco morto; **brain- —,** esaurimento nervoso, *m.*; **— end,** mozzicone, *m.*; coda, fine, estremità, *f.*
faggot, fagot [ˈfægət], *n.* Fascina, *f.*, fascio, fastello, *m.* || *v.t.* Affastellare, legare insieme.
fail [feil], *v.i.* Fallire; (*to miss*) mancare, venir meno; riuscire male, fare fiasco; (*fig.*) naufragare, andare a vuoto; decadere, indebolirsi; (*Comm.*) far fallimento; *v.i.* mancare a, far diffetto a; (*to desert*) abbandonare. **I shall not — to come,** non mancherò di venire; **words — me,** le parole mi mancano; **he is gradually failing,** si indebolisce gradualmente; **my memory fails me,** la memoria mi fa difetto; **to — an exam,** essere respinto a un esame.
failing, *n.* Difetto, fallo, *m.*, mancanza, debolezza, *f.* || *prep.* In mancanza di, venendo meno. || *a.* Debole. **Never- —,** inesauribile.
failure [ˈfeiliəɹ], *n.* Insuccesso, fiasco, *m.*; difetto, *m.*; mancanza, insufficienza, *f.*; indebolimento, *m.*; (*Comm.*) fallimento, *m.*, bancarotta, *f.*; (*person*) uomo fallito, *m.*

fain [fein], *a.* Contento, soddisfatto. || *adv.* Di buon grado, volontieri. **I — would come,** verrei volontieri, sarei contento di venire.
faint [feint], *a.* Debole, languido, fievole, fiacco; indistinto, pallido. || *n.* Deliquio, svenimento, *m.* || *v.i.* Svenire, venir meno. **— green,** verde pallido; **to feel —,** sentirsi svenire; (*of sound*) **to grow fainter,** andar svanendo; **to — away,** cadere in deliquio; **— -hearted,** timido, pusillanime, pauroso; **— -heartedness,** timidità, pusillanimità, *f.*
faintly, *adv.* Debolmente. **To breathe —,** respirare appena.
faintness, *n.* Debolezza, fiacchezza, languidezza, *f.*; pallidezza, *f.*
fair (1) [fɛəɹ], *n.* Fiera, *f.*, mercato, *m.*
fair (2), *a.* Bello, chiaro; (*complexion*) biondo; (*weather*) buono; (*dealing*) giusto, imparziale; onesto; (*moderate*) discreto, abbastanza buono. || *adv.* Bene, cortesemente, dolcemente; lealmente. **— and square,** apertamente, sinceramente; **a — price,** un giusto prezzo, *m.*; **to be in a — way,** essere bene avviato; **to bid — to,** promettere di; **to make a — copy,** fare una bella copia; **— speeches,** parole insincere, *f.pl.*; **a — field,** un campo libero, *m.*; **by — means or by foul,** colle buone o colle brutte; **— play,** lealtà, giustizia, *f.*; giuoco pulito, *m.*; **a — wind,** un vento propizio, *m.*; **to fight —,** combattere lealmente; **the — sex,** il bel sesso, *m.*; **— -complexioned,** di carnagione bianca, biondo; **— -dealing,** lealtà, buona fede, *f.*; **— -haired,** dai capelli biondi; **— -spoken,** dalla parola melata; **fair's fair,** siamo giusti!
fairing, *n.* Regalo portato da una fiera, *m.*
fairish, *a.* Discreto, abbastanza buono.
fairly, *adv.* Bene, onestamente; abbastanza.
fairness, *n.* Bellezza, beltà, *f.*; biondezza, *f.*; imparzialità, buona fede, probità, *f.* **In — to him,** per essere giusto con lui.
fairway, *n.* (*of river*) Via navigabile, *f.*; (*Golf*) percorso regolare, *m.*, via tagliata, *f.*
fairy [ˈfɛəri], *n.* Fata, *f.* || *a.* Delle fate. **— -land,** il regno delle fate, *m.*; **— -like,** come una fata; **— -ring,** aiuola erbosa, *f.*; **— -tale,** fiaba, fola, *f.*; **— -cycle,** bicicletta da bambini, *f.*; **— light,** lampada cinese, *f.*
faith [feiθ], *n.* Fede, fedeltà, fiducia, *f.*; credenza, *f.* **Breach of —,** mancanza di parola, *f.*; **in good —,** in buona fede; **to put — in,** avere fede in; **to pin one's — to,** attaccarsi disperatamente a; **to pledge one's —,** promettere sulla fede; **to keep —,** stare alla parola, mantenere la promessa; **to break —,** mancare alla parola data; **— -healing,** cura per mezzo della fede, *f.*
faithful, *a.* Fedele, costante. || *n.* Fedele, credente, *m.*
faithfulness, *n.* Fedeltà, costanza, *f.*
faithless, *a.* Infedele, perfido, sleale, miscredente.
faithlessness, *n.* Infedeltà, perfidia, incostanza, lealtà, *f.*; miscredenza, *f.*
fake [feik], *v.t.i.* Falsificare, truccare. || *n.* Trucco, *m.*; contraffazione, *f.*; falso, *m.*
fakir [fəˈkiːɹ], *n.* Fachiro, *m.*
falchion [fɔːltʃən], *n.* Scimitarra, *f.*
falcon [ˈfɔːlkən], *n.* (*Zool.*) Falco, falcone, *m.*
falconer, *n.* Falconiere. *m.*
falconet, *n.* Falchetto; falconetto, *m.*
falconry, *n.* Falconeria, *f.*
faldstool [ˈfɔːldstuːl], *n.* (*Eccles.*) Faldistorio, *m.*
fall [fɔːl], *v.i.* Cadere, cascare; abbassarsi; (*of prices*) diminuire, ribassare; soccombere, perire, morire; avvenire, accadere; spettare, toccare a; pendere, staccarsi. || *n.* Caduta, *f.*; (*season*) autunno, *m.*; (*water*) cascata, *f.* (*in ground*) pendio, declivio, *m.*; (*of prices*) ribasso, *m.*, diminuzione, *f.*; (*of flood, etc.*) abbassamento, *m.*; (*veil*) veletta, *f.*; (*tackle*) catena di comando, *f.* **To — out with,** litigare; **to — away,** dimagrire, deperire; **to — away from,** abbandonare; **to — back,** rinculare, indietreggiare; **to — back upon,** far ricorso a; **to — down,** cadere in terra, prostarsi; **to — due,** scadere; **to — foul of,** urtarsi con, inimicarsi con; **to — in,** crollare, scadere, (*Mil.*) adunarsi, formare le righe; **to — in with,** incontrare, (*fig.*) accordarsi con; **to — off,** cadere da, (*fig.*) mancare a; **to — short,** difettare, mancare; **to — through,** fallire, andare a vuoto; **it falls to me,** tocca a me; **we fell to with a good appetite,** ci mettemmo a mangiare con buon appetito; **to — to blows,** venire alle mani; **to — upon,** attaccare; **the Thames falls into the North Sea,** il Tamigi sbocca nel mare del Nord; **there has been a — of snow,** c'è stata una nevicata; (*Theat.*) **the — of the curtain,** la calata del sipario, *f.*; **to — asleep,** addormentarsi; **to — in love,** innamorarsi.
fallacious [fəˈleiʃəs], *a.* Fallace, ingannevole, falso.
fallaciousness, *n.* Fallacia, falsità, *f.*
fallacy, *n.* Fallacia, *f.*; sofisma, errore, *m.*
fal-lal [ˈfælæl], *n.* Falpalà, *f.*; ninnolo, *m.*
fallibility [fæliˈbiliti], *n.* Fallibilità, *f.*
fallible, *a.* Fallibile.
falling [ˈfɔːliŋ], *n.* Caduta, *f.* || *a.* Cadente. **— away,** dimagramento, *m.*; apostasia, *f.*; **— in,** crollo, sprofondamento, *m.*; **— off,** diminuzione, *f.*; **— out,** dissenso, dissidio, *m.*; **— star,** stella cadente, *f.*
fallow [ˈfælou], *a.* Incolto, a maggese; (*colour*) rossiccio. || *v.t.* Maggesare, lasciare incolto. **— field,** maggese, *m.*; **to lie —,** stare a maggese; **to let —,** mettere a maggese; **— deer,** daino, *m.*
false [fɔːls], *a.* Falso; mendace, bugiardo; erroneo, sbagliato; spurio, finto, artificiale, posticcio. **— bottom,** fondo doppio, *m.*; **— teeth,** denti artificiali, *m.pl.*; **— hair,** capelli posticci, *m.pl.*; **to play —,** ingannare; **— imprisonment,** detenzione illegale, *f.*; **— hearted,** perfido, sleale.
falsehood, *n.* Falsità, menzogna, bugia, *f.*
falsely, *adv.* Falsamente.
falseness, *n.* Falsità, perfidia, doppiezza, *f.*
falsetto [fɔːlˈsetou], *n.a.* (*Mus.*) Falsetto, *m.*
falsification [fɔːlsifiˈkeiʃən], *n.* Falsificazione, *f.*
falsifier, *n.* Falsificatore, falsario, contraffattore, *m.*
falsify [ˈfɔːlsifai], *v.t.* Falsificare, contraffate, falsare, alterare; ingannare, deludere.
falsity, *n.* Falsità, perfidia, doppiezza, *f.*
falter [ˈfɔːltəɹ], *v.i.* Vacillare, esitare; balbettare.
faltering, *n.* Esitazione, *f.*
falteringly, *adv.* Con esitazione, balbettante.
fame [feim], *n.* Fama, rinomanza, celebrità, gloria, *f.* **Of ill —,** di mala fama, di dubbia fama; **house of ill —,** bordello, *m.*

F H

famed, *a.* Famoso, rinomato, celebre.
familiar [fə'miljəɹ], *a.* Familiare, intimo; esperto, pratico. || *n.* Amico intimo, *m.*; demone, *m.* **To be — with,** essere familiare con; (*of languages, etc.*) essere pratico di; **to grow — with,** familiarizzarsi con; **to make oneself — with,** prendere familiarità con, impratichirsi di; **a — spirit,** demone, spirito familiare, *m.*
familiarity [fəmili'æriti], *n.* Familiarità, intimità, domestichezza, *f.*, conoscenza, *f.*
familiarize [fə'miljəraiz], *v.t.* Far conoscere, ambientare, familiarizzarsi.
familiarly, *adv.* Familiarmente, alla buona.
family ['fæmili], *n.* Famiglia, *f.*; razza, *f.*; gruppo, *m.* **To come of good —,** essere di buona famiglia; **to be one of the —,** essere di famiglia; **a — likeness,** un'aria di famiglia, *f.*; **a friend of the —,** un amico di casa, *m.*; **— tree,** albero genealogico, *m.*
famine ['fæmin], *n.* Carestia, *f.*; fame, *f.*
famish ['fæmiʃ], *v.t.i.* Affamare.
famished, *a.* Affamato, famelico.
famous ['feiməs], *a.* Famoso, celebre, illustre, rinomato, insigne.
famously, *adv.* Famosamente; (*colloq.*) benissimo.
fan (1) [fæn], *n.* Ventaglio, *m.* || *v.t.* Sventolare, ventilare, far vento a; (*a flame*) soffiare su; (*fig.*) eccitare, stimolare. **Electric —,** ventilatore, *m.*; **to — oneself,** farsi vento; **— -light,** lunetta, imposta, *f.*; **— -like,** a ventaglio; **— -tail** (*Zool.*) piccione con coda a ventaglio.
fan (2), *n.* (*colloq.*) Ammiratore, *m.*, ammiratrice, *f.*, tifoso, *m.* **— -mail,** lettere estatiche dagli ammiratori, *f.pl.*
fanatic [fə'nætik], *n.* Fanatico, *m.*
fanatical, fanatic, *a.* Fanatico.
fanaticism, *n.* Fanatismo, *m.*
fanaticize, *v.t.* Fanatizzare.
fancied ['fænsid], *a.* Immaginato, immaginario, supposto, fittizio.
fancier, *n.* Amatore, collezionista, *m.*; negoziante, *m.*
fanciful, *a.* Fantastico, immaginoso; capriccioso, bizzarro.
fancifulness, *n.* Fantasia, immaginazione, *f.*; capricciosità, *f.*
fancy, *n.* Fantasia, immaginazione, *f.*; idea, *f.*; pensiero, *m.*; capriccio, gusto, desiderio, *m.* || *a.* Di fantasia; fantastico. || *v.t.* Immaginare, pensare; amare, avere una simpatia per, aver gusto per. || *v.i.* immaginarsi, figurarsi, credere, persuadersi. **To take a — to,** invaghirsi di, trovare simpatico; **I took a — to visit her,** mi venne l'idea di andarla a trovare; **— dress ball,** ballo in costume, ballo mascherato, *m.*; **— bread,** pasticceria, *f.*; **at a — price,** a un prezzo favoloso; **— goods,** articoli di lusso, *m.pl.*; **— needlework,** ricamo, *m.*; **Just —!** Immaginatevi!, Figuratevi! **to — oneself,** avere una buona opinione di se stesso; **— -free,** col cuore libero.
fane [fein], *n.* Tempio, *m.*
fanfare ['fænfɛəɹ], *n.* (*Mus.*) Fanfara, *f.*
fanfaronade [fænfərə'neid], *n.* Fanfaronata, millanteria, *f.*
fang [fæŋ], *n.* Zanna, *f.*; (*of snake*) dente, *m.*; (*of tooth*) radice, *f.*
fanged, *a.* Zannuto, dentato.
fantasia [fæn'teiziə], *n.* (*Mus.*) Fantasia, *f.*
fantastic [fæn'tæstik], *a.* Fantastico, bizzarro, strano, capriccioso.
fantasticalness, *n.* Fantasticaggine, bizzarria, *f.*
fantasy, *n.* Fantasia, *f.*
far [fɑːɹ], *a.* Lontano, distante, discosto, remoto, allontanato. || *adv.* Lontano, lungi, distante; molto, di molto. **The — side,** la parte più lontana, *f.*; **as — as I know,** per quanto mi risulta; **as — as the eye can see,** a perdita d'occhio; **let us go as — as the station,** andiamo fino alla stazione; **by —,** di gran lunga, di molto; **— and near,** dappertutto, per ogni dove; **from — and wide,** da tutti i lati; **Far be it from me!** Dio me ne guardi! **few and — between,** pochissimi; **— from,** lontano da; **— from it,** tutt'al contrario; **— inferior,** molto inferiore; **How — is it from here to London ?** Quanto dista Londra da qui? **How — have you got in this book ?** Quanto avete letto di questo libro? **as — as that goes,** quanto a ciò; **to go so — as to,** arrivare fino al punto di; **so — so good,** fin qui va bene; **the night was — spent,** la notte era molto avanzata; **to go too —,** esagerare, andar troppo oltre; **— -famed,** celeberrimo, rinomato; **— -fetched,** ricercato, affettato, fantastico, stiracchiato; **— -gone,** molto avanzato; **— -reaching,** di lunga portata, di larga influenza; **far-seeing, — sighted,** previdente, preveggente, chiaroveggente, perspicace, cauto; (*of vision*) presbite.
farad ['færəd], *n.* (*Elec.*) Farad, *f.*
farce (1) [fɑːɹs], *n.* Farsa, *f.*
farce (2), *v.t.* Gonfiare, riempire, stagionare.
farceur [fɑːɹ'səːɹ], *n.* Buffone, *m.*
farcical, *a.* Farsesco, comico, burlesco.
farcy ['fɑːɹsi], *n.* (*Med.*) Scabbia, *f.*
fardel ['fɑːɹdəl], *n.* (*obs.*) Fardello, peso, *m.*
fare [fɛəɹ], *n.* Prezzo della corsa, prezzo del viaggio, *m.*; (*food*) cibo, *m.*, tavola, *f.*; (*person*) viaggiatore, *m.*, viaggiatrice, *f.* || *v.i.* Passarsela, trovarsi; vivere; mangiare. **To — badly,** trovarsi male; **How did you — yesterday ?** Come ve la passaste ieri? **good —,** buon cibo, *m.*; **bill of —,** lista delle vivande, *f.*; **Fares, please!** Signori, il biglietto; **return —,** prezzo di andata e ritorno, *m.*
farewell, *n.* Addio, *m.* || *inter.* Addio! Arrivederla! Arrivederci! **To bid — to,** dire addio a, accommiatarsi, prender congedo.
farina [fə'riːnə], *n.* Farina, *f.*
farinaceous [færi'neiʃəs], *a.* Farinaceo.
farm [fɑːɹm], *n.* Podere, *m.*, fattoria, tenuta, *f.* || *v.t.i.* Coltivare; affittare; utilizzare, sfruttare. **— -house,** cascina, casa colonica, *f.*; masseria, *f.*; **to — out,** dare in affitto, appaltare; **— -bailiff,** fattore, castaldo, *m.*; **— -buildings,** cascine, *f.pl.*; **— labourer,** contadino, bracciante, *m.*; **— -yard,** cortile, corte, *m.*, aia, *f.*
farmer, *n.* Coltivatore, colono, agricoltore, mezzadro, affittuario, *m.*
farming, *n.* Agricoltura, *f.*
farmstead, *n.* Cascina, *f.*; cascinale, *m.*
farrago [fə'rɑːgou], *n.* Farragine, *f.*
farrier ['færiəɹ], *n.* Maniscalco, *m.*
farriery, *n.* Maniscalcia, *f.*
farrow ['færou], *n.* Figliata di una scrofa, *f.* || *v.t.i.* Figliare.

farther [ˈfɑːɹðəɹ], *a.adv.* Più lontano, più al di là, ulteriore, più oltre.
farthest, *a.adv.* Il più lontano, più lontano. **At the —,** al più.
farthing [ˈfɑːɹðiŋ], *n.* Quattrino, soldo, *m.* **To pay to the last —,** pagare fino all'ultimo soldo.
farthingale [fɑːɹðiŋˈgeil], *n.* (*obs.*) Guardinfante, *m.*
fasces [ˈfæsiːz], *n.pl.* (*Hist.*) Fascio, *m.*
fascicle [ˈfæsikl], *n.* Fascetto, fastello, *m.*
fascinate [ˈfæsineit], *v.t.* Affascinare, incantare, cattivare.
fascinating, *a.* Affascinante, seducente, fascinatore. **A—look,** uno sguardo affascinante, *m.*
fascination, *n.* Fascino, incanto, *m.*; seduzione, *f.*
fascine [fæˈsiːn], *n.* (*Mil.*) Fascina, *f.*
Fascism [ˈfæʃizm], *n.* (*Hist.*) Fascismo, *m.*
Fascist, *n.a.* Fascista, *m.f.*
fashion [ˈfæʃən], *n.* Moda, voga, foggia, *f.*; (*way*) maniera, *f.*, uso, modo, *m.*; genere, *m.* || *v.t.* Formare, foggiare, modellare, adattare. **In a —, after a —,** in certo modo; **in —,** di moda; **in the English —,** all'inglese; **it is the —,** è la moda; **out of —,** fuor di moda; **people of —,** gente di mondo, gente alla moda, *f.*; **to bring into —,** metter di moda, dar voga a; **to come into —,** divenire di moda; **to go out of —,** uscir di moda; **to set the —,** introdurre la moda; **— book, — plate,** giornale di mode, figurino, *m.*
fashionable, *a.* Di moda, alla moda, elegante. **— society,** bel mondo, gran mondo, *m.*; **— man,** uomo elegante, *m.*; **a — audience,** un uditorio scelto.
fashionableness, *n.* Eleganza, *f.*
fashionably, *adv.* Alla moda, elegantemente.
fast (1) [fɑːst], *n.* Digiuno, *m.* || *v.i.* Digiunare, fare il digiuno **— -day,** giorno di digiuno, giorno di magro, *m.*
fast (2), *a.* (*quick*) Rapido, celere, veloce; (*fixed*) fermo, saldo, fisso, fissato; (*faithful*) fedele, costante; (*colour*) solido; (*knot*) stretto, serrato; (*Naut.*) ormeggiato; (*of door*) ben chiuso; (*fig.*) dissoluto. || *adv.* Fermo; presto, rapidamente; bene. **A — friend,** un amico intimo, *m.*; **a — train,** un treno diretto, *m.*; **to make —,** attaccare, serrare, (*Naut.*) ormeggiare; **to rain —,** piovere dirottamente; **— asleep,** profondamente, addormentato; **to play — and loose,** fare a tira e molla; **to hold —,** tener fermo, tener saldo; **to stand —,** star saldo, star fermo, tener duro; **— shut,** ben serrato; **my watch is ten minutes —,** il mio orologio va avanti di dieci minuti.
fasten [fɑːsən], *v.t.i.* Attaccare; allacciare, abbottonare; legare, fissare; chiudere, serrare. **To — a window,** chiudere una finestra; **to — a door,** chiudere una porta a chiave; **to — one's dress,** allacciare l'abito; **to — together,** legare insieme; **to — in,** rinserrare, rinchiudere; **to — on,** attaccare, attaccarsi a, aggrapparsi a; **to — (something) on (someone),** accusare di, imputare a.
fastener, fastening, *n.* Fermaglio, legaccio, *m.*; legame, *m.*; attacco, *m.*; (*door*) chiavistello, *m.*; (*window*) spagnoletta, *f.*
fastidious [fəˈstidiəs], *a.* Meticoloso, sofistico; difficile, ritroso, schifiltoso, incontentabile.
fastidiousness, *n.* Meticolosità, ritrosia, incontentabilità, *f.*
fasting, *n.* Digiuno, *m.*
fastness [fɑːstnəs], *n.* Fermezza, sicurezza, *f.*; fortezza, *f.*; luogo fortificato, rifugio, *m.*
fat [fæt], *a.* Grasso, pingue, adiposo; fertile, fecondo. || *n.* Grasso, *m.* **To grow —,** ingrassare; **to live on the — of the land,** nuotare nell'abbondanza; **a — living,** una prebenda, *f.*; **a — job,** un posto lucroso, *m.*; (*colloq.*) **— -head,** stupido, scioccone, *m.*
fatal [feitəl], *a.* Fatale, funesto; mortale.
fatalism, *n.* Fatalismo, *m.*
fatalist, *n.* Fatalista, *m.*
fatality, *n.* Fatalità, *f.*, morte violenta, *f.*
fate [feit], *n.* Fato, destino, *m.*, sorte, *f.*; (*Myth.*) parca, *f.* **The Three Fates,** Le Tre Parche, *f.pl.*
fated, *a.* Destinato, condannato. **Ill- —,** sventurato.
fateful, *a.* Fatale, funesto.
father [ˈfɑːðəɹ], *n.* Padre, *m.* || *v.t.* Adottare, riconoscere; generare. **Fathers,** antenati, maggiori, padri, *m.pl.*; **The Father Almighty,** Il Padre Eterno, *m.*; **the Holy Father,** il Santo Padre, il Papa, *m.*; **— -in-law,** suocero, *m.*; **god-father,** padrino, *m.*; **grandfather,** nonno, *m.*; **step- —,** patrigno, *m.*; **the Early Fathers,** i padri della Chiesa, *m.pl.*; **to act as a —,** far da padre; **to — on,** attribuire la paternità a.
fatherhood, *n.* Paternità, *f.*
fatherland, *n.* Patria, *f.*
fatherless, *a.* Orfano, orfano di padre.
fatherlessness, *n.* Orfanezza, *f.*
fatherliness, *n.* Amore paterno, *m.*
fatherly, *a.* Paterno, di padre. || *adv.* Da padre, paternamente.
fathom [ˈfæðəm], *n.* (*measure*) Braccio, *m.* || *v.t.* Sondare, scandagliare; (*fig.*) approfondire, capire bene. **I can't — it,** non riesco a capirlo.
fathomless, *a.* Senza fondo; (*fig.*) impenetrabile, incomprensibile.
fatidical [fəˈtidikl], *a.* Fatidico.
fatigue [fəˈtiːg], *n.* Fatica, stanchezza, *f.* || *v.t.* Faticare, affaticare, stancare. (*Mil.*) **— dress,** tenuta di fatica, *f.*; **— -duty,** corvé, *f.*; **— -party,** drappello id lavoratori, *m.*; **to be worn out with —,** essere spossato dalla fatica, essere stanco morto.
fatiguing, *a.* Faticoso, affaticante, molesto.
fatling [ˈfætliŋ], *n.* Bestia ingrassata, *f.*
fatness, *n.* Grassezza, pinguedine, corpulenza, *f.*
fatten [ˈfætən], *v.t.i.* Ingrassare, impinguare; (*fig.*) arricchire, arricchirsi.
fattener, *n.* Ingrassatore, *m.*
fattening, *a.* Ingrassante. || *n.* Ingrassamento, *m.*
fattiness, *n.* Untuosità, *f.*
fattish, *a.* Grassino, grassotto.
fatty, *a.* Unto, untuoso.
fatuity, fatuousness [fəˈtjuːiti. ˈfætjuːəsnəs], *n.* Fatuità, stoltezza, scempiaggine, *f.*
fatuous [ˈfætjuːəs], *a.* Fatuo, stolto, scemo, sciocco.
fauces [ˈfɔːsiːz], *n.pl.* (*Anat.*) Fauci, *f.pl.*
faucet [ˈfɔːset], *n.* Cannello, *m.*; spillo, *m.*
fault [fɔːlt], *n.* Colpa, *f.*, fallo, difetto, *m.*; sbaglio, errore, *m.*; menda, magagna, macchia,

f ; (*Geol.*) frattura, *f.*, **At —,** in difetto; **generous to a —,** di troppo buon cuore; **to find — with,** criticare, riprendere, biasimare; **Whose — is it?** Di chi è la colpa?; **it is my —,** è colpa mia; **— -finder,** critico, biasimatore, censuratore, *m.*; **— -finding,** biasimo, rimprovero, *m.*
faultily, *adv.* Imperfettamente, male.
faultiness, *n.* Imperfezione, *f.*
faultless, *a.* Perfetto; irreprensibile.
faultlessness, *n.* Perfezione, *f.*
faulty, *a.* Difettoso, deficiente, imperfetto, scorretto, errato, pieno di errori.
faun [fɔ:n], *n.* Fauno, *m.*
fauna, *n.* Fauna, *f.*
favour [ˈfeivəɹ], *n.* Favore, *m.*; simpatia, *f.*; grazia, cortesia, *f.*; indulgenza, parzialità, benevolenza, *f.*; (*Comm.*) gradita lettera, *f.*; fiocco, *m.*, colori, *m.pl.* ‖ *v.t.* Favorire, proteggere, aiutare; rassomigliare. **By — of,** col favore di; **in his —,** a suo favore; **to ask a — of,** domandare un favore a; **to be in — with,** essere in grazia di; **I have a — to ask you,** debbo domandarvi un favore; **to keep in — with,** conservare la benevolenza di; **your esteemed — to hand,** ci è pervenuta la gradita vostra; **to wear a —,** portare i colori (di una squadra); **to curry — with,** insinuarsi nelle grazie di; **he favours his father,** egli rassomiglia a suo padre.
favourable, *a.* Favorevole, propizio, vantaggioso.
favourableness, *n.* Favore, *m.*
favourably, *adv.* Favorevolmente.
favoured, *a.* Favorito. **Ill- —,** brutto.
favourite [ˈfeivərit], *n.* Favorito, *m.*, favorita, *f.*; prediletto, beniamino, *m.* ‖ *a.* Favorito, prediletto, preferito. **To be a great —,** essere molto benvisto; **a — author,** un autore prediletto; (*Racing*) **the —,** il cavallo preferito, *m.*
favouritism, *n.* Favoritismo, *m.*
fawn [fɔ:n], *n.* (*Zool.*) Daino, cerbiatto, *m.* ‖ *a.* Fulvo. ‖ *v.i.* (*of deer*) Figliare. **To — upon,** adulare, corteggiare, piaggiare.
fawning, *a.* Strisciante, servile.
fawningly, *adv.* Servilmente.
fay [fei], *n.* Fata, *f.*
fealty [ˈfi:əlti], *n.* Fedeltà, *f.* **To swear — to,** giurare fedeltà a.
fear [fiəɹ], *n.* Paura, tema, *f.*, timore, spavento, terrore, *m.*; apprensione, *f.* ‖ *v.t.i.* Aver paura, temere, spaventarsi. **For — of,** per timore di; **for — that,** per tema che; **No —!** Non c'è pericolo! **there's no — that,** non c'è da temere che; **to be in — of one's life,** temere per la propria vita; **Never —!** State tranquilli! Niente paura!
fearful, *a.* Terribile, spaventevole; pauroso, timido, apprensivo.
fearfully, *adv.* Terribilmente; (*colloq.*) molto, eccessivamente.
fearfulness, *n.* Terribilità, *f.*; timidità, apprensione, *f.*
fearless, *a.* Senza paura, intrepido.
fearlessness, *n.* Intrepidità, *f.*
feasibility [fi:ziˈbiliti], *n.* Possibilità, praticabilità, *f.*
feasible, *a.* Fattibile, possibile, praticabile.
feast [fi:st], *n.* Festa, *f.*; banchetto, convito, *m.* ‖ *v.t.* Festeggiare; *v.i.* banchettare, far festa. **— -day,** giorno festivo, *m.*; **movable —,** festa mobile, *f.*
feaster, *n.* Festeggiatore, festaiuolo, *m.*
feasting, *n.* Festeggiamento, *m.*; baldoria, *f.*
feat [fi:t], *n.* Fatto, *m.*, impresa, azione insigne, *f.* **Feats,** gesta, *f.pl.*; **feats of arms,** fatti d'arme, *m.pl.*
feather [ˈfeðəɹ], *n.* Penna, piuma, *f.*; (*plumes*) pennacchio, *m.* ‖ *v.t.* Piumare, fornir di piume; (*rowing*) spalare i remi. **A — in one's cap,** un onore, una distinzione, *f.*; **in full —,** piumato, (*fig.*) in pompa magna; **to show the white —,** mostrarsi vigliacco; **— -bed,** letto di piume, *m.*; **— -brained,** dal cervello leggero, spensierato; **— grass,** stipa pennuta, *f.*; **— -duster,** spazzolino di piume, *m.*; **— -stitch,** punto mosca, punto di piuma, *m.*
feathered, *a.* Pennuto, piumato.
feathery, *a.* Pennuto, piumato; leggero, soffice, morbido.
feature [ˈfi:tʃəɹ], *n.* Caratteristica, *f.*, segno, *m.*; tratto distintivo, *m.*; aspetto, *m.* ‖ *v.t.* Ritrarre, rappresentare. **Features,** fattezze, *f.pl.*; lineamenti, tratti, *m.pl.*; the **features of a country,** la configurazione di un paese, *f.*
featured, *a.* Rappresentato. **Hard- —,** dal viso duro; **ill- —,** brutto.
featureless, *a.* Informe.
febrifuge [ˈfebrifju:dʒ], *n.* (*Med.*) Febbrifugo, *m.*
febrile [ˈfi:brail], *a.* Febbrile.
February [ˈfibru:əri], *n.* Febbraio, *m.*
fecal [cp. **faecal**].
feckless [ˈfekles], *a.* Incapace, inabile, inetto.
fecklessness, *n.* Incapacità, inabilità, *f.*
fecula [ˈfekju:lə], *n.* (*Chem.*) Fecola, *f.*
fecund [ˈfekʌnd], *a.* Fecondo.
fecundate, *v.t.* Fecondare.
fecundation, *n.* Fecondazione, *f.*
fecundity, *n.* Fecondità, *f.*
federal [ˈfedərəl], *a.* Federale.
federalism, *n.* Federalismo, *m.*
federalist, *n.* Federalista, *m.*
federate, *a.* Federato, alleato. ‖ *v.t.i.* Confederare, confederarsi.
federation, *n.* Federazione, confederazione, lega, *f.*
fee [fi:], *n.* Compenso, prezzo, *m.*; onorario, *m.*; tassa, *f.*; diritto, *m.* ‖ *v.t.* Pagare, rimunerare. **Consular fees,** diritti consolari, *m.pl.*; **entrance —,** tassa d'ammissione, *f.*; **a lawyer's fees,** l'onorario d'un avvocato, *f.pl.*; (*Law*) **an estate in — simple,** beni in proprietà assoluta, *m.pl.*
feeble [ˈfi:bəl], *a.* Debole, fievole, fiacco. **To grow —,** indebolirsi; **— -minded,** ebete, idiota.
feebleness, *n.* Debolezza, fiacchezza, *f.*
feed [fi:d], *n.* Pasto, *m.*, mangiata, *f.*; pascolo, foraggio, *m.*; (*Mech.*) rifornimento, *m.* ‖ *v.t.* Nutrire, alimentare, cibare, dar da mangiar a; pascolare; *v.i.* nutrirsi, alimentarsi; pascere, pascolare. **A — of oats,** l'avena, *f.*; (*colloq.*) **to be off one's —,** mancare d'appetito; **out at —,** al pascolo; **he cannot — himself,** non può nutrirsi da solo; **— -pump,** pompa d'alimentazione, *f.*; **to — up** (*an animal*), ingrassare.
feeder, *n.* Nutritore, mangiatore, *m.*; (*tributary*) affluente, *m.*; (*Mech.*) alimentatore, *m.*; (*bib*) bavaglino, *m.*

feeding, *n.* Pasto, cibo, alimento, nutrimento, *m.* **— -bottle**, poppatoio, *m.*
feel [fi:l], *v.t.* Tastare, toccare, palpare; sentire, provare, percepire; ritenere; *v.i.* sentirsi; trovarsi; ritenere; sembrare. || *n.* Tatto, *m.*; sensazione, *f.* **To — a pulse**, tastare il polso; **to — one's way**, andare brancolando, andare tastoni; **to — pain**, soffrire, sentir dolore; **to — cold**, aver freddo; **to — for**, sentire simpatia per; **this cloth feels rough**, questa tela è ruvida al tatto; **this room feels damp**, questa stanza sembra umida; **I — like doing nothing to-day**, non ho voglia di far nulla oggi; **by the —**, al tatto; **how do you — ?** come stai? come ti senti?
feeler, *n.* (*of insect*) Antenna, *f.*; tentacolo, *m.*; (*fig.*) sondaggio, *m.*
feeling, *n.* Sentimento, *m.*; (*physical*) sensazione, *f.*; emozione, sensibilità, *f.*; tasto, tatto, *m.* *a.* Sensitivo, sensibile, commovente. **— of cold**, sensazione di freddo, *f.*; **— of pity**, sentimento di pietà, *m.*; **ill- —**, rancore, *m.*; **to have no —**, mancare di sensibilità; **to hurt someone's feelings**, urtare i sentimenti di qualcuno; **he spoke in a — manner**, parlò in un modo commoventissimo.
feelingly, *adv.* Sensibilmente, con emozione, con simpatia.
feign [fein], *v.t.* Fingere, simulare, far vista di, far finta di; *v.i.* fingersi, rappresentarsi, simulare. **To — indifference**, ostentare un'aria indifferente, far finta di nulla.
feigned, *a.* Finto, simulato, contraffatto. **In a — hand**, con scrittura contraffatta.
feignedly, *adv.* Fintamente.
feigning, *n.* Dissimulazione, *f.*
feint, *n.* Finta, *f.*
feldspar ['felspɑ:ɹ], *n.* (*Geol.*) Feldispato, *m.*
felicitate [fe'lisiteit], *v.t.* Felicitare.
felicitation, *n.* Felicitazione, *f.*
felicitous, *a.* Felice; squisito, grazioso, garbato. **A very — expression**, un'espressione molto calzante, *f.*
felicity, *n.* Felicità, contentezza, *f.*
feline ['fi:lain], *a.* Felino, di gatto.
fell (1) [fel], *n.* Pelle, *f.*, vello, *m.*
fell (2), *a.* Crudele, truce, fiero, feroce.
fell (3), *v.t.* Abbattere, atterrare; ribattere.
fell (4), *n.* Monte, *m.*, collina, *f.*
fell (5), *past* of **fall.**
felling, *n.* Abbattimento, taglio, *m.*
felloe ['felou], *n.* Cerchio di ruota, segmento, *m.*
fellow ['felou], *n.* Compagno, socio, *m.*; camerata, collega, *m.f.*; pari, simile, *m.*; uomo, individuo, *m.*; tipo, compare, *m.*; (*of university*) aggregato, socio, *m.*; (*of club, etc.*) membro, *m.* **A fine —**, un bel carattere, *m.*; **a good —**, un buon diavolo, *m.*; **a worthless —**, un cattivo soggetto, *m.*; **an old —**, un vecchione, *m.*; **Poor — !** Povero diavolo! *m.*; **a queer —**, un originale, *m.*; **school- —**, compagno di scuola, *m.*; **— -citizen**, concittadino, *m.*; **— -countryman**, compatriotta, *m.f.*; **— -creature**, simile, *m.f.*; **— feeling**, simpatia, *f.*
fellowship, *n.* Compagnia, colleganza, società, confraternita, *f.*; cameratismo, *m.*, amicizia, *f.* **Good —**, socievolezza, cordialità, *f.*; **research —**, pensionato per ricerche.
felly [cp. **felloe**].
felo-de-se [feloudi'si:], *n.* (*Law*) Suicida, *m.*
felon ['felən], *n.* Fellone, malfattore, criminale, *m.*; traditore, *m.* || *a.* Fellone, malvagio, reo.
felonious, *a.* Cattivo, malvagio, delittuoso.
feloniously, *adv.* Delittuosamente.
felony, *n.* Fellonia, *f.*
felspar [cp. **feldspar**].
felt (1) [felt], *n.* Feltro, *m.* *v.t.* Feltrare. **— hat**, cappello di feltro, *m.*
felt (2) *past* **feel.**
felting, *n.* Feltratura, *f.*
female ['fi:meil], *a.* Femminile, femmineo. || *n.* Femmina, donna, *f.* **— screw**, vite femmina, *f.*
feminine ['feminin], *a.* Femminino, femminile. **Of the — gender**, di genere femminile.
feminineness, femininity, *n.* Femminilità, *f.*
feminism, *n.* Femminismo, *m.*
feminist, *n.* Femminista, *m.f.*
feminize, *v.t.* Effeminare.
femoral ['femərəl], *a.* (*Anat.*) Femorale.
femur ['fi:məɹ], *n.* (*Anat.*) Femore, *m.*
fen [fen], *n.* Pantano, palude, *m.*; maremma, *f.*
fence (1) [fens], *n.* Steccato, riparo, recinto, *m.*, palizzata, *f.*; (*colloq.*) ricettatore, *m.* || *v.t.* Cingere, chiudere. (*fig.*) **To sit on the —**, rimanere neutrale (*in una disputa*); **to — in**, ricingere, circondare.
fence (2), *v.t.* Tirare di scherma, schermire; difendersi. || *n.* Scherma, *f.*
fencer, *n.* Schermitore, *m.*
fencibles ['fensəbls], *n.pl.* (*Hist.*) Guardia nazionale, *f.*
fencing (1), *n.* Recinto, *m.*; materiale per fare steccati, *m.*
fencing (2), *n.* Scherma, *f.* **— -master**, maestro di scherma, *m.*; **— -match**, torneo di scherma, *m.*, gara di scherma, *f.*; **— -school**, sala di scherma, *f.*
fend [fend], *v.t.i.* Parare, scansare; difendersi da. **To — off**, sviare, parare; **to — for oneself**, arrangiarsi, provvedersi.
fender, *n.* Parafuoco, *m.*; (*Naut.*) guardalato, parabordo, *m.*; (*Am.Motor.*) parafango, *m.*
fennel ['fenəl], *n.* (*Bot.*) Finocchio, *m.*
fenny, *a.* Palustre, pantanoso.
fenugreek ['fenju:gri:k], *n.* (*Bot.*) Fieno greco, *m.*
feoff [fi:f, fef], *v.t.* (*Law*) Dare in feudo.
feoffee [fe'fi:], *n.* (*Law*) Feudatario, *m.*; donatario, *m.*
feracious [fe'reiʃəs], *a.* Ferace.
feral [fi:rəl], *a.* Ferale.
ferment (1) ['fəɹment], *n.* Fermento, *m.*; (*fig.*) agitazione, *f.*
ferment (2) [fəɹ'ment], *v.i.* Fermentare; *v.t.* far fermentare.
fermentation, *n.* Fermentazione, *f.*; lievito, *m.*
fern [fəɹn], *n.* (*Bot.*) Felce, *f.* **— -brake**, felceto, *m.*
fernery, *n.* Felceto, *m.*
ferocious [fə'rouʃəs], *a.* Feroce, fiero, crudele.
ferociousness, ferocity [fe'rouʃəsnis, fe'rɔsiti], *n.* Ferocia, crudeltà, *f.*
ferreous, *a.* Ferreo, ferrigno.
ferret ['feret], *n.* (*Zool.*) Furetto, *m.* || *v.t.i.* Cacciare col furetto. **To — out**, snidare; **to — about**, cercare, frugare.
ferric ['ferik], *a.* (*Chem.*) Ferrico.
ferriferous, *a.* Ferrifero.
ferro-concrete [ferou'kɔnkri:t], *n.* Cemento armato, *m.*

ferro-cyanide [ferouˈsaiənaid], *n.* Cianuro di ferro, *m.*
ferruginous [feˈruːdʒinəs], *a.* Ferruginoso.
ferrule [ˈferjuːl], *n.* Ghiera, *f.*, puntale, *m.*
ferry [ˈferi], *v.t.i.* Traghettare. || *n.* Passo, traghetto, tragitto, *m.* **— -boat,** nave-traghetto, traghetto, *m.*; **— -man,** battelliere, traghettiere, *m.*
fertile [ˈfəːɹtail], *a.* Fertile, fecondo, ferace, fruttifero.
fertility, fertileness, *n.* Fertilità, feracità, *f.*; fecondità, *f.*
fertilize, *v.t.* Fertilizzare.
fertilizer, *n.* (*Agric.*) Concime, letame, fertilizzante, *m.*
ferula [ˈferjuːlə], *n.* (*Bot.*) Ferula, *f.*
ferule, *n.* Ferula, *f.* **Schoolmaster's —,** ferula di pedagogo, *f.*
fervency [ˈfəːɹvənsi], *n.* Fervore, calore, ardore, *m.*
fervent, *a.* Fervente, ardente, caloroso, fervido.
fervid, *a.* Fervido, caloroso, ardente, caldo.
fervidness, fervour [ˈfəːɹvidnis, ˈfəːɹvəɹ], *n.* Fervore, ardore, impeto, *m.*; veemenza, *f.*
fescue [ˈfeskjuː], *n.* Stecchetto, *m.*; bacchetta, *f.* **— -grass,** festuca, *f.*
fesse [fes], *n.* (*Heraldry*) Fascia, *f.*
festal [ˈfestəl], *a.* Festivo, di festa.
fester [ˈfestəɹ], *v.i.* Suppurare, maturare, ulcerarsi; (*fig.*) corrompersi. || *n.* Ascesso, *m.*; postema, *f.*
festival [ˈfestəvəl], *a.* Festivo, di festa; gioioso, lieto. || *n.* Festa, *f.*
festive, *a.* Festivo, festoso, lieto.
festivity, *n.* Festività, *f.*; gaiezza, *f.*, brio, *m.*
festoon [fesˈtuːn], *n.* Festone, *m.* || *v.t.* Festonare; ornare di festoni.
fetch, *v.t.* Andare a prendere, andare a cercare, portare, riportare; (*a sigh*) trarre; (*one's breath*) prendere; (*a price*) ottenere, produrre, valere. **These goods — a high price,** queste merci raggiungono un alto prezzo; **to — away,** portar via; **to — back,** (*a person*) ricondurre, (*a thing*) riportare; **to — down,** fare scendere; **to — in,** fare entrare; **to — out,** portar fuori, fare uscire; **to — up with,** raggiungere; **to — and carry,** fare il servitore.
fetching, *a.* Attraente, seducente.
fête [feit], *n.* Festa, *f.* || *v.t.* Fare festa a.
fetid [ˈfetid], *a.* Fetido.
fetidity, fetidness, *n.* Fetidume, fetore, *m.*
fetish [ˈfetiʃ], *n.* Feticcio, *m.*
fetishism, *n.* Feticismo, *m.*
fetlock [ˈfetlɔk], *n.* Garetto, *m.*; barbetta, *f.*
fetter [ˈfetəɹ], *v.t.* Incatenare, inceppare; (*a horse*) impastoiare. || *n.* Catena, *f.*; ferro, *m.* **— -lock,** pastoia, *f.*; **fetters,** catene, *f.pl.*, ceppi, *m.pl.*; (*fig.*) schiavitù, *f.*
fettle [fetl], *n.* Ordine, stato, *m.*; condizione, *f.* **In fine —,** in ottimo stato.
fetus [cp. **foetus**].
feud (1) [fjuːd], *n.* Querela, lotta, ostilità, contesa, *f.* **A deadly —,** una lotta mortale, *f.*
feud (2), *n.* (*Hist.*) Feudo, *m.*
feudal, *a.* Feudale.
feudalism, *n.* Feudalismo, *m.*
feudatory, *n.a.* Feudatario, *m.*
fever [ˈfiːvəɹ], *n.* Febbre, *f.* **To be in a —,** avere la febbre; **— heat,** calore febbrile, *m.*; **— -hospital,** ospedale per malattie contagiose, *m.*; **— -stricken,** febbricitante, febbroso.
feverish, *a.* Febbricitante, febbrile.
feverishly, *adv.* Febbrilmente.
feverishness, *n.* Febbrilità, *f.*
feverfew [ˈfiːvəɹfjuː], *n.* (*Bot.*) Camomilla, matricaria, *f.*
few [fjuː], *a.* Pochi, *m.pl.*, poche, *f.pl.*, qualche, *m.f.* || *n.* Pochi, *m.pl.*, poche, *f.pl.*, alquanti, *m.pl.*, alquante, *f.pl.* **— people think thus,** poche persone pensano così; **give me a — of those apples,** datemi qualche mela di quelle; **some —,** alcuni, alquanti, *m.pl.*; **a good —,** parecchi, *m.pl.*; **not a —,** non pochi, alcuni; **the —,** la minoranza, *f.*, i pochi, *m.pl.*
fewer, *a.* Meno, non tanto.
fewness, *n.* Scarsità, *f.*
fiancé, *m.*; **fiancée,** *f.*, fidanzato, *m.*; fidanzata, *f.*
fiasco [fiˈæskou], *n.* Fiasco, *m.*
fiat [ˈfaiət], *n.* Decreto, ordine, comando, *m.*
fib [fib], *n.* Fandonia, frottola, bugia, *f.* || *v.i.* Contare fandonie, dir bugie.
fibber, *n.* Bugiardo, *m.*
fibre [ˈfaibəɹ], *n.* Fibra, *f.*; tiglio, *m.*
fibril, *n.* Fibrilla, *f.*
fibrillar [ˈfibriləɹ], *a.* Fibrillare.
fibrillous, *a.* Filamentoso.
fibrin, *n.* Fibrina, *f.*
fibrinous, *a.* Fibrinoso.
fibrous, *a.* Fibroso.
fibula [ˈfibjuːlə], *n.* (*Anat.*) Fibula, *f.*; peroneo, *m.*
fichu [ˈfiʃuː], *n.* Fisciù, scialletto, *m.*
fickle [fikl], *a.* Mobile, instabile, volubile, incostante.
fickleness, *n.* Incostanza, mutabilità, *f.*
fictile [ˈfiktail], *a.* Fittile, d'argilla.
fiction [ˈfikʃən], *n.* Finzione, *f.*; menzogna, *f.*; romanzo, *m.* **Work of —,** narrativa, *f.*
fictional, *a.* Immaginario, finto.
fictitious, *a.* Finto, fittizio, falso, simulato.
fictitiousness, *n.* Falsità, *f.*
fictive, *a.* Fittizio.
fid [fid], *n.* (*Naut.*) Caviglia, *f.*
fiddle [ˈfidl], *n.* (*Mus.*) Violino, *m.*; (*Naut.*) passerino, cordone, *m.* || *v.i.* Suonare il violino; (*fig.*) baloccarsi, gingillarsi; (*colloq.*) manipolare, falsificare. **— stick,** archetto, *m.* **Fiddle-sticks! Fiddle-de-dee!** Sciocchezze! **— -string,** corda di violino, *f.*
fiddler, *n.* Violinista, *m.f.*
fiddling, *n.* Il suonare il violino, *m.* || *a.* Frivolo; vano, leggero.
fidelity [faiˈdeliti], *n.* Fedeltà, *f.*
fidget [ˈfidʒət], *n.* Agitazione, irrequietezza, *f.*; persona irrequieta, *f.* || *v.i.* Agitarsi, dimenarsi, inquietarsi. **It gives me the fidgets,** mi fa impazientire; **What a — you are!** Come sei irrequieto!
fidgety, *a.* Irrequieto, agitato, inquieto. **To be —,** stare sulle spine, essere irrequieto.
fiduciary [faiˈdjuːʃəri], *n.a.* Fiduciario, *m.*
Fie! [fai], *inter.* Vergogna! Oibò!
fief [fiːf], *n.* Feudo, *m.*
field [fiːld], *n.* Campo, prato, terreno, *m.*; (*of ice*) banco, *m.*; (*hunting*) caccia, *f.*; (*Heraldry*) campo, *m.*; (*Mil.*) campagna, *f.* **Battle- —,** campo di battaglia, *m.*; **to take the —,** entrare in campagna; **a wide — of vision,** un largo campo di visione, *m.* **supreme in**

his own —, ottimo nel suo campo; **— -artillery,** artiglieria da campagna, *f.*; **— -day,** giornata campale, *f.*; **— -dressing,** pacco di medicazioni, *m.*; **— -glasses,** binocolo da campagna, *m.*; **— -marshal,** maresciallo, *m.*; **— -mouse,** arvicola, *f.*; **— -officer,** ufficiale di stato maggiore; **— -sports,** giuochi all'aria aperta, *m.pl.*

fiend [fi:nd], *n.* Demonio, diavolo, *m.*

fiendish, *a.* Diabolico, infernale.

fiendishness, *n.* Malizia infernale, diabolicità, *f.*

fierce [fiəɹs], *a.* Feroce, fiero, crudo, crudele, furioso, spietato.

fierceness, *n.* Ferocia, fierezza, crudeltà *f.*; furia, impetuosità, *f.*

fieriness ['fairinis], *n.* Ardore, *m.*; foga, impetuosità, *f.*

fiery, *a.* Di fuoco, ardente, focoso.

fife [faif], *n.* (*Mus.*) Piffero, *m.* || *v.i.* Suonare il piffero.

fifer, *n.* Pifferaro, *m.*

fifteen [fif'ti:n], *n.a.* Quindici, *m.*

fifteenth, *a.* Decimoquinto, quindicesimo. || *n.* La quindicesima parte, *f.*, il quindicesimo, *m.*

fifth ['fifθ], *n.a.* Quinto; la quinta parte, *f.*; (*Mus.*) quinta, *f.* **Charles the Fifth,** Carlo quinto, *m.*

fifthly, *adv.* In quinto luogo.

fiftieth ['fiftiəθ], *n.a.* Cinquantesimo, *m.*

fifty, *n.a.* Cinquanta, *m.* **About —,** una cinquantina, *f.*

fig [fig], *n.* (*tree and fruit*) Fico, *m.* **I don't care a —,** non me ne importa un fico; **in full —,** in vestito di gala, in ghingheri; **not worth a —,** non vale niente; (*Zool.*) **— -eater,** beccafico, *m.*; **— -leaf,** foglia di fico, (*Art*) foglia d'acanto, *f.*

fight [fait], *v.i.* Combattere, battersi, lottare, battagliare, fare a pugni; *v.t.* combattere, contrastare con, dare battaglia. || *n.* Combattimento, *m.*, battaglia, *f.*; pugna, lotta, *f.*; mischia, zuffa, *f.*; contesa, *f.* **To — shy of,** schivare, scansare; **let them — it out themselves,** lasciate che se la sbrighino da soli; **to — one's way through,** aprirsi una via combattendo; **to — hand to hand,** combattere corpo a corpo; **in the thick of the —,** nel folto della mischia; **to show —,** mostrare i denti; **rough and tumble —,** rissa violenta, *f.*; **to keep up a running —,** ritirarsi combattendo.

fighter, *n.* Combattente, guerriero, *m.*; (*Aviat.*) apparecchio da caccia, *m.*

fighting, *n.* Combattimento, *m.*; battaglia, lotta, *f.* || *a.* Combattente, lottante, battagliero. **— line,** prima linea, *f.*

figment ['figmənt], *n.* Finzione, invenzione, fantasia, *f.*

figurable ['figju:rəbl], *a.* Figurabile, immaginabile.

figurant ['figju:rənt], *n.* (*Theat.*) Ballerino, figurante, *m.*

figuration, *n.* Figurazione, rappresentazione, *f.*

figurative, *a.* Figurato, traslato, allegorico, metaforico. **In a — sense,** in senso figurato.

figuratively, *adv.* Metaforicamente.

figurativeness, *n.* Senso figurato, *m.*

figure ['figəɹ], *n.* Figura, forma, *f.*; aria, *f.*; aspetto, *m.*; disegno, *m.*; prezzo, *m.*; (*Arith.*) cifra, *f.*, numero, *m.*; tipo, *m.* || *v.t.i.* Figurare, far figura, rappresentare; (*fig.*) immaginare. **A — of speech,** un traslato, *m.*, una metafora, *f.*; **a fine —,** una bella figura, *f.*; **lay- —,** manichino, fantoccio, *m.*; **to cut a —,** fare una figura; **to cut a poor —,** fare una brutta figura; **to — to oneself,** immaginarsi, figurarsi; **to — up,** calcolare; **to — as,** sembrare, passare per; **— -head,** (*Naut.*) polena, *f.*, figura di prua, (*fig.*) prestanome, uomo di paglia, figurante, *m.*; **in round figures,** in cifra tonda.

figured, *a.* Figurato, impresso, stampato a figure. **— satin,** raso impresso, *m.*

figurine, *n.* Figurina, statuetta, *f.*

figurist, *n.* Figurista, *m.*

Fiji ['fi:dʒi:], *n.* (*Geog.*) Le isole Figi, *f.pl.*

filament ['filəmənt], *n.* Filamento, *m.*

filamentous, *a.* Filamentoso.

filbert ['filbəɹt], *n.* (*Bot.*) (*nut*) Avellana, nocciuola, *f.*; (*tree*) avellano, nocciuolo, *m.*

filch [filtʃ], *v.t.* Rubare, rubacchiare, involare, commettere furto.

filcher, *n.* Ladro, mariuolo, *m.*

file (1) [fail], *n.* (*tool*) Lima, *f.* || *v.t.* Limare. **— -dust,** limatura, *f.*; **a cunning old —,** un furbacchione, *m.*

file (2), *n.* (*for papers*) Filza, *f.*; (*of papers*) incartamento, *m.* || *v.t.* Registrare, schedare, infilzare; (*Law*) presentare. **To — for reference,** schedare, registrare.

file (3), *n.* (*line*) Fila, *f.*; coda, *f.* || *v.i.* Sfilare. **In single —,** in fila, in fila indiana; **to stand in —,** far la coda; **— -leader,** capofila, *m.*

filial ['filiəl], *a.* Filiale.

filiation, *n.* Filiazione, *f.*

filibuster ['filibʌstəɹ], *n.* Filibustiere, *m.* || *v.i.* Fare il filibustiere.

filigree ['filigri:], *n.* Filigrana, *f.*

filigreed, *a.* Filigranato.

filing, *n.* (*Mech.*) Limatura, *f.*; (*papers*) collezione, *f.* **Filings,** limatura, *f.*; **— -cabinet** schedario, *m.*

fill [fil], *v.t.* Empiere, empire, riempire; colmare, caricare; (*a post, etc.*) occupare, tenere; (*a tooth*) otturare. || *n.* Sufficienza, *f.*; (*of a pipe*) pipata, *f.* **To — a pipe** caricare una pipa; **to — a tooth,** piombare un dente, otturare un dente; **to — in a name,** inserire un nome; **to — in a form,** riempire un modulo; **to — up,** colmare; **to — up one's time with,** impiegare il tempo a; **the wind fills the sails,** il vento gonfia le vele; **to — out** (*with plumpness*), ingrassare; **to — out a cheque,** riempire un assegno; **to — someone's place,** supplire qualcuno; **to eat one's —,** mangiare a sufficienza; **a — of tobacco,** una pipata di tabacco, *f.*

filler, *n.* Empitore, *m.*; (*Mech.*) imbuto, *m.*

fillet ['filit], *n.* Benda, *f.*; (*of meat, etc.*) filetto, *m.* **To — fish,** disossare; **— steak,** bistecca di filetto, *f.*; **— of beef,** filetto di bue, *m.*; **filleted sole,** filetto di sogliola, *m.*

filling, *n.* Riempitura, *f.*, riempimento, *m.*; (*of tooth*) otturazione, *f.* || *a.* Sazievole.

fillip ['filip], *n.* Stimolo, incitamento, *m.*; buffetto, *m.* **To give a — to,** stimolare, incoraggiare.

filly ['fili], *n.* Puledra, cavallina, *f.*

film [film], *n.* (*Anat.*) Membrana, *f.*; pellicola, film, *f.*; (*fig.*) nebbia, *f.*, velo, *m.* || *v.t.* Rappresentare in un film, adattare per il cinema; fare un film, filmare. **A — of mist,** un velo di nebbia, *m.*; **— rights,** diritto d'adattazione cinematografica, *m.*; **— star,** divo, diva dello schermo, *m.f.*; **— -fan,** tifoso del cinema, *m.*; **— director,** regista, *m.*; **the — industry,** l'industria cinematografica, *f.*

filminess, *n.* Trasparenza, *f.*

filmy, *a.* Trasparente.

filter ['filtəɹ], *n.* Filtro, *m.*; (*Phot.*) filtro luce, *m.* || *v.t.i.* Filtrare. **— -bed,** strato filtrante, *m.*

filth [filθ], *n.* Sudiciume, *m.*, sozzura, lordura, sporcizia, *f.*

filthily, *adv.* Sozzamente.

filthiness, *n.* Sporcizia, *f.*

filthy, *a.* Sporco, sudicio, sozzo, lordo; (*fig.*) osceno. **— lucre,** danaro, *m.*

filtration [fil'treiʃən], *n.* Filtrazione, *f.*

fin [fin], *n.* Pinna, aletta, *f.*; (*of aquatic animals*) natatoia, *f.*

finable, *a.* Soggetto a multa.

final ['fainəl], *a.* Finale, ultimo; decisivo, conclusivo, definitivo. (*Sport*) **— heat,** prova decisiva, *f.*

finale [fi'nɑːli], *n.* (*Mus.*) Finale, *m.*

finalist, *n.* (*Sport*) Finalista, *m.*

finality, *n.* Finalità, *f.*

finally, *adv.* Finalmente, conclusivamente.

finance [fai'næns], *n.* Finanza, *f.*; finanze, *f.pl.* || *v.t.* Finanziare, sovvenzionare.

financial, *a.* Finanziario.

financier, *n.* Finanziere, *m.*

finch [fintʃ], *n.* (*Zool.*) Fringuello, cardellino, *m.*

find [faind], *v.t.* Trovare, scoprire; fornire; (*Law*) dichiarare; ottenere, guadagnare. || *n.* Scoperta, trovata, *f.*; oggetto trovato, *m.* **To — out,** scoprire; indovinare; **to — again,** ritrovare; **I found him in food,** gli ho fornito del cibo; **I could — it in my heart to weep,** ho voglia di piangere; **to — one's way,** trovare la via; **to — one's feet,** sistemarsi.

finder, *n.* Scopritore, *m.*; trovatore, inventore, *m.*; (*camera*) mirino, *m.*; (*telescope*) cercatore, *m.*

finding, *n.* Scoperta, *f.*; ritrovamento, *m.*; (*Law*) verdetto, *m.*, sentenza, *f.*

fine (1) [fain], *n.* Multa, ammenda, contravvenzione, *f.* || *v.t.* Multare, fare una contravvenzione. **They fined him £5,** gli hanno fatto una contravvenzione di cinque sterline.

fine (2), *a.* Fino, sottile, delicato, squisito, raffinato; bello; acuto; buono, eccellente; (*of weather*) bello. || *v.t.* Chiarificare. || *adv.* Bene, elegantemente. **The weather's —,** fa bel tempo; **that's all very —, but,** tutto ciò va benissimo, ma; **— -arts,** belle arti, *f.pl.*; **— -drawn,** sottile; magro; tirato; **— spoken,** fiorito; **— -spun,** filato fino; **one of these — days,** un giorno o l'altro, un bel giorno.

fine (3), **In —,** in fine.

finely, *adv.* Bene, squisitamente, sottilmente.

fineness, *n.* Finezza, delicatezza, squisitezza, bellezza, *f.*; sottigliezza, *f.*

finery, *n.* Fronzoli, ninnoli, *m.pl.*

finesse [fi'nes], *n.* Sottigliezza, *f.* || *v.t.* Sottilizzare.

finger ['fiŋgəɹ], *n.* Dito, *m.* || *v.t.* Toccare, tastare; (*Mus.*) diteggiare. **Little —,** mignolo, *m.*; **fore- —,** indice, *m.*; **ring —,** anulare, *m.*; **middle —,** medio, *m.*, **to have a finger in every pie,** avere le mani in ogni pasta; **to have at one's — -ends,** sapere a menadito, avere sulla punta delle dita; **to point at with one's —,** mostrare a dito; **not to lift a —,** non muovere un dito; **— -board** (*of violin*), manico, *m.*; **— -bowl,** sciacquadita, *m.*; **— -mark,** ditata, *f.*; **— -nail,** unghia, *f.*; **— -post,** palo indicatore, *m.*; **— -print,** impronta digitale, *f.*; **— -stall,** ditale di protezione, *m.*; **— -plate,** placca, *f.*

fingering, *n.* Il tastare, il tasteggiare, *m.*; (*Mus.*) diteggio, tocco, *m.*

finial ['finiəl], *n.* (*Arch.*) Vertice ornamentale, *m.*

finical, finicking, finicky ['finikəl, 'finikiŋ, 'finiki], *a.* Meticoloso, pedante, affettato, ritroso, sofistico.

fining ['fainiŋ], *n.* (*of metals*) Raffinatura, *f.*; (*of liquors*) chiarificazione, *f.*

finis ['finis], *n.* Fine, *f.*

finish ['finiʃ], *v.t.* Finire, terminare, compiere, completare, conchiudere, concludere, ultimare, condurre a fine; *v.i.* finire, terminare, cessare. || *n.* Fine, *f.*, compimento, *m.*, finitezza, *f.*; rifinitura, *f.* **To fight to a —,** combattere a oltranza.

finished, *a.* Finito; perfetto, raffinato; (*iron.*) matricolato, di tre cotte.

finisher, *n.* Rifinitore, *m.*

finishing, *a.* Ultimo. || *n.* Rifinitura, *f.* **— stroke,** ultimo colpo, colpo di grazia, *m.*; ultima mano, *f.*

finite ['fainait], *a.* Limitato, circoscritto; (*Gram.*) finito.

finiteness, *n.* Limitatezza, *f.*

Finland ['finlənd], *n.* (*Geog.*) Finlandia, *f.*

finless, *a.* Senza pinne.

Finn, Finnish, *n.a.* Finlandese, *m.*

finny, *a.* Con pinne. **The — tribe,** i pesci, *m.*

fir, fir-tree [fəːɹ, 'fəːɹtriː], *n.* (*Bot.*) Abete, *m.* **— -cone,** pigna, *f.*; **— -plantation,** abetina, *f.*

fire [faiɹ], *n.* Fuoco, *m.*; (*house on fire*) incendio, *m.*; (*fig.*) ardore, slancio, *m.*, foga, *f.* || *v.t.* Mettere fuoco a, appiccare il fuoco a, incendiare, accendere; (*gun, etc.*) sparare; (*fig.*) infiammare, avvampare, accendere, eccitare; (*colloq.*) congedare, licenziare; *v.i.* prender fuoco, incendiarsi, accendersi; (*Mil.*) sparare. (*Mil.*) **Fire!** Fuoco! Al fuoco! **to be on —,** essere in fiamme; **to catch —,** pigliar fuoco, prender fuoco; **to make a —,** far fuoco; **to put out a —,** spegnere un fuoco, spegnere un incendio; **to set on —,** dare fuoco a; **between two fires,** tra due fuochi; **to stir the —,** attizzare il fuoco; **under —,** sotto il fuoco; **to — off,** sparare, scaricare; **to cease —,** cessare il fuoco; **to hang —,** far cilecca; (*fig.*) **to — up,** infiammarsi; (*colloq.*) **Fire away!** Cominciate! **to add fuel to the —,** gettare olio sul fuoco; **to fall from the frying-pan into the —,** cascar dalla padella nella brace; **to go through — and water for someone,** farsi in pezzi per qualcuno; **to — with passion,** infiammare di passione; **— -alarm,** segnale d'allarme, *m.*; **— -arms,** armi da fuoco, *f.pl.*; **— -ball,**

(*Astron.*) meteora, *f.*, (*Mil.*) palla di cannone, granata, *f.*; (*Rail.*) **— -box,** fornello, *m.*; **— -brand,** tizzone, *m.*, (*fig.*) testa calda, *f.*; **— -brick,** mattone refrattario, *m.*; **— -brigade,** corpo di pompieri, *m.*, vigili del fuoco, *m.pl.*; **— -bucket,** secchio da incendio, *m.*; **— -clay,** argilla refrattaria, *f.*; **— -damp,** gas esplosivo delle miniere, *m.*; **— -dog,** alare, *m.*; **— -eater,** millantatore, spaccone, *m.*; **— -engine,** pompa d'incendio, *f.*; **— -escape,** apparecchio di salvataggio per incendio, *m.*; **— -extinguisher,** estintore, *m.*; **— -fly,** lucciola, *f.*; **— -grate,** grata del focolare, *f.*; **— -guard,** parafuoco, *m.*; **— -hose,** tubo da getto, *m.*; **— -insurance,** assicurazione contro l'incendio, *f.*; **— -lighter,** accendifuoco, *m.*; **— -lock,** moschetto, *m.*; **— -man,** (*Rail.*) fochista, *m.*, (*brigade*) pompiere, *m.*; **— -place,** focolare, *m.*; **— -proof,** resistente al fuoco, incombustibile; **— -screen,** parafuoco, *m.*; **— -ship,** brulotto, *m.*; **— -side,** focolare, *m.*, intimità familiare, *f*; **— -station,** caserma dei pompieri, *f.*; **— worship,** culto del fuoco, *m.*

firewood, *n.* Legna da fuoco, *f.*

fireworks, *n.pl.* Fuochi artificiali, *m.pl.* **To let off —,** fare fuochi artificiali.

firing, *n.* Il far fuoco, *m.*; (*Mil.*) sparo, *m.*, sparatoria, scarica, *f.*; (*heating*) riscaldamento, *m.*; (*fuel*) combustibili, *m.pl.* **— -party,** plotone d'esecuzione, *m.*

firkin [ˈfəːɹkin], *n.* Quartarolo, barilotto, *m.*

firm (1) [fəːɹm], *n.* Ditta, casa commerciale, compagnia, società, *f.* **Publishing —,** casa editrice, *f.*; **to establish a —,** fondare una ditta.

firm (2), *a.* Fermo, saldo, solido; costante, stabile.

firmament [ˈfəːɹməmənt], *n.* Firmamento, cielo, *m.*

firman [ˈfəːɹmæn], *n.* Firmano, *m.*

firmness, *n.* Fermezza, saldezza, *f.*; stabilità, consistenza, *f.*

first [fəːɹst], *a.* Primo, primario, principale. || *adv.* Prima, in prima, dapprima. || *n.* Il primo, il principio, *m.* **He is always the — to complain,** è sempre il primo a lamentarsi; **in the — place,** in primo luogo; **the — -comer,** il primo venuto, *m.*; **at —,** prima, dapprima; **— and last,** tutto considerato; **— or last,** o presto o tardi; **from the very — I suspected it,** fin dal primo momento lo sospettavo; **When did you see him — ?** Quando l'avete visto per la prima volta? **— -aid,** primo soccorso, *m.*; **— -born,** primogenito, pronto nato; **— -class, — -rate,** di prima qualità, di prim'ordine, eccellente; **to travel — class,** viaggiare in prima classe; **— -fruits,** primizie, *f.pl.*; **— -hand,** di prima mano; **from the —,** dal principio.

firstling, *n.* (*of animals*) Primo nato, *m.*

firth, frith [fəːɹθ], *n.* (*Geog.*) Estuario, *m.*

fisc [fisk], *n.* Fisco, *m.*

fiscal, *n.a.* Fiscale, *m.*

fish [fiʃ], *n.* Pesce, *m.* || *v.t.i.* Pescare; trarre fuori; (*fig.*) cercare, scoprire, trovare. (*fig.*) **A pretty kettle of —,** un bel pasticcio, *m.*; **to be like a — out of water,** essere come un pesce fuor d'acqua; **to have other — to fry,** aver ben altro per il capo; **all's — that comes to his net,** fa di ogni erba un fascio; **neither — nor fowl,** nè carne nè pesce; **to — out,** trarre fuori; **to — for compliments,** cercare dei complimenti; **to — in troubled waters,** pescare nel torbido; **— -bone,** spina, lisca, *f.*; **— -hook,** amo, *m.*; **— -kettle,** pesciaiuola, *f.*; **— -knife,** coltello da pesce, *m.*; **— -pond,** vivaio, *m.*, peschiera, *f.*; **— -wife,** pescivendola, pesciaia, *f.*; (*Rail.*) **— -plate,** stecca a ganascia, *f.*

fisher, fisherman, *n.* Pescatore, *m.*

fishery, *n.* Pesca, *f.* **Herring —,** pesca delle aringhe, *f.*

fishiness, *n.* Sapore di pesce, *m.*; (*colloq.*) ambiguità, *f.*; equivoco, *m.*

fishing, *n.* Pesca, *f.* **— boat,** barca da pesca, *f.*; peschereccio, *m.*; **— -line,** lenza, *f.*; **— -net,** rete, *f.*; **— -rod** canna da pesca, *f.*; **— -tackle,** attrezzi pescherecci, *m.pl.*

fishmonger [ˈfiʃmʌŋgəɹ], *n.* Pescivendolo, pesciaio, *m.*

fishy, *a.* Pescoso, di pesce; (*colloq.*) ambiguo, equivoco. **To smell —,** saper di pesce.

fissiparous [fiˈsipərəs], *a.* (*Zool.*) Fissipari.

fissiped, *a.* Fissipede.

fissure [ˈfiʃəɹ], *n.* Fessura, *f.*; spaccatura, fenditura; (*Med.*) ragade, *f.* || *v.t.* Spaccare, fendere; *v.i.* fendersi.

fist [fist], *n.* Pugno, *m.*; (*colloq. writing*) calligrafia, *f.* **Close-fisted,** avaro, tirchio.

fisticuffs [ˈfistikʌfs], *n.pl.* Pugni, *m.pl.* lotta coi pugni, *f.*

fistula [ˈfistjuːlə], *n.* (*Med.*) Fistola, *f.*

fistulous, *a.* Fistoloso.

fit (1) [fit], *n.* Attacco, accesso, parossismo, *m.*; convulsione, *f.*; (*fig.*) capriccio, ticchio, umore, *m.*; (*Mech.*) montaggio, *m.* **A — of laughter,** un convulso di riso, *f.* **— of rage,** parossismo d'ira, *m.*; **if the — takes me,** se mi salta il ticchio; **by fits and starts,** a capriccio, a sbalzi.

fit (2), *a.* Atto, adatto a, capace di; conveniente, calzante, giusto; degno; buono; sano; in istato di, in forma, idoneo. || *v.t.i.* Adattare; adattarsi a; fornire; (*of clothes*) star bene a, essere attillato, abbigliare. **— for use,** usabile, atto all'uso; **— to eat,** buono da mangiare; **he thought — to,** gli sembrò giusto di; **— as a fiddle,** sano come un pesce; **I'm not — to go out,** non sono in condizione di uscire; **— for service,** atto al servizio; **to keep —,** tenersi in forma; **to — in with the others,** accordarsi con gli altri; **to — up,** preparare, arredare, montare; **that coat is a splendid —,** quell'abito vi sta benissimo.

fitchew, fitch [ˈfitʃjuː, fitʃ], *n.* (*Zool.*) Puzzola, *f.*

fitful, *a.* Spasmodico, capriccioso, irregolare, vacillante, saltuario.

fitfully, *adv.* A salti, a sbalzi. **A light gleamed — from a window,** una luce guizzava a tratti da una finestra.

fitly, *adv.* Convenevolmente, giustamente.

fitness, *n.* Convenienza, disposizione, attitudine, *f.*

fitted, *a.* Atto, adatto a, capace di.

fitter, *n.* (*Mech.*) Aggiustatore, montatore, *m.*

fitting, *a.* Conveniente, convenevole, giusto. || *n.* Aggiustamento, *m.* **Fittings,** arredo, guarnimento, *m.*; mobilia, *f.* (*Naut.*) **— out,** armamento, *m.*

five [faiv], *n.a.* Cinque.

fivefold, *a.* Quintuplo, quintuplice. || *adv.* Cinque volte.
fiver, *n.* (*colloq.*) Biglietto da cinque sterline, *m.*
fives, *n.pl.* Giuoco della palla al muro, *m.*
fix [fiks], *v.t.* Fissare, fermare, attaccare; stabilire, determinare, convenire; (*in the mind*) ribadire; *v.i.* fissarsi, stabilirsi. || *n.* Difficoltà, *f.*, dilemma, *m.*; imbarazzo, *m.* **To — one's eyes on,** fissare l'occhio su; **to — in advance,** prestabilire; **to — upon,** scegliere; **he is fixed in his determination,** egli è fermo nella sua risoluzione; (*colloq.*) **to be in a —,** essere in un ginepraio; (*Mil.*) **Fix bayonets!** Baionet-can!
fixable, *a.* Fissabile.
fixation, *n.* Fissazione, *f.*
fixative, *n.a.* Fissativo, *m.*
fixed, *a.* Fisso, stabilito, convenuto.
fixedness, fixity, *n.* Fissità, stabilità, *f.*
fixer, *n.* Fissatore, *m.*
fixing, *n.* (*Phot.*) Fissaggio, *m.* **— solution,** fissatore, *m.*
fixture, *n.* Infisso, affisso, *m.*; (*Sport*) data fissa, *f.* **Fixtures in a house,** infissi d'una casa; **he seems to be a — there,** sembra diventato un mobile di casa.
fizz [fiz], *v.i.* Spumare, spumeggiare. || *n.* Spuma, *f.*; (*colloq.*) sciampagna, *f.*
fizzle ['fizl], *v.i.* Spumeggiare; fischiare. **To — out,** non riuscire, fare fiasco.
flabbergast ['flæbəɹgɑːst], *v.t.* Stupire, intontire, sbalordire.
flabbiness ['flæbinis], *n.* Flaccidità, *f.*; fiacchezza, *f.*; languidezza, *f.*
flabby, *a.* Floscio, cascante, fiacco, flaccido, molle.
flaccid ['flæsid], *a.* Fiacco, flaccido.
flaccidity, *n.* Fiacchezza, languidezza, *f.*
flag (1) [flæg], *n.* Bandiera, insegna, *f.*, vessillo, stendardo, *m.*; pavese, *m.*; (*Bot.*) iride, *f.*, giaggiolo, *m.*; (*stone*) lastrico, *m.* || *v.t.* Lastricare: far segno con una bandiera. **— of truce,** bandiera bianca, *f.*; **to hoist the —,** issare la bandiera; **to strike the —,** ammainare la bandiera; **to dress a ship with flags,** pavesare; **—-officer,** ufficiale ammiraglio, *m.*; **—-lieutenant,** ufficiale di bandiera, *m.*
flag (2), *v.i.* Pendere; languire, allentarsi, affievolirsi, venir meno.
flagellant ['flædʒilənt], *n.* Flagellante, *m.*
flagellate ['flædʒileit], *v.t.* Flagellare.
flagellation, *n.* Flagellazione, *f.*
flagellator, *n.* Flagellatore, *m.*
flageolet ['flædʒiolet], *n.* (*Mus.*) Clarinetto, *m.*; zufolo, *m.*
flagging ['flægiŋ], *a.* Languido, affievolito, fiacco.
flagitious [flə'dʒiʃəs], *a.* Scellerato, malvagio, infame, atroce.
flagitiousness, *n.* Scelleratezza, malvagità, *f.*
flagon [flægən], *n.* Flacone, *m.*; boccetta, *f.*, bottiglietta, *f.*
flagrancy ['fleigrənsi], *n.* Flagranza, *f.*; evidenza, *f.*
flagrant, *a.* Flagrante; palese, manifesto.
flagrantly, *adv.* Notoriamente.
flagship, *n.* (*Naut.*) Nave ammiraglia, *f.*
flagstaff, *n.* Asta di bandiera, *f.*
flagstone, *n.* Lastra di pietra, *f.*
flail [fleil] *n.* Correggiato, *m.*
flair [flɛəɹ], *n.* Fiuto, acume, *m.*
flake [fleik], *n.* (*of snow*) Falda, *f.*, fiocco, *m.*; scaglia, lamina, *f.* || *v.t.* Sfaldare; *v.i.* sfaldarsi, scagliarsi.
flaky, *a.* A falde, scaglioso, fioccoso. **— pastry,** pasta sfoglia, *f.*
flambeau ['flæmbou], *n.* Fiaccola, *f.*
flamboyant [flæm'bɔiənt], *a.* Sfavillante, fiammeggiante.
flame [fleim], *n.* Fiamma, vampa, *f.*; fuoco, *m.*; (*fig.*) ardore, *m.* || *v.i.* Fiammeggiare, avvampare, ardere. **To — up,** avvampare; **—-coloured,** color fiamma.
flamen ['flæmen], *n.* (*Hist.*) Flamine, *m.*
flaming, *a.* Fiammeggiante, fiammante; (*fig.*) ardente, violento, focoso.
flamingo [flə'miŋgou], *n.* (*Zool.*) Fenicottero, *m.*
Flanders ['flɑːndəɹz], *n.* (*Geog.*) Le Fiandre, *f.pl.*
flange [flændʒ], *n.* Flangia, *f.*; orlo, risalto, sporto, *m.*
flank [flæŋk], *n.* Fianco, lato, *m.* || *v.t.* (*Mil.*) Affiancare, fiancheggiare. **In —,** di fianco.
flanker, *n.* Fiancheggiatore, *m.*
flanking, *n.* Fiancheggiamento, *m.* **— fire,** fuoco d'infilata, *m.*
flannel ['flænəl], *n.* Flanella, *f.* || *a.* Di flanella.
flannelette, *n.* Flanella di cotone, *f.*
flap [flæp], *v.t.* Sventolare; battere, agitare; *v.i.* agitarsi, penzolare, dondolare. || *n.* Falda, *f.*; (*of hat*) tesa, *f.*; (*of desk*) ribalta, *f.*; (*of pocket*) risvolto, *m.*; (*for flies*) scacciamosche, *m.*; (*of wings*) colpo d'ala, *m.* **To — the wings,** battere le ali, aleggiare; **to — away flies,** scacciare le mosche; **—-eared,** orecchiuto; (*colloq.*) **to get in a —,** essere agitato.
flapdoodle [flæp'duːdl], *n.* Sciocchezze, *f.pl.*
flapper, *n.* (*of seals, etc.*) Pinna, *f.*; (*for flies*) scacciamosche, *m.*; (*colloq.*) donzella, donzelletta, ragazza, *f.*
flapping, *n.* Sventolio, *m.*
flare [flɛəɹ], *v.i.* Fiammeggiare, scintillare, ardere, sfolgorare; (*of a lamp*) sfilare. || *n.* Fulgore, chiarore, *m.*; fiammata, vampa, *f.*; (*signal*) razzo, *m.*
flaring, *a.* Lucente, abbagliante, sfolgorante.
flash [flæʃ], *n.* Lampo, bagliore, fulgore, splendore, sprazzo di luce, *m.* || *v.i.* Brillare, scintillare, sfolgorare, lampeggiare, balenare; *v.t.* lampeggiare. || *a.* Falso. **A — of lightning,** un lampo, un baleno, *m.*; **in a —,** in un lampo; **to — past,** passare come un lampo; **a — of wit,** un tratto di spirito, *m.*; **it flashed upon me that,** mi balenò in mente che; **his eyes flashed fire,** i suoi occhi mandavano fuoco; **his eyes flashed,** gli brillavano gli occhi; **—-lamp,** lampada elettrica portatile, *f.*; (*Phot.*) **—-light,** lampo al magnesio, *m.*
flashing, *a.* Scintillante, lampeggiante, rilucente.
flashy, *a.* Abbagliante, vistoso, volgare.
flask [flɑːsk], *n.* Fiasco, *m.*; bottiglia, *f.* **Pocket —, hip —,** fiaschetta, *f.*
flat [flæt], *a.* Piatto; piano; eguale, uniforme; (*of wine*) guasto; (*in taste*) insipido; (*Mus.*) bemolle; (*fig.*) netto, chiaro, franco; noioso. || *n.* Piatto; (*dwelling*) appartamento, *m.*; pianura, *f.*; (*Mus.*) bemolle, *m.* **To fall — on the ground,** cadere disteso; (*fig.*) **to fall —,** far fiasco, andare a vuoto; **to lay —,** stendere

al suolo; **to lie —**, stendersi a terra, giacere supino; **to sing —**, stonare; **a — nose**, un naso camuso, *m.*; (*Racing*) **— -race**, corsa piana, *f.*; **— -iron**, ferro da stiro, *m.*; **— -footed**, dai piedi piatti.
flatly, *adv.* Nettamente, chiaramente, recisamente.
flatness, *n.* Piattezza, pianezza, *f.*; (*fig.*) banalità, trivialità, *f.*, tedio, *m.*
flatten [flætən], *v.t.* Appiattire, spianare, livellare; (*Mus.*) calare di un semitono. **To — oneself against the wall**, serrarsi al muro.
flatter [ˈflætəɹ], *v.t.* Adulare, lusingare, accarrezzare, blandire. **To — oneself**, lusingarsi.
flatterer, *n.* Adulatore, *m.*
flattering, *a.* Lusinghiero; adulatorio.
flattery, *n.* Adulazione, lusinga, *f.*; blandizie, *f.pl.*
flatulence, flatulency [ˈflætju:ləns, ˈflætju:lənsi], *n.* (*Med.*) Flatulenza, *f.*; (*fig.*) fatuità, *f.*
flatulent, *a.* Flatulento; (*fig.*) vacuo, fatuo, stolto.
flaunt [flɔ:nt], *v.i.* Pavoneggiarsi, gloriarsi; *v.t.* far mostra di, ostentare, sfoggiare.
flaunting, *a.* Vanitoso, pomposo.
flautist [ˈflɔ:tist], *n.* (*Mus.*) Flautista, *m.*
flavour [ˈfleivəɹ], *n.* Sapore, gusto, aroma, profumo, *m.* || *v.t.* Condire, rendere saporito.
flavouring, *n.* Condimento, *m.*
flavourless, *a.* Insipido.
flaw [flɔ:], *n.* Difetto, guasto, *m.*, tacca, magagna, *f.*; (*crack*) incrinatura, *f.*; (*Naut.*) folata di vento, *f.*; (*Law*) causa di nullità, *f.*
flawless, *a.* Perfetto, senza difetto; intatto.
flawlessness, *n.* Perfezione, interezza, purità, *f.*
flax [flæks], *n.* (*Bot.*) Lino, *m.* **— -comb**, cardo, scardasso, *m.*; **— -dresser**, cardatore di lino, *m.*; **— -seed**, seme di lino, *m.*
flaxen, *a.* (*of the hair*) Biondissimo; di lino.
flay [flei], *v.t.* Scorticare, scuoiare.
flayer, *n.* Scorticatore, *m.*
flaying, *n.* Scorticamento, *m.*
flea [fli:], *n.* (*Zool.*) Pulce, *f.* **— -bite**, puntura, morsicatura di pulci, *f.*; (*fig.*) un nonnulla, un niente, *m.*; **— -bitten**, morsicato dalle pulci; (*fig.*) macchiettato; (*Bot.*) **— -bane**, pulicaria, erba pulce, *f.*
fleam [fli:m], *n.* Lancetta, *f.*
fleck [flek], *n.* Macchiolina, *f.*; (*of light*) chiazza, *f.*
fledge [fledʒ], *v.t.* Coprir di penne, piumare.
fledged, *a.* Pennato, piumato.
fledgling, *n.* Uccellino, pennuto, *m.*
flee [fli:], *v.i.* Fuggire, scappare; *v.t.* fuggire, schivare, scansare.
fleece [fli:s], *n.* Vello, tosone, *m.* || *v.t.* Tosare; (*fig.*) scorticare, spogliare, pelare.
fleecy, *a.* Lanoso, velloso, lanuto; (*fig.*) spumoso; fioccoso. **— clouds**, pecorelle, *f.pl.*
fleer [fliəɹ], *v.i.* Motteggiare, sogghignare; *v.t.* beffarsi di, deridere, schernire. || *n.* Sogghigno, dileggio, *m.*
fleet (1) [fli:t], *n.* Flotta, *f.*
fleet (2), *a.* Rapido, veloce, agile.
fleeting, *a.* Fuggitivo, fugace, transitorio.
fleetness, *n.* Rapidità, agilità, *f.*
Fleming [ˈflemiŋ], *n.* Fiammingo, *m.*
Flemish, *a.* Fiammingo.
flesh [fleʃ], *n.* Carne, *f.* || *v.t.* (*Hunting*) Accanire, aizzare. **In the —**, in carne e ossa; **to make one's — creep**, fare accapponare la pelle; **to put on —**, rimettersi in carne; **— -brush**, spazzola per frizioni, *f.*; **— -coloured**, color di carne, carnicino; **— -pots**, la buona tavola, *f.*; **— -tights, fleshings**, maglia color carne, *f.*; **— wound**, ferita superficiale, *f.*
fleshiness, *n.* Grassezza, carnosità, *f.*
fleshless, *a.* Scarno, magro.
fleshliness, *n.* Carnalità, *f.*
fleshly, *a.* Carnale, sensuale, mondano.
fleshy, *a.* Carnoso.
fleur-de-lis [flə:ɹdəˈli:], *n.* Giglio, fiordaliso, *m.*
flex [fleks], *v.t.* Piegare, flettere. ||*n.* (*Elec.*) Filo, cordone, *m.*
flexibility [fleksiˈbiliti], *n.* Flessibilità, *f.*
flexible, *a.* Flessibile.
flexion, *n.* Flessione, *f.*; piegamento, *m.*
flexor, *n.* (*Anat.*) Flessore, *m.*
flexure, *n.* Flessura, *f.*
flick [flik], *n.* Colpettino, *m.*, frustata, frustatina, *f.* || *v.t.* Dare un colpetto a.
flicker [ˈflikəɹ], *v.i.* Tremolare, guizzare; (*of light*) vacillare. || *n.* Guizzo, *m.*
flickering, *a.* Vacillante, guizzante.
flicks, *n.pl.* (*colloq.*) Cinema, *m.*
flier [ˈflaiˈəɹ], *n.* Aviatore, *m.*, aviatrice, *f.*
flight [flait], *n.* Fuga, *f.*; (*of birds*) volo, stormo, *m.*; (*of time*) corso, *m.*; (*of projectile*) traiettoria, *f.*; (*of stairs*) rampa di scale, *f.*; (*of steps*) scalinata, *f.*; (*fig.*) slancio, trasporto, *m.*; (*Aviat.*) volo, *m.*, volata, *f.* **In —**, in fuga; **to put to —**, mettere in fuga; **to take —**, pigliar la fuga; (*Aviat.*) **— -commander**, comandante di squadriglia, *m.*
flightiness, *n.* Leggerezza, incostanza, volubilità, *f.*
flighty, *a.* Leggero, incostante, volubile.
flimsiness [flimzinis], *n.* Leggerezza, frivolezza, inconsistenza, *f.*
flimsy, *a.* Leggero, fiacco, debole; frivolo.
flinch [flintʃ], *v.i.* Ritirarsi, titubare, esitare, rinculare, cedere. **I shall not — from my duty**, non verrò meno al mio dovere; **without flinching**, senza esitare.
fling [fliŋ], *v.t.* Lanciare, scagliare, gettare, buttare; *v.i.* lanciarsi, precipitarsi. || *n.* Colpo, getto, tiro, *m.* **To — away**, buttar via; **to — down**, gettare a terra; **to — out**, gettar fuori; **to — up**, buttare all'aria, abbandonare; **he flung out of the room**, si precipitò fuori dalla stanza; **to have a — at**, lanciare un frizzo a; **to have one's —**, darsi buon tempo; **the Highland —**, un ballo scozzese, *m.*
flint [flint], *n.* Selce, silice, *f.*; pietra focaia, *f.* **— and steel**, acciarino, *m.*; **to set one's face like a —**, fare il muso duro; **— glass**, cristallo di rocca, *m.*; **— -lock**, fucile a acciarino, *m.*
flinty, *a.* Siliceo; pietroso; (*fig.*) duro, spietato.
flip [flip], *v.t.* Dare un buffetto a, dare una ditata a. || *n.* Buffetto, *m.*, ditata, *f.* **Egg- —**, zabaione, *m.* [cp. **flick**].
flippancy [ˈflipənsi], *n.* Leggerezza, volubilità, *f.*
flippant, *a.* Leggero, volubile, frivolo.
flipper, *n.* Pinna, *f.*, natatoia, *f.*
flirt [flə:ɹt], *v.i.* Flirtare, amoreggiare, civettare. || *n.* Civetta, *f.*; fraschetta, *f.*; uomo galante, *m.*

flirtation, *n.* Flirt, *m.*, civetteria, *f.*
flirtatious, *a.* Civettuolo, galante.
flit [flit], *v.i.* Fuggire; svolazzare, volteggiare; sloggiare, sgombrare, traslocare. *n.* Traslocamento, *m.* **Moonlight —,** partire di notte senza aver pagato la pigione, *m.*; **to — about,** svolazzare; **to — by,** passare rapidamente.
flitch [flitʃ], *n.* Lardo, *m.*, fianco di lardo, *m.*
flitter-mouse [ˈflitəɹmaus], *n.* (*Zool.*) Pipistrello, *m.*
flitting, *n.* Fuga, *f.*; trasloco, *m.*
float [flout], *v.i.* Galleggiare, stare a galla; (*Swimming*) fare il morto; *v.t.* Far galleggiare; inondare; (*Comm.*) lanciare. || *n.* (*raft*) Zattera, *f.* (*vehicle*) carretto, *m.*; (*cork*) sughero, *m.*; (*Theat.*) luci della ribalta, *f.pl.*
floater, *n.* Galleggiante, *m.*; (*Comm.*) promotore di società anonima, *m.*
floating, *a.* Galleggiante, fluttuante. **— -bridge,** ponte galleggiante, *m.*; **— -dock,** bacino galleggiante, *m.*; **— population,** popolazione fluttuante, *f.* (*Comm.*) **— capital,** capitale circolante, *m.*; **— debt,** debito fluttuante, *m.*
flocculent [ˈflɔkju:lənt], *a.* Fioccoso.
flock (1) [flɔk], *n.* (*of sheep*) Gregge, *m.*; (*of cattle*) mandra, *f.*, armento, *m.*; (*of birds*) stormo, *m.*; (*of people*) stuolo, *m.*, truppa, folla, *f.* || *v.i.* Congregarsi, adunarsi, affollarsi, accalcarsi.
flock (2), *n.* Fiocco, bioccolo, *m.*, borra, *f.*
floe [flou], *n.* Banco di ghiaccio, lastra di ghiaccio, *m.* **— ice,** ghiaccio galleggiante, *m.*
flog [flɔg], *v.t.* Frustare, sferzare, staffilare, flagellare; (*colloq.*) vendere. **To — a dead horse,** fare un lavoro inutile.
flogging, *n.* Frustatura, sferzata, fustigazione, *f.* **He deserves a —,** egli si merita una sferzata.
flood [flʌd], *n.* Allagamento, diluvio, *m.*, innondazione, *f.*; (*of a river*) straripamento, *m.*; flusso, torrente, *m.*; (*of tide*) flusso, *m.* (*fig.*) ondata, *f.*; abbondanza, *f.* || *v.t.* Inondare, diluviare, sommergere; allagare, straripare. **At the — tide,** a marea alta; **a — of tears,** un torrente di lagrime, *m.*; **— -lighting,** illuminazione con proiettori, *f.*
floor [flɔ:ɹ], *n.* Pavimento, suolo, *m.*; (*storey*) piano, *m.*; fondo, tavolato, *m.* || *v.t.* Pavimentare; (*fig.*) gettare a terra, ridurre al silenzio. **Inlaid —,** parquet, *m.*; **on the first —,** al primo piano; **on the ground —,** a terreno, a pianterreno; **— -board,** asse del pavimento, *m.*; **— -cloth,** linoleum, *m.*
flop [flɔp], *v.t.i.* Buttar giù; piombare, precipitarsi; (*colloq. theatr.*) far fiasco. || *n.* (*colloq.*) Insuccesso, *m.* **To — about,** dimenarsi; **to — down,** buttarsi giù.
flora [ˈflɔ:rə], *n.* (*Bot.*) Flora, *f.*
floral, *a.* Floreale, florale.
Florence [ˈflɔrəns], *n.* (*Geog.*) Firenze, *f.*
Florentine [ˈflɔrəntain], *n.a.* Fiorentino, *m.*
florescence [flɔˈresəns], *n.* (*Bot.*) Efflorescenza, *f.*
floriculture [ˈflɔrikʌltʃəɹ], *n.* Fioricultura, *f.*
florid [ˈflɔrid], *a.* Florido, fiorente, fiorito.
floridity, floridness [flɔˈriditi, ˈflɔridnis], *n.* Floridezza; freschezza, *f.*
florilegium [floriˈli:dʒiəm], *n.* (*Lit.*) Florilegio, *m.*
florin [ˈflɔrin], *n.* Fiorino, *m.*
florist, *n.* Fioraia, *f.*, fiorista, *m.*
floss [flɔs], *n.* Cascame di seta, *m.*, piumino, *m.*, borra, bavella, *f.*; (*of plants*) lanugine, *f.* **— -silk,** filaticcio, *m.*
flossy, *a.* Lanuginoso; vellutato.
flotation, *n.* (*Comm.*) Lancio d'un impresa, *m.*, fluttazione, *f.*
flotilla [floˈtilə], *n.* (*Naut.*) Flottiglia, *f.*
flotsam [ˈflɔtsəm], *n.* Relitti, *m.pl.* **— and jetsam,** rottami galleggianti, *m.pl.*
flounce [flauns], *n.* Balza, balzana, piega, *f.*; falpalà, *f.* || *v.t.* Ornare di gale; *v.i.* dimenarsi, dibattersi. **To — out,** precipitarsi fuori.
flounder (1) [ˈflaundəɹ], *n.* (*Zool.*) Passerino, *m.*
flounder (2), *v.i.* Dimenarsi, dibattersi; impappinarsi.
flour [ˈflauəɹ], *n.* Farina, *f.* || *v.t.* Infarinare. **— bin,** madia, *f.*; **— -dredger,** polverizzatore, *m.*; **— -merchant, — dealer,** farinaiuolo, *m.*; **— -mill,** mulino, *m.*
flourish [ˈflʌriʃ], *v.t.* Prosperare; (*a weapon*) brandire; *v.i.* fiorire, prosperare; vantarsi, gloriarsi. || *n.* (*in writing*) Ghirigoro, arabesco, *m.*, paraffo, *m.*; (*of trumpets*) fanfara, *f.*; (*Mus.*) fioritura *f.*
flourishing, *a.* Fiorente, rigoglioso, prosperoso.
floury, *a.* Farinoso, coperto di farina.
flout [flaut], *v.t.* Beffarsi di, schernire, deridere, disprezzare.
flow [flou], *v.i.* Fluire, scorrere; (*of blood*) circolare; (*tide*) montare; (*fig.*) emanare, derivare. || *n.* Flusso, corso, *m.*; scorrimento, *m.*; corrente, *f.*, torrente, *m.*; abbondanza, *f.*; (*of words*) facilità, *f.* **To — back,** rifluire; **to — down,** scorrere; (*fig.*) **to — from,** derivare da; **to — over,** straripare; **ebb and —,** flusso e riflusso; **a — of talk,** un fiume di parole, *m.*; **— of spirits,** indole allegra, *f.*; **the stream flows from the mountains,** il ruscello sgorga dalla montagna.
flower [ˈflauəɹ], *n.* Fiore, *m.*; (*Print.*) fiorone, *m.* || *v.i.* Fiorire, far fiori; *v.t.* ornare di fiori. **— -bed,** aiuola, *f.*; **— -garden,** giardino, *m.*; **— pot,** vaso da fiori, *m.*; **— -girl,** fioraia, *f.*; **— -show,** esposizione di fiori, *f.*; **— -stand,** giardiniera, *f.*
flowered, *a.* Fiorito, a fiorami, a fiori. **— material,** stoffa a fiori, *f.*
flowering, *a.* Fiorito. || *n.* Fioritura, *f.*
flowery, *a.* Infiorato; in fiore; (*of language*) fiorito.
flowing, *a.* Scorrevole, fluente; (*of tide*) montante. || *n.* Corso, flusso, *m.*
flowingly, *adv.* Scorrevolmente, facilmente.
flown, *a.* (*obs.*) Gonfio, tronfio. **High —,** ampolloso.
flu [flu:], *n.* (*colloq. Med.*) Influenza, *f.*
fluctuate [ˈflʌktju:eit], *v.i.* Fluttuare, oscillare.
fluctuating, *a.* Fluttuante, incostante, oscillante.
fluctuation, *n.* Fluttuazione, *f.* **Fluctuations of the money market,** oscillazioni del mercato monetario, *f.pl.*
flue [flu:], *n.* Tubo, condotto, *m.*; (*of chimney*) gola, *f.*
fluency [ˈflu:ənsi], *n.* Facilità, scorrevolezza, *f.*
fluent, *a.* Fluente, corrente, scorrente, fecondo.
fluently, *adv.* Correntemente.

fluff, *n.* Borra, *f.*; (*on floor*) lanugine, peluria, *f.*
fluffy, *a.* Coperto di peluria. **— hair**, capelli soffici, capelli vellutati, *m.pl.*
fluid ['flu:id], *n.a.* Fluido, *m.*; liquido, *m.*
fluidity, *n.* Fluidezza, *f.*; fluidità, *f.*
fluke (1) [flu:k], *n.* (*Naut.*) Marra, *f.*
fluke (2), *n.* (*chance*) Colpo di fortuna, *m.*, caso inaspettato, *m.*
fluke (3), *n.* (*Zool.*) (*fish*) Passerino, *m.*; (*parasite*) linguattola, *f.*
flummery ['flʌməri], *n.* Fandonie, chiacchiere, *f.pl.*
flunkey ['flʌŋki], *n.* Lacchè; (*colloq.*) tirapiedi, *m.*
fluor ['flu:ɔɹ], *n.* (*Chem.*) Fluoro, *m.* **—spar**, spato fluore, *m.*; fluorite, *f.*
fluorescence, *n.* Fluorescenza, *f.*
fluorescent, *a.* Fluorescente.
fluorine, *n.* Fluorina, *f.*
flurry ['flʌri], *n.* Trambusto, *m.*, agitazione, *f.*; (*of wind*) folata, *f.* ‖ *v.t.* Agitare, inquietare, turbare. **In a terrible —**, in gran trambusto.
flush [flʌʃ], *n.* Rossore, *m.*, (*fig.*) trasporto, accesso, *m.*, ebbrezza, *f.*; (*of colour*) vampa, *f.*; (*Cards*) flusso, *m.* ‖ *v.t.* Far arrossire; (*fig.*) esaltare, rallegrare; (*shooting game*) levare; (*drains*) ripulire, risciacquare; *v.i.* arrossire. ‖ *a.* Ripieno; (*fig.*) ben provveduto; a livello, a fiore. **He flushed deeply**, diventò rosso come un peperone; **to be — of money**, essere ben provveduto di danaro; **— with**, a livello con.
flushing, *n.* Rossore; (*of drains*) nettamento, *m.*
Flushing ['flʌʃiŋ], *n.* (*Geog.*) Flessinga, *f.*
fluster, *v.t.* Agitare, turbare, scompigliare. ‖ *n.* Agitazione, *f.*, scompiglio, trambusto, *m.*
flute [flu:t], *n.* Flauto, *m.*; (*Arch.*, *etc.*) scanalatura, *f.* ‖ *v.t.* Suonare il flauto; scanalare. **— -player, flautist**, flautista, *m.*
fluted, *a.* Scanalato.
fluting, *n.* Scanalatura, *f.*
flutter ['flʌtəɹ], *n.* (*of birds*) Svolazzamento, frullio, battito, *m.*; tremito, tremore, *m.*; agitazione, *f.*; (*colloq.*) speculazione, *f.* ‖ *v.t.* Agitare, turbare, scompigliare; (*of flags*) sventolare; *v.i.* svolazzare, aleggiare; dimenarsi; palpitare. **She was all of a —**, era tutta agitata; **to put into a —**, agitare, turbare, metter sossopra.
fluttering, *a.* Palpitante. **A — pulse**, un polso irregolare, *m.*
fluvial ['flu:viəl], *a.* Fluviale.
flux [flʌks], *n.* Flusso, corso, *m.* ‖ *v.t.i.* Fluire, fondere, fondersi. **In a state of —**, fluttuante.
fluxion, *n.* Flussione, *f.*
fly [flai], (1) (*pl.* **flies**) *n.* (*Zool.*) Mosca, *f.* **Spanish —**, cantaride, *f.*; **— -blow**, uovo di mosca, *m.pl.*; **— -blown**, sporcato, guasto dalle mosche; (*Zool.*) **— -catcher**, pigliamosche, *f.*; **— -fishing**, pesca colla lenza, *f.*; **— -flap**, scacciamosche, *m.*; **— -paper**, carta moschicida, *f.*; (*Bot.*) **— -trap**, dionea, *f.*; (*Sport*) **— -weight**, peso mosca, *m.*
fly (2) (*pl.* **flys**), *n.* Vettura da nolo, *f.*; (*trouser*) sparato, *m.*
fly (3), *v.i.* Volare; fuggire, sfuggire, scappare; involarsi, sparire; correre; *v.t.* (*a flag*) battere, sventolare; (*a kite*) lanciare. **To — asunder**, spezzarsi, schiantarsi; **to — at**, lanciarsi addosso a, avventarsi su *or* contro; **to — away**, scappare, volar via; (*of spring, etc.*) **to — back**, scattare; **to — for refuge**, ricoverarsi; **to — from justice**, sottrarsi alla giustizia; **to — in the face of**, disubbidire a; (*fig.*) **to — high**, ambire a grandi cose; **to — into a passion**, montare in collera; **to — over**, sorvolare; **to let —**, lanciare, scagliare; **to — up on high**, innalzarsi a volo; **to — the country**, fuggire dal paese; **— -leaf**, foglio di guardia, *m.*; **— -sheet**, foglio volante, *m.*
flying, *a.* Volante; fuggente; a volo. ‖ *n.* Aviazione, *f.*, volo, volare, *m.* **— -column**, colonna volante, *f.*; **— colours**, bandiere spiegate, *f.pl.*; **— buttress**, arco a sprone, *m.*; **— -jump**, salto di volata, *m.*; **— -ace**, asso d'aviazione, *m.*; **— boat**, idroplano, idrovolante, *m.*; (*Zool.*) **— -fish**, pesce rondine, pesce volante, *m.*; (*Aviat.*) **— -ground**, aerodromo, aeroscalo, *m.*, campo d'aviazione, *m.*; (*police*) **— squad**, squadra mobile, *f.*; **a — visit**, una rapida visita, *f.*
foal [foul], *n.* Puledro, *m.*, puledra, *f.*; asinello, *m.* ‖ *v.i.* Figliare.
foam [foum], *n.* Spuma, schiuma, *f.* ‖ *v.i.* Spumare, schiumare; spumeggiare. **He was foaming at the mouth with anger**, dalla rabbia gli veniva la bava alla bocca; **the foaming waves**, le onde spumeggianti, *f.pl.*
foamy, *a.* Spumante, spumeggiante, spumoso.
fob [fɔb], *n.* Taschino per l'orologio, *m.* ‖ *v.t.* Ingannare, gabbare; affibbiare. **To — off with**, rimandare indietro con.
focal ['foukəl], *a.* Focale.
focalization, *n.* Concentrazione, *f.*
fo'c'sle [cp. **forecastle**].
focus ['foukəs], *n.* Foco, fuoco, *m.*; centro, *m.* ‖ *v.t.* Mettere a fuoco; concentrare. **In —**, a fuoco, a foco; **the — of a parabola**, fuoco della parabola, *m.*; **the — of a disease**, il focolare d'una malattia, *m.*; **to bring into —**, mettere a fuoco; **out of —**, sfuocato.
fodder ['fɔdəɹ], *n.* Foraggio, *m.* ‖ *v.t.* Dar foraggio a, foraggiare.
foe [fou], *n.* Nemico, avversario, antagonista, *m.*
foetus ['fi:təs], *n.* Feto, *m.*
foetal, *a.* Fetale.
fog [fɔg], *n.* Nebbia, *f.*; (*fig.*) oscurità, perplessità, *f.*; (*Phot.*) velo, *m.* ‖ *v.t.* Annebbiare, oscurare, offuscare; (*Phot.*) velare. **A thick —**, un nebbione; (*fig.*) **in a —**, molto perplesso; **— -horn**, sirena, *f.*; **— -signal**, segnale da nebbia, *m.*
fogginess ['fɔginis], *n.* Nebbiosità; (*fig.*) oscurità, perplessità, *f.*
foggy, *a.* Nebbioso, fosco, offuscato, brumoso. **It's —**, c'è la nebbia.
fogy, fogey ['fougi], *n.* **Old —**, vecchione, vecchiotto, *m.*
foible ['fɔibl], *n.* Debole, *m.* **It is one of my foibles**, è un mio debole.
foil [fɔil], *n.* (*of metal*) Foglia, lamina, *f.*; (*Arch.*) fogliame, *m.*; (*Fencing*) fioretto, *m.*; (*fig.*) contrasto, *m.* ‖ *v.t.* Frustrare, deludere, render vano. **Gold- —**, orpello, *m.*; **tin- —**, stagnola, *f.*; **to act as a — to**, dar rilievo a, mettere in contrasto.
foist [fɔist], *v.t.* Affibbiare, imporre. **To — upon**, insinuare, imporre a.

fold [fould], *v.t.* Piegare; (*in the arms*) stringere; (*sheep*) addiacciare, stabbiare, chiudere nell'ovile. || *n.* Piega, piegatura, *f.*; (*for sheep*) ovile, *m.* **To — back,** piegare indietro; **to — up,** avvolgere, ripiegare; **to — one's arms,** incrociare le braccia; **to — the hands,** intrecciare le mani, giungere le mani.
folder, *n.* Piegatore, *m.*; (*Mech.*) macchina piegatrice, *f.*
folding, *a.* Pieghevole. || *n.* Piegatura. **— -bed,** letto pieghevole, letto da campo, *m.*; **— -chair,** sedia pieghevole, *f.*; **— -doors,** porta a due battenti, *f.*; **— -screen,** paravento, *m.*; **— -camera,** apparecchio fotografico pieghevole, *m.*
foliaceous [fouliˈeiʃəs], *a.* (*Bot.*) Fogliaceo.
foliage [ˈfouliədʒ], *n.* Fogliame, *m.*
foliate, *v.t.* Laminare; ornare di foglie. || *a.* Fogliato.
foliation, *n.* Fogliazione, *f.*
folio [ˈfouliou], *n.* (*Print.*) Folio, *m.*; (*book*) in-folio, *m.*
folk [fouk], *n.* Gente, *f.*, popolo, *m.* **The old folks,** i vecchi, *m.pl.*; **the little folks,** i bambini, *m.pl.*
folklore, *n.* Folklore, *m.*, tradizioni popolari, *f.pl.*
folklorist, *n.* Folklorista, *m.*; studente di folklore, *m.*
follicle [ˈfɔlikl], *n.* (*Anat.*) Follicolo, *m.*
follicular, *a.* Follicolare.
folliculous, *a.* Follicoloso.
follow [ˈfɔlou], *v.t.* Seguire, inseguire, seguitare; imitare, copiare; (*a custom*) conformarsi a; (*a profession*) esercitare; *v.i.* conseguire, risultare, derivare. **To — suit,** imitare, far lo stesso, (*Cards*) rispondere al colore; **to — up,** proseguire, approfittare di; **to — in the wake of,** calcare le orme di; **as follows,** come segue; **it follows that,** risulta che.
follower, *n.* Seguace, compagno, partigiano, *m.*; (*colloq.*) innamorato, *m.*
following, *a.* Seguente, successivo, prossimo. || *n.* Seguito, corteo, *m.* **The year —,** l'anno dopo, *m.*; **in the — manner,** nel modo seguente; **the — persons,** i sottoscritti, i sottonominati, *m.pl.*
folly [ˈfɔli], *n.* Follia, stoltezza, sventatezza, sciocchezza, *f.*, l'assurdo, *m.*
foment [fəˈment], *v.t.* Fomentare, applicare un fomento.
fomentation, *n.* (*Med.*) Fomento, *m.*, fomentazione, *f.*
fomenter, *n.* Istigatore, *m.*
fond [fɔnd], *a.* Amorevole, affezionato, tenero; appassionato; svagato; (*of hopes*) caro; credulo. **To be — of,** voler bene a, amare; **he's very — of music,** è appassionato per la musica.
fondle [ˈfɔndl], *v.t.* Accarezzare, vezzeggiare, coccolare.
fondly, *adv.* Teneramente.
fondness, *n.* Amorevolezza, affezione, tenerezza, *f.*; inclinazione, *f.*, gusto, *m.*
font [fɔnt], *n.* Fonte battesimale, *f.*; (*Print.*) corpo, *m.*
food [fu:d], *n.* Cibo, nutrimento, alimento, *m.*, viveri, *m.pl.*; vitto, mangiare, *m.*; (*of animals*) pascolo, *m.*, pastura, *f.*; (*fig.*) materia, *f.*, soggetto, argomento, *m.* **Article of —,** commestibile, *m.*; **— -stuffs,** derrate alimentari, *f.pl.*, generi alimentari, *m.pl.*; **— and drink,** il bere e il mangiare; **to give — for thought,** dare da pensare.
fool [fu:l], *n.* Sciocco, stolto, scimunito, imbecille, pazzo, *m.*; (*jester*) buffone, *m.* || *v.t.* Ingannare, truffare, burlarsi di; *v.i.* fare il buffone. **— -proof,** perfettamente sicuro; **to play the —,** far lo stupido; **to live in a fool's paradise,** vivere in un paradiso artificiale; **to make a fool of someone,** far passare qualcuno da sciocco.
foolery, *n.* Follia, *f.*; scempiaggine, *f.*; sciocchezze, inezie, *f.pl.*
foolhardiness, *n.* Temerità, avventatezza, *f.*
foolhardy, *a.* Temerario, avventato.
fooling, *n.* Buffonate, *f.pl.*
foolish, *a.* Scemo, sciocco, imbecille; insensato.
foolishness, *n.* Follia, scempiaggine, scemenza, sciocchezza, *f.*; imprudenza, *f.*
foolscap, *n.* Carta protocollo, *f.*
foot (*pl.* **feet**) [fut, fi:t], *n.* Piede, *m.*; (*of animals*) zampa; (*Mil.*) fanteria, *f.*; base, parte inferiore, *f.* || *v.t.* (*a stocking*) Rifare il piede; (*a bill*) pagare. **To — it,** andare a piedi, farlo a piedi; **— -bath,** pediluvio, *m.*; **— -board,** predellino, *m.*, pedana, *f.*; **— -boy,** paggio, *m.*; **— -bridge,** passerella, *f.*, ponticello, *m.*; (*Mil.*) **— -guards,** guardie a piedi, *f.pl.*; **— -pace,** passo lento; **— -passenger,** pedone, *m.*; **— -path,** sentiero, *m.*, marciapiede, *m.*; **— -print,** impronta, *f.*; **— -race,** corsa a piedi, corsa podistica, *f.*; **— rest,** predellino, sgabello, *m.*; **— -rule,** regolo, *m.*: **— -soldier,** fantaccino, fante, *m.*
footage, *n.* (*Cinema.*) Metraggio, *m.*
football, *n.* (*game*) Giuoco del calcio, *m.*; (*ball*) pallone, *m.*, palla, *f.* **Rugby —,** pallone ovale, *m.*
footballer, *n.* Calciatore, *m.*
footed, *a.* Con piedi. **Four- —,** quadrupede.
footfall, *n.* Passo, *m.*
foothold, *n.* Appiglio, *m.* **To gain a —,** trovare un appiglio.
footing, *n.* Piede, sostegno, *m.*; (*fig.*) appoggio, principio, *m.*; (*Arch.*) base, basamento, *m.* **He missed his —,** mise il piede in fallo; **on an equal —,** alla pari; **on a war —,** in assetto di guerra; **on the same — as,** al pari di; **to get a —,** stabilirsi, prender piede.
footle [ˈfu:tl], *v.i.* (*colloq.*) Gingillarsi, perdere il tempo.
footlights, *n.pl.* Lumi della ribalta, *m.pl.*
footman, *n.* Valletto, *m.*
footmark, *n.* Orma, pedata, *f.*
footnote, *n.* Nota a pie di pagina, *f.*
footpad, *n.* Grassatore, *m.*
footplate, *n.* (*Rail.*) Piattaforma, *f.*
footstep, *n.* Passo, *m.*, pedata, orma, traccia, *f.*; vestigio, *m* **To follow in someone's footsteps,** seguire le orme di qualcuno.
footstool, *n.* Sgabello, *m.*
footwarmer, *n.* Scaldapiedi, *m.*
fop [fɔp], *n.* Bellimbusto, damerino, zerbinotto, *m.*
foppery, foppishness, *n.* Fatuità, smanceria, *f.*
foppish, *a.* Attillato, azzimato; fatuo.
for [fɔ:ɹ], *prep.* Per, da, durante; a favore di, in cambio di; a causa di, malgrado. || *conj.* Perchè, a cagione che, imperocchè. **As — me,** per me, in quanto a me; **— all that,** nonostante ciò; **— aught we know,** per quanto ne

sappiamo noi; **— more than a month past,** da più di un mese; **— oneself,** per sè; **— pity's sake,** per pietà; **— the present,** per ora; **— your sake,** per amor vostro; **I did it — his good,** l'ho fatto per suo bene; **in exchange —,** in cambio di; **it is not — you to,** non tocca a voi di; **— and against,** pro e contro; **word — word,** parola per parola; (*colloq.*) **to go — someone,** attaccare qualcuno; **he sits — Birkenhead,** è deputato di Birkenhead.

forage [ˈfɔridʒ], *n.* Foraggio, *m.* || *v.i.* Foraggiare. **— -cap,** beretto di fatica, *m.*

forager, *n.* Foraggiere, *m.*

foraging, *n.* Foraggiamento, *m.*

foraminate, foraminated [fəˈræmineit, fəˈræmineitəd], *a.* Foraminoso.

forasmuch as, *conj.* Giacchè, visto che, poichè.

foray [ˈfɔrei], *n.* Scorreria, *f.* || *v.i.* Fare una scorreria.

forbear [fɔɹˈbɛəɹ], *v.t.i.* Fare a meno di, astenersi da; evitare, risparmiare; pazientare.

forbearance, *n.* Pazienza, indulgenza, tolleranza, *f.*

forbearingly, *adv.* Pazientemente, con indulgenza.

forbears [cp. **forebears**].

forbid [fəɹˈbid], *v.t.* Vietare, interdire, proibire. **God —!** Dio me ne guardi! **he is forbidden to,** gli è vietato di; **I forbade him to go,** gli ho proibito di andare.

forbidding, *a.* Antipatico, scostante, repellente, arcigno.

force [fɔːɹs], *n.* Forza, potenza, violenza, *f.*; vigore, *m.*; validità, *f.*; energia, *f.* || *v.t.* Forzare, sforzare, costringere, obbligare; aprire con forza; (*plants*) far maturare in serra. (*Law*) **In —,** in vigore; **land and sea forces,** forze di terra e di mare, *f.pl.*; **the — of circumstances,** la forza delle circostanze, *f.*; **there is — in what you say,** ciò che voi dite non è privo di valore; **by —,** per forza, a forza; **by main —,** a viva forza; **to — a passage,** aprirsi un passaggio colla forza; **to — back,** respingere, ricacciare; **to — down,** far discendere a forza; **to — one's way,** aprirsi a forza la via; **to — open,** forzare, scassinare; **to — someone's hand,** forzare la mano a qualcuno; **to — the pace,** forzare il passo; **— -pump,** pompa premente, *f.*

forced, *n.* Forzato, costretto, obbligato. **A — laugh,** un riso forzato, *m.*

forceful, *a.* Forte, vigoroso, possente.

forcemeat, *n.* Ripieno, *m.*

forceps [ˈfɔːɹseps], *n.* (*Med.*) Forcipe, *m.*

forcible, *a.* Efficace, energico, forte; forzato, violento.

forcibly, *a.* Energicamente, con efficacia, con forza.

forcing, *n.* Forzamento, *m.* **— -house,** serra, *f.*

ford [fɔːɹd], *n.* Guado, *m.* || *v.t.* Guadare, passare a guado.

fordable, *a.* Guadabile.

fore [fɔːɹ], *a.* Anteriore, di fronte; (*Naut.*) di prora, di prua, di trinchetto. || *adv.* Anteriormente, prima, avanti. || *inter.* (*Golf*) Attenti! || *n.* Davanti, *m.*; (*Naut.*) prua, *f.* **— and aft,** da poppa a prua; **to come to the —,** divenire d'attualità.

forearm [ˈfɔːɹɑːɹm], *n.* Avambraccio, cubito, *m.* || *v.t.* [fɔːˈrɑːɹm], Premunire.

forebears, *n.pl.* Antenati, *m.pl.*

forebode, *v.t.* Presagire, presentire, pronosticare.

foreboding, *n.* Presentimento, presagio, *m.*

forecast, *n.* Previsione, *f.*, pronostico, *m.* || *v.t.* Prevedere, pronosticare. **Weather —,** previsioni meteorologiche, *f.pl.*

forecastle, fo'c'sle [ˈfouksl], *n.* (*Naut.*) Castello di prua, *m.*

foreclose, *v.t.* (*Law*) Ipotecare.

foreclosure, *n.* Ipoteca, *f.*

forecourt, *n.* Atrio, *m.*

foredeck, *n.* (*Naut.*) Ponte di prua, *m*

foredoom, *v.t.* Predestinare.

forefather, *n.* Antenato, avo, *m.*

forefinger [ˈfɔːɹfiŋgəɹ], *n.* Indice, *m.*

forefront, *n.* La parte anteriore, *f.*, il davanti, *m.* **In the — of the battle,** nelle prime linee, in prima linea.

forego (1), *v.t.i.* Precedere.

forego (2) [cp. **forgo**].

foregoing, *n.a.* Precedente, anteriore. *m.*

foregone, *a.* Preconcetto, predeterminato. **A — conclusion,** una conclusione prevista, *f.*

foreground, *n.* Primo piano, il davanti, *m.* **He's always in the —,** è sempre molto in vista.

forehand, *n.* Parte d'un cavallo anteriore al cavaliere, *f.*; (*Tennis*) **— stroke,** colpo diritto, *m.*

forehead [ˈfɔred], *n.* (*Anat.*) Fronte, *f.*

foreign [ˈfɔrin], *a.* Straniero, estero, estraneo; alieno; esotico. **— products,** merci estere, *f.pl.*; **in — parts,** all'estero; **that is — to his nature,** quello gli è proprio alieno; **Foreign Office,** Ministero degli Affari Esteri, *m.*; **a — body,** un corpo estraneo, *m.*

foreigner, *n.* Straniero, *m.*, straniera, *f.*; forestiere, *m.f.*

forejudge, *v.t.* Giudicare in avanzo.

foreknow, *v.t.* Preconoscere, prevedere.

foreknowledge, *n.* Preconoscenza, prescienza, *f.*

foreland [ˈfɔːɹlənd], *n.* (*Geog.*) Promontorio, capo, *m.*

foreleg, *n.* (*Anat.*) Gamba anteriore, *f.*

forelock, *n.* Ciuffo, *m.* **To take time by the —,** prender la fortuna per il ciuffo.

foreman (*pl.* **foremen**) [ˈfɔːɹmən], *n.* Capo operaio, capotecnico, capomastro, *m.* **— of the jury,** capo dei giurati, capo della giuria, *m.*

foremast, *n.* (*Naut.*) Albero di trinchetto, *m.*

forementioned, *a.* Suddetto, summenzionato.

foremost, *n.* Il primo, il più avanti, *m.*; il migliore, *m.* **First and —,** prima di tutto, anzitutto, a bella prima; **to be —,** essere il primo, essere tra i primi.

forenamed, *a.* Soprannominato.

forenoon, *n.* Mattina, mattinata, *f.*

forensic [fəˈrensik], *a.* Forense, legale. **— medicine,** medicina legale, *f.*

fore-ordain [fɔːrɔːɹˈdein], *v.t.* Preordinare predestinare.

forepart, *n.* Fronte, parte anteriore, *f.*

forepaw, *n.* Zampa anteriore, *f.*

forepeak, *n.* (*Naut.*) Gavone di prua, *m.*

forerunner, *n.* Precursore, *m.*

foresail, *n.* (*Naut.*) Vela di trinchetto, *f.*; fiocco, *m.*

foresee, *v.t.* Prevedere; presentire.

foreshadow, *v.t.* Prefigurare; adombrare, far presentire.
foreshore, *n.* Spiaggia, *f.*
foreshorten, *v.t.* Dipingere in iscorcio.
foreshortening, *n.* Scorcio, *m.*
foreshow, *v.t.* Predire, prefigurare.
foresight, *n.* Previdenza, preveggenza, *f.*; (*of a gun*) mirino, *m.*
foreskin, *n.* (*Anat.*) Prepuzio, *m.*
forest [ˈfɔrest], *n.* Foresta, selva, *f.*, bosco, *m.* || *a.* Forestale. **— laws,** leggi forestali, *f.pl.*; **— tree,** albero d'alto fusto, *m.*
forestall [fɔːɹˈstɔːl], *v.t.* Anticipare, prevenire; accaparrare.
forestaller, *n.* Incettatore, accaparratore, *m.*
forestalling, *n.* Accaparramento, *m.*
forested, *a.* Boscoso.
forester, *n.* Guardaboschi, *m.*
forestry, *n.* Selvicoltura, *f.*
foretaste, *n.* Pregustazione, *f.* || *v.t.* Pregustare, assaggiare.
foretell, *v.t.* Predire.
foretelling, *n.* Predizione, *f.*
forethought, *n.* Previsione, previdenza, *f.*; premeditazione, *f.*
foretoken, *v.t.* Pronosticare. || *n.* Pronostico, presagio, *m.*
foretop, *n.* (*Naut.*) Alberetto di trinchetto, *m.*
forewarn, *v.t.* Prevenire, avvertire.
foreword, *n.* Prefazione, *f.*; proemio, *m.*
forfeit [ˈfɔːɹfit], *n.* Multa, ammenda, *f.*; pena, *f.*; (*Law*) confisca, *f.*, fio, *m.*; (*wager*) posta, *f.*, pegno, *m.* || *v.t.* Confiscare, perdere per sequestro; mancare a; demeritare, privarsi di. || *a.* Confiscato; (*fig.*) perduto. **His life was the —,** pagò il fio colla propria vita; **to play at forfeits,** giuocare a pegni; **to — one's word,** mancare di parola.
forfeitable, *a.* Confiscabile.
forfeiture, *n.* Confisca, perdita, *f.*; (*Law*) decadenza, *f.*
forfend [fɔːɹˈfend], *v.t.* Stornare. **Heaven —!** Dio ne guardi!
forgather [fɔːiɹˈgæðəɹ], *v.i.* Adunarsi, raccogliersi.
forge [fɔːɹdʒ], *n.* Fucina, *f.* || *v.t.* Fucinare, fabbricare; contraffare, falsificare. **To — a signature,** falsificare una firma; **to — ahead,** tirare avanti.
forged, *a.* Contraffatto.
forger, *n.* Falsario, contraffattore, *m.*
forgery, *n.* Falsificazione, *f.*; falso, *m.*; (*Law*) reato di falso, *m.*
forget [fɔːɹˈget], *v.t.* Dimenticare scordare, scordarsi. **To — oneself,** dimenticarsi, comportarsi indecorosamente; perdere il controllo; **let's forget it,** lasciamo perdere, non ne parliamo più.
forgetful, *a.* Dimentico, immemore, incurante, noncurante. **— of his honour,** noncurante dell'onore.
forgetfulness, *n.* Dimenticanza, trascuratezza, noncuranza, smemoratezza, *f.*, oblio, *m.*
forget-me-not, *n.* (*Bot.*) Non-ti-scordar-di-me, miosotide, *m.*
forgive [fɔːɹˈgiv], *v.t.* Perdonare, rimettere, condonare. **God — me!** Dio mi perdoni! **— him for having hurt you,** perdonategli di avervi fatto male.
forgiveness, *n.* Perdono, *m.*, remissione, *f.*
forgiving, *a.* Clemente, indulgente, mite.
forgo, *v.t.* Rinunciare a, astenersi da.
fork [fɔːɹk], *n.* (*for the table*) Forchetta, *f.*; (*Agric.*) forca, *f.*; (*in roads*) bivio, *m.*, biforcazione, *f.*; (*Mech.*) forcella, *f.*; (*tree*) forcella, *f.*, ramo biforcato, *m.* || *v.t.* Portare colla forca, inforcare; *v.i.* biforcarsi. (*colloq.*) **To — out,** pagare.
forked, *a.* Forcuto, biforcato, a forca; (*Zool.*) biforcuto. **— lightning,** folgore, fulmine a zig-zag, *m.*
forlorn [fɔːɹˈlɔːɹn], *a.* Abbandonato, derelitto, disperato, perduto, solitario; sconsolato. **A — hope,** un caso disperato, *m.*
forlornness, *n.* Abbandono, *m.*, condizione disperata, miseria, *f.*
form [fɔːɹm], *n.* Forma, figura, *f.*; formalità, cerimonia, *f.*; formula, *f.*; (*in school*) classe, *f.*; (*seat*) panca, *f.*, banco, *m.*; (*of hare*) covo, *m.*; (*printed*) modulo, *m.* || *v.t.* Formare, figurare, fare; costituire, ordinare; *v.i.* formarsi, prendere forma. **In bad —,** sconveniente; **in due —,** nella debita forma; **good —,** buona creanza, *f.*; **in —,** in vena; **a telegram —,** un modulo per telegramma, *m.*; **empty forms,** formule vane, *f.pl.*; **to — an idea of,** figurarsi, formarsi un' idea di; **to — a society,** costituire una società; **to — part of,** far parte di; (*Mil.*) **to — fours,** mettersi per quattro; **to — up,** mettersi in fila.
formal, *a.* Formale, di forma; ceremonioso; ufficiale; esplicito.
formalism, *n.* Formalismo, *m.*
formalist, *n.* Formalista, *m.*
formality, *n.* Formalità, cerimonia, *f.*
formalize, *v.t.* Formulare.
formally, *adv.* Formalmente.
formation, *n.* Formazione, costituzione, creazione, struttura, *f.*; (*Mil.*) ordine, *m.*, formazione, *f.* (*Mil.*) **Close —,** ordine chiuso, *m.*
formative, *a.* Formativo.
forme [fɔːɹm], *n.* (*Print.*) Forma, *f.*
former, *a.* Precedente, primo; passato. **In — times,** nei tempi passati; **the —, the latter,** quello, questo; l'uno, l'altro; il primo, il secondo; **she is like her — self,** è tornata quella che era.
formerly, *adv.* Altre volte, anticamente, anteriormente, già, un tempo, tempo addietro, precedentemente.
formic [ˈfɔːɹmik], *a.* (*Chem.*) Formico.
formidable [ˈfɔːɹmidəbl], *a.* Formidabile, spaventoso.
formidableness, *n.* Formidabilità, spaventosità, *f.*
formless, *a.* Informe, amorfo.
formula (*pl.* **formulae**) [ˈfɔːɹmjuːlə], *n.* Formula, *f.*
formulary, *n.* Formulario, *m.*
formulate, *v.t.* Formulare.
formulation, *n.* Formulazione, *f.*
fornicate [ˈfɔːɹnikeit], *v.i.* Fornicare.
fornication, *n.* Fornicazione, *f.*
fornicator, *n.* Fornicatore, *m.*, fornicatrice, *f.*
forsake [fɔːɹˈseik], *v.t.* Abbandonare, lasciare, rinunziare a. **To — one's colours,** disertare la propria bandiera.
forsaking, *n.* Abbandono, *m.*
forsooth [fɔːɹˈsuːθ], *adv.* In verità, davvero, veramente.

forswear [fɔːɹˈswɛəɹ], *v.t.* Abiurare, rinunziare, disdire; rinunciare a. **To — oneself,** spergiurare, giurare il falso.
fort [fɔːɹt], *n.* Forte, *m.*, fortezza, *f.*
forte [ˈfɔːɹti], *n.* Forte, *m.* || *adv.* (*Mus.*) Forte. **Punctuality is not my —,** la puntualità non è il mio forte.
forth [fɔːɹθ], *adv.* Fuori, avanti, innanzi. **Back and —,** avanti e indietro; **from this time —** d'ora innanzi; **and so —,** e così via; **from that time —,** da allora in poi.
forthcoming, *a.* Prossimo, pronto, entrante, futuro. **The money shall be —,** il danaro sarà pronto.
forthright, *a.* Franco, schietto, onesto, esplicito.
forthwith, *adv.* Immediatamente, subito.
fortieth [ˈfɔːɹtieθ], *n.a.* Quarantesimo, *m.*
fortifiable [fɔːɹtiˈfaiəbl], *a.* Fortificabile.
fortification, *n.* Fortificazione, *f.*; (*of wine*) alcoolizzazione, *f.*
fortify [ˈfɔːɹtifai], *v.t.* Fortificare, rafforzare, munire. **To — oneself,** fortificarsi, irrobustirsi.
fortifying, *a.* Fortificante, corroborante.
fortitude, *n.* Fortezza, forza d'animo, fermezza, *f.*; magnanimità, *f.*; coraggio, *m.*
fortnight [ˈfɔːɹtnait], *n.* Quindici giorni, *m.pl.*; una quindicina, *f.*; due settimane, *f.pl.* **A — ago,** due settimane fa; **a — ago yesterday,** quindici giorni ieri; **to-day —,** oggi a quindici.
fortnightly, *a.* Quindicinale, bisettimanale. || *adv.* Ogni due settimane, due volte al mese.
fortress, *n.* Fortezza, piazzaforte, *f.*
fortuitous [fɔːɹˈtjuːitəs], *a.* Fortuito, accidentale, casuale.
fortunate [ˈfɔːɹtjuːnit], *a.* Fortunato, felice.
fortunately, *adv.* Fortunatamente, per buona fortuna.
fortune [ˈfɔːɹtjuːn], *n.* Fortuna, ventura, *f.*; sorte, *f.*; ricchezze, *f.pl.*; oroscopo, *m.*; caso, *m.*; patrimonio, *m.* **Good —,** buona fortuna, *f.*; **by good —,** fortunatamente, per fortuna; **to have one's — told,** farsi dire la buona ventura; **to tell a —,** dire la buona ventura; **to go to seek one's —,** andare a cercare fortuna; **a stroke of —,** un colpo di fortuna, *m.*; **— -hunter,** cacciatore di dote, *m.*; **— -teller,** indovino, chiromante, *m.*; **— -telling,** sortilegio, *m.*
forty [ˈfɔːɹti], *n.a.* Quaranta, *m.* **About —,** una quarantina, *f.*; (*colloq.*) **— winks,** un pisolino, *m.*
forum [ˈfɔːɹəm], *n.* Foro, *m.*
forward [ˈfɔːɹwəd], *a.* Avanzato, inoltrato; precoce; (*of fruit, etc.*) primaticcio; pronto, sollecito; (*of a child*) vivace, sbarazzino. || *adv.* Avanti, in avanti, in evidenza. || *v.t.* Spedire, inviare, (*letters*) far seguire, inoltrare; assecondare. || *n.* (*Football*) Centro attacco, *m.* **— delivery,** a futura consegna; **from this day —,** d'ora in poi; **to look — to,** anticipare, pregustare; **to bring oneself —,** mettersi avanti; **to be well —,** essere avanti; **straight —,** difilato; **please — (letters),** favorite far seguire, con preghiera di inoltro, si prega di far recapitare.
forwarder, *n.* Promotore, fautore; (*Comm.*) mittente speditore, *m.*
forwarding, *n.* Spedizione, *f.* **— agent,** spedizioniere, *m.*
forwardness, *n.* Progresso, *m.*; precocità, *f.*; impertinenza, *f.*
fosse [fɔs], *n.* Fossa, *f.*
fossil [ˈfɔsəl], *n.a.* Fossile, *m.*
fossilization, *n.* Fossilizzazione, *f.*
fossilize, *v.t.* Fossilizzare; *v.i.* fossilizzarsi.
foster [ˈfɔstəɹ], *v.t.* Nutrire, allevare; (*fig.*) proteggere, favorire, incoraggiare, sostentare. **— -brother,** fratello di latte, *m.*; **— -child,** bambino adottato, *m.*; **— -father,** padre adottivo, *m.*; **— -mother,** balia, nutrice; madre adottiva, *f.*; **— -sister,** sorella di latte, *f.*
fostering, *n.* Allevamento, *m.*, protezione, *f.* || *a.* Materno, paterno, protettore.
foul [faul], *a.* Sporco, immondo, impuro; fetido, infetto; corrotto; sconcio; (*of language*) osceno; (*of water*) torbido; (*of weather*) cattivo, brutto; (*of wind*) contrario; (*fig.*) sleale, disonesto, vergognoso, vile. || *v.t.* Sporcare, imbrattare, infettare; macchiare; contaminare; disonorare; impigliare, intrigare; intorbidare; *v.i.* impigliarsi (*of anchor*). || *adv.* Slealmente, disonestamente. || *n.* Collisione, *f.* ; urto, *m.*; (*Football*) fallo, *m.* **A — deed,** un'azionaccia, *f.*; **— language,** parole sconcie, *f.pl.*, mala lingua, *f.*; **— play,** trucco, *m.*, condotta sleale, *f.*; **a — anchor,** un'ancora impigliata, *f.*; **a — stroke,** un colpo mancino, *m.*; **— weather,** brutto tempo, *m.*; **to fall — of someone,** urtarsi con qualcuno; **a — slander,** una calunnia vergognosa, *f.*; **— faced,** brutto; **— -mouthed,** osceno, sboccato.
foully, *adv.* Crudelmente, slealmente. **He was — murdered,** fu vilmente ammazzato.
foulness, *n.* Sporcizia, bruttura, oscenità, *f.*; malvagità, nequizia, *f.*
found (1) [faund], *v.t.* Fondare, stabilire; originare, iniziare; (*to cast*) fondere. **To — oneself on,** fondarsi su; **well-founded,** fondato, ben fondato, sicuro.
found (2), *past* of **find.**
foundation, *n.* Fondamento, *m.*; (*Arch.*) fondamenta, *f.pl.*, base, *f.* **To lay the —,** porre le fondamenta, gettare le basi; **— -stone,** prima pietra, *f.*, pietra angolare, *f.*; **— scholar,** titolare di una borsa di studio, borsista, *m.*
founder (1), *n.* Fondatore, *m.*; (*of metals*) fonditore, *m.*
founder (2), *v.t.* (*Vet.*) Storpiare; (*Naut.*) fare affondare; *v.i.* (*Vet.*) storpiarsi; (*Naut.*) affondare.
foundered, *a.* Storpiato; affondato.
foundling, *n.* Trovatello, *m.*, trovatella, *f.*
foundress, *n.* Fondatrice, *f.*
foundry, *n.* Fonderia, *f.*
fount [faunt], *n.* Fonte, sorgente, *f.*; (*Print.*) corpo di caratteri, *m.*
fountain [ˈfauntin], *n.* Fontana, fonte, sorgente, *f.*; getto d'acqua, *m.* **— -head,** sorgente, *m.*; **— -pen,** penna stilografica, *f.*
four [fɔːɹ], *n.a.* Quattro, *m.* **A carriage and —,** tiro a quattro, *m.*; **on all fours,** carponi; **on all fours with,** pari a, simile a; **— -cornered,** quadrangolare; **— -fold,** quadruplo, quadruplice; quattro volte; **— -footed,** quadrupede; **— -in-hand,** tiro a quattro, *m.* **— -poster,** letto a colonne, *m.*; **— -wheeled,** a quattro ruote.
fourscore, *n.a.* Ottanta, *f.*

foursome, *n.* Partita di quattro giuocatori, *f.*
fourteen, *n.a.* Quattordici, *m.*
fourteenth, *n.a.* Quattordicesimo, decimoquarto, *m.*
fourth [fɔːɹθ], *n.a.* Quarto, *m.*; (*Mus.*) quarta, *f.* **The — part,** il quarto, *m.*, la quarta parte, *f.*; **— finger,** dito mignolo, *m.*
fourthly, *adv.* In quarto luogo.
fowl, *n.* Pollo, *m.*; uccello, *m.* || *v.t.* Uccellare, andare a caccia. **Fowls,** pollame, *m.*, uccelli, *m.pl.* **— -house, — -run,** pollaio, *m.*
fowler, *n.* Uccellatore, cacciatore, *m.*
fowling, *n.* Caccia agli uccelli, *f.* **— -piece,** fucile da caccia, *m.*
fox [fɔks], *n.* Volpe, *f.*; (*fig.*) persona astuta, *f.* **A sly —,** volpone, *m.*; **— -cub,** volpacchiotto, volpicino, *m.*; **— -earth,** tana di volpe, *f.*; **— -hound,** cane da caccia, *m.*; **— -hunt, — -hunting,** caccia alla volpe, *f.*; **— -hunter,** cacciatore di volpi, *m.*; **— -terrier,** terrier, *m.*
fox, *v.t.* dissimulare, scolorire, inacidire.
foxglove, *n.* (*Bot.*) Digitale, *f.*
foxtail, *n.* (*Bot.*) Codino di prato, *m.*, coda di volpe, *f.*
foxy, *a.* Volpino; astuto, scaltro.
foyer [ˈfɔiəɹ], *n.* Ridotto, *m.*
fracas [ˈfrækɑː], *n.* Fracasso, chiasso, *m.*
fraction [ˈfrækʃən], *n.* Frazione, *f.* **Vulgar fractions,** frazioni ordinarie, *f.pl.*
fractional, *a.* Frazionario.
fractious, *a.* Stizzoso; permaloso; (*of a child*) piagnucoloso.
fractiousness, *n.* Stizzosaggine, permalosità, *f.*
fracture [ˈfræktʃəɹ], *n.* (*Med.*) Frattura, *f.* || *v.t.* Fratturare, rompere, spezzare. **Compound —,** frattura composta, *f.*
fragile [ˈfrædʒail], *a.* Fragile.
fragility, *n.* Fragilità, *f.*
fragment [ˈfrægmənt], *n.* Frammento, pezzo, pezzettino, *m.*
fragmentary, *a.* Frammentario.
fragrance [ˈfreigrəns], *n.* Fragranza, *f.*, profumo, *m.*
fragrant, *a.* Fragrante, odoroso, profumato.
fragrantly, *adv.* Soavemente.
frail (1) [freil], *a.* Fragile, debole, delicato.
frail (2), *n.* Cesto, *m.*, sporta, *f.*
frailness, frailty, *n.* Fralezza, fragilità, debolezza, *f.*
frame [freim], *n.* Forma, figura, *f.*; costituzione, struttura, *f.*; corpo, *m.*; (*of building*) armatura, *f*; (*of picture*) cornice, *f.*; (*Mech.*) telaio, *m.*; ossatura, *f.*; (*of umbrella*) fusto, *m.* || *v.t.* Formare, costituire; adattare a; incorniciare, comporre; tramare, inventare; immaginare, concepire. **Door- —,** stipite di porta, *m.*; **— of mind,** stato d'animo, *m.*; **a man of gigantic —,** un uomo gigantesco, *m.*; (*colloq.*) **to — up,** fabbricare una situazione incriminante; **— work,** intelaiatura, struttura, ossatura, armatura, *f.*
framer, *n.* Artifice, autore, creatore, *m.* **Picture- —,** corniciaio, *m.*
framing, *n.* Intelaiatura, *f.*; incorniciatura, *f.*
franc [fræŋk], *n.* Franco, *m.*
France [frɑːns], *n.* (*Geog.*) Francia, *f.*
Frances [ˈfrɑːnsez], *n.* Francesca, *f.*
franchise [ˈfræntʃaiz], *n.* Franchigia, *f.*, privilegio, *m.*; diritto di voto, *m.*
Francis [ˈfrɑːnsis], *n.* Francesco, *m.*
Franciscan [frænˈsiskən], *n.a.* Francescano, *m.*
Francophile [fræŋkoˈfail], *n.a.* Francofilo, gallofilo, *m.*
Francophobe [fræŋkoˈfoub], *n.a.* Francofobo, gallofobo, *m.*
frangible [ˈfrændʒibl], *a.* Frangibile.
Frank [fræŋk], *n.* (*Hist.*) Franco, francese, *m.*
frank, *a.* Franco, sincero, schietto. || *v.t.* Affrancare.
Frankfort [ˈfræŋkfɔːɹt], *n.* (*Geog.*) Francoforte, *f.*
frankincense [ˈfræŋkinsens], *n.* Incenso, *m.*
frankness, *n.* Franchezza, sincerità, *f.*
frantic [ˈfræntik], *a.* Frenetico, furioso, folle. **— with joy,** ebbro di gioia.
frap [fræp], *v.t.* (*Naut.*) Imbrigliare.
fraternal [frəˈtəːɹnəl], *a.* Fraterno.
fraternally, *adv.* Fraternamente.
fraternity, *n.* Fraternità, fratellanza, *f.*
fraternize [ˈfrætəɹnaiz], *v.i.* Fraternizzare.
fratricide, *n.* (*crime*) Fratricidio, *m.*; (*criminal*) fratricida, *m.*
fratricidal, *a.* Fratricida.
fraud [frɔːd], *n.* Frode, *f.*; dolo, inganno, *m.*; impostura, *f.*; (*person*) truffatore, *m.* **By —,** con mezzi dolosi; **that man is a perfect —,** quell'uomo è un vero impostore; **a pious —,** un pietoso inganno, *m.*
fraudulence, *n.* Frodolenza, *f.*
fraudulent, *a.* Frodolento, doloso, disonesto.
fraught [frɔːt], *a.* Carico, pieno, pregno. **— with danger,** pieno di pericoli; **— with meaning,** denso di significato.
fray (1) [frei], *n.* Combattimento, *m.*; lotta, contesa, zuffa, mischia, *f.* **In the thick of the —,** nel folto della mischia; **eager for the —,** pronto alla lotta.
fray (2), *v.t.i.* Sfregare, consumare, logorarsi, sfilacciare, sfilacciarsi.
fraying, *n.* Sfilacciatura, *f.*
freak [friːk], *n.* Capriccio, ticchio, ghiribizzo, *m.* **A — of nature,** un aborto di natura, uno scherzo della natura, *m.*
freakish, *a.* Capriccioso, bizzarro, fantastico; strano, curioso; anormale.
freakishness, *n.* Capricciosità, bizzarria, fantasticheria, *f.*
freckle [frekl], *n.* Lentiggine, *f.* || *v.t.* Coprire di lentaggini.
freckled, *a.* Lentigginoso.
free [friː], *a.* Libero, esente; gratuito; franco; volontario; familiare; scevro, privo; sciolto, slegato; ingenuo, sincero, aperto. || *adv.* Gratis, gratuitamente, a ufo. || *v.t.* Liberare, affrancare, esentare; svincolare, sbarazzare, esonerare. **— and easy,** senza cerimonie; **duty —,** esente da imposta; **a — fight,** una zuffa generale, *f.*; **a — hand,** una mano libera, *f.*; **— -trade,** libero scambio, *m.*; **— wheel,** ruota libera, *f.*; **— will,** libero arbitrio, *m.*; **of one's own — will,** di spontanea volontà; **to make — with,** prendersi troppa libertà con; **to set —,** liberare; **— with his money,** prodigo di danaro; **to make someone — of the house,** aprire le porte di casa a qualcuno; (*Theat.*) **— -list,** le entrate di favore, *f.pl.*; (*Comm.*) **— on board,** franco a bordo; **— on rail,** franco vagone.
freebooter, *n.* Pirata, predone, *m.*
freeborn, *a.* Nato libero.
freedman, *n.* (*Hist.*) Liberto, *m.*

freedom, *n.* Libertà, indipendenza, *f.*; franchezza, schiettezza, *f.*; familiarità, *f.*; facilità, speditezza, *f.*; (*from duty*) esenzione, *f.*; (*of a city*) cittadinanza, *f.* — **of speech,** libertà di parola.
freehand, *a.* (*Art*) A mano libera.
freehold, *n.* (*Law*) Proprietà fondiaria assoluta, *f.*
freeholder, *n.* Chi possiede beni in proprietà assoluta, *m.*
freely, *adv.* Liberamente, francamente, volontieri; liberalmente, generosamente.
freeman, *n.* Cittadino, *m.*
Freemason, *n.* Frammassone, *m.*
Freemasonry, *n.* Frammassoneria, massoneria, *f.*
freeness, *n.* Sincerità, *f.*; generosità, liberalità, *f.*
freesia, *n.* (*Bot.*) Fresia, *f.*
freestone, *n.* Pietra da taglio, *m.*
freethinker, *n.* Libero pensatore, *m.*
freethought, *n.* Libero pensiero, *m.*
freeze, *v.t.i.* Gelare, congelare, agghiacciare; assiderare, gelarsi, agghiacciarsi; (*prices etc.*) bloccare. **To — to death,** morire assiderato, morire per assideramento.
freezing, *n.* Congelamento, *m.*, congelazione, *f.* || *a.* Glaciale, assiderante. — **-point,** punto di congelazione, *m.*; — **-mixture,** miscela frigorifera, *f.*
freight [freit], *n.* Carico, *m.*; (*cost*) nolo, *m.* || *v.t.* Caricare, noleggiare.
freighter, *n.* Noleggiatore, *m.*; (*Naut.*) nave da carico, *f.*
freighting, *n.* Noleggiamento, *m.*
French [frentʃ], *a.* Francese. || *n.* (*language*) Francese, *m.* **In the — fashion,** alla francese; — **beans,** fagiolini, *m.pl.*; — **chalk,** gesso da sarti, *m.*; (*Mus.*) — **horn,** corno inglese, *m.*; — **plum,** prugna secca, *f.*; — **polish,** vernice all'alcool, *m.*; — **-window,** finestra a porta, *f.*; — **roll,** panino, *m.*; **to take — leave,** andarsene senza permesso, partire all'inglese.
Frenchify [ˈfrentʃifai], *v.t.* Infrancesare, gallicizzare.
Frenchman (*pl.* **Frenchmen**), *n.* Francese, *m.*
Frenchwoman (*pl.* **Frenchwomen**), *n.* Francese, *f.*
frenzied [ˈfrenzid], *a.* Forsennato, frenetico, furioso.
frenzy, *n.* Forsennatezza, frenesia, pazzia, *f.*
frequence, frequency [ˈfri:kwəns, fri:kwənsi], *n.* Frequenza, *f.*; ricorrenza, ripetizione, *f.*
frequent [ˈfri:kwənt], *a.* Frequente, spesso.
frequent [friˈkwent], *v.t.* Frequentare.
frequentative, *n.a.* (*Gram.*) Frequentativo, *m.*
frequenter, *n.* Frequentatore, *m.*
frequently, *adv.* Frequentemente, spesso.
fresco [ˈfreskou], *n.* (*Art*) Affresco, *m.* **To paint in —,** affrescare.
fresh [freʃ], *a.* Fresco; recente, nuovo; (*not salt*) dolce; inesperto, imperito; (*cheeky*) brillo; (*fig.*) vigoroso, gagliardo, vegeto. || *adv.* Di fresco, recentemente, da poco. — **complexion,** tinta fresca, *f.*; — **horses,** cavalli di ricambio, *m.pl.*; (*not salt*) — **water,** acqua dolce, *f.*; (*just drawn*) **fresh water,** acqua fresca, *f.*; **a — supply,** un nuovo rifornimento, *m.* **To feel as — as a daisy,** sentirsi fresco come una rosa.
freshen, *v.t.i.* Rinfrescare. **The wind freshens,** il vento rinfresca.
freshet, *n.* Piena, *f.*
freshly, *adv.* Di fresco, di recente, di bel nuovo.
freshman, *n.* Studente di primo anno, matricolino, *m.*
freshness, *n.* Freschezza, novità, *f.*; vigore, *m.*
freshwater, *a.* D'acqua dolce.
fret [fret], *v.t.* Sfregare, corrodere, consumare, logorare; irritare, corrucciare; inquietare; cesellare, scolpire, escoriare; (*water*) increspare; *v.i.* agitarsi, affliggersi, crucciarsi, irritarsi. || *n.* Corruccio, *m.*; inquietudine, ansietà, *f.* **To — inwardly,** consumarsi di rabbia; **to — one's life out,** logorarsi la vita.
fretful, *a.* Stizzoso, irritato, inquieto, scontroso.
fretfulness, *n.* Stizza, irritabilità, *f.*
fretsaw, *n.* Sega da traforo, *f.*
fretting, *n.* Sfregamento, logorio, *m.*
fretwork, *n.* Traforo, *m.*
Freudian, *a.* freudiano.
friability, friableness [fraiəˈbiliti, ˈfraiəbəlnis], *n.* Friabilità, *f.*
friable, *a.* Friabile.
friar [ˈfraiəɹ], *n.* Frate, *m.* **Black Friar,** Domenicano, *m.*; **White Friar,** Carmelitano, *m.*; **Grey Friar,** Francescano, *m.*; **friar's balsam,** tintura di benzoino, *f.*
friary, *n.* Convento, monastero, *m.*
fricassee [frikəˈsi:], *n.* Fricassea, *f.*
fricative, *n. a.* (*Gram.*) Fricativo, *m.*
friction [ˈfrikʃən], *n.* Frizione, *f.*, fregamento, *m.*; (*Mech.*) attrito, *m.*; — **clutch,** innesto a frizione, *m.*; — **gearing,** trasmissione ad attrito, *f.*
Friday [ˈfraidi], *n.* Venerdì, *m.* **Good —,** Venerdì Santo, *m.*
fried [fraid], *a.* Fritto. — **fish,** pesce fritto, *m.*
friend [frend], *n.* Amico, *m.*, amica, *f.*; (*Eccles.*) Quacquero, Quacchero, *m.* **A — in need is a — indeed,** un vero amico si conosce nel bisogno; **a bosom —,** un amico intimo, *m.*; **a — of the family,** un amico di casa, *m.*; **to make friends,** diventare amici; **to keep friends with,** mantenersi amico di.
friendless, *a.* Senza amici; abbandonato.
friendliness, *n.* Amichevolezza, simpatia, benevolenza, *f.*
friendly, *a.* Amichevole, simpatico; amico, fautore di; favorevole a. — **society,** società di mutuo soccorso, *f.*; **in a — way,** amichevolmente; **to be on — terms with,** avere rapporti amichevoli con.
friendship, *n.* Amicizia, *f.*
frieze [fri:z], *n.* Tela di Frisia, *f.*; (*Arch.*) fregio, *m.*
frigate [ˈfrigət], *n.* (*Naut.*) Fregata, *f.* (*Zool.*) — **-bird,** fregata, *f.*
fright [frait], *n.* Spavento, terrore, *m.*, paura, *f.* **To take —,** spaventarsi; **What a — you are!** Come vi siete conciata male!
frighten, *v.t.* Spaventare, impaurire, intimorire. **To — to death,** far morire di paura.
frightful, *a.* Spaventevole, spaventoso, orribile.
frightfully, *adv.* Terribilmente; (*colloq.*) molto, eccessivamente.

frightfulness, *n.* Spavento, terrore, *m.*; orribilità, *f.*; terrorismo, *m.*
frigid [ˈfridʒid], *a.* Frigido, ghiacciato, glaciale, freddo. **— zone,** zona glaciale, *f.*
frigidity, frigidness [friˈdʒiditi, fridʒidnis], *n.* Frigidezza, freddezza, *f.*; frigidità, *f.*
frigidly, *adv.* Freddamente, frigidamente.
frill [fril], *n.* Gala, trina, *f.*, fronzolo, *m.* || *v.t.* Ornare di gale; increspare, arricciare.
fringe [frindʒ], *n.* Frangia, *f.*; bordo, orlo, *m.*, estremità, *f.* || *v.t.* Ornare di frange, orlare, guarnire.
frippery [ˈfripəri], *n.* Fronzoli, *m.pl.*, cianfrusaglie, *f.pl.*; roba usata, *f.*
Frisian [ˈfriʒən], *n.a.* Frisone, *m.*
frisk [frisk], *n.* Salto, sgambettio, *m.* || *v.i.* Saltellare, balzellare, sgambettare; folleggiare; (*colloq.*) cercare armi nascoste nei vestimenti d'una persona.
friskiness, *n.* Vivacità, sveltezza, *f.*
frisky, *a.* Vispo, pazzerello, svelto, saltellante.
frit [frit], *n.* Fritta, *f.*
frith [cp. **firth**].
fritillary [friˈtiləri], *n.* (*Bot.*) Fritillaria, *f.*; (*Zool.*) specie di farfalla, *f.*
fritter [ˈfritəɹ], *n.* Frittella, *f.* || *v.t.* Sminuzzare. **To — away,** dissipare, disperdere, sprecare.
frivolity [friˈvɔliti], *n.* Frivolezza, *f.*
frivolous, *a.* Frivolo.
frizz, frizzle (1) [friz, frizl], *v.t.* (*the hair*) Arricciare.
frizzle (2), *v.t.* (*bacon, etc.*) Cuocere sulla graticola *or* alla griglia.
frizzy, *a.* Arricciato, crespo, riccio.
fro [frou], *adv.* Indietro. **To go to and —,** andare e venire, andar su e giù; **to walk to and —,** camminare in lungo e in largo.
frock [frɔk], *n.* Vestina, veste, *f.*; costume, *m.*; (*child's*) vestitino, *m.*; (*smock*) camiciotto, *m.*; (*monk's*) tonaca, *f.* **— -coat,** redingote, *m.*, finanziera, *f.*
frog (1) [frɔg], *n.* (*Zool.*) Rana, *f.*, ranocchio, *m.*
frog (2), *n.* (*trimming*) Alamaro, *m.*
frog (3), *n.* (*Rail.*) Raccordo di rotaie, *m.*, incrocio, *m.*
frogged, *a.* Con alamari.
froggery [ˈfrɔgəri], *n.* Ranocchiaia, *f.*
frolic [ˈfrɔlik], *n.* Trastullo, scherzo, *m.*, scappatella, *f.* || *v.i.* Giocare, scherzare, folleggiare, trastullarsi.
frolicsome, *a.* Giocoso, allegro, festevole, pazzerello.
frolicsomeness, *n.* Allegria, gaiezza, *f.*
from [frɔm], *prep.* Da, per, di, dopo; fino da; a causa di; a contare da; da parte di. **— abroad,** dall'estero; **— afar,** da lontano; **— among,** d'infra; **— day to day,** di giorno in giorno; **— time to time,** di quando in quando, di tanto in tanto; **— behind,** dal didietro; **— beneath,** da sotto, dal disotto; **— henceforth,** d'ora innanzi; **tell him — me,** ditegli da parte mia; **a sketch — nature,** un abbozzo dal vero; **we saw — fifteen to twenty,** ne vedemmo da quindici a venti; **apart —,** a parte; **he is suffering — typhoid,** è malato di tifo; **his illness prevented him — working,** la malattia gli impedì di lavorare; **Where are you —?** Di dove siete? **— without,** dal di fuori.
frond [frɔnd], *n.* (*Bot.*) Fronda, *f.*
front [frʌnt], *n.* Davanti, *m.*; fronte, faccia, *f.*; facciata, *f.*; (*colloq.*) audacia, *f.* || *a.* Anteriore, dal davanti; primo; frontale. || *v.t.* Far fronte a, fronteggiare, tener testa a; guardare su. **In — of,** di fronte a; **to show a bold —,** mostrar il viso; **a change of —,** un cambiamento di fronte, *m.*; **to come to the —,** mettersi in vista; **the house fronts the sea,** la casa guarda sul mare; (*Mil.*) **Eyes —!** Fissi!; (*warfare*) **at the —,** alla fronte, al fronte; **shirt- —,** davanti di camicia, *m.*; **shop- —,** vetrina d'un negozio, *f.*; **— room,** stanza sul davanti, *f.*; (*hair*) **false —,** frontino, *m.*; **— -door,** porta d'entrata, *f.*
frontage [ˈfrʌntidʒ], *n.* Facciata, *f.*; (*extent*) lunghezza della facciata, *f.*
frontal, *n.* (*Eccles.*) Paliotto, *m.* || *a.* (*Anat.*) Frontale.
frontier [ˈfrʌntiəɹ], *n.* Frontiera, *f.*; confine, *m.* || *a.* Limitrofo, di frontiera. **A — town,** una città di confine, *m.*
frontiersman, *n.* Abitante in zone di confine, *m.*
fronting, *prep.* In faccia a, di fronte a.
frontispiece [ˈfrʌntispiːs], *n.a.* Frontespizio, *m.*
frontlet, *n.* Frontale, *m.*
frost [frɔːst], *n.* Gelo, *m.*, gelata, *f.*; freddo, *m.*; (*colloq.*) fiasco, *m.* || *v.t.* Gelare; (*with sugar*) candire. **— -bite,** congelamento, *m.*; **— -bitten,** gelato, congelato; **hoar —,** brinata; brina, *f.*
frosted, *a.* Brinato; (*of sweets*) candito; (*of glass*) smerigliato.
frostily, *adv.* Freddamente, gelidamente.
frostiness, *n.* Freddo glaciale, gelo, *m.*
frosty, *a.* Gelato, brinato, glaciale. **It is —,** è brinato, fa gelo.
froth [frɔːθ], *n.* Schiuma, spuma, *f.* || *v.i.* Schiumare, spumare, spumeggiare; *v.t.* far spumare.
frothily, *adv.* Con spuma; (*fig.*) frivolmente, con leggerezza.
frothy, *a.* Spumante, spumeggiante; (*fig.*) vano, frivolo.
froward [ˈfrouəɹd], *a.* Arcigno, burbero, caparbio, indocile.
frowardness, *n.* Caparbietà, ostinazione, indocilità, *f.*
frown [fraun], *n.* Cipiglio, *m.*; viso arcigno, sguardo cruccioso, *m.* || *v.i.* Aggrottare le ciglia, accigliarsi, aggrondarsi, corrugare la fronte; (*fig.*) minacciare. **To — upon,** disapprovare, essere contrario a; **to — down,** atterrire con lo sguardo; **to — at,** guardare in cagnesco.
frowning, *a.* Accigliato, arcigno; minaccioso, rannuvolato.
frowningly, *adv.* Arcignamente, minacciosamente.
frowzy [frauzi], *a.* Sporco, muffito, pien di tanfo, lezzoso.
frozen [ˈfrouzən], *a.* Gelato, ghiacciato.
fructiferous [frʌkˈtifərəs], *a.* (*Bot.*) Fruttifero.
fructification, *n.* Fruttificazione, *f.*
fructify [ˈfrʌktifai], *v.t.i.* Fruttificare; fertilizzare.
fructuous [ˈfrʌktjːəs], *a.* Fruttuoso.
frugal [ˈfruːgəl], *a.* Frugale, parco, sobrio, economo.

frugality [fru:ˈgæliti], *n.* Frugalità, parsimonia, *f.*; sobrietà, *f.*
frugally, *adv.* frugalmente.
fruit [fru:t], *n.* Frutto, *m.*; frutta, *f.pl.*; (*fig.*) risultato, profitto, *m.*; frutti, *m.pl.* || *a.* Di frutto. || *v.i.* Fruttare. **First fruits,** primizie, *f.pl.*; **the fruits of education,** i frutti dell'educazione, *m.pl.*; **— -bowl,** fruttiera, *f.*; **— -cake,** dolce con frutta, *m.*; **— -salad,** macedonia di frutta, *f.*; **— -tree,** albero fruttifero, albero da frutto, *m.*
fruiterer, *n.* Fruttivendolo, fruttaiuolo, *m.*
fruitful, *a.* Fruttuoso, fertile, fecondo, fruttifero, utile, profittevole.
fruitfulness, *n.* Fecondità, fertilità, *f.*; utilità, *f.*
fruition [fru:ˈiʃən], *n.* Adempimento, *m.*; soddisfazione, *f.*
fruitless, *a.* Sterile; vano, inutile.
fruitlessly, *adv.* Vanamente.
fruity, *a.* Di frutto; (*of wine*) saporito.
frump [frʌmp], *n.* Vecchia sciattona, *f.*; vecchia pettegola.
frustrate [frʌsˈtreit], *v.t.* Frustrare, deludere, rendere vano.
frustration, *n.* Delusione, frustrazione, *f.*; insuccesso, *m.*
frustum [ˈfrʌstəm], *n.* Tronco, *m.*
frutescent [fru:ˈtesənt], *a.* (*Bot.*) Fruticoso.
frutex [ˈfru:teks], *n.* (*Bot.*) Frutice, *m.*
fry [frai], *v.t.* Friggere, far friggere; *v.i.* friggersi. || *n.* (*Zool.*) Pesciolini, *m.pl.*; (*cooking*) frittura, *f.*, fritto, *m.* **Small —,** pescheria minuta, *f.*; **fried potatoes,** patate fritte, *f.pl.*; **frying-pan,** padella, *f.*; **to fall from the frying-pan into the fire,** cascar dalla padella nella brace.
fuchsia [ˈfju:ʃə], *n.* (*Bot.*) Fucsia, *f.*
fucus [ˈfju:kəs], *n.* (*Bot.*) Fuco, *m.*
fuddle [fʌdl], *v.t.i.* Ubbriacare, ubbriacarsi.
fuddled, *a.* Brillo, ubbriaco.
fudge [fʌdʒ], *inter.* Sciocchezze! Frottole! Baie! || *n.* Specie di confetto, *f.* || *v.t.* Falsificare.
fuel [ˈfju:əl], *n.* Combustibile, *m.*; (*Aviat.*) carburante, *m.*; (*fig.*) alimento, *m.*, esca, *f.* || *v.t.* Riscaldare. **To add — to,** alimentare; **to add — to the flames,** aggiungere esca al fuoco; **— oil,** petrolio da ardere, *m.*; **— -tank,** cisterna per carburanti, *f.*
fugacious [fju:ˈgeiʃəs], Fugace, fuggevole, transitorio.
fugitive [ˈfju:dʒitiv], *a.* Fugace, fuggitivo; effimero, temporaneo. || *n.* Fuggitivo, fuggiasco, disertore, *m.*
fugleman [ˈfju:gəlmən], *n.* Guida, *f.*, capofila, *m.*; fautore, esponente, *m.*
fugue [fju:g], *n.* (*Mus.*) Fuga, *f.*
fulcrum (*pl.* **fulcra**) [ˈfʌlkrəm], *n.* Fulcro, punto d'appoggio, *m.*
fulfil [fulfil], *v.t.* Adempiere, compire, eseguire; mantenere; effettuare, soddisfare, esaudire. **To — a promise,** mantenere una promessa; **to — a desire,** esaudire un desiderio; **to — a purpose,** effettuare un disegno; **to — one's expectations,** corrispondere all'aspettativa.
fulfilment, *n.* Adempimento, *m.*, esecuzione, soddisfazione, *f.*
fulgent [ˈfʌldʒənt], *a.* Fulgente, risplendente.
fuliginous [fju:ˈlidʒinəs], *a.* Fuligginoso.
full (1) [ful], *a.* Pieno, ripieno, riempito, colmo; compito, compiuto, perfetto, intero; ampio; (*of age*) maturo. || *adv.* Molto, affatto, perfettamente, bene. || *n.* Pieno, colmo, *m.*, pienezza, *f.* **At — speed,** a tutta velocità; **to fill —,** colmare; **a — meal,** un pasto copioso, *m.*; **— up,** ripieno; **— of years,** carico d'anni; **to give — details,** fornire ogni particolare; **a — supply,** una buona provvista, *f.*; **in —,** per esteso; **to the —,** appieno; **— stop,** punto fermo, *m.*; **in — view,** in piena vista; **— age,** età maggiore, *f.*; **receipt in —,** ricevuta a saldo, *f.*; **in — swing,** in pieno sviluppo, al colmo; **— in one's face,** proprio nella faccia; **she is — twenty years of age,** ha venti anni compiuti; **I know — well,** io so benissimo; **the moon is at the —,** la luna è al pieno; **to cite a passage in —,** citare un brano per intiero; **to the —,** completamente; **to give one's — name,** dare il nome e cognome; **— -blooded,** sanguigno, esuberante; **— -blown,** in pieno fiore; **— -bodied,** corpulento, pastoso; **— -faced,** grassotto, paffuto; **— -grown,** adulto, cresciuto; **— -length,** di grandezza naturale; **— steam,** a tutto vapore; **— -tilt,** a briglia sciolta.
full (2), *v.t.* Follare, gualcare.
fuller, *n.* Follatore, *m.* **Fuller's earth,** terra da purgo, *f.*
fulling, *n.* Follatura, *f.* **— -mill,** gualchiera, *f.*
fullness, *n.* Pienezza, abbondanza, ampiezza, completezza, *f.*; sazietà, *f.* **In the — of time,** a tempo opportuno, a cose mature.
fully, *adv.* Pienamente, ampiamente, bene, perfettamente.
fulminant [ˈfʌlminənt], *a.* Fulminante.
fulminate [ˈfʌlmineit], *v.t.i.* Fulminare. || *n.* (*Chem.*) Fulminato, *m.*
fulmination, *n.* Fulminazione, *f.*
fulsome [ˈfulsəm], *a.* Servile, basso, disgustoso, nauseante.
fulsomeness, *n.* Bassezza, servilità, *f.*
fumble [fʌmbl], *v.i.* Armeggiare, annaspare, frugare, cercare a tastoni.
fumbler, *n.* Armeggiatore, annaspone, *m.*
fumblingly, *adv.* Goffamente.
fume [fju:m], *n.* Fumo, vapore, *m.*; (*fig.*) collera, rabbia, *f.* || *v.i.* Fumare, esalare; (*fig.*) arrabbiarsi, adirarsi, smaniare; *v.t.* affumicare, offuscare; profumare.
fumigate [ˈfju:migeit], *v.t.* Disinfettare, suffumicare.
fumigation, *n.* Fumigazione, *f.*, suffumigio, *m.*
fumigator, *n.* Che fa suffumigi, *m.*
fumitory [ˈfju:mitəri], *n.* (*Bot.*) Fumaria, *f.*
fumy, *a.* Fumoso.
fun [fʌn], *n.* Divertimento, spasso, scherzo, *m.*, gaiezza, *f.*; bel tempo, *m.*; baia, burla, celia, giocosità, *f.* **For —,** per ridere, per celia; **he is full of —,** è pieno d'allegria; **to have plenty of —,** divertirsi molto; **to make — of,** burlarsi di, prender in giro; **I don't see the — of it,** non ci vedo niente da ridere.
funambulist [fju:næmbju:list], *n.* Funambolo, *m.*
function [ˈfʌŋkʃən], *n.* Funzione, mansione, incombenza, *f.*; cerimonia, pompa, *f.*; ricevimento ufficiale, *m.* || *v.i.* Funzionare, agire.
functional, *a.* Funzionale.
functionary, *n.* Funzionario, *m.*

fund [fʌnd], *n.* Fondo, capitale, *m.*, cassa, *f.* || *v.t.* Investire nei fondi pubblici. **Funds,** titoli, *m.pl.*, rendita, *f.*, denaro, *m.*; (*Comm.*) **sinking —,** fondo d'ammortamento, *m.*; **public funds,** fondi pubblici, *m.pl.*; **trust —,** fondo di garanzia, *m.*

fundamental [fʌndəˈmentəl], *a.* Fondamentale, essenziale, basilare. || *n.* Base, *f.*, fondamento, *m.*

fundamentally, *adv.* Fondamentalmente, essenzialmente.

funded, *a.* (*Comm.*) Consolidato.

funeral [ˈfjuːnərəl], *n.* Funerale, ufficio funebre, *m.*, esequie, *f.pl.* || *a.* Funebre, funerario, funereo.

funereal [fjuːˈniəriəl], *a.* Funereo, funebre; lugubre, triste.

fungous [ˈfʌngəs], *a.* Fungoso.

fungus [ˈfʌngəs], *n.* (*Bot.*) Fungo, *m.*

funicular [fjuːˈnikjuːləɹ], *n.a.* Funicolare, *m.*

funk [fʌŋk], *n.* (*colloq.*) Fifa, *f.*; tremarella, *f.* || — *v.t.* Aver paura di. **To be in a blue —,** aver fifa.

funnel [ˈfʌnəl], *n.* Imbuto, *m.*; (*of steamer*) fumaiolo, *m.*; ciminiera, *f.*

funny [ˈfʌni], *a.* Divertente, buffo, faceto, ridicolo, comico, lepido; curioso, strano. **— bone,** nervo cubitale, nervo del gomito, *m.*; **it's — that I have not heard from you,** è strano che non abbia avuto vostre notizie; **the — part of it is,** il comico è; (*Theat.*) **— man,** comico, *m.*

fur [fəːɹ], *n.* Pelliccia, *f.*, pelo, *m.*; (*on animals*) pelame, *m.*; (*in a kettle*) incrostatura, *f.* || *v.i.* Incrostarsi. **— -lined,** foderato di pelliccia; **wrapped in furs,** impellicciato; **— -trade** pellicceria, *f.*, commercio delle pellicce, *m.*

furbelow [ˈfəːɹbilou], *n.* Falpalà, *m.*; balzana, *f.*

fur-coat, *n.* pelliccia, *f.*

furbish [ˈfəːɹbiʃ], *v.t.* Forbire, lucidare. **To — one's knowledge,** rinfrescare la conoscenza, *f.*

furbisher, *n.* Forbitore, *m.*

furcation [fəɹˈkeiʃən], *n.* Biforcazione, *f.*

furious [ˈfjuːriəs], *a.* Furioso, iracondo, violento; concitato. **The fun was fast and —,** si faceva un chiasso tremendo.

furiously, *adv.* Furiosamente.

furiousness, *n.* Furia, violenza, *f.*

furl [fəːɹl], *v.t.* Ammainare, calare; chiudere.

furlong [ˈfəːɹlɔŋ], *n.* Misura di lunghezza ($\frac{1}{8}$ *mile*).

furlough [ˈfəːɹlou], *n.* (*Mil.*) Congedo, *m.*, licenza, *f.* **On —,** in licenza; **sick —,** licenza per malattia, *f.*

furnace [ˈfəːɹnis], *n.* Fornace, *f.*; forno, *m.*; (*of an engine*) fornello, *m.*

furnish [ˈfəːɹniʃ], *v.t.* Fornire, munire, provvedere di; mobiliare, ammobiliare.

furnished, *a.* Ammobiliato. **— rooms,** stanze ammobiliate, *f.pl.*

furnisher, *n.* Fornitore, *m.*

furnishing, *n.* Fornitura, *f.*, arredamento, ammobiliamento, *m.*

furniture [ˈfəːɹnitʃəɹ], *n.* Mobilia, *f.*, mobili, *m.pl.*, contenuto, *m.* (*of a horse*) finimenti, *m.pl.*; (*Print.*) fraschetta, *f.* **A piece of —,** un mobile, *m.*; **— -broker,** rigattiere, *m.*; **— -warehouse,** deposito per mobili, *m.*; **— -remover,** agenzia di trasporti, *f.*; **— -van,** furgone da traslochi, *m.*

furred, *a.* Guarnito di pelliccia; (*of the tongue*) patinata.

furrier, *n.* Pellicciaio, *m.*

furriery, *n.* Pellicceria, *f.*

furrow [ˈfʌrou], *n.* Solco, *m.*; (*of the face*) grinza, ruga, *f.* || *v.t.* Solcare, arare; scanalare, incavare.

furrowed, *a.* Rugoso.

furry [ˈfəːri], *a.* Di pelliccia, coperto di pelliccia; (*of tongue*) carica, patinosa.

further [ˈfəːɹðəɹ], *a.* Più lontano, ulteriore; altro; nuovo. || *adv.* Più lontano, ulteriormente, ancora, di più, più in là, più oltre; per di più, oltre a ciò. || *v.t.* Avanzare, agevolare, promuovere, favorire, secondare. **until — orders,** fino a nuovo ordine; **the — end,** l'altra estremità, *f.*

furtherance, *n.* Avanzamento, *m.*; promozione, *f.*

furthermore, *adv.* Ancora, di più, inoltre, oltre a ciò.

furthermost, *n.* Il più lontano, *m.*

furthest, *a.* Il più lontano, ultimo, estremo.

furtive [ˈfəːɹtiv], *a.* Furtivo, clandestino, occulto.

furuncle [ˈfjuːrʌŋkl], *n.* (*Med.*) Foruncolo, *m.*

fury [ˈfjuri], *n.* Furia, *f.*; furore, *m.*; smania, *f.* **She's a perfect —,** è una vera furia; **to run like —,** correre furiosamente.

furze [fəːɹz], *n.* (*Bot.*) Ginestrone, *m.*

fuse [fjuːz], *v.t.i.* Fondere, liquefare, liquefarsi. || *n.* Miccia, *f.*; spoletta, *f.*; (*Elec.*) valvola fusibile, *f.*, piombo fusibile, *m.* **Time —,** spoletta a tempo, *f.*

fusee [fjuːˈziː], *n.* (*of clock*) Piramide, *f.*

fuselage [ˈfjuːzilidʒ], *n.* (*Aviat.*) Fusoliera, *f.*

fusibility [fjuːziˈbiliti], *n.* Fusibilità, *f.*

fusible, *a.* Fusibile.

fusilier [fjuːzəˈliəɹ], *n.* (*Mil.*) Fuciliere, *m.*

fusillade, *n.* Fucileria, *f.*

fusion [ˈfjuːʒən], *n.* Fusione, assimilazione, *f.*

fuss [fʌs], *n.* Chiasso, rumore, *m.*; scalpore, trambusto, tramestio, imbarazzo, *m.*; difficoltà, briga, *f.*; storie, cerimonie, *f.pl.* || *v.i.* Darsi briga, fare tante storie, fare scalpore. **Please don't make such a —,** non far tanti complimenti, ti prego; non fare tante storie.

fussiness, *n.* Meticolosità, puntigliosità, *f.*; scalpore, *m.*

fussy, *a.* Puntiglioso, meticoloso, storioso.

fustian [ˈfʌstʃən], *n.* Fustagno, *m.*; (*fig.*) discorso ampolloso, *m.* || *a.* Di fustagno; (*fig.*) ampolloso, gonfio.

fustigate [ˈfʌstigeit], *v.t.* Fustigare.

fustiness [ˈfʌstinis], *n.* Odore di muffa, tanfo, *m.*

fusty, *a.* Muffito; (*fig.*) antiquato, vieto.

futile [ˈfjuːtail], *a.* Futile, inutile, vano; frivolo, leggiero.

futility, *n.* Futilità, inutilità, *f.*

future [ˈfjuːtʃəɹ], *a.* Futuro, da venire, venturo. || *n.* Futuro, avvenire, *m.*; (*Gram.*) futuro, *m.*; (*Comm.*) contratto per consegna futura, *m.* **For the —,** pel futuro, in avvenire; **he has a great —,** ha un grande avvenire; (*Comm.*) **futures,** operazioni a termine, *f.pl.*

futurism, *n.* (*Art*) Futurismo, *m.*

futurist, *n.* Futurista, *m.*

futurity [fjuːˈtjuːriti], *n.* Avvenire, *m.*

fuzzy [ˈfʌzi], *a.* (*hair*) Increspato, arricciato (*image*) impalpabile, indistinto.

G

G, g [dʒiː], Settima lettera dell'alfabeto inglese; (*Mus.*) sol, *m.*
gab [gæb], *n.* (*colloq.*) Chiacchiere, ciancie, *f.pl.*, cicaleccio, *m.* **To have the gift of the —,** avere lo scilinguagnolo, avere la lingua sciolta.
gabble [gæbl], *v.i.* Chiacchierare, ciarlare, cianciare, blaterare; *v.t.* pronunziare troppo rapidamente. || *n.* Chiacchierio, cicaleccio, mormorio, *m.*
gabbler, *n.* Chiacchierone, *m.*
gaberdine ['gæbəɹdiːn], *n.* (*garment*) Gabbano, *m.*; (*material*) gaberdina, *f.*
gable [geibl], *n.* (*Arch.*) Frontone. **— -roof,** tetto a più spioventi, comignolo, *m.*
gad [gæd], *v.i.* Gironzare, girellare. **To — about,** vagare, correre qua e là. || *n.* Giramondo, *m.*
gadfly ['gædflai], *n.* (*Zool.*) Tafano, *m.*
gadget ['gædʒit], *n.* Dispositivo, piccolo congegno, ordigno, *m.*; aggeggio, *m.*; accessorio di macchina, *m.*
Gael [geil], *n.* Celta gaelico, *m.*
Gaelic, *n.a.* Gaelico, *m.*
gaff [gæf], *n.* (*Naut.*) Picco di randa, *m.*; (*spear*) uncino, graffio, *m.* (*colloq.*) **To blow the —,** rivelare un segreto.
gaffer, *n.* Compare, *m.*
gag [gæg], *n.* Bavaglio, *m.*; (*Theat.*) frizzo improvvisato, *m.* || *v.t.* Mettere il bavaglio, imbavagliare; *v.i.* (*Theat.*) interpolare parole, improvvisare battute.
gage [geidʒ], *n.* (1) Pegno, *m.*; arra, caparra, *f.* || *v.t.* Impegnare.
gage, *n.* (2) Susina, prugna.
gaggle [gægl], *v.i.* Schiamazzare. || *n.* Stormo di oche, *m.*
gaiety ['geiiti], *n.* Gaiezza, allegria, giocondità, *f.*
gaily, *adv.* Allegramente, gaiamente.
gain [gein], *n.* Guadagno, profitto, vantaggio, acquisto, compenso, *m.* || *v.t.* Guadagnare, acquistare, ottenere; *v.i.* (*of clock*) avanzare; guadagnare; progredire. **He has nothing to — by it,** non ci guadagna niente; **to — friends,** farsi degli amici; **to — ground,** guadagnar terreno; **to — admittance,** ottenere l'accesso; **to — the day,** guadagnar la giornata; **to — upon,** avvicinarsi a, raggiungere; **ill-gotten gains,** guadagni illeciti.
gainer, *n.* Vincente, *m.*; vincitore, *m.* **To be a — by,** guadagnare a.
gainful, *a.* Profittevole, lucrativo, vantaggioso.
gainings, *n.pl.* Guadagni, profitti, utili, *m.pl.*
gainsay [gein'sei], *v.t.* Contraddire, dire di no.
gainsaying, *n.* Contraddizione, *f.* **There's no — it,** non si può negarlo.
gait [geit], *n.* Andatura, *f.*, passo, portamento, *m.*
gaiter, *n.* Ghetta, *f.*
gala ['geilə], *n.* Gala, *f.* || *a.* Di gala. **— night,** serata di gala, *f.*
galactic [gə'læktik], *a.* (*Astron.*) Della Via Lattea.
galaxy ['gæləksi], *n.* (*Astron.*) Via Lattea, *f.*; galassia, *f.*
gale [geil], *n.* Burrasca, tempesta, *f.*, fortunale, *m.*; procella, *f.*; uragano, *m.*
galena [gə'liːnə], *n.* (*Min.*) Galena, *f.*, solfuro di piombo, *m.*
Galilean [gæli'liːən], *m.a.* Galileiano; (*Bible*) Galileo.
gall [gɔːl], *n.* Fiele, *m.*, bile, *f.*; (*sore*) scorticatura, vescica, *f.*; (*Bot.*) galla, gallozzola, *f.*; (*fig.*) rancore, sdegno, *m.*, amarezza, *f.*; sfacciataggine, *f.* || *v.t.* Scorticare, fregare; irritare, infastidire. **— bladder,** vescica del fiele, *f.*; **— stone,** calcolo biliare, *m.*, calcolo vescicale, *m.*
gallant ['gælənt], *a.* Prode, valoroso, coraggioso, bravo; (*to women*) galante, cavalleresco, cortese, grazioso. || *n.* Galante, innamorato, *m.*
gallantly, *adv.* Valorosamente; galantemente.
gallantry, *n.* Coraggio, *m.*, prodezza, *f.*; galanteria, *f.*
galleon ['gæliən], *n.* Galeone, *m.*
gallery ['gæləri], *n.* Galleria, *f.* (*Theat.*) loggione, *m.*, galleria, *f.* **Art —,** pinacoteca, *f.*
galley ['gæli], *n.* (*ship*) Galea, galera, *f.*; (*cookhouse*) cucina di bordo, cucina, *f.*; (*Print.*) vantaggio, *m.* **— -proof,** bozza di stampa, *f.*; **— -slave,** galeotto, *m.*
galliard ['gæliəɹd], *n.* (*obs.*) Gagliarda, *f.*
Gallic ['gælik], *a.* Gallico, francese.
Gallican, *n.a.* Gallicano, *m.*
Gallicism ['gælisizm], *n.* Gallicismo, francesismo, *m.*
gallicize, *v.t.* Gallicizzare, francesizzare.
gallimaufry [gæli'mɔːfri], *n.* Guazzabuglio, *m.*, mescolanza, *f.*
gallinaceous [gæli'neiʃəs], *a.* Gallinaceo.
galling ['gɔːliŋ], *a.* Irritante, seccante, molesto.
galliot ['gæliɔt], *n.* Galeotta, *f.*
gallipot ['gælipɔt], *n.* Barattolo, *m.*
gallivant [gæli'vænt], *v.i.* Andar a zonzo, bighellonare.
gallon ['gælən], *n.* Gallone, *m.* (misura di capacità 4.54 litri).
galloon [gə'luːn], *n.* Gallone, *m.* **To bind with —,** gallonare.
gallop ['gæləp], *v.i.* Galoppare. || *n.* Galoppo, *m.* **Full —,** gran galoppo, *m.*; **hand —,** piccolo galoppo, *m.*; **to — off,** partire a galoppo; (*Med.*) **galloping consumption,** tisi galoppante, *f.*
Gallophile ['gælofail], *n.a.* Gallofilo, *m.*, francofilo, *m.*
Gallophobe ['gælofoub], *n.a.* Gallofobo, *m.*
gallows ['gælouz], *n.pl.* Patibolo, *m.*, forca, *f.* **— -bird,** uomo da forca, *m.*, roba da forca, *f.*
galore [gə'lɔːɹ], *adv.* In abbondanza, a bizzeffe, a iosa.
galosh [gə'lɔʃ], *n.* Galoscia, soprascarpa, *f.*
galvanic [gæl'vænik], *a.* Galvanico.
galvanism ['gælvənizm], *n.* Galvanismo, *m.*
galvanization, *n.* Galvanizzazione, *f.*
galvanize, *v.t.* Galvanizzare.
galvanometer [gælvə'nɔmətəɹ] *n.* Galvanometro, *m.*
galvanoplasty, *n.* Galvanoplastica, *f.*
gambit ['gæmbit], *n.* Gambitto, *m.*
gamble [gæmbl], *v.i.* Giuocare d'azzardo; scommettere; speculare. || *n.* Giuoco d'azzardo, *m.*; speculazione, *f.* **He gambled away his money,** sperperò il suo danaro al giuoco.
gambler, *n.* Giuocatore, biscazziere, *m.*; speculatore, *m.*

gambling, *n.* Giuoco d'azzardo, *m.* **— -house**, Casa di giuoco, bisca, *f.*, casino, *m.*; **— -table**, tavolino da giuoco, *m.*

gamboge [gæm'bu:ʒ], *n.* Gomma gutta, *f.*; pigmento di color giallo, *m.*

gambol ['gæmbɔl], *v.i.* Saltellare, sgambettare, far capriole. || *n.* Capriola, *f.*, sgambetto, salto, *m.*

game (1) [geim], *n.* Selvaggina, *f.* || *a.* Coraggioso; pronto; sportivo. **— -bag**, carniere, *m.*; **— -cock**, gallo da combattimento, *m.*; **— -laws**, leggi sulla caccia, *m.pl.*; **big — hunting**, caccia grossa, *f.*

game (2), *n.* Giuoco, *m.*, partita, *f.*; scherzo, *m.*; burla, *f.*; (*dodge*) sotterfugio, trucco, *m.* || *v.i.* Giuocare d'azzardo. **A — of cards**, una partita a carte, *f.*; **a drawn —**, una partita indecisa, una partita alla pari, *f.*; pareggio, *m.*; **to play a double —**, fare il doppio giuoco; **to play the —**, giuocare lealmente, essere onesto; **to die —**, morire da forte; **to give up the —**, abbandonare la partita; **to make — of**, burlarsi; **to play a losing —**, giuocare una partita disperata.

game (3), *a.* Zoppo.

gamekeeper, *n.* Guardacaccia, *m.*

gameness, *n.* Coraggio, *m.*

gamesome, *a.* Allegro, gaio, scherzevole.

gamesomeness, *n.* Allegria, gaiezza, *f.*

gamester, *n.* Giuocatore, biscazziere, *m.*

gaming, *n.* Giuoco, giocare, *m.* **— -house**, casa da giuoco, *f.*; **— -table**, tavola da giuoco, *f.*

gammer ['gæməɹ], *n.* Comare, *f.*; vecchia donna, *f.*

gammon ['gæmən], *n.* (*of bacon*) Quarto salato, prosciutto salato, *m.*; (*colloq.*) fandonia, *f.* || *v.t.* (*colloq.*) Corbellare, bluffare.

gammy, *a.* (*colloq.*) Zoppo; leso, malato.

gamp [gæmp], *n.* (*colloq.*) Ombrello, ombrellaccio, *m.*

gamut ['gæmʌt], *n.* Gamma, *f.*; (*fig.*) scala, serie, *f.*

gamy, gamey ['geimi], *a.* Abbondante di selvaggina; avente il gusto o sapore di selvaggina.

gander ['gændəɹ], *n.* Maschio dell'oca, *m.*

gang [gæŋ], *n.* Combriccola, banda, masnada, *f.*, branco, *m.*; (*of workmen*) squadra, *f.* **A — of thieves**, una masnada di ladri, *f.*

ganger, *n.* Capo squadra, *m.*

Ganges ['gændʒi:z], *n.* (*Geog.*) Gange, *m.*

ganglion (*pl.* **ganglia**) ['gæŋgliən], *n.* (*Anat.*) Ganglio, *m.*

gangrene ['gæŋgri:n], *n.* (*Med.*) Cancrena, *f.* || *v.i.* Cancrenarsi, incancrenire.

gangrened, *a.* Cancrenato, incancrenito.

gangrenous, *a.* Cancrenoso.

gangster ['gæŋstəɹ], *n.* Bandito, malvivente, *m.*

gangue [gæŋ], *n.* (*Geol.*) Ganga, *f.*

gangway ['gæŋwei], *n.* Passaggio, andito, corridoio, *m.*; (*Naut.*) pontile, barcarizzo, passavanti, *m.*; passerella, *f.*, plancia da sbarco, *f.*

gannet ['gænit], *n.* (*Zool.*) Gabbiano, *m.*

gantry ['gæntri], *n.* Gru a cavalletto, *f.*; cavalletto, *m.*

gaol, jail [dʒeil], *n.* Carcere, *m.*, prigione, *f.*; galera, *f.* **— -bird**, galeotto, *m.*

gaoler, *n.* Carceriere, *m.*

gap [gæp], *n.* Apertura, breccia, *f.*; vuoto, intervallo, *m.*; lacuna, *f.*; (*gorge*) burrone, *m.* **To fill a —**, colmare una lacuna; **his death has left a —**, la sua morte ha lasciato un vuoto.

gape [geip], *v.i.* Sbadigliare; aprirsi, spaccarsi; spalancare la bocca; meravigliarsi, stupirsi. || *n.* Sbadiglio, *m.* **To stand gaping**, restare a bocca aperta.

gaper, *n.* Chi sbadiglia; chi si meraviglia.

gaping, *a.* Sbadigliante; stupito, stordito.

garage ['gærɑ:ʒ], *n.* Garage, *m.*, autorimessa, *f.* || *v.t.* Mettere in rimessa.

garb [gɑ:ɹb], *n.* Costume, abbigliamento, *m.*, foggia del vestire, *f.* || *v.t.* Vestire, abbigliare.

garbage ['gɑ:ɹbidʒ], *n.* Frattaglie, *f.pl.*, rifiuto, *m.*, immondizie, *f.pl.*; porcheria, robaccia, *f.* **— -heap**, mondezzaio, *m.*

garble [gɑ:ɹbl], *v.t.* Falsificare, mutilare, alterare, troncare, dare una versione storpiata.

garboard ['gɑ:ɹbəd], *n.* (*Naut.*) Torello, *m.* **— strake**, travatura di torelli, *f.*

garden ['gɑ:ɹdən], *n.* Giardino, *m.* || *v.t.* Coltivare un giardino, fare il giardiniere. **Kitchen —**, orto, *m.*; **botanical gardens**, giardino botanico, *m.*; **— city**, città giardino, *f.*; **— frame**, serra, *f.*; **— -party**, merenda in giardino, *f.*; **— -seat**, panca da giardino, *f.*; **— -flower**, fiore da giardino, *m.*; **— -hose**, pompa per innaffiare, *f.*; **— -plot**, aiuola, *f.*; **— -roller**, rullo da giardino, *m.*

gardener, *n.* Giardiniere, *m.*, giardiniera, *f.*; ortolano, *m.*

gardenia [gɑ:ɹ'di:niə], *n.* (*Bot.*) Gardenia, *f.*

gardening, *n.* Giardinaggio, *m.*, orticultura, *f.*

garfish ['gɑ:ɹfiʃ], *n.* (*Zool.*) Aguglia, *f.*, luccio, *m.*

gargantuan, *a.* Smisurato, immenso.

gargle [gɑ:ɹgl], *v.t.* Gargarizzare. || *n.* Gargarismo, *m.*

gargoyle ['gɑ:ɹgɔil], *n.* (*Arch.*) Gronda sporgente scolpita, *f.*

garish ['gɛəriʃ], *a.* Abbagliante, vistoso, sfarzoso.

garishness, *n.* Barbaglio, *m.*, vistosità, *f.*

garland ['gɑ:ɹlənd], *n.* Ghirlanda, *f.*, serto, *m.* || *v.t.* Inghirlandare.

garlic ['gɑ:ɹlik], *n.* Aglio, *m.* **Clove of —**, capo d'aglio, *m.*

garment ['gɑ:ɹmənt], *n.* Vestimento, abbigliamento, indumento, *m.*

garner ['gɑ:ɹnəɹ], *v.t.* Raggranellare, raccogliere, ammassare, riunire, mettere insieme. *n.* Granaio, *m.*

garnet ['gɑ:ɹnət], *n.* Granato, *m.*

garnish ['gɑ:ɹniʃ], *v.t.* Guarnire, ornare, abbellire. || *n.* Guarnizione, *f.*; (*cooking*) contorno, *m.*

garnishing, garniture, *n.* Guarnizione, *f.*, ornamento, *m.*

Garonne [gə'rɔn], *n.* (*Geog.*) Garonna, *f.*

garret ['gærət], *n.* Solaio, *m.*, soffitta, *f.*

garrison ['gærisən], *n.* Guarnigione, *f.*; presidio, *m.* || *v.t.* Guarnire, munire, presidiare. **— artillery**, artiglieria di piazza, *f.*; **— town**, città che è sede di un presidio.

garrisoned, *a.* Guarnito, munito. **To be — at**, essere di guarnigione a.

garrotte [gəˈrɔt], *v.t.* Strangolare. || *n.* Garrotta, *f.*
garrulity [gəˈru:liti], *n.* Loquacità, garrulità, *f.*
garrulous [ˈgærju:ləs], *a.* Garrulo, loquace, ciarliero.
garter [ˈgɑ:ɹtər], *n.* Giarrettiera, *f.*, legaccio, *m.* **Order of the Garter,** Ordine della Giarrettiera, *m.*
garters, *n.pl.* Elastici, *m.pl.*
garth [gɑ:ɹθ], *n.* Recinto, cortile, chiuso, *m.*
gas (*pl.* **gases**) [gæs, ˈgæsiz], *n.* Gas, *m.*; (*American usage*) benzina, *f.* || *v.t.* Gasare; (*Mil.*) attaccare con gas, distruggere coi gas; *v.i.* (*colloq.*) ciarlare. **Asphyxiating —,** gas asfissiante, *m.*; **tear- —,** gas lacrimogeno, *m.*; **— -bomb,** bomba a gas, *f.*; **— -burner,** becco a gas, *m.*; **— -bag,** (*colloq.*) bagolone, *m.*; **— -engine,** motore a gas, *m.*; **— -man, — -fitter,** gasista, *m.*; **— -lighter,** accenditore a gas, *m.*; **— -lighting,** illuminazione a gas, *f.*; **— -main,** condotto principale del gas, *m.*; **— meter,** contatore del gas, *m.*; **— -mask,** maschera contro i gas, *f.*; **— -pipe,** tubo del gas, *m.*; **— -stove,** cucina a gas, stufa a gas, *f.*; **— -works,** officina del gas, *f.*; **— -fire,** radiatore a gas, *m.* (*Phot.*) **— -light paper,** carta lenta ad impressionarsi con luce artificiale, *f.*; **— ring,** fornello, *m.*
Gascon [ˈgæskən], *n.a.* Guascone, *m.*
gasconade [gæskəˈneid], *n.* Guasconata, *f.*
gaseous [ˈgæsiəs], *a.* Gassoso.
gash [gæʃ], *n.* Sfregio, taglio, *m.*, incisione, *f.*; ferita, *f.* || *v.t.* Sfregiare, incidere, tagliare.
gasiform [ˈgæsifɔɹm], *a.* Gasiforme.
gasify, *v.t.* Convertire in gas, volatilizzare.
gasket [ˈgæskit], *n.* Guarnizione, *f.*; (*Mech.*) guarnitura di uno stantuffo, *f.*; (*Naut.*) garzetta, *f.*, gerlo, *m.*
gasogene [ˈgæsodʒi:n], *n.* Gasogeno, *m.*
gasolene [ˈgæsoli:n], *n.* Benzina, *f.*
gasometer [gæsˈɔmitəɹ], *n.* Gasometro, *m.*
gasp [gɑ:sp], *v.i.* Ansare, ansimare, respirare con affanno, anelare. || *n.* Respiro affannoso, anelito, *m.* **To — for breath,** ansimare; **at the last —,** agli estremi, all'ultimo respiro.
gasper, *n.* Chi ansima, *m.*; (*colloq.*) sigaretta, *f.*
gasping *a.* Ansimante, anelante, affannoso. || *n.* Ansito, affanno, *m.*
gassy [ˈgæsi], *a.* Gassoso; pieno di gas; (*colloq.*) verboso.
gasteropod [ˈgæstəropɔd], *n.* (*Zool.*) Gasteropode, *m.*
gastralgia [gæsˈtrældʒiə], *n.* (*Med.*) Gastralgia, *f.*
gastric, *a.* Gastrico.
gastritis [gæsˈtraitis], *n.* (*Med.*) Gastrite, *f.*
gastronome, gastronomist [ˈgæstrənoum, gəˈtrɔnəmist], *n.* Gastronomo, *m.*
gastronomic, *a.* Gastronomico.
gastronomy, *n.* Gastronomia, *f.*
gate, [geit], *n.* Porta, *f.*; portone, *m.*; cancello, *m.*; barriera, *f.* **Sluice- —,** caterrata, *f.*; **— -keeper,** portiere, portinaio, *m.*, (*Rail.*) guardabarriere, *m.*; **— -money,** prezzo d'ingresso, *m.*, ingressi, *m.pl.*; **— post,** pilastro, *m.*; **— -crasher,** intruso, *m.*, intrusa, *f.*
gateway, *n.* Portone, passaggio, ingresso, *m.*
gather [ˈgæðəɹ], *v.t.* Ammassare, raccogliere; cogliere, radunare; desumere, dedurre; argomentare, conchiudere; prendere, acquistare; (*needlework*) increspare, pieghettare; *v.i.* riunirsi, adunarsi, raccogliersi; (*Med.*) suppurare. || *n.* Piega, crespa, *f.* **To — breath,** riprender fiato; **to — oneself together,** riunire tutte le proprie forze; **to — strength,** ristabilirsi, rimettersi; **to — grapes,** vendemmiare; **to — taxes,** riscuotere imposte; **try to — what his intentions are,** provate a scandagliare le sue intenzioni; **the hedgehog gathers itself into a ball,** il riccio si appallottola; **a rolling stone gathers no moss,** pietra mossa non fa musco.
gatherer, *n.* Raccoglitore, adunatore, *m.*; (*of taxes*) esattore, *m.*
gathering, *n.* Adunanza, riunione, *f.*; raccolta, *f.*; adunata, *f.*; (*Med.*) suppurazione, postema, *f.*
gathers, *n.pl.* Pieghe, crespe, *f.pl.*
gaud [gɔ:d], *n.* (*obs.*) Ninnolo, fronzolo, *m.*
gaudiness, *n.* Sfarzo, sfoggio, fasto, *m.*
gaudy, *a.* Sfarzoso, fastoso, vistoso.
gauffer [cp. **goffer**].
gauge [geidz], *v.t.* Misurare; stazzare, stimare; apprezzare, scandagliare. || *n.* Stazza, misura, norma, *f.*; livello, scandaglio, *m.*; manometro, indicatore, *m.*; (*Rail.*) larghezza, *f.*, scartamento, *m.* (*Rail.*) **Narrow —,** scartamento ridotto, *m.*
gauger, *n.* Stazzatore, *m.*
gauging, *n.* Stazzatura, *f.* **— -rod,** stazza. asta di sonda, *f.*
Gaul (1) [gɔ:l], *n.* (*Geog.*) Gallia, *f.*
Gaul (2), *n.a.* Gallo, *m.*
Gaulish, *a.* Gallico, gallo.
gaunt [gɔ:nt], *a.* Magro, scarno, sparuto.
gauntlet [ˈgɔ:ntlet], *n.* Guanto lungo, *m.*; manopola, *f.*; (*fig.*) sfida, *f.* **To run the —,** esporsi agli attacchi, sfidare; **to throw down the —,** gettare il guanto; **to take up the —,** accettare la sfida, raccogliere il guanto.
gauze [gɔ:z], *n.* Garza, *f.*; velo, *m.*
gauzy, *a.* Leggero come un velo.
gavelkind [ˈgævəlkaind], *n.* (*Law*) Spartimento eguale d'un'eredità, *m.*
gavotte [gəˈvɔt], *n.* Gavotta, *f.*
gawk [gɔ:k], *n.* Balordo, minchione, *m.*
gawkiness, *n.* Goffaggine, sguaiataggine, *f.*
gawky, *a.* Goffo, sguaito, balordo.
gay [gei], *a.* Gaio, allegro, giocondo, ridente, lieto, leggiadro, vivace. **As — as a lark,** allegro come una pasqua.
gayety [cp. **gaiety**].
gaze [geiz], *v.i.* Guardar fisso, fissare, mirare, contemplare. || *n.* Sguardo, sguardo fisso, *m.* **To — at a man,** fissare un uomo.
gazelle [gəˈzel], *n.* (*Zool.*) Gazzella, *f.*
gazer, *n.* Spettatore, contemplatore, *m.*
gazette [gəˈzet], *n.* Gazzetta, *f.*, giornale, foglio, *m.* || *v.t.* Pubblicare sul bollettino ufficiale. **his appointment is not yet gazetted,** la sua nomina non è ancora divenuta ufficiale.
gazetteer [gæzəˈtiəɹ], *n.* Dizionario geografico, *m.*
gazogene [cp. **gasogene**].
gear [giəɹ], *n.* Arredo, *m.*; arnesi, *m.pl.*; corredo, *m.*; masserizie, *f.pl.*; (*fig.*) roba, *f.*; (*Mech.*) congegno, meccanismo, ingranaggio, *m.*; (*of a cycle*) moltiplica, *f.*, sviluppo di velocità, *m.* **To put in —,** ingranare; **— -case,** scatola dell'ingranaggio, *f.*; **— -box,** scatola del cambio di velocità, *f.*; **to be out**

of —, essere fuori posto; **to throw out of —,** guastare; **head- —,** copricapo, *m.*; **— lever,** leva di comando, *f.*
gearing, *n.* Meccanismo, ingranaggio, *m.*
Gee-up! [ˈdʒiːʌp], *inter.* Arri!, Ih!, Op!
Gehenna [giˈhenə], *n.* Inferno, *m.*
geisha [ˈgeiʃə], *n.* Gheiscia, *f.*
gelatine [ˈdʒelətiːn], *n.* Gelatina, *f.*
gelatinize, *v.t.* Convertire in gelatina.
gelatinous, *a.* Gelatinoso.
geld [geld], *v.t.* Castrare.
gelder, *n.* Castratore, *m.*
gelding, *n.* Castrone, cavallo castrato, *m.*; castrazione, *f.*
gem [dʒem], *n.* Gemma, gioia, *f.*; gioiello, *m.* ‖ *v.t.* Ingemmare.
gemmiferous, *a.* Gemmifero.
gemmation [dʒeˈmeiʃən], *n.* (*Bot.*) Gemmazione, *f.*
gemmule, *n.* (*Bot.*) Gemmula, *f.*
Gemini [ˈdʒemini], *n.* (*Astron.*) Gemini, *m.pl.*
gendarme [ˈʒendɑːɹm], *n.* Gendarme, *m.*; carabiniere, *m.*
gender [ˈdʒendəɹ], *n.* Genere, *m.*
genealogical [dʒiːniəˈlɔdʒikəl], *a.* Genealogico.
genealogist [dʒiːniˈælodʒist], *n.* Genealogista, *m.*
genealogy, *n.* Genealogia, *f.*
general [ˈdʒenərəl], *a.* Generale, comune; generico, vago; l'insieme di, collettivo. ‖ *n.* (*Mil., etc.*) Generale, *m.* **Attorney General,** procuratore generale, *m.*; **for — use,** per uso comune; **as a — rule,** generalmente, per lo più; **— practitioner,** dottore di famiglia, *m.*; **— servant,** donna di servizio, *f.*; medico non specialista; **the — welfare,** il bene pubblico, *m.*; **the General Post Office,** l'ufficio postale centrale, *m.*; **the — effect,** l'insieme, *m.*; **by — request,** a richiesta generale; (*Mil.*) **lieutenant-general,** tenente generale, *m.*
generalissimo [dʒenərəˈlisimou], (*Mil.*) Generalissimo, *m.*
generality [dʒenəˈræliti], *n.* Generalità, moltitudine, maggioranza, *f.*
generalization [dʒenərəlaiˈzeiʃən], *n.* Generalizzazione, *f.*
generalize, *v.t.i.* Generalizzare.
generally, *adv.* Generalmente, in generale, comunemente. **— speaking,** parlando in generale.
generalship, *n.* Generalato, *m.*; strategia, tattica, *f.*
generate [ˈdʒenəreit], *v.t.* Generare, procreare, produrre.
generating, *a.* Generativo. (*Elec.*) **— station,** centrale elettrica, *f.*
generation, *n.* (*in all senses*) Generazione, *f.*
generative, *a.* Generativo, generatore.
generator, *n.* Generatore, *m.*
generic, generical [dʒeˈnerik, dʒeˈnerikəl], *a.* Generico.
generosity [dʒenəˈrɔsiti], *n.* Generosità, liberalità, magnanimità, *f.*
generous [ˈdʒenərəs], *a.* Generoso, liberale, magnanimo; fertile, ricco.
generousness, *n.* Generosità, *f.*
genesis [ˈdʒenisis], *n.* Genesi, origine, *f.* **The Book of Genesis,** la Genesi, *f.*
genet [ˈdʒenet], *n.* (*Zool.*) Genetta, *f.*
Geneva (1) [dʒəˈniːvə], *n.* (*Geog.*) Ginevra, *f.*
geneva (2), *n.* Ginepro, spirito di ginepro, *m.*
Genevan, Genevese [dʒeˈniːvən, dʒeneˈviːz], *a.* Ginevrino.
genial [ˈdʒiːniəl], *a.* Allegro, piacevole, simpatico, buontempone; mite, clemente, (*of climate*) benigno.
geniality [dʒiːniˈæliti], *n.* Piacevolezza, *f.*; mitezza, clemenza, *f.*
genie [ˈdʒiːni], *n.* Genio, demonio, *m.*
genital [ˈdʒenitəl], *a.* Genitale. **The genitals,** i genitali, *m.pl.*
genitive [ˈdʒenitiv], *n.a.* (*Gram.*) Genitivo, *m.*
genius [ˈdʒiːniəs], *n.* Genio, ingegno, indole, temperamento, *m.*; propensione, *f.*
Genoa [ˈdʒenoə], *n.* (*Geog.*) Genova, *f.*
Genoese [dʒenoˈiːz], *n.a.* Genovese, *m.*
genteel [dʒenˈtiːl], *a.* (*colloq.*) Manieroso, snob.
genteelness, *n.* Gentilezza, signorilità, *f.*
gentian [ˈdʒenʃən], *n.* (*Bot.*) Genziana, *f.*
gentile [ˈdʒentail], *n.a.* Gentile, *m.f.*, non ebreo; pagano, *m.*
gentility [dʒenˈtiliti], *n.* Gentilezza, raffinatezza, distinzione, *f.*; nascita elevata, *f.*
gentle [dʒentl], *a.* Gentile, bennato; dolce, amabile, tenero, buono, benigno. **Of — birth,** di qualità, bennato; **a — heat,** un dolce tepore, *m.*
gentlefolk [ˈdʒentlfouk], *n.pl.* Gente di qualità, gente distinta, *f.*; gente per bene, *f.*
gentleman (*pl.* **gentlemen**) [ˈdʒentlmən], *n.* Gentiluomo, signore, *m.* **A perfect —,** un perfetto signore, *m.*; **a young —,** un signorino, *m.*; **— -farmer,** gentiluomo di campagna, *m.*; **— -in-waiting,** gentiluomo del sovrano, *m.*; **to play the fine —,** darsi arie da signore; **gentlemen's agreement,** accordo che si basa solo sul rispetto della parola data.
gentlemanliness, *n.* Signorilità, *f.*, modi gentili, *m.pl.*
gentlemanly, *a.* Signorile, distinto, gentile.
gentleness, *n.* Gentilezza, dolcezza, bontà, amabilità, tenerezza, *f.*
gentlewoman (*pl.* **gentlewomen**), *n.* Gentildonna, signora, *f.*
gently, *adv.* Dolcemente, teneramente, soavemente.
gentry, *n.* Gente per bene, *f.*; nobilità campagnuola, *f.*; proprietari terrieri, *m.pl.*; (*ironically*) gente, *f.*
genuflexion [dʒenjuːˈflekʃən], *n.* (*Eccles.*) Genuflessione, *f.*
genuine [ˈdʒenjuːin], *a.* Genuino, schietto, puro, autentico, sincero.
genuineness, *n.* Genuinità, autenticità, schiettezza, sincerità, *f.*
genus (*pl.* **genera**) [ˈdʒiːnəs, ˈdʒenərə], *n.* Genere, *m.*
geocentric [dʒiːouˈsentrik], *a.* (*Astron.*) Geocentrico.
geodesy [dʒiːˈɔdəsi], *n.* Geodesia, *f.*
geodetic [dʒiːouˈdetik], *a.* Geodetico.
geodynamic, *a.* Geodinamico.
geognosy [dʒiːˈɔgnosi], *n.* Geognosia, *f.*
geographer [dʒiːˈɔgrəfəɹ], *n.* Geografo, *m.*
geographical, *a.* Geografico.
geography, *n.* Geografia, *f.*

geological [dʒi:ou'lɔdʒikəl], *a.* Geologico.
geologist [dʒi:'ɔlədʒist], *n.* Geologo, *m.*
geology, *n.* Geologia, *f.*
geomancer, *n.* Geomante, *m.*
geomancy, *n.* Geomanzia, *f.*
geometer, geometrician, *n.* Geometra, *m.*
geometric, geometrical, *a.* Geometrico.
geometry, *n.* Geometria, *f.*
George ['dʒɔ:ɹdʒ], *n.* Giorgio, *m.* **By —!** Per Bacco!
Georgics, *n.pl.* (*Poet.*) Georgiche, *f.pl.*
geranium [dʒə'reiniəm], *n.* (*Bot.*) Geranio, *m.*
gerfalcon ['dʒəɹfɔ:kən], *n.* (*Zool.*) Girifalco, *m.*
germ [dʒəɹm], *n.* Germe, *m.*; germoglio, embrione, *m.*
german (1) ['dʒəɹmən], *a.* Germano. **Cousin —**, cugino germano, *m.*
German (2), *n.* Tedesco, *m.*, tedesca, *f.*; (*language*) tedesco, *m.* || *a.* Tedesco. **— measles**, rosolia, *f.*; **— silver**, argentone, *m.*
germander [dʒəɹ'mændəɹ], *n.* (*Bot.*) Camedrio, *m.*; quercinola, *f.*
germane [dʒəɹ'mein], *a.* Pertinente, relativo.
Germanic [dʒəɹ'mænik], *a.* Germanico, tedesco.
germanize, *v.t.i.* Germanizzare.
Germany ['dʒəɹməni], *n.* Germania, *f.*
germinal ['dʒəɹminəl], *n.a.* Germinale, *m.*
germinate ['dʒəɹmineit], *v.i.* Germinare, germogliare.
germination, *n.* Germinazione, *f.*
germinative, *a.* Germinativo.
gerund ['dʒerʌnd], *n.* (*Gram.*) Gerundio, *m.*
gerundive, *n.a.* Gerundivo, *m.*
gestation [dʒes'teiʃən], *n.* Gestazione, *f.*
gestatorial [dʒestə'tɔ:riəl], *a.* (*Eccles.*) Gestatorio. **— chair**, sedia gestatoria, *f.*
gesticulate [dʒes'tikju:leit], *v.i.* Gesticolare.
gesticulation, *n.* Gesticolazione, *f.*, gesti, *m.pl.*
gesticulatory, *a.* Gesticolante.
gesture ['dʒestʃəɹ], *n.* Gesto, atto, *m.* || *v.i.* Gesticolare, gestire. **A noble —**, un bel gesto, *m.*
get [get], *v.t.* Ottenere, procurarsi, acquistare; (*to receive*) ricevere; guadagnare; avere; afferrare, prendere, pigliare; (*to buy*) comprare; (*an illness*) contrarre; imparare; fare; *v.i.* divenire, diventare; dare. **I got him to write a letter**, gli ho fatto scrivere una lettera; **I cannot — a living here**, non posso trovare da vivere qui; **he has got the upper hand**, ha preso il sopravvento; **to — the start of somebody**, avere il vantaggio su qualcuno; **Get out!** Andatevene! Vattene! **I cannot — it into my head that**, non posso convincermi che; **to — down**, scendere; **to — away**, allontanarsi; **to — hold of**, afferrare; **to — in**, entrare; **the thieves got into the bank**, i ladri penetrarono nella banca; **to — into trouble**, mettersi nei pasticci; **to — married**, sposarsi; **to — out of the way**, tenersi alla larga; **to — the worst of it**, perdere la partita, avere la peggio; **she gets on my nerves**, ella mi dà sui nervi; **it has got to be done**, deve essere fatto; **to — ready**, preparare, prepararsi; **to — over**, sormontare, rimettersi da; **to — rid of**, sbrigarsi di, sbarazzarsi di; **to — up**, alzarsi; **to — up steam**, riscaldare; **it is getting late**, si fa tardi; **he can't — about**, non può muoversi; **a rumour has got around**, corre voce; **to—ahead of**, sorpassare; **to — along**, avanzare, procedere, tirare innanzi; **to — back**, tornare, riavere; **to — behind**, arretrarsi; **to — by heart**, imparare a mente; **to — drunk**, ubbriacarsi; **to — hot**, riscaldarsi; **to —better**, migliorare; **to — made**, far fare; **to — old**, invecchiare; **to — on**, riuscire; **it is getting on for 6 o'clock**, sono quasi le sei; **to — rich**, arricchirsi; **to — tired**, faticarsi, stancarsi; **to — together**, adunarsi, riunirsi; **to — wet**, bagnarsi.
getaway ['getəwei], *n.* Fuga, *f.*
get-up ['getʌp], *n.* Costume, *m.*; formato, *m.*
gew-gaw ['gju:gɔ:], *n.* Ninnolo, gingillo, fronzolo, *m.*, cianfrusaglia, *f.*
geyser ['gi:zəɹ], *n.* (*Geol.*) Geyser, *m.*, sorgente calda, *f.*; (*Mech.*) stufa da bagno a gas, *f.*
ghastliness ['gɑ:stlinis], *n.* Orrore, squallore, *m.*; pallidezza, *f.*
ghastly, *a.* Orribile, spaventoso; orrendo; spettrale, pallido, squallido, smorto.
Ghent [gent], *n.* (*Geog.*) Gand, *f.*
gherkin ['gəːɹkin], *n.* Cetriuolo, cetriolino, *m.*
ghetto ['getou], *n.* Ghetto, *m.*
ghost [goust], *n.* Spettro, fantasma, *m.*; larva, ombra, apparizione, *f.*; anima, *f.* **The Holy Ghost**, lo Spirito Santo, *m.*; **to give up the —**, rendere l'anima, spirare.
ghostlike, *a.* Spettrale.
ghostly, *a.* Spettrale; spirituale, religioso.
ghoul [gu:l], *n.* Mostro che divora i cadaveri, *m.*; (*fig.*) chi si diletta di orrori.
ghoulish, *a.* Mostruoso; macabro.
giant ['dʒaiənt], *n.* Gigante, *m.* || *a.* Gigantesco.
giantess, *n.* Gigantessa, *f.*
giantlike, *a.* Gigantesco, mostruoso.
giaour [dʒauɹ], *n.* Giaurro, *m.*
gibber ['dʒibəɹ], *v.i.* Barbugliare, cianciare, straparlare, borbottare.
gibberish ['gibəriʃ], *n.* Ciancia, tiritera, *f.*; parole inintelligibili, *f.pl.*
gibbet ['dʒibit], *n.* Patibolo, *m.*, forca, *f.* || *v.t.* Impiccare; (*fig.*) mettere alla berlina.
gibbon ['gibən], *n.* (*Zool.*) Gibbone, *m.*
gibbous ['gibəs], *a.* Gibboso; gobbo.
gibe [dʒaib], *v.i.* Schernire, beffarsi di. || *n.* Scherno, *m.*, derisione, beffa, *f.* **To — at**, farsi beffa di.
gibingly, *adv.* Con scherno, derisoriamente.
giblets ['dʒiblits], *n.pl.* Rigaglie, frattaglie, *f.pl.*
Gibraltar [dʒi'brɔ:ltəɹ], *n.* (*Geog.*) Gibilterra, *f.*
giddily ['gidili], *adv.* Vertiginosamente, stordi-tamente.
giddiness, *n.* Vertigine, *f.*; capogiro, *m.*; stordimento, *m.*, storditezza, sbadataggine, *f.*; negligenza, *f.*
giddy, *a.* Vertiginoso; (*fig.*) stordito, sbadato, scervellato, spensierato. **I feel —**, ho il capogiro; **it makes me feel —**, mi fa venir le vertigini; **she's a — young thing**, è una stordita.
gift [gift], *n.* Dono, regalo, presente, *m.*; (*fig.*) dono, talento, *m.*; dote, *f.* (*Law*) **Deed of —**, contratto di donazione, *m.*; **— of the gab**, parlantina, *f.*; **do not look a — horse in the mouth**, a caval donato non si guarda in bocca; **the living is in the — of the earl**, il benefizio è di spettanza del conte.

gifted, *a.* Di gran talento, d'ingegno, pieno di doti.
gig [gig], *n.* Biroccino, calessino, *m.*; (*Naut.*) lancia, iole, iolla, *f.*
gigantic [dʒaiˈgæntik], *a.* Gigantesco.
giggle [ˈgigl], *v.i.* Ridacchiare, ridere stupidamente. || *n.* Risolino, *m.*
giggler, *n.* Ridanciano, *m.*, ridanciana, *f.*
gild [gild], *v.t.i.* Dorare, indorare.
gilded, *a.* Dorato.
gilder, *n.* Doratore, *m.*
gilding, *n.* Doratura, *f.*
gill (1) [gil], *n.* (*Zool.*) Branchia, *f.*
gill (2) [gil], *n.* (*ravine*) Burrone, *m.*
gill (3) [dʒil], *n.* Misura inglese di capacità (0.142 litri).
gillie [ˈgili], *n.* Servo scozzese, *m.*
gillyflower [ˈdʒiliflauəɹ], *n.* Garofano, *m.*
gilt [gilt], *n.* Doratura, indoratura, *f.* || *a.* Dorato, indorato. **— -edged** (*book*), dorato sul taglio; **— -edged securities**, titoli di prim'ordine, *m.pl.*
gimcrack [ˈdʒimkræk], *a.* Vistoso ma senza valore; da dozzina. || *n.* Bagattella, *f.*; ninnolo, *m.*
gimlet [ˈgimlit], *n.* Succhiello, *m.*
gimp [gimp], *n.* Cordoncino, passamano, *m.*
gin (1) [dʒin], *n.* Gin, liquore di ginepro, *m.* **— -shop, — -palace**, taverna, bettola, *f.*, debito di liquori, *m.*
gin (2), *n.* Trappola, *f.*; (*crane*) gru, *f.*
gin (3), *v.t.* Sgranare. **Cotton- —**, sgranatoio per cotone, *m.*
ginger [ˈdʒindʒəɹ], *n.* Zenzero, *m.* **— -ale, — -beer, — -pop**, gassosa allo zenzero; **— -bread**, pane pepato, panforte, *m.*; **— -nut**, dolce di panpepato, *m.*; **— -hair**, capelli rossicci, *m.pl.*; **— group**, attivisti, propagandisti, agitatori, *m.pl.*
gingerly, *adv.* Con molta cautela, pian piano.
gingham [ˈgiŋəm], *n.* Percallina, *f.*
gingival [dʒinˈdʒaivəl], *a.* (*Anat.*) Gengivale.
ginseng [dʒinˈseŋ], *n.* (*Bot.*) Ginseng, *m.*
gipsy [ˈdʒipsi], *n.* Zingaro, *m.*, zingara, *f.*
giraffe [dʒiˈrɑːf], *n.* (*Zool.*) Giraffa, *f.*
girandole [dʒirənˈdoul], *n.* Girandola, *f.*; candeliere a bracci, *m.*
gird [gəːɹd], *v.t.* Cingere, circondare, investire; *v.i.* schernire. **To — on one's sword**, cingersi la spada; **to — at**, schernire, beffarsi di.
girder [ˈgəːɹdəɹ], *n.* Trave, sbarra, traversa, *f.*
girdle [gəːɹdl], *n.* Cintola, cintura, *f.*, cinturino, *m.* || *v.t.* Cingere, circondare.
girl [gəːɹl], *n.* Fanciulla, ragazza, giovinetta, *f.*; signorina, *f.* **Little —**, fanciulletta, ragazzina, *f.*; **Girl Scout**, Giovine Esploratrice, *f.*; **call —**, ragazza-squillo, *f.*
girlhood, *n.* Giovinezza, adolescenza, *f.*
girlish, *a.* Fanciullesco, femminile, di ragazza.
girlishly, *adv.* Da ragazza.
girth [gəːɹθ], *n.* Circonferenza, *f.*, giro, *m.*; (*harness*) sottopancia, *f.* **In —**, di giro, di circonferenza.
gist [dʒist], *n.* Essenza, *f.*, punto, succo, *m.*; essenziale, *m.*
give [giv], *v.t.* Dare; donare, consegnare; largire; concedere, accordare; fare; dedicare; *v.i.* cedere, piegare. **— and take**, compromesso, *m.*; **to — as good as one gets**, rendere pan per focaccia; **to — someone his due**, dare il dovuto a qualcuno; **— him my compliments**, salutatelo da parte mia; **he gave me to understand**, mi fece capire; **to — oneself airs**, darsi delle arie; **I gave myself an hour to do it**, risolsi di farlo in un' ora; **to — a piece of one's mind**, fare una lavata di capo a; **to — ear**, prestare l'orecchio; (*of dogs*) **to — tongue**, latrare; **to — place**, cedere il posto, far posto; **to — rise to**, cagionare, suscitare; **to — way**, cedere, ritirarsi; **to — away**, dare, dare via, presentare; **to — the show away**, rivelare il segreto; **to — back**, ridare, restituire, rendere; **to — in**, cedere; **to — out**, annunciare, far correre la voce, essere esausto, emettere; **to — off**, emettere; **to — up**, abbandonare, desistere da, rinunciare a; **to — oneself up to**, darsi a; **to — one's mind to**, applicare la mente a; **to — vent to**, sfogare, dare sfogo a.
given, *a.* Dato, convenuto, stabilito; disposto. **In a — time**, in un dato tempo; **— to**, dedito a.
giver, *n.* Datore, *m.*, datrice, *f.*; donatore, *m.*, donatrice, *f.*
giving, *n.* Il dare, *m.*
gizzard [ˈgizəɹd], *n.* Ventriglio, *m.*
glacial [ˈgleiʃəl, ˈglæsiəl], *a.* Glaciale.
glacier [ˈglæsiəɹ], *n.* Ghiacciaio, *m.*
glacis [ˈglæːsi], *n.* (*Mil.*) Spalto, *m.*
glad [glæd], *a.* Contento, soddisfatto, lieto, felice. **I'm — to hear it**, sono lieto di sentirlo; **I should be — to know**, mi piacerebbe sapere; **to be —**, rallegrarsi.
gladden, *v.t.* Rallegrare, dilettare, allietare. **It gladdens my eyes**, mi rallegra la vista.
glade [gleid], *n.* Radura, *f.*
gladiator [ˈglædieitəɹ], *n.* Gladiatore, *m.*
gladiatorial, *a.* Gladiatorio.
gladiolus [glædiˈouləs], *n.* (*Bot.*) Gladiolo, *m.*
gladly, *adv.* Con piacere, volentieri, di buon grado, di buona voglia.
gladness, *n.* Contentezza, letizia, *f.*, piacere, *m.*
gladsome, *a.* Lieto, gaio, giocondo, allegro.
gladstone-bag [ˈglædstən bæg], *n.* Valigia, *f.*
glair [glɛəɹ], *n.* Albume, *f.*, bianco dell'uovo, *m.*
glaireous, glairy, *a.* Albuminoso.
glamour [ˈglæməɹ], *n.* Malia, *f.*, incanto, fascino, *m.* **To cast a — over**, circondar d'aureola; **— girl**, una ragazza affascinante, una diva, *f.*
glance [glɑːns], *n.* Sguardo, *m.*; occhiata, guardata, *f.*; colpo d'occhio. || *v.i.* Dare un'occhiata, dare uno sguardo; balenare. **At first —**, a prima vista; **to — off**, sfiorare, strisciare; **to — at**, accennare con lo sguardo; **to — over**, scorrere, dare una scorsa a; **to — up**, alzare lo sguardo.
glancingly, *adv.* Di striscio, di scorsa.
gland [glænd], *n.* Glandola, ghiandola, *f.*
glanders, *n.* Cimurro, *m.*
glandiferous [glænˈdifəɹəs], *a.* (*Bot.*) Ghiandifero.
glandular, *a.* (*Anat.*) Glandoloso.
glare [glɛəɹ], *n.* Bagliore, splendore, barbaglio, *m.*; sguardo di fuoco, sguardo penetrante, *m.* || *v.i.* Splendere, sfolgorare; gettare uno sguardo di fuoco, guardare con occhio torvo; guardare fissamente.
glaring, *a.* Abbagliante, sfolgorante, splendente; manifesto, evidente, patente. **A — mistake**, uno sbaglio patente, un errore madornale, *m.*

glass [glɑ:s], *n.* Vetro, *m.*; cristallo, *m.*; (*receptacle*) bicchiere, *m.*; barometro, *m.*; specchio, *m.* || *a.* Di vetro. **Glasses,** occhiali, *m.pl.*, lenti, *f.pl.*; **cut —,** cristallo tagliato, *m.*; **— case,** vetrina, *f.*; **— door,** porta a vetri, *f.*; **— -house,** serra, *f.*; **— -paper,** carta vetrata, *f.*; **— -ware,** vetrame, *m.*; vetrerie, *f.pl.*; **looking- —,** specchio, *m.*; **plate- —,** cristallo, cristallo in lastre, *m.* **ground- —,** vetro smerigliato, *m.*; **stained- —,** vetrate dipinte, *f.pl.*; **weather- —,** barometro, *m.*; **magnifying- —,** lente d'ingrandimento, *f.*; **opera- —,** binocolo, *m.*; **— -blower,** vetraio, soffiatore di vetro, *m.*; **he's had a glass too much,** ha bevuto un bicchiere di troppo.

glassiness, *n.* Vetrosità, *f.*; trasparenza, *f.*

glassy, *a.* Trasparente, vitreo, cristallino. **— eyes,** occhi vitrei, *m.pl.*

glaucoma [glɔ:ˈkoumə], *n.* (*Med.*) Glaucoma, *f.*

glaucous, *a.* Glauco.

glaze [gleiz], *v.t.* (*to varnish*) Verniciare; (*pottery*) smaltare; (*a window*) invetriare; (*pastry*) candire. || *n.* Smalto, *m.*; vernice, *f.*

glazier, *n.* Vetraio, *m.*

glazing, *n.* (*of windows*) L'invetriare, *f.*; invetriatura, *f.*; smaltatura, *f.*

gleam [gli:m], *n.* Barlume, raggio, *m.*; sprazzo di luce, *m.* || *v.i.* Raggiare, scintillare, luccicare.

gleaming, *a.* Lucente, risplendente, brillante, luccicante.

glean [gli:n], *v.t.i.* Spigolare, raccogliere; racimolare, spicciolare.

gleaner, *n.* Spigolatore, *m.*, spigolatrice, *f.*

gleaning, *n.* Spigolatura, *f.*

glebe [gli:b], *n.* Gleba, *f.*; podere di proprietà ecclesiastica, *m.*

glee [gli:], *n.* Gioia, gaiezza, allegrezza, *f.*; (*Mus.*) canto a ripresa, *m.*; canzone a parecchie voci, *f.*

gleeful, *a.* Gaio, allegro.

glen [glen], *n.* Valletta, *f.*

glib [glib], *a.* Scorrevole, loquace, facondo, sciolto di lingua. **A — tongue,** una lingua lunga, una lingua sciolta, *f.*

glibness, *n.* Volubilità, loquacità, scioltezza di lingua, *f.*

glide [glaid], *v.i.* Scivolare, strisciare; insinuarsi in; sdrucciolare; (*Aviat.*) volare con aliante. || *n.* Scivolamento, *m.*, scivolata, *f.*; (*dancing*) valzer strisciato, *m.*

glider, *n.* (*Aviat.*) Aliante, *m.*

gliding, *n.* (*Aviat.*) Volo a vela, *m.*

glidingly, *adv.* Scivolando, scorrevolmente.

glimmer [glimər], *n.* Luccichio, barlume, chiarore, *m.*, luce fioca, *f.* || *v.i.* Tralucere, luccicare; (*of the dawn*) albeggiare.

glimmering, *n.* Luccichio, *m.*; (*fig.*) barlume, *m.* || *a.* Debole, fioco. **A — of hope,** un barlume di speranza, *m.*

glimpse [glimps], *n.* Sguardo passeggero, occhiata di sfuggita, *f.* || *v.t.i.* Intravedere; far capolino. **To catch a — of,** veder di sfuggita.

glint [glint], *n.* Scintilla, *f.*, scintillamento, *m.*; riflesso, *m.*; barlume, *m.* || *v.t.* Scintillare, brillare.

glisten [ˈglisn], *v.i.* Luccicare, brillare, sfavillare.

glitter [ˈglitər], *v.i.* Brillare, splendere, luccicare, scintillare. || *n.* Luccichio, lustro, scintillio, *m.*

glittering, *a.* Lucente, brillante, scintillante.

gloaming [ˈgloumiŋ], *n.* Crepuscolo, *m.*

gloat [glout], *v.i.* Divorare con gli occhi; gongolare. **To — over someone's troubles,** gongolare per le disgrazie di qualcuno.

globe [gloub], *n.* Globo, orbe, *m.*, sfera, *f.* **— -trotter,** giramondo, *m.*

globular [ˈglobju:lər], *a.* Globulare, sferico.

globule [ˈglobju:l], *n.* Globulo, *m.*

glomerule [ˈglɔməru:l], *n.* (*Anat.Bot.*) Glomerulo, *m.*

gloom [glu:m], *n.* Oscurità, *f.*, tenebre, *f.pl.*; tetraggine, tristezza, melanconia, *f.* **To throw a — over,** rattristare.

gloomily, *adv.* Tetramente; malinconicamente.

gloominess [cp. **gloom**].

gloomy, *a.* Oscuro, tetro, melanconico, fosco. **— weather,** tempo fosco, *m.*

glorification [glɔ:rifiˈkeiʃən], *n.* Glorificazione, *f.*

glorify [ˈglɔ:rifai], *v.t.* Glorificare; celebrare.

glorious [ˈglɔ:riəs], *a.* Glorioso, illustre, preclaro, nobile, splendido.

glory [ˈglɔ:ri], *n.* Gloria, fama, *f.* || *v.i.* **To — in,** gloriarsi di, vantarsi di.

gloss [glɔs], *n.* Lucidità, lucentezza, *f.*, lustro, *m.*; (*fig.*) glossa, chiosa, *f.* || *v.t.* Lustrare, lucidare; glossare, chiosare. **To — over,** palliare, mascherare, cercar di scusare.

glossary [ˈglɔsəri], *n.* Glossario, *m.*

glossiness, *n.* Lustro, *m.*, lucentezza, *f.*

glossography [glɔsˈɔgrəfi], *n.* Glossografia, *f.*

glossy, *a.* Lucido, lucente, brillante.

glottis [ˈglɔtis], *n.* (*Anat.*) Glottide, *f.*

glove [glʌv], *n.* Guanto, *m.* || *v.t.* Inguantare, fornire di guanti. **To fit like a —,** calzare bene; **to be hand in — with,** essere in lega con; **to put on one's gloves,** mettersi i guanti.

glover, *n.* Guantaio, *m.*

glow [glou], *v.i.* Ardere, bruciare; (*fig.*) ardere, struggersi, infiammarsi di; rosseggiare. || *n.* Ardore, calore, fuoco, *m.*, incandescenza, *f.* **The — of health,** il fiore della salute; **to be in a —,** essere accaldato; **to set in a —,** riscaldare, animare; **to feel a pleasant —,** sentire un calore per tutto il corpo; **— -worm,** lucciola, *f.*; **— -lamp,** lampada incandescente, *f.*

glowing, *a.* Brillante, ardente, fervente, cocente; acceso, animato. **A — description,** una descrizione entusiastica, *f.*; **that girl is — with health,** quella ragazza scoppia di salute.

glower at [ˈglauər æt], *v.i.* Guardare in cagnesco, guardare torvamente.

gloxinia [glɔkˈsiniə], *n.* (*Bot.*) Gloscinia, *f.*

gloze [glouz], *v.t.* Palliare, mascherare. **To — over,** palliare, attenuare.

glucose [ˈglu:kous], *n.* Glucosio, *m.*

glue [glu:], *n.* Colla, *f.*, colla forte, *f.* || *v.t.* Incollare, attaccare con la colla. **— -pot,** vaso da colla, *m.*

gluey [ˈglu:i], *a.* Glutinoso, viscoso, tenace, colloso.

glum [glʌm], *a.* Arcigno, cupo, triste.

glume [glu:m], *n.* (*Bot.*) Gluma, *f.*
glut [glʌt], *v.t.* Saziare, satollare; ingombrare, inondare. || *n.* Eccesso, *m.*, sovrabbondanza, sazietà, *f.* **To — oneself,** saziarsi; **to — the market,** inondare il mercato.
gluten [ˈglu:tən], *n.* Glutine, *m.*
glutinous, *a.* Glutinoso.
glutton [ˈglʌtən], *n.* Ghiottone, goloso, mangione, *m.*
gluttonous, *a.* Ghiotto, goloso.
gluttony, *n.* Ghiottoneria, golosità, *f.*
glycerine [ˈglisəri:n], *n.* Glicerina, *f.*
glyptics [ˈgliptiks], *n.pl.* Glittici, *m.pl.*
gnarl [nɑ:ɹl], *n.* Nodo, nocchio, *m.*
gnarled, *a.* Nodoso, nocchioso.
gnash [næʃ], *v.t.i.* Digrignare i denti, arrotare i denti.
gnashing, *n.* Digrignamento, ringhio, arrotamento, *m.*
gnat [næt], *n.* (*Zool.*) Moscerino, *m.*, zanzara, *f.*
gnaw [nɔ:], *v.t.* Rodere, rosicchiare; corrodere, consumare.
gnawer, *n.* Roditore, *m.*
gnawing, *n.* Rodimento, rosicchio, *m.*, rosicatura, *f.*; corrosione, *f.* || *a.* Rodente, rosicante.
gnome (1) [noum], *n.* Gnomo, *m.*
gnome (2), *n.* (*Lit.*) Massima, *f.*; aforisma, *m.*
gnomon [ˈnoumən], *n.* (*Geom.*) Gnomone, *m.*
gnosis [ˈnousis], *n.* Gnosi, *f.*
gnostic [ˈnɔstik], *n.a.* Gnostico, *m.*
gnosticism [ˈnɔstisizm], *n.* Gnosticismo, *m.*
gnu [nju:], *n.* (*Zool.*) Gnu, *m.*
go [gou], *v.i.* Andare, partire, camminare; trarre; passare; riuscire, diventare. || *n.* Moda, voga, *f.*; energia, attività, *f.*; vigore, spirito, *m.* **As times —,** per i tempi che corrono; **Go ahead!** Avanti! **to — about,** andar quà e là, andar attorno; **I'll — about it at once,** mi occuperò subito di ciò; (*Naut.*) **to — about,** virare; **to — abroad,** andare all'estero; **to — ahead,** progredire, andare avanti; **to — astray,** fuorviarsi, perder la strada giusta, smarrirsi; **to — back,** tornare, ritornare; **to — backwards,** retrocedere, rinculare; **to — backwards and forwards,** andare innanzi e indietro; andare e venire; **to — beyond,** oltrepassare; **to — down,** discendere, (*fig.*) decadere, declinare, (*Naut.*) naufragare, affondare; **to — far to,** contribuire molto a; **to — forth,** uscire, andar fuori; **to — forward,** avanzare, far progressi; **to — near,** avvicinarsi a, essere sul punto di, correre il rischio di; **to — on,** avanzare, continuare, condursi, comportarsi; **to — one's way,** fare a modo proprio; **to — out of one's way to help,** scomodarsi per aiutare; **to — over,** ripassare, esaminare, verificare; **to — to sleep,** addormentarsi; **to — without,** astenersi da, far senza; **to — out,** uscire, (*of a light*) spegnersi; **to — through with,** finire, condurre a buon fine; **I — by my own watch,** io mi regolo sul mio orologio; **I'll — for him,** andrò a cercarlo; (*fig.*) gli darò una sgridata; **I shall not — from my word,** non mancherò alla mia parola; (*colloq.*) **to — the whole hog,** andar fino in fondo; **he has no facts to — upon,** non ha nulla su cui fondarsi; **to — with the times,** camminare coi tempi; **to — in rags,** vestirsi di cenci; **to — armed,** portare armi; **to — hungry,** aver fame; **Who goes there?** Chi va là? **the story goes,** si dice; **to — mad,** impazzire; **to — on the stage,** fare l'attore; **his sight is going,** la sua vista si indebolisce; **Where does this road — to?** Dove mena questa strada? **to — to war,** entrare in guerra; **he will — to all lengths,** non tralascierà niente; **to — one better,** superare, vincere; **at one —,** di getto; **it's no —,** non è possibile; **to be always on the —,** essere sempre in ballo, darsi sempri daffare; **I'll have a — at it,** tenterò di farlo; **—-ahead,** intraprendente, fattivo; **—-between,** mediatore, mezzano, intermediario, *m.*; **to give the —-by,** girare al largo; **—-cart,** carrozzina, *f.*, girello, *m.*
goad [goud], *n.* Pungolo, *m.*; (*fig.*) stimolo, *m.* || *v.t.* Pungere; spronare; stimolare.
goal [goul], *n.* Meta, *f.*, scopo, termine, *m.*; traguardo, *m.*; (*Football*) porta, rete, *f.*; gol, *m.*, **To score a —,** segnare gol, fare rete; **—-keeper,** portiere, *m.*; **—-kick,** rimessa del portiere, *f.*; **—-post,** palo della porta, *m.*
goat [gout], *n.* Capra, *f.*, capro, caprone, *m.* **He-—, billy-—,** capro, becco, *m.*; **nanny-—,** capra, *f.*; **—-herd,** capraio, *m.*, capraia, *f.*
goatee [gouˈti:], *n.* Barba caprina, *f.*, pizzo, *m.*
goatish, *a.* Caprino.
goatsucker, *n.* (*Zool.*) Caprimulgo, *m.*
gobbet [ˈgɔbit], *n.* Boccone, *m.*
gobble [gɔbl], *v.t.* Ingollare, ingoiare, trangugiare, ingozzare, ingurgitare; *v.i.* (*of turkeys*) chiocciare.
gobbler, *n.* Ghiottone, mangione, *m.*; (*colloq.*) tacchino, *m.*
goblet [ˈgɔblit], *n.* Bicchiere, calice, *m.*, coppa, tazza, *f.*
goblin [ˈgɔblin], *n.* Folletto, spirito maligno, fantasma, *m.*
God (1) [gɔd], *n.* Dio, Iddio, *m.* **If — wills,** se Dio vuole, se piace a Dio; **in the name of —,** in nome di Dio; **for the love of —,** per amor di Dio; **Would to —!** Dio volesse!
god (2), *n.* Dio, *m.* **The gods of Greece,** gli dei della Grecia, *m.pl.*; (*Theat.*) **a seat in the gods,** un posto nel loggione, *m.*
godchild, *n.* Figlioccio, *m.*, figlioccia, *f.*
goddaughter, *n.* figlioccia, *f.*
goddess, *n.* Dea, *f.*
godfather, *n.* Padrino, *m.*
Godhead, *n.* Divinità, *f.*
godless, *a.* Ateo, empio.
godlike, *a.* Divino.
godliness, *n.* Devozione, santità, pietà, *f.*
godly, *a.* Pio, devoto.
godmother, *n.* Madrina, *f.*
godown [goˈdaun], *n.* Deposito, magazzino, *m.*
godson, *n.* figlioccio, *m.*
goer [ˈgouəɹ], *n.* Camminatore, *m.* **A good —,** un buon camminatore, un cavallo corridore, *m.*
goffer, gopher, gauffer [ˈgɔfəɹ, ˈgoufəɹ], *v.t.* Stirare a cannoncini, cannettare, pieghettare, increspare. **Goffering iron,** ferro da arricciare.
goggle [gɔgl], *v.i.* Stralunare gli occhi. **— eyes,** occhi stralunati, *m.pl.*; **—-eyed,** dagli occhi stralunati.
goggles, *n.pl.* Occhialoni, occhiali di protezione, *m.pl.*
going [gouiŋ], *n.* Andata, *f.*, andare, andamento, *m.*; andatura, partenza, *f.* **The — was good**

on that road, era un gran bell'andare su quella strada; **goings and comings,** viavai, *m.pl.*; **— in,** entrata, *f.*; **— out,** uscita *f.*; **a — concern,** un'azienda attiva, *f.*

goitre ['gɔitəɹ], *n.* (*Med.*) Gozzo, *m.*

goitrous, *a.* Gozzuto.

gold [gould], *n.* Oro, *m.* || *a.* Aureo, d'oro. **As good as —,** buonissimo; **to be worth its weight in —,** essere venduto a peso d'oro; **— -beater,** battiloro, *m.*; **— -beater's skin,** membrana sottilissima usata dai battiloro, *f.*; **— -digger,** cercatore d'oro, *m.*; **— -dust,** polvere d'oro, *f.* ; **— -field,** terreno aurifero, *m.*; **— -leaf,** oro in foglia, *m.*; **gold-mine,** *n.* miniera d'oro, *f.*; (*Geog.*) **the Gold Coast,** la Costa d'Oro, *f.*; **all is not — that glitters,** non è tutto oro quel che riluce.

golden, *a.* Aureo, d'oro. **— wedding,** nozze d'oro, *f.pl.*; (*Bot.*) **— -rod,** verga d'oro, *f.*

goldfinch, *n.* (*Zool.*) Cardellino, *m.*

goldfish, *n.* (*Zool.*) Pesce dorato, *m.*, orata, *f.*

goldsmith, *n.* Orefice, *m.* **Goldsmith's work,** oreficeria, *f.*

golf, *n.* Golf, *m.* **— -course, — -links,** campo di golf, *m.*; **— -club,** mazza da golf, *f.*, bastone, *m.*; **— -ball,** una palla da golf, *f.*; **a round of —,** una partita di golf, *f.*

golfer, *n.* Giuocatore di golf, *m.*, giuocatrice di golf, *f.*

golliwog ['gɔliwɔg], *n.* Fantoccio grottesco, *m.*

golosh [cp. **galosh**].

gondola ['gɔndələ], *n.* Gondola, *f.*; (*Aviat.*) navicella, *f.*

gondolier [gɔndə'liəɹ], *n.* Gondoliere, *m.*

gone [gɔn], *p.p.a.* Andato, partito; perduto, sparito; morto, estinto; (*at auctions*) aggiudicato. **Far —,** avanzato; **in days — by,** nei tempi passati, in giorni lontani; **Going, going, — !** Uno, due e tre, aggiudicato!

gonfalon [gɔnfələn], *n.* (*Hist.*) Gonfalone, *m.*

gong [gɔŋ], *n.* Gong, *m.*

goniometer [gɔni'ɔmitəɹ], *n.* (*Geom.*) Goniometro, *m.*

goniometry, *n.* Goniometria, *f.*

gonorrhoea [gɔnə'riə], *n.* (*Med.*) Gonorrea, blenorragia, *f.*

good [gud], *a.* Buono; dabbene; utile, atto; genuino, valido; bello; bravo; favorevole; vantaggioso. || *n.* Bene, buono, vantaggioso, *m.*; utilità, *f.* || *inter.* Bene! || *adv.* Bene, benissimo. **A — deal,** molto, assai; **as — as,** quasi, come; **be so — as to,** abbiate la bontà di; **— humour,** buon umore, *m.*; **— luck** buona fortuna, *f.*; **— nature,** bontà, gentilezza, *f.*; **Good day!** Buon giorno! **in — earnest,** seriamente; **it's as — as done,** la cosa è quasi fatta; **it's no — asking me that,** non serve chiedermi questo; **Be a — girl!** Sta buona! **it's no —,** non vale niente; **that's as — as saying,** vale quanto dire; **to make — a promise,** mantenere la promessa; **to make —,** riuscir bene; **to stand —,** esser valido; **a — turn,** un servizio, *m.*; **I thought — to do this,** pensai che fosse bene fare questo; **it is — to be here,** mi trovo bene qui; **Much — may it do you!** Buon pro vi faccia! **this will do you —,** questo vi farà bene; **my — angel,** l'angelo custode, *m.*; **— breeding,** buone maniere, *f.pl.*; **a — ear for music,** un orecchio musicale, *m.*; **— offices,** servigi, buoni uffici, *m.pl.*; **for — and all,** per sempre; **— and evil,** il bene e il male; **so much to the —,** tanto di guadagnato; **a power for —,** una buona influenza, *f.*; **he will come to no —,** egli finirà male; **I can do no — with that man,** non riesco a farne nulla di quell'uomo. **What's the — ?** A che pro? **Good-bye!** Addio! **Good-bye for the present!** Arrivederci!

goodliness, *n.* Bellezza, *f.*

goodly, *a.* Bello, buono, grande. **A — number,** un gran numero, *m.*

goodman, *n.* Compare, *m.* **The — of the house,** il padron di casa, *m.*

goodness, *n.* Bontà, benignità, *f.*; gentilezza, cortesia, *f.* **Goodness knows!** Dio sa! **Thank —!** Grazie a Dio!

goods, *n.pl.* Beni, effetti, *m.pl.*; merci, *f.pl.* **— -lift,** montacarichi, *m.*; **— -train,** treno merci, *m.*; **— delivery office,** ufficio consegna, *m.*; **— receiving office,** ufficio accettazione merci, *m.*

goodwill, *n.* Benevolenza, buona volontà, gentilezza, *f.*; (*Comm.*) avviamento, *m.*

goody, *n.* Comare, *f.*; (*a sweet*) caramella, *f.* **Goodies,** chicche, *f.pl.*, dolci, *m.pl.*

goose (1) (*pl.* **geese**) [gu:s, gi:s], *n.* Oca, *f.*; (*fig.*) sciocco, tonto, *m.*; **— -flesh,** pelle d'oca, *f.*; **— -quill,** penna d'oca, *f.*; (*Mil.*) **— -step,** passo da parata, passo romano, *m.*; **to go on a wild — chase,** imbarcarsi in un'impresa folle.

goose (2), (*pl.* **gooses**), *n.* **Tailor's —,** ferro da sarto, *m.*

gooseberry ['guzbəri], *n.* (*Bot.*) Uva spina, *f.*; ribes, *m.* **To play —,** reggere il moccolo, far lume.

Gordian ['gɔ:ɹdiən], *a.* **— knot,** nodo gordiano, *m.*

gore (1) [gɔ:ɹ], *n.* Sangue, sangue coagulato, *m.* || *v.t.* Trafiggere, ferir con le corna.

gore (2), *n.* Gherone, *m.*

gorge [gɔ:ɹdʒ], *n.* Gola, forra, stretta, *f.*, burrone, *m.* || *v.t.i.* Rimpinzarsi, saziarsi. **One's — rises at the thought,** vien la nausea a pensarvi.

gorgeous ['gɔ:ɹdʒəs], *a.* Sontuoso, sfarzoso, magnifico, pomposo, fastoso, ricco.

gorgeousness, *n.* Sontuosità, magnificenza, pompa, fastosità, *f.*

gorget ['gɔ:ɹdʒit], *n.* Gorgiera, *f.*

Gorgon ['gɔ:ɹgən], *n.* (*Myth.*) Gorgone, *m.*

gorilla [gə'rilə], *n.* (*Zool.*) Gorilla, *m.*

gormandize ['gɔ:ɹməndaiz], *v.i.* Impinzarsi, ingurgitare.

gormandizing, *n.* Ghiottoneria, ingordigia, golosità, *f.*

gorse [gɔ:ɹs], *n.* (*Bot.*) Ginestrone, *m.*, ginestra spinosa, *f.*

gory ['gɔ:ri], *a.* Sanguinoso, insanguinato, coperto di sangue.

goshawk ['gɔshɔ:k], *n.* (*Zool.*) Astore, *m.*

gosling ['gɔzliŋ], *n.* Papero, paperetto, *m.*

gospel ['gɔspəl], *n.* Vangelo, evangelo, *m.* **— oath,** giuramento sul vangelo, *m.*; **— truth,** verità sacra, *f.*, vangelo, *m.*; **to take for —,** considerare come vangelo.

gossamer ['gɔsəməɹ], *n.* Garza sottile, *f.*; ragnatela, *f.*, filo della Madonna, *m.*

gossip ['gɔsip], *n.* (*talk*) Ciarla, chiacchiera, *f.*; pettegolezzo, *m.*; (*person*) pettegolo, *m.*, pettegola, *f.*; (*obs.*) comare, *f.* || *v.i.* Ciarlare, pettegolare.

gossiping, *n.* Ciarle, chiacchiere, *f.pl.*, pettegolezzi, *m.pl.*
Goth [gɔθ], *n.* Goto, *m.*; (*fig.*) barbaro, *m.*
Gothic, *a.* Gotico; (*Arch.*) ogivale.
gouache [gu:ˈɑ:ʃ], *n.* (*Art*) Guazzo, *m.*
gouge [gaudʒ], *n.* Sgorbia, *f.*, scalpello, *m.* || *v.t.* Sgorbiare, scalpellare.
gourd [gu:ɹd], *n.* (*Bot.*) Zucca, cucurbita, *f.*
gourmand [ˈgu:ɹmənd], *n.* Ghiottone, goloso, *m.*
gourmet [ˈgu:ɹmei], *n.* Bongustaio, *m.*
gout [gaut], *n.* Gotta, podagra, *f.*
gouty, *a.* Gottoso.
govern [ˈgʌvəɹn], *v.t.* Governare, reggere, dirigere. **To — oneself**, governarsi.
governable, *a.* Governabile.
governance, *n.* Governo, *m.*
governess, *n.* Governante, istitutrice, *f.*
governing, *a.* Governante, dirigente, dominante. **The — classes**, le classi dirigenti, *f.pl.*
government, *n.* Governo, *m.*, amministrazione, *f.*
governor, *n.* Governatore, amministratore, *m.*; direttore, *m.*; (*Mech.*) regolatore, *m.*; (*colloq.*) padrone, padre, *m.*
governorship, *n.* Governatorato, *m.*
gowan [ˈgauən], *n.* Margheritina, *f.*
gown [gaun], *n.* Veste, *f.*, vestito, *m.*; abito, *m.*; (*cassock*) zimarra, *f.*; (*university*) toga, cappa, *f.* **Dressing- —**, veste da camera, *f.*
gowned, *a.* Togato.
gownsman (*pl.* **gownsmen**), *n.* Membro dell'Università di Oxford o di Cambridge.
grab [græb], *v.t.* Afferrare, arraffare, agguantare. || *n.* (*Mech.*) Benna, *f.*
grabber, *n.* Arraffone, *m.*
grabble, *v.i.* Andar carponi.
grace [greis], *n.* Grazia, *f.*, favore, *m.*; perdono, *m.*; eleganza, leggiadria, *f.*; (*before meal*) benedicite, *m.* || *v.t.* Ornare, abbellire; onorare, illustrare. **The Three Graces**, le Tre Grazie, *f.pl.*; **to say —**, dire il benedicite; **with a good —**, garbatamente; **to be in someone's good graces**, essere nelle buone grazie di qualcuno; **His Grace**, Sua Grazia, *f.*; (*Mus.*) **— -notes**, **gruppetti**, *m.pl.*, fioritura, *f.*; (*Comm.*) **days of —**, giorni di grazia, *m.pl.*
graceful, *a.* Grazioso, leggiadro, elegante.
gracefulness, *n.* Grazia, leggiadria, garbatezza, *f.*
graceless, *a.* Sgarbato, sgraziato, perverso, scellerato.
gracious [ˈgreiʃəs], *a.* Grazioso, buono, benigno, gentile, favorevole. **Good —!** Mio Dio!
graciousness, *n.* Grazia, bontà, benignità, indulgenza, *f.*
gradation [grəˈdeiʃən], *n.* Gradazione, *f.*
grade [greid], *n.* Grado, *m.*, pendenza, *f.* || *v.t.* Graduare, classificare. (*fig.*) **On the up —**, in rialzo.
graded, *a.* Graduato, classificato.
gradient, *n.* Pendenza, salita, *f.*; discesa, china, inclinazione, *f.*
gradual [ˈgrædju:əl], *a.* Graduale.
gradually, *adv.* Poco a poco, gradualmente.
graduate (1) [ˈgrædju:eit], *v.t.* Graduare; *v.i.* laurearsi.
graduate (2) [ˈgrædju:it], *n.* Laureato, *m.*, laureata, *f.*; (*Chem.*) bicchiere graduato, *m.*
graduation, *n.* Graduazione, *f.*
graffito (*pl.* **graffiti**) [grəˈfi:tou], *n.* Graffito, *m.*
graft [grɑ:ft], *v.t.* Innestare, trapiantare. || *n.* Innesto, *m.*; (*Med.*) trapiantamento, *m.* (*colloq.*) corruzione.
grafter, *n.* Innestatore, *m.*
grafting, *n.* Innestatura, *f.*; (*knitting*) ricucitura, *f.*
grain [grein], *n.* Grano, *m.*, granaglie, *f.pl.*, cereali, *m.pl.*; (*in wood*) filo, *m.*, vena, *f.* (*stone*) grana, *f.*; (*weight*) grano, *m.*; granello, granellino, chicco, *m.* || *v.t.* Granare, tingere in grana. **A — of coffee**, un chicco di caffè, *m.*; **a — of sand**, un granello di sabbia, *m.*; **against the —**, contro genio, a malvoglia.
grained, *a.* Granato, granito; (*painting*) verniciato. **Coarse- —**, di grana grossa, grossolano; **cross- —**, nodoso; bisbetico.
graining, *n.* Venatura, granitura, *f.*
grains, *n.* (*fishing*) Arpione, *m.*
gramineous, **graminaceous** [grəˈminiəs, græmiˈneiʃəs], *a.* (*Bot.*) Graminaceo.
graminivorous [græmiˈnivərəs], *a.* (*Zool.*) Erbivoro.
grammalogue [ˈgræməlɔg], *n.* Stenogramma, *m.*
grammar [ˈgræməɹ], *n.* Grammatica, *f.* **That is bad —**, ciò è sgrammaticato; **— school**, ginnasio, *m.*
grammarian, *n.* Grammatico, *m.*
grammatical, *a.* Grammaticale.
gramme [græm], *n.* Grammo, *m.*
gramophone [ˈgræməfoun], *n.* Grammofono, fonografo, *m.* **— -needle**, puntina di grammofono, *f.*; **— -record**, disco, *m.*
grampus [ˈgræmpəs], *n.* (*Zool.*) Orca, balena, *f.*
Granada [grəˈnɑ:də], *n.* (*Geog.*) Granata, *f.*
granadilla [grænəˈdilə], *n.* (*Bot.*) Granadiglia, *f.*
granary [ˈgrænəri], *n.* Granaio, *m.*
grand [grænd], *a.* Grande; magnifico, superbo; stupendo. **— piano**, pianoforte a coda, *m.*; **— staircase**, scala d'onore, *f.*; **— -stand**, tribuna; **— total**, somma, *f.*
grandad, *n.* (*colloq.*) Nonno, *m.*
grandchild, *n.* Nipote, *m.f.*
granddaughter, *n.* Nipote, nipotina, *f.*
grandee [grænˈdi:], *n.* Grande di Spagna, *m.*
grandeur [ˈgrændjəɹ], *n.* Grandiosità, bellezza, magnificenza, *f.*; lusso, fasto, *m.*; elevatezza, *f.*
grandfather, *n.* Nonno, *m.* **— clock**, orologio a pendolo, *m.*
grandiloquence [grænˈdiləkwəns], *n.* Magniloquenza, grandiloquenza, *f.*
grandiloquent, *a.* Magniloquente.
grandiose, *a.* Grandioso.
grandmother, *n.* Nonna, *f.*
grandson, *n.* Nipote, nipotino, *m.*
grange [greindʒ], *n.* Cascina, fattoria, masseria, casa colonica, *f.*
graniferous [græˈnifərəs], *a.* (*Bot.*) Granifero.
granite [ˈgrænit], *n.* (*Geol.*) Granito, *m.*
granivorous [græˈnivərəs], *a.* (*Zool.*) Granivoro.
granny [ˈgræni], *n.* (*colloq.*) Nonna, vecchia, *f.* **— knot**, nodo falso, *m.*
grant [grɑ:nt], *v.t.* Accordare, concedere, esaudire; consentire, permettere; assegnare. || *n.* Concessione, *f.*, dono, *m.* **God — it!** Dio lo voglia! **granted that it be true,**

supposto che sia vero; **to — a pardon,** concedere la grazia; **to — a request,** esaudire una richiesta; **to — a pension,** assegnare una pensione; **to take for granted,** ritenere per certo, ritenere ovvio.
grantee [grɑːnˈtiː], *n.* (*Law*) Concessionario, assegnatario, *m.*
grantor, *n.* (*Law*) Concedente, *m.*
granular [ˈgrænjuləɹ], *a.* Granulato, granulare.
granulate, *v.t.i.* Granulare.
granulated, *a.* Granulato. **— sugar,** zucchero cristallizzato, *m.*
granulation, *n.* Granulazione, *f.*
granule, *n.* Granule, granello, *m.*
granulous, *a.* Granuloso.
grape [greip], *n.* Uva, *f.*, chicco d'uva, acino d'uva, *m.* **— -gatherer,** vendemmiatore, *m.*, vendemmiatrice, *f.*; **a bunch of grapes,** un grappolo d'uva, *m.*; **— -harvest,** vendemmia, *f.*; **— -stone,** vinacciolo, *m.*; **— -shot,** mitraglia, *f.*; **— -fruit,** pompelmo, *m.*
graph [græf], *n.* (*Math.*) Grafico, *m.*
graphic, *a.* Grafico; pittoresco, vivido.
graphically, *adv.* Graficamente.
graphite, *n.* Grafite, *f.*
graphology [grəˈfɔlədʒi], *n.* Grafologia, *f.*
grapnel [ˈgræpnəl], *n.* Grappino, uncino, *m.*
grapple [græpl], *v.t.* Abbrancare, agguantare, afferrare; (*Naut.*) uncinare, abbrancarsi; *v.i.* lottare corpo a corpo, avvinghiarsi. **To — with,** venire alle prese con, aggrapparsi a; **grappling-irons,** grappini, *m.pl.*
grasp [grɑːsp], *v.t.* Afferrare, impugnare, abbracciare; stringere; (*fig.*) capire. || *n.* Stretta, presa, *f.*, pugno, *m.*; (*fig.*) comprensione, *f.*, potere, *m.* **To — at,** afferrare, abbrancare; **— all, lose all,** chi troppo abbraccia, nulla stringe; **to loose one's —,** allentare la stretta; **to lose one's —,** lasciare la stretta; **within one's —,** in pugno, in proprio potere.
grasping, *a.* Avaro, avido, cupido.
grass [grɑːs], *n.* Erba, *f.* **To turn out to —,** mettere a erba; **Keep off the —!** È vietato calpestare i tappeti verdi! (*Tennis*) **— -court,** l'erba, *f.*; **— -land,** prateria, *f.*; **— plot,** praticello, tappeto, *m.*; **— -snake,** biscia, *f.*; **— widow,** donna maritata il cui marito è assente, sposa a spasso;divorziata, *f.*
grassiness, *n.* Erbosità, *f.*
grassy, *a.* Erboso, pieno d'erba.
grate (1) [greit], *n.* Grata, inferriata, *f.*; fornello, focolare, *m.*
grate (2), *v.t.* Raspare, fregare, grattare; grattugiare; *v.i.* stridere. **To — the teeth,** digrignare i denti; **to — upon the ear,** lacerare gli orecchi.
grated, *a.* A griglia, a grata; grattugiato. **A — window,** una finestra a griglia, *f.*; **— cheese,** formaggio grattugiato, *m.*; **— bread-crumbs,** pangrattato, *m.*
grateful, *a.* Grato, riconoscente; gradevole, piacevole. **I am very — to you,** vi sono molto riconoscente.
gratefully, *adv.* Gratamente.
gratefulness, *n.* Gratitudine, riconoscenza, *f.*; gradevolezza, *f.*
grater, *n.* Grattugia, *f.*; raspa, *f.*
gratification [grætifiˈkeiʃən], *n.* Gratificazione, *f.*; soddisfazione, *f.*; compiacimento, piacere, *m.*; ricompensa, *f.*
gratify [ˈgrætifai], *v.t.* Soddisfare, accontentare, appagare; gratificare, compensare.
gratifying, *a.* Soddisfacente, piacevole, gradito.
grating, *n.* Griglia, grata, inferriata, cancellata, *f.*; stridore, stridio, *m.* || *a.* Stridente, dissonante, aspro, lacerante.
gratingly, *adv.* Stridentemente.
gratis [ˈgreitis], *adv.* Gratis, gratuitamente, a ufo.
gratitude [ˈgrætitjuːd], *n.* Gratitudine, riconoscenza, *f.*, riconoscimento, *m.*
gratuitous [grəˈtjuːitəs], *a.* Gratuito; senza motivo. **A — insult,** un'offesa gratuita, *f.*
gratuitousness, *n.* Gratuità, *f.*
gratuity, *n.* Gratificazione, *f.*; mancia, ricompensa, *f.*; indennità, *f.*
gravamen [grəˈveimən], *n.* (*Law*) Gravame, *m.*
grave (1) [greiv], *n.* Tomba, fossa, sepoltura, *f.*, sepolcro, *m.* **As secret as the —,** segreto come una tomba; **— -clothes,** lenzuolo funebre, *m.*; **— -digger,** beccamorto, becchino, affossatore, *m.*; **— -stone,** pietra sepolcrale, lapide, *f.*; **— -yard,** cimitero, camposanto, *m.*
grave (2), *a.* Grave, serio; composto, austero.
grave (3), *v.t.* Scolpire, incidere; (*Naut.*) carenare, riparare, raddobbare.
gravel [ˈgrævəl], *n.* Ghiaia, *f.*; sabbia grossa, *f.*; (*Med.*) renella, *f.*, calcoli, *m.pl.* || *v.t.* Inghiaiare. **— -pit,** cava di ghiaia, *f.*; **— -walk,** viale ghiaiato, *m.*
graven [ˈgreivən], *a.* Scolpito, inciso, tagliato. **A — image,** una figura scolpita, *f.*
graveness, gravity [ˈgreivnis, ˈgræviti], *n.* Gravità, serietà, austerità, *f.*
graver [ˈgreivəɹ], *n.* Incisore, *m.*; (*instrument*) bulino, *m.*
gravid [ˈgrævid], *a.* Incinta, gravida.
graving [ˈgreiviŋ], *n.* Incisione, *f.*; (*Naut.*) carenaggio, *m.* **— -dock,** bacino di raddobbo, bacino di carenaggio, *m.*; **— -tool,** bulino, *m.*
gravitate [ˈgræviteit], *v.i.* Gravitare; propendere.
gravitation, *n.* Gravitazione, *f.*
gravity [ˈgræviti], *n.* Gravità, austerità, serietà, *f.*; peso, *m.* **The law of —,** la legge di gravità, *f.*
gravy [ˈgreivi], *n.* Sugo, intinto, *m.*, salsa, *f.* **— -boat,** salsiera, *f.*
gray [cp. **grey**].
grayling [ˈgreiliŋ], *n.* (*Zool.*) Temolo, *m.*
graze [greiz], *v.t.* Sfiorare, scalfire; rasentare, radere, pascere, pascolare; *v.i.* pascere, pascolare. || *n.* (*scratch*) Scalfittura, *f.*; escoriazione, *f.* **Grazing land,** pascolo, *m.*
grazier, *n.* Allevatore di bestiame, *m.*
grease (1) [griːs], *n.* Grasso, unto, *m.*; sugna, *f.* **— -box,** scatola lubrificatrice, *f.*; (*Theat.*) **— -paint,** belletto, *m.*; **— -proof paper,** carta pergamenata, *f.*
grease (2) [griːz], *v.t.* Ungere, untare, spalmare, ingrassare. **To — the wheels,** ungere le ruote; **to — someone's palm,** untare la mano a qualcuno.
greaser [griːzəɹ], *n.* Lubrificatore, ingrassatore, *m.*; (*Am. colloq. off.*) messicano, *m.*
greasiness [ˈgriːzinis], *n.* Grassezza, untuosità, *f.*; oleosità, *f.*
greasy [ˈgriːzi], *a.* Grasso, unto, oleoso, untuoso; sudicio.

great [greit], *a.* Grande, grosso; superiore, principale; sommo, supremo; forte; alto; lungo. || *n.pl.* I grandi, *m.pl.* **A — many,** molti, un gran numero, *m.*; **it's no — matter,** poco importa; **a — while ago,** molto tempo fa; **he lived to a — age,** visse fino a tarda età; **— -granddaughter,** pronipote, *f.*; **— -grandfather,** bisnonno, *m.*; **— -grandmother,** bisnonna, *f.*; **— -grandson,** pronipote, *m.*; **— -aunt,** prozia, *f.*; **— -uncle,** prozio, *m.*; **— -coat,** soprabito, *m.*, cappotto, *m.*; **Great Britain,** Gran Bretagna, *f.*; **— -toe,** pollice del piede, alluce, *m.*; **— -hearted,** magnanimo.
greatly, *adv.* Grandemente, molto; nobilmente, magnanimamente.
greatness, *n.* Grandezza, altezza, *f.*, nobiltà, eccellenza, *f.*
greave [gri:v], *n.* (*Hist.*) Gambale, *m.*
grebe [gri:b], *n.* (*Zool.*) Colimbo, *m.*
Grecian ['gri:ʃən], *n.a.* Greco, *m.*
Greece [gri:s], *n.* (*Geog.*) Grecia, *f.*
greed, greediness [gri:d, 'gri:dinis], *n.* Cupidigia, avidità, ingordigia, bramosia, *f.*; ghiottoneria, golosità, *f.*
greedily, *adv.* Avidamente.
greedy, *a.* Cupido, ingordo, bramoso; ghiotto, goloso; avido. **— of gain,** avido di danaro.
Greek [gri:k], *n.a.* Greco, *m.* **— fire,** fuoco greco, *m.*; **he speaks —,** parla il greco; **it's all — to me,** questo è turco per me.
green [gri:n], *a.* Verde; (*fig.*) fresco, nuovo, giovane, immaturo; ingenuo, inesperto; (*fruit*) immaturo, acerbo. || *n.* Verde, *m.*; (*Golf*) prato, praticello, *m.*; (*village*) prato pubblico, praticello, *m.* **Bottle- —,** verde bottiglia; **emerald- —,** verde smeraldo; **a — old age,** una vecchiezza verde, *f.*; **a — wound,** una ferita fresca, *f.*; **sea —,** verdemare; **— -eyed,** dagli occhi verdi; (*fig.*) geloso; **— -eyed monster,** gelosia, *f.*; **— -fly,** (*Zool.*) afide, gorgoglione, *m.*; **— finch,** (*Zool.*) verdone, *m.*; (*Theat.*) **— -room,** camerino, *m.*; **— wood,** foresta, *f.*
greenback, *n.* Biglietto di banca degli Stati Uniti, *m.*
greenery, *n.* Verzura, verdura, *f.*
greengage, *n.* Susina verde, susina claudia, *f.*
greengrocer, *n.* Erbivendolo, fruttaiolo, fruttivendolo, *m.*
greenhorn, *n.* Semplicione, novizio, *m.*
greenhouse, *n.* Serra, *f.*
greenish, *a.* Verdognolo, verdastro.
Greenland ['gri:nlənd], *n.* (*Geog.*) Groenlandia, *f.*
greenness, *n.* Verdezza, *f.*; freschezza, *f.*; inesperienza, *f.*
greens, *n.pl.* Erbaggi, ortaggi, *m.pl.*, erbe, *f.pl.*, verdura, *f.*
greensward, *n.* Tappeto verde, *m.*
greet (1) [gri:t], *v.t.* Salutare, riverire, ossequiare, complimentare, dare il benvenuto a.
greet (2), *v.i.* Piangere.
greeting, *n.* Saluto, *m.*, accoglianza, salutazione, *f.* **The season's greetings,** gli auguri di stagione, *m.pl.*
gregarious [gre'gɛəriəs], *a.* Gregario, socievole.
Gregorian [gre'gɔ:riən], *a.* Gregoriano.
Grenada [gre'neidə], *n.* (*Geog.*) Granata, *f.*
grenade [gre'neid], *n.* (*Mil.*) Granata, *f.* **Hand- —,** granata a mano, bomba a mano, *f.*
grenadier [grenə'diəɹ], *n.* Granatiere, *m.*
grenadine ['grenədi:n], *n.* Granatina, *f.*
grey, gray [grei], *a.* Grigio, bigio. **Iron- —,** grigio ferro; **pearl- —,** grigio perla; (*of hair*) **to grow —,** diventar grigio; (*Eccles.*) **— friar,** francescano, *m.*; **— -eyed,** dagli occhi bigi; **— matter** (*of brain*) sostanza grigia del cervello, *f.*; **— -haired,** grigio di capelli, brizzolato.
greybeard, *n.* Vecchione, *m.*
greyhound, *n.* Levriere, *m.* **— -racing,** corse di levrieri, *f.pl.*
greyish, *a.* Grigiastro.
greyness, *n.* Tinta grigia, *f.*, grigio, *m.*
grid [grid], *n.* Grata, *f.*; (*Radio*) griglia di valvola, *f.*; (*Elec.*) sistema per la diffusione di elettricità nella campagna, *f.*
griddle [gridl], *n.* Tegamino, *m.*; piastra per cuocere dolci, *f.*
gridiron ['gridaiəɹn], *n.* Graticola, gratella, *f.*
grief [gri:f], *n.* Dolore, cordoglio, *m.*, afflizione, pena, angoscia, *f.*; rammarico, *m.* **To come to —,** andare in malora, andar a rotoli; **overcome by —,** abbattuto dal dolore.
grievance ['gri:vəns], *n.* Rancore, risentimento, *m.*; ruggine, *f.*; torto, *m.*; gravame, reclamo, *m.* **To have a — against,** nutrire risentimento per, avercela con.
grieve [gri:v], *v.t.* Affliggere, addolorare, attristare; *v.i.* affliggersi, addolorarsi, attristarsi, crucciarsi.
grievous, *a.* Doloroso, angoscioso; enorme, atroce, terribile.
grievously, *adv.* Dolorosamente.
grievousness, *n.* Gravezza, enormità, *f.*
griffin, griffon, gryphon ['grifin, 'grifən], *n.* Grifo, grifone, *m.*
grig [grig], *n.* (*Zool.*) Anguilla piccola, *f.* **As merry as a —,** gaio come un grillo.
grill [gril], *v.t.* Cuocere alla graticola; (*fig.*) tormentare, tormentare con questioni. || *n.* Gratella, graticola; (*meat*) arrosto ai ferri. **— -room,** rosticceria, *f.*
grille, *n.* Inferriata, *f.*; cancello, *m.*
grilse [grils], *n.* (*Zool.*) Salmoncino, *m.*
grim [grim], *a.* Arcigno, torvo, feroce, truce, orrendo, orribile. **A — smile,** un sogghigno truce, *m.*
grimace [gri'meis], *n.* Smorfia, boccaccia, *f.* || *v.i.* Fare smorfie, storcer la bocca, far boccacce.
grimalkin [gri'mɔ:lkin], *n.* Gattomammone, *m.*, gattaccia, *f.*
grime [graim], *n.* Sudiciume, *m.*, sporcizia, *f.*, nero, *m.*; fuliggine, *m.* || *v.t.* Sporcare, annerire.
griminess, *n.* Nerezza, sporcizia, *f.*
grimly, *adv.* Torvamente, trucemente.
grimness, *n.* Terribilità, *f.*, aspetto truce, *m.*
grimy ['graimi], *a.* Sudicio; fuligginoso, nero.
grin [grin], *n.* Ghigno, sogghigno, *m.*, smorfia, *f.* || *v.i.* Ghignare, sogghignare. **A hideous —,** un ghigno torvo, *m.*; **to — and bear it,** soffrire senza lagnarsi.
grind [graind], *v.t.* Macinare, stritolare; frantumare; (*knife*) affilare, arrotare; (*glass*) levigare; (*the teeth*) digrignare; (*barrel-organ*) suonare; *v.i.* sgobbare, fare il ripetitore. || *n.* (*colloq.*) Fatica, *f.* **To — down,**

triturare, (*fig.*) opprimere; **to — the faces of the poor**, opprimere i poveri; **he ground his heel into it**, egli vi affondò il tallone; **the ship was grinding on the rocks**, la nave si sfracellava sugli scogli.

grinder, *n.* Macinatore, *m.*; (*tooth*) molare, *m.* **Organ- —**, suonatore d'organetto, *m.*

grindery, *n.* Arnesi di calzolaio, *m.pl.*

grinding, *n.* Macinazione, *f.*; arrotatura, *f.*; digrignamento, *m.*; politura, *f.*

grindstone, *n.* Mola, macina, *f.*

grinning ['griniŋ], *a.* Ghignante. || *n.* Ghigno, *m.*

grip [grip], *n.* Presa, stretta, *f.*; (*fig.*) dominio, *m.*, padronanza, *f.* || *v.t.* Afferrare, stringere, impugnare. **To come to grips**, venire alle prese; **he has a perfect — of the situation**, conosce benissimo le circostanze, ha in pugno la situazione; **to — someone's hand**, dare una stretta di mano a qualcuno.

gripe [graip], *v.t.* Stringere, afferrare; dare i crampi, lacerare. || *n.* Stretta, *f.* **Gripes**, colica, *f.*, crampo di stomaco, *m.*

griping, *a.* Avaro, rapace; lacerante.

grippe [grip], *n.* (*Med.*) Influenza, *f.*

griskin ['griskin], *n.* Coscia di maiale, *f.*

grisly ['grizli], *a.* Spaventoso, orribile.

Grisons ['gri:zɔn], *n.pl.* (*Geog.*) Grigioni, *m.pl.*

grist [grist], *n.* Grano da macinare, frumento, *m.* **To bring — to one's mill**, tirar l'acqua al proprio mulino; **all's — to his mill**, tutto è buono per lui.

gristle [grisl], *n.* Cartilagine, *f.*

gristly, *a.* Cartilaginoso.

grit [grit], *n.* Tritume di pietra, *m.*, sabbia, arenaria, *f.*; (*fig.*) coraggio, *m.*; fermezza, *f.*, fegato sano, *m.*

gritstone, *n.* (*Geol.*) Pietra da macina, arenaria, *f.*, macigno, *m.*

grittiness, *n.* Arenosità, ghiaiosità, *f.*

gritty, *a.* Ghiaioso, granuloso, sabbioso, renoso.

grizzled ['grizld], *a.* Grigio, brizzolato.

grizzly, *a.* Grigio, grigiastro, brizzolato. **— bear**, orso americano, orso grigio, orso grizzly, *m.*

groan [groun], *n.* Gemito, lamento, sospiro, *m.* || *v.i.* Gemere, mandar gemiti, lamentarsi.

groat [grout], *n.* (*obs.*) Moneta inglese di otto soldi, *f.*

groats, *n.pl.* Farina d'avena, *f.*; tritello d'avena, *m.*

grocer ['grousəɹ], *n.* Droghiere, *m.*

grocery, *n.* Drogheria, *f.*, negozio di commestibili, *m.*; commestibili, alimentari, *m.pl.*

grog [grɔg], *n.* Grog, ponce, *m.* **— -blossom**, naso come un peperone, *m.*, naso d'un bevitore, *m.*; **— -shop**, bettola, *f.*

groggy, *a.* Malfermo, debole; vacillante; ubbriaco.

grogram ['grɔgrəm], *n.* Grossagrana, *f.*

groin [grɔin], *n.* (*Anat.*) Inguine, *m.*, anguinaia, *f.*; (*Arch.*) lunetta, nervatura, *f.*, costolone, *m.* **A groined roof**, un tetto a costoloni, *m.*

groom [grum], *n.* Stalliere, palafreniere, mozzo di stalla, *m.*; sposo, *m.* || *v.t.* Strigliare. **Well-groomed**, azzimato, elegante, pulito.

grooming, *n.* Governo, *m.*

groomsman, *n.* Paraninfo dello sposo, *m.*, testimonio, *m.*, paggio d'onore, *m.*

groove [gru:v], *n.* Scanalatura, *f.*, incastro, solco, *m.*; (*fig.*) vecchia abitudine, *f.* || *v.t.* Scanalare, incavare, solcare. **In the same old —**, alle solite.

grope [group], *v.i.* Brancolare, andar a tastoni, andar tentoni. **To — for**, cercare a tastoni, cercar tastando.

gropingly, *adv.* Tastando, brancolando, a tastoni.

grosbeak ['grousbi:k], *n.* (*Zool.*) Frusone, *m.*

gross [grous], *a.* Grosso, spesso, rozzo, grossolano; (*Comm.*) lordo, complessivo; (*fig.*) grave, volgare, osceno, indecente. || *n.* (144) Grossa, *f.*, grosso, *m.* **— weight**, peso lordo, *m.*; **in the —**, in generale, in grosso, all'ingrosso; **— negligence**, negligenza grave, *f.*; **— income**, entrata lorda, *f.*

grossly, *adv.* Grossamente, volgarmente.

grossness, *n.* Grossezza, grossolanità, *f.*

grotesque [grou'tesk], *n.a.* Grottesco, *m.*

grotto, grot ['grɔtou, grɔt], *n.* Grotta, *f.*

ground (1) [graund], *a.* Macinato, frantumato; affilato; (*sharpened*) arrotato. **— glass**, vetro smerigliato, *m.*

ground (2), *n.* Terra, *f.*; terreno, suolo, *m.*; area, *f.*; campo, fondo, sfondo, *m.*; fondamento, motivo, *m.*, ragione, *f.* || *v.t.* Porre a terra, metter giù; fondare, basare; istruire nei primi elementi; (*Elec.*) mettere a terra; (*Naut.*) fare incagliare, dare in secco; *v.i.* (*Naut.*) incagliarsi, arenarsi. **The grounds of the mansion**, il parco, *m.*, i giardini, *m.pl.*; **fishing- —**, località pescosa, *f.*; **coffee grounds**, fondo di caffè, *m.*; **to fall to the —**, cadere a terra; **on the — of**, per motivo di; **to have no — for complaint**, non aver motivo di lagnarsi; **to be on sure —**, camminare sul solido, sentirsi sicuri; **to dispute the —**, contendere il terreno; **to gain —**, acquistare terreno; **to lose —**, perdere terreno; **forbidden —**, terreno proibito, *m.*; **to keep one's —**, star saldo; **— floor**, pian terreno, *m.*; **— sman**, guardiano del terreno, *m.*; **— -nut**, arachide, *f.*; **— -ash**, alberello di frassino, *m.*; **— -ivy**, edera terrestre, *f.*; **— -landlord**, proprietario del suolo, *m.*; **— -plan**, pianta, sezione orizzontale, *f.*; **— -rent**, rendita fondiaria, *f.*; **— -swell**, maremoto, *m.*

grounded, *a.* Fondato, basato; istruito; (*Naut.*) arenato. **Well- —**, ben fondato; **well- — in Italian**, ben ferrato in Italiano.

grounding, *n.* Prima mano, *f.*; istruzione, *f.*; (*Naut.*) incagliamento, *m.*

groundless, *a.* Senza base, infondato.

groundlessness, *n.* Mancanza di fondamento, *m.*

groundlessly, *adv.* Senza ragione.

groundsel ['graundsəl], *n.* (*Bot.*) Senecione, *m.*

groundwork, *n.* Base, *f.*, fondamento, *m.*

group [gru:p], *n.* Gruppo, *m.*, brigata, *f.* || *v.t.* Raggruppare, radunare. **To form a —**, raggrupparsi.

grouping, *n.* Raggruppamento, *m.*

grouse (1) (*pl.* **grouse**) [graus], *n.* (*Zool.*) Starna di montagna, *f.*

grouse (2), *v.i.* Brontolare.

grout, grouting [graut, 'grautiŋ], *n.* (*Arch.*) Malta, *f.*; colamento, *m.*

grove [grouv], *n.* Boschetto, *m.*, piantagione, *f.* **Oak- —**, querceto, *m.*

grovel ['grɔvəl], *v.i.* Strisciare; abbassarsi, umiliarsi, avvilirsi.
groveller, *n.* Persona abietta, *f.*
grovelling, *a.* Strisciante, vile, abietto. || *n.* Bassezza, *f.*
grow [grou], *v.i.* Crescere, ingrandire, svilupparsi, svolgersi, venir su; divenire, farsi; germinare, allignare; *v.t.* coltivare, far crescere. **To — again,** ricrescere; **to — better,** migliorare; **to — big,** ingrandire; **to — cold,** raffreddarsi; **to — fat,** ingrassare; **to — hot,** riscaldarsi; **to — into,** divenire, diventare; **to — less,** diminuire, scemare; **to — old,** invecchiare; **to — older,** diventare più vecchio; **to — poor,** impoverirsi; **to — rich,** arricchirsi; **to — thin,** dimagrare, dimagrire; **to — ugly,** abbruttirsi, abbruttire; **to — up,** crescere, ingrandire, venire a maturità; **to — worse,** peggiorare; **to — young again,** ringiovanire; **this picture grows on me,** questo quadro mi piace sempre più.
grower, *n.* Coltivatore, piantatore, *m.*
growing, *a.* Crescente. || *n.* Crescenza, coltivazione, *f.*
growl [graul], *v.i.* Ringhiare, brontolare, borbottare. || *n.* Ringhio, brontolio, *m.*
grown, *a.* Cresciuto, adulto, fatto. **— -up,** adulto, maturo; **English- —,** di provenienza inglese.
growth [grouθ], *n.* Crescita, *f.*, accrescimento, aumento, sviluppo, progresso, *m.*; coltivazione, *f.*; prodotto, *m.*; (*Med.*) escrescenza, *f.*, tumore, *m.*
groyne [grɔin], *n.* Paraonde, *m.*, riparo contro l'alta marea, *m.*
grub [grʌb], *n.* Verme, bruco, *m.*; larva, *f.*; (*colloq.*) cibo, *m.* || *v.t.* Estirpare, sradicare; *v.i.* zappare; (*colloq.*) mangiare. **To — up,** sradicare; **to — along,** sgobbare.
grubber, *n.* Sterpatore, raccoglitore, *m.*
grubbiness, *n.* Sporcizia, *f.*
grubby, *a.* Sporco, sudicio; (*wormy*) verminoso, bacato.
grudge [grʌdʒ], *n.* Malanimo, risentimento, rancore, *m.*, ruggine, *f.*; animosità. || *v.t.* Dare controvoglia, invidiare a. **To bear a — against,** avere rancore con; **I've got a — against you,** io l'ho con Lei.
grudgingly, *adv.* Controvoglia, malvolentieri, a malincuore.
gruel ['gru:əl], *n.* Farina d'avena cotta nell'acqua.
gruelling, *n.* Maltrattamento, *m.* || *a.* Faticoso, duro.
gruesome ['gru:səm], *a.* Spaventevole, orrendo, raccapricciante.
gruff [grʌf], *a.* Burbero, aspro, arcigno, rozzo.
gruffly, *adv.* Burberamente, aspramente.
gruffness, *n.* Asprezza, burbanza, rozzezza, *f.*
grumble ['grʌmbəl], *v.i.* Brontolare, borbottare, mormorare, lagnarsi.
grumbler, *n.* Brontolone, borbottone, *m.*
grumbling, *a.* Querulo, brontolone. || *n.* Borbottamento, brontolio, mormorio, *m.*
grumbling, *adv.* Di mala voglia, brontolando.
grume [gru:m], *n.* (*Med.*) Grumo, *m.*
grumous, *a.* Grumoso.
grumpy ['grʌmpi], *a.* Arcigno, burbero, ritroso, scontroso.
grunt [grʌnt], *v.i.* Grugnire; (*fig.*) lagnarsi. || *n.* Grugnito, *m.*
grunter, *n.* Grugnitore, *m.*; porco, *m.*
grunting, *n.* Grugnito, *m.*
gruntling, *n.* Porcellino, maialino, *m.*
Gruyère ['gru:iɛəɹ], *n.* (*cheese*) Gruera, *f.*
guaiacum ['gwaiəkəm], *n.* (*Bot.*) Guaiaco, *m.*
guano ['gwɑ:nou], *n.* Guano, *m.*
guarantee [gærən'ti:], *n.* Garanzia, *f.* || *v.t.* Garantire.
guarantor, *n.* Garante, mallevadore, *m.*
guaranty [cp. **guarantee**].
guard [gɑ:ɹd], *n.* Guardia, *f.*; guardiano, protettore, *m.*; (*Rail.*) capotreno, conduttore, *m.*; custode, *m.* || *v.t.i.* Guardare, custodire, difendere, curare, salvaguardare, proteggere. **On —,** in guardia, sulla difesa; **to be on one's —,** stare in guardia; **to be caught off one's —,** esser preso all'improvviso; **to mount —,** montar la guardia; **Lifeguards,** Guardie del corpo, *f.pl.*; **— -boat,** guardacoste, *m.*; **— -house,** corpo di guardia; (*Rail.*) **guard's van,** furgone del conduttore, *m.*; (*Rail.*) **— -rail,** controrotaia, *f.*
guarded, *a.* Prudente, circospetto, cauto.
guardedness, *n.* Prudenza, circospezione, cautela, *f.*
guardian, *n.* Guardiano, custode, *m.*; (*of minor*) tutore, *m.*, tutrice, *f.* || *a.* Tutelare. **— angel,** angelo custode, *m.*
guardianship, *n.* Tutela, *f.*; difesa, protezione, *f.*
guava ['gwɑ:və], *n.* Guaivo, *m.*; (*fruit*) guaiva, *f.*
gudgeon ['gʌdʒən], *n.* (*Zool.*) Ghiozzo, *m.*; (*Mech.*) chiavarda, *f.*, perno, *m.*
guelder-rose ['geldəɹrouz], *n.* (*Bot.*) Viburno, *m.*; pallone di neve, *m.*
guerdon ['gə:ɹdən], *n.* Guiderdone, *m.*, ricompensa, *f.*
guerrilla [gə'rilə], *n.* Guerriglia, *f.*, partigiano, *m.* **— warfare,** guerriglia, guerra di scaramucce, *f.*
guernsey ['gə:ɹnzi], *n.* Camiciotto di lana, *m.*
guess [ges], *v.t.i.* Indovinare, congetturare; supporre, credere. || *n.* Congettura, supposizione, *f.* **At a rough —,** a un dipresso, a lume di naso; **to make a good —,** coglier nel segno, azzeccare giusto.
guesswork, *n.* Congettura, *f.*, fare a indovinare, *m.*
guest [gest], *n.* Ospite, *m.f.*; convitato, invitato, *m.*, convitata, invitata, *f.* **Paying —,** ospite pagante, dozzinante, pensionante, *m.f.*; **— -chamber,** camera degli ospiti, *f.*; **— -house,** albergo, *m.*; **— of honour,** convitato d'onore, *m.*
guffaw [gʌ'fɔ:], *n.* Risata, *f.*, scoppio di risa, *m.* || *v.i.* Scoppiare in una risata.
guidance ['gaidəns], *n.* Guida, scorta, condotta, *f.*; norma, *f.*; governo, *m.* **For your —,** per vostra norma.
guide [gaid], *n.* Guida, *f.*; conduttore, cicerone, *m.*; scorta, *f.* || *v.t.* Guidare, condurre; dirigere; scortare. **— -book,** guida, *f.*; **— -post,** palo indicatore, *m.*; **— -rope,** fune di sicurezza, *f.*, (*Aviat.*) stabilizzatore, *m.*
guided, *a.* Condotto. **— missile,** siluro volante, *m.*
guiding, *a.* Dirigente. **— principle,** regola, norma, *f.*
guild [gild], *n.* Corporazione, associazione, *f.*; maestranza, *f.*
guildhall, *n.* Palazzo municipale, *m.*

guilder ['gildəɹ], *n.* Fiorino, *m.*
guile [gail], *n.* Astuzia, scaltrezza, frode, *f.*
guileful, *a.* Astuto, scaltro.
guileless, *a.* Ingenuo, schietto, semplice.
guilelessness, *n.* Ingenuità, schiettezza, semplicità, *f.*
guillotine ['giləti:n], *n.* Ghigliottina, *f.* || *v.t.* Ghigliottinare.
guilt [gilt], *n.* Colpa, colpabilità, reità, *f.*
guiltily, *adv.* Colpevolmente, delittuosamente.
guiltiness, *n.* Colpabilità, reità, *f.*
guiltless, *a.* Innocente, senza colpa. **To hold —,** dichiarare innocente.
guiltlessness, *n.* Innocenza, *f.*
guilty, *a.* Colpevole, reo; responsabile. **The — party,** il colpevole, il reo, *m.*; (*Law*) **to find —,** convincere di un reato; (*Law*) **to plead —,** dichiararsi colpevole.
guinea ['gini], *n.* Ghinea, *f.* **— -fowl,** faraona, gallina di Faraone, *f.*; **— -pig,** porcellino d'India, *m.*, cavia, *f.*
guise [gaiz], *n.* Guisa, forma, sembianza, *f.*
guitar [gi'tɑ:ɹ], *n.* Chitarra, *f.*
gules [gju:lz], *n.a.* (*Heraldry*) Color rosso, *m.*
gulf [gʌlf]. *n.* (*Geog.*) Golfo, *m.*; (*fig.*) abisso, baratro, *m.*; vortice, *m.*; grande intervallo, *m.* **The Gulf Stream,** La Corrente del Golfo, *f.*; **Gulf of the Lion,** Golfo del Leone, *m.*
gull [gʌl], *n.* (*Zool.*) Gabbiano, *m.*; (*fig.*) gonzo, minchione, semplicione, *m.* || *v.t.* Minchionare, canzonare, darla da bere a.
gullet, *n.* (*Anat.*) Gola, *f.*, esofago, *m.*
gullibility [gʌli'biliti], *n.* Credulità, *f.*
gullible, *a.* Credulo, credulone, ingannabile.
gully ['gʌli], *n.* Burrone, *m.*; cunicolo, condotto, *m.*; fossetto di scolo, *m.* **— -hole,** chiavica, *f.*, tombino, *m.*
gulp [gʌlp], *v.t.* Trangugiare, tracannare. || *n.* Sorso, boccone, fiato, *m.* **To — down,** ingozzare, mandar giù; **at a —,** d'un sol fiato, in un boccone.
gum (1) [gʌm], *n.* Gomma, *f.* || *v.t.* Ingommare. **— arabic,** gomma arabica, *f.*; **— resin,** gomma resina, *f.*; **— -tree,** eucalipto, albero della gomma, *m.*
gum (2), *n.* (*Anat.*) Gengiva, *f.* **— -boil,** ascesso alle gengive, *m.*, postema, *f.*
gumminess, *n.* Gommosità, *f.*
gummy, *a.* Gommoso, aderente.
gumption ['gʌmʃən], *n.* (*colloq.*) Sagacità, accortezza, *f.*; tatto, senno, comprendonio, *m.*
gun [gʌn], *n.* Fucile, schioppo, *m.*; cannone, *m.* (*fig.*) **He's a big —,** è un pezzo grosso; **to stick to one's guns,** star saldo, tener duro; (*colloq.*) **son of a —,** birbante, mascalzone, *m.*; (*of wind*) **to blow great guns,** soffiar forte; **— -barrel,** canna di fucile, *f.*; **— -carriage,** *n.* affusto di cannone, *m.*; **— -cotton,** cotone fulminante, fulmicotone, *m.*; **— -fire,** sparo del cannone, *m.*; **— -licence,** porto d'armi, permesso di caccia, *m.*; **— -maker,** armaiuolo, *m.*; **— -metal,** lega di bronzo, *f.*; **— -room,** (*Naut.*) quadrato dei subalterni, *m.*; **— -runner,** contrabbandiere di armi, *m.*; **— -running,** contrabbando di armi, *m.*; **— -stock,** fusto di fucile, *m.*; **— -layer,** puntatore, *m.*
gunboat, *n.* (*Naut.*) Cannoniera, *f.*
gunnel [cp. **gunwale**].
gunner, *n.* Cannoniere, artigliere, *m.*
gunnery, *n.* Artiglieria, balistica, *f.* **— -lieutenant,** tenente d'artiglieria, *m.*; **— -practice,** esercizi di tiro, tiri d'artiglieria, *m.pl.*
gunny ['gʌni], *n.* Tela da sacchi, tela d'iuta, *f.*
gunpowder, *n.* Polvere da cannone, polvere da sparo, polvere nera, *f.* **The Gunpowder Plot,** La Congiura delle Polveri, *f.*
gunshot, *n.* (*range*) Tiro di fucile, tiro di cannone, *m.*; (*wound*) colpo di fucile, *m.*, fucilata, *f.* **Within —,** a portata di fucile, a tiro di cannone.
gunsmith, *n.* Armaiuolo, *m.*
gunter, Gunter's scale ['gʌntəɹ, 'gʌntəɹz 'skeil], *n.* (*Math.*) Guntero, *m.*
gunwale, gunnel ['gʌnəl], *n.* (*Naut.*) Capo di banda, *m.*
gurgle [gə:ɹgl], *v.i.* Gorgogliare.
gurgling, *n.* Gorgoglio, *m.* || *a.* Gorgogliante.
gurnard, gurnet ['gə:ɹnəd, 'gə:ɹnit], *n.* (*Zool.*) Capone, *m.*
gush [gʌʃ], *n.* Getto, scoppio, zampillo, fiotto, *m.*; effusione, *f.* || *v.i.* Sgorgare, zampillare, scaturire; (*fig.*) entusiasmarsi troppo. **To — out,** scaturire.
gushing, *a.* Sgorgante; (*fig.*) espansivo.
gushingly, *adv.* Espansivamente, con entusiasmo.
gusset ['gʌsit], *n.* Gherone, *m.*; (*Mech.*) bazzoletto, *m.*
gust [gʌst], *n.* Colpo di vento, *m.*, raffica, ventata, *f.*; (*fig.*) accesso, trasporto, *m.*
gusty, *a.* Burrascoso, ventoso, tempestoso.
gustation, *n.* Gustazione, *f.*
gusto ['gʌstou], *n.* Gusto, trasporto, *m.* **With great —,** con grande entusiasmo.
gut [gʌt], *n.* Budello, intestino, *m.*; (*Naut.*) gola, *f.*; (*fishing-line*) crine di Firenze, *m.* || *v.t.* Sventrare, sviscerare; (*fig.*) saccheggiare. **Guts,** intestini, *m.pl.*; (*fig.*) coraggio, *m.*, determinazione, *f.*; **the house was gutted by fire,** la casa fu smantellata dal fuoco.
gutta-percha [gʌtə'pə:ɹtʃə], *n.* Guttaperga, guttaperca, *f.*
gutter ['gʌtəɹ], *n.* (*on roof*) Grondaia, gronda, *f.*; (*in road*) cunetta, fossetta, *f.*, rigagnolo, *m.*; (*conduit*) canale; (*fig.*) fango. || *v.t.* Scanalare, solcare; *v.i.* (*of a candle*) colare, sgocciolare. **The — press,** la stampa prezzolata, *f.*; **— -snipe,** birichino, *m.*
guttural ['gʌtərəl], *a.* Gutturale. || *n.* Suono gutturale, *m.*
guy (1) [gai], *n.* (*rope*) Ritenuta, *f.*
guy (2), *n.* Spauracchio, *m.*, caricatura, *f.*; figura fantastica, *f.*; (*colloq. American*) uomo, individuo, tipo, *m.* || *v.t.* Mostrare in effigie; canzonare. (*colloq.*) **To do a —,** scappare.
guzzle [gʌzl], *v.t.i.* Gozzovigliare, trincare, trangugiare, tracannare, satollarsi.
guzzler, *n.* Ghiottone, crapulone, *m.*
gymkhana [dʒim'kɑ:nə], *n.* Gimkana, gymkana, *f.*
gymnasium [dʒim'neiziəm], *n.* Palestra, scuola di ginnastica, *f.*
gymnast, *n.* Ginnasta, *m.*
gymnastic, *a.* Ginnastico.
gymnastics, *n.pl.* Ginnastica, *f.*
gymnosophist [dʒim'nɔsəfist], *n.* Ginnosofista, *m.*
gymnosophy, *n.* Ginnosofia, *f.*
gymnosperm, *n.* (*Bot.*) Gimnosperme, *f.*

gynaecological [gainikə'lɔdʒikəl], *a.* Ginecologico.
gynaecologist, *n.* Ginecologo, *m.*
gynaecology, *n.* Ginecologia, *f.*
gynandrous [dʒai'nændrəs], *a.* (*Bot.*) Ginandrico.
gypseous ['dʒipsiəs], *a.* Gessoso.
gypsum ['dʒipsəm], *n.* Gesso, *m.*
Gypsy [cp. **Gipsy**].
gyrate [dʒai'reit], *v.i.* Girare, roteare.
gyration, *n.* Giro, giramento, *m.*
gyratory, *a.* Rotatorio.
gyroscope ['dʒairəskoup], *n.* Giroscopio, *m.*
gyve [dʒaiv], *v.t.* Incatenare. **Gyves,** ferri, ceppi, *m.pl.*

H

H, h [eitʃ]. Ottava lettera dell'alfabeto inglese, *f.* **To drop one's aitches,** non pronunciare l'acca, parlare incorrettamente; **H-bomb,** bomba all'idrogeno, *f.*
Ha! [hɑ:] *inter.* Ah!
haberdasher ['hæbəɹdæʃəɹ], *n.* Merciaio, *m.*, merciaia, *f.*
haberdashery, *n.* Merceria, *f.*
habiliment [hæ'bilimənt], *n.* Abbigliamento. **Habiliments,** vestiti, abiti, *m.pl.*
habit ['hæbit], *n.* Abitudine, *f.*, vezzo, uso, *m.*; stato, *m.*; temperamento, *m.*; (*costume*) abito, costume, *m.* **Habits,** abitudini, modi, *m.pl.*; **— of mind,** mentalità, *f.*, temperamento, *m.*; **— of body,** complessione, *f.*; **to be in the — of,** avere l'abitudine di, aver l'uso di, solere; **to get into the — of,** prendere l'abitudine di, assuefarsi a; **to break oneself of a —,** disassuefarsi; **riding- —,** amazzone, *f.*
habitable, *a.* Abitabile.
habitant, *n.* Abitante, *m.f.*
habitat ['hæbitæt], *n.* Dimora, *f.*; (*Zool.*) habitat, *m.*
habitation, *n.* Abitazione, dimora, *f.*
habitual [hə'bitju:əl], *a.* Abituale, consueto, solito. **— criminal,** recidivo, *m.*
habitually, *adv.* Abitualmente.
habituate [hə'bitju:eit], *v.t.* Abituare, avvezzare. **To — oneself,** abituarsi, assuefarsi.
habitude ['hæbitju:d], *n.* Abitudine, consuetudine, *f.*, costume, uso, *m.*
hack (1) [hæk], *v.t.* Tagliuzzare, mutilare, sminuzzare; tirare calci nello stinco d'un avversario; *v.i.* tossicchiare. **A hacking cough,** una tosse secca, *f.*
hack (2), *n.* Taglio, *m.*, lacerazione, *f.* **— -saw,** seghetto, *m.*, sega per metalli, *f.*
hack (3), *n.* Cavallo da nolo, *m.*, ronzino, *m.*; cavallaccio, *m.* **— -writer,** imbrattacarte, scribacchino, scrittoruccio, *m.*; **— -work,** lavoro mercenario, *m.*
hackle [hækl], *n.* Gorgiera d'un gallo, *f.*; pettine pel lino, *f.* || *v.t.* (*flax*) Pettinare.
hackney ['hækni], *n.* Cavallo da nolo, *m.* **— -carriage,** carrozza da nolo, *f.*
hackneyed, *a.* Banale, comune, trito, vieto.
haddock ['hædək], *n.* (*Zool.*) Specie di merluzzo, *m.* **Dried —,** baccalà, *m.*
Hades ['heidi:z], *n.* Inferno, Ade, *m.*
haematite ['hemətait], *n.* (*Min.*) Ematite, *f.*
haematuria [hemə'tju:riə], *n.* (*Med.*) Ematuria, *f.*
haemorrhage ['hemərid3], *n.* (*Med.*) Emorragia, *f.*
haemorrhoids ['hemərɔidz], *n.pl.* Emorroidi, *f.pl.*
haft [hɑ:ft], *n.* Manico, *m.* || *v.t.* Fornire di manico.
hag [hæg], *n.* Vecchiaccia, strega, *f.* **— -ridden,** oppresso dall'incubo.
haggard ['hægəɹd], *a.* Sparuto, smunto, allampanato.
haggardness, *n.* Sparutezza, *f.*; pallore, *f.*; magrezza, *f.*
haggis ['hægis], *n.* (*Cooking*) Un piatto scozzese, *m.*
haggle [hægl], *v.i.* Lesinare, stiracchiare, mercanteggiare. **To — about the price,** lesinare sul prezzo.
hagiographer [hægi'ɔgrəfəɹ], *n.* Agiografo, *m.*
hagiology, *n.* Agiologia, *f.*
Hague [heig], **The,** *n.* (*Geog.*) L'Aia, *f.*
ha-ha ['hɑ:hɑ:], *n.* Fosso di cinta, *m.*
hail (1) [heil], *n.* Grandine, *f.* || *v.i.* Grandinare. **— -storm,** grandinata, *f.*; **— -stone,** chicco di grandine, *m.*
hail (2), *n.* Saluto, *m.*; chiamata, *f.*; appello, *m.*; accoglienza, *f.* || *v.t.* Salutare, chiamare, accogliere. || *inter.* Salve! Salute! **Within —,** a portata di voce; **to be — fellow-well-met,** essere familiare, essere amico di tutti; **they hailed him king,** lo salutarono re; **Hail Mary!** Ave Maria! **he hails from Scotland,** viene dalla Scozia, è scozzese.
hair [hεəɹ], *n.* Pelo, capello, *m.*, capelli, *m.pl.*; chioma, *f.*; crine, *m.*, crini, *m.pl.*; capigliatura, *f.* **Head of —,** capigliatura, *f.*; **to a —,** esattamente, a capello, appuntino; **to comb one's —,** pettinarsi; **to do one's —,** acconciarsi i capelli; **to dress someone's —,** pettinare qualcheduno; **to have one's — cut,** farsi tagliare i capelli; **to make one's — stand on end,** far rizzare i capelli; **to put up one's —,** farsi su i capelli; **to let down one's —,** sciogliersi i capelli; **to have a — -do,** avere una pettinatura; **to dye one's —,** tingere i capelli; **to split hairs,** guardare per il sottile, cercare il pelo nell'uovo; **— -splitting,** pedanteria, meticolosità, *f.*; **not to turn a —,** non scomporsi; **to tear one's —,** strapparsi i capelli; **— -comb,** pettine, *m.*; **— -drier,** apparecchio per asciugare i capelli, *m.*; **— -net,** reticella, rete per i capelli, *f.*; **— -pin,** forcellina, *f.*; **— -pin bend,** brusca volta, curva a forcella, *f.*; **— -mattress,** materasso di crine, *m.*; **— -slide,** ferma capelli, *m.*; **— -wash,** lozione per capelli, *f.*; **— -shirt,** cilicio, *m.*; **— -spring,** molla capillare, *f.*; **— -trigger,** grilletto doppio, *m.*; **— grip,** molletta, *f.*
hairbreadth, hair's breadth, *n.* (*fig.*) Pelo, *m.* **He had a — escape,** mancò un pelo che non fosse ucciso.
hairdresser, *n.* Parrucchiere, barbiere, *m.*; pettinatrice, *f.*, parrucchiere per signore, *m.*
haired, *n.* Capelluto. **Red- —,** dai capelli rossi.
hairiness, *n.* Pelosità, *f.*
hairless, *a.* Senza capelli, calvo, imberbe.
hairy, *a.* Peloso, capelluto.
hake [heik], *n.* (*Zool.*) Nasello, *m.*
halation [hə'leiʃən], *n.* (*Phot.*) Alone, *m.*
halberd ['hælbəɹd], *n.* Alabarda, *f.*

halberdier [hælbəɹ'diəɹ], *n.* Alabardiere, *m.*
halcyon ['hælsiən], *n.* Alcione, *m.* **— days,** giorni di bonaccia, giorni sereni, *m.pl.*
hale (1) [heil], *a.* Arzillo, sano, robusto, vigoroso, gagliardo. **To be — and hearty,** essere arzillo e vegeto, essere in gamba.
hale (2), *v.t.* Trascinare, tirare.
half [hɑ:f], *n.* Metà, *f.*, mezzo, *m.*, mezza, *f.* || *a.* Mezzo, semi-. || *adv.* A metà, a mezzo. **— a loaf,** la metà d'un pane, *f.*, un mezzo pane, *m.*; **— an hour,** una mezz'ora, *f.*; **— as much,** una metà, *f.*; **— as much again,** una metà di più, *f.*; **an hour and a —,** un'ora e mezza, *f.*; **to divide in halves,** dividere per metà, dividere a mezzo; **to go halves with,** fare a metà con; **too long by —,** troppo lungo; **he never does things by halves,** non fa mai le cose a mezzo; (*Football*) **— -back,** mediano, sostegno, *m.*; **— -mast high,** a mezz'albero; **at — -price,** a metà prezzo; **— -light,** mezza luce, penombra, *f.*; **— -binding,** mezza tela, *f.*; **— -bound,** in mezza legatura; **— -breed,** meticcio, *m.*; **— -caste,** uomo di sangue misto, *m.*; **— -brother,** fratello uterino, fratellastro, *m.*; **— -dead,** mezzo morto, semivivo; **— -done,** mezzo fatto, cotto a metà; **— -hearted,** indifferente, apatico; **— -heartedness,** indifferenza, apatia, *f.*; **— -holiday,** mezza festa, *f.*; **— moon,** mezza luna, *f.*; **— -mourning,** mezzo lutto, *m.*; **— -length,** a mezzo busto; **— -pay,** mezza paga, *f.*; **— -sister,** sorella uterina, sorellastra, *f.*; (*Print.*) **— -title,** titolo abbreviato, *m.*; (*Print.*) **— -tone,** a mezza tinta; **— -tone block,** cliché a mezza tinta, *m.*; **— -way,** a mezza strada; **— -way up the hill,** a metà della collina; **— -witted,** ebete, idiota; **— -year,** semestre, *m.*; **— -yearly,** semestrale, a semestri; (*colloq.*) **not —!** altro che!
halfpenny (*pl.* **halfpence**) ['heipni, 'heipəns], *n.* Soldo, *m.*
halibut ['hælibət], *n.* (*Zool.*) Grosso rombo, ippoglosso, *m.*
hall [hɔ:l], *n.* Sala, aula, *f.*; salone, *m.*; atrio, vestibolo, *m.* **Dining- —,** refettorio, *m.*; **town- —,** palazzo municipale, *m.*; **— -porter,** portinaio, *m.*; portiere, *m.*; **— -stand,** attaccapanni, *m.*; **— -mark,** marca ufficiale per il vero oro e argento.
hallelujah [hæli'lu:jə], *n.* Alleluia, *f.*
halliard [cp. **halyard**].
Hallo! [hə'lou], *inter.* Olà!, Ohè! (*at telephone*) Pronto!, Pronti!
halloo [hə'lu:], *v.t.i.* Gridare, vociare; incitare, aizzare. *n.* Grido di caccia, *m.*, Hallalì!
hallow ['hælou], *v.t.* Santificare, consacrare, dedicare.
Hallowe'en [hælou'i:n], *n.* Vigilia di Ognissanti, *f.*
Hallowmas, All Hallows ['hælouməs, ɔ:l 'hælouz], *n.* Ognissanti, *m.*
hallucinate [hə'lu:sineit], *v.t.* Allucinare.
hallucination, *n.* Allucinazione, *f.*
halo ['heilou], *n.* Alone, *m.*; aureola, *f.*
halt (1) [hɔ:lt], *n.* Fermata, sosta, *f.*; alto, *m.* || *v.i.* Fermarsi, arrestarsi; (*Mil.*) fare alt; *v.t.* far fermare. || *inter.* Alto!, Alt!, Alto là! **halting-place,** posto di tappa, *m.*
halt (2), *a.* Zoppo, storpiato. || *v.i.* Zoppicare; (*fig.*) vacillare, esitare. **To — between two opinions,** star dubbioso fra due opinioni; **to enter life —,** entrar nella vita zoppo.
halter, *n.* Cavezza, *f.*; (*for hanging*) capestro, *m.*, forca, *f.*
halting, *a.* Esitante; zoppicante.
halve [hɑ:v], *v.t.* Dividere per metà, dimezzare, smezzare.
halyard ['hæliəɹd], *n.* Drizza, *f.*; sagola, *f.*
ham [hæm], *n.* Prosciutto, *m.*; (*of person*) natica, *f.* **— and eggs,** prosciutto e uova.
hamadryad [hæmə'draiəd], *n.* (*Myth.*) Amadriade, *f.*
Hamburg ['hæmbə:ɹg], *n.* (*Geog.*) Amburgo, *m.*
hamlet ['hæmlet], *n.* Casale, piccolo villaggio, *m.*; frazione di campagna, *f.*
Hamlet, *n.* (*Lit.*) Amleto, *m.*
hammer [hæməɹ], *n.* Martello, *m.*; (*Mech.*) pilone, *m.*; (*of gun*) cane, *m.*; (*auctioneer's*) asta, *f.* || *v.t.* Martellare; battere, picchiare. **— and tongs,** con violenza; **— and sickle,** falce e martello; **to bring under the —,** mettere all'incanto; **sledge- —,** mazza, mazzetta, *f.*; **steam- —,** maglio a vapore, *m.*; **to — out an idea,** escogitare un'idea; **to — away,** perseverare, lavorare senza riposo; **— -cloth,** gualdrappa sul sedile del cocchiere, *f.*; **— -head,** ferro del martello, *m.*
hammering, *n.* Martellio, martellamento, *m.*, martellata, *f.*
hammock ['hæmək], *n.* Amaca, *f.*
hamper (1) ['hæmpəɹ], *v.t.* Impedire, intralciare, inceppare, imbarazzare.
hamper (2), *n.* Cesto, paniere, canestro, *m.* (*Naut.*) **Top- —,** attrezzatura ingombrante, *f.*
hamster ['hæmstəɹ], *n.* (*Zool.*) Criceto, *m.*
hamstring ['hæmstriŋ], *v.t.* Sgarettare, tagliare i garetti a. || *n.* Tendine del garetto, *m.*
hand [hænd], *n.* Mano, *f.*; pugno, *m.*; (*writing*) scrittura, calligrafia, *f.*; (*cards*) mano, *f.*; (*clock*) lancetta, *f.*; (*workman*) operaio, equipaggio, *m.*; (*side*) parte, *f.*, canto, *m.*; (*measure*) palmo, *m.* || *v.t.* Consegnare, porgere, dare, rimettere; (*Naut.*) ammainare; aiutare. **First- —,** di prima mano; **at —,** a portata di mano, vicino; **by —,** a mano; **cash in —,** avanzo di cassa, *m.*; **from — to —,** di mano in mano; **from — to mouth,** alla giornata; **— to — fight,** un combattimento corpo a corpo; **Hands off!** Giù le mani! **Hands up!** Mani in alto! **off- —,** brusco, subito, sui due piedi; **on all hands,** da tutti i lati, da ogni mano; **to have on —,** occuparsi di, avere alla mano; **on one's hands,** sulle braccia; **on the other —,** d'altra parte; **out of —,** fuori controllo; **second- —,** di seconda mano; **to be — in glove with,** essere due anime in un nocciolo; **to bear a —,** prestare mano a; **to be a good — at,** aver la mano a; **to bring up by —,** allattare artificialmente; **with a high —,** in modo prepotente; **to change hands,** cambiar mani; **to get one's — in,** impratichirsi, farsi la mano; **to get the upper —,** prendere il sopravvento; **to have a — in,** prendere parte a, aver una mano in; **to have one's hands full,** avere troppe cose sulle braccia; **to lay hands on,** mettere le mani su, trovare; **to lay violent hands on oneself,** attentare alla propria vita; **to play into each other's hands,** tenersi mano, intendersela; **to shake hands with,** stringer la mano a;

to show one's —, rivelarsi, scoprir il proprio giuoco; **to take in —**, mettere mano a; **with both hands**, con tutt'e due le mani; **he handed her into the carriage**, la aiutò a montare in carrozza; **to — round**, far circolare, far girare; **to — down**, trasmettere per successione; **to — over**, consegnare; **— -bag**, borsetta, *f.*; **— -barrow**, carretto a mano, *m.*, carriola, *f.*; **— -bill**, annunzio, avviso, *m.*; **— -gallop**, piccolo galoppo, *m.*; **— -grenade**, bomba a mano, *f.*; **— -made**, fatto a mano; **— -rail**, ringhiera, *f.*; **— saw**, sega a mano.

handbook ['hændbuk], *n.* Manuale, prontuario, *m.*; guida, *f.*

handcuffs, *n.pl.* Manette, *f.pl.* **To handcuff**, ammanettare, mettere le manette a.

handful, *n.* Manata, manciata, *f.*, pugno, *m.*; manipolo, gruppetto, *m.*

handicap ['hændikæp], *n.* (*Sport*) Handicap, *m.*; abbuono, *m.*, corsa a ragguagli, *f.*; (*fig.*) svantaggio, intralcio, ostacolo, *m.* || *v.t.* Regolare un handicap; (*fig.*) intralciare, svantaggiare.

handicraft ['hændikrɑːft], *n.* Mestiere, *m.*, arte, *f.*

handicraftsman, *n.* Artigiano, *m.*

handily, *adv.* Destramente; convenientemente.

handiness, *n.* Maneggevolezza, *f.*; convenienza, *f.*

handiwork, *n.* Fattura, *f.*; lavoro manuale, *m.*

handkerchief ['hæŋkəɹtʃif], *n.* Fazzoletto, *m.*

handle [hændl], *n.* Manico, *m.*; (*of vase, etc.*) ansa, *f.*; (*of sword, etc.*) impugnatura, *f.*; (*of door*) maniglia, *f.*; (*Mech.*) manovella, *f.* || *v.t.* Maneggiare, manipolare; toccare, tastare, trattare; (*fig.*) svolgere. **A — to one's name**, un titolo, *m.*; (*Motor.*) **starting- —**, manovella di avviamento, *f.*; (*fig.*) **to give a — to**, dare un pretesto a; **to — carefully**, manipolare con cura; **to — roughly**, trattare male, malmenare; **— -bar** (*of cycle*), manubrio, *m.*

handling, *n.* Maneggio, *m.*, manipolazione, *f.*; svolgimento, trattamento, *m.*

handmaid ['hændmeid], *n.* Serva, fantesca, ancella, *f.*

handsel ['hænsəl], *n.* Strenna, *f.*; (*fig.*) saggio, *m.* || *v.t.* Dare una strenna; saggiare.

handsome ['hænsəm], *a.* Bello, avvenente; (*fig.*) generoso, liberale; grande, splendido. **A — present**, un regalo splendido, un bel dono, *m.*

handsomely, *adv.* Elegantemente; generosamente, gentilmente.

handsomeness, *n.* Beltà, eleganza, generosità, *f.*

handspike ['hændspaik], *n.* Leva, *f.*

handwriting, *n.* Scrittura, calligrafia, *f.*

handwritten, *a.* Scritto a mano.

handy ['hændi], *a.* Destro, abile, servizievole; maneggevole, a portata di mano. **— -man**, fasservizi, *m.*

hang (1) (*p.* and *p.p.* **hanged**) [hæŋ], *v.t.* (*as capital punishment*) Impiccare. (*colloq.*) **I'll be hanged if I will**, preferisco crepare piuttosto di.

hang (2) (*p.* and *p.p.* **hung**), *v.t.* Impiccare; sospendere, appendere; (*wall-paper*) attaccare; (*the head*) chinare, abbassare; (*necklace, etc.*) ornare di; *v.i.* pendere, penzolare, star sospeso. (*colloq.*) **Hang it!** Accidenti! Alla malora! **to — about**, ciondolare, bighellonare; **to — back**, esitare; **time hangs heavy on his hands**, la vita gli pesa; **his life hangs on a thread**, la sua vita pende da un filo; **to — over**, star sospeso sopra, minacciare; (*colloq.*) **— -over**, mal di capo dopo una bevuta, *m.*; **to — out washing**, stendere la biancheria all'aria; **to — together**, unirsi, stringersi insieme; (*of an argument*) essere coerente; **to — out flags**, issare le bandiere; **— -dog**, basso, abbattuto; degno di forca; **a — -dog look**, faccia patibolare, *f.*

hangar ['hæŋəɹ], *n.* (*Aviat.*) Capannone, *m.*, tettoia, aviorimessa, *f.*

hanger, *n.* Coltellaccio, *m.* **Coat- —**, attaccapanni, ometto, *m.*; **— -on**, parassita, scroccone, *m.*

hanging, *a.* Sospeso, pendente, pensile. || *n.* (*punishment*) Impiccagione, *f.* **— -lamp**, lampada a sospensione, *f.*; **— -garden**, giardino pensile, *m.*

hangings, *n.pl.* Tappezzerie, tendine, *f.pl.*, cortinaggi, *m.pl.*

hangman, *n.* Boia, carnefice, *m.*

hank [hæŋk], *n.* Matassa, *f.*, pugno, *m.*; (*Naut.*) garzetta, *f.*

hanker, *v.i.* **To — after**, bramare, agognare a.

hankering, *n.* Bramosia, brama, *f.*

Hanoverian [hæno'viəriən], *n.a.* Annoveriano, *m.*

Hanseatic [hænzi'ætik], *a.* (*Hist.*) Anseatico.

hansom, hansom cab ['hænsəm, hænsəm 'kæb], *n.* Cab, calessino, *m.*

hap (1) [hæp], *n.* Caso, *m.*; incidente, *m.* || *v.i.* Accadere per caso.

hap (2), *v.i.* **To — up**, avvolgersi, coprirsi.

haphazard [hæp'hæzəɹd], *n.* Caso, accidente, *m.* || *a.* Casuale, accidentale. || *adv.* Per caso, accidentalmente; alla buona, alla carlona.

hapless, *a.* Sfortunato, infelice.

haply, *adv.* Per caso, forse.

happen ['hæpən], *v.i.* Accadere, avvenire, succedere, capitare. **A man happened to pass**, un uomo passava per caso; **as if nothing had happened**, come se nulla fosse accaduto; **Happen what may!** Avvenga che può! **if he happened to come**, se gli accadesse di venire; **it is to be hoped that this will not — again**, è da sperare che questo non abbia più da verificarsi; **Do you — to have a pen?** Avete per caso una penna? **I happened upon this book at the hotel**, trovai questo libro per caso nell'albergo.

happening, *n.* Avvenimento, *m.*; vicenda, *f.*

happily ['hæpili], *adv.* Fortunatamente, felicemente.

happiness, *n.* Felicità, *f.*

happy, *a.* Felice, fortunato; lieto, contento. **To a — issue**, ad un buon risultato; **a — medium**, un giusto mezzo, *m.*; **I'm — to**, sono lieto di; **a — New Year**, buon Capodanno; **— -go-lucky**, spensierato, imprevidente.

harangue [hæ'ræŋ], *n.* Arringa, *f.* || *v.t.i.* Arringare, esortare.

harass ['hærəs], *v.t.* Molestare, irritare, tormentare, frustrare.

harassed, *a.* Affaticato; tormentato; vessato.

harbinger ['hɑːɹbindʒəɹ], *n.* Foriere, precursore, messaggero, *m.*

harbour ['hɑːɹbəɹ], *n.* Porto, *m.*; asilo, ricovero, rifugio, *m.* || *v.t.* Albergare, alloggiare; (*fig.*) nutrire, intrattenere, covare; (*a criminal*) proteggere; *v.i.* venire a porto. **To — evil thoughts,** covare cattivi pensieri; **— dues,** diritti di porto, *m.pl.*; **— -master,** capitano di porto, *m.*
harbourage, *n.* Rifugio, asilo, *m.*
hard [hɑːɹd], *a.* Duro, fermo, sodo; difficile, penoso; gravoso, oneroso; rigoroso, crudele. || *adv.* Forte, fortemente; difficilmente, a stento, a fatica, a pena, male, troppo. **— and fast rule,** regola immutabile, *f.*; **— frost,** gelo intenso, *m.*; **— labour,** lavoro forzato, *m.*; **— of belief,** incredulo; **— of hearing,** duro d'orecchio; **— to please,** difficile da contentare; **— up,** al verde, alle strette, nei guai; **— water,** acqua dura, *f.*; **— words,** parole ingiuriose, *f.pl.*; **— cash,** contanti, *m.pl.*; **that's — lines on you,** questo è un bel guaio, è una bella disdetta; **a — nut to crack,** un osso duro da rodere; **to be a — drinker,** essere un gran bevitore; **— by,** vicinissimo; **to look — at,** guardare fissamente; **to rain —,** piovere dirottamente; **to work —,** lavorare indefessamente; **— -bitten,** risoluto; **— -boiled egg,** uovo sodo; (*colloq.*) **that girl is — -boiled,** quella ragazza è molto sofisticata; (*Tennis*) **— court,** terra battuta, *f.*; **— roe,** uova, *f.*; **— -earned,** guadagnato a fatica; **— -fisted,** avaro; **— -hearted,** duro, crudele, inumano; **— -mouthed,** duro di bocca; **— -working,** laborioso.
harden, *v.t.* Indurire, indurare, temperare; *v.i.* indurirsi.
hardened, *a.* Indurito.
hardening, *n.* Indurimento, *m.*; (*Mech.*) tempera, *f.*
hardihood ['hɑːɹdihud], *n.* Audacia, intrepidità, *f.*, coraggio, *m.*
hardily, *adv.* Audacemente.
hardiness, *n.* Vigore, *m.*, robustezza, *f.*
hardly, *adv.* Appena, a fatica, a stento; quasi, poco; duramente, severamente; **— ever,** quasi mai.
hardness, *n.* Durezza, fermezza, rigidezza, *f.*; difficoltà, severità, *f.* **— of heart,** insensibilità, *f*; durezza di cuore, *f.*
hardship, *n.* Stento, *m.*, fatica, privazione, pena, *f.*; ingiustizia, *f.*
hardware, *n.* Chincaglieria, *f.*, articoli di metallo, *m.pl.*; ferramenta, *f.pl.*
hardwareman, *n.* Negoziante di ferramenta, *m.*
hardy, *a.* Ardito, coraggioso; forte, robusto; (*Bot.*) resistente, selvatico.
hare [hɛəɹ], *n.* (*Zool.*) Lepre, *f.* **A young —,** un leprotto; **to run with the — and hunt with the hounds,** tenere il piede in due scarpe; **as mad as a March —,** matto da legare; (*game*) **— and hounds,** caccia alla lepre; **— -brained,** scervellato, stordito; **— -lip,** labbro leporino, *m.*; (*Bot.*) **hare's-foot,** piede di lepre, *m.*
harebell, *n.* (*Bot.*) Campanellina, campanula, *f.*
harem ['hɛəɹəm], *n.* Arem, *m.*
haricot ['hærikou], *n.* Fagiuolo secco, *m.*
hark [hɑːɹk], *v.t.i.* Ascoltare. || *inter.* Ascolta!, Ascoltate! **To — back,** ritornare su.
harlequin ['hɑːɹlikwin], *n.* Arlecchino, *m.*
harlequinade, *n.* Arlecchinata, *f.*
harlot ['hɑːɹlət], *n.* Meretrice, puttana, prostituta, *f.*
harlotry, *n.* Prostituzione, *f.*
harm [hɑːɹm], *n.* Male, danno, pregiudizio, *m.* || *v.t.* Far male a, far torto a, nuocere, recar danno a, danneggiare. **Out of harm's way,** al sicuro; **there's no — in him,** è un uomo inoffensivo; **there's no — in that,** non c'è nulla di male in ciò; **bodily —,** vie di fatto.
harmful, *a.* Nocivo, dannoso.
harmfulness, *n.* Dannosità, *f.*, danno, *m.*
harmless, *a.* Innocente, innocuo, inoffensivo.
harmlessness, *n.* Innocenza, innocuità, *f.*
harmonic [hɑːɹ'mɔnik], *n.a.* Armonico, *m.*
harmonica, *n.* Armonica, *f.*
harmonious, *a.* Armonioso.
harmonist, *n.* Armonista, *m.*
harmonium, *n.* Armonium, *m.*
harmonize, *v.t.* Armonizzare; *v.i.* armonizzare, concordare, essere in armonia.
harmonizing, *a.* Armonioso, concordante, consenziente.
harmony, *n.* Armonia, *f.*, accordo, *m.*
harness ['hɑːɹnis], *n.* Bardatura, *f.*, finimenti, *m.pl.*; armatura, *f.* || *v.t.* Bardare; attaccare; metter i finimenti; (*waterfall*) usare per la forza elettrica. **To die in —,** morire sulla breccia, morire sul lavoro; **— -maker,** sellaio, *m.*
harp [hɑːɹp], *n.* (*Mus.*) Arpa, *f.* || *v.i.* Suonare l'arpa, arpeggiare. **Jew's —,** scacciapensieri, *m.*; (*fig.*) **to — on,** ripetere, tornare sull'argomento, insistere; **to — on the same string,** tornare sempre allo stesso argomento.
harper, harpist, *n.* Arpista, *m.f.*
harpoon [hɑːɹ'puːn], *n.* Rampone, *m.*, fiocina, *f.* || *v.t.* Ramponare.
harpooner, *n.* Ramponiere, *m.*
harpsichord ['hɑːɹpsikɔːɹd], *n.* (*Mus.*) Clavicembalo, *m.*
harpy ['hɑːɹpi], *n.* Arpia, *f.*
harquebus ['hɑːɹkwibəs], *n.* Archibugio, *m.*
harridan ['hæridən], *n.* Vecchiaccia, *f.*
harrier ['hæriəɹ], *n.* (*Zool.*) Levriere, *m.*
harrow ['hærou], *n.* (*Agric.*) Erpice, *m.* || *v.t.* Erpicare; (*fig.*) straziare, tormentare.
harrowing, *n.* Erpicatura, *f.* || *a.* (*fig.*) Straziante, atroce.
harry ['hæri], *v.t.* Saccheggiare, devastare.
harsh [hɑːɹʃ], *a.* Ruvido, aspro, duro; severo, acerbo, crudele; (*voice*) rauco; (*taste*) acre.
harshly, *adv.* Aspramente; severamente, crudelmente.
harshness, *n.* Ruvidezza, asprezza, acerbità, *f.*; crudeltà, *f.*
hart [hɑːɹt], *n.* Cervo, *m.* (*Bot.*) **Hart's tongue,** lingua cervina, *f.*
hartshorn ['hɑːɹtshɔːɹn], *n.* Ammoniaca liquida, *f.*
harum-scarum ['hɛərəm 'skɛərəm], *n.a.* Scervellato, stordito, sventato, *m.*
harvest ['hɑːɹvest], *n.* Raccolto, *m.*, messe, mietitura, raccolta, *f.* || *v.t.* Mietere, raccogliere, fare il raccolto. **— -home,** festa della mietitura, *f.*, festa del raccolto, *f.*; **— moon,** luna della mietitura, *f.*; **to get in the —,** fare il raccolto; **— -bug,** falangio, *m.*
harvester, *n.* Mietitore, *m.*, mietitrice, *f.*; (*Mech.*) mietitrice, *f.*

hash [hæʃ], *n.* (*cooking*) Guazzetto, ragù, *m.*; (*fig.*) guazzabuglio, *m.* || *v.t.* Sminuzzare, tagliuzzare, tritare. **To make a — of,** fare un bel pasticcio di, impasticciare.
hashish [ˈhæʃiʃ], *n.* Hascisc, *m.*
haslet [ˈheizlət], *n.* (*cooking*) Frattaglie, *f.pl.*
hasp [hɑːsp], *n.* Fermaglio, serramento, *m.* || *v.t.* Agganciare.
hassock [ˈhæsək], *n.* Inginocchiatoio, cuscino, *m.*
haste [heist], *n.* Fretta, furia, precipitazione, *f.*; sollecitudine, celerità, *f.* **In great —,** in gran fretta; **to make —,** affrettarsi, sbrigarsi; **in hot —,** in fretta e in furia; **more — less speed,** chi ha fretta vada adagio.
hasten, *v.t.* Affrettare, sollecitare, accelerare, sbrigare; *v.i.* affrettarsi, darsi fretta, spicciarsi. **To — away,** andar via in fretta, filar via; **to — back,** tornare in fretta, accorrere.
hastily, *adv.* In fretta, frettolosamente.
hastiness, *n.* Fretta, precipitazione, *f.*; irritabilità, *f.*
hasty, *a.* Frettoloso, affrettato; irascibile, irritabile.
hat [hæt], *n.* Cappello, *m.* **Top- —,** cappello a cilindro, *m.*, tuba, *f.*; **felt —,** cappello di feltro; **bowler- —,** cappello duro, *m.*, bombetta, *f.*; **straw —,** cappello di paglia, *m.*; **to pass round the —,** fare una colletta, *f.*; **Hats off!** Giù i cappelli! **— -stand,** attaccapanni, *m.*; **— -band,** nastro di cappello, *m.*; **— -brush,** spazzola per cappelli, *f.*; **— -maker,** cappellaio, *m.*; **— -shop,** cappelleria, *f.*; **— -peg,** portacappelli, *m.*
hatch (1) [hætʃ], *n.* (*of chicken*) Covata, *f.* || *v.t.* Covare; (*fig.*) macchinare, tramare, congiurare, complottare; *v.i.* uscire dall'uovo, schiudersi. **Don't count your chickens before they're hatched,** non vender la pelle dell'orso prima d'averlo preso.
hatch (2), **hatchway,** *n.* (*Naut.*) Boccaporto, *m.*; mezza porta, *f.* (*Naut.*) **Under hatches,** al riparo, in stiva.
hatch (3), *v.t.* (*Art*) Tratteggiare, ombreggiare.
hatchet [ˈhætʃit], *n.* Accetta, ascia, *f.* **To bury the —,** riconciliarsi; **— -faced,** affilato, scarno.
hatching, *n.* (*Art*) Tratteggio, *m.*, ombreggiatura, *f.*
hatchment [ˈhætʃmənt], *n.* (*Heraldry*) Stemma, *m.*
hatchway [cp. **hatch** (2)].
hate [heit], *n.* Odio, *m.*, avversione, *f.* || *v.t.* Odiare, detestare, avere in odio.
hateful, *a.* Odioso, detestabile.
hatefulness, *n.* Odiosità, *f.*
hater, *n.* Odiatore, nemico, *m.* **To be a good —,** essere un nemico senza compassione.
hatred [ˈheitrid], *n.* Odio, *m.*, avversione, inimicizia, *f.*
hatter [ˈhætəɹ], *n.* Cappellaio, *m.* **Mad as a —,** proprio matto.
hauberk [ˈhɔːbəɹk], *n.* Usbergo, *m.*
haughtily [ˈhɔːtili], *adv.* Altezzosamente, orgogliosamente, fieramente.
haughtiness, *n.* Alterigia, boria, superbia, *f.*; orgoglio, *m.*
haughty, *a.* Altezzoso, superbo, orgoglioso, borioso.
haul [hɔːl], *v.t.* Tirare, trarre; (*Naut.*) rimorchiare; trasportare. || *n.* (*of fish*) Retata, *f.* **To — in,** tirar dentro; (*Naut.*) **to — down sail,** ammainare; (*Naut.*) **to — upon the wind,** orzare; **to — over the coals,** sgridare, dare una lavata di testa a; **at a —,** con una sola retata; (*fig.*) **a good —,** un buon profitto, *m.*
haulage [ˈhɔːlidʒ], *n.* Alaggio, rimorchio, *m.* **— contractor,** imprenditore di trasporti, *m.*
haulm [hɔːm], *n.* Stelo, *m.*; stoppia, *f.*
haunch [hɔːntʃ], *n.* (*Anat.*) Anca, *f.*; (*of meat*) coscia, *f.*, quarto, *m.*
haunt [hɔːnt], *n.* Ricovero, soggiorno, ritiro, *m.*; (*of thieves*) covo, *m.* || *v.t.* Frequentare, visitare, praticare; (*fig.*) tormentare, perseguitare, infestare. **That house is haunted,** quella casa è infestata dagli spiriti; **I am haunted by the idea that,** sono perseguitato dall'idea che.
hautboy [ˈhoubɔi], *n.* (*Mus.*) Oboe, *m.*
Havana [həˈvænə], *n.* (*Geog.*) Avana, *f.* **— cigar,** avana, *f.*, sigaro avana, *m.*
have [hæv], *v.t.aux.* Avere, possedere, contenere; fare; dovere; ottenere; prenderei **Had all the soldiers fought,** se tutti i soldati avessero combattuto; **had it not been that I was too busy,** se io non fossi stato troppo occupato; **he will — it that the news is true,** insiste che le notizie sono vere; **he will — his room arranged thus,** vuole che la sua camera sia ordinata così; **I had as lief go as stay,** vorrei tanto andare che rimanere; **I had rather,** preferirei; **I — to be home by ten,** devo tornare a casa alle dieci; **just let me — that book for a minute,** datemi quel libro per un momento; **I won't — anything to do with her,** non voglio avere nulla da fare con lei; **I — done with him,** l'ho fatta finita con lui; **this may be had at,** questo s'ottiene da; **to — breakfast,** far colazione; **I — it from a reliable source,** l'ho da fonte attendibile; **let us — him in,** facciamolo entrare; **I — got a coat on,** porto un abito; **as Shakespeare has it,** come dice Shakespeare; **he has no English,** non parla inglese; **you had better go,** fareste meglio ad andare; **he had his leg broken,** si è rotta la gamba; **they had him up in court,** l'hanno fatto comparire in giudizio; **to — a walk,** fare una passeggiata; (*colloq.*) **you've had it,** è finito; stai fresco!
haven [ˈheivən], *n.* Porto, *m.*; (*fig.*) rifugio, asilo, *m.*
haversack [ˈhævəɹsæk], *n.* Bisaccia, *f.*, tascapane, *m.*
having, *a.* Avente.
havoc [ˈhævək], *n.* Danno, *m.*, rovina, distruzione, *f.*
haw (1) [hɔː], *n.* (*Bot.*) Bacca del biancospino, *f.*
haw (2), *v.i.* Esitare nel parlare, balbettare. **To hum and —,** titubare.
hawfinch [ˈhɔːfintʃ], *n.* (*Zool.*) Becco duro, frosone, *m.*
hawk [hɔːk], *n.* (*Zool.*) Falco, falchetto, falcone, *m.* || *v.i.* Cacciare col falcone; scatarrare, scaracchiare; *v.t.* portare in giro per la vendita, rivender merci al minuto. **— -eyed,** dagli occhi grifagni; **— -nosed,** dal naso aquilino.

hawker, *n.* Girovago, merciaio ambulante, *m.*
hawking, *n.* Falconeria, *f.*; rivendita al minuto, *f.*
hawse-hole [ˈhɔːzhoul], *n.* (*Naut.*) Occhio di prua, occhio di cubia, *m.*
hawser, *n.* Alzana, *f.*, gherlino, cavo, *m.*, gomena, *f.*
hawthorn [ˈhɔːθɔːɹn], *n.* (*Bot.*) Biancospino, *m.*
hay [hei], *n.* Fieno, *m.* **To make —,** far fieno; (*fig.*) **to make — of,** mettere in disordine, scompigliare. **—-cock,** mucchio di fieno, *m.*; **—-fever,** febbre del fieno, *f.*; **—-harvest,** fienagione, *f.*; **—-market,** mercato del fieno, *m.*; **—-rake,** rastrello per fieno, *m.*; **—-rick, —-stack,** mucchio di fieno, fienile, *m.*; **to make — while the sun shines,** battere il ferro mentre è caldo.
haymaker, *n.* Falciatore, *m.*, falciatrice, *f.*
haymaking, *n.* Falciatura, fienagione, *f.*
hazard [ˈhæzəɹd], *n.* Azzardo, rischio, pericolo, repentaglio, *m.*; caso, *m.*; sorte, *f.*; (*Golf*) ostacolo, *m.* || *v.t.* Azzardare, arrischiare. **At all hazards,** a qualunque costo; **to run the —,** correre il rischio; **to put to —,** mettere a rischio, mettere a repentaglio.
hazardous, *a.* Azzardato, arrischiato, rischioso, temerario.
haze [heiz], *n.* Bruma, nebbia, foschia, *f.*; nebbiosità, *f.* || *v.t.* (*colloq.*) Malmenare.
hazel [ˈheizl], *n.* (*Bot.*) Nocciuolo, avellano, *m.* || *a.* Nocciuolo, bruno, chiaro. **—-eyed,** con gli occhi color nocciuola; **—-nut,** nocciuola, *f.*
hazily, *adv.* Indistintamente.
haziness, *n.* Nebbiosità, *f.*
hazy, *a.* Caliginoso, nebbioso, fosco; (*fig.*) confuso, indistinto, vago.
he [hiː], *pron.* Egli, esso; colui, quegli, costui; lui. **He and I,** lui ed io; **he who,** colui che, chi.
he-, *prefix.* Maschio. **He-goat,** capro, becco, *m.*
head [hed], *n.* Testa, *f.*; capo, *m.*; origine, *f.*; termine, *m.*; estremità, *f.*; fondo, *m.*; (*Naut.*) prora, *f.*; (*summit*) cima, *f.*; (*of river*) sorgente, *f.*; (*on liquor*) spuma, *f.*; (*of pin, nail, etc.*) capocchia, *f.*; (*of axe, spear, etc.*) punta, *f.*; (*of hair*) capigliatura, *f.*; (*of bed*) capezzale, *m.*; (*of steam*) pressione, *f.*; (*of coin*) faccia, *f.* || *v.t.* Mettersi a capo di, guidare, capeggiare, capitanare, dirigere; intestare, intitolare. || *a.* Capo, primo, principale. **A —, per —,** a testa; **at the — of the table,** a capo tavola; **from — to foot,** da capo a piedi; **— foremost,** a capofitto; **— over heels,** capovolto, a capitombolo, a gambe levate; **heads or tails,** faccia o pila, testa o croce; **taller by a —,** più alto di tutta la testa; **I cannot make — or tail of it,** non ci trovo nè capo nè coda; **to bring to a —,** portare a compimento; **to come into one's —,** venire alla mente; **to take into one's —,** cacciarsi in testa; **to go to one's —,** dare alla testa; **over — and ears in debt,** indebitato fino ai capelli; **to come to a —,** raggiungere il colmo, (*Med.*) suppurare; **let's lay our heads together,** intendiamoci; **the music runs in my —,** la musica mi torna sempre a mente; **to take it into one's —,** mettersi in testa; **to trouble one's — about,** inquietarsi per, rompersi il capo per; **off one's —,** fuori di sè; **out of one's own —,** di propria testa; **to keep one's —,** non perder la testa, tener la testa a posto; **to talk a person's — off,** romper la testa a; **to make — against,** avanzare contro; **to win by a —,** vincere per una testa; **to run one's — against,** dar di testa contro, picchiar la testa; **to — off,** stornare, deviare; **—-band,** benda, *f.*; **—-dress,** acconciatura, *f.*; (*Motor.*) **—-light,** faro, fanale, *m.*; **—-line,** intestazione, intitolazione, *f.*; **—-man,** capo, *m.*; **—-piece,** elmo, *m.*, (*Print.*) testata, *f.*; **—-phone,** cuffia, *f.*, microfono, *m.*; **—-rest,** poggiacapo, *m.*; **—-stall,** testiera, cavezza, *f.*; (*Naut.*) **—wind,** vento di prua, *m.*; **—-work,** lavoro mentale, *m.*; **—-on collision,** urto frontale, *m.*
headache, *n.* Mal di testa, mal di capo, *m.*
headed, *a.* Capeggiato; diretto.
header, *n.* Mattone posto per il taglio, *m.* **To take a —,** tuffarsi a capofitto.
headiness, *n.* Impetuosità, *f.*
heading, *n.* Titolo, *m.*; intestazione, rubrica, *f.*
headland, *n.* Capo, promontorio, *m.*
headless, *a.* Senza testa, senza capo.
headlong, *adv.* A capofitto; precipitatamente. || *a.* Violento, avventato, impetuoso.
headmost [cp. **foremost**].
headquarters, *n.pl.* Quartier generale, *m.*; **— staff,** ufficiali di stato maggiore, *m.pl.*
headship, *n.* Primato, *m.*; autorità suprema, *f.*
headsman, *n.* Boia, *m.*
headstone, *n.* Lapide, *f.* **Head stone,** pietra angolare, *f.*
headstrong, *a.* Ostinato, caparbio, testardo.
headway, *n.* Progresso, cammino, *m.* **To make —,** far strada, progredire.
heady, *a.* (*of wine*) Che dà alla testa, inebriante.
heal [hiːl], *v.t.* Guarire, risanare, sanare; rimediare; *v.i.* guarire, guarirsi, rimettersi; rimarginarsi; (*of wounds*) cicatrizzarsi.
healer, *n.* Risanatore, guaritore, *m.*
healing, *a.* Salutare, curativo, salubre. || *n.* Guarigione, *f.*, risanamento, *m.*
health [helθ], *n.* Salute, sanità, *f.*; (*toast*) brindisi, *m.* **— resort,** stazione climatica, *f.*, luogo di cura, *m.*; **—-officer,** ufficiale sanitario, *m.*; **bill of —,** patente di sanità, *f.*
healthful, *a.* Sano, salubre.
healthfulness, *n.* Sanità, *f.*
healthily, *adv.* Salubremente, salutarmente.
healthiness, *n.* Sanità, salubrità, *f.*
healthy, *a.* Sano, salutare, salubre; igienico; vigoroso, robusto. **To be —,** esser sano.
heap [hiːp], *n.* Mucchio, monte, cumulo, ammasso, *m.*, congerie, catasta, massa, *f.* || *v.t.* Ammucchiare, ammassare, accumulare, accatastare. **To — the measure,** colmare la misura; **to — up,** ammucchiare.
hear [hiəɹ], *v.t.i.* Sentire, udire, intendere; (*to listen*) ascoltare; (*to grant*) esaudire; (*Law*) esaminare; (*to learn*) apprendere; (*news*) ricevere notizie. **Hear! hear!** Bene!, Bravo! **Hear him!** Ascoltatelo! **please — him say his lesson,** favorite fargli ripetere la lezione; **I never heard of such a thing,** non ho mai sentito una cosa simile; **let me — from you,** datemi vostre notizie.
hearer, *n.* Uditore, ascoltatore, *m.*, ascoltatrice, *f.*
hearing, *n.* (*sense of*) Udito, *m.*; udienza, *f.*; (*Law*) esami di testimoni, *m.* **To be hard of —,** essere duro d'orecchio; **he said it in my —,** io lo sentii dirlo; **to get a —,** ottenere

un'udienza; **to give a —,** dare udienza; **within —,** a portata d'orecchio.

hearken [ˈhɑːɹkən], *v.i.* Ascoltare, stare attento.

hearsay [ˈhiəɹsei], *n.* Diceria, *f.*, sentito dire, *m.* **By —,** per sentito dire.

hearse [həːɹs], *n.* Carro funebre, *m.*

heart [hɑːɹt], *n.* Cuore, *m.*; (*fig.*) animo, coraggio, *m.*; centro, mezzo, *m.*; (*of cabbage, etc.*) grumolo, *m.* **At —,** in cuor suo, in fondo; **by —,** a mente; **in one's — of hearts,** nell'intimo del cuore; **to be out of —,** essere scoraggiato; **to break one's —,** spezzare il cuore; **to have at —,** avere a cuore; **to have the — to,** bastare il cuore di; **to keep a good —,** farsi cuore; **to lay to —,** essere molto commosso da, chiudersi in cuore; **tc one's heart's content,** con gioia di cuore, a piacimento; **with all my —,** di tutto cuore; **to set one's — on,** avere il cuore a; **to take — of grace,** farsi cuore; **to take to —,** prendere a cuore, dolersi assai di; **— -break,** crepacuore, *m.*; **— -breaking, — -rending,** straziante; **— -broken,** addolorato, afflitto, straziato; **— -disease,** malattia di cuore, *f.*; **— -sick,** afflitto, abbattuto; **— -sore,** accorato; **— -strings,** fibre del cuore, *f.pl.*; **— -whole,** col cuore libero.

heartache, *n.* Crepacuore, mal di cuore, *m.*, angoscia, *f.*

heartburn, *n.* (*Med.*) Bruciore di stomaco, *m.*

heartburning, *n.* Rancore, risentimento, *m.*

hearten, *v.t.* Incoraggiare, incuorare.

heartfelt, *a.* Profondamente sentito, vivo, sincero, di cuore.

hearth [hɑːɹθ], *n.* Focolare, camino, fuoco, *m.* **— -rug,** tappeto pel focolare, *m.*

hearthstone, *n.* Pietra del focolare, *f.*

heartily, *adv.* Cordialmente, di cuore; con appetito.

heartiness, *n.* Cordialità, sincerità, *f.*

heartless, *a.* Senza cuore, crudele, insensibile.

heartlessness, *n.* Insensibilità, mancanza di cuore, *f.*

hearty, *a.* Cordiale, caloroso, sincero; vigoroso; (*of meals*) abbondante. **A — laugh,** una grossa risata, una risata di cuore, *f.*; **to be a — eater,** mangiare con appetito, essere una buona forchetta; **hale and —,** sano e rubizzo.

heat (1) [hiːt], *n.* Caldo, calore, *m.*; fervore, impeto, ardore, *m.*; afa, *f.*; temperatura, *f.*; (*anger*) collera, *f.*; foga, *f.*; (*of animals*) eccitamento sessuale, *m.* ‖ *v.t.* Scaldare, riscaldare, infiammare; *v.i.* scaldarsi, infiammarsi. **To get into a —,** scaldarsi; **in the — of passion,** a sangue caldo; **— -stroke,** colpo di sole, *m.*; **— -spot,** macchia di calore sulla pelle, *f.*; **— -wave,** *n.* ondata di caldo, *f.*

heat (2), *n.* (*Sport*) Prova, volata, eliminatoria, gara preliminare, *f.* **A dead —,** una corsa alla pari, *f.*

heater, *n.* Scaldatore, riscaldatore, *m.*; scaldabagno, scaldino, scaldapiedi, *m.*; (*for food*) scaldavivande, scaldapiatti, *m.*

heath [hiːθ], *n.* (*Bot.*) Erica, scopa, *f.*; (*land*) brughiera, landa, *f.* (*Zool.*) **— -cock,** gallo di montagna, gallo di brughiera, *m.*

heathen [ˈhiːðən], *n.a.* Pagano, *m.*, pagana, *f.*

heathendom, *n.* Paganità, *f.*

heathenish, *a.* Pagano, paganeggiante.

heathenism, *n.* Paganesimo, *m.*

heather [ˈheðəɹ], *n.* (*Bot.*) Erica, scopa, *f.*

heathery, *a.* Coperto di eriche.

heating [ˈhiːtiŋ], *n.* Riscaldamento, *m.* **Central —,** riscaldamento centrale, *m.*; **— furnace, — apparatus,** calorifero, termosifone, *m.*

heave [hiːv], *n.* Sollevamento, sussulto, *m.*; sforzo, *m.* ‖ *v.t.* Sollevare, elevare; gettare, lanciare; (*Naut.*) issare, virare; *v.i.* sollevarsi, ondulare, palpitare; (*retch*) recere, sentire nausea. **To — a sigh,** sospirare, emettere un sospiro; (*Naut.*) **to — the anchor,** levare l'ancora; **to — in sight,** apparire all'orizzonte, spuntare; (*Naut.*) **to — to,** mettere in panna; **to — down,** carenare.

heaven [ˈhevən], *n.* Cielo, *m.*, cieli, *m.pl.*; paradiso, *m.* **Look to the heavens and see,** considera i cieli e vedi; **— -born,** celeste; **Good heavens!** Dio mio! **For Heaven's sake!** Per amor del cielo!

heavenly, *a.* Celeste, divino. **— -minded,** puro, santo.

heavily [ˈhevili], *adv.* Pesantemente, gravemente; assai, molto; tristemente.

heaviness, *n.* Pesantezza, gravezza, *f.*; (*fig.*) tristezza, malinconia, *f.*; languore, *m.*; gravedine, *f.*

heavy [ˈhevi], *a.* Pesante, grave, carico; (*of the sea*) grosso; noioso, molesto; triste, malinconico; (*of a road*) fangoso; (*expense*) forte, gravoso; (*of eyes*) assopito. **A — task,** un lavoro gravoso, *m.*; (*Sport*) **— -weight,** peso, peso massimo, *m.*; **to lie —,** essere di peso; **— -handed,** goffo, maldestro; **— -headed,** stupido, balordo; **— -hearted,** malinconico, triste; **— -laden,** sovraccaricato; **heavier-than-air machine,** aeroplano, apparecchio più pesante dell'aria, *m.*

hebdomadal [hebˈdɔmədəl], *a.* Ebdomadario.

Hebe [ˈhiːbi], *n.* (*Myth.*) Ebe, *f.*

Hebraic [heˈbreiik], *a.* Ebraico.

Hebraist, *n.* Ebraista, *m.*

Hebrew [ˈhiːbruː], *n.a.* Ebreo, *m.*, ebrea, *f.* **The — language,** l'ebraico, *m.*, la lingua ebraica, *f.*

Hebrides [ˈhebridiːz], *n.pl.* (*Geog.*) Ebridi, *f.pl.*

Hecate [ˈhekəti], *n.* (*Myth.*) Ecate, *f.*

hecatomb [ˈhekətɔm], *n.* Ecatombe, *f.*

heckle [hekl], *v.t.* (*flax*) Pettinare, cardare; (*fig.*) interrompere, rivolgere domande imbarazzanti.

heckler, *n.* Interruttore importuno, *m.*

hectic [ˈhektik], *a.* (*Med.*) Etico, tisico; (*colloq.*) tumultuoso, agitante.

hectogram [ˈhektəgræm], *n.* Ettogrammo, etto, *m.*

hectolitre, *n.* Ettolitro, *m.*

hectometre, *n.* Ettometro, *m.*

Hector [ˈhektəɹ], *n.* Ettore, *m.*

hector, *n.* Millantatore, spaccamonte, bravaccione, *m.* ‖ *v.t.i.* Insolentire, soverchiare, malmenare; fare lo spaccone.

hectoring, *a.* Prepotente.

hedge [hedʒ], *n.* Siepe, *f.*; barriera, protezione, *f.* ‖ *v.t.* Assiepare, circondare d'una siepe; *v.i.* fare siepi; (*fig.*) evadere una domanda, mettersi al coperto, ripararsi. **To — a bet,** scommettere pro e contro; **to — in,**

assiepare, circondare; **— -alehouse,** bettola, *f.*; **— -bill,** ronca, roncola, *f.*; (*Bot.*) **— -hyssop,** graziola, *f.*; **— -school,** scuola all'aperto, *f.*; (*Zool.*) **— -sparrow,** scopaiola, *f.*
hedgehog, *n.* (*Zool.*) Riccio, istrice, *m.*
hedger, *n.* Tagliatore di siepi, *m.*
hedgerow, *n.* Siepe, *f.*
heed [hi:d], *n.* Attenzione, cura, *f.*; precauzione, *f.* || *v.t.* Badare a, dare retta a, prestare attenzione a. **To give —,** fare attenzione, ascoltare, dar retta; **to take —,** badare, stare attento.
heedful, *a.* Attento, accorto, sollecito.
heedfulness, *n.* Attenzione, cura, sollecitudine, vigilanza, *f.*
heedless, *a.* Stordito, disattento, noncurante, negligente, trascurato.
heedlessness, *n.* Disattenzione, sbadataggine, negligenza, *f.*
heel (1) [hi:l], *n.* Calcagno, tallone, *m.*; (*of shoe*) tacco, *m.* || *v.i.* (*Naut.*) sbandarsi; *v.t.* (*shoes*) rattacconare, metter tacchi a. **To be at someone's heels,** essere alle calcagna di qualcuno; **to be down at —,** essere scalcagnato; **head over heels,** sottosopra, a capitombolo; **to turn head over heels,** capovolgersi, fare i capitomboli; **to show a clean pair of heels, to take to one's heels,** battere il tacco, svignarsela; **to tread on someone's heels,** stare ai calcagni di qualcuno; **to turn on one's —,** voltar le spalle, girare sui tacchi; **to lay by the heels,** imprigionare; **— -taps,** goccia di vino in fondo a un bicchiere, *f.*
heel (2), *n.* (*colloq.*) Mascalzone, *m.*
heeling, *n.* Il rifare i tacchi, *m.*
hefty [ˈhefti], *a.* Robusto, vigoroso, gagliardo.
hegemony [heˈgeməni], *n.* Egemonia, *f.*
Hegira [ˈhedʒirə], *n.* (*Hist.*) Egira, *f.*
heifer [ˈhefəɹ], *n.* Giovenca, *f.*
Heigh-ho! [heiˈhou], *inter.* Ahimè!, Ohimè!
height [hait], *n.* Altezza, altitudine, *f.*; altura, cima, *f.*; statura, *f.*; (*fig.*) colmo, apice, *m.* **The — of summer,** il colmo dell'estate, *m.*; **the — of perfection,** l'apice della perfezione, *m.*; **the — of presumption,** il colmo della presunzione, *m.*; **of medium —,** di media statura.
heighten, *v.t.* Innalzare; accrescere, aumentare; (*fig.*) ingrandire, esagerare; esaltare; mettere in rilievo.
heinous [heinəs], *a.* Atroce, nefando, odioso, enorme.
heinously, *adv.* Atrocemente.
heinousness, *n.* Atrocità, odiosità, *f.*
heir [ɛəɹ], *n.* Erede, *m.* (*Law*) **— apparent,** erede diretto, *m.*; **— -at-law,** erede legittimo, *m.*
heiress, *n.* Erede, ereditiera, *f.*
heirless, *a.* Senza eredi.
heirloom, *n.* Oggetto di famiglia, mobile inalienabile, *m.*
heirship, *n.* Eredità, *f.*
Helen [ˈhelen], *n.* Elena, *f.*
heliacal [heˈlaiəkəl], *a.* (*Astron.*) Eliaco.
helianthus [hi:liˈænθəs], *n.* (*Bot.*) Elianto, *m.*
helicopter [ˈhelikɔptəɹ], *n.* (*Aviat.*) Elicottero, *m.*
heliocentric, heliocentrical, *a.* (*Astron.*) Eliocentrico.
heliograph [ˈhi:liougræf], *n.* Eliografo, *m.*
helioscope, *n.* Elioscopio, *m.*
heliotrope, *n.* (*Bot.*) Eliotropio, *m.*
helium [ˈhi:liəm], *n.* Elio, *m.*
helix (*pl.* **helices**) [hi:liks], *n.* Elica, spirale, *f.*; (*Anat.*) elice, *f.*
hell [hel], *n.* Inferno, *m.* **Gambling —,** bisca, *f.*; **— -cat,** furia, strega, *f.*; **— -hound,** diavolo, demonio, *m.*
hellebore [ˈhelibɔ:ɹ], *n.* (*Bot.*) Elleboro, *m.*
Hellene [ˈheli:n], *n.* Elleno, *m.*
Hellenic [helˈenik], *a.* Ellenico
Hellenism, *n.* Ellenismo, *m.*
Hellenist, *n.* Ellenista, *m.*
hellish, *a.* Infernale.
hellishly, *adv.* Infernalmente.
hellishness, *n.* Infernalità, *f.*
Hello! [heˈlou], *inter.* (*Telephone*) Pronti!, Pronto!
helm [helm], *n.* Timone, *m.*; barra del timone, *f.*; (*fig.*) guida, *f.* **Helmsman, man at the —,** timoniere, *m.*
helmet, helm [ˈhelmit, helm], *n.* Elmo, casco, *m.*
helot [ˈhelət], *n.* (*Hist.*) Ilota, *m.*
helotism, *n.* Ilotismo, *m.*
help [help], *n.* Aiuto, soccorso, *m.*, assistenza, *f.*; rimedio, *m.*; domestico, *m.*, domestica, *f.*, servo, *m.*, serva, *f.* || *v.t.* Aiutare, soccorrere, assistere, giovare; (*at table*) servire; rimediare a; (*prevent*) impedire; (*avoid*) evitare. **Help!** Aiuto! **there is no — for it,** non c'è rimedio, non c'è da far niente; **to cry for —,** gridare al soccorso, gridare aiuto; **with the — of,** coll'aiuto di; **she is a great — to me,** essa mi giova assai, mi è di aiuto; **God — you!** Dio vi aiuti! **How can I — it?** Che cosa volete che io faccia?; **I can't — it,** non è colpa mia; **I cannot — thinking,** non posso fare a meno di pensare; **don't be longer than you can —,** fate il più presto possibile; **to — down,** aiutare a scendere; **to — forward,** avanzare; **to — out of a difficulty,** aiutare a trarsi d'impaccio; **to — oneself to,** servirsi di; **So — me God!** Dio è il mio testimonio! **Help yourself!** Servitevi!
helper, *n.* Aiutante, assistente, aiuto, *m.*, aiutatore, *m.*, aiutatrice, *f.*
helpful, *a.* Utile; servizievole, giovevole.
helping, *a.* Utile, soccorrevole. || *n.* (*of food*) Porzione, *f.* **To lend a — hand to,** porgere una mano soccorrevole a.
helpless, *a.* Senz'aiuto, indifeso; debole, impotente, inetto, incapace.
helplessly, *adv.* Debolmente, impotentemente.
helplessness, *n.* Irrimediabilità, incapacità, *f.*
helpmate, helpmeet, *n.* Consorte, *m.f.*, marito, *m.*, moglie, *f.*; socio, *m.*
helter-skelter [ˈheltəɹ ˈskeltəɹ], *adv.* Alla rinfusa, scompigliatamente.
helve [helv], *n.* Manico, *m.*
Helvetian [helˈvi:ʃən], *a.* Elvetico, svizzero.
hem (1) [hem], *n.* Orlo, *m.*, orlatura, bordura, *f.* || *v.t.* Orlare. **To — in,** cingere, circondare, investire.
hem (2), *v.i.* Schiarirsi la voce, tossicchiare; titubare, esitare nel parlare. || *inter.* **Hem!** Ehm!
hematite [hemətait], *n.* Ematite, *f.*
hemicycle [ˈhemisaikl], *n.* Emiciclo, *m.*
hemiplegia, *n.* (*Med.*) Emiplegia, *f.*
hemisphere, *n.* Emisfero, *m.*

hemispheric, hemispherical, *a.* Emisferico.
hemistich ['hemistik], *n.* (*Poet.*) Emistichio, *m.*
hemlock ['hemlɔk], *n.* (*Bot.*) Cicuta, *f.*
hemorrhage ['hemərid ʒ], *n.* Emorragia, *f.*
hemorrhoids ['hemərɔidz], *n.pl.* Emorroidi, *f.pl.*
hemp [hemp], *n.* (*Bot.*) Canapa, *f.* **— -dresser,** canapaio, *m.*; **— -field,** canapaia, *f.*; **— -seed,** canapuccia, *f.*; seme di canapa, *m.*
hempen, *a.* Canapino, di canapa.
hemstitch ['hemstitʃ], *n.* Orlo a giorno, punto d'orlo, *m.* || *v.t.* Orlare a giorno.
hen [hen], *n.* Gallina, chioccia, *f.*; (*of birds in general*) femmina, *f.* **— -coop,** stia, gabbia, *f.*; **— -house,** pollaio, *m.*; **— -roost,** pollaio, posatoio, *m.*; **— -pecked,** bistrattato dalla moglie; **— pheasant,** fagiana, *f.*
hence [hens], *adv.* (*of place*) Di qua; (*of time*) da ora; (*in consequence*) perciò. **A week —,** oggi a otto.
henceforth, henceforward [hens'fɔːɹθ, hens'fɔːɹwəɹd], *adv.* D'ora innanzi, d'ora in avanti, ormai.
henchman ['hentʃmən], *n.* Servo, paggio, *m.*; partigiano, *m.*; accolito, *m.*
hendecagon [hen'dekəgən], *n.* (*Geom.*) Endecagono, *m.*
hendecasyllable [hendekə'siləbl], *n.* (*Poet.*) Endecasillabo, *m.*
henna ['henə], *n.* Ennè, *m.*
hepatic [he'pætik], *a.* (*Anat.*) Epatico.
hepatica, *n.* (*Bot.*) Epatica, *f.*
heptagon ['heptəgən], *n.* (*Geom.*) Ettagono, *m.*
her [həːɹ], *pron.a.* La, lei; le, a lei; il suo, la sua, i suoi, di lei.
herald ['herəld], *n.* Araldo, *m.*; (*fig.*) precursore, foriere, *m.* || *v.t.* Annunziare, proclamare.
heraldic, *a.* Araldico.
heraldry, *n.* Araldica, *f.*
herb [həːɹb], *n.* Erba, *f.* **Pot-herbs,** erbaggi, ortaggi, *m.pl.*; **sweet herbs,** erbe aromatiche, *f.pl.*
herbaceous [həɹ'beiʃəs], *a.* Erbaceo. **— border,** aiuola, *f.*; bordura di fiori vivaci, *f.*
herbage ['həːɹbidʒ], *n.* Erbaggio, *m.*; pastura, *f.*
herbal, *n.* Erbario, *m.*; elenco di erbe medicinali, *m.* || *a.* Erbario.
herbalist, *n.* Erbaiuolo, erbalista, *m.*
herbarium (*pl.* **herbaria**) [həɹ'bɛəɹiəm], *n.* Erbario, *m.*
herbivorous [həɹ'bivərəs], *a.* Erbivoro. **A — animal,** un erbivoro, *m.*
herborization, *n.* Erborazione, *f.*
herborize, *v.t.* Erborare, erborizzare.
herby, *a.* Erboso.
Herculaneum [həɹkjuː'leiniəm], *n.* (*Geog.*) Ercolano, *m.*
Herculean [həɹ'kjuːliən], *a.* Erculeo.
Hercules ['həːɹkjuːliːz], *n.* (*Myth.*) Ercole, *m.*
herd [həːɹd], *n.* Gregge, *m.*; mandra, *f.* || *v.t.* Custodire; *v.i.* far gregge, attrupparsi. **The common —,** il volgo, il gregge del popolo, *m.*, la plebe, *f.*; **the — instinct,** il sentimento gregario, *m.*; **to — together,** mescolarsi, vivere in gregge.
herdsman, herd, *n.* Pastore, mandriano, *m.*
here [hiəɹ], *adv.* Qui, ci, qua, di qui, di qua. **Here!** Presente! **— and there,** qua e là; **— below,** quaggiù; **— he comes,** eccolo che viene; **Here's to you!** Alla vostra salute! **— they are,** eccoli; **I am —,** eccomi; **neither — nor there,** di poca importanza; **Look —!** Bada qui! **Here goes!** Pronti!, Incominciamo!
hereabout, hereabouts, *adv.* Qui vicino, qui presso.
hereafter, *adv.* Nell'avvenire, nel futuro; nel mondo di là || *n.* L'al di là, l'altro mondo, *m.*
hereat, *adv.* A questo, a ciò.
hereby, *adv.* Per questo mezzo; con la presente.
hereditable [he'reditəbl], *a.* Ereditabile.
hereditament [here'ditəmənt], *n.* (*Law*) Proprietà ereditabile, *f.*
hereditary [he'reditəri], *a.* Ereditario.
heredity, *n.* Eredità, *f.*
herein, *adv.* Qui, in questo.
hereinafter, *adv.* D'ora innanzi.
hereof, *adv.* Di questo, di ciò.
heresiarch [he'riːziaːɹk], *n.* Eresiarca, *m.*
heresy ['herisi], *n.* Eresia, *f.*
heretic, *n.* Eretico, *m.*
heretical, *a.* Eretico, ereticale.
hereto, *adv.* Fino ad ora, fin qui.
heretofore, *adv.* In altri tempi, fin qui.
hereupon, *adv.* Con ciò, su ciò.
herewith, *adv.* Qui accluso; con ciò, con questo.
hereunder, *adv.* (*at foot of page*) Qui in calce.
heritable ['heritəbl], *a.* Ereditario.
heritage ['heritidʒ], *n.* Eredità, *f.*; (*fig.*) retaggio, *m.*
heritor, *n.* Erede, *m.*
hermaphrodite [həɹ'mæfroudait], *n.* Ermafrodito, *m.*
hermaphroditism, *n.* Ermafrodismo, *m.*
hermeneutic [həɹmen'juːtik], *a.* Ermeneutico.
hermeneutics, *n.pl.* Ermeneutica, *f.*
hermetic [həɹ'metik], *a.* Ermetico.
hermetically, *adv.* Ermeticamente.
hermit ['həːɹmit], *n.* Eremita, romito, *m.* (*Zool.*) **— -crab,** paguro, *m.*
hermitage, *n.* Eremitaggio, romitorio, *m.*
hernia ['həːɹniə], *n.* (*Med.*) Ernia, *f.*
hero [hiərou], *n.* Eroe, *m.*; (*Theat.*) protagonista, *m.* **— -worship,** culto degli eroi, *m.*
Herod ['herəd], *n.* (*Hist.*) Erode, *m.*
Herodias [he'roudiəs], *n.* (*Hist.*) Erodiade, *f.*
heroic, heroical [he'rouik, he'rouikl], *a.* Eroico. **Heroics,** *n.pl.* Eroismo vanaglorioso, *m.*
heroicomic [heroui'kɔmik], *a.* (*Lit.*) Eroicomico.
heroin ['herouin], *n.* Eroina, *f.* (un narcotico).
heroine ['herouin], *n.* Eroina, *f.*
heroism, *n.* Eroismo, *m.*
heron, hern ['herən], *n.* (*Zool.*) Airone, *m.*
heronry, *n.* Nidiata di aironi, *f.*
herpes ['həːɹpiːz], *n.* (*Med.*) Erpete, *m.*
herpetology [həːɹpe'tɔlədʒi], *n.* Erpetologia, *f.*
herring ['heriŋ], *n.* (*Zool.*) Aringa, *f.* **Red —,** aringa affumicata, *f.*, (*fig.*) traccia falsa, *f.*; **— -boat,** barca da pesca per le aringhe, *f.*; **— -bone,** (*stitch*) punto incrociato, *m.*
hers [həːɹz], *pron.* Il suo, la sua, i suoi, le sue; di lei. **A book of —,** uno dei suoi libri.
herself, *pron.* Ella stessa, essa medesima, sè, sè stessa. **All by —,** tutta sola; **she did it by —,** l'ha fatto da sè; **she has hurt —,** si è fatta male.

hesitancy, hesitation [ˈhezitənsi, heziˈteiʃən], *n.* Esitazione, *f.*
hesitate, *v.i.* Esitare; essere incerto; titubare.
hesitating, *a.* Esitante.
Hesse [ˈhesi], *n.* (*Geog.*) Assia, *f.*
heteroclite [ˈhetərouklait], *a.* (*Gram.*) Eteroclito.
heterodox [ˈhetəroudɔks], *a.* Eterodosso.
heterodoxy, *n.* Eterodossia, *f.*
heterogeneity, heterogeneousness [hetərodʒiːniəti, hetəroˈdʒiːniəsnəs], *n.* Eterogeneità, *f.*
heterogeneous, *a.* Eterogeneo.
hetman [ˈhetmæn], *n.* Etmano, *m.*
hew [hjuː], *v.t.* Tagliare, spaccare, fendere. **To — wood,** spaccare la legna; **to — down,** abbattere.
hewer, *n.* Tagliatore, spaccalegna, taglialegna, *m.* **Hewers of wood and drawers of water,** spaccalegna e acquaioli, *m.pl.*
hewing, *n.* Taglio, spaccamento, *m.*
hexachord [ˈheksəkɔːɹd], *n.* Esacordo, *m.*
hexagon [ˈheksəgən], *n.* Esagono, *m.*
hexagonal, *a.* Esagonale.
hexameter [heksˈæmitəɹ], *n.* Esametro, *m.*
hey! [hei], **hi!** [hai], *inter.* Olà!, Ohi là!
heyday [ˈheidei], *n.* Bei giorni, *m.pl.*; (*fig.*) primavera, *f.*, fiore, mattino, *m.* **The — of youth,** il mattino della vita, *m.*, i bei giorni di gioventù, *m.pl.*
hiatus [haiˈeitəs], *n.* Iato, *m.*; (*fig.*) lacuna, *f.*
hibernate [ˈhaibəɹneit], *v.i.* Svernare, passare l'inverno in letargo.
hibernation, *n.* Ibernazione, *f.*
Hibernian [haiˈbəːɹniən], *n.a.* Irlandese, *m.*
hibiscus [hiˈbiskəs], *n.* (*Bot.*) Ibisco, *m.*
hiccough, hiccup [ˈhikʌp], *n.* Singhiozzo, singulto, *m.* || *v.i.* Avere il singulto.
hickory [ˈhikəri], *n.* (*Bot.*) Noce bianco americano, *m.*
hidden [ˈhidən], *a.* Nascosto, celato; (*fig.*) segreto, occulto.
hide (1) [haid], *v.t.* Nascondere, celare; *v.i.* nascondersi, celarsi. **— and seek,** rimpiattino, *m.*, rimpiatterello, *m.*
hide (2), *n.* Pelle, *f.*, pellame, cuoio, *m.* **—-bound,** di mente ristretta, gretto.
hideous [ˈhidiəs], *a.* Brutto, orrendo, laido, ripulsivo.
hideousness, *n.* Bruttezza, *f.*, orrore, *m.*
hiding [ˈhaidiŋ], *n.* Nascondimento, *m.*; (*colloq.*) bastonatura, *f.*, legnate, *f.pl.* **To give someone a good —,** dare un fracco di legnate a qualcuno.
hiding-place [ˈhaidiŋ pleis], *n.* Nascondiglio, *m.*
hie [hai], *v.i.* Affrettarsi, spicciarsi.
hierarch [ˈhairɑːɹk], *n.* Gerarca, *m.*
hierarchic, hierarchical, *a.* Gerarchico.
hierarchy, *n.* Gerarchia, *f.*
hieratic [haiəˈrætik], *a.* Ieratico.
hieroglyph [ˈhairouglif], *n.* Geroglifico, *m.*
hieroglyphic, hieroglyphical, *n.a.* Geroglifico, *m.*
hierophant, *n.* Gerofante, *m.*
higgle [higl], *v.i.* Lesinare sul prezzo [cp. **haggle**].
higgledy-piggledy [ˈhigldi ˈpigldi], *adv.* Alla rinfusa, a catafascio.
high [hai], *a.* Alto, elevato, superiore; (*fig.*) grande, sublime; fiero, orgoglioso; eminente; forte, violento; (*of price*) caro; (*of meat, etc.*) passato, frollo; (*colloq.*) brillo. || *adv.* In alto; molto, forte, fortemente. **On —,** in alto; **— and dry,** a secco, in secco; **— and low,** gente di ogni condizione, *f.*; **— life,** gran vita, *f.*, gran mondo, *m.*; **— noon,** pieno mezzogiorno, *m.*; **High Mass,** messa alta, *f.*; **—-road,** strada maestra, via maestra, *f.*; **— street,** via principale, *f.*; **— water,** alta marea, *f.*; **—-water mark,** limite d'alta marea, *m.*; **— and mighty,** arrogante; **four feet —,** alto quattro piedi; **the Most High,** l'Altissimo, *m.*; **it is — time to go,** è ormai tempo di andare; **to rule with a — hand,** tiranneggiare; **to play —,** giocare forte; **the sea runs —,** il mare è grosso; **to aim —,** mirare all'alto; **—-born,** d'alto lignaggio; **—-class,** di prim'ordine; **—-coloured,** di colore vivo; **— dive,** tuffo da una grande altezza, *m.*; **—-flier,** (*fig.*) ambizioso, *m.*; **—-flown,** ampolloso, gonfio, turgido; (*Elect.*) **— frequency,** alta frequenza, *f.*; (*Motor.*) **— gear,** quarta velocità, presa diretta, *f.*; **— jump,** salto in altezza, *m.*; **—-mettled,** focoso, ardente, veemente; **—-minded,** magnanimo, nobile, di mente elevata; **—-mindedness,** magnanimità, *f.*; **—-pressure,** ad alta pressione; **— priest,** arciprete, *m.*; **— seas,** alto mare, *m.*; **—-sounding,** pomposo, altisonante; **—-speed,** rapidissimo, velocissimo; **at — speed,** a gran velocità; **—-spirited,** coraggioso, animoso, ardito; **— treason,** alto tradimento, *m.*, lesa maestà, *f.*; (*colloq.*) **— brow,** saccentone, l'intellettuale, *m.f.*
higher, *a.* Più alto, più elevato, superiore. **A — class,** una classe superiore, *f.*; **— education,** insegnamento superiore, *m.*; **— mathematics,** matematica superiore, *f.*
highest, *a.* Il più alto, il più elevato, altissimo, massimo. **The — bidder,** il miglior offerente, *m.*
highlander, *n.* Montanaro, *m.*
highlands, *n.pl.* Le montagne, *f.pl.*, paese montagnoso, *m.* **The Highlands,** la parte nord-occidentale della Scozia, *f.*
highlights, *n.pl.* (*Art*) Lumi, lumeggiamenti, *m.pl.*; (*fig.*) punti salienti.
highly, *adv.* Altamente, caldamente, vivamente; molto, forte, bene. **— recommended,** caldamente raccomandato; **— coloured,** (*fig.*) dipinto di colori smaglianti; **to speak — of,** parlar bene di; **— strung,** eccitabile.
highness, *n.* Altezza, *f.*; elevatezza, *f.* **His Highness,** Sua Altezza, *f.*
hight [hait], *a.* (*obs.*) Chiamato.
highway, *n.* Via maestra, strada pubblica, *f.* **— code,** codice stradale, *m.*; **— robbery,** grassazione, *f.*
highwayman, *n.* Ladrone, bandito, grassatore, *m.*
hike [haik], *v.i.* Far un escursione a piedi, vagabondare. **Hitch- —,** viaggiare con l'autostop.
hiker, *n.* Escursionista a piedi, *m.f.*
hilarious [hiˈlɛəriəs], *a.* Ilare.
hilarity [hiˈlæriti], *n.* Ilarità, *f.*
hill [hil], *n.* Collina, *f.*, colle, poggio, *m.*; altura, *f.* **Up — and down dale,** da monte a valle; **up —, down —,** in salita, in discesa.
hilliness, *n.* Montuosità, *f.*

hillock, *n.* Monticello, poggio, *m.*, collinetta, *f.*
hilly, *a.* Montagnoso, montuoso; disuguale, accidentato.
hilt [hilt], *n.* Impugnatura, elsa, *f.* **Up to the —,** fino all'elsa, completamente.
hilum ['hailəm], *n.* (*Bot.*) Ilo, *m.*
him [him], *pron.* Lo, lui; gli; colui; quello.
Himalaya [himə'leijə], *n.* (*Geog.*) Imalaia, *f.*
himself [him'self], *pron.* Sè, sè stesso, egli stesso, egli medesimo. **By —,** da sè; **all by —,** solo soletto, tutto solo.
hind (1) [haind], *n.* (*Zool.*) Daina, cerva, *f.*
hind (2), *n.* (*obs.*) Contadino; bracciante; (*fig.*) zotico, rozzo, *m.*
hind (3), *a.* Posteriore, dietro, di dietro. **— legs,** gambe posteriori, *f.pl.*; **— quarters,** quarti di dietro, *m.pl.*
hinder (1) ['haindəɹ], *a.* Dietro, di dietro.
hinder (2) ['hindəɹ], *v.t.* Impedire, ostacolare, inceppare, impacciare; ritardare. **You are hindering him from working,** voi gli impedite di lavorare.
hinderer, *n.* Impeditore, *m.*
hindmost, hindermost, *n.a.* Ultimo, *m.*
hindrance ['hindrəns], *n.* Impedimento, ostacolo, impaccio, *m.*
Hindu, Hindoo [hin'du:], *n.* Indù, indiano, *m.*
Hindustani [hindu:'stɑ:ni], *n.* Indostano, *m.*
hinge [hindʒ], *n.* Cardine, ganghero, *m.*; perno, *m.* || *v.i.* Imperniarsi, girare su; (*fig.*) dipendere su; *v.t.* incardinare. **To be off the hinges,** essere fuori dai cardini, essere scardinato.
hinged, *a.* Incardinato.
hinny ['hini], *n.* Mulo, muletto, bardotto, *m.* || *v.i.* Nitrire.
hint [hint], *n.* Accenno, cenno, indizio, avvertimento, avviso, *m.*; insinuazione, *f.*; allusione, *f.* || *v.i.* Accennare, alludere; suggerire, insinuare. **To take a —,** intendere a volo; **to — at,** suggerire, insinuare.
hinterland ['hintəɹlənd], *n.* Retroterra, *m.*
hip (1) [hip], *n.* (*Anat.*) Anca, *f.*; fianco, *m.*; (*Arch.*) padiglione, *m.* **— -bath,** semicupo, mezzo bagno, *m.*; **— -bone,** anca, *f.*; **— -joint,** giuntura femorale, *f.*; (*Arch.*) **— -roof,** tetto a padiglione, *m.*
hip (2), *n.* (*Bot.*) Frutto della rosa canina, *m.*
hip, hip, hurrah! [hip hip hu'rɑ:], *inter.* Evviva!
hipped, *a.* Tetro, ipocondriaco, malinconico.
hippic, *a.* Ippico.
hippocampus [hipou'kæmpəs], *n.* (*Zool.*) Ippocampo, cavalluccio marino, *m.*
hippocras ['hipoukræs], *n.* Ippocrasso, *m.*
hippocrene ['hipoukri:n], *n.* (*Myth.*) Ippocrene, *f.*
hippodrome ['hipədroum], *n.* Ippodromo, *m.*
hippopotamus (*pl.* **hippopotami, hippopotamuses**) [hipə'pɔtəməs, hipə'pɔtəmai], *n.* (*Zool.*) Ippopotamo, *m.*
hire ['haiəɹ], *n.* Nolo, noleggio, *m.*; affitto, fitto, *m.*; pigione, *f.* || *v.t.* Noleggiare, dare a nolo, prendere a nolo; affittare; salariare, stipendiare; prezzolare. **For —,** da nolo; **on —,** a nolo; **— -purchase,** vendita a rate, *f.*; **to — out,** dare a nolo.
hired, *a.* Noleggiato, affittato, appigionato. **— ruffians,** sicari prezzolati, *m.pl.*; **— soldiers,** mercenari, *m.pl.*; **— carriage,** carrozza da nolo, vettura da nolo, *f.*
hireling, *n.a.* Mercenario, prezzolato, *m.*
hirer, *n.* Noleggiatore, *m.*, noleggiatrice, *f.*
hiring, *n.* Nolo, noleggiamento, *m.*
hirsute ['hə:ɹsju:t], *a.* Irsuto, ispido, irto, peloso.
his [hiz], *pron.a.* Il suo, la sua, i suoi, le sue; di lui, a lui. **Is this book his or hers?** Questo libro è di lui o di lei?
Hispanic [his'pænik], *a.* Ispanico.
hispid ['hispid], *a.* (*Bot. Zool.*) Ispido.
hiss [his], *v.t.i.* Fischiare, sibilare. || *n.* Fischio, sibilo, *m.* **To — a play,** fischiare una commedia o un dramma.
hissing, *n.* Fischio, sibilo, *m.* || *a.* Fischiante, sibilante.
hist! [hist], *inter.* Zitto! Silenzio!
histology [his'tɔlədʒi], *n.* Istologia, *f.*
histological [histə'lɔdʒikəl], *a.* Istologico.
historian [his'tɔ:riən], *n.* Storico, storiografo, *m.*
historic, historical [his'tɔrik, his'tɔrikəl], *a.* Storico.
historiographer [histɔri'ɔgrəfəɹ], *n.* Storiografo, *m.*
history ['histəri], *n.* Storia, *f.*
histrion ['histriən], *n.* Istrione, *m.*
histrionic [histri'ɔnik], *a.* Istrionico.
hit [hit], *v.t.* Colpire, battere, picchiare, percuotere; ferire; danneggiare; *v.i.* urtarsi contro. || *n.* Colpo, *m.*, botta, percossa, ferita, *f.*; (*fig.*) successo, *m.* **To — it off well with someone,** andar d'accordo con qualcuno; (*fig.*) **to — the nail on the head,** indovinare, azzeccare, imbroccar giusto; (*fig.*) **to — someone hard,** colpire qualcuno nel vivo; **he is hard — by the strike,** ha subito gravi danni per lo sciopero; **to — upon,** trovare, escogitare; **a lucky —,** un colpo di fortuna, un buon colpo, *m.*; **a nasty —,** un frizzo mordace, *m.*, una frecciata, una bottata, *f.*; **to make a —,** fare colpo, avere un buon successo; **— or miss,** checchè avvenga.
hitch (1) [hitʃ], *v.t.i.* Attaccare, legare. || *n.* (*Naut.*) Nodo, groppo, *m.* **To — up,** tirar su; agganciare, strappare. **To — -hike,** viaggiare con l'autostop.
hitch (2), *n.* Ostacolo, intoppo, impedimento, *m.*, difficoltà, *f.* **Without a —,** senza intoppi, senza il minimo guaio, liscio liscio.
hither ['hiðəɹ], *adv.* Qui, qua, di qui, da qua. **— and thither,** qua e là. || *a.* Citeriore; più vicino, più prossimo.
hithermost, *a.* Il più vicino, il più prossimo.
hitherto, *adv.* Fin qui, finora.
hitherward, *adv.* Da questa parte.
hive [haiv], *n.* Alveare, *m.*, arnia, *f.*; sciame, *m.* || *v.t.* Porre in un alveare; *v.i.* vivere in un alveare; vivere insieme.
hives [haivz], *n.* (*Med.*) Specie d'eruzione cutanea, *f.*
ho!, hoa! [hou], *inter.* Oh!, Olà!, Ohè!
hoar [hɔ:ɹ], *a.* Bianco; (*fig.*) canuto. **— -frost,** brina, brinata, *f.*
hoard [hɔ:ɹd], *n.* Ammasso, mucchio, *m.*; gruzzolo, peculio, *m.* || *v.t.* Ammassare, accumulare; economizzare.
hoarder, *n.* Risparmiatore, *m.*, risparmiatrice, *f.*; incettatore, *m.*
hoarding, *n.* Accumulazione, incetta, *f.*, risparmio, *m.*; (*for notices, etc.*) assito per affissi, *m.*

hoariness, *n.* Canizie, bianchezza, *f.*
hoarhound [ˈhɔːɹhaund], *n.* (*Bot.*) Marrubio, *m.* [cp. **horehound**].
hoarse [hɔːɹs], *a.* Rauco, fioco.
hoarseness, *n.* Raucedine, fiocaggine, *f.*
hoary, *a.* Bianco; canuto, incanutto; vecchio.
hoax [houks], *n.* Beffa, burla, canzonatura, *f.*; inganno, *m.*; mistificazione, *f.* ‖ *v.t.* Beffare, canzonare, corbellare.
hoaxer, *n.* Ingannatore, mistificatore, *m.*
hob [hɔb], *n.* Piastra del focolare, *f.*
hobble [hɔbl], *v.i.* Zoppicare, andar zoppo; *v.t.* (*a horse*) impastoiare. ‖ *n.* Zoppicamento, *m.*; imbarazzo, impaccio, *m.*; pastoia, *f.*
hobbledehoy [ˈhɔbldihɔi], *n.* Giovanotto adolescente, goffo, *m.*
hobby [ˈhɔbi], *n.* Passione, mania, *f.*; passatempo favorito, svago; ticchio, pallino; (*Zool.*) falco, *m.*; ronzino, *m.* **His — is stamp-collecting,** la filatelia è il suo svago; **fishing is his —,** la pesca è la sua passione; **—-horse,** cavalluccio di legno, *m.*
hobgoblin [hɔbˈgɔblin], *n.* Folletto, *m.*; spauracchio, *m.*
hobnail [ˈhɔbneil], *n.* Chiodo a capocchia grossa usato per scarpa, *m.*
hobnailed, *a.* Chiodato. **— shoes,** scarpe coi chiodi, *f.pl.*
hobnob [hɔbˈnɔb], *v.i.* Bere insieme, famigliarizzarsi con, dare del tu a.
hobo [ˈhoubou], *n.* Vagabondo, *m.*
Hobson's choice [ˈhɔbsəns tʃɔis], *n.* Scelta forzata, *f.*
hock (1) [hɔk], *n.* Garetto, *m.* ‖ *v.t.* Tagliare i garetti a.
hock (2), *n.* Specie di vino del Reno, *f.*
hockey [ˈhɔki], *n.* Hockey, *m.*; palla al maglio, *f.* **— stick,** bastone da hockey, *m.*; **ice-—,** disco sul ghiaccio, *m.*
hocus [ˈhoukəs], *v.t.* Ingannare; intossicare, fatturare, adulterare. **—-pocus,** gherminella, *f.*, giuoco di prestigio, *m.*
hod [hɔd], *n.* Trogolo, giornello, portatile da calcina, *m.*
hodden-grey [hɔdnˈgrei], *a.* Di lana greggia.
Hodge [hɔdʒ], *n.* Nome dato ad un campagnuolo, *m.*
hodge-podge [cp. **hotch-potch**].
hodman, *n.* Manovale, *m.*
hodometer [hɔˈdɔmitəɹ], *n.* Odometro, *m.*
hoe [hou], *n.* Zappa, marra, *f.* ‖ *v.t.-i.* Zappare.
hoeing, *n.* Zappatura, *f.*
hog [hɔg], *n.* Porco, maiale, *m.* ‖ *v.t.* (*horse's mane*) Tosare; (*colloq.*) ammassare egoisticamente. **—-backed,** inarcato, a schiena d'asino; **—-wash,** lavatura di piatti, *f.*
hoggish [ˈhɔgiʃ], *a.* Porcino; (*fig.*) bestiale, sporco.
hoggishness, *n.* Porcheria, *f.*; ghiottoneria, golosità, *f.*
hogshead [ˈhɔgzhed], *n.* Botte, *f.*
hoist [hɔist], *v.t.* Issare, inalberare; inalzare, sollevare. ‖ *n.* Spinta, *f.*; montacarichi, ascensore, *m.* **To — a flag,** issare una bandiera.
hoisting, *n.* Issamento, alzamento, *m.*
hoity-toity [hɔitiˈtɔiti], *inter.* Oibò!, Vergogna!
hokey-pokey [houkiˈpouki], *n.* Gelato, *m.*
hold [hould], *n.* Presa, stretta, *f.*; appiglio, *m.*; appoggio, sostegno, *m.*; influenza, *f.*, predominio, *m.*; (*Mil.*) rocca, fortezza, *f.*; (*Naut.*) stiva, *f.*; (*Boxing*) presa, *f.* ‖ *v.t.* Tenere, ritenere; trattenere; contenere; capire; occupare, possedere; considerare; tenere per; stimare; *v.i.* rimanere, durare. **To take — of,** afferrare, dar di piglio a; **to have a — on,** far presa su; **to have — of,** avere presa su, avere in pugno; **to let go one's —,** allentare la presa; (*telephone*) **to — the line,** rimanere all' apparecchio, tenere la comunicazione; **to — back,** trattenere, nascondere, esitare; **to — by,** attenersi a; **to — fast,** tenere fermo, tener saldo; **to — forth,** offrire, promettere, parlare, declamare; **to — good,** rimaner vero, essere valido; **to — in,** frenare, impedire; **to — off,** tenere a distanza, tenersi a distanza; **to — on,** star fermo; **to — one's own,** mantenere la propria posizione, tener duro; **to — one's nose,** turarsi il naso; **to — one's tongue,** tacere, star zitto; **to — out,** offrire, promettere, resistere, durare; **to — over,** aggiornare, posporre; **to — up,** sostenere, aggredire, attaccare, fermare per rubare; **to — up to ridicule,** mettere in ridicolo; **to — one's hand,** astenersi; **to — together,** stringersi insieme, stare uniti; **to — with,** approvare, parteggiare per; **the rain holds off,** la pioggia non viene; **Hold on!, Hold hard!** Fermatevi!, Smettetela! **I can't — up any longer,** non posso reggermi più; **—-all,** valigia, sacca, *f.*; **—-up,** furto con violenza, *f.*
holder, *n.* Manico, *m.*, presa, *f.*; fodero, *m.*; guaina, *f.*; reticolo, *m.*; (*Comm.*) portatore, *m.*, portatrice, *f.*; possessore, *m.f.*; (*Sport*) primatista, *m.f.*; latore, *m.* **Paper-—,** portacarte, *m.*; **pen-—,** portapenne, *m.*
holding, *n.* Tenuta, *f.*, podere, *m.* **Small-—,** piccola proprietà, *f.*; **I have holdings in three companies,** io ho azioni in tre società.
hole [houl], *n.* Buco, foro, pertugio, *m.*; buca, apertura, *f.*; caverna, *f.*, antro, *m.*; (*of animals*) tana, *f.*; (*Golf*) buca, *f.* ‖ *v.t.* Bucare, forare; mettere in una buca; (*Golf*) fare entrare nella buca. **To make a — in,** usare molto di, fare un bel vuoto in; **to pick holes in,** criticare, trovare da ridire; **full of holes,** bucato, pieno di buchi; **I'm in a —,** mi trovo in imbarazzo; **with a — in it,** bucato, forato; **—-and-corner,** segreto, nascosto.
holiday [ˈhɔlədi], *n.* Festa, *f.*, giorno festivo, *m.*; vacanza, *f.*, vacanze, *f.pl.*; villeggiatura, *f.* ‖ *a.* Festivo, di festa, di vacanza. **Christmas holidays,** vacanze di Natale, *f.pl.*; **for the holidays,** in vacanza, per le vacanze; **—-camp,** colonia di vacanze, *f.*; **—-resort,** luogo di villeggiatura, *m.*
holily [ˈhoulili], *adv.* Santamente.
holiness, *n.* Santità, *f.* **His Holiness,** Sua Santità, *f.*
Holland (1) [ˈhɔlənd], *n.* (*Geog.*) Olanda, *f.*
holland (2), *n.* Tela d'olanda, olanda, *f.*
hollands, *n.* Gin d'Olanda, ginepro olandese, *m.*
hollo, holloa [həˈlou], *v.i.* Gridare, vociare [cp. **halloo**].
hollow [ˈhɔlou], *a.* Cavo, incavato; vuoto; cupo; (*sound*) sordo; (*fig.*) falso, insincero,

vano. || *n.* Cavo, *m.*, cavità, *f.*; depressione, *f.*; conca, *f.* || *v.t.* Cavare, scavare. **To beat someone —,** sorpassare qualcuno di gran lunga; **a — excuse,** un pretesto insincero, *m.*; **to — out,** incavare, scanalare; **— -eyed,** dagli occhi infossati.

hollowness, *n.* Cavo, *m.*; (*fig.*) falsità, insincerità, *f.*

holly ['hɔli], *n.* (*Bot.*) Agrifoglio, *m.*

hollyhock ['hɔlihɔk], *n.* (*Bot.*) Malvarosa, alcea, *f.*

holm [houm], *n.* Isoletta di fiume, golena, *f.*

holm-oak, *n.* (*Bot.*) Leccio, *m.*

holocaust ['hɔləkɔ:st], *n.* Olocausto, *m.*

holograph ['hɔləgræf], *n.* Olografo, *m.*

holothurian [holə'θju:riən], *n.* (*Zool.*) Oloturia, *f.*

holster ['houlstəɹ], *n.* Fonda, fondina, *f.*

holy ['houli], *a.* Santo, sacro, benedetto, consecrato. **— of holies,** santo dei santi, *m.*; **the Holy Ghost,** lo Spirito Santo, *m.*; **the Holy Land,** la Terra Santa, *f.*; **— water,** acqua benedetta, acqua santa, *f.*; **Holy Week,** la settimana santa, *f.*; **— writ,** le sacre scritture, *f.pl.*; **— orders,** ordini sacri, *m.pl.*

homage ['hɔmidʒ], *n.* Omaggio, ossequio, *m.* **To pay — to,** rendere omaggio a.

home [houm], *n.* Casa, dimora, *f.*, domicilio, *m.*; focolare domestico, *m.*; patria, *f.*; asilo, *m.* || *a.* Casalingo, domestico; nostrano, indigeno, interno, nazionale. || *adv.* A casa, nel suo paese; (*fig.*) direttamente. **At —,** a casa; **away from —,** lontano da casa; **to come —,** tornare a casa; (*fig.*) **to come — to,** toccare nel vivo; **to feel oneself at —,** sentirsi come a casa propria; **to make oneself at —,** fare come a casa propria; **to set up a — of one's own,** metter su casa; **to bring — to someone,** fare che qualcuno capisca; **to strike —,** colpire nel vivo; **a — truth,** una verità amara, *f.*; **a — thrust,** un colpo nel vivo, *m.*; **Home Office,** ministero dell'interno, *m.*; (*Pol.*) **— rule,** autonomia, *f.*; **one's long —,** la tomba, *f.*; **— -bred,** domestico, del paese; **— -brewed,** fatto in casa; **— -coming,** ritorno a casa, *m.*; **— -grown,** nostrano; **— -made,** casalingo, di produzione nazionale; **— -made bread,** pane casalingo, *m.*; **— -made frock,** veste casalinga, *f.*

homeless, *a.* Senza casa, senza tetto.

homelike, *a.* Comodo, intimo.

homeliness, *n.* Semplicità, *f.*; bruttezza, *f.*

homely, *a.* Semplice; bruttino.

Homer ['houməɹ], *n.* Omero, *m.*

homeric [hou'merik], *a.* Omerico.

homesick, *a.* Nostalgico.

homesickness, *n.* Nostalgia, *f.*

homespun, *a.* Fatto in casa, casalingo; semplice.

homestead, *n.* Cascina, casa colonica, masseria, *f.*

homeward, homewards ['houmwəd, 'houmwədz], *adv.* Verso casa, verso il proprio paese. **Homeward bound,** in viaggio di ritorno.

homicidal [hɔmi'saidəl], *a.* Micidiale.

homicide ['hɔmisaid], *n.* (*crime*) Omicidio, *m.*; (*person*) omicida, *m.f.*

homily ['hɔmili], *n.* Omelia, *f.*; sermoncino, predicozzo, *m.*

homing pigeon, homer [houmiŋ 'pidʒən, 'houməɹ], *n.* Colombo messagero, piccione viaggiatore, *m.*

homœopath, homœopathist ['houmiəpæθ, houmi'ɔpəθist], *n.* Omeopatista, *m.f.*, medico omeopatico, *m.*

homœopathic, *a.* Omeopatico.

homœopathy [homi'ɔpəθi], *n.* Omeopatia, *f.*

homogeneity, homogeneousness [hougə'ni:iti, houmou'dʒi:niəsnis], *n.* Omogeneità, *f.*

homogeneous [houmou'dʒi:niəs], *a.* Omogeneo.

homologate [hɔ'mɔlougeit], *v.t.* Omologare.

homologation, *n.* Omologazione, *f.*

homologous [hɔ'mɔləgəs], *a.* Omologo.

homonym ['hɔmɔnim], *n.* Omonimo, *m.*

homonymous [hɔ'mɔniməs], *a.* Omonimo.

homonymy, *n.* Omonimia, *f.*

homosexual [hɔmou'sekʃu:əl], *a.* Omosessuale.

homosexuality [hɔmousekʃu:'æliti], *n.* Omosessualità, *f.*

homunculus [hɔ'mʌŋkju:ləs], *n.* Omuncolo, omicciattolo, *m.*

hone [houn], *n.* Cote, *f.* || *v.t.* Affilare con cote.

honest ['ɔnest], *a.* Onesto, probo, integro, leale; dabbene, di buona fede, sincero. **An — man,** un galantuomo, *m.*

honesty, *n.* Onestà, probità, buona fede, sincerità, *f.*; (*Bot.*) lunaria, *f.* **Tried —,** onestà a tutta prova.

honey ['hʌni], *n.* Miele, *m.*; (*colloq.*) carino, *m.*, carina, *f.* **— -bee,** pecchia, ape operaia, ape domestica, *f.*; **— -mouthed,** mellifluo; (*Zool.*) **— -buzzard,** falco pecchiaiolo, *m.*; (*Bot.*) **— -dew,** melata, *f.*

honeycomb ['hʌnikoum], *n.* Favo, *m.* || *v.t.* Crivellare.

honeycombed, *a.* Bucherellato, reticolato.

honeyed ['hʌnid], *a.* Dolce, melato; mellifluo, lusinghiero.

honeymoon ['hʌnimu:n], *n.* Luna di miele, *f.*

honeysuckle ['hʌnisʌkl], *n.* (*Bot.*) Caprifoglio, *m.*

honorarium (*pl.* **honorariums, honoraria**) [ɔnə'rɛəriəm, ɔnə'rɛəriə], *n.* Onorario, *m.*

honorary ['ɔnərəri], *a.* Onorario, onorifico, senza stipendio.

honour ['ɔnəɹ], *n.* Onore, pregio, *m.*; dignità, *f.*; stima, *f.*; onorificenza, *f.* || *v.t.* Onorare, fare onore a, venerare; festeggiare; (*Comm.*) accettare. **On my —,** parola d'onore; **to swear on one's —,** giurare sull'onore; **to do the honours of the house,** fare gli onori di casa; **he got honours in his exams,** ha avuto distinzione negli esami; **he is an — to the profession,** fa onore alla sua professione; **the last honours,** gli estremi onori, *m.pl.*; **to be bound in — to,** essere vincolato dall'onore a; **his — is concerned,** ne va del suo onore; **to come off with —,** cavarsela con onore; **an honours student,** uno studente specializzato in una data materia, *m.*; **— -bright,** parola d'onore, *f.*; (*Comm.*) **to — a bill,** accettare una cambiale.

honourable, *a.* Onorevole, onorando, pregevole; onesto. **Right Honourable,** Onorevole.

honoured, *a.* Onorato, rispettato.

hood [hud], *n.* Cappuccio, *m.*; (*of motor, carriage, etc.*) mantice, soffietto, *m.*, cofano, *m.*

hoodwink ['hudwiŋk], *v.t.* Bendare gli occhi a; ingannare, infinocchiare.
hoof (*pl.* **hoofs**) [hu:f], *n.* Zoccolo, *m.*, unghia, *f.* **To — it,** camminare a piedi.
hoofed, *a.* Unghiato, ungulato.
hook [huk], *n.* Uncino, gancio, *m.*; (*fishing*) amo, *m.*; (*sickle*) falcetto; (*Boxing*) hook, *m.* || *v.t.* Uncinare; agganciare; prendere all'amo. **— and eye,** gancio ad occhio, *m.*; **by — or by crook,** con le buone o le cattive, di riffa o di raffa; (*colloq.*) **on one's own —,** per conto proprio; (*colloq.*) **to — it,** svignarsela; **to — on to,** unirsi a, attaccarsi a; **— -nosed,** dal naso aquilino.
hookah ['huːkɑː], *n.* Pipa turca, *f.*, narghilè, *m.*
hooked, *a.* Uncinato; curvato; (*of nose*) aquilino.
hooker, *n.* (*Naut.*) Battello da pesca, *m.*
hooligan ['huːligən], *n.* Predone, giovinastro, teppista, facinoroso, *m.*
hoop [hu:p], *n.* Cerchio, cerchione, anello, *m.*, reggetta, *f.*; (*skirt*) guardinfante, *m.*, crinolina, *f.* || *v.t.* Cerchiare; circondare. **To bowl a —,** giuocare al cerchio.
hooping-cough ['huːpiŋkɔf], *n.* (*Med.*) Tosse canina, ipertosse, *f.*
hoopoe ['huːpou], *n.* (*Zool.*) Upupa, *f.*
hoot [hu:t], *v.i.* Gridare; (*of owls*) ululare; (*Motor.*) suonare il clacson; *v.t.* fischiare, gridare dietro. || *n.* Urlo, fischio. **I don't care a —,** non m'importa niente.
hooter, *n.* Tromba, *f.*; (*Motor.*) clacson, *m.*
hooting, *n.* Fischiata, *f.*; strombettio, *m.*
hop (1) [hɔp], *n.* Salto, salterello, *m.*; salto su una gamba, *m.*; danza, *f.* || *v.i.* Saltellare, salterellare; ballare.
hop (2), *n.* (*Bot.*) Luppolo, *m.* || *v.i.* Raccogliere luppoli. **— -field,** luppoliera, *f.*; **— -picking,** raccolta dei luppoli, *f.*; **— -pole,** pertica da luppolo, *f.*
hope [houp], *n.* Speranza, speme, *f.* || *v.t.i.* Sperare, confidare, aspettare, aver fiducia. **I am in hopes that,** nutro la speranza che; **to live in —,** vivere di speranza; **I — to see you again shortly,** spero rivedervi fra poco; **I — he will come at once,** spero che venga subito.
hopeful, *a.* Pieno di speranza, speranzoso; promettente; fiducioso. **A — outlook,** una prospettiva promettente, *f.*
hopefully, *adv.* Speranzosamente.
hopefulness, *n.* Buona speranza, *f.*; aspettazione, *f.*
hopeless, *a.* Senza speranza, disperato; irreparabile, irremediabile.
hopelessness, *n.* Disperazione, *f.*
hopper, *n.* Raccoglitore di luppoli, *m.*; (*Mech.*) tramoggia, *f.*
hopscotch ['hɔpskɔtʃ], *n.* Giuoco fanciullesco dove si saltella.
Horace ['hɔrəs], *n.* Orazio, *m.*
horary ['hɔrəri], *a.* Orario.
horde [hɔːɹd], *n.* Orda, moltitudine, *f.*
horehound ['hɔːɹhaund], *n.* (*Bot.*) Marrubio, *m.*
horizon [hə'raizən], *n.* Orizzonte, *m.* **On the —,** all'orizzonte; **the sun is high above the —,** il sole è alto sull'orizzonte.
horizontal [hɔri'zɔntəl], *a.* Orizzontale.
horn [hɔːɹn], *n.* Corno, *m.*; (*Motor.*) tromba, *f.*; (*Mus.*) corno, *m.*; (*gramophone*) braccio acustico, *m.* || *a.* Di corno, corneo. **— of plenty,** cornucopia, *f.*; **to blow the —,** suonare il corno; **to sound the (motor) —,** strombettare; **to draw in one's horns,** ritirare le corna; **the horns of a deer,** la cornatura d'un daino, *f.*
hornbeam, *n.* (*Bot.*) Carpino, *m.*
hornbill, *n.* (*Zool.*) Bucero, *m.*
hornbook, *n.* Abbecedario, *m.*
horned, *a.* Cornuto, cornifero. **— cattle,** grosso bestiame, *m.*; **— owl,** gufo, *m.*
hornet, *n.* (*Zool.*) Calabrone, *m.* (*fig.*) **Hornets' nest,** vespaio, *m.*
hornpipe ['hɔːɹnpaip], *n.* (*Mus.*) Cornamusa, *f.*; specie di danza, *f.*
hornstone, *n.* (*Min.*) Selce cornea, *f.*
horny, *a.* Corneo, calloso, indurito. **— -handed,** dalle mani callose.
horology [hɔ'rɔlədʒi], *n.* Orologeria, *f.*
horoscope ['hɔrəskoup], *n.* Oroscopo, *m.*
horrible ['hɔribl], *a.* Orribile, orrendo, spaventevole.
horribleness, *n.* Orribilità, atrocità, *f.*
horribly, *adv.* Orribilmente; (*colloq.*) molto.
horrid, *a.* Orrido, spaventoso; (*colloq.*) antipatico.
horridness, *n.* Orrore, *m.*, orribilità, *f.*
horror, *n.* Orrore, spavento, *m.* **To have a — of,** avere in orrore, sentire orrore di; **the horrors,** delirio alcoolico, *m.*
hors-d'œuvre [ɔːdəːvr], *n.* Antipasto, *m.*
horse [hɔːɹs], *n.* Cavallo, *m.*; cavalli, *m.pl.*; (*trestle*) cavalletto, *m.* || *v.t.* Fornire di un cavallo. **Led —,** cavallo condotto a mano, *m.*; (*fig.*) **to ride the high —,** darsi aria d'importanza, essere prepotente; **to work like a —,** lavorare come un cane; (*Mil.*) **light —,** cavalleria leggiera, *f.*; (*Mil.*) **— -artillery,** artiglieria a cavallo, *f.*; (*Bot.*) **— -bean,** specie di fava per cavalli, *f.*; **— -block,** montatoio, cavalcatoio, *m.*; **— -box,** cassone, vagone per trasporto dei cavalli, *m.*; **— -boy,** garzone di stalla, mozzo di stalla, *m.*; **— -breaker,** scozzone, domatore, *m.*; **— -chestnut,** ippocastano, castagno d'India, *m.*; **— -cloth,** gualdrappa, groppiera, *f.*; **— -dealer, — -coper,** sensale di cavalli, cavallaro, *m.*; **— -doctor,** veterinario, *m.*; **— -fair,** fiera di cavalli, *f.*; **— -flesh,** carne di cavallo, *f.*; **— -box,** vagone scuderia, cassone, *m.*; **— -fly,** tafano, *m.*; **— -laugh,** riso sgangherato, *m.*, risataccia, *f.*; **— -leech,** veterinario, *m.*; mignatta del cavallo, *f.*; **— -pistol,** pistola da sella, *f.*; **— -race,** corsa dei cavalli, corsa ippica, *f.*, concorso ippico, *m.*; **— -radish,** rafano, *m.*; **— -sense,** buon senso, *m.*; **— -show,** mostra equina, *f.*; **— -soldier,** cavalleggero, *m.*; (*Bot.*) **— -tail,** coda di cavallo, *f.*
horseback, *adv.* A cavallo. **To ride on —,** cavalcare, andare a cavallo; **to get on —,** montare a cavallo.
horsehair, *n.* Crine, *m.*
horseman (*pl.* **horsemen**), *n.* Cavaliere, cavallerizzo, cavalcatore, *m.* **To be a good —,** essere un buon cavallerizzo.
horsemanship, *n.* Equitazione, cavallerizza, *f.*
horseplay, *n.* Scherzi rozzi, giuochi di mano, *m.pl.*
horsepower, *n.* Cavallo vapore, cavallo motore, *m.* (*Motor.*) **A 10-h.p. car,** un'auto a dieci cavalli, *m.*

horseshoe, *n.* Ferro di cavallo, *m.* || *a.* A ferro di cavallo.
horsewhip, *n.* Sferza, frusta, *f.*, staffile, frustino, *m.* || *v.t.* Sferzare, frustare, staffilare.
horsewoman, *n.* Cavalcatrice, amazzone, *f.*
horsy, *a.* Di cavallo, amatore di cavalli.
hortatory [ˈhɔːɹtətəri], *a.* Esortatorio.
horticultural [hɔːɹtiˈkʌltjuːrəl], *a.* D'orticoltura.
horticulture [ˈhɔːɹtikʌltʃəɹ], *n.* Orticoltura, *f.*
horticulturist, *n.* Orticoltore, *m.*
Hosanna [houˈzænə], *n.* Osanna, *m.*
hose (1) [houz], *n.pl.* Calze, calzette, *f.pl.*; calzeria, *f.*
hose (2) (*pl.* **hoses**), *n.* Tubo di gomma, tubo flessibile, *m.*, manica, *f.*
hosier [ˈhouʒəɹ], *n.* Calzettaio, *m.*
hosiery [ˈhouʒəri], *n.* Maglieria, calzeria, *f.*
hospice [ˈhɔspis], *n.* Ospizio, *m.*
hospitable [ˈhɔspitəbl], *a.* Ospitale.
hospitably, *adv.* Ospitalmente.
hospital, *n.* Ospedale, *m.* **— nurse, — attendant,** infermiere, *m.*, infermiera, *f.*; **— service,** servizio ospitaliere, *m.*; **— -ship,** nave ospedale, *f.*; **— -train,** treno ospedale, *m.*
hospitality, *n.* Ospitalità, *f.*
host (1) [houst], *n.* Ospite, *m.*; (*of inn, etc.*) oste, *m.*
host (2), *n.* Oste, *f.*, esercito, *m.*; folla, moltitudine, *f.*
Host (3), *n.* (*Eccles.*) Ostia, *f.*
hostage [ˈhɔstidʒ], *n.* Ostaggio, *m.*
hostel [ˈhɔstəl], *n.* Pensione, casa, *f.*, ospizio, ostello, *m.* **University —,** casa degli studenti, *f.*
hostelry, *n.* Albergo, *m.*, osteria, *f.*
hostess, *n.* Ospite, ostessa, *f.*; (*Aviat.*) hostess, *f.*
hostile [ˈhɔstail], *a.* Ostile, nemico; contrario, avverso.
hostility [hɔsˈtiliti], *n.* Ostilità, inimicizia, *f.*
hostler, *n.* Stalliere, *m.*
hot [hɔt], *a.* Caldo, ardente; rovente, bruciante, infuocato; (*to taste*) piccante; (*fig.*) fervido, caloroso, impetuoso. **All —,** caldo caldo; **boiling —,** bollente; **to be burning —,** bruciare; **to be —, to feel —,** aver caldo; **to get —,** scaldarsi, riscaldarsi; **to make —,** scaldare; **to make it — for,** dare filo da torcere a; **in — haste,** in fretta e furia; **— -blooded,** ardente, impetuoso; **— -headed,** focoso, eccitabile; **— -house,** serra, *f.*; **— -spring,** sorgente termale, *f.*; **— -water bottle,** borsa dell'acqua calda, *f.*
hotbed, *n.* Concimaio, *m.*; (*fig.*) covo, fomite, *m.* **— of vice,** fomite di vizio, *m.*
hotchpotch [ˈhɔtʃpɔtʃ], *n.* (*Cooking*) Carne in umido con legumi, *m.*; (*fig.*) miscuglio, guazzabuglio, *m.*
hotel [houˈtel], *n.* Albergo, *m.* **— -keeper,** albergatore, *m.*, albergatrice, *f.*
hotly, *adv.* Caldamente, vivamente; violentemente.
hotness, *n.* Calore, *m.*
Hottentot [ˈhɔtəntɔt], *n.* Ottentotto, *m.*
hough [hɔk], *n.* Garetto, *m.* || *v.t.* Tagliare i garetti a.
hound [haund], *n.* Cane da caccia, bracco, segugio, *m.*; levriere, *m.* || *v.t.* Cacciare. **A pack of hounds,** una muta di cani, *f.*; **to — on,** incitare, aizzare; **to — out,** cacciar via; (*Bot.*) **hound's-tongue,** cinoglossa, *f.*
hour [auɹ], *n.* Ora, *f.* **An — ago,** un'ora fa; **an — and a quarter,** un'ora e un quarto; **half an —,** mezz'ora; **at the eleventh —,** all'ultimo momento, all'ultima ora; **to keep late hours,** far le ore piccole; **the small hours,** le ore piccole, *f.pl.*; **a question of the —,** una cosa d'attualità, *f.*; **in an evil —,** in una cattiva ora; **by the —,** all'ora; **— -glass,** orologio a polvere, *m.*; (*of clock, etc.*) **— -hand,** lancetta delle ore, *f.*
hourly, *a.* Continuo, che accade ogni ora. || *adv.* D'ora in ora, ogni ora, di continuo.
house (1) [haus], *n.* Casa, *f.*; dimora, abitazione, *f.*; domicilio, *m.*; famiglia, casata, *f.*; (*Pol.*) camera, *f.*; (*Theat.*) teatro, *m.*, sala, *f.* **At one's —,** a casa propria; **from — to —,** di casa in casa; (*Theat.*) **full —,** teatro esaurito, *m.*, sala al completo, *f.*; **public —,** osteria, taverna, bettola, *f.*; **to keep —,** tener casa; **to keep open —,** tener casa aperta; **to move —,** sgombrare, traslocare; **to get on like a — on fire,** far grandi progressi; **a commercial —,** una casa di commercio; **— agent,** agente d'immobili, *m.*; **— -breaker,** (*thief*) scassinatore, ladro, *m.*, (*workman*) demolitore di case vecchie, *m.*; **— -breaking,** (*robbery*) scasso, *m.*; **— -dog,** cane da guardia, *m.*; **— -fly,** mosca domestica, *f.*; **— -leek,** barba di Giove, *f.*, semprevivo, *m.*; **— -martin,** rondinella, *f.*; **— -painter,** imbianchino, verniciatore, *m.*; **— -property,** proprietà immobiliare, *f.*; **—-rent,** pigione, *f.*; **— -room,** spazio in casa, posto in casa, *m.*; **— -sparrow,** passero, *m.*; **— -surgeon,** chirurgo d'ospedale, *m.*; **— -warming,** inaugurazione di residenza in una casa, *f.*
house (2) [hauz], *v.t.* Alloggiare, albergare; ricoverare, ricettare, riporre; (*Mech.*) incassare.
household, *n.* Casa, famiglia, *f.* || *a.* Casalingo, di casa, di famiglia, domestico. **— gods,** penati, *m.pl.*; **— goods,** mobilia, *f.*, mobili di casa, *m.pl.*; **a — word,** una parola comune, *f.*
householder, *n.* Capo di famiglia, *m.*
housekeeper, *n.* Massaia, governante, *f.*
housekeeping, *n.* Faccende di casa, *f.pl.*; gestione della casa, *f.*, andamento di casa, *m.* **To start —,** metter su casa; **good —,** buon governo della casa, *m.*
houseless, *a.* Senza casa, senza tetto.
housemaid, *n.* Cameriera, donna di servizio, domestica, *f.*
housetop, *n.* Tetto, *m.* **To proclaim from the housetops,** predicare sui tetti.
housewife, *n.* Madre di famiglia, massaia, padrona di casa, *f.*
housewifery, *n.* Economia domestica, *f.*
housing [ˈhauziŋ], *n.* Alloggio, *m.*; (*horse-cloth*) gualdrappa, *f.* **The — problem,** la crisi degli alloggi, *f.*
hovel [ˈhɔvəl], *n.* Capanna, bicocca, casupola, *f.*; tugurio, *m.*
hover [ˈhɔvəɹ], *v.i.* Librarsi a volo, sorvolare, volteggiare. **To — over,** librarsi su; **to — about,** bighellonare, aggirarsi intorno a.
how [hau], *adv.* Come, in che modo. **How lovely!** Com'è bello! **How do you do?** Come sta? **How far are you going?** Fin dove andate? **How is it that . . . ?** Come avviene che . . . ? **How long is your garden?** Quanto è lungo il vostro giardino? **How long have**

you been here ? Da quanto tempo siete qui? **How old is he ?** Quanti anni ha?; **the — and the why,** il come e il perchè, il perchè e il percome.

howbeit, *adv.* Nondimeno.

however [hau'evəɹ], *conj.* Pure, nondimeno, tuttavia. || *adv.* In ogni modo, per tanto, comunque, per quanto, come mai. **— late he may come,** per quanto tardi egli venga; **— rich he may be,** per quanto ricco egli sia; **— that may be,** comunque ciò sia; **he, —, has arrived,** egli, tuttavia, è arrivato; **However did you get here ?** Come mai siete venuto qui?

howitzer ['hauitzəɹ], *n.* (*Mil.*) Obice, *m.*

howl [haul], *n.* Urlo, grido, mugolio, *m.*; lamento, *m.* || *v.i.* Urlare, gridare, ululare, mugolare; lamentarsi, gemere.

howler, *n.* Urlatore, *m.*; (*fig.*) sproposito, strafalcione, *m.*; errore grossolano, *m.*

howling, *n.* Ululato, gridio, gemito, mugolio, *m.* || *a.* Urlante.

howsoever, *adv.* In qualunque modo.

hoy (1) [hɔi], *n.* (*Naut.*) Maona, chiatta, *f.*

hoy ! (2) *inter.* Olà!

hoyden ['hɔidən], *n.* Sfacciatella, maschietta chiassona, *f.*

hoydenish, *a.* Sguaiato.

hub [hʌb], *n.* (*of wheel*) Mozzo, *m.*; centro, *m.* **— -brake,** freno sul mozzo, *m.*

hubbub ['hʌbʌb], *n.* Schiamazzo, strepito, tafferuglio, baccano, chiasso, *m.*; baraonda, *f.*

huckaback ['hʌkəbæk], *n.* Tela operata, *f.* **— towel,** salvietta a nido d'api.

huckle [hʌkl], *n.* Anca, *f.* **— -backed,** gobbo.

huckster, *n.* Rivendugliolo, merciaiuolo, *m.*; trafficante, *m.*

huckstering, *n.* Commercio al minuto, *m.*

huddle [hʌdl], *v.t.* Ammucchiare, pasticciare, scompigliare; *v.i.* affollarsi, accalcarsi. || *n.* Folla, calca, *f.*; confusione, *f.* **To — oneself up,** rannicchiarsi; **to — on one's clothes,** infagottarsi.

hue (1) [hju:], *n.* Colore, *m.*, tinta, sfumatura, *f.* **Dark-hued,** di tinta scura, *f.*

hue (2), *n.* **— and cry,** grido di 'Dalli! Dalli!' *m.* **To raise a — and cry after,** gridar la croce addosso a.

huff [hʌf], *n.* Sfuriata, stizza, *f.* || *v.t.i.* Affrontare, offendere; (*at draughts*) buffare, soffiare. **He is in a —,** si è stizzito.

huffily, *adv.* Con sdegno.

huffiness, *n.* Sdegnosità, alterigia, *f.*

huffy, huffish, *a.* Sdegnato, indignato; collerico.

hug [hʌg], *v.t.* Abbracciare, stringere fra le braccia; (*fig.*) nutrire, serbare; (*Naut.*) accostarsi a, rasentare. || *n.* Abbraccio, amplesso, *m.*, stretta, *f.* **To — oneself,** felicitarsi, congratularsi; (*Naut.*) **to — the shore,** serrare la terra; **to — the wind,** serrare il vento, stringere il vento.

huge [hju:dʒ], *a.* Vasto, immenso, enorme, smisurato.

hugely, *adv.* Enormemente.

hugeness, *n.* Vastità, immensità, *f.*

hugger-mugger ['hʌgəɹmʌgər], *n.* Segretezza, *f.*; confusione, *f.* || *a.* Segreto; negligente. || *adv.* Segretamente, di nascosto; negligentemente. **In — fashion,** negligentemente.

Huguenot ['hju:gənɔt], *n.* (*Hist.*) Ugonotto, *m.*

hulk [hʌlk], *n.* (*Naut.*) Scafo, *m.*; carcassa, *f.* **The Hulks,** galera, *f.*, bagno penale, *m.*

hulking, *a.* Grosso, goffo, grossolano. **A great — fellow,** un omaccione, *m.*

hull [hʌl], *n.* (*of peas, etc.*) Guscio, *m.*; (*of nuts*) mallo, *m.*; (*Naut.*) scafo, *m.*, carena, *f.* || *v.t.* Sgusciare; (*Naut.*) cannoneggiare in pieno.

hullabaloo [hʌləbə'lu:], *n.* Baccano, schiamazzo, *m.*

hullo ! [hə'lou], *inter.* Olà!; (*at telephone*) Pronto!

hum [hʌm], *v.t.i.* Cantarellare, borbottare; (*of insects*) ronzare. || *n.* Mormorio, ronzio, *m.* || *inter.* Uhm! **To — and haw,** esitare, titubare; **to make things —,** suscitare le attività.

human ['hju:mən], *n.a.* Umano, *m.* **A — being,** un essere umano, *m.*; **— beings,** gli umani, *m.pl.*

humane [hju:'mein], *a.* Umano, mite, compassionevole, pietoso.

humanist ['hju:mənist], *n.* Umanista, *m.*

humanitarian [hju:məni'tɛəriən], *n.a.* Umanitario, *m.*

humanity [hju:'mæniti], *n.* Umanità, *f.*

humanize, *v.t.* Umanizzare.

humankind, *n.* Umanità, *f.*

humble [hʌmbl], *a.* Umile, dimesso. || *v.t.* Umiliare, avvilire, mortificare. **To eat — pie,** umiliarsi, scusarsi umilmente. **— -bee,** calabrone, *m.*

humbleness, *n.* Umiltà, *f.*

humbly, *adv.* Umilmente.

humbug ['hʌmbʌg], *n.* Inganno, imbroglio, trucco, *m.*; ciurmeria, corbellatura, impostura, *f.*; gabbamondo, ciarlatano, impostore, *m.*; (*sweet*) dolce di menta, *m.* || *v.t.* Ingannare, corbellare, imbrogliare. || *inter.* Fandonie!; Sciocchezze!

humdrum ['hʌmdrʌm], *a.* Monotono, uniforme, meschino, banale. **A — existence,** una vita meschina, *f.*

humeral ['hju:mərəl], *a.* (*Anat.*) Omerale.

humerus, *n.* (*Anat.*) Omero, *m.*

humid ['hju:mid], *a.* Umido.

humidity [hju:'miditi], *n.* Umidità, *f.*

humiliate [hju:'milieit], *v.t.* Umiliare, avvilire.

humiliating, *a.* Umiliante.

humiliation, *n.* Umiliazione, *f.*

humility, *n.* Umiltà, *f.*; sottomissione, *f.*

humming ['hʌmiŋ], *n.* Ronzio, mormorio, rombo, *m.* (*Zool.*) **— -bird,** colibrì, *m.*; **— -top,** trottola sonante, *f.*

hummock ['hʌmək], *n.* Collina, *f.*, poggio, greppo, *m.*

humoral ['hju:mərəl], *a.* (*Med.*) Umorale.

humorist ['hju:mərist], *n.* Umorista, *m.*; persona faceta, *f.*, comico, *m.*

humorous, *a.* Umoristico, spiritoso, brioso, comico, faceto; caustico.

humorously, *adv.* Con umore, facetamente.

humorousness, *n.* Comicità, *f.*, brio, *m.*; gaiezza, *f.*; capriccio, *m.*

humour ['hjuməɹ], *n.* Umore, *m.*, disposizione, *f.*, stato d'animo, *m.*; brio, spirito, *m.*, vena, fantasia, *f.* || *v.t.* Soddisfare, lasciar fare a, adattarsi a. **In — for,** disposto a, in vena di; **to be in a good —,** essere di buon umore; **out of —,** di cattivo umore; **it is just a — of mine,** è un puro capriccio da parte mia.

humoured, *a.* D'umore. **Good- —,** di buon umore.
humourless, *a.* Senza umore, senza vivacità.
humoursome, *a.* Capriccioso, petulante.
hump [hʌmp], *n.* Gobba, gibbosità, *f.*, bernoccolo, *m.* (*colloq.*) **To have the —,** essere di malumore, essere triste.
humpback, *n.* Gobbo, *m.*, gobba, *f.*
humpbacked, *a.* Gobbo.
humph! [hʌmf], *inter.* Auf!
Hun [hʌn], *n.* (*Hist.*) Unno, *m.*
hunch [hʌntʃ], *n.* Pezzo, tozzo, *m.*; (*colloq.*) nozione, idea, *f.*
hunchback [cp. **humpback**].
hundred [ˈhʌndrəd], *n.a.* Cento, *m.*; centinaio, *m.*; (*Hist.*) distretto, *m.* **In hundreds,** a centinaia.
hundredfold, *n.a.* Centuplo, *m.* ‖ *adv.* Cento volte.
hundredth, *n.a.* Centesimo, *m.*
hundredweight, *n.* Misura di peso (50.8 chili).
Hungarian [hʌnˈgɛəriən], *n.a.* Ungherese, *m.*
Hungary [ˈhʌŋgərɪ], *n.* (*Geog.*) Ungheria, *f.*
hunger [ˈhʌŋgəɹ], *n.* Fame, *f.* ‖ *v.i.* Aver fame, affamare, patir fame. **To feel the pangs of —,** sentire gli stimoli della fame; **— is the best sauce,** a chi ha fame è buono ogni pane; **to satisfy one's —,** cavarsi la fame; **to — after,** bramare, agognare; **— -strike,** sciopero della fame, *m.*
hungrily, *adv.* Ingordamente, famelicamente.
hungry [ˈhʌŋgri], *a.* Affamato, famelico, bramoso; macilento; (*of soil*) magro. **To be —,** aver fame; **to be as — as a hunter,** aver una fame da lupi.
hunk [hʌŋk], *n.* Pezzo, tocco, tozzo, *m.*
hunks, *n.* Avaro, taccagno, *m.*
hunt [hʌnt], *v.t.* Cacciare; perseguitare; scacciare; *v.i.* andare a caccia, cacciare. ‖ *n.* Caccia, *f.*; inseguimento, *m.*; (*Sport*) caccia alla volpe, *f.* **To — down,** perseguitare; **to — for,** cercare, andare in cerca di; **to — out,** snidare, scovare; **to — up,** cercare.
hunter, *n.* Cacciatore, *m.*; cavallo da caccia, *m.*; (*watch*) orologio a doppia cassa, *f.*
hunting, *n.* Caccia, *f.* ‖ *a.* Da caccia. **— -box,** padiglione da caccia, *m.*; **— -crop,** frustino, *m.*; **— -ground,** terreno da caccia, *m.*; (*fig.*) campo d'azione, *m.*; **— -horn,** corno; da caccia, *m.*
huntress, *n.* Cacciatrice, *f.*
huntsman (*pl.* **huntsmen**), *n.* Cacciatore, *m.*; capocaccia, *m.*
huntsmanship, *n.* L'arte della caccia, l'arte venatoria, *f.*
hurdle [ˈhəːɹdl], *n.* Graticcio, *m.*, barriera, *f.*; (*Sport*) ostacolo, steccato, *m.* **— -race,** corsa a ostacoli, *f.*; **— -fence,** barriera portatile, *f.*
hurdler, *n.* (*Sport*) Ostacolista, *m.*
hurdy-gurdy [ˈhəːɹdigəːɹdi], *n.* Organetto a manovella, *m.*
hurl [həːɹl], *v.t.* Lanciare, scagliare, vibrare. **To — oneself,** lanciarsi, precipitarsi.
hurler, *n.* Lanciatore, *m.*
hurley, *n.* (*Sport*) Hockey irlandese, *m.*
hurling, *n.* Lanciamento, lancio, *m.*
hurly-burly [ˈhəːɹlibəːɹli], *n.* Tumulto, tafferuglio, chiasso, baccano, *m.*
hurrah, hurray [huˈrɑː, huˈrei], *v.i.* Gridare evviva. ‖ *inter.* Alalà!, Evviva!, Urrah!
hurricane [ˈhʌrikən], *n.* Uragano, *m.*, bufera, *f.* **— -lamp,** lanterna di sicurezza, lampada chiusa, *f.*; (*Naut.*) **— -deck,** ponte di manovra, *m.*
hurried [ˈhʌrid], *a.* Affrettato, frettoloso, precipitato.
hurriedly, *adv.* In fretta, frettolosamente.
hurriedness, *n.* Fretta, precipitazione, *f.*
hurry, *n.* Fretta, furia, premura, *f.*; sollecitudine, *f.*; disordine, confusione, *f.* ‖ *v.t.* Affrettare, accelerare, precipitare; sbrigare; incalzare, spingere; *v.i.* affrettarsi, sbrigarsi, spicciarsi, far presto. **To — away,** andarsene in fretta, svignarsela; **to — along,** camminare in fretta; **to — up,** sbrigarsi, spicciarsi; **to be hurried into doing something,** essere incalzato a far qualcosa; **to — back,** tornare in fretta; **to — on,** affrettare, affrettarsi; **I'm in a —,** ho fretta; **Hurry up!** Spicciatevi!
hurt (*p.* and *p.p.* **hurt**) [həːɹt], *v.t.* Far male a; ferire, urtare; (*fig.*) offendere, addolorare; danneggiare, nuocere, pregiudicare; *v.i.* far male, dolere. ‖ *n.* Male, *m.*, ferita, *f.*; danno, *m.* **To — oneself,** farsi male; **to — someone's feelings,** urtare i sentimenti di qualcuno; **it does not —,** non fa male; **my head hurts,** mi duole la testa.
hurtful, *a.* Nocivo, dannoso, pernicioso; (*fig.*) pregiudizievole.
hurtfully, *adv.* Nocivamente, dannosamente.
hurtfulness, *n.* Perniciosità, dannosità, *f.*
hurtle [həːɹtl], *v.i.* Urtarsi, agitarsi, precipitarsi.
husband [ˈhʌzbənd], *n.* Marito, sposo, *m.* ‖ *v.t.* Economizzare, risparmiare. **We must — our resources,** dobbiamo risparmiare sulle spese.
husbandman (*pl.* **husbandmen**), *n.* Agricoltore; contadino; colono, *m.*
husbandry, *n.* Agricoltura, *f.*; economia, *f.*, risparmio, *m.*; lavoro dei campi, *m.*
hush [hʌʃ], *v.t.* Far tacere; calmare, assopire; *v.i.* tacere, far silenzio. ‖ *n.* Silenzio, *m.*, calma, *f.* ‖ *inter.* Zitto! Silenzio! **To — to sleep,** ninnare, cullare; **to — a matter up,** metter in silenzio una cosa, nascondere una cosa; **— -money,** prezzo del silenzio, *m.*
hushaby! [ˈhʌʃəbai], *inter.* Ninna nanna!
husk [hʌsk], *n.* Guscio, *m.*, buccia, pellicola, *f.*; involucro, *m.* ‖ *v.t.* Sbucciare, pelare, mondare.
husked, *a.* Sbucciato, ondato.
huskiness, *n.* Raucedine, *f.*
husky, *a.* Rauco, roco, fioco; (*Zool.*) cane eskimese.
hussar [huˈzɑːɹ], *n.* (*Mil.*) Ussero, ussaro, *m.*
hussy [ˈhʌzi], *n.* Sfacciatella, donna impertinente, *f.*
hustings [ˈhʌstiŋz], *n.pl.* Piattaforma elettorale, tribuna, *f.*
hustle [hʌsl], *v.t.i.* Spingere, spintonare, urtare; spicciarsi, sbrigarsi. ‖ *n.* Spinta, fretta, *f.*
huswife, hussif [ˈhʌzif], *n.* Astuccio per aghi, *m.*
hut [hʌt], *n.* Capanna, *f.*; tugurio, *m.*; baracca, cabina, *f.* ‖ *v.t.* (*Mil.*) Alloggiare in baracche.
hutch [hʌtʃ], *n.* Capanna, *f.*, tugurio, *m.*; (*for rabbits*) conigliera, *f.*

hutment, *n.* Baraccamento, *m.*
huzza [cp. **hurrah**].
hyacinth ['haiəsinθ], *n.* (*Bot.*) Giacinto, *m.*
hyaline ['haiəlin], *a.* (*Min.*) Ialino.
hybrid ['haibrid], *n.a.* Ibrido, *m.*
hydra ['haidrə], *n.* (*Myth.*) Idra, *f.*
hydrangea [hai'dreindʒə], *n.* (*Bot.*) Ortensia, *f.*
hydrant, *n.* Idrante, *m.*
hydrate ['haidreit], *n.* Idrato, *m.*
hydraulic [hai'drɔ:lik], *a.* Idraulico.
hydraulics, *n.pl.* Idraulica, *f.*
hydride, *n.* (*Chem.*) Idruro, *m.*
hydrocarbon, *n.* Idrocarburo, *m.*
hydrocephalus [haidrou'sefələs], *n.* (*Med.*) Idrocefalo, *m.*
hydrochlorate, *n.* Idroclorato, *m.*
hydrochloric, *a.* Idroclorico.
hydrodynamic, *a.* Idrodinamico.
hydroelectric, *a.* Idroelettrico.
hydrogen ['haidrədʒən], *n.* Idrogeno, *m.*
hydrographer [hai'drɔgrəfəɹ], *n.* Idrografo, *m.*
hydrometer [hai'drɔmitər], *n.* Idrometro, *m.*
hydropathic [haidrou'pæθik], *a.* Idropatico.
hydropathy [hai'drɔpəθi], *n.* Idropatia, idroiatria, *f.*
hydrophobia [haidrou'foubiə], *n.* Idrofobia, *f.*
hydrophobic, *a.* Idrofobo.
hydroplane, *n.* (*Aviat.*) Idroplano, idrovolante, *m.*
hydrostatic, *a.* Idrostatico.
hydrostatics, *n.pl.* Idrostatica, *f.*
hydrotherapeutics [haidrouθerə'pju:tiks], *n.pl.* Idroterapeutica, idroterapia, *f.*
hyena [hai'i:nə], *n.* (*Zool.*) Iena, *f.*
hygiene, hygienics [hai'dʒi:n, hai'dʒi:niks], *n.* Igiene, *f.*
hygienic, *a.* Igienico.
hygrometer [hai'grɔmitəɹ], *n.* Igrometro, *m.*
hygrometry, *n.* Igrometria, *f.*
hymen ['haimen], *n.* Imeneo, *m.*; (*Anat.*) imene, *m.*
hymeneal, *a.* Nuziale.
hymenoptera [haimən'ɔptərə], *n.pl.* (*Zool.*) Imenotteri, *m.pl.*
hymn [him], *n.* Inno, canto sacro, canto spirituale, *m.*; carme, *m.* || *v.i.* Inneggiare, cantare inni. **— -book, hymnal,** raccolta di inni, *f.*, libro di inni, *m.*
hymnody, *n.* Innodia, *f.*
hyoid ['haiɔid], *a.* (*Anat.*) Ioide. **— bone,** osso ioide, *m.*
hyperbola, hyperbole [hai'pə:ɹbolə, hai'pə:ɹboli], *n.* Iperbole, *f.*
hyperborean [haipəɹ'bɔ:riən], *a.* Iperboreo.
hypercritical [haipəɹ'kritikəl], *a.* Ipercritico.
hyphen ['haifən], *n.* Lineetta, *f.*; tratto, trattino, *m.*
hypnosis [hip'nousis], *n.* Ipnosi, *f.*
hypnotic, *a.* Ipnotico.
hypnotism ['hipnɔtizm], *n.* Ipnotismo, *m.*
hypnotist, *n.* Ipnotista, *m.*
hypnotize, *v.t.* Ipnotizzare.
hypochondria [haipou'kɔndriə], *n.* Ipocondria, *f.*
hypochondriac [haipou'kɔndriək], *n.a.* Ipocondriaco, *m.*, ipocondriaca, *f.*
hypocrisy [hi'pɔkrəsi], *n.* Ipocrisia, *f.*
hypocrite ['hipɔkrit], *n.* Ipocrita, *m.f.*
hypocritical, *a.* Ipocrito.
hypodermic, *a.* Ipodermico. **— syringe,** siringa ipodermica, *f.*
hypogastric, *a.* Ipogastrico.
hypostasis [hi'pɔstəsis], *n.* (*Med.Eccles.*) Ipostasi, *f.*
hypostatic, *a.* Ipostatico.
hyposulphite, *n.* Iposolfito, *m.*
hypotenuse [hai'pɔtənju:z], *n.* (*Geom.*) Ipotenusa, *f.*
hypothecate [hai'pɔθikeit], *v.t.* Ipotecare.
hypothecation, *n.* Ipoteca, *f.*
hypothesis (*pl.* **hypotheses**) [hai'pɔθisis, hai'pɔθisi:z], *n.* Ipotesi, *f.*
hypothetic, hypothetical [haipə'θetik, haipə'θetikəl], *a.* Ipotetico.
hyssop ['hisəp], *n.* (*Bot.*) Issopo, *m.*
hysteria [his'tiəriə], *n.* Isteria, *f.*; isterismo, *m.*
hysteric, hysterical, *a.* Isterico.
hysterics, *n.pl.* Attacco d'isteria, accesso di isterismo, *m.*
hysterotomy [histə'rɔtəmi], *n.* (*Med.*) Isterotomia, *f.*

I

I, i [ai], Nona lettera dell'alfabeto inglese, *f.*
I [ai], *pron.* Io. **It is I,** sono io; **Here I am!** Eccomi!
iambic [ai'æmbik], *a.* (*Poet.*) Giambico. || *n.* Giambo, *m.*
Iberian [ai'bɛəriən], *a.* Iberico.
ibex ['aibeks], *n.* (*Zool.*) Stambecco, *m.*
ibis ['aibis], *n.* (*Zool.*) Ibi, ibis, *m.*
ice [ais], *n.* Ghiaccio, *m.*; (*ice-cream*) gelato, *m.* || *v.t.* Ghiacciare, gelare; (*a cake*) candire; (*wine*) mettere in ghiaccio. **— -age,** epoca glaciale, *f.*; **— -axe,** piccozza, *f.*; **— -bound,** serrato fra i ghiacci; **— -box,** ghiacciaia, *f.*; **— -blink,** riflesso del ghiaccio, *m.*; (*Naut.*) **— -breaker,** nave rompighiaccio, *f.*; **— -cream,** gelato, *m.*; **— -cream vendor,** gelatiere, *m.*, gelatiera, *f.*; **— -floe, — -field,** campo di ghiaccio, *m.*; **— -hockey,** disco sul ghiaccio, *m.*; **— -house,** refrigeratore, frigorifero, *m.*
iceberg ['aisbə:ɹg], *n.* Ghiaccio galleggiante, *m.*; montagna galleggiante di ghiaccio, *f.*
iced, *a.* Ghiacciato, gelato; con ghiaccio; candito.
Iceland ['aislənd], *n.* (*Geog.*) Islanda, *f.*
Icelander, *n.* Islandese, *m.f.*
Icelandic, *a.* Islandese.
ichneumon [ik'nju:mɔn], *n.* (*Zool.*) Icneumone, *m.*
ichnographic [iknə'græfik], *a.* Icnografico.
ichnography [ik'nɔgrəfi], *n.* Icnografia, *f.*
ichor ['aikɔ:ɹ], *n.* (*Myth.*) Icore, *m.*
ichthyological [ikθiə'lɔdʒikəl], *a.* Ittiologico.
ichthyologist, *n.* Ittiologo, *m.*
ichthyology, *n.* Ittiologia, *f.*
ichthyosaurus [ikθio'sɔ:rəs], *n.* (*Zool.*) Ittiosauro, *m.*
icicle ['aisikl], *n.* Ghiacciuolo, diacciuolo, *m.*
icily, *adv.* Glacialmente, frigidamente.
iciness, *n.* Freddo glaciale, *m.*, gelidità, *f.*
icing, *n.* (*cooking*) Zuccheratura, *f.*
icon ['aikɔn], *n.* Icona, *f.*
iconoclast [ai'kɔnəklæst], *n.* Iconoclasto, *m.*
iconography, *n.* Iconografia, *f.*
iconology, *n.* Iconologia, *f.*

icosahedron [aikosə'hedrən], *n.* (*Geom.*) Icosaedro, *m.*
icy ['aisi], *a.* Ghiacciato, gelato; glaciale, frigido.
idea [ai'diə], *n.* Idea, *f.* **What an —!** Che idea! **to form an —,** farsi un idea; **a man of great ideas,** un uomo di larghe vedute, *m.*; **I had no — that she was ill,** non avevo la minima idea che essa fosse malata; **to cherish an —,** vagheggiare un'idea; **to get rid of an —,** cavarsi un'idea dalla mente.
ideal, *n.a.* Ideale, *m.*
idealism, *n.* Idealismo, *m.*
idealist, *n.* Idealista, *m.f.*
ideality, *n.* Idealità, *f.*
idealization, *n.* Idealizzazione, *f.*
idealize, *v.t.i.* Idealizzare.
ideally, *adv.* Idealmente.
identic, identical [ai'dentik, ai'dentikəl], *a.* Identico, uguale. **Identical twins,** gemelli monozigotici, *m.pl.*
identification, *n.* Identificazione, *f.* (*Motor.*) numero di circolazione, *m.*
identify [ai'dentifai], *v.t.* Identificare, riconoscere. **To — oneself with,** identificarsi con, dare il proprio appoggio a.
identity, *n.* Identità, *f.* **— disk,** piastrina di riconoscimento, *f.*; **— card,** carta d'identità, *f.*
ideographic [idio'græfik], *a.* Ideografico.
ideography, *n.* Ideografia, *f.*
ideological [aidio'lɔdʒikəl], *a.* Ideologico.
ideologist [aidi'ɔlədʒist], *n.* Ideologo, *m.*
ideology, *n.* Ideologia, *f.*
Ides [aidz], *n.pl.* (*Hist.*) Idi, *m.pl.*
idiocy ['idiəsi], *n.* Idiozia, imbecillità, *f.*, ebetismo, cretinismo, *m.*
idiom ['idiəm], *n.* (*language*) Idioma, *m.*; (*phrase*) idiotismo, modo di dire, *m.*, locuzione, *f.*
idiomatic, idiomatical, *a.* Idiomatico, fraseologico. **— expression,** idiotismo, modo di dire, *m.*
idiopathy [idi'ɔpəθi], *n.* (*Med.*) Idiopatia, *f.*
idiosyncrasy [idio'sinkrəsi], *n.* Idiosincrasia, *f.*
idiot ['idiət], *n.* Idiota, imbecille, ebete, *m.f.*, cretino, *m.*, cretina, *f.*
idiotic [idi'ɔtik], *a.* Stupido, imbecille.
idle [aidl], *a.* Pigro, ozioso, neghittoso, infingardo, sfaccendato; (*fig.*) vano, inutile, frivolo, futile. || *v.t.i.* Oziare, impigrire. **An — fellow,** un fannullone, uno sfaccendato, *m.*; **— hours,** ore oziose, *f.pl.*; **an — tale,** un racconto futile, *m.*; **an — fancy,** una fantasia, *f.*; **— talk,** discorsi oziosi, *m.pl.*, baie, *f.pl.*; **to — away one's time,** passare il tempo nell'ozio, perdere il tempo, stare con le mani in mano.
idleness, *n.* Pigrizia, scioperataggine, infingardaggine, *f.*, ozio, *m.*; inutilità, frivolezza, futilità, *f.*
idler, *n.* Pigro, infingardo, fannullone, ozioso, *m.*
idly, *adv.* Pigramente, inutilmente, oziosamente.
idol ['aidəl], *n.* Idolo, *m.* **—-worship,** culto degli idoli, *m.*
idolator, idolatress, *n.* Idolatra, *m.f.*
idolatrous, *a.* Idolatra, idolatrico.
idolatry, *n.* Idolatria, *f.*
idolization [aidəlai'zeiʃən], *n.* Idolatramento, *m.*
idolize, *v.t.* Idolatrare, idoleggiare.
idyll, idyl ['idil], *n.* Idillio, *m.*
idyllic, *a.* Idillico, idilliaco.
if [if], *conj.* Se; posto che, dato che; quando, qualora, quand'anche, seppure. **As if,** come se; **even if it were true,** quand'anche fosse vero; **if he would but come quickly,** se venisse presto; **if I were you,** se io fossi in voi; **they look as if they are tired,** hanno l'aria di essere stanchi; **he is a fool if ever there was one,** è un imbecille se mai ce ne fu uno; **if necessary,** se ce n'è bisogno, se è necessario; **if possible,** se possibile, purchè sia possibile; **if so,** se è così; **If you only knew!** Se sapeste!
igneous ['igniəs], *a.* Igneo.
ignis fatuus (*pl.* **ignes fatui**) ['ignis 'fætju:əs, igni:z 'fætju:ai], *n.* Fuoco fatuo, *m.*
ignite [ig'nait], *v.t.* Accendere, infiammare; *v.i.* accendersi, infiammarsi, prendere fuoco.
ignition [ig'niʃən], *n.* Accendimento, *m.*; (*Motor.*) accensione, *f.*
ignoble [ig'noubl], *a.* Ignobile; vile, turpe.
ignobleness, *n.* Ignobiltà, bassezza, *f.*
ignobly, *adv.* Ignobilmente.
ignominious [igno'miniəs], *a.* Ignominioso, infamante.
ignominiously, *adv.* Ignominiosamente.
ignominy ['ignəmini], *n.* Ignominia, *f.*
ignoramus [ignə'reiməs], *n.* Ignorante, *m.f.*; zotico, asino, *m.*
ignorance ['ignərəns], *n.* Ignoranza, *f.* **Out of —,** per ignoranza.
ignorant, *a.* Ignorante, ignaro. **To be — of,** ignorare, essere ignaro di.
ignorantly, *adv.* Ignorantemente.
ignore, *v.t.* Passare sotto silenzio; fingere di non sapere, ignorare; fingere di non riconoscere.
iguana [ig'wɑ:nə], *n.* (*Zool.*) Iguana, *f.*
iguanodon [ig'wɑ:nədən], *n.* (*Zool.*) Iguanodonte, *m.*
ilex ['aileks], *n.* (*Bot.*) Elce, *f.*
Iliad ['iliəd], *n.* (*Poet.*) Iliade, *f.*
ilium ['iliəm], *n.* (*Anat.*) Ilio, *m.*
ilk [ilk], *a.* (*Scots*) Lo stesso. **Of that —,** dello stesso nome.
ill [il], *a.* Cattivo, nocivo, dannoso; ammalato, malato, infermo; infelice. || *n.* Male, danno, *m.* || *adv.* Male, malamente; poco, scarsamente. **To fall —,** ammalarsi; **— at ease,** imbarazzato, a disagio; **to take it —,** prender in mala parte; **— to please,** difficile da contentare; **— able to,** poco capace a; **it went — with him,** non ebbe fortuna; **—-advised,** malavveduto, malaccorto; **—-assorted,** poco adatto, mal accoppiato; **—-bred,** sgarbato, grossolano, maleducato; **—-considered,** sconsigliato; **—-affected,** mal disposto, ostile; **—-conditioned,** in cattive condizioni, maleducato; **—-contrived,** mal combinato, mal ideato; **—-deserved,** immeritato; **—-disposed,** mal disposto, sfavorevole; **—-famed,** malfamato; **house of — fame,** bordello, *m.*; **—-fated,** sfortunato, infelice, malavventurato; **—-favoured,** brutto, sgraziato; **—-feeling,** malumore, rancore, *m.*, inimicizia, *f.*; **—-gotten,** mal acquistato; **—-health,** salute malferma, *f.*; **—-luck,** sfortuna, mala sorte, *f.*; **—-mannered,** sgarbato, scostumato; **—-meaning,** male intenzionato; **—-nature,** umore cattivo, *m.*; **—-natured,** cattivo, malvagio, bisbetico;

— -omened, malaugurato, nefasto, sinistro; **— -pleased,** scontento, malcontento; **— -qualified,** impreparato, inadatto, inetto; **— -starred,** sfortunato, infelice, sventurato; **— -tempered,** collerico, irritabile, stizzoso, bisbetico; **— -timed,** inopportuno, intempestivo; **to — -treat, to — use,** maltrattare, bistrattare, usar male; **— -will,** malvolere, malanimo, *m.*; **to bear — -will,** voler male a.
illation [iˈleiʃən], *n.* Illazione, *f.*
illative [ˈilətiv], *a.* Illativo.
illegal [iˈli:gəl], *a.* Illegale; illecito.
illegality [iliˈgæliti], *n.* Illegalità, *f.*
illegally, *adv.* Illegalmente, illecitamente.
illegibility [iledʒiˈbiliti], *n.* Illeggibilità, *f.*
illegible, *a.* Illeggibile.
illegibly, *adv.* Illeggibilmente.
illegitimacy [iliˈdʒitiməsi], *n.* Illegittimità, *f.*
illegitimate, *a.* Illegittimo.
illiberal [iˈlibərəl], *a.* Illiberale; meschino, avaro.
illicit [iˈlisit], *a.* Illecito, vietato.
illicitly, *adv.* Illecitamente.
illimitable [iˈlimitəbl], *a.* Illimitato, sconfinato.
illiteracy [iˈlitərəsi], *n.* Analfabetismo, *m.*
illiterate, *a.* Illetterato, analfabeta.
illiterately, *adv.* Ignorantemente.
illness, *n.* Malattia, infermità, indisposizione, *f.*
illogical [iˈlɔdʒikəl], *a.* Illogico.
illogicalness, illogicality, *n.* Illogicità, *f.*
illude [iˈlju:d], *v.t.* Illudere.
illuminant [iˈlju:minənt], *n.* Lume, *m.*
illuminate [iˈlju:mineit], *v.t.* Illuminare, rischiarare; *(Art)* miniare.
illumination, *n.* Illuminazione, *f.*; *(Art)* miniatura, *f.*
illuminative, *a.* Illuminativo.
illuminator, *n.* Illuminatore, *m.*; miniatore, *m.*
illumine [iˈlju:min], *v.t.* Illuminare, rischiarare.
illusion [iˈlju:ʒən], *n.* Illusione, *f.*
illusionist, *n.* Illusionista, *m.*
illusive, illusory, *a.* Illusorio.
illusiveness, *n.* Illusorietà, *f.*
illustrate [ˈiləstreit], *v.t.* Illustrare; *(fig.)* spiegare, schiarire, dilucidare.
illustration, *n.* Illustrazione, spiegazione, *f.*, esempio, *m.*; incisione, immagine, tavola, *f.* **In — of my meaning,** per spiegare ciò che voglio dire.
illustrative, *a.* Illustrativo.
illustrator, *n.* Illustratore, *m.*
illustrious [iˈlʌstriəs], *a.* Illustre, famoso, insigne, celebre, rinomato. **To make —,** render illustre.
illustriously, *adv.* Insignemente.
illustriousness, *n.* Fama, gloria, rinomanza, *f.*
image [ˈimidʒ], *n.* Immagine, *f.*; idolo, *m.*; ritratto, *m.*, figura, *f.* || *v.t.* Ritrarre, rappresentare; riflettere, rispecchiare; immaginarsi. **She is the — of her mother,** essa è il ritratto di sua madre; **— -worship,** idolatria, *f.*
imagery, *n.* Immagini, statue, *f.pl.*; figure retoriche, *f.pl.*
imaginable [iˈmædʒinəbl], *a.* Immaginabile.
imaginary, *a.* Immaginario.
imagination, *n.* Immaginazione, fantasia, *f.*
imaginative, *a.* Immaginativo, fantastico.
imagine, *v.t.i.* Immaginare, figurare; immaginarsi, figurarsi; avere un'idea di, farsi un'idea di.
imago (*pl.* **imagines**) [iˈmeigou, imˈædʒini:z], *n.* *(Zool.)* Insetto allo stato perfetto, *m.*
imam [imˈɑ:m], *n.* Imamo, *m.*
imbecile [ˈimbəsi:l], *n.a.* Imbecille, ebete, *m.f.*, scemo, *m.*
imbecility [imbəˈsiliti], *n.* Imbecillaggine, imbecillità, *f.*; sciocchezza, scemenza, *f.*; ebetismo, *m.*
imbed [cp. **embed**].
imbibe [imˈbaib], *v.t.* Imbevere, assorbire, assimilare.
imbricate [ˈimbrikeit], *v.t.* Sovrapporre; mettere degli embrici.
imbroglio [imˈbrouliou], *n.* Imbroglio, *m.*
imbrue [imˈbru:], *v.t.* Bagnare, tuffare in, immergere.
imbue [imˈbju:], *v.t.* Imbevere, assorbire; istillare, infondere.
imbued, *a.* Imbevuto, ispirato; impregnato. **To be — with,** essere imbevuto di.
imitate [ˈimiteit], *v.t.* Imitare; contraffare.
imitation, *n.* Imitazione, *f.*; contraffazione, *f.* || *a.* Falso, contraffatto; artificiale, posticcio. **In — of,** ad imitazione di.
imitative, *a.* Imitativo.
imitativeness, *n.* Mimetismo, *m.*, facoltà imitativa, *f.*
imitator, *n.* Imitatore, contraffatore, *m.*, imitatrice, contraffatrice, *f.*
immaculate [iˈmækju:lit], *a.* Immacolato, incontaminato. **The Immaculate Conception,** l'Immacolata Concezione, *f.*
immaculateness, *n.* Purità, purezza, immacolatezza, *f.*
immanence [ˈimənəns], *n.* Immanenza, *f.*
immanent, *a.* Immanente.
immaterial, *a.* Immateriale; indifferente. **It is — to me,** mi è indifferente, poco m'importa.
immaterialism, *n.* Immaterialismo, *m.*
immaterialist, *n.* Immaterialista, *m.*
immature, *a.* Immaturo.
immaturity, *n.* Immaturità, *f.*
immeasurable, *a.* Immisurabile; immenso, smisurato.
immeasurably, *adv.* Immisurabilmente, immensamente.
immediate [iˈmi:diət], *a.* Immediato; urgente; prossimo, vicino.
immediately, *adv.* Immediatamente, subito, all'istante, d'un tratto.
immediateness, *n.* Immediatezza, *f.*
immemorial [imeˈmɔ:riəl], *a.* Immemorabile. **From time —,** da tempo immemorabile.
immense [iˈmens], *a.* Immenso, smisurato.
immensely, *adv.* Immensamente; *(colloq.)* molto.
immensity, *n.* Immensità, smisuratezza, *f.*
immerse [iˈmə:ɹs], *v.t.* Immergere, tuffare, affondare.
immersion, *n.* Immersione, *f.*
immigrant [ˈimigrənt], *n.a.* Immigrante, *m.f.*
immigrate, *v.i.* Immigrare.
immigration, *n.* Immigrazione, *f.*
imminence [ˈiminəns], *n.* Imminenza, *f.*

Unless otherwise indicated, the pronunciation of words compounded with the prefixes "im", "in", "inter" or "ir" can be ascertained by reference to the unprefixed word in its alphabetical position in this dictionary.

imminent, *a.* Imminente, prossimo.
immiscible [iˈmisibl], *a.* Che non può mischiarsi.
immitigable [iˈmitigəbl], *a.* Immitigabile.
immobile, *a.* Immobile.
immobility, *n.* Immobilità, *f.*
immobilization, *n.* Immobilizzazione, *f.*
immobilize, *v.t.* Immobilizzare.
immoderate, *a.* Immoderato, smoderato, eccessivo, smodato.
immoderately, *adv.* Immoderatamente.
immoderation, *n.* Immoderatezza, *f.*
immodest, *a.* Immodesto, impudico, spudorato, sfacciato.
immodestly, *adv.* Immodestamente, impudicamente.
immodesty, *n.* Immodestia, impudicizia, spudoratezza, *f.*
immolate [ˈimoleit], *v.t.* Immolare, sacrificare.
immolation, *n.* Immolazione, *f.*
immolator, *n.* Immolatore, *m.*
immoral, *a.* Immorale.
immorality, *n.* Immoralità, *f.*
immortal, *a.* Immortale; perpetuo, eterno, perenne.
immortality, *n.* Immortalità, *f.*
immortalization, *n.* Immortalizzazione, *f.*
immortalize, *v.t.* Immortalare, immortalizzare.
immortally, *adv.* Immortalmente, perpetuamente.
immortelle [imɔːɹˈtel], *n.* (*Bot.*) Sempreviva, *f.*
immovability, immovableness [imuvəˈbiliti, iˈmuvəblnis], *n.* Irremovibilità, *f.*
immovable, *a.* Irremovibile, fermo, fisso; (*Law*) inamovibile; (*fig.*) insensibile, impassibile.
immovably, *adv.* Irremovibilmente.
immune [iˈmjuːn], *a.* Immune, esente.
immunity, *n.* Immunità, *f.*
immunize, *v.t.* Immunizzare.
immure [iˈmjuːɹ], *v.t.* Imprigionare, rinchiudere. **To — oneself,** rinchiudersi.
immutability [imjuːtəˈbiliti], *n.* Immutabilità, *f.*
immutable, *a.* Immutabile.
immutably, *adv.* Immutabilmente.
imp [imp], *n.* Diavoletto, demonietto, folletto, *m.*; (*urchin*) birichino, *m.*
impact [ˈimpækt], *n.* Urto, cozzo, *m.*; collisione, *f.* || *v.t.* Ficcare, configgere.
impair [imˈpɛəɹ], *v.t.* Menomare, danneggiare, pregiudicare, diminuire, intaccare; peggiorare, deteriorare. **To become impaired,** deperire, guastarsi; **his health was seriously impaired,** la sua salute fu seriamente menomata.
impairment, *n.* Menomazione, *f.*; deterioramento, peggioramento, *m.*
impale [imˈpeil], *v.t.* Impalare.
impalement, *n.* Impalamento, *m.*, impalatura, *f.*
impalpability, *n.* Impalpabilità, *f.*
impalpable, *a.* Impalpabile.
impanel [cp. **empanel**].
impart [imˈpɑːɹt], *v.t.* Impartire, distribuire; trasmettere; comunicare, far partecipe. **To — knowledge,** impartire nozioni.
impartial, *a.* Imparziale, disinteressato, equo.
impartiality, *n.* Imparzialità, *f.*
impartially, *adv.* Imparzialmente.
impassable, *a.* (*of a road*) Impraticabile; (*of a river*) inguadabile, invarcabile.
impassibility, impassibleness [impɑːsəˈbiliti, imˈpɑːsəblnis], *n.* Impassibilità, *f.*
impassible, *a.* Impassibile, imperturbato.
impassion, *v.t.* Appassionare, commuovere.
impassioned, *a.* Appassionato, commosso, infiammato.
impassive, *a.* Impassibile.
impassiveness, impassivity, *n.* Impassibilità, *f.*
impasto [imˈpæstou], *n.* (*Art*) Impasto, *m.*
impatience, *n.* Impazienza, *f.*
impatient, *a.* Impaziente, insofferente, intollerante. **To get —,** impazientirsi.
impatiently, *adv.* Impazientemente, con impazienza.
impeach [imˈpiːtʃ], *v.t.* Accusare, denunziare; incriminare, metter in stato d'accusa.
impeachment, *n.* Accusa, denunzia, incriminazione, *f.*; messa in istato d'accusa, *f.*
impeccability [impekəˈbiliti], *n.* Impeccabilità, *f.*
impeccable, *a.* Impeccabile.
impeccably, *adv.* Impeccabilmente.
impecuniosity [impekjuːniˈɔsiti], *n.* Mancanza di danaro, povertà, *f.*
impecunious [impeˈkjuːniəs], *a.* Senza danaro, povero, indigente.
impede [imˈpiːd], *v.t.* Impedire, inceppare, ritardare, ostacolare.
impediment [imˈpedimənt], *n.* Impedimento, ostacolo, impaccio, *m.* **To have an — in one's speech,** aver un difetto di pronuncia.
impedimenta, *n.pl.* Bagagli, *m.pl.*
impel [imˈpel], *v.t.* Spingere, costringere, forzare.
impellent, impelling, *a.* Impellente.
impend [imˈpend], *v.i.* Soprastare, incombere, minacciare, essere imminente.
impendence, impendency, *n.* Imminenza, *f.*
impendent, impending, *a.* Imminente, soprastante, incombente.
impenetrability, impenetrableness, *n.* Impenetrabilità, *f.*
impenetrable, *a.* Impenetrabile.
impenetrably, *adv.* Impenetrabilmente.
impenitence, *n.* Impenitenza, *f.*
impenitent, *a.* Impenitente, indurito.
imperative [imˈperətiv], *a.* Imperativo; urgente; imperioso. || *n.* (*Gram.*) Imperativo, *m.*
imperceptible, *a.* Impercettibile.
imperceptibleness, *n.* Impercettibilità, *f.*
imperceptibly, *adv.* Impercettibilmente.
imperfect, *a.* Imperfetto, difettoso, incompleto, manchevole. || *n.* (*Gram.*) Imperfetto, *m.*
imperfection, *n.* Imperfezione, *f.*
imperforate, *a.* Imperforato.
imperforation, *n.* Imperforazione, *f.*
imperial [imˈpiəriəl], *a.* Imperiale; sovrano, supremo; maestoso, grandioso. || *n.* (*beard*) Pizzo *m.*; (*on carriage*) imperiale, *m.*
imperialism, *n.* Imperialismo, *m.*

Unless otherwise indicated, the pronunciation of words compounded with the prefixes "im", "in", "inter" or "ir" can be ascertained by reference to the unprefixed word in its alphabetical position in this dictionary.

imperialist, *n.* Imperialista, *m.f.*
imperialistic, *a.* Imperialistico.
imperil, *v.t.* Mettere in pericolo, arrischiare, azzardare; compromettere.
imperious [im'piəriəs], *a.* Imperioso; urgente, impellente.
imperiousness, *n.* Imperiosità, arroganza, *f.*
imperishable, *a.* Indistruttibile, imperituro.
impermanence, *n.* Instabilità, *f.*
impermanent, *a.* Temporaneo, non permanente.
impermeability, *n.* Impermeabilità, *f.*
impermeable, *a.* Impermeabile.
impersonal, *a.* Impersonale.
impersonate, *v.t.* Impersonare, personificare; (*Theat.*) impersonare, interpretare.
impersonation, *n.* Personificazione, rappresentazione, *f.*; (*Law*) supposizione di persona, *f.*
impertinence [im'pə:ɹtinəns], *n.* Impertinenza, sconvenienza, insolenza, *f.*
impertinent, *a.* Impertinente, sconveniente, insolente, sfacciato.
impertinently, *adv.* Impertinentemente.
imperturbability [impəɹtə:ɹbə'biliti], *n.* Imperturbabilità, *f.*
imperturbable [impəɹ'tə:ɹbəbl], *a.* Imperturbabile.
imperturbably, *adv.* Imperturbabilmente.
impervious [im'pə:ɹviəs], *a.* Impervio, impenetrabile, inaccessibile. **— to reason,** inaccessibile alla ragione.
imperviousness, *n.* Impenetrabilità, inaccessibilità, *f.*
impetigo [impə'taigou], *n.* (*Med.*) Impetiggine, *f.*
impetrate ['impitreit], *v.t.* Impetrare.
impetration, *n.* Impetrazione, *f.*
impetuosity, impetuousness [impetju:'ɔsiti, im'petju:əsnis], *n.* Impetuosità, *f.*
impetuous, *a.* Impetuoso.
impetus ['impitəs], *n.* Impeto, impulso, *m.*, foga, *f.*; slancio, *m.*
impiety, *n.* Empietà, *f.*
impinge [im'pindʒ], *v.t.i.* **To — upon,** urtare contro, percuotere.
impious ['impiəs], *a.* Empio.
impish ['impiʃ], *a.* Indiavolato, birichino, sbarazzino, malizioso.
implacability [implækə'biliti], *n.* Implacabilità, *f.*
implacable, *a.* Implacabile, spietato.
implant [im'plɑ:nt], *v.t.* Piantare; (*fig.*) imprimere, inculcare, istillare.
implement ['implimənt], *n.* Ordigno, strumento, utensile, arnese, *m.* || *v.t.* Effettuare, adempiere; completare. **Implements,** masserizie, *f.pl.*, attrezzi, *m.pl.*
implicate ['implikeit], *v.t.* Implicare, coinvolgere, compromettere. **To be implicated in a crime,** essere implicato in un delitto.
implication, *n.* Implicazione, *f.* **By —,** implicitamente, per induzione.
implicit [im'plisit], *a.* Implicito; compreso in.
implicitness, *n.* Implicazione, *f.*
implied [im'plaid], *a.* Implicito, implicato, tacito, sottinteso.
implore [im'plɔ:ɹ], *v.t.* Implorare, supplicare, impetrare.
imploringly, *adv.* Supplichevolmente.
imply [im'plai], *v.t.* Implicare, voler dire, significare, suggerire, insinuare.
impolite, *a.* Scortese, sgarbato, villano, maleducato.
impoliteness, *n.* Scortesia, villania, sgarbatezza, maleducazione, *f.*
impolitic, *a.* Impolitico, imprudente, inopportuno.
imponderability [impɔndərə'biliti], *n.* Imponderabilità, *f.*
imponderable, *a.* Imponderabile.
import (1) ['impɔ:ɹt], *n.* (*meaning*) Significato, senso, valore, *m.*; importanza, *f.*; (*Comm.*) importazione, *f.* **Of great —,** di gran momento.
import (2) [im'pɔ:ɹt], *v.t.* Significare, indicare, importare; (*Comm.*) importare, introdurre.
importance [im'pɔ:ɹtəns], *n.* Importanza, *f.*
important, *a.* Importante, rilevante, grave. **The — point,** l'importante, *m.*
importantly, *adv.* In modo importante.
importation, *n.* Importazione, *f.*
importer, *n.* Importatore, *m.*
importunate [im'pɔ:ɹtju:nit], *a.* Importuno, indiscreto, noioso, seccante, molesto.
importunately, *adv.* Importunamente.
importune [im'pɔ:ɹtju:n], *v.t.* Importunare, seccare, molestare.
importunity [impɔɹ'tju:niti], *n.* Molestia, insistenza, *f.*
impose [im'pouz], *v.t.* Imporre; *v.i.* imporsi. **To — upon someone,** ingannare qualcuno.
imposing, *a.* Imponente, grandioso. **An — appearance,** un aspetto imponente.
imposingly, *adv.* Grandiosamente.
imposingness, *n.* Imponenza, *f.*
imposition [impə'ziʃən], *n.* Imposizione, soperchieria, *f.*; inganno, *m.*, impostura, *f.*; (*school*) penso, *m.*
impossibility [impɔsi'biliti], *n.* Impossibilità, *f.* **There's no doing impossibilities,** nessuno è tenuto all'impossibile.
impossible, *a.* Impossibile; assurdo, stravagante. **It is — for him to go,** è impossibile che egli vada.
impossibly, *adv.* Impossibilmente, assurdamente.
impost ['impoust], *n.* Imposta, tassa, *f.*, balzello, *m.*; (*Arch.*) pietra di spalla, *f.*
impostor [im'pɔstəɹ], *n.* Impostore, *m.*, impostora, *f.*
imposture, *n.* Impostura, frode, *f.*, inganno, *m.*
impotence, impotency ['impətəns, 'impətənsi], *n.* Impotenza, *f.*
impotent, *a.* Impotente, debole, incapace; (*Med.*) impotente.
impotently, *adv.* Impotentemente.
impound [im'paund], *v.t.* (*Law*) Confiscare, sequestrare; rinchiudere.
impoverish [im'pɔvriʃ], *v.t.* Impoverire, immiserire.
impoverished, *a.* Impoverito.
impoverishment, *n.* Impoverimento, *m.*
impracticability, *n.* Impraticabilità, inattuabilità, impossibilità, *f.*

Unless otherwise indicated, the pronunciation of words compounded with the prefixes "im", "in", "inter" or "ir" can be ascertained by reference to the unprefixed word in its alphabetical position in this dictionary.

impracticable, *a.* Impraticabile, inattuabile; intrattabile.
imprecate ['imprikeit], *v.t.* Imprecare, maledire.
imprecation, *n.* Imprecazione, maledizione, bestemmia, *f.* **A fierce —,** un' imprecazione orribile, *f.*
imprecatory, *a.* Imprecativo.
impregnable [im'pregnəbl], *a.* Imprendibile; inespugnabile.
impregnably, *adv.* Imprendibilmente.
impregnate ['impregneit], *v.t.* Impregnare, fecondare, imbevere. **This wood is impregnated with creosote,** questo legno è iniettato di creosoto.
impregnation, *n.* Impregnazione, fecondazione, *f.*
impresario [impre'zɑ:riou], *n.* (*Theat.*) Impresario, *m.*
imprescriptible [impre'skriptəbl], *a.* Imprescrittibile.
impress (1) [im'pres], *v.t.* Imprimere, stampare; impressionare, colpire; arruolare per forza. **I was impressed by his words,** fui impressionato dalle sue parole.
impress (2) ['impres], *n.* Impressione, impronta, *f.*
impression [im'preʃən], *n.* Impressione, impronta, *f.*; (*fig.*) idea, *f.*; (*Print.*) impressione, *f.* **I was under the — that,** avevo l'idea che; **to create an —,** fare un'impressione.
impressionable, *a.* Impressionabile.
impressionism, *n.* (*Art*) Impressionismo, *m.*
impressionist, *n.* (*Art*) Impressionista, *m.f.*
impressive, *a.* Impressionante, emozionante, commovente, solenne.
impressively, *adv.* Solennemente, imponentemente.
impressiveness, *n.* Forza, imponenza, potenza, *f.*; solennità, *f.*
impressment, *n.* Requisizione, *f.*; arruolamento a forza, *m.*
imprest ['imprest], *n.* (*Comm.*) Anticipazione, *f.*; prestito, *m.*
imprimatur [impri'meitəɹ], *n.* (*Eccles.*) Imprimatur, *m.*; (*fig.*) sanzione, *f.*
imprint (1) [im'print], *v.t.* Imprimere, stampare; (*fig.*) fissare.
imprint (2) ['imprint], *n.* Impronta, *f.* **Publisher's —,** impresa editoriale, *f.*
imprison, *v.t.* Imprigionare; (*fig.*) rinchiudere, confinare.
imprisonment, *n.* Imprigionamento, arresto, *m.*, carcerazione, prigionia, *f.* **A year's —,** un anno di prigione, *m.*
improbability, *n.* Improbabilità, *f.*
improbable, *a.* Improbabile, inverosimile.
improbably, *adv.* Improbabilmente.
improbity [im'proubiti], *n.* Improbità, *f.*
impromptu [im'prɔmtju:], *a.* Improvvisato, estemporaneo. || *adv.* all'improvviso, estemporaneamente. || *n.* Improvvisazione, *f.*
improper, *a.* Improprio; sconveniente, indecente; erroneo, disdatto. (*Math.*) **— fractions,** frazioni improprie, *f.pl.*
improperly, *adv.* Impropriamente; erroneamente.
impropriate [im'prouprieit], *v.t.* (*Eccles.* Appropriarsi, secolarizzare.
impropriety, *n.* Sconvenienza, indecenza, *f.*; erroneità, *f.*; (*Gram.*) improprietà, *f.*
improvable [im'pru:vəbl], *a.* Perfezionabile, migliorabile.
improve [im'pru:v], *v.t.* Migliorare, correggere, perfezionare; abbellire; aumentare; *v.i.* migliorare, avvantaggiarsi, star meglio; avanzare, aumentarsi; (*Comm.*) essere in rialzo. **To — the occasion,** profittare dell'occasione; **to — on,** perfezionare, fare meglio di; **to — a tract of land,** bonificare un terreno; **he has improved in looks,** egli è imbellito; **to — on acquaintance,** guadagnare ad esser conosciuto.
improvement, *n.* Miglioramento, progresso, *m.*, (*of land, houses, etc.*) miglioria, bonificazione, *f.*; perfezionamento, aumento, *m.*; profitto, avanzamento, *m.*
improvements, *n.pl.* Migliorie, *f.pl.*
improver, *n.* Apprendista che si perfeziona in un'arte, assistente, *m.*, lavorante, *m.f.*
improvidence, *n.* Imprevidenza, imprudenza, *f.*
improvident, *a.* Imprevidente, imprudente.
improvidently, *adv.* Imprevidentemente.
improvisation [imprəvai'zeiʃən], *n.* Improvvisazione, *f.*
improvise ['improvaiz], *v.t.* Improvvisare.
improvised, *a.* Improvvisato, improvviso.
imprudence, *n.* Imprudenza, *f.*
imprudent, *a.* Imprudente, incauto.
imprudently, *adv.* Imprudentemente.
impudence ['impju:dəns], *n.* Impudenza, sfacciataggine, *f.*
impudent, *a.* Impudente, sfacciato, sfrontato.
impudently, *adv.* Impudentemente.
impudicity, *n.* Impudicizia, *f.*
impugn [im'pju:n], *v.t.* Impugnare, contraddire, attaccare, accusare.
impugnable, *a.* Impugnabile.
impugnment, *n.* Impugnamento, *m.*, impugnazione, *f.*
impulse ['impʌls], *n.* Impulso, urto, *m.*; spinta, *f.*; motivo, stimolo, impeto, *m.*; (*Mech.*) impulsione, *f.*
impulsion, *n.* Impulsione, spinta, *f.*
impulsive, *a.* Impulsivo.
impulsively, *adv.* Impulsivamente.
impulsiveness, *n.* Impulsività, *f.*
impunity [im'pju:niti], *n.* Impunità, *f.* **With —,** impunemente.
impure, *a.* Impuro, immondo, disonesto, impudico.
impurity, *n.* Impurità, *f.*; impudicizia, disonestà, *f.*
imputable [im'pju:təbl], *a.* Imputabile.
imputation, *n.* Imputazione, accusa, *f.*; addebito, *m.*
impute, *v.t.* Imputare, attribuire, ascrivere. **To — as a crime,** imputare a colpa.
in [in], *prep.* In, entro, dentro. || *adv.* Dentro, entro. || *a.* Interno. **In the house,** nella casa; **dressed in white,** vestito di bianco; **he was in brown boots,** aveva scarpe gialle; **not one in a hundred,** non uno fra cento; **he is in the army,** è soldato; **in my opinion,** nella mia

Unless otherwise indicated, the pronunciation of words compounded with the prefixes "im", "in", "inter" or "ir" can be ascertained by reference to the unprefixed word in its alphabetical position in this dictionary.

opinione; **in good health,** bene in salute, in buona salute; **the fire is still in,** il fuoco vive ancora, il fuoco non è spento; **in fashion,** alla moda, di moda; **that man is in liquor,** quell'uomo è ubbriaco; **in passing,** passando, di passaggio; **in dozens,** a dozzine; **in the night,** di notte; **in the daytime,** di giorno; **in three months,** fra tre mesi; **it is good in itself,** è buono per se stesso; **as far as in me lies,** per quanto sta in me; **to put in one's pocket,** mettersi in tasca; **cut it in half,** tagliatelo per metà; **this boy is weak in Latin,** questo ragazzo è deboluccio in latino; **he is wanting in courage,** gli manca il coraggio; **a change in the government,** un cambiamento di governo; **six in number,** in sei; **in that,** perchè; **in black and white,** per iscritto, nero sul bianco; **in Paris,** a Parigi; **Is she in ?** È in casa? **let us have him in,** fatelo entrare; **lock him in,** serratelo dentro; **the ins and outs of the matter,** tutti i dettagli della faccenda.

inability, *n.* Inabilità, incapacità, *f.*

inaccessibility, *n.* Inaccessibilità, *f.*

inaccessible, *a.* Inaccessibile.

inaccuracy, *n.* Inesattezza, *f.*

inaccurate, *a.* Inesatto, inaccurato.

inaccurately, *adv.* Inesattamente.

inaction, *n.* Inazione, inerzia, *f.*

inactive, *a.* Inattivo, inoperoso.

inactively, *adv.* Inoperosamente.

inactivity, *n.* Inattività, inoperosità, *f.*

inadaptability, *n.* Inadattabilità, *f.*

inadaptable, *a.* Inadattabile.

inadequacy, inadequateness, *n.* Insufficienza, manchevolezza, inettitudine, *f.*

inadequate, *a.* Inadeguato, insufficiente; inetto, inesperto.

inadequately, *adv.* Insufficientemente.

inadmissibility, *n.* Inammissibilità, *f.*

inadmissible, *a.* Inammissibile.

inadvertence, *n.* Inavvertenza, sbadataggine, disattenzione, *f.*

inadvertent, *a.* Disattento, incauto; impremeditato.

inadvertently, *adv.* Inavvertitamente.

inalienability, *n.* Inalienabilità, *f.*

inalienable, *a.* Inalienabile.

inalterability, *n.* Inalterabilità, immutabilità, *f.*

inalterable, *a.* Inalterabile, immutabile.

inane [inˈein], *a.* Inane, vacuo, vuoto, vano. || *n.* Vuoto, *m.*

inanition [inəˈniʃən], *n.* Inanizione, *f.*

inanity [inˈæniti], *n.* Inanità, vacuità, *f.*

inanimate, *a.* Inanimato, esanime.

inappeasable, *a.* Implacabile; insaziabile.

inappetence [inˈæpitəns], *n.* (*Med.*) Inappetenza, *f.*

inapplicability, *n.* Inapplicabilità, *f.*

inapplicable, *a.* Inapplicabile.

inapposite, *a.* Inapplicabile, improprio, non appropriato.

inappositely, *adv.* Male a proposito.

inappreciable, *a.* Impercettibile, inapprezzabile.

inapprehensible, *a.* Inapprensibile.

inapproachable, *a.* Inaccessibile, inaccostabile.

inappropriate, *a.* Improprio, inacconcio, disadatto.

inappropriately, *adv.* Impropriamente.

inappropriateness, *n.* Improprietà, disadattezza, *f.*

inapt, *a.* Inetto, disadatto, inabile, sciatto, maldestro.

inaptitude, inaptness, *n.* Inettitudine, incapacità, *f.*

inaptly, *adv.* Sciattamente, inettamente.

inarticulate, *a.* Inarticolato.

inarticulateness, *n.* Inarticolazione, *f.*; pronuncia poco distinta, *f.*

inartistic, *a.* Inartistico.

inasmuch as [inəzˈmʌtʃ æz], *adv.* Giacchè, poichè, dacchè.

inattention, *n.* Inattenzione, disattenzione, trascuratezza, *f.*

inattentive, *a.* Disattento, distratto, trascurato.

inaudible, *a.* Inaudibile.

inaudibility, *n.* Inaudibilità, *f.*

inaugural, *a.* Inaugurale.

inaugurate, *v.t.* Inaugurare.

inauguration, *n.* Inaugurazione, *f.*

inauguratory, *a.* Inaugurale.

inauspicious, *a.* Inauspicato, malaugurato, infausto, infelice.

inauspiciously, *adv.* Malauguratamente.

inauspiciousness, *n.* Cattivi auspici, *m.pl.*, malaugurio, *m.*; infelicità, *f.*

inboard, *a.adv.* (*Naut.*) A bordo.

inborn, inbred, *a.* Innato, naturale, congenito.

incalculability, *n.* Incalcolabilità, *f.*

incalculable, *a.* Incalcolabile.

incandescence [inkənˈdesəns], *n.* Incandescenza, *f.*

incandescent, *a.* Incandescente. **— lamp,** lampada a incandescenza, *f.*; **— burner,** becco incandescente, *m.*

incantation [inkænˈteiʃən], *n.* Incanto, incantesimo, *m.*; magia, *f.*

incapability, *n.* Incapacità, inettitudine, *f.*

incapable, *a.* Incapace, inabile, inetto.

incapably, *adv.* Inabilmente.

incapacitate, *v.t.* Inabilitare, incapacitare.

incapacitation, *n.* Incapacità, *f.*; inabilitazione, squalifica, *f.*

incapacity, *n.* Incapacità, inabilità, *f.*

incarcerate, *v.t.* Incarcerare, carcerare.

incarceration, *n.* Incarcerazione, *f.*

incarnate, *a.* Incarnato.

incarnation, *n.* Incarnazione, *f.*

incautious, *a.* Incauto, imprudente, sconsiderato.

incautiously, *adv.* Incautamente.

incautiousness, *n.* Imprudenza, sconsideratezza, *f.*

incendiarism, *n.* Delitto d'incendio, incendio doloso, *m.*

incendiary, *n.a.* Incendiario, *m.*

incense (1) [ˈinsens], *n.* Incenso, *m.* || *v.t.* Incensare. **— -burner,** incensiere, turibolo, *m.*

incense (2) [inˈsens], *v.t.* Irritare, provocare, esasperare.

incentive [inˈsentiv], *n.* Incentivo, stimolo, incitamento, motivo, movente, *m.* || *a.* Stimolante.

Unless otherwise indicated, the pronunciation of words compounded with the prefixes "im", "in", "inter" or "ir" can be ascertained by reference to the unprefixed word in its alphabetical position in this dictionary.

inception [in'sepʃən], *n.* Principio, inizio, *m.*
inceptive, *a.* Principiante; (*Gram.*) incoativo.
incertitude, *n.* Incertezza, dubbiosità, *f.*
incessant [in'sesənt], *a.* Incessante, continuo, ininterotto.
incessantly, *adv.* Incessantemente.
incest ['insest], *n.* Incesto, *m.*
incestuous [in'sestju:əs], *a.* Incestuoso.
inch [intʃ], *n.* Pollice, dito, *m.* **To die by inches,** morire a poco a poco; **— by —,** poco a poco; **within an — of,** a un pelo di; **not to yield an —,** non cedere di un pollice; **every —,** da cima a fondo.
inchoate ['inkoueit], *a.* Appena cominciato, iniziale, rudimentale.
incidence ['insidəns], *n.* Incidenza, *f.*
incident, *n.* Incidente, caso, episodio, *m.* || *a.* Incidente.
incidental, *a.* Casuale, fortuito, accessorio, secondario; eventuale, inerente. **— expenses,** spese eventuali, *f.pl.*
incidentally, *adv.* Incidentalmente, per caso.
incinerate, *v.t.* Incenerire.
incineration, *n.* Incenerimento, *m.*
incinerator, *n.* Inceneritore, *m.*
incipient [in'sipiənt], *a.* Incipiente, iniziale.
incise [in'saiz], *v.t.* Incidere, intagliare.
incision [in'siʒən], *n.* Incisione, *f.*
incisive [in'saisiv], *a.* Incisivo, acuto.
incisor [in'saizəɹ], *n.* (*Anat.*) Dente incisivo, *m.*
incite [in'sait], *v.t.* Incitare, istigare, spingere, stimolare, spronare.
incitement, *n.* Incitamento, stimolo, *m.*
inciter, *n.* Incitatore, istigatore, *m.*
incivility, *n.* Villania, scortesia, *f.*
incivism [in'sivizm], *n.* (*Pol.*) Incivismo, *m.*
inclemency, *n.* Inclemenza, asprezza, *f.*, rigore, *m.*
inclement, *a.* Inclemente, aspro, duro.
inclinable [in'klainəbl], *a.* Inclinabile, inchinevole, propenso, proclive.
inclination [inkli'neiʃən], *n.* Inclinazione, pendenza, *f.*; disposizione, attitudine, propensione, *f.*; simpatia, *f.*; (*of head*) cenno, *m.* By —, di preferenza, per simpatia.
incline (1) ['inklain], *n.* Pendio, declivio (*down*), *m.*; (*up*) salita, *f.*
incline (2) [in'klain], *v.t.* Inclinare, chinare; indurre, disporre; *v.i.* inclinare, pendere; propendere, essere disposto, aver voglia; (*of colour*) tendere a.
inclined, *a.* Propenso, proclive, disposto; inclinato, chinato. **Do you feel — to come ?** Avete voglia di venire ?; **an — plane,** un piano inclinato, *m.*
inclinometer, *n.* Inclinometro, *m.*
include [in'klu:d], *v.t.* Includere, accludere; comprendere, racchiudere.
included, *a.* Incluso, inchiuso; compreso.
including, *a.* Compreso.
inclusion, *n.* Inclusione, *f.*
inclusive, *a.* Totale, completo, incluso; tutto compreso. **— of all charges,** tutto compreso; **— charge,** prezzo inclusivo.
incognito [in'kɔgnitou], *n.a.adv.* Incognito, *m.* **To travel —,** viaggiare in incognito.
incognizant [in'kɔgnizənt], *a.* Inconsapevole, inconscio.
incoherence, *n.* Incoerenza, *f.*
incoherent, *a.* Incoerente, incongruo, sconnesso.
incoherently, *adv.* Incoerentemente.
incombustibility, incombustibleness, *n.* Incombustibilità, *f.*
incombustible, *a.* Incombustibile.
income ['inkʌm], *n.* Reddito, *m.*; rendita, entrata, *f.*, entrate, *f.pl.* **—-tax,** imposta sul reddito, *f.*; **earned —,** rendita del lavoro, *f.*; **unearned —,** rendita patrimoniale, *f.*
incomer, *n.* Sopravvenuto, immigrante, *m.*; intruso, *m.*
incoming, *a.* Nuovo, sopravveniente, entrante; in arrivo; (*tide*) montante. **The — tenant,** l'inquilino subentrante, *m.*
incommensurability, *n.* Incommensurabilità, *f.*
incommensurable, *a.* Incommensurabile.
incommensurate, *a.* Sproporzionato, insufficiente, inadeguato.
incommode, *v.t.* Incomodare, scomodare, annoiare.
incommodious, *a.* Incomodo, scomodo.
incommodiousness, *n.* Incomodità, *f.*
incommunicability, *n.* Incomunicabilità, *f.*
incommunicable, *a.* Incomunicabile.
incommunicative, *a.* Riservato.
incommunicativeness, *n.* Riservatezza, *f.*, riserbo, *m.*
incommutable, *a.* Incommutabile.
incompact, *a.* Incompatto.
incomparable, *a.* Incomparabile.
incomparableness, *n.* Incomparabilità, *f.*
incompatibility, *n.* Incompatibilità, *f.*
incompatible, *a.* Incompatibile, contraddittorio.
incompetence, incompetency, *n.* Incompetenza, *f.*
incompetent, *a.* Incompetente, incapace, inetto.
incomplete, *a.* Incompleto, incompiuto, imperfetto.
incompletely, *adv.* Incompletamente.
incompleteness, *n.* Imperfezione, manchevolezza, *f.*
incompletion, *n.* L'essere incompleto, imperfezione, *f.*
incomprehensibility, *n.* Incomprensibilità, *f.*
incomprehensible, *a.* Incomprensibile.
incomprehension, *n.* Incomprensione, *f.*
incompressibility, *n.* Incompressibilità, *f.*
incompressible, *a.* Incompressibile.
incomputable, *a.* Incomputabile, incalcolabile.
inconceivable, *a.* Inconcepibile.
inconclusive, *a.* Inconcludente, inconclusivo.
inconclusiveness, *n.* Inconclusività, *f.*
incongruity, *n.* Incongruenza, *f.*; assurdità, *f.*
incongruous, *a.* Incongruente, incongruo; assurdo.
inconsecutive, *a.* Non consecutivo.
inconsequence, *n.* Inconseguenza, *f.*
inconsequent, *a.* Inconseguente, illogico, sconnesso.
inconsequential, *a.* Inconseguente, illogico.
inconsiderable, *a.* Inconsiderabile, trascurabile, di poco valore, di poco entità.

Unless otherwise indicated, the pronunciation of words compounded with the prefixes "im", "in", "inter" or "ir" can be ascertained by reference to the unprefixed word in its alphabetical position in this dictionary.

inconsiderableness, *n.* Trascurabilità, *f.*
inconsiderably, *adv.* Inconsiderabilmente.
inconsiderate, *a.* Inconsiderato, sconsiderato, irreflessivo, senza riguardi, poco simpatico.
inconsiderateness, inconsideration, *n.* Inconsideratezza, irriflessione, mancanza di riguardi, *f.*
inconsistency, *n.* Inconsistenza, incompatibilità, *f.*
inconsistent, *a.* Inconsistente, incompatibile, contradditorio, incongruente. **To be — with,** esser contrario a, esser incompatibile con.
inconsolable, *a.* Inconsolabile.
inconsonance, *n.* Discordanza, *f.*, disaccordo, *m.*
inconsonant, *a.* Inconsonante, discordante, contrario.
inconspicuous, *a.* Incospicuo; minuto, piccolo.
inconspicuously, *adv.* Incospicuamente.
inconspicuousness, *n.* Minutezza, piccolezza, *f.*
inconstancy, *n.* Incostanza, instabilità, mutabilità, *f.*
inconstant, *a.* Incostante, instabile, mutabile, variabile.
incontestable, *a.* Incontestabile, incontrastabile.
incontinence, incontinency, *n.* Incontinenza, *f.*
incontinent, *a.* Incontinente, sregolato.
incontinently, *adv.* Subito, immediatamente.
incontrovertible, *a.* Incontrovertibile, incontestabile.
inconvenience, *n.* Inconveniente, disturbo, *m.*; noia, *f.*, incomodo, *m.* || *v.t.* Recare disturbo a, disturbare, incomodare, annoiare.
inconvenient, *a.* Scomodo, incomodo, molesto. **If it is — to you,** se vi torna incomodo; **to come at an — time,** venire a un'ora scomoda.
inconvertible, *a.* Inconvertibile.
inconvincible, *a.* Inconvincibile.
incorporate, *v.t.* Incorporare; *v.i.* incorporarsi.
incorporation, *n.* Incorporazione, *f.*
incorporeal, *a.* Incorporeo.
incorrect, *a.* Incorretto, scorretto, inesatto, sbagliato.
incorrectly, *adv.* Scorrettamente.
incorrectness, *n.* Incorrettezza, inesattezza, scorrettezza, *f.*; erroneità, *f.*
incorrigibility, *n.* Incorreggibilità, *f.*
incorrigible, *a.* Incorreggibile.
incorrigibly, *adv.* Incorreggibilmente.
incorrupt, incorrupted, *a.* Incorrotto, puro, integro.
incorruptibility, incorruptibleness, *n.* Incorruttibilità, *f.*
incorruptible, *a.* Incorruttibile.
incorruptibly, *adv.* Incorruttibilmente.
incorruption, *n.* Incorruzione, *f.*
incorruptness, *n.* Integrità, *f.*
increase (1) [inˈkriːs], *v.t.* Aumentare, ingrandire, accrescere; *v.i.* aumentare, crescere, estendersi, moltiplicarsi.
increase (2) [ˈinkriːs], *n.* Aumento, incremento, accrescimento, ingrandimento, *m.*, crescenza, *f.* **On the —,** in aumento.
increasing, *a.* In aumento, crescente. **To go on —,** aumentare sempre.
increasingly, *adv.* Più e più, sempre più.
incredibility, incredibleness, *n.* Incredibilità, *f.*
incredible, *a.* Incredibile.
incredibly, *adv.* Incredibilmente.
incredulity, *n.* Incredulità, *f.*
incredulous, *a.* Incredulo.
incredulously, *adv.* Incredulamente.
increment [ˈinkrimənt], *n.* Incremento, aumento, *m.*
incriminate, *v.t.* Incriminare, imputare, incolpare.
incriminating, incriminatory, *a.* Incriminante.
incrust [cp. **encrust**].
incrustation, *n.* Incrostazione, incrostatura, *f.*
incubate [ˈinkjuːbeit], *v.t.* Covare; incubare.
incubation, *n.* Incubazione, *f.*
incubator, *n.* Incubatrice, *f.*
incubus [ˈinkjuːbəs], *n.* Incubo, *m.*
inculcate [ˈinkʌlkeit], *v.t.* Inculcare, istillare, imprimere.
inculcation, *n.* Inculcazione, *f.*
inculpate [ˈinkʌlpeit], *v.t.* Incolpare, incriminare.
inculpatory, *a.* Incolpatore, accusatorio.
incumbency [inˈkʌmbənsi], *n.* Beneficio ecclesiastico, *m.*, prebenda, *f.*
incumbent, *a.* Appoggiato a; obbligatorio. || *n.* (*Eccles.*) Beneficiato, titolare d'una prebenda, *m.* **To be — upon,** incombere a; **it is — upon me to,** mi incombe l'obbligo di.
incunabula [inkjuːˈnæbjuːlə], *n.pl.* Incunaboli, *m.pl.*
incur [inˈkəːɹ], *v.t.* Incorrere in, esporsi a, attirarsi; (*debts*) contrarre.
incurable, *a.* Incurabile, insanabile, cronico. **Hospital for Incurables,** Gli Incurabili, I Cronici, *m.pl.*
incurious, *a.* Incurioso; negligente, trascurato.
incuriosity, *n.* Incuriosità, *f.*
incursion, *n.* Incursione, irruzione, scorreria, *f.*
incurvation, *n.* Incurvazione, *f.*; incurvamento, *m.*
incurve [inˈkəːɹv], *v.t.* Incurvare, curvare, piegare.
indebted, *a.* Indebitato; obbligato, tenuto. (*Comm.*) **— to,** debitore di; **heavily — to a bank,** gravemente indebitato con una banca; **I'm deeply — to you for your kindness,** Le sono molto tenuto per la Sua gentilezza.
indebtedness, *n.* Debito, obbligo, *m.*; obbligazione, *f.* **To acknowledge one's —,** riconoscersi debitore, sentirsi obbligato.
indecency, *n.* Indecenza, sconvenienza, *f.*
indecent, *a.* Indecente, sconveniente.
indecently, *adv.* Indecentemente.
indecipherable, *a.* Indecifrabile, illeggibile.
indecision, *n.* Indecisione, esitanza, irresolutezza, *f.*
indecisive, *a.* Non decisivo; indeciso, dubbioso.
indecisively, *adv.* Indecisamente.
indecisiveness, *n.* Indecisione, *f.*
indeclinable, *a.* Indeclinabile.

Unless otherwise indicated, the pronunciation of words compounded with the prefixes "im", "in", "inter" or "ir" can be ascertained by reference to the unprefixed word in its alphabetical position in this dictionary.

indecorous, *a.* Indecoroso, sconveniente.
indecorousness, indecorum, *n.* Sconvenienza, indecorosità, indecenza, *f.*
indeed [in'di:d], *adv.* Davvero, in verità, realmente, infatti, veramente. || *inter.* Davvero!
indefatigable, *a.* Infaticabile, instancabile.
indefatigably, *adv.* Instancabilmente.
indefeasible, *a.* Inalienabile, inattaccabile, imprescrittibile.
indefectible, *a.* Indefettibile.
indefensible, *a.* Insostenibile, indifendibile.
indefinable, *a.* Indefinibile.
indefinably, *adv.* Indefinibilmente.
indefinite, *a.* Indefinito, indeterminato.
indefinitely, *adv.* Indefinitamente.
indefiniteness, *n.* Indefinitezza, indeterminatezza, *f.*
indelible, *a.* Indelebile, incancellabile.
indelicacy, *n.* Indelicatezza, sconvenienza, grossolanità, *f.*
indelicate, *a.* Indelicato, grossolano, sconveniente.
indelicately, *adv.* Grossolanamente.
indemnification, *n.* Indennizzo, risarcimento, *m.*
indemnify, *v.t.* Indennizzare, risarcire.
indemnity, *n.* Indennità, *f.*, risarcimento, *m.* **Act of —,** amnistia, *f.*
indemonstrable, *a.* Indimostrabile, evidente, assiomatico.
indent (1) [in'dent], *v.t.* Intaccare; (*coastline*) frastagliare; incidere; requisire. **An indented coast,** una costa frastagliata, *f.*
indent (2) ['indent], *n.* Tacca, intaccatura, *f.*; (*Comm.*) acquisto, prelievo.
indentation, *n.* Tacca, intaccatura, *f.*; (*Geog.*) frastagliatura, insenatura, *f.*; dentellatura, *f.*
indention, *n.* (*Print.*) Capolinea, *m.*
indenture, *n.* Assunzione d'un apprendista, *f.*, contratto di lavoro, *m.*; (*Law*) contratto, contratto bilaterale, *m.* || *v.t.* Collocare.
independence, *n.* Indipendenza, *f.*, stato indipendente, *m.*
independent, *a.* Indipendente, libero. **To be — of,** essere indipendente da; **person of — means,** persona fornita di mezzi, *f.*
independently, *adv.* Indipendentemente. **— of that,** all'infuori di ciò.
indescribable, *a.* Indescrivibile, indicibile.
indestructibility, *n.* Indistruttibilità, *f.*
indestructible, *a.* Indistruttibile.
indeterminable, *a.* Indeterminabile.
indeterminate, *a.* Indeterminato, vago, astratto.
indeterminateness, *n.* Indeterminatezza, *f.*
index ['indeks], *n.* Indice, *m.*; indicatore, *m.*; segno, indizio, *m.*; ago, *m.*, lancetta, *f.* || *v.t.* Fornire di un indice; metter nell'indice. **— finger,** indice, *m.*; (*Eccles.*) **— expurgatorius,** indice dei libri proibiti, *m.*
India ['indiə], *n.* (*Geog.*) India, *f.* **— paper,** carta bibbia, carta d'India, *f.*; **— rubber,** caucciù, *m.*, gomma elastica, *f.*; **—-rubber stamp,** timbro di gomma, *m.*
Indiaman, *n.* (*Naut.*) Nave per il traffico delle Indie, *f.*
Indian, *n.* Indiano, *m.*, indiana, *f.* **Red —,** Pellirossa, *m.*
Indian, *a.* Indiano. **— club,** clava, *f.*; **— corn,** granturco, *m.*; **—-ink,** inchiostro di Cina, *m.*; **— summer,** estate di San Martino, *f.*; **in — file,** in fila indiana, **— Ocean,** Oceano Indiano, Mare delle Indie, *m.*
indicate ['indikeit], *v.t.* Indicare, mostrare, additare, accennare.
indication, *n.* Indicazione, *f.*, segno, cenno, *m.*
indicative [in'dikətiv], *n.a.* Indicativo, *m.* **To be — of,** indicare.
indicator, *n.* Indicatore, *m.* (*Mech.*) **Speed —,** indicatore della velocità, tachimetro, *m.*
indicatory, *a.* Indicativo, indicatorio.
indict [in'dait], *v.t.* Incriminare, accusare; (*Law*) mettere in istato d'accusa, processare.
indictable [in'daitəbl], *a.* Punibile dalla legge, processabile. **An — offence,** un atto passibile di pena, *m.*
indiction [in'dikʃən], *n.* (*Hist.*) Indizione, *f.*
indictment [in'daitmənt], *n.* Accusa, imputazione, *f.* **Bill of —,** atto d'accusa, *m.*; **count of an —,** capo d'accusa, *m.*
indifference, *n.* Indifferenza, apatia, insensibilità, neutralità, *f.*
indifferent, *a.* Indifferente, apatico, neutrale, imparziale; (*of health*) cagionevole. **With — success,** con poco successo.
indifferentism, *n.* Indifferentismo, *m.*
indifferently, *adv.* Indifferentemente; imparzialmente; nè bene nè male.
indigence ['indidʒəns], *n.* Indigenza, povertà, *f.*
indigenous [in'didʒənəs], *a.* Indigeno, nativo.
indigent ['indidʒənt], *a.* Indigente, bisognoso.
indigestible, *a.* Indigeribile, indigesto.
indigestion, *n.* Indigestione, dispepsia, *f.*
indign [in'dain], *a.* (*obs.*) Indegno.
indignant [in'dignənt], *a.* Indignato, sdegnato, adirato; sdegnoso.
indignantly, *adv.* Con indignazione.
indignation, *n.* Indignazione, *f.*; sdegno, *m.* **To give vent to one's —,** sfogare la propria indignazione.
indignity, *n.* Indegnità, *f.*, oltraggio, affronto, *m.*
indigo ['indigou], *n.* Indaco, *m.* **—-plant,** indigofera, *f.*; **—-blue,** azzurro d'indaco, *m.*
indirect, *a.* Indiretto, obliquo, traverso. (*Gram.*) **— speech,** discorso indiretto, *m.*; (*Mil.*) **— fire,** tiro indiretto, *m.*
indirectness, *n.* Obliquità, *f.*
indiscernible, *a.* Indiscernibile, impercettibile.
indiscipline, *n.* Indisciplina, *f.*
indiscoverable, *a.* Introvabile, irreperibile.
indiscreet, *a.* Indiscreto, imprudente, sventato, sconsiderato, leggiero.
indiscreetly, *adv.* Indiscretamente.
indiscretion, *n.* Indiscrezione, imprudenza, sconsideratezza, *f.* **To commit an —,** commettere un'indiscrezione.
indiscriminate, *a.* Confuso, indiscriminato, caotico, senza discernimento.
indiscriminately, *adv.* Confusamente, indiscriminatamente.
indiscriminating, *a.* Che non discerne, approssimativo, confusionario.
indiscrimination, *n.* Mancanza di discernimento, indiscriminazione, *f.*

Unless otherwise indicated, the pronunciation of words compounded with the prefixes "im", "in", "inter" or "ir" can be ascertained by reference to the unprefixed word in its alphabetical position in this dictionary.

indispensable, *a.* Indispensabile, necessario.
indispensableness, *n.* Indispensabilità, necessità, *f.*
indispose, *v.t.* Indisporre; indispettire, disgustare.
indisposed, *a.* Indisposto; ammalato, infermiccio. **Not — to yield,** non avverso al cedere.
indisposition, *n.* (*health*) Indisposizione, *f.*; avversione, *f.*, disgusto, *m.*
indisputable, *a.* Indisputabile, indiscutibile, incontestabile.
indisputability, *n.* Incontestabilità, *f.*
indissolubility, *n.* Indissolubilità, *f.*
indissoluble, *a.* Indissolubile.
indistinct, *a.* Indistinto, vago, confuso.
indistinctness, *n.* Indistinzione, confusione, oscurità, *f.*
indistinguishable, *a.* Indistinguibile, indiscernibile.
indite [in'dait], *v.t.* Scrivere, redigere.
individual [indi'vidju:əl], *a.* Individuale, solo, singolo, personale. || *n.* Individuo, *m.*
individualism, *n.* Individualismo, *m.*
individualist, *n.* Individualista, *m.f.*
individualistic, *a.* Individualistico.
individuality [individju:'æliti], *n.* Individualità, *f.*
individualization, *n.* Individuazione, individualizzazione, *f.*
individualize, *v.t.* Individuare, individualizzare.
indivisibility, *n.* Indivisibilità, *f.*
indivisible, Indivisibile.
indivisibly, *adv.* Indivisibilmente.
Indo-China [indou'tʃainə], *n.* (*Geog.*) Indocina, *f.*
indocile, *a.* Indocile, riottoso, recalcitrante.
indocility, *n.* Indocilità, *f.*
indoctrinate, *v.t.* Addottrinare.
indoctrination, *n.* Addottrinamento, *m.*
Indo-European [indouju:rə'pi:ən], *n.a.* Indoeuropeo, *m.*
indolence ['indoləns], *n.* Indolenza, neghittosità, *f.*
indolent, *a.* Indolente, neghittoso.
indolently, *adv.* Indolentemente.
indomitable, *a.* Indomabile; ferreo, forte.
indomitably, *adv.* Indomabilmente.
indoor [in'dɔ:ɹ], *a.* Domestico, intimo, casalingo. **— games,** giuochi da sala, *m.pl.*
indoors, *adv.* In casa, al coperto, all'interno. **To stay —,** stare in casa; **— and out,** dentro e fuori.
indorse [cp. **endorse**].
indubitable, *a.* Indubitabile, certo, indubbio.
indubitably, *adv.* Indubitabilmente.
induce [in'dju:s], *v.t.* Indurre, persuadere, incitare, invogliare, spingere a; produrre, cagionare; (*Elect.*) indurre. (*Elect.*) **Induced current,** corrente indotta, *f.*
inducement, *n.* Allettamento, *m.*, lusinga, *f.*; movente, incentivo, stimolo, *m.*; persuasione, *f.*
induct [in'dʌkt], *v.t.* Introdurre, insediare, installare.
inductile, *a.* Non duttile.
induction, *n.* (*Lit.*) Introduzione, iniziazione, *f.*; (*Elect.*) induzione, *f.*; (*Amer.*) chiamata, *f.* **— -coil,** rocchetto d'induzione, *m.*
inductive, *a.* Induttivo.
inductor, *n.* Induttore, *m.*
indue [cp. **endue**].
indulge [in'dʌldʒ], *v.t.* Soddisfare, appagare, contentare; (*fig.*) accarezzare; *v.i.* abbandonarsi a, indulgere in, lasciarsi andare a. **To — oneself,** amare i propri comodi; **to — someone with,** permettere a qualcuno; **to — in,** permettersi il lusso di.
indulgence, *n.* Indulgenza, condiscendenza; rilassatezza, *f.*
indulgent, *a.* Indulgente, benevolo, compiacente.
indulgently, *adv.* Indulgentemente.
indult ['indʌlt], *n.* (*Eccles.*) Indulto, *m.*
indurate ['indju:reit], *v.t.i.* Indurire, irrigidire.
indurated, *a.* Indurito, ostinato.
induration, *n.* Indurimento, *m.*, ostinazione, *f.*
industrial [in'dʌstriəl], *a.* Industriale. **— disease,** malattia di occupazione, malattia professionale, *f.*
industrialism, *n.* Industrialismo, *m.*
industrialist, *n.* Industrialista, *m.*
industrious, *a.* Industrioso, industre; diligente, laborioso, attivo.
industriously, *adv.* Industriosamente, laboriosamente.
industry ['indəstri], *n.* Industria, manifattura, *f.*; diligenza, operosità, assiduità, attività, *f.* **The textile —,** l'industria tessile, *f.*
indwell, *v.t.i.* Essere insito, essere immanente, risiedere.
indwelling, *a.* Interiore, intimo, insito, immanente.
inebriate (1) [in'i:brieit], *v.t.* Ubbriacare, inebbriare.
inebriate (2) [in'i:briət], *a.* Brillo, alticcio, ubbriaco. || *n.* Ubbriacone, *m.*, ubbriacona, *f.*
inebriation, inebriety, *n.* Ebbrezza, ubbriachezza, *f.*
inedible, *a.* Immangiabile.
inedited, *a.* Inedito.
ineffability, ineffableness, *n.* Ineffabilità, *f.*
ineffable, *a.* Ineffabile.
ineffably, *adv.* Ineffabilmente.
ineffaceability, *n.* Incancellabilità, *f.*
ineffaceable, *a.* Incancellabile, indelebile.
ineffective, *a.* Inefficace.
ineffectively, *adv.* Inefficacemente.
ineffectual, *a.* Inefficace, inutile, vano.
ineffectually, *adv.* Inutilmente.
ineffectualness, *n.* Inefficacia, inutilità, *f.*
inefficacious, *a.* Inefficace.
inefficacy, *n.* Inefficacia, *f.*
inefficiency, *n.* Inefficienza, incapacità, *f.*
inefficient, *a.* Inefficiente, incapace, inabile.
inefficiently, *adv.* Inefficientemente, inabilmente.
inelastic, *a.* Non elastico, senza elasticità.
inelasticity, *n.* Mancanza d'elasticità, *f.*
inelegance, *n.* Ineleganza, *f.*
inelegant, *a.* Inelegante.
inelegantly, *adv.* Inelegantemente.

Unless otherwise indicated, the pronunciation of words compounded with the prefixes "im", "in", "inter" or "ir" can be ascertained by reference to the unprefixed word in its alphabetical position in this dictionary.

ineligibility, *n.* Ineleggibilità, *f.*
ineligible, *a.* Ineleggibile.
ineluctable, *a.* Ineluttabile.
inept [in'ept], *a.* Inetto, inabile, incapace, fatuo, sciocco.
ineptitude, ineptness, *n.* Inettitudine, insipienza, incapacità, fatuità, *f.*
ineptly, *adv.* Inettamente.
inequality, *n.* Ineguaglianza, disuguaglianza, *f.*; irregolarità, *f.*
inequitable, *a.* Ingiusto.
inequitably, *adv.* Ingiustamente.
inequity, *n.* Ingiustizia, *f.*
ineradicable, *a.* Inestirpabile.
ineradicably, *adv.* Inestirpabilmente.
inert [i'nəːɹt], *a.* Inerte; pigro, indolente.
inertia [i'nəːɹʃə], *n.* Inerzia, *f.*
inertness, *n.* Inerzia, *f.*
inescapable, *a.* Inevitabile.
inescapably, *adv.* Inevitabilmente.
inessential, *n.a.* Non essenziale, *m.*
inestimable, *a.* Inestimabile, incalcolabile.
inestimably, *adv.* Inestimabilmente.
inevitability, inevitableness, *n.* Inevitabilità, *f.*
inevitable, *a.* Inevitabile.
inevitably, *adv.* Inevitabilmente.
inexact, *a.* Inesatto, scorretto.
inexactitude, inexactness, *n.* Inesattezza, *f.*
inexactly, *adv.* Inesattamente.
inexcusable, *a.* Inescusabile, imperdonabile.
inexcusably, *adv.* Inescusabilmente.
inexecutable, *a.* Ineseguibile.
inexhaustible, *adv.* Inesauribile.
inexorability, *n.* Inesorabilità, *f.*
inexorable, *a.* Inesorabile, implacabile.
inexorably, *adv.* Inesorabilmente.
inexpediency, *n.* Inopportunità, impraticità, inutilità, *f.*
inexpedient, *a.* Inopportuno, inutile, inefficace, impratico.
inexpensive, *a.* Poco costoso, economico.
inexpensively, *adv.* A buon mercato, economicamente.
inexperience, *n.* Inesperienza, imperizia, *f.*
inexperienced, *a.* Inesperto; imperito; ingenuo, semplice.
inexpert, *a.* Inesperto, imperito, inabile.
inexpertly, *adv.* Inespertamente.
inexplicable, *a.* Inesplicabile.
inexplicit, *a.* Non esplicito, oscuro.
inexplosive, *a.* Non esplosivo, inesplosivo.
inexpressible, *a.* Inesprimibile. (*obs. colloq.*) **Inexpressibles,** calzoni, *m.pl.*
inexpressibly, *adv.* Inesprimibilmente.
inexpressive, *a.* Inespressivo.
inexpugnable, *a.* Inespugnabile, invincibile.
inextinguishable, *a.* Inestinguibile.
inextricable, *a.* Inestricabile.
inextricably, *adv.* Inestricabilmente.
infallibility, infallibleness, *n.* Infallibilità, *f.*
infallible, *a.* Infallibile, immancabile.
infallibly, *adv.* Infallibilmente.
infamous ['infəməs], *a.* Infame, scellerato, tristo.
infamously, *adv.* Infamemente.
infamy, *n.* Infamia, scelleratezza, *f.*, vituperio, *m.*
infancy ['infənsi], *n.* Infanzia, *f.*; (*Law*) minorità, *f.*
infant ['infənt], *n.* Infante, *m.f.*, bambino, *m.*, bambina, *f.*; (*Law*) minorenne, *m.f.* || *a.* Infantile; (*fig.*) nascente, nuovo. **— in arms,** bambino in braccio, *m.*; **an — industry,** un'industria nascente, *f.*; **— school,** asilo infantile, *m.*; **— mortality,** mortalità infantile, *f.*; **— prodigy,** prodigio infantile, *m.*
infanticide [in'fæntisaid], *n.* (*crime*) Infanticidio, *m.*; (*criminal*) infanticida, *m.f.*
infantile, infantine, *a.* Infantile, bambinesco, puerile.
infantry, *n.* (*Mil.*) Fanteria, *f.* **Light —,** fanteria leggiera, *f.*; bersaglieri, *m.pl.*
infantryman (*pl.* **infantrymen**) ['infəntrimən], *n.* (*Mil.*) Fante, soldato di fanteria, *m.*
infatuate [in'fætjuːeit], *v.t.* Infatuare, far impazzire; esaltare. **To become infatuated with,** infatuarsi, far pazzie per, infiammarsi per.
infatuation, *n.* Infatuazione, follia, esaltazione, *f.*
infect [in'fekt], *v.t.* Infettare; corrompere; appestare.
infection, *n.* Infezione, *f.*, contagio, *m.*
infectious, *a.* Infettivo, contagioso; (*fig.*) attaccaticcio, appiccicaticcio, contagioso.
infectiously, *adv.* Contagiosamente.
infectiousness, *n.* Infezione, infettività, *f.*
infelicitous, *a.* Infelice; stonato, improprio.
infelicitously, *adv.* Infelicemente.
infelicity, *n.* Infelicità, improprietà, *f.*
infer [in'fəːɹ], *v.t.* Inferire; dedurre, desumere, argomentare, arguire.
inferable, *a.* Deducibile, desumibile.
inference ['infərəns], *n.* Inferenza, illazione, *f.*
inferential, *a.* Deduttivo.
inferentially, *adv.* Deduttivamente.
inferior [in'fiəriəɹ], *a.* Inferiore, disotto. || *n.* Inferiore, *m.f.*, subordinato, *m.*
inferiority [infiəri'ɔriti], *n.* Inferiorità, *f.*
inferiorly, *adv.* Inferiormente.
infernal [in'fəːɹnəl], *a.* Infernale, diabolico. **The — regions,** l'Inferno, *m.*; **— machine,** macchina infernale, *f.*
inferno [in'fəːɹnou], *n.* Inferno, *m.*
infertile, *a.* Sterile, infruttifero.
infertility, *n.* Sterilità, *f.*
infest [in'fest], *v.t.* Infestare, devastare; molestare.
infestation, *n.* Infestamento, *m.*, infestazione, *f.*
infidel ['infidəl], *n.a.* Infedele, *m.f.*; eretico, *m.*
infidelity [infi'deliti], *n.* Infedeltà, *f.*; incredulità, *f.*; scetticismo, *m.*
infiltrate, *v.t.i.* Infiltrare, filtrare, infiltrarsi.
infiltration, *n.* Infiltrazione, *f.*
infinite ['infinit], *n.a.* Infinito, *m.*
infinitely, *adv.* Infinitamente.
infinitesimal [infini'tesiməl], *a.* Infinitesimale.
infinitive [in'finitiv], *n.a.* (*Gram.*) Infinito, *m.*
infinitude, *n.* Infinitudine, *f.*
infinity, *n.* Infinità, *f.*; (*Math.Phot.*) l'infinito, *m.*
infirm, *a.* Infermo, debole, malato; (*fig.*) fiacco, malfermo. **— of purpose,** irresoluto, indeciso.

Unless otherwise indicated, the pronunciation of words compounded with the prefixes "im", "in", "inter" or "ir" can be ascertained by reference to the unprefixed word in its alphabetical position in this dictionary.

infirmary, *n.* Infermeria, *f.*, ospedale, *m.*
infirmity, *n.* Infermità, malattia, *f.*; fiacchezza, *f.*
infix, *v.t.* Infiggere, ficcare.
inflame, *v.t.* Infiammare; accendere, eccitare; *v.i.* infiammarsi.
inflammability, inflammableness, *n.* Infiammabilità, *f.*
inflammable, *a.* Infiammabile.
inflammation, *n.* (*Med.*) Infiammazione, *f.* **— of the lungs,** polmonite, *f.*
inflammatory, *a.* Infiammatorio; (*fig.*) incendiario, sedizioso.
inflate [in'fleit], *v.t.* Gonfiare, dilatare; enfiare, ingrandire.
inflated, *a.* Gonfiato; (*fig.*) gonfio, turgido.
inflation, *n.* Enfiagione, *f.*, gonfiamento, *m.*; (*Comm.*) inflazione, *f.*
inflect [in'flekt], *v.t.* Inflettere; (*the voice*) modulare.
inflection, inflexion, *n.* Inflessione, modulazione, flessione, *f.*
inflexibility, *n.* Inflessibilità, *f.*
inflexible, *a.* Inflessibile.
inflexibly, *adv.* Inflessibilmente.
inflict [in'flikt], *v.t.* Infliggere, imporre; (*pain*) fare.
infliction, *n.* Inflizione, *f.*; (*fig.*) noia, *f.*, fastidio, *m.* **What an —!** Che noia!
inflorescence, *n.* (*Bot.*) Infiorescenza, *f.*
inflow, *n.* Influsso, afflusso, *m.* || *v.i.* Affluire.
influence ['influ:əns], *n.* Influenza, *f.*, ascendente, *m.* || *v.t.* Influire su, influenzare. **Influenced by,** influenzato da.
influential, *a.* Influente, autorevole.
influenza, flu [influ:'enzə, flu:], *n.* (*Med.*) Influenza, *f.*
influx, *n.* Affluenza, *f.*; invasione, *f.*, concorso, *m.*
infold, *v.t.* Avvolgere, avvoltolare.
inform [in'fɔ:ɹm], *v.t.* Informare; ragguagliare, istruire, avvertire, far sapere a. **To — against,** accusare, incolpare, denunziare; **to — oneself about,** informarsi circa, informarsi di.
informal, *a.* Non ufficiale, senza formalità; irregolare; senza cerimonie.
informality, *n.* Irregolarità, *f.*; mancanza di cerimonie, *f.*
informally, *adv.* Senza cerimonie, alla buona.
informant, *n.* Informatore, *m.*, informatrice, *f.*
information, *n.* Informazione, notizia, conoscenza, *f.*; (*Law*) accusa, denunzia, delazione, *f.*; sapere, *m.*; scienza, *f.*; ragguagli, *m.pl.* **A great desire for —,** una grande avidità di sapere, *f.*; **to get — on,** procurarsi informazioni circa; **to lay an —,** accusare qualcuno; **to seek —,** informarsi.
informer, *n.* Spia, *f.*; delatore, *m.*, delatrice, *f.*
infraction, *n.* Infrazione, violazione, *f.*; contravvenzione, *f.*
infrangible, *a.* Infrangibile.
infrequency, *n.* Infrequenza, *f.*
infrequent, *a.* Infrequente, scarso, rado, raro.
infrequently, *adv.* Infrequentemente, raramente.
infringe [in'frindʒ], *v.t.* Infrangere, violare, trasgredire; contravvenire.
infringement, *n.* Infrazione, violazione, trasgressione, contravvenzione, *f.* **— of copyright,** contraffazione letteraria, *f.*
infringer, *n.* Contravventore, trasgressore, *m.*
infuriate [in'fju:rieit], *v.t.* Infuriare.
infuriated, *a.* Furibondo, furente, furioso.
infuse [in'fju:z], *v.t.* Infondere; ispirare, istillare. **To — tea,** fare un' infusione di tè.
infusibility, *n.* Infusibilità, *f.*
infusible, *a.* Infusibile.
infusion, *n.* Infusione, *f.*; (*fig.*) infondimento, *m.*, ispirazione, *f.*
infusoria [infju:'zɔ:riə], *n.pl.* (*Zool.*) Infusori, *m.pl.*
ingathering, *n.* Raccolto, *m.*, messe, *f.*
ingenious, *a.* Ingegnoso; abile.
ingeniously, *adv.* Ingegnosamente.
ingenuity [indʒe'nju:iti], *n.* Ingegnosità, *f.*
ingenuous [in'dʒenju:əs], *a.* Ingenuo, schietto, semplice, sincero.
ingenuously, *adv.* Ingenuamente.
ingenuousness, *n.* Ingenuità, schiettezza, sincerità, *f.*
ingle-nook ['iŋglnuk], *n.* Cantuccio del focolare, *m.*
inglorious, *a.* Inglorioso, ignobile; oscuro.
ingloriously, *adv.* Ingloriosamente.
ingloriousness, *n.* Ignominia, *f.*; oscurità, *f.*
ingoer [i'ngouəɹ], *n.* Entrante, *m.*
ingoing, *n.* Entrata, *f.* || *a.* Entrante, nuovo.
ingot ['iŋgɔt], *n.* Lingotto, *m.*; (*of gold*) verga, *f.*
ingraft [cp. **engraft**].
ingrained [in'greind], *a.* Inveterato, inerente; matricolato.
ingrate ['ingreit], *n.a.* Ingrato, *m.*
ingratiate [in'greiʃieit], *v.r.* **To — oneself with,** ingraziarsi con, entrare nella grazia di.
ingratiating, *a.* Insinuante.
ingratiatingly, *adv.* Insinuantemente.
ingratitude, *n.* Ingratitudine, *f.*
ingredient [in'gri:diənt], *n.* Ingrediente, *m.*
ingress ['ingres], *n.* Ingresso, *m.*, entrata, *f.*
ingrowing, *a.* Incarnato. **— nail,** unghia incarnata, *f.*
inguinal ['iŋgwinəl], *a.* (*Anat.*) Inguinale.
ingulf [cp. **engulf**].
ingurgitate, *v.t.* Ingurgitare.
ingurgitation, *n.* Ingurgitamento, *m.*
inhabit [in'hæbit], *v.t.* Abitare, abitare in.
inhabitable, *a.* Abitabile.
inhabitancy, *n.* Abitazione, *f.*
inhabitant, *n.* Abitante, abitatore, *m.*
inhabitation, *n.* Abitazione, *f.*
inhabited, *a.* Abitato.
inhalation, *n.* Inalazione, *f.*
inhale, *v.t.* Inalare, aspirare.
inhaler, *n.* (*Med.*) Inalatore, *m.*
inharmonic, *a.* Inarmonioso, inarmonico.
inharmonious, *a.* Inarmonioso.
inharmoniousness, *n.* Disarmonia, *f.*
inhere [in'hiəɹ], *v.i.* Essere inerente, esser proprio di.
inherence, *n.* Inerenza, *f.*
inherent, *a.* Inerente a.
inherit [in'herit], *v.t.i.* Ereditare.
inheritable, *a.* Ereditario.
inheritance, *n.* Eredità, *f.*; retaggio, patrimonio, *m.*

Unless otherwise indicated, the pronunciation of words compounded with the prefixes "im", "in", "inter" or "ir" can be ascertained by reference to the unprefixed word in its alphabetical position in this dictionary.

inheritor, inheritrix, inheritress, *n.* Erede, *m.f.*
inhesion, *n.* Inerenza, *f.*
inhibit [in'hibit], *v.t.* Inibire; proibire.
inhibition, *n.* Inibizione, proibizione, *f.*; divieto, *m.*
inhibitory, *a.* Inibitorio.
inhospitable, *a.* Inospitale.
inhospitableness, inhospitality, *n.* Inospitalità, *f.*
inhuman, *a.* Inumano, crudele, barbaro.
inhumanity, *n.* Inumanità, crudeltà, *f.*
inhumanly, *adv.* Inumanamente, crudelmente.
inhumation, *n.* Inumazione, *f.*
inhume, *v.t.* Inumare, sotterrare.
inimical [i'nimikəl], *a.* Ostile, contrario, nemico, avverso.
inimically, *adv.* Ostilmente, contrariamente.
inimitable [in'imitəbl], *a.* Inimitabile, inarrivabile.
inimitableness, *n.* Inimitabilità, *f.*
inimitably, *adv.* Inimitabilmente.
iniquitous [in'ikwitəs], *a.* Iniquo, ingiusto.
iniquitously, *adv.* Iniquamente, ingiustamente.
iniquity [in'ikwiti], *n.* Iniquità, *f.*
initial [in'iʃəl], *a.* Iniziale, primo. || *n.* Iniziale, *f.* || *v.t.* Firmare con le iniziali, apporre le iniziali a.
initially, *adv.* Inizialmente, al principio.
initiate (1) [in'iʃieit], *v.t.* Iniziare; incominciare, fare il primo passo.
initiate (2) [in'iʃiət], *n.* Iniziato, *m.*, iniziata, *f.*
initiation, *n.* Iniziazione, *f.*
initiative, *n.* Iniziativa, *f.* **To take the —,** prendere l'iniziativa; **he has no —,** è senza iniziativa.
initiator, *n.* Iniziatore, *m.*
initiatory, *a.* Iniziativo.
inject [in'dʒekt], *v.t.* Iniettare.
injection, *n.* (*Med.*) Iniezione, *f.*
injector, *n.* (*Mech.*) Iniettore, *m.*
injudicious, *a.* Poco giudizioso, sventato, imprudente, insensato.
injudiciously, *adv.* Imprudentemente.
injudiciousness, *n.* Insensatezza, *f.*
injunction [in'dʒʌŋkʃən], *n.* Ingiunzione, *f.*, comando, *m.*; (*Law*) ingiunzione, *f.*
injure ['indʒəɹ], *v.t.* Nuocere a, danneggiare, far male a; guastare, ledere; menomare; far torto a, pregiudicare; ferire. **To — one's health,** guastarsi la salute; **the injured party,** la parte lesa, *f.*; **fatally injured,** ferito mortalmente.
injured, *a.* Offeso; ferito; (*of tone of voice*) piagnucoloso.
injurious [in'dʒju:riəs], *a.* Nocivo, dannoso, lesivo.
injury ['indʒəri], *n.* Male, torto, danno, *m.*; ingiustizia, offesa, lesione, ferita, piaga, *f.* **To the — of,** di pregiudizio a, con pregiudizio di.
injustice, *n.* Ingiustizia, *f.* **To do someone an —,** far torto a qualcuno.
ink [iŋk], *n.* Inchiostro, *m.* || *v.t.* Inchiostrare, macchiare d'inchiostro. **Copying- —,** inchiostro copiativo, *m.*; **in red —,** con inchiostro rosso; **marking- —,** inchiostro indelebile, inchiostro per la biancheria, *m.*; **printer's —,** inchiostro da stampa, *m.*; **invisible —,** inchiostro simpatico, *m.*; **to — oneself,** inchiostrarsi, macchiarsi d'inchiostro; **to — over,** dar l'inchiostro a; **— -bag,** (*of cuttle-fish*) tasca del nero, *f.*; **— -bottle,** bottiglia d'inchiostro, *f.*; **— -eraser,** gomma per l'inchiostro; **— -horn,** calamaio, *m.*; **— -pad,** tampone per timbro, cuscinetto per timbri, *m.*; **— -well,** calamaio, *m.*
inker, *n.* (*Print.*) Rullo inchiostratore, *m.*
inkiness, *n.* Nerezza, *f.*, nero d'inchiostro, *m.*
inkling ['iŋkliŋ], *n.* Sentore, sospetto, *m.*
inkstand, *n.* Calamaio, *m.*
inky, *a.* Sporco d'inchiostro, nero come l'inchiostro; inchiostroso.
inlaid [in'leid], *a.* Intarsiato, impresso. **— work,** intarsiatura, *f.*, intarsio, *m.*; **— linoleum,** linoleo incrostato, *m.*
inland ['inlənd,'inlænd], *a.* Interno, entroterra. || *adv.* All'interno, dell'interno. || *n.* L'interno del paese, l'entroterra, *m.* **— revenue,** fisco, *m.* **— postage,** servizio postale interno, *m.*
inlay (1) [in'lei], *v.t.* Intarsiare, intagliare.
inlay (2) ['inlei], *n.* Intarsiatura, *f.*, intaglio, *m.*
inlet ['inlet], *n.* (*Mech.*) Immissione, *f.*; (*Geog.*) braccio di mare, *m.*; baia, insenatura, *f.*
inly, *adv.* Internamente, nel cuore.
inmate ['inmeit], *n.* Abitante, *m.f.*; ospite, *m.f.*; inquilino, *m.*, inquilina, *f.* **The inmates of the house,** gli abitanti della casa, (*tenants*) gli inquilini della casa, *m.pl.*
inmost ['inməst], *a.* Il più intimo, il più segreto, il più riposto. **In one's — heart,** nel profondo del cuore.
inn [in], *n.* Albergo, *m.*, locanda, *f.*; osteria, *f.* **To put up at an —,** scendere ad un albergo; **— -yard,** cortile d'albergo.
innate [i'neit], *a.* Innato, ingenito.
innately, *adv.* Innatamente.
inner ['inəɹ], *a.* Interno, interiore; segreto, intimo. (*colloq.*) **The — man,** appetito, stomaco, *m.*; (*Motor, etc.*) **— tube,** camera d'aria, *f.*, tubo, *m.*
innermost, *a.* Il più segreto, il più intimo.
innings ['iniŋz], *n.* (*Sport*) Volta, *f.*, turno, *m.*; periodo, *m.*
innkeeper, *n.* Albergatore, *m.*, albergatrice, *f.*; locandiere, *m.*, locandiera, *f.*, oste, *m.*, ostessa, *f.*
innocence ['inosəns], *n.* Innocenza, *f.*
innocent, *a.* Innocente; semplice, ingenuo || *n.* Innocente, *m.f.* (*fig.*) **— of,** senza.
innocently, *adv.* Innocentemente.
innocuous [in'ɔkju:əs], *a.* Innocuo, inoffensivo.
innocuously, *adv.* Innocuamente.
innocuousness, *n.* Innocuità, *f.*
innominate [i'nɔmineit], *a.* (*Anat.*) Innominato.
innovate ['inəveit], *v.i.* Innovare.
innovation, *n.* Innovazione, novità, *f.*
innovator, *n.* Innovatore, *m.*
innoxious [i'nɔkʃəs], *a.* Innocuo, inoffensivo.
innuendo [inju:'endou], *n.* Insinuazione, malignazione, *f.*

Unless otherwise indicated, the pronunciation of words compounded with the prefixes "im", "in", "inter" or "ir" can be ascertained by reference to the unprefixed word in its alphabetical position in this dictionary.

innumerable, *a.* Innumerevole.
inobservable, *a.* Inosservabile.
inobservance, *n.* Inosservanza, *f.*
inoculate [in'ɔkju:leit], *v.t.* Inoculare; (*Bot.*) innestare.
inoculation, *n.* Inoculazione, *f.*; (*Bot.*) innesto, *m.*
inoculator, *n.* Inoculatore, *m.*
inodorous, *a.* Inodoro.
inoffensive, *a.* Inoffensivo, innocuo.
inoffensively, *adv.* Inoffensivamente.
inoffensiveness, *n.* Inoffensività, *f.*
inofficious, *a.* (*Law*) Inofficioso.
inoperative, *a.* Inefficace, senza effetto.
inopportune, *a.* Inopportuno, intempestivo.
inopportunely, *adv.* Inopportunamente.
inopportuneness, *n.* Inopportunità, *f.*
inordinate [in'ɔ:ɹdineit], *a.* Smoderato, eccessivo; disordinato, sregolato.
inordinately, *adv.* Smoderatamente.
inordinateness, *n.* Smoderatezza, *f.*, eccesso, *m.*, disordine, sregolatezza, *f.*
inorganic, *a.* Inorganico.
inorganically, *adv.* Inorganicamente.
in-patient ['inpeiʃənt], *n.* (*Med.*) Interno, ammalato ricoverato all'ospedale, *m.*
inpouring, *n.* Versamento, *m.*
inquest ['inkwest], *n.* Inchiesta, *f.* **Coroner's —,** inchiesta giudiziaria in caso di morte repentina, *f.*; **to hold an —,** fare un'inchiesta su.
inquietude, *n.* Inquietudine, *f.*
inquire [in'kwaiɹ], *v.t.* Domandare, chiedere, cercare informazioni; *v.i.* informarsi; indagare, investigare. **To — after a friend's health,** domandar della salute d'un amico; **to — the price,** chiedere il prezzo; **to — at the post office,** rivolgersi all'ufficio postale; **I will — about it,** me ne informerò; **we will — from our friends,** ci informeremo presso i nostri amici; **— within,** rivolgersi all'interno.
inquirer, *n.* Indagatore, investigatore, *m.*
inquiring, *a.* Curioso, indagatore, investigatore, scrutatore. **He has a very — mind,** ha una mente avida di sapere; **an — look,** uno sguardo indagatore, *m.*
inquiringly, *adv.* Interrogativamente, con sguardo scrutatore.
inquiry [in'kwairi], *n.* Domanda, *f.*; ricerca, investigazione, indagine, *f.*; (*Law*) inchiesta, *f.* **— office,** ufficio informazioni, *m.*; **on —,** dopo debite ricerche; **to make inquiries about,** chiedere notizie di, domandare informazioni su; **court of —,** commissione d'inchiesta, *f.*; (*Telephone*) **— operator,** operatrice per informazioni, *f.*
inquisition [inkwi'ziʃən], *n.* (*Eccles.*) Inquisizione, *f.*; investigazione, ricerca, *f.*
inquisitive [in'kwizitiv], *a.* Curioso, inquisitivo, inquisitorio.
inquisitively, *adv.* Inquisitivamente.
inquisitiveness, *n.* Curiosità, *f.*
inquisitor, *n.* (*Eccles.*) Inquisitore, *m.*
inquisitorial, *a.* Inquisitoriale.
inroad, inrush ['inroud, 'inrʌʃ], *n.* Incursione, irruzione, invasione, *f.*
insalubrious, *a.* Insalubre, malsano.
insalubrity, *n.* Insalubrità, *f.*
insane, *a.* Pazzo, matto, folle, demente, alienato. **Insane asylum,** manicomio, *m.*
insanitary, *a.* Insalubre, malsano, antigienico.
insanity, *n.* Pazzia, follia, demenza, *f.*; (*folly*) stoltezza, pazzia, *f.*
insatiability [inseiʃə'biliti], *n.* Insaziabilità, *f.*
insatiable [in'seiʃəbl], *a.* Insaziabile, ingordo.
insatiably, *adv.* Insaziabilmente.
insatiate [in'seiʃiət], *a.* Insaziato, insaziabile.
inscribe [in'skraib], *v.t.* Inscrivere; scolpire, incidere; dedicare, intitolare.
inscription [in'skripʃən], *n.* Iscrizione, *f.*; dedica, *f.*; (*Law*) inscrizione, *f.*
inscrutability [inskru:tə'biliti], *n.* Inscrutabilità, imperscrutabilità, *f.*
inscrutable, *a.* Inscrutabile, imperscrutabile.
insect ['insekt], *n.* Insetto, *m.* **— powder,** polvere insetticida, *f.*
insecticide, *n.a.* Insetticida, *m.*
insectivora [insek'tivərə], *n.pl.* Insettivori, *m.pl.*
insectivorous, *a.* Insettivoro.
insecure, *a.* Malsicuro; traballante; malfermo.
insecurely, *adv.* Malsicuramente, dubbiosamente.
insecurity, *n.* Mancanza di sicurezza, incertezza, *f.*, rischio, *m.*
insensate [in'sensit], *a.* Insensato.
insensately, *adv.* Insensatamente.
insensibility, *n.* Insensibilità, *f.*
insensible, *a.* Insensibile, indifferente, impassibile; inanimato, svenuto.
insensibly, *adv.* Insensibilmente.
insensitive, *a.* Insensitivo.
insentient, *a.* Inanimato.
inseparability, inseparableness, *n.* Inseparabilità, *f.*
inseparable, *n.a.* Inseparabile, indivisibile, *m.f.*
inseparably, *adv.* Inseparabilmente.
insert [in'sə:ɹt], *v.t.* Inserire, introdurre, intercalare.
insertion [in'sə:ɹʃən], *n.* Inserzione, aggiunta, *f.*
inset (1) [in'set], *v.t.* Inserire; aggiungere.
inset (2) ['inset], *n.* Inserzione, *f.*, inserto, riquadro, *m.*
inshore [in'ʃɔ:ɹ], *adv.* Presso la riva, sulla riva. **— fishing,** pesca costiera, *f.*
inshrine [cp. **enshrine**].
inside ['insaid], *n.* L'interno, il didentro, *m.*; parte interna. || *a.* Interno, dell'interno, interiore. || *adv. prep.* [in'said], Dentro, entro. **— out,** a rovescio; **to turn — out,** mettere a rovescio, rivoltare; **— passenger,** passeggero nell'interno; **— knowledge,** conoscenza intima, *f.*; (*Skating*) **— -edge,** curva interna, *f.*
insidious [in'sidiəs], *a.* Insidioso, ingannevole, perfido.
insidiously, *adv.* Insidiosamente.
insidiousness, *n.* Insidia, perfidia, astuzia, *f.*
insight, *n.* Penetrazione, veggenza, *f.*; acume, intendimento, discernimento, *m.* **To afford an — into,** lasciar vedere addentro in.
insignia [in'signiə], *n.pl.* Insegne, *f.pl.*, distintivo, *m.*

Unless otherwise indicated, the pronunciation of words compounded with the prefixes "im", "in", "inter" or "ir" can be ascertained by reference to the unprefixed word in its alphabetical position in this dictionary.

insignificance, *n.* Piccolezza, esiguità, *f.*; futilità, *f.*
insignificant, *a.* Insignificante, inconcludente, futile, di nessun conto.
insignificantly, *adv.* Insignificantemente.
insincere, *a.* Insincero, bugiardo, falso, finto, simulato, ipocrita.
insincerely, *adv.* Insinceramente.
insincerity, *n.* Insincerità, falsità, ipocrisia, *f.*
insinuate [in'sinju:eit], *v.t.* Insinuare, dare ad intendere, far credere; *v.i.* insinuarsi, infiltrarsi.
insinuating, *a.* Insinuante, subdolo; persuasivo, suggestivo.
insinuatingly, *adv.* Insinuantemente.
insinuation, *n.* Insinuazione, *f.*
insinuative, *a.* Insinuativo.
insipid [in'sipid], *a.* Insipido, insulso, scipito, sciocco.
insipidity, insipidness, *n.* Insipidità, insulsaggine, scipitaggine, sciocchezza, *f.*
insipidly, *adv.* Insipidamente.
insist [in'sist], *v.i.* Insistere, persistere; sostenere. **To — on,** insistere in, insistere per, sostenere che; **to — on saying,** insistere a dire; **to — on having,** esigere.
insistence, insistency, *n.* Insistenza, *f.*
insistent, *a.* Insistente, persistente.
insistently, *adv.* Insistentemente.
insnare [cp. **ensnare**].
insobriety, *n.* Intemperanza, ubbriachezza, *f.*
insolation, *n.* Insolazione, *f.*, colpo di sole, *m.*
insolence ['insələns], *n.* Insolenza, impertinenza, arroganza, *f.*
insolent, *a.* Insolente, impertinente, arrogante.
insolently, *adv.* Insolentemente.
insolubility, insolubleness, *n.* Insolubilità, *f.*
insoluble, *a.* Insolubile.
insolvency, *n.* Insolvenza, *f.*; fallimento, *m.*
insolvent, *a.* Insolvente, insolvibile. || *n.* Debitore insolvente, *m.* **To become —,** fallire.
insomnia [in'sɔmniə], *n.* Insonnia, *f.*
insomuch [insou'mʌtʃ], *adv.* A tal punto, talmente che.
insouciant [in'su:siənt], *a.* Spensierato, noncurante.
inspect [in'spekt], *v.t.* Ispezionare, esaminare, visitare, verificare; (*Mach.*) collaudare.
inspection, *n.* Ispezione, *f.*, esame, *m.*; visita, *f.* **On closer —,** dopo accurato esame.
inspector, *n.* Ispettore, *m.*
inspectorship, *n.* Ispettorato, *m.*
inspiration [inspi'reiʃən], *n.* Ispirazione, *f.*; respirazione, *f.*, respiro, *m.*
inspiratory [inspi'reitəri], *a.* Ispiratore.
inspire [in'spaiɹ], *v.t.* Ispirare; infondere, incutere. **To be inspired by,** ispirarsi a; **to be inspired with,** essere ispirato da.
inspiring, *a.* Ispirato, ispiratore. **An — speech,** un discorso ispirato, un discorso animatore, *m.*
inspirit [in'spirit], *v.t.* Animare, incoraggiare.
inspiriting, *a.* Ispirante, incoraggiante.
inspissate [ins'piseit], *v.t.* Inspessire, condensare.
instability, *n.* Instabilità, incostanza, *f.*
install [in'stɔ:l], *v.t.* Installare, insediare, collocare.
installation [instə'leiʃən], *n.* Installazione, *f.*, impianto, *m.* **Electric light —,** impianto della luce elettrica, *m.*
instalment, *n.* (*of money*) Rata, *f.*; (*of serial, etc.*) fascicolo, *m.*, puntata, *f.* **— plan,** vendita a rate, con pagamenti rateali, *m.pl.*
instance ['instəns], *n.* Esempio, caso, *m.*; domanda, istanza, richiesta, *f.* || *v.t.* Citare ad esempio, menzionare. **For —,** per esempio; **in the first —,** nel primo caso; **at the — of,** a domanda di, ad istanza di; **in the present —,** in questo caso.
instancy, *n.* Istanza, persistenza, insistenza, *f.*
instant ['instənt], *a.* Corrente, presente; immediato, urgente; (*date*) corrente. || *n.* Istante, momento, attimo, *m.* **In an —,** in un batter d'occhio; **the — that,** al momento in cui; **this —,** subito, all'istante.
instantaneous [instən'teiniəs], *a.* Istantaneo.
instantaneousness, *n.* Istantaneità, *f.*
instanter [in'stæntəɹ], *adv.* (*colloq.*) Subito, senza indugio.
instantly, *adv.* Immediatamente, subito, istantaneamente.
instead [in'sted], *adv.* Invece, in luogo, anzichè. **— of,** in luogo di; **to act — of,** fare le veci di.
instep ['instep], *n.* Collo del piede, tarso, *m.*
instigate ['instigeit], *v.t.* Istigare, incitare, spingere, fomentare; promuovere.
instigation, *n.* Istigazione, *f.*, incitamento, *m.*
instigator, *n.* Istigatore, incitatore, *m.*
instil [in'stil], *v.t.* Istillare, instillare, infondere, inculcare.
instillation, *n.* (*Med.*) Instillazione, *f.*
instinct ['instiŋkt], *n.* Istinto, *m.* || *a.* Imbevuto, penetrato; pieno; animato di. **By —,** per istinto; **— with life,** pieno di vita.
instinctive, *a.* Istintivo, impulsivo, spontaneo.
instinctively, *adv.* Istintivamente.
institute ['institju:t], *n.* Istituto, *m.*, istituzione, *f.* || *v.t.* Istituire, stabilire, fondare; iniziare, piantare; costituire, nominare; (*Law*) intentare (una causa).
institution, *n.* Istituzione, fondazione, *f.*; istituto, *m.*
institutor, *n.* Istitutore, fondatore, *m.*
instruct [in'strʌkt], *v.t.* Istruire, ammaestrare, insegnare; informare, comandare.
instruction, *n.* Istruzione, *f.*, ammaestramento, insegnamento, *m.*; comando, ordine, *m.*
instructional, *a.* Educativo.
instructive, *a.* Istruttivo.
instructor, *n.* Istruttore, *m.*; istitutore, *m.*
instructress, *n.* Istruttrice, istitutrice, insegnante, *f.*
instrument ['instru:mənt], *n.* Strumento, arnese, ordigno, utensile, *m.*; (*Law*) istrumento, atto, documento, *m.*; (*fig.*) agente, mezzano, *m.* || *v.t.* (*Mus.*) Strumentare. **Musical —,** strumento musicale, *m.*; **wind —,** strumento a fiato, *m.*; **stringed —,** strumento a corda, *m.*
instrumental [instru:'mentəl], *a.* Strumentale. **To be — in,** contribuire a.

Unless otherwise indicated, the pronunciation of words compounded with the prefixes "im", "in", "inter" or "ir" can be ascertained by reference to the unprefixed word in its alphabetical position in this dictionary.

instrumentalist, *n.* Strumentista, *m.*
instrumentality, *n.* Aiuto, *m.*, mezzi, *m.pl.*; intercessione, *f.*
instrumentation, *n.* (*Mus.*) Strumentazione, *f.*
insubordinate, *a.* Insubordinato, indisciplinato.
insubordination, *n.* Insubordinazione, indisciplinatezza, *f.*
insubstantial, *a.* Inconsistente.
insufferable, *a.* Insoffribile, insopportabile.
insufferably, *adv.* Insoffribilmente.
insufficiency, *n.* Insufficienza, *f.*
insufficient, *a.* Insufficiente.
insufficiently, *adv.* Insufficientemente.
insufflator ['insʌfleitəɹ], *n.* Spruzzatore, polverizzatore, *m.*
insular ['insju:ləɹ], *a.* Insulare; (*fig.*) di mente ristretta, limitato.
insularity, *n.* Insularità, *f.*; (*fig.*) limitatezza, *f.*
insulate ['insju:leit], *v.t.* Isolare, separare, staccare.
insulation, *n.* Isolamento, *m.*; separazione, *f.*; staccamento, allontanamento, *m.*
insulator, *n.* Isolatore, *m.*
insulin ['insju:lin], *n.* Insulina, *f.*
insult (1) [in'sʌlt], *v.t.* Insultare, vituperare, ingiurare, insolentire, oltraggiare.
insult (2) ['insʌlt], *n.* Insulto, *m.*; ingiuria, offesa, villania, insolenza, *f.*
insulting, *a.* Insultante, ingiurioso, insolente.
insultingly, *adv.* Insultantemente.
insuperable, *a.* Insuperabile, invincibile.
insuperably, *adv.* Insuperabilmente.
insupportable, *a.* Insopportabile, insoffribile, intollerabile.
insupportableness, *n.* Insopportabilità, *f.*
insupportably, *adv.* Insopportabilmente.
insurable, *a.* Assicurabile.
insurance, *n.* Assicurazione, *f.* **Fire —,** assicurazione contro gli incendi, *f.*; **life- —,** assicurazione sulla vita, *f.*; **— agent,** agente d'assicurazione, *m.*; **— office,** ufficio d'assicurazione, *m.*; **— policy,** polizza d'assicurazione, *f.*; **— premium,** premio d'assicurazione, *m.*; **— company,** società d'assicurazione, *f.*
insure, *v.t.* Assicurare, accertare, garantire; *v.i.* assicurarsi.
insured, *a.* Assicurato. ‖ *n.* (*person*) Assicurato, *m.*, assicurata, *f.*
insurer, *n.* Assicuratore, *m.*
insurgent, *n.a.* Insorgente; insorto, ribelle, *m.*
insurmountable, *a.* Insormontabile, insuperabile, invincibile.
insurrection, *n.* Insurrezione, sollevazione, *f.*; sommossa, *f.* **To rise in —,** sollevarsi, ribellarsi.
insurrectionary, *a.* Insurrezionale.
insusceptibility, *n.* Insuscettibilità, *f.*
intact, *a.* Intatto, intero.
intaglio, *n.* Intaglio, *m.*
intake, *n.* Immissione, *f.*; presa (d'acqua), *f.*; (*Mech.*) energia assorbita, *f.*; aspirazione, *f.*
intangibility, *n.* Intangibilità, *f.*
intangible, *a.* Intangibile.
integer, *n.* (*Math.*) Numero intero, *m.*
integral, *a.* Integro, integrale, compiuto, totale; necessario. (*Math.*) **— calculus,** calcolo integrale, *m.*; **an — part,** una parte integrante, *f.*
integrant, *a.* Integrante.
integrate, *v.t.* Integrare; completare.
integration, *n.* Integrazione, *f.*
integrity, *n.* Integrità, *f.*; lealtà, *f.*; probità, *f.*; purità, *f.*
integument, *n.* Integumento, *m.*
intellect, *n.* Intelletto, intendimento, *m.*, intelligenza, *f.*
intellectual, *a.* Intellettuale; intelligente.
intellectually, *adv.* Intellettualmente.
intelligence, *n.* Intelligenza, *f.*, perspicacia, sagacia, *f.*; giudizio, comprendonio, *m.*; informazioni, notizie, *f.pl.*, avvisi, *m.pl.* **— bureau,** ufficio d'informazioni, *m.*; **latest —,** ultime notizie, *f.pl.*
intelligencer, *n.* Informatore, *m.*; messaggero, *m.*
intelligent, *a.* Intelligente, perspicace, sagace.
intelligibility, intelligibleness, *n.* Intelligibilità, chiarezza, *f.*
intelligible, *a.* Intelligibile, comprensibile.
intelligibly, *adv.* Intelligibilmente.
intemperance, *n.* Intemperanza, *f.*, alcoolismo, *m.*
intemperate, *a.* Intemperato, sfrenato, smodato, immoderato, sregolato; alcoolizzato, ubbriaco.
intemperately, *adv.* Intemperatamente.
intend [in'tend], *v.t.* Intendere, disegnare, proporsi, stabilire; volere, aver l'intenzione di; destinare, riservare. **The book intended for you,** il libro a voi destinato.
intendant, *n.* Intendente, amministratore, *m.*
intended, *a.* Intenzionale, deliberato. ‖ *n.* (*colloq.*) Promesso sposo, fidanzato, *m.*, fidanzata, *f.*
intense, *a.* Intenso; veemente, vivo, eccessivo.
intensely, *adv.* Intensamente.
intenseness, intensity, *n.* Intensità, forza; violenza, fierezza, *f.*
intensification, *n.* Intensificazione, *f.*
intensify, *v.t.* Intensificare; (*Phot.*) rinforzare.
intensive, *a.* Intensivo.
intensively, *adv.* Intensivamente.
intent [in'tent], *a.* Intento, attento, assorto; fisso. ‖ *n.* Intento, scopo, proposito, *m.*; fine, *f.* **— on,** intento a, assorto in; **to all intents and purposes,** sotto tutti i rapporti; **with — to,** allo scopo di.
intention, *n.* Intenzione, *f.*, proposito, proponimento, disegno, *m.*
intentional, *a.* Intenzionale, premeditato, deliberato, fatto ad arte.
intentionally, *adv.* Apposta, con intenzione, deliberatamente.
intentioned, *a.* Intenzionato. **Ill- —,** male intenzionato; **well- —,** ben intenzionato.
intently, *adv.* Intentamente.
intentness, *n.* Applicazione, attenzione, *f.*; preoccupazione, *f.*
inter [in'tə:ɹ], *v.t.* Seppellire, sotterrare, inumare.
interact [intər'ækt], *v.i.* Reagire reciprocamente.
interaction, *n.* Azione reciproca, *f.*
interbreed, *v.t.* Incrociare, allevare ibridi.

Unless otherwise indicated, the pronunciation of words compounded with the prefixes "im", "in", "inter" or "ir" can be ascertained by reference to the unprefixed word in its alphabetical position in this dictionary.

intercalary [intəɹˈkæləri], *a.* Intercalare.
intercalate, *v.t.* Intercalare.
intercalation, *n.* Intercalazione, *f.*
intercede [intəɹˈsi:d], *v.i.* Intercedere. **To — with,** intercedere presso; **to — for,** intercedere per.
intercept [intəɹˈsept], *v.t.* Intercettare; arrestare, fermare.
interception, *n.* Intercettamento, *m.*
intercession [intəɹˈseʃən], *n.* Intercessione, *f.*; intervento, *m.*
intercessor, *n.* Intercessore, *m.*
intercessory, *a.* Intercedente.
interchange, *v.t.* Scambiare, ricambiare, contraccambiare, alternare. || *n.* Scambio, ricambio, *m.*; alternazione, *f.*
interchangeable, *a.* Scambievole, vicendevole, reciproco.
intercommunicate, *v.i.* Intercomunicare.
intercommunication, *n.* Intercomunicazione, *f.*
intercostal [intəɹˈkɔstəl], *a.* (*Med.*) Intercostale.
intercourse [ˈintəɹkɔ:ɹs], *n.* Comunicazione, *f.*, relazioni, *f.pl.*, rapporti, *m.pl.*; commercio, *m.*, pratica, *f.*; coito, *m.*
interdependent, *a.* Interdipendente.
interdict (1) [intəɹˈdikt], *v.t.* Interdire, vietare, proibire.
interdict (2), **interdiction** [ˈintəɹdikt, intəɹˈdikʃən], *n.* Interdetto, divieto, *m.*, interdizione, *f.*
interdictory, *a.* Interdittorio, interdicente.
interest [ˈintərest], *v.t.* Interessare, destare interesse. || *n.* Interesse, *m.*; interessamento, vantaggio, profitto, tornaconto, *m.* **To — oneself in,** interessarsi a; **the brewing —,** gli interessi dei birrai, *m.pl.*; **at —,** a frutto; **compound —,** interesse composto, *m.*; **simple —,** interesse semplice, *m.*; **to bear —,** fruttare interesse, dare interesse; **to have — with,** avere influenza presso; **to put out to —,** dare a interesse, porre ad interesse; **to repay with —,** pagare con gli interessi.
interested, *a.* Interessato. **— party,** parte interessata, *f.*
interesting, *a.* Interessante. (*colloq.*) **In an — condition,** incinta.
interfere [intəɹˈfiəɹ], *v.i.* Interferire, intromettersi; inframmettersi, immischiarsi in, ingerirsi. **To — with someone,** immischiarsi con alcuno; **Don't —!** Non immischiatevi!
interference, *n.* Inframmettenza, ingerenza, intromissione, *f.*; (*Elec.Radio, etc.*) interferenza, *f.*
interfuse, *v.t.i.* Mischiare, mischiarsi, fondere, infondere.
interfused, *a.* Mischiato, fuso.
interim [ˈintərim], *a.* Provvisorio, temporaneo, interinale. || *n.* Interim, interinato, *m.*; frattempo, intervallo, *m.* (*Comm.*) **— dividend,** dividendo provvisorio, *m.*; **in the —,** frattanto, intanto.
interior [inˈtiəriəɹ], *n.a.* Interiore, interno, *m.*
interjacent [intəɹˈdʒeisənt], *a.* Intermediario.
interject [intəɹˈdʒekt], *v.t.* Interporre, intercalare, interloquire; esclamare, interrompere.
interjection, *n.* Interiezione, *f.*
interlace [intəɹˈleis], *v.t.* Intrecciare, allacciare.
interlacing, *n.* Intreccio, allacciamento, incrocio, *m.*
interlard, *v.t.* Lardellare. **To — with quotations,** lardellare di citazioni.
interleave, *v.t.* Interfogliare.
interline, *v.t.* Interlineare.
interlinear, *a.* Interlineare. **— translation,** traduzione interlineare, *f.*
interlineation, *n.* Interlineazione, *f.*
interlock, *v.i.* Concatenare, connettere, collegare.
interlocution, *n.* Interlocuzione, *f.*; dialogo, *m.*
interlocutor [intəɹˈlɔkju:təɹ], *n.* Interlocutore, *m.*
interlocutory, *a.* Interlocutorio.
interloper [ˈintəɹloupəɹ], *n.* Intruso, estraneo, *m.*; contrabbandiere, *m.*
interlude [ˈintəɹlju:d], *n.* Intervallo, *m.*; (*Mus.*) intermezzo, interludio, *m.*
intermarriage, *n.* Matrimonio tra parenti, *m.*; matrimonio tra diverse razze o famiglie, *m.*
intermarry, *v.i.* Sposarsi tra parenti.
intermeddle [intəɹˈmedl], *v.i.* Immischiarsi, intromettersi.
intermeddler, *n.* Intrigante, ficcanaso, *m.*
intermeddling, *n.* Intervento, *m.*, intromissione, *f.*
intermediary, *n.a.* Intermediario, mediatore, *m.*
intermediate, *n.a.* Intermedio, frapposto, *m.*
interment [inˈtə:ɹmənt], *n.* Seppellimento, sotterramento, *m.*, inumazione, *f.*
intermezzo, *n.* (*Mus.*) Intermezzo, *m.*
intermigration, *n.* Emigrazione scambievole, *f.*
intermuscular, *a.* (*Anat.*) Intermuscolare.
intern [inˈtə:ɹn], *v.t.* Internare, confinare.
internal [inˈtə:ɹnəl], *a.* Interno, interiore; intimo, domestico, intrinseco. **— evidence,** evidenza interna, *f.*; **— combustion engine,** motore a scoppio, *m.*
internally, *adv.* Internamente.
international, *a.* Internazionale, *a.*
internationale, *n.* (*hymn*) Internazionale, *f.*
internationalism, *n.* Internazionalismo, *m.*
internationalist, *n.a.* Internazionalista, *m.f.*
internationalize, *v.t.* Internazionalizzare.
internecine [intəɹˈni:sain], *a.* Micidiale, mortale. **— strife,** guerra micidiale, *f.*
internee [intə:ɹˈni:], *n.* Internato, *m.*, internata, *f.*
internment, *n.* Internamento, confino, *m.* **— camp,** campo di concentramento, *m.*
interpellate [inˈtə:ɹpəleit], *v.t.* (*Pol.*) Interpellare.
interpellation, *n.* Interpellanza, *f.*
interpellator, *n.* Interpellante, interpellatore, *m.*
interplanetary, *a.* (*Astron.*) Interplanetario.
interpolate [inˈtə:ɹpəleit], *v.t.* Interpolare, inserire, intercalare.
interpolation, *n.* Interpolazione, inserzione, *f.*
interpolator, *n.* Interpolatore, *m.*

Unless otherwise indicated, the pronunciation of words compounded with the prefixes "im", "in", "inter" or "ir" can be ascertained by reference to the unprefixed word in its alphabetical position in this dictionary.

interpose [intəɹ'pouz], *v.t.* Interporre, frapporre, inserire; *v.i.* interporsi, frapporsi, intervenire.
interposition, *n.* Interposizione, *f.*, intervento, *m.*; intercessione, *f.*
interpret [in'tə:ɹpret], *v.t.* Interpretare; spiegare, palesare, chiarire.
interpretation, *n.* Interpretazione, spiegazione, *f.*
interpretative, *a.* Interpretativo.
interpreter, *n.* Interprete, *m.f.*
interregnum [intəɹ'regnəm], *n.* Interregno, *m.*
interrelation, *n.* Relazione, *f.*, rapporto, *m.*
interrogate [in'terəgeit], *v.t.* Interrogare, chiedere, domandare.
interrogation, *n.* Interrogazione, domanda, *f.* **Note of —,** punto interrogativo, *m.*
interrogative, *n.a.* Interrogativo, *m.*
interrogator [in'terəgeitəɹ], *n.* Interrogatore, interrogante, *m.*
interrogatory, *n.* Interrogatorio, esame, *m.* || *a.* Interrogatorio.
interrupt [intə'rʌpt], *v.t.* Interrompere, troncare, sospendere.
interruptedly, *adv.* Interrottamente, saltuariamente.
interrupter, *n.* Interruttore, *m.*, interruttrice, *f.*; (*Elec.*) interruttore, *m.*
interruption, *n.* Interruzione, *f.*, interrompimento, *m.*; cessazione, sospensione, *f.*
intersect [intəɹ'sekt], *v.t.* Intersecare; incrociare; *v.i.* intersecarsi, incrociarsi.
intersection, *n.* Intersezione, intersecazione, *f.*
interspace, *n.* Spazio, intervallo, *m.*
intersperse [intəɹ'spə:ɹs], *v.t.* Cospargere, seminare; alternare.
interstellar [intəɹ'steləɹ], *a.* (*Astron.*) Interstellare.
interstice [in'tə:ɹstis], *n.* Interstizio, *m.*
intertwine, *v.t.* Intrecciare, intessere.
interval ['intəɹvəl], *n.* Intervallo, spazio, *m.*
intervene [intəɹ'vi:n], *v.i.* Intervenire; interporsi, ingerirsi; accadere, avvenire; (*of time*) trascorrere, intercorrere.
intervening, *a.* (*Law*) Interveniente; intermedio, frapposto, intercorrente. **In the — time,** nel frattempo.
intervention, *n.* Intervento, *m.*, interposizione, mediazione, *f.*
interview ['intəɹvju:], *n.* Intervista, *f.*; abboccamento, colloquio, *m.*; udienza, *f.* || *v.t.* Intervistare; abboccarsi con.
interviewer, *n.* Intervistatore, *m.*
interweave, *v.t.* Intessere, intrecciare.
interweaving, *n.* Intessitura, *f.*
interworking, *n.* Azione reciproca, *f.*
intestacy [in'testəsi], *n.* Mancanza di testamento, *f.*, il morire intestato.
intestate [in'testət], *a.* Senza testamento, intestato.
intestinal [in'testinəl], *a.* Intestinale.
intestine [in'testin], *n.* (*Anat.*) Intestino, *m.* || *a.* Intestino, interiore, interno. **— warfare,** guerre intestine, *f.pl.*
intimacy ['intiməsi], *n.* Intimità, domestichezza, *f.*
intimate (1) ['intimit], *n.a.* Intimo, familiare.
intimate (2) ['intimeit], *v.t.* Intimare, notificare; ammonire; dichiarare, accennare.
intimately, *adv.* Intimamente, familiarmente.
intimation, *n.* Intimazione, notifica, *f.*; avviso, *m.*
intimidate [in'timideit], *v.t.* Intimidire.
intimidation, *n.* Intimidazione, *f.*
into ['intu:], *prep.* In, dentro. **— the bargain,** per soprammercato, per giunta; **far — the night,** a notte avanzata.
intolerable, *a.* Intollerabile, insopportabile.
intolerableness, *n.* Intollerabilità, *f.*
intolerably, *adv.* Intollerabilmente.
intolerance, *n.* Intolleranza, *f.*
intolerant, *a.* Intollerante, intransigente.
intolerantly, *adv.* Intollerantemente.
intonation [intə'neiʃən], *n.* Intonazione, *f.*
intone [in'toun], *v.t.* Intonare.
intoxicant [in'tɔksikənt], *n.* Bevanda alcoolica, *f.*, liquore, *m.*
intoxicate, *v.t.* Ubbriacare, intossicare, inebriare.
intoxicated, *a.* Ubbriaco, ebbro.
intoxication, *n.* Ebbrezza, *f.*, inebbriamento, *m.*; ubbriachezza, *f.*
intractability, *n.* Intrattabilità, *f.*
intractable, *a.* Intrattabile, scontroso.
intractably, *adv.* Intrattabilmente.
intrados [in'treidɔs], *n.* (*Arch.*) Intradosso, *m.*
intransigence [in'trænzidʒəns], *n.* Intransigenza, *f.*
intransigent, *n.a.* Intransigente, *m.f.*
intransitive, *a.* (*Gram.*) Intransitivo.
intrench, *v.t.* Trincerare.
intrepid [in'trepid], *a.* Intrepido, impavido, imperterrito.
intrepidity [intre'piditi], *n.* Intrepidezza, *f.*, coraggio, *m.*
intrepidly, *adv.* Intrepidamente.
intricacy ['intrikəsi], *n.* Intrico, groviglio, viluppo, *m.*; complicazione, oscurità, difficoltà, *f.*
intricate, *a.* Intricato, imbrogliato; oscuro, difficile.
intricately, *adv.* Intricatamente.
intrigue [in'tri:g], *n.* Intrigo, raggiro, maneggio, *m.*; tresca, *f.* || *v.i.* Intrigare; *v.t.* (*colloq.*) stuzzicare, incuriosire.
intriguer, *n.* Intrigante, *m.f.*
intriguing, *a.* Intrigante; (*coll.*) interessante.
intrinsic [in'trinsik], *a.* Intrinseco, essenziale, vero.
intrinsically, *adv.* Intrinsecamente.
introduce [intro'dju:s], *v.t.* Introdurre; presentare, far conoscere; cominciare. **To — oneself,** presentarsi, farsi conoscere.
introducer, *n.* Introduttore, *m.*, introduttrice, *f.*, presentatore, *m.*, presentatrice, *f.*
introduction, *n.* Introduzione, presentazione, *f.*; (*of a speech*) esordio, *m.* **Letter of —,** lettera di presentazione, *f.*
introductory, *a.* Introduttivo, introduttorio, preliminare.
introit [in'trouit], *n.* (*Eccles.*) Introito, *m.*
intromission, *n.* Intromissione, *f.*
introspection [intro'spekʃən], *n.* Introspezione, *f.*
introspective, *a.* Introspettivo.

Unless otherwise indicated, the pronunciation of words compounded with the prefixes "im", "in", "inter" or "ir" can be ascertained by reference to the unprefixed word in its alphabetical position in this dictionary.

introvert [intro'vəːɹt], *v.t.* Volgere in dentro, introvertere, ripiegare in se stesso. || *n.* (*Psychology*) Introspettivo, introverso, *m.*
intrude [in'truːd], *v.i.* Intrudersi, immischiarsi, intromettersi, interporsi; *v.t.* intromettere, interporre. **To — on,** importunare, incomodare, disturbare; **to — into,** immischiarsi in.
intruder, *n.* Intruso, *m.*, intrusa, *f.*, importuno, *m.*, importuna, *f.*
intrusion, *n.* Intrusione, importunità, *f.*
intrusive, *a.* Intruso, importuno.
intrust [cp. **entrust**].
intuition [intjuː'iʃən], *n.* Intuizione, *f.*, intuito, *m.*
intuitive [in'tjuːitiv], *a.* Intuitivo.
intuitively, *adv.* Intuitivamente.
intumescence [intjuː'mesəns], *n.* (*Med.*) Intumescenza, *f.*
inundate ['inʌndeit], *v.t.* Inondare, allagare, sommergere.
inundation, *n.* Inondazione, *f.*, allagamento, *m.*
inure [injuːɹ], *v.t.* Abituare, assuefare, avvezzare, indurire, temprare.
inurement, *n.* Assuefazione, *f.*
inutility, *n.* Inutilità, *f.*
inutile, *a.* Inutile, vano.
invade [in'veid], *v.t.* Invadere, assalire, usurpare, violare.
invader, *n.* Invasore, *m.*
invading, *a.* Invadente, invasore.
invalid (1) [in'vælid], *a.* Invalido, nullo.
invalid (2) ['invəliːd], *a.* Infermo, malato, debole, invalido. || *n.* Malato, infermo, invalido, *m.*, malata, inferma, invalida, *f.*
invalidate [in'vælideit], *v.t.* Invalidare, rendere nullo.
invalided, *a.* Invalido, malato; (*Mil.*) riformato.
invalidity [invə'liditi], *n.* Invalidità, infermità, debolezza, *f.*
invaluable, *a.* Inestimabile, prezioso, incalcolabile.
invariableness, invariability, *n.* Invariabilità, *f.*
invariable, *a.* Invariabile, costante, fisso.
invariably, *adv.* Invariabilmente, sempre.
invasion [in'veiʒən], *n.* Invasione, *f.*; (*fig.*) violazione, usurpazione, *f.*
invective [in'vektiv], *n.* Invettiva, *f.*
inveigh [in'vei], *v.i.* Inveire, sfogarsi contro. **To — against,** apostrofare, ingiuriare.
inveigle [in'veigl], *v.t.* Sedurre, allettare, tentare.
inveiglement, *n.* Seduzione, lusinga, *f.*, allettamento, *m.*
invent [in'vent], *v.t.* Inventare.
invention, *n.* Invenzione, *f.*
inventive, *a.* Inventivo.
inventor, *n.* Inventore, *m.*, inventrice, *f.*
inventory ['invəntəri], *n.* Inventario, *m.* || *v.t.* Inventariare, far l'inventario di.
inverness [invəɹ'nes], *n.* Un mantello pesante, *m.*
inverse [in'vəːɹs], *a.* Inverso. **In — ratio,** in ragione inversa.
inversion, *n.* Inversione, *f.*, rovesciamento, *m.*
invert [in'vəːɹt], *v.t.* Invertire, rovesciare, capovolgere; trasporre.
invertebrate, *n.a.* (*Zool.*) Invertebrato, *m.*
inverted, *a.* Rovesciato. **— commas,** virgolette, *f.pl.*
invertedly, *adv.* A rovescio, contrariamente.
invest [in'vest], *v.t.* Investire, rivestire; impiegare, collocare; (*Mil.*) investire, assediare, bloccare.
investigate [in'vestigeit], *v.t.* Investigare, esplorare, indagare.
investigation, *n.* Investigazione, ricerca, indagine, *f.*
investigative, investigatory, *a.* Investigativo, investigatore.
investigator, *n.* Investigatore, indagatore, *m.*
investiture [in'vestitʃəɹ], *n.* Investitura, *f.*
investment, *n.* (*Comm.*) Investimento, impiego, *m.*, collocazione, *f.*; (*Mil.*) investimento, blocco, assedio, *m.*
investor, *n.* Azionista, risparmiatore, *m.*
inveteracy, inveterateness, *n.* Tenacia, ostinazione, *f.*; incancrenamento, *m.*
inveterate, *a.* Inveterato, radicato, ostinato.
inveterately, *adv.* Inveteratamente.
invidious [in'vidiəs], *a.* Irritante, antipatico, spiacevole, odioso, ingiusto. **An — distinction,** una distinzione antipatica, *f.*
invidiousness, *n.* Odiosità, spiacevolezza, *f.*
invigilate [in'vidʒileit], *v.t.* Invigilare, sorvegliare.
invigilator, *n.* Invigilatore, ispettore, *m.*
invigorate [in'vigəreit], *v.t.* Rinvigorire, rianimare, rinforzare, fortificare.
invigorating, *a.* Rinforzante, fortificante, corroborante.
invincibility, invincibleness [invinsi'biliti, in'vinsəblnis], *n.* Invincibilità, *f.*
invincible, *a.* Invincibile, insuperabile.
invincibly, *adv.* Invincibilmente.
inviolability, *n.* Inviolabilità, *f.*
inviolable, *a.* Inviolabile.
inviolate, *a.* Inviolato, illeso, integro, intero, intatto.
invisibility, invisibleness, *n.* Invisibilità, *f.*
invisible, *a.* Invisibile, impercettibile.
invisibly, *adv.* Invisibilmente, impercettibilmente.
invitation [invi'teiʃən], *n.* Invito, *m.*, offerta, *f.*
invitatory, *a.* Invitatorio.
invite [in'vait], *v.t.* Invitare; domandare; offrire, attrarre; provocare.
inviting, *a.* Attraente, seducente, invitante.
invitingly, *adv.* In modo attraente.
invitingness, *n.* Attrattiva, seduzione, *f.*, fascino, *m.*
invocation, *n.* Invocazione, supplica, *f.*, appello, *m.*
invoice ['invɔis], *n.* (*Comm.*) Fattura, *f.* || *v.t.* Fatturare, mandare la fattura. **—-clerk,** contabile, *m.*
invoke [in'vouk], *v.t.* Invocare, implorare, impetrare.
involucre ['invəluːkəɹ], *n.* (*Bot.*) Involucro, *m.*
involuntarily, *adv.* Involontariamente.
involuntariness, *n.* Involontarietà, *f.*
involuntary, *a.* Involontario.
involute, *n.* (*Bot.*) Involuta, *f.*
involuted, involutive, *a.* Involuto, involutivo.

Unless otherwise indicated, the pronunciation of words compounded with the prefixes "im", "in", "inter" or "ir" can be ascertained by reference to the unprefixed word in its alphabetical position in this dictionary.

involution, *n.* Involuzione, *f.*, involgimento, *m.*
involve [in'vɔlv], *v.t.* Involgere, coinvolgere; implicare, comprendere; richiedere, cagionare; imbrogliare, complicare. **To — expense,** richiedere gravi spese; **he is involved in debt,** è carico di debiti; **to be involved in difficulties,** essere involto nelle difficoltà; **to be involved in bankruptcy,** essere coinvolto in un fallimento.
involved, *a.* Implicato, coinvolto. **— speech,** discorso involuto, *m.*
involvement, *n.* Imbarazzo pecunario, dissesto, *m.*
invulnerability, *n.* Invulnerabilità, *f.*
invulnerable, *a.* Invulnerabile.
invulnerably, *adv.* Invulnerabilmente.
inward ['inwəɹd], *a.* Interiore, interno, intimo.
inwardly, inward, *adv.* Interiormente, nell'intimo dell'anima, fra sè, intimamente.
inwardness, *n.* Interiorità, intimità, *f.*
inwards, *adv.* Al di dentro, interiormente, verso l'interno, nell'interno. || *n.pl.* Visceri, *m.pl.*
inweave, *v.t.* Intrecciare, intessere.
inwrought, *a.* Figurato; ricamato; (*fig.*) connesso, commisto.
iodic [ai'ɔdik], *a.* (*Chem.*) Iodico.
iodiferous [aiou'difərəs], *a.* Iodifero.
iodine [aiou'dain], *n.* Iodio, *m.*
iodize, *v.t.* Iodare.
iodoform [ai'oudofɔːɹm], *n.* Iodoformio, *m.*
ion ['aiɔn], *n.* Iono, *m.*
Ionian, Ionic [ai'ouniən, ai'ɔnik], *a.* Ionio, Ionico.
iota [ai'outə], *n.* Iota, *f.*
I.O.U. [aiou'juː], *abbrev.* **I owe you,** *n.* Io vi devo; dichiarazione di debito, *f.*
ipecacuanha [ipikækjuː'ɑːnə], *n.* (*Bot.*) Ipecacuana, *f.*
Iranian [ai'reniən], *a.* Iranico.
irascibility [iræsi'biliti], *n.* Irascibilità, irritabilità, *f.*
irascible, *a.* Irascibile, irritabile.
irascibly, *adv.* Irascibilmente.
irate [ai'reit], *a.* Irato, iroso, incollerito.
irately, *adv.* Iratamente.
ire ['aiəɹ], *n.* Ira, collera, *f.*, sdegno, corruccio, *m.*
ireful, *a.* Collerico, adirato, cruccioso.
Ireland ['aiəɹlənd], *n.* (*Geog.*) Irlanda, *f.*
iridescence [iri'desəns], *n.* Iridescenza, *f.*
iridescent, *a.* Iridescente, cangiante.
iridium [i'ridiəm], *n.* (*Min.*) Iridio, *m.*
iris ['airis], *n.* (*Anat., Bot., etc.*) Iride, *f.*
Irish, *a.* Irlandese. || *n.* (*language*) Irlandese, gaelico, *m.*
Irishism, *n.* Locuzione irlandese, *f.*
Irishman, Irishwoman, *n.* Irlandese, *m.f.*
irk [əːɹk], *v.t.* Affliggere, turbare, annoiare.
irksome, *a.* Fastidioso, seccante, tedioso, increscioso.
irksomeness, *n.* Fastidio, tedio, *m.*, noia, *f.*
iron [aiɹən], *n.* Ferro, *m.* || *a.* Ferreo, di ferro. || *v.t.* (*linen*) Stirare; (*fetter*) mettere ai ferri; rivestire di ferro, guarnire di ferro, ferrare. **Cast- —,** ghisa, *f.*; **sheet- —,** lamiera di ferro, *f.*; **wrought- —,** ferro battuto, *m.*; **galvanized- —,** ferro galvanizzato, *m.*; **pig- —,** pane di ghisa, lingotto, *m.*; **to put in irons,** mettere ai ferri; **the Iron Age,** L'Età del Ferro, *f.*; **old —,** ferraccio, *m.*; (*fig.*) **to strike the — while it is hot,** battere il ferro quando è caldo; **to have too many irons in the fire,** avere troppa carne al fuoco; **he has got an — constitution,** gode di una salute di ferro; **— -bound,** cerchiato di ferro, ferrato, dirupato; **an — -bound coast,** una costa dirupata, *f.*; **— -founder,** fonditore in ferro, *m.*; **— -foundry,** fonderia, *f.*; **— -grey,** grigio ferro; **— -mould,** macchia di ruggine, *f.*; **— ore,** minerali di ferro, *m.pl.*, ganga, *f.*; **— -stone,** minerale di ferro, *m.*; **— wire,** filo di ferro, *m.*; (*Mil.*) **— rations,** viveri di riserva, *m.pl.*
ironclad, *n.* (*Naut.*) Nave corazzata, *f.*
ironer, *n.* Stiratore, *m.*, stiratrice, *f.*
ironic, ironical [ai'rɔnik, ai'rɔnikəl], *a.* Ironico.
ironing, *n.* Stiratura, *f.*
ironmaster, *n.* Padrone di ferriera, *m.*
ironmonger ['aiɹnmʌŋgəɹ], *n.* Negoziante di ferramenta, *m.*
ironmongery, *n.* Ferramenta, *f.pl.*, ferrareccia, *f.*, articoli in ferro, *m.pl.*
ironwork, *n.* Ferro battuto, *m.*, lavori in ferro, *m.pl.*, ferrame, *m.*
ironworks, *n.pl.* Ferriera, *f.*
irony, *n.* Ironia, *f.*
irradiance, *n.* Irradiazione, *f.*, irraggiamento, *m.*
irradiate, *v.t.* Irradiare, illuminare, rischiarare.
irradiation, *n.* Irradiazione, *f.*, irraggiamento, *m.*; illuminazione, *f.*
irrational, *a.* Irrazionale, irragionevole; (*Math.*) irrazionale.
irrationality, *n.* Irrazionalità, irragionevolezza, assurdità, *f.*
irreclaimable, *a.* Incorreggibile.
irreconcilable, *a.* Irreconciliabile, inconciliabile. **— enemies,** avversari implacabili, *m.pl.*
irreconcilability, *n.* Irreconciliabilità, *f.*
irrecoverable, *a.* Inesigibile, irrecuperabile, irreparabile.
irredeemable, *a.* Irredimibile; incorreggibile.
irredentism [iri'dentizm], *n.* (*Pol.*) Irredentismo, *m.*
irredentist, *n.* (*Pol.*) Irredentista, *m.f.*
irreducible, *a.* Irriducibile.
irreducibly, *adv.* Irriducibilmente.
irreformable, *a.* Irriformabile, incorreggibile.
irrefragable, *a.* Irrefragabile, inconfutabile.
irrefutable, *a.* Irrefutabile.
irregular, *a.* Irregolare, anormale; (*of surface*) disuguale; (*of conduct*) sregolato, sconveniente. || *n.* (*Mil.*) Soldato irregolare, *m.*
irregularity, *n.* Irregolarità, anormalità, *f.*; ineguaglianza, *f.*; sregolatezza, sconvenienza, *f.*; disordine, *f.*
irregularly, *adv.* Irregolarmente.
irrelative, *a.* Non connesso, senza relazione.
irrelevance, *n.* Irrilevanza, *f.*
irrelevant, *a.* Fuori di proposito, insignificante, irrilevante, inconcludente.

Unless otherwise indicated, the pronunciation of words compounded with the prefixes "im", "in", "inter" or "ir" can be ascertained by reference to the unprefixed word in its alphabetical position in this dictionary.

irreligion, *n.* Irreligione, *f.*
irreligious, *a.* Irreligioso.
irreligiousness, *n.* Irreligiosità, empietà, *f.*
irremediable, *a.* Irrimediabile.
irremediably, *adv.* Irrimediabilmente.
irremissible, *a.* Irremissibile, imperdonabile.
irremovable, *a.* Inamovibile; irremovibile.
irreparable [i'repərəbl], *a.* Irreparabile, irrimediabile.
irreparably, *adv.* Irreparabilmente.
irreplaceable, *a.* Irreparabile, insostituibile.
irrepressible, *a.* Irrepressibile, irrefrenabile.
irreproachable, *a.* Irreprensibile, incensurabile.
irresistibility, *n.* Irresistibilità, *f.*
irresistible, *a.* Irresistibile; (*fig.*) affascinante.
irresolute, *a.* Irresoluto, indeciso.
irresolution, irresoluteness, *n.* Irresolutezza, indecisione, perplessità, *f.*
irresolvable, *a.* Insolubile.
irrespective, *a.* Indipendente. **— of,** astraendo, all'infuori di, senza riguardo a, astrazione fatta da.
irrespectively, *adv.* Indipendentemente.
irresponsibility, *n.* Irresponsabilità, *f.*
irresponsible, *a.* Irresponsabile.
irresponsibly, *adv.* Irresponsabilmente.
irretrievable, *a.* Irreparabile, irrimediabile.
irreverence, *n.* Irriverenza, irreligiosità, empietà, *f.*; insolenza, sfacciataggine, *f.*
irreverent, *a.* Irriverente, irreligioso, empio; insolente, sfacciato.
irreverently, *adv.* Irriverentemente.
irreversible, *a.* Irrevocabile, immutabile.
irrevocability [irevoukə'biliti], *n.* Irrevocabilità, *f.*
irrevocable [i'revəkəbl], *a.* Irrevocabile.
irrevocably, *adv.* Irrevocabilmente.
irrigable ['irigəbl], *a.* Irrigabile.
irrigate ['irigeit], *v.t.* Irrigare, inaffiare.
irrigation, *n.* Irrigazione, *f.*, inaffiamento, *m.*
irrigator, *n.* Irrigatore, *m.*
irritability [iritə'biliti], *n.* Irritabilità, irascibilità, *f.*
irritable ['iritəbl], *a.* Irritabile, permaloso.
irritably, *adv.* Irritabilmente, permalosamente.
irritant, *a.* Irritante.
irritate, *v.t.* Irritare, stuzzicare. **To be irritated,** irritarsi, adirarsi, sdegnarsi.
irritation, *n.* Irritazione, *f.*; provocazione, *f.*, sdegno, *m.*; ira, *f.*
irruption [i'rʌpʃən], *n.* Irruzione, *f.*; incursione, scorreria, *f.*
isagogic [aizə'gɔgik], *a.* Induttivo.
Isaiah [ai'zaiə], *n.* Isaia, *m.*
Ishmaelite ['iʃməlait], *n.* Ismaelita, *m.*
isinglass ['aiziŋglæs], *n.* Colla di pesce, *f.*
Islam [iz'lɑ:m], *n.* Islam, Islamismo, *m.*
Islamic, *a.* Islamitico.
Islamism, *n.* Islamismo, *m.*
island ['ailənd], *n.* Isola, *f.* **Traffic —,** salvagente, *m.*
islander, *n.* Isolano, *m.*, isolana, *f.*
isle [ail], *n.* Isola, *f.*
islet ['ailet], *n.* Isoletta, *f.*, isolotto, *m.*
isochromatic [aisoukrou'mætik], *a.* Isocromatico.
isochronous [ai'zɔkrənəs], *a.* Isocrono.
isoclinal [aisou'klainəl], *a.* Isoclino.
isodynamic [aisoudai'næmik], *a.* Isodinamico.
isolate ['aisouleit], *v.t.* Isolare.
isolated, *a.* Isolato.
isolation, *n.* Isolamento, *m.*
isomeric [aisou'merik], *a.* Isomerico.
isosceles [ai'sɔsəli:z], *a.* (*Geom.*) Isoscele.
isothermic [aisou'θə:ɹmik], *a.* Isoterma, isotermica.
Israel ['izreil], *n.* (*Geog.*) Israele, *m.*
Israelite, *n.* Israelita, *m.f.*
Israelitish, *a.* Israelitico.
issue ['iʃu:, 'isju:, 'iʃju:], *n.* (*egress*) Uscita, *f.*; (*outcome*) esito, risultato, *m.*, riuscita, fine, *f.*; (*progeny*) discendenza, figliuolanza, prole, *f.*; (*Comm.*) emissione, *f.*; (*publication*) pubblicazione, stampa, edizione, *f.*; (*Med.*) scolo, *m.*; (*Law*) questione, *f.* || *v.t.* Pubblicare, emettere; (*ticket, etc.*) rilasciare; spedire; *v.i.* uscire, venir fuori; risultare, originare, provenire, scaturire, sgorgare. **It appeared in yesterday's — of the newspaper,** si leggeva nel numero di ieri del giornale; **at —,** in lite, in contestazione; **to join — with,** esser d'altra opinione.
isthmus ['isməs], *n.* (*Geog.*) Istmo, *m.*
it [it], *pron.* Lo, esso, *m.*, la, essa, *f.*; gli, *m.*, le, *f.*; ci; ciò. **It is I,** sono io; **it is you,** siete voi; **it is said that,** si dice che; **it is believed,** si crede; **it must be so,** dev'essere così; **it is ten o'clock,** sono le dieci; **of it, for it, from it,** ne; **What is it you want?** Che cosa volete? **you will find it difficult to do,** troverete difficile farlo.
Italian [i'tæliən], *n.a.* Italiano, *m.*, italiana, *f.*; (*language*) italiano, *m.*
Italianize, *v.t.* Italianizzare.
italic [i'tælik], *a.* Italico. **Italics,** caratteri corsivi, *m.pl.*
italicize, *v.t.* Stampare in corsivo; (*fig.*) accentuare.
Italy ['itəli], *n.* (*Geog.*) Italia, *f.*
itch [itʃ], *n.* Prurito, pizzicore, *m.*; (*Med.*) scabbia, rogna, *f.* || *v.i.* Prudere, pizzicare; (*fig.*) aver voglia di. **My hand itches,** mi prude la mano.
itching, *n.* Prurito, pizzicore, *m.*
itchy, *a.* Rognoso, che prude.
item ['aitəm], *n.* Articolo, *m.*, voce, *f.*; (*of programme*) numero, *m.* || *adv.* Item, parimenti, similmente. **— of expenditure,** capo di spesa, *m.*
iterant ['itərənt], *a.* Iterativo.
iterate, *v.t.* Iterare, ripetere, reiterare.
iteration, *n.* Iterazione, ripetizione, *f.*
iterative, *a.* Iterativo, frequentativo.
itinerant [ai'tinərənt], *a.* Ambulante, girovago.
itinerary [ai'tinərəri], *n.* Itinerario, *m.*
its [its], *pron.* Il suo, *m.*, la sua, *f.*, i suoi, *m.pl.*, le sue, *f.pl.*, ne.
itself [it'self], *pron.* Esso stesso, esso medesimo, *m.*, essa stessa, essa medesima, *f.*, se stesso, lui stesso. **It goes of —,** va da se; **by —,** da solo; **he is goodness —,** è la bontà in persona.
ivied ['aivid], *a.* Coperto d'edera.

Unless otherwise indicated, the pronunciation of words compounded with the prefixes "im", "in", "inter" or "ir" can be ascertained by reference to the unprefixed word in its alphabetical position in this dictionary.

ivory ['aivəri], *n.* Avorio, *m.* || *a.* D'avorio, eburneo.
ivy ['aivi], *n.* (*Bot.*) Edera, *f.* **—-mantled,** coperto d'edera.
izard ['aizəɹd], *n.* (*Zool.*) Isardo, *m.*
izzard ['izɑːɹd], *n.* (*obs.*) La lettera zeta.

J

J, j [dʒei], Decima lettera dell'alfabeto inglese.
jab [dʒæb], *v.t.* Punzecchiare, colpeggiare, stilettare, vibrare colpi a. || *n.* Punzecchiamento, *m.*, puntata, stoccata, *f.*; pugno, *m.*
jabber, *v.i.* Ciarlare, chiacchierare; cicalare; borbottare; parlare incoerentemente. || *n.* Ciarla, chiacchiera, *f.*
jabberer, *n.* Ciarlone, chiacchierone, *m.*
jabbering, *n.* Ciarlio, chiacchierio, cicalio, *m.*
jacinth ['dʒæsinθ], *n.* Giacinto, *m.*
Jack (1) [dʒæk], *n.* Giovannino, *m.*
jack (2), *n.* (*Mech.*) Martinetto, cricco, *m.*, binda, *f.*; (*Zool.*) luccio, *m.*; (*Cards*) fante, *m.*; (*spit*) girarrosto, *m.*; (*Bowls*) boccino, pallino, *m.*; (*Naut.*) bandiera, *f.* || *v.t.* Levare. **Hydraulic —,** arganetto idraulico, *m.*; **—-in-office,** funzionario che si dà delle arie, *m.*; **— of all trades,** factotum, *m.*; **— o' lantern,** fuoco fatuo, *m.*; **boot-—,** cavastivali, *m.*; **cheap-—,** merciaio ambulante; **Jack Ketch,** il boia, *m.*; **before you can say Jack Robinson,** in un batter d'occhio, in men che non si dica; **—-in-the-box,** saltamartino, fantoccio a molla, *m.*; **—-boot,** stivalone, *m.*; **—-knife,** coltello a serramanico, *m.*; **—-plane,** pialletto, *m.*; **—-pudding,** buffone, pagliaccio, *m.*; **Jack-tar,** marinaio, *m.*; **—-towel,** bandinella, *f.*, asciugamano, *m.*
jackal ['dʒækɔːl], *n.* (*Zool.*) Sciacallo, *m.*
jackanapes ['dʒækəneips], *n.* Vanesio, sfacciatello, *m.*; sciocco, *m.*
jackass ['dʒækæs], *n.* Asino, ciuco, somaro, *m.*; (*fig.*) asino, imbecille, *m.*
jackdaw ['dʒækdɔː], *n.* (*Zool.*) Taccola, *f.*
jacket ['dʒækit], *n.* Giacchetta, giacca, giubba, *f.*; (*Mech.*) fasciatura, camicia, *f.*; (*book*) copertina, *f.*
Jacob ['dʒeikəb], *n.* Giacobbe, *m.* **Jacob's ladder,** *n.* scala biscaglina, *f.*
Jacobean [dʒækə'biən], *n.* Dell'epoca di Giacomo I d'Inghilterra, giacomiano.
Jacobin ['dʒækəbin], *n.* (*Hist.,Pol.*) Giacobino, *m.*
Jacobite ['dʒækobait], *n.* (*Hist.*) Giacobita, *m.*
jaconet ['dʒækənet], *n.* Giaconetto, *m.*
jade (1) [dʒeid], *n.* (*woman*) Donnaccia, sgualdrina, megera, *f.*; (*horse*) rozza, *f.*, ronzino, *m.*
jade (2), *n.* (*Min.*) Giada, *f.*
jade (3), *v.t.* Spossare, sovraccaricare di lavoro, affaticare.
jaded, *a.* Spossato, affaticato.
jag [dʒæg], *n.* Tacca, intaccatura, *f.*, dente, *m.* || *v.t.* Frastagliare, dentellare, seghettare.
jagged ['dʒægid], *a.* Intaccato, dentellato.
jaggedness, *n.* Intagliamento, *m.*, seghettatura, *f.*
jaguar ['dʒægjuːəɹ], *n.* (*Zool.*) Giaguaro, *m.*
jail, gaol [dʒeil], *n.* Prigione, *f.*, carcere, *m.* **—-bird,** galeotto, pezzo da galera, *m.*; **—-delivery,** rifiuto di galera, *m.*; **—-fever,** tifo, *m.*
jailer, *n.* Carceriere, *m.*
jalap ['dʒæləp], *n.* (*Bot.*) Gialappa, *f.*
jam (1) [dʒæm], *n.* (*Cooking*) Marmellata, conserva di frutta, *f.*; **—-pot,** vasetto da conserva, *m.*
jam (2), *v.t.* Pigiare, comprimere, premere, stringere; (*Radio*) disturbare; *v.i.* (*Mech.*) inceppare, incantarsi. || *n.* Inceppamento, *m.*; incaglio, blocco, *m.*; (*fig.*) calca, folla, *f.* (*colloq.*) **To be in a —,** essere nelle difficoltà.
Jamaica [dʒə'meikə], *n.* (*Geog.*) Giamaica, *f.*
jamb [dʒæm], *n.* Stipite, pilastro, *m.*
jamboree [dʒæmbə'riː], *n.* Raduno sportivo dei Giovani Esploratori, *m.*
James [dʒeimz], *n.* Giacomo, *m.*
Jane [dʒein], *n.* Giovanna, *f.*
jangle [dʒæŋgl], *v.t.* (*bells*) Scampanellare; stonare, fare discordare; *v.i.* stonare; (*fig.*) altercare, litigare, far baruffa.
jangling ['dʒæŋgliŋ], *n.* Baruffa, contesa, *f.*, alterco, *m.*; disputa, *f.* || *a.* Stridente, stonato.
janitor ['dʒænitəɹ], *n.* Portinaio, portiere, custode, *m.*
janizary ['dʒænizəri], *n.* (*Hist.*) Giannizzero, *m.*
jannock ['dʒænək], *a.* (*Dialect.*) Integro, tutto d'un pezzo, schietto, genuino.
Jansenism ['dʒænsənizm], *n.* (*Eccles.*) Giansenismo, *m.*
Jansenist, *n.* Giansenista, *m.*
January ['dʒænjuri], *n.* Gennaio, *m.*
Japan (1) [dʒə'pæn], *n.* (*Geog.*) Giappone, *m.*
japan (2), *n.* Lacca giapponese, *f.* || *v.t.* Verniciare con lacca giapponese, inverniciare, laccare.
Japanese [dʒæpə'niːz], *n.a.* Giapponese, *m.f.*
japanning, *n.* Lacca, vernice, *f.*; verniciatura, *f.*
jape [dʒeip], *n.* Scherzo, *m.* || *v.i.* Scherzare.
jar (1) [dʒɑːɹ], *n.* Vaso, *m.*, giara, *f.*; brocca, *f.*; boccale, *f.*
jar (2), *v.i.* Stonare, dissonare, scordare; urtare; litigare, urtarsi. || *n.* Vibrazione, scossa, *f.*, urto, *m.*; bega, disputa, *f.*; stonatura, dissonanza, *f.* **To — one's nerves,** urtare i nervi; **their opinions —,** le loro opinioni cozzano; **family jars,** beghe di famiglia, *f.pl.*
jar (3), *n.* **The door is on the —,** la porta è socchiusa.
jardiniere [dʒɑːɹdini'ɛəɹ], *n.* Portafiori, *m.*
jargon ['dʒɑːɹgən], *n.* Gergo, *m.*; linguaggio professionale, *m.*
jarring, *n.* Stonatura, *f.*; vibrazione, *f.*; litigio, *m.* || *a.* Stonato, stridente, scordato, discordante.
jarringly, *adv.* In modo stridente.
jarvey ['dʒɑːɹvi], *n.* (*obs.*) Vetturino, *m.*
jasmine ['dʒæzmin], *n.* (*Bot.*) Gelsomino, *m.*
jasper ['dʒæspəɹ], *n.* (*Min.*) Diaspro, *m.*
jaundice ['dʒɔːndis], *n.* (*Med.*) Itterizia, *f.*
jaundiced, *a.* Itterico; (*fig.*) fegatoso, geloso, invidioso. **To take a jaundiced view,** prendere un atteggiamento fegatoso.
jaunt [dʒɔːnt], *n.* Gita, escursione, *f.* || *v.i.* Fare una gita, andare a spasso.
jauntily, *adv.* Gaiamente.
jauntiness, *n.* Gaiezza, lepidezza, *f.*

jaunting-car [ˈdʒɔːntiŋ kɑːɹ], *n.* Specie di carrozza irlandese.
jaunty (1), *a.* Gaio, lepido; attillato, azzimato.
jaunty (2) [cp. **jonty**].
Java [ˈdʒɑːvə], *n.* (*Geog.*) Giava, *f.*
javelin [ˈdʒævlin], *n.* Giavellotto, *m.*
jaw [dʒɔː], *n.* Mascella, ganascia; mandibola, *f.*; bocca, gola, *f.*; fauci, *f.pl.*; porte, *f.pl.*; (*colloq.*) cicaleccio, *m.* ‖ *v.i.* (*colloq.*) Ciarlare, chiacchierare; sermoneggiare. **—-bone**, mascella, *f.*
jay [dʒei], *n.* (*Zool.*) Ghiandaia, *f.* **—-walker**, pedone disattento, *m.*
jazz [dʒæz], *n.* Jazz, *m.*
jealous [ˈdʒeləs], *a.* Geloso; invidioso; sospettoso.
jealously, *adv.* Gelosamente.
jealousy, *n.* Gelosia, *f.*
jean [dʒiːn], *n.* (*cloth*) Traliccio, *m.* **Jeans**, tuta di traliccio, *f.*
jeep [dʒiːp], *n.* Camionetta, *f.*, gip, *m.*
jeer [dʒiəɹ], *v.t.i.* Schernire, dileggiare, deridere, beffarsi. ‖ *n.* Beffa, canzonatura, *f.* **To — at**, beffarsi di.
jeering, *a.* Derisorio, beffardo. ‖ *n.* Dileggio, scherno, *m.*
Jehovah [dʒiˈhouvə], *n.* Geova, *m.*
jehu [ˈdʒiːhjuː], *n.* (*colloq.*) Cocchiere, vetturino, *m.*
jejune [dʒeˈdʒjuːn], *a.* Magro, gramo; (*fig.*) arido, vacuo, sterile, meschino.
jejuneness, *n.* Magrezza, *f.*; meschinità, *f.*
jelly [ˈdʒeli], *n.* Gelatina, *f.*; conserva, *f.* (*Zool.*) **—-fish**, medusa, *f.*
jemmy [ˈdʒemi], *n.* Grimaldello, *m.*
jennet [ˈdʒenet], *n.* Ginnetto, *m.*
jenny [ˈdʒeni], *n.* Macchina filatrice, *f.*; asina, *f.*
jeopardize [ˈdʒepədaiz], *v.t.* Arrischiare, azzardare, cimentare, mettere a repentaglio.
jeopardy, *n.* Rischio, azzardo, repentaglio, cimento, *m.*
jerboa [dʒəɹˈbouə], *n.* (*Zool.*) Gerboa, *f.*
jeremiad [dʒeriˈmaiəd], *n.* Geremiade, *m.*
Jeremiah [dʒeriˈmaiə], *n.* Geremia, *m.*
Jericho [ˈdʒerikou], *n.* (*Geog.*) Gerico, *m.* **Go to —!** Va a farti benedire!
jerk [dʒəːɹk], *n.* Scossa, *f.*, urto, *m.*; spinta, *f.*, scatto, balzo, strappo, *m.*; tirata, *f.*; tremito, *m.* ‖ *v.t.* Spingere, tirare, lanciare; *v.i.* scattare, balzare.
jerkily, *adv.* Irregolarmente.
jerkin [ˈdʒəːɹkin], *n.* Giustacuore, *m.*
jerky, *a.* A scatti, a scosse; irregolare.
jerry-builder [ˈdʒeribildəɹ], *n.* Costruttore di case per speculazione, *m.*
jerry-built, *a.* Malcostruito, costruito in fretta. **A — house**, una casa malcostruita, *f.*
jersey [ˈdʒəːɹzi], *n.* Giacchetta a maglia, *f.*
Jerusalem [dʒəˈruːsələm], *n.* (*Geog.*) Gerusalemme, *f.* **— artichoke**, topinambur, carciofo di Giudea, *m.*
jess, *n.* Geto, *m.*
jessamine [ˈdʒesəmin], *n.* Gelsomino, *m.*
jest [dʒest], *n.* Scherzo, *m.*, burla, facezia, celia, canzonatura, *f.*; (*laughing-stock*) ludibrio, *m.*; motteggio, frizzo, *m.* ‖ *v.i.* Scherzare, burlare, celiare, beffare, motteggiare. **—-book**, raccolta di facezie, *f.*
jester, *n.* Burlone, celiatore, *m.*; (*at court*) buffone, *m.*; beffatore, canzonatore, schernitore, *m.*
jesting, *a.* Scherzoso, faceto, burlevole, beffardo. ‖ *n.* Scherzo, *m.*, burle, beffe, *f.pl.*
jestingly, *adv.* Per ischerzo.
Jesuit [ˈdʒezjuːit], *n.* Gesuita, *m.*
Jesuitical [dʒezjuːˈitikəl], *a.* Gesuitico.
Jesus [ˈdʒiːzəs], *n.* Gesù, *m.* **Jesus Christ**, Gesù Cristo, *m.*
jet (1) [dʒet], *n.* (*Min.*) Giavazzo, gè, *m.*, ambra nera, *f.* **—-black**, nero come ebano.
jet (2), *n.* Getto, zampillo, *m.*; (*gas*) becco, *m.*; tubo di scarico, *m.* ‖ *v.i.* Zampillare, scaturire, sgorgare. **Gas-—**, becco a gas, *m.*; (*Aviat.*) **—-plane**, aeroplano a reazione, *m.*; **—-propulsion**, propulsione a reazione, *f.*
jetsam [ˈdʒetsəm], *n.* Gettito, *m.*, relitto di mare, *m.*
jettison, *n.* Gettito in mare, *m.* ‖ *v.t.* Fare gettito, gettare fuori bordo.
jetty, *n.* Molo, *m.*, banchina, gettata, *f.*; pontile, *m.*
Jew [dʒuː], *n.* Ebreo, israelita, giudeo, *m.* **Jew's harp**, scacciapensieri, *m.*
jewel [ˈdʒuːəl], *n.* Gioia, *f.*, gioiello, *m.*; (*in watch*) rubino, *m.* ‖ *v.t.* Ingemmare, ingioiellare. **—-case**, astuccio dei gioielli, scrigno, *m.*
jeweller, *n.* Gioielliere, *m.*
jewellery, **jewelry**, *n.* Gioielli, *m.pl.*, gioie, *f.pl.*, gioielleria, *f.*
Jewess [ˈdʒuːes], *n.* Ebrea, israelita, giudea, *f.*
Jewish [ˈdʒuːiʃ], *a.* Ebreo, giudeo; giudaico, israelita.
Jewry, *n.* Gli Ebrei, *m.pl.*; il ghetto, *m.*
Jezebel [ˈdʒezəbel], *n.* Izebel, *f.*; (*fig.*) megera, *f.*
jib (1) [dʒib], *n.* (*Naut.*) Flocco, *m.*; (*Mech.*) braccio (di gru), *m.* **—-boom**, bompresso di flocco, *m.*, asta del flocco, *f.*
jib (2), *v.i.* Ricalcitare, impennarsi. **To — at**, ricalcitrare a.
jibe [cp. **gibe**].
jiffy [ˈdʒifi], *n.* (*colloq.*) Batter d'occhio, istante, momentino, *m.* **In a —**, in un batter d'occhio; **Wait a —!** Aspetta un momentino!
jig [dʒig], *n.* (*dance*) Giga, *f.* ‖ *v.i.* Saltellare, saltarellare. (*Mech.*) **—-saw**, sega verticale, *f.*; **—-saw puzzle**, giuoco da mettere insieme dei pezzi irregolari per fare un disegno, *m.*; **to — about**, saltellare attorno.
jigger [ˈdʒigəɹ], *n.* (*Zool.*) Pulce tropicale, *f.*; (*Naut.*) bozzello, *m.*; (*colloq.*) aggeggio, *m.*; (*Min.*) crivello, *m.*
jiggered [ˈdʒigəɹd], *adv.* (*colloq.*) **I'm —!** Caspita!
jiggle [dʒigl], *v.t.i.* Scuotere, urtare; dimenarsi, agitarsi.
jilt [dʒilt], *v.t.* Civettare, mancare di promessa di matrimonio, farsi giuoco di, piantare in asso. ‖ *n.* Civetta, fraschetta, *f.*
jingle [dʒiŋgl], *v.t.* Far tintinnare; *v.i.* tintinnare, risuonare, squillare. ‖ *n.* Tintinnio, squillo, *m.*; (*Poet.*) rima senza significato, *f.*
jingo [ˈdʒiŋgou], *n.* Sciovinista, *m.* **By Jingo!** Per Bacco!
jingoism, *n.* Sciovinismo, *m.*
jinks [dʒiŋks], *n.pl.* **High —**, allegria, baldoria, *f.*
jinricksha [dʒinˈrikʃɔː], *n.* Risciò, *m.*
jinx [dʒiŋks], *n.* (*colloq.*) Persona o cosa che porta mala fortuna, *f.*; menagramo, iettatore, *m.*

jitters ['dʒitəɹz], *n.pl.* (*colloq.*) Paura, nervosismo, *m.*
jittery, *a.* (*colloq.*) Nervoso.
jive [dʒaiv], *n.* Specie di jazz.
jiu-jitsu [dʒuː'dʒitsuː], *n.* Lotta giapponese, *f.*
Job [dʒoub], *n.* Giobbe, *m.* **Job's comforter,** consolatore con parole inette; falso amico che fa proteste di simpatia.
job [dʒɔb], *n.* Lavoro, mestiere, *m.*; opera, *f.*; compito, *m.*; affare, *m.*; posto, impiego, *m.* || *v.t.* Noleggiare, dare in affitto, dare lavoro; *v.i.* speculare in borsa; dare a nolo, lavorare a cottimo. **Have you got a good —?** Avete un buon impiego?; **it is a bad — for him,** è un affare serio per lui; **it's a good — that,** è una buona cosa che, meno male che; **a — lot,** una cosa a buon mercato; **to work by the —,** lavorare a cottimo; **I give it up as a bad —,** lo lascio come un caso disperato.
jobation jɔb'eiʃən], *n.* (*colloq.*) Ramanzina, *f.*
jobber, *n.* Noleggiatore, *m.*; cottimista, *m.*; (*Comm. Am.*) grossista, *m.*
jobbery, *n.* Affarismo, *m.*
jobbing, *a.* Avventizio.
jobmaster ['dʒɔbmɑːstəɹ], *n.* Noleggiatore di cavalli e carrozze, *m.*
jockey ['dʒɔki], *n.* Fantino. *m.* || *v.t.i.* Ingannare, truffare, gabbare. (*Radio*) **Disk- —,** persona che fa un programma coi dischi fonografici.
jocose [dʒə'kous], *a.* Giocoso, faceto, scherzoso, allegro.
jocosely, *adv.* Giocosamente.
jocoseness, *n.* Giovialità, giocondità, *f.*
jocular ['dʒɔkjuːləɹ], *a.* Faceto, scherzoso, burlesco, gaio, allegro.
jocularity [dʒɔkjuː'læriti], *n.* Giocondità, allegria, *f.*
jocularly, *adv.* Facetamente.
jocund ['dʒɔkənd], *a.* Giocondo, lieto, gioioso, allegro.
jocundity, *n.* Giocondità, letizia, allegrezza, *f.*
jog [dʒɔg], *v.t.* Spingere, dar di gomito, urtare; (*memory*) stimolare; sballottare, sballottolare; *v.i.* andare via lentamente; andarsene. || *n.* Scossa, spinta, *f.*, urto, *m.*; gomitata, *f.* **To — along,** avviarsi, trotterellare; **to be jogged about,** essere sballottato; **— -trot,** piccolo trotto, trotterello, *m.*
joggle [dʒɔgl], *v.t.* Scuotere leggermente. || *n.* Leggera scossa, *f.*; (*Arch.*) immorsatura, *f.*
John [dʒɔn], *n.* Giovanni, *m.* **— Dory,** pesce di San Pietro, *m.*
johnny, *n.* (*colloq.*) Giovanotto, *m.*
join [dʒɔin], *v.t.* Congiungere, connettere, unire; accoppiare; raggiungere; associarsi; entrare a far parte; *v.i.* riunirsi, unirsi; essere contiguo; associarsi. || *n.* Giuntura, *f.* **To — hands,** venire ad un accordo; **he joined our party this morning,** raggiunse la nostra comitiva stamattina; **to — in,** prendere parte a; **to — together in,** mettersi insieme per, accordarsi per.
joiner, *n.* Falegname, *m.*; legnaiuolo, *m.*
joinery, *n.* Falegnameria, *f.*
joint [dʒɔint], *n.* Giuntura, unione, congiunzione, connessione, *f.*; (*Anat.*) articolazione, *f.*; (*Bot.*) nodo, *m.*; (*Cooking*) arrosto, *m.*; (*Geol.*) fessura, fenditura, *f.* || *v.t.* (*a fowl, etc.*) Smembrare; (*to assemble*) congiungere. || *a.* Riunito, unito, comune, in comune, associato. **Out of —,** slogato, spostato; (*fig.*) disordinato, sconquassato, squinternato; **with — consent,** di comune consenso; **our — efforts,** i nostri sforzi riuniti; **— ownership,** proprietà in comune, *f.*; **— command,** comando unico, *m.*; **— -heir,** coerede, *m.*; **— -stock,** capitale sociale, *m.*; **— -stock company,** società anonima, *f.*; **— tenant,** coinquilino, *m.*
jointed, *a.* Articolato, fatto a giunture.
jointly, *adv.* Insieme, d'accordo, in comune.
jointure, *n.* (*Law*) Beni dotali, *m.pl.*
joist [dʒɔist], *n.* Trave, *f.*
joke [dʒouk], *n.* Scherzo, *m.*, facezia, celia, barzelletta, arguzia, canzonatura, *f.* || *v.i.* Scherzare, celiare, motteggiare, canzonare. **A practical —,** una burla, una beffa, *f.*; un tiro birbone, *m.*; **a poor —,** uno scherzo mediocre, *m.*; **in —,** per ischerzo, per ridere, per burla; **it is no —,** non c'è nulla da ridere, c'è poco da scherzare; **to crack a —,** dire una facezia; **a standing —,** una burletta, *f.*, uno zimbello, *m.*
joker, *n.* Burlone, *m.*; (*Cards*) buffone, *m.*
joking, *a.* Faceto, scherzoso.
jollification [dʒɔlifi'keiʃən], *n.* Festa, baldoria, *f.*
jolliness, *n.* Allegria, *f.*
jollity, *n.* Allegrezza, baldoria, *f.*
jolly ['dʒɔli], *a.* Allegro, gaio; giocondo, ridente; festoso, ilare, divertente; (*colloq.*) brillo. (*colloq.*) **— good,** proprio buono; **— well,** veramente bene; **he came home from the party rather —,** è tornato dalla festa un po' brillo; (*Naut.*) **— -boat,** canotto, *m.*, lancia, *f.*
jolt [dʒoult], *n.* Scossa, *f.*, sobbalzo, sbalzo, *m.*; (*shock*) sorpresa dispiacevole, *f.* || *v.t.i.* Scuotere, sobbalzare, sballottare, sballottolare.
jolting, *n.* Scuotimento, sballottolio, *m.*
Jonah ['dʒounə], *n.* Giona, *m.*; (*fig.*) iettatore, *m.*
Jonathan ['dʒɔnəθən], *n.* Gionata, *m.*
jonquil [dʒɔŋkwil], *n.* (*Bot.*) Giunchiglia, *f.*
jonty, jaunty [dʒɔnti, dʒɔːnti], *n.* (*Naut.*) Poliziotto navale, *m.*
Jordan ['dʒɔːɹdən], *n.* (*Geog.*) Giordano, *m.*
Joseph ['dʒouzef], *n.* Giuseppe, *m.*
Josephine ['dʒouzəfiːn], *n.* Giuseppina, *f.*
joss [dʒɔs], *n.* Idolo cinese. **— -house,** tempio cinese, *m.*; **— -stick,** specie d'incenso, *f.*
jostle [dʒɔsl], *v.t.* Spingere, pigiare, urtare, dar di gomito; *v.i.* spingersi, pigiarsi, urtarsi, affollarsi.
jostling, *n.* Calca, *f.*, pigia-pigia, *m.*
jot [dʒɔt], *n.* Iota, un nulla, *m.*; particella, *f.* || *v.t.* **To — down,** annotare, prendere appunti, prendere nota di.
journal ['dʒəːɹnəl], *n.* Giornale, diario, *m.*; periodico, *m.*; (*Mech.*) perno, *m.*; collo d'asse, *m.*
journalese, *n.* Lingua giornalistica, *f.*, linguaggio bolso, *m.*
journalism, *n.* Giornalismo, *m.*
journalist, *n.* Giornalista, *m.f.*
journalistic, *a.* Giornalistico.
journey ['dʒəːɹni], *n.* Viaggio, tragitto, *m.* || *v.i.* Viaggiare; trasferirsi, recarsi. **A day's —,** un giorno di viaggio, *m.*; **Pleasant —!** Buon viaggio! **to go on a —,** andare in viaggio; **the — out,** il viaggio di andata, *m.*

journeyman (*pl.* **journeymen**), *n.* operaio avventizio, *m.*
joust [dʒaust], *n.* Giostra, *f.*, torneo, *m.* || *v.i.* Giostrare, torneare.
Jove [dʒouv], *n.* (*Myth.*) Giove, *m.* **By —!** Per Bacco!
jovial [ˈdʒouviəl], *a.* Gioviale, lieto, allegro, gaio.
joviality, *n.* Giovialità, allegrezza, *f.*
jovially, *adv.* Giovialmente.
jowl [dʒaul], *n.* Guancia, mascella, gota, *f.* **Cheek by —**, allato, vicinissimo, guancia a guancia.
joy [dʒɔi], *n.* Gioia, allegrezza, contentezza, felicità, *f.*, gaudio, *m.* **To jump for —**, saltare dalla gioia; **to be beside oneself with —**, non stare in sè dalla gioia; **to wish someone —**, rallegrarsi con qualcuno; **— -bells**, campane a festa, *f.pl.*
joyful, *a.* Allegro, giocondo, lieto, gioioso.
joyfully, *adv.* Allegramente.
joyfulness, *n.* Gioia, allegrezza, *f.*
joyless, *a.* Triste, melanconico, mesto.
joylessly, *adv.* Tristemente.
joylessness, *n.* Tristezza, melanconia, mestizia, *f.*
joyous, *a.* Allegro, lieto.
joyousness, *n.* Allegrezza, *f.*
jubilant [ˈdʒu:bilənt], *a.* Giubilante, esultante.
jubilate, *v.i.* Giubilare, far festa.
jubilation, *n.* Giubilo, *m.*, esultanza, *f.*
jubilee [ˈdʒu:bili:], *n.* Giubileo, cinquantenario, *m.*; (*fig.*) festa, allegrezza, *f.* **— year**, anno del giubileo, *m.*
Judaea [dʒu:ˈdiə], *n.* (*Geog.*) Giudea, *f.*
Judaean, *a.* Giudaico.
Judaic, Judaical, *a.* Giudeo; della Giudea.
Judaism [ˈdʒu:deiizm], *n.* Giudaismo, *m.*
Judaize, *v.t.* Ebraizzare.
Judas [ˈdʒu:dəs], *n.* Giuda, *m.*; (*fig.*) traditore, *m.* **— kiss**, bacio di Giuda, *m.*; (*Bot.*) **— -tree**, albero di Giuda, *m.*
judge [dʒʌdʒ], *n.* Giudice, arbitro, *m.*; intenditore, esperto, *m.* || *v.t.* Giudicare; stimare, ritenere, valutare, reputare. **To be a — of**, intendersi di; **judging from**, giudicando da; **you must — for yourself**, dovete giudicare per conto vostro.
Judges, *n.pl.* **The Book of —**, il Libro dei Giudici, *m.*
judgeship, *n.* Ufficio di giudice, *m.*
judgment, judgement, *n.* Giudizio, parere, *m.*; criterio, senno, discernimento, *m.*; (*Law*) sentenza, *f.* **In my —**, a mio parere, secondo me; **an error of —**, un errore di calcolo, *m.*; **to have a sound —**, giudicare con discernimento; **the Last Judgment**, il Giudizio Universale, *m.*; **Judgment Day**, il giorno del Giudizio; **— -seat**, tribunale, *m.*
judicature [ˈdʒu:dikətʃəɹ], *n.* Giudicatura, magistratura, *f.*; corte di giustizia, *f.*; ordinamento giudiziario, *m.*
judicial [dʒu:ˈdiʃəl], *a.* Giudiziario; giudiziale. **— murder**, delitto giudiziario, *m.*; **— separation**, separazione legale, *f.*
judiciary [dʒu:ˈdiʃiəri], *n.* Giudicatura, *f.* || *a.* Giudiziario.
judicious, *a.* Giudizioso, savio, prudente, accorto, assennato.
judiciously, *adv.* Saviamente, prudentemente.
judiciousness, *n.* Giudizio, senno, *m.*, prudenza, saggezza, *f.*
judo [ˈdʒu:dou], *n.* Specie di lotta giapponese, *f.*
jug [dʒʌg], *n.* Brocca, *f.*, boccale, *m.*; caraffa, *f.* || *v.t.* (*cooking*) Mettere in salmì. **Jugged hare**, lepre in salmì, *f.*
juggle [dʒʌgl], *v.t.i.* Giocare ai bussolotti, giocolare; ingannare, gabbare, imbrogliare. **To — with facts**, travisare i fatti; **to — with words**, equivocare, giuocare con le parole.
juggler, *n.* Prestigiatore, giocoliere, giocatore di bussolotti, *m.*; impostore, *m.*
jugglery, juggling, *n.* Giuochi di prestigio, *m.pl.*; trucco, *m.*, gherminelle, *f.pl.*, impostura, *f.*
Jugo-Slav [cp. **Yugoslav**].
Jugo-Slavia [cp. **Yugoslavia**].
jugular [ˈdʒʌgju:ləɹ], *n.a.* (*Anat.*) Giugulare, *f.*
juice [dʒu:s], *n.* Sugo, succo, *m.*
juiceless, *a.* Senza sugo.
juiciness, *n.* Sugosità, *f.*; succosità, *f.*
juicy, *a.* Sugoso, succoso.
jujube [ˈdʒu:dʒu:b], *n.* (*Bot.*) Giuggiola, *f.*; (*shrub*) giuggiolo, *m.*; (*sweetmeat*) pasticca, pastiglia, *f.*
julep [ˈdʒu:ləp], *n.* Giulebbe, *m.*
Julian [ˈdʒu:liən], *n.* Giuliano, *m.*
July [dʒu:ˈlai], *n.* Luglio, *m.*
jumble [dʒʌmbl], *v.t.* Confondere, mischiare, ammucchiare, gettare alla rinfusa. || *n.* Confusione, mescolanza, *f.*, miscuglio, guazzabuglio, *m.* **— sale**, vendita di roba spaiata, *f.*; bazar (di beneficenza), *m.*
jump [dʒʌmp], *n.* Salto, *m.*; balzo, sbalzo, *m.* || *v.i.* Saltare; balzare, sbalzare; scavalcare; slanciarsi; sussultare, sobbalzare, trasalire; *v.t.* far saltare. **To — at an offer**, affrettarsi ad accettare un'offerta; **to — on**, lanciarsi su; **to — out of bed**, saltare dal letto; **to — up**, saltar su; **to — to a conclusion**, affrettarsi a concludere; **he made me —**, mi fece trasalire.
jumper, *n.* Saltatore, *m.*; (*garment*) giubbettino, golf, *m.*
jumping, *n.* Salto, *m.* || *a.* Saltatore. **A — pain**, un dolore pulsante, *m.*; **— -jack**, saltamartino, *m.*; **— -ladder**, biscaglina, *f.*
jumpy, *a.* (*colloq.*) Agitato; instabile.
junction [dʒʌŋkʃən], *n.* Congiunzione, *f.*; (*Rail.*) biforcazione, *f.*, nodo ferroviario, *m.*; diramazione, *f.*
juncture, *n.* Congiuntura, *f.*; punto, momento, frangente, *m.*
June [dʒu:n], *n.* Giugno, *m.*
jungle [dʒʌŋgəl], *n.* Giungla, *f.*
junior [ˈdʒu:niəɹ], *a.* Più giovane, meno anziano, minore; cadetto, iuniore. || *n.* Iuniore, cadetto, *m.*; figlio, *m.* **He is my —**, è più giovane di me; **— partner**, socio più recente, *m.*; (*Mil.*) **— officer**, ufficiale dipendente, ufficiale subalterno.
juniper [ˈdʒu:nipəɹ], *n.* (*Bot.*) Ginepro, *m.*
junk [dʒʌŋk], *n.* (*Naut.*) Giunca, *f.*; vecchio cordame, *m.*; (*rubbish*) roba di rifiuto, *f.*
junket, *n.* Giuncata, *f.* || *v.i.* Festeggiare.
junketing, *n.* Festa, *f.*, trattenimento, *m.*
junta [dʒʌnta], *n.* (*Pol.*) Giunta, *f.*
Jurassic [dʒu:ˈræsik], *a.* (*Geol.*) Giurassico.
juridical [dʒu:ˈridikəl], *a.* Giuridico.
jurisconsult [ˈdʒu:riskɔnsʌlt], *n.* Giureconsulto, *m.*

jurisdiction, *n.* Giurisdizione, competenza, *f.*
jurisdictional, *a.* Giurisdizionale.
jurisprudence, *n.* Giurisprudenza, *f.*
jurist, *n.* Giurista, *m.*
juror, juryman ['dʒu:rəɹ, 'dʒu:rimən], *n.* Giurato, *m.*
jury, *n.* Giuria, *f.*, giurati, *m.pl.*, giurì, *m.* **Foreman of the —,** presidente della giuria, *m.*; **—-box,** banco della giuria, *m.*; (*Naut.*) **—-mast,** albero di fortuna, *m.*
just [dʒʌst], *a.* Giusto, imparziale, equo, retto, equanime; esatto, preciso. || *adv.* Esattamente, precisamente; appunto, per l'appunto; soltanto, solamente. **— one,** uno soltanto; **— now,** proprio ora, or ora, un momento fa; **— as,** nel momento stesso che; **— at present,** proprio ora; **you are — in time,** siete venuto giusto in tempo; **Just imagine!** Immaginatevi! **— let us see,** vediamo un poco; **— so,** precisamente; **that was — like him,** era proprio da lui; **he has — gone,** è appena partito; **I — managed to catch the train,** sono appena riuscito a prendere il treno.
justice ['dʒʌstis], *n.* Giustizia, *f.*; (*judge*) giudice, *m.* **— of the peace,** giudice conciliatore, *m.*; **to do — to,** fare giustizia a, riconoscere; **to do — to a dinner,** fare onore ad un pranzo; **to do oneself —,** fare una buona figura.
justiciary [dʒʌs'tiʃəri], *n.* Amministratore della giustizia, *m.*
justifiable [dʒʌsti'faiəbl], *a.* Giustificabile, scusabile, lecito, permesso.
justifiably, *adv.* Scusabilmente.
justification, *n.* Giustificazione, scusa, *f.*
justify ['dʒʌstifai], *v.t.* Giustificare, difendere, scusare, assolvere. **To — oneself,** giustificarsi; **I feel justified in . . .,** ho buone ragioni per . . .
justly, *adv.* Giustamente, con ragione, a buon diritto.
justness, *n.* Giustezza, *f.*; precisione, esattezza, *f.*
jut [dʒʌt], *v.i.* Sporgere, protendersi. **To — out,** sporgere in fuori, protendersi.
jute [dʒu:t], *n.* Iuta, *f.*
jutting, *a.* Sporgente.
juvenile ['dʒu:vənail], *a.* Giovanile, giovane; (*Law*) minorenne. || *n.* Giovane, *m.f.*; (*book*) libro per la gioventù. **— offender,** imputato minorenne, *m.*
juvenility, *n.* Giovinezza, gioventù, *f.*
juxtapose [dʒʌkstə'pouz], *v.t.* Porre vicino, apporre, giustapporre.
juxtaposition [dʒʌkstəpə'ziʃən], *n.* Giustapposizione, contiguità, *f.* **In —,** contiguo, a contatto.

K

K, k [kei], Undicesima lettera dell'alfabeto inglese.
Kaffir ['kæfəɹ], *n.a.* Cafro, *m.*
kaiser ['kaizəɹ], *n.* Imperatore, kaiser, *m.*
kale [keil], *n.* Cavolo riccio, *m.* **Sea- —,** cavolo marino, *m.*
kaleidoscope [kə'laidoskoup], *n.* Caleidoscopio, *m.*
kalendar [cp. **calendar**].
kalends ['kælendz], *n.pl.* Calende, *f.pl.* **Greek —,** calende greche, *f.pl.*
Kalif [cp. **Caliph**].
kangaroo [kæŋgə'ru:], *n.* (*Zool.*) Canguro, *m.*
Kantian ['kæntiən], *n.a.* Cantiano, *m.*
kaolin ['keioulin], *n.* (*Min.*) Caolino, *m.*
kapok ['keipɔk], *n.* Capoc, *m.*
kedge [kedʒ], *n.* (*Naut.*) Ancorotto, *m.*
kedgeree ['kedʒəri:], *n.* (*Cooking*) Carne o pesce cotto con riso.
keel [ki:l], *n.* (*Naut.*) Chiglia. **To — over,** capovolgere.
keelhaul ['ki:lhɔ:l], *v.t.* (*Naut.*) Tuffare un marinaio per punizione.
keelson, kelson ['ki:lsən, 'kelsən], *n.* Paramezzale, *m.*
keen [ki:n], *a.* Acuto, affilato, aguzzo, tagliente; (*fig.*) entusiasta, ardente, vivace; profondo; buono. **A — edge,** un taglio acuto, *m.*; **a — disappointment,** un vivo disappunto, *m.*; (*colloq.*) **to be — on,** amare molto, aver una gran voglia di; **the boy has a — appetite,** il ragazzo ha un buon appetito; **—-eyed,** dalla vista acuta; **—-witted,** acuto, sagace, scaltro.
keenly, *adv.* Vivamente, acutamente.
keenness, *n.* Acutezza, sottigliezza, penetrazione, *f.*, ardore, *m.*; vivacità, *f.*
keep [ki:p], *n.* (*castle*) Torrione; (*board*) sostentamento, mantenimento, vitto, *m.* || *v.t.* Tenere, ritenere; serbare, conservare; attenersi a, osservare, stare a; proteggere; mantenere, sostentare; *v.i.* stare, continuare; tenersi, mantenersi, serbarsi; (*of food*) durare. **To — in prison,** tenere in prigione; **to — from,** preservare da, impedire di; **to — one's own counsel,** nascondere i propri pensieri; **to — one's bed,** stare a letto; **to — the house,** stare in casa; **to — house,** mantenere casa; **to — in good health,** conservarsi in salute; (*fig.*) **to — cool,** mantenersi calmo; **she keeps on laughing,** essa continua a ridere; **I can't — going any longer,** non posso più tenermi in piedi; **to — the law,** rispettare la legge; **to — the Commandments,** osservare i Comandamenti; **to — oneself to oneself,** star sulle sue, tenersi in disparte; **to — from** (*abstain*), astenersi da; **to — back,** ritrarre, trattenere, tenere indietro; **to — down,** tener basso, abbassare; **to — in,** tener dentro, tener chiuso; **to — in with someone,** conservare l'amicizia di qualcuno; **to — off,** tenere lontano, tenersi lontano; **to — under,** tenere a freno; **to — up,** mantenere, tenere su; **to — up appearances,** salvare le apparenze; **you must — up your Italian,** dovete tenervi in esercizio col vostro italiano; **he kept me up all night,** mi fece star desto tutta la notte; (*Comm.*) **to — the books,** tenere la contabilità; **to — one's counsel,** tacere, nascondere i propri pensieri; **to — one's temper,** non adirarsi, star tranquillo; **the clock keeps good time,** l'orologio va molto bene; **to — watch,** stare in guardia; **to — a woman,** mantenere una donna; **to earn one's —,** guadagnarsi il sostentamento; (*colloq.*) **he gave me this for keeps,** m'ha regalato questo; **— off the grass,** è vietato camminare sull'erba.

keeper, *n.* Custode, guardiano, *m.*, guardia, *f.*; vigile, sorvegliante, inserviente, *m.*; guardacaccia, *m.* **— of a museum,** conservatore d'un museo, *m.*

keeping, *n.* Guardia, custodia, cura, *f.*; armonia, *f.*, accordo, *m.* **In — with,** in armonia con, d'accordo con; **in safe —,** in buona guardia.

keepsake, *n.* Ricordo, pegno d'amicizia, *m.*, pegno d'affetto, *m.*

keg [keg], *n.* Barilotto, botticello, *m.*

kelp [kelp], *n.* (*Chem.*) Soda greggia tratta da alghe, *f.*; fuco, *m.*

kelson [cp. **keelson**].

ken [ken], *n.* Vista, conoscenza, *f.*; comprensione, *f.* **Beyond one's —,** fuori di vista, al di là della propria comprensione.

kennel [ˈkenəl], *n.* Canile, covo, *m.*; (*pack of hounds*) muta, *f.*; (*gutter*) rigagnolo, *m.*, grondaia, *f.* || *v.i.* Accovacciarsi; *v.t.* mettere in canile, mandare a cuccia.

Kenya [ˈkiːniə], *n.* (*Geog.*) Chenia, *f.*

kerb [kəːɹb], *n.* Orlo del marciapede, *m.* **—-stone,** gradino del marciapede, *m.*

kerchief [ˈkəːɹtʃif], *n.* Fazzoletto da capo, fisciù, *m.*; fazzoletto, *m.*

kern [kəːɹn], *n.* (*Hist.*) Fantaccino irlandese, *m.*

kernel [ˈkəːɹnəl], *n.* Nocciolo, gheriglio, *m.*; mandorla, *f.*; nucleo, nodo, *m.*; essenza, sostanza, *f.*

kerosene [ˈkerousiːn], *n.* Petrolio illuminante, *m.*

kersey [ˈkəːɹzi], *n.* Stoffa di lana, *f.*

kestrel [ˈkestrəl], *n.* (*Zool.*) Gheppio, *m.*

ketch [ketʃ], *n.* Tartana, *f.*

ketchup[ketʃəp],*n.*Salsa di funghi e pomodori,*f.*

kettle [ketl], *n.* Caldaia, caldaietta, *f.*, bollitore, *m.*; calderotto, bricco, *m.* (*fig.*) **A pretty — of fish,** un bel pasticcio, *m.*; **—-drum,** timpano, *m.*; **—-drummer,** timpanista, *m.*; **—-holder,** presa, *f.*

key [kiː], *n.* Chiave, *f.*; (*of piano*) tasto, *m.*; (*of watch*) chiavetta, *f.*; (*Mus.*) chiave, *f.*; (*Mech.*) chiavetta, bietta, *f.* || *v.t.* Chiudere a chiave; (*Mus.*) intonare, accordare. **Under lock and —,** sotto chiave; (*colloq.*) **to have the — of the street,** essere lasciato a ciel sereno; **to — up,** stimolare, aizzare; (*Mus.*) **—-board,** tastiera, *f.*; **—-bugle,** cornetto a pistone, *f.*; **—-hole,** buco della serratura, *m.*; **—-industry,** industria chiave, *f.*; (*Mus.*) **—-note,** tonica, *f.*; nota dominante, *f.*; **—-ring,** anello per le chiavi, *m.*; (*Arch.*) **—-stone,** chiave di volta, *f.*

khaki [ˈkɑːki], *n.a.* Kaki, *m.*

khan [kæn, kɑːn], *n.* (*Hist.*) Can, *m.*

khedive [keˈdiːv], *n.* Kedive, *m.*

kibble [kibl], *n.* (*Min.*) Secchia di ferro, *f.*

kick [kik], *n.* Calcio, *m.*, pedata, *f.*; colpo di piede, *m.*; (*of horse*) calcio, *m.*; (*of gun*) rinculo, *m.* || *v.t.* Dar dei calci, cacciar a calci, prendere a calci; (*a goal*) segnare; *v.i.* rinculare, tirare calci, scalciare. **To — against the pricks,** dibattersi; **to — one's heels,** stare ad aspettare, battere i piedi; **to — out,** cacciar a calci; (*Football*) **—-off,** calcio d'inizio, *m.*; **to — off,** dare il primo calcio; **penalty- —,** calcio di rigore, *m.*; **free- —,** calcio di punizione, *m.*; **corner- —,** calcio d'angolo, *m.*; **to — up a row,** fare chiasso, fare una scenata.

kicker, *n.* Cavallo che tira calci, *m.*

kicking, *n.* Calcio, lo scalciare, *m.* **—-strap,** paracalci, *m.*

kickshaw [ˈkikʃɔː], *n.* Leccornia, ghiottoneria, *f.*, manicaretto, *m.*

kid (1) [kid], *n.* Capretto, *m.* || *a.* Di capretto. **— gloves,** guanti di pelle, *m.pl.*

kid (2), *n.* (*colloq.*) Piccino, bimbo, *m.*, piccina, bimba, *f.*

kid (3), *v.t.* (*colloq.*) Gabbare, ingannare.

kiddy, *n.* (*colloq.*) Bambino, *m.*, bambina, *f.*

kidnap [ˈkidnæp], *v.t.* Rapire, rubare (un bambino); portare via a forza.

kidnapper, *n.* Rapitore, *m.*

kidney [ˈkidni], *n.* (*Anat.*) Rene, *m.*; (*of animals*) rognone, arnione, *m.*; (*fig.*) tempra, specie, sorta, disposizione, *f.* **A man of that —,** un uomo di quella sorta, *m.*; **—-bean,** fagiuolo; **—-shaped,** reniforme.

kilderkin [ˈkildəɹkin], *n.* (*Measure*) Mezzo barile, barilotto, *m.*

kill [kil], *v.t.* Uccidere, ammazzare, trucidare; assassinare; distruggere. || *n.* Uccisione, *m.* **To be killed on the spot,** essere ucciso sul posto; **to — oneself,** uccidersi, suicidarsi; **to — time,** passare il tempo, ammazzare il tempo; **to — with kindness,** sopraffare di cortesie; **to — oneself with laughter,** crepare dalle risa; **he was killed in action,** fu ucciso in combattimento; **his son was among the killed,** suo figlio era fra i caduti.

killer, *n.* Uccisore, *m.*; assassino, *m.*

killing, *n.* Uccisione, *f.*, assassinio, *m.*; strage, *f.* || *a.* Mortale; (*colloq.*) irresistibile, affascinante; grave, pesante.

kill-joy, *n.* Guastafeste, *m.*

kiln [kiln], *n.* Forno, *m.*, fornace, *f.* **Brick- —,** fornace da mattoni, *f.*; **lime- —,** fornace da calce, *f.*; **to —-dry,** seccare al forno.

kilo, kilogramme [ˈkiːlou, ˈkilogræm], *n.* Chilo, chilogramma, *m.*

kilocycle [ˈkilosaikl], *n.* (*Radio*) Chilociclo, *m.*

kilolitre [ˈkiloliːtəɹ], *n.* Chilolitro, *m.*

kilometre [ˈkilomiːtəɹ], *n.* Chilometro, *m*

kilometric, *a.* Chilometrico.

kilowatt [ˈkilowɔt], *n.* Chilowatt, *m.*

kilt [kilt], *n.* Gonnellino, *m.*; gonnella degli Scozzesi, *f.* || *v.t.* Raccogliere in pieghe.

kimono [kiˈmounou], *n.* Chimono, *m.*

kin [kin], *n.* Parentela, *f.*, parenti, *m.f.pl.*, congiunti, *m.pl.* **Next of —,** il parente più prossimo, *m.*; **of — to,** affine a; **kith and —,** amici e parenti, *m.pl.*

kind (1) [kaind], *a.* Buono, gentile, benevolo; compiacente, cortese; tenero; indulgente. **A — word,** una buona parola, *f.*; **— regards,** saluti cordiali, *m.pl.*; **be so — as to,** abbiate la gentilezza di; **to be — to someone,** essere buono con qualcuno; **it is very — of you,** è molto gentile da parte vostra.

kind (2), *n.* Genere, *m.*, sorta, specie, *f.*; natura, *f.* **They act after their —,** agiscono secondo la loro natura; **payment in —,** pagamento in natura, *m.*; **to differ in —,** essere di diversa specie; **nothing of the —,** niente del genere; **he is a — of writer,** è una specie di scrittore.

kindergarten [ˈkindəɹgɑːɹtən], *n.* Asilo infantile, giardino d'infanzia, *m.*

kindhearted, *a.* Buono, benevolo.

kindheartedness, *n.* Bontà, *f.*

kindle [kindl], *v.t.* Accendere, dar fuoco a; (*fig.*) eccitare, provocare; destare, suscitare, infiammare; *v.i.* accendersi, prender fuoco.
kindliness, *n.* Gentilezza, amabilità, affabilità, *f.*
kindling, *n.* Accensione; legna minuta per accendere, *f.*
kindly, *a.* Gentile, amabile, affabile, buono. ‖ *adv.* Gentilmente.
kindness, *n.* Benevolenza, bontà, gentilezza, *f.*, beneficio, piacere, *m.* **To do a —,** fare una gentilezza.
kindred [ˈkindrid], *n.* Parentela, *f.*, parenti, *m.pl.* ‖ *a.* Imparentato, affine, simile; analogo.
kine [kain], *n.pl.* Vacche, *f.pl.* [cp. **cow**].
kinematograph [cp. **cinematograph**].
kinetic [kaiˈnetik], *a.* Cinetico.
king [kiŋ], *n.* Re, *m.*; (*draughts*) dama, *f.* (*Mech.*) **—-bolt,** perno, *m.*; (*Bot.*) **—-cup,** bottone d'oro, *m.*; (*Arch.*) **— -post,** trave maestra, *f.*; **king's evil,** scrofola, *f.*
kingcraft, *n.* L'arte di regnare, *f.*
kingdom, *n.* Regno, reame, *m.* **The animal —,** il regno animale, *m.*; **the United Kingdom,** il Regno Unito, *m.*; (*colloq.*) **— come,** mondo dell'al di là, *m.*
kingfisher, *n.* (*Zool.*) Martin pescatore, *m.*
kinglike, kingly, *a.* Reale, regale, sovrano, augusto.
kingship, *n.* Regalità, *f.*, potere sovrano, *m.*
kink [kiŋk], *n.* Nodo, cappio, *m.*; attorcigliamento, *m.*; (*fig.*) ghiribizzo, grillo, *m.* ‖ *v.i.* Annodare, attorcigliare. **To have a — in one's brain,** aver dei grilli per la testa.
kinsfolk [ˈkinzfouk], *n.* Parentela, *f.*, parentado, *m.*
kinship, *n.* Parentela, *f.* **To claim — with,** allegare una parentela.
kinsman [ˈkinzmən], *n.* Parente, congiunto, *m.*
kinswoman, *n.* Parente, congiunta, *f.*
kiosk [ˈkiːɔsk], *n.* Chiosco, *m.*; (*news-stall*) edicola, *f.*
kipper [ˈkipəɹ], *n.* Aringa affumicata, *f.* ‖ *v.t.* Affumicare pesce.
kirk [kəːɹk], *n.* (*Scottish*) Chiesa, *f.*
kirtle [kəːɹtl], *n.* (*obs.*) Sottana, *f.*
kiss [kis], *n.* Bacio, *m.* ‖ *v.t.* Baciare. **To — each other,** baciarsi; **to keep on kissing,** baciucchiare; **to — hands,** (*on appointment*) baciare le mani a; **to — one's hand to,** mandare un bacio a; **to — the dust,** mordere la polvere.
kissing, *n.* Il baciare, *m.*, baci, *m.pl.* **— of hands,** baciamano, baciamani, *m.*
kit [kit], *n.* Corredo, *m.*, arnesi, *m.pl.*; (*Mil.*) equipaggiamento, *m.* **—-bag,** zaino, *m.*, valigia inglese, *f.*
kitchen [ˈkitʃin], *n.* Cucina, *f.* **—-garden,** orto, *m.*; **—-maid,** serva di cucina, *f.*; **—-range,** cucina economica, *f.*; fornelli, *m.pl.*; **—-utensils,** batteria di cucina, *f.*
kitchener, *n.* Fornello da cucina, *m.*, cucina economica, *f.*
kite [kait], *n.* (*Zool.*) Nibbio, *m.*; (*toy*) aquilone, *m.*; cervo volante, *m.*; (*Comm.*) cambiale di comodo, *f.*
kith [kiθ], *n.* **Kith and kin,** parenti e amici, *m.pl.*
kitten [ˈkitən], *n.* Gattino, micino, miciolino, *m.* ‖ *v.i.* Figliare dei gattini.
kittenish, *a.* Simile ad una gattina.
kittiwake [ˈkitiweik], *n.* (*Zool.*) Gabbiano terragnolo, *m.*
kleptomania [kleptouˈmeiniə], *n.* Cleptomania, *f.*
kleptomaniac, *n.* Cleptomane, *m.f.*
knack [næk], *n.* Arte, abilità, destrezza, scaltrezza, *f.*; abitudine, *f.* **He has a — of irritating me,** ha la specialità di irritarmi.
knacker, *n.* Macellatore di cavalli, *m.* **Knacker's yard,** mattatoio, *m.*
knag [næg], *n.* Nocchio, nodo nel legno, *m.*
knapsack, *n.* Sacco, zaino, *m.*
knave [neiv], *n.* Briccone, birbante, furfante, furbone, mariuolo, *m.*; (*Cards*) fante, *m.*
knavery, *n.* Bricconeria, furfanteria, *f.*
knavish, *a.* Briccone, birbone, furfantesco, disonesto, furbo.
knavishness, *n.* Furfanteria, *f.*
knead [niːd], *v.t.* Intridere, impastare. **Kneading trough,** madia, *f.*
knee [niː], *n.* Ginocchio, *m.* ‖ *v.t.* Dare una ginocchiata a. **On one's knees,** ginocchioni; **to bring to one's knees,** far piegare le ginocchia; **on one's —,** in ginocchio; (*of horses*) **broken knees,** piaghe dei ginocchi, *f.pl.*; **Down on your knees!** In ginocchio! **— -breeches,** calzoni corti, *m.pl.*; (*Anat.*) **—-cap,** rotula, *f.*; (*for horses*) ginocchiello, *m.*; **—-deep,** fino alle ginocchia; **—-hole,** (*in a desk*) posto pei ginocchi, *m.*; **—-joint,** giuntura del ginocchio, *f.*
kneel, kneel down [niːl, niːl ˈdaun], *v.i.* Inginocchiarsi, genuflettersi.
kneeling, *n.* Inginocchiamento, *m.* ‖ *a.* ginocchioni, genuflesso. **— -stool,** inginocchiatoio, *m.*
knell [nel], *n.* Rintocco funebre, suono a morto, *m.* ‖ *v.t.i.* Rintoccare.
knickerbockers [ˈnikəɹbɔkəɹz], *n.pl.* Calzoni corti, *m.pl.*
knickers, *n.pl.* Calzoncini, *m.pl.*, mutandine, *f.pl.*
knick-knack [ˈniknæk], *n.* Ninnolo, *m.*, bagatella, *f.* **Knick-knacks,** chincaglieria, cianfrusaglia, *f.*
knife (*pl.* **knives**) [naif, naivz], *n.* Coltello, *m.* ‖ *v.t.* Dare una coltellata a, pugnalare. **Carving-—,** trinciante, *m.*; **flick-—,** coltello a molla, *m.*; **— and fork,** posate, *f.pl.*; **—-basket,** cestello delle posate, *m.*; **paper-—,** tagliacarte, *m.*; **pen-—,** temperino, *m.*; **pruning-—,** falcetto, *m.*; **table-—,** coltello da tavola, *m.*; **to have one's — into someone,** averla con qualcuno; **war to the —,** guerra a coltello, *f.*; **before you can say —,** in un batter d'occhio; **—-grinder,** arrotino, *m.*; **—-blade,** lama di coltello, *f.*; **—-board,** asse per coltelli, *m.* **— -rest,** reggiposata, *m.*; **— -sharpener, —-steel,** affilacoltelli, *m.*
knight [nait], *n.* Cavaliere, *m.*; (*Chess*) cavallo, *m.* ‖ *v.t.* Creare cavaliere. **—-errant,** cavaliere errante, *m.*
knighthood, *n.* Cavalleria, *f.*
knightliness, *n.* Carattere cavalleresco, *m.*
knightly, *a.* Cavalleresco.
knit [nit], *v.t.i.* Fare a maglia, lavorare a maglia, far la calza; (*the brow*) aggrottare le ciglia; (*fig.*) unire, legare, attaccare; (*of bones*) saldarsi; congiungersi, combaciare. **The bone is knitting,** l'osso si salda; **a well-**

— **frame,** una corporatura robusta, *f.*; **to — up,** annodare.
knitted, *a.* Fatto a maglia, lavorato a maglia.
knitter, *n.* Tessitore a maglia, *m.*, magliaia, *f.*
knitting, *n.* Lavoro a maglia, *m.*, maglieria, *f.* **— -machine,** macchina da calze, *f.*; **— -needle,** ferro da calza, *m.*
knitwear [ˈnitwɛəɹ], *n.* Lavori a maglia, *m.pl.*
knob [nɔb], *n.* Protuberanza, bozza, *f.*; (*of stick*) pomo, *m.*; (*in wood*) nodo, *m.*; (*Radio*) manopola, *f.* **Door- —,** maniglia, *f.*
knobbiness, *n.* Nodosità, *f.*
knobby, *a.* Nodoso, gibboso.
knock [nɔk], *v.t.i.* Colpire, battere, picchiare, percuotere, urtare; (*at a door*) bussare. ‖ *n.* Colpo, urto, picchio, *m.*; percossa, botta, bussata, *f.* **To — at the door,** bussare all'uscio; **to — a person on the head,** colpire qualcuno alla testa; **to — one's head against,** battere la testa contro; **to — about,** bistrattare; girellare, girondolare; **— -about comedian,** buffone, *m.*; **to — down,** atterrare, gettare a terra, **to — in,** ficcare, forzare, rompere; **to — off,** far saltare, cessare, fare presto; **to — out,** vincere, sopraffare; **to — up,** svegliare, dare la sveglia; **to be knocked up,** essere strapazzato, essere estenuato; essere svegliato; **— -kneed,** colle gambe storte.
knocker, *n.* Martello della porta, battente, *m.*
knocking, *n.* Colpi, *m.pl.*, picchio, *m.*; bussata, botta, *f.*
knoll [noul], *n.* Monticello, poggetto, *m.*, collinetta, *f.*
knot [nɔt], *n.* Nodo, *m.*; gruppo, crocchio, *m.*; groviglio, *m.*; difficoltà, *f.*; imbarazzo, imbroglio, *m.*; (*Naut.*) nodo, *m.* ‖ *v.t.* Annodare, legare, aggrovigliare. (*Naut.*) **To make eight knots,** fare otto nodi all'ora; **to — one's brows,** accigliarsi, corrugar la fronte.
knotted, *a.* Nodoso, annodato, nocchieruto. **To get —,** annodarsi, aggrovigliarsi.
knottiness, *n.* Nodosità, *f.*; difficoltà, complessità, *f.*
knotty, *a.* Nodoso; (*fig.*) difficile, imbrogliato, intricato; spinoso.
knout [naut], *n.* Knut, *m.*
know [nou], *v.t.i.* Sapere, intendersene; conoscere, riconoscere; comprendere, discernere. ‖ *n.* Conoscenza, *f.* **I knew him at once,** lo riconobbi subito; **I — her by sight,** la conosco di vista; **he does not — fear,** egli non conosce paura; **Do you — French?** Sapete il francese? **he does not — how to write,** non sa scrivere; **I — more than that,** io ne so di più; **not that I — of,** non che io sappia; **to — what's what,** sapere barcarmenarsi, saperla lunga; **to — of,** sapere di; **to be in the —,** essere a conoscenza; **to — by heart,** sapere a memoria; **to let someone — something,** far sapere qualcosa a qualcuno; **to make known,** rendere noto; **to make oneself known,** rendersi noto; **you ought to — better than that,** dovreste avere più criterio.
knowable, *a.* Conoscibile.
knowing, *a.* Intelligente, scaltro, astuto, sagace; furbo.
knowingly, *adv.* Astutamente; consapevolmente, scientemente.
knowledge [ˈnɔledʒ], *n.* Conoscenza, cognizione, scienza, dottrina, *f.*; sapere, *m.*; conoscimento, *m.*, consapevolezza, *f.* **To the best of my —,** per quanto io sappia; **to his —,** a sua conoscenza; **without my —,** a mia insaputa.
known, *a.* Noto; conosciuto.
knuckle [nʌkl], *n.* (*Anat.*) Nocca, *f.*; (*of meat*) garretto, *m.* ‖ *v.t.* Battere con le nocche. **To rap over the knuckles,** battere sulle nocche; (*fig.*) sgridare, riprendere severamente; **to — under,** arrendersi, cedere, sottomettersi; (*game*) aliossi, *m.pl.*; **— -duster,** pugno di ferro, *m.*; (*Mech.*) **— -joint,** giunto a cerniera, *m.*
knurl [nəːɹl], *v.t.* Godronare, zigrinare. ‖ *n.* Godronatura, *f.*
kohlrabi [koulˈrɑːbi], *n.* (*Bot.*) Cavolrapa, *f.*
Koran [kɔˈrɑːn], *n.* Corano, *m.*
Korea [kɔˈriə], *n.* (*Geog.*) Corea, *f.*
kosher [ˈkouʃəɹ], *a.* Puro secondo la legge ebraica. ‖ *n.* Cibo preparato secondo la legge ebraica, *m.*
kraal [krɑːl], *n.* Capanna ottentotta, *f.*
kudos [ˈkjuːdɔs], *n.* Fama, gloria, *f.*
kursaal [ˈkuːɹsɑːl], *n.* Casino, *m.*

L

L, l [el], Dodicesima lettera dell'alfabeto inglese.
la [lɑː], *n.* (*Mus.*) La, *m.*
label [leibl], *n.* Etichetta, *f.*, cartellino, *m.* ‖ *v.t.* Mettere un'etichetta; (*fig.*) catalogare, incasellare, descrivere.
labial [ˈleibiəl], *a.* Labiale.
laboratory [ˈlæbərətəri], *n.* Laboratorio, *m.*; officina, *f.*
laborious [ləˈbɔːriəs], *a.* Laborioso; faticoso, penoso.
laboriously, *adv.* Laboriosamente.
laboriousness, *n.* Laboriosità, *f.*; fatica, *f.*
labour [ˈleibəɹ], *n.* Lavoro, *m.*, fatica, pena, *f.*; impresa, *f.*; mano d'opera, *f.*; (*Med.*) travaglio del parto, *m.*; (*Pol.*) il partito socialista, *m.* ‖ *v.t.i.* Lavorare, affaticarsi, travagliarsi; angustiarsi; sforzarsi; tentare. (*Law*) **Hard —,** lavori forzati, *m.pl.*; **manual —,** lavoro manuale, *m.*; **the labours of Hercules,** le fatiche d'Ercole, *f.pl.*; **to have one's — for one's pains,** perdere il tempo e la fatica; **the — question,** la questione operaia, *f.*; **— exchange,** camera del lavoro, *f.* (*Med.*) **to be in —,** aver le doglie; **— -saving,** che fa risparmiar fatica; **to — under a delusion,** essere nell'errore; **to — the point,** insistere sopra un punto.
laboured, *a.* Elaborato, stentato. **— breathing,** respiro difficile, *m.*
labourer, *n.* Operaio, lavoratore, manovale, *m.*; giornaliero, *m.* **Farm- —,** lavoratore agricolo, *m.*; **day- —,** operaio avventizio, giornaliero, bracciante, *m.*
labouring, *a.* Lavorante. **The — class,** la classe operaia, *f.*; **a — man,** un operaio, *m.*
laburnum [ləˈbʌɹnəm], *n.* (*Bot.*) Orno, ornello, laburno, *m.*
labyrinth [ˈlæbirinθ], *n.* Labirinto, *m.*
labyrinthine, *a.* Labirintico; intricato.

lac (1) [læk], *n.* Lacca, *f.*
lac (2), *n.* **— of rupees**, centomila rupie, *f.pl.*
lace [leis], *n.* Merletto, pizzo, *m.*, trina, *f.*; gallone, *m.*; stringa, *f.*; (*of shoes*) laccio. || *v.t.* Allacciare; merlettare, gallonare; battere, bastonare, randellare, strigliare. **To — oneself tight**, serrarsi; **— -maker**, trinaia, *f.*; **— -frame**, telaio da merletti, *m.*; **— -pillow**, tombolo, *m.*; **— -work**, merletti, pizzi, *m.pl.*
lacerable [ˈlæsərəbl], *a.* Lacerabile.
lacerate [ˈlæsəreit], *v.t.* Lacerare, strappare, stracciare, squarciare. || *a.* Lacerato, lacero.
lacerated, *a.* Lacero, lacerato, strappato, stracciato.
laceration, *n.* Lacerazione, *f.*, strappo, *m.*
lachrymal [ˈlækriməl], *a.* Lagrimale.
lachrymatory [lækriˈmeitəri], *a.* Lagrimatorio.
lachrymose [ˈlækrimouz], *a.* Lagrimoso, doloroso.
laciniate, laciniated [ləˈsinieit], *a.* (*Bot., Zool.*) Laciniato.
lack [læk], *n.* Mancanza, *f.*; bisogno, difetto, *m.*; scarsità, *f.* || *v.t.i.* Mancare, scarseggiare di, far difetto. **To — money**, mancare di danaro; **time is lacking**, manca il tempo; **I — the courage**, mi manca il coraggio.
lackadaisical [lækəˈdeizikəl], *a.* Lezioso, sentimentale, svenevole.
lackey [ˈlæki], *n.* Lacchè, valletto, *m.*
lack-lustre [ˈlæklʌstəɹ], *a.* Smorto, spento, appannato. **— eyes**, occhi spenti, *m.pl.*
laconic [ləˈkɔnik], *a.* Laconico.
laconicism [ləˈkɔnisizm], *n.* Laconismo, *m.*, laconicità, *f.*
lacquer [ˈlækəɹ], *n.* Lacca, *f.*, vernice, *m.* || *v.t.* Verniciare, laccare. **— work**, lacca, *f.*
lacquering, *n.* Laccatura, *f.*
lacrosse [lɑːˈkrɔs], *n.* (*Sport*) Lacrosse, *f.*
lactation [lækˈteiʃən], *n.* Lattazione, *f.*, allattamento, *m.*
lacteal [ˈlæktiəl], *a.* Latteo.
lactescence, *n.* Lattescenza, *f.*
lacteous, *a.* Latteo.
lactic, *a.* Lattico.
lactiferous, *a.* Lattifero.
lactose, *n.* (*Chem.*) Lattosio, *m.*
lacuna (*pl.* **lacunae**) [ləˈkjuːnə, ləˈkjuːniː], *n.* Lacuna, *f.*, vuoto, *m.*
lacustral, lacustrine [ləˈkʌstrəl, ləˈkʌstrain], *a.* Lacustre.
lad [læd], *n.* Giovinetto, giovanotto, ragazzo, *m.* **Look here, my —!** Bada, ragazzo mio!
ladder [ˈlædəɹ], *n.* Scala (a piuoli), *f.*; (*Mil.*) scala d'assalto, *f.*; (*in stocking*) sfilatura, maglia caduta, *f.* || *v.i.* (*of stocking*) Smagliarsi. **— -proof**, indemagliabile; **to mend ladders in a stocking**, rimagliare una calza.
lade [leid], *v.t.* Caricare; travasare, immettere.
lading, *n.* Caricamento, carico, *m.* **Bill of —**, polizza di carico, *f.*
ladle [leidl], *n.* Cucchiaione, mestolo, *m.* || *v.t.* Scodellare.
ladleful, *n.* Cucchiaiata, mestolata, *f.*
lady [ˈleidi], *n.* Signora, dama, gentildonna, padrona di casa, *f.* **Ladies and gentlemen!** Signore e signori!; (*address*) **my —**, eccellenza, vossignoria, *f.*; **young —**, signorina, giovane signora, *f.*; **Our Lady**, La Madonna, *f.*; **ladies first**, prima le signore; **ladies' man**, damerino, *m.*; **lady-bird**, coccinella, gallinella *f.*; **Lady Day**, festa dell'Annunciazione, *f.*; **— doctor**, dottoressa *f.*; **— -help**, governante, *f.*; **his — -love**, donna dei suoi pensieri, *f.*; **lady's maid**, cameriera, *f.*; **lady's-smock**, (*Bot.*) billeri, *m.*
ladylike, *a.* Fine, distinta, signorile.
ladyship, *n.* Signoria, *f.* **Your —**, sua eccellenza, vossignoria, signora, *f.*
lag (1) [læg], *v.i.* Restare indietro, ritardare, attardarsi, trascinarsi; tentennare; *v.t.* fasciare, foderare.
lag (2), *n.* (*colloq.*) Forzato, *m.*
laggard [ˈlægəɹd], *n.* Infingardo, ritardatario, indolente, *m.*
lagging, *a.* Lento, tardivo, indolente. || *n.* Fasciame, *m.*
lager-beer [lɑːgəɹˈbiəɹ], *n.* Birra tedesca, *f.*
lagoon [ləˈguːn], *n.* Laguna, *f.*
laic [ˈleiik], *n.a.* Laico, *m.*
laicization [leiisaiˈzeiʃən], *n.* Laicizzazione, *f.*
laicize, *v.t.* Laicizzare.
laid [leid], (*p.* of **lay**), **Laid up**, ammalato, obbligato a tenere il letto; (*Naut.*) disarmato, in disarmo.
lair [lɛəɹ], *n.* Tana, *f.*, nascondiglio, covo, *m.*
laird [lɛəɹd], *n.* Possidente scozzese, *m.*
laity [ˈleiiti], *n.* Laicato, *m.*, laici, *m.pl.*
lake (1) [leik], *n.* Lago, *m.* **— dwelling**, abitazione lacustre, *f.*
lake (2), *n.* Color cremisi, rosso scuro, *m.*
lakelet, *n.* Laghetto, *m.*
lama [ˈlɑːmə], *n.* Lama, *m.* **The Grand Lama**, Il Gran Lama, *m.*
lamb [læm], *n.* Agnello, *m.* || *v.t.* Figliare (agnelli). **— -like**, timido, dolce, mansueto; **lamb's skin**, pelle d'agnello, *f.*; **lamb's wool**, lana agnellina, lana d'agnello, *f.*
lambent [ˈlæmbənt], *a.* Lambente, sfiorante, guizzante, scintillante; (*fig.*) sottile.
lambkin [ˈlæmkin], *n.* Agnelletto, agnellino, *m.*
lame [leim], *a.* Zoppo; storpio, storpiato; (*fig.*) imperfetto, difettoso, dubbioso, incerto. || *v.t.* Storpiare, azzoppare. **A — excuse**, una scusa magra, *f.*; **to walk —**, zoppicare, andar zoppo.
lamella (*pl.* **lamellae**) [ləˈmelə, ləˈmeliː], *n.* Lamella, *f.*
lamelliform, *a.* Lamelliforme.
lamely, *adv.* Zoppicando; (*fig.*) imperfettamente.
lameness, *n.* Zoppaggine, *f.*; (*fig.*) difettosità; imperfezione *f.*
lament [ləˈment], *v.t.i.* Lamentare, deplorare, lamentarsi, piangere, dolersi, lagnarsi. || *n*, Lamento, lagno, gemito, pianto, *m.* **To — one's lot**, lagnarsi della propria sorte; **to — over someone**, piangere qualcuno.
lamentable [ˈlæmentəbl], *a.* Lamentevole, deplorevole.
lamentation [læmenˈteiʃən], *n.* Lamentazione, *f.*, lamento, *m.*; querimonia, *f.*
lamented, *a.* Deplorato, compianto. **The late —**, il compianto, *m.*, la compianta, *f.*
lamina (*pl.* **laminae**) [ˈlæminɑ, ˈlæminiː], *n.* Lamina, *f.*
laminar, laminate, *a.* Laminare.
laminate, *v.t.* Laminare.
Lammas [ˈlæməs], *n.* Il primo agosto, *m.*

lammergeier [ˈlæməɹgaiəɹ], *n.* (*Zool.*) Avvoltoio barbuto, *m.*
lamp [læmp], *n.* Lampada, lanterna, lucerna, *f.*; (*on vessels. etc.*) fanale, *m.*; (*street*) lampione, *m.*; (*fig.*) lume, *m.* **Arc —**, lampada ad arco, *f.*; **incandescent —**, lampada a incandescenza, *f.*; **safety-—**, lampada di sicurezza, *f.*; **—-black**, nerofumo, *m.*; **—-bracket**, braccio per lampada, *m.*; **—-post**, lampione, *m.*; **—-room**, lampisteria, *f.*; **—-shade**, paralume, *m.*; **—-stand**, piede di lampada, *m.*; **—-oil**, olio per lampade, *m.*; **—-lighter**, lampionaio, *m.*
lampoon [læmˈpuːn], *n.* Pasquinata, satira, *f.*, libello, *m.* || *v.t.* Satireggiare.
lampooner, *n.* Libellista, scrittore di pasquinate, *m.*
lamprey [ˈlæmprei], *n.* (*Zool.*) Lampreda, *f.*
lance [lɑːns], *n.* Lancia, *f.* || *v.t.* (*Med.*) Lancettare.
lanceolate [ˈlænsiouleit], *a.* (*Bot.*) Lanceolato.
lancer, *n.* (*Mil.*) Lanciere, *m.* **Lancers** (*dance*) lancieri, *m.pl.*
lancet, *n.* (*Med.*) Lancetta, *f.*, bisturì, *m.* (*Arch.*) **— window**, finestra ogivale, *f.*
land [lænd], *n.* Terra, *f.*; paese, *m.*; patria, *f.*; contrada, proprietà, *f.* || *v.i.* (*Naut.*) Sbarcare; (*Aviat.*) atterrare, prender terra; *v.t.* metter a terra. **—-agent**, agente fondiario, amministratore, fattore, *m.*; **—-breeze**, brezza da terra, *f.*; **—-jobber**, speculatore sui beni immobili, *m.*; **—-laws**, leggi terriere, *f.pl.*; **—-locked**, circondato da terra; **—-lubber**, marinaio d'acqua dolce, *m.*; **—-surveyor**, agrimensore, *m.*; **—-tax**, imposta fondiaria, *f.*
landau [ˈlændou], *n.* Landò, *m.*
landed, *a.* Fondiario, terriero, agricolo. **— interest**, interessi agricoli, interessi fondiari, *m.pl.*; **— property**, proprietà fondiaria, *f.*, beni fondiari, *m.pl.*
landfall, *n.* (*Naut.*) Approdo, *m.*
landgrave, *n.* Langravio, *m.*
landholder, *n.* Padrone di fondi, possidente, *m.*
landing, *n.* (*Arch.*) Pianerottolo, ripiano, *m.*; (*Naut.*) sbarco, approdo, *m.*; (*Aviat.*) atterraggio, *m.* (*Aviat.*) **—-ground**, campo d'atterraggio; **—-stage**, imbarcadero, scalo, pontile, *m.*; **—-net**, piccola rete a mano, *f.*; **—-ticket**, biglietto di sbarco, *m.*
landlady, *n.* Proprietaria, padrona, albergatrice, affittacamere, *f.*
landlord, *n.* Proprietario, padrone, albergatore, oste, locandiere, *m.*
landmark, *n.* Limite, *m.*; pietra miliare, pietra di confine, *f.*; punto di riferimento, *m.*; (*fig.*) segnacolo, contrassegno, *m.*
landowner, *n.* Proprietario terriero, latifondista, *m.*
landrail, *n.* (*Zool.*) Specie di quaglia, *f.*
landscape, *n.* Paesaggio, *m.* **— gardener**, giardiniere artista, *m.*; **— painter**, paesista, *m.f.*
landslide, landslip, *n.* Frana, *f.*, franamento, *m.*
landsman, *n.* Uomo della terraferma, *m.*
landward, *adv.* Verso terra.
lane [lein], *n.* Vicolo, *m.*, viottola, viuzza, stradicciuola, *f.*; (*Sport*) corridoio, *m.*
language [ˈlæŋgwidʒ], *n.* Lingua, *f.*; linguaggio, *m.*; idioma, parlata, favella, *f.* **Bad —**, parolacce, *f.pl.*, turpiloquio, *m.*
languid [ˈlæŋgwid], *a.* Languido, fiacco, spossato, snervato.
languidly, *adv.* Languidamente.
languidness, *n.* Languore, fiacchezza, *f.*
languish [ˈlæŋgwiʃ], *v.i.* Languire, struggersi, affievolirsi.
languishing, *a.* Languente, languido. **— eyes**, occhi languidi, *m.pl.*
languishingly, *adv.* Languidamente.
languor [ˈlæŋgəɹ], *n.* Languore, *f.*
languorous, *a.* Languido; svenevole; seducente.
laniard [cp. **lanyard**].
laniferous, lanigerous [lænˈifərəs, lænˈidʒərəs], *a.* Lanifero, lanoso.
lank [læŋk], *a.* Magro, sparuto, scarno, smilzo, macilento; (*hair*) capelli lisci, *m.pl.*
lankness, *n.* Magrezza, sparutezza, macilenza, *f.*
lanky, *a.* Magro, sparuto, scarno.
lanner [ˈlænəɹ], *n.* (*Zool.*) Specie di falco.
lanoline [ˈlænolin], *n.* Lanolina, *f.*
lansquenet [ˈlænskənet], *n.* Lanzichenecco, *m.*
lantern [ˈlæntəɹn], *n.* Lanterna, *f.*; (*Naut.*) fanale, faro, *m.* **Dark —**, lanterna cieca, *f.*; **magic —**, lanterna magica, *f.* **Chinese —**, palloncino cinese, *m.*; **—-jawed**, con le guancie infossate, macilento; **—-slide**, diapositiva, *f.*; lastra per proiezioni, *f.*
lanthorn [ˈlæntəɹn], *n.* Lanterna, *f.*
lanyard [ˈlæniəɹd], *n.* Rizza, cordicella, *f.*
lap (1) [læp], *n.* (*of person*) Grembo, *m.*; (*of coat, etc.*) falda, piega, *f.* || *v.t.* Avvolgere, piegare; *v.i.* piegarsi, ripiegarsi. **In his mother's —**, in grembo alla madre; **—-dog**, cagnolino, *m.*, cagnetta, *f.*; **— of the ear**, lobo dell'orecchio, *m.*
lap (2), *v.t.* Leccare, lambire, lappare. **The cat laps up milk**, il gatto lappa il latte; **the lapping waves**, le onde lambenti, *f.pl.*
lap (3), *n.* (*Sport*) Giro, *m.*
lapel [ləˈpel], *n.* Risvolto, rovescio, *m.*
lapidary [ˈlæpidəri], *n.a.* Lapidario, *m.*
lapis lazuli [læpis ˈlæzjuːlai], *n.* Lapislazzuli, *m.*
Lapland [ˈlæplənd], *n.* (*Geog.*) Lapponia, *f.*
Laplander, Lapp, *n.a.* Lappone, *m.*
lappet [læpit], *n.* Falda, *f.*, lembo, *m.*
lapse [læps], *n.* Decorrenza, *f.*; decorso, *m.*; (*of time*) intervallo, *m.*; (*expiration*) decadenza, *f.*; (*of judgment*) errore, sbaglio, *m.*; fallo, *m.*; mancanza, caduta, *f.* || *v.i.* Decadere, ricadere, mancare a; (*of time*) passare, trascorrere. **To — back into poverty**, ricadere nella povertà; **he lapsed into silence**, si immerse nel silenzio; **the inheritance lapsed to a cousin**, l'eredità passò a un cugino.
lapwing [ˈlæpwiŋ], *n.* (*Zool.*) Pavoncella, *f.*
larboard [ˈlɑːɹbəd], *n.* (*Naut.*) Babordo, *m.*
larceny [ˈlɑːɹsəni], *n.* Furto, ladrocinio, *m.* **Petty —**, piccolo furto, *m.*
larch [lɑːɹtʃ], *n.* (*Bot.*) Larice, *m.*
lard [lɑːɹd], *n.* Strutto, *m.*, sugna, *f.* || *v.t.* Lardellare. **Larding-needle, larding-pin**, lardatoio, *m.*
larder, *n.* Dispensa, *f.*; guardavivande, *m.*
lares [ˈlɛəriːz], *n.pl.* (*Myth.*) Lari, *m.pl.*

large [lɑːɹdʒ], *a.* Grande, grosso; ampio, largo, esteso; abbondante; spazioso; considerevole. **As — as life,** a grandezza naturale; **at —,** in libertà, in generale, nell'insieme; **a — sum,** una buona somma, *f.*; **the world at —,** il mondo in genere, *m.*; **to grow —,** ingrossarsi, ingrandire; (*Naut.*) **to sail —,** prendere il largo.
largely, *adv.* Largamente; in gran parte.
largeness, *n.* Grandezza, grossezza, ampiezza, larghezza, *f.*
largesse [lɑːɹdʒˈes], *n.* Liberalità, *f.*, dono, regalo, *m.*
largish, *a.* Larghetto, abbastanza grande.
lark (1) [lɑːɹk], *n.* (*Zool.*) Allodola, *f.*
lark (2), *n.* Scherzo, *m.*, scappatella, birichinata, *f.* || *v.i.* Fare una scappatella. **To — about,** divertirsi.
larkspur, *n.* (*Bot.*) Consolida reale, *f.*, fior capriccio, *m.*
larrikin [ˈlærikin], *n.* Giovinastro, *m.*
larrup [ˈlærəp], *v.t.* Staffilare; bastonare.
larva (*pl.* **larvae**) [ˈlɑːɹvə, ˈlɑːɹviː], *n.* Larva, *f.*
laryngeal [ləˈrindʒiəl], *a.* (*Anat.*) Laringeo.
laryngitis, *n.* (*Med.*) Laringite, *f.*
larynx (*pl.* **larynges**) [ˈlæriŋks, ləˈrindʒiːz], *n.* (*Anat.*) Laringe, *f.*
lascar [ˈlæskɑːɹ], *n.* Lascaro, marinaio delle Indie orientali, *m.*
lascivious [ləˈsiviəs], *a.* Lascivo, impudico, sensuale.
lasciviously, *adv.* Lascivamente.
lasciviousness, *n.* Lascivia, *f.*
lash [læʃ], *n.* Sferza, frusta, *f.*; corda, striscia, *f.*; (*cut with whip*) sferzata, *f.*; (*of eye*) ciglio, *m.*; (*fig.*) flagello, *m.* || *v.t.i.* Frustare, sferzare, scudisciare; (*to tie*) legare con fune. **To — out,** menar colpi alla cieca, (*of horse*) sferrare calci; **the rebuke lashed him to fury,** il rimprovero lo fece montare in furia.
lasher, *n.* (*of river*) Cateratta, rapida, *f.*; frustatore, *m.*
lashing, *n.* Battitura, *f.*; (*fig.*) castigo, *m.*, flagellazione, *f.*; (*Naut.*) canapo, *m.*, gomena, *f.*
lass, lassie [læs, læsi], *n.* Ragazza, giovanetta, *f.*
lassitude [ˈlæsitjuːd], *n.* Stanchezza, lassitudine, *f.*; sfinimento, accasciamento, *m.*
lasso [læˈsuː], *n.* Laccio, *m.* || *v.t.* Acchiappare col laccio.
last (1) [lɑːst], *a.* Ultimo; estremo; passato, scorso. || *adv.* Finalmente, l'ultima volta. || *n.* Fine, ultima volta, *f.* || *v.i.* Durare, conservarsi, andare in lungo. **I have been here for the — hour,** è un' ora che sono qui; **— but not least,** ultimo ma non da meno; **— but one,** penultimo; **— night,** la notte scorsa; **the — time,** l'ultima volta, *f.*; **this day — year,** l'anno scorso come oggi; **as a — resource,** come ultimo scampo; **he would be the — to do that,** egli sarebbe l'ultima persona a fare questo; **to have the — word,** aver l'ultima parola; **the — straw,** il colmo, *m.*; **the — word in fashion,** la perfezione di gran moda, *f.*; **to breathe one's —,** trarre l'ultimo respiro; **at —,** finalmente; **When did you — see her?** Quando la vedeste l'ultima volta?; **these gloves will — me a year,** questi guanti mi dureranno un anno.
last (2), *n.* (*for shoes*) Forma, *f.*
lasting, *a.* Durevole, durabile.
lastingness, *n.* Durabilità, *f.*
lastly, *adv.* Finalmente, alla fine, ultimamente.
latch [lætʃ], *n.* Saliscendi, chiavistello, *m.*; (*of gate*) stanghetta, *f.* || *v.t.* Chiudere con chiavistello.
latchet, *n.* Stringa, *f.*
latchkey, *n.* Chiave di casa, *f.*
late [leit], *a.* Tardo, tardivo, in ritardo; ultimo, estremo; (*deceased*) fu, defunto; (*former*) già, ex-; (*recent*) recente. || *adv.* Tardi, ultimamente; già. **Of —,** ultimamente, recentemente; **of — years,** in quest'ultimi anni; **the — king,** il defunto re, l'ultimo re; **he was — for dinner,** era in ritardo per il pranzo; **I am always —,** vengo sempre tardi, son sempre in ritardo; **to keep — hours,** rientrare ad ora tarda, coricarsi tardi; **better — than never,** meglio tardi che mai; **it is getting —,** si fa tardi; **it is very —,** è molto tardi; **— in the day,** ad un' ora avanzata del giorno, tardi.
lateen-sail [ləˈtiːnseil], *n.* (*Naut.*) Vela latina, *f.*
lately, *adv.* Ultimamente, di recente, poco fa, già.
lateness, *n.* Ritardo, indugio, *m.* **The — of the hour,** l'ora avanzata, *f.*
latent [ˈleitənt], *a.* Latente, nascosto; potenziale.
later [ˈleitəɹ], *a.* Più recente, più avanzato, posteriore. || *adv.* Più tardi. **Sooner or —,** presto o tardi; **I will see you —,** ci vedremo più tardi.
lateral [ˈlætərəl], *a.* Laterale.
laterally, *adv.* Lateralmente.
Lateran [ˈlætərən], *a.* (*Geog.*) Laterano. **The — Palace,** il Palazzo Laterano, *m.*; **St. John —,** San Giovanni Laterano, *m.*
latest, *a.* Ultimo, recentissimo. **The — news,** le notizie recentissime, *f.pl.*; **on Tuesday at —,** martedì al più tardi.
latex [ˈleiteks], *n.* Lattice, *m.*
lath [lɑːθ], *n.* Assicella, *f.*, listello, *m.* || *v.t.* Coprire di assicelle. **As thin as a —,** magro come un chiodo.
lathe [leið], *n.* Tornio, *m.* **—-bed,** banco del tornio, *m.*
lather [ˈlɑːðəɹ], *n.* Saponata, schiuma, *f.* || *v.t.* Insaponare, schiumare; (*colloq.*) bastonare.
Latin [ˈlætin], *n.a.* Latino, *m.*
Latinist, *n.* Latinista, *m.*
Latinity, *n.* Latinità, *f.*
latish [ˈleitiʃ], *a.* Tardetto, un po' in ritardo. || *adv.* Un po' tardi.
latitude [ˈlætitjuːd], *n.* (*Geog.*) Latitudine, *f.*; larghezza, *f.*, libertà di azione, *f.*
latitudinal, *a.* Latitudinale.
latitudinarian [lætitjuːdiˈnɛəriən], *n.a.* Latitudinario, *m.*
latrine [ləˈtriːn], *n.* Latrina, *f.*
latten [ˈlætən], *n.* Ottone, *m.*
latter [ˈlætəɹ], *a.* Posteriore, più recente; quest'ultimo. **In these — days,** in questi giorni; **the — end,** la fine, *f.*; la morte, *f.*; **the —,** questi, quest'ultimo, *m.*; **the former . . . the —,** quello . . . questo, l'uno . . . l'altro; **Latter Day Saints,** i Mormoni, *m.pl.*
latterly, *adv.* Di recente, ultimamente.
lattice [ˈlætis], *n.* Graticcio, traliccio, *m.*, grata, *f.* || *v.t.* Ingraticciare, intrecciare. **—-window,** finestra a vetriate, *f.*; **—-work,** graticolato, graticcio, traliccio, *m.*

Latvia [ˈlætviːə], *n.* (*Geog.*) Lettonia, *f.*
Latvian, *n.a.* Lettone, *m.f.*
laud [lɔːd], *v.t.* Lodare, elogiare. || *n.* Lode, laude, *f.* **To — to the skies,** portare alle stelle.
laudable, *a.* Lodabile, lodevole.
laudably, *adv.* Lodevolmente.
laudanum [ˈlɔdnəm], *n.* Laudano, *m.*
laudatory [lɔːˈdeitəri], *a.* Laudativo, laudatorio.
laugh [lɑːf], *n.* Riso, *m.*, risata, *f.* || *v.i.* Ridere, ridersi di. **A loud —,** una sonora risata, *f.*; **to burst into a —,** dare in uno scoppio di risa, scoppiare a ridere; **to force a —,** ridere in modo forzato; **to have the — of,** avere buona ragione di ridere; **he laughs best who laughs last,** ride bene che ride l'ultimo; **to — at,** ridersi di, beffarsi di; **to — down,** deridere; **to — in one's sleeve,** ridere in cuor suo; **to — in someone's face,** ridere in faccia a qualcuno; **there's nothing to — at,** non c'è nulla da ridere; **I could not help laughing,** non potevo tenermi dal ridere.
laughable, *a.* Ridevole, risibile.
laughably, *adv.* Ridevolmente.
laughing, *a.* Ridente, allegro, gioioso. **It's no — matter,** non c'è da ridere; **—-stock,** zimbello, *m.*; **—-gas,** gas esilarante, *m.*
laughingly, *adv.* Ridendo.
laughter [ˈlɑːftəɹ], *n.* Risata, *f.*, riso, *m.* **A burst of —,** uno scoppio di risa, *m.*; **to burst with —,** crepare dalle risa; **Homeric —,** una risata omerica, *f.*
launch [lɔːntʃ], *v.t.* Lanciare, scagliare; (*Naut.*) varare; (*an attack*) sferrare; *v.i.* lanciarsi, gettarsi; imbarcarsi. || *n.* (*boat*) Lancia, *f.*; (*of a ship*) varo, *m.* **To — a blow,** vibrare un colpo; **to — forth on an enterprise,** avventurarsi in un'impresa.
launching, *n.* Lancio, avvio, *m.*; (*Naut.*) varo, *m.*
launder [ˈlɔːndəɹ], *v.t.* Lavare i panni.
laundress, *n.* Lavandaia, stiratrice, *f.*
laundry, *n.* (*place*) Lavanderia, *f.*; (*linen*) bucato, *m.*
laundryman, *n.* Lavandaio, *m.*
laureate [ˈlɔːrieit], *a.* Coronato d'alloro. **Poet —,** poeta cesareo, *m.*
laurel [ˈlɔrəl], *n.* (*Bot.*) Alloro, lauro, *m.* **— wreath,** corona d'alloro; **to rest on one's laurels,** dormire sugli allori.
laurelled, *a.* Coronato d'alloro.
laurustinus [lɔːrəsˈtainəs], *n.* (*Bot.*) Viburno, *m.*
lava [ˈlɑːvə], *n.* (*Geol.*) Lava, *f.*
lavatory [ˈlævətəri], *n.* Lavatoio, *m.*; gabinetto di toeletta, *m.*, ritirata, *f.*
lave [leiv], *v.t.* Lavare, bagnare.
lavender [ˈlævəndəɹ], *n.* (*Bot.*) Lavanda, *f.*, spiganardo, *m.* **—-water,** acqua di lavanda, *f.*
laver [ˈleivəɹ], *n.* Lavabo, *m.*; fonte, *f.*
lavish [ˈlæviʃ], *a.* Prodigo, sciupone, scialacquatore; generoso, largo, liberale. || *v.t.* Prodigare; sprecare, scialacquare; dar largamente.
lavishly, *adv.* Prodigalmente.
lavishness, *n.* Prodigalità, profusione, *f.*; sciupio, *m.*
law [lɔː], *n.* Legge, *f.*; diritto, *m.*; giurisprudenza, *f.*; decreto, statuto, *m.*; giustizia, *f.* **Civil —,** diritto civile, *m.*; **commercial —,** diritto commerciale, *m.*; **criminal —,** diritto penale, *m.*; **— case,** causa civile, *f.*; **— charges,** spese di giudizio, *f.pl.*; **court of —,** tribunale, *m.*; **— of nations,** diritto internazionale, *m.*; **— of the land,** la legge nazionale, *f.*; **a point of —,** una questione di diritto, *f.*; **to lay down the —,** stabilire la legge, (*fig*). dettar legge; **necessity knows no —,** la necessità non ha legge; **learned in the —,** dotto in giurisprudenza; **bred to the —,** avviato all'avvocatura; **to go to —,** ricorrere alla legge; **to have the — of someone,** intentar lite contro qualcuno; **to take the — into one's own hands,** farsi giustizia da sè; **—-abiding,** ubbidiente alla legge; **—-book,** trattato di legge, *m.*; **—-breaker,** violatore della legge, *m.*; **—-list,** albo degli avvocati, *m.*; **—-maker,** legislatore, *m.*; **—-writer,** scrivano, copista, *m.*
lawful, *a.* Legittimo, lecito, legale; permesso.
lawfulness, *n.* Legittimità, legalità, *f.*
lawless, *a.* Senza legge; (*fig.*) sfrenato, sregolato.
lawlessness, *n.* Licenza, sfrenatezza, *f.*, disordine, *m.*
lawn (1) [lɔːn], *n.* Praticello, tappeto verde, *m.*, radura, *f.* **—-mower,** falciatrice da prato, *f.*; **—-tennis,** tennis, *m.*
lawn (2), *n.* Rensa, *f.* || *a.* Di rensa.
lawsuit [ˈlɔːsjuːt], *n.* Causa, lite, querela, *f.*
lawyer [ˈlɔːiəɹ], *n.* Avvocato, legale, giurista, *m.* **To consult a —,** rivolgersi ad un avvocato; **a pettifogging —,** un azzeccagarbugli, *m.*
lax [læks], *a.* Trascurato, negligente, inesatto, vago; molle, fiacco, rilassato, snervato, immorale. **— morals,** morale rilassata, *f.*
laxative, *n.* (*Med.*) Lassativo, *m.*
laxity, laxness, *n.* Trascuratezza, negligenza, *f.*; inesattezza, mollezza, fiacchezza, *f.*; immoralità, *f.*
laxly, *adv.* Trascuratamente.
lay (1) [lei], *v.t.* Posare, mettere, porre; (*stretch*) stendere; (*to bet*) scommettere; (*eggs*) fare; (*a snare*) tendere; (*dust*) ammorzare; (*to calm*) calmare. **To — a fire,** preparare un fuoco; **to — a gun,** puntare un cannone; **to — the blame on,** dare il biasimo a; **to — aside,** mettere da parte, abbandonare; **to — before,** presentare a, esporre; **to — bare,** mettere a nudo; **to — down,** (*arms*) deporre, (*a principle*) stabilire, (*a ship*) impostare, (*a rule*) formulare, dettare, (*on the ground*) coricare, (*life*) dare sacrificio di; **to — hold of,** pigliare, impadronirsi di; **to — in,** provvedere, procurare; **to — on,** imporre, applicare, (*gas, etc.*) installare; **to — open,** esporre; **to — out,** (*money*) spendere, sborsare; (*a corpse*) vestire, (*clothes, etc.*) stendere; **to — a snare,** tendere un laccio; **to — to heart,** prendere a cuore; **to — about one,** menar colpi dappertutto; **to — the table,** apparecchiare la tavola; **to — waste,** devastare.
lay (2), *n.* (*Poet.*) Ballata, canzone, *f.*
lay (3), *a.* Laico, secolare; profano. **— brother,** frate laico, *m.*; **— clerk,** cantore, *m.*
lay-day, *n.* (*Naut.*) Stallia, *f.*
layer, *n.* (*bed*) Strato, *m.*; (*of rails, etc.*) montatore, *m.*; (*of carpets*) tappezziere, *m.*; (*Agric.*) margotta, *f.* **A good — (*of eggs*),** una gallina che fa le uova regolarmente.

layette [lei'et], *n.* Corredino, *m.*
lay figure, *n.* Manichino, fantoccio, *m.*
laying, *n.* Messa, postazione, *f.*; (*of eggs*) il fare, *m.*, covata, *f.* (*Eccles.*) **— on of hands,** imposizione delle mani, *f.*
layman (*pl.* **laymen**) ['leimən], *n.* Laico, *m.*; profano, *m.*
layout ['leiaut], *n.* Disegno, piano, *m.*; progetto, *m.*
lazaretto, lazaret [læzə'retou, 'læzəret], *n.* Lazzaretto, *m.*
laze [leiz], *v.i.* Oziare, vivere nell'inerzia.
lazily, *adv.* Pigramente, indolentemente.
laziness, *n.* Pigrizia, indolenza, infingardaggine, ignavia, *f.*
lazy, *a.* Pigro, infingardo, ignavo, indolente. **A — fellow,** un fannullone, un fiaccone, *m.*
lazybones, *n.* Fannullone, infingardo, *m.*
lea [li:], *n.* (*Poet.*) Prato, campo, *m.*, prateria, *f.*
leach [li:tʃ], *n.* Lisciva, *f.*, ranno, *m.* || *v.t.i.* Lisciviare.
lead (1) [led], *n.* (*Min.*) Piombo, *m.*; (*Naut.*) piombino, scandaglio, *m.*; (*Print.*) interlinea, *f.*; (*for pencils*) grafite, matita, *f.* || *v.t.* Impiombare; (*Print.*) interlineare. **Red —,** rosso di piombo, minio, *m.*; **white —,** bianco di piombo, *m.*, biacca, *f.*; (*Naut.*) **to heave the —,** gettare lo scandaglio; **—-pencil,** matita, *f.*, lapis, *m.*; **—-poisoning,** colica saturnina; **—-work,** impiombatura, *f.*
lead (2) [li:d], *v.t.* Condurre, guidare, dirigere, menare, portare; capeggiare, comandare; indurre, spingere; *v.i.* (*Cards*) cominciare; (*Mil.*) comandare. || *n.* Direzione, *f.*, comando, *m.*; esempio, *m.*; (*Cards*) mano, *f.*; (*Theat.*) primo attore, *m.*; (*for dogs*) guinzaglio, laccio, *m.* **To — about,** menare dappertutto; **to — astray,** traviare, sviare; **to — back,** ricondurre, riportare; **to — on,** spingere, indurre; **to — up to,** risultare in; **to — someone to believe,** far credere a qualcuno; **to — the way,** andare innanzi, mostrare la via; **to — a miserable life,** menare una vita misera; **to — someone a dance,** dare un sacco di noie a qualcuno; **to — by the nose,** menare per il naso; **to — off,** cominciare; (*Cards*) **it's your —,** è a lei la mano, tocca a lei; **to take the —,** prendere il comando, capeggiare; **to follow someone's —,** seguire l'esempio di qualcuno; **to give a —,** far da guida, instradare, dar la spinta.
leaded ['ledid], *a.* Piombato; (*Print.*) Interlineato.
leaden ['ledən], *a.* Di piombo, plumbeo; pesante. **A — sky,** un cielo plumbeo, *m.*
leader ['li:dəɹ], *n.* Capo, duce, *m.*, guida, *f.*; comandante, capitano, *m.*; (*Pol.*) capopartito, *m.*; (*newspaper*) articolo di fondo, *m.*; (*horse*) cavallo di testa, *m.*; (*Mus.*) primo violino, *m.*; (*Sport*) **team —,** capitano della squadra, *m.*
leadership, *n.* Direzione, guida, condotta, *f.*, comando, primato, *m.*, supremazia, *f.*
leading ['li:diŋ], *a.* Principale, preminente, primo, primario. **— article,** articolo di fondo, *m.*; **— man,** persona autorevole, *f.*; (*Theat.*) **— lady,** prima attrice, *f.*; **— question,** domanda capziosa, domanda suggestiva, *f.*; **— seaman,** marinaio scelto, *m.*; **—-rein,** corda per guidare, *f.*; **—-strings,** dande, *f.pl.*
leadsman ['ledzmən], *n.* (*Naut.*) Scandagliatore, *m.*
leaf [li:f], *n.* (*of plant*) Foglia, *f.*; (*of book, etc.*) foglio, *m.*, pagina, *f.*; (*of door*) battente, *m.*; (*of table*) aggiunta, *f.*; (*of rifle*) alzo, *m.* (*of spring*) lamina, *f.* || *v.i.* Frondeggiare. **To turn over a new —,** cominciare una vita nuova; **to turn over the leaves of a book,** sfogliare un libro; **in —,** coperto di foglie; **—-gold,** oro in foglie, *m.*; **—-mould,** terriccio, *m.*
leafage, *n.* Fogliame, *m.*
leafless, *a.* Senza foglie.
leaflet, *n.* (*Bot.*) Foglina, fogliolina, *f.*; (*printed*) foglietto, volantino a stampa, *m.*
leafy, *a.* Foglioso, frondoso, fronzuto.
league (1) [li:g], *n.* Lega, associazione, alleanza, unione, *f.*; società, *f.* || *v.t.* Allearsi, confederarsi. **In —,** in lega; **leagued together,** alleati, confederati.
league (2), *n.* (*distance*) Lega, *f.*
leaguer, *n.* Alleato, confederato, *m*; (*Hist.*) assedio, *m.*
leak [li:k], *n.* Falla, fuga, *f.*; fenditura, perdita, *f.*; scolo; ammanco, *m.* || *v.i.* Colare, perdere, far acqua; sfuggire, spandersi; trapelare. **To spring a —,** fare acqua, avere una falla; (*fig.*) **to — out,** trapelare.
leakage, *n.* Fuga (di gas); falla, *f.*, scolo, *m.*; colatura, perdita, *f.*, infiltramento, *m.*
leaky, *a.* Che fa acqua, che cola; che perde.
lean (1) [li:n], *a.* Magro, sparuto, scarno, smilzo; povero, sterile. || *n.* Magro, *m.*, carne magra, *f.*
lean (2), *v.i.* Appoggiarsi; pendere, inclinare; (*fig.*) propendere, esser propenso a; *v.t.* appoggiare. **To — on,** appoggiarsi a; **to — one's head back,** piegare la testa indietro; **to — out,** sporgersi; **to — a ladder against the wall,** appoggiare una scala al muro.
leaning, *n.* Inclinazione, propensione, tendenza, *f.* **— tower,** torre pendente, *f.*
leanness, *n.* Magrezza, sparutezza, *f.*
lean-to, *n.* Baracchino, *m.*, tettoia, *f.*
leap [li:p], *n.* Salto, balzo, sbalzo, *m.* || *v.t.i.* Saltare, saltellare, sbalzare, balzare, lanciarsi. **A — in the dark,** un salto nel buio; **by leaps and bounds,** a passi di gigante, a salti e a sbalzi; **—-frog,** saltamontone, *m.*, cavallina, *f.*; **— year,** anno bisestile, *m.*
leaper, *n.* Saltatore, *m.*
leaping, *a.* Saltante, saltellante. **—-board,** trampolino, *m.*
learn [lə:ɹn], *v.t.i.* Imparare, apprendere, studiare; venir a sapere, istruirsi.
learned ['lə:ɹnid], *a.* Dotto, erudito, istruito, savio, saggio, sapiente. **A — profession,** una professione liberale, *f.*
learnedly, *adv.* Dottamente, eruditamente.
learner, *n.* Scolaro, affitto, *m.*; apprendista, *m.*
learning, *n.* Sapere, *m.*, scienza, erudizione, cultura, dottrina, *f.*
lease [li:s], *n.* Contratto d'affitto, *m.*, affittanza, locazione, *f.* || *v.t.* Affittare, dare in affitto, prendere in affitto. **On a —,** in affitto; **long —,** enfiteusi, *m.*; **to take a new — of life,** cominciare una vita nuova.
leasehold, *n.* Proprietà fondiaria in affitto, *f.*
leaseholder, *n.* Locatario, affittuario, *m.*

leash [liːʃ], *n.* Guinzaglio, laccio, *m.*; (*of dogs*) muta, *f.* || *v.t.* Tenere col guinzaglio. **To hold in —,** frenare al guinzaglio.
least [liːst], *a.* Il più piccolo, il minimo. || *adv.* Il meno. **At —,** almeno, per lo meno; **not in the —,** niente affatto, in nessun modo, per nulla; **to say the — of it,** a dir poco, per limitarsi al minimo.
leat [liːt], *n.* Canale di diversione, *m.*; gora, *f.*
leather [ˈleðəɹ], *n.* Cuoio, *m.*, pelle, *f.*; corame, *m.* || *v.t.* (*colloq.*) Conciare, fustigare, staffilare. **— dressing,** concia del cuoio, *f.*
leatherette [leðərˈet], *n.* Finto cuoio, *m.*
leathern, *a.* Di cuoio, di pelle.
leathery, *a.* Coriaceo, duro come il cuoio.
leave [liːv], *n.* Permesso, *m.*, licenza, *f.*; congedo, *m.* || *v.t.i.* Lasciare; (*to depart*) partire; (*to desert*) abbandonare; (*to bequeath*) legare. **On —,** in licenza; **to give —,** permettere, concedere; **sick- —,** licenza per malattia, *f.*; **to take French —,** andarsene insalutato ospite; **to take one's —,** congedarsi, accomiatarsi, dire addio; **to take — of one's senses,** perdere il ben dell'intelletto; **By your —!** Permesso! Con vostro permesso! **I have nothing left,** non mi rimane niente; **I — that to you,** me ne rimetto a voi; **— it to me,** lasciate fare a me; **— well alone,** lasciare com'è; **to be left,** rimanere; **to be left till called for,** fermo in posta; **to — alone,** lasciar solo, lasciar stare; **to — behind,** lasciar dietro di sè; **to — hold of,** rilasciare; **to — off a garment,** smettere un vestito; **to — off,** cessare di, finire di; **to — out,** omettere, tralasciare; **to — over,** posporre; **to — no stone unturned,** fare tutto il possibile; **to — word,** lasciar detto; **he left yesterday,** partì ieri; **— -taking,** commiato, congedo, *m.*
leaven [ˈlevən], *n.* Lievito, *m.* || *v.t.* Lievitare; (*fig.*) temperare.
leavings [ˈliːviŋz], *n.pl.* Avanzi, rimasugli, *m.pl.*
lecher [ˈletʃəɹ], *n.* Libertino, *m.*
lecherous, *a.* Libertino, lascivo, impudico.
lechery, *n.* Lascivia, *f.*, libertinaggio, *m.*
lectern [ˈlektəɹn], *n.* (*Eccles.*) Leggio, *m.*
lector [ˈlektəɹ], *n.* Lettore, *m.*
lecture [ˈlektʃəɹ], *n.* Conferenza, *f.*; lezione, lettura, *f.*; discorso, *m.*; (*fig.*) predicozzo, *m.*, ramanzina, *f.* || *v.t.* Rimproverare, ammonire; *v.i.* tener conferenze, far conferenze; sermoneggiare, predicare. **A course of lectures,** un corso di conferenze, *m.*; **to give a —,** fare una conferenza; **— -room,** sala di conferenze, *f.*
lecturer, *n.* Conferenziere, *m.*; lettore, *m.*
led [led], *a.* **A — horse,** un cavallo a mano, *m.* [cp. **lead** (2)].
ledge [ledʒ], *n.* Sporgenza, *f.*, risalto, orlo, bordo, *m.*; ripiano, *m.*; (*window*) davanzale, *m.*; (*mountain*) cornice, *f.*; (*Geol.*) strato, *m.*
ledger [ˈledʒəɹ], *n.* Libro mastro, *m.* || *a.* (*Mus.*) Sopra il rigo. **— lines,** note sopra il rigo, *f.pl.*
lee [liː], *n.* (*Naut.*) Luogo protetto, luogo sottovento, *m.* || *a.* Riparato, sottovento.
leech [liːtʃ], *n.* (*Zool.*) Sanguisuga, mignatta, *f.*; (*fig.*) chirurgo, flebotomo, *m.* **To cling like a —,** attaccarsi come una sanguisuga.
leechcraft, *n.* L'arte medica, *f.*
leek [liːk], *n.* (*Bot.*) Porro, *m.*
leer [liəɹ], *v.i.* Sbirciare, guardare con la coda dell'occhio. || *n.* Sbirciata, *f.*, sguardo furbo, lascivo, di trionfo, *m.* **To — at,** sogguardare, sbirciare.
leeringly, *adv.* Sbirciando, con la coda dell'occhio.
lees [liːz], *n.pl.* Feccia, *f.*, sedimento, *m.*
leeward [ˈluːəɹd, ˈliːwəɹd], *a.adv.* A sottovento. **The Leeward Islands,** Le Isole Sottovento, *f.pl.*
leeway [ˈliːwei], *n.* Deriva, *f.*
left (1) [left], *a.* Sinistro, manco, mancino; (*colloq.*) ultra socialista. || *adv.* A sinistra. || *n.* Sinistra, mano sinistra, *f.* **— -handed,** mancino, (*fig.*) ambiguo, equivoco; **a — -handed compliment,** un complimento ambiguo; **— -handedly,** goffamente; **— -handedness,** uso della mano sinistra, *m.*, (*fig.*) goffaggine, *f.*
left (2) **To be —,** restare; **— -luggage office,** consegna dei bagagli, *f.*; **— -overs,** rimasugli, *m.pl.* [cp. **leave**].
leg [leg], *n.* Gamba, *f.*; (*of fowls*) coscia, *f.*; (*of animals, etc.*) zampa, *f.*; (*of furniture*) piede, *m.*; (*of stocking, boot*) forma, *f.* **He has not a — to stand on,** egli non ha ragione di sorte; **to stand on one —,** stare su una gamba sola; **to give a — up to,** dare una spinta in su a; (*colloq.*) **to shake a —,** ballare; **to be on one's legs again,** rimettersi in gamba; **to get one's sea legs,** abituarsi al mare; **he's on his last legs,** è al lumicino, è ai mali passi; **to stand on one's own legs,** essere indipendente; **to walk someone off his legs,** far correre qualcuno; **to make a —,** fare una riverenza; **— -guard,** gambale, *m.*; **— -rest,** appoggio per le gambe, *m.*
legacy [ˈlegəsi], *n.* Lascito, legato, *m.* **— duty,** imposta di successione, *f.*
legal [ˈliːgəl], *a.* Legale, giuridico, legittimo. (*Comm.*) **To be — tender,** aver corso legale; **— -aid,** assistenza legale, *f.*; **— charges,** spese giudiziali, *f.pl.*
legality, *n.* Legalità, *f.*
legalization, *n.* Legalizzazione, *f.*
legalize, *v.t.* Legalizzare, legittimare.
legate [ˈlegət], *n.* (*Eccles.*) Legato, *m.*
legatee [legəˈtiː], *n.* Legatario, *m.*, erede di beni mobili, *m.*
legation, *n.* Legazione, *f.*
legend [ˈledʒənd], *n.* Leggenda, *f.*, mito, *m.*
legendary, *a.* Leggendario, mitico.
legendry, *n.* Leggenda, *f.*
legerdemain [ˈledʒəɹdəmein], *n.* Giuoco di prestigio, giuoco di mano, *m.* **Feat of —,** gherminella, *f.*
legged [ˈlegid], *a.* Con gambe. **Four- —** quadrupede; **two- —,** bipede.
leggings, *n.pl.* Gambali, ghette, *m.f.pl.*
leggy [ˈlegi], *a.* Con le gambe lunghe.
Leghorn [leˈgɔːɹn], *n.* (*Geog.*) Livorno, *f.*; cappello di paglia di Firenze, *m.*; una qualità di pollame, *f.*
legibility [ledʒiˈbiliti], *n.* Leggibilità, *f.*
legible, *a.* Leggibile.
legibly, *adv.* Leggibilmente.
legion [ˈliːdʒən], *n.* Legione, *f.* **Their name is —,** sono legione.
legionary, *n.* Legionario, *m.*
legislate [ˈledʒisleit], *v.i.* Legiferare, far leggi.

legislation, *n.* Legislazione, *f.*
legislative, *a.* Legislativo.
legislator, *n.* Legislatore, *m.*
legislature ['ledʒislətʃəɹ], *n.* Legislatura, *f.*, corpo legislativo, *m.*
legist, *n.* Legista, *m.*
legitimacy [le'dʒitiməsi], *n.* Legittimità, *f.*
legitimate [le'dʒitimit], *a.* Legittimo, lecito; giusto; autentico. || *v.t.* [le'dʒitimeit], Legittimare.
legitimation, *n.* Legittimazione, *f.*
legitimist, *n.* Legittimista, *m.*
legitimize, *v.t.* Legittimare.
legume, legumen ['legju:m, le'gju:men], *n.* (*Bot.*) Legume, *m.*
leguminous, *a.* Leguminoso.
leisure ['leʒəɹ], *n.* Agio, comodo, riposo, svago, *m.* **To be at —,** esser libero, esser a proprio agio; **at your —,** con tutto comodo, a vostro agio.
leisured, *a.* Libero, disoccupato, comodo.
leisurely, *adv.a.* Con agio, con comodo; tardivo, lento. **In a — way,** senza fretta, a bell'agio; **a — man,** un uomo tranquillo.
leitmotiv, leitmotif ['laitmoutiv], *n.* Tema, tema conducente, *m.*
lemma ['lemə], *n.* (*Math.*) Lemma, *f.*
lemon ['lemən], *n.* Limone, *m.* **— ice,** gelato al limone, *m.* **—-peel,** scorza di limone, *f.*; **—-squash,** spremuta di limone, *f.*; **—-squeezer,** schiaccialimoni, strizzalimoni, spremilimoni, *m.*; **—-tree,** limone, *m.*; (*Zool.*) **—-sole,** sogliola, *f.*
lemonade [lemə'neid], *n.* Limonata, *f.*; gazzosa, *f.*
lemur ['li:məɹ], *n.* (*Zool.*) Lemuro, *m.*
lend [lend], *v.t.* Prestare, imprestare, dare in prestito; fornire, dare. **To — a hand,** prestar man forte.
lender, *n.* Prestatore, *m.*
lending, *n.* Prestito, l'imprestare, *m.* **—-library,** biblioteca circolante, *f.*
length [leŋθ], *n.* Lunghezza, *f.*; (*of time*) durata, *f.*; estensione, distanza, *f.*; (*of cloth*) taglio, *m.*; **To fall full —,** stramazzare, cadere lungo disteso; **to keep at arm's —,** tenere a debita distanza; **to go all lengths,** far tutto il possibile; **at —,** finalmente, alla fine; **at some —,** abbastanza, distesamente; **two feet in —,** due piedi di lunghezza; **a full- — portrait,** un ritratto in piedi; **— of service,** anzianità, *f.*
lengthen, *v.t.* Allungare, prolungare, distendere; *v.i.* allungarsi, prolungarsi, distendersi. **The days are lengthening,** i giorni si allungano.
lengthening, *n.* Allungamento, prolungamento, distendimento, *m.*
lengthiness, *n.* Lunghezza, *f.*; lungaggine, prolissità, *f.*
lengthways, lengthwise, *adv.* Nel senso della lunghezza, per il lungo.
lengthy, *a.* Lungo, prolisso; prolungato.
leniency ['li:niənsi], *n.* Indulgenza, mitezza, benevolenza, *f.*
lenient, *a.* Indulgente, benevolo, dolce, mite.
leniently, *adv.* Indulgentemente.
lenitive ['lenitiv], *n.a.* (*Med.*) Lenitivo, calmante, *m.*
lenity, *n.* Indulgenza, bontà, mitezza, *f.*
lens [lenz], *n.* Lente, *f.*; obiettivo, *m.*
Lent [lent], *n.* Quaresima, *f.* **To keep —,** far quaresima; (*Bot.*) **— lily,** narciso dei prati, *m.*
Lenten, *a.* Quaresimale, magro.
lenticular [len'tikju:ləɹ], *a.* Lenticolare.
lentil ['lentl], *n.* (*Bot.*) Lenticchia, lente, *f.*
lentisk, *n.* (*Bot.*) Lentischio, *m.*
Leo ['li:ou], *n.* (*Astron.*) Il Leone, *m.*
leonine ['li:ounain], *a.* Leonino.
leopard ['lepəɹd], *n.* (*Zool.*) Leopardo, *m.*
leopardess, *n.* Leopardo femmina, *f.*
leper ['lepəɹ], *n.* Lebbroso, *m.*, lebbrosa, *f.* **— hospital,** lebbrosario, *m.*
Lepidoptera [lepi'dɔptərə], *n.pl.* (*Zool.*) Lepidotteri, *m.pl.*
leprosy ['leprəsi], *n.* (*Med.*) Lebbra, *f.*
leprous, *a.* Lebbroso.
lesbian ['lezbiən], *a.* Lesbico. || *n.* Tribade, *f.*
lesbianism, *n.* Amore saffico, *m.*
lesion ['li:ʒən], *n.* Lesione, *f.*
less [les], *a.* Minore, più piccolo, inferiore, meno. || *adv.* Meno. || *n.* Meno, *m.* || *prep.* Meno. **To grow —,** rimpicciolirsi, diminuire; **Drink — wine!** Bevete meno vino!; **a man —,** un uomo di meno; **for — than,** per meno di; **none the —,** nondimeno; **— and —,** di meno in meno; **no — a person than,** niente di meno che; **so much the —,** tanto meno; **the — . . . the —,** meno . . . meno; **in — than no time,** in men che non si dica; **a year — four days,** un anno meno quattro giorni.
lessee [le'si:], *n.* (*Law*) Affittuario, locatario, *m.*
lessen, *v.t.i.* Diminuire, menomare, scemare, impicciolire.
lessening, *n.* Diminuzione, *f.*
lesser, *a.* Più piccolo, minore, minimo.
lesson ['lesən], *n.* Lezione, *f.*, compito, esempio, *m.*
lessor, *n.* (*Law*) Locatore, *m.*
lest [lest], *conj.* Per tema che, per paura che, affinchè non. **— we forget,** per non dimenticare.
let (1) [let], *v.t.* Lasciare, permettere; fare; (*a house*) affittare, appigionare. (*Med.*) **To — blood,** salassare; **to — be, to — alone,** lasciare stare; **— alone,** senza dire, prescindendo da; **to — down,** calare, lasciar discendere, (*fig.*) piantare in asso; abbandonare nelle difficoltà; **a — down,** un disappunto, *m.*; **to — go,** lasciare andare, (*drop*) allentare, rilasciare, (*rope*) mollare; **to — drop an opinion,** emettere un'opinione; **to — go the anchor,** affondare l'ancora; **to — in,** lasciare entrare, far entrare; **to — oneself in,** entrare in casa; **to — in for,** obbligare a; **to — loose,** sciogliere, rilasciare, scatenare; **to — off,** (*a gun*) sparare, (*pardon*) perdonare; (*colloq.*) **to — on,** divulgare una cosa; **to — out,** lasciare uscire, far uscire, (*a secret*) divulgare, (*a dress*) allargare; **to — slip an opportunity,** lasciarsi sfuggire un'occasione; **house to —,** casa da affittare; **to — know,** far sapere a; **Let us go!** Andiamo!; **to — things slide,** lasciar andare le cose a rotoli; **to — the fire out,** lasciar spegnere il fuoco.
let (2), *v.t.* Impedire. || *n.* Impedimento, *m.*; (*Tennis*) colpo nullo, *m.* **Without — or hindrance,** senza impedimenti.
lethal ['li:θəl], *a.* Letale, mortale, micidiale.
lethargic [le'θɑ:ɹdʒik], *a.* Letargico.
lethargy ['leθəɹdʒi], *n.* Letargia, *f.*, letargo, *m.*

Lethe ['li:θi], *n.* (*Myth.*) Lete, *m.*
letter ['letəɹ], *n.* Lettera, *f.*; epistola, missiva, *f.*; carattere, segno, *m.* || *v.t.* (*Print.*) Mettere il titolo a, intitolare; imprimere lettere. **— of attorney,** mandato di procura; (*Comm.*) **— of advice,** notificazione, *f.*; **— of credit,** lettera di credito, *f.*; **letters patent,** brevetto d'invenzione, *m.*; **registered —,** lettera raccomandata, *f.*; **dead —,** lettera morta, *f.* **—-book,** copialettere, *m.*; **—-box,** cassetta per le lettere, buca delle lettere, *f.*; **—-carrier,** postino, *m.*; **—-case,** portafoglio, *m.*; **—-paper,** carta da lettera, *f.*; **—-press,** copialettere, *m.*; **—-writer,** epistolografo, *m.*
lettered, *a.* Istruito, colto, dotto, letterato.
lettering, *n.* Iscrizione, *f.*; lettere, *f.pl.*
letters, *n.pl.* Belle lettere, *f.pl.*, letteratura, *f.*
letting, *n.* Locazione, affittanza, pigione, *f.*
lettuce ['letəs], *n.* (*Bot.*) Lattuga, *f.* **Wild —,** lattuga romana, *f.*; **cabbage —,** lattuga cappuccia, *f.*
leucocyte ['lju:kəsait], *n.* (*Anat.*) Leucocite, *m.*
leucorrhoea [lju:kə'riə], *n.* (*Med.*) Leucorrea, *f.*
Levant (1) [le'vænt], *n.* (*Geog.*) Levante, *m.*
levant (2), *v.i.* Prendere la fuga.
Levantine, *n.a.* Levantino, *m.*
levee (1) ['levi], *n.* Ricevimento a corte, ricevimento reale, *m.*
levee (2) [le'vi:], *n.* Diga, *f.*, argine, *m.*
level ['levəl], *a.* A livello, piano, piatto, spianato, orizzontale; eguale; (*fig.*) equo, giusto, imparziale. || *n.* Livello, *m.*; grado, piano, *m.*; spianata, *f.* || *v.t.* Livellare, spianare; aggiustare; (*a blow*) vibrare; (*a gun*) puntare. (*Rail.*) **—-crossing,** passaggio a livello, *m.*; **— with,** a livello con; **to do one's — best,** fare il possibile; **to have a — head,** avere una buona testa; **on the same — as,** allo stesso livello di; **a dead —,** una piatta monotonia, *f.*; **to find one's —,** trovare il proprio ambiente; **at sea —,** sul livello di mare; **to — down,** abbassare allo stesso livello; **to — at,** prender di mira, puntar contro; **to — to the ground,** radere al suolo; **to — distinctions,** abolire le distinzioni; **to — an accusation,** lanciare un'accusa.
levelling, *n.* Livellamento, *m.*; puntamento, *m.*
lever ['li:vəɹ], *n.* Leva, *f.*; manubrio, *m.* || *v.t.* Sollevare per mezzo d'una leva. **—-watch,** orologio ad ancora, *m.*
leverage ['li:vəridʒ], *n.* Potenza d'una leva, *f.*; sostegno, punto d'appoggio, *m.*; (*fig.*) influenza, *f.*, vantaggio, *m.*
leveret ['levəret], *n.* (*Zool.*) Leprotto, *m.*
leviable ['leviəbl], *a.* Imponibile.
leviathan [le'vaiəθən], *n.* Leviatano, *m.*
levigate ['levigeit], *v.t.* Levigare, lisciare, polverizzare.
levitation [levi'teiʃən], *n.* Levitazione, *f.*
Levite ['li:vait], *n.* Levita, *m.*
Levitical [le'vitikəl], *a.* Levitico.
Leviticus, *n.* Il Levitico, *m.*
levity ['leviti], *n.* Leggerezza, spensieratezza, frivolezza, *f.*
levy ['levi], *n.* (*Mil.*) Leva, *f.*; (*taxes*) imposizione, *f.*; raccolta, *f.* || *v.t.* Levare, percepire, imporre; raccogliere. **Capital —,** imposta sul capitale, *f.*; **to — a tax,** imporre un tributo.
lewd [lju:d], *a.* Dissoluto, lascivo, impudico, libidinoso.
lewdly, *adv.* Lascivamente.
lewdness, *n.* Dissolutezza, lascivia, libidine, *f.*
lexicographer [leksi'kɔgrəfəɹ], *n.* Lessicografo, *m.*
lexicography, *n.* Lessicografia, *f.*
lexicology, *n.* Lessicologia, *f.*
lexicon ['leksikən], *n.* Lessico, vocabolario, dizionario, *m.*
Leyden ['laidən], *n.* (*Geog.*) Leida, *f.*
liability [laiə'biliti], *n.* Responsabilità, *f.*; disposizione, suscettibilità, *f.*; (*Comm.*) obblighi, debiti, impegni, *m.pl.*, passivo, *m.*, passività, *f.* **Assets and liabilities,** attivo e passivo; **to meet one's liabilities,** soddisfare agli impegni.
liable ['laiəbl], *a.* Soggetto (a), esposto (a), suscettibile (di); responsabile (di), impegnato (in).
liaison [li:'eizən], *n.* Relazione amorosa, *f.*; legame, *m.*; relazione, *f.* (*Mil.*) **— officer,** ufficiale di collegamento, *m.*
liar ['laiəɹ], *n.* Bugiardo, mentitore, *m.*, bugiarda, mentitrice, *f.*
lias ['laiəs], *n.* (*Geol.*) Lias, *m.*
libation [lai'beiʃən], *n.* Libazione, *f.*
libel ['laibəl], *n.* Diffamazione, *f.*, libello, oltraggio, *m.*; calunnia, *f.* || *v.t.* Diffamare, calunniare. **Action for —,** causa per diffamazione, *f.*
libeller, *n.* Diffamatore, calunniatore, *m.*
libelling, *n.* Diffamazione, *f.*
libellous, *a.* Diffamatorio, calunnioso.
liberal ['libərəl], *a.* Liberale, generoso, largo; abbondante, ampio, copioso. || *n.* (*Pol.*) Liberale, *m.*
liberalism, *n.* Liberalismo, *m.*
liberality [libə'ræliti], *n.* Liberalità, munificenza, *f.*
liberalize, *v.t.* Rendere liberale.
liberate, *v.t.* Liberare, redimere, affrancare.
liberation, *n.* Liberazione, *f.*, affrancamento, *m.*
liberator, *n.* Liberatore, *m.*
libertine ['libəɹti:n], *n.a.* Libertino, vizioso, *m.*
libertinism, libertinage, *n.* Libertinaggio, *m.*, sregolatezza, *f.*
liberty ['libəɹti], *n.* Libertà, *f.* **To be at —,** essere libero; **to set at —,** mettere in libertà; **to take the — of,** prendersi la libertà di; **to take liberties with,** trattare con soverchia libertà, prendersi delle libertà con.
libidinous [li'bidinəs], *a.* Libidinoso, lascivo.
librarian [lai'brɛəriən], *n.* Bibliotecario, *m.*, bibliotecaria, *f.*
library ['laibrəri], *n.* Biblioteca, *f.*; libreria, *f.*
librate [lai'breit], *v.i.* Librarsi, oscillare, bilanciarsi.
libration, *n.* Librazione, *f.*; ondeggiamento, *m.*
libretto [li'bretou], *n.* Libretto, *m.*
lice [cp. **louse**].
licence ['laisəns], *n.* Licenza, *f.*, permesso, *m.*; autorizzazione, *f.*; brevetto, patente, *m.*; eccesso, *m.* (*Motor.*) **Driving- —,** patente di guida (per condurre automobili), *m.*; **car- —,** patente di circolazione, *f.*; **gun —,** porto d'armi, *m.*; **marriage —,** consenso di matrimonio, *m.*
license ['laisəns], *v.t.* Licenziare, dar permesso, autorizzare.
licensed, *a.* Autorizzato, brevettato.
licensee [laisən'si:], *n.* Autorizzato alla vendita di bevande alcooliche, *m.*

licentiate [lai'senʃiət], *n.* Licenziato, *m.*
licentious, *a.* Licenzioso, scostumato, indecente.
licentiously, *adv.* Licenziosamente.
licentiousness, *n.* Licenziosità, licenza, scostumatezza, *f.*
lichen [laikin], *n.* (*Bot.*) Lichene, *m.*
lich-gate, porta del cimitero.
licit ['lisit], *a.* Lecito, permesso.
lick [lik], *v.t.* Leccare, lambire; (*colloq.*) vincere, bastonare. || *n.* Leccata, *f.* **To — into shape,** foggiare, plasmare, dar forma a; **to — up,** leccare; **to — one's lips,** leccarsi le labbra; **to — the dust,** mordere la polvere.
licking, *n.* Leccamento, *m.*; bastonatura, *f.*, busse, *f.pl.*
lictor ['liktəɹ], *n.* (*Hist.*) Littore, *m.*
lid [lid], *n.* Coperchio, *m.*; (*of eye*) palpebra, *f.*; (*Zool.Bot.*) opercolo, *m.*
lie (1), *n.* Bugia, menzogna, *f.*; falsità, fandonia, *f.* || *v.i.* (*p.pp.* **lied**) Mentire, dire bugie. **A white —,** una bugia veniale; **to give the —,** dare una smentita; **a tissue of lies,** un tessuto di menzogne, *m.*; **to — unblushingly,** mentire spudoratamente.
lie (2), *v.i.* (*p.* **lay,** *pp.* **lain**). Giacere, star disteso, riposare; stare, trovarsi; (*Law*) essere luogo a procedere. || *n.* Disposizione, postura, posizione, situazione, *f.*; (*Golf*) posizione, *f.* **Let sleeping dogs —,** non toccare il can che dorme; **to — in state,** venir esposto (*of corpse*); **to — in prison,** essere in prigione; **to — in ruins,** giacere in rovina; **the road lies through a wood,** la strada traversa un bosco; (*Naut.*) **to — at anchor,** stare all'ancora; **the choice lies between these two,** la scelta sta fra questi due; **he knows where his interest lies,** egli sa dove sta il suo interesse; **here lies,** qui giace; **it lies with you to do it,** tocca a voi di farlo; **his death lies at your door,** voi siete responsabile della sua morte; **to — about,** esser disperso quà e là; **to — by,** esser messo in serbo; **to — close,** star vicino a; **to — down,** stendersi, sdraiarsi, coricarsi; **to take something lying down,** lasciarsi maltrattare senza reagire; (*fig.*) **to — heavy upon,** pesare su, essere di peso a; **to — in wait,** stare in agguato; (*Naut.*) **to — off,** stare al largo; **to — over,** essere rimandato, essere rinviato; (*Naut.*) **to — to,** essere in panna; **to — under suspicion,** essere sospetto; **to — up,** stare in letto; **to — dormant,** essere in giacenza; **to — idle,** starsene in ozio, restare ozioso; **the — of the land,** la configurazione del terreno, *f.*
lief [li:f], *adv.* Volentieri. **I would as — go as stay,** m'è indifferente l'andare o lo stare.
liege [li:dʒ], *n.* Vassallo, *m.* || *a.* Sovrano; ligio, fedele. **— lord,** signore, *m.*
lien ['li:ən], *n.* (*Law*) Diritto di sequestro, diritto di rivalsa, *m.*
lieu [lju:], *n.* Luogo, *m.* **In — of,** in luogo di, invece di.
lieutenancy [lef'tenənsi], *n.* Tenenza, *f.*
lieutenant [lef'tenənt], *n.* Tenente, luogotenente, *m.* (*Mil.*) **First —,** tenente, *m.*; **second —,** sottotenente, *m.*; (*Naut.*) [le'tenənt] tenente di vascello, *m.*; (*Mil.*) **—-colonel,** tenente colonnello, *m.*; **—-general,** tenente generale, *m.*; (*Naut.*) **—-commander,** capitano di corvetta, *m.*; **—-governor,** vicegovernatore, *m.*; **Lord —,** luogotenente generale.
life [laif], *n.* Vita, esistenza, *f.*; energia, *f.*, vigore, *m.*; vivacità, *f.*; (*Art*) naturale, *m.* **A matter of — and death,** una questione di vita o di morte, *f.*; **to come to —,** ritornare in vita; **to bring to —,** vivificare, render vivo; **to lay down one's — for,** dar la vita per; **to escape with one's —,** salvarsi la vita; **risk to — and limb,** rischio per l'incolumità personale; **a great sacrifice of —,** un gran sacrificio di vite umane, *f.*; **to run for one's —,** salvarsi con la fuga; **Upon my —!** Alla grazia! Caspita!; **he was the — and soul of the party,** era l'anima della compagnia; **taken from the —,** ritratto dal vero; **to portray to the —,** ritrarre al vivo; **a — sentence,** condanna a vita; **expectation of —,** probabilità di vivere, *f.*; **never in my —,** mai in vita mia; **at his time of —,** alla sua età; **where there's — there's hope,** quando c'è vita c'è speranza; **the single —,** la vita da celibe; **to depart this —,** morire, passare a miglior vita; **—-annuity,** vitalizio, *m.*; **—-belt,** salvagente, *m.*, cinta di salvataggio, *f.*; **—-boat,** battello di salvataggio, *m.*; **—-buoy,** gavitello di salvataggio, *m.*; **—-giving,** vivificante, animatore; **—-assurance,** assicurazione sulla vita, *f.*; **—-interest,** rendita vitalizia, *f.*; **—-line,** canapo di salvataggio, *m.*; **—-size,** al naturale, al vero; grandezza naturale, *f.*; **—-work,** lavoro di tutta una vita, *m.*
lifeguards ['laifgɑ:ɹdz], *n.pl.* (*Mil.*) Guardie del corpo, *f.pl.*
lifeless, *a.* Senza vita, inanimato, esanime; (*fig.*) inerte, freddo, snervato.
lifelessness, *n.* Mancanza di vita, *f.*; inerzia, *f.*; freddezza, *f.*
lifelike, *a.* Verosimile, parlante.
lift [lift], *n.* Sollevamento, *m.*, spinta, alzata, *f.*; ascensore, elevatore, *m.*; gesto, cenno, *m.* || *v.t.* Levare, elevare, alzare, sollevare; (*steal*) rubare. **To give a — to,** fare montare con sè, (*fig.*) dare una spinta a; **Can you give me a —?** Potete darmi un passaggio?; **— attendant,** addetto all'ascensore, *m.f.*
lifting, *n.* Sollevamento, *m.*, alzata, *f.* **—-power** massima portata, *f.*; **—-jack,** cricco, martinetto, *m.*
ligament 'ligəmənt], *n.* (*Anat.*) Legamento, *m.*
ligature ['ligətʃəɹ], *n.* Legatura, *f.*
light (1) [lait], *n.* Luce, *f.*; lume, *m.*; chiarore, splendore, *m.*; fanale, *m.*; lampada, *f.*; (*fig.*) aspetto, punto di vista, *m.* || *v.t.* Accendere; illuminare, dar lume a; rischiarare; *v.i.* illuminarsi. || *a.* Pieno di luce, luminoso. **By the — of a lamp,** a lume di lampada; **by the — of the moon,** al chiaro di luna; **in its true —,** sotto il vero aspetto, nella vera luce; **don't stand in my —,** non to ietemi la luce; (*fig.*) **to stand in one's own —,** nuocere a sè stesso; **to bring to —,** mettere in luce; **to come to —,** venire in luce, manifestarsi; **to give — to,** dar luce a; **to see the —,** veder la luce; **the — of one's eyes,** la luce degli occhi; **to throw — on a subject,** gettar luce su un soggetto; **in the — of these facts,** alla luce di questi fatti; **to strike a —,** accendere un fiammifero; **Have you a —?**

Avete un fiammifero? **to — the streets,** illuminare le strade; **to — up,** accendere, rischiarare; **his face lit up,** il suo viso s'illuminò.
light (2), *a.* Leggero; (*complexion*) biondo; (*colour*) chiaro; (*fig.*) incostante, frivolo; divertente, gaio; (*Naut.*) senza carico, in zavorra. (*Mil.*) **— -horse,** cavalleria leggera, *f.*; **a — hand,** una mano leggera, *f.*; **to make — of,** far poco conto di; **— of foot,** snello, agile; **— -fingered,** lesto di mano; **— -handed,** destro; **— -headed,** sventato; **— -hearted,** gaio, allegro; **— -heartedness,** gaiezza, allegria, *f.*; **— -minded,** frivolo, sventato, leggero.
light (3), *v.i.* **To — upon,** imbattersi in, incontrare a caso.
lighten (1), *v.t.* Illuminare, rischiarare; *v.i.* balenare, lampeggiare.
lighten (2), *v.t.* Alleggerire; sollevare, mitigare.
lighter (1), *n.* Accenditore, *m.*
lighter (2), *n.* (*Naut.*) Chiatta, *f.*, pontone, *m.*
lighterage, *n.* Prezzo di scarico, scaricamento, *m.*
lighterman, *n.* Scaricatore, chiattaiuolo, *m.*
lighthouse, *n.* Faro, *m.*
lighting, *n.* Illuminazione, *f.*; accensione, *f.* **— -up time,** l'ora d'accendere le luci, *f.*
lightly, *adv.* Leggermente; lievemente. **To sleep —,** dormir leggero, aver il sonno leggero.
lightness, *n.* Leggerezza, *f.*
lightning, *n.* Baleno, lampo, *m.* **A flash of —,** un lampo, *m.*; **— war,** guerra lampo, *f.*; **to be killed by —,** essere fulminato; **— -conductor,** parafulmine, *m.*; **— strike,** sciopero lampo, *m.*
lights, *n.pl.* (*of animals*) Polmoni, *m.pl.*, corata, *f.*
lightship, *n.* Battello faro, *m.*
lightsome, *a.* Leggero, grazioso; allegro, giocondo; snello.
lightsomeness, *n.* Leggerezza, allegrezza, agilità, *f.*
light-weight ['laitweit], *n.* (*Sport*) Peso leggero, *m.*
ligneous ['ligniəs], *a.* (*Bot.*) Ligneo.
lignite ['lignait], *n.* (*Geol.*) Lignite, *f.*
lignum vitae ['lignəm 'vaiti:], *n.* (*Bot.*) Guiaco, *m.*
likable, likeable ['laikəbl], *a.* Simpatico, amabile.
like (1) [laik], *a.* Simile, somigliante, pari, eguale, conforme; tale, stesso, medesimo. || *n.* Uguale, pari, simile, *m.f.* || *prep.* Come, da, alla maniera di. **— father, — son,** qual padre, tale figlio; **— master, — man,** tale abate, quali monaci; **he is very — his father,** somiglia molto al padre; **they are as — as two peas,** si somigliano come due gocce d'acqua; **to look —,** somigliare a, rassomigliare a; **What is he — ?** Che tipo è? Che aspetto ha?; **we collected something — a pound,** abbiamo raccolto qualcosa come una sterlina; **it's — his cheek,** è la sua solita sfacciataggine; **I have never seen his —,** non ho mai visto il suo uguale; **and the —,** e così via, e simili; **he will never do the — again,** non farà mai più una simile cosa; (*colloq.*) **the likes of me,** i miei simili, *m.pl.*; **I can't speak French — you,** non posso parlare francese come voi; **don't talk — that,** non parlate così; **she acted — a brave woman,** si comportò da donna coraggiosa.
like (2), *v.t.* Amare, aver caro, voler bene a; piacere a; volere, desiderare. **As you —,** come vi piace; **Do you — London ?** Vi piace Londra? **I should — to come,** mi piacerebbe venire; **he will do as he likes,** farà come vorrà; **if you —,** se vi piace, se vi pare; **I should — nothing better,** non vorrei niente di meglio; **I should — to have seen it,** avrei voluto vederlo; **I — this best,** preferisco questo.
likeable, likable, *a.* Simpatico, amabile.
likelihood ['laiklihud], *n.* Probabilità, *f.*; apparenza, verosimiglianza, *f.* **In all —,** con ogni probabilità.
likely, *a.* Probabile. || *adv.* Probabilmente. **Very —,** è molto probabile; **it is not —,** non è probabile; **they called at every — house,** visitarono le case che davano affidamento; **three — young men,** tre giovani promettenti; **Where is the likeliest place to find him ?** Dov'è il posto più probabile per trovarlo?
liken, *v.t.* Rassomigliare; paragonare, comparare.
likeness ['laiknis], *n.* Rassomiglianza, somiglianza, *f.*; ritratto, *m.*; sembianza, *f.* **To have one's — taken,** farsi fare il ritratto; **an enemy in the — of a friend,** un nemico in sembianza d'amico.
likewise, *adv.* Anche, inoltre; del pari, similmente.
liking, *n.* Gusto, *m.*; affetto, *m.*; simpatia, inclinazione, *f.* **To have a — for,** aver una simpatia per; **to take a — to,** prender gusto a; **that is to my —,** ciò mi va a genio.
lilac ['lailək], *n.* (*Bot.*) Lilla, *f.* **— -coloured,** color lilla.
liliaceous [lili'eiʃəs], *a.* (*Bot.*) Liliaceo.
Lilliputian [lili'pju:ʃən], *a.* Lillipuziano.
lilt [lilt], *n.* Ritmo, *m.*, cadenza, *f.*; canzonetta, carola, *f.* || *v.t.i.* Cantare, gorgheggiare.
lily ['lili], *n.* (*Bot.*) Giglio, *m.* **— of the valley,** mughetto, *m.*
limb [lim], *n.* (*of body*) Membro, *m.*; (*of tree*) ramo, *m.*; (*of cross*) braccio, *m.*; (*Astron. Math.*) limbo, *m.*; (*fig.*) diavoletto, *m.*
limbed, *a.* Membrato. **Strong- —,** membruto.
limber (1) ['limbəɹ], *a.* Flessibile, agile.
limber (2), *n.* (*Mil.*) Avantreno, *m.* **To — up,** attaccare all'avantreno.
limbless ['limlis], *a.* Senza membra.
limbo ['limbou], *n.* Limbo, *m.*
lime (1) [laim], *n.* (*fruit*) Cedro, *m.*; (*tree*) tiglio, *m.* **— -juice,** acqua di cedro, *f.*, succo di limone, *m.*
lime (2), *n.* Calce, calcina, *f.* || *v.t.* (*Agric.*) concimare con calce. **Bird- —,** vischio, *m.*, pania, *f.*; **— -kiln,** fornace da calce, *f.*; **— -burner,** fornaciaio, *m.*; **— -pit,** buca della calcina, *f.*; **— -water,** acqua di calce, *f.*
limelight, *n.* Luce bianca, *f.* **In the —,** alla luce della ribalta, in evidenza.
limestone, *n.* (*Geol.*) Calcare, *m.*; pietra calcarea, *f.*

limit ['limit], *n.* Limite, confine, termine, *m.*; fine, *f.*; perimetro, *m.* || *v.t.* Limitare, confinare, circoscrivere. (*colloq.*) **It's the —!** È il colmo!
limitable, *a.* Limitabile.
limitation [limi'teiʃən], *n.* Limitazione, riserva, *f.*, limite, *m.* **He has his limitations,** esso hai suoi limiti.
limitative, *a.* Limitativo.
limited, *a.* Limitato, ristretto; scarso; (*Comm.*) anonimo. **A — company,** una società anonima, *f.*; **— monarchy,** monarchia costituzionale, *f.*
limitless, *a.* Illimitato.
limn [lim], *v.t.* Dipingere.
limner, *n.* Pittore, *n.m.*
limousine ['limu:zi:n], *n.* Limousine, *f.*
limp [limp], *a.* Fiacco, floscio, cascante, molle. || *v.i.* Zoppiccare, andar zoppo. || *n.* Zoppicamento, *m.*
limpet ['limpit], *n.* (*Zool.*) Patella, *f.*
limpid, *a.* Limpido, chiaro; terso.
limpidity, limpidness, *n.* Limpidezza, limpidità, *f.*
limpingly, *adv.* Zoppicando, zoppiconi.
limy ['laimi], *a.* Calcareo; viscoso.
linchpin ['lintʃpin], *n.* Chiodo del mozzo, *m.*, caviglia, *f.*
linden ['lindən], *n.* (*Bot.*) Tiglio, *m.*
line (1) [lain], *n.* Linea, riga, *f.*; tratto, *m.*; (*fishing*) lenza, *f.*; (*string*) corda, *f.*; (*row*) fila, *f.*; (*series*) serie, *f.*; (*ancestry*) discendenza, *f.*; (*poetry*) verso, *m.*; (*wrinkle*) ruga, *f.*; (*of business*) genere di affari, *m.* || *v.t.* Allineare, rigare, segnare. **The Line,** l'Equatore, *m.*, la linea equatoriale, *f.*; **on the same lines,** nello stesso modo; **to draw the —,** segnare il limite; **I draw the — at that,** quello è proprio contro la mia coscienza; **to come into —,** mettersi d'accordo; **to draw up in —,** allineare; **all along the line,** in tutta la linea; **just a — to tell you,** soltanto due righe per dirvi; (*Theat.*) **to learn one's lines,** imparar la propria parte; **to take one's own —,** battere la propria strada; **it is hard lines,** è una sfortuna, è un guaio; **it is not in my —,** non è di mia competenza; **a face lined with wrinkles,** una faccia solcata di rughe; (*Mil.*) **— of march,** direzione di marcia, *f.*; **lines of communication,** linee di comunicazione, *.pl.*; **— of battle,** ordine di battaglia, *m.*; **— of fire,** linea di tiro, *f.*; **troops of the —,** reggimenti di linea, *m.pl.*; (*Rail.*) **main —,** linea principale, *f.*; **branch —,** linea secondaria, *f.*; **loop —,** diversione, linea di scambio, *f.*; **— engraving,** incisione, *f.*; **— block,** cliché al tratto, *m.*
line (2), *v.t.* (*garments, etc.*) Foderare.
lineage ['liniədʒ], *n.* Lignaggio, *m.*, stirpe, razza, *f.*
lineal, *a.* Lineare, in linea retta. **A — descendant,** discendente in linea retta, *m.f.*
lineally, *adv.* Linearmente.
lineament ['liniəmənt], *n.* Lineamento, *m.*, fattezza, *f.*; tratto, *m.*
linear, *a.* Lineare.
linen ['linin], *n.* Tela di lino, *f.*, pannolino, *m.*; (*sheets, etc.*) biancheria, *f.* || *a.* Di tela, di lino. **Clean —,** biancheria pulita, *f.*; **a change of —,** biancheria di ricambio, *f.*, un cambio di biancheria, *m.*; **baby —,** corredino per neonato; **—-draper,** mercante di tela, *m.*; **—-drapery,** teleria, *f.*; **— thread,** filo di lino, refe, *m.*
liner ['lainəɹ], *n.* (*Naut.*) Transatlantico, *m.* **Air- —,** aeroplano di linea, *m.*
linesman ['lainzmən], *n.* (*Football*) Guardalinee, arbitro, *m.*; (*Rail.*) guardalinea, *m.*; (*Teleg.Teleph.*) guardafili, *m.*; (*Mil.*) soldato di fanteria, *m.*
ling [liŋ], *n.* (*Bot.*) Erica, *f.*; (*Zool.*) merluzzo, *m.*
linger ['liŋgəɹ], *v.i.* Tardare, attardarsi, indugiare, soffermarsi; esitare. **To — over a subject,** dilungarsi su un argomento; **to — on,** languire, struggersi; **to — behind,** restare indietro.
lingerer, *n.* Ritardatario, *m.*
lingerie ['lɑ̃:ʒəri:], *n.* Biancheria, *f.*
lingering, *n.* Ritardo, indugio, *m.*, lentezza, lungaggine, *f.* || *a.* Tardo, lento; languente, esitante. **A — illness,** una malattia prolungata, *f.*; **a — death,** una morte lenta, *f.*
lingo ['liŋgou], *n.* (*colloq.*) Gergo, *m.*, lingua barbara, *f.*
lingual ['liŋgwəl], *a.* (*Anat.*) Linguale.
linguiform ['liŋgwifɔ:ɹm], *a.* Linguiforme.
linguist ['liŋgwist], *n.* Linguista, *m.f.*
linguistic, *a.* Linguistico.
linguistically, *adv.* Linguisticamente.
linguistics, *n.pl.* Linguistica, *f.*
liniment ['linimənt], *n.* (*Med.*) Linimento, unguento, *m.*
lining ['lainiŋ], *n.* Fodera, foderatura, *f.*; rivestimento, *m.*; (*of hat*) guarnizione, *f.*
link (1) [liŋk], *n.* Anello, *m.*, maglia, *f.*; giuntura, congiunzione, *f.*; vincolo, legame, *m.* (*Mech.*) biella, bielletta, *f.*, giunto, uncino, *m.* || *v.t.i.* Collegare, congiungere, unire, connettere; unirsi, congiungersi, legarsi.
link (2), *n.* (*obs.*) Fiaccola, *f.* **—-boy,** portafiaccola, *m.*
links, *n.pl.* Landa, *f.*, terreno aperto; (*Golf.*) campo, terreno, *m.*
linnet ['linit], *n.* (*Zool.*) Fanello, *m.*
linoleum, lino [lin'ouliəm, 'lainou], *n.* Linoleum, *m.*, tela cerata, *f.*
linotype ['lainoutaip], *n.* Linotipo, *m.*; linotipia, *f.*
linseed ['linsi:d], *n.* Seme di lino, *m.*; linosa, *f.* **—-oil,** olio di linosa, olio di lino, *m.*; **—-poultice,** cataplasma di linosa, *m.*
linsey-woolsey [linzi 'wulzi], *n.* Mezzalana, *f.*
lint [lint], *n.* Filaccia, garza, *f.*
lintel ['lintəl], *n.* (*Arch.*) Architrave, listello, *m.*
lion ['laiən], *n.* (*Zool.*) Leone, *m.*; (*fig.*) celebrità, *f.* **The lion's share,** la parte del leone, *f.*; **lion's cub,** leoncello, leoncino, *m.*; **—-hearted,** dal cuor di leone.
lioness, *n.* Leonessa, *f.*
lionize ['laiənaiz], *v.i.t.* Trattare come una celebrità, adulare.
lip [lip], *n.* Labbro, *m.*; orlo, bordo, *m.* (*Mech.*) coprimozzo, *m.*; (*colloq.*) impertinenza. **To bite one's lips,** mordersi le labbra; **to curl one's —,** increspar il labbro; **to lick one's lips,** leccarsi le labbra; **to open one's lips,** aprire le labbra; **— -salve,** unguento per le labbra; **—-stick,** rossetto, *m.*; **—-service,** consentimento a parole soltanto, *m.*; **—-reading,** il capire dal moto delle labbra, *m.*

liquation [liˈkweiʒən], *n.* (*Chem.*) Liquazione, *f.*
liquefaction [likwiˈfækʃən], *n.* Liquefazione, *f.*
liquefiable, *a.* Liquefabile.
liquefy [ˈlikwifai], *v.t.i.* Liquefare, liquefarsi.
liquescent [liˈkwesənt], *a.* Liquescente.
liqueur [liˈkju:əɹ], *n.* Liquore, *m.* **— brandy,** cognac fino, *m.*
liquid [ˈlikwid], *a.* Liquido, fluido, scorrevole; trasparente, lucente. || *n.* Liquido, *m.* **— ammonia,** spirito d'ammoniaca, *m.*; (*Comm.*) **— assets,** attività liquide, *f.pl.*; **— paraffin,** olio di paraffina, *m.*
liquidate [ˈlikwideit], *v.t.* (*Comm.*) Liquidare.
liquidation, *n.* Liquidazione, *f.*
liquidator, *n.* Liquidatore, *m.*
liquidity, liquidness, *n.* Liquidità, *f.*
liquor [ˈlikəɹ], *n.* Liquore, *m.* **In —,** ubbriaco.
liquorice [ˈlikəris], *n.* (*Bot.*) Liquirizia, *f.*
Lisbon [ˈlizbən], *n.* (*Geog.*) Lisbona, *f.*
lisp [lisp], *v.t.i.* Parlare bleso, biascicare, balbettare. || *n.* Balbuzie, *f.pl.*
lisping, *a.* Balbuziente.
lispingly, *adv.* Biascicando, scilinguando.
lissom [ˈlisəm], *a.* Flessibile, pieghevole, agile, snello, svelto.
list (1) [list], *n.* Lista, *f.*, elenco, catalogo, listino, *m.*; tavola, *f.*; inventario, *m.* || *v.t.* Elencare, catalogare. **Civil —,** lista civile, *f.*; **price —,** distinta dei prezzi, *f.*; **on the retired —,** in ritiro.
list (2), *v.i.* (*Naut.*) Sbandare. || *n.* Sbandamento, *m.*
list (3), *n.* (*selvedge*) Vivagno, *m.*
list (4), (*obs.*) *v.t.* Volere, desiderare; ascoltare.
listen [ˈlisn], *v.i.* Ascoltare, sentire, porgere orecchio. (*Radio*) **To — in,** ascoltare.
listener, *n.* Ascoltatore, uditore, *m.*
listless, *a.* Languido, disattento, sbadato, svogliato, indifferente.
listlessness, *n.* Sbadataggine, svogliatezza, indifferenza, *f.*
lists, *n.pl.* Lizza, arena, *f.* **To enter the —,** scendere in lizza.
litany [ˈlitəni], *n.* Litania, *f.*
literal [ˈlitərəl], *a.* Letterale, alla lettera. || *n.* (*Print.*) Errore di stampa, *m.*
literally, *adv.* Letteralmente.
literary [ˈlitərəri], *a.* Letterario. **A — man,** un letterato, *m.*
literate, *a.* Letterato, erudito.
literature, *n.* Letteratura, *f.*
litharge [ˈliθɑ:ɹdʒ], *n.* (*Chem.*) Litargirio, *m.*
lithe, lithesome [laið, ˈlaiðsəm], *a.* Pieghevole, flessibile, snello, svelto.
litheness, *n.* Pieghevolezza, flessibilità, *f.*
lithia [ˈliθiə], *n.* Litina, *f.* **— water,** l'acqua litina, *f.*
lithium, *n.* Litio, *m.*
lithograph [ˈliθougræf], *n.* Litografia, *f.* || *v.t.* Litografare.
lithographer [liˈθɔgrəfəɹ], *n.* Litografo, *m.*
lithographic [liθouˈgræfik], *a.* Litografico.
lithography, *n.* Litografia, *f.*
Lithuania [liθju:ˈeiniə], *n.* (*Geog.*) Lituania, *f.*
litigant [ˈlitigənt], *n.* Litigante, *m.f.* || *a.* Litigante, litigioso,
litigate [ˈlitigeit], *v.t.i.* Litigare, disputare.
litigation, *n.* Lite, *f.*, litigio, *m.*; contestazione, vertenza, *f.*; processo, *m.*
litigious [liˈtidʒəs], *a.* Litigioso.
litigiousness, *n.* Litigiosità, *f.*
litmus [ˈlitməs], *n.* (*Chem.*) Tornasole, *m.* **— -paper,** carta di tornasole, *f.*
litotes [ˈlaitouti:z], *n.* (*Gram.*) Litote, *f.*
litre [ˈli:təɹ], *n.* Litro, *m.*
litter (1) [ˈlitəɹ], *n.* (*of animals*) Figliata, ventrata, *f.* || *v.t.* Figliare.
litter (2), *n.* Disordine, confusione, *f.*, scompiglio, *m.*; (*in stables*) strame, *m.*, lettiera, *f.* || *v.t.* Sparpagliare, lordare, ingombrare di cartaccia. **To — down a horse,** far la lettiera a un cavallo.
litter (3), *n.* Lettiga, barella, *f.*
little [ˈlitl], *a.* Piccolo, piccino; minimo; esiguo, scarso; breve, corto; meschino, gretto. || *adv.* Poco. || *n.* Poco, po', pochino, *m.* **A — chap, a — one,** un piccino, *m.*; **a — mind,** una mente ristretta, *f.*; **big and —,** grandi e piccini, *m.pl.*; **we know his — ways,** conosciamo le sue graziette; **wait a — while,** aspettate un pochino; **every — difficulty,** ogni minima difficoltà, *f.*; **— finger,** mignolo, dito mignolo, *m.*; **I like him —,** mi piace poco; **— by —,** a poco a poco; **give me a — bread,** datemi un po' di pane; **— or nothing,** poco o niente; **not a —,** non poco; **as — as possible,** il meno possibile; **Little Red Riding-Hood,** Cappuccetto Rosso, *m.*
littleness, *n.* Piccolezza, pochezza, scarsezza, *f.*
littoral [ˈlitərəl], *n.a.* Littorale, litorale, *m.*
liturgic [liˈtə:ɹdʒik], *a.* Liturgico.
liturgy [ˈlitəɹdʒi], *n.* Liturgia, *f.*
live (1) [liv], *v.t.i.* Vivere, esistere; (*reside*) dimorare, abitare; nutrirsi, alimentarsi, sostentarsi. **To — on,** nutrirsi di, vivere di; **enough to — on,** di che vivere; **— and let —,** vivi e lascia vivere; **to — from hand to mouth** vivere alla giornata; **as long as I —,** finchè vivrò; **Long — the Queen!** Evviva la regina! **to — well,** vivere nell'abbondanza; **to — down a slander,** sfatare coi fatti una calunnia; **he will not — through the night,** egli non passerà la notte; **his memory lives,** la sua memoria sopravvive.
live (2) [laiv], *a.* Vivo, vivente, vitale; ardente; (*Elect.*) sottotensione. **A — coal,** un carbone ardente; (*Elec.*) **a — wire,** un filo carico di corrente, *m.*, (*fig.*) un animatore, *m.*; **a — issue,** una questione vitale, *f.*; **— -stock,** bestiame, *m.*
livelihood [ˈlaivlihud], *n.* Vita, sussistenza, *f.* **To earn one's —,** guadagnarsi la vita.
liveliness, *n.* Vivacità, vivezza, *f.*, brio, *m.*; animazione, *f.*; attività, *f.*
livelong [ˈlivlɔŋ], *a.* Lungo, eterno. **All the — day,** tutto il santo giorno.
lively [ˈlaivli], *a.* Vivo, vivace, brioso, allegro; (*colloq.*) difficile. **To make things — for someone,** dare del filo da torcere a qualcuno.
liven [ˈlaivn], *v.t.* **To — up,** ravvivare, animare.
liver [ˈlivəɹ], *n.* (*Anat.*) Fegato, *m.* **— -coloured** rosso bruno; **— -complaint,** mal di fegato, *m.*
liverish, *a.* Fegatoso, bilioso.
liverwort, *n.* (*Bot.*) Fegatella, *f.*
livery [ˈlivəri], *n.* Livrea, *f.* **In —,** in livrea; **— -stable,** scuderia, *f.*; **— -servant,** cameriere in livrea, valletto, *m.*
liveryman (*pl.* **liverymen**) [ˈlivərimən], *n.* Membro di una corporazione della città di Londra, *m.*

livid [livid], *a.* Livido.
lividity, *n.* Lividezza, *f.*, lividore, *m.*
lividly, *adv.* Lividamente.
living, *n.* Vita, sussistenza, *f.*; (*Eccles.*) beneficio, *m.*; prebenda, *f.* || *a.* Vivente, vivo. **To earn one's —,** guadagnarsi la vita, guadagnare di che vivere, guadagnarsi il pane; **a fat —,** una grassa prebenda; **he enjoys good —,** ama una buona tavola; **a — wage,** salario che dà da vivere; **the land of the —,** il paese dei viventi, *m.*; **—-room,** stanza di soggiorno, *f.*; **within — memory,** a memoria d'uomo.
lixiviate [lik'sivieit], *v.t.* (*Chem.*) Lisciviare.
lizard ['lizəɹd], *n.* (*Zool.*) Lucertola, *f.* **Lounge —,** cicisbeo, *m.*
llama ['lɑ:mə], *n.* (*Zool.*) Lama, *m.*
lo! [lou], *inter.* Ecco! **Lo and behold!** Veh! Vedi!
loach [loutʃ], *n.* (*Zool.*) Ghiozzo, *m.*
load [loud], *n.* Carico, *m.*, soma, *f.*; peso, fardello, *m.* || *v.t.* Caricare; (*fig.*) gravare, opprimere; colmare. (*Naut.*) **— draught,** pescaggio con carico, *m.*; **—-line,** linea di carico, *f.*; **to — with favours,** colmare di benefizi; **to — the dice,** falsare i dadi; **—-star** stella polare, buona stella, *f.*; **to — a gun,** caricare un fucile, *m.*; **to take in a —,** fare il carico.
loader, *n.* Caricatore, *m.*
loading, *n.* Caricamento. **A ship in —,** un battello in carico, *m.*
loadstone, *n.* Calamita, *f.*
loaf (1) [louf], *n.* Pane, *m.*; pagnotta, *f.* **—-sugar,** pan di zucchero, *m.*
loaf (2), *v.i.* Oziare, bighellonare, vagabondare.
loafer, *n.* Fannullone, bighellone, *m.*
loam [loum], *n.* Terra grassa, argilla, *f.*; terriccio, *m.*; marna, *f.*
loamy, *a.* Marnoso.
loan [loun], *n.* Prestito, imprestito, *m.*; (*Comm.*) mutuo, prestito, *m.* || *v.t.* Prestare, imprestare, dare in prestito; dare a mutuo. **May I have the — of,** favorite prestarmi; **to raise a —,** emettere un prestito.
loath, loth [louθ], *a.* Avverso, contrario, sfavorevole, poco disposto. **To be — to,** aver poco voglia di, esser restio a; **nothing —,** molto volentieri.
loathe [louð], *v.t.* Detestare, odiare, aborrire; provare ripugnanza, aver a nausea, avere in fastidio.
loathing ['louðiŋ], *n.* Disgusto, odio, aborrimento, *m.*
loathsome, *a.* Detestabile, odioso, disgustoso, schifoso.
loathsomeness, *n.* Detestabilità, odiosità, schifosità, *f.*
lob [lɔb], *v.t.* (*Sport*) Tirare alto. || *n.* (*Tennis*) Pallonetto, *m.*, candela, *f.*
lobate ['loubeit], *a.* Lobato.
lobby ['lɔbi], *n.* Corridoio, vestibolo, atrio, *m.*; (*fig. Pol.*) corridoio, *m.*; (*Theat.*) ridotto, *m.* || *v.i.* (*Pol.*) Sollecitar voti.
lobbying, *n.* (*Pol.*) Mene di corridoio, *f.pl.*
lobe [loub], *n.* (*Anat.Bot.*) Lobo, *m.*
lobed, *a.* Lobato.
lobelia [lou'bi:liə], *n.* (*Bot.*) Lobelia, *f.*
lobster ['lɔbstəɹ], *n.* (*Zool.*) Aragosta, *f.*, gambero di mare, *m.*; **—-pot,** nassa, *m.*
lobular ['lɔbju:ləɹ], *a.* Lobulare.
local ['loukəl], *a.* Locale, del luogo; di campanile. || *n.* (*colloq.*) Bettola, osteria, *f.* **— colour,** colore locale, *m.*; **— time,** ora locale, *f.*
locality [lou'kæliti], *n.* Località, *f.* **Bump of —,** facoltà d'orientarsi, *f.*
localization, *n.* Localizzazione, *f.*
localize, *v.t.* Localizzare.
locally, *adv.* Localmente.
locate [lou'keit], *v.t.* Situare, piazzare, fissare, collocare; individuare. **We located the enemy's camp,** individuammo il campo nemico.
location, *n.* Situazione, posizione, *f.*; sito, *m.*; locazione, *f.*
locative ['lɔkətiv], *a.* (*Gram.*) Locativo.
loch [lɔk], *n.* Lago, *m.*
lock (1) [lɔk], *n.* (of hair) Riccio, ricciolo, *m.*; (*of wool*) fiocco, *m.* **Her long locks,** i suoi riccioloni, *m.pl.*; le sue trecce, *f.pl.*
lock (2), *n.* (*of door, etc.*) Serratura, *f.*; (*of gun*) congegno di sparo, scatto, *m.*; (*on canal*) cateratta, chiusa, conca, *f.* || *v.t.* Chiudere a chiave, serrare, rinserrare, sprangare; (*Mech.*) congiungere; **—, stock and barrel,** con tutto l'armamentario; **a double —,** una serratura a doppio giro, *f.*; **to — in,** rinchiudere, rinserrare; **to — out,** serrar fuori, chiuder fuori; **a —-out,** una serrata, *f.*; **to — up,** chiudere, nascondere; **to be locked up,** essere imprigionato, esser chiuso dentro; **under — and key,** sotto chiave; (*Mech.*) **—-nut,** controdado, *m.*; **—-chain,** catenella d'arresto, *f.*; **—-gate,** chiusa, porta di conca, *f.*; (*Med.*) **—-jaw,** tetano, trisma, *m.*; **—-keeper,** guardaconca, *m.*; **—-stitch,** punto a filo doppio, *m.*; **—-up,** guardina, prigione, *f.*; **—-up shop,** bottega senza abitazione vicina, *f.*
Lock (3), *n.* **— hospital,** Sifilicomio, *m.*
lockage, *n.* Diritto di passaggio da una chiusa, *m.*
locker, *n.* Armadietto, ripostiglio, cassone, *m.* **I haven't a shot in my —,** non mi resta più niente.
locket, *n.* Medaglione fermaglio, *m.*
locksmith, *n.* Magnano, fabbro ferraio, *m.*
locomotion [loukə'mouʃən], *n.* Locomozione, *f.*
locomotive, *n.* Locomotiva, *f.* || *a.* Locomotivo, locomotore.
locomotor, *n.* (*Med.*) **— ataxy,** atassia locomotrice, *f.*
loculus [lɔ'kju:ləs], *n.* Alveolo, loculo, *m.*
locum tenens ['loukəm 'ti:nenz], *n.* Supplente, *m.f.*; sostituto, *m.*
locus ['loukəs], *n.* (*Geom.*) Luogo, *m.*
locust ['loukəst], *n.* (*Zool.*) Locusta, cavalletta, *f.*; **—-tree,** carrubo, *m.*; **—-bean,** carruba, *f.*
locution [lə'kju:ʃən], *n.* Locuzione, *f.*, modo di dire, *m.*
lode [loud], *n.* Filone, *m.*, vena, corrente, *f.*
lodestone [cp. **loadstone**].
lodge [lɔdʒ], *n.* Casetta, villetta, *f.*; dipendenza, *f.*, annesso, *m.*; (*porter's*) portineria, *f.*; (*Masonic*) loggia, *f.* || *v.t.* Alloggiare, albergare; deporre, mettere; situare, collocare; (*a complaint*) presentare; piantare, fissare; *v.i.* alloggiare, dimorare, abitare; conficcarsi. **—-keeper,** custode, portinaio, *m.*; **shooting-—,** casina da caccia, *f.*; **the bullet lodged in his brain,** la palla gli si conficcò nel cervello.

lodger, *n.* Pigionante, pensionante, inquilino, *m.*
lodging, *n.* Alloggio, appartamento, *m.*, camera, residenza, pensione, *f.* **Board and —,** vitto e alloggio; **a night's —,** alloggio per una notte, *m.*; **furnished lodgings,** camere ammobigliate, *f.pl.*; **— -house,** casa di camere ammobigliate, pensione, *f.*; **— -house keeper,** padrone, *m.*, padrona, *f.*
lodgment, *n.* Deposito, *m.*; alloggio, alloggiamento, *m.*
loft [lɔft], *n.* Granaio, solaio, *m.*, piccionaia, soffitta, tribuna, *f.* || *v.t.* (*Golf*) Mandare in aria.
loftily, *adv.* Altamente, superbamente, arrogantemente.
loftiness, *n.* Altezza, elevatezza, *f.*; nobilità, grandezza, *f.*
lofty, *a.* Alto, elevato; nobile, grande, sublime; superbo, arrogante.
log [lɔg], *n.* Ceppo, ciocco, tronco, *m.*; (*Naut.*) scandaglio, *m.* || *v.t.* (*Naut.*) Iscrivere nel giornale di bordo. **— -book,** giornale di bordo **— -cabin,** capanna di tronchi d'albero, *f.*; (*Naut.*) **— -line,** sagola dello scandaglio, *f.*; **— -rolling,** (*fig.*) mutuo soccorso, *m.*
loganberry [ˈlougənberi], *n.* (*Bot.*) Specie di lampone.
logan-stone [ˈlougənstoun], *n.* Macigno pencolante, *m.*
logarithm [ˈlɔgəriðm], *n.* (*Math.*) Logaritmo, *m.*
logarithmic, *a.* Logaritmico.
loggerheads, *n.* **To be at —,** essere in lite, essere alle prese, essere come cani e gatti; **to set at —,** mettere in disaccordo.
logic [ˈlɔdʒik], *n.* Logica, *f.*
logical, *a.* Logico.
logicality, *n.* Logicità, *f.*
logically, *adv.* Logicamente.
logician [louˈdʒiʃən], *n.* Logico, *m.*
logistics [louˈdʒistiks], *n.pl.* (*Mil.*) Logistica, *f.*
logomachy [lɔˈgouməki], *n.* Logomachia, *f.*
logwood, *n.* (*Bot.*) Legno di campeggio, *m.*
loin [lɔin], *n.* (*Anat.*) Lombo, *m.*; (*of meat*) lombata, *f.* **The loins,** i reni, i fianchi, i lombi, *m.pl.*; **— -cloth,** fascia attorno ai fianchi, *f.*; **— -chop,** braciola di filetto, *f.*
loiter [ˈlɔitəɹ], *v.t.i.* Oziare, attardarsi, bighellonare, gironzolare. **To — away one's time,** perdere il tempo, baloccarsi.
loiterer, *n.* Bighellone, fannullone, perdigiorno, *m.*
loitering, *n.* L'andare a zonzo; l'attardarsi.
loiteringly, *adv.* Lentamente, pigramente.
loll [lɔl], *v.i.* Pencolare, pendere, penzolare, stendersi, sdraiarsi; *v.t.* (*of tongue*) lasciar penzolare.
lollipop [ˈlɔlipɔp], *n.* Caramella, *f.*
Lollard [ˈlɔləɹd], *n.* (*Hist.*) Lollardo, *m.*
Lombard [ˈlɔmbəɹd], *n.a.* Lombardo, *m.*; (*Hist.*) Longobardo, *m.*
Lombardy, *n.* (*Geog.*) Lombardia, *f.*
London [ˈlʌndən], *n.* (*Geog.*) Londra, *f.* (*Bot.*) **— pride,** sassifraga ombrosa, *f.*
Londoner, *n.* Londinese, *m.f.*
lone [loun], *a.* Solo, isolato, solitario, abbandonato.
loneliness [ˈlounlinis], *n.* Solitudine, *f.*, isolamento, *m.*
lonely, lonesome, *a.* Solitario, isolato, deserto, abbandonato; fuor di mano; solingo.
long (1) [lɔŋ], *v.i.* Anelare, bramare, desiderare ardentemente. **To — for,** desiderare vivamente, struggersi per; **to — to,** aver gran voglia di, non veder l'ora di, sospirare di.
long (2), *a.* Lungo, esteso; prolungato; lento, tardo, tedioso; di lunghezza. || *adv.* Lungo tempo, a lungo, lungamente. **To make a — arm,** stendere il braccio; **a — time ago,** molto tempo fa; **he is — in coming,** è ben lento a venire; **in the — run,** a lungo andare, alla lunga; **to pull a — face,** fare il muso lungo; **to take a — view,** (*fig.*) veder lontano; **to be a — business,** andare per le lunghe; **it is four feet —,** è lungo quattro piedi; **of — standing,** di lunga data; **all night —,** tutta la notte; **before —,** fra non molto, fra poco; **How — have you been here?** Da quanto tempo siete qui? **How — will it take?** Quanto tempo ci vorrà? **Has he been here —?** È qui da molto tempo? **as — as I live,** finchè io vivrò; **not — ago,** non molto tempo fa; **not — after,** poco tempo dopo; **he is not — for this world,** non vivrà a lungo; **— -boat** (*Naut.*) lancia, scialuppa, *f.*; **— -cloth,** calico, *m.*; **— -forgotten,** dimenticato da lungo tempo; **— -headed,** dolicocefalo, (*fig.*) sagace, scaltro; **— -legged,** con le gambe lunghe; **— -lived,** longevo, di vita lunga; **— -lost,** perduto da molto tempo; **— -sighted,** presbite; (*fig.*) chiaroveggente, perspicace; **— -suffering,** *a.* longanime, indulgente; *n.* longanimità, indulgenza, *f.*; **— -winded,** prolisso, stiracchiato; **— -distance race,** corsa di fondo, *f.*; **— jump,** salto in lunghezza, *m.*; **the — and short of it is,** per farla breve.
longanimity [lɔŋgəˈnimiti], *n.* Longanimità, *f.*
longbow, *n.* Arco, *m.* (*fig.*) **To draw the —,** sballarne delle grosse.
longer [ˈlɔŋgəɹ], *a.* Più lungo. || *adv.* Più, più a lungo.
longevity [lɔnˈdʒeviti], *n.* Longevità, *f.*
longing [ˈlɔŋiŋ], *n.* Brama, *f.*, desiderio, *m.*; bramosia, voglia, *f.*
longingly, *adv.* Con desiderio ardente, bramosamente.
longish [ˈlɔŋiʃ], *a.* Lunghetto, piuttosto lungo.
longitude [ˈlɔndʒitjuːd], *n.* Longitudine, *f.*
longitudinal, *a.* Longitudinale.
longshoreman [ˈlɔŋʃɔːɹmən], *n.* Scaricatore, facchino del porto, *m.*
loo [luː], *n.* (*Cards*) Bestia, *f.*
loofah [ˈluːfə], *n.* Luffa, *f.*
look [luk], *v.i.t.* Guardare, mirare, vedere; sembrare, parere, aver l'aria di, apparire; badare. || *n.* Sguardo, *m.*, occhiata, *f.*; aspetto, *m.*, aria, apparenza, cera, *f.* **How does it —?** Che aspetto ha? **Look here!** Guardate! Badate! **Look out!** Guardatevi! Badate! **Look sharp!** Spicciatevi! **she looks miserable,** essa ha l'aria infelice; **— before you leap,** badate prima di saltare; **he looks well, he looks ill,** ha buona cera, ha cattiva cera; **to — at him,** a vederlo; **to — at,** guardare, esaminare, considerare; **to — someone through and through,** penetrare qualcuno con lo sguardo; **the house looks on to a field,** la casa dà su un campo; **it looks as if,** sembra che; **it looks like rain,** il tempo

minaccia pioggia; **it looks like being fine,** sembra una bella giornata; **he looks his age,** dimostra i suoi anni; **to — after** (*care for*) badare a, custodire, curare, occuparsi di, sorvegliare; **to — askance at,** guardare di sbieco; **to — away,** girar gli occhi; **to — back upon** (*remember*) ricordarsi di; **to — down upon,** guardare d'alto in basso, (*fig.*) disprezzare; **to — for,** cercare, aspettare; **to — forward to,** aspettare con piacere, pregustare; **to — in on someone,** fare una visitina a qualcuno; **to — like,** somigliare, rassomigliare a; **to — out of the window,** guardare dalla finistra; **to — over a book,** scorrere un libro; **to — over a lesson,** ripassare una lezione; **the room looks to the south,** la camera è esposta a mezzogiorno; **to — up,** levare gli occhi, (*a friend*) andare a trovare, (*Comm.*) essere in rialzo; **to — upon,** considerare, riguardare, stimare; **to — up to** (*in respect*), rispettare; **by the — of it,** secondo le apparenze; **good looks,** bell'aspetto, *m.*, bella presenza, *f.*; **to take a good — at it,** guardarlo bene; **—-out,** guardia, *f.*; **to be on the —-out,** stare in guardia; **that's my —-out,** ciò spetta a me; **to keep a good —-out,** stare all'erta.

looker ['lukəɹ], *n.* (*colloq.*) **A good-—,** una bella donna, *f.*; **—-on,** spettatore, astante, *m.*; **—-in,** (*Television*) televisore, *m.*

looking-glass ['lukiŋglɑːs], *n.* Specchio, *m.*; psiche, *f.*

looks, *n.pl.* Aspetto, *m.*

loom (1) [luːm], *n.* Telaio, *m.*

loom (2), *v.i.* Apparire in lontananza, profilarsi. **To — large,** grandeggiare.

loon [luːn], *n.* (*obs.*) Fannullone, birbone, *m.*; (*Zool.*) smergo, *m.*

loop [luːp], *n.* Cappio, cappiello, *m.*; nodo scorsoio, *m.*; alamaro, *m.*; laccio, *m.*; ripiegatura, *f.* || *v.t.i.* Annodare. **A — of hair,** una treccia, *f.*; **a — in the road,** un rigiro nella strada, *m.*; **to — up,** tirar su; **looping the —,** il cerchio della morte, *m.*; **—-hole,** feritoia, apertura, *f.*; scappatoia, *f.*, espediente, *m.*

loose [luːs], *a.* Sciolto, slegato; discinto; dissoluto, sfrenato, licenzioso; vago, scorretto, inesatto; staccato, disgiunto; rilassato, allentato. || *v.t.* Sciogliere, slegare, slacciare, snodare; liberare, svincolare; (*an arrow*) lanciare; staccare; allentare, rilassare. || *n.* Corso, sfogo, *m.* **— cash,** spiccioli, *m.pl.*; **at a — end,** sfaccendato; **to break —,** staccarsi, scappare, scatenarsi, liberarsi; **with a — rein,** a briglia sciolta; **of — build,** dinoccolato; **a — thinker,** una mente disordinata, *f.*; (*colloq.*) **on the —,** a zonzo; **to — one's hold,** allentare la presa; **to give a — to one's feelings,** dar sfogo ai propri sentimenti; **—-leaf ledger,** mastro a fogli staccati, *m.*

loosen ['luːsn], *v.t.i.* Sciogliere, sciogliersi, rilasciare, rilasciarsi.

loosely, *adv.* Scioltamente, liberamente.

looseness, *n.* Scioltezza, *f.*; sfrenatezza, *f.*; scorrettezza, inesattezza, *f.*; allentamento, *m.*; (*of bowels*) diarrea, *f.*

loosestrife ['luːstraif], *n.* (*Bot.*) Lisimachia, *f.*

loot [luːt], *v.t.* Saccheggiare, predare. || *n.* Bottino, *m.*, preda, *f.*

looter, *n.* Saccheggiatore, predatore, predone, *m.*

looting, *n.* Saccheggio, *m.*

lop [lɔp], *v.t.* Mozzare, recidere; sfrondare, potare. **To — off,** mozzare; **—-eared,** con gli orecchi penzoloni; **—-sided,** pendente, pencolante; asimetrico.

loquacious [lou'kweiʃəs], *a.* Loquace, garrulo.

loquaciousness, loquacity [lou'kweiʃəsnis, lou'kwæsiti], *n.* Loquacità, garrulità, *f.*

lord [lɔːɹd], *n.* Signore, padrone, *m.*; lord (titolo inglese), *m.* || *v.t.i.* **To — it over someone,** spadroneggiare qualcuno, signoreggiare, tiranneggiare; **House of Lords,** Camera dei Lordi, *f.*; **Lord's Day,** domenica, *f.*; **the Lord's Supper,** la cena eucaristica, *f.*; **the Lord's Prayer,** il Paternostro, *m.*; **the year of Our Lord,** l'anno di grazia, *m.*; **to live like a —,** vivere da gran signore; **—-lieutenant,** governatore, *m.*; **— mayor,** sindaco, *m.*

lordliness, *n.* Alterigia, superbia, *f.*, orgoglio, *m.*; fasto, sfarzo, *m.*

lordling, *n.* Signorotto, tirannello, *m.*

lordly, *a.* Altero, superbo, orgoglioso; arrogante; nobile, magnifico, sfarzoso, fastoso.

lordship, *n.* Signoria, *f.*; potere, *m.*; padronanza, *f.*; dominio, *m.* **Your —,** vostra Signoria, vostra Eccellenza, *f.*

lore [lɔːɹ], *n.* Sapere, *m.*, scienza, sapienza, erudizione, *f.*

lorgnette [lɔːɹ'njet], *n.* Occhialetto, occhialino col manico, *m.*

loris ['lɔris], *n.* (*Zool.*) Lori, *m.*

lorn [lɔːɹn], *a.* Solingo, solitario, deserto.

Lorraine [lɔ'rein], *n.* (*Geog.*) Lorena, *f.*

lorry ['lɔri], *n.* Carro, autocarro, camion, *m.* **—-driver,** camionista, *m.*

lose [luːz], *v.t.* Perdere, smarrire; sprecare, sciupare; *v.i.* perdere, scapitare; (*of clocks*) ritardare. **To — one's head,** perdere la testa, sbigottirsi; **to — one's heart to,** innamorarsi di; **to — one's way,** smarrirsi; **to — sight of,** perder di vista; **to be lost,** andare smarrito, perdersi; **you shall not — by it,** non ci perderete niente.

loser, *n.* Perditore, perdente, *m.*, vinto, *m.*; giuocatore, *m.*

loss [lɔs], *n.* Perdita, *f.*; svantaggio, *m.*, mancanza, *f.*; scapito, danno, *m.* **I am at a — to know,** non riesco a sapere; **to sell at a —,** vendere con perdita; **to make good a —,** compensare una perdita; **a dead —,** una perdita totale, *f.*; **— of appetite,** inappetenza, *f.*

lost, *p.p.a.* Perduto, perso, smarrito; rovinato, dannato.

lot [lɔt], *n.* Sorte, *f.*, destino, *m.*; ventura, *f.*; (*share*) parte, *f.*; (*amount*) quantità, *f.*; (*land*) lotto, *m.*; (*goods*) partita, *f.* **To draw lots,** tirare a sorte; **to throw in one's lot with,** correr la stessa ventura con; **I'll have no part nor lot in it,** non avrò nulla a che fare con ciò; **it fell to my —,** mi capitò; (*colloq.*) **he's a bad —,** è una pelle grama, *f.*; **all the —,** tutti quanti.

loth [cp. **loath**].

lotion ['louʃən], *n.* (*Med.*) Lozione, *f.*

lottery ['lɔtəri], *n.* Lotteria, *f.*, lotto, *m.*, estrazione a sorte, *f.* **—-ticket,** biglietto di lotteria, *m.*

lotto, *n.* (*game*) Lotto, *m.*
lotus [ˈloutəs] *n.* (*Bot.*) Loto *m.*
loud (1) [laud], *a.* Alto, forte; sonoro, rumoroso; (*noisy*) chiassoso; (*of appearance*) vistoso, sgargiante. **—-speaker,** altoparlante, *m.*; **— cheers,** grande applauso, *m.*; (*Mus.*) **— pedal,** pedale forte, *m.*
loud (2), **loudly,** *adv.* Alto, ad alta voce, forte, fortemente.
louden, *v.t.* (*the voice*) Alzare.
loudness, *n.* Forza, sonorità, *f.*; (*of dress*) vistosità, *f.*
lough [lɔk], *n.* Lago, *m.*
Louis [ˈlu:i], *n.* Luigi, *m.*
Louisa [lu:ˈi:zə], *n.* Luigia, *f.*
Louisiana [lu:i:ziˈænə], *n.* (*Geog.*) Luisiana, *f.*
lounge [laundʒ], *n.* (*in house*) Salotto, *m.*; (*in hotel*) vestibolo, *m.*, sala di ritrovo, *f.* || *v.i.* Oziare, poltrire, gironzare, bighellonare. **To — about,** andare a zonzo, bighellonare; **to — away the time,** passare il tempo in ozio; **—-suit,** abito completo, abito da passeggio, *m.*; **—-chair,** poltrona a sdraio, *f.*
lounger, *n.* Fannullone, perdigiorno, *m.*
loungingly, *adv.* Oziosamente, bighellonando.
lour, lower [louəɹ], *v.i.* Oscurarsi; (*of sky*) annuvolarsi. **To — upon,** guardare in cagnesco.
louring, *a.* Oscuro, annuvolato; aggrondato, minaccioso.
louringly, *adv.* Oscuramente, minacciosamente.
louse (*pl.* **lice**) [laus, lais], *n.* (*Zool.*) Pidocchio, *m.*
lousy [ˈlauzi], *a.* Pidocchioso; (*fig.*) ignobile, abbietto, cattivo.
lout [laut], *n.* Zotico, villano, *m.*
loutish, *a.* Zotico, rozzo, villano, sguaiato, goffo, maleducato.
loutishness, *n.* Rozzezza, sguaiataggine, *f.*
lovable [ˈlʌvəbl], *a.* Caro, gentile, simpatico, amabile.
lovableness, *n.* Bontà, amabilità, *f.*; fascino, *m.*
love [lʌv], *v.t.* Amare, aver caro, voler bene a. || *n.* Amore, *m.*; affetto, *m.*, affezione, *f.* carità, *f.*; (*person*) amante, *m.f.* **For — of,** per amor di; **for the — of God,** per l'amor di Dio; **give my — to her,** salutatela da parte mia; **to fall in —,** innamorarsi, invaghirsi; **to be in — with,** essere innamorato di; **I — you,** io ti voglio bene; **to make — to,** far la corte a, corteggiare; **a labour of —,** lavore fatto con gioia, *m.*; **to play for —,** giuocare per amore; (*Tennis*) **— all,** zero pari; **—-affair,** amoruccio, *m.*, passioncella, *f.*; **—-bird,** *n.* specie di piccolo pappagallo; **—-child,** figlio illegittimo, *m.*; **—-knot,** nodo d'amore, *m.*; **—-letter,** lettera amorosa, *f.*; **—-making,** amoreggiamento, *m.*; **—-match,** matrimonio d'amore, *m.*; **—-potion,** filtro, *m.*; **—-song,** canzone d'amore, *m.*; **—-token,** pegno d'amore, *m.*; **—-lock,** ciuffetto, ricciolo, *m.*; **—-story, —-tale,** storia d'amore, *f.*, romanzo, *m.*; (*Bot.*) **—-in-a-mist,** fior del finocchio, *m.*
loveless, *a.* Senz'amore.
loveliness, *n.* Bellezza, *f.*; grazia, soavità, leggiadria, *f.*, incanto, *m.*
lovelorn, *a.* Infelice in amore.
lovely, *a.* Bello, grazioso, soave, vezzoso; incantevole; piacevole.
lover, *n.* Amante, *m.f.*, innamorato, amoroso, *m.*, innamorata, amorosa, *f.*
loving, *a.* Amoroso, amorevole, affetuoso, tenero. **—-kindness,** bontà, carità, misericordia, *f.*; **—-cup,** antico costume di bere in una coppa cogli ospiti.
lovesick, *a.* Innamorato.
low (1) [lou], *a.* Basso; di bassa condizione, vile, abbietto; volgare; profondo; (*weak*) debole; (*of speed*) lento. || *adv.* Basso; piano, sotto voce; a basso prezzo. **A — dress,** un vestito scollato, *m.*; **in a — voice,** a voce bassa; **— tide, — water,** bassa marea, *f.*; **in — spirits,** abbattuto; **of — stature,** di statura bassa; (*fig.*) **in — water,** in male acque; **on — diet,** a dieta magra; **at a — price,** a prezzo basso; **to have a — opinion of,** aver cattiva opinione di; (*Motor.*) **— gear,** prima velocità, *f.*; **to lie —,** nascondersi, stare tranquillo; **to lay —,** vincere; **to bring —,** ridurre a mal partito; **funds are running —,** i fondi scarseggiano; **to make a — bow,** fare un inchino profondo; **—-born,** di nascita bassa; (*Eccles.*) **Low Mass,** Messa bassa, *f.*; **speak —,** parlate piano; **—-down,** vile, meschino, abbietto.
low (2), *v.i.* Muggire, mugghiare.
lower (1) [ˈlouəɹ], *a.* Più basso, inferiore, di sotto. || *adv.* Più basso. **The — part of the building,** la parte inferiore dell'edifizio; (*Print.*) **— case,** minuscolo; **speak —,** parlate più basso.
lower (2), *v.t.* Abbassare, diminuire, ridurre; calare; degradare, umiliare; (*Naut.*) ammainare. **He lowered the bucket,** calò la secchia; **to — oneself,** umiliarsi, abbassarsi, degradarsi.
lower (3) [cp. **lour**].
lowering, *n.* Abbassamento, *m.*, diminuzione, *f.* || *a.* Umiliante.
lowland [ˈloulənd], *n.* Pianura, *f.*, bassopiano, *m.* || *a.* Della pianura.
lowlander, *n.* Abitante della pianura *m.f.*
lowliness, *n.* Umiltà, modestia, *f.*
lowly, *a.* Umile, modesto.
lowness, *n.* Bassezza, *f.*; (*fig.*) pochezza, *f.*; avvilimento, *m.*; miseria, volgarità, *f.*; profondità, *f.*; debolezza, *f.*
loyal [ˈlɔiəl], *a.* Leale, fedele, ligio, fido.
loyalism, *n.* Lealismo, *m.*
loyalist, *n.* Realista, monarchico, *m.*
loyalty, *n.* Lealtà, fedeltà, *f.*
lozenge [ˈlɔzindʒ], *n.* Pastiglia, pasticca, *f.*; (*Geom., Heraldry*) losanga, *f.*
lubber [ˈlʌbəɹ], *n.* Villanzone, rusticone, goffone, zoticone, *m.*; (*Naut.*) marinaio d'acqua dolce, *m.*
lubberly, *a.* Maldestro, goffo, villano, rustico.
lubricant [ˈlu:brikənt], *n.* Lubrificante, *m.*
lubricate, *v.t.* Lubrificare. **Lubricating oil,** olio lubrificante, *m.*
lubrication, *n.* Lubrificazione, *f.*
lubricator, *n.* Lubrificatore, *m.*
lubricity [lju:ˈbrisiti], *n.* Lubricità, scurrilità, *f.*
Lucca [ˈlʌkə], *n.* (*Geog.*) Lucca, *f.* || *a.* Lucchese.
luce [lu:s], *n.* (*Zool.*) Luccio, *m.*
Lucerne (1) [lu:ˈsə:ɹn], *n.* (*Geog.*) Lucerna, *f.* **Lake of —,** lago di Lucerna, lago dei Quattro Cantoni, *m.*
lucerne (2), *n.* (*Bot.*) Trifoglio, *m.*, erba medica, *f.*

lucid ['lu:sid], *a.* Lucido, limpido, terso; (*Poet.*) lustro, lucente, brillante.
lucidity, lucidness [lu:'siditi, 'lu:sidnis], *n.* Lucidità, chiarezza, *f.*; lucentezza, *f.*
lucidly, *adv.* Lucidamente, chiaramente.
Lucifer ['lu:sifəɹ], *n.* Lucifero, *m.* — **match,** zolfanello, *m.*
luck [lʌk], *n.* Fortuna, sorte, ventura, *f.*, caso, azzardo, *m.* **By good —,** per fortuna, per buona sorte; **by ill —,** per sfortuna, disgraziatamente; **Good —!** Buona fortuna! **Bad — to him!** Maledizione a lui! **down on one's —,** accasciato; **a stroke of —,** un colpo di fortuna, *m.*; **to take pot- —,** mangiare quel che offre il convento; **to bring good —,** portar buona fortuna; **as — would have it,** la fortuna volle che; **I give you this for —,** vi do questo per portafortuna.
luckiness, *n.* Fortuna, buona fortuna, *f.*
luckless, *a.* Infelice, sfortunato, sventurato, disgraziato.
lucky, *a.* Fortunato, felice. **Lucky you!** Beato voi! **my — star,** la mia buona stella.
lucrative ['lu:krətiv], *a.* Lucrativo, proficuo, lucroso.
lucre [lu:kəɹ], *n.* Lucro, guadagno, *m.* **Filthy —,** danaro, *m.*
lucubration [lu:kju:'breiʃən], *n.* Elucubrazione, *f.*
lucubrate, *v.i.* Elucubrare.
ludicrous ['lu:dikrəs], *a.* Assurdo, ridicolo, comico.
ludicrousness, *n.* Assurdità, ridicolaggine, comicità, *f.*
luff [lʌf], *v.i.* (*Naut.*) Orzare, andare all'orza. || *n.* Orzata, *f.*
lug [lʌg], *v.t.* Tirare, strascinare. || *n.* Strappata, tirata, *f.* **To — away,** strascinar via; **to — in,** far entrare per forza, tirar dentro; **— -worm,** specie di verme marino; **— -sail,** vela quadra, vela aurica, *f.*
luge [lu:ʒ], *n.* Piccola slitta, *f.* || *v.i.* Slittare.
luggage ['lʌgidʒ], *n.* Bagaglio, *m.* **— -office,** ufficio bagagli, *m.*; **— -ticket,** scontrino di bagaglio, *m.*; **— -van,** bagagliaio, *m.*; **— carrier, — grid,** porta-bagagli, *m.*
lugger ['lʌgəɹ], *n.* (*Naut.*) Trabaccolo, *m.*
lugubrious [lu:'gju:briəs], *a.* Lugubre, tetro, cupo.
lugubriously, *adv.* Lugubremente.
lugubriousness, *n.* L'essere lugubre, *m.*
lukewarm ['lu:kwɔ:ɹm], *a.* Tiepido; (*fig.*) indifferente. **To become —,** intiepidire, intiepidirsi.
lukewarmness, *n.* Tiepidezza, indifferenza, *f.*
lull [lʌl], *v.t.* Cullare, addormentare, calmare, acquietare. || *n.* Momento di calma, *m.*, sosta, bonaccia, *f.* **To — to sleep,** addormentare, ninnare, assopire; **to — suspicion,** dissipare i sospetti; **the storm was lulled,** la tempesta si calmò.
lullaby ['lʌləbai], *n.* Ninna nanna, cantilena, *f.*
lumbago [lʌm'beigou], *n.* (*Med.*) Lombaggine, *f.*
lumbar ['lʌmbɑ:ɹ], *a.* (*Anat.*) Lombale.
lumber (1) ['lʌmbəɹ], *n.* Ferravecchi, *m.pl.*, cianfrusaglie, *f.pl.*; cose non usate, *f.pl.*, robaccia, *f.* || *v.t.* Ingombrare, ammucchiare, accatastare. **— room,** ripostiglio, *m.*, soffitta, *f.*; **to — about,** camminare dinocolato.
lumber (2), *n.* Legname, *m.* || *v.i.* Tagliar legna. **— -jack, — man,** boscaiuolo, *m.*
lumberer, *n.* Tagliaboschi, *m.*
lumbering, *a.* Pesante, ingombrante.
luminary ['lu:minəri], *n.* Luminare, *m.*; astro, lume, corpo luminoso, *m.*
luminous ['lu:minəs], *a.* Luminoso.
luminosity, luminousness [lu:mi'nɔsiti, 'lu:minəsnis], *n.* Luminosità, *f.*
lump [lʌmp], *n.* Massa, *f.*, blocco, *m.*; boccone, *m.*; zolletta, *f.*; nodo, groppo, *m.*; grumo, *m.*; (*of sugar*) pezzo, *m.*; (*swelling*) enfiagione, *f.*, gonfiore, *m.* || *v.t.* Mettere insieme, ammassare, accozzare, prendere all'ingrosso; trattare senza distinzione. **— sum,** somma complessiva, somma pagata tutt'in una volta, *f.*; **in the —,** in blocco; all'ingrosso; **a — in the throat,** un nodo alla gola; **— sugar,** zucchero in pezzi, *m.*
lumpish, *a.* Grosso, pesante; tonto, balordo.
lumpy, *a.* Grumoso, spesso.
lunacy ['lu:nəsi], *n.* Alienazione mentale, *f.*; follia, pazzia, *f.*
lunar ['lu:nəɹ], *a.* Lunare.
lunate ['lu:neit], *a.* (*Zool.Bot.*) Lunato.
lunatic ['lu:nətik], *n.* Matto, pazzo, *m.*, matta, pazza, *f.*; alienato, *m.*, alienata, *f.* || *a.* Matto, pazzo, alienato, folle; lunatico. **— asylum,** manicomio, *m.*
lunation [lu:'neiʃən], *n.* (*Astron.*) Lunazione, *f.*
lunch, luncheon [lʌntʃ, 'lʌntʃən], *n.* Colazione, *f.* **To lunch,** far colazione; **lunch-time,** ora di colazione, *f.*; **— -basket,** cestino da viaggio, *m.*
lunette [lu:'net], *n.* (*Arch.*) Lunetta, *f.*
lung [lʌŋ], *n.* (*Anat.*) Polmone, *m.*
lunge [lʌndʒ], *n.* (*Fencing*) Botta, *f.* || *v.i.* Dare una botta.
lungwort, *n.* (*Bot.*) Polmonaria, *f.*
lunisolar [lu:ni'souləɹ], *a.* (*Astron.*) Lunisolare.
lupin, lupine ['lu:pin], *n.* (*Bot.*) Lupino, *m.*
lupine ['lu:pain], *a.* Lupesco.
lupus ['lu:pəs], *n.* (*Med.*) Lupus, *m.*
lurch [lə:ɹtʃ], *n.* Trabalzo, sobbalzo, traballio, *m.* || *v.i.* Traballare, barcollare, vacillare, rullare. **To give a —,** dare una scossa; **to leave in the —,** lasciar nelle peste, lasciare in asso, piantare.
lurcher, *n.* (*Zool.*) Specie di cane da caccia, *m.*
lure [lju:ɹ], *n.* Esca, *f.*, allettamento, fascino, *m.*; lusinga, *f.* || *v.t.* Adescare, allettare, affascinare.
lurid ['lju:rid], *a.* Livido, fosco; scuro, triste; terribile; sconcio, scandaloso.
luridly, *adv.* Lividamente.
lurk [lə:ɹk], *v.i.* Nascondersi, appiattarsi, tenersi da parte, stare in agguato. **Lurking-place,** nascondiglio, *m.*
luscious ['lʌʃəs], *a.* Delizioso; voluttuoso; succolento; melato.
lusciously, *adv.* Deliziosamente.
lusciousness, *n.* Voluttuosità, *f.*; stucchevolezza, *f.*
lush [lʌʃ], *a.* Lussureggiante, rigoglioso; sugoso.
lust [lʌst], *n.* Lussuria, *f.*; concupiscenza, sensualità, *f.*; brama, avidità, *f.* || *v.i.* Bramare ardentemente. **To — after,** bramare, agognare.

lustful, *a.* Lussurioso, sensuale, libidinoso, lascivo; bramoso, avido.
lustily, *adv.* Con grande vigore.
lustiness [ˈlʌstinis], *n.* Vigore, *m.*, forza, gagliardia, robustezza, *f.*
lustral [ˈlʌstrəl], *a.* Lustrale.
lustration, *n.* Lustrazione, *f.*
lustre (1) [ˈlʌstəɹ], *n.* Lustro, splendore, decoro, *m.*, gloria, ceramica iridiscente, *f.* ‖ *v.t.* Lustrare, verniciare.
lustre (2), **lustrum,** *n.* (*period of* 5 *years*) Lustro, *m.*
lustreless, *a.* Senza lustro, appannato.
lustrine [ˈlʌstri:n], *n.* Lustrina (sorta di seta).
lustrous, *a.* Lustro, lucente, brillante.
lusty, *a.* Vigoroso, robusto, forte, gagliardo.
lutanist [ˈlju:tənist], *n.* Liutista, *m.*
lute (1) [lju:t], *n.* (*Mus.*) Liuto, *m.* **— maker,** liutaio, *m.*
lute (2), *n.* (*cement*) Luto, *m.* ‖ *v.t.* Lutare.
Lutheran [ˈlu:θərən], *n.a.* Luterano, *m.*
luxate [ˈlʌkseit], *v.t.* (*Med.*) Lussare.
luxation, *n.* Lussazione, *f.*
Luxemburg [ˈlʌksəmbə:ɹg], *n.* (*Geog.*) Lussemburgo, *m.*
luxuriance [lʌkˈsju:riəns], *n.* Rigoglio, *m.*, sovvrabbondanza, esuberanza, abbondanza, *f.*; (*of vegetation*) rigogliosità, *f.*
luxuriant, *a.* Rigoglioso, sovvrabbondante, esuberante, lussureggiante, copioso. **— hair** una folta chioma, *f.*
luxuriate [lʌkˈʒju:rieit], *v.i.* Lussureggiare. **To — in,** godere, abbandonarsi a.
luxurious, *a.* Lussuoso, sfarzoso, sontuoso; voluttuoso.
luxuriously, *adv.* Lussuosamente.
luxuriousness, *n.* Sfarzo, sfoggio, lusso, *m.*, sontuosità, *f.*
luxury, *n.* Lusso, *m.*; profusione, sontuosità, *f.*; voluttà, *f.*
lycanthropy [laiˈkænθroupi], *n.* Licantropia, *f.*
lyceum [laiˈsi:əm], *n.* Liceo, *m.*
lychnis [ˈliknis], *n.* (*Bot.*) Licnide, *m.*
lycopod, lycopodium [ˈlaikopɔd, laikoˈpoudiəm], *n.* (*Bot.*) Licopodio, *m.*
Lyddite [ˈlidait], *n.* (*Chem.*) Liddite, *f.*
Lydian [ˈlidiən], *n.a.* Lidio, *m.*
lye [lai], *n.* Liscivia, *f.*, soda caustica, *f.*
lying (1) [ˈlaiiŋ], *n.* Menzogna, bugia, *f.* ‖ *a.* Menzognero, bugiardo.
lying (2), *a.* Steso; situato; giacente. **— -in,** parto, puerperio, *m.*; **— -in hospital,** casa di maternità, *f.*
lymph [limf], *n.* Linfa, *f.*; (*Med.*) vaccino, *m.*; (*Poet.*) acqua pura, *f.*
lymphatic [limˈfætik], *a.* Linfatico.
lynch [lintʃ], *v.t.* Linciare. **— law,** legge di Lynch, *f.*
lynching, *n.* Linciaggio, *m.*
lynx [liŋks], *n.* (*Zool.*) Lince, *f.*, lupo cerviero, *m.* **— -eyed,** dagli occhi di lince, linceo.
lyre [laiɹ], *n.* (*Mus.*) Lira, *f.* (*Zool.*) **— -bird,** uccello lira, *m.*; **Aeolian —,** arpa eolia, *f.*
lyric [lirik], *n.* Lirica, *f.*
lyrical, lyric, *a.* Lirico.
lyricism, *n.* Lirismo, *m.*
lyrist [ˈlairist], *n.* (*Poet.*) Lirico, *m.*; suonatore di lira, *m.*

M

M, m [em], *n.* Tredicesima lettera dell'alfabeto inglese.
ma'am [ˈmæm], *n.* (*mode of address*) Signora, *f.*
macabre [məˈkɑ:bəɹ], *a.* Macabro.
macaco, macaque [məˈkeikou, məˈkeik], *n.* (*Zool.*) Macaco, *m.*
macadam [məˈkædəm], *n.* Macadam, *m.*
macadamize, *v.t.* Macadamizzare.
macaroni [mækəˈrouni], *n.* Maccheroni, spaghetti, *m.pl.*; pasta, *f.*
macaronic [mækəˈrɔnik], *a.* (*Lit.*) Maccheronico.
macaroon [mækəˈru:n], *n.* Amaretto, *m.*
macaw [məˈkɔ:], *n.* (*Zool.*) Ara, *f.*, macao, *m.*
mace (1) [meis], *n.* Mazza, *f.* **— -bearer,** mazziere, *m.*
mace (2), *n.* (*spice*) Macis, mace, *m.*
macerate [ˈmæsəreit], *v.t.* Macerare.
maceration, *n.* Macerazione, *f.*
Machiavellian [mækiəˈveliən], *a.* Machiavellico; astuto, scaltro.
Machiavellism, *n.* Machiavellismo, *m.*
machicollation [məˈtʃikəleiʃən], *n.* (*Mil.*) Piombatoio, *m.*, feritoia, *f.*
machinate [ˈmækineit], *v.i.* Macchinare, tramare.
machination, *n.* Macchinazione, *f.*, macchinamento, *m.*; trama, insidia, *f.*
machine [məˈʃi:n], *n.* Macchina, *f.* ‖ *v.t.* Eseguire a macchina, cucire a macchina; (*Print.*) stampare, tirare. **— -gun,** mitragliatrice, *f.*; **— -gunner,** mitragliere, *m.*; **— -made,** fatto a macchina; **— -tool,** macchina utensile, *f.*; **— -oil,** olio da macchinario, *m.*
machinery [məˈʃi:nəri], *n.* Macchinario, meccanismo, *m.*; congegno, *m.*; macchine, *f.pl.*, apparecchi, *m.pl.*; procedimento, *m.*
machining, *n.* (*Print.*) Tiratura, *f.*
machinist, *n.* Macchinista, meccanico, *m.*; lavorante a macchina, punteggiatrice, *f.*
mackerel [ˈmækərəl], *n.* (*Zool.*) Scombro, sgombro, *m.* **— sky,** cielo a pecorelle, *m.*
mackintosh, mack [ˈmækintɔʃ, mæk], *n.* Impermeabile, *m.*
macrocosm [ˈmækroukɔzm], *n.* Macrocosmo, *m.*
macula (*pl.* **maculae**) [ˈmækju:lə, ˈməkju:li:], *n.* Macchia, *f.*
mad [mæd], *a.* Pazzo, matto, folle, alienato, demente, insano; insensato; furibondo, forsennato, arrabbiato. **To be — after something,** andar pazzo di qualcosa; **— as a hatter, — as a March hare,** pazzo da catena; **to run like —,** correre come un matto; **he's — with me,** è furioso contro me; **— with grief,** pazzo di dolore; **to drive —,** far impazzire; **to go —,** impazzire, ammattire; **a — dog,** un cane arrabbiato, *m.*
madam [ˈmædəm], *n.* Signora, *f.*
madcap [ˈmædkæp], *n.* Scervellato, impulsivo, *m.*
madden, *v.t.* Far impazzire, far ammattire.
maddening, *a.* Da far impazzire.
madder [ˈmædəɹ], *n.* (*Bot.*) Robbia, *f.*
made [meid], *a.* Fatto, eseguito. **Ready- —,** bell'e fatto, confezionato; **a — man,** un uomo arrivato, *m.*; **a self- — man,** un uomo fattosi da sè, *m.*; **— up,** artificiale, falso; (*of the face*) imbellettato, truccato [cp. **make**].

Madeira [mə'diərə], *n.* (*Geog.*) Madera, *f.*; (*wine*) vino di Madera, *m.*
madhouse ['mædhaus], *n.* Manicomio, *m.*
madly, *adv.* Pazzamente, insensatamente, da pazzo. **To be — in love,** esser innamorato pazzo.
madman (*pl.* **madmen**), *n.* Pazzo, folle, matto, demente, alienato, *m.*
madness, *n.* Pazzia, demenza, follia, mania, *f.*; stravaganza, *f.*; rabbia, *f.*
Madonna [mə'dɔnə], *n.* Madonna, *f.*
madrepore ['mædripɔːɹ], *n.* (*Zool.*) Madrepora, *f.*
madrigal ['mædrigəl], *n.* Madrigale, *m.*
madwoman (*pl.* **madwomen**), *n.* Pazza, matta, alienata, *f.*
maelstrom ['meilstrɔm], *n.* Malstrom, gorgo, vortice, *m.*
maenad ['miːnæd], *n.* (*Myth.*) Menade, *f.*
magazine [mægə'ziːn], *n.* (*Mil.*) Magazzino militare, *m.*; deposito, fondaco, *m.*; (*Lit.*) rivista, *f.*, periodico, *m.*; **—-rifle,** fucile a ripetizione, *m.*; (*Phot.*) **—-camera,** macchina fotografica a magazzino, *f.*; **powder —,** polveriera, *f.*
Magdalen ['mægdəlen, (*Oxford & Cambridge*) 'mɔːdlin], *n.* Maddalena, *f.*
magenta [mə'dʒentə], *n.* Magenta, cremisi, *m.*
maggot ['mægət], *n.* (*Zool.*) Verme, baco, *m.*; (*fig.*) capriccio, grillo, *m.*, ubbia, *f.* **To have a — in one's brain,** avere grilli per il capo.
maggoty, *a.* Verminoso, bacato.
Magi ['meidʒai], *n.pl.* I Re Magi, *m.pl.*
magian ['meidʒən], *n.a.* Mago, *m.*
magic ['mædʒik], *n.* Magia, arte magica, *f.*; incanto, *m.*, fattucchieria, malia, *f.* || *a.* Magico; meraviglioso. **— lantern,** lanterna magica, *f.*; **— wand,** bacchetta magica, *f.*
magical, *a.* Magico.
magically, *adv.* Magicamente.
magician [mə'dʒi'ʃən], *n.* Mago, stregone, indovino, negromante, *m.*
magisterial [mædʒis'tiəriəl], *a.* Magistrale, autoritario; di magistrato.
magistracy ['mædʒistrəsi], *n.* Magistrato, *m.*, magistratura, *f.*
magistrate ['mædʒistrit], *n.* Magistrato, giudice, pretore, *m.* **Examining —,** giudice istruttore, *m.*
magistrature, *n.* Magistrato, *m.*, magistratura, *f.*
magnanimity [mægnə'nimiti], *n.* Magnanimità, *f.*
magnanimous [mæg'næniməs], *a.* Magnanimo.
magnanimously, *adv.* Magnanimamente.
magnate ['mægneit], *n.* Magnate, maggiorente, *m.*, notabilità, *f.*; (*colloq.*) pezzo grosso, *m.*
magnesia [mæg'niːʒə], *n.* (*Chem.*) Magnesia, *f.*
magnesian, *a.* Magnesiaco.
magnesium, *n.* (*Min.*) Magnesio, *m.* **— light,** luce al magnesio, *f.*
magnet ['mægnit], *n.* Calamita, *f.*, magnete, *m.*
magnetic [məg'netik], *a.* Magnetico; attraente, attrativo. **— -bar, — needle,** ago magnetico, *m.*
magnetics, *n.pl.* Magnetismo, *m.*
magnetism ['mægnitizm], *n.* Magnetismo, *m.*
magnetist, *n.* Magnetista, *m.*
magnetize, *v.t.* Magnetizzare, calamitare.
magnetizer, *n.* Magnetizzatore, *m.*
magneto [mæg'niːtou], *n.* Magnete, spinterogeno, *m.* **— electric,** magnete-elettrico.
magnetometer [mægni'tɔmitəɹ], *n.* Magnetometro, *m.*
magnificence [mæg'nifisəns], *n.* Magnificenza, *f.*; lusso, sfarzo, *m.*
magnificent, *a.* Magnifico, splendido.
magnificently, *adv.* Magnificamente.
magnified ['mægnifaid], *p.p.a.* Ingrandito; esagerato.
magnifier, *n.* Lente d'ingrandimento, *f.*; (*fig.*) esaltatore, panegirista, *m.*
magnify, *v.t.* Ingrandire; esagerare; (*fig.*) magnificare, esaltare, celebrare.
magnifying, *n.* Ingrandimento, *m.* || *a.* Ingranditore. **—-glass,** lente d'ingrandimento, lente ingranditrice, *f.*
magniloquence [mæg'nilokwəns], *n.* Magniloquenza, ampollosità, *f.*
magniloquent, *a.* Magniloquente, ampolloso.
magnitude ['mægnitjuːd], *n.* Grandezza, *f.*; importanza, *f.* **Of the first —,** di somma importanza.
magnolia [mæg'nouliə], *n.* (*Bot.*) Magnolia, *f.*
magot ['mægət], *n.* (*Zool.*) Macaco, *m.*
magpie ['mægpai], *n.* (*Zool.*) Gazza, *f.*
Magyar ['mɔdʒɑːɹ], *n.a.* Magiaro, *m.*
mahlstick [cp. **maulstick**].
mahogany [mə'hɔgəni], *n.* Mogano, *m.* || *a.* Di mogano.
mahout [mə'hout], *n.* Conduttore d'elefanti, *m.*
maid [meid], *n.* Ragazza, fanciulla, giovanetta, *f.*; nubile, vergine, *f.*; zitella, *f.*; (*servant*) cameriera, serva, domestica, donna di servizio, *f.*; (*Lit.*) pulcella, donzella, *f.* **— of all work,** donna a tuttofare, *f.*; **old —,** zitellona, *f.*; **— of honour,** damigella, *f.*; **the Maid of Orleans,** la Pulcella d'Orleans, *f.*
maiden, *n.* Fanciulla, ragazza, *f.*; vergine, *f.* || *a.* Di fanciulla, di ragazza; verginale, nubile. **— name,** nome di fanciulla, nome da signorina, *m.*; **— speech,** primo discorso d'un deputato, *m.*; (*Naut.*) **— voyage,** primo viaggio, *m.*; **— lady,** signorina, zitella, *f.*
maidenhair, *n.* (*Bot.*) Capelvenere, *m.*
maidenhead, maidenhood, *n.* Verginità, *f.*
maidenlike, *a.* Verginale, casto, puro, pudico.
maidenliness, *n.* Pudore, *m.*, modestia, *f.*
maidenly, *a.* Verginale.
mail (1) [meil], *n.* (*armour*) Maglia di ferro, cotta di maglia, *f.* **Coat of —,** corazza a maglia, *f.*
mail (2), *n.* Corriere, *m.*; posta, corrispondenza, *f.*, lettere, *f.pl.* || *v.t.* Impostare. **—-bag,** valigia postale, *f.*, sacco di corrispondenza, *m.*; (*child's*) **—-cart,** carrozzina, *f.*; **—-coach,** corriera, diligenza postale, vettura della posta, *f.*; **—-boat, —-packet, —-steamer,** vapore postale, piroscafo postale, *m.*; **—-train,** treno postale, *m.*; **—-order business,** ordinazioni per posta, *f.pl.*
mailed, *a.* Corazzato. **The — fist,** il pugno di ferro, *m.*
maim [meim], *v.t.* Mutilare, storpiare, amputare.
maiming, *n.* Mutilazione, *f.*
main [mein], *a.* Principale, primario, precipuo; essenziale; grande, grosso; maggiore. || *n.* (*sea*) L'alto mare, *m.*; (*cockfighting*) combattimento di galli, *m.*; (*water, gas, etc.*) conduttura principale, *f.*; (*Elec.*) conduttore

MO

principale. (*Naut.*) **—-brace,** gomena, *f.*; (*fig.*) **to splice the —-brace,** fare una bicchierata; **by — force,** a viva forza; **the — point,** il punto principale, *m.*; (*Rail.*) **— line,** linea principale, *f.*; **to have an eye on the — chance,** attendere ai propri interessi; **by might and —,** con tutta la sua forza; **in the —,** per lo più, in generale; **the — idea,** il concetto generale, *m.*; (*Naut.*) **—-deck,** ponte principale, *m.*; **—-top,** gabbia grande, *f.*; **— yard,** antenna maestra, *f.*

mainland [ˈmeinlənd], *n.* Continente, *m.*, terraferma, *f.*

mainly, *adv.* Principalmente, in generale, per lo più.

mainmast [ˈmeinməst], *n.* (*Naut.*) Albero maestro, *m.*

mainsail [ˈmeinsəl], *n.* (*Naut.*) Vela maestra, *f.*

mainspring, *n.* Molla dell'orologio, molla principale, *f.*; (*fig.*) agente principale, *m.*, causa prima, *f.*

mainstay, *n.* (*Naut.*) Straglio di maestra, *m.*; (*fig.*) sostegno principale, appoggio principale, *m.*

maintain [meinˈtein], *v.t.* Mantenere, sostentare; conservare, sostenere; dichiarare, affermare.

maintainable, *a.* Sostenibile, mantenibile.

maintenance [ˈmeintənəns], *n.* Mantenimento, sostentamento, *m.*, conservazione, *f.*; (*Law*) alimenti, *m.pl.*; (*Mech.*) manutenzione, *f.*

Mainz, Mayence [maints, meiˈjɔns], *n.* (*Geog.*) Magonza, *f.*

maisonette [meizəˈnet], *n.* Casetta, *f.*; appartamento a due piani, *m.*

maize [meiz], *n.* Granturco, mais, *m.*

majestic [məˈdʒestik], *a.* Maestoso.

majestically, *adv.* Maestosamente.

majesty, *n.* Maestà, *f.* **His Majesty, Her Majesty,** Sua Maestà, *f.*

majolica [məˈjɔlikə], *n.* Maiolica, *f.*

major [ˈmeidʒəɹ], *a.* Più grande, maggiore; anziano, più anziano. || *n.* (*Mil.*) Maggiore; (*Law*) maggiorenne, *m.f.* **— road,** strada maestra, *f.*; **—-general,** maggior generale, *m.*; (*Mus.*) **— key,** tono maggiore, *m.*

Majorca [məˈdʒɔːɹkə], *n.* (*Geog.*) Maiorca, *f.*

majordomo [meidʒəˈdoumou], *n.* Maggiordomo, *m.*

majority [məˈdʒɔriti], *n.* Maggioranza, *f.*, i più, *m.pl.*, la parte più grande, *f.*; (*Law*) età maggiore, *f.*; (*Mil.*) grado di maggiore, *m.*

make [meik], *v.t.i.* Fare, creare, produrre, fabbricare; costringere; assumere. || *n.* Fabbricazione, fabbrica, *f.*; forma, fattura, *f.*; marca, *f.* **I don't know what to — of it,** non ne capisco niente; **to — away with,** distruggere, spacciare, dissipare, scialacquare; **to — believe,** fingere, far finta, dare a intendere; **to — someone believe,** dare ad intendere a qualcuno; **to — bold to,** osare; **to — fast,** attaccare, (*Naut.*) ammarrare; **to — free with,** prendersi delle libertà con ; **to — good an assertion,** giustificare un'asserzione; **to — good a loss,** risarcire un danno; **to — good,** compensare, riparare, (*fig.*) succedere; **to — good a promise,** mantenere una promessa; **to — head, to — headway,** far progresso, avanzare; **to — hay,** raccogliere il fieno; **to — hay while the sun shines,** battere il ferro mentre è caldo; **to — known,** far conoscere; (*Naut.*) **to — land,** approdare, toccar terra; **to — light of,** far poco caso di, prendere alla leggera; **to — much of,** far gran caso di, carezzare; **to — no difference,** non importare; **to — oneself heard, known, understood, etc.,** farsi intendere, conoscere, capire, etc.; **to — out,** capire, decifrare, scoprire; **How do you — that out ?** Come spiegate questo? **to — over to,** cedere a; **to — ready,** preparare; **—-up** (*for face*) imbellettatura, *f.*; (*lie*) truccatura, *f.*; **to — up a quarrel,** riconciliarsi; **to — up one's face,** tingersi, imbellettarsi; **to — up,** comporre, raccogliere, completare, supplire a, risarcire, fabbricare, (*Print.*) impaginare; (*Theat.*) **to — up for a part,** truccarsi, travestirsi; **to — water,** orinare; **to — against,** nuocere a; **to — as if to,** far sembianza di, far finta di; **to — for,** dirigersi verso, tendere verso, assalire; **to — off,** scappare, andarsene, fuggire; **to — up to someone,** corteggiare qualcuno; **to — up for lost time,** riguadagnare il tempo perduto; **to — one of the party,** essere della comitiva; **this makes pleasant reading,** questo fa piacere a leggerlo; **he will — a good husband,** egli sarà un buon marito; **What time do you — it ?** Che ora fate? **this is of English —,** questo è di fabbrica inglese; **Is this your own — ?** È fatto in casa? È di vostra fattura? **—-believe,** finta, sembianza, *f.*; **—-weight,** riempitivo; **this is by way of —-weight,** questo è per far peso; **Has he made his will ?** Ha fatto testamento? **he is always making faces,** fa sempre le smorfie.

maker, *n.* Fattore, creatore, artefice, *m.*; (*Comm.*) fabbricante, *m.*

makeshift [ˈmeikʃift], *n.* Espediente, ripiego, *m.* || *a.* Improvvisato, temporaneo.

making, *n.* Fabbricazione, *f.* **He has the makings of a poet,** ha la stoffa d'un poeta; **it was the — of him,** è ciò che ha fatto la sua fortuna; (*Comm.*) **—-up price,** prezzo corrente al giorno di riporto.

malachite [ˈmæləkait], *n.* (*Min.*) Malachite, *f.*

maladjustment [mæləˈdʒʌstmənt], *n.* Aggiustatura difettosa, *f.*

maladministration [mælədminisˈtreiʃən], *n.* Malgoverno, *m.*

maladroit [ˈmælədrɔit], *a.* Malaccorto.

malady [ˈmælədi], *n.* Malattia, *f.*

Malaga [ˈmæləgə], *n.* (*Geog. and wine*) Malaga, *f.*

Malagasy [mæləˈgæsi], *n.a.* Malagascio, *m.*

malapert [ˈmæləpəɹt], *a.* Impertinente, sfacciato, sfrontato.

malapropism [ˈmæləprɔpizm], *n.* Incongruità di parole, *f.*

malar [ˈmeilɑːɹ], *n.* (*Anat.*) Osso della guancia, *m.*

malaria [məˈlɛiriə], *n.* (*Med.*) Malaria, *f.*

malarial, *a.* Malarico.

Malayan, Malay [məˈleiən, məˈlei], *n.a.* Malese, *m.*

Malaysia [məˈleiziə], *n.* (*Geog.*) Malesia, *f.*

malcontent [ˈmælkəntent], *n.a.* Malcontento, *m.*

male [meil], *n.* Maschio, *m.* || *a.* Maschio, virile, maschile. **In the — line,** nella discendenza maschile; **— nurse,** infermiere, *m.*

malediction [mæli'dikʃən], *n.* Maledizione, *f.*
malefactor ['mælifæktəɹ], *n.* Malfattore, *m.*
maleficence [mə'lefisəns], *n.* Malignità, cattiveria, *f.*
maleficent, *a.* Malefico, cattivo, maligno.
malevolence [mə'levələns], *n.* Malevolenza, *f.*
malevolent, *a.* Malevole, invido, maligno.
malformation [mælfɔːɹ'meiʃən], *n.* Malformazione, deformità, *f.*
malformed, *a.* Deforme.
malice ['mælis], *n.* Malizia, malignità, cattiveria, *f.*; (*Law*) premeditazione, *f.* **To bear — towards,** voler male a; **with — aforethought,** con premeditazione.
malicious [mə'liʃəs], *a.* Maligno, malevolo.
maliciousness, *n.* Maliziosità, malignità, *f.*
malign [mə'lain], *a.* Maligno, malevolo, malvagio. || *v.t.* Calunniare, diffamare.
malignant [mə'lignənt], *a.* Maligno, malevolo, cattivo, nocivo.
malignity, malignancy, *n.* Malignità, malvagità, *f.*
malinger [mə'liŋgəɹ], *v.i.* Fingere una malattia, darsi malato.
malingerer, *n.* Finto malato, fiaccone, *m.*
mall [mæl, mɔːl], *n.* (*Hist.*) Maglio, *m.*
mallard ['mælɑːɹd], *n.* (*Zool.*) Anitra selvatica, *f.*, mallardo, *m.*
malleability [mæliə'biliti], *n.* Malleabilità, *f.*
malleable ['mæliəbl], *a.* Malleabile.
mallet ['mælit], *n.* Maglio, martello di legno, *m.*
mallow ['mælou], *n.* (*Bot.*) Malva, *f.*
malmsy ['mɑːmzi], *n.* Malvasia, *f.*
malnutrition [mælnjuː'triʃən], *n.* Malnutrizione, denutrizione, *f.*
malodorous [mæl'oudərəs], *a.* Puzzolente.
malpractice [mæl'præktis], *n.* Abuso, malcostume, misfatto, *m.*; (*Law*) malversazione, *f.*; (*Med.*) cura sbagliata, *f.*
malt [mɔːlt], *n.* Malto, *m.* || *v.t.* Trasformare in malto. **—-house, —-kiln,** distilleria di malto, *f.*, germinatoio, *m.*
Maltese [mɔːl'tiːz], *n.a.* Maltese, *m.f.* **— cross,** croce di Malta, *f.*
Malthusian [mæl'θuːʒən], *a.* Maltusiano.
maltreat [mæl'triːt], *v.t.* Maltrattare, bistrattare, malmenare.
maltreatment, *n.* Maltrattamento, bistrattamento, *m.*
maltster, *n.* Distillatore di malto, *m.*, fabbricante di malto, *m.*
malversation [mælvəɹ'seiʃən], *n.* (*Law*) Malversazione, *f.*
mameluke ['mæmiluːk], *n.* (*Hist.*) Mammaluco, *m.*
mamillary ['mæmiləri], *a.* (*Anat.*) Mammillare.
mamma, mama [mə'mɑː], *n.* Mamma, *f.*
mammal ['mæməl], *n.* (*Zool.*) Mammifero, *m.*
mammalia [mə'meiliə], *n.pl.* Mammiferi, *m.pl.*
mammon ['mæmən], *n.* Mammone, *m.*
mammoth ['mæməθ], *n.* (*Zool.*) Mammut, *m.*
man (*pl.* **men**) [mæn, men], *n.* Uomo, *m.*; servo, domestico, *m.*; operaio, lavorante, impiegato, *m.*; il genere umano, *m.*; (*Chess*) pezzo, *m.*; (*Draughts*) pedina, *f.* || *v.t.* (*Naut.*) Equipaggiare; (*Mil.*) fornire di guarnigione. **A dead —,** un morto, *m.*; **the inner —,** l'io interiore, *m.*, (*fig.*) lo stomaco, *m.*; **What can a — do?** Che si può fare? **a bad —,** un omaccio, *m.*; **a fine —,** un bell'uomo, un brav'uomo, *m.*; **a little —,** un ometto, un omettino, *m.*; **between — and —,** da uomo a uomo; **— and wife,** marito e moglie; **man's estate,** età virile, *f.*; **no —,** nessuno; **the — in the street,** l'uomo qualunque, *m.*; **I'm your — for that job!** Son io l'uomo che ci vuole per voi! **a — of the world,** un uomo di mondo, *m.*; **—-of-all-work,** factotum, *m.*; **a — of deeds,** un uomo d'azione, *m.*; **a — of fashion,** un elegante, *m.*; **a — of substance,** un uomo agiato, *m.*; **—-at-arms,** soldato, *m.*; **—-child,** maschietto, *m.*; **to —-handle,** maltrattare, bistrattare; **—-hole,** tombino, *m.*; **—-killer,** (*murderer*) omicida, *m.*, (*animal*) uccisore d'uomini; (*Naut.*) **—-of-war,** nave da guerra, *f.*; **—-trap,** tagliola, *f.*
manacle ['mænəkl], *v.t.* Ammanettare, incatenare. || *n.* **Manacles,** manette, *f.pl.*
manage ['mænidʒ], *v.t.* Maneggiare (*to handle*); dirigere, condurre; amministrare, governare, reggere; sistemare, arrangiare; *v.i.* combinare; riuscire, venire a capo di, fare in modo di, destreggiarsi, sbrigarsi. **Can you —?** Riuscite?
manageable, *a.* Maneggiabile, trattabile, docile.
management, *n.* Direzione, amministrazione, gestione, *f.*; artificio, inganno, *m.*
manager, *n.* Direttore, *m.*, direttrice, *f.*; amministratore, *m.*, amministratrice, *f.*; gerente, *m.*; (*Theat.*) impresario, *m.*; (*housewife*) massaia, *f.*; (*farm*) massaio, massaro, *m.* **General —,** direttore generale, *m.*; **she is a good —,** è una buona massaia; (*Theat.*) **actor- —,** capocomico, *m.*
manageress, *n.* Direttrice, *f.*; economa, *f.*
managership, *n.* Direzione, gerenza, amministrazione, *f.*
managing, *a.* Gerente, delegato. **— director,** amministratore delegato, *m.*
manatee [mænə'tiː], *n.* (*Zool.*) Lamantino, *m.*
manchineel [mæntʃi'niːl], *n.* (*Bot.*) Mancinella, *f.*
Manchuria [mæn'tʃjuːriə], *n.* (*Geog.*) Manciuria, *f.*
manciple ['mænsipl], *n.* (*of colleges, etc.*) Economo, *m.*
mandamus [mæn'deiməs], *n.* (*Law*) Ordine, *m.*
mandarin ['mændərin], *n.* Mandarino, *m.* **— orange,** mandarino, *m.*
mandatary ['mændətəri], *n.* (*Law*) Mandatario, *m.*
mandate ['mændeit], *n.* (*Pol.*) Mandato, *m.*; comando, ordine, *m.*
mandator, *n.* Mandante, *m.*
mandatory, *n.* Mandatore, mandatario, *m.*
mandible ['mændibl], *n.* Mandibola, *f.*
mandolin, mandoline ['mændəlin], *n.* (*Mus.*) Mandolino, *m.*
mandrake, mandragora ['mændreik, mæn'drægərə], *n.* (*Bot.*) Mandragola, mandragora, *f.*
mandrel ['mændrəl], *n.* (*Mach.*) Mandrino, *m.*
mandril ['mændril], *n.* (*Zool.*) Mandrillo, *m.*
mane [mein], *n.* Criniera, *f.*; (*of lion*) giubba, *f.*
maneater ['mæniːtəɹ], *n.* Antropofago, *m.*; cannibale, *m.*
manège [mə'neiʒ], *n.* Maneggio, *m.*
manes ['meiniːz], *n.pl.* (*Myth.*) Mani, *m.pl.*

manful ['mænful], *a.* Coraggioso, ardito; virile.
manfully, *adv.* Coraggiosamente, da uomo, virilmente.
manfulness, *n.* Coraggio, *m.*, arditezza, *f.*
manganese [mæŋgə'ni:z], *n.* (*Min.*) Manganese, *m.*
mange [meindʒ], *n.* Rogna, scabbia, *f.*
mangel-wurzel, mangel ['mæŋgəlwə:ɹzl, mæŋgl], *n.* (*Bot.*) Barbabietola campestre, *f.*
manger ['meindʒəɹ], *n.* Mangiatoia, greppia, *f.*; (*Eccles.*) presepio, *m.*
mangle (1) [mæŋgl], *n.* Mangano, *m.* ‖ *v.t.* (*clothes*) Manganare.
mangle (2), *v.t.* Sbranare, mutilare, lacerare, stracciare, squarciare; (*fig.*) maltrattare.
mangler, *n.* Manganatore, *m.*, manganatrice, *f.*
mangling, *n.* Cilindratura, *f.*; lacerazione, *f.*
mango ['mæŋgou], *n.* (*Bot.*) Mango, *m.*
mangosteen ['mæŋgosti:n], *n.* (*Bot.*) Mangostana, *f.*
mangrove ['mæŋgrouv], *n.* (*Bot.*) Rizoforea, *f.*
mangy ['meindʒi], *a.* Rognoso, scabbioso.
manhood ['mænhud], *n.* Virilità, maschilità, *f.*; età virile, *f.*; coraggio, *m.*, intrepidezza, *f.*; **— suffrage,** suffragio universale, *m.*
mania ['meiniə], *n.* Mania, follia, pazzia, *f.*
maniac (1) ['meiniæk], *n.* Maniaco, *m.*
maniac (2) **maniacal** ['meiniæk, mə'naiəkəl], *a.* Maniaco, furioso, folle.
Manichæism ['mæniki:izm], *n.* Manicheismo, *m.*
Manichee [mæni'ki:], *n.* (*Eccles.*) Manicheo, *m.*
manicure ['mænikju:ɹ], *n.* Manicura, *f.* ‖ *v.t.* Fare una manicura. **— set,** astuccio da manicura, *f.*
manifest ['mænifest], *v.t.* Manifestare, mostrare, dimostrare, rivelare. ‖ *a.* Manifesto, palese, chiaro, ovvio, evidente. ‖ *n.* (*Naut.*) Manifesto, *m.*, nota di carica, *f.* **To — oneself,** rivelarsi, mostrarsi, scoprirsi.
manifestation, *n.* Manifestazione, *f.*
manifestly, *adv.* Manifestamente, palesemente.
manifesto [mæni'festou], *n.* Manifesto, *m.*
manifold ['mænifould], *a.* Molteplice, vario, diverso, multiforme. ‖ *v.t.* Moltiplicare; poligrafare. **— -book,** copialettere, *m.*; **— -writer** poligrafo, *m.*
manifoldness, *n.* Molteplicità, varietà, *f.*
manikin ['mænikin], *n.* Omino, ometto, omuncolo, *m.*; (*model*) manichino, fantoccio, *m.*
Manilla, Manila [mə'nilə], *n.* (*Geog.*) Manilla, *f.*; (*cheroot*) manilla, *f.*; (*rope*) canapo di Manilla, *m.*; carta grezza, *f.*
manioc ['mæniɔk], *n.* (*Bot.*) Manioc, *f.*
maniple ['mænipl], *n.* (*Eccles.*) Manipolo, *m.*
manipulate [mə'nipju:leit], *v.t.* Manipolare, maneggiare, lavorare; abbindolare.
manipulation, *n.* Manipolazione, lavorazione, *f.*
manipulator, *n.* Manipolatore, *m.*
mankind [mæn'kaind], *n.* Umanità, *f.*, genere umano, *m.*; gli uomini, *m.pl.*
manlike ['mænlaik], *a.* Virile, maschile, simile a uomo. **A — woman,** una donna maschile, *f.*
manliness, *n.* Coraggio, *m.*, arditezza, intrepidezza, *f.*
manly, *a.* Virile, ardito, coraggioso.
manna ['mænə], *n.* Manna, *f.*
mannequin ['mænikin], *n.* Indossatrice, modella, *f.* **— parade,** sfilata di modelle, *f.*
manner ['mænəɹ], *n.* Maniera, *f.*, modo, *m.*; specie, sorte, *f.*; abitudine, usanza, *f.*, costume, *m.* **After the — of,** alla maniera di; **all — of things,** ogni sorta di cose; **good manners,** buone maniere, *f.pl.*; **bad manners,** cattive maniere, *f.pl.*; **in a —,** in qualche modo; **in like —,** nello stesso modo; **manners and customs,** costumi, *m.pl.*; **to have no manners,** non aver creanza; **in a particular —,** in modo speciale.
mannered, *a.* Manierato, affettato, ricercato.
mannerism, *n.* Manierismo, *m.*, affettazione, leziosaggine, *f.*
mannerliness, *n.* Gentilezza, urbanità, cortesia, *f.*
mannerly, *a.* Gentile, urbano, cortese.
mannish, *a.* (*applied to women*) Maschile.
mannishness, *n.* Maschilità, mascolinità, *f.*
manœuvre [mə'nu:vəɹ], *n.* Manovra, *f.*; maneggio, raggiro, *m.* ‖ *v.t.i.* Manovrare; maneggiare, destreggiarsi.
manœuvrer, *n.* (*fig.*) Destreggiatore, *m.*
manometer [mə'nɔmitəɹ], *n.* Manometro, *m.*
manor ['mænəɹ], *n.* Maniero, *m.*; (*house*) villa, casa signorile, *f.*; (*Law*) feudo, *m.* **— -house,** casa signorile, *f.*
manorial [mə'nɔ:riəl], *a.* Feudale.
mansard roof ['mænsɑ:rd ru:f], *n.* (*Arch.*) Mansarda, *f.*, abbaino, *m.*
manse [mæns], *n.* Casa parocchiale di ministro presbiteriano, *f.*
manservant ['mænsə:ɹvənt], *n.* Servo, domestico, *m.*
mansion ['mænʃən], *n.* Palazzo, castello, *m.*; sede, residenza, *f.*; **— -house,** casa signorile, *f.*; palazzo municipio a Londra, *m.*
mansions, *n.pl.* Casamenti, appartamenti, *m.pl.*; case d'affitto, *f.pl.*
manslaughter ['mænslɔ:təɹ], *n.* (*Law*) Omicidio colposo, omicidio preterintenzionale, *m.*
mantelet ['mæntlit], *n.* Mantellina, *f.*
mantelpiece, mantel ['mæntlpi:s, mæntl], *n.* Mensola del camino, *f.*, caminetto, *m.*
mantelshelf, *n.* Cappa del camino, *f.*
mantilla [mæn'tilə], *n.* Mantiglia, *f.*
mantis ['mæntis], *n.* (*Zool.*) Mantide, *f.*
mantissa [mæn'tisə], *n.* (*Math.*) Mantissa, *f.*
mantle [mæntl], *n.* Mantello, *m.*; (*gas*) reticella, *f.* ‖ *v.t.* Ammantellare, coprire, velare; *v.i.* soffondere; coprirsi. **The blood mantled in her cheeks,** il sangue le salì alle gote.
Mantua ['mæntju:ə], *n.* (*Geog.*) Mantova, *f.*
mantua-maker, mantle-maker ['mæntju:ə meikəɹ], *n.* Sarta, *f.*
Mantuan, *a.* Mantovano.
manual ['mænju:əl], *a.* Manuale, delle mani. ‖ *n.* Manuale, *m.*; (*Mus.*) tastiera, *f.*; (*Mil.*) **— exercise,** esercizi colle armi, *m.pl.*, maneggio delle armi, *m.*
manufactory [mænju:'fæktəri], *n.* Fabbrica, *f.*, opificio, stabilimento, *m.*
manufacture [mænju:'fæktʃəɹ], *n.* Manifattura, industria, *f.*; prodotto, *m.* ‖ *v.t.* Fabbricare, produrre, confezionare. **Manufactures,** manufatti, prodotti, *m.pl.*
manufacturer, *n.* Fabbricante, industriale, *m.*
manufacturing, *a.* Manifatturiero, industriale.

manumission [mænju:ˈmiʃən], *n.* (*Hist.*) Manomissione, affrancazione, *f.*
manumit, *v.t.* Manomettere, emancipare.
manure [məˈnju:əɹ], *n.* Concime, letame, *m.* || *v.t.* Concimare.
manuring, *n.* Concimazione, *f.*
manuscript [ˈmænju:skript], *n.a.* Manoscritto, *m.*
Manx [mæŋks], *a.* (*Geog.*) Dell'isola di Man.
many [ˈmeni], *a.* Molti; numerosi; parecchi. || *n.* Numero, *m.*, moltitudine, *f.*; popolo, *m.*, folla, *f.* **— a time,** molte volte, *f.pl.*; **How — ?** Quanti? **as — as you like,** quanti ne volete; **three mistakes in as — lines,** tre sbagli in tre righe; **one too —,** uno di troppo; **he was one too — for me,** era troppo forte per me; **How — more are coming ?** Quanti altri verranno? **too —,** troppi; **however — they are,** per quanto numerosi siano; **a great —,** un gran numero, *m.*, moltissimi, *m.pl.*; **a good —,** parecchi, *m.pl.*; **the —,** la moltitudine, *f.*, i più, *m.pl.*; **—-coloured,** molticolore; **—-sided,** moltilatero.
map [mæp], *n.* Mappa, carta geografica, *f.*; (*of a city*) pianta, *f.*; (*of the world*) mappamondo, *m.*; (*of the heavens*) carta celeste, *f.* || *v.t.* Fare una carta di. **—-maker,** cartografo, *m.*; **road- —,** carta stradale, *f.*; **to — out,** tracciare; **—-making,** cartografia, *f.*
maple [meipl], *n.* (*Bot.*) Acero, *m.* **—-sugar,** zucchero d'acero, *m.*
mar [mɑ:ɹ], *v.t.* Guastare; sconciare, sfigurare; danneggiare.
marabou [ˈmærəbu:], *n.* (*Zool.*) Marabù, *m.*
marabout [ˈmærəbu:t], *n.* (*Moslem*) Marabutto, marabut, *m.*
maraschino [mærəˈski:nou], *n.* Maraschino, *m.*
marasmus [məˈræzməs], *n.* (*Med.*) Marasma, *m.*
marathon [ˈmærəθən], *n.* (*Sport*) Corsa di Maratona, *f.*
maraud [məˈrɔ:d], *v.i.* Predare, saccheggiare.
marauder, *n.* Predatore, predone, saccheggiatore, *m.*
marauding, *n.* Saccheggio, predamento, ladroneggio, *m.*
marble [mɑ:ɹbl], *n.* (*stone*) Marmo, *m.*; (*toy*) pallina, *f.* || *a.* Di marmo. || *v.t.* Marmorare, marmorizzare, marezzare. **To play at marbles** giuocare alle palline; **—-quarry,** cava di marmo, *f.*; **—-mason,** marmista, *m.*
marbled, *a.* Marmorato, marmorizzato, marezzato.
marbling, *n.* Marezzamento, marezzo, *m.*
marc [mɑ:ɹk], *n.* (*fruit refuse*) Fondaccio, *m.*
marcasite [ˈmɑ:ɹkəsait], *n.* (*Min.*) Marcassite, *f.*
March (1) [mɑ:ɹtʃ], *n.* Marzo, *m.*
march (2), *n.* Marcia, *f.*; (*boundary*) frontiera, *f.*, confine, *m.*; (*fig.*) corso, progresso, *m.* || *v.i.* Marciare, camminare, procedere; essere contiguo. **A day's —,** una giornata di marcia, *f.*; **the — of time,** il corso del tempo, *m.*; **the — of intellect,** il progresso intellettuale, *m.*; **the dead —,** la marcia funebre, *f.*; **— past,** sfilata, *f.*; (*Mil.*) **Quick —!** Avanti marc! **to steal a — on someone,** prendere il vantaggio su qualcuno; **to — abreast,** camminare in fila; **to — off,** mettersi in marcia; allontanarsi.
marching, *a.* Di marcia. **In — order,** in ordine di marcia.
marchioness [ˈmɑ:ɹʃənes], *n.* Marchesa, *f.*
marchpane [ˈmɑ:ɹtʃpein], *n.* Marzapane, *m.*
mare [mɛəɹ], *n.* Cavalla, cavallina, puledra, giumenta, *f.* **Shanks's —,** il cavallo di San Francesco, *m.*; (*fig.*) **mare's nest,** scoperta illusoria, *f.*; (*Bot.*) **mare's-tail,** coda cavallina, *f.*
margarine [ˈmɑ:ɹdʒəri:n, ˈmɑ:ɹgəri:n], *n.* Margarina, *f.*
margin, marge [ˈmɑ:ɹdʒin], *n.* Margine, bordo, orlo, *m.* || *v.t.* Provvedere di margine, marginare.
marginal, *a.* Marginale.
margrave [ˈmɑ:ɹgreiv], *n.* (*Hist.*) Margravio, *m.*
marguerite [ˈmɑ:ɹgəri:t], *n.* (*Bot.*) Margherita, *f.*
marigold [ˈmærigould], *n.* (*Bot.*) Fiorrancio, *m.*, calendula, *f.*
marine [məˈri:n], *a.* Marino, di mare, marittimo, navale. || *n.* (*Mil.*) Soldato di marina, *m.*; marina, *f.* **— store-dealer,** rivendugliolo, rigattiere, *m.*; (*colloq.*) **tell that to the Marines,** vallo a contare a chi vuoi, non sballarle grosse.
mariner [ˈmærinəɹ], *n.* Marinaio, *m.* **Master —,** capitano mercantile, *m.*; **mariner's compass,** bussola, *f.*
Mariolatry [mɛəriˈɔlətri], *n.* (*Eccles.*) Mariolatria, *f.*
marionette [mæriəˈnet], *n.* Marionetta, *f.*
marital [ˈmæritəl], *a.* Maritale.
maritime [ˈmæritaim], *a.* Marittimo.
marjoram [ˈmɑ:ɹdʒərəm], *n.* (*Bot.*) Maggiorana, *f.*
mark [mɑ:ɹk], *n.* Segno, *m.*, marca, *f.*; marchio, *m.*, impronta, *f.*; importanza, distinzione, *f.*; (*of esteem*) distinzione, *f.*; (*at school*) punto, *m.*; (*target*) punto di mira, bersaglio, *m.* || *v.t.* Segnare, marcare, bollare, marchiare; osservare, notare. **I am not up to the — to-day,** oggi sto poco bene; **a man of —,** un uomo notabile, *m.*; **to make one's — in the world,** farsi una posizione nel mondo; **to miss one's —,** fallire il colpo; **to hit the —,** colpire nel segno; **that's beside the —,** questo è fuori dell'argomento; **to overshoot the —,** andare al di là, varcare i limiti; **— my words,** notate bene ciò che dico; **to — out,** segnalare, designare, destinare, contraddistinguere; **to — time,** segnare il passo; **book- —,** segnalibro, *m.*; **low water —,** linea di fondo, *f.*; **trade —,** marca di fabbrica, *f.*
marked, *a.* Marcato, segnato; notevole. **A — accent,** uno spiccato accento, *m.*; **a — man,** una persona sospetta, *f.*; **with — attention,** con viva attenzione; **— cards,** carte segnate, *f.pl.*
marker, *n.* Marcatore, *m.*; (*counter*) gettone, *m.* **Billiard- —,** segnapunti, *m.*; **book- —,** segnalibro, *m.*
market [ˈmɑ:ɹkit], *n.* Mercato, *m.*, piazza, *f.*; sbocco, *m.*; (*sale*) vendita, *f.*; (*Comm.*) borsa, *f.* || *v.t.i.* Vendere al mercato, comprare al mercato; far mercato; mercanteggiare. **On the —,** sul mercato; **to find new markets,** trovare nuovi sbocchi, trovare nuovi mercati; **to put on the —,** lanciare sul

mercato; **to go marketing**, andare a far le spese; **—-day**, giorno di mercato, *m.*; **—-garden**, orto, *m.*; **—-gardener**, ortolano, *m.*; **covered —**, mercato coperto, *m.*; **—-place**, piazza del mercato, *f.*; **—-town**, borgo, *m.*, borgata, *f.*; **—-woman**, mercantina, *f.*; (*Comm.*) **— price**, prezzo di mercato, *m.*; **black —**, borsa nera, *f.*

marketable, *a.* Vendibile, commerciabile.

marketing, *n.* Mercatura, *f.*, commercio, traffico, *m.*

marking, *n.* Segno, *m.*, traccia, tiratura, *f.*; strisce, *f.pl.* **—-ink**, inchiostro indelebile, *m.*

marksman, *n.* Tiratore, buon tiratore, *m.*

marksmanship, *n.* Abilità al tiro, *f.* **Good —**, buona mira, *f.*

marl [mɑːɹl], *n.* (*Geol.*) Marna, *f.* || *v.t.* Marnare. **—-pit**, marniera, *f.*

marline [ˈmɑːɹlin], *n.* (*Naut.*) Merlino, *m.* **—-spike**, punterolo per funi, *m.*, caviglia da impiombare, *f.*

marly, *a.* Marnoso.

marmalade [ˈmɑːɹməleid], *n.* Marmellata d'arancie, *f.*

Marmora [ˈmɑːɹmərə], *n.* (*Geog.*) Marmara, *f.*

marmoreal [mɑːɹˈmɔːriəl], *a.* Marmoreo.

marmoset [ˈmɑːɹməzet], *n.* (*Zool.*) Uistiti, *f.*

marmot [ˈmɑːɹmɔt], *n.* (*Zool.*) Marmotta, *f.*

Marne [mɑːɹn], *n.* (*Geog.*) Marna, *f.*

Maronite [ˈmærənait], *n.* (*Eccles.*) Maronita, *m.*

maroon (1) [məˈruːn], *a.* Marrone, rossastro. || *n.* Colore marrone, *m.*

maroon (2), *n.* (*firework*) Mortaretto, *m.*, castagnola, *f.*

maroon (3), *v.t.* Abbandonare in un'isola deserta.

maroon (4), *n.* Schiavo fuggitivo, *m.*

marplot [ˈmɑːɹplɔt], *n.* Guastamestieri, intruso, *m.*

marque [mɑːɹk], *n.* **Letters of —**, patente di corso, *m.*

marquee [mɑːɹˈkiː], *n.* Tenda, *f.*, padiglione, *m.*

marquess, marquis [ˈmɑːɹkwis], *n.* Marchese, *m.*

marquetry [ˈmɑːɹkitri], *n.* Intarsio, *m.*, intarsiatura, *f.*

marquisate, *n.* Marchesato, *m.*

marriage [ˈmæridʒ], *n.* Matrimonio, sposalizio, *m.*, nozze, *f.pl.*, sponsali, *m.pl.* **To give in —**, dare in moglie; **—-bed**, letto nuziale, *m.*; **—-contract**, contratto di matrimonio, *m.*; **—-portion**, dote, *f.*; **—-settlement**, contratto di matrimonio, *m.*; **—-licence**, dispensa di matrimonio, *f.*; **—-tie**, vincolo coniugale, *m.*; **sister by —**, sorella acquistata, *f.*

marriageable, *a.* Nubile, da marito.

married, *a.* (*of woman*) Maritata, (*of man*) ammogliato; coniugale. **— couple**, coniugi, *m.pl.*, marito e moglie; **— life**, vita coniugale, *f.*; **newly- — couple**, sposini, *m.pl.*

marrow (1) [ˈmærou], *n.* (*Anat.*) Midollo, *m.*, midolla, fibra, *f.* **—-bone**, ossobuco, *m.*

marrow (2), *n.* (*Bot.*) Zucca ovifera, *f.*

marrowfat, *n.* (*Bot.*) Specie di pisello primaticcio.

marrowy, *a.* Midolloso.

marry (1) [ˈmæri], *v.t.* Sposare; maritare, ammogliare; maritarsi con, ammogliarsi con; (*fig.*) unire, congiungere. || *v.i.* maritarsi, ammogliarsi. **To — again**, risposarsi, passare a seconde nozze; **to — into a family**, imparentarsi con una famiglia.

marry! (2), *inter.* (*obs.*) Davvero! In verità!

Mars [mɑːɹz], *n.* (*Myth.Astron.*) Marte, *m.*

Marseillaise [mɑːɹsəˈleiz], *n.* (*hymn*) Marsigliese, *f.*

Marseilles [mɑːɹˈseilz], *n.* (*Geog.*) Marsiglia, *f.*

marsh [mɑːɹʃ], *n.* Palude, *f.*, stagno, *m.* **—-fever**, Malaria, *f.*, paludismo, *m.*; **—-gas**, metano, *m.*; **— mallow**, altea, bismalva, *f.*; **—-marigold**, fiorrancio delle paludi, *m.*

marshal [ˈmɑːɹʃəl], *n.* Maresciallo, *m.*; prefetto, *m.*; cerimoniere, *m.* || *v.t.* Ordinare, schierare.

marshalship, *n.* Maresciallato, *m.*

marshy, *a.* Paludoso, palustre, pantanoso.

marsupial [mɑːɹˈsuːpiəl], *n.a.* (*Zool.*) Marsupiale, *m.*

mart [mɑːɹt], *n.* Mercato, emporio, *m.*, fiera, *f.*; sala di vendita all'incanto, *f.*

martello tower [mɑːɹˈtelou ˈtauəɹ], *n.* Torrione per guardia delle coste, *m.*

marten [ˈmɑːɹtin], *n.* (*Zool.*) Martora, faina, *f.*

martial [ˈmɑːɹʃəl], *a.* Marziale, guerresco, bellicoso. **— law**, legge marziale, *f.*, stato d'assedio, *m.*; **— array**, ordine di battaglia, *m.*

Martian [ˈmɑːɹʃən], *n.* Marziano, *m.*

martin [ˈmɑːɹtin], *n.* (*Zool.*) Rondine, rondinella, *f.*

martinet [mɑːɹtiˈnet], *n.* Ufficiale rigorista, *m.*

martingale [ˈmɑːɹtiŋgeil], *n.* Martingala, *f.*

Martinmas [ˈmɑːɹtinməs], *n.* Il Martino, *m.*, festa di San Martino, *f.*

martlet [ˈmɑːɹtlit], *n.* Rondine, *f.*; (*Her*). rondine senza piedi, *f.*

martyr [ˈmɑːɹtəɹ], *n.* Martire, *m.f.* || *v.t.* Martirizzare. **A — to rheumatism**, vittima del reumatismo, *f.*; **to make a — of oneself**, fare il martire, atteggiarsi a martire.

martyrdom, *n.* Martirio, *m.*

martyrize, *v.t.* Martirizzare, martoriare, tormentare.

martyrologist, *n.* Martirologista, *m.*

martyrology, *n.* Martirologio, *m.*

marvel [ˈmɑːɹvəl], *n.* Meraviglia, maraviglia, *f.*, prodigio, *m.* || *v.i.* Maravigliarsi, meravigliarsi. **To — at**, maravigliarsi di.

marvellous, *a.* Maraviglioso, meraviglioso, mirabile, straordinario.

marvellously, *adv.* Maravigliosamente.

marvellousness, *n.* Maraviglia, maravigliosità, *f.*

marzipan [ˈmɑːɹzipæn], *n.* Marzapane, *m.*

mascot [ˈmæskət], *n.* Mascotte, *f.*, portafortuna, *m.f.*, talismano, *m.*

masculine [ˈmæskjuːlin], *a.* Maschile, maschio, mascolino; (*Gram.*) maschile, genere maschile. **In the —**, al maschile.

masculinity, *n.* Maschiezza, maschilità, virilità, mascolinità, *f.*

mash [mæʃ], *n.* Mescolanza, miscela, *f.*, miscuglio, *m.*; (*for cattle*) beverone, pastone, *m.*; (*for poultry*) pastone, *m.*; (*cooking*) passata, *f.* || *v.t.* Mescolare, mischiare, pestare; schiacciare. **Mashed potatoes**, purè di patate, *m.*; **—-tub**, tino, *m.*, bigoncia, *f.*

masher, *n.* (*obs. colloq.*) Elegante, *m.*

mask [mɑːsk], *n.* Maschera, *f.*; (*of fox*) testa, *f.*; (*Arch.*) mascherone, *m.*; (*Phot.*) velo di carta, *m.* || *v.t.* Mascherare, nascondere, dissimulare, travestire. **To throw off the —**,

levarsi la maschera; **a masked ball,** un ballo in maschera, *m.*
masker, masquer, *n.* Maschera, *f.*
masochism ['mæsokizm], *n.* (*Med.*) Masochismo, *m.*
mason ['meisən], *n.* Muratore, *m.* **Freemason,** frammassone, massone, franco muratore, *m.*; **master —,** maestro muratore, capomastro, *m.*
masonic [mə'sɔnik], *a.* Massonico.
masonry ['meisənri], *n.* Muratura, *f.*; massoneria, frammassoneria, *f.*
masque [mɑ:sk], *n.* (*Lit.*) Spettacolo allegorico, *m.*; balletto, trionfo, *m.*
masquerade [mɑ:skə'reid], *n.* Mascherata, *f.* || *v.t.* Mascherarsi, travestirsi. **To — as,** mascherarsi da.
masquerader, *n.* Maschera, *f.*
mass (1) [mæs], *n.* Massa, *f.*, ammasso, *m.*; moltitudine, folla, *f.*; quantità grande, *f.* || *v.t.i.* Radunare, radunarsi; ammassare, ammassarsi, aggruppare. **The masses,** le masse, *f.pl.*, il popolo, *m.*; **he was a — of bruises,** era tutto ammaccato; **in the —,** in complesso; **— production,** produzione in serie, *f.*; **— -meeting,** comizio, *m.*
Mass (2), *n.* (*Eccles.*) Messa, *f.* **High —,** messa grande, messa cantata, *f.*; **Low —,** messa bassa, messa piana, *f.*; **to hear —,** udir messa, sentir messa; **to go to —,** andare a messa. **— -book,** libro da messa, *m.*
massacre ['mæsəkəɹ], *n.* Massacro, *m.*, strage, *f.*; macello, *m.* || *v.t.* Massacrare, trucidare.
massage [mə'sɑ:ʒ], *n.* (*Med.*) Massaggio, *m.* || *v.t.* Massaggiare, frizionare, fregare.
masseur [mæ'sə:ɹ], *n.* Masseur, massaggiatore, *m.*
masseuse [məs'əɹz], *n.* Masseuse, massaggiatrice, *f.*
massif [mæsi:f], *n.* (*Geol.*) Massiccio, *m.*
massive, massy ['mæsiv, 'mæsi], *a.* Massiccio, pesante, solido.
massively, *adv.* Pesantemente.
massiveness, *n.* Solidità, pesantezza, *f.*
mast (1) [mɑ:st], *n.* Albero, *m.*, alberatura, *f.* || *v.t.* Alberare. **Foremast,** albero di trinchetto, *m.*; **jury —,** albero di fortuna, *m.*; **mizen- —,** albero di mezzana, *m.*; **— -head,** coffa, *f.*
mast (2), *n.* (*Bot.*) (*beech*) Faggiuola, *f.*; (*oak*) ghianda, *f.*
master ['mɑ:stəɹ], *n.* Maestro, *m.*; capo, *m.*; (*employer*) padrone, *m.*; (*head of house*) padrone, *m.*; (*school*) maestro, professore, *m.*; (*boy*) signorino, *m.*; (*Naut.*) capitano, *m.* || *v.t.* Dominare, vincere, sormontare, reprimere; impadronirsi di, padroneggiare, comandare. **Head- —,** direttore, *m.*; **— -hand** mano maestra, *f.*; **Master of Arts,** dottore in lettere, *m.*; **Master of the Horse,** Grande Scudiere, *m.*; **to be one's own —,** essere indipendente; **to be — in one's own house,** esser padrone in casa propria; **to be thoroughly — of,** conoscere a fondo; **to make oneself — of,** farsi padrone di; **— -card,** carta maestra, *f.*; **— -builder,** capomastro, *m.*; **— -key,** chiave maestra, *f.*, passapertutto, *m.*, **— -mind,** genio, *m.*; **— -stroke,** colpo maestro, *m.*; **— mariner,** capitano di nave mercantile, *m.*; **— of hounds,** capocaccia, *m.*; **— of ceremonies,** maestro del cerimoniale, *m.*
masterful, *a.* Imperioso, prepotente.
masterfulness, *n.* Imperiosità, *f.*
masterless, *a.* Senza padrone, senza maestro.
masterly, *a.* Da maestro, abilissimo; magistrale.
masterpiece, *n.* Capolavoro, *m.*
mastership, *n.* Dominio, potere, *m.*; ufficio di maestro di scuola, *m.*
mastery, *n.* Padronanza, *f.*, possesso, *m.*; (*skill*) maestria, *f.* **To contend for the — of,** disputare il possesso di; **to gain the —,** acquistare la padronanza.
mastic ['mæstik], *n.* Mastice, *m.* **— -tree,** lentischio, *m.*
masticate ['mæstikeit], *v.t.* Masticare.
mastication, *n.* Masticazione, *f.*
masticatory [mæsti'keitəri], *a.* Masticatorio.
mastiff ['mæstif], *n.* (*Zool.*) Mastino, *m.*
masting, *n.* Alberatura, *f.*
mastodon ['mæstodɔn], *n.* (*Zool.*) Mastodonte, *m.*
mastitis [mæs'taitis], *n.* (*Med.*) Mastite, *f.*
mastoid ['mæstɔid], *a.* (*Anat.*) Mastoideo. **— bone,** mastoide, *f.*
mat (1), **matt** [mæt], *a.* Appannato, opaco, ruvido, smorto.
mat (2), *n.* Stuoia, *f.*, stoino, zerbino, *m.*; sottopiatto, sottovaso, *m.* || *v.t.* Coprire con stuoie; intrecciarsi. **Door- —,** zerbino, *m.*; **matted hair,** capelli arruffati, *m.pl.*
matador ['mætədɔ:ɹ], *n.* Matador, *m.*
match (1) [mætʃ], *n.* Fiammifero, zolfanello, cerino, *m.*; (*fuse*) miccia, *f.* **— box,** scatola di fiammiferi, *f.*; **— -lock,** fucile a miccia, *m.*
match (2), *n.* Simile, pari, eguale, *m.*; partito matrimoniale, *m.*; lotta, gara, *f.*; partita, *f.*; (*Football*) partita, *f.* || *v.t.i.* Accoppiare, unire; tener testa a, esser della forza di; appaiarsi; misurarsi con; combaciare, corrispondere, andar bene insieme; pareggiare, eguagliare. **To be a good —,** intonarsi, andar bene; **to make a good —,** far un buon matrimoniale; **to be a — for,** esser pari a, far fronte a; **to meet one's —,** trovare pane per i propri denti; **— -board,** assi gemelle, *f.pl.*; **— -maker,** combinatore di matrimoni, *m.*; **— -making,** il combinar matrimoni, *m.*; (*Golf.*) **— play,** partita a buche, *f.*
matchless, *a.* Impareggiabile, incomparabile.
matchlessness, *n.* Incomparabilità, *f.*
mate [meit], *n.* Compagno, *m.*, camerata, *m.f.*; sposo, *m.*, sposa, *f.*; (*Naut.*) secondo di bordo, *m.*; (*Chess*) scaccomatto, *m.* || *v.t.* Accoppiare, unire, appaiare; (*Chess*) dare scaccomatto a.
maté ['mætei], *n.* (*drink*) Mate, *f.*
mateless, *a.* Senza sposo, senza sposa, senza compagno, solitario.
mater ['meitəɹ], *n.* (*colloq.*) Madre, *f.*
material [mə'tiəriəl], *a.* Materiale, rozzo, grossolano; corporeo; importante, essenziale. || *n.* Materia, *f.*; stoffa, *f.*, panno, tessuto, *m.* **Materials,** materiali, oggetti, *m.pl.*; **building materials,** materiale di costruzione, materiale laterizio, *m.*; **raw materials,** materie prime, *f.pl.*; **writing-materials,** l'occorrente per scrivere; **made-up materials,** confezioni, *f.pl.*
materialism, *n.* Materialismo, *m.*
materialist, *n.* Materialista, *m.*
materiality, *n.* Materialità, *f.*

materialize, *v.t.i.* Materializzare; avverarsi, realizzarsi.
maternal [mə'tə:ɹnəl], *a.* Materno.
maternity, *n.* Maternità, *f.*
mathematical [mæθə'mætikəl], *a.* Matematico; geometrico.
mathematician [mæθəmə'tiʃən], *n.* Matematico, *m.*
mathematics, *n.pl.* Matematica, *f.*
matinee ['mætinei], *n.* (*Theat.*) Mattinata, *f.*
matins ['mætinz], *n.pl.* (*Eccles.*) Mattutino, *m.*
matriarch ['meitriɑ:ɹk], *n.* Materfamilias, *f.*
matriarchy, *n.* Matriarcato, *m.*
matricide ['mætrisaid], *n.* (*criminal*) Matricida, *m.f.*; (*crime*) matricidio, *m.*
matriculate [mə'trikju:leit], *v.t.* Immatricolare, matricolare, iscrivere; *v.i.* matricolarsi, iscriversi.
matriculation, *n.* Immatricolazione, matricolazione, iscrizione, *f.*
matrimonial [mætri'moniəl], *a.* Matrimoniale, coniugale.
matrimony ['mætriməni], *n.* Matrimonio, *m.*
matrix ['mætriks], *n.* Matrice, *f.*
matron ['meitrən], *n.* Matrona, signora anziana, *f.*; direttrice, *f.*; capoinfermiera, *f.*
matronhood, *n.* Matronato, *m.*
matronly, *a.* Matronale, da matrona.
matronship, *n.* Direzione, *f.*; direttorato, *m.*
matted, *a.* Intrecciato, arruffato.
matter ['mætəɹ], *n.* Materia, sostanza, *f.*; soggetto, contenuto, *m.*; cosa, faccenda, *f.*; affare, *m.*; (*Med.*) pus, *m.*; (*fig.*) importanza, *f.* || *v.i.* Importare, avere importanza. **It is a — for regret,** c'è da rammaricarsi; **printed —,** stampe, *f.pl.*; **No —!** Non importa! **money matters,** affari di danaro, *m.pl.*; **that is a — of habit,** è una questione d'abitudine; **for that —,** in quanto a ciò; **a — of five weeks,** quasi cinque settimane; **in the — of,** in quanto a; **a — of course,** una cosa naturale, *f.*; **as a — of fact,** in realtà, in verità; **a small —,** una cosa di nessun'importanza, un'inezia, *f.*; **as matters stand,** mentre le cose stanno così; **Is anything the — ?** È successo qualche cosa? **What is the — ?** Di che cosa si tratta? Cosa c'è? **he has something the — with his leg,** ha male alla gamba; **a —-of-fact person,** una persona prosaica, *f.*; **it doesn't —,** non importa, non fa nulla; **it matters little,** importa poco; **What does it — ?** Che importa?
Matterhorn ['mætəɹhɔ:ɹn], *n.* (*Geog.*) Monte Cervino, *m.*
matting, *n.* Stuoia, *f.*; stuoiame, paglericcio, *m.*; fibra di cocco, *f.*
mattins ['mætinz], *n.pl.* (*Eccles.*) Mattutino, *m.*
mattock ['mætək], *n.* Zappa, *f.*
mattress ['mætris], *n.* Materasso, *m.* **Spring —,** materasso elastico, *m.*; **—-maker,** materassaio, *m.*
maturation [mætju:'reiʃən], *n.* (*Med.*) Maturazione, suppurazione, *f.*
mature [mə'tju:əɹ], *a.* Maturo. || *v.t.i.* Maturare, maturarsi; (*Comm.*) scadere.
matureness, maturity, *n.* Maturità, *f.*; (*Comm.*) scadenza, *f.*
matutinal [mætju:'tainəl], *a.* Mattutino, mattinale, mattiniero.
maudlin ['mɔ:dlin], *a.* Brillo, alticcio; lagrimoso, lezioso, sentimentale.
maul [mɔ:l], *n.* Mazza, *f.* || *v.t.* Battere, bastonare; malmenare, bistrattare.
maul-stick, mahl-stick ['mɔ:lstik], *n.* (*Art*) Appoggiamano, *m.*
maunder ['mɔ:ndəɹ], *v.i.* Borbottare, mormorare, brontolare.
Maundy Thursday ['mɔ:ndi 'θə:ɹsdi], *n.* Giovedì santo, *m.*
Mauritius [mə'riʃəs], *n.* (*Geog.*) Maurizio, *m.*
mausoleum [mɔ:so'liəm], *n.* Mausoleo, *m.*
mauve [mouv], *n.a.* Color malva, *m.*, malva, *f.*
mavis ['meivis], *n.* (*Zool.*) Tordo, *m.*
maw [mɔ:], *n.* Stomaco, *m.*; (*of birds*) gozzo, *m.* **—-worm,** verme intestinale, *m.*
mawkish ['mɔ:kiʃ], *a.* Sdolcinato, lezioso, insipido.
mawkishly, *adv.* Insipidamente.
mawkishness, *n.* Sdolcinatezza, leziosaggine, *f.*
maxilla [mək'zilə], *n.* (*Anat.*) Mascella, *f.*
maxillary, *a.* Mascellare.
maxim (1) ['mæksim], *n.* Massima, *f.*; sentenza, *f.*, precetto, *m.*
maxim (2), *n.* (*Mil.*) Mitragliatrice maxim, *f.*
maximum (*pl.* **maxima**) ['mæksiməm, 'mæksimə], *n.* Massimo, *m.*
May (1) [mei], *n.* Maggio, *m.* || *a.* Maggese, di Maggio. **— Day,** il primo Maggio, calendimaggio, *m.*; **— queen,** regina del Maggio, *f.*; (*Zool.*) **—-fly,** effimera, *f.*; **maypole,** il maggio, l'albero di maggio, *m.*
may (2), *n.* (*Bot.*) Biancospino, *m.* **—-blossom** biancospino, fiore di maggio, *m.*
may (3), *v.aux.* Potere, esser possibile. **— I come in ?** Posso entrare? **I — as well go,** potrei anche andare; **it — be that,** può darsi che; **it might happen that,** potrebbe accadere che; **it might have been better if,** sarebbe stato meglio se; **— be,** forse; **that — be so,** può darsi; **you — have seen this,** avete forse visto ciò; **if I — say so,** se mi è permesso di dirlo; **be that as it —,** sia come si vuole; **it — not be true,** forse non è vero; **you might offer to help,** potreste offrirvi di aiutare; **— it please you,** vi possa piacere; **you might have told me,** potreste avermelo detto.
maybe, *adv.* Forse.
mayonnaise [meijo'neiz], *n.* Maionese, salsa maionese, *f.*
mayor [mɛəɹ], *n.* Sindaco, podestà, *m.*
mayoral, *a.* Sindacale.
mayoralty ['mɛərəlti], *n.* Sindacato, *m.*, podesteria, *f.*
mayoress, *n.* Moglie del sindaco, *f.*; una donna che tiene l'ufficio di sindaco, *f.*
maze [meiz], *n.* Labirinto, dedalo, *m.*; (*fig.*) imbroglio, *m.*, perplessità, confusione, *f.*
mazurka [mə'zə:ɹkə], *n.* (*Mus.*) Mazurca, mazurka, *f.*
mazy, *a.* Labirintico; perplesso, confuso, sconcertato.
me [mi:], *pron.* Mi, me. **Of me,** di me; **with me,** meco, con me.
mead (1) [mi:d], *n.* (*drink*) Idromele, *m.*
mead (2), *n.* (*Poet.*) Prato, *m.*
meadow ['medou], *n.* Prato, *m.*, prateria, *f.* **—-land,** praterie, *f.pl.*, pascoli, *m.pl.*; (*Bot.*) **—-saffron,** colchico, *m.*; **—-sweet,** spirea, regina dei prati, *f.*
meadowy, *a.* Prativo, pratoso, erboso.

meagre ['mi:gəɹ], *a.* Magro, povero, scarso.
meagrely, *adv.* Magramente.
meagreness, *n.* Magrezza, povertà, *f.*
meal (1) [mi:l], *n.* Farina, *f.* **—-tub,** madia, *f.*
meal (2), *n.* Pasto, *m.* **—-time,** ora del pasto, *f.*
mealies, *n.pl.* Granturco, *m.*
mealiness, *n.* Farinosità, *f.*
mealy, *a.* Farinoso. (*fig.*) **—-mouthed,** schivo, schifiltoso nel parlare.
mean (1) [mi:n], *a.* Basso, vile, gretto, servile; povero, insignificante, inferiore, mediocre; meschino; avaro. **A — trick,** un colpo mancino, *m.*, una meschinità, *f.*; **of — birth,** d'umile origine; **—-spirited,** vile, meschino.
mean (2), *n.* Medio, mezzo, *m.*; mediocrità, *f.*; (*Math.*) media, *f.* || *a.* Medio. **A man of private means,** un uomo che vive del proprio; **by all means,** ad ogni costo; **by fair means or by foul,** per dritto o per rovescio, con le buone o le cattive; **by means of,** per mezzo di; **by some means or other,** in una maniera o nell'altra; **by this means,** in questo modo; **the golden —,** il giusto mezzo, *m.*; l'aurea mediocrità, *f.*; **to live on one's means,** vivere del proprio; **Greenwich — time,** il tempo secondo la longitudine di Greenwich.
mean (3), *v.t.i.* Significare, voler dire; spiegarsi, intendere, proporsi, aver intenzione di, destinare a. **Do you — it ?** Parlate sul serio? **I did not — to do it,** non avevo intenzione di farlo; **he meant the book for me,** destinò il libro a me; **What does this word — ?** Che cosa significa questa parola? **What do you — ?** Che cosa volete dire? **What does this — ?** Che vuol dire questo? **to — well by someone,** voler bene a qualcuno; **What do you — by such conduct ?** Cosa intendete fare con questa condotta?
meander [mi'ændəɹ], *v.i.* Serpeggiare, vagare. || *n.* Meandro, serpeggiamento, *m.*, giravolta, *f.*
meandering, *a.* Serpeggiante, tortuoso.
meaning, *n.* Significato, senso, *m.* || *a.* Significativo. **A double —,** un doppio senso, *m.*; **that is not my —,** non è ciò che voglio dire; **Do I make my — clear ?** Mi spiego? Parlo chiaro? **a — look,** uno sguardo significativo, *m.*; **ill-—,** male intenzionato; **well-—** ben intenzionato.
meaningless, *a.* Insignificante.
meanness ['mi:nnis], *n.* Bassezza, meschinità, *f.*; mediocrità, *f.*; grettezza, *f.*
meantime, meanwhile [mi:n'taim, mi:n'wail], *adv.* Intanto, frattanto. **In the meantime,** nel frattempo.
measles ['mi:zlz], *n.* (*Med.*) Morbillo, *m.* **German —,** rosolia, *f.*
measly, *a.* Morbilloso; (*colloq.*) meschino.
measurable ['meʒərəbl], *a.* Misurabile.
measurably, *adv.* Moderatamente.
measure ['meʒəɹ], *n.* Misura, *f.*; limite, *m.*; proporzione, *f.*; capacità, *f.*; (*Poet.*) metro, ritmo, *m.*; (*Pol.*) progetto di legge, *m.*; (*Geol.*) strato, *m.* || *v.t.* Misurare; valutare, giudicare; (*for clothes*) prendere le misure. **Tape-—,** nastro, *m.*; **beyond —,** oltre misura, oltre modo; **to give good —, to give short —** dare buona misura, dare scarsa misura; **made to —,** fatto su misura; **in great —,** in larga misura; **in some —,** in parte; **to take measures,** prendere misure; **to take legal measures,** aver ricorso alle vie legali; **to take someone's —,** prendere le misure a qualcuno, (*fig.*) pesare qualcuno; **it measures three feet,** ha tre piedi di lunghezza; **to — one's length on the ground,** cader lungo disteso; **to — with the eye,** misurare a occhio; **to — one's strength against another's,** misurarsi con un altro; **to — one's words,** misurare le parole.
measured, *a.* Misurato; moderato, temperato. **In no — terms,** in termini eccessivi; **a — tread,** un passo regolare, un passo cadenzato, *m.*
measureless, *a.* Senza misura, smisurato, sterminato, illimitato.
measurement, *n.* Misurazione, misura, *f.*
measurer, *n.* Misuratore, *m.*
measuring, *n.* Misuramento, *m.*, misurazione, *f.*
meat [mi:t], *n.* Carne, *f.*; cibo, pasto, alimento, *m.*; vivande, *f.pl.* **Butcher's —,** carne macellata, *f.*; **boiled —,** carne lessa, *f.*; **roast —,** arrosto, *m.*; **canned —, tinned —,** carne in iscatola, *f.*; (*Eccles.*) **— day,** giorno di grasso, *m.*; **—-safe,** guardavivande, *m.*, dispensa, moscheruola, *f.*
meaty, *a.* Carnoso; (*fig.*) sostanzioso.
mechanic [me'kænik], *n.* Meccanico, macchinista, *m.*; artigiano, artefice, *m.*
mechanical, *a.* Meccanico, macchinale. **— drawing,** disegno d'officina, *m.*; **— engineer,** ingegnere meccanico, *m.*; **— engineering,** ingegneria meccanica, *f.*
mechanically, *adv.* Meccanicamente.
mechanicalness, *n.* Meccanicità, *f.*
mechanician [mekə'niʃən], *n.* Meccanico, *m.*
mechanics, *n.pl.* Meccanica, *f.*
mechanism ['mekənizm], *n.* Meccanismo, *m.*; congegno, *m.*
mechanization, *n.* Meccanizzazione, *f.*
mechanize, *v.t.* Meccanizzare.
Mechlin, Mechlin lace ['meklin, meklin 'leis], *n.* Merletto di Malines, *m.*
medal ['medəl], *n.* Medaglia, *f.* **— collection,** medagliere, *m.*; **to award a — to,** conferire una medaglia; (*Golf.*) **— play,** partita alla medaglia, *f.*
medalled, *a.* Decorato di medaglie.
medallion [me'dæliən], *n.* Medaglione, *m.*
medallist, *n.* Medaglista, *m.*; premiato con medaglia, *m.*
meddle [medl], *v.i.* Immischiarsi, intromettersi, ingerirsi. **To — with,** toccare.
meddler, *n.* Intrigante, faccendiere, faccendone, ficcanaso, affannone, *m.*
meddlesome, *a.* Intrigante, pettegolo. **A — person,** un ficcanaso, *m.*
meddling, *a.* Intrigante.
mediaeval, medieval [medi'i:vəl], *a.* Medioevale, del medio evo.
mediaevalist, *n.* Studioso della storia medioevale, *m.*
medial ['mi:diəl], *a.* Medio.
mediant, *n.* (*Mus.*) Mediante, *m.*
mediate (1) ['mi:dieit], *v.i.* Interporsi, intercedere, far da mediatore.
mediate (2) ['midiit], *a.* Mediato, intermediario.
mediation [mi:di'eiʃən], *n.* Mediazione, intercessione, *f.*

mediatization, *n.* (*Hist.*) Annessione, *f.*
mediatize, *v.t.* (*Hist.*) Annettere.
mediator ['mi:dieitəɹ], *n.* Mediatore, intercessore, *m.*
mediatorial, mediatory, *a.* Mediatore.
mediatrix, *n.* Mediatrice, *f.*
medicable ['medikəbl], *a.* Medicabile, guaribile, sanabile.
medical ['medikəl], *a.* Medico, di medicina. **— man,** medico, dottore, *m.*; **— officer,** ufficiale sanitario, *m.*; **the — profession,** la professione medica, *f.*; **— student,** studente di medicina, *m.*; **— jurisprudence,** medicina legale, *f.*; **to take — advice,** ricorrere al medico.
medicament [me'dikəmənt], *n.* Medicamento, rimedio, farmaco, *m.*
medicate, *v.t.* Medicare, curare.
medicated, *a.* Medicato.
medication, *n.* Medicatura, cura, *f.*
medicative, *a.* Medicinale, medicamentoso.
Medicean [medi'si:ən], *a.* (*Hist.*) Mediceo.
medicinal [me'disinəl], *a.* Medicinale.
medicinally, *adv.* Medicinalmente.
medicine ['medsən], *n.* Medicina, *f.*, medicamento, farmaco, rimedio, *m.* **— chest, — cabinet,** armadietto farmaceutico, *m.*; **— -man,** stregone, *m.*
medieval [cp. **mediaeval**].
mediocre ['mi:dioukəɹ], *a.* Mediocre.
mediocrity [medi'ɔkriti], *n.* Mediocrità, *f.*; (*person*) mediocre, *m.*
meditate ['mediteit], *v.t.i.* Meditare su, contemplare; macchinare, tramare.
meditation, *n.* Meditazione, *f.*
meditative, *a.* Meditativo, pensieroso, cogitabondo.
Mediterranean [meditə'reiniən], *a.* (*Geog.*) Mediterraneo. **The — Sea,** Il mare mediterraneo, il Mediterraneo, *m.*
medium (*pl.* **mediums, media**) ['mi:diəm], *n.* Mezzo, espediente, veicolo, *m.*; (*Math.*) numero medio; (*agent*) intermediario, mezzano, *m.*; (*Spiritualism*) medium, *m.* || *a.* Medio, mediano, intermedio. **— of circulation,** mezzo circolante, *m.*; **the happy —,** il giusto mezzo, *m.*; **through the — of,** per mezzo di.
mediumistic, *a.* Di un medium.
medlar ['medlər], *n.* (*Bot.*) Nespola, *f.* **— -tree,** nespolo, *m.*
medley ['medli], *n.* Miscuglio, *m.*, mescolanza, accozzaglia, *f.*; guazzabuglio, zibaldone, *m.* || *a.* Misto, mescolato.
medulla [me'dʌlə], *n.* (*Anat.*) Midollo, *m.*
medullary, *a.* Midollare.
Medusa [me'dju:zə], *n.* (*Myth.Zool.*) Medusa, *f.*
meed [mi:d], *n.* (*Poet.*) Ricompensa, *f.*
meek [mi:k], *a.* Mansueto, mite, umile, dimesso, bonario.
meekly, *adv.* Umilmente.
meekness, *n.* Mansuetudine, mitezza, umiltà, bonarietà, *f.*
meerschaum ['miərʃəm], *n.* Schiuma di mare, *f.*; pipa di schiuma, *f.*
meet (1) [mi:t], *v.t.* Incontrare, trovare, andare incontro a, imbattersi in; coprire, far fronte a, soddisfare, far onore a; contentare, accordarsi con; *v.i.* incontrarsi, trovarsi, imbattersi, adunarsi, raccogliersi, riunirsi; far la conoscenza. || *n.* (*hunt*) Riunione, *f.*, raduno, *m.* **To — someone half-way,** venire a un compromesso; **to go out to — someone,** andare incontro a qualcuno; **to — the eye,** saltare all'occhio; **to — someone's eye,** guardare in viso a qualcuno; **to — one's engagements,** soddisfare gl'impegni; **to make ends —,** sbarcare il lunario; **extremes —,** gli estremi si toccano; **he met with an accident,** gli accadde una disgrazia; **to — with,** incontrare, trovare; **When shall we — again?** Quando ci rivedremo? **I met her in Naples.** l'ho conosciuta a Napoli.
meet (2), *a.* Conveniente, adatto, convenevole; appropriato, ragionevole.
meeting, *n.* Incontro, *m.*; adunanza, assemblea, riunione, *f.*; seduta, *f.*; (*of rivers*) confluenza, *f.*; (*duel*) duello, *m.*; (*political*) comizio, *m.* **To call a —,** convocare un'adunanza; **right of public —,** diritto di adunanza, *m.*; **— -house,** casa di riunione, *f.*; **— -place,** ritrovo, luogo di riunione, *m.*
meetness, *n.* Convenienza, convenevolezza, *f.*
megacephalic [megəse'fælik], *a.* Megacefalo.
megacycle ['megəsaikl], *n.* Megaciclo, *m.*
megalith, *n.* Megalite, *m.*
megalithic, *a.* Megalitico.
megalomania [megəlou'meiniə], *n.* Megalomania, *f.*
megalomaniac, *n.* Megalomane, *m.*
megaphone ['megəfoun], *n.* Megafono, portavoce, *m.*
megapod ['megəpɔd], *n.* (*Zool.*) Megapode, *m.*
megatherium [megə'θiəriəm], *n.* (*Zool.*) Megaterio, *m.*
megrim ['mi:grim], *n.* Emicrania, *f.*, capriccio, *m.* **Megrims,** malinconia, *f.*, malumore, *m.*
melancholia [melən'kouliə], *n.* Malinconia, *f.*
melancholic, melancholy [melən'kɔlik], *a.* Malinconico, triste, mesto.
melancholy ['melənkəli], *n.* Malinconia, tristezza, mestizia, *f.*
melanism ['melənizm], *n.* (*Bot.Zool.*) Melanismo, *m.*
melilot ['melilou], *n.* (*Bot.*) Meliloto, *m.*
melliferous [me'lifərəs], *a.* Mellifоro, mellifero.
mellifluence [me'liflu:əns], *n.* Mellifluità, *f.*
mellifluent, mellifluous, *a.* Mellifluo, dolce, melato, soave.
mellow ['melou], *a.* Maturo; polposo; generoso; brillo, alticcio. || *v.t.i.* Maturare, ammollire, ammollirsi.
mellowness, *n.* Maturità, *f.*; dolcezza, *f.*
melodeon [me'loudiən], *n.* (*Mus.*) Melodion, *m.*, fisarmonica, *f.*
melodic [me'lɔdik], *a.* (*Mus.*) Melodico.
melodious [me'loudiəs], *a.* Melodico, melodioso.
melodiously, *adv.* Melodiosamente.
melodiousness, *n.* Melodiosità, *f.*
melodist ['melədist], *n.* Melodista, *m.*
melodrama ['meloudrɑ:mə], *n.* Melodramma, *m.*; drammone sensazionale, *m.*
melodramatic [meloudrə'mætik], *a.* Melodrammatico, sensazionale.
melodramatically, *adv.* Melodrammaticamente.
melodramatist, *n.* Autore di melodrammi, *m*
melody ['meloudi], *n.* Melodia, *f.*, canto, *m.*
melon ['melən], *n.* (*Bot.*) Melone, popone, *m.* **Water- —,** cocomero, *m.*; **— -bed,** melonaio, *m.*

melt [melt], *v.t.i.* Sciogliere, fondere, liquefare, struggere; (*fig.*) intenerire, intenerirsi. **To — away,** fondersi, dissiparsi, sparire; **to — into tears,** sciogliersi in lagrime; **to — in the mouth,** sciogliersi in bocca; **to — down,** fondere.
melting, *a.* Caldo, afoso; commovente. || *n.* Fusione, liquefazione, *f.* **—-point,** punto di fusione, *m.*; **—-pot,** crogiuolo, *m.*
meltingly, *adv.* Teneramente, in modo commovente.
member [ˈmembəɹ], *n.* (*limb*) Membro, *m.*; (*of parliament*) membro, deputato, *m.*; (*of a society, club, etc.*) socio, associato, *m.*; rappresentante, *m.* **— of a congress,** congressista, *m.*
membered, *a.* Che ha membra. **Large-—,** membruto.
membership, *n.* Funzione di membro, *f.*; insieme dei membri, *m.*
membrane [ˈmembrein], *n.* (*Anat.*) Membrana, *f.*
membraneous [memˈbreiniəs], *a.* Membranaceo.
memento [meˈmentou], *n.* Memento, ricordo, *m.*
memoir [ˈmemwɑːɹ], *n.* (*Lit.*) Memoria, storia, biografia, *f.* **Memoirs,** memorie, ricordanze, *f.pl.*; ricordi, *m.pl.*
memorable [memərəbl], *a.* Memorabile.
memorably, *adv.* Memorabilmente.
memorandum (*pl.* **memoranda**) [meməˈrændəm], *n.* Nota, *f.*, appunto, avviso, promemoria, *m.* **—-book,** taccuino, *m.*, agenda, *f.*; (*Comm.*) **— of association,** atto costitutivo d'una società anonima, *m.*
memorial [meˈmɔːriəl], *n.* Ricordo, *m.*, commemorazione, memoria, *f.*; monumento, *m.*; (*petition*) memoriale, *m.* || *a.* Commemorativo, in memoria.
memorialize, *v.t.* Presentare un memoriale.
memorize [ˈmeməraiz], *v.t.* Imparare a mente, imparare a memoria; ricordare, commemorare.
memory, *n.* Memoria, ricordanza, rimembranza, *f.*, ricordo, *m.* **To have a good —,** aver buona memoria; **to have happy memories of,** serbare lieta ricordanza di; **within the — of man,** a memoria d'uomo; **from —,** a mente, a memoria; **in — of,** in memoria di, in ricordo di; **within my own —,** a mia memoria; **to the best of my —,** per quanto io me ne ricordo.
men [cp. **man**].
menace [ˈmenəs], *n.* Minaccia, *f.* || *v.t.* Minacciare. **A public —,** un malfattore pubblico, *m.*
menacing, *a.* Minaccioso, minacciante.
menacingly, *adv.* Minacciosamente.
menagerie [məˈnædʒəri], *n.* Serraglio, *m.*
mend [mend], *v.t.* Aggiustare, riparare, rattoppare, rammendare, racconciare, raccomodare, riattare; (*fig.*) migliorare, emendare, rettificare; *v.i.* migliorare, rimettersi, ristabilirsi, rasserenarsi. **To — one's ways,** cambiar vita, correggersi; **to — a fire,** racconciare il fuoco; **to — matters,** accomodar le cose; **to — one's pace,** affrettarsi.
mendable, *a.* Riparabile; emendabile, correggibile.
mendacious [menˈdeiʃəs], *a.* Mendace, bugiardo, menzognero.
mendacity [menˈdæsiti], *n.* Menzogna, mendacia, falsità, *f.*
mender, *n.* Riparatore, *m.*, riparatrice, *f.*, racconciatore, *m.*, racconciatrice, *f.*
mendicancy, mendicity [ˈmendikənsi, menˈdisiti], *n.* Mendicità, *f.*, accattonaggio, *m.*
mendicant [ˈmendikənt], *n.* Mendicante, pitocco, accattone, *m.*, pezzente, *m.f.* || *a.* Mendicante, mendico.
mending, *n.* Riparazione, aggiustatura, racconciatura, rammendatura, *f.* **I have a lot of — to do,** ho molte aggiustature da fare.
menhir [ˈmenhiəɹ], *n.* Menhir, *m.*
menial [ˈmiːniəl], *a.* Servile, domestico. || *n.* Domestico, *m.*, domestica, *f.*, servo, *m.*, serva, *f.*
meningitis [meninˈdʒaitis], *n.* (*Med.*) Meningite, *f.*
meninx [ˈmeniŋks], *n.* (*Anat.*) Meninge, *f.*
menopause [ˈmenopɔːz], *n.* Menopausa, *f.*
menorrhagia [menəˈreidziə], *n.* (*Med.*) Menorragia, *f.*
menorrhoea [menəˈriə], *n.* Menorrea, *f.*
menses [mensiːz], *f.pl.* (*Med.*) Mestrui, *m.pl.*
menstrual [ˈmenstruːəl], *a.* Mestruale.
menstruate, *v.i.* Mestruare.
menstruation, *n.* Mestruazione, *f.*
mensurable [ˈmenʃuːrəbl], *a.* Misurabile.
mensuration [mensuːˈreiʃən], *n.* Misurazione, *f.*, misuramento, *m.*
mental [ˈmental], *a.* Mentale; intellettuale. **— arithmetic,** calcolo mentale, *m.*; **— reservation,** restrizione mentale, riserva mentale, *f.*; **—-hospital,** manicomio, *m.*, casa di alienati, *f.*; **— patient,** alienato, *m.*, alienata, *f.*; **— specialist,** alienista, *m.*
mentality [menˈtæliti], *n.* Mentalità, *f.*
mentally, *adv.* Mentalmente. **— deficient,** un deficiente.
menthol [ˈmenθəl], *n.* (*Chem.*) Mentolo, *m.*
mention [ˈmenʃən], *n.* Menzione, *f.*, cenno, *m.*; allusione, *f.* || *v.t.* Menzionare, nominare, far menzione di, accennare a, dire. **He mentioned that,** egli disse che; **Don't — it!** Non ne parlate! Prego! **not to —,** tralasciando; **the above-mentioned person,** la persona sopramenzionata, *f.*; **mentioned below,** sottocitato.
mentor [ˈmentɔːɹ], *n.* Mentore, *m.*
menu [ˈmenjuː], *n.* Lista del pranzo, carta delle vivande, *f.*, menu, *m.*
Mephistophelean [mefistəˈfiːliən], *a.* Mefistofelico.
Mephistopheles [mefiˈstɔfiliːz], *n.* Mefistofele, *m.*
mephitic [meˈfitik], *a.* Mefitico.
mephitis [meˈfaitis], *n.* Mefite, *f.*
mercantile [ˈməːɹkəntail], *a.* Mercantile, commerciale. **— marine,** marina mercantile, *f.*
mercantilism, *n.* Mercantilismo, *m.*
Mercator's Projection [məɹˈkeitəɹz prouˈdʒekʃən], *n.* (*Geog.*) Carta Mercatore, *f.*
mercenariness [ˈməːɹsinərinis], *n.* Venalità, *f.*
mercenary, *a.* Mercenario, venale, prezzolato. || *n.* Mercenario, *m.*
mercer [ˈməːɹsəɹ], *n.* Merciaio, mercante di seterie, *m.*
mercerize, *v.t.* Mercerizzare.
mercerized, *a.* Mercerizzato.
merchandise [ˈməːɹtʃəndaiz], *n.* Mercanzia, merce, derrata, *f.*

merchant, *n.* Mercante, negoziante, commerciante, *m.* || *a.* Mercantile, commerciale. **The — class,** il ceto commerciale, *m.*; (*Naut.*) **— -ship, merchantman,** nave mercantile, *f.*; (*Naut.*) **— -service,** marina mercantile, *f.*; **— -tailor,** sarto negoziante, *m.*
merciful [ˈmə:ɹsifəl], *a.* Misericordioso, pietoso.
mercifully, *adv.* Misericordiosamente.
mercifulness, *n.* Misericordia, compassione, pietà, *f.*
merciless, *a.* Spietato, implacabile, inesorabile.
mercurial [mə:ɹˈkju:riəl], *a.* Mercuriale; vivace, allegro, vivo, irrequieto. **A — temperament,** un temperamento vivace, *m.*; **a — barometer,** un barometro a mercurio, *m.*
mercury [ˈmə:ɹkju:ri], *n.* (*Min.*) Mercurio, *m.*; (*Bot.*) mercuriale, *f.* (*Myth.Astron.*) **Mercury,** Mercurio, *m.*
mercy [ˈmə:ɹsi], *n.* Misericordia, compassione, pietà, clemenza, grazia, indulgenza, *f.* **At the — of,** in balia di, in potere di; **For mercy's sake!** Per grazia! **Mercy on us!** Per pietà! **left to the tender mercies of,** lasciato alle buone grazie di; (*Law*) **recommendation to —,** raccomandazione per la grazia; **Sisters of Mercy,** Suore di Carità, *f.pl.*; **to beg for —,** implorare grazia; **to have — on,** usar misericordia verso, perdonare; **— -seat,** trono di Dio, *m.*
mere (1) [miəɹ], *a.* Mero, puro, semplice; niente altro che. **By — chance,** per mero caso; **— nonsense,** niente altro che sciocchezze; **a — nothing,** niente, nulla, un nonnulla, *m.*
mere (2), *n.* Lago, stagno, laghetto, *m.*
merely, *adv.* Meramente, puramente, soltanto, solamente.
meretricious [meriˈtriʃəs], *a.* Falso, finto, artificiale, attraente.
meretriciousness, *n.* Artificio, *m.*
merge [mə:ɹdʒ], *v.t.* Confondere, mescolare, unire, fondere; *v.i.* confondersi, unirsi, fondersi. **To — into,** fondersi con.
merger, *n.* Fusione, *f.*, (*Comm.*) trust, *m.*
meridian [məˈridiən], *a.* Meridiano. || *n.* (*Geog.*) Meridiano, *m.*; (*Astron.*) meridiana, *f.*; (*fig.*) apogeo, *m.*
meridional, *a.* Meridiano.
meringue [məˈræŋ], *n.* Meringa, *f.*
merino [məˈri:nou], *n.* Merino, *m.*
merit [ˈmerit], *n.* Merito, valore, pregio, *m.* || *v.t.* Meritare. **To — well of,** meritar bene di; **to make a — of,** farsi merito di.
meritorious [meriˈtɔ:riəs], (*of actions*) Meritorio; (*of persons*) meritevole.
meritoriousness, *n.* Merito, *m.*
Merlin (1) [ˈmə:ɹlin], *n.* Merlino, *m.*
merlin (2), *n.* (*Zool.*) Smeriglio, *m.*
mermaid [ˈmə:ɹmeid], *n.* Sirena, *f.*
merman [ˈmə:ɹmən], *n.* Tritone, *m.*
merrily [ˈmerili], *adv.* Allegramente, gaiamente.
merriment, *n.* Allegria, baldoria, festevolezza, giocondità, *f.*
merry, *a.* Allegro, giocondo, festevole, faceto; brillo. **The more the merrier,** più siamo più si sta allegri; **to make —,** far festa, far baldoria; **to make — over,** farsi beffa di, ridersi di; **— -andrew,** buffone, pagliaccio, *m.*; **Merry Christmas!** Buon Natale! Felice Natale! **— -go-round,** carosello, *m.*; giostra con cavalli di legno, *f.*; **— -making,** festa, baldoria, *f.*, divertimento, *m.*; **— -thought,** sterno di pollo, *m.*
mesenteric [mesenˈterik], *a.* (*Anat.*) Mesenterico.
mesentery, *n.* (*Anat.*) Mesenterio, *m.*
mesh [meʃ], *n.* Maglia, *f.* || *v.i.* Ingranare. (*Mech.*) **In —,** in ingranaggio.
mesmeric [mezˈmerik], *a.* Mesmerico, magnetico.
mesmerism [ˈmezmərizm], *n.* Mesmerismo, *m.*
mesmerist, *n.* Mesmerista, *m.f.*
mesmerize, *v.t.* Ipnotizzare, magnetizzare.
mesocarp [mesouˈkɑ:ɹp], *n.* (*Bot.*) Mesocarpo, *m.*
mesozoic [mesouˈzouik], *a.* (*Geol.*) Mesozoico.
mess [mes], *n.* (*portion*) Piatto, *m.*, porzione, *f.*; (*Mil.Naut.*) tavola, mensa, *f.*, rancio, *m.*; (*dirt*) porcheria, sporcizia, *f.*; (*muddle*) impiccio, imbroglio, pasticcio, *m.* || *v.i.* Mangiare insieme; *v.t.* sporcare, imbrogliare. (*Mil.*) **— allowance,** indennità di mensa, *f.*; **— -tin,** gavetta, gamella, *f.*; (*fig.*) **a fine —,** un bell'imbroglio, un bel pasticcio, *m.*; **to make a — of things,** imbrogliare, arruffar le cose; **he has made a — of it,** ha fatto fiasco, ha combinato un bel pasticcio; **to — about,** gingillarsi; **to — up,** guastare, pasticciare, metter sottosopra.
message [ˈmesidʒ], *n.* Messaggio, avviso, annunzio, *m.*; commissione, *f.*
messenger [ˈmesendʒəɹ], *n.* Messaggero, messo, *m.*; corriere, *m.*
Messiah [meˈsaiə], *n.* Messia, *m.*
messianic [mesiˈænik], *a.* Messianico.
messmate [ˈmesmeit], *n.* Commensale, compagno di tavola, *m.*
Messrs. [ˈmesəɹz], *n.pl.* Signori, *m.pl.*
messuage [ˈmesju:idʒ], *n.* Casa e dipendenze, *f.pl.*
messy, *a.* Sporco, sudicio, imbrattato.
metabolic [metəˈbɔlik], *a.* Metabolico.
metabolism [meˈtæbəlizm], *n.* Metabolismo, *m.*
metacarpus [metəˈkɑ:ɹpəs], *n.* (*Anat.*) Metacarpo, *m.*
metal [metl], *n.* Metallo, *m.*; (*for roads*) brecciame, pietrisco, *m.*, ciottoli, *m.pl.* || *v.t.* (*a road*) Inghiaiare, massicciare, ricoprire con brecciame. (*Rail.*) **Metals,** rotaie, *f.pl.*
metallic [meˈtælik], *a.* Metallico.
metalliferous [metəˈlifərəs], *a.* Metallifero.
metallization, *n.* Metallizzazione, *f.*
metallize, *v.t.* Metallizzare.
metallography [metəˈlɔgrəfi], *n.* Metallografia, *f.*
metallurgist [meˈtæləɹdʒist], *n.* Metallurgico, *m.*
metallurgy [meˈtæləɹdʒi], *n.* Metallurgia, *f.*
metamorphic [metəˈmɔ:ɹfik], *a.* (*Geol.*) Metamorfico.
metamorphose [metəˈmɔ:ɹfouz], *v.t.* Metamorfosare, trasformare.
metamorphosis [metəˈmɔ:ɹfousis], *n.* Metamorfosi, *f.*
metaphor [ˈmetəfəɹ], *n.* Metafora, *f.*
metaphoric, metaphorical, *a.* Metaforico.
metaphorically, *adv.* Metaforicamente.
metaphysical [metəˈfizikəl], *a.* Metafisico.
metaphysician [metəfiˈziʃən], *n.* Metafisico, *m.*

metaphysics, *n.pl.* Metafisica, *f.*
metaplasm ['metəplæzm], *n.* Metaplasma, *m.*
metatarsus [metə'tɑːɹsəs], *n.* (*Anat.*) Metatarso, *m.*
metathesis [me'tæθisis], *n.* (*Gram.*) Metatesi, *f.*
métayage [me'teijɑːʒ], *n.* Mezzadria, *f.*
mete ['miːt], *v.t.* Misurare. **To — out justice,** distribuire la giustizia.
metempsychosis metemsai'kousis], *n.* Metempsicosi, *f.*
meteor ['miːtiəɹ], *n.* Meteora, *f.*
meteoric, *a.* Meteorico.
meteorite ['miːtiərait], *n.* Meteorite, *f.*
meteorological [miːtiərə'lɔdʒikl], *a.* Meteorologico.
meteorologist, *n.* Meteorologo, *m.*
meteorology, *n.* Meteorologia, *f.*
meter ['miːtəɹ], *n.* Contatore, misuratore, *m.* **Gas —,** contatore del gas, *m.*; **electric —,** contatore della luce elettrica, *m.*
methinks [mi'θiŋks], *v.i.* (*obs.*) Mi pare, penso che.
method ['meθəd], *n.* Metodo, *m.*; modo, *m.*, maniera, *f.*
methodical [me'θɔdikəl], *a.* Metodico; ben regolato.
methodically, *adv.* Metodicamente.
Methodism ['meθədizm], *n.* (*Eccles.*) Metodismo, *m.*
Methodist, *n.* Metodista, *m.f.*
methodize, *v.t.* Metodizzare, sistematizzare.
methyl ['meθil], *n.* (*Chem.*) Metile, *m.* **Methylated spirit,** alcool metilico, alcool denaturato, *m.*
meticulous [me'tikjuːləs], *a.* Meticoloso.
metonymy [me'tɔnimi], *n.* Metonimia, *f.*
metope ['metopi], *n.* (*Arch.*) Metope, *f.*
metre ['miːtəɹ], *n.* (*unit of length*) Metro, *m.*; (*Poet.*) metro, verso, *m.*
metric, metrical ['metrik, 'metrikəl], *a.* Metrico. **Metric system,** sistema metrico decimale, *m.*
metrics, *n.pl.* Metrica, *f.*
metrology, *n.* Metrologia, *f.*
metronome ['metrənoum], *n.* (*Mus.*) Metronomo, *m.*
metropolis [me'trɔpəlis], *n.* Metropoli, *f.*
metropolitan [metro'pɔlitən], *a.* Metropolitano. || *n.* (*Eccles.*) Metropolitano, metropolita, *m.*
mettle [metl], *n.* Fegato, coraggio, ardore, slancio, animo, *m.* **To put someone on his —,** metter qualcuno alla prova; **to show one's —,** mostrar la propria fibra.
mettlesome, *a.* Coraggioso, focoso, ardente. **A — horse,** un cavallo focoso, *m.*
mew (1) [mjuː], *n.* (*Zool.*) Gabbiano, *m.*
mew (2), *n.* (*cage*) Gabbia, *f.* || *v.t.* Rinchiudere. **To — up,** confinare, imprigionare.
mew (3), *v.i.* (*of cat*) Miagolare. || *n.* Miao, miagolio, *m.*
mewing, *n.* Miagolio, *m.*
mews [mjuːz], *n.* Scuderie, *f.pl.*, stallaggio, *m.*
Mexican ['meksikən], *n.a.* Messicano, *m.*
Mexico ['meksikou], *n.* (*Geog.*) (*country*) Il Messico, *m.*; (*city*) Messico, *f.*
mezzanine ['mezənain], *n.* (*Arch.*) Mezzanino, *m.*
mezzo-rilievo [medzourili'eivou], *n.* (*Art.*) Mezzo-rilievo, *m.*
mezzotint ['medzoutint], *n.* Acquaforte, *m.*, mezzatinta, *f.*
miaow [mi'au], *n.* Miao, *m.* || *v.i.* Miagolare.
miasma [mai'æsmə], *n.* Miasma, *m.*
miasmatic, *a.* Miasmatico.
mica ['maikə], *n.* (*Min.*) Mica, *f.* **—-schist,** micaschisto, *m.*
micaceous [mi'keiʃəs], *a.* Micaceo.
mice [cp. **mouse**].
Michael ['maikəl], *n.* Michele, *m.*
Michaelmas ['miklməs], *n.* Il San Michele, giorno di San Michele, *m.* (*Bot.*) **— daisy,** aster, astro, *m.*, ottobrina, *f.*
mickle [mikl], *n.a.* (*Scots*) Molto, un gran numero, *m.*
microbe ['maikroub], *n.* Microbo, microbio, *m.*
microbial, *a.* Microbico.
microbiology [maikroubai'ɔlədʒi], *n.* Batteriologia, *f.*
microcephalic, microcephalous [maikrouse'feilik, maikrou'sefələs], *a.* Microcefalo.
microcosm ['maikroukɔzm], *n.* Microcosmo, *m.*
micrology [mi'krɔlədʒi], *n.* Micrologia, *f.*
micrometer [mai'krɔmitəɹ], *n.* Micrometro, *m.*
microphone ['maikroufoun], *n.* Microfono, *m.*
microscope ['maikrouskoup], *n.* Microscopio, *m.*
microscopic, microscopical [maikro'skɔpic], *a.* Microscopico.
microscopically, *adv.* Microscopicamente, col microscopio.
microscopist, *n.* Microscopista, *m.*
microscopy [mai'krɔscəpi], *n.* Microscopia, *f.*
micturition [miktjuː'reiʃən], *n.* (*Med.*) Diuresi, *f.*
mid [mid], *a.* Mezzo, di mezzo. **In — career,** nel bello della carriera; **—-air,** atmosfera, *f.*, cielo, *m.*; **in —-air,** a mezz'aria; **in —-Channel,** nel mezzo della Manica; **—-Lent,** mezza Quaresima, *f.*
midday ['middei], *n.* Mezzogiorno, mezzodì, *m.* || *a.* Di mezzogiorno. **The — meal,** il pasto del mezzogiorno, *m.*
middle [midəl], *n.* Mezzo, centro, *m.*, metà, *f.*; (*waist*) vita, cintura. || *a.* Medio, intermedio, mezzano, di mezzo. **In the — of,** nel mezzo di, a metà di; **right in the — of,** nel bel mezzo di; **up to one's — in mud,** fino alla cintola nel fango; **—-age,** mezza età, *f.*; **the Middle Ages,** il Medioevo, *m.*; **of — stature,** di media statura; **the Middle Classes,** il ceto medio, *m.*, la borghesia, *f.*; **to take a — course,** prendere una via di mezzo; (*Art*) **— distance,** secondo piano; **— finger,** dito medio, *m.*; **—-sized,** di media grandezza, di media statura.
middleman, *n.* Intermediario, sensale, *m.*
middlemost [cp. **midmost**].
middling, *a.* Mediocre, passabile; (*of health*) benino; (*Comm.*) dozzinale, da dozzina. **Middlings,** cascami, *m.pl.*
middy [cp. **midshipman**].
midge ['midʒ], *n.* Moscerino, *m.*
midget ['midʒit], *n.* Nano, nanerottolo, *m.*
midland ['midlənd], *a.* Interiore, interno, centrale. **The Midlands,** regione centrale d'Inghilterra, *m.*
midmost, middlemost, *a.* Il più centrale.

midnight, *n.* Mezzanotte, *f.* || *a.* Di mezzanotte.
midrib, *n.* Nervatura mediana, *f.*
midriff, *n.* (*Anat.*) Diaframma, *m.*
midship, *n.* (*Naut.*) Centro d'un bastimento, *m.*
midshipman, middy, *n.* (*Naut.*) Aspirante di marina, *m.*
midst [midst], *n.* Mezzo, *m.* **In the — of**, fra, tra; **in our —**, fra noi.
midstream [mid'stri:m], *n.* Mezzo della corrente, *m.* **In —**, nel mezzo della corrente.
midsummer, *n.* Mezza estate, *f.*, mezzo dell'estate, *m.* **Midsummer Day**, il San Giovanni, *m.*; **Midsummer Eve**, la vigilia di San Giovanni, *f.*
midway, *adv.* A mezzo del cammino, a mezza strada, a metà strada.
midwife ['midwaif], *n.* Levatrice, ostetrica, *f.*
midwifery ['midwifri], *n.* Ostetricia, *f.*
midwinter, *n.* Cuore dell'inverno, *m.*
mien [mi:n], *n.* Aria, cera, maniera, *f.*; fare, *m.*
miff [mif], *n.* (*colloq.*) Stizza, *f.* **To get in a —**, stizzirsi.
might (1) [mait], *n.* Potere, *m.*, forza, possa, possanza, potenza, *f.* **With — and main**, con ogni possa, a corpo morto, con tutte le forze; **— versus right**, forza contro diritto.
might (2), *p.* of **may**.
mightily, *adv.* Possentemente; (*colloq.*) estremamente.
mightiness, *n.* Possanza, potenza, grandezza, *f.*
mighty, *a.* Possente, poderoso, forte; vasto, enorme, tremendo. || *adv.* (*colloq.*) Molto, estremamente. **High and —**, prepotente.
mignonette [minjə'net], *n.* (*Bot.*) Reseda, *f.*
migrant ['maigrənt], *n.* Uccello migratore, *m.* || *a.* Migratore.
migrate [mai'greit], *v.i.* Migrare.
migration, *n.* Migrazione, *f.*
migratory, *a.* Migratorio.
mikado [mi'kɑ:dou], *n.* Micado, *m.*
milage ['mailidʒ], *n.* Chilometraggio, *m.*; indennità di percorso, *f.*
Milan [mi'læn], *n.* (*Geog.*) Milano, *f.*
Milanese [milə'ni:z], *n.a.* Milanese, *m.f.*
milch [miltʃ], *a.* Lattifero. **— -cow**, mucca, vacca lattifera, vacca da latte, *f.*
mild [maild], *a.* Dolce, mite, mansueto; (*of punishment*) lieve; (*of weather*) dolce, mite; (*of medicine*) blando; (*of drink or tobacco*) leggiero.
mildew ['mildju:], *n.* Muffa, *f.*; (*on plants*) ruggine, *f.* || *v.i.* Ammuffire, prendere la ruggine; *v.t.* corrodere.
mildness, *n.* Dolcezza, leggerezza, mitezza, *f.*
mile [mail], *n.* Miglio, *m.* **A — off**, lontano un miglio.
Milesian [mai'li:ʒən], *n.a.* Irlandese, *m.f.*
milestone, *n.* Pietra miliare, *f.*
milfoil ['milfɔil], *n.* (*Bot.*) Millefoglie, *f.*
miliary ['miliəri], *a.* (*Med.*) Migliare.
militant ['militənt], *n.a.* Militante, *m.f.*
militarism, *n.* Militarismo, *m.*
militarist, *n.* Militarista, *m.*
military, *a.* Militare. || *n.* I militari, *m.pl.* **— law**, codice militare, *m.*; **a — man**, un militare, *m.*
militarize, *v.t.* Militarizzare.
militarization, *n.* Militarizzazione, *f.*
militate, *v.i.* Militare. **To — against**, militare contro.
militia [mi'liʃə], *n.* Milizia, *f.*
militiaman, *n.* Milite, *m.*
milk [milk], *n.* Latte, *m.* || *v.t.* Mungere. (*fig.*) **— and water**, insipido, sciocco; **skim- —**, latte scremato, *m.*; **condensed —**, latte condensato, *m.* **— -chocolate**, cioccolata al latte, *f.*; **a — diet**, una dieta lattea, *f.*; **— -can**, vaso da latte, pentolino da latte, *m.*; **— -fever**, febbre di latte, *f.*; **— -jug**, lattiera, *f.*; **— -pail**, secchio da latte, *m.*; **— -tooth**, dente di latte, *m.*; **— -white**, bianco come il latte; **to give —**, allattare.
milker, *n.* (*person*) Mungitore, *m.*, mungitrice, *f.*; (*cow*) vacca da latte, *f.*
milkiness, *n.* Lattiginosità, *f.*
milking, *n.* Mungitura, *f.*
milkmaid, *n.* Lattaia, *f.*
milkman, *n.* Lattaio, lattivendolo, *m.*
milksop, *n.* Uomo effeminato, *m.*
milkwoman, *n.* Lattaia, lattivendola, *f.*
milky, *a.* Latteo. **The Milky Way**, la Via Lattea, *f.*
mill [mil], *n.* Mulino, *m.*; fabbrica, *f.*, opificio, *m.*; (*cotton*) filanda, *f.* || *v.t.* (*corn, etc.*) Macinare; (*cloth*) follare, feltrare; (*a coin*) granire; *v.i.* (*of cattle*) attrupparsi; (*to fight*) prendere a pugni. **— -board**, cartone, cartone forte, *m.*; **— -dam**, cateratta, chiusa d'un mulino, *f.*; **— -pond**, gora del mulino, *f.*; **— -race**, corrente del mulino, *m.*; **— -owner**, proprietario di mulino, proprietario di fabbrica, *m.*; **— -hand**, operaio, *m.*, operaia, *f.*; **to bring grist to the —**, tirare l'acqua al mulino.
milled, *a.* (*cloth*) Follato; (*grain*) macinato; (*coin*) granito.
millenarian [mili'nɛəriən], *n.a.* Millenario, *m.*
millenarianism, *n.* Fede nel Millennio, *f.*
millenary, *n.* Millenario.
millennial, *a.* Millenne.
millennium, *n.* Il Millennio, *m.*
millepede ['milipi:d], *n.* (*Zool.*) Millepiedi, *m.*
miller, *n.* Mugnaio, *m.* **The miller's wife**, la mugnaia, *f.*
millesimal [mi'lezimәl], *n.a.* Millesimo, *m.*
millet ['milit], *n.* (*Bot.*) Miglio, *m.*
milliard ['miliərd], *n.* Miliardo, *m.*
milliner ['milinəɹ], *n.* Modista, crestaia, *f.* **Milliner's shop**, modisteria, *f.*
millinery, *n.* Generi di modisteria, *m.pl.*
milling, *n.* (*flour*) Macinatura, *f.*; (*cloth*) feltratura, *f.*; (*metal*) fresatura, *f.*; (*ore*) martellatura, *f.*; (*coin*) granitura, *f.*
million, *n.* Milione, *m.* **The —**, il popolo, *m.*, la massa, *f.*
millionaire [miliən'ɛəɹ], *n.* Milionario, *m.* **A multi- —**, un miliardario, *m.*
millionth, *n.a.* Milionesimo, *m.*
millstone, *n.* Macina, *f.*
milt [milt], *n.* (*in animals*) Milza, *f.*; (*fish*) latte di pesce, *m.*
mime [maim], *n.* (*Theat.*) Mimo, *m.*, mima, *f.* || *v.i.* Imitare, esprimersi coi gesti.
mimetic [mi'metik], *a.* Mimetico.
mimic ['mimik], *n.* Mimo, imitatore, *m.*, mima, imitatrice, *f.* || *a.* Mimico, imitativo. || *v.t.* Imitare, contraffare, scimmiottare.
mimicry, *n.* Mimica, pantomima, imitazione, parodia, *f.*; (*Zool.*) mimetismo, *m.*, mimesi, *f.*
mimosa [mi'mouzə], *n.* (*Bot.*) Mimosa, *f.*
mimulus ['mimju:ləs], *n.* (*Bot.*) Mimolo, *m.*

minaret [ˈminəret], *n.* Minareto, *m.*
minatory [ˈminətəri], *a.* Minatorio.
mince [mins], *v.t.* Tagliuzzare, tritare, sminuzzare; *v.i.* parlare affettato, far lo smorfioso, far smancerie, camminare impettito. || *n.* Carne tritata, *f.* **— -pie,** tortina di frutta; **mincemeat,** miscuglio di frutta secca, mele, ecc., *m.*; (*fig.*) **to make mincemeat of,** fare una frittata di, stritolare.
mincing, *a.* Affettato, manierato, lezioso. **— -machine,** tritacarne, *m.*
mind [maind], *n.* Mente, intelligenza, *f.*, intelletto, *m.*; voglia, inclinazione, volontà, *f.*; opinione, *f.*, parere, *m.*; memoria, *f.* || *v.t.i.* Badare, attendere, considerare; custodire, curare; stare attento, star in guardia; importare. **To keep in —,** tenere in mente; **to call to —,** rammentarsi di; **to speak one's —,** parlare chiaro e tondo; **time out of —,** da tempo immemorabile; **to give someone a piece of one's —,** cantarla chiara e tonda, dirne quattro, vuotare il sacco; **to be of one —,** essere d'accordo; **to my —,** a mio parere; **to know one's own —,** saper bene ciò che si vuole; **to make up one's —,** decidersi; **to change one's —,** cambiar d'opinione, cangiar mente; **to have a good — to,** esser disposto a; **to have half a — to,** essere mezzo disposto a; **to set one's — on,** mettersi in testa di; **to give one's — to,** dar mente a; **it is not to my —,** non mi piace, non è di mio genio; **a frame of —, a state of —,** uno stato d'animo, *m.*; **the mind's eye,** gli occhi della mente; **it has quite gone out of my —,** mi è proprio scappato dalla mente; **of sound —,** sano di mente; **to be out of one's —,** essere fuori di sè, aver perso la ragione; **that puts me in — of,** ciò mi rammenta di; **Never —!** Non importa! **I do not — the expense,** non bado alle spese; **he does not — what anyone says,** non gli importa ciò che si dice; **Do you — helping me a little?** Volete avere la gentilezza di aiutarmi un po? **if you don't —,** se non vi dispiace; **Mind what you are about!** State attenti a ciò che fate! **Mind your own business!** Badate ai fatti vostri! **Never — him!** Non badate a lui! **I should not — at all,** non me ne darei il minimo pensiero; **I shouldn't — a cup of tea,** non mi spiacerebbe una tazza di tè; **Mind and bring me that book!** Rammentatevi di portarmi quel libro!
minded, *a.* Disposto a, incline a; di mente. **If you are so —,** se siete disposto; **right- —,** di mente retta.
mindful, *a.* Attento a, sollecito di.
mindfulness, *n.* Attenzione, sollecitudine, *f.*
mine (1) [main], *pron. poss.* Il mio, *m.*, la mia, *f.*, i miei, *m.pl.*, le mie, *f.pl.*; mio, *m.*, mia, *f.*, miei, *m.pl.*, mie, *f.pl.* **A book of —,** un mio libro, *m.*; **this is —,** questo è mio.
mine (2), *n.* Miniera, *f.*; (*Mil.Naut.*) mina, *f.* || *v.t.* Scavare; minare. **— -layer,** posamine, *m.*; **— -sweeper,** dragamine, spazzamine, *m.*; **— -crater,** cavità, *f.*
miner, *n.* Minatore, *m.*
mineral [ˈminərəl], *n.a.* Minerale, *m.* **— water,** acqua minerale, acqua gazosa, *f.*
mineralization, *n.* Mineralizzazione, *f.*
mineralize, *v.t.* Mineralizzare.
mineralogical, *a.* Mineralogico.
mineralogist, *n.* Mineralogista, mineralogo, *m.*
mineralogy, *n.* Mineralogia, *f.*
mingle [ˈmiŋgəl], *v.t.* Mescolare, mischiare, confondere; *v.i.* mescolarsi, mischiarsi, confondersi, unirsi. **To — with,** mescolarsi a.
mingling [ˈmiŋgliŋ], *n.* Mescolamento, miscuglio, *m.*, mescolanza, miscela, mistura, commistione, *f.*
mingy [ˈmindʒi], *a.* (*colloq.*) Spilorcio.
miniature [ˈminiətʃəɹ], *n.* Miniatura, *f.*, ritratto in miniatura, *m.* || *a.* In miniatura, in piccolo.
miniaturist, *n.* Miniaturista, *m.f.*
minim [ˈminim], *n.* (*Med.*) Goccia, *f.*; (*Mus.*) minima, *f.*
minimize, *v.t.* Ridurre al minimo, attenuare.
minimum (*pl.* **minima**), *n.* Minimo, *m.*
mining [ˈmainiŋ], *n.* Sfruttamento delle miniere, *m.*; scavi di miniere, *m.pl.* || *a.* Minerario, di miniera. **— industry,** industria mineraria, *f.*; **— -engineer,** ingegnere minerario, *m.*
minion [ˈminiən], *n.* Favorito, schiavo, *m.*; (*Print.*) mignone, *m.* **— of the Law,** assistente giudiziario, *m.*
minister [ˈministəɹ], *n.* Ministro, *m.*; ambasciatore, *m.*; (*Eccles.*) pastore, *m.* || *v.t.* Servire a; contribuire a; (*Eccles.*) ufficiare, celebrare. **Ministering angel,** angelo di bontà, *m.*; **— of State,** ministro di Stato, *m.*; **to — to,** venire in soccorso a; **to — to someone's wants,** provvedere ai bisogni di qualcuno.
ministerial [minisˈtiəriəl], *a.* Ministeriale.
ministration, *n.* Somministrazione, *f.*; servigio, aiuto, intervento, *m.*
ministry, *n.* Ministero, *m.*; sacerdozio, *m.*
miniver, minever [ˈminivəɹ], *n.* (*Zool.*) Vaio, *m.*; pelliccia di vaio, *f.*
mink [miŋk], *n.* (*Zool.*) Visone, *m.*; pelliccia di visone, *f.*
minnow [ˈminou], *n.* (*Zool.*) Pesciolino, ghiozzetto, *m.*
minor [ˈmainəɹ], *a.* Minore, più piccolo, di second'ordine; minuto, piccolo; poco importante. || *n.* Minore, minorenne, *m.f.*; (*Mus.*) minore, *m.* **In a — key,** in tono minore; **Friar Minor,** Frate Minore, *m.*
minority [miˈnɔɹiti], *n.* Minorità, *f.*; minoranza, *f.*; età minore, *f.*
Minotaur [ˈminotɔːɹ], *n.* (*Myth.*) Minotauro, *m.*
minster [ˈminstəɹ], *n.* Cattedrale, *f.*, duomo, *m.*; badia, *f.*
minstrel [ˈminstrəl], *n.* (*Hist.*) Giullare, menestrello, *m.*; cantore, *m.*
minstrelsy, *n.* Giulleria, *f.*; canzoni giulleresche, *f.pl.*
mint (1) [mint], *n.* (*Bot.*) Menta, *f.* **— -sauce,** salsa di menta, *f.*
mint (2), *n.* Zecca, *f.*; (*fig.*) tesoro, *m.* || *v.t.* Coniare, monetare, batter moneta. **To have a — of money,** aver una miniera d'oro; **Master of the Mint,** Direttore della Zecca, *m.*
mintage, *n.* Conio, *m.*
minter, *n.* Coniatore, *m.*
minuet [minjuːˈet], *n.* (*Mus.*) Minuetto, *m.*
minus [ˈmainəs], *a. prep.* Meno, privo, mancante; negativo. || *n.* Meno, *m.* **A — quantity,** una quantità negativa, *f.*; **four — two,** quattro meno due; **— sign,** segno di sottrazione, *m.*

minuscule ['minəskju:l], *n.a.* Minuscolo, *m.*
minute (1) [mai'nju:t], *a.* Minuto, esiguo, piccolissimo; minuzioso, meticoloso, scrupoloso, dettagliato.
minute (2) ['minit], *n.* (*of time*) Minuto, momento, istante, *m.*; (*record*) minuta, nota, *f.*; processo verbale, *m.* || *v.t.* Minutare, fare la minuta di. **In a —,** in un istante, in un subito; **this —,** immediatamente; **I expect him every —,** lo aspetto da un momento all'altro; **to make a — of,** far la minuta di; **to draw up the minutes,** scrivere il verbale, stendere il verbale; **— -book,** libro di verbale, *m.*; **— -hand** (*of clock*), lancetta dei minuti, *f.*; **— -gun,** cannonata a salve, *f.*
minutely [mai'nju:tli], *adv.* Minutamente, minuziosamente.
minuteness [mai'nju:tnis], *n.* Minutezza, esiguità, *f.*; minuziosità, meticolosità, scrupolosità, *f.*
minutia (*pl.* **minutiae**) [min'ju:ʃə], *n.* Minuzia, *f.*
minx [miŋks], *n.* Civetta, fraschetta, birichina, birbona, *f.*
minxish, *a.* Come una birbona.
Miocene ['maiosi:n], *n.* (*Geol.*) Miocene, *m.*
miracle ['mirəkəl], *n.* Miracolo, *m.*, meraviglia, *f.* **By a —,** per miracolo; **— -play,** sacra rappresentazione, *f.*, mistero, *m.*
miraculous [mi'rækju:ləs], *a.* Miracoloso, meraviglioso.
miraculously, *adv.* Miracolosamente.
miraculousness, *n.* Miracolosità, *f.*
mirage [mi'rɑ:ʒ], *n.* Miraggio, *m.*
mire [maiɹ], *n.* Melma, mota, *f.*, fango, *m.* || *v.t.* Infangare, inzaccherare, sporcare di mota. **To sink in the —,** affondare nel fango.
miriness ['mairinis], *n.* Fangosità, immondizia, *f.*
mirror ['mirəɹ], *n.* Specchio, *m.*, psiche, *f.* || *v.t.* Rispecchiare, riflettere.
mirth [mə:ɹθ], *a.* Allegria, baldoria, *f.*; riso, chiasso, *m.*
mirthful, *a.* Allegro, gaio, festivo, chiassoso, ridente.
mirthfully, *adv.* Allegramente.
mirthfulness, *n.* Allegria, *f.*
miry ['mairi], *a.* Melmoso, fangoso.
misadventure, *n.* Sfortuna, *f.*, infortunio, *m.*; contrattempo, *m.*, disgrazia, *f.*
misalliance, *n.* Matrimonio sconveniente, *m.*, unione sfortunata, *f.*
misanthrope, misanthropist ['misənθroup, mi'sænθrəpist], *n.* Misantropo, *m.*
misanthropic, misanthropical, *a.* Misantropico.
misanthropy [mi'sænθrəpi], *n.* Misantropia, *f.*
misapplication, *n.* Uso erroneo, *m.*; (*of funds*) uso abusivo, *m.*
misapply, *v.t.* Usare abusivamente, usare erroneamente. **To — a sum of money,** distrarre una somma di danaro.
misapprehend, *v.t.* Fraintendere.
misapprehension, *n.* Malinteso, equivoco, *m.*
misappropriate, *v.t.* Appropriarsi fraudolentemente; dilapidare.
misappropriation, *n.* Appropriazione indebita, *f.*
misbecome, *v.t.* Sconvenire a, star male a.
misbecoming, *a.* Sconveniente, indegno.
misbegotten, *a.* Illegittimo; malnato, malcreato, sciagurato.
misbehave, *v.i.* Condursi male, comportarsi male.
misbehaviour, *n.* Cattiva condotta, villania, *f.*
misbelief, *n.* Miscredenza, empietà, *f.*
misbeliever, *n.* Miscredente, empio, *m.*
misbelieving, *a.* Miscredente, empio.
miscalculate, *v.t.* Calcolare male.
miscalculation, *n.* Calcolo sbagliato, errore di calcolo, *m.*
miscall, *v.t.* Dare un nome sbagliato a, chiamare impropriamente.
miscarriage, *n.* Insuccesso, fallimento, *m.*; (*Med.*) aborto, *m.*; (*of letter*) disguido, *m.* **— of justice,** smarrimento giudiziario, *m.*
miscarry, *v.i.* Fallire, mancare allo scopo; (*Med.*) abortire; (*of letter*) smarrirsi.
miscasting, *n.* Errore di calcolo, *m.*; (*Theat.*) distribuzione erronea delle parti, *f.*
miscellanea [misə'leiniə], *n.* Miscellanea, *f.*
miscellaneous [misə'leiniəs], *a.* Miscellaneo; diversi.
miscellanist [mi'selənist], *n.* (*Lit.*) Autore di miscellanea, *m.*
miscellany [mi'seləni], *n.* Miscellanea, mescolanza, *f.*
mischance, *n.* Sfortuna, disgrazia, *f.*, infortunio, *m.*
mischief ['mistʃif], *n.* Male, malfare, danno, torto, *m.*; malizia, cattiveria, *f.*; discordia, *f.*; birichinata, *f.* **To make —,** metter male, creare dei guai; **— -maker,** mettimale, accattabrighe, *m.f.*; **— -making,** *a.* intrigante, arruffone, *n.*, malignità, *f.*, il metter male, *m.*; **the — of it is that,** il male è che, il guaio è che; **out of pure —,** per pura cattiveria; **to get into —,** fare delle birichinate; **to do —,** far male; **he means —,** vuol fare un tiro birbone.
mischievous ['mistʃivəs], *a.* Nocivo, dannoso; malizioso, furbo; (*child*) birichino.
mischievousness, *n.* Maliziosità, furberia, *f.*
miscible ['misibl], *a.* Mescolabile.
misconceive, *v.t.i.* Giudicar male; fraintendere.
misconception, *n.* Idea erronea, idea sbagliata, *f.*, fraintendimento, malinteso, *m.*
misconduct [mis'kɔndəkt], *n.* Cattiva condotta, *f.*; adulterio, *m.* || *v.t.* [miskən'dʌkt] Condurre male, dirigere male. **To — oneself,** condursi male.
misconstruction, *n.* Interpretazione erronea, *f.*, controsenso, *m.*
misconstrue, *v.t.* Interpretare male, interpretare in cattivo senso; fraintendere.
miscount, *v.t.* Contar male. || *n.* Conto sbagliato, *m.*
miscreant ['miskriənt], *n.* Scellerato, malvagio, briccone, *m.*
miscue, *n.* (*Billiards*) Colpo sbagliato, *m.*
misdate, *v.t.* Mettere una data erronea.
misdeal, *v.t.* (*Cards*) Distribuire male. || *n.* Distribuzione erronea, *f.*
misdeed, *n.* Misfatto, *m.*
misdeliver, *v.t.* Distribuire in errore, distribuire a un indirizzo sbagliato.

For pronunciation of words with prefix "mis" see the root words in their proper place in the dictionary.

misdemeanant [misdi'mi:nənt], *n.* Trasgressore, *m.*
misdemeanour [misdi'mi:nəɹ], *n.* Trasgressione, offesa, *f.*, fallo, *m.*
misdirect, *v.t.* Informar male, disorientare; (*of letters*) sbagliare l'indirizzo di.
misdirection, *n.* Indicazione erronea, *f.*; (*of a jury*) il traviare la giuria, *m.*
misdoing, *n.* Misfatto, *m.*
miser ['maizəɹ], *n.* Avaro, *m.*, avara, *f.*
miserable ['mizərəbl], *a.* Misero, afflitto, disgraziato; meschino, miserabile, povero. **To make someone's life —,** rendere misera la vita a qualcuno.
miserably, *adv.* Miserabilmente, meschinamente.
misere [mi'zɛəɹ], *n.* (*Cards*) Miseria, *f.*
miserere [mizə'riəri], *n.* (*Eccles.*) Miserere, *m.*
misericord ['mizərikɔ:ɹd], *n.* Misericordia, *f.*
miserly ['maizəɹli], *a., adv.* Avaro, tirchio, taccagno, sordido.
misery ['mizəri], *n.* Infelicità; miseria, *f.*; tormento, supplizio, *m.*; povertà, indigenza, *f.* **To put a cat out of its —,** metter fine alle sofferenze d'un gatto.
misestimate, *v.t.* Apprezzar male.
misfeasance [mis'fi:zəns], *n.* (*Law*) Abuso di autorità, *m.*
misfire, *v.i.* Scattare a vuoto, fallire il colpo, far cilecca. || *n.* Scatto a vuoto, *m.*, cilecca, *f.*
misfit, *n.* Abito che non calza, *m.*; (*fig.*) pesce fuor d'acqua, *m.*
misfortune, *n.* Sfortuna, sventura, *f.*, infortunio, *m.*; disgrazia, *f.*; male, malanno, *m.* **Misfortunes never come singly,** un male attira l'altro.
misgive, *v.t.* Ispirare sospetto a, inspirare paura a. **My mind misgives me that,** ho un presentimento che.
misgiving, *n.* Presentimento, dubbio, timore, *m.*
misgovern, *v.t.* Governar male, amministrar male.
misgovernment, *n.* Malgoverno, *m.*, cattiva amministrazione, *f.*
misguidance, *n.* Traviamento, pervertimento, *m.*
misguide, *v.t.* Corrompere, traviare, pervertire.
misguided, *a.* Traviato, pervertito, fuorviato.
mishap [mis'hæp], *n.* Infortunio, *m.*, disgrazia, *f.*; contrattempo, *m.*
mishear [mis'hiəɹ], *v.t.* Udire male, intendere male.
misinform, *v.t.* Informare male, dare informazioni false a, fuorviare.
misinformation, *n.* Informazioni false, notizie false, *f.pl.*
misinformed, *a.* Mal informato.
misinterpret, *v.t.* Interpretare male, interpretare in cattivo senso, fraintendere.
misinterpretation, *n.* Falsa interpretazione, *f.*, controsenso, *m.*
misjudge, *v.t.* Giudicar male; formare un'idea falsa di.
misjudgment, *n.* Giudizio erroneo, *m.*
mislay, *v.t.* Smarrire.
mislead, *v.t.* Sviare, traviare, fuorviare; ingannare, indurre in errore.
misleading, *a.* Ingannevole, ingannatore, disorientante, sconcertante.
mismanage, *v.t.* Dirigere male, amministrar male.
mismanagement, *n.* Cattiva amministrazione, *f.*
misnamed, *a.* Chiamato a torto, denominato erroneamente.
misnomer [mis'noumaɹ], *n.* Errore di nome, nome falso, *m.*; termine improprio, *m.*
misogamist [mai'sɔgəmist], *n.* Misogamo, *m.*
misogynist [mai'sɔdʒənist], *n.* Misogino, *m.*
misogyny [mai'sɔdʒəni], *n.* Misoginia, *f.*
misplace, *v.t.* Collocar male, spostare. **Misplaced affections,** amore male speso, *m.*
misplacement, *n.* Spostamento, *m.*
misprint ['misprint], *n.* Errore di stampa, errore tipografico, refuso, *m.*
misprision [mis'priʒən], *n.* (*Law*) Connivenza, *f.*
misprize, *v.t.* Sprezzare, svalutare.
mispronounce, *v.t.* Pronunciare male.
mispronunciation, *n.* Pronuncia scorretta, *f.*
misquotation, *n.* Citazione scorretta, citazione sbagliata, *f.*
misquote, *v.t.* Citare scorrettamente.
misreckon, *v.t.* Calcolar male.
misreckoning, *n.* Errore di calcolo, *m.*
misreport, *v.t.* Riferire inesattamente.
misrepresent, *v.t.* Travisare, svisare, storcere, snaturare.
misrepresentation, *n.* Travisamento, *m.*
misrule, *n.* Malgoverno, *m.*
Miss (1) [mis], *n.* Signorina, *f.*
miss (2), *n.* Colpo mancato, fallo, colpo a vuoto, *m.* || *v.t.i.* Mancare, tralasciare, omettere; perdere, smarrire, non trovare più; rimpiangere, sentir la mancanza di; fallire il segno, sgarrare. **I — my friend terribly,** mi sento sperso senza l'amico mio; **he missed the train,** perdette il treno; **no one will — him,** nessuno lo rimpiangerà; **to — the mark,** fallire il colpo; **to — out,** omettere, tralasciare; **to be missing,** mancare; **he missed writing last week,** la settimana passata tralasciò di scrivere; **to — the point,** tralasciare l'essenziale.
missal ['misəl], *n.* (*Eccles.*) Messale, *m.*
missel thrush ['misəl θrʌʃ], *n.* (*Zool.*) Tordella, *f.*
misshapen [mis'ʃeipən], *a.* Deforme.
missile ['misail], *n.* Proiettile, *m.*
missing, *a.* Mancante, perduto; (*after battle*) disperso; assente. **There is a page —,** manca una pagina; **to be —,** mancare, esser disperso; **the — link,** l'anello mancante, *m.*
mission ['miʃən], *n.* Missione, *f.*, mandato, scopo, *m.*; ambasciata, *f.* **To have a — in life,** avere una missione nella vita.
missionary, *n.* Missionario, *m.*, missionaria, *f.* || *a.* Missionario.
missioner, *n.* Missionario, *m.*
missive ['misiv], *a.* Missiva, lettera, *f.*
misspell [mis'spel], *v.t.* Compitar male.
misspelling, *n.* Errore di ortografia, *m.*
misspend [mis'spend], *v.t.* Spendere male, sprecare, vivere male.
misspent, *a.* (*of life*) Mal vissuta.
misstate [mis'steit], *v.t.* Riferir male, travisare.

For pronunciation of words with prefix "mis" see the root words in their proper place in the dictionary.

misstatement, *n.* Affermazione sbagliata, una cosa per l'altra, una bugia, *f.*
mist [mist], *n.* Nebbia, nebbietta, nebbiolina, *f.*; (*at sea*) foschia, *f.*
mistakable [mi'steikəbl], *a.* Confondibile, scambiabile.
mistake [mi'steik], *n.* Sbaglio, errore, fallo, *m.*; (*oversight*) svista, *f.*; (*blunder*) cantonata, *f.*; strafalcione, sproposito, *m.* || *v.t.* Errare, sbagliare; intender male, scambiare, ingannarsi su, confondere. **To be mistaken,** sbagliare, sbagliarsi, errare, ingannarsi; **he mistook her for me,** la scambiò per me; **if I — not,** se non sbaglio, se non mi sbaglio; **there is no mistaking the fact that,** non si può negare il fatto che; **to make a terrible —,** prendere una cantonata; **And no —!** E non si sbaglia! **by —,** per isbaglio, per errore; **to make a —,** commettere uno sbaglio; **Make no —!** Non vi ingannate!
mistaken, *a.* Sbagliato, erroneo, falso, errato. **It is a — kindness,** è gentilezza fuori di proposito, è un eccesso di bontà.
Mister, Mr. ['mistəɹ], *n.* Signore, Signor, *m.*
mistime [mis'taim], *v.t.* Sbagliare il momento per.
mistimed, *a.* Inopportuno, intempestivo.
mistiness ['mistinis], *n.* Nebbiosità, *f.*
mistletoe ['misəltou], *n.* (*Bot.*) Vischio, *m.*
mistral ['mistrəl], *n.* (*wind*) Maestrale, *m.*
mistranslate, *v.t.* Tradurre male, tradurre erroneamente.
mistranslation, *n.* Traduzione inesatta, versione errata, *f.*, errore di traduzione, *m.*
mistress ['mistris], *n.* (*of house*) Padrona, *f.*; (*teacher*) maestra, *f.*; (*lover*) amante, *f.* **To be — of the situation,** dominar la situazione; **to be one's own —,** essere padrona di sè stessa, essere indipendente; **head- —,** direttrice, *f.*
mistrust, *v.t.* Diffidare di, non fidarsi di, sospettare. || *n.* Diffidenza, sfiducia, *f.*, sospetto, *m.*
mistrustful, *a.* Diffidente, timoroso; sospettoso.
mistrustfulness, *n.* Diffidenza, *f.*
misty, *a.* Nebbioso, vaporoso; (*fig.*) oscuro, vago, confuso.
misunderstand, *v.t.* Fraintendere, capir male, intender male, ingannarsi su, prender in senso erroneo.
misunderstanding, *n.* Malinteso, equivoco, *m.*; disaccordo, *m.* **To give rise to misunderstandings,** far nascere malintesi; **to clear up a —,** chiarire un malinteso.
misunderstood, *a.* Incompreso.
misuse [mis'ju:s], *n.* Abuso, cattivo uso, *m.*; maltrattamento, bistrattamento, *m.* || *v.t.* [mis'ju:z] Abusare di, far cattivo uso di; maltrattare, bistrattare.
mite [mait], *n.* (*child*) Piccino, *m.*, piccina, *f.*; (*little bit*) pochino, *m.*; (*coin*) obolo, *m.*; (*Zool.*) baco, acaro, *m.*
mitigate ['mitigeit], *v.t.* Mitigare, lenire, disacerbare, alleviare.
mitigation, *n.* Mitigazione, *f.*, lenimento, alleviamento, *m.*
mitre ['maitəɹ], *n.* (*Eccles.*) Mitra, mitria, *f.*; (*Carpenter's*) ugnatura, *f.* || *v.t.* Commettere a ugna, commettere a triangolo. **— -joint,** ugna, ugnatura, *f.*
mitred, *a.* Mitrato; ugnato.
mitt, mitten [mit, mitn], *n.* Mezzo guanto, *m.*
mittimus ['mitiməs], *n.* (*Law*) Mandato di cattura, *m.*
mix [miks], *v.t.i.* Mischiare, mescolare, confondere, frammischiare; mischiarsi, mescolarsi. **To get mixed up with,** esser coinvolto in; **I won't be mixed up in it,** non mi ci mischio, non ho nulla a che vederci.
mixed, *a.* Misto, mescolato; (*fig.*) promiscuo, confuso; (*Chem.*) composto. **— marriage,** matrimonio misto, *m.*; **— school,** scuola mista, *f.*; **— bathing,** bagni misti, *m.pl.*; (*Tennis*) **— double,** doppio misto, *m.*; **— metaphor,** metafora incoerente, *f.*
mixture ['mikstʃəɹ], *n.* Mistura, mescolanza, *f.*, miscuglio, *m.*; (*Med.*) mistura, pozione, *f.*; (*blend*) miscela, *f.*
mizen, mizzen ['mizən], *n.* (*Naut.*) Mezzana. **— -mast,** albero di mezzana, *m.*; **— -top,** contromezzana, *m.*; **— -sail,** mezzana, vela di mezzana, *f.*
mizzle ['mizəl], *v.i.* Piovigginare; (*colloq.*) scappare. || *n.* Pioggerella, pioggia fine, *f.*
mnemonic [ne'mɔnik], *a.* Mnemonico.
mnemonics, *n.pl.* Mnemonica, *f.*
mo' [mou], *n.* (*colloq. abbrev.* **moment**) Momentino, *m.*
moan [moun], *n.* Lamento, gemito, *m.*; pianto, *m.* || *v.i.* Gemere, piangere, lamentarsi. **The moans of the wounded,** i gemiti dei feriti, *m.pl.*
moat [mout], *n.* Fosso, fossato, *m.* || *v.t.* Circondare di un fosso.
mob [mɔb], *n.* Folla, calca, moltitudine, *f.*; popolaccio, *m.*, plebe, plebaglia, marmaglia, *f.* || *v.t.* Attaccare, assalire, linciare; *v.i.* affollarsi, accalcarsi. **— -law,** legge della folla, *f.*, linciaggio, *m.*
mob-cap, *n.* Specie di cuffia, *m.*
mobile ['moubail], *a.* Mobile.
mobility, *a.* Mobilità, *f.*
mobilization [mɔbilai'zeiʃən], *n.* Mobilitazione, *f.*
mobilize, *v.t.* Mobilitare, mobilizzare.
moccasin ['mɔkəsin], *n.* Moccasino, *m.*, babbuccia, *f.*
Mocha ['moukə], *n.* (*Geog.*) Moca, *f.* **— coffee,** moca, caffè moca, *m.*
mock [mɔk], *v.t.i.* Beffarsi di, deridere, burlarsi di, prendersi giuoco di; ingannare, deludere, (*imitate*) scimmiottare. || *a.* Falso, imitato, contraffatto. **To — at,** schernire, deridere, dileggiare; **— -heroic,** eroicomico; **— -sun,** parelio, *m.*; **— -turtle soup,** minestra di testa di vitello, *f.*
mocker, *n.* Schernitore, dileggiatore, beffatore, burlone, *m.*
mockery, *n.* Scherno, dileggio, *m.*, derisione, *f.*; scimmiottatura, *f.*; ludibrio, *m.*
mocking, *a.* Derisorio, beffardo. (*Zool.*) **— -bird,** mimo, merlo poliglotta, *m.*
modal ['moudəl], *a.* (*Gram.Mus.*) Modale.
modality [mou'dæliti], *n.* Modalit à, *f.*
mode [moud], *n.* (*method*) Modo, *m.*, maniera, *f.*; (*fashion*) moda, *f.*; (*Mus.*) modo, *m.*

For pronunciation of words with prefix "mis" see the root words in their proper place in the dictionary.

model ['mɔdəl], *n.* Modello, esempio, *m.*; campione, *m.*; tipo, *m.* || *v.t.* Modellare; (*in clay*) plasmare. **To — oneself on,** modellarsi su, conformarsi a, seguire come esempio.
modeller, *n.* Modellatore, *m.*, modellatrice, *f.*
modelling, *n.* Modellatura, *f.*
moderate (1) ['mɔdərit], *a.* Moderato, temperato; parco, modico, discreto. || *n.* (*Pol.*) Moderato, *m.*
moderate (2) ['mɔdəreit], *v.t.i.* Moderare, temperare, mitigare; presedere. **To — oneself,** moderarsi, contenersi.
moderateness, *n.* Moderatezza, *f.*
moderation, *n.* Moderazione, temperanza, misura, *f.* **In —,** con moderazione; **Moderations,** esame preliminare di laurea all'università di Oxford, *m.*
moderator, *n.* Moderatore, *m.*; (*Eccles.*) presidente della chiesa Presbiteriana, *m.*
modern ['mɔdəɹn], *n.a.* Moderno, *m.* **— language,** lingua vivente, lingua moderna, *f.*
modernism, *n.* Modernismo, *m.*
modernist, *n.* Modernista, *m.*
modernity, *n.* Modernità, *f.*
modernization, *n.* Rimodernamento, *m.*, modernizzazione, *f.*
modernize, *v.t.* Modernizzare, rimodernare.
modernness, *n.* Modernità, *f.*
modest ['mɔdist], *a.* Modesto; pudico; onesto; parco, semplice.
modestly, *adv.* Modestamente; semplicemente.
modesty, *n.* Modestia, *f.*
modicum ['mɔdikəm], *n.* Pochino, *m.*, piccola quantità, porzioncella, *f.*
modifiable [mɔdi'faiəbl], *a.* Modificabile.
modification, *n.* Modificazione, modifica, *f.*
modificative, *a.* Modificativo.
modify, *v.t.* Modificare.
modillion [mɔ'diliən], *n.* (*Arch.*) Modiglione, *f.*
modish ['moudiʃ], *a.* Alla moda, di moda, elegante.
modishly, *adv.* Alla moda.
modishness, *n.* Eleganza, *f.*
modulate ['mɔdju:leit], *v.t.* Modulare.
modulating, *a.* Modulante.
modulation, *n.* Modulazione, *f.*
module ['mɔdju:l], *n.* (*Arch.*) Modulo, *m.*
modus operandi ['moudəs ɔpə'rændai], *n.* Modo d'operazione, *m.*
Mogul [mo'gʌl], *n.* (*Hist.*) Mogol, *m.*
mohair ['mouhɛəɹ], *n.* Pelo della capra d'Angora, *m.*
Mohammed [mo'hæmid], *n.* Maometto, *m.*
Mohammedan, *n.a.* Maomettano.
Mohammedanism, *n.* Maomettismo, islamismo, *m.*
moiety ['mɔ:iəti], *n.* Metà, *f.*
moil [mɔ:il], *v.i.* Sgobbare, sfacchinare, affaticarsi.
moire, moiré [mwɑ:ɹ, mɔ:irei], *n.a.* Moerro, *m.*, seta marezzata, *f.*
moist [mɔ:ist], *a.* Umido, bagnato, madido, umidiccio.
moisten, *v.t.* Umettare, inumidire.
moisture, moistness, *n.* Umido, *m.*, umidità, umidezza, *f.*
moke [mouk], *n.* (*colloq.*) Asino, *m.*
molar ['mouləɹ], *n.a.* Molare, *m.*
molasses [mo'læsiz], *n.* Melassa, *f.*
mole (1) [moul], *n.* (*Zool.*) Talpa, *f.* **—-catcher,** cacciatore di talpe; **—-hill,** tana di talpa, *f.*; **—-skin,** pelle di talpa, *f.*, fustagno forte, *m.*
mole (2), *n.* (*on skin*) Neo, *m.*; verruca, *f.*
mole (3), *n.* (*jetty*) Molo, *m.*, diga, gettata, *f.*
molecular [mə'lekju:ləɹ], *a.* Molecolare.
molecule ['mɔlikju:l], *n.* Molecola, *f.*
molest [mə'lest], *v.t.* Molestare, far male a, malmenare, maltrattare.
molestation, *n.* Molestia, *f.*; offesa, *f.*; oltraggio, *m.*
mollification [mɔlifi'keiʃən], *n.* Mollificazione. *f.*
mollify ['mɔlifai], *v.t.* Mollificare, addolcire, placare.
mollusc ['mɔlʌsk], *n.* (*Zool.*) Mollusco, *m.*
molly ['mɔli], *n.* Effeminato, baggeo, *m.* **—-coddle,** donnetta, *f.*, (*colloq.*) pulcino bagnato, *m.*
molten ['moultən], *a.* Fuso.
Moluccas [mə'lʌkəz], *n.pl.* (*Geog.*) Le Molucche, *f.pl.*
moment ['moumənt], *n.* Momento, istante, attimo, minuto, *m.*; importanza, *f.*, peso, *m.* **Half a —!** Un momentino! **Come here this —!** Venite qua subito! **the very — that,** proprio nell'attimo che; **I was busy at the —,** ero occupato in quel momento; **he will come in a —,** verrà a momenti; **of no —,** di poca importanza, di nessun peso; **he stops every —,** si ferma ad ogni momento; **at the — of coming out,** al momento di uscire.
momentary, *a.* Momentaneo, passeggiero.
momentous [mo'mentəs], *a.* Di gran momento grave, importante.
momentously, *adv.* Importantemente.
momentum [mo'mentəm], *n.* (*Mech.*) Momento, impulso, *m.*; (*impetus*) impeto, slancio, *m.*
monachal ['mɔnəkl], *a.* Monacale.
monad ['mounəd], *n.* (*Chem., etc.*) Monade, *f.*
monadic, *a.* Monadico.
monadism, *n.* Monadismo, *m.*
monadelphous [mɔnə'delfəs], *a.* (*Bot.*) Monadelfo.
monarch ['mɔnɑ:ɹk], *n.* Monarca, *m.f.*, sovrano, re, *m.*, sovrana, regina, *f.*
monarchic, monarchical, *a.* Monarchico.
monarchism, *n.* Monarchismo, *m.*
monarchist, *n.* Monarchico, *m.*
monarchy, *n.* Monarchia, *f.*
monastery ['mɔnəstri], *n.* Monastero, convento, *m.*
monastic [mo'næstik], *a.* Monastico.
monasticism [mo'næstisizm], *n.* Monasticismo, *m.*
Monday ['mʌndi], *n.* Lunedì, *m.*
monetary ['mʌnitəri], *a.* Monetario.
monetization, *n.* Monetazione, *f.*
monetize, *v.t.* Monetare.
money (*pl.* **moneys**) ['mʌni], *n.* Danaro, denaro, *m.*, valuta, *f.*; (*coins*) monete, *f.pl.*, quattrini, *m.pl.*; fondi, *m.pl.* **Paper —,** valuta cartacea, carta moneta, *f.*; **time is —,** il tempo è danaro; **counterfeit —,** monete false, *f.pl.*; **to make —,** far denari; **to be made of —,** nuotare nell'oro; **ready- —,** denaro contante; **to be short of —,** essere a corto di denaro; **public —,** fondi pubblici,

m.pl.; **silver —,** valuta in argento, *f.*; **to put — to interest,** impiegare danaro; **to get one's money's worth,** avere l'equivalente del proprio danaro; **—-bag,** borsa, *f.*, borsellino, *m.*; (*Pol.*) **—-bill,** legge finanziaria *f.*; **—-box,** salvadanaro, *m.*; **—-changer,** cambiavalute, *m.*; **—-grubber,** avaro, strozzino, *m.*; **—-lender,** usuraio, strozzino, *m.*; **—-market,** mercato del danaro, *m.*, Borsa, *f.*; **—-order,** vaglia, *m.*

moneyed, *a.* Danaroso, ricco.

moneyless, *a.* Senza danaro, povero, squattrinato.

moneywort, *n.* (*Bot.*) Nummolaria, erba quattrina, *f.*

monger [ˈmʌŋgəɹ], *suffix.* Mercante, negoziante, *m.*

Mongol [ˈmɔŋgɔl], *n.* Mongolo, *m.* || *a.* Mongolico.

mongoose (*pl.* **mongooses**) [ˈmɔnguːs], *n.* (*Zool.*) Mangusta, *f.*

mongrel [ˈmʌŋgrəl], *n.* Ibrido, *m.*, meticcio, *m.*, meticcia, *f.*, bastardo, *m.*, bastarda, *f.* || *a.* Ibrido, di razza incrociata, meticcio. **— dog,** cane di razza mista, *m.*

monism [ˈmounizm], *n.* Monismo, *m.*

monist, *n.* Monista, *m.*

monition [mɔˈniʃən], *n.* (*Law*) Ammonizione, *f.*; avviso, avvertimento, *m.*

monitor [ˈmɔnitəɹ], *n.* (*school*) Capoclasse, *m.*; (*Naut.*) monitore, *m.*; (*Radio*) monitore, *m.*

monitorial, *a.* Monitorio.

monitory, *a.* Monitorio. (*Eccles.*) **— letter,** lettera monitoria, *f.*

monk [mʌŋk], *n.* Monaco, *m.* (*Bot.*) **Monk's-hood,** aconito, *m.*

monkery, *n.* Vita monastica, *f.*, monachismo, *m.*

monkhood, *n.* Monachismo, *m.*

monkish, *a.* Monastico, monacale.

monkey [ˈmʌŋki], *n.* Scimmia, *f.*; (*Mech.*) battipalo, *m.* **She- —,** scimmia, bertuccia, *f.*; **—-trick,** birbonata, *f.*; (*Bot.*) **—-puzzle,** araucaria, *f.*; **—-house,** gabbia delle scimmie, *f.*; (*Mech.*) **— wrench,** chiave inglese, *f.*

monobasic [mɔnouˈbeisik], *a.* (*Chem.*) Monobasico.

monocarpous, *a.* (*Bot.*) Monocarpico.

monochord, *n.* (*Mus.*) Monocordo, *m.*

monochrome [ˈmɔnokroum], *n.a.* Monocromo, *m.*

monocle [ˈmɔnəkl], *n.* Monocolo, *m.*, caramella, *f.*

monocotyledon [mɔnokɔtiˈliːdən], *n.* (*Bot.*) Monocotiledone, *f.*

monody, *n.* Monodia, *f.*

monogamist [məˈnɔgəmist], *n.* Monogamo, *m.*

monogamous, *a.* Monogamo.

monogamy, *n.* Monogamia, *f.*

monogenesis, *n.* Monogenesi, *f.*

monogenetic, *a.* Monogenico.

monogram, *n.* Monogramma, *m.*

monograph, *n.* Monografia, *f.*

monolith, *n.* Monolito, *m.*

monolithic, *a.* Monolito, monolitico.

monologize, *v.i.* Monologare.

monologue, *n.* Monologo, *m.*

monomania, *n.* Monomania, *f.*

monomaniac, *n.* Monomaniaco, *m.*

monometallism, *n.* Monometallismo, *m.*

monometrical, *a.* (*Poet.*) Monometrico.

monomial, *a.* (*Math.*) Monomiale.

monopetalous, *a.* (*Bot.*) Monopetalo.

monoplane, *n.* (*Aviat.*) Monoplano, *m.*

monopolist [məˈnɔpəlist], *n.* Monopolista, accaparratore, *m.*

monopolize, *v.t.* Monopolizzare, accaparrare.

monopoly, *n.* Monopolio, *m.*

monosyllabic, *a.* Monosillabico.

monosyllable, *n.* Monosillabo, *m.*

monotheism, *n.* Monoteismo, *m.*

monotheist, *n.* Monoteista, *m.*, *f.*

monotone [ˈmɔnətoun], *n.* Monotonia, *f* **To speak in a —,** parlare con monotonia.

monotonous, *a.* Monotono.

monotony, *n.* Monotonia, *f.*

monotype, *n.* (*Print.*) Monotipo, *m.*

monsoon [mɔnˈsuːn], *n.* Monsone, *m.*

monster [ˈmɔnstəɹ], *n.a.* Mostro, *m.*

monstrance [ˈmɔnstrəns], *n.* (*Eccles.*) Ostensorio, *m.*

monstrosity [mɔnˈstrɔsiti], *n.* Mostruosità, *f.*

monstrous, *a.* Mostruoso; enorme; deforme; straordinario; atroce. **A — crime,** un delitto atroce, *m.*

monstrously, *adv.* Mostruosamente.

monstrousness, *n.* Mostruosità, enormità, *f.*

montage [ˈmɔntɑːʒ], *n.* (*Cinema.*) Montaggio, *m.*

Mont Blanc *n.* (*Geog.*) Monte Bianco, *m.*

Montenegrin [mɔntiˈniːgrin], *n.a.* Montenegrino, *m.*

month [mʌnθ], *n.* Mese, *m.* **Calendar —,** mese solare, *m.*; **lunar —,** mese lunare, *m.*; **What is the day of the —?** Quanti ne abbiamo del mese? **month's salary, month's rent, etc.,** il mensile, *m.*

monthly, *a.* Mensile. || *adv.* Ogni mese, al mese, mensilmente. **A — magazine,** una rivista mensile, *f.*; **— nurse,** levatrice, *f.*; (*Comm.*) **— statement,** bilancio mensile, *m.*

monument [ˈmɔnjuːmənt], *n.* Monumento, *m.*

monumental, *a.* Monumentale. **— mason,** marmista, lavoratore in marmo, *m.*

moo [muː], *v.i.* Mugghiare, muggire. || *n.* Mugghio, muggito, *m.*

mood [muːd], *n.* Umore, *m.*, inclinazione, disposizione, *f.*; (*Gram.*) modo, *m.* **To be in the — for,** essere disposto a; **to be in a bad —,** essere di cattivo umore.

moodiness, *n.* Malinconia, *f.*, malumore, *m.*

moody, *a.* Malinconico, triste; di malumore, imbronciato, cupo.

moon (1) [muːn], *n.* Luna, *f.* **By the light of the —,** al chiaro di luna; **full —,** plenilunio, *m.*; **new —,** novilunio, *m.*, luna nuova, *f.*; **—-calf,** imbecille, idiota, *m.*; **—-flower,** margherita, *f.*, occhio di bove, *m.*; **to believe the — is made of green cheese,** prendere lucciole per lanterne.

moon (2), *v.i.* **To — about,** bighellonare, gironzare, stare a far niente; **to — away the time,** gingillarsi, oziare.

moonbeam, *n.* Raggio lunare, raggio di luna, *m.*

moonless, *a.* Senza luna, illune.

moonlight, *n.* Chiaro di luna, *m.*

moonlit, *a.* Rischiarato dalla luna.

moonshine, *n.* (*fig.*) Baie, fandonie, *f.pl.* **It's all —!** Le son baie! Son tutte fandonie!

moonstone, *n.* Pietra di luna, lunaria, *f.*

moonstruck, *a.* Lunatico.

moonwort, *n.* (*Bot.*) Lunaria, *f.*

moony, *a.* Lunatico, imbecille; visionario, stravagante.
Moor (1) [muːɹ], *n.* Moro, Saraceno, *m.*
moor (2), *n.* Landa, brughiera, *f.* **— -cock,** gallo di montagna, gallo di brughiera, *m.*; **— -hen,** gallinella d'acqua, *f.*; **moorland —,** brughiera, *f.*
moor (3), *v.t.* (*Naut.*) Ormeggiare, amarrare.
moorage, *n.* (*Naut.*) Ormeggio, ancoraggio, *m.*
mooring, *n.* Ormeggio, ancoraggio, *m.* **To break from the moorings,** rompere gli ormeggi.
Moorish, *a.* Moresco.
moose [muːs], *n.* (*Zool.*) Alce, alce americano, *m.*
moot [muːt], *v.t.* Sollevare, dibattere, tirare in campo. ‖ *a.* Discutibile, dubbio, controverso. **To — a question,** sollevare una questione; **a — point,** un punto controverso.
mooted, *a.* Dibattuto, discusso.
moot-hall [muːtˈhɔːl], *n.* Municipio, *m.*
mop (1) [mɔp], *n.* Scopa a frangie, radazza, *f.*; (*of hair*) zazzera, massa compatta, *f.* ‖ *v.t.* Pulire, asciugare. **To — up,** rasciugare; **to — one's face,** asciugarsi la faccia.
mop (2), *v.i.* **To — and mow,** fare smorfie.
mope [moup], *v.i.* Annoiarsi, stuccarsi; immusonirsi; essere depresso.
mopish [moupiʃ], *a.* Annoiato, depresso.
mopishness, *n.* Noia, *f.*
moraine [məˈrein], *n.* (*Geol.*) Morena, *f.*
moral [ˈmɔrəl], *a.* Morale, etico, virtuoso. ‖ *n.* Morale, *f.*; costumi, *m.pl.*, moralità, *f.*; etica, *f.* **— courage,** coraggio civile, *m.*
morale [məˈrɑːl], *n.* Morale, *m.* **The — of the army,** il morale dell'esercito.
moralist, *n.* Moralista, *m.*
morality, *n.* Moralità, *f.*
moralization, *n.* Moralizzazione, *f.*
moralize, *v.t.i.* Moralizzare. **To — on a subject,** far la morale su qualcosa.
morally, *adv.* Moralmente; praticamente. **It is — certain,** è praticamente sicuro.
morass [məˈræs], *n.* Palude, *f.*, pantano, acquitrino, *m.*
moratorium [mɔrəˈtɔːriəm], *n.* Moratoria, *f.*
Moravian [məˈreiviən], *n.a.* Moravo, *m.*
morbid [ˈmɔːɹbid], *a.* Morboso, malsano, malaticcio.
morbidity, morbidness [mɔːɹˈbiditi, ˈmɔːɹbidnis], *n.* Morbosità, *f.*
morbidly, *adv.* Morbosamente.
morbific, *a.* Morbifico, morbifero.
mordacious [mɔːɹˈdeiʃəs], *a.* Mordace, mordente, caustico, tagliente.
mordacity, mordancy [mɔːɹˈdæsiti, ˈmɔːɹdənsi], *n.* Mordacità, asprezza, acrimonia, *f.*
mordant, *a.* Mordace, mordente. ‖ *n.* (*Chem.*) Mordente, *m.*
more [mɔːɹ], *a.* Più, maggiore, più numeroso. ‖ *adv.* Di più, più, in più, maggiormente, ancora. **Bring some — money,** portate più danaro; **— than one person has been,** più di una persona è venuta; **give me one —,** datemene uno di più; **they are — than we,** sono più di noi; **many —,** molti di più; **— or less,** più o meno; **— and —,** più e più; **never —,** mai più; **once —,** ancora una volta; **so much the —,** tanto più; **he is — frightened than hurt,** ha più paura che altro; **he is no —,** è morto, non è più.
moreen [məˈriːn], *n.* Damasco di lana, *m.*
morel [məˈrel], *n.* (*Bot.*) Morchella, *f.*
morello [məˈrelou], *n.* (*Bot.*) Ciliegia amarena, *f.*
moreover [mɔːɹˈouvəɹ], *adv.* Poi, di più, inoltre, oltre a questo.
Moresque [məˈresk], *a.* Moresco.
morganatic [mɔːɹgəˈnætik], *a.* Morganatico.
moribund [ˈmɔɹibənd], *a.* Moribondo, morente.
morion [ˈmɔːriən], *n.* (*Hist.*) Morione, *m.*
Morisco [məˈriskou], *a.* Moresco. ‖ *n.* Moro, *m.*
Mormon [ˈmɔːɹmən], *n.a.* Mormone, *m.*
Mormonism, *n.* Mormonismo, *m.*
morn [mɔːɹn], *n.* (*Poet.*) Mattino, *m.*, aurora, *f.*
morning [ˈmɔːɹniŋ], *n.* Mattina, *f.*, mattino, *m.*; mattinata, *f.* **Good —!** Buon giorno! **all the —,** tutta la mattina; **every —,** ogni mattina; **from — till night,** da mattina a sera, dal mattino alla sera; **in the —, to-morrow —,** domani mattina; **the — before,** la mattina prima; **the next —,** la mattina dopo; **this —,** stamattina; **— -dress,** vestito da passaggio, dorsè, *m.*; **— call,** visita di mattina, *f.*; **— -room,** salottino, *m.*; **the — star,** l'astro del mattino, *m.*, la stella mattutina, *f.*
Moroccan [məˈrɔkən], *a.* Marocchino. ‖ *n.* Marocchino, *m.*, Marocchina, *f.*
Morocco [məˈrɔkou], *n.* (*Geog.*) Marocco, *m.* **— -leather,** marocchino, *m.*
morose [məˈrous], *a.* Tetro, cupo, malinconico, stizzoso.
morosely, *adv.* Tetramente, cupamente.
moroseness, *n.* Tetraggine, malinconia, *f.*
Morpheus [ˈmɔːɹfjuːs], *n.* (*Myth.*) Morfeo, *m.*
morphia, morphine ˈmɔːɹfiə, mɔːɹfiːn], *n.* (*Chem.*) Morfina, *f.*
morphinism, *n.* Morfinismo, *m.*
morphinomania, *n.* Morfinomania, *f.*
morphinomaniac, *n.* Morfinomane, *m.f.*
morphological [mɔːɹfəˈlɔdʒikəl], *a.* Morfologico.
morphologist, *n.* Morfologista, *m.*
morphology, *n.* Morfologia, *f.*
morris, morris dance [ˈmɔris, ˈmɔris dɑːns], *n.* Danza moresca, antica danza rurale degli inglesi, *f.*
morrow [ˈmɔrou], *n.* Il giorno seguente, l'indomani, *m.* **Good —!** Buon giorno!
morse [mɔːɹs], *n.* (*Zool.*) Tricheco, *m.*
morsel [ˈmɔːɹsəl], *n.* Pezzo, pezzetto, *m.*; (*mouthful*) boccone, *m.*; (*crust*) tozzo, *m.*
mortal [ˈmɔːɹtəl], *a.* Mortale, umano; fatale, letale, funesto; a morte, ad oltranza. ‖ *n.* Mortale, *m.* **A — combat,** un duello mortale, *m.*; **in — agony,** agonizzante; (*colloq.*) **for three — hours,** per tre interminabili ore; **Poor little —!** Povero piccino! **we poor mortals,** noi miseri mortali.
mortality [mɔːɹˈtæliti], *n.* Mortalità, caducità, *f.*
mortally, *adv.* Mortalmente, fatalmente.
mortar [ˈmɔːɹtəɹ], *n.* (*for crushing*) Mortaio, *m.*; (*Mil.*) mortaio, *m.*; (*in building*) malta, calcina, *f.* **Trench —,** bombarda, *f.*; **— -board,** cappello accademico, *m.*
mortgage [ˈmɔːɹgidʒ], *n.* Ipoteca, *f.* ‖ *v.t.* Ipotecare. **— deed,** contratto ipotecario, *m.*; **to pay off a —,** estinguere un'ipoteca.
mortgagee [mɔːɹgəˈdʒiː], *n.* Creditore ipotecario, *m.*

mortgagor [ˈmɔːɹgədʒəɹ], *n.* Debitore ipotecario, *m.*
mortification [mɔːɹtifiˈkeiʃən], *n.* Mortificazione, *f.*; (*Med.*) cancrena, *f.*
mortify [ˈmɔːɹtifai], *v.t.* Mortificare, umiliare, abbassare; *v.i.* cancrenarsi, incancrenire.
mortifying, *a.* Mortificante.
mortise, mortice [ˈmɔːɹtis], *n.* Incavo, incastro, *m.*, mortisa, *f.* || *v.t.* Incastrare, congiungere a mortisa. **—-lock**, serratura incastrata, *f.*
mortmain [ˈmɔːɹtmein], *n.* (*Law*) Manomorta, *f.*
mortuary [ˈmɔːɹtjuːəri], *n.* Stanza mortuaria, camera mortuaria, *f.* || *a.* Mortuario. **— chapel**, cappella mortuaria, *f.*
Mosaic (1) [moˈzeiik], *a.* Mosaico, di Mosè. **— law**, legge mosaica, *f.*
mosaic (2), *n.* Mosaico, *m.*
Moscow [ˈmɔskou], *n.* (*Geog.*) Mosca, *f.*
Moslem, Muslim [ˈmɔzlem, ˈmʌzlim], *n.a.* Mussulmano, maomettano, *m.*
mosque [mɔsk], *n.* Moschea, *f.*
mosquito [məsˈkiːtou], *n.* (*Zool.*) Zanzara, *f.* **—-bite**, morsicatura di zanzara; **—-net, —-curtain**, zanzariera, *f.*
moss (1) [mɔs], (*Bot.*) Musco, muschio, *m.*, borracina, *f.* || *v.t.* Coprire di muschio. **—-grown**, coperto di muschio; **— rose**, rosa muschiosa, *f.*
moss (2), *n.* Palude, torbiera, *f.* (*Hist.*) **—-trooper**, bandito, brigante, *m.*
mossiness, *n.* Muschiosità, *f.*
mossy, *a.* Muschioso, coperto di muschio.
most [moust], *a.* Il più, il maggior numero, il più grande. || *adv.* Il più, più, molto. || *n.* La più gran parte, *f.*; il più gran numero, *m.*; la maggioranza, *f.* **You have made — mistakes,** voi avete fatto il maggior numero di sbagli; **that child makes the — noise of all,** quel bambino fa più chiasso di tutti; **— people,** il più della gente; **the — part,** la maggior parte; **a — beautiful day,** una giornata bellissima, *f.*; **what — annoys me,** ciò che mi secca più; **— likely,** molto probabilmente; **he is the — honourable man in the world,** egli è l'uomo più onesto del mondo; **to make the — of it,** tirare il miglior partito da; **— of all,** soprattutto.
mostly, *adv.* Per lo più, principalmente.
mote [mout], *n.* (*in the eye*) Festuca, pagliuzza, *f.*; (*of dust*) atomo, *m.* **To see the — in another's eye,** vedere la festuca nell'occhio altrui.
motel [mouˈtel], *n.* Albergo stradale per automobilisti, autostello, *m.*
motet [mouˈtet], *n.* (*Mus.*) Mottetto, *m.*
moth [mɔθ], *n.* (*Zool.*) Farfalla notturna, farfalla crepuscolare, falena, *f.*; (*Aviat.*) aeroplano tignola, *m.* **Clothes- —**, tignola, tarma, *f.*; **—-eaten,** tarmato.
mother (1) [ˈmʌðəɹ], *n.* Madre, mamma, *f.* || *a.* Madre, materno. || *v.t.* Fare da madre a, adottare. **— Church,** Madre Chiesa, chiesa metropolitana, *f.*; **— earth,** madre terra, *f.*; **— country,** patria, *f.*; paese nativo, *m.*; **— superior,** madre superiore, *f.*; **— tongue,** lingua materna, madre lingua, *f.*; (*Zool.*) **Mother Cary's chicken,** procellaria, *f.*; **—-in-law,** suocera, *f.*; **step- —**, matrigna, *f.*; **—-of-pearl,** madreperla, *f.*; **—-wit,** senso comune, *m.*
mother (2), *n.* (*mould*) Muffa, *f.* || *v.i.* Far la muffa.
motherhood, *n.* Maternità, *f.*
motherless, *a.* Senza madre, orfano.
motherly, *a.* Materno, di madre, da madre.
mothproof, *a.* Antitarmico. **— bag,** tessilsacco, *m.*
mothy [ˈmɔθi], *a.* Pieno di tignole.
motif [mouˈtiːf], *n.* Motivo, *m.*; tema, *m.*; argomento, *m.*
motion [ˈmouʃən], *n.* Moto, movimento, *m.*; (*at a meeting*) mozione, *f.*; (*sign*) cenno, *m.*; (*of bowels*) andata di corpo, *m.*, scarica, *f.* || *v.t.* Far cenno a, fare segno. **Perpetual —,** moto perpetuo, *m.*; **in —,** in moto; **to set in —,** mettere in moto; **to put a —,** mettere ai voti una mozione; **the — was carried,** la mozione fu approvata; **he motioned me away,** mi fece cenno d'andar via.
motionless, *a.* Immobile, fermo.
motivate, *v.t.* Motivare.
motive [ˈmoutiv], *a.* Motivo, movente; motore, motrice. || *n.* Motivo, *m.*, causa, *f.*; ragione, *f.* **— power,** forza motrice, *f.*
motley [ˈmɔtli], *a.* Screziato, variopinto; diverso, vario, misto. || *n.* Screziatura, *f.*; abito da buffone *or* arlecchino, *m.*
motor [ˈmoutəɹ], *n.* Motore, *m.*; automobile, auto, *m.f.*, macchina, *f.* || *v.i.* Andare in automobile. **—-boat,** motoscafo, *m.*; **—-ship,** motonave, *m.*; **—-bus,** autobus, *m.*; **—-cycle,** motocicletta, *f.*, motociclo, *m.*; **—-cyclist,** motociclista, *m.f.*; **—-coach,** torpedone, autosalone, autobus, *m.*; **—-lorry,** autocarro, camion, *m.*; **—way,** autostrada, *f.*; **—-scooter,** motopattino; **—-man** (*on train*) macchinista, *m.*; **—-show,** mostra automobilistica, *f.*; **—-horn,** clacson, *m.*
motoring, *n.* Automobilismo, *m.*
motorist, *n.* Automobilista, motorista, *m.f.*
motorize, *v.t.* Motorizzare.
mottle [mɔtl], *v.t.* Marmorizzare, marezzare, screziare, variegare.
mottled, *a.* Macchiato, chiazzato, screziato, variegato. **— soap,** sapone marmorizzato, *m.*
motto (*pl.* **mottoes**) [ˈmɔtou, ˈmɔtouz], *n.* Motto, *m.*, divisa, *f.*; epigrafe, *f.*; (*Mus.*) motivo, *m.*
moufflon [ˈmuːflɔŋ], *n.* (*Zool.*) Mufflone, *m.*
mould [mould], *n.* (*earth*) Terriccio, *m.*; (*decay*) muffa, *f.*; (*shape*) forma, *f.*, modello, *m.*, carattere, *m.*, stampo, *m.* || *v.t.* Formare, modellare, plasmare; *v.t.* muffire, ammuffire. **A man of heroic —,** un uomo di stampo eroico, *m.*
moulder (1) [ˈmouldəɹ], *v.i.* Polverizzarsi, consumarsi; ridursi in polvere.
moulder (2), *n.* Modellatore, gettatore, *m.*
mouldering, *a.* Crollante, rovinante.
mouldiness, *n.* Muffa, *f.*
moulding, *n.* Modanatura, *f.*; (*act of*) modellatura, *f.*
mouldy, a. Muffito, ammuffito; (*colloq.*) cattivo, miserabile. **To turn —,** muffire, ammuffire; **it smells —,** sente di muffa.
moult [moult], *v.t.i.* Mudare, mutare le penne, spiumarsi, perdere il pelo.
moulting, *a.* Muda, *f.*

mound [maund], *n.* Monticello, tumulo, rialzo, *m.* || *v.t.* Formare in monticello.
mount (1), [maunt], *n.* Monte, *m.* **Mount Vesuvius,** Monte Vesuvio, *m.*
mount (2), *n.* Cavallo da sella, *m.*; cavalcatura, *f.*; monta, *f.* || *v.t.* Montare.
mount (3), *n.* (*picture*) Cartone, *m.* || *v.t.* (*picture*) Montare; (*a gun*) montare; (*a gem*) incastonare; (*Mech.*) montare; (*Theat.*) mettere in scena.
mountain ['mauntin], *n.* Montagna, *f.*, monte, *m.* || *a.* Di montagna, montano, montanaro, montagnuolo. (*Bot.*) **— -ash,** sorbo selvatico, *m.*; **— sickness,** mal di montagna, *m.* **— -dweller,** montanaro, *m.*; **the Rocky Mountains,** le Montagne Rocciose, *f.pl.*; **— dew,** whisky di contrabbando, *m.*
mountaineer [mauntə'niəɪ], *n.* Alpinista, *m.f.*; montanaro, *m.*, montanara, *f.*
mountaineering, *n.* Alpinismo, *m.*
mountainous, *a.* Montagnoso, montuoso, alpestre; enorme.
mountebank ['mauntibæŋk], *n.* Saltimbanco; ciarlatano, *m.*
mounted, *a.* Montato, a cavallo. **— police,** polizia a cavallo, *f.*
mounter, *n.* Montatore, *m.*, montatrice, *f.*
mounting, *n.* Montaggio, *m.*; montatura, incastonatura, *f.*; (*Theat.*) messa in scena, *f.*
mourn [moəɹn, mɔːɹn], *v.t.i.* Piangere, rimpiangere, lamentare, lamentarsi, addolorarsi. **To — a friend,** pianger un amico, rimpiangere un amico.
mourner, *n.* Chi segue un funerale; dolente. **Hired —,** prefica, *f.*; **chief —,** parente stretto a un funerale, *m.*; **to be one of the mourners,** essere uno dei presenti a un funerale.
mournful ['mɔːɹnful], *a.* Triste, lugubre, doloroso, luttuoso.
mournfully, *adv.* Lugubremente.
mournfulness, *n.* Tristezza, *f.*
mourning, *n.* (*clothes*) Lutto, *m.*; (*grief*) lamentazione, *f.* || *a.* Triste, afflitto. **Deep —,** lutto pesante, *m.*; **half- —,** mezzo lutto; **to go into —,** prendere il lutto; **dressed in —,** vestito a lutto; **to be in —,** essere in lutto; **— -coach,** carro funebre, *m.*
mouse (*pl.* **mice**) [maus, mais] *n.* (*Zool.*) Topo, topolino, sorcio, *m.* || *v.i.* Prendere topi. **Field-—,** topolino delle messi, *m.*; **— -trap,** trappola per topi, *f.*; **— -hole,** buco di topo, *m.*; **— -coloured,** grigio topo.
mouser, *n.* Gatto buono a prender i topi, *m.*
moustache [məs'tɑːʃ], *n.* Baffi, mustacchi, *m.pl.*
mousy, *a.* Grigio topo; quietissimo.
mouth [mauθ], *n.* Bocca, *f.*; gola, *f.*; foce, imboccatura, entrata, *f.*; orifizio, *m.*; smorfia, *f.* || *v.t.* [mauð] Declamare ampollosamente, vociare; *v.i.* parlare gonfio, parlare ore rotundo. **— -organ,** armonica, *m.*; **— -piece,** imboccatura, *f.*; (*fig.*) portavoce, *m.*
mouthed, *a.* A bocca. **Hard- —,** duro di bocca; **open- —,** a bocca aperta.
mouthful, *n.* Boccata, *f.*, boccone, *m.* **At a —,** in un boccone.
mouthless, *a.* Senza bocca.
mouthwash, *n.* Acqua dentifricia, *f.*
mouthy, *a.* Ampolloso, smanceroso.
movable ['muːvəbl], *a.* Mobile, movibile. || *n.* Mobile, *m.* **Movables,** mobili, *m.pl.*; (*furniture*) mobilia, *f.*; beni mobili, *m.pl.*
movability, *n.* Mobilità, *f.*
move [muːv], *v.t.* Muovere; spostare; portare, trasportare; agitare, eccitare, commuovere; spingere; proporre; *v.i.* muovere, muoversi, partire, allontanare; spostarsi; (*at chess, etc.*) giuocare; (*furniture*) sgombrare. || *n.* Mossa, *f.*, moto, *m.*; (*Chess, etc.*) turno, *m.* **To — away,** portar via; **to — back,** mettere a posto, spingere indietro; **to — heaven and earth,** far ogni sforzo; **to — out,** portar fuori; **to — to laughter,** far ridere; **I was much moved,** fui molto commosso; **Move on, please!** Via via! Largo largo! **to — about,** andare qua e la, andare intorno; **to — away,** andar via, partire; **to — backwards,** indietreggiare, rinculare; **to — into a new house,** entrare in una nuova casa; **to — in good society,** praticare l'alta società; **to — on,** avanzare, andare innanzi; **to — out one's furniture,** sgombrare i mobili; **to — up,** salire, passare davanti; **to — forward,** avanzare, procedere; **it is your —,** tocca a voi a giuocare; **to give checkmate in three moves,** dare scacco in tre turni; **he's always on the —,** è sempre in moto; **a false —,** una mossa falsa, *f.*; **to make a —,** muovere, muoversi, giuocare; **What is our next — ?** Che faremo adesso?
movement, *n.* Movimento, moto, *m.*, mossa, *f.*; gesto, cenno, *m.*
mover, *n.* Motore, *m.*; fautore, promotore, *m.*; (*of resolution*) proponente, *m.* **Prime —,** iniziatore, *m.*; forza motrice, *f.*
movies ['muːviz], *n.pl.* (*colloq.*) Il cinema, *m.*; **movie-man,** operatore cinematografico, *m.*; **movie-star,** stella del cinema, *f.*
moving, *a.* Movente, mobile; commovente. || *n.* Movimento, *m.*; (*removal*) sgombro, *m.*; spostamento, *m.* **— -pictures,** il cinema, *m.*
movingly, *adv.* Teneramente, pateticamente, commoventemente.
mow (1) [mou], *v.t.* Falciare, mietere; (*the lawn*) tagliare. || *n.* Mucchio di fieno, *m.*
mow (2) [cp. **mop** (2)].
mower, *n.* Falciatore, mietitore, *m.*; (*Mech.*) falciatrice, *f.* **Lawn- —,** falciatrice da prato, *f.*
mowing, *n.* Falciatura, mietitura, *f.* **— -machine,** falciatrice, mietitrice, *f.*
Mr. ['mistəɹ], *n.* Signor, *m.*
Mrs. ['misiz], *n.* Signora, *f.*
much [mʌtʃ], *a.adv.* Molto, assai; grande, di molto, a lungo, bene. **How — ?** Quanto? **so —,** tanto; **I am — about the same,** sto quasi lo stesso, son sempre allo stesso punto; **they are — of a size,** sono press'a poco della stessa grandezza; **he's not — of a scholar,** non è uno studioso; **— of a muchness,** press'a poco la stessa cosa; **nothing —,** niente d'importante; **So — for that!** Basta per ciò! **so — more,** tanto più; **so — so that,** in tal modo che; **so — the better,** tanto meglio; **to make — of,** stimare, voler bene a, fare gran caso di; **too —,** troppo.
mucilage ['mjuːsilədʒ], *n.* Mucillaggine, *f.*
mucilaginous, *a.* Mucillagginoso.
muck [mʌk], *n.* Fango, *m.*; letame, sterco, *m.*; porcheria, *f.* || *v.t.* Sporcare, lordare, insudiciare; (*fig.*) guastare; (*colloq.*) **To — about,**

gingillarsi; **— -heap,** letamaio, *m.*; **— -rake,** rastrello per il concime, *m.*
muckiness, *n.* Fango, *m.*, porcheria, *f.*
mucky, *a.* Fangoso, sporco, lurido, sudicio.
muckle [ˈmʌkəl], *n.a.* (*Scots*) Molto, una grande quantità, *f.*
mucous [ˈmju:kəs], *a.* Mucoso. **— membrane,** mucosa, *f.*
mucus, *n.* Muco, mucco, *m.*
mud [mʌd], *n.* Fango, *m.*, mota, melma, fanghiglia, poltiglia, *f.*; limo, *m.* **To throw — at,** (*fig.*) denigrare; **— -guard,** parafango, *m.*; **— -lark,** birichino di strada, monello, *m.*; **— bath,** bagno di fango, *m.*
muddiness, *n.* Fangosità, *f.*
muddle [mʌdl], *v.t.* Turbare, intontire, confondere; far pasticci, impasticciare; (*with drink*) inebriare, stupidire. || *n.* Confusione, *f.*, disordine, *m.*; imbroglio, pasticcio, viluppo, *m.* **He always muddles his money away,** spreca sempre il suo danaro; **to make a — of a thing,** imbrogliare una faccenda; **to — along,** tirare avanti; **to — through,** arrabattarsi, arrangiarsi; **to — up,** impasticciare; **— -headed,** confusionario.
muddled, *a.* Confuso; imbrogliato, avviluppato, mescolato; (*with drink*) brillo.
muddler, *n.* Imbroglione, confusionario, guastamestieri, *m.*
muddy, *a.* Fangoso; infangato, inzaccherato; oscuro; (*fig.*) confuso. || *v.t.* Infangare, inzaccherare; intorbidare.
muezzin [mu:ˈezin], *n.* Muezzino, *m.*
muff [mʌf], *n.* Manicotto, *m.*; (*fig.*) balordo, grullo, *m.*, persona maldestra, *f.* || *v.t.* Far fiasco, far cilecca, mancare il colpo.
muffin [ˈmʌfin], *n.* Tartina per tè, *f.*, specie di focaccina, *f.*
muffle [mʌfl], *v.t.* Imbacuccare, avviluppare; camuffare; ammorzare; (*drum*) velare; (*bell*) legare; (*oars*) assordare. || *n.* (*Chem.*) Muffola, *f.* **To — oneself up,** imbacuccarsi.
muffler, *n.* Sciarpa, sciarpa da collo, *f.*
mufti (1) [ˈmʌfti], *n.* Mufti, *m.*
mufti, (2), *n.* Abito borghese, *m.* **Dressed in —,** vestito in borghese.
mug [mʌg], *n.* Gotto, *m.*; bicchiere, *m.*, tazza, *f.*; boccale, *m.*; (*colloq.*) muso, grugno, *m.*; sciocco, semplicione, *m.*
muggy [ˈmʌgi], *a.* Umido, afoso.
mugwump [ˈmʌgwʌmp], *n.* (*colloq.*) Pezzo grosso, caporione, *m.*
mulatto [mjuˈlætou], *n.* Mulatto, *m.*, mulatta, *f.* || *a.* Mulatto.
mulberry [ˈmʌlbəri], *n.* (*Bot.*) Mora, gelsa mora, *f.* **— -tree,** gelso, *m.*
mulch [mʌltʃ], *n.* Strame, *m.*, paglia, *f.*, letame, *m.* || *v.t.* Impagliare.
mulct [mʌlkt], *n.* Multa, *f.* || *v.t.* Multare; privare di.
mule [mju:l], *n.* (*Zool.*) Mulo, *m.*, mula, *f.*; (*slipper*) ciabatta, *f.* **Stubborn as a —,** caparbio come un mulo; **— -track,** mulattiera, *f.*; **— -driver, muleteer,** mulattiere, *m.*; (*Mech.*) **— -jenny,** specie di telaio.
muleteer, *n.* Mulattiere, *m.*
mulish, *a.* Mulesco; caparbio, ostinato.
mulishness, *n.* Caparbietà, ostinatezza, *f.*
mull [mʌl], *v.t.* Scaldare e condire vino con spezie.
mullein [ˈmʌlin] *n* (*Bot.*) Verbasco, *m.*
muller, *n.* (*Min.*) Macinello, *m.*
mullet [ˈmʌlit], *n.* (*Zool.*) (*grey*) Muggine, *m.*; (*red*) triglia, *f.*
mulligrubs [ˈmʌligrʌbz], *n.pl.* (*colloq.*) Colica, *f.*; malumore, *m.*
mullion [ˈmʌljən], *n.* (*Arch.*) Regolo, *m.*, traversa, *f.*
mullioned, *a.* A regoli.
multangular [mʌlˈtæŋgju:ləɹ], *a.* Poligonale.
multicoloured [ˈmʌltikʌləɹd], *a.* Multicolore, variopinto.
multifarious [mʌltiˈfɛəriəs], *a.* Multiforme, vario, diverso.
multifariousness, *n.* Varietà, diversità, *f.*
multifid, *a.* (*Zool.Bot.*) Multifido.
multiform, *a.* Multiforme.
multiformity, *n.* Varietà, molteplicità, *f.*
multilateral [mʌltiˈlætərəl], *a.* Multilatero.
multi-millionaire [mʌltimiliənˈɛəɹ], *n.* Multi-milionario, miliardario, *m.*
multiple [ˈmʌltipl], *n.* Multiplo, *m.* || *a.* Multiplo, molteplice.
multiplex, *a.* Molteplice.
multiplicand [ˈmʌltiplikənd], *n.* (*Math.*) Moltiplicando, *m.*
multiplication, *n.* Moltiplicazione, *f.* **— -table,** tavola pitagorica, *f.*
multiplicative, *a.* Moltiplicatore.
multiplicity [mʌltiˈplisiti], *n.* Molteplicità *f.*
multiplier, *n.* Moltiplicatore, *m.*
multiply, *v.t.* Moltiplicare; *v.i.* moltiplicarsi.
multitude, *n.* Moltitudine, *f.*
multitudinous, *a.* Molteplice, numeroso.
multitudinousness, *n.* Molteplicità, *f.*
mum [mʌm], *a.* Muto. **To be —,** avere la bocca chiusa; **Mum's the word!** Zitto! Acqua in bocca!
mumble [ˈmʌmbl], *v.t.i.* Mormorare, borbottare, biascicare.
mumbler, *n.* Mormoratore, borbottatore, biascicone, *m.*
mummer [ˈmʌməɹ], *n.* Maschera, *f.*; attore, commediante, *m.*
mummery, *n.* Mascherata, pagliacciata, *f.*
mummification [mʌmifiˈkeiʃən], *n.* Mummificazione, *f.*
mummify [ˈmʌmifai], *v.t.* Mummificare.
mummy (1), *n.* Mummia, *f.*
mummy (2), *n.* Mamma, mammina, *f.*
mump [mʌmp], *v.i.* (*obs.*) Mendicare; imbronciarsi.
mumper, *n.* Mendicante, *m.*
mumps, *n.pl.* (*Med.*) Orecchioni, *m.pl.*; (*fig.*) broncio, *m.*, musoneria, *f.*
munch [mʌntʃ], *v.t.i.* Masticare, sbatter la bocca, divorare; sgretolare.
mundane [mʌnˈdein], *a.* Mondano.
mundaneness, *n.* Mondanità, *f.*
Munich [ˈmju:nik], *n.* (*Geog.*) Monaco, Monaco di Baviera, *f.*
mungoose [cp. **mongoose**].
municipal [mju:ˈnisipəl], *a.* Municipale. **— law,** diritto amministrativo, *m.*, legge comunale, *f.*
municipality [mju:nisiˈpæliti], *n.* Municipalità, *f.*
munificence [mju:ˈnifisəns], *n.* Munificenza, *f.*
munificent, *a.* Munificente, munifico, largo, liberale.
muniment [ˈmju:nimənt], *n.* Carta, *f.*, documento, titolo, *m.* **— -room,** archivio, *m.*

munition [mju:ˈniʃən], *n.* Munizione, *f.* || *v.t.* Fornire di munizioni, munire. **Munitions of war,** munizioni da guerra, *f.pl.*; **—-worker,** operaio alle munizioni, *m.*
mural [ˈmju:rəl], *a.* Murale. **— painting,** pittura a fresco, *f.*, affresco, *m.*
muraena [mju:ˈri:nə], *n.* (*Zool.*) Murena, *f.*
murder [ˈmə:ɹdəɹ], *n.* Omicidio, assassinio, *m.* || *v.t.* Assassinare, uccidere; massacrare. **Murder!** All'assassino! Aiuto!, (*colloq.*) Accidenti! **wilful —,** omicidio premeditato, *m.*; **the — is out,** il segreto è scoperto.
murderer, *n.* Omicida, assassino, *m.*
murderess, *n.* Omicida, assassina, *f.*
murderous, *a.* Assassino, micidiale, massacrante.
murex [ˈmju:reks], *n.* (*Zool.*) Murice, *m.*
muriate [ˈmju:riət], *n.* (*Chem.*) Muriato, *m.*
muriatic, *a.* Muriatico.
murkiness [ˈmə:ɹkinis], *n.* Oscurità, nerezza, *f.*
murky, *a.* Oscuro, tenebroso, buio, nero. **— darkness,** buio fitto, *m.*
murmur [ˈmə:ɹməɹ], *n.* Mormorio, borbottamento, borbottio, *m.*; lagnanza, *f.* || *v.t.i.* Mormorare, borbottare, brontolare; lagnarsi.
murmuring, murmurous, *a.* Mormorante, borbottante.
murrain [ˈmʌrin], *n.* (*Med.*) Afta epizootica, *f.*
murrey [ˈmʌri], *a.* (*obs.*) Rosso scuro.
murrhine [ˈmʌrain], *a.* Murrino.
muscat, muscatel, muscadel [ˈmʌskæt, mʌskəˈtel, mʌskəˈdel], *n.* (*wine*) Moscato, *m.* **Muscatel grape,** moscatello, *m.*
muscle [ˈmʌsəl], *n.* (*Anat.*) Muscolo, *m.*
Muscovite [ˈmʌskovait], *n.a.* Moscovita, russo, *m.*
muscular, *a.* Muscolare; muscoloso; robusto.
muscularity, *n.* Muscolosità, robustezza; gagliardia, *f.*
musculature, *n.* Muscolatura, *f.*
Muse (1) [mju:z], *n.* (*Myth.*) Musa, *f.*
muse (2), *v.i.* Meditare, riflettere, pensare. || *n.* Meditazione, *f.* **To — on,** riflettere, pensare; **to be in a —,** stare in meditazione, essere assorto.
museum [mju:ˈziəm], *n.* Museo, *m.* **Natural history —,** museo di storia naturale, *m.*
mush [mʌʃ], *n.* Pappa, *f.*; poltiglia, *f.*
mushroom [ˈmʌʃrum], *n.* Fungo, *m.*, fungo mangereccio, fungo prataiolo, *m.* || *a.* Effimero, di un giorno, come funghi. **To spring up like mushrooms,** venir su come i funghi; **—-growth,** sviluppo rapido; **—-bed,** fungaia, *f.*; **— spawn,** micelio, *m.*
music [ˈmju:zik], *n.* Musica, *f.* **To set to —,** mettere in musica; **—-master,** maestro di musica, *m.*; **—-room,** sala da musica, *f.*; **—-stand,** leggio, *m.*; **—-stool,** sgabello per piano, *m.*; **—-case,** portamusica, *m.* **—-hall,** teatro di varietà, *m.*
musical, *a.* Musicale; armonioso, melodioso; (*of a person*) amante della musica. **— instrument,** strumento musicale, *m.*; **—-box,** scatola armonica, *f.* **—-director,** capomusica, direttore d'orchestra, *m.*; **— play,** operetta, *f.*; **to be —,** amar la musica.
musically, *adv.* Melodiosamente.
musician [mju:ˈziʃən], *n.* Musicista, *m.f.*, musico, *m.*; musicante, *m.f.*
musicology, *n.* Musicologia, *f.*
musing [ˈmju:ziŋ], *n.* Meditazione, *f.*
musk [mʌsk], *n.* Muschio, *m.*; (*Bot.*) erba del muschio, *f.* (*Zool.*) **—-deer,** mosco, cervo muschio, *m.*, capra muschiata, *f.*; **—-ox,** bue muschiato, *m.*; **—-rat,** ondatra, *f.*, miogale muschiato, *m.*; **—-rose,** rosa muschiata, *f.*; **to perfume with —,** muschiare.
musket [ˈmʌskit], *n.* Moschetto, fucile, *m.* **—-ball,** palla di fucile, *f.*; **—-shot,** moschettata, *f.*
musketeer, *n.* Moschettiere, *m.*
musketry, *n.* Moschetteria, fucileria, *f.*, tiro, *m.* **—-fire,** fuoco di moschetteria, *m.*; **— instructor,** istruttore di tiro, *m.*
musky, *a.* Muschiato.
Muslim, Moslem [ˈmʌzlim, ˈmɔzləm], *n.a.* Maomettano, *m.*
muslin [ˈmʌzlin], *n.* Mussolina, *f.* || *a.* Di mussolina.
musquash [ˈmʌskwɔʃ], *n.* (*Zool.*) Ondatra, *f.*; (*fur*) pelle d'ondatra, *f.*
mussel [ˈmʌsəl], *n.* (*Zool.*) Dattero di mare, *m.*; mitilo, *m.*
Mussulman (*pl.* **Mussulmans**) [ˈmʌslmən], *n.a.* Mussulmano, *m.*
must (1) [mʌst], *v.aux.* Dovere, bisognare, occorrere. **You — go away,** dovete andar via; **it — be found,** bisogna trovarlo; **he — come,** bisogna ch'egli venga; **I — have some money,** mi occorre del danaro; **you — have known what I meant,** dovevate sapere ciò che io volevo dire; **it — be so,** dev'essere così.
must (2), *n.* (*new wine*) Mosto, *m.*
must (3), *n.* Muffa, *f.*
must (4), *n.* Frenesia di certi animali con eccitamento sessuale.
mustang [ˈmʌstæŋ], *n.* Mustango, *m.*
mustard [ˈmʌstəɹd], *n.* (*Bot.*) Senapa, *f.*; (*condiment*) senape, mostarda, *f.* **— plaster,** senapismo, *m.*; **—-pot,** mostardiera, *f.*; **— seed,** semi di senapa, *m.pl.*; **—-sauce,** salsa di mostarda, *f.*; **—-gas,** iprite, *f.*
muster [ˈmʌstəɹ], *n.* Appello, *m.*, rivista, adunata, *f.*; assembramento, *m.*, assemblea, *f.* || *v.t.i.* Passare in rivista; riunire, riunirsi, assembrare. **—-roll,** ruolo, appello, ruolino, *m.*; **to — up courage,** farsi coraggio.
mustiness, *n.* Muffa, muffosità, *f.*, tanfo, *m.*
musty, *a.* Muffito, stantio.
mutability [mju:təˈbiliti], *n.* Mutabilità, incostanza, *f.*
mutable, *a.* Mutabile, incostante, volubile.
mutation, *n.* Mutazione, *f.*, mutamento, *m.*
mute [mju:t], *a.* Muto, taciturno, silenzioso. || *n.* Muto, *m.*, muta, *f.*; (*on violin*) sordina, *f.*; (*Gram.*) lettera muta, *f.*; (*at funerals*) piagnone, *m.* || *v.t.* (*Mus.*) Metter la sordina. **Deaf —,** sordomuto, *m.*, sordomuta, *f.*
mutely, *adv.* Mutamente, senza parole, in silenzio.
muteness, *n.* Mutezza, *f.*
mutilate [ˈmju:tileit], *v.t.* Mutilare, mozzare, troncare.
mutilated, *a.* Mutilato; (*of MSS, etc.*) mutilo.
mutilation, *n.* Mutilazione, *f.*, mozzamento, troncamento, *m.*
mutilator, *n.* Mutilatore, *m.*
mutineer [mju:tiˈniəɹ], *n.* Ammutinato, rivoltoso, ribelle, *m.*
mutinous, *a.* Ammutinato, ribelle.

mutiny, *n.* Ammutinamento, *m.*, rivolta, sedizione, *f.* || *v.i.* Ammutinarsi, ribellarsi. **The Indian Mutiny,** l'ammutinamento nelle Indie (1857–58), *m.*
mutism, *n.* Mutismo, silenzio, *m.*
mutter ['mʌtəɹ], *v.t.i.* Mormorare, borbottare, brontolare, bisbigliare; (*of thunder*) rumoreggiare.
muttering, *n.* Mormorio, borbottio, brontolio, bisbiglio, *m.*
mutton ['mʌtən], *n.* Montone, castrato, *m.* **— -chop, — cutlet,** costoletta di castrato, *f.*; **— -chop whiskers,** favoriti, *m.pl.*, basette, *f.pl.*
mutual ['mju:tju:əl], *a.* Mutuo, scambievole, reciproco; comune. **— association,** mutualità, società di mutuo soccorso, *f.*; **on — terms,** alla pari.
mutuality, *n.* Mutualità, *f.*
mutule ['mju:tju:l], *n.* (*Arch.*) Modiglione, *m.*
muzzle ['mʌzəl], *n.* (*of animals*) Muso, *m.*; (*of a gun*) bocca, *f.*; (*for dog*) museruola, *f.*; (*to prevent speech*) bavaglio, *m.* || *v.t.* Mettere la museruola a; (*fig.*) imbavagliare, far tacere. **— -loader,** cannone ad avancarica.
my [mai], *a.pron.* Il mio, mio, *m.*, la mia, mia, *f.*, i miei, *m.pl.*, le mie, *f.pl.* || *inter.* Santo cielo! Perbacco!
mycology [mai'kɔlədʒi], *n.* Micologia, *f.*
mycologist, *n.* Micologo, *m.*
myelitis [maiə'laitis], *n.* (*Med.*) Mielite, *f.*
mylodon ['mailədɔn], *n.* (*Zool.*) Milodonte, *m.*
myocarditis [maioukɑ:ɹ'daitis], *n.* (*Med.*) Miocardite, *f.*
myope ['maıoup], *n.a.* Miope, *m.f.*
myopia, myopy, *n.* Miopia, *f.*
myopic, *a.* Miope.
myosotis [maio'soutis], *n.* (*Bot.*) Miosotide, *f.*
myriad ['miriəd], *n.* Miriade, *f.*
myriapod ['miriəpɔd], *n.* (*Zool.*) Miriapode, *m.*
myrmidon ['mə:ɹmidən], *n.* Mirmidone, *m.*; (*fig.*) sbirro, *m.* **The myrmidons of the law,** gli sbirri, *m.pl.*
myrrh [mə:ɹ], *n.* (*Bot.*) Mirra, *f.*
myrtle ['mə:ɹtl], *n.* (*Bot.*) Mirto, *m.* **— -berry,** bacca di mirto, *f.*, mirtillo, *m.*
myself [mai'self], *pron.* Io stesso, io, me. **I was by —,** ero tutto solo; **I have lost —,** ho perduto la via; **I have hurt —,** mi son fatto male; **I am not — to-day,** oggi non mi sento troppo bene, oggi non sono io.
mystagogue ['mistəgɔg], *n.* Mistagogo, *m.*
mysterious [mis'tiəriəs], *a.* Misterioso, oscuro, arcano.
mysteriously, *adv.* Misteriosamente, oscuramente.
mysteriousness, *n.* Misteriosità, *f.*
mystery ['mistəri], *n.* Mistero, *m.* **To make a — of,** far mistero di; **wrapt in —,** avvolto in mistero; (*Hist.*) **— play,** mistero, *m.*
mystic ['mistik], *n.* (*Eccles.*) Mistico, *m.*, mistica, *f.*
mystical, mystic, *a.* Mistico.
mysticalness, *n.* Misticità, *f.*
mysticism ['mistisizm], *n.* Misticismo, *m.*
mystification, *n.* Mistificazione, *f.*
mystifier, *n.* Mistificatore, *m.*
mystify, *v.t.* Mistificare, ingannare.
myth [miθ], *n.* Mito, *m.*
mythical, mythic, *a.* Mitico.
mythography [mi'θɔgrəfi], *n.* Mitografia.
mythological [miθə'lɔdʒikəl], *a.* Mitologico.
mythologist, *n.* Mitologista, mitologo, *m.*
mythology, *n.* Mitologia, *f.*

N

N, n [en], *n.* Quattordicesima lettera dell'alfabeto inglese (*Math.*) **nth,** ennesimo; **the nth power,** l'ennesima potenza, *f.*
nab [næb], *v.t.* Afferrare, acchiappare.
nabob ['neibɔb], *n.* Nabab, nababbo, *m.*
nacre ['neikəɹ], *n.* Madreperla, *f.*
nacreous, *a.* Madreperlaceo.
nadir ['nædəɹ], *n.* Nadir, *m.*; punto più basso, *m.*
naevus ['ni:vəs], *n.* Neo, *m.*, voglia, *f.*
nag (1) [næg], *n.* Ronzino, cavallino, *m.*
nag (2), *v.t.i.* Sgridare, criticare, annoiare, rimbrottare, infastidire.
nagging ['nægiŋ], *a.* Bisbetico, seccante; irritante.
naiad ['naiəd], *n.* (*Myth.*) Naiade, *f.*
nail [neil], *n.* Chiodo, *m.*; (*of finger*) unghia, *f.*; (*of animal*) artiglio, *m.* || *v.t.* Inchiodare; chiodare, fornire di chiodi; (*fig.*) afferrare, acchiappare. **To bite one's nails,** mangiarsi le unghie; **to cut one's nails,** tagliarsi le unghie; **to drive in a —,** conficcare un chiodo; (*fig.*) **to hit the — on the head,** colpire nel segno; **to pay on the —,** pagare a contanti; **hard as nails,** muscoloso, durissimo; **tooth and —,** con tutta l'anima, con ogni possa; **to — up,** inchiodare; **— -brush** spazzolino per le unghie, *m.*; **— -head,** capocchia di chiodo, *f.*; **— -maker,** chiodaiuolo, chiodaio, *m.*; **— -scissors,** forbici per le unghie; **— -file,** lima per le unghie, *f.*
nailery, nail-works, *n.* Chioderia, *f.*
nainsook ['neinsu:k], *n.* Specia di battista, *f.*
naïve, naïf ['nɑ:i:f, 'neiv, nɑ:'if], *a.* Ingenuo, semplice, candido.
naïvely, *adv.* Ingenuamente.
naïveté, naïvety [nɑ:'i:vti], *n.* Ingenuità, semplicità, *f.*
naked ['neikid], *a.* Nudo, ignudo, spoglio, spogliato; inerme, sguernito; (*defenceless*) disarmato; (*fig.*) semplice, schietto. **The — truth,** la nuda verità, *f.*; **with the — eye,** ad occhio nudo; **stark —,** tutto nudo, nudo come la mano.
nakedly, *adv.* Nudamente, allo scoperto.
nakedness, *n.* Nudità, *f.*
namby-pamby ['næmbi 'pæmbi], *a.* Sentimentale, affettato, sdolcinato. || *n.* Sentimentalità, *f.*; una persona sentimentale, *f.*
name [neim], *n.* Nome, *m.*; denominazione, *f.*, titolo, *m.*; rinomanza, reputazione, *f.* || *v.t.* Nominare, chiamare, denominare; menzionare, ricordare; indicare, parlare di. **Another — for,** sinonimo di; **assumed —,** pseudonimo, *m.*; **by —,** di nome, per nome, chiamato; **Christian —,** nome proprio, nome di battesimo, *m.*; **family —,** cognome, *m.*; **in the — of,** in nome di; **to call someone names,** ingiurare qualcuno; **What is your — ?** Come vi chiamate? **my — is John,** mi chiamo Giovanni; **to be named,** chiamarsi; **he has a — for honesty,** è reputato

onesto; **she is named after her godmother,** ha il nome della madrina; **the above-named,** il suddetto, il summenzionato, *m.*; **— -day,** giorno onomastico, *m.*; **— -plate,** targa, targhetta, *f.*
nameless, *a.* Senza nome; anonimo; sconosciuto.
namely, *adv.* Cioè, vale a dire.
namesake, *n.* Omonimo, *m.*
nankeen [næn'kiːn], *n.* Tela di Nanking, nanchina, *f.*
nanny ['næni], *n.* (*colloq.*) Bambinaia, balia, *f.*; (*goat*) capra, capretta, *f.*
nap (1) [næp], *n.* (*sleep*) Sonnellino, pisolino, *m.*, siesta, dormitina, *f.* || *v.i.* Appisolarsi, fare una dormitina. **To catch someone napping,** prendere qualcuno alla sprovvista.
nap (2), *n.* (*of cloth*) Pelo, *m.*, peluria, *f.*
nap (3), *n.* Specie di giuoco alle carte.
napalm [næ'pælm], *n.* Napalm, *m.*
nape [neip], *n.* (*Anat.*) Nuca, *f.*; (*colloq.*) collottola, *f.*
napery, n. Biancheria, *f.*
naphtha ['næfθə], *n.* (*Chem.*) Nafta, *f.*
naphthaline, naphthalene, *n.* Naftalina, *f.*
naphthol, *n.* Naftolo, *m.*
napkin ['næpkin], *n.* Tovagliuolo, *m.*; salvietta, *f.* **— ring,** anello del tovagliuolo, *m.*
Naples ['neiplz], *n.* (*Geog.*) Napoli, *f.*
napless, *a.* Senza pelo, raso.
nappy ['næpi], *n.* (*baby's*) Pannicello, pannolino, *m.*
Napoleonic [nəpouli'ɔnik], *a.* Napoleonico.
narcissus [nɑːɹ'sisəs], *n.* (*Bot.*) Narciso, *m.*
narcotic [nɑːɹ'kɔtik], *n.a.* Narcotico, *m.*
narcotism, *n.* Narcotismo, *m.*
narcotize, *v.t.* Narcotizzare.
nard [nɑːɹd], *n.* (*Bot.*) Nardo, *m.*
narghile [nɑːɹ'gili], *n.* Narghilè, *m.*
narrate [nə'reit], *v.t.* Narrare, raccontare.
narration, *n.* Narrazione, *f.*, racconto, *m.*
narrative ['nærətiv], *n.* Narrativa, *f.* || *a.* Narrativo.
narrator, *n.* Narratore, raccontatore, *m.*, narratrice, raccontatrice, *f.*
narrow ['nærou], *a.* Stretto; ristretto, angusto, limitato, esiguo; meschino. || *v.t.* Restringere, limitare, accorciare, diminuire; *v.i.* restringersi, diminuire. **A — mind,** una mente ristretta, *f.*; **to keep within — bounds,** restringere, circoscrivere; **to be in — circumstances,** vivere in ristrettezze; **to have a — escape,** scamparla bella; **a — scrutiny,** un esame meticoloso, *m.*; **narrows,** (*of water*) stretto, *m.*, (*of land*) gola, stretta, *f.*; **— -brimmed,** a tesa stretta; **— -minded,** di mente ristretta, gretto; (*Rail.*) **— -gauge,** a scartamento ridotto.
narrowly, *adv.* Strettamente; attentamente, accuratamente.
narrowness, *n.* Strettezza, *f.*; angustia, limitatezza, *f.*; esiguità, *f.*; meschineria, grettezza, *f.*
narthex ['nɑːɹθeks], *n.* (*Arch.*) Nartece, *m.*
narwhal ['nɑːɹwəl], *n.* (*Zool.*) Narvalo, *m.*
nasal ['neizəl], *a.* Nasale, di naso. || *n.* (*Gram.*) Suono nasale, *m.*, lettera nasale, *f.*
nasality, *n.* Nasalità, *f.*
nasalize, *v.t.* Nasalizzare.
nascent ['næsənt], *a.* Nascente.
nastily, *adv.* Bruttamente, sconciamente.
nastiness ['nɑːstinis], *n.* Sporcizia, *f.*; villania, *f.*, grossolanità, oscenità, *f.*; cattivo gusto, *m.*, disgustosità, *f.*
nasturtium [nə'stəːɹʃəm], *n.* (*Bot.*) Nasturzio, *m.*
nasty ['nɑːsti], *a.* Sporco, sudicio; villano, grossolano; nauseante, disgustoso, sgradevole; brutto, cattivo; (*of weather*) tempestoso; dispettoso, offensivo. **A — cold,** un brutto raffreddore, *m.*; **a — day,** una giornataccia, *f.*; **to taste —,** aver cattivo sapore; **a — wound,** una ferita grave, *f.*; (*colloq.*) **a — one,** un colpo mancino, *m.*, una partaccia, *f.*
natal ['neitəl], *a.* Natale, natalizio. **— day,** giorno natalizio, *m.*
natation [nə'teiʃən], *n.* Nuoto, *m.*
natatorial, natatory, *a.* Natatorio.
nation ['neiʃən], *n.* Nazione, *f.*, popolo, *m.*
national ['næʃənəl], *a.* Nazionale. **— debt,** debito pubblico, *m.*
nationalism, *n.* Nazionalismo, *m.*
nationalist, *n.* Nazionalista, *m.f.* || *a.* Nazionalista.
nationality [næʃə'næliti], *n.* Nazionalità, *f.*
nationalization, *n.* Nazionalizzazione, *f.*
nationalize, *v.t.* Nazionalizzare.
nationally, *adv.* Nazionalmente.
nationals, *n.pl.* Connazionali, *m.pl.*
native ['neitiv], *a.* Nativo, natio; indigeno; naturale, innato; schietto, semplice; (*of language*) materno. || *n.* Nativo, indigeno, naturale, *m.*; nativa, indigena, *f.* **— place,** luogo natio, *m.*; **— land,** patria, *f.*, paese natio, *m.*; **— tongue,** lingua materna, *f.*; **a — of Rome,** un nativo di Roma, *m.*
nativity [nə'tiviti], *n.* Natività, nascita, *f.*; (*Astrol.*) oroscopo, *m.*; (*Eccles.*) Natività, *f.*
natterjack ['nætəɹdʒæk], *n.* (*Zool.*) Specie di rospo, *m.*
natty ['næti], *a.* Attillato, lindo; svelto, ben tenuto.
natural ['nætʃjuːrəl], *a.* Naturale, reale; ingenito, nativo; schietto, semplice; illegittimo. || *n.* Idiota, *m.f.*; (*Mus.*) bequadro, *m.* **— history museum,** museo di storia naturale.
naturalist, *n.* Naturalista, *m.f.*
naturalistic, *a.* Naturalistico.
naturalization, *n.* Naturalizzazione, *f.* **— papers,** lettere di naturalizzazione, *f.pl.*
naturalize, *v.t.* Naturalizzare.
naturally, *adv.* Naturalmente; semplicemente.
naturalness, *n.* Naturalezza, *f.*; disinvoltura, *f.*
nature ['neitʃəɹ], *n.* Natura, *f.*; disposizione, indole, *f.*; carattere, temperamento, *m.* **Good —,** bontà, *f.*; (*Art*) **from —,** dal vero, dal naturale; **to pay the debt of —,** morire, pagare il tributo alla natura; **it is in the — of things that,** è naturale che; **by —,** per natura, naturalmente; **in a state of —,** allo stato di natura.
naught [nɔːt], *n.* Niente, nulla, *m.*; (*Math.*) zero, *m.* **To set at —,** far poco caso di, sprezzare; **to bring to —,** far fallire; **a thing of —,** una cosa inutile, *f.*
naughtily, *adv.* Male, malvagiamente.
naughtiness, *n.* Cattiveria, malvagità, indecenza, *f.*
naughty, *a.* Cattivo, malizioso, malvagio; indecente, grossolano. **Naughty boy!** Birichino!, Cattivello!; **a — trick,** una birichinata, *f.*

nausea ['nɔːsiə], *n.* Nausea, *f.*; avversione, noia, *f.*; fastidio, disgusto, *m.*
nauseate ['nɔːsieit], *v.t.i.* Nauseare, disgustare.
nauseating, nauseous, *a.* Nauseante, nauseabondo, nauseoso.
nauseousness ['nɔːsiəsnis], *n.* Nausea, *f.*
nautical ['nɔːtikəl], *a.* Nautico, marinaresco, navale. **— almanac,** effemeridi astronomiche, *f.pl.*; **— mile,** miglio nautico, *m.*; **— science,** nautica, *f.*
nautilus ['nɔːtiləs], *n.* (*Zool.*) Nautilo, *m.*
naval ['neivəl], *a.* Navale; marittimo; di marina, della marina. **— architect,** architetto navale, *m.*; **— dockyard,** arsenale marittimo, *m.*; **— base, — station,** porto militare, *m.*, stazione navale, *f.*; **— cadet,** allievo della scuola navale, *m.*; **— forces,** marina, *f.*, forze navali, *f.pl.*; **— officer,** ufficiale di marina, *m.*; **— engagement,** battaglia navale, *f.*
nave (1) [neiv], *n.* (*Arch.*) Navata centrale, *f.*
nave (2), *n.* (*of wheel*) Mozzo, *m.*
navel ['neivəl], *n.* (*Anat.*) Umbilico, ombelico, *m.* **— cord, — string,** cordone ombelicale, *m.*
navicert ['nævisəɹt], *n.* (*Naut.*) Certificato di navigazione, *m.*
navigability, *n.* Navigabilità, *f.*
navigable ['nævigəbl], *a.* Navigabile.
navigate, *v.t.i.* Navigare, governare, dirigere.
navigation, *n.* Navigazione, *f.* **Aerial —,** navigazione aerea, *f.*; **internal —,** navigazione interna, *f.*
navigator, *n.* Navigatore, *m.*
navvy ['nævi], *n.* Sterratore, terrazziere, badilante, *m.*; (*Mech.*) macchina scavatrice, *f.*
navy ['neivi], *n.* Marina, *f.*; **Royal Navy,** Regia Marina, *f.*; **— list,** annuario della Marina, *m.*; **— yard,** arsenale marittimo, *m.*; **— -blue,** blu marino, *m.*
nay [nei], *adv.* No; anzi. || *n.* No, *m.* **To say someone —,** negare qualcosa a qualcuno; **he won't take — for an answer,** non vuol aver un rifiuto.
Nazarene [næzə'riːn], *n.a.* Nazareno, *m.*
Nazareth ['næzərəθ], *n.* (*Geog.*) Nazaret, *f.*
Nazarite, *n.a.* Nazareno, *m.*
Neapolitan [niːə'pɔlitən], *n.* Napoletano, *m.*, napoletana, *f.* || *a.* Napoletano.
neap tide [niːp taid], *n.* Bassa marea, *f.*
near [niəɹ], *a.* Vicino, prossimo; (*of time*) imminente; (*miserly*) meschino, tirchio; (*of friends*) caro, fedele; (*left*) sinistro. || *adv.* Presso, vicino, dappresso, quasi, circa. || *prep.* Presso, vicino, presso a, vicino a, accanto a. || *v.i.* Avvicinarsi. **A — relative,** un parente prossimo, *m.*; **to give a — guess,** indovinare press'a poco; **a — resemblance,** una rassomiglianza quasi perfetta, *f.*; **the nearest way,** la più breve strada, *f.*; **the Near East,** il Levante, *m.*; **— relationship,** parentela stretta, *f.*; **— -sighted,** miope; (*Naut.*) **— the wind,** stretto al vento.
nearly, *adv.* Quasi, press'a poco; dappresso; strettamente; da vicino. **He examined it —,** lo esaminò da vicino; **this concerns me —,** ciò mi tocca da vicino; **not — enough,** non proprio abbastanza; **it is — noon,** è quasi mezzogiorno; **he — had an accident,** mancò poco che gli accadesse una disgrazia; **I — missed the train,** ho quasi perduto il treno.
nearness, *n.* Prossimità, vicinanza, *f.*; intimità, *f.*; tirchieria, meschinità, *f.*
neat (1) [niːt], *a.* Netto, pulito, lindo; elegante; (*undiluted*) puro; nitido, terso; destro, abile. **— -handed,** destro, svelto.
neat (2), *n.* Bestiame grosso, *m.*; bove, *m.*, bovini, *m.pl.*; vacca, *f.* **— -herd,** vaccaio, vaccaro, *m.*; **neat's tongue,** lingua di bue, *f.*; **neat's-foot oil,** olio di piede di bue, *m.*
neatness, *n.* Nettezza, pulizia, proprietà, *f.*; nitidezza, tersezza, *f.*; destrezza, *f.*
neath [cp. **beneath**].
neb [neb], *n.* (*obs.*) Becco, *m.*
nebula ['nebjuːlə], *n.* (*Astron.*) Nebulosa, *f.*
nebulosity, *n.* Nebulosità, *f.*
nebulous, *a.* Nebuloso; (*fig.*) incerto, vago.
necessaries ['nesisəriz], *n.pl.* Cose necessarie, necessità, *f.pl.*, necessario, *m.*
necessarily, *adv.* Necessariamente, di necessità.
necessary, *a.* Necessario. || *n.* Necessario, *m.* **If —,** se ce n'è bisogno, se è necessario; **to be —,** bisognare, occorrere.
necessitate [ni'sesiteit], *v.t.* Necessitare, costringere, rendere necessario.
necessitous, *a.* Bisognoso, indigente, povero.
necessity, *n.* Necessità, *f.*; indigenza, povertà, *f.* **From —,** per necessità; **of —,** necessariamente; **to make a virtue of —,** fare di necessità virtù; **— knows no law,** la necessità non ha legge; **to be under the — of,** essere costretto a.
neck [nek], *n.* (*Anat.*) Collo, *m.*; (*of land*) lingua, *f.*; (*of sea*) braccio, *m.*; (*of bottle*) collo, *m.*; (*of violin*) manico, *m.*; (*Racing*) incollatura, *f.* **To break one's —,** rompersi il collo; **to save one's —,** sottrarsi alla morte; (*Sport*) **to win by a —,** vincere per un'incollatura; **— and crop,** a capofitto; **— or nothing,** o morte o nulla; **— and —,** alla pari; **a stiff —,** un torcicollo, *m.*; **— -tie,** cravatta, *f.*; **— measurement,** giro del collo, *m.*
neckband, *n.* Accollatura, *f.*, colletto, collarino, *m.*
neckcloth, *n.* Cravatta, *f.*
necked, *a.* Dal collo. **Long- —,** dal collo lungo; **short- —,** dal collo corto; (*fig.*) **stiff- —,** ostinato, testardo.
neckerchief ['nekəɹtʃif], *n.* Fazzoletto da collo, *m.*
necklace ['nekləs], *n.* Collana, *f.*
necklet, *n.* Collana, *f.*, collarino, *m.*
necrological [nekro'lɔdʒikəl], *a.* Necrologico.
necrologist, *n.* Necrologista, *m.f.*
necrology, *n.* Necrologia, *f.*; necrologio, registro dei morti, *m.*
necromancer ['nekromænsəɹ], *n.* Negromante, *m.f.*
necromancy, *n.* Negromanzia, *f.*
necromantic, *a.* Negromantico.
necropolis [ne'krɔpolis], *n.* Necropoli, *f.*
necrosis [ne'krousis], *n.* (*Med.*) Necrosi, *f.*
nectar ['nektəɹ], *n.* Nettare, *m.*
nectareous, *a.* Nettareo.
nectarine ['nektərin], *n.* (*Bot.*) Pesca noce, *f.*
nectary, *n.* (*Bot.*) Nettario, *m.*
Ned, Neddy [ned, 'nedi], *n.* (*colloq.*) Edoardo, *m.*

née [nei], *a.* (*maiden name of married woman*) Nata.
need [ni:d], *n.* Bisogno, *m.*, necessità, *f.*; povertà, indigenza, *f.* || *v.t.i.* Bisognare, aver bisogno di; dovere; occorrere, esser necessario. **If — be,** se ce n'è bisogno, al bisogno; **there is no —,** non c'è bisogno; **to have — of,** avere bisogno di; **you had — remember,** voi dovete ricordarvi; **to be in — of,** essere bisognoso, aver bisogno di; **in case of —,** in caso di bisogno; **he — not go,** non è necessario che vada; **Why — he say that?** Perchè deve dir ciò? **this child needs care,** questo bambino ha bisogno di molta cura; **don't be away longer than you —,** non state via più che non sia necessario; **there is — of,** c'è bisogno di; **you needn't laugh,** non c'è di che ridere; **he needn't write to me,** è inutile che egli mi scriva.
needful, *a.* Necessario, indispensabile, occorrente. || *n.* (*colloq.*) Il fabbisogno, il necessario, *m.*
neediness, *n.* Bisogno, *m.*, povertà, indigenza, *f.*
needle [ni:dl], *n.* Ago, *m.*; (*gramophone*) puntina per grammofono, *f.*; (*knitting*) ferro, ago da calza, *m.* **Eye of a —,** cruna, *f.*; **to thread a —,** infilare un ago; **—-case,** astuccio per aghi, *m.*, agoraio, *m.*; **—-gun,** fucile ad ago, *m.*
needleful, *n.* Gugliata, agugliata, *f.*
needless ['ni:dles], *a.* Inutile, superfluo, non necessario. **It is — to say that,** va da sè che, è inutile dire che.
needlessness, *n.* Inutilità, superfluità, *f.*
needlewoman, *n.* Cucitrice, *f.*
needlework, *n.* Lavoro d'ago, ricamo, *m.*
needs, *adv.* **I — must,** devo assolutamente, devo proprio.
needy, *a.* Bisognoso, indigente, povero.
ne'er [nɛəɹ], *adv.* (*Poet.*) Mai, giammai. **—-do-well,** buono a nulla, fannullone, *m.* [cp. **never**].
nefarious [ne'fɛəriəs], *a.* Cattivo, scellerato, iniquo.
nefariously, *adv.* Scelleratamente, iniquamente.
nefariousness, *n.* Scelleratezza, nequizia, *f.*
negate [ne'geit], *v.t.* Negare.
negation, *n.* Negazione, *f.*
negative ['negətiv], *n.* Negativa, *f.* || *a.* Negativo. || *v.t.* Negare, rigettare, dare il veto a; neutralizzare. **The answer is in the —,** la risposta è No.
neglect [ne'glekt], *n.* Negligenza, trascuratezza, trascuranza, *f.*; noncuranza, disattenzione, *f.*; abbandono, oblio, *m.* || *v.t.* Trascurare, tralasciare, mancare di, negligere; dimenticare.
neglectful [cp. **negligent**].
négligé ['negli:dʒei], *n.* Abito da camera, *m.*
negligence ['neglidʒəns], *n.* Negligenza, trascuranza, *f.*; oblio, abbandono, *m.*
negligent, neglectful, *a.* Negligente, trascurato, disattento, svogliato, indifferente.
negligently, *adv.* Negligentemente.
negligible, *a.* Trascurabile, negligibile. **A — quantity,** una quantità trascurabile, *f.*
negotiability [negouʃə'biliti], *n.* (*Comm.*) Negoziabilità, *f.*
negotiable [ne'gouʃəbl], *a.* Negoziabile.
negotiate [ne'gouʃieit], *v.t.i.* Negoziare.
negotiation, *n.* Negoziazione, trattativa, *f.*
negotiator, *n.* Negoziatore, *m.*
negotiatress, negotiatrix, *n.* Negoziatrice, *f.*
Negress ['ni:gres], *n.* (*off.*) Negra, *f.*
Negrillo, *n.* Negretto, *m.*
Negrito, *n.* Negrita, *m.*
Negro ['ni:grou] *n.m.* or *f.* (*pl.* **Negroes**) Negro, *m.*, negra, *f.* || *a.* Negro, nero.
Negroid ['ni:grɔid], *a.* Negroide.
negus (1) ['ni:gəs], *n.* Vino riscaldato, *m.*
Negus (2), *n.* L'imperatore di Etiopia, *m.*
neigh [nei], *v.i.* Nitrire. || *n.* Nitrito, *m.*
neighbour ['neibəɹ], *n.* Vicino, prossimo, *m.*, vicina, prossima, *f.* || *a.* Vicino, prossimo. || *v.t.i.* Esser vicino a, toccare, confinare. **One's next door neighbours,** i vicini di casa, *m.pl.*
neighbourhood, *n.* Vicinanza, *f.*, dintorni, *m.pl.*, vicinato, *m.*; pressi, *m.pl.*, quartiere, *m.*
neighbouring, *a.* Vicino, adiacente, contiguo, confinante; (*country*) limitrofo, *m.*
neighbourly, *a.* Socievole, gentile, compagnevole. **To be —,** essere buon vicino; **in a — way,** da buon vicino.
neither ['naiðəɹ, 'ni:ðəɹ], *a.pron.* Nè l'uno nè l'altro, *m.*, nè l'una nè l'altra, *f.*, nè gli uni, nè gli altri, *m.pl.*, nè le une nè le altre, *f.pl.*, nessun dei due. || *adv.* Neanche, nemmeno. || *conj.* nè, neppure.
Nemesis ['nemisis], *n.* (*Myth.*) Nemesi, *f.*
nenuphar ['nenju:fɑ:ɹ], *n.* (*Bot.*) Nenufaro, *m.*
neolithic [ni:o'liθik], *a.* (*Geol.*) Neolitico.
neological [ni:o'lɔdʒikəl], *a.* Neologico.
neologism [ni:'ɔlodʒizm], *n.* Neologismo, *m.*
neon ['ni:ən], *n.* Neon, *m.* **— light,** luce di neon, *f.*; **— lamp,** lampada di neon, *f.*
neophyte ['ni:ofait], *n.* Neofito, *m.*, neofita, *f.*
neoplatonism [ni:o'pleitənizm], *n.* Neoplatonismo, *m.*
neoplatonist, *n.* Neoplatonico, *m.*
nepenthe [ne'penθi], *n.* (*Bot.*) Nepente, *m.*
nephew ['nevju:], *n.* Nipote, *m.* **Great- —,** pronipote, *m.*
nephritic [ne'fritik], *a.* (*Med.*) Nefritico.
nephritis, *n.* Nefrite, *f.*
nepotism ['ni:potizm], *n.* Nepotismo, *m.*
Neptune ['neptju:n], *n.* (*Myth. Astron.*) Nettuno, *m.*
Neptunian, *a.* Nettuniano.
Nereid ['nɛərəid], *n.* (*Myth.*) Nereide, *f.*
nervate ['nə:ɹvit], *a.* (*Bot.*) Nervato.
nerve [nə:ɹv], *n.* (*Anat.*) Nervo, *m.*; (*sinew*) nerbo, *m.*; (*courage*), coraggio, nerbo, *m.*; (*Bot.*) nervatura, *f.*; (*impudence*) audacia, *f.* || *v.t.* Fortificare, rinvigorire, rafforzare, temprare. **A fit of nerves,** un attacco di nervi, *m.*; **he has iron nerves,** ha nervi d'acciaio; **it gets on my nerves,** mi dà ai nervi, mi irrita; **to — oneself,** prendere animo, rinfrancarsi, ritemprarsi. **—-centre,** ganglio nervoso, *m.*; **— specialist,** neurologo, *m.*
nerveless, *a.* Snervato, sfibrato, debole; (*Bot.*) senza nervatura.
nervine, *a.* (*Med.*) Nervino.
nervous ['nə:ɹvəs], *a.* Nervoso, timido, eccitabile; energico; (*Anat.*) nerveo.
nervously, *adv.* Timidamente.
nervousness, *n.* Nervosità, timidità, *f.*; apprensione, *f.*

nervure, *n.* (*Bot.*) Nervatura, *f.*
nervy, *a.* Nervoso. (*Am. colloq.*) sfacciato.
nescience [ˈneʃiəns], *n.* Nescienza, *f.*
nesh [neʃ], *a.* Friabile.
ness [nes], *n.* (*Geog.*) Promontorio, capo, *m.*
nest [nest], *n.* Nido, *m.*; (*fig.*) riparo, covo, covile, *m.* || *v.i.* Nidificare; annidarsi. **— -egg,** endice, uovo finto, *m.*; (*money*) gruzzolo, *m.*; danaro risparmiato, *m.*; **— of drawers,** piccolo cassettone, *m.*
nestful, *n.* Nidiata, *f.*
nestle [nesl], *v.i.* Annidarsi, accomodarsi, adagiarsi, rannicchiarsi, accoccolarsi. **To — down,** rannicchiarsi; **to — close,** tenersi stretto, stringersi a.
nestling, *n.* Uccellino di nido, nidiace, *m.*
Nestor [ˈnestɔːɹ], *n.* Nestore, *m.*
Nestorian [nesˈtɔːriən], *n.a.* Nestoriano, *m.*
Nestorianism, *n.* Nestorianismo, *m.*
net (1) [net], *n.* Rete, *f.*; (*for hair*) reticella, *f.*; (*fig.*) laccio, *m.*, trappola, *f.* || *v.t.* (*to catch*) Irretire; (*to snare*) accalappiare; (*Comm.*) guadagnare, ricavare; *v.i.* lavorare a rete. **Drag- —,** tramaglio, *m.*; **sweep- —,** giacchio, *m.*; **— -bag,** rete per le spese, *f.*
net (2), *a.* (*Comm.*) Netto. **— profit,** utile netto, *m.*
netful, *n.* Retata, *f.*
nether [ˈneðəɹ], *a.* Più basso, inferiore. **— regions,** inferno, *m.*
Netherlander [ˈneðəɹləndəɹ], *n.* Olandese, *m.f.*
Netherlands, *n.pl.* (*Geog.*) I Paesi Bassi, *m.pl.*, l'Olanda, *f.*
nethermost [ˈneðəɹmost], *a.* Il più basso.
netting, *n.* Lavoro a rete, *m.* **— needle,** spola, *f.*; **wire- —,** reticolato, *m.*, rete metallica, *f.*
nettle [netl], *n.* (*Bot.*) Ortica, *f.* || *v.t.* Esasperare, pungere. **— -rash,** orticaria, *f.*
network, *n.* Reticolato, retato, *m.*, rete, *f.*
neuralgia [njuːˈrældʒə], *n.* (*Med.*) Nevralgia, *f.*
neuralgic, *a.* Nevralgico.
neurasthenia [njuːrəsˈθiːniə], *n.* (*Med.*) Nevrastenia, *f.*
neurasthenic, *a.* Nevrastenico.
neuritis [njuːˈraitis], *n.* (*Med.*) Neurite, *f.*
neurologist [njuːˈrɔlədʒist], *n.* Neurologo, *m.*
neurology, *n.* Neurologia, *f.*
neuropathology [njuːropəˈθɔlədʒi], *n.* Neuropatologia, *f.*
neuropterous [njuːˈrɔptərəs], *a.* (*Zool.*) Neurottero.
neurosis [njuːˈrousis], *n.* (*Med.*) Nevrosi, *f.*
neurotic, *a.* Nevrotico.
neurotomy, *n.* Nevrotomia, *f.*
neuter [ˈnjuːtəɹ], *n.a.* Neutro, *m.*, genere neutro, *m.*
neutral, *n.a.* Neutrale, *m.*; (*Chem.Elec.*) neutro.
neutrality [njuːˈtræliti], *n.* Neutralità, *f.*
neutralization, *n.* Neutralizzazione, *f.*
neutralize, *v.t.* Neutralizzare.
never [ˈnevəɹ], *adv.* Mai, non . . . mai; giammai, non . . . giammai. **Never again!** Mai più! **Never!** Giammai! **he will — come back,** non tornerà mai; **I — saw such a thing,** non vidi mai una simil cosa; **Never mind!** Non importa! (*colloq.*) **Well, I —!** Non è possibile! **— a word,** non una parola; **now or —,** ora o mai più; **better late than —,** meglio tardi che mai; **— -ending,** interminabile, infinito; **— -failing,** infallibile, immancabile; **— -to-be-forgotten,** indimenticabile.
nevermore, *adv.* Mai più.
nevertheless, *conj.adv.* Tuttavia, nondimeno, contuttociò; ad ogni modo, pure, pertanto.
new [njuː], *a.* Nuovo, novello, recente; fresco. **As good as —,** come nuovo; **there's nothing — under the sun,** non c'è nulla di nuovo sotto il sole; **brand- —,** nuovo di zecca, nuovo fiammante; **— bread,** pane fresco, *m.*; **— potatoes,** patate novelle, *f.pl.*; **— -laid eggs,** uova fresche, *f.pl.*; **— -comer,** nuovo venuto, *m.*; **New Testament,** Nuovo Testamento, *m.*; **New Year's Day,** capo d'anno, capodanno, *m.*; **New Year's gift,** strenna, *f.* **— -fashioned,** d'attualità, alla moda; **New South Wales,** Nuova Galles del Sud, *f.*; **New Zealand,** Nuova Zelanda, *f.*
newel [ˈnjuːəl], *n.* Fusto d'una scala a chiocciola, nocciolo, *m.*
Newfoundland [ˈnjuːfənlænd, njuːˈfaundlənd], *n.* (*Geog.*) Terranova, *f.* **— dog,** terranova, *m.*
newly, *adv.* Recentemente, di fresco, di recente.
newness, *n.* Novità, *f.*; freschezza, *f.*
news [njuːz], *n.* Notizie, nuove, novelle, *f.pl.* notizia, nuova, *f.*; informazioni, *f.pl.*; (*Cinema*) attualità, *f.* **No — is good —,** nessuna nuova buona nuova; **What's the —?** Che c'è di nuovo? **the latest —,** le recentissime, *f.pl.*; **bad —,** brutta notizia, *f.*; **— -agency,** agenzia di informazioni, *f.*; **— -agent,** venditore di giornali, *m.*; **— -boy,** giornalaio, strillone, *m.*; (*Radio*) **— -bulletin,** giornale radio, *m.*; (*Cinema*) **— -film,** film d'attualità, *m.*; **— -room,** gabinetto di lettura, *m.*
newsmonger [ˈnjuːzmʌŋgəɹ], *n.* Chiacchierone, pettegolo, *m.*
newspaper, *n.* Giornale, foglio, *m.*, gazzetta, *f.*
newsreel [ˈnjuːzriːl], *n.* (*Cinema*) Notiziario, *m.*, le attualità della settimana, *f.pl.*
newt [njuːt], *n.* (*Zool.*) Tritone, *m.*; salamandra, acquaiola, *f.*
Newtonian [njuːˈtouniən], *n.a.* Neutoniano, *m.*
next [nekst], *a.* Vicino, accanto, contiguo; prossimo, seguente, successivo, venturo. || *adv.* Dopo, poi, in seguito, appresso. **— day,** l'indomani, il giorno seguente, *m.*; **— time,** la prossima volta, *f.*; **— year,** l'anno venturo, *m.*; **Tuesday —,** martedì prossimo, *m.*; **— -door to,** accanto a, vicino a; **— to nothing,** quasi niente; **ask the — man you see,** domandate al primo uomo che vedrete; **— but one,** il secondo, il penultimo, *m.*; **— of kin,** parenti prossimi, *m.pl.*; **the — world,** l'altro mondo, il mondo di là, l'al di là, *m.*; **Who comes —?** Chi vien dopo? **What —?** E poi?
nib [nib], *n.* Pennino, *m.*, punta, *f.*
nibbed, *a.* Con punta, con pennino. **A broad- — pen,** una penna a pennino largo, *f.*
nibble [nibl], *v.t.i.* Rosicchiare, morsicare; mangiucchiare; sgranocchiare; (*of sheep*) brucare; (*of fish*) abboccare. || *n.* Bocconcino, *m.*
nibbler, *n.* Roditore, *m.*

nice (1) [nais], *a.* Buono, gentile, amabile, simpatico; piacevole, dilettevole; minuzioso, scrupoloso, delicato, puntiglioso; fino, sottile; squisito. **A — distinction,** una sottile distinzione, *f.*; **a — ear,** un orecchio fino, *m.*; **a — experiment,** un esperimento difficile, *m.*; **a — fellow,** un simpaticone, *m.*; **Here's a — mess!** Ecco un bel pasticcio!

Nice (2) [ni:s], *n.* (*Geog.*) Nizza, *f.*

nicely, *adv.* Molto bene, gradevolmente; esattamente; benino. **This will do —,** questo andrà proprio bene.

Nicene [nai'si:n], *a.* (*Eccles.*) Di Nicea. **The — Creed,** il simbolo di Nicea, *m.*

niceness, *n.* Bontà, piacevolezza, *f.*; scrupolosità, finezza, *f.*

nicety, *n.* Finezza, sottigliezza, *f.*; esattezza, precisione, *f.* **Niceties,** minuzie, *f.pl.*, dettagli, *m.pl.*; sottigliezze, *f.pl.* **To a —,** esattamente; **the niceties of a language,** le finezze di una lingua, *f.pl.*; **to fit to a —,** andare a cappello.

niche [nitʃ], *n.* Nicchia, *f.*

nick (1) [nik], *n.* Intaccatura, tacca, *f.* || *v.t.* Intaccare, fare una tacca. **In the — of time,** al momento preciso, in buon punto, all'ultimo istante.

Nick (2), *abbrev.* Nicola, *m.* **Old Nick,** il diavolo, *m.*

nickel ['nikəl], *n.* (*Min.*) Nichel, nichelio, *m.* || *v.t.* Nichelare. **—-plated,** nichelato; **—-silver,** argentone, *m.*; **—-steel,** acciaio nichelato, *m.*

nick-nack ['niknæk], *n.* Ninnolo, gingillo, *m.* [cp. **knick-knack**].

nickname ['nikneim], *n.* Nomignolo, soprannome, *m.* || *v.t.* Soprannominare, dare un nomignolo.

nicotine ['nikoti:n], *n.* Nicotina, *f.*

nicotinism, *n.* (*Med.*) Nicotinismo, *m.*

nicotinize, *v.t.* Impregnare di nicotina.

nictate, nictitate ['nikteit, 'niktiteit], *v.i.* Battere gli occhi, palpebrare. **Nictitating membrane,** terza palpebra degli uccelli, *f.*

nidification [nidifi'keiʃən], *n.* Nidificazione, *f.*

nidify ['nidifai], *v.t.* Nidificare.

niece [ni:s], *n.* Nipote, *f.* **Grand- —,** pronipote, *f.*

niello [ni'elou], *n.* Niello, *m.*

niggard ['nigəɹd], *n.a.* Avaro, tirchio, taccagno, gretto, spilorcio, *m.*

niggardliness, *n.* Avarizia, taccagneria, *f.*

niggardly, *a.* Gretto, avaro, spilorcio. || *adv.* Avaramente.

nigger ['nigəɹ], *n.* (*off.*) Negro, *m.*, negra, *f.*

niggling ['nigliŋ], *a.* Insignificante, minuto.

nigh [nai], *adv.* Vicino, prossimo. **To draw —,** avvicinarsi; **well —,** quasi, ormai.

night [nait], *n.* Notte, *f.*; nottata, *f.*; sera, serata, *f.* **Good- —!** Buona notte! **all —,** tutta la notte; **at —,** di notte; **last —,** la notte scorsa, ieri sera; (*Theat.*) **first —,** première, *f.*; **— after —,** una sera dopo l'altra, *f.*; **late at —,** a tarda notte, a notte inoltrata; **to- —,** stanotte, stasera, *f.*; **to turn — into day,** fare di notte giorno; **he stayed here two nights,** passò due notti qui; **Did you have a good —?** Ha dormito bene? (*colloq.*) **to make a — of it,** fare nottata; **to have a — out,** fare nottata, passar fuori la sera; **in the dead of —,** nel cuor della notte; **—-attire,** veste da notte, *f.*; **—-bird,** uccello notturno, *m.*, (*fig.*) nottambulo, *m.*; **—-blindness,** nictalopia, emeralopia, *f.*; **—-call** (*Telephone*) telefonata notturna, *f.*; **—-club,** tabarin, *m.*, ritrovo notturno, *m.*; **—-light,** lumino da notte, *m.*; (*Art*) **—-piece,** effetto notturno, effetto serale, *m.*; **—-school,** scuola serale, *f.*; **—-nurse,** infermiera di notte, *f.*; **—-nursing,** veglia notturna, *f.*; **— stool,** seggetta, *f.*; **—-time,** notte, *f.*; **in the —-time,** durante la notte, di nottetempo; **—-watchman,** guardia notturna, *f.*, guardiano notturno, *m.*; **—-work,** lavoro notturno, *m.*

nightcap, *n.* Berretto da notte, *m.*; (*drink*) bevanda prima di andar a letto, *f.*

nightdress, nightgown, *n.* Camicia da notte, *f.*

nightfall, *n.* Crepuscolo, tramonto, *m.* **At —,** sul far della notte.

nightingale ['naitiŋgeil], *n.* (*Zool.*) Usignuolo, *m.*

nightjar ['naitdʒɑ:ɹ], *n.* (*Zool.*) Nottolone, *m.*

nightlong, *a.* Per l'intera notte.

nightly, *a.* Notturno, di notte, di ogni notte. || *adv.* Tutte le notti.

nightmare, *n.* Incubo, *m.*, oppressione, *f.*

nightmarish, *a.* Opprimente, angoscioso, ossessionante, orribile.

nightshade, *n.* (*Bot.*) Morella, *f.* **Woody —,** dulcamara, *f.*; **deadly —,** belladonna, *f.*

nigrescence, *n.* Nereggiamento, *m.*

nigrescent [ni'gresənt], *a.* Nericcio, nereggiante, nerastro.

Nihilism ['naihilizm], *n.* (*Pol.*) Nichilismo, *m.*

Nihilist, *n.* Nichilista, *m.f.*

nil [nil], *n.* Niente, nulla, *m.*

Nile [nail], *n.* (*Geog.*) Nilo, *m.*

nilometer [nai'lɔmitəɹ], *n.* Nilometro, *m.*

Nilotic [ni'lɔtik], *a.* Del Nilo, nilotico.

nimble ['nimbəl], *a.* Agile, leggiero, lesto, svelto. **—-footed,** agile, lesto; **—-witted,** svelto, pronto.

nimbleness, *n.* Agilità, lestezza, sveltezza, *f.*

nimbly, *adv.* Agilmente, lestamente.

nimbus ['nimbəs], *n.* Aureola, *f.*, nimbo, *m.*; (*rain-cloud*) nembo, *m.*

niminy-piminy ['nimini 'pimini], *a.* Lezioso.

nincompoop ['ninkəmpu:p], *n.* Imbecille, *m.*; zuccone, balordo, stupido, *m.*

nine [nain], *n.a.* Nove, *m.* **A — days' wonder,** un fuoco di paglia, *m.*; **— times out of ten,** nove volte su dieci; **dressed up to the nines,** azzimato, in ghingheri; **—-score,** cento ottanta; (*Golf*) **—-hole course,** percorso di nove buchi, *m.*

ninefold, *a.* Nove volte tanto.

ninepins, *n.pl.* Birilli, *m.pl.*

nineteen [nain'ti:n], *n.a.* Diciannove, *m.*

nineteenth, *n.a.* Diciannovesimo, decimonono, *m.*

ninetieth ['naintiəθ], *n.a.* Novantesimo, *m.*

ninety ['nainti], *n.a.* Novanta, *m.* **Ninety-one, ninety-two,** *etc.*, novantuno, novantadue, *ecc.*

Nineveh ['ninivə], *n.* (*Geog.*) Ninive, *f.*

ninny ['nini], *n.* Imbecille, zuccone.

ninth [nainθ], *n.a.* Nono, *m.* **Pius IX,** Pio Nono, *m.*

ninthly ['nainθli], *adv.* In nono luogo.

nip [nip], *n.* Pizzico, pizzicotto, morso, *m.*; (*of cold*) gelo, abbruciamento, *m.*; (*fig.*) sarcasmo, *m.*; (*drink*) grappino, bicchierino, *m.* || *v.t.* Pizzicare, morsicare; gelare, assiderare. **To — about,** correre qua e là; **to — in the bud,** distruggere in germe, arrestare all'inizio; **to be nipped by frost,** prendere il gelo.

nipper, *n.* (*colloq.*) Ragazzino, biricchino, *m.*

nippers, *n.pl.* Pinze, pinzette, *f.pl.*; (*of crabs, etc.*) chele, *f.pl.*; tenaglie, *f.pl.*

nipping, *a.* Pungente, frizzante, mordente.

nipple [ˈnipəl], *n.* (*Anat.*) Capezzolo, *m.*, poppa, *f.*; (*of baby's bottle*) poppatoio, *m.*; (*of gun*) mirino, luminello, *m.*

nipplewort, *n.* (*Bot.*) Lassana, *f.*

nippy, *a.* Agile, lesto, svelto; mordace.

ni rvana [niəɹˈvɑːnə], *n.* Nirvana, *m.*

nit [nit], *n.* (*Zool.*) Lendine, *m.*

nitrate [ˈnaitreit], *n.* (*Chem.*) Nitrato, azotato, *m.*

nitre [ˈnaitəɹ], *n.* Nitro, *m.*

nitric, *a.* Nitrico, azotico.

nitrify, *v.t.* Nitrificare.

nitrogen [ˈnaitrədʒən], *n.* Nitrogeno, azoto, *m.*

nitrogenous, *a.* Nitrogenoso.

nitroglycerine [naitrouˈglisəriːn], *n.* Nitroglicerina, *f.*

nitrous, *a.* Nitroso.

nit-wit [ˈnitwit], *n.* (*colloq.*) Imbecille, stupido, *m.*

no [nou], *a.adv.* No, non, punto, mica, non . . . più, nessuno. || *n.* No, *m.* **He has no relations,** non ha parenti; **I have no books at all,** non ho punti libri; **he is no doctor,** non è affatto dottore; **no doubt,** senza dubbio; **No matter!** Non importa! **No more!** Basta! **he is no more,** è morto, non è più; **no one,** nessuno; **no sooner said than done,** detto fatto; **No such thing!** Non è vero! **there is no avoiding a disaster,** è impossibile di evitare un disastro; **there is no sense in it,** non c'è senso, è ridicolo; **tell me whether or no,** ditemelo in ogni modo; **Are you no better ?** Non state meglio? **he gave me no less than £100**; mi ha dato la bellezza di cento sterline; **let us read no more,** non leggiamo più; **he is no more a scholar than I am,** è dotto come lo sono io; **no more can I,** neanche io, nemmeno io; **no admittance,** è vietato l'ingresso; **no entry** (*one-way street*), senso unico; **no parking,** divieto di sosta; (*Telephone*) **no reply,** non risponde; **no thoroughfare,** divieto di transito.

Noachian [noˈeikiən], *a.* Noetico.

Noah [ˈnouə], *n.* Noè, *m.* **Noah's Ark,** l'arca di Noè, *f.*

nob [nɔb], *n.* (*colloq.*) Pezzo grosso, *m.*; testa, zucca, *f.*

nobby, *a.* (*colloq.*) Elegante, azzimato.

nobiliary [noˈbiliəri], *a.* Nobiliare.

nobility [noˈbiliti], *n.* Nobiltà, *f.*; eccellenza, elevatezza, *f.*

noble [ˈnoubəl], *n.* Nobile, signore, *m.* || *a.* Nobile, gentile, signorile, elevato. **— -minded,** generoso, magnanimo, elevato; **— -mindedness,** generosità, magnanimità, *f.*

nobleman, *n.* Nobile, nobiluomo, *m.*

nobleness, *n.* Nobiltà, *f.*

noblewoman, *n.* Nobildonna, signora, *f.*

nobly, *adv.* Nobilmente.

nobody [ˈnoubədi], *n.* Nessuno, *m.* **I have seen —,** non ho visto nessuno; **— knows,** nessuno sa niente, chi lo sa? **— else,** nessun'altro; **he's a mere —,** è una nullità.

noctambulist [nɔkˈtæmbjuːlist], *n.* Nottambulo, *m.*, nottambula, *f.*

nocturnal [nɔkˈtəːɹnəl], *a.* Notturno, di notte.

nocturnally, *adv.* Notturnamente.

nocturne [ˈnɔktəːɹn], *n.* (*Mus.*) Notturno, *m.*

nocuous [ˈnɔkjuːəs], *a.* Nocivo, dannoso.

nod [nɔd], *n.* Inchino, cenno, segno, *m.* || *v.t.i.* Inchinare la testa, accennare col capo; (*drop asleep*) sonnecchiare, dormicchiare; tentennare. **To — assent,** assentire; **to — to a friend,** salutare un amico; **nodding plumes,** pennacchi svolazzanti, *m.pl.*

noddle [nɔdl], *n.* (*colloq.*) Testa, zucca, *f.*

node [noud], *n.* (*Bot.*) Nocchio, *m.*; (*Anat.*) nodo, *m.*

nodose, *a.* Nocchioso, nodoso.

nodule [ˈnɔdjuːl], *n.* Nodulo, *m.*

noggin [ˈnɔgin], *n.* Bicchierino, boccaletto, *m.*; settima parte d'un litro, *f.*

noise [nɔiz], *n.* Rumore, fragore, strepito, schiamazzo, chiasso, frastuono, *m.*; baccano, fracasso, *m.*; tumulto, *m.*; (*in ears*) ronzio, *m.* || *v.t.* **To — abroad,** strombazzare, divulgare. **Hold your —!** Tacete! **to make a —,** strepitare, rumoreggiare, far rumore; **to make a — in the world,** levar rumore, destar rumore, far chiasso; **What a —!** Che chiasso! Che rumore!

noiseless, *a.* Silenzioso.

noiselessness, *n.* Silenzio, *m.*, silenziosità, *f.*

noisily, *adv.* Rumorosamente, strepitosamente.

noisiness, *n.* Rumorosità, *f.*, rumore, fragore, *m.*

noisome [ˈnɔisəm], *a.* Nocivo, malsano; fetido, infetto.

noisomeness, *n.* Fetidezza, *f.*

noisy [ˈnɔizi], *a.* Rumoroso, fragoroso, chiassoso, tumultuoso.

nolens volens [ˈnoulenz ˈvoulenz], *adv.* Volente o nolente.

nomad [ˈnoumæd], *n.* Nomade, *m.*

nomadic, *a.* Nomade.

nom de plume [nɔm də ˈpluːm], *n.* Pseudonimo, *m.*

nomenclator [ˈnoumenkleitəɹ], *n.* Nomenclatore, *m.*

nomenclature, *n.* Nomenclatura, *f.*

nominal [ˈnɔminəl], *a.* Nominale; di nome, nominativo.

nominate [ˈnɔmineit], *v.t.* Nominare, designare; proporre come candidato.

nomination, *n.* Nomina, *f.*; (*for parliament*) candidatura, *f.*

nominative, *n.a.* (*Gram.*) Nominativo, *m.*

nominator, *n.* Nominatore, *m.*

nominee [nɔmiˈniː], *n.* Persona nominata, persona designata a qualche ufficio, *f.*, candidato, *m.*

non, non- [nɔn], *prefix. negative.*

non-acceptance, *n.* Rifiuto di accettare, *m.*

nonage [ˈnɔnidʒ, ˈnounidʒ], *n.* Minorità, età minore, *f.*

nonagenarian [nɔnədʒəˈnɛəriən], *n.a.* Nonagenario, *m.*

non-alcoholic, *a.* Nonalcoolico. **— drink,** bevanda nonalcoolica.

non-appearance, *n.* (*Law*) Mancata comparizione, assenza, *f.*
non-attendance, *n.* Assenza, *f.*
nonce [nɔns], *n.* **For the —,** per questo caso, per questa volta.
nonchalance [ˈnɔnʃæləns], *n.* Noncuranza, indifferenza, *f.*
nonchalant, *a.* Noncurante, indifferente.
nonchalantly, *adv.* Svogliatamente.
non-combattant, *n.a.* Non-combattente, *m.*
non-commissioned, *a.* (*Mil.*) Senza brevetto. **— officer,** sottufficiale, *m.*
non-committal, *a.* Che rifiuta d'impegnarsi. **To be —,** non dire nè sì nè no.
non-compliance, *n.* Rifiuto di ubbidire, *m.*, inadempienza, *f.*
non-conducting, *a.* (*Phys.Elect.*) Non conduttore, cattivo conduttore.
nonconformist, *n.a.* Non-conformista, *m.f.*; dissidente dalla chiesa stabilita.
nonconformity, *n.* Dissidenza dalla chiesa stabilita, *f.*
nondescript [ˈnɔndiskript], *a.* Indefinito, indefinibile; imprecisabile; strambo, bizzarro; scadente.
none [nʌn], *pron.* Nessuno, nulla, veruno, niente. || *a.* Nessuno. || *adv.* Non, punto, mica. **I have —,** non ne ho; **— the less,** nondimeno; **None of your impudence!** Sfacciato! **— but fools believe that,** soltanto gli sciocchi lo credono; **my sight is — of the clearest,** i miei occhi non sono troppo forti; **he was — the worse for it,** non stava peggio per ciò.
nonentity [nɔnˈentiti], *n.* Inesistenza, *f.*; (*fig.*) uomo da nulla, *m.*; nullità, *f.*; uno zero, *m.*
nones [nounz], *n.pl.* (*Hist.*) None, *f.pl.*; (*Eccles.*) nona, *f.*
non-essential [nɔniˈsenʃəl], *a.* Inutile, inessenziale.
nonesuch [ˈnʌnsʌtʃ], *n.* Cosa senza pari, *f.*, cosa impareggiabile, *f.*
non-execution, *n.* Mancata esecuzione, *f.*
non-existence, *n.* Inesistenza, *f.*
non-existent, *a.* Inesistente.
non-interference, non-intervention, *n.* Neutralità, *f.*, non-intervento, *m.*
non-juror, *n.* (*Hist.*) Chi non voleva prestar fedeltà al re Guglielmo III nel 1689.
non-moral, *a.* Non-morale, amorale.
non-observance, *n.* Inosservanza, *f.*
nonpareil [nɔnpəˈrel], *a.* Senza pari, incomparabile.
non-party, *a.* Indipendente.
non-payment, *n.* Mancato pagamento, *m.*
non-performance, *n.* Inesecuzione, *f.*
nonplus [nɔnˈplʌs], *n.* Imbarazzo, *m.*, perplessità, *f.* || *v.t.* Imbarazzare, confondere, sconcertare, impacciare. **At a —,** perplesso, alle strette, impacciato; **I was absolutely nonplussed,** ero proprio sconcertato.
non-professional, *a.* Dilettante.
non-resident, *n.a.* Assente, *m.f.*
non-resistance, *n.* Ubbidienza passiva, *f.*
nonsense [ˈnɔnsəns], *n.* Assurdità, insensatezza, *f.*, nonsenso, controsenso, *m.*; bagattelle, frottole, *f.pl.* || *inter.* Macchè! Che sciocchezze!
nonsensical [nɔnˈsensikəl], *a.* Assurdo, scipito, sciocco, insensato.
nonsensicalness, *n.* Assurdità, scipitezza, insensatezza, sciocchezza, *f.*
non-skid, *a.* Antisdrucciolevole.
non-stop, *a.* Continuo; (*Rail.*) diretto; (*Aviat.*) senza scalo.
non-success, *n.* Insuccesso, *m.*
nonsuch [cp. **nonesuch**].
nonsuit, *n.* (*Law*) Non luogo a procedere. || *v.t.* Mettere fuori ruolo.
non-union, *a.* Che non appartiene a sindicato.
noodle [nuːdl], *n.* Semplicione, imbecille, scimunito, *m.*
noodles, *n.pl.* Pasta, *f.*, tagliatelli, *m.pl.*
nook [nuk], *n.* Angolo, canto, *m.*; ritiro, cantuccio, *m.*; ripostiglio, *m.*
noon, noonday, noontide [nuːn, ˈnuːndei, ˈnuntaid], *n.* Mezzogiorno, mezzodì, *m.* **At noon,** a mezzogiorno; **the noonday heat,** il caldo meridiano, *m.*
noose [nuːs], *n.* Laccio, nodo scorsoio, cappio, *m.* || *v.t.* Prendere al laccio, accalappiare.
nopal [noupl], *n.* (*Bot.*) Nopale, *m.*
nor [nɔːɹ], *adv.conj.* Nè; nè . . . nè, neanche, nemmeno. **Neither you nor they,** nè voi nè loro; **nor shall I ever go,** e non andrò mai; **nor I neither,** e nemmeno io; **nor was this all,** e ciò non era tutto.
Nordic [ˈnɔːɹdik], *a.* Nordico.
norm [nɔːɹm], *n.* Norma, *f.*; modello, tipo, *m.*
normal, *a.* Normale.
normally, *adv.* Normalmente.
Norman [ˈnɔːɹmən], *n.a.* Normanno, *m.*
Normandy [ˈnɔːɹməndi], *n.* (*Geog.*) Normandia, *f.*
Norse [nɔːɹs], *a.* Scandinavo, Norvegese. **— language,** lingua scandinava antica, *f.*
Norseman, *n.* Scandinavo, norvegese, *m.*
north [nɔːɹθ], *n.* Nord, settentrione, *m.*, tramontana, *f.* || *a.* Nordico, settentrionale. || *adv.* A nord, verso nord. **North Star,** stella polare, *f.*; **— wind,** tramontana, *f.*, vento di tramontana, *m.*; **—-east,** nord-est, *m.*; **— west,** nord-ovest, *m.*; **North America,** America del Nord, *f.*; **North Britain,** Scozia, *f.*
northerly, *a.* Settentrionale, del nord. || *adv.* Verso nord.
northern, *a.* Nordico, settentrionale, del nord. **— lights,** aurora boreale, *f.*
northward, northwards, *a.adv.* Verso nord, al nord.
Norway [ˈnɔːɹwei], *n.* (*Geog.*) Norvegia, *f.*
Norwegian [nɔːɹˈwiːdʒən], *n.a.* Norvegese, *m.f.*
nose [nouz], *n.* (*Anat.*) Naso, *m.*; (*of animal*) muso, *m.*; (*of bellows, etc.*) tubo, *m.*, canna, *f.*; (*for scent*) fiuto, odorato, *m.*; (*Mech.*) becco, *m.* || *v.t.i.* Odorare, annusare, fiutare; scoprire. **A Roman —,** un naso aquilino, *m.*; **turn-up —,** naso all'insù, *m.*; **to bleed at the —,** far sangue dal naso; **to blow one's —,** soffiarsi il naso; **to make a long —,** fare marameo; **not to see beyond one's —,** non veder più in là del naso; **to lead by the —,** menare per il naso; **to put someone's — out of joint,** dare lo sgambetto a qualcuno; **to speak through the —,** parlar nel naso; **to turn one's — up at,** arricciare il naso a; **as plain as the — on your face,** chiaro come la luce del sole; **to follow one's —,** seguire il proprio naso, andar diritto; **to pay through**

the —, pagare profumatamente; **under one's —,** sotto il naso; **to — about,** cercare, metter il naso negli affari altrui; **—-bag,** sacchetto per la biada, sacchetto mangiatoia, *m.*; **—-band,** museruola, *f.*; (*Aviat.*) **—-dive,** picchiata, *f.*, *v.i.* scendere in picchiata, calare a picco.

nosegay, *n.* Mazzo, mazzetto, mazzolino di fiori, *m.*

noseless, *a.* Senza naso, senza odorato.

nose-ring, *n.* Anello per il naso, *m.*, nasiera, *f.*

nosography [noˈsɔgrəfi], *n.* Nosografia, *f.*

nosology, *n.* Nosologia, *f.*

nostalgia [nɔsˈtældʒə], *n.* Nostalgia, *f.*

nostalgic, *a.* Nostalgico.

nostril [ˈnɔstril], *n.* (*Anat.*) Narice, *f.*; (*of horse*) frogia, *f.*

nostrum [ˈnɔstrəm], *n.* Panacea, *f.*, rimedio sovrano, *m.*

not [nɔt], *adv.* Non, non . . . punto, non . . . mica. **I know not,** io non so; **say not so,** non ditelo; **not at all,** punto, niente affatto; **not a few,** non pochi; **Is it not?** Non è vero? **not but that,** non che; **I think not,** credo di no; **the lady is not at home,** la signora non è in casa; **not guilty,** non colpevole, innocente; (*Med.*) **not to be taken,** per uso esterno; **not to be confused with,** da non confondersi con.

notability [noutəˈbiliti], *n.* Notabilità, *f.*, maggiorente, *m.*

notable [ˈnoutəbl], *a.* Notevole, notabile; insigne, segnalato; considerevole. || *n.* Notabile, *m.*, notabilità, *f.*

notably, *adv.* Notevolmente.

notarial [noˈtɛəriəl], *a.* Notarile.

notary [ˈnoutəri], *n.* (*Law*) Notaro, notaio, *m.* **— public,** pubblico notaio, *m.*

notation [noˈteiʃən], *n.* (*Mus.*) Notazione, *f.*; (*Math.*) numerazione, *f.*

notch [nɔtʃ], *n.* Tacca, intaccatura, *f.*, intaglio, incavo, *m.* || *v.t.* Intaccare, intagliare, incavare.

note [nout], *n.* Nota, *f.*, appunto, *m.*; (*comment*) postilla, chiosa, *f.* (*letter*) biglietto, *m.*; (*Mus.*) nota, *f.*; distinzione, reputazione, *f.*; tono accento, *m.*; (*Gram.*) punto, *m.* || *v.t.* Notare, osservare, prendere una nota di, registrare. **— of exclamation,** punto esclamativo, *m.*; (*Comm.*) **— of hand,** cambiale, *m.*; **to make notes of,** prendere delle note di; **to take — of,** prendere nota di; **a man of —,** un uomo di riguardo; **to — down,** annotare; **—-book,** taccuino, *m.*; **—-paper,** carta da lettera, *f.*

noted, *a.* Distinto, eminente, notevole, celebre.

noteworthy, *a.* Degno di nota, notevole.

nothing [ˈnʌθiŋ], *n.* Niente, nulla, *m.*; zero, *m.*; nessuna cosa, *f.* || *adv.* Niente affatto, in nessun modo. **A mere —,** un bel nulla, proprio nulla, *m.*; **— of the kind,** niente affatto; **there is — good in him,** non c'è nulla di buono in lui; **he has — in him,** è un uomo da nulla, è un inconcludente; **— else than,** nient'altro che; **there is — for it but,** non c'è altro rimedio che; **he is — if not critical,** vuol sempre criticare; **this is — to you,** ciò non vi tocca; **to make — of,** non far caso di; **he thinks — of walking twenty miles,** per lui è niente fare venti miglia; **I can make — of this book,** non ci cavo niente da questo libro; **to come to —,** finire in niente; andare a monte; **to have — to do with,** non aver che fare con; **little nothings,** inezie, *f.pl.*; **there is — to laugh at,** non c'è nulla da ridere; **not for —,** non per nulla; **there is — much the matter,** non c'è nulla di grave.

nothingness, *n.* Niente, nulla, *m.*, inesistenza, *f.*, oblio, *m.*

notice [ˈnoutis], *n.* Avviso, *m.*, notizia, *f.*; annunzio, *m.*; conoscenza, osservazione, attenzione, *f.*; (*in newspaper*) articolo, *m.*, recensione, *f.*; notifica, *f.*; preavviso, *m.*; (*dismissal*) licenziamento, *m.*; (*to quit*) disdetta, *f.* || *v.t.* Osservare, notare; accorgersi di, prender conoscenza di; occuparsi di, fare attenzione a. **Without —,** senza preavviso; **at short —,** con breve preavviso, a breve scadenza; **biographical —,** notizia biografica; **to attract —,** tirare l'attenzione; **to bring to —,** far notare; **to give — to,** licenziare, disdire, dar la disdetta, dar avviso a, prevenire; **until further —,** fino a nuov'ordine; **beneath one's —,** non degno d'attenzione; **Take —!** Attenzione!

noticeable, *a.* Percettibile, notevole, apparente.

notifiable [noutiˈfaiəbl], *a.* Notificabile.

notification, *n.* Notifica, *f.*; (*Law*) denunzia, *f.*

notify [ˈnoutifai], *v.t.* Notificare, deferire, denunziare; informare. **Please — me of his arrival,** favorite informarmi del suo arrivo.

notion [ˈnouʃən], *n.* Nozione, idea, *f.*, concetto, *m.* **He has no — of obedience,** non sa cos'è ubbidienza; **I haven't the haziest —,** non ne ho la minima nozione; **it is a common —,** è un'idea corrente.

notoriety [noutəˈraiiti], *n.* Notorietà, *f.*

notorious [nəˈtɔːriəs], *a.* Notorio, famigerato.

notoriously, *adv.* Notoriamente.

notwithstanding [nɔtwiðˈstændiŋ], *prep. adv.conj.* Malgrado, nonostante, a dispetto di, nulladimeno.

nought [nɔːt], *n.* Nulla, *m.* [cp. **naught**].

noun [naun], *n.* (*Gram.*) Sostantivo, nome, *m.*

nourish [ˈnʌriʃ], *v.t.* Nutrire, alimentare; (*fig.*) covare, serbare, custodire.

nourishing, *a.* Nutriente.

nourishment, *n.* Nutrimento, alimento, cibo, *m.*

nous [naus], *n.* Senso comune, *m.*; intelletto, spirito, *m.*

novel [ˈnɔvəl], *a.* Nuovo, recente, insolito, strano. || *n.* Romanzo, *m.*

novelette [nɔvəˈlet], *n.* Romanzetto popolare, *m.*, novella, *f.*

novelist [ˈnɔvəlist], *n.* Romanziere, *m.*

novelty, *n.* Novità, attualità, *f.*; cosa di attualità, *f.*

November [noˈvembəɹ], *n.* Novembre, *m.*

novice [ˈnɔvis], *n.* Novizio, *m.*, novizia, *f.*

novitiate [nɔˈviʃiət], *n.* Noviziato, *m.*; tirocinio, *m.*

now [nau], *adv.* Adesso, ora, presentemente, al presente; allora, dunque. || *conj.* Ora che. || *n.* Il presente, tempo attuale, *m.* || *inter.* Oibò! Via! Macchè! **Just —,** or ora; **before —,** prima d'ora; **— and then, every — and then,** di quando in quando; **— or never,** ora o mai; **now's the time,** è l'ora; **till —,** fino ad ora; **Now then!** Ebbene! **from — until tomorrow,** di qui a domani.

nowadays [nauəˈdeiz], *adv.* Oggi, al giorno d'oggi, oggidì, oggigiorno.
nowhere [ˈnouwεəɹ], *adv.* In nessun luogo, da nessuna parte.
nowise [ˈnouwaiz], *adv.* In nessun modo.
noxious [ˈnɔkʃəs], *a.* Nocivo, dannoso, pernicioso.
noxiously, *adv.* Nocivamente.
noxiousness, *n.* Dannosità, *f.*
noyau [ˈnwɑjou], *n.* Acqua di nocciolo, *f.*
nozzle [nɔzl], *n.* Becco, *m.*; tubo, *m.*; naso, *m.*
nuance [ˈnju:əns], *n.* Sfumatura, *f.*
nubile [ˈnju:bil, ˈnju:bail], *a.* Nubile.
nucleus [ˈnju:kliəs], *n.* Nucleo, *m.*
nude [nju:d], *a.* Nudo, ignudo. || *n.* Nudo, *m.*
nudge [nʌdʒ], *n.* Gomitata, *f.* || *v.t.* Dare una gomitata, toccare col gomito.
nudist, *n.* Nudista, *m.f.*
nudity, *n.* Nudità, *f.*
nugatory [ˈnju:gətəri], *a.* Frivolo, vano; inetto, futile.
nugget [ˈnʌgit], *n.* Pepita, *f.*
nuisance [ˈnju:səns], *n.* Noia, seccatura, molestia, *f.*, fastidio, *m.*; (*Law*) danno, *m.*, molestie, *f.pl.*; (*person*) seccatore, *m.*, seccatrice, *f.* **What a —!** Che seccatura! Che noia! **to be a — to,** dar fastidio a, riuscir molesto a; **a public —,** un inconveniente, *m.*, una peste, *f.*
null [nʌl], Nullo. **— and void,** nullo, annullato.
nullify [ˈnʌlifai], *v.t.* Annullare, invalidare.
nullity, *n.* (*Law*) Nullità, *f.*
numb [nʌm], *a.* Intirizzito, torpido, intorpidito, intormentito. || *v.t.* Intirizzire, intorpidire, intormentire.
number [ˈnʌmbəɹ], *n.* Numero, *m.*; cifra, *f.*; quantità, *f.*; puntata, dispensa, *f.*; (*of periodical*) numero, fascicolo, *m.* || *v.t.* Numerare, contare, annoverare, enumerare. **A — of,** parecchi; **cardinal, ordinal —,** numero cardinale, ordinale, *m.*; **odd, even —,** numero dispari, pari, *m.*; **in great numbers,** in gran numero; **a back —,** un arretrato, *m.* (*fig.*) un parruccone, *m.*; **without —,** senza numero, innumerevole; **he is not of our —,** non è con noi; **three in —,** tre di numero; **to the — of fifty,** in numero di cinquanta; **his days are numbered,** ha i giorni contati; **to — among,** includere tra; **the town numbers 6,000 inhabitants,** la città conta 6,000 abitanti.
numbering, *n.* Numerazione, *f.* **— -machine,** numeratrice, *f.*
numberless, *a.* Senza numero, innumerevole.
numbness [ˈnʌmnis], *n.* Intirizzimento, intorpidimento, torpore, *m.*
numeral [ˈnju:mərəl], *n.* Numero, *m.*, cifra, *f.* || *a.* Numerale.
numerary, *a.* Numerario.
numeration, *n.* Numerazione, *f.*
numerator, *n.* (*Math.*) Numeratore, *m.*
numerical [nju:ˈmerikəl], *a.* Numerico.
numerically, *adv.* Numericamente.
numerous, *a.* Numeroso.
numerousness, *n.* Numerosità, *f.*
numismatic [nju:misˈmætik], *a.* Numismatico.
numismatics, *n.pl.* Numismatica, *f.*
numismatist [nju:ˈmismətist], *n.* Numismatico, *m.*
nummulite [ˈnʌmju:lait], *n.* (*Geol.*) Nummolite, *m.*
numskull [ˈnʌmskʌl], *n.* Imbecille, testone, sciocco, minchione, *m.*
nun [nʌn], *n.* Monaca, suora, religiosa, *f.* **— -like,** monacale.
nunciature [ˈnʌnsiətju:ɹ], *n.* (*Eccles.*) Nunziatura, *f.*
nuncio, *n.* Nunzio, *m.*
nuncupative [ˈnʌŋkju:pətiv], *a.* (*Law*) Nuncupativo.
nunnery [ˈnʌnəri], *n.* Convento, monastero, *m.*
nuptial [ˈnʌpʃəl], *a.* Nuziale, di nozze.
nuptials, *n.pl.* Nozze, *f.pl.*
Nuremberg [ˈnju:rəmbə:ɹg], *n.* (*Geog.*) Norimberga, *f.*
nurse [nə:ɹs], *n.* (*children's*) Nutrice, balia, bambinaia, *f.*; (*for the sick*) infermiera, *f.*, infermiere, *m.* || *v.t.* (*to suckle*) Nutrire, allattare; (*the sick*) far da infermiere a; (*fig.*) nutrire, covare, fomentare. **Wet —,** balia, *f.*; **to put out to —,** mettere a balia.
nursery [ˈnə:ɹsri], *n.* Stanza da bambini, *f.*; (*horticultural*) semenzaio, vivaio, orto, *m.*, ortaglia, serra, *f.* **Day- —,** asilo infantile, *m.*; **— rhyme,** poesia per bambini, *f.*; **— tale,** fiaba, *f.*; **— -garden,** ortaglia, serra, *f.*; **— -maid,** bambinaia, *f.*
nurseryman, *n.* Ortolano, *m.*
nursing, *n.* (*suckling*) Allattamento, *m.*; (*the sick*) fare l'infermiera, *m.*; **— -home,** clinica, casa di salute, *f.*
nursling, *n.* Lattante, poppante; (*fig.*) beniamino, prediletto, *m.*
nurture [ˈnə:ɹtʃəɹ], *n.* Educazione, *f.*; alimento, nutrimento, *m.* || *v.t.* Educare; nutrire.
nut [nʌt], *n.* Noce, nocciuola, *f.*; (*Mech.*) madrevite, dado, *m.*; (*of violin*) capotasto, *m.*; (*coal*) carbone in piccoli pezzi, *m.*; (*colloq.*) damerino, *m.* (*fig.*) **A — to crack,** del filo a torcere; **to go nutting,** andare a coglier nocciuole; (*colloq.*) **to be nuts on,** andar pazzo per; **— -brown,** color nocciuola; **— -crackers,** schiaccianoci, *m.*; **— -cracker face,** faccia tosta, *f.*; **— -gall,** galla della quercia, *f.*; **— tree,** noce, *m.*
nutation [nju:ˈteiʃən], *n.* (*Bot.Astron.*) Nutazione, *f.*
nuthatch [ˈnʌthætʃ], *n.* (*Zool.*) Picchio, *m.*
nutmeg [ˈnʌtmeg], *n.* Noce moscata, *f.*
nutrient [ˈnju:triənt], *a.* Nutriente, nutritivo.
nutriment, *n.* Nutrimento, alimento, cibo, *m.*
nutritious, nutritive, *a.* Nutritivo, nutriente.
nutshell [ˈnʌtʃel], *n.* Guscio di noce, *m.* (*fig.*) **In a —,** in noce, in essenza.
nutting, *n.* Raccolta delle noci, *f.*, abbacchiamento delle noci, *m.*
nutty, *a.* Che sa di noce.
nux vomica [nʌks ˈvɔmikə], *n.* (*Bot.*) Noce vomica, *f.*
nuzzle [nʌzl], *v.t.i.* Annusare, fiutare; annidarsi, accoccolarsi; grufolarsi; rannicchiarsi. **To — against,** grufolare, annusare.
nyctalopia [niktəˈloupiə], *n.* (*Med.*) Nictalopia, *f.*
nymph [nimf], *n.* Ninfa, *f.*
nympha, *n.* (*Zool.*) Crisalide, *f.*
nymphean, nymphlike, *a.* Ninfeo, ninfale.
nymphomania, *n.* (*Med.*) Ninfomania, *f.*

O

O, o [ou], Quindicesima lettera dell'alfabeto inglese.
O [ou], *inter.* **O dear!** Dio mio! **O king, live for ever,** O re, possa tu vivere in perpetuo.
oaf [ouf], *n.* Zotico, tanghero, *m.*
oafish, *a.* Zotico, rozzo, incolto.
oafishness, *n.* Zoticaggine, rozzezza, *f.*
oak [ouk], *n.* (*tree*) Quercia, *f.*; (*wood*) legno di quercia, *m.* **— -apple, — gall,** galla della quercia, *f.*; **— -grove,** querceto, *m.*
oaken, *a.* Di quercia.
oakling, *n.* Querciuolo, *m.*
oakum [ˈoukəm], *n.* Stoppa, *f.* **To pick —,** far stoppa.
oar [ɔːɹ], *n.* Remo, *m.* || *v.i.* Remare. **A stroke of the —,** una remata, *f.*; **muffled oars,** remi assorditi, *m.pl.*
oared, *a.* A remi. **A four- — boat,** un canotto a quattro remi, *m.*
oarsman, *n.* Rematore, vogatore, canottiere, *m.*
oarsmanship, *n.* L'arte del remare, *f.*
oarswoman, *n.* Rematrice, *f.*
oasis [ouˈeisis], *n.* Oasi, *f.*
oast, oast-house [oust, ousthaus], *n.* Forno da luppoli, *m.*
oat [cp. **oats**].
oatcake [ˈoutkeik], *n.* Focaccia di avena, *f.*
oaten, *a.* Di avena.
oath [ouθ], *n.* Giuramento, *m.*; bestemmia, imprecazione, *f.* **On —,** sotto giuramento; **to put on —,** far giurare; **to break one's —,** violare il giuramento, mancare al giuramento; **to rap out an —,** prorompere in un'imprecazione, tirare un moccolo; **to tender the — to,** prestare giuramento a; **to take an —, to swear an —,** giurare; **a terrible —,** una solenne bestemmia, *f.*; un solenne giuramento, *m.*
oatmeal [ˈoutmiːl], *n.* Farina d'avena, *f.*
oats [outs], *n.pl.* Avena, *f.* **To sow one's wild —,** correre la cavallina.
obduracy [ˈɔbdjuːrəsi], *n.* Durezza, ostinazione, caparbietà, *f.*; impenitenza, *f.*
obdurate, *a.* Duro, ostinato, caparbio, testardo; impenitente.
obdurately, *adv.* Caparbiamente.
obedience [oˈbiːdiəns], *n.* Ubbidienza, obbedienza, *f.*; docilità, sottomissione, *f.* **In — to,** in ubbidienza a.
obedient, *a.* Ubbidiente, obbediente; docile, sottomesso; rispettoso.
obediently, *adv.* Ubbidientemente.
obeisance [oˈbeisəns], *n.* Riverenza, *f.*, inchino, *m.*
obelisk [ˈɔbəlisk], *n.* Obelisco, *m.*; (*Print.*) croce, *f.*
obese [oˈbiːz], *a.* Obeso, corpulento, pingue.
obesity, obeseness [oˈbiːziti, oˈbiːznis], *n.* Obesità, corpulenza, pinguedine, *f.*
obey [oˈbei], *v.t.* Ubbidire a, obbedire a; *v.i.* ubbidire, obbedire.
obfuscate [ˈɔbfʌskeit], *v.t.* Offuscare, oscurare.
obfuscation, *n.* Offuscazione, *f.*
obituary [oˈbitjuːəri], *a.* Necrologico. || *n.* Necrologia, *f.* **— notice,** necrologia, notizia necrologica.
object (1) [ˈɔbdʒekt], *n.* Oggetto, *m.*; scopo, intento, *m.*; mira, *f.*, fine, *m.*; (*fig.*) orrore, *m.*; (*Gram.*) complemento oggetto, *m.* **To gain one's —,** raggiungere lo scopo, ottenere lo scopo; **money is no — to him,** il danaro non lo attira; **with the — of,** con intento di; **What an —!** Che orrore! **— -glass,** obbiettivo, lente obbietiva, *f.*; **— -lesson,** esempio pratico, *m.*
object (2) [ɔbˈdʒekt], *v.t.i.* Obbiettare, opporre; fare obbiezione, opporsi, ripugnare, resistere, protestare. **I — to being treated like this,** mi ripugna d'esser trattato così.
objection [ɔbˈdʒekʃən], *n.* Obbiezione, difficoltà, *f.*; inconveniente, *m.* **Have you any — ?** Avete da ridire? Avete qualche obbiezione? **I have no —,** non mi spiace, non ho niente in contrario; **to raise objections,** sollevare obbiezioni.
objectionable, *a.* Riprovevole, riprensibile, biasimevole; ripugnante, spiacevole.
objectionably, *adv.* Biasimevolmente.
objective [ɔbˈdʒektiv], *a.* Obbiettivo; (*Gram.*) oggettivo. || *n.* Obbietivo, scopo, proposito, *m.*
objectiveness, objectivity [ɔbˈdʒektivnis, ɔbdʒekˈtiviti], *n.* Obbiettività, oggettività, *f.*
objectivism, *n.* Obbiettivismo, *m.*
objectless, *a.* Senza oggetto *or* scopo, inutile.
objector, *n.* Oppositore, *m.* **Conscientious —,** obbiettore di coscienza, *m.*
objurgation [ɔbdʒəːˈgeiʃən], *n.* Rimprovero, *m.*, sgridata, *f.*
objurgatory, *a.* Riprensivo, riprensorio.
oblate (1) [ˈɔbleit], *n.* (*Eccles.*) Oblato, *m.*, oblata, *f.*
oblate (2), *a.* (*Geom.*) Sferoidale, compresso ai poli.
oblation, *n.* Oblazione, offerta, *f.*
obligate [ˈɔbligeit], *v.t.* Obbligare.
obligation, *n.* Obbligazione, *f.*, obbligo, impegno, *m.* **To be under an — to,** avere un obbligo con; **to put under an —,** rendere un vero servigio a; **to repay an —,** restituire un favore.
obligatory, *a.* Obbligatorio.
oblige [ɔbˈlaidʒ], *v.t.* Obbligare, costringere; far piacere a, contentare, soddisfare. **Please — me by,** favorite farmi il piacere di; **I am greatly obliged to you,** vi sono proprio obbligatissimo; **I am obliged to go,** sono costretto ad andare.
obliging, *a.* Compiacente, gentile, servizievole, cortese.
obligingly, *adv.* In modo compiacente.
obligingness, *n.* Compiacenza, gentilezza, cortesia, *f.*
oblique [oˈbliːk], *a.* Obliquo.
obliquely, *adv.* Obliquamente.
obliqueness, obliquity, *n.* Obliquità, *f.*
obliterate [oˈblitəreit], *v.t.* Obliterare, cancellare, distruggere.
obliteration, *n.* Obliterazione, distruzione, *f.*
oblivion [oˈbliviən], *n.* Oblio, *m.*, dimenticanza, *f.* (*Hist.*) **Act of —,** amnistia, *f.*; **to fall into —,** cadere in oblio.
oblivious, *a.* Dimentico, immemore, oblioso.
oblong [ˈɔblɔŋ], *a.* Oblungo, bislungo. || *n.* Figura oblunga, *f.*, rettangolo, *m.*
obloquy [ˈɔbləkwi], *n.* Onta, infamia, *f.*; vituperio, *m.*; vergogna, *f.*, ingiuria, censura, *f.*
obnoxious [ɔbˈnɔkʃəs], *a.* Odioso, molesto, noioso, nocivo, pernicioso.

obnoxiously, *adv.* Odiosamente.
obnoxiousness, *n.* Molestia, noia, perniciosità, *f.*
oboe [ˈoubou], *n.* (*Mus.*) Oboe, *m.*
oboist, *n.* Oboista, *m.f.*
obol [ˈɔbəl], *n.* (*Hist.*) Obolo, *m.*
obscene [ɔbˈsiːn], *a.* Osceno, turpe, disonesto, impudico.
obscenely, *adv.*, Oscenamente.
obsceneness, obscenity [ɔbˈsiːnnis, ɔbˈseniti], *n.* Oscenità, *f.*; turpitudine, disonestà, impudicizia, *f.*
obscuration [ɔbskjuːˈreiʃən], *n.* Oscuramento, *m.*; (*Astron.*) oscurazione, *f.*
obscure [ɔbˈskjuːəɹ], *a.* Oscuro; (*fig.*) nascosto; umile. || *v.t.* Oscurare, abbuiare, ottenebrare; ecclissare.
obscurely, *adv.* Oscuramente.
obscureness, obscurity, *n.* Oscurità, *f.*, buio, *m.*; tenebre, *f.pl.*
obsequies [ˈɔbsikwiz], *n.pl.* Esequie, *f.pl.*
obsequious [ɔbˈsiːkwiəs], *a.* Servile; ossequioso, riverente.
obsequiously, *adv.* Servilmente; ossequiosamente.
obsequiousness, *n.* Servilità, *f.*; ossequiosità, *f.*
observable [ɔbˈzəːɹvəbl], *a.* Osservabile, notevole.
observably, *adv.* Notevolmente.
observance [ɔbˈzəːɹvəns], *n.* Osservanza, *f.*, compimento, *m.*; usanza, *f.*; rito, *m.*; pratica, *f.*
observant, *a.* Osservatore, perspicace, attento; esatto. || *n.* Osservante, *m.* **A very — child,** un ragazzo a cui nulla sfugge.
observation, *n.* Osservazione, considerazione, *f.*
observatory [ɔbˈzəːɹvətəri], *n.* Osservatorio, *m.*, specola, *f.*, posto di osservazione, *m.*
observe [ɔbˈzəːɹv], *v.t.* Osservare, notare, rimarcare; mantenere, adempiere; celebrare, praticare.
observer, *n.* Osservatore, *m.*, osservatrice, *f.*
observing, *a.* Osservatore, indagatore, attento.
observingly, *adv.* Attentamente.
obsess [obˈses], *v.t.* Ossessionare, opprimere. **To be obsessed by,** essere ossessionato da.
obsessed, *a.* Ossesso, ossessionato.
obsession, *n.* Ossessione, *f.*
obsidian [ɔbˈsidiən], *n.* (*Geol.*) Ossidiana, *f.*
obsolescent [ɔbsəˈlesənt], *a.* Che cade in disuso.
obsolete [ˈɔbsoliːt], *a.* Disusato, vieto, antiquato.
obstacle [ˈɔbstəkl], *n.* Ostacolo, impedimento, *m.* **— race,** corsa a ostacoli, *f.*
obstetric, obstetrical [ɔbˈstetrik, ɔbˈstetrikəl], *a.* Ostetrico.
obstetrician [ɔbstetˈriʃən], *n.* Ostetrico, *m.*
obstetrics, *n.pl.* Ostetrica, *f.*
obstinacy, obstinateness [ˈɔbstinəsi, ˈɔbstinətnis], *n.* Ostinatezza, ostinazione, caparbietà, pervicacia, *f.*; accanimento, *m.*
obstinate, *a.* Ostinato, inflessibile, caparbio, testardo, cocciuto; accanito.
obstinately, *adv.* Ostinatamente.
obstreperous [ɔbˈstrepərəs], *a.* Turbolento, tumultuoso, clamoroso; insofferente di disciplina.
obstreperousness, *n.* Turbolenza, *f.*
obstruct [ɔbˈstrʌkt], *v.t.* Ostruire, chiudere; (*Med.*) ostruire, occludere; impedire, inceppare, ritenere, ritardare; (*Pol.*) ricorrere all'ostruzionismo. **To — the light,** intercettare la luce; **to — the passage,** ostruire il passaggio.
obstruction, *n.* Ostacolo, impedimento, *m.*; (*Med.*) ostruzione, *f.*
obstructionist [obˈstrʌkʃənist], *n.* Ostruzionista, *m.*
obstructive, *a.* Ostruttivo; (*Med.*) ostruente.
obtain [obˈtein], *v.t.* Ottenere, guadagnare; conseguire, raggiungere; *v.i.* prevalere, essere in voga, usare, esistere.
obtainable, *a.* Ottenibile, conseguibile, raggiungibile.
obtainment, *n.* Ottenimento, conseguimento, *m.*
obtrude [obˈtruːd], *v.t.* Mettere avanti, intromettere. **To — oneself,** imporsi, farsi valere, farsi avanti, intromettersi.
obtrusive [obˈtruːziv], *a.* Importuno, molesto, indiscreto, inframettente.
obturator [ˈɔbtjuːreitəɹ], *n.* Otturatore, *m.*
obtuse [obˈtjuːs], *a.* (*in all senses*) Ottuso; smussato, spuntato; stupido, poco penetrante. **— angle,** angolo ottuso, *m.*
obtuseness, *n.* Ottusità, *f.*; stupidità, stolidità, *f.*
obverse [ˈɔbvəːɹs], *n.* Faccia, *f.*, diritto, *m.*; (*of page*) retto, *m.*
obviate [ˈɔbvieit], *v.t.* Ovviare a, evitare.
obvious, *a.* Ovvio, evidente, manifesto, chiaro. **It is —,** è evidente, salta agli occhi.
obviously, *adv.* Evidentemente.
obviousness, *n.* Evidenza, *f.*, l'essere ovvio, *m.*
occasion [oˈkeiʃən], *n.* Occasione, *f.*; cagione, causa, *f.*; motivo, *m.*; bisogno, uopo, *m.* || *v.t.* Occasionare, cagionare, dar luogo a. **For the —,** per l'occasione; **should — arise,** all'occasione; **there is no — to,** non c'è bisogno di; **to give — to,** dare occasione a; **to rise to the —,** essere all'altezza della situazione; **this is a great —,** questo è un grande avvenimento; **to profit by the —,** profittare dell'occasione.
occasional, *a.* Occasionale, casuale, fortuito; di tempo in tempo.
occasionally, *adv.* Qualche volta, di tempo in tempo; di quando in quando, saltuariamente.
occident [ˈɔksidənt], *n.* Occidente, *m.*
occidental, *a.* Occidentale.
occipital [ɔkˈsipitəl], *a.* (*Anat.*) Occipitale.
occiput [ˈɔksipət], *n.* Occipite, *m.*
occult [ɔˈkʌlt], *a.* Occulto, arcano, segreto, nascosto. || *v.t.* Occultare. **Occulting light,** luce intermittente, *f.*
occultation, *n.* (*Astron.*) Occultazione, *f.*
occultism, *n.* Occultismo, *m.*
occultness, *n.* Occultezza, *f.*
occupancy [ˈɔkjuːpənsi], *n.* Occupazione, *f.*
occupant [ˈɔkjuːpənt], *n.* Occupante, abitante, *m.f.*; (*tenant*) locatario, *m.*, locataria, *f.*; (*of a post*) titolare, *m.*
occupation [ɔkjuːˈpeiʃən], *n.* Occupazione, *f.*, impiego, lavoro, *m.*; possesso, *m.*
occupational, *a.* Appartenente ad un'occupazione. **— disease,** malattia del lavoro, *f.*
occupier [ˈɔkjuːpaiəɹ], *n.* Occupante, abitante, *m.f.*, locatario, *m.*, locataria, *f.*

occupy ['ɔkju:pai], *v.t.* Occupare; impiegare; abitare. **To be occupied in,** occuparsi di.
occur [o'kə:ɹ], *v.i.* Occorrere, accadere, arrivare, succedere, capitare. **It occurred to me,** mi venne in mente; **Has an accident occurred?** È successa qualche disgrazia? **it shall not — again,** non accadrà più.
occurrence [o'kʌrəns], *n.* Avvenimento, evento, fatto, caso, *m.*, occorrenza, *f.* **It is of frequent —,** accade spesso; **in any —,** all'occorrenza.
ocean ['ouʃən], *n.* Oceano, *m.* || *a.* Oceanico. **—-going vessel,** nave di lungo corso, *f.*; (*fig.*) **— greyhound,** transatlantico veloce, *m.*
Oceania [ouʃi'einiə], *n.* (*Geog.*) Oceania, *f.*
oceanic [ouʃi'ænik], *a.* Oceanico.
oceanography [ouʃən'ɔgrəfi], *n.* Oceanografia, *f.*
ocelot ['ousilɔt], *n.* (*Zool.*) Tigre-gatto, *m.*
ochre ['oukəɹ], *n.* (*Min.*) Ocra, *f.*
ochreous, *a.* Ocraceo.
o'clock [ə'klɔk], *n.* Ora, *f.*, ore, *f.pl.* **What — is it?** Che ora è? **it is three —,** sono le tre.
octagon ['ɔktəgən], *n.* Ottagono, *m.*
octagonal [ɔk'tægənəl], *a.* Ottagono, ottagonale.
octahedron [ɔktə'hi:drən], *n.* Ottaedro, *m.*
octangular [ɔk'tæŋgju:ləɹ], *a.* Ottangolo.
octant ['ɔktənt], *n.* (*Astron.*) Ottante, *m.*
octave ['ɔktiv], *n.* (*Mus.*) Ottava, *f.*
octavo [ɔk'teivou], *n.a.* Ottavo, in ottavo, *m.*
octennial [ɔk'teniəl], *a.* Ottenne, ottennale.
October [ɔk'toubəɹ], *n.* Ottobre, *m.*
octogenarian [ɔktodʒe'nɛəriən], *n.a.* Ottuagenario, ottantenne, *m.*
octopus ['ɔktəpəs], *n.* (*Zool.*) Ottopode, polipo, *m.*, piovra, *f.*
octoroon [ɔktə'ru:n], *n.* Figlio di un meticcio e di una bianca, *m.*, persona con un ottavo di sangue negro, *f.*
octosyllabic [ɔktosi'læbik], *n.a.* Ottosillabo, ottonario, *m.*
octroi ['ɔktrwɑ:], *n.* Dazio, *m.*
octuple [ɔk'tju:pl], *a.* Ottuplo. || *v.t.* Ottuplicare.
ocular ['ɔkju:ləɹ], *a.* Oculare.
oculist, *n.* Oculista, *m.*
odalisque ['oudəlisk], *n.* Odalisca, *f.*
odd [ɔd], *a.* (*of numbers*) Dispari, impari; (*of pair, set*) spaiato, scompagnato; (*queer*) originale, eccentrico, strano, bizzarro; in soprappiù, in soprannumero. **An — fellow,** un originale, *m.*; **forty —,** circa quaranta, una quarantina; **the — change,** il resto; **— jobs,** occupazioni casuali, *f.pl.*, lavoretti, *m.pl.*; **at — moments,** nei momenti di ozio, di quando in quando; **—-looking,** strano, bizzarro.
oddity, *n.* Stranezza, stravaganza, eccentricità, *f.*; (*person*) originale, *m.*
oddly, *adv.* Stranamente.
oddments, *n.pl.* Pezzi spaiati, scampoli, *m.pl.*
oddness, *n.* Disparità, imparità, *f.*; stranezza, stravaganza, eccentricità, *f.*
odds, *n.pl.* Probabilità, *f.pl.*, vantaggio, *m.*; avversità, *f.* **What's the —?** Che cosa importa? **to be at — with,** contendere con; **the — are against us,** il giuoco è contro di noi; **to lay — of ten to one,** scommettere dieci contro uno; **to fight against great —,** battersi contro un numero soverchiante, lottare contro gravi ostacoli; **to give —,** dar punti di vantaggio; **the — are that,** è probabile che; **— and ends,** pezzi e bocconi, ritagli, scampoli, *m.pl.*, una miscellanea, *f.*, un po' di tutto, *m.*; **— and evens,** pari e caffo, pari e dispari; **to set at —,** imbrogliare, metter negli imbrogli; **to lay —,** fare una scommessa ineguale.
ode [oud], *n.* Ode, *f.*
odious ['oudiəs], *a.* Odioso.
odiously, *adv.* Odiosamente.
odiousness, *n.* Odiosità, *f.*
odium ['oudiəm], *n.* Odio, *m.*, avversione, detestazione, *f.*; colpa, *f.*
odometer [ɔ'dɔmitəɹ], *n.* Odometro, *m.*
odontoid [o'dɔntɔid], *a.* Odontoide.
odontology [odɔn'tələdʒi], *n.* Odontologia, *f.*
odoriferous [oudə'rifərəs], *a.* Odorifero.
odoriferousness, *n.* Odore, *m.*, odorosità, *f.*
odour ['oudəɹ], *n.* Odore, *m.*; fragranza, *f.*, profumo, *m.*; (*fig.*) sentore, indizio, *m.*, riputazione, *f.* **To be in bad — with,** essere mal visto da; **in the — of sanctity,** in odore di santità.
odourless, *a.* Inodoro.
Odyssey ['ɔdisi], *n.* Odissea, *f.*
œcology [i:'kɔlədʒi], *n.* Ecologia, *f.*
œcumenical [i:kju:'menikəl], *a.* (*Eccles.*) Ecumenico.
œdema [i:'di:mə], *a.* (*Med.*) Edema, *m.*
o'er [cp. **over**].
œsophagus [i:'sɔfəgəs], *n.* (*Anat.*) Esofago, *m.*
œstrum ['i:strəm], *n.* (*Zool.*) Estro, *m.*
of [ɔv], *prep.* Di; a; da, fra; per. **It is very kind of you,** siete molto gentile; **I should like it of all things,** mi piacerebbe più di tutto; **of late,** ultimamente; **of old,** anticamente; **the second of May,** il due di Maggio, il due Maggio; **he's the best of men,** è la miglior pasta del mondo; **of course,** per certo, beninteso, naturalmente; **of an evening,** la sera; **Saint Anthony of Padua,** Sant'Antonio da Padova; **short of cash,** a corto di quattrini.
off [ɔ:f, ɔf], *adv.* Lontano, distante, lungi, via. || *prep.* Da, giù da, fuori di; (*Naut.*) all'altezza di. || *a.* Più distante, più lontano; (*side*) destro; laterale. **Two miles —,** lontano due miglia; **Hands —!** Giù le mani! **Hats —!** Giù i cappelli! **I'm —!** Io me ne vado! Io me la svigno! **— and on,** di tempo in tempo, saltuariamente; **Off with you!** Via di lì! Fuori dai piedi! **the meeting is —,** l'adunanza non avrà luogo; **to be — colour,** stare poco bene, essere indisposto; **they are very well —,** sono ricchi; **his house is a mile —,** la sua casa dista un miglio; **he has come — very well,** l'ha scampata bella; **to put —,** rimandare, rinviare; **to take —,** svestirsi di, levarsi, (*colloq.*) imitare; (*fig.*) **to fall —,** deteriorare, degenerare; **to pay —,** congedare pagando il saldo, liquidare, fare l'ultimo pagamento; **to show —,** mettere in mostra, pavoneggiarsi; **the gas is —,** manca il gas; **he fell — a ladder,** cadde da una scala; **it is — the beaten track,** è fuori di mano; **he eats — a silver plate,** mangia su un piatto d'argento; **— duty,** libero; **a street — the Corso,** una strada che sbocca nel Corso; **— one's head,** pazzo, matto,

delirante, fuori di sè, fuori dei gangheri; **the door is — the hinges,** la porta è fuori dei cardini; **— Naples,** al largo di Napoli; **this dish is —,** questo piatto è esaurito; **we dined — roast mutton,** mangiammo un arrosto di castrato; **this is an — day,** oggi è giorno libero; **an — chance,** una possibilità, *f.*; **— -scourings,** rifiuto, scarto, *m.* **— side,** lato destro, *m.*, (*Football*) fuori giuoco; (*Golf*) **1 — 3,** meno 3.

offal [ˈɔfəl], *n.* Frattaglie, *f.pl.*, rimasugli, rifiuti, *m.pl.*; (*carrion*) malacarne, *f.*

offence [ɔˈfens], *n.* Offesa, *f.*, oltraggio, insulto, *m.*; ingiuria, *f.*; contravvenzione, trasgressione, *f.*, delitto, reato, *m.* **No — was meant,** non c'era nessun'intenzione di offendere; **to give —,** offendere; **to take — at,** recarsi a offesa, ritenere come un'offesa; **an indictable —,** un reato, *m.*; **weapons of —,** armi offensive, *f.pl.*

offend, *v.t.i.* Offendere, oltraggiare, insultare; trasgredire, violare, spiacere. **To — against the law,** trasgredire la legge; **to — against morality,** offendere la moralità; **it offends my sense of justice,** va contro il mio senso di giustizia; **to feel offended,** offendersi, recarsi a offesa, impermalirsi.

offended, *a.* Offeso, oltraggiato, disgustato, impermalito. **The — party,** la parte lesa, *f.*

offendedly, *adv.* Con aria impermalita, con aria offesa.

offender, *n.* Offensore, *m.*; colpevole, delinquente, *m.f.*; reo, *m.*, rea, *f.* **Juvenile —,** delinquente minorenne, *m.f.*; **an old —,** un recidivo, *m.*

offensive, *a.* Offensivo, aggressivo, oltraggioso, ingiurioso; spiacevole, nauseante, nocivo. ‖ *n.* Offensiva, *f.* **— language,** turpiloquio, *m.*; **to take the —,** prendere l'offensiva.

offensively, *adv.* Offensivamente.

offensiveness, *n.* Offensività, offesa, ingiuria, *f.*

offer [ˈɔfəɹ], *v.t.i.* Offrire, offrirsi, porgere, proferire, proferirsi. ‖ *n.* Offerta, proposta, *f.*; tentativo, *m.* **To — oneself,** offrirsi; **to — an opinion,** dare un'opinione; **to — goods for sale,** offrire roba da vendere; **to — resistance,** resistere, opporsi; **as opportunity offers,** secondo l'occasione, se l'occasione si presenta; **to — to,** offrire di; (*Comm.*) **on —,** in vendita; **an — of marriage,** un'offerta di matrimonio, *f.*; **to — up,** offrire, rendere.

offering, *n.* Offerta, *f.*; oblazione, *f.*, sacrificio, *m.* **Votive —,** ex voto, *m.*

offertory, *n.* (*Eccles.*) Offertorio, *m.*, colletta, questua, *f.*

offhand, *a.* Subito, senza preparazione; disinvolto, indifferente, sfrontato, noncurante.

offhanded, *a.* Noncurante. **To treat in an — manner,** trattare con noncuranza.

offhandedly, *adv.* Con disinvoltura.

offhandedness, *n.* Disinvoltura, noncuranza, *f.*

office [ˈɔfis], *n.* Ufficio, uffizio, dovere, obbligo, incarico, *m.*; carica, funzione, *f.*; gabinetto, studio, ufficio, *m.*; (*Eccles.*) servizio divino, *m.*, preghiere del giorno, *f.pl.* **Thanks to the kind offices of,** mercè i buoni uffici di; **— hours,** ore di ufficio, *f.pl.*; **to take —,** entrare in carica, assumere l'ufficio; **the Holy Office,** il Santo Uffizio, *m.*; (*Eccles.*) **to say the —,** dire l'uffizio.

officer, *n.* Ufficiale, *m.*; funzionario, agente, *m.*; usciere, *m.* ‖ *v.t.* Fornire d'ufficiali, fornire i quadri, inquadrare. **Staff —,** ufficiale di stato maggiore, *m.*; **the officers of a society,** le cariche d'una società, *f.pl.*

officered, *a.* Comandato.

official [oˈfiʃəl], *a.* Ufficiale, pubblico. ‖ *n.* Ufficiale, funzionario, impiegato, *m.* **— gazette,** gazzetta ufficiale, *f.*; **in an — capacity,** in forma ufficiale.

officialdom, *n.* Burocrazia, *f.*, funzionarismo, *m.*

officiate [oˈfiʃieit], *v.i.* (*Eccles.*) Officiare, celebrare. **To — as,** fare le funzioni di, officiare da.

officiating, *a.* Celebrante. **The — priest,** il celebrante, *m.*

officinal [oˈfisinəl], *a.* (*Med.*) Officinale.

officious [oˈfiʃəs], *a.* Ufficioso, inframmettente. **An — person,** un ficcanaso, *m.*; **— adviser,** consigliere, *m.*

offing [ˈɔfiŋ, ˈɔːfiŋ], *n.* (*Naut.*) Largo, mare aperto, *m.* **In the —,** al largo.

offset [ˈɔfset, ˈɔːfset], *a.n.* Compenso, equivalente, *m.*; (*Agric.*) rampollo, germoglio, *m.*; (*Print.*) rotocalcografia, *f.*

offshoot, *n.* Rampollo, germoglio, *m.*

offside, *adv.* (*Football*) Fuori giuoco.

offspring [ˈɔːfspriŋ], *n.* Figli, *m.pl.*, progenie, *f.*, discendenti, *m.pl.*, figliuolanza, *f.*; prodotto, risultato, *m.*

often, oft [ɔːfn, ɔfn, ɔft], *adv.* Sovente, spesso, frequentemente, molte volte, spesse volte. **How often?** Quante volte? **too often,** troppe volte, troppo spesso; **very often,** spessissimo; **oft-told,** detto e ridetto.

ofttimes [ˈɔftaimz], *adv.* Spesso, frequentemente.

ogee [ouˈdʒiː], *n.* (*Arch.*) Cimasa, *f.*

ogival [ouˈdʒaivəl], *a.* Ogivale.

ogive [ˈoudʒaiv], *n.* Ogiva, *f.*

ogle [ougl], *v.t.* Adocchiare, occhieggiare, vagheggiare, sbirciare, far l'occhiolino. ‖ *n.* Occhiata, *f.*

ogler, *n.* Occhieggiatore, *m.*

ogling, *n.* Occhieggiamento, vagheggiamento, *m.*

ogre [ˈougəɹ], *n.* Orco, gigante favoloso, mostro, *m.*

ogress, *n.* Orchessa, gigantessa, *f.*

oh! [ou], *inter.* Oh! Ah! Ahimè! Ahi!

ohm [oum], *n.* (*Elec.*) Ohm, *m.*

oil [ɔil], *n.* Olio, *m.*, essenza, *f.*; petrolio, *m.* ‖ *v.t.* Lubrificare, ungere, spalmare. (*Art*) **In oils,** a olio; **in —,** sott'olio; **to pour — on the flames,** gettar olio sulle fiamme; **— -can,** latta di petrolio, *f.*, bidone, *m.*; (*Art*) **— -colour,** colore a olio, *m.*; **— -field,** giacimento di petrolio, *m.*; **— -lamp,** lampada a olio, *f.*; **— -painting,** pittura ad olio, *f.*; **— -engine,** motore a petrolio, *m.*; **— -fuel,** petrolio combustibile, *m.*; **— -heater** stufa a petrolio, *f.*; **— -hole,** buco ingrassatore, *m.*; **— -paper,** carta oliata, *f.*; **— -mill, — -press,** torchio per olio, *m.*; **— -ship,** nave cisterna, *f.*; **— -shop,** magazzino d'olio, *m.*; **— -silk,** seta cerata, *f.*; **— -field,** campo petrolifero, *m.*; **— -well,** pozzo d'olio, *m.*; **castor- —,** olio di ricino, *m.*; **cooking- —,** olio commestibile, *m.*

oilcake, *n.* Pan di sesamo, panello, *m.*

oilcloth, *n.* Tela cerata, *f.*
oiled, *a.* Lubrificato; (*colloq.*) ubbriaco.
oiler, *n.* Oliatore, *m.*; lubricatoio, *m.*
oiliness, *n.* Oleosità, untuosità, *f.*
oiling, *n.* Lubrificazione, *f.*
oilman, *n.* Mercante d'olio, *m.*
oilnut, *n.* Noce oleosa, *f.*
oilskins, *n.pl.* Incerato, *m.*; impermeabile, *m.*
oily, *a.* Oleoso, untuoso.
ointment [ˈɔintmənt], *n.* Unguento, *m.*
okay, o.k. [ouˈkei], *inter.* (*colloq.*) Va bene! || *n.* approvazione, *f.*,
old [ould], *a.* Vecchio, antico, antiquato, vieto, vetusto. **An — man,** un vecchio, un vegliardo, *m.*; **an — woman,** una vecchia, *f.*; **at five years —,** all'età di cinque anni; **How — are you ?** Quanti anni avete? **I am twenty years —,** ho venti anni, sono ventenne; **of —,** anticamente; **— age,** la vecchiaia, *f.*; **he's — enough to know better,** ha anni abbastanza per capir la ragione; **as — as the hills,** vecchio come Matusalemme; **the — world,** il mondo antico; **— in crime,** birbante matricolato, *m.*; **an — hand,** abituato, esperto, perito; **an — family,** una famiglia antica, *f.*; **Old Nick,** il diavolo, *m.*; **to grow —,** invecchiare; **— clothes,** abiti usati, *m.pl.*; **—-established,** esistente da lungo tempo, di lunga mano; **—-fashioned,** antiquato, vecchio stile, fuori moda, all'antica; (*of children*) birichino; **Old chap!, Old fellow!** Caro mio! **— iron,** rottami di ferro, *m.pl.* (*Art*) **— master,** antico maestro, *m.*; **the Old Testament,** l'Antico Testamento, *m.*; **—-womanish, —-womanly,** timido; **—-world,** antico, dei tempi passati, vecchio stile.
olden, *a.* Vecchio, antico. **In — times,** nei tempi antichi.
oldish, *a.* Vecchietto, vecchiotto, piuttosto vecchio.
oldness, *n.* Vecchiezza, *f.*
oleaginous [oliˈædʒinəs], *a.* Oleoso.
oleander [oliˈændəɹ], *n.* (*Bot.*) Oleandro, *m.*
oleaster [oliˈæstæɹ], *n.* (*Bot.*) Oleastro, olivastro, *m.*
oleograph [ˈouliogræf], *n.* Oleografia, *f.*
olfactory [ɔlˈfæktəri], *a.* Olfattivo, olfattorio.
olibanum [oˈlibənəm], *n.* (*Bot.*) Olibano, *m.*
oligarch [ˈɔligɑːɹk], *n.* Oligarca, *m.*
oligarchical, *a.* Oligarchico.
oligarchy [ˈɔligɑːɹki], *n.* Oligarchia, *f.*
olivaceous [ɔliˈveiʃəs], *a.* Ulivaceo, olivastro.
olive [ˈɔliv], *n.* (*fruit*) Oliva, uliva, *f.*; (*tree*) olivo, *m.*; (*colour*) verde oliva, *m.*; **Mount of Olives,** Monte Oliveto, *m.*; **—-branch,** ramo d'olivo, ramoscello d'olivo, *m.*; **an — complexion,** una carnagione olivastra, *f.*; **—-grove,** oliveto, uliveto, *m.*; **—-oil,** olio d'oliva, *m.*
Olympiad [oˈlimpiəd], *n.* Olimpiade, *f.*
Olympian, Olympic, *a.* Olimpiaco, olimpico. **— Games,** giuochi olimpici, *m.pl.*
Olympus [oˈlimpəs], *n.* (*Geog.*) Olimpo, *m.*
ombre [ˈɔmbəɹ], *n.* Specie di giuoco alle carte.
omega [ˈoumegə], *n.* Omega, *m.*
omelet, omelette [ˈɔmlet], *n.* Omelette, frittata, *f.*
omen [ˈoumen], *n.* Augurio, presagio, pronostico, segno, indizio, *m.*
omened, *a.* Di augurio, presagito. **Ill- —,** di cattivo augurio, di malaugurio, sfortunato.
omentum [oˈmentəm], *n.* (*Anat.*) Omento, *m.*
ominous [ˈɔminəs], *a.* Di cattivo augurio, sinistro, malaugurato.
ominously, *adv.* Malauguratamente, minaccevolmente.
omissible [oˈmisəbl], *a.* Tralasciabile.
omission [oˈmiʃən], *n.* Omissione, *f.*, tralasciamento, *m.*; lacuna, *f.*
omit [oˈmit], *v.t.* Omettere, tralasciare.
omnibus [ˈɔmnibəs], *n.* Omnibus, autobus, *m.* **—-conductor,** bigliettaio, *m.*
omnifarious [ɔmniˈfɛəriəs], *a.* Di ogni sorta, svariato.
omnipotence [ɔmˈnipətəns], *n.* Onnipotenza, *f.*
omnipotent, *a.* Onnipotente.
omnipresence [ɔmniˈpresəns], *n.* Onnipresenza, *f.*
omnipresent, *a.* Onnipresente.
omniscience [ɔmˈniʃəns], *n.* Onniscienza, *f.*
omniscient, *a.* Onnisciente.
omnivorous [ɔmˈnivərəs], *a.* Onnivoro.
omoplate [ˈoumoupleit], *n.* (*Anat.*) Omoplata, *m.*, scapola, *f.*
on [ɔn], *prep.* Su, sopra; da; in; a; per; dopo. || *adv.* Avanti, via, sempre. **A ring on the finger,** un anello in dito; **on hearing that,** udito ciò; **on entering we saw,** entrati che fummo vedemmo, nell'entrare vedemmo; **on fire,** in fiamme; **on foot,** a piedi; **to keep on one's feet,** reggersi in piedi; **on hand,** alla mano, in magazzino; **on high,** in alto; **on my honour,** sul mio onore; **on my side,** da parte mia; **on that day,** in quel giorno; **on the right, on the left,** a destra, a sinistra; **Have you any money on you ?** Avete danaro addosso? **to fall on one's feet,** cadere in piedi; **he dropped the book on the floor,** lasciò cadere a terra il libro; **on the first floor,** al primo piano; **on the cheap,** a buon mercato; **to be mad on,** essere pazzo per; **bent on,** risoluto a; **he writes on economics,** scrive d'economia; **and so on,** e così via; **far on in the night,** a notte avanzata; **put on your hat,** mettete il cappello; **On!** Avanti! **please read on,** favorite continuare a leggere; **he keeps on saying 'no',** continua a dire di 'No'; **getting on for four o'clock,** verso le quattro; **What's on at the theatre ?** Che cosa si dà al teatro? **on-coming,** che si avvicina; **on-looker,** spettatore, *m.*; **on-lookers,** astanti, *m.pl.*
onager [ˈɔnəgəɹ], *n.* (*Zool.*) Onagro, *m.*
once [wʌns], *adv.* Una volta, una sola volta; altrevolte, un tempo, già. **All at —,** ad un tratto; **at —,** subito; **— before,** già una volta; **— for all,** una volta per sempre; **— upon a time there was,** c'era una volta; **just this —,** questa volta soltanto; **when — I have learned it,** una volta che l'avrò imparato; **at — strong and gentle,** forte e mite allo stesso tempo; **— a year,** una volta all'anno.
one [wʌn], *n.a.* Uno, *m.*, una, *f.*, l'uno, *m.*, l'una, *f.*, il solo, *m.*, la sola, *f.*, unico, *m.* || *pron.* L'uno, *m.*, l'una, *f.*, altri, chi, si. **All, as — man,** tutti, come un sol'uomo; **we are at —,** siamo d'accordo; **four ones are four,** quattro per uno fa quattro; **I have but**

— **book,** non ho che un libro; **it's all — to me,** è tutt'uno per me, non mi fa nè caldo nè freddo; **— and all,** tutti quanti; **I bet ten to —,** scommetto dieci contro uno; **every — of you,** voi tutti; **he is — who,** è un uomo che; **she's the — who did it,** è colei che l'ha fatto; **it does — good to go out,** fa bene uscire; **the — . . . the other,** l'uno . . . l'altro, chi . . . chi; **How does — open this door?** Come si fa ad aprire questa porta? **no —,** nessuno; **by ones and twos,** uno o due alla volta; **— by —,** a uno a uno, uno dopo l'altro; **I never saw — like it,** non vidi mai una cosa simile; **he is — of us,** è dei nostri; **— of themselves,** uno di loro; **such a —,** un tale, *m.*; **— sees that,** si vede che; **it makes — gasp,** fa mancare il fiato; leva il respiro; **the little ones,** i piccini, *m.pl.*; **the only — who,** il solo che; **— Thomas Jones,** un certo Tommaso Jones; **we were talking about — thing and another,** parlavamo di diverse cose; parlavamo del più e del meno; **—-armed,** monco d'un braccio; **—-eyed,** che ha un solo occhio; **—-handed,** monco d'una mano; **—-horse,** con un cavallo solo; (*fig.*) povero, meschino, insignificante; **—-legged,** mutilato d'una gamba; **—-man,** in mano di una persona sola; **—-price,** a prezzo unico; **—-sided,** unilaterale, (*fig.*) parziale, ingiusto; **— way street,** via a senso unico; **—-way traffic,** circolazione a senso unico.

oneness ['wʌnnes], *n.* Unità, unione, *f.*; singolarità, *f.*

onerous ['ounərəs], *a.* Oneroso, grave.

onerousness, *n.* Gravezza, *f.*

one's [wʌnz], *pron.* Suo, *m.*, sua, *f.*, suoi, *m.pl.*, sue, *f.pl.*, proprio, *m.*, propria, *f.*, propri, *m.pl.*, proprie, *f.pl.*

oneself, *pron.* Sè, se stesso, *m.*, se stessa, *f.*; si.

onion ['ʌniən], *n.* Cipolla, *f.* **—-bed,** cipollaio, *m.*; **—-skin,** buccia di cipolla, *f.*

only ['ounli], *a.* Solo, unico || *adv.* Solamente, soltanto, unicamente; non . . . che. || *conj.* Ma. **That — makes matters worse,** ciò non fa che peggiorar le cose; **if —,** se almeno; **I have — just arrived,** sono appena arrivato; **— too glad,** proprio contento; **Only think!** Immaginatevi! Figuratevi!

onomastic [ɔno'mæstik], *a.* Onomastico.

onomatopœia [ɔnomæto'pi:ɑ], *n.* Onomatopea, *f.*

onomatopœic, *a.* Onomatopeico.

onrush, onslaught ['ɔnrʌʃ, 'ɔnslɔ:t], *n.* Assalto, urto, *m.*, carica, *f.*

onset ['ɔnset], *n.* Assalto, attacco, urto, *m.*, carica, *f.* **At the first —,** al primo attacco.

ontogenesis [ɔnto'dʒenisis], *n.* Ontogenesi, *f.*

ontology [ɔn'tɔlədʒi], *n.* Ontologia, *f.*

onus ['ounəs], *n.* Onere, peso, carico, obbligo, impegno, *m.* **— of proof,** onere della prova, *m.*

onward, onwards ['ɔnwəɹd, 'ɔnwəɹdz], *adv.a.* Avanti, in avanti, innanzi, oltre; (*of time*) in poi. **From now —,** da ora in poi; **to go onward,** avanzare, andare innanzi, procedere.

onyx ['ɔniks], *n.* Onice, *m.*

oof [u:f], *n.* (*colloq.*) Danaro, *m.*, quattrini, *m.pl.*

oolite ['ouəlait], *n.* (*Geol.*) Oolite, *f.*

oolitic, *a.* Oolitico.

ooze [u:z], *n.* Limo, fango, *m.*, melma, *f.*; (*of liquid*) filtramento, *m.* || *v.t.* Filtrare, stillare, gemere, traspirare, trapelare. **The secret oozed out,** il segreto trapelò; **to — away,** sparire.

oozing, *n.* Filtrazione, *f.*, stillamento, trapelamento, *m.*

oozy, *a.* Limoso, fangoso, melmoso.

opacity [o'pæsiti], *n.* Opacità, *f.*

opal ['oupəl], *n.* Opale, *m.*

opalescence [opə'lesəns], *n.* Opalescenza, *f.*

opalescent, *a.* Opalescente.

opaline ['oupəlain], *a.* Opalino.

opaque [o'peik], *a.* Opaco.

opaqueness, *n.* Opacità, *f.*

open ['oupən], *v.t.i.* Aprire, aprirsi, schiudere, schiudersi; cominciare, iniziare; allargare, allargarsi; sturare, rivelare, palesare, schiarire; (*a letter*) dissuggellare; (*a bottle*) stappare, sturare; (*oysters*) sgusciare; (*of flower*) sbocciare, schiudersi. || *a.* Aperto, dischiuso, schiuso, allargato, spalancato; nudo, scoperto, esposto; chiaro, manifesto, evidente; (*of weather*) mite; franco, sincero. **To — wide,** spalancare; **to — fire,** aprire il fuoco; **to — one's eyes,** spalancare gli occhi; (*fig.*) **that will — his eyes,** ciò gli aprirà gli occhi; **the room opens on a passage,** la camera dà su un corridoio; **to — the ball,** iniziare la danza; **it opens up brighter prospects for us,** ci schiude un avvenire più lieto; **Open sesame!** Sesamo, apriti! **in the — air,** all'aria aperta, a cielo scoperto; **half- —,** socchiuso, mezz'aperto; **wide- —** spalancato; **an — boat,** un'imbarcazione scoperta, *f.*; **an — scandal,** uno scandalo pubblico, *m.*; un'onta pubblica, *f.*; **the — country,** l'aperta campagna, *f.*; **their position is — to attack,** la loro posizione è esposta alla critica; **I am always — to argument,** sono sempre pronto a ricredermi; **in the — sea,** in alto mare; **Are you — for a job?** Siete liberi ad assumere un impegno? **with — arms,** a braccia aperte; **I will be — with you,** vi parlerò francamente; **it is an — question,** è una questione insoluta, *f.*; **he is an — enemy,** è un avversario dichiarato; **I have an — mind,** ho la mente aperta; **—-eared,** con gli orecchi tesi, attento; **—-eyed,** con gli occhi spalancati; **—-handed,** generoso, liberale, largo di mano; **—-hearted,** franco, sincero, leale, genuino; **—-minded,** liberale, spregiudicato; **—-mouthed,** a bocca aperta; **—-work,** punto a giorno, lavoro a traforo, *m.*

opener, *n.* Apritore, *m.*, apritrice, *f.*; (*for cans, etc.*) arnese per aprire, apritrice, *f.* **An eye- —,** una rivelazione, *f.*

opening, *n.* Apertura, *f.*; cominciamento, principio, inizio, *m.*; occasione, *f.*; (*Comm.*) sbocco, *m.* || *a.* Inaugurale, primo; (*Med.*) lassativo.

openly, *adv.* Apertamente, francamente, pubblicamente.

openness, *n.* Franchezza, sincerità, *f.*

opera ['ɔpərə], *n.* (*Mus.*) Opera, *f.* **Grand —,** opera, *f.*; **comic —,** opera comica, opera buffa, *f.*; **—-cloak,** sortita, sortie, *f.*; **—-glasses,** binocolo da teatro, *m.*; **—-hat,** gibus, *m.*; **—-house,** opera, *f.*, teatro dell'opera, *m.*

operate [ˈɔpəreit], *v.t.i.* Operare, agire, produrre. **To — on,** operare.
operatic [ɔpəˈrætik], *a.* D'opera, lirico.
operating [ˈɔpəreitiŋ], *a.* Operativo, attivo, operante. **— theatre,** sala d'operazioni, *f.*
operation, *n.* Operazione, azione, *f.* **In —,** in azione, in atto, in attuazione, all'atto pratico.
operative [ˈɔpərətiv], *a.* Operativo, attivo, efficace; manuale, operaio, lavorante. || *n.* Operaio, *m.*, operaia, *f.*, lavorante, *m.f.*
operator [ˈɔpəreitəɹ], *n.* Operatore, *m.*, operatrice, *f.*; autore, *m.*; (*Med.*) operatore, chirurgo, *m.*; (*Comm.*) borsista, *m.*; (*Telephone*) centralinista, *m. f.*
operculum [oˈpəːɹkjuːləm], *n.* Opercolo, *m.*
operetta [ˈɔpəretə], *n.* Operetta, *f.*
ophicleide [ˈɔfiklaid], *n.* (*Mus.*) Oficleide, *m.*
ophidian [oˈfidiən], *n.* (*Zool.*) Ofidio, *m.*
ophthalmia [ofˈθælmiə], *n.* (*Med.*) Oftalmia, *f.*
ophthalmic, *a.* Oftalmico.
opiate [ˈoupiət], *n.* Narcotico, sonnifero, *m.* || *a.* Narcotico, sonnifero, soporifero.
opine [oˈpain], *v.t.* Opinare, pensare, stimare.
opinion [oˈpiniən], *n.* Opinione, idea, credenza, *f.*; parere, avviso, pensiero, giudizio, concetto, *m.*; sentenza, *f.*, consiglio, *m.* **In my —,** a mio parere; **in the — of,** secondo l'opinione di; **that is a matter of —,** è questione d'opinione; **to have a great — of oneself,** avere grande opinione di sè; **to be of the — that,** essere d'opinione che; **according to public —,** nell'opinione degli uomini, secondo l'opinione pubblica; **to yield to —,** arrendersi all'opinione generale; **to act up to one's opinions,** seguire le proprie opinioni; **to take counsel's —,** consultare un avvocato.
opinionated, opinionative, *a.* Ostinato, dogmatico; intransigente.
opium [ˈoupiəm], *n.* Oppio, *m.* **— addict,** oppiomane, *m.*; **— den,** casa per fumatori d'oppio; **— poppy,** papavero sonnifero, *m.*
opossum [oˈpɔsəm], *n.* (*Zool.*) Opossum, *m.*
opponent [oˈpounənt], *n.* Opponente, oppositore, avversario, *m.* || *a.* Contrario, opposto.
opportune [ˈɔpɔɹtjuːn], *a.* Opportuno, conveniente, propizio.
opportunely, *adv.* Opportunamente, a proposito.
opportuneness, *n.* Convenienza, opportunità, *f.*
opportunism, *n.* Opportunismo, *m.*
opportunist, *n.* Opportunista, *m f.*
opportunity, *n.* Occasione; opportunità, *f.* **To take the —,** cogliere l'occasione; **to let the — slip,** perdere l'occasione.
oppose [oˈpouz], *v.t.* Opporre, opporsi a, combattere, contrastare, contestare.
opposed, *a.* Contrario.
opposing, *a.* Opposto, avverso.
opposite [ˈɔpəzit], *a.* Opposto, contrario, diverso; altro. || *n.* L'opposto, il contrario, *m.* **The — side of the road,** il lato opposto della strada, *m.*; **to go — ways,** andarsene per vie opposte; **they are absolute opposites,** sono l'opposto, sono agli antipodi; **the — sex,** l'altro sesso, *m.*; **— to,** di fronte a, in faccia a, dirimpetto a.
opposition [ɔpəˈziʃən], *n.* Opposizione, resistenza, *f.*; contrasto, *m.*; (*competition*) concorrenza, *f.* **In — to,** in opposizione a; **to be in the —,** essere all'opposizione; **to set up in — to,** entrare in concorrenza con; **Her Majesty's Opposition,** l'opposizione parlamentare, *f.*
oppress [oˈpres], *v.t.* Opprimere, gravare, sopraffare; tribolare, vessare, angariare.
oppression [oˈpreʃən], *n.* Oppressione, vessazione, *f.*; angoscia, stretta, *f.*, peso, *m.*, ansia, *f.*
oppressive, *a.* Oppressivo; accasciante.
oppressively, *adv.* Oppressivamente.
oppressiveness, *n.* Tirannia, oppressività, *f.*; (*of weather*), afa, *f.*, oppressione, calura, *f.*
oppressor, *n.* Oppressore, tiranno, soverchiatore, *m.*
opprobrious [oˈproubriəs], *a.* Obbrobrioso, vituperevole, vergognoso.
opprobriously, *adv.* Obbrobriosamente.
opprobriousness, opprobrium [oˈproubriəsnis, oˈproubriəm], *n.* Obbrobrio, vituperio, *m.*
oppugn [oˈpjuːn], *v.t.* Oppugnare, impugnare.
optative [ˈɔptətiv], *a.* (*Gram.*) Ottativo.
optic, optical [ˈɔptik, ˈɔptikəl], *a.* Ottico.
optician [opˈtiʃən], *n.* Ottico, *m.*
optics, *n.pl.* Ottica, *f.*
optimism [ˈɔptimizm], *n.* Ottimismo, *m.*
optimist, *n.* Ottimista, *m.f.*
optimistic, *a.* Ottimistico.
optimistically, *adv.* Ottimisticamente.
option [ˈɔpʃən], *n.* Scelta, *f.*; opzione, *f.*; facoltà, libertà, *f.*; (*Comm.*) contratto a premio, *m.* **We had no — but to,** non potevamo fare altro che.
optional, *a.* Facoltativo.
opulence [ˈɔpjuːləns], *n.* Opulenza, *f.*
opulent, *a.* Opulento.
opulently, *adv.* Opulentemente.
opuscule, opusculum [ˈɔpəskjuːl, oˈpʌskjuːləm], *n.* Opuscolo, *m.*
or (1) [ɔːɹ], *conj.* O, ovvero, ossia, oppure. **Either . . . or,** o . . . o, sia . . . sia; **or else,** altrimente, oppure.
or (2), *n.* (*Heraldry*) Oro, *m.*
oracle [ˈɔrəkəl], *n.* Oracolo, *m.*
oracular [oˈrækjuːləɹ], *a.* D'oracolo, da oracolo; autoritario, magistrale.
oracularly, *adv.* Oracolamente.
oral [ˈɔːrəl], *a.* Orale. **— examination,** esame orale, *m.*
orally, *adv.* Oralmente.
orange [ˈɔrindʒ], *n.* Arancia, *f.*; (*colour*) arancio, color d'arancia, *m.* **—-blossom,** fiore d'arancio, *m.*; **—-peel,** scorza d'arancia, buccia d'arancia, *f.*; **—-tree,** arancio, *m.*; **—-marmalade,** marmellata d'arancia, *f.*
orangeade [ɔrindʒˈeid], *n.* Aranciata, *f.*
orangery, *n.* Aranciera, *f.*; aranceto, *m.*
Orangeman [ˈɔrindʒmən], *n.* (*Hist.Pol.*) Protestante irlandese, *m.*
orang-outang [oˈræŋ uˈtæŋ], *n.* (*Zool.*) Orang-utan, orango, *m.*
oration [oˈreiʃən], *n.* Orazione, *f.*; arringa, *f.*; discorso, *m.*
orator [ˈɔrətəɹ], *n.* Oratore, *m.*
oratorical, *a.* Oratorico.
oratorio [ɔrəˈtɔːriou], *n.* (*Mus.*) Oratorio, *m.*
oratory (1) [ˈɔrətəri], *n.* Oratoria, eloquenza, *f.*
oratory (2), *n.* (*Eccles.*) Oratorio, *m.*

orb [ɔːɹb], *n.* Orbe, globo, mondo, *m.*, sfera, *f.*; (*Poet.*) occhio, *m.*
orbicular [ɔːɹ'bikjuːləɹ], *a.* Orbicolare, orbicolato.
orbicularity, *n.* Sfericità, *f.*
orbit ['ɔːɹbit], *n.* (*Astron.*) Orbita, *f.*
orbital, *a.* Orbitale.
orc [ɔːɹk], *n.* (*Myth. Zool.*) Orca, *f.*; (*Myth.*) orco, *m.*
orchard ['ɔːɹtʃəɹd], *n.* Frutteto, *m.*
orchestra ['ɔːɹkestrə], *n.* Orchestra, *f.* **— stall,** poltrona, *f.*
orchestral, *a.* Orchestrale.
orchestrate, *v.t.* Orchestrare.
orchestration, *n.* Orchestrazione, *f.*
orchid, orchis ['ɔːɹkid, 'ɔːɹkis], *n.* (*Bot.*) Orchidea, *f.*
orchil ['ɔːɹkil], *n.* (*Chem.*) Orchilia, *f.*
ordain [ɔːɹ'dein], *v.t.* Decretare, ordinare, stabilire; (*Eccles.*) ordinare, consacrare.
ordainer, *n.* (*Eccles.*) Ordinante, *m.*
ordainment, *n.* Decreto, *m.*, ordinanza, *f.*; ordinamento, *m.*
ordeal [ɔːɹ'diːl], *n.* Prova, *f.*, travaglio, cimento, *m.*; traversia, *f.*; (*Hist.*) ordalie, *f.pl.*, giudizio di Dio, *m.*
order ['ɔːɹdəɹ], *n.* Ordine, *m.*, serie, fila, *f.*; grado, ceto, *m.*; ordinanza, *f.*, ordinamento, *m.*; (*Comm.*) ordinazione, *f.*; (*Law*) mandato, *m.*; genere, *m.* || *v.t.* Ordinare, comandare; disporre, regolare, collocare; dirigere, condurre. **By —,** per ordine; **in good —,** in buon ordine; **in — that,** affinchè, acciocchè; **in — to,** affine di, allo scopo di; (*Mil.*) **open, close —,** ordine sparso, chiuso, *m.*; (*Eccles.*) **to take orders,** prendere gli ordini; **made to —,** fatto su ordinazione; **the lower orders,** il ceto basso, *m.*; **— of the day,** ordine del giorno, *m.*; **out of —,** guasto; **until further orders,** fino a nuov'ordine; **Order!** Silenzio! Ordine!; **a point of —,** una questione di procedura, *f.*; **to rise to a point of —,** sollevare una questione di procedura; **to call to —,** richiamare all'ordine; **postal- —,** cartolina vaglia, *f.*; (*Comm.*) **to cancel an —,** annullare un'ordinazione; **to get out of —,** cessare di funzionare, guastarsi, incepparsi; **to keep in —,** tenere in ordine; **to keep —,** mantenere l'ordine; (*Comm.*) **bill payable to —,** cambiale all'ordine; **to — dinner,** ordinare il pranzo; **we were ordered to leave,** ci ordinarono di andare; **to — away,** far partire, dar ordine di partire; (*colloq.*) **to — about,** mandare qua e là; **to — in,** comandare di entrare.
ordering, *n.* Disposizione, *f.*
orderliness, *n.* Regolarità, compostezza, correttezza, *f.*, ordine, *m.*; buona condotta, *f.*
orderly, *a.* Ordinato, regolato, regolare, metodico; in buone ordine; composto, corretto; pacifico, tranquillo. || *n.* (*Mil.*) Ordinanza, *f.*; attendente, *m.* **— officer,** ufficiale d'ordinanza, *m.*; **— -room,** fureria, *f.*, ufficio di campagnia, *m.*; **hospital —,** inserviente.
ordinal ['ɔːɹdinəl], *a.* Ordinale. || *n.* Numero ordinale, *m.*
ordinance ['ɔːɹdinəns], *n.* Ordinanza, *f.*, decreto, regolamento, *m.*; rito, *m.*, cerimonia, *f.*
ordinand, *n.* (*Eccles.*) Candidato per ordinazione, *m.*
ordinary ['ɔːɹdinəri], *a.* Ordinario, consueto, solito, normale. || *n.* (*Eccles.*) Vescovo, *m.*; (*at inn*) tavola comune, *f.* **Out of the —,** straordinario; **— seaman,** marinaio semplice, *m.*
ordinate ['ɔːɹdineit], *n.* (*Geom.*) Ordinata, *f.*
ordination, *n.* Ordinazione, *f.*
ordnance ['ɔːɹdnəns], *n.* Artiglieria, *f.* **— survey,** ufficio cartografico, *m.*; **— map,** carta ufficiale, carta dello Stato Maggiore, *f.*; **— surveyor,** topografo militare, *m.*
ordure ['ɔːɹdjuːɹ], *n.* Sporcizia, lordura, *f.*, escremento, *m.*; oscenità, *f.*
ore [ɔːɹ], *n.* Minerale, *m.* **Iron- —,** minerale di ferro, *m.*
oread ['ɔːriəd], *n.* (*Myth.*) Oreade, *f.*
organ ['ɔːɹgən], *n.* (*all senses*) Organo, *m.*; (*fig.*) voce, *f.* **Barrel —,** organetto, *m.*; **— -grinder,** suonatore d'organetto, *m.*; **mouth- —,** armonica, *f.*; **— -blower,** tiramantici, *m.*; **— -builder,** fabbricante di organi, *m.*; **— -loft,** tribuna dell'organo, *f.*; **— -pipe,** canna d'organo, *f.*; **— -stop,** registro d'organo, *m.*
organdie ['ɔːɹgəndi], *n.* Organdisse, organdi, *m.*
organic [ɔːɹ'gænik], *a.* Organico.
organically, *adv.* Organicamente.
organism ['ɔːɹgənizm], *n.* Organismo, *m.*
organist, *n.* Organista, *m.f.*
organization [ɔːɹgənai'zeiʃən], *n.* Organizzazione, *f.*; ordinamento, *m.*
organize, *v.t.* Organizzare, ordinare.
organizer, *n.* Organizzatore, *m.*, organizzatrice, *f.*
organon, organum ['ɔːɹgənən, 'ɔːɹgənəm], *n.* Organo, *m.*
orgasm ['ɔːɹgæzm], *n.* Orgasmo, *m.*
orgy ['ɔːɹdʒi], *n.* Orgia, *f.*
oriel ['ɔːriəl], *n.* (*Arch.*) Finestra sporgente, *f.*
orient ['ɔːriənt], *n.* Oriente, levante, *m.* || *a.* D'oriente, orientale.
oriental, *a.* Orientale. || *n.* Orientale, asiatico, *m.*
orientalism, *n.* Orientalismo, *m.*
orientalist, *n.* Orientalista, *m.f.*
orientate ['ɔːriənteit], *v.t.* Orientare.
orientation, *n.* Orientazione, *f.*
orifice ['ɔrifis], *n.* Orifizio, *m.*, apertura, bocca, *f.*
oriflamme ['ɔriflæm], *n.* Orifiamma, *f.*
origin ['ɔridʒin], *n.* Origine, sorgente, cominciamento, principio, *m.*, provenienza, *f.*
original, *a.* Originale; nuovo; singolare. || *n.* Originale, *m.*
originality, *n.* Originalità, *f.*
originally, *adv.* Originalmente.
originate [ə'ridʒineit], *v.t.i.* Originare, produrre, cagionare; originarsi, derivare. **To — from,** provenire da, derivare da.
originating, *a.* Originario, derivante.
origination, *n.* Originazione, derivazione, *f.*
originator, *n.* Originatore, autore, iniziatore, *m.*
oriole ['ɔrioul], *n.* (*Zool.*) Rigogolo, *m.*
Orion [ə'raiən], *n.* (*Myth.Astron.*) Orione, *m.*
orison ['ɔrizən], *n.* Preghiera, orazione, *f.*
Orkneys ['ɔːɹkniz], *n.pl.* (*Geog.*) Le Orcadi, *f.pl.*

Orleans [ɔːɹˈliːənz], *n.* (*Geog.*) Orleans, *f.*
orlop [ˈɔːɹlɔp], *n.* (*Naut.*) Ponte a cassa, falso ponte, *m.*
ormolu [ˈɔːɹməluː], *n.* Bronzo dorato, *m.*
ornament [ˈɔːɹnəmənt], *n.* Ornamento, *m.*; ninnolo, *m.* || *v.t.* [ˈɔɹnəment] Ornare, abbellire, guarnire, decorare.
ornamental [ɔːɹnəˈmentəl], *a.* Ornamentale, decorativo.
ornamentally, *adv.* Decorativamente.
ornamentation, *n.* Ornamentazione, *f.*, abbellimento, *m.*
ornamentor, *n.* Ornamentatore, *m.*
ornate [ɔːɹˈneit], *a.* Ornato, adorno, abbellito, elaborato.
ornately, *adv.* Ornatamente.
ornateness, *n.* Ornatezza, *f.*
ornithological [ɔːɹniθəˈlɔdʒikəl], *a.* Ornitologico.
ornithologist [ɔːɹniˈθɔlədʒist], *n.* Ornitologo, *m.*
ornithology, *n.* Ornitologia, *f.*
ornithorhyncus [ɔːɹniθəˈriŋkəs], *n.* (*Zool.*) Ornitorinco, *m.*
orography [ɔˈrɔgrəfi], *n.* Orografia, *f.*
orphan [ˈɔːɹfən], *n.* Orfano, *m.*, orfana, *f.* || *a.* Orfano. || *v.t.* Rendere orfano. — **asylum,** orfanotrofio, *m.*
orphanage, *n.* Orfanotrofio, *m.*
Orphean, Orphic [ɔːɹˈfiːən, ˈɔːɹfik], *a.* Orfico.
Orpheus [ˈɔːɹfjuːs], *n.* Orfeo, *m.*
orpiment [ˈɔːɹpimənt], *n.* Orpimento, *m.*
orpine [ˈɔːɹpain], *n.* (*Bot.*) Favagello, *m.*
orrery [ˈɔrəri], *n.* (*Astron.*) Planetario, *m.*
orris [ˈɔris], *n.* Iris, giaggiolo, *m.* — **-root,** radice di giaggiolo, *f.*
orthodox [ˈɔːɹθədɔks], *a.* Ortodosso.
orthodoxy [ˈɔːɹθədɔksi], *n.* Ortodossia, *f.*
orthoepic [ɔːɹθouˈepik], *a.* Ortoepico.
orthoepy, *n.* Ortoepia, *f.*
orthographic, orthographical [ɔːɹθəˈgræfik, ɔːɹθəˈgræfikəl], *a.* Ortografico.
orthography [ɔːɹˈθɔgrəfi], *n.* Ortografia, *f.*
orthopaedic [ɔːɹθoˈpiːdik], *a.* Ortopedico.
orthopaedy [ˈɔːɹθopiːdi], *n.* Ortopedia, *f.*
ortolan [ˈɔːɹtələn], *n.* (*Zool.*) Ortolano, *m.*
orts [ɔːɹts], *n.pl.* Rifiuti, resti, *m.pl.*
oscillate [ˈɔsileit], *v.i.* Oscillare; vacillare.
oscillating, *a.* Oscillante; (*Elec.*) — **current,** corrente oscillatoria, *f.*
oscillation, *n.* Oscillazione, *f.*
oscillatory, *a.* Oscillatorio.
osculation [ɔskjuːˈleiʃən], *n.* Baciamento, *m.*, osculazione, *f.*; (*Geom.*) combaciamento, *m.*
osculatory, *a.* Osculatorio. || *n.* (*Eccles.*) Osculatorio, *m.*
osier [ˈouʒəɹ], *n.* (*Bot.*) Vimine, vinco, *m.* — **-bed,** canneto, vincheto, *m.*
osmium [ˈɔzmiəm], *n.* Osmio, *m.*
osprey [ˈɔsprei], *n.* (*Zool.*) Ossifraga, *f.*, falco pescatore, *m.*
osseous [ˈɔsiəs], *a.* Osseo.
ossicle [ˈɔsikəl], *n.* (*Anat.*) Ossicolo, ossicino, *m.*
ossification, *n.* Ossificazione, *f.*
ossify [ˈɔsifai], *v.t.i.* Ossificare, ossificarsi.
ossuary [ˈɔsjuːəri], *n.* Ossario, *m.*
Ostend [ɔsˈtend], *n.* (*Geog.*) Ostenda, *f.*
ostensible [ɔsˈtensibl], *a.* Ostensibile, preteso.
ostensibly, *adv.* Ostensibilmente.
ostensory [ɔsˈtensəri], *n.* (*Eccles.*) Ostensorio, *m.*
ostentation [ɔstenˈteiʃən], *n.* Ostentazione, mostra, pompa, *f.*; fasto, *m.*
ostentatious [ɔstenˈteiʃəs], *a.* Vanitoso, pomposo, fastoso.
osteoblast [ˈɔstioblɑːst], *n.* Osteoblasti, *m.pl.*
osteoclasis [ɔstioˈklæsis], *n.* (*Med.*) Osteoclasia, *f.*
osteology [ɔstiˈɔlədʒi], *n.* Osteologia, *f.*
osteotomy [ɔstiˈɔtəmi], *n.* Osteotomia, *f.*
ostler [ˈɔsləɹ], *n.* Stalliere, mozzo di stalla, *m.*
ostracism [ˈɔstrəsizm], *n.* Ostracismo, *m.*
ostracize, *v.t.* Ostracizzare.
ostrich [ˈɔstritʃ], *n.* (*Zool.*) Struzzo, *m.* — **feather,** piuma di struzzo, *f.*
Oswald [ˈɔzwəld], *n.* Osvaldo, *m.*
Othello [ɔθˈelou], *n.* Otello, *m.*
other [ˈʌðəɹ], *a.* Altro, diverso. || *pron.* Altro, l'altro. **Every — day,** ogni due giorni; — **people,** altri, *m.pl.*; **quite —,** ben diverso, affatto diverso, tutt'altra cosa; **all the others,** tutti gli altri; **each —,** l'un l'altro; **someone or —,** qualcuno; **on the — hand,** d'altra parte; **in — respects,** sotto altri riguardi.
otherwise [ˈʌðəɹwaiz], *adv.* Altrimenti, se no; diversamente, d'altronde.
other-worldliness [ʌðəɹˈwɔːɹldlinis], *n.* Spiritualità, *f.*, transcendentalismo, *m.*
otherworldly, *a.* Spirituale, religioso; apocalittico.
otiose [ˈoutiouz], *a.* Ozioso.
otter [ˈɔtəɹ], *n.* (*Zool.*) Lontra, *f.*
Ottoman [ˈɔtomən], *a.* Ottomano. || *n.* (Turk) Ottomano, *m.*
ottoman *n.* Ottomana, *f.*, divano, *m.*
otto [cp. **attar**].
oubliette [uːbliˈet], *n.* Trabocchetto, carcere perpetuo, *m.*
ought (1) [ɔːt], *v.aux.* Dovere, bisognare. **It — not to be allowed,** non si dovrebbe permettere; **you — to go away,** dovreste andar via; **I — to have known,** avrei dovuto saperlo.
ought (2) [cp. **aught**].
ounce (1) [auns], *n.* Oncia, *f.*
ounce (2), *n.* (*Zool.*) Lince, lonza, pantera dei monti, *m.*
our [auɹ], *a.* Nostro, il nostro, *m.*, nostra, la nostra, *f.*; nostri, i nostri, *m.pl.*, nostre, le nostre, *f.pl.* **Our Lord,** Nostro Signore; **Our Lady,** Nostra Signora, La Madonna, *f.*; **at — house,** in casa nostra.
ours [auɹz], *pron.* Il nostro, *m.*, la nostra, *f.*, i nostri, *m.pl.*, le nostre, *f.pl.*, di noi.
ourselves, *pron.* Noi, noi stessi, *m.pl.*, noi, noi stesse, *f.pl.*; ci.
ousel [ˈuːzəl], *n.* (*Zool.*) Merlo, *m.*
oust [aust], *v.t.* Sloggiare, cacciare, espellere, spodestare.
out [aut], *adv.* Fuori, via. || *a.* Di fuori; assente; spento, sbocciato, pubblicato; nell'errore; in isciopero. **To go —,** andar fuori, uscire; **his elbow is —,** si è slogato il gomito; **he is — in Canada,** si trova nel Canada; **Get —!** Fuori! Via! **the voyage —,** il viaggo di andata, *m.*; **the miners are — on strike,** i minatori sono in isciopero; **the fire is —,** il fuoco è spento; **hear me —,** sentitemi sino alla fine; **Out with him!** Cacciatelo fuori! **Out with it!** Parlate! **the book is —,** il

libro è uscito adesso; **the secret is —,** il segreto è scoperto; **the flowers are all —,** i fiori sono tutti sbocciati; **murder will —,** la luce sarà fatta, ogni nodo viene al pettine; **tired —,** stanco morto; **we must have our talk — tomorrow,** dobbiamo finire la nostra chiacchierata domani; **before the year is —,** prima che finisca l'anno; **— and —,** da cima a fondo; **— and away the best,** di gran lunga il migliore; **to speak — loud,** parlare ad alta voce; **I'm very put —,** sono proprio scontento; **she is not yet —,** non è ancora entrata in società; **he laughed right —,** scoppiò a ridere; **Speak —!** Parlate liberamente! Parlate più forte! **to be — in one's reckoning,** calcolare male; **— size,** misura massima.

out of, *prep.* Fuori, fuori di, oltre. **To come —,** uscire da, venir fuori di; **— doors,** all'aria aperta, all'aperto; **you must choose — these,** dovete scegliere fra questi; **— sight,** fuori di vista; **— breath,** anelante, ansante, trafelato; **— work,** senza lavoro, disoccupato; **we are — tea,** non abbiamo più tè; **— kindness,** per gentilezza; **— print,** esaurito, fuori stampa; **— action,** fuori servizio, fuori di combattimento; **— bounds,** oltre i limiti; **— commission,** (*Naut.*) in disarmo, (*Mech.*) fuori servizio; **— date,** disusato, non più di moda, troppo vecchio; **— hand,** indisciplinato; subito; **times — number,** volte innumerevoli, tante e tante volte; **— doubt,** fuori dubbio; **— danger,** fuori pericolo; **— one's element,** spostato, pesce fuori d'acqua; **— order,** in cattivo stato, guasto; **— place,** (*fig.*) male a proposito; **to be — stock of,** essere a corto di; **— the common,** raro; **— drawing,** mal disegnato; **I am — pocket,** sono in perdita, ci rimetto del mio; **I wish him well — it,** spero che se la cavi bene; **— favour,** uscito di grazia; **— the way,** lontano, fuori di mano, straordinario; **to feel — it,** sentirsi trascurato; **to drink — a glass,** bere da un bicchiere; **— sorts,** indisposto, malaticcio; **— tune,** stonato, fuori d'accordo; **— sight — mind,** lontano dagli occhi lontano dal cuore.

outbalance, *v.t.* Pesare di più, sorpassare di peso.

outbid, *v.t.* Offrire di più di, fare un'offerta superiore.

outboard, *a.adv.* Fuori bordo. **— motor,** motore fuoribordo, *m.*

outbreak, *n.* (*of war,*) Scoppio, *m.*; (*of a volcano*) eruzione, *f.*; (*of a disease*) epidemia, *f.*; (*revolt*) insurrezione, *f.*; (*of fire*) incendio, *m.*

outbuilding, *n.* Annesso, *m.*, dipendenza, *f.*

outburst, *n.* Scoppio, *m.*, esplosione, *f.*; (*of emotion*) trasporto, *m.*, tirata, *f.*

outcast, *a.* Proscritto, bandito, cacciato. || *n.* Proscritto, esule, *m.*; vagabondo, paria, *m.*

outclass, *v.t.* Superare.

outcome, *n.* Risultato, *m.*, riuscita, *f.*; esito, *m.*; conseguenza, *f.*

outcrop, *n.* (*Geol.*) Affioramento, *m.*

outcry, *n.* Grido, clamore, *m.*

outdare, *v.t.* Sorpassare in coraggio; sfidare.

outdistance, *v.t.* Sorpassare, lasciar indietro.

outdo, *v.t.* Sorpassare, superare, vincere.

outdoor, *a.* Di fuori, esterno, all'aperto.

outdoors, *adv.* Fuori, fuori di casa, all'aria aperta, all'aperto.

outed, *a.* Espulso, cacciato fuori.

outer, *a.* Esterno, esteriore. (*of tyre*) **— cover,** copertone, *m.*

outermost, *a.* Il più esterno, l'estremo.

outface, *v.t.* Bravare, affrontare, far fronte a, far abbassare gli occhi a.

outfall, *n.* Scarico, *m.*; (*of river, sewer, etc.*) imboccatura, foce, *f.*

outfit, *n.* Corredo, arredo, *m.*; equipaggiamento, fornimento, *m.*

outfitter, *n.* Fornitore, provveditore, negoziante di corredi, *m.*

outflank, *v.t.* Girare, aggirare.

outflow, *n.* Uscita, *f.*, sbocco, *m.*

outgeneral, *v.t.* Superare nella tattica.

outgoing, *a.* In partenza, partente.

outgoings, *n.pl.* Spese, *f.pl.*

outgrow, *v.t.* Divenire più grande di, diventare troppo grande per. **To — one's clothes,** divenire troppo grande per i propri vestiti; **to — a habit,** disfarsi di un'abitudine.

outgrowth, *n.* Prodotto, frutto, *m.*; risultato, *m.*

out-Herod, *v.t.* **To — Herod,** superare in violenza o prepotenza.

outhouse ['authaus], *n.* Tettoia, *f.*; capanna, *f.*, rimessa, *f.*

outing, *n.* Gita, escursione, *f.*, viaggetto, *m.*

outlandish, *a.* Strano, esotico, straniero, fantastico, bizzarro.

outlast, *v.t.* Sorpassare in durata, durare oltre, sopravvivere a.

outlaw, *n.* Proscritto, bandito, brigante, fuorilegge, *m.* || *v.t.* Bandire, proscrivere.

outlawry, *n.* Bando, *m.*, proscrizione, *f.*

outlay, *n.* Sborso, *m.*, spesa, *f.* **Initial —,** spese d'impianto, *f.pl.*

outlet, *n.* Uscita, *f.*; apertura, *f.*; sbocco, *m.*; (*fig.*) sfogo, *m.*

outline, *n.* Contorni, profilo, *m.*; schizzo, abbozzo, *m.* || *v.t.* Abbozzare, tracciare a grandi linee, delineare. **— drawing,** sagoma, *f.*; disegno lineare, *m.*; **in —,** a grandi linee.

outlive, *v.t.* Sopravvivere a.

outlook, *n.* Prospetto, *m.*, prospettiva, *f.*; veduta, *f.*; avvenire, *m.*

outlying, *a.* Esteriore, esterno; isolato, distante, remoto; (*Mil.*) avanzato.

outmanœuvre, *v.t.* Sorpassare in astuzia; sventare, manovrare più abilmente di.

outmarch, *v.t.* Sorpassare, lasciare indietro, sopravanzare.

outnumber, *v.t.* Superare in numero, sorpassare in numero, essere più numeroso di.

outpace, *v.t.* Sorpassare, distanziare.

out-patient, *n.* Malato esterno, *m.*

outpost, *n.* Avamposto, *m.*

outpouring, outpour, *n.* Effusione, *f.*

output, *n.* Produzione, *f.*, gettito, *m.*

outrage, *n.* Oltraggio, *m.*, ingiuria, violenza, *f.*; attentato, *m.* || *v.t.* Oltraggiare, fare oltraggio a; violare.

outrageous, *a.* Oltraggioso, ingiurioso, violento, offensivo; (*colloq.*) esorbitante, eccessivo.

outrageously, *adv.* Oltraggiosamente.

outrelief, *n.* Sussidio, *m.*

outrider, *n.* Battistrada, *m.*

outrigger, *n.* (*Naut.*) Barca da corsa a scalmi esterni, *f.*; buttafuori, *m.*

outright, *adv.* Subito, senz'indugio, senz'altro, immediatamente; affatto, interamente, completamente; apertamente. || *a.* Completo, matricolato. **An — payment,** un pagamento in blocco, *m.*
outrival, *v.t.* Sorpassare in merito, oltrepassare.
outrun, *v.t.* Sorpassare in velocità, oltrepassare, distanziare.
outset, *n.* Principio, cominciamento, inizio, *m.* **At the very —,** fin dal principio.
outshine, *v.t.* Ecclissare, sorpassare in splendore, brillare più di.
outside, *a.* Esterno, esteriore, di fuori, estraneo. || *adv.* Fuori, di fuori, al di fuori. || *prep.* Fuori di. || *n.* Il di fuori, l'esterno, *m.*, la superficie, *f.* **An — opinion,** un'opinione spregiudicata, *f.*; **to be — politics,** esser estraneo alla politica; **the — of an omnibus,** l'imperiale, *f.*, l'esterno d'un omnibus, *m.*; **at the —,** tutt'al più, al massimo.
outsider, *n.* Estraneo, *m.*; (*Racing*) cavallo non classificato, *m.*
outsize, *n.* Taglia fuori misura, *m.*
outskirts, *n.pl.* Orlo, bordo, *m.*; confine, *m.*; sobborghi, dintorni, *m.pl.*; periferia, *f.*
outspan, *v.t.* Staccare i cavalli.
outspoken, *a.* Franco, chiaro, esplicito; retto.
outspokenness, *n.* Franchezza, *f.*
outspread, *a.* Steso, disteso, spiegato.
outstanding, *a.* Eminente, prominente, segnalato; in pendenza, arretrato, insoluto, in sospeso. **— bills,** effetti in circolazione, *m.pl.*; **— debts,** crediti attivi, *m.pl.*
outstare, *v.t.* Soggiogare con lo sguardo.
outstay, *v.t.* **To — one's welcome,** trattenersi più del necessario.
outstretch, *v.t.* Distendere; dispiegare.
outstretched, *a.* Steso, disteso, allungato.
outstrip, *v.t.* Sorpassare, oltrepassare, distanziare.
out-turn, *n.* Rendimento, *m.*
outvote, *v.t.* Vincere nella votazione, mettere in minoranza.
outward, *a.* Esteriore, esterno; estrinseco, apparente, superficiale.
outward, outwards, *adv.* Al di fuori, all'esterno. **Outward bound,** in partenza.
outwardly, *adv.* Al di fuori, all'esterno.
outweigh, *v.t.* Sorpassare in peso; sorpassare in importanza.
outwit, *v.t.* Acchiappare, sorpassare in finezza, truffare, mettere in sacco.
outwork, *n.* Opera avanzata, *f.*, lavoro esterno, *m.*
ouzel [ˈuːzəl], *n.* (*Zool.*) Merlo, *m.*
oval [ˈouvəl], *n.a.* Ovale, *m.*
ovariotomy [ovəriˈɔtəmi], *n.* (*Med.*) Ovariotomia, *f.*
ovary [ˈouvəri], *n.* (*Anat.*) Ovaia, *f.*; (*Bot.*) ovario, *m.*
ovate, *a.* Ovato.
ovation, *n.* Ovazione, *f.*
oven [ˈʌvən], *n.* Forno, fornello, *m.*; stufa, *f.* **Field- —,** forno da campo, *m.*
ovenful, *n.* Fornata, infornata, *f.*
over (1) [ˈouvəɹ], *prep.* Sopra, su; attraverso, attraverso a; più di; al di là di, oltre, dal altra parte di; da; durante. || *adv.* Al di sopra, di sopra; al di là; per soprappiù; oltre, troppo. **— three pounds,** più di tre libbre; **I shall take an hour — the job,** ne avrò per un ora; **he jumped — the table,** saltò la tavola; **— the water,** al di là del mare; **the mud came — my ankles,** ero infangato fin sopra le caviglie; **he walked — two fields,** attraversò due campi; **he fell — the precipice,** cadde nel precipizio; **to fall — an obstacle,** inciampare in un ostacolo; **— the way,** dall'altra parte della strada; **all —,** dappertutto, per tutto, in ogni parte; **all the world —,** in tutto il mondo; **he is — from abroad,** è venuto dall'estero; **to hear —,** sentire dal principio alla fine; **— again,** ancora una volta, nuovamente; **— and above,** inoltre, di più, per soprammercato; **— and — again,** ripetutamente, a più riprese; **all — mud,** tutto infangato; **to have something —,** aver qualcosa d'avanzo; **— against,** opposto a; **I don't feel — well,** mi sento poco bene; **the struggle is —,** la lotta è finita; **it's all — with him,** è bell'e spacciato; **the danger is —,** non c'è più pericolo; **the rain is —,** è finito di piovere; **the crisis is —,** la crisi è passata.
over (2), *n.* (*Cricket*) Sei mandate palle successive di cui dispone il lanciatore.
overact, *v.t.* Esagerare la parte.
overall, *n.* (*woman's*) Grembiulone, copritutto, *m.*; (*doctor's*) camice, *m.*; (*workman's*) tuta, *f.* || *a.* Totale.
overarch, *v.t.* Coprire con una volta, gettare un arco.
overarm, *a.* **Overarm stroke,** taglio, *m.*
over-assess, *v.t.* Tassare eccessivamente.
over-assessment, *n.* Sopratassa, *f.*
overawe, *v.t.* Intimidire, mettere in soggezione.
overbalance, *v.t.* Sorpassare in peso; *v.i.* sbilanciarsi, perdere l'equilibrio.
overbearing, *a.* Arrogante, prepotente, altezzoso, borioso.
overboard, *adv.* (*Naut.*) In mare, fuori bordo.
overburden, *v.t.* Sovraccaricare, opprimere, accasciare.
overbuy, *v.t.* Comprare in quantità eccessiva.
over-capitalize, *v.t.* (*Comm.*) Impiegare un capitale troppo grande.
over-careful, *a.* Troppo premuroso.
overcast, *v.t.* Annuvolare; cucire a sopraffilo. || *a.* Coperto, chiuso, annuvolato.
overcautious, *a.* Troppo prudente, timido.
overcharge, *v.t.* Sovraccaricare; far pagare troppo caro. || *n.* Prezzo eccessivo, sovraccarico, *m.*
overcloud, *v.t.* Annuvolare, oscurare.
overcoat, *n.* Soprabito, cappotto, *m.*
overcolour, *v.t.* Esagerare, accentuare.
overcome, *v.t.* Sormontare, superare, vincere. || *a.* Sopraffatto, esausto; emozionato, commosso. **— by drink,** ubbriaco.
over-confident, *a.* Troppo sicuro, presuntuoso.
overcrowd, *v.t.* Stipare, affollare, ingombrare.
overcrowding, *n.* Affollamento, ammassamento, *m.*
overdo, *v.t.* Esagerare, strafare, eccedere stracuocere. **To — oneself,** strapazzarsi.
overdone, *a.* Esagerato; troppo cotto.
overdose, *n.* Dose troppo forte, *f.*
overdraft, *n.* (*Comm.*) Scoperto, credito allo scoperto, *m.*

overdraw, *v.t.* Esagerare; (*Comm.*) eccedere, oltrepassare, trarre allo scoperto. **To — one's account,** trarre un assegno per una somma superiore ai fondi depositati.
overdress, *v.i.* Vestirsi con troppo lusso.
overdrive, *v.t.* Strapazzare, esaurire, affaticare.
overdue, *a.* In ritardo; scaduto, arretrato.
overeat, *v.t.* Mangiare troppo, rimpinzarsi.
over-elaborate, *v.t.* Sforzare; rifinire.
over-estimate, *v.t.* Sopravalutare, stimare in eccesso.
overexcite, *v.t.* Sovreccitare.
over-expose, *v.t.* (*Phot.*) Esporre troppo.
overexposure, *n.* Eccesso di posa, *m.*
overfeed, *v.t.* Dare troppo da mangiare, rimpinzare.
overflow, *v.t.i.* Inondare, allagare, traboccare. || *n.* Inondazione, *f.*; sovrabbondanza, *f.*; traboccamento, *m.*; (*fig.*) sfogo, *m.* **— meeting,** assemblea supplementare, *f.*
overflowing, *a.* Inondato, straripante, traboccante; sovrabbondante. || *n.* Inondazione, *f.* traboccamento, *m.* **Full to —,** strabocchevole, ricolmo, ripieno, pieno zeppo.
overfond, *a.* Pazzo per.
overgrow, *v.t.* Ricoprire; *v.i.* crescere troppo, crescere sopra.
overgrown, *a.* Coperto; cresciuto troppo.
overgrowth, *n.* Crescita eccessiva, *f.*
overhand, *a.* A braccio alto.
overhang, *v.t.* Sporgere, strapiombare, pendere; incombere, sovrastare.
overhanging, *a.* Sporgente; imminente, incombente.
overhaul, *v.t.* Esaminare, ispezionare; raggiungere; (*overtake*) sorpassare; restaurare.
overhead, *a.* Di sopra, aereo, di soffitto. || *adv.* In alto, in cielo, in su. **— expenses,** spese generali, spese vive, *f.pl.*
overheads, *n.pl.* Spese generali, *f.pl.*
overhear, *v.t.* Sentire per caso, udire di sfuggita; sorprendere.
overheat, *v.t.* Riscaldare troppo, surriscaldare.
overheated, *a.* Surriscaldato.
overindulgence, *n.* Intemperanza, *f.*
overjoyed, *a.* Lietissimo, felicissimo, colmo di gioia.
overladen, *a.* Sovraccarico.
overland, *adv. a.* Per via di terra, per terra, di terra.
overlap, *v.t.* Ricoprire, sovrapporre, combaciare; *v.i.* sovrapporsi.
overlapping, *a.* Sovrapposizione, *f.*
overlay, *v.t.* Coprire, ricoprire; soffocare. || *n.* Coperta da letto, *f.*
overleaf, *adv.* Al rovescio, retro. **See —,** vedi retro.
overleap, *v.t.* Saltare oltre.
overlie, *v.t.* Soffocare.
overload, *v.t.* Sovraccaricare. || *n.* Sovraccarico, *m.*
overlook, *v.t.* Dare su, dominare; sorvegliare; chiudere gli occhi a, passare sopra, perdonare, condonare; non vedere, trascurare.
overlooker, *n.* Soprintendente, ispettore, *m.*
overlord, *n.* Signore supremo, *m.*
overmantel, *n.* Specchiera, *f.*, intelaiatura sopra il camino, *f.*
overmatch, *v.t.* Vincere, superare.
overmuch, *a.adv.* Troppo, all'eccesso.
overnice, *a.* Troppo delicato, schifiltoso.
overnight, *adv.* Durante la notte; ieri sera.
overpass, *v.t.* Traversare, valicare, passare sopra.
overpay, *v.t.* Pagare troppo, strapagare, pagare troppo caro.
overpeopled, *a.* Troppo popolato.
overpersuade, *v.t.* Costringere a persuadersi.
overplus, *n.* Soprappiù, eccesso, *m.*
over-polite, *a.* Cerimonioso.
overpower, *v.t.* Dominare, opprimere, soggiogare.
overpowering, *a.* Opprimente, schiacciante, irresistibile.
overpraise, *v.t.* Lodare all'eccesso.
overproduction, *n.* Sovraproduzione, *f.*
overrate, *v.t.* Sopravalutare, stimare più del valore, far troppo caso di.
overreach, *v.t.* Ingannare, abbindolare, oltrepassare. **To — oneself,** darsi la zappa sui piedi.
override, *v.t.* Strapazzare; sopraffare; calpestrare, calcare; passare sopra; (*a horse*) affaticare.
overripe, *a.* Troppo maturo, strafatto.
overrule, *v.t.* Prevalere su; annullare; scartare un'obbiezione; dominare, governare.
overrun, *v.t.* Invadere, infestare, devastare; percorrere; (*Print.*) rimaneggiare.
oversea, overseas, *a.* D'oltremare. || *adv.* Oltremare.
oversee, *v.t.* Sorvegliare, soprintendere a.
overseer, *n.* Soprintendente, direttore, *m.*
overset, *v.t.* Rovesciare, capovolgere, mettere sossopra.
oversewing, *n.* Sopraggitto, *m.*
overshadow, *v.t.* Ombreggiare; (*fig.*) oscurare, ecclissare.
overshoes, *n.pl.* Soprascarpe, galosce, *f.pl.*
overshoot, *v.t.* Oltrepassare, portare al di là. **To — the mark,** oltrepassare il segno.
oversight, *n.* Svista, *f.*, sbaglio, *m.*; sorveglianza, *f.*
oversleep, *v.i.* Dormire oltre l'ora giusta.
overspend, *v.t.* Spendere troppo.
overspread, *v.t.* Spargere, cospargere, coprire.
overstate, *v.t.* Esagerare.
overstatement, *n.* Esagerazione, *f.*
overstep, *v.t.* Oltrepassare, eccedere, trasgredire.
overstock, *v.t.* Ingombrare, approvvigionare ad eccesso. || *n.* Soprappiù, *m.*
overstrain, *v.t.* Strapazzare, affaticare, sforzare.
overstrung, *a.* Sovreccitato.
overt [ˈouvəɹt], *a.* Aperto, evidente, manifesto, palese.
overtake, *v.t.* Raggiungere, sopraggiungere; sorprendere; oltrepassare.
overtask, *v.t.* Sovraccaricare.
overtax, *v.t.* Sovraccaricare; abusare di; gravare di imposte.
overthrow, *v.t.* Rovesciare, abbattere, gettare a terra; vincere, sconfiggere; distruggere, disfare. || *n.* Disfatta, sconfitta, distruzione, caduta, *f.*
overtime, *n.* Ore supplementari, ore straordinarie, *f.pl.*
overtire, *v.t.* Strapazzare.
overtop, *v.t.* Elevarsi al disopra di, soprastare, dominare.

overtraining, *n.* Allenamento eccessivo, *m.*
overture, *n.* Proposta, offerta, *f.*; (*Mus.*) preludio, *m.*
overturn, *v.t.* Rovesciare, capovolgere; abbattere, distruggere; *v.i.* capovolgersi.
overvalue, *v.t.* Valutare troppo.
overweening, *a.* Arrogante, presuntuoso.
overweight, *n.* Eccesso di peso, soprappeso, *m.*
overwhelm, *v.t.* Opprimere, sopraffare, schiacciare, accasciare; (*with kindness*) colmare.
overwhelming, *a.* Opprimente, schiacciante, trabordante, strabocchevole.
overwork, *v.t.* Affaticare, far lavorare troppo, strapazzare; *v.i.* affaticarsi, strapazzarsi. ‖ *n.* Eccesso di lavoro, *m.*
overwrought, *a.* Sovreccitato.
ovine [ˈouvain], *a.* Ovino.
oviparous [oˈvipərəs], *a.* Oviparo.
ovoid [ˈouvɔid], *n.a.* Ovoide, *m.*
ovolo [ˈouvəlou], *n.* (*Arch.*) Ovolo, *m.*
ovule, *n.* (*Zool.*) Ovulo, *m.*
ovum (*pl.* **ova**) [ˈouvəm, ˈouvə], *n.* Uovo, *m.*
owe [ou], *v.t.i.* Dovere, essere in debito per, essere debitore di. **I — you for that book,** vi devo pagare quel libro; **I — no one anything,** non devo niente a nessuno.
owing, *a.* Dovuto; scaduto, arretrato; a cagione di, a motivo di, grazie a. **Pay what is —,** pagate ciò che è dovuto; **— to the weather,** a causa del tempo.
owl [aul], *n.* (*Zool.*) Gufo, *m.*, civetta, *f.*; barbagianni, *m.*
owlet, *n.* Civettino, *m.*
owlish, *a.* Di gufo, da gufo.
own (1) [oun], *a.* Proprio, particolare. **I heard it with my — ears,** lo sentii coi miei orecchi; **a poor thing but mine —,** una povera cosa ma mia propria; **the view has a beauty all its —,** la vista ha una bellezza tutta sua; **to be one's — master,** essere padrone di sè stesso; **to do as one likes with one's —,** disporre del proprio come si vuole; **I have no money of my —,** non ho denaro del mio; **with one's — hand,** colle proprie mani; **to hold one's —,** cavarsela bene, far valere i propri diritti.
own (2), *v.t.* Possedere, avere; riconoscere, accettare; confessare, ammettere, concedere. **To — up,** confessare.
owner, *n.* Possessore, *m.f.*; proprietario, *m.*, proprietaria, *f.*; padrone, *m.*, padrona, *f.* **The rightful —,** il proprietario vero, *m.*; (*Motor.*) **— -driver,** proprietario conducente, *m.*; **at owner's risk,** a rischio e pericolo del destinatario (o proprietario).
ownership, *n.* Possesso, dominio, *m.*, proprietà, *f.*
ox (*pl.* **oxen**) [ɔks, ˈɔksən], *n.* Bue, bove, *m.* **— -eye daisy,** margherita dei campi, *f.*
oxalic [ɔksˈælik], *a.* (*Chem.*) Ossalico.
oxherd, *n.* Bovaro, *m.*
oxhide, *n.* Pelle di bue, *f.*
oxidation, *n.* Ossidazione, *f.*
oxide, *n.* Ossido, *m.*
oxidization, *n.* Ossidazione, *f.*
oxidize, *v.t.* Ossidare.
Oxonian [ɔkˈzouniən], *n.* *a.* (Studente) dell'università di Oxford.
oxtail, *n.* Coda di bue, *f.*
oxygen [ˈɔksidʒən], *n.* Ossigeno, *m.*
oxygenate, *v.t.* Ossigenare.
oxygenous, *a.* D'ossigeno.
oxyhydrogen [ɔksiˈhaidrodʒən], *a.* Ossidrico.
oxytone [ˈɔksitoun], *n.* (*Gram.*) Ossitono, *m.*
Oyez! [ouˈjes], *inter.* Udite! Silenzio!
oyster [ˈɔistəɹ], *n.* (*Zool.*) Ostrica, *f.* **Close as an —,** muto come un pesce; **— -bed,** ostricaio, *m.*; **— -knife,** coltello per le ostriche, *m.*; **— -man,** ostricaio, ostricaro, *m.*; **— -shell,** conchiglia d'ostrica, *f.*
ozone [ouˈzoun], *n.* (*Chem.*) Ozono, *m.*

P

P, p [piː], *n.* Sedicesima lettera dell'alfabeto inglese. **To mind one's ps and qs,** comportarsi bene.
Pa [pɑː], *n.* (*colloq.*) Papà, *m.*
pabulum [ˈpæbjuːləm], *n.* Pabolo, alimento, *m.*
pace [peis], *n.* Passo, *m.*, andatura, *f.*; velocità, *f.* ‖ *v.i.* Passeggiare, camminare; *v.t.* misurare coi passi. **At a foot's —,** di passo; **at a great —,** di buon passo, a gran passi; **to keep — with,** camminare di pari passo con; (*fig.*) **to put someone through his paces,** mettere alla prova qualcuno; (*fig.*) **to go the —,** correre la cavallina; **to mend one's —,** affrettarsi, cambiare il passo; **to — up and down,** camminare su e giù.
pacemaker, *n.* (*Sport*) Allenatore, *m.*; (*Racing*) cavallo che dà l'andatura di partenza, *m.*
pacha [cp. **pasha**].
pachyderm [ˈpækidəɹm], *n.* (*Zool.*) Pachiderma, *m.*
pacific [pəˈsifik], *a.* Pacifico. **Pacific Ocean,** il Pacifico, *m.*
pacification [pæsifiˈkeiʃən], *n.* Pacificazione, *f.*
pacificatory, *a.* Pacificativo, conciliativo.
pacifier, *n.* Paciere, pacificatore, *m.*
pacifist, *n.a.* Pacifista, *m.f.*
pacify [ˈpæsifai], *v.t.* Pacificare, calmare, sedare.
pacifying, *a.* Pacificatore.
pack [pæk], *n.* Pacco, fardello, fagotto, peso, *m.*; (*of cards*) mazzo, *m.*; (*of hounds*) muta, *f.*; (*of ice*) ammasso, lastrone, *m.*; (*of thieves*) mano, banda, masnada, *f.*; (*of lies*) mucchio, *m.*; (*Med.*) impacco, *m.* ‖ *v.t.* Imballare, involtare, impaccare; incassare; mettere in scatole; riempire; pigiare, serrare, stringere; (*Naut.*) spiegare; *v.i.* far le valigie, fare i bagagli. **A — of nonsense,** un mucchio di spropositi, *m.*; (*Naut.*) **to — on all sail,** spiegare tutte le vele; **to — a jury,** manipolarsi una giuria favorevole; **to — off,** andar via, filar via; **to send someone packing,** mandar via qualcuno armi e bagagli, cacciar via qualcuno; **to — up,** far le valigie, finire il lavoro; **— -horse,** cavallo da soma, *m.*; **— -saddle,** basto, *m.*; **— -ice,** banco di ghiaccio, *m.*; banchisa, *f.*
package [ˈpækidʒ], *n.* Pacco, involto, *m.*, balla, *f.*; collo, *m.*
packed, *a.* Impaccato, disposto in pacchi. **The room was —,** la stanza era piena zeppa.
packer, *n.* Imballatore, impaccatore, *m.*, impaccatrice, *f.*

packet, *n.* Pacchetto, involto, *m.*; (*Naut.*) vapore postale, *m.*
packing, *n.* Imballaggio, *m.*; (*Mech.*) guarnizione. **—-case**, cassa d'imballaggio, *f.*; **—-needle**, ago per imballaggio, *m.*; **—-paper**, carta d'imballaggio, *f.*
packman, *n.* Merciaiolo ambulante, *m.*
packthread, *n.* Spago, filo, *m.*, cordicella, *f.*
pact [pækt], *n.* Patto, *m.*
pad [pæd], *n.* Cuscinetto, guancialetto, *m.*; tampone, battufolo, *m.*; (*Med.*) stuello, *m.*; (*of fox, etc.*) zampa, *f.* || *v.i.* Andare a piedi, far strada; *v.t.* imbottire, ovattare; riempire. **Blotting —**, cartella di carta sugante, *f.*; **writing- —**, blocco di carta da lettere, *m.*; sottomano, *m.*; **padded cell**, stanza imbottita, *f.*
padding, *n.* Imbottitura, *f.*, riempitivo, *m.*; borra, ovatta, *f.*
paddle ['pædəl], *n.* (*of canoe, etc.*) Pagaia, *f.*, remo, *m.*; (*of water-wheel*) pala, *f.*; (*board*) pala, paletta, *f.* || *v.t.* Pagaiare, remare; *v.i.* sguazzare, diguazzare. **To — one's own canoe**, essere indipendente, sbrigarsi da sè; **—-board**, paletta di ruota, *f.*; **—-boat**, nave a ruote, *f.*; **—-box**, tamburo, *m.*; **—-wheel**, ruota a pale, *f.*
paddler, *n.* Pagaiatore, rematore, *m.*
paddling, *n.* (*in the sea*) Guazzamento, diguazzare, *m.*; (*in a canoe*) navigazione con la pagaia, *f.*
paddock ['pædək], *n.* Recinto, chiuso, *m.*; (*Racing*) passeggiatoio, *m.*
paddy (1) ['pædi], *n.* (*colloq.*) Irlandese, *m.*
paddy (2), *n.* (*in India*) Riso, *m.*
padishah ['pɑ:diʃə], *n.* Padiscià, *m.*
padlock ['pædlɔk], *n.* Lucchetto, catenaccio, *m.* || *v.t.* Allucchettare, chiudere con lucchetto.
padre ['pɑ:dri], *n.* (*colloq.*) Cappellano militare, prete, *m.*
Padua ['pædju:ə], *n.* (*Geog.*) Padova, *f.*
paduasoy ['pædju:əsɔi], *n.* Seta di Padova, *f.*
paean ['pi:ən], *n.* Peana, *m.*
pagan ['peigən], *n.a.* Pagano, *m.*
pagandom, *n.* Paganismo, *m.*
paganish, *a.* Paganesco, paganizzante.
paganism, *n.* Paganismo, *m.*
paganize, *v.t.i.* Rendere pagano, paganizzare.
page (1) [peidʒ], *n.* Pagina, *f.* || *v.t.* Numerare le pagine di. **Left-hand —**, verso, *m.*; **right-hand —**, recto, *m.* **—-proof**, messa in pagina, *f.*
page (2), *n.* Paggio, *m.*; fattorino, *m.* || *v.t.* Chiamare per mezzo d'un paggio.
pageant ['pædʒənt], *n.* Spettacolo, *m.*; corteo storico, *m.*; parata, processione, *f.*; sfilata, sagra, *f.*
pageantry, *n.* Parata, *f.*, fasto sfarzo, *m.*
paginal ['pædʒinəl], *a.* Paginale.
paginate, *v.t.* Impaginare.
pagination, paging [pædʒi'neiʃən, 'peidʒiŋ], *n.* (*Print.*) Impaginazione, *f.*
pagoda [pə'goudə], *n.* Pagoda, *f.*
pah! [pɑ:], *inter.* Via, via!
paid [peid], *p.p.a.* Pagato, saldato; versato. **— with thanks**, per quietanza; **carriage- —**, franco di porto; (*Comm.*) **—-up capital**, capitale versato, *m.*
pail [peil], *n.* Secchia, *f.*; bigonciolo, *m.*
pailful, *n.* Secchiata, *f.*
paillasse [cp. **palliasse**].
pain [pein], *n.* Dolore, male, *m.*; pena, cura, *f.*; tormento, *m.*, sofferenza, *f.* || *v.t.* Far male a, far soffrire; dolere, addolorare, affliggere, attristare. **To take pains**, affannarsi, darsi pena, darsi da fare; **a — in the chest**, un male al petto, *m.*; **to be in —**, soffrire, aver male; **under — of death**, sotto pena di morte; **to have one's labour for one's pains**, essere mal ricompensato; **to give someone —**, far soffrire qualcuno, addolorare qualcuno; **it pains me**, mi duole.
painful, *a.* Doloroso, penoso, molesto.
painfully, *adv.* Dolorosamente.
painfulness, *n.* Dolore, *m.*, pena, molestia, *f.*
painless, *a.* Senza dolore.
painstaking, *a.* Laborioso, accurato, diligente, sollecito.
paint [peint], *n.* Colore, *m.*; vernice, *f.*; (*for face*) belletto, rossetto, *m.* || *v.t.* Verniciare, dipingere, pitturare; colorare; (*face*) imbellettare. **—-box**, scatola di colori, *f.*; **—-brush**, pennello, *m.*
painter (1), *n.* (*artist*) Pittore, *m.*; (*house*) verniciatore, imbianchino, *m.*
painter (2), *n.* (*Naut.*) Ormeggio, *m.*, barbetta, *f.*
painting, *n.* Pittura, *f.*, quadro, *m.*; verniciatura, *f.*
pair [pɛəɹ], *n.* Paio, *m.*, coppia, *f.*; (*of horses*) pariglia, *f.* || *v.t.* Appaiare, accoppiare; maritare, unire; *v.i.* appaiarsi, accoppiarsi; (*Pol.*) accordarsi con un membro dell'opposizione per astenersi dal voto. **A — of steps**, una scala doppia, *f.*; (*fig.*) **another — of shoes**, un altro paio di maniche, *m.*; **to sell in pairs**, vendere a paia; **a — of compasses**, un compasso, *m.*; **a — of scissors**, un paio di forbici, *m.*; **a — of trousers**, calzoni, *m.pl.*; (*Naut.*) **—-oar**, a due remi; **to — off**, mettersi per due, andare in due.
pairing, *n.* Appaiamento, abbinamento, accoppiamento, *m.*
pal [pæl], *n.* (*colloq.*) Amico, compagno, *m.*
palace ['pæləs], *n.* Palazzo, *m.* **Royal —**, reggia, *f.*, palazzo reale, *m.*; **bishop's —**, vescovato, *m.*
paladin ['pælədin], *n.* (*Hist.*) Paladino, *m.*
palaeographer [pæli'ɔgrəfəɹ], *n.* Paleografo, *m.*
palaeography [pæli'ɔgrəfi], *n.* Paleografia, *f.*
palaeontology [peiliɔn'tɔlədʒi], *n.* Paleontologia, *f.*
palaestra [pə'lestrə], *n.* Palestra, *f.*
palankeen, palanquin ['pælənkin], *n.* Palanchino, *m.*
palatable ['pælətəbl], *a.* Saporito, appetitoso; benaccetto, gradito, piacevole.
palatal ['pælətəl], *a.* (*Gram.*) Palatale.
palate ['pælət], *n.* (*Anat.*) Palato, *m.*; (*fig.*) gusto, *m.* **To have a vitiated —**, aver il palato guasto.
palatial [pə'leiʃəl], *a.* Da palazzo, magnifico, grandioso.
Palatinate [pə'lætinət], *n.* (*Hist.*) Palatinato, *m.*
Palatine ['pælətain], *a.* Palatino.
palaver [pə'lɑ:vəɹ], *n.* Chiacchiere, *f.pl.*, vaniloquio, cicaleccio, *m.*; conferenza, discussione, *f.* || *v.i.* Cicalare, chiacchierare, confabulare.

pale (1) [peil], *a.* Pallido, smorto, scolorito; sbiadito, scialbo, biondo. || *v.t.i.* Impallidire, render pallido. **To grow —,** impallidire; **— -faced,** pallido, smorto, dalla faccia pallida.
pale (2) *n.* Palo, *m.*, asse, *f.*; limite, termine, confine, *m.* **Beyond the —,** impossibile; scomunicato.
palely, *adv.* Pallidamente.
paleness, *n.* Pallidezza, *f.*, pallore, *m.*
Palestine ['pælestain], *n.* (*Geog.*) Palestina, *f.*
paletot ['pælətou], *n.* Soprabito, cappotto, *m.*
palette ['pælit], *n.* Tavolozza, *f.* **— -knife,** spatola, *f.*, mestichino, *m.*
palfrey ['pɔ:lfri], *n.* Palafreno, *m.*
palimpsest ['pælimpsest], *n.* Palinsesto, *m.*
paling ['peiliŋ], *n.* Palizzata, *f.*, steccato, *m.*; impalancato, *m.*
palinode ['pælinoud], *n.* Palinodia, *f.*
palisade [pæli'seid], *n.* Stecconaia, palizzata, *f.* || *v.t.* Stecconare, circondare con una palizzata.
palish ['peiliʃ], *a.* Pallidino, pallidetto, palliduccio.
pall (1) [pɔ:l], *n.* Drappo funebre, *m.*; (*Eccles.*) pallio, *m.*; mantello, *m.* **— -bearer,** che regge i cordoni a un funerale.
pall (2), *v.i.* Divenire insipido, svaporare; saziare, satollare.
palladium [pə'leidiəm], *n.* Palladio, *m.*
pallet ['pælet], *n.* Lettuccio, giaciglio, *m.*; paglericcio, *m.*
palliasse ['pæliæs], *n.* Paglione, paglericcio, *m.*
palliate ['pælieit], *v.t.* Palliare, attenuare.
palliation, *n.* Palliazione, attenuazione, *f.*
palliative, *n.a.* Palliativo, *m.*
pallid ['pælid], *a.* Pallidetto, smunto.
pallium ['pæliəm], *n.* (*Hist.Eccles.*) Pallio, *m.*
pall-mall [pel'mel], *n.* (*Hist.*) Pallamaglio, *m.*
pallor ['pælər], *n.* Pallore, *m.*
palm [pɑ:m], *n.* (*Bot.*) Palma, *f.*; (*of hand*) palma, *f.*; palmo, *m.*; (*fig.*) mancia, *f.* || *v.t.* Palpare, toccare; nascondere in mano. **To bear the —,** portar la palma; **Palm Sunday,** Domenica delle Palme; **date —,** palma a datteri, *f.*; palmizio, *m.*; **— -grove,** palmeto, *m.*; **— -house** serra per palme, *f.*; **— oil,** olio di palma, *m.*; **to — off,** far credere a, imporre colla frode, far passare per.
palmar, *a.* Palmare.
palmary, *a.* Palmare.
palmate, *a.* Palmato.
palmer ['pɑ:mər], *n.* (*Hist.*) Palmiere, pellegrino, *m.*
palmetto [pæl'metou], *n.* (*Bot.*) Palmetto, palmizio, *m.*
palmiped ['pælmiped], *n.* (*Zool.*) Palmipede, *m.*
palmist ['pɑ:mist], *n.* Chiromante, *m.f.*
palmistry, *n.* Chiromanzia, *f.*
palmy ['pɑ:mi], *a.* Bello, glorioso, felice. **In the — days of,** nei giorni fausti di.
palp, palpus [pælp, 'pælpəs], *n.* Palpo, *m.*
palpability, *n.* Palpabilità, *f.*
palpable ['pælpəbl], *a.* Palpabile, evidente, chiaro.
palpably, *adv.* Evidentemente.
palpate ['pælpeit], *v.t.* (*Med.*) Palpare.
palpation, *n.* Palpazione, *f.*
palpebral ['pælpebrəl], *a.* (*Anat.*) Palpebrale.
palpitate ['pælpiteit], *v.i.* Palpitare.
palpitation, *n.* Palpitazione, *f.*
palsied [pɔ:lzid], *a.* Paralitico.
palsy ['pɔ:lzi], *n.* (*Med.*) Paralisi, *f.*
palter ['pɔ:ltər], *v.i.* Equivocare, tergiversare. **To — with someone,** non essere franco con qualcuno.
paltriness ['pɔ:ltrinis], *n.* Meschinità, grettezza, miseria, *f.*
paltry, *a.* Meschino, gretto, misero; dappoco. **A — gift,** un dono meschino, *m.*
pampas ['pæmpəs], *n.pl.* (*Geog.*) Pampa, *f.*
pamper ['pæmpər], *v.t.* Accarezzare, lusingare, viziare.
pamphlet ['pæmflet], *n.* Opuscolo, libretto, *m.*; libello, *m.*
pamphleteer [pæmfle'tiər], *n.* Scrittore di opuscoli, *m.*; libellista, *m.*
pan [pæn], *n.* Tegame, *m.*, casseruola, *f.*; padella, *f.*; teglia, terrina, *f.*; (*of scales*) piatto, *m.*; (*of firearms*) focone, *m.* **Brain- —,** cranio, *m.*; **frying- —** padella, *f.*; **a flash in the —,** un colpo a vuoto, un fuoco di paglia, *m.*
panacea [pænə'siə], *n.* Panacea, *f.*
panama, panama hat ['pænəmɑ:], *n.* Panama, *m.*
pancake ['pænkeik], *n.* Frittella, *f.*
pancreas ['pænkriæs], *n.* (*Anat.*) Pancreas, *m.*
pancreatic [pænkri'ætik], *a.* Pancreatico.
Pandean [pæn'di:ən], *a.* (*Myth.*) Del dio Pan, panico.
pandects ['pændekts], *n.pl.* (*Law*) Pandette, *f.pl.*
pandemonium [pændi'mouniəm], *n.* Pandemonio, *m.*
pander ['pændər], *n.* Mezzano, ruffiano, *m.* || *v.t.i.* Far da mezzano; (*fig.*) adulare, lusingare, prestarsi a, fare il compiacente.
Pandora's box [pæn'dɔrəs bɔks], *n.* (*Myth.*) Vaso di Pandora, *m.*
pane [pein], *n.* (*of glass*) Vetro, *m.*; lastra, *f.*; faccetta, *f.*; (*of hammer*) penna, *f.*
panegyric [pæni'dʒirik], *n.* Panegirico, *m.*
panegyrical, *a.* Panegirico.
panegyrist, *n.* Panegirista, *m.f.*
panegyrize, *v.t.* Lodare, elogiare.
panel ['pænəl], *n.* Pannello, *m.*; riquadro, scomparto, *m.*; (*of jury*) lista, *f.*; (*painting*) tavola, *f.*; (*Radio*) cassa. || *v.t.* Pannellare, scompartire, squadrare; rivestire di legno. **Oak-panelled,** rivestito di quercia; **— -envelope,** busta a cellofane, *f.*
panelling, *n.* Pannelli, *m.pl.*, rivestimento, *m.*
pang [pæŋ], *n.* Dolore acuto, spasimo, *m.*; angoscia, *f.*; tormento, *m.* **Pangs,** doglie, *f.pl.*
Pan-Germanism [pæn'dʒə:rmənizm], *n.* Pangermanesimo, *m.*
pangolin ['pæŋgolin], *n.* (*Zool.*) Pangolino, *m.*
Panhellenism [pæn'helenizm], *n.* Panellenismo, *m.*
panic ['pænik], *n.a.* Panico, *m.* || *v.i.* Essere colto dal panico. **— -monger,** allarmista, *m.f.*; **— -stricken,** spaventato, assalito da panico, esterrefatto; **— -grass,** panìco, *m.*
panicky, *a.* Timido, pauroso.
panicle ['pænikl], *n.* (*Bot.*) Pannocchia, spiga, *f.*
panification [pænifi'keiʃən], *n.* Panificazione, *f.*
Panislamism [pæn'izləmizm], *n.* Panislamismo, *m.*

panjandrum [pæn'dʒændrəm], *n.* (*colloq.*) Pezzo grosso, *m.*; funzionario arrogante, *m.*
pannier ['pænjəɹ], *n.* Paniere, corbello, cesto, *m.*; gerla, *f.*
pannikin ['pænikin], *n.* Piccolo tegame, *m.*; tazza di latta, *f.*; pentolino, *m.*
panoply ['pænəpli], *n.* Panoplia, *f.*
panorama [pænə'rɑːmə], *n.* Panorama, *m.*
panoramic, *a.* Panoramico.
Panslavism [pæn'slɑːvizm], *n.* Panslavismo, *m.*
pansy ['pænzi], *n.* (*Bot.*) Viola del pensiero, *f.*
pant [pænt], *v.i.* Ansare, anelare, ansimare. || *n.* Anelito, palpito, ansito, *m.* **To — after,** anelare a, bramare, aspirare a.
Pantaloon [pæntə'luːn], *n.* (*Theat.*) Pantalone, *m.*; buffone, *m.*
pantaloons, *n.pl.* Pantaloni, calzoni, *m.pl.*
pantechnicon [pæn'teknikən], *n.* Furgone, *m.*
pantheism ['pænθiizm], *n.* Panteismo, *m.*
pantheist, *n.* Panteista, *m.*
pantheistic, *a.* Panteistico.
Pantheon ['pænθiən], *n.* Panteon, *m.*
panther ['pænθəɹ], *n.* (*Zool.*) Pantera, *f.*
pantile ['pæntail], *n.* Specie di tegola, *f.*
panting, *a.* Anelito, ansito, affanno.
pantingly, *adv.* Affannosamente.
pantograph ['pæntogræf], *n.* Pantografo, *m.*
pantomime ['pænto'maim], *n.* Pantomima, mimica, *f.*
pantomimic, *a.* Pantomimico.
pantomimist, *n.* Pantomimo, *m.*
pantry ['pæntri], *n.* Dispensa, *f.*
pants [pænts], *n.pl.* Mutande, *f.pl.*; calzoni, *m.pl.*
pap [pæp], *n.* Panbollito, *m.*, pappa, *f.*; (*nipple*) capezzolo, *m.*
papa [pə'pa:], *n.* Papà, babbo, *m.*
papacy ['peipəsi], *n.* Papato, *m.*
papal ['peipəl], *a.* Papale, pontificio, papalino. **The Papal States,** gli Stati Pontifici, *m.pl.*, lo Stato Pontificio, *m.* **— nuncio,** nunzio apostolico *or* pontificio, *m.*
papalism, *n.* Papismo, *m.*
papalist, *n.* Papista, papalino, *m.*
papaverous [pə'peivərəs], *a.* (*Bot.*) Papaveraceo, papaverico.
papaw [pə'pɔː], *n.* (*Bot.*) Papaia, *f.*
paper ['peipəɹ], *n.* Carta, *f.*; (*newspaper*) giornale, *m.*; documento, *m.*; (*wallpaper*) tappezzeria, *f.*; (*exam.*) foglio di esame, *m.*, tema, *f.*, esercizio, *m.*; (*voting*) scheda di votazione, *f.*; (*money*) carta moneta, *f.*, valori, biglietti di banca, *m.pl.*; (*learned*) saggio, studio, trattato, *m.*, dissertazione, *f.*; (*Law*) incartamento, carteggio, *m.* || *a.* Cartaceo. || *v.t.* Tappezzare con carta, coprire di carta. **Brown —,** carta scura, *f.*; **comic —,** giornale a fumetti, *m.*; **foreign —,** carta fina, *f.*; **note-—,** carta da lettera, *f.*; **waste —,** carta straccia, *f.*; **to send in one's papers,** dare le dimissioni; (*fig.*) **— warfare,** polemica giornalistica, *f.*; (*Sport*) **—-chase,** finta caccia alla volpe, *f.*; **—-fastener, —-clip,** serracarte, fermacarte, *m.*; **—-hanger,** decoratore, tappezziere, *m.*; **—-knife,** tagliacarte, *m.*; **— lantern,** lanternino di carta, *m.*; **—-maker,** fabbricante di carta, cartaio, *m.*; **—-making,** fabbricazione della carta, *f.*; **—-mill,** cartiera, *f.*; **—-weight,** fermacarte, calcafogli, *m.*
papered, *a.* Tappezzato.
papier mâché ['pæpieimæʃei], *n.* Cartapesta, *f.*
papilla [pə'pilə], *n.* (*Anat.*) Papilla, *f.*
papillary, *a.* Papillare.
papism, papistry ['peipizm, 'peipistri], *n.* Papismo, *m.*
papist, *n.* Papista, *m.f.*; cattolico, *m.*, cattolica, *f.*
papistical, *a.* Papistico.
pappus ['pæpəs], *n.* (*Bot.*) Pappo, *m.*
papyrus (*pl.* **papyri**) [pə'pairəs, pə'pairai], *n.* Papiro, *m.*
par [pɑːɹ], *n.* Pari, *f.*; (*Print.*) paragrafo, *m.* **On a — with,** pari a; **— of exchange,** parità di cambio, *f.*; **at —,** alla pari; **above —,** sopra la pari; **below —,** sotto la pari.
parabasis [pə'ræbəsis], *n.* (*Lit.*) Parabasi, *f.*
parable ['pærəbl], *n.* Parabola, *f.*
parabola [pə'ræbələ], *n.* (*Geom.*) Parabola, *f.*
parabolic, parabolical, *a.* Parabolico; allegorico.
parachute ['pærəʃuːt], *n.* Paracadute, *m.*
parachutist, *n.* Paracadutista, *m.*
Paraclete ['pærəkliːt], *n.* (*Eccles.*) Paracleto, *m.*
parade [pə'reid], *n.* Parata, mostra, *f.*, sfoggio, *m.*; ostentazione, *f.*; (*mannequin*) mostra, sfilata, *f.*; spianata, *f.*; passeggiata pubblica, *f.* || *v.t.* Mettere in mostra; far pompa di; *v.i.* sfilare in parata. **On —,** in parata, all'adunata; **to make a — of,** mettere in mostra; **—-ground,** piazza d'armi, *f.*
paradigm ['pærədaim], *n.* (*Gram.*) Paradigma, *m.*
paradise ['pærədais], *n.* Paradiso, *m.* **Bird of —,** uccello di paradiso, *m.*; **the earthly —,** il paradiso terrestre, *m.*
paradisiacal [pærədi'zeiikəl], *a.* Paradisiaco.
parados ['pærədɔs], *n.* (*Mil.*) Spalletta, *f.*
paradox ['pærədɔks], *n.* Paradosso, *m.*
paradoxical, *a.* Paradossale.
paraffin ['pærəfin], *n.* Petrolio combustibile, *m.* **— wax,** paraffina, *f.*
paragoge [pærə'goudʒi], *n.* (*Gram.*) Paragoge, *f.*
paragon ['pærəgən], *n.* Campione, modello, *m.*; (*of a person*) persona esemplare, *f.*
paragraph ['pærəgrɑːf], *n.* Paragrafo, *m.*; alinea, *m.*; capoverso, *m.* || *v.t.* Paragrafare. **— writer,** cronista, *m.f.*
parakeet ['pærəkiːt], *n.* (*Zool.*) Parrocchetto, *m.*
parallactic [pærə'læktik], *a.* (*Astron.*) Parallattico.
parallax ['pærəlæks], *n.* Parallasse, *f.*
parallel ['pærəlel], *a.* Parallelo; simile, analogo. || *n.* (*Geom.*) Parallela, *f.*; (*Geog.*) parallelo, *m.*; (*comparison*) parallelo, confronto, paragone, *m.* || *v.t.* Paragonare, comparare, confrontare; eguagliare, essere parallelo a. **To run — with,** essere parallelo a; (*fig.*) **to draw a —,** istituire un parallelo; **— bars,** parallele, *f.pl.*; **— ruler,** regolo per tracciare parallele, *m.*
parallelepiped [pærəle'lepiped], *n.* Parallelepipedo, *m.*
parallelogram [pærə'lelogræm], *n.* Parallelogramma, *m.*
paralogism [pæ'rælodʒizm], *n.* Paralogismo, *m.*
paralysis [pə'rælisis], *n.* (*Med.*) Paralisi, *f.*

paralytic, *n.a.* Paralitico, *m.* — **stroke,** colpo di paralisi, *m.*
paralyse [ˈpærəlaiz], *v.t.* Paralizzare.
paramount [ˈpærəmaunt], *a.* Sovrano; supremo, sommo, eminente. — **lord,** signore sovrano, *m.*; **of — importance,** di somma importanza.
paramour [ˈpærəmur], *n.* Amante, *m.f.*, drudo, *m.*, druda, *f.*
paranoia [pærəˈnɔiə], *n.* (*Med.*) Paranoia, *f.*
paranymph [ˈpærənimf], *n.* Paraninfo, *m.*
parapet [ˈpærəpet], *n.* Parapetto, *m.*
paraphernalia [pærəfəɹˈneiliə], *n.pl.* Arnesi, oggetti, *m.pl.*, roba, *f.*; armamentario, *m.*, accessori, *m.pl.*
paraphrase [ˈpærəfreiz], *n.* Parafrasi, *f.* || *v.t.i.* Parafrasare.
paraphrastic [pærəˈfræstik], *a.* Parafrastico.
paraplegia [pærəˈpliːdʒə], *n.* (*Med.*) Paraplegia, *f.*
parasite [ˈpærəsait], *n.* Parassita, *m.f.*; cortigiano, adulatore, *m.*
parasitic [pærəˈsitik], *a.* Parassitico, parassitario; parassita.
parasitism, *n.* Parassitismo, *m.*
parasol [ˈpærəsɔl], *n.* Parasole, ombrellino, *m.*
paratroops [ˈpærətruːps], *n.pl.* (*Mil.*) Reparti di paracadutisti, *m.pl.*
parboil [ˈpɑːɹbɔil], *v.t.* Far bollire a metà; riscaldare, sobbollire.
parbuckle [ˈpɑːɹbʌkl], *n.* Lentia, braca da botte, *f.*; treviro, *m.* || *v.t.* Lentiare.
parcel [ˈpɑːɹsəl], *n.* Pacco, involto, collo, *m.*; (*of land*) pezzo, *m.* || *v.t.* Impaccare, impacchettare, involtare. — **post,** servizio dei pacchi postali, *m.*; **by — post,** per pacco postale; **parcels office,** ufficio di messaggeria, *m.*; **part and — of,** parte integrante di; **to — out,** spartire, dividere, distribuire.
parch [pɑːɹtʃ], *v.t.* Arsicciare, arrostire, essicare; abbruciare; *v.i.* essicare, disseccarsi. **Parched with thirst,** riarso di sete; **the parched earth,** la terra riarsa, *f.*; **parched peas,** piselli secchi, *m.pl.*
parchment, *n.* Pergamena, cartapecora, *f.*
pard [pɑːɹd], *n.* (*Zool.*) Leopardo, pardo, *m.*
pardon [ˈpɑːɹdən], *n.* Perdono, *m.*, grazia, amnistia, *f.*; (*Eccles.*) indulgenza, *f.* || *v.t.* Perdonare, scusare; graziare. **I beg your —!** Scusi! Scusate! **to ask someone's —,** chiedere perdono a qualcuno; **to — someone for an error,** perdonare a qualcuno un errore, perdonare qualcuno d'un errore; **I will never — him for it,** non gliela perdonerò mai.
pardonable, *a.* Perdonabile, scusabile.
pardonableness, *n.* Scusabilità, *f.*
pardonably, *adv.* Scusabilmente.
pardoner, *n.* (*Hist.*) Distributore di indulgenze, *m.*
pare [pɛəɹ], *v.t.* (*fruit*) Sbucciare, pelare; (*the nails*) tagliarsi (le unghie).
paregoric [ˈpærigɔrik], *n.a.* (*Med.*) Paregorico, *m.*
parenchyma [pæˈreŋkimə], *n.* (*Anat.*) Parenchima, *m.*
parent [ˈpɛərənt], *n.* Genitore, *m.*, genitrice, *f.*, padre, *m.*, madre, *f.*; origine, fonte, sorgente, *f.* || *a.* D'origine. **Parents,** genitori, *m.pl.*
parentage [ˈpɛərəntidʒ], *n.* genitori, *m.pl.*; lignaggio, *m.*, nascita, *f.*; famiglia, *f.*
parental [pəˈrentəl], *a.* Dei genitori; paterno, materno.
parenthood [ˈpɛərənthud], *n.* Genitura, *f.*; paternità, maternità, *f.*
parenthesis (*pl.* **parentheses**) [pəˈrenθəsis, pəˈrenθəsiːz], *n.* Parentesi, *f.* **In —,** fra parentesi.
parenthetic, parenthetical [pærenˈθetik, pærenˈθetikəl], *a.* Fra parentesi, parentetico.
parenthetically, *adv.* Per parentesi.
parget [ˈpɑːɹdʒet], *n.* Gesso, *m.* || *v.t.* Ingessare.
parhelion [pɑːɹˈhiːliən], *n.* (*Astron.*) Parelio, *m.*
pariah [ˈpɑːriə], *n.* Paria, *m.f.*
parietal [pəˈraiətəl], *a.* (*Anat.*) Parietale.
paring [ˈpɛəriŋ], *n.* Pelatura, *f.*; ritagliamento, *m.*; buccia, *f.*
Paris [ˈpæris], *n.* (*Geog.*) Parigi, *f.*
parish [ˈpæriʃ], *n.* (*civil*) Comune, municipio, *m.*; (*Eccles.*) parrocchia, *f.* || *a.* Comunale, parrocchiale. — **church,** parrocchia, pieve, *f.*; — **priest,** parroco, pievano, *m.*; — **clerk,** sagrestano, *m.*; — **register,** libro parrocchiale, *m.*
parishioner [pəˈriʃənəɹ], *n.* Parrocchiano, *m.*, parrocchiana, *f.*
Parisian [pəˈriziən], *a.* Parigino, di Parigi. || *n.* Parigino, *m.*, Parigina, *f.*
parisyllabic [pærisiˈlæbik], *a.* (*Gram.*) Parisillabo.
parity [ˈpæriti], *n.* Parità, *f.*
park [pɑːɹk], *n.* Parco, *m.*; bosco, *m.* || *v.t.* (*to enclose*) Chiudere in un parco; (*vehicles*) parcare, posteggiare, stazionare. — **-keeper,** guardiano di parco, *m.*
parking, *n.* Parcheggio, *m.* — **-place,** posteggio, *m.*; **no —,** proibizione di sosta, *f.*; divieto di sosta, *m.*
parlance [ˈpɑːɹləns], *n.* Lingua, *f.*, linguaggio, *m.* **In common —,** nel linguaggio corrente.
parley [ˈpɑːɹli], *n.* Colloquio, *m.*, conferenza, *f.*; abboccamento, *m.* (*Mil.*) parlamento, *m.* || *v.i.* Conferire, abboccarsi; parlamentare.
parliament [ˈpɑːɹləmənt], *n.* Parlamento, *m.*, camera dei deputati, *f.* **Act of Parliament,** decreto, *m.*, atto del parlamento, *m.*; **Houses of Parliament,** le due Camere, *f.pl.*
Parliamentarian, *n.* (*Hist.*) Parlamentare, *m.*
parliamentary, *n.* Parlamentare. — **language,** linguaggio corretto, *m.*; — **division,** circoscrizione elettorale, *f.*
parlour [ˈpɑːɹləɹ], *n.* Salotto, salottino, *m.*; (*in convent*) parlatorio, *m.* — **boarder,** pensionante, dozzinante, *m.f.*; — **game,** giuoco di sala, *m.*; — **-maid,** cameriera, *f.*; (*Rail.*) — **-car,** vagone di lusso, *m.*, vettura-salon, *f.*
parlous [ˈpɑːɹləs], *a.* Pericoloso.
Parmesan [ˈpɑːɹmizən], *n.a.* Parmigiano, *m.* — **cheese,** formaggio parmigiano, *m.*; grana, *m.*
Parnassian [pɑːɹˈnæsiən], *a.* Parnassico; Parnassiano.
Parnassus, *n.* Parnasso, Parnaso, *m.*
parochial [pəˈroukiəl], *a.* Comunale; (*Eccles.*) parrocchiale; (*fig.*) di campanile.
parochialism, *n.* Campanilismo, *m.*
parodist [ˈpærodist], *n.* Parodista, *m.f.*
parody [ˈpærədi], *n.* Parodia, *f.* || *v.t.* Parodiare.
parole [pəˈroul], *n.* Parola, parola d'onore, *f.* **To be on —,** essere lasciato libero sulla parola.

paronomasia [pærəno'meiziə], *n.* (*Gram.*) Paronomasia, *f.*, bisticcio, *m.*
paroquet [cp. **parakeet**].
parotid [pə'rɔtid], *a.* (*Anat.*) Parotide.
paroxysm ['pærəksizm], *n.* Parossismo, accesso, *m.*
paroxytone [pə'rɔksitoun], *n.a.* (*Gram.*) Parossitono, *m.*
parquet ['pɑ:ɹkei], *n.* Pavimento di legno lucido, *m.* || *v.t.* Pavimentare di legno.
parricidal [pæri'saidəl], *a.* Parricida.
parricide, *n.* (*crime*) Parricidio, *m.*; (*criminal*) parricida, *m.f.*
parrot ['pærət], *n.* (*Zool.*) Pappagallo, *m.*, pappagallo femmina, *f.* || *v.t.i.* Ripetere da pappagallo. **— -cry,** grido popolare, *m.*
parry ['pæri], *v.t.* Parare, scansare, stornare; evitare, schivare; ribattere. || *n.* (*Fencing*) Parata, *f.*; (*fig.*) risposta, *f.*
parrying, *n.* Parata, *f.*
parse [pɑ:ɹz], *v.t.* (*Gram.*) Analizzare.
Parsee [pɑ:ɹ'si:], *n.* Parso, Parsì, *m.*
parsimonious [pɑ:ɹsi'mouniəs], *a.* Parsimonioso, parco, frugale, economo.
parsimoniously, *adv.* Frugalmente.
parsimoniousness, parsimony [pɑ:ɹsi'mouniəsnis, 'pɑ:ɹsiməni], *n.* Parsimonia, *f.*
parsing ['pɑ:ɹziŋ], *n.* (*Gram.*) Analisi, *f.*
parsley ['pɑ:ɹsli], *n.* (*Bot.*) Prezzemolo, *m.*
parsnip ['pɑ:ɹsnip], *n.* (*Bot.*) Pastinaca, *f.*
parson ['pɑ:ɹsən], *n.* Parroco, prete, curato, *m.*; (*Protestant*) pastore, ministro, *m.* **Parson's nose,** groppone di pollo, *m.*
parsonage ['pɑ:ɹsənidʒ], *n.* Presbiterio, *m.*, casa parrocchiale, *f.*
part [pɑ:ɹt], *n.* Parte, porzione, *f.*; pezzo, *m.*; località, *f.*; (*of book*) fascicolo, *m.*, dispensa, *f.*; regione, *f.*, luogo, *m.*; (*Theat.*) parte, *f.* || *v.t.* Separare, dividere, spartire, sceverare; *v.i.* dividersi, separarsi, lasciarsi. **To have neither — nor lot in,** non avere nè arte nè parte; **it was not my — to interfere,** non spettava a me framettermi nella faccenda; **I have done my —,** ho fatto la mia parte; **to play a —,** fare una parte; **a man of parts,** un uomo di molti numeri; **for the most —,** per la maggior parte; **to take — in,** prendere parte a; **to take someone's —,** sostenere le parti di qualcuno; **to take in good —,** prendere in buona parte; **on my —,** da parte mia; **from all parts,** da ogni lato; **in foreign parts,** all'estero; **published in parts,** pubblicato a dispense; (*Mech.*) **spare parts,** pezzi di ricambio, *m.pl.*; (*Theat.*) **to take the — of,** rappresentare, impersonare; **to — with,** disfarsi di; **to — company,** separarsi; **let us — friends,** dividiamoci da buoni amici; **to — one's hair,** farsi la scriminatura; **— -owner,** comproprietario, *m.*; (*Mus.*) **— -song,** canto a varie voci, *m.*
partake [pɑ:ɹ'teik], *v.t.i.* Partecipare a, prendere parte a; dividere il pasto, sapere di, sentire di. **He partook of our meal,** egli mangiò con noi; **his methods — of the tyrant,** i suoi modi sentono del tiranno.
partaker, *n.* Partecipante, *m.f.*
parterre [pɑ:ɹ'tɛəɹ], *n.* Parterre, *m.*, aiuola, *f.*
parthenogenesis [pɑ:ɹθeno'dʒenisis], *n.* Partenogenesi, *f.*
Parthian ['pɑ:ɹθiən], *n.* Partico. (*fig.*) **— shot,** freccia del Parto, *f.*
partial ['pɑ:ɹʃəl], *a.* Parziale; ineguale, ingiusto. **To be — to,** avere un debole per.
partiality [pɑ:ɹʃi'æliti], *n.* Parzialità *f.*; preferenza, predilezione, *f.*; debole, *m.*
partially, *adv.* Parzialmente.
participant [pɑ:ɹ'tisipənt], *n.* Partecipante, *m.f.*
participate, *v.t.i.* Partecipare a, prendere parte a; partecipare di. **He participates in the faults of his father,** partecipa dei difetti del padre.
participation, *n.* Partecipazione, *f.*
participial [pɑ:ɹti'sipiəl], *a.* (*Gram.*) Participiale.
participle, *n.* (*Gram.*) Participio, *m.*
particle ['pɑ:ɹtikl], *n.* Particola, particella, *f.*; (*fig.*) grano, granello, *m.* **A — of common sense,** un grano di buon senso, *m.*
particoloured ['pɑ:ɹtikʌləɹd], *a.* Variegato, variopinto.
particular [pɑ:ɹ'tikju:ləɹ], *a.* Particolare, speciale; preciso, esatto, minuzioso, meticoloso, scrupoloso; difficile, schizzinoso; fastidioso, esigente. || *n.* Particolare, dettaglio, *m.*; particolarità, *f.* **Particulars,** dettagli, particolari, *m.pl.*, informazioni, *f.pl.*; **to give full particulars,** dare ampi dettagli; **I took — trouble,** feci uno sforzo speciale; **a — friend of mine,** un mio amico intimo, *m.*; **he is not — to an hour or two,** non fa caso per un'ora più o meno; **nothing —,** niente di particolare; **for no — reason,** per nessuna ragione speciale; **— in one's dress,** ricercato nel vestire; **in —,** in particolare.
particularity, *n.* Particolarità, *f.*
particularize, *v.t.* Particolareggiare, dettagliare.
particularly, *adv.* Particolarmente, in particolare.
parting ['pɑ:ɹtiŋ], *n.* Separazione, *f.*; divisione, *f.*; (*of hair*) scriminatura, *f.* || *a.* D'addio, ultimo. **The — of the ways,** il bivio, *m.*; **a — kiss,** un bacio d'addio, *m.*; **a — injunction,** un ultimo comando, *m.*
partisan (1) ['pɑ:ɹtizən], *n.* Partigiano, *m.*
partisan (2), *n.* (*weapon*) Partigiana, *f.*
partition [pɑ:ɹ'tiʃən], *n.* Partizione, spartizione, ripartizione, *f.* (*in room*) tramezzo, *m.* || *v.t.* Separare, dividere; tramezzare; dividere in lotti. **To — off part of a room,** tramezzare una stanza.
partitioned, *a.* Intramezzato, suddiviso.
partitive ['pɑ:ɹtitiv], *a.* (*Gram.*) Partitivo.
partly, *adv.* In parte, parzialmente.
partner ['pɑ:ɹtnəɹ], *n.* (*Comm.*) Socio, *m.*; (*Sport, etc.*) compagno, *m.*, compagna, *f.*; (*husband, wife*) compagno, *m.*, compagna, *f.*; (*Dancing*) cavaliere, *m.*, dama, *f.* || *v.t.* Menare, condurre, ballare con. (*Comm.*) **Sleeping —,** socio accomandante, *m.*
partnership, *n.* Società, associazione, *f.* **To enter into — with,** entrare in società con.
partridge ['pɑ:ɹtridʒ], *n.* (*Zool.*) Pernice, *f.*
parturient [pɑ:ɹ'tju:riənt], *a.* Partoriente.
parturition [pɑ:ɹtju:'riʃən], *n.* Parto, *m.*
party ['pɑ:ɹti], *n.* (*political, etc.*) Partito, *m.*; (*social*) partita, festa, comitiva, compagnia, *f.*; gruppo, crocchio, *m.*; (*Mil.*) plotone, distaccamento, *m.*; (*Law*) parte, *f.*; (*colloq.*) persona, *f.*, individuo, *m.* **— spirit,** spirito di parte, *m.*; **a dinner —,** un pranzo, *m.*; **an**

evening —, una serata, *f.*; **a tea —,** un tè, *m.*; **a pleasure —,** una partita di piacere, *f.*; **to be a — to,** prendere parte a; **to be of the —,** essere della compagnia; **to be a — to a crime,** essere complice in un delitto; **—-man,** partigiano, *m.*; **—-wall,** muro divisorio, *m.*; **—-coloured,** screziato, variopinto.

parvenu ['pɑːɹvenuː], *n.* Parvenu, *m.*; arricchito, *m.*; pescecane, *m.*

pas [pɑː], *n.* Passo, *m.* **To give the — to,** dare la precedenza a; (*Dancing*) **a — seul,** un passo a solo, *m.*

paschal ['pæskəl], *a.* (*Eccles.*) Pasquale.

pasha ['pæʃəː], *n.* Pascià, *m.*

pasque-flower ['pæskflauəɹ], *n.* (*Bot.*) Anemone, *m.*

pasquinade [pæskwi'neid], *n.* Pasquinata, *f.*

pass [pɑːs], *v.t.* Passare; traversare; sorpassare; ammettere; adottare, prendere; approvare; collaudare, verificare; *v.i.* passare, andare oltre; morire; aver luogo, succedere, accadere. || *n.* Passo, *m.*; (*mountain*) gola, *f.*; (*permit*) lasciapassare, salvacondotto, permesso, *m.*; (*in exam.*) approvazione, *f.*; (*Fencing*) passata, stoccata, *f.*; (*fig.*) condizione, estremità, *f.* **It passes my comprehension,** non arrivo a capire; **to — in review,** passare in rivista; **to — one's word,** promettere; **to — on,** passare; **to — the time,** passare il tempo; **to — the time of day,** intrattenersi; **to — sentence on,** giudicare, pronunziare una sentenza su; **to — a criticism on,** criticare; **to — something off as,** far passare qualcosa per; **to — over,** omettere, passare sotto silenzio; **to — along,** passar oltre, andare avanti; **to come to —,** accadere, capitare; **to — away,** morire, sparire; **to — by,** passare; **to — for,** passare per; **to — on,** andare avanti; **to — off,** sparire, dileguare; **to — out,** uscire, svenire; **to — through,** attraversare, soffrire, sopportare; **no words passed between us,** non scambiammo una sola parola; **to — by the name of,** essere conosciuto dal nome di; **to — hence,** passare da questa vita; **let such remarks — unnoticed,** non fate attenzione a tali osservazioni; **he saw all that passed,** vide tutto ciò che accadde; **things have come to a pretty —,** le cose sono giunte ai mali passi; **to bring to —,** adempire; **to — for payment,** dar l'ordine di pagare; **—-book,** *m.*, libretto; **—-key,** chiave comune, *f.*

passable, *a.* Passabile, tollerabile, mediocre; praticabile, navigabile.

passably, *adv.* Passabilmente.

passage ['pæsidʒ], *n.* (*in a building*) Passaggio, corridoio, *m.*; (*by sea*) traversata, *m.*, viaggio, tragitto, *m.*; (*in book, etc.*) brano, passo, squarcio, *m.* **To book one's —,** comprare il biglietto di viaggio; **to force a —,** aprirsi un passaggio; **a bird of —,** un uccello di passaggio, un uccello migratorio, *m.*; **—-money,** prezzo della traversata, *m.*

passenger ['pæsendʒəɹ], *n.* Viaggiatore, *m.*, viaggiatrice, *f.*, passeggero, *m.*, passeggera, *f.* **— train,** treno passeggieri, *m.*; **— ship,** piroscafo passeggeri, *m.*; **—-lift,** ascensore, *m.*; **— traffic,** movimento di viaggiatori, *m.*

passer-by (*pl.* **passers-by**), *n.* Passante, viandante, *m.f.*

passerine ['pæsərain], *a.* (*Zool.*) Passeraceo.

passibility [pɑːsibiliti], *n.* Passibilità, *f.*

passible, *a.* Passibile.

passibly, *adv.* Passibilmente.

passing ['pɑːsiŋ], *a.* Passeggiero, transitorio, effimero, fugace. || *adv.* Molto, estremamente. || *n.* Passaggio, *m.*; (*death*) trapasso, decesso, *m.*, morte, *f.*; (*of time*) decorso, *m.*; (*of a parliamentary bill*) approvazione, *f.* **—-bell,** rintocco funebre, *m.*; **— events,** attualità, *f.*; **a — fancy,** un capriccio, *m.*; (*Mus.*) **—-note,** nota di passaggio, *f.*

passion ['pæʃən], *n.* Passione, *f.*; (*of anger*) collera, *f.*, corruccio, *m.* **To have a — for,** avere una passione per; **to fly into a —,** montare in collera; (*Theat.*) **— play,** mistero della Passione, *m.*; rappresentazione della Passione, *f.*; **Passion Week,** Settimana Santa, *f.*; (*Bot.*) **—-flower,** passiflora, *f.*, fior di passione, *m.*

passionate, *a.* Appassionato, ardente; irascibile, collerico, iracondo, veemente.

passionately, *adv.* Appassionatamente. **— fond of,** che ama alla follia.

passionateness, *n.* Appassionatezza, veemenza, *f.*; passione, irascibilità, *f.*

Passionist, *n.* (*Eccles.*) Passionista, *m.*

passionless, *a.* Impassibile, calmo.

passive, *a.* Passivo. *n.* (*Gram.*) Passivo, *m.*

passiveness, passivity, *n.* Passività, *f.*

passman ['pɑːsmən], *n.* Studente universitario che non si specializza in alcuna materia, *m.f.*

Passover ['pɑːsouvəɹ], *n.* Pasqua degli Ebrei, *f.*

passport ['pɑːspɔːɹt], *n.* Passaporto, *m.*

password ['pɑːswəːɹd], *n.* Parola d'ordine, *f.*

past [pɑːst], *a.* Passato, trascorso, scorso; finito; ultimo. || *prep.* (*of time*) dopo; (*of place*) oltre. || *n.* Passato, *m.* **The — week,** la settimana scorsa, *f.*; **half- — two,** le due e mezzo; **he ran — the house,** passò la casa correndo; **he is — seventy,** ha più di settant'anni; **it is — eleven o'clock,** sono le undici passate; **it is — bearing,** è insopportabile; **he is — praying for,** è incorreggibile; **in times —,** in tempi passati, nel passato; **for some time —,** da qualche tempo; **—-master,** maestro perfetto, *m.* (*colloq.*) matricolato.

paste [peist], *n.* (*for sticking*) Colla, *f.*; (*Cooking*) pasta, *f.*; (*jewellery*) strasse, *m.*, diamante artificiale, *m.* || *v.t.* Incollare, appiccicare. **To — up,** affissare, affiggere; **—-pot,** vaso da colla, *m.*

pasteboard, *n.* Cartone, *m.* || *a.* Di cartone.

pastel ['pæstel], *n.* Pastello, *m.*

pastellist, *n.* Pastellista, *m.f.*

pastern ['pæstəɹn], *n.* (*Anat.*) Pasturale, pastoia, *f.*

pasteurize ['pɑːstəːraiz], *v.t.* Pastorizzare.

pastiche [pæs'tiːʃ], *n.* Zibaldone, *m.*, farragine, *f.*

pastille ['pæstil], *n.* Pasticca, pastiglia, *f.*

pastime ['pɑːstaim], *n.* Passatempo, svago, trastullo, divertimento, *m.*, distrazione, *f.*

pastor ['pɑːstəɹ], *n.* Pastore, *m.*

pastoral, *n.a.* Pastorale, *m.*

pastorate ['pɑːstəreit], *n.* (*Eccles.*) Ufficio di pastore, *m.*

pastry [ˈpeistri], *n.* Pasticceria, *f.*; paste, *f.pl.*, pasticcio, pasticcino, *m.* **—-cook,** pasticciere, *m.*; **—-shop,** pasticceria, *f.*; **—-board,** tavola per fare la pasticceria, *f.*, spianatoia, *f.*
pasturable [ˈpɑːstjuːrəbl], *a.* Pascolabile, pascolativo.
pasturage [ˈpɑːstjuːridʒ], *n.* Pascolo, *m.*, pastura, *f.*
pasture [ˈpɑːstjuːɹ], *n.* Pascolo, *m.*, pastura, *f.* || *v.t.i.* Pascolare, pascere. **He maketh me to lie down in green pastures,** Egli mi fa giacere in verdeggianti paschi.
pasty (1) [ˈpeisti], *a.* Pastoso; (*of complexion*) pallido.
pasty (2) [ˈpɑːsti], *n.* (*Cooking*) Pasticcio, *m.*
pat [pæt], *n.* Colpettino, colpetto, *m.*, carezza, *f.*; (*of butter*) panetto *m.* || *adv.* A punto, a proposito. || *a.* Pronto, esatto, opportuno. || *v.t.* Dare un colpetto a, accarezzare. **To — oneself on the back,** lodarsi, essere contento di se stesso.
Patagonian [pætəˈgouniən], *n.a.* Patagone, *m.*
patch [pætʃ], *n.* Pezza, toppa, *f.*; (*of land*) pezzo, appezzamento, *m.*; (*on face*) neo, *m.*; (*on tyre*) rappezzatura, *f.*, impiastro di gomma, *m.* || *v.t.* Rappezzare, rattoppare, raccomodare. **To — up,** rammendare, aggiustare, accomodare; (*colloq.*) **cross- —,** brontolone, bisbetico, *m.*; (*fig.*) **not a — on,** molto inferiore a.
patcher, *n.* Rappezzatore, rattoppatore, *m.*, rappezzatrice, rattoppatrice, *f.*
patching, *n.* Rappezzatura, rattoppatura, *f.*
patchouli [ˈpætʃuːli], *n.* Pasciulì, *m.*
patchwork, *n.* Rappezzamento, rattoppamento, *m.*; (*fig.*) mosaico, zibaldone, miscuglio, *m.* **A — quilt,** una coperta a scacchi, *f.*
patchy, *a.* Rattoppato, mal combinato; variegato; inuguale.
pate [peit], *n.* Testa, zucca, *f.* **Shallow-pated,** vanesio.
patella [pəˈtelə], *n.* (*Anat.*) Patella, *f.*
paten [ˈpætən], *n.* (*Eccles.*) Patena, *f.*; disco, *m.*
patent [ˈpætənt, ˈpeitənt], *n.* Brevetto, *m.*; patente, *f.*, titolo, diploma, *m.*; invenzione brevettata, *f.* || *a.* Patente, aperto, ovvio. || *v.t.* Brevettare. **To take out a —,** prendere un brevetta d'invenzione; (*fig.*) **a — of gentility,** una patente di nobiltà, *f.*; **letters —,** patente, *f.*; **— food,** specialità alimentare, *f.*; **— leather,** cuoio verniciato; **— medicine,** specialità farmaceutica, *f.*; **— office,** ufficio brevetti, *m.*
patented, *a.* Brevettato.
patentee [pætənˈtiː], *n.* Concessionario di brevetto, *m.*
patently, *adv.* Evidentemente, chiaramente.
pater [ˈpeitəɹ], (*colloq.*) Padre, babbo, *m.*
paterfamilias [pætəɹfəˈmiliəs], *n.* Padre di famiglia, *m.*
paternal [pəˈtəːɹnəl], *a.* Paterno.
paternally, *adv.* Paternamente.
paternity, *n.* Paternità, *f.*
paternoster [pætəɹˈnɔstəɹ], *n.* (*Eccles.*) Paternostro, *m.*; una lenza con molti ami, *f.*
path [pɑːθ], *n.* Sentiero, *m.*, viottola, stradicciuola, *f.*; cammino, *m.*; (*fig.*) via, strada, *f.*; (*Astron.*) corso, cammino, *m.*; traiettoria, *f.* **The beaten —,** il cammino battuto, il metodo usuale, *m.*; **bye- —,** via traversa, strada secondaria, *f.*; **the — of glory,** la via della gloria, *f.*; **the — of the storm,** il corso dell'uragano, *m.*
pathetic [pəˈθetik], *a.* Patetico, commovente, pietoso.
pathetically, *adv.* Pateticamente.
pathless, *a.* Senza sentiero; sconosciuto, impenetrabile.
pathogenesis [pæθoˈdʒenesis], *n.* (*Med.*) Patogenesi, *f.*
pathogenic, *a.* Patogenico.
pathological [pæθoˈlɔdʒikəl], *a.* Patologico.
pathologically, *adv.* Patologicamente.
pathologist [pəˈθɔlodʒist], *n.* Patologo, *m.*
pathology, *n.* Patologia, *f.*
pathos [ˈpeiθɔs, ˈpæθɔs], *n.* Patos, patetico, *m.*
pathway [cp. **path**].
patience [ˈpeiʃəns], *n.* Pazienza, *f.*; (*Cards*) solitario, *m.* **To be out of — with,** essere impaziente di; **to have no — with,** non aver pazienza con; **to lose —,** perder la pazienza, impazientirsi.
patient [ˈpeiʃənt], *a.* Paziente, tollerante. || *n.* Paziente, *m.f.*, malato sotto cura, *m.*, infermo, *m.*, inferma, *f.* **To be —,** pazientare.
patiently, *adv.* Pazientemente.
patina [ˈpætinə], *n.* Patina, *f.*
patly, *adv.* A proposito.
patness, *n.* Esattezza, *f.*
patriarch [ˈpeitriɑːɹk], *n.* Patriarca, *m.*
patriarchal, *a.* Patriarcale.
patriarchate, *n.* (*Eccles.*) Patriarcato, *m.*
patrician [pəˈtriʃən], *n.a.* Patrizio, nobile, *m.*
patrimonial [pætriˈmouniəl], *a.* Patrimoniale.
patrimony [ˈpætriməni], *n.* Patrimonio, *m.*
patriot [ˈpætriət, ˈpeitriət], *n.* Patriota, patriotta, *m.f.*
patriotic, *a.* Patriottico.
patriotically, *adv.* Patriotticamente.
patriotism, *n.* Patriottismo, *m.*
patristic, *a.* Patristico.
patrol [pəˈtroul], *n.* Pattuglia, *f.*; ronda, *f.* || *v.i.* Pattugliare, andare di pattuglia, far la ronda; (*Naut.*) perlustrare.
patron [ˈpætrən, ˈpeitrən], *n.* Patrono, protettore, patrocinatore, *m.*; (*customer*) avventore, compratore, *m.* **— saint,** patrono, *m.*, patrona, *f.*; **— saint's day,** festa patronale, *f.*
patronage, *n.* Protezione, *f.*, patronato, patrocinio, *m.*; (*of customers*) avviamento, *m.*
patroness, *n.* Patronessa, protettrice, patrocinatrice, *f.*
patronize, *v.t.* Patrocinare, proteggere, favorire, incoraggiare; (*a shop*) frequentare.
patronized, *a.* (*of a shop*) Avviato. **Well —,** ben avviato.
patronizing, *a.* Di condiscendenza.
patronizingly, *adv.* Con aria protettrice, con fare condiscendente.
patronymic [pætrəˈnimik], *n.a.* Patronimico, *m.*
patten [ˈpætən], *n.* Soprascarpa, *f.*; (*Arch.*) zoccolo, *m.*
patter [ˈpætəɹ], *n.* Rumore, scroscio, scalpito, *m.*; (*Theat.*) cicalio, cicaleccio, *m.* || *v.i.* Scalpicciare; (*of rain*) picchiettare.
pattern [ˈpætəɹn], *n.* (*sample*) Campione, *m.*; modello, *m.*; (*design*) disegno, *m.*; esempio, *m.* || *v.t.* Modellare. **To cut to —,** tagliar sul modello; **to take — by,** modellarsi su; **—-maker,** modellatore, *m.*; **—-making,** modellamento, *m.*; **—-book, —-card,** campionario, *m.*

patty [ˈpæti], *n.* Pasticcino, pasticcetto, *m.* **—-pan,** forma da pasticcino, *f.*

paucity [ˈpɔːsiti], *n.* Pochezza, scarsezza, *f.*, mancamento, *m.*

Paul [pɔːl], *n.* Paolo, *m.* **— Pry,** Ficcanaso, *m.*

paunch [ˈpɔːntʃ], *n.* Pancia, *f.*

paunchy, *a.* Panciuto.

pauper [ˈpɔːpəɹ], *n.* Povero, *m.*, povera, *f.*, indigente, *m.f.*, mendicante, *m.f.*

pauperism, *n.* Povertà, indigenza, penuria, *f.*, pauperismo, *m.*

pauperize, *v.t.* Ridurre all'indigenza; creare del pauperismo.

pause [pɔːz], *n.* Pausa, fermata, sosta, *f.*; intervallo, *m.*; (*Mus.*) pausa, *f.* || *v.i.* Far pausa, interrompersi, fermarsi, aspettare, arrestarsi. **To give — to,** rendere incerto, rendere indeciso; **I — for a reply,** aspetto la vostra risposta; **to — upon a word,** soffermarsi su una parola.

pavan [pəˈvɑːn], *n.* Pavana, *f.*

pave [peiv], *v.t.* Lastricare, pavimentare. (*fig.*) **To — the way for someone,** far la via a qualcuno.

pavement, *n.* Lastrico, lastricato, selciato, pavimento, suolo, *m.*; (*in street*) marciapiede, *m.*; (*outside a café*) terrazza, *f.*; (*of bricks*) ammattonato, *m.*

paver, paviour [ˈpeivəɹ, ˈpeiviəɹ], *n.* Lastricatore, pavimentatore, *m.*

pavilion [pəˈviljən], *n.* Padiglione, *m.*; tenda, *f.*, tendone, *m.* || *v.t.* Fornire di tende.

paving, *n.* Lastricamento, *m.*, pavimentazione, *f.* **— -stone,** lastra di pietra, *f.*, calce, *m.*

pavonine [pəˈvounain], *a.* Iridescente, paonazzo.

paw [pɔː], *n.* Zampa, *f.* (*colloq.*) mano, *f.* || *v.t.* Zampare; (*to handle*) maneggiare, toccare; *v.i.* zampare. **To — the ground,** scalpitare.

pawky [ˈpɔːki], *a.* Scaltro, astuto, furbo.

pawl [pɔːl], *n.* (*Mech.*) Dente d'arresto, *m.*

pawn (1) [pɔːn], *n.* (*Chess*) Pedina, *f.*

pawn (2), *v.t.* Impegnare, dare in pegno, pignorare. || *n.* Pegno, *m.* **In —,** in pegno; **to take out of —,** riscattare; **—-broker,** prestatore su pegni, *m.*; **—-shop,** Monte di Pietà, *m.*; **—-ticket,** polizza di pegno, *f.*

pax [pæks], *n.* (*Eccles.*) Pace, *f.*

pay [pei], *n.* Paga, *f.*, soldo, salario, stipendio, *m.*; ricompensa, *f.* || *v.t.* Pagare, saldare; ricompensare, soddisfare, risarcire; (*compliment, attention, etc.*) fare; (*respect*) portare; (*a visit*) fare; *v.i.* fruttare, rendere. **To — an account,** saldare un conto; **to — back,** rimborsare; **to — down,** pagare a contanti; **to — for,** pagare; **to — homage,** rendere omaggio; **to — in,** versare; **to — off,** (*a debt*) estinguere, ammortizzare, (*an employee*) licenziare, (*a ship*) disarmare; **to — out,** sborsare, (*a rope*) filare; **to — someone out,** vendicarsi di qualcuno, farla pagare; **to — someone in his own coin,** rendere pan per focaccia; **to — one's way,** sbarcare il lunario; **to — dearly for,** pagarla cara; **it does not — me,** non mi mette conto, non mi conviene; **the business does not —,** il negozio non rende; **—-day,** giorno di paga, *m.*; **—-roll,** distinta dei salarii, *f.*

payable, *a.* Pagabile, esigibile. **— to bearer,** pagabile al portatore.

payee [peiˈiː], *n.* Beneficiario, *m.*, beneficiaria, *f.*; (*on cheque*) portatore, latore, *m.*

payer, *n.* Pagatore, *m.*, pagatrice, *f.*

paying, *a.* Fruttifero, produttivo, lucrativo. **— guest,** pensionario, *m.*, pensionaria, *f.*, pensionante, *m.f.*; **—-in slip,** cedola di versamento, *f.*

paymaster, *n.* Pagatore, *m.*; (*Mil.*) ufficiale pagatore, *m.*

payment, *n.* Pagamento, *m.*; rimborso, *m.*, ricompensa, *f.*; versamento, *m.* **Part-—,** acconto, *m.*; **— in full,** pagamento a saldo, *m.*; **— in advance,** pagamento anticipato, *m.*

paynim [ˈpeinim], *n.* (*obs.*) Saraceno, pagano, *m.*

pea (*pl.* **peas, pease**) [piː, piːz], *n.* Pisello, *m.* **As like as two peas,** come due goccie d'acqua; **—-green,** verde pisello; **—-shooter,** cerbottana, *f.*; **—-soup,** consommé di piselli, *m.*, passata di piselli, *f.*; **—-stick,** palo, *m.*

peace [piːs], *n.* Pace, *f.*; tranquillità, *f.*; ordine pubblico, *m.* **At —,** in pace; **breach of the —,** attentato contro l'ordine pubblico, *m.*; **— of mind,** tranquillità d'animo, *f.*; **to hold one's —,** tacere; **to keep the —,** mantenere l'ordine pubblico; **to make one's — with,** riconciliarsi con; **—-offering,** sacrifizio propiziatorio.

peaceable, *a.* Pacifico.

peaceful, *a.* Pacifico; quieto, tranquillo.

peacefully, *adv.* Quietamente, tranquillamente.

peacefulness, *n.* Quiete, tranquillità, *f.*

peacemaker, *n.* Paciere, pacificatore, *m.*

peacemaking, *n.* Pacificazione, *f.*

peach (1) [piːtʃ], *n.* Pesca, *f.* **—-tree,** pesco, *m.*

peach (2), *v.i.* (*colloq.*) Tradire, denunciare.

peacock [ˈpiːkɔk], *n.* (*Zool.*) Pavone, *m.* **To strut like a —,** pavoneggiarsi; **— butterfly,** pavoncella, *f.*

peahen, *n.* Pavona, pavonessa, *f.*

peajacket, *n.* Giacchetta alla marinara, *f.*

peak (1) [piːk], *n.* Cima, vetta, sommità, *f.*; (*mountain*) picco, *m.*; (*of cap*) visiera, *f.*; (*Naut.*) picco, *m.*; punta, estremità, *f.* **— hours,** ore di punta, *f.pl.*

peak (2), *v.i.* Languire, struggersi, affievolirsi.

peaked, *a.* Appuntito, affilato; (*of cap*) con visiera.

peaky, *a.* Languente, scarno.

peal [piːl], *n.* (*of bells*) Scampanio, *m.*; (*of thunder*) scoppio, rumore, rimbombo, *m.*; (*of laughter*) scroscio, scoppio, *m.* || *v.i.* Scampanare, sonare a distesa; tuonare, rumoreggiare; *v.t.* far risonare.

peanut [ˈpiːnʌt], *n.* Arachide, *f.*

pear [pɛəɹ], *n.* Pera, *f.* **—-tree,** pero, *m.*; **— orchard,** pereto, *m.*

pearl [pəːɹl], *n.* Perla, *f.*; (*Print.*) perla, *f.* || *v.i.* Pescare perle; *v.t.* imperlare; perlare. **—-ash,** carbonato potassico, *m.*; **—-barley,** orzo perlato, *m.*; **—-diver, —-fisher,** pescatore di perle, *m.*; **—-fishery,** pesca di perle, *f.*; **—-grey,** grigio perla; **—-oyster,** meleagrina, ostrica perlifera, *f.*; **mother of —,** madreperla, *f.*; **— knitting,** punto rovescio, *m.*

pearled, *a.* Irrorato, perlato.

pearly, *a.* Perlato, perlaceo.

pearmain ['pɛəɹmein], *n.* (*Bot.*) Specie di mela, *f.*
peasant ['pezənt], *n.* Contadino, *m.*, contadina, *f.*, campagnuolo, *m.*, campagnuola, *f.* || *a.* Contadinesco. **—-proprietor,** colono agricoltore, *m.*
peasantry, *n.* Contadini, *m.pl.*; rurali, *m.pl.*
pease [cp. **pea**].
peat [pi:t], *n.* Torba, *f.*; formella, *f.* **—-bog,** torbiera, *f.*
peaty, *a.* Torboso.
pebble [pebəl], *n.* Ciottolo, sasso, sassolino, *m.*
pebbly, *a.* Ciottoloso.
peccable ['pekəbl], *a.* Peccabile.
peccadillo [pekə'dilou], *n.* Peccatuccio, *m.*
peccant ['pekənt], *a.* Errante.
peccary ['pekəri], *n.* (*Zool.*) Pecari, *m.*
peccavi [pe'keivai], *n.* **To cry —,** dire "mea culpa".
peck (1) [pek], *n.* Misura di capacità, *f.*; (*fig.*) moltitudine. **A — of troubles,** un sacco di guai, *m.*
peck (2), *n.* Beccata, *f.*, colpo di becco, *m.* || *v.t.i.* Beccare, dare colpi di becco. **To — a hole,** fare un buco; **to — out,** beccare; (*fig.*) **to — at,** biasimare, criticare, mangiare delicatamente.
pecker, *n.* (*colloq.*) Coraggio, *m.* **To keep one's — up,** non perder coraggio.
peckish, *a.* (*colloq.*) Che ha fame.
pecten ['pektən], *n.* Pettine, *m.*
pectoral ['pektərəl], *a.* (*Med.*) Pettorale. (*Eccles.*) **— cross,** croce pettorale, *f.*
peculate ['pekju:leit], *v.t.* Appropriarsi.
peculation, *n.* Peculato, *m.*
peculator, *n.* Malversatore, *m.*
peculiar [pe'kju:liəɹ], *a.* Peculiare, particolare, speciale; singolare, strano, bizzarro.
peculiarity, *n.* Particolarità, singolarità, *f.*
peculiarly, *adv.* Specialmente; stranamente.
pecuniary [pe'kju:niəri], *a.* Pecuniario.
pedagogic [pedə'gɔgik], *a.* Pedagogico.
pedagogue ['pedəgɔg], *n.* Pedagogo, *m.*
pedagogy ['pedəgɔgi], *n.* Pedagogia, *f.*
pedal ['pedəl], *n.* Pedale, *m.* (*Mus.*) **Loud —, soft —,** pedale del forte, pedale del piano, *m.* || *v.i.* Pedalare; (*Mus.*) pedaleggiare.
pedant ['pedənt], *n.* Pedante, *m.*
pedantic [pe'dæntik], *a.* Pedantesco; (*of a person*) pedante.
pedantically, *adv.* Pedantescamente.
pedantry, *n.* Pedanteria, *f.*
peddle ['pedəl], *v.t.i.* Fare il merciaiuolo, vendere in piccola quantità, vendere al dettaglio, vendere al minuto.
peddling, *n.* Meschino, gretto, *m.*
pedestal ['pedestəl], *n.* Piedestallo, *m.*; piede, *m.*; zoccolo, *m.* (*fig.*) **To place on a —,** mettere su di un piedestallo; **—-table,** tavola a piede centrale, *f.*
pedestrian [pe'destriən], *n.* Pedone, viandante, *m.* || *a.* Pedestre; prosaico, comune. **— crossing,** passaggio per pedoni, *m.*
pedicular [pe'dikju:ləɹ], *a.* Pedicolare.
pedigree ['pedigri:], *n.* Genealogia, *f.*; albero genealogico, *m.*
pediment ['pedimənt], *n.* (*Arch.*) Frontone, *m.*
pedlar ['pedləɹ], *n.* Merciaiuolo ambulante, girovago, *m.*
pedometer [pe'dɔmitəɹ], *n.* Pedometro, *m.*
peduncle [pe'dʌŋkl], *n.* (*Bot.*) Peduncolo, *m.*
peel (1) [pi:l], *n.* Buccia, scorza, pelle, *f.* || *v.t.* Pelare, sbucciare, mondare; *v.i.* pelarsi.
peel (2), *n.* (*Hist.*) Torre fortificata, *f.*
peeler, *n.* (*colloq.*) Poliziotto, *m.*
peelings, *n.pl.* Mondatura, *f.*; bucce, *f.pl.*
peep (1) [pi:p], *v.i.* Spiare, sbirciare; far capolino, spuntare, apparire. || *n.* Capolino, *m.*, sbirciata, occhiata, *f.*, sguardo furtivo, *m.* **At — of day,** allo spuntar del giorno; **to take a — at,** dar un'occhiata a; **—-hole,** spiraglio, pertugio, *m.*; **—-show,** diorama, *m.*
peep (2), *v.i.* Pigolare.
peer (1) [pɛəɹ], *n.* Pari, *m.*; uguale, pari, simile, *m.*
peer (2), *v.i.* Guardare, scuriosare. **To — at,** adocchiare, sbirciare; **to — into,** scrutare, guardare curiosamente.
peerage, *n.* I pari, *m.pl.*, dignità di pari, *f.*; almanacco nobiliare, *m.*, consulta araldica, *f.*
peeress, *n.* Moglie d'un pari, nobildonna, *f.*
peerless, *a.* Impareggiabile, incomparabile, senza pari.
peerlessness, *n.* Incomparabilità, *f.*
peeve [pi:v], *v.t.* (*colloq.*) Irritare, provocare.
peevish, *a.* Querulo, permaloso, irritabile.
peevishly, *adv.* Querulamente.
peevishness, *n.* Permalosità, irritabilità, *f.*
peewit ['pi:wit], *n.* (*Zool.*) Pavoncella, *f.*, vanello, *m.*
peg [peg], *n.* Caviglia, *f.*, cavicchio, *m.*; piuolo, gancio, infisso, *m.*; appiglio, *m.*; (*degree*) grado, punto, *m.*; (*drink*) bevanda spiritosa, *f.*; (*of violin*) bischero, *m.* || *v.t.* Incavigliare, incavicchiare, infiggere; (*Comm.*) stabilizzare. **To take down a —,** far abbassar la cresta, umiliare; **to — away,** lavorare sodo, perseverare; **to — out a claim,** accaparrarsi un diritto; (*colloq.*) **to — out,** morire; **—-top,** trottola, *f.*; **—-top trousers,** calzoni a sbuffo, *m.pl.*
Pegasus ['pegəsəs], *n.* (*Myth.*) Pegaso, *m.*
pegging ['pegiŋ], *n.* Incavigliatura, *f.*
pejorative ['pi:dʒəreitiv], *a.* Peggiorativo.
Peking [pi:'kiŋ], *n.* (*Geog.*) Pechino, *f.*
pekinese, peke [pi:ki'ni:z, pi:k], *n.* (*Zool.*) Cane pechinese, *m.*
Pelagian [pe'leidʒiən], *a.* (*Eccles.*) Pelagiano.
pelagic [pe'leidʒik], *a.* Marino.
pelargonium [pelɑ:ɹ'gouniəm], *n.* (*Bot.*) Pelargonio, *m.*
Pelasgic [pe'læsdʒik], *a.* (*Hist.*) Pelasgico.
pelerine ['pelərin], *n.* Pellegrina, *f.*
pelf [pelf], *n.* Danaro, lucro, guadagno, *m.*; ricchezze, *f.pl.*, quattrini, *m.pl.*
pelican ['pelikən], *n.* (*Zool.*) Pellicano, *m.*
pelisse [pe'li:s], *n.* Pelliccia, *f.*, mantello, *m.*
pellagra [pe'lægrə], *n.* (*Med.*) Pellagra, *f.*
pellet ['pelet], *n.* Pallottola, pallina, *f.*; (*pill*) pillola, *f.*
pellicle ['pelikl], *n.* Pellicola, *f.*
pell-mell [pel'mel], *adv.* Alla rinfusa; promiscuamente.
pellucid [pe'lu:sid], *a.* Pellucido, trasparente, chiaro, limpidissimo.
pellucidity [pelu:'siditi], *n.* Trasparenza, chiarezza, *f.*
pelmet ['pelmet], *n.* Pendaglio al di sopra delle tende, *m.*
Peloponnesian [pelɔpə'ni:ʒən], *a.* Peloponnesiaco.

pelt (1), *v.t.i.* Assalire a colpi, battere. **To — with stones,** lapidare; **the rain is pelting down,** piove dirottamente; **at full —,** a gambe levate; **pelting rain,** pioggia a secchie, pioggia a catinelle, *f.*

pelt (2), *n.* Pelliccia, pelle greggia, *f.*; pelle col pelo, *f.*

peltry, *n.* Pelliccie, *f.pl.*, pelleteria, *f.*

pelvic [ˈpelvik], *a.* (*Anat.*) Pelvico. **— girdle,** cintura pelvica, *f.*

pelvis, *n.* (*Anat.*) Pelvi, *f.*

pemmican [ˈpemikən], *n.* Pemmican, *m.*, carne seccata, *f.*

pen (1) [pen], *n.* Chiuso, recinto, *m.*; (*for sheep*) ovile, *m.*; (*for fowls*) pollaio, *m.* ‖ *v.t.* Chiudere. **To — in,** rinchiudere.

pen (2), *n.* Penna, *f.* ‖ *v.t.* Scrivere; comporre. **— -and-ink drawing,** schizzo a penna, *m.*; **— -holder,** portapenne, cannello, *m.*; **— -wiper,** nettapenne, *m.*; **fountain —,** penna stilografica, *f.*; **quill —,** penna d'oca, *f.*; **— -name,** pseudonimo, *m.*

penal [ˈpiːnəl], *a.* Penale. **— servitude,** lavori forzati, *m.pl.*

penalization, *n.* Penalizzazione, *f.*

penalize [ˈpiːnəlaiz], *v.t.* Punire, esigere una pena.

penalty [ˈpenəlti], *n.* Pena, *f.*; penalità, multa, *f.*; (*fig.*) svantaggio, *m.* **To pay the —,** pagare la pena, pagare il fio; (*Comm.*) **— clause,** clausola penale, *f.* (*Football*) **— -kick,** calcio di rigore, *m.*

penance [ˈpenəns], *n.* Penitenza, *f.* **To do —,** far penitenza.

penates [peˈneitiːz], *n.pl.* (*Myth.*) Penati, *m.pl.*

pence [pens], *n.pl.* Denari, *m.pl.* [cp. **penny**].

pencil [ˈpensəl], *n.* Lapis, *m.*, matita, *f.*; (*of rays*) fascio, *m.* ‖ *v.t.* Scrivere a matita; disegnare a matita, tratteggiare. **Drawing- —,** matita da disegno, *f.*; **— -case,** portalapis, portamatite, *m.*; **— -sharpener,** temperalapis, taglialapis, *m.*; **pencilled eyebrows,** sopracciglia dipinte, *f.pl.*

pendant [ˈpendənt], *n.* Pendente, pendaglio, *m.*; orecchino, *m.*; (*Naut.*) fiamma, banderuola, *f.* ‖ *a.* Pendente; sospeso; indeciso.

pendency [ˈpendənsi], *n.* (*Law*) Pendenza, *f.*

pending, *a.* Pendente, indeciso, non risolto. ‖ *prep.* Durante, in attesa di.

pendulous [ˈpendjuːləs], *a.* Pendulo, pendente, sospeso.

pendulum [ˈpendjuːləm], *n.* Pendolo, *m.* **The swing of the —,** il moto del pendolo, *m.*; **— clock,** pendola, *f.*

penetrability [penetrəˈbiliti], *n.* Penetrabilità, *f.*

penetrable, *a.* Penetrabile.

penetralia, *n.pl.* Penetrali, *m.pl.*

penetrate, *v.t.i.* Penetrare.

penetrating, *a.* Penetrante.

penetration, *n.* Penetrazione, *f.*

penful, *n.* Pennata, *f.*

penguin [ˈpengwin], *n.* (*Zool.*) Pinguino, *m.*

penicillin [peniˈsilin], *n.* Penicillina, *f.*

peninsula [peˈninsjuːlə], *n.* (*Geog.*) Penisola, *f.*

peninsular, *a.* Peninsulare.

penitence [ˈpenitəns], *n.* Penitenza, *f.*, pentimento, *m.*

penitent, *n.a.* Penitente, *m.f.*

penitential [peniˈtenʃəl], *a.* Penitenziale.

penitentiary [peniˈtenʃəri], *n.* (*prison*) Penitenziario, *m.*; (*Eccles.*) penitenziere, *m.* ‖ *a.* Penitenziario.

penitently, *adv.* Penitentemente.

penknife [ˈpennaif], *n.* Temperino, *m.*

penman, *n.* Calligrafo, *m.*

penmanship, *n.* Calligrafia, *f.*

pennant [ˈpenənt], *n.* Orifiamma, banderuola, *f.*; pennone, *m.*

penniform [ˈpenifɔːɹm], *a.* (*Zool.Bot.*) Penniforme.

penniless [ˈpeniles], *a.* Senza un soldo, senza quattrini, spiantato, povero, indigente.

pennon [ˈpenən], *n.* Pennone, *m.*, orifiamma, *f.*

Pennsylvania [pensilˈveiniə], *n.* (*Geog.*) Pensilvania, *f.*

penny (*pl.* **pennies, pence**) [ˈpeni, ˈpeniz, pens], *n.* Penny, *m.*, due soldi, *m.pl.*; denaro, soldo, *m.* **To turn an honest —,** guadagnarsi il pane; **a pretty —,** un prezzo salato, *m.*; **— -a-liner,** scrittorello, *m.*; **— -in-the-slot-machine,** macchina automatica, *f.*; **— -dreadful,** romanzo da due soldi, *m.*; **to be — -wise,** badare al soldo.

pennyroyal [peniˈrɔiəl], *n.* (*Bot.*) Puleggio, *m.*

pennyweight [ˈpeniweit], *n.* Peso di $1\frac{1}{2}$ grammi.

pennywort, *n.* (*Bot.*) Cotiledone, *m.*

pennyworth [ˈpeniwəɹθ, ˈpenəθ], *n.* Due soldi, *m.pl.*, pel valore di due soldi. **A — of sweets,** un soldo di caramelle, *m.*

pensile [ˈpensail], *a.* Pensile, sospeso.

pension [ˈpenʃən], *n.* Pensione, *f.* ‖ *v.t.* Pensionare. **Old-age —,** pensione per la vecchiaia, *f.*; **to — off,** giubilare, mettere in ritiro *or* in pensione.

pensioner, *n.* Pensionario, pensionato, *m.*; (*Mil.*) invalido, *m.*

pensive [ˈpensiv], *a.* Pensieroso, cogitabondo, soprappensiero.

pensively, *adv.* Pensierosamente.

pensiveness, *n.* Pensosità, *f.*

penstock, *n.* (*of sluice*) Chiusa, *f.*

pent [pent], *a.* Rinchiuso; rattenuto. **— -up feelings,** sentimenti repressi, *m.pl.*

pentagon [ˈpentəgən], *n.* Pentagono, *m.*

pentagonal, *a.* Pentagonale.

pentagram, *n.* Pentagramma, *m.*

pentameter [penˈtæmitəɹ], *n.* (*Poet.*) Pentametro, *m.*

Pentateuch [ˈpentətjuːk], *n.* Pentateuco, *m.*

Pentecost [ˈpentikɔst], *n.* (*Eccles.*) Pentecoste, *f.*

pentecostal, *a.* Della Pentecoste.

penthouse [ˈpenthaus], *n.* Tettoia, *f.*

penultimate [peˈnʌltimit], *a.* Penultimo. ‖ *n.* Penultima, *f.*

penumbra [peˈnʌmbrə], *n.* (*Astron.*) Penombra, *f.*

penurious [peˈnjuːriəs], *a.* Parsimonioso, gretto, avaro, meschino; povero indigente; scarso.

penury [ˈpenjuːri], *n.* Penuria, indigenza, *f.*; scarsità, *f.*

peony [ˈpiːəni], *n.* (*Bot.*) Peonia, *f.*

people [ˈpiːpəl], *n.* Popolo, *m.*, razza, nazione, gente, *f.*; (*the crowd*) folla, moltitudine, *f.*; (*relatives*) famiglia, *f.*, parenti, *m.pl.*; persone, *f.pl.* ‖ *v.t.* Popolare. **His —,** i suoi, *m.pl.*; **— say,** si dice; **many — say,** molti dicono; **the old —,** i vecchi, *m.pl.*; **they are good —,** sono buona gente.

pep [pep], *n.* (*colloq.*) Energia, *f.*, vigore, *m.*; entusiasmo, *m.*
pepper ['pepəɹ], *n.* Pepe, *m.* || *v.t.* Pepare; (*fig.*) assalire, crivellare. **— -box, — -caster,** pepaiuola, *f.*; **— -mill,** macinino da pepe, *m.*, pepaiuola, *f.*; **— -plant,** pepe, albero del pepe, *m.*
peppercorn, *n.* Granello di pepe, *m.*
peppermint, *n.* Menta peperina, *f.*; (*sweet*) pasticca di menta, *f.*, mentino, *m.*
peppery, *a.* Pepato, acre, pungente; (*fig.*) irascibile.
peppy, *a.* (*colloq.*) Pieno di energia.
pepsin ['pepsin], *n.* Pepsina, *f.*
per [pə:ɹ], *prep.* Per, per mezzo di, secondo. **— annum,** per anno, all'anno; **— cent,** per cento; **a shilling — man,** uno scellino a testa; (*Comm.*) **as — invoice,** come da fattura; **— contra,** in contropartita.
peradventure [pə:rəd'ventʃəɹ], *adv.* Forse, caso mai, per avventura. || *n.* Dubbio, *m.* **Beyond —,** fuor di dubbio.
perambulate [pə'ræmbju:leit], *v.t.* Girellare, girare, bighellonare, percorrere a piedi.
perambulation, *n.* Passeggiata, *f.*, giro, passeggio, *m.*
perambulator, pram [pə'ræmbju:leitəɹ, præm], *n.* Carrozzino, *m.*, carrozzella, *f.*
percale [pəɹ'keil], *n.* Percalle, *m.*
perceive [pəɹ'si:v], *v.t.* Percepire, apprendere; osservare, vedere, scorgere, scoprire; comprendere, capire.
percentage [pəɹ'sentidʒ], *n.* Percentuale, *f.*
perceptibility [pəɹsepti'biliti], *n.* Percettibilità, *f.*
perceptible, *a.* Percettibile, visibile, sensibile.
perceptibly, *adv.* Visibilmente.
perception [pəɹ'sepʃən], *n.* Percezione, nozione, concezione, *f.*; sensibilità, *f.*
perch (1) [pə:ɹtʃ], *n.* (*Zool.*) Pesce persico, *m.*
perch (2), *n.* (*for bird*) Posatoio, bastoncino, *m.*; (*measure of length*) pertica, *f.* || *v.i.* Appollaiarsi, collocarsi, posarsi.
perchance [pəɹ'tʃɑ:ns], *adv.* Forse, per caso.
percipient [pəɹ'sipiənt], *a.* Percettivo.
percolate ['pə:ɹkoleit], *v.t.i.* Filtrare, stillare, colare.
percolation, *n.* Filtrazione, *f.*
percolator, *n.* Filtro, colatoio, *m.*
percussion [pəɹ'kʌʃən], *n.* Percussione, *f.*; percossa, *f.* **— -cap,** capsula di percussione, spoletta, *f.*; (*Mus.*) **— instruments,** strumenti a percussione, *m.pl.*
percussive, *a.* Percussivo.
perdition [pəɹ'diʃən], *n.* Perdizione, rovina, *f.*, danno, *m.*
peregrinate ['perigrineit], *v.i.* Peregrinare, viaggiare.
peregrination, *n.* Peregrinazione, *f.*, viaggio, *m.*
peregrine falcon ['perigrin 'fælkən], *n.* (*Zool.*) Falcone pellegrino, *m.*
peremptorily, *adv.* Perentoriamente.
peremptoriness [pe'remptərinis], *n.* Perentorietà, imperiosità, *f.*
peremptory, *a.* Perentorio, decisivo, positivo.
perennial [pe'reniəl], *a.* Perenne; perpetuo, eterno; (*Bot.*) perenne. || *n.* (*Bot.*) Pianta perenne, *f.*
perennially, *adv.* Perennemente.
perfect ['pə:ɹfekt], *a.* Perfetto; compiuto, completo, intero. || *v.t.* Perfezionare, compire; terminare, finire. || *n.* (*Gram.*) Tempo perfetto, *m.* **A — stranger,** del tutto estraneo; **a — nuisance,** una vera seccatura, *f.*; (*Gram.*) **the — tense,** il passato perfetto, il passato remoto, *m.*
perfectibility, *n.* Perfezionabilità, *f.*
perfectible, *a.* Perfettibile.
perfection [pəɹ'fekʃən], *n.* Perfezione, *f.* **It succeeded to —,** è riuscito a perfezione.
perfectly, *adv.* Perfettamente.
perfectness, *n.* Perfezione, *f.*
perfervid [pəɹ'fə:ɹvid], *a.* Fervidissimo.
perfidious [pəɹ'fidiəs], *a.* Perfido.
perfidiously, *adv.* Perfidamente.
perfidiousness, perfidy [peɹ'fidiəsnis, 'pə:ɹfidi], *n.* Perfidia, *f.*
perforate ['pə:ɹforeit], *v.t.* Perforare, traforare, trapanare. **To — into,** penetrare in; (*Mech.*) **perforating-machine,** macchina perforatrice, *f.*
perforation, *n.* Perforazione, *f.*, foro, buco, *m.*
perforative, *a.* Perforante.
perforce [pəɹ'fɔ:ɹs], *adv.* Per forza, per necessità.
perform [pəɹ'fɔ:ɹm], *v.t.i.* Eseguire, compiere, effettuare; (*Theat.*) rappresentare, recitare; (*to fulfil*) adempiere; (*Mus.*) eseguire. **To — a promise,** adempiere una promessa; **to — on the piano,** suonare il pianoforte; **to — a sonata on the piano,** eseguire una sonata al pianoforte; **to — a part,** rappresentare una parte; **performing animals,** animali ammaestrati, *m.pl.*
performable, *a.* Eseguibile, effettuabile, praticabile.
performance, *n.* Esecuzione, effettuazione, *f.*, adempimento, *m.*; (*Theat.*) rappresentazione, *f.*; (*Cinema.*) spettacolo, *m.*; (*Sport*) forma, *f.*; (*deed*) atto, fatto, *m.*, azione, *f.*
performer, *n.* Esecutore, *m.*, esecutrice, *f.*; attore, *m.*, attrice, *f.*; artista, musicante, *m.f.*
perfume ['pə:ɹfju:m], *n.* Profumo, *m.*, fragranza, *f.*; olezzo, *m.* || *v.t.* Profumare.
perfumer, *n.* Profumiere, *m.*
perfumery, *n.* Profumeria, *f.*
perfunctoriness [pəɹ'fʌŋktərinis], *n.* Negligenza, superficialità, *f.*
perfunctory, *a.* Negligente, superficiale.
pergola ['pə:ɹgolə], *n.* Pergola, *f.*
perhaps [pəɹ'hæps, præps], *adv.* Forse, per caso, probabilmente, possibilmente. **— not,** forse no.
peri ['piəri], *n.* (*Myth.*) Fata, *f.*
perianth ['periænθ], *n.* (*Bot.*) Perianto, *m.*
pericardium [peri'kɑ:ɹdiəm], *n.* (*Anat.*) Pericardio, *m.*
pericarp ['perikɑ:ɹp], *n.* (*Bot.*) Pericarpio, *m.*
perigee ['peridʒi:], *n.* (*Astron.*) Perigeo, *m.*
perihelion [peri'hi:liən], *n.* (*Astron.*) Perielio, *m.*
peril ['peril], *n.* Pericolo, rischio, cimento, *m.* **In — of,** in pericolo di; **at your —,** a vostro rischio e pericolo.
perilous, *a.* Pericoloso, rischioso.
perilously, *adv.* Pericolosamente.
perilousness, *n.* Pericolo, rischio, *m.*
perimeter [pe'rimitəɹ], *n.* Perimetro, *m.*
perineum [peri'ni:əm], *n.* (*Anat.*) Perineo, *m.*

period [ˈpiəriəd], *n.* Periodo, *m.*; tempo, *m.*, epoca, *f.*; durata, *f.*; fine, *f.*, termine, *m.*; (*Gram.*) punto, *m.*; (*menses*) mestruo, *m.* **To put a — to,** porre fine a.
periodic [piəriˈɔdik], *a.* Periodico.
periodical, *a.* Periodico. || *n.* Periodico, giornale, *m.*, rivista, *f.*
peripatetic [peripəˈtetik], *n.a.* Peripatetico, *m.*
periphery [peˈrifəri], *n.* Periferia, *f.*
periphrasis (*pl.* **periphrases**) [peˈrifrəsis, peˈrifrəsi:z], *n.* Perifrasi, *f.*
periphrastic, *a.* Perifrastico, indiretto.
peripteral [peˈriptərəl], *a.* (*Arch.*) Perittero.
periscope [ˈperiskoup], *n.* Periscopio, *m.*
perish [ˈperiʃ], *v.i.* Perire, morire; deperire, deteriorare, guastarsi. **To be perished with cold,** morire dal freddo; **to — by the sword,** morire di spada; **to — with hunger,** sentirsi morir di fame; **Perish the thought!** Via questo brutto pensiero!
perishable, *a.* Deperibile. **— goods,** merci deperibili, *m.pl.*
perishing, *n.* Deperimento, *m.* || *a.* Assiderante.
peristaltic [periˈstæltik], *a.* (*Anat.*) Peristaltico.
peristyle [ˈperistail], *n.* (*Arch.*) Peristilio, *m.*
peritoneum [peritoˈni:əm], *n.* (*Anat.*) Peritoneo, *m.*
peritonitis [peritoˈnaitis], *n.* Peritonite, *f.*
periwig [ˈperiwig], *n.* Parrucca, *f.*
periwinkle [ˈperiwiŋkəl], *n.* (*Bot.*) Pervinca, *f.*; (*Zool.*) littorina, *f.*
perjure [ˈpə:ɹdʒəɹ], *v.r.* Spergiurare, giurare il falso.
perjured, *p.p.a.* Spergiuro, spergiurato.
perjurer, *n.* Spergiuratore, spergiuro, *m.*
perjury, *n.* Spergiuramento, *m.*; mendacio, *m.*
perk [pə:ɹk], *v.t.i.* **To — up,** sollevare, innalzare, buttarsi avanti.
perkily, *adv.* Insolentemente, con aria disinvolta.
perky, *a.* Sfacciatello, impertinente; vivace; civettuolo.
perm [pə:ɹm], *v.t.* (*colloq.*) Fare la permanente. || *n.* La permanente, *f.* **She had her hair permed,** si fece fare la permanente.
permanence, permanency [ˈpə:ɹmənəns, ˈpə:ɹmənənsi], *n.* Permanenza, *f.*; (*situation*) posto fisso, *m.*
permanent, *a.* Permanente, stabile, durevole. (*Rail.*) **— way,** via rotabile, *f.*, rotaie, *f.pl.*; **— wave, perm,** ondulazione permanente, *f.*
permanently, *adv.* Permanentemente, in permanenza.
permanganate [pəɹˈmæŋgəneit], *n.* Permanganato, *m.*
permeability [pə:ɹmiəˈbiliti], *n.* Permeabilità, *f.*
permeable [ˈpə:ɹmiəbl], *a.* Permeabile, penetrabile.
permeate, *v.t.* Permeare, penetrare.
permeation, *n.* Penetrazione, *f.*
permissible [pəɹˈmisibl], *a.* Permissibile.
permissibly, *adv.* Permissibilmente.
permission [pəɹˈmiʃən], *n.* Permesso, *m.*, licenza, *f.*
permissive, *a.* Permissivo.
permit [ˈpə:ɹmit], *n.* Permesso, *m.*, licenza, *f.*; lasciapassare, *m.* || *v.t.* [pəɹˈmit], Permettere, lasciare, concedere a; soffrire; tollerare. **— me to say,** permetta che io dica; **it does not — of alteration,** non permette cambiamento.
permutation [pə:ɹmju:ˈteiʃən], *n.* Permutazione, *f.*
permute [pəɹˈmju:t], *v.t.* Permutare.
pernicious [pəɹˈniʃəs], *a.* Pernicioso, malefico, funesto, dannoso.
perniciously, *adv.* Perniciosamente.
perniciousness, *n.* Perniciosità, dannosità, *f.*
perorate [ˈperoreit], *v.i.* Perorare.
peroration [perəˈreiʃən], *n.* Perorazione, *f.*
peroxide [pəˈrɔksaid], *n.* (*Chem.*) Perossido, *m.*
perpendicular [pə:ɹpənˈdikju:ləɹ], *n.a.* Perpendicolare, *f.*
perpendicularity, *n.* Perpendicolarità, *f.*
perpendicularly, *adv.* Perpendicolarmente.
perpetrate [ˈpə:ɹpetreit], *v.t.* Perpetrare, commettere.
perpetration, *n.* Perpetrazione, *f.*
perpetrator, *n.* Autore, *m.*
perpetual [pəɹˈpetju:əl], *a.* Perpetuo, continuo, incessante.
perpetually, *adv.* Perpetuamente, continuamente.
perpetuate [pəɹˈpetju:eit], *v.t.* Perpetuare, eternare.
perpetuation, *n.* Perpetuazione, *f.*
perpetuity [pə:ɹpiˈtju:iti], *n.* Perpetuità, *f.* **In —,** in perpetuo.
perplex [pəɹˈpleks], *v.t.* Confondere, sbalordire, imbarazzare; imbrogliare.
perplexed, *a.* Perplesso, incerto.
perplexing, *a.* Imbarazzante.
perplexity, *n.* Perplessità, irresoluzione, *f.*, imbarazzo, *m.*
perquisite [ˈpə:ɹkwizit], *n.* Gratificazione, *f.*, emolumento casuale, *m.*; mancia, *f.*; spettanze, *f.pl.*
perroquet [cp. **parakeet**].
persecute [ˈpə:ɹsikju:t], *v.t.* Perseguitare, vessare, molestare; (*fig.*) importunare.
persecution, *n.* Persecuzione, *f.*
persecutor, *n.* Persecutore, *m.*, persecutrice, *f.*
perseverance [pəɹseˈviərəns], *n.* Perseveranza, *f.*
persevere [pəɹseˈviəɹ], *v.i.* Perseverare.
persevering, *a.* Perseverante.
perseveringly, *adv.* Perseverantemente.
Persian [ˈpə:ɹʃən], *n.a.* Persiano, *m.* **— blind,** persiana, gelosia, *f.*; **— carpet,** tappeto persiano, *m.*; **— cat,** gatto persiano, gatto d'angora, *m.*; (*Geog.*) **Persian Gulf,** Golfo Persico.
persicaria [pəɹsiˈkɛəriə], *n.* (*Bot.*) Persicaria, *f.*
persiflage [ˈpə:ɹsiflɑ:ʒ], *n.* Facezie, burlette, *f.pl.*, ironia, *f.* **A piece of —,** una spiritosaggine, *f.*
persist [pəɹˈsist], *v.i.* Persistere; perseverare; ostinarsi. **He persists in saying that,** persiste a dire che; **to — in an opinion,** persistere in un opinione.
persistence, persistency, *n.* Persistenza, *f.*
persistent, *a.* Persistente, tenace, caparbio.
persistently, *adv.* Persistentemente.
person [ˈpə:ɹsən], *n.* Persona, *f.*; figura, *f.* **I know no such —,** non conosco tale persona; **in —,** in persona; **in the third —,** in terza persona; **to address in the second — singular,** dare del tu a; **a — of independent means,** una persona abbiente, *f.*

personable, *a.* Bello, ben fatto.
personage, *n.* Personaggio, *m.*
personal, *a.* Personale. — **property,** beni mobili, *m.pl.*; proprietà personale, *f.*
personality [pəːɹsəˈnæliti], *n.* Personalità, *f.*
personalization, *n.* Personificazione, *f.*
personally, *adv.* Personalmente.
personalty, *n.* (*Law*) Beni mobili, *m.pl.*
personate [ˈpəːɹsəneit], *v.t.* Personificare; impersonare; (*for fraudulent purposes*) spacciarsi per.
personation, *n.* Personificazione, *f.*
personator, *n.* Impersonatore, *m.*, impersonatrice, *f.*
personification, *n.* Personificazione, *f.*
personify [pəɹˈsɔnifai], *v.t.* Personificare.
personnel [pəːɹsəˈnel], *n.* Personale, *m.*
perspective [pəɹˈspektiv], *n.* Prospettiva, *f.*; scorcio, *m.*, veduta, *f.* || *a.* Prospettivo. — **glass,** cannocchiale, *m.*; **in —,** in prospettiva, in scorcio.
perspicacious [pəːɹspiˈkeiʃəs], *a.* Perspicace, acuto, chiaroveggente, sagace, scaltro.
perspicaciously, *adv.* Perspicacemente.
perspicacity [pəːɹspiˈkæsiti], *n.* Perspicacia, acutezza, sagacia, *f.*
perspicuity, perspicuousness [pəːɹspiˈkjuːiti, pəɹsˈpikjuːəsnes], *n.* Perspicuità, *f.*; chiarezza, *f.*
perspicuous [pəɹsˈpikjuːəs], *a.* Perspicuo, evidente, chiaro.
perspicuously, *adv.* Perspicuamente.
perspiration [pəːɹspəˈreiʃən], *n.* Sudore, *m.*, traspirazione, *f.* **To be bathed in —,** essere madido di sudore.
perspire [pəɹsˈpaiɹ], *v.i.* Sudare, traspirare.
persuadable [pəɹˈsweidəbəl], *a.* Persuadibile, persuasibile.
persuade [pəɹˈsweid], *v.t.* Persuadere, indurre. **We persuaded him to come,** lo persuademmo a venire; **to — oneself,** persuadersi.
persuasible [pəɹˈsweizibəl], *a.* Persuasibile.
persuasion [pəɹˈsweiʒən], *n.* Persuasione, *f.*; (*creed*) setta, *f.*
persuasive, *a.* Persuasivo.
persuasively, *adv.* Persuasivamente.
persuasiveness, *n.* Persuasività, *f.*
pert [pəːɹt], *a.* Impudente, sfacciato, insolente.
pertly, *adv.* Impudentemente, insolentemente.
pertain [pəɹˈtein], *v.i.* Appartenere; riguardare, concernere.
pertinacious [pəɹtiˈneiʃəs], *a.* Pertinace, ostinato, caparbio.
pertinaciously, *adv.* Ostinatamente.
pertinaciousness, pertinacity, *n.* Pertinacia, ostinazione, caparbietà, *f.*
pertinence, pertinency [ˈpəːɹtinəns, ˈpəːɹtinənsi], *n.* Pertinenza, *f.*
pertinent, *a.* Pertinente, relativo.
pertness, *n.* Impertinenza, *f.*; vivacità, *f.*
perturb [pəɹˈtəːɹb], *v.t.* Perturbare, turbare, confondere, sconcertare, agitare.
perturbation [pəːɹtəɹˈbeiʃən], *n.* Perturbazione, confusione, agitazione, *f.*, turbamento, *m.*
perturbed, *a.* Turbato, confuso, agitato.
Peru [pəˈruː], *n.* (*Geog.*) Perù, *m.*
peruke [pəˈruːk], *n.* Parrucca, *f.*
perusal [pəˈruːzəl], *n.* Lettura, *f.*, esame, *m.*
peruse [pəˈruːz], *v.t.* Leggere; esaminare.
Peruvian [pəˈruːviən], *n.a.* Peruviano, *m.* — **bark,** china, *f.*
pervade [pəɹˈveid], *v.t.* Pervadere, penetrare in; diffondersi in, spargersi per.
pervasion, *n.* Penetrazione, diffusione, *f.*
pervasive, *a.* Penetrante, diffuso.
pervasiveness, *n.* Diffusione, *f.*
perverse [pəɹˈvəːɹs], *a.* Perverso; cattivo, reo, malvagio.
perverseness, perversity, *n.* Perversità, cattiveria, malvagità, *f.*
perversion, *n.* Perversione, *f.*, pervertimento, *m.*
pervert [pəɹˈvəːɹt], *v.t.* Pervertire, guastare, corrompere, depravare. || *n.* [ˈpəːɹvəɹt] Pervertito, apostata, *m.*
perverter, *n.* Pervertitore, corruttore, *m.*
pervious [ˈpəːɹviəs], *a.* Accessibile, aperto, pervio, permeabile.
perviousness, *n.* Penetrabilità, permeabilità, accessibilità, *f.*
pessary [ˈpesəri], *n.* (*Med.*) Pessario, *m.*
pessimism [ˈpesimizm], *n.* Pessimismo, *m.*
pessimist, *n.* Pessimista, *m.f.*
pessimistic, *a.* Pessimistico.
pessimistically, *adv.* Pessimisticamente.
pest [pest], *n.* Peste, pestilenza, *f.*; (*fig.*) flagello, *m.*; seccatura, noia, *f.*
pester [ˈpestəɹ], *v.t.* Tormentare, annoiare, molestare, seccare, importunare.
pestiferous [pesˈtifərəs], *a.* Pestifero; noioso, molesto.
pestilence [ˈpestiləns], *n.* Peste, pestilenza, *f.*
pestilent, *a.* Pestilente, pernicioso, nocivo; noioso, molesto.
pestilential [pestiˈlenʃəl], *a.* Pestilenziale, pernicioso, nocivo.
pestle [ˈpestəl], *n.* Pestello, *m.* || *v.t.* Pestare.
pet (1) [pet], *n.* Favorito, *m.*, favorita, *f.*, beniamino, *m.*; animale favorito, *m.* || *a.* Favorito, preferito, prediletto. || *v.t.* Accarezzare, viziare, coccolare. **My little —!** Cocco mio! **a — lamb,** un agnellino, *m.*; **a — name,** un nomignolo, *m.*; **— argument,** argomento prediletto, *m.*; **— aversion,** antipatia, *f.*; **— theory,** fissazione, *f.*
pet (2), *n.* Stizza, *f.*, accesso di malumore, *m.* **To be in a —,** essere stizzito, essere arrabbiato.
petal [ˈpetəl], *n.* Petalo, *m.*
petard [peˈtɑːɹd], *n.* (*Mil.*) Petardo, *m.* **To be hoist with one's own —,** darsi la zappa sui piedi.
Peter [ˈpiːtəɹ], *n.* Pietro, *m.* **Peter's Pence,** l'obolo di San Pietro, *m.*
petiole [ˈpetioul], *n.* (*Bot.*) Picciuolo, *m.*
petite [pəˈtiːt], *a.* Piccolina, carina.
petition [pəˈtiʃən], *n.* Petizione, domanda, istanza, supplica, preghiera, *f.*; ricorso, *m.* || *v.t.* Supplicare, domandare, sollecitare, rivolgere un'istanza, presentare una petizione.
petitionary, *a.* Supplicante.
petitioner, *n.* Supplicante, richiedente, postulante, *m.f.*
petrel [ˈpetrəl], *n.* (*Zool.*) Procellaria, *f.*
petrifaction [petriˈfækʃən], *n.* Pietrificazione, *f.*
petrify, *v.t.* Pietrificare; (*fig.*) stupefare, stupire, sbalordire.

petrography [pe'trɔgrəfi], *n.* Pietrografia, *f.*
petrol ['petrəl], *n.* Petrolio, *m.*; (*for motors*) benzina, *f.* — **tank**, serbatoio di benzina, *m.*; — **tin**, bidone da benzina, *m.*
petroleum [pe'trouliəm], *n.* Petrolio, *m.*
petrous ['petrəs], *a.* Pietroso, lapideo.
petticoat ['petikout], *n.* Gonnella, sottana, *f.*; sottoveste, *f.* — **government**, regime muliebre, governo delle donne, *m.*
pettifogger ['petifɔgəɹ], *n.* Leguleio, causidico, mozzorecchi, azzeccagarbugli, *m.*
pettifoggery, *n.* Sofisticheria, *f.*, cavilli, *m.pl.*, litigiosità, *f.*
pettifogging, *a.* Cavilloso, sofistico.
pettiness, *n.* Piccolezza, meschinità, *f.*
pettish, *a.* Irritabile, permaloso, di cattivo umore.
pettishly, *adv.* Di cattivo umore, lunatico.
pettishness, *n.* Irritabilità, permalosità, *f.*
pettitoes ['petitouz], *n.pl.* Piedi di porco, *m.pl.*
petty ['peti], *a.* Piccolo, di poca importanza, insignificante; meschino, gretto, triviale. — **cash**, spese minute, *f.pl.*; — **jury**, giuria ordinaria, *f.*; — **prince**, principotto, *m.*; — **officer**, sottufficiale di marina, *m.*
petulance ['petju:ləns], *n.* Petulanza, irritabilità, *f.*
petulant, *a.* Petulante, capriccioso, irritabile.
petunia [pe'tju:niə], *n.* (*Bot.*) Petunia, *f.*
pew [pju:], *n.* Panca di chiesa, *f.*
pewit, peewit ['pi:wit], *n.* (*Zool.*) Pavoncella, fifa, *f.*
pewter ['pju:təɹ], *n.* Peltro, *m.* — **pot**, vaso di peltro, *m.*
pewterer, *n.* Stagnaio, *m.*
phaeton ['feitən], *n.* Carrozza scoperta a quattro ruote, *f.*, carrozzino, *m.*
phagocyte ['fægosait], *n.* Fagocito, *m.*
phalange ['fælændʒ], *n.* (*Anat.*) Falange, *f.*
phalanger ['fælændʒəɹ], *n.* (*Zool.*) Falangista, *f.*
phalanstery [fə'lænstəri], *n.* Falansterio, *m.*
phalanx ['fælæŋks], *n.* Falange, *f.*
phallic ['fælik], *a.* Fallico.
phallus, *n.* Fallo, *m.*
Phanariot [fə'næriət], *n.* (*Hist.*) Fanariota, *m.*
phantasm ['fæntæzm], *n.* Fantasma, spettro, *m.*, visione, illusione, *f.*
phantasmagoria [fæntæzmə'gɔ:riə], *n.* Fantasmagoria, *f.*
phantasmagorical, *a.* Fantasmagorico.
phantasmal [fæn'tæzməl], *a.* Spettrale, fantasmagorico.
phantasy ['fæntəzi], *n.* Fantasia, *f.*
phantom ['fæntəm], *n.* Fantasma, spettro, *m.*, larva, ombra, *f.*; apparizione, *f.* ‖ *a.* Spettrale, irreale; fantastico.
Pharaoh ['fɛərou], *n.* (*Hist.*) Faraone, *m.*
Pharaonic, *a.* Faraonico.
pharisaic, pharisaical [færi'zeiik], *a.* Farisaico.
Pharisee ['færisi:], *n.* Fariseo, *m.*
pharmaceutical [fɑ:ɹmə'sju:tikəl], *a.* Farmaceutico.
pharmaceutics, *n.pl.* Farmaceutica, *f.*
pharmacist, *n.* Farmacista, *m.f.*
pharmacologist, *n.* Farmacologo, *m.*
pharmacology, *n.* Farmacologia, *f.*
pharmacopoeia [fɑ:ɹməkə'pi:ə], *n.* Farmacopea, *f.*
pharmacy, *n.* Farmacia, *f.*
Pharos ['fɛərɔs], *n.* Faro, *m.*
pharyngitis [færin'dʒaitis], *n.* (*Med.*) Faringite, *f.*
pharynx ['færiŋks], *n.* (*Anat.*) Faringe, *f.*
phase [feiz], *n.* Fase, *f.*, aspetto, *m.* **The phases of the moon**, le fasi della luna, *f.pl.*
pheasant ['fezənt], *n.* (*Zool.*) Fagiano, *m.* **Hen-** —, fagiana, *f.*; **young** —, fagianotto, *m.*; — **-shooting**, caccia al fagiano, *f.*
pheasantry, *n.* Fagianaia, *f.*
phenacetin [fe'næsitin], *n.* (*Chem.*) Fenacetina, *f.*
phenol ['fenɔl], *n.* (*Chem.*) Fenolo, *m.*
phenology [fe'nɔlədʒi], *n.* Fenologia, *f.*
phenomenal [fe'nɔminəl], *a.* Fenomenale.
phenominalism, *n.* Fenomenalismo, *m.*
phenomenon (*pl.* **phenomena**) [fe'nɔmenɔn, fe'nɔmenə], *n.* Fenomeno, *m.*
phenyl ['fenil], *n.* (*Chem.*) Fenile, *m.*
phial ['fail], *n.* Fiala, *f.*; boccetta, *f.*
Phidias ['fidiæs], *n.* (*Hist.*) Fidia, *m.*
Philadelphia [filə'delfiə], *n.* (*Geog.*) Filadelfia, *f.*
philander [fi'lændəɹ], *v.i.* Civettare, fare il galante.
philanderer, *n.* Donnaiuolo, damerino, galante, *m.*
philanthropic, philanthropical [filən'θrɔpik, filən'θrɔpikəl], *a.* Filantropico.
philanthropist, *n.* Filantropo, *m.*, filantropa, *f.*
philanthropy, *n.* Filantropia, *f.*
philatelic [filə'telik], *a.* Filatelico.
philatelist [fi'lætəlist], *n.* Filatelico, *m.*, filatelica, *f.*
philately, *n.* Filatelia, filatelica, *f.*
philharmonic [filhɑ:ɹ'mɔnik], *a.* Filarmonico.
Philhellene ['filheli:n], *n.* Filelleno, *m.*
Philhellenism, *n.* Filellenismo, *m.*
philippic [fi'lipik], *n.* Filippica, *f.*
Philistine ['filistain], *n.* (*in all senses*) Filisteo, *m.*
philological [filo'lɔdʒikəl], *a.* Filologico.
philologist [fi'lɔlədʒist], *n.* Filologo, *m.*
philology, *n.* Filologia, *f.*
Philomel, Philomela ['filomel, filo'melə], *n.* Filomela, *f.*; usignuolo, *m.*
philoprogenitive [failopro'dʒenitiv], *a.* Prolifero.
philosopher [fi'lɔsəfəɹ], *n.* Filosofo, *m.* **Natural** —, naturalista, *m.*; **philosopher's stone**, pietra filosofale, *f.*; **doctor of** —, dottore in filosofia, *m.*
philosophical [filo'sɔfikəl], *a.* Filosofico; calmo, temperato.
philosophically, *adv.* Calmamente.
philosophize [fi'lɔsəfaiz], *v.i.* Filosofare.
philosophy [fi'lɔsəfi], *n.* Filosofia, *f.* **Natural** —, fisica, *f.*
philotechnic [failo'teknik], *a.* Filotecnico.
philtre, philter ['filtəɹ], *n.* Filtro, *m.*
phiz [fiz], *n.* (*colloq.*) Fisonomia, faccia, *f.*
phlebitis [fle'baitis], *n.* (*Med.*) Flebite, *f.*
phlebotomist [fle'bɔtəmist], *n.* Flebotomo, salassatore, *m.*
phlebotomy, *n.* Flebotomia, *f.*
phlegm [flem], *n.* Muco, *m.*; (*characteristic*) flemma, *f.*, sangue freddo, *m.*
phlegmatic [fleg'mætik], *a.* Flemmatico; tardo, calmo, freddo. — **disposition**, temperamento flemmatico, *m.*

phlegmon [ˈflegmɔn], *n.* (*Med.*) Flemmone, *m.*
phlogistic [floˈdʒistik], *a.* (*Med.*) Flogistico.
phlogiston, *n.* Flogisto, *m.*
phlox [flɔks], *n.* (*Bot.*) Flos, *m.*, flosside, *f.*
Phocian [ˈfouʃən], *a.* Focese.
Phoebus [ˈfiːbəs], *n.* (*Myth.*) Febo, *m.*; il sole, *m.*
Phoenician [fiˈniːʃən], *n.a.* Fenicio, *m.*
phoenix [ˈfiːniks], *n.* Fenice, *f.*
phone [foun], *n.* (*colloq.*) Telefono, *m.* || *v.t.i.* Telefonare.
phonetic [foˈnetik], *a.* Fonetico.
phonetics, *n.pl.* Fonetica, *f.*
phonogram [ˈfounogræm], *n.* Fonogramma, *m.*
phonograph [ˈfounogræf], *n.* Fonografo, *m.*
phonographic, *a.* Fonografico.
phonography, *n.* Fonografia, *f.*
phonology, *n.* Fonologia, *f.*
phosphate [ˈfɔsfeit], *n.* (*Chem.*) Fosfato, *m.*
phosphite [ˈfɔsfait], *n.* (*Chem.*) Fosfito, *m.*
phosphoresce [fɔsfəˈres], *v.i.* Fosforeggiare.
phosphorescence, *n.* Fosforescenza, *f.*
phosphorescent, *a.* Fosforescente.
phosphoric, *a.* Fosforico.
phosphorism, *n.* (*Med.*) Fosforismo, *m.*
phosphorous, *a.* Fosforoso.
phosphorus, *n.* Fosforo, *m.*
phosphuretted, *a.* Fosforato.
photograph [ˈfoutogræf], *n.* Fotografia, *f.* || *v.t.* Fotografare. **I always — badly,** non mi riesce di fotografare bene; **—frame,** cornice, *f.*
photographer [foˈtɔgræfəɹ], *n.* Fotografo, *m.*
photographic [fotoˈgræfik], *a.* Fotografico.
photography, *n.* Fotografia, *f.*
photogravure [fotogrəˈvjuːɹ], *n.* Fotoincisione, *f.*
photolithography [fotoliθˈɔgrəfi], *n.* Fotolitografia, *f.*
photometer [foˈtɔmetəɹ], *n.* Fotometro, *m.*
phrase [freiz], *n.* Frase, locuzione, *f.*; modo di dire, *m.* (*Mus.*) frase, *f.* || *v.t.* Esprimere, formulare, dire; (*Mus.*) fraseggiare. **Set phrases,** frasi fatte, *f.pl.*
phraseology [freiziˈɔlədʒi], *n.* Fraseologia, *f.*
phrenetic [freˈnetik], *a.* Frenetico, furioso, folle.
phrenic, *a.* (*Anat.*) Frenico.
phrenological [frenoˈlɔdʒikəl], *a.* Frenologico.
phrenologist [freˈnɔlədʒist], *n.* Frenologo, *m.*
phrenology, *n.* Frenologia, *f.*
Phrygia [ˈfridʒiə], *n.* (*Geog.*) Frigia, *f.*
Phrygian, *a.* Frigio. **— cap,** berretto frigio, *m.*
phthisical [ˈθizikəl, ˈfθizikəl], *a.* (*Med.*) Tisico, etico.
phthisis [ˈθaisis, ˈfθaisis], *n.* (*Med.*) Tisi, etisia, *f.*
phut [fʌt](*slang*) **To go —,** Avere un collasso, finire subitamente.
phylactery [fiˈlæktəri], *n.* Filatterio, *m.*
phylloxera [fiˈlɔksərə, filɔkˈsiːrə], *n.* (*Agric.*) Fillossera, *f.*
physic [ˈfizik], *n.* Medicina, *f.*, medicamento, farmaco, *m.*; (*fig.*) rimedio, *m.* || *v.t.* Dare una medicina.
physical, *a.* Fisico.
physically, *adv.* Fisicamente.
physician [fiˈziʃən], *n.* Medico, *m.*
physicism [ˈfizisizm], *n.* Materialismo, naturalismo, *m.*
physicist, *n.* Fisico, *m.*; materialista, *m.*
physics, *n.pl.* Fisica, *f.*
physiognomic [fizioˈnɔmik], *a.* Fisionomico.
physiognomist [fiziˈɔnəmist], *n.* Fisionomista, *m.*
physiognomy [fiziˈɔnəmi], *n.* Fisionomia, *f.*; faccia, *f.*, viso, *m.*
physiographical [fizioˈgræfikəl], *a.* Fisiografico.
physiographer [fiziˈɔgrəfəɹ], *n.* Fisiografo, *m.*
physiological [fizioˈlɔdʒikəl], *a.* Fisiologico.
physiologist [fiziˈɔlədʒist], *n.* Fisiologo, *m.*
physiology, *n.* Fisiologia, *f.*
physique [fiˈziːk], *n.* Fisico, *m.*, costituzione, *f.*
pia mater [ˈpaiə ˈmeitəɹ], *n.* (*Anat.*) Pia madre, *f.*
pianist [ˈpiːənist], *n.* Pianista, *m.f.*
piano, pianoforte [piˈænou, piænoˈfɔːɹte], *n.* Pianoforte, *m.* **Grand piano,** pianoforte a coda, *m.*; **cottage piano, upright —,** pianoforte verticale, *m.*; **— string,** corda del pianoforte, *f.*; **piano-player,** pianoforte meccanico, *m.*; **to play the piano,** suonare il pianoforte; **piano-tuner,** accordatore, *m.*
piastre [piˈæstəɹ], *n.* Piastra, *f.*
piazza [piˈætzə], *n.* Veranda, *f.*, piazza, *f.*
pibroch [ˈpiːbrɔk], *n.* (*Mus.*) Specie di cornamusa.
pica [ˈpaikə], *n.* (*Print.*) Pica, *f.*, paragone, *m.*
picaresque [pikəˈresk], *a.* Picaresco.
picaroon [pikəˈruːn], *n.* Manigoldo, furfante, *m.*; pirata, *m.*
piccaninny[ˈpikənini], *n.*(*off.*) Bambino negro.
piccolo [ˈpikolou], *n.* (*Mus.*) Ottavino, *m.*
pick [pik], *n.* (*tool*) Piccone, *m.*; (*choice*) scelta, *f.*; il fiore, *m.* || *v.t.i.* (*with tool*) Picconare, scavare; (*the teeth*) stuzzicare; (*a bone*) pulire; (*to gather*) cogliere; (*to select*) scegliere; (*a lock*) aprire, scassinare; (*a quarrel*) cercare contesa; (*fruit*) piluccare, cogliere. (*fig.*) **To — holes in,** criticare; **to — one's way,** camminare con cautela; **to — a quarrel,** attaccar lite; **to — a pocket,** borseggiare; **to — to pieces,** fare a pezzi; **to — off,** spiccare; **to — out,** scegliere, trascegliere; **to — out a tune,** suonare un motivo a orecchio; **to — up,** raccogliere, pigliar su, riprendere vigore, (*Radio*) captare; **the — of the basket,** il fior fiore, *m.*
pick-a-back [ˈpikəbæk], *adv.* Addosso, sulle spalle, sul dorso.
pickaxe [ˈpikæks], *n.* Piccone, *m.*
picked, *a.* Scelto; colto, raccolto; distinto; mondato, pulito.
picker, *n.* Raccoglitore, *m.*, raccoglitrice, *f.*; pulitore, *m.*, pulitrice, *f.*
pickerel [ˈpikərəl], *n.* (*Zool.*) Piccolo luccio, *m.*
picket [ˈpikit], *n.* Palo, picchetto, *m.*; (*Mil.*) picchetto, *m.* || *v.t.i.* (*a horse*) Attaccare ad un palo; circondare con pali; picchettare.
picking [ˈpikiŋ], *n.* Raccolta, scelta, *f.*; mondatura, *f.*
pickings, *n.pl.* Guadagni casuali, *m.pl.*
pickle [pikəl], *n.* Salamoia, *f.*; (*plight*) imbroglio, imbarazzo, *m.*; (*child*) birichino, *m.* || *v.t.* Salare, mettere sotto aceto, conservare in salamoia; marinare. **He's in a fine —,** è

in un bell'imbarazzo; **I have a rod in — for you!** Ho una tirata d'orecchi in serbo per voi!
pickled, *a.* In aceto, sotto aceto; salato; (*colloq.*) ubbriaco.
pickles, *n.pl.* Sottaceti, *m.pl.*
picklock [ˈpiklɔk], *n.* Grimaldello, *m.*
pick-me-up [ˈpikmiʌp], *n.* Cordiale, ristorativo, *m.*
pickpocket [ˈpikpɔkit], *n.* Borsaiuolo, *m.*
picnic [ˈpiknik], *n.* Merenda in campagna, scampagnata, *f.* || *v.i.* Fare merenda, merendare, fare una scampagnata. **—-basket,** cestino, *m.*
picot [ˈpi:kou], *n.* Picot, *m.* || *v.t.* Picchettare.
picotee [pikəˈti:], *n.* (*Bot.*) Specie di garofano, *m.*
picric [ˈpikrik], *a.* (*Chem.*) Picrico.
pictograph [ˈpiktogræf], *n.* Geroglifico, *m.*
pictorial [pikˈtɔ:ɹiəl], *a.* Pittorico; illustrato; figurato. || *n.* Giornale illustrato, *m.*
pictorially, *adv.* Con illustrazioni.
Picts [pikts], *n.pl.* (*Hist.*) I Pitti, *m.pl.*
picture [ˈpiktʃəɹ], *n.* Quadro, *m.*, pittura, *f.*; dipinto, *m.*; tela, *f.*; (*fig.*) ritratto, *m.*, immagine, *f.* || *v.t.* Dipingere; descrivere al vivo; figurare, immaginare. **He looks the — of health,** è la salute in persona; **— post-card,** cartolina illustrata, *f.*; **—-book,** libro con figurine, libro illustrato, *m.*; **—-frame,** cornice, *f.*; **—-gallery,** galleria di quadri, pinacoteca, *f.*; **— writing,** geroglifici, *m.pl.*; **—-palace,** cinema, *m.*
pictures, *n.pl.* Il cinema, *m.*
picturesque [piktʃəˈresk], *a.* Pittoresco.
picturesqueness, *n.* Il pittoresco, *m.*
piddle [ˈpidəl], *v.i.* Orinare. || *n.* Orina, *f.*
piddling, *a.* Insignificante; meschino.
pidgin [ˈpidʒin], *n.* (*colloq.*) Affare, *m.* **That's not my —,** non è affare mio, non tocca a me; **—-English,** gergo anglo-cinese, *m.*
pie (1) [pai], *n.* (*meat*) Pasticcio, *m.*; (*fruit*) torta, crostata, *f.* **To eat humble —,** umiliarsi; **to have a finger in every —,** avere le mani in ogni pasta; **—-crust,** crosta di pasticcio; **—-dish,** tortiera, terrina, *f.*
pie (2), *n.* (*Print.*) Refusi, caratteri confusi, *m.pl.*
pie (3), *n.* (*Zool.*) Gazza, *f.*
piebald [ˈpaibɔ:ld], *a.* Pezzato.
piece [pi:s], *n.* Pezzo, frammento, brano, *m.*; parte, *f.*; (*of cloth*) pezza, *f.*; (*Theat.*) dramma, *m.* || *v.t.* Rattoppare, rabberciare, rappezzare. **In pieces,** a pezzi, rotto; **to break in pieces,** rompere in pezzi, fare a pezzi; **to fall to pieces,** cascare a pezzi; **a fine — of work,** un bel lavoro, *m.*; **a — of impudence,** una bella sfacciataggine, *f.*; **all of a —,** tutto d'un pezzo; **a penny —,** un soldone, *m.*; **to sell by the —,** vendere al pezzo; **to take to pieces,** smontare; **to pay by the —,** pagare a cottimo, pagare un tanto al pezzo; **a — of business,** un affare, *m.*; **a — of news,** notizia, *f.*; **a — of poetry,** una poesia, *f.*; **a — of furniture,** un mobile, *m.*; **—-goods,** stoffa in pezze, *f.*; **—-work,** lavoro a cottimo, *m.*
piecemeal [ˈpi:smi:l], *adv.* A spizzico, a bocconcini, pezzo a pezzo.
pied [paid], *a.* Screziato, variegato.
Piedmont [ˈpi:dmont], *n.* (*Geog.*) Piemonte, *m.*
Piedmontese [pi:dmonˈti:z], *n.a.* Piemontese, *m.f.*
pier (1) [piəɹ], *n.* (*landing-stage*) Pontile, *m.*; gettata, *f.*, molo, *m.*; (*Arch.*) pilastro, *m.*; (*of bridge*) pilone, *m.* **—-head,** testa di molo, *m.*; **—-dues,** diritto di banchina, *m.*
pier (2), *n.* **—-glass,** specchio, *m.*, specchiera, *f.*
pierce [ˈpiəɹs], *v.t.i.* Penetrare, perforare, trafiggere; (*fig.*) pungere, straziare.
piercing, *a.* Penetrante, acuto; pungente, straziante; (*sound*) squillante.
piercingly, *adv.* Acutamente.
piercingness, *n.* Penetrazione, acutezza, *f.*
Pierian [paiˈiəriən], *a.* (*Myth.*) Delle Pieridi, pierio.
pierrot [ˈpiərou], *n.* Pagliaccio, *m.*
pietist [ˈpaiətist], *n.* Pietista, *m.*; bacchettone, *m.*
piety [ˈpaiiti], *n.* Divozione, religiosità, *f.*; pietà, riverenza, *f.*
piffle [ˈpifəl], *n.* (*colloq.*) Inezie, sciocchezze, *f.pl.*
piffling, *a.* Futile. **I don't want to do — jobs,** non voglio occuparmi di cose futili.
pig [pig], *n.* Porco, maiale, *m.*; (*iron*) lingotto, *m.* || *v.t.i.* Figliare. **Sucking- —,** porcellino, *m.*; **to — it,** vivere alla carlona; **to buy a — in a poke,** comprare la gatta nel sacco; **to bring one's pigs to the wrong market,** prendere un granchio; **—-breeding,** allevamento suino, *m.*; **— iron,** ghisa, *f.*
pigeon [ˈpidʒin], *n.* Piccione, *m.*, colomba, *f.* **—-breasted,** col petto a sterno convesso; **carrier —,** piccione viaggiatore, *m.* **—-hole,** casella, *f.*; **—-house,** colombaia, piccionaia, *f.*; **—-shooting,** tiro al piccione, *m.*
piggery [ˈpigəri], *n.* Porcile, *m.*; porcheria, *f.*
piggish, *a.* Porcino, da porco, ghiotto.
pigheaded [pigˈheded], *a.* Ostinato, caparbio, testardo, cocciuto.
pigheadedness, *n.* Ostinatezza, caparbietà, *f.*
piglet, *n.* Porcellino, *m.*
pigmean [ˈpigmiən], *a.* Pigmeo.
pigmeat [ˈpigmi:t], *n.* Carne di maiale, carne di porco, *f.*
pigment, *n.* Pigmento, colore, *m.*
pigmy [cp. **pygmy**].
pigskin, *n.* Pelle di porco, *f.*
pigsty [ˈpigstai], *n.* Porcile, *m.*
pigtail, *n.* (*of hair*) Treccia, *f.*
pigwash, *n.* Brago, *m.*
pike (1) [paik], *n.* (*Zool.*) Luccio, *m.*
pike (2), *n.* Picca, *f.*
pikeman, *n.* Alabardiere, *m.*
pikestaff, *n.* Asta di picca, *f.* **Plain as a —,** chiaro come la luce del sole.
pilaster [piˈlæstəɹ], *n.* (*Arch.*) Pilastro, *m.*
Pilate [ˈpailət], *n.* Pilato, *m.*
pilau [piˈlau], *n.* (*Cooking*) Pilao, *m.*
pilchard [ˈpiltʃəɹd], *n.* (*Zool.*) Sardella, *f.*
pile (1) [pail], *n.* Mucchio, ammasso, *m.*; edificio, *m.*; casamento, *m.*; (*Elect.*) pila, *f.*; (*on cloth*) pelo, *m.* || *v.t.* Ammucchiare, ammassare, ammonticchiare. **Funeral —,** rogo, *m.*; **wood- —,** catasta, *f.*; (*fig.*) **to make one's —,** fare fortuna, farsi un gruzzolo; (*Mil.*) **to — arms,** mettere le armi in fascio; (*colloq.*) **to — it on,** esagerare.
pile (2), *n.* Palo, *m.*, palafitta, *f.* **To drive a —,** piantar un palo; **—-driver,** battipalo, *m.*

piles, *n.pl.* (*Med.*) Emorroidi, *f.pl.*
pilework, *n.* Palafitta, *f.*
pilfer ['pilfəɹ], *v.t.* Rubacchiare, frodare.
pilferer, *n.* Ladroncello, ladruncolo, *m.*
pilfering, *n.* Ladroneccio, furto, *m.*
pilgrim ['pilgrim], *n.* Pellegrino, *m.*, pellegrina, *f.*
pilgrimage ['pilgrimidʒ], *n.* Pellegrinaggio, *m.*
piling, *n.* L'ammucchiare; palafittata, *f.*
pill [pil], *n.* Pillola, *f.* **To gild the —,** indorare la pillola; **—-box,** scatoletta per pillole, *f.*, (*Mil.*) fortino in cemento, *m.*
pillage ['pilidʒ], *n.* Saccheggio, sacco, *m.* || *v.t.* Saccheggiare, dare il sacco a, mettere a ruba, predare.
pillager, *n.* Saccheggiatore, predatore, *m.*
pillar ['piləɹ], *n.* Colonna, *f.*, pilastro, *m.*; (*fig.*) appoggio, sostegno, *m.* **—-box,** buca delle lettere, *f.*
pillau [cp. **pilau**].
pillion ['piljən], *n.* Sella di donna, *f.*; (*Cycling*) sedile di tandem, cuscinetto, *m.*
pillory ['pilәri], *n.* Gogna, berlina, *f.* || *v.t.* (*in all senses*) Mettere alla gogna, mettere alla berlina.
pillow ['pilou], *n.* Guanciale, cuscino, *m.* || *v.t.* Posare, appoggiare, adagiare. **The child pillowed his head on her breast,** il bimbo posò il capo sul suo seno; **—-case, —-slip,** federa, *f.*; **lace-making —,** tombolo, *m.*; **—-lace,** merletto a tombolo.
pilose, pilous ['pailouz, 'pailəs], *a.* Peloso.
pilot ['pailət], *n.* Pilota, *m.*; (*fig.*) guida, *f.* || *v.t.* Guidare; pilotare; condurre, dirigere. **—-boat,** battello pilota, *m.*; **—-cloth,** stoffa di lana pesante, *f.*; (*Zool.*) **—-fish,** pesce pilota, *m.*; **—-balloon,** pallone di prova, *m.*
pilotage ['pailətidʒ], *n.* Pilotaggio, *m.*
pilule, pillule ['pilju:l], *n.* Pillola, pillolina, *f.*
pimento [pi'mentou], *n.* (*Bot.*) Pimento, *m.*
pimp [pimp], *n.* Mezzano, *m.* || *v.t.* Ruffianeggiare.
pimpernel ['pimpəɹnel], *n.* (*Bot.*) Anagallide, *f.*; pimpinella, *f.*
pimple ['pimpəl], *n.* Pustoletta, pustola, vescichetta, *f.*; bitorzolo, *m.*
pimpled, pimply, *a.* Pustoloso, bitorzoluto.
pin [pin], *n.* Spillo, *m.*; (*peg*) cavicchio, *m.*; (*Mech.*) pernio, asse, *m.*; (*Mus.*) bischero, *m.*; (*fig.*) bagatella, *f.* || *v.t.* Appuntare, puntare, attaccare con uno spillo, fissare, imperniare. **I don't care a —,** non me ne importa un fico; **to have pins and needles in one's foot,** avere un piede informicolato; (*fig.*) **to be on pins,** essere sulle spine; (*colloq.*) **quick on his pins,** vispo, snello; **to — down,** agguantare, legare con una promessa; **to — together,** unire con spilli; **—-cushion,** portaspilli, *m.*; **—-head,** capocchia dello spillo, *f.*; **—-money,** danaro per le spesuccie, spillatico, *m.*; **—-prick,** colpo di spillo, *m.*, puntata di spillo, *f.*; **—-table,** biliardino, flipper, *m.*; **drawing- —,** puntina, *f.*
pinafore ['pinəfɔɹ], *n.* Grembiule, grembiulino, *m.*
pince-nez ['pɑ:nsnei], *n.* Lenti a molla, *m.pl.*
pincers ['pinsəɹz], *n.pl.* Tenaglie, *f.pl.*
pinch [pintʃ], *n.* (*of salt*) Pizzico, *m.*; (*of snuff*) presa, *f.*; pizzicotto, *m.*; (*fig.*) strettezza, angustia, *f.* || *v.t.i.* Pizzicare; stringere, serrare; far soffrire; ridurre alle strettezze; (*colloq.*) rubare. **The — of hunger,** gli stimoli della fame, *m.pl.*; **at a —,** in caso di bisogno, in caso d'urgenza; **pinched for money,** corto a quattrini; **pinched for room,** senza spazio sufficiente; **to — oneself,** tenersi a stecchetto.
pinchbeck ['pintʃbek], *n.* Similoro, princisbecco, *m.*
pinched, *a.* (*face*) Sparuto.
Pindaric [pin'dɑ:rik], *a.* (*Poet.*) Pindarico.
pine (1) [pain], *n.* (*Bot.*) Pino, *m.*; **—-cone,** pigna, pina, *f.*, pinocchio, *m.*; **—-wood,** pineto, *m.*, pineta, *f.*
pine (2), *v.i.* Languire, struggersi, consumarsi. **To — away,** struggersi, consumarsi; **to — after,** sospirare per.
pineal ['painiәl], *a.* Pineale.
pineapple ['painæpl], *n.* Ananasso, ananas, *m.*
pinery, *n.* Serra di ananas, *f.*
pinfold ['pinfould], *n.* Chiuso, recinto, *m.*
ping [piŋ], *n.* (*of a bullet, etc.*) Sibilo, *m.*
ping-pong ['piŋpɔŋ], *n.* Tennis da tavola, *m.*
pining, *n.* Languore, deperimento, *m.*; struggimento, *m.*; nostalgia, *f.*
pinion ['pinjən], *n.* Ala, *f.*; punta dell'ala, *f.*; vanni, *m.pl.*; (*Mech.*) pignone, rocchetto, *m.* || *v.t.* Tarpare le ali a; legare, inceppare.
pink (1) [piŋk], *n.* (*Bot.*) Garofano, *m.*
pink (2), *a.* Rosa, colore di rosa, roseo. || *n.* (*fig.*) Il fiore, *m.* **The — of elegance,** il fiore dell'eleganza, *m.*; **in the — of condition,** in condizione ideale.
pink (3), *v.t.* Trafiggere, bucare; traforare.
pinkish, *a.* Rosato, roseo.
pinnace ['pinəs], *n.* (*Naut.*) Scialuppa, *f.*
pinnacle ['pinәkl], *n.* (*Arch.*) Pinnacolo, *m.*; (*fig.*) colmo, *m.*, cima, sommità, *f.*; sommo, apogeo, *m.*
pinnate ['pineit], *a.* (*Bot.*) Pennato.
pint [paint], *a.* Pinta, *f.*; mezzo litro, *m.*
pintle ['pintәl], *n.* Cardine, *m.*; spillo del perno, *m.*; (*Naut.*) agugliotto, *m.*
piny ['paini], *a.* Pinoso, coperto di pini.
pioneer [paiә'niәɹ], *n.* Pioniere, *m.*; precursore, *m.*; (*Mil.*) zappatore, *m.* || *v.t.* Preparare la via.
pious ['paiәs], *a.* Pio, religioso, devoto.
piously, *adv.* Piamente, religiosamente.
pip [pip], *n.* Granello, seme, acino, chicco, *m.*; (*on cards*) punto, *m.*; (*bird disease*) pipita, *f.*; (*Mil.*) stelletta, *f.*
pipe [paip], *n.* Tubo, condotto, *m.*, canna, *f.*; (*tobacco*) pipa, *f.*; (*measure of capacity*) pipa, *f.*; (*Mus.*) piffero, zufolo, flauto, *m.*; (*Naut.*) fischio, *m.*; (*of birds*) fischiettio. || *v.t.i.* Sonare il piffero; fischiare, fischiettare, zufolare. **To fill one's —,** caricar la pipa; **—-line,** condotto di petrolio, *m.*; **—-rack,** portapipe, *m.*; (*colloq.*) **to — one's eye,** piangere; **—-lighter,** fiammifero per accendere la pipa, accendisigaro, *m.*
pipeclay ['paipklei], *n.* Argilla plastica, argilla per pipe, *f.*
piper, *n.* Pifferaro, *m.*
piping, *n.* Tubatura, *f.*; (*sewing*) bordura, *f.* || *a.* Stridulo. (*fig.*) **—-hot,** bollentissimo, caldo caldo; **the — days of peace,** l'epoca serenissima della pace.
pipit ['pipit], *n.* (*Zool.*) Calandro, *m.*, pispola, *f.*

pipkin ['pipkin], *n.* Pignatta, pentola, *f.*, tegame, pentolino, *m.*
pippin ['pipin], *n.* Mela renetta, *f.*
piquancy ['pi:kənsi], *n.* Gusto piccante, *m.*; (*fig.*) sale, piccante, *m.*; mordacità, *f.*
piquant ['pi:kənt], *a.* Piccante, pungente, frizzante; arguto, spiritoso.
pique [pi:k], *n.* Picca, irritazione, *f.*, risentimento, puntiglio, *m.* || *v.t.* Offendere; irritare. **Out of —,** per picca; **to feel piqued,** piccarsi, risentirsi, impermalirsi; **to — oneself on,** piccarsi di, vantarsi di.
piquet [pi'ket], *n.* (*Cards*) Picchetto, *m.*
piracy ['pairəsi], *n.* Pirateria, *f.*; contraffazione, *f.*
Piraeus [pai'riəs], *n.* (*Geog.*) Pireo, *m.*
pirate ['pairət], *n.* Pirata, *m.* || *v.t.* (*fig.*) Pubblicare alla macchia; *v.i.* pirateggiare.
piratical [pai'rætikəl], *a.* Piratico, piratesco.
pirogue [pi'roug], *n.* (*Naut.*) Piroga, *f.*
pirouette [piru'et], *n.* Piroetta, piroletta. || *v.i.* Piroettare.
piscatorial, piscatory [piskə'tɔ:riəl, pis'keitəri], *a.* Piscatorio.
Pisces ['pisi:z], *n.pl.* (*Astron.*) Pesci, *m.pl.*
pisciculture ['pisikʌltʃəɹ], *n.* Piscicoltura, *f.*
piscina, piscine [pi'si:nə], *n.* Piscina, *f.*
piscine ['pisain], *a.* Pescino.
pish! [piʃ], *inter.* Oibò! Via!
pismire ['pismaiɹ], *n.* (*Zool.*) Formica, *f.*
piss [pis], *v.t.i.* Pisciare, orinare. *n.* Orina, *f.*
pistachio [pis'tɑ:ʃou], *n.* (*Bot.*) Pistacchio, *m.*
pistil ['pistil], *n.* (*Bot.*) Pistillo, *m.*
pistol ['pistəl], *n.* Pistola, *f.* || *v.t.* Pistolettare, sparare. (*fig.*) **To hold a — at one's head,** rivolgere una minaccia a; **within —-shot,** a tiro di pistola.
pistole [pis'toul], *n.* (*Hist.*) Pistola, *f.*
piston ['pistən], *n.* (*Mech.*) Stantuffo, pistone, *m.* **—-rod,** asta dello stantuffo, *f.*; **—-packing,** baderna, *f.*
pit [pit], *n.* Fossa, buca, *f.*; pozzo, *m.*; cava, *f.*; (*mine*) miniera, *f.*; (*Theat.*) platea, *f.*; (*of stomach*) bocca, *f.*; (*Med.*) buttero, *m.*, cicatrice, *f.*; (*in metal*) forellino, *m.* || *v.t.* Butterare; infossare. **To — one against the other,** aizzare l'un contro l'altro; **pitted by smallpox,** butterato dal vaiuolo.
pit-a-pat ['pitəpæt], *n.* Palpito, palpitio, batticuore, *m.*; stropiccio, *m.* **To go —,** palpitare.
pitch (1) [pitʃ], *n.* Punto, grado, *m.*; (*of roof, etc.*) pendenza, inclinazione, *f.*; (*Mus.*) tono, *m.*; (*Sport*) terreno fra le due porte nel giuoco del cricket, *m.*; (*of streetvendor*) posteggio, *m.* || *v.t.* Gettare, lanciare, scagliare (*to fix*) fissare, piantare, rizzare; (*Mus.*) accordare; (*fig.*) esprimere, dare il tono; *v.i.* cadere, stramazzare; (*of a boat*) beccheggiare. **To — a yarn,** contar delle storie; **to — on one's head,** cadere a capofitto; (*colloq.*) **to — into someone,** urtare qualcuno, dare una botta a qualcuno; **to — upon,** scegliere; **—-pipe,** diapason a fiato, *m.*; **—-and-toss,** giuoco di testa e croce, *m.*
pitch (2), *n.* Pece, *f.* || *v.t.* Impeciare. **— dark,** buio pesto; **—-blende,** pechblenda, *f.*; **—-pine,** Pino americano, pichpine, abete rosso, *m.*
pitched, *a.* Campale. **A — battle,** una battaglia campale, *f.*
pitcher, *n.* Brocca, secchia, *f.*
pitchfork ['pitʃfɔ:ɹk], *n.* Forca, *f.*, forcone, *m.* || *v.t.* Muover con la forca. **To — someone into a job,** far far carriera a qualcuno.
pitching, *n.* (*of a boat*) Beccheggio, *m.*
pitchy, *a.* Pecioso, piceo; (*fig.*) nero, buio.
piteous ['pitiəs], *a.* Doloroso, lagrimevole, compassionevole, pietoso, commovente.
piteously, *adv.* Dolorosamente, pietosamente.
piteousness, *n.* Pietosità, *f.*
pith [piθ], *n.* Midollo, *m.*; (*fig.*) essenziale, *m.*, essenza, sostanza, forza, energia, *f.* **A — helmet,** un casco coloniale, *m.*
pithily, *adv.* Energicamente, efficacemente; tersamente.
pithiness, *n.* Forza, energia, sostanza, efficacia, *f.*; intensità, *f.*; tersezza, *f.*
pithy, *a.* Midolloso; forte, energico, efficace; terso.
pitiable, pitiful ['pitiəbl, 'pitiful], *a.* Pietoso, compassionevole, misericordioso; lagrimevole.
pitiableness, pitifulness, *n.* Pietosità, *f.*
pitifully, *adv.* Pietosamente.
pitiless, *a.* Spietato.
pitilessly, *adv.* Spietatamente.
pitilessness, *n.* Spietatezza, crudeltà, *f.*
pittance ['pitəns], *n.* Compenso, donativo, *m.*, paga, *f.*; pietanza, piccola porzione, *f.* **A mere —,** una paga irrisoria, *f.*
pituitary [pi'tju:itəri], *a.* (*Anat.*) Pituitario.
pituitous, *a.* Pituitoso.
pity ['piti], *n.* Pietà, compassione, misericordia, *f.* || *v.t.* Aver pietà, aver compassione di, compatire, compassionare. **What a —!** Che peccato! **for pity's sake,** per pietà; **the more's the —,** tanto peggio; **to have — on,** aver pietà di.
pityingly, *adv.* Compassionevolmente.
pivot ['pivət], *n.* Perno, pernio, *m.*; asse, *f.*, cardine, *m.* || *v.t.* Impernare, imperniare; *v.i.* imperniarsi, girare su; dipendere da.
pixy ['piksi], *n.* Fata, *f.*
placability [plækə'biliti], *n.* Placabilità, *f.*
placable, *a.* Placabile.
placard ['plækɑ:ɹd], *n.* Affisso, cartellone, *m.* || *v.t.* Affiggere, attaccare; coprire di affissi.
placate [plə'keit], *v.t.* Placare, calmare, pacificare.
place [pleis], *n.* Luogo, posto, *m.*, località, *f.*; (*employment*) posto, impiego, *m.*; posizione, *f.*, rango, *m.*; dimora, residenza, casa, *f.* || *v.t.* Porre, mettere, collocare, posare. **— of amusement,** luogo di divertimento, *m.*; **a sore — on one's foot,** un male al piede, *m.*; (*fig.*) **to know one's —,** star al proprio posto; **in the first —,** in primo luogo; **I know his face but I can't — him,** lo conosco di vista ma non ricordo dove l'ho incontrato; **Is there a — for me?** C'è posto per me? **in — of,** invece di, al posto di; **out of —,** inopportuno, fuori di posto; **out of its —,** spostato; **in —,** a posto; **to give — to,** cedere il posto a; **to take —,** accadere, succedere, aver luogo; **a watering- —,** una stazione balneare, *f.*
placeman, *n.* Funzionario, ufficiale pubblico, *m.*
placenta [plə'sentə], *n.* (*Anat.*) Placenta, *f.*
placer, *n.* (*Mining*) Giacimento aurifero alluvionale, placer, *m.*

placid [ˈplæsid], *a.* Placido, tranquillo, quieto, sereno.
placidity, *n.* Placidità, tranquillità, calma, *f.*
placidly, *adv.* Placidamente, serenamente.
placket [ˈplækit], *n.* apertura di sottana, *f.*
plagal [ˈpleigəl], *a.* (*Mus.*) Plagale.
plagiarism [ˈpleidʒərizm], *n.* Plagio, *m.*
plagiarist, plagiary, *n.* Plagiario, *m.*
plagiarize, *v.t.* Plagiare, spacciare per proprio.
plague [pleig], *n.* Peste, pestilenza, *f.*; (*fig.*) rovina, calamità, *f.*; flagello, tormento, *m.*; seccatura, noia, *f.* || *v.t.* Tormentare, vessare, importunare, molestare. **—-spot,** focolare d'infezione, *m.*; **—-stricken,** colpito dalla peste.
plaguey [ˈpleigi], *a.* (*colloq.*) Maledetto, calamitoso.
plaice [pleis], *n.* (*Zool.*) Passerino, *m.*; pianuzza, *f.*
plaid [plæd, pleid], *n.* Plaid, *m.*; mantello scozzese a scacchi, *m.*
plain [plein], *a.* Chiaro, evidente; semplice, puro, schietto, aperto; (*of looks*) bruttino; comune, ordinario. || *n.* Piano, *m.*, pianura, *f.* **In — clothes,** in borghese; **in — English,** a dirla schietta, in buon italiano; **all is now — sailing,** ora andiamo col vento in poppa; **the — truth,** la pura verità, *f.*; **— dealing,** patti chiari, *m.pl.*; franchezza, *f.*; **—-chant, —-song,** canto fermo, *m.*; **— speaking,** franchezza, schiettezza, sincerità, *f.*, parole chiare, *f.pl.*; **—-spoken,** franco, schietto, sincero; **— cooking,** cucina casalinga, *f.*; **in —-language,** in termini chiari.
plainly, *adv.* Chiaramente, evidentemente, visibilmente; francamente; semplicemente; alla buona; al naturale.
plainness, *n.* Chiarezza, evidenza, *f.*; semplicità, schiettezza, *f.*; bruttezza, *f.*
plaint [pleint], *n.* Lagnanza, *f.*; lamento, *m.*
plaintiff [ˈpleintif], *n.* (*Law*) Parte civile, parte querelante, *f.*; attore, *m.*, attrice, *f.*
plaintive [ˈpleintiv], *a.* Flebile, triste, mesto, lamentevole, querulo.
plaintively, *adv.* Flebilmente, querulamente.
plaintiveness, *n.* Tono lamentevole, *m.*
plait [plæt], *n.* Piega, pieghetta, *f.*; (*of hair*) treccia, *f.* || *v.t.* Piegare, pieghettare; intrecciare.
plan [plæn], *n.* Piano, disegno, progetto, proposito, *m.*; (*Arch.*) pianta, *f.* || *v.t.* Disegnare; progettare, prestabilire, fissare.
plane (1) [plein], *a.* Piano. || *n.* (*Geom.*) Piano, *m.*; (*tool*) pialla, *f.* || *v.t.* Piallare; spianare. **Planing-machine,** piallatrice meccanica, *f.*
plane (2), *n.* (*Bot.*) Platano, *m.*
plane (3), *n.* Aeroplano, *m.*
planet [ˈplænit], *n.* (*Astron.*) Pianeta, *m.*
planetarium [plænəˈtɛəriəm], *n.* Planetario, *m.*
planetary, *a.* Planetario.
plangent [ˈplændʒənt], *a.* Sonoro, rumoroso.
planish [ˈplæniʃ], *v.t.* Appiattire; piallare; martellare; cilindrare (metalli).
plank [plæŋk], *n.* Asse, trave, tavola, *f.*; (*Pol.*) caposaldo, *m.* || *v.t.* Impalcare, intavolare. **He planked down a shilling,** buttò giù uno scellino; **a — in the party platform,** una parte del programma del partito, *f.*
planking, *n.* Impalcatura, intavolatura, *f.*, assito, *m.*
plankton [ˈplæŋktən], *n.* Plankton, *m.*
planner [ˈplænəɹ], *n.* Progettista, autore d'un piano, *m.*
planning, *n.* Concezione, invenzione, *f.*, piano, progetto, *m.*; pianificazione, *f.* **Town-—,** piano regolatore, *m.*; urbanistica, *f.*
plant [plɑ:nt], *n.* (*Bot.*) Pianta, *f.*; (*Mech.*) impianto, materiale, *m.*, attrezzi, arnesi, *m.pl.*; (*colloq.*) inganno, *m.*, frode, *f.* || *v.t.* Piantare, impiantare; fermare, stabilire, fissare; (*a blow*) affibbiare (un colpo). **To — out,** trapiantare; **—-life,** vita vegetale, *f.*; **—-pot,** vaso da pianta, *m.*
plantain [ˈplæntin], *n.* (*Bot.*) Piantaggine, petacciuola, *f.*; (*tree*) banano, *m.*, musa, *f.*
plantation [plænˈteiʃən], *n.* Piantagione, *f.*; albereto, boschetto, *m.*; (*Hist.*) colonia, *f.*
planter [ˈplɑ:ntəɹ], *n.* Colono, *m.*; piantatore, *m.*
plantigrade [ˈplæntigreid], *n.* (*Zool.*) Plantigrado, *m.*
planting, *n.* Piantagione, *f.*; (*Arch.*) posa, *f.*
plaque [plɑ:k], *n.* Placca, lastra, *f.*
plash [plæʃ], *n.* Pozza, pozzanghera, *f.* || *v.t.i.* Schizzare, zampillare; intrecciare.
plasm [plæzm], *n.* (*Zool. Anat.*) Plasma, *f.*
plaster [ˈplɑ:stəɹ], *n.* Gesso, intonaco, *m.*; (*Med.*) impiastro, *m.*, cataplasma, *f.* || *v.t.* Impiastrare, ingessare, intonacare, mettere un impiastro a. **To — up,** incerottare, ingessare; **sticking-—,** sparadrappo, *m.*, taffetà inglese, *f.*; **— of Paris,** gesso, *m.*; **mustard-—,** senapismo, *m.*; **—cast,** gesso, *m.*
plastered, *a.* Intonacato; (*colloq.*) ubbriaco.
plasterer, *n.* Intonacatore, *m.*
plastic [ˈplæstik], *a.* Plastico.
plasticity [plæsˈtisiti], *n.* Plasticità, *f.*
plastics, *n.pl.* Plastici, *m.pl.*; materie plastiche, *f.pl.*
plat (1) [plæt], *n.* Aiuola, *f.*, pezzo di terra, *m.*
plat (2), *n.* Treccia, *f.* || *v.t.* Intrecciare [cp. **plait**].
plate [pleit], *n.* (*dish*) Piatto, *m.*; (*of metal, etc.*) piastra, placca, lastra, lamina, *f.*; (*gold and silver ware*) argenteria, *f.*; (*illustration*) incisione, illustrazione, *f.*; (*Phot.*) lastra, negativa, *f.*; (*Racing*) coppa, *f.*; (*door*) targhetta, *f.* || *v.t.* Placcare, laminare; dorare, indorare, inargentare; (*Naut.*) corazzare. **—-basket,** cesto per posate, *m.*; **—-glass,** cristallo, cristallo in lastre, *m.*; (*Rail.*) **fish-—,** ganascia, *f.*; **—-layer,** guardalinea, *m.*; **—-powder,** polvere per l'argenteria, *f.*; **—-rack,** portapiatti, *m.*
plateau [plæˈtou], *n.* Altipiano, *m.*
plateful [ˈpleitful], *n.* Piatto colmo, *m.*
platen [ˈplætən], *n.* (*Print.*) Pirrone, *m.*; (*of typewriter*) rullo, *m.*
platform [ˈplætfɔ:ɹm], *n.* Piattaforma, tribuna, terrazza, *f.*; (*Theat.*) palcoscenico, *m.*; (*Rail.*) marciapiedi, *m.*, banchina, *f.*; (*Pol.*) programma, *m.*, piattaforma, *f.*
platiniferous [plætiˈnifərəs], *a.* Platinifero.
platinotype [ˈplætinotaip], *n.* Platinotipia, *f.*
platinum [ˈplætinəm], *n.* (*Min.*) Platino, *m.*
platitude [ˈplætitju:d], *n.* Banalità, *f.*; luogo comune, *m.*
platitudinous [plætiˈtju:dinəs], *a.* Banale.
Plato [ˈpleitou], *n.* Platone, *m.*
platonic [pləˈtɔnik], *a.* Platonico.
Platonism [ˈpleitənizm], *n.* Platonismo, *m.*

Platonist, *n.* Platonista, *m.*
platoon [plə'tu:n], *n.* Plotone, *m.*
platter ['plætəɹ], *n.* Piatto, *m.*; gavetta, *f.*
plaudit ['plɔ:dit], *n.* Plauso, applauso, *m.*
plausibility [plɔ:zə'biliti], *n.* Plausibilità, *f.*
plausible ['plɔ:zəbl], *a.* Plausibile.
plausibleness, *n.* Plausibilità, *f.*
plausibly, *adv.* Plausibilmente.
play [plei], *n.* Giuoco, *m.*, ricreazione, *f.*; azione, *f.*, movimento, scopo, slancio, *m.*; (*Theat.*) dramma, *m.*; rappresentazione, commedia, *f.* || *v.t.i.* Giuocare a; scherzare, trastullarsi, baloccarsi; (*Mus.*) suonare; (*Theat.*) rappresentare; (*at chess, etc.*) muovere. **A — upon words,** un giuoco di parole, *m.*; **— of fancy,** fantasticaggine, *f.*; **in —,** per ischerzo; **to give full — to,** dare libero campo a, dare sfogo a; **to call into —,** tirare in campo, tirare in ballo, mettere in giuoco; **a smile played on his lips,** un sorriso gli sfiorò le labbra; **to — a trick on someone,** giocare un tiro a qualcuno; (*fig.*) **to — the game,** stare al giuoco, comportarsi lealmente; **to — into the hands of,** esser lo strumento di; **to — someone off,** giuocare una persona; **to — upon someone's fears,** profittare della paura di qualcuno; **to — up to someone,** tener bordone a qualcuno; **to — high,** giuocare forte; **to — low,** giuocare prudente; **to — fair,** giuocare pulito; (*fig.*) **to — one's cards well,** giuocar bene le proprie carte; **to — a fish,** tirare la lenza; **—-bill,** avviso di teatro, programma di spettacolo, *m.*; **—-debt,** debito di giuoco, *m.*; **—-boy,** birichino, furfantello, vitaiolo, *m.*
player, *n.* Giocatore, giuocatore, *m.*, giocatrice, giuocatrice, *f.*; (*Theat.*) attore, *m.*, attrice, *f.*; (*Mus.*) suonatore, *m.*, suonatrice, *f.* **—-piano,** pianoforte meccanico, *m.*
playfellow, *m.* Compagno di giuoco, *m.*, compagna di giuoco, *f.*
playful, *a.* Scherzoso, scherzevole, festevole, festoso, allegro, giocondo.
playfully, *adv.* Scherzosamente.
playfulness, *n.* Scherzosità, festosità, letizia, *f.*
playgoer, *n.* Frequentatore di teatri, *m.*
playground, *n.* Campo di giuoco, *m.*, cortile di ricreazione, *f.*
playhouse, *n.* Teatro, *m.*
playmate [cp. **playfellow**].
plaything, *n.* Giocattolo, giocherello, balocco, *m.*
playtime, *n.* Ora della ricreazione, *f.*
playwright, *n.* Drammaturgo, commediografo, *m.*
plea [pli:], *n.* Scusa, difesa, *f.*, pretesto, *m.*; istanza, supplica, *f.*; (*Law*) causa, difesa, *f.* **A — for mercy,** una domanda di grazia, *f.*
plead [pli:d], *v.t.i.* Allegare, dichiarare; perorare, sostenere, patrocinare. **To — for,** perorare a favore di; **to — with,** intercedere presso; **to — against,** appellarsi contro; **to — guilty,** dichiararsi colpevole; **to — someone's cause,** perorare la causa di qualcuno.
pleader, *n.* Avvocato difensore, *m.*; intercessore, *m.*
pleading, *n.* (*Law*) Difesa, perorazione, *f.*
pleasant ['plezənt], *a.* Gradevole, piacevole, ameno, dilettevole; amabile.
pleasantly, *adv.* Gradevolmente, amabilmente.
pleasantness, *n.* Gradevolezza, piacevolezza, amenità, *f.*
pleasantry, *n.* Facezia, *f.*; burla, *f.*, scherzo, *m.*
please [pli:z], *v.t.i.* Piacere a, soddisfare, contentare, compiacere. **To be pleased,** compiacersi, rallegrarsi, essere contento, essere lieto; **to — oneself,** fare ciò che accomoda; **as you —,** come vi piace; **If you —!** Per piacere! Per favore! Prego! **May it — your Majesty,** Piaccia alla Sua Maestà; **Please go away!** Favorite andarvene!
pleased, *a.* Contento, soddisfatto, lieto.
pleasing, *a.* Piacevole, gradevole; attraente; ameno.
pleasurable ['pleʒərəbl], *a.* Gradevole, piacevole.
pleasure ['pleʒəɹ], *n.* Piacere, diletto, *m.*; divertimento, spasso, *m.*; buonvolere, *m.* **I shall not consult his —,** gli piaccia o non gli piaccia; **it can be altered at —,** si può cambiarlo a volontà; **it is a — to see you,** è un piacere vedervi; **do me the — of,** fatemi il favore di; **—-boat,** canotto di piacere, *m.*, barca da passeggio, *f.*; **—-ground,** parco, *m.*; **—-party,** comitiva, *f.*; **—-resort,** luogo di ricreazione, *m.*; **—-trip,** gita di piacere, *f.*
pleat [pli:t], *n.* Piega, pieghetta, ripiegatura, *f.* || *v.t.* Piegare, pieghettare.
plebeian [ple'bi:ən], *a.* Plebeo. || *n.* Plebeo.
plebiscite ['plebisit], *n.* Plebiscito, *m.*
pledge [pledʒ], *n.* Pegno, impegno, *m.*; garanzia, promessa, *f.*; (*toast*) brindisi, *m.*; (*teetotal*) voto di temperanza, *m.* || *v.t.* Impegnare, pignorare; far brindisi a. **Under — of secrecy,** sotto suggello di segretezza; **to hold in —,** tenere come garanzia; **to — one's honour,** impegnare l'onore.
Pleiades ['plaiədi:z], *n.pl.* (*Astron.*) Pleiadi, *f.pl.*
plenary ['pli:nəri], *a.* Pieno, compiuto, assoluto; (*Eccles.*) plenario.
plenipotentiary [plenipə'tenʃəri], *n.a.* Plenipotenziario, *m.*
plenitude ['plenitju:d], *n.* Pienezza, *f.*
plenteous, plentiful ['plentiəs, 'plentifəl], *a.* Abbondante, copioso. **To be plentiful,** abbondare.
plentifully, *adv.* Copiosamente.
plentifulness, *n.* Abbondanza, *f.*
plenty, *n.* Abbondanza, copia, *f.* **Horn of —,** cornucopia, *f.*; **there's — of time,** c'è tanto tempo.
plenum ['pli:nəm], *n.* Pieno, *m.*; adunanza plenaria, *f.*
pleonasm ['pli:onæzm], *n.* Pleonasmo, *m.*
pleonastic [pli:o'næstik], *a.* Pleonastico.
plesiosaurus [pli:sio'sɔ:rəs], *n.* (*Zool.*) Plesiosauro, *m.*
plethora ['pleθərə], *n.* Pletora, *f.*
plethoric [ple'θɔrik], *a.* Pletorico.
pleura ['plu:rə], *n.* (*Anat.*) Pleura, *f.*
pleurisy, *n.* (*Med.*) Pleurite, *f.*
pleuro-pneumonia [plu:ronju:'mouniə], *n.* (*Med.*) Pleuropolmonite, *f.*
plexus ['pleksəs], *n.* (*Anat.*) Plesso, *m.*
pliability, pliableness, pliancy [plaiə'biliti, 'plaiəblnis, 'plaiənsi], *n.* Pieghevolezza, flessibilità, arrendevolezza, *f.*
pliable, pliant ['plaiəbl, 'plaiənt], *a.* Pieghevole, piegabile, flessibile; arrendevole.

pliers ['plaiəɹz], *n.pl.* Pinze, tenaglie, *f.pl.*

plight (1) [plait], *n.* Stato, *m.*, condizione, *f.* **In a sore —**, in uno stato pietoso.

plight (2), *v.t.* Impegnare, dare la parola d'onore. **To — one's troth**, impegnarsi, dar la parola.

plimsolls ['plimsəlz], *n.pl.* Scarpe da tennis, *f.pl.*; scarpe di tela gommata, *f.pl.*

plinth [plinθ], *n.* (*Arch.*) Plinto, *m.*

Pliocene ['plaiosi:n], *a.* (*Geol.*) Pliocenico. || *n.* Pliocene, *m.*

plod [plɔd], *v.i.* Tirare avanti, arrancare; sfacchinare, sgobbare. **To — along**, camminare a fatica.

plodder, *n.* Sgobbone, lavoratore assiduo, *m.*

plodding, *a.* Laborioso.

ploddingly, *adv.* Laboriosamente.

plomb [plɔm], *n.* Piombo, *m.* || *v.t.* Piombare.

plot (1) [plɔt], *n.* Complotto, *m.*, cospirazione, congiura, *f.*; intrigo, *m.*, trama, *f.* || *v.t.* Complottare, macchinare, congiurare; progettare, fare un piano di. **The — of a novel**, l'intreccio di un romanzo, *m.*; **to lay a —**, ordire una congiura.

plot (2), *n.* Appezzamento, *m.* **A grass —**, un pezzo di terreno erboso, *m.*

plotter, *n.* Cospiratore, *m.*, cospiratrice, *f.*, intrigante, *m.f.*

plough [plau], *n.* Aratro, *m.* || *v.t.* Arare, solcare; (*at exams*) bocciare. **To put one's hand to the —**, intraprendere un lavoro; **to — up**, arare; **to — through**, solcare; **snow —**, spartineve, *m.*

ploughboy, ploughman, *n.* Aratore, *m.*

ploughing, *n.* Aratura, *f.*

ploughland, *n.* Terreno arabile, *m.*

ploughshare, *n.* Vomere, *m.*

plover ['plʌvəɹ], *n.* (*Zool.*) Piviere, *m.*, pavoncella, *f.*

pluck (1) [plʌk], *n.* Coraggio, fegato, *m.*, audacia, *f.*; (*entrails*) frattaglie, *f.pl.*

pluck (2) *v.t.* (*flowers, etc.*) Cogliere; (*poultry*) spennare; (*to pull*) tirare, svellere, strappare; (*at an exam.*) bocciare. || *n.* Tirata, strappata, *f.* **To — away**, strappare; **to — up**, sradicare, svellere; **to — up courage**, riprendere coraggio.

pluckily, *adv.* Coraggiosamente.

plucky, *a.* Coraggioso, audace, di fegato.

plug [plʌg], *n.* Tappo, tampone, turacciolo, zaffo, *m.*; valvola, *f.*; (*Elec.*) spina, *f.*; (*Motor.*) candela, *f.*; (*Med.*) tampone, stuello, *m.*, spina, *f.*; (*in tobacco pipe*) deposito, grumo, *m.* || *v.t.* Tamponare, tappare; stoppare, zaffare; otturare; (*Radio*) ripetere una canzone incessantemente. **Spark —**, candela, *f.*; **—-hole**, presa d'acqua, *f.*

plum [plʌm], *n.* Susina, prugna, *f.* **Dried —**, prugna secca, *f.*; **—-cake**, plum-cake, *m.*; **—-pudding**, budino all'inglese, *m.*; **—-tree**, susino, prugno, *m.*

plumage ['plu:midʒ], *n.* Piumaggio, *m.*, penne, piume, *f.pl.*

plumb [plʌm], *n.* Piombo, filo a piombo, *m.* || *v.t.* Piombare; (*Naut.*) scandagliare. || *adv.* A piombo. **—-line**, filo a piombo, scandaglio, *m.*

plumbago [plʌm'beigou], *n.* (*Min.*) Piombaggine, *f.*

plumbeous, *a.* Piomboso, plumbeo.

plumber ['plʌməɹ], *n.* Idraulico, tubista, trombaio, stagnaio, *m.*

plumbiferous [plʌm'bifərəs], *a.* (*Min.*) Piombifero.

plumbing, *n.* Piombatura, impiombatura, opera del trombaio, *f.*

plumbism ['plʌmbizm], *n.* (*Med.*) Saturnismo, *m.*

plume [plu:m], *n.* Penna, piuma, *f.*, pennacchio, *m.* || *v.t.* Piumare, impennacchiare. **To — oneself on**, vantarsi di, farsi bello con; **to — its feathers**, pulirsi le penne.

plumeless, *a.* Spiumato, spennato.

plummer-block ['plʌməɹblɔk], *n.* Cuscinetto di perno, *m.*

plummet ['plʌmit], *n.* Scandaglio, filo a piombo, piombino, contrappeso, *m.*

plumose ['plu:mouz], *a.* Piumoso.

plump (1) [plʌmp], *a.* Grassoccio, paffuto, tondo, rotondo, grasso. || *v.t.i.* Far ingrassare.

plump (2), *v.t.i.* Piombare, cadere a piombo, gettare giù. || *n.* Tonfo, *m.* || *adv.* A piombo, di peso. **To — for a candidate**, dare tutti i voti ad un candidato.

plumper, *n.* Voto dato ad un sol candidato, *m.*; voto in massa, *m.*

plumpness, *n.* Grassezza, rotondità, *f.*

plumy ['plu:mi], *a.* Piumoso, pennuto.

plunder ['plʌndəɹ], *v.t.* Saccheggiare, rubare, spogliare, mettere a sacco. || *n.* Bottino, *m.*, preda, *f.*; saccheggio, *m.*

plunderer, *n.* Saccheggiatore, predatore, *m.*

plunge [plʌndʒ], *v.t.i.* Tuffare, tuffarsi; precipitare, lanciarsi, scagliarsi; (*gaming*) giuocare grosso. || *n.* Tuffo. **To take the —**, fare il primo passo, romper gl'indugi, saltare il fosso.

plunger ['plʌndʒəɹ], *n.* Tuffatore; (*Comm.*) speculatore rischioso, *n.*; (*Mech.*) stantuffo, pistone, *m.*

pluperfect [plu:'pə:ɹfəkt], *n.* (*Gram.*) Passato anteriore, piuccheperfetto, *m.*

plural ['plu:rəl], *n.a.* Plurale, *m.*

pluralism, *n.* Pluralismo, *m.*

plurality [plu:'ræliti], *n.* Pluralità, *f.*

plus [plʌs], *prep.a.* Più; con l'aggiunta di. **That boy is 12 —**, quel ragazzo ha 12 anni passati; **the — sign**, segno più, simbolo più, *m.*

plush [plʌʃ], *n.* Felpa, *f.*, peluzzo, *m.*

Pluto ['plu:tou], *n.* (*Myth.*) Plutone, *m.*

plutocracy [plu:'tɔkrəsi], *n.* Plutocrazia, *f.*

plutocratic [plu:to'krætik], *a.* Plutocratico.

Plutonian [plu:'tounіən], *a.* (*Geol.*) Plutoniano.

pluvial ['plu:viəl], *a.* Pluviale.

pluvious, *a.* Pluvio, piovoso. **Jupiter Pluvius**, Giove Pluvio, *m.*

ply (1) [plai], *n.* Spessore, *m.*; piega, *f.*; **—-wood**, legno compensato, *m.*

ply (2), *v.t.* Adoperare, maneggiare, usare; esercitare, fare, manipolare. **To — someone with drink**, offrire da bere a qualcuno; **to — with questions**, assalire di domande; **the boat plies between London and Southend**, il vapore fa la spola fra Londra e Southend; **to — for hire**, offrirsi a nolo.

pneumatic [nju:'mætik], *a.* Pneumatico. **— tyre**, pneumatico, *m.*, gomma, *f.*

pneumatics, *n.pl.* Pneumatica, *f.*

pneumonia [nju:'mouniə], *n.* (*Med.*) Polmonite, *f.*

pneumonic [nju:ˈmɔnik], *a.* Pneumonico, polmonare.
Po [pou], *n.* (*Geog.*) Po, *m.* **North of the Po,** Traspadano.
poach (1) [poutʃ], *v.t.i.* Cacciar di frodo, frodare, rubare. **To — on someone's preserves,** invadere il campo di qualcuno.
poach (2), *v.t.* Affogare. **Poached eggs,** uova in camicia, uova affogate, *f.pl.*
poacher, *n.* Bracconiere, cacciatore di frodo, *m.*
poaching, *n.* Caccia di frodo, *f.*
pochard [ˈpɔtʃɑ:ɹd], *n.* Specie di anitra, *f.*
pock [pɔk], *n.* (*Med.*) Pustola, *f.*; cicatrice, *f.* **—-marked,** butterato.
pocket [ˈpɔkit], *n.* Tasca, *f.*; saccoccia, *f.*; (*Billiards*) buca, *f.*; (*Geol.*) cavità, *f.*; (*air*) vuoto, *m.*, sacca, *f.* || *v.t.* Intascare; appropriarsi; involare, mandar giù; imbucare. **To be in — by,** guadagnare a; **I am out of — by it,** ci rimetto del mio; **to have someone in one's —,** avere in mano qualcuno; **to fill one's pockets,** empirsi le tasche; **—-book,** portafoglio, *m.*; **—-handkerchief,** fazzoletto da tasca, *m.*; **—-knife,** temperino, *m.*; **—-money,** spiccioli, *m.pl.*, danaro per le spese minute, *m.*; **— edition,** edizione tascabile, *f.*
pocketful, *n.* Tascata, *f.*
pod [pɔd], *n.* Baccello, guscio, *m.*
podagra [poˈdægrə], *n.* (*Med.*) Podagra, *f.*
podgy [ˈpɔdʒi], *a.* Paffuto, grassotto, tondo.
poem [ˈpouem], *n.* (*epic, narrative, etc.*) Poema, *m.*; (*lyric*) poesia, *f.*
poesy [cp. **poetry**].
poet [ˈpouet], *n.* Poeta, *m.*
poetaster [poueˈtæstəɹ], *n.* Poetastro, *m.*
poetess, *n.* Poetessa, *f.*
poetic, poetical [pouˈetik, pouˈetikəl], *a.* Poetico.
poetics, *n.pl.* Poetica, *f.*
poetize, *v.t.i.* Poetizzare.
poetry, *n.* Poesia, *f.*
poignancy [ˈpɔinənsi], *n.* Acutezza, cocentezza, intensità, violenza, *f.*
poignant [ˈpɔinənt], *a.* Pungente, cocente, acuto; intenso; penoso.
poignantly, *adv.* Cocentemente.
point [pɔint], *n.* (*locality*) Punto, *m.*; (*sharp end*) punta, *f.*; (*of compass*), quarto, grado, *m.*; (*Rail.*) ago dello scambio, *m.*; (*Print.*) punto, *m.*; (*full-stop*) punto, *m.*; (*Naut.*) gaschetta, *f.*; (*Geog.*) promontorio, *m.* || *v.t.* (*to sharpen*) Affilare, appuntare, aguzzare; (*to indicate*) additare, mostrare, indicare; (*firearms*) puntare; (a wall) stuccare i giunti; (*fig.*) illustrare; *v.i.* dirigere; (*of dogs*) puntare. **A — of conscience,** un caso di coscienza, *m.*; **at the — of death,** in punto di morte; **to give points to,** dare dei punti a; **at boiling- —,** al punto di ebullizione; **when it comes to the —,** quando si viene al fatto; **his strong —,** il suo forte, *m.*; **that is just the —,** questo è il punto; **to make a — of,** farsi un dovere di; **I don't see the —,** non afferro l'idea; **to the —,** appropriato, calzante, a proposito, opportuno; **a case in —,** un esempio tipico, *m.*; **in — of fact,** per la verità, di fatto, difatti, nel caso speciale; **a — of honour,** un punto d'onore, *m.*; **the — of view,** il punto di vista, *m.*; **to gain one's —,** ottenere l'intento; **to stretch a —,** fare un'eccezione, lasciar correre; **to be on the — of,** essere sul punto di; **the main —,** l'essenziale, *m.*; **he has many good points,** ha molti meriti; **armed at all points,** armato di tutto punto; **—-blank,** a bruciapelo, diretto, categorico; **—-duty,** servizio di traffico, *m.*; **flash- —,** punto d'infiammabilità, *m.*; **starting- —,** punto di partenza, *m.*; (*Math*) **six — five,** sei virgola cinque.
pointed, *a.* Appuntato, aguzzo, acuto; (*fig.*) mordace, pungente; allusivo, ovvio; (*Arch.*) ogivale.
pointer, *n.* Indice, *m.*, lancetta, *f.*; bacchetta, *f.*; (*dog*) cane da punta, cane da fermo, *m.*
pointing, *n.* (*of walls*) Cementatura, *f.*; (*punctuation*) interpunzionare, *f.*; (*of a gun*) puntamento, *m.*
pointless, *a.* Spuntato; insignificante, inutile, insulso.
pointlessly, *adv.* Inutilmente.
pointsman, *n.* (*Rail.*) Scambista, deviatore, *m.*
poise [pɔiz], *n.* Equilibrio, *m.*; portamento, *m.*; contrappeso, *m.* || *v.t.i.* Bilanciare, equilibrare; equilibrarsi, librarsi.
poison [ˈpɔizən], *n.* Veleno, tossico, *m.* || *v.t.* Avvelenare, attossicare. **—-gas,** gas asfissiante, gas velenoso, *m.*
poisoner, *n.* Avvelenatore, *m.*, avvelenatrice, *f.*
poisoning, *n.* Avvelenamento, *m.*
poisonous, *a.* Velenoso.
poke (1) [pouk], *n.* Colpo, *m.*, puntata, botta, spinta, *f.* || *v.t.i.* Colpire, urtare, dare una botta a, dare un colpo a; ficcare, configgere. **To — the fire,** attizzare il fuoco; **to — fun at,** beffare, dileggiare, deridere; **to — one's head out,** cacciar fuori la testa; **to — one's nose in,** ficcare il naso in; **to — about,** frugare, frugacchiare.
poke (2), *n.* Tasca, *f.*, sacco, *m.* **To buy a pig in a —,** comprare la gatta nel sacco, comprare alla cieca.
poker, *n.* Attizzatoio, *m.*; (*Cards*) poker, *m.* **—-work,** pirografia, *f.*
poky, *a.* Piccolo, meschino. **A — little room,** una cameruccia, *f.*
Poland [ˈpoulənd], *n.* (*Geog.*) Polonia, *f.*
polar [ˈpouləɹ], *a.* Polare. (*Zool.*) **— bear,** orso bianco, *m.*
polarity [poˈlæriti], *n.* Polarità, *f.*
polarization, *n.* Polarizzazione, *f.*
polarize, *v.t.* Polarizzare, polarizzarsi.
pole (1) [poul], *n.* Palo, *m.*, pertica, *f.*; (*carriage*) timone, *m.*; (*measure*) pertica, *f.* **The greasy —,** l'albero della cuccagna, *m.*
pole (2), *n.* (*Geog.Astron.*) Polo, *m.* **The Pole Star,** la stella polare, *f.*; **poles apart,** molto differente.
Pole (3), *n.* Polacco, *m.*, Polacca, *f.*
pole-axe [ˈpoulæks], *n.* Ascia del beccaio, mazza piombata, *f.*; (*Hist.*) azza, *f.*
polecat [ˈpoulkæt], *n.* (*Zool.*) Puzzola, *f.*
polemic, polemical [poˈlemik, poˈlemikəl], *a.* Polemico.
polemics, *n.pl.* Polemica, *f.*
police [poˈli:s], *n.* Polizia, *f.*; gendarmeria, *f.* *v.t.* Presidiare con polizia; sorvegliare, vigilare. **—-court,** tribunale correzionale, *m.*; **—-office,** questura, *f.*; **—-station,** ufficio di polizia, posto di polizia, *m.*; **— spy, — informer,** spia, *f.*; informatore, *m.*

policeman, *n.* Agente di polizia, carabiniere, *m.*, guardia, *f.*; poliziotto, *m.*
policy ['pɔlisi], *n.* Politica, *f.*; linea di condotta, *f.*, sistema, piano, *m.*; prudenza, tattica, sagacità, *f.*; (*insurance*) polizza, *f.*
polio, poliomyelitis ['pouliou, pouliou-maie'laitis], *n.* (*Med.*) Paralisi infantile, poliomelite, *f.*
Polish (1) ['pouliʃ], *n.a.* Polacco, *m.*
polish (2) ['pɔliʃ], *v.t.* Pulire; (*to smooth*) lisciare, levigare; (*to brighten*) lustrare, lucidare, verniciare; (*fig.*) raffinare, ingentilire. || *n.* Lustro, lucido, *m.*; (*for shoes*) crema, *f.*; vernice, *f.*; (*fig.*) squisitezza, finezza, raffinatezza, *f.* **To — off,** sbrigare; sbarazzarsi di.
polished, *a.* Lucido, lustro; (*fig.*) raffinato, squisito, fino.
polisher, *n.* Pulitore, *m.*
polishing, *n.* Verniciatura, lucidatura, *f.*
polite [po'lait], *a.* Cortese, gentile, garbato. **— literature,** belle lettere, *f.pl.*
politely, *adv.* Cortesemente.
politeness, *n.* Cortesia, gentilezza, garbatezza, eleganza, *f.*
politic ['politik], *a.* Politico; (*of persons*) sagace, prudente; (*of actions*) utile, giovevole. **The body —,** lo stato, *m.*
political, *a.* Politico.
politically, *adv.* Politicamente.
politician [pɔli'tiʃən], *n.* Politico, politicante, *m*
politics, *n.pl.* Politica, *f.* **To talk —,** parlare di politica.
polity, *n.* Stato, governo, *m.*, la cosa pubblica, *f.*
polka ['pɔlkə], *n.* Polca, *f.*
poll [poul], *n.* Elezione, votazione, *f.*; scrutinio, *m.*; voti, *m.pl.*; testa, *f.* || *v.t.i.* (*trees*) Potare, svettare; (*votes*) ottenere; (*to vote*) votare. **— -tax,** Testatico, *m.*; **polling-booth,** cabina elettorale, *f.*; **— -station,** sezione elettorale, sala di votazione, *f.*
pollack, pollock ['pɔlək], *n.* (*Zool.*) Gado, *m.*
pollard ['pɔlɑːɹd], *n.* Capitozza, *f.*, albero a capitozzo. || *v.t.* Potare, capitozzare, svettare, dicimare, scamozzare.
pollen ['pɔlən], *n.* (*Bot.*) Polline, *m.*
polling ['pouliŋ], *n.* Votazione, *f.*, ballottaggio, *m.*
pollock [cp. **pollack**].
pollute [po'luːt], *v.t.* Contaminare, infettare; corrompere, violare.
pollution, *n.* Contaminazione, infezione, *f.*; corruzione, *f.*
polo ['poulou], *n.* Polo, *m.* **— collar,** polo, *m.*
polonaise [pɔlə'neiz], *n.* (*Mus.*) Polacca, polonese, *f.*
polony [pə'louni], *n.* Specie di salsiccia, mortadella, *f.*
poltroon [pɔl'truːn], *n.* Codardo, vigliacco, *m.*
poltroonery, *n.* Codardia, vigliaccheria, *f.*
polyandrous [pɔli'ændrəs], *a.* Poliandro.
polyandry, *n.* Poliandria, *f.*
polyanthus [pɔli'ænθəs], *n.* (*Bot.*) Polianto, *m.*
polychromatic [pɔlikrou'mætik], *a.* Policromo.
polyclinic [poli'klinik], *n.* Policlinico, *m.*
polygamist [pə'ligəmist], *n.* Poligamo, *m.*
polygamous, *a.* Poligamo.
polygamy [pə'ligəmi], *n.* Poligamia, *f.*
polyglot ['pɔliglɔt], *n.a.* Poliglotta, *m.f.*
polygon ['pɔligən], *n.* (*Geom.*) Poligono, *m.*
polygonal, *a.* Poligonale.
polygraph ['pɔligræf], *n.* Poligrafo, *m.*
polyhedron [pɔli'hiːdrən], *n.* (*Geom.*) Poliedro, *m.*
Polynesia [pɔli'niːʒə], *n.* (*Geog.*) Polinesia, *f.*
polyp ['pɔlip], *n.* (*Zool.*) Polipo, *m.*
polypetalous [pɔli'petələs], *a.* (*Bot.*) Polipetalo.
polyphonic [pɔli'fɔnik], *a.* Polifonico.
polypus ['pɔlipəs], *n.* (*Med.*) Polipo, *m.*
polysyllabic [pɔlisi'læbik], *a.* Polisillabo.
polysyllable, *n.* Polisillabo, *m.*
polytechnic [pɔli'teknik], *n.a.* Politecnico, *m.*
polytheism ['pɔliθiːizm], *n.* Politeismo, *m.*
polytheist, *n.* Politeista, *m.f.*
pomace ['pʌmis], *n.* Tritume di mele (residuo del sidro), *m.*
pomade [po'mɑːd], *n.* Pomata, *f.* || *v.t.* Impomatare.
pomander [po'mændəɹ], *n.* Palla di profumo, *f.*
pomatum [po'meitəm], *n.* Pomata, *f.*
pomegranate ['pɔmgrænit], *n.* Melagrana, *f.* **— -tree,** melagrano, *m.*
Pomeranian [pɔmə'reiniən], *a.* Della Pomerania. **— dog, pom,** cane di Pomerania, pomer, *m.*
pommel ['pʌməl], *n.* Pomo, pomolo, *m.* || *v.t.* Battere, percuotere, dare pugni a.
pommelling, *n.* Bastonatura, *f.*
pomp [pɔmp], *n.* Pompa, *f.*, sfarzo, fasto, *m.*
Pompeii [pom'peii], *n.* (*Geog.*) Pompei, *f.*
pompon ['pɔmpɔn], *n.* Fiocco, *m.*, nappa, *f.*
pomposity, pompousness [pɔm'pɔsiti, 'pɔmpəsnis], *n.* Pomposità, burbanza, *f.* (*of style*) ampollosità, *f.*
pompous ['pɔmpəs], *a.* Pomposo, affettato, ampolloso.
pompously, *adv.* Pomposamente.
poncho ['pɔntʃou], *n.* Poncio, *m.*
pond [pɔnd], *n.* Stagno, laghetto, *m.*; peschiera, *f.* **— -weed,** alghe, erbacce, *f.pl.*
ponder ['pɔndəɹ], *v.t.i.* Ponderare, considerare, riflettere.
ponderable, *a.* Ponderabile.
ponderingly, *adv.* Ponderatamente.
ponderous ['pɔndrəs], *a.* Ponderoso, pesante.
ponderousness, *n.* Ponderosità, pesantezza, *f.*
poniard ['pɔniəɹd], *n.* Pugnale, *m.* || *v.t.* Pugnalare.
pontiff ['pɔntif], *n.* Pontefice, *m.* **The Sovereign Pontiff,** il Sommo Pontefice, *m.*
pontifical [pɔn'tifikəl], *a.* Pontificale.
pontificals, *n.pl.* Pontificale, *m.*
pontificate, *n.* Pontificato, *m.*
pontoon [pɔn'tuːn], *n.* Pontone, *m.*, chiatta, *f.* **— -bridge,** ponte di barche, ponte di barconi, ponte di chiatte, *m.*
pony ['pouni], *n.* Cavallino, cavalluccio, *m.*; (*colloq.*) 25 lire sterline, *f.pl.*
poodle [puːdl], *n.* Can barbone, cane maltese, *m.*
pooh! [pu], *inter.* Poh! Oibò! Auf!
pooh-pooh [puː'puː], *v.t.* Dileggiare, prendere alla leggiera, ridersene di.
pool [puːl], *n.* Stagno, *m.*, pozzanghera, *f.*; (*bathing*) piscina, *f.*; (*Cards*) banco, pool, *m.*; (*Comm.*) fondo comune, consorzio, sindacato, *m.* || *v.t.* Metter in comune, consorziare.
poop [puːp], *n.* (*Naut.*) Poppa, *f.*

poor [puːɹ], *a.* Povero, indigente, bisognoso; scarso, meschino, misero; disgraziato; infelice, afflitto. || *n.pl.* I poveri. **A — excuse,** una scusa meschina, *f.*; **a — consolation,** una magra consolazione, *f.*; **— fare,** cibo povero, *m.*; **Poor little chap!** Poverino! **—-box,** cassetta dell'elemosina, cassetta dei poveri, *f.*; **—-house,** ricovero, ospizio, *m.*; **—-law,** legge per l'assistenza ai poveri, *f.*; **—-rate,** tassa a beneficio dei poveri; **—-spirited,** pusillanime, timido, dappoco; **— health,** salute malferma, cattiva salute, *f.*

poorly, *adv.* Male, scarsamente. || *a.* Malaticcio, indisposto. **He is — to-day,** sta poco bene oggi.

poorness, *n.* Scarsezza, povertà, magrezza, mediocrità, *f.*

pop [pɔp], *n.* Schiocco, scatto, *m.*; (*colloq.*) gassosa, *f.* || *v.t.i.* Schioccare; esplodere. **Off he pops,** è scappato; **to — in,** far capolino, fare una visita senza cerimonia; **to — out,** far una corsa fuori; **to — up,** balzar fuori; **—-gun,** schioppetto ad aria compressa, *m.*

pope [poup], *n.* (*Eccles.*) Papa, *m.* **— Joan,** specie di giuoco di carte.

popery, *n.* Papismo, *m.*

popinjay [ˈpɔpindʒei], *n.* (*Hist.*) Pappagallo, *m.*; zerbinotto, damerino, *m.*

popish [ˈpoupiʃ], *a.* Papistico.

poplar [ˈpɔpləɹ], *n.* (*Bot.*) Pioppo, *m.*

poplin [ˈpɔplin], *n.* Poplina, *f.*

poppet [ˈpɔpit], *n.* Bambino, *m.*, bambina, *f.*, piccino, *m.*, piccina, *f.*

poppy [ˈpɔpi], *n.* (*Bot.*) Papavero, *m.* **—-head,** testa di papavero, *f.*

populace [ˈpɔpjuːlis], *n.* Popolo, volgo, *m.*, plebe, plebaglia, *f.*

popular [ˈpɔpjuːləɹ], *a.* Popolare, in voga, alla moda; ad uso popolare; (*well-liked*) ben voluto; popolaresco.

popularity [pɔpjuːˈlæriti], *n.* Popolarità, voga, *f.*

popularize, *v.t.* Popolarizzare, volgarizzare.

popularly, *adv.* Popolarmente.

populate [ˈpɔpjuːleit], *v.t.* Popolare.

population [pɔpjuːˈleiʃən], *n.* Popolazione, *f.*

populous [ˈpɔpjuːləs], *a.* Popolato, popoloso.

populousness, *n.* Popolosità, *f.*

porcelain [ˈpɔːɹslin], *n.* Porcellana, *f.*

porch [pɔːɹtʃ], *n.* Vestibolo, portico, *m.*; atrio, *m.*

porcine [ˈpɔːɹsain], *a.* Porcino, suino.

porcupine [ˈpɔːɹkjuːpain], *n.* (*Zool.*) Porcospino, *m.*

pore (1) [pɔːɹ], *n.* (*Anat.*) Poro, *m.*

pore (2), *v.t.i.* Studiare, meditare. **To — over,** studiare attentamente, sgobbare su.

pork [pɔːɹk], *n.* Carne di maiale, carne suina, *f.* **—-butcher,** pizzicagnolo, salumiere, *m.*; **—-chop,** costoletta di maiale, *f.*; **—-pie,** pasticcio di carne di maiale, *m.*

porker, *n.* Maiale, porco, *m.*

pornographic [pɔːɹnoˈgræfik], *a.* Pornografico.

pornography [pɔːɹˈnɔgrəfi], *n.* Pornografia, *f.*

porosity, porousness [pɔːrˈɔsiti, ˈpɔːrəsnis], *n.* Porosità, *f.*

porous [ˈpɔːrəs], *a.* Poroso.

porphyry [ˈpɔːɹfiri], *n.* (*Min.*) Porfirio, porfido, *m.*

porpoise [ˈpɔːɹpəs], *n.* (*Zool.*) Marsovino, porco marino, *m.*

porridge [ˈpɔridʒ], *n.* Farinata, farinata di avena, zuppa di avena, *f.*

porringer [ˈpɔrindʒəɹ], *n.* Scodella, *f.*

port (1) [pɔːɹt], *n.* (*harbour*) Porto, *m.* **— of call,** approdo, porto di scalo, *m.*; **— of registry,** porto d'iscrizione, *m.*; **—-admiral,** comandante di piazza marittima, *m.*; **—-dues,** diritti di porto, *m.pl.*

port (2), **porthole** [pɔːɹt, ˈpɔːɹthoul], *n.* Boccaporto, oblò, *m.*

port (3), *n.* (*bearing*) Portamento, incesso, *m.*

port (4), *n.* (*Naut.*) Babordo, *m.*, sinistra, *f.* ||*v.t.* **To — the helm,** mettere la barra a sinistra, portare la barra a sinistra; virare (la nave) a destra; *v.i.* virare a sinistra.

port (5), *n.* Vino di Oporto, *m.* **—-wine mark,** macchia di vino, *f.*

portability [pɔːɹtəˈbiliti], *n.* Portabilità, trasportabilità, *f.*

portable [ˈpɔːɹtəbl], *a.* Portabile, portatile.

portage [ˈpɔːɹtidʒ], *n.* (*Comm.*) Porto, trasporto, *m.*; trasporto d'una barca oltre una rapida, *m.*

portal [ˈpɔːɹtəl], *n.* Portale, *m.* **— vein,** vena porta, *f.*

portcullis [pɔːɹtˈkʌlis], *n.* Saracinesca, *f.*

Porte [pɔːɹt], *n.* (*Geog.Hist.*) Porta, *f.* **The Sublime —,** la Sublime Porta, *f.*

portend [pɔːɹˈtend], *v.t.* Predire, prenunziare, presagire.

portent [ˈpɔːɹtənt], *n.* Portento, prodigio, *m.*; pronostico, augurio, *m.*

portentous [pɔːɹˈtentəs], *a.* Portentoso; presago, ammonitore; funesto.

porter [ˈpɔːɹtəɹ], *n.* Facchino, portabagagli, *m.*; (*at door*) portinaio, portiere, *m.*; specie di birra nera, *f.*

porterage, *n.* Porto, trasporto, *m.*

portfolio [pɔːɹtˈfouliou], *n.* Cartella, busta, *f.*; (*Pol.*) portafoglio, *m.*

portico [ˈpɔːɹtikou], *n.* Portico, *m.*, colonnata, *f.*

portion [ˈpɔːɹʃən], *n.* Porzione, parte, *f.*; dote, *f.* || *v.t.* Dividere, ripartire; dotare. **To — out,** spartire, distribuire.

portionless, *a.* Senza dote.

portliness [ˈpɔːɹtlinis], *n.* Corpulenza, grassezza, *f.*

portly, *a.* Corpulento; prestante; maestoso.

portmanteau [pɔːɹtˈmæntou], *n.* Valigia, *f.*; baule, *m.*

portrait [ˈpɔːɹtrit], *n.* Ritratto, *m.*, pittura, *f.*; descrizione, *f.* **A speaking —,** un ritratto parlante; **to have one's — taken,** farsi fare il ritratto; **—-painter,** ritrattista, *m.f.*

portraiture [ˈpɔːɹtritʃjuːɹ], *n.* Ritratto, *m.*, arte di ritrarre, *f.*; descrizione, *f.*

portray [pɔːɹˈtrei], *v.t.* Ritrattare, dipingere; rappresentare, descrivere.

portress [ˈpɔːɹtres], *n.* Portinaia, portiera, *f.*

Portugal [ˈpɔːɹtjuːgəl], *n.* (*Geog.*) Portogallo, *m.*

Portuguese [pɔːɹtjuːˈgiːz], *n.a.* Portoghese, *m.f.*

pose [pouz], *v.t.* Asserire, affermare; (*a question*) proporre; *v.i.* atteggiarsi, posare, assumere una posa. || *n.* Posa, *f.*, atteggiamento, *m.*; affettazione, *f.* **To — someone** (*with a problem*), ammutolire qualcuno; **to — as a martyr,** atteggiarsi a martire; **his kindness is a mere —,** la sua gentilezza è pura posa.

poser, *n.* Enigma, problema, *m.*, domanda imbarazzante, *f.*
poseur [pouˈzəːɹ], *n.* Posatore, *m.*
posh [pɔʃ], *a.* (*colloq.*) Elegante. **To — oneself up,** mettersi in ghingheri.
position [poˈziʃən], *n.* Posizione, situazione, postura, *f.*; grado, rango, *m.*; impiego, *m.*; (*Sport*) classifica, *f.* || *v.t.* Collocare. **In a false —,** in una falsa posizione; **in a — to,** in condizione di.
positive [ˈpɔzitiv], *a.* Positivo, esplicito, concreto; certo, sicuro, convinto; (*colloq.*) vero. || *n.* Positivo, *m.*; (*Phot.*) positiva, *f.* **A — nuisance,** una vera seccatura, *f.*
positively, *adv.* Positivamente, assolutamente.
positiveness, *n.* Positività, *f.*; certezza, sicurezza, *f.*
positivism, *n.* Positivismo, *m.*
positivist, *n.* Positivista, *m.f.*
posse [ˈpɔsi], *n.* Drappello, *m.*, squadra, compagnia, *f.*
possess [poˈzes], *v.t.* Possedere, tenere, avere; invadere, occupare. **To — oneself of,** impossessarsi di; **What possessed you to do that?** Che cosa vi spinse a far ciò? **to — one's soul in patience,** armarsi di pazienza.
possessed, *a.* (*demoniacally*) Posseduto, indemoniato, ossesso.
possession [poˈzeʃən], *n.* Possessione, *f.*, possedimento, possesso, *m.*; ossessione, *f.* **British possessions,** possedimenti britannici, *m.pl.*; **to enter into —, of,** venire in possesso di; **to put into —,** mettere in possesso; **to take —,** prender possesso.
possessive, *n.a.* Possessivo, *m.*
possessor, *n.* Posseditore, *m.*, posseditrice, *f.*
possessory, *a.* Possessorio.
posset [ˈpɔsit], *n.* Bevanda di latte caldo con vino.
possibility [pɔsiˈbiliti], *n.* Possibilità, *f.*
possible [ˈpɔsibl], *a.* Possibile. **As soon as —,** quanto prima, al più presto possibile; **as far as —,** nei limiti del possibile; **It's —!** Può darsi!
possibly, *adv.* Forse, possibilmente, può darsi. **He cannot — come,** non è possibile che venga; **How can she — walk so far?** Come mai può andare così lontano?
post [poust], *n.* (*in ground*) Palo, pilastro, *m.*, colonna, *f.*; (*place*) posto, *m.*, situazione, *f.*; (*job*) impiego, *m.*; (*mail*) posta, *f.*, ufficio postale, *m.*; corrispondenza, *f.* || *v.t.* (*letters*) Impostare, imbucare, inviare per posta; (*affix*) affiggere; (*Bookkeeping*) registrare a mastro; (*Mil.*) appostare. || *v.i.* posteggiare, viaggiare in diligenza. **To send by —,** spedire per la posta; **by return of —,** a posta corrente, a volta di corriere, a giro di posta; **I missed the —,** ho impostato in ritardo; **to ride —,** correr le poste; **to — up,** aggiornare, mettere al corrente; metter al giorno; **to be posted up in,** essere al corrente di; **to go — haste,** andare in gran fretta; **—-bag,** sacco postale, *m.*; **—-boy,** messaggero, *m.*; **—-chaise,** diligenza postale, *f.*; **—-free,** porto franco; **—-horse,** cavallo da posta, *m.*; **—-house,** posta, *f.*; **—-office,** posta, *f.*, ufficio postale, *m.*; **—-office savings bank,** cassa di risparmio postale, *f.*; **—-paid,** porto pagato; (*Sport*) **winning-—,** traguardo, *m.*
postage [ˈpoustidʒ], *n.* Porto, *m.*, affrancatura, francatura, *f.*, spese postali, *f.pl.*; **—stamp,** francobollo, *m.*
postal, *a.* Postale. **— order,** vaglia, vaglia postale, *m.*
postcard, *n.* Cartolina, cartolina postale, *f.*
post-communion [poustkoˈmjuːniən], *n.* (*Eccles.*) Postcommunio, *m.*
post-date [poustˈdeit], *v.t.* Posdatare.
poster [ˈpoustəɹ], *n.* Affisso, avviso, manifesto, *m.*
poste restante [poustˈrestɑ̃ːt], *a.* Fermo in posta.
posterior [pɔsˈtiəriəɹ], *a.* Posteriore. || *n.* Deretano, *m.*
posterity [pɔsˈteriti], *n.* Posterità, *m.*, i posteri, *m.pl.*
postern [ˈpɔstəɹn], *n.* Porticciuola, *f.*; pusterla, *f.* || *a.* Di dietro.
posthumous [ˈpɔstjuːməs], *a.* Postumo.
posthumously, *adv.* Dopo la morte.
postillion [pɔsˈtiljən], *n.* Postiglione, *m.*
posting [ˈpoustiŋ], *n.* (*letters*) Impostazione, *f.*; (*notices*) affissione, *f.*; (*Bookkeeping*) registrazione a mastro; (*of sentry*) posa, *f.*
postman [ˈpoustmən], *n.* Postino, *m.*
postmaster, postmistress, *n.* Capo d'ufficio postale, *m.*, direttore, direttrice d'ufficio postale, *m.f.*
postmeridian [poustməˈridiən], *a.* Pomeridiano.
post meridiem, p.m. [poustməˈridiəm, piːˈem], *n.* Pomeriggio, *m.*
post-mortem [poustˈmɔːɹtem], *n.* Autopsia, *f.*
post-obit [poustˈɔbit], *n.* (*Law*) Anticipo sopra un'eredità, *m.*
postpone [poustˈpoun], *v.t.* Posporre, differire, rimandare.
postponement, *n.* Posponimento, differimento, *m.*, dilazione, *f.*
postprandial [poustˈprændiəl], *a.* Dopopranzo, conviviale.
postscript, P.S. [ˈpoustskript, piːˈes], *n.* Poscritto, *m.*
postulant [ˈpɔstjuːlənt], *n.* Postulante, *m.f.*
postulate [ˈpɔstjuːleit], *v.t.i.* Postulare, domandare, richiedere. *n.* [ˈpɔstjuːlit] Postulato, *m.*
posture [ˈpɔstʃəɹ], *n.* Positura, postura, posa, *f.*, atteggiamento, *m.*; stato, *m.*, condizione, *f.*
posturer, *n.* Acrobata, *m.f.*; tipo affettato, *m.*
post-war [poustˈwɔːɹ], *a.* Di dopoguerra, posbellico.
posy [ˈpouzi], *n.* Mazzetto di fiori, *m.*; motto, *m.*
pot [pɔt], *n.* Vaso, *m.*, brocca, *f.*; boccale, *m.*; pentola, marmitta, pignatta, *f.* || *v.t.* Conservare in vaso; piantare in vaso; (*colloq.*) fucilare. **—-bellied,** panciuto, corpacciuto; **—-boy, —-man,** cameriere di bettola, *m.* **—-hat,** cappello a bombetta, *m.*; **—-hole,** (*Geol.*) marmitta, *f.*, (*in road*) buca, *f.*; **to take —-luck,** contentarsi di un piatto alla buona; (*colloq.*) **to go to —,** rovinarsi, andare in rovina; **—-valiant,** eroe a stomaco pieno; **—-roast,** arrosto in pentola, *m.*; **chamber- —,** vaso da notte, *m.*; **melting —,** crogiuolo, *m.*
potable [ˈpoutəbl], *a.* Potabile.
potash [ˈpɔtæʃ], *n.* Potassa, *f.*
potassium [pɔˈtæsiəm], *n.* Potassio, *m.*

potation [po'teiʃən], *n.* Bevuta, libazione, *f.*
potato (*pl.* **potatoes**) [po'teitou], *n.* Patata, *f.* **Boiled potatoes,** patate lesse, *f.pl.*; **mashed potatoes,** purè di patate, *m.*
potency ['potənsi], *n.* Potenza, forza, efficacia, *f.*
potent, *a.* Potente, forte, efficace. **A — wine,** un vino forte, *m.*
potentate ['poutənteit], *n.* Potentato, *m.*
potential [po'tenʃəl], *n.a.* Potenziale, *m.*
potentiality [potenʃi'æliti], *n.* Potenzialità, *f.*
potentially, *adv.* Potenzialmente.
potentilla [poten'tilə], *n.* Potentilla, *f.*, fragolaria, *f.*
potful, *n.* Pentolata, *f.*
pother ['pɔðəɹ], *n.* Chiasso, rumore, *m.*, tumulto, *m.*; confusione, *f.*
potherbs ['pɔthəːɹbz], *n.pl.* Erbaggio, ortaggio, *m.*
pothook ['pɔthuk], *n.* (*in writing*) Asta, *f.*
pothouse ['pɔthaus], *n.* Bettola, *f.*
potion ['pouʃən], *n.* Pozione, *f.*; bevanda, *f.*
potsherd ['potʃəɹd], *n.* Frammento di vaso, coccio, *m.*
pottage ['pɔtidʒ], *n.* Zuppa, *f.* **A mess of —,** un piatto di lenticchie, *m.*
potted, *a.* Conservato in scatola. **— meat,** carne conservata, carne in scatola, *f.*
potter (1) ['pɔtəɹ], *n.* Vasaio, *m.*; pentolaio, *m.* **Potter's wheel,** ruota del vasaio, *f.*
potter (2), *v.i.* **To — about,** gingillarsi; **to — at,** occuparsi di; **to — away one's time,** perdere il tempo in inezie.
pottery, *n.* Terraglia, ceramica, *f.*, stoviglie, *f.pl.*; industria della ceramica, *f.*
pottle ['pɔtəl], *n.* Cestellino, *m.*
potty [pɔti], *a.* (*colloq.*) Piccolo, insignificante; pazzo. **To be — on someone,** amare qualcuno alla follia.
pouch [pautʃ], *n.* Borsa, *f.*, sacchetto, *m.*; carniera, *f.*; (*Mil.*) cartucciera, giberna, *f.*; (*of kangaroo*) borsa, *f.* ‖ *v.t.* Intascare; *v.i.* assumere forma di sacco. **Tobacco —,** borsa del tabacco, borsetta, *f.*
pouf [puːf], *n.* Puf, *m.*
poult [poult], *n.* Pollastro, pollastrino, pollo, *m.* **Turkey —,** tacchinotto, *m.*
poulterer, *n.* Pollaiuolo, pollivendolo, *m.*
poultice ['poultis], *n.* Cataplasma, impiastro, *m.*; (*colloq.*) polentina, *f.* ‖ *v.t.* Mettere un cataplasma a.
poultry, *n.* Pollame, *m.* **— yard, — -house,** pollaio, *m.*; **— -farming,** allevamento di pollame, *m.*
pounce (1) [pauns], *n.* (*powder*) Spolvero, polverino, *m.* ‖ *v.t.* Spolverare.
pounce (2), *v.t.i.* Piombare su, gettarsi addosso. ‖ *n.* Artiglio, *m.* **He pounced on my mistake,** colse a volo il mio errore.
pound (1) [paund], *n.* (*weight*) Libbra, *f.*; (*money*) lira sterlina, *f.* **He paid five shillings in the —,** pagò cinque scellini su una sterlina.
pound (2), *v.t.* Polverizzare, stritolare; battere, colpire. **To — along,** andare di gran carriera; **to — to a jelly,** conciar male.
pound (3), *n.* Deposito di animali rinvenuti o sequestrati, *m.*; chiuso, *m.*
poundage ['paundidʒ], *n.* Percentuale, *f.*; commissione, *f.*; tassa per l'emissione di un vaglia, *f.*
pounder, *n.* (*Mil.*) Pezzo, cannone, *m.* **A sixty- —,** un pezzo da sessanta, *m.*
pour [pɔːɹ], *v.t.* Versare, spargere, spandere; *v.i.* riversare, riversarsi; piovere dirottamente. ‖ *n.* Diluvio, *m.* (*fig.*) **To — cold water on,** scoraggiare, raffreddare; **to — out money,** scialacquare danaro; (*fig.*) **to — oil on the waves,** calmare, tranquillizzare; **the people poured in from all sides,** la folla affluì da tutte le parti; **it was pouring with rain,** pioveva a dirotto.
pouring, *a.* (*of rain*) Torrenziale.
pout [paut], *v.i.* Imbronciarsi, fare il broncio, fare il muso lungo, fare il grugno. ‖ *n.* Broncio, grugno, *m.*
pouter, pouter-pigeon, *n.* Piccione cavaliere, *m.*
pouting, *a.* Imbronciato.
poverty ['pɔvəɹti], *n.* Povertà, miseria, indigenza, *f.*; inopia, scarsezza, *f.* **To come to —,** cadere in miseria; **— -stricken,** misero, indigente, miserabile.
powder ['paudəɹ], *n.* Polvere, polverina, *f.*; (*for face*) cipria, *f.* ‖ *v.t.* Impolverare, spargere di polvere, spolverizzare, incipriare. **To keep one's — dry,** tenere asciutte le polveri; **food for —,** carne di cannone, *f.*; **— -blue,** blu elettrico, *m.*; **— -flask, — -horn,** fiaschetta della polvere, *f.*; **— -magazine,** polveriera, *f.*; (*Naut.*) santabarbara, *f.*; **— -mill,** polverificio, *m.*; **— -monkey,** ragazzo addetto alle munizioni, *m.*; **— -puff,** piumino per la cipria, *m.*
powdered, *a.* Polverizzato, in polvere; impolverato, incipriato. **— -sugar,** zucchero al velo, *m.*
powderiness, *n.* Friabilità, *f.*
powdering, *n.* Spolveratura, *f.*
powdery, *a.* Polveroso, friabile; polverizzato, in polvere.
power ['pauəɹ], *n.* Potere, *m.*, potenza, *f.*; capacità, potestà, *f.*; facoltà, possibilità, *f.*; forza, *f.*, vigore, *m.*; (*Elec.*) corrente industriale, *m.* **I have done all in my —,** ho fatto il possibile; **to tax one's powers to the uttermost,** usare al massimo le proprie forze; **heating —,** potere calorifico, *m.*; **the powers that be,** le autorità costituite, *f.pl.*; **to have full powers,** avere pieni poteri; **the Great Powers,** le grandi potenze, *f.pl.*; (*Math.*) **to raise to the fourth —,** elevare alla quarta potenza; **the balance of —,** l'equilibrio politico, *m.*; **— -house,** centrale elettrica, *m.*; **— -loom,** telaio meccanico, *m.*; **— of attorney,** procura, *f.*
powerful, *a.* Potente, vigoroso, valido, forte, efficace.
powerfully, *adv.* Potentemente, vigorosamente.
powerless, *a.* Senza potere, debole, fiacco, impotente, incapace.
powerlessness, *n.* Impotenza, incapacità, *f.*
pow-wow ['pau-wau], *n.* (*colloq.*) Colloquio, ragionamento, *m.*
pox [pɔks], *n.* Sifilide, *f.*
pozzuolana [pɔtswo'lɑːnə], *n.* Pozzolana, *f.*
practicability [præktikə'biliti], *n.* Praticabilità, *f.*
practicable ['præktikəbl], *a.* Praticabile, fattibile.

practical ['præktikəl], *a.* Pratico; positivo. **A — man,** un uomo pratico, *m.*; **— joke,** burla beffa, *f.*; **— joker,** burlone, corbellatore, *m.*
practically, *adv.* Praticamente, in effetto; quasi. **The job is — finished,** il lavoro è quasi finito; **he is — in control of the business,** ha effettivo controllo degli affari.
practice ['præktis], *n.* Pratica, *f.*, uso, esercizio, *m.*; abitudine, *f.* (*of doctors, etc.*) clientela, pratica, *f.*; (*Sport*) allenamento, *m.*; (*Arith.*) metodo delle parti aliquote, *m.* **In —,** in pratica; **— makes perfect,** la pratica val più che la grammatica; **the doctor has sold his —,** il dottore ha venduto la sua pratica; **to put into —,** mettere in pratica; **to be out of —,** essere fuori esercizio; **to make a — of,** aver l'uso di, solere; **to keep in —,** stare in esercizio.
practician [præk'tiʃən], *n.* Praticante, *m.*
practise ['præktis], *v.t.i.* Praticare, esercitare, usare, operare; professare; (*Mus.*) esercitarsi; addestrarsi, impratichirsi, far pratica. **To — the piano,** esercitarsi al piano; **to — upon someone,** influenzare qualcuno.
practised, *a.* Esperto, provetto, pratico.
practising, *a.* Professante, praticante.
practitioner, *n.* Professionista, praticante, *m.*; medico, *m.*
Praetorian [pri'tɔːriən], *a.* Pretoriano.
pragmatic, pragmatical [præg'mætik, præg'mætikəl], *a.* Prammatica. (*Hist.*) **Pragmatic Sanction,** prammatica sanzione, *f.*
pragmatism ['prægmətizm], *n.* Pragmatismo, *m.*
pragmatist, *n.* Pragmatista, *m.*
Prague [prɑːg], *n.* (*Geog.*) Praga, *f.*
prairie ['prɛəri], *n.* Prateria, *f.*
praise [preiz], *n.* Lode, *f.*, elogio, *m.* ‖ *v.t.* Lodare, approvare, elogiare, vantare. **In — of,** in lode di; **to sing the praises of,** celebrare le lodi di.
praiseworthily, *adv.* Lodevolmente.
praiseworthiness, *n.* Lodevolezza, *f.*
praiseworthy, *a.* Lodevole, lodabile.
pram [cp. **perambulator**].
prance [prɑːns], *v.i.* (*of horse*) Impennarsi; (*of child*) saltellare, saltare; pavoneggiarsi.
prancing, *n.* Impennata, *f.*
prank (1) [præŋk], *n.* Monelleria, birichinata, *f.*; beffa, burla, *f.*; tiro, *m.* **To play a — on,** fare un tiro a; **to play one's pranks,** farne di tutti i colori.
prank (2) [cp. **prink**].
prankish, *a.* Birichino, sbarazzino.
prate [preit], *v.i.* Ciarlare, cicalare, pettegolare, chiacchierare.
prater, *n.* Chiacchierone, cicalone, *m.f.*
pratique [præ'tiːk], *n.* Libera pratica, *f.*
prattle [prætl], *v.i.t.* Chiacchierare, cianciare, ciarlare, cinguettare. ‖ *n.* Chiacchierio, *m*, ciancia, ciarlata, *f.*, cicaleccio, *m.*
prattler, *n.* Chiacchierone, *m.*, chiacchierona, *f.*
prawn [prɔːn], *n.* (*Zool.*) Palemone, *m.*
praxis ['præksis], *n.* Prassi, *f.*
pray [prei], *v.t.i.* Pregare, supplicare, implorare, impetrare. **To — for,** pregare per; **to — to God,** pregare Dio; **Pray tell me!** Ditemi, vi prego! **Pray be seated!** Si accomodi, prego!
prayer ['prɛəɹ], *n.* Preghiera, supplica, istanza, *f.*; orazione, *f.*; domanda, *f.* **The Lord's Prayer,** la preghiera domenicale, *f.*, il paternostro, *m.*; **—-book,** libro di preghiere, *m.*; **—-wheel,** cilindro girevole, *m.*
prayerful, *a.* Fervente, divoto.
prayerfulness, *n.* Fervore, *m.*, divozione, *f.*
preach [priːtʃ], *v.t.i.* Predicare. (*fig.*) **To — at someone,** fare una predica a qualcuno.
preacher, *n.* Predicatore, *m.*; (*Protestant*) pastore, *m.*
preaching, *n.* Predica, *f.*, sermone, *m.*
preacquaint [priːə'kweint], *v.t.* Preavvertire, preavvisare.
preadamic, preadamite [priːə'dæmik, priː'ædəmait], *a.* Preadamitico.
preadmonish [priːəd'mɔniʃ], *v.t.* Preavvertire, prevenire.
preadmonition, *n.* Premonizione, *f.*, preavviso, *m.*
preamble ['priːæmbl], *n.* Preambolo, *m.*
prebend ['prebənd], *n.* (*Eccles.*) Prebenda, *f.*
prebendal, *a.* Prebendato.
prebendary, *n.* Prebendario, *m.*
precarious [pre'kɛəriəs], *a.* Precario; incerto, aleatorio.
precariously, *adv.* Precariamente.
precariousness, *n.* Precarietà, alea, *f.*
precaution [pre'kɔːʃən], *n.* Precauzione, *f.* **With due —,** con le debite precauzioni.
precautionary, *a.* Precauzionale.
precede [pre'siːd], *v.t.* Precedere.
precedence ['presidəns, pri'siːdəns], *n.* Precedenza, *f.* **To give — to,** dare la precedenza a.
precedent ['presidənt], *n.* Precedente, *m.* **Without —,** senza precedenti.
preceding, *a.* Precedente.
precentor [pri'sentəɹ], *n.* (*Eccles.*) Primo cantore, capocoro, precentore, *m.*
precept ['priːsept], *n.* Precetto, *m.*
preceptor, *n.* Precettore, *m.*
preceptorial [presep'tɔːriəl], *a.* Precettivo.
preceptorship, *n.* Ufficio di precettore, *m.*
preceptress, *n.* Istitutrice, *f.*
precession [pri'seʃən], *n.* (*Astron.*) Precessione, *f.*
prechristian [priː'kristʃən], *a.* Avanti Cristo.
precinct ['priːsiŋkt], *n.* Recinto, *m.* **Precincts,** limiti, confini, *m.pl.*
preciosity [presi'ɔsiti], *n.* Preziosità, *f.*
precious ['preʃəs], *a.* Prezioso; (*colloq.*) famoso; (*of style*) ricercato. **They've made a — mess of it,** l'hanno conciato proprio male.
preciously, *adv.* Preziosamente.
preciousness, *n.* Preziosità, *f.*, pregio, valore, *m.*
precipice ['presipis], *n.* Precipizio, *m.*
precipitable [pre'sipitəbl], *a.* (*Chem.*) Precipitabile.
precipitance, precipitancy, *n.* Precipitazione, fretta, *f.*
precipitant, *n.a.* Precipitante, *m.*
precipitate (1) [pri'sipitit], *a.* Precipitato, affrettato.
precipitate (2) [pri'sipiteit], *v.t.* Precipitare.
precipitately, *adv.* Precipitatamente.
precipitation, *n.* Fretta, *f.*; (*Chem.*) precipitazione, *f.*

precipitous, *a.* Precipitoso, ripido, erto, scosceso.
precipitously, *adv.* Precipitosamente.
precipitousness, *n.* Ripidezza, ertezza, *f.*
precis ['preisi:], *n.* Sunto, *m.*
precise [pri'sais], *a.* Preciso, esatto; puntiglioso, scrupoloso, sollecito, attento. **At the — moment that,** proprio al momento che.
precisely, *adv.* Precisamente.
preciseness, *n.* Precisione, esattezza, *f.*; scrupolosità, sollecitudine, *f.*
precisian [pri'siʒən], *n.* Formalista, *m.f.*
precision, *n.* Precisione, esattezza, *f.*
preclude [pri'klu:d], *v.t.* Precludere, impedire, vietare.
preclusive [pri'klu:ziv], *a.* Impeditivo, ostacolante.
precocious [pri'kouʃəs], *a.* Precoce; scaltro; (*Bot.*) con sviluppo precoce.
precociously, *adv.* Precocemente.
precociousness, precocity [pri'kouʃəsnis, pri'kɔsiti], *n.* Precocità, *f.*
precognition, *n.* Precognizione, preconoscenza, *f.*
preconceive [pri:kən'si:v], *v.i.* Formare in anticipo un'opinione, preconcepire.
preconceived, *a.* Preconcetto.
preconception, *n.* Preconcetto, pregiudizio, *m.*
preconcert [pri:kən'sə:ɹt], *v.t.* Predisporre, preordinare, prestabilire.
preconcerted, *a.* Preconcetto.
preconize ['pri:kənaiz], *v.t.* Preconizzare; proclamare.
precursor [pri:'kə:ɹsəɹ], *n.* Precursore, *m.*
precursory, *a.* Precorritore, foriero.
predatory ['predətəri], *a.* Predace, predatorio, rapace.
predecease [pri:di'si:s], *v.i.* Premorire a. || *n.* (*Law*) Premorienza, *f.*
predecessor [pr:di'sesəɹ], *n.* Predecessore, *m.*
predestinate (1) [pri:'destinit], *a.* Predestinato.
predestinate, predestine [pri:'destineit, pri:'destin], *v.t.* Predestinare.
predestination, *n.* Predestinazione, *f.*
predetermine [pri:di'tə:ɹmin], *v.t.* Predeterminare.
predicable ['predikəbl], *a.* Predicabile.
predicament [pre'dikəmənt], *n.* Imbarazzo, imbroglio, *m.*; mal passo, *m.*, situazione difficile, *f.*; (*Logic*) predicato, *m.*, categoria.
predicate ['predikeit], *v.t.* Predicare, affermare. || *n.* (*Gram.*) ['predikit], Predicato, *m.*
predication, *n.* Predicazione, *f.*
predict [pri'dikt], *v.t.* Predire, presagire.
prediction, *n.* Predizione, profezia, *f.*, pronostico, *m.*
predictor, *n.* Profeta, *m.*
predigestion [pri:di'dʒestʃən], *n.* Predigestione, *f.*
predilection [pri:di'lekʃən], *n.* Predilezione, *f.*
predispose [pri:dis'pouz], *v.t.* Predisporre. **To be predisposed in someone's favour,** essere ben predisposto in favore di qualcuno.
predisposition, *n.* Predisposizione, *f.*
predominance [pri'dɔminəns], *n.* Predominio, *m.*
predominant, *a.* Predominante, prevalente.
predominate [pri'dɔmineit], *v.i.* Predominare, prevalere.
pre-elect [pri:e'lekt], *v.t.* Preeleggere.
pre-eminence [pri:'eminəns], *n.* Preminenza, *f.*
pre-eminent, *a.* Preminente.
pre-eminently, *adv.* Preminentemente.
pre-empt [pri:'emt], *v.t.* Esercitare il diritto di prelazione nell'acquisto.
pre-emption, *n.* Prelazione, *f.*; preacquisto, *m.*
preen [pri:n], *v.t.* Lisciarsi le penne; pulire, adornare.
pre-engage, *v.t.* Prenotare.
pre-establish, *v.t.* Prestabilire.
pre-exist, *v.i.* Preesistere.
pre-existence, *n.* Preesistenza, *f.*
pre-existent, *a.* Preesistente.
preface ['prefəs], *n.* Prefazione, introduzione, *f.*, proemio, *m.* || *v.t.* Premettere, anteporre, fare la prefazione a.
prefatory ['prefətəri], *a.* Preliminare, introduttivo, proemiale.
prefect ['pri:fekt], *n.* (*Hist.Pol.*) Prefetto, *m.*; (*in school*) capoclasse, *m.*
prefectorial [prefek'tɔ:riəl], *a.* Prefettizio.
prefecture ['prefektʃu:ɹ], *n.* Prefettura, *f.*
prefer [pri'fə:ɹ], *v.t.* Preferire, preporre, prescegliere; promuovere, avanzare, elevare; sollevare. **To — to a living,** nominare ad un benefizio; **to — a charge,** sollevar un'accusa.
preferable ['prefərəbl], *a.* Preferibile.
preferably, *adv.* Preferibilmente.
preference, *n.* Preferenza, *f.* **By —,** a preferenza; (*Comm.*) **— share,** azione privilegiata, *f.*
preferential [prefə'renʃəl], *a.* Preferenziale, privilegiato.
preferment [pre'fə:ɹmənt], *n.* Promozione, *f.*, avanzamento, *m.*
prefix ['pri:fiks], *n.* (*Gram.*) Prefisso, *m.* || *v.t.* [pri'fiks] Premettere, anteporre; mettere come prefisso.
pregnable ['pregnəbl], *a.* Prendibile, espugnabile.
pregnancy ['pregnənsi], *n.* Gravidanza, *f.* (*fig.*) significanza, *f.*
pregnant, *a.* (*of woman*) Incinta; (*of animal*) gravida; (*fig.*) pregnante, pregno, pieno, intenso, fecondo, fertile.
prehensile [pri:'hensail], *a.* Prensile.
prehension, *n.* Prensione, *f.*
prehistoric [pri:his'tɔrik], *a.* Preistorico.
prehistory [pri:'histəri], *n.* Preistoria, *f.*
prejudge [pri:'dʒʌdʒ], *v.t.* Giudicare prematuramente.
prejudgment, *n.* Giudizio prematuro, *m.*
prejudice ['predʒu:dis], *v.t.* Pregiudicare, danneggiare, nuocere. || *n.* Pregiudizio, danno. **To the — of,** con pregiudizio di; **without —,** senza pregiudizio.
prejudiced, *a.* Prevenuto, danneggiato.
prejudicial, *a.* Pregiudizievole, dannoso.
prelacy ['preləsi], *n.* Prelatura, *f.*
prelate ['prelət], *n.* Prelato, *m.*
prelatic, prelatical [pre'lætik, pre'lætikəl], *a.* Prelatizio.
prelector [pre'lektəɹ], *n.* Professore, lettore, *m.*
preliminary [pre'liminəri], *n.a.* Preliminare, *m.*; introduzione, *f.*
prelude ['prelju:d], *n.* Preludio, *m.* || *v.t.i.* Preludere, preannunziare.

premature ['prematʃju:ɹ], *a.* Prematuro; precoce, anticipato, intempestivo.
prematurely, *adv.* Prematuramente.
prematureness, prematurity, *n.* Prematurità, *f.*; precocità, *f.*
premeditate [pri:'mediteɪt], *v.t.* Premeditare.
premeditated, *a.* Premeditato.
premeditation, *n.* Premeditazione, *f.*
premier ['premiəɹ], *a.* Primo, primario. || *n.* (*Pol.*) Primo ministro, *m.*
premiership, *n.* Presidenza del consiglio, *f.*
première [premi'ɛəɹ], *n.* (*Theat.Cinema.*) Prima, *f.*
premise (1) [pri'maiz], *v.t.* Premettere.
premise (2), **premiss** ['premis], *n.* Premessa, *f.*
premises ['premisiz], *n.pl.* Locali, *m.pl.*, casa e le sue attinenze; (*Logic*) premesse, *f.pl.*
premium ['pri:miəm], *n.* Premio, *m.*, ricompensa, *f.*; (*insurance*) premio d'assicurazione, *m.* **At a —,** con profitto, sopra la pari; **a high —,** un forte premio, *m.*; **to put a — on,** incoraggiare, favorire.
premonition [pri:mə'niʃən], *n.* Premonizione, *f.*, presentimento, *m.*
premonitory [pri'mɔnitəri], *a.* Premonitorio.
preoccupation [pri:ɔkju:'peiʃən], *n.* Preoccupazione, *f.*
preoccupied, *a.* Preoccupato.
preoccupy, *v.t.* Preoccupare; dominare, signoreggiare.
preordain [pri:ɔ:ɹ'dein], *v.t.* Preordinare, prestabilire.
prepaid [pri:'peid], *a.* Franco, porto franco.
preparation [prepə'reiʃən], *n.* Preparazione, *f.*; preparativo, allestimento, *m.*; (*Med.*) preparato, *m.*; (*lessons*) ore di studio, *f.pl.* **Preparations for the journey,** preparativi per viaggio, *m.pl.*
preparative [pre'pærətiv], *n.a.* Preparativo, *m.*
preparatory, *a.* Preparatorio. **— school,** scuola elementare *f.*
prepare [pri'pɛəɹ], *v.t.i.* Preparare, apparecchiare, allestire; prepararsi, apparecchiarsi, disporsi. **To be prepared to,** essere pronto a, essere disposto a.
prepared, *a.* (*ready*) Pronto.
preparedness, *n.* L'essere preparato; preparazione, *f.*
prepay [pri:'pei], *v.t.* Pagare in anticipo; (*letter*) affrancare.
prepayment, *n.* Pagamento anticipato, *m.*; (*of letter*) affrancatura, *f.*
prepense [pri'pens], *a.* (*Law*) Premeditato.
preponderance [pri'pɔndərəns], *n.* Preponderanza, *f.*
preponderant, *a.* Preponderante, predominante.
preponderate [pri'pɔndəreit], *v.i.* Preponderare, predominare. **To — over,** superare, pesare più di.
preposition [prepo'ziʃən], *n.* (*Gram.*) Preposizione, *f.*
prepositional, *a.* Preposizionale.
prepossess [pri:po'zes], *v.t.* Predisporre, preoccupare; impressionare. **I was prepossessed in his favour,** ero interamente predisposto in suo favore.
prepossessing, *a.* Simpatico, attraente, insinuante.
prepossession, *n.* Preoccupazione, *f.*; pregiudizio, *m.*
preposterous [pri'pɔstərəs], *a.* Assurdo, sciocco, irragionevole.
preposterousness, *n.* Assurdità, sciocchezza, *f.*
Pre-Raphaelite, *n.a.*, Preraffaelita.
prerequisite [pri:'rekwizit], *n.* Requisito indispensabile, *m.*
prerogative [pri'rɔgətiv], *n.* Prerogativa, *f.*, privilegio, *m.*
presage ['presidʒ], *n.* Presagio, pronostico, presentimento, *m.*; profezia, *f.* || *v.t.* [pri:'seidʒ], Presagire, pronosticare, presentire.
presbyopia [prezbi'oupiə], *n.* Presbiopia, *f.*
presbyter ['prezbitəɹ], *n.* (*priest*) Prete, *m.*; sacerdote presbiteriano; (*elder*) anziano, *m.*
Presbyterian [prezbi'tiəriən], *n.a.* Presbiteriano, *m.*
Presbyterianism, *n.* Presbiterianismo, *m.*
presbytery ['prezbitəri], *n.* Presbiterio, *m.*
prescience ['preʃəns], *n.* Prescienza, *f.*
prescient ['preʃənt], *a.* Presciente.
prescind [pre'sind], *v.t.i.* Prescindere, prescindere da.
prescribe [pre'skraib], *v.t.i.* Prescrivere, ordinare; (*Med.*) ordinare, dare una ricetta.
prescript ['pri:skript], *n.* Prescritto, precetto, *m.*, norma, *f.*
prescription [pre'skripʃən], *n.* (*Med.*) Ricetta, *f.*; prescrizione, *f.*
prescriptive, *a.* Prescrittivo. **A — right,** un diritto consuetudinario, *m.*
presence ['prezəns], *n.* Presenza, *f.*; aspetto, *m.*, aria, *f.*; portamento, *m.* **In the — of,** alla presenza di, al cospetto di; **a fine —,** un bel portamento, un bell'aspetto, *m.*; **— of mind,** presenza di spirito, *f.*; **— -chamber,** sala di udienza, *f.*
present (1) ['prezənt], *a.* Presente, attuale; corrente. || *n.* Presente, dono, regalo, *m.* **The — queen,** l'attuale regina, *f.*; **to be — at,** assistere a; **in the — fashion,** alla moda di oggi; **at —,** al presente, ora, adesso; **for the —,** per ora, pel momento; **to make a — of,** regalare.
present (2) [pri'zent], *v.t.* Presentare, porgere, consegnare, offrire; introdurre; regalare. **To — with,** regalare, donare, offrire in dono a; **to — oneself,** presentarsi, comparire; (*Mil.*) **Present arms!** Presentat-arm!
presentable [pre'zentəbl], *a.* Presentabile.
presentation [prezen'teiʃən], *n.* Presentazione, offerta, *f.*; (*Theat.*) rappresentazione, *f.* **— copy,** copia in omaggio, *f.*
presentee [prezen'ti:], *n.* Presentato, *m.*
presentiment [pre'zentimənt], *n.* Presentimento, *m.* **To have a — of,** presentire.
presently, *adv.* Fra poco, a momenti, dopo; subito, adesso.
presentment [pre'zentmənt], *n.* Presentazione, rappresentazione, *f.*; resoconto, *m.*; descrizione, *f.*
preservable [pre'zə:ɹvəbl], *a.* Conservabile.
preservation [prezəɹ'veiʃən], *n.* Preservazione, conservazione, *f.*; salvezza, *f.*, salvamento, scampo, *m.* **In a good state of —,** ben conservato.
preservative [pre'zə:ɹvətiv], *n.a.* Preservativo, preservante, *m.*

preserve, *n.* (*jam*) Conserva, marmellata, composta di frutta, *f.*; (*for game*) riserva, bandita, *f.*; (*for fish*) vivaio, *m.*, peschiera, *f.* || *v.t.* Preservare, salvare; conservare, serbare.
preserved, *a.* Conservato. — **fruit,** frutta candita, *f.*; — **meat,** carne in conserva, *f.*
preserver, *n.* Salvatore, *m.*; conservatore, *m.*
preside [preˈzaid], *v.i.* Presiedere a, tener la presidenza di. **To — at a meeting,** presiedere ad un'adunanza.
presidency [ˈprezidənsi], *n.* Presidenza, *f.*
president, *n.* Presidente, *m.*; (*of college, etc.*) preside, *m.*
presidential [preziˈdenʃəl], *a.* Presidenziale.
presiding [preˈzaidiŋ], *prep.p.a.* Alla presidenza, sotto la presidenza. **The vice-president —,** sotto la presidenza del vice-presidente.
press (1) [pres], *v.t.i.* Premere, comprimere; pigiare, calcare; stringere; pressare; urgere, spingere, urtare; far accettare. **To be pressed for time,** aver poco tempo; **she pressed his hand,** essa gli strinse la mano; **it presses on my mind,** mi pesa; **to — for an answer,** insistere per una risposta; **to — a gift on someone,** far accettare un dono a qualcuno; **the crowd pressed round,** la folla si accalcò intorno; **to — forward,** spingere, spingersi avanti; **time presses,** il tempo incalza.
press (2), *n.* (*crowd*) Calca, folla, *f.*; (*urgency*) fretta, premura, *f.*; (*Mech.*) torchio, *m.*; (*cupboard*) armadio, *m.*; (*newspapers*) stampa, *f.*; giornalismo, *m.*; (*of sail*) forza, *f.* **The — of events,** l'incalzare degli avvenimenti, *m.*; (*Print.*) **to go to —,** andare in stampa; **in the —,** in corso di stampa; **—-agency,** agenzia d'informazioni, *f.*; **—-cutting,** ritaglio di giornale, *m.*; **—-man,** giornalista, *m.*, (*Print.*) macchinista, *m.*; **—-mark,** segno indicatore del libro.
pressed, *a.* Compresso, premuto. — **beef,** carne di bue conservata, *f.*
pressing, *a.* Urgente, pressante, incalzante. || *n.* Pressione, *f.* **A — need,** un bisogno urgente, *m.*; **a — invitation,** un invito caloroso, *m.*; **he does not need much —,** non ha bisogno d'esser pregato.
pressure [ˈpreʃəɹ], *n.* Pressione, costrizione, *f.*; insistenza, *f.*; fretta, urgenza, *f.* **Financial —,** strettezze finanziarie, *f.pl.* — **of business,** cumulo di lavoro, *m.*; **to yield under —,** esser forzato a cedere; **to bring — to bear,** far pressione; **high, low —,** alta, bassa pressione, *f.*; **—-gauge,** manometro, *m.*
prestidigitator [prestiˈdidʒiteitəɹ], *n.* Prestidigitatore, *m.*
prestige [ˈpresti:ʒ], *n.* Prestigio, *m.*
presto [ˈprestou], *adv.* (*Mus.*) Presto. || *inter.* **Hey —!** Ecco! Vedete!
presumable [priˈzju:məbl], *a.* Presumibile.
presumably, *adv.* Presumibilmente.
presume [preˈzju:m], *v.t.i.* Presumere, immaginarsi, supporre; arrogarsi, ardire, prendersi la libertà, avvantaggiarsi. **To — on one's position,** abusare della propria posizione.
presumingly, *adv.* Presuntuosamente.
presumption [preˈzʌmʃən], *n.* Presunzione, *f.*; congettura, *f.*; arroganza, *f.*
presumptive, *a.* Presuntivo, presunto. **Heir —,** erede presunto, *m.*
presumptuous [preˈzʌmptju:əs], *a.* Presuntuoso, arrogante.
presumptuousness, *n.* Presuntuosità, arroganza, *f.*
presuppose [pri:səˈpouz], *v.t.* Presupporre.
presupposition [pri:sʌpəˈziʃən], *n.* Presupposizione, *f.*
pretence [preˈtens], *n.* Pretesa, pretensione, *f.*; finzione, mostra, *f.*; pretesto, *m.*, scusa, *f.* **Devoid of all —,** senza pretese; **on the slightest —,** alla minima scusa; **under the — of,** col pretesto di, facendo finta di; **false pretences,** millantato credito.
pretend, *v.t.i.* Pretendere; fingere, far finta, far mostra, far le viste. **He does not — to be a scholar,** non pretende di essere erudito; **to — ignorance,** fingere di esser ignorante.
pretended, *a.* Preteso, supposto, ritenuto, finto.
pretender, *n.* Pretendente, *m.f.*
pretension, *n.* Pretensione, pretesa, *f.* **Of great pretensions,** di molte pretese; **to have pretensions,** aver molte pretese.
pretentious [preˈtenʃəs], *a.* Pretenzioso; arrogante; vanitoso, ostentato.
pretentiousness, *n.* Pretenziosità, ostentazione, arroganza, *f.*
preterhuman [pri:təɹˈhju:mən], *a.* Sovrumano.
preterit [ˈpretərit], *n.* (*Gram.*) Preterito, *m.*
pretermission [pri:təɹˈmiʃən], *n.* Omissione, *f.* **Without —,** senza cessare, senza requie.
preternatural [pri:təɹˈnætʃurəl], *a.* Preternaturale.
pretext [ˈpri:tekst], *n.* Pretesto, *m.*, scusa, *f.* **To offer a —,** dar appiglio, fornir un pretesto.
prettily [ˈpritili], *adv.* Graziosamente; gentilmente.
prettiness [ˈpritinis], *n.* Graziosità, leggiadria, eleganza, *f.*
pretty [ˈpriti], *a.* Bellino, carino, grazioso, leggiadro, delizioso. || *adv.* Abbastanza, quasi; passibilmente. **A — wit,** un tipo spiritoso, *m.*; (*fig.*) **a — mess,** un bell'imbroglio, *m.*; **I am — well,** sto benino; — **much the same,** quasi lo stesso; — **—,** lezioso, sdolcinato; — **nearly,** quasi, press'a poco.
prevail [preˈveil], *v.i.* Prevalere, vincere, superare; predominare; persuadere. **Cold winds — here,** venti freddi predominano qui; **I prevailed on him to come,** lo persuasi a venire; **to — over,** prevalere su, vincerla su.
prevailing, *a.* Prevalente, predominante; generale.
prevalence [ˈprevələns], *n.* Prevalenza, predominanza, *f.*
prevalent, *a.* Prevalente, predominante; generale, diffuso.
prevaricate [preˈværikeit], *v.i.* Prevaricare; uscire dai limiti.
prevarication, *n.* Prevaricazione, *f.*
prevaricator, *n.* Prevaricatore, *m.*
prevent [priˈvent], *v.t.* Impedire, inceppare, ostacolare.
preventable, preventible, *a.* Evitabile.
prevention, *n.* Prevenzione, *f.*, l'impedire, *m.*
preventive, *n.a.* Preventivo, *m.*

previous ['pri:viəs], *a.* Previo, precedente, antecedente. **— to,** prima di, avanti che; **the — speaker,** l'oratore precedente, *m.*; (*colloq.*) **to be —,** anticipare.
previously, *adv.* Dapprima, prima, anteriormente.
prevision [pri:'viʒən], *n.* Previsione, *f.*
pre-war ['pri:'wɔ:ɹ], *a.* D'anteguerra.
prey [prei], *n.* Preda, rapina, *f.* || *v.i.* Far preda di, saccheggiare, predare. **Bird of —,** uccello di rapina, *m.*; **a — to,** in preda a; **to fall a — to,** darsi in preda a; **to — upon someone's mind,** ossessionare qualcuno.
preyer, *n.* Predone, predatore, *m.*
price [prais], *n.* Prezzo, costo, *m.* || *v.t.* Valutare, mettere il prezzo a; domandare il prezzo di. **At any —,** ad ogni costo, a qualunque prezzo; **at reduced prices,** a prezzi ribassati; **at half —,** a mezzo costo; **cost —,** prezzo di costo, *m.*; **high —,** prezzo alto, *m.*; **beyond —,** inestimabile, inapprezzabile; **trade —,** prezzo di fabbrica, *m.*; **below cost —,** sotto costo; **to rise in —,** aumentare di prezzo; **to set a — on someone's head,** mettere una taglia su qualcuno; **market —,** prezzo corrente, *m.*; **— list,** listino dei prezzi, *m.*; distinta, tariffa, *f.*
priceless, *a.* Inestimabile, senza prezzo, impagabile.
prick [prik], *n.* Puntura, *f.*, pungolo, *m.* || *v.t.* Pungere, punzecchiare; spronare; segnare con un punto. **The — of conscience,** lo stimolo della coscienza, rimorso, *m.*; **to kick against the pricks,** ribellarsi al proprio destino; **to — out seedlings,** trapiantare piantine; **to — up one's ears,** tendere gli orecchi, drizzare gli orecchi.
pricker, *n.* Punteruolo, bulino, *m.*
pricking, *n.* Puntura, *f.*, pizzicore, *m.* || *a.* Pungente.
prickle ['prikl], *n.* Spina, *f.*, aculeo, *m.*
prickliness, *n.* Spinosità, *f.*
prickly, *a.* Spinoso, pungente; difficile, scabroso. (*Med.*) **— heat,** calore, *m.*, infiammazione, *f.*; (*Bot.*) **— pear,** fico d'India, *m.*
pride (1) [praid], *n.* Superbia, fierezza, *f.*, orgoglio, *m.* || *v.r.* Piccarsi di, inorgoglirsi, vantarsi di. **Proper —,** amor proprio, *m.*, fierezza, *f.*; **false —,** falso orgoglio, *m.*; **to humble someone's —,** far cader l'orgoglio a qualcuno; **to take a — in,** avere la fierezza di, essere fiero di; **to — oneself on,** vantarsi di, farsi gloria di.
pride (2), *n.* (*of lions*) Gruppo, *m.*
priest [pri:st], *n.* Prete, sacerdote, chierico, *m.* **High —,** sommo sacerdote, *m.*; **parish —,** parroco, *m.*; **— -ridden,** governato dai preti.
priestcraft ['pri:stkrɑ:ft], *n.* Impostura pretesca, *f.*; gesuiteria, *f.*
priestess, *n.* Sacerdotessa, *f.*
priesthood ['pri:sthud], *n.* Sacerdozio, clero, *m.*
priestlike, *a.* Sacerdotale, pretesco.
priestliness, *n.* Pretismo, sacerdozio, *m.*
priestling, *n.* Pretino, *m.*
priestly, *a.* Sacerdotale, pretesco.
prig [prig], *n.* Saccente, pedante, saputello, *m.*; persona pretenziosa, *f.* || *v.t.* (*colloq.*) Rubare.
priggish ['prigiʃ], *a.* Saputello, pretenzioso.
priggishness, *n.* Saccenteria, pretenziosità, *f.*
prim [prim], *a.* Formale, preciso, affettato, tirato ai quattro spilli.
primacy ['praiməsi], *n.* (*Eccles.*) Primazia, *f.*; (*supremacy*) primato, *m.*, supremazia, *f.*
prima donna ['pri:mədɔnə], *n.* Prima donna, diva, *f.*
prima facie [praimə'feiʃi], *a.* Prima facie, a prima vista.
primage ['praimidʒ], *n.* (*Naut.*) Cappa, *f.*; tassa di carico, *f.*
primal, primary ['praiməl, 'praiməri], *a.* Primario, primo, elementare, fondamentale. **Primary school,** scuola primaria, *f.*
primate ['praimit], *n.* (*Eccles.*) Primate, *m.*
primates [prai'meiti:z], *n.pl.* (*Zool.*) Primati, *m.pl.*
prime [praim], *a.* Primo, principale; di prima qualità, eccellente, ottimo. || *n.* Colmo, fiore, *m.*; (*Math.*) numero primo, *m.*; (*Eccles.*) prima, *f.*; (*Fencing*) prima, *f.* || *v.t.* (*a gun*) Caricare; (*woodwork*) mesticare, dare la mestica a; (*a pump*) adescare, proiettare acqua nel cilindro; (*instruct*) istruire, preparare, mettere al corrente; (*with drink*) far sbevazzare. **— cost,** prezzo di costo, costo di produzione, *m.*; **— minister,** primo ministro, *m.*; **— mover,** promotore, *m.*; causa prima, *f.*; **the — of life,** la primavera della vita, *f.*; **in the — of life,** nel fiore della vita; **in its —,** nel suo fiore; **in one's —,** nel fiore dell'età.
primeness, *n.* Eccellenza, *f.*
primer (1) ['praiməɹ], *n.* Primo libro, sillabario, *m.*; manuale, *m.*; (*of fuse*) innesco, *m.* **Latin —,** primo libro di latino, *m.*
primer (2) ['priməɹ], *n.* (*Print.*) Garamone, *m.*, carattere corpo 10.
primeval [praim'i:vəl], *a.* Primevo, primordiale, primitivo.
priming ['praimiŋ], *n.* (*of gun*) Innesco, polverino, *m.*; (*of paint*) prima mano, *f.*
primitive ['primitiv], *a.* Primitivo. || *n.* (*Art*) Primitivo, *m.*
primitiveness, *n.* Primitività, *f.*
primness, *n.* Formalità, *f.*; affettazione, *f.*
primogeniture [praimo'dʒenitʃu:ɹ], *n.* Primogenitura, *f.*
primordial [praim'ɔ:ɹdiəl], *a.* Primordiale.
primrose ['primrouz], *n.* (*Bot.*) Primula, primaverina, *f.*
prince [prins], *n.* Principe, *m.*
princedom, *n.* Principato, *m.*
princelike, *a.* Di principe, principesco.
princeliness, *n.* Nobiltà, maestà, *f.*
princely, *a.* Principesco, magnifico, splendido.
princeship, *n.* Principato, *m.*
princess, *n.* Principessa, *f.*
principal ['prinsipəl], *a.* Principale, primo, primario, precipuo. || *n.* Capo, direttore; principale, padrone; (*Comm.*) capitale, *m.*
principality [prinsi'pæliti], *n.* Principato, *m.* **The Principality,** il Galles, *m.*
principally, *adv.* Principalmente.
principalship, *n.* Direzione, presidenza, *f.*
principle ['prinsipəl], *n.* Principio, *m.* **Of no —,** senza principii; **on —,** per principio; **well-principled,** di buoni principii.
prink [priŋk], *v.t.i.* Attillarsi, pavoneggiarsi.
print [print], *v.t.* Stampare, imprimere, improntare. || *n.* Stampa, impronta, impressione, *f.*; (*Phot.*) prova, *f.*; (*cotton material*) indiana, tela stampata, *f.*; (*lettering*) carat-

teri, *m.pl.*; (*engraving*) incisione, stampa, *f.* **Small —,** stampa piccola; **in —,** stampato, in stampa; **out of —,** esaurito; **to come out in —,** uscire per le stampe; **printed matter,** stampato, *m.*; **— -seller,** mercante di incisioni, *m.*; **— -shop,** negozio di incisioni, *m.*; **— -works,** fabbrica di tessuti stampati, *f.*; **finger- —,** impronta digitale, *f.*

printer, *n.* Stampatore, tipografo, *m.* **Printer's devil,** ragazzo di tipografia, *m.*; **printer's ink,** inchiostro da stampa, inchiostro tipografico, *m.*; **printer's error,** errore tipografico, errore di stampa, *m.*

printing, *n.* Tipografia, *f.*; stampatura, tiratura, *f.* **— -works,** tipografia, *f.*, stabilimento tipografico, *m.*; (*Phot.*) **— -frame,** torchietto, *m.*; **— -out paper,** carta ad annerimento diretto, *f.*; **— press,** torchio, *m.*, macchina tipografica, *f.*

prior (1) ['praiəɹ], *a.adv.* Anteriore a, avanti di, antecedente, previo.

prior (2), *n.* (*Eccles.*) Priore, *m.*

prioress, *n.* Priora, badessa, *f.*

priority [prai'ɔːriti], *n.* Anteriorità, priorità, *f.*

priorship, *n.* Priorato, *m.*

priory ['praiəri], *n.* Prioria, *f.*

prise [praiz], *n.* Leva, *f.* || *v.t.* Far leva su. **To — open,** forzare, scoperchiare.

prism [prizm], *n.* Prisma, *m.*

prismatic [priz'mætik], *a.* Prismatico.

prison ['prizən], *n.* Prigione, *f.*, carcere, *m.* **In —,** in prigione; **out of —,** fuori di prigione; **to break —,** scappare di prigione, evadere; **— breaker,** evaso dal carcere; **— -van,** vettura cellulare, *f.*

prisoner, *n.* Prigioniero, *m.*, prigioniera, *f.*, detenuto, *m.*, detenuta, *f.* **— at the bar,** imputato, *m.*, imputata, *f.*; **to take —,** far prigioniero, catturare; **to be kept a close —,** essere prigioniero sotto stretta sorveglianza.

pristine ['pristin], *a.* Pristino, primiero.

prithee! ['priði], *obs. inter.* Di grazia! Prego!

privacy ['praivəsi, 'privəsi], *n.* Ritiro, isolamento, *m.*, solitudine, *f.*; intimità, *f.*; privatezza, *f.* **In —,** in privato, appartatamente, per conto proprio.

private ['praivit], *a.* Privato, particolare, personale; segreto, nascosto, celato; confidenziale; solitario; (*on door*) è proibito l'ingresso. || *n.* Soldato semplice, *m.* **To keep a matter —,** tener nascosta una cosa; **— reasons,** ragioni personali, *m.pl.*; **a — boarding-house,** una pensione, *f.*; **— theatricals,** una recita in famiglia, *f.*; **his — property,** la sua proprietà privata, *f.*; **a — conversation,** una conversazione a quattr'occhi; **a letter marked —,** una lettera segnata confidenziale, *f.*; **privates,** parti genitali, *f.pl.*; (*Art*) **— view,** anteprima, *f.*; **by — treaty,** per accordo privato.

privateer [praivə'tiəɹ], *n.* Corsaro patentato, *m.*

privateering, *n.* Il corseggiare, *m.*

privately, *adv.* Privatamente, in forma privata, personalmente.

privation [prai'veiʃən], *n.* Privazione, *f.*; disagio, *m.*, mancanza, *f.*

privative ['privətiv], *a.* Privativo, negativo.

privet ['privit], *n.* (*Bot.*) Ligustro, *m.*

privilege ['privilidʒ], *n.* Privilegio, *m.*; prerogativa, *f.* || *v.t.* Privilegiare.

privileged, *a.* Privilegiato.

privily ['privili], *adv.* Segretamente, in segreto.

privity, *n.* Comunicazione confidenziale, *f.*

privy ['privi], *a.* Nascosto, segreto, privato. || *n.* Latrina, ritirata, *f.*, cesso, *m.* **— purse,** lista civile del sovrano, *f.*; **Privy Councillor,** membro del consiglio privato, *m.*; **to be — to,** aver cognizione di.

prize [praiz], *n.* Premio, *m.*, ricompensa, *f.*; (*naval*) cattura, preda, *f.*; (*lottery*) premio, lotto, *m.* || *v.t.* Apprezzare, valutare, stimare, far caso di. **— poem,** poema premiato, *m.*; **to make — of,** catturare, far bottino; **to become lawful —,** cader preda, venir catturato; **— court,** tribunale delle prede, *m.*; **— -fight,** pugilato, *m.*, partita di pugilato, *f.*; **— -fighter,** pugile, pugilatore, *m.*; **— -giving,** distribuzione dei premi, *f.*; **— -list,** elenco dei premiati; **— -money,** decima di preda, taglia, *f.*

prizeman, *n.* Premiato, laureato; detentore di un premio, *m.*

prizewinner, *n.* Premiato, vincitore, *m.*

pro [prou], *prep.* Per, pro. **The pros and cons,** il pro e il contro, *m.*

probability [prɔbə'biliti], *n.* Probabilità, *f.* **In all —,** probabilmente.

probable ['prɔbəbəl], *a.* Probabile.

probably, *adv.* Probabilmente.

probate ['proubeit], *n.* (*Law*) Verificazione d'un testamento, *f.*; omologazione, autenticazione, *f.* **— duty,** tassa di successione, *f.*

probation [pro'beiʃən], *n.* Periodo di prova, *m.*; tirocinio, noviziato, *m.*; prova, *f.*; (*Eccles.*) noviziato, *m.* **On —,** in prova, in esame.

probationary, *a.* Probatorio, probativo.

probationer, *n.* Candidato, novizio, *m.*

probationership, *n.* Candidatura, *f.*, noviziato, *m.*

probe [proub], *v.t.* Sondare, esplorare; (*fig.*) approfondire, esaminare a fondo. || *n.* Sonda, *f.*, (*Med.*) specillo, *m.*

probity ['proubiti], *n.* Probità, integrità, *f.*

problem ['prɔbləm], *n.* Problema, *m.* **— play,** dramma a tesi, *m.*

problematic, problematical, *a.* Problematico.

proboscis (*pl.* **proboscides**) [pro'bɔsis, pro'bɔsidiːz], *n.* Proboscide, *f.*

pro-British [prou'britiʃ], *a.* Anglofilo.

procedure [pro'siːdjuːɹ], *n.* Procedura, *f.*, procedimento, *m.*

proceed [pro'siːd], *v.i.* Procedere, avanzare, camminare; seguitare, continuare; venire, derivare, provenire; fare. **How shall we —?** Che cosa faremo adesso? **to — to extremities,** andare agli estremi; **to — with,** continuare, a, agire verso; (*Law*) **to — against,** procedere contro, intentare processo a.

proceeding, *a.* Azione, *f.*; procedimento, *m.*

proceedings, *n.pl.* Atti, rendiconti, *m.pl.*; (*Law*) processo, *m.* **The — of a society,** gli atti d'una società.

proceeds ['prousiːdz], *n.pl.* Profitti, *m.pl.*, ricavo, *m.*; incassi, *m.pl.*

process ['prouses], *n.* Processo, *m.*; procedimento, corso, *m.*; (*Law*) processo, *m.*, citazione, *f.* || *v.i.* [pro'ses], (*colloq.*) Andare in processione; *v.t.* ['prouses], preparare, processare. **In — of time,** con il tempo; **— engraving,** fotoincisione, *f.*

procession, *n.* Processione, *f.*, corteo, *m.* **To walk in —,** sfilare in corteo.
processional, *a.* Processionale, di corteo.
proclaim [pro'kleim], *v.t.* Proclamare, dichiarare, render pubblico. **To — queen,** proclamare regina.
proclamation [prɔklə'meiʃən], *n.* Proclamazione, dichiarazione, pubblicazione, *f.*
proclivity [pro'kliviti], *n.* Proclività, inclinazione, propensione, *f.*
proconsul [prou'kɔnsəl], *n.* Proconsole, *m.*
proconsular, *a.* Proconsolare.
procrastinate [pro'kræstineit], *v.i.* Procrastinare, temporeggiare, indugiare.
procrastination, *n.* Procrastinazione, *f.*, temporeggiamento, indugio, *m.*
procrastinator, *n.* Procrastinatore, *m.*
procreate ['proukrieit], *v.t.* Procreare, generare.
procreative, *a.* Generativo, fecondo.
procreativeness, *n.* Fecondità, *f.*
Procrustean [pro'krʌstiən], *a.* Di Procuste. **A — bed,** un letto di Procuste, *m.*
proctor ['prɔktəɹ], *n.* (*Law*) Procuratore legale, *m.*; (*University*) censore, funzionario incaricato della disciplina, *m.*
proctorial, *a.* Censorio.
proctorship, *n.* funzioni di censore, *f.pl.*
procumbent [pro'kʌmbənt], *a.* Prostrato; procombente.
procurable [pro'kju:rəbl], *a.* Ottenibile.
procuration [prɔkju:'reiʃən], *n.* Procurazione, *f.* (*Law*) procura, *f.*; (*of women*) ruffianeria, *f.*, prossenetismo, *m.*
procurator, *n.* (*Law*) Procuratore, *m.*; **— Fiscal,** procuratore fiscale (in Scozia), *m.*
procure [pro'kju:ɹ], *v.t.* Procurare, provvedere, procacciare; *v.i.* (*women*) fare il mezzano.
procurement, *n.* Procurazione, *f.*
procurer, *n.* Mezzano, ruffiano, *m.*
procuress, *n.* Mezzana, ruffiana, *f.*
prod [prɔd], *v.t.* Pungere; spronare, stimolare. || *n.* Pungolo, *m.*
prodigal ['prɔdigəl], *a.* Prodigo, scialacquatore; generoso, largo, liberale. || *n.* Prodigo, scialacquatore, *m.* **The — son,** il figliuol prodigo, *m.*
prodigality [prɔdi'gæliti], *n.* Prodigalità, *f.*
prodigious [pro'didʒəs], *a.* Prodigioso, miracoloso, portentoso.
prodigiously, *adv.* Prodigiosamente.
prodigiousness, *n.* Prodigiosità, *f.*
prodigy ['prɔdidʒi], *n.* Prodigio, portento, miracolo, *m.*
produce (1) ['prɔdju:s], *n.* Prodotto, frutto, *m.*; profitto, *m.* **—-broker,** agente di produzione, *m.*; **— market,** mercato commerciale, *m.*
produce (2) [pro'dju:s], *v.t.* Produrre; fornire; esibire; fabbricare; pubblicare, esporre; (*Theat.*) mettere in scena, rappresentare; (*Geom.*) prolungare.
producer, *n.* Produttore, *m.*; (*Theat.*) direttore, impresario, *m.*; (*Cinema*) produttore, *m.*
producibility, *n.* Producibilità, *f.*; (*Geom.*) prolungabilità, *f.*
producible, *a.* Producibile; prolungabile.
product ['prɔdʌkt], *n.* Prodotto, frutto, *m.*
production [pro'dʌkʃən], *n.* Produzione, *f.*; prodotto, *m.*; (*Theat.*) messa in scena, *f.*
productive, *a.* Produttivo, fruttifero, fertile. **— of great annoyance,** causa di gran fastidio, *f.*
productiveness, *n.* Produttività, *f.*
proem ['prouem], *n.* Proemio, esordio, *m.*, prefazione, *f.*
profanation [prɔfə'neiʃən], *n.* Profanazione, *f.*
profane [pro'fein], *a.* Profano. || *v.t.* Profanare, violare.
profanely, *adv.* Profanamente.
profaneness, profanity [pro'feinnes, pro'fæniti], *n.* Profanità, *f.*; bestemmia, *f.*; irriverenza, *f.*
profaner, *n.* Profanatore, *m.*
profess [pro'fes], *v.t.i.* Professare, dichiarare, pretendere, far professione di. **To — friendship,** far professione di amicizia; **to — oneself,** professarsi, dichiararsi.
professed, *a.* Professato, dichiarato, preteso.
professedly, *adv.* Dichiaratamente, apertamente.
profession, *n.* Professione, *f.*; mestiere, *m.* **By —,** di mestiere.
professional, *a.* Professionale, di mestiere. **A — man,** un professionista, *m.*
professionally, *adv.* Efficientemente, abilmente.
professor, *n.* Professore di università, *m.*
professorial [prɔfe'sɔ:riəl], *a.* Professorale.
professorship, *n.* Professorato, *m.*, cattedra, *f.*
proffer ['prɔfəɹ], *v.t.* Offrire; proferire. || *n.* Profferta, offerta, *f.*
proficiency [pro'fiʃənsi], *n.* Abilità, efficenza, *f.*; profitto, *m.*
proficient, *a.* Esperto, provetto, abile, bravo.
proficiently, *adv.* Espertamente.
profile ['proufail, 'proufi:l], *n.* Profilo, *m.* || *v.t.* Profilare. **In —,** in profilo, di profilo.
profit ['prɔfit], *n.* Profitto, utile, guadagno, frutto, *m.*; progresso, vantaggio, *m.* || *v.t.i.* Profittare, approfittare; avvantaggiarsi, valersi, avvalersi. **— and loss,** profitti e perdite; **to make a — on,** guadagnare da; **What will it — him?** Che vantaggio ne avrà? **to — by,** trarre profitto da; **—-sharing,** compartecipazione agli utili, *f.*
profitable, *a.* Profittevole, utile, fruttuoso.
profitableness, *n.* Utilità, *f.*, vantaggio, *m.*
profitably, *adv.* Profittevolmente.
profiteer [profi'tiəɹ], *n.* Affarista, profittatore, *m.*
profitless, *a.* Inutile, senza profitto, senza vantaggio.
profitlessness, *n.* Inutilità, *f.*
profligacy ['prɔfligəsi], *n.* Dissolutezza, sfrenatezza, *f.*, libertinaggio, *m.*
profligate, *a.* Dissoluto, sfrenato, sregolato, libertino. || *n.* Libertino, prodigo, *m.*
profound [pro'faund], *a.* Profondo; immenso, intenso.
profoundly, *adv.* Profondamente.
profoundness, profundity [pro'faundnis, pro'fʌnditi], *n.* Profondità, *f.*
profuse [pro'fju:s], *a.* Profuso, abbondante; prodigo, copioso. **— in promises,** prodigo di promesse.
profusely, *adv.* Profusamente, a profusione.
profuseness, profusion [pro'fju:snis, pro'fju:ʒən], *n.* Profusione, abbondanza, prodigalità, *f.*
progenitor [pro'dʒenitəɹ], *n.* Progenitore, *m.*, progenitrice, *f.*, antenato, capostipite, *m.* **Our progenitors,** i nostri avi, *m.pl.*

progeny ['prɔdʒəni], *n.* Progenie, discendenza, *f.*; prole, figliuolanza, *f.*, stirpe, *f.*
prognathous [prɔg'neiθəs], *a.* Prognato.
prognosis [prɔg'nousis], *n.* (*Med.*) Prognosi, *f.*
prognostic [prɔg'nɔstik], *n.* Pronostico, *m.*
prognosticate, *v.t.* Pronosticare.
prognostication, *n.* Pronosticazione, *f.*
prognosticator, *n.* Pronosticatore, *m.*
programme ['prougræm], *n.* Programma, *m.*
progress (1) ['prougres], *n.* Progresso, corso, avanzamento, *m.*; viaggio, cammino, progredimento, *m.* **Work in —,** lavori in corso, *m.pl.*; **to make —,** far progressi; **to report —,** riferire sull'andamento.
progress (2) [pro'gres], *v.i.* Progredire, procedere, avanzare. **How is your work progressing?** Come va il lavoro? **to — well,** progredire bene.
progression, *n.* Progresso; (*Math.Mus.*) progressione, *f.* **Mode of —,** modo di progredire.
progressive, *a.* Progressivo. || *n.* Progressista, *m.*
progressiveness, *n.* Progressività, *f.*
prohibit [pro'hibit], *v.t.* Proibire, vietare, interdire.
prohibition [prohi'biʃən], *n.* Proibizione, *f.*, divieto, *m.*
Prohibitionism, *n.* Proibizionismo, *m.*
prohibitive [pro'hibitiv], *a.* Proibitivo.
prohibitory, *a.* Proibitorio.
project (1) ['prɔdʒekt], *n.* Progetto, disegno, piano, *m.*
project (2) [pro'dʒekt], *v.t.i.* Progettare, disegnare; gettare, proiettare; sporgersi, proiettarsi.
projectile, *n.* Proiettile, proietto, *m.*
projecting, *a.* Sporgente.
projection, *n.* Proiezione, prominenza, *f.*; sporgenza, *f.*
projector, *n.* Progettista, *m.*; (*instrument*) proiettore, *m.*
prolapse ['proulæps], *n.* (*Med.*) Prolasso, *m.*
prolegomena [prole'gɔmenə], *n.pl.* Prolegomeni, *m.pl.*
proletarian [prouli'tɛəriən], *n.a.* Proletario.
proletariat, *n.* Proletariato, *m.*
proliferate [pro'lifəreit], *v.i.* Prolificare.
proliferation, *n.* Proliferazione, *f.*
prolific [pro'lifik], *a.* Prolifico, fecondo, fertile.
prolificness, *n.* Fecondità, fertilità, *f.*
prolix ['prouliks], *a.* Prolisso, diffuso.
prolixity, *n.* Prolissità, *f.*
prologue ['proulɔg], *n.* Prologo, *m.*
prolong [pro'lɔŋ], *v.t.* Prolungare, allungare; ritardare. **To — matters,** tirare in lungo.
prolongation [prɔlɔŋ'geiʃən], *n.* Prolungamento, *m.*, prolungazione, *f.*
promenade ['prɔmenɑ:d], *n.* Passeggiata, *f.*, corso, *m.* || *v.i.* Fare una passeggiata, passeggiare. **— deck,** prima coperta, *f.*; **— concert,** concerto popolare, *m.*
promenader, *n.* Passeggiatore, *m.*
promethean [pro'mi:θiən], *a.* Prometeico.
Prometheus [pro'mi:θju:s], *n.* Prometeo, *m.*
prominence ['prɔminəns], *n.* Prominenza, sporgenza, *f.*; eminenza, importanza, *f.*, risalto, *m.*
prominent, *a.* Prominente, sporgente; eminente, importante; cospicuo, notevole. **A — position,** una posizione importante, *f.*; **— eyes,** occhi sporgenti.
prominently, *adv.* Prominentemente, notevolmente.
promiscuity [promis'kju:iti], *n.* Promiscuità, confusione, *f.*
promiscuous, *a.* Promiscuo.
promiscuously, *adv.* Promiscuamente.
promise ['prɔmis], *n.* Promessa, *f.*; (*fig.*) speranze, *f.pl.* || *v.t.i.* Promettere, fare una promessa; predire, dare a sperare. **A youth of great —,** un giovane promettente, *m.*; **to break one's —,** mancare alla promessa; **to keep one's —,** mantenere la promessa, adempiere la promessa; **it promises to be fine,** promette una bella giornata; **to — well,** prometter bene; **to — greatly,** promettere grandi cose; **I — you it won't be easy,** vi assicuro che non sarà facile; **the promised land,** la terra promessa, *f.*
promising, *a.* Promettente.
promissory [pro'misəri], *a.* Promissorio. (*Comm.*) **— note,** pagherò, cambiale, *m.*
promontory ['prɔməntəri], *n.* (*Geog.*) Promontorio, *m.*
promote [pro'mout], *v.t.* Promuovere, favorire, stimolare, provocare. **He was promoted colonel,** fu promosso colonnello; **to — someone's interests,** favorire l'interesse di qualcuno.
promoter, *n.* Promotore, iniziatore, fautore, *m.* **Company —,** affarista, *m.*
promotion, *n.* Promozione, *f.*, avanzamento, *m.*; (*of a company*) lancio, *m.*
prompt [prɔmt], *a.* Pronto, svelto, rapido, lesto, alacre; (*Comm.*) a contanti, pronta cassa. || *v.t.* Spingere, urgere, stimolare, indurre; ispirare; (*Theat.*) suggerire. (*Theat.*) **— -book,** libro del suggeritore, *m.*; **— -box,** buca del suggeritore, *f.*
prompter, *n.* Suggeritore, *m.*
prompting, *n.* Stimolo, impulso, *m.*, suggestione, instigazione, *f.*; (*Theat.*) il suggerire, *m.*
promptness, promptitude ['prɔmtnis, 'prɔmtitju:d], *n.* Prontezza, sveltezza, alacrità, *f.*
promulgate ['prɔməlgeit], *v.t.* Promulgare.
promulgation, *n.* Promulgazione, *f.*
prone [proun], *a.* Prono, prostrato; incline, propenso, proclive, disposto a. || *adv.* Bocconi.
proneness, *n.* Inclinazione, propensione, proclività, *f.*
prong [prɔŋ], *n.* Rebbio, dente, *m.*, punta, *f.*
pronged, *a.* Con denti, con rebbi. **A three- — fork,** una forchetta a tre denti, *f.*
pronominal [pro'nɔminəl], *a.* (*Gram.*) Pronominale.
pronoun ['prounaun], *n.* (*Gram.*) Pronome, *m.*
pronounce [pro'nauns], *v.t.i.* Pronunziare, pronunciare, proferire, dire; dichiarare, esprimere. **To — an opinion,** emettere un giudicio; **the doctor pronounces him cured,** il medico lo dichiara guarito.
pronounceable, *a.* Pronunziabile.
pronounced, *a.* Pronunziato, marcato, rilevato, spiccato.
pronouncement, *n.* Dichiarazione, asserzione, *f.*
pronunciation [pronʌnsi'eiʃən], *n.* Pronunzia, pronuncia, *f.*

proof [pru:f], *n.* Prova, *f.*; assaggio, esperimento, *m.*; (*of alcohol*) grado, *m.*; (*Print.*) bozza, *f.* || *v.t.* Rendere impermeabile; (*Print.*) tirare una bozza. **As a — of,** in prova di; **to be — against,** poter resistere a; **to put to the —,** mettere alla prova; **to stand —,** reggere alla prova; **bomb- —,** a prova di bomba; **— -reader,** correttore di bozze, *m.*; **— -reading,** correzione delle bozze, *f.*
proofless, *a.* Senza prova.
prop [prɔp], *n.* Puntello, *m.*; appoggio, *m.*; sostegno, *m.* || *v.t.* Puntellare; sorreggere, sostenere.
propaganda [prɔpə'gændə], *n.* Propaganda, *f.*
propagandist, *n.* Propagandista, *m.f.*
propagate ['prɔpəgeit], *v.t.* Propagare; diffondere, spargere; (*Bot.*) propagginare.
propagation, *n.* Propagazione, *f.*
propagator, *n.* Propagatore, *m.*
proparoxytone [proupə'rɔksitoun], *a.* (*Gram.*) Proparossitono.
propel [pro'pel], *v.t.* Spingere innanzi, mettere in moto, avviare, propulsare.
propeller, *n.* Propulsore, *m.*; (*Naut.Aviat.*) elica, *f.*
propelling, *a.* Propulsore, motore. **— force,** forza motrice, *f.*
propensity [pro'pensiti], *n.* Propensione, tendenza, *f.*
proper ['prɔpəɹ], *a.* Proprio, particolare; vero, corretto, esatto, giusto; conveniente, convenevole. **— name,** nome proprio, *m.*; **in the — sense of the word,** nel senso proprio della parola; **at the — time,** nel momento buono; **it is — to,** conviene; **when I think —,** quando mi sembra bene.
properly, *adv.* Bene, giustamente, a rigore. **He very — refused,** molto giustamente egli ricusò; **— speaking,** a dir il vero, a rigore; **to behave —,** comportarsi bene; **I was — puzzled,** ero proprio imbarazzato.
property, *n.* Proprietà, *f.*, possesso, *m.*; beni, *m.pl.*, possedimento, *m.*, tenuta, *f.*; (*Theat.*) fabbisogno, vestiario, *m.* **A man of —,** un possidente, *m.*; **personal —,** beni mobili, *m.pl.*; **real —,** beni immobili, *m.pl.*; **to become public —,** divenir di dominio pubblico; **this house is my —,** questa casa appartiene a me; **— -tax,** imposta fondiaria, *f.*; (*Theat.*) **— -man,** trovarobe, *m.*; **— market,** mercato immobiliare, *m.*
prophecy ['prɔfisi], *n.* Profezia, *f.*
prophesy ['prɔfisai], *v.t.i.* Profetare, profetizzare, predire, preannunziare.
prophet ['prɔfit], *n.* Profeta, *m.*
prophetess, *n.* Profetessa, *f.*
prophetic, prophetical, *a.* Profetico.
prophylactic [proufi'læktic], *n.a.* (*Med.*) Profilattico, *m.*
prophylaxis, *n.* Profilassi, *f.*
propinquity, *n.* (*of place*) Vicinanza, *f.*; propinquità, affinità, *f.*; (*relationship*) parentela, *f.*
propitiate [pro'piʃieit], *v.t.* Propiziare, placare.
propitiation, *n.* Propiziazione, *f.*
propitiator, *n.* Propiziatore, *m.*
propitiatory, *a.* Propiziatorio.
propitious [pro'piʃəs], *a.* Propizio, favorevole, benigno.
propitiously, *adv.* Propiziamente.
propitiousness, *n.* Disposizione propizia, *f.*
proportion [pro'pɔːɹʃən], *n.* Proporzione, *f.*; parte, *f.* || *v.t.* Proporzionare. **In — as,** a misura che; **in — to,** in proporzione di; **out of —,** sproporzionato, fuor di misura.
proportionable, *a.* Proporzionabile.
proportional, *a.* Proporzionale; eguale. (*Pol.*) **— representation,** rappresentanza proporzionale, *f.*
proportionate, *a.* Proporzionato, adeguato, conforme.
proportionately, *adv.* Proporzionatamente.
proportionateness, *n.* Proporzionalità, *f.*
proposal [pro'pouzəl], *n.* Proposta, offerta, *f.* **A — of marriage,** una proposta di matrimonio, *f.*
propose, *v.t.i.* Proporre, suggerire, offrire; proporsi. **To — a toast,** fare un brindisi; **to — as a member,** proporre come socio; **to — to,** fare una proposta di matrimonio a, domandare la mano di.
proposer, *n.* Proponitore, *m.*
proposition [prɔpo'ziʃən], *n.* Proposizione, *f.*; (*colloq.*) proposta, *f.*, progetto, suggerimento, *m.*
propositional, *a.* Proposizionale.
propound [pro'paund], *v.t.* Proporre, presentare, mettere in campo.
proprietary [pro'praiətəri], *a.* Proprietario; di brevetto, brevettato. || *n.* Proprietario, *m.* **— rights,** diritti proprietari, *m.pl.*; **— medicine,** specialità farmaceutica, *f.*
proprietor, *n.* Proprietario, *m.*
proprietress, *n.* Proprietaria, *f.*
propriety, *n.* Proprietà, *f.*, decoro, garbo, *m.*; convenienza, *f.* **To observe the proprieties,** serbare le convenienze; **a breach of —,** una sconvenienza, *f.*
props [prɔps], *n.pl.* (*colloq.Theat.*) Fabbisogno, *m.*; oggetti teatrali, *m.pl.*
propulsion [pro'pʌlʃən], *n.* Propulsione, *f.* **Jet —,** propulsione a reazione, *f.*
propulsive, *a.* Propulsivo.
pro rata [prou'rɑːtə], *adv.* In proporzione.
prorogation [proro'geiʃən], *n.* Proroga, prorogazione, *f.*
prorogue [pro'roug], *v.t.* Prorogare, dilazionare, differire.
prosaic [pro'zeiik], *a.* Prosaico.
prosaically, *adv.* Prosaicamente.
prosaicness, *n.* Prosaicismo, *m.*
proscenium [pro'siːniəm], *n.* Proscenio, *m.*
proscribe [pro'skraib], *v.t.* Proscrivere; bandire, esiliare.
proscription [pro'skripʃən], *n.* Proscrizione, *f.*, bando, esilio, *m.*
proscriptive, *a.* Proscrittivo.
prose [prouz], *n.* Prosa, *f.* || *v.i.* Proseggiare; scrivere prolissamente. **— writer,** prosatore, *m.*; **— writings,** opere in prosa, *f.pl.*
prosecute ['prɔsikjuːt], *v.t.* Perseguire; continuare; (*Law*) processare, querelare, perseguire a termini di legge. **To — one's claims,** rivendicarsi i propri diritti.
prosecution, *n.* Prosecuzione, continuazione, *f.*; (*Law*) processo, *m.*, querela, parte civile, *f.*
prosecutor, *n.* (*Law*) Accusatore, attore, *m.* **Public —,** pubblico ministero, *m.*
prosecutrix, *n.* Accusatrice, *f.*
proselyte [prosə'lait], *n.* Proselito, seguace, *m.*

proselytize, *v.t.* Convertire, far proseliti.
proser ['prouzəɹ], *n.* Parolaio, ciarlone, *m.*
prosiness ['prouzinis], *n.* Verbosità, *f.*; prosaicismo, *m.*
prosodical [pro'zɔdikəl], *a.* Prosodico.
prosody ['prouzədi], *n.* Prosodia, *f.*
prospect (1) ['prɔspekt], *n.* Prospetto, *m.*; veduta, *f.*; (*fig.*) speranza, aspettazione, prospettiva, *f.* **There is no — of success,** non c'è speranza di riuscire; **it offers a fine — for the future,** presenta una bella prospettiva per l'avvenire; **to have in —,** avere in vista, avere in prospetto.
prospect (2) [pro'spekt], *v.i.* Esplorare; fare assaggi. **To — for,** andare alla ricerca di.
prospective [pro'spektiv], *a.* Prospettivo; futuro, avvenire, anticipato. **The — bridegroom,** il futuro sposo, *m.*; **this law is —,** questa legge ha decorrenza avvenire.
prospector, *n.* Cercatore, prospettore, *m.*
prospectus, *n.* Prospetto, programma, manifesto, *m.*
prosper ['prɔspəɹ], *v.i.* Prosperare, riuscire; *v.t.* far riuscire, favorire.
prosperity, *n.* Prosperità, *f.*
prosperous, *a.* Prospero, felice, fortunato, fiorente.
prosperously, *adv.* Prosperamente, fortunatamente.
prostate, prostate gland ['prɔsteit, prɔsteit 'glænd], *n.* (*Anat.*) Prostata, *f.*
prostatic [pro'stætik], *a.* Prostatico.
prostitute ['prostitju:t], *n.* Meretrice, prostituta, *f.* ‖ *v.t.* Prostituire. **To — one's talents,** prostituire l'ingegno.
prostitution, *n.* Prostituzione, *f.*
prostrate (1) ['prɔstreit], *a.* Prostrato, prosternato; abbattuto. **To be — with fatigue,** essere prostrato dalla fatica.
prostrate (2) [prɔs'treit], *v.t.* Prostrare, prosternare; abbattere, accasciare, infiacchire. **To — oneself before,** prostrarsi di pronte a.
prostration, *n.* Prostrazione, *f.*, abbattimento, *m.*
prostyle ['prostail], *n.* (*Arch.*) Prostilo, *m.*
prosy ['prouzi], *a.* Parolaio, verboso, loquace, tedioso.
protagonist [pro'tægənist], *n.* Protagonista, *m.f.*
protean ['proutiən], *a.* Proteiforme.
protect [pro'tekt], *v.t.* Proteggere, difendere, salvaguardare, riparare. **To — one's interests,** salvaguardare i propri interessi; **to — from the rain,** riparare dalla pioggia.
protection, *n.* Protezione, difesa, *f.*; (*patronage*) patrocinio, *m.*
protectionism, *n.* (*Pol.*) Protezionismo, *m.*
protectionist, *n.* (*Pol.*) Protezionista, *m.*
protective, *a.* Protettivo, protettore. **— colouring,** mimetismo, *m.*
protector, *n.* Protettore, difensore, patrono, *m.*
protectorate, *n.* Protettorato, *m.*
protectress, *n.* Protettrice, *f.*
protégé ['prɔteiʒei], *n.* Protetto, *m.*
protein ['prouti:n], *n.* (*Chem.*) Proteina, *f.*
pro tempore, pro tem. [prou 'tempɔri, prou'tem], *adv.* In via provvisoria.
protest (1) ['proutest], *n.* Protesta, *f.*; (*Law, Comm.*) protesto, *m.* **Under —,** protestando; **to enter a —,** protestare, fare una protesta.
protest (2) [pro'test], *v.t.i.* Protestare; dichiarare, attestare. **To — a bill,** protestare una cambiale; **to — one's innocence,** protestare la propria innocenza.
Protestant ['prɔtestənt], *n.a.* (*Eccles.*) Protestante, *m.f.*
Protestantism, *n.* Protestantesimo, Protestantismo, *m.*
protestation [prɔtes'teiʃən], *n.* Protestazione, protesta, *f.*
protester, *n.* Protestatore, *m.*
Proteus ['proutju:s], *n.* Proteo, *m.*
protocol ['proutokɔl], *n.* Protocollo, *m.*
protomartyr [proutɔ'mɑ:ɹtəɹ], *n.* Protomartire, *m.*
protonotary, *n.* Protonotario, *m.*
protoplasm ['proutoplæzm], *n.* Protoplasma, *m.*
prototype ['proutotaip], *n.* Prototipo, *m.*
Protozoa [prouto'zouə], *n.pl.* (*Zool.*) Protozoi, *m.pl.*
protract [pro'trækt], *v.t.* Protrarre, prolungare.
protractedly, *adv.* A lungo.
protractile [pro'træktail], *a.* (*Zool.*) Prolungabile.
protraction, *n.* Protrazione, prolungazione, *f.*
protractor, *n.* (*Geom.*) Rapportatore, goniometro, *m.*
protrude [pro'tru:d], *v.t.i.* Sporgere, spingersi fuori; uscire, proiettare.
protrusion, *n.* Prominenza, *f.*
protrusive, *a.* Prominente.
protuberance [pro'tju:bərəns], *n.* Protuberanza, *f.*
protuberant, *a.* Protuberante, prominente.
proud [praud], *a.* Orgoglioso, altero, fiero; superbo, arrogante; (*fig.*) bello, grande, nobile, splendido. **To become —,** insuperbire; **to be — of,** essere fiero di; **too — to complain,** troppo fiero per lagnarsi; **a — day for us,** un bel giorno per noi; (*Med.*) **— flesh,** suppurazione, *f.*
proudly, *adv.* Orgogliosamente, superbamente.
provable ['pru:vəbl], *a.* Provabile.
prove [pru:v], *v.t.* Provare, dimostrare; esperimentare, mettere alla prova; (*a will*) omologare, verificare; autenticare; *v.i.* mostrarsi, rivelarsi. **He will — to be a hero,** si mostrerà un eroe; **as it proved,** come s'è visto.
proved, *a.* Provato, sperimentato, riconosciuto. **Of — honour,** di provata onestà.
proven, *a.* Provato. (*Law*) **Not —,** non provata reità.
provenance ['prɔvenəns], *n.* Provenienza, *f.*
Provençal [pro'vɔnsɑ:l], *n.a.* Provenzale, *m.f.*
Provence [pro'vɔns], *n.* (*Geog.*) Provenza, *f.*
provender ['prɔvendəɹ], *n.* Foraggio, nutrimento, *m.*, provvigioni, *m.pl.*
proverb ['prɔvəɹb], *n.* Proverbio, *m.*
proverbial [pro'vəɹbiəl], *a.* Proverbiale.
proverbially, *adv.* Proverbialmente.
provide [pro'vaid], *v.t.* Provvedere a; procurare, fornire, procacciare; (*Law*) stipulare. **To — oneself with,** fornirsi di; **to — for,** provvedere a; **to — against,** premunirsi contro.
provided, *conj.* Purchè. **— that,** purchè, a condizione che.

providence ['prɔvidəns], *n.* Provvidenza, *f.*; previdenza, prudenza, *f.*; (*divine*) Provvidenza, *f.*
provident, *a.* Provvido, previdente, prudente. **— society,** società di mutuo soccorso, *f.*; **— fund,** fondo di previdenza, *m.*
providential [provi'denʃəl], *a.* Provvidenziale.
provider, *n.* Provveditore, fornitore, *m.*
province ['prɔvins], *n.* Provincia, *f.*; (*fig.*) affare, *m.*, competenza, *f.* **It is not within my —,** non è di mia competenza.
provincial, *n.a.* Provinciale, *m.f.*
provincialism, *n.* Provincialismo, *m.*
provision, *n.* Provvisione, *f.*; stipulazione, *f.*; (*Law*) provvedimento, *m.* || *v.t.* Approvvigionare. **Provisions,** viveri, commestibili, *m.pl.*, vettovaglie, *f.pl.*; **to make — for,** provvedere a; **—-dealer,** mercante di commestibili, *m.*; **— warehouse,** negozio di commestibili, *m.*
provisional, *a.* Provvisorio.
provisionally, *adv.* Provvisoriamente.
provisionment, *n.* Approvvigionamento, *m.*
proviso, *n.* Stipulazione, clausola, *f.* **With the — that,** a condizione che.
provisory, *a.* Provvisorio, condizionale.
provocation, *n.* Provocazione, *f.*
provocative, *a.* Provocativo, provocatore. || *n.* (*Med.*) Stimolante, *m.*
provoke, *v.t.* Provocare, eccitare, stimolare, irritare, stuzzicare. **To — indignation,** provocar l'ira.
provoking, *a.* Provocante, irritante; noioso, seccante, fastidioso.
provost ['prɔvɔst], *n.* (*Eccles.*) Prevosto, *m.*; (*university*) rettore, *m.*; (*in Scotland*) podestà, *m.*
provost-marshal, *n.* (*Mil.*) Capo della polizia militare, *m.*
provostship, *n.* Ufficio di prevosto, *m.*; rettorato, *m.*; podesteria, *f.*
prow, *n.* (*Naut.*) Prora, prua, *f.*
prowess, *n.* Valore, *m.*, bravura, prodezza, *f.*
prowl, *v.i.* Gironzare, girellare, vagolare, andare in busca. **He is always prowling about here,** gironza sempre da queste parti; **the tiger prowls by night,** la tigre vagola nella notte.
prowler, *n.* Predone, girellone, *m.*
proximate, *a.* Prossimo, immediato, vicino; approssimato.
proximity, *n.* Prossimità, vicinanza, *f.*
proximo, *adv.* (*Comm.*) Del mese venturo.
proxy, *n.* Procura, *f.*, mandato, *m.*; procuratore, *m.* **By —,** per procura.
prude, *n.* Persona eccessivamente pudibonda, *f.*
prudence, *n.* Prudenza, *f.*
prudent, *a.* Prudente, cauto, savio.
prudential, *a.* Prudenziale.
prudently, *adv.* Prudentemente.
prudery, *n.* Santimonia, pudicizia affettata, *f.*
prudish, *a.* Schizzinoso, schifiltoso, pudico, pudibondo, timorato.
prune (1) [pru:n], *n.* Prugna secca, pruna, *f.*
prune (2), *v.t.* Potare, troncare, mondare; (*fig.*) scemare, diminuire.
prunella [pru:'nelə], *n.* Prunella, *f.*
pruning, *n.* Potatura, *f.* **—-hook,** ronca, roncola, *f.*, potatoio, falcetto, *m.*; **—-knife,** coltello per potare, *m.*; **—-shears,** forbici da giardino, *f.pl.*
prurience, pruriency ['pru:riəns, 'pru:riənsi] *n.* Lascivia, lubricità, *f.*; sensualità, *f.*
prurient, *a.* Lascivo, lubrico, libidinoso.
prurigo [pru:'raigou], *n.* Prurigine, *f.*
pruritus [pru:'raitəs], *n.* (*Med.*) Prurito, *m.*
Prussia ['prʌʃə], *n.* (*Geog.*) Prussia, *f.*
Prussian, *n.a.* Prussiano, *m.* **— blue,** blu di Prussia.
prussic ['prʌsik], *a.* Prussico. **— acid,** acido prussico, *m.*
pry [prai], *v.i.* Spiare, scrutare, rovistare, indagare. **To — into,** frugare, rovistare, immischiarsi in, ficcare il naso; **to — about,** ficcare il naso dappertutto; **a Paul Pry,** un ficcanaso, *m.*
prying, *a.* Indagatore, curioso. || *n.* Curiosità, *f.*
psalm [sɑ:m], *n.* Salmo, cantico, *m.* **—-book,** libro dei salmi, *m.*; **—-singing,** salmodia, *f.*; (*fig.*) ipocrizia, *f.*
psalmist, *n.* Salmista, *f.*
psalmody, *n.* Salmodia, *f.*
psalter ['sɔ:ltəɹ], *n.* Salterio, libro dei salmi, *m.*
psaltery, *n.* (*Mus.*) Salterio, *m.*
pseudonym ['sju:donim], *n.* Pseudonimo, *m.*
pseudonymous [sju:'donimǝs], *a.* Pseudonimo.
pshaw! [pʃɔ:], *inter.* Puh! Oibò!
psoriasis [sɔri'eisis], *n.* (*Med.*) Psoriasi, *f.*
Psyche ['saiki], *n.* (*Myth.*) Psiche, *f.*
psychiatrist [sai'kaiətrist], *n.* Psichiatra, *m.*
psychic, psychical, *a.* Psichico.
psycho-analysis [saikouə'nælisis], *n.* Psicoanalisi, *f.*
psycho-analyst, *n.* Psicoanalista, *m.f.*
psychologic, psychological [saiko'lɔdʒik, saiko'lɔdʒikəl], *a.* Psicologico.
psychologist, *n.* Psicologo, *m.*
psychology, *n.* Psicologia, *f.*
psychometry [sai'kɔmetri], *n.* Psicometria, *f.*
psychopathy ['saikopæθi], *n.* Psicopatia, *f.*
psychophysics [saiko'fiziks], *n.pl.* Psicofisica, *f.*
psychosis [sai'kousis], *n.* Psicosi, *f.*
ptarmigan ['tɑ:ɹmigən], *n.* (*Zool.*) Pernice di montagna, *f.*
pterodactyl [tero'dæktil], *n.* (*Zool.*) Pterodattilo, *m.*
ptolemaic [tɔli'meiik], *a.* Tolemaico.
Ptolemy ['toləmi], *n.* (*Hist.*) Tolomeo, *m.*
ptomaine [to'mein], *n.* Ptomaina, *f.* **— poisoning,** intossicazione intestinale, *f.*
pub [pʌb], *n.* (*colloq.*) Bettola, *f.* [cp. **public-house**].
puberty ['pju:bəɹti], *n.* Pubertà, *f.*
pubescent [pju:'besənt], *a.* Pubescente, pubere.
public ['pʌblik], *a.* Pubblico. || *n.* Pubblico, *m.*, clientela, *f.* **In —,** in pubblico; **— school,** collegio, *m.*; **— spirit,** senso civico, *m.*, **a — protest,** una protesta pubblica, *f.*; **to make —,** pubblicare, render di pubblica ragione; **— assistance,** assistenza pubblica, *f.*; **— convenience,** latrina pubblica, *f.*; **— holiday,** giorno di festa, *m.*; **—-house,** bettola, osteria, *f.*
publican, *n.* Oste, bettoliere, *m.*; (*Bible*) pubblicano, *m.*
publication, *n.* Pubblicazione, *f.*
publicist ['pʌblisist], *n.* Pubblicista, *m.*

publicity, *n.* Pubblicità, *f.*
publicize, *v.t.* Pubblicare, render pubblico.
publish, *v.t.* Pubblicare; promulgare; render pubblico. **Just published,** appena uscito, novità editoriale, *f.*
publisher, *n.* Editore, *m.*
publishing, *n.* Pubblicazione, *f.* **— house,** casa editrice, *f.*
puce [pju:s], *a.* Color pulce.
puck [pʌk], *n.* Folletto, demonietto, *m.*; (*Sport*) disco, *m.*
pucker [ˈpʌkəɹ], *v.t.* Raggrinzare, corrugare, increspare; *v.i.* raggrinzarsi, corrugarsi, incresparsi. || *n.* Grinza, crespa, ruga, *f.*
puckering, *n.* Raggrinzamento, *m.*, corrugazione, *f.*
puckish, *a.* Furbetto, maliziosetto.
pudding [ˈpudiŋ], *n.* Bodino, *m.* (*Geol.*) **—-stone,** puddinga, *f.*
puddle [pʌdl], *n.* Pozza, pozzanghera, *f.* || *v.t.i.* Sguazzare; intorbidire; (*clay*) rimescolare, impastare; (*metal*) pudellare, affinare.
puddler, *n.* Affinatore, *m.*
puddling, *n.* Affinamento, *m.*, pudellatura, *f.*
puerile [ˈpju:ərail], *a.* Puerile, fanciullesco.
puerility [pju:ˈriliti], *n.* Puerilità, fanciullaggine, *f.*
puerperal [pju:ˈə:ɹpərəl], *a.* Puerperale. **— fever,** febbre puerperale, *f.*
puff [pʌf], *n.* Soffio, sbuffo, *m.*, buffata, *f.*; (*Cooking*) sfogliata, *f.*; (*powder*) piumino, *m.*; (*of hair*) ciuffo, *m.*; (*advertisement*) réclame, gonfiatura, montatura, *f.* || *v.t.i.* Soffiare, sbuffare; (*of wind*) spirare; gonfiare, distendere. **To — out,** gonfiare; **to — and blow,** sbuffare, ansimare; **to be puffed up with pride,** esser gonfio di boria, schiattar di superbia; **—-ball,** vescica di lupo, *f.*; **—-paste,** pasta sfoglia, *f.*
puffer, *n.* Fanfarone, *m.*; (*childish*) locomotiva, *f.*
puffin [ˈpʌfin], *n.* (*Zool.*) Puffino, *m.*
puffiness [ˈpʌfinis], *n.* Ansamento, *m.*; turgidezza, gonfiezza, *f.*
puffy, *a.* Sbuffante, ansante; gonfiato, gonfio; tumido, turgido.
pug (1) [pʌg], *n.* (*Zool.*) Cagnolino, cane bolognese, *m.* **—-nose,** naso camuso, *m.*
pug (2), *n.* (*clay*) Argilla, impastata, *f.* || *v.t.* Impastare, murare alla grossa.
puggaree [ˈpʌgəri:], *n.* Velo intorno al casco, *m.*
pugilism [ˈpju:dʒilizm], *n.* Pugilato, *m.*, pugilistica, *f.*
pugilist, *n.* Pugilatore, *m.*
pugilistic, *a.* Pugilistico.
pugnacious [pʌgˈneiʃəs], *a.* Pugnace, combattivo.
pugnaciously, *adv.* Combattivamente.
pugnaciousness, pugnacity [pʌgˈneiʃəsnis, pʌgˈnæsiti], *n.* Pugnacità, combattività, *f.*
puisne [ˈpju:ni], *a.* (*Law*) Inferiore, menoanziano. **— judge,** giudice del tribunale, *m.*
puissant [ˈpju:sənt], *a.* Potente.
puke [pju:k], *v.i.* Vomitare, rigettare.
pule [pju:l], *v.i.* Strillare, piagnucolare.
pull [pul], *v.t.i.* Tirare, trarre, trascinare; togliere; strappare; estrarre; vogare, remare. || *n.* Tirata, strappata, *f.*, strappo, *m.*; (*fig.*) vantaggio, *m.*; (*Print.*) bozza, *f.*; (*drink*) sorsata, *f.*; (*rope, etc.*) cordone, *m.* **To — someone by the ear,** tirare qualcuno per l'orecchio; **to — someone by the sleeve,** tirar per la manica; **to — off one's hat,** togliersi il cappello, scappellarsi; **to — on one's stockings,** mettersi le calze; **to — to pieces,** fare a pezzi; (*colloq.*) **to — someone's leg,** prender in giro qualcuno; **this horse pulls well,** questo cavallo tira bene; **to — at a pipe,** tirare alla pipa; **to — to the shore,** remare verso la sponda; **to — faces,** far boccacce, far smorfie; **to — about,** trascinare qua e la, maltrattare; **to — down,** demolire, abbattere, tirare giù; **to — off,** togliere, cavare; (*in traffic*) **to — to one side,** tirare da parte; **to — through an illness,** rimettersi da una malattia; (*fig.*) **to — oneself together,** farsi coraggio, calmarsi; **to — together,** mettersi d'accordo; **to — up,** (*to reprimand*) sgridare; (*to stop*) fermare, fermarsi; (*to recover*) riprendersi; (*to root up*) strappare, sradicare; **he took a — at his glass,** bevve una sorsata; (*fig.*) **to have the — of,** avere il vantaggio su.
puller, *n.* Tiratore, *m.*; tiratoio, *m.*
pullet [ˈpulit], *n.* Pollastra, pollastrella, *f.*
pulley [ˈpuli], *n.* Puleggia, *f.*; carrucola, *f.* **—-block,** paranco, *m.*
Pullman, Pullman car [ˈpulmən kɑ:ɹ], *n.* (*reg. trade name*) (*Rail.*) Vettura Pullman, *f.*
pullover, *n.* Pullover, maglione, *m.*
pullulate [ˈpʌlju:leit], *v.i.* Pullulare, germogliare, germinare.
pullulation, *n.* Pullulazione, germinazione, *f.*
pulmonary [ˈpʌlmənəri], *a.* Polmonare.
pulp [pʌlp], *n.* Polpa, *f.*; (*paper*) pasta, *f.* || *v.t.* Ridurre in polpa; ridurre in pasta.
pulpiness, *n.* Polposità, pastosità, *f.*
pulpit [ˈpulpit], *n.* Pulpito, *m.* **— eloquence,** oratoria sacra, *f.*
pulpy, *a.* Polposo, polputo.
pulsate [pʌlˈseit], *v.i.* Pulsare, battere, palpitare.
pulsation, *n.* Pulsazione, *f.*
pulsatory, *a.* Pulsatorio.
pulse (1) [pʌls], *n.* (*Anat.*) Polso, *m.* **Irregular, weak —,** polso irregolare, debole, *m.*; **to feel the —,** tastare il polso.
pulse (2), *n.* (*food*) Piante leguminose, *f.pl.*
pulsometer [pʌlˈsɔmitəɹ], *n.* Pulsometro, *m.*
pulverizable [pʌlvəˈraizəbl], *a.* Polverizzabile.
pulverization, *n.* Polverizzazione, *f.*
pulverizator, *n.* Polverizzatore, *m.*
pulverize, *v.t.* Polverizzare.
puma [pju:mə], *n.* (*Zool.*) Puma, coguaro, *m.*
pumice [ˈpʌmis], *n.* (*Geol.*) Pomice, *f.* || *v.t.* Fregare con la pomice.
pummel [cp. **pommel**].
pump (1) [pʌmp], *n.* Pompa, *f.* || *v.t.* Pompare; (*fig.*) cavare informazioni, sondare, tastare. **Air- —,** pompa ad aria, *f.*; **fire- —,** pompa da incendio, *f.*; **suction- —,** pompa aspirante, *f.*; **to — up a tyre,** gonfiare una gomma; **—-handle,** manovella di pompa, *f.*; **—-room,** sala della pompa, *f.*
pump (2), *n.* (*shoe*) Scarpetta di vernice da sera, *f.*
pumpkin [ˈpʌmpkin], *n.* (*Bot.*) Zucca, *f.*, popone, *m.*
pun [pʌn], *n.* Bisticcio, *m.*; giuoco di parole, *m.*; freddura, *f.* || *v.i.* Far dei bisticci, equivocare.

punch (1) [pʌntʃ], *n.* (*Mech.*) Punzone, *m.*; punteruolo, *m.*; (*blow*) colpo di pugno, *m.* || *v.t.* Punzonare, forare; dare un pugno a.
punch (2), *n.* (*drink*) Ponce, *m.* **—-bowl,** tazza da ponce, *f.*
Punch (3), *n.* Pulcinella, *f.* **— and Judy show,** la baracca dei burattini, *f.*; i burattini, *m.pl.*
puncheon ['pʌntʃən], *n.* Botte, *f.*
punching-ball ['pʌntʃiŋ bɔ:l], *n.* Pallone elastico da pugilato, *m.*
punctate ['pʌŋktit], *a.* (*Zool.*) Puntato.
punctilio [pʌŋk'tiliou], *n.* Puntiglio, scrupolo, *m.*, esattezza, formalità, *f.* **To stand upon —,** star sul puntiglio, impuntigliarsi.
punctilious, *a.* Puntiglioso, scrupoloso, esatto, meticoloso.
punctiliousness, *n.* Scrupolosità, esattezza, *f.*
punctual [pʌŋktju:əl], Puntuale, esatto.
punctuality [pʌŋktju:'æliti], *n.* Puntualità, *f.*
punctually, *adv.* Puntualmente.
punctuate, *v.t.* Punteggiare.
punctuation, *n.* Punteggiatura, interpunzione, puntuazione, *f.*
puncture ['pʌŋktʃəɹ], *n.* Puntura, *f.*, (*of tyre*) bucatura, *f.*; foratura, *f.* || *v.t.* Forare, bucare. **He has had a —,** ha bucato, ha avuto una bucatura.
pundit ['pʌndit], *n.* Bramino, *m.*; (*fig.*) sapientone, dotto, *m.*
pungency ['pʌndʒənsi], *n.* Acrimonia, asprezza, *f.*
pungent, *a.* Pungente, mordente, frizzante, acre, aspro.
Punic ['pju:nik], *a.* (*Hist.*) Punico.
puniness ['pju:ninis], *n.* Piccolezza, debolezza, esilità, *f.*; gracilità, *f.*
punish ['pʌniʃ], *v.t.* Punire, castigare.
punishable, *a.* Punibile.
punisher, *n.* Punitore, castigatore, *m.*
punishment, *n.* Punizione, pena, *f.*, castigo, *m.* **Capital —,** pena capitale, *f.*
punitive ['pju:nitiv], *a.* Punitivo.
punnet ['pʌnit], *n.* Cestino per frutta, *f.*
punning, *n.* Bisticcio, *m.*, freddura, *f.*
punster, *n.* Freddurista, *m.f.*
punt (1) [pʌnt], *n.* (*boat*) Zatta, zattera, *f.*, sandalo, *m.* || *v.t.* Puntare, spinger la barca puntando.
punt (2), *v.t.* (*Football*) Dare un calcio al pallone lasciandolo cadere dalle mani.
punt (3), *v.i.* (*Cards, etc.*) Puntare; scommettere. || *n.* Puntatore, *m.*; scommettitore, *m.*
puny ['pju:ni], *a.* Piccolo, debole, gracile, mingherlino, esile.
pup [pʌp], *n.* Cagnolino, cucciolo, *m.* || *v.i.* Figliare. (*fig.*) **To sell a —,** raggirare.
pupa (pl. **pupae**) ['pju:pə, 'pju:pi:], *n.* (*Zool.*) Crisalide, *f.*
pupil ['pju:pəl], *n.* Scolaro, alunno, allievo, *m.*; (*Law*) pupillo, *m.*; (*of the eye*) pupilla, *f.* **—-teacher,** tirocinante, *m.*
pupilage, *n.* (*Law*) Minorità, *f.*
pupillary ['pju:piləri], *a.* (*Anat.*) Pupillare.
puppet ['pʌpit], *n.* Marionetta, *f.*, burattino, *m.* **—-show,** teatro delle marionette, *m.*
puppy ['pʌpi], *n.* Cagnolino, cane lattante, *m.* [cp. **pup**].
puppyhood, *n.* Giovinezza, *f.*
purblind ['pə:ɹblaind], *a.* Miope, mezzo orbo; ottuso.
purblindness, *n.* Miopia, *f.*
purchasable ['pə:ɹtʃəsəbl], *a.* Comperabile.
purchase ['pə:ɹtʃis], *n.* Compera, compra, *f.*, acquisto, *m.*; (*Mech.*) presa, *f.*; (*tackle*) paranco, *m.* || *v.t.* Comprare, comperare, acquistare. **His life is not worth an hour's —,** non ha un'ora di vita; **—-block,** paranco di puleggia, *m.*; (*Comm.*) **—-deed,** contratto di compera, *m.*; **—-money,** prezzo di acquisto, *m.*
purchaser, *n.* Compratore, *m.*, compratrice, *f.*, acquirente, *m.f.*
pure ['pju:əɹ], *a.* Puro, schietto.
purely, *adv.* Puramente.
pureness, *n.* Purità, schiettezza, *f.*
purgation [pəɹ'geiʃən], *n.* Purgazione, *f.*
purgative, *a.* Purgativo. || *n.* Purgativo, *m.*, purga, *f.*
purgatorial [pəɹgə'tɔ:riəl], *a.* Purgatorio.
purgatory ['pə:ɹgətəri], *n.* Purgatorio, *m.*
purge [pə:ɹdʒ], *v.t.* Purgare, purificare; (*Med.*) purgare. || *n.* Purga, *f.*, purgante, *m.*
purification [pju:rifi'keiʃən], *n.* Purificazione, *f.*
purify ['pju:rifai], *v.t.* Purificare.
purism, *n.* Purismo, *m.*
purist, *n.* Purista, *m.*
Puritan ['pju:ritən], *n.* Puritano, *m.*
puritanical [pju:ri'tænikəl], *a.* Puritano.
Puritanism, *n.* Puritanismo, *m.*
purity ['pju:riti], *n.* Purità, purezza, *f.*; castità, *f.*
purl (1) [pə:ɹl], *n.* (*knitting*) Smerlo, *m.* || *v.t.* Smerlare.
purl (2), *v.i.* Mormorare, borbottare, sussurare. || *n.* Mormorio, borbottio, *m.*
purl (3), *n.* Bevanda di ginepro e birra, *f.*
purlieu [pə:ɹlju:], *n.* Confine, orlo, *m.* **Purlieus,** vicinanze, *f.pl.*, dintorni, *m.pl.*
purlin ['pə:ɹlin], *n.* (*Arch.*) Corrente, *f.*, trave, *m.*
purloin [pəɹ'lɔ:in], *v.t.* Rubacchiare, sottrarre, involare; plagiare.
purple ['pə:ɹpl], *n.* Porpora, *f.* || *a.* Purpureo. || *v.t.* Porporeggiare, imporporare. **Raised to the —,** innalzato alla porpora; **born in the —,** di sangue reale.
purplish, *a.* Porporino.
purport ['pə:ɹpɔɹt], *n.* Senso, significato, valore, *m.*, portata, *f.* || [pəɹ'pɔɹt], *v.t,* Significare, dare a intendere, far apparire; aver per scopo. **A letter purporting to be written by him,** una lettera che si faceva apparire scritta da lui.
purpose ['pə:ɹpəs], *n.* Proposito, disegno, *m.*, intenzione, mira, fine, *f.*; scopo, *m.* || *v.t.* Proporsi, intendere, volere, mirare a. **To serve one's —,** andare a proposito, fare al caso proprio; **on —,** di proposito, apposta; **he lacks —,** gli manca la fermezza; **a novel with a —,** un romanzo a tesi, *m.*; **to the —,** a proposito; **to no —,** senza scopo; **to some —,** molto a proposito; **to be at cross purposes,** fraintendersi, essere in contrasto.
purposeful, *a.* Fermo, risoluto, tenace.
purposefulness, *n.* Fermezza, risoluzione, tenacità, *f.*
purposeless, *a.* Incerto, irresoluto.
purposely, *adv.* Di proposito, apposta, intenzionalmente.
purr, purring ['pə:ɹ, 'pə:ɹriŋ], *n.* Fusa, *f.* **To purr,** far le fusa.

purse [pəːɹs], *n.* Borsa, *f.*; (*fig.*) danaro, *m.*, averi, *m.pl.* || *v.t.i.* (*the lips*) Stringere, increspare, fare il bocchino bello. **—-bearer,** tesoriere, *m.* **—-proud,** soddisfatto dei propri quattrini; **to have a common —,** far borsa comune; **to have a long —,** aver piena la borsa; **the public —,** l'erario, *m.*; (*fig.*) **to hold the —-strings,** tenere i cordoni della borsa.

purser, *n.* (*Naut.*) Ufficiale commissario, *m.*

pursiness, *n.* L'esser asmatico, *m.*

purslane [ˈpəːɹslein], *n.* (*Bot.*) Portulaca, porcellana, *f.*

pursuance [pəɹˈsjuːəns], *n.* **In — of,** in esecuzione di, conformemente a.

pursuant, *adv.* **— to,** In conformità con, facendo seguito a.

pursue [pəɹˈsjuː], *v.t.i.* Perseguire, perseguitare, incalzare, inseguire; seguire, proseguire, cercare; cacciare; continuare. **To — an aim,** perseguire un fine; **to — pleasure,** cercare il piacere; **to — gain,** inseguire il guadagno; **to — a hare,** cacciare una lepre; **to — one's studies,** continuare gli studi.

pursuer, *n.* Inseguitore, cacciatore, *m.*

pursuit [pəɹˈsjuːt], *n.* Inseguimento, *m.*, caccia, *f.*; ricerca, *f.*; occupazione, *f.* **To go in —,** inseguire; **in — of one's profession,** nell'esercizio della professione.

pursuivant [ˈpəːɹswivənt], *n.* Messaggero di Stato, *m.*; valletto d'arme, *m.*; araldo inferiore, *m.*

pursy [ˈpəːɹsi], *a.* Asmatico, bolso, sbuffante; corpulento, panciuto.

purulence, purulency [ˈpjuːruːləns, ˈpjuːruːlənsi], *n.* Purulenza, *f.*

purulent, *a.* Purulento.

purvey [pəɹˈvei], *v.t.i.* Provvedere, fornire, approvvigionare.

purveyance, *n.* Provvigioni, *f.pl.*, fornimento, approvvigionamento, *m.*

purveyor, *m.* Fornitore, *m.* **— to the Royal Household,** fornitore della Real Casa, *m.*

purview [ˈpəːɹvjuː], *n.* Scopo, *m.*, mira, intenzione, *f.*; intento, *m.*; portata, *f.*; (*Law*) testo di una legge, *m.*

pus [pʌs], *n.* (*Med.*) Pus, *m.*, marcia, *f.*

push [puʃ], *v.t.i.* Spingere, urtare; pigiare, premere; promuovere. || *n.* Spinta, *f.*, urto, impulso, *m.*; sforzo, *m.* **To — out roots,** metter fuori radici; (*Naut.*) **to — off,** spingere al largo; **to — one's way,** aprirsi la via a forza, farsi largo; **to — on,** affrettarsi, avanzarsi; **to — a matter through,** sbrigare un affare; **to — one's fortune,** cercar fortuna; **to — about,** spingere qua e la; **—-bike,** bicicletta, *f.*; **—-button,** pulsante, *m.*; **—-cart,** carretto a mano, *m.*

pushing, *a.* Intraprendente, energico.

pusillanimity [pjuːsiləˈnimiti], *n.* Pusillanimità, viltà, timidezza, *f.*

pusillanimous, *a.* Pusillanime, timido, dappoco, vile.

puss [pus], *n.* (*cat*) Micio, micino, *m.*; (*hare*) lepre, *f.*; (*girl*) fanciulla, birichina, *f.* **Puss in Boots,** Il Gatto con gli Stivali, *m.*

pussy, *n.* Micino, *m.*

pustule [ˈpʌstjuːl], *n.* (*Med.*) Pustola, bolla, *f.*

pustular, pustulous, *a.* Pustoloso.

put (1) [put], *v.t.i.* Mettere, porre, collocare; proporre, offrire, presentare. || *n.* (*Sport*) Lancio, *m.* **To — away,** mettere via, mettere da parte, conservare; (*Naut.*) **to — about,** virare di bordo, (*to circulate*) mettere in giro; **to — back,** ritardare, rimettere a posto; **to — by,** (*money*) mettere da parte, (*a question*) evadere; **to — down,** (*to deposit*) deporre, (*a rebellion*) sopprimere, (*to write*) scrivere, (*to attribute*) attribuire; **to — one's foot down,** tener duro, imporsi; **to — forth,** produrre, mettere, (*strength, etc.*) esercitare; **to — forward,** avanzare, proporre, tirar fuori; **to — oneself forward,** mettersi avanti; **to — in,** metter dentro, introdurre, inserire; **to — in an appearance,** mostrarsi, farsi vedere, far atto di presenza; **to — in one's oar,** inframettersi, ingerirsi; **to — off,** posporre, rinviare; **to — off from,** dissuadere; **to — on,** indossare, mettere; **to — on the clock,** far avanzare l'orologio; **to — on flesh,** ingrassare; **to — out,** (*a joint*) slogare, (*a fire*) spegnere, (*money*) mettere ad interesse, (*annoy*) sconcertare, irritare, annoiare; **to — through,** eseguire; **to — together,** mettere insieme; **to — up,** (*price*) aumentare, (*a prayer*) innalzare, (*for election*) proporre, proporsi, (*to pack*) imballare, (*at an inn*) alloggiare; **to — up with,** soffrire, sopportare, rassegnarsi; **to — someone up to something,** istigare qualcuno a fare qualcosa; **I won't be — upon,** non voglio sottomettermi; **to — someone's back up,** stizzire qualcuno; (*Sport*) **to — the weight,** lanciare il peso; (*Naut.*) **to — out to sea,** prendere il largo; **to — new life into,** infondere nuova vita in; **I will — the matter before him,** gli esporrò la questione; **— the matter into my hands,** lasciate fare a me; **I — her age at twenty,** le do venti anni; **to — into words,** esprimere in parole; **to — to a good use,** porre a buon uso; **to — an end to,** porre fine a, dar fine a; **to — into shape,** formare, plasmare; **to — in the wrong,** mettere dalla parte del torto; **to — to death,** dar morte a, mettere a morte, uccidere; **to — someone through his paces,** metter alla prova qualcuno; **to be hard — to it,** aver grande difficoltà di; **to — to flight,** fugare, mettere in fuga; **a —-up job,** un inganno, *m.*, una frode, *f.*; un colpo preparato, *m.*

put (2), **putt** [pʌt], *v.t.i.* (*Golf*) Imbucare la palla; colpire leggermente la palla. || *n.* Colpo leggero per far entrare la palla nella buca, *m.*

putative [ˈpjuːtətiv], *a.* Putativo.

puteal [ˈpjuːtiəl], *n.* (*Arch.*) Puteale, *m.*

putlog [ˈpʌtlɔg], *n.* (*Arch.*) Traversa orizzontale, *f.*

putrefaction [pjuːtriˈfækʃən], *n.* Putrefazione, corruzione, *f.*

putrefactive, *a.* Putrefattivo.

putrefy [ˈpjuːtrifai], *v.t.* Putrefare, corrompere, *v.i.* putrefarsi, corrompersi, marcire, imputridire.

putrescence [pjuːˈtresəns], *n.* Putrescenza, *f.*

putrescent, *a.* Putrescente.

putrid [ˈpjuːtrid], *a.* Putrido, marcio, imputridito, putrefatto; corrotto.

putridity, putridness, *n.* Putridità, putredine, *m.*, marciume, *m.*

putt [cp. **put** (2)].

puttee [ˈpʌtiː], *n.* Mollettiere, *f.*

putter, *n.* (*Golf*) Mazza per far arrivare la palla nella buca, *f.*
putty ['pʌti], *n.* Stucco, mastice, *m.* || *v.t.* Immasticare, stuccare.
puzzle [pʌzəl], *n.* Enigma, indovinello, rompicapo, *m.* || *v.t.* Imbarazzare, confondere, sbalordire. **To — out,** districare, scoprire stillandosi il cervello.
puzzled, *a.* Perplesso, sconcertato.
puzzlement, *n.* Sbalordimento, *m.*, confusione, *f.*
puzzler, *n.* Enigma, *m.*; imbarazzo, *m.*
pyaemia [pai'i:mə], *n.* (*Med.*) Piemia, *f.*
pygmy, pigmy ['pigmi], *n.a.* Pigmeo, *m.*
pyjamas [pi'dʒɑ:məz], *n.pl.* Pigiama, *f.*
pylon ['pailɔn], *n.* Pilone, *m.*
pylorus [pai'lɔ:rəs], *n.* (*Anat.*) Piloro, *m.*
pyorrhoea [paiə'ri:ə], *n.* (*Med.*) Piorrea alveolare, *f.*
pyramid ['pirəmid], *n.* Piramide, *f.*
pyramidal, *a.* Piramidale.
pyre [paiəɹ], *n.* Pira, *f.*
Pyrenees [pirə'ni:z], *n.pl.* (*Geog.*) Pirenei, *m.pl.*
pyrethrum [pai'ri:θrəm], *n.* (*Bot.*) Pilatro, iperico, *m.*
pyretic [pai'retik], *a.* (*Med.*) Piretico.
pyrites [pai'raiti:z], *n.* Pirite, *f.*
pyritic, *a.* Piritico.
pyrometer [pai'rɔmitəɹ], *n.* Pirometro, *m.*
pyrotechnics [pairo'tekniks], *n.pl.* Pirotecnica, *f.*
pyrotechnist, *n.* Pirotecnico, *m.*
pyroxylin [pai'rɔksilin], *n.* Pirossilina, *f.*
Pyrrhic ['pirik], *a.* (*Hist.*) Pirrico. **A — victory,** una vittoria di Pirro, *f.*
Pythagoras [pai'θægɔrəs], *n.* Pitagora, *m.*
Pythagorean [paiθægə'riən], *n.a.* Pitagorico, *m.*
python ['paiθɔn], *n.* (*Zool.*) Pitone, *m.*
pythoness, *n.* Strega, pitonessa, *f.*
pyx [piks], *n.* (*Eccles.*) Pisside, coppella, *f.*, ciborio, *m.*

Q

Q, q [kju:], *n.* Diciasettesima lettera dell'alfabeto inglese.
qua [kwei], *conj.* Come, in qualità di.
quack (1) [kwæk], *v.i.* (*of ducks and geese*) Gracidare, gridare. || *n.* Gracidio, grido, *m.*
quack (2), *n.* Ciarlatano, impostore, gabbamondo, empirico, *m.* **— doctor,** ciarlatano, medicastro, empirico, *m.*; **— medicine,** rimedio segreto, *m.*, panacea, *f.*
quackery, *n.* Ciarlatanismo, *m.*, ciarlataneria, impostura, *f.*; empirismo, *m.*
quacking, *n.* Gracidio, *m.*
quad [kwɔd], *n.* (*colloq.*) Quadrangolo, *m.*, corte, *f.*
Quadragesima [kwɔdrə'dʒesimə], *n.* (*Eccles.*) Quadragesima, *f.*
quadrangle ['kwɔdræŋgl], *n.* Quadrangolo, *m.*
quadrangular, *a.* Quadrangolare.
quadrant ['kwɔdrənt], *n.* (*Geom.Naut.*) Quadrante, *m.*
quadrat ['kwɔdrət], *n.* (*Print.*) Quadrato, *m.*
quadrate ['kwɔdreit], *a.* (*Anat.*) Quadrato. || *v.t.* (*Math.*) Quadrare.
quadratic [kwɔd'rætik], *n.a.* (*Math.*) Quadratico, *m.*
quadrature ['kwɔdrətʃu:ɹ], *n.* (*Math.*) Quadratura, *f.*
quadrennial [kwɔd'reniəl], *a.* Quadriennale.
quadrilateral [kwɔdri'lætərəl], *n.a.* Quadrilatero, *m.*
quadroon [kwɔd'ru:n], *n.* Meticcio, quarterone, *m.*
quadrumanous [kwɔdru:mənəs], *a.* (*Zool.*) Quadrumane.
quadruped ['kwɔdruped], *n.a.* Quadrupede, *m.*
quadruple ['kwɔdru:pl], *v.t.* Quadruplicare. || *n.a.* Quadruplo, *m.*
quadruplets, quads, *n.pl.* Parto quadrigemino, *m.*, quattro nati in un solo parto.
quaestor ['kwestɔɹ], *n.* (*Hist.*) Questore, *m.*
quaff [kwɑ:f], *v.t.i.* Bere, tracannare.
quagga ['kwægə], *n.* (*Zool.*) Quagga, *f.*
quagmire ['kwægmaiɹ], *n.* Pantano, *m.*, palude, *f.*
quail (1) [kweil], *n.* (*Zool.*) Quaglia, *f.*
quail (2), *v.i.* Tremare, aver paura, sgomentarsi, turbarsi, perdersi l'animo.
quaint [kweint], *a.* Fantastico, bizzarro, originale, strano, singolare.
quaintly, *adv.* Bizzarramente.
quaintness, *n.* Bizzarria, singolarità, stranezza, *f.*
quake [kweik], *v.i.* Tremare, trepidare; tremolare, vacillare; oscillare; scuotersi, agitarsi.
Quaker, *n.* (*Eccles.*) Quacchero, *m.*
Quakeress, *n.* Quacchera, *f.*
Quakerism, *n.* Quaccherismo, *m.*
quakingly, *adv.* Tremebondo.
qualifiable [kwɔli'faiəbl], *a.* Qualificabile.
qualification [kwɔlifi'keiʃən], *n.* Qualifica, qualificazione, *f.*, titolo, attributo, *m.*; modifica, modificazione, *f.*; restrizione, diminuzione, *f.* **The statement requires —,** occorre precisare.
qualified ['kwɔlifaid], *a.* Qualificato; capace, atto, competente; condizionale, con riserva.
qualify ['kwɔlifai], *v.t.i.* Qualificare, abilitare; moderare, temperare, mitigare.
qualifying, *a.* Qualificativo. (*Sport*) **— competition,** eliminatoria, *f.*
qualitative ['kwɔlitətiv], *a.* Qualitativo.
quality ['kwɔliti], *n.* Qualità, proprietà, *f.*, pregio, attributo, *m.*; capacità, *f.*, carattere, *m.* **Of the best —,** di prima qualità; **to give a taste of one's —,** dar saggio di sè; **in his — as professor,** in qualità di professore.
qualm [kwɑ:m, kwɔ:m], *n.* Nausea, *f.*; malessere, *m.*; (*fig.*) scrupolo, *m.* **Without a —,** senza scrupolo.
quandary ['kwɔndəri], *n.* Imbarazzo, impaccio, dubbio, *m.*; situazione difficile, *f.* **To be in a —,** trovarsi in imbarazzo, essere nei pasticci.
quantitative ['kwɔntitətiv], *a.* Quantitativo.
quantity ['kwɔntiti], *n.* Quantità, *f.*; abbondanza, *f.*; estensione, grandezza, *f.*, numero, *m.*; (*Poet.*) quantità, *f.* **In quantities,** in quantità; **— surveyor,** misuratore, *m.*
quantum ['kwɔntəm], *n.* Quanto, *m.*, sufficenza, *f.* **— theory,** teoria dei quanta, *f.*
quarantine ['kwɔrənti:n], *n.* Quarantena, *f.* || *v.t.* Fare la quarantena. **To put into —,** mettere in quarantena; **— station,** lazzaretto, *m.*

quarrel (1) ['kwɔrəl], *n.* Lite, contesa, questione, *f.*, contrasto, *m.*, disputa, *f.*; rissa, *f.* || *v.i.* Litigare, altercare, questionare, disputare, attaccar briga; biasimare, trovare a ridire. **To — with one's bread and butter,** guastarsi la posizione; **to pick a — with,** attaccar briga, attaccar lite; **I have no — against her,** non ho niente contro di lei; **to espouse someone's —,** sposare la causa di qualcuno.

quarrel (2), *n.* (*Hist.*) Quadrello, *m.*, freccia, saetta, *f.*

quarrelsome, *a.* Litigioso, attaccabrighe, attaccalite.

quarrelsomeness, *n.* Litigiosità, *f.*

quarry (1) ['kwɔri], *n.* Preda, *f.*

quarry (2), *n.* Cava, petraia, *f.* || *v.t.i.* Scavare pietre; (*fig.*) estrarre.

quarryman, *n.* Cavatore, *m.*

quart [kwɔ:ɹt], *n.* Misura di capacità per liquidi (1.14 litri).

quartan ['kwɔ:ɹtən], *a.* Quartana. **— ague,** febbre quartana, *f.*

quarter ['kwɔ:ɹtəɹ], *n.* Quarta, *f.*; (*fourth part*) quarto, *m.*; (*of a year*) trimestre, *m.*; (*Heraldry*) quarto, *m.*; (*dry measure*) quarta, *f.*; (*mercy*) grazia, *f.* || *v.t.* Squartare, dividere in quarti; (*Heraldry*) squartare, portare arme a quartieri; (*Mil.*) alloggiare. (*Mil.*) **Quarters,** quartieri, *m.pl.*, accantonamento, *m.*; **a — of a century,** un quarto di secolo, *m.*; **a bad — of an hour,** un brutto quarto d'ora; **What — is the wind in ?** Da che punto viene il vento? **from that —,** da quella parte; **to give no —,** non dar quartiere; **at close quarters,** corpo a corpo, dappresso; **—-day,** giorno della pigione, giorno di paga, *m.*; (*Naut.*) **—-deck,** cassero, *m.*; **—-master,** (*Mil.*) furiere, commissario, intendente, *m.*, (*Naut.*) second capo timoniere, **-sessions,** (*Law*) sessioni trimestrali, *f.pl.*

quarterly, *a.* Trimestrale.

quartern, quartern loaf ['kwɔ:ɹtəɹn 'louf], *n.* Pane di quattro libbre, *m.*

quarterstaff, *n.* Bastone adoperato dai contadini, *m.*

quartet, quartette [kwɔ:ɹ'tet], *n.* Quartetto, *m.*

quarto, 4to ['kwɔ:tou], *n.a.* In-quarto, 4to.

quartz [kwɔ:ɹts], *n.* (*Min.*) Quarzo, *m.*

quash [kwɔʃ], *v.t.* Annullare, cassare, invalidare.

quasi ['kweizai, 'kweizi], *conj.prep.* Quasi, come se, poco meno che; finto.

quassia ['kwæsiə, 'kwɔʃə], *n.* (*Bot.*) Quassia, *f.*

quaternary [kwɔ'tə:ɹnəri], *a.* (*Geol.*) Quaternario.

quatrain ['kwɔtrein], *n.* (*Poet.*) Quartina, *f.*

quaver ['kweivəɹ], *n.* Tremolo, *m.*; (*Mus.*) croma, *f.* || *v.t.i.* Tremolare, trillare. **To — out,** parlare con voce tremante.

quaveringly, *adv.* Con voce tremante.

quavery, quavering, *a.* Tremante, tremolante.

quay [ki:], *n.* Molo, *m.*, banchina, *f.*

quean [kwi:n], *n.* Sgualdrina, *f.*

queasiness ['kwi:zinis], *n.* Schizzinosità, *f.*

queasy ['kwi:zi], *a.* Nauseante, nauseabondo; schizzinoso, delicato, schifiltoso. **A — stomach,** uno stomaco delicato, *m.*

queen [kwi:n], *n.* Regina, *f.* (*Cards, Chess*) regina, donna, *f.* || *v.t.i.* Far regina; (*Chess*) far dama. **To — it,** far la regina. **—-dowager, —-mother,** regina madre, *f.*; **—-bee,** ape regina, *f.*

queencake, *n.* Specie di torta, *f.*

queenship, *n.* Regalità, *f.*

queenlike, queenly, *a.* Da regina, reale, regale.

queer ['kwiəɹ], *a.* Strano, singolare, curioso, bizzarro; sospetto, sospettoso; indisposto. || *v.t.* Guastare. **To feel —,** sentirsi male; **a — fellow,** un tipo strano, *m.*; **to — the pitch,** guastar le uova nel paniere.

queerly, *adv.* Stranamente, curiosamente.

queerness, *n.* Stranezza, singolarità, curiosità, bizzarria, *f.*

quell [kwel], *v.t.* Reprimere, raffrenare, domare.

quench [kwentʃ], *v.t.* Spegnere, smorzare, estinguere; calmare. **To — one's thirst,** dissetarsi, cavarsi la sete.

quenchable, *a.* Estinguibile.

quenchless, *a.* Inestinguibile, perenne, perpetuo.

querist ['kwiərist], *n.* Interrogatore, *m.*

quern [kwə:ɹn], *n.* Macinatoio, *m.*

querulous ['kwerju:ləs], *a.* Querulo, lamentoso, dolente, lagnoso.

querulousness, *n.* Lamentosità, querimonia, *f.*

query ['kwiəri], *n.* Questione, domanda, interrogazione, *f.*, quesito, *m.*; punto interrogativo, *m.* || *v.t.* Domandare, indagare; obiettare, muovere un dubbio; segnare con punto interrogativo.

quest [kwest], *n.* Cerca, ricerca, *f.* || *v.t.i.* Cercare, andare in cerca di, ricercare. **In — of,** in cerca di.

question ['kwestʃən], *n.* Domanda, interrogazione, *f.*; tema, soggetto, *m.*; dubbio, *m.*, questione, disputa, controversia, *f.* || *v.t.* Interrogare, domandare a; mettere in dubbio, negare; dubitare di, eccepire su. **He allowed it without —,** non ci fece nessuna obiezione; **beyond all —,** fuor di dubbio; **to call in —,** mettere in dubbio; **there is no — but that,** non c'è dubbio che; **to ask a —,** fare una domanda; **a — of time,** una questione di tempo, *f.*; **the person in —,** la persona in questione, *f.*; **out of the —,** impossibile, fuori discussione; **to put the —,** venire ai voti; **an open —,** una questione pendente, *f.*; **I — his honesty,** dubito della sua onestà.

questionable, *a.* Discutibile, insoluto, dubbioso, ambiguo.

questionably, *adv.* Discutibilmente.

questioner, *n.* Interrogatore, *m.*, interrogatrice, *f.*

questioningly, *adv.* Interrogativamente.

queue [kju:], *n.* Coda, *f.*; (*of hair*) codino, *m.* || *v.i.* Far coda, mettersi in coda.

quibble ['kwibl], *n.* Equivoco, cavillo, arzigogolo, *m.*; scappatoia, *f.*; sotterfugio, *m.* || *v.i.* Cavillare, equivocare, arzigogolare, sottilizzare.

quibbler, *n.* Equivocatore, cavillatore, sofista, *m.*

quibbling, *n.* Equivocazione, sofisticheria, *f.*

quick [kwik], *a.* Celere, rapido, veloce, presto; pronto, vivace, sveglio, desto; intelligente; svelto, lesto; vivo. || *n.* Vivo, *m.* || *adv.* Presto, subito. **A — eye,** un occhio vivace, *m.*; **— to take offence,** pronto a impermalirsi; **to touch to the —,** toccare sul vivo;

the — of the nails, il vivo delle unghie, *m.* **Be —!** Spicciatevi! Fate presto! (*Mil.*) **Quick march!** March! Fuori il passo! (*Theat.*) **—-change**, di trasformista; **—-change artist**, trasformista, *m.f.*; **—-firing**, a tiro rapido; **—-tempered**, irascibile, impulsivo; **—-witted**, acuto, perspicace, sagace; **the — and the dead**, i vivi e i morti.
quicken, *v.t.i.* Vivificare, ravvivare, ravvivarsi.
quicklime, *n.* Calce viva, *f.*
quickly, *adv.* Presto, subito, rapidamente.
quickness, *n.* Rapidità, celerità, prestezza, velocità, *f.*; prontezza, vivacità, sveltezza, intelligenza, *f.* **— of temper**, irascibilità, impulsività, *f.*
quicksand, *n.* Sabbia mobile, *f.*
quicksilver, *n.* Mercurio, argento vivo, *m.*
quid [kwid], *n.* (*of tobacco*) Cicca, *f.*; (*colloq.*) una sterlina, *f.*
quiddity ['kwiditi], *n.* Quiddità, *f.*
quidnunc ['kwidnʌŋk], *n.* Pettegolo, saccente, *m.*; chiacchierone, *m.*
quid pro quo [kwid prou kwou], *n.* Scambio, compenso, *m.*, ricompensa, *f.*
quiescence [kwai'esəns], *n.* Quiescenza, inerzia, *f.*
quiescent, *a.* Quiescente, inerte.
quiet ['kwaiət], *n.* Quiete, tranquillità, pace, *f.*; silenzio, *m.*; calma, *f.* || *a.* Quieto, tranquillo, cheto, zitto, placido; modesto, semplice, dimesso. || *v.t.* Tranquillizzare, calmare, quietare, pacificare. **A — laugh**, una risatina, *f.*; **on the —**, quatto quatto, furtivamente; **Be —!** State quieti! Zitti! Tacete! **to — down**, calmare; calmarsi, placarsi, rasserenarsi.
quieten [cp. **quiet**].
quietism ['kwaiətizm], *n.* (*Eccles.*) Quietismo, *m.*
quietist, *n.* Quietista, *m.f.*
quietly, *adv.* Quietamente. **To dress —**, vestirsi in modo serio, vestirsi semplicemente.
quietness, quietude ['kwaiətnis, 'kwaiitju:d] *n.* Quiete, calma, tranquillità, *f.*; silenzio, riposo, *m.*
quietus [kwai'i:təs], *n.* Colpo di grazia, *m.*
quill [kwil], *n.* (*feather*) Penna, *f.*; (*pen*) penna d'oca, *f.*; (*of porcupine*) spina, punta, *f.*; (*Mus.*) plettro, *m.* **—-driver**, scrittorello, imbrattacarte, *m.*
quilt [kwilt], *n.* Coltre, coperta, *f.*; piumino, *m.* || *v.t.* Trapuntare, imbottire.
quilting, *n.* Imbottitura, *f.*
quince [kwins], *n.* (*Bot.*) Cotogna, *f.* **—-tree**, cotogno, *m.*; **— marmelade**, cotognata, *f.*
quincentenary [kwinsen'ti:nəri], *n.* Quingentenario, *m.*
quincunx ['kwinkʌŋks], *n.* (*Geom.*) Quinconce, *f.*
quinine [kwi'ni:n], *n.* China, chinina, *f.*, chinino, *m.*
quinquagenarian [kwiŋkwədʒe'nεəriən], *n.a.* Cinquantenne, *m.f.*
Quinquagesima [kwiŋkwə'dʒesimə], *n.* (*Eccles.*) Quinquagesima, *f.*
quinquennial [kwin'kweniəl], *a.* Quinquenhale.
quinquennium [kwin'kweniəm], *n.* Quinquennio, *m.*
quinsy ['kwinzi], *n.* (*Med.*) Angina, squinanzia, *f.*
quint [kwint], *n.* Quinta, *f.*
quintain ['kwintən], *n.* (*Hist.*) Quintana, *f.*
quintal ['kwintəl], *n.* Quintale.
quintessence [kwin'tesəns], *n.* Quintessenza, *f.*
quintet, quintette, *n.* (*Mus.*) Quintetto, *m.*
quintuple ['kwintju:pl], *n.a.* Quintuplo, *m.*
quip [kwip], *n.* Frizzo, *m.*, arguzia, bottata, *f.*; bisticcio, *m.*; equivoco, cavillo, *m.*
quire (1) [kwaiəɹ], *n.* Quinterno, *m.*
quire (2) [cp. **choir**].
Quirinal ['kwirinəl], *n.* Quirinale, *m.*
quirk [kwə:ɹk], *n.* Frizzo, *m.*, arguzia, *f.*; ticchio, vezzo, *m.*; (*in writing*) ghirigoro, *m.*
quit [kwit], *a.* Liberato, sbarazzato, sdebitato. || *v.t.* Lasciare, abbandonare; partire; *v.r.* condursi, comportarsi. **To be — of**, liberarsi di, sbarazzarsi di; **— you like men**, comportatevi da uomini; **notice to —**, disdetta, *f.*
quitclaim, *n.* Rinuncia di diritto, *f.*
quite [kwait], *adv.* Tutto, in tutto, affatto, interamente, completamente, proprio. **— by myself**, tutto solo, solo soletto; **— other**, tutto diverso; **he — likes it**, gli piace proprio; **it is — the thing now**, adesso è proprio la moda; **— two years ago**, almeno due anni fa.
quitrent, *n.* (*Law*) Livello, *m.*
quits [kwits], *a.* Pari, pari e patta. **To be — with**, esser pari con; **to cry —**, riconciliarsi.
quittance ['kwitəns], *n.* Ricevuta, *f.*; quietanza, *f.*
quiver (1) ['kwivəɹ], *n.* Faretra, *f.*, turcasso, *m.*
quiver (2), *v.i.* Tremare, tremolare, vacillare, aver i brividi.
quivering, *a.* Tremebondo. || *n.* Tremito, fremito, *m.*
quiveringly, *adv.* Tremante.
qui vive [ki:'vi:v], *n.* **On the —**, all'erta.
Quixote ['kwikzət], *n.* Don Chisciotte, *m.*
quixotic [kwik'zɔtik], *a.* Donchisciottesco, stravagante.
quixotism, *n.* Donchisciottismo, *m.*
quiz [kwiz], *n.* Burlone, beffardo, canzonatore, *m.*; questionario, *m.* || *v.t.* Burlarsi di, dileggiare, canzonare, satireggiare; sogguardare, sbirciare.
quizzical, *a.* Beffardo, satirico.
quizzingly, *adv.* Beffardamente.
quod [kwɔd], *n.* (*colloq.*) Prigione, *f.*
quoin [kwɔin], *n.* Spigolo, cantone, *m.*; (*Print.*) cuneo, *m.*
quoit [kwɔit], *n.* Disco, cerchietto, *m.*
quondam ['kwɔndæm], *a.* Antico, ex-, già.
quorum ['kwɔ:rəm], *n.* Numero legale (d'un comitato), *m.*
quota ['kwoutə], *n.* Quota, rata, porzione, *f.*; contribuzione, *f.*
quotable ['kwoutəbl], *a.* Citabile, adducibile.
quotation [kwo'teiʃən], *n.* (*Lit.*) Citazione, *f.*, brano, citato, *m.*; (*Comm.*) quotazione, *f.*; (*Print.*) quadrato, *m.* **— marks, quotes**, virgolette, *f.pl.*
quote, *v.t.* Citare, addurre, allegare; (*Comm.*) quotare.
quoth [kwouθ, kwɔθ], *v.t.* **— I**, dissi; **— he, — she**, disse.
quotidian [kwo'tidiən], *a.* Quotidiano, giornaliero.
quotient ['kwouʃənt], *n.* (*Math.*) Quoziente, *m.*

R

R, r [ɑːɹ], *n.* Diciottesima lettera dell'alfabeto inglese.
rabbet ['ræbit], *n.* Scanalatura, *f.* **— plane,** pialletto per scanalare, *m.*
rabbi ['ræbai], *n.* Rabbino, *m.*
rabbinical [rə'binikəl], *a.* Rabbinico.
rabbit ['ræbit], *n.* (*Zool.*) Coniglio, *m.*; (*at sport*) schiappa, *f.* || *v.i.* Cacciare i conigli. **—-hutch,** conigliera, *f.*; **—-burrow,** tana di coniglio, *f.*; **—-warren,** covo di coniglio, *m.*
rabbitry, *n.* Conigliera, *f.*
rabble [ræbl], *n.* Folla, calca, *f.*; maramaglia, canaglia, gentaglia, razzumaglia, *f.*
Rabelaisian [ræbə'leiʒən], *a.* Rabelesiano.
rabid ['ræbid], *a.* Furioso, furente, arrabbiato; (*of dog*) rabbioso, idrofobo. **— hatred,** odio fanatico, *m.*
rabidity, rabidness, *n.* Rabbia, furia, *f.*, furore, *m.*
rabies ['reibiːz], *n.* Rabbia, *f.*; idrofobia, *f.*
raccoon [rə'kuːn], *n.* (*Zool.*) Procione, *m.*
race (1) [reis], *n.* Corsa, gara, *f.* || *v.t.* Far correre in una corsa, mettere in gara; sopravanzare; correre, gareggiare con. **To — someone,** superare qualcuno nella corsa; **they raced their horses,** fecero correre i loro cavalli; **horse- —,** corsa ippica, *f.*; **boat- —,** gara di canottaggio, *f.*; **—-card,** programma di corse, *m.*; **—-meeting,** concorso ippico, *m.*; **—-track,** pista, *f.*
race (2), *n.* Razza, schiatta, stirpe, discendenza, *f.*
racecourse ['reiskɔːɹs], *n.* Ippodromo, campo di corse, *m.*, pista, *f.*
racehorse, *n.* Cavallo da corsa, *m.*
raceme ['ræsiːm], *n.* (*Bot.*) Racemo, *m.*
racemose, *a.* Racemoso.
racer, *n.* Corridore, cavallo da corsa, *m.*
rachis ['reikis], *n.* (*Bot.*) Rachide, *f.*
rachitis [rə'kaitis], *n.* (*Med.*) Rachitide, *f.*
racial ['reiʃəl], *a.* Di razza, di stirpe; razziale.
raciness ['reisinis], *n.* Brio, *m.*, mordacità, vivacità, *f.*
racing, *n.* Corse, *f.pl.* **Horse- —,** corse ippiche, *f.pl.*; **—-calendar,** calendario delle corse, *m.*; **—-cyclist,** corridore ciclista, *m.*; (*Motor.*) **—-car,** automobile da corsa, *m.*
rack (1) [ræk], *n.* (*of clouds*) Nuvolaglia, *f.*
rack (2), *n.* Rovina, malora, *f.* **To go to — and ruin,** andare in rovina, andare in malora.
rack (3), *n.* (*for fodder*) Rastrelliera, grata, *f.*; (*for plates, etc.*) scolapiatti, scolabottiglie, *m.*; (*Mech.*) cremagliera, dentiera, ruota dentata, *f.*; (*for luggage*) rete, reticella, *f.*; (*for letters*) portacarte, portabiglietti, *m.*; (*for torture*) ruota, *f.*, cavalletto, *m.* || *v.t.* Arrotare, mettere alla ruota, torturare, tormentare, angariare. **On the —,** torturato, sulle spine; **to — one's brains,** stillarsi il cervello; **—-rent,** pigione eccessiva, *f.*; **—-railway,** ferrovia a cremagliera, *f.*; **— and pinion,** ingranaggio a dentiera, *m.*
racket (1) ['rækit], *n.* Chiasso, rumore, baccano, fracasso, *m.* || *v.i.* Fare il chiasso, far baccano, far fracasso. **To — about,** divertirsi, darsi buon tempo; **to stand the —,** pagare il fio.
racket (2), **racquet,** *n.* Racchetta, *f.* (*Sport*) **Rackets,** le racchette, *f.pl.*
racketeer [rækə'tiəɹ], *n.* Imbroglione; ricattatore, *m.*
racketeering, *n.* Ricatto, *m.*
rackety, *a.* Chiassoso, rumoroso.
racoon [cp. **raccoon**].
racy ['reisi], *a.* Brioso, frizzante, vivace, piccante.
radar ['reidɑːɹ], *n.* Radar, *m.* **— station,** posto radar, *m.*
raddle [rædl], *n.* Ocra rossa, *f.* || *v.t.* Colorire di ocra rossa; (*the face*) imbellettare. **A raddled face,** un viso imbellettato, *m.*
radial ['reidiəl], *a.* Radiale.
radiance, radiancy, *n.* Radiosità, radiazione, irradiazione, *f.*, splendore, *m.*
radiant, *a.* Radiante, raggiante, irradiato; splendido, sfavillante, brillante, esultante. **— heat,** calore raggiante, *m.*; **— with joy,** raggiante di gioia.
radiate, *v.t.* Raggiare, emanare, irradiare, irraggiare, diffondere.
radiation, *n.* Radiazione, irradiazione, *f.*
radiator, *n.* Radiatore, calorifero, *m.*
radical ['rædikəl], *n.a.* Radicale, *m.*
radio ['reidiou], *n.* Radio, *f.*; apparecchio radio, *m.*
radioactive [reidiou'æktiv], *a.* Radioattivo.
radioactivity, *n.* Radioattività, *f.*
radiogram, *n.* Radiogramma, *m.*
radiogramophone, *n.* Radiogrammofono, *m.*
radiograph, *n.* Radiografo, *m.*
radiography, *n.* Radiografia, *f.*
radiolocation, *n.* Radiolocazione, *f.*
radioscopy, *n.* Radioscopia, *f.*
radiotelegraphy, *n.* Radiotelegrafia, *f.*
radiotelephony, *n.* Radiotelefonia, *f.*
radiotherapy, *n.* Radioterapia, *f.*
radish ['rædiʃ], *n.* (*Bot.*) Rafano, ravanello, *m.*
radium ['reidiəm], *n.* Radio, *m.*
radius 'reidiəs], *n.* (*Geom.*) Raggio, *m.*; (*Anat.*) radio, *m.* **Within a — of,** entro un raggio di.
radix (pl. **radices**) ['reidiks, 'reidisiːz], *n.* (*Math.*) Base, radice, *f.*
raffia ['ræfiə], *n.* (*Bot.*) Rafia, *f.* **—-work,** lavoro in rafia, *m.*
raffish ['ræfiʃ], *a.* Discolo, vizioso, corrotto.
raffle [ræfl], *n.* Riffa, lotteria privata, estrazione a sorte, *f.* || *v.t.* Mettere in lotteria, estrarre a sorte.
raft [rɑːft], *n.* Zattera, chiatta, *f.* || *v.t.* Trasportare con zattera.
rafter, *n.* Trave, *f.*, puntone, *m.*
rafting, *n.* Trasporto con zattere, *m.*
raftsman, *n.* Zatteriere, chiattaiuolo, *m.*
rag [ræg], *n.* Cencio, straccio, brandello, *m.*; (*colloq.*) festa di studenti, *f.*; (*colloq.*) giornalaccio, *m.* || *v.t.i.* Prendere in giro, fare un tiro bribone a; far chiasso. **In rags,** logoro, in brandelli, sbrindellato; **—, tag and bobtail,** plebaglia, *f.*; **—-picker, —-and-bone man,** cenciaiuolo, straccivendolo, *m.*; (*Mus.*) **—-time,** musica sincopata, *f.*
ragamuffin ['rægəmʌfin], *n.* Straccione, pezzente, *m.*; birichino, ragazzaccio, *m.*
rage [reidʒ], *n.* Collera, ira, rabbia, furia, *f.*; furore, *m.*, stizza, *f.*; corruccio, sdegno, *m.*; (*fig.*) mania, passione, *f.*; moda, *f.* || *v.i.* Infuriare, smaniare, dar nelle furie; infierire, imperversare. **To fly into a —,** montare in

furia, montare in collera; **a — for collecting books,** una mania pei libri; **all the —,** di moda; **to — against,** inveire contro; **the storm has raged itself out,** la tempesta si è sfogato.
ragged ['rægid], *a.* Aspro, ruvido, scabroso; lacero, logoro, cencioso, stracciato, sbrindellato; frastagliato. (*Bot.*) **—-robin,** erba San Giacomo, *f.*
raggedly, *adv.* Ruvidamente.
raggedness, *n.* Asprezza, ruvidezza, scabrosità, *f.*; imperfezione, incompiutezza, *f.*
raging ['reidʒiŋ], *a.* Furioso, furibondo, violento. **A — fever,** una febbre ardente, *f.*; **— toothache,** forte dolor di denti, *m.*
raglan coat ['ræglən kout], *n.* Soprabito raglan, *m.*
ragout [ræg'u:], *n.* Intingolo, ragù, *m.*
ragwort, *n.* (*Bot.*) Erba di San Giacomo, *f.*
raid [reid], *n.* Razzia, scorreria, incursione, *f.* || *v.t.* Fare una scorreria in, far razzia; rubare, saccheggiare, predare. **A police- —** una retata della polizia, *f.*; **air- —,** incursione aerea, *f.* **air- — precautions,** protezione antiaerea, *f.*
raider, *n.* Razziatore, predatore, predone, *m.*
rail (1) [reil], *n.* Piuolo, *m.*, sbarra, asta, traversa, *f.*; (*of banisters, etc.*) ringhiera, *f.*; (*Rail.*) ferrovia, *f.*; (*line*) rotaia, *f.*; (*Naut.*) battagliola, *f.* || *v.t.* Ingraticolare, chiudere con cancellata; (*Rail.*) fornire di rotaie. **By —,** per ferrovia; **to go off the rails,** deviare, deragliare, (*fig.*) andar fuori strada, uscire dalle rotaie.
rail (2), *n.* (*Zool.*) Gallinella, *f.*
rail (3), *v.i.* Brontolare. **To — at,** ingiuriare, insultare.
railer, *n.* Brontolone, *m.*
railing (1), *n.* Cancellata, inferriata, ringhiera, *f.*
railing (2), *n.* Ingiurie, *f.pl.*
raillery, *n.* Motteggio, scherno, *m.*, derisione, beffa, *f.*
railway, railroad ['reilwei, 'reilroud], *n.* Ferrovia, strada ferrata, *f.* **—-line,** binario, *m.*, linea ferroviaria, *f.*; **— company,** società delle strade ferrate, *f.*; **— accident,** disastro ferroviario, *m.*; **—-engine,** locomotiva, *f.*; **—-train,** treno, *m.*; **— station,** stazione, *f.*; **—-carriage,** vettura, *f.*, vagone, *m.*; **— system,** rete ferroviaria, *f.*
railwayman, *n.* Ferroviere, impiegato ferroviario, *m.*
raiment ['reimənt], *n.* Vestimenti, *m.pl.*, abbigliamento, *m.*
rain [rein], *n.* Pioggia, *f.* || *v.i.* Piovere; spargersi, versarsi; *v.t.* piovere; spargere, versare. **It is raining,** piove; **it looks like —,** sembra che voglia piovere; **it is raining cats and dogs,** piove a catinelle; **it never rains but it pours,** nessun due senza tre; **tears rained down her cheeks,** le sue guancie erano cosparse di lagrime; **he rained kindness upon them,** li colmò di gentilezze; **—-gauge,** pluviometro, *m.*
rainbow, *n.* Arcobaleno, *m.*
raindrop, *n.* Goccia di pioggia, *f.*
rainfall, *n.* Pioggia, caduta di pioggia, *f.*; precipitazione, *f.*
rainproof, *n.a.* Impermeabile, *m.*
rainwater, *n.* Acqua piovana, *f.*
rainy, *a.* Piovoso, umido, di pioggia. **— weather,** tempo piovoso. **To put aside for a — day,** risparmiare per i tempi difficili.
raise [reiz], *v.t.* Levare, elevare, sollevare, alzare, innalzare; rizzare, erigere; creare; gettare, dare; (*hat*) levarsi; (*flag*) issare; (*money*) procurare, procurarsi; (*objections*) muovere. **He raised her from her knees,** la sollevò da in ginocchio; **to — from the dead,** risuscitare; **to — the country,** sollevare il paese; **to — a dust,** sollevare polvere, (*fig.*) far chiasso; **to — a family,** allevare una famiglia; **to — a hymn,** innalzare un inno; **to — a controversy,** sollevare una controversia; **to — a claim,** avanzare una domanda; **to — a question,** sollevare una questione; **to — a laugh,** suscitare il riso; **to — one's voice,** alzare la voce; **to — one's glass to,** fare un brindisi a, alzare il bicchiere a; **to — a siege,** levare l'assedio; **to — a sum of money,** raccogliere una somma di denaro; (*fig.*) **to — Cain,** far tumulto, sollevare un pandemonio.
raised, *a.* In rilievo, rilevato.
raisin ['reizən], *n.* Uva secca, uva passa, *f.*
rajah ['rɑ:dʒɑ:], *n.* Raià, *m.*
rake (1) [reik], *n.* Rastrello, *m.* || *v.t.i.* Rastrellare; raccogliere, riunire; frugare, frugacchiare. **To — out the fire,** spegnere il fuoco; **I was raking about among old letters,** stavo frugando tra vecchie lettere; (*Mil.*) **a raking fire,** un tiro radente.
rake (2), *n.* Scapestrato, libertino, discolo, *m.*
rake (3), *v.i.* (*Naut.*) Inclinarsi. || *n.* Inclinazione, *f.*
rakish (1), *a.* Dissoluto, licenzioso, scapestrato.
rakish (2), *a.* (*Naut.*) Inclinato; svelto, slanciato.
rakishness, *n.* Libertinaggio, *m.*
rallier ['ræliəɹ], *n.* Beffeggiatore, *m.*
rally (1) ['ræli], *n.* Ripresa, *f.*; radunanza, riunione, *f.*, raduno, *m.*; (*Tennis*) ripresa, *f.*; (*of health*) ricupero di forze, *m.* || *v.t.i.* Raccogliere, radunare, riunire; riprendersi, rimettersi, ristabilirsi, riaversi. **His party rallied round him,** il suo partito si raccolse intorno a lui.
rally (2), *v.t.* Deridere, canzonare, beffeggiare.
rallying, *n.* Adunata, *f.* **—-point,** luogo del raduno, *m.*
ram [ræm], *n.* (*Zool.*) Montone, *m.*; (*Astron.*) ariete, *m.*; (*Mech.*) battipolo, maglio, mazzapicchio, *m.*, berta, *f.*; (*Naut.*) sperone, *m.* || *v.t.* Assodare, battere, sfondare, martellare, ficcare, conficcare; (*Naut.*) speronare. **To — in,** conficcare, cacciar dentro; **to — one's hat on one's head,** cacciarsi il cappello in testa; **to — one's head against a brick wall,** sbattere la testa contro il muro; **to — one's argument home,** dar forza alle proprie parole.
ramble ['ræmbəl], *n.* Passeggiata, gita, escursione, *f.*, giro, *m.* || *v.i.* Vagare, andare a zonzo; (*in speech*) divagare; (*in the mind*) delirare, vaneggiare.
rambler, *n.* Girovago, *m.*; gitante, escursionista, *m.f.* **— rose,** rosaio rampicante, *m.*
rambling, *a.* Errante; saltuario, sconnesso, incoerente; (*of plants*) rampicante.

ramification [ræmifiˈkeiʃən], *n.* Ramificazione, *f.*
ramify [ˈræmifai], *v.t.i.* Ramificarsi, diramarsi; suddividere.
rammer, *n.* Ariete, maglio, *m.*; (*for soil*) mazzeranga, berta, *f.*; (*for gun*) bacchetta, *f.*, calcatoio, *m.*
ramose [rəˈmous], *a.* (*Bot.*) Ramoso.
ramp [ræmp], *n.* Salita, rampa, *f.*, pendio, *m.*; (*colloq.*) raggiro, *m.* ‖ *v.i.* Imperversare; smaniare, dar nelle furie.
rampage [ræmˈpeidʒ], *v.i.* Smaniare, scalmanarsi, dar nelle furie. **To be on the —,** essere scalmanato, essere accalorato, avere i fumi.
rampageous, *a.* Furibondo.
rampant, *a.* (*Heraldry*) Rampante; (*fig.*) predominante, imperversante, sfrenato. **Drunkenness is — here,** l'ubriacchezza imperversa qui.
rampart [ˈræmpɑːɹt], *n.* Bastione, baluardo, *m.*; difesa, *f.* ‖ *v.t.* Bastionare.
rampion [ˈræmpiən], *n.* (*Bot.*) Raperonzolo, *m.*
ramrod [ˈræmrɔd], *n.* Bacchetta, *f.*, calcatoio, *m.*
ramshackle [ˈræmʃækl], *a.* Sgangherato, sconquassato, rovinato, diroccato.
ranch [ræntʃ, rɑːntʃ], *n.* Rancio, podere, *m.*, fattoria, *f.* ‖ *v.i.* Tenere una fattoria.
rancher, *n.* Padrone di un rancio, *m.*
rancid [ˈrænsid], *a.* Rancido, stantio.
rancidity, rancidness, *n.* Rancidezza, *f.*
rancorous [ˈræŋkərəs], *a.* Acrimonioso, maligno, pieno di rancore.
rancour [ˈræŋkəɹ], *n.* Rancore, risentimento, *m.*, acrimonia, *f.*
random [ˈrændəm], *a.* Casuale, a caso, fortuito. **At —,** a casaccio, alla rinfusa, alla cieca; **a — shot,** un colpo a caso, *m.*
randy, *a.* Rumoroso, chiassoso.
ranee [ˈrɑːniː], *n.* Moglie di un raià, *f.*
range [reindʒ], *n.* Portata, *f.*; serie, *f.*, ordine, *m.*; area, sfera, *f.*; direzione, *f.*; campo, spazio, *m.*; (*of mountains*) catena, *f.*; (*of land*) tratto, *m.*; (*shooting*) campo di tiro, *m.*; (*kitchen*) fornello, *m.*, cucina economica, *f.*; (*Mus.*) tastiera, estensione, *f.* ‖ *v.t.i.* Schierare ordinare; disporre; estendersi, vagare, divagare. **The whole — of literature,** tutto il campo della letteratura; **the — of his voice,** l'estensione della sua voce, *f.*; **studies of very wide —,** studi di ampia portata, *m.pl.*; **out of my —,** fuori della mia portata; (*Mil.*) **to find the —,** regolare il tiro; **within —,** a tiro; **—-finder,** telemetro, *m.*
ranger, *n.* Guardaboschi, *m.*, guardia forestale, *f.*
ranging, *n.* Allineamento, *m.*, classificazione, *f.*; schieramento, *m.*
Rangoon [ræŋgˈuːn], *n.* (*Geog.*) Rangun, *f.*
rank (1) [ræŋk], *n.* Rango, grado, ordine, ceto, *m.*; (*status*) condizione, *f.*; (*Mil.*) rango, *m.*; fila, schiera, *f.* (*cab*) posteggio, *m.*, stazione, *f.* ‖ *v.t.* Schierare; classificare, ordinare; *v.i.* schierarsi; prender posto, occupare un posto. **The — and file,** militari di truppa, (*fig.*) i gregari, *m.pl.*; **to rise from the ranks,** venire dalla gavetta; **to keep the ranks,** tenersi in fila, stare nei ranghi; **people of all ranks,** persone di ogni ceto, *f.pl.*; **of high —,** di alto rango; **to close the ranks,** serrare le file; **to — as,** passare per, esser quotato come; **to — after,** venir dopo.
rank (2), *a.* (*of growth*) Rigoglioso; ricco, fertile; (*of smell, taste*) rancido, stantio; corrotto, schifoso; grossolano; eccessivo. **— pedantry,** gretta pedanteria, *f.*
ranker, *n.* (*Mil.*) Ufficiale che viene dai ranghi, *m.*
rankle [ræŋkl], *v.i.* Inasprire, infiammarsi, struggersi, rodersi. **Envy rankles in his breast,** si strugge d'invidia, l'invidia lo invelenisce.
rankling, *n.* Irritazione, *f.*
rankly, *adv.* Rigogliosamente; rancidamente.
rankness, *n.* Esuberanza, ricchezza, fertilità, *f.*; rancidità, *f.*; corruzione, *f.*
ransack [ˈrænsæk], *v.t.* Frugare, frugacchiare, rovistare; predare, saccheggiare.
ransom [ˈrænsəm], *n.* Riscatto, *m.*, redenzione, *f.*; (*blackmail*) ricatto, *m.* ‖ *v.t.* Riscattare, ricomprare, redimere. **To hold to —,** tenere in ostaggio.
rant [rænt], *n.* Concione, cicalata, *f.*, discorso ampolloso, *m.* ‖ *v.i.* Declamare, concionare, inveire, smaniare, scalmanarsi.
ranter, *n.* Declamatore, retore, *m.*; cialtrone, energumeno, *m.*
ranting, *a.* Stravagante, scalmanato.
ranunculus [rəˈnʌŋkjuːləs], *n.* (*Bot.*) Ranuncolo, *m.*
rap [ræp], *n.* Colpo, colpetto, *m.*, picchiata, *f.* ‖ *v.t.* Battere, picchiare, bussare. **I don't care a —,** me ne infischio, non m'importa un fico; **to — on the door,** battere all'uscio, bussare; **to — out an oath,** lanciare una bestemmia.
rapacious [rəˈpeiʃəs], *a.* Rapace, avido.
rapaciousness, rapacity, *n.* Rapacità, avidità, *f.*
rape (1) [reip], *n.* Violazione, *f.*, stupro; rapimento, ratto, *m.* ‖ *v.t.* Violare, stuprare, violare carnalmente; rapire.
rape (2), *n.* (*Bot.*) Colza, rapa, *f.*
Raphaelesque [ræfeiəˈlesk], *a.* Raffaellesco.
rapid [ˈræpid], *a.* Rapido, veloce, celere, lesto; (*of pulse*) frequente. ‖ *n.* (*of river*) Rapida, *f.*
rapidity, *n.* Rapidità, velocità, celerità, *f.*
rapidly, *adv.* Rapidamente.
rapier [ˈreipiəɹ], *n.* Stocco, *m.*, spada, *f.*; spadino, *m.* **—-thrust,** colpo di spada, *m.*, stoccata, *f.*
rapine [ˈræpin], *n.* Rapina, *f.*
rapparee [ræpəˈriː], *n.* Vagabondo, *m.*
rappee [rəˈpiː], *n.* Rapè, *m.*
rapscallion [ræpsˈkæliən], *n.* Furfante, birbante, mascalzone, *m.*
rapt [ræpt], *a.* Rapito, trasportato, estasiato, estatico.
raptorial [ræpˈtɔːriəl], *a.* (*Zool.*) Predatorio.
rapture [ˈræptʃəɹ], *n.* Trasporto, entusiasmo, *m.*, estasi, *f.*
rapturous, *a.* Rapito, estatico, estasiato; entusiastico.
rapturously, *adv.* Estaticamente.
rare [rɛəɹ], *a.* Raro; rado, scarso, tenue; infrequente, insolito; singolare, prezioso, scelto, eccelente; poco cotto.
rarebit [cp. **welsh rabbit**].
raree-show [ˈrɛəriːʃou], *n.* Teatrino ambulante, *m.*, mostra delle curiosità, *f.*
rarefaction [rɛəriˈfækʃən], *n.* Rarefazione, *f.*
rarefactive [rɛəriˈfæktiv], *a.* Rarefattivo.

rarefy ['rɛərifai], *v.t.* Rarefare; *v.i.* rarefarsi.
rarely ['rɛəɹli], *adv.* Raramente, rade volte, di rado; ottimamente.
rareness, rarity, *n.* Rarezza, radezza, *f.*; rarità, *f.* **A rarity,** una rarità, *f.*; **the rarity of the air,** la rarefazione dell'aria, *f.*
rascal ['rɑːskəl], *n.* Briccone, furfante, birbante, mascalzone, *m.*
rascality [rɑːs'kæliti], *n.* Bricconeria, furfanteria, birbanteria, *f.*
rascally, *a.* Mascalzonesco, furfantesco, canagliesco.
rase [cp. **raze**].
rash (1) [ræʃ], *n.* (*Med.*) Eruzione, *f.*
rash (2), *a.* Precipitoso, avventato, inconsiderato, imprudente.
rasher, *n.* Fetta di lardo, fetta di prosciutto, *f.*
rashly, *adv.* Inconsideratamente, imprudentemente.
rashness, *n.* Imprudenza, avventatezza, inconsideratezza, *f.*
rasp [rɑːsp], *n.* Raspa, grattugia, *f.* || *v.t.* Raspare, grattare, grattugiare.
raspberry ['rɑːzbəri], *n.* (*Bot.*) Lampone, *m.*; (*colloq.*) suono grossolano con la bocca, *m.* **— -cane,** pianta di lampone, *f.*
rasping, *a.* (*of voice*) Rauco. **Raspings,** pane grattugiato, *m.*
rat [ræt], *n.* (*Zool.*) Topo, ratto, sorcio, *m.*; (*fig.*) crumiro, rinnegato, *m.*; (*Pol.*) girella, *f.* || *v.i.* Far la caccia ai topi; (*of dog*) cacciare i topi; (*Pol.*) abbandonare il proprio partito, voltar casacca. (*fig.*) **To smell a —,** aver qualche sospetto, mangiar la foglia; (*colloq.*) **Rats!** Che sciocchezza! **— -catcher,** prenditore di topi; **— -trap,** trappola per topi, *f.*; (*Cycling*) **— -trap pedal,** pedale a sega, *m.*
ratable, rateable ['reitəbl], *a.* Tassabile, gravabile; (*of land*) catastale.
ratafia [rætə'fiə], *n.* Ratafia, *f.*
ratchet ['rætʃit], *n.* Dente d'arresto, rocchetto, *m.* **— brace,** trapano a cricco, *m.*; **— -wheel,** ruota d'arresto, *f.*
rate (1) [reit], *n.* Proporzione, media, *f.*; prezzo, *m.*; velocità, *f.*; (*Comm.*) corso, *m.*; (*of interest*) saggio, tasso, *m.*; tassa comunale, imposta comunale, *f.*; (*quality*) grado, *m.*, qualità, *f.* || *v.t.* Stimare, valutare, quotare, apprezzare; considerare, riguardare; tassare; *v.i.* essere classificato. **At a cheap —,** a buon mercato; **at a great —,** a gran velocità; **at any —,** in ogni modo, insomma, comunque; (*colloq.*) **at that —,** in quel caso, di quel passo; **at the — of 2/-,** al prezzo di due scellini; **at the — of 4 miles an hour,** alla velocità di quattro miglia all'ora; **— of interest,** tasso d'interesse, *m.*; **railway rates,** tariffe ferroviarie, *f.pl.*; **to — high,** stimare molto; **these houses are too highly rated,** queste case sono tassate troppo forte; **death —,** mortalità, *f.*; **— -payer,** contribuente, *m.*; **— -collector,** esattore comunale, *m.*
rate (2), *v.t.* Sgridare, rimproverare, rampognare.
rateable [cp. **ratable**].
rather ['rɑːðəɹ], *adv.* Piuttosto, alquanto; discretamente; abbastanza. **— pretty than beautiful,** più grazioso che bello; **anything — than,** tutto piuttosto che; **the — that,** tanto più che; **I — think,** ho l'idea, immagino; **I would — not,** preferisco di no; **she would — die than give in,** vorrebbe piuttosto morire che cedere; **Rather!** Sicuro! Certo! Sfido!
ratification [rætifi'keiʃən], *n.* Ratifica, *f.*
ratify ['rætifai], *v.t.* Ratificare.
rating (1) ['reitiŋ], *n.* Stima, valutazione, *f.*; ripartizione delle imposte, *f.*; grado, rango, *m.*; (*Naut.*) marinaio semplice, *m.*
rating (2), *n.* Sgridata, lavata di capo, *f.*
ratio (pl. **ratios**) ['reiʃiou, 'reiʃiouz], *n.* Ragione, proporzione, *f.*, rapporto, *m.* **In the — of,** in ragione di; **inverse —,** ragione inversa, *f.*
ratiocinate [ræti'ɔsineit], *v.i.* Raziocinare.
ratiocination, *n.* Raziocinazione, *f.*, ragionamento, *m.*
ration ['ræʃən], *n.* Razione, *f.* || *v.t.* Razionare. **Rations,** viveri, *m.pl.*, razione, *f.*; **to put on rations,** mettere a razione, razionare; **— -book,** libretto d'alimentazione, *m.*; **— -card,** tessera annonaria, *f.*
rational ['ræʃənəl], *a.* Razionale, ragionevole.
rationale [ræʃiou'nɑːli], *n.* (*Logic*) Ragione, base, *f.*
rationalism, *n.* Razionalismo, *m.*
rationalist, *n.* Razionalista, *m.f.*
rationality, *n.* Razionalità, *f.*
rationalize, *v.t.* Razionalizzare.
rationalization, *n.* Razionalizzazione, *f.*
rationally, *adv.* Razionalmente.
rationing, *n.* Razionamento, *m.*
ratlines ['rætlinz], *n.pl.* (*Naut.*) Griselle, *f.pl.*
rattan ['rætən], *n.* (*Bot.*) Canna d'India, *f.*
rat-tat-tat [rætæt'æt], *n.* (*on door*) Picchio, colpo, *m.*
ratter, *n.* Cane da topi, *m.*
ratting, *n.* Caccia ai topi, *f.*; (*fig.*) defezione, *f.*
rattle [rætl], *v.t.i.* Sbatacchiare, strepitare, risonare; far tintinnare, far risonare. || *n.* (*for baby*) Sonaglio, *m.*; (*sound*) strepito, fracasso, rumore, tintinnio, *m.*; (*chatter*) cicaleccio, *m.* **To — away,** chiacchierare, ciarlare, cicalare; prender la corsa; **to — along,** rintronare, andar rotolando; **to — off,** recitare; **death- —,** rantolo, *m.*; **— -brained,** scervellato.
rattlesnake ['rætlsneik], *n.* (*Zool.*) Serpente a sonagli, crotalo, *m.*
rattletrap, *n.* Macchina guasta, *f.* || *a.* Sconquassato, scassinato. **Rattletraps,** cianfrusaglie, *f.pl.*
rattling, *a.* (*colloq.*) Eccellente, ottimo. **A — good story,** una storiella gustosa, *f.*
raucous ['rɔːkəs], *a.* Rauco.
raucously, *adv.* Raucamente.
ravage ['rævidʒ], *v.t.i.* Devastare rovinare, saccheggiare.
ravages, *n.pl.* Danni, *m.pl.*, rovine, *f.pl.* **The — of time,** le ingiurie degli anni, *f.pl.*
rave [reiv], *v.i.* Delirare, vaneggiare, farneticare. **To — about,** andar pazzo di.
ravel ['rævəl], *v.t.i.* Imbrogliare, avviluppare, arruffare; confondere, complicare; imbrogliarsi, avvilupparsi, distrigare, sciogliere, sbrogliare.
raven (1) ['reivən], *n.* (*Zool.*) Corvo, *m.*
raven (2) ['rævən], *v.t.* Divorare; *v.i.* cercare preda, andar predando.
ravenous, ravening, *a.* Vorace, ingordo, insaziabile, affamato.
ravenously, *adv.* Voracemente.
ravenousness, *n.* Voracità, ingordigia, insaziabilità, *f.*

ravine [rə'vi:n], *n.* Burrone, *m.*; borro, *m.*, fossa, *f.*
raving ['reiviŋ], *a.* Delirio, vaneggiamento, *m.* || *a.* Furioso, frenetico. **— mad,** pazzo da catena.
ravish ['ræviʃ], *v.t.* Rapire, violare, stuprare; incantare, trasportare di gioia.
ravisher, *n.* Violatore, *m.*
ravishing, *a.* Incantevole.
ravishingly, *adv.* Incantevolmente, d'incanto.
ravishment, *n.* Estasi, *f.*, incanto, incantamento, *m.*
raw [rɔ:], *a.* Crudo; greggio, rozzo; spellato, scorticato; (*of weather*) freddo e umido; (*of meat*) sanguinante; (*inexperienced*) immaturo, inesperto; zotico. || *n.* Vivo, *m.* **A — hand,** un novizio, *m.*; **— materials,** materie gregge, materie prime, *f.pl.*; **to touch on the —,** toccare sul vivo; **—-boned,** scarno, ossuto.
rawness, *n.* Crudezza, *f.*; rozzezza, *f.*; immaturità, ineducazione, inesperienza, *f.*; umidità, *f.*
ray (1) [rei], *n.* Raggio, *m.* || *v.i.* Radiare, raggiare.
ray (2), *n.* (*Zool.*) Razza, *f.*
rayless, *a.* Senza raggio, tetro, buio, oscuro, cieco.
rayon ['reijɔn], *n.* Raion, *m.*
raze, rase [reiz], *v.t.* Radere, abbattere, spianare. **To — to the ground,** radere al suolo.
razor ['reizəɹ], *n.* Rasoio, *m.* **Safety-—,** rasoio di sicurezza, *m.*; **dry —,** rasoio elettrico, *m.*; **—-backed,** a lama di rasoio; (*Zool.*) **—-bill,** pinguino comune; **—-shell,** cappalunga, *f.*; **—-edge,** filo di rasoio, *m.*; **—-blade,** lametta, *f.*
razzle [ræzl], *n.* (*colloq.*) Scappata, baldoria, *f.*
reabsorb [ri:əb'sɔ:ɹb], *v.t.* Riassorbire.
reach [ri:tʃ], *n.* Portata, *f.*, accesso, *m.*; capacità, *f.*; (*of a river*) tratto, *m.*; penetrazione, *f.* || *v.t.* Arrivare a, pervenire a, raggiungere, porgere; *v.i.* stendersi. **Within —,** a portata di mano; **within easy — of town,** a comoda distanza dalla città; **out of —,** fuori di mano; **it is out of my —,** non riesco ad arrivarci; **to — out an arm,** stendere un braccio; **to — after,** cercare di arrivare a.
react (1) [ri:'ækt], *v.i.* Reagire.
react (2), *v.t.* Rappresentare ancora, ridare.
reaction, *n.* Reazione, *f.*
reactionary, *n.a.* (*Pol.*) Reazionario, *m.*
reactive, *a.* Reattivo.
read [ri:d], *v.t.* Leggere; dare lettura di; (*Univ.*) studiare; (*fig.*) indovinare, interpretare, spiegare; (*a meter*) rilevare. **To — aloud,** leggere ad alta voce; **to — between the lines,** leggere tra le righe; **to — over,** scorrere; **to — a subject up,** fare uno studio speciale di un soggetto; **to — about,** leggere di; **to — music at sight,** leggere la musica a prima vista; **to — someone to sleep,** addormentare uno colla lettura; **it does not — very well,** non suona bene alla lettura.
readable, *a.* Leggibile, piacevole a leggersi.
readableness, *n.* Leggibilità, *f.*
readdress [ri:ə'dres], *v.t.* Rindirizzare, rispedire.
reader ['ri:dəɹ], *n.* Lettore, *m.*, lettrice, *f.*; (*schoolbook*) libro di lettura, *m.*; (*Print.*) correttore, *m.*
readership, *n.* Lettorato, *m.*
readily ['redili], *adv.* Volentieri, prontamente; facilmente, correntemente.
readiness ['redinis], *n.* Prontezza, sollecitudine, prestezza, *f.*; buona volontà, *f.*; premura, *f.* **In —,** pronto, alla mano; in assetto.
reading ['ri:diŋ], *n.* Lettura, *f.*; lezione, *f.*; (*textual*) variante, *f.*; interpretazione, *f.* **A man of vast —,** un uomo di vaste letture; **there is plenty of — in this book,** c'è molto da leggersi in questo libro; **this is good —,** fa piacere leggerlo; **—-book,** libro da lettura, *m.*; **—-desk,** leggio, *m.*; **—-room,** gabinetto di lettura, *m.*, sala di lettura, *f.*; **—-glass,** lente biconvessa, *f.*; **—-lamp,** lampada da studio, *f.*
readjourn [ri:ə'dʒə:ɹn], *v.t.* Aggiornare ancora, rimandar di nuovo.
readjust [riə'dʒʌst], *v.t.* Raggiustare.
readjustment, *n.* Raggiustamento, *m.*
readmission, readmittance, *n.* Riammissione, *f.*
readmit [ri:əd'mit], *v.t.* Riammettere.
ready ['rədi], *a.* Pronto, preparato, disposto; franco, svelto, abile; alla mano; (*of money*) liquido, contante. **To get —,** prepararsi, apparecchiarsi; **he is too — to interfere,** è troppo pronto a frammettersi; **— to hand,** alla mano; **— money,** contanti, *m.pl.*, pronta cassa, *f.*; **—-made,** confezionato, bell'e fatto; **—-reckoner,** tabella dei calcoli, *f.*, libretto calcolatore, *m.*; **—-witted,** dallo spirito pronto, dall'ingegno vivace.
reaffirm [ri:ə'fə:ɹm], *v.t.* Riaffermare, riconfermare.
reaffirmation, *n.* Riconferma, riaffermazione, *f.*
reagent [ri:'eidʒənt], *n.* (*Chem.*) Reagente, *m.*
real ['ri:əl], *a.* Reale; genuino, vero, effettivo, attuale; (*Law*) immobile. **In — earnest,** proprio sul serio; **— estate,** beni immobili, *m.pl.*
realism ['ri:əlizm], *n.* Realismo, *m.*
realist, *n.* Realista, *m.f.*
realistic, *a.* Realistico.
realistically, *adv.* Realisticamente.
reality [ri:'æliti], *n.* Realtà, verità, *f.*
realizable [riə'laizəbl], *a.* Concepibile, realizzabile, effettuabile.
realization, *n.* Percezione, concezione, realizzazione, *f.*; (*Comm.*) realizzo, *m.*
realize, *v.t.* Rendersi conto, percepire, concepire; realizzare, effettuare, attuare.
really ['ri:əli], *adv.* Realmente, veramente, in verità, proprio. || *inter.* Davvero!
realm [relm], *n.* Regno, *m.*; reame, dominio, *m.*
realty [ri:'ælti], *n.* (*Law*) Beni immobili, *m.pl.*
ream [ri:m], *n.* Risma, *f.* || *v.t.* Alesare.
reamer, *n.* Alesatore, *m.*
reanimate [ri:'ænimeit], *v.t.* Rianimare.
reanimation, *n.* Rianimazione, *f.*
reannex [ri:ə'neks], *v.t.* Riannettere.
reap [ri:p], *v.t.* Mietere, falciare; (*fig.*) raccogliere. **To — the harvest,** mietere il grano; **to — where others have sown,** mietere l'altrui campo.
reaper, *n.* Mietitore, *m.*, mietitrice, *f.*
reaping, *n.* Mietitura, *f.* **—-hook,** falce, *f.*; **—-machine,** mietitrice, *f.*; **combined harvester, reaper and thresher,** mietitrice-trebbiatrice, *f.*

reapparel [ri:əˈpærəl], *v.t.* Rivestire.
reappear [ri:əˈpiəɹ], *v.i.* Riapparire.
reappearance, *n.* Ricomparsa, *f.*
reappoint [ri:əˈpɔint], *v.t.* Rinominare, rieleggere.
reappointment, *n.* Rielezione, *f.*
rear (1) [riəɹ], *n.* Il di dietro, il tergo, il dietro, *m.*; coda, *f.*; (*Mil.*) retroguardia, *f.* **To stay in the —,** stare alla retroguardia; **at the — of the house,** dietro la casa; **at the —, in the —,** a tergo, alle spalle, per di dietro; **— -lamp,** fanalino posteriore, *m.*; **— rank,** ultima fila, *f.*; **— admiral,** contrammiraglio, *m.*; **the — seats,** i sedili posteriori, *m.pl.*
rear (2), *v.t.* Innalzare, elevare; *v.i.* (*of a horse*) impennarsi.
rear (3), *v.t.* (*young*) Allevare, coltivare.
rearing, *n.* Allevamento, *m.*
rearm [ri:ˈɑːɹm], *v.t.* Riarmare.
rearmament, *n.* Riarmamento, riarmo, *m.*
rearrangement [ri:əˈreindʒmənt], *n.* Riordinamento, *m.*
rearward [ˈriəɹwəd], *a.* Di dietro, a tergo.
rearwards, *adv.* Di dietro, a tergo.
reascend [ri:əˈsend], *v.i.* Riascendere.
reason [ˈri:zən], *n.* Ragione, causa, cagione, *f.*, motivo, *m.* ‖ *v.t.i.* Ragionare, argomentare, discorrere. **By — of,** per causa di; **to give reasons for,** render ragioni di; **for the same —,** per la stessa ragione; **with —,** a ragione, giustamente; **it stands to — that,** va senza dire che; **there is every — to believe,** c'è ragione di credere; **to bring to —,** ridurre alla ragione; **to listen to —,** ascoltare la ragione; **to lose one's —,** perder la ragione; **to — something out,** escogitare, farsi una ragione; **we reasoned him out of his fears,** lo persuademmo a non aver più paura; **to state the — for,** motivare.
reasonable, *a.* Ragionevole; giusto, conveniente.
reasonableness, *n.* Ragionevolezza, *f.*
reasonably, *adv.* Ragionevolmente; giustamente.
reasoner, *n.* Ragionatore, *m.*, ragionatrice, *f.*
reasoning, *n.* Ragionamento, raziocinio, *m.*, argomentazione, *f.*
reasonless, *a.* Irragionevole, irrazionale.
reassemble [ri:əˈsembl], *v.t.* Adunare ancora; *v.i.* adunarsi ancora.
reassert [ri:əˈsəːɹt], *v.t.* Riaffermare.
reassess [ri:əˈses], *v.t.* Fissare di nuovo la tassa.
reassessment, *n.* Riagiudicazione, *f.*
reassign [ri:əˈsain], *v.t.* Riassegnare.
reassurance [ri:əˈʃju:rəns], *n.* Riassicurazione, *f.*; rassicurazione, *f.*
reassure, *v.t.* Riassicurare, rassicurare.
reassuring, *a.* Rassicurante.
reattach [ri:əˈtætʃ], *v.t.* Riattaccare.
rebate (1) [ˈri:beit], *n.* Ribasso, sconto, *m.*, bonifica, *f.*
rebate (2) [ˈræbit], [cp. **rabbet**].
rebeck [ˈri:bek], *n.* Ribeca, *f.*
rebel [ˈrebəl], *n.* Ribelle, *m.f.* ‖ *v.i.* [riˈbel], Ribellarsi, rivoltarsi, insorgere.
rebellion [reˈbeljən], *n.* Ribellione, rivolta, insurrezione, *f.*
rebellious, *a.* Ribelle, riottoso, disubbidiente.
rebelliousness, *n.* Riottosità, *f.*
rebind [ri:ˈbaind], *v.t.* Rilegare.
rebound (1) [ri:ˈbaund], *v.i.* Rimbalzare. ‖ *n.* Rimbalzo, contraccolpo. **To take someone on the —,** agire sui sentimenti di riazione di qualcuno.
rebound (2) [ri:ˈbaund], *p.p.a.* Rilegato.
rebuff [riˈbʌf], *n.* Ripulsa, *f.*, rifiuto, *m.* ‖ *v.t.* Respingere, dare una repulsa, sconfessare.
rebuild [ri:ˈbild], *v.t.* Riedificare, ricostruire.
rebuilding, *n.* Riedificazione, ricostruzione, *f.*
rebuke [riˈbju:k], *n.* Rimprovero, biasimo, *m.*, riprensione, sgridata, *f.* ‖ *v.t.* Rimproverare, biasimare, riprendere.
rebukingly, *adv.* Rimproverando.
rebus [ˈri:bəs], *n.* Rebus, *m.*
rebut [riˈbʌt], *v.t.* Ributtare, confutare, respingere.
rebuttal, *n.* Ributtamento, *m.*, confutazione, *f.*
recalcitrant [riˈkælsitrənt], *a.* Ricalcitrante, restio. ‖ *n.* Ricalcitrante, *m.f.*
recall [riˈkɔ:l], *n.* Richiamo, *m.* ‖ *v.t.* Richiamare, revocare; rammentarsi di, ricordarsi. **Past —,** irrevocabile.
recant [riˈkænt], *v.t.* Ritrattare, disdire; *v.i.* ritrattarsi, disdirsi, cantare la palinodia.
recantation, *n.* Ritrattazione, palinodia, *f.*
recapitulate [ri:kəˈpitju:leit], *v.t.* Ricapitolare.
recapitulation, *n.* Ricapitulazione, *f.*
recapture [ri:ˈkæptʃəɹ], *v.t.* Riprendere. ‖ *n.* Ripresa, riconquista, *f.*
recast [ri:ˈkæst], *v.t.* Rifondere; rimaneggiare, ricomporre.
recede [riˈsi:d], *v.i.* Recedere, ritirarsi, farsi indietro, indietreggiare.
receding, *a.* Indietreggiante, ritirantesi; (*chin*) fuggente.
receipt [riˈsi:t], *n.* Ricevuta, quietanza, *f.*; (*act of*) ricevimento, *m.*; (*recipe*) ricetta, *f.* ‖ *v.t.* Quietanzare. **To acknowledge — of,** accusare ricevuta di; **I am in — of,** ho ricevuto; **on — of your letter,** a riscontro della vostra lettera; **— stamp,** marca da bollo, *f.*; **— -book,** libro di ricevute, *m.*
receipted, *a.* Quietanzato.
receivable [reˈsi:vəbl], *a.* Ricevibile.
receive [reˈsi:v], *v.t.* Ricevere, accogliere, accettare; sostenere; (*money*) riscuotere; (*stolen goods*) ricettare. **I will stay here and — him,** starò qui a riceverlo.
receiver, *n.* Ricevitore, destinatario, recipiente, *m.*; (*of stolen goods*) ricettatore, *m.*; (*Telephone*) ricevitore, *m.*; (*Tennis*) ribattitore, *m.*, ribattitrice, *f.* **Official —,** curatore, *m.*
receiving, *n.* (*Law*) Ricettazione, *f.*
recension [reˈsenʃən], *n.* Recensione, *f.*
recent [ˈri:sənt], *a.* Recente, nuovo, fresco.
recently, *adv.* Recentemente, poco fa.
receptacle [reˈseptəkl], *n.* Recipiente, recettacolo, *m.*
reception [reˈsepʃən], *n.* Ricevimento, *m.*, accoglienza, *f.*; (*Radio*) ricezione, *f.* **To give a —,** dare un ricevimento.
receptive, *a.* Recettivo.
receptiveness, receptivity, *n.* Recettività, *f.*
recess [riˈses], *n.* Nicchia, rientranza, alcova, *f.*; recesso, *m.*; (*holidays*) vacanze, *f.pl.* ‖ *v.t.* Sfondare.
recession, *n.* Recessione, *f.*
recharge [ri:ˈtʃɑːɹdʒ], *v.t.* Ricaricare.
recipe [ˈresipi], *n.* Ricetta, *f.*; (*Med.*) formula, *f.*

recipient [re'sipiənt], *n.* Ricevitore, *m.*, ricevitrice, *f.*, recipiente, *m.f.*
reciprocal [re'siprokəl], *a.* Reciproco. || *n.* (*Math.*) Numero reciproco, *m.*
reciprocate, *v.t.* Reciprocare, contraccambiare; *v.i.* alternarsi, avvicendarsi. **I — your good wishes,** contraccambio i vostri buoni auguri.
reciprocating, *a.* (*Mech.*) Alternativo.
reciprocity [resi'prɔsiti], *n.* Reciprocanza, reciprocità, *f.*
recital [ri'saitəl], *n.* Relazione, narrazione, *f.*, referto, rapporto, *m.*; (*of drama, etc.*) recita, *f.*; (*of music*) concerto, *m.*, recita, *f.*; (*of poems*) recitazione, *f.*
recitation, *n.* Recitazione, recita, *f.*
recitative, *n.* (*Mus.*) Recitativo, *m.*
recite [ri'sait], *v.t.* Recitare; narrare, enumerare.
reciter, *n.* Recitatore, *m.*, recitatrice, *f.*
reck [rek], *v.t.i.* Far caso di, curarsi di. **He recks not of it,** non ne fa caso, non gli importa.
reckless, *a.* Temerario, imprudente; inconsiderato, avventato.
recklessly, *adv.* Temerariamente, inconsideratamente.
recklessness, *a.* Temerità, imprudenza, inconsideratezza, avventatezza, *f.*
reckon ['rekən], *v.t.* Contare, calcolare, computare; stimare, reputare, giudicare. **Reckoning from to-day,** a contare da oggi; **to — up,** computare; **to — in,** includere nel conto; **to — upon,** contare su.
reckoner, *n.* Contatore, computista, *m.*
reckoning, *n.* Conto, calcolo, computo, *m.*; retribuzione, *f.*; (*Naut.*) stima, *f.* **Short reckonings make long friends,** patti chiari amici cari; **to be out in one's —,** far male i suoi conti; **a day of —,** un giorno di retribuzione, *m.*
reclaim [ri'kleim], *v.t.* Correggere, raddrizzare, emendare; (*land*) prosciugare, bonificare.
reclaimable, *a.* Correggibile; bonificabile.
reclaiming, reclamation, *n.* Correzione, *f.*, prosciugamento, *m.*, bonifica, *f.*
recline [ri'klain], *v.t.* Appoggiare, adagiare, reclinare; *v.i.* appoggiarsi, adagiarsi, sdraiarsi.
reclining, *a.* Adagiato, sdraiato.
recluse [re'klu:z], *n.* Solitario, eremita, anacoreta, *m.*
reclusion, *n.* Reclusione, *f.*
recoal [ri:'koul], *v.i.* Far carbone.
recognition [rekɔg'niʃən], *n.* Riconoscenza, *f.*, riconoscimento, *m.*
recognizable [rekɔg'naizəbl], *a.* Riconoscibile.
recognizance [re'kɔnisəns], *n.* (*Law*) Malleveria, garanzia, *f.*; scrittura d'obbligo, *f.*
recognize ['rekɔgnaiz], *v.t.* Riconoscere; ammettere.
recoil [re'kɔil], *n.* Rinculo, indietreggiamento, *m.*; rimbalzo, *m.* || *v.i.* Rinculare, indietreggiare, rimbalzare; rifuggere a. **I — from the thought,** mi ripugna il pensiero.
recoin [ri:'kɔin], *v.t.* Riconiare.
recollect [rekə'lekt], *v.t.* Ricordarsi di, rammentarsi di.
recollection, *n.* Ricordanza, rimembranza, memoria, *f.*, ricordo, *m.*; riflessione, *f.* **I have no — of it,** non lo ricordo; **to the best of my —,** per quanto io ricordo; **I have some slight — of it,** ne ho qualche rimembranza.
recolonization [ri:kɔlənai'zeiʃən], *n.* Nuova colonizzazione, *f.*
recommence [ri:kə'mens], *v.t.i.* Ricominciare.
recommend [rekə'mend], *v.t.* Raccomandare; proporre. **Can you — me a book?** Potete consigliarmi un libro?
recommendable, *a.* Raccomandabile.
recommendation [rekəmen'deiʃən], *n.* Raccomandazione, *f.*; proposta, *f.* **Letter of —,** lettera di raccomandazione, *f.*
recommender, *n.* Proponente, presentatore, *m.*
recommit [ri:kə'mit], *v.t.* Rimandare in prigione.
recommitment, recommittal, *n.* Rinvio in prigione, *m.*
recompense ['rekəmpens], *n.* Ricompensa, rimunerazione, *f.*, risarcimento, *m.* || *v.t.* Ricompensare, rimunerare; risarcire.
recompose [ri:kəm'pouz], *v.t.* Ricomporre.
reconcilable [rekən'sailəbl], *a.* Riconciliabile.
reconcilability, *n.* Riconciliabilità, *f.*
reconcile ['rekənsail], *v.t.* Riconciliare, ravvicinare, armonizzare. **To become reconciled,** riconciliarsi; **to — oneself to,** rimettersi a, riconciliarsi con.
reconcilement, *n.* Riconciliazione, *f.*, ravvicinamento, *m.*
reconciler, *n.* Riconciliatore, *m.*, riconciliatrice, *f.*
reconciliation, *n.* Riconciliazione, *f.*
reconciliatory, *a.* Riconciliatorio.
recondite ['rekəndait], *a.* Recondito, nascosto, celato, occulto.
reconduct [ri:kən'dʌkt], *v.t.* Ricondurre.
reconnaissance [re'kɔnisəns], *n.* (*Mil.*) Esplorazione, ricognizione, *f.*
reconnoitre [rekə'nɔitəɹ], *v.t.i.* Esplorare, perlustrare, fare una ricognizione.
reconnoitring, *a.* Esplorativo, riconoscitivo. **— party,** pattuglia di ricognizione, *f.*
reconquer [ri:'kɔŋkəɹ], *v.t.* Riconquistare.
reconsider [ri:kən'sidəɹ], *v.t.* Riconsiderare, rivedere; riesaminare. **To — a decision,** ritornare su una decisione.
reconsideration, *n.* Riesame, *m.*
reconstitute [ri:'kɔnstitju:t], *v.t.* Ricostituire.
reconstitution, *n.* Ricostituzione, *f.*
reconstruct, *v.t.* Ricostruire.
reconstruction, *n.* Ricostruzione, *f.*; ricostituzione, *f.*
record (1) [re'kɔ:ɹd], *v.t.* Notare, registrare, segnalare; (*vote*) votare.
record (2) ['rekɔ:ɹd], *n.* Ricordo, *m.*; documento, registro, *m.*; (*Sport*) record, primato, *m.*; (*gramophone*) disco, *m.*; stato di servizio; protocollo, *m.* **Records,** archivi, *m.pl.*, atti, *m.pl.* **He has a good —,** ha un buon stato di servizio; **it is on — that,** risulta che, è documentato che; **public records,** archivi, *m.pl.*; **— office,** archivio di stato; (*Sport*) **to break the —,** battere il primato; **at — speed,** a velocità di primato; **— library,** discoteca, *m.*; **long-playing —,** microsolco, *m.*
recorder, *n.* Archivista, *m.*; narratore, *m.*; (*Law*) giudice, *m.*

recount [re'kaunt], *v.t.* Narrare, raccontare, riferire.
re-count [ri:'kaunt], *v.t.* Ricontare, contare di nuovo. || *n.* Nuovo conto, *m.*
recoup [ri'ku:p], *v.t.* Rimborsare, compensare, ricuperare. **To — oneself,** rimborsarsi, rifarsi di.
recoupment, *n.* Rimborso, *m.*, compensazione, *f.*
recourse [re'kɔ:ɹs], *n.* Ricorso, *m.* **To have — to,** far ricorso a.
recover [re'kʌvəɹ], *v.t.* Ricuperare, riavere, riacquistare, riprendere; salvare; *v.i.* ristabilirsi, rimettersi, guarire; reintegrare. **To — oneself,** rimettersi, riaversi; **to — one's breath,** riprendere fiato; **to — from an illness,** rimettersi da una malattia.
re-cover [ri:'kʌvəɹ], *v.t.* Coprire di nuovo, ricoprire.
recoverable, *a.* Ricuperabile; reintegrabile.
recovery [re'kʌvəri], *n.* Ricupero, ristabilimento, *m.*, guarigione, *f.*; (*Sport*) ripresa, *f.* **Past —,** incurabile, insanabile, senza rimedio.
recreant ['rekriənt], *n.* Traditore, apostata, *m.* || *a.* Vigliacco, codardo.
recreate ['rekrieit], *v.t.* Ricreare, divertire, svagare.
re-create ['ri:kri'eit], *v.t.* Ricreare, creare di nuovo.
recreation [rekri'eiʃən], *n.* Ricreazione, *f.*, divertimento, svago, passatempo, *m.*
recreative [rekri'eitiv], *a.* Ricreativo.
recriminate [re'krimineit], *v.i.* Recriminare.
recrimination, *n.* Recriminazione, *f.*
recross [ri:'krɔs], *v.t.* Riattraversare, ritraversare. **To cross and —,** traversare in tutti i sensi.
recrudescence [ri:kru:'desəns], *n.* Recrudescenza, *f.*
recrudescent, *a.* Rincrudito.
recruit [re'kru:t], *n.* Recluta, *f.* || *v.t.* Reclutare, arruolare; ristabilire, rinvigorire, rimettere; *v.i.* far reclute; ristabilirsi, rimettersi. **A raw —,** un coscritto, un novizio, *m.*; **to — oneself,** ristabilirsi, rimettersi in salute.
recruiting, recruitment, *n.* Reclutamento, *m.* **— sergeant,** sottufficiale di reclutamento, *m.*
rectal ['rektəl], *a.* (*Anat.*) Del retto.
rectangle ['rektæŋgl], *n.* (*Geom.*) Rettangolo, *m.*
rectangular [rekt'æŋgju:ləɹ], *a.* Rettangolare.
rectifiable [rekti'faiəbl], *a.* Corregibile.
rectification [rektifi'keiʃən], *n.* Rettificazione, *f.*; rettifica, *f.*
rectifier ['rektifaiəɹ], *n.* Rettificatore, *m.*
rectify ['rektifai], *v.t.* Rettificare, correggere.
rectilinear, rectilineal [rekti'liniəɹ, rekti'liniəl], *a.* Rettilineo.
rectitude ['rektitju:d], *n.* Rettitudine, *f.*
recto ['rektou], *n.* Recto, retto, *m.*
rector, *n.* (*Eccles.*) Pievano; rettore, *m.*
rectorate, rectorship, *n.* Rettorato, *m.*
rectorial, *a.* Rettorale.
rectory ['rektəri], *n.* Presbiterio, *m.*, pievania, *f.*
rectum ['rektəm], *n.* (*Anat.*) Retto, *m.*
recumbency [re'kʌmbənsi], *n.* Sdraio, *m.*, giacitura, *f.*
recumbent, *a.* Sdraiato, disteso, giacente.
recuperate [re'kju:pəreit], *v.i.* Ricuperare, ricuperarsi, rifarsi.
recuperation, *n.* Ricupero, *m.*
recuperative, *a.* Ricuperativo.
recur [re'kə:ɹ], *v.i.* Ricorrere, ritornare; riaccadere, succedere ancora.
recurrence [re'kʌrəns], *n.* Ricorrenza, *f.*, ritorno, *m.* **He has had a — of his illness,** ha avuto una ripresa della sua malattia.
recurrent, recurring, *a.* Ricorrente, periodico. **— decimal,** frazione periodica, *f.*
recurve [ri:'kə:ɹv], *v.t.* Ricurvare; *v.i.* ricurvarsi.
recusance, recusancy ['rekju:zəns, 'rekju:zənsi], *n.* (*Hist.*) Nonconformismo, *m.*
recusant, *n.* (*Hist.*) Nonconformista, *m.f.*
recut [ri:'kʌt], *v.t.* Ritagliare.
red [red], *a.* Rosso, rossiccio; fulvo. || *n.* Rosso, *m.* **Blood-—,** rosso sangue; **fiery —,** rosso fuoco; **deep —,** rosso scuro; **—-letter day,** un giorno fausto, *m.*; (*fig.*) **to see —,** vedere rosso; (*colloq.*) **to be in the —,** essere in deficit; **the Red Cross,** la Croce Rossa, *f.*; **a —-faced man,** un rubicondo, *m.*; **—-hot,** rovente; **—-handed,** in flagrante; (*fig.*) **a — herring,** una traccia falsa, *f.*; **redskin, red Indian,** pellirossa, *m.f.*; **— lead,** minio, *m.*; (*Zool.*) **— mullet,** triglia, *f.*; **— pepper,** pepe di Caienna, *m.*; **the Red Sea,** il Mare Rosso, *m.*; (*fig.*) **— tape,** burocrazia, *f.*; (*fig.*) **— light,** pericolo, *m.*
redact [re'dækt], *v.t.* Redigere.
redaction, *n.* Redazione, *f.*
redan [re'dæn], *n.* (*Mil.*) Barbacane, saliente, risalto, *m.*
redbreast ['redbrest], *n.* (*Zool.*) Pettirosso, *m.*
redcoat, *n.* (*colloq.*) Soldato inglese, *m.*
redden ['redən], *v.t.i.* Arrossire.
reddish, *a.* Rossiccio, rossastro.
redeem [re'di:m], *v.t.* Redimere, riscattare; liberare, affrancare; (*a promise*) mantenere, adempiere; (*from pawn*) ritirare. **To — one's honour,** riscattare l'onore.
redeemable, *a.* Redimibile.
Redeemer, *n.* (*Eccles.*) Il Redentore, *m.*
redeeming, *a.* Compensatore. **He has one — feature,** ha una qualità che lo salva.
redemption [re'demʃən], *n.* Redenzione, *f.*, riscatto, *m.*; ritiro, *m.*, ricupero, *m.*; (*of a mortgage, etc.*) estinzione, *f.*, ammortamento, *m.*
redintegrate [re'dintegreit], *v.t.* Reintegrare.
redintegration, *n.* Reintegrazione, *f.*
rediscover [ri:dis'kʌvəɹ], *v.t.* Riscoprire.
redistribute [ri:dis'tribjut], *v.t.* Ridistribuire.
redistribution, *n.* Ridistribuzione, *f.*
redness ['rednis], *n.* Rossezza, *f.*; rossore, *m.*
redolence ['redoləns], *n.* Odore, profumo, *m.*
redolent, *a.* Odoroso, fragrante, olezzante.
redouble [ri:'dʌbl], *v.t.* Raddoppiare.
redoubt [re'daut], *n.* (*Mil.*) Ridotto, *m.*
redoubtable, *a.* Formidabile, terribile, temibile.
redoubted, *a.* Temuto.
redound [re'daund], *v.t.* Ridondare, tornare. **To — to someone's credit,** ridondare ad onore di qualcuno.
redpoll ['redpoul], *n.* (*Zool.*) Fanello, *m.*

redraft [riː'drɑːft], *v.t.* Redigere di nuovo, fare un nuovo progetto.
redress [re'dres], *v.t.* Riaggiustare, riparare, rettificare, correggere. || *n.* Riparazione, *f.*, risarcimento, *m.*; soddisfazione, *f.*; rimedio, *m.* **To — the balance,** ristabilire l'equilibrio; **to — a grievance,** riparare un'ingiustizia.
redshank ['redʃæŋk], *n.* (*Zool.*) Albastrello, *m.*
redskin, *n.* Pellirossa, *m.f.*
redstart, *n.* (*Zool.*) Codirosso, *m.*
reduce [re'djuːs], *v.t.* Ridurre, convertire, scemare, diminuire; dimagrare. **To — to practice,** mettere in pratica; (*Mil.*) **to — to the ranks,** degradare; **in reduced circumstances,** in strettezze; **to — a salary,** ridurre uno stipendio; **to — one's weight,** dimagrarsi.
reducible, *a.* Riducibile.
reduction [re'dʌkʃən], *n.* Riduzione, diminuzione, *f.*
redundance [re'dʌndəns], *n.* Ridondanza, *f.*
redundant, *a.* Ridondante; superfluo.
reduplicate [riː'djuːplikeit], *v.t.* Raddoppiare, duplicare.
reduplication, *n.* Raddoppiamento, *m.*
redwing ['redwiŋ], *n.* (*Zool.*) Tordo rosso, *m.*
re-echo [riː'ekou], *v.t.i.* Riecheggiare; rimbombare, risonare.
reed [riːd], *n.* (*Bot.*) Canna, *f.*, giunco, *m.*; (*pipe*) zampogna, fistola, *f.*; (*Mus.*) linguetta, ancia, *f.*; (*weaver's*) pettine, *m.* (*fig.*) **A broken —,** una canna fessa, *f.* **— -bed,** canneto, *m.*; **— -pipe,** zampogna, *f.* (*Zool.*) **— -warbler,** verdone, *m.*
reedy, *a.* Coperto di canna; (*of a voice*) stridulo.
reef (1) [riːf], *n.* (*rocky*) Scoglio, *m.*, scogliera, *f.*; (*of coral*) banco, *m.*; (*Geol.*) vena, *f.*
reef (2), *n.* (*Naut.*) Terzaruolo, *m.* || *v.t.* Far terzaruolo. **To take in a —,** far terzaruolo, terzaruolare; **— -knot,** nodo piatto, nodo piano, nodo di terzaruolo, *m.*
reefer, *n.* Giacchetta, giubba, *f.*
reek [riːk], *n.* Fumo, vapore, puzzo, *m.*, esalazione, *f.* || *v.i.* Puzzare.
reel [riːl], *n.* Rocchetto, *m.*; aspo, guindolo, *m.*; gomitolo, *m.*, bobina, *f.*; (*film*) rotolo, *m.*; (*dance*) trescone scozzese, *m.* || *v.t.i.* Aggomitolare, annaspare; barcollare, vacillare. **To — off a story,** snocciolare una storiella, ripetere tutto d'un fiato; **my head reels,** mi gira la testa.
re-elect [riːe'lekt], *v.t.* Rieleggere.
re-election, *n.* Rielezione, *f.*
re-embark [riːem'bɑːɹk], *v.t.* Rimbarcare; *v.i.* rimbarcarsi.
re-embarkation, *n.* Rimbarco, *m.*
re-embody [riːem'bɔdi], *v.t.* Rincorporare.
re-emerge [riːem'əːɹdʒ], *v.i.* Riemergere.
re-employ [riːem'plɔi], *v.t.* Rimpiegare.
re-enable [riːen'eibl], *v.t.* Ridare la possibilità.
re-enact [riːen'ækt], *v.t.* Rimettere in vigore, promulgare di nuovo.
re-enactment, *n.* Rimessa in vigore, *f.*
re-engage [riːen'geidʒ], *v.t.* Rimpegnare.
re-enlist [riːen'list], *v.i.* Riarruolarsi.
re-enter [riː'entəɹ], *v.t.* Rientrare in; *v.i.* reintrare.
re-entrance [riː'entrəns], *n.* Rientrata, *f.*
re-entrant, *a.* Rientrante.
re-entry [riː'entri], *n.* Rientrata, *f.*
re-equip [riːek'wip], *v.t.* Rifornire, riequipaggiare.
re-establish [riːes'tæbliʃ], *v.t.* Ristabilire.
re-establishment, *n.* Ristabilimento, *m.*
reeve (1) [riːv], *v.t.* (*Naut.*) Infilare, passare; assicurare.
reeve (2), *n.* (*Hist.*) Castaldo, *m.*
re-examination [riːekzæmin'eiʃən], *n.* Nuovo esame, riesame, *m.*
re-examine, *v.t.* Riesaminare; rinterrogare.
re-export [riːeks'pɔːɹt], *v.t.* Riesportare.
re-exportation, *n.* Riesporto, *m.*
refection [re'fekʃən], *n.* Refezione, *f.*
refectory [re'fektəri], *n.* Refettorio, *m.*
refer [re'fəːɹ], *v.t.i.* Riferire, attribuire, ascrivere; rimettere; riferirsi, rivolgersi; alludere; consultare. **He referred to his notebook,** consultò il suo taccuino; **— to the office,** rivolgetevi all'ufficio; **let us — the matter to an arbitrator,** rimettiamo la cosa ad un arbitro.
referable ['refərəbl], *a.* Riferibile, attribuibile.
referee [refə'riː], *n.* Arbitro, *m.* || *v.t.* Arbitrare.
reference ['refərəns], *n.* Riferimento, *m.*; riguardo, rapporto, *m.*; relazione, *f.*; allusione, *f.*; referenza, raccommandazione, *f.* **To ask for references,** domandare referenze; **in — to,** in rapporto a, rispetto a; **to have — to,** aver relazione con; **to make a — to,** fare allusione a; **to go for a — to,** rivolgersi per informazioni a; **book of —,** libro di consultazione, *m.*; **— library,** biblioteca di consultazione, *f.*; **cross —,** richiamo, *m.*
referendum [refə'rendəm], *n.* Referendum, plebiscito, *m.*
refill [riː'fil], *v.t.* Riempire, rifornire. || *n.* Rifornimento, *m.*
refine [re'fain], *v.t.* Raffinare, purificare; *v.i.* raffinarsi. **To — upon,** sottilizzare.
refined, *a.* Raffinato; colto, fino, elegante; puro, delicato.
refinement, *n.* Raffinamento, *m.*; raffinatezza, squisitezza, finezza, *f.*; sottigliezza, *f.*
refiner, *n.* Raffinatore, *m.*
refinery, *n.* Raffineria, *f.*
refit [riː'fit], *v.t.* Riparare, riattare; (*Naut.*) raddobbare.
reflect [re'flekt], *v.t.* Riflettere, riverberare; *v.i.* riflettere; pensare, ponderare, meditare; riflettersi. **To — discredit on,** gettare discredito su; **to — blame on,** biasimare; **to — upon,** riflettere su; **the light is reflected from the mirror,** la luce si riflette dallo specchio.
reflection, *n.* Riflessione, *f.*; riflesso, *m.*; biasimo, rimprovero, *m.* **On —,** pensandoci sopra.
reflective, *a.* Riflessivo, riflettente; cogitabondo, meditabondo, pensieroso.
reflector, *n.* Riflettore, *m.*
reflex ['riːfleks], *n.a.* Riflesso, *m.* (*Phot.*) **— camera,** camera riflessa, *f.*
reflexibility, *n.* Riflessibilità, *f.*
reflexible, *a.* Riflessibile.
reflexion, *n.* Riflessione, *f.*
reflexive, *a.* (*Gram.*) Riflessivo.
refloat [riː'flout], *v.t.* Rimettere a galla.
refluent ['refluːənt], *a.* Rifluente.
reflux ['riːflʌks], *n.* Riflusso, *m.*

reform [re'fɔːɹm], *n.* Riforma, *f.* || *v.t.* Riformare; emendare, correggere; *v.i.* riformarsi, correggersi.
re-form [riː'fɔːɹm], *v.t.* Riformare, rimodellare.
reformation [refɔːɹ'meiʃən], *n.* Riforma, riformazione, *f.* **The Reformation,** la Riforma, *f.*
reformative, *a.* Riformativo.
reformatory [re'fɔːɹmətəri], *n.* Casa di correzione, *f.*, riformatorio, *m.*
reformer, *n.* Riformatore, *m.*, riformatrice, *f.*
refract [re'frækt], *v.t.* Rifrangere.
refraction, *n.* Rifrazione, *f.*
refractive, *a.* Rifrattivo.
refractor, *n.* Rifrattore, *m.*
refractoriness, *n.* Indocilità, *f.*; riottosità, *f.*
refractory, *a.* Indocile, riottoso, ricalcitrante, ribelle.
refrain (1) [re'frein], *v.i.* Frenarsi, trattenersi, astenersi. **To — from,** astenersi da.
refrain (2), *n.* Ritornello, *m.*, ripresa, *f.*; aria, cantilena, *f.*
refrangibility [refrængi'biliti], *n.* Rifrangibilità, *f.*
refresh [re'freʃ], *v.t.* Rinfrescare; ristorare, rinnovare. **To — oneself,** ristorarsi, rinfrescarsi, rifocillarsi; **to — one's memory,** rinfrescare la memoria.
refresher, *n.* (*colloq.*) Bibita, *f.*; (*Law*) parcella, *f.*
refreshing, *a.* Rinfrescante.
refreshment, *n.* Rinfresco, *m.*; riposo, ristoro, *m.* **Refreshments,** rinfresco, *m.*, rinfreschi, *m.pl.*; **—-room,** buffè, *m.*; caffè, ristorante, *m.*; **—-bar,** mescita, *f.*
refrigerant [re'fridʒərənt], *n.a.* Refrigerante, *m.*
refrigerate [re'fridʒəreit], *v.t.* Refrigerare.
refrigeration, *n.* Refrigerazione, *f.*
refrigerator, *n.* Frigorifero, refrigerante, *m.*, ghiacciaia, cella frigorifera, *f.*
refuel [riː'fjuːəl], *v.t.i.* Rifornirsi di combustibile; (*Aviat.*) rifornire di carburante.
refuge ['refjuːdʒ], *n.* Rifugio, asilo, *m.* **To take —,** rifugiarsi; **to take — with,** trovar rifugio presso; **street —,** salvagente, *m.*; **house of —,** casa di ricovero, *f.*
refugee [refjuː'dʒiː], *n.* Rifugiato, *m.*, rifugiata, *f.*, esule, *m.f.*; profugo, *m.*
refulgence [re'fʌldʒəns], *n.* Rifulgenza, *f.*
refulgent, *a.* Rifulgente, splendente.
refund [re'fʌnd], *v.t.* Rimborsare, rifondere; restituire. || *n.* ['riːfʌnd], Rimborso, *m.*
refurnish [riː'fəːɹniʃ], *v.t.* Rifornire, ammobigliare di nuovo.
refusal [re'fjuːzəl], *n.* Rifiuto, *m.* **To have the — of,** avere il diritto di scelta da; **to meet with a —,** subire un rifiuto.
refuse (1) [re'fjuːz], *v.t.i.* Rifiutare, respingere, ricusare. **To — obedience,** rifiutare di ubbidire; **to — admittance,** vietare l'entrata, non lasciare entrare.
refuse (2) ['refjuːs], *n.* Rifiuti, avanzi, *m.pl.*, feccia, *f.*, immondizie, *f.pl.* **— dump,** mondezzaio, *m.*
re-fuse [riː'fjuːz], *v.t.* Rifondere.
refutable ['refjuːtəbl], *a.* Confutabile.
refutation [refjuː'teiʃən], *n.* Confutazione, *f.*
refute, *v.t.* Confutare; ribattere; dimostrare falso.
regain [riː'gein], *v.t.* Riguadagnare, riprendere, ripigliare, riacquistare.
regal ['riːgəl], *a.* Regale, reale.
regale [re'geil], *v.t.* Festeggiare, intrattenere. **To — oneself,** trattarsi bene.
regalia [re'geiliə], *n.pl.* Insegne regie, *f.pl.*; distintivi, *m.pl.* decorazioni, *f.pl.*
regard [re'gɑːɹd], *n.* Riguardo, *m.*; cura, attenzione, *f.*; stima, considerazione, *f.*; rispetto, *m.*; (*look*) sguardo, *m.* || *v.t.* Riguardare, osservare; stimare, considerare. **Kind regards,** cordiali saluti, complimenti, *m.pl.*; **in — to,** riguardo a; **out of — for,** per riguardo a; **to — kindly,** voler bene a, aver caro.
regardful, *a.* Attento, riguardoso, rispettoso.
regardless, *a.* Indifferente, noncurante, negligente, sbadato. **— of,** indifferente a, noncurante di, senza far caso di.
regardlessness, *n.* Indifferenza, negligenza, noncuranza, sbadataggine, *f.*
regatta [re'gætə], *n.* Regata, *f.*
regency ['riːdʒənsi], *n.* Reggenza, *f.*
regenerate [ri'dʒenərit], *a.* Rigenerato. *v.t.* [riː'dʒenereit], Rigenerare.
regeneration, *n.* Rigenerazione, *f.*
regenerator, *n.* Rigeneratore, *m.*
regent ['riːdʒənt], *n.* Reggente, *m.f.*
regerminate [riː'dʒəːɹmineit], *v.i.* Rigerminare.
regicidal [redʒi'saidəl], *a.* Regicida.
regicide, *n.* (*criminal*) Regicida, *m.f.*; (*crime*) regicidio, *m.*
regild [riː'gild], *v.t.* Ridorare.
regimen ['redʒimen], *n.* Regime, *m.*, dieta, *f.*
regiment ['redʒimənt, 'redgmənt], *n.* Reggimento, *m.* || *v.t.* Reggimentare.
regimental, *a.* Reggimentale.
regimentals, *n.pl.* Uniforme, *f.* **In full —,** in alta divisa, *f.*
regimentation, *n.* Reggimentazione, *f.*
region ['riːdʒən], *n.* Regione, *f.*; contrada, *f.*; (*fig.*) campo, *m.*
regional, *a.* Regionale.
register ['redʒistəɹ], *n.* Registro, *m.*; libro, *m.*; matricola, *f.*; (*Pol.*) lista elettorale, *f.* || *v.t.* Registrare; (*letters*) raccomandare; indicare, mostrare; depositare.
registered, *a.* (*letter, etc.*) Raccomandato. (*Naut.*) **— tonnage,** tonnellaggio netto, *m.*; **— trade-mark,** marca depositata, *f.*
registrar, *n.* Segretario, *m.*; cancelliere, *m.*; attuario, *m.*; archivista, *m.*; ufficiale dello Stato civile, *m.*
registration, *n.* Registrazione, *f.*; (*of letters*) raccomandazione, *f.*
registry, registry office, *n.* Ufficio dello Stato civile, *m.*; (*for servants*) ufficio di collocamento, *m.*
regnant ['regnənt], *a.* Regnante.
regrate [riː'greit], *v.t.* Incettare.
regrater, regrator, *n.* Incettatore, *m.*
regress [ri'gres], *n.* Regresso, *m.* || *v.i.* Regredire, retrocedere.
regression [reg'reʃən], *n.* Regressione, *f.*
regressive, *a.* Regressivo.
regret [re'gret], *n.* Rammarico, rincrescimento, dispiacere, *m.* || *v.t.* Rimpiangere, deplorare, dolersi di, spiacere, dispiacere di, rincrescere di, rammaricarsi di, pentirsi di. **With profound —,** con profondo rammarico; **much to my —,** con mio vivo rammarico; **I — to say,** mi spiace dire; **I — his loss,**

rimpiango la sua morte; **it is to be regretted,** è da deplorare.
regretful, *a.* Dolente, addolorato, spiacente.
regretfully, *adv.* Con rincrescimento, con dispiacere.
regrettable, *a.* Spiacevole, increscioso, deplorevole.
regrettably, *adv.* Deplorevolmente.
regretted, *a.* Rimpianto.
regular [ˈregju:ləɹ], *a.* Regolare, uniforme, normale; regolato, ordinato, usuale; (*colloq.*) perfetto, completo, matricolato. || *n.* (*Eccles.*) Regolare, *m.*; (*Mil.*) soldato di professione, *m.* **To keep — hours,** mantenere l'orario, tenere le ore; **— features,** lineamenti regolari, *m.pl.*; **a — villain,** un birbante matricolato, *m.*; **as — as clockwork,** esatto come un orologio; (*Mil.*) **the — army,** l'esercito regolare, *m.*; **through — channels,** per vie regolari.
regularity [regju:ˈlæriti], *n.* Regolarità, *f.*
regularization, *n.* Regolarizzazione, *f.*
regularize, *v.t.* Regolarizzare.
regularly, *adv.* Regolarmente.
regulate [ˈregju:leit], *v.t.* Regolare.
regulation, *n.* Regolamento, *m.*; ordine, *m.*, norma, regola, *f.*; ordinanza, *f.* || *a.* Regolamentare, conforme al regolamento.
regulator, *n.* Regolatore, *m.*
regurgitate [ri:ˈgə:ɹdʒiteit], *v.i.* Rigurgitare.
regurgitation, *n.* Rigurgito, *m.*
rehabilitate [ri:həˈbiliteit], *v.t.* Riabilitare.
rehabilitation, *n.* Riabilitazione, *f.*
rehandle [ri:ˈhændl], *v.t.* Rimaneggiare.
rehear [ri:ˈhiəɹ], *v.t.* Riudire.
rehearsal [riˈhə:ɹsəl], *n.* Ripetizione, *f.*; (*Theat.*) prova, *f.* **Dress —,** prova generale, *f.*
rehearse, *v.t.* Ripetere, recitare, narrare; (*Theat.*) provare, far le prove di.
rehousing [ri:ˈhauziŋ], *n.* Rialloggiamento, rialloggiare, *m.*
reign [rein], *n.* Regno, *m.* || *v.i.* Regnare. **In the — of,** sotto il regno di.
reigning, *a.* Regnante; attuale; (*fig.*) predominante, dominante.
reimburse [ri:imˈbə:ɹs], *v.t.* Rimborsare, rifondere.
reimbursement, *n.* Rimborso, *m.*
reimport [ri:imˈpɔ:ɹt], *v.t.* Reimportare, importare di nuovo.
reimpose [ri:imˈpouz], *v.t.* Reimporre, imporre di nuovo.
rein [rein], *n.* Redine, briglia, *f.*; (*fig.*) freno, *m.* || *v.t.* Frenare, raffrenare, imbrigliare; contenere, governare. **To give — to,** allentare il freno a, lasciar le redini a; **to draw —,** tirar le redini; **to assume the reins,** prendere le redini; **to keep a tight — over,** tenere a freno; **to — in,** frenare.
reincarnate [ri:ˈinkɑ:ɹneit], *v.t.* Rincarnare.
reincarnation, *n.* Rincarnazione, *f.*
reindeer [ˈreindiəɹ], *n.* (*Zool.*) Renna, *f.*
reinforce [ri:inˈfɔ:ɹs], *v.t.* Rinforzare; (*Mech.*) rafforzare; (*concrete*) armare. **Reinforced concrete,** cemento armato, *m.*
reinforcement, *n.* Rinforzo, rinforzamento, *m.*; consolidamento, *m.*; armatura, *f.*; (*Mil.*) rinforzo, *m.*
reinsert [ri:inˈsə:ɹt], *v.t.* Inserire di nuovo.
reinstate [ri:inˈsteit], *v.t.* Restituire, reintegrare, ristabilire.
reinstatement, *n.* Restituzione, reintegrazione, *f.*
reinsurance [ri:inˈʃu:rəns], *n.* Riassicurazione, *f.*
reinsure, *v.t.* Riassicurare.
reinter [ri:inˈtə:ɹ], *v.t.* Risotterrare.
reinvest [ri:inˈvest], *v.t.* (*Comm.*) Rinvestire, riimpiegare.
reinvestment, *n.* Rinvestimento, rimpiego, *m.*
reinvigorate [ri:inˈvigoreit], *v.t.* Rinvigorire.
reissue [ri:ˈiʃju:], *v.t.* (*a book*) Ripubblicare, ristampare; (*Comm.*) (*of shares*) emettere ancora. || *n.* (*of book*) Ristampa, nuova edizione, *f.*; (*Comm.*) (*of shares*) nuova emissione, *f.*
reiterate [ri:ˈitəreit], *v.t.* Reiterare.
reiteration, *n.* Reiterazione, *f.*
reject [reˈdʒekt], *v.t.* Rigettare, rifiutare, respingere. || *n.* [ˈri:dʒekt], Un rifiuto, *m.*
rejection, *n.* Rifiuto, rigetto, *m.*
rejector, *n.* Respingitore, repulsore, *m.*
rejoice [reˈdʒɔis], *v.t.* Rallegrare, dilettare, allietare; *v.i.* rallegrarsi, allietarsi, gioire, godere. **I am rejoiced to see you,** sono lieto di vedervi.
rejoicing, *n.* Giubilo, *m.*, gioia, esultanza, *f.*; allegrezza, festa, *f.* **Rejoicings,** feste, *f.pl.* festeggiamenti, *m.pl.*
rejoin (1) [riˈdʒɔin], *v.t.i.* Rispondere, ribattere, replicare.
rejoin (2) [ri:ˈdʒɔin], *v.t.i.* Riunirsi a, ricongiungere, raggiungere, ricongiungersi a.
rejoinder, *n.* Risposta, replica, *f.*
rejuvenate [ri:ˈdʒu:vəneit], *v.t.* Ringiovanire.
rejuvenescence [ri:dʒu:vəˈnesəns], *n.* Ringiovanimento, *m.*
rekindle [ri:ˈkindl], *v.t.* Riaccendere.
relapse [reˈlæps], *n.* Ricaduta, *f.*; caduta, *f.*; (*into crime*) recidiva, *f.* || *v.i.* Ricadere in, ricascare.
relate [reˈleit], *v.t.* Raccontare, narrare; rapportare, riferire; *v.i.* concernere, riguardare, aver rapporto.
related, *a.* Connesso; parente, consanguineo, congiunto. **To be — to,** esser parente di.
relater, *n.* Narratore, raccontatore, *m.*
relating, *a.* Relativo, concernente.
relation, *n.* Relazione, narrazione, *f.*, referto, rapporto, *m.*; rapporto, rispetto, *m.*; parente, congiunto, *m.* **Relations are strained,** le relazioni sono tese; **distant relations,** parenti lontani, *m.pl.*; **near relations,** stretti parenti, *m.pl.*; **in — to,** in rapporto a, in quanto a.
relationship, *n.* Parentela, affinità, *f.*; connessione, *f.*
relative [ˈrelətiv], *a.* Relativo, concernente; rispettivo; (*Gram.*) relativo. || *n.* Parente, *m.f.*, congiunto, *m.*, congiunta, *f.*
relatively, *adv.* Relativamente.
relativeness, *n.* Relatività, *f.*
relativity [reləˈtiviti], *n.* Relatività, *f.*
relax [reˈlæks], *v.t.* Rilassare, rilasciare, allentare; sollevare, riposare, ricreare; sciogliere; *v.i.* rilassarsi, allentarsi, riposarsi, infiacchirsi. **To — one's grasp,** rilassare la stretta; **to — one's efforts,** rallentare gli sforzi; **to — one's mind,** distrarsi, ricrearsi.
relaxation, *n.* Rilassamento, rilassarsi, *m.*; ricreazione, *f.*, sollievo, riposo, svago, *m.* **— of a penalty,** diminuzione di una pena.

relaxing, *a.* (*of climate*) Snervante; debilitante; rilassante; (*Med.*) calmante, rilassante.
relay [ri'lei, 'ri:lei], *n.* Ricambio, cambio, *m.*; (*of horses*) muta, posta, *f.*; (*Elec.*) relè, *m.*; (*Radio*) trasmissione, *f.* || *v.t.* (*horses*) Cambiare; (*Radio*) ritrasmettere.
re-lay [ri:'lei], *v.t.* Posare di nuovo, ricollocare.
release [re'li:s], *v.t.* Liberare, rilasciare, sciogliere; sollevare, esonerare; lanciare. || *n.* Liberazione, esenzione, *f.*; esonero, *m.*; (*Law*) cessione, *f.*; (*of pigeons*) lanciare, *m.*; (*Mech.*) scarico, *m.*
relegate ['relegeit], *v.t.* Relegare.
relegation, *n.* Relegazione, *f.*
relent [ri'lent], *v.i.* Piegarsi, cedere, placarsi, pentirsi.
relentless, *a.* Inflessibile, inesorabile, severo, rigido, implacabile.
relentlessly, *adv.* Inflessibilmente, implacabilmente.
relentlessness, *n.* Inflessibilità, inesorabilità, implacabilità, *f.*
re-let [ri:'let], *v.t.* Affittare di nuovo, riaffittare.
reletting, *n.* Riaffitto, *m.*
relevancy ['relivənsi], *n.* Rapporto, *m.*, relazione, applicabilità, *f.*
relevant, *a.* Relativo, applicabile, a proposito, pertinente.
reliability [relaiə'biliti], *n.* Attendibilità, fidatezza, *f.*; sicurezza, certezza, esattezza, *f.*; credibilità, *f.*; solidità, saldezza, *f.* (*Motor.*) **— trials,** prove di collaudo, prove di resistenza, *f.pl.*
reliable [re'laiəbl], *a.* (*of person*) Fidato; (*of information*) attendibile; sicuro, certo, esatto; solido, resistente.
reliably, *adv.* Fidatamente.
reliance, *n.* Confidenza, fede, fiducia, *f.* **To place — on,** aver fiducia in.
relic ['relik], *n.* Reliquia, *f.*; resto, avanzo, *m.*; cimelio, *m.*
relict ['relikt], *n.* Vedova, *f.*
relief [re'li:f], *n.* Sollievo, ristoro, conforto, *m.*; assistenza, *f.*, soccorso, aiuto, sussidio, *m.*; (*Art*) rilievo, risalto, *m.*; (*Mil.*) cambio, *m.*; (*of tax*) esenzione, *f.*, abbattimento, *m.* **To bring —,** dar sollievo; **by way of —,** per variare, per cambiare; **— fund,** fondo d'assistenza, *m.*; **to bring out in —,** mettere in rilievo, dar risalto a; (*Mil.*) **— party,** colonna di soccorso, truppa di cambio, *f.*; (*Rail.*) **— train,** treno supplementare, *m.*
relieve [re'li:v], *v.t.* Sollevare, mitigare, alleviare; dispensare, esonerare; aiutare, soccorrere; mettere in rilievo; (*Mil.*) rilevare, dare il cambio a. **I am relieved to hear it!** Che sollievo! Che bella notizia! **to — one's feelings,** dar sfogo ai propri sentimenti; **to — oneself,** defecare, orinare.
relight [ri:'lait], *v.t.* Riaccendere.
religion [re'lidʒən], *n.* Religione, *f.*
religionist, *n.* Bigotto, fanatico, *m.*
religiosity [relidʒ'ɔsiti], *n.* Religiosità, *f.*
religious [re'lidʒəs], *a.* Religioso, pio, devoto. || *n.* Religioso, *m.*, religiosa, *f.* **A — book,** un libro di devozione, *m.*
religiously, *adv.* Religiosamente; meticolosamente.
religiousness, *n.* Religiosità, devozione, *f.*
relinquish [re'liŋkwiʃ], *v.t.* Abbandonare, rinunziare.
relinquishment, *n.* Abbandono, *m.*, rinunzia, *f.*
reliquary ['relikwəri], *n.* Reliquario, *m.*
relish ['reliʃ], *n.* Gusto, sapore, *m.*; appetito, *m.*; condimento, *m.*; attrattiva, *f.* || *v.t.* Gustare, godere, assaporire; condire; *v.i.* sapere di, aver il gusto di. **To eat with —,** mangiare di gusto, mangiare con appetito; **life has no — for him,** la vita non ha attrattiva per lui; **to give a — to,** dar sapore a; **I do not — the prospect,** la prospettiva non mi va a genio.
relive [ri:'liv], *v.i.* Rivivere.
reload [ri:'loud], *v.t.* Ricaricare.
reluctance [re'lʌktəns], *n.* Riluttanza, ripugnanza, avversione, *f.*
reluctant, *a.* Riluttante, avverso, alieno, poco disposto. **I am — to,** mi ripugna di, sono riluttante a.
reluctantly, *adv.* A malincuore, di controgenio.
rely [re'lai], *v.i.* Contare su, fidarsi di, fare assegnamento sopra.
remain [re'mein], *v.i.* Rimanere, restare, stare; (*in letters*) rassegnarsi. **It remains for me to,** spetta a me; **that remains to be seen,** ciò è ancora da vedere; **much remains for us to do,** ci resta molto da fare; **I — yours faithfully,** mi rassegno suo devmo; **to — over,** avanzare.
remainder, *n.* Rimanente, resto, avanzo, residuo, *m.*; (*Law*) riversibilità, *f.*; (*Math.*) avanzo, *m.* **A publisher's —,** un fondo di magazzino, un libro di fondo, *m.*
remaining, *a.* Rimanente.
remains, *n.pl.* Resto, avanzi, rimasugli, *m.pl.*; ceneri, spoglie, *f.pl.*; (*Lit.*) opere postume, *f.pl.* **The mortal —,** la spoglia mortale, la salma, *f.*
remake [ri:'meik], *v.t.* Rifare.
remand [re'mɑ:nd], *v.t.* (*Law*) Rinviare. || *n.* Rinvio, *m.*
remark [re'mɑ:ɹk], *n.* Osservazione, nota, *f.*, commento, *m.* || *v.t.* Notare, osservare, rilevare, rimarcare. **Without —,** senza commento; **worthy of —,** degno di nota; **to pass a —,** fare un'osservazione; **to — upon,** menzionare, accennare a, far osservare, commentare.
re-mark [ri:'mɑ:ɹk], *v.t.* Rimarcare, marcare di nuovo.
remarkable, *a.* Rimarchevole, notevole; straordinario, cospicuo.
remarkableness, *n.* Straordinarietà, *f.*
remarkably, *adv.* Notevolmente.
remarry [ri:'mæri], *v.t.* Rimaritare, risposare; *v.i.* rimaritarsi, risposarsi.
remediable [re'mi:diəbl], *a.* Rimediabile.
remedial [re'mi:diəl], *a.* Riparatore, curativo.
remedy ['remedi], *n.* Rimedio, *m.*; (*Law*) azione, *f.*; ricorso, mezzo giuridico, *m.* || *v.t.* Rimediare a, riparare.
remember [re'membəɹ], *v.t.* Ricordarsi di, rammentare, rammentarsi di, rimembrare, sovvenirsi di. **If I — rightly,** se mi ricordo bene; **— me to him,** salutatelo da parte mia.
remembrance [re'membrəns], *n.* Ricordo, *m.*, memoria, rimembranza, *f.* **In — of,** in memoria di; **to bring to one's —,** richiamare alla memoria; **my remembrances to,** i miei saluti a, i miei rispetti a.
remembrancer, *n.* (*Law*) Agente del fisco, *m.*

remind [reˈmaind], *v.t.* Rammentare, ricordare, richiamare alla mente. **That reminds me,** a proposito, questo mi richiama alla mente; **— me of my promise,** rammentatemi la mia promessa; **he reminds me of his father,** mi rammenta il padre.
reminder, *n.* Ricordo, memento, *m.* **As a — of,** per rammentare, come svegliarino, come richiamo.
reminiscence [remiˈnisəns], *n.* Reminiscenza, *f.*
reminiscent, *a.* Che rammenta.
remiss [reˈmis], *a.* Negligente; disattento, trascurato, svogliato.
remissible [reˈmisəbl], *a.* Remissibile.
remission [reˈmiʃən], *n.* Remissione, *f.*, perdono, *m.*
remissness, *n.* Negligenza, disattenzione, trascuratezza, svogliatezza, *f.*
remit [reˈmit], *v.t.i.* Rinviare, rimandare, rimettere; perdonare condonare; inviare; diminuire, ridurre, scemare.
remittal, *n.* Remissione, *f.*
remittance, *n.* (*of money*) Rimessa, *f.*
remitter, *n.* Mittente, *m.f.*
remnant [ˈremnənt], *n.* Avanzo, rimasuglio, ritaglio, *m.*; (*of cloth*) scampolo, *m.*
remodel [riːˈmɔdəl], *v.t.* Rimodellare, riplasmare.
remonstrance [reˈmɔnstrəns], *n.* Rimostranza, *f.*
remonstrant, *n.* Rimostrante, *m.f.*
remonstrate [reˈmɔnstreit], *v.i.* Rimostrare, protestare, far delle rimostranze. **To — with,** fare delle rimostranze a.
remorse [reˈmɔːɹs], *n.* Rimorso, *m.*
remorseful, *a.* Pieno di rimorso, contrito.
remorsefully, *adv.* Contritamente.
remorseless, *a.* Spietato, senza rimorso.
remorselessly, *adv.* Spietatamente.
remorselessness, *n.* Spietatezza, *f.*
remote [reˈmout], *a.* Remoto, lontano; (*fig.*) alieno, estraneo.
remotely, *adv.* Remotamente.
remoteness, *n.* Lontananza, distanza, *f.*
remould [riːˈmould], *v.t.* Rimaneggiare, rifondere, rimodellare.
remount [riːˈmaunt], *v.t.i.* Rimontare. || *n.* Rimonta, *f.*, cavallo di rimonta, *m.*
removability [rimuːvəˈbiliti], *n.* Amovibilità, *f.*, trasferimento, *m.*
removable, *a.* Rimovibile, trasferibile.
removal, *n.* Spostamento, trasporto, trasferimento, *m.*; (*from house*) trasloco, sgombero, *m.*; (*from employment*) destituzione, rimozione, *f.*
remove [reˈmuːv], *n.* Promozione, *f.*; grado, *m.*; distanza, *f.* || *v.t.* Spostare, trasportare, trasferire; allontanare, rimuovere; eliminare, tagliare via; destituire; *v.i.* sgombrare, traslocare; allontanarsi, trasferirsi, spostarsi. **To — all doubts,** eliminare ogni dubbio.
removed, *a.* Lontano, discosto, allontanato. **Cousin once —,** cugino in secondo grado, *m.*
remover, *n.* Sgombratore, *m.*
remunerate [reˈmjuːnəreit], *v.t.* Rimunerare, ricompensare.
remuneration, *n.* Rimunerazione, ricompensa, *f.*
remunerative, *a.* Rimunerativo.
Renaissance [reˈneisəns], *n.* (*Hist.*) Rinascenza, *f.*, Rinascimento, *m.*
renal [ˈriːnəl], *a.* (*Anat.*) Renale.
rename [riːˈneim], *v.t.* Rinominare.
renard [cp. **reynard**].
renascence [reˈneisəns], *n.* Rinascenza, *f.*, rinascimento, *m.*
renascent, *a.* Rinascente.
rencounter [renˈkauntəɹ], *n.* Incontro, *m.*; scontro, urto, *m.*
rend [rend], *v.t.* Lacerare, stracciare, squarciare. **To — away,** strappare; **to — the heart,** straziare il cuore; **to — asunder,** fendere in due.
render, *v.t.* Rendere; restituire, ridare; dare, pagare; (*Theat.*) rappresentare; (*Mus.*) eseguire; (*Art*) rendere, interpretare; (*Arch.*) arricciare, incalcinare; (*Cooking*) struggere. **To — down,** fondere, far sciogliere; **to — void,** rendere nullo, annullare; (*Comm.*) **to — an account,** rimettere un conto.
rendering, *n.* Restituzione, *f.*; rappresentazione, esecuzione, interpretazione, *f.*; traduzione, *f.*; (*accounts*) rendimento, *m.*; (*plaster*) spalmo, *m.*
rendezvous [ˈrɔndeivuː], *n.* Appuntamento, *m.*; convegno, ritrovo, *m.* **To give —,** dare un appuntamento.
rendition [renˈdiʃən], *n.* (*surrender*) Resa, *f.*; (*Theat.Mus.*) esecuzione, rappresentazione, *f.*
renegade [ˈrenigeid], *n.* Rinnegato, *m.*
renew [reˈnjuː], *v.t.* Rinnovare, ripristinare; rinnovellare, rimettere a nuovo; sostituire.
renewable, *a.* Rinnovabile.
renewal, *n.* Rinnovamento, *m.*; ripresa, *f.*
rennet (1) [ˈrenet], *n.* Caglio, presame, *m.*
rennet (2), *n.* (*Bot.*) Mela ranetta, *f.*
renounce [reˈnauns], *v.t.* Rinunciare, rinunziare, ricusare; ripudiare. **To — the crown,** rinunciare la corona; **to — pleasure,** rinunciare ai piaceri.
renouncement, *n.* Rinuncia, rinunzia, *f.*
renovate [ˈrenoveit], *v.t.* Rinnovare, ripristinare.
renovation, *n.* Rinnovamento, ripristino, *m.*, riparazione, *f.*
renown [reˈnaun], *n.* Rinomanza, fama, nominanza, *f.*
renowned, *a.* Rinomato, famoso, celebre.
rent (1) [rent], *n.* (*tear*) Squarcio, strappo, *m.*, lacerazione, *f.*; spacco, *m.*, spaccatura, rottura, *f.*
rent (2), *n.* (*of house*) Affitto, *m.*, pigione, *f.*; (*hire*) nolo, *m.* || *v.t.* Affittare, prendere in affitto, appigionare. **A high —,** una pigione cara, *f.*, un affitto forte, *m.*; **a low —,** una pigione discreta, *f.*, un affitto modesto, *m.*; **—-free,** libero da affitto; **—-roll,** lista delle rendite, *f.*
rent (3), *p.* and *pp.* **rend.**
rental, *n.* Affitto, *m.*; valore locativo, *m.*
renter, *n.* Inquilino, affittuario, pigionale, *m.*
renumber [riːˈnʌmbəɹ], *v.t.* Rinumerare.
renunciation [renʌnsiˈeiʃən], *n.* Rinuncia, rinunzia, *f.*
reoccupation [riːɔkjuːˈpeiʃən], *n.* Rioccupazione, *f.*
reoccupy [riːˈɔkjuːpai], *v.t.* Rioccupare.
reopen [riːˈoupən], *v.t.i.* Riaprire, riaprirsi.
reopening, *n.* Riapertura, *f.*, riaprimento, *m.*
reorganization [riːɔːɹgənaiˈzeiʃən], *n.* Riorganizzamento, *m.*, riorganizzazione, *f.*
reorganize, *v.t.* Riorganizzare.

repack [riː'pæk], *v.t.* Imballare di nuovo; *v.i.* rifare la valigia.
repaint [riː'peint], *v.t.* Ridipingere; rinverniciare.
repair [ri'pɛəɹ], *v.t.* Riparare, rifare; aggiustare, raccomodare, rammendare; *v.i.* riparare, rifugiarsi, recarsi. || *n.* Riparazione, *f.*, restauro, *m.*; stato, *m.*; (*Naut.*) raddobbo, *m.* **To — a wrong,** riparare un torto; **in good —,** in buono stato; **out of —,** guasto, in cattivo stato; **to keep in —,** mantenere; **a place of —,** un riparo, *m.*
repairer, *n.* Aggiustatore, racconciatore, *m.*; rammendatore, *m.*
reparable ['repərəbl], *a.* Riparabile.
reparation [repə'reiʃən], *n.* Riparazione, aggiustatura, *f.*; soddisfazione, *f.*, riscatto, compenso, *m.*
repartee [repɑːɹ'tiː], *n.* Risposta mordace, replica, *f.*, frizzo, *m.*; risposta pronta, *f.*
repass [riː'pɑːs], *v.t.i.* Ripassare.
repast [ri'pɑːst], *n.* Pasto, *m.*; banchetto, *m.*
repatriate [riː'pætrieit], *v.t.i.* Rimpatriare.
repatriation, *n.* Rimpatrio, *m.*
repave [riː'peiv], *v.t.* Rilastricare.
repay [riː'pei], *v.t.* Rimborsare, restituire; ricompensare, ripagare; ricambiare; valere la pena di. **It well repays reading,** vale la pena di leggere.
repayable, *a.* Rimborsabile, restituibile.
repayment, *n.* Rimborso, *m.*, restituzione, ricompensa, *f.*, contraccambio, *m.*
repeal [re'piːl], *v.t.* Abrogare, revocare, annullare. || *n.* Abrogazione, revoca, *f.*, annullamento, *m.*
repeat [re'piːt], *v.t.* Ripetere, rifare; reiterare; ripetere a memoria; *v.i.* ripetersi, rinnovarsi, ricorrere; (*of food*) tornare a gola. || *n.* Ripetizione; (*Mus.*) replica, *f.* (*Theat.*) **A — performance,** una replica, *f.*
repeatedly, *adv.* Ripetutamente, frequentemente.
repeater, *n.* (*watch*) Orologio a ripetizione, *m.*
repeating, *a.* Periodico, a ripetizione. **— decimal,** frazione periodica, *f.*
repel [re'pel], *v.t.* Respingere.
repellent, *a.* Repellente, repulsivo.
repent [re'pent], *v.t.i.* Pentirsi di, pentirsi. **You will not — it,** non avrete a pentirvene.
repentance, *n.* Pentimento, *m.*, penitenza, contrizione, *f.*
repentent, *a.* Penitente, pentito, contrito.
repeople [riː'piːpl], *v.t.* Ripopolare.
repeopling, *n.* Ripopolamento, *m.*
repercussion [riːpəɹ'kʌʃən], *n.* Ripercossa, ripercussione, *f.*
repertory ['repəɹtəri], *n.* Repertorio, *m.* **— theatre,** teatro a largo repertorio, *m.*
reperusal [riːpə'ruːzəl], *n.* Nuova lettura, *f.*
reperuse, *v.t.* Leggere di nuovo, rileggere.
repetend [repi'tend], *n.* (*Math.*) Decimale ricorrente, periodo, *m.*
repetition [repi'tiʃən], *n.* Ripetizione, *f.*; copia, *f.*; replica, *f.*, recitazione, *f.*
repine [re'pain], *v.i.* Dolersi, lagnarsi, lamentarsi; mormorare.
repiningly, *adv.* Lagnosamente, lamentosamente.
replace [riː'pleis], *v.t.* Ricollocare, restituire, rimettere; sostituire.
replaceable, *a.* Restituibile; sostituibile.
replacement, *n.* Restituzione, *f.*; sostituzione, *f.*
replant [riː'plɑːnt], *v.t.* Ripiantare.
replantation, *n.* Ripiantamento, *m.*
replay [riː'plei], *v.t.* Giocare di nuovo, ripetere una partita; suonare di nuovo.
replenish [re'pleniʃ], *v.t.* Riempire, rifornire.
replenishment, *n.* Riempimento, *m.*
replete [re'pliːt], *a.* Riempito, pieno, zeppo; satollo, gonfio.
repletion, *n.* Pienezza, sazietà, *f.*
replevin [re'plevin], *n.* (*Law*) Riconsegna di beni mobili, *f.*; reintegrazione, *f.*
replica ['replikə], *n.* Replica, copia, *f.*, facsimile, *m.*
reply [re'plai], *n.* Risposta, replica, *f.* || *v.t.i.* Rispondere, replicare. **In — to,** in risposta a; **— -paid,** con risposta pagata.
repolish [riː'pɔliʃ], *v.t.* Riforbire.
repopulate [riː'pɔpjuːleit], *v.t.* Ripopolare.
repopulation, *n.* Ripopolamento, *m.*
report [re'pɔːɹt], *v.t.* Riferire, riportare, rapportare, raccontare, comunicare; (*a speech*) stenografare; fare la cronaca di; *v.i.* far un rapporto, dar comunicazione, fare il cronista. || *n.* Rapporto, *m.*, relazione, *f.*; rendiconto, *m.*; (*Law*) referto, *m.*; notizia, voce, diceria, *f.*; riputazione, fama, *f.*; (*school*) pagella, *f.*; (*sound*) sparo, colpo, scoppio, *m.*, detonazione, *f.* **It is reported,** si dice, corre voce; **to — oneself** (*to the police, etc.*) presentarsi; **I shall — you to,** vi deferirò a; **of good —,** di buona riputazione; **to draw up a —,** stendere un rapporto.
reporter, *n.* Rapportatore, *m.*; redattore, cronista, *m.* **Reporters' gallery,** tribuna della stampa, *f.*
reporting, *n.* Servizio d'informazione, cronaca, *f.*
reposal [re'pouzəl], *n.* Fiducia, *f.*
repose [re'pouz], *v.i.* Riposare, riposarsi; appoggiarsi, fondarsi; *v.t.* avere, riporre. || *n.* Riposo, *m.*, calma, tranquillità, *f.* **To — confidence,** aver fiducia, nutrire fiducia; **to — faith in,** riporre fede in.
reposeful, *a.* Calmo, tranquillo, riposante.
repository [re'pɔzitəri], *n.* Deposito, magazzino, *m.*; negozio, *m.*
repossess [riːpo'zes], *v.t.* Ripossedere.
repot [riː'pɔt], *v.t.* Rinvasare.
repoussé work [re'puːsei wəːɹk], *n.* Lavoro a sbalzo, lavore di rilievo, *m.*
reprehend [repri'hend], *v.t.* Riprendere, ammonire, riprovare, biasimare, censurare.
reprehensible [repri'hensibl], *a.* Riprensibile, biasimevole, riprovevole.
reprehensibleness, *n.* Riprensibilità, *f.*
reprehensibly, *adv.* Riprensibilmente.
reprehension, *n.* Riprensione, *f.*, biasimo, *m.*
reprehensive, *a.* Biasimevole.
represent [repre'zent], *v.t.* Rappresentare.
representation, *n.* Rappresentazione, *f.*, rapporto, *m.* **According to his own representations,** secondo ciò che dice lui; **to make representations,** far osservare.
representative [repre'zentətiv], *a.* Rappresentativo. || *n.* Rappresentante, *m.f.*; deputato, *m.* **A — body,** una rappresentanza, *f.*
repress [re'pres], *v.t.* Reprimere, comprimere.

repression, *n.* Repressione, *f.*
repressive, *a.* Repressivo.
reprieve [re'pri:v], *n.* Dilazione, proroga, sospensione, *f.*; grazia, *f.* || *v.t.* Graziare, sospendere l'esecuzione. **To — a condemned man,** graziare un condannato.
reprimand ['reprimɑ:nd], *v.t.* Rimproverare, sgridare; ammonire. || *n.* Ramanzina, sgridata, lavata di testa, *f.*, rimprovero, *m.*
reprint, *v.t.* [ri:'print], Ristampare. || *n.* ['ri:print] Ristampa, *f.*
reprisal [re'praizəl], *n.* Rappresaglia, *f.* **By way of —,** per rappresaglia; **to take reprisals,** usare rappresaglie.
reproach [re'proutʃ], *n.* Rimprovero, biasimo, *m.*; vergogna, onta, *f.*, sconcio, *m.* || *v.t.* Rimproverare, biasimare, rimbrottare, sgridare. **To be a — to,** essere una vergogna a; **to — with,** rimproverare a.
reproachful, *a.* Di rimprovero; lagnoso, querulo, scontento; ingiurioso.
reproachfully, *adv.* In tono di rimprovero.
reproachless, *a.* Irreprensibile.
reprobate ['reprobeit], *n.* Reprobo, *m.* || *v.t.* Riprovare.
reprobation, *n.* Riprovazione, *f.*
reproduce [ri:pro'dju:s], *v.t.* Riprodurre.
reproducer, *n.* Riproduttore, *m.*
reproducible, *a.* Riproducibile.
reproduction [ri:pro'dʌkʃən], *n.* Riproduzione, *f.*
reproductive, reproductory, *a.* Riproduttivo.
reproof [re'pru:f], *n.* Biasimo, rimprovero, *m.*, sgridata, riprensione, *f.*
reprove [re'pru:v], *v.t.* Biasimare, sgridare, rimproverare, riprendere, censurare.
reprovingly, *adv.* Con biasimo, rimproverando.
reptile ['reptail], *n.a.* Rettile, *m.*
reptilian [rep'tiliən], *a.* Rettile, strisciante.
republic [re'pʌblik], *n.* Repubblica, *f.*
republican, *n.a.* Repubblicano, *m.*
republicanism, *n.* Repubblicanismo, *m.*
republication [ri:pʌbli'keiʃən], *n.* Ripubblicazione, *f.*
republish, *v.t.* Ripubblicare.
repudiate [re'pju:dieit], *v.t.* Ripudiare; disconoscere, sconfessare.
repudiation, *n.* Ripudio, *m.*, sconfessione, *f.*
repugnance [re'pʌgnəns], *n.* Ripugnanza, avversione, *f.*
repugnant, *a.* Ripugnante, contrario, avverso. **It is — to me,** mi ripugna.
repulse [re'pʌls], *v.t.* Repellere, respingere, rigettare, ricusare. || *n.* Ripulsa, *f.*, rifiuto, rabbuffo, *m.*; sconfitta, *f.* **To meet with a —,** ricevere una ripulsa.
repulsion, *n.* Ripulsione, ripugnanza, *f.*, disgusto, *m.*
repulsive, *a.* Ributtante, ripugnante, schifoso; ripulsivo.
repulsiveness, *n.* Disgustosità, *f.*
repurchase [ri:'pə:ɹtʃis], *v.t.* Ricomprare, ricomperare. || *n.* Ricompera, *f.*
reputable ['repju:təbl], *a.* Onorevole, di buona fama, reputato, stimabile.
reputation, *n.* Riputazione, fama, *f.*, nome, *m.*; onore, *m.* **Of good —,** reputato, quotato bene; **he has a bad —,** è un uomo di cattiva fama; **to have the — of,** essere reputato, aver fama di; **to get a —,** farsi una riputazione.
repute [re'pju:t], *v.t.* Reputare, stimare, credere. || *n.* Riputazione, fama, *f.*, nome, *m.* **Ill —,** dubbia fama, *f.*, cattivo nome, *m.*; **good —,** bella fama, *f.*, buon nome, *m.*; **of —,** rinomato.
reputed, *a.* Reputato; putativo. **— father,** padre putativo, *m.*
reputedly, *adv.* Secondo l'opinione generale.
request [re'kwest], *n.* Richiesta, domanda, preghiera, *f.*; invito, *m.* || *v.t.* Richiedere, chiedere, domandare, pregare, invitare. **At the — of,** a richiesta di; **in —,** in voga, alla moda, richiesto; **to make a —,** fare una domanda; **it is requested that,** si prega di; **he requested her to go,** la pregò di andare; **to — an answer,** richiedere una risposta.
requicken [ri:'kwikən], *v.t.* Ravvivare, rianimare.
requiem ['rekwiem], *n.* Requie, *f.*, requiem, *m.*
require [re'kwaiɹ], *v.t.* Richiedere, esigere; domandare; aver bisogno di, volere. **To — an answer,** esigere una risposta; **the child requires care,** il bambino ha bisogno di cura; **to be required,** occorrere; mancare.
requirement, *n.* Bisogno, *m.*, esigenza, necessità, *f.*; requisito, *m.*; condizione richiesta, *f.*
requisite ['rekwizit], *a.* Necessario, richiesto, indispensabile. || *n.* Requisito, attributo, elemento necessario, *m.*; fabbisogno, occorrente, *m.*
requisition [rekwi'ziʃən], *n.* Richiesta, domanda, *f.*; requisizione, *f.* || *v.t.* Requisire. **To call into —,** richiedere.
requital [re'kwaitəl], *n.* Ricompensa, *f.*, contraccambio, *m.*; vendetta, *f.*, rappresaglia, *f.*
requite, *v.t.* Ricompensare, rimunerare, contraccambiare, rendere. **To — with good,** rendere bene per male.
re-read [ri:'ri:d], *v.t.* Rileggere.
reredos ['riəɹdɔs], *n.* (*Arch.*) Dossale, *m.*
resale [ri:'seil], *n.* Rivendita, *f.*
rescind [re'sind], *v.t.* Rescindere, annullare, abrogare.
rescission [re'siʒən], *n.* Rescissione, *f.*, annullamento, *m.*; abrogazione, *f.*
rescript ['ri:skript], *n.* Rescritto, *m.*
rescue ['reskju:], *n.* Salvamento, salvataggio, *m.*, liberazione, *f.*; scampo, *m.*; soccorso, aiuto, *m.* || *v.t.* Salvare, liberare; soccorrere, aiutare. **To come to the —,** venire in soccorso.
rescuer, *n.* Salvatore, liberatore, *m.*
research [re'sə:ɹtʃ], *n.* Ricerca, indagine, *f.*; inchiesta, *f.*; studio, *m.* || *v.i.* Far ricerche, indagare. **To — into,** ricercare, indagare.
researcher, research worker, *n.* Ricercatore, investigatore, *m.*, ricercatrice, investigatrice, *f.*
reseat [ri:'si:t], *v.t.* Riporre a sedere; rifornire di sedia; rimettere un nuovo fondo a.
reseda [re'si:də], *n.* (*Bot.*) Reseda, *f.* || *a.* Color reseda.
reseize [ri:'si:z], *v.t.* Ripigliare, riafferrare.
resell [ri:'sel], *v.t.* Rivendere.
resemblance [re'zembləns], *n.* Rassomiglianza, somiglianza, *f.*
resemble, *v.t.* Rassomigliare a, somigliare a.

resent [reˈzent], *v.t.* Risentirsi di, offendersi per, prendere in mala parte, arrabbiarsi per.
resentful, *a.* Acrimonioso, permaloso.
resentfully, *adv.* Acrimoniosamente.
resentment, *n.* Risentimento, sdegno, *m.*
reservation [rezəɹˈveiʃən], *n.* Riserva, restrizione, eccezione, *f.*; (*of seats*) prenotazione, *f.* **Mental —,** restrizione mentale, *f.*; **Indian —,** terreno riservato ai Pellirosse, *m.*
reserve [reˈzəːɹv], *n.* Riserbo, *m.*, riservatezza, reticenza, *f.*; riguardo, *m.*; riserva, *f.* || *v.t.* Riserbare, riservare; ritenere; locare. **With due —,** con le dovute riserve; **— price,** prezzo minimo, *m.*; **— fund,** fondo di riserva; (*Mil.*) **the reserves,** le riserve, *f.pl.*; **to — for oneself,** riservarsi.
reserved, *a.* Riservato; circospetto, sostenuto, cauto. **— seat,** posto riservato, *m.*
reservedly, *adv.* Con riserbo.
reservist, *n.* Riservista, *m.*
reservoir [ˈrezəɹvwɑːɹ], *n.* Serbatoio, *m.*, cisterna, *f.*; recipiente, *f.*
reset [riːˈset], *v.t.* (*jewels*) Rincastonare; (*Print.*) ricomporre.
resetting, *n.* (*Print.*) Ricomposizione, *f.*
resettle [riːˈsetl], *v.t.* Ristabilire, riassettare; *v.i.* ristabilirsi.
resettlement, *n.* Ristabilimento, riassettamento, riordinamento, *m.*
reship [riːˈʃip], *v.t.* Rimbarcare, rispedire.
reshipment, *n.* Rimbarco, *m.*, rispedizione, *f.*
reshuffle [riːˈʃʌfl], *v.t.* Rimescolare.
reside [reˈzaid], *v.i.* Abitare, risiedere, dimorare, stare.
residence [ˈrezidəns], *n.* Abitazione, residenza, dimora, *f.*; soggiorno, *m.*; casa, *f.*, domicilio, *m.* **Board and —,** vitto e alloggio, pensione.
residency, *n.* Palazzo governativo, *m.*, residenza, *f.*
resident, *n.* Residente, abitante, *m.f.* || *a.* Residente, domiciliato; (*fig.*) inerente.
residential [reziˈdenʃəl], *a.* D'abitazione, residenziale.
residual [reˈzidjuːəl], *a.* Residuale.
residuary, *a.* Residuale, rimanente. (*Law*) **— legatee,** erede universale, *m.*
residue [ˈrezidjuː], *n.* Residuo, resto, avanzo, rimanente, *m.*
residuum [reˈzidjuːəm], *n.* Residuo, *m.*
resign [reˈzain], *v.t.* Dimettersi da, rinunciare a, abbandonare, lasciare; *v.i.* dimettersi, dare le dimissioni, rassegnare le dimissioni, rassegnarsi. **To — oneself to,** rassegnarsi a.
resignation [rezigˈneiʃən], *n.* Rassegnazione, pazienza, *f.*; abbandono, *m.*; (*from office*) dimissione, *f.* **To send in one's —,** dare le dimissioni.
resigned [reˈzaind], *a.* Rassegnato; dimissionario.
resignedly [reˈzainedli], *adv.* Rassegnatamente.
resilience, resiliency [reˈziliəns, reˈziliənsi], *n.* Elasticità, *f.*
resilient, *a.* Elastico; rimbalzante.
resin [ˈrezin], *n.* (*Bot.*) Resina, *f.*; (*for violin*) colofonia, *f.*
resinous, *a.* Resinoso.
resist [reˈzist], *v.t.* Resistere a, opporsi a, respingere; rifiutarsi di; *v.i.* resistere, reggere.
resistance, *n.* Resistenza, *f.*
resistant, *a.* Resistente.
resistible, *a.* Resistibile.
resistless, *a.* Irresistibile.
resole [riːˈsoul], *v.t.* Risolare, rimettere le suole a.
resoluble [ˈrezɔljuːbl], *a.* Risolubile.
resolute [ˈrezoljuːt], *a.* Risoluto, animoso, deciso, determinato.
resolutely, *adv.* Risolutamente.
resolution, *n.* Risoluzione, determinazione, decisione, deliberazione, *f.* **To pass a —,** prendere una deliberazione; **to come to a —,** decidere.
resolvable [reˈzɔlvəbl], *a.* Risolubile.
resolve [reˈzɔlv], *n.* Risoluzione, intenzione, *f.*, proposito, disegno, *m.* || *v.t.* Risolvere; dissolvere, sciogliere, chiarire, spiegare; decidere, determinare; deliberare; *v.i.* risolversi, decidere; dissolversi, sciogliersi, dissiparsi. **It was unanimously resolved that,** venne deliberato all'unanimità; **to — oneself into,** costituirsi in; **to — upon,** decidersi, risolversi.
resolved, *a.* Risoluto, risolto, determinato.
resolvent, *a.* (*Med.*) Risolvente.
resonance [ˈrezonəns], *n.* Risonanza, *f.*
resonant, *a.* Risonante, sonoro.
resort [reˈzɔːɹt], *n.* Ricorso, *m.*, risorsa, *f.*; convegno, ritrovo, *m.*; stazione, *f.* || *v.i.* Ricorrere a; recarsi a; frequentare. **In the last —,** come ultima risorsa; **to have — to,** aver ricorso a, ricorrere a; **a — of scholars,** un ritrovo di eruditi, *m.*; **a place of great —,** un luogo molto frequentato, *m.*; **a health —,** (*in mountains*) stazione climatica, *f.*, (*watering-place*) stazione balneare *or* termale, *f.*
resound [reˈzaund], *v.i.* Risonare, echeggiare, rimbombare, ripercuotersi; *v.t.* far risonare, far echeggiare. **To — with,** risonare di.
resounding, *a.* Risonante, sonoro.
resource [reˈsɔːɹs], *n.* Risorsa, *f.*; ripiego, espediente, *m.*; mezzo, *m.* **To be at the end of one's resources,** essere alla fine delle proprie risorse.
resourceful, *a.* Pieno di risorse, intraprendente.
resourcefulness, *n.* Intraprendenza, *f.*
resow [riːˈsou], *v.t.* Riseminare.
respect [reˈspekt], *n.* Rispetto, riguardo, *m.*; stima, considerazione, *f.*, conto, *m.* || *v.t.* Rispettare, stimare, tenere da conto. **To pay one's respects,** presentare i rispetti a; **with — to,** circa, quanto a; **to pay — to,** portar rispetto a; **without — to,** senza riguardo a; **in — of,** riguardo a, in quanto a; **in some respects,** in certo modo, in qualche modo; **in this —,** per questo riguardo; **in one —,** sotto un aspetto, in una cosa; **to have a great — for,** avere molto rispetto per; **with due —,** coi debiti riguardi, col dovuto rispetto.
respectability [respektəˈbiliti], *n.* Rispettabilità, *f.*
respectable [resˈpektəbl], *a.* Rispettabile, considerevole, ragguardevole; discreto. **A — number,** un numero discreto, *m.*
respectably, *adv.* Rispettabilmente; decentemente.
respecter, *n.* **I am no — of persons,** non ho rispetti umani.
respectful, *a.* Rispettoso.

respectfully, *adv.* Rispettosamente.
respectfulness, *n.* Rispetto, *m.*, deferenza, *f.*
respecting, *prep.* Circa, quanto a, in rapporto a, riguardo a.
respective, *a.* Rispettivo, proprio.
respectively, *adv.* Rispettivamente.
respiration [respi'reiʃən], *n.* Respirazione, *f.*
respirator, *n.* Respiratore, *m.*
respiratory, *a.* Respiratorio.
respire, *v.i.t.* Respirare.
respite ['respit], *v.t.* Dar respiro a, accordare un respiro, accordare una dilazione a. ‖ *n.* Respiro, sollievo, riposo, *m.*; dilazione, *f.*
resplendence, resplendency [re'splendens, re'splendənsi], *n.* Risplendenza, *f.*, splendore, *m.*
resplendent, *a.* Risplendente.
respond [re'spɔnd], *v.t.i.* Rispondere; ubbidire; reagire.
respondent, *a.* Rispondente. ‖ *n.* (*Law*) Prevenuto, convenuto, imputato, *m.* **Co-—,** coimputato, *m.*, coimputata, *f.*
response, *n.* Risposta, *f.*; (*Eccles.*) responso, *m.*
responsibility [respɔnsi'biliti], *n.* Responsabilità, *f.* **On my own —,** sotto la mia responsabilità.
responsible, *a.* Responsabile.
responsive, *a.* Responsivo; (*fig.*) simpatico.
responsory, *n.* (*Eccles.*) Responsorio, *m.*
rest (1) [rest], *n.* Riposo, *m.*, (*shelter*) rifugio, asilo, *m.*; (*pause*) posa, sosta, *f.*; (*support*) sostegno, appoggio, *m.*; (*Mus.*) pausa, *f.*; (*Billiards*) ponticino, *m.*; (*for lance*) resta, *f.* *v.i.* Riposare, riposarsi; appoggiarsi, sostenersi; fermarsi; stare; *v.t.* far riposare; appoggiare. **To retire to —,** andare a letto, coricarsi; **a good night's —,** una buona notte, *f.*; **at —,** in riposo; **to set someone's mind at —,** mettere in pace qualcuno; **never to have a moment's —,** non aver mai tregua; **it rests with you,**, sta a voi; **to — assured,** essere sicuro; **the matter cannot — here,** non si può lasciar cadere la cosa; **to come to —,** fermarsi.
rest (2), *n.* Resto, rimanente, avanzo, residuo, *m.*; (*remainder*) restante, *m.*; (*the others*) gli altri, *m.pl.* **All the — of it,** eccetera, e così via.
re-stage [ri:'steidʒ], *v.t.* Rimettere in scena.
restart [ri:'stɑ:ɹt], *v.t.i.* Ricominciare; riavviarsi, ripartire.
restate [ri:'steit], *v.t.* Dichiarare di nuovo, riesporre, riaffermare.
restaurant ['restərɔnt], *n.* Ristorante, *m.*; trattoria, *f.*
restful, *a.* Calmo, tranquillo, quieto, riposante.
rest-harrow [rest'hærou], *n.* (*Bot.*) Restabue, *f.*
resting, *a.* In riposo. **—-place,** luogo di riposo, *m.*; **the last —-place,** il sepolcro, *m.*, la tomba, *f.*
restitch [ri:'stitʃ], *v.t.* Ricucire.
restitution [resti'tju:ʃən], *n.* Restituzione, *f.*
restive ['restiv], *a.* Restio, irrequieto; ritroso. **A — horse,** un cavallo restio, *m.*
restiveness, *n.* Irrequietezza, *f.*
restless, *a.* Irrequieto, inquieto, turbato, agitato. **A — night,** una notte insonne, *f.*
restlessly, *adv.* Irrequietamente.
restlessness, *n.* Irrequietezza, inquietezza, inquietudine, agitazione, *f.*
restock [ri:'stɔk], *v.t.* Rifornire.
restorable [re'stɔ:rəbl], *a.* Restaurabile.
restoration [restɔ:'reiʃən], *n.* Restaurazione, *f.*, ristabilimento, *m.*; restituzione, *f.*; (*Arch.*) restauro, *m.* **The — of the Bourbons,** la restaurazione dei Borboni, *f.*
restorative [res'tɔ:rətiv], *n.a.* Ristorativo, ristoratore, *m.*
restore [re'stɔ:ɹ], *v.t.* Restaurare, ristorare, ristabilire; restituire; rimettere, rendere. **To — to health,** rimettere in salute.
restorer, *n.* Restauratore, *m.*
restrain [re'strein], *v.t.* Trattenere, frenare; limitare, reprimere, dominare. **To — from,** impedire di; **to — oneself,** frenarsi, trattenersi; **to — one's anger,** reprimere l'ira.
restrainable, *a.* Raffrenabile, reprimibile.
restraining, *a.* Restrittivo, limitativo.
restraint, *n.* Costringimento, *m.*, restrizione, *f.*; freno, ritegno, riserbo, *m.*; detenzione, *f.* **Under —,** sotto vigilanza, privo della libertà; **to keep under —,** contenere, trattenere; **to place under —,** mettere sotto controllo.
restrict [re'strikt], *v.t.* Restringere, limitare.
restricted, *a.* Ristretto.
restriction, *n.* Restrizione, limitazione, *f.*
restrictive, *a.* Restrittivo.
restring [ri:'striŋ], *v.t.* (*violin, etc.*) Rimettere le corde a.
result [re'zʌlt], *n.* Risultato, effetto, esito, *m.*, conseguenza, *f.* ‖ *v.i.* Risultare, seguire, riuscire. **What is the — ?** Che ne risulta? A che prò? Con che risultato?; **to — in,** risultare in.
resultant, *a.* Risultante.
resumable [re'zju:məbl], *a.* Riassumibile.
resume [re'zju:m], *v.t.* Riprendere, riassumere, ripigliare; *v.i.* ricominciare, ricapitolare.
résumé [re'zju:mei], *n.* Sunto, riassunto, *m.*
resumption [re'zʌmʃən], *n.* Riassunzione, ripresa, *f.*
resurgent [re'sə:ɹdʒənt], *a.* Rinascente, risorgente.
resurrection [resə'rekʃən], *n.* Risurrezione, *f.*
resurrectionist, *n.* Disseppellitore di cadaveri, *m.*
resurvey [ri:sə:ɹ'vei], *v.t.* Riesaminare, riconsiderare. ‖ *n.* Riesame, *m.*
resuscitate [re'sʌsiteit], *v.t.i.* Risuscitare.
resuscitation, *n.* Risuscitazione, *f.*, risuscitamento, *m.*
ret [ret], *v.t.* Macerare.
retail ['ri:teil], *n.* Minuto, dettaglio, *m.*; vendita al dettaglio, vendita al minuto, *f.* ‖ *a.* Al dettaglio, al minuto. ‖ *v.t.* [re'teil], Vendere al minuto; (*fig.*) dettagliare, particolareggiare. **— price,** prezzo al minuto, *m.*; **— trade,** commercio al dettaglio, *m.*
retailer, *n.* Venditore al minuto, dettagliante, *m.*
retain [re'tein], *v.t.* Ritenere, trattenere, serbare; (*Law*) accaparrarsi un difensore.
retainer, *n.* Dipendente, servitore, *m.*; (*Law*) onorario, *m.*, caparra, *f.* **Retainers,** seguaci, vassalli, gregari, *m.pl.*
retaining, *a.* D'appoggio, di sostegno. **— wall,** muro di sostegno, *m.*; (*Law*) **— fee,** onorario anticipato, anticipo, *m.*
retake [ri:'teik], *v.t.* Riprendere, ripigliare.
retaliate [re'tælieit], *v.i.* Rendere la pariglia, usare rappresaglie; ribattere, rivalersi; *v.t.* ritorcere, ribattere.

retaliation, *n.* Rappresaglia, rivalsa, vendetta, *f.*; contraccambio, *m.* **By way of —,** per rappresaglia.
retaliatory [reˈtæliətəri], *a.* Di rappresaglia.
retard [reˈtɑːɹd], *v.t.i.* Ritardare, rallentare, tirare in lungo, indugiare; trattenere; essere in ritardo, far tardi. **To — payment,** rimandare il pagamento.
retardation, *n.* Ritardo, indugio, *m.*, ritardazione, *f.*; ritardamento, *m.*
retarding, *a.* Ritardativo, ritardatore.
retch [riːtʃ], *v.i.* Recere, vomitare.
retching, *n.* Conato di vomito, vomito, *m.*
retell [riːˈtel], *v.t.* Ridire, ripetere.
retention [reˈtenʃən], *n.* Ritenzione, *f.*; conservazione, *f.*
retentive [reˈtentiv], *a.* Ritentivo.
retentiveness, *n.* Ritentiva, *f.*
reticence [ˈretisəns], *n.* Reticenza, *f.*
reticent, *a.* Reticente, evasivo.
reticle [ˈretikl], *n.* Reticolo, *m.*, reticella, *f.*
reticulate [reˈtikjuːlət], *a.* Reticolare, reticolato.
reticulation, *n.* Reticolazione, *f.*
reticule [ˈretikjuːl], *n.* Borsetta, *f.*
retiform [ˈretifɔːɹm], *a.* (*Anat.*) Retiforme.
retina [ˈretinə], *n.* Retina, *f.*
retinue [ˈretinjuː], *n.* Seguito, corteo, corteggio, *m.*
retire [reˈtaiɹ], *v.t.* Ritirare, collocare a riposo; congedare; *v.i.* ritirarsi; dimettersi; indietreggiare.
retired, *a.* Ritirato, appartato, nascosto; privato, solitario; collocato a riposo, pensionato, in ritiro. **On the — list,** in ritiro, in pensione; giubilato; **— officer,** ufficiale in ritiro.
retirement, *n.* Ritiro, riposo, *m.*; (*colloq.*) giubilazione, *f.*; (*fig.*) solitudine, *f.*
retiring, *a.* Ritirato, riservato; solitario; timido, modesto; uscente. **—-pension,** pensione, *f.*
retort [reˈtɔːɹt], *n.* Ritorsione, replica, *f.*, rimbecco, *m.*; (*Chem.*) storta, *f.* || *v.t.* Ribattere, ritorcere; rispondere, replicare; *v.i.* rimbeccare.
retouch [riːˈtʌtʃ], *v.t.* Ritoccare.
retouching, *n.* Ritocco, *m.*, ritoccatura, *f.*
retrace [riːˈtreis], *v.t.* Rintracciare, riandare, ripassare. **To — one's steps,** rifare la strada, ritornare sui propri passi.
retract [reˈtrækt], *v.t.* Ritirare, revocare; ritrattare, disdire; *v.i.* ritrattarsi, disdirsi.
retractable, *a.* Ritrattabile, revocabile.
retractation [retrækˈteiʃən], *n.* Ritrattazione, *f.*
retractile [reˈtræktail], *a.* Retrattile.
retraction, *n.* Contrazione, *f.*
retransfer [riːtrɑːnsˈfəɹ], *v.t.* Ritrasferire.
retranslate [riːtrɑːnsˈleit], *v.t.* Ritradurre.
retread [riːˈtred], *v.t.* Ricalcare.
retreat [reˈtriːt], *n.* Ritiro, ricovero, asilo, *m.*; (*Mil.*) ritirata, *f.* || *v.i.* Ritirarsi, indietreggiare; (*Mil.*) ripiegare. **To beat a —,** ritirarsi, andarsene, battere in ritirata; **to sound the —,** battere la ritirata.
retreating, *a.* Ritirante, ripiegante. **— chin,** mento sfuggente, *m.*
retrench [reˈtrentʃ], *v.t.* Ridurre, scemare, diminuire; *v.i.* economizzare, ridurre le spese.
retrenchment, *n.* Economia, *f.*, risparmio, *m.*
retribution [retriˈbjuːʃən], *n.* Retribuzione, ricompensa, *f.*; castigo, *m.*, punizione, *f.*
retributive, *a.* Retribuente, compensativo.
retrievable [reˈtriːvəbl], *a.* Ricuperabile, riparabile.
retrieve [reˈtriːv], *v.t.* Ricuperare, ritrovare, riacquistare, riprendere; riparare; richiamare; (*game*) riportare. **To — one's fortunes,** rifarsi dalle perdite.
retriever, *n.* Cane da caccia, cane da fermo, *m.* **That dog is a good —,** quel cane riporta bene.
retroaction [retrouˈækʃən], *n.* Retroazione, *f.*
retroactive, *a.* Retroattivo.
retroactivity, *n.* Retroattività, *f.*
retrocede [retrouˈsiːd], *v.i.* Retrocedere, rinculare.
retrocession, *n.* Retrocessione, *f.*
retrogradation [retrougrəˈdeiʃən], *n.* (*Astron.*) Retrogradazione, *f.*
retrograde [ˈretrougreid], *v.i.* Retrogradare. || *a.* Retrogrado.
retrogression, *n.* Retrogressione, *f.*
retrogressive, *a.* Regressivo.
retrospect [ˈretrouspekt], *n.* Sguardo retrospettivo, *m.*, visuale del passato, vista d'insieme, *f.* **In —,** guardando indietro, guardando in scorcio.
retrospection, *n.* Retrospezione, *f.*
retrospective, *a.* Retrospettivo; (*of a law, etc.*) retroattivo.
retroversion [retrouˈvəːɹʃən], *n.* (*Med.*) Retroversione, *f.*
rettery [ˈretəri], *n.* Maceratoio, macero, *m.*
return [reˈtəːɹn], *v.i.* Ritornare, tornare, rivenire; riapparire; rispondere; ricorrere; *v.t.* (*to give back*) rendere, ritornare, restituire; (*to send back*) rimandare, rinviare; (*to put back*) rimettere indietro; (*to reciprocate*) ricambiare, contraccambiare; (*a candidate*) eleggere; (*Tennis*) ribattere, rimandare. || *n.* Ritorno, *m.*; (*giving back*) restituzione, *f.*; (*sending back*) rinvio, *m.*; (*an account*) rendiconto, rapporto, *m.*; (*election*) elezione, *f.*; (*profit*) compenso, guadagno, *m.* **To — to the subject,** tornare a bomba; **to — home,** tornare a casa; **to — like for like,** rendere la pariglia; **to — thanks,** rendere grazie; **to — a greeting,** ricambiare un saluto; **to — a profit,** fruttare; **by — of post,** a volta di corriere, a volta di posta; **a — ticket,** un biglietto di andata e ritorno, *m.*; **many happy returns of the day,** mille di questi giorni, tanti auguri; **in — for,** in contraccambio di; **on my —,** al mio ritorno; **on sale or —,** da vendere o rimandare; **— journey,** viaggio di ritorno, *m.*; (*Sport*) **— match,** rivincita, *f.*; (*Comm.*) **returned empties,** vuoti di ritorno, *m.pl.*; (*Pol.*) **returning officer,** scrutinatore in un'elezione, *m.*
returnable, *a.* Restituibile, di rimando; (*Law*) di rinvio.
reunion [riːˈjuːniən], *n.* Riunione, adunanza, *f.*
reunite [riːjuːˈnait], *v.t.* Riunire; *v.i.* riunirsi.
revaccinate [riːˈvæksineit], *v.t.* Rivaccinare.
reveal [reˈviːl], *v.t.* Rivelare, svelare, palesare, manifestare. || *n.* (*Arch.*) Strombatura, *f.*
reveille [reˈvæli], *n.* (*Mil.*) Sveglia, diana, *f.* **To sound the —,** suonare la sveglia, battere la diana.

revel [ˈrevəl], *n.* Festa, *f.*; baldoria, crapula, *f.* ‖ *v.i.* Divertirsi, festeggiare; far baldoria, bagordare, gozzovigliare. **To — in,** divertirsi di, godere, gongolare.
revelation [revəˈleiʃən], *n.* Rivelazione, *f.* (*Bible*) **Book of Revelations,** l'Apocalisse, *f.*
reveller [ˈrevələɹ], *n.* Festaiuolo, crapulone, gozzovigliatore, *m.*
revelry [ˈrevəlri], *n.* Festeggiamento, *m.*; bagordo, *m.*, gozzoviglia, crapula, baldoria, *f.*
revendication [riːvendiˈkeiʃən], *n.* Rivendicazione, *f.*
revenge [reˈvendʒ], *n.* Vendetta, *f.*; (*games*) rivincita, *f.* ‖ *v.t.* Vendicare, vendicarsi di. **To be revenged on,** vendicarsi con; (*games*) **to have one's —,** prendere la rivincita.
revengeful, *a.* Vendicativo.
revengefulness, *n.* Spirito vendicativo.
revenger, *n.* Vendicatore, *m.*
revenue [ˈrevenjuː], *n.* Entrata, rendita, *f.*, reddito, *m.*; fisco, erario, *m.* **Public —,** tributo fiscale, *m.*; **— cutter,** barca doganiera, *f.*; **inland —,** fisco, *m.*
reverberant [reˈvəːɹbərənt], *a.* Risonante, riverberante.
reverberate [reˈvəːɹbəreit], *v.t.i.* Riverberare, riverberarsi, rupercuotere, riflettere; rimbombare, risonare.
reverberation, *n.* Riverberazione, *f.*
reverberatory, *a.* A riverbero. ‖ *n.* Forno a riverbero, *m.*
revere [reˈviəɹ], *v.t.* Riverire, venerare, onorare.
reverence [ˈrevərəns], *n.* Riverenza, *f.* ‖ *v.t.* Riverire. **Your Reverence,** Vostra Riverenza, *f.*
reverend, *a.* Reverendo, venerabile. **Most Reverend,** Reverendissimo; **— sir,** signore reverendo.
reverent, *a.* Reverente, riverente.
reverential [revəˈrenʃəl], *a.* Riverenziale, riverente.
reverentially, *adv.* Riverenzialmente.
reverently, *adv.* Reverentemente, riverentemente.
reverie [ˈrevəri], *n.* Meditazione, *f.*; fantasticheria, *f.*
revers (pl. **revers**) [reˈviəɹ], *n.* (*of coat, etc.*) Rovescio, *m.*
reversal [reˈvəːɹsəl], *n.* Inversione, *f.*, rovesciamento, *m.*; annullamento, *m.*, revoca, cassazione, *f.*
reverse [reˈvəːɹs], *n.* Rovescio, contrario, opposto, *m.*; rovescio di fortuna, *m.* ‖ *a.* Inverso, a rovescio; contrario, opposto. ‖ *v.t.* Rivoltare, riversare; annullare, revocare, cassare; (*Motor, etc.*) cambiare marcia. **Quite the —,** tutto l'opposto; **the — way,** in senso inverso; **the — of the medal,** il rovescio della medaglia, *m.*
reversible, *a.* Riversibile, invertibile; (*of cloth*) a due diritti; (*Law*) revocabile.
reversibility, *n.* Riversibilità, *f.*
reversing gear [reˈvəːɹsiŋ giəɹ], *n.* (*Mech.*) Meccanismo d'inversione, *m.*
reversion [reˈvəːɹʃən], *n.* Ritorno, *m.*, riversione, *f.*; atavismo, *m.*, regressione, *f.*
reversionary, *a.* Regressivo.
revert [reˈvəːɹt], *v.i.* Ritornare; rivolgersi.
revertible, *a.* Riversibile.
revet [reˈvet], *v.t.* (*Mil.*) Rivestire.
revetment, *n.* Rivestimento, *m.*
revictual [riːˈvitəl], *v.t.* Vettovagliare di nuovo, rifornire di viveri.
revictualling, *n.* Rifornimento, *m.*
review [reˈvjuː], *n.* Rivista, *f.*; (*of book*) recensione, *f.*; (*Law*) revisione, *f.* ‖ *v.t.* Rivedere, ripassare, riesaminare; (*Mil.*) passare in rivista; (*books*) recensire, criticare. **To pass in —,** esaminare, rivedere, passare in rivista.
reviewer, *n.* Recensore, critico, *m.*
revile [reˈvail], *v.t.* Ingiuriare, oltraggiare, svillaneggiare, vituperare, insultare, sparlare di.
reviler, *n.* Ingiuriatore, oltraggiatore, detrattore, *m.*
reviling, *n.* Ingiurie, *f.pl.*, oltraggio, *m.*, vituperi, *m.pl.* ‖ *a.* Oltraggioso, ingiurioso.
revisal [reˈvaizəl], *n.* Revisione, *f.*
revise [reˈvaiz], *v.t.* Rivedere, correggere. ‖ *n.* (*Print.*) Seconda bozza, *f.*; **second —,** terza bozza, *f.*
reviser, *n.* Revisore, correttore, *m.*
revision [reˈviʒən], *n.* Revisione, correzione, *f.*
revisit [riːˈvizit], *v.t.* Rivisitare.
revival [reˈvaivəl], *n.* Risveglio, risorgimento, rinnovamento, *m.*; rinascenza, rinascita, *f.*; ravvivamento, *m.*; risveglio religioso, *m.*; (*Theat.*) ripresa, *f.*
revive [reˈvaiv], *v.t.* Ravvivare, rinnovare, ristabilire; *v.i.* rivivere, risuscitare; ravvivarsi, rianimarsi, rinascere, rimettere in vigore.
reviver, *n.* Ravvivatore, *m.*; (*colloq.*) bevanda ristorativa, *f.*
revivification [riːvivifiˈkeiʃən], *n.* Ravvivamento, *m.*
revivify [riːˈvivifai], *v.t.* Ravvivare.
revocable [ˈrevəkəbl], *a.* Revocabile.
revocation, *n.* Revoca, abrogazione, *f.*
revoke [reˈvouk], *v.t.* Revocare, annullare; *v.i.* (*Cards*) rifiutare.
revolt [reˈvoult], *n.* Rivolta, ribellione, sommossa, *f.* ‖ *v.i.t.* Rivoltarsi, ribellarsi, sollevarsi; disgustare, nauseare. **To — at,** disgustarsi di, sentir fastidio di.
revolting, *a.* Nauseante, ripugnante, disgustoso, ributtante.
revolution [revoˈluːʃən, revoˈljuːʃən], *n.* Rivoluzione, *f.*; giro, *m.* **100 revolutions per minute,** cento giri al minuto.
revolutionary, *n.a.* Rivoluzionario, *m.*
revolutionist, *n.* Rivoluzionario, *m.*
revolutionize, *v.t.* Rivoluzionare.
revolve [reˈvɔlv], *v.i.* Girare, roteare; (*Astron.*) rotare; *v.t.* rivolgere, considerare, ponderare. **To — in one's mind,** rivolgere in mente.
revolver, *n.* Rivoltella, *f.*, revolver, *m.*
revolving, *a.* Girevole, girante, rotante, roteante. **— light,** faro girevole, faro girante, *m.* **— book-case,** scaffaletto girevole, *m.*
revue [reˈvjuː], *n.* Rivista, *f.*; (*Theat.*) spettacolo di varietà, *f.*
revulsion [reˈvʌlʃən], *n.* (*Med.*) Revulsione, *f.*; ripugnanza, *f.*
revulsive, *a.* (*Med.*) Revulsivo.
reward [reˈwɑːrd], *n.* Ricompensa, *f.*, compenso, premio, *m.* ‖ *v.t.* Ricompensare, rimeritare, rimunerare, retribuire, premiare.
rewarding, *a.* Di ricompensa.

rewrite [riː'rait], *v.t.* Riscrivere.
reynard ['reinɑːɹd], *n.* (*Lit.*) La volpe, *f.*
rhabdomancy ['ræbdomænsi], *n.* Rabdomanzia, *f.*
rhabdomancer, *n.* Rabdomante, *m.*
rhapsodical [ræp'sɔdikəl], *a.* Rapsodico; stravagante, ampolloso.
rhapsodist, *n.* Rapsodista, rapsodo, *m.*
rhapsodize, *v.t.i.* Scrivere rapsodie, cantare rapsodie.
rhapsody ['ræpsədi], *n.* Rapsodia, *f.*
Rheims [riːmz], *n.* (*Geog.*) Reims, *f.*
Rhenish ['reniʃ], *a.* Del Reno. || *n.* Vino del Reno, *m.*
rheometer ['riːomiːtəɹ], *n.* Reometro, *m.*
rheostat ['riːostæt], *n.* Reostato, *m.*
rhetoric ['retorik], *n.* Retorica, rettorica, *f.*
rhetorical [re'tɔrikəl], *a.* Retorico, rettorico.
rhetorician [retə'riʃən], *n.* Retore, *m.*
rheum ['ruːm], *n.* Catarro, *m.*
rheumatic [ruː'mætik], *a.* Reumatico.
rheumatics, *n.pl.* (*colloq.*) Reumatismo, *m.*
rheumatism, *n.* Reumatismo, *m.*
rheumatoid ['ruːmətɔid], *a.* Reumatoide.
Rhine [rain], *n.* (*Geog.*) Reno, *m.*
Rhineland ['rainlənd], *n.* (*Geog.*) Renania, *f.*
rhinitis [rai'naitis], *n.* (*Med.*) Rinite, *f.*
rhino ['rainou], *n.* (*colloq.*) Danaro, *m.*, quattrini, *m.pl.*
rhinoceros (pl. **rhinoceroses**) [rai'nɔsərəs, rai'nɔsərəsiz], *n.* (*Zool.*) Rinoceronte, *m.*
rhinology [rai'nɔlədʒi], *n.* Rinologia, *f.*
rhizome ['raizoum], *n.* (*Bot.*) Rizoma, *m.*
rhizopod ['raizopɔd], *n.* (*Zool.*) Rizopode, *m.*
Rhodes [roudz], *n.* (*Geog.*) Rodi, *m.*
rhododendron [roudo'dendrən], *n.* (*Bot.*) Rododendro, *m.*
rhomb, rhombus [rɔmb, 'rɔmbəs], *n.* (*Geom.*) Rombo, *m.*
rhomboid, *n.* Romboide, *m.*
Rhone [roun], *n.* (*Geog.*) Rodano, *m.*
rhubarb ['ruːbɑːɹb], *n.* (*Bot.*) Rabarbaro, *m.*
rhyme [raim], *n.* Rima, *f.*; poesia, *f.*, versi, *m.pl.* || *v.t.i.* Rimare, versificare. **In —**, in rima; **to put in —**, mettere in rima; **to — with**, rimare con.
rhymer, rhymster, *n.* Rimatore, poetastro, *m.*
rhythm [riðm], *n.* Ritmo, *m.*
rhythmic, rhythmical, *a.* Ritmico.
rib [rib], *n.* (*Anat.*) Costola, costa, *f.*; (*of umbrella*) stecca, *f.*; (*Bot.Arch.*) nervatura, *f.*; (*Naut.*) costa, corba, *f.*
ribald ['ribəld], *a.* Scurrile, licenzioso, scostumato, osceno.
ribaldry, *n.* Scurrilità, scostumatezza, *f.*
riband [cp. **ribbon**].
ribbed, *a.* Fatto a costole, fornito di costole; (*Arch.*) con nervatura, cordonato.
ribbon ['ribən], *n.* Nastro, *m.*; (*decoration*) nastrino, *m.*; (*shred*) brandello, straccio, *m.* **To tear to ribbons**, stracciare, fare a brandelli; (*colloq.*) **ribbons** (*reins*), redini, *m.pl.*; (*Bot.*) **—-grass**, erba nastro, *f.*; **—-weaver**, nastraio, *m.*
ribboned, *a.* Ornato di nastri.
rice [rais], *n.* Riso, *m.* **— field, —-swamp**, risaia, *f.*; **ground —**, farina di riso, *f.*; **—-pudding**, riso al latte, *m.*; **—-paper**, carta cinese, *f.*
rich [ritʃ], *a.* Ricco; fertile, fecondo; ghiotto, saporito, condito, drogato; costoso, magnifico, prezioso; dolce, delizioso, squisito. || *n.* I ricchi, *m.pl.* **A — colour**, un colore brillante, *m.*; **a — harvest**, una messe abbondante, *f.*; **to grow —**, arricchire, arricchirsi; (*colloq.*) **That's —!** Questo è buffo!
Richard ['ritʃəɹd], *n.* Riccardo, *m.*
riches, *n.pl.* Ricchezze, *f.pl.*
richly, *adv.* Molto. **He — deserves it**, l'ha proprio meritato.
richness, *n.* Ricchezza, abbondanza, copia, *f.*; fertilità, *f.*; sontuosità, opulenza, *f.*
rick (1) [rik], *n.* (*of hay*) Mucchio di fieno, pagliaio, *m.*; catasta, *f.* **—-cloth**, coperta da pagliaio, *f.*
rick (2) [cp. **wrick**].
rickets ['rikits], *n.pl.* (*Med.*) Rachitide, *f.*, rachitismo, *m.*
rickety, *a.* Rachitico; (*fig.*) malfermo, zoppicante, sconquassato, sgangherato. **A — chair**, una seggiola zoppa, *f.*
rickshaw ['rikʃɔː], *n.* Risciò, *m.*
ricochet ['rikoʃei], *n.* Rimbalzo, *m.* || *v.i.* Rimbalzare.
rid [rid], *v.t.* Liberare, disfare, sbarazzare. **To get — of**, liberarsi da, sbarazzarsi di, disfarsi di.
riddance, *n.* Liberazione, *f.*, disbrigo, *m.* **Good —!** Una bella liberazione!
riddle (1) ['ridəl], *n.* Indovinello, enigma, *m.* **To speak in riddles**, parlare enigmaticamente.
riddle (2), *v.t.* (*to sieve*) Crivellare, vagliare. || *n.* Crivello, vaglio, *m.* **To be riddled with bullets**, essere crivellato di ferite.
ride [raid], *v.i.t.* (*horse*) Cavalcare, montare; (*bicycle*) montare; (*to float*) galleggiare; andare a cavallo, passeggiare a cavallo, passeggiare in carrozza. || *n.* Passeggiata a cavallo, *m.*, cavalcata, *f.*; corsa, *f.* **To — horseback**, cavalcare, andare a cavallo; **to — in a motor-car**, andare in auto; **to — a bicycle**, andare in bicicletta; **he rode three miles**, cavalcò tre miglia; **to — full speed**, andare a gran galoppo; **to — to hounds**, dar la caccia alla volpe; (*fig.*) **to — for a fall**, andare a rompicollo; **ridden by fears**, tormentato dalla paura; (*Naut.*) **to — at anchor**, essere all'ancora; (*fig.*) **to — rough-shod over**, tiranneggiare; **to — over**, percorrere a cavallo; (*fig.*) **to — the high horse**, darsi delle grandi arie; **to — side-saddle**, montare da amazzone; (*fig.*) **to — to death**, abusare.
rider, *n.* Cavaliere, cavallerizzo, cavalcatore, *m.*; (*jockey*) fantino, *m.*; (*Math.*) corollario, *m.*; (*Law*) clausola addizionale, aggiunta, *f.*; poscritto, *m.*
ridge [ridʒ], *n.* (*mountain*) Cresta, cima, costa, *f.*, rialzo, risalto, *m.*; giogaia, catena, *f.*; (*of roof*) comignolo, colmo, *m.*; (*Agric.*) solco, *m.*, colmo, *m.*; (*between furrows*) porca, *f.* || *v.t.* (*Agric.*) Solcare, rincalzare. (*Arch.*) **—-tree, —-piece**, trave del comignolo, *f.*; **—-tile**, tegola del comignolo, *f.*
ridicule ['ridikjuːl], *n.* Ridicolo, *m.*; scherno, *m.* || *v.t.* Mettere in ridicolo, porre in ridicolo, beffeggiare. **To bring into —**, mettere in ridicolo, canzonare.
ridiculous [ri'dikjuːləs], *a.* Ridicolo.
ridiculously, *adv.* Ridicolamente.
ridiculousness, *n.* Comicità, ridicolaggine, *f.*, ridicolo, *m.*

riding ['raidiŋ], *n.* Equitazione, cavallerizza, *f.*, maneggio, *m.*; corsa, *f.* **— -breeches,** calzoni da equitazione, *m.pl.*; **— -boots,** stivali da equitazione, *m.pl.*; **— -habit,** amazzone, *f.*; **— -master,** cavallerizzo, maestro d'equitazione, *m.*; **— -school,** scuola d'equitazione, *f.*; **— -whip,** frustino, scudiscio, *m.*; **Little Red Ridinghood,** Cappuccetto Rosso, *m.*

rife [raif], *a.* Abbondante, prevalente, comune, generale; pieno di. **To be —,** imperversare; **disorder is —,** la discordia regna; **to be — with,** abbondare di.

riff-raff ['rifræf], *n.* Canaglia, ciurmaglia, plebaglia, *f.*

rifle (1) ['raifəl], *n.* Fucile, *m.*, carabina, *f.* **Rifles,** moschettieri, fucilieri, *m.pl.*; **— -range,** campo di tiro, tiro a segno, *m.*; **— shot,** colpo di fucile, *m.*, fucilata, *f.*

rifle (2), *v.t.* Svaligiare, saccheggiare, rubare; rigare.

rifleman, *n.* Bersagliere, fuciliere, *m.*

rift [rift], *n.* Fessura, fenditura, spaccatura, *f.*, spacco, *m.* **A — in the clouds,** uno spiraglio nelle nubi; (*fig.*) **a — in the lute,** un dissenso, *m.*, una divisione, *f.*

rig [rig], *v.t.* Allestire, armare, equipaggiare; guarnire. ‖ *n.* Arnese, *m.*; (*Naut.*) attrezzatura, *f.*; (*trick*) tiro, *m.* **To — oneself out,** provvedersi, fornirsi; **to — up,** allestire, impiantare; (*Comm.*) **to — the market,** controllare il mercato.

rigger ['rigəɹ], *n.* Operaio allestitore, *m.*; (*Aviat.*) montatore, *m.*

rigging ['rigiŋ], *n.* Attrezzatura, *f.*, sartiame, *m.*

right [rait], *a.* Giusto, retto, corretto, regolare; diritto, dritto; buono, conveniente; opportuno; dovuto; (*direction*) destro; (*Geom.*) retto. ‖ *adv.* Diritto, dirittamente; immediatamente, subito; tutto; proprio, bene, molto; veramente, giustamente; a destra. ‖ *n.* Diritto, *m.*; giustizia, *f.*, ragione, *f.*; (*side*) destra, *f.* ‖ *v.t.* Correggere, rettificare, raddrizzare, drizzare. **All —!** Benissimo! **Is that —?** Va bene? **— hand,** mano destra, destra, *f.*; **to the —,** a destra; **the — moment,** il momento propizio, *m.*; **Is this the — train for London?** È il treno giusto per Londra? Va bene questo treno per Londra? **to be —,** aver ragione; **to be in the —,** avere ragione, esser nel giusto; **to go the — way to work,** saper barcamenarsi; **to set —,** rettificare, raddrizzare; **to come —,** rimettersi; **a — angle,** un angolo retto, *m.*; **it is only — to tell you,** è giusto dirvi; **the — way,** il modo giusto, il modo buono, *m.*; **the — side** (*of cloth, etc.*) il dritto, *m.*; **— -minded,** retto, ben pensante; **the — time,** l'ora giusta, *f.*; **it serves him —,** se l'è meritato, ben gli sta; **Right away!** Andiamo! Via! Subito! **— off,** addirittura; **— or wrong,** bene o male, giusto o sbagliato; **to do —,** far bene; (*Mil.*) **Right-about turn!** Dietro front! **by rights,** a rigore; **in one's own —,** di proprietà assoluta; **to have a — to,** avere il diritto di; **by — of,** per diritto di; **to set to rights,** metter in ordine; **to know the rights of,** conoscere la verità di; **to — oneself,** farsi giustizia; **a fault that will — itself,** un errore che si correggerà da sè; (*Law*) **— of way,** diritto di passaggio, *m.*; **— -about,** la direzione opposta, *f.*, **to send to the — -about,** congedare senza cerimonie; **— -angled,** rettangolare.

righteous ['raitʃəs], *a.* Giusto, retto; santo, virtuoso.

righteously, *adv.* Giustamente; rettamente; santamente.

righteousness, *n.* Giustizia, rettitudine, *f.*; santità, *f.*

rightful ['raitfəl], *a.* Legittimo, vero, giusto, equo.

rightfully, *adv.* Legittimamente, veramente.

rightfulness, *n.* Legittimità, verità, giustezza, *f.*

rightly, *adv.* Bene, giustamente, con giusto titolo, correttamente.

rightness, *n.* Giustezza, rettitudine, correttezza, *f.*

rigid ['ridʒid], *a.* Rigido; severo, inflessibile.

rigidity, rigidness [ri'dʒiditi, 'ridʒidnis], *n.* Rigidezza, rigidità, *f.*; severità, inflessibilità, *f.*

rigidly, *adv.* Rigidamente.

rigmarole ['rigmərəul], *n.* Tiritera, cantilena, *f.*, guazzabuglio di parole, *m.*

rigor [raigɔːɹ], *n.* (*Med.*) Rigidità, *f.*, brividi, *m.pl.* **— mortis,** rigidità cadaverica, *f.*

rigorous ['rigərəs], *a.* Rigoroso, rigido, severo.

rigorously, *adv.* Rigorosamente.

rigour ['rigəɹ], *n.* Rigore, severità, asprezza, *f.*

rile [rail], *v.t.* (*colloq.*) Irritare, arrabbiare.

rill [ril], *n.* Ruscelletto, *m.*

rim [rim], *n.* Orlo, margine, *m.*; (*of wheel*) cerchione, quarto, *m.* ‖ *v.t.* Orlare, bordare. **— brake,** freno sul cerchione, *m.*; **— lock,** serratura a cassetta, *f.*; **— -less spectacles,** occhialini senza montatura, *m.pl.*

rime [raim], *n.* Brina, *f.* ‖ *v.t.* Brinare.

rimose, rimous ['raimouz, 'raiməs], *a.* (*Bot.*) Rimoso.

rimy ['raimi], *a.* Brinato.

rind [raind], *n.* (*of fruit*) Buccia, scorza, *f.*; (*of cheese*) crosta, *f.*; (*of bacon*) cotenna, *f.*

rinderpest ['rindəɹpest], *n.* Peste bovina, *f.*

ring (1) [riŋ], *n.* (*for finger*) Anello, *m.*; (*circle*) cerchio, circolo, *m.*; (*circus*) arena, *f.*; (*Sport*) recinto, ring, *m.*; (*of people*) gruppo, crocchio, *m.*, cricca, combriccola, *f.*; (*Comm.*) sindacato, *m.* **In a —,** in circolo; **wedding —,** anello nuziale, *m.*, vera, *f.*; **— -finger,** dito anulare, *m.*; (*Zool.*) **— -dove,** piccione selvatico, *m.*; **— -master,** direttore di circo, *m.*; **— -shaped,** anellato, circolare.

ring (2) (p. and pp. **ringed**), *v.t.* Circondare, accerchiare, cerchiare; (*bull, etc.*) mettere un anello a.

ring (3) (p. **rang,** pp. **rung**), *v.i.* Suonare, risonare; squillare; scampanellare, tinnire; *v.t.* suonare. ‖ *n.* Suono, squillo, tintinno, tintinnio, *m.*; risonanza, *f.*, sonata, *f.* **To make one's head —,** intronare il capo; **to — for dinner,** suonare per il pranzo; **to — true,** suonare vero; **to — for the chambermaid,** suonare per la cameriera, chiamare la cameriera; **to — at the door,** suonare alla porta; **the song rings in my head,** la canzone mi ronza nel capo; **to — off at the telephone,** interrompere la comunicazione; **to — up,** chiamare al telefono; **to — a bell,** suonare un campanello; **to — a coin,** far risonare una

moneta; **a — of the bell,** una sonata di campanello; **a — of bells,** un suono (*or* concerto) di campane, *m.*
ringer [ˈriŋəɹ], *n.* Campanaro, *m.*
ringing [ˈriŋiŋ], *n.* Suono, tintinno, *m.*; scampanata, *f.* || *a.* Risonante, sonoro, tinnulo. **A — in the ears,** un tintinno negli orecchi, un ronzio negli orecchi, *m.*; **a — laugh,** una risata sonora, *f.*
ringleader [ˈriŋliːdəɹ], *n.* Caporione, agitatore, *m.*
ringlet, *n.* Ricciolino, *m.*
ringworm, *n.* (*Med.*) Tigna, empetigine, *f.*
rink [riŋk], *n.* Impiantito di pattinaggio, *m.*, pista, *f.*
rinse [rins], *v.t.* Sciacquare, risciacquare. || *n.* Sciacquata, *f.*
rinsing, *n.* Sciacquatura, risciacquatura, *f.* **Rinsings,** risciacquate, *f.pl.*
riot [ˈraiət], *n.* Sommossa, sollevazione, *f.*, tumulto, *m.*; sedizione, *f.*; (*fig.*) baccano, eccesso, *m.*, orgia, *f.*; stravizio, *m.*, gozzoviglia, *f.* || *v.i.* Tumultuare, sollevarsi; gozzovigliare, far baccano, bagordare. **A — of colour,** uno splendore di colori, *m.*; **a — of emotion,** uno scoppio d'emozione, *m.*; **to run —,** dare in eccessi; (*Law*) **Riot Act,** ordine di scioglimento dato ad una folla.
rioter, *n.* Ribelle, sedizioso, rivoltoso, *m.*
riotous, *a.* Tumultuante, turbolento, sedizioso, riottoso, indocile, recalcitrante; libertino, licenzioso.
riotousness, *n.* Turbolenza, *f.*; libertinaggio, *m.*
rip [rip], *v.t.* Fendere, spaccare; squarciare, squartare, lacerare; *v.i.* squarciarsi, spaccarsi; andare a grande velocità, filar via. || *n.* Lacerazione, *f.*, squarcio, strappo, *m.*; (*colloq.*) furfante, birbante, mascalzone, *m.* **To — off,** strappare; **to — open,** sventrare, squartare, sdrucire.
riparian [raiˈpɛəriən], *a.* Rivierasco.
ripe [raip], *a.* Maturo; compiuto, perfetto, idoneo.
ripen, *v.t.i.* Maturare; maturarsi.
ripeness, *n.* Maturità, *f.*; perfezione, *f.*
ripening, *n.* Maturazione, *f.*
riposte [riˈpɔst], *n.* Risposta, *f.* || *v.t.* Rispondere, rendere colpo per colpo.
ripping, *a.* (*colloq.*) Buonissimo, eccellente, magnifico, splendido.
ripple [ˈripəl], *v.i.* Incresparsi; *v.t.* increspare. || *n.* Increspamento, *m.*; mormorio, *m.*
rise [raiz], *v.i.* (*to stand up*) Levarsi, alzarsi, sorgere, rizzarsi; (*to terminate a meeting*) separarsi, sciogliersi; salire; (*to rebel*) sollevarsi, insorgere; (*to increase*) crescere, aumentare; (*to originate*) nascere, derivare, provenire; (*of rivers, etc.*) sorgere, scaturire; (*of sun*) levarsi; (*of bread*) lievitare. || *n.* (*of sun*) Levata, *f.*; (*of ground*) salita, ascesa, elevazione, *f.*; (*of prices*) aumento, rialzo, *m.*; (*of rivers*) sorgente, origine, *m.*; (*in status*) avanzamento, progresso, *m.*, promozione, *f.*; (*of a step*) altezza di gradino, *f.*; (*of a fish*) presentarsi d'un pesce, *m.*; (*of salary*) aumento, *m.* **To — again,** risorgere; **to — from table,** levarsi da tavola; **he rises at seven o'clock,** si alza alle sette; **to — to power,** salire al potere; **Parliament rises tomorrow,** la Camera si chiude domani; **the hair rose on his head,** i capelli gli si rizzarono in testa; **my gorge rises against it,** ciò mi disgusta; **to — in price,** rincarare; **an idea rises before my mind,** un'idea mi si presenta; **to — in the world,** farsi strada, guadagnarsi una posizione nel mondo; **the wind is rising,** il vento si leva; (*Comm.*) **funds are rising,** i fondi sono in aumento; **the — of the tide,** il flusso della marea, *m.*; (*colloq.*) **to take a — out of someone,** stuzzicare qualcuno; **to give — to,** far nascere, dare origine a; **to take its —,** originare, derivare, sorgere; **a — of temperature,** un aumento di temperatura, *m.*; **a fish is rising,** un pesce viene a fior d'acqua.
riser, *n.* Chi si alza, *m.*; (*of step*) altezza d'un gradino, *f.* **An early —,** una persona mattiniera, *f.*; **a late —,** un dormiglione, *m.*; una persona che si alza tardi, *f.*
risibility [raizəˈbiliti], *n.* Risibilità, *f.*
risible, *a.* Risibile.
rising [ˈraiziŋ], *a.* Nascente, sorgente, crescente; (*fig.*) promettente. || *n.* (*of sun*) Levata, *f.*; (*of tide*) flusso, *m.*; (*of assembly*) levata, *f.*; (*rebellion*) sollevamento, *m.*, ribellione, sommossa, *f.* **The — sun,** il sole nascente, il sole levante, *m.*; **the — tide,** la marea crescente, *m.*, il flusso, *m.*; **the — generation,** la generazione, *f.*; **a — man** un uomo nuovo, un uomo che ha un avvenire, *m.*
risk [risk], *n.* Rischio, *m.* || *v.t.* Arrischiare, avventurare, azzardare. **To run a —,** correre un rischio; **at one's own —,** a proprio rischio e pericolo; **at the — of,** a rischio di.
riskiness, *n.* Pericolo, *m.*, rischiosità, *f.*
risky, *a.* Arrischiato, pericoloso, rischioso, azzardoso.
rissole [ˈrisoul], *n.* Polpetta, crocchetta, frittella, *f.*
rite [rait], *n.* Rito, *m.*, cerimonia, *f.*
ritual [ˈritjuːəl], *n.* Rituale, cerimoniale, *m.* || *a.* Rituale.
ritualist, *n.* (*Eccles.*) Ritualista, *m.f.*
rival [ˈraivəl], *n.a.* Rivale, *m.f.* || *v.t.i.* Rivaleggiare con, eguagliare.
rivalry, *n.* Rivalità, emulazione, *f.*
rive [raiv], *v.t.* Spaccare, fendere; *v.i.* fendersi.
river [ˈrivəɹ], *n.* Fiume, *m.*, riviera, *f.* || *a.* Fluviale. **Down —,** ingiù del fiume, a valle; **up —,** insù del fiume, a monte; **—-god,** deità fluviale, *f.*; **—-bank,** argine, *m.*; **—-head,** sorgente, *f.*
riverside, *n.* Riva del fiume, sponda del fiume, *f.* || *a.* Rivierasco.
rivet [ˈrivit], *n.* Chiodo ribadito, bullone, *m.* || *v.t.* Ribadire, inchiodare, ficcare; (*fig.*) concentrare, fissare.
riveting, *n.* Ribadimento, *m.*, chiodatura, ribaditura, *f.* **—-machine,** ribaditoio, *m.*
riveter, *n.* Ribaditore, *m.*
rivulet [ˈrivjuːlet], *n.* Ruscelletto, *m.*
roach [routʃ], *n.* (*Zool.*) Lasca, *f.*
road [roud], *n.* Via, strada, *f.*, cammino, *m.*; stradone, viale, *m.*; (*Naut.*) rada, *f.* **By- —,** via traversa, *f.*; **carriage- —,** strada carrozzabile, *f.*; **cross-roads,** crocicchio, *m.*, crocevia, *f.*; **high —,** strada maestra, *f.*; **on the —,** in cammino, lungo la strada; **to take the —,** mettersi in cammino; **to take to the —,** darsi alla strada; (*Naut.*) **in the roads,** in

rada; **the — to ruin,** la via della perdizione, *f.*; **the rule of the —,** il codice stradale, il codice della strada, *m.*; **— -book,** itinerario, *m.*; **— -hog,** conducente sconsiderato, *m.*; **— -mender,** cantoniere, *m.*; **— -map,** carta stradale, *f.*; **— metal,** inghiaiata, massicciata, *f.*; **— -side,** margine della strada, *m.*; *a.* sulla strada; **— -side station,** stazione di passeggio, *f.*; **— house,** locanda sulla strada, *f.*

roadster, *n.* (*Motor.*) Spyder, spider, *m.*

roadway, *n.* Via di transito, *f.*, stradale, *m.*; carreggiata, *f.*

roadworthy, *a.* Atto a prender la strada.

roam [roum], *v.i.* Errare, vagare, vagolare, ramingare, girovagare.

roamer, *n.* Vagabondo, *m.*

roan [roun], *a.* (*of horse*) Roano, rovano; (*of shoe*) uso marocchino. || *n.* (*horse*) Roano, *m.*; (*leather*) alluda, *f.*; bazzana, *f.*

roar [rɔːɹ], *n.* (*of wild beast*) Urlo, ruggito, *m.*; (*of sea*) muggito, *m.*; (*of laughter*) scroscio, *m.*; (*of thunder, etc.*) rombo, scoppio, *m.* || *v.t.* Urlare, ruggire, muggire; scrosciare, scoppiare. **To — out,** vociferare, vociare.

roaring, *a.* Ruggente; scrosciante, sonante. **To drive a — trade,** fare affaroni; **a — fire,** un bel fuoco crepitante, *m.*

roast [roust], *v.t.* (*meat*) Arrostire; (*coffee*) tostare, torrefare; (*fig.*) beffare, dileggiare. || *n.* Arrosto, *m.* || *a.* Arrostito. **— beef,** rosbif, manzo arrosto, *m.*; **— mutton,** arrosto di castrato, *m.*

roasting, *n.* Arrostimento, *m.* **— -jack,** girarrosto, *m.*

rob [rɔb], *v.t.* Rubare, derubare, spogliare, svaligiare; privare. **To — a house,** rubare in una casa; **to — someone,** rubare a qualcuno.

robber, *n.* Ladro, brigante, *m.*; masnadiero, *m.*

robbery, *n.* Ruberia, ladreria, *f.*, svaligiamento, saccheggio, *m.*; furto, *m.*; ladrocinio, *m.* **— with violence,** furto a mano armata, *m.*; **highway —,** grassazione, aggressione, *f.*

robe [roub], *n.* (*academic*) Toga, *f.*; (*woman's*) vestito da signora, *m.*, veste, *f.* || *v.t.* Vestire la toga. **Robing-room,** vestiario, *m.*

Robert [ˈrɔbəɹt], *n.* Roberto, *m.*

robin, robin redbreast [ˈrɔbin, rɔbin ˈredbrest], *n.* (*Zool.*) Pettirosso, *m.*

robot [ˈroubɔt], *n.* Automa, *m.*

robust [roˈbʌst], *a.* Robusto, forte, vigoroso, gagliardo.

robustness, *n.* Robustezza, gagliardia, *f.*

rochet [ˈrɔtʃit], *n.* (*Eccles.*) Rocchetto, roccetto, *m.*

rock (1) [rɔk], *n.* Roccia, *f.*, sasso, *m.*; rupe, balza, *f.*; scoglio, *m.*; (*sweetmeat*) specie di torrone. **To run upon a —,** urtare in uno scoglio; (*colloq.*) **to be on the rocks,** essere al verde; **— crystal,** cristallo di rocca, *m.*; **— drill,** macchina perforatrice, *f.*; **— -hewn,** scolpito nella roccia; **— -pigeon,** colomba sassarola, *f.*; **— -rose,** cisto, *m.*, imbrentina, *f.*; **— -garden,** giardino alpino, *m.*; **— -salt,** salgemma, *m.*

rock (2), *v.t.* Cullare, dondolare; *v.i.* barcollare; vacillare; oscillare. **To — oneself to and fro,** dondolarsi, cullarsi.

rocker, *n.* Dondola, culla, *f.*; basculla, *f.*

rockery, *n.* Roccia artificiale, *f.*, giardino alpino, *m.*

rocket [ˈrɔket], *n.* Razzo, *m.*; (*Bot.*) ruchetta, *f.* || *v.i.* Rimbalzare, balzare in cielo.

rockiness, *n.* Rocciosità, *f.*

rocking, *n.* Oscillazione, *f.*; dondolio, barcollamento, *m.*; vacillazione, *f.* **— -chair,** dondola, sedia a dondolo, *f.*; **— -horse,** cavallo a dondolo, *m.*; **— -stone,** roccia instabile, *f.*

rocky, *a.* Roccioso, sassoso, scoglioso. **The Rocky Mountains,** le Montagne Rocciose, *f.pl.*

rococo [roˈkoukou], *n.a.* Rococò, *m.*

rod [rɔd], *n.* Bacchetta, verga, barra, stecca, *f.*; (*curtain*) asta, *f.*; (*Mech.*) biella, *f.*; (*fishing*) canna per pescare, *f.*; (*measure of length*) pertica, *f.* **Spare the — and spoil the child,** con le buone non si ottien nulla; **I have a — in pickle for you,** ve la serbo io, vi do io una lavata di testa; (*fig.*) **to kiss the —,** prender la punizione allegramente.

rode, *p.* of **ride.**

rodent [ˈroudənt], *n.* (*Zool.*) Roditore, rosicante, *m.* || *a.* Rodente, roditore, rosicante. **A — ulcer,** un'ulcera roditrice, *f.*

rodomontade [rodomɔnˈteid], *n.* Rodomontata, spacconata, *f.*

roe [rou], *n.* Fregola, *f.* **Hard —,** uova, *f.pl.*; **soft —,** latte di pesce, *m.*

roebuck [ˈroubʌk], *n.* (*Zool.*) Capriolo, *m.*

roedeer, roe-doe, *n.* Capriola, *f.*

rogation [roˈgeiʃən], *n.* (*Eccles.*) Rogazione, *f.*

Roger [ˈrɔdʒəɹ], *n.* Ruggiero, *m.*

rogue [roug], *n.* Briccone, furfante, birbante, *m.*; (*Law*) vagabondo, *m.*; (*child*) birichino, rubacuori, *m.* **— elephant,** elefante feroce, *m.*

roguery [ˈrougəri], *n.* Bricconeria, furfanteria, birbanteria, *f.*

roguish, *a.* Furfante; furbo, malizioso, mariuolo.

roguishness, *n.* Furfanteria, *f.*; furberia, malizia, *f.*

roister [ˈrɔistəɹ], *v.i.* Far baldoria, fare il diavolo a quattro, schiamazzare.

roisterer, *n.* Schiamazzatore, *m.*

roistering, *n.* Schiamazzo, *m.*, baldoria, *f.*

Roland [ˈroulənd], *n.* Orlando, *m.* **To give a — for an Oliver,** rendere pan per focaccia.

roll [roul], *n.* (*of paper*) Rotolo, *m.*; (*list*) elenco, *m.*, lista, *f.*; (*movement of ship*) rullio, *m.*; (*of drums*) rullo, *m.*; (*of bread*) panino, *m.*; (*of sea, thunder, etc.*) mormorio, *m.*; (*record*) registro, ruolo, *m.*, archivi, *m.pl.*; (*of honour*) ruolo d'onore, *m.* || *v.t.* Rotolare, ruzzolare, voltolare, avvoltolare; rullare; (*cigarette*) arrotolare; *v.i.* rotolare, rotolarsi; rotare; ondeggiare, oscillare; rullare. **To call the —,** fare l'appello; **to strike off the rolls,** cancellare dal novero; **a — of butter,** un panetto di burro, *m.*; **to — a stone,** far ruzzolare un sasso; **to — up,** ravvolgere; **to — pastry,** spianare la pasta; **to — oneself up,** raggomitolarsi, ravvolgersi; **to — one's eyes,** storcere gli occhi, stralunare gli occhi; **to — out a song,** cantare a pieni polmoni una canzone; **to — into a ball,** aggomitolare; **the carriage rolled along,** la carrozza rotolò via; **to — away,** rotolar via; **the years — by,** gli anni scorrono; **— -call,** appello, *m.*; **— -top desk,** scrittoio americano, *m.*; (*Phot.*) **— -film camera,** macchina fotografica per pellicole su rocchetti, *f.*; **rolled gold,** oro laminato, *m.*

roller, *n.* Rullo, *m.*; cilindro, *m.*; laminatoio, *m.*; (*garden*) cilindro, *m.*; (*wave*) cavallone, *m.*; **—-skates,** pattini a rotelle, *m.pl.*; **—-skating,** pattinaggio a rotelle, *m.*; **—-towel,** bandinella, *f.*, asciugamano a rotolo, *m.*; **—-bandage,** benda arrotolata, *f.*
rollick ['rɔlik], *v.i.* Far festa, folleggiare, darsi buon tempo, gozzovigliare.
rollicking, *a.* Festoso, brioso, buontempone.
rolling ['rouliŋ], *n.* Rotolamento, *m.*; (*of ship*) rullio, *m.*; **—-mill,** laminatoio, *m.*; **—-pin,** matterello, spianatoio, *m.*; (*Rail.*) **—-stock,** materiale rotabile, *m.*; **— in wealth,** ricchissimo.
roly-poly ['rouli 'pouli], *n.* Specie di bodino fatto con marmellata.
Roman ['roumən], *a.* Romano, romanesco; (*nose*) aquilino. || *n.* Romano, *m.*, Romana, *f.*; (*Print.*) caratteri romani, *m.pl.* **— Catholic,** cattolico; **—-candle,** candela romana, *f.*
romance (1) [ro'mæns], *n.* Romanzo, idillio, *m.*; favola, *f.*; (*Mus.*) romanza, *f.* || *v.i.* Favoleggiare, inventare, esagerare. **—-writer** narratore di romanzi, romanziere, *m.*
Romance (2), *a.* Romanzo, neolatino. **— languages,** lingue romanze, lingue neolatine, *f.pl.*
romancer, *n.* Romanziere, favoleggiatore, *m.*
Romanesque [romə'nesk], *a.* Romanico.
Romansch [ro'mænʃ], *n.a.* Romanico, Retico romano, *m.*; Ladino, *m.*
Romanism ['romənizm], *n.* (*Eccles.*) Cattolicismo, *m.*
Romanist, *n.* Cattolico, *m.*
romantic [ro'mæntik], *a.* Romantico; romanzesco.
romantically, *adv.* Romanticamente.
romanticism, *n.* Romanticismo, *m.*
Romany ['roumәni], *n.a.* Zingaro, *m.*
Rome [roum], *n.* (*Geog.*) Roma, *f.*
Romish, *a.* Papistico.
romp [rɔmp], *v.i.* Ruzzare, folleggiare; far chiasso. || *n.* Trambusto, gioco chiassoso; monella chiassosa. (*colloq.*) **To — home,** vincere facilmente nella corsa.
rompers, *n.pl.* Grembiule da bambino, *m.*
rondeau ['rɔndou], *n.* (*Poet.*) Rondò, *m.*
rondo ['rɔndou], *n.* (*Mus.*) Rondò, *m.*
Röntgen rays ['rʌntjən reiz], *n.pl.* Raggi X, *m.pl.*
rood [ru:d], *n.* Crocifisso, *m.*, croce, *f.*; misura di 40 pertiche quadrate, *f.* **—-screen,** balconcino o galleria dove si esponeva il crocifisso.
roof (pl. **roofs**) [ru:f, ru:fs], *n.* Tetto, *m.*; volta, *f.*; cielo, *m.*; (*of mouth*) palato, *m.*; (*of omnibus*) imperiale, *m.* || *v.t.* Coprire con tetto, coprire, mettere il tetto a. **—-tree,** trave del comignolo, *f.*; tetto, *m.*; **—-garden,** giardino pensile, *m.*
roofing, *n.* Copertura del tetto, *f.*
roofless, *a.* Senza tetto.
rook [ruk], *n.* (*Zool.*) Cornacchia, *f.*; (*Chess*) torre, *f.*, rocco, *m.*; (*card-sharper*) baro, *m.* || *v.t.* (*colloq.*) Barrare, truffare.
rookery, *n.* Nidi di cornacchie, *m.pl.*, cornacchiaia, *f.*
room [rum], *n.* (*apartment*) Stanza, camera, sala, *f.*; (*space*) spazio, posto, *m.*; (*fig.*) luogo, agio, *m.*; motivo, *m.* **Rooms,** appartamento, *m.*; **a back —,** una camera sul retro, *f.*; **a front —,** una camera sulla strada, *f.*; **in — of,** in luogo di, in vece di; **there is no —,** non c'è posto; **it leaves — for improvement,** lascia a desiderare; **to make — for,** far posto per; **I prefer his — to his company,** non gradisco la sua compagnia; **to do a —,** fare la camera; **boiler- —,** locale caldaie, *m.*; **engine- —,** sala macchine, *f.*; **spare- —,** camera disponibile, *f.*; **Make —!** Fate luogo! **standing- — only,** soltanto posti in piedi.
roomful, *n.* Stanza piena, gente in una camera, *f.*
roominess, *n.* Spaziosità, *f.*
roomy, *a.* Spazioso, ampio, vasto.
roost [ru:st], *n.* Posatoio, pollaio, *m.* || *v.i.* Appollaiarsi, essere a pollaio. **To go to —,** andare a dormire; (*colloq.*) andare a nanna.
rooster, *n.* Gallo, *m.*
root [ru:t], *n.* (*in all senses*) Radice, *f.* || *v.t.i.* Radicare, fissare, piantare; radicarsi, abbarbicarsi, appigliarsi. **— and branch,** radicalmente, totalmente; (*Math.*) **cube —, square —,** radice cubica, radice quadrata, *f.*; **to take —,** radicarsi, abbarbicarsi, appigliarsi, metter radice; **to — out,** sradicare, estirpare; **these plants — freely,** queste piante attaccano bene; **to — about,** frugacchiare.
rooted, *a.* Radicato; profondo; inveterato. **A — objection,** una profonda ripugnanza, *f.*
rootedness, *n.* Profondità, radicatezza, *f.*
rootlet, *n.* Radicetta, radichetta, *f.*
rootstock, *n.* (*Bot.*) Rizoma, *f.*
rope [roup], *n.* Corda, fune, *f.*; cavo, *m.*; canapo, *m.*; capestro, *m.* || *v.t.* Legare, cingere con corda. **A — of pearls,** un filo di perle, *m.*, una filza di perle, *f.*; **to — up a trunk,** legare un baule; (*mountaineering*) **to — together,** fare una cordata; (*fig.*) **to know the ropes,** essere pratico e astuto, saperla lunga; **to give someone plenty of —,** dar corda a qualcuno, lasciarlo fare fino alla fine; **—-dancer,** funambolo, *m.*, funambula, *f.*; **— ladder,** scala di corda, *f.*; **—-maker,** cordaio, funaio, funaiuolo, *m.*; **—-walk,** corderia, *f.*, canapificio, *m.*; **—-walker,** funambolo, *m.*, funambola, *f.*
ropiness, *n.* Viscosità, viscidità, *f.*
ropy, *a.* Viscido, viscoso; inspessito.
rorqual ['rɔ:ɹkwæl], *n.* (*Zool.*) Balenottera, *f.*
rosaceous [ro'zeiʃəs], *a.* (*Bot.*) Rosaceo.
rosary ['rouzəri], *n.* Rosario, *m.*, corona, *f.*
rose (1) [rouz], *n.* Rosa, *f.* **Every — has its thorn,** non c'è rosa senza spine; **under the —,** segretamente; **a path strewn with roses,** un cammino sparso di rose, *m.*; **—-bed,** rosaio, roseto, *m.*; **—-bush,** rosaio, *m.*; **—-colour,** colore di rosa, rosa; **to see things through —-coloured spectacles,** veder tutto color di rosa; **—-garden,** roseto, *m.*; **—-leaf,** petalo di rosa; **—-pink,** roseo, rosato, color rosa; **—-tree,** rosaio, *m.*; **—-water,** acqua di rose, *f.*; **—-window,** rosone, *m.*
rose (2), *p.* of **rise.**
roseate ['rouziət], *a.* Rosa, rosato, roseo.
rosebud ['rouzbʌd], *n.* Bottone di rosa, *m.*
rosemary ['rouzməri], *n.* (*Bot.*) Rosmarino, *m.*
roseola [rou'zi:olə], *n.* (*Med.*) Roseola, *f.*
rosery, *n.* Roseto, *m.*
rosette [ro'zet], *n.* Rosetta, *f.*, nastrino, *m.*; coccarda, *f.*

rosewood, *n.* Legno di rosa, palissandro, *m.*
Rosicrucian [rɔzi'kru:ʃən], *n.a.* Rosacroce, *m.*
rosin ['rɔzin], *n.* Resina, ragia, *f.*; (*for stringed instruments, etc.*) colofonia, *f.* || *v.t.* Strofinare con la pece.
roster ['roustəɹ], *n.* (*Mil.*) Ruolino, *m.*; turno di servizio, *m.*
rostrum ['rɔstrəm], *n.* Tribuna, *f.*, rostro, *m.*
rosy ['rouzi], *a.* Roseo, colore di rosa, rosato.
rot [rɔt], *n.* Marciume, putridume, *m.*; carie, *f.*; (*sheep*) moria, *f.*; (*colloq.*) sciocchezze, *f.pl.* || *v.t.* Putrefare, corrompere, guastare; *v.i.* putrefarsi, corrompersi, imputridire, marcire; cariare.
rota ['routə], *n.* (*Eccles.*) Ruota, *f.*; (*Mil.*) ruolino, *m.*; lista, *f.*
rotary ['routəri], *a.* Rotatorio, rotante, girevole.
rotate [ro'teit], *v.i.t.* Rotare, roteare; (*Agric.*) avvicendare.
rotation, *n.* Rotazione, *f.*; avvicendamento, *m.*; giro, *m.*; successione, *f.* — **of crops,** avvicendamento di colture, *m.*, giro delle sementi, *m.*; **in —,** successivamente, in rotazione.
rotatory, *a.* Rotatorio.
rote [rout], *n.* **By —,** a memoria.
rotifer ['routifəɹ], *n.* (*Zool.*) Rotifero, *m.*
rotten ['rɔtən], *a.* Corrotto, putrefatto, marcio, putrido, fradicio, guasto; cariato; (*colloq.*) pessimo, spregevole, seccante.
rottenness, *n.* Corruzione, putrefazione; meschinità, *f.*
rottenstone, *n.* (*Geol.*) Tripoli, *m.*
rotter, *n.* (*colloq.*) Cialtrone, *m.*
rotting, *a.* Marcio, putrefatto, guasto.
rotund [ro'tʌnd], *a.* Rotondo, tondo.
rotunda [ro'tʌndə], *n.* Rotonda, *f.*
rotundity, *n.* Rotondità, *f.*
rouble [ru:bl], *n.* Rublo, *m.*
rouge [ru:ʒ], *n.* Belletto, rossetto, *m.* || *v.i.* Imbellettarsi; *v.t.* imbellettare. — **et noir,** trenta e quaranta.
rough [rʌf], *a.* Ruvido, scabro, aspro; rozzo, zotico, sgarbato; (*of sea, weather*) agitato, tempestoso; (*of road*) malagevole, difficile, faticoso; (*not exact*) approssimativo; violento, severo; greggio, crudo; inesperto. || *n.* Stato greggio; (*fellow*) chiasone, giovinastro sregolato, *m.*; (*Golf*) erba lunga. || *v.t.* Rendere ruvido, irruvidire. **A — diamond,** un diamante greggio, *m.*; **in the —,** abbozzato; — **and ready,** all'ingrosso, improvvisato; **a — draft,** un abbozzo, *m.*, una minuta, *f.*; **a — estimate,** una stima approssimativa, *f.*; **at a — estimate,** all'ingrosso; **to be — with,** maltrattare, trattare duramente; **to cut up —,** mostrare i denti; **a — district,** una parte turbolenta della città, *f.*; **to have a — time,** essere trattato male, soffrire disagi; **a — passage,** una traversata tempestosa; — **justice,** giustizia sommaria, *f.*; **to take the — with the smooth,** prendere il buono e il cattivo; **to — out,** abbozzare, sbozzare; **to — it,** soffrire disagi, menar vita dura, passarla grama; **—-cast,** arricciato, incalcinato; arricciatura, *f.*; **—-and-tumble,** zuffa, mischia, rissa, baruffa, *f.* **to —-hew,** digrossare, sbozzare; **—-rider,** domatore di cavalli, scozzone, cavallerizzo, *m.*; **—-shod,** ferrato a ghiaccio; **to ride —-shod over,** calpestare, passare sul corpo di; **—-spoken,** aspro, ruvido nel parlare.
roughen, *v.t.* Rendere ruvido, irruvidire; disordinare, arruffare; *v.i.* agitarsi, ingrossarsi; irruvidirsi.
roughness, *n.* Ruvidezza, scabrosità, *f.*; rozzezza, villania, sgarbatezza, *f.*; agitazione, burrascosità, *f.*; malagevolezza, *f.*; sprezza, severità, *f.*
round [raund], *a.* Tondo, rotondo; circolare, sferico; (*fig.*) compiuto, perfetto, intiero. || *adv.* In giro, in cerchio; attorno, intorno. || *prep.* Intorno a, nei dintorni di. || *n.* Tondo, cerchio, circolo, *m.*, sfera, circonferenza, *f.*; (*movement*) giro, *m.*; (*of ladder*) scalino, *m.*; (*of applause*) salva, *f.*, scoppio, *m.*; (*of ammunition*) caricatore, *m.*; (*slice*) fetta, *f.*; (*tour*) giro, *m.*; (*Sport*) partita, volta, *f.*; (*Boxing*) ripresa, *f.*, assalto, *m.* || *v.t.i.* Arrotondare; doppiare, andare in giro. **In — numbers,** in cifra tonda; — **cheeks,** guancie paffute, *f.pl.*; — **robin,** petizione con le firme poste in cerchio, *f.*; **a — game,** giuoco in circolo, *m.*; — **dance,** ballo tondo, *m.*; **all —,** tutto attorno, per tutti; **all the year —,** durante tutto l'anno; **six feet —,** sei piedi di giro; **to sleep the clock —,** dormire dodici ore; **to win —,** guadagnare il favore di; **to get —,** persuadere, mettersi d'accordo, piegarsi; **to come —,** riaversi, rimettersi; **a long way —,** un lungo giro, *m.*; **to show someone —,** portare uno in giro; **we went — the park,** facemmo il giro del parco; **seated — the table,** seduti intorno alla tavola; **a — of beef,** una rotella di manzo, *f.*; **a — of toast,** un crostino, *m.*; **the doctor is on his rounds,** il dottore è in giro; **to — off,** completare, perfezionare; **to — up cattle,** riunire il bestiame; **to — a cape,** doppiare un capo; (*colloq.*) **to — on,** denunciare; **—-hand,** calligrafia rotonda, *f.*; **—-up,** raduno, *m.*, accolta, *f.*
roundabout ['raundəbaut], *a.* Indiretto, obliquo, storto. || *n.* Giostra, carosella, *f.*; (*traffic*) senso giratorio, *m.*
roundelay ['raundilei], *n.* Canzonetta, *f.*
rounders, *n.pl.* Specie di giuoco alla palla.
Roundhead, *n.* (*Hist.*) Puritano inglese del Seicento, *m.*
roundish, *a.* Rotondetto, tondetto.
roundly, *adv.* (*fig.*) Francamente, chiaro e tondo.
roundness, *n.* Tondezza, rotondità, *f.*
roundsman ['raundzmən], *n.* Distributore, fattorino, *m.*
roup [ru:p], *n.* Pipita, *f.*
rouse [rauz], *v.t.* Svegliare, destare; provocare, eccitare, suscitare; *v.i.* svegliarsi, destarsi.
rousing, *a.* Eccitante, stimolante, animatore. **A — cheer,** un'ovazione travolgente, *f.*
rout [raut], *n.* Folla, *f.*; tumulto, *m.*; sommossa, *f.*; sconfitta, *f.*; (*obs.*) riunione, *f.* || *v.t.* Sconfiggere, sbaragliare, vincere, mettere in fuga. **To put to —,** sconfiggere; **to — out,** scavare, scoprire; buttar fuori.
route [ru:t], *n.* Via, rotta, direzione strada, *f.*, itinerario, *m.*; cammino, viaggio, *m.* || *v.t.* Avviare, incamminare. **—-march,** marcia di addestramento, *f.*
routine [ru:'ti:n], *n.* Uso, *m.*, abitudine, usanza, *f.* || *a.* D'uso, abitudinario.

rove (1) [rouv], *v.i.* Errare, vagare, vagolare, andare ramingo, girovagare.
rove (2), *v.t.* Infilare, torcere il filo.
rover, *n.* Girovago, vagabondo, *m.*; pirata, corsaro, *m.*
roving, *a.* Errante, vagabondo, ramingo.
row (1) [rau], *n.* Chiasso, rumore, strepito, *m.*; tafferuglio, *m.*, baruffa, lite, *f.* (*colloq.*) **To kick up a —,** fare una lite.
row (2) [rou], *n.* Fila, riga, *f.*; (*of trees*) filare, *m.*; riga, fila, *f.*, rango, *m.*; (*Knitting*) giro, *m.* **In a —,** in fila; **in rows,** in file.
row (3) [rou], *v.i.t.* Remare, vogare. ‖ *n.* Escursione in barca, remata, *f.* **To — a boat,** remare; **to go for a —,** andare in barca; **— -boat, rowing- —,** barca, *f.*, canotto a remi, *m.*
rowan [ˈrouən, ˈrauən], *n.* (*Bot.*) Frassino di montagna, *m.*
rowdiness [ˈraudinis], *n.* Turbolenza, *f.*
rowdy [ˈraudi], *a.* Tumultuoso, turbolento, scalmanato, facinoroso. ‖ *n.* Teppista, *m.*
rowdyism [ˈraudiizm], *n.* Teppismo, *m.*
rowel [ˈrauəl], *n.* Rotella, spronella, *f.*
rower [ˈrouəɹ], *n.* Rematore, canottiere, *m.*
rowing [ˈrouiŋ], *n.* Canottaggio, *m.* **— -club,** circolo dei canottieri, *m.*; **— -match,** gara di canottaggio, *f.*
rowlock [ˈrʌlək], *n.* Scalmo, *m.*, scalmiera, *f.*
royal [ˈrɔiəl], *a.* Reale, regale, regio. ‖ *n.* (*Naut.*) Controvelaccio, *m.* **His Royal Highness,** sua Altezza Reale, *f.*; **a battle —,** mischia, zuffa, baruffa.
royalist, *n.* Realista, *m.f.*
royally, *adv.* Regalmente.
royalty, *n.* (*persons*) I reali, *m.pl.*; (*royalness*) regalità, *f.*; dignità reale, *f.*; (*author's*) diritti d'autore, *m.pl.*; (*rent*) diritto, censo, *m.*
rub [rʌb], *v.t.* Fregare, sfregare, strofinare, stropicciare; (*inscriptions*) improntare; (*Med.*) far frizioni a. ‖ *n.* Fregamento, strofinamento, stropicciamento, *m.*; (*Med.*) frizione, *f.*; (*fig.*) pasticcio, impiccio, *m.* **To — shoulders with, to — up against,** venire in contatto con; **to — up the wrong way,** offendere, andar contrappelo a; **to — out,** cancellare; **to — in,** frizionare con, (*fig.*) imprimere; **to — along,** campare, tirare avanti; **to — down a horse,** strigliare un cavallo; **to — off,** cancellare; **there's the —,** qui sta il busillis, qui sta il punto.
rubber, *n.* Gomma, *f.*, caucciù, *m.*; (*Cards*) partita, *f.*; fregatore, *m.* **Indiarubber,** gomma elastica, *f.*; **— heels,** salvatacchi, *m.pl.*; **— -stamp,** stampino di gomma, *m.*; **— -tyre,** pneumatico, *m.*
rubbing, *n.* Fregamento, sfregamento, *m.*; (*Med.*) frizione, *f.*
rubbish [ˈrʌbiʃ], *n.* Immondizia, *f.*, sudiciume, *m.*; robaccia, roba di scarto, *f.*; (*fig.*) sciocchezze, corbellerie, *f.pl.* **Good riddance to bad —,** un buon repulisti, *m.*; **— -cart,** carro della spazzatura, *m.*
rubbishy, *a.* Senza valore, di scarto; infimo, stupido.
rubble [ˈrʌbəl], *n.* Pietrisco, *m.*, pietrame grezzo, *m.* **— work,** costruzione a secco, *f.*
rubicund [ˈru:bikənd], *a.* Rubicondo.
rubric [ˈru:brik], *n.* Rubrica, *f.*
rubricate [ˈru:brikeit], *v.t.* Rubricare.
ruby [ˈru:bi], *n.* Rubino, *m.* ‖ *a.* Di rubino, vermiglio. **— lips,** labbra vermiglie, *f.pl.*
ruche [ru:ʃ], *n.* Gala, *f.*
ruck (1) [rʌk], *n.* Gregge, *m.*, folla, *f.*
ruck (2), *n.* Grinza, piega, *f.* ‖ *v.i.* Raggrinzarsi, corrugarsi.
rucksack [ˈruksæk], *n.* Sacco da montagna, zaino, *m.*
rudder [ˈrʌdəɹ], *n.* Timone, *m.*
ruddiness [ˈrʌdinis], *n.* Rossezza, floridezza, freschezza, *f.*
ruddy, *a.* Rosso, fresco, florido, rubizzo, vermiglio.
rude [ru:d], *a.* Rozzo, rude, informe, grossolano; semplice, primitivo; scortese, villano, incivile; duro, severo, aspro; (*of health*) robusto. **A — awakening,** un crudele disinganno, *m.*
rudely, *adv.* Rozzamente, grossolanamente.
rudeness, *n.* Rozzezza, grossolanità, *f.*; scortesia, villania, inciviltà, *f.*; semplicità, *f.*; durezza, severità, *f.*
rudiment [ˈru:dimənt], *n.* Rudimento, *m.* **Rudiments,** elementi, *m.pl.*
rudimentary, *a.* Rudimentale.
rue (1) [ru:], *v.t.* Pentirsi di, rammaricarsi di, deplorare.
rue (2), *n.* (*Bot.*) Ruta, *f.*
rueful, *a.* Triste, malinconico, afflitto, dolente, addolorato.
ruefully, *adv.* Malinconicamente.
ruefulness, *n.* Tristezza, afflizione, *f.*
ruff [rʌf], *n.* Gorgiera, *f.*
ruffian [ˈrʌfiən], *n.* Furfante, ribaldo, scellerato, *m.*; ruffiano, *m.*
ruffianism, *n.* Scelleratezza, ribalderia, malvagità, *f.*
ruffianly, *a.* Scellerato, malvagio, brutale.
ruffle [rʌfl], *n.* (*dress*) Manicotto, *m.*, gala, *f.*; (*on water*) crespa, *f.*, crespamento, *m.* ‖ *v.t.* (*on water*) Increspare; (*hair*) arruffare; (*fig.*) turbare, agitare, irritare; *v.i.* vantarsi, fare il fanfarone.
rufous [ˈru:fəs], *a.* Rosso, rosso di capelli.
rug [rʌg], *n.* (*on floor*) Tappeto, tappetino, *m.*; (*travelling*) coperta da viaggio, *f.*; (*bedside*) scendiletto, *m.*
Rugby football [rʌgbiˈfutbɔ:l], *n.* (*game*) Giuoco del pallone ovale, *m.*; (*ball*) palla ovale, *f.*
rugged [ˈrʌgid], *a.* (*uneven*) Ineguale, ruvido, scabro; aspro, rozzo; austero, severo. **— features,** fattezze rudi, *f.pl.*; **— honesty,** rozza onestà, *f.*
ruggedness, *n.* Inegualità, ruvidezza, scabrosità, *f.*; asprezza, rozzezza, *f.*; austerità, *f.*
rugose [ˈru:gouz], *a.* (*Zool.Bot.*) Rugoso.
rugosity, *n.* Rugosità, *f.*
ruin [ˈru:in], *n.* Rovina, *f.*; disgrazia, *f.*; crollo, disastro, *m.*; rudero, *m.* ‖ *v.t.* Rovinare. **To go to —,** andare in rovina; **to lie in ruins,** stare in rovina; **to bring to —,** cagionar la rovina di, mandare in rovina.
ruination, *n.* Rovina, *f.*
ruinous, *a.* Rovinato, diroccato, fracassato; disastroso, rovinoso, dannoso. **To prove — to,** essere rovinoso per.
ruinousness, *n.* Rovina, *f.*; dannosità, *f.*
rule [ru:l], *n.* Regola, formula, massima, *f.*; governo, dominio, impero, potere, *m.*; (*instrument*) regolo, *m.*, riga, *f.*; (*Print.*)

filetto, *m.* || *v.t.* Regolare; dirigere, governare, reggere; rigare; (*Law*) decidere; *v.i.* regnare. **As a —,** generalmente, d'ordinario; **— of thumb,** regola empirica, *f.*; (*Math.*) **— of three,** regola del tre, *f.*; **by —,** secondo le regole; **hard and fast —,** formula prescritta, *f.*; **— of the road,** regolamento stradale, *m.*

ruler, *n.* Re, sovrano, governatore, dominatore, *m.*; (*for measuring, etc.*) riga, *f.*, regolo, *m.*

ruling, *a.* Dominante, dirigente. || *n.* Rigatura, *f.*; (*Law*) decisione, *f.*

rum (1) [rʌm], *n.* Rum, *m.* **— -punch,** ponce al rum, *m.*

rum (2), *a.* (*colloq.*) Strano, strambo, bizzarro, originale.

Rumania, Roumania [ru:ˈmeiniə], *n.* (*Geog.*) Romania, Rumenia, *f.*

rumble (1) [rʌmbl], *v.i.* Rimbombare, rintronare, risuonare, rumoreggiare; (*of bowels*) gorgogliare. || *n.* Rimbombo, rumore.

rumble (2), *n.* Sedile posteriore di una carrozza, *m.*

rumbling, *n.* Rimbombo, rumorio, *m.* || *a.* Rimbombante, risonante.

ruminant [ˈru:minənt], *n.* (*Zool.*) Ruminante, *m.* || *a.* Ruminante; (*fig.*) meditabondo, pensieroso.

ruminate, *v.i.* Ruminare; meditare. **To — on,** mulinare, meditare su.

rumination, *n.* Ruminazione, *f.*; elucubrazione, meditazione, *f.*

rummage [ˈrʌmidʒ], *v.t.i.* Frugare in, frugacchiare in, rovistare. || *n.* Frugata, *f.*, rovistio, *m.* **— -sale,** vendita di roba usata, *f.*

rummer [ˈrʌməɹ], *n.* Bicchierone, *m.*, tazza, *f.*

rumour [ˈru:məɹ], *n.* Diceria, voce, *f.*; rumore, *m.* || *v.t.* Far correre voce, sparger notizia. **There is a —,** corre voce, si dice; **it is rumoured that,** corre voce che, si dice che.

rump [rʌmp], *n.* Culatta, groppa, *f.*; (*colloq.*) culo, deretano, *m.*; (*of bird*) codione, *m.* **— -steak,** romstek, *m.*

rumple [rʌmpl], *v.t.* Raggrinzare, sgualcire, accartocciare, arruffare, scompigliare.

rumpus [ˈrʌmpəs], *n.* (*colloq.*) Chiasso, rumore, strepito, *m.*; tafferuglio, *m.*, baruffa, *f.*; scandalo, *m.*

run [rʌn], *v.i.t.* Correre, fuggire; (*to extend*) stendersi; (*of water*) scorrere, colare, fluire; (*to melt*) fondere, struggersi; (*of eyes*) piangere, lagrimare; (*of wounds*) suppurare; (*of machine*) funzionare; (*of colour*) spandere; (*sewing*) imbastire; colare, versare, gocciolare, stillare; condurre, tenere, esercire. || *n.* Corsa, *f.*, corso, *m.*; traversata, *f.*, viaggio, *m.*; (*Mus.*) fioritura, *f.*; serie, *f.*, seguito, *m.*; gita, *f.*; ritmo, *m.*; voga, durata, domanda, *f.* **To — across,** traversare correndo, incontrare, imbattersi in; **to — after,** correr dietro, perseguire; **to — against,** incontrare; **to — up against,** aver disaccordo con; **to — at,** correre su, attaccare, precipitarsi su; **to — into debt,** indebitarsi; **to — into,** urtare, investire, incontrare; **the book ran into five editions,** il libro raggiùnse la quinta edizione; **to — on,** continuare, occuparsi di; **to — over,** (*of liquid*) traboccare, (*of vehicle*) investire, (*peruse*) scorrere, percorrere; **to — through,** (*examine*) scorrere, percorrere, (*money*) consumare, scialacquare, (*with sword*) trafiggere; **to — to,** arrivare a, (*amount*) raggiungere, (*of money*) bastare per; **to — to seed,** sementire, far seme; **to — about,** correre qua e là; **to — away,** fuggire, scappare; **to — away with,** rapire, consumare; **to — away with an idea,** mettersi un'idea nella testa; **to — down,** (*of vehicle*) investire, (*of clock*) fermarsi, (*to disparage*) parlar male di, (*to track*) trovare il nascondiglio di; **to — out of,** esaurire, finire; **to — up,** montare, far montare, rincarare; **to — for Parliament,** farsi portar deputato; **the ship runs before the wind,** la nave fugge dinanzi alla tempesta; **that tune runs in my head,** quel motivo mi torna sempre in mente; **the contract runs for three years,** il contratto è valido per tre anni; **the play ran a month,** la commedia venne data per un mese; **inquisitiveness runs in the family,** la curiosità è una caratteristica della famiglia; **the bus runs between the two towns,** l'autobus fa la spola fra le due città; **to — one's eyes over something,** scorrere qualcosa; **feeling ran high,** si riscaldarono molto; **it makes one's blood — cold,** fa rabbrividire; **to — dry,** esaurirsi; **to — to extremes,** andare troppo oltre; **prices — high,** i prezzi aumentano; **the disease must — its course,** la malattia deve fare il suo corso; **to — someone close,** esser vicino a vincere qualcuno; **she runs the shop herself,** essa stessa dirige il negozio; **to — a horse,** far correre un cavallo; **she ran a needle into her finger,** si infilzò un ago nel dito; **a — on the bank,** un assedio alla banca, *m.*; **on the —,** in fuga; **at a —,** correndo; **a — of luck,** un seguito di successi, *m.*; **in the long —,** a lungo andare; **the play had a long —,** la commedia ebbe lungo successo; **he has the — of my house,** ha libero accesso alla mia casa; **to — the risk,** correre il rischio; **to — riot,** fare il diavolo a quattro.

runabout [ˈrʌnəbaut], *n.* (*Motor.*) Vetturetta, *f.*; discolo, *m.*, discola, *f.*

runaway, *n.* Fuggitivo, fuggiasco, disertore, *m.* **A — match,** un matrimonio clandestino, *m.*; **a — horse,** un cavallo in fuga, *m.*

rune [ru:n], *n.* Runa, *f.*; carattere runico, *m.*

rung [rʌŋ], *n.* Piuolo, *m.*

runlet [ˈrʌnlet], *n.* Ruscello, *m.*

runnel [ˈrʌnl], *n.* Ruscelletto, rigagnolo, *m.*

runner [ˈrʌnəɹ], *n.* (*Sport*) Corridore, *m.*; (*messenger*) fattorino, messaggero, *m.*; (*tout*) piazzista, *m.*; (*millstone*) macina superiore, *f.*; (*Bot.*) tralcio, pollone, rampollo, *m.*; (*bean*) fagiuolo rampicante, *m.*; (*of sledge*) chiglia, *f.*, pattino, *m.* **Scarlet —,** fagiuolo rampicante, fagiuolo di Spagna, *m.*; **— -up,** il secondo in una gara, *m.*

running, *n.* Corsa, *f.*, corso, *m.*; rincorsa, *f.*; marcia, *f.*; funzionamento, *m.* || *a.* Corrente, consecutivo; scorsoio; scorrente, colante. **To make the —,** correre nella corsa, succedere; battere il passo; **out of the —,** fuori gara; **three days —,** tre giorni consecutivi; **a — jump,** un salto con rincorsa, *m.*; (*Radio*) **a — commentary,** una cronaca radiofonica, *f.*; **— fire,** fuoco a volontà, fuoco continuo, *m.*; (*Motor.*) **— -board,** montatoio, *m.*; (*Mech.*) **— gear,** parti mobili di una macchina, *f.pl.*; **— hand,** corsivo carattere, *m.*

runt [rʌnt], *n.* Animale nano; (*fig.*) omiciattolo, *m.*
runway [ˈrʌnwei], *n.* (*Aviat.*) Pista di decollo, pista di lancio, *f.*
rupee [ru:ˈpi:], *n.* Rupia, *f.*
rupture [ˈrʌptʃəɹ], *n.* Rottura, *f.*; (*Med.*) ernia, *f.* ‖ *v.t.* Rompere. **To be ruptured,** avere un'ernia.
rural [ˈru:rəl], *a.* Rurale, campestre.
ruralize [ˈru:rəlaiz], *v.t.* Ruralizzare.
ruse [ru:z], *n.* Artificio, trucco, stratagemma, *m.*
rush (1) [rʌʃ], *n.* (*Bot.*) Giunco, *m.* **It is not worth a —,** non vale un fico; **—-light,** lumicino, *m.*; **—-chair,** sedia impagliata, *f.*
rush (2), *n.* Impeto, *m.*, fretta, furia, ressa, *f.*; slancio, *m.*; trambusto, traffico, *m.*; assalto, attacco, *m.*; corsa impetuosa, *f.* ‖ *v.i.* Precipitarsi, accorrere, affrettarsi, slanciarsi, avventarsi; *v.t.* spingere, indurre, stimolare; (*colloq.*) far pagare. **There was a — for the front seats,** ci fu grande ricerca pei primi posti; **the — hours,** le ore di punta, le ore di maggior traffico, *f.pl.*; **a — of blood to the head,** congestione cerebrale, *f.*; **to — down,** precipitarsi giù.
rushing, *a.* Impetuoso, furioso, precipitoso.
rusk [rʌsk], *n.* Biscotto, *m.*
russet [ˈrʌsit], *a.* Rossiccio, rossetto. ‖ *n.* (*colour*) rossetto, *m.*; (*apple*) ranetta, *f.*
Russia [ˈrʌʃə], *n.* (*Geog.*) Russia, *f.* **— leather,** cuoio di Russia, *m.*
Russian [ˈrʌʃən], *n.a.* Russo, *m.*
rust [rʌst], *n.* Ruggine, *f.* ‖ *v.i.t.* Arrugginire, arrugginirsi.
rustic [ˈrʌstik], *a.* Rustico, campagnuolo, rurale, agreste. ‖ *n.* Contadino, zoticone, *m.*
rusticate [ˈrʌstikeit], *v.i.* Villeggiare, vivere in campagna; *v.t.* sospendere per cattiva condotta, espellere.
rustication, *n.* Sospensione, espulsione, relegazione, *f.*
rusticity [rʌsˈtisiti], *n.* Rustichezza, rusticità, *f.*
rustiness [ˈrʌstinis], *n.* Rugginosità, *f.*
rustle [rʌsl], *v.i.* Frusciare; stormire; far fruscio. ‖ *n.* Fruscio, stormire, mormorio, *m.*
rustler, *n.* Rubatore di bestiame, *m.*
rustless, *a.* Inossidabile.
rustling, *a.* Frusciante, sussurrante.
rusty, *a.* Rugginoso; antiquato; (*of voice*) rauco. **My Italian is rather —,** il mio Italiano non è forbito; **to get —,** irrugginire.
rut (1) [rʌt], *n.* Carreggiata, *f.*; rotaia, *f.*; solco, *m.*; scanalatura, *f.* ‖ *v.t.* Solcare.
rut (2), *n.* (*of animals*) Frega, *f.*, calore, *m.*
ruthless [ˈru:θles], *a.* Spietato, crudele, implacabile, inesorabile.
ruthlessness, *n.* Spietatezza, crudeltà, *f.*
rye [rai], *n.* (*Bot.*) Segala, *f.* **—-bread,** pan di segala, *m.*; **— grass,** spelta, *f.*, loglio, *m.*

S

S, s [es], Diciannovesima lettera dell'alfabeto inglese.
sabbatarian [sæbəˈtɛəriən], *n.a.* Sabatario, sabatino, *m.*
sabbatarianism, *n.* Sabateismo, *m.*
sabbath [ˈsæbəθ], *n.* (*Jewish*) Sabato, *m.*; (*Christian*) domenica, *f.* **—-breaker,** violatore del sabato, *m.*
sabbatic, sabbatical [sæˈbætik, səˈbætikəl] *a.* Sabatico. **— year,** ogni settimo anno, anno di riposo, *m.*
sable [ˈseibəl], *n.* (*Zool.*) Zibellino, *m.*; (*fur*) zibellino, *m.*; (*Heraldry*) nero; (*fig.*) abito di lutto, *m.* ‖ *a.* Di zibellino; (*fig.*) nero.
sabotage [sæbəˈtɑ:ʒ], *n.* Sabotaggio, *m.* ‖ *v.t.* Sabotare.
sabre [ˈseibəɹ], *n.* Sciabola, *f.* ‖ *v.t.* Sciabolare. **—-cut,** sciabolata, *f.*
sabretache [ˈsæbəɹtæʃ], *n.* (*Mil.*) Borsetta, *f.*
sac [sæk], *n.* (*Anat.*) Sacco, *m.*
sacchariferous [sækəˈrifərəs], *a.* Saccarifero.
saccharify [ˈsækərifai], *v.t.* Saccarificare.
saccharimeter [sækəˈrimitəɹ], *n.* Saccarimetro, *m.*
saccharine [ˈsækərin], *n.* Saccarina, *f.* ‖ *a.* Saccarino.
sacciform [ˈsæksifɔ:ɹm], *a.* A forma di sacco.
sacerdotal [sæsəɹˈdoutəl], *a.* Sacerdotale.
sacerdotalism, *n.* Pretismo, clericalismo, *m.*
sachet [ˈsæʃei], *n.* Sacchetto, *m.*; cuscinetto di profumi, *m.*
sack (1) [sæk], *n.* Sacco, *m.* (*colloq.*) **To get the —,** essere licenziato; **to give the — to,** licenziare, mandare a spasso; **—-race,** corsa nel sacco, *f.*
sack (2), *n.* Saccheggio, *m.* ‖ *v.t.* Rubare, saccheggiare.
sack (3), *n.* Vino bianco, *m.*
sackcloth, *n.* Tela da sacco, *f.* **In — and ashes,** in cilicio, con aria penitente.
sackful, *n.* Saccata, *f.*
sacking, *n.* Tela da sacco, *f.*
sacral [ˈseikrəl], *a.* (*Anat.*) Sacro.
sacrament [ˈsækrəmənt], *n.* Sacramento, *m.* **To receive the —,** ricevere i sacramenti.
sacramental [sækrəˈmentəl], *n.a.* Sacramentale, *m.*
sacramentarian, sacramentary, *n.* (*Hist.*) Sacramentario, *m.*
sacrarium [səˈkrɛəriəm], *n.* (*Eccles.*) Sacrario, *m.*
sacred [ˈseikred], *a.* Sacro, consacrato; inviolabile; santo. **— to,** sacro a.
sacredly, *adv.* Sacramente.
sacredness, *n.* Santità, inviolabilità, *f.*
sacrifice [ˈsækrifais], *v.t.i.* Sacrificare; immolare; abbandonare. ‖ *n.* Sacrificio, *m.*, offerta, *f.* **To sell at a —,** vendere con perdita.
sacrificial [sækriˈfiʃəl], *a.* Di sacrificio, espiatorio.
sacrilege [ˈsækriledʒ], *n.* Sacrilegio, *m.*
sacrilegious, *a.* Sacrilego.
sacristan [ˈsækristən], *n.* Sagrestano, *m.*
sacristy, *n.* Sagrestia, *f.*
sacrosanct [ˈsækrosæŋkt], *a.* Sacrosanto.
sacrum [ˈseikrəm], *n.* (*Anat.*) Sacro, osso sacro, *m.*
sad [sæd], *a.* Triste, mesto, malinconico, addolorato, afflitto; doloroso, pietoso; (*to be pitied*) penoso; (*Cooking*) grave, pesante; (*of colour*) oscuro; (*fig.*) matricolato, incorreggibile. **To grow —,** attristarsi, rattristarsi; **he is a — coward,** è un vero vigliacco.
sadden, *v.t.* Attristare, rattristare; *v.i.* attristarsi, rattristarsi.
saddle [sædl], *n.* Sella, *f.*; (*mountain*) cresta, giogaia, *f.*; gola, *f.* ‖ *v.t.* Sellare, accollare a, appioppare a. **In the —,** in sella; **to put the — on the wrong horse,** dare la colpa ad

altri; **to — with a responsibility**, accollare una responsabilità a; **—-bag**, bisaccia, *f.*, tascapane, *m.*; **—-bow**, arcione, *m.*; **—-cloth**, gualdrappa, *f.*; **—-horse**, cavallo da sella, *m.*; **—-room**, selleria, *f.*; **—-tree**, fusto della sella.

saddlebacked, *a.* Sellato.

saddler, *n.* Sellaio, *m.*

saddlery, *n.* Selleria, *f.*

Sadducee [ˈsædjuːsiː], *n.* Sadduceo, *m.*

sadly, *adv.* Tristemente, dolorosamente.

sadness, *n.* Tristezza, *f.*

safe [seif], *a.* Salvo, sicuro, fuori di pericolo; sano, intero, intatto, incolume. ‖ *n.* Cassaforte, *f.*; (*for food*) guardavivande, *m.* **It is not — to touch it**, è pericoloso toccarlo; **— and sound**, sano e salvo; **— from harm**, al sicuro, sicuro da pericolo; **in — custody**, sotto buona guardia; al sicuro, sotto chiave; **to be on the — side**, essere al sicuro, essere a scanso di pericoli; **it is — to say**, si può dire con sicurezza; **—-conduct**, salvacondotto, *m.*; **—-keeping**, custodia, sicurezza, *f.*; **—-deposit**, camera di sicurezza, *f.*

safeguard, *n.* Salvaguardia, *f.* ‖ *v.t.* Salvaguardare; proteggere.

safely, *adv.* In salvo, felicemente; con sicurezza, senza pericolo.

safeness, *n.* Salvezza, sicurezza, *f.*

safety [ˈseifti], *n.* Sicurezza, salvezza, *f.*, salvamento, *m.* **Public —**, sicurezza pubblica, *f.*; **to play for —**, giuocare al sicuro; **—-lamp**, lampada di sicurezza, *f.*; **—-match**, fiammifero svedese, *m.*; **—-belt**, cintura di salvataggio, *f.*; **—-catch**, dente d'arresto, *m.*; sicura, *f.*; **—-curtain**, sipario di sicurezza, *m.*; **—-pin**, spillo di sicurezza, *m.*; **—-razor**, rasoio di sicurezza, *m.*; **—-valve**, valvola di sicurezza, *f.*

safflower [ˈsæflauɹ], *n.* (*Bot.*) Cartamo, *m.*

saffron [ˈsæfrən], *n.* (*Bot.*) Zafferano, *m.* ‖ *a.* Color zafferano.

sag [sæg], *v.i.* Cedere, ripiegarsi, ricascare; penzolare; abbassarsi. ‖ *n.* Depressione, insellatura, *f.*

saga [ˈsɑːgə], *n.* (*Lit.*) Saga, *f.*

sagacious [səˈgeiʃəs], *a.* Sagace, accorto, scaltro.

sagaciousness, sagacity [səˈgeiʃəsnis, səˈgæsiti], *n.* Sagacia, sagacità, *f.*

sage (1) [seidʒ], *n.* (*Bot.*) Salvia, *f.*

sage (2), *a.* Savio, saggio, prudente. ‖ *n.* Savio, *m.*

sagging, *a.* Cascante, spiegazzato. ‖ *n.* Abbassamento, *m.*

Sagittarius [sædʒiˈtɛəriəs], *n.* (*Astron.*) Sagittario, *m.*

sago [ˈseigou], *n.* (*Bot.*) Sagù, sago, *m.* **—-palm**, palma di sagù, *f.*

said [sed], *n.* Detto, suddetto, sopradetto, *m.*

sail [seil], *n.* Vela, *f.*; viaggio per mare, *m.*; (*of windmill*) ala, *f.*; (*fig.*) bastimento, *m.* ‖ *v.i.* Navigare, veleggiare, salpare; partire, imbarcarsi; *v.t.* navigare, correre, percorrere. **To go for a —**, andare in gita sull'acqua; **a day's — from Naples**, un viaggio d'un giorno da Napoli; **to set —**, salpare, imbarcarsi; **to strike —**, ammainare; **under —**, sotto vela; **to shorten —**, terzaruolare; **to crowd —**, spiegar le vele; **to lower —**, calare le vele; **to hoist —**, issare le vele; **to — along the coast**, costeggiare; **to — close to the wind**, serrare il vento, orzare, (*fig.*) rasentare il precipizio; **—-cloth**, tela da vele, *f.*; **—-maker**, velaio.

sailable, *a.* Navigabile.

sailer, *n.* Veliero, *m.*, nave a vela, *f.*

sailing, *n.* Navigazione, *f.*; imbarco, *m.*; partenza, *f.* ‖ *a.* A vela, veliero. **—-boat**, barca a vela, *f.*; **—-ship**, nave a vela, *f.*, veliero, *m.*

sailor, *n.* Marinaio, *m.* **To be a good —**, non soffrire il mal di mare; **—-suit**, costume da marinaio, *m.*; **—-hat**, cappello alla marinara, *m.*

sainfoin [ˈseinfɔin], *n.* (*Bot.*) Lupinello, *m.*, cedrangolo, *f.*

saint [seint], *n.* Santo, *m.*, santa, *f.* ‖ *a.* Santo. **All Saints' Day**, l'Ognissanti, *m.*; **a saint's day**, una festa, *f.*; **St. John's wort**, erba di San Giovanni, *f.*; **St. Vitus's dance**, ballo di San Vito, *m.*, corea, *f.*; **St. Bernard dog**, cane di San Bernardo, *m.*

sainted, *a.* Santo, sacro, canonizzato.

sainthood, saintship, *n.* Santità, *f.*

saintliness, *n.* Santità, *f.*

saintly, *a.* Santo, esemplare, pio, devoto.

sake [seik], *n.* Causa, ragione, *f.*; riguardi, amore, *m.* **For my —**, per amor mio; **for conscience's —**, per scrupolo, per scrupolo di coscienza; **for all our sakes**, nell'interesse di tutti noi; **for pity's —**, per pietà; **for form's —**, per la forma.

sal [sæl], *n.* (*Chem.*) Sale, *m.* **— ammoniac**, sale ammoniaco, *m.*; **— volatile**, sale volatile, *m.*

salaam [səˈlɑːm], *n.* Salamelecco, *m.*

salable [ˈseiləbl], *a.* Vendibile.

salacious [səˈleiʃəs], *a.* Salace, sboccato.

salacity [səˈlæsiti], *n.* Salacità, *f.*

salad [ˈsæləd], *n.* Insalata, *f.* **—-bowl**, insalatiera, *f.*; **—-dressing**, condimento per l'insalata, *m.*; **—-oil**, olio d'oliva, olio da tavola, *m.*; (*fig.*) **—-days**, anni di inesperienza, *m.pl.*

salamander [ˈsæləmændəɹ], *n.* (*Zool.*) Salamandra, *f.*

salaried [ˈsælərid], *a.* Salariato, stipendiato.

salary [ˈsæləri], *n.* Stipendio, *m.*; salario, soldo, *m.*, paga, *f.*; onorario, *m.* ‖ *v.t.* Stipendiare, salariare.

sale, *n.* Vendita, *f.*; spaccio, smercio, *m.* **Clearance —**, liquidazione, messa in vendita, *f.*; **for —**, da vendere; **on —**, in vendita; **— by auction**, vendita all'asta; **deed of —**, contratto di vendita, *m.*; **on — or return**, da vendere o rimandare; **ready —**, pronta vendita; **it has little —**, ha poco smercio, va poco; **—-room**, sala di vendita, *f.*

salesman [ˈseilzmən], *n.* Commesso, venditore, *m.*; piazzista, *m.*

salesmanship, *n.* L'arte di vendere, *f.*

saleswoman, *n.* Commessa, *f.*

Salic [ˈsælik], *a.* (*Hist.*) Salico.

salient [ˈseiliənt], *a.* Saliente, sporgente; importante, notevole, prominente. ‖ *n.* Saliente, *m.*

saliferous [sæliˈfərəs], *a.* (*Geol.*) Salifero.

saline [ˈseilain], *a.* (*Chem.*) Salino.

saliva [səˈlaivə], *n.* Saliva, *f.*

salivary, *a.* Salivare.

salivate, *v.i.* Salivare.

salivation, *n.* Salivazione, *f.*
sallow (1) ['sælou], *a.* Pallido, scialbo, giallíccio.
sallow (2), *n.* (*Bot.*) Salcio, salice, *m.*
sally ['sæli], *n.* (*Mil.*) Sortita, *f.*; scappata, escursione, *f.*; (*fig.*) motto, *m.*, facezia, *f.*; frizzo, *m.* || *v.i.* Fare una sortita. **To — forth,** andar fuori, uscire, balzar fuori.
salmi ['sælmi:], *n.* Salmì, *m.*
salmon ['sæmən], *n.* (*Zool.*) Salmone, *m.*; (*young*) salmoncino, *m.* **— -fishery,** pesca dei salmoni, *f.*; **— -pink,** rosa salmone, color salmone, *m.*; **— -trout,** trota salmonata, *f.*
Salonica [sælou'ni:kə], *n.* (*Geog.*) Salonicco, *m.*
saloon [sə'lu:n], *n.* Salone, *m.*; bar, *m.* **— -car,** vagone salotto, *m.*, vettura salone, *f.*; **— -passenger,** viaggiatore di prima classe, *m.*; **— -bar,** bar, *m.*
salsify ['sælsifi], *n.* (*Bot.*) Sassefrica, *f.*
salt [sɔlt, sɔ:lt], *n.* Sale, *m.* || *a.* Salato, salso. || *v.t.* Salare. **Table —,** sale fino, *m.*; **a pinch of —,** un pizzico di sale, *m.*; **Epsom salts,** sale inglese, *m.*; **to eat someone's —,** essere ospite di qualcuno; **not to be worth one's —,** non valere il pan che si mangia; **to put — on a bird's tail,** mettere il sale sulla coda dell'uccello; **to take with a grain of —,** prendere con un grano di sale; (*fig.*) **an old —,** un lupo di mare, *m.*; **salts of lemon,** acido citrico, *m.*; **— -box,** scatola per sale, *f.*; **— -cellar,** saliera, *f.*; **— -marsh, — pan,** salina, *f.*; **— -spoon,** cucchiaino per sale, *m.*; **— -water,** acqua salsa, acqua di mare, *f.*; **— -water fish,** pesce di mare, *m.*; **— -works,** salina, *f.*
saltatory ['sæltətəri], *a.* Saltatorio.
salted, *a.* Salato.
salter, *n.* Salinaio, salatore, *m.* **Dry- —,** droghiere, *m.*
salting, *n.* Salatura, salata, *f.*, il salare, *m.*; (*place*) salina, *f.*
saltiness, saltness, *n.* Salsedine, salsezza, *f.*
saltpetre [sɔlt'pi:təɹ], *n.* Salnitro, *m.*
salty, *a.* Salato, salso.
salubrious [sə'lu:briəs], *a.* Salubre.
salubrity [sə'lu:briti], *n.* Salubrità, *f.*
saluki [sə'lu:ki], *n.* (*Zool.*) Levriere d'Africa, *m.*
salutary ['sælju:təri], *a.* Salutare.
salutation [sælju:'teiʃən], *n.* Saluto, *m.*, salutazione, *f.*; inchino, *m.*, riverenza, *f.*
salute [sə'lu:t, sə'lju:t], *n.* Saluto, *m.*; (*of guns*) salva, *f.* || *v.t.* Salutare; inchinarsi a. **To fire a —,** sparare a salva.
salvage ['sælvidʒ], *n.* Salvataggio, ricupero, *m.* || *v.t.* Salvare, ricuperare. **— money,** compenso di salvataggio, *m.*, diritti di ricupero, *m.pl.*
salvation [sæl'veiʃən], *n.* Salvazione, salvezza, *f.*, salvamento, salute, *m.* **Salvation Army,** Esercito della Salute, *m.*
salve [sælv], *n.* Unguento, balsamo, *m.*, pomata, *f.*; rimedio, *m.* || *v.t.* Ungere, impomatare, spalmare d'unguento; (*fig.*) placare, quietare; salvare.
salver ['sælvəɹ], *n.* Vassoio, *m.*, sottocoppa, *m.*
salvo (1) ['sælvou], *n.* (*salute*) Salva, *f.*
salvo (2), *n.* Riserva, *f.*, pretesto, *m.*; scusa, *f.*
salvor ['sælvəɹ], *n.* Salvatore, ricuperatore, *m.*
Salzburg ['sælzbəɹg], *n.* (*Geog.*) Salisburgo, *m.*
Samaritan [sə'mæritən], *n.a.* Samaritano, *m.*
same [seim], *a.* Stesso, medesimo; monotono, uniforme. || *n.* Lo stesso, il medesimo, *m.*, la stessa cosa, *f.* **All the —,** nondimeno, lo stesso; **it's all the — to me,** per me è tutt'uno, per me è lo stesso; **he is just the — as ever,** è sempre lo stesso; **much about the —,** quasi lo stesso; **the — to you,** altrettanto; **it is the very —,** è proprio lo stesso; **at the — time,** ciò nonostante, contuttociò, pure.
sameness, *n.* Identità, identicità, somiglianza, *f.*; uniformità, monotonia, *f.*
samphire ['sæmfaiɹ], *n.* (*Bot.*) Finocchio marino, *m.*
sample [sɑ:mpl], *n.* Campione, *m.*; modello, *m.*; saggio, esempio, esemplare, *m.* || *v.t.* Assaggiare; gustare. **— -book, — -card,** campionario, *m.*; **— -fair,** fiera campionaria, *f.*
sampler, *n.* Modello di ricamo, quadro ricamato, *m.*; assaggiatore, *m.*
Samson ['sæmsən], *n.* Sansone, *m.*
sanative, sanatory ['sænətiv, 'sænətəri], *a.* Sanativo.
sanatorium [sænə'tɔ:riəm], *n.* Sanatorio, *m.*, casa di salute, *f.*
sanctification [sæŋktifi'keiʃən], *n.* Santificazione, *f.*
sanctified ['sæŋktifaid], *a.* Santificato, consacrato.
sanctify ['sæŋktifai], *v.t.* Santificare.
sanctifying ['sæŋktifaiiŋ], *a.* Santificante.
sanctimonious [sæŋkti'mouniəs], *a.* Santocchio, bigotto, untuoso, ipocrita.
sanctimoniousness, *n.* Santimonia, ipocrisia, *f.*
sanction ['sæŋkʃən], *n.* (*Law*) Sanzione, approvazione, *f.*, permesso, *m.*; (*Law*) pena, sanzione, *f.* || *v.t.* Sanzionare; permettere, approvare.
sanctity ['sæŋktiti], *n.* Santità, *f.*
sanctuary ['sæŋktju:əri], *n.* Santuario, *m.*; asilo, rifugio, *m.* **Right of —,** diritto d'asilo, *m.*; **to take —,** rifiugiarsi, trovare un rifugio; **to claim —,** invocare il diritto d'asilo.
sanctum ['sæŋktəm], *n.* Santuario, *m.*; (*colloq.*) gabinetto di lavoro, *m.*, camera privata, *f.*
sand [sænd], *n.* Sabbia, rena, arena, *f.* || *v.t.* Sabbiare, insabbiare, sparger di sabbia. **Sands,** spiaggia, *f.*; **on the sands,** sulla spiaggia; **— -bag,** sacco a terra, *m.*; **— -blast,** getto di sabbia, *m.*; (*Rail.*) **— -box,** sabbiera, *f.*; **— -glass,** clessidra, *f.*, oriolo a polvere, *m.*; **— -hill,** duna, *f.*; (*Zool.*) **— -martin,** rondine delle rive, *m.*; (*Zool.*) **— -piper,** piovanello, *m.*; **— -pit,** cava di rena, *f.*; **— -shoes,** scarpe di gomma, *f.pl.*; **— -storm,** bufera di sabbia, *f.*
sandal ['sændəl], *n.* Sandalo, *m.* **— -wood,** legno di sandalo, *m.*
sandbank, *n.* Banco di sabbia, *m.*
sandfly, *n.* (*Zool.*) Specie di moscerino.
sandiness, *n.* Arenosità, sabbiosità, *f.*
sandpaper, *n.* Carta vetrata, *f.*
sandwich [sændwitʃ], *n.* Panino gravido, *m.*, tartina, *f.* **— -man,** uomo reclame, *m.* || *v.t.* Stringere in mezzo, serrare.
sandy, *a.* Sabbioso, arenoso. **— -haired,** biondiccio.
sane [sein], *a.* Sano di mente, equilibrato, posato, ragionevole.
sanguinary ['sæŋgwinəri], *a.* Sanguinario.

sanguine [ˈsæŋgwin], *a.* Sanguigno; ardente, fiducioso. **I am not very — of success,** non ho grande speranza di riuscire; **— hopes,** vive speranze, *f.pl.*
sanguineous [sæŋˈgwiniəs], *a.* Sanguigno.
Sanhedrin [ˈsænidrin], *n.* (*Hist.*) Sinedrio, *m.*
sanitary [ˈsænitəri], *a.* Sanitario, igienico. **— dustbin,** secchia igienica; **— inspector,** ispettore sanitario, *m.*; **— towel,** pannilino, assorbente igienico, *m.*
sanitation [sæniˈteiʃən], *n.* Regime sanitario, *m.*, igiene, *f.*
sanity [ˈsæniti], *n.* Sanità di mente, *f.*, equilibrio, discernimento, *m.*
Sanskrit [ˈsænskrit], *n.a.* Sanscrito, *m.*
Santa Claus [sæntəˈklɔːz], *n.* Befana, *f.*, Babbo natale, *m.*
sap (1) [sæp], *n.* Succhio, *m.*, linfa, *f.*; succo, sugo, *m.*; (*colloq.*) imbecille. **— wood,** alburno, *m.*
sap (2), *v.t.i.* Zappare, minare, scavar trincee; (*fig.*) insidiare, sovvertire. ‖ *n.* Trincea, *f.*, scavo d'approccio, *m.*
sapid [ˈsæpid], *a.* Sapido, saporoso.
sapidity, *n.* Sapidità, *f.*
sapience [sæpiəns, ˈseipiəns], *n.* Sapienza, *f.*
sapient, *a.* Sapiente.
sapling, *n.* Arboscello, *m.*
saponaceous [sæpəˈneiʃəs], *a.* Saponaceo.
saponification, *n.* Saponificazione, *f.*
saponify [səˈpɔnifai], *v.t.* Saponificare.
sapper, *n.* (*Mil.*) Zappatore, *m.* **The Sappers,** il Genio, *m.*
Sapphic [ˈsæfik], *n.a.* Saffico, *m.*
sapphire [ˈsæfaiɹ], *n.* Zaffiro, *m.*
Sappho [ˈsæfou], *n.* Saffo, *f.*
sappiness [ˈsæpinis], *n.* Succosità, *f.*
sappy, *a.* Succoso, sugoso.
saraband [ˈsærəbænd], *n.* Sarabanda, *f.*
Saracen [ˈsærəsən], *n.a.* Saraceno, *m.*
sarcasm [ˈsɑːɹkæzm], *n.* Sarcasmo, *m.*
sarcastic [sɑːɹˈkæstik], *a.* Sarcastico.
sarcastically, *adv.* Sarcasticamente.
sarcenet [ˈsɑːɹsənet], *n.* Taffetà, *m.*
sarcology [sɑːɹˈkɔlədʒi], *n.* Sarcologia, *f.*
sarcoma [sɑːɹˈkoumə], *n.* (*Med.*) Sarcoma, *m.*
sarcophagus [sɑːɹˈkɔfəgəs], *n.* Sarcofago, *m.*
sardine [sɑːɹˈdiːn], *n.* (*Zool.*) Sardina, *f.*
Sardinia [sɑːɹˈdiniə], *n.* (*Geog.*) Sardegna, *f.*
Sardinian, *n.a.* Sardo, *m.*
sardonic [sɑːɹˈdɔnik], *a.* Sardonico.
sardonically, *adv.* Sardonicamente.
sardonyx [ˈsɑːɹdəniks], *n.* Sardonice, *m.*
Sargasso Sea [sɑːɹˈgæsou ˈsiː], *n.* (*Geog.*) Il mare dei sargassi, *m.*
sarsaparilla [sɑːɹsəpəˈrilə], *n.* Salsapariglia, *f.*
sarsenet [cp. **sarcenet**].
sartorial [sɑːɹˈtɔːriəl], *a.* Del sarto.
sash (1) [sæʃ], *n.* Sciarpa, fascia, *f.*; (*belt*) cintura, *f.*
sash (2), *n.* (*of window*) Telaio, intelaio, *m.* **— -frame,** imposta di finestra, *f.*; **— -window,** finestra a ghigliottina, finestra all'inglese, *f.*
sassafras [ˈsæsəfræs], *n.* (*Bot.*) Sassafrasso, *m.*
sat *p.* of **sit.**
Satan [ˈseitən], *n.* Satana, *m.*
satanic [səˈtænik], *a.* Satanico.
Satanism, *n.* Satanismo, *m.*
satchel [ˈsætʃəl], *n.* Sacchetto, *m.*, borsa, *f.*
sate [seit], *v.t.* Saziare, satollare.
sateen [səˈtiːn], *n.* Raso di cotone, rasato, satinato, *m.*
satellite [ˈsætəlait], *n.* Satellite, *m.*
satiate [ˈseiʃeit], *v.t.* Saziare, satollare.
satiety [səˈtaiəti], *n.* Sazietà, *f.*, satollamento, *m.*
satin [ˈsætin], *n.* Raso, *m.* ‖ *a.* Di raso. **— -stitch,** punto a raso, *m.*; **— -wood,** legno satinato, *m.*
satiny [ˈsætini], *a.* Rasato, lustro.
satire [ˈsætaiɹ], *n.* Satira, *f.*
satiric, satirical [səˈtirik, səˈtirikəl], *a.* Satirico.
satirically, *adv.* Satiricamente.
satirist, *n.* Satirico, scrittore di satire, *m.*
satirize, *v.t.* Satireggiare.
satisfaction [sætisˈfækʃən], *n.* Soddisfazione, contentezza, *f.*; pagamento, *m.*; riparazione, *f.*; appagamento, *m.* **To demand —,** domandare soddisfazione; **to give —,** dare soddisfazione a, contentare.
satisfactorily, *adv.* Soddisfacentemente.
satisfactoriness, *n.* Stato soddisfacente, *m.*
satisfactory, *a.* Soddisfacente.
satisfy [ˈsætisfai], *v.t.* Soddisfare, appagare, contentare; persuadere; *v.i.* soddisfare, dare soddisfazione. **To be satisfied with,** essere soddisfatto di, contentarsi di; **to be satisfied of,** essere convinto di; **to — one's appetite,** saziare l'appetito.
satisfying, *a.* Soddisfacente. **A — meal,** un pasto sufficiente, *m.*
satrap [ˈsætrəp], *n.* (*Hist.*) Satrapo, *m.*
saturable [ˈsætjuːrəbl], *a.* Saturabile.
saturate [ˈsætjuːreit], *v.t.* Saturare.
saturation, *n.* Saturazione, *f.*
Saturday [ˈsætəɹdi], *n.* Sabato, *m.*
Saturn [ˈsætəɹn], *n.* (*Myth.Astron.*) Saturno, *m.*
saturnalia [sætəɹˈneiliə], *n.pl.* Saturnali, *m.pl.*
saturnalian, *a.* Saturnale.
saturnine [ˈsætəɹnain], *a.* Fosco, cupo, taciturno, tetro; malinconico; (*Med.*) saturnino.
saturnism, *n.* (*Med.*) Saturnismo, *m.*
satyr [ˈsætəɹ], *n.* Satiro, *m.*
satyric [səˈtirik], *a.* Satiresco.
sauce [sɔːs], *n.* Salsa, *f.*; condimento, *m.*; (*colloq.*) insolenza, impertinenza, *f.* ‖ *v.t.* (*colloq.*) Dire impertinenze a, insultare. **— -boat,** salsiera, *f.*; (*colloq.*) **— -box,** sfacciatello, *m.*; **mint- —,** salsa di menta, *f.*
saucepan, *n.* Casseruola, pentola, *f.*, tegame, *m.*
saucer, *n.* Sottocoppa, piattino, piattello, *m.*
saucily, *adv.* Impertinentemente.
sauciness, *n.* Insolenza, impertinenza, sfacciataggine, *f.*
saucy, *a.* Insolente, impertinente, sfacciato.
sauerkraut [ˈsauəɹkraut], *n.* Salcrautte, *m.*
saunter [ˈsɔːntəɹ], *v.i.* Gironzare, girellare, girovagare, andare a zonzo, fare una passeggiatina.
sauntering, *n.* Girandolamento, girovagare, *m.*, passeggiata oziosa, *f.*
saurian [ˈsɔːriən], *n.* (*Zool.*) Sauriano, *m.*
sausage [ˈsɔsidʒ], *n.* (*fresh*) Salsiccia, *f.*; (*smoked*) salame, *m.* **Sausages,** salumi, *m.pl.*; salsiccie, *f.pl.*; **Bologna —,** mortadella, *f.*; **— -meat,** carne da salsiccia, *f.*
savage [ˈsævidʒ], *a.* Selvaggio, selvatico; feroce, crudele; barbaro; orrido. ‖ *n.* Selvaggio, *m.*, selvaggia, *f.*, barbaro, *m.*, barbara, *f.* ‖ *v.t.* Attaccare; mordere, calpestare.

savagely, *adv.* Ferocemente.
savageness, savagery, *n.* Selvatichezza, *f.*; ferocia, crudeltà, *f.*; barbarità, *f.*; orrore, *m.*
savannah [sə'vænə], *n.* Savana, *f.*
savant ['sævɔnt], *n.* Sapiente, dotto, erudito, *m.*
save [seiv], *v.t.* (*from danger*) Salvare, preservare, scampare; (*to keep*) serbare, conservare, preservare; (*to spare*) risparmiare; (*to avoid*) evitare; *v.i.* economizzare, risparmiare. || *prep.conj.* Eccetto, eccettuato, salvo, tranne, fuorchè. **God — the Queen!** Evviva la regina! **to — appearances,** salvare le apparenze; **to — one's breath,** risparmiare il fiato; **to — the situation,** salvare la situazione; **to — one's strength,** risparmiare le forze.
saver, *n.* Economizzatore, risparmiatore, *m.*; liberatore, *m.*
saveloy ['sævəlɔi], *n.* Cervellata, *f.*
saving, *n.* Risparmio, *m.*, economia, *f.*; preservazione, *f.* || *a.* Economo, economico, frugale; (*fig.*) di riserva. || *prep.* Eccetto, tranne. **— clause,** riserva, *f.*; **— grace,** grazia giustificante, *f.*; **savings-bank,** cassa di risparmio, *f.*; **— your presence,** con rispetto parlando.
saviour ['seiviəɹ], *n.* Salvatore, *m.* **The Saviour,** il Redentore, *m.*
savory ['seivəri], *n.* (*Bot.*) Savore, *m.*, santoreggia, *f.*
savour ['seivəɹ], *n.* Sapore, gusto, *m.* || *v.t.* Assaporare, assaggiare, gustare; *v.i.* sapere di, sentire di.
savouriness, *n.* Saporosità, *f.*
savoury, *a.* Saporoso, saporito, condito; soave. || *n.* Piatto salato, *m.*; vivanda servita alla fine del pranzo, *f.*; **— omelette,** frittata di verdura, *f.*
Savoy (1) [sə'vɔi], *n.* (*Geog.*) Savoia, *f.*
savoy (2), *n.* (*cabbage*) Cavolo cappuccio, *m.*
Savoyard [sə'vɔijɑːɹd], *a.* Savoiardo, sabaudo. || *n.* Savoiardo, *m.*
saw (1) [sɔː], *n.* (*tool*) Sega, *f.* || *v.t.* Segare. **—-fish,** pesce sega, *m.*; **—-mill,** segheria, *f.*; **—-pit,** fossa del segatore, *f.*
saw (2), *n.* Detto, proverbio, *m.*
saw (3), *p.* of **see.**
sawbones ['sɔːbounz], *n.* (*colloq.*) Chirurgo, *m.*
sawder, *n.* **Soft —,** Moine, piaggerie, *f.pl.*; complimenti, *m.pl.*
sawdust ['sɔːdʌst], *n.* Segatura, *f.*
sawing, *n.* Segatura, *f.*
sawyer ['sɔːjəɹ], *n.* Segatore, *m.*
saxhorn ['sækshɔːɹn], *n.* (*Mus.*) Saxcorno, *m.*, basso tuba, *f.*
saxifrage ['sæksifridʒ], *n.* (*Bot.*) Sassifraga, *f.*
Saxon ['sæksən], *n.a.* Sassone, *m.f.*
Saxony, *n.* (*Geog.*) Sassonia, *f.*
saxophone ['sæksəfoun], *n.* (*Mus.*) Sassofono, *m.*
say [sei], *v.t.* Dire; dichiarare; recitare; parlare. || *n.* Detto, dire, *m.*; discorso, *m.*, parola, *f.* **Be it said,** sia detto; **to — nay,** dir di no; **I dare —,** credo bene; **that is to —,** cioè a dire, vale a dire, sarebbe a dire; **to — a good word for someone,** parlare bene di qualcuno; **to — out,** esprimere; **to — one's —,** dire la propria; **to — a lesson,** dire la lezione; **I —!** Senta! Senti! Dica! Dimmi un po'! Ascoltate! **it is said,** si dice; **it goes without saying,** ciò va da sè; **You don't — so!** Non è possibile! Non mi far celia! **You may well — so!** Altro che! Sfido! **— it were so, would it matter?** posto che fosse così, cosa importerebbe? **it is hard to —,** è difficile dire; **give me, —, a shilling,** datemi, diciamo, uno scellino; **to — nothing of,** senza parlare di; **to have one's —,** dire la sua; **he has no — in the matter,** non tocca a lui decidere la questione; **What do you — to a glass of wine?** Che ne dite di un bicchiere?
saying, *n.* Detto, motto, adagio, proverbio, *m.*; massima, sentenza, *f.*, precetto, *m.* **As the — goes,** come si suol dire, come dice l'adagio.
scab [skæb], *n.* Crosta, *f.*; (*Med.*) crosta, tigna, *f.*; (*of sheep*) scabbia, *f.*; (*on plant*) rogna, *f.*; (*blackleg*) crumiro, *m.*
scabbard ['skæbəɹd], *n.* Fodero, *m.*, guaina, *f.*
scabbiness, *n.* Rognosità, *f.*
scabby, *a.* Coperta di croste; rognoso; scabbioso.
scabious ['skeibiəs], *n.* (*Bot.*) Scabbiosa, *f.*
scabrous ['skæbrəs], *a.* Scabroso.
scaffold ['skæfold], *n.* Palco, ponteggio, *m.*; patibolo, *m.*
scaffolding, *n.* Impalcatura, *f.*, ponte, *m.* **—-pole,** antenna, *f.*
scalable ['skeiləbl], *a.* Salibile, scalabile.
scald (1) [skɔːld], *n.* (*Lit.*) Scaldo, *m.*
scald (2), *n.* Scottata, scottatura, *f.* || *v.t.* Scottare. **Scalding hot,** scottante.
scalding, *n.* Scottatura, *f.*
scale (1) [skeil], *n.* (*of fish, snake, etc.*) Scaglia, squama, *f.*; (*of metal*) piastra, *f.* || *v.t.* Squamare; *v.i.* squamarsi, sfaldarsi.
scale (2), *n.* (*of balance*) Piatto della bilancia, *m.*; bascula, *f.* **To turn the —,** dare il crollo alla bilancia.
scale (3), *n.* Scala, *f.*; (*Mus.*) gamma, scala, *f.*; (*ruler*) regolo, *m.* || *v.t.* Scalare, graduare. **To draw to —,** disegnare in proporzione, disegnare secondo la scala; **on a large —,** su larga scala; **a — of 1 to 100,** una scala di uno a cento; **to — up,** ingrandire a gradi.
scale (4), *v.t.* (*a wall*) Scavalcare, arrampicarsi su. **Scaling-ladder,** scala d'assedio, *f.*
scalene ['skeiliːn], *a.* (*Geom.*) Scaleno.
scallop ['skæləp], *n.* (*Zool.*) Petonchio, *m.*; pettine, *m.*; (*decoration*) smerlo, *m.*, dentellatura, *f.* || *v.t.* Smerlare, festonare.
scalloped, *a.* A smerli.
scalloping, *n.* Smerlatura, *f.*
scallywag ['skæliwæg], *n.* Discolo, scioperato, mascalzone, *m.*
scalp [skælp], *n.* (*Anat.*) Cuoio capelluto, *m.*, cotenna, cuticagna, *f.*; (*trophy*) cotenna, *f.* || *v.t.* Scotennare. **—-wound,** ferita al cuoio capelluto, *m.*; **—-massage,** frizione, *f.*
scalpel ['skælpəl], *n.* Scalpello, *m.*
scaly ['skeili], *a.* Squamoso, scaglioso.
scamp [skæmp], *n.* Briccone, furfante, birbante, discolo, *m.* || *v.t.* Abborracciare, acciabattare.
scamper ['skæmpəɹ], *v.i.* Sgambettare, scorrazzare, correre, saltellare. || *n.* Corserella, scappata, *f.* **To — about,** saltarellare; **to — away,** svignarsela, darsela a gambe.
scan [skæn], *v.t.* Scrutare, misurare a occhio, esaminare; (*Poet.*) scandire; *v.i.* tornare. **These lines do not —,** questi versi non tornano.

scandal ['skændəl], *n.* Scandalo, *m.*; onta, *f.*; maldicenza, *f.*; vergogna, *f.* **To give rise to —,** dar luogo alla maldicenza; **to talk —,** sparlare; **—-monger,** maldicente, *m.f.*, malalingua, *f.*
scandalize ['skændəlaiz], *v.t.* Scandalizzare, disgustare. **To be scandalized,** scandalizzarsi.
scandalous, *a.* Scandaloso, vergognoso; calunnioso.
scandalously, *adv.* Scandolosamente.
scandalousness, *n.* Scandalosità, vergogna, *f.*; maldicenza, *f.*
Scandinavian [skændi'neiviən], *n.a.* Scandinavo, *m.*
scansion ['skænʃən], *n.* (*Poet.*) Scansione, *f.*
scant [skænt], *a.* Scarso, insufficiente; magro, povero; sommario.
scantiness, *n.* Scarsezza, insufficienza, *f.*; meschinità, *f.*
scantling ['skæntliŋ], *n.* (*Arch.*) Travicello, *m.*; pezzo di legno, *m.*
scanty, *a.* Scarso, poco, manchevole, insufficiente; magro, povero, meschino; (*of hair*) rado.
scape [skeip], *n.* (*Bot.Arch.*) Scapo, *m.*
scapegoat ['skeipgout], *n.* Capro espiatorio, *m.*
scapegrace, *n.* Scapestrato, cattivo soggetto, *m.*; (*child*) birichino, *m.*
scapula ['skæpju:lə], *n.* (*Anat.*) Scapola, *f.*
scapular, scapulary, *n.* (*Eccles.*) Scapolare, *m.*
scar (1) [skɑ:ɹ], *n.* Cicatrice, *f.*, sfregio, *m.* ‖ *v.t.* Cicatrizzare; sfregiare; *v.i.* cicatrizzarsi.
scar, scaur (2), *n.* Rupe scoscesa, balza, *f.*
scarab ['skærəb], *n.* Scarabeo, *m.*
scaramouch ['skærəmautʃ], *n.* Smargiasso, *m.*
scarce [skɛəɹs], *a.* Raro; rado, scarso, insufficiente; breve. **To make oneself —,** scappare, battersela.
scarcely, *adv.* Quasi, appena; scarsamente. **— anyone,** quasi nessuno; **— anywhere,** in quasi nessun luogo; **— ever,** quasi mai.
scarceness, *n.* Rarità, scarsezza, *f.*
scarcity, *n.* Scarsezza, carestia, *f.*
scare [skɛəɹ], *n.* Spavento, sgomento, panico, *m.*, paura, *f.* ‖ *v.t.* Spaventare, sgomentare, sbigottire, impaurire.
scarecrow, *n.* Spauracchio, *m.*
scaremonger ['skɛəɹmʌŋgəɹ], *n.* Allarmista, *m.f.*
scarf (pl. **scarfs, scarves**) [skɑ:ɹf], *n.* Sciarpa, *f.*; cravatta, *f.* (*Tech.*) **—-joint,** giuntura a denti, *f.*; **—-pin,** spilla per la cravatta, *f.*; (*Anat.*) **—-skin,** epidermide, *f.*
scarfwise, *adv.* A guisa di cintura, a cintura.
scarification [skærifi'keiʃən], *n.* Scarificazione, *f.*
scarify ['skærifai], *v.t.* Scarificare.
scarlatina [skɑ:ɹlə'ti:nə], *n.* (*Med.*) Scarlattina, *f.*
scarlet ['skɑ:ɹlet], *n.a.* Scarlatto, *m.* **—-fever,** scarlattina, *f.*; **—-runner,** fagiuolo di Spagna, *m.*
scarp [skɑ:ɹp], *n.* Scarpa, *f.*, scarpata, [pendice, *f.*
scarred, *a.* Segnato di cicatrici.
scatheless ['skeiðles], *a.* Illeso, incolume, senza danno.
scathing ['skeiðiŋ], *a.* Scottante, rovente, mordace, feroce. **A — attack,** una stroncatura, *f.*
scatter ['skætəɹ], *v.t.* Sparpagliare, spargere, disperdere, diffondere, disseminare; *v.i.* sparpagliarsi, spargersi, disperdersi. **—-brained,** scervellato, balordo.
scatterbrain, *n.* Scervellato, imprudente, *m.*
scattering, *n.* Sparpagliamento, *m.*, dispersione, *f.*
scavenge ['skævendʒ], *v.t.* Spazzare, scopare.
scavenger, *n.* Spazzino, spazzaturaio, *m.*
scenario [se'nɑ:riou], *n.* Scenario, *m.*; canovaccio, *m.*
scene [si:n], *n.* Scena, *f.*; spettacolo, *m.*; (*stage*) palcoscenico, *m.*; veduta, *f.*, colpo d'occhio, *m.* **Behind the scenes,** dietro le scene; **the — is laid in Rome,** la scena è a Roma; (*fig.*) **to make a —,** fare una scenata; **the — of the battle,** il teatro del combattimento; **—-painter,** scenografo, *m.*; **—-shifter,** macchinista, *m.*
scenery ['si:nəri], *n.* Paesaggio, *m.*, veduta, *f.*; (*Theat.*) scenario, *m.*
scenic ['senik], *a.* Scenico. **— railway,** montagne russe, *f.pl.*
scenographer [se'nɔgrəfəɹ], *n.* Scenografo, *m.*
scent [sent], *n.* Odore, profumo, olezzo, *m.*, fragranza, *f.*; fiuto, odorato, *m.* ‖ *v.t.* Profumare, olezzare; (*of animals*) fiutare. **On the right —,** sulla buona pista; **on the wrong —,** su una falsa strada; **to put off the —,** stornare, sviare; **to throw off the —,** far perdere la traccia a; **—-bottle,** boccetta di profumo, *f.*
scented, *a.* Profumato, odoroso.
scentless, *a.* Inodoro.
sceptic ['skeptik], *n.* Scettico, *m.*
sceptical, *a.* Scettico.
sceptically, *adv.* Scetticamente.
scepticism ['skeptisizm], *n.* Scetticismo, *m.*
sceptre ['septəɹ], *n.* Scettro, *m.*
sceptred, *a.* Scettrato.
Schaffhausen [ʃəf'hauzen], *n.* (*Geog.*) Sciaffusa, *f.*
schedule ['ʃedju:l], *n.* Prospetto, specchietto, *m.*; lista, *f.*, orario, *m.*; cedola, scheda, *f.* ‖ *v.t.* Schedare, notare, registrare, fissare, programmare.
Scheldt [skelt], *n.* (*Geog.*) Schelda, *f.*
schema (pl. **schemata**) ['ski:mə], *n.* Schema, *m.*
schematic [ske'mætik], *a.* Schematico.
scheme [ski:m], *n.* Schema, disegno, piano, progetto, *m.*; combinazione, disposizione, *f.* ‖ *v.t.* Disegnare, progettare; *v.i.* far progetti; intrigare, macchinare. **Colour- —,** combinazione di colori, *f.*
schemer, *n.* Intrigante, *m.f.*
scheming, *a.* Intrigante, astuto. ‖ *n.* Progetti, *m.pl.*
schism [sizm], *n.* Scisma, *m.*
schismatic [siz'mætik], *a.* Scismatico.
schist [ʃist], *n.* (*Geol.*) Schisto, *m.*
schistose ['ʃistouz], *a.* Schistoso.
schizophrenia [skizou'fri:niə], *n.* Schizofrenia, *f.*
schizophrenic, *n.a.* Schizofrenico, *m.*
scholar ['skɔləɹ], *n.* (*pupil*) Scolaro, allievo, alunno, *m.*, scolara, allieva, alunna, *f.*; (*learned person*) erudito, letterato, studioso, *m.*, erudita, letterata, studiosa, *f.* **Classical —,** umanista, classicista, *m.f.*; **day- —,** scolaro esterno, *m.*; **he is no —,** non è uno studioso, non è un dotto.

scholarly, *a.* Erudito, dotto.
scholarship, *n.* Erudizione, scienza, dottrina, coltura, *f.*; (*grant*) borsa di studio, *f.*
scholastic [skɔ'læstik], *a.* Scolastico.
scholasticism [skɔ'læstisizm], *n.* Scolasticismo, *m.*
school [sku:l], *n.* Scuola, *f.*; collegio, liceo, ginnasio, *m.*, seminario, *m.*; convitto, *m.*; (*of music*) conservatorio, *m.*; (*of whales, etc.*) frotta, *f.*, banco, *m.* || *v.t.* Istruire; disciplinare, ammaestrare. **At —,** a scuola, in collegio; **evening —,** scuola serale, *f.*; **high —,** scuola secondaria, *f.*, liceo, *m.*; **infant —,** asilo infantile, *m.*; **—-book,** libro scolastico, *m.*; **—-fellow,** compagno di scuola, condiscepolo, *m.*; **to — oneself,** disciplinarsi.
schoolboy, *n.* Scolaro, scolaretto, *m.* || *a.* Scolaresco, da scolaretto.
schoolgirl, *n.* Scolara, *f.*
schooling, *n.* Istruzione, educazione, *f.*, insegnamento, *m.*
schoolman, *n.* Filosofo scolastico, *m.*
schoolmaster, *n.* Maestro di scuola, *m.*
schoolmistress, *n.* Maestra di scuola, *f.*
schoolroom, *n.* Classe, aula, *f.*
schooner ['sku:nəɹ], *n.* (*Naut.*) Goletta, *f.*
sciatic [sai'ætik], *a.* (*Anat.*) Sciatico.
sciatica, *n.* (*Med.*) Sciatica, *f.*
science ['saiəns], *n.* Scienza, *f.*
scientific [saiən'tifik], *a.* Scientifico.
scientifically, *adv.* Scientificamente.
scientist, *n.* Scienziato, *m.*, scienziata, *f.*
Scilly Isles ['sili ailz], *n.* (*Geog.*) Isole Sorlinghe, *f.pl.*
scimitar ['simitɑ:ɹ], *n.* Scimitarra, *f.*
scintilla [sin'tilə], *a.* Scintilla, *f.*
scintillate ['sintileit], *v.i.* Scintillare.
scintillation, *n.* Scintillazione, *f.*
sciolist ['saiolist], *n.* Saputello, saccente, *m.*
scion ['saiən], *n.* Rampollo, discendente; *m.*; (*Bot.*) pollone, *m.*
scirrhous ['sirəs], *a.* (*Med.*) Scirroso.
scirrhus ['sirəs], *n.* (*Med.*) Scirro, tumore, *m.*
scissile ['sisail], *a.* Scissile.
scission ['siʃən], *n.* Scissione, *f.*
scissors ['sizəɹz], *n.pl.* Forbici, *f.pl.*; cesoie, *f.pl.* **A pair of —,** un paio di forbici, *m.*; **—-case,** astuccio per forbici, *m.*
sclerosis [skle'rousis], *n.* (*Med.*) Sclerosi, *f.*
sclerotic [skle'rɔtik], *a.* (*Anat.*) Sclerotico. **— membrane,** sclerotica, *f.*
scoff (1) [skɔf], *n.* Scherno, *m.*, beffa, *f.*; cileggio, *m.* || *v.i.* Schernire, beffare, dileggiare, deridere. **To — at,** beffarsi di, deridere, ganzonare.
scoff (2), *v.i.* Mangiare ghiottamente.
scoffer, *n.* Schernitore, dileggiatore, derisore, *m.*
scoffing, *n.* Scherno, *m.*, derisione, *f.* || *a.* Derisorio, beffardo.
scoffingly, *adv.* Beffardamente.
scold [skould], *v.t.* Sgridare, riprendere, rimproverare; *v.i.* strillare, brontolare, schiamazzare. || *n.* Brontolona, megera, donna bisbetica, *f.*
scolding, *n.* Sgridata, *f.* **To give a — to,** dare una lavata di testa a, dare una ramanzina a.
scollop [cp. **scallop**].
scolopendrium [skɔlo'pendriəm], *n.* (*Bot.*) Scolopendrio, *m.*
sconce [skɔns], *n.* Lanterna, *f.*, candelabro, braccio di candeliere, *m.*; mensola, *f.*; canna di candeliere, *f.*; (*colloq.*) zucca, *f.*
scone [skoun, skɔn], *n.* Focaccina, *f.*
scoop [sku:p], *n.* (*for dry goods*) Benna, *f.*; (*for liquids*) cucchiaione, ramaiolo, *m.*; (*journalistic*) colpo, *m.* || *v.t.* Scavare, svuotare. **To make a —,** fare un bel colpo; **to — out,** scucchiaiare, scodellare; **to — up,** raccogliere, tirar su.
scoot [sku:t], *v.i.* (*colloq.*) Scappare, battersela, filar via, svignarsela.
scooter, *n.* (*child's*) Monopattino, *m.*; (*motor*) motopattino, *m.*
scope [skoup], *n.* Portata, sfera, attribuzione, *f.*, campo, *m.*; obiettivo, scopo, *m.* **To give full — to,** dar campo libero a; **to have — for one's energies,** aver campo libero alle proprie energie; **that is beyond my —,** ciò è di là delle mie attribuzioni.
scorbutic [skɔ:ɹ'bju:tik], *a.* (*Med.*) Scorbutico.
scorch [skɔ:ɹtʃ], *v.t.* Bruciare, arrostire, abbrustolire, abbruciacchiare, scottare; *v.i.* abbruciacchiarsi; (*colloq.*) pedalare a furia.
scorcher, *n.* (*colloq.*) Pedalatore, velocipedastro, *m.*
scorching, *a.* Bruciante, scottante.
score [skɔ:ɹ], *n.* (*mark*) Tacca, linea, tratta, *f.*; (*reckoning*) conto, debito, *m.*; (*20*) venti, *m.*, una ventina, *f.*; (*Sport*) punteggio, *m.*, punti, *m.pl.*; (*Mus.*) partitura, orchestrazione, *f.*; (*fig.*) ragione, *f.*, riguardo, rispetto, *m.* || *v.t.* (*to mark*) Intagliare, graffiare, intaccare, marcare, segnare; (*points*) notare; fare punti; raggiungere; (*Mus.*) orchestrare. **To — out,** cancellare; **to — under,** sottolineare; **to — up against,** addebitare a; **to — off someone,** vincerla alle spese di qualcuno.
scorer, *n.* (*Sport*) Chi segna i punti, marcatore, *m.*
scoria (pl. **scoriae**) ['skɔ:riə], *n.* Scoria, *f.*
scorify ['skɔ:rifai], *v.t.* Ridurre in scorie.
scoring ['skɔ:riŋ], *n.* (*Sport*) Punti, *m.pl.*, punteggio, *m.*; (*Mus.*) orchestrazione, *f.* **—-board,** pallottoliere, *m.*; (*Golf*) **—-card,** carta di risultati, *f.*
scorn [skɔ:ɹn], *v.t.* Sdegnare, sprezzare, spregiare. || *n.* Sdegno, disprezzo, sprezzo, spregio, *m.*; noncuranza, *f.*; scorno, ludibrio, *m.* **I would — to do it,** sdegnerei di farlo; **to laugh to —,** deridere, farsi beffa di.
scorner, *n.* Schernitore, *m.*, schernitrice, *f.*
scornful, *a.* Sdegnoso, sprezzante, derisorio, beffardo.
scornfully, *adv.* Sdegnosamente.
scornfulness, *n.* Sdegnosità, *f.*
scorpion ['skɔ:ɹpiən], *n.* (*Zool.*) Scorpione, *m.*
scot (1) [skɔt], *n.* (*Hist.*) Scotto, conto, *m.* **To pay — and lot,** pagare lo scotto; **to get off — free,** passarla liscia; andarsene senza pagare lo scotto.
Scot (2), *n.* Scozzese, *m.f.*; (*Hist.*) Scoto, *m.*
Scotch (1) [skɔtʃ], *a.* Scozzese. || *n.* Whisky, whisky scozzese, *m.*; **— mist,** nebbia spessa, *f.*; **—-broth,** zuppa con orzo e legumi, *f.*
scotch (2), *v.t.* Intagliare, intaccare; sfregiare; sopprimere.
Scotchman, Scotchwoman, *n.* Scozzese, *m.f.*
scoter ['skoutəɹ], *n.* (*Zool.*) Specie di anitra, *f.*
Scotland ['skɔtlənd], *n.* (*Geog.*) Scozia, *f.*
Scots, *a.* Scozzese.

Scotsman, *n.* Scozzese, *m.*
scotticism ['skɔtisizm], *n.* Idiotismo scozzese, *m.*
Scottish, *a.* Scozzese.
scoundrel ['skaundrəl], *n.* Scellerato, malvagio, mascalzone, *m.*
scoundrelism, *n.* Scelleratezza, *f.*
scoundrelly, *a.* Scellerato, malvagio, infame, tristo.
scour [skauɹ], *v.t.* Ripulire, forbire, nettare, fregare; percorrere, perlustrare; *v.i.* correre; vagare, vagabondare. **To — the country,** battere la campagna, correre il paese.
scourer, *n.* Cavamacchie, smacchiatore, *m.*
scourge [skəːɹdʒ], *n.* Flagello, *m.*, sferza, *f.*; frusta, *f.* || *v.t.* Sferzare,, flagellare.
scourging, *n.* Flagellazione, *f.*
scouring ['skauriŋ], *n.* Ripulitura, pulitura, forbitura, *f.*
scout [skaut], *n.* Esploratore, *m.*; (*Naut.*) vedetta, nave in vedetta, *f.* || *v.i.* Esplorare, perlustrare, riconoscere il terreno; *v.t.* respingere, scartare, smentire. **Boy Scout,** Giovane Esploratore, *m.*; **Scout-master,** Capo Esploratore, *m.*
scow [skau], *n.* (*Naut.*) Chiatta, *f.*
scowl [skaul], *v.i.* Aggrottare le ciglia, accigliarsi, imbronciarsi. || *n.* Cipiglio, sguardo torvo, aspetto minaccioso, *m.*
scowling, *a.* Torvo, minaccioso, accigliato.
scowlingly, *adv.* Con cipiglio.
scrag [skræg], *n.* (*of mutton*) Collottola, *f.* **— -end,** collo, *m.*
scragginess ['skrægines], *n.* Magrezza, *f.*
scraggy ['skrægi], *a.* Magro, scarno, affilato, smilzo.
scramble [skræmbl], *v.i.* Arrancare, sgambare, dibattersi, urtarsi, inerpicarsi. || *n.* Parapiglia, mischia, baruffa, confusione, zuffa, *f.*; (*for place*) lotta, *f.* **Scrambled eggs,** uova strapazzate, *f.pl.*; **to — for,** azzuffarsi per; **to — up,** arrampicarsi su, inerpicarsi.
scrap [skræp], *n.* Pezzetto, frammento, *m.*; squarcio, brano, *m.*; briciola, *f.*; (*colloq.*) rissa, zuffa, baruffa, *f.* || *v.t.* Rigettare, gettare al rottame; *v.i.* (*colloq.*) altercare. **— -book,** album, *m.*; **— -iron,** ferraccio, *m.*
scrape [skreip], *v.t.* Raschiare, raspare, grattare, scrostare; spillaccherare; (*Golf*) scalfire; *v.i.* economizzare. || *n.* Raschiata, *f.*; (*fig.*) imbarazzo, imbroglio, impaccio, *m.*, difficoltà, *f.* **To — acquaintance with,** insinuarsi presso; **to — one's feet,** stropicciare i piedi; **to — together,** ammucchiare, raccogliere; **to bow and —,** fare salamelecchi; **to — through,** cavarsela; **to get into a —,** mettersi in un imbroglio; **to get out of a —,** cavarsela, tirarsi d'impaccio; **a — of the pen,** un tratto di penna, *m.*
scraper, *n.* Raschino, raschietto, raschiatoio, *m.*; puliscipiedi, *m.*; (*colloq.*) grattatore di violino, *m.*
scrapings, *n.pl.* Raschiature, spazzature, *f.pl.*; risparmi, *m.pl.*, economie, *f.pl.*
scratch [skrætʃ], *n.* Graffio, *m.*, graffiatura, *f.*; scalfittura, *f.*; (*Sport*) linea di partenza, *f.* || *v.t.* Graffiare, scalfire, grattare; (*Sport*) ritirare; *v.i.* (*Sport*) ritirarsi; (*of pen*) intaccare. **He hasn't got a —,** non si è fatto una graffiatura; **a — team,** un'accozzaglia, una squadra improvvisata, *f.*; **to come up to —,** mettersi al cimento; **— -race,** scratch, *m.*; **to — out someone's eyes,** cavare gli occhi a qualcuno; **to — one's head,** grattarsi la testa; **to — out a word,** cancellare una parola; (*Art*) **— -work,** graffiti, *m.pl.*
scratching, *n.* Graffiatura, *f.*
scratchy, *a.* Ruvido, scabroso; stridulo.
scrawl [skrɔːl], *n.* Scarabocchio, *m.* || *v.t.i.* Scarabocchiare, fare scarabocchi.
scrawler, *n.* Scarabocchiatore, *m.*
scream [skriːm], *n.* Grido, strillo, *m.*; (*colloq.*) cosa molto divertente. || *v.i.* Gridare, strillare; vociare, schiamazzare. **To — with laughter,** ridere sguaiatamente.
screaming, *a.* Strillante, stridulo. || *n.* Gridio, strillio, *m.* **A — farce,** una farsa buffa, *f.*
scree [skriː], *n.* Breccia, *f.*
screech [skriːtʃ], *n.* Strillo, *m.* || *v.t.* Strillare; miagolare. (*Zool.*) **— -owl,** barbagianni, *m.*, civetta, *f.*
screen [skriːn], *n.* Riparo, *m.*; parafuoco, *m.*; paravento, *m.*; coperta, *f.*; (*sieve*) crivello, *m.*; (*Arch.*) tramezzo, *m.* (*Cinema.Television*) schermo, *m.* || *v.t.* Nascondere, coprire; proteggere, difendere; (*sift*) crivellare; (*Cinema.*) proiettare, cinematografare. **Under — of night,** col favore della notte; **a — hero,** un eroe dello schermo; **to — from punishment,** sottrarre alle pene.
screenings, *n.pl.* Mondiglia, *f.*
screw (1) [skruː], *n.* Vite, *f.*; (*Naut.*) elica, *f.*; (*on ball*) effetto, *m.*; (*twist of paper*) cartoccio, *m.*; (*miser*) avaro, taccagno, spilorcio, *m.* (*colloq. wages*) stipendio, *m.*, paga, *f.* || *v.t.* Avvitare; torcere, storcere; (*fig.*) opprimere, costringere; *v.i.* girare, voltare. || *a.* Ad elica. **A turn of the —,** un giro della vite, *m.*; **female —,** madrevite, chiocciola, *f.*; (*colloq.*) **he has a — loose,** ne ha un ramo, è un po' tocco; **to — down a lid,** avvitare un coperchio; **to — up one's courage,** farsi coraggio, farsi animo; **to — money out of someone,** estorcere denari a qualcuno; **to — up one's eyes,** aguzzar gli occhi; **to — up one's face,** distorcere il viso; **to — up one's lips,** storcere la bocca; **— -coupling,** accoppiamento a vite, *m.*; **— -driver,** cacciavite, *m.*; **— -jack,** cricco, martinetto, martinetto a vite, *m.*; **— -nut,** dado, *m.*, madrevite, *f.*; **— -wrench,** chiave inglese, *f.*; **— -steamer,** vapore ad elica, *m.*
screw (2), *n.* (*horse*) Rozza, *f.*
screwed, *a.* (*colloq.*) Brillo, ubbriaco.
scribble [skribl], *n.* Scarabocchio, *m.* || *v.t.i.* Scarabocchiare, scribacchiare.
scribbler, *n.* Scarabocchiatore, scribacchiatore, *m.*; scribacchino, scrittoruccio, scrittorello, *m.*
scribe [skraib], *n.* Scriba, scrivano, *m.*
scrimmage ['skrimidʒ], *n.* Parapiglia, *f.*, tafferuglio, *m.*; zuffa, rissa, *f.*
scrimp [cp. **skimp**].
scrip [skrip], *n.* (*Comm.*) Certificato provvisorio, *m.*; titoli, valori, *m.pl.*; (*obs.*) bisaccia, *f.*
script [skript], *n.* Scritto, *m.*, scrittura, *f.*; scrittura molto chiara, *f.*
scriptural ['skriptjuːrəl], *a.* Scritturale, biblico.
Scripture ['skriptʃəɹ], *n.* Sacra Scrittura, la Bibbia, *f.* **— history,** storia sacra, *f.*

scrivener ['skrivənəɹ], *n.* Scrivano, *m.*; notaio, *m.*
scrofula ['skrɔfju:lə], *n.* (*Med.*) Scrofola, *f.*
scrofulous, *a.* Scrofoloso.
scroll [skroul], *n.* (*of paper*) Rotolo, *m.*; (*Arch.*) voluta, *f.*; (*handwriting*) arabesco, ghirigoro, *m.*; (*bearing motto*) drappello, nastro, *m.*
scrotal ['skroutəl], *a.* Scrotale.
scrotum, *n.* (*Anat.*) Scroto, *m.*
scrounge [skraundʒ], *v.t.i.* (*colloq.*) Guadagnucchiare, mendicare, sottrarre, scroccare.
scrounger, *n.* Mendicante, rigattiere, scroccone, *m.*
scrub (1) [skrʌb], *v.t.* Strofinare, fregare, sfregare stropicciare; pulire, lustrare. || *n.* Strofinata, *f.*; (*fig.*) persona taccagna, *f.*, nanerottolo, *m.*
scrub (2), *n.* (*brushwood*) Macchia, *f.*
scrubber, *n.* Spazzolone, spazzola da strofinare, *f.*; lavatore, pulitore, *m.*
scrubbing, *n.* Strofinatura, pulitura, *f.* —**-brush,** spazzola da strofinare, spazzola dura, *f.*
scrubby, *a.* Malcresciuto, meschino, stentato.
scruff [skrʌf], *n.* **The — of the neck,** la nuca, la collottola, *f.*
scrum, scrummage [skrʌm, 'skrʌmidʒ], *n.* Mischia, *f.*, scompiglio, *m.*; (*Rugby*) zuffa, *f.*
scrumptious ['skrʌmpʃəs], *a.* (*colloq.*) Magnifico, stupendo, splendido.
scrunch [skrʌntʃ], *v.t.* Schiacciare, sgretolare.
scruple [skru:pl], *n.* Scrupolo, *m.* || *v.i.* Farsi scrupolo, avere scrupolo. **Without a —,** senza scrupolo.
scrupulous ['skru:pju:ləs], *a.* Scrupoloso.
scrupulously, *adv.* Scrupolosamente.
scrupulousness, *n.* Scrupolosità, *f.*
scrutator [skru:'teitəɹ], *n.* Investigatore, *m.*
scrutineer [skru:ti'niəɹ], *n.* Scrutinatore, *m.*
scrutinize ['skru:tinaiz], *v.t.* Scrutare, scrutinare, investigare, indagare.
scrutiny ['skru:tini], *n.* Esame, ricerca, investigazione, *f.*; (*of votes*) scrutinio, *m.*
scud [skʌd], *n.* (*of clouds*) Nuvolaglia, *f.*; corsa rapida, *f.* || *v.i.* Fuggire. **To — before the wind,** fuggire dinanzi alla tempesta, correre la fortuna.
scuffle [skʌfl], *n.* Baruffa, zuffa, *f.*, tafferuglio, *m.*; rissa, *f.* || *v.i.* Azzuffarsi, venire a baruffa, accapigliarsi.
scull [skʌl], *n.* Remo, *m.*, pagaia, *f.*; remo a pertica, *m.* || *v.i.* Remare, vogare all'inglese.
sculler, *n.* Rematore, *m.*
scullery ['skʌləri], *n.* Retrocucina, acquaio, *m.* —**-maid,** sguattera, lavapiatti, *f.*
scullion ['skʌliən], *n.* Sguattero, *m.*
sculptor ['skʌlptəɹ], *n.* Scultore, *m.*
sculptress, *n.* Scultrice, *f.*
sculpture ['skʌlptʃəɹ], *n.* Scultura, *f.* || *v.t.* Scolpire.
sculptured, *a.* Scolpito.
scum [skʌm], *n.* Schiuma, spuma, *f.*; (*fig.*) feccia, *f.*, rifiuto, *m.* || *v.t.* Schiumare. **The — of the earth,** il rifiuto della società, *m.*
scumble [skʌmbl], *v.t.* (*Art*) Attenuare le tinte. || *n.* Smorzatura di tinte, *f.*
scupper ['skʌpəɹ], *n.* (*Naut.*) Ombrinale, *m.* || *v.t.* Affondare.
scurf [skə:ɹf], *n.* (*in hair*) Forfora, *f.*; (*on skin*) crosta, *f.*
scurfiness, *n.* Forfora, *f.*
scurfy, *a.* Forforoso.
scurrility, scurrilousness [skʌ'riliti, 'skʌriləsnes], *n.* Scurrilità, *f.*
scurrilous, *a.* Scurrile, grossolano, oltraggioso, basso, volgare.
scurrilously, *adv.* Scurrilmente.
scurry ['skʌri], *v.i.* Affrettarsi, sgambare.
scurvied ['skə:ɹvid], *a.* Scorbutico.
scurvily, *adv.* Bassamente, vilmente.
scurviness, *n.* Bassezza, meschinità, grettezza, *f.*
scurvy ['skə:ɹvi], *n.* (*Med.*) Scorbuto, *m.* || *a.* Basso, meschino, gretto. (*Bot.*) —**-grass,** coclearia, *f.*
scut [skʌt], *n.* (*of rabbit, etc.*) Coda, *f.*
scutch [skʌtʃ], *n.* (*Mach.*) Gramola, *f.* || *v.t.* Gramolare.
scutcheon, escutcheon ['skʌtʃən, es'kʌtʃən], *n.* Stemma, scudo, *m.*
scuttle [skʌtl], *n.* (*for coal*) Secchio, *m.*; (*Naut.*) boccaporto, *m.* || *v.t.* (*Naut.*) Affondare; *v.i.* affrettarsi, correre, fuggire alla chetichella. **To — away,** scappare.
scuttleful, *n.* Secchiata, *f.*
scuttling, *n.* Affondamento, *m.*
scythe [saið], *n.* Falce, *f.* || *v.t.* Falciare.
Scythia ['siðiə], *n.* (*Geog.*) Scizia, *f.*
Scythian, *n.a.* Scito, *m.*
sea [si:], *n.* Mare, *m.*; colpo di mare, maroso, *m.*; ondata, *f.*; (*fig.*) moltitudine, massa, *f.* **At —,** in mare, (*fig.*) perplesso; **beyond the seas,** oltre il mare, oltremare; (*fig.*) **half-seas over,** brillo; **a heavy —,** un mare grosso, *m.*; **a choppy —,** un mare corto, un mare agitato, *m.*; **in the open —, on the high seas,** in alto mare; **to follow the —,** fare il marinaio; **to put out to —,** prendere il mare; **to go to —,** farsi marinaio; **to stand out to —,** guadagnare l'alto mare; —**-bathing,** bagni di mare, *m.pl.*; —**-beast,** mostro marino, *m.*; —**-boots,** stivaloni impermeabili, *m.pl.*; —**-breeze,** brezza marina, *f.*; —**-calf,** foca, *f.*; —**-change,** trasformazione, *f.*; —**-chest,** cassa di mare, *f.*; —**-coast,** littorale, *m.*, costa del mare, *f.*; —**-dog,** (*sailor*) lupo di mare, *m.*; —**-fight,** battaglia navale, *f.*; —**-fog,** foschia, caligine sul mare, *f.*; —**-fowl,** uccello marino, *m.*; —**-front,** marina, *f.*; —**-girt,** circondato dal mare; —**-green,** color verde mare, verdazzurro; (*colloq.*) — **lawyer,** marinaio capzioso, *m.*; —**-level,** livello del mare, *m.*; (*Zool.*) —**-lion,** otaria leonina, *f.*; —**-mark,** meda, *f.*, faro, *m.*; (*Zool.*) —**-mew,** gabbiano, *m.*; —**-nymph,** ninfa di mare, nereide, *f.*; —**-piece,** marina, *f.* —**-room,** il largo, *m.*; —**-salt,** sale marino, *m.*; —**-serpent,** serpente di mare, *m.*; —**-shell,** conchiglia marina, *f.*; —**-trout,** trota salmonata, *f.*; —**-wall,** diga, *f.*; —**-way,** corso d'una nave, *m.*
seabird, *n.* Uccello marino, *m.*
seaboard, *n.* Costa, costiera, spiaggia, riviera, *f.*
seaborne, *a.* Portato dal mare; trasportato per mare.
seafarer, seafaring man, *n.* Navigatore, marinaio, *m.*
seagoing, *a.* **— ship,** nave di mare, *f.*
seagull ['si:gʌl], *n.* (*Zool.*) Gabbiano, *m.*

seahorse, *n.* (*Zool.*) Cavalluccio marino, ippocampo, *m.*
seakale ['si:keil], *n.* (*Bot.*) Cavolo marino, *m.*
seal (1) [si:l], *n.* (*Zool.*) Foca, *f.* || *v.i.* Cacciare le foche.
seal (2), *n.* Sigillo, suggello, *m.*; (*fig.*) impronta, *f.*; segno, marchio, *m.* || *v.t.* Sigillare, suggellare; chiudere. **Under — of confession,** sotto sigillo di confessione; **to set one's — to,** autorizzare; **to affix the seals,** apporre i sigilli; **my lips are sealed,** ho il sigillo alla bocca; **hermetically sealed,** chiuso ermeticamente; **it is a sealed book to me,** è un libro chiuso per me; **his fate is sealed,** la sua sorte è decisa; **to — up,** sigillare.
sealing, *n.* Sigillazione, *f.*, suggellamento, *m.* **—-wax,** ceralacca, *f.*
sealskin, *n.* Pelle di foca, *f.*
seam [si:m], *n.* Costura, cucitura, *f.*; (*Geol.*) vena, *f.*, filone, strato, *m.*; (*scar*) cicatrice, sutura, *f.* || *v.t.* Cucire, fare una costura a.
seaman ['si:mən], *n.* Marinaio, *m.*
seamanlike, *a.* Da marinaio, marinaresco.
seamanship, *n.* Nautica, marineria, arte marinaresca, *f.*
seamless ['si:mles], *a.* Senza costure, senza cucitura.
seamstress ['semstres], *n.* Cucitrice, *f.*
seamy, *a.* **The — side,** il lato brutto, il rovescio, *m.*
seaplane, *n.* Idroplano, idrovolante, *m.*
seapower, *n.* Potere sul mare, *m.*, potenza marittima, *f.*
sear [siəɪ], *a.* Secco, appassito. || *v.t.* Bruciare, cauterizzare; insecchire, fare appassire. **Searing-iron,** cauterio, *m.*
search [sə:ɪtʃ], *n.* Ricerca, cerca, *f.*; (*Law*) perquisizione, *f.*; (*Customs*) visita, *f.* || *v.t.i.* Cercare, ricercare; tastare, frugare; fare una perquisizione, perquisire. **A vain —,** una vana ricerca, *f.*; **right of —,** diritto di perquisizione, *m.*; **to be in — of,** essere in cerca di, cercare; **to — a wound,** sondare una ferita; **to — about,** frugacchiare, frugare; **to — out,** ricercare, scoprire; **to — after,** ricercare, indagare; **to — for,** cercare; **to — into,** approfondire, scovare; **—-warrant,** mandato di perquisizione, *m.*
searcher, *n.* Cercatore, ricercatore, investigatore, *m.*; (*Customs*) doganiere, *m.*
searching, *a.* Penetrante, scrutatore; minuzioso. || *n.* Ricerca, cerca, *f.* **A — examination,** un esame rigoroso, *m.*; **searchings of the heart,** introspezione, *f.*
searchlight, *n.* Proiettore, *m.*, riflettore, *m.*
seashore, *n.* Lido, *m.*, spiaggia, *f.*
seasickness, *n.* Mal di mare, *m.* **To be seasick,** avere il mal di mare.
seaside, *n.* Marina, spiaggia, *f.* **A — resort,** una stazione balneare, *f.*
season ['si:zən], *n.* Stagione, *f.*; (*fig.*) tempo, momento opportuno, *m.* || *v.t.* (*food*) Condire; (*wood*) stagionare, acclimare; (*fig.*) abituare, avvezzare; moderare, temprare; *v.i.* acclimarsi, stagionarsi. **A word in —,** una parola opportuna, *f.*; **in — and out of —,** a proposito e a sproposito; **strawberries are in —,** le fragole sono di stagione; **—-ticket,** tessera, *f.*, abbonamento, *m.*
seasonable, *a.* Di stagione; opportuno, a proposito; tempestivo.
seasonableness, *n.* Tempestività, *f.*
seasonably, *adv.* A proposito.
seasonal, *a.* Di stagione, stagionale.
seasoned, *a.* (*of food*) Condito; (*of wood*) stagionato; avvezzato; (*of soldiers*) agguerrito.
seasoning, *n.* (*of food*) Condimento, *m.*; (*of wood*) stagionamento, *m.*
seat [si:t], *n.* Posto a sedere, *m.*; (*chair*) sedia, *f.*; (*of chair, trousers, etc.*) fondo, *m.*; (*of body*) sedere, *m.*; (*of war*) teatro, *m.*; (*mansion*) castello, *m.*; (*in parliament, etc.*) seggio, *m.*; (*of a disease*) sede, *f.* || *v.t.* Porre a sedere, far sedere, provvedere posti a sedere; mettere un fondo a; installare, fissare. **Pray take a —!** Accomodatevi! **a — of learning,** un ateneo, *m.*; **to book seats at the theatre,** prenotare posti al teatro; **the hall seats a thousand,** l'aula è provvista di mille posti a sedere; **to — oneself,** accomodarsi, sedersi, mettersi a sedere.
seated, *a.* Seduto. **A cane- — chair,** una sedia a fondo di canna, *f.*; **a deep- — disease,** un male profondamente radicato, *m.*
seater, *a.* A posti. **A four- — car,** un auto a quattro posti, *m.*
seating, *n.* Posti a sedere, *m.pl.*
seaward, *a.adv.* Verso il mare.
seawater, *n.* Acqua di mare, *f.*
seaweed, *n.* (*Bot.*) Alga, *f.*
seaworthiness, *n.* Navigabilità, *f.*
seaworthy, *a.* In buono stato, che tiene il mare.
sebaceous [se'beiʃəs], *a.* Sebaceo.
secant ['si:kənt], *n. a.* (*Math.*) Secante, *f.*
secede [se'si:d], *v.i.* Separarsi da, staccarsi da.
seceder, *n.* Secessionista, separatista, *m.f.*
secession [se'seʃən], *n.* Secessione, *f.*
seclude [se'klu:d], *v.t.* Separare, ritirare, rimuovere, allontanare. **To — oneself,** ritirarsi, allontanarsi.
secluded, *a.* Ritirato, solitario.
seclusion, *n.* Ritiro, *m.*; allontanamento, *m.*; solitudine, *f.*
second ['sekənd], *a.* Secondo. || *n.* (*of time*) Secondo, *m.*; appoggio, protettore, *m.*; (*duel*) padrino, *m.*; (*Boxing*) secondo, *m.* || *v.t.* Assecondare, secondare, aiutare; sostenere, appoggiare, fare da padrino; [se'kɔnd] (*Mil.*) mettere in disponibilità. **Every — day,** ogni due giorni; **in the — place,** in secondo luogo; **— to none,** non secondo a nessuno; **the — floor,** il secondo piano, *m.*; **— in command,** secondo, *m.*; **habit is — nature,** l'abitudine è una seconda natura; **on — thoughts,** ripensandoci bene; **at — hand,** di seconda mano, per sentita dire; **—-hand books,** libri usati, *m.pl.*; **to come off — best,** averne la peggio; **to — a resolution,** appoggiare una risoluzione; **his — best suit** suo vestito di riserva; **— cousin,** cugino in secondo grado, *m.*; **—-sight,** prescienza, *f.*; **— childhood,** senilità, *f.*; **— finger,** dito medio, *m.*; **the — of March,** il due marzo; **—-rate,** inferiore, di second'ordine, scadente.
secondary, *a.* Secondario.
seconder, *n.* Chi appoggia, secondatore, *m.*
secondly, *adv.* Secondamente, in secondo luogo.
secrecy ['si:krisi], *n.* Segretezza, *f.*; riserbo, segreto, *m.*; discrezione, *f.* **You can rely upon his —,** potete affidarvi alla sua discrezione.

secret ['si:kret], *a.* Segreto, occulto, nascosto; ritirato, privato, appartato. || *n.* Segreto, *m.* **— drawer,** cassetto segreto, *m.*; **— service money,** fondi segreti, *m.pl.*; **to keep —,** tenere segreto; **an open —,** il segreto di Pulcinella, *m.*; **in —,** in segreto; **to keep a —,** mantenere un segreto, serbare un segreto.
secretaire ['sekretɛəɹ], *n.* Scrittoio, *m.*
secretarial [sekri'tɛəriəl], *a.* Segretariale.
secretariat, *n.* Segretariato, *m.*
secretary ['sekritəri], *n.* Segretario, *m.*, segretaria, *f.* **Home Secretary,** Ministro dell'Interno, *m.*; **Secretary of State,** Segretario di Stato, *m.*; **Foreign Secretary,** Ministro degli Affari Esteri, *m.*; **private —,** segretario privato, *m.*; (*Zool.*) **— bird,** serpentario, *m.*
secretaryship, *n.* Segretariato, *m.*
secrete [se'kri:t], *v.t.* Nascondere, segregare; secernere.
secretion, *n.* Secrezione, *f.*
secretive ['si:kritiv, se'kri:tiv], *a.* Segreto; secretivo.
secretory [se'kri:təri], *a.* Secretorio.
secretly ['si:krətli], *adv.* Segretamente, in segreto, di nascosto.
sect [sekt], *n.* Setta, *f.*
sectarian [sek'tɛəriən], *n.a.* Settario, *m.*
sectarianism, *n.* Spirito settario, *m.*
sectary, *n.* Settario, *m.*
sectile ['sektail], *a.* Segabile.
section ['sekʃən], *n.* Sezione, *f.*; divisione, *f.*; spaccato, taglio, *m.*; rubrica, *f.* **Cross- —,** sezione trasversale, *f.*
sectional, *a.* Di sezione, parziale.
sector ['sektəɹ], *n.* (*Geom.*) Settore, *m.*; (*instrument*) compasso di proporzione, *m.*
secular ['sekju:ləɹ], *a.* Secolare; laico, civile, mondano. || *n.* (*Eccles.*) clero secolare, *m.*
secularism, *n.* Secolarismo, *m.*
secularist, *n.* Secolarista, *m.*
secularity [sekju:'læriti], *n.* Secolarità, mondanità, *f.*
secularization, *n.* Secolarizzazione, *f.*
secularize, *v.t.* Secolarizzare.
secure [se'kju:əɹ], *a.* Sicuro, certo; al sicuro, in sicurezza; salvo. || *v.t.* Assicurare, mettere al sicuro; afferrare, chiudere, serrare; rinchiudere; (*to get*) ottenere. **A — foundation,** un fondamento sicuro, *m.*; **we have got him —,** lo abbiamo qui al sicuro; **he is — of victory,** è sicuro di vincere; **— from interruption,** sicuro da interruzione; **to — oneself against damage,** assicurarsi contro il danno.
securely, *adv.* Sicuramente.
security [se'kju:riti], *n.* Sicurezza, *f.*; (*Law*) garanzia, cauzione, *f.*, pegno, *m.* (*Comm.*) **Securities,** titoli, valori, *m.pl.*; **gilt-edged securities,** titoli di primissimo ordine, *m.pl.*; **in — for,** in pegno di, in cauzione di; **collective —,** sicurezza collettiva, *f.*
sedan chair [se'dæn tʃɛəɹ], *n.* Portantina, *f.*
sedate [se'deit], *a.* Composto, contegnoso, calmo, placido.
sedately, *adv.* Compostamente.
sedateness, *n.* Compostezza, *f.*
sedative ['sedətiv], *a.* Sedativo, calmante. || *n.* Calmante, *m.*
sedentary ['sedentəri], *a.* Sedentario.
sedge [sedʒ], *n.* (*Bot.*) Carice, *f.*, giunco, *m.* (*Zool.*) **— -warbler,** re di macchia, *m.*, capinera dei giunchi, *f.*
sediment ['sedimənt], *n.* Sedimento, deposito, *m.*
sedimentary, *a.* Sedimentario.
sedition [se'diʃən], *n.* Sedizione, *f.*
seditious [se'diʃəs], *a.* Sedizioso.
seditiousness, *n.* Sedizione, *f.*
seduce [se'dju:s], *v.t.* Sedurre.
seducer, *n.* Seduttore, *m.*, seduttrice, *f.*
seduction [se'dʌkʃən], *n.* Seduzione, *f.*
seductive, *a.* Seduttore, seducente, attraente.
sedulity, sedulousness [se'dju:liti, 'sedju:ləsnes], *n.* Diligenza, assiduità, *f.*
sedulous ['sedju:ləs], *a.* Diligente, assiduo.
sedulously, *adv.* Assiduamente.
see (1) [si:], *v.t.i.* Vedere; accorgersi di; (*fig.*) intendere, comprendere, capire. **Fit to be seen,** presentabile; (*fig.*) **to — stars,** veder le stelle; **I cannot — my way to doing it,** non posso risolvermi a farlo; **to — the sights,** vedere i monumenti; **to — a thing done,** far fare qualcosa; **she cannot — a joke,** non può capire uno scherzo; **Do you — what I mean ?** Capite ciò che voglio dire? **as far as I can —,** per quanto io vedo; **he has seen better days,** ha visto tempi migliori; **to — something through,** vedere che una cosa sia fatta; **to — someone home,** accompagnare a casa qualcuno; **to — someone off,** vedere partire qualcuno; **to — about, to — to,** occuparsi di, aver cura di; **See to it that . . .!** Badate bene che . . .! **you must — into this,** dovete occuparvi di questo; **Let us —!** Vediamo! **come and — us,** venite a trovarci; **to — over,** visitare; **I will — to it!** Me ne occuperò io! Lasciate fare a me!
see (2), *n.* (*Eccles.*) Sedia episcopale, *f.*; vescovado, *m.*, arcivescovado, *m.* **The Holy See,** La Santa Sede, *f.*
seed [si:d], *n.* Seme, *m.*; semenza, *f.*; chicco, granello, *m.*, discendenza, *f.*; (*fig.*) origine, *f.*; progenie, *f.* || *v.i.* Sementire; seminare; *v.t.* sgranare. **To go to —,** sementire; **to sow the — of discord,** gettare il seme della discordia; **— -bed,** semenzaio, *m.*; **— -corn,** semente, *f.*; **— -pearl,** perla minuta, *f.*; **— -time,** seminagione, *f.*; **— -vessel,** pericarpio, *m.*
seedling, *n.* Pianticella, *f.*
seedsman, *n.* Mercante di semi, granaiolo, *m.*
seedy, *a.* Malconcio, male in arnese, logoro; indisposto, infermiccio.
seeing ['si:iŋ], *n.* Vista, veduta, *f.*, vedere, *m.* || *conj.* Visto che, considerato che. **— -in,** televisione, *f.*; **— the state of affairs,** visto lo stato delle cose; **— that,** visto che.
seek [si:k], *v.t.i.* Cercare, ricercare; procacciare, tentare, procurare. **To — someone's life,** voler uccidere qualcuno; **to — out,** cercare, andare cercando; **to — to,** tentare di.
seeker, *n.* Cercatore, ricercatore, *m.*, cercatrice, ricercatrice, *f.*
seem [si:m], *v.i.* Sembrare, parere. **It seems,** pare; **it seems to me,** mi pare, mi sembra; **he seems to be ill,** sembra malato; **it seemed good to him to . . .,** gli sembrava bene di . . .
seeming, *n.* Sembianza, apparenza, *f.*; sembiante, aspetto, *m.* || *a.* Apparente, ostensibile. **With — truth,** sotto le sembianze del vero, con apparente verità.

seemingly, *adv.* Apparentemente.
seemliness ['si:mlines], *n.* Convenienza, decenza, *f.*, decoro, *m.*
seemly, *a.* Conveniente, decente.
seer [siəɹ], *n.* Veggente, profeta, *m.*
seesaw ['si:sɔ:], *n.* Altalena, *f.* ‖ *v.i.* Altalenare, fare all'altalena; (*fig.*) vacillare, barcamenarsi.
seethe [si:ð], *v.t.* Far bollire, lessare; *v.i.* bollire; agitarsi, fermentare, ribollire. **The country is seething with unrest,** c'è un gran fermento nel paese.
segment ['segmənt], *n.* Segmento, *m.*; porzione, *f.*, pezzo, *m.*
segregate ['segre'geit], *v.t.* Segregare.
segregation, *n.* Segregazione, *f.*
Seidlitz powder ['sedlitz paudəɹ], *n.* Polvere di Sedlitz, *f.*
seine (1) [sein], *n.* Sagena, sciabica, *f.*
Seine (2), *n.* (*Geog.*) Senna, *f.*
seisin ['si:zin], *n.* (*Law*) Possesso, *m.*
seismic ['saizmik], *a.* Sismico.
seismograph ['saizmogræf], *n.* Sismografo, *m.*
seizable ['si:zəbl], *a.* Afferrabile; confiscabile.
seize [si:z], *v.t.* Afferrare, prendere, pigliare, impossessarsi di, impadronarsi di; confiscare; legare; *v.i.* (*Mech.*) grippare, ingranarsi.
seizin [cp. **seisin**].
seizure ['si:ʒəɹ], *n.* Afferramento, *m.*, presa, *f.*; confisca, *f.*; (*Med.*) attacco, accesso, *m.*
selachian [se'leikiən], *n.a.* (*Zool.*) Selachio, *m.*
seldom ['seldəm], *adv.* Raramente, di rado, rare volte.
select [se'lekt], *v.t.* Scegliere, eleggere; (*Sport*) selezionare. ‖ *a.* Scelto, prescelto, eletto, distinto. — **committee,** commissione d'inchiesta, *f.*
selection [se'lekʃən], *n.* Scelta, *f.*, selezione, *f.*; raccolta, *f.* **Natural —,** selezione naturale, *f.*
selectivity [selek'tiviti], *n.* (*Radio*) Selettività, *f.*
selenite ['selinait], *n.* (*Min.*) Selenite, *f.*; (*Astron.*) selenite, *m.*
selenium [se'li:niəm], *n.* (*Min.*) Selenio, *m.*
self (pl. **selves**) [self, selvz], *n.a.* Persona, *f.*, individuo, *m.*; stesso, io stesso, sè stesso, *m.*, l'io, *m.* **I myself,** io stesso; **I did it by myself,** l'ho fatto da me stesso; **I was all by myself,** ero tutto solo; **oneself,** sè stesso, sè; **he cares for nothing but self,** pensa soltanto a sè stesso.
self-, *prefix.* Sè stesso, stesso. **—-abasement,** umiliazione, *f.*; **—-abuse,** onanismo, *m.*; **—-acting,** automatico, semovente; **—-assertion,** autoritarietà, prepotenza, *f.*; **—-assertive,** autoritario, prepotente; **—-centred,** egotistico, egocentrico; **—-coloured,** di un sol colore; **—-command,** dominio di sè stesso, *m.*; **—-communion,** meditazione, *f.*; **—-conceit,** presunzione, *f.*; **—-confidence,** sicurezza di sè, *f.*; **—-confident,** sicuro di sè; **—-conscious,** preoccupato di sè; **—-consciousness,** autocoscienza, *f.*; **—-contained,** completo, raccolto, compatto, (*fig.*) riservato; **—-control,** padronanza di sè, *f.*; **—-defence,** legittima difesa, difesa personale, *f.*; **in —-defence,** per defendersi; **the art of —-defence,** il pugilato, *m.*; **—-denial,** abnegazione, astinenza, *f.*; **—-denying,** disinteressato; **—-destruction,** suicidio, *m.*; **—-determination,** autodecisione, *f.*; **—-discipline,** autodisciplina, *f.*; **—-educated,** autodidatta; **—-esteem,** amor proprio, *m.*; **—-evident,** evidente, manifesto; **—-governing,** autonomo, indipendente; **—-government,** autonomia, indipendenza, *f.*; **—-help,** il fare da sè, *m.*; **—-importance,** boria, presunzione, *f.*, sussiego, *m.*; **—-important,** borioso; **—-indulgence,** indulgenza con sè stesso, *f.*; **—-interest,** interesse personale, *m.*; **—-inflicted,** inflitto da sè stesso; **—-made,** fatto da sè; **a —-made man,** un uomo che s'è fatto da sè; figlio del proprio lavoro; **—-opinionated,** testardo, caparbio; **—-possessed,** calmo, tranquillo, composto; **—-possession,** sangue freddo, *m.*, padronanza di sè, *f.*; **—-propelled,** automotore, semovente; **—-reliance,** fiducia in sè, *f.*; **—-reliant,** fiducioso in sè; **—-respect,** dignità, *f.*, amor proprio, *m.*; **—-respecting,** dignitoso; **—-restraint,** contenutezza, riservatezza, *f.*; **—-sacrifice,** abnegazione, *f.*, sacrificio di sè, *m.*; **—-same,** proprio lo stesso; **—-satisfied,** soddisfatto di sè, vanesio; **—-seeker,** egoista, *m.*; **—-styled,** sedicente; **—-sufficient,** borioso, bastante a sè; **—-supporting,** indipendente; **—-taught** autodidatta; **—-will,** ostinazione, caparbietà, *f.*; **—-willed,** ostinato, caparbio.
selfish, *a.* Egoista, egoistico; interessato.
selfishly, *adv.* Egoisticamente.
selfishness, *n.* Egoismo, *m.*
selfless, *a.* Disinteressato.
sell [sel], *v.t.* Vendere, smerciare, spacciare; alienare; cedere, realizzare; (*colloq.*) ingannare; *v.i.* vendersi, spacciarsi. ‖ *n.* (*colloq.*) Inganno, *m.*, disillusione, *f.* **To be sold,** da vendere; **to — one's life dearly,** vendere cara la vita; (*fig.*) **to — oneself,** prostituirsi; **these books — well,** questi libri hanno facile smercio; **to — off,** liquidare; **to — out,** vendere tutto; **to — by auction,** vendere all'asta, vendere all'incanto; (*colloq.*) **I was thoroughly sold,** m'hanno proprio preso in giro.
seller, *n.* Venditore, *m.* **Best-—,** scrittore (*or* libro) a gran tiratura; libro di successo, *m.*
selling, *n.* Vendita, *f.* **—-off,** liquidazione, *f.*; **—-price,** prezzo di vendita, *m.*
seltzer, seltzer water ['seltzəɹ, 'seltzəɹ wɔ:təɹ], *n.* Acqua di seltz, *f.*
seltzogene ['seltzodʒi:n], *n.* Seltzogeno, *m.*
selvage, selvedge ['selvidʒ], *n.* Vivagno, orlo, *m.*, cimosa, *f.*
semantics [se'mæntiks], *n.pl.* Semantica, semasiologia, *f.*
semaphore ['seməfɔ:ɹ], *n.* Semaforo, *m.*
semblance ['sembləns], *n.* Sembianza, apparenza, figura, *f.*, sembiante, aspetto, *m.*
semen ['si:men], *n.* (*Anat.*) Sperma, *f.*
semester [se'mestəɹ], *n.* Semestre, *m.*
semi- ['semi], *prefix.* Semi, mezzo. **—-annual,** semestrale; **—-detached houses,** case gemelle, case accoppiate, *f.pl.*; **—-diameter,** semidiametro, *m.*; (*Sport*) **—-final,** semifinale; **—-official,** semiufficiale; **—-precious** (*of jewels*) duro.
semibreve ['semibri:v], *n.* (*Mus.*) Semibreve, *f.*

semicircle ['semisə:ɹkl], *n.* Semicerchio, semicircolo, *m.*
semicircular, *a.* Semicircolare.
semicolon [semi'koulən], *n.* Punto e virgola, *m.*
seminal ['seminəl], *n.a.* Seminale, *m.*
seminarist ['seminərist], *n.* Seminarista, *m.*
seminary, *n.* Seminario, *m.*
semination [semi'neiʃən], *n.* Semina, disseminazione, *f.*
seminiferous [semi'nifərəs], *a.* Seminifero.
semiology [si:mi'ɔlədʒi], *n.* Semiologia, *f.*
semiquaver ['semikweivəɹ], *n.* (*Mus.*) Semicroma, biscroma, *f.* — **rest,** pausa di semicroma, *f.*
Semite ['semait], *n.* (*Hist.*) Semita, *m.*
Semitic [se'mitik], *a.* Semitico.
semitone ['semitoun], *n.* (*Mus.*) Semitono, *m.*
semolina [semo'li:nə], *n.* Semolino, *m.*
sempiternal [sempi'tə:ɹnəl], *a.* Sempiterno.
sempstress ['sempstres], *n.* Sarta, cucitrice, *f.*
senate ['senət], *n.* Senato, *m.* **—-house,** palazzo del senato, *m.*
senator, *n.* Senatore, *m.*
senatorial, *a.* Senatorio.
senatorship, *n.* Senatorato, *m.*
send [send], *v.t.* Mandare, inviare, spedire; lanciare. **To be sent about one's business,** esser mandato fuor dei piedi; **to — away,** mandar via, licenziare, rimandare; **to — back,** rimandare; **to — for,** mandare per, far venire; **to — forth,** mandar fuori, metter fuori; emettere, emanare; **to — in,** fare entrare, mandare, servire; **to — off,** mandar via, spedire, congedare; **to — on,** trasmettere, mandare oltre; **to — out,** mandar fuori, spedire, esalare; (*fig.*) **to — packing,** mandare a farsi benedire; **he sent to tell me,** mandò a dirmi; **to — after,** mandare a cercare; **God — it may be so!** Dio voglia che sia vero! **to — to sleep,** addormentare; (*Univ.*) **to — down,** espellere, scacciare.
sender, *n.* Mittente, speditore, *m.*
sending, *n.* Spedizione, *f.*, invio, *m.*
send-off, *n.* Commiato, *m.*
senescence [se'nesəns], *n.* Senescenza, *f.*
seneschal ['seneʃəl], *n.* Siniscalco, maggiordomo, *m.*
senile ['si:nail], *a.* Senile. **— decay,** decrepitezza, senilità, *f.*
senility [se'niliti], *n.* Senilità, *f.*
senior ['si:niəɹ], *a.* Maggiore, più anziano, più vecchio, seniore. || *n.* Seniore, anziano, *m.*, maggiore, *m.f.* **He is ten years my —,** ha dieci anni più di me; **— partner,** socio più anziano, socio dirigente, *m.*; **Mr Brown, —,** il signor Brown padre.
seniority [si:ni'ɔriti], *n.* Anzianità, *f.*
senna ['senə], *n.* (*Bot.*) Senna, *f.*
sennight ['senait], *n.* (*obs.*) Settimana, *f.*
sensation [sen'seiʃən], *n.* Sensazione, impressione, *f.* **To make a —,** causare sensazione, fare impressione.
sensational, *a.* Sensazionale, a sensazione.
sensationalism, *n.* Sensazionalismo, *m.*
sense [sens], *n.* Senso, discernimento, *m.*; buon senso, senso comune, *m.*; sentimento, *m.*; opinione, *f.*; significato, senso, *m.*; sensazione, *f.* || *v.t.* Presentire, indovinare. **Keen senses,** sensi acuti, *m.pl.*; **a dull — of smell,** un ottuso senso olfattivo, *m.*; **to be out of one's senses,** esser fuori di sè, essere fuori di mente; **to bring someone to his senses,** ricondurre uno alla ragione; **to come to one's senses,** tornare in sè, ravvedersi; **to be frightened out of one's senses,** perdere la ragione per paura; **to talk —,** parlare da senno; **a — of humour,** una vena d'umorismo, *f.*; **a keen — of honour,** un vivo sentimento dell'onore, *m.*; **to have the — to,** avere il buon senso di; **now you are talking —,** adesso parlate sensatamente; **it does not make —,** ciò non fa senso; **to take the — of the meeting,** consultare l'assemblea; **in the best — of the word,** nel miglior senso della parola.
senseless, *a.* Insensato, scemo, stupido, assurdo; insensibile, senza conoscenza.
senselessly, *adv.* Insensatamente.
senselessness, *n.* Assurdità, insensatezza, mancanza di buon senso, *f.*, insensibilità, *f.*
sensibility [sensi'biliti], *n.* Sensibilità, impressionabilità, *f.*
sensible ['sensibl], *a.* Assennato, ragionevole, saggio; sensibile; rilevante; impressionabile. **— to the eye,** sensibile all'occhio; **a — difference,** una differenza sensibile; **I am — of your kindness,** sono grato della vostra gentilezza; **that is very — of you,** siete molto ragionevole.
sensibleness, *n.* Senso, buon senso, *m.*, ragionevolezza, *f.*
sensibly, *adv.* Sensibilmente; assennatamente.
sensitive ['sensitiv], *a.* Sensibile, sensitivo; suscettibile; (*touchy*) permaloso.
sensitiveness, sensitivity, *n.* Sensitività, sensibilità, *f.*
sensitize ['sensitaiz], *v.t.* Rendere sensitivo, sensibilizzare.
sensitized, *a.* (*Phot.*) Sensibile.
sensorial, sensory [sen'sɔ:riəl, 'sensəri], *a.* Sensorio.
sensual ['senʃu:əl], *a.* Sensuale, carnale.
sensualism, *n.* Sensualismo, *m.*
sensualist, *n.* Sensualista, *m.f.*
sensuality [senʃju:'æliti], *n.* Sensualità, *f.*
sensually, *adv.* Sensualmente.
sensuous ['sensju:əs], *a.* Sensuoso.
sentence ['sentəns], *n.* (*Gram.*) Frase, *f.*, periodo, *m.*; (*Law*) sentenza, *f.*, giudizio, *m.*; condanna, *f.* || *v.t.* Condannare, pronunciare la sentenza. **To pass — on,** condannare.
sententious [sen'tenʃəs], *a.* Sentenzioso.
sententiousness, *n.* Sentenziosità, *f.*
sentient ['senʃənt], *a.* Sensibile, senziente, cosciente.
sentiment ['sentimənt], *n.* Sentimento, senso, *m.*; opinione, *f.*, parere, *m.*
sentimental, *a.* Sentimentale.
sentimentalism, *n.* Sentimentalismo, *m.*
sentimentalist, *n.* Sentimentale, *m.f.*, romantico, *m.*, romantica, *f.*
sentimentality [sentimen'tæliti], *n.* Sentimentalità, *f.*
sentimentally, *adv.* Sentimentalmente.
sentinel, sentry ['sentinəl, 'sentri], *n.* Sentinella, guardia, *f.* **To be on sentry duty,** far la sentinella, montar la guardia; **to stand sentinel,** star di sentinella; **to relieve a sentry,** mutar la guardia; **sentry-box,** garitta, *f.*; **sentry-go,** guardia, *f.*
sepal ['sepəl], *n.* (*Bot.*) Sepalo, *m.*

separable [ˈsepərəbl], *a.* Separabile.
separate [ˈsepəreit], *v.t.* Separare, disgiungere, disunire; *v.i.* separarsi, disgiungersi, disunirsi. ‖ *a.* Separato, diviso, disgiunto, disunito, distinto.
separately, *adv.* Separatamente.
separateness, *n.* Separatezza, *f.*
separation [sepəˈreiʃən], *n.* Separazione, disgiunzione, disunione, *f.* **Judicial —,** separazione legale, *f.*
separatism, *n.* Separatismo, *m.*
separator, *n.* (*Mech.*) Scrematrice, *f.*
sepia [ˈsiːpiə], *n.* Nero di seppia, *m.*
sepoy [ˈsiːpɔi], *n.* Cipai, *m.*
sepsis [ˈsepsis], *n.* (*Med.*) Sepsi, *f.*
sept [sept], *n.* Tribù, *m.*
septangular [septˈæŋgjuːləɹ], *a.* (*Geom.*) Ettagonale.
September [sepˈtembəɹ], *n.* Settembre, *m.*
septenary [sepˈtiːnəri], *a.* Settenario.
septennial [sepˈteniəl], *a.* Settenale.
septet [sepˈtet], *n.* (*Mus.*) Settimino, *m.*
septic [ˈseptik], *a.* (*Med.*) Settico.
septuagenarian [septjuːədʒeˈnɛəriən], *n.a.* Settantenne, settuagenario, *m.*
Septuagesima [septjuːəˈdʒesimə], *n.* (*Eccles.*) Settuagesima, *f.*
Septuagint [ˈseptjuːədʒint], *n.* (*Eccles.*) Versione della Bibbia dei Settanta, *f.*
septum [ˈseptəm], *n.* (*Anat.*) Setto, *m.*
septuple [ˈseptjuːpl], *a.* Settuplo. ‖ *v.t.* Settuplicare.
sepulchral [seˈpʌlkrəl], *a.* Sepolcrale.
sepulchre [ˈsepəlkəɹ], *n.* Sepolcro, *m.*
sepulture [ˈsepəltjuːɹ], *n.* Sepoltura, *f.*
sequel [ˈsiːkwəl], *n.* Seguito, *m.*, conseguenza, continuazione, sequela, *f.* **In the —,** in conseguenza, in seguito.
sequence [ˈsiːkwəns], *n.* Seguito, *m.*, sequela, serie, successione, *f.*; (*Mus.Cards*) sequenza, *f.*
sequester [seˈkwestəɹ], *v.t.* Allontanare, separare, appartare, ritirare. **To — oneself,** allontanarsi, appartarsi.
sequestered, *a.* Allontanato, appartato; (*Law*) sotto sequestro.
sequestrate [seˈkwestreit], *v.t.* (*Law*) Sequestrare, mettere sotto sequestro.
sequestration [siːkwesˈtreiʃən], *n.* Allontanamento, *m.*, sequestrazione, *f.*; (*Law*) sequestro, *m.*
sequestrator, *n.* Sequestratore, *m.*
sequin [ˈsiːkwin], *n.* (*ornament*) Lustrino, *m.*; (*coin*) zecchino, *m.*
seraglio [seˈrɑːljou], *n.* Serraglio, harem, *m.*
seraph (pl. **seraphim, seraphs**) [ˈserəf], *n.* Serafino, *m.*
seraphic [seˈræfik], *a.* Serafico.
Serbia [ˈsəːɹbiə], *n.* (*Geog.*) Serbia, *f.*
Serb, Serbian, *n.a.* Serbo, *m.*
sere [siəɹ], *a.* Secco, disseccato, adusto. [cp. **sear**].
serenade [serəˈneid], *n.* Serenata, *f.* ‖ *v.t.* Cantare una serenata, fare una serenata a.
serene [seˈriːn], *a.* Sereno, quieto, tranquillo, calmo. **His Serene Highness,** sua Altezza Serenissima, *f.*; **All —!** Tutto va bene!
serenely, *adv.* Serenamente, tranquillamente.
sereneness, serenity [seˈriːnnis, seˈreniti], *n.* Serenità, tranquillità, *f.*
serf [səːɹf], *n.* Servo della gleba, schiavo, *m.*
serfdom, *n.* Servitù, schiavitù, *f.*, servaggio, *m.*
serge [səːɹdʒ], *n.* Rascia, saia, *f.*
sergeant [ˈsɑːɹdʒənt], *n.* (*Mil.*) Sergente, *m.*; (*Police*) brigadiere, *m.* **Colour- —,** portabandiera, *m.*; **— -at-arms,** usciere, cancelliere, *m.*; **— -major,** sergente maggiore, *m.*; **lance- —,** caporale maggiore, *m.*; (*Hist.*) **— -at-law,** avvocato di prima classe, *m.*
serial [ˈsiəriəl], *a.* Periodico, di serie; a puntate, a dispense; pubblicato a fascicoli. ‖ *n.* Romanzo a puntate, romanzo d'appendice, *m.* **— rights,** diritti di riproduzione nei giornali, ecc.
serialize, *v.t.* Pubblicare in una pubblicazione periodica.
serially, *adv.* A puntate, a dispense.
seriatim [seriˈeitim], *adv.* In serie, successivamente.
sericulture [ˈserikʌltʃəɹ], *n.* Sericoltura, *f.*
sericulturist, *n.* Sericoltore, *m.*
series [ˈsiəriːz], *n.* Serie, *f.*, seguito, *m.*; successione, *f.*
serio-comic [siəriouˈkɔmik], *a.* Semiserio, tragicomico.
serious [siəriəs], *a.* Serio, grave. **Are you — ?** Parlate sul serio? **a — illness,** una malattia grave, *f.*
seriously, *adv.* Sul serio; seriamente, gravemente. **To take —,** prendere sul serio.
seriousness, *n.* Serietà, gravità, *f.*
serjeant [cp. **sergeant**].
sermon [ˈsəːɹmən], *n.* Sermone, *m.*, predica, *f.*
sermonize, *v.t.i.* Sermoneggiare, predicare.
sermonizer, *n.* Predicatore, *m.*
serosity [seˈrɔsiti], *n.* Sierosità, *f.*
serous [ˈsiərəs], *a.* Sieroso.
serpent [ˈsəːɹpənt], *n.* Serpente, *m.*, serpe, *f.*; (*Mus.*) serpentone, *m.* **— -like,** serpentino.
serpentine [ˈsəːɹpəntain], *a.* Serpentino, di serpente, sinuoso. ‖ *n.* (*Min.*) Serpentino, *m.*
serpiginous [səːɹˈpidʒinəs], *a.* (*Med.*) Serpiginoso.
serrate [ˈsereit], *a.* (*Bot.*) Dentellato.
serration, *n.* Dentellatura, *f.*
serrated, *a.* Dentellato, a denti di sega.
serried [ˈserid], *a.* Serrato, folto, compatto, fitto. **— ranks of soldiers,** schiere serrate di soldati, *f.pl.*
serum [ˈsiərəm], *n.* Siero, *m.*
servant [ˈsəːɹvənt], *n.* Servo, servitore, domestico, *m.*; fante, *m.*; famiglio, *m.*; impiegato, *m.*; attendente, *m.* **General —,** donna di servizio, *f.*; **— girl,** domestica, fantesca, *f.*; **indoor servants,** servi di casa, *m.pl.*; **civil —,** impiegato statale, *m.*
serve [səːɹv], *v.t.i.* Servire, servire da, servire di; giovare, bastare; (*a sentence*) subire, scontare; (*a ball*) mandare; (*at table*) portare; (*a notice*) intimare a; (*apprenticeship*) fare; (*Naut.*) far la manica a. **To — a purpose,** servire ad uno scopo; **to — one's own ends,** fare i propri interessi; **it serves my turn,** serve al caso mio; **as occasion serves,** all'occasione; **to — a sentence,** scontare una pena; **dinner is served,** il pranzo è servito; **he has served me badly,** mi ha trattato male; **it serves you right,** ben vi sta; **to — someone out,** rendere la pariglia a qualcuno; **to — out,** servire, distribuire; **to — as an excuse,** servire di scusa; (*Law*) **to — a warrant,** presentare un mandato di cattura.

server, *n.* (*Tennis*) Battitore, mandatore, *m.*
Servian [cp. **Serbian**].
service [ˈsəːɹvis], *n.* Servizio, *m.*; impiego, *m.*; (*favour*) servigio, *m.*; vantaggio, *m.*, utilità, *f.*; beneficio, favore, *m.*; (*Law*) citazione, notificazione, *f.*; (*Eccles.*) ufficio divino, *m.*, messa, *f.*; (*domestic*) servitù, *f.*, servizio, *m.*; (*china, etc.*) servizio, vasellame, *m.*; (*Tennis*) servizio, *m.* ‖ *v.t.* Mantenere in ordine, mettere in ordine. **At your —,** servo vostro, ai vostri ordini; **divine —,** servizio divino, *m.*; **foreign —,** servizio estero, *m.*; **in —,** al servizio, appadronato; **at the — of,** al servizio di; **of —,** utile, giovevole; **on active —,** in servizio attivo; **to do someone a —,** rendere un servigio a qualcuno; **civil —,** pubblica amministrazione, *f.*; **— -book,** rituale, *m.*; **— -pipe,** condotto dell'acqua, *m.*; **— -hatch,** sportello della credenza, *m.*; **— -lift,** montavivande, *m.*; (*Tennis*) **— -line,** linea di servizio, *m.*; (*Bot.*) **— -tree,** sorbo, *m.*
serviceable, *a.* Utile, pratico; durabile, durevole, resistente.
serviceableness, *n.* Utilità, durabilità, *f.*
serviceably, *adv.* Utilmente, durevolmente.
serviette [səːɹviˈet], *n.* Tovagliuolo, *m.*
servile [ˈsəːɹvail], *a.* Servile.
servileness, servility [ˈsəːɹvailnes, səːɹˈviliti], *n.* Servilità, *f.*
serving-maid, *n.* Cameriera, fantesca, *f.* **Serving-man,** servo, domestico, *m.*
servitor, *n.* Servitore, cameriere, *m.* (*Oxford Univ.*) studente con borsa di studio, *m.*
servitude [ˈsəːɹvitjuːd], *n.* Servitù, soggezione, schiavitù, *f.* **Penal —,** lavori forzati, *m.pl.*
sesame [ˈsesəmi], *n.* (*Bot.*) Sesamo, *m.* **Open, —!** Apriti, sesamo!
sesquipedalian [seskwipeˈdeiliən], *a.* Sesquipedale.
sessile [ˈsesail], *a.* (*Bot.*) Sessile.
session [ˈseʃən], *n.* Sessione, *f.*; seduta, *f.*; (*Law*) **Sessions,** assise, *f.pl.* **Quarter-sessions,** assise trimestrali, *f.pl.*
sestet [sesˈtet], *n.* (*Mus.*) Sestetto, *m.*
set (1) [set], *v.t.* Mettere, porre, disporre, locare; fissare, ficcare, stabilire; piantare; seminare; (*Print.*) comporre; (*Med.*) aggiustare; (*tools*) affilare; (*jewels*) incastonare; *v.i.* solidificarsi, coagulare, rapprendersi; formarsi; rassodarsi; indurire; (*of sun*) tramontare. **To — about,** cominciare, mettersi a, accingersi a; **to — against,** opporre a, contrapporre a, aizzare, influenzare contro; **to — apart, to — by,** mettere a parte, riservare; **to — aside,** mettere a parte, (*Law*) annullare; **to — a clock,** regolare un orologio; **to — an alarum clock at 5 o'clock,** metter la sveglia sulle cinque; **to — at defiance,** sfidare; **to — at ease,** rassicurare; **to — back,** far indietreggiare, impedire; **to — down,** porre giù, mettere in iscritto; **to — down to,** attribuire a; **to — down as,** spiegare come; **to — eyes on,** metter gli occhi su; **to — foot on,** metter piede su; **to — on foot,** cominciare; **to — forth,** mostrare, dimostrare, esporre, mettersi in via; **to — forward,** andare avanti, aiutare, promuovere; **to — in,** cominciare, stabilirsi; **it — in wet,** cominciò a piovere; **to — off,** ornare, abbellire, far valere, dar risalto a, compensare, far cominciare; **to — on,** istigare, stimolare, spingere, attaccare; **to — one's hand to,** dar mano a, formare; **to — out,** mostrare, esporre, spiegare, mettersi in via, partire; **to — a hen,** far covare una gallina; **to — one's heart on,** aver gran voglia di; **to — over,** dare autorità a; **to — right,** sorreggere, rettificare, mettere a posto; **to — someone's mind at rest,** tranquillizzare qualcuno; **to — sail,** veleggiare; **to — one's teeth,** serrare i denti; **to — one's teeth on edge,** allegare i denti; **to — to,** applicarsi, cominciare a battersi; **to — to work,** mettersi al lavoro; **to — up,** erigere, innalzare, stabilire, dar luogo a; **to — up as,** spacciarsi per; **to — up someone in business,** avviare qualcuno negli affari; **to — one's face against,** opporsi a; **to — going,** porre in moto, avviare; **to — someone laughing,** far ridere qualcuno; **to — the fashion,** introdurre la moda; **to — to music,** mettere in musica, musicare; **opinion is setting against him,** l'opinione gli è divenuta contraria; **to — someone on his feet again,** rimettere qualcuno in salute, ristabilire qualcuno; **to — a task,** assegnare un compito; **to — up for,** spacciarsi per; **the current sets westward,** la corrente volge ad ovest; **to — to partners,** riprendere il compagno; **that dress sets badly,** quell'abito s'attaglia male; **rain is setting in,** il tempo si è messo alla pioggia; **to — the hair,** mettere in piega i capelli.
set (2), *n.* Serie, *f.*; collezione, *f.*; fornimento, assortimento, *m.*; (*of china*) servizio, *m.*; (*of ornaments*) guarnizione, *f.*; (*Elec.Radio*) apparecchio, *m.*; (*of current*) moto, *m.*; (*Theat.*) scenario, *m.*; (*Tennis*), set, *m.*, partita, *f.*; (*Bot.*) pianticella, *f.* **A fine — of men,** un bel insieme di uomini; **the — of public feeling,** la direzione dell'opinione pubblica, *f.*; **a — of (natural) teeth,** dentatura, *f.*; **a — of (artificial) teeth,** una dentiera, *f.*; **to make a dead — at,** far una guerra sorda a; **the smart —,** il bel mondo, *m.*; **the — of the saw,** l'allicciatura della sega, *f.*; **— -back,** regresso, intoppo, arretramente, *m.* (*of illness*) ricaduta, *f.*; **— -down,** affronto, *m.*; **— -off,** compenso, contrappeso, *m.*, ornamento, *m.*; **— -out,** mostra, *f.*; **— -square,** squadra, *f.*; **— -to,** zuffa, *f.*, lite, *f.*; **— -up,** sistemazione, messa a punto, *f.*, portamento, *m.*
set (3), *a.* Messo, posto, collocato; fisso, fermo; regolare, determinato, stabilito; studiato, preparato. **A — smile,** un sorriso fisso, *m.*; **at a — time,** ad un'ora determinata; **of — purpose,** apposta, con intenzione, di proposito; **to be dead — on a thing,** essere impuntato in una cosa; **a sky — with stars,** un cielo cosparso di stelle; **— fair,** messo al bello; **a — phrase,** una frase stereotipata, *f.*; **a — speech,** un discorso preparato, *m.*
setaceous [seˈteiʃəs], *a.* Setoloso.
seton [ˈsiːtən], *n.* (*Med.*) Setone, *m.*
sett [set], *n.* Pietra da lastricare, *f.*, quadrello, *m.*
settee [seˈtiː], *n.* Canapè, divano, *m.*, sofà, *f.*
setter, *n.* Cane da fermo, *m.* **— on,** istigatore, *m.*
setting, *n.* Messa, positura, *f.*; postura, *f.* (*of sun*) tramonto, *m.*; (*Mus.*) messa in musica,

f.; (*of gem*) incastonatura, *f.*; (*of tools*) affilatura, *f.*; (*Theat.*) messa in scena, *f.*; (*Print.*) composizione, *f.* **—-free,** liberazione, *f.*; **—-in,** inizio, principio, *m.*; **—-off,** partenza, *f.*; **—-up,** stabilimento, *m.*; montaggio, *m.*; (*Print.*) composizione, *f.*; (*Print.*) **—-stick,** compositoio, *m.*; **— aside,** lasciando stare, astrazione fatta da.

settle (1) [setl], *n.* Panca, *f.*, sedile, *m.*; sgabellino, *m.*

settle (2), *v.t.* Fissare, stabilire, determinare; (*to decide*) decidere, risolvere; (*to colonize*) colonizzare; (*a difference*) comporre; (*to pay*) pagare; (*to adjust*) accomodare, aggiustare; (*to arrange*) sistemare; (*of property*) intestare; *v.i.* fissarsi, stabilirsi; domiciliarsi; sposarsi, metter su casa; (*of liquids*) depositare; (*to sink*) affondare; (*of weather*) mettersi al bello; (*of ground*) cedere, avvallarsi. **To — oneself in a chair,** adagiarsi in una sedia; **to — the day,** fissare la data; **to — a quarrel,** comporre una lite; **to — someone's debts,** pagare i debiti di qualcuno; **that settles the matter,** ciò decide la questione; **to — one's affairs,** regolare i propri affari; **to — down,** metter su casa, stabilirsi; calmarsi, tranquillarsi; **to — down to, to — to,** applicarsi a, mettersi a; **he settled an annuity on her,** le assegnò una rendita; **to — up,** pagare, liquidare; **to — on,** posarsi su, determinare; **it was settled that,** fu convenuto che.

settled, *a.* Fisso, stabilito; stanziato; (*Comm.*) saldato; sereno, costante. **— habit,** abitudine radicata, *f.*; **— price,** prezzo fisso, *m.*

settlement, *n.* Stabilimento, assestamento, *m.*; decisione, risoluzione, *f.*; (*colony*) colonia, *f.*; (*Law*) assegno, *m.*; (*annuity*) rendita, *f.*; (*of accounts*) quietanza, *f.*, saldo, *m.*; (*Stock Exchange*) liquidazione, *f.* **marriage —,** contratto di matrimonio, *m.*

settler, *n.* Colono, *m.*

settling, *n.* Stabilimento, *m.* (*Comm.*) **—-day,** giorno di liquidazione, *m.*; **—-up,** regolamento, *m.*, liquidazione dei conti, *f.*

seven [ˈsevən], *n.a.* Sette, *m.* **The Seven Sleepers,** I Sette Dormienti, *m.pl.*; **the — deadly sins,** i sette peccati mortali, *m.pl.*

sevenfold, *a.* Settuplo. || *adv.* Sette volte.

seventeen [sevənˈtiːn], *n.a.* Diciassette, *m.* **— years old,** diciassettenne.

seventeenth, *n.a.* Decimosettimo, diciassettisimo, *m.*

seventh, *n.a.* Settimo, *m.*

seventieth [ˈsevəntiəθ], *n.a.* Settantesimo, *m.*

seventy, *n.a.* Settanta, *m.* **A man of —,** un settantenne.

sever [ˈsevəɹ], *v.t.* Separare, dividere, distaccare, disgiungere; tagliare. **To — one's connection with,** separarsi da, staccarsi da.

several [ˈsevərəl], *a.* Parecchi; separato, diverso, distinto, diviso; particolare, proprio. **They went their — ways,** ciascuno andò per la propria via.

severally, *adv.* Separatamente, individualmente.

severance, *n.* Separazione, divisione, disgiunzione, *f.*; taglio, distacco, *m.*

severe [seˈviəɹ], *a.* Severo, duro, austero; (*of weather*) rigido; (*of pain*) acuto, vivo, violento. **A — winter,** un inverno rigido, *m.*

severity [seˈveriti], *n.* Severità, durezza, austerita, *f.*; rigidezza, *f.*; acutezza, violenza, *f.*

Seville [ˈsevil, seˈvil], *n.* (*Geog.*) Siviglia, *f.* **— orange,** arancia amara, *f.*

sew [sou], *v.t.* Cucire.

sewage [ˈsjuːidʒ], *n.* Fognatura, scolatura, *f.* **—-farm,** cascina che utilizza i detriti di fogna quale concime.

sewed [ˈsoud], *a.* Cucito.

sewer (1) [ˈsouəɹ], *n.* Cucitore, *m.*, cucitrice, *f.*

sewer (2) [ˈsjuːəɹ], *n.* Fogna, cloaca, *f.* **—-gas,** gas di fognatura, *m.*

sewerage [cp. **sewage**].

sewerman, *n.* Fognaiuolo, *m.*

sewing [ˈsouiŋ], *n.* Cucito, *m.*, cucitura, *f.* **—-cotton,** cotone da cucire, *m.*; **—-machine,** macchina da cucire, *f.*

sex [seks], *n.* Sesso, *m.* **The fair —,** il gentil sesso, *m.*; **— appeal,** attrazione del sesso, *f.*, fascino muliebre, *m.*

sexagenarian [seksədʒeˈnɛəriən], *n.a.* Sessagenario, *m.*

sexagenary, *a.* Sessantenne, sessagenario.

Sexagesima [seksəˈdʒesimə], *n.* (*Eccles.*) Sessagesima, *f.*

sexennial [sekˈseniəl], *a.* Sessennale.

sexless, *a.* Senza sesso, senza l'attrazione del sesso.

sextant [ˈsekstənt], *n.* Sestante, *m.*

sextet [seksˈtet], *n.* (*Mus.*) Sestetto, *m.*

sexton [ˈsekstən], *n.* Necroforo, becchino, *m.*; sagrestano, *m.*

sextuple [ˈsekstjuːpl], *a.* Sestuplo.

sexual [ˈseksjuːəl], *a.* Sessuale.

sexuality [seksjuːˈæliti], *n.* Sessualità, *f.*

sexually, *adv.* Sessualmente.

shabbily [ˈʃæbili], *adv.* Meschinamente; male. **— dressed,** male in arnese.

shabbiness, *n.* Straccioneria, scompostezza, *f.*; (*meanness*) meschineria, grettezza, *f.*

shabby, *a.* Male in arnese, mal vestito, scalcagnato; frusto, malconcio, logoro, sciupato; meschino, gretto, tirchio. **A — trick,** un brutto tiro, un brutto scherzo, *m.*, una birbonata, *f.*

shack [ʃæk], *n.* Capanna, baracca, *f.*

shackle [ʃækl], *v.t.* Incatenare, inceppare; (*fig.*) impedire, imbrogliare, inceppare. || *n.* (*Mech.*) Anello di trazione, *m.*; (*Naut.*) maniglia, *f.* **Shackles,** ceppi, legami, *m.pl.*, pastoie, *f.pl.* **The shackles of convention,** le pastoie delle convenzioni, *f.pl.*

shad [ʃæd], *n.* (*Zool.*) Alosa, *f.*

shaddock [ˈʃædək], *n.* (*Bot.*) Pampelimosa, *f.*

shade [ʃeid], *n.* (*from light*) Ombra, oscurità, *f.*; (*of colour*) tinta, sfumatura, gradazione, *f.*; (*for lamp*) paralume, *m.*; (*for eyes*) paraluce, *m.*; (*ghost*) ombra, fantasma, *f.*, spettro, spirito, *m.* || *v.t.* Ombreggiare; oscurare, ottenebrare, offuscare; parare, riparare, difendere proteggere; sfumare. **The shades of night,** le ombre notturne, *f.pl.*; **in the —,** all'ombra; **he is a — better to-day,** oggi sta un' ombra meglio; **to throw into the —,** eclissare, oscurare.

shaded, *a.* All'ombra; ombroso, ombreggiato; sfumato.

shadeless, *a.* Senza ombra.

shadiness, *n.* Ombra, ombrosità, *f.*; (*fig.*) dubbia fama, loschezza, *f.*

shading, *n.* Sfumatura, gradazione dei colori, *f.*
shadow [ˈʃædou], *n.* Ombra, *f.*; riflessione, *f.*, riflesso, *m.*; oscurità, *f.*; (*fig.*) compagno inseparabile, *m.* || *v.t.* Ombreggiare, oscurare; sorvegliare, tener d'occhio, spiare; pedinare. **To — forth**, adombrare; **— boxing**, pugilato finto, *m.*
shadowy, *a.* Ombroso; scuro, tenebroso; oscuro, irreale, chimerico.
shady [ˈʃeidi], *a.* Ombroso, ombreggiato, folto, oscuro; losco, sospetto, di dubbia fama. **The — side of the street**, il lato ombroso della strada, *m.*; **to be on the — side of fifty**, avere oltrepassato la cinquantina.
shaft [ʃɑːft], *n.* (*of lance*) Asta, *f.*; (*of arrow*) freccia, saetta, *f.*, dardo, strale, *m.*; (*of column*) fusto, *m.*; (*of lightning*) fulmine, *m.*; (*of carriage*) timone, *m.*; (*of chimney*) camino, *m.*; (*of cart*) stanga, *f.*; (*of mine, lift, etc.*) pozzo, *m.*; (*Mech.*) asse, albero, manico, *m.* **The shafts of ridicule**, le frecciate del ridicolo, *f.pl.*; **a — of light**, un fascio di luce, *m.*; **driving- —**, albero motore, *m.*; **connecting- —**, albero di trasmissione, *m.*; **— -horse**, cavallo a stanga, cavallo da tiro, *m.*; **ventilating- —**, pozzo di aerazione, *m.*
shafting, *n.* (*Mech.*) Trasmissione, *f.*
shag [ʃæg], *n.* Vello, pelo, *m.*; specie di tabacco da fumare, *f.*
shagginess [ˈʃægines], *n.* Ruvidezza, asprezza, *f.*
shaggy [ˈʃægi], *a.* Velloso, peloso, irsuto, ispido; ruvido, scabro, aspro.
shagreen [ʃəˈgriːn], *n.* Zigrino, *m.* || *a.* Di zigrino.
shah [ʃɑː], *n.* Scià, *m.*
shake [ʃeik], *n.* Scossa, *f.*, urto, crollo, *m.*; (*of hand*) stretta, *f.*; (*of head*) cenno, *m.*; (*Mus.*) trillo, *m.*, cadenza, *f.*; (*in wood*) screpolatura, *f.* || *v.t.* Scuotere, riscuotere, agitare, sbattere; infiacchire, indebolire; (*Mus.*) trillare; commuovere, agitare; *v.i.* tremare, tremolare; barcollare, traballare, vacillare; agitarsi. **To — hands with someone**, stringere la mano ad uno; **to — down**, far cadere, (*fig.*) adattarsi; **to — off**, scuotere di dosso, disfarsi di, sbarazzarsi di; **to — one's fist at someone**, mostrare il pugno ad uno; **to — one's head**, scuotere la testa; **it shook his composure**, scosse la sua impassibilità; **to — off the yoke**, liberarsi dal giogo; **to — oneself free from**, liberarsi da; **to — one's sides with laughter**, tenersi i fianchi dal ridere; **to — to pieces**, spezzettare, sbriciolare; **to — up**, sbattere, scuotere; **my hand shakes**, mi trema la mano; **to — like a leaf**, tremare come una foglia; **to — with cold**, tremare dal freddo; **to — with laughter**, spanciarsi dal ridere; **all of a —**, tremolante, barcollante; (*colloq.*) **no great shakes**, una cosa da poco, *f.*; **— -down**, letto improvvisato, *m.*
shaking, *n.* Scossa, *f.*, scuotimento, *m.*; tremore, *m.*, vibrazione, agitazione, *f.* **To give someone a good —**, dare uno scossone a qualcuno.
shako [ˈʃækou], *n.* Cheppì, *m.*
shaky [ˈʃeiki], *a.* Tremante, barcollante, vacillante; malfermo, scosso, debole. **A — table**, una tavola traballante, *f.*; **a — old man**, un vecchio barcollante, *m.*; **he looks very —**, pare molto scosso; **his Latin is very —**, il suo latino è molto debole.
shale [ʃeil], *n.* (*Geol.*) Schisto argilloso, *m.*, argilla friabile, *f.* **— -oil**, olio minerale, *m.*
shall [ʃæl], *v.aux.* Dovere. (Usually expressed in Italian by future tense). **We — see!** Vedremo! **I say you — do it**, dico io che dovrete farlo; **Shall I open the door?** Devo aprire la porta? **Why should I go?** Perchè dovrei andare?
shalloon [ʃəˈluːn], *n.* Saia, *f.*
shallop [ˈʃæləp], *n.* (*Naut.*) Scialuppa, *f.*
shallot [ʃəˈlɔt], *n.* (*Bot.*) Scalogno, *m.*
shallow [ˈʃælou], *a.* Poco profondo; basso; (*fig.*) superficiale, frivolo, leggiero. || *n.* (*Naut.*) Bassofondo, *m.*, secca, *f.* **— -brained**, vuoto, scervellato, frivolo.
shallowness, *n.* Poca profondità, bassezza, *f.*; superficialità, frivolezza, leggerezza, *f.*
sham [ʃæm], *a.* Finto, falso, fittizio. || *n.* Finzione, simulazione, *f.*, infingimento, inganno, *m.* || *v.t.i.* Fingere, simulare, fingersi. **A — fight**, una finta battaglia, *f.*; **to — illness**, fingere un'infermità, fingersi malato; **he is only shamming**, egli fa finta.
shamble [ʃæmbl], *v.i.* Camminare dinoccolato.
shambles, *n.pl.* Macello, *m.*; disordine, *m.*
shambling, *a.* Dinoccolato. **A — gait**, un'andatura dinoccolata, *f.*
shame [ʃeim], *n.* Onta, vergogna, infamia, ignominia, *f.*; obbrobrio, vituperio, *m.*; (*modesty*) pudore, *m.* || *v.t.* Vituperare, umiliare, svergognare, disonorare; far arrossire. **For —!** Vergogna! **out of —**, per pudore; **to be lost to all —**, aver perduto il pudore; **cheeks flushed with —**, guance rosse di vergogna; **to bring — on**, recare onta a; **to put someone to —**, svergognare uno; **to cry — on**, gettar la vergogna su.
shamefaced, *a.* Vergognoso, timido, pudibondo.
shamefacedly, *adv.* Timidamente.
shamefacedness, *n.* Timidità, modestia, *f.*
shameful, *a.* Vergognoso; infame, disonorevole.
shamefully, *adv.* Vergognosamente.
shameless, *a.* Svergognato, sfrontato, impudente, spudorato.
shamelessly, *adv.* Svergognatamente, sfacciatamente, sfrontatamente.
shamelessness, *n.* Impudenza, spudoratezza, *f.*
shammer, *n.* Simulatore, fintone, impostore, *m.*
shammy, shammy leather [ˈʃæmi, ʃæmi ˈleðəɹ], *n.* Pelle di camoscio, *f.*
shampoo [ʃæmˈpuː], *n.* (*wet*) Shampoo, *m.*; (*dry*) frizione, *f.* || *v.t.* Fare uno shampoo, fare una frizione.
shamrock [ˈʃæmrɔk], *n.* (*Bot.*) Trifoglio d'Irlanda, *m.*
shandy, shandygaff [ˈʃændi, ʃændiˈgæf], *n.* Bibita fatta di birra e di gassosa, *f.*
Shanghai [ʃæŋˈhai], *n.* (*Geog.*) Sciangai, *f.*
shank [ʃæŋk], *n.* (*leg*) Gamba, *f.*; (*leg-bone*) tibia, *f.*, stinco, *m.*; (*of flower, leaf, button, etc.*) gambo, *m.*; (*of anchor*) fuso, *m.*; (*of pillar*) fusto, *m.* **Shanks's mare**, il cavallo di San Francesco, *m.*
shanty (1) [ˈʃænti], *n.* Capanna, baracca, *f.*

shanty (2), *n.* Canzone marinesca, *f.*
shape [ʃeip], *n.* Forma, figura, fattezza, statura, *f.*; tipo, modello, *m.* ‖ *v.t.* Formare, modellare, plasmare; adattare, regolare, dirigere; concepire; *v.i.* prender forma. **In the — of,** a forma di; **to get out of —,** perdere la forma; **to take —,** prender forma; **to get into —,** ordinare, disporre, allestire; **he shapes well,** va avanti bene.
shapeless, *a.* Informe; confuso, caotico.
shapelessness, *n.* Informità, deformità, mancanza di forma, *f.*
shapeliness, *n.* Simmetria, bellezza di forma, *f.*
shapely, *a.* Simmetrico; ben fatto, bello.
shard [ʃɑːɹd], *n.* Coccio, *m.*; elitra, *f.*
share [ʃɛəɹ], *n.* Parte, porzione, quota, *f.*; (*Comm.*) azione, *f.*, titolo, valore, *m.*; ‖ *v.t.i.* Dividere, spartire; partecipare, prender parte, condividere. **To go shares in,** dividere egualmente; **a fair —,** una porzione giusta, *f.*; **the lion's —,** la parte del leone, *f.*; (*Comm.*) **preference shares,** azioni preferenziali, *f.pl.*; **to have shares in,** avere azioni in; **to — in,** prender parte a; **to — out,** distribuire; **to — and — alike,** prendere parti eguali; **I — your opinion,** condivido la vostra opinione; (*Comm.*) **— capital,** capitale azionario, *m.*; **— -pusher,** piazzista, *m.*
shareholder, *n.* Azionista, *m.f.*
sharer, *n.* Partecipante, *m.* **To be a — in,** partecipare a, prender parte a, condividere.
sharing, *n.* Distribuzione, divisione, *f.*; spartizione, *f.*
shark [ʃɑːɹk], *n.* (*Zool.*) Squalo, pescecane, *m.*; (*fig.*) pescecane, *m.*; scroccone, *m.*
sharp [ʃɑːɹp], *a.* Acuto, affilato, aguzzo, tagliente; penetrante, fino, sottile; piccante, pungente, frizzante; perspicace; mordace; astuto, malizioso, furbo; aspro, severo. ‖ *n.* (*Mus.*) diesis, *m.* ‖ *adv.* Preciso, in punto; presto. **A — appetite,** un appetito gagliardo, *m.*; **a — outline,** un contorno netto, *m.*; **— features,** fattezze affilate, *f.pl.*; **a — tongue,** una lingua mordace, *f.*; **a — temper,** un temperamento collerico, *m.*; **a — attack of influenza,** un forte attacco d'influenza, *m.*; **— practice,** furberia, *f.*; **to keep a — look-out,** stare all'erta; **he was too — for me,** era troppo furbo per me; **to take a — walk,** far una lesta camminata; **Look —!** Presto; Sbrigatevi! **at ten o'clock —,** alle dieci precise, alle dieci in punto; **— -edged,** affilato; **— -set,** affamato; **— -sighted,** dalla vista acuta, oculato; **— -witted,** di mente acuta; **— -shooter,** tiratore scelto, *m.*
sharpen, *v.t.* Affilare, aguzzare, appuntare; arrotare; stimolare; (*Mus.*) diesare.
sharpener, *n.* Affilatoio, arrotino, *m.*; (*Mech.*) affilatrice, *f.*
sharper, *n.* Scroccone, truffatore, *m.*
sharply, *adv.* Acutamente; aspramente, severamente; nettamente. **The road turns — to the right,** la strada piega bruscamente a destra; **— -outlined,** nettamente profilato; **to answer —,** rispondere vivacemente.
sharpness, *n.* Acutezza, *f.*; penetrazione, finezza, *f.*; sottigliezza, *f.*; perspicacia, *f.*; mordacità, *f.*; astuzia, furberia, *f.*; asprezza, severità, *f.*
shatter [ˈʃætəɹ], *v.t.* Fracassare, spezzare, fare in pezzi, frantumare; distruggere, rovinare. **Shattered health,** salute rovinata, *f.*; **shattered hopes,** speranze rovinate, *f.pl.*
shave [ʃeiv], *v.t.* Radere, sbarbare, fare la barba a; (*to graze*) sfiorare; *v.i.* farsi la barba, radersi, sbarbarsi. **To get shaved,** farsi sbarbare, farsi far la barba; (*colloq.*) **to have a close —,** scamparla bella.
shaveling, *n.* Tonsurato, chierico, *m.*
shaver, *n.* Barbiere, *m.*; (*colloq.*) monello, *m.*
shaving, *n.* Raditura, *f.*, radere, radersi, *m.*; (*of wood*) truciolo, ritaglio, *m.* **— -brush,** pennello da barba, *m.*; **— -soap,** sapone per la barba; **— -cream,** crema per rasarsi *f.*; **— -stick,** bastoncello di sapone per la barba, *m.*
shawl [ʃɔːl], *n.* Scialle, sciallo, *m.*
shawm [ʃɔːm], *n.* (*obs. Mus.*) Chiarina, cennamella, *f.*
she [ʃiː], *pron.* Essa, ella, lei; colei; quella. **It is —,** è lei; **Is the child a he or a she?** Il bambino è un maschio o una femmina? **— -ass,** asina, *f.*; **— -bear,** orsa, *f.*; **— -cat,** gatta, *f.*; **— -devil,** diavola, diavolessa, *f.*; **— -goat,** capra, *f.*; **— -monkey,** bertuccia, scimmia, *f.*; **— -wolf,** lupa, *f.*
sheaf (pl. **sheaves**) [ʃiːf, ʃiːvz], *n.* Covone, *m.*; fascio, *m.* ‖ *v.t.* Abbarcare, accovonare; affastellare, ammontare.
shear [ʃiəɹ], *v.t.* Tosare, tondere; scorticare; tagliare, spaccare. **To — the sheep,** tosare le pecore; (*Zool.*) **— -water,** puffino, *m.*
shearer, *n.* Tosatore, *m.*; macchina tosatrice, *f.*
shearing, *n.* Tosatura, *f.* **— -machine,** tosatrice, *f.*; **— -time,** tempo della tosatura, *m.*
shearling, *n.* Pecora tosata una volta sola, *f.*
shears, *n.pl.* Forbici grosse, cesoie, *f.pl.*
sheath (pl. **sheaths**) [ʃiːθ], *n.* Guaina, *f.*; fodero, *m.*; (*case*) astuccio, *m.*; (*of insects*) elitra, *f.*
sheathe [ʃiːð], *v.t.* Rinfoderare, ringuainare, foderare, rivestire di. **To — the sword,** rinfoderar la spada.
sheathing, *n.* (*Mech.*) Fodera, *f.*, rivestimento, *m.*
sheave [ʃiːv], *n.* Carrucola, puleggia, *f.*
shed (1) [ʃed], *n.* Tettoia, rimessa, *f.*; hangar, capannone, *m.*; tugurio, *m.*
shed (2), *v.t.* Versare, spargere, spandere; lasciar cadere; (*of trees*) perdere; (*of skin*) spogliarsi di. **To — tears,** versare lagrime; **the snake sheds its skin,** il serpente si spoglia della pelle; **to — one's blood for one's country,** dare il sangue per la patria; **to — light,** spargere luce.
shedding, *n.* Spargimento, versamento, *m.*; effusione, *f.*; perdita, *f.*
sheen [ʃiːn], *n.* Splendore, *m.*, lucentezza, *f.*
sheeny, *a.* Lustro, lucido, lucente.
sheep (pl. **sheep**) [ʃiːp], *n.* Pecora, *f.*, pecore, *f.pl.* (*fig.*) **Black —,** pecora segnata, pecora nera, *f.*; **to cast sheep's eyes at,** fare il cascamorto a, far l'occhiolino a; **lost —,** pecorella smarrita, *f.*; **— -cote, — -fold,** ovile, chiuso, *m.*; **— -dip, — -wash,** lavatura disinfettante, *f.*; **— -dog,** cane da pastore, *m.*; **— -farmer,** allevatore di pecore, pecoraio, *m.*; **— -run, — -walk,** pascolo di pecore, *m.*; **— -hook,** bastone del pastore, vincastro, *m.*; **— -shearer,** tosatore, *m.*; **— -shearing,** tosatura, *f.*

sheepish, *a.* Impacciato, imbarazzato, tonto, melenso, confuso, stordito.
sheepishly, *adv.* Imbarazzatamente.
sheepskin, *n.* Pelle di pecora, pelle di montone, *f.*
sheer (1) [ʃiəɹ], *a.* Puro, semplice, mero; netto, affatto; perpendicolare, a picco; diafano, trasparente. **— nonsense,** un puro nonsenso, *m.*; **— waste,** puro sperpero, *m.*; **a — drop,** uno strapiombo, *m.*
sheer (2), *n.* (*Naut.*) Curvatura, *f.*; virata, *f.* || *v.i.* Virare, scartare. **To — off,** scappare, svignarsela, dileguarsi; prendere il largo; **— -hulk,** pontone a biga, *m.*
sheers, *n.pl.* (*Naut.*) Biga, *f.*; argano, *m.*
sheet [ʃi:t], *n.* (*on bed*) Lenzuolo, *m.*; (*of paper*) foglio, *m.*; (*of metal*) lamiera, lastra, piastra, *f.*; (*of water*) specchio, *m.*; (*newspaper*) giornale, *m.*; (*Naut.*) corda, *f.*; (*of flame*) fiammata, *f.* || *v.t.* Coprire di lenzuolo, avvolgere in lenzuolo. **— -anchor,** ancora di fortuna, *f.*; **— -copper,** rame in lastre, *m.*; **— -iron,** lamiera, *f.*; **— -lightning,** baleno a secco, lampeggio, *m.*; **— -glass,** lastra di vetro, cristallo, *m.*
sheeting, *n.* Tela per lenzuola, *f.*; (*Mech.*) blindaggio, *m.*
sheik [ʃi:k, ʃek], *n.* Sceicco, *m.*
shekel [ˈʃekəl], *n.* Siclo, *m.* (*colloq.*) **Shekels,** danaro, *m.*, quattrini, *m.pl.*
sheldrake [ˈʃeldreik], *n.* (*Zool.*) Volpoca, anitra selvatica, *f.*
shelf (pl. **shelves**) [ʃelf, ʃelvz], *n.* (*of book-case*) Palchetto, *m.*; (*ledge*) sporgenza, *f.*; (*of rock*) scogliera, *f.*; asse, *m.* **A set of shelves,** uno scaffale, *m.*; (*fig.*) **to be put on the —,** andare a riposo.
shell [ʃel], *n.* Conchiglia, conca, corazza, *f.*, guscio, *m.*; baccello, *m.*; (*of building*) ossatura, *f.*; fodera, *f.*; (*coffin*) cassa, *f.*; (*Mil.*) granata, bomba, *f.*, proiettile, *m.*; (*fig.*) esterno, *m.*, apparenza, *f.*; contorno, *m.* || *v.t.* Sgusciare, sgranare, sbaccellare; (*Mil.*) bombardare, cannoneggiare. (*fig.*) **To come out of one's —,** uscire dal guscio; (*colloq.*) **to — out,** sborsare; **— -hole,** cratere di granata, *m.*; **— -proof,** a prova di bomba; **— -shock,** commozione, psicosi traumatica, *f.*
shellac [ˈʃelæk], *n.* Gomma lacca, *f.*, scaglie di lacca, *f.pl.*
shellfish, *n.* Mollusco, crostaceo, *m.*
shelter [ˈʃeltəɹ], *n.* Riparo, ricovero, rifugio, schermo, asilo, *m.*; difesa, protezione, *f.*; (*in street*) tettoia, *f.* || *v.t.i.* Riparare, coprire, proteggere, difendere; ripararsi, ricoverarsi, rifiugiarsi. **To take —,** ripararsi; **to reach —,** giungere al coperto; **to — from the rain,** ripararsi dalla pioggia; **to — in a doorway,** ricoverarsi in un portone; **under —,** al coperto.
sheltered, *a.* Al coperto, al riparo; protetto, riparato. **A — life,** una vita ritirata, *f.*
shelterless, *a.* Senza asilo, senza tetto.
shelve [ʃelv], *v.t.* Mettere in uno scaffale; fornire di palchetti; (*fig.*) mettere da parte, rimandare; *v.i.* inclinarsi, essere in pendenza.
shelving, *a.* In pendenza, in declivio.
shepherd [ˈʃepəɹd], *n.* Pastore, pecoraio, *m.* || *v.t.* Custodire; condurre, guidare. **Shepherd's crook,** bastone del pastore, vincastro, *m.*; (*Bot.*) **shepherd's purse,** borsa di pastore, *f.*
shepherdess, *n.* Pastora, pastorella, *f.*
sherbet [ˈʃəːɹbət], *n.* Sorbetto, *m.*
sherd [cp. **shard**].
sheriff [ˈʃerif], *n.* Sceriffo, *m.* **Sheriff's officer,** usciere prefettizio, *m.*
sherry [ˈʃeri], *n.* Vino di Xeres, *m.*
shew [cp. **show**].
shibboleth [ˈʃibəleθ], *n.* Formula, parola d'ordine, *f.*
shield [ʃi:ld], *n.* Scudo, *m.*; schermo, *m.*; protettore, *m.*, difesa, *f.*; (*Heraldry*) scudo, *m.*, stemma, *f.* || *v.t.* Difendere, proteggere, far scudo a. **— -bearer,** scudiero, *m.*
shift (1) [ʃift], *n.* Camicia, *f.*
shift (2), *n.* Cambiamento, mutamento, *m.*; (*expedient*) espediente, ritrovato, *m.*; sotterfugio, inganno, *m.*; (*of wind*) salto, *m.*; (*of workmen*) turno, *m.*, squadra, *f.* || *v.t.i.* Cambiare, muovere, trasferire, spostare; muoversi, spostarsi. **To make — to,** aggiustarsi alla meglio a; **to make — with,** contentarsi di, adattarsi a; **to — about,** spostarsi, vacillare; **to — for oneself,** fare da sè; **to — responsibility,** evitare la responsabilità; **the wind has shifted to the east,** il vento è voltato ad est; **the scene shifts,** la scena cambia; (*fig.*) **to — one's ground,** portare la questione su un terreno diverso.
shiftiness, *n.* Furberia, *f.*
shifting, *n.* Cambiamento, mutamento, spostamento, *m.* || *a.* Instabile, incerto, mutevole.
shiftless, *a.* Inetto, inconcludente, incapace.
shifty, *a.* Furbo, scaltro, astuto. **— eyes,** occhi sfuggenti, *m.pl.*
shillelagh [ʃiˈleilə], *n.* Bastone degli Irlandesi, *m.*
shilling [ˈʃiliŋ], *n.* Scellino, *m.*
shilly-shally [ˈʃiliʃæli], *n.* Esitazione, irresolutezza, titubanza, *f.* || *v.i.* Esitare, vacillare, titubare.
shimmer [ˈʃiməɹ], *n.* Luccicchio, scintillio, bagliore, *m.* || *v.i.* Brillare, luccicare, scintillare.
shin [ʃin], *n.* (*Anat.*) Stinco, *m.*; (*of beef*) garretto, *m.* **— -bone,** tibia, *f.*; **— guard,** gambale, ghettone, *m.*; **to — up,** arrampicarsi.
shindy [ˈʃindi], *n.* Schiamazzo, baccano, strepito. **To kick up a —,** fare un gran baccano.
shine [ʃain], *v.i.* Brillare, risplendere, splendere, rifulgere, raggiare; *v.t.* pulire. || *n.* Splendore, fulgore, lustro, *m.*; bel tempo, *m.* **He does not — in conversation,** non brilla nella conversazione; **the sun shines,** splende il sole; **to take the — out of,** eclissare.
shingle [ʃiŋgl], *n.* (*roofing*) Assicella, *f.*; (*on beach*) ghiaia, *f.*, ciottoli, *m.pl.*; (*hair*) capelli a zazzera, *m.pl.* || *v.t.* Coprire di assicelle; (*hair*) tagliare i capelli alla garçonne.
shingles, *n.pl.* (*Med.*) Erpete, *m.*; fuoco di Sant' Antonio, *m.*
shingly, *a.* Coperto di ciottoli, ghiaioso.
shining, shiny [ˈʃainiŋ, ˈʃaini], *a.* Brillante, lucente, sfolgorante.
ship [ʃip], *n.* Nave, *f.*, bastimento, *m.*, vascello, naviglio, battello, *m.* || *v.t.* Imbarcare, mettere a bordo; spedire; armare; *v.i.* imbarcarsi. **Merchant- —,** nave mercantile, *f.*; **sailing- —,** nave a vela, *f.*; **on board —, on shipboard,** a bordo; **to take —,** imbarcarsi;

ship's papers, carte di bordo, *f.pl.*; **to — the oars,** disarmare i remi; **to — a heavy sea,** imbarcare un'ondata; **to — the rudder,** montare il timone; **— biscuit,** biscotto di mare, *m.*; **—-broker,** agente marittimo, *m.*; **—-builder,** costruttore di navi, *m.*; **—-building,** costruzione di navi, *f.*; **—-canal,** canale navigabile, *m.*; **—-chandler,** fornitore marittimo, *m.*; **ship's husband,** raccomandatario di una nave, *m.*

shipmate, *n.* Compagno di bordo, *m.*

shipment, *n.* Carico, *m.*; spedizione, *f.*, invio, *m.*

shipowner, *n.* Armatore, *m.*

shipper, *n.* Esportatore, spedizioniere, *m.*

shipping, *n.* Navi, *f.pl.*, naviglio, *m.*; marina mercantile, *f.*; invio, *m.*, spedizione, *f.*, traffico marittimo, *m.* || *a.* Marittimo, navale. **—-agent,** agente marittimo, *m.*; **—-office,** agenzia marittima, *f.*; **— charges,** spese di spedizione, *f.pl.*

shipshape, *a.* In ordine, bene assettato.

shipwreck, *n.* Naufragio, *m.* || *v.t.* Far naufragare, mandare a picco. **To be shipwrecked,** naufragare.

shipwrecked, *a.* Naufragato, rovinato.

shipwright, *n.* Costruttore di navi, *m.*

shipyard, *n.* Cantiere navale, arsenale, *m.*

shire [ʃaiɹ], *n.* Contea, *f.*

shirk [ʃəːɹk], *v.t.* Evitare, schivare, scansare, sottrarsi a; *v.i.* imboscarsi. **To — one's work,** sottrarsi al lavoro.

shirker, *n.* Scansafatiche, *m.*; imboscato, *m.*

shirt [ʃəːɹt], *n.* Camicia, *f.* **Night-—,** camicia da notte, *f.*; **—-collar,** collo di camicia, colletto, *m.*; **—-front,** sparato, *m.*; **—-sleeves,** maniche di camicia, *f.pl.*

shirting, *n.* Tela per camicia, *f.*

shirty, *a.* (*colloq.*) Irascibile, irritabile.

shiver [ˈʃivəɹ], *v.t.* Fracassare, frantumare, spezzare, fare in pezzi; *v.i.* rabbrividire, tremare. || *n.* Brivido, tremito, *m.* **To — with cold,** tremare di freddo; **to have the shivers,** rabbrividire, avere i brividi.

shivering, *a.* Tremante. || *n.* Brivido, tremore, *m.*

shiveringly, *adv.* Tremando, con brividi.

shivery, *a.* Freddoloso.

shoal [ʃoul], *n.* (*of fish*) Frotta, *f.*; moltitudine, folla, *f.*; (*shallow*) bassofondo, *m.*, secca, *f.* || *v.i.* (*of fish*) Raggrupparsi. **In shoals,** in folla.

shoaly, *a.* Pieno di secche, poco profondo.

shock (1) [ʃɔk], *n.* Urto, cozzo, *m.*, scossa, *f.*; colpo, *m.*; impressione, *f.*; (*Med.*) collasso, shock, *m.* || *v.t.* Urtare, scuotere; impressionare, offendere, ferire. **The news was a great — to me,** la notizia mi ha impressionato molto; **an electric —,** una scossa elettrica, *f.*; **—-absorber,** para-urti, paracolpi, *m.*; (*Mil.*) **— troops,** arditi, *m.pl.*

shock (2), *n.* (*of corn*) Mucchio, covone, *m.*; (*of hair*) zazzera, massa, *f.* || *v.t.* Ammucchiare. **—-headed,** arruffato, scompigliato, dai capelli arruffati.

shocker, *n.* (*colloq.*) Romanzo sensazionale, *m.*

shocking, *a.* Disgustoso, indecente, ripugnante; orribile, terribile.

shockingly, *adv.* Terribilmente; offensivamente.

shockingness, *n.* Orrore, spavento, *m.*

shod [ʃɔd], *a.* (*of horses*) Ferrato; (*of persons*) calzato; (*Mech.*) ferrato [cp. **shoe**].

shoddy [ˈʃɔdi], *n.* Robaccia, *f.*; cascame, *m.*; ritagli, panni sfilacciati, *m.pl.* || *a.* Di scarto, scadente. **— goods,** robaccia, roba scadente, *f.*

shoe [ʃuː], *n.* Scarpa, *f.*; (*of horse*) ferro, *m.*; (*wooden*) zoccolo, *m.*; (*brake*) martinicca, *f.* || *v.t.* Calzare; ferrare. **Shoes down at heel,** scarpe scalcagnate, *f.pl.*; (*fig.*) **to be in someone's shoes,** essere nei panni di qualcuno; (*fig.*) **another pair of shoes,** un altro paio di maniche, *m.*; (*fig.*) **to put the — on the right foot,** mettere il dito sulla piaga; **to take off one's shoes and stockings,** scalzarsi; **to provide with shoes,** calzare; **—-black, —-shine,** lustrascarpe, lustrino, *m.*; **—-brush,** spazzola per scarpe, *f.*; **—-buckle,** fibbia di scarpa, *f.*; **—-horn,** calzatoia, *f.*; **—-lace, —-string,** stringa per scarpa, *f.*; **—-leather,** cuoio per scarpe, *m.*, (*fig.*) scarpe, *f.pl.*

shoeing [ˈʃuːiŋ], *n.* Ferratura di cavalli, *f.* **—-forge,** fucina del fabbro; **—-smith,** maniscalco, *m.*

shoeless, *a.* Scalzo, senza scarpe.

shoemaker, *n.* Calzolaio, *m.*

shoemaking, *n.* Calzoleria, *f.*

shone, *p.* of **shine.**

shook, *p.* of **shake.**

shoot [ʃuːt], *v.t.* Tirare, sparare, scagliare, lanciare, scoccare, gettare; scaricare; colpire; (*to hit*) ferire; (*to kill*) fucilare; (*rapids*) scendere; (*Cinema.*) filmare, girare; (*to tip out*) rovesciare; *v.i.* guizzare, scattare, balzare; (*hunt*) cacciare; (*of stars*) filare; (*Bot.*) germogliare; saettare, dardeggiare; (*Football*) tirare un colpo secco, tirare un calcio secco; (*of pain*) dare un dolore lancinante. || *n.* (*of plant*) Rampollo, pollone, *m.*; (*hunting*) caccia, *f.*, partita di caccia, *f.*; (*at butts*) gara di tiro, *f.*; (*rapids*) rapido, *m.*; (*of pain*) puntura, fitta, *f.* **To — out, to — forth,** guizzar fuori, balzar avanti; **a flash shot across the sky,** un lampo saettò attraverso il cielo; **the boat shot along the river,** la barca guizzò lungo il fiume; **the boy shot ahead of his competitors,** il fanciullo oltrepassò i suoi competitori; **to — an arrow,** scoccare una saetta; **to — rubbish,** scaricare immondizie; **the sun shoots its rays,** il sole lancia i suoi raggi; **he cannot — straight,** non sa sparar dritto; **to go shooting,** andare a caccia; **he had his arm shot off,** un colpo gli asportò il braccio; **to — forth leaves,** metter fuori le foglie; **to — up,** crescere; **the pain shoots through my nerves,** il dolore mi lacera i nervi.

shooting, *n.* Tiro, *m.*; caccia, *f.*; fucilazione, *f.* || *a.* (*of pain*) Lancinante; (*of stars*) filante, cadente. **—-boots,** stivali da caccia, *m.pl.*; **—-box,** villino da caccia, *m.*; **—-gallery,** tiro al bersaglio, *m.*; **—-jacket,** cacciatora, *f.*; **—-match,** gara di tiro, *f.*; **—-range,** tiro al bersaglio, tiro a segno, *m.*; **—-star,** stella cadente, stella filante, *f.*; **—-stick,** bastone sedile, *m.*; (*Mil.*) **a shooting party,** un plotone d'esecuzione, *m.*

shop [ʃɔp], *n.* Bottega, *f.*, negozio, spaccio, magazzino, fondaco, *m.*; (*workshop*) officina, *f* || *v.i.* Fare le spese, girar le botteghe. **To keep —,** tenere bottega; (*fig.*) **to talk —,**

parlare d'affari; **to shut up —,** chiudere bottega; **wine-—,** spaccio di vini, *m.*; **—-bell,** campanello di bottega, *m.*; **—-boy,** giovane di negozio, *m.*; **—-girl,** commessa, *f.*; **—-lifter,** taccheggiatore, *m.*; **—-lifting,** taccheggiamento, *m.*; **—-soiled,** sciupato, guasto per lo stare in vetrina; **—-walker,** capo riparto, *m.*; **—-window,** vetrina, *f.*

shopkeeper, *n.* Bottegaio, *m.*, negoziante, *m.f.*

shopman, *n.* Commesso di negozio, *m.*

shopping, *n.* **To go —,** andare a far acquisti; **to do one's —,** fare le provviste; **—-bag,** borsa per la spesa, *f.*

shore (1), [ʃɔːɹ], *n.* Spiaggia, *f.*, lido, littorale, *m.*; riva, sponda, *f.* **Along the —,** lungo la spiaggia; **to hug the —,** stare a riva, tenersi a riva; **to go on —,** sbarcare.

shore (2), *v.t.* Puntellare. || *n.* Puntello, *m.*; sostegno, appoggio, *m.* **To — up a wall,** puntellare un muro.

shorn, *p.* of **shear.**

short [ʃɔːɹt], *a.* Corto, breve; piccolo, basso; insufficiente; (*of pastry*) frollo, croccante; (*incivil*) brusco, incivile. || *adv.* Corto. **In —,** in breve, in poche parole; **we are — of bread,** ci manca il pane; **— sight,** miopia, *f.*; **the long and the — of it is,** insomma; **to cut the matter —,** a farla corta, alle corte; **to make — work of,** sbarazzarsi senz'altro di; **a — time ago,** poco fa; **a — story,** una novella; **he has a — temper,** è molto collerico; **to give — weight,** dare peso scarso; **at — range,** a breve distanza; **— memory,** memoria corta, *f.*; **we call him Jack for —,** lo chiamiamo Jack per abbreviazione; **nothing — of marvellous,** niente di meno che meraviglioso; **— of money,** corto a quattrini; **it falls — of perfection,** non arriva alla perfezione; **to cut —,** tagliar corto; **to stop —,** arrestarsi di colpo, fermarsi su due piedi; **to stop — of,** fermarsi davanti a; **she took him up —,** essa lo interruppe bruscamente; **— of explaining everything,** senza spiegare tutto; (*Elec.*) **—-circuit,** corto circuito, *m.*; **—-cut,** scorciatoia, *f.*; **—-dated,** a breve scadenza; **—-haired,** dal pelo raso, dal pelo corto; **—-handed,** a corto di personale; **—-horn,** bue a corna corte, *m.*; **—-lived,** di breve vita, di poca durata; **—-necked,** dal collo corto; **—-sighted,** miope, corto di vista, (*fig.*) imprevidente; **—-sightedness,** miopia, *f.*; (*fig.*) imprevidenza, *f.*; **—-tempered,** collerico, stizzoso; **—-winded,** affannoso; (*Radio*) **— wave,** onde corte, *f.pl.*

shortage [ˈʃɔːɹtidʒ], *n.* Mancanza, scarsità, *f.*

shortbread, shortcake, *n.* Pasta frolla, *f.*

shortcoming, *n.* Deficienza, manchevolezza, *f.*

shorten, *v.t.* Raccorciare, abbreviare, scorciare; diminuire; *v.i.* raccorciarsi, diminuire. (*Naut.*) **To — sail,** far terzaruolo, ridurre le vele.

shortening, *n.* Raccorciamento, abbreviamento, *m.*; diminuzione, *f.*

shorthand [ˈʃɔːɹthænd], *n.* Stenografia, *f.* **To take down in —,** stenografare. **—-writer,** stenografo, *m.*, stenografa, *f.*; **—-typist,** stenodattilografo, *m.*, stenodattilografa, *f.*

shortly, *adv.* Presto, tosto, fra poco; in breve, brevemente, in poche parole.

shortness, *n.* Brevità, cortezza, *f.*; piccolezza, *f.*; mancanza, scarsità, *f.* **— of breath,** respiro affannoso, *m.*; **— of memory,** mancanza di memoria, *f.*

shorts, *n.pl.* Calzoncini, *m.pl.*

shot (1) [ʃɔt], *p.*, *pp.* of **shoot.**

shot (2), *n.* Colpo, tiro, *m.*; tratto, *m.*; (*bullet*) palla, *f.*; proiettile, *m.*; pallini, *m.pl.*; (*shooter*) tiratore, *m.* (*fig.*) **To have a good — at,** tentare di indovinare, azzeccare, indovinare bene; **a flying —,** un colpo sperso, *m.*; **he is a crack —,** è un valente tiratore; **he was off like a —,** scappò come un dardo; **to fire a — at,** sparare un colpo a; **without firing a —,** senza colpo ferire; **—-gun,** schioppo, fucile da caccia, *m.*; **—-proof,** a prova di palle, impenetrabile.

shot (3), *a.* (*of material*) Cangiante.

should, *v.aux.* (*p.* of **shall** used as sign of conditional). **I — go away if I were you,** se io fossi in voi me ne andrei; **Should I read this book ?** Dovrei leggere questo libro ?

shoulder [ˈʃouldəɹ], *n.* Spalla, *f.*; omero, *m.*; (*Mech.*) spallamento. || *v.t.* Mettere sulle spalle, caricarsi di; (*to push*) spingere; (*fig.*) sobbarcarsi, assumersi. **To lay the blame on the right shoulders,** dare il torto a chi spetta; **to shrug one's shoulders,** alzare le spalle; **over the —,** ad armacollo; **round shoulders,** spalle curve, *f.pl.*; **— to —,** d'accordo; **broad shoulders,** spalle larghe, *f.pl.*; (*fig.*) **to put one's — to the wheel,** mettersi all'opera, darsi attorno; **to give the cold — to,** trattare dall'alto in basso; **to — one's way through,** farsi largo colle spalle; (*Mil.*) **Shoulder arms !** Spall'arm ! **—-belt,** bandoliera, tracolla, *f.*; **—-blade,** scapola, *f.*; **—-knot,** spallina, *f.*, cordone, *m.*; **—-strap,** spallina, *f.*

shout [ʃaut], *v.t.i.* Gridare; urlare, strillare, strepitare, schiamazzare. || *n.* Grido, urlo, strillo, *m.*; suono, *m.*; (*of laughter*) scroscio, *m.* **To — for joy,** esultare di gioia; **to — at,** gridare a; **to — down,** far tacere a forza di grida; **shouts of applause,** scrosci d'applauso, *m.pl.*

shouting, *n.* Gridio, *m.*, grida, *f.*; acclamazioni, *f.pl.*

shove [ʃʌv], *v.t.i.* Spingere, urtare, sospingere; spingersi, sospingersi. || *n.* Spinta, *f.*, urto, impulso, *m.* **To — away,** respingere; **to — forward,** spingere avanti, spingersi avanti; **to give a — to,** dare una spinta a; **to — off,** spingere dalla riva, spingersi al largo.

shovel, *n.* Pala, *f.* || *v.t.* Spalare, badilare. **Fire-—,** paletta, *f.*; **to — away the snow,** spalare la neve; **—-hat,** cappello a larghe tese portato dal clero anglicano, *m.*

shovelboard, *n.* Giuoco delle piastrelle, *m.*

shovelful, *n.* Palata, *f.*

show [ʃou], *v.t.* Mostrare; indicare, additare; dimostrare, provare; rivelare, palesare, esporre; *v.i.* mostrarsi, apparire, farsi vedere. || *n.* Apparenza, mostra, ostentazione, pompa, *f.*; esposizione, *f.*; (*colloq.*) affare, *m.*; (*colloq.*) spettacolo al teatro, dramma, *m.* **To — in,** introdurre, fare entrare, far accomodare; **to — off,** mettere in mostra, ostentare; **to — out,** condurre alla porta; **to — over a house,** far vedere una casa; **to — fight,** mostrarsi bellicoso; **to — the white feather,** mostrarsi codardo; **to — one's hand,** mostrare il proprio giuoco; **it only shows how**

silly he is, ciò dimostra la sua scemenza; **to — up,** metter a nudo, smascherare, (*display*) far risaltare; **cattle- —,** esposizione di bestiame, *f.*; **in dumb- —,** in pantomima; **for —,** per mostra; **to make a — of,** ostentare, vantare; **a — of hands,** un voto a mano levata; **— -card,** cartello, *m.*; **— -case,** vetrina, *f.*; **— -place,** monumento, *m.*; **— -window,** vetrata, *f.*; **— -room,** sala di esposizione, *f.*

show-down ['ʃoudaun], *n.* Carte in tavola, *f.pl.* **If it comes to a —,** se si arriverà al momento di prendere partito.

shower ['ʃauəɹ], *n.* Acquazzone, rovescio di pioggia, *m.*; (*of blows*) scarica, grandinata, *f.* ‖ *v.i.* Piovere, diluviare; *v.t.* grandinare; inondare di. **An April —,** un acquazzone d'aprile, *m.*; **a heavy —,** un diluvio, *m.*; **to — gifts on someone,** inondare qualcuno di regali; **— -bath,** doccia, *f.*

showery, *a.* Piovoso.

showily ['ʃouili], *adv.* Con pompa, vistosamente.

showiness, *n.* Ostentazione, appariscenza, pompa, *f.*, fasto, *m.*; vistosità, *f.*

showing, *n.* Rappresentazione, *f.* **On his own —,** a sentir lui, a detta di lui.

showy, *a.* Vistoso, fastoso, pomposo, appariscente.

shrapnel ['ʃræpnəl], *n.* (*Mil.*) Shrapnel, *m.*; granata a pallette, *f.*

shred [ʃred], *n.* Brandello, brindello, brendolo, cencio, straccio, *m.* ‖ *v.t.* Sbrindellare, tagliuzzare, stracciare. **To tear to shreds,** fare a brandelli, sbrindellare.

shrew [ʃru:], *n.* Bisbetica, megera, *f.* **The taming of the —,** la bisbetica domata; **— -mouse,** musaragno, toporagno, *m.*

shrewd, *a.* Accorto, scaltro, sagace, perspicace.

shrewdly, *adv.* Scaltramente, sagacemente.

shrewdness, *n.* Accortezza, scaltrezza, sagacità, penetrazione, *f.*

shrewish, *a.* Bisbetico, brontolone, borbottone.

shrewishness, *n.* Malumore, *m.*; cattiveria, acrimonia, *f.*

shriek [ʃri:k], *n.* Grido, urlo, strillo, *m.* ‖ *v.i.t.* Gridare, urlare, strillare. **To — out,** emettere grida, strillare.

shrieking, *n.* Grida, *f.pl.*, urlio, gridio, strillio, *m.*

shrievalty ['ʃri:vəlti], *n.* Grado di sceriffo, *m.*; giurisdizione di sceriffo, *f.*

shrift [ʃrift], *n.* Confessione, assoluzione, *f*

shrike [ʃraik], *n.* (*Zool.*) Velia, *f.*

shrill [ʃril], *a.* Stridulo, acuto, lacerante. ‖ *v.t.i.* Stridere, strillare.

shrillness, *n.* Stridore, stridio, *m.*, acutezza, *f.*

shrilly, *adv.* Stridulamente.

shrimp [ʃrimp], *n.* (*Zool.*) Gamberetto di mare, *m.*; (*fig.*) omiciattolo, minuzzolo, *m.* ‖ *v.i.* Prendere gamberetti.

shrimper, *n.* Gamberaio, *m.*

shrimping, *n.* Pesca dei gamberetti, *f.*

shrine [ʃrain], *n.* Sacrario, santuario, *m.*; tempio, altare, luogo sacro, reliquario, *m.*

shrink [ʃriŋk], *v.i.* Diminuire, contrarsi, aggrinzarsi, restringersi, accorciarsi, ritirarsi; rinculare, indietreggiare, ritrarsi; *v.t.* raccorciare, diminuire, far restringere. **To — back,** rinculare, indietreggiare; **to — from,** rifuggire da, indietreggiare davanti a, ritrarsi da; **to — up,** accartocciarsi; **he shrinks from any kind of fuss,** rifugge da ogni ostentazione.

shrinkable, *a.* Restringibile.

shrinkage, *n.* Diminuzione, contrazione, *f.*, restringimento, accorciamento, *m.*; (*Mech.*) ritiro, *m.*; (*Comm.*) calo, *m.*

shrinking, *n.* Diminuzione, contrazione, *f.*, l'indietreggiare, il rifuggire, *m.*

shrinkingly, *adv.* Timidamente, con ripugnanza.

shrive [ʃraiv], *v.t.* Confessare ed assolvere, ascoltare la confessione.

shrivel ['ʃrivəl], *v.i.* Contrarsi, aggrinzarsi, raggrinzarsi; *v.t.* aggrinzare, raggrinzare; abbruciacchiare, disseccare, inaridire. **To — up,** raggrinzarsi.

shroud (1) [ʃraud], *n.* Sudario, lenzuolo funebre, *m.* ‖ *v.t.* Avvolgere in un lenzuolo; (*fig.*) coprire, nascondere, ricoprire, drappeggiare, annebbiare.

shroud (2), *n.* (*Naut.*) Sartia, *f.*

Shrovetide ['ʃrouvtaid], *n.* Ultimi giorni di carnevale, *m.pl.* **Shrove Tuesday,** martedì grasso, *m.*

shrub (1) [ʃrʌb], *n.* Arbusto, arboscello, *m.*

shrub (2), *n.* Bevanda fatta di liquori e sciroppo di frutta, *f.*

shrubbery, *n.* Boschetto, *m.*, piantagione di arbusti, *f.*

shrubby, *a.* Cespuglioso, pieno di arbusti.

shrug [ʃrʌg], *n.* Alzata di spalla, *f.* ‖ *v.t.* **To — one's shoulders,** alzare le spalle, scrollare le spalle, stringersi nelle spalle.

shudder ['ʃʌdəɹ], *v.i.* Rabbrividire, raccapricciare, fremere. ‖ *n.* Brivido, tremito, *m.*

shudderingly, *adv.* Con brividi, tremando.

shuffle [ʃʌfl], *v.t.* Mischiare, mescolare; trascinare, strascinare; *v.i.* trascinarsi, strascinarsi, muoversi a fatica; (*fig.*) tergiversare, cavillare, prevaricare. ‖ *n.* Confusione, *f.*, scompiglio, *m.*; inganno, equivoco, artifizio, *m.*, evasione, *f.*; (*Dancing*) passo doppio, *m.* **To — the cards,** mescolare le carte; **to — off the responsibility,** sbarazzarsi della responsabilità; **to — with one's feet,** stropicciare i piedi; **the old man shuffles along,** il vecchio si strascina a stento.

shuffler, *n.* Furbone, cavillatore, gabbamondo, *m.*; mescolatore delle carte, *m.*

shuffling, *a.* Evasivo; trasandato, strascicato, dinoccolato. ‖ *n.* Andatura trasandata, *f.*, passo strascinante, *m.*

shun [ʃʌn], *v.t.* Evitare, schivare, scansare, fuggire, rifuggire.

shunt [ʃʌnt], *v.t.i.* (*Rail.*) Smistare, scambiare; (*Elec.*) derivare. ‖ *n.* (*Elect.*) Derivazione, *f.*

shunter, *n.* Smistatore, deviatore, *m.*

shunting, *n.* Smistamento, cambiamento di binario, *m.*

shut [ʃʌt], *v.t.i.* Chiudere, serrare; chiudersi. **To — one's teeth,** serrare i denti; **to — a knife,** chiudere un coltello; **to — in,** rinchiudere dentro; **to — off** (*gas, steam, etc.*) chiudere, (*fig.*) allontanare, interdire; **to — out,** chiuder fuori, nascondere; **to — out from,** escludere da; **to — up,** (*house*) serrare, (*a person*) rinchiudere, (*be silent*) far tacere, chiudere la bocca; **Shut up!** Tacete! Zitti! **to — up shop,** chiudere la bottega.

shutter, *n.* Imposta, *f.*, scuro, *m.*; persiana, gelosia, *f.*; (*Phot.*) otturatore, *m.*
shuttle [ʃʌtl], Spola, navicella, navetta, *f.* (*Rail., etc.*) **—-service,** servizio avanti e indietro fra due stazioni, *m.*
shuttlecock, *n.* Volano, volante, *m.*
shy (1) [ʃai], *a.* Timido, vergognoso, diffidente; schivo, guardingo; pauroso, ombroso. **To fight — of,** schivare, evitare; (*fig.*) **to be — of money,** essere a corto di danaro.
shy (2), *v.i.* (*of horse*) Adombrarsi; *v.t.* gettare, lanciare, scagliare. || *n.* Colpo, *m.* **To have a — at,** tirare un sasso a; (*fig.*) tentare di.
shyly, *adv.* Timidamente.
shyness, *n.* Timidità, vergogna, diffidenza, *f.*
Siamese [saiə'mi:z], *n.a.* Siamese, *m.* **— cat,** gatto del Siam, *m.*; **— twins** fratelli siamesi, *m.*, gemelli siamesi, *m.pl.*
Siberian [sai'biəriən], *n.a.* Siberiano, *m.*
sibilance, sibilancy, *n.* Sibilazione, *f.*
sibilant ['sibilənt], *n.a.* Sibilante, *f.*
sib yl ['sibil], *n.* Sibilla, *f.*
sib ylline ['sibilain], *a.* Sibillino.
siccative ['sikətiv], *a.* Seccativo, essicante. || *n.* Vernice seccativa, *f.*
Sicilian [si'siliən], *n.a.* Siciliano, *m.*; Siciliana, *f.*
Sicily ['sisili], *n.* (*Geog.*) Sicilia, *f.*
sick [sik], *a.* Ammalato, malato, infermo; nauseato, disgustato. || *n.pl.* I malati, *m.pl.* **I feel —,** mi sento nausea, ho nausea; **a — headache,** un'emicrania, *f.*; **— of,** infastidito di, stufo di, seccato di; **I am — and tired of it,** ne sono stanco morto; **— of a fever,** malato di febbre; **a — man,** un malato, *m.*; **— unto death,** malato da morire; **to be — at heart,** aver la morte nel cuore; **—-bay,** infermeria di bordo, *f.*; **—-bed,** letto di dolore, *m.*; **—-leave,** congedo per malattia, *m.*; **—-list,** lista degli ammalati, *f.*; **on the —-list,** malato, indisposto; **—-nurse,** infermiera, *f.*; **—-room,** camera del malato.
sicken, *v.i.* Ammalare, ammalarsi; sentir nausea; (*fig.*) infastidirsi, annoiarsi; *v.t.* far nausea a; (*fig.*) infastidire, annoiare, disgustare; ripugnare. **The child is sickening for something,** quel ragazzo sta covando un malanno; **it sickened him to see it,** gli ripugnò a vederlo.
sickener, *n.* Causa di disgusto, *f.*
sickening, *a.* Nauseante, nauseoso, nauseabondo; (*fig.*) disgustoso, sgradevole.
sickish, *a.* Un po' malato, indisposto.
sickle [sikl], *n.* Falce, *f.*, falcetto, *m.*
sickliness, *n.* Salute malferma, *f.*; (*of situation*) insalubrità, *f.*
sickly, *a.* Malaticcio, malatuccio; malsano, malfermo in salute, debole; insalubre, malsano; sdolcinato.
sickness, *n.* Malattia, *f.*, male, *m.*; nausea, *f.*
side [said], *n.* Lato, fianco, canto, *m.*, banda, parte, *f.*; (*edge*) margine, orlo, bordo, *m.*; (*in quarrel, etc.*) parte, fazione, *f.*, partito, *m.*; (*of river*) riva, sponda, *f.*; (*relationship*) linea, *f.*; (*of question*) aspetto, *m.*; (*colloq.*) boria, *f.* || *a.* Di fianco, di lato, laterale; indiretto, obliquo; in profilo. || *v.t.* Parteggiare. **To — with,** tener da, prendere le parti di; **his blind —,** il suo lato debole, *m.*; **by his —,** accanto a lui, vicino a lui; **by the — of the river,** in riva al fiume, sulla sponda del fiume; **by the — of the road,** sul margine della via; **the near —,** il lato sinistro, *m.*, la parte più vicina, *f.*; **the off —,** la parte più lontana, *f.*, il lato destro, *m.*; **—-arms,** armi bianche, *f.pl.*; **— -dish,** piatto secondario, *m.*; **— -note,** nota marginale, *f.*; **— -path,** sentiero, *m.*; **—-saddle,** sella da donna, *f.*; **— -show,** baraccone, *m.*, (*fig.*) azione secondaria, *f.*; **— slip,** (*Motor.*) slittamento, *m.*; (*Aviat.*) **to — -slip,** scivolare d'ala; **— -splitting,** da tenersi i fianchi; **to —-step,** fare un passo obliquo, tirarsi in disparte; **—-track,** (*Rail.*) smistare, (*fig.*) posporre; **— stroke,** nuotata sul fianco, *f.*; **—-wind,** vento di traverso, *m.*; **—-whiskers,** fedine, *f.pl.*
sideboard, *n.* Buffè, *m.*, credenza, *f.*
sidecar, *n.* (*Motor.*) Side-car, motocarrozzino, *m.*
sided, *a.* Da lati. **Two- —,** da due lati.
sidelight, *n.* Riflesso, *m.*, illustrazione, *f.*
sidelong, *a.* Obliquo, laterale, di fianco. || *adv.* Obliquamente, a sghembo; di sottecchi. **A — glance,** uno sguardo furtivo, *m.*
sidereal [said'iəriəl], *a.* (*Astron.*) Siderale, sidereo.
sidesman, *n.* Laico sagrestano, *m.*
sidewalk, *n.* Marciapiede, *m.*
sideways, *adv.* Obliquamente, a sghembo, storto. **To walk —,** camminare storto.
siding, *n.* (*Rail.*) Binario morto, *m.*
sidle [saidl], *v.i.* Andare a sghembo, camminare storto. **To — up,** accostarsi con esitazione.
siege [si:dʒ], *n.* Assedio, *m.* **To lay — to,** assediare; **to raise the —,** levare l'assedio; **— gun,** pezzo d'assedio, *m.*; **—-train,** artiglieria d'assedio, *f.*
sienna [si'enə], *n.* (*paint*) Terra di Siena, *f.*
siesta [sı:'estə], *n.* Siesta, *f.* **To take a —,** fare la siesta.
sieve [siv], *n.* Vaglio, *m.*; staccio, crivello, *m.*; buratto, *m.*; setaccio, *m.* || *v.t.* Vagliare, stacciare, crivellare.
sift [sift], *v.t.* Vagliare, stacciare, crivellare; spargere; (*fig.*) esaminare, investigare, approfondire. **To — the evidence,** vagliare le testimonianze.
sifting, *n.* Vagliatura, investigazione, *f.*, esame, *m.* **Siftings,** mondiglia, vagliatura, stacciatura, *f.*
sigh [sai], *n.* Sospiro, *m.* || *v.i.* Sospirare. **To — after,** sospirare; **to — over,** sospirare per.
sighing, *n.* Sospiri, *m.pl.*
sight [sait], *n.* Vista, veduta, *f.*; visione, *f.*; spettacolo, *m.*; mira, *f.*; (*of gun*) mirino, *m.*; (*colloq.*) quantità, *f.* || *v.t.* Avvistare; aggiustare la mira di. **A — to see,** una cosa da vedere, *f.*; **at first —,** a prima vista; **at —,** a vista; **by —,** di vista; **I loathe the — of it,** non posso vederlo; **the ship is in —,** la nave è in vista; **in the — of,** al cospetto di, innanzi a, in presenza di; **near —,** miopia, *f.*; **do not lose — of him,** non perdetelo di vista; **out of —,** fuori di vista; **out of — out of mind,** lontano dagli occhi lontano dal cuore; **to catch — of,** vedere per un momento; **to have a — of,** prendere visione di; **to keep out of —,** tenersi nascosto; **to lose one's —,** perdere la vista; **What a — !** Che spettacolo!

to do what is right in one's own —, fare ciò che pare buono; **to — land,** avvistare la terra; (*Mil.*) **line of —,** linea di mira; **—-seer,** turista, *m.f.*; **—-seeing,** visita ai monumenti, *f.*; giro, *m.*, gita, *f.*
sighted, *a.* Avvistato, visto.
sightless, *a.* Cieco, orbo.
sightlessness, *n.* Cecità, orbezza, *f.*
sightliness, *n.* Bellezza, avvenenza, *f.*
sightly, *a.* Bello, avvenente.
sign [sain], *n.* Segno, indizio, cenno, *m.*; portento, miracolo, *m.*; (*signboard*) insegna, *f.*; sintomo, *m.* || *v.t.* Firmare; sottoscrivere, ratificare, sanzionare; *v.i.* fare segno a, accennare. **A — of the times,** un segno dei tempi, *m.*; **to give signs of,** dar segno di; **to make signs to,** far cenni a; **to give no — of life,** non dar segno di vita; **to make the — of the cross,** farsi il segno della croce, segnarsi; **to — away,** cedere, alienare; **to — on,** ingaggiarsi per un lavoro, far la firma; **I — myself,** mi firmo.
signal ['signəl], *n.* Segnale, segno, cenno, *m.*; (*traffic, Rail.*) semaforo, *m.* || *a.* Segnalato, insigne, cospicuo, notabile. || *v.i.* Fare segnalazioni. **— of distress,** segnale di pericolo, segnale d'allarme, *m.*; **—-box,** cabina dei segnali, *f.*; **—-gun,** cannoncino; **—-light,** fanale, *m.*; **—-post,** palo da segnali, *m.*
signalize ['signəlaiz], *v.t.* Segnalare.
signaller, *n.* Segnalatore, *m.*
signally, *adv.* Segnalatamente.
signatory ['signətəri], *n.* Firmatario, *m.*
signature ['signətʃjuːɹ], *n.* Firma, *f.*; segnatura, *f.*; (*Mus.*) indicazione del tempo, indicazione del tono, *f.*
signboard, *n.* Insegna, *f.*
signer, *n.* Firmatario, *m.*
signet ['signet], *n.* Sigillo, *m.* **Writer to the Signet,** avvocato scozzese, *m.*; **—-ring,** anello con sigillo, *m.*
significance [sig'nifikəns], *n.* Significato, senso, *m.*; rilievo, *m.*; importanza, *f.*; peso, *m.*
significant, *a.* Significativo, espressivo; importante.
significantly, *adv.* Espressivamente.
signification, *n.* Significato, senso, *m.*
signify ['signifai], *v.t.* Voler dire, significare; esprimere, indicare; importare. **It does not —,** non importa, non significa niente.
signpost ['sainpoust], *n.* Palo indicatore, *m.*
silage ['sailidʒ], *n.* (*Agric.*) Foraggio conservato in un silo.
silence ['sailəns], *n.* Silenzio, *m.*; taciturnità, *f.* || *v.t.* Ridurre al silenzio, far tacere; arrestare, far cessare. **A dead —,** un silenzio di tomba, *m.*; **to keep —,** serbare il silenzio; **to pass over in —,** passare sotto silenzio; **to reduce to —,** mettere in silenzio; **— is consent,** chi tace consente; **to — complaints,** mettere fine alle lagnanze.
silencer, *n.* Silenziatore, smorzatore, *m.*
silent, *a.* Silenzioso; taciturno; muto. **Keep —!** Tacete! **to be —,** tacere, far silenzio.
silently, *adv.* Silenziosamente, taciturnamente.
Silenus [sai'liːnəs], *n.* (*Myth.*) Sileno, *m.*
Silesia [sai'liːʒə], *n.* (*Geog.*) Slesia, *f.*
silhouette [siluː'et], *n.* Siluetta, *f.*, contorno, profilo, *m.* || *v.t.* Profilare, siluettare.
silica ['silikə], *n.* (*Min.*) Silice, *f.*
silicate, *n.* Silicato, *m.*
silicon, *n.* Silicio, *m.*
silk [silk], *n.* Seta, *f.* || *a.* Di seta, serico. **Raw —,** seta greggia, *f.*; **spun —,** seta filata, *f.*; **shot —,** seta cangiante, *f.*; **thrown —,** organzino, *m.*; **to dress in —,** vestire di seta; **—-handkerchief,** fazzoletto di seta a colori, *m.*; **— goods,** seterie, *f.pl.*; **—-hat,** cilindro, *m.*; **—-spinner,** setaiuolo, filandiere, *m.*; **—-thrower,** torcitore d'organzino, *m.*; **—-weaver,** tessitore di seta, *m.*
silken, *a.* Di seta, serico; (*fig.*) dolce.
silkiness, *n.* Setosità, *f.*
silkworm, *n.* Baco da seta, *m.* **— breeder,** sericoltore, *m.*; **—-breeding,** serocultura, *f.*; **—-nursery,** bigattiera, *f.*
silky, *a.* Setaceo, serico, di seta; (*fig.*) soave, dolce.
sill [sil], *n.* (*of window*) Davanzale, *m.*; (*of door*) soglia, *f.*
silliness ['silines], *n.* Sciocchezza, stupidità, imbecillità, *f.*
silly, *a.* Sciocco, stupido, scemo, imbecille. || *n.* Sciocco, *m.*; stupido, *m.*, stupida, *f.* **Don't be —!** Non fare sciocchezze!
silo ['sailou], *n.* Silo, *m.* || *v.t.* Mettere nel silo.
silt [silt], *v.t.* Colmare di sabbia. || *n.* Sabbia, *f.* **To — up,** insabbiare; **silting-up,** insabbiamento, *m.*
Silurian [sai'ljuːriən], *a.* (*Geol.*) Siluriano.
silvan [cp. **sylvan**].
silver ['silvəɹ], *n.* Argento, *m.*; (*plate*) argenteria, *f.*; (*money*) moneta d'argento, *f.* || *a.* D'argento, argenteo; argentino. || *v.t.* Inargentare. **German —,** argentone, *m.*; **— hair,** canizie, *f.*, capelli inargentati, *m.pl.*; **he has a — tongue,** è una lingua d'oro; **— lace,** gallone d'argento, *m.*; **— plate,** argenteria, *f.*; **to be born with a — spoon in one's mouth,** nascere vestito; (*Tech.*) **—-bath,** bagno di argentatura, *m.*; (*Zool.*) **— fox,** volpe argentata, *f.*; **—-gilt,** argento dorato, *m.*; **—-grey,** grigio d'argento; **—-haired,** dai capelli argentei; **—-mounted,** montato in argento; **—-paper,** carta stagnola, carta d'argento, *f.*; **—-point,** punta secca, *f.*; **—-sand,** sabbia bianca, *f.*; **— thaw,** nevischio, *m.*
silverside, *n.* Girello di bue, *m.*
silversmith, *n.* Argentiere, *m.*
silverware, *n.* Argenteria, *f.*, vasellame d'argento, *m.*
silverweed, *n.* (*Bot.*) Argentina, *f.*
silvering, *n.* Argentatura, stagnatura, *f.*
silvery, *a.* Argenteo, argentino; argentato.
simian ['simiən], *a.* (*Zool.*) Scimmiesco. || *n.* Scimmia, *f.*
similar ['similəɹ], *a.* Simile, somigliante; pari, analogo, eguale.
similarity [simi'læriti], *n.* Somiglianza, rassomiglianza, similitudine, *f.*
similarly, *adv.* Similmente.
simile ['simili], *n.* Similitudine, *f.*; comparazione, *f.*, paragone, *m.*
simmer ['siməɹ], *v.t.i.* Bollire, sobbollire, gorgogliare.
simmering, *n.* Bollore, bollimento, *m.*
simnel ['simnəl], *n.* Specie di torta dolce mangiata verso Pasqua.
simoniacal [simon'aiəkəl], *a.* (*Eccles.*) Simoniaco.
simonist, *n.* Simoniaco, *m.*

simony, *n.* Simonia, *f.*
simoom, simoon [saiˈmuːm, saiˈmuːn], *n.* Simun, *m.*
simper [ˈsimpəɹ] *n.* Smorfia *f.* sorriso affettato *m.* || *v.i.* Smorfiare, civettare, far vezzi.
simperer, *n.* Smorfioso, lezioso, affettato, *m.*
simpering, *n.* Smorfie, *f.pl.*
simple (1) [simpl] *a.* Semplice, puro; innocente, ingenuo, credulo; (*foolish*) scemo; umile, basso. **— -minded, — -hearted,** ingenuo, aperto, candido, schietto; **— -mindedness,** ingenuità, *f.*
simple (2), *n.* (*Bot.*) Semplice, *m.*
simpleness, *n.* Semplicità, *f.*; schiettezza, ingenuità, *f.*
simpleton, *n.* Semplicione, scimunito, *m.*
simplicity [simˈplisiti], *n.* Semplicità, *f.*
simplification [simplifiˈkeiʃən], *n.* Semplificazione, *f.*
simplify [ˈsimplifai], *v.t.* Semplificare.
Simplon [ˈsæmplɔŋ], *n.* (*Geog.*) Sempione, *m.*
simply, *adv.* Semplicemente, schiettamente, puramente.
simulacrum [siməlˈeikrəm], *n.* Simulacro, *m.*
simulate [ˈsimjuːleit], *v.t.* Fingere, simulare.
simulation, *n.* Simulazione, finzione, *f.*; infingimento, *m.*
simultaneous [siməlˈteiniəs], *a.* Simultaneo.
simultaneousness, simultaneity, *n.* Simultaneità, *f.*
sin [sin], *n.* Peccato, fallo, *m.*; colpa, *f.*; delitto, errore, *m.* || *v.i.* Peccare, trasgredire. **As ugly as —,** brutto come il peccato.
sinapism [ˈsinəpizm], *n.* (*Med.*) Senapismo, *m.*
since [sins], *conj.* Poichè, dacchè, giacchè, dopo che. || *prep.* Da. || *adv.* Dopo, di poi. **How long is it — you saw him?** Quanto tempo è che non l'avete visto? **I have not seen him — he was last at home,** non lo vidi da che ripartì; **— there is no help for it,** dacchè non c'è rimedio; **I have heard nothing — last Monday,** non ho sentito niente da lunedì scorso; **she has been ill ever —,** è stata malata d'allora in poi; **the building has — been pulled down,** lo stabile è stato poi abbattuto; **I saw him not long —,** l'ho visto or non è molto.
sincere [sinˈsiəɹ], *a.* Sincero, franco.
sincerely, *adv.* Sinceramente. **Yours —,** con sincera stima, Suo; distinti saluti, Suo.
sincereness, sincerity, *n.* Sincerità, franchezza, *f.*
sine [sain], *n.* (*Math.*) Seno, *m.*
sinecure [ˈsainikjuːɹ], *n.* Sinecura, *f.*
sinecurist, *n.* Chi ha una sinecura, *m.*
sinew [ˈsinjuː], *n.* (*Anat.*) Tendine, *m.*; (*colloq.*) nervo, nerbo, *m.*, fibra, *f.*; (*in meat*) muscolo, *m.* **The sinews of war,** il nerbo della guerra, *m.*
sinewy, *a.* Nerboruto, robusto, gagliardo.
sinful [ˈsinful], *a.* Peccaminoso, colpevole; iniquo, cattivo.
sinfully, *adv.* Peccaminosamente, colpevolmente.
sinfulness, *n.* Colpevolezza, colpabilità, nequizia, cattiveria, *f.*
sing [siŋ], *v.t.i.* Cantare; (*of kettle*) borbottare. **To — the praises of someone,** enumerare le lodi di qualcuno; **to make someone — small,** fare che qualcuno si confessi vinto; **to — to sleep,** addormentare cantando; **to — in tune,** cantare intonato; **to — out of tune,** cantare stonato; **to — out,** gridare.
singable, *a.* Cantabile.
singe [sindʒ], *v.t.* Abbruciacchiare, abbruciare, scottare. || *n.* Abbruciatura, scottatura, *f.*
singer [ˈsiŋəɹ], *n.* Cantante, cantore, cantatore, *m.*, cantatrice, *f.*
singing, *n.* Canto, il cantare, *m.*; (*in the ears*) ronzio, tintinnio, *m.* || *a.* Cantante, cantatore. **— -bird,** uccello cantore, *m.*; **— -book,** quaderno di canto, *m.*; **— -master, — -mistress,** maestro, maestra di canto, *m.f.*
single [ˈsiŋgl], *a.* Solo, singolo, unico; celibe; solitario; (*fig.*) sincero, schietto. || *v.t.* Scegliere. **— -blessedness,** il celibato, *m.*; **— combat,** duello, *m.*; **the — life,** il celibato, *m.*, la vita celibe, *f.*; **a — man,** un celibe, *m.*; **a — woman,** una zitella, *f.*; **a — ticket,** un biglietto di sola andata, *m.*; **a — bedroom,** una camera da un letto, *f.*; **a — bed,** un letto a uno; **to — out,** trascegliere, tirar fuori; (*Mech.*) **— -acting,** a semplice effetto; **— -barrelled,** ad una sola canna; **— -breasted,** ad un petto; **— -handed,** da sè, senza aiuto; **— -hearted,** sincero, ingenuo, schietto; **— -oar,** remo corto, *m.*; **— -stick,** bastone, giuoco del bastone, *m.*; (*Sport*) **singles,** partita semplice, *f.*
singleness, *n.* Celibato, *m.* **— of purpose,** sincerità, schiettezza, *f.*
singlet [ˈsiŋglet] *n.* Sottoveste *m.*, maglietta sulla pelle, *f.*
singly [ˈsiŋgli], *adv.* Solamente; ad uno ad uno, separatamente.
singsong [ˈsiŋsɔŋ], *a.* Monotono. || *n.* Canto monotono, *m.*; cantilena, *f.*; (*colloq.*) riunione per il canto, *f.*
singular [ˈsiŋgjuːləɹ], *a.* Singolare, solo; raro, unico; insolito, strano; eccentrico; (*Gram.*) singolare.
singularity [siŋgjuːˈlæriti], *n.* Singolarità, novità, stranezza, *f.*; eccentricità, *f.*
singularize [ˈsiŋgjuːləraiz], *v.t.* Singolarizzare.
singularly, *adv.* Singolarmente.
sinister [ˈsinistəɹ], *a.* Sinistro, funesto, di cattivo augurio; torto, storto, contrario. **Bar —,** sbarra sinistra, *f.*
sink (1) [siŋk], *n.* (*in scullery*) Acquaio, lavatoio, scolatoio, *m.*; (*fig.*) sentina, *f.* **A — of iniquity,** una sentina di vizi, *f.*
sink (2), *v.i.* Affondare, sommergersi, andare a fondo, colare a fondo; penetrare, internarsi; inchinarsi; (*to grow weak*) indebolirsi, infiacchirsi; (*of the sun*) tramontare; (*of wind, etc.*) abbassarsi, calare; *v.t.* affondare, sprofondare; (*a well*) scavare, infossare; (*money*) investire; (*a die*) incidere; (*a debt*) ammortizzare. **My heart sank,** mi sentii cascare le braccia; **the ship sank,** la nave affondò; **he is sinking rapidly,** è agli estremi; **to — back,** ricadere, ricascare; **to — low,** abbassarsi, degenerare; **to — under,** soccombere a, cedere a; **to — in someone's estimation,** decadere nella stima di qualcuno; **his voice sank to a whisper,** la sua voce si ridusse ad un bisbiglio; **the ground sinks here,** il suolo sprofonda qui; **to — a ship,** mandare a picco una nave, affondare una nave; **to — one's own interests,** non badare

al proprio interesse; **to — money in an undertaking,** investire denaro in un'azienda; **sinking-fund,** fondo d'ammortizzamento, *m.*
sinker, *n.* (*on fishing-line*) Piombo, *m.*; (*of well*) scavatore, *m.*
sinking, *n.* (*of wells*) Scavatura, *f.*; (*lowering*) abbassamento, *m.*; ammortizzamento, *m.*
sinless, *a.* Senza peccato, innocente, puro.
sinlessness, *n.* Innocenza, *f.*
sinner, *n.* Peccatore, *m.*, peccatrice, *f.*
sinologist, sinologue [si'nɔlədʒist, 'sainolɔg], *n.* Sinologo, *m.*
sinuosity [sinju:'ɔsiti], *n.* Sinuosità, *f.*
sinuous, *a.* Sinuoso, tortuoso.
sinus ['sainəs], *n.* (*Anat.*) Seno, *m.*, cavità, *f.*
sip [sip], *n.* Sorso, *m.* || *v.t.i.* Sorseggiare, centellinare, bere a sorsi.
siphon ['saifən], *n.* Sifone, *m.* || *v.t.* Sifonare.
sippet ['sipit], *n.* Fettina, *f.*
sir [sə:ɹ], *n.* Signore, cavaliere, *m.*; (*title*) Sir, *m.*
sire [saiɹ], *n.* Padre, antenato, *m.*; (*royalty*) Sire, Signore, *m.*, Maestà, *f.*; (*horse*) stallone, *m.* || *v.t.* Generare.
siren ['sairən], *n.* (*Myth.Mech.*) Sirena, *f.*
Sirius ['siriəs], *n.* (*Astron.*) Sirio, *m.*
sirloin ['sə:ɹlɔin], *n.* Lombo di manzo, *m.*
sirocco [si'rɔkou], *n.* Scirocco, *m.*
sir rah ['sira:], *n.* (*obs.*) Birbante, furfante, *m.*
siskin ['siskin], *n.* (*Zool.*) Lucarino, *m.*
sister ['sistəɹ], *n.* Sorella, *f.*; suora, monaca, *f.*; suora infermiera, *f.* **—-in-law,** cognata, *f.*; **— ships,** navi gemelle, *f.pl.*
sisterhood, *n.* Comunità di monache, *f.*
sisterly, *a.* Sorellevole. || *adv.* Da sorella, sorellevolmente.
sit [sit], *v.i.* Sedere, sedersi; star seduto; (*for portrait*) posare; (*in court, etc.*) tener seduta; (*of hen*) covare; *v.t.* far sedere, mettere a sedere. **To — down,** sedersi, accomodarsi, porsi a sedere; **to — on a matter,** investigare un affare; (*colloq.*) **to — on someone,** trattare qualcuno dall'alto in basso; **I will — it out,** ne vedrò la fine; **to — up,** tenersi diritto; **to — up late,** andare tardi a coricarsi; (*colloq.*) **to make someone — up,** dare una lavata di capo a qualcuno; **to — in judgement,** giudicare; **to — for an exam,** dare un esame; **to — up for someone,** star alzato ad aspettare qualcuno; **Parliament is now sitting,** Il Parlamento è aperto; **to — still,** star fermo; **to — tight,** non lasciarsi smuovere; **to — a horse well,** star bene a cavallo.
site [sait], *n.* Sito, *m.*; situazione, posizione, *f.* **Building —,** terreno fabbricabile. || *v.t.* Scegliere un sito.
sitter ['sitəɹ], *n.* Modello, *m.*, modella, *f.*; chi posa, *m.f.*; (*hen*) chioccia, *f.*
sitting, *n.* Seduta, adunanza, *f.*; posa, *f.*; covata, chioccia, *f.*; (*in church*) posto riservato, *m.* **—-hen,** chioccia, *f.*; **—-room,** salotto, *m.*
situate, situated ['sitju:eit, 'sitju:eitəd], *a.* Situato, posto, collocato. **I am awkwardly —,** mi trovo in imbarazzo.
situation [sitju:'eiʃən], *n.* Sito, posto, *m.*, posizione, situazione, *f.*; impiego, *m.* **A fine —,** un bel posto, *m.*; **a difficult —,** un bell'imbroglio, *m.*; **to apply for a —,** domandare un impiego; **to have a good —,** avere un buon posto.
sitz-bath ['sitsba:θ], *n.* Semicupio, *m.*
six [siks], *n.a.* Sei, *m.* **— of one and half a dozen of the other,** se non è zuppa è pan bagnato; **at sixes and sevens,** in disordine.
sixfold, *a.* Sestuplo. || *adv.* Sei volte.
sixpence ['sikspəns], *n.* Sei soldoni, *m.pl.*, un mezzo scellino, *m.*
sixpenny, *a.* Del valore di mezzo scellino.
sixteen [siks'ti:n], *n.a.* Sedici, *m.*; (*Print.*) **—-mo,** in sedicesimo.
sixteenth, *a.* Sedicesimo. **On the —,** il giorno sedici.
sixth [siksθ], *n.a.* Sesto, *m.*; (*Mus.*) sesta, *f.*
sixthly, *a.* In sesto luogo.
sixtieth ['sikstiəθ], *a.* Sessantesimo.
sixty, *n.a.* Sessanta, *m.* **A man of —,** un sessantenne, *m.*
sizable ['saizəbl], *a.* Abbastanza grande.
sizar ['saizəɹ], *n.* Detentore d'una borsa di studio alle università di Cambridge e Dublino.
size (1) [saiz], *n.* Dimensione, misura, *f.*; statura, grandezza, *f.*, numero, *m.*; formato, *m.*; taglia, *f.* || *v.t.* Graduare secondo la misura. **Life —,** di grandezza naturale; **these gloves are a — too large,** questi guanti sono troppo grandi di un numero; **a man of his —,** un uomo di quella taglia; (*fig.*) **to — someone up,** giudicare qualcuno, pesare qualcuno.
size (2), *n.* Colla, bozzina, *f.* || *v.t.* Incollare, imbozzinare.
sizing, *n.* Incollatura, imbozzinatura, *f.*
sizzle [sizl], *v.i.* Friggere. || *n.* Friggio, *m.*
skate (1) [skeit], *n.* Pattino, *m.* || *v.i.* Pattinare. **Roller-—,** pattino a rotelle, *m.*; (*fig.*) **to — on thin ice,** camminare su un terreno sdrucciolevole.
skate (2), *n.* (*Zool.*) Razza, *f.*
skater, *n.* Pattinatore, *m.*, pattinatrice, *f.*
skating, *n.* Pattinaggio, *m.* **—-rink,** campo di pattinaggio, *m.*
skedaddle [ske'dædl], *v.i.* Scapparsene, darsela a gambe.
skein [skein], *n.* Matassa, *f.* **A tangled —,** una matassa arruffata, *f.*
skeleton ['skeletən], *n.* Scheletro, *m.*; (*Tech.*) scheletro, *m.*, ossatura, *f.* **A — in the cupboard,** una segreta onta, *f.*; **—-key,** grimaldello, *m.*
skep [skep], *n.* Cesta, *f.*; (*for bees*) alveare, *m.*
sketch [sketʃ], *n.* Schizzo, abbozzo, disegno, *m.*; (*Theat.*) macchietta, commedietta, *f.* || *v.t.i.* Schizzare, disegnare, abbozzare. **To go out sketching,** andar a prender schizzi; **—-book,** album di schizzi, *m.*; **—-map,** carta muta, *f.*
sketcher, *n.* Disegnatore, *m.*
sketchy, *a.* Appena abbozzato, vago, incompleto.
skew [skju:], *a.* Obliquo, storto, a sghembo, sbieco.
skewbald, *a.* Pomellato.
skewer, *n.* Spiedo, spiedino, stecco, *m.* || *v.t.* Infilzare con stecchi.
ski (pl. **skis**) [ski:, ski:z], *n.* Sci, *m.* || *v.i.* Sciare. **— stick,** bastone da sci.
skid [skid], *n.* Martinicca, scarpa, *f.*; (*slip*) slittamento, *m.*, slittata, *f.*; (*Aviat.*) pattino, *m.* || *v.i.* Slittare, scivolare.
skier ['ski:əɹ], *n.* Sciatore, *m.*, sciatrice, *f.*

skiff [skif], *n.* (*Naut.*) Schifo, singolo, *m.*, barchettina, *f.*
skiing ['ski:iŋ], *n.* Corse con gli sci, *f.pl.*
skilful ['skilfəl], *a.* Abile, esperto, destro.
skilfully, *adv.* Abilmente, destramente.
skilfulness, *n.* Abilità, destrezza, *f.*
skill [skil], *n.* Abilità, destrezza, perizia, maestria, *f.*
skilled, *a.* Perito, esperto, pratico. **— labour,** mano d'opera specializzata; **— in,** esperto in.
skillet ['skilit], *n.* Casseruola con lungo manico, *f.*
skilly ['skili], *n.* Brodaglia, *f.*, brodo lungo, *m.*
skim [skim], *v.t.i.* Schiumare; spannare, scremare; sfiorare, rasentare. **To — over,** sfiorare; **to — a book,** scorrere un libro; **— milk,** latte spannato, latte scremato, *m.*
skimmer, *n.* Schiumatoio, schiumaruolo, *m.*; spanattoia, *f.*
skimmings, *n.pl.* Schiuma, *f.*
skimp [skimp], *v.t.i.* Tenere a stecchetto, lesinare; restringere.
skimpy, *a.* Scarso, meschino.
skin [skin], *n.* Pelle, *f.*; cute, derma, epidermide, *f.*; cuoio, *m.*; (*rind*) buccia, *f.* ‖ *v.t.* Scorticare; pelare; sbucciare; *v.i.* coprirsi di pelle, cicatrizzarsi. **To save one's —,** salvar la pelle; **to be nothing but — and bone,** essere pelle e ossa; **I wouldn't like to be in his —,** non vorrei essere nei suoi panni; **to escape by the — of one's teeth,** uscire pel rotto della cuffia; **to have a fair —,** avere la carnagione bionda; **wet to the —,** bagnato fino alle ossa; **—-deep,** leggiero, superficiale; (*fig.*) **to be thin-skinned,** essere suscettibile; **—-disease,** malattia cutanea, *f.*; **—-grafting,** innesto epidermico, *m.*
skinflint, *n.* Taccagno, spilorcio, *m.*
skinful, *n.* Scorpacciata, *f.* **He has had a —,** è ubbriaco.
skinless, *a.* Senza pelle, senza buccia.
skinner, *n.* Scorticatore, *m.*; pellicciaio, pellaio, *m.*
skinniness, *n.* Magrezza, macilenza, *f.*; (*fig.*) meschinità, grettezza *f.*
skinny, *a.* Magro, scarno, macilente; (*fig.*) meschino, gretto.
skip [skip], *n.* Salto, balzo, sgambetto, *m.* ‖ *v.i.t.* Saltare, saltellare, balzare; svolazzare; omettere. **To — a chapter,** saltare un capitolo; **to — with a rope,** saltare alla corda.
skipper, *n.* Padrone, capitano, *m.*
skipping, *n.* Il saltare, *m.* **—-rope,** corda per saltare, *f.*
skirl [skə:ɹl], *n.* Suono delle zampogne, *m.*
skirmish ['skə:ɹmiʃ], *n.* (*Mil.*) Scaramuccia, *f.*; (*fig.*) schermaglia, *f.* ‖ *v.i.* Scaramucciare.
skirmisher, *n.* Scaramucciatore, *m.*
skirret ['skiret], *n.* (*Bot.*) Sedano d'acqua, *m.*
skirt [skə:ɹt], *n.* Sottana, gonna, *f.*; (*of coat*) falda, *f.*; margine, orlo, *m.*, estremità, *f.* ‖ *v.t.* Rasentare, costeggiare, appressarsi a, accostarsi a. **Outskirts,** sobborghi, *m.pl.*; **to — along,** andare lungo, costeggiare.
skirting, skirting-board, *n.* Zoccolo, zoccolino, *m.*
skit [skit], *n.* Satira, pasquinata, burla, *f.*
skittish, *a.* Capriccioso, affettato, smorfioso; (*of horse*) ombroso.
skittishly, *adv.* Affettatamente.
skittishness, *n.* Affettazione, smorfiosaggine, *f.*
skittles ['skitlz], *n.pl.* Birilli, *m.pl.* **—-alley,** andito per giuocare ai birilli, *m.*
skua ['skju:ə], *n.* (*Zool.*) Specie di gabbiano.
skulk [skʌlk], *v.i.* Nascondersi, rintanarsi, accovacciarsi. **To — in the shadows,** ritrarsi nell'ombra.
skulker, *n.* Scansapericolo, scansafatiche, *m.*
skull [skʌl], *n.* Teschio, cranio, *m.* **—-cap,** papalina, calotta, *f.*
skunk [skʌŋk], *n.* (*Zool.*) Moffetta, *f.*; (*fur*) pelliccia di moffetta, *f.*; (*fig.*) tipaccio, vigliacco, farabutto, *m.*
sky [skai], *n.* Cielo, firmamento, *m.* ‖ *v.t.* Levare in alto, (*of a picture*) appendere in alto. **Under the open —,** a cielo scoperto; **to laud to the skies,** innalzare al cielo, portare alle stelle; **—-blue,** celeste, turchino; **—-high,** altissimo, fino al cielo; **to blow up —-high,** far saltare in aria; **—-line,** orizzonte, *m.*; (*colloq.*) **—-pilot,** prete, *m.*; **—-rocket,** razzo volante, *m.*
skylark, *n.* (*Zool.*) Allodola, *f.* ‖ *v.i.* Scherzare, giuocare.
skylarking, *n.* Beffe, celie, *f.pl.*
skylight, *n.* Lucernario, *m.*
skysail, *n.* (*Naut.*) Pappafico, velaccio, *m.*
skyscraper, *n.* Grattacielo, grattanuvole, *m.*
skyward, *adv.* Verso il cielo.
slab [slæb], *n.* Lastra, piastra, *f.*; tavola, *f.*; pezzo, *m.*
slack [slæk], *a.* Lento, allentato, disteso; languido, fiacco; inattivo, negligente, incurante, trasandato. ‖ *n.* Carbone minuto, *m.*; (*of rope*) imbando, *m.* ‖ *v.t.* Allentare. **Business is —,** gli affari languono; **the — season,** la stagione morta, *f.*; **— water,** marea bassa, *f.*; **to — off,** allentarsi, rilassarsi.
slacken, *v.t.* Allentare, rilassare; diminuire, scemare; *v.i.* allentarsi, rilassarsi; diminuire, scemare, calare. **To — speed,** rallentare; **to — lime,** spegnere la calce.
slackening, *n.* Allentamento, *m.*, diminuzione, *f.*; rallentamento, *m.*
slacker, *n.* Scansafatiche, fannullone, *m.*
slackly, *adv.* Lentamente, languidamente, negligentemente.
slackness, *n.* Lentezza, fiacchezza, inattività, *f.*; negligenza, incuranza, *f.*; allentamento, *m.*
slacks, *n.pl.* Calzoni, *m.pl.*
slag [slæg], *n.* Scoria, *f.*
slake [sleik], *v.t.* Spegnere, estinguere; dissetare, appagare. **To — one's thirst,** dissetarsi; **to — lime,** spegnere la calce.
slaking, *n.* Spegnimento, *m.*
slam [slæm], *v.t.* Sbattere, chiudere con forza; *v.i.* sbattersi. ‖ *n.* Sbattuta, *f.*; (*Cards*) cappotto, *m.*
slander ['slɑ:ndəɹ], *n.* Maldicenza, calunnia, *f.*; (*Law*) diffamazione, *f.* ‖ *v.t.* Calunniare; diffamare. **An action for —,** una querela per diffamazione, *f.*
slanderous, *a.* Maldicente, calunnioso; diffamativo.
slanderously, *adv.* Calunniosamente.
slang [slæŋ], *n.* Gergo, *m.* ‖ *v.t.* Insultare, vituperare; usare idiotismi propri di una classe.
slangy ['slæŋi], *a.* Di gergo.
slant [slɑ:nt], *v.i.* Pendere, inclinarsi; *v.t.* far pendere, rendere obliquo. ‖ *n.* Inclinazione, pendenza, *f.*; (*fig.*) punto di vista, *m.*

slanting, *a.* Inclinato, obliquo, pendente.
slantingly, slantwise, *adv.* Obliquamente, a sghembo.
slap [slæp], *n.* Schiaffo, ceffone, *m.*; colpo, *m.* || *v.t.* Battere, schiaffeggiare, percuotere. || *adv.* Di colpo. **To — someone's face,** dare uno schiaffo a qualcuno; **he ran — into me,** mi venne addosso di colpo; **he hit me — in the eye,** mi diede un colpo all'occhio; **— -bang,** d'impeto, a capofitto; **— -up,** ottimo, coi fiocchi, di prim'ordine; (*Theat. Cinema.*) **— -stick,** scena comica, *f.*
slapdash [ˈslæpdæʃ], *a.* Noncurante, disinvolto, sventato. || *adv.* Senza riguardi.
slash [slæʃ], *n.* Taglio, *m.*; (*in the face*) sfregio, *m.*; (*in dress*) apertura, *f.*, spacco, *m.*; (*with whip*) sferzata, frustata, *f.* || *v.t.* Tagliare, tagliuzzare; sfregiare; *v.i.* menar colpi. **To — about,** colpire a casaccio; **to — someone with a whip,** sferzare qualcuno; **a slashing criticism,** una stroncatura, *f.*
slat [slæt], *n.* Stecca, *f.*; assicella, *f.*
slate (1) [sleit], *n.* Ardesia, *f.*; (*for writing on*) lavagna, *f.*; (*for roof*) tegola d'ardesia, *f.* || *v.t.* Coprire di ardesia. **— -coloured,** del colore d'ardesia; **— -pencil,** matita d'ardesia, *f.*; **— -quarry,** cava d'ardesia, *f.*
slate (2), *v.t.* (*colloq.*) Sgridare, stroncare.
slater, *n.* Conciatetti, *m.*
slating, *n.* (*colloq.*) Stroncatura, *f.*
slattern [ˈslætəɹn], *n.* Sudiciona, sporcacciona, *f.*
slatternliness, *n.* Sudiceria, trascuratezza, *f.*
slatternly, *a.* Sciatto, sudicio, sporco, trascurato.
slaty [ˈsleiti], *a.* Lavagnino, schistoso; di color ardesia.
slaughter [ˈslɔːtəɹ], *n.* Strage, *f.*, massacro, macello, *m.*; carneficina, *f.*, eccidio, *m.* || *v.t.* Massacrare, trucidare, ammazzare; macellare. **— -house,** macello, mattatoio, ammazzatoio, *m.*
slaughterer, slaughterman, *n.* Macellaio, abbattitore, *m.*
slaughterous, *a.* Micidiale.
Slav [slæv, slaːv], *n.a.* Slavo, *m.*
slave [sleiv], *n.* Schiavo, *m.*, schiava, *f.* || *v.i.* Lavorare come uno schiavo, sgobbare. **A — of prejudice,** uno schiavo di pregiudizi, *m.*; **— -trade,** tratta dei negri, *f.*; **— -dealer,** mercante di schiavi, *m.*; **— -driver,** negriero, *m.*; tiranno, *m.*; **white- — traffic,** tratta delle schiave bianche, *f.*
slaver (1) [ˈsleivəɹ], *n.* Negriero, *m.*
slaver (2) [ˈslævəɹ], *v.i.* Far la bava, sbavare, salivare. || *n.* Bava, saliva, *f.*
slavery (1) [ˈsleivəri], *n.* Schiavitù, *f.*
slavery (2) [ˈslævəri], *a.* Bavoso.
slavey [ˈsleivi], *n.* (*obs.*) Serva, *f.*
slavish [ˈsleiviʃ], *a.* Servile, basso; (*fig.*) pedissequo.
slavishly, *adv.* Servilmente.
slavishness, *n.* Servilità, *f.*
Slavonic [sləˈvɔnik], *a.* Slavo.
slay [slei], *v.t.* Uccidere, ammazzare, trucidare; sacrificare.
slayer, *n.* Uccisore, assassino, *m.*
slaying, *n.* Uccisione, *f.*, assassinio, *m.*
sledge (1) [sledʒ], *n.* Slitta, *f.*; treggia, *f.*; traino, *m.* || *v.t.* Slittare, andare in slitta.
sledge (2), **sledge-hammer,** *n.* Martello da fabbro, *m.*, mazza, *f.*; maglio, *m.*
sledging, *n.* Lo slittare, l'andare in slitta, *m.*
sleek [sliːk], *a.* Liscio, lucente, lustro, lucido. || *v.t.* Lisciare, pettinare.
sleekness, *n.* Lisciezza, levigatezza, lucentezza, *f.*
sleep [sliːp], *n.* Sonno, *m.*; riposo, *m.* || *v.i.* Dormire; riposarsi; alloggiare. **Beauty —,** primo sonno, *m.*; **I have not had a wink of —,** non ho potuto chiuder occhio; **overcome with —,** cascando di sonno, vinto dal sonno; **the — of the just,** il sonno del giusto, *m.*; **to go to —,** addormentarsi; **to send to —,** far dormire; **to wake from —,** svegliarsi dal sonno; **to lose one's —,** perdere il sonno; **to have a good —,** far un bel sonno; **let us — on the matter,** dormiamoci sopra; **to — like a log,** dormire come un macigno; **to — like a top,** dormire come un ghiro; **to — soundly,** dormire profondamente; **— -walker,** sonnambulo, *m.*, **— -walking,** sonnambulismo, *m.*
sleeper, *n.* Dormiente, dormiglione, *m.*, (*Rail.*) vagone letto, *m.* **A light —,** uno che dorme leggiero, *m.*; **a heavy —,** uno che dorme sodo, *m.*
sleepily, *adv.* D'un'aria sonnolente.
sleepiness, *n.* Sonnolenza, *f.*
sleeping, *n.* Sonno, riposo, *m.* || *a.* Dormiente, addormentato, assonnato. **— partner,** socio accomandante, *m.*; **— -bag,** sacco a pelo, *m.*; **The Sleeping Beauty,** la Bella Addormentata, *f.*; **— -berth,** cuccetta, *f.*; **— -car,** vagone letto, *m.*; **— -draught,** sonnifero, *m.*; **— -sickness,** malattia del sonno, *f.*; **— -suit,** pigiama, *m.*
sleepless, *a.* Insonne.
sleeplessness, *n.* Insonnia, *f.*
sleepy, *a.* Sonnacchioso, assonnato, soporifico; (*of fruit*) mezzo. **To feel —,** aver sonno; **— -head,** dormiglione, *m.*; **— sickness,** encefalite letargica, *f.*
sleet [sliːt], *n.* Nevischio, *m.* || *v.i.* Cader nevischio, nevischiare.
sleety, *a.* Nevischioso.
sleeve [sliːv], *n.* Manica, *f.*; (*Mech.*) manicotto, *m.* **To laugh in one's —,** ridere sotto i baffi; **— -board,** stiramaniche, *m.*; **— -links,** bottoni da polsino, *m.*, gemelli da polsino, *m.pl.*
sleeveless, *a.* Senza maniche.
sleigh [slei], *n.* Slitta leggera, *f.*
sleighing, *n.* Andare in slitta, *m.*
sleight [slait], *n.* **— of hand,** giuoco di prestigio, giuoco di mano, *m.*
slender [ˈslendəɹ], *a.* Smilzo, sottile, snello, esile, magro, esiguo, scarso; fiacco, debole. **A — girl,** una fanciulla esile, *f.*; **— hopes,** speranze fragili, *f.pl.*; **— means,** mezzi scarsi, *m.pl.*; **a — repast,** un desinare parco, *m.*; **a — waist,** una vita sottile, una vita snella, *f.*
slenderness, *n.* Sottigliezza, esilità, magrezza, tenuità, *f.*; esiguità, scarsezza, *f.*; debolezza, *f.*
sleuth, sleuth-hound [sljuːθ, ˈsljuːθhaund], *n.* Segugio, *m.*
slew (1) *p.* and *pp.* of **slay.**
slew (2), **slue** [sluː], *v.t.* Girare, rotare.

slice [slais], *n.* Fetta, *f.*; (*fig.*) parte, porzione, *f.* || *v.t.* Affettare, tagliare a fetta; (*a ball*) tagliare. **Fish- —,** tagliapesce, *m.*; **a — of bread,** una fettina di pane, *f.*; **a — of bread and butter,** una fetta di pane e burro, una tartina, *f.*

slick [slik], *a.* (*colloq.*) Destro, abile, svelto; fluido, scorrevole. || *adv.* Destramente, abilmente; pronto.

slide [slaid], *n.* Sdrucciolo, *m.*, scivolo, *m.*, scivolata, *f.*; inclinazione, pendenza, *f.*; (*Photo.*) lastra, *f.*, vetro, *m.*, proiezione, *f.* || *v.i.* Scivolare, sdrucciolare, sfuggire, dileguarsi; scorrere; *v.t.* fare scivolare, fare scorrere; tirare. **Land- —,** frana, *f.*; **to let things —,** lasciare correre le cose; **to — down,** scivolare giù; **he slid the drawer out of the table,** tirò fuori il cassetto dalla tavola; **— -rule,** regolo calcolatore, *m.*; **— -valve,** valvola a cassetto, *f.*; **— -rest,** sostegno scorrevole, *m.*; **a lecture with slides,** una conferenza con proiezioni, *f.*

slider, *n.* Scivolatore, *m.*

sliding, *n.* Scivolata, *f.*; lo scivolare, lo sdrucciolare, *m.* || *a.* Scorrevole, mobile. **— -door,** porta scorrevole, *f.*; **— scale,** scala mobile; **— -roof,** tetto mobile, *m.*; (*in boat*) **— -seat,** sedile scorrevole, *m.*

slight [slait], *a.* Smilzo, sottile, snello, esile, magro, tenue; scarso; leggiero, superficiale, insignificante; piccolo, poco. || *n.* Mancanza di rispetto, *f.*, dispetto, affronto, sfregio, *m.*, ingiuria, offesa, *f.* || *v.t.* Sfregiare, disprezzare, far poco caso di; mancare di rispetto a, ingiuriare. **A — wound,** una ferita leggiera, *f.*; **a — cold,** un po' di raffreddore, *m.*; **there is not the slightest excuse,** non c'è la minima scusa; **to put a — upon,** far un affronto a.

slightingly, *adv.* Senza riguardo, con disprezzo.

slightly, *adv.* Leggermente, superficialmente, poco, un poco.

slightness, *n.* Sottigliezza, snellezza, *f.*; magrezza, *f.*; leggerezza, *f.*

slily ['slaili], *adv.* Scaltramente, furbamente.

slim [slim], *a.* Smilzo, sottile, snello, esile, magro; (*colloq.*) furbo, scaltro. || *v.i.* Dimagrire.

slime [slaim], *n.* Limo, *m.*, melma, poltiglia, fanghiglia, *f.*; (*of snails*) bava, *f.*, limaccio, *m.*

sliminess, *n.* Viscosità, *f.*

slimness ['slimnis], *n.* Sottigliezza, snellezza, esilità, *f.*

sling [sliŋ], *n.* Fionda, *f.*; frombola, *f.*; (*for rifle*) cinghia, *f.*; (*for broken limb*) fascia, *f.*; (*hoist*) braca, ghia, *f.* || *v.t.* Lanciare, scagliare; sospendere, appendere; (*Naut.*) imbracare. **To — a hammock,** sospendere un'amaca; **to — over one's shoulder,** portare ad armacollo; **to — a stone,** lanciare una pietra con la fionda.

slink [sliŋk], *v.i.* Sgattaiolare. **To — away,** filar via; **to — by,** strisciare presso; **to — out,** svignarsela, battersela.

slip [slip], *v.i.t.* Scivolare, sdrucciolare; scorrere, correre; (*to come undone*) sciogliersi; (*to mistake*) sbagliare, fare una svista; (*to loose*) sciogliere; (*to lose*) perdere, lasciare, scappare; (*to escape*) scappare; (*Naut.*) filare, infilare. || *n.* Scivolata, *f.*, scivolone sdrucciolone, *m.*; (*error*) sbaglio, errore, *m.*, svista, *f.*; (*for pillow*) federa, *f.*; (*underskirt*) combinazione, *f.*; (*leash*) guinzaglio; (*Bot.*) rampollo, innesto, *m.*; (*of paper*) striscia, *f.*, pezzetto, *m.*; (*Naut.*) scalo, *m.*; (*Boxing*) scanso, *m.*; (*Theat.*) quinte, *f.pl.* **Land- —,** frana, *f.*; **his foot slipped,** gli mancò il piede; **the blanket slipped off the bed,** la coperta scivolò giù dal letto; **she slipped off the ring,** si tolse l'anello; **to let something — through one's fingers,** lasciare scappare qualcosa; **to — out of the room,** scivolar fuori dalla stanza; **to — off, to — away,** scappare, andarsene, svignarsela; **I'll — across to the shop,** faccio un salto fino al negozio; **she slipped on her frock,** si infilò il vestito; **to let — an observation,** lasciare scappare un'osservazione; **to let — an opportunity,** lasciarsi sfuggire l'occasione; **a — of the tongue,** uno scorso di lingua, *m.*; **to give someone the —,** evitare qualcuno; **a — of a girl,** una giovinetta, *f.*; **there's many a — 'twixt the cup and the lip,** dal dire al fare c'è di mezzo il mare; (*Rail.*) **— -carriage,** vagone staccato, *m.*; **— -knot,** nodo scorsoio, *m.*; (*Print.*) **— -proof,** bozza, *f.*

slipper, *n.* Pantofola, ciabatta, pianella, *f.*, (*for wheel*) scarpa, *f.*

slipperiness ['slipərinis], *n.* Sdrucciolosità, incertezza, instabilità, *f.*

slippery, *a.* Sdrucciolevole, sdruccioloso; lubrico; incerto, malsicuro, instabile; difficile. (*fig.*) **A — customer,** una persona evasiva, *f.*; **the pavement is very —,** il lastrico è sdruccioloso; **as — as an eel,** guizzante come un'anguilla.

slips, *n.pl.* Mutandine da bagno, *f.pl.*

slipshod ['slipʃɔd], *a.* Trasandato, trascurato, negligente, incurante; scalcagnato.

slipslop, *n.* Risciacquatura, *f.*

slipway, *n.* (*Naut.*) Scalo, *m.*

slit [slit], *v.t.* Fendere, spaccare; *v.i.* fendersi. || *n.* Fessura, fenditura, spaccatura, *f.*

slither ['sliðəɹ], *v.i.* (*colloq.*) Scivolare, sdrucciolare.

sliver ['slivəɹ], *v.t.* Scheggiare. || *n.* Scheggia, *f.*

slobber ['slɔbəɹ], *v.i.* Sbavare, fare la bava, salivare. || *n.* Bava, *f.*

sloe [slou], *n.* (*Bot.*) Prugnola, *f.*, prugna selvatica, *f.* **— -tree,** prugnolo, *m.*; **— -gin,** liquore di prugnola, *m.*

slog [slɔg], *v.i.t.* Dare dei pugni, picchiare; lavorare di sgobbo, faticare.

slogan ['slougən], *n.* Divisa di pubblicità, *f.*; slogan, motto, *m.*; grido di guerra scozzese, *m.*

sloop [slu:p], *n.* (*Naut.*) Sloop, *m.*, scialuppa, *f.*

slop [slɔp], *v.t.* Versare, far cadere, spargere. || *n.* (*colloq.*) Poliziotto, *m.* **To — over,** traboccare; **— -basin,** tazza per versare gli avanzi del tè, *f.*; **— -pail,** secchio per l'acqua sporca, *m.*; **— -shop,** bottega da rigattiere, *f.* [cp. **slops**].

slope [sloup], *n.* Pendio, *m.*, pendenza, costa salita, *f.*; declivio, *m.*, pendice, *f.* || *v.i.* Pendere, inclinare, piegarsi; (*colloq.*) scappare, svignarsela; *v.t.* inclinare, abbassarsi.

sloping, *a.* Obliquo, inclinato, in isbieco, in pendenza, in declivio.

sloppiness ['slɔpinis], *n.* Umidità, *f.*; (*fig.*) svenevolezza, sciattaggine, *f.*

sloppy, *a.* Umido, bagnato, guazzoso; fangoso; (*fig.*) sdolcinato, svenevole; abborracciato.
sloppily, *adv.* Sdolcinatamente.
slops [slɔps], *n.pl.* Pappa, *f.*, cibo liquido, *m.*; (*refuse*) lavatura, risciacquatura, acqua sporca, *f.*; (*clothes*) vestiti bell'e fatti, *m.pl.*
slot [slɔt], *n.* Apertura, *f.*, foro, buco, *m.*; traccia di cervo, pesta, *f.* || *v.t.* Fare buchi in, fare aperture in. **—-machine,** distributore automatico, *m.*; **—-meter,** contatore a pagamento anticipato, *m.*
sloth [slouθ], *n.* Pigrizia, ignavia, infingardaggine, accidia, indolenza, *f.*; (*Zool.*) bradipo, *m.*
slothful, *a.* Pigro, ignavo, infingardo, poltrone, accidioso.
slothfully, *adv.* Pigramente.
slothfulness, *n.* Pigrizia, *f.*
slouch [slautʃ], *v.i.* Penzolare, ciondolare, camminare dinoccolato. **—-hat,** cappello a cencio, *m.*
slouching, *a.* Trasandato, dinoccolato.
slough (1) [slau], *n.* Pantano, palude, *m.*, pozzanghera, *f.*
slough (2) [slʌf], *v.t.* (*of snake*) Spogliarsi. || *n.* Spoglia, *f.*; (*Med.*) crosta, *f.*
sloven ['slʌvən], *n.* Sudicione, sporcaccione, *m.*
slovenliness, *n.* Sudiceria, sciatteria, negligenza, trascuratezza, *f.*
slovenly, *a.* Trasandato, trascurato, sciatto, sudicio, sporco.
slow [slou], *a.* Lento, tardo; (*dull*) ottuso; (*tardy*) tardivo; (*of clocks*) in ritardo; (*inactive*) pigro, inerte, infingardo; (*tedious*) noioso, monotono. || *adv.* Lento, lentamente. || *v.t.i.* Rallentare. **— and steady wins the race,** chi va piano va sano e va lontano; **a — march,** una marcia lenta, *f.*; **he was not — to defend himself,** non tardò a difendersi; **a — fire,** un fuoco lento, *m.*; **—-coach,** trottapiano, posapiano, pigrone, perdigiorno, *m.*; **—-combustion stove,** stufa a combustione continua, *f.*; (*Cinema.*) **—-motion picture,** film al rallentatore, *m.*; (*traffic*) **Go —!** Rallentare! **to — down,** rallentare.
slowly, *adv.* Lento, lentamente.
slowness, *n.* Lentezza, *f.*; pigrizia, *f.*; monotonia, *f.*; ritardo, indugio, *m.*
slow-worm ['slouwəːɹm], *n.* (*Zool.*) Orbettino, *m.*
sludge [slʌdʒ], *n.* Fango, *m.*, fanghiglia, *f.*; fognatura, *f.*
slue [sluː], *v.t.* Far girare; *v.i.* girare.
slug [slʌg], *n.* (*Zool.*) Lumaca, *f.*; (*metal*) lingotto, *m.*; (*Print.*) pallottola, *f.*; (*bullet*) pallottola, *f.*
sluggard ['slʌgəɹd], *n.* Pigrone, dormiglione, infingardo, *m.*
sluggish ['slʌgiʃ], *a.* Pigro, tardo, lento, inerte, infingardo.
sluggishly, *adv.* Pigramente, lentamente.
sluggishness, *n.* Pigrizia, lentezza, *f.*
sluice [sluːs], *n.* Chiusa, cateratta, *f.*, canale, *m.* || *v.t.* Inondare, allagare; bagnare, risciacquare. **—-gate,** saracinesca, cateratta, *f.*
slum [slʌm], *n.* Quartiere basso, *m.*; catapecchie, *f.pl.*; tuguri, angiporti, *m.pl.* || *v.i.* Visitare i quartieri poveri d'una città.
slumber ['slʌmbəɹ], *n.* Sonno, sonnellino, riposo, *m.* || *v.i.* Dormire, dormicchiare, sonnecchiare.
slumberer, *n.* Dormiente, *m.f.*
slumbering, *a.* Dormiente, addormentato.
slump [slʌmp], *v.i.* (*of prices*) Ribassare, rinvilire, abbassarsi. || *n.* Abbassamento generale, ribasso improvviso, *m.*
slur [sləːɹ], *n.* Macchia, taccia, imputazione, *f.*; (*Mus.*) legatura, *f.* || *v.t.* Articolare male; (*Mus.*) legare. **To cast a — upon,** calunniare, diffamare; **to — over,** passar sopra, lasciar passare.
slurring, *n.* (*Mus.*) Legatura, *f.*
slush [slʌʃ], *n.* Fango, *m.*, fanghiglia, *f.*; neve disciolta, *f.*
slut [slʌt], *n.* Sudiciona, sporcacciona, *f.*; sgualdrina, *f.*
sluttish, *a.* Sudicio, sporco, trascurato.
sluttishly, *adv.* Trascuratamente.
sluttishness, *n.* Sporcizia, trascuratezza, negligenza, *f.*
sly [slai], *a.* Scaltro, furbo, astuto, avveduto, accorto, sornione. **On the —,** di nascosto, alla chetichella; **a — dog,** un sornione, un furbacchione, *m.*
slyboots, *n.* Sornione, *m.*; maliziosetto, *m.*
slyly, *adv.* Scaltramente, furbamente.
slyness, *n.* Scaltrezza, furberia, astuzia, accortezza, *f.*
smack (1) [smæk], *n.* Colpo, *m.*; schiaffo, ceffone, *m.*; scapaccione, scappellotto, *m.*; (*of whip*) schiocco, *m.*; (*kiss*) bacione, *m.*; (*flavour*) gusto, sapore, *m.* || *v.t.* Schiaffeggiare, schioccare, fare schioccare; battere; *v.i.* sentire di, sapere di. || *adv.* In pieno. **His ways smacked of the tyrant,** i suoi modi sentivano del tiranno; **to — one's lips,** schioccare le labbra.
smack (2), *n.* (*Naut.*) Barca da pesca, paranza, *f.*
smacking, *n.* Busse, botte, *f.pl.*, picchiata, *f.* || *a.* Sonoro.
small [smɔːl], *a.* Piccolo, piccino; scarso, esiguo; umile, basso; meschino, gretto. || *n.* La parte più sottile. **A — farmer,** un colono, un piccolo proprietario, *m.*; **to think no — beer of oneself,** avere un concetto elevato di sè stesso; **— blame to him,** una colpa da poco a suo carico; **—-talk,** chiacchiere, banalità, *f.pl.*; **they live in a — way,** vivono molto modestamente; **— change,** spiccioli, *m.pl.*; **the — hours,** le ore piccole, *f.pl.*; **he was made to look —,** gli fecero far una brutta figura; **the — of the back,** le reni, *f.pl.*; **—-arms,** armi da fuoco; **—-hand,** scrittura ordinaria, *f.*; **—-minded,** gretto, meschino, piccino; **—-sword,** spadino, *m.*
smallish, *a.* Piuttosto piccolo, piccoletto.
smallness, *n.* Piccolezza, *f.*, scarsezza, esiguità, *f.*; meschineria, grettezza, *f.*
smallpox, *n.* (*Med.*) Vaiolo, *m.*; **— patient,** vaioloso, *m.*
smalt [smɔːlt], *n.* (*Chem.*) Smalto, *m.*
smart (1) [smɑːɹt], *a.* Acuto; vivo, vivace; bravo, accorto, intelligente, scaltro, destro; elegante, attillato, bene in arnese; mordace, frizzante, pungente. **A — rap on the knuckles,** una picchiatina sulle nocche, *f.*; **a — saying,** una frase mordace; **the — set,** il bel mondo, *m.*
smart (2), *n.* Bruciore, dolore, *m.* || *v.i.* Bruciare, sentire un vivo dolore, far male. **My finger smarts,** ho un bruciore al dito; **you shall — for this,** pagherete il fio di questo.

smarten, *v.t.* Abbellire, farsi bello. **To — oneself up,** attillarsi.

smarting, *n.* Bruciore, *m.* || *a.* Cocente, bruciante, doloroso.

smartly, *adv.* Vivamente, scaltramente; spiritosamente, elegantemente.

smartness, *n.* Accortezza, intelligenza, *f.*; scaltrezza, destrezza, *f.*; eleganza, attillatezza, *f.*; prontezza, *f.*

smash [smæʃ], *v.t.* Spezzare, fracassare, frantumare; (*fig.*) rovinare; *v.i.* fallire. || *n.* Sconquasso, *m.*, rovina, distruzione, *f.*; fallimento, *m.*; disastro, *m.*, collisione, *f.* **To — into,** urtare in, imbattersi in; **to go to —,** andare in rovina, andare in malora.

smatter [ˈsmætəɹ] *v.i.* Parlare a sproposito.

smatterer, *n.* Saccentino, saputello, *m.*

smattering, *n.* Infarinatura, conoscenza superficiale, *f.*

smear [smiəɹ], *v.t.* Spalmare; ungere, imbrattare. || *n.* Macchia, patacca, spalmata, *f.*; calunnia, *f.*; dubbio, *m.*

smeary, *a.* Macchiato, imbrattato, sporco.

smell [smel], *n.* Odore, *m.*; profumo, olezzo, *m.*; fragranza, *f.*; (*sense of smell*) odorato, fiuto, *m.* || *v.t.* Sentire l'odore di, odorare, fiutare; annusare; *v.i.* odorare; sentire, sapere, dare odore. **A bad —,** un puzzo, *m.*; **to take a — at something,** fiutare qualchecosa; (*fig.*) **to — a rat,** fiutare l'imbroglio; **I can — gas,** sento un odore di gas; **to — out,** scoprire; **to — nasty,** puzzare; **to — stuffy,** sapere di chiuso; **to — nice,** avere un buon odore, saper di buon; **the milk smells sour,** il latte sa di acido, *m.*; **smelling-bottle,** boccettina d'odori, *f.*; **smelling-salts,** i sali, *m.pl.*

smelly, *a.* Puzzolente, fetente.

smelt (1) [smelt], *v.t.* Fondere.

smelt (2), *n.* (*Zool.*) Eperlano, *m.*

smelt (3) *pp.* of **smell.**

smelter, *n.* Fonditore, *m.*

smelting, *n.* Fusione, *f.* **— -furnace,** forno fusorio, alto forno, *m.*; **— -works,** fonderia, *f.*

smilax [ˈsmailæks], *n.* (*Bot.*) Smilace, *f.*

smile [smail], *n.* Sorriso, *m.* || *v.i.* Sorridere. **To — bitterly,** sorridere amaramente; **to — on,** sorridere a; **to — at a girl,** sorridere ad una ragazza; **to — at a joke,** sorridere di una facezia.

smiling, *a.* Sorridente.

smilingly, *adv.* Sorridentemente.

smirch [sməːɹtʃ], *v.t.* Macchiare, imbrattare, sporcare; (*fig.*) macchiare, deturpare.

smirk [sməːɹk], *v.i.* Fare smorfie, civettare. || *n.* Sorriso affettato, *m.*

smirking, *a.* Smorfioso.

smite [smait], *v.t.* Battere, colpire, picchiare, percuotere; castigare; uccidere; *v.i.* urtare, battere. **To be smitten with a girl,** essere innamorato di una ragazza; **smitten with plague,** colpito dalla peste; **I was smitten with a desire to run away,** fui preso dal desiderio di svignarmela; **the sound smote upon my ear,** il suono mi ferì l'orecchio.

smith [smiθ], *n.* Fabbro, *m.*; magnano, *m.*; fabbro ferraio, *m.*

smithereens [smiðəˈriːnz], *n.pl.* Pezzi, frammenti, *m.pl.* **To smash to —,** fare in cento pezzi, sfracellare, frantumare.

smithy, *n.* Fucina, ferriera, *f.*

smitten [cp. **smite**].

smock [smɔk], *n.* Camiciotto, *m.*, blusa, sopravveste, *f.* **— -frock,** camiciotto da contadino, *m.*

smocking, *n.* Ricamo pieghettato, *m.*

smoke [smouk], *n.* Fumo, *m.*, fumata, *f.* || *v.i.* Fumare; *v.t.* fumare, affumicare. **To end in —,** finire in fumo; **to have a —,** fumare, fare una fumatina; **to — out,** cacciar via col fumo; **this chimney smokes,** questo camino butta fumo; **the lamp is smoking,** la lampada fila; **— -consuming,** fumivoro; **— -dried,** affumicato; **— -helmet,** maschera contro il fumo, *f.*; **— -jack,** girarrosto, *m.*; **— -stack,** fumaiuolo, camino, *m.*

smoked, *a.* Affumicato. **— herring,** aringa affumicata, *f.*

smokeless, *a.* Senza fumo.

smoker, *n.* Fumatore, *m.*, fumatrice, *f.*

smokiness, *n.* Fumosità, *f.*

smoking, *n.* Il fumare, il fumo, *m.* || *a.* Fumante, fumoso, da fumo. **No — allowed,** vietato fumare; (*Rail.*) **— -carriage,** compartimento per fumatori, *m.*; **— -mixture,** tabacco per la pipa, *m.*; **— -room,** fumatoio, *m.*

smoky, *a.* Fumoso; affumicato, nero. **A — chimney,** un camino che butta fumo, *m.*

smooth [smuːð], *a.* Liscio, levigato; piano, eguale; facile, scorrevole; sdolcinato. || *v.t.* Lisciare, levigare; spianare, appianare; calmare; stirare. **A — passage,** una traversata calma, *f.*; **to — away,** spianare; **the sea has smoothed down,** il mare si è calmato; **to — the way,** spianare la via; **a — -bore gun,** un fucile a canna liscia, *m.*; **— -faced,** imberbe, glabro, (*fig.*) untuoso; **— -spoken, — -tongued,** lusinghiero, mellifluo, insinuante.

smoothing, *n.* Spianatura, *f.* **— -iron,** ferro da stirare, *m.*; **— -plane,** pialla, *f.*

smoothly, *adv.* Lisciamente, facilmente, dolcemente. **All has gone —,** tutto è andato bene.

smoothness, *n.* Lisciezza, levigatezza, *f.*; pianezza, *f.*; facilità, scorrevolezza, *f.*; (*of sea*) calma, *f.*

smother [ˈsmʌðəɹ], *v.t.* Soffocare; affogare, reprimere, nascondere; colmare; spegnere, estinguere. **To — with kisses,** soffocare di baci.

smoulder [ˈsmouldəɹ], *v.i.* Bruciare senza fiamma, covare.

smouldering, *a.* Che cova, sopito. **— hatred,** odio sopito.

smudge [smʌdʒ], *v.t.* Sgorbiare, scarabocchiare, macchiare, imbrattare. || *n.* Macchia, macchia d'inchostro, *f.*; sgorbio, *m.*

smudgy, *a.* Macchiato, imbrattato.

smug [smʌg], *a.* Affettato, soddisfatto di sè stesso, vanitoso.

smuggle [smʌgl], *v.t.* Contrabbandare, frodare; *v.i.* esercitare il contrabbando, far contrabbando. **To — in,** fare entrare di contrabbando, introdurre di frodo, fare entrare di nascosto.

smuggled, *a.* Contrabbando.

smuggler, *n.* Contrabbandiere, *m.*

smuggling, *n.* Contrabbando, frodo, *m.*

smut [smʌt], *n.* Fuliggine, *f.*, fiocco di fuliggine, *m.*; (*Agric.*) golpe, fuliggine, *f.*; (*fig.*) oscenità, *f.* ‖ *v.t.* Sporcare di fuliggine, annerire; infettare colla golpe; *v.i.* ingolpare.
smuttily, *adv.* Sporcamente, oscenamente.
smuttiness, *n.* Nerezza, *f.*; oscenità, *f.*
smutty, *a.* Fuligginoso, nero; sporco; ingolpato; (*fig.*) sconcio, osceno.
Smyrna [ˈsməːɹnə], *n.* (*Geog.*) Smirne, *f.*
snack [snæk], *n.* Spuntino, bocconcino, *m.*, merenda, *f.* **To take a —,** mangiare un boccone, fare uno spuntino; **— -bar,** ristorante a bar, *m.*, tavola calda, *f.*
snaffle [snæfl], *n.* Morso snodato, *m.* ‖ *v.t.* (*colloq.*) Rubare.
snag [snæg], *n.* Nodo, groppo, troncone, *m.*; (*fig.*) ostacolo, impedimento, intoppo, inciampo, *m.*
snail [sneil], *n.* (*Zool.*) Chiocciola, lumaca, *f.* **At a snail's pace,** a passo di lumaca.
snake [sneik], *n.* (*Zool.*) Serpente, *m.*, serpe, *f.*; biscia, *f.* **A — in the grass,** un serpente tra l'erbe, un tranello, *m.*; **— -charmer,** incantatore di serpenti, *m.*; (*Bot.*) **— -root,** serpentaria.
snaky, *a.* Serpentino, tortuoso; (*fig.*) scaltro, furbo, astuto.
snap [snæp], *v.t.i.* Morsicare, tentare di mordere; agguantare, afferrare; rompere, spezzare; spezzarsi; schioccare; (*Phot.*) prendere un istantanea di. ‖ *n.* Scatto, schiocco, scoppio; morsicata, *f.*, morso, *m.*; molla, molletta, *f.*; rottura subitanea, *f.*; specie di giuoco alle carte. **A cold —,** un periodo freddo, *m.*; (*Pol.*) **a — division,** una votazione improvvisa, *f.*; (*colloq.*) **to — out of it,** prendere controllo di sè stesso; **to — one's fingers at,** schernire, farsi beffe di; **to — up,** chiappare, rubare; **— -lock,** serratura a molla, *f.*
snapdragon, *n.* (*Bot.*) Bocca di leone, *f.*, antirrino, *m.*; giuoco familiare a Natale, *m.*
snappish, *a.* (*of dogs*) Disposto a mordere; (*fig.*) bisbetico, brusco, aspro.
snappishness, *n.* Umore bisbetico, *m.*, bruschezza, *f.*
snappy, *a.* Bisbetico, brusco; (*colloq.*) brioso, vivace. **Make it — !** Sbrigatevi !
snapshot, *v.t.i.* (*Phot.*) Scattare un'istantanea. ‖ *n.* Istantanea, *f.*
snare [snɛəɹ], *n.* Laccio, lacciuolo, *m.*, rete, trappola, *f.*; (*Mus.*) timbro, tamburo, *m.* ‖ *v.t.* Prendere al laccio, pigliare col laccio, accalappiare; (*fig.*) ingannare, truffare. **To lay a —,** tendere il laccio.
snarl (1) [snɑːɹl], *v.i.* Ringhiare; brontolare, mormorare. ‖ *n.* Ringhio, *m.*
snarl (2), *v.t.i.* Aggrovigliare, aggrovigliarsi. ‖ *n.* Groviglio, *m.*
snarling, *a.* Ringhioso, brontolone.
snatch [snætʃ], *v.t.* Afferrare, dar di piglio a, carpire, ghermire, agguantare. ‖ *n.* Pezzetto, frammento, brano, *m.* **To — at,** afferrare; **to — away,** rapire; **to — a kiss,** strappare un bacio; **to — from,** strappare da; **to — up,** agguantar su, afferrare; **to — a few moments' sleep,** carpire qualche minuto di sonno; **by snatches,** a salti, a sbalzi; **a — of song,** uno spunto di canzone, *m.*
sneak [sniːk], *v.i.* Strisciare; spiare, far la spia; rifischiare, dare informazioni di nascosto. ‖ *n.* Spia, *f.*; sornione, trappolone, *m.*; rifischione, *m.* **To — away,** svignarsela, andarsene di nascosto.
sneakers, *n.pl.* Scarpe di gomma, *f.pl.*
sneaking, *a.* Vile, abietto; servile, basso; meschino, celato, nascosto. **To have a — affection for,** avere del tenero per.
sneakingly, *adv.* Furtivamente, di nascosto, di soppiatto; vilmente.
sneer [sniəɹ], *n.* Ghigno, sogghigno, riso di scherno, *m.* ‖ *v.i.* Ghignare, sogghignare, sghignazzare. **To — at,** deridere, beffarsi di, sbeffare.
sneering, *a.* Beffardo, derisorio.
sneeringly, *adv.* Sogghignando.
sneeze [sniːz], *n.* Starnuto, sternuto, *m.* ‖ *v.i.* Starnutare, sternutire. **Not to be sneezed at,** non disprezzabile.
sniff [snif], *v.i.* Fiutare, annusare. ‖ *n.* Fiutata, *f.* **To — at,** fiutare; **to — up,** aspirare.
sniffy, *a.* (*colloq.*) Sdegnoso, superbietto; puzzolente.
snigger [ˈsnigəɹ], *v.i.* Ridacchiare, ridere sotto i baffi.
snip [snip], *v.t.* Tagliuzzare, tagliare con le forbici. ‖ *n.* Ritaglio, *m.*; brandello, pezzettino, *m.*; (*colloq.*) buon affare, *m.*
snipe (1) [snaip], *n.* (*Zool.*) Beccaccino, *m.*
snipe (2), *v.t.* Sparare da luogo sicuro, cecchinare.
sniper, *n.* (*Mil.*) Cecchino, tiratore isolato, *m.*
snippet [ˈsnipit], *n.* Pezzettino, *m.*
snivel [ˈsnivəl], *v.i.* Moccicare; piagnucolare, frignare.
sniveller, *n.* Moccicone, moccioso, *m.*; piagnucolone, *m.*
snivelling, *a.* Moccicoso, piagnucoloso. ‖ *n.* Piagnucolio, *m.*
snob [snɔb], *n.* Millantatore, snob, parassita, *m.*; ciabattino, *m.*
snobbish, *a.* Snobistico.
snobbishness, *n.* Snobismo, *m.*
snood [snud, snuːd], *n.* Benda, *f.*; rete per i capelli, *m.*
snooze [snuːz], *n.* Pisolino, *m.*, dormitina, *f.* ‖ *v.i.* Dormicchiare, sonnecchiare. **To have a —,** fare una dormitina.
snore [snɔːɹ], *v.i.* Russare. ‖ *n.* Il russare, *m.*
snorer, *n.* Russatore, *m.*, russatrice, *f.*
snoring, *n.* Russio, *m.*
snort [snɔːɹt], *v.i.* Sbuffare, soffiare. ‖ *n.* Sbuffo, *m.*, sbuffata, *f.*
snorting, *n.* Sbuffamento, *m.* ‖ *a.* Sbuffante.
snout [snaut], *n.* Muso, ceffo, *m.*; (*of pig*) grugno, *m.*; (*of boar*) grifo, *m.*; (*of bellows*) cannello, *m.*
snow [snou], *n.* Neve, *f.* ‖ *v.i.* Nevicare, far la neve; *v.t.* nevicare, spargere. **A fall of —,** una nevicata, *f.*; **snowed up,** bloccato dalla neve; **— -blindness,** cecità da neve, ambliopia, *f.*; **— -bound,** bloccato dalla neve; **— -capped,** coronato di neve, nevoso; **— -line,** limite delle nevi perpetue, *m.*; **— -shoes,** racchette per la neve, *f.pl.*; **— -plough,** spazzaneve, spartineve, *m.*; **— -white,** bianco come la neve, niveo.
snowball, *n.* Palla di neve, *f.* ‖ *v.t.* Lanciare palle di neve. **— -tree,** viburno, *m.*
snowboots, *n.pl.* Scarpe da neve, *f.pl.*
snowdrift, *n.* Ammasso di neve, banco di neve, *m.*
snowdrop, *n.* (*Bot.*) Bucaneve, *m.*

snowfall, *n.* Nevosità, nevicata, *f.*
snowflake, *n.* Fiocco di neve, *m.*, falda di neve, *f.*
snowstorm, *n.* Tempesta di neve, tormenta, *f.*
snowy, *a.* Nevoso, di neve, niveo; bianco come la neve; (*fig.*) puro, immacolato. **— weather,** tempo nevoso, *m.*
snub (1) [snʌb], *n.* Affronto, rabbuffo, rimprovero, *m.* || *v.t.* Offendere, fare un affronto, umiliare, respingere sgarbatamente.
snub (2), *a.* Camuso, rincagnato. **— -nosed,** dal naso camuso.
snuff [snʌf], *n.* Tabacco da naso. tabacco da fiuto, *m.*; (*of candle*) moccolo, *m.*, moccolatura, *f.* || *v.t.* (*a candle*) Smoccolare; (*to smell at*) annusare, fiutare; aspirare, respirare. **A pinch of —,** una presa di tabacco, *f.*; (*colloq.*) **to be up to —,** avere buon fiuto; **to take —,** prender tabacco; **to — out,** spegnere, estinguere, (*fig.*) morire; **— -box,** tabacchiera, *f.*; **— -coloured,** color tabacco.
snuffers, *n.pl.* Smoccolatoio, *m.*
snuffle [snʌfl], *v.i.* Parlare nel naso.
snuffler, *n.* Biascicone, *m.*; bacchettone, baciapile, *m.*
snuffling, *n.* Nasalità, *f.*
snuffy, *a.* Tabaccoso.
snug [snʌg], *a.* Comodo, ben fatto, agevole; raccolto, intimo; compatto, bene assestato; nascosto, ritirato. **A — little house** una bella casetta, *f.*; **a — little income,** una comodissima rendita, *f.*; **to lie — in bed,** star ben accucciato in letto.
snuggle [snʌgl], *v.i.* Accostarsi, stringersi, rannicchiarsi.
snugly, *adv.* Comodamente, adagio, a bell'agio.
snugness, *n.* Comodità, *f.*
so [sou], *adv.* Così, in questo modo; tanto, talmente. || *conj.* Purchè, a condizione che. **And so on,** e così via; **Be it so!** Così sia! **How so?** Ma come? **so to speak,** per dir così; **I am afraid so,** temo di sì; **I do not say so,** non dico ciò; **if so,** se è così; **I think so,** lo credo, credo di sì; **I am so pleased to see you,** mi fa tanto piacere vederla; **Mr So-and-So,** il Signor tal dei tali; **so do I,** anch'io; **so far,** finora; **so far so good,** finora tutto va bene; **in so far as,** per quanto; **so it is,** così è, tant'è; **so long as,** finchè; **so much the better,** tanto meglio; **so many men so many minds,** tante teste tanti pareri; **so many, so much,** tanto; **so saying,** a tali parole; **so then,** così, dunque; **You don't say so!** Proprio così? Davvero! **Why so?** E perchè? **I am so glad,** sono tanto lieto; **I told you so,** l'avevo detto io; **it is better so,** è meglio così! **Quite so! Just so!** È proprio così! **give me a dozen or so,** datemi circa una dozzina; **so that,** di maniera che, cosicchè; **so-called,** cosiddetto; **so-so,** passabile, mediocre, così così, passabilmente.
soak [souk], *v.t.* Bagnare, inzuppare, immollare; *v.i.* bagnarsi, inzupparsi, imbeversi; (*colloq.*) bere come una spugna. || *n.* Bagno, *m.*, bagnata, inzuppata, *f.*; (*colloq.*) ubbriacone, *m.* **I am soaked to the skin,** sono tutto bagnato; **to — up,** assorbire, imbeversi di; **to — through,** penetrare, infiltrare, inzuppare; **to — into,** penetrare in.
soaker, *n.* Pioggia dirotta, *f.*, acquazzone, rovescio di pioggia, *m.*; ubbriacone, sbevazzatore, *m.*
soaking, *a.* Dirotto, scrosciante. || *n.* Bagno, *m.*
soap [soup], *n.* Sapone, *m.* || *v.t.* Insaponare. **Mottled —,** sapone marezzato, *m.*; **scented —,** sapone profumato, *m.*; **shaving- —,** sapone per la barba, *m.*; **soft —,** sapone tenero, *m.*, (*fig.*) adulazione, *f.*; **washing- —,** sapone pel bucato, *m.*; **a cake of —,** un pezzo di sapone, *m.*, una saponetta, *f.*; **— -box,** saponiera, *f.*; **— -bubble,** bolla di sapone, *f.*; **— -dish,** portasapone, *m.*; **— -stone,** steatite, *f.*; **— -suds,** saponata, *f.*; **— -works,** saponeria, *f.*
soapy, *a.* Insaponato; saponoso, saponaceo; (*fig.*) lusinghiero.
soar [sɔːɹ], *v.i.* Ascendere, montare, innalzarsi a volo, levarsi in alto, spiccare il volo, spaziare, prender l'aria.
soaring, *a.* Ascendente, sorgente; sublime, eccelso.
soaringly, *adv.* A volo.
sob [sɔb], *v.i.* Singhiozzare. || *n.* Singhiozzo, singulto, *m.* **— -stuff,** racconto piagnucoloso, *m.*
sobbing, *n.* Singhiozzio, *m.*
sober ['soubəɹ], *a.* Sobrio, temperante, moderato; composto, contegnoso; calmo, tranquillo, quieto; savio, assennato, serio; oscuro. || *v.t.i.* Moderare, calmare, rendere sobrio. **He is not —,** è ubbriaco; **to — down,** smaltire la sbornia, calmarsi, metter la testa a segno; **— -minded,** sobrio, assennato, serio; **— -sides,** musoduro, *m.*
soberly, *adv.* Moderatamente, seriamente, con calma.
soberness, sobriety ['soubəɹnis, sou'braiiti], *n.* Sobrietà, moderazione, assennatezza, serietà, *f.*
sobriquet ['sobrikei], *n.* Soprannome, nomignolo, *m.*
sociability, sociableness [souʃə'biliti, 'souʃəblnes], *n.* Sociabilità, socievolezza, *f.*
sociable ['souʃəbl], *a.* Sociabile, socievole, affabile. || *n.* (*carriage*) Giardiniera, *f.*; (*settee*) divano a forma di esse, *m.*
sociably, *adv.* Socievolmente.
social ['souʃəl], *a.* Sociale. || *n.* Trattenimento, *m.*, veglia, serata, *f.* **— happenings,** mondanità, *f.*
socialism ['souʃəlizm], *n.* Socialismo, *m.*
socialist, *n.* Socialista, *m.f.*
socialistic, *a.* Socialistico.
socialize, *v.t.* Socializzare.
socially, *adv.* Socialmente.
society [so'saieti], *n.* Società, *f.*; ordine sociale, *m.*; compagnia, lega, *f.*; (*fashionable world*) bel mondo, *m.* || *a.* Di società, di mondo. **High —,** l'alta società, *f.*, il bel mondo, *m.*; **a learned —,** un'accademia; **to go into —,** andare in società; **a charitable —,** una società di beneficenza, *f.*; **a secret —,** una setta, una società segreta, *f.*; **a — lady,** una donna di mondo, *f.*; **— gossip,** ciarle del bel mondo.
sociological [souʃə'lɔdʒikəl], *a.* Sociologico.
sociologist, *n.* Sociologo, *m.*
sociology, *n.* Sociologia, *f.*
sock [sɔk], *n.* Calzetta, calza, *f.*; calzino, *m.*; **— -suspenders,** giarrettiere, *f.pl.*; **shoe- —, boot- —,** soletta, *f.*
socket ['sɔkit], *n.* Incavo, incastro, cannello, tubo, *m*; manico, *m.*; (*of candlestick*)

bocciolo, *m.*; (*of eye*) orbita, occhiaia, *f.*; (*of tooth*) alveolo, *m.* **— -joint**, collegamento ad incastro, manicotto, *m.*
socketed, *a.* Incastrato.
socle [sɔkl], *n.* (*Arch.*) Zoccolo, *m.*
Socrates [ˈsɔkrəti:z], *n.* Socrate, *m.*
socratic [soˈkrætik], *a.* Socratico.
sod [sɔd], *n.* Piota, zolla erbosa, *f.* || *v.t.* Coprire di zolle.
soda [ˈsoudə], *n.* (*Chem.*) Soda, *f.*; (*colloq.*) acqua di seltz, *f.* **Soda-water**, acqua di seltz, acqua gassosa, *f.*
sodden [ˈsɔdən], *a.* Bagnato, inzuppato; non soffice, molle; pesante; (*fig.*) brillo.
soddenness, *n.* Umidore, *m.*
sodium [ˈsoudiəm], *n.* Sodio, *m.*
sodomite [ˈsɔdəmait], *n.* Sodomita, *m.*
sodomy, *n.* Sodomia, *f.*
soever [soˈevəɹ], *adv.* Che sia, qualunque. **Whatsoever**, checchessia, qualunque sia.
sofa [ˈsoufə], *n.* Sofà, canapè, divano, *m.* **— -bed**, sofà a letto, *m.*
soft [sɔft, sɔ:ft], *a.* Molle; soffice, morbido; tenero, dolce, soave, mite; debole, effeminato; (*fig.*) scemo, sciocco, stupido. || *adv.* Piano, sommessamente, adagio. **A — colour**, un colore pastoso, *m.*; **— goods**, tessuti, *m.pl.*; **the — palate**, il palato molle, *m.*; **— air**, aria dolce, *f.*; **a — voice**, una voce sommessa, *f.*; **to get —**, rammollirsi, (*fig.*) rimbecillire, divenire fiacco; **— -boiled** (*of eggs*), al latte, bazzotte; **a — collar**, un colletto morbido, *m.*; **a — hat**, un feltro floscio, *m.*; **— -headed**, imbecille, sciocco; **— -hearted**, dal cuoro tenero; **a — job**, un impiego facile; **— nothings**, paroline, *f.pl.*; **— -pedal**, sordina, *f.*; **— roe**, latte di pesce, *m.*; **— -sawder**, piaggeria, *f.*; **— -spoken**, mite, affabile, dalla voce soave.
soften, *v.t.* Ammollire, mollificare, ammorbidire; addolcire, intenerire, lenire, placare, mitigare, moderare; attenuare; *v.i.* ammollirsi, addolcirsi; placarsi; attenuarsi.
softening, *n.* Addolcimento, *m.*; rammollimento, *m.* **— of the brain**, rammollimento cerebrale, *m.*
softish, *a.* Molliccio; teneruccio; piuttosto sciocco.
softly, *adv.* Pian piano, adagio; teneramente, soavemente, dolcemente.
softness, *n.* Mollezza, dolcezza, morbidezza, *f.*; debolezza, *f.*; effeminatezza, *f.*; sciocchezza, stupidaggine, *f.*
soggy [ˈsɔgi], *a.* Bagnato, inzuppato.
soho! [souˈhou], *inter.* (*obs.*) Olà! Ohì la!
soil [sɔil], *n.* Suolo, terreno, *m.*, terra, *f.*; (*stain*) macchia, *f.*, sudiciume, *m.* || *v.t.* Sporcare, insudiciare, imbrattare, lordare. **Rich —**, suolo fertile, *m.*; **one's native —**, il suolo natio, *m.*
soiled, *a.* (*linen*) Sudicio; (*goods*) appassito, sbiadito.
soirée [ˈswɑ:rei], *n.* Serata, veglia, *f.*, trattenimento, *m.*
sojourn [ˈsʌdʒəɹn], *n.* Soggiorno, *m.*, dimora, *f.* || *v.i.* Soggiornare, dimorare.
sojourner, *n.* Residente, *m.*
solace [ˈsɔleis], *n.* Conforto, sollievo, *m.*, consolazione, *f.* || *v.t.* Confortare, consolare, sollevare.
solan, solan goose [ˈsoulən, ˈsoulən gu:s], *n.* (*Zool.*) Sula, *f.*
solanum [soˈleinəm], *n.* (*Bot.*) Solano, *m.*
solar [ˈsouləɹ], *a.* Solare. **— plexus**, plesso solare, *m.*
solatium [soˈleiʃiəm], *n.* Compenso, *m.*
sold [sould], *p.* and *p.p.* of **sell**.
solder [ˈsɔldəɹ, ˈsɔ:dəɹ], *n.* Saldatura, *f.* || *v.t.* Saldare.
soldering, *n.* Saldatura, *f.* **— -iron**, saldatoio, *m.*
soldier [ˈsouldjəɹ], *n.* Soldato, milite, militare, *m.* **A private —**, un soldato semplice, *m.*; **to go for a —**, fare il soldato, andar soldato; **to play at soldiers**, giuocare ai soldati; **the Unknown Soldier**, il milite ignoto, *m.*
soldier-like, soldierly, *a.* Soldatesco, militare, marziale.
soldiery, *n.* Truppa, *f.*; soldatesca, *f.*, militari, *m.pl.*
sole (1) [soul], *a.* Solo, unico; esclusivo; tutto. **— agent**, agente esclusivo, *m.*
sole (2), *n.* (*of foot*) Pianta, *f.*; (*of shoe*) suola, *f.*; fondo, *m.*, base, *f.* || *v.t.* Solare, risolare.
sole (3), *n.* (*Zool.*) Sogliola, *f.*
solecism [ˈsɔlesizm], *n.* Solecismo, *m.*
solemn [ˈsɔləm], *a.* Solenne; grave, serio. **A — oath**, un giuramento solenne, *m.*; **to put on a — face**, darsi un'aria solenne, mettersi in sussiego.
solemnity [sɔˈlemniti], *n.* Solennità, *f.*; pompa, *f.*; serietà, gravità, *f.*
solemnization [sɔlemnaiˈzeiʃən], *n.* Solennità, celebrazione, *f.*
solemnize, *v.t.* Solennizzare, celebrare.
solemnly [ˈsɔləmli], *adv.* Solennemente, seriamente.
sol-fa [sɔlˈfɑ:], *n.* (*Mus.*) Solfeggio, *m.*, solfa, *f.* || *v.t.i.* Solfeggiare.
solicit [sɔˈlisit], *v.t.* Sollecitare, invitare; attirare; (*of prostitutes*) importunare.
solicitation, *n.* Sollecitazione, *f.*, invito, *m.*; importunità, *f.*
solicitor, *n.* Avvocato, legale, notaio, *m.* **Solicitor General**, Procuratore Generale, *m.*
solicitous, *a.* Sollecito; desideroso, premuroso, ansioso. **He is very — for her comfort**, ha gran cura del di lei benessere; **he is — of quiet**, è desideroso di quiete.
solicitously, *adv.* Sollecitamente, con cura.
solicitude [sɔˈlisitju:d], *n.* Sollecitudine, premura, *f.*
solid [ˈsɔlid], *a.* Solido, sodo, massiccio; saldo, compatto; (*fig.*) serio, posato, grave. || *n.* Solido, *m.* **A man of — build**, un uomo massiccio, *m.*; **of — silver**, d'argento massiccio; **a — vote**, un voto unanime, *m.*; **to go — for**, votare unanimamente; **— sense**, buon senso, *m.*; **to become —**, solidificarsi; **the — rock**, la roccia viva, *f.*
solidarity [sɔlidˈæriti], *n.* Solidarietà, *f.*
solidification [sɔlidifiˈkeiʃən], *n.* Solidificazione, *f.*
solidify [sɔˈlidifai], *v.t.* Solidificare; indurire; *v.i.* solidificarsi.
solidity, solidness, *n.* Solidità, saldezza, *f.*
soliloquize [sɔˈlilokwaiz], *v.i.* Fare un soliloquio, *m.*
soliloquy [sɔˈlilokwi], *n.* Soliloquio, monologo, *m.*
soling [ˈsouliŋ], *n.* (*of shoes*) Solatura, *f.*

soliped ['sɔliped], *n.* (*Zool.*) Solipedo, solidungolo, *m.*
solitaire ['sɔlitɛəɹ], *n.* Solitario, *m.*
solitariness ['sɔlitərines], *n.* Solitudine, *f.*
solitary ['sɔlitəri], *a.* Solitario, solo, solingo; unico. — **confinement,** segregazione cellulare, *f.*
solitude ['sɔlitju:d], *n.* Solitudine, *f.*
solo ['soulou], *n.* (*Mus.*) Solo, *m.*; (*Cards*) specie di whist.
soloist ['soulouist], *n.* Solista, *m.f.*
Solomon ['sɔləmən], *n.* Salomone, *m.* (*Bot.*) **Solomon's Seal,** sigillo di Salomone, *m.*
solstice ['sɔlstis], *n.* (*Astron.*) Solstizio, *m.*
solubility [sɔlju:'biliti], *n.* Solubilità, *f.*
soluble ['sɔlju:bl], *a.* Solubile.
solution, *n.* Soluzione, *f.*, scioglimento, *m.*; risoluzione, *f.*
solvable ['sɔlvəbl], *a.* Solubile.
solve, *v.t.* Risolvere, sciogliere, spiegare. **To — a problem,** sciogliere un problema.
solvency ['sɔlvənsi], *n.* Solvibilità, *f.*
solvent, *a.* (*Chem.*) Solvente; (*Comm.*) solvente, solvibile. || *n.* (*Chem.*) Solvente, dissolvente, *m.*
somatology [soumə'tɔlədʒi], *n.* Somatologia, *f.*
sombre ['sɔmbəɹ], *a.* Oscuro, fosco, tetro, tenebroso; triste.
sombrely, *adv.* Oscuramente; tristemente.
sombreness, *n.* Tetraggine, cupezza, *f.*
some [sʌm], *a.* Qualche, alcuno, poco; del, dello, *m.*, della, *f.*, dei, degli, *m.pl.*, delle, *f.pl.*; certi, parecchi. || *pron.* Alcuni, certuni, *m.pl.*, alcune, certune, *f.pl.* || *adv.* Quasi, circa; un poco. — **books,** dei libri, *m.pl.*; **I saw it in — book or other,** l'ho letto in qualche libro; — **people say,** alcuni dicono; **we waited — hours,** aspettammo qualche ora; — **ten years ago,** circa dieci anni fa; — **few,** alcuni, alcuni pochi; **give me —,** datemene; **here are — of your books,** ecco alcuni dei vostri libri; **I have —,** ne ho un po', ne ho alcuni; — **of us,** alcuni di noi; **there are — who say,** ci sono alcuni che dicono.
somebody ['sʌmbɔdi], *n.* Qualcuno, qualcheduno, uno, *m.* — **else,** qualcun'altro; **to be a —,** essere qualcuno; **to think oneself —,** credere d'essere qualcheduno.
somehow, *adv.* In un modo o nell'altro, in qualche modo, tanto bene che male.
someone, *n.* Qualcuno, qualcheduno, uno, *m.*
somersault ['sʌməɹsɔlt], *n.* Capitombolo, *m.*, ruzzolone, *f.*; salto mortale, *m.*; capriola, *f.* **To turn a —,** capitombolare, fare un salto mortale.
something ['sʌmθiŋ], *n.* Qualchecosa, qualcosa, *f.* || *adv.* Alquanto, un poco. **There is — nice about him,** c'è qualcosa di molto simpatico in lui; — **else,** qualcos'altro; — **good,** qualcosa di buono; **there's — in that,** c'è qualcosa in questo; **it looked — like a book,** sembrava un libro; (*colloq.*) **That's — like!** Questo va un po' meglio!
sometime ['sʌmtaim], *adv.* Già, altra volta. **My — friend,** il mio amico d'altri tempi, *m.*; — **or other,** una volta o l'altra, uno di questi giorni.
sometimes, *adv.* Qualche volta, talvolta, talora, di quando in quando.
somewhat ['sʌmwɔt], *adv.* Un poco, alquanto, qualche poco.
somewhere ['sʌmwɛəɹ], *adv.* In qualche luogo, in qualche parte. — **else,** altrove.
somnambulism [sɔm'næmbju:lizm], *n.* Sonnambulismo, *m.*
somnambulist, *n.* Sonnambulo, *m.*, sonnambula, *f.*
somniferous [sɔm'nifərəs], *a.* Sonnifero.
somnolence ['sɔmnoləns], *n.* Sonnolenza, *f.*
somnolent, *a.* Sonnolente.
son [sʌn], *n.* Figlio, figliuolo, *m.*; discendente, *m.* — **-in-law,** genero, *m.*
sonata [sɔn'ɑ:tə], *n.* (*Mus.*) Sonata, *f.*
song [sɔŋ], *n.* Canto, *m.*, canzone, *f.*; cantico, inno, *m.*; romanza, aria, *f.* **Renowned in —,** cantato in poesia; **I bought it for an old —,** lo comprai per una bagatella; **a — without words,** una romanza senza parole, *f.*; (*fig.*) **to make a — about it,** farne una questione; — **-book,** libro di canti, canzoniere, *m.*; (*Zool.*) — **-thrush,** tordo, *m.*
songster, songstress, *n.* Cantante, *m.f.*, cantatore, *m.*, cantatrice, *f.*
sonnet ['sɔnet], *n.* Sonetto, *m.*
sonneteer [sɔne'tiəɹ], *n.* Sonettista, *m.f.*
sonorous [so'nɔ:rəs], *a.* Sonoro.
sonorousness, sonority, *n.* Sonorità, *f.*
sonship ['sʌnʃip], *n.* Qualità di figlio, *f.*
soon [su:n], *adv.* Presto, subito; di buon'ora; tosto; prossimamente. **As — as,** appena che, subito che; **as — as possible,** appena possibile, al più presto possibile; **How —?** Quando? **he would as — stay in as go out,** vorrebbe tanto stare in casa che uscire; — **after,** poco dopo, subito dopo; **too —,** troppo presto; **very —,** molto presto, fra poco.
sooner, *adv.* Piuttosto, più; più presto, prima. — **or later,** o presto o tardi; **no — said than done,** detto fatto; — **than do that I would . . .** piuttosto che fare ciò vorrei . . .; **the — the better,** più presto è meglio è.
soonest, *adv.* Il più presto. **At the —,** al più presto; **Which would you — do?** Che cosa preferireste fare? **least said — mended,** meno si parla meglio è.
soot [sut], *n.* Fuliggine, *f.*
sooth [su:θ], *n.* (*obs.*) Verità, *f.* **In —,** veramente.
soothe [su:ð], *v.t.* Blandire, calmare; mitigare, attenuare, lenire; placare, lusingare; soddisfare.
soothing, *a.* Calmante, lenitivo; consolante; lusinghiero.
soothingly, *adv.* Con blandizie, dolcemente.
soothsay ['su:θsei], *v.i.* Predire, profetare, profetizzare.
soothsayer, *n.* Indovino, *m.*
soothsaying, *n.* Divinazione, *f.*
sootiness ['sutines], *n.* Nerezza, *f.*
sooty ['suti], *a.* Fuligginoso; (*fig.*) nero, oscuro.
sop [sɔp], *n.* Panata, pappa, pane inzuppato, *m.*; (*fig.*) offa, *f.* || *v.t.* Inzuppare, bagnare. **To throw a — to,** gettare l'offa a.
sophism ['sɔfizm], *n.* Sofisma, sofismo, *m.*
sophist, *n.* Sofista, *m.f.*
sophisticate [sɔ'fistikeit], *v.i.* Sofisticare, cavillare, sottilizzare; *v.t.* snaturare, adulterare.
sophistication, *n.* Sofisticheria, sofisticazione, *f.*

sophisticated, *a.* Affettato, adulterato.
sophistry, *n.* Sofisticheria, *f.*
sophomore ['sɔfəmɔːɹ], *n.* Studente del second'anno in una università americana.
soporific [sɔpə'rifik], *n.a.* Soporifico, *m.*
sopping, *a.* Bagnato.
soppy, *a.* Bagnato; (*fig.*) effeminato, sentimentale.
soprano [so'prɑːnou], *n.* (*Mus.*) Soprano, *m.*
sorb [sɔːɹb], *n.* (*Bot.*) Sorbo, *m.*, sorba, *f.* **—-apple,** sorbo, *m.*
sorcerer ['sɔːɹsərəɹ], *n.* Stregone, mago, maliardo, negromante, *m.*
sorceress, *n.* Strega, maliarda, fattucchiera, *f.*
sorcery, *n.* Stregoneria, malia, fattucchieria, *f.*
sordid ['sɔːɹdid], *a.* Sordido, meschino, gretto; basso, vile.
sordidly, *adv.* Sordidamente.
sordidness, *n.* Sordidezza, meschinità, grettezza, bassezza, viltà, *f.*
sore [sɔːɹ], *a.* Doloroso, dolente; infiammato; severo, grave, crudele; sensitivo, permaloso; irritato; addolorato. ‖ *n.* Piaga, *f.*, male, *m.* **He has a — finger,** ha male al dito; **he is very — about his failure,** è molto addolorato del suo insuccesso; **a — subject,** un argomento delicato, *m.*; **in — distress,** addoloratissimo, in gran pena; **to make —,** irritare, far male a.
sorely, sore, *adv.* Molto, gravemente, severamente.
soreness, *n.* Dolore, male, *m.*; (*fig.*) irritazione, *f.*
sorghum ['sɔːɹgəm], *n.* (*Bot.*) Sorgo, *m.*
sorority [sɔ'rɔriti], *n.* Comunità di donne, *f.*; società accademica delle studenti nelle università americane.
sorrel (1) ['sɔrəl], *n.* (*Bot.*) Acetosa, *f.*
sorrel (2), *a.* Sauro. ‖ *n.* Sauro, cavallo sauro, *m.*
sorrily ['sɔrili], *adv.* Poveramente, meschinamente, miseramente.
sorrow ['sɔrou], *n.* Dolore, *m.*, pena, afflizione, *f.*; affanno, cordoglio, *m.*; travaglio, *m.* ‖ *v.i.* Affliggersi, addolorarsi, piangere, crucciarsi. **She is in great —,** è molto addolorata; **to my —,** con mio dolore; **to — for someone,** piangere per qualcuno.
sorrowful, *a.* Afflitto, triste, addolorato, abbattuto; doloroso, penoso, triste.
sorrowfully, *adv.* Dolorosamente, tristemente.
sorrowfulness, *n.* Tristezza, afflizione, *f.*, dolore, *m.*
sorrowing, *a.* Addolorato, afflitto.
sorry ['sɔri], *a.* Dolente, spiacente; meschino, povero, misero; pietoso. **I am — for you,** mi rincresce per voi; **you will be — for it some day,** un giorno ve ne pentirete; **I am — to hear it,** mi spiace udirlo, mi rincresce udirlo; **a — excuse,** una scusa meschina; **in a — plight,** conciato male, in mille guai; **Sorry!** Scusate! Scusa! Scusi!
sort [sɔːɹt], *n.* Sorta, specie, *f.*; genere, *m.*; maniera, *f.*; modo, *m.* ‖ *v.t.* Assegnare, distribuire, classificare, scegliere. **A good — of man,** un uomo di buona pasta, *m.*; **one of the right —,** un brav'uomo, *m.*; **in some —,** in qualche modo; **nothing of the —,** niente del genere; **out of sorts,** indisposto, depresso; **What — of book is this?** Che specie di libro è questo? **to — out,** scegliere, trascegliere; (*Print.*) **sorts,** assortimento, *m.*
sortable, *a.* Classificabile.
sorted, *a.* Assortito, scelto.
sorter, *n.* Distributore, *m.*; cernitore, *m.*; classificatore, *m.*
sortie ['sɔːɹti], *n.* Sortita, *f.*
sortilege ['sɔːɹtiledʒ], *n.* Sortilegio, *m.*
sorting, *n.* Assortimento, *m.*
so-so [cp. **so**].
sot [sɔt], *n.* Ubbriacone, *m.*, ubbriacona, *f.*
sottish, *a.* Ubbriaco; inebetito, stupido.
sottishness, *n.* Ubbriacchezza, *f.*; stupidaggine, *f.*
sou [suː], *n.* Soldo, *m.*
sough [sʌf, sau], *v.i.* Mormorare, sussurrare. ‖ *n.* Mormorio, sussurrio, *m.*
sought, *a.* Cercato. **— after,** ricercato [cp. **seek**].
soul [soul], *n.* Anima, *f.*, spirito, *m.*; (*fig.*) persona, creatura, *f.*; essenza, *f.* **All Soul's Day,** il giorno dei morti, *m.*; **I have not seen a —,** non ho visto un'anima; **the life and — of the party,** l'anima della compagnia, *f.*; **a good —,** una buona creatura, *f.*; **the — of honour,** l'onore stesso, *m.*; **with all my —,** con tutta l'anima; **—-destroying,** che perde l'anima; **—-felt,** profondamente sentito; **—-stirring,** commovente, emozionante.
soulful, *a.* Appassionato, sentimentale.
soulfulness, *n.* Sentimentalità, *f.*
soulless, *a.* Senz'anima.
soullessness, *n.* Mancanza d'anima, *f.*
soulfully, *adv.* Sentimentalmente.
sound (1) [saund], *a.* Sano, valido, intero, perfetto; (*of sleep*) profondo; (*of argument*) sodo, solido, valido, forte, efficace; (*Comm.*) solvente, solvibile. **Safe and —,** sano e salvo; **— views,** idee sane, *f.pl.*; **a — sleeper,** uno che dorme sodo; **a — flogging,** un fracco di legnate, *m.*; **of — mind,** di mente sana; **a — argument,** un argomento solido, *m.*
sound (2), *v.t.* Suonare, far risuonare; proclamare, celebrare; sondare; ascoltare; *v.i.* suonare, risuonare, dar suono; sembrare, parere, apparire. ‖ *n.* Suono, *m.*, rumore, strepito, rimbombo, *m.*; tocco, rintocco, *m.* **That sounds like thunder,** sembra che tuoni; **that sounds well,** ciò suona bene, pare che vada bene; **his excuses — lame,** le sue scuse sembrano magre; **to — the alarm,** suonare a stormo; **to — the retreat,** battere la ritirata; (*fig.*) **to — someone,** sondare l'animo di qualcuno, tastare qualcuno; **not a — was heard,** non s'udiva il minimo rumore; (*Cinema.*) **—-film,** film sonoro, *m.*; (*Cinema.*) **—-track,** colonna sonora, *f.*; **—-hole** (*of violin*) esse, *m.*; **—-post,** (*of violin*) anima, *f.*; **—-proof,** impenetrabile al suono; **—-wave,** onda sonora, *f.*
sound (3), *v.t.* (*Med.*) Sondare; (*Naut.*) scandagliare; ascoltare. ‖ *n.* Sonda, *f.*
sound (4), *n.* (*Geog.*) Stretto, *m.*
sound (5), *n.* (*of fish*) Vescica natatoria, *f.*
sounder, *n.* Risuonatore, *m.*; mandra di maiali, *f.*
sounding (1), *n.* (*Med.*) Sondaggio, *m.*; (*Naut.*) scandaglio, *m.* **To take soundings,** far scandagli; **—-line,** scandaglio, *m.*, sonda, *f.*; **—-rod,** sonda di pompa, *f.*

sounding (2), *a.* Sonante, risonante, sonoro. ‖ *n.* Suono, *m.*, risonanza, sonorità, *f.*; (*Med.*) auscultazione, *f.* **— -board,** tavola armonica, *f.*; (*Eccles.*) tetto di pulpito, *m.*
soundless, *a.* Senza suono, muto.
soundlessly, *adv.* Silentemente.
soundly, *adv.* Bene; fortemente, severamente; giustamente, sanamente; profondamente.
soundness, *n.* Buono stato, *m.*; sanità, *f.*; validità, correttezza, *f.*; solvibilità, *f.*
soup [su:p], *n.* Minestra, zuppa, *f.*; brodo, *m.* **Thick —,** minestra spessa, *f.*; **clear —,** minestrina brodosa, *f.*; **vegetable —,** minestrone, *m.*; **— -kitchen,** cucina popolare, *f.*; **— -ladle,** cucchiaione, *m.*; mestolo, *m.*; **— -plate,** scodella, *f.*; **— -tureen,** zuppiera, *f.*
soupçon ['su:psɔŋ], *n.* Pizzico, tantino, *m.*
sour [sauɹ], *a.* Agro, acido, acre, aspro; aspro, bisbetico, acerbo, brusco. ‖ *v.t.* Inacidire; acidificare; inasprire, inacerbire. **To make —,** inacerbire, inasprire; **to turn —,** inacidire; **— milk,** latte acido; **to taste —,** saper di agro, saper d'acido.
source [sɔ:ɹs], *n.* Sorgente, fonte, *f.*; origine, *f.*
sourish ['sauriʃ], *a.* Acidulo, acidetto, aspretto.
sourly, *adv.* Acerbamente, aspramente.
sourness, *n.* Agrezza, acidità, *f.*; acredine, asprezza, *f.*; acerbità, *f.*
souse [saus], *v.t.* Tuffare, bagnare, sommergere; marinare, mettere in salamoia. ‖ *n.* Salamoia, *f.*
soutane [su:'tɑ:n], *n.* (*Eccles.*) Abito talare, *m.*
south [sauθ], *n.* Sud, meridione, mezzogiorno, mezzodì, *m.* ‖ *a.* Del sud, meridionale, del mezzogiorno. ‖ *adv.* Verso il sud, al sud. **South Pole,** Polo Sud, polo antartico, polo australe, *m.*; **South Africa,** l'Africa del Sud, *f.*; **South African,** sud-africano; **South America,** l'America del Sud, *f.*; **South American,** sud-americano; **— -east,** sud-est; **— west,** sud-ovest.
southerly ['sʌðəɹli], *a.* dal sud; meridionale. ‖*adv.* Verso il sud.
southern ['sʌðəɹn], *a.* Del sud, meridionale. (*Astron.*) **The Southern Cross,** la Croce del Sud, *f.*; **the — hemisphere,** l'emisfero australe, *m.*
southerner, *n.* Meridionale, *m.f.*
southernmost, *a.* Il più al sud.
southernwood, *n.* (*Bot.*) Abrotano, *m.*
southing ['sauθiŋ], *n.* (*Naut.*) Differenza di latitudine verso il sud.
southward ['sauθwəd], *adv.* Verso il sud, al sud.
souvenir ['su:vəniəɹ], *n.* Ricordo, *m.*
sou'wester [sau'westəɹ], *n.* Cappello a gronda, *m.*; vento di sud-ovest, libeccio, *m.*
sovereign ['sɔvrin], *a.* Sovrano, sommo. ‖ *n.* Sovrano, re, *m.*, sovrana, regina, *f.*; (*coin*) sterlina, *f.* **A — remedy,** un rimedio sovrano, *m.*
sovereignty ['sɔvrinti], *n.* Sovranità, *f.*
Soviet ['sɔviət], *n.* Soviet, *m.* ‖ *a.* Sovietico.
sow (1) [sau], *n.* Scrofa, troia, *f.* **— -thistle,** cicerbita, *f.*
sow (2) [sou], *v.t.* Seminare; disseminare, spargere, spandere; *v.i.* seminare, far la semina.
sower ['souəɹ], *n.* Seminatore, *m.*
sowing ['souiŋ], *n.* Seminatura, semina, sementa, *f.* **— -time,** seminagione, stagione della semina, *f.*; **— -machine,** seminatrice, *f.*
soya, soya bean ['sɔiə, 'sɔiəbi:n], *n.* Soia, *f.*
spa [spɑ:], *n.* Stazione termale, stazione balneare, *f.*; terme, *f.pl.*, bagni, *m.pl.*
space [speis], *n.* Spazio, *m.*, estensione, *f.*; intervallo, *m.*; vuoto, *m.*; (*Mus.*) spazio, *m.* ‖ *v.t.* Spaziare, diradare; (*Print.*) spaziare. (*Print.*) **— -line,** interlinea, *f.*; **to — out,** disporre ad intervalli; **— -ship,** apparecchio per navigare nello spazio.
spacing, *n.* Divisione, *f.*; (*Print.*) spaziatura, *f.*
spacious ['speiʃəs], *a.* Spazioso, ampio, vasto.
spaciousness, *n.* Spaziosità, ampiezza, *f.*
spade [speid], *n.* Vanga, *f.*; badile, *m.*; (*Cards*) picche, *f.* ‖ *v.t.* Vangare, badilare. **To call a — a —,** dire pane al pane; (*fig.*) **— -work,** opera preparatoria, *f.*
spadeful, *n.* Vangata, badilata, *f.*
spadille [spə'dil], *n.* (*Cards*) Asso di picche, *m.*
spadix ['speidiks], *n.* (*Bot.*) Spadice, *m.*
Spain [spein], *n.* (*Geog.*) Spagna, *f.*
spalpeen [spæl'pi:n], *n.* Furfante, birbante, *m.*
span [spæn], *n.* (*length of hand*) Spanna, *f.*, palmo, *m.*; (*extent*) portata, larghezza, ampiezza, *f.*; (*of bridge*) arco, *m.*; (*of oxen, etc.*) paio, *m.*; (*of time*) durata, *f.* ‖ *v.t.* Attraversare, stare attraverso a, stendersi attraverso; misurare a spanna; abbracciare. **A short — of life,** una vita breve, *f.*; **his life spans nearly a century,** la sua vita abbraccia quasi un secolo; (*Aviat.*) **wing —,** larghezza d'ala, apertura d'ali, *f.*
spandrel ['spændrəl], *n.* (*Arch.*) Timpano, *m.*
spangle [spæŋgl], *n.* Lustrino, *m.*, paglietta, *f.* ‖ *v.t.* Ornare di lustrini.
spangled, *a.* Ornato con lustrini, ornato di stelle, stellato.
Spaniard ['spænjəɹd], *n.* Spagnolo, *m.*, Spagnola, *f.*
spaniel ['spænjəl], *n.* Bracco spagnolo, *m.*
Spanish ['spæniʃ], *a.* Spagnolo, di Spagna. ‖ *n.* Spagnolo, *m.* **The — language,** la lingua spagnola, *f.*; **— wines,** vini di Spagna, *m.pl.*; **— -fly,** cantaride, *f.*; **— mahogany,** acagiù delle Antille, *m.*; **— onion,** cipolla dolce di Spagna, *f.*; **— grass,** sparto, *m.*
spank [spæŋk], *v.t.* Sculacciare; schiaffeggiare; *v.i.* (*of horse*) trottare serrato.
spanker, *n.* (*Naut.*) Randa, *f.*; (*colloq.*) cavallo veloce, *m.*
spanking, *a.* Forte, vigoroso; ottimo, bellissimo. **A — breeze,** un vento forte, *m.*; **to go at a — pace,** trottare serrato.
spanner, *n.* Chiave inglese, *f.*; chiave a viti, *f.* **Box- —,** chiave a dadi, *f.*
spar (1) [spɑ:ɹ], *n.* (*Naut.*) Albero, *m.*, stanga, *f.*; antenna, *f.*
spar (2), *n.* (*Min.*) Spato, *m.*
spar (3), *v.i.* Battersi, picchiarsi, fare a pugni, esercitarsi al pugilato; (*fig.*) disputare, litigare.
spare [spɛəɹ], *v.t.i.* Risparmiare; lesinare, economizzare; fare a meno di, far senza di; dare, accordare; aver riguardo a, salvare. ‖ *a.* Magro, parco, frugale; scarno, sparuto; affilato, smilzo; di riserva, di ricambio; libero, disponibile; d'avanzo. **To — no expense,** non badare a spese; **Can you — me a moment?** Potete accordarmi un momento? **I cannot — her just now,** al

momento non posso fare a meno di lei; — **me these excuses,** risparmiami queste scuse; — **my blushes,** non fatemi arrossire; **she never spares his feelings,** essa non ha riguardo dei suoi sentimenti; **I cannot — the time,** non posso trovare il tempo; **he never spares himself,** non si risparmia mai; **I will — you the trouble,** vi risparmierò il disturbo; **I have enough and to —,** ne ho da vendere, ne ho più che abbastanza; **we have no time to —,** non abbiamo tempo da perdere; **a man of — build,** un uomo smilzo, *m.*; — **cash,** denaro disponibile, *m.*; **a — bed,** un letto in più; **a — room,** una camera in più, una camera degli ospiti, *f.*; — **parts,** pezzi di ricambio, *m.pl.*; **a — pair of shoes,** scarpe di ricambio, *f.pl.*; — **moments,** ritagli di tempo, *m.pl.*; (*Motor.*) — **wheel,** ruota di ricambio, *f.*

spare-rib [spɛərib], *n.* Costoletta di maiale, *f.*

spareness, *n.* Scarnezza, sparutezza, magrezza, *f.*

sparing, *a.* Economo, parsimonioso, frugale, sobrio, parco. — **of speech,** sobrio nel parlare, parco di parole.

sparingly, *adv.* Frugalmente, parcamente, di rado.

spark [spɑːɹk], *n.* Scintilla, favilla, *f.*; (*fig.*) damerino, bellimbusto. ‖ *v.i.* Scintillare, sprizzare scintille. (*Motor.*) **Sparking-plug,** candela d'accensione, *f.*

sparkish, *a.* Elegante, galante.

sparkle [spɑːɹkl], *n.* Lustro, splendore, scintillio, sfavillo, *m.* ‖ *v.i.* Scintillare, sfavillare; (*of wine*) spumare.

sparkling, *a.* Scintillante, sfavillante, raggiante, splendente; spumante.

sparklingly, *adv.* Sfavillantemente.

sparring [ˈspɑːriŋ], *n.* (*Sport*) Allenamento di pugilatori, *m.*; (*fig.*) disputa, contesa, *f.*

sparrow [ˈspærou], *n.* (*Zool.*) Passero, *m.* **Young —,** passerotto, *m.*; **— -hawk,** sparviere, *m.*

sparse [spɑːɹs], *a.* Scarso, rado. — **hair,** capelli radi, *m.pl.*

sparsely, *adv.* Scarsamente.

sparseness, *n.* Scarsezza, scarsità, radezza, *f.*

Spartan [ˈspɑːɹtən], *n.a.* Spartano, *m.*

spasm [spæzm], *n.* Spasimo, *m.*

spasmodic [spæzˈmɔdik], *a.* Spasmodico, spasimoso; intermittente.

spasmodically, *adv.* Spasmodicamente.

spat (1) [spæt], *n.* Uosa, ghetta, ghetta di città, *f.*

spat (2), *p.* and *p.p.* of **spit.**

spatchcock [cp. **spitchcock**].

spate [speit], *n.* Piena, *f.* **A river in —** un fiume in piena, *m.*

spathe [speiθ], *n.* (*Bot.*) Spata, *f.*

spathic [ˈspæθik], *a.* Spatico, *f.*

spatter [ˈspætəɹ], *v.t.* Spruzzare spargere; inzaccherare.

spatula [ˈspætjuːlə] *n.* (*Med.*) Spatola, spatula, *f.*

spavin [ˈspævin], *n.* Spavenio, *m.*

spavined, *a.* Affetto da spavenio.

spawn [spɔːn], *n.* (*of fish*) Uova, *f.pl.*; (*of mushroom*) bianco, *m.*; (*fig.*) razza, prole, progenie, *f.* ‖ *v.t.i.* Deporre le uova; generare, far nascere; nascere. **Spawning-time,** fregola, *f.*, tempo della fregola, *m.*

speak [spiːk], *v.i.t.* Parlare, dire; discorrere, favellare, trattare; pronunciare, esprimere. **To — about,** parlare di; **that speaks for itself,** si raccomanda da sè; **so to —,** per così dire; **it speaks well for his honesty,** fa onore alla sua onestà; **to — highly of,** parlar bene di; **to — out,** parlare chiaro; **to — up,** parlare forte; **to — Italian,** parlare italiano; **to — up for,** parlare a favore di; **to — with,** parlare con, (*a ship*) parlamentare; **strictly speaking,** per esser precisi; **to — like a book,** parlare come un libro stampato; **her look spoke volumes,** il suo sguardo era molto eloquente; **to — to** (*in support*), portar testimonianza a, testimoniare di; **nothing to — of,** niente d'importante; **I have heard — of it,** ne ho sentito parlare; **English spoken,** si parla inglese; **to my shame be it spoken,** sia detto a mio disdoro; **to — one's mind,** dire il fatto suo, parlare fuori dai denti; **to — the truth,** dire la verità; — **-easy,** bettola illegale, *f.*

speaker, *n.* Parlatore, oratore, *m.*; (*in dialogue*) interlocutore, *m.*; (*in Parliament*) presidente, *m.* **The last —,** il preopinante, *m.*; (*Radio*) **loud- —,** altoparlante, *m.*

speaking, *n.* Il parlare, *m.*, parola, *f.*; parlata, parlatura, *f.*; discorso, *m.* ‖ *a.* Parlante. — **of,** a proposito di; **they are not on — terms,** non sono in buoni rapporti; **a — likeness,** un ritratto parlante, *m.*; — **trumpet,** portavoce, *m.*; **— -tube,** tubo acustico, *m.*; (*Telephone*) **John Smith —,** parla John Smith.

spear [spiəɹ], *n.* Lancia, *f.*; asta, *f.*; (*for fish*) fiocina, *f.*; (*for hunting*) spiedo, *m.* ‖ *v.t.* Trafiggere; ferire con una lancia, uccidere con una lancia; **— -head,** punta di lancia, *f.*; (*Bot.*) **— -grass,** gramigna, *f.*

spearmint, *n.* (*Bot.*) Menta verde, *f.*

spec [spek], *n.* (*colloq.*) Speculazione, *f.*

special [ˈspeʃəl], *a.* Speciale, particolare; espresso; straordinario. **What is your — work?** Che genere di lavoro fate? — **instructions,** istruzioni particolari, *f.pl.*; **I have taken — trouble,** ho avuto cura speciale; — **train,** treno speciale, *m.*; — **constable,** agente volontario, *m.*; — **edition,** supplemento, *m.*, edizione speciale, *f.*; **nothing —,** nulla di particolare; — **correspondent,** inviato speciale, *m.*

specialist, *n.* Specialista, *m.f.*

speciality [speʃiˈæliti], *n.* Specialità, *f.*, prodotto speciale, *m.*

specialization, *n.* Specializzazione, *f.*

specialize [ˈspeʃəlaiz], *v.t.* Specializzare; *v.i.* specializzarsi.

specially, *adv.* Specialmente, in ispecie.

specie [ˈspiːʃiː], *n.* Numerario, *m.*, denaro contante, *m.*, moneta metallica, *f.*

species, *n.* Specie, *f.*; genere, sorte, qualità, classe, *f.*

specific [speˈsifik], *n.a.* Specifico, *m.* — **gravity,** peso specifico, *m.*

specification [spesifiˈkeiʃən], *n.* Specificazione, *f.*; descrizione, *f.*; specifica, *f.*

specify [ˈspesifai], *v.t.* Specificare, indicare, fissare, particolareggiare. **He specified four o'clock,** fissò le quattro.

specimen [ˈspesimən], *n.* Esemplare, campione, modello, saggio, *m.*; (*Print.*) — **page,** foglio di prova, *m.*

specious ['spi:ʃəs], *a.* Specioso, di apparenza, plausibile.
speciousness, *n.* Speciosità, *f.*
speck [spek], *n.* Chiazza, macchietta, *f.*; punto, *m.*; particella, *f.*
speckle, *v.t.* Chiazzare, macchiettare.
speckled, *a.* Chiazzato, macchiettato, variegato; picchiettato, moschettato.
specks (*colloq.*) [cp. **spectacles**].
spectacle ['spektəkl], *n.* Spettacolo, *m.*
spectacles, *n.pl.* Occhiali, *m.pl.* **To put on one's —,** inforcare gli occhiali; **spectacle-case,** astuccio per occhiali, *m.*; **spectacle-maker,** occhialaio, ottico, *m.*
spectacled, *a.* Che porta occhiali, occhialuto.
spectacular [spek'tækju:ləɹ], *a.* Spettacoloso; teatrale, vistoso.
spectator [spek'teitəɹ], *n.* Spettatore, *m.*; astante, *m.*
spectral ['spektrəl], *a.* Spettrale, di spettro.
spectre ['spektəɹ], *n.* Spettro, fantasma, *m.*
spectroscope ['spektroskoup], *n.* Spettroscopio, *m.*
spectroscopic, *a.* Spettroscopico.
spectrum (pl. **spectra**) ['spektrəm, 'spektrə], *n.* Spettro, *m.* **— analysis,** analisi spettrale, *f.*
speculate ['spekju:leit], *v.i.* Speculare; considerare, meditare. **To — in stocks,** speculare in titoli; **to — on,** meditare su.
speculation, *n.* Speculazione, *f.*; meditazione, *f.*; congettura, supposizione, *f.* **On —, on spec,** per speculazione.
speculative ['spekju:lətiv], *a.* Speculativo; di speculazione.
speculator, *n.* Speculatore, *m.*
speculum (pl. **specula**) ['spekju:ləm, 'spekju:lə], *n.* Specchio, *m.*; (*Med.*) specolo, *m.*
speech [spi:tʃ], *n.* Parola, *f.*; parlata, favella, *f.*; discorso, *m.*, orazione, arringa, *f.* **Extempore —,** discorso improvvisato, *m.*; **set —,** discorso preparato, *m.*; **figure of —,** figura retorica, *f.*; **to lose one's —,** perdere la parola; **to be slow of —,** parlare lento; **the parts of —,** le parti del discorso, *f.pl.*; **— for the defence,** arringa, *f.*; **— -day,** distribuzione dei premi, *f.*; **— -maker,** oratore, parlatore, *m.*
speechifier ['spi:tʃifaiəɹ], *n.* Oratore da strapazzo, *m.*
speechify ['spi:tʃifai], *v.i.* Fare sproloqui, concionare.
speechifying, *n.* Sproloquio, *m.*
speechless, *a.* Muto, senza parola. **To be struck —,** rimaner muto, restar senza parole; **— with rage,** muto per la rabbia.
speechlessness, *n.* Mutismo, silenzio, *m.*
speed [spi:d], *n.* Velocità, rapidità, celerità, *f.*; prestezza, fretta, premura, sollecitudine, *f.* ‖ *v.t.* Spedire, accomiatare; *v.i.* affrettarsi, accelerare, andar rapido; riuscire, prosperare. **At full —,** a tutta corsa, a tutta velocità, a briglia sciolta, a gran carriere; (*of trains*) a tutto vapore; **at the top of one's —,** a tutta velocità, a rotta di collo, al più presto possibile; **with all —,** in tutta fretta; **more haste less —,** chi ha fretta vada adagio; **to wish God- —,** augurare felice esito; **God — you!** Dio v'accompagni! **to — the parting guest,** accomiatare l'ospite; **to — up,** accelerare; (*Motor.*) 3- **— gear,** ingranaggio a tre velocità, *m.*
speedboat, *n.* Motoscafo; fuori bordo, *m.*
speedily, *adv.* In fretta, subito, presto.
speediness, *n.* Celerità, rapidità, *f.*; fretta, premura, sollecitudine, *f.*
speedometer, *n.* Tachimetro, contagiri, *m.*
speedway, *n.* Pista, *f.*; autostrada, *f.*
speedwell, *n.* (*Bot.*) Veronica, *f.*
speedy, *a.* Celere, veloce, rapido; frettoloso; pronto, spiccio.
spell (1) [spel], *n.* (*magic*) Malia, *f.*, incanto, fascino, *m.*; sortilegio, *m.* **To break the —,** rompere l'incanto; **to cast a — on,** incantare, affascinare, stregare, ammaliare; **— -bound,** incantato, affascinato, ammaliato.
spell (2), *n.* Periodo, tempo, *m.*; intervallo, *m.*; turno di servizio, *m.*
spell (3), *v.t.* Compitare, sillabare, alfabetare; scrivere, scrivere correttamente; (*fig.*) significare, voler dire. **This spells ruin to me,** ciò vuol dire che sono rovinato; **to — out,** compitare per lettera; **How do you — it?** Come si scrive?
spelling, *n.* Compitazione, *f.*; ortografia, *f.* **— mistake,** errore di ortografia, *m.*; **— -bee,** gara d'ortografia, *f.*; **— -book,** sillabario, abbecedario, *m.*
spelt [spelt], *n.* (*Bot.*) Farro, *m.*, spelta, *f.*
spelter, *n.* (*Min.*) Zinco, *m.*
spencer ['spensəɹ], *n.* Giacchetta, *f.*, panciotto, *m.*; spenser, *m.*
spend [spend], *v.t.* Spendere; impiegare; consumare, esaurire; (*time*) passare; *v.i.* spendere danaro; consumarsi, esaurirsi. **The storm has spent itself,** la tempesta s'è calmata; **to — one's holidays,** passare le vacanze.
spender, *n.* Spenditore, *m.*
spending, *n.* Lo spendere, *m.*
spendthrift ['spendθrift], *n.* Scialacquatore, *m.* ‖ *a.* Spendereccio, prodigo.
spent, *a.* Speso; esaurito, esausto; (*of bullet*) morta, fredda.
sperm [spəːɹm], *n.* Sperma, *m.* **— -oil,** spermaceti, *m.*; **— -whale,** capodoglio, *m.*
spermaceti [spəːɹmə'seti], *n.* Spermaceti, *m.pl.*, bianco di balena, *m.*
spermatic [spəːɹ'mætik], *a.* Spermatico.
spermatology [spəːɹmə'tələdʒi], *n.* Spermatologia, *f.*
spermatozoon (pl. **spermatozoa**) [spəːɹmətə'zouən], *n.* Spermatozoo, *m.*
spew [spju:], *v.t.* Vomitare.
sphenoid ['sfenɔid], *n.a.* (*Anat.*) Sfenoide, *m.*
sphere [sfiəɹ], *n.* Sfera, *f.*, globo, circolo, *m.* **— of influence,** sfera d'influenza, *f.*; **celestial —,** sfera celeste, *f.*
spherical ['sferikəl], *a.* Sferico.
spherics, *n.pl.* (*Geom.*) Teoria della sfera, *f.*
spheroid ['sfiərɔid], *a.* Sferoide.
spheroidal, *a.* Sferoidale.
sphincter ['sfiŋktəɹ], *n.* (*Anat.*) Sfintere, *m.*
sphinx [sfiŋks], *n.* Sfinge, *f.*
spice [spais], *n.* Spezie, droga, *f.*; (*fig.*) pochino, tantino, pizzico, *m.* ‖ *v.t.* Condire. **Dealer in spices,** droghiere, *m.*
spiciness, *n.* Sapore piccante, *f.*; aroma, *m.*; (*fig.*) oscenità, *f.*
spick and span ['spik ənd 'spæn], *a.* Attillato, tirato ai quattro spilli; nuovo di zecca.
spicy, *a.* Piccante, saporito, frizzante, pungente; aromatico, odoroso; (*colloq.*) piccante.

spider [ˈspaidəɹ], *n.* (*Zool.*) Ragno, *m.* **Spider's web,** ragnatelo, *m.*, ragnatela, *f.*
spidery, spider-like, *a.* Come un ragno.
spigot [ˈspigət], *n.* Zipolo, tappo, *m.*; turacciolетto, *m.*
spike [spaik], *n.* Punta, *f.*, puntone, *m.*; bullone, chiodo grosso, *m.*; caviglia, *f.*; (*of corn*) spiga, *f.* || *v.t.* Inchiodare, ferrare, armar di punte; infilare, infilzare. **To — a gun,** inchiodare un cannone; (*fig.*) **to — an opponent's guns,** rendere impotente un avversario; (*Bot.*) **—-lavender,** spigo, spigonardo, *m.*
spiked, *a.* Con chiodi, chiodato.
spikenard [ˈspaiknɑːɹd], *n.* (*Bot.*) Spigonardo, nardo, *m.*
spiky, *a.* A punte, a chiodi, chiodato.
spill (1) [spil], *v.t.* Versare, spargere, spandere, far cadere; perdere; *v.i.* cadere, spargersi, spandersi. || *n.* Caduta, *f.*, capitombolo, *m.* **He had a nasty —,** ha fatto una brutta caduta.
spill (2), *n.* Striscia di carta per dar fuoco, *f.*, legnetto, *m.*
spillikins [ˈspilikinz], *n.pl.* Stecchi, *m.pl.*, giuoco di stecchi, *m.*
spin [spin], *n.* Giro, *m.*; biciclettata, gita in bicicletta, automobilata, *f.*; (*Aviat.*) avvitamento, *m.* || *v.t.* (*thread, etc.*) Filare; (*a top*) far girare, far trottolare; *v.i.* girare, trottolare. (*fig.*) **To — a yarn,** raccontare una storia; **to — out,** allungare, prolungare, menare per le lunghe; **to — round and round,** girare e rigirare.
spinach, spinage [ˈspinidʒ], *n.* (*Bot.*) Spinacio, spinace, *m.*; (*Cooking*) gli spinaci, *m.pl.*
spinal [ˈspainəl], *a.* (*Anat.*) Spinale. **— column,** spina dorsale, *f.*; **—-cord,** midollo spinale, *m.*; **— curvature,** lussazione, deviazione spinale, *f.*
spindle [spindl], *n.* Fuso, *m.*; asse, perno, *m.* **—-shanked,** dalle gambe sottili; **—-shaped,** fusiforme; (*Bot.*) **—-tree,** fusaggine, *f.*
spindrift, *n.* Spruzzaglia delle onde, *f.*
spine [spain], *n.* (*Anat.*) Spina dorsale, colonna vertebrale, *f.*; (*Bot.*) spina, *f.*; (*of book*) dorso, *m.*
spinel [ˈspinəl], *n.* (*Min.*) Spinello, *m.*
spineless [ˈspainles], *a.* Senza spina dorsale; (*fig.*) debole, fiacco, slombato.
spinet [ˈspinet, spiˈnet], *n.* (*Mus.*) Spinetta, *f.*
spiniferous [spaiˈnifərəs], *a.* Spinoso.
spinnaker [ˈspinəkəɹ], *n.* (*Naut.*) Controranda, *f.*
spinner, *n.* Filatore, *m.*, filatrice, *f.*
spinney [ˈspini], *n.* Boschetto, *m.*
spinning, *n.* Filatura, *f.* || *a.* Girante. **—-frame, —-jenny,** filatoio, *m.*, filatrice meccanica, *f.*; **—-mill,** filatoio, *m.*, filanda, *f.*; **—-top,** trottola, *f.*; **—-wheel,** filatoio, *m.*; ruota da filare, *f.*
spinster [ˈspinstəɹ], *n.* Zitella, *f.*; donna nubile, *f.*
spiny [ˈspaini], *a.* Spinoso; (*fig.*) difficile, spinoso.
spiracle [ˈspairəkəl], *n.* (*of whales*) Sfiatatoio, *m.*
spiræa [spaiˈriə], *n.* (*Bot.*) Spirea, *f.*
spiral [ˈspairəl], *a.* Spirale; (*of staircase*) a chiocciola. || *n.* Spirale, *f.*
spirant [ˈspairənt], *a.* (*Gram.*) Spirante.
spire [spaiɹ], *n.* (*steeple*) Guglia, *f.*; campanile, *m.*; (*Bot.*) gambo, *m.*, spira, *f.*
spirit, *n.* Spirito, *m.*, anima, *f.*; ardore, ardimento, coraggio, *m.*; brio, *m.*, vivacità, *f.*; spettro, fantasma, *m.*; alcool, liquore, *m.*; umore, *m.* || *v.t.* Animare, incoraggiare. **Spirits,** liquori alcoolici, *m.pl.*, bevande spiritose, *f.pl.*; **a meeting of choice spirits,** una riunione di spiriti superiori; **a master- —,** un genio, *m.*; **Do show a little —!** Fatti coraggio! **he took it in the wrong —,** lo prese in mala parte; **a — of mischief,** un demonio; **the — of the age,** lo spirito del tempo, *m.*; **animal spirits,** spiriti animali, *m.pl.*; **in high spirits,** vivace, animato, di buon umore; **in low spirits,** triste, abbattuto, scoraggiato; **party —,** spirito di parte, *m.*, partigianeria, *f.*; **proof —,** alcool di prova, *m.*; **raw spirits,** liquori puri, *m.pl.*; **to recover one's spirits,** riprendere coraggio; **spirits of wine,** spirito di vino, *m.*; **to raise a —,** evocare uno spirito; **to raise someone's spirits,** riconfortare gli spiriti di qualcuno; **to — away,** far sparire per incanto, trafugare; **—-lamp,** lampada a spirito, *f.*; **—-level,** livello ad aria, *m.*; **—-rapping,** spiritismo, *m.*; **—-trade,** commercio di liquori, *m.*
spirited, *a.* Animato, vivace, brioso, vivo; ardente, coraggioso; focoso. **A — horse,** un cavallo focoso, *m.*; **high- —,** ardente, focoso; **low- —,** abbattuto, triste, melanconico; **mean- —,** meschino, gretto; **poor- —,** abietto, fiacco, vile.
spiritedly, *adv.* Vivacemente, con brio; ardentemente, coraggiosamente.
spiritedness, *n.* Animazione, vivacità, *f.*; ardore, coraggio, *m.*, foga, *f.*
spiritless, *a.* Avvilito, scoraggiato; debole, fiacco, abbattuto.
spiritual [ˈspiritjuːəl], *a.* Spirituale.
spiritualism, spiritism [ˈspiritjuːəlizm, ˈspiritizm], *n.* Spiritismo, *m.*; spiritualismo, *m.*
spiritualist, spiritist, *n.* Spiritista, *m.f.*; spiritualista, *m.f.*
spiritualistic, *a.* Spiritistico.
spirituality [spiritjuːˈæliti], *n.* Spiritualità, *f.*
spiritualize, *v.t.* Spiritualizzare.
spiritually, *adv.* Spiritualmente.
spirituous [ˈspiritjuːəs], *a.* Alcoolico. **— liquors,** liquori, *m.pl.*
spirituousness, *n.* Alcoolicità, *f.*
spirometer [spaiˈrɔmetəɹ], *n.* Spirometro, *m.*
spirt, spurt [spəːɹt], *n.* Getto, *m.* || *v.i.* Schizzare, spruzzare; sprizzare.
spit (1) [spit], *n.* (*for roasting*) Spiedo, schidione, *m.*; (*of land*) lingua di terra, *f.* || *v.t.* Schidionare; trafiggere.
spit (2), *n.* Sputo, *m.*, saliva, *f.* || *v.i.t.* sputare. **He is the very — of his father,** è suo padre nato sputato; **to — in someone's face,** sputare in viso a qualcuno; **to — out,** sputare, buttar fuori.
spit (3), *n.* (*of soil*) Vangata, badilata, *f.*
spitch-cock, spatch-cock [ˈspitʃkɔk, ˈspætʃkɔk], *v.t.* Arrostire sulla graticola.
spite [spait], *n.* Dispetto, spregio, odio, rancore, *m.*, ruggine, *f.* || *v.t.* Far dispetto a, vessare, contrariare, tormentare. **In — of,** a dispetto di, malgrado; **out of —,** per dispetto, per picca; **to have a — against,** aver della ruggine con, aver del rancore con.

spiteful, *a.* Dispettoso, malevolo, malizioso, maligno, malvagio.
spitefully, *adv.* Malevolmente.
spitefulness, *n.* Malizia, cattiveria, malignità, malvagità, *f.*
spitfire ['spitfaiɹ], *n.* Persona irascibile, *f.*, rabbiosetto, zolfino, stizzoso, *m.* ; (*Aviat.*) spitfire, *m.*
spitter, *n.* Sputatore, *m.*
spitting, *n.* Lo sputare, *m.* **No —,** è vietato sputare.
spittle, *n.* Sputo, *m.*, saliva, *f.*
spittoon [spi'tu:n], *n.* Sputacchiera, *f.*
splanchnic ['splæŋknik], *a.* (*Anat.*) Splancnico.
splash [splæʃ], *v.t.i.* Schizzare, sprizzare, spruzzare; sciabordare, sciaguattare; infangare, inzaccherare. || *n.* Schizzo, spruzzo, *m.*, zacchera, chiazza, pillacchera, *f.*, sciaguattio, tonfo, *m.*; (*fig.*) mostra, parata, *f.* **He was splashing about in the water,** diguazzava nell'acqua; **splashed all over,** tutto inzaccherato; (*fig.*) **to make a —,** fare un effettone, fare colpo, far furore; **—-board,** parafango, *m.*; **a — of colour,** una chiazza di colore, *f.*
splashing, *n.* Schizzata, spruzzata, *f.*, spruzzamento, *m.*
splashy, *a.* Fangoso.
splay [splei], *v.t.* (*Arch.*) Strombare, sguanciare; (*dislocate*) slogare, spallare. || *n.* (*Arch.*) Strombo, *m.*, strombatura, *f.* **—-footed,** coi piedi aperti.
spleen [spli:n], *n.* (*Anat.*) Milza, *f.*; (*fig.*) ipocondria, *f.*; malinconia, *f.*; dispetto, rancore, malumore, *m.* **A fit of —,** un accesso di malumore; **to vent one's — on,** sfogare il fiele su.
spleenful, spleenish, *a.* Malinconico, atrabiliare, bilioso, irritabile.
spleenwort, *n.* (*Bot.*) Asplenio, *m.*
splendid ['splendid], *a.* Splendido, risplendente, rilucente; suntuoso, magnifico.
splendidly, *adv.* Splendidamente; magnificamente; (*colloq.*) benissimo.
splendour ['splendəɹ], *n.* Splendore, fulgore, *m.*, lucentezza; suntuosità, magnificenza, *f.*
splenetic [sple'netik], *a.* Splenetico, atrabiliare.
splenitis [spli:'naitis], *n.* (*Med.*) Splenite, *f.*
splice [splais], *n.* (*Naut.*) Impiombatura, intrecciatura, *f.*; (*Tech.*) unione, intrecciatura, *f.* || *v.t.* Impiombare, unire, accoppiare, riunire; (*colloq.*) sposare. **To get spliced,** sposarsi.
splint [splint], *n.* Stecca, assicella, *f.*; (*Anat.*) stinco, *m.*, fibula, incannucciata, *f.* || *v.t.* Incannucciare.
splinter, *n.* Scheggia, *f.* || *v.t.* Scheggiare, spaccare, frantumare; *v.i.* scheggiarsi, frantumarsi. **—-bar,** bilancino, *m.*; **—-bone,** fibula, *f.*
splintery, *a.* Scheggioso, scheggiato, pieno di schegge.
split [split], *v.t.i.* Fendere, spaccare; scindere; dividere, ripartire; fendersi, spaccarsi; scoppiare; (*colloq.*) divulgare un segreto. || *n.* Fessura, crepa, fenditura, spaccatura, *f.*, crepaccio, *m.*; scissione, divisione, *f.*; scisma, *m.*, separazione, *f.* **To — the difference,** fare a metà; **to — hairs,** cavillare, guardare per il sottile; **to — into fragments,** frantumare; **to — off,** staccare, staccarsi; **my head is splitting,** la mia testa scoppia; **to — one's sides laughing,** sbellicarsi dalle risa; **to — on a rock,** infrangersi su uno scoglio; **— peas,** piselli spaccati, *m.pl.*; **—-ring,** anello doppio, *m.*; **a splitting headache,** un mal di testa da impazzire, *m.*
splotch, splodge [splɔtʃ, splɔdʒ], *n.* Chiazza, macchia, *f.*
splurge [splə:ɹdʒ], *n.* Sfoggio, colpo, furore, effettone, *m.*
splutter, sputter ['splʌtəɹ, 'spʌtəɹ], *n.* Barbugliamento, *m.* || *v.i.* Barbugliare, sputacchiare parlando.
spoil (1) [spɔil], *v.t.* Guastare, sciupare, rovinare; predare, rubare, saccheggiare, (*children*) viziare; *v.i.* guastarsi, sciuparsi; (*of fruit*) infracidirsi; deperire, deteriorare, andare a male. || *n.* Preda, *f.*, bottino, *m.*, spoglie, *f.pl.* **Spoils,** profitto, vantaggio, utile, guadagno, *m.*; **to — sport,** guastare la festa; **a —-sport,** un guastafeste, *m.*; **to — the Egyptians,** spogliare i nemici vinti; **he is spoiling for a fight,** brucia dalla voglia di battersi; **fish spoils by keeping,** il pesce si guasta se è tenuto.
spoil (2), *n.* Terra scavata, *f.*
spoiled, *a.* Guasto, rovinato, sciupato; (*of children*) viziato.
spoiler, *n.* Saccheggiatore, predatore, spogliatore, *m.*
spoiling, *n.* Saccheggio, *m.*, spoliazione, *f.*; guasto, guastamento, *m.*; rovina, corruzione, deteriorazione, *f.*
spoke [spouk], *n.* Raggio, *m.* **—-shave,** pialla, *f.* **To put a — in someone's wheel,** mettere un bastone nelle ruote.
spoken, *a.* Parlato, orale. **Soft-—,** affabile, mellifluo; **well-— of,** ben quotato.
spokesman ['spoukzmən], *n.* Rappresentante, esponente, portavoce, *m.*
spoliation [spouli'eiʃən], *n.* Spoliazione, estorsione, *f.*
spoliator, *n.* Spogliatore, *m.*
spondee ['spɔndi:], *n.* (*Poet.*) Spondeo, *m.*
spondyl ['spɔndil], *n.* (*Anat.*) Spondilo, *m.*
sponge [spʌndʒ], *n.* Spugna, *f.* || *v.t.i.* Ripulire con spugna; scroccare. **To throw up the —,** confessarsi vinto, darsi per vinto; **to — out,** espungere, cancellare; **to — down,** fare una spugnatura a; **to — on someone,** vivere alle spalle altrui; **—-bag,** sacchetto da spugna, *m.*; **—-basket,** portaspugne, *m.*; **—-bath,** semicupio, *m.*, spugnatura, *f.*; **—-cake,** pan di Spagna, biscotto spugnoso, *m.*
sponger ['spʌndʒəɹ], *n.* Scroccone, *m.*
sponginess, *n.* Spugnosità, *f.*
sponging, *n.* Spugnatura, *f.*; scroccheria, *f.* **—-house,** prigione provvisoria per debitori, *f.*
spongy ['spʌndʒi], *a.* Spugnoso.
sponsor ['spɔnsəɹ], *n.* Garante, mallevadore, *m.*; (*Eccles.*) padrino, *m.*, madrina, *f.*, compare, *m.f.* || *v.t.* Garantire, essere mallevadore di.
sponsorship, *n.* Uffizio di compare, *m.*; garanzia, malleveria, *f.*
spontaneity [spɔntein'i:iti], *n.* Spontaneità, *f*
spontaneous [spɔn'teiniəs], *a.* Spontaneo.
spontaneously, *adv.* Spontaneamente.

spontaneousness, *n.* Spontaneità, *f.*
spontoon [spɔn'tu:n], *n.* Spuntone, *m.*, alabarda, *f.*
spook [spu:k], *n.* Spettro, fantasma, *m.*
spool [spu:l], *n.* Rocchetto, cannello, *m.*, bobina, *f.* || *v.t.* Bobinare, incannare.
spoon [spu:n], *n.* Cucchiaio, *m.*; (*fig.*) innamorato, *m.*, cascamorto, *m.* || *v.i.* Amoreggiare, flirtare. **To be born with a silver — in one's mouth,** essere nato vestito; **to — out,** versare col cucchiaio, scucchiaiare; **to — up,** pigliare col cucchiaio; **—-meat,** cibo liquido, *m.*; **—-brake,** freno sul pneumatico, *m.*
spoonbill, *n.* (*Zool.*) Spatola, *f.*
spoonerism ['spu:nərizm], *n.* Papera, *f.*, confusione nel parlare, *f.*
spoonful, *n.* Cucchiaiata, *f.*
spoony, *a.* Svenevole, sentimentale.
spoor [spu:ɹ], *n.* Traccia, *f.*
sporadic [spɔ'rædik], *a.* Sporadico.
spore [spɔ:ɹ], *n.* (*Bot.*) Spora, *f.*
sporran ['spɔrən], *n.* Borsa portata dai montanari scozzesi, *f.*
sport [spɔ:ɹt], *n.* Giuoco, scherzo, diporto, trastullo, svago, divertimento, passatempo, *m.*; lo sport, *m.*; (*Bot.Zool.*) deviazione del tipo normale, *f.* || *v.i.* Divertirsi, svagarsi, giuocare, spassarsi; *v.t.* portare. **To make — of,** beffarsi di, prendere in giro; **athletic sports,** atletica, *f.*; **in sport,** per divertimento, per burla; **to be the — of,** essere il trastullo di; (*colloq.*) **to be a —,** esser generoso, essere leale; **to have good —,** far buona caccia; **he was sporting a new hat,** portava un cappello nuovo; **sports editor,** redattore sportivo, *m.*; **sports-ground,** campo di calcio, campo dello sport, *m.*; **sports suit,** completo da sport, *m.*; **sports wear,** vestiti sportivi, *m.pl.*
sporting, *a.* Sportivo. **A — man,** uno sportsman, uno sportivo, *m.*; **a — offer,** un'offerta giusta, *f.*; **the — press,** la stampa sportiva, *f.*; **a — chance,** una mera possibilità, *f.*; **—-dog,** cane da caccia, *m.*; **—-gun,** fucile da caccia, *m.*
sportive ['spɔ:ɹtiv], *a.* Scherzoso, scherzevole, faceto, allegro, gaio.
sportiveness, *n.* Allegria, gaiezza, *f.*
sportsman, *n.* Cacciatore, sportivo, sportsman, *m.*
sportswoman, *n.* Cacciatrice, amazzone, donna sportiva, *f.*
sporty, *a.* Gentile, cortese; sportivo.
spot [spɔt], *n.* (*stain*) Macchia, macchiolina, *f.*; (*dot*) punto, *m.*, picchiettatura, *f.*; (*place*) punto, luogo, posto, *m.*; (*Billiards*) segno, *m.* || *v.t.* (*to stain*) Macchiare, chiazzare; (*to dot*) picchiettare, punteggiare; (*to discover*) scoprire, osservare, riconoscere. || *a.* (*Comm.*) Pronto per consegna immediata. **On the —,** subito, lì per lì, senz'altro, sul posto; **to be killed on the —,** restar morto sul colpo; **a weak —,** un punto debole.
spotless, *a.* Senza macchia; immacolato, puro.
spotlessness, *n.* Pulizia, *f.*; purità, *f.*
spotlight, *n.* Proiettore orientabile, *m.*; (*Theat.*) luce di proscenio, *f.*
spotted, *a.* Macchiato, macchiettato, chiazzato, punteggiato, picchiettato. **—-fever,** meningite cerebro-spinale, *f.*
spottiness, *n.* Chiazzatura, *f.*
spotty, *a.* Macchiato, chiazzato; coperto di bollicine.
spouse [spauz], *n.* Sposo, marito, *m.*, sposa, moglie, *f.*
spout [spaut], *n.* Tubo, *m.*, canna, *f.*; becco beccuccio, *m.*; grondaia, *f.*; getto zampillo, *m.* || *v.t.* Gettare, lanciare, schizzare; (*fig.*) declamare; *v.i.* sgorgare, schizzare, scaturire; (*fig.*) perorare, concionare. (*colloq.*) **Up the —,** al monte di pietà.
spouter, *n.* Oratore, declamatore, *m.*
spouting, *n.* Sgorgo, getto, *m.*; (*fig.*) declamazione, *f.*
sprain [sprein], *n.* (*Med.*) Storta, distorsione, *f.* || *v.t.* Storcere, stortare; lussare. **To — one's ankle,** stortarsi una caviglia.
sprang, *p.* of **spring.**
sprat [spræt], *n.* (*Zool.*) Spratto, *m.* **To throw a — to catch a whale,** dare un uovo per aver un bue.
sprawl [sprɔ:l], *v.i.* Sdraiarsi, abbandonarsi, stendersi lungo disteso. **To send someone sprawling,** mandare qualcuno a gambe all'aria.
spray (1) [sprei], *n.* (*of liquid*) Spruzzo, *m.*, spruzzi, *m.pl.*, spruzzata, spruzzaglia, *f.*; (*squirt*) vaporizzatore, spruzzatore, *m.* || *v.t.* Spruzzare; aspergere, cospargere, innaffiare; vaporizzare.
spray (2), *n.* (*of flowers, etc.*) Frasca, fraschetta, *f.*, ramoscello, *m.*; rama, *f.*; (*of jewels*) spiga, *f.*
sprayer, *n.* Spruzzatore, vaporizzatore, *m.*
spread [spred], *v.t.* Spiegare, stendere, spandere; spalmare; propagare, diffondere; coprire; *v.i.* stendersi, estendersi, spaziare; diffondersi, spandersi, propagarsi. || *n.* Estensione, dimensione, *f.*; diffusione, *f.*; (*colloq.*) festa, *f.*, banchetto, *m.* **To — a rumour,** diffondere una diceria; **to — abroad,** divulgare, propalare; **to — over,** stendersi sopra; **—-eagle,** aquila colle ali stese.
spreading, *n.* Propagazione, diffusione, *f.* || *a.* Esteso, largo, ampio.
spree [spri:], *n.* Baldoria, *f.*, bagordo, *m.*; scappata, *f.* **To go on the —,** far baldoria, gozzovigliare.
sprig [sprig], *n.* Ramoscello, rametto, *m.*; rampollo, *m.*
sprightliness ['spraitlines], *n.* Vivacità, allegria, *f.*, brio, *m.*
sprightly, *a.* Vivace, allegro, lesto, gaio, brioso.
spring (1) [spriŋ], *n.* Primavera, *f.* **A — day,** un giorno primaverile, *m.*; **—-chicken,** pulcino, *m.*; **—-cleaning,** gran pulizia, *f.*; **—-onion,** cipollina, *f.*
spring (2), *v.i.* (*to jump*) Saltare, balzare; (*to arise from*) sorgere, nascere; venire, provenire; (*to gush forth*) scaturire, zampillare; (*of wood*) incrinarsi, storcersi; *v.t.* fare scattare, mettere in moto; (*of wood*) incrinare, storcere; (*of game*) far levare; (*a leak*) aprire; (*a mine*) far esplodere. || *n.* (*leap*) Salto, balzo, slancio *m.*; (*elasticity*) elasticità, *f.*; (*recoil*) molla, *f.*; (*of water*) sorgente, *f.*; (*backward movement*) rinculo, *m.*; (*cause*) origine, causa, sorgente, *f.*, motivo, *m.* **To — up,** balzare su, (*grow*) crescere, (*arise*) nascere; **to — down,** saltare giù; **to —**

back, rinculare, indietreggiare, arretrarsi, scattare; **he sprang to her aid,** balzò ad aiutarla; **the door sprang to,** la porta sbattè; **a breeze sprang up,** sorse un venticello; **Where did you — from?** Da dove siete venuto? **to — forward,** slanciarsi avanti; **to — a leak,** aprire una falla; **to — a surprise,** fare una sorpresa; (*Naut.*) **to — a mast,** drizzare un albero; **hot springs,** sorgenti termali, *f.pl.*; **he has no — in him,** non ha elasticità; **to take a —,** spiccare un salto; **— -balance,** bilancia a molla, *f.*; **— -blind,** tendina a molla, *f.*; **— -board,** trampolino, *m.*; **— knife,** coltello a molla, *m.*; **— -mattress,** materasso elastico, *m.*; **— tide,** marea alta di plenilunio, marea massima, *f.*; **— -water,** acqua sorgiva, *f.*

springbok ['spriŋbɔk], *n.* (*Zool.*) Gazzella africana, *f.*

springe [sprindʒ], *n.* Calappio, *m.*, trappola, *f.*

springer ['spriŋəɹ], *n.* (*Arch.*) Imposta, *f.*

springiness ['spriŋines], *n.* Elasticità, *f.*

springing, *n.* Lo slanciarsi, il balzare, *m.* **— back,** arretramento, rinculo, *m.*; **— up,** il sorgere, lo scaturire.

springlike, *a.* Primaverile.

springtime, *n.* Primavera, stagione primaverile, *f.*

springy ['spriŋi], *a.* Elastico.

sprinkle [spriŋkl], *v.t.* Spruzzare, inaffiare, aspergere; cospargere; *v.i.* piovigginare. **A sky sprinkled with stars,** un cielo cosparso di stelle, *m.*

sprinkler, *n.* Spruzzatore, *m.*; (*Eccles.*) aspersorio, *m.*

sprinkling, sprinkle, *n.* Spruzzo, *m.*, spruzzaglia, *f.*; (*of rain*) acquerugiola, *f.*; piccola quantità, *f.*, pizzico, *m.*

sprint [sprint], *v.i.* Correr di volata. || *n.* Corsa di volata, volata, *f.*, scatto, *m.*

sprinter, *n.* Velocista, podista, scattista, *m.*

sprit [sprit], *n.* (*Naut.*) Struzza, *f.* **— -sail,** tarchia, civada, *f.*

sprite [sprait], *n.* Folletto, genietto, *m.*

sprocket ['sprɔket], *n.* (*Mech.*) Dente di ruota, *m.* **— -wheel,** ruota dentata per catena, *f.*, rocchetto a denti, *m.*

sprout [spraut], *n.* Germoglio, rampollo, *m.* || *v.i.* Germogliare, germinare, rampollare; *v.t.* germinare, generare, produrre. **Brussels sprouts,** cavoli di Brusselle, broccoletti di Brusselle, *m.pl.*

sprouting, *n.* Germinazione, *f.*

spruce (1) [spru:s], *a.* Attillato, lindo, elegante. **To — up,** attillarsi.

spruce (2), *n.* (*Bot.*) Abete rosso, *m.*

spruceness, *n.* Attillatezza, eleganza, *f.*

sprung [sprʌŋ], *a.* A molle.

spud [spʌd], *n.* (*Agric.*) Zappetta, *f.*, sarchio, *m.*; (*colloq.*) patata, *f.*

spume [spju:m], *n.* Spuma, schiuma, *f.* || *v.i.* Spumare, schiumare.

spumy, *a.* Spumoso.

spun, *a.* Filato. **— -silk,** seta filata, *f.*; **— -gold,** oro filato, *m.*

spunk [spʌŋk], *n.* (*colloq.*) Fegato, coraggio, *m.*

spunky, *a.* Di fegato, coraggioso.

spur [spə:ɹ], *n.* Sprone, sperone, *m.*; (*of cock*) spronetto, *m.*; (*fig.*) stimolo, incitamento, *m.*; (*Arch.*) sprone, *m.*; (*of mountain*) contrafforte. || *v.t.i.* Spronare; (*fig.*) stimolare, incalzare, incitare. **On the — of the moment,** sui due piedi, lì per lì; **to put spurs to one's horse,** dare di sprone al cavallo; **to win one's spurs,** vincer la prova; **to — on, to — forward,** spronare, spingere avanti; (*Mech.*) **— -gearing,** ingranaggio di rinvio, *m.*; **— -wheel,** ruota dentata, *f.*

spurge [spə:ɹdʒ], *n.* (*Bot.*) Euforbia, *f.* **— -laurel,** laureola, *f.*

spurious ['spju:riəs], *a.* Spurio, falso.

spuriousness, *n.* Falsità, *f.*

spurn [spə:ɹn], *v.t.* Respingere, rifiutare, rigettare; sdegnare.

spurning, *n.* Rifiuto, respingimento, *m.* sdegno, *m.*

spurred [spə:ɹd], *a.* Speronato, spronato.

spurrier ['spʌriəɹ], *n.* Spronaio, *m.*

spurry, spurrey ['spʌri], *n.* (*Bot.*) Spergula, *f.*

spurt [spə:ɹt], *v.i.* Spruzzare, zampillare, schizzare; *v.t.* spruzzare, far zampillare. || *n.* Getto, zampillo, spruzzo, *m.*; (*fig.*) sforzo, *m.*; scatto, *m.*, volata, *f.* **To make a —,** fare uno sforzo.

sputter ['spʌtəɹ], *v.t.i.* Sputacchiare; schizzare; borbottare, biascicare. || *n.* Borbottamento, *m.*; spruzzo, *m.*

sputum ['spju:təm], *n.* (*Med.*) Sputo, *m.*

spy [spai], *n.* Spia, *f.*; (*police*) spione, delatore, *m.* || *v.t.i.* Spiare, far la spia; scorgere. **To — out,** scorgere, scoprire, trovare; esplorare; **to — into,** scrutare, investigare; **— -glass,** cannocchiale, *m.*; **— -system,** spionaggio, *m.*; **— -hole,** spioncino, *m.*

squab [skwɔb], *n.* (*young pigeon*) Piccioncino, *m.*; (*cushion*) cuscino imbottito, *m.* || *a.* Grassotto, grassoccio, paffuto; implume.

squabble [skwɔbl], *n.* Alterco, contrasto, *m.*, lite, *f.* || *v.i.* Altercare, litigare, questionare.

squabbler, *n.* Litigone, attaccabrighe, *m.*

squabbling, *n.* Litigio, *m.* || *a.* Litigante.

squad [skwɔd], *n.* Squadra, *f.*, drappello, *m.* **The awkward —,** la squadra dei coscritti, *f.*

squadron ['skwɔdrən], *n.* (*Mil.*) Squadrone, *m.*; (*Naut.*) squadra, squadriglia, *f.*; (*Aviat.*) squadriglia, *f.*

squalid ['skwɔlid], *a.* Squallido, sordido, misero.

squalidness [cp. **squalor**].

squall [skwɔ:l], *n.* (*wind*) Raffica, *f.*, turbine, *m.*; (*cry*) grido, strillo, *m.* || *v.i.* Sbraitare, vociare, strillare. **To look out for squalls,** stare all'erta.

squalling, *n.* Urlio, *m.*

squally, *a.* Burrascoso, tempestoso, turbinoso.

squalor ['skwɔləɹ], *n.* Squallidezza, *f.*, squallore, *m.*; sordidezza, *f.*; sudiciume, *m.*

squamous ['skweiməs], *a.* Squamoso.

squander ['skwɔndəɹ], *v.t.* Dissipare, scialacquare, sperperare.

squanderer, *n.* Scialacquatore, sperperatore, *m.*

squandering, *n.* Sperperio, *m.*; dissipazione, *f.*, scialacquio, *m.*

square [skwɛəɹ], *a.* Quadrato, quadro, quadrangolare, tozzo, tarchiato; (*not round*) angolare; (*arranged*) assettato, ordinato, corretto; completo, pieno; fermo, saldo; (*fig.*) giusto, leale, onesto. || *n.* Quadrato, *m.* (*open space*) piazza, *f.*; (*Math.*) quadrato, *m.*; (*on chessboard*) scacco, *m.* || *v.t.* Quadrare, squadrare; aggiustare, regolare, adattare; pagare; (*colloq.*) corrompere con danaro; *v.i.* essere d'accordo con, convenire. **A — meal,** un pasto sostanzioso, *m.*; **— measure,** misura di superficie, *f.*; **to get things —,** assettare le cose; **a — refusal,** un rifiuto netto, *m.*; **to get — with one's creditors,** sdebitarsi; **a — metre of ground,** un metro quadrato di terreno, *m.*; **a set- —,** una squadra, *f.*; **out of the —,** obliquo, fuori squadra; **on the —,** giustamente, lealmente; **his practice does not — with his principles,** la sua pratica non è d'accordo con i suoi principi; **to — accounts with,** regolare i conti con; **to — up to,** darsi un'aria bellicosa verso; **— -built,** quadro, quadrato, tozzo, tarchiato; (*Naut.*) **— -rigged,** a vele quadre; **— -shouldered,** dalle spalle quadre; (*fig.*) **— -toes,** saputello, bacchettone, *m.*

squarely, *adv.* Giustamente, lealmente; in pieno.

squareness, *n.* Quadratura, *f.*; lealtà, onestà, *f.*

squaring, *n.* Quadratura, *f.*

squash (1) [skwɔʃ], *v.t.* Schiacciare, spremere, pigiare, pestare, (*fig.*) ridurre al silenzio. ‖ *n.* Schiacciamento, *m.*; (*crowd*) calca, folla, ressa, *f.*, pigia pigia, *m.* **Lemon- —,** spremuta di limone, limonata, *f.*

squash (2), *n.* (*Bot.*) Zucca, *f.*

squash (3), *n.* Un gioco della palla, *m.*

squat [skwɔt], *a.* Tozzo, tarchiato. ‖ *v.i.* Accoccolarsi, accosciarsi; accovacciarsi, rannicchiarsi, star coccoloni.

squatter, *n.* Intruso, chi occupa terreno non suo, primo occupante, *m.*; chi sta coccoloni, *m.*

squaw [skwɔ:], *n.* Moglie di un Pellirossa, *f.*

squeak [skwi:k], *n.* (*of animals*) Guaito, pigolio, *m.*; (*of voice*) strillo, *m.*; (*of objects*) cigolio, scricchiolio, *m.* ‖ *v.i.* Squittire, guaire; cigolare, scriccholare; strillare.

squeaker, *n.* Cosa o persona che cigola, *f.*; (*colloq.*) spia, *f.*, delatore, *m.*

squeaking, squeaky, *a.* Stridulo.

squeal [skwi:l], *v.i.* Strillare, guaire; lamentarsi; (*colloq.*) denunciare un complice. ‖ *n.* Strillo, guaito, *m.*, grido di dolore, *m.*

squeamish [ˈskwi:miʃ], *a.* Schifiltoso, schizzinoso.

squeamishness, *n.* Schizzinosità, schifiltà, *f.*

squeegee [skwi:ˈdʒi:], *n.* Asciugatoio di gomma, *m.*

squeeze [skwi:z], *v.t.i.* Spremere, premere, pigiare, comprimere, stringere, strizzare. ‖ *n.* Stretta, pigiata, *f.*; pressione, compressione, *f.* **To — someone's hand,** stringere la mano a qualcuno; **to — into,** pigiare dentro; **to — through a crowd,** cacciarsi tra la folla pigiando; **to — out,** spremere; **to — money out of someone,** estorcere danaro da qualcuno; **a tight —,** un pigia pigia, *m.*

squelch [skweltʃ], *v.t.* (*colloq.*) Schiacciare; ridurre al silenzio.

squib [skwib], *n.* Razzo, razzetto, *m.*; (*fig.*) pasquinata, satira, *f.*; libello, *m.*

squid [skwid], *n.* (*Zool.*) Calamaro, *m.*, seppia, *f.*

squill [skwil], *n.* (*Bot.*) Scilla, *f.*

squint [skwint], *v.i.* Esser strabico, guardare guercio. ‖ *n.* Sguardo guercio, sguardo losco, *m.*; (*Med.*) strabismo. **— -eyed,** strabico, losco; guercio.

squinter, *n.* Guercio, *m.*, guercia, *f.*

squinting, *n.* (*Med.*) Strabismo, *m.* ‖ *a.* Guercio, strabico.

squire [skwaiɹ], *n.* Possidente, proprietario di terre, *m.*; gentiluomo di campagna, *m.*; (*of lady*) cavaliere, *m.*; (*Hist.*) scudiero, *m.* ‖ *v.t.* Accompagnare una signora.

squirearchy [ˈskwairɑ:ɹki], *n.* Ceto dei proprietari, *m.*

squireen [skwaiˈri:n], *n.* Piccolo proprietario, *m.*

squirm [skwə:ɹm], *v.i.* Torcersi, storcersi, dimenarsi.

squirrel [ˈskwirəl], *n.* (*Zool.*) Scoiattolo, *m.*

squirt [skwə:ɹt], *n.* Siringa, *f.*, schizzetto, schizzatoio, *m.*; getto, zampillo, *m.* ‖ *v.t.* Schizzare, sprizzare; *v.i.* schizzare, zampillare.

stab [stæb], *n.* Pugnalata, coltellata, stilettata, *f.* ‖ *v.t.* Pugnalare, accoltellare, stilettare. **To — someone in the back,** pugnalare qualcuno alle spalle, (*fig.*) calunniare qualcuno.

stability [stəˈbiliti], *n.* Stabilità, fermezza, saldezza, *f.*

stabilization [stæbilaiˈzeiʃən], *n.* Consolidamento, *m.*, stabilizzazione, *f.*

stabilize, *v.t.* Consolidare, stabilizzare.

stable (1) [steibl], *a.* Stabile, fermo, fisso, solido, saldo; costante, risoluto.

stable (2), *n.* (*for horses*) Scuderia, *f.*; (*for cattle*) stalla, *f.* ‖ *v.t.* Mettere nella scuderia, mettere nella stalla. **— -boy,** mozzo di stalla, *m.*; **— -manure,** concime di stalla, *m.*; **— -yard,** cortile di scuderia, *m.*

stabling, *n.* Stallaggio, *m.*

stablish [cp. **establish**].

stack [stæk], *n.* (*of hay, etc.*) Mucchio, *m.*; (*of grain*) bica, *f.*; (*of wood*) catasta; (*of guns*) fascio, *m.*; (*of chimney*) camino, *m.*; ammasso, *m.*, gran quantità, *f.* ‖ *v.t.* Ammucchiare, accatastare; metter in fascio; abbicare. **— -yard,** cortile, *m.*, aia, *f.*

stacking, *n.* Ammucchiamento, accatastamento, *m.*

stadholder [ˈstɑ:thouldəɹ], *n.* (*Hist.*) Statolder *m.*

stadium [ˈsteidiəm], *n.* (*Sport*) Stadio, *m.*

staff (1) (pl. **staffs, staves**) [stɑ:f, steivz], *n.* Bastone, *m.*, asta, *f.*; (*pilgrim's*) bordone, *m.*; (*pole*) asta, *f.*; (*fig.*) sostegno, appoggio, *m.* **Bread is the — of life,** il pane è il sostegno della vita; **a bishop's —,** il pastorale d'un vescovo, *m.*

staff (2) (pl. **staffs**), *n.* (*Mil.*) Stato maggiore, *m.*; personale, *m.*; impiegati, *m.pl.* **Chief of —,** capo di stato maggiore, *m.*; **— officer,** ufficiale di stato maggiore, *m.*; **editorial —,** redazione, *f.*; **teaching —,** personale insegnante, *m.*

staff (3) (pl. **staves**), *n.* (*Mus.*) Rigo, *m.* **— notation,** notazione musicale, *f.*

stag [stæg], *n.* Cervo, *m.* **A young —,** un cerbiatto, *m.*; **— -beetle,** cervo volante, *m.*; **— -hound,** cane da caccia al cervo, *m.*; **— -hunt,** caccia al cervo, *f.*; **— party,** riunione di uomini soli, *f.*

stage [steidʒ], *n.* Punto, *m.*, fase, tappa, *f.*; grado, periodo, *m.*; (*Theat.*) palcoscenico, *n.*, scena, *f.*, teatro, *m.*; (*scaffolding*) palco, *m.*, impalcatura, *f.*; (*on journey*) posta, *f.* ‖ *v.t.* Mettere in scena, rappresentare, inscenare.

To go on the —, fare l'attore, andare sul teatro; **the English —,** il teatro inglese, *m.*; **at this — of the proceedings,** a questo punto del procedimento; **by easy stages,** a piccole tappe; **—-whisper,** a parte; **to speak in a — whisper,** mormorare in modo da essere intesi; **—-box,** palco di proscenio, *m.*; **—-carpenter,** macchinista, *m.*; **—-coach,** diligenza, *f.*; **—-craft,** arte scenica, scenotecnica, *f.*; **—-directions,** didascalie, *f.pl.*; **—-effect,** effetto scenico, *m.*; **—-fright,** paura, *f.*; **—-manager,** direttore di scena, *m.*; **—-name,** nome di teatro, *m.*; **—-properties,** arredi scenici, *m.pl.*; **—-struck,** attratto verso il teatro.

stager, *n.* Praticone, *m.*, una persona scaltrita, *f.* **An old —,** una volpe vecchia, *f.*

stagger ['stægəɪ], *v.i.* Barcollare, vacillare, titubare; *v.t.* far barcollare; (*fig.*) scuotere, commuovere, impressionare; (*fig.*) mettere una cosa avanti un'altra. || *n.* Barcollamento, *m.* **The staggers,** vertigini, *f.pl.*, (*Vet*). vermocane, *m.*

staggerer, *n.* (*fig.*) Domanda imbarazzante, *f.*

staggering, *n.* Barcollio, *m.*, vacillazione, *f.*, vacillamento, *m.* || *a.* Barcollante, vacillante, travolgente. **A — blow,** un colpo terribile, *m.*

staggeringly, *adv.* Barcollando.

staging ['steidʒiŋ], *n.* (*scaffolding*) Impalcatura, *f.*, ponteggio, *m.*; (*Theat.*) messa in scena, *f.*

stagnancy ['stægnənsi], *n.* Ristagno, ristagnamento, *m.*

stagnant, *a.* Stagnante, ristagnante; inattivo, languido.

stagnate [stæg'neit], *v.i.* Stagnare, ristagnare.

stagnation, *n.* Ristagno, *m.*, inattività, *f.*

stagy ['steidʒi], *a.* Teatrale.

staid [steid], *a.* Posato, contegnoso, grave, serio, sobrio.

staidly, *adv.* Posatamente.

staidness, *n.* Posatezza, serietà, *f.*

stain [stein], *n.* Macchia, chiazza, *f.*; colore, *m.*, tinta, *f.*; sfregio, *m.*, taccia, *f.* || *v.t.* Macchiare, tingere; *v.i.* macchiarsi, tingersi. **Without a — on one's character,** senza macchia.

stained, *a.* Macchiato, tinto; sfregiato. **—-glass,** vetro dipinto, vetro colorato, *m.*; **—-glass window,** vetrata dipinta, *f.*

staining, *n.* Tintura, *f.*, coloramento, *m.*

stainless, *a.* Senza macchia; (*fig.*) immacolato; (*of steel*) inossidabile.

stair [stɛəɪ], *n.* Gradino, scalino, *m.*; grado, *m.* **Stairs,** scale, *f.pl.*, scala, *f.*; scalinata, *f.* **A flight of stairs,** una scalinata, *f.*; **below stairs,** di sotto, nelle stanze di servizio; **downstairs,** giù, dabbasso; **upstairs,** disopra; **to go upstairs,** andar su; **winding —,** scala a chiocciola, *f.*; **—-carpet,** tappeto per le scale, *m.*, passatoia, *f.*; **—-head,** capo di scala, *m.*; **—-rod,** bacchetta per fissare le passatoie, *f.*

staircase, *n.* Scala, *f.*, scale, *f.pl.*, scalone, *m.*

stake [steik], *n.* Palo, paletto, steccone, *m.*; (*martyr's*) rogo, *m.*; (*bet*) scommessa, posta, *f.* || *v.t.* Scommettere, giuocare, arrischiare; fissare con stecconi. **His life is at —,** ce ne va della sua vita; **he died at the —,** morì sul rogo; **he has no — in his country,** non ha legami col suo paese; **to — out,** segnare con stecconi; **—-holder,** chi prende le scommesse; **to — out a claim,** pretendere a, reclamare.

stalactite ['stæləktait], *n.* (*Geol.*) Stalattite, *f.*

stalagmite ['stæləgmait], *n.* (*Geol.*) Stalagmite, *f.*

stale [steil], *a.* Vecchio; stantio; (*of bread*) raffermo. || *n.* (*of horse*) orina, *f.* || *v.i.* (*of horse*) Orinare.

stalemate ['steilmeit], *n.* (*Chess*) Stallo, *m.*; (*fig.*) punto morto, *m.* || *v.t.* Far stallo.

staleness, *n.* Vecchiezza, *f.*

stalk (1) [stɔːk], *n.* Stelo, gambo, *m.*; picciuolo, *m.*; torsolo, *m.*; (*of wine-glass*) piede, *m.*

stalk (2), *v.t.* Cacciare all'agguato, inseguire; *v.i.* camminare a lunghi passi, camminare impettito.

stalker, *n.* Cacciatore, *m.*

stalking, *n.* La caccia, *f.* **— -horse,** pretesto, *m.*

stall (1) [stɔːl], *n.* (*stable*) Stalla, *f.*; (*in market*) baracca, *f.*; (*for newspapers*) chiosco, *m.*; (*Theat.*) poltrona, *f.*; (*in church*) stallo, *m.* || *v.t.* Mettere nella stalla. **—-holder,** mercatino, *m.*

stall (2) *v.t.* Fermarsi, non andare innanzi; posporre; (*Aviat.*) avvitarsi, andare al disotto della velocità che consente il controllo dell'apparecchio. **To — for time,** posporre attività.

stallion ['stæliən], *n.* Stallone, *m.*

stalwart ['stɔːlwəɪt], *a.* Forte, robusto, gagliardo, vigoroso, nerboruto. || *n.* Aderente fidato, *m.*

stamen ['steimen], *n.* (*Bot.*) Stame, *m.*

stamina ['stæminə], *n.* Vigore, *m.*, fibra, robustezza, *f.*; forza di resistenza, *f.*

stammer ['stæməɪ], *v.t.i.* Balbettare, tartagliare.

stammerer, *n.* Tartaglione, balbettatore, balbuziente, *m.*

stammering, *n.* Balbuzie, *f.*

stammeringly, *adv.* Balbettando.

stamp [stæmp], *v.t.* (*to print*) Imprimere, improntare, stampare; (*letters*) affrancare; (*documents*) bollare; (*with the foot*) pestare; (*of a horse*) calpestare; *v.i.* scalpitare; pestare i piedi, battere i piedi. || *n.* Impressione, impronta, *f.* (*implement*) stampiglia, stampa, *f.*; conio, *m.*, ponzone, *m.*; (*on documents*) bollo, *m.*; (*postage*) francobollo, *m.*; (*fig.*) marchio, segno, *m.*; stampo, *m.*, sorta, specie, tempra, *f.*; colpo di piede, *m.* **To — upon,** calpestare, pestare; **to — out,** estirpare, distruggere, sradicare; **this stamps the story as untrue,** ciò mostra che la storia non è vera; **stamped paper,** carta bollata, *f.*; **it bears the — of genius,** porta l'impronta del genio; **I don't like men of his —,** non mi piacciono gli uomini del suo stampo; **receipt —,** bollo di quietanza, *m.*; **stamped addressed envelope,** busta affrancata, *f.*; **—-album,** album per i francobolli, *m.*; **—-collector,** filatelico, *m.*, filatelica, *f.*; **—-collecting,** filatelia, *f.*; **—-duty,** tassa di bollo, *f.*; **—-office,** ufficio del bollo, *m.*

stampede [stæm'piːd], *n.* Fuggi fuggi, serra serra, *m.*, fuga precipitosa, *f.* || *v.i.* Fuggire in disordine; *v.t.* far fuggire.

stamping, *n.* Impressione, *f.*; bollatura, *f.*; affrancatura, *f.*; (*of feet*) calpestio, *m.*

stanch [cp. **staunch**].
stanchion [ˈstæntʃən], *n.* Puntello, appoggio, sostegno, *m.*
stand [stænd], *v.i.* Stare, essere, trovarsi; stare in piedi, star ritto, tenersi in piedi; rizzarsi, alzarsi; rimanere, durare, esistere; stazionare; (*Pol.*) presentarsi come candidato. ‖ *n.* (*stop*) Pausa, sosta, fermata, *f.*; (*position*) posizione, resistenza, *f.*, posto, *m.*; (*stall*) banco, stand, *m.*; (*platform*) tavolato, palco, *m.*; (*support*) appoggio, sostegno, *m.*; (*Sport*) tribuna, *f.*, stand, *m.* **Tell me how matters —,** ditemi come stanno le cose; **How do we — as regards money ?** Come si va a danari? **he is standing at the door,** sta alla porta; **she stood watching him,** stava in piedi a guardarlo; **it stands to reason that,** va da sè che, è ovvio che; **he stands convicted,** è colpevole; **Stand back!** Indietro! State indietro! (*Mil.*) **Stand at ease!** Riposo! **to — in someone's light,** intercettare la luce a qualcuno, fare ombra a qualcuno; **this colour will —,** questo colore è solido; **to — in the way,** impedire il passaggio; **to — in the way of,** opporsi a, fare ostacolo a; **to — aside,** tenersi da parte; **to — aloof, to — off,** tenersi lontano, allontanarsi; **to — back,** tenersi indietro, rinculare; **to — by,** star vicino, assistere; **to — by someone,** aiutare qualcuno, sostenere qualcuno; **to — fast, to — firm,** tener fermo, tener duro; **to — for,** significare, voler dire; presentarsi come candidato; sostenere, favorire; **to — good,** essere vero, esser valido; (*Naut.*) **to — in for the shore,** dirigersi verso la costa; **he stood on a chair,** salì su una sedia; **to — out,** staccarsi, spiccare, risaltare; **to — out against,** opporsi a; **to — out from,** distinguersi fra; **to — over,** essere posposto, essere rinviato; **he stood over me while I did it,** stette a guardarmi mentro lo facevo; **to — still,** star fermo, star quieto; **to — to a promise,** aderire ad una promessa; **to — together,** tenersi insieme, stare uniti, accordarsi; **to — up,** tenersi ritto, alzarsi in piedi; **to — on end,** rizzarsi; **to — up for someone,** difendere qualcuno; **to — well with someone,** essere nelle buone grazie di qualcuno; **Will you — in with us ?** Volete associarvi con noi? **he stood to it that his story was true,** sosteneva che ciò che diceva era vero; **to — up to someone,** far fronte a qualcuno; **to remain standing,** rimanersi in piedi; (*Naut.*) **to — off and on,** bordeggiare; **Stand the jug on the table!** Mettete la brocca sulla tavola! **he stands no nonsense,** non tollera sciocchezze; **I cannot — the strain,** non reggo allo sforzo, non supporto lo strapazzo; **I cannot — him,** non posso soffrirlo; **to — the test,** subire la prova; **to — one's ground,** star saldo, star fermo; **he stood his trial yesterday,** fu processato ieri; **to — fatigue,** reggere alle fatiche; **to — heat,** resistere al caldo; **to — pain,** sopportare il dolore; **to make a — against,** resistere a, opporsi a, far fronte a; **to make a — for,** sostenere, appoggiare; **take my — on the truth,** mi fondo sulla verità; **hat-—,** portacappelli, *m.*; **to come to a —,** far sosta, fermarsi; **—-offish,** altezzoso; **—-offishness,** alterigia, *f.*; **—-up fight,** zuffa accanita, *f.*; **—-up collar,** colletto alto, *m.*
standard [ˈstændəɹd], *n.* Bandiera, *f.*, stendardo, *m.*; insegna, *f.*; tipo, modello, *m.*, norma, *f.*; grado, livello, tenore, *m.* ‖ *a.* Che serve di modello; normale, usuale, medio; definitivo; fissato. **A — work,** un'opera classica, *f.*, un libro fondamentale, *m.*; **a — lamp,** una torcera, una lampada a piede, *m.*; **— prices,** prezzi normali, *m.pl.*; **— rose-tree,** una rosa ad albero, *f.*; **—-bearer,** portabandiera, alfiere, *m.*
standardize, *v.t.* Unificare, standardizzare; (*Chem.*) titolare.
standing, *n.* Lo stare in piedi, *m.*; posizione, condizione, riputazione, *f.*; rango, grado, *m.*; (*duration*) durata, *f.* ‖ *a.* Permanente, stabilito, fisso. **A man of high —,** un uomo di alto rango, un uomo di grande integrità, *m.*; **a dispute of long —,** una disputa di lunga durata, *f.*; **a — rule,** una regola fissa, *f.*; **a — joke,** una barzelletta comune, *f.*; **a — army,** un esercito permanente, *m.*; **— orders,** regolamenti permanenti, *m.pl.*; **— corn,** grano in erba, grano non falciato, *m.*; **a — jump,** un salto a pie'pari, *m.*; **— water,** acqua stagnante, *f.*; **a long- — account,** un conto di vecchia data, *m.*; **a — dish,** un piatto giornaliero, *m.*; **Standing room only!** Soltanto posti in piedi!
standish, *n.* Calamaio, *m.*
standpoint, *n.* Punto di vista, *m.*, visuale, *f.*
standstill, *n.* Arresto, ristagno, *m.*, inazione, fermata, *f.* **I am now brought to a —,** sono adesso ridotto all'inazione; **trade is at a —,** c'è un ristagno negli affari; **to be at a —,** essere inattivo, essere in ristagno, essere a un punto morto.
stanhope [ˈstænəp], *n.* Specie di carrozza leggera, *f.*
stannary [ˈstænəri], *n.* Miniera di stagno, *f.*
stannic [ˈstænik], *a.* (*Chem.*) Stannico.
stanza [ˈstænzə], *n.* Strofa, stanza, *f.*
staple (1) [ˈsteipəl], *n.* Derrata principale, *f.*, prodotto principale, *m.*; (*of cotton, wool*) fiocco, *m.*; (*raw material*) materia prima, *f.*; (*fig.*) soggetto principale. ‖ *a.* Principale, stabilito, fisso. **— commodities,** merci di prima necessità, *f.pl.*; **— industry,** industria base, *f.*; **— of conversation,** soggetto principale della conversazione, *m.*
staple (2), *n.* (*of lock*) Toppa, staffa, *f.*; (*in wall*) grappa, *f.*; (*for nailing down*) gancio, *m.*; chiodo a U, *m.*
star [stɑːɹ], *n.* Stella, *f.*; astro, *m.*; (*fig.*) celebrità, *f.*; (*Cinema.*) divo, *m.*, diva, *f.*; (*Theat.*) stella, *f.*; (*Print.*) stella, *f.*; asterisco, *m.* ‖ *v.t.* Stelleggiare, seminare di stelle, spargere di stelle; (*Print.*) mettere un asterisco; *v.i.* (*Theat.Cinema.*) primeggiare, far la parte di protagonista. **Evening —,** espero, *m.*; **North Star,** stella polare, *f.*; **guiding —,** stella guidatrice, *f.*; **—-gazer,** astronomo, *m.*; **—-shell,** razzo luminoso, *m.*; (*Bot.*) **— of Bethlehem,** stella di Betlemme, *f.*, latte di gallina, *m.*; **—-spangled,** stellato; (*Theat.*) **the — turn,** il numero principale, *m.*
starboard [ˈstɑːɹbəd], *n.* (*Naut.*) Tribordo, *m.*, destra, *f.* ‖ *a.* Di tribordo.

starch [stɑːɹtʃ], *n.* Amido, *m.*; (*fig.*) rigidezza, sostenutezza, *f.* || *v.t.* Inamidare.
starched, *a.* Inamidato.
starchiness, *n.* Inamidatezza, *f.*; (*fig.*) sostenutezza, *f.*
starchy, *a.* Inamidato, amidoso; amidaceo; (*fig.*) rigido, sostenuto.
stare [stɛəɹ], *v.i.* Guardare fisso, fissare gli occhi, spalancare gli occhi, sbarrare gli occhi. || *n.* Sguardo fisso, *m.* **To — at,** guardare, fissare; **he stared her out of countenance,** le fece abbassare gli occhi collo sguardo; **to — someone in the face,** guardare fisso ad alcuno; **ruin stares him in the face,** la rovina gli sovrasta; **the truth stares us in the face,** la verità ci salta agli occhi; **What are you staring at ?** Che cosa guardate così fisso? **it made him —,** gli fece spalancare gli occhi.
starfish [ˈstɑːɹfiʃ], *n.* (*Zool.*) Stella di mare, *f.*
staring [ˈstɛəriŋ], *n.* Il guardare, *m.* || *a.* Chiassoso, vistoso, sguaiato.
staringly, *adv.* Fissamente, con tanto d'occhi.
stark [stɑːɹk], *a.* Rigido, inflessibile. || *adv.* Tutto, affatto, tutt'affatto, completamente. **— naked,** nudo nato; **— staring crazy,** pazzo da catena, pazzo da legare.
starlight [ˈstɑːɹlait], *n.* Luce stellare, luce delle stelle, *f.* || *a.* Stellato. **A — night,** una notte stellata, *f.*
starlike [ˈstɑːɹlaik], *a.* Come una stella; brillante, lucente.
starling [ˈstɑːɹliŋ], *n.* (*Zool.*) Storno, stornello, *m.*
starlit, *a.* Stellato, illuminato dalle stelle.
starred, *a.* Stellato, ornato di stelle; segnato con una stelletta; **Ill- —,** malaugurato.
starry, *a.* Stellato, seminato di stelle, sparso di stelle, lucente.
start [stɑːɹt], *v.i.* (*to begin*) Cominciare, mettersi a; (*to jump*) trasalire, sussultare, sobbalzare; (*to set out*) partire, avviarsi, prendere le mosse; (*to give way*) disgiungersi, staccarsi; *v.t.* (*to begin*) cominciare, principiare; (*game*) levare, scovare; (*to send off*) far partire, mettere in moto; (*to found*) fondare; (*a question*) sollevare; (*of timbers, etc.*) far staccare, far disgiungere. || *n.* (*jump*) Sussulto, balzo, sbalzo, *m.*, scossa, *f.*; (*beginning*) principio, cominciamento, inizio, primo passo, *m.*; (*of journey*) partenza, *f.*; (*in race*) vantaggio, *m.*; avviamento, *m.* **To — again,** ricominciare, ripartire; **to — aside,** balzare da una parte, fare uno scarto; **to — back,** rinculare, balzare indietro; **to — off,** partire; **to — out of one's sleep,** svegliarsi di soprassalto; **to — up,** balzar su, (*fig.*) far nascere, far funzionare; **to — with,** per cominciare; **to — a newspaper,** fondare un giornale; **to — a shop,** aprire un negozio; **to — a controversy,** sollevare una controversia; **by fits and starts,** a salti, a sbalzi, saltuariamente; **a false —,** un passo falso, un cattivo inizio, *m.*, (*Sport*) una falsa partenza, *f.*; **to get the — of,** prendere il vantaggio su; **to give a —,** sussultare, trasalire; **to give someone a — in life,** avviare qualcuno in una carriera; **we shall make an early —,** partiremo di buon'ora.
starter, *n.* Iniziatore, autore, inventore, *m.*; (*Sport*) mossiere, *m.*; (*horse, runner, etc.*) partente, *m.*; (*Elec.*) avviatore, *m.*
starting, *n.* Sussulto, *m.*; partenza, *f.*; inizio, *m.*; avviamento, *m.*; (*Mech.*) messa in moto, *f.* **—-line,** linea di partenza, *f.*; **—-post,** palo di partenza, *m.*
startle [stɑːɹtl], *v.t.* Far trasalire, far sussultare; spaventare, sorprendere.
startling, *a.* Sorprendente, emozionante; spaventevole, terribile.
startlingly, *adv.* Sorprendentemente.
starvation [stɑːɹˈveiʃən], *n.* Fame, inanizione, inedia, *f.*; (*with cold*) assideramento, *m.*
starve [stɑːɹv], *v.t.* Affamare, far morire di fame; (*with cold*) assiderare; (*fig.*) privare di; morire di fame, aver fame; morire di freddo, assiderare. **To — someone to death,** far morire qualcuno di fame; **to — into surrender,** prendere per fame; **to — out,** affamare; **she is starving for a little affection,** è assetata di un po' d'amore.
starveling, *n.* Affamato, famelico, *m.*
starving, *a.* Affamato, famelico.
starwort [ˈstɑːɹwəːɹt], *n.* (*Bot.*) Astero, *m.*
state [steit], *n.* Stato, *m.*, condizione, *f.*; (*body politic*) stato, *m.*; (*rank*) rango, *m.*; (*pomp*) pompa, parata, cerimonia, *f.* || *a.* Dello stato, di stato, statale. || *v.t.* Esporre, affermare, dichiarare, formulare, spiegare; fissare, determinare, stabilire; enunciare. **In a — of,** in uno stato di; (*colloq.*) **he was in quite a — about it,** era tutt'eccitato; **he arrived in great —,** arrivò con grande pompa; **to lie in —,** essere esposto nella camera ardente; **in the present — of affairs,** nelle circostanze attuali; **robes of —,** abiti di parata, *m.pl.*; **a state ball,** un ballo di corte, *m.*; **State Church,** Chiesa di Stato, *f.*; **— documents,** documenti politici, *m.pl.*; **a — prisoner,** un prigioniero di stato; **a — trial,** un processo politico, *m.*; (*Naut.*) **— room,** cabina di lusso, *f.*; **—-controlled,** statizzato; **— insurance,** previdenza sociale, *f.*; **a — reception,** un ricevimento solenne, *m.*; **— apartments,** grandi appartamenti, *m.pl.*; **States General,** Stati generali, *m.pl.*
statecraft [ˈsteitkrɑːft], *n.* Politica, arte dı governo, *m.*
stated, *a.* Fisso, determinato, stabilito.
stateliness, *n.* Maestà, nobiltà, imponenza, *f.*
stately, *a.* Maestoso, nobile, imponente, grandioso, solenne.
statement, *n.* Esposizione, dichiarazione, *f.*; asserzione, affermazione, *f.*; (*Comm.*) rendiconto, rapporto, *m.*; distinta, *f.* **The — is unfounded,** l'asserzione è infondata; **according to his —,** secondo ciò che dice lui; (*Law*) **— of claim,** comparsa, memoria, *f.*; (*Comm.*) **— of affairs,** bilancio, *m.*
statesman [ˈsteitsmən], *n.* Uomo di stato, statista, *m.*
statesmanlike, *a.* Politico, da uomo di stato.
statesmanship, *n.* Politica, arte di governo, *f.*
static, statical [ˈstætik, ˈstætikəl], *a.* Statico.
statics, *n.pl.* Statica, *f.*
station [ˈsteiʃən], *n.* (*position*) Posto, *m.*, posizione, *f.*; (*rank*) rango, grado, stato, *m.*; (*Rail.*) stazione, *f.*; (*Mil.*) guarnigione, *f.*; (*Eccles.*) stazione, *f.*; (*police*) questura, *f.* || *v.t.* Collocare, appostare, mettere. **Coastguard —,** stazione di salvataggio, *f.*; **fire —,** caserma dei pompieri; **to take up one's —,** prendere il proprio posto;

(*Rail.*) **— -master,** capo-stazione, *m.*; **goods- —,** scalo merci, *m.*; (*Mil.*) **to be stationed at,** essere di guarnigione a; **to — sentries,** mettere sentinelle.
stationary [ˈsteiʃənəri], *a.* Stazionario, fisso.
stationer [ˈsteiʃənəɹ], *n.* Cartolaio, *m.* **Stationer's shop,** cartoleria, *f.*
stationery, *n.* Cartoleria, *f.* **— -case,** portafogli, *m.*; **— -rack,** portacarte, *m.*
statist [ˈstætist], *n.* Statistico, esperto di statistica, *m.*
statistic, statistical, *a.* Statistico.
statistician [stætisˈtiʃən], *n.* Statistico, *m.*
statistics, *n.pl.* Statistica, *f.*
statuary [ˈstætjuːəɹi], *n.* Statuaria, scultura, *f.* || *a.* Statuario.
statue [ˈstætjuː], *n.* Statua, *f.*
statuesque [stætjuːˈesk], *a.* Scultorio, come una statua.
statuette [stætjuːˈet], *n.* Figurina, *f.*, stucchino, *m.*
stature [ˈstætjuːɹ], *n.* Statura, *f.*
status [ˈsteitəs], *n.* Rango, *m.*, categoria, condizione, posizione, *f.* **Legal —,** condizione giuridica, *f.*
statute [ˈstætjuːt], *n.* Statuto, *m.*, legge, *f.* **— law,** legge statutaria, *f.*; **— -barred,** caduco, decaduto; **— book,** codice, *m.*
statutory, *a.* Statutario, statutale, prescritto dalla legge.
staunch, stanch [stɔːntʃ], *a.* Fermo, devoto, fido. || *v.t.* Ristagnare; levarsi, estinguere.
stave [steiv], *n.* (*of cask*) Doga, *f.*; (*of ladder*) piuolo, *m.*; (*Poet.*) versetto, *m.*, strofa, *f.*; (*Mus.*) rigo, *m.* || *v.t.* Dogare, fornire di doghe. **To — in,** sfondare; **to — off,** evitare, scansare, allontanare, respingere, ritardare.
stavesacre [ˈsteivzeikəɹ], *n.* (*Bot.*) Stafisagria, *f.*
stay [stei], *v.i.* Stare, rimanere, trattenersi; dimorare, trovarsi; fermarsi, arrestarsi; aspettare; resistere, reggere, durare; *v.t.* (*to stop*) arrestare; (*to postpone*) differire; (*to prop*) puntellare; (*one's hunger*) calmare, soddisfare; (*Naut.*) sostenere con stragli. **To — at home,** stare in casa; **— -at-home,** casalingo, domestico; **to — with a friend,** stare presso un amico; **to — away,** assentarsi; **to — in,** stare in casa; **Stay a minute!** Aspettate un momento! **How long are you staying here?** Quanto tempo vi trattenete qui? **a — -in strike,** uno sciopero bianco, *m.*; **to — the course,** finire la corsa; **staying-power,** resistenza *f.*
stays [steiz], *n pl.* Busto, *m.*; corsetto, *m.* **Stay-lace,** cordoncino da busto, *m.*; **staymaker,** bustaia, *f.*
stead [sted], *n.* Luogo, posto, *m.*; vece, *f.* **In his —,** invece di lui, in suo luogo; **to stand in good —,** giovare molto a, essere utilissimo a.
steadfast [ˈstedfɑːst], *a.* Costante, stabile, fermo, risoluto.
steadfastly, *adv.* Saldamente, costantemente.
steadfastness, *n.* Costanza, fermezza, risoluzione, *f.*
steadily [ˈstedili], *adv.* Fermamente, stabilmente, costantemente; seriamente.
steadiness, *n.* Fermezza, stabilità, costanza, *f.*; serietà, sobrietà, *f.*; regolarità, *f.*
steady, *a.* Fermo, saldo; stabile, costante; serio, sobrio, industrioso; uniforme, regolare; (*of wind*) costante. || *v.t.* Render fermo, tener fermo. **He is not — on his legs,** non è fermo sulle gambe, ha il passo malfermo; **at a — pace,** di buon passo; **to keep —,** tener fermo; **to have a — hand,** aver la mano ferma; **to — down,** mettere la testa a segno; (*Mil.*) **Steady!** Fermi! Fissi!
steak [steik], *n.* Costoletta, fetta, *f.* **Beef —,** bistecca, *f.*
steal [stiːl], *v.t.i.* Rubare, derubare, involare; (*fig.*) guadagnare, cattivare. **To — a kiss,** rubare un bacio; **to — a march on someone,** prendere vantaggio di qualcuno; **they have stolen my purse,** mi hanno rubato la borsa; **to — away,** andarsene di nascosto; **she stole silently up to me,** essa mi s'avvicinò senza rumore; **to — in,** entrare alla chetichella; **time steals on,** il tempo passa; **the mist is stealing over the valley,** la nebbia dilaga nella valle.
stealer, *n.* Ladro, rubatore, *m.* **A — of hearts,** un rubacuori, *m.*
stealing, *n.* Furto, *m.*, ruberia, rapina, ladreria, *f.*
stealth [stelθ], *n.* Segreto, *m.* **By —,** di soppiatto, di nascosto, alla sordina.
stealthily, *adv.* Di soppiatto, furtivamente.
stealthy, *a.* Furtivo, clandestino, nascosto, segreto.
steam [stiːm], *n.* Vapore, *m.* || *v.t.* Vaporizzare; (*Cooking*) cuocere a vapore; *v.i.* fumare; esalare; navigare a vapore. **At full —,** a tutto vapore; **full — ahead,** avanti a tutto vapore; **by —,** a vapore; **to get up —,** caricare la macchina; **to let off —,** scaricare il vapore, (*fig.*) sfogarsi; **under —,** sotto vapore; **to — away,** (*evaporate*) evaporare, (*of ship*) allontanarsi; **to — ahead,** (*fig.*) lavorare a tutta forza; **— -box, — -chest,** cilindro, *m.*; **— -engine,** macchina a vapore, *f.*; **— -gauge,** manometro, *m.*; **— -heating,** riscaldamento a vapore, *m.*; **— -launch,** lancia a vapore, *f.*; **— -pipe,** tubo del vapore, *m.*; **— -power,** forza vapore, *f.*; **— -roller,** rullo compressore, *m.*; **— -tight,** ermetico; **— -tug,** rimorchiatore, *m.*
steamer, steamship, *n.* Piroscafo, bastimento a vapore, *m.*, nave a vapore, *f.*; (*Cooking*) marmitta a vapore, autoclave, *f.*
steaming, *a.* Fumante.
steamy, *a.* Pieno di vapore, vaporoso; appannato. **— windows,** vetri appannati, *m.pl.*
stearic [ˈstiərik], *a.* (*Chem.*) Stearico.
stearin [ˈstiːərin], *n.* Stearina, *f.*
steatite [ˈstiːətait], *n.* (*Geol.*) Steatite, *f.*
steed [stiːd], *n.* (*Poet.*) Cavallo, destriero, *m.*
steel [stiːl], *n.* Acciaio, *m.* (*for sharpening*) acciaiuolo, *m.*; (*of tinder-box*) acciarino, *m.*; (*of corsets*) stecca, *f.* || *v.t.* Indurire, indurare; fortificare, temprare. || *a.* D'acciaio, di ferro. **Cast —,** acciaio fuso, *m.*; **mild —,** acciaio dolce, *m.*; **tempered —,** acciaio temprato, *m.*; **a — pen,** un pennino; **— -clad,** corazzato; **— -engraving,** incisione su acciaio, *f.*; **— -plated,** corazzato, rivestito d'acciaio; **— works,** acciaieria, *f.*
steeliness, *n.* Durezza, inflessibilità, *f.*
steely, *a.* Acciaiato; duro, inflessibile, ferreo.

steelyard, *n.* Stadera.
steep (1) [stiːp], *a.* Ripido, erto; (*colloq.*) ingiusto, salato. || *n.* Erta, salita, costa, *f.*, scoscendimento, precipizio, *m.*
steep (2), *v.t.* Bagnare, inzuppare, infondere, imbevere, saturare; (*fig.*) immergere. **To be steeped in,** essere imbevuto di, essere immerso in; **steeped in slumber,** immerso nel sonno.
steeping, *n.* Bagnatura, *f.*, inzuppamento, *m.*
steeple [ˈstiːpəl], *n.* Campanile, *m.*, guglia, *f.* **—-jack,** conciatetti, *m.*
steeplechase, *n.* Steeplechase, *m.*, corsa ad ostacoli, *f.*
steeply, *adv.* Ripidamente.
steepness, *n.* Ripidezza, ertezza, *f.*
steer (1) [stiəɹ], *v.t.* Timonare, timoneggiare, governare, dirigere, guidare, condurre; (*Motor.*) guidare; *v.i.* sterzare. **To — for,** dirigersi verso; **to — clear of,** scansare, evitare, sterzare.
steer (2), *n.* Giovenco, bue giovine, *m.*
steerage [ˈstiəridʒ], *n.* (*Naut.*) Viraggio, *m.*; timoneria, *f.*; (*class*) posti di terza classe, *m.pl.*; quartieri di prua, *m.pl.* **—-way,** abbrivo, *m.*
steering, *n.* Direzione, *f.*; (*Naut.*) governo, (*Motor.*) **—-wheel,** volante, sterzo, *m.*; (*Naut.*) ruota del timone, *f.*; **— compass,** bussola di rotta, *f.*
steersman, *n.* Timoniere, *m.*
stele [ˈstiːliː], *n.* Stela, stele, *f.*
stellar [ˈsteləɹ], *a.* Stellare.
stellate, stellated [ˈsteleit, ˈsteleited], *a.* Stellato.
stem [stem], *n.* Stelo, gambo, *m.*; (*of tree*) fusto, ceppo, tronco, *m.*; (*of wine-glass*) stelo, gambo, *m.*; (*Mus.*) gamba, *f.*; (*Gram.*) radice, *f.*; (*of tobacco-pipe*) cannello, *m.*; (*Naut.*) prua, *f.*; (*of family*) ramo, *m.* || *v.t.* Arrestare, impedire; arginare; resistere a, opporsi a, lottare contro. **From — to stern,** da prua a poppa; **to — the tide,** resistere alla marea.
stench [stentʃ], *n.* Puzzo, fetore, *m.*
stencil [ˈstensəl], *n.* Stampino, *m.*; (*typing*) stencil, *m.* || *v.t.* Stampinare, imprimere collo stampino.
stenographer [stenˈɔgrəfəɹ], *n.* Stenografo, *m.*, stenografa, *f.*
stenographic, *a.* Stenografico.
stenography, *n.* Stenografia, *f.*
stentorian [stenˈtɔːriən], *a.* Stentoreo.
step [step], *v.i.* Fare un passo; camminare, andare, venire; *v.t.* misurare coi passi; (*Naut.*) drizzare; ballare. || *n.* Passo, *m.*; (*of stairs*) gradino, scalino, *m.*; (*of ladder*) piuolo, *m.*; (*of vehicle*) predellino, montatoio, *m.*; (*of door*) soglia, *f.*; (*fig.*) passo, grado, *m.* **A pair of steps,** una scala doppia, *f.*; **to — across the road,** traversare la strada; **to — aside,** andare in disparte, farsi da un lato; **to — back,** fare un passo indietro; **to — down,** scendere; **to — forward,** avanzarsi, andare avanti, farsi avanti; **to — in,** entrare; intervenire; **he stepped into the car,** salì nell'auto; **he stepped into the boat,** scese nella barca; **Step this way!** Venite qui! Accomodatevi qui! **to — out,** uscire, allungare il passo, affrettare il passo; **to — over,** passare, attraversare; (*of horse*) **to — high,** andare a passo di parata; **— by —,** a passo a passo, passo passo; **to turn one's steps towards,** dirigersi verso; **I know his —,** riconosco il suo passo; **in —,** a passo; **out of —,** fuori passo, **to keep —,** andare di pari passo; **to break —,** cambiare il passo; **to take steps in a matter,** prendere le debite misure in un affare; **a good — away,** assai lontano; **a — in the right direction,** un passo sulla via giusta; **to retrace one's steps,** tornare sui propri passi; **—-ladder,** scala a gradini, *f.*
stepbrother, *n.* Fratellastro, *m.*
stepchild, *n.* Figliastro, *m.*, figliastra, *f.*
stepdaughter, *n.* Figliastra, *f.*
stepfather, *n.* Patrigno, *m.*
Stephen [ˈstiːvən], *n.* Stefano, *m.*
stepmother, *n.* Matrigna, *f.*
steppe [step], *n.* (*Geog.*) Steppa, *f.*
stepping, *n.* Andatura, *f.* **—-stone,** pietra a guado, *f.*, (*fig.*) gradino, marciapiede, *m.*
stepsister, *n.* Sorellastra, *f.*
stepson, *n.* Figliastro, *m.*
stercoraceous [stəːɹkəˈreiʃəs], *a.* Stercoraceo.
stereographic [sterioˈgræfik], *a.* Stereografico.
stereoscope [ˈsterioskoup], *n.* Stereoscopio, *m.*
stereotype [ˈsteriotaip], *n.* Stereotipo, *m.* || *v.t.* Stereotipare.
stereotyped, *a.* Stereotipato.
stereotypy, *n.* Stereotipia, *f.*
sterile [ˈsterail], *a.* Sterile, infecondo.
sterility [steˈriliti], *n.* Sterilità, infecondità, *f.*
sterilize, *v.t.* Sterilizzare.
sterilization, *n.* Sterilizzazione, *f.*
sterling [ˈstəːɹliŋ], *a.* Genuino, puro; di buona lega. **A pound —,** una sterlina, *f.*; **of — worth,** di valore intrinseco.
stern (1) [stəːɹn], *a.* Severo, arcigno, austero, rigido; spietato, implacabile, aspro.
stern (2), *n.* (*Naut.*) Poppa, *f.*; (*colloq.*) deretano, *m.* **—-fast,** ormeggio di poppa, *m.*; **— -post,** dritto di poppa, *m.*; **— -sheets,** poppa, camera, *f.*; **— -tube,** tubo dell'elica, *m.*
sternly, *adv.* Severamente, duramente, aspramente.
sternmost, *a.* (*Naut.*) Il più indietro.
sternness, *n.* Severità, durezza, austerità, rigidezza, *f.*
sternum [ˈstəːɹnəm], *n.* (*Anat.*) Sterno, *m.*
sternutation [stəːɹnjuːˈteiʃən], *n.* Starnutazione, *f.*
stertorous [ˈstəːɹtərəs], *a.* (*Med.*) Stertoroso.
stet [stet], *v.t.* Cancellare una correzione.
stethoscope [ˈsteθoskoup], *n.* Stetoscopio, *m.*
stevedore [ˈstiːvidɔːɹ], *n.* Stivatore, *m.*
stevedoring, *n.* Lo stivare, *m.*
stew [stjuː], *n.* (*Cooking*) Umido, stufato, intingolo, stracotto, *m.*; (*fig.*) impiccio, grattacapo; bordello, *m.* || *v.t.i.* Stufare, cuocere in umido. (*fig.*) **In a —,** nell'imbarazzo, ansioso; **Irish —,** umido di montone e patate, *m.*; **to — in one's own juice,** cuocere nel proprio brodo, frigger nel proprio olio; **—-pan,** casseruola, *f.*, tegame, *m.*
stewed, *a.* Stufato, stracotto, cotto. **— fruit,** frutta cotta, composta di frutta.
stewing, *n.* Il cuocere in umido. || *a.* (*fig.*) Caldissimo. **— pears,** pere da cuocere.

steward [ˈstjuːəɹd], *n.* Fattore, castaldo, agente, *m.*; maggiordomo, *m.*; economo, *f.*; (*Naut.*) cambusiere, dispensiere, *m.*; cameriere, *m.*; (*at function*) cerimoniere, *m.*
stewardess, *n.* (*Naut.*) Cameriera, *f.*
stewardship, *n.* Posto di fattore, *m.*; amministrazione, *f.*
stick (1) [stik], *n.* Bastone, bastoncino, *m.*; (*cudgel*) mazza, *f.*; (*wand*) bacchetta, *f.*; (*cane*) canna, *f.*; (*prop*) puntello, *m.* || *v.t.* Pungere, ferire, trafiggere; mettere, porre. **A — of shaving-soap,** un bastoncino di sapone da barba, *m.*; **a — of sealing-wax,** una stecca di ceralacca, *f.*; **to pick up sticks,** raccogliere legna; (*fig.*) **to get hold of the wrong end of the —,** prender lucciole per lanterne; **to — a pin in,** pungere con uno spillo; **he stuck a flower in his hat,** gli puntò un fiore sul cappello; **to — one's head out of the window,** sporgere la testa dalla finestra; **to — out one's chest,** stare impettito, andar pettoruto.
stick (2), *v.t.* Mettere, porre, fissare, conficcare; attaccare, ingommare, appiccicare; *v.i.* aderire, tenere, attaccarsi, appigliarsi, attenersi; stare, rimanere; fermarsi, arrestarsi. **Stick no bills!** Vietata l'affissione! **to — stamps on a letter,** attaccare francobolli ad una lettera; **Stick close to me!** Tienti vicino! Stammi attaccato! **to — in the mud,** impantanarsi, restare fitto nel fango; **he sticks to it that it is true,** persiste a dire che è vero; **to — to a friend,** mantenersi fedele ad un amico; **to — on,** aderire, attaccarsi, stare; attaccare; **to — out,** sporgere; tener duro; **to — to,** aderire, attaccarsi, perseverare, ostinarsi, stare a; **to — up,** alzarsi, star dritto; **to — up for,** parlare in difesa di; **to — out for better terms,** pretendere condizioni migliori; **the door has stuck,** la porta si è ingranata; **— -in-the-mud,** trottapiano, *m.*; **sticking-plaster,** cerotto adesivo, *m.*, taffetà inglese, *f.*; **sticking-point,** punto di fermata, *m.*
stickiness, *n.* Viscosità, tenacità, *f.*
stickleback [ˈstikəlbæk], *n.* (*Zool.*) Spinarello, *m.*
stickler, *n.* Rigido, pedante, *m.* **He is a great — for propriety,** tiene molto alla convenienza.
sticky, *a.* Appiccicaticcio, attaccaticcio, viscoso, tenace; colloso; (*fig.*) difficile.
stiff [stif], *a.* Rigido, irrigidito; duro, forte; intirizzito, indolenzito; impalato, stecchito; (*fig.*) rigido, severo, rigoroso; stentato, difficile. **As — as a poker,** dritto come un palo; **a — price,** un prezzo salato, *m.*; **a — breeze,** una brezza tesa, *f.*; **to keep a — upper lip,** star duro, tener duro; **— manners,** modi sostenuti, *m.pl.*; **a — bow,** un inchino contegnoso, *m.*; **a — examination,** un esame difficile, *m.*; **a — neck,** un torcicollo, *m.*; **— -necked,** ostinato, caparbio.
stiffen, *v.t.i.* Irrigidire, indurire; intirizzire, rassodare; irrigidirsi, indurirsi; rassodarsi.
stiffening, *n.* Irrigidimento, indurimento, intirizzimento, rassodamento, *m.*; (*lining*) anima, *f.*; armatura, imbottitura, *f.*
stiffly, *adv.* Rigidamente, duramente, severamente; con stento, con difficoltà.
stiffness, *n.* Rigidezza, durezza, severità, rigorosità, difficoltà, *f.*; consistenza, *f.*
stifle [staifl], *v.t.i.* Soffocare, strangolare; (*fig.*) reprimere attutire. **To — a yawn,** soffocare uno sbadiglio.
stifling, *a.* Soffocante.
stigma (1) (pl. **stigmas**) [ˈstigmə], *n.* Stigma, macchia, *f.*; marchio d'infamia, *m.*
stigma (2) (pl. **stigmata**), *n.* (*Eccles.Med.*) Stimmata, stimata, *f.pl.*
stigmatize [ˈstigmətaiz], *v.t.* Stigmatizzare, stimatizzare.
stile [stail], *n.* Barriera, *f.*, cavalcasiepe, cancello, steccato, *m.*
stiletto [stiˈletou], *n.* Stiletto, *m.*; punteruolo, *m.*
still (1) [stil], *a.* Fermo, tranquillo, quieto, cheto, calmo; silenzioso; immobile; (*of drinks*) non spumante. || *v.t.* Calmare, tranquillare, placare, appagare. **— -born,** nato morto; **— waters run deep,** le acque chete rovinano i ponti; **Keep —!** State fermi! **to stand stock- —,** stare completamente immobile; (*Art*) **— life,** natura morta, *f.*
still (2), *n.* Lambicco, *m.* **— -room,** dispensa, cantina, *f.*
still (3), *adv.* Ancora, anche; sempre; nondimeno, tuttavia, pure. **— less,** ancora meno; **— more,** ancor più, a più forte ragione.
stillage [ˈstilidʒ], *n.* Cavalletto per botte, *m.*
stillness, *n.* Immobilità, quiete, calma, *f.*
stilly [ˈstili], *a.* Tranquillo, silenzioso.
stilt [stilt], *n.* Trampolo, *m.* **To walk on stilts,** camminare sui trampoli.
stilted, *a.* Pomposo, affettato, ampolloso.
stimulant [ˈstimjuːlənt], *n.* Stimolante, *m.*
stimulate [ˈstimjuːleit], *v.t.* Stimolare, eccitare.
stimulating, *a.* Stimolante.
stimulation, *n.* Stimolazione, *f.*
stimulus, *n.* Stimolo, *m.*
sting [stiŋ], *n.* (*of insect*) Pungiglione, *f.*, aculeo, *m.*; puntura, *f.*; (*of nettle*) orticata, *f.*; (*fig.*) stimolo, pungolo, *m.* || *v.t.i.* Pungere; offendere, mordere, ferire. **The stings of conscience,** il pungolo del rimorso, *m.*; **stung to the quick,** punto sul vivo.
stingily [ˈstindʒili], *adv.* Meschinamente, grettamente.
stinginess [ˈstindʒines], *n.* Meschinità, grettezza, tirchieria, taccagneria, spilorceria, *f.*
stinging [ˈstiŋiŋ], *n.* Puntura, *f.* || *a.* Pungente, mordente; frizzante. **— nettle,** ortica, ortica bruciante, *f.*
stingy [ˈstindʒi], *a.* Gretto, taccagno, spilorcio, tirchio.
stink [stiŋk], *n.* Puzzo, fetore, *m.* || *v.i.* Puzzare. **— -pot,** cosa puzzolente, *f.*
stinking, *a.* Puzzolente, fetente.
stint (1) [stint], *v.t.* Tenere a stecchetto, limitare, restringere, privare. || *n.* Limite, *m.*, restrizione, *f.*; **To — oneself,** stare a stecchetto; **to — oneself of food,** privarsi del cibo necessario; **without —,** liberalmente, abbondantemente, senza restrizione.
stint (2), *n.* Compito, lavoro, *m.*; compito assegnato, *m.*
stipend [ˈstaipend], *n.* Stipendio, *m.*
stipendiary, *n.a.* Stipendiato, *m.* **— magistrate,** magistrato, *m.*
stipple [stipl], *v.t.* Punteggiare.
stippling, *n.* Punteggiatura, *f.*
stipulate [ˈstipjuːleit], *v.i.t.* Stipulare. **To — for,** stipulare.

stipulation, *n.* Stipulazione, *f.*
stipule ['stipju:l], *n.* (*Bot.*) Stipola, *f.*
stir [stə:ɹ], *v.t.* Muovere, agitare, eccitare, animare; irritare; mescolare; (*the fire*) attizzare; (*the blood*) far bollire; *v.i.* muoversi, scuotersi, agitarsi. ‖ *n.* Movimento, moto, *m.*; trambusto, scompiglio, *m.*; agitazione, *f.* **To — the soup,** rimestare la minestra; **he never stirs a foot,** non si muove mai; **to — up,** eccitare, suscitare; **to — someone's curiosity,** eccitare la curiosità di qualcuno; **to be stirred,** essere emozionato, essere impressionato; **Do not —!** Non disturbatevi! **he is not stirring yet,** non è ancora alzato; **to — abroad,** andar fuori, uscire; **it has made a great —,** ha fatto una grande sensazione; **there is a great — in the town,** la città è tutta in subbuglio.
stirring ['stə:riŋ], *a.* Stimolante, eccitante, emozionante, commovente. **A — speech,** un discorso elettrizzante, *m.*; **— times,** tempi agitati, *m.pl.*
stirrup ['stirəp], *n.* Staffa, *f.* **—-cup,** bicchiere della staffa, *m.*; **—-leather,** staffile, *m.*
stitch [stitʃ], *n.* Punto, *m.*; (*knitting*) maglia, *f.* ‖ *v.t.* Cucire; (*leather*) impuntire. **A — in the side,** una puntura al fianco, *f.*; **to drop a —,** lasciar scappare una maglia; **to take up a —,** ripigliare una maglia; (*Med.*) **to put stitches in,** dare dei punti a; **he has not got a dry — on him,** è bagnato fino alle ossa; **buttonhole- —,** punto a smerlo, *m.*; **to — up,** appuntare, cucir su; **a — stitch in time saves nine,** chi non cuce buchino cuce bucone.
stitching, *n.* Cucitura, *f.*
stithy ['stiði], *n.* (*obs.*) Fucina, incudine, *f.*
stiver ['staivəɹ], *n.* Quattrino, centesimo, *m.*
stoat [stout], *n.* (*Zool.*) Donnola, *f.*
stock [stɔk], *n.* (*of tree, etc.*) Ceppo, tronco, *m.*; (*of gun*) fusto, *m.*; (*of family*) razza, famiglia, schiatta, *f.*; (*of anchor*) ceppo, *m.*; (*die*) filiera, *f.*; (*of plant*) innesto, *m.*, mazza, *f.*; (*flower*) violaciocca, *f.*; (*of goods*) assortimento, *m.*, scorta, *f.*; materiale, *m.*; (*necktie*) cravattone, *m.*; (*Comm.*) valore, titolo, *m.*; (*Cooking*) brodo, consumato, *m.* ‖ *v.t.* Fornire, provvedere, approvvigionare; tenere in magazzino; immettere, popolare. **In —,** in magazzino, disponibile; **live —,** bestiame, *m.*; **rolling —,** materiale rotabile, *m.*; **—-in-trade,** mercanzie, *f.pl.*; **a great — of information,** una quantità d'informazione, *f.*; **to lay in a — of,** fare provvista di; **to take — of,** fare l'inventario di, misurare la capacità di; **—-book,** libro inventarii, *m.*; **—-breeder,** allevatore, *m.*; **—-broker,** agente di cambio, *m.*; **—-jobber,** aggiotatore, speculatore di borsa, *m.*; **—-market,** borsa, *f.*; (*Theat.*) **—-piece,** pezzo di repertorio, *m.*; **—-pot,** marmitta, *f.*; **—-rider,** buttero, *m.*; **—-still,** immobile; **—-taking,** compilazione dell'inventario, *f.*; **—-yard,** recinto pel bestiame, *m.* [cp. **stocks**].
stockade [stɔk'eid], *n.* Stecconata, palizzata, *f.* ‖ *v.t.* Stecconare.
stockdove, *n.* Colombo selvatico, *m.*
stockfish, *n.* Stoccafisso, baccalà, *m.*
stockholder, *n.* Azionista, possessore di titoli, *m.*
stockinet [stɔki'net], *n.* Tessuto elastico, tessuto a maglia, *m.*
stocking, *n.* Calza (lunga), calzetta, *f.* **Nylon stockings,** calze di nailon, *f.pl.*
stocks, *n.pl.* (*Comm.*) Titoli, fondi, valori, *m.pl.*; (*Naut.*) cantiere, *m.*; (*for punishment*) ceppi, *m.pl.*; **— and dies,** filiera guarnita, *f.*; **— and shares,** titoli ed azioni, *m.pl.*
stocky, *a.* Tozzo, tarchiato.
stodgy ['stɔdʒi], *a.* Pesante; indigesto, ingombrante.
Stoic ['stouik], *n.a.* Stoico, *m.*
stoical, *a.* Stoico.
stoicism ['stouisizm], *n.* Stoicismo, *m.*
stoke [stouk], *v.t.* Attizzare, scaldare, alimentare. **—-hold, —-hole,** camera delle caldaie, *f.*
stoker, *n.* Fochista, *m.*
stole (1) [stoul], *n.* Stola, *f.*
stole (2), *p.* of **steal.**
stolen ['stoulən], *a.* Rubato, derubato. **A — glance,** un'occhiata di sottecchi, *f.*
stolid ['stɔlid], *a.* Flemmatico, lento, tardo; stupido.
stolidity [stɔ'liditi], *n.* Flemma, lentezza, stupidità, stolidità, *f.*
stolidly, *adv.* Stolidamente.
stomach ['stʌmək], *n.* Stomaco, *m.*; (*fig.*) cuore, *m.*, voglia, *f.*; appetito, *m.*, fame, *f.* ‖ *v.t.* Mangiare, digerire; (*fig.*) ingoiare. **To have no — for,** non avere lo stomaco per; **on an empty —,** a digiuno; **to turn one's —,** nauseare, far stomaco a; **to — an affront,** ingoiare un'ingiuria; **—-ache,** mal di stomaco, mal di pancia, *m.*; **—-pump,** pompa stomacale, *f.*
stomacher, *n.* Pettorina, *f.*
stomachic [stɔ'mækik], *a.* Stomatico.
stomatitis [stɔmə'taitis], *n.* (*Med.*) Stomatite, *f.*
stone [stoun], *n.* Pietra, *f.*, sasso, *m.*; sassolino, ciottolo, *m.*; (*of fruit*) nocciolo, *m.*; (*of grape*) granello, vinacciuolo, *m.*; (*Med.*) calcolo, *m.*; (*weight*) peso di 14 libbre, *m.* ‖ *a.* Di pietra, di sasso, di laveggio. ‖ *v.t.* Lapidare; (*roads*) acciottolare; (*fruit*) snocciolare; pulire con una pietra speciale. **To have a heart of —,** essere un sasso, avere un cuore di pietra; **meteoric —,** meteorite, aerolito, *m.*; **to leave no — unturned,** non lasciare nulla d'intentato; **the — age,** l'età della pietra, *f.*; **to draw blood from a —,** cavar sangue da una rapa; **to kill two birds with one —,** fare un viaggio e due servizi, prender due piccioni a una fava; **—-blind,** completamente cieco; (*Zool.*) **—-chat,** culbianco, *m.*; **—-cold,** freddo come ghiaccio; **—-cutter** tagliapietra, scalpellino, *m.*; **—-dead,** morto stecchito; **—-deaf,** sordo come una talpa, sordo come una campana; **—-fruit,** frutta a nocciolo, *f.*; **—-mason,** scalpellino, muratore, *m.*; **—-pine,** pino da pinocchi, *m.*; **stone's throw,** tiro di pietra, *m.*; **within a stone's-throw,** a un tiro di pietra; **—-ware,** laveggio, *m.*; **—-work,** muratura, *f.*, lavori in muratura, *m.pl.*
stonily, *adv.* Impassibilmente.
stoniness, *n.* Pietrosità, *f.*; (*fig.*) durezza, insensibilità, *f.*
stoning, *n.* Lapidazione, *f.*
stony, *a.* Pietroso, sassoso; (*fig.*) duro, insensibile. **— -hearted,** duro di cuore, insensibile.

stood, *p.* and *p.p.* of **stand.**
stook [stuːk], *n.* (*Agric.*) Fascio di covoni. || *v.t.* Mettere in covoni.
stool [stuːl], *n.* Sgabello, *m.*; scanno, *m.*; (*Med.*) evacuazione, *f.*, feci, *m.pl.* **Foot-—,** sgabello per i piedi, *m.*; (*fig.*) **to fall between two stools,** fare come l'asino di Buridano; **—-pigeon,** zimbello, *m.*
stoop [stuːp], *v.i.* Piegarsi, chinarsi, inchinarsi, abbassarsi, curvarsi; accondiscendere, cadere; *v.t.* piegare, inchinare, curvare. || *n.* Curvatura, *f.*, ingobbimento, *m.* **She stoops to conquer,** si abbassa per salire; **he stooped to pick it up,** si abbassò per raccoglierlo; **he stoops a good deal,** è molto curvo; **Don't — your head so much!** Non chinare tanto la testa; **he walks with a —,** cammina curvo.
stooping, *a.* Curvo. **— shoulders,** spalle incurvate, *f.pl.*
stoopingly, *adv.* Curvamente.
stop [stɔp], *n.* Pausa, sosta, interruzione, *f.*; (*of trains*) fermata, *f.*; (*punctuation*) punto, *m.*; (*Mus.*) registro, *m.*; (*Mech.*) arresto, *m.*; (*Phot.*) diaframma, *m.*, apertura, *f.* || *v.t.* Arrestare, fermare, trattenere, far cessare, metter fine a; chiudere, turare; (*a wound*) stagnare; (*a tooth*) otturare, piombare; (*payment*) cessare, sospendere; (*wages*) trattenere; (*to intercept*) intercettare; *v.i.* fermarsi, arrestarsi; stare, rimanere, trattenersi. **Full —,** punto fermo, *m.*; **to put a — to,** porre fine a; (*for trams, etc.*) **optional —, request —,** fermata facoltativa, *f.*; **I shall — him from doing that,** gl'impedirò di far ciò; **to — payment,** cessare i pagamenti; **to — the engine,** fermare la macchina; **Stop thief!** Al ladro! **—-gap,** stoppabuchi, riempitivo, *m.*; **—-press,** recentissime, *f.pl.*; **—-watch,** cronometro, *m.*; (*in telegrams*) stop.
stoppage [ˈstɔpidʒ], *n.* Interruzione, pausa, sosta, fermata, *f.*; ostruzione, *f.*, impedimento, *m.*; sciopero, *m.*
stopper, *n.* Turacciolo, tappo, *m.* || *v.t.* Turare, tappare.
stopping, *n.* Riempitura, *f.*; (*of teeth*) piombatura, *f.*
storage [ˈstɔːridʒ], *n.* Magazzinaggio, *m.* **— battery,** accumulatore, *m.*
store [stɔːɹ], *n.* Provvista, provvisione, *f.*; quantità, abbondanza, *f.*; riserva, *f.*, deposito, *m.*; (*shop*) negozio, *m.*, bottega, *f.*; (*fig.*) tesoro, *m.* || *v.t.* Fornire, approvvigionare, munire; conservare, immagazzinare, metter in serbo, tesoreggiare. **To — up,** accumulare, ammassare; **in —,** in riserva, da parte, in serbo; **there's a surprise in — for you,** c'è una sorpresa in serbo per voi; **to lay in a — of,** fare una provvista di; **to set — by,** far gran caso di; **—-house,** deposito, magazzino, *m.*; (*fig.*) tesoro, *m.*; **—-keeper,** magazziniere, dispensiere, *m.*; negoziante, *m.*; **—-room,** dispensa, guardarobe, *f.*; (*Naut.*) **—-ship,** nave trasporto, *f.*
storey, story [ˈstɔːri], *n.* Piano, *m.*
storied (1), *a.* Con piani. **A 4- — house,** una casa di quattro piani, *f.*
storied (2), *a.* Istoriato.
stork [stɔːɹk], *n.* (*Zool.*) Cicogna, *f.* **Stork's-bill,** geranio, *m.*
storm [stɔːɹm], *n.* Tempesta, *f.*, temporale, *m.*; bufera, procella, burrasca, *f.*; uragano, *m.* || *v.t.* (*Mil.*) Dare l'assalto a, assalire, prendere d'assalto; *v.i.* infierire, imperversare; infuriare, smaniare. **A — in a teacup,** una burrasca in un bicchiere, *f.*; **—-beaten,** sbattuto dalla tempesta; **—-belt,** zona delle tempeste, *f.*; **—-bound,** in preda alla tempesta; **—-centre,** zona tempestosa, *f.*, focolaio, *m.*; **—-cloud,** nube tempestosa, *f.*, nembo, *m.*; (*Zool.*) **—-cock,** tordo, *m.*; **—-cone,** banderuola, *f.*, anemoscopio. *m.*; (*Naut.*) **—-sail,** vela di fortuna, *f.*; **—-signal,** segnale di tempesta, *m.*
stormily, *adv.* Violentemente.
storminess, *n.* Tempestosità, *f.*
storming, *n.* Assalto, *m.*; (*fig.*) violenza, furia, *f.* **—-party,** colonna d'assalto, *f.*
stormy, *a.* Tempestoso, burrascoso, procelloso; fortunoso. (*Zool.*) **— petrel,** procellaria, *f.*; **a — life,** una vita fortunosa, *f.*
story (1) [ˈstɔːri], *n.* (*history*) Storia, *f.*; (*narrative*) racconto, *m.*, narrazione, *f.*; fiaba, storiella, novella, *f.*; aneddoto, *m.*; (*falsehood*) bugia, fandonia, *f.*; (*plot*) intreccio,. *m.* **To make a long — short,** per farla breve; **that is quite another —,** è un altro paio di maniche; **the — goes,** si dice, raccontano che; **a short —,** una novella, *f.*; **a funny —,** un aneddoto divertente, *m.*, una storiella, *f.*; **always the same —,** la solita storia, *f.*; **to tell stories,** dir fandonie, contarle grosse; **—-book,** libro di racconti, *m.*; **—-teller,** narratore, novelliere, *m.*; bugiardo, *m.*
story (2) [cp. **storey**].
stoup [stuːp], *n.* Boccale, *m.*; acquasantiere, *f.*
stout (1) [staut], *a.* Forte, robusto, gagliardo; grasso, corpulento, pingue; coraggioso. **To grow —,** ingrassare; **—-hearted,** coraggioso.
stout (2), *n.* Birra nera, *f.*, stout, *m.*
stoutly, *adv.* Vigorosamente, fortemente, coraggiosamente.
stoutness, *n.* (*of body*) Corpulenza, pinguedine, *f.*; (*of heart*) robustezza, gagliardia, *f.*
stove [stouv], *n.* Stufa, *f.*, fornello, *m.*; (*for central-heating*) calorifero, *m.* **Gas- —,** stufa a gas, *f.*; **oil- —,** stufa a olio, *f.*; **—-pipe,** tubo della stufa, *m.*; **—-pipe hat,** cappello a cilindro, *m.*
stow [stou], *v.t.* Assettare, stivare; mettere, mettere via; (*Naut.*) stivare; (*colloq.*) smettere, finire.
stowage, *n.* Assettatura, collocazione, *f.*; (*Naut.*) stivaggio, *m.*
stowaway, *n.* (*Naut.*) Passeggiero clandestino, *m.* || *v.i.* Imbarcarsi clandestinamente.
strabismus [stræˈbizməs], *n.* (*Med.*) Strabismo, *m.*
straddle [strædl], *v.t.* Mettersi a cavalcioni, inforcare; *v.i.* allargare le gambe, stare a cavalcioni.
straggle [strægl], *v.i.* Sparpagliare, spargersi, dilungarsi, sbandarsi, smarrirsi; arrabattarsi; allungarsi.
straggler, *n.* Sbandato, fuorviato, spedato, *m.*
straggling, straggly, *a.* Sparpagliato, sparso. **A — village,** un paese sparso.
straggling, *adv.* Fuori via, sbandatamente.
straight [streit], *a.* Dritto, diritto; ritto, eretto; giusto, onesto, vero, schietto. || *adv.*

Dritto, direttamente, difilato; addiritura. **— hair,** capelli lisci, *m.pl.*; **to put —,** mettere in assetto, ordinare, accomodare; **that picture is not —,** quel quadro non è diritto; **to hit — from the shoulder,** essere molto franco; **I told him — out,** glielo dissi francamente; **he cannot see —,** non può veder bene; **— away,** subito, presto, immediatamente; **I cannot tell you — off,** non posso dirvelo così subito; **keep — on,** andate dritto; (*Boxing*) **a — left,** un sinistro diritto; **a — line,** una linea retta, *f.* **— -edge,** regolo, *m.*

straighten, *v.t.* Assettare, aggiustare; accomodare; drizzare, raddrizzare. **To — oneself up,** raddrizzarsi.

straightforward [streit'fɔːrwəd], *a.* Franco, onesto, schietto, retto, chiaro; semplice.

straightforwardly, *adv.* Schiettamente.

straightforwardness, *n.* Franchezza, onestà, schiettezza, *f.*

straightness, *n.* Dirittura, *f.*; rettitudine, *f.*

straightway, *adv.* Subito, presto, immediatamente.

strain (1) [strein], *v.t.* Tendere, forzare, sforzare; violentare, costringere; (*to hug*) serrare; (*to sprain*) storcere; (*the eyes*) far male a; *v.i.* sforzarsi, affaticarsi, ingegnarsi. ‖ *n.* Sforzo, *m.*, tensione, *f.*; storcimento, *m.* **To — every nerve,** fare ogni sforzo; **to — one's eyes,** affaticarsi gli occhi; **the rowers — at the oars,** i rematori arrancano furiosamente; **to — at the leash,** tirare il guinzaglio; **on the —,** teso.

strain (2), *v.t.* (*a liquid*) Colare, filtrare.

strain (3), *n.* Razza, famiglia, schiatta, *f.*; ritmo, motivo, *m.* **In the same —,** nello stesso tono; **there is a — of cruelty in him,** c'è qualchecosa di crudele in lui; **these dogs are of the same —,** questi cani sono della stessa razza.

strained, *a.* Sforzato, teso. **— relations,** rapporti tesi, *m.pl.*

strainer, *n.* Colatoio, colino, filtro, *m.*

straining, *n.* Tensione, *f.*, sforzo, *m.*; esagerazione, *f.*; colatura, *f.*

strait [streit], *a.* Stretto, serrato, angusto. **— -laced,** rigido, severo, rigoroso, inflessibile; **— -jacket, — -waistcoat,** camicia di forza, *f.*

straiten, *v.t.* Ristringere. **In straitened circumstances,** in ristrettezze.

straitness, *n.* Strettezza, *f.*

straits, *n.pl.* Strette, strettezze, difficoltà, *f.pl.*; (*Geog.*) braccio di mare, stretto, *m.* **The Straits of Dover,** il passo di Calais, *m.*; **the Straits of Gibraltar,** lo stretto di Gibilterra, *m.*

strand [strænd], *n.* Spiaggia, *f.*, lido, *m.*; sponda, *f.*; (*of rope*) filo, *m.* ‖ *v.t.i.* Incagliare, arenare; arenarsi, dare in secco. **To be stranded,** essere a secco, essere arenato, essere incagliato.

strange [streindʒ], *a.* Strano, strambo, singolare, curioso, straordinario; straniero; non pratico, non abituato; sconosciuto. **He is very — in his manner,** ha dei modi strani; **truth is stranger than fiction,** la verità è più straordinaria d'un romanzo; **I am quite — to the place,** sono poco pratico del luogo; **Strange to say!** Cosa strana!

strangely, *adv.* Stranamente, curiosamente, straordinariamente.

strangeness, *n.* Stranezza, singolarità, straordinarietà, *f.*

stranger, *n.* Un estraneo; forestiero, sconosciuto, *m.*; forestiera, sconosciuta, *f.* **He is a — to me,** mi è sconosciuto; **I am a — here,** non sono pratico di questi luoghi; **to make a — of someone,** trattare qualcuno da estraneo; **he is a — to fear,** non conosce la paura; **you are quite a —,** voi non vi fate mai vedere.

strangle [stræŋgl], *v.t.* Strangolare, strozzare, soffocare.

strangler, *n.* Strangolatore, *m.*; strozzatore, *m.*

strangles, *n.pl.* (*Vet.*) Stranguglione, *m.*

strangling, *n.* Strangolatura, *f.*; soffocazione, *f.*

strangulated ['stræŋgjuːleited], *a.* Strangolato, strozzato. **— hernia,** ernia strozzata, *f.*

strangulation, *n.* Strangolatura, strozzatura, *f.*

strangury ['stræŋgjuːri], *n.* (*Med.*) Stranguria, *f.*

strap [stræp], *n.* Cinghia, coreggia, *f.*; bandella, *f.*; guinzaglio, *m.* ‖ *v.t.* Cinghiare, cingere, stringere con cinghia, attaccare con cinghia; (*to flog*) sferzare. **To — up a wound,** fasciare una ferita.

strapper, *n.* Un pezzo d'uomo, *m.*

strapping, *a.* Grande, robusto, gagliardo. **A — girl,** una ragazzona, *f.*, un pezzo di ragazza, *m.*; **a — young fellow,** un giovanottone, *m.*

Strasbourg ['stræzbəːɹg], *n.* (*Geog.*) Strasburgo, *m.*

stratagem ['strætədʒəm], *n.* Stratagemma, *m.*

strategic, strategical [strə'tiːdʒik, strə'tiːdʒikəl], *a.* Strategico.

strategist, *n.* Stratega, *m.*

strategy, *n.* Strategia, *f.*

stratification [strætifi'keiʃən], *n.* Stratificazione, *f.*

stratified ['strætifaid], *a.* Stratificato.

stratiform, *a.* Stratiforme.

stratify ['strætifai], *v.t.* Stratificare.

stratocruiser [stræto'kruːzəɹ], *n.* Grande aeroplano da trasporto, *m.*

stratosphere ['strætosfiəɹ], *n.* Stratosfera, *f.*

stratum (pl. **strata**) ['streitəm streitə], *n.* Strato, *m.*

straw [strɔː], *n.* Paglia, *f.*; festuca, *f.* ‖ *a.* Di paglia. **This is the last —,** questo è il colmo; **not to be worth a —,** non valer nulla; **I don't care a —,** non me ne importa nulla; **a man of —,** un uomo di paglia, un prestanome, *m.*; **— -bottomed,** col fondo di paglia; **— -coloured,** color paglia, paglierino; **— -hat,** cappello di paglia, *m.*, paglietta, *f.*; **— -mat,** stuoia, *f.*; **— -mattress,** paglericcio, *m.*

strawberry, *n.* Fragola, *f.* **— -bed,** fragoleto, *m.*; **— -plant,** fragola, *f.*

strawboard, *n.* Cartone di paglia, *m.*

stray [strei], *v.i.* Fuorviarsi, sviarsi, smarrirsi, sperdersi. ‖ *a.* Smarrito, disperso, sperso; (*fig.*) fortuito, casuale; randagio. **To — from,** allontanarsi da, dilungarsi da; **a — dog,** un cane randagio, *m.*

streak [striːk], *n.* Striscia, stria, linea, riga, *f.*; (*fig.*) vena, *f.*, tantino, *m.* ‖ *v.t.* Striare, screziare. **Like a — of lightning,** come un lampo, comme un razzo.

streaked, *a.* Striato, screziato.
streaky, *a.* Striato, screziato; (*of meat*) lardellato.
stream [stri:m], *n.* Corrente, *f.*; ruscello, corso d'acqua, fiume, torrente, *m.*; (*fig.*) fiume, profluvio, *m.*; marea, valanga, *f.* ‖ *v.i.* Scorrere; sgorgare, scaturire; irraggiare; ondeggiare; sventolare. **Against the —,** contro corrente; **to go with the —,** seguir la corrente; **to — with blood,** grondare sangue; **to — with perspiration,** colare sudore; **the flag streamed in the wind,** la bandiera ondeggiava al vento; **—-lined,** affusolato, aerodinamico; (*Motor.*) **— line,** linea slanciata, *f.* **—-lining,** aerodinamismo, *m.*
streamer, *n.* Banderuola, *f.*, pennoncello, *m.*
streaming, *a.* Bagnato, grondante.
streamlet, *n.* Ruscelletto, *m.*
street [stri:t], *n.* Strada, via, *f.* **The high —,** la strada principale, *f.*; **to go down the —,** andar giù per la strada; **to walk the streets,** battere la città; **to pick up out of the —,** raccattare nella strada; **— cries,** grida di venditori ambulanti, *m.pl.*; **— arab,** monello, birichino, *m.*; **—-car,** tram, *m.*; **—-lamp,** lampione, *m.*; **—-organ,** organetto, *m.*; **—-sweeper,** spazzino, *m.*, macchina spazzatrice, *f.*; **—-walker,** prostituta, *f.*
strength [streŋθ], *n.* Forza, potenza, energia, *f.*, potere, vigore, *m.*; (*of materials*) resistenza, *f.*; (*of troops, etc.*) effettivi, *m.pl.* **On the — of,** in forza di; **that is beyond my —,** ciò è al di là delle mie forze; **in full —,** al completo; **by sheer — of will,** per pura forza di volontà; **to regain —,** riprendere le forze, rimettersi, ristabilirsi.
strengthen, *v.t.* Fortificare, rinforzare, rafforzare, corroborare, rinvigorire; rinforzare.
strengthening, *a.* Fortificante, rinforzante; (*Med.*) corroborante.
strenuous [ˈstrenjuːəs], *a.* Strenuo, energico, vigoroso, gagliardo; attivo, intenso.
strenuously, *adv.* Strenuamente, energicamente.
strenuousness, *n.* Strenuità, energia, *f.*, vigore, *m.*
streptomycine [streptouˈmaisiːn], *n.* Streptomicina, *f.*
stress [stres], *n.* Forza, *f.*, sforzo, *m.*; enfasi, *f.*; (*Med.*) tensione, *f.*; (*Gram.*) accento tonico, *m.*; (*Mech.*) pressione, *f.*; (*of weather*) violenza, *f.* ‖ *v.t.* Dar forza a, insistere su, accentuare; (*Mus.*) scandire. **To lay — on,** insistere sopra.
stretch [stretʃ], *v.t.* Tendere, tirare; distendere stendere; forzare, sforzare; allargare, ampliare, ingrandire; esagerare, stiracchiare; *v.i.* stendersi, estendersi, allungarsi, spaziare; allargarsi, ampliarsi, ingrandirsi. ‖ *n.* Estensione, distesa, *f.*; tensione, *f.*, sforzo, *m.*; tratto, spazio, *m.*; (*colloq.*) incarceramento, *m.* **To — a point,** fare un'eccezione, lasciar correre; **to — oneself,** stirarsi; **to — out at full length,** sdraiarsi, giacere lungo disteso; **to — one's legs,** sgranchire le gambe; **to — out one's hand,** stendere la mano; **to — trousers,** stirare i calzoni; **to — away to,** stendersi verso; **it stretches like elastic,** si allunga come l'elastico; **by no — of the imagination,** neanche per sogno; **two hours at a —,** due ore di seguito; **on the —,** teso; **a — of sea,** un tratto di mare, *m.*; **at a —,** d'un tratto.
stretcher, *n.* (*for the injured*) Barella, *f.*; (*in rowing-boat*) pedagna, *f.*; (*for gloves*) allargaguanti, *m.*; (*for shoes*) forma, *f.* **—-bearer,** portabarelle, portaferiti, *m.*
stretching, *n.* Allargamento, ingrandimento, *m.*
strew [stru:], *v.t.* Spargere, sparpagliare, seminare.
stria (pl. **striae**) [ˈstraiə, ˈstraii:], *n.* Stria, *f.*
striated, *a.* Striato.
striation, *n.* Striazione, striatura, *f.*
strickle [strikl], *n.* (*Mech.*) Rasiera, *f.*
strict [strikt], *a.* Esatto, stretto, preciso; severo, rigido, austero, rigoroso.
strictly, *adv.* Esattamente, strettamente, severamente. **— speaking,** a dire il vero, in senso stretto.
strictness, *n.* Esattezza, strettezza, precisione, *f.*; severità, rigidezza, austerità, *f.*, rigore, *m.*
stricture [ˈstriktʃəɹ], *n.* Rimprovero, biasimo, *m.*, censura, *f.*; (*Med.*) restringimento, *m.*
stride [straid], *n.* Passo lungo, *m.*, andatura, *f.* ‖ *v.i.* Camminare a passi lunghi, sgambare; inforcare. (*fig.*) **To make rapid strides,** far gran progresso; **with giant strides,** a passi di gigante; **to take in one's —,** fare una cosa facilmente, come bere un bicchiere d'acqua; **with rapid strides,** di buon passo, a passo accelerato; **to — over,** scavalcare.
strident, *a.* Stridente.
stridulant, *a.* Stridulo.
strife [straif], *n.* Lotta, contesa, *f.*, conflitto, *m.*
strike [straik], *v.t.* Battere, picchiare, colpire, percuotere; (*the hour*) suonare; (*a balance*) stabilire; (*a bargain*) conchiudere; (*a light*) fare; (*a match*) accendere; (*a tent*) levare; (*a flag*) ammainare; (*dumb, etc.*) rendere; *v.i.* (*of workmen*) scioperare; (*of clock*) suonare; (*Bot.*) attecchiare, abbarbicare. ‖ *n.* Sciopero, *m.* **To — one's hand on the table,** battere il pugno sulla tavola; **he struck the weapon aside,** deviò l'arma con un colpo; **the ship struck on a rock,** la nave urtò uno scoglio; **I struck upon an idea,** mi venne un'idea; **it struck me that . . .,** mi venne in mente che . . .; **How does it — you ?** Come vi pare? (*fig.*) **to — at the root of,** scuotere le basi di; **to — the track,** trovare la traccia; **to — sparks out of,** fare sprizzare scintille da; **to — someone blind,** acciecare qualcuno; **to — out a line for oneself,** farsi una via propria; **to — dumb,** ammutolire, ridurre al silenzio; **to — an attitude,** darsi una posa; **to — up an acquaintance with,** fare la conoscenza di; **to — work,** cessare di lavorare, scioperare; **to — root,** attecchire, metter radici; (*fig.*) **I was struck all of a heap,** fui proprio sbalordito; **to — down,** abbattere, atterrare; **to — in,** interporre, interrompere; **to — off,** (*cancel*) cancellare, (*to cut off*) tagliare, mozzare; (*Print.*) tirare; **to — oil,** trovare petrolio; **to — up,** cominciare a suonare; **to — through,** penetrare; **I was much struck by . . .,** rimasi molto colpito da . . .; **to — at,** tentare di colpire; **to — home,** colpire nel segno, colpire in pieno; **to — out,**

cancellare, lanciarsi, estendersi, menar colpi, mettersi a nuotare; **on —,** in sciopero; **to go on —,** scioperare; **stay-in- —,** sciopero bianco, *m.*; **— -breaker,** crumiro, *m.*

striker, *n.* (*workman*) Scioperante, *m.*; (*of firearm*) percussore, *m.*

striking, *a.* Sorprendente, straordinario, impressionante. (*Mil.*) **— -force,** massa d'attacco, *f.*; **— -clock,** orologio a suoneria, *m.*

strikingly, *adv.* Singolarmente, meravigliosamente.

string [striŋ], *n.* (*for parcels, etc.*) Spago, *m.*, corda, *f.*; (*of musical instrument*) corda, *f.*; (*of apron, etc.*) cintura, *f.*; (*of beads*) filza, *f.*, filo, *m.*; (*a row*) fila, *f.* || *v.t.* Legare con spago; fornire di corde; infilare; (*violin, etc.*) mettere le corde a. **To harp on one —,** toccare sempre la stessa corda; **to have two strings to one's bow,** tenere il piede in due scarpe; (*fig.*) **to pull the strings,** tirare i fili; **tied to his mother's apron-strings,** attaccato alle gonne della mamma; **to — up,** impiccare; **to — up one's nerves,** tendere i nervi; **— -bag,** borsa a rete, *f.*; (*Mus.*) **— band,** orchestra di strumenti a corda, *f.*; (*Mus.*) **the strings,** le corde, *f.pl.*; (*Arch.*) **— -board,** traversa delle scale, *f.*; (*Arch.*) **— -course,** cordone, *m.*

stringed, *a.* A corda.

stringency ['strindʒənsi], *n.* Rigore, *m.*, severità, *f.*; urgenza, *f.*

stringent, *a.* Rigoroso, severo, stretto, stringente; urgente.

stringless, *a.* Senza corda.

stringy, *a.* Fibroso; filamentoso.

strip [strip], *v.t.* Denudare, spogliare; (*to rob*) svaligiare; (*a tree*) sfogliare, sfrondare; (*Naut.*) smontare, disattrezzare; privare di; *v.i.* spogliarsi, svestirsi. || *n.* Striscia, lista, banda, *f.*; nastro, *m.* **A — of land,** una striscia di terra, *f.*; **to — off,** toglier via, strappare; **to — of,** spogliare di.

stripe [straip], *n.* Riga, lista, stria, striscia, *f.*; (*with whip*) sferzata, staffilata, *f.*; (*Mil.*) gallone, *m.*

striped, *a.* Rigato, listato, a righe.

stripling ['stripliŋ], *n.* Giovinetto, adolescente, *m.*

stripping, *n.* Spogliamento, *m.*

strive [straiv], *v.i.* Sforzarsi, ingegnarsi; lottare, combattere; contendere. **To — against,** lottare contro; **to — with,** lottare con, contendere con; **to — hard to,** fare ogni sforzo per.

striving, *n.* Lotta, *f.*, sforzi, *m.pl.*

strode *p.* of **stride.**

stroke [strouk], *n.* Colpo, *m.*; tratto, *m.*; pennellata, *f.*; (*Swimming*) bracciata, *f.*; (*in writing*) asta, *f.*; (*an animal*) lisciata, carezza, *f.*; (*in boat's crew*) capovoga, *m.*; (*in rowing*) palata, remata, *f.*; (*Med.*) colpo apoplettico, *m.* || *v.t.* Lisciare, accarezzare, dare una lisciata a, passare la mano sopra. **At a —,** d'un tratto; **a bold —,** un colpo ardito, *m.*; **on the — of midnight,** al batter della mezzanotte; **a — of luck,** un colpo di fortuna, *m.*; **a — of bad luck,** un colpo di sfortuna, *m.*; **to row —,** fare il capovoga; **a — of the oar,** una remata, *f.*; (*Swimming*) **breast- —,** nuoto a rana, *m.*; **side- —,** nuoto alla marinara, *m.*; **a piston —,** una corsa di stantuffo, *f.*; (*fig.*) **to — someone the wrong way,** andare a contrappelo a qualcuno.

stroking, *n.* Accarezzamento, *m.*, carezze, *f.pl.*; lisciatina, *f.*

stroll [stroul], *n.* Passeggiatina, giratina, *f.* || *v.i.* Andare a zonzo, girellare, girovagare. **To go for a —,** fare una passeggiatina, fare due passi; **to — about,** girellare qua e là, bighellonare.

stroller, *n.* Girandolone, *m.*

strolling, *a.* Ambulante, girovago, errante. **— players,** attori girovaghi, comici vaganti, *m.pl.*

strong [strɔŋ], *a.* Forte, robusto, gagliardo, valido, potente; vigoroso, energico; solido, sodo, fermo; duro, resistente; (*of liquor*) alcoolico; (*of tea*) nero; (*of butter, etc.*) rancido; (*of cheese*) piccante; (*Gram.*) forte, irregolare. **An army 3,000 strong,** un esercito di tre mila, *m.*; **a — light,** una luce vivida, *f.*; **— in the arm,** forte di braccio; **with a — hand,** con una mano forte; **to smell —,** sapere di rancido; **Are you quite — again ?** Siete proprio rimesso? **he is very — in Italian,** è molto forte in Italiano; **— language,** parole grosse, *f.pl.*; parole ferme, *f.pl.*; (*colloq.*) **going —,** arzillo, vegeto, vigoroso; **one's — point,** il forte di uno; **— -box,** forziere, *m.*, cassa forte, *f.*; **— -minded,** di mente virile, ardito, risoluto; **— -room,** camera di sicurezza, camera blindata, *f.*

stronghold, *n.* Fortezza, *f.*; (*fig.*) roccaforte, *f.*

strongly, *adv.* Forte, fortemente, energicamente.

strontium ['strɔnʃəm], *n.* (*Min.*) Stronzio, *m.*

strop [strɔp], *n.* Cuoio da rasoio, *m.*, coramella, *f.* || *v.t.* Affilare, ripassare.

strophe ['stroufi], *n.* (*Poet.*) Strofa, *f.*

strove, *p.* of **strive.**

struck, *p.* of **strike.**

structural ['strʌktʃju:rəl], *a.* Strutturale.

structure ['strʌktʃəɹ], *n.* Struttura, *f.*; costruzione, fabbrica, *f.*; edifizio, monumento, *m.*; (*fig.*) impalcatura, *f.*

struggle [strʌgl], *n.* Lotta, *f.*, sforzo, *m.* || *v.i.* Lottare, combattere; dimenarsi, dibattersi. **The — for existence,** la lotta per l'esistenza, *f.*; **he was struggling to speak,** si sforzava di parlare; **to — with an illness,** lottare contro una malattia.

struggler, *n.* Lottatore, combattente, *m.*

struggling, *n.* Lotta, *f.* || *a.* Lottante, di lotta.

strum [strʌm], *v.i.* Strimpellare.

strumming, *n.* Strimpellamento, *m.*

strumpet ['strʌmpet], *n.* Prostituta, meretrice, *f.*

strut (1) [strʌt], *v.i.* Pavoneggiarsi, andar impettito, incedere tronfio. || *n.* Tronfiezza, *f.*, modo impettito, *m.*

strut (2), *n.* Puntello, *m.*; pezzo di rinforzo, *m.*; (*Aviat.*) montante, *m.*

struttingly, *adv.* Pavoneggiandosi, tronfiamente.

strychnin, strychnine ['striknin], *n.* (*Chem.*) Stricnina, *f.*

stub [stʌb], *n.* Ceppo, troncone, *m.*; (*of pencil, cigar, etc.*) mozzicone, *m.*; (*of cheque, etc.*) *etc.*) madre, *f.* || *v.t.* Sradicare; urtare contro. **To — out,** estinguere.

stubble [stʌbl], *n.* Stoppia, *f.* **—-field,** campo di stoppie, *m.*
stubbly, *a.* Pieno di stoppie, stoppioso.
stubborn [ˈstʌbəɹn], *a.* Ostinato, caparbio, testardo, duro, inflessibile, pertinace; refrattario.
stubbornly, *adv.* Ostinatamente.
stubbornness, *n.* Ostinatezza, ostinazione, *f.*; caparbietà, testardaggine, *f.*; inflessibilità, tenacia, *f.*
stucco, stucco-work [ˈstʌkou, ˈstʌkouwəːɹk], *n.* (*Arch.*) Stucco, *m.*
stuck [stʌk], *p.* and *p.p.* of **stick. —-up,** arrogante, borioso.
stud (1) [stʌd], *n.* (*for shirt*) Bottoncino, *m.*; (*ornament*) borchia, *f.*; (*nail*) chiodo, *m.* || *v.t.* Guarnire di borchie. **Studded crossing,** passaggio tracciato da chiodi, *m.*
stud (2), *n.* Scuderia, *f.*; stabilimento di allevamento, *m.* **—-book,** registro di animali di puro sangue, *m.*; **—-farm,** scuderia di allevamento, *f.*; **—-groom,** capo allevatore, *m.*; **—-horse,** stallone, cavallo da razza, *m.*
studding-sail [ˈstʌnsəl], *n.* (*Naut.*) Coltellaccio, *m.*
student [ˈstjuːdənt], *n.* Studente, *m.*, studentessa, *f.*; allievo, *m.*; allieva, *f.*; studioso, *m.*
studied [ˈstʌdid], *a.* Studiato, ricercato; premeditato, calcolato; affettato, manierato.
studio [ˈstjuːdiou], *n.* Studio, *m.*
studious [ˈstjuːdiəs], *a.* Studioso; diligente, attento, sollecito, premuroso; premeditato. **With — care,** con sollecitudine; **— to please,** sollecito a compiacere.
studiously, *adv.* Studiosamente, diligentemente; con sollecitudine, con premura.
studiousness, *n.* Studiosità, applicazione, *f.*, studio, *m.*
study [ˈstʌdi], *n.* Studio, *m.*; gabinetto, *m.* || *v.t.* Studiare, meditare, riflettere; industriarsi sforzarsi, ingegnarsi. **To — one's own interests,** attendere ai propri interessi; **to — for the bar,** studiare legge; **to — economy,** mirare all'economia; **to — the comfort of,** cercare il benessere di; **in a brown —,** soprapensiero.
stuff [stʌf], *n.* Stoffa, *f.*, tessuto, *m.*; roba, robaccia, *f.*; materiali, *m.pl.*; (*fig.*) sciocchezze, *f.pl.* || *v.t.* Riempire; imbottire; turare; (*a skin*) impagliare; (*Cooking*) infarcire; (*fig.*) ingannare, prendere in giro; *v.i.* rimpinzarsi. **Stuff and nonsense!** Che sciocchezze! **garden- —,** verdura, *f.*; **Take this — away!** Portate via questa roba! **this is poor —,** questa è roba scadente; **he has good — in him,** ha della stoffa; **my nose is stuffed up,** ho il naso intasato; **a head stuffed with nonsense,** una testa rimpinzata di sciocchezze; **to — up,** ostruire, tappare, intasare; **to — in,** spingere dentro.
stuffing, *n.* Imbottitura, riempitura, *f.*, ripieno, *m.*; impagliatura, *f.*
stuffy, *a.* Mal ventilato, afoso, senz'aria. **To smell —,** saper di rinchiuso.
stultify [ˈstʌltifai], *v.t.* Render nullo, invalidare; infirmare; neutralizzare, render inefficace.
stum [stʌm], *n.* Mosto, *m.*
stumble [stʌmbl], *v.i.* Inciampare, incespicare, intoppare. || *n.* Passo falso, *m.*, inciampata, *f.* **To — in one's speech,** intopparsi nel parlare; **to — over,** inciampare in; **to — upon,** incontrare per caso, imbattersi in.
stumbling, *n.* Inciampamento, *m.*; (*fig.*) errore, *m.* **—-block,** ostacolo, inciampo, intoppo, *m.*
stumblingly, *adv.* Barcollando.
stump [stʌmp], *n.* (*of tree*) Ceppo, troncone, *m.*; (*of limb*) moncone, moncherino, *m.*; (*of pencil, etc.*) mozzicone, *m.*; (*cricket*) sbarra, *f.*; (*of tooth*) dente rotto, *m.*; (*Art*) sfumino, *m.* || *v.t.* Confondere con una questione; *v.i.* camminare. **Stir your stumps!** Affrettati! Spicciati! **to — the country,** percorrere il paese facendo discorsi politici; **—-orator,** oratore da piazza, *m.*; **to — along,** camminare con passo cadenzato; (*colloq.*) **to — up,** pagare in contanti.
stumpy, *a.* Tozzo.
stun [stʌn], *v.t.* Stordire, intronare, sbalordire, intontire, istupidire. **I was stunned by the news,** rimasi stordito alla notizia.
stunning, *a.* Assordante; (*colloq.*) deliziosissimo, bellisimo, stupefacente. **A — blow,** un colpo che stordisce.
stunsail [cp. **studding-sail**].
stunt (1) [stʌnt], *v.t.* Rendere stentato; opprimere.
stunt (2), *n.* Tentativo, *m.*; bravata, *f.*; montatura (giornalistica), *f.*; (*Aviat.*) acrobazia, *f.* || *v.i.* (*Aviat.*) Fare delle acrobazie.
stunted, *a.* Stentato, mal cresciuto.
stupefaction [stjuːpiˈfækʃən], *n.* Stupefazione, *f.*, stupore, *m.*
stupefy [ˈstjuːpifai], *v.t.* Stupefare, stordire, sbalordire, istupidire.
stupefying, *a.* Stupefacente.
stupendous [stjuːˈpendəs], *a.* Stupendo, meraviglioso, sorprendente.
stupendously, *adv.* Stupendamente.
stupendousness, *n.* Meraviglia, *f.*
stupid [ˈstjuːpid], *a.* Stupido, sciocco, stolto, ottuso, scimunito, melenso. || *n.* Stupido, sciocco, *m.* **To become —,** istupidire; **a — thing,** una stupidaggine, una sciocchezza, *f.*
stupidity, *n.* Stupidità, stupidaggine, scempiaggine, scemenza, *f.*
stupidly, *adv.* Stupidamente.
stupor [ˈstjuːpəɹ], *n.* Torpore, *m.*
sturdily [ˈstəːɹdili], *adv.* Vigorosamente, energicamente.
sturdiness, *n.* Robustezza, gagliardia, fortezza, *f.*, vigore, *m.*
sturdy, *a.* Robusto, gagliardo, forte, vigoroso.
sturgeon [ˈstəːɹdʒən], *n.* (*Zool.*) Storione, *m.*
stutter [ˈstʌtəɹ], *v.i.t.* Tartagliare, balbettare.
stutterer, *n.* Tartaglione, *m.*, tartagliona, *f.*, balbuziente, *m.f.*
stuttering, *n.* Il balbettare, il tartagliare, *m.*; balbuzie, *f.pl.*
stutteringly, *adv.* Balbettando.
sty (1) [stai], *n.* Porcile, *m.*
sty (2), **stye,** *n.* (*Med.*) Orzaiuolo, *m.*
Stygian [ˈstidʒən], *a.* Stigio.
style [stail], *n.* Stile, *m.*; titolo, nome, *m.*; specie, tipo, *m.*; modo, costume, *m.*; (*instrument*) stile, stilo, *m.*; (*of firm*) ragione sociale, *f.* || *v.t.* Chiamare, nominare, definire, dare il titolo di, intitolare. **In the — of,** al modo di, **there is no — about her,** essa non ha stile; **to do a thing in —,** fare una cosa

con stile; **in fine —,** magnificamente, in perfetto stile; **in the French —,** alla francese; **to — oneself,** intitolarsi.
stylish, *a.* Elegante, fine; stilizzato.
stylishly, *adv.* Elegantemente.
stylishness, *n.* Eleganza, *f.*, stile, *m.*
stylist, *n.* Stilista, *m.f.*
stylistic, *a.* Stilistico.
stylite ['stailait], *n.* (*Eccles.*) Stilita, *m.*
styptic ['stiptik], *a.* Astringente.
suability [sju:ə'biliti], *n.* Processabilità, *f.*
suable ['sju:əbl], *a.* Processabile.
suasion ['sweiʒən], *n.* Persuasione, *f.*
suasive ['sweiziv], *a.* Persuasivo.
suave [sweiv], *a.* Soave.
suavely, *adv.* Soavemente.
suavity, *n.* Soavità, *f.*
sub- [sʌb], *prefix.* Sotto, vice; quasi.
subacid [sʌb'æsid], *a.* Subacido, acidetto, agrodolce.
subagent, *n.* Subagente, *m.*
subalpine, *a.* Subalpino.
subaltern ['sʌbəltəɹn], *n.a.* Subalterno, *m.*
sub-committee, *n.* Sottocomitato, *m.*, sottocommissione, *f.*
subcontract, *n.* Subappalto, *m.*
subcontractor, *n.* Subappaltatore, *m.*
subcutaneous, *a.* Sottocutaneo.
subdeacon, *n.* (*Eccles.*) Suddiacono, *m.*
subdivide, *v.t.* Suddividere.
subdivision, *n.* Suddivisione, *f.*
subdominant, *n.* (*Mus.*) Sottodominante, *f.*
subduable [səb'dju:əbl], *a.* Vincibile, superabile, sottomettibile.
subdue, *v.t.* Vincere, superare, assoggettare, sottomettere, soggiogare; mitigare, addolcire, abbassare, attutire. **A subdued light,** una luce tenue, una luce moderata, *f.*; **to — one's voice,** abbassare la voce; **to — one's satisfaction,** frenare la soddisfazione.
sub-edit, *v.t.* Redigere.
sub-editor, *n.* Vice-direttore, *m.*; redattore assistente, *m.*
sub-heading, *n.* Sottotitolo, *m.*
sub-inspector, *n.* Sottoispettore, *m.*
subjacent, *a.* Soggiacente.
subject (1) ['sʌbdʒekt], *a.* Soggetto, suddito, soggiogato; esposto a. || *n.* (*of the state*) Suddito, *m.*; (*of conversation, etc.*) soggetto, argomento, tema, *m.*; oggetto, *m.* **To change the —,** cambiar soggetto; **a — for pity,** un oggetto di compassione, *m.*; **—-matter,** argomento, *m.*, materia, *f.*
subject (2) [səb'dʒekt], *v.t.* Soggiogare, assoggettare; sottomettere, sottoporre, esporre. **To — oneself to,** esporsi a, sottomettersi a.
subjection [səb'dʒekʃən], *n.* Soggezione, sottomissione, *f.*; assoggettamento, *m.* **To bring into —,** assoggettare.
subjective, *n.a.* Soggettivo, *m.*
subjectively, *adv.* Soggettivamente.
subjectivism, *n.* Soggettivismo, *m.*
subjectivity [sʌbdʒek'tiviti], *n.* Soggettività, *f.*
subjoin, *v.t.* Soggiungere, aggiungere; (*Comm.*) accludere.
subjoined, *a.* Soggiunto.
subjugate ['sʌbdʒju:geit], *v.t.* Soggiogare, debellare, vincere.
subjugation, *n.* Soggiogazione, *f.*
subjunctive [səb'dʒʌŋktiv], *a.* (*Gram.*) Soggiuntivo, congiuntivo.
sub-kingdom, *n.* (*Zool.*) Sottoregno, *m.*
sub-lease, *n.* Subaffitto, *m.*
sub-let, *v.t.* Subaffittare.
sub-lieutenant [sʌble'tenənt], *n.* Sottotenente, *m.*
sublimate (1) ['sʌblimeit], *v.t.* Sublimare.
sublimate (2) ['sʌblimit], *n.* (*Chem.*) Sublimato, *m.*
sublime [sə'blaim], *a.* Sublime, eccelso, elevato, maestoso. || *n.* Sublime, *m.*
sublimely, *adv.* Sublimemente.
sublimity [sə'blimiti], *n.* Sublimità, elevatezza, maestà, *f.*
subliminal [səb'liminəl], *a.* Subconscio.
sublunar, sublunary [səb'lu:nəɹ, səb'lju:nəri], *a.* Sublunare.
sub-manager, *n.* Sottodirettore, *m.*
submarine ['sʌbməri:n], *a.* Sottomarino. || *n.* Sommergibile, *m.*
submerge [səb'mə:ɹdʒ], *v.t.* Sommergere.
submergence, *n.* Sommersione, *f.*, sommergimento, *m.*
submission [səb'miʃən], *n.* Sommissione, sottomissione, umiltà, rassegnazione, *f.*
submissive, *a.* Sommesso, umile, rassegnato.
submissiveness, *n.* Sommissione, *f.*
submit, *v.t.* Sottomettere a, fare presente; *v.i.* sottomettersi, sottoporsi a, ubbidire.
subnormal, *a.* Subnormale.
subordinate [səb'ɔ:ɹdinit], *a.* Subordinato, soggetto, dipendente. || *n.* Subordinato, subalterno, *m.* || [səb'ɔ:ɹdineit], *v.t.* Subordinare.
subordination, *n.* Subordinazione, dipendenza, sottomissione, *f.*
suborn [sə'bɔ:ɹn], *v.t.* Subornare, sedurre.
suborner, *n.* Subornatore, *m.*
subpoena [səb'pi:nə], *n.* (*Law*) Citazione, *f.* || *v.t.* Citare come testimonio.
sub-prefect, *n.* Sottoprefetto, *m.*
sub-prefecture, *n.* Sottoprefettura, *f.*
subprior, *n.* (*Eccles.*) Sottopriore, *m.*
subreption [səb'repʃən], *n.* (*Law*) Surrezione, *f.*
subrogate ['sʌbrougeit], *v.t.* Surrogare.
subscribe [səb'skraib], *v.t.* Sottoscrivere; abbonarsi a; aderire a, approvare di; contribuire. **To — a pound to,** sottoscrivere una sterlina a; **to — oneself,** firmarsi; **I cannot — to that view,** io non sono di quella opinione, non posso sottoscrivere a tale idea.
subscriber, *n.* Sottoscrittore, *m.*; abbonato, *m.*
subscription, *n.* Sottoscrizione, firma, *f.*; contribuzione, quota, *f.*; abbonamento, *m.* **To raise a —,** iniziare una sottoscrizione.
subsection, *n.* Sottodivisione, sottosezione, *f.*
subsequence ['sʌbsikwəns], *n.* Susseguenza, *f.*
subsequent, *a.* Susseguente, seguente; ulteriore.
subsequently, *adv.* Dopo, susseguentemente.
subserve [səb'sə:ɹv], *v.t.* Giovare a, servire a, contribuire a.
subservience, subserviency [səb'sə:ɹviəns, səb'sə:ɹviənsi], *n.* Utilità, *f.*, giovamento, *m.*; (*fig.*) ossequiosità, arrendevolezza, *f.*
subservient, *a.* Giovevole; ossequente, arrendevole. **To make — to,** fare servire a.
subside [səb'said], *v.i.* (*of ground*) Cedere, sprofondare, avvallarsi; (*of flood*) decrescere; (*of wind*) diminuire, calmarsi, cessare. **To — into,** sprofondare in.

subsidence ['sʌbsidəns], *n.* Avvallamento, cedimento, *m.*; abbassamento, *m.*, diminuzione, *f.*
subsidiary [səb'sidiəri], *n.a.* Sussidario, *m.*
subsidize ['sʌbsidaiz], *v.t.* Sussidiare, sovvenzionare.
subsidy ['sʌbsidi], *n.* Sussidio, aiuto, rinforzo, *m.*, assistenza, *f.*
subsist [səb'sist], *v.i.* Sussistere, esistere, sostenersi, vivere. **To — on,** vivere di.
subsistence, *n.* Sussistenza, *f.*; alimento, *m.*, viveri, *m.pl.* **— allowance,** indennità di trasferta, *f.*
subsistent, *a.* Sussitente, esistente.
subsoil ['sʌbsɔil], *n.* Sottosuolo, *m.*
subspecies, *n.* Sottospecie, *f.*
substance ['sʌbstəns], *n.* Sostanza, *f.*; essenza, *f.*; contenuto, *m.*; realtà, *f.*; corpo, *m.*; (*wealth*) averi, beni, *m.pl.* **To take the shadow for the —,** prendere l'ombra pel corpo; **a man of —,** un uomo ricco, *m.*; **to waste one's —,** consumare le proprie sostanze.
substantial [səb'stænʃəl], *a.* Sostanziale, sostanzioso, solido, reale, vero; ricco, agiato. **A — meal,** un pasto sostanzioso, *m.*; **— proof,** prova sostanziale, *f.*; **— progress,** vero progresso, *m.*
substantiality, *n.* Sostanzialità, *f.*
substantially, *adv.* Sostanzialmente, realmente, veramente.
substantiate, *v.t.* Provare, stabilire, confermare.
substantive ['sʌbstəntiv], *n.a.* Sostantivo, *m.*
substantively, *adv.* Sostantivamente.
substitute ['sʌbstitju:t], *v.t.* Sostituire a. || *n.* Sostituto, supplente, *m.*
substitution, *n.* Sostituzione, *f.*
substratum (pl. **substrata**) [sʌb'streitəm, sʌb'streitə], *n.* Sostrato, substrato, *m.*; fondo, *m.*
substructure [sʌb'strʌktʃəɹ], *n.* Sostruzione, *f.*; fondamenta, *f.pl.*; piano di posa, *m.*
subtenant, *n.* Subaffittuario, *m.*
subtend [səb'tend], *v.t.* (*Geom.*) Sottendere.
subterfuge ['sʌbtəɹfju:dʒ], *n.* Sotterfugio, pretesto, *m.*; equivoco, *m.*
subterranean, subterraneous [sʌbtə'reiniən, sʌbtə'reiniəs], *a.* Sotterraneo.
subtilize ['sʌtilaiz], *v.t.i.* Sottilizzare; assottigliare, affinare.
subtilty, subtlety ['sʌtlti], *n.* Sottigliezza, sottilità, *f.*; finezza, tenuità, *f.*; sagacia, sagacità, penetrazione, astuzia, *f.*
subtitle, *n.* Sottotitolo, *m.*
subtle ['sʌtl], *a.* Sottile, fino, tenue; sagace, penetrante, acuto.
subtly, *adv.* Sottilmente.
subtract [səb'trækt], *v.t.* Sottrarre, dedurre.
subtraction, *n.* Sottrazione, *f.*
subtrahend ['sʌbtrəhend], *n.* Sottraendo, *m.*
subtropical, *a.* Quasi tropicale.
suburb ['sʌbəɹb], *n.* Sobborgo, suburbio, *m.*
suburban [sʌ'bə:ɹbən], *a.* Suburbano.
subvention [səb'venʃən], *n.* Sovvenzione, *f.*, sussidio, *m.*
subversion [səb'və:ɹʃən], *n.* Sovversione, *f.*, sovvertimento, *m.*
subversive, *a.* Sovversivo.
subvert, *v.t.* Sovvertire, rovesciare.
subway ['sʌbwei], *n.* Sottopassaggio, *m.*
succedaneous [sʌkse'deiniəs], *a.* Succedaneo.
succeed [sək'si:d], *v.i.* Succedere a, seguire, sottentrare a; riuscire, aver successo. **He succeeded to the throne,** egli succedette al trono; **he succeeded in obtaining it,** riuscì a ottenerlo; **to — each other,** succedersi; **day succeeds day,** i giorni si succedono.
succeeding, *a.* Succedente, successivo, seguente, susseguente, futuro.
success [sək'ses], *n.* Successo, *m.*, riuscita, *f.*; buona fortuna, *f.* **Without —,** senza successo; **spoilt by —,** guastato dal successo; **to be a great — as . . .,** riuscire benissimo come . . .
successful, *a.* Felice, fortunato, prospero, vittorioso, riuscito. **To be —,** aver successo, riuscire.
successfully, *adv.* Felicemente, vittoriosamente.
successfulness, *n.* Buona fortuna, riuscita, prosperità, *f.*
succession [sək'seʃən], Successione, *f.*; serie, sequela, *f.*; eredi, successori, *m.pl.* **In —,** di seguito, successivamente; (*Law*) **— duty,** imposta di successione, *f.*; **second in the —,** secondo alla successione, *m.*
successive, *a.* Successivo, seguente, consecutivo.
successively, *adv.* Successivamente.
successor, *n.* Erede, successore, *m.*
succinct [sʌk'siŋkt], *a.* Succinto, breve, conciso.
succinctly, *adv.* Succintamente, in succinto.
succinctness, *n.* Brevità, concisione, *f.*
succory ['sʌkəri], *n.* (*Bot.*) Cicoria, *f.*
succour ['sʌkəɹ], *v.t.* Soccorrere, aiutare. || *n.* Soccorso, aiuto, *m.*
succuba, succubus ['sʌkju:bə, 'sʌkju:bəs], *n.* Succubo, *m.*
succulence ['sʌkju:ləns], *n.* Sugosità, succolenza, *f.*
succulent, *a.* Succolento, succoso, sugoso.
succumb [sə'kʌm], *v.i.* Soccombere; cedere.
such [sʌtʃ], *a.* Tale, simile, tanto, così, siffatto. || *pron.* Tale, *m.f.*, tali, *m.f.pl.*; cotale, *n.f.*, cotali, *m.f.pl.* **I don't like — people,** non mi piace tal gente; **— kindness as hers is rare,** gentilezza come la sua è rara; **— flowers as you never saw,** fiori che voi non avete mai visto i simili; **there are no — things,** non ci sono cose siffatte; **at — a time as this,** in un tempo come questo; **it happened — a long time ago,** accadde tanto tempo fa; **in — weather as this,** con tempo come questo; **no — thing,** niente di simile, in nessun modo; **— and —,** un tale, *m.*; **— as it is,** tale qual'è, così com'è; **tears — as angels weep,** lagrime da angeli; **we have had — a lovely walk,** abbiamo fatto una così bella passeggiata; **it is — a bore,** è tanto noioso; **in — a way,** in tal modo; **in — wise,** in tal guisa, siffattamente.
suck [sʌk], *v.t.* Succhiare, succiare; assorbire, imbevere; (*at the breast*) poppare; *v.i.* succhiare, poppare. || *n.* Succiata, succhiata, *f.* **To — down,** ingoiare, trangugiare; **to — dry,** esaurire; **to — in,** sorbire, assorbire; **to — at a pipe,** succhiare la pipa; **to give — to,** allattare.
sucker, *n.* Succhiatore, *m.*; (*Mech.*) stantuffo, *m.*; (*Bot.*) succhione, pollone, rampollo, *m.*;

(*Zool.*) ventosa, *f.*, succhiatoio, *m.*; (*of insect*) tromba, proboscide, *f.*; (*colloq.*) gonzo, *m.*, vittima di un inganno, *f.*
sucking, *n.* Succhiamento, *m.* || *a.* Lattante, poppante. **— -pig,** porcellino lattante, *m.*
suckle [sʌkl], *v.t.* Allattare.
suckling, *n.* Allattamento, *m.*; (*child*) lattante, poppante, *m.f.*
suction [ˈsʌkʃən], *n.* Succhiamento, *m.*, aspirazione, *f.* **— -pump,** pompa aspirante, *f.*; **— -pipe,** tubo d'aspirazione, *m.*
sudation [sjuːˈdeiʃən], *n.* Il sudore, *m.*, sudata, *f.*
sudden [ˈsʌdən], *a.* Subito, repentino, subitaneo; improvviso, inatteso, inaspettato. **All of a —,** ad un tratto, di colpo; **— death,** morte improvvisa, *f.*; **a — change,** un cambiamento inaspettato, *m.*; **a — bend in the road,** una curva improvvisa, *f.*
suddenly, *adv.* Improvvisamente, ad un tratto, di colpo, subito.
suddenness, *n.* Subitaneità, repentinità, *f.*
sudoriferous [sjuːdəˈrifərəs], *a.* Sudorifico.
sudorific, *a.* Sudorifico.
suds [sʌdz], *n.pl.* Saponata, acqua saponata, *f.*
sue [sjuː], *v.t.* Chiamare in giudizio, citare; querelare; chiedere, domandare; *v.i.* sollecitare, supplicare. **To — for damages,** citare per danni; **to — for libel,** querelare per diffamazione; **to — for peace,** chiedere la pace, sollecitare la pace.
suède [sweid], *a.* Di camoscio, scamosciato. **— gloves,** guanti scamosciati, *m.pl.*
suet [ˈsjuːet], *n.* Grasso di bue, *m.*
suffer [ˈsʌfəɹ], *v.t.* (*to bear*) Soffrire, subire, patire; sopportare, comportare, tollerare; (*to allow*) permettere, lasciare; (*to die*) morire; *v.i.* soffrire, patire. **I should not — it for a moment,** non lo permetterei affatto; **to — losses,** subire danni; **to — punishment,** soffrire la pena; **he was suffered to go,** gli si permise di andare; **to — hunger,** patire la fame; **he was suffering from consumption,** egli soffriva di tisi; **your reputation will —,** la vostra riputazione ne avrà scapito; **you will — for it,** voi ne pagherete il fio, voi ci andrete di mezzo.
sufferable, *a.* Soffribile, tollerabile, sopportabile, comportabile.
sufferance, *n.* Tolleranza, *f.* **On —,** per tolleranza.
sufferer, *n.* Sofferente, paziente, *m.*, vittima, *f.* **Fellow- —,** compagno di dolore, *m.*; **to be a — by,** essere la vittima di; **I am the — in this matter,** sono io che ci rimetto, sono io che ci vado di mezzo.
suffering, *n.* Sofferenza, *f.*, patimento, dolore, *m.* || *a.* Sofferente.
suffice [səˈfais], *v.t.i.* Bastare, essere bastante, essere sufficiente. **Very little food suffices him,** pochissimo cibo gli basta; **— it to say,** basta il dire; **your word will —,** la vostra parola sarà sufficiente.
sufficiency [səˈfiʃensi], *n.* Sufficienza, bastevolezza, *f.* **A — of,** abbastanza di.
sufficient, *a.* Sufficiente, bastante, bastevole, adeguato. **I had not — courage,** non mi bastava il coraggio; **more than —,** più che abbastanza; **that is —,** basta, basta così.
sufficiently, *adv.* Abbastanza.
suffix [ˈsʌfiks], *n.* (*Gram.*) Suffisso, *m.*
suffocate [ˈsʌfokeit], *v.t.* Soffocare; asfissiare.
suffocating, *a.* Soffocante.
suffocatingly, *adv.* Da soffocare, oppressivamente.
suffocation, *n.* Soffocazione, *f.*, soffocamento, *m.*; asfissia, *f.*
suffragan [ˈsʌfrəgən], *n.a.* Suffraganeo, *m.* **— bishop,** vescovo suffraganeo, *m.*
suffrage [ˈsʌfridʒ], *n.* Suffragio, *m.*, diritto di voto, *m.*
suffragette [sʌfrəˈdʒet], *n.* Suffragetta, *f.*
suffuse [sʌˈfjuːz], *v.t.* Spargere, diffondere, soffondere, coprire, spandere sopra; bagnare. **Cheeks suffused with blushes,** guance soffuse di rossore; **his eyes were suffused with tears,** le lagrime gli bagnavano gli occhi.
suffusion, *n.* Diffusione, soffusione, *f.*, spargimento, *m.*
sugar [ˈʃugəɹ], *n.* Zucchero, *m.* || *v.t.* Inzuccherare, zuccherare. **Brown, raw, moist —,** zucchero greggio, *m.*; **(caster) powdered —,** zucchero in polvere, *m.*; **granulated —,** zucchero granulato, *m.*; **a lump of —,** un quadretto di zucchero, *m.*; **lump —,** zucchero in zollette, *m.*; **loaf —,** zucchero in pani, *m.*; **beet —,** zucchero di barbabietole, *m.*; **— -basin,** zuccheriera, *f.*; **— -candy,** zucchero candito, *m.*; (*Bot.*) **— -beet,** barbabietola da zucchero, *f.*; **— -cane,** canna da zucchero, *f.*; **— -maple,** acero da zucchero, *m.*; **— -plum,** zuccherino, *m.*, chicca, *f.*, confetto, *m.*; **— -refiner,** raffinatore di zucchero, *m.*; **— -refinery,** raffineria di zucchero, *f.*; **— -sifter,** inzuccheratore, *m.*; **— tongs,** mollette per lo zucchero, *f.pl.*
sugared, *a.* Inzuccherato, zuccherato.
sugariness, *n.* Zuccherosità, *f.*; dolcezza, mellifluità, *f.*
sugary, *a.* Zuccherino, zuccheroso; dolce, melato, mellifluo; edulcorato.
suggest [sʌˈdʒest], *v.t.* Suggerire, proporre; suggestionare, insinuare. **To — itself,** presentarsi, venire in mente.
suggestion [sʌˈdʒestʃən], *n.* (*advice*) Suggerimento, consiglio, *m.*; (*insinuation*) proposta, suggestione, instigazione, *f.* **To make a —,** dare un suggerimento, fare una proposta; **on his —,** seguendo il suo suggerimento.
suggestive, *a.* Allusivo, insinuante; indicativo; (*colloq.*) salace.
suicidal [suːiˈsaidəl], *a.* Suicida; fatale. **It would be — to do that,** sarebbe fatale fare ciò.
suicide [ˈsuːisaid], *n.* (*act*) Suicidio, *m.*; (*person*) suicida, *m.f.* **To commit —,** suicidarsi, uccidersi.
suit [sjuːt, suːt], *n.* (*request*) Richiesta, preghiera, petizione, *f.*; (*courtship*) corte, *f.*, corteggiamento, *m.*; (*Law*) lite, causa, *f.*; (*clothes*) abito completo, *m.*; (*Cards*) seme, *m.* || *v.t.* Adattare, accomodare; soddisfare, contentare, piacere a; convenire a, andare bene a; *v.i.* adattarsi, convenire, accordarsi, piacere. **To press one's —,** fare la corte; (*Law*) **to bring a —,** intentar lite, far causa; **a — of armour,** un'armatura completa, *f.*; **a dress —,** un abito da sera, *m.*; (*Cards*) **to follow —,** rispondere alla carta del compagno, (*fig.*) fare lo stesso, fare altrettanto; **this dress**

does not — me, questo vestito non mi va bene; **— yourself,** fate come vi piace; **that just suits me,** ciò mi conviene benissimo, ciò mi fa comodo; **cold weather does not — him,** il freddo gli fa male.

suitability, suitableness, *n.* Convenienza, convenevolezza, opportunità, *f.*

suitable, *a.* Adatto, atto, conveniente, convenevole, opportuno. **At a — moment,** ad un momento opportuno; **a very — match,** un partito molto conveniente, *m.*

suitably, *adv.* Convenevolmente, convenientemente.

suite [swi:t], *n.* (*of people*) Seguito, corteggio, corteo, *m.*; (*of furniture*) arredo, mobilio, ammobiliamento, *m.*, mobilia, *f.*; (*of rooms*) appartamento, *m.* **A drawing-room —,** un mobilio da sala, *m.*

suitings [ˈsju:tiŋz], *n.pl.* Tessuti per vestiti, *m.pl.*

suitor [ˈsju:təɹ], *n.* Postulante, petente, richiedente, *m.*; (*Law*) litigante, *m.*; (*wooer*) pretendente, aspirante, *m.*

sulk [sʌlk], *v.i.* Essere di malumore, imbronciarsi, accigliarsi, tenersi il broncio. **To — at,** tenere il broncio a.

sulkily, *adv.* Con malumore.

sulkiness, *n.* Malumore, *m.*, musoneria, *f.*

sulks, *n.pl.* Malumore, *m.*, musoneria, *f.* **A fit of the —,** un accesso di malumore, *m.*; **to be in the —,** tenere il broncio, portare il broncio.

sulky (1), *a.* Imbronciato, di cattivo umore, burbero, arcigno, accigliato, ingrugnito.

sulky (2), *n.* Vettura a due ruote per una sola persona, *f.*

sullen [ˈsʌlən], *a.* Tetro, cupo; burbero, accigliato, imbronciato, arcigno.

sullenly, *adv.* Burberamente, di malumore, malvolentieri.

sullenness, *a.* Malumore, *m.*, musoneria, *f.*

sully [ˈsʌli], *v.t.* Macchiare, insudiciare; sporcare. **To — one's reputation,** macchiare la propria riputazione.

sulphate [ˈsʌlfeit], *n.* (*Chem.*) Solfato, *m.* **— of copper,** solfato di rame, *m.*

sulphide [ˈsʌlfaid], *n.* (*Chem.*) Solfuro, *m.*

sulphite [ˈsʌlfait], *n.* (*Chem.*) Solfito, *m.*

sulphonal [ˈsʌlfənəl], *n.* (*Med.*) Sulfonale, *m.*

sulphur [ˈsʌlfəɹ], *n.* Solfo, zolfo, *m.* **Flowers of —,** fiori di zolfo, *m.pl.*; **— bath,** bagno solforoso, *m.*; **— mine,** miniera di zolfo, zolfatara, *f.*

sulphurate, *v.t.* Solforare.

sulphureous, *a.* Sulfureo.

sulphuretted, *a.* Solforato. **— hydrogen,** idrogeno solforato, *m.*

sulphuric [sʌlˈfju:rik], *a.* Solforico.

sulphurous [ˈsʌlfərəs], *a.* Sulfureo.

sultan [ˈsʌltən], *n.* Sultano, *m.*; (*Hist.*) soldano, *m.*

sultana [sʌlˈtɑ:nə], *n.* Sultana, *f.*; (*fruit*) sultanina, uva secca, *f.*

sultriness [ˈsʌltrines], *n.* Afa, afosità, *f.*

sultry, *a.* Afoso, soffocante. **How — it is!** Che afa!

sum [sʌm], *n.* (*of money*) Somma, *f.*; (*amount*) totale, importo, complesso, ammontare, *m.*, cifra, *f.*; sommo, colmo, *m.*; (*Math.*) problema, calcolo, conto, *m.*, operazione, *f.* ‖ *v.t.i.* Sommare, addizionare; riassumere. **The — total,** la somma totale, *f.*; **to do sums,** computare, calcolare, fare i conti; **to set a —,** dar da fare un'operazione; **to work out a —,** fare un calcolo, fare un conto; **the — and substance of,** la sostanza di; **a round —,** una cifra tonda, *f.*; **to — up,** riassumere; riassumendo, in conclusione, insomma; (*Law*) **summing-up,** riassunto, *m.*

sumac, sumach [ˈsju:mæk, ˈʃu:mæk], *n.* (*Bot.*) Sommacco, *m.*

summarily [ˈsʌmərili], *adv.* Sommariamente, per sommi capi.

summarize [ˈsʌməraiz], *v.t.* Riassumere, fare un sunto di.

summary, *n.* Sunto, compendio, sommario, epitome, *m.* ‖ *a.* Sommario, compendioso, abbreviato. **— jurisdiction,** giudizio sommario, *m.*

summer [ˈsʌməɹ], *n.* Estate, *f.* ‖ *v.i.* Passare l'estate. ‖ *a.* D'estate, estivo. **In —,** nell'estate **— heat,** caldo estivo, *m.*; **— clothes,** abito d'estate, *m.*; **— season,** stagione estiva, *f.*; **— -house,** chiosco, cupolino, bersò, padiglione, *m.*; **— time,** stagione estiva, *f.*; (*Legal*) ora estiva, *f.*; **— resort,** stazione estiva, *f.*; **— -lightning,** balenare a secco, *m.*

summit [ˈsʌmit], *n.* Sommità, cima, *f.*; vertice, *m.*, colmo, *m.*

summon [ˈsʌmən], *v.t.* Chiamare, invitare; (*Law*) citare, chiamare; (*to call together*) convocare; (*to call to surrender*) intimare. **To — up courage,** farsi coraggio; **they were summoned to surrender,** fu intimata loro la resa; **he was suddenly summoned away,** fu inaspettatamente chiamato altrove.

summons, *n.* Chiamata, *f.*, invito, appello, *m.*; (*Law*) citazione, comparizione, *f.* **To issue a —,** mandare una comparizione; **to take out a — against,** far citare in giudizio; **to answer a —,** comparire in giudizio; **to serve a — on,** citare in giudizio.

sump [sʌmp], *n.* (*in mine*) Pozzo di scarico, *m.*; (*Mech.*) scodellino, raccoglitore d'olio, *m.*

sumpter [ˈsʌmptəɹ], *n.* Bestia da soma, *f.*, somiero, *m.* **— -horse,** cavallo da soma, *m.*; **— -mule,** mulo da soma, somaro, somiero, *m.*

sumptuary [ˈsʌmptjuːəri], *a.* Suntuario.

sumptuous [ˈsʌmptjuːəs], *a.* Suntuoso, sontuoso.

sumptuously, *adv.* Suntuosamente.

sumptuousness, *n.* Suntuosità, *f.*, lusso, *m.*

sun [sʌn], *n.* Sole, *m.* **In the —,** al sole; **the — is high,** il sole è alto; **the — is up,** il sole è levato; **to rise with the —,** alzarsi col sole; **the midnight —,** il sole di mezzanotte, *m.*; **to let in the —,** lasciar entrare il sole; **there's nothing new under the —,** nulla di nuovo sotto il sole; **the rising —,** il sole nascente, *m.*; **to — oneself,** soleggiare, stare al sole, riscaldarsi al sole; **— -bath,** bagno di sole, *m.*; **— -blind,** tenda, *f.*; **— -bonnet,** cappello da sole; **— -dried,** seccato al sole; **— -helmet,** casco, *m.*; **— -worship,** culto del sole, *m.*; **—-suit,** prendisole, *m.*

sunbeam, *n.* Raggio di sole, *m.*

sunburn, *n.* Abbronzatura, *f.*

sunburned, sunburnt, *a.* Abbronzato, adusto, bruciato da sole.

sundae [ˈsʌndei], *n.* Tipo di cassata con crema.

Sunday [ˈsʌndi], *n.* Domenica, *f.* ‖ *a.* Domenicale, di domenica, da domenica. **To keep —,** osservare la domenica; **— -school,**

scuola domenicale, *f.* (*colloq.*) **a month of Sundays,** una quaresima, *f.*
sunder ['sʌndəɹ], *v.t.* Separare, spartire, disgiungere, disunire.
sundew ['sʌndju:], *n.* (*Bot.*) Rosolida, *f.*
sundial ['sʌndail], *n.* Meridiana, *f.*
sundown, *n.* Tramonto, *m.* **At —,** al tramonto.
sundries [['sʌndriz], *n.pl.* Cose diverse, *f.pl.*, articoli diversi, *m.pl.*; (*Comm.*) spese diverse, spese casuali, *f.pl.*
sunfish, *n.* (*Zool.*) Mola, *f.*; pesce luna, *f.*
sunflower, *n.* (*Bot.*) Girasole, *m.*
sunken ['sʌŋkən], *a.* Infossato, incavato. **— eyes,** occhi infossati, *m.pl.*
sunless, *a.* Senza sole.
sunlight, *n.* Luce del sole, *f.*; (*Med.*) **— treatment,** cura del sole, *f.*
sunlit, *a.* Soleggiato.
sunny, *a.* Esposto al sole, soleggiato; aprico, solatio; (*fig.*) lieto, allegro, felice. **It is —,** fa sole; **to look on the — side,** guardar le cose dal lato buono.
sunrise, *n.* Levata del sole, *f.*; alba, aurora, *f.*
sunset, *n.* Tramonto, *m.*
sunshade, *n.* Parasole, *m.*
sunshine, *n.* Luce del sole, *f.*, sole, *m.*; splendore, calore, *m.* **In the —,** al sole, in pieno sole; (*Motor.*) **— roof,** tetto mobile, tetto scorrevole, *m.*; (*Med.*) **— treatment,** elioterapia, *f.*
sunshiny, *a.* Soleggiato, pieno di sole. **A — day,** un giorno di sole, *m.*
sunspot, *n.* Macchia solare, *f.*
sunstroke, *n.* Insolazione, *f.*, colpo di sole, *m.*
sunsuit ['sʌnsju:t], *n.* Prendisole, *m.*
sup [sʌp], *n.* Sorso, *m.* ‖ *v.t.* Sorseggiare; (*to drink*) bere; (*to take supper*) cenare; *v.i.* cenare.
super ['sju:pəɹ], *prefix.* Sopra, sovra.
super, *n.* (*Theat.*) Comparsa, *f.*, figurante, *m.f.*
superable ['sju:pərəbl], *a.* Superabile.
superabound, *v.i.* Sovrabbondare.
superabundance, *n.* Sovrabbondanza, *f.*
superabundant, *a.* Sovrabbondante.
superabundantly, *adv.* Sovrabbondantemente.
superadd, *v.t.* Aggiungere in più.
superannuate [sju:pəɹ'ænju:eit], *v.t.* Pensionare, giubilare.
superannuated, *a.* Pensionato, giubilato.
superannuation, *n.* Pensione, giubilazione, *f.*, collocamento a riposo, *m.* **— fund,** fondo pensione, *m.*, cassa pensioni, *f.*
superb [sju:'pə:ɹb], *a.* Superbo, maestoso, imponente, grandioso.
superbly, *adv.* Superbamente.
supercargo ['sju:pəɹkɑ:ɹgou], *n.* (*Naut.*) Sovraccarico, *m.*
supercilious [sju:pəɹ'siliəs], *a.* Arrogante, arcigno, borioso, altezzoso.
superciliously, *adv.* Arrogantemente.
superciliousness, *n.* Arroganza, alterigia, boria, *f.*
supererogation [sju:pəɹerou'geiʃən], *n.* Supererogazione, *f.*
superfatted, *a.* (*of soap*) Raffinato.
superficial [sju:pəɹ'fiʃəl], *a.* Superficiale.
superficiality, *n.* Superficialità, *f.*
superficially, *adv.* Superficialmente.
superficies [sju:pəɹ'fisii:z], *n.* Superficie, *f.*
superfine, *a.* Sopraffino, finissimo.
superfluity, superfluousness [sju:pəɹ'flu:iti, sju:'pə:ɹflu:əsnes], *n.* Superfluità, *f.*, superfluo, *m.*
superfluous, [sju:'pə:ɹflu:əs] *a.* Superfluo, inutile, soverchio.
superfluously, *adv.* Superfluamente.
superheat, *v.i.* Surriscaldare.
superheated, *a.* Surriscaldato, sopraccaldo.
superhuman, *a.* Sovrumano.
superhumanly, *adv.* Sovrumanamente.
superimpose, *v.t.* Sovrapporre, sovrimporre.
superimposition, *n.* Sovrapponimento, *m.*
superinduce, *v.t.* Soprindurre.
superintend, *v.t.* Soprintendere, sorvegliare, vigilare.
superintendence, *n.* Soprintendenza, sorveglianza, vigilanza, cura, *f.*
superintendent, *n.* Soprintendente, *m.*; capo, ispettore, direttore, *m.*; (*of police*) commissario, *m.*
superior [sju:'piəriəɹ], *n.a.* Superiore, *m.* **Mother —,** madre superiora, *f.*
superiority, *n.* Superiorità, *f.*
superlative [sju:'pə:ɹlətiv], *n.a.* Superlativo, *m.*
superlatively, *adv.* Superlativamente.
superman, *n.* Superuomo, *m.*
supermundane, *a.* Oltremondano.
supernal [sju:'pə:ɹnəl], *a.* Superno.
supernatural, *n.a.* Soprannaturale.
supernaturally, *adv.* Soprannaturalmente.
supernumerary [sju:pəɹ'nju:mərəri], *n.a.* Soprannumerario, *m.*; (*Theat.*) comparsa, *f.*
superscribe [sju:pəɹ'skraib], *v.t.* Scrivere sopra.
superscription, *n.* Soprascritta, *f.*, indirizzo, *m.*
supersede [sju:pəɹ'si:d], *v.t.* Soppiantare, sostituire, surrogare, rimpiazzare. **To be superseded,** passare di moda, diventare antiquato, esser rimpiazzato.
supersensitive, *a.* Ipersensitivo.
supersession, *n.* Soppiantamento, *m.*, sostituzione, *f.*
superstition [sju:pəɹ'stiʃən], *n.* Superstizione, *f.*
superstitious, *a.* Superstizioso.
superstitiousness, *n.* Superstiziosità, *f.*
superstructure, *n.* Soprastruttura, *f.*
super-tax, *n.* Sopratassa, *f.*
supertonic, *n.* (*Mus.*) Supertonico, sopramodale, *m.*
supervene [sju:pəɹ'vi:n], *v.i.* Sopravvenire, sopraggiungere.
supervise [sju:pəɹ'vaiz], *v.t.* Sorvegliare, ispezionare, soprintendere.
supervision [sju:pəɹ'viʒən], *n.* Sorveglianza, supervisione, soprintendenza, ispezione, *f.*
supervisor, *n.* Ispettore, soprintendente, controllore, *m.*
supine ['sju:pain], *a.* Supino; (*fig.*) negligente, pigro, ignavo. ‖ *n.* (*Gram.*) Supino, *m.*
supinely, *adv.* Supinamente.
supineness, *n.* Posizione supina, *f.*; (*fig.*) supinità, *f.*; negligenza, trascuratezza, *f.*
supper ['sʌpəɹ], *n.* Cena, *f.* **The Lord's Supper,** La Cena, *f.*; **to have —,** cenare; **— -time,** ora di cena, *f.*
supperless, *a.* Senza cena.
supplant, *v.t.* Soppiantare, dare lo sgambetto.

supplanter, *n.* Soppiantatore, *m.*
supple [ˈsʌpəl], *a.* Flessibile, pieghevole; (*fig.*) arrendevole, molle, cedevole, lusinghiero. **To make —,** rendere flessibile; **to become —,** divenire flessibile.
supplement [ˈsʌplimənt], *n.* Supplemento, *m.*; (*Geom.*) angolo supplementare, *m.* || *v.t.* Integrare, completare, aggiungere.
supplemental, supplementary, *a.* Supplementare.
suppleness, *n.* Flessibilità, pieghevolezza, *f.*; (*fig.*) mollezza, arrendevolezza, *f.*
suppliant [ˈsʌpliənt], *a.* Supplicante, supplichevole. || *n.* Supplicante, *m.f.*
supplicate, *v.t.i.* Supplicare, scongiurare.
supplication, *n.* Supplicazione, supplica, *f.*
supplicatory, *a.* Supplicatorio, supplichevole.
supplier [sʌˈplaiəɹ], *n.* Fornitore, *m.*
supply [sʌˈplai], *n.* Provvista, *f.*, approvvigionamento, *m.*; provvisione, scorta, *f.* || *v.t.* Fornire, provvedere, munire di; supplire, colmare, soddisfare; completare. **Supplies,** viveri, *m.pl.*; (*Pol.*) sussidi, fondi, *m.pl.*; **— and demand,** offerta e domanda; **to cut off supplies,** tagliare i viveri; **a good — of bread,** una buona provvista di pane, *f.*; **to stop supplies,** cessare i rifornimenti; **to lay in a — of,** approvvigionarsi di; **to — with goods,** fornire di merci; **to — a want,** soddisfare a un bisogno; **to — a deficiency,** colmare una deficienza; **supplied with food,** munito di vettovaglie.
support [sʌˈpɔːɹt], *v.t.* Sostenere, reggere, appoggiare, sopportare, resistere a, durare; mantenere, sostentare, nutrire; confermare, convalidare, rafforzare; rappresentare; (*Mil.*) rincalzare. || *n.* Sostegno, appoggio, puntello, aiuto, *m.*; sostentamento, mantenimento, nutrimento, *m.*; puntello, *m.* **To — oneself,** sostentarsi, guadagnarsi la vita; **to — an assertion,** convalidare un'asserzione; **to — a candidate,** appoggiare un candidato; **in — of,** a sostegno di.
supportable, *a.* Sopportabile, tollerabile, comportabile; sostenibile.
supporter, *n.* Sostenitore, difensore, propugnatore, *m.*; aderente, fautore, *m.*; sostentatore, mantenitore, *m.*; (*Heraldry*) sostegno, *m.*
supposable [sʌˈpouzəbl], *a.* Supponibile.
suppose [sʌˈpouz], *v.t.* Supporre, immaginare, pensare, credere. **Let us — it is so,** supponiamo che sia così; **— we read this,** leggiamo questo; **— anyone came,** per caso qualcuno venisse; **it is not to be supposed that,** non è da supporre che; **What do you — it means ?** Che cosa credete che voglia dire? **— that it were so,** se puta caso fosse così.
supposed, *a.* Supposto, immaginato, putativo. **His — brother,** suo fratello putativo.
supposing, *conj.* Supposto che, puta caso che, dato che.
supposition [sʌpəˈziʃən], *n.* Supposizione, ipotesi, congettura, *f.*
supposititious, [sʌpɔsiˈtiʃəs] *a.* Suppositizio, falso, spurio.
suppository [sʌˈpɔzitəri], *n.* (*Med.*) Supposta, *f.*
suppress [sʌˈpres], *v.t.* (*to put down*) Sopprimere, reprimere, domare; (*to check*) trattenere, soffocare, reprimere, attutire; (*to hide*) nascondere, celare. **To — a rebellion,** reprimere una ribellione; **to — a groan,** reprimere un gemito; **to — evidence,** far scomparire le prove; **to — a newspaper,** sopprimere un giornale.
suppressed, *a.* Soffocato, represso, domato, contenuto. **A — laugh,** un riso soffocato; **— anger,** ira repressa, *f.*
supressible, *a.* Sopprimibile.
suppression, *n.* Soppressione, repressione, *f.*
suppurate [ˈsʌpjuːreit], *v.i.* (*Med.*) Suppurare.
suppuration, *n.* Suppurazione, *f.*
suppurative, *a.* Suppurativo.
supra [ˈsjuːprə], *prefix.* Al di sopra di.
suprarenal [sjuːprəˈriːnəl], *a.* (*Anat.*) Surrenale.
supremacy [sjuːˈpreməsi], *n.* Supremazia, *f.*, primato, *m.*
supreme [sjuːˈpriːm], *a.* Supremo, sommo, altissimo.
supremely, *adv.* Supremamente.
surcease [səɹˈsiːs], *v.i.* Cessare; *v.t.* mettere fine a. || *n.* Cessazione, *f.*
surcharge [ˈsəːɹtʃɑːɹdʒ], *n.* Sovraccarico, *m.*, maggiorazione, sopratassa, *f.*; supplemento, *m.* || *v.t.* Sovraccaricare, far pagare in più, maggiorare.
surcingle [ˈsəːɹsiŋgl], *n.* Sopraccinghia, cinghia, *f.*
surcoat, *n.* (*Hist.*) Cotta d'arme, *f.*
surd [səːɹd], *a.* (*Math.*) Irrazionale; (*Gram.*) sordo. || *n.* Numero irrazionale, *m.*; (*Gram.*) consonante sorda, *f.*
sure [ʃuːɹ], *a.* Sicuro, certo; vero, verace, indubitabile; (*expert*) provetto, esperto; assicurato. **To be — of,** essere sicuro di; **I'm — I can't say,** non ne so niente davvero; **To be —!** Senza dubbio! **be — not to tell,** abbiate cura di non dirlo; **be — to come,** non mancate di venire; **to make — of,** assicurarsi di; **to have a — hand,** avere la mano sicura; **to feel — of oneself,** sentirsi sicuro di sè; **a — shot,** un tiratore esperto, *m.*; **to make — of a fact,** assicurarsi d'un fatto, appurare un fatto; **— footed,** di piede fermo.
surely, sure *adv.* Sicuramente, certamente.
sureness, *n.* Sicurezza, certezza, *f.*
surety [ˈʃjuːɹti], *n.* (*Law*) Mallevadore, garante, *m.*; cauzione, *f.*; certezza, *f.* **Of a —,** certamente; **to stand — for,** garantire, farsi garante di.
suretyship, *n.* Garanzia, malleveria, *f.*
surf [səːɹf], *n.* Risacca, *f.*, risucchio, *m.*; frangenti, *m.pl.* **— -board,** scì acquatico *or* idroscì, *m.*; **— -boat,** piroga, *f.*, canotto da costa, *m.*; **— -riding,** lo sport dell'idroscì, *m.*
surface [ˈsəːɹfis], *n.* Superficie, faccia, *f.*, esterno, *m.* **On the —,** superficiale, esterno, esteriore; **to rise to the —,** venire a galla; **— -mine,** cava a cielo aperto, *f.*; (*Mech.*) **— -plate,** piano di riscontro, *m.*
surfeit [ˈsəːɹfit], *n.* Eccesso, rimpinzamento, *m.*, sazietà, indigestione, *f.* || *v.t.* Satollare, saziare; (*fig.*) nauseare, annoiare, disgustare. **To have a — of,** saziarsi di; **to — oneself,** satollarsi, rimpinzarsi.
surfeiting, *n.* Eccesso, *m.*, indigestione, *f.*
surge [səːɹdʒ], *n.* Maroso, *m.*, ondata, *f.*; fiotto, flutto, *m.* || *v.i.* Ondeggiare, agitarsi, sollevarsi; rifluire.

surgeon [ˈsəːɹdʒən], *n.* Chirurgo, *m.* — **-dentist**, chirurgo dentista, *m.*
surgery, *n.* (*Art*) Chirurgia, *f.*; (*place*) gabinetto medico, *m.*, infermeria, clinica, *f.*
surgical, *a.* Chirurgico. — **instruments**, strumenti chirurgici, *m.pl.*
surging, *a.* Ondeggiante, agitato.
surlily [ˈsəːɹlili], *adv.* Burberamente, rozzamente.
surliness, *n.* Scontrosità, *f.*
surly, *a.* Burbero, scontroso, arcigno; rozzo, zotico; (*of dogs*) ringhioso.
surmise [səɹˈmaiz], *n.* Supposizione, congettura, *f.*, sospetto, *m.* || *v.t.i.* Supporre, congetturare, sospettare.
surmount [səɹˈmaunt], *v.t.* Sormontare, superare, vincere, sorpassare.
surmountable, *a.* Superabile.
surname [ˈsəːɹneim], *n.* Cognome, *m.*; soprannome, *m.*; nome di famiglia, *m.*
surpass [səɹˈpɑːs], *v.t.* Sorpassare, superare.
surpassing, *a.* Eccellente, superiore, raro.
surpassingly, *adv.* Eccellentemente, straordinariamente.
surplice [ˈsəːɹplis], *n.* Cotta, *f.*; roccetto, *m.*
surpliced, *a.* In cotta.
surplus [ˈsəːɹpləs], *n.* Soprappiù, soverchio, eccesso, *m.*; avanzo, *m.*; eccedenza, *f.* || *a.* Di soprappiù, soverchio. — **stock**, rimanenze, *f.pl.*, saldo, *m.*, scampoli, *m.pl.*; — **population**, eccesso di popolazione, *m.*; — **energy**, energia sovrabbondante, *f.*
surplusage, *n.* Soprappiù, eccesso, *m.*, superfluità, *f.*
surprise [səɹˈpraiz], *n.* Sorpresa, meraviglia, *f.*; stupore, *m.* || *v.t.* Sorprendere, cogliere all'improvviso; colpire di meraviglia, stupire. **To be taken by** —, essere preso di sorpresa, esser colto all'improvviso; **to recover from one's** —, riaversi dalla sorpresa; **to my great** —, con mia grande sorpresa; **to give someone a** —, fare una sorpresa a qualcuno, fare un'improvvisata a qualcuno; **a pleasant** —, una sorpresa gradita, *f.*; **a — visit**, una visita inaspettata, *f.*; **to be surprised**, essere sorpreso, sorprendersi; **I am not surprised at it**, non mi sorprende; **to — in the act**, cogliere in fallo, sorprendere in flagrante.
surprising, *a.* Sorprendente, meraviglioso.
surprisingly, *adv.* Sorprendentemente.
surrender [sʌˈrendəɹ], *n.* Resa, capitolazione, *f.*; abbandono, *m.*; cessione, consegna, *f.*; (*insurance*) riscatto, *m.* || *v.t.* Consegnare, cedere, abbandonare; rinunciare a, concedere; *v.i.* arrendersi, capitolare. **To — one's freedom**, rinunciare alla propria libertà; **to — oneself to justice**, costituirsi all'autorità; (*Law*) — **of property**, cessione di beni, *f.*; **to — an insurance policy**, riscattare una polizza d'assicurazione.
surreptitious [sʌrepˈtiʃəs], *a.* Furtivo, clandestino, nascosto.
surreptitiously, *adv.* Furtivamente, clandestinamente, di nascosto, in segreto.
surrogate [ˈsʌrogeit], *n.* Sostituto, *m.*; delegato, surrogato, *m.*
surround [sʌˈraund], *v.t.* Circondare, cingere, accerchiare, circuire, attorniare. || *n.* Contorno, *m.*
surrounding, *a.* Circondante, circostante, circonvicino, vicino.
surroundings, *n.pl.* Dintorni, *m.pl.*, ambiente, *m.*
surtax [ˈsəːɹtæks], *n.* Sopratassa, *f.* || *v.t.* Sopratassare.
surtout [ˈsəːɹtuː], *n.* Soprabito, *m.*
surveillance [səɹˈveiləns], *n.* Sorveglianza, *f.*
survey (1) [ˈsəːɹvei], *n.* Veduta, vista, *f.*; stima, valutazione, *f.*; scorsa, *f.*, colpo d'occhio, panorama, *m.*; esame, *m.*, ispezione, *f.*; perizia, *f.*; (*of land*) agrimensura, *f.*; levata, *f.*; (*map*) mappa catastale, *f.* **A — of literature**, una valutazione della letteratura, *m.*; **an official** —, un catasto, *m.*; **to make a** —, far una perizia; pigliare i rilievi; esaminare, dare uno sguardo d'insieme.
survey (2) [səɹˈvei], *v.t.* Osservare, esaminare; valutare, stimare, far perizia di; misurare, levare i piani di, rilevare; contemplare, considerare.
surveying, *n.* Agrimensura, *f.*
surveyor, *n.* Agrimensore, *m.*; (*of land*) geometra, *f.*; (*of taxes*) esattore, controllore, *m.*; perito, *m.*; topografo, *m.* **Quantity** —, misuratore, *m.*; — **of roads**, ispettore stradale, *m.*
survival [səɹˈvaivəl], *n.* Sopravvivenza, *f.*
survive [səɹˈvaiv], *v.i.* Sopravvivere, campare; *v.t.* sopravvivere a.
surviving, *a.* Sopravvivente, superstite.
survivor, *n.* Sopravvivente, superstite, *m.f.*
susceptibility [sʌseptiˈbiliti], *n.* Suscettibilità, permalosità, *f.*
susceptible [sʌˈseptəbl], *a.* Suscettibile; permaloso, impressionabile.
susceptive, *a.* Suscettivo.
suspect [sʌsˈpekt], *v.t.* Sospettare, dubitare, diffidare di. || [sˈʌspekt] *n.* Persona sospetta, *f.*, sospetto, *m.* || *a.* Sospetto. **To — danger**, sospettare pericolo; **I suspected as much**, ho sospettato altrettanto.
suspend [sʌsˈpend], *v.t.* Sospendere; appendere; (*postpone*) sospendere, differire. **To — judgement**, sospendere il giudizio; **to — payment**, sospendere i pagamenti.
suspended, *a.* Sospeso, differito. (*Med.*) — **animation**, stato comatoso, *m.*
suspenders, *n.pl.* (*for stockings*) Giarrettiere, *f.pl.*; (*braces*) bretelle, *f.pl.*; **sock-** —, giarrettiere, *f.pl.*; **suspender belt**, cinta portabretelle, *f.*
suspense [sʌsˈpens], *n.* Incertezza, *f.*, dubbio, *m.*; sospensione d'animo, *f.*; (*Law*) sospensione, *f.* **In** —, in sospeso, nell'incertezza; **to keep in** —, tenere in sospeso; (*Comm.*) — **account**, conto crediti contestati, *m.*
suspension, *n.* Sospensione, *f.*; dilazione, *f.*, differimento, *m.* — **bridge**, ponte sospeso, *m.*
suspensory, *a.* Sospensorio. — **bandage**, sospensorio, *m.*
suspicion [sʌsˈpiʃən], *n.* Sospetto, dubbio, *m.*; (*small amount*) tantino, pochino, *m.* **Above** —, fuori di ogni sospetto; **to have suspicions**, nutrire sospetti; **under — of**, sospetto di, sospettato di.
suspicious, *a.* Sospettoso, diffidente; sospetto, sospettabile, sospettato. **He became** —, cominciò a sospettare; **under — circumstances**, in circostanze sospette.
suspiciously, *adv.* Sospettamente; con diffidenza, sospettosamente.

suspiciousness, *n.* Diffidenza, sospettosità, sfiducia, *f.*
suspire [sʌsˈpaiɹ], *v.i.* Sospirare.
sustain [sʌsˈtein], *v.t.* Sostenere, sostentare; sopportare, provare, subire, durare, resistere a; soffrire; difendere, propugnare. **To — an objection,** sollevare un incidente; **to — a theory,** sostenere una teoria.
sustaining, *a.* Nutriente, corroborante.
sustenance [ˈsʌstənəns], *n.* Nutrimento, alimento, cibo, *m.*
sustentation [sʌstenˈteiʃən], *n.* Sostentazione, *f.*, mantenimento, *m.*
susurration [sʌsjuːˈreiʃən], *n.* Susurro, sussurro, *m.*
sutler [ˈsʌtləɹ], *n.* Vivandiere, *m.*
suttee, sati [sʌˈtiː], *n.* Sacrificio d'una vedova indiana alla morte del marito, *m.*
suture [ˈsuːtjuːɹ], *n.* Sutura, *f.*
suzerain [ˈsuːzərein], *n.* Sovrano, signore, *m.* || *a.* Sovrano.
suzerainty, *n.* Signoria, *f.*
swab [swɔb], *n.* Strofinaccio, *m.*; (*Naut.*) radazza, *f.*; (*Med.*) compressa, *f.*, tampone, *m.* || *v.t.* Pulire, lavare. **To — the decks,** radazzare i ponti.
Swabian [ˈsweibiən], *a.* (*Hist.*) Svevo.
swaddle [swɔdl], *v.t.* Fasciare. **Swaddling clothes,** fasce, *f.pl.*
swag [swæg], *n.* (*colloq.*) Bottino, *m.*; pacco, fardello, *m.*
swage [sweidʒ], *n.* (*Mech.*) Stampo, *m.* || *v.t.* stampare.
swagger [ˈswægəɹ], *v.i.* Vantarsi, gloriarsi, ringalluzzirsi, far lo spavaldo, far lo spaccone. || *n.* Spavalderia, bravata, fanfaronata, vanagloria, *f.* || *a.* Elegante. **To — along,** camminare pavoneggiandosi.
swaggerer, *n.* Spaccone, smargiasso, fanfarone, millantatore, bravaccio, *m.*
swaggeringly, *adv.* Pavoneggiandosi.
swain [swein], *n.* Contadino, pastorello, *m.*; amante, *m.*
swallow (1) [ˈswɔlou], *v.t.* Inghiottire, ingoiare, mandar giù, trangugiare, ingozzare. || *n.* Gola, *f.*, gorgozzule, *m.*; gorgata, ingozzata, sorsata, *f.* **To be swallowed up,** inabissarsi, sommergersi; **to — down,** trangugiare, mandar giù; **he will — anything you tell him,** è pronto a beversi tutto; **to — insults,** inghiottire ingiurie.
swallow (2), *n.* (*Zool.*) Rondine, rondinella, *f.* **— -tail coat,** abito a coda di rondine, *m.*, marsina, *f.*; **— -tail butterfly,** macaone, *m.*
swam [swæm], *p.* of **swim.**
swamp [swɔmp], *n.* Pantano, *m.*, palude, *f.*; acquitrino, *m.* || *v.t.* Impantanare, sprofondare; travolgere, sommergere, inondare, allagare; (*a boat*) riempire di acqua; colmare. **To be swamped with letters,** essere inondato di lettere.
swampy, *a.* Paludoso, pantanoso.
swan [swɔn], *n.* (*Zool.*) Cigno, *m.* **— -song,** canto del cigno, *m.*; **swan's down,** piuma di cigno, *f.*, panno di vigogna, *m.*
swank [swæŋk], *n.* (*colloq.*) Alterigia, vanagloria, *f.* || *v.t.* Ostentare, gloriarsi, darsi delle arie.
swap [swɔp], *v.t.* (*colloq.*) Scambiare, barattare.
sward [swɔːɹd], *n.* Erba, *f.*, tappeto verde, *m.*; erbetta, *f.*
swarded, *a.* Erboso.
swarm (1) [swɔːɹm], *n.* Sciame, *m.*; moltitudine, folla, *f.* || *v.i.* Sciamare; affollarsi, accalcarsi; brulicare, formicolare. **A — of bees,** uno sciame di api, *m.*; **in swarms,** a sciami; **to — with,** brulicare di, formicolare di.
swarm (2), *v.i.* **To — up,** arrampicarsi su.
swarming, *n.* Sciamatura, *f.*
swarthiness, *n.* Carnagione bruna, brunezza, *f.*
swarthy, swart, *a.* Bruno, abbronzato, nericcio.
swash [swɔʃ], *v.t.i.* Schiaffeggiare; scrosciare, sciacquare.
swashbuckler [ˈswɔʃbʌkləɹ], *n.* Smargiasso, spaccone, fanfarone, mangiacristiani, millantatore, *m.*
swastika [ˈswɔstikə], *n.* Croce uncinata, *f.*
swat [swɔt], *v.t.* (*flies*) Uccidere. **Fly-swatter,** scacciamosche, *m.*
swath [swɔθ], *n.* Falciata, *f.*, mannello, *m.*
swathe [sweið], *v.t.* Fasciare, avvolgere. || *n.* Fascia, *f.*
sway [swei], *v.t.* Dondolare, sballottare, agitare; brandire, maneggiare; dirigere, reggere; influenzare, guidare; *v.i.* oscillare, traballare, barcollare, vacillare, titubare. || *n.* Dominio, potere, governo, *m.*; influenza, *f.* **To bear —,** dominare, governare, reggere.
swaying, *n.* Oscillazione, *f.*, traballio, barcollamento, *m.*
swear [swɛəɹ], *v.t.* Giurare, far giurare; *v.i.* giurare; bestemmiare, imprecare. || *n.* Bestemmia, *f.* (*Law*) **To — in,** far prestare il giuramento; (*Law*) **to be sworn,** prestare giuramento; **to — off,** rinunciare a; **to — obedience,** giurare ubbidienza; **to — by,** giurare su; **to — falsely,** spergiurare; **to — like a trooper,** bestemmiare come un Turco; **to — at someone,** imprecare contro alcuno; **I won't — to it,** non vorrei giurarlo; **— -word,** bestemmia, *f.*
swearer, *n.* Giuratore, *m.*; bestemmiatore, *m.*
swearing, *n.* Il giurare, *m.*; il bestemmiare, *m.*
sweat [swet], *n.* Sudore, *m.*, traspirazione, *f.*; sudata, *f.*; (*colloq.*) fatica, *f.* || *v.t.i.* Sudare, trasudare; affaticarsi; far sudare; sfruttare. **In a —,** sudato, tutto in un'acqua; **by the — of one's brow,** col proprio sudore; **in a cold —,** sudando freddo; **dripping with —,** grondante di sudore; **to have a —,** fare una sudata; **to — out a cold,** sfogare un raffreddore sudando; **sweated labour,** lavoro sfruttato, *m.*
sweater, *n.* (*exploiter*) Sfruttatore, *m.*; (*garment*) maglia, *f.*; maglia a maniche lunghe, *f.*, maglione, corpetto a maglia, *m.*
sweatiness, *n.* Sudore, *m.*
sweating, *n.* Il sudare, *m.*; sfruttamento, *m.* **— bath,** bagno a vapore, *m.*
sweaty, *a.* Sudato, coperto di sudore, grondante di sudore.
Swede (1) [swiːd], *n.* Svedese, *m.f.*
swede (2), *n.* Rapa svedese, *f.*
Sweden [ˈswiːdən], *n.* (*Geog.*) Svezia, *f.*
Swedish, *n.a.* Svedese, *m.*
sweep [swiːp], *v.t.* Spazzare, scopare; passare sopra, sfiorare; (*to dredge*) dragare; percorrere, scorrere; *v.i.* passare, scorrere via, scivolar via; incedere; camminare maestosa-

mente; spaziare; stendersi. || *n.* (*with brush*) Scopata, spazzata, *f.*; (*with oar*) remata, *f.*; (*chimney-sweep*) spazzacamino, *m.*; (*of road*) tratto, *m.*, curva, distesa, *f.*; (*of arm*) gesto, *m.*; (*oar*) remo, *m.*; (*range*) portata, *f.* **A dress that sweeps the ground,** un abito che strascica; **to — the strings of a harp,** scorrer le corde d'un' arpa; **his eyes swept the horizon,** i suoi occhi percorsero l'orizzonte; **to — along,** sfilare; **to — away, to — off,** portar via; **to — up the snow,** spazzare la neve; **she swept out of the room,** uscì impettita dalla stanza; **their foes swept over them,** i nemici si rovesciarono su di essi; **with a — of the hand,** con un gesto della mano; **a — of mountain country,** una distesa di montagne, *f.*; **to make a clean —,** far repulisti, far piazza pulita, far tavola rasa; **to — the board,** raccogliere le poste; **— -net,** giacchio, *m.*

sweeper, *n.* Scopa da tappeto, *f.*; spazzatrice meccanica, *f.* **Chimney- —,** spazzacamino, *m.*; **street- —,** spazzino, *m.*

sweeping, *n.* Spazzatura, scopatura, *f.* || *a.* Travolgente, rapido, impetuoso, irresistibile; (*fig.*) completo, generale. **Sweepings,** spazzature, immondizie, *f.pl.*

sweepingly, *adv.* Irresistibilmente, di colpo.

sweepstake, *n.* Lotteria, *f.*

sweet [swi:t], *a.* Dolce, soave; fragrante, profumato; zuccherino; dolce, melodioso. || *n.* Dolce, *m.*; confetto, zuccherino, *m.*, caramella, chicca, *f.* **Sweets,** dolci, *m.pl.*; piaceri, diletti, *m.pl.*; **to taste —,** saper di dolce, avere un sapore dolce; **to smell —,** saper di buono; **— water,** acqua dolce, *f.*; **to keep —,** conservarsi bene; **a — temper,** un'indole mite, *f.*; **to have a — tooth,** avere una buona bocca per i dolci; **— sleep,** sonno tranquillo, *m.*; **— -pea,** pisello odoroso, *m.*; **— -potato,** patata dolce, *f.*; **— nothings,** nonnulla, inezie, paroline dolci, *f.pl.*; (*colloq.*) **to be — on,** essere innamorato di; (*Bot.*) **— -brier,** rosa selvatica, *f.*; **— -oil,** olio d'oliva, *m.*; **— -scented, — smelling,** fragrante, profumato, odoroso; **— -shop,** confetteria, *f.*; **— -stuff,** dolciumi, *m.pl.*; **— -tempered,** dall'indole dolce; (*Bot.*) **— -william,** dianto, *m.*, garofolini, *m.pl.*

sweetbread, *n.* Animella, *f.*

sweeten, *v.t.* Addolcire; inzuccherare; purificare, disinfettare; temperare, ingentilire.

sweetening, *n.* Addolcimento, inzuccheramento, *m.*

sweetheart [ˈswi:thɑ:ɹt], *n.* Innamorato, *m.*, innamorata, *f.*, amoroso, *m.*, amorosa, *f.*

sweetish, *a.* Dolcetto, dolcigno.

sweetly, *adv.* Dolcemente, soavemente, piacevolmente, graziosamente; melodiosamente.

sweetmeat, *n.* Dolce, confetto, zuccherino, *m.*, caramella, chicca, *f.*

sweetness, *n.* Dolcezza, soavità, gentilezza, *f.*; fragranza, *f.*, profumo, *m.*

swell (1) [swel], *v.i.* Gonfiare, gonfiarsi, enfiare, dilatarsi; ingrossare, inturgidire, intumidire; crescere, aumentare; *v.t.* gonfiare, dilatare, distendere, ingrossare; aumentare; ingrandire, accrescere. || *n.* (*of sea*) Ondeggiamento, ondulamento, *m.*; (*of ground*) elevazione, *f.*; (*thick part*) grosso, *m.* **To — out,** gonfiarsi, intumidire, enfiarsi; **his wrist swelled up,** gli si enfiò il polso; **to — with pride,** insuperbire, inorgoglirsi.

swell (2), *n.* (*colloq.*) Elegante, damerino, *m.*; pezzo grosso, gran signore, *m.* || *a.* Elegante, bello, alla moda. **You are a —!** Come siete elegante! Che lusso! **— clothes,** vestiti eleganti, *m.pl.*; **— mobsman,** borsaiuolo elegante, *m.*

swelling, *n.* Enfiagione, gonfiezza, *f.*, gonfiore, gonfiamento, rigonfiamento, *m.* || *a.* Gonfio, grosso. **A — on the neck,** un gonfiore al collo, *m.*; **with a — heart,** col cuore gonfio.

swelter [ˈsweltəɹ], *v.i.* Arrostire, scoppiare, soffocare dal caldo, essere molle di sudore. || *n.* Afa, *f.*

swerve [swə:ɹv], *v.i.* Deviare; scartare, sterzare; allontanarsi, piegare; traviare, errare. || *n.* sterzata, *f.*, deviamento, *m.*, scarto, *m.* **To — from one's duty,** mancare al proprio dovere.

swift (1) [swift], *a.* Rapido, veloce, celere, presto; pronto, immediato, repentino. || *adv.* Presto, subito, rapidamente. **— -footed,** agile, di pie' veloce, a piede leggero.

swift (2), *n.* (*Zool.*) Rondone, *m.*

swiftly, *adv.* Rapidamente, velocemente, celermente.

swiftness, *n.* Rapidità, velocità, celerità, *f.*

swig [swig], *v.t.i.* Tracannare, bere d'un fiato. || *n.* Sorso, *m.*, sorsata, *f.*

swill [swil], *v.t.* Lavare, risciacquare; tracannare, bere; *v.i.* sbevazzare. || *n.* Lavatura, risciacquatura, *f.*; lavata, *f.* **— -tub,** mastello da lavatura, *m.*

swiller, *n.* Sbevazzatore, beone, *m.*

swim [swim], *v.i.* Nuotare; (*to float*) galleggiare; (*of the head*) girare; essere bagnato, essere inondato; *v.t.* traversare a nuoto. || *n.* Nuotata, *f.* **To — across,** traversare a nuoto; **to — out to sea,** nuotare al largo; **he cannot — a stroke,** nuota come un mattone; **my head swims,** mi gira la testa; **swimming with water,** inondata di acqua; **to go for a —,** andare a nuotare, fare una nuotata; (*colloq.*) **in the —,** al corrente, aggiornato, all'avanguardia.

swimmer, *n.* Nuotatore, *m.*, nuotatrice, *f.* **He is a good —,** è un valente nuotatore.

swimming, *n.* Nuoto, *m.* **— of the head,** vertigine, *f.*; **— -bath,** vasca da nuoto, *f.*; piscina, *f.*; **— -bladder,** vescica natatoria; **— -pool,** piscina, *f.*

swimmingly, *adv.* Benissimo, a meraviglia.

swimsuit [ˈswimsju:t], *n.* Costume da bagno, *m.*

swindle [swindl], *v.t.* Truffare, frodare, raggirare, imbrogliare. || *n.* Truffa, frode, *f.*, raggiro, imbroglio, *m.*

swindler, *n.* Truffatore, imbroglione, impostore, *m.*

swindling, *n.* Truffa, *f.*, imbroglio, raggiro, *m.*

swine (pl. **swine**) [swain], *n.* Porco, maiale, *m.* **— -fever,** febbre suina contagiosa, *f.*; **— -herd,** porcaio, porcaro, *m.*

swing [swiŋ], *v.i.* Oscillare; dondolarsi; penzolare, star penzoloni; (*fig.*) esser impiccato; *v.t.* dondolare, agitare; vibrare, maneggiare, brandire. || *n.* Oscillazione, *f.*, dondolio, *m.*; vibrazione, *f.*; (*swinging seat*) altalena, *f.*; (*fig.*) attività, *f.*, libero corso, *m.*, slancio, *m.* **To — round,** voltarsi di scatto; (*Naut.*) **to — at anchor,** girare sull'ancora;

to — **one's arms,** agitare le braccia; **he sat on the table swinging his legs,** sedette sul tavolo con le gambe penzoloni; (*colloq.*) **to go with a —,** avere un bel ritmo; **in full —,** in piena attività; **— -boat,** altalena, *f.*; **— -bridge,** ponte girevole, *m.*; **— -door,** porta battente, *f.*

swingeing ['swindʒiŋ], *a.* Fortissimo, grandissimo.

swinging ['swiŋiŋ], *n.* Oscillazione, *f.*, dondolio, dondolamento, *m.* || *a.* Ritmico, cadenzato; oscillante, fluttuante; pendente. **A — trot,** un trotto serrato, *m.*

swingle [swiŋgl], *n.* Maciulla, *f.* **— -tree,** bilancino di carrozza, *m.*

swinish ['swainiʃ], *a.* Porcino; schifoso, sozzo, sudicio, bestiale.

swinishly, *adv.* Sozzamente, bestialmente.

swipe [swaip], *n.* (*colloq.*) Cazzotto, *m.*; botta, *f.* || *v.t.i.* Cazzottare, batter sodo.

swipes, *n.pl.* (*colloq.*) Birra cattiva, *f.*

swirl [swəːɹl], *v.i.* Turbinare. || *n.* Turbine, vortice, *m.*

swish [swiʃ], *v.t.* Sferzare; agitare, vibrare; maneggiare; *v.i.* scrosciare. || *n.* Sferzata, *f.*, scroscio, *m.*

Swiss [swis], *n.a.* Svizzero, *m.*

switch [switʃ], *n.* Bacchetta, verghetta, *f.*; (*Rail.*) scambio, deviatoio, *m.*; (*Elec.*) interruttore, *m.*, chiavetta, *f.* || *v.t.i.* Sferzare; voltarsi di scatto; afferrare, agguantare; (*Rail.*) deviare; dimenare. **To — off the light,** spegnere la luce; **to — off the current,** chiudere la corrente, rompere il circuito; **to — on the light,** accendere la luce; **to — on the current,** aprire la corrente; **— -board,** quadro di distribuzione, *m.*

switchback, switchback railway, *n.* Montagne russe, *f.pl.*

Switzerland ['switzəɹlənd], *n.* (*Geog.*) Svizzera, *f.*

swivel ['swivəl], *n.* Perno, mulinello, anello girevole, *m.* || *v.i.* Girare, imperniarsi. **— -eyed,** guercio, bircio, losco; **— -gun,** cannone girevole, *m.*

swollen ['swoulən], *a.* Gonfiato.

swoon [swuːn], *v.i.* Svenire, venir meno, tramortire, perdere i sensi. || *n.* Svenimento, deliquio, *m.*

swoop [swuːp], *v.i.* Piombare, slanciarsi, avventarsi. || *n.* Slancio, balzo, colpo, *m.* **To — down upon,** piombare su, avventarsi su, assalire all'improvviso; **at one fell —,** d'un sol colpo.

swop [cp. **swap**].

sword [sɔːɹd], *n.* Spada, *f.*; sciabola, *f.*; ferro, *m.* **To cross swords with,** incrociar la spada con; **to draw one's —,** sguainare la spada; **to put to the —,** mettere a fil di spada; **fire and —,** ferro e fuoco; **— -arm,** la mano destra, *f.*; **— -bayonet,** sciabola baionetta, *f.*; **— -bearer,** portaspada, *m.*; **— -belt,** cinturino, *m.*; **— -blade,** lama della spada, *f.*; **— -cane,** stocco, *m.*; **— -dance,** danza della spada, *f.*; (*Zool.*) **— -fish,** pesce spada, *m.*; (*Bot.*) **— -grass,** spadacciuola, *f.*, gladiolo, *m.*; **— hilt,** elsa della spada, *f.*; **— -knot,** dragona, *f.*; **— -stick,** stocco, bastone animato, *m.*; **— -thrust,** stoccata, *f.*

swordsman, *n.* Spadaccino, schermitore, *m.*

swordsmanship, *n.* Scherma, *f.*

sworn [swɔːɹn], *a.* Giurato; devoto; accanito. **— friends,** amici devoti, *m.pl.*; **— enemies,** nemici giurati, *m.pl.*

swot [swɔt], *v.i.* (*colloq.*) Sgobbare. || *n.* Sgobbone, *m.*

sybarite ['saibərait], *n.* Sibarita, *m.*

sycamore ['sikəmɔːɹ], *n.* (*Bot.*) Sicomoro, *m.*

sycophancy ['sikofənsi], *n.* Delazione, venalità, *f.*

sycophant, *n.* Sicofante, parassita, *m.f.*

sycophantic, *a.* Venale, corrotto.

syllabary ['siləbəri], *n.* Sillabario, *m.*

syllabic [si'læbik], *a.* Sillabico.

syllabically, *adv.* Sillaba per sillaba.

syllabification, *n.* Sillabazione, *f.*

syllable ['siləbl], *n.* Sillaba, *f.*

syllabus ['siləbəs], *n.* Sommario, compendio, *m.*; programma, *m.*, lista, *f.*; (*Eccles.*) sillabo, *m.*

syllogism ['silodʒizm], *n.* Sillogismo, *m.*

syllogistic, *a.* Sillogistico.

syllogize ['silodʒaiz], *v.t.i.* Sillogizzare.

sylph [silf], *n.* Silfo, *m.*, silfide, *f.*

sylvan ['silvən], *a.* Silvano, silvestre, boschereccio.

symbiosis [simbai'ousis], *n.* Simbiosi, *f.*

symbol ['simbəl], *n.* Simbolo, *m.*

symbolic, symbolical [sim'bɔlik, sim'bɔlikəl], *a.* Simbolico.

symbolically, *adv.* Simbolicamente.

symbolism ['simbolizm], *n.* Simbolismo, *m.*

symbolize, *v.t.* Simboleggiare, simbolizzare.

symmetrical [si'metrikəl], *a.* Simmetrico.

symmetrically, *adv.* Simmetricamente.

symmetrize, *v.t.* Simmetrizzare, porre in simmetria.

symmetry ['simetri], *n.* Simmetria, *f.*

sympathetic [simpə'θetik], *a.* Simpatizzante, amichevole, cordiale; comprensivo, simpatico.

sympathetically, *adv.* Cordialmente, teneramente.

sympathize ['simpəθaiz], *v.i.* Simpatizzare, compatire, partecipare. **To — with,** simpatizzare con, compatire.

sympathizer, *n.* Simpatizzante, *m.f.*

sympathy, *n.* Compassione, *f.*, rammarico, *m.*; condoglianza, *f.*; simpatia, comprensione, *f.*

symphonic [sim'fɔnik], *a.* Sinfonico.

symphony, *n.* Sinfonia, *f.*

symposium [sim'pouziəm], *n.* Simposio, *m.*

symptom ['simptəm], *n.* Sintomo, *m.*

symptomatic, *a.* Sintomatico.

symptomatology [simptəmə'tɔlɔdʒi], *n.* Sintomatologia, semeiotica, *f.*

synæresis [sinə'riːsis], *n.* (*Gram.*) Sineresi, *f.*

synagogue ['sinəgɔg], *n.* Sinagoga, *f.*

synchronous ['sinkronəs], *a.* Sincrono, sincronico.

synchronously, *adv.* Sincronicamente.

synchronism, *n.* Sincronismo, *m.*

synchronization [sinkronai'zeiʃən], *n.* Sincronizzazione, *f.*

synchronize, *v.t.* Sincronizzare.

syncopate ['sinkopeit], *v.t.* Sincopare.

syncopation, *n.* Sincopatura, *f.*

syncope ['sinkopi], *n.* (*Med.*) Sincope, *f.*

syndic ['sindik], *n.* Sindaco, *m.*

syndicalism, *n.* (*Pol.*) Sindacalismo.

syndicate ['sindikeit], *n.* Sindacato, *m.* || *v.t.* Riunire in sindacato.

synod [ˈsinəd], *n.* Sinodo, *m.*
synodal, *a.* Sinodale.
synodic, synodical, *a.* Sinodico.
synonym [ˈsinonim], *n.* Sinonimo, *m.*
synonymity, *n.* Sinonimia, *f.*
synonymous, *a.* Sinonimo.
synonymously, *adv.* Sinonimamente.
synopsis (pl. **synopses**) [siˈnɔpsis, siˈnɔpsi:z], *n.* Sinossi, *f.*, sommario, *m.*; prospetto, *m.*
synoptic, synoptical, *a.* Sinottico. **The — gospels,** i vangeli sinottici, *m.pl.*
synovitis [sainoˈvaitis], *n.* (*Med.*) Sinovite, *f.*
syntax [ˈsintæks], *n.* Sintassi, *f.*
synthesis (pl. **syntheses**) [ˈsinθesis, ˈsinθesi:z] *n.* Sintesi, *f.*
synthesize [ˈsinθesaiz], *v.t.* Sintetizzare.
synthetic, synthetical [sinˈθetik, sinˈθetikəl], *a.* Sintetico.
synthetically, *adv.* Sinteticamente.
syphilis [ˈsifilis], *n.* (*Med.*) Sifilide, *f.*
syphilitic [sifiˈlitik], *a.* Sifilitico.
Syracuse [ˈsairəkju:z], *n.* (*Geog.*) Siracusa, *f.*
Syria [ˈsiriə], *n.* (*Geog.*) Siria, *f.*
Syriac, *a.* Siriaco. || *n.* Lingua siriaca, *f.*
Syrian [ˈsiriən], *n.a.* Siriano, *m.*
syringa [siˈriŋgə], *n.* (*Bot.*) Salindia, *f.*, gelsomino della Madonna, *m.*
syringe [ˈsirindʒ], *n.* Siringa, *f.* || *v.t.* Siringare, fare un'inezione. **Garden —,** canna da inaffiamento, *f.*
syrinx [ˈsiriŋks], *n.* Siringa, fistola, *f.*; (*Anat.*) siringe, *f.*
syrup [ˈsirəp], *n.* Sciroppo, *m.*; (*treacle*) melassa, *f.* **Golden —,** melassa raffinata, *f.*
syrupy, *a.* Sciropposo.
system [ˈsistəm], *n.* Sistema, *m.*; (*Rail., etc.*) rete, *f.*; metodo, *m.* **Railway —,** rete ferroviaria, *f.*; **telephone —,** rete telefonica, *f.*; **digestive —,** sistema digestivo, *m.*; **he lacks —,** non ha sistema, non ha metodo; **heating —,** impianto di riscaldamento, *m.*
systematic [sisteˈmætik], *a.* Sistematico, metodico.
systematically, *adv.* Sistematicamente.
systematization [sistemətaiˈzeiʃən], *n.* Sistemazione, *f.*
systematize, *v.t.* Sistemare.
systole [ˈsistouli], *n.* (*Anat.*) Sistole, *f.*
syzygy [ˈsizidʒi], *n.* (*Astron.*) Sizigia, *f.*

T

T, t [ti:], Ventesima lettera dell'alfabeto inglese. **That suits me to a T,** ciò mi va benissimo; **he hit it off to a T,** lo espresse esattamente; **T-square,** squadra a T, *f.*
tab [tæb], *n.* Striscettina, *f.*; (*of shoe*) linguetta, *f.*; (*of lace*) puntale, aghetto, *m.*; segnalibro, *m.*
tabard [ˈtæbəɹd], *n.* Cotta d'arme, *f.*
tabaret [ˈtæbəret], *n.* Specie di raso rigato.
tabby, tabby cat [ˈtæbi, tæbi ˈkæt], *n.* Gatto soriano, gatto tigrato, *m.*
tabefaction [tæbiˈfækʃən], *n.* (*Med.*) Consumazione, *f.*, dimagramento, *m.*
tabernacle [ˈtæbəɹnækl], *n.* (*Eccles.*) Tabernacolo, *m.*
tabes [ˈteibi:z], *n.* (*Med.*) Tabe, *f.*
tabetic, *a.* Tisico, infetto di tabe.
tablature [ˈtæblətʃju:ɹ], *n.* (*Art*) Affresco, *m.*
table [ˈteibəl], *n.* Tavola, *f.*, tavolo, *m.*; (*of figures*) tabella, *f.*; indice, prospetto, *m.* || *v.t.* Posporre, differire, mettere innanzi, intavolare; (*Mech.*) incastrare. **Folding —,** tavola pieghevole, *f.*; **kitchen —,** tavolo da cucina, *m.*; **the tables are turned,** le cose hanno cambiato aspetto; (*Pol.*) **to be laid upon the —,** essere proposto; **to sit at —,** sedere a tavola; **to clear the —,** sparecchiare la tavola; **to keep a good —,** far buona tavola; **to lay the —,** apparecchiare la tavola: **to rise from —,** alzarsi da tavola; **to sit down to —,** mettersi a tavola; **to put on the —,** intavolare; **the multiplication —,** la tavola pitagorica, *f.*; **— -beer,** birra leggera, *f.*; **— centre,** centro da tavola, *m.*; **— -cloth,** tovaglia, *f.*; **— -cover** tappeto, *m.*; **— -flap,** ribalta del tavolo, *f.*; **— -knife,** coltello da tavola, *m.*; **— -linen,** biancheria da tavola, *f.*; **— -mat,** sottopiatto, *m.*; **— -napkin,** tovagliolo, *m.*; **— -spoon,** cucchiaio da tavola, *m.*; **— spoonful,** cucchiaiata, *f.*; **— -talk,** conversazione famigliare, *f.*; **— -ware,** servizio da tavola, *m.*; **— -water,** acqua minerale, *f.*; **— -rapping, — turning,** battere del tavolo, giro del tavolo, *m.*
tableau [ˈtæblou], *n.* Quadro plastico, tablò, *m.*
tableful, *n.* Tavolata, *f.*
tableland, *n.* (*Geog.*) Altipiano, *m.*
tablet [ˈtæblet], *n.* Tavoletta, *f.*; pasticca, pastiglia, *f.*; lapide, *f.*
tabloid [ˈtæblɔid], *n.* Marca di fabbrica di certi prodotti chimici; (*colloq.*) pasticca, *f.*; giornale sensazionale, *m.*
taboo [təˈbu:], *n.* Tabù, *m.* || *v.t.* Proibire, vietare, interdire.
tabor [ˈteibɔɹ], *n.* (*Mus.*) Specie di tamburo.
tabouret [ˈtæbəret], *n.* Sgabello, *m.*
tabular [ˈtæbju:ləɹ], *a.* Tavolare, di tavola, di tabelle. **Arranged in — form,** in forma di tavola.
tabulate, *v.t.* Disporre in tavole sinottiche, prospettare, catalogare, disporre in tabelle.
tabulation, *n.* Disposizione in tavole, catalogazione, *f.*
tachometer [təˈkɔmetəɹ], *n.* Tachimetro, *m.*
tachygraphy [təˈkigrəfi], *n.* Tacheografia, stenografia, *f.*
tachymeter, tacheometer, *n.* Tacheometro, *m.*
tacit [ˈtæsit], *a.* Tacito, implicito.
tacitly, *adv.* Tacitamente, implicitamente.
taciturn [ˈtæsitə:ɹn], *a.* Taciturno.
taciturnity [tæsiˈtə:ɹniti], *n.* Taciturnità, *f.*
taciturnly, *adv.* Taciturnamente.
tack (1) [tæk], *n.* Bulletta, *f.*, chiodetto, *m.*; (*stitch*) punto lungo, *m.* || *v.t.* Chiodare; (*to sew*) imbastire. **To — on,** aggiungere.
tack (2), *n.* (*Naut.*) (*direction*) Bordata, *f.*; (*rope*) mura, *f.*; (*fig.*) strada, via, *f.*; (*colloq.*) cibo, *m.* || *v.i.* Bordeggiare, virare di bordo. **To be on the right —,** essere sulla buona via; **to change —,** bordeggiare; **to sail on the port —,** virare a babordo; (*colloq.*) **hard —,** biscotti, *m.pl.*
tacking, *n.* (*sewing*) Imbastitura, *f.*; (*Naut.*) bordeggiamento, viramento, *m.* **— cotton,** cotone da imbastire, *m.*
tackle, *n.* (*Mech.*) Paranco, *m.*; arnesi attrezzi, strumenti, *m.pl.*; (*Football*) arresto, *m.* || *v.t.*

Affrontare; afferrare, venire alle prese con; (*to undertake*) cominciare, mettersi a, intraprendere; (*Football*) arrestare. **Fishing-—**, arnese da pesca, *m.*; **—-block,** puleggia, *f.*
tacky, *a.* Viscoso, attaccaticcio, tenace.
tact [tækt], *n.* Tatto, *m.*, accortezza, *f.*; riguardo, *m.*
tactful, *a.* Pieno di tatto, accorto, premuroso.
tactical ['tæktikəl], *a.* Tattico.
tactically, *adv.* Tatticamente.
tactician [tæk'tiʃən], *n.* Tattico, *m.*
tactics, *n.pl.* Tattica, *f.*
tactile, tactual ['tæktail, 'tæktju:əl], *a.* Tattile.
tactless, *a.* Senza tatto, malaccorto.
tadpole ['tædpoul], *n.* (*Zool.*) Girino, *m.*
taenia ['ti:niə], *n.* (*Zool.*) Tenia, *f.*
taffeta ['tæfetə], *n.* Taffetà, *m.*
taffrail ['tæfril], *n.* (*Naut.*) Coronamento della poppa, *m.*
Taffy ['tæfi], *n.* (*colloq.*) Un Gallese, *m.*
tag [tæg], *n.* (*of lace, etc.*) Puntale, aghetto, *m.*; (*label*) etichetta, *f.*; (*of boot*) tirante, *m.*; (*of song, etc.*) ritornello; (*phrase*) frase fatta, espressione bell'e fatta, *f.*; (*child's game*) il giuocare a prendersi, *m.* || *v.t.* Mettere il puntale a; aggiungere; (*colloq.*) seguire, star dietro a. **Rag, — and bobtail,** canaglia, *f.*; **to — after someone,** star dietro a qualcuno.
Tagus ['teigʌs], *n.* (*Geog.*) Tago, *m.*
Tahiti [tɑ:'hi:ti], *n.* (*Geog.*) Taiti, *m.*
tail [teil], *n.* Coda, *f.*; estremità, fine, *f.*; (*of coat*) falda, coda, *f.*; (*of coin*) rovescio, *m.*; (*Aviat.*) coda, *f.* **To turn —,** battersela, darsela a gambe; **with his — between his legs,** con le pive nel sacco; **—-board,** ribalta d'un carro, *f.*; **—-coat, tails,** (*evening*) abito a coda di rondine, *m.*; (*morning*) abito a falda, *m.*, marsina, *f.*; **—-piece,** vignetta, *f.*; **—-race,** acqua di scarico del mulino, *f.*
tailed, *a.* Codato, caudato.
tailings, *n.pl.* (*grain*) Mondiglia, lolla, *f.*; rifiuti di miniera, *m.pl.*
tailor ['teilər], *n.* Sarto, *m.* **Lady's —,** sarto per signore, *m.*; **—-made,** tailleur; **—-made costume,** abito tailleur; (*Zool.*) **—-bird,** uccello sarto, *m.*
tailoress, *n.* Sarta, sartina, *f.*
tailoring, *n.* Sartoria, *f.*
taint [teint], *v.t.* Guastare, infettare, corrompere; macchiare, lordare; *v.i.* guastarsi, corrompersi. || *n.* Corruzione, infezione, *f.*; macchia, taccia, *f.* **A — of insanity,** un'ombra di pazzia, *f.*; **a reputation without —,** una riputazione immacolata, *f.*
tainted, *a.* (*of food*) Guastato, corrotto.
taintless, *a.* Immacolato, senza macchia, puro.
take [teik], *v.t.* Prendere, togliere; (*to lead*) menare, condurre, portare; (*to seize*) afferrare, pigliare; (*to accept*) accettare, ricevere; (*to gain*) guadagnare; (*to charm*) cattivare, incantare; (*to consider*) prendere, ritenere, considerare; (*to hold*) contenere; (*a walk*) fare; *v.i.* riuscire, avere successo; aver presa, attaccare, attecchire; fare, andare. || *n.* Presa, *f.*; quantità, *f.* **How long does it — to go there?** Quanto tempo ci vuole a andarci? **How old do you — me to be?** Quanti anni mi date? **— this book to her,** portatele questo libro; **he took him by the throat,** lo prese alla gola; **to — the bit between one's teeth,** mordere il freno; **to — prisoner,** fare prigioniero; **to — someone in the act,** cogliere qualcuno in flagrante; **to — a holiday,** andare in vacanza, far vacanza; **to — a seat,** accomodarsi, porsi a sedere; **to — seats at the theatre,** prenotare posti al teatro; **to — legal advice,** consultare un avvocato; **to — someone to task,** rimproverare qualcuno; **to — someone in hand,** far filar dritto qualcuno; **I do not — your meaning,** non riesco a capirvi; **I — it that he is not coming,** ritengo che non venga; **to — it easy,** fare i propri comodi, prendersela comoda; **Do you — 'The Times'?** Siete abbonato al 'Times'? **I should take it kindly if you would . . .,** vi sarei obbligato se voleste . . .; **to — it ill,** prendere in mala parte; **you must — us as you find us,** dovete prenderci come siamo; **to — one's chance,** arrischiare, tentar la sorte; **to — earth,** rintanarsi; **to — one's life in one's hand,** rischiare la vita; **to — place,** aver luogo, verificarsi; **to be taken giddy,** esser preso da vertigini; **to be taken ill,** ammalarsi, sentirsi male; **to give and —,** dare e togliere; **to — aback,** sconcertare, prendere di sorpresa; (*fig.*) **to — a back seat,** prendere un posto secondario, venir messo da parte; **to — away,** portar via, togliere, sparecchiare, rimuovere; **to — away from,** dedurre, detrarre; **to — back,** riprendere, riportare; **to — back one's words,** disdire le proprie parole; **to — breath,** prender fiato, ripigliar fiato; **to — down,** (*to humble*) umiliare, abbassare; (*to swallow*) inghiottire, ingoiare; (*to write*) scrivere, prender nota di; (*to demolish*) atterrare, demolire; **to — farewell of,** dire addio a, accomiatarsi da; **to — for,** scambiare con, confondere con; **to — for a walk,** condurre a fare una passeggiata; **to — from,** diminuire, indebolire, derogare a; **to — away from,** togliere a; **to — in,** (*guests*) ricevere; (*to comprise*) comprendere, contenere; (*a dress*) restringere; (*sail*) serrare; (*to understand*) capire; (*to deceive*) ingannare; **to — into one's confidence,** prendere in confidenza; **to — in washing,** fare la lavandaia; **to — in hand,** intraprendere; **to — into account,** tenere presente, tener conto di, aver riguardo a; **to — it into one's head that . . .,** mettersi in testa che . . .; **to — it out in . . .,** farsi pagare in . . .; **to — off,** (*clothes*) levarsi; (*to lead away*) condurre via, portare via; (*to reduce*) dedurre; (*to mimic*) imitare, burlarsi di; (*Aviat.*) decollare; (*to jump*) spiccare; **to — on,** assumere, intraprendere; **to — someone on at golf,** far una partita di golf con qualcuno; **to — oneself off,** andarsene, scappare, battersela, svignarsela; **to — out,** (*to remove*) rimuovere; (*to abstract*) portar fuori, far uscire; (*a stain*) smacchiare; (*a patent*) prendere; **to — out of,** portar fuori di, rimuovere da; **to — the nonsense out of,** togliere i grilli dalla testa a; **to — over a business,** rilevare un'azienda; **to — it out of someone,** vendicarsi con qualcuno, spossare qualcuno; **to — pity on,** avere pietà di; **to — someone's life,** uccidere qualcuno, togliere la vita a qualcuno; **to — to heart,** affliggersi di, prendere a cuore; **to — up,** (*to lift*) raccogliere, sollevare; (*to absorb*)

assorbire; (*space*) occupare, ingombrare; (*time*) consumare; (*passengers*) far salire; (*to arrest*) arrestare; (*an enquiry*) perseguire; (*a dropped stitch*) ripigliare; (*a profession*) entrare in; (*a bill*) pagare; **to — upon oneself,** incaricarsi di, impegnarsi di, assumersi, prendersi a carico; **What do you — me for?** Per chi mi prendete? **he took her for her sister,** la scambiò colla sua sorella; **— it or leave it,** prendere o lasciare, o dentro o fuori; **the novel did not —,** il romanzo non ebbe successo; **the vaccine did not —,** il siero non ha attaccato; **to — after,** somigliare a; (*colloq.*) **to — on,** lamentarsi, dolersi, affliggersi; **to — to,** (*begin to*) cominciare a, mettersi a; (*to have recourse to*) darsi a, correre a; (*to take refuge*) rifugiarsi in; (*to like*) voler bene a, prendere una simpatia per; **to — up with,** fare amicizia con; **to — to pieces,** smontare; **Take your seats!** A posto! In vettura! **—-off,** caricatura, imitazione, *f.*; (*Aviat.*) decollo, *m.*; **a —-in,** un inganno, *m.*, una frode, *f.*

taker, *n.* (*Sport*) Chi accetta una scommessa; prenditore, *m.*

taking, *n.* Presa, *f.* || *a.* Attraente, seducente, simpatico. **Takings,** incasso, *m.*; (*Aviat.*) **—-off,** decollo, *m.*

takingness, *n.* Attrattiva, *f.*; simpatia, *f.*

talc [tælk], *n.* (*Geol.*) Talco, *m.*

tale [teil], *n.* Storia, *f.*, racconto, *m.*; narrazione, novella, *f.*; romanzo, *m.*; numero, *m.* **A silly —,** una fandonia, *f.*; **it tells its own —,** si spiega da sè; **to tell tales out of school,** fare la spia, riportare; **— bearer,** spifferone, *m.*, spia, *f.*; **—-bearing,** delazione, *f.*; **—-teller,** bugiardo, *m.*; raccontatore, narratore, *m.*

talent [ˈtælənt], *n.* Talento, ingegno, *m.*, attitudine, *f.* **A — for languages,** un'attitudine per le lingue, *f.*

talented, *a.* Di talento, d'ingegno, abile.

tales [ˈteiliːz], *n.pl.* (*Law*) Giurati supplenti, *m.pl.*

talion [tæliən], *n.* Taglione, *m.*

talisman (pl. **talismans**) [ˈtælizmən], *n.* Talismano, *m.*

talk [tɔːk], *v.i.* Parlare; discorrere, ragionare, conversare; ciarlare, chiacchierare; *v.t.* parlare, dire. || *n.* Discorso, *m.*, conversazione, *f.*; ragionamento, *m.*; colloquio, abboccamento, *m.*; ciarla, chiacchiera, *f.* cicaleccio, *m.*; diceria, voce, *f.* **What are you talking about?** Di che parlate? **to — at someone,** farla capire a qualcuno; **to — away the time,** passare il tempo discorrendo; **to — back,** ribattere; **to — down,** stordire uno colle chiacchiere; **to — down to someone,** parlare in lingua semplice; **to — to oneself,** parlare a se stesso; **to — nonsense,** parlare a vanvera; **to — oneself hoarse,** spolmonarsi, sfiatarsi; **to — over,** discutere; **to — someone over,** persuadere qualcuno; **to be the — of the town,** essere sulla bocca di tutti; **small-—,** banalità, *f.* inezie *f.pl.*; **there is — that . . .,** corre voce che . . . si dice che . . . .

talkative [ˈtɔːkətiv] *a.* Loquace, ciarliero, chiacchierone.

talkativeness, *n.* Loquacità, *f.*

talker, *n.* Parlatore, *m.*; chiacchierone, ciarlone, cicalone, *m.*; millantatore, *m.*

talkie [ˈtɔːki], *n.* (*colloq.*) Film parlato, *m.*

talking, *n.* Conversazione, *f.*, ciarle, chiacchiere, *f.pl.* || *a.* Parlante. **To give a —-to,** dare una ramanzina.

tall [tɔːl], *a.* Grande, alto. **A — fellow,** un pezzo d'uomo, *m.*; **a — hat,** un cappello a cilindro, *m.*, una tuba, *f.*; (*colloq.*) **a — story,** una panzana, una frottola; (*colloq.*) **a — order,** un affare serio, un affare difficile, *m.*; **—-boy,** canterano, *m.*; (*colloq.*) **to talk —,** esagerare, sballarle grosse.

tallith [ˈtæliθ], *n.* (*Eccles.*) Taled, *m.*

tallness, *n.* Grandezza, altezza, *f.*; statura, *f.*

tallow [ˈtælou], *n.* Sego, *m.* || *v.t.* Impiastrare di sego. **—-candle,** candela di sego, *f.*; **—-chandler,** candelaio, *m.*; **—-faced,** pallido, *a.*

tallowy, *a.* Segoso.

tally [ˈtæli], *n.* (*check*) Riscontro, *m.*; (*stick*) taglia, *f.*; (*label*) etichetta, *f.* || *v.t.* Intaccare, intagliare; *v.i.* accordarsi, coincidere. **To — with,** accordarsi con, coincidere con.

tally-ho! [tæliˈhou], *inter.* Dallì dallì!

tallyman [ˈtælimæn], *n.* Mercante che vende a credito, *m.*

Talmud [ˈtælmʌd], *n.* (*Eccles.*) Talmud, *m.*

Talmudist, *n.* Talmudista, *m.*

talon [ˈtælən], *n.* Artiglio, *m.*; (*counterfoil*) madre, matrice, *f.*

talus [ˈteiləs], *n.* (*Anat.*) Talo, *m.*; scarpata, *f.*, pendio, *m.*

tamarind [ˈtæmərind], *n.* (*Bot.*) Tamarindo, *m.*

tamarisk [ˈtæmərisk], *n.* (*Bot.*) Tamerice, *f.*, tamerisco, *m.*

tambour [ˈtæmbəɹ], *n.* (*Mus.*) Tamburo, *m.*; tombolo, telaio da ricamo, *m.* **—-frame,** telaino da ricamo, *m.*; **—-work,** ricamo, *m.*

tambourine [ˈtæmbəriːn], *n.* (*Mus.*) Tamburello, *m.*

tame [teim], *a.* Domestico, addomesticato; docile, mansueto; insipido, insulso, sbiadito; sommesso, umile. || *v.t.* Domare, addomesticare, ammansire, soggiogare, vincere.

tameable, *a.* Domabile, addomesticabile, addomestichevole.

tamely, *adv.* Docilmente; insipidamente, sommessamente.

tameness, *n.* Docilità, mansuetudine, *f.*; insipidità, insulsaggine, *f.*; sommissione, umiltà, *f.*

tamer, *n.* Domatore, *m.*, domatrice, *f.*

taming, *n.* Soggiogamento, ammansimento, *m.* **The Taming of the Shrew,** La Bisbetica Domata, *f.*

Tamil [ˈtæmil], *n.a.* (*Geog.*) Tamulo, Tamilo, *m.* **— language,** lingua tamulica, *f.*

tammy [ˈtæmi], *n.* Filtro, *m.*; staccio, *m.*

tam o'shanter [tæmoˈʃæntəɹ], *n.* Berretto di lana, berretto scozzese, *m.*

tamp [tæmp], *v.t.* Turare, tappare; battere, pestare.

tamper [ˈtæmpəɹ], *v.i.* Immischiarsi, frammettersi. **To — with,** (*document, etc.*) falsificare, alterare; (*a lock*) forzare; (*food, etc.*) adulterare, contaminare; (*to bribe*) corrompere, subornare.

tampering, *n.* Intrighi, *m.pl.*, macchinazioni, mene, *f.pl.*

tamping, *n.* Il turare, il tappare, *m.*; il battere, *m.*

tampon, *n.* Tampone, stuello, *m.*

tan [tæn], *n.* (*for tanning*) Concia, *f.*; (*colour*) color marrone, tane, *m.*; (*sunburn*) tinta abbronzata, *f.* || *v.t.* Conciare; abbronzare, abbrunire; (*colloq.*) sferzare, sonarle (a uno); **— -yard,** conceria, *f.*
tanager [ˈtænədʒəɹ], *n.* (*Zool.*) Tanagra, *f.*
tandem [ˈtændəm], *n.* (*horses*) Tiro a freccia, *m.*; (*bicycle*) tandem, *m.* || *a.adv.* In fila.
tang [tæŋ], *n.* Gusto, sapore piccante, *m.*, salsedine, *f.*; (*sound*) rumore, *m.*; (*shank*) codolo, *m.* **There's a — in the air,** l'aria è frizzante.
tangent [ˈtændʒənt], *n.a.* (*Geom.*) Tangente, *f.* **To fly off at a —,** deviare, scantonare, filare per la tangente.
tangential, *a.* Tangenziale.
tangerine [ˈtændʒəriːn], *n.* (*orange*) Mandarino, *m.*
tangibility [ˈtændʒiˈbiliti], *n.* Tangibilità, *f.*
tangible [ˈtændʒibl], *a.* Tangibile; sicuro, manifesto.
Tangier [tænˈdʒiəɹ], *n.* (*Geog.*) Tangeri, *f.*
tangle [tæŋgl], *n.* Groviglio, garbuglio, viluppo, arruffio, *m.*; intrigo, *m.*, confusione, *f.*; imbroglio, *m.* || *v.t.* Ingarbugliare, aggrovigliare, avviluppare, arruffare, intricare, intralciare; confondere, imbrogliare. **To be in a —,** essere in un groviglio; (*fig.*) essere negli impicci.
tango [ˈtæŋgou], *n.* Tango, *m.*
tank [tæŋk], *n.* Cisterna, *f.*, serbatoio, *m.*; (*Mil.*) carro armato, *m.*; (*Rail.*) **— -engine,** locomotiva tender, *f.*; (*Naut.*) **— -steamer, tanker,** nave cisterna, *f.*
tankard [ˈtæŋkəɹd], *n.* Boccale, *m.*
tanker, *n.* (*Naut.*) Nave cisterna, nave petroliera, petroliera, *f.*; autobotte, *f.*
tanner (1) [ˈtænəɹ], *n.* Conciapelli, conciatore, *m.*
tanner (2), *n.* (*colloq.*) Mezzo scellino, *m.*
tannery, *n.* Conceria, *f.*
tannic, *a.* (*Chem.*) Tannico.
tannin, *n.* (*Chem.*) Tannino, *m.*
tanning, *n.* Concia, *f.*; (*colloq.*) sferzata, *f.*
tansy [ˈtænzi], *n.* (*Bot.*) Tanaceto, *m.*
tantalization [tæntəlaiˈzeiʃən], *n.* Tentazione, *f.*
tantalize [ˈtæntəlaiz], *v.t.* Tentare fortemente; frustrare, tormentare col supplizio di Tantalo.
tantalizing, *a.* Tentante, seducente; tormentoso.
tantalum [ˈtæntələm], *n.* (*Min.*) Tantalio, *m.*
Tantalus [ˈtæntələs], *n.* (*Myth.*) Tantalo, *m.*; (*decanter-holder*) cassettina da liquori, *f.*, portabottiglie, *m.*
tantamount [ˈtæntəmaunt], *a.* Equivalente, eguale. **That is — to saying that . . .,** vale a dire che, ciò è quanto dire che. . . .
tantivy! [tænˈtivi], *inter.* (*obs.*) Olà; || *adv.* A briglia sciolta, ventre a terra.
tantrum [ˈtæntrəm], *n.* Malumore, *m.*, furia, *f.* **To get into a —,** montare in furia; **a fit of the tantrums,** nervi, *m.pl.*, burrasche, *f.pl.*
tap (1) [tæp], *n.* (*knock*) Colpetto, colpettino, picchio, *m.* || *v.t.* Dare un colpetto a, picchiare, battere; *v.i.* picchiare, percuotere, battere. **To — on the door,** bussare alla porta; **he tapped me on the shoulder,** mi battè sulla spalla.
tap (2), *n.* (*for water, gas, etc.*) Rubinetto, *m.*; (*of cask*) cannella, *f.*; (*tap-room*) bar, *m.* || *v.t.* (*a cask*) Spillare; (*to draw*) cavare, prendere (*a tree*) incidere; (*Med.*) fare la paracentesi a, cavar del liquido a. **On —,** di botte, dalla spina; **an excellent —,** un'ottima qualità, *f.*; **to — a telephone wire,** intercettare una telefonata; (*colloq.*) **he tapped me for a pound,** m'ha chiesto in prestito una sterlina; **— -dance** punta e tacco, *m.*; **— -room,** sala d'osteria, *f.*, bar, *m.*; **— -root,** fittone, *m.*, radice principale, *f.*
tape [teip], *n.* Fettuccia, spighetta, *f.*, nastrino, *m.* || *v.t.* (*colloq.*) Misurare la capacità di. **Red —,** burocrazia, *f.*; lungaggini burocratiche, *f.pl.*; **— -measure,** metro a nastro; **— -machine,** telescrivente, *f.*; (*Zool.*) **— -worm,** tenia, *f.*
taper, *n.* Cero, *m.*, piccola candela, *f.*; moccolo, *m.* || *v.t.* Affusolare, affilare, assottigliare; *v.i.* affusolarsi, assottigliarsi. **It tapers to a point,** finisce a punta.
tapering, *a.* Affusolato; conico, a punta. **— fingers,** dita affusolate, *f.pl.*
tapestried [ˈtæpestrid], *a.* Tappezzato.
tapestry [ˈtæpestri], *n.* Tappezzeria, *f.*; paramenti, arazzi, *m.pl.* **— -worker,** ricamatrice, *f.*
tapioca [tæpiˈoukə], *n.* Tapioca, *f.*
tapir [ˈteipəɹ], *n.* (*Zool.*) Tapiro, *m.*
tapis [ˈtæpiː], *n.* Tappeto, *m.* **To be on the —,** essere in discussione.
tappet [ˈtæpet], *n.* (*Mech.*) Castagnola, *f.*
tapping [ˈtæpiŋ], *n.* Picchio, colpo, *m.*; (*of tree*) incisione, *f.*; (*Med.*) paracentesi, *f.*
tapster [ˈtæpstəɹ], *n.* Garzone di osteria, *m.*
tar [tɑːɹ], *n.* Catrame, *m.*; (*colloq.*) marinaio, *m.* || *v.t.* Incatramare, spalmare di catrame. **To — and feather,** impeciare e coprir di penne; **tarred with the same brush,** della stessa razza; **— -barrel,** botte di catrame, *f.*; **— -macadam,** macadam al catrame, *m.*; **— -spraying,** incatramazione, incatramatura, *f.*
taradiddle [ˈtærədidl], *n.* (*colloq.*) Piccola bugia, *f.*
tarantella [tærənˈtelə], *n.* Tarantella, *f.*
tarantism [ˈtærəntizm], *n.* (*Med.*) Tarantolismo, *m.*
tarantula [təˈræntjuːlə], *n.* (*Zool.*) Tarantola, *f.*
tardigrade [ˈtɑːɹdigreid], *a.* (*Zool.*) Tardigrado.
tardily [ˈtɑːɹdili], *adv.* Tardi.
tardiness, *n.* Tardità, lentezza, *f.*; indugio, ritardo, *m.*
tardy, *a.* Tardo, lento; in ritardo; tardivo.
tare (1) [tɛəɹ], *n.* (*Bot.*) Loglio, *m.*, veccia, *f.*
tare (2), *n.* (*Comm.*) Tara, *f.* || *v.t.* Computare la tara di. **Average —,** tara media, *f.*
target [ˈtɑːɹget], *n.* Bersaglio, segno, *m.*; (*fig.*) scopo, obiettivo, *m.* **— -practice,** tiro al bersaglio, tiro a segno, *m.*
tariff [ˈtærif], *n.* Tariffa, *f.*; listino dei prezzi, *m.* || *v.t.* Tariffare. (*Hist.*) **Tariff Reform,** Protezionismo, *m.*
tarlatan [ˈtɑːɹlətən], *n.* Tarlatana, *f.*
tarn [tɑːɹn], *n.* Laghetto in montagna, *m.*
tarnish [ˈtɑːɹniʃ], *v.t.* Annerire, appannare, offuscare; (*fig.*) macchiare; *v.i.* annerire, appannarsi, offuscarsi.
taroc, tarot [ˈtærɔk, ˈtærou], *n.* (*Cards*) Tarocchi, *m.pl.*

tarpaulin [tɑːɹˈpɔːlin], *n.* Tela incatramata, *f.*; copertone, *m.*
Tarpeian [tɑːɹˈpiːən], *a.* (*Hist.*) Tarpeo. **The — Rock,** la Rupe Tarpea, *f.*
tarragon [ˈtærəgɔn], *n.* (*Bot.*) Targone, dragoncello, *m.*
tarry (1) [ˈtɑːri], *a.* Catramato, incatramato.
tarry (2) [ˈtæri], *v.i.* Stare, dimorare, trattenersi; aspettare; indugiare, tardare.
tarsal [ˈtɑːɹsəl], *a.* (*Anat.*) Tarsale.
tarsus, *n.* (*Anat.*) Tarso, *m.*
tart (1) [tɑːɹt], *n.* (*Cooking*) Torta, *f.*; crostata, *f.*
tart (2) *n.* (*Colloq.*) Donna di malaffare, meretrice, *f.*
tart (3), *a.* Acido, agro, acerbo; (*fig.*) mordace, aspro, mordente.
tartan (1) [ˈtɑːɹtən], *n.* Tessuto di lana scozzesse a vari colori e in quadri.
tartan (2), *n.* (*Naut.*) Tartana, *f.*
Tartar (1), **Tatar** [ˈtɑːɹtəɹ], *n.* (*Hist.*) Tartaro, *m.* **To catch a —,** imbattersi in un muso duro.
tartar (2), *n.* (*Chem.*) Tartaro, *m.*
tartaric [tɑːɹˈtærik], *a.* (*Chem.*) Tartarico.
Tartarus [ˈtɑːɹtərəs], *n.* (*Myth.*) Tartaro, *m.*
tartlet, *n.* Tortina, *f.*, pasticcino, *m.*
tartly, *adv.* Acerbamente, aspramente.
tartness, *n.* Acidità, agrezza, *f.*; acredine, *f.*; mordacità, asprezza, *f.*
tartrate [ˈtɑːɹtreit], *n.* (*Chem.*) Tartrato, *m.*
Tartuffe [ˈtɑːɹtuf], *n.* Tartufo, ipocrita, *m.*
task [tɑːsk], *n.* Compito, lavoro, *m.*; incarico, dovere, *m.*; mansione, *m.* || *v.t.* Dare un lavoro a, assegnare un compito a; affaticare, sforzare, esaurire. **To set a —,** assegnare un compito; **to take to —,** fare una ramanzina a, riprendere; **the work tasked his powers,** il lavoro gli costò un grande sforzo.
taskmaster, *n.* Padrone, *m.*
tassel [ˈtæsəl], *n.* Fiocco, fiocchetto, *m.*, nappina, *f.*
tasselled, *a.* Infiocchettato.
taste [teist], *n.* Gusto, sapore, *m.*; (*mouthful*) bocconcino, *m.* (*small quantity*) un tantino, un pochino, *m.*; disposizione, attitudine, *f.* || *v.t.* Gustare, assaporare, assaggiare; degustare; (*fig.*) sentire, provare; *v.i.* sapere di, sentire di, aver sapore. **Tastes differ,** tutti i gusti son gusti; **a man of —,** un uomo di buon gusto, *m.*; **to have good taste, bad taste,** aver buon gusto, cattivo gusto; **Is it to your —?** È di vostro gusto? Vi va a genio? **there is no accounting for tastes,** dei gusti non si discute; **Will you have a — of this?** Volete un tantino di questo? **to dress with —,** vestire con gusto; **to — good,** avere un buon sapore; **to — of,** sapere di, sentire di.
tasteful, *a.* Di buon gusto.
tastefully, *adv.* Con gusto.
tastefulness, *n.* Buon gusto, *m.*
tasteless, *a.* Insipido; di cattivo gusto.
tastelessness, *n.* Insipidità, *f.*
taster, *n.* Gustatore, assaggiatore, degustatore, *m.*
tasting, *n.* Gustamento, assaporamento, *m.*; degustazione, *f.*
tasty, *a.* Saporito, saporoso, gustoso.
tata! [tæˈtɑː], *inter.* (*child's talk*) Addio! Ciao!
tatter [ˈtætəɹ], *n.* Cencio, straccio, brandello, *m.* **In tatters,** logoro, stracciato, sbrindellato.
tatterdemalion [tætəɹdeˈmeiliən], *n.* Straccione, *m.*
tattered, *a.* Logoro, stracciato, a brandelli.
tatting, *n.* Merletto, *m.*
tattle [tætəl], *n.* Ciancie, ciarle, chiacchiere, *f.pl.* || *v.i.* Cianciare, ciarlare, chiacchierare.
tattler, *n.* Ciarlone, chiacchierone, *m.*
tattling, *a.* Ciarliero, chiacchierone.
tattoo (1) [təˈtuː], *n.* (*Mil.*) Ritirata, *f.*; rivista militare, *f.* **To beat the —,** battere la ritirata; **to beat the devil's —,** sonare il tamburino; **torchlight —,** fiaccolata militare, *f.*
tattoo (2), *n.* Tatuaggio, *m.* || *v.t.* Tatuare.
tattooing, *n.* Tatuaggio, *m.*
taught, *p.* of **teach.**
taunt [tɔːnt], *n.* Rinfacciamento, rimprovero, *m.*, rampogna, *f.*; ingiuria, *f.*, insulto, *m.* || *v.t.* Rimproverare; ingiuriare, insultare. **To — someone with cowardice,** dar del vigliacco a qualcuno.
tauntingly, *adv.* Ingiuriosamente; sarcasticamente.
tauromachy [tɔːˈrɔməki], *n.* Tauromachia, giostra dei tori, *f.*
Taurus [ˈtɔːrəs], *n.* (*Astron.*) Il Tauro, *m.*
taut [tɔːt], *a.* Teso, rigido.
tauten, *v.t.* Tendere, irrigidire.
tautness, *n.* Tensione, *f.*
tautological [tɔːtoˈlɔdʒikəl], *a.* Tautologico.
tautology [tɔːˈtɔlɔdʒi], *n.* Tautologia, *f.*
tavern [ˈtævəɹn], *n.* Taverna, bettola, trattoria, *f.*; osteria, mescita, *f.* **— -keeper,** taverniere, oste, *m.*
taw [tɔː], *v.t.* Conciare pelli con allume, allumare.
tawdrily [ˈtɔːdrili], *adv.* Vistosamente.
tawdriness, *n.* Vistosità, *f.*
tawdry, *a.* Vistoso, pretenzioso, di cattivo gusto, sgargiante.
tawer, *n.* Conciatore, *m.*
tawing, *n.* Conciatura, *f.*
tawny, *a.* Fulvo; bruno, abbronzato.
tax [tæks], *n.* Imposta, tassa, *f.*; dazio, *m.* balzello, *m.*; (*fig.*) peso, carico, *m.*, molestia, *f.* || *v.t.* Tassare, sottoporre a tassa; daziare; (*fig.*) accusare; faticare, sforzare, gravare, logorare. **Land —,** imposta fondiaria, *f.*; **income —,** imposta sul reddito, *f.*; **a — on one's energies,** un logorio di forze, *m.*; **to — with,** accusare di; **to — heavily,** gravare di balzelli; **— -collector,** esattore delle imposte, *m.*; **— -free,** esente da tassa; **— -payer,** contribuente, *m.f.*; **— -dodger,** chi evita di pagare una tassa.
taxable, *a.* Tassabile, imponibile, gravabile.
taxation, *n.* Tassazione, *f.*, tasse, imposte, *f.pl.*
taxi [ˈtæksi], *v.i.* (*Aviat.*) Rullare, (*seaplane*) galleggiare; (*Colloq.*) andare in tassì. || *n.* Tassì, *m.*, autopubblica, *f.* **— -driver, — -man,** autista di tassì, *m.*
taxidermist [tækˈsidəɹmist], *n.* Impagliatore, *m.*
taxidermy [tækˈsidəɹmi], *n.* Tassidermia, *f.*
taximeter [ˈtæksimiːtəɹ], *n.* Tassametro, *m.*
tea [tiː], *n.* Tè, *m.* **High —,** tè completo, *m.*; (*colloq.*) **that's just my cup of —,** è proprio un affare che mi va a genio; **— -caddy,** scatola da tè, *f.*; **— -chest,** cassa da tè, *f.*; **— -cake,** specie di focaccia; (*colloq.*) **— -fight,** tè, *m.*; **— -garden,** giardino da tè, *m.*; **— -gown,** vestito da casa, *m.*, vestaglia, *f.*; **— -kettle,**

bollitore, *m.*; **—-leaf,** foglia di tè, *f.*; **—-party,** tè, *m.*; **—-plant,** pianta del tè, *f.*; **—-planter,** piantatore di tè, *m.*; **—-pot,** teiera, *f.*; **—-room, —-rooms,** sala da tè, *f.*; **—-rose,** rosa tè, *f.*; **—-service, —-set,** servizio da tè, *m.*; **—-strainer,** colino, *m.*; **—-table,** tavola da tè, *f.*; **—-time,** ora del tè, *f.*; **—-tray,** vassoio da tè, *m.*; **—-urn,** samovar, *m.*

teach [ti:tʃ], *v.t.* Insegnare, istruire, ammaestrare, addottrinare; mostrare, spiegare; *v.i.* insegnare, dar lezioni. **To — how to write,** insegnare a scrivere; **to — someone to write,** insegnare a qualcuno a scrivere; **to — a lesson,** dare una lezione; **that will — him a lesson,** ciò gli servirà di lezione.

teachable [ˈtitʃəbl], *a.* Insegnabile; docile, disposto a imparare.

teachableness, *n.* Docilità, disposizione a imparare, *f.*

teacher, *n.* Maestro, *m.*, maestra, *f.*, insegnante, *m.f.*, professore, *m.*, professoressa, *f.*

teaching, *n.* Insegnamento, *m.*, istruzione, *f.*; dottrina, *f.*

teacup [ˈti:kʌp], *n.* Tazza da tè, *f.* **A storm in a —,** molto rumore per nulla, una tempesta in un bicchier d'acqua.

teak [ti:k], *n.* (*Bot.*) Teak, tec, *m.*

teal [ti:l], *n.* (*Zool.*) Alzavola, *f.*

team [ti:m], *n.* (*of horses*) Tiro, *m.*; (*of men*) squadra, *f.*; (*pair*) pariglia, *f.* **A football —,** una squadra calcistica, *f.*; **a — of four horses,** un tiro a quattro, *m.*; **— -spirit,** spirito di corpo, *m.*; **—-work,** sforzo combinato, lavoro in squadra, *m.*

teamster, *n.* Carrettiere, *m.*

tear (1) [tiəɹ], *n.* Lagrima, lacrima, *f.*; (*big tear*) luccicone, *m.* **Tears,** lagrime, *f.pl.*, pianto, *m.*; **in tears,** piangendo; **to move to tears,** muovere al pianto; **her eyes were bathed in tears,** i suoi occhi erano bagnati di lagrime; **to burst into tears,** scoppiare in lagrime; **to shed tears,** versare lagrime, piangere; **—-drop,** lagrima, *f.*; **—-stained,** rigato dal pianto; **— -gas,** gas lacrimogeno, *m.*

tear (2) [tɛəɹ], *v.t.* Lacerare, strappare, stracciare, squarciare, logorare, rompere; (*fig.*) straziare; *v.i.* strapparsi, stracciarsi; correre velocemente. || *n.* Rottura, *f.*, squarcio, strappo, *m.* **To — in two pieces,** stracciare in due pezzi; **to — asunder,** strappare l'uno dall'altro, distaccare; **to — away, to — out,** strappare, strappar via; **to — down,** strappar giù; **to — up,** squarciare, spezzare, sradicare; **I could not — myself away,** non potevo staccarmi; **this paper tears easily,** questa carta si strappa facilmente; **the runner tore past,** il corridore passò come un razzo; **he tore off,** andò come il vento; (*fig.*) **to — one another to pieces,** dilaniarsi l'un l'altro; **wear and —,** logorio, deterioramento, *m.*, (*Mech.*) usura, *f.*

tearful [ˈtiəɹful], *a.* Lagrimoso, pieno di lagrime.

tearfully, *adv.* Piangendo.

tearless, *a.* Senza lagrime.

tease [ti:z], *v.t.* Stuzzicare, tormentare; seccare, annoiare, irritare, vessare, importunare; (*wool.*) cardare, scardassare. || *n.* Seccatore, *m.*

teasel [ti:zl], *n.* Cardo, *m.*; scardasso, *m.*

teaser, *n.* Seccatore, *m.*, seccatrice, *f.*; questione difficile, *f.*; domanda imbarazzante, *f.*

teasing, *n.* Seccatura, seccaggine, *f.*, fastidio, *m.*; malizia, *f.* || *a.* Seccante, irritante, importuno.

teaspoon [ˈti:spu:n], *n.* Cucchiaino, *m.*

teaspoonful, *n.* Cucchiainata, *f.*

teat [ti:t], *n.* Capezzolo, *m.*, mammella, poppa, tetta, *f.*; (*of rubber*) poppatoio, *m.*

teazel [cp. **teasel**].

technical [ˈteknikəl], *a.* Tecnico. **— school** scuola tecnica, *f.*

technicality [tekniˈkæliti], *a.* Tecnicismo, termine tecnico, *m.*

technically, *adv.* Tecnicamente.

technician [tekˈniʃən], *n.* Tecnico, *m.*; perito, *m.*

technics, *n.pl.* Tecnica, *f.*

technique [tekˈni:k], *n.* Tecnica, *f.*; arte, *f.*

technological [teknoˈlɔdʒikəl], *a.* Tecnologico.

technology, *n.* Technologia, *f.*

techy [cp. **tetchy**].

tectology [tekˈtɔlədʒi], *n.* Morfologia, *f.*

tectonic [tekˈtɔnik], *a.* Tettonico.

tectonics, *n.pl.* Tettonica, *f.*

ted [ted], *v.t.* (*hay*) Spandere, stendere, rivoltare.

teddy bear [tediˈbɛəɹ], *n.* Orso di felpa, *m.*

tedious [ˈti:diəs], *a.* Tedioso, noioso, fastidioso, uggioso.

tediously, *adv.* Tediosamente.

tediousness, tedium [ˈti:diəsnes, ˈti:diəm], *n.* Tediosità, noia, *f.*, fastidio, tedio, *m.*; uggia, *f.*

tee [ti:], *n.* (*letter*) Ti, T., *m.*; (*Golf*) tee, monticello, mucchietto di rena per la partenza della palla, *m.* || *v.t.* (*Golf*) Mettere la palla sul tee; **teeing ground,** piazzuola di partenza, *f.*

teem [ti:m], *v.t.i.* Generare; abbondare. **To — with,** abbondare in, formicolare di, brulicare di.

teeming, *a.* Che abbonda in, formicolante di.

teenager [ti:nˈeidʒəɹ], *n.* Adolescente, *m.f.*

teens [ti:nz], *n.pl.* L'età da tredici anni a venti. **In his (her) —,** adolescente, *m.f.*, giovinetto, *m.*, giovinetta, *f.*

teethe [ti:ð], *v.i.* Mettere i denti, spuntare i denti.

teething [ˈti:ðiŋ], *n.* Dentizione, *f.*

teetotal [ti:ˈtoutəl], *a.* Non-alcoolico; astinente, astemio.

teetotalism, *n.* Astinenza da bevande alcooliche, *f.*

teetotaller, *n.* Astemio, *m.*, astemia, *f.*

teetotum [ti:ˈtoutəm], *n.* Trottolino, *m.*

teg [teg], *n.* Agnello, *m.*

tegular [ˈtegju:ləɹ], *a.* Di tegolo.

tegument [ˈtegju:mənt], *n.* Tegumento, *m.*

tegumentary, *a.* Tegumentare.

telecast [ˈteleka:st], *v.t.* Trasmettere per televisione.

telecommunication, *n.* Telecomunicazione, *f.*

telegram [ˈtelegræm], *n.* Telegramma, dispaccio, *m.*

telegraph [ˈtelegræf], *n.* Telegrafo, *m.* || *v.t.i.* Telegrafare. **— clerk,** telegrafista, *m.f.*; **— office,** ufficio del telegrafo, *m.*; **—-boy,** fattorino telegrafico, *m.*; (*Sport*) **— board,** indicatore, *m.*; **—-pole,** palo del telegrafo, *m.*; **— -line, —-wire,** filo telegrafico, *m.*

telegraphese [telegrə'fi:z], *n.* Linguaggio telegrafico, stile telegrafico, *m.*
telegraphic, *a.* Telegrafico.
telegraphically, *adv.* Telegraficamente.
telegraphist, *n.* Telegrafista, *m.f.*
telegraphy [te'legrəfi], *n.* Telegrafia, *f.* **Wireless —,** telegrafia senza fili, radiotelegrafia, *f.*
teleological [teleo'lɔdʒikəl], *a.* Teleologico.
teleology, *n.* Teleologia, *f.*
telepathic [tele'pæθik], *a.* Telepatico.
telepathy [te'lepəθi], *n.* Telepatia, *f.*
telephone ['telefoun], *n.* Telefono, *m.* || *v.t.i.* Telefonare. **— exchange,** centralino, *m.*; **— -box,** cabina telefonica, *f.*; **— operator,** telefonista, *m.f.*
telephonic [tele'fɔnik], *a.* Telefonico.
telephonist [te'lefonist], *n.* Telefonista, *m.f.*
telephony [te'lefoni], *n.* Telefonia, *f.*
telephotograph, telephotography, *n.* Telefotografia, *f.*
teleprinter, *n.* Telescrivente, *m.*
telescope ['teleskoup], *n.* Telescopio, *m.*; cannocchiale, *m.* || *v.t.* Investire, sfondare; *v.i.* sfondare, incastrarsi, inserirsi, infilarsi.
telescopic, *a.* Telescopico.
televise ['televaiz], *v.t.* Trasmettere per televisione.
television ['televiʒən], *n.* Televisione, *f.*; **— set,** televisore, *m.*
televisor, *n.* Televisore, *m.*
tell (1) [tel], *v.t.* Dire; narrare, raccontare; parlare; sapere; scoprire, distinguere, riconoscere; assicurare; confessare; *v.i.* fare effetto, produrre effetto. **— me about it,** raccontatemi tutto; **to — a lie,** mentire; **to — you the truth,** a dire il vero; **you cannot — them apart,** si rassomigliano come due gocce d'acqua, non si può distinguere l'uno dall'altro; **to — off for duty,** dar un'ordine a; *(colloq.)* **to — off,** fare una ramanzina a; **I am told,** mi si dice; **he has told everything,** ha confessato tutto; **I cannot —,** non saprei dire; **you cannot — by appearances,** non si può giudicare dalle apparenze; **the strain is telling on him,** egli tradisce lo sforzo; **every blow tells,** ogni colpo influisce; **to — of someone,** denunciare qualcuno; **— -tale,** malalingua, *f.*, delatore, denunciatore, *m.*; *(Mech.)* contatore meccanico, *m.*; *(Naut.)* assiometro del timone, *m.*; *a.* rivelatore.
tell (2), *v.t.* Contare, numerare. **To — one's beads,** recitare il rosario; **all told,** tutto sommato.
teller, *n.* Raccontatore, narratore, *m.*; *(in bank)* cassiere, *m.*; *(of votes)* scrutatore, *m.*
telling, *a.* Efficace, energico; espressivo. **There is no —,** non si sa, non si può sapere; *(colloq.)* **— -off,** ramanzina, *f.*
telpher ['telfəɹ], *n.* Teleferica, *f.*
temerarious [temə'rɛəriəs], *a.* Temerario.
temerity [te'meriti], *n.* Temerità, *f.*
temper ['tempəɹ], *n.* *(disposition)* Temperamento, *m.*, indole, *f.*; umore, *m.*; *(anger)* stizza, collera, ira, *f.*; *(of metal)* tempera, *f.* || *v.t.* *(to mingle)* Temperare, mescolare; *(steel)* temperare; *(to mitigate)* temperare, raddolcire, mitigare, moderare; *(Mus.)* modulare. **A placid —,** un temperamento calmo, *m.*; **in a good —,** di buon umore; **in a bad —, out of —,** di malumore, stizzito; **a fit of —,** un accesso di malumore, *m.*; **to get into a —,** adirarsi, montare in collera; **to keep one's —,** serbare la calma; **to lose one's —,** adirarsi, arrabbiarsi, uscir dai gangheri, perder le staffe; **to put out of —,** stizzire; **bad-tempered,** irascibile; **good-tempered,** di buona pasta, bonaccione.
tempera ['tempərə], *n.* *(Art)* Tempera, *f.*
temperament ['tempərəmənt], *n.* Temperamento, *m.*, indole, *f.*, carattere, *m.*
temperamental [tempərə'mentəl], *a.* Temperamentale, capriccioso.
temperance, temperateness, *n.* Temperanza, moderazione, *f.*; astinenza (dall'alcool), *f.* **— society,** società che consiglia l'astensione dall'alcool.
temperate ['tempərit], *a.* Temperato, moderato, sobrio. **The — zone,** la zona temperata, *f.*
temperature ['tempərətʃju:ɹ], *n.* Temperatura, *f.* **To take the —,** misurare la temperatura; **he has a slight —,** ha un po' di febbre; **his — has dropped (risen),** gli è diminuita (aumentata) la febbre.
tempest ['tempest], *n.* Tempesta, *f.*, temporale, uragano, *m.*; burrasca, *f.* **— -tossed,** sballottato dalla tempesta.
tempestuous [tem'pestju:əs], *a.* Tempestoso, procelloso, burrascoso.
tempestuousness, *n.* Tempestosità, *f.*
Templar ['templəɹ], *n.* Templare, *m.*; *(Law)* avvocato, studente in legge, *m.*
template, templet ['templeit], *n.* *(Mech.)* Sagoma, forma, *f.*; sostegno, cuscino d'appoggio, *m.*
temple ['tempəl], *n.* Tempio, *m.*; *(Anat.)* tempia, *f.*; *(Mech.)* tempiale, *m.*
temporal ['tempərəl], *a.* Temporale.
temporality [tempə'ræliti], *n.* Temporalità, *f.*
temporally, *adv.* Temporalmente.
temporarily, *adv.* Temporaneamente, provvisoriamente.
temporariness, *n.* Temporaneità, *f.*
temporary, *a.* Temporaneo, provvisorio.
temporization [tempɔrai'zeiʃən], *n.* Temporeggiamento, *m.*
temporize ['tempɔraiz], *v.i.* Temporeggiare.
temporizer, *n.* Temporeggiatore, *m.*
temporizing, *a.* Temporeggiante.
tempt [tempt], *v.t.* Tentare, istigare, provocare; attrarre, sedurre, allettare, invitare. **I am tempted to deny that,** sono incline a negare ciò.
temptation, *n.* Tentazione, *f.* **To lead into —,** indurre in tentazione; **to resist —,** resistere alla tentazione; **to yield to —,** cedere alla tentazione, cadere in tentazione.
tempter, *n.* Tentatore, *m.*
tempting, *a.* Allettante, seducente, attraente, invitante; appetitoso.
temptingly, *adv.* Seducentemente.
temptress, *n.* Tentatrice, *f.*
ten [ten], *n.a.* Dieci, *m.* **About —,** una diecina, *f.*; **it is — to one that . . .,** ci son nove probabilità su dieci che . . .; **— -gallon hat,** cappello americano a larghe tese, *m.*
tenable ['tenəbl], *a.* Tenibile, detenibile; sostenibile.
tenacious [ten'eiʃəs], *a.* Tenace; ostinato. **— of,** tenace in; **to be — of life,** essere attaccato alla vita.

tenaciously, *adv.* Tenacemente.
tenacity [te'næsiti], *n.* Tenacia, ostinazione, perseveranza, *f.*
tenancy ['tenənsi], *n.* Affitto, *m.*, locazione, *f.*; usufrutto, *m.*
tenant, *n.* Inquilino, locatario, affittuario, pigionale, *m.*; (*of farm*) fittaiuolo, *m.* **— farmer,** fittaiuolo, mezzadro, *m.*
tenantable, *a.* Abitabile.
tenanted, *a.* Occupato, abitato.
tenantless, *a.* Disoccupato, libero, disaffittato.
tenantry, *n.* I fittaiuoli, i mezzadri, *m.pl.*
tench [tentʃ], *n.* (*Zool.*) Tinca, *f.*
tend (1) [tend], *v.t.* Curare, prendere cura di, sorvegliare, vegliare su.
tend (2), *v.i.* Tendere, piegare, inclinare, aver tendenza. **The road tends towards the coast,** la via piega verso la costa; **he tends to be too modest,** tende a essere troppo modesto.
tendency, *n.* Tendenza, propensione, inclinazione, *f.*
tendentious [ten'denʃəs], *a.* Tendenzioso.
tender (1) ['tendəɹ], *a.* Tenero, dolce, affettuoso, amorevole; sensitivo, sensibile; difficile, scabroso. **— meat,** carne tenera, *f.*; **a — conscience,** una coscienza troppo delicata, *f.*; **to be — of,** essere sollecito di; **of — age,** di tenera età; **—-hearted,** sensibile; **—-heartedness,** sensibilità, *f.*
tender (2), *n.* Offerta, *f.*; proposta, *f.*; (*Naut.*) nave ausiliaria, *f.*; (*Rail.*) tender, carro di scorta, *m.* || *v.t.* Offrire; deferire. **Legal —,** valuta legale, *f.*, corso legale, *m.*; **to be legal —,** aver corso; **the lowest —,** l'offerta più bassa, *f.*; **to — one's services,** offrire i propri servigi; **to — for a contract,** fare un'offerta per un contratto.
tenderfoot, *n.* (*colloq.*) Nuovo venuto, *m.*
tenderly, *adv.* Teneramente, amorevolmente, compassionevolmente.
tenderness, *n.* Tenerezza, *f.*; compassione, *f.*; sensibilità, *f.*; fragilità, *f.*
tendon ['tendən], *n.* (*Anat.*) Tendine, *m.*; **Achilles' —,** il tallone di Achille.
tendril ['tendril], *n.* (*Bot.*) Viticcio, *m.*; pampino, *m.*
tenebrous ['tenebrəs], *a.* Tenebroso, oscuro.
tenement ['tenemənt], *n.* Tenuta, *f.*, possesso, *m.*; casa, abitazione, *f.*; appartamento di basso valore, *m.*; (*Law*) fondo enfiteutico, *m.*; **—-house,** casamento, *m.*, casa popolare.
Teneriffe ['tenəri:f], *n.* (*Geog.*) Teneriffa, *f.*
tenet ['ti:net, 'tenet], *n.* Dogma, canone, *m.*, dottrina, *f.*
tenfold ['tenfould], *a.* Decuplo. || *adv.* Dieci volte.
tenner, *n.* (*colloq.*) Un biglietto da dieci sterline, *m.*
tennis ['tenis], *n.* Tennis, *m.*, pallacorda, *f.* **—-court,** campo di tennis, tennis, *m.*; **—-ball,** palla da tennis, *f.*; **—-racquet,** racchetta da tennis, *f.*; **—-player,** tennista, *m.f.*, giuocatore di tennis, *m.*
tenon ['tenən], *n.* Cavicchio, dente d'incastro, *m.* **—-saw,** sega per incastri, seghetta, *f.*
tenor ['tenəɹ], *n.* Tenore, andamento, corso, *m.*; (*Mus.*) tenore, *m.*; (*Comm.*) scadenza, *f.* (*Mus.*) **— clef,** chiave di do, chiave di tenore, *f.*
tense (1) [tens], *n.* (*Gram.*) Tempo, *m.*
tense (2), *a.* Teso; intento, attento; sforzato.
tensely, *adv.* Sforzatamente.
tenseness, *n.* Tensione, *f.*; rigidezza, *f.*
tensile ['tensail], *a.* Di tensione.
tension ['tenʃən], *n.* Tensione, *f.*
tensor ['tensəɹ], *n.* (*Anat.*) Tensore, *m.*
tent [tent], *n.* Tenda, *f.*, padiglione, *m.*; (*Med.*) tenta, sonda, tasta, *f.*, specillo, *m.* || *v.t.* Sondare. **—-bed,** letto a baldacchino, *m.*; **—-peg,** picchetto da tenda, *m.*; **—-pegging,** esercizio d'equitazione consistente nell'infilare i picchetti con le lance, *m.*; **—-pole,** palo da tenda, *m.*
tentacle ['tentəkl], *n.* Tentacolo, *m.*
tentative ['tentətiv], *a.* Di prova, sperimentale, tentativo. **In a — way,** tentativamente, in via provvisoria; **a — effort,** un tentativo, *m.*
tented, *a.* Coperto di tende.
tenterhook ['tentəɹhuk], *n.* Uncino per stendere, *m.* **To be on tenterhooks,** essere sulle spine, essere sui carboni ardenti.
tenth [tenθ], *a.* Decimo. || *n.* Decimo, *m.*, decima parte, *f.* **The — of May,** il dieci maggio.
tenthly, *adv.* In decimo luogo.
tenuity [ten'ju:iti], *n.* Tenuità, sottigliezza, *f.*
tenuous ['tenju:əs], *a.* Tenue, sottile, esile, leggiero.
tenure ['tenju:ɹ], *n.* Tenuta, *f.*, possesso, *m.*; occupazione, *f.*; permanenza, *f.*; gestione, *f.* **— of office,** permanenza nell'ufficio, *f.*; **to hold on a precarious —,** avere poca presa su; **during his — of office,** durante l'esercizio delle sue funzioni.
tepid ['tepid], *a.* Tiepido, tepido.
tepidity, tepidness [te'piditi, 'tepidnes], *n.* Tiepidezza, tepidità, *f.*
teratology [terə'tɔlədʒi], *n.* Teratologia, *f.*
tercentenary [tə:ɹsen'ti:nəri], *n.* Terzo centenario, *m.*
terebene ['terebi:n], *n.* (*Chem.*) Terebene, *m.*
terebinth ['terebinθ], *n.* (*Bot.*) Terebinto, *m.*
teredo [te'ri:dou], *n.* (*Zool.*) teredine, *f.*
tergiversation [tə:ɹdʒivəɹ'seiʃən], *n.* Tergiversazione, *f.*
term [tə:ɹm], *n.* Termine, *m.*; (*duration*) durata, *f.*, periodo, *m.*; (*Law*) sessione, *f.*; (*school*) trimestre, *m.* || *v.t.* Chiamare, nominare, definire. **For a — of years,** per un certo numero di anni; **to set a — to,** porre un termine a.
termagant ['tə:ɹməgənt], *n.* Megera, virago, *f.*
terminable ['tə:ɹminəbl], *a.* Terminabile.
terminal ['tə:ɹminəl], *n.* (*Elec.*) Terminale, morsetto, serrafilo, *m.* || *a.* Terminale.
terminate ['tə:ɹmineit], *v.t.* Terminare, finire, conchiudere; *v.i.* terminare.
termination, *n.* Terminazione, fine, conclusione, *f.*; (*Gram.*) desinenza, *f.*
terminology [tə:ɹmin'ɔlədʒi], *n.* Terminologia, *f.*
terminus ['tə:ɹminəs], *n.* Limite, termine, *m.*; (*Rail.*) stazione capolinea, *f.*
termite ['tə:ɹmait], *n.* (*Zool.*) Termite, *f.*
terms, *n.pl.* Termini, *m.pl.*; condizioni, *f.pl.*; relazioni, *f.pl.*; rapporti, *m.pl.* **To be on good — with,** essere in buone relazioni con, avere buoni rapporti con; **in plain —,** in parole povere; **liberal —,** offerte vantaggiose, *f.pl.*; **in the most flattering —,** nei termini più lusinghieri; **What are his —?**

Che cosa domanda? Quali sono le sue condizioni? **to reduce to its lowest —,** ridurre ai minimi termini; **to be on bad — with,** avere rapporti tesi con; **we are not on speaking terms,** non ci parliamo; **to come to —,** accordarsi, venire a patti; **to make —,** venire a patti, porre delle condizioni; **not on any —,** a nessun patto; **on equal —,** del pari.

tern [tə:ɹn], *n.* (*Zool.*) Rondine di mare, *m.*, sterna, *f.*

ternary [ˈtə:ɹnəri], *a.* Ternario.

terrace [ˈterəs], *n.* Terrazza, terrazzina, *f.*; terrapieno, ripiano, *m.* || *v.t.* Terrazzare, disporre in ripiani.

terracotta [terəˈkɔtə], *n.* Terracotta, *f.*

terrapin [ˈterəpin], *n.* (*Zool.*) Tartaruga acquatica, *f.*

terraqueous [teˈreikwiəs], *a.* Terracqueo.

terrene [ˈteri:n], *a.* Terreo; terrestre, terreno.

terrestrial [teˈrestriəl], *a.* Terrestre.

terrible [ˈterəbl], *a.* Terribile, spaventoso, orrendo.

terribleness, *n.* Terribilità, *f.*

terribly, *adv.* Terribilmente; (*colloq.*) molto.

terrier (1) [ˈteriəɹ], *n.* (*Zool.*) Terrier, *m.*

terrier (2), *n.* (*Hist.*) Registro d'una signoria feudale, *m.*

terrific [teˈrifik], *a.* Terribile, spaventevole, spaventoso.

terrifically, *adv.* Terribilmente; (*colloq.*) molto.

terrify [ˈterifai], *v.t.* Spaventare, atterrire, sbigottire, sgomentare.

territorial [teriˈtɔ:riəl], *a.* Territoriale. **— army,** milizia territoriale, *f.*

territoriality, *n.* Territorialità, *f.*

territorially, *adv.* Territorialmente.

territory, *n.* Territorio, *m.*

terror [ˈterəɹ], *n.* Terrore, spavento, sgomento, *m.* **To strike — into,** incutere timore a, atterrire; **that child is a perfect —,** quel ragazzo è proprio un diavoletto; **— struck,** atterrito, spaventato.

terrorism, *n.* Terrorismo, *m.*

terrorist, *n.* Terrorista, *m.*

terrorize [ˈterɔraiz], *v.t.* Terrorizzare, atterrire, intimidire.

terse [tə:ɹs], *a.* Terso, netto, lucido, conciso.

tersely, *adv.* Tersamente, nitidamente, concisamente.

terseness, *n.* Tersezza, nitidezza, *f.*; concisione, *f.*

tertian [ˈtə:ɹʃən], *a.* Terzana, ogni tre giorni. **— ague,** terzana, *f.*

tertiary [ˈtə:ɹʃəri], *a.* Terziario.

tessellated [ˈteseleited], *a.* Di mosaico, a mosaico. **— pavement,** pavimento a mosaico, *m.*

test [test], *n.* Prova, *f.*, esperimento, *m.*; cimento, paragone, criterio, *m.*, norma, *f.*; (*Chem.*) reagente, *f.*; saggio, *m.*, esame, *m.* || *v.t.* Provare, mettere alla prova, verificare; saggiare; controllare; collaudare. **To put to the —,** mettere alla prova; **to stand the —,** reggere alla prova; **— -tube,** provino, *m.*; (*Chem.*) **— -paper,** carta reattiva, *f.*

testaceous [tesˈteiʃəs], *a.* Testaceo.

testament [ˈtestəmənt], *n.* Testamento, *m.* **New, Old Testament,** Nuovo, Vecchio Testamento, *m.*

testamentary, *a.* Testamentario.

testator [tesˈteitɔɹ], *n.* Testatore, *m.*

testatrix, *n.* Testatrice, *f.*

tester [ˈtestəɹ], *n.* Baldacchino, *m.* **— -bed,** letto con baldacchino, *m.*

testicle [ˈtestikl], *n.* (*Anat.*) Testicolo, coglione, *m.*

testify [ˈtestifai], *v.t.* Testificare, dimostrare, far testimonianza di, attestare; *v.i.* testificare, testimoniare. **To — in favour of,** testimoniare a favore di; **to — against,** testimoniare contro.

testily, *adv.* Stizzosamente, irascibilmente.

testimonial [testiˈmouniəl], *a.* (*of character*) Benservito, attestato di buona condotta, *m.*; (*of esteem*) dichiarazione, testimonianza, *f.*

testimony, *n.* Testimonianza, attestazione, *f.* **To bear — to,** far testimonianza di, attestare; (*Law*) **in — whereof,** in fede di che.

testiness, *n.* Irascibilità, *f.*

testing, *n.* Prova, *f.*, saggio, collaudo, *m.*

testy, *a.* Irascibile, stizzoso.

tetanic [ˈtetənik], *a.* Tetanico.

tetanus [ˈtetənəs], *n.* (*Med.*) Tetano, *m.*

tetchily [tetʃili], *adv.* Irascibilmente.

tetchiness, *n.* Irascibilità, irritabilità, *f.*

tetchy, *a.* Irascibile, irritabile, permaloso.

tête-à-tête [ˈteitɑ:ˈteit], *n.* Colloquio a quattr'occhi, abboccamento, *m.*

tether [teðəɹ], *v.t.* Impastoiare, legare, costringere. || *n.* Pastoia, *f.*; limite, termine, *m.* **To be at the end of one's —,** essere agli sgoccioli, essere agli estremi.

tetrachord [ˈtetrəkɔɹd], *n.* (*Mus.*) Tetracordo, *m.*

tetragon, *n.* (*Geom.*) Tetragono, *m.*

tetrarch, *n.* (*Hist.*) Tetrarca, *m.*

Teuton [ˈtju:tən], *n.* Teutone, *m.*

Teutonic [tju:ˈtɔnik], *a.* Teutonico.

text [tekst], *n.* Testo, *m.* **— -hand,** scrittura grossa, *f.*; **— -book,** manuale, libro di testo, *m.*

textile [ˈtekstail], *a.* Tessile. || *n.* Tessuto, *m.*

textual [ˈtekstju:əl], *a.* Testuale. **— criticism,** critica del testo, *f.*

textually, *adv.* Testualmente.

texture [ˈtekstʃju:ɹ], *n.* Tessitura, *f.*, tessuto, *m.*; struttura, composizione, *f.*

thalamus [ˈθæləməs], *n.* (*Bot. Anat.*) Talamo, *m.*

thaler [ˈtɑ:ləɹ], *n.* (*Hist.*) Tallero, *m.*

thallium [ˈθæliəm], *n.* (*Min.*) Tallio, *m.*

thallus [ˈθælʌs], *n.* (*Bot.*) Tallo, *m.*

Thames [temz], *n.* (*Geog.*) Tamigi, *m.* **He'll never set the — on fire,** non è mica un genio, non fa miracoli.

than [ðæn], *conj.* Che; di. **You are older — he,** siete più vecchio di lui; **rather — do that,** piuttosto che fare ciò; **the town is further away — I thought,** la città è più distante che non credevo; **better late — never,** meglio tardi che mai; **no other —,** nessun altro che, niente altro che.

thane [θein], *n.* (*Hist.*) Barone, *m.*

thank [θæŋk], *v.t.* Ringraziare di, render grazie di. **Thank you!** Grazie! **Thank God!** Grazie a Dio! **I will — you to leave me alone,** favorite lasciarmi stare; **— -offering,** oblazione, *f.*

thankful, *a.* Riconoscente, grato. **I am — to say that . . .,** sono contento di dire che . . ., mi è grato il dire che .

thankfully, *adv.* Con gratitudine.
thankfulness, *n.* Riconoscenza, gratitudine, *f.*
thankless, *a.* Ingrato; sgradevole. **A — task,** un ingrato lavoro, *m.*
thanklessness, *n.* Ingratitudine, *f.*
thanks, *n.pl.* Grazie, *f.pl.*, ringraziamento, *m.* **To give —,** rendere grazie; **accept my —,** vi prego gradire i miei ringraziamenti; **— to you,** grazie a voi; **to return — to,** ringraziare; **— to him,** mercè sua, grazie a lui.
thanksgiving, *n.* Rendimento di grazie, *m.*
that (1) [ðæt], *a.pron.* Quello, quel, *m.*, quella, *f.*, cotesto, *m.*, cotesta, *f.*; ciò, *m.*; che, *m.f.*, il quale, *m.*, la quale, *f.* **For all —,** con tutto ciò, nonostante, nondimeno; **Has it come to — ?** È giunto a questo? **on —,** con ciò, al che; **that is . . .,** cioè, ossia, vale a dire; **— I will not,** ciò non farò mai; **that's all,** ecco tutto; **that's he,** eccolo; **What of — ?** Che cosa importa? **with —,** con ciò; **What noise is — ?** Che rumore è quello? **that's right,** va bene; **That's a good girl!** Che brava ragazza! **talking of this and —,** discorrendo del più e del meno; **and that's —!** Punto e basta!
that (2), *conj.* Che; perchè; acciochè, affinchè. **It is hoped — all goes well,** si spera che tutto vada bene; **not — I don't like it,** non che io non l'ami; **come tomorrow so — we can talk it over,** venite domani e parleremo delle nostre faccende.
thatch [θætʃ], *n.* Paglia, stoppia, *f.* ‖ *v.t.* Coprire di paglia. **A thatched roof,** un tetto di paglia, *m.*
thatcher, *n.* Chi fa coperture di paglia, *m.*
thaumaturgical [θɔːməˈtəːɹdʒikəl], *a.* Taumaturgico.
thaumaturgy, *n.* Taumaturgia, *f.*
thaw [θɔː], *n.* Disgelo, sgelo, *m.* ‖ *v.t.i.* Disgelare, disgelarsi, sgelare, sgelarsi; (*fig.*) sciogliere, sciogliersi, intenerire, intenerirsi.
the [ðiː, ðə], *def.art.* Il, lo, *m.*, la, *f.*, i, gli, *m.pl.*, le, *f.pl.* **Of the,** del, dello, della, dei, degli, delle; **to the, at the,** al, allo, alla, ai, agli, alle; **the sooner the better,** più presto è meglio è; **the more he has the more he wants,** più egli ha più egli desidera.
Theatin [ˈθiːətin], *n.* (*Eccles.*) Teatino, *m.*
theatre [ˈθiətəɹ], *n.* Teatro, *m.*; scena, *f.* **The English —,** il teatro inglese, *m.*; **the — of war,** il teatro della guerra, *m.*; **— -goer,** frequentatore di teatro, *m.*
theatrical [θiˈætrikəl], *a.* Teatrale, scenico, di teatro.
theatrically, *adv.* Teatralmente.
theatricals, *n.pl.* Rappresentazioni teatrali, *f.pl.*, recita, *f.*
Thebaid [ˈθiːbeiid], *n.* (*Geog.*) Tebaide, *f.*
Theban, *a.* Tebano.
Thebes [θiːbz], *n.* (*Geog.*) Tebe, *f.*
thee [ðiː], *pron.* Te, ti.
theft [θeft], *n.* Furto, ladrocinio, *m.*, ruberia, *f.*
their, theirs [ðeəɹ, ðeəɹz], *a.poss.pron.* Il loro, *m.*, la loro, *f.*, i loro, *m.pl.*, le loro, *f.pl.*
theism [ˈθiːizm], *n.* Teismo, *m.*
theist, *n.* Teista, *m.f.*
theistic, *a.* Teistico.
them [ðem], *pron.* Li, loro, essi, *m.pl.*; le, loro, esse, *f.pl.*; ci, vi, ne. **Have you seen — ?** Li avete veduti? **I shall not speak to —,** io non parlerò loro; **I sent — to her,** glieli ho mandati; **she gave me three of —,** me ne diede tre.
theme [θiːm], *n.* Tema, soggetto, *m.*; (*Mus.*) tema, motivo, *m.*
themselves [ðemˈselvz], *pron.* Essi stessi, loro stessi, *m.pl.*, esse stesse, loro stesse, *f.pl.*; se, *pl.* **By —,** soli, *m.pl.*; **to keep to —,** tenersi in disparte.
then [ðen], *adv.* Allora, in quel tempo; poi, dopo, quindi, poscia; dunque, così. ‖ *conj.* Dunque, quindi. **He was too busy just —,** allora era troppo occupato; **you must — return home,** e poi dovete tornare a casa; **now and —,** di quando in quando; **Well then, you should have said so!** Ebbene, avreste dovuto dirmelo! **Then why did you do it ?** Perchè dunque, l'avete fatto? **till —,** fino allora; **What —!** E poi! **Now —, what are you doing ?** Macchè, cosa state facendo? **— and there,** subito.
thence [ðens], *adv.* Quindi, ne, perciò, per questa ragione; di là, di lì. **It — appears that,** ne resulta che.
thenceforth, thenceforward, *adv.* D'allora in poi.
theocracy [θiːˈɔkrəsi], *n.* Teocrazia, *f.*
theocratic [θiːoˈkrætik], *a.* Teocratico.
theodicy [θiːˈɔdisi], *n.* Teodicea, *f.*
theodolite [θiːˈɔdolait], *n.* Teodolite, *f.*
theogony [θiːˈɔgəni], *n.* Teogonia, *f.*
theologian [θiːˈoloudʒiən], *n.* Teologo, *m.*
theological, *a.* Teologico.
theology [θiːˈɔlɔdʒi], *n.* Teologia, *f.*
theorbo [θiˈɔːɹbou], *n.* (*Mus.*) Tiorba, *f.*
theorem [ˈθiːərem], *n.* Teorema, *m.*
theoretic, theoretical, *a.* Teoretico, teorico.
theoretically, *adv.* Teoreticamente.
theorist, *n.* Teorico, dottrinario, *m.*
theorize [ˈθiːoraiz], *v.i.* Teorizzare.
theory, *n.* Teoria, ipotesi, *f.*
theosophist [θiːˈɔsofist], *n.* Teosofista, *m.f.*
theosophy, *n.* Teosofia, *f.*
therapeutic [θerəˈpjuːtik], *a.* Terapeutico.
therapeutics, *n.pl.* Terapeutica, *f.*
therapeutist, *n.* Terapeutico, *m.*
therapy, *n.* Terapeutica, *f.*
there [ðeəɹ], *adv.* Là, lì; colà, costà, costì, ivi; ci, vi; ecco. **Down —,** laggiù; **here and —,** qua e là; **I shall be —,** ci sarò io; **in —,** lì dentro; **over —,** colà, costì; **— and then,** subito, su due piedi, su di ciò; **There he comes!** Eccolo che viene! **There he is!** Eccolo! **— is,** c'è, v'è; **— are,** ci sono, vi sono; **there's many a slip 'twixt the cup and the lip,** dal dire al fare c'è di mezzo il mare; **up —,** lassù; **I passed by — yesterday,** sono passato lì vicino ieri. **There, there, never mind!** Or su, coraggio!
thereabout, thereabouts, *adv.* Lì presso, lì vicino, all'intorno, all'incirca, giù di lì.
thereafter, *adv.* Poscia, d'allora in poi, d'allora innanzi.
thereat, *adv.* A ciò, su di ciò.
thereby, *adv.* Da ciò, per ciò, così, con tale mezzo.
therefor, *adv.* Per ciò.
therefore, *adv.* Dunque, perciò, quindi.
therefrom, *adv.* Da ciò.
therein, *adv.* In ciò, vi, là dentro.

thereon, *adv.* Lassù, su di ciò, a tal proposito.
thereto, thereunto, *adv.* A ciò, vi, ci.
thereupon, *adv.* Su di ciò, su questo, in conseguenza, immediatamente dopo.
therewith, *adv.* Con ciò, insieme a ciò.
therewithal, *adv.* Inoltre, in più, con tutto questo, nello stesso tempo.
theriac [ˈθiəriæk], *n.* (*Chem.*) Teriaca, *f.*
therm [θəːɹm], *n.* Unita termica, *f.*
thermae [ˈθəːɹmiː], *n.pl.* (*Hist.*) Terme, *f.pl.*
thermal, *a.* Termale.
thermic, *a.* Termico.
thermo-chemistry [θəːɹmoˈkemistri], *n.* Termochimica, *f.*
thermo-dynamics, *n.pl.* Termodinamica, *f.*
thermometer [θəɹˈmɔmetəɹ], *n.* Termometro, *m.*
thermostat [ˈθəːɹmostæt], *n.* Termostato, *m.*
thermostatic, *a.* Termostatico.
these [ðiːz], *pron.* Questi, *m.pl.*, queste, *f.pl.*; cotesti, *m.pl.*, coteste, *f.pl.* **We have been waiting — three hours,** sono tre ore che attendiamo; **— are his,** questi sono i suoi.
thesis (pl. **theses**) [ˈθiːsis, ˈθiːsiːz], *n.* Tesi, *f.*
Thespian [ˈθespiən], *a.* Di Tespi.
Thessalonian [θesəˈlouniən], *n.a.* Tessalonico, Tessalonicese, *m.*
theurgic [θiːˈəːɹdʒik], *a.* Teurgico.
theurgy, *n.* Teurgia, teurgica, *f.*
thews [θjuːz], *n.pl.* Muscoli, tendini, nervi, *m.pl.*; forza muscolare, *f.*; (*fig.*) forza mentale *or* morale.
they [ðei], *pron.* Essi, *m.pl.*, esse, *f.pl.*; coloro, *m.f.pl.*, si. **— say,** si dice; **it is —,** sono loro.
thick [θik], *a.* (*solid*). Spesso, denso; grosso, solido, sodo; (*thickly growing*) folto, fitto; (*not clear*) torbido, fosco; (*stupid*) stupido, sciocco; (*of voice*) fioco, rauco; (*colloq.*) intimo. ‖ *adv.* Spesso; densamente, fitto; fiocamente, raucamente. ‖ *n.* Grosso, *m.*; folto, *m.* **As — as thieves,** legati a doppio filo; **— hair,** capelli folti, *m.pl.*; **two inches —,** dello spessore di due pollici, alto due pollici; **a — paste,** una pasta densa, *f.*; **in the — of the fight,** nel folto della mischia; **through — and thin,** malgrado tutto, attraverso ogni ostacolo; **snow was falling —,** la neve cadeva fitta; **— -headed,** stupido, ottuso; **— -lipped,** dalle labbra grosse; **— -skinned,** (*fig.*) di pelle dura.
thicken, *v.t.* Addensare, condensare; indurire; spessire, ispessire, infittire; *v.i.* addensarsi, condensarsi; indurirsi; ispessirsi, infittirsi. **The plot thickens,** l'intreccio s'imbroglia.
thickening, *n.* Addensamento, ispessimento, indurimento, *m.*; legamento, *m.*
thicket, *n.* Macchia, boscaglia, *f.*, boschetto, *m.*; selva, *f.*
thickish, *a.* Piuttosto fitto, denso.
thickly, *adv.* Spesso, densamente; fiocamente; raucamente.
thickness, *n.* Spessore, *m.*, grossezza, densità, *f.*; consistenza, *f.*; foltezza, *f.*; oscurità, *f.*
thickset, *a.* Denso, folto, fitto; tarchiato; ben piantato.
thief [θiːf], *n.* Ladro, *m.*, ladra, *f.*; ladrone, ladruncolo, *m.* **Stop —!** Al ladro! **a thieves' kitchen,** un covo di ladri, *m.*
thieve [θiːv], *v.i.* Rubare.
thieving, thievery, *n.* Ladreria, ruberia, *f.* ladrocinio, *m.*
thievish, *a.* Ladro, ladresco.
thievishly, *adv.* Ladramente, furtivamente.
thievishness, *n.* Ladroneria, *f.*
thigh [θai], *n.* (*Anat.*) Coscia, *f.*; cosciotto, *m.* **— -bone,** femore, *m.*; **— -boots,** cosciali, *m.pl.*
thill [θil], *n.* Stanga, *f.*; (*of cart*) timone, *m.*
thimble [θimbl], *n.* Ditale, anello da cucire, *m.*; (*Naut.*) radancia, *f.*; **— -rig,** giuoco dei bussolotti, *m.*
thimbleful, *n.* Ditalata, *f.*, dito, *m.* **A — of wine,** un dito di vino, *m.*
thin [θin], *a.* Sottile, fino; (*lean*) tenue, fievole, magro, smilzo, esile, scarno; (*not dense*) rado, raro; sparso, scarso; (*weak*) debole, fiacco; (*of liquid*) leggiero. ‖ *v.t.* Assottigliare, attenuare; ridurre; (*hair*) sfoltire, diradare; (*to prune*) sfrondare, diramare; (*a liquid*) allungare. **— as a lath,** secco come un chiodo; **— broth,** brodo lungo, *m.*; **— blood,** sangue povero, *m.*; **a — disguise,** una maschera trasparente; **to grow —,** dimagrire, dimagrare; **— -skinned,** (*fig.*) sensibile, suscettibile, permaloso; **a — slice,** una fettuccina.
thine [ðain], *poss.pron.* Il tuo, *m.*, la tua, *f.*, i tuoi, *m.pl.*, le tue, *f.pl.*; a te.
thing [θiŋ], *n.* Cosa, *f.*; affare, oggetto, *m.*; essere, *m.*, creatura, *f.* **Above all things,** soprattutto; **anything,** qualchecosa; qualunque cosa; **for one —,** prima di tutto; **it's a bad — for her,** è molto male per lei; **it's a very good — that,** meno male che; **Poor —!** Poverino! *m.*, Poverina! *f.*; **things are looking up,** gli affari vanno meglio; **to make a mess of things,** fare un bell'imbroglio; **the latest — in frocks,** l'ultima moda in vestiti; **it is not the — to behave so,** non ci si deve comportare così; **no such —,** non è vero, niente affatto; **I don't feel at all the —,** sto poco bene; **that's quite another —,** è un altro paio di maniche; **to pack up one's things,** fare le valigie.
thingummy, thingumajig [ˈθiŋʌmi, ˈθiŋəmədʒig], *n.* Quella roba, *f.*; (*of person*) quel tale, *m.*
think [θiŋk], *v.t.i.* Pensare; (*to believe*) credere; (*to imagine*) immaginare, figurarsi; (*to judge*) giudicare, stimare, ritenere; considerare, meditare; sembrare, parere. **Do as you — best,** fate quel che vi pare; **I thought better of it,** cambiai di proposito, ci ho pensato meglio; **I — it a shame to . . .,** mi pare un peccato che . . .; **he little thinks that . . .,** non se lo sogna che . . .; **he thinks nothing of walking twenty miles,** non ci mette nè uno nè due a far venti miglia; **I — nothing of that book,** non faccio il minimo caso di quel libro; **he thinks very highly of it,** ne fa gran caso; **I — so,** credo di sì; **I thought as much,** lo pensavo; **to tell someone what one thinks of him,** dire il fatto suo a qualcuno; **to — about,** pensare a; **to — over,** riflettere su, pensarci su; **What do you — of it ?** Che ve ne pare ?
thinkable, *a.* Pensabile, concepibile, immaginabile.
thinker, *n.* Pensatore, *m.*
thinking, *n.* Pensiero, *m.*; parere, avviso, *m.*; opinione, *f.* ‖ *a.* Pensante, prudente, savio. **To my way of —,** a mio avviso, a mio parere.

thinly, *adv.* Sottilmente, magramente; leggermente; scarsamente. **The performance was — attended,** c'era un pubblico scarso; **— -clad,** leggermente vestito; **— -sown,** seminato rado.
thinness, *n.* Sottigliezza, tenuità, *f.*; magrezza, radezza, *f.*; rarità, *f.*
thinnish, *a.* Magretto, minghelino.
third [θəːɹd], *a.* Terzo. ‖ *n.* Terza parte, *f.*, terzo, *m.*; (*Mus.*) terza, *f.* **A — party,** un terzo, *m.*; **the — finger,** il dito anulare, *m.*; (*Gram.*) **— person,** terza persona, *f.*; **the — of March,** il tre marzo, *m.*
thirdly, *adv.* In terzo luogo.
thirst [θəːɹst], *n.* Sete, *f.* ‖ *v.i.* Aver sete di. **The — for power,** la sete del potere; **to quench one's —,** dissetarsi, appagare la sete.
thirstily, *adv.* Avidamente.
thirstiness, *n.* Sete, *f.*
thirsty, *a.* Assetato, sitibondo; avido, bramoso; arido. **I am —,** ho sete; **the heat makes one —,** il caldo fa venir sete.
thirteen [θəːɹˈtiːn], *n.a.* Tredici, *m.* **— -year-old,** tredicenne, *m.f.*
thirteenth, *n.a.* Tredicesimo, decimoterzo, *m.*
thirtieth [ˈθəːɹtiəθ], *n.a.* Trentesimo, *m.*
thirty, *n.a.* Trenta, *m.*, trentina, *f.* **— years old,** trentenne, di trentanni; **— years of service,** un trentennio di servizio, *m.*; **— -one,** trentuno.
this [ðis], *a.pron.* Questo, *m.*, questa, *f.*, codesto, *m.*, codesta, *f.*; ciò; (*of persons*) costui, *m.*, costei, *f.* **At — moment,** al presente, al momento; **by — time,** a quest'ora; **— is our house,** questa è casa nostra; **just for — once,** per questa volta soltanto; **— day week,** oggi a otto; **upon —,** con questo, con ciò; **What's —?** Che cosa è questo? Cosa succede? **talking of — and that,** discutendo del più e del meno. **This way!** Di qui! Di qua! **— way and that,** qua e là.
thistle [θisl], *n.* (*Bot.*) Cardo, cardone, *m.*
thistledown, *n.* Lanugine del cardo, *f.*
thither [ˈðiðəɹ], *adv.* Là, colà, vi, ci. **Hither and —,** qua e là.
thole (1), **thole-pin** [θoul, ˈθoulpin], *n.* Scalmo, *m.* (*Naut.*).
thole (2), *v.t.* Soffrire, sopportare.
Thomas [ˈtɔməs], *n.* Tommaso, *m.*
thong (θɔŋ], *n.* Correggia, *f.*, corregiuolo, *m.*; striscia di cuoio, cinghia, *f.*
thoracic [θɔˈræsik], *a.* Toracico.
thorax [ˈθɔːræks], *n.* (*Anat.*) Torace, *m.*
thorn [θɔːɹn], *n.* Spina, *f.* **No rose without a —,** non c'è rosa senza spine; **a — in one's flesh,** una spina nel fianco, *f.*, un fastidio, *m.*; **I have a — in my finger,** ho una spina nel dito; (*Zool.*) **— -back,** specie di razza, *f.*; **— -bush,** spino, spineto, rovo, *m.*; **to be on thorns,** essere sui carboni ardenti.
thorny, *a.* Spinoso.
thorough [ˈθʌrʌ], *a.* Intero, completo, esauriente; perfetto; profondo; matricolato, solenne, famoso. **His work is not —,** il suo lavoro è trascurato; **he's a — rogue,** è un birbante matricolato.
thoroughbass, *n.* (*Mus.*) Basso continuo, *m.*, armonia, *f.*
thoroughbred, *a.* Di puro sangue, di razza; genuino, schietto.
thoroughfare, *n.* Via pubblica, strada, *f.*, passaggio, *m.*, diritto di passaggio. **No —,** vietato il passaggio, divieto di transito.
thoroughgoing, *a.* Esauriente; dichiarato, riconosciuto; matricolato.
thoroughly, *adv.* Completamente, profondamente, a fondo; pienamente.
thoroughness, *n.* Perfezione, *f.*; completezza, *f.*
thoroughpaced, *a.* Franco, schietto; matricolato, di tre cotte.
those [ðouz], *a.* Quei, quegli, *m.pl.*, quelle, *f.pl.*, cotesti, *m.pl.*, coteste, *f.pl.* ‖ *pron.* Quelli, *m.pl.*, quelle, *f.pl.* **Bring me — books,** portatemi cotesti libri; **— are the best,** quelli sono i migliori.
thou [ðau], *pron.* Tu. **To thee and —,** dare del tu.
though [ðou], *conj.* Benchè, quantunque, sebbene, ancorchè; nondimeno, pure, tuttavia. **As —,** come se; **even —,** benchè, quantunque, sebbene; **— it was late,** benchè fosse tardi.
thought (1) [θɔːt], *p.* and *pp.* of **think.**
thought (2), *n.* Pensiero, *m.*; idea, opinione, *f.*, sentimento, *m.*; riflessione, *f.*; cura, *f.* **A happy —,** una buona idea, *f.*; **on second thoughts,** ripensandoci; **to collect one's thoughts,** riaversi, riprendersi; **to take — for,** inquietarsi di; **without —,** senza riflettere; **quick as —,** ratto come il pensiero; **— -reader,** lettore del pensiero, *m.*
thoughtful, *a.* Pensieroso, cogitabondo; soprappensiero, preoccupato, pensoso, attento, sollecito, premuroso; gentile, buono. **— of,** attento a, sollecito a, sollecito di.
thoughtfully, *adv.* Pensatamente, saggiamente, premurosamente, gentilmente.
thoughtfulness, *n.* Meditazione, *f.*, raccoglimento, *m.*; attenzione, premura, *f.*
thoughtless, *a.* Spensierato, leggiero, sventato, incosciente.
thoughtlessly, *adv.* Spensieratamente.
thoughtlessness, *n.* Spensieratezza, leggerezza, incoscienza, trascuratezza, *f.*
thousand [ˈθauzənd], *a.* Mille. ‖ *n.* Mille, migliaio, *m.* **About a —,** un migliaio, *m.*; **the year one — nine hundred and fifty-seven,** l'anno mille novecento cinquantasette; **he is one in a —,** è una mosca bianca; **a — thanks,** mille grazie; **in thousands,** a migliaia; **thousands of,** migliaia di.
thousandth, *n.a.* Millesimo, *m.*
Thrace [θreis], *n.* (*Geog.*) Tracia, *f.*
Thracian, *n.a.* Trace, *m.*
thraldom [ˈθrɔːldəm], *n.* Schiavitù, soggezione, *f.*
thrall, *n.* Schiavo, *m.*, schiava, *f.*
thrash [θræʃ], *v.t.* Battere, percuotere; bastonare, sferzare, fustigare. **To — out a question,** discutere a fondo una questione.
thrashing, *n.* Bastonatura, *f.*, busse, botte, *f.pl.*; sferzata, *f.*
thread [θred], *n.* Filo, refe, *m.*; corda, *f.*; (*of screw*) filetto, *m.*; (*screw pitch*) pane, *m.* ‖ *v.t.* Infilare, infilzare. **To lose the — of one's discourse,** perdere il filo del discorso; **to — one's way through a crowd,** passare attraverso una folla, infilarsi nella folla; (*Zool.*) **— -worm,** ossiuro.
threadbare, *a.* Frusto, liso, consumato, logoro; (*fig.*) trito, vieto.

threadbareness, *n.* Logoratezza, *f.*
thready, *a.* Pieno di fili, filamentoso, fibroso.
threat [θret], *n.* Minaccia, *f.*
threaten, *v.t.i.* Minacciare. **To — with death,** minacciare di morte; **it threatens to rain,** minaccia pioggia, minaccia di piovere.
threatening, *a.* Minaccioso, minacciante. **— words,** parole minacciose, *f.pl.*
threateningly, *adv.* Minacciosamente, con minacce.
three [θri:], *n.a.* Tre, *m.* **The rule of —,** la regola del tre, *f.*; **it is — o'clock,** sono le tre; **— -cornered,** triangolare; **— -cornered hat,** tricorno, nicchio, *m.*; (*Pol.*) **— -cornered contest,** lotta elettorale con tre candidati, *f.*; **— -legged,** a tre gambe, a tre piedi; **a — -legged stool,** uno sgabello a tre piedi; (*Naut.*) **— -master,** trealberi, *m.*; **— -ply wood,** legno compensato a tre strati; **— -ply wool,** lana di tre fili, *f.*; **— -quarter,** di tre quarti; (*Football*) terzino, *m.*; **— -quarter length,** lungo tre quarti; **— -colour process,** tricromia; (*Motor., etc.*) **— -speed gear,** cambio a tre velocità, *m.*
threefold, *a.* Triplice, triplo.
threepence [ˈθrepəns], *n.pl.* Un quarto di uno scellino.
threepenny, *a.* **A — bit,** un pezzo di threepence, *m.*
threescore, *a.* Sessanta. || *n.* Sessanta, sessantina, *f.* **He has passed —,** ha varcata la sessantina.
threesome [ˈθri:səm], *n.* (*Golf, etc.*) Partita di tre persone, *f.*
threnody [ˈθrenodi], *n.* Trenodia, *f.*
thresh [θreʃ], *v.t.* Battere, trebbiare.
thresher, *n.* Trebbiatore, *m.*
threshing, *n.* Trebbia, trebbiatura, *f.* **— -machine,** trebbiatrice, *f.*; **— -floor,** aia, *f.*
threshold [ˈθreʃhould], *n.* Soglia, *f.* **To cross the —,** varcare la soglia; **on the — of life,** sulla soglia della vita.
thrice [θrais], *adv.* Tre volte.
thrift (1) [θrift], *n.* (*Bot.*) Pianta della famiglia delle plumbaginee, *f.*, spilletone, *m.*
thrift (2), *n.* Economia, frugalità, *f.*, risparmio, *m.*
thriftily, *adv.* Economicamente.
thriftiness, *n.* Economia, frugalità, *f.*, risparmio, *m.*
thriftless, *a.* Prodigo, scialacquatore.
thriftlessness, *n.* Prodigalità, *f.*
thrifty, *a.* Economo, frugale, parco, risparmiatore.
thrill [θril], *n.* Emozione, *f.*, fremito, sussulto, *m.*; trepidazione, *f.* || *v.t.* Far trasalire, commuovere, emozionare, elettrizzare; *v.i.* rabbrividire, fremere, trepidare. **He was thrilled with horror,** rabbrividì di terrore; (*colloq.*) **thrilled to death,** lietissimo, colmo di gioia.
thriller, *n.* Racconto sensazionale, romanzo giallo, romanzo poliziesco, *m.*
thrilling, *a.* Emozionante, elettrizzante.
thrive [θraiv], *v.i.* Prosperare, fiorire, crescere; riuscire; attecchire, allignare. **To — on,** nutrirsi di.
thriving, *a.* Prospero, prosperoso, fiorente; robusto, vigoroso.
thrivingly, *adv.* Prosperamente, con successo.
thro', thro [cp. **through**].
throat [θrout], *n.* Gola, *f.*; canna, strozza, *f.*, gorgozzule, *m.*; (*neck*) collo, *m.* **A sore —,** male alla gola, mal di gola, *m.*; **to cut someone's —,** scannare qualcuno; **to cut one's —,** tagliarsi la gola; **a lump in one's —,** un nodo alla gola, *m.*; **to seize by the —,** prendere per la gola.
throaty, *a.* Gutturale, di gola.
throb [θrɔb], *v.i.* Battere, palpitare, pulsare; spasimare. || *n.* Palpito, sussulto, spasimo, *m.*, pulsazione, fitta, *f.*
throbbing, *n.* Palpitazione, pulsazione, *f.*, battito, *m.* || *a.* Palpitante, pulsante.
throe [θrou], *n.* Travaglio, tormento, *m.*, pena, agonia, *f.* **Throes,** doglie, pene, angosce, *f.pl.*
thrombosis [θrɔmˈbousis], *n.* (*Med.*) Trombosi, *f.*
throne [θroun], *n.* Trono, soglio, *m.*; (*Eccles.*) cattedra, *f.* **— -room,** sala del trono, *f.*
throng [θrɔŋ], *n.* Folla, calca, *f.*; torma, moltitudine, *f.* || *v.i.* Affollarsi, accalcarsi, pigiarsi; *v.t.* affollare, riempire.
throstle [θrɔsl], *n.* (*Zool.*) Tordo, *m.*
throttle [θrɔtl], *v.t.* Strangolare, strozzare; (*Mech.*) regolare la pressione del vapore. || *n.* Strozza, *f.*; (*Mech.*) Glifo, *m.*, valvola d'immissione, *f.*
through [θru:], *prep.* Attraverso, per; per mezzo di; per causa di; per colpa di. || *a.* (*of trains, etc.*) Diretto. || *adv.* Da parte a parte, dal principio alla fine; a buon fine, completamente. **We walked — the town,** camminammo attraverso la città; **to see — a telescope,** guardare in un telescopio; **to look — a window,** guardare dalla finestra; **to get — an exam,** passare un esame; **he did it — ignorance,** l'ha fatto per ignoranza; **it was all — you,** accadde per colpa vostra; **a — train,** un treno diretto, *m.*; **they would not let us —,** non ci lasciarono passare; **I have read the book —,** ho letto il libro dal principio alla fine; **he looked me — and —,** mi guardò in fondo agli occhi; **to be wet —,** essere bagnato fino alle ossa; (*of a project*) **to fall —,** andare a monte, fallire; **to go — with,** condurre a fine. (*Rail.*) **a — rate,** una tariffa per trasporti in servizio cumulativo, *f.*
throughout, *prep.* In tutto, durante, per tutto. || *adv.* Dappertutto, in ogni parte, interamente.
throw [θrou], *v.t.* Gettare, buttare, scagliare, lanciare; atterrare, abbattere; (*silk*) torcere; *v.i.* gettare, lanciare. || *n.* Gettata, *f.*, getto, tiro, lancio, *m.* **To — aside,** gettare da parte; **to — at,** gettare a; **to — away,** gettare via, buttare via, (*to lose*) perdere, (*to waste*) sperperare, scialacquare; **to — back,** rigettare, gettare indietro, (*to reflect*) riflettere, (*to delay*) ritardare; **to — down,** atterrare, abbattere, gettare giù; **to — in,** gettare dentro, (*to give over and above*) dare per soprammercato, frammettere; **to — off,** gettar via, (*a garment*) levare, (*to get rid of*) liberarsi di, disfarsi di, scuotere; **to — off the scent,** far perdere le tracce; **to — oneself into,** abbandonarsi a, buttarsi in; **to — open,** aprire, spalancare; **to — out,** gettare via, (*to suggest*) insinuare, suggerire; (*to emit*) metter fuori, emettere; **to — out of the window,** gettare dalla finestra; **to — up,** gettare

in su; (*to abandon*) abbandonare, rinunciare a, (*to vomit*) rigettare, (*a window*) aprire; **to — wide open,** spalancare; **to be within a stone's —,** essere a un tiro di pietra, a un tiro di schioppo, a due passi.

throwing, *n.* Lanciamento, *m.*

throwster, *n.* Torcitore di seta, *m.*

thrum [θrʌm], *v.i.* Strimpellare.

thrush [θrʌʃ], *n.* (*Zool.*) Tordo, *m.*; (*Med.*) afte, *f.pl.*

thrust [θrʌst], *v.t.* Spingere, cacciare, ficcare, conficcare; *v.i.* cacciare, cacciarsi. ‖ *n.* Colpo, *m.*, botta, puntata, stoccata, spinta, *f.* **To — back,** respingere, spingere indietro; **to — in,** spingere dentro, cacciare dentro; **to — out,** spingere fuori, cacciar fuori, metter fuori; **to — oneself forward,** spingersi avanti, lanciarsi avanti; **he — through the crowd,** egli si cacciò tra la folla; si aprì una strada in mezzo alla folla; **a home- —,** un colpo in pieno.

thud [θʌd], *n.* Tonfo, colpo sordo, *m.*

thug [θʌg], *n.* Strangolatore, sicario, *m.*

thumb [θʌm], *n.* (*Anat.*) Pollice, *m.* ‖ *v.t.* Maneggiare, lasciare ditate su. **By rule of —,** per praticaccia, a lume di naso; **to be under someone's —,** essere sotto il dominio di qualcuno; **—-mark, —-print,** impronta del pollice; **—-screw,** strumento di tortura; **—-nut,** dado ad alette, *m.*; **—-stall,** ditale, *m.*; (*colloq.*) **Thumbs up!** Tutto va bene!

thump [θʌmp], *v.t.* Battere, picchiare, tirare pugni a, sferrare pugni a. ‖ *n.* Colpo, *m.*, pugno, *m.*

thumper, *n.* (*colloq.*) Cosa enorme, *f.*; grossa bugia, bomba, *f.*

thumping, *a.* (*colloq.*) Grande, enorme, madornale.

thunder [ˈθʌndəɹ], *n.* Tuono, *m.*; (*fig.*) fragore, strepito, *m.* ‖ *v.t.i.* Tuonare; rombare. **A peal of —,** un tuono, un rombo di tuono, *m.*; **— of applause,** scrosci d'applausi, *m.pl.* **it thunders,** tuona; **the cavalry thundered past,** la cavalleria passò rombando; **—-clap,** colpo di tuono, *m.*; **—-cloud,** nuvolone, nembo, *m.*; **—-shower,** acquazzone, *m.*; **—-storm,** temporale, *m.*; **—-struck,** (*fig.*) attonito, stupefatto, meravigliato.

thunderbolt, *n.* Fulmine, *m.*

thunderer, *n.* Tuonatore, *m.*; **the —,** Giove.

thundering, *a.* Tuonante; (*colloq.*) enorme, terribile.

thunderous, thundery, *a.* Temporalesco.

thurible [ˈθjuːribl], *n.* (*Eccles.*) Turibolo, *m.*

thurifer [ˈθjuːrifəɹ], *n.* (*Eccles.*) Turiferario, *m.*

Thursday [ˈθəːɹsdi], *n.* Giovedì, *m.*

thus [ðʌs], *adv.* Così, in questo modo. **— far,** fin qui; **— much,** tanto.

thuya, thuja [ˈθuːiə], *n.* (*Bot.*) Tuia, *f.*

thwack [θwæk], *n.* Colpo, *m.*, botta, *f.* ‖ *v.t.* Colpire, bastonare, bussare, percuotere.

thwacking, *n.* Bastonata, *f.* **A good —,** un sacco di legnate, *m.*

thwart (1) [θwɔːɹt], *v.t.* Attraversare, contrariare, opporre, contrastare. ‖ *adv.* Attraverso.

thwart (2), *n.* (*Naut.*) Banco del rematore, *m.*

thy [ðai], *a.* Il tuo, *m.*, la tua, *f.*, i tuoi, *m.pl.*, le tue, *f.pl.*

thyme [taim], *n.* (*Bot.*) Timo, *m.*; serpillo, *m.*

thyroid [ˈθairɔid], *n.a.* (*Anat.*) Tiroide, *f.* **— gland,** glandola tiroidea, *f.*

thyrsus [ˈθəːɹsəs], *n.* (*Myth.*) Tirso, *m.*

thyself [ðaiˈself], *pron.* Te stesso, *m.*, te stessa, *f.*

tiara [tiːˈɑːrə], *n.* Tiara, *f.*

Tiber [ˈtaibəɹ], *n.* (*Geog.*) Tevere, *m.*

tibia [ˈtibiə], *n.* (*Anat.*) Tibia, *f.*, stinco, *m.*

tic [tik], *n.* (*Med.*) Tic, ticchio, *m.*

tick (1) [tik], *n.* (*sound*) Tic, tic-tac, battito, *m.* ‖ *v.i.* Battere, far tic-tac, ticchettare. **Tick-tock,** tic-tac, *m.*; (*Mech.*) **to — over,** girare adagio; (*colloq.*) **in two ticks,** subito.

tick (2), *v.t.* Segnare, notare con un punto. ‖ *n.* Segno, punto, *m.* **To — off,** contrassegnare; (*fig.*) biasimare, fare una ramanzina.

tick (3), *n.* (*Zool.*) Acaro, *m.*, zecca, *f.*

tick (4), **ticking,** *n.* Fodera di materasso, *f.*

tick (5), *n.* (*colloq.*) Credito, *m.* **On —,** a credito.

ticket [ˈtikit], *n.* Biglietto, *m.*; etichetta, *f.*, cartellino, *m.*; carta, tessera, *f.* ‖ *v.t.* Metter l'etichetta, etichettare. **Return —,** biglietto di andata e ritorno, *m.*; **season —,** abbonamento, *m.*; **season — holder,** abbonato, *m.*; (*colloq.*) **that's the —,** ecco ciò che occorre; **—-collector,** controllore, *m.*; **—-office,** ufficio biglietti, *m.*; biglietteria, *f.*; **—-window,** sportello, *m.*

tickle [tikl], *v.t.* Solleticare, vellicare, titillare; (*fig.*) divertire, vellicare, stimolare, eccitare; *v.i.* pizzicare.

tickling, *n.* Solleticamento, vellicamento, *m.*

ticklish, *a.* Solleticoso; (*fig.*) difficile, delicato, scabroso.

ticklishness, *n.* Solletico, *m.*; (*fig.*) difficoltà, *f.*

tidal [ˈtaidəl], *a.* Di marea. **— basin,** porto soggetto alla marea, *m.*; **— wave,** maremoto, *m.*; **— water,** acque a marea, *f.pl.*

tide [taid], *n.* Marea, *f.*, flutto, *m.*; corrente, *f.*; tempo, *m.*, stagione, *f.*; periodo, *m.* ‖ *v.i.* Andare colla marea. **To — over,** sormontare, superare, campare; **high —, flood —,** alta marea, *f.*; **low —, ebb —,** bassa marea, *f.*; **carried along by the —,** portato dalla corrente; **the rising —,** il montare della marea, *m.*; **the turn of the —,** il cambiamento della marea, *m.*; **to go with the —,** andare con la corrente; **Eastertide,** la stagione di Pasqua; **—-gauge,** mareografo, *m.*; **—-table,** tavola della marea, *f.*; **—-waiter,** doganiere, *m.*; **—-way,** corrente della marea, *f.*, filo di corrente, *m.*

tidily [ˈtaidili], *adv.* In buon ordine, nettamente.

tidiness, *n.* Buon ordine, *m.*, nettezza, *f.*; proprietà, pulitezza, *f.*

tidings [ˈtaidiŋz], *n.pl.* Notizie, *f.pl.*

tidy [ˈtaidi], *a.* Ordinato, pulito, lindo, in buon ordine. ‖ *v.t.* Assettare, acconciare, metter in ordine, ordinare. ‖ *n.* Copertura di seggiola, *f.* **To — oneself up,** mettersi in ordine, fare toletta; (*colloq.*) **a — sum,** una bella sommetta, *f.*

tie [tai], *v.t.* Legare, attaccare; (*to knot*) annodare; *v.i.* (*Sport*) esser pari, pareggiare. ‖ *n.* Legame, vincolo, *m.*; (*knot*) nodo, *m.*; (*for shoe*) stringa, *f.*; (*necktie*) cravatta, *f.*; (*Arch.*) chiavarda, *f.*; (*Mus.*) legatura, *f.*; (*Sport*) partita nulla, *f.*, pareggio, *m.* **To — down,** legare; (*fig.*) costringere, obbligare;

to — up, legare, (*fig.*) assicurare; (*Football*) **cup- —,** campionato, *m.*; (*Arch.*) **— -beam,** rampone, *m.*; chiavarda, *f.*; **— -pin,** spillo per la cravatta, *m.*
tier [tiəɹ], *n.* Fila, *f.*, ordine, piano, gradino, palco, *m.* **In tiers,** a gradini, a piani, a palchi; **— upon —,** piano su piano, in vari ordini.
tierce [tiəɹs], *n.* (*cask*) Barilotto, *m.*; (*Fencing*) terza, *f.*; (*Mus.*) terza, *f.*
Tierra del Fuego [ti'erə del 'fweigou], *n.* (*Geog.*) Terra del Fuoco, *f.*
tiff [tif], *n.* Battibecco, bisticcio, malumore, *m.*
tiffin ['tifin], *n.* Colazione, *f.*
tiger ['taigəɹ], *n.* (*Zool.*) Tigre, *f.* **— -cat,** gatto selvaggio, gatto tigre, *m.*; **— -cub,** tigretto, tigrotto, *m.*; (*Bot.*) **— -lily,** giglio variegato, giglio tigrino, *m.*
tight [tait], *a.* Stretto, serrato; teso; chiuso; ermetico, stagno; (*colloq.*) brillo, ubbriaco. ‖ *adv.* Fortemente, strettamente, fermo. **This jacket is too —,** questa giacchetta è troppo stretta; **— shoes,** scarpe strette, *f.pl.*; **a — squeeze,** un serra serra, una pigiata, *f.*; **money is —,** il denaro è scarso; **to keep a — hand on,** comandare a bacchetta; **to be in a — place,** essere in una situazione difficile; **to hold — to,** tenersi fermo a, appigliarsi a, stare attaccato a; **to squeeze —,** stringere fortemente; **air- —,** a tenuta d'aria, a chiusura ermetica; **— -fitting,** attillato; **— -fisted,** avaro; **— -rope,** corda, *f.*
tighten, *v.t.* Serrare, stringere, restringere. **He tightened his grip on her arm,** le strinse sempre più il braccio.
tightly, *adv.* Strettamente, fortemente.
tightness, *n.* Strettezza, *f.*; (*of rope*) tensione, *f.*; (*of chest*) oppressione, *f.*; (*of money*) scarsezza, *f.*
tights, *n.pl.* Maglia, *f.*; magliette aderenti da ballerine, *f.pl.*
tigress, *n.* (*Zool.*) Tigre, *f.*
Tigris ['taigris], *n.* (*Geog.*) Tigri, *m.*
tile [tail], *n.* (*roofing*) Tegolo, embrice, *m.*; (*for floor*) mattonella, *f.* ‖ *v.t.* Coprire di tegoli, coprire di mattonelle. **— -flooring,** ammattonato, *m.*; **— -works,** tegolaia, *f.*
tiler, *n.* Conciatetti, *m.*; mosaicista, *m.*; (*Freemasonry*) custode della porta, *m.*
tiling, *n.* Tegolato, mosaico, *m.*
till (1) [til], *n.* Cassetto (per denaro), *m.*
till (2), *v.t.* Coltivare, lavorare.
till (3), *prep.* Fino a, sino a, insino a. ‖ *conj.* Finchè, fintantochè, fino a che. **— tomorrow,** fino a domani; **— death,** fino alla morte.
tillable, *a.* Coltivabile.
tillage, *n.* Coltivazione, agricoltura, *f.*
tiller (1), *n.* Coltivatore, agricoltore, *m.*
tiller (2), *n.* (*Naut.*) Barra del timone, *f.*
tilling, *n.* Coltivazione, *f.*
tilt [tilt], *v.t.* Inclinare, far pendere, abbassare; scaricare; *v.i.* inclinare, pendere; (*to joust*) giostrare, torneare. ‖ *n.* (*slope*) Inclinazione, *f.*; (*jousting*) torneo, *m.*, giostra, *f.*; (*hammer*) maglio, *m.*; (*for cart*) tendone, copertone, *m.* **Full —,** a briglia sciolta, di gran carriera; **to — up,** far saltare su; **to — at,** assalire, attaccare, prender di mira; **— -cart,** carro con tenda, *m.*; **— -yard,** lizza, *f.*, campo chiuso, *m.*
tilted, *a.* Inclinato; con tenda.
tilth [tilθ], *n.* Coltivazione, *f.*
tilting, *n.* Giostra, *f.*
timber ['timbəɹ], *n.* Legname, *m.*, alberi da legname, *m.pl.*; boschi, *m.pl.*; (*Naut.*) ossatura, ordinata, costola, *f.*, trave, *m.* **Building —,** legname da costruzione; **seasoned —,** legname stagionato; (*Naut.*) **— -head,** bittone, *m.*; **— -tree,** albero d'alto fusto, *m.*; **— -work,** costruzione in legno, *f.*; **— -yard,** cantiere, *m.*, segheria, *f.*
timbered, *a.* Costrutto in legno, coperto di legno; alberato, piantato d'alberi. **Half- —,** mezzo in legno.
timbering, *n.* Alberatura, *f.*
timbre ['tæmbəɹ], *n.* Timbro, *m.*
timbrel, *n.* (*Mus.*) Tamburello, *m.*
Timbuctoo [timbʌk'tuː], *n.* (*Geog.*) Timbuktu, *f.*
time [taim], *n.* Tempo, *m.*; epoca, *f.*, periodo, *m.*; (*occasion*) volta, *f.*; (*hour*) ora, *f.*; (*moment*) momento, *m.*; (*Mus.*) tempo, *m.*, misura, *f.* ‖ *v.t.* Scegliere il momento, fare a proposito, fare al momento buono, cogliere il momento opportuno; regolare, accomodare; misurare il tempo impiegato, cronometrare. **After a —,** dopo qualche tempo; **all the —,** sempre, tutto il tempo; **another —,** un' altra volta, *f.*; **as times go,** dati i tempi; **at all times,** sempre, in ogni tempo; **any —,** a qualsiasi ora; **at a — when,** in un'ora in cui; **at such a — as this,** in un tal momento; **at my — of life,** alla mia età; **at no —,** in nessun tempo, non . . . mai; **at that —,** a quel tempo, a quell'epoca; **from — to —,** di tempo in tempo, di quando in quando, volta a volta; **some — or other,** una volta o l'altra; **this — last year,** un anno fa; **this — next week,** oggi a otto; **six times,** sei volte; **till the end of —,** eternamente; (*Mus.*) **to beat —,** segnare il tempo, battere il tempo; (*Mus.*) **to keep —,** andare a tempo; (*of clock*) **to keep good —,** tenere il tempo giusto; **to have a good —,** darsi buon tempo, divertirsi; **to lose —,** perdere tempo; **to serve one's —,** fare il tirocinio; **up to the present —,** fino ad ora; **What — is it ? What is the — ?** Che ora è? Che ore sono? **times out of number,** moltissime volte; **— and again,** ripetutamente; **at the present —,** ora, adesso, al presente; **at the same —,** nello stesso tempo; **at times,** alle volte; **to work against —,** lavorare d'urgenza, lavorare coll'acqua alla gola; **ahead of —,** di buon'ora, prima del tempo; **behind —,** tardi, in ritardo; **every —,** ogni volta, tutte le volte; **from that — on,** d'allora in poi; **I must bide my —,** debbo aspettare il momento opportuno; **he has had a bad — lately,** è stato sfortunato in questi ultimi tempi; **in a short —,** fra poco, in poco tempo, in breve tempo; **in a month's —,** fra un mese; **in course of —,** col tempo, coll'andar di tempo; **all in good —,** ogni cosa a suo tempo; **he came in good —,** venne a tempo; **in no —,** in un attimo; **in its proper — and place,** a tempo e luogo; **in the — of,** al tempo di, all'epoca di; **in —,** a tempo; **in the process of —,** in processo di tempo; **in — to come,** per l'avvenire; **it is — we went,** è tempo di andare; **mean —,** tempo medio, *m.*; **next —,** la prossima volta, *f.*; **now's the —,** ecco il momento; **once upon a — there was . . .,** c'era una volta . . .; (*Mus.*)

out of —, fuori tempo; **three at a —,** tre alla volta; **to pass the — of day with,** intrattenersi con; **hard times,** tempi difficili; **to take one's — over something,** fare con tutto comodo qualcosa; **he timed his visit well,** arrivò molto a proposito; **— presses,** il tempo incalza; **ill-timed,** male a proposito, inopportuno; **— -fuse,** spoletta a tempo, *f.*; **— -honoured,** venerabile, venerato; **— -server,** opportunista, *m.*; **— -sheet,** foglio di presenza, *m.*; **— -table,** orario, *m.*; **— -work,** lavoro a ora, *m.*; **—-worn,** vecchio, usato, logoro, sdruscito.

timekeeper, *n.* (*in works*) Controllore dell'orario, *m.*; (*Sport*) cronometrista, *m.*; (*watch*) pendola, *f.*, cronometro, *m.*

timeliness, *n.* Convenienza, tempestività, *f.*

timely, *a.* Opportuno, tempestivo, conveniente, a proposito.

timepiece, *n.* Orologio, cronometro, *m.*

timid ['timid], *a.* Timido, pauroso, timoroso.

timidity, *n.* Timidità, timidezza, *f.*

timidly, *adv.* Timidamente, timorosamente.

timing ['taimiŋ], *n.* Tempo, *m.*, messa a tempo, regolazione, *f.*

timorous ['timərəs], *a.* Timoroso, pauroso.

timorously, *adv.* Timorosamente.

timorousness, *n.* Timidità, timorosità, *f.*

Timothy ['timəθi], *n.* Timoteo, *m.*

tin [tin], *n.* (*Min.*) Stagno, *m.*, latta, *f.*; (*tin box*) scatola di latta, *f.*; (*colloq.*) denari, quattrini, *m.pl.* || *v.t.* Stagnare; mettere in scatola. || *a.* Di stagno, di latta. **Tinned salmon,** salmone in scatola, *m.*; **— -foil,** stagnola, *f.*; **— -mine,** miniera di stagno, *f.*; **— -plate,** latta, latta stagnata, *f.*; **— -tack,** chiodetto, *m.*, bulletta, *f.*; **— -opener,** apriscatole, *m.*; (*colloq.*) **— hat,** elmetto, *m.*

tincture ['tiŋktʃəɹ], *n.* Tintura, *f.*; (*fig.*) tinta, tintura, infarinatura, *f.* || *v.t.* Tingere. **To be tinctured with,** avere una tintura di.

tinder ['tindəɹ], *n.* Esca, *f.* **— -box,** scatola per l'esca, *f.*, acciarino, *m.*

tine [tain], *n.* Rebbio, *m.*, punta, *f.*; (*of deer*) palco, *m.*

ting [tiŋ], *v.i.* Tintinnare, tintinnire, tinnire. || *n.* Tintinnio, *m.*

tinge [tindʒ], *n.* Tinta, tintura, *f.*; pizzico, *m.* || *v.t.* Tingere, colorire; mischiare, permeare. **Admiration tinged with envy,** ammirazione mista a invidia, *f.*

tingle ['tiŋgəl], *v.i.* Prudere, informicolare, sentir bruciore; fremere. **To — with indignation,** fremere di sdegno.

tingling ['tiŋgliŋ], *a.* Formicolio, prurito, bruciore, *m.*

tinker ['tiŋkəɹ], *n.* Calderaio ambulante, magnano, *m.* || *v.t.* Stagnare. **To — up,** raccomodare, rattoppare, rabberciare; **to — at,** affaccendarsi, arrabattarsi intorno; **I don't give a —'s dam,** non me ne importa niente.

tinkering, *n.* Stagnatura, *f.*; rattoppatura, aggiustatura, *f.*

tinkle ['tiŋkəl], *v.i.* Tintinnare, risonare, squillare; *v.t.* far tintinnare, suonare. || *n.* Tintinnio, squillo, *m.*

tinkling, *n.* Tintinnio, *m.* || *a.* Tinnulo, squillante, risonante.

tinman, *n.* Stagnaio, stagnino, lattoniere, *m.*

tinny, *a.* Ricco di stagno; (*of sound*) metallico.

tinsel ['tinsəl], *n.* Orpello, *m.*; (*fig.*) orpello, *m.*, finzione, *f.* || *a.* D'orpello; falso, artificiale. || *v.t.* Inorpellare.

tint, *n.* Tinta, sfumatura, *f.*, colore, *m.* || *v.t.* Tingere, colorire.

tinware ['tinwεəɹ], *n.* Articoli di latta, *m.pl.*, chincaglieria, *f.*

tiny ['taini], *a.* Piccolino, piccino, minuto. **A — bit,** un pochino, un tantino, *m.*; **a — drop,** una gocciolina, *f.*

tip [tip], *n.* Punta, estremità, *f.*; (*ferrule, etc.*) ghiera, *f.*; (*gratuity*) mancia, *f.*; (*information*) consiglio, *m.*, informazione privata, *f.*; (*for refuse*) terreno da scarico, *f.*; (*of billiard cue*) cuoio, *m.* || *v.t.* Aguzzare, appuntare, fornire d'una punta; toccare leggermente; dare una mancia a; inclinare; dare, lanciare. **To — off,** avvertire, informare, prevenire; **to — over,** rovesciare, far rovesciare; **to — up,** inclinare, far piegare; **to — the wink,** fare un cenno; **clouds tipped with gold,** nubi dorate, nubi sfumate d'oro, *f.pl.*; **— -cart,** carro a bilico, *m.*; **— -cat,** lippa, *f.*; **— -top** colmo, *m.*, cima, *f.*; (*colloq.*) ottimo, eccellente, di prim'ordine; **to have something on the — of one's tongue,** avere qualcosa nella punta della lingua.

tippet, *n.* Pellegrina, *f.*

tipple ['tipəl], *v.i.* Bere, sbevazzare. || *n.* Bevanda, *f.*

tippler, *n.* Sbevazzatore, beone, ubbriacone, *m.*

tippling, *n.* Ubbriacchezza, *f.*

tipstaff ['tipstɑːf], *n.* Usciere, *m.*

tipster ['tipstəɹ], *n.* (*Sport*) Chi da consiglio alle corse.

tipsy, *a.* Brillo, alticcio, ubbriaco, avvinazzato; da ubbriaco. **A — voice,** voce d'avvinazzato, *f.*; **to get —,** ubbriacarsi; **— -cake,** zuppa inglese, *f.*

tiptoe ['tiptou], *n.* Punta di piedi, *f.* || *v.i.* Camminare in punta di piedi. **On —,** in punta di piedi.

tirade [ti'reid], *n.* Tirata, tiritera, *f.*

tire (1), **tyre** [taiəɹ], *n.* Cerchione, *m.*; copertone, *m.*; gomma, *f.*; pneumatico, *m.* **To change a —,** cambiare una gomma; **to put on a new —,** applicare una gomma ad una ruota; **to puncture a —,** forare una gomma.

tire (2), *v.t.* Faticare, stancare; spossare; annoiare, seccare; *v.i.* affaticarsi, stancarsi, annoiarsi. **I am tired out,** sono spossato, sono stanco morto; **to get tired,** affaticarsi, stancarsi, annoiarsi.

tired, *a.* Stanco, spossato, esaurito, affaticato.

tiredness, *n.* Stanchezza, spossatezza, *f.*, esaurimento, *m.*

tiresome, *a.* Noioso, fastidioso, seccante.

tiresomeness, *n.* Noia, *f.*, fastidio, *m.*

tiring, *a.* Stanchevole, faticoso.

tiro, tyro ['tairou], *n.* Novizio, *m.*

tissue ['tisjuː, 'tiʃuː, 'tiʃjuː], *n.* Tessuto, *m.*; ordito, *m.* **A — of lies,** un tessuto di bugie, *m.*; **adipose —,** tessuto adiposo, *m.*; **— -paper,** carta velina, *f.*

tit (1) [tit], *n.* (*Zool.*) Cingallegra, *f.*

tit (2), *n.* **To give — for tat,** dare pan per focaccia.

tit (3), *n.* Mammella, *f.*

tit (4), *n.* (*obs.*) Ronzino, *m.*

Titan ['taitən], *n.* (*Myth.*) Titano, *m.*

titanic, *a.* Titanico.
titanium [ti'teiniəm], *n.* Titanio, *m.*
titbit ['titbit], *n.* Bocconcino, boccone squisito, *m.*, leccornia, *f.*
tithable ['taiðəbl], *a.* Prediale, soggetto alla decima.
tithe [taið], *n.* Decima, *f.* || *v.t.* Mettere la decima sopra.
tithing, *n.* Riscuotimento delle decime, *m.*
titillate ['titileit], *v.t.* Titillare, solleticare, vellicare.
titillating, *a.* Titillatorio.
titillation, *n.* Titillazione, *f.*, solletico, *m.*
titivate ['titiveit], *v.t.i.* Attillare; attillarsi.
titlark ['titlɑːɹk], *n.* (*Zool.*) Calandra, allodola, *f.*
title [taitl], *n.* Titolo, nome, *m.*, denominazione, *f.*; (*fig.*) diritto, *m.* || *v.t.* Intitolare, chiamare. **—-deed,** titolo, documento, *m.*; **—-page,** frontispizio, *m.*; **—-role,** parte principale, *f.* ; **the — of this book is,** questo libro si intitola.
titmouse (pl. **titmice**) ['titmaus, 'titmais], *n.* (*Zool.*) Cincia, *f.*
titter ['titəɹ], *v.t.* Sogghignare, ridacchiare. || *n.* Sogghigno, risolino, *m.*
tittle [titl], *n.* Ette, iota, *m.* **Not one jot or —,** non un'iota, non un ette.
tittle-tattle ['titltætl], *n.* Chiacchiere, ciarle, *f.pl.*, pettegolezzi, *m.pl.* || *v.i.* Chiacchierare, ciarlare.
titular ['titjuːləɹ], *n.a.* Titolare, *m.*
titularly, *adv.* Titolarmente.
to [tuː], *prep.* A, di; per, affinchè, onde; in, verso, di, in confronto a, a paragone di. **Ten minutes to six,** le sei meno dieci; **from time to time,** di quando in quando; **from room to room,** da una camera all'altra; **his kindness to me,** la sua gentilezza con me; **your duty to your parents,** il vostro dovere verso i genitori; **the heir to the throne,** l'erede al trono, *m.*; **Is this the way to the village ?** E questa la strada che va al villaggio? **on the way to London,** in viaggio per Londra; **to and fro,** qua e là, su e giù; **to apply to,** rivolgersi a; **to fall to ruins,** rovinare, cadere in rovina; **to go to France,** andare in Francia; **to go to Paris,** andare a Parigi; **to put to flight,** porre in fuga, mettere in fuga; **I told him to his face,** glielo dissi in faccia; **to this day,** fino ad oggi; **explain it to me,** spiegatemelo; **it seems to me,** mi pare; **to my mind, to my way of thinking,** a parer mio; **try to explain,** tentate di spiegare; **he began to sing,** cominciò a cantare; **I had work to do,** avevo un lavoro da fare; **I had no time to do it,** non ebbi tempo per farlo; **to measure,** su misura; **to boot,** per di più, per giunta; **to wit,** cioè, nominatamente.
toad [toud], *n.* (*Zool.*) Rospo, *m.* **—-eater,** parassita, adulatore, leccapiatti, *m.*; **— flax,** linaiola, *f.*
toadstone, *n.* (*Geol.*) Batrachite, *f.*
toadstool, *n.* (*Bot.*) Fungo velenoso, *m.*
toady, *n.* Parassita, sicofante, leccapiatti, *m.*
toadyism, *n.* Parassitismo, *m.*, piaggeria, servilità, *f.*
toast (1) [toust], *n.* Pane abbrustolito, pane tostato, tosto, crostino, *m.* || *v.t.* Abbrustolire, tostare; riscaldare. **—-rack,** portatosti, portacrostini, *m.*; **toasting-fork,** forchettone per crostini, *m.*
toast (2), *n.* Brindisi, *m.* || *v.t.* Fare un brindisi a. **To drink a — to,** bere alla salute di, fare un brindisi a; **—-master,** direttore dei brindisi, maestro di cerimonie, *m.*
toaster, *n.* Graticola, *f.* ; tostino, *m.*
tobacco [to'bækou], *n.* Tabacco, *m.* **—-box,** tabacchiera, *f.*; **—-jar,** vaso da tabacco, *m.*; **—-pipe,** pipa, *f.*; **—-pouch,** borsa da tabacco, *f.*
tobacconist, *n.* Tabaccaio, *m.* **Tobacconist's shop,** tabaccheria, *f.*, spaccio di tabacchi, *m.*
Tobias [to'baiəs], *n.* Tobia, *m.*
toboggan [to'bɔgən], *n.* Toboga, *m.*; slitta, *f.* || *v.t.* Slittare. **— run,** pista di toboga, *f.*
tobogganing, *n.* Lo slittare, *m.*
Toby ['toubi], *n.* Tobia, *m.* **—-jug,** boccale a forma di testa di vecchio, *m.*
tocsin ['tɔksin], *n.* Campana a martello, *f.*, segno d'allarme, *m.* **To sound the —,** suonare a stormo, suonare a martello.
to-day [tə'dei], *n.adv.* Oggi, oggidì, oggigiorno, il giorno d'oggi, *m.* **— week,** oggi a otto.
toddle [tɔdl], *v.i.* Sgambettare, trotterellare; (*colloq.*) partire, andar via.
toddler, *n.* Bambino, piccino, *m.*, bambina, piccina, *f.*
to-do [tə'duː], *n.* Commozione, agitazione, *f.*, gran daffare, *m.*; rumore, chiasso, *m.* **There'll be such a —,** ci sarà un baccano infernale, ci sarà un putiferio.
toe [tou], *n.* Dito del piede, *m.*; (*of shoe or stocking*) punta, *f.* **To tread on someone's toes,** pestare i piedi a qualcuno; **to — the line,** stare in riga; (*colloq.*) **to turn up one's toes,** morire; **big —,** pollice del piede, alluce, *m.*; **little —,** mignolo del piede, *m.*; **—-cap,** mascherina, *f.*; **—-nail,** unghia del piede, *f.*; **from top to —,** da capo a piedi.
toff [tɔf], *n.* (*colloq.*) Elegantone, *m.*
toffee, toffy ['tɔfi], *n.* Caramella, *f.*, zuccherino, *m.*
toga ['tougə], *n.* (*Hist.*) Toga, *f.*
together [tə'geðəɹ], *adv.* Insieme, d'accordo, unitamente; di seguito, consecutivamente. **To live —,** abitare insieme; **to gather —,** raccogliere, radunare; **— with,** insieme a; **for days —,** molti giorni di seguito.
toggle [tɔgl], *n.* (*Naut.*) Coccinello, perno, cavicchio, *m.*
togs [tɔgz], *n.pl.* (*colloq.*) Vestiti, panni, *m.pl.*
toil (1) [tɔil], *n.* Lavoro, travaglio, *m.*, fatica, pena, *f.* || *v.t.* Lavorare, affaticarsi, tribolare, affanarsi, sgobbare, sfacchinare. **To — along,** camminare a stento, arrancare; **to — up,** sormontare con fatica; **—-worn,** logoro, sfinito dal lavoro.
toil (2), *n.* Rete, trappola, *f.* **Toils,** trappole, *f.pl.* **To be in the toils,** essere preso in trappola.
toiler, *n.* Lavoratore, lavorante, *m.*
toilet ['tɔilet], *n.* Toletta, *f.*; (*w.c.*) gabinetto, *m.* **— -paper,** carta igienica, *f.*; **— roll,** rotolo igienico, *m.*; **—-set,** servizio da toletta; **—-soap,** saponetta; **— -powder,** cipria, *f.*
toiling, *n.* Lavoro, *m.*, pena, *f.*
toilsome, *a.* Laborioso, faticoso, penoso.
toilsomeness, *n.* Fatica, pena, *f.*
Tokay [tɔ'kei], *n.* Tocai, *m.*

token [ˈtoukən], *n.* Segno, contrassegno, pegno, *m.*, prova, *f.*; omaggio, *m.*; ricordo, *m.*; (*coin*) gettone, *m.*
told, *p.* and *pp.* of **tell.**
tolerable [ˈtɔlərəbl], *a.* Tollerabile, sopportabile; passabile.
tolerableness, *n.* Tollerabilità, *f.*
tolerably, *adv.* Tollerabilmente; benino, così così.
tolerance, *n.* Tolleranza, *f.*
tolerate, *v.t.* Tollerare.
toleration, *n.* Tolleranza, *f.*
toll (1) [toul], *n.* Tassa, *f.*, dazio, *m.*; pedaggio, *m.* (*Telephone*) **—-call,** chiamata interurbana, *f.*; **—-bar, —-gate,** barriera di pedaggio, *f.*; **—-bridge,** ponte di pedaggio, *m.*; **—-house,** ufficio del pedaggio, dazio, *m.*
toll (2), *v.t.* Suonare a rintocchi; *v.i.* suonare a rintocchi, suonare a morto, rintoccare.
tolling, *n.* Rintocco, *m.*
tollbooth [ˈtoulbu:ð], *n.* (*Scots*) Prigione, *f.*
Tom [tɔm], *n.* Tommaso, *m.* **—-cat,** gatto, gattone, *m.*
tomahawk [ˈtɔməhɔ:k], *n.* Accetta dei Pellirosse, *f.*
tomato (pl. **tomatoes**) [təˈmɑ:tou], *n.* Pomodoro, pomidoro, *m.* **—-sauce,** salsa di pomidoro, *f.*
tomb [tu:m], *n.* Tomba, *f.*, sepolcro, *m.*
tomboy [ˈtɔmbɔi], *n.* Maschiotta, ragazzona, *f.*
tombstone [ˈtu:mstoun], *n.* Lapide, pietra sepolcrale, pietra tombale, *f.*
tome [toum], *n.* Tomo, volume, *m.*
tomfool [tɔmˈfu:l], *n.* Minchione, semplicione, babbeo, *m.*
tomfoolery, *n.* Minchioneria, *f.*, buffonate, *f.pl.*
Tommy (1) [ˈtɔmi], *n.* Tommaso, *m.* **— Atkins, Tommy,** soldato semplice inglese, *m.*
tommy (2), **tommy bar,** *n.* Spillo, fermaglio, *m.* **—-gun,** fucile mitragliatore, *m.*
to-morrow [təˈmɔrou], *n.adv.* Domani, *m.* **— morning,** domani mattina, domattina; **the day after —,** posdomani, doman l'altro, dopodomani.
tompion [ˈtɔmpiən], *n.* Turacciolo, *m.*; (*Print.*) tampone, stampo, *m.*
tomtit [tɔmˈtit], *n.* (*Zool.*) Cingallegra, *f.*
tomtom [ˈtɔmtɔm], *n.* Tam-tam, *m.*
ton [tʌn], *n.* Tonnellata, *f.* (1016 chilogrammi).
tone [toun], *n.* Tono, suono, accento, *m.*; tonalità, voce, *f.*; registro, *m.*; (*Phot.*) intonazione, *f.* || *v.t.* (*Phot.*) Virare, intonare; dare il tono a. **In a mocking — of voice,** in un tono canzonatorio; **to give — to,** dare tono a, tonificare; dar lustro a; **to speak in a loud —,** parlare ad alta voce; **to — down,** smorzare, attenuare, raddolcire; **to — with,** armonizzare con, intonarsi con.
toneless, *a.* Senza tono, piatto.
tongs [tɔŋz], *n.pl.* Molle, *f.pl.*, pinze, *f.pl.*; tenaglie, *f.pl.*
tongue [tʌŋ], *n.* Lingua, *f.*; (*of shoe*) linguetta, *f.*; (*of buckle*) puntale, *m.*; (*of bell*) battaglio, *m.* **Hold your —!** Tacete! Taci! **it was a slip of the —,** mi è scappato di bocca; (*of hounds*) **to give —,** latrare; **to have a glib —,** aver la lingua sciolta; **to have on the tip of one's —,** avere sulla punta della lingua; **the mother —,** la lingua materna, *f.*; **to find one's —,** snodare la lingua; **—-tied,** scilinguato, bleso; ridotto al silenzio, ammutolito.
tongued, *a.* Dalla lingua.
tonic [ˈtɔnik], *a.* Tonico. (*Mus.*) **— sol-fa,** solfa tonica, *f.* || *n.* (*Med.*) Tonico, ricostituente, *m.*; (*Mus.*) tonica, *f.*
tonicity [təˈnisiti], *n.* Tonicità, *f.*
to-night [təˈnait], *n.adv.* Questa sera, stasera; questa notte, stanotte, *f.*
toning [ˈtouniŋ], *n.* (*Phot.*) Viraggio, *m.*
tonnage [ˈtʌnidʒ], *n.* Tonnellaggio, *m.*; (*Naut.*) stazza, *f.*
tonneau [ˈtɔnou], *n.* (*Motor.*) Carrozzeria, *f.*
tonsil [ˈtɔnsəl], *n.* (*Anat.*) Tonsilla, *f.*
tonsilitis [tɔnsilˈaitis], *n.* (*Med.*) Tonsillite, *f.*
tonsorial [tɔnˈsɔ:riəl], *a.* Del parrucchiere.
tonsure [ˈtɔnʃəɹ], *n.* Tonsura, chierica, *f.* || *v.t.* Tonsurare.
tonsured, *a.* Tonsurato.
Tony [ˈtouni], *n.* Tonio, Antonio, *m.*
too [tu:], *adv.* Troppo; anche, pure, altresì, ancora. **This is too much for me,** per me è troppo; **too much of a good thing is good for nothing,** il troppo stroppia; **it is too good to be true,** è troppo bello per esser vero; **take this book too,** prendete anche questo libro.
took, *p.* of **take.**
tool (1) [tu:l], *n.* Strumento, arnese, utensile, attrezzo, ordigno, *m.*; agente, fautore, *m.* || *v.t.* Lavorare; (*Bookbinding*) bulinare. **Tools,** ferri, arnesi, *m.pl.*; **the tools of the trade,** i ferri del mestiere, *m.pl.*; **a set of tools,** un assortimento di attrezzi, *m.*; **—-bag,** borsa per attrezzi, *f.*; **—-chest, —-box,** cassetta per attrezzi, cassetta dei ferri, *f.*; **—-shed,** baracca per gli attrezzi, *f.*; **—-maker,** fabbroferraio, *m.*
tool (2), *v.i.* Trottare.
tooling, *n.* (*Bookbinding*) Fregiatura, ornamentazione, *f.*
toot [tu:t], *v.t.* Suonare il corno. || *n.* Suono del corno, *m.*
tooth (pl. **teeth**) [tu:θ, ti:θ], *n.* Dente, *m.* || *v.t.* Dentellare. **Back —,** dente molare, *m.*; **eye —,** dente canino, *m.*; **milk teeth,** denti di latte, *m.pl.*; **false teeth,** denti artificiali, denti posticci, *m.pl.*; **a set of false teeth,** una dentiera, *f.*; **a fine set of teeth,** una bella dentatura, *f.*; **in the teeth of,** malgrado, a dispetto di; **to fight — and nail,** battersi accanitamente; **to cast in someone's teeth,** gettare in faccia a; (*of a child*) **to cut teeth,** spuntare i denti; **to set the teeth on edge,** dare ai nervi; **to show one's teeth,** mostrare i denti; **wisdom —,** dente del giudizio, *m.*; **—-brush,** spazzolino da denti, *m.*; **—-paste, —-powder,** dentifricio, *m.*
toothache [ˈtu:θeik], *n.* Mal di denti, *m.* **I have the —,** ho il mal di denti.
toothed, *a.* Dentellato; dentato.
toothless, *a.* Sdentato.
toothpick, *n.* Stuzzicadenti, stecchino, *m.*
toothsome [ˈtu:θsəm], *a.* Saporito, saporoso, ghiotto, appetitoso.
toothsomeness, *n.* Saporosità, *f.*
toothy, *a.* Dentato.
tootle [tu:tl], *v.i.* Suonare un flauto.
top (1) [tɔp], *n.* Cima, vetta, sommità, *f.*; apice, culmine, vertice, *m.*; cocuzzolo, capo,

m., testa, *f.*; coperchio, *m.*; (*of bus*) imperiale, *m.*; (*Naut.*) gabbia, coffa, *f.* || *a.* Primo, principale; il più alto. || *v.t.* Coronare, sovrastare a, sormontare; sorpassare; svettare; raggiungere la cima di; (*Naut.*) cicognare. **At the — of the hill,** in cima alla collina; (*fig.*) **at the — of the tree,** arrivato al culmine; **at the — of his voice,** a squarciagola, a perdifiato; **at — speed,** di tutta corsa, a tutta velocità; **from — to toe,** da capo a piedi; **he fell on — of me,** mi cadde addosso; **to — off,** finire, dare l'ultimo colpo a; **to — up,** riempire completamente; **— -boots,** stivali a risvolta, stivaloni, *m.pl.*; **— -coat,** soprabito, *m.*; (*Agric.*) **— -dressing,** concime, *m.*; **— -hat,** cappello a cilindro, *m.*, tuba, *f.*; **— -heavy,** strapiombante; **— -knot,** ciuffo di penne, fiocco di nastro, *m.*

top (2), *n.* (*toy*) Trottola, *f.*

topaz [ˈtoupæz], *n.* (*Min.*) Topazio, *m.*

tope [toup], *v.i.* Sbevazzare, trincare.

toper, *n.* Sbevazzatore, beone, ubriacone, *m.*

topgallant [tɔpˈgælənt, təˈgælənt], *a.* (*Naut.*) Di parrocchetto. || *n.* Parrocchetto, *m.*, vela di parrocchetto, *f.*

topic [ˈtɔpik], *n.* Soggetto, argomento, *m.*, questione, *f.*

topical, *a.* D'attualità; locale. **— film,** film di attualità, *m.*

topmast [ˈtɔpməst], *n.* (*Naut.*) Albero di gabbia, *m.*

topmost [ˈtɔpmost], *a.* Il più alto, il sommo, il più elevato.

topographer [təˈpɔgrəfəɹ], *n.* Topografo, *m.*

topographic, topographical [tɔpoˈgræfik, tɔpoˈgræfikəl], *a.* Topografico.

topography [təˈpɔgrəfi], *n.* Topografia, *f.*

topper, *n.* (*colloq.*) Cappello a cilindro, *m.*, tuba, *f.*

topping, *a.* (*colloq.*) Ottimo, stupendo.

topple [tɔpl], *v.i.* Capitombolare, ruzzolare. **To — over,** rovesciarsi, ribaltare; cadere giù.

topsail [ˈtɔpsəl], *n.* (*Naut.*) Vela di gabbia, *f.* **— schooner,** goletta a gabbiola, *f.*

topsyturvy [tɔpsiˈtəːɹvi], *adv.* Sottosopra, sossopra, a catafascio, in confusione, in scompiglio.

toque [touk], *n.* (*hat*) Toque, *m.*

tor [tɔːɹ], *n.* Altura, *f.*, costone, *m.*; collina, *f.*

torch [tɔːɹtʃ], *n.* Fiaccola, torcia, *f.*; face, *f.* **Electric —,** lampadina tascabile, *f.*; **— -bearer,** portafiaccola, *m.*; **— -light,** lume di torcia, *m.*; **— -light procession,** una fiaccolata, *f.*

tore, *p.* of **tear.**

torment [ˈtɔːɹment], *n.* Tormento, *m.*, tortura, *f.*; supplizio, strazio, *m.*, pena, *f.* || *v.t.* [tɔːɹˈment], Tormentare, torturare; molestare, vessare.

tormentil [ˈtɔːɹmentil], *n.* (*Bot.*) Tormentilla, *f.*

tormenting, *a.* Tormentoso, torturante, straziante; molesto.

tormentor, *n.* Tormentatore, *m.*, tormentatrice, *f.*

torn, *p.p.* of **tear.**

tornado (pl. **tornadoes**) [tɔːɹˈneidou], *n.* Uragano, ciclone, turbine, *m.*

torpedo (pl. **torpedoes**) [tɔːɹˈpiːdou], *n.* (*Naut.*) Torpedine, siluro, *m.*; (*Zool.*) torpedine, *m.* || *v.t.* Torpedinare, silurare. **— -boat,** torpediniera, *f.*, silurante, *m.*; **— -tube,** tuba, lanciasiluri, *m.*

torpid [ˈtɔːɹpid], *a.* Torpido, intorpidito; tardo, pigro.

torpidity, torpidness, torpor [tɔːɹˈpiditi, ˈtɔːɹpidnes, ˈtɔːpəɹ], *n.* Torpore, intorpidimento, *m.*, pigrizia, *f.*

torrefaction [tɔriˈfækʃən], *n.* Torrefazione, *f.*

torrent [ˈtɔrənt], *n.* Torrente, *m.* **In torrents,** a torrenti.

torrential [təˈrenʃəl], *a.* Torrenziale.

torrid [ˈtɔrid], *a.* Torrido, caldissimo, bruciante, ardente.

torridness, torridity [ˈtɔridnes, təˈriditi], *n.* Calore, bruciore, *m.*

torsion [ˈtɔːɹʃən], *n.* Torsione, *f.*

torso [ˈtɔːɹsou], *n.* Torso, *m.*

tort [tɔːɹt], *n.* (*Law*) Torto, delitto civile, *m.*

tortoise [ˈtɔːɹtəs], *n.* (*Zool.*) Testuggine, tartaruga, *f.* **— -shell,** tartaruga, *f.*, di tartaruga; **— -shell cat,** gatto giallonero, gatto di Spagna, *m.*; **— -shell butterfly,** tartaruga, *f.*

tortuosity, tortuousness [tɔːɹtjuːˈɔsiti, ˈtɔːɹtjuːəsnes], *n.* Tortuosità, *f.*

tortuous, *a.* Tortuoso, bistorto; obliquo, perverso.

tortuously, *adv.* Tortuosamente.

torture [ˈtɔːɹtʃəɹ], *n.* Tortura, *f.*, supplizio, strazio, tormento, *m.* || *v.t.* Torturare, tormentare; angariare.

torturer, *n.* Boia, tormentatore, aguzzino, *m.*

torus (pl. **tori**) [ˈtɔːrəs, ˈtɔːrai], *n.* (*Arch.*) Toro, *m.*

Tory [ˈtɔːri], *n.* (*Pol.*) Tory, conservatore, *m.*

tosh [tɔʃ], *n.* (*colloq.*) Sciocchezze, *f.pl.*

toss [tɔs], *n.* Scossa, *f.*, urto, *m.* || *v.t.* Gettare, lanciare in aria; scuotere, palleggiare, sballottare; *v.i.* agitarsi, scuotersi, ballonzolare. **A — of the head,** una scossa della testa, *f.*; **to win the —,** fare a testa o croce; **to — off,** bere in un sorso, tracannare; **— -up,** testa o croce, palle e santi, sorteggio, (*fig.*) puro caso, *m.*; **it is a — -up whether,** è un mero caso se; **to — up,** far a testa o croce, tirare a sorte, sorteggiare; **to — about,** dimenarsi.

tossing, *n.* Sballottamento, sballottio, *m.*

tot, *n.* (*colloq.*) Gocciolo, *m.*; (*child*) frugolino, minuzzolo, *m.* **To — up,** addizionare, ammontare a.

total [ˈtoutəl], *n.* Totale, ammontare, *m.*, somma, *f.* || *a.* Totale, completo, intiero. || *v.t.* Ammontare a, sommare a. **Those present totalled a hundred,** i presenti ammontavano a cento.

totality [toˈtæliti], *n.* Totalità, *f.*

totalizator, totalizer, *n.* Totalizzatore, *m.*

totalize, *v.t.* Totalizzare, sommare.

totally, *adv.* Totalmente, interamente, affatto.

totem [ˈtoutem], *n.* Totem, *m.*

totemism, *n.* Totemismo, *m.*

totter [ˈtɔtəɹ], *v.i.* Barcollare, traballare, vacillare, titubare, tentennare. **To — away,** andare via barcollando; **to — to one's feet,** alzarsi barcollando.

tottering, *n.* Barcollamento, barcollio, *m.* || *a.* Barcollante.

totteringly, *adv.* Barcollando.

tottery, *a.* Barcollante, traballante.
toucan [ˈtuːkən], *n.* (*Zool.*) Tucano, *m.*
touch [tʌtʃ], *v.t.* Toccare; (*to handle*) tastare, palpare, maneggiare; (*to reach*) arrivare a; (*to concern*) toccare a, importare a; (*to move*) commuovere, intenerire; *v.i.* toccare; toccarsi. || *n.* (*sense of touch*) Tatto, *m.*; (*stroke*) toccata, *f.*, tocco, *m.*; (*small amount*) pizzico, pochino, tantino, *m.*; (*Mus.*) tocco, *m.*; (*contact*) contatto, *m.*; (*of illness*) attacco leggero, *m.* **To — off,** (*a gun*) sparare; **to — one's hat to,** salutare, levarsi il cappello a; **to — up,** ritoccare, ripassare; **to — at,** toccare, approdare, accostarsi a; **to — upon,** toccare, sfiorare; **a — of,** un tantino di, *m.*; **it was — and go whether he recovered,** sembrava che non si rimetesse più; **to give the finishing — to,** dare l'ultimo tocco a; **to keep in — with,** non perder di vista, stare a contatto con; **to lose — with,** perder di vista; **to get into — with,** mettersi in contatto con; **hard to the —,** duro al tatto; **to — for money,** chiedere quattrini; **—-hole,** focone, *m.*; (*Football*) **—-lines,** linee di fuori giuoco, *f.pl.*
touchable, *a.* Toccabile, tangibile.
touchily, *adv.* Suscettibilmente, permalosamente.
touchiness, *n.* Permalosità, suscettibilità, suscettività, *f.*
touching, *a.* Commovente. || *prep.* Quanto a, riguardo a.
touchingly, *adv.* Commoventemente.
touchstone, *n.* Paragone, *m.*, pietra di paragone, *f.*
touchwood, *n.* Esca, *f.*
touchy, *a.* Permaloso, suscettibile, suscettivo.
tough [tʌf], *a.* Duro, resistente, tenace; fermo, sodo, solido; coriaceo, tiglioso; (*fig.*) difficile, duro. || *n.* (*colloq.*) Teppista, *m.* **— meat,** carne dura, carne tigliosa, *f.*; **a — job,** un lavoro difficile, *m.*; **— luck,** sorte crudele, disdetta, *f.*
toughen, *v.t.* Indurire, rassodare; temprare; *v.i.* indurirsi, temprarsi, rinvigorirsi.
toughly, *adv.* Duramente, tenacemente.
toughness, *n.* Durezza, sodezza, resistenza, tenacità, *f.*; fermezza, *f.*
Toulon [tuːlɔ̃], *n.* (*Geog.*) Tolone, *m.*
toupee [ˈtuːpei], *n.* Riccioli finti, *m.pl.*, ciuffo, toppè, *m.*
tour [tuːɹ], *n.* Giro, viaggio, *m.* || *v.t.* Percorrere, viaggiare, girare; *v.i.* viaggiare, far un giro.
touring, *n.* Turismo, *m.* || *a.* Turistico. **— car,** vettura da turismo, *f.*, torpedone, *m.*
tourist, *n.* Turista, *m.f.* **— agency,** ufficio viaggi, *m.*, agenzia di turismo, *f.*; **— ticket,** biglietto circolare, biglietto turistico, *m.*
tourmaline [ˈtuːɹməlin], *n.* (*Min.*) Tormalina, *f.*
tournament [ˈtuːɹnəmənt], *n.* Torneo, *m.*; (*Sport*) concorso, *m.*, gara, *f.* **Tennis —,** gara di tennis, *f.*
tourney, *n.* Torneo, *m.*
tourniquet [ˈtuːɹniket], *n.* (*Med.*) Tornichetto, *m.*, pinza emostatica, *f.*
tournure [tuːrˈnjuːɹ], *n.* Contorno, *m.*, forma, *f.*
tousle [tauzl], *v.t.* Disordinare, arruffare, scompigliare. **Tousled hair,** capelli arruffati, *m.pl.*
tout [taut], *v.i.* Sollecitare, cercare clienti. || *n.* Sollecitatore, piazzista, galoppino, *m.*
touting, *n.* Sollecitazione, *f.*
tow (1) [tou], *n.* Stoppa, *f.*
tow (2), *n.* Rimorchio, alaggio, *m.* || *v.t.* Rimorchiare, trainare, tirare, strascinare. **In —,** a rimorchio; **—-boat,** rimorchiatore, *m.*; **—-line,** rimorchio, *m.*, fune da rimorchio, *f.*; **—-path,** banchina di rimorchio, *f.*
towage, *n.* Rimorchio, alaggio, *m.*, spesa di rimorchio, *f.*
toward, towards [tɔːɹdz, təˈwɔːdz], *prep.* Verso, verso di, alla volta di; presso, circa; per. **Towards seven o'clock,** verso le sette; **towards me,** verso di me.
towel [ˈtauəl], *n.* Asciugamano, *m.*, salvietta, *f.* || *v.t.i.* Asciugare. **—-horse, —-rail,** porta asciugamani, *m.*; **sanitary —,** salviettina igienica, *f.*
towelling, *n.* Tela per asciugamani, *f.*
tower [ˈtauəɹ], *n.* Torre, *f.* || *v.i.* Torreggiare. **A — of strength,** un carattere forte, *m.*, una persona fidata, *f.*; **to — above,** dominare su, torreggiare su.
towered, *a.* Turrito, coronato di torri.
towering, *a.* Torreggiante; (*fig.*) violentissimo. **A — rage,** una collera pazza, *f.*
towing [cp. **tow** (2)].
town [taun], *n.* Città, *f.*; (*country town*) borgo, *m.* **County —,** città di provincia, *f.*; **in —,** in città; **out of —,** in campagna; **to go to —,** andare in città; **— house,** casa di città, *f.*; **a man about —,** un mondano, *m.*; **—-clerk,** segretario municipale, *m.*; **—-council,** consiglio municipale, *m.*; **—-councillor,** consigliere municipale, *m.*; **—-crier,** banditore pubblico, *m.*; **—-planning,** piano regolatore *m.*; **it is the talk of the —,** è sulla bocca di tutti, tutta la città ne parla.
township, *n.* Comune, *m.*
townsman, *n.* Cittadino, borghese, *m.* **Fellow-—,** concittadino, *m.*
townspeople, townsfolk, *n.pl.* Cittadinanza, *f.*
towny, *a.* Urbano.
toxic [ˈtɔksik], *a.* Velenoso.
toxicology [tɔksiˈkɔlədʒi], *n.* Tossicologia, *f.*
toxin, *n.* Tossina, *f.*
toy [tɔi], *n.* Giocattolo, giocherello, balocco, *m.*; bagatella, *f.*; trastullo, *m.* || *v.i.* Giocherellare; trastullarsi, divertirsi. **To — with,** giocherellare con; **—-shop,** bottega di giocattoli, *f.*
trabecula [trəˈbekjuːlə], *n.* (*Anat.*) Trabecola, *f.*
trace (1) [treis], *n.* Traccia, orma, *f.*, vestigio, (*small quantity*) tantino, pochino, *m.* || *v.t.* Tracciare; abbozzare, disegnare, scrivere; ricalcare; rintracciare. **To — out,** rintracciare; **to — the origin of,** scoprire l'origine di.
trace (2), *n.* Tirella, *f.* **In the traces,** coi finimenti; **to kick over the traces,** scuotere il giogo, ribellarsi.
traceable, *a.* Rintracciabile; attribuibile.
tracer, *n.* Rintracciatore, *m.*
tracery, *n.* (*Arch.*) Traforo, intaglio, *m.*
trachea [trəˈkiə], *n.* (*Anat.*) Trachea, *f.*
tracheal, *a.* Tracheale.
tracheotomy, *n.* Tracheotomia, *f.*
tracing [ˈtreisiŋ], *n.* Tracciamento, *m.*; ricalco, *m.*, ricalcatura, *f.* **—-paper,** carta per ricalcare, carta da calco, *f.*

track [træk], *n.* (*of footsteps*) Traccia, *f.*, peste, orme, *f.pl.*; (*of ship*) scia, *f.*, solco, *m.*; (*on road*) carreggiata, *f.*; (*path*) sentiero, *m.*; (*Sport*) pista, *f.*; (*Rail.*) binario, *m.*; (*Astron.*) orbita, *f.* || *v.t.* Inseguire, pedinare, seguire le orme, rintracciare, scoprire; rimorchiare. **To follow the beaten —,** seguire la strada battuta; **to make tracks for,** andarsene in fretta verso; **off the —,** fuori di strada; **to — down game,** scovare; **to — down a criminal,** snidare un criminale.
trackage, *n.* (*Rail.*) Binari, *m.pl.*, rotaie, *f.pl.*; (*towing*) rimorchio, *m.*
tracking, *n.* Inseguimento, *m.*
trackless, *a.* Senza sentieri.
tract (1) [trækt], *n.* Tratto, *m.*, estensione, *f.*, spazio, *m.*, regione, *f.*
tract (2), *n.* Libretto, opuscolo, *m.*
tractability, tractableness [træktə'biliti, 'træktəblnes], *n.* Trattabilità, docilità, arrendevolezza, *f.*
tractable, *a.* Trattabile, docile, arrendevole, remissivo.
tractably, *adv.* Docilmente.
Tractarian [træk'teəriən], *n.* (*Eccles.Hist.*) Aderente all'Oxford movement.
tractate ['trækteit], *n.* Trattato, *m.*
traction ['trækʃən], *n.* Trazione, *f.* **Steam —,** trazione a vapore, *f.*; **—-engine,** trattrice, locomobile, *f.*
tractor, *n.* Trattrice, *f.*; trattore, *m.* **Caterpillar- —,** trattrice a cingoli, *f.*; **—-driver,** trattorista, *m.*
trade [treid], *n.* Commercio, traffico, *m.*; negozio, *m.*; scambio, *m.*; (*calling*) mestiere, *m.*; (*business*) affari, *m.pl.* || *v.i.* Commerciare, far affari, negoziare, trafficare, mercanteggiare. **Board of Trade,** Ministero del Commercio, *m.*; **a carpenter by —,** un falegname di mestiere; **free —,** libero scambio, *m.*; **in —,** negli affari, in commercio; **to be in the —,** essere del mestiere; **to do a roaring —,** far affari d'oro; **to learn a —,** imparare un mestiere; **— is bad,** gli affari vanno male; **foreign —,** commercio estero, *m.*; **to ply one's —,** fare il proprio mestiere; **— price,** prezzo all'ingrosso, *m.*; **to — upon,** trarre vantaggio da; **to — with,** commerciare con, far affari con; **— allowance,** sconto di rivendita, *m.*; **— mark,** marca di fabbrica, *f.*; **— route,** rotta commerciale, *f.*; **— union,** sindacato operaio, *m.*, società operaia, *f.*; camera del lavoro, *f.*; **— unionist,** membro di un sindacato, sindacalista, *m.*; **— wind,** vento aliseo, *m.*
trader, *n.* Negoziante, commerciante, mercante, *m.*
tradesman, *n.* Bottegaio, fornitore, *m.*; artigiano, *m.*
tradespeople, *n.pl.* Fornitori, bottegai, *m.pl.*
trading, *n.* Negozio, commercio, traffico, *m.* || *a.* Commerciale, mercantile.
tradition [trə'diʃən], *n.* Tradizione, *f.*
traditional, *a.* Tradizionale.
traditionally, *adv.* Tradizionalmente.
traduce [trə'dju:s], *v.t.* Diffamare, calunniare.
traducer, *n.* Diffamatore, *m.*, diffamatrice, *f.*
traffic ['træfik], *n.* Traffico, viavai, movimento, *m.*; (*trade*) commercio, *f.*; trasporto, *m.* || *v.i.* Trafficare, commerciare. **— lights,** semaforo, *m.*; (*Rail.*) **— manager,** capo traffico, *m.*; **— circle,** piazza a traffico circolare, *f.*; **—-sign,** segnale di traffico, *m.*; **—-policeman,** vigile, *m.*
trafficator, *n.* (*Motor.*) Indicatore di direzione, *f.*
trafficker, *n.* Commerciante, mercante, *m.*; trafficante, *m.*
tragacanth ['trægəkænθ], *n.* (*Med.*) Dragante, *m.*
tragedian [trə'dʒi:diən], *n.* Tragico, tragediografo, autore di tragedie, *m.*; attore tragico, *m.*
tragedienne [trədʒi:di'en], *n.* Attrice tragica, *f*
tragedy, *n.* Tragedia, *f.*
tragic, tragical, *a.* Tragico.
tragically, *adv.* Tragicamente.
tragi-comedy, *n.* Tragicommedia, *f.*
tragicomic, *a.* Tragicomico.
trail [treil], *n.* Strascico, *m.*, traccia, *f.*; striscia, *f.*; pista, traccia, *f.*; piste, orme, *f.pl.*; (*Mil.*) coda d'affusto, *f.* || *v.i.* Camminare a stento; strascinarsi, strascicare; pendere, spenzolare; *v.t.* strascicare, strascinare; rintracciare, inseguire, ormeggiare, seguire le piste di. **To get on the — again,** rintracciar la pista; **to get on someone's —,** mettersi dietro le piste di qualcuno; **—-net,** strascino, *m.*; (*Aviat.*) **—-rope,** fune di pallone, *f.*
trailer, *n.* Carro rimorchiato, rimorchio, *m.*; (*Cinema.*) pezzo di richiamo, *m.*
trailing, *a.* Strisciante.
train [trein], *n.* Treno, convoglio, *m.*; seguito, corteo, accompagnamento, *m.*; serie, sequela, *f.*; traccia, *f.*; (*of dress*) strascico, *m.*; (*of comet*) coda, *f.* || *v.t.* Ammaestrare, abituare; educare, istruire, disciplinare, addestrare, preparare; (*Sport*) allenare; (*of plants*) far salire; (*of horses*) domare; *v.i.* andare col treno; allenarsi. **Armoured —,** treno blindato, *m.*; **breakdown —,** treno di soccorso, *m.*; **corridor —,** treno comunicante, *m.*; **excursion —,** treno festivo, *m.*; **express —,** treno direttissimo, *m.*; **local —,** treno accelerato; **fast —,** treno rapido, *m.*; **goods —,** treno merci, *m.*; **passenger —,** treno viaggiatori, *m.*; **to bring in its —,** essere seguito da, avere al proprio seguito; **to — a gun upon,** puntare un cannone contro; **— band,** milizia cittadina, *f.*; **— -bearer,** paggio, valletto, *m.*; (*Eccles.*) caudatario, *m.*; **— oil,** olio di balena, *m.*; **— ferry,** pontone trasbordatore, *m.*
trainer, *n.* (*Sport*) Allenatore, *m.*
training, *n.* Educazione, istruzione, disciplina, *f.*, addestramento, ammaestramento, *m.*; (*Sport*) allenamento, *m.* **— college,** scuola normale, *f.*; **—-ship,** nave scuola, *f.*
traipse, trapse [treips], *v.i.* (*Colloq.*) Andare a zonzo, girovagare.
trait [trei], *n.* Caratteristica, *f.*, tratto, *m.*
traitor, *n.* Traditore, *m.*
traitorous, *a.* Traditore, perfido, sleale, proditorio.
traitorously, *adv.* A tradimento, perfidamente.
traitress, *n.* Traditrice, *f.*
trajectory [trə'dʒektəri], *n.* Traiettoria, *f.*
tram, tram-car [træm, 'træmkɑ:ɹ], *n.* Tram, tranvai, *m.* **— service,** servizio

tranviario, *m.*; **— -conductor,** bigliettario, *m.*; **— -driver,** guidatore, manovratore, *m.*; **— -line, tramway,** tranvia, *f.*
trammel ['træməl], *n.* Tramaglio, *m.*; pastoia, *f.* || *v.t.* Impedire, impacciare, impastoiare, inceppare.
tramontane [trɑ:mɔn'tein], *a.* Oltramontano.
tramp [træmp], *v.i.* Calpestare; marciare, camminare, viaggiare a piedi; vagabondare; *v.t.* percorrere a piedi; calpestare. || *n.* (*walk*) Passeggiata, *f.*, calpestio, *m.*; (*vagabond*) vagabondo, girovago, camminante, *m.* **— steamer,** vapore senza linea regolare, *m.*
trample, *v.t.* Calpestare, metter sotto i piedi; conculcare.
trampling, *n.* Calpestamento, calpestio, *m.*
trance [trɑ:ns], *n.* Estasi, *f.*, (*hypnotic*) stato ipnotico, *m.*; catalessi.
tranquil ['trænkwil], *a.* Tranquillo, quieto, calmo.
tranquillity, tranquilness, *n.* Tranquillità, *f.*
tranquillization, *n.* Tranquillamento, *m.*
tranquillize, *v.t.* Tranquillare, tranquillizzare.
tranquilly, *adv.* Tranquillamente.
transact [træns'ækt], *v.t.* Trattare, fare, sbrigare. **To — business,** sbrigare un affare.
transaction, *n.* Affare, *m.*, operazione, transazione, *f.*; negozio, disbrigo, *m.* **Transactions,** atti, rendiconti, *m.pl.*
transactor, *n.* Negoziatore, *m.*
transalpine [træns'ælpain], *a.* (*Geog.*) Transalpino.
transatlantic [trænsət'læntik], *a.* Transatlantico.
transcend [træn'send], *v.t.* Trascendere, oltrepassare, superare.
transcendence, transcendency, *n.* Trascendenza, *f.*
transcendent, *a.* Trascendente, eccellente.
transcendently, *adv.* Eccellentemente, ottimamente.
transcendental [trænsen'dentəl], *a.* Trascendentale.
transcendentalism, *n.* Trascendentalismo, *m.*
transcendentally, *adv.* Trascendentalmente.
transcribe [træn'skraib], *v.t.* Trascrivere, copiare.
transcriber, *n.* Trascrittore, *m.*
transcript, transcription, *n.* Trascrizione, *f.*
transept ['trænsept], *n.* Transetto, *m.*
transfer [træns'fə:ɹ], *v.t.* Trasferire, trasportare; cedere; (*Art*) riportare, ricalcare. || *n.* ['trænsfəɹ], Trasferimento, trasporto, *m.*; (*Law*) trapasso, *m.*, cessione, *f.*; disegno da ricalcare, *m.*; corrispondenza, *f.*
transferable, *a.* Trasferibile, trasportabile. (*of tickets*) **Not —,** personale, non cedibile, non trasferibile.
transferee [trænsfər'i:], *n.* (*Law*) Cessionario, *m.*
transference, *n.* Trasferimento, *m.*
transferrer, transferor, *n.* Cedente, *m.*
transfiguration [trænsfigju:'reiʃən], *n.* Trasfigurazione, *f.*
transfix [træns'fiks], *v.t.* Trafiggere.
transform [træns'fɔ:ɹm], *v.t.* Trasformare, cambiare.
transformation, *n.* Trasformazione, metamorfosi, *f.*, cambiamento, *m.*
transformable, *a.* Trasformabile.
transformer, *n.* Trasformatore, *m.*
transfuse [træns'fju:z], *v.t.* Trasfondere, trasmettere.
transfusion, *n.* Trasfusione, *f.* **Blood —,** trasfusione di sangue, *f.*
transgress [træns'gres], *v.t.* Trasgredire, violare; *v.i.* errare, peccare.
transgression, *n.* Trasgressione, violazione, *f.*; colpa, *f.*
transgressor, *n.* Trasgressore, violatore, *m.*; peccatore, *m.*
tranship [træn'ʃip], *v.t.* Trasbordare; *v.i.* trasbordarsi.
transhipment, *n.* Trasbordo, *m.*
transience, transiency ['trænsiəns, 'trænsiənsi], *n.* Momentaneità, temporaneità, *f.*; corta durata, caducità, *f.*
transient, *a.* Transitorio, temporaneo, passeggiero, caduco, labile, momentaneo.
transiently, *adv.* Transitoriamente.
transire [træn'zairi], *n.* (*at Customs*) Lasciapassare, *m.*
transit ['trænzit], *n.* Transito, passaggio, *m.*; traversata, *f.* **In —,** in transito, di passaggio; (*Astron.*) **— -instrument,** equatoriale, *m.*
transition, *n.* Transizione, *f.*
transitional, *a.* Di transizione.
transitive ['trænzitiv], *a.* (*Gram.*) Transitivo.
transitory, *a.* Transitorio, temporaneo.
translatable [træns'leitəbl], *a.* Traducibile.
translate [træns'leit], *v.t.* Tradurre; trasferire; **— into English,** tradurre in inglese.
translation, *n.* Traduzione, *f.*; trasferimento, *m.*
translator, *n.* Traduttore, *m.*, traduttrice, *f.*
transliterate [træns'litəreit], *v.t.* Trascrivere.
translucence, translucency [træns'lu:səns, træns'lu:sənsi], *n.* Translucidità, *f.*
translucent, *a.* Translucido, diafano.
transmigrate [træns'maigreit], *v.i.* Trasmigrare.
transmigration, *n.* Trasmigrazione, *f.*
transmissibility [trænsmisi'biliti], *n.* Trasmissibilità, *f.*
transmissible, *a.* Trasmissibile.
transmission, *n.* Trasmissione, *f.*
transmit, *v.t.* Trasmettere.
transmitter, *n.* Trasmettitore, *m.*
transmutability [trænsmju:tə'biliti], *n.* Trasmutabilità, *f.*
transmutable, *a.* Trasmutabile.
transmutation, *n.* Trasmutazione, trasformazione, *f.*, cambiamento, *m.*
transmute, *v.t.* Trasmutare, trasformare, cambiare.
transmuter, *n.* Trasmutatore, *m.*
transoceanic [trænsouʃi'ænik], *a.* Transoceanico.
transom ['trænsəm], *n.* Traversa, *f.*, listello, *m.*, (*Naut.*) barra d'arcaccia, *f.*
transparence, transparency [træns'pærəns, træns'pærənsi], *n.* Trasparenza, *f.*; trasparente, *m.*
transparent, *a.* Trasparente, diafano.
transparently, *adv.* Chiaramente, evidentemente, ovviamente.
transpierce [træns'piərs], *v.t.* Trafiggere.
transpiration [trænspai'reiʃən], *n.* Traspirazione, *f.*

transpire, *v.i.* Traspirare; (*fig.*) trapelare, manifestarsi; (*colloq.*) accadere, succedere.
transplant, *v.t.* Trapiantare.
transplantation, *n.* Trapiantamento, *m.*
transplanter, *n.* Trapiantatore, *m.*; (*tool*) trapiantatoio, *m.*
transport [ˈtrænspɔːɹt], *n.* Trasporto, *m.*; (*Naut.*) nave trasporto, *m.*; (*fig.*) trasporto, accesso, *m.*; (*Hist.*) forzato, *m.* *v.t.* [træns-ˈpɔːɹt], Trasportare, trasferire; deportare, relegare. **A — of rage,** un accesso di rabbia, *m.*; **to be transported with joy,** lasciarsi trasportare dalla gioia.
transportable, *a.* Trasportabile.
transportation, *n.* Trasportazione, *f.*; (*Law*) deportazione, relegazione, *f.*
transportingly, *adv.* Con trasporto.
transposal, transposition, *n.* Trasposizione, *f.*, spostamento, *m.*
transpose, *v.t.* Trasporre, trasportare; (*Mus.*) trasportare.
transubstantiation [trænsʌbstænʃiˈeiʃən], *n.* Transustanziazione, *f.*
transudation, *n.* Trasudazione, *f.*, trasudamento, *m.*
transversal [trænsˈvəːɹsəl], *a.* Traversale.
transversely, *adv.* Traversalmente.
transverse, *a.* Traverso, obliquo.
trap [træp], *n.* Trappola, *f.*, laccio, *m.*; (*fig.*) tranello, *m.*; inganno, *m.*; insidia, *f.*; (*vehicle*) carrozzetta, *f.*; (*drain*) valvola, *f.*, sifone, *m.* || *v.t.* Trappolare, prendere in trappola; ingannare, truffare. **—-door,** trabocchetto, *m.*; **to be caught in a —,** essere preso in trappola; **to set a —,** mettere una trappola, tendere un laccio; **to pack up one's traps,** far fagotto.
trapeze [trəˈpiːz], *n.* Trapezio, *m.*
trapper, *n.* Cacciatore di pelli, *m.*
trappings, *n.pl.* Paramenti, ornamenti, *m.pl.*; guarnimenti, *m.pl.*, guarnizioni, *f.pl.*
Trappist [ˈtræpist], *n.* (*Eccles.*) Trappista, *m.*
trapse [cp. **traipse**].
trash [træʃ], *n.* Robaccia, *f.*, rifiuti, *m.pl.*; sciocchezze, *f.pl.*; porcheria, birbonata, *f.*; futilità, *f.*
trashiness, *n.* Meschinità, nullaggine, *f.*
trashy, *a.* Di nessun valore, di scarto, da nulla.
trauma [ˈtrɔːmə], *n.* (*Med.*) Trauma, *m.*
traumatic, *a.* Traumatico.
travail [ˈtræveil], *n.* Doglie del parto, *f.pl.*; (*obs.*) travaglio, *m.*, pena, *f.* || *v.i.* Sforzarsi, affaticarsi, darsi pena. **In —,** di parto, sotto le doglie.
travel [ˈtrævəl], *v.i.* Viaggiare, far viaggio, esser in viaggio; andare, circolare, diffondersi; percorrere. || *n.* Il viaggiare. **To — on foot,** andare a piedi, viaggiare a piedi; **to — by train,** viaggiare in treno; **to — over,** percorrere; **to — a great distance,** venire da lontano, andare lontano, fare un lungo viaggio; **—-stained,** sciupato dal viaggio.
travelled, *a.* Che ha molto viaggiato.
traveller, *n.* Viaggiatore, *m.*, viaggiatrice, *f.*; (*Comm.*) commesso viaggiatore, piazzista, *m.* **Traveller's cheque,** assegno turistico, *m.*; (*Bot.*) **traveller's joy,** vitalba, *f.*
travelling, *n.* Il viaggiare, *m.* || *a.* Viaggiante; da viaggio, di viaggio. **—-expenses,** spese di viaggio, *f.pl.*; **—-companion,** compagno di viaggio, *m.*; **—-bag,** valigia, *f.*; **—-rug,** coperta da viaggio, *f.*; (*Mech.*) **—-crane,** gru a ponte, gru mobile, *f.*
traverse [ˈtrævəɹs], *v.t.* Attraversare, traversare; (*in climbing*) obliquare; opporsi a, impedire; (*Law*) contestare, negare; (*Mil.*) puntare; (*fig.*) discutere, considerare; *v.i.* girare. || *a.* Traverso, obliquo. || *n.* Traversa, *f.*; (*Naut.*) bordata, *f.*; (*Law*) contestazione, *f.*; (*Alpinism*) traversata, *f.*
travesty [ˈtrævesti], *n.* Travestimento, *m.*, travestitura, truccatura, *f.* || *v.t.* Travestire, svisare, parodiare, truccare.
trawl [trɔːl], *n.* Strascico, giacchio, *m.*, rete a strascico, draga, *f.* || *v.t.* Pescare a rete, giacchiare.
trawler, *n.* Nave da pesca a strascico, *f.*; peschereccio, *m.*
trawling, *n.* Pesca col giacchio, *f.*
tray [trei], *n.* Vassoio, *m.*; (*Phot.*) bacinella *f.*; **—-cloth,** tovagliolino, *m.*
trayful, *n.* Vassoiata, *f.*
treacherous [ˈtretʃərəs], *a.* Perfido, sleale, traditore; proditorio.
treacherously, *adv.* Perfidamente, proditoriamente.
treachery, *n.* Perfidia, slealtà, *f.*, tradimento, *m.*
treacle [triːkl], *n.* Melassa, *f.*, sciroppo di zucchero, *m.*
treacly, *a.* Sciropposo, sciroppato.
tread [tred], *v.i.* Camminare, andare a piedi, porre il piede, procedere; *v.t.* calcare, pigiare, pestare. || *n.* Passo, *m.*; (*of stair*) gradino, scalino, *m.* **To — in the footsteps of,** procedere sulle tracce di, pestare l'orme di; **to — on,** camminare sopra, calpestare; **to — down,** calpestare, pigiare, calcare; **to — lightly,** camminare pian piano; (*Theat.*) **to — the boards,** calcare le scene; **to — grapes,** pigiare l'uva; **to — water,** nuotare ritto, nuotare in piedi; **the — of a tyre,** il battistrada, *m.*
treading, *n.* Passo, *m.*, andatura, *f.*; (*of grapes*) pigiatura, *f.*
treadle, *n.* (*of sewing-machine, cycle, etc.*) Pedale, *m.*; (*of loom*) calcola, *f.*
treadmill, *n.* Mola per tortura, *f.*; (*fig.*) lavoro monotono, *m.*
treason [ˈtriːzən], *n.* Tradimento, *m.*
treasonable, *a.* Di tradimento, proditorio, sedizioso.
treasonably, *adv.* A tradimento, sediziosamente.
treasure [ˈtreʒəɹ], *n.* Tesoro, *m.* || *v.t.* Tesoreggiare; (*fig.*) stimare, apprezzare, far tesoro di. **To — up,** tesoreggiare; **—-house,** tesoro, *m.*, tesoreria, *f.*; **—-trove,** tesoro trovato, *m.*
treasurer, *n.* Tesoriere, *m.*
treasury, *n.* Tesoreria, *f.*, erario, tesoro, *m.*; cassa, *f.*, fisco, *m.* **The Treasury,** il Tesoro, l'Erario dello Stato, *m.*; **First Lord of the Treasury,** Presidente del Consiglio dei Ministri, *m.*; (*Pol.*) **Treasury bench,** banchi ministeriali, *m.pl.*; **— note,** biglietto di banca, *m.*; **— bond,** buono del Tesoro, *m.*
treat [triːt], *v.t.* Trattare; *v.i.* trattare, venire a patti, venire a trattative, negoziare. || *n.* Piacere, *m.*, festa, *f.*; trattenimento, divertimento, *m.* **To — kindly,** trattare dolcemente; **to — of,** trattare di; **to — to a drink,** pagare

da bere, offrire una bibita a; **to — with,** trattare con; **the doctor treated him for rheumatism,** il dottore l'ha curato di reumatismo; **it was a great — for us,** era un gran piacere per noi; **a school- —,** una festa scolastica, *f.*; **to stand —,** pagare le spese; **I'll stand for —,** pago io, offro io.

treatise [ˈtri:tiz], *n.* Trattato, *m.*

treatment, *n.* Trattamento, *m.*; (*Med.*) cura, *f.*; accoglienza, *f.*; (*Art, Mus.*) esecuzione, *f.* **To have —,** fare una cura.

treaty, *n.* Trattato, *m.*; patto, contratto, *m.* **— of peace,** trattato di pace, *m.*; **by private —,** per patto privato, all'amichevole; **to be in — for,** negoziare la compera di, essere in trattative per.

treble (1) [ˈtrebəl], *v.t.i.* Triplicare. || *n.* Triplo, *m.* || *a.* Triplice.

treble (2), *n.* (*Mus.*) Soprano, *m.*, voce di soprano, *f.* || *a.* Soprano acuto; cantabile. **— clef,** chiave di sol; chiave di violino, *f.*

trebling, *n.* Triplicazione, *f.*, triplo, *m.*

trebly, *adv.* Tre volte, triplicemente.

tree [tri:], *n.* Albero, *m.*; (*for boots*) gambale, *m.* || *v.t.* Far salire su di un albero. **Genealogical —,** albero genealogico, *m.*; (*colloq.*) **to be up a —,** essere nell'imbarazzo; **— -fern,** felce arborea, *f.*

treeless, *a.* Senza alberi.

treenail [ˈtrenəl, ˈtri:neil], *n.* Caviglia, *f.*, cavicchio, *m.*

trefoil [ˈtrefɔil], *n.* (*Bot.*) Trifoglio, *m.*

trek [trek], *n.* Tappa, *f.*; viaggio in carro, *m.* || *v.i.* Viaggiare.

trellis [ˈtrelis], *n.* Graticolato, reticolato di legno, *m.*, graticciata, *f.* || *v.t.* Ingraticciare. **— -work,** traliccio, graticcio, *m.*

tremble [ˈtrembəl], *v.i.* Tremare; fremere; trepidare. **To — with fear,** tremar di paura; **to — with rage,** fremere d'ira; **to — in every limb,** tremar come una foglia.

trembler, *n.* (*Elec.*) Interruttore, *m.*

trembling, *n.* Tremito, fremito, tremore, *m.*, trepidazione, *f.* || *a.* Tremante, fremente; tremolo.

tremblingly, *adv.* Tremando, trepidando.

trembly, *a.* Tremolo, tremante.

tremendous [treˈmendəs], *a.* Tremendo; terribile, spaventoso; (*colloq.*) straordinario.

tremendously, *adv.* Tremendamente, straordinariamente.

tremendousness, *n.* Terribilità, spaventosità, *f.*

tremolo [ˈtremolou], *n.* (*Mus.*) Tremolo, *m.*

tremor [ˈtreməɹ], *n.* Tremore, tremito, *m.*

tremulous [ˈtremju:ləs], *a.* Tremolo, tremolante; (*fig.*) timido, pauroso.

tremulously, *adv.* Tremolando, timidamente.

tremulousness, *n.* Tremore, *m.*, paura, trepidazione, *f.*

trench [trentʃ], *n.* Trincea, *f.*; scavo, *m.*, fossa, *f.* || *v.t.* Scavare fosse in; solcare; (*Mil.*) trincerare. (*Mil.*) **Communication —,** camminamento, *m.*; **— warfare,** guerra di trincea, *f.*; **— -mortar,** lanciabombe, *m.*; **to — upon,** invadere; rasentare.

trenchant [ˈtrentʃənt], *a.* Tagliente, acuto, penetrante, incisivo.

trencher, *n.* Tagliere, *m.*; berretto universitario, *m.*

trencherman, *n.* Mangiatore, *m.*

trend, *n.* Direzione, tendenza, *f.*, orientamento, *m.* || *v.i.* Dirigersi, tendere verso, stendersi verso. **The — of opinion,** l'orientamento dell'opinione, *m.*

trental [ˈtrentəl], *n.* (*Eccles.*) Trigesimo, *m.*

trepan (1) [treˈpæn], *n.* (*Med.*) Trapano, *m.* || *v.t.* Trapanare.

trepan (2), *v.t.* Ingannare, truffare.

trepanning, *n.* Trapanamento, *m.*, trapanazione, *f.*

trepidation [trepiˈdeiʃən], *n.* Trepidazione, trepidanza, *f.*; (*Med.*) tremito, *m.*

trespass [ˈtrespəs], *n.* Intrusione, offesa, colpa, *f.*; violazione di proprietà, *f.*; prevaricazione, trasgressione, *f.* || *v.i.* Oltrepassare, violare, trasgredire; contravvenire a, abusare di; oltrepassare un confine, far torto a. **To — upon,** abusare di; **to — against,** offendere, violare; **— -offering,** sacrificio espiatorio, *m.*

trespasser, *n.* Trasgressore, peccatore, *m.*; contravventore, *m.* **Trespassers will be prosecuted,** divieto di transito, vietato l'ingresso, i contravventori saranno puniti a termini di legge.

tress [tres], *n.* Treccia, *f.*; ciocca, *f.*, ricciolo, *m.* || *v.t.* Intrecciare.

trestle [tresl], *n.* Cavalletto, trespolo, *m.*; traliccio, *m.* **— -bridge,** ponte a trespolo, *m.*

tret [tret], *n.* (*Comm.*) Deduzione di parte del peso, *f.*

Treves [tri:vz], *n.* (*Geog.*) Treviri, *f.*

trews [tru:z], *n.pl.* Calzoni, *m.pl.*

trey [trei], *n.* (*Cards, Dice*) Tre, *m.*

triad [ˈtraiəd], *n.* Triade, *f.*

trial [ˈtraiəl], *n.* Saggio, collando, *m.*, prova, *f.*; esperimento, *m.*; dolore, *m.*, sofferenza, *f.*; (*Law*) processo, *m.*, causa, lite, *f.* || *a.* Di prova, di saggio, sperimentale. **To make — of,** mettere alla prova; **to employ on —,** prendere in prova; (*colloq.*) **a terrible —,** una dura prova, *f.*; **on one's —,** sotto processo; **he stood his —,** fu processato; **— -trip,** viaggio di prova, *m.*; (*Comm.*) **— balance,** bilancio di verificazione, *m.*; **— and error,** tastoni, tentoni, *m.pl.*

triangle [ˈtraiæŋgl], *n.* Triangolo, *m.*

triangular [traiˈæŋgju:ləɹ], *a.* Triangolare.

triangulate, *v.t.* Triangolare.

triangulation, *n.* Triangolazione, *f.*

tribal [ˈtraibəl], *a.* Di tribù, tribale.

tribe, *n.* Tribù, *f.*; famiglia, razza, *f.*

tribesman, *n.* Membro di tribù, *m.*

tribulation [tribju:ˈleiʃən], *n.* Tribolazione, *f.*, patimento, *m.*

tribunal [traiˈbju:nəl], *n.* Tribunale, *m.*

tribune [ˈtribju:n], *n.* (*Hist.*) Tribuno, *m.*; (*platform*) tribuna, *f.*

tributary, *a.* Tributario. || *n.* (*Geog.*) Affluente, *m.*

tribute [ˈtribju:t], *n.* Tributo, *m.* **To pay — to,** pagare un tributo a, (*fig.*) fare un elogio di; **— -money,** tributo, *m.*

trice (1) [trais], *n.* Batter d'occhio, istante, *m.* **In a —,** in un attimo, in un batter d'occhio.

trice (2), *v.t.* (*Naut.*) Issare.

triceps [ˈtraiseps], *n.* (*Anat.*) Tricipite, *m.*

trick [trik], *n.* Tiro, artificio, inganno, trucco, *m.*, frode, *f.*; (*Cards*) plico, *m.*, bazza, *f.*; (*habit*) abitudine, *f.*, vezzo, *m.*; (*knack*) abilità, destrezza, *f.* || *v.t.* Ingannare, gabbare; frodare; giuocare un tiro a, turlupinare, raggirare. **I know a — worth two of that,** io la so più lunga ancora, io ne so una migliore; **a shabby —,** un tiro birbone, *m.*; **the tricks of the trade,** i segreti del mestiere, *m.pl.*; **he is at his tricks again,** ne fa ancora delle sue; **to do the —,** ottenere l'effetto voluto; **to play someone a —,** giuocare un tiro a qualcuno; **she has a — of giggling,** ha il vizio di ridacchiare; **a — cyclist,** un ciclista acrobata, *m.*; **to — out,** ornare, adornare.

trickery, *n.* Furberia, frode, astuzia, malizia, *f.*

trickish, *a.* Furbo, astuto.

trickle [trikl], *v.i.* Gocciolare, stillare, trapelare. || *n.* Filo d'acqua, *m.*; gocciolio, *m.*, ruscelletto, *m.*

trickling, *n.* Gocciolio, *m.*

trickster, *n.* Mariuolo, gabbamondo, furbone, raggiratore, *m.*

tricky, *a.* Infido, imbrogliato; complicato.

tricolour [ˈtraikʌləɹ], *n.* Tricolore, *m.* || *a.* Tricolore. **The — flag,** la bandiera tricolore, *f.*

tricycle [ˈtraisikl], *n.* Triciclo, *m.*

tricyclist, *n.* Triciclista, *m.*

trident [ˈtraidənt], *n.* Tridente, *m.*

tried [traid], *a.* Provato. **A — friend,** un vero amico, un amico provato, *m.*

triennial [traiˈeniəl], *a.* Triennale.

triennially, *adv.* Ogni tre anni.

trier [ˈtraiəɹ], *n.* Esperimentatore, *m.*; (*colloq.*) persona volonterosa, *f.*

trifle [ˈtraifəl], *n.* Bagattella, bazzecola, *f.*; inezia, minuzia, *f.*; nonnulla, *f.*; pochino, tantino, *m.*; (*Cooking*) zuppa inglese, *f.* || *v.i.* Baloccarsi, frivoleggiare, gingillarsi. **To waste time on trifles,** perdere il tempo in inezie, **he seems a — vexed,** pare un po' seccato; **to — away one's time,** sprecare il tempo in sciocchezze; **he is not to be trifled with,** non c'è da scherzare con lui.

trifler, *n.* Perdigiorno, sfaccendato, *m.*

trifling, *n.* Frivolezze, *f.pl.* || *a.* Insignificante, da nulla. **A — matter,** una cosa da nulla, *f.*

triforium [traiˈfɔːɹiəm], *n.* (*Arch.*) Galleria, *f.*, triforio, *m.*

trig [trig], *n.* Scarpa di carro, martinicca, *f.* || *a.* Lindo, attillato.

trigger [ˈtrigəɹ], *n.* Grilletto, *m.*; scatto, *m.* **—-guard,** guardamacchia, *f.*

triglyph [ˈtraiglif], *n.* Triglifo, *m.*

trigonometrical [trigənɔˈmetrikəl], *a.* Trigonometrico.

trigonometry [trigoˈnɔmetri], *n.* Trigonometria, *f.*

trill [tril], *n.* Trillo, *m.* || *v.i.* Trillare.

trillion, *n.* Trilione, *m.*

trilogy [ˈtrilodʒi], *n.* Trilogia, *f.*

trim [trim], *v.t.* Assettare, aggiustare, sistemare; (*wick*) smoccolare; (*hedge, etc.*) tagliare, potare; (*hair*) spuntare, regolare; (*to ornament*) guarnire, ornare; (*Naut.*) stivare, bilanciare; (*sails*) orientare; *v.i.* temporeggiare, tergiversare; barcarmenarsi. || *a.* Netto, lindo, ben messo, attillato, azzimato. || *n.* Stato, ordine, grado, *m.*, condizione, *f.*; assetto, *m.* **To — oneself up,** attillarsi, azzimarsi, farsi bello; **to — off,** ritagliare; **in good —,** assettato, ordinato, in ottimo stato; **in fighting —,** in assetto di guerra.

trimly, *adv.* Nettamente, lindamente, elegantemente.

trimmer, *n.* Ornatore, decoratore; (*fig.*) girella, voltafaccia, opportunista, *m.*; (*Naut.*) fochista, *m.*

trimming, *n.* Guarnizione, guarnitura, *f.*; contorno, *m.*

trimness, *n.* Nettezza, lindura, attillatura, *f.*, buon ordine, *m.*

trine [train], *a.* Trino, triplice.

Trinidad [ˈtrinidæd], *n.* (*Geog.*) La Trinità, *f.*

trinitarian [triniˈtɛəriən], *n.* (*Eccles.*) Trinitario, *m.*

Trinity [ˈtriniti], *n.* Trinità, *f.* **— Sunday,** domenica della Trinità, *f.*

trinket [ˈtriŋkit], *n.* Gingillo, ciondolo, ninnolo, fronzolo, *m.*

trinomial [traiˈnoumiəl], *a.* (*Math.*) Trinomio.

trio [ˈtriːou], *n.* Trio, terzetto, *m.*

trip [trip], *v.i.* Inciampare, intoppare, incespicare; sbagliare, errare; saltellare, ballare; *v.t.* fare inciampare, far cadere; cogliere in fallo; (*Naut.*) spedare. || *n.* Gita, *f.*, viaggio, giro, *m.*; escursione, *f.*; passo falso, *m.* **To — along,** andare saltellando; **to — over a stone,** inciampare in un sasso; **to — up,** far cadere; **pleasure —,** gita di piacere, *f.*

tripartite [traiˈpɑːɹtait], *a.* Tripartito.

tripe [traip], *n.* Trippa, *f.*

triphthong [ˈtrifθɔŋ], *n.* (*Gram.*) Trittongo, *m.*

triplane [ˈtraiplein], *n.* (*Aviat.*) Triplano, *m.*

triple [tripl], *a.* Triplo, triplice. || *v.t.* Triplicare.

triplet, *n.* (*Poet.*) Terzina, *f.*; (*Mus.*) tripletta, *f.* **Triplets,** fratelli trigemini, *m.pl.*, un parto trigemino, *m.*

triplicate [ˈtriplikeit], *v.t.* Triplicare. || [ˈtriplikət], *a.* Triplicato, triplo. || *n.* Triplo, *m.* **In —,** in triplo, in triplice copia.

triplication, *n.* Triplicazione, *f.*

triply, *adv.* Triplicemente.

tripod [ˈtraipɔd], *n.* Tripode, *m.*

tripos [ˈtraipɔs], *n.* (*Univ. Cambridge*) Esame di laurea, *m.*

tripper, *n.* Escursionista, gitante, *m.*

tripping, *n.* Passo falso; sbaglio, errore; passo leggero, ballo leggero, *m.* || *a.* Lesto, snello, svelto, agile.

trippingly, *adv.* Lestamente, sveltamente.

triptych [ˈtriptik], *n.* Trittico, *m.*

trisect [traiˈsekt], *v.t.* Dividere in tre parti, tripartire.

trisection, *n.* Trisezione, *f.*

trite [trait], *a.* Trito, usato, banale, comune, stantio.

tritely, *adv.* Banalmente.

triteness, *n.* Banalità, *f.*

Triton [ˈtraitən], *n.* (*Myth.*) Tritone, *m.*

tritone [ˈtraitoun], *n.* (*Mus.*) Tritono, *m.*

triturate [ˈtritjuːreit], *v.t.* Tritare, triturare.

trituration, *n.* Tritatura, *f.*

triumph [ˈtraiʌmf], *n.* Trionfo, *m.* || *v.i.* Trionfare; vincere. **To — over,** trionfare di.

triumphal, *a.* Trionfale, di trionfo.

triumphant, *a.* Trionfante; superbo, altero.

triumphantly, *adv.* Trionfalmente; superbamente, alteramente.

triumvir [traiˈʌmvəɹ], *n.* (*Hist.*) Triumviro, *m.*

trivet [ˈtrivit], *n.* Treppiede, *m.* **As right as a —,** benissimo, alla perfezione.

trivial [ˈtriviəl], *a.* Insignificante, inconcludente, futile, da nulla, banale.

trivially, *adv.* Banalmente.
trivialness, triviality, *n.* Futilità, vacuità, banalità, *f.*
trochaic [trou'keiik], *a.* (*Poet.*) Trocaico.
trochee ['trouki:], *n.* (*Poet.*) Trocheo, *m.*
trod, trodden, *p.* and *p.p.* of **tread.**
troglodyte ['trɔglodait], *n.* Troglodito, *m.*
Trojan ['troudʒən], *n.a.* Troiano, *m.* **To work like a —,** sgobbare come un somaro.
troll (1) [troul], *v.t.* Cantare.
troll (2), *v.t.* Pescare con esca girante.
troll (3), *n.* (*Myth.*) Gnomo, nano, *m.*; gigante, *m.*
trolley, trolly ['trɔli], *n.* Carrello, *m.*, carretta, *f.*; (*Elec.*) asta di presa, *f.*, trolle, *m.*, puleggia, *f.* **— -bus,** filobus, *m.*
trolling ['trouliŋ], *n.* Pesca con esca girante, *f.*
trollop ['trɔləp], *n.* Sudiciona, *f.*; sgualdrina, *f.*
trombone ['trɔmboun], *n.* (*Mus.*) Trombone, *m.*
troop [tru:p], *n.* Truppa, banda, schiera, *f.*, squadrone, *m.* ‖ *v.i.* Schierarsi, raccogliersi, adunarsi, riunirsi, affollarsi; *v.t.* adunare, schierare. **To — along,** sfilare; **to — in,** ammassarsi, affollarsi; **— -ship,** trasporto, *m.*; **— -train,** treno militare, *m.*; **trooping the colours,** sfilamento in parata, *m.*, rivista militare, *f.*
trooper, *n.* Soldato di cavalleria, *m.*
trope [troup], *n.* (*Gram.*) Tropo, *m.*
trophied ['troufid], *a.* Ornato di trofei.
trophy, *n.* Trofeo, *m.*
tropic ['trɔpik], *n.* (*Geog.*) Tropico, *m.* **— of Cancer,** tropico del Cancro, *m.*
tropical, *a.* Tropicale; caloroso, fervido; metaforico.
trot [trɔt], *v.i.* Trottare, andar di trotto; *v.t.* far andare di trotto. ‖ *n.* Trotto, *m.*, trottata, *f.* **To go at a gentle —,** trottellare; **to put a horse to the —,** far trottare un cavallo; **at a jog- —,** a piccolo trotto; **to go for a —,** fare una trottata.
troth [trouθ], *n.* Verità, fede, *f.* **In troth,** in fede mia; **to plight one's —,** fidanzarsi.
trotter, *n.* (*Sport*) Trottatore, *m.* **Trotters,** zamponi, piedi, *m.pl.*
trotting, *n.* Trotto, *m.* ‖ *a.* Trottatore. **— -match,** corsa al trotto, *f.*
troubadour ['tru:bədɔ:ɹ], *n.* Trovadore, trovatore, *m.*
trouble [trʌbl], *v.t.* Agitare, turbare, disturbare; *v.i.* disturbarsi, incomodarsi; prendersi la pena, darsi la pena. ‖ *n.* Pena, noia, molestia, *f.*, fastidio, incomodo, *m.*; afflizione, *f.*, dolore, guaio, *m.*; disturbo, *m.*; imbroglio, imbarazzo, *m.* **I will not — you,** non voglio disturbarvi; **May I — you for a match?** Mi favorite un fiammifero? **he is troubled with neuralgia,** è tormentato dalla nevralgia; **I am sorry to — you,** mi duole disturbarvi; **don't — about it,** non disturbatevi per questo; **he did not — to apologize,** non si è nemmeno dato la pena di scusarsi; **it is not worth the —,** non vale la pena; **to get into —,** cacciarsi in un imbroglio; **to be in —,** essere in imbarazzo, avere dei guai.
troubled, *a.* Agitato, turbato; inquieto, ansioso, afflitto. **To fish in — waters,** pescare nel torbido; **a — countenance,** una faccia turbata, *f.*; **to be — about,** inquietarsi di, preoccuparsi di; **to be — with money matters,** essere in difficoltà finanziarie.
troublesome, *a.* Noioso, fastidioso, seccante, molesto, incomodo, importuno; penoso, doloroso. **A — child,** un bambino noioso, *m.*
troublesomely, *adv.* Noiosamente, molestamente.
troublesomeness, *n.* Noia, *f.*, fastidio, *m.*; molestia, importunità, *f.*
troublous, *a.* Agitato, inquieto, turbato. **— times,** tempi difficili, *m.pl.*
trough [trɔf, trɔ:f], *n.* Trogolo, *m.*; vasca, *f.*, abbeveratoio, *m.*; madia, *f.* **In the — of the sea,** fra i marosi.
trounce [trauns], *v.t.* Castigare, punire; bastonare; malmenare.
troupe [tru:p], *n.* Compagnia, *f.*
trousering ['trauzəriŋ], *n.* Stoffa per calzoni, *f.*
trousers, *n.pl.* Calzoni, pantaloni, *m.pl.* **Trouser-clip,** molletta per calzoni, *f.*; **trouser-press,** stiracalzoni, *m.*; (*colloq.*) **wife who wears the —,** moglia che porta i pantaloni.
trousseau ['tru:sou], *n.* Corredo per una sposa, *m.*
trout [traut], *n.* (*Zool.*) Trota, *f.* **— -fishing,** pesca delle trote, *f.*; **— -stream,** vivaio di trote, *m.*
trove [cp. **treasure**].
trover, *n.* (*Law*) Domanda per riacquistare la proprietà, *f.*
trowel ['trauəl], *n.* (*mason's*) Mestola, cazzuola, *f.*; (*gardening*) vanghetta, *f.*, spiantatore, *m.*
Troy [trɔi], *n.* (*Hist.*) Troia, *f.*
troy-weight ['trɔiweit], *n.* Peso per i metalli preziosi, *m.*
truancy ['tru:ənsi], *n.* Mancanza, assenza, *f.*; vagabondaggio, *m.*
truant, *n.* Fiaccone, pigrone, bighellone, *m.* ‖ *a.* Pigro, ozioso; vagabondo. **To play —,** marinare la scuola, batter la fiacca.
truce [tru:s], *n.* Tregua, *f.*, armistizio, *m.* **Flag of —,** bandiera bianca, *f.*
truck (1) [trʌk], *n.* Carro, carretto, *m.*; (*Rail.*) carro, vagone, *m.*; carrello, *m.*; (*Naut.*) pomo d'albero, *m.* ‖ *v.t.* Carreggiare. **Cattle- —,** carro bestiame.
truck (2), *n.* Scambio, baratto, *m.*; roba, robaccia, *f.* **To have no — with,** non aver niente a che fare con, evitar di trattare con; **— -system,** il sistema di pagare gli operai in natura, *m.*
truckle [trʌkl], *v.i.* Umiliarsi, abbassarsi, avvilirsi, sottomettersi.
truckle-bed, *n.* Letticciuolo su rotelle, *m.*, branda, *f.*
truckling, *n.* Abbassamento, avvilimento, *m.*, umiliazione, sottomissione, *f.*
truculence, truculency ['trʌkju:ləns, 'trʌkju:lənsi], *n.* Trucolenza, *f.*
truculent, *a.* Trucolento; terribile, feroce.
trudge [trʌdʒ], *v.i.* Camminare a stento, trascinarsi, camminare a fatica.
trudgen ['trʌdʒən], *n.* (*Swimming*) Nuoto a doppio braccetto, nuoto all'indiana, *m.*
true [tru:], *a.* Vero, verace; certo, reale; veridico, veritiero; giusto, genuino, sincero, leale; conforme; esatto; intonato. **To be — to,** essere fedele a; **it is only too —,** è

purtroppo vero; **strange but —,** incredibile ma vero; **to prove —,** avverarsi, realizzarsi, verificarsi; **—-blue,** leale, fedele; **—-born,** legittimo; **— -bred,** di buona razza, di puro sangue; **—-hearted,** leale, sincero, onesto; **—-heartedness,** lealtà, sincerità, onestà, *f.*; **—-love,** innamorato, amoroso, *m.*, amorosa, bella, *f.*; **—-lover's knot,** nodo d'amore, *m.*; **— to life,** al naturale; **to come —,** avverarsi.

truffle [ˈtrʌfəl, ˈtru:fl], *n.* (*Bot.*) Tartufo, *m.*

truism [ˈtru:izm], *n.* Verità evidente, *f.*, truismo, *m.*, verità banale, *m.*

truly, *adv.* Veramente, realmente; sinceramente; lealmente, fedelmente. **Yours —,** vostro devotissimo.

trump (1) [trʌmp], *n.* Tromba, *f.* **The last —,** la tromba del giudizio universale, *f.*

trump (2), *n.* (*Cards*) Briscola, *f.*, trionfo, *m.*; (*colloq.*) simpaticone, brav'uomo, *m.* || *v.t.* Prendere con briscola. **— card,** trionfo, *m.*; **to — up,** inventare, manipolare.

trumpery, *n.* Fronzoli, gingilli, *m.pl.*; robaccia, *f.*; sciocchezze, frottole, *f.pl.* || *a.* Senza valore, da nulla, meschino, insignificante, inetto. **— arguments,** ragioni inconcludenti, *m.pl.*

trumpet [ˈtrʌmpet], *n.* Tromba, *f.* || *v.t.* Annunciare a suon di tromba, strombazzare, strombettare; *v.i.* (*of elephant*) barrire. **Ear- —,** corno acustico, *m.*; **speaking- —,** megafono, portavoce, *m.*; **to blow one's own —,** cantare le proprie lodi; **— -call,** squillo di tromba; (*Bot.*) **—-flower,** bignonia, *f.*

trumpeter, *n.* Trombettiere, *m.*

truncate [trʌŋˈkeit], *v.t.* Troncare, mozzare.

truncated, *a.* Troncato.

truncheon [ˈtrʌntʃən], *n.* Mazza, *f.*, randello, bastone, *m.*

trundle [trʌndl], *v.t.* Rotolare, ruzzolare. || *n.* Rotella, ruzzola, *f.* **To — a hoop,** far correre un cerchio.

trunk [trʌŋk], *n.* (*of tree*) Tronco, fusto, *m.*; (*box*) baule, *m.*; (*of body*) torso, *m.*; (*of elephant*) proboscide, *f.* **— -call,** (*Telephone*) comunicazione intercomunale, *f.*; comunicazione interurbana, *f.*; **—-line,** linea principale, *f.*; (*Telephone*) linea interurbana, *f.*; **— road,** strada maestra, *f.*; **— -maker,** valigiaio, *m.*

trunnion [ˈtrʌniən], *n.* Orecchione, *m.*

truss [trʌs], *n.* (*of hay*) Fascio, *m.*; (*Med.*) cinto ernario, *m.*; (*framework*) travata, travatura, *f.*; (*prop*) puntello, *m.* || *v.t.* Affastellare; legare, allacciare; puntellare. **To — up,** legare; **to — a fowl,** preparare un pollo.

trust [trʌst], *n.* Fiducia, confidenza, *f.*; credito, *m.*; (*Law*) legato, lascito, *m.*; (*obligation*) carico, obbligo, *m.*; (*care*) cura, protezione, *f.*; (*Comm.*) trust, cartello, sindacato, consorzio, *m.* || *v.t.i.* Fidare, affidare; fidarsi, affidarsi; confidare, credere; sperare; contare, far assegnamento sopra. **Breach of —,** abuso di confidenza, *m.*, violazione di fidecommesso, *f.*; **on —,** a credito; **to hold in —,** tenere in deposito, custodire, avere in custodia; **to put — in,** aver fiducia in; **to fulfil one's —,** compiere il proprio incarico; **a situation of —,** un posto di fiducia; **he is to be trusted,** è degno di fiducia, ci si può fidare di lui; **I — the child to your care,** affido il bambino a voi; **we — that . . .,** speriamo che; **—-deed,** atto fiduciario, *m.*

trusted, *a.* Fidato, di fiducia.

trustee [trʌsˈti:], *n.* Curatore, amministratore, *m.*; depositario, fiduciario, *m.*; tutore, *m.* **In the hands of trustees,** in mano dei curatori.

trusteeship, *n.* Amministrazione, *f.*; tutela, *f.*; curatela, procura, *f.* **Trusteeship territory,** amministrazione fiduciaria, *f.*

trustful, *a.* Fiducioso, confidente.

trustfully, *adv.* Fiduciosamente.

trustily, *adv.* Fedelmente.

trustiness, trustworthiness, *n.* Fidatezza, *f.*

trustworthy, *a.* Fidato, sicuro.

trusty, *a.* Fidato, fedele, sicuro.

truth [tru:θ], *n.* Verità, *f.*, il vero, *m.*; veracità, *f.*; sincerità, lealtà, onestà, *f.* **In —,** veramente, davvero; infatti; **the honest —,** la pura verità; **there is — in what he says,** è vero ciò che dice; **home truths,** la dura verità, *f.*; **to tell you the —,** a dire il vero.

truthful, *a.* Verace, veridico, veritiero, vero.

truthfully, *adv.* Veracemente, veramente.

truthfulness, *n.* Veracità, *f.*

truthless, *a.* Falso, sleale, senza fede.

try [trai], *v.t.i.* Tentare, cercare, provare; (*to taste*) assaggiare, sentire; (*Law*) giudicare, processare; (*to tire*) affaticare, stancare. || *n.* Prova, *f.*, tentativo. **To — one's hand at,** tentare di fare; **his patience was sorely tried,** la sua pazienza fu messa a dura prova; **to — one's eyes,** affaticare gli occhi; **to — for,** cercare di ottenere, concorrere a; **to — on a dress,** provare un vestito; **to have a —,** provare, fare un tentativo.

trying, *a.* Difficile, penoso, faticoso, duro; noioso, fastidioso. **A — day,** un giorno faticoso; **it is very —,** è molto noioso; (*of clothes*) **—-on,** prova, *f.*

tryst [trist, traist], *n.* Convegno, appuntamento, *m.* **To break —,** mancare al convegno; **to keep —,** tenere un appuntamento; **trysting-place,** convegno, *m.*

tsar [zɑ:ɹ, tsɑ:ɹ], *n.* (*Hist.*) Zar, czar, *m.*

tsetse [ˈtsetsi], *n.* (*Zool.*) Mosca tsè-tsè, *f.*

tub [tʌb], *n.* Tino, *m.*, tinozza, botte, *f.*; vasca da bagno, *f.*; cassetta, *f.* || *v.t.* Bagnare, lavare. (*colloq.*) **An old —,** un bastimento logoro, *m.*, una vecchia carcassa, *f.*; **— -thumper,** demagogo, *m.*

tuba [ˈtju:bə], *n.* (*Mus.*) Tuba, *f.*

tubby, *a.* Grasso, paffuto, grassoccio, obeso.

tube [tju:b], *n.* Tubo, *m.*; canale, *m.*; condotto, *m.*; canna, *f.* (*Rail.*) ferrovia sotterranea, *f.* (*of tyre*) **Inner —,** camera d'aria, *f.*

tuber [ˈtju:bəɹ], *n.* (*Bot.*) Tubero, *m.*

tubercle, *n.* Tubercolo, *m.*

tubercular, tuberculous, *a.* Tubercolare.

tuberculosis [tju:bəɹkju:ˈlousis], *n.* (*Med.*) Tuberculosi, *f.*

tuberose [ˈtju:bəɹrouz], *n.* (*Bot.*) Tuberosa, *f.*

tuberous, *a.* Tuberoso.

tubing, *n.* Tubatura, *f.*, tubi, *m.pl.*

tubular [ˈtjubju:ləɹ], *a.* Tubolare, tubulare.

tuck (1) [tʌk], *n.* Piega, piegatura, *f.* || *v.t.* Piegare, ripiegare. **To — in the bedclothes,** rincalzare le coperte; **to — up in bed,** coricare, mettere a letto; **to — up one's skirts,** alzare le gonnelle; (*colloq.*) **to — in,** mangiare ingordamente.

tuck (2), *n.* (*colloq.*) Cibo, *m.*, pasticcini, *m.pl.* **To — in,** fare una scorpacciata; **a —-in,** una scorpacciata, *f.*; **—-shop,** confetteria, pasticceria, *f.*
tucker, *n.* Camicetta, *f.*, collettino, *m.*
Tuesday [ˈtju:zdei], *n.* Martedì, *m.* **Shrove —,** martedì grasso, *m.*
tufa, tuff [ˈtju:fə, tʌf], *n.* (*Geol.*) Tufo, *m.*
tuft [tʌft], *n.* Ciuffo, ciuffetto, *m.*; (*of hair*) ciocca, *f.*; (*of wool*) fiocco, *m.*; (*of bird*) cresta, *f.* ‖ *v.t.* Formare in ciocche; fiocchettare; trapuntare. **—-hunter,** parassito, cortigiano, *m.*
tufted, *a.* Fiocchettato; crestato.
tug [tʌg], *v.t.* Turare, strascinare; rimorchiare; strappare. ‖ *n.* Strappo, *m.*, tirata, *f.*; (*Naut.*) rimorchiatore. **To — at someone's hair,** strappare i capelli a qualcuno; **— of war,** tiro alla fune; **to give a good —,** dare una buona strappata.
tuition, *n.* Istruzione, *f.*, insegnamento, *m.*
tulip [ˈtju:lip], *n.* (*Bot.*) Tulipano, *m.* **—-tree,** tulipifero, *m.*
tulle [tu:l], *n.* Tulle, *m.*
tumble [tʌmbl], *n.* Caduta, *f.*, capitombolo, *m.*; ruzzolata, *f.* ‖ *v.i.* Cadere, capitombolare, ruzzolare; agitarsi, sobbalzare; saltare; dimenarsi; *v.t.* arruffare, disordinare; gettar giù, rovesciare, mandar sossopra. **To — down,** crollare, stramazzare; cader giù; **to — downstairs,** ruzzolare dalle scale; **—-down,** crollante, caduco, diroccato; **to — out of bed,** ruzzolare dal letto.
tumbler, *n.* (*glass*) Bicchiere, *m.*; (*acrobat*) saltimbanco, acrobata, *m.*; (*pigeon*) piccione tomboliere.
tumblerful, *n.* Contenuto di un bicchiere, *m.*
tumbrel, *n.* Carro, *m.*; furgone, *m.*
tumefaction [tju:miˈfækʃən], *n.* (*Path.*) Tumefazione, *f.*
tumid [ˈtju:mid], *a.* Tumido, gonfio, enfiato.
tumidness, tumidity, *n.* Tumidità, *f.*
tumify, *v.t.* (*Med.*) Tumefare.
tummy [ˈtʌmi], *n.* (*colloq.*) Ventre, *m.* **To begin to get a —,** metter su pancia.
tumour [ˈtjuməɹ], *n.* (*Med.*) Tumore, *m.*
tumult [ˈtju:mʌlt], *n.* Tumulto, *m.*; scompiglio, *m.*, sommossa, sollevazione, *f.*
tumultuary, *a.* Tumultuario.
tumultuous, *a.* Tumultuoso, agitato, turbolento.
tumultuously, *adv.* Tumultuosamente.
tumulus (pl. **tumuli**) [ˈtju:mju:ləs, ˈtju:mju:lai], *n.* Tumulo, *m.*
tun [tʌn], *n.* Botte, *f.*, barile, *m.* ‖ *v.t.* Imbottare. **—-bellied,** panciuto, corpacciuto.
tunable [ˈtju:nəbl], *a.* Accordabile, che si può accordare.
tune [tju:n], *n.* Motivo, *m.*, aria, melodia, *f.*; tono, accordo, *m.* ‖ *v.t.* Accordare, metter d'accordo. **In —,** intonato, armonico; **out of —,** stonato; **to get out of —,** stonare; **to the — of £5,** alla bellezza di cinque sterline; **to — a piano,** accordare un piano.
tuner, *n.* Accordatore, *m.*
tuneful, *a.* Melodioso, armonioso, intonato.
tuneless, *a.* Scordato.
tungsten [ˈtʌŋstən], *n.* (*Min.*) Tungsteno, *m.*
tunic [ˈtjunik], *n.* Tunica, *f.*
tuning, *n.* Accordatura, *f.* **—-fork,** diapason, *m.*, corista, *f*

Tunis [ˈtju:nis], *n.* (*Geog.*) (*town*) Tunisi, *f.*
Tunisia [tju:ˈniziə], *n.* (*state*) Tunisia, *f.*
Tunisian, *a.* Tunisino. ‖ *n.* Tunisino, *m.*, Tunisina, *f.*
tunnel [ˈtʌnəl], *n.* Galleria, *f.*, traforo, *m.* ‖ *v.t.* Traforare.
tunnelling, *n.* Traforo, *m.*
tunny [ˈtʌni], *n.* (*Zool.*) Tonno, *m.*
tup [tʌp], *n.* Montone, *m.*; (*Mech.*) berta, *f.*, battipalo, *m.*
turban [ˈtə:ɹbən], *n.* Turbante, *m.*
turbid [ˈtə:ɹbid], *a.* Torbido; agitato, turbato.
turbidness, turbidity, *n.* Torbidezza, *f.*
turbinate [ˈtə:ɹbineit], *a.* Turbinato.
turbine [ˈtə:ɹbain], *n.* (*Mech.*) Turbina, *f.*
turbo-jet [tə:ɹbouˈdʒet], *a.* **— engine,** motore a reazione, *m.*; **— plane,** aeroplano a reazione, *m.*, turboreattore, *m.*
turbot [ˈtə:ɹbət], *n.* (*Zool.*) Rombo, *m.*
turbulence, turbulency [ˈtə:ɹbju:ləns, ˈtə:ɹbju:lənsi], *n.* Turbolenza, agitazione, riottosità, *f.*
turbulent, *a.* Turbolento, turbulento, facinoroso, riottoso.
turbulently, *adv.* Turbolentemente.
tureen [tju:ˈri:n], *n.* (*for soup*) Zuppiera, *f.*; (*for sauce*) salsiera, *f.*
turf [tə:ɹf], *n.* Zolla erbosa, piota, *f.*; cotica erbosa, *f.*; torba, *f.*; (*Racing*) turf, campo delle corse, *m.*; le corse, *f.pl.*; il mondo ippico, *m.* ‖ *v.t.* Coprire di zolle erbose; **—-cutter,** tagliazolle, *m.*; **—-moss,** torbiera, *f.*
turfiness, *n.* Erbosità, *f.*
turfy, *a.* Erboso, torboso.
turgescence, turgescency [tə:ɹˈdʒesəns, tə:ɹˈgesənsi], *n.* Turgidezza, *f.*; (*fig.*) gonfiezza, ampollosità, *f.*
turgid [ˈtə:ɹdʒid], *a.* Turgido, gonfio; (*fig.*) ampolloso, gonfio, turgido.
turgidity, turgidness, *n.* Turgidezza, *f.*; (*fig.*) enfasi, ampollosità, gonfiezza, *f.*
turgidly, *adv.* Turgidamente.
Turin [tju:ˈrin], *n.* (*Geog.*) Torino, *f.*
Turk [tə:ɹk], *n.* Turco, *m.*, Turca, *f.* (*fig.*) **He's a young —,** è un diavoletto.
Turkey (1) [ˈtə:ɹki], *n.* (*Geog.*) Turchia, *f.* **A — carpet,** un tappeto turco, *m.*; **— red,** rosso di robbia.
turkey (2), *n.* (*Zool.*) Tacchino, *m.* **—-hen,** tacchina, *f.* **— poult,** tacchinotto, *m.*
Turkish, *a.* Turco. **— bath,** bagno turco, *m.*; **— slipper,** babbuccia, *f.*; **— towel,** asciugamano arricciato, *m.*
Turkoman [ˈtə:ɹkomæn], *n.* Turcomanno, *m.*
turmeric [ˈtə:ɹmərik], *n.* (*Bot.*) Curcuma, *f.*; (*Chem.*) curcumina, *f.*
turmoil [ˈtə:ɹmɔil], *n.* Tumulto, scompiglio, *m.*, agitazione, confusione, baraonda, *f.*
turn [tə:ɹn], *v.t.* Girare, volgere, voltare; rivolgere, rivoltare; agitare, sconvolgere; (*blade*) smussare; (*wood, etc.*) tornire; *v.i.* girare, volgere, volgersi, rivolgersi, rivoltarsi. ‖ *n.* Giro, *m.*, volta, *f.*; voltata, curva, svolta, *f.*, piega, direzione, *f.*; temperamento, *m.*; vicenda, *f.*, turno, *m.*; scopo, *m.*; fine, tiro, servizio, *m.*; (*of tide*) cambiamento, *m.*; (*Mus.*) fioritura, *f.*; (*Theat.*) numero, *m.* **A turned-up nose,** un naso all'insù, *m.*; **he is turned twenty,** ha più di vent'anni; **to — about,** rivoltare, voltarsi indietro; **to —**

adrift, respingere, mettere alla porta, piantare in asso; **to — an honest penny,** fare un onesto guadagno; **to — against,** inimicarsi, voltarsi contro; **to — aside,** stornare, sviare; **to — away,** mandar via, cacciare, congedare, licenziare; scostarsi, allontanarsi, andare da un'altra parte; **to — back,** far tornare, tornar indietro, volgersi indietro; **to — down,** (*the light*) abbassare, (*a page, etc.*) ripiegare; (*a proposal*) respingere, rigettare; **to — down a street,** imboccare una strada; **to — from,** stornare da, distogliere da; scostarsi da; **to — in,** ripiegare; andare a letto, coricarsi, rientrare; **to — in at,** entrare; **to — into,** cambiare, trasformare, mutare, tradurre; cambiarsi in, trasformarsi in; **to — off,** (*a tap*) chiudere; (*a servant*) mandar via, congedare; produrre, finire; **to — on,** (*a tap*) aprire; (*water*) far correre; (*a light*) accendere; dipendere da, mostrare risentimento verso; **to — out,** uscire, alzarsi dal letto; provare, tornare, riuscire, diventare; mettere alla porta, far uscire; rovesciare, vuotare; **it has turned out very well,** è riuscito bene; **he turned out to be a rascal,** risultò essere una canaglia; **to — over,** dar volta, voltarsi, cambiar partito, rovesciare, rivoltare; **to — over and over,** volgere e rivolgere; **to — over a new leaf,** cambiar vita, metter giudizio; **to — over to,** trasferire a, consegnare a; **to — round,** girare, voltare, voltarsi, volgersi indietro; **to — round and round,** girare e rigirare; **to — tail,** darsi alla fuga, ritirarsi; **to — to,** rivolgersi a, mettersi al lavoro; **to — to the left,** girare a sinistra; **to — to account,** far valere, trarre profitto da; **to — up,** arrivare, presentarsi; accadere, succedere, venir trovato; volgere in su, accorciare, trovare; **to — up one's nose at,** arricciare il naso a; **to — upside down,** capovolgere, rovesciare, mettere sossopra, capovolgersi; **to — one's hand to,** metter mano a; **not to — a hair,** non batter ciglio; **to — a dress,** rivoltare un vestito; **to — the scale,** far traboccare; **success has turned his head,** il successo gli ha montato la testa; **to — one's stomach,** rivoltare lo stomaco; **to — a phrase,** tornire una frase; **not to know which way to —,** non sapere a che santo votarsi, non sapere dove batter il capo; **to do someone a good —,** fare un buon servizio a qualcuno; **at every —,** in ogni occasione, ad ogni piè sospinto; **by turns,** a vicenda, a turno, successivamente; **cooked to a —,** cotto a perfezione; **it is your —,** tocca a voi; **to take it in turns,** fare per turno; **the milk is on the —,** il latte si guasta; **to take a — in the garden,** fare un giro nel giardino; **—-down,** rovesciato; **—-out,** equipaggio, *m.*; assemblea, adunanza, *f.*; **—-over,** (*Comm.*) giro d'affari, *m.*; (*Cooking*) pasticcio, *m.*; **—-screw,** cacciavite, *m.*; (*Rail.*) **—-table,** piattaforma, *f.*, (*of gramophone*) piatto girevole, *m.*

turncoat, *n.* Voltacasacca, *m.*, girella, *f.*

turncock, *n.* Fontaniere, *m.*

turner, *n.* Tornitore, *m.*

turnery, *n.* Tornitura, *f.*

turning, *n.* (*bend*) Curva, svolta, *f.*, giro, *m.*; (*street*) cantonata, *f.*; (*at lathe*) tornitura, *f.*, il tornire, *m.* **—-about,** giravolta, *f.*; **—-point,** svolta, *f.*, punto di cambiamento, *m.*; momento critico, *m.*; **—-lathe,** tornio, *m.*

turnip [ˈtəːɹnip], *n.* (*Bot.*) Rapa, *f.* **—-tops,** foglie di rapa, *f.pl.*

turnkey, *n.* Carceriere, secondino, *m.*

turnpike, *n.* Barriera, *f.*

turnspit, *n.* Girarrosto, *m.*

turnstile, *n.* (*on post*) Cancelletto, *m.*; (*at entrance*) barriera girevole, *f.*, contagente, *m.*

turpentine [ˈtəːɹpentain], *n.* Trementina, *f.*

turpitude [ˈtəːɹpitjuːd], *n.* Turpitudine, *f.*

turquoise [ˈtəːɹkwɔiz], *n.* Turchese, *f.*

turret [ˈtʌrit], *n.* Torretta, torricella, *f.*; (*Naut.*) torre, torretta, *f.* **— ship,** nave con torrette, *f.*

turtle [təːɹtl], *n.* (*Zool.*) Tartaruga, *f.*; testuggine di mare, *f.* **—-dove,** tortora, *f.*; **—-soup,** zuppa di tartaruga, *f.*; **to turn —,** capovolgersi.

Tuscan [ˈtʌskən], *n.a.* Toscano, *m.*, Toscana, *f.*

Tuscany, *n.* (*Geog.*) Toscana, *f.*

tusk [tʌsk], *n.* Zanna, *f.*

tusked, *a.* Zannuto.

tussle [tʌsl], *n.* Lotta, rissa, baruffa, zuffa, *f.* || *v.i.* Lottare, rissare, azzuffarsi.

tussock [ˈtʌsək], *n.* Ciuffo di erba, *m.* **—-grass,** festuca antartica, *f.*

tussore [tʌˈsɔːɹ], *n.* Tussore, stoffa di seta, *f.*

tut ! [tʌt], *inter.* Oibò! Pst!

tutelage [ˈtjuːtilidʒ], *n.* Tutela, *f.*

tutelary, *a.* Tutelare.

tutor [ˈtjuːtəɹ], *n.* Istitutore, precettore; insegnante privato; ripetitore, *m.* || *v.t.* Istruire, insegnare, ammaestrare.

tutorial [tjuːˈtɔːriəl], *a.* Didattico, d'istruzione, di studio. || *n.* Lezione privata.

tutoring, *n.* Istruzione, *f.*, ammaestramento, insegnamento, *m.*

tutorship, *n.* Tutela, *f.*, insegnamento, *m.*

tutsan [ˈtʌtsæn], *n.* (*Bot.*) Tuttasana, *f.*

tutty, *n.* (*Chem.*) Tuzia, *f.*

twaddle [twɔdl], *n.* Chiacchiere, ciarle, frottole, *f.pl.*; stupidaggine, *f.* || *v.i.* Chiacchierare.

twaddler, *n.* Chiacchierone, ciarlone, *m.*

twain [twein], *n.* Due, *m.*

twang [twæŋ], *n.* Tintinnio, strimpellio, suono acuto, *m.*; accento nasale, *m.* || *v.t.i.* Strimpellare, tintinnare; parlare nel naso, naseggiare; pizzicare le corde di.

tweak [twiːk], *v.t.* Pizzicare, pizzicottare, tirare. || *n.* Pizzicotto, *m.*

tweed [twiːd], *n.* Tessuto di lana, *m.*, stoffa scozzese, *f.*

'tween decks [twiːn ˈdeks], *n.* (*Naut.*) Fra i ponti, sottocoperta, *f.*

tweezers [ˈtwiːzəɹz], *n.pl.* Pinzette, *f.pl.*

twelfth [twelfθ], *n.a.* Dodicesimo, *m.* **Twelfth Night,** la notte dell'epifania, la notte dei re.

twelve [twelv], *n.a.* Dodici, *m.* **— o'clock noon,** le dodici, *f.pl.*, mezzogiorno, mezzodì; **— o'clock at night,** le ventiquattro, *f.pl.*, mezzanotte, *f.*

twelvemonth, *n.* Anno, *m.* **To-day —,** fra un anno.

twentieth [ˈtwentiəθ], *n.a.* Ventesimo, *m.*

twenty, *n.a.* Venti, *m.* **—-one,** ventuno; **— first,** ventunesimo, ventesimo primo.

twice [twais], *adv.* Due volte. **— as much,** due volte tanto, il doppio.

twiddle [twidl], *v.t.* Far girare.

twig (1) [twig], *n.* Ramoscello, *m.*, verga, verghetta, *f.*
twig (2), *v.t.i.* (*colloq.*) Capire, afferrare l'idea.
twilight [ˈtwailait], *n.* Crepuscolo, *m.*, chiaroscuro, *m.* || *a.* Crepuscolare; oscuro, offuscato. — **sleep**, anestesia (per il parto), *f.*
twill [twil], *n.* Saia, *f.*, tessuto incrociato, tessuto spigato, *m.* || *v.t.* Spigare.
twilled, *a.* A spiga, spigato.
twin [twin], *a.* Gemello, doppio. || *n.* Gemello, *m.*, gemella, *f.* **Twins,** gemelli, *m.pl.*; — **-screw,** a due eliche.
twine [twain], *n.* Spago, *m.*, corda, cordicella, *f.* || *v.t.* Torcere, attortigliare; intrecciare, tessere; *v.i.* torcersi, attorcigliarsi. **To — around,** avvolgere.
twinge [twindʒ], *n.* Fitta, puntura, *f.* || *v.i.* Dolere, pungere.
twining [ˈtwainiŋ], *a.* (*Bot.*) Rampicante.
twinkle [twiŋkl], *v.i.* Scintillare, sfavillare, brillare, ammiccare, occhieggiare, strizzare gli occhi. || *n.* Scintillio, sfavillio, ammicco, *m.*, strizzatina, *f.*
twinkling, *a.* Scintillante, sfavillante, brillante. || *n.* Scintillio, sfavillio, *m.* **In the — of an eye,** in un batter d'occhio.
twirl [twəːɹl], *v.t.* Far roteare, far girare, mulinare; attorcigliare, arricciare; *v.i.* girare attorno, piroettare. || *n.* Mulinello, *m.*, rotazione, piroetta, *f.*
twist [twist], *v.t.* Torcere, storcere; strizzare; attorcere, contorcere; attorcigliare; intrecciare, *v.i.* torcersi, contorcersi, attorcigliarsi; avvolgersi. || *n.* Torsione, *f.*, torcimento, *m.*; cordoncino, filo ritorto, *m.*; vergola, *f.*; piega, voltata, curva, *f.*, giro, *m.*; tendenza, inclinazione, *f.*; contorsione, *f.* **To give a — to,** torcere, dare una strizzatina a **to — someone's words,** cambiar le carte in tavola.
twisted, *a.* Torto, ritorto; storto, contorto.
twister, *n.* Torcitore, *m.*; (*colloq.*) truffatore, *m.*
twisting, *n.* Torcitura, torsione, *f.*
twit [twit], *v.t.* Rimproverare, riprendere, biasimare. **To — with,** rimproverare di.
twitch [twitʃ], *n.* Spasimo, *m.*, contrazione, *f.*; strappo, *m.*, strappata, tirata, *f.* || *v.t.* Strappare, tirare; *v.i.* contrarsi, storcersi, contorcersi.
twitching, *n.* Spasimo, *m.*; contrazione, *f.* || *a.* Palpitante.
twitter, *v.i.* Cinguettare, pigolare. || *n.* Cinguettio, pigolio, *m.*; (*colloq.*) ansia, agitazione, *f.*
two [tuː], *n.a.* Due, *m.* **One or —,** pochi, *m.pl.*, uno o due; **in twos,** due a due, per due; — **heads are better than one,** due teste valgon più d'una; **to put — and — together,** procedere a fil di logica, vedere che due e due fanno quattro; **you have found that — can play at that game,** avete trovato pane pei vostri denti; **— -edged,** a due tagli, a doppio taglio; **— -handed,** a due mani; **— -legged,** bipede, a due gambe; (*Naut*) **— -master,** a due alberi; **— -seater,** biposto, *m.*; — **-way switch,** interruttore bipolare, *m.*
twofold, *a.* Doppio. || *adv.* Due volte.
twopence [ˈtʌpəns], *n.pl.* Quattro soldi, *m.pl.*
twopenny [ˈtʌpəni], *a.* Di quattro soldi; (*fig.*) povero, meschino.
tycoon [taiˈkuːn], *n.* Taicun, *m.*; (*colloq.*) grosso uomo d'affari, *m.*
tympan, tympanum [ˈtimpən, ˈtimpənəm], *n.* Timpano, *m.*
type [taip], *n.* Tipo, modello, emblema, *m.*; (*Print.*) carattere tipografico, *m.* || *v.t.i.* Scrivere a macchina, dattilografare. (*Print.*) **— -face,** occhio dei caratteri, *m.*; **— -founder,** fonditore di caratteri, *m.*; **— -metal,** metallo per caratteri, *m.*; **— -script,** dattiloscritto, *m.*; **— -setter,** compositore, *m.*; **— -setting,** composizione, *f.*; **to set up in —,** comporre.
typewrite, *v.t.* Scrivere a macchina, dattilografare.
typewriter, *n.* Macchina da scrivere, *f.*
typewriting, *n.* Dattilografia, *f.*
typewritten, *a.* Scritto a macchina, dattilografato.
typhoid [ˈtaifɔid], *n.* (*Med.*) Tifoide, *f.*
typhoon [taiˈfuːn], *n.* Tifone, *m.*
typhus [ˈtaifəs], *n.* (*Med.*) Tifo, *m.*
typical [ˈtipikəl], *a.* Tipico.
typically, *adv.* Tipicamente.
typify [ˈtipifai], *v.t.* Figurare, rappresentare, impersonare, simbolizzare.
typist [ˈtaipist], *n.* Dattilografo, *m.*, dattilografa, *f.*
typographer [taiˈpɔgrəfəɹ], *n.* Tipografo, *m.*
typographic, typographical [taipoˈgræfik, taipoˈgræfikəl], *a.* Tipografico.
typography [taiˈpɔgrəfi], *n.* Tipografia, *f.*
tyrannic, tyrannical [tiˈrænik, tiˈrænikəl], *a.* Tirannico.
tyrannically, *adv.* Tirannicamente.
tyrannicide [tiˈrænisaid], *n.* (*act*) Tirannicidio, *m.*; (*person*) tirannicida, *m.*
tyrannize [ˈtirənaiz], *v.i.* Tiranneggiare. **To — over,** tiranneggiare.
tyranny [ˈtirəni], *n.* Tirannia, *f.*
tyrant [ˈtairənt], *n.* Tiranno, *m.* **Petty —,** tirannello, *m.*
tyre, tire [taiɹ], *n.* (*pneumatic*) Pneumatico, *m.*, gomma, *f.*; copertone, *m.* **The — is punctured,** il pneumatico è forato; **to put on a —,** mettere una gomma.
tyro [cp. **tiro**].
Tyrol [ˈtirəl], *n.* (*Geog.*) Tirolo, *m.*
Tyrolese [tirəˈliːz], *n.a.* Tirolese, *m.f.*
Tyrrhene, Tyrrhenian [tiˈriːn, tiˈriːniən], *a.* (*Geog.*) Tirreno, tirrenico.
Tzigany [ˈtzigəni], *n.a.* Zingaro, *m.*, Zingara, *f.*

U

U, u [juː], Ventunesima lettera dell'alfabeto inglese.
ubiquitous [juːˈbikwitəs], *a.* Onnipresente.
ubiquity, *n.* Ubiquità, *f.*
udal [ˈjuːdəl], *a.* (*Law*) Allodiale.
udder [ˈʌdəɹ], *n.* Mammella, poppa, *f.*
udometer [juːˈdɔmetəɹ], *n.* Udometro, *m.*
ugh! [uː], *inter.* Puh! Oibò!
uglily [ˈʌglili], *adv.* Bruttamente.
ugliness, *n.* Bruttezza, deformità, *f.*
ugly, *a.* Brutto; laido; deforme; turpe. **As — as sin,** brutto come il peccato; **to grow —,** imbruttire; **— weather,** brutto tempo, *m.*; **an — scene,** una brutta scenata, *f.*
uhlan [ˈuːlɑːn], *n.* (*Mil.*) Ulano, *m.*
ukase [juːˈkeiz], *n.* Decreto, editto, *m.*
ukulele [juːkəˈleili], *n.* Ukulele, *m.*, chitarra delle Hawai, *f.*

ulcer [ˈʌlsəɹ], *n.* (*Med.*) Ulcera, *f.*
ulcerate, *v.t.* Ulcerare; *v.i.* ulcerarsi.
ulceration, *n.* Ulcerazione, *f.*
ulcered, *a.* Ulcerato.
ulcerous, *a.* Ulceroso.
uliginose [juːˈlidʒinəs], *a.* Acquoso.
ullage [ˈʌlidʒ], *n.* Quantità di liquido per completare una botte, *f.*
ulna [ˈʌlnə], *n.* (*Anat.*) Ulna, *f.*
ulster [ˈʌlstəɹ], *n.* Ulster, cappotto lungo, *m.*
ulterior [ʌlˈtiəriəɹ], *a.* Ulteriore. **With — motives,** con un secondo fine.
ulteriorly, *adv.* Ulteriormente.
ultimate [ˈʌltimit], *a.* Ultimo, estremo, finale, definitivo.
ultimately, *adv.* Ultimamente, alla fine.
ultimatum (pl. **ultimata**) [ʌltiˈmeitəm, ʌltiˈmeitə], *n.* Ultimatum, *m.*
ultimo, ult. [ˈʌltimou, ʌlt], *adv.* Scorso, del mese passato.
ultra [ˈʌltrə], *a.* Ultra.
ultramarine [ʌltrəməˈriːn], *n.a.* Oltremarino, oltremare; azzurro oltremare, *m.*
ultramontane [ʌltrəmɔnˈtein], *a.* (*Eccles.*) Oltremontano.
ultramundane [ʌltrəmʌnˈdein], *a.* Oltremondano.
ultra-violet [ʌltrəˈvaiolet], *a.* Ultravioletto. **— rays,** raggi ultravioletti, *m.pl.*
ultravires [ʌltrəˈvairiːz], *adv.* In eccesso di potere.
ululate [ˈʌljuːleit], *v.i.* Ululare.
ululation, *n.* Ululato, *m.*
Ulysses [juːˈlisiːz], *n.* Ulisse, *m.*
umbel [ˈʌmbəl], *n.* (*Bot.*) Umbella, ombrella, *f.*
umbelliferous [ʌmbelˈifərəs], *a.* Umbellifere, ombrellifere.
umber [ˈʌmbəɹ], *n.* Terra d'ombra, *f.*; (*Zool.*) ombrino, *m.*
umbilical [ʌmˈbilikəl], *a.* Ombilicale. **— cord,** cordone umbilicale, *m.*
umbilicate, *a.* Ombilicato.
umbilicus [ʌmbiˈlaikəs], *n.* (*Anat.*) Umbilico, ombelico, *m.*
umbrage [ˈʌmbridʒ], *n.* Offesa, *f.*; ombra, *f.* **To take — at,** offendersi per, inalberarsi per, prender ombra per; **to give — to,** offendere, dare ombra a.
umbrageous [ʌmˈbreidʒəs], *a.* Ombroso, ombreggiante.
umbrella [ʌmˈbrelə], *n.* Ombrello, *m.*; paracqua, *m.* **— -frame,** armatura d'ombrello, *f.*; **— -ring,** ghiera d'ombrello, *f.*; **— stick,** *n.* bastone d'ombrello, *m.*; **— -stand,** portaombrelli, *m.*
Umbrian [ˈʌmbriən], *a* (*Geog.*) Umbro.
umpire [ˈʌmpaiɹ], *n.* Arbitro, *m.* ‖ *v.t.i.* Arbitrare, fare da arbitro.
un- [ʌn], *prefix.* Non-, in-, s-, senza, dis-.
unabashed, *a.* Svergognato, senza vergogna.
unabated, *a.* Non scemato, sostenuto; infaticabile; implacato, inesorabile.
unable, *a.* Incapace, inabile. **To be — to,** non potere, non essere capace di, non essere in grado di; **I am — to come,** non posso venire.
unabridged, *a.* Intero, completo.
unaccented, *a.* Senza accento; (*Gram.*) atono.
unacceptable, *a.* Inaccettabile.
unacceptableness, *n.* Inaccettabilità, *f.*
unaccepted, *a.* (*Comm.*) Respinto.
unaccommodating, *a.* Scortese, poco condiscendente.
unaccompanied, *a.* Senza compagno; (*Mus.*) senza accompagnamento.
unaccomplished, *a.* Incompiuto.
unaccountable, *a.* Inesplicabile; strano, bizzarro.
unaccountableness, *n.* Inesplicabilità, *f.*; stranezza, bizzarria, *f.*
unaccountably, *adv.* Inesplicabilmente; stranamente.
unaccredited, *a.* Non accreditato, non autorizzato.
unaccustomed, *a.* Insolito, poco abituato; straordinario. **To be — to,** non essere abituato a.
unacknowledged, *a.* Non riconosciuto; (*of letters*) senza risposta.
unacquainted, *a.* Ignaro di; poco abituato a; poco pratico di. **To be — with someone,** non conoscere qualcuno.
unacquired, *a.* Naturale.
unactable, *a.* Irrecitabile.
unadapted, *a.* Inadatto, non adattato.
unaddressed, *a.* Senza indirizzo.
unadjusted, *a.* Non aggiustato, non assestato.
unadmonished, *a.* Senza rimprovero.
unadorned, *a.* Disadorno, senz'ornamenti; naturale, semplice.
unadulterated, *a.* Non adulterato, non sofisticato, schietto, puro.
unadvisable, unadvised, *a.* Sconsigliabile, imprudente, inconsulto, sconveniente.
unaffected, *a.* Non affettato, inaffettato; disinvolto, sincero, semplice.
unaffectedly, *adv.* Semplicemente; sinceramente.
unaffectedness, *n.* Disinvoltura, semplicità, sincerità, *f.*
unafraid, *a.* Senza paura.
unaided, *a.* Solo, senza aiuto.
unalienable, *a.* Inalienabile.
unallayed, *a.* Non placato, non diminuito.
unalloyed, *a.* Senza lega; puro.
unalterable, *a.* Inalterabile, immutabile.
unalterably, *adv.* Inalterabilmente.
unaltered, *a.* Inalterato, immutato, costante.
unambiguous, *a.* Senza ambiguità, senza equivoco, inequivocabile.
unambiguously, *adv.* Chiaramente, inequivocabilmente.
unambitious, *a.* Senza ambizioni, modesto.
unamiable, *a.* Poco amabile, burbero.
unanimity [juːnəˈnimiti], *n.* Unanimità, *f.*
unanimous [juːˈnæniməs], *a.* Unanime.
unanimously, *adv.* Unanimemente, all'unanimità. **Carried —,** approvato all'unanimità.
unannounced, *a.* Senza preavviso, improvviso, imprevisto.
unanswerable, *a.* Irrefutabile, innegabile, incontestabile.
unanswerably, *adv.* Irrefutabilmente.
unanswered, *a.* Senza risposta.
unappeased, *a.* Insoddisfatto.
unappetizing, *a.* Poco appetitoso.

Unless otherwise indicated, the pronunciation of words prefixed by "un" can be ascertained by reference to the unprefixed words or their derivatives in their alphabetical position in this dictionary.

unappreciated, *a.* Inapprezzato, incompreso, svalutato.
unapprehensive, *a.* Non apprensivo, inapprensivo.
unapproachable, *a.* Inaccessibile, inaccostabile, inabbordabile.
unarm, *v.t.* Disarmare.
unarmed, *a.* Inerme, indifeso.
unascertainable, *a.* Inaccertabile.
unascertained, *a.* Inappurato.
unashamed, *a.* Senza vergogna, svergognato, spudorato.
unasked, *a.* Senza invito, non richiesto; spontaneo. || *adv.* Spontaneamente.
unaspiring, *a.* Poco ambizioso.
unassailable, *a.* Inattaccabile; incontestabile.
unassisted, *a.* Senza aiuto, tutto solo.
unassuming, *a.* Senza pretesa, modesto, alla buona.
unassured, *a.* Non assicurato.
unatoned, *a.* Inespiato.
unattached, *a.* Libero; (*Mil.*) in disponibilità.
unattainable, *a.* Irraggiungibile, inaccessibile.
unattempted, *a.* Intentato.
unattended, *a.* Solo, senza seguito; incustodito; negletto. **To leave a car —,** lasciar l'auto incustodita.
unattested, *a.* Non comprovato.
unattractive, *a.* Poco attraente, antipatico.
unauthentic, *a.* Non autentico, spurio, falso.
unauthenticated, *a.* Non autenticato.
unauthorized, *a.* Non autorizzato; illecito, illegale, abusivo.
unavailable, *a.* Indisponibile, occupato, impegnato.
unavailing, *a.* Inutile, vano, inefficace.
unavenged, *a.* Non vendicato, impunito.
unavoidable, *a.* Inevitabile.
unavoidableness, *n.* Inevitabilità.
unavoidably, *adv.* Inevitabilmente. **— absent,** assente per forza maggiore.
unaware, *a.* Inconsapevole, ignaro. **To be — of,** ignorare, non sapere.
unawares, *adv.* Alla sprovvista, improvvisamente, di sorpresa, impensatamente. **To be taken —,** essere preso alla sprovvista.
unbacked, *a.* Senza appoggio.
unbaked, *a.* Non cotto, malcotto.
unbalanced, *a.* Squilibrato.
unbandage, *v.t.* Sbendare, togliere la benda a.
unbaptized, *a.* Non battezzato.
unbar, *v.t.* Aprire, disserrare, levare le barre a.
unbearable, *a.* Insopportabile, intollerabile.
unbearably, *adv.* Insopportabilmente.
unbeaten, *a.* Invitto, insuperato; non frequentato.
unbecoming, *a.* Sconveniente, indecoroso, disdicevole, sconvenevole; (*of clothes*) che non sta bene.
unbecomingly, *adv.* Sconvenientemente; goffamente.
unbefitting, *a.* Sconvenevole, disdicevole.
unbefriended, *a.* Senza amici.
unbeknownst [ʌnbiˈnounst], *a.* All'insaputa di.
unbelief, *n.* Incredulità, mancanza di fede, *f.*; scetticismo, *m.*, miscredenza, *f.*
unbeliever, *n.* Incredulo, scettico, miscredente, *m.*
unbend, *v.t.* (*to straighten*) Raddrizzare; rilassare, stendere; (*Naut.*) sciogliere; *v.i.* raddrizzarsi, stendersi; (*fig.*) rilassarsi, spianare la fronte, raddolcirsi, divenire affabile.
unbending, *a.* Inflessibile, austero, rigido.
unbendingly, *adv.* Inflessibilmente.
unbiased, *a.* Imparziale, spregiudicato.
unbidden, *adv.* Spontaneamente, volontariamente; senza invito. || *a.* Volontario; senza invito.
unbind, *v.t.* Slegare, sciogliere.
unblamable, *a.* Irreprensibile.
unbleached, *a.* Greggio, non imbiancato.
unblemished, *a.* Senza taccia; puro, perfetto, intatto.
unblest, *a.* Senza benedizione; infelice, sfortunato; maledetto.
unblotted, *a.* Non asciugato.
unblushing, *a.* Sfacciato, spudorato, senza vergogna, svergognato.
unblushingly, *adv.* Sfacciatamente, senza vergogna.
unbolt, *v.t.* Disserrare, aprire, levare il catenaccio.
unbolted, *a.* Disserrato, aperto; (*of flour*) non stacciato, non abburattato.
unborn, *a.* Non nato; futuro, da venire; di là da venire. **Innocent as a babe —,** innocente come una creatura non ancora nata.
unbosom, *v.t.* Scoprire, svelare, rivelare. **To —oneself,** sfogarsi, sbottonarsi, confidarsi con.
unbound, *a.* Slegato, sciolto; liberato, libero; (*of books*) non legato, non rilegato.
unbounded, *a.* Illimitato, smisurato, sconfinato, infinito; libero, sciolto; sfrenato.
unbowed [ʌnˈbaud], *a.* Invitto, indomito.
unbreakable, *a.* Infrangibile.
unbreathable, *a.* Irrespirabile.
unbred, *a.* Maleducato.
unbreeched, *a.* Senza calzoni.
unbribable, *a.* Incorruttibile.
unbridled, *a.* Sfrenato, sbrigliato.
unbroken, *a.* Intatto; invitto; ininterrotto, continuo; inviolato; (*of horse*) indomato, indomabile.
unbrotherly, *a.* Poco fraterno.
unbuckle, *v.t.* Sfibbiare.
unburden, *v.t.* Scaricare, sgravare. **To — oneself,** sfogarsi.
unburied, *a.* Insepolto.
unbusinesslike, *a.* Poco pratico, senza metodo, sconclusionato.
unbutton, *v.t.* Sbottonare.
uncage, *v.t.* Sgabbiare, liberare.
uncalled, *a.* Non chiamato. **— for,** non necessario, gratuito, immeritato, fuor di proposito.
uncancelled, *a.* Non annullato.
uncandid, *a.* Poco franco, insincero.
uncanny, *a.* Soprannaturale, strano, fantastico, magico.
uncap, *v.i.* Scappellarsi.
uncapsizable, *a.* Che non si può capovolgere.
uncared-for, *a.* Negletto, in abbandono, trascurato.
uncarpeted, *a.* Senza tappeto.
uncaught, *a.* Libero, in libertà.

Unless otherwise indicated, the pronunciation of words prefixed by "un" can be ascertained by reference to the unprefixed words or their derivatives in their alphabetical position in this dictionary.

unceasing, *a.* Incessante, continuo.
unceasingly, *adv.* Incessantemente, continuamente.
uncensured, *a.* Incensurato.
unceremonious, *a.* Poco cerimonioso, spicciativo.
unceremoniously, *adv.* Senza cerimonie.
uncertain, *a.* Incerto, dubbio, malsicuro, indeciso, ambiguo; (*of footsteps*) barcollante.
uncertainly, *a.* Incertamente, dubbiamente.
uncertainty, *n.* Incertezza, *f.*, dubbio, *m.*; indecisione, *f.*
unchain, *v.t.* Scatenare, sciogliere, liberare.
unchangeable, *a.* Immutabile, costante, inalterabile.
unchangeableness, *n.* Immutabilità, costanza, inalterabilità, *f.*
unchangeably, *adv.* Immutabilmente, costantemente.
unchanged, *a.* Immutato, inalterato.
unchanging, *a.* Invariabile, costante.
uncharged-for, *a.* Gratuito, gratis; (*Comm.*) franco.
uncharitable, *a.* Incaritatevole; aspro, duro.
uncharitableness, *n.* Mancanza di carità, asprezza, durezza, *f.*
uncharitably, *adv.* Aspramente, duramente.
uncharted, *a.* Non registrato nelle carte geografiche.
unchaste, *a.* Non casto, impuro, impudico, lascivo.
unchastely, *adv.* Impudicamente.
unchecked, *a.* Sfrenato, sbrigliato; incontrollato, non verificato.
unchivalrous, *a.* Poco cavalleresco, poco generoso; villano, scortese.
unchristian, *a.* Poco cristiano, barbaro, inumano; pagano; incaritatevole.
uncial [ˈʌnsiəl], *n.a.* Onciale, *m.*
uncircumcised, *a.* Incirconciso.
uncircumscribed, *a.* Non circoscritto.
uncircumspect, *a.* Imprudente, disavveduto.
uncivil, *a.* Scortese, grossolano, villano.
uncivilized, *a.* Incivile, barbaro, selvaggio.
uncivilly, *adv.* Scortesemente.
unclad, *a.* Nudo.
unclaimed, *a.* Non reclamato.
unclasp, *v.t.* Sfibbiare; staccare, mollare.
uncle [ʌŋkl], *n.* Zio, *m.* (*colloq.*) **I'm going to uncle's,** vado al monte di pietà.
unclean, *a.* Sporco, sudicio; impudico; impuro, immondo.
uncleanly, *a.* Sporco, sudicio.
uncleanness, *n.* Sporcizia, sudiceria, *f.*; impudicizia, *f.*
uncleansed, *a.* Non pulito.
unclench, *v.t.* Disserrare, aprire.
unclipped, *a.* Non tagliato; non tosato.
uncloak, *v.t.* Levare il manto; scoprire; smascherare.
unclothe, *v.t.* Svestire; *v.i.* svestirsi.
unclothed, *a.* Spogliato, svestito, nudo.
unclouded, *a.* Senza nuvole, sereno.
uncock, *v.t.* (*a gun*) Disarmare, scaricare.
uncoil, *v.t.* Svolgere, spiegare, snodare.
uncollected, *a.* Non raccolto, sparso; non riscosso, non ricevuto.
uncoloured, *a.* Incoloro, senza colore; naturale, semplice.
uncombed, *a.* Arruffato, in disordine.
uncomeatable [ʌnkʌmˈætəbl], *a.* (*colloq.*) Inaccessibile.
uncomely, *a.* Brutto, bruttino, sgraziato; sconvenevole.
uncomfortable, *a.* Scomodo, incomodo; non a suo agio, a disagio; fuori di posto, inquieto; penoso, increscioso. **I am very — here,** non mi trovo bene qui.
uncomfortably, *adv.* Scomodamente.
uncommercial, *a.* Non commerciale.
uncommitted, *a.* Non commesso.
uncommon, *a.* Raro, non comune, straordinario.
uncommonly, *adv.* Singolarmente, straordinariamente; assai, molto.
uncommonness, *n.* Rarità, singolarità, *f.*
uncommunicative, *a.* Taciturno, riservato, chiuso.
uncommunicativeness, *n.* Taciturnità, riservatezza, *f.*
uncompanionable, *a.* Insocievole.
uncomplaining, *a.* Rassegnato.
uncomplainingly, *adv.* Rassegnatamente, senza lagnarsi.
uncompleted, *a.* Incompiuto.
uncomplicated, *a.* Senza complicazioni, semplice.
uncomplimentary, *a.* Poco lusinghiero.
uncompromising, *a.* Intransigente, irriducibile, inflessibile.
uncompromisingly, *adv.* Inflessibilmente.
unconcealed, *a.* Aperto, manifesto.
unconcern, *n.* Noncuranza, indifferenza, *f.*
unconcerned, *a.* Indifferente, noncurante.
unconcernedly, *adv.* Indifferentemente.
unconciliatory, *a.* Poco conciliativo.
uncondemned, *a.* Non condannato.
unconditional, *a.* Incondizionato, assoluto, senza condizioni. **— surrender,** resa incondizionata, resa senza condizioni.
unconditionally, *adv.* Assolutamente, senza condizioni.
unconfined, *a.* Libero; illimitato.
unconfirmed, *a.* Non confermato.
unconformable, *a.* Incompatibile con, contrario a.
uncongenial, *a.* Antipatico, incompatibile; spiacevole, noioso.
unconnected, *a.* Estraneo a; separato, distaccato.
unconquerable, *a.* Invincibile, insuperabile; indomabile.
unconquerably, *adv.* Invincibilmente.
unconquered, *a.* Invitto, insuperato; indomito, indomato.
unconscionable [ʌnˈkɔnʃənəbl], *a.* Eccessivo, esorbitante, smisurato.
unconscionably, *adv.* Eccessivamente.
unconscious, *a.* Inconscio, inconsapevole, ignaro; incosciente, privo di coscienza, svenuto. **He lay — for two hours,** rimase privo di coscienza per due ore; **— of one's fate,** inconsapevole della propria sorte.
unconsciously, *adv.* Inconsciamente, inconsapevolmente, senza saperlo.
unconsciousness, *n.* Inconsapevolezza, ignoranza, *f.*, svenimento, *m.*

Unless otherwise indicated, the pronunciation of words prefixed by "un" can be ascertained by reference to the unprefixed words or their derivatives in their alphabetical position in this dictionary.

unconsecrated, *a.* Non consacrato, non sacro.
unconsenting, *a.* (*Law*) Non consenziente.
unconsidered, *a.* Sprezzato; trascurato, negletto.
unconstitutional, *a.* Incostituzionale.
unconstrained, *a.* Libero, spontaneo, disinvolto, naturale.
unconstrainedly, *adv.* Liberamente, spontaneamente.
unconstraint, *n.* Disinvoltura, scioltezza, *f.*, abbandono, *m.*
unconsumed, *a.* Non consumato, non mangiato.
uncontaminated, *a.* Incontaminato.
uncontemplated, *a.* Inaspettato, imprevisto.
uncontested, *a.* Incontrastato, incontestato.
uncontradicted, *a.* Non contraddetto, senza contraddizione.
uncontrollable, *a.* Indomabile, irrefrenabile; inestinguibile, incontrollabile.
uncontrollably, *adv.* Irrefrenabilmente.
uncontrolled, *a.* Libero, sfrenato.
unconventional, *a.* Non convenzionale; disinvolto.
unconverted, *a.* Non convertito.
unconvinced, *a.* Non convinto, non persuaso.
unconvincing, *a.* Non convincente, non persuasivo.
uncooked, *a.* Crudo.
uncord, *v.t.* Slegare.
uncork, *v.t.* Sturare, stappare.
uncorrected, *a.* Non corretto.
uncorroborated, *a.* Non-comprovato.
uncorrupted, *a.* Incorrotto, incontaminato.
uncounted, *a.* Non numerato.
uncouple, *v.t.* Staccare, sconnettere, disgiungere.
uncourtly, *a.* Scortese, sgarbato, rozzo.
uncouth [ʌn'ku:θ], *a.* Goffo, impacciato, rozzo, grossolano; strano.
uncouthness, *n.* Goffaggine, grossolanità rozzezza, *f.*
uncover, *v.t.* Scoprire, spogliare, denudare; *v.i.* scappellarsi. **With head uncovered,** a capo scoperto.
uncreated, *a.* Increato, non creato.
uncritical, *a.* Accontentabile.
uncross, *v.t.* Disincrociare (le gambe).
uncrossed, *a.* Non traversato; aperto; (*of cheque*) non sbarrato.
uncrowned, *a.* Senza corona.
unction ['ʌŋkʃən], *n.* Unzione, *f.*; fervore, *m.*; gusto, *m.*, soddisfazione, *f.*
unctuous, *a.* Untuoso.
unctuously, *adv.* Untuosamente.
uncultivated, *a.* Incolto.
uncultured, *a.* Incolto.
uncurbed, *a.* Sfrenato, indomito.
uncurl, *v.t.i.* Disfare, disfare i ricci, disfarsi.
uncurtailed, *a.* Non raccorciato; non scemato, non diminuito.
uncushioned, *a.* Senza cuscini.
uncustomary, *a.* Insolito, inusato.
uncustomed, *a.* (*Comm.*) Non dichiarato in dogana; esente da dazio.
uncut, *a.* Non tagliato; intero; (*of book*) intonso.
undamaged, *a.* Intatto; non guasto, in buone condizioni; non avariato.
undamped, *a.* Non smorzato, non scemato, non diminuito; non scoraggiato.
undated, *a.* Senza data, non datato.
undaunted, *a.* Intrepido, imperterrito.
undauntedly, *adv.* Intrepidamente.
undauntedness, *n.* Intrepidezza, *f.*
undeceive, *v.t.* Disingannare, sgannare, disilludere.
undecided, *a.* Indeciso, incerto; irresoluto, vacillante.
undecipherable, *a.* Indecifrabile.
undefended, *a.* Indefeso; senza difensore.
undefiled, *a.* Incorrotto, immacolato, puro.
undefinable, *a.* Indefinibile.
undefined, *a.* Indefinito, indeterminato.
undelivered, *a.* Non recapitato.
undemonstrable, *a.* Indimostrabile.
undemonstrative, *a.* Riservato, chiuso.
undeniable, *a.* Innegabile, incontrastabile.
undenominational, *a.* Laico, neutro.
under ['ʌndəɹ], *prep.* Sotto, disotto a, al disotto di, inferiore a; a meno di, meno di. ‖ *adv.* Sotto, abbasso, di sotto. ‖ *a.* Inferiore, di sotto, sotto, subalterno. **You cannot buy it — a pound,** non si può comprarlo a meno di una sterlina; **he will be back in — an hour,** sarà di ritorno in meno di un'ora; **to speak — one's breath,** parlare sottovoce; **to be — an obligation to,** avere un obbligo con, essere in obbligo verso; **to sell — price,** vendere sotto prezzo; **the house is — repair,** la casa è in riparazione; **to be — a delusion,** avere un'allucinazione, avere un'idea falsa; **— age,** minorenne; **— arms,** sotto le armi; **— consideration,** in esame; **— cover of night,** col favore della notte; (*fig.*) **— cover of,** sotto colore di, sotto il pretesto di; **— fire,** esposto al fuoco, sotto il fuoco; (*Naut.*) **— sail,** sotto vela; **— separate cover,** sotto fascia; **to go —,** soccombere, andar sotto; **to keep —,** contenere, reprimere.
underact, *v.t.* (*Theat.*) Recitare freddamente.
underbelly, *n.* Pancia (degli animali), *f.*
underbid, *v.t.* Fare offerta più bassa di.
underbred, *a.* Maleducato, malcreato.
under-carriage, *n.* (*Aviat.*) Carrello di atterraggio, *m.*
underclothes ['ʌndəɹklouðz], *n.pl.* Sottovesti, *f.pl.*
underclothing ['ʌndəɹklouðiŋ], *n.* Biancheria, *f.*
undercrust ['ʌndəɹkrʌst], *n.* Crosta di sotto, *f.*
undercurrent ['ʌndəɹkʌrənt], *n.* Sottocorrente, *f.*; corrente secondaria, *f.*; influsso segreto, *m.*
undercut ['ʌndəɹkʌt], *n.* (*of meat*) Filetto, *m.*; (*Boxing*) colpo di taglio, *m.*
underdone [ʌndəɹ'dʌn], *a.* Poco cotto, al sangue.
underestimate [ʌndəɹ'estimeit], *v.t.* Svalutare, sminuire, deprezzare.
under-expose [ʌndəɹeks'pouz], *v.t.* (*Phot.*) Dare posa insufficiente a.
under-exposure, *n.* (*Phot.*) Posa insufficiente, *f.*
underfed [ʌndəɹ'fed], *a.* Denutrito.
underfoot [ʌndəɹ'fut], *adv.* Sotto i piedi. **To trample —,** calpestare.

Unless otherwise indicated, the pronunciation of words prefixed by "un" can be ascertained by reference to the unprefixed words or their derivatives in their alphabetical position in this dictionary.

under-gardener ['ʌndəɹgɑːɹdənəɹ], *n.* Aiutante giardiniere, *m.*
undergarment ['ʌndəɹgɑːɹmənt], *n.* Sottoveste, *f.*
undergo [ʌndəɹ'gou], *v.t.* Subire, patire, soffrire, sottoporsi a. **To — an operation,** subire un'operazione.
undergraduate [ʌndəɹ'grædjuːeit], *n.* Studente universitario, *m.*
underground ['ʌndəɹgraund], *a.* Sotterraneo. || *adv.* Sotterra. || *n.* (*Rail.*) Ferrovia sotterranea, *f.*
undergrowth ['ʌndəɹgrouθ], *n.* Boscaglia, *f.*, sterpi, arbusti, *m.pl.*
underhand ['ʌndəɹhænd], *adv.* Clandestinamente, sottomano, di soppiatto, segretamente, di nascosto. || *a.* Clandestino, segreto, nascosto; furbo; astuto; (*Tennis*) inverso. **— dealings,** mene segrete, *f.pl.*
underhung [ʌndəɹ'hʌŋ], *a.* Sporgente.
underlay [ʌndəɹ'lei], *v.t.* Metter sotto. *n.* ['ʌndəɹlei], (*Print.*) Alzo, *m.*
underlease ['ʌndəɹliːs], *n.* Subaffitto, *m.*
underlet [ʌndəɹ'let], *v.t.* Subaffittare.
underlie [ʌndəɹ'lai], *v.i.* Stare sotto, sottostare; (*fig.*) star alla base di, formar la base di.
underline [ʌndəɹ'lain], *v.t.* Sottolineare.
underlinen ['ʌndəɹlinin], *n.* Biancheria personale, *f.*
underling ['ʌndəɹliŋ], *n.* Subalterno, inferiore, *m.*; agente, strumento, *m.*
underlying [ʌndəɹ'laiiŋ], *a.* Basilare, angolare, sotterraneo, fondamentale; sottostante.
underman [ʌndəɹ'mæn], *v.t.* Equipaggiare scarsamente; fornire di personale insufficiente.
undermentioned [ʌndəɹ'menʃənd], *a.* Sottomenzionato, sottoindicato.
undermine [ʌndəɹ'main], *v.t.* Sottominare, minare; (*fig.*) scalzare, minare, scardinare. **To — confidence in,** far perdere fiducia in.
undermost ['ʌndəɹmoust], *a.* Il più basso, l'ultimo.
underneath [ʌndəɹ'niːθ], *prep.* Sotto, di sotto. || *adv.* Sotto, abbasso, al di sotto. **From —,** dal di sotto di.
underpay [ʌndəɹ'pei], *v.t.* Pagare insufficientemente, pagar male.
underpin [ʌndəɹ'pin], *v.t.* Puntellare, sottomurare.
underproduction [ʌndəɹpro'dʌkʃən], *n.* Sottoproduzione, produzione insufficiente, *f.*
underprop [ʌndəɹ'prɔp], *v.t.* Puntellare.
underrate [ʌndəɹ'reit], *v.t.* Svalutare, sminuire, deprezzare, tenere in poco conto.
under-ripe [ʌndəɹ'raip], *a.* Immaturo, acerbo.
underscore [ʌndəɹ'skɔːɹ], *v.t.* Sottolineare.
under-sea ['ʌndəɹsiː], *a.* Sottomarino.
under-secretary [ʌndəɹ'sekretəri], *n.* Sottosegretario, *m.*
undersell [ʌndəɹ'sel], *v.t.* Svendere, vendere meno caro di.
under-servant ['ʌndəɹsəːɹvənt], *n.* Domestico, *m.*
under-sheriff [ʌndəɹ'ʃerif], *n.* Sottosceriffo, *m.*
undershot ['ʌndəɹʃɔt], *a.* (*of mill wheel*) A pala.
underside ['ʌndəɹ'said], *n.* Disotto, *m.*; rovescio, *m.*
undersigned [ʌndəɹ'saind], *n.a.* Sottoscritto, *m.*
undersized [ʌndəɹ'saizd], *a.* Di statura bassa, piccolo, stentato.
underskirt ['ʌndəɹskəːɹt], *n.* Sottogonna, *f.*
understand [ʌndəɹ'stænd], *v.t.* Capire, comprendere, intendere; pensare, credere, essere informato di; sottintendere. **Am I to — that . . .?** Devo credere che . . .? **Do you — ?** Avete capito? Capite? **it is understood that . . .,** s'intende che . . ., resta inteso che . . .; **there is no understanding his motives,** non si riesce a capire i suoi moventi; **to give to —,** far sapere, informare; **to make oneself understood,** farsi capire; **they — one another,** essi si capiscono; **I don't — anything about it,** non mi ci raccapezzo.
understandable, *a.* Intelligibile, comprensibile.
understanding, *n.* Intelligenza, comprensione, *f.*; intelletto, *m.*; giudizio, *m.*; accordo, *m.*; intesa, *f.* **A good —,** una intelligenza fine, *f.*; **there is an — between them,** se la intendono, sono d'accordo, c'è un'intesa fra loro; **on the — that,** a condizione che, restando inteso che; **to come to an — with,** intendersi con, accordarsi con, venire a un accordo.
understandingly, *adv.* Intelligentemente; simpaticamente.
understate [ʌndəɹ'steit], *v.t.* Dir meno del vero, attenuare.
understatement, *n.* Attenuazione, reticenza, parsimonia verbale, *f.*; affermazione incompleta, *f.*
understood [ʌndəɹ'stud], *a.* Inteso, compreso, capito, sottinteso.
understrapper ['ʌndəɹstræpəɹ], *n.* Impiegato subalterno, *m.*; (*vulg.*) tirapiedi, *m.*
understudy ['ʌndəɹstʌdi], *n.* (*Theat.*) Sostituto, attore supplente, *m.*, attrice supplente, *f.* || *v.t.* Fare da supplente.
undertake [ʌndəɹ'teik], *v.t.* Intraprendere, incaricarsi di, impegnarsi a, obbligarsi a, assumere. **I will — to say,** non ho paura di dire; **I will — that you will be safe,** m'incarico io della vostra sicurezza.
undertaker ['ʌndəɹteikəɹ], *n.* Agente di pompe funebri, *m.*
undertaking [ʌndəɹ'teikiŋ], *n.* Impresa, *f.* impegno, *m.* **To give an —,** impegnarsi; **a written —,** un impegno scritto, *m.*
under-tenant ['ʌndəɹtenənt], *n.* Subaffittuario, *m.*
undertone ['ʌndəɹtoun], *n.* Tono basso. **In an —,** sottovoce.
undertow ['ʌndəɹtou], *n.* Risucchio, *m.*, risacca, *f.*
undervaluation [ʌndəɹvæljuː'eiʃən], *n.* Svalutazione, *f.*
undervalue [ʌndəɹ'væljuː], *v.t.* Svalutare, deprezzare, sminuire, far poco conto di.
undervest ['ʌndəɹvest], *n.* Maglia, camiciuola, *f.*
underwear [cp. **underclothing**].
underworld ['ʌndəɹwəːɹld], *n.* Inferno, *m.*; (*colloq.*) i bassi fondi, *m.pl.*, la mala vita, *f.*
underwrite [ʌndəɹ'rait], *v.t.* Sottoscrivere, sottoscrivere per; garantire, assicurare.
underwriter ['ʌndəɹraitəɹ], *n.* Assicuratore, *m.*; mallevadore, garante, *m.*

Unless otherwise indicated, the pronunciation of words prefixed by "un" can be ascertained by reference to the unprefixed words or their derivatives in their alphabetical position in this dictionary.

underwriting, *n.* Sottoscrizione, assicurazione, *f.*
undeserved, *a.* Immeritato.
undeservedly, *adv.* Immeritatamente, immeritamente.
undeserving, *a.* Immeritevole, indegno.
undesigned, *a.* Involontario.
undesignedly, *adv.* Involontariamente, senza volerlo.
undesigning, *a.* Innocente, franco, schietto, leale.
undesirable, *a.* Non desiderabile, indesiderabile. **An — person,** una persona sgradita, *f.*
undesired, *a.* Non desiderato.
undesirous, *a.* Non desideroso, poco disposto a.
undetected, *a.* Non scoperto, non individuato.
undetermined, *a.* Indeterminato, indefinito; indeciso, irresoluto.
undeterred, *a.* Non spaventato, imperturbato.
undeveloped, *a.* Non sviluppato, incolto.
undeviating, *a.* Dritto, diretto; costante, fermo.
undigested, *a.* Non digerito, non assimilato, crudo.
undignified, *a.* Poco dignitoso, senza dignità.
undiminished, *a.* Intero, non diminuito.
undiplomatic, *a.* Poco diplomatico.
undirected, *a.* Senza direzione, senza indirizzo.
undiscerned, *a.* Inosservato.
undiscernible, *a.* Impercettibile.
undiscerning, *a.* Poco giudizioso.
undisciplined, *a.* Indisciplinato.
undisclosed, *a.* Segreto, nascosto.
undiscoverable, *a.* Introvabile, irreperibile.
undiscovered, *a.* Sconosciuto, inesplorato.
undisguised, *a.* Non mascherato; aperto, manifesto, evidente.
undismayed, *a.* Senza paura, imperterrito. **— by difficulties,** imperterrito dinanzi alle difficoltà.
undisputed, *a.* Indubitato, incontrastato, indiscusso.
undissolved, *a.* Non fuso, non sciolto.
undistinguished, *a.* Senza distinzione, poco distinto.
undistorted, *a.* Non distorto; vero, verace.
undistracted, *a.* Non distratto.
undisturbed, *a.* Imperturbato, tranquillo, calmo.
undivided, *a.* Indiviso, intero.
undo, *v.t.* Disfare, sfare; slacciare, slegare, sciogliere; distruggere, rovinare. **To come undone,** sciogliersi, slegarsi; **to leave undone,** tralasciar di fare; **to leave nothing undone,** non lasciar nulla di intentato.
undoing, *n.* Rovina, perdita, *f.*, sfacelo, *m.*
undoubted, *a.* Indubbio, indubitato, certo.
undoubtedly, *adv.* Senza dubbio, indubbiamente, certamente.
undoubting, *a.* Convinto, senza sospetto; credulo.
undraped, *a.* Non drappeggiato.
undreamed-of, *a.* Incredibile, impensato.
undress, *v.t.* Spogliare, svestire; *v.i.* spogliarsi, svestirsi. || *n.* (*Mil.*) Bassa tenuta, piccola divisa, *f.*
undressed, *a.* Spogliato, svestito; crudo, greggio, grezzo.
undrinkable, *a.* Imbevibile; non potabile.
undue, *a.* Eccessivo, smoderato; indebito, sconveniente.
undulate ['ʌndju:leit], *v.i.* Ondeggiare, ondulare. || *a.* Ondulato.
undulating, *a.* Ondeggiante, ondulato.
undulation, *n.* Ondeggiamento, *m.*, ondulazione, *f.*
undulatory, *a.* Ondulatorio.
unduly, *adv.* Eccessivamente, smoderatamente; indebitamente, sconvenientemente.
undutiful, *a.* Non riguardoso, irrispettoso, irriverente.
undutifulness, *n.* Irriverenza, *f.*
undying, *a.* Eterno, immortale, imperituro.
unearned, *a.* Non guadagnato; immeritato. **— increment,** plus-valore, *m.*
unearth, *v.t.* Disottoterrare; scoprire, trovare.
unearthly, *a.* Non terreno; soprannaturale, spettrale; strano.
uneasily, *adv.* Inquietamente, a disagio.
uneasiness, *n.* Inquietudine, irrequietezza, *f.*; agitazione, *f.*, turbamento, *m.*; ansia, *f.*
uneasy, *a.* Inquieto, agitato, turbato; incomodo, scomodo, disagevole, molesto, penoso.
uneatable, *a.* Immangiabile.
unedifying, *a.* Poco edificante.
uneducated, *a.* Incolto, ignorante, senza istruzione.
unembarrassed, *a.* Non imbarazzato; disinvolto; senza debiti.
unemotional, *a.* Impassibile.
unemployable, *a.* Inabile al lavoro.
unemployed, *a.* Disoccupato; sfaccendato; inoperoso, inerte, ozioso. **The —,** i disoccupati, *m.pl.*
unemployment, *n.* Disoccupazione, *f.* **— benefit,** indennità di disoccupazione, *f.*; **— insurance,** assicurazione contro la disoccupazione, *f.*
unenclosed, *a.* Aperto.
unencumbered, *a.* Libero; non gravato da ipoteche.
unending, *a.* Eterno, senza fine, interminabile.
unendorsed, *a.* (*Comm.*) Senza girata, non controfirmato.
unendowed, *a.* Senza dote.
unendurable, *a.* Insopportabile, insoffribile.
un-English, *a.* Non inglese, indegno d'un Inglese.
unenlightened, *a.* Ignorante.
unenterprising, *a.* Poco intraprendente, senza iniziative.
unenthusiastic, *a.* Senza entusiasmo.
unenviable, *a.* Da non invidiarsi, poco invidiabile.
unequal, *a.* Ineguale, disuguale; incapace, inabile. **He is — to his work,** non è all'altezza del suo compito.
unequalled, *a.* Senza pari, incomparabile.
unequally, *adv.* Inegualmente.
unequivocal, *a.* Non equivoco, inequivocabile, chiaro, schietto, franco.
unequivocally, *adv.* Chiaramente, schiettamente.

Unless otherwise indicated, the pronunciation of words prefixed by "un" can be ascertained by reference to the unprefixed words or their derivatives in their alphabetical position in this dictionary.

unerring [ʌn'əːɹriŋ], *a.* Infallibile, certo.
unerringly, *adv.* Infallibilmente.
uneven, *a.* Ineguale, irregolare; scabroso; impari. — **numbers,** numeri dispari, *m.pl.*
unevenly, *adv.* Ineguaglianza, diseguaglianza, irregolarmente.
unevenness, *n.* Inegualità, irregolarità, *f.*
uneventful, *a.* Monotono, senza incidenti, calmo.
uneventfulness, *n.* Monotonia, *f.*
unexampled, *a.* Senza esempio, singolare, inaudito.
unexcelled, *a.* Senza pari, insuperato, incomparabile.
unexceptionable, *a.* Ineccepibile, irreprensibile.
unexceptionably, *adv.* Irreprensibilmente.
unexhausted, *a.* Inesausto.
unexpected, *a.* Inaspettato, inatteso, improvviso, impensato.
unexpectedly, *adv.* Inaspettatamente, all'improvviso.
unexpired, *a.* (*Comm.*) Non ancora scaduto.
unexplained, *a.* Inesplicato, non spiegato.
unexplored, *a.* Inesplorato.
unexposed, *a.* Non esposto.
unexpressed, *a.* Non espresso, sottinteso, inespresso.
unexpurgated, *a.* Inespurgato, integrale.
unfadable, *a.* Inalterabile, non scolorabile.
unfading, *a.* Inalterabile, immutabile; (*fig.*) imperituro, immortale.
unfailing, *a.* Infallibile, sicuro; immancabile, inesauribile.
unfailingly, *adv.* Infallibilmente, immancabilmente, senza fallo.
unfair, *a.* Ingiusto; sleale, disonesto.
unfairly, *adv.* Ingiustamente, a torto; slealmente, disonestamente.
unfairness, *n.* Ingiustizia, *f.*, torto, *m.*; slealtà, disonestà, *f.*
unfaithful, *a.* Infedele.
unfaithfully, *adv.* Infedelmente.
unfaithfulness, *n.* Infedeltà, *f.*
unfaltering, *a.* Fermo, fisso, costante; risoluto, deciso.
unfamiliar, *a.* Poco familiare, estraneo, sconosciuto, poco pratico. **I am — with this district,** sono poco pratico di questi luoghi.
unfamiliarity, *n.* Mancanza di familiarità, stranezza, *f.*
unfashionable, *a.* Fuori moda, inelegante.
unfashionably, *adv.* Fuori moda.
unfashioned, *a.* Informe.
unfasten, *v.t.* Aprire, disfare; sciogliere, slegare; slacciare, sfibbiare.
unfathomable, *a.* Senza fondo, insondabile, impenetrabile; (*fig.*) inscrutabile.
unfathomably, *adv.* Impenetrabilmente.
unfathomed, *a.* Non scandagliato, insondato.
unfavourable, *a.* Sfavorevole, contrario; negativo. **In an — light,** in una cattiva luce.
unfavourableness, *n.* Condizione sfavorevole, *f.*, sfavore, *m.*
unfavourably, *adv.* Sfavorevolmente, contrariamente.
unfeasible, *a.* Infattibile, inattuabile.
unfeathered, *a.* Senza penne, implume.
unfed, *a.* Senza cibo.
unfeeling, *a.* Insensibile, duro, arido, crudele.
unfeelingly, *adv.* Crudelmente.
unfeelingness, *n.* Insensibilità, aridità, crudeltà, *f.*
unfeigned, *a.* Non finto, sincero, reale.
unfeignedly, *adv.* Sinceramente.
unfeignedness, *n.* Sincerità, *f.*
unfelt, *a.* Non sentito.
unfeminine, *a.* Poco femminile; indegno di una donna.
unfenced, *a.* Indifeso, aperto, senza chiusa, senza muri, senza siepi.
unfermented, *a.* Non fermentato.
unfertile, *a.* Infruttifero, sterile.
unfettered, *a.* Libero, sciolto, senza ceppi, senza impedimenti; (*fig.*) illimitato.
unfilial, *a.* Poco filiale.
unfilled, *a.* Vuoto, non riempito; libero; vacante.
unfiltered, *a.* Non filtrato.
unfinished, *a.* Incompiuto, non terminato.
unfit, *a.* Disadatto, inadatto, inetto, inabile, incapace; sconvenevole, indegno. — **for service,** inabile al servizio; **food — to eat,** cibo immangiabile; **the —,** gli inabili.
unfitly, *adv.* Sconvenevolmente; ingiustamente, a torto.
unfitness, *n.* Inettitudine; inabilita, incapacità, *f.*; indegnità, sconvenevolezza, *f.*
unfitting, *a.* Sconveniente, sconvenevole.
unfix, *v.t.* Staccare; togliere, levare.
unfixed, *a.* Staccato, sciolto; incostante, incerto. **To come —,** staccarsi, sciogliersi.
unflagging [ʌn'flægiŋ], *a.* Instancabile, indefesso, infaticabile.
unflattering, *a.* Poco lusinghiero.
unfledged, *a.* Senza penne, implume; (*fig.*) immaturo, inesperto, in erba.
unflinching, *a.* Risoluto, fermo, inflessibile, irremovibile.
unflinchingly, *adv.* Irremovibilmente, risolutamente.
unfold, *v.t.* Spiegare, distendere, stendere, allargare; (*fig.*) scoprire, rivelare, svelare; *v.i.* spiegarsi, stendersi, allargarsi.
unfolding, *n.* Spiegamento, allargamento, *m.*; (*fig.*) scoprimento, *m.*, rivelazione, *f.*
unforced, *a.* Spontaneo, libero; naturale; facile.
unfordable, *a.* Inguadabile.
unforeseeing, *a.* Imprevidente.
unforeseen, *a.* Imprevisto, inaspettato, inatteso.
unforgettable, *a.* Indimenticabile.
unforgivable, *a.* Imperdonabile.
unforgiven, *a.* Non perdonato.
unforgiving, *a.* Implacabile, inesorabile.
unforgotten, *a.* Non dimenticato, inobliato.
unformed, *a.* Informe, amorfo; immaturo.
unfortified, *a.* Non fortificato, indifeso, senza difesa, aperto.
unfortunate, *a.* Sfortunato, sventurato, disgraziato, infelice.
unfortunately, *adv.* Purtroppo, sfortunatamente, sventuratamente.
unfounded, *a.* Infondato, senza base, ingiustificato.
unframed, *a.* Senza cornice.

Unless otherwise indicated, the pronunciation of words prefixed by "un" can be ascertained by reference to the unprefixed words or their derivatives in their alphabetical position in this dictionary.

unfrequented, *a.* Non frequentato, poco praticato.
unfriendliness, *n.* Ostilità, inimicizia, scortesia, *f.*
unfriendly, *a.* Poco amichevole, mal disposto, ostile; contrario; scortese.
unfrock, *v.t.* (*Eccles.*) Spretare, sfratare.
unfruitful, *a* Non fertile, infruttifero, sterile, infecondo; infruttuoso.
unfruitfulness, *n.* Sterilità, infecondità, *f.*; infruttuosità, *f.*
unfulfilled, *a.* Inadempiuto, incompiuto.
unfunded, *a.* (*Comm.*) Non consolidato. — **debt,** debito fluttuante, *m.*
unfurl, *v.t.* Spiegare.
unfurnished, *a.* Non ammobiliato; sfornito; — **with,** sprovvisto di.
ungainliness, *n.* Goffaggine, sguaiatezza, *f.*
ungainly, *a.* Goffo, sgraziato, sguaiato.
ungallant, *a.* Poco galante, scortese.
ungarnished, *a.* Sguarnito; disadorno.
ungathered, *a.* Non colto, non raccolto.
ungauged, *a.* Non misurato.
ungenerous, *a.* Poco generoso, ingeneroso, meschino.
ungenerously, *adv.* Ingenerosamente, meschinamente.
ungenial, *a.* Antipatico, freddo; inclemente, aspro, rigido.
ungenteel, *a.* Rozzo, incivile, scortese; inelegante, goffo.
ungentle, *a.* Duro, aspro; sgarbato, scortese.
ungentlemanly, *a.* Maleducato, grossolano, scortese; volgare, basso.
ungentleness, *n.* Durezza, asprezza, *f.*
ungently, *adv.* Duramente.
ungifted, *a.* Senza ingegno.
ungird, *v.t.* Scingere, discingere. **To — one's sword,** scingersi la spada.
unglazed, *a.* Senza vetri, non invetriato; non lucido; non verniciato.
ungodliness, *n.* Empietà, irreligiosità, *f.*
ungodly, *a.* Empio, irreligioso.
ungovernable, *a.* Sfrenato, riottoso; ingovernabile; indisciplinato, sregolato, disordinato.
ungovernably, *adv.* Sfrenatamente, sregolatamente.
ungraceful, *a.* Sgraziato, goffo; senza grazia; sgarbato, scortese.
ungracefully, *adv.* Sgarbatamente; senza grazia, goffamente.
ungracefulness, *n.* Sgarbatezza, *f.*; goffaggine, ineleganza, *f.*
ungracious, *a.* Villano, scortese, sgarbato, incivile.
ungraciously, *adv.* Scortesemente, villanamente.
ungrammatical, *a.* Sgrammaticato, scorretto.
ungrammatically, *adv.* Scorettamente, non correttamente. **To speak (or write) —,** sgrammaticare.
ungrateful, *a.* Ingrato; spiacevole, sgradevole.
ungratefully, *adv.* Ingratamente.
ungratefulness, *n.* Ingratitudine, *f.*
ungratified, *a.* Non appagato, insoddisfatto.
ungrounded, *a.* Infondato.
ungrudging, *a.* Generoso, liberale, di buon cuore, volonteroso.
ungrudgingly, *adv.* Di buon cuore, volentieri.
ungual [ˈʌŋgwəl], *a.* Ungulato.
unguarded, *a.* Indifeso, incostudito; imprudente, indiscreto, incauto. **In an — moment,** in un momento di disattenzione.
unguardedly, *adv.* Imprudentemente.
unguent [ˈʌŋgwənt], *n.* Unguento, *m.*
unguided, *a.* Non guidato, senza guida.
ungulate [ˈʌŋgjuːleit], *a.* Ungulato.
unhallowed, *a.* Profano; sacrilego, scellerato.
unhampered, *a.* Non imbarazzato, disimpacciato, libero.
unhandily, *adv.* Maldestramente, goffamente.
unhandsome, *a.* Brutto; meschino, gretto; scortese.
unhandsomely, *adv.* Meschinamente; scortesemente.
unhandsomeness, *n.* Bruttezza, *f.*; meschinità, grettezza, *f.*; scortesia, *f.*
unhandy, *a.* Maldestro, goffo, impacciato, inesperto; scomodo.
unhang, *v.t.* Staccare, spiccare. **To — a picture,** staccare un quadro; **to — a door,** scardinare una porta.
unhappily, *adv.* Purtroppo; sfortunatamente.
unhappiness, *n.* Infelicità, *f.*; sfortuna, disgrazia, *f.*
unhappy, *a.* Infelice, sfortunato, disgraziato, misero, afflitto.
unharmed, *a.* Sano e salvo, illeso, incolume.
unharness, *v.t.* Staccare, levare i finimenti.
unhatched, *a.* Non covato, non schiuso.
unhealthily, *adv.* Insalubremente, malsanamente.
unhealthiness, *n.* Insalubrità, *f.*; morbosità, *f.*
unhealthy, *a.* Malsano, insalubre; infermo, malaticcio.
unheard, *a.* Non udito, non sentito. **— of,** inaudito, incredibile.
unheated, *a.* Non riscaldato
unheeded, *a.* Inascoltato, inesaudito; negletto, poco riguardato.
unheedful, unheeding, *a.* Disattento, negligente, sbadato, trascurato.
unhelped, *a.* Senza aiuto.
unhelpful, *a.* Inutile, non giovevole.
unheroic, *a.* Non eroico.
unhesitating, *a.* Fermo, risoluto, deciso, pronto.
unhesitatingly, *adv.* Senza esitazione, prontamente, risolutamente.
unhewn, *a.* Greggio, non tagliato.
unhindered, *a.* Non impedito, senz'impedimenti, sciolto.
unhinge, *v.t.* Scardinare, sgangherare, sconnettere; (*fig.*) disordinare. **His mind is unhinged,** è fuori di sè; (*colloq.*) il suo cervello non è a posto.
unhitch, *v.t.* Staccare.
unholiness, *n.* Empietà, *f.*; profanazione, *f.*
unholy, *a.* Empio, sacrilego; profano.
unhonoured, *a.* Inonorato, non apprezzato.
unhook, *v.t.* Sganciare, staccare; slacciare, sfibbiare.
unhoped, unhoped for, *a.* Insperato, inaspettato.

Unless otherwise indicated, the pronunciation of words prefixed by "un" can be ascertained by reference to the unprefixed words or their derivatives in their alphabetical position in this dictionary.

unhorse, *v.t.* Smontare, scavalcare.
unhouseled [ʌnˈhauzld], *a.* (*obs.*) Senza aver ricevuto i sacramenti.
unhung, *a.* Non appeso; non impiccato. (*colloq.*) **The biggest rogue —,** un tipo da forca, *m.*
unhurt, *a.* Sano e salvo, illeso, incolume.
unicellular [ju:niˈselju:ləɹ], *a.* Unicellulare.
unicorn [ˈju:nikɔ:ɹn], *n.* (*Myth.*) Unicorno, liocorno, *m.* (*Zool.*) narvalo, *m.*
unification [ju:nifiˈkeiʃən], *n.* Unificazione, *f.*
uniform [ˈju:nifɔ:ɹm], *n.* Uniforme, divisa, tenuta, *f.*; abito, *m.* || *a.* Uniforme. **In full —,** in alta tenuta.
uniformity [ju:niˈfɔ:ɹmiti], *n.* Uniformità, *f.*
uniformly, *adv.* Uniformemente; regolarmente.
unify [ˈju:nifai], *v.t.* Unificare.
unilateral [ju:niˈlætərəl], *a.* Unilaterale.
unimaginable, *a.* Inimmaginabile, inconcepibile.
unimaginably, *adv.* Inconcepibilmente.
unimaginative, *a.* Poco immaginativo, senza immaginazione.
unimagined, *a.* Inimmaginato, impensato.
unimpaired, *a.* Intatto, inalterato, in pieno vigore.
unimpeachable, *a.* Incensurabile, irreprensibile, inattaccabile, indiscutibile.
unimpeded, *a.* Senza ostacoli.
unimportant, *a.* Insignificante, poco importante, di poco valore.
unimposed, *a.* Volontario.
unimposing, *a.* Poco imponente.
unimpressed, *a.* Non commosso, non impressionato.
unimpressionable, *a.* Poco impressionabile.
unimpressive, *a.* Poco commovente, poco impressionante.
unimproved, *a.* Non corretto; non migliorato.
uninfected, *a.* Non infetto.
uninflammable, *a.* Non infiammabile.
uninfluenced, *a.* Non influenzato.
uninfluential, *a.* Senza influenza.
uninformed, *a.* Ignorante, poco istruito, ignaro. **To be — of,** ignorare.
uninhabitable, *a.* Inabitabile.
uninhabited, *a.* (*of a house*) Disabitato; (*of a country, etc.*) inabitato.
uninitiated, *a.* Non iniziato.
uninjured, *a.* Illeso, incolume; intatto.
uninspired, *a.* Non ispirato, senza ispirazione.
uninstructed, *a.* Poco istruito, ignorante, incolto.
uninsured, *a.* Non assicurato.
unintelligent, *a.* Poco intelligente, stupido, ottuso.
unintelligible, *a.* Inintelligibile.
unintelligibly, *adv.* Inintelligibilmente.
unintended, unintentional, *a.* Non intenzionale, non premeditato, involontario.
unintentionally, *adv.* Senza intenzione, involontariamente.
uninterested, *a.* Non interessato, indifferente, incurante.
uninterestedly, *adv.* Indifferentemente.
uninteresting, *a.* Poco interessante.
uninterestingly, *adv.* In modo poco interessante.
uninterrupted, *a.* Ininterrotto, continuo, incessante.
uninterruptedly, *adv.* Ininterrottamente, senza interruzione.
uninvited, *a.* Non invitato, senza invito.
uninviting, *a.* Poco invitante, poco attraente, poco allettante; poco appetitoso.
union [ˈju:niən], *n.* Unione, società, alleanza, *f.*; (*Mech.*) raccordo, collegamento, *m.* **— is strength,** l'unione fa la forza; **the Union Jack,** la bandiera inglese, *f.*; **the Union of South Africa,** l'Unione sud-africana, *f.*; **Union of Soviet Socialist Republics, (U.S.S.R.),** Unione delle Repubbliche Socialiste Sovietiche (U.R.S.S.); **trade —,** camera del lavoro, *f.*, sindacato operaio, *m.*
unionist, *n.* Unionista, *m.f.*
uniparous [ju:ˈnipərəs], *a.* Uniparo.
unipartite [ju:niˈpɑ:ɹtait], *a.* Indiviso.
unipolar [ju:niˈpouləɹ], *a.* Unipolare.
unique [ju:ˈni:k], *a.* Unico, solo. **— of its kind,** unico nel suo genere.
uniquely, *adv.* Unicamente.
unisexual [ju:niˈseksju:əl], *a.* Unisessuale.
unison [ˈju:nizən], *n.* Unisono, *m.* **In —,** all'unisono.
unit [ˈju:nit], *n.* Unità, *f.*; (*Mil.*) unità, *f.*, reparto, *m.*
Unitarian [ju:niˈtɛəriən], *n.a.* (*Eccles.*) Unitario, *m.*
unite [ju:ˈnait], *v.t.* Unire; congiungere, connettere, riunire; accoppiare; *v.i.* unirsi; congiungersi, riunirsi.
united [ju:ˈnaited], *a.* Unito; congiunto, riunito. **Our — efforts,** i nostri sforzi uniti; **— Kingdom,** Regno Unito, *m.*; **United States,** Stati Uniti, *m.pl.*; **United Nations (U.N.),** Nazioni Unite (N.U.)., *f.pl.*
unitedly, *adv.* Unitamente, insieme, d'accordo.
unity [ˈju:niti], *n.* Unità, *f.*, concordia, unione, armonia, *f.*
universal [ju:niˈvə:ɹsəl], *n.a.* Universale, *m.*
universality [ju:nivə:ɹˈsæliti], *n.* Universalità, *f.*
universally, *adv.* Universalmente, da per tutto, per ogni dove.
universe [ˈju:nivə:ɹs], *n.* Universo, *m.*
university [ju:niˈvə:ɹsiti], *n.* Università, *f.* || *a.* Universitario. **— degree,** laurea, *f.*; **— teaching,** insegnamento universitario, *m.*
unjoyful, unjoyous, *a.* Triste.
unjust, *a.* Ingiusto, iniquo.
unjustifiable, *a.* Ingiustificabile.
unjustifiably, *adv.* Ingiustificabilmente.
unjustified, *a.* Ingiustificato.
unjustly, *adv.* Ingiustamente.
unkempt [ʌnˈkempt], *a.* Arruffato, spettinato, scarmigliato; disordinato, trascurato, maltenuto.
unkind, *a.* Poco gentile, sgarbato; poco buono; cattivo, malevolo, crudele, aspro, duro. **— to animals,** crudele verso gli animali.
unkindliness, *n.* Durezza, malevolenza, crudeltà, *f.*
unkindly, *a.* Poco gentile; cattivo. || *adv.* Crudelmente, duramente, senza benevolenza. **I shall take it very — if . . .,** me l'avrò a male se . . .

Unless otherwise indicated, the pronunciation of words prefixed by "un" can be ascertained by reference to the unprefixed words or their derivatives in their alphabetical position in this dictionary.

unkindness, *n.* Asprezza, durezza, malevolenza, *f.*
unkingly, *a.* Indegno d'un re.
unknit, *v.t.* Disfare, snodare, slegare.
unknot, *v.t.* Snodare, slegare, slacciare.
unknowable, *a.* Inconoscibile.
unknowing, *a.* Ignorante, inconsapevole.
unknowingly, *adv.* Inconsapevolmente.
unknown, *a.* Ignoto, sconosciuto. **— to me,** a mia insaputa; **an — person,** uno sconosciuto, *m.*, una sconosciuta, *f.* **The Unknown Soldier,** il Milite Ignoto, *m.*
unlabelled, *a.* Senz'etichetta.
unlaboured, *a.* Spontaneo, naturale.
unlace, *v.t.* Slacciare.
unlading [ʌn'leidiŋ], *n.* Scarico, scaricamento, *m.*
unladylike, *a.* Indegno d'una signora, grossolano, volgare.
unlamented, *a.* Incompianto, illacrimato.
unlatch, *v.t.* Aprire, schiudere, disserrare; levare il saliscendi.
unlawful, *a.* Illegale, illecito, illegittimo.
unlawfully, *adv.* Illegalmente, illecitamente, illegittimamente.
unlawfulness, *n.* Illegalità, *f.*
unlearn, *v.t.* Disimparare.
unlearned, *a.* Ignorante, illetterato.
unleash, *v.t.* Sguinzagliare.
unleavened, *a.* Senza lievito; azzimo. **— bread,** pane azzimo, *m.*
unless [ʌn'les], *conj.* A meno che, se non, eccetto che, salvo che. **— he comes,** a meno che egli non venga; **do not come — sent for,** non venire se non sei chiamato.
unlet, *a.* Disaffittati, disoccupato, vuoto, senza inquilini.
unlettered, *a.* Analfabeta.
unlicensed, *a.* Senza licenza, senza patente.
unlicked, *a.* (*fig.*) Sgarbato, maleducato.
unlike, *a.* Dissimile, diverso, vario. || *prep.* A differenza di; all'inverso di, tutto al contrario di. **He was totally — his father,** non somigliava in niente a suo padre.
unlikelihood, unlikeliness, *n.* Inverosimiglianza, *f.*; improbabilità, *f.*
unlikely, *a.* Inverosimile; improbabile; poco promettente. **It is very — that,** è molto improbabile che.
unlimber, *v.t.* (*Mil.*) Staccare l'avantreno.
unlimited, *a.* Illimitato, sconfinato, immenso.
unlimitedness, *n.* Immensità, *f.*
unlined, *a.* Non foderato; (*paper*) senza righe; (*face*) senza rughe.
unlink, *v.t.* Disfare, staccare, disgiungere.
unlit, *a.* Non acceso; non illuminato.
unload, *v.t.* Scaricare; sgravare; (*Comm.*) disfarsi di.
unloading, *n.* Scarico, scaricamento, *m.*
unlock, *v.t.* Disserrare, aprire, schiudere.
unlooked-for, *a.* Inatteso, inaspettato, improvviso, impensato.
unloose, unloosen, *v.t.* Sciogliere, slegare; scatenare; sguinzagliare, lasciare andare.
unlovable, *a.* Non amabile, antipatico, spiacevole.
unloved, *a.* Non amato.
unlovely, *a.* Brutto, antipatico, non attraente.
unloving, *a.* Insensibile, freddo, poco affettuoso.
unluckily, *adv.* Sfortunatamente, disgraziatamente.
unluckiness, *n.* Sfortuna, disgrazia, sventura, *f.*
unlucky, *a.* Sfortunato, disgraziato, sventurato; malaugurato, nefasto.
unmade, *a.* Non fatto; disfatto. **An — road,** una strada non lastricata.
unmaidenly, *a.* Indecoroso, inverecondo; vergognoso.
unmake, *v.t.* Disfare; distruggere, rovinare, abbattere.
unman [ʌn'mæn], *v.t.* Scoraggiare, snervare, indebolire; abbattere, accasciare; (*Naut.*) disarmare.
unmanageable, *a.* Intrattabile, scontroso, riottoso, ribelle; ingovernabile.
unmanliness, *n.* Codardia, viltà, *f.*; effeminatezza, debolezza, *f.*
unmanly, *a.* Codardo; effeminato, debole, pusillanime.
unmannerliness, *n.* Sgarbatezza, grossolanità, scortesia, *f.*
unmannerly, *a.* Sgarbato, grossolano, scortese; maleducato. || *adv.* Sgarbatamente, scortesemente.
unmanufactured, *a.* Greggio, crudo.
unmarked, *a.* Non marcato, senza marca; inosservato.
unmarketable, *a.* Invendibile, incommerciabile.
unmarried, *a.* Non sposato; (*of a woman*) nubile, zitella; (*of a man*) celibe, scapolo. **An — man,** uno scapolo, *m.*; **an — woman,** una zitella, *f.*
unmask, *v.t.* Smascherare; palesare; *v.i.* smascherarsi.
unmastered, *a.* Indomato, indomito.
unmatched, *a.* Impareggiabile, incomparabile.
unmeaning, *a.* Senza significato; insignificante; vacuo, inane.
unmeant, *a.* Non intenzionale, involontario.
unmeasured, *a.* Non misurato; smisurato, grandissimo.
unmelodious, *a.* Discordante, scordato, stonato, senza melodia.
unmelted, *a.* Non fuso; non intenerito.
unmentionable, *a.* Innominabile, da non menzionarsi. (*obs.*) **Unmentionables,** calzoni, *m.pl.*
unmerciful, *a.* Spietato, crudele, senza pietà, implacabile.
unmercifully, *adv.* Spietatamente, crudelmente, senza pietà.
unmerited, *a.* Immeritato.
unmethodical, *a.* Senza metodo, senza sistema, non sistematico.
unmethodically, *adv.* Senza metodo.
unmindful, *a.* Dimentico, immemore; incurante. **— of his obligations,** incurante dei suoi doveri.
unmindfully, *adv.* Disattentamente, noncurantemente.
unmindfulness, *n.* Dimenticanza, *f.*; incuranza, *f.*
unmingled, *a.* Puro, non mischiato, non mescolato.

Unless otherwise indicated, the pronunciation of words prefixed by "un" can be ascertained by reference to the unprefixed words or their derivatives in their alphabetical position in this dictionary.

unmistakable, *a.* Da non sbagliarsi, lampante, chiaro, evidente, manifesto.
unmistakably, *adv.* Chiaramente, evidentemente.
unmitigated, *a.* Non mitigato; assoluto, totale; (*colloq.*) inqualificabile, solenne, matricolato. **An — fool,** un solenne imbecille, *m.*
unmixed, *a.* Puro, non mischiato; scevro di.
unmodified, *a.* Non modificato.
unmoor, *v.t.* (*Naut.*) Disormeggiare.
unmotherly, *a.* Non materno, poco materno.
unmounted, *a.* A piedi, appiedato; (*of a picture*) senza incorniciatura; (*of a gem*) non incastonato.
unmourned, *a.* Incompianto, illagrimato.
unmoved, *a.* Immobile, immoto, fisso; (*fig.*) non commosso, impassibile, calmo.
unmurmuring, *a.* Rassegnato, sottomesso.
unmusical, *a.* Discordante, scordato, inarmonioso; poco musicale.
unmuzzle, *v.t.* Togliere la muserola a.
unnameable, *a.* Innominabile.
unnamed, *a.* Innominato; anonimo.
unnatural, *a.* Contro natura, non naturale, snaturato, inumano; sforzato, affettato.
unnaturally, *adv.* Contro natura, snaturatamente; sforzatamente, affettatamente.
unnavigable, *a.* Innavigabile.
unnecessarily, *adv.* Senza necessità, inutilmente.
unnecessary, *a.* Non necessario, inutile, superfluo.
unnegotiable, *a.* (*Comm.*) Non negoziabile.
unneighbourly, *a.* Poco amichevole, scortese, sgarbato. || *adv.* Scortesemente, non da buon vicino.
unnerve, *v.t.* Snervare, infiacchire, indebolire; scoraggiare.
unnoted, unnoticed, *a.* Inosservato, negletto. **To pass —,** passare inosservato; **to leave unnoticed,** passare sotto silenzio.
unnumbered, *a.* Non numerato, innumerabile.
unobjectionable, *a.* Ineccepibile, irreprensibile.
unobjectionably, *adv.* Irreprensibilmente.
unobscured, *a.* Non oscurato, chiaro.
unobservant, *a.* Inosservante, disattento; poco osservatore.
unobserved, *a.* Inosservato.
unobstructed, *a.* Non impedito.
unobtainable, *a.* Inottenibile; irraggiungibile.
unobtrusive, *a.* Non importuno, non impacciante, discreto, modesto, riservato.
unobtrusively, *adv.* Discretamente, modestamente.
unobtrusiveness, *n.* Discrezione, modestia, *f.*, riserbo, *m.*
unoccupied, *a.* Disoccupato; libero, vacante, vuoto, disponibile.
unoffending, *a.* Inoffensivo, innocuo, innocente.
unoffered, *a.* Non offerto.
unofficial, *a.* Non ufficiale, ufficioso. **An — communication,** una communicazione ufficiosa, *f.*
unofficially, *adv.* Non ufficialmente; ufficiosamente.
unopened, *a.* Chiuso; non aperto, non dissigillato.
unopposed, *a.* Incontestato, incontrastato, senza opposizione.
unorganized, *a.* Non organizzato, disorganizzato.
unoriginal, *a.* Non originale, derivato, di seconda mano.
unornamental, *a.* Poco ornamentale, brutto.
unornamented, *a.* Disadorno.
unorthodox, *a.* Eterodosso.
unorthodoxy, *n.* Eterodossia, *f.*
unostentatious, *a.* Senz'ostentazione, non ostentato, senza fasto; semplice, modesto.
unostentatiously, *adv.* Senza pretese, semplicemente, senza ostentazione, senza fasto, modestamente.
unostentatiousness, *n.* Semplicità, modestia, *f.*
unowned, *a.* Senza proprietario; non reclamato.
unpack, *v.t.* Disfare, sballare, disimballare, spacchettare.
unpacked, *a.* Non imballato, aperto.
unpacking, *n.* Disimballaggio, *m.*
unpaid, *a.* Non pagato, irremunerato, irretribuito; (*of debt*) non saldato; (*of postage*) non affrancato.
unpainted, *a.* Non dipinto.
unpalatable, *a.* Sgradevole al gusto; sgradevole, spiacevole.
unparalleled, *a.* Impareggiabile, incomparabile, senza pari, senza precedenti.
unpardonable, *a.* Imperdonabile, inescusabile.
unpardonably, *adv.* Imperdonabilmente, inescusabilmente.
unpardoned, *a.* Non perdonato, senza perdono.
unparliamentary, *a.* Poco parlamentare, poco civile, rude.
unpatriotic, *a.* Poco patriottico, non patriottico.
unpatriotically, *adv.* Poco patriotticamente.
unpaved, *a.* Non lastricato, senza selciato.
unpeaceful, *a.* Poco tranquillo, inquieto, agitato, turbato.
unpeeled, *a.* Non pelato, non sbucciato.
unpeg, *v.t.* Schiodare, staccare.
unpeopled, *a.* Spopolato.
unperceived, *a.* Inosservato.
unperformed, *a.* Ineseguito, non fatto.
unpersuaded, *a.* Non persuaso.
unperturbed, *a.* Imperturbato, tranquillo, sereno.
unphilosophical, *a.* Poco filosofico.
unpick, *v.t.* Scucire; disfare.
unpicked, *a.* Non scelto; non colto, non raccolto.
unpicturesque, *a.* Poco pittoresco.
unpin, *v.t.* Togliere gli spilli a, disfare.
unpitied, *a.* Non compatito.
unpitying, *a.* Spietato, senza pietà.
unplaced, *a.* (*Racing*) Non piazzato, non fra i tre primi alle corse.
unplait, *v.t.* Disfare le treccie.
unpleasant, *a.* Spiacevole, spiacente, sgradito, antipatico, noioso.
unpleasantly, *adv.* Spiacevolmente, sgradevolmente.
unpleasantness, *n.* Spiacevolezza, *f.*; malinteso, disaccordo, *m.*

Unless otherwise indicated, the pronunciation of words prefixed by "un" can be ascertained by reference to the unprefixed words or their derivatives in their alphabetical position in this dictionary.

unpleasing, *a.* Spiacevole, antipatico.
unpliable, unpliant, *a.* Rigido, inflessibile.
unploughed, *a.* Non arato, incolto.
unplucked, *a.* Non colto, non raccolto.
unplumbed, *a.* Non scandagliato, insondato, inesplorato.
unpoetical, *a.* Poco poetico, impoetico.
unpolished, *a.* Non pulito, non lustrato; greggio, crudo; (*fig.*) rozzo, grossolano, inelegante.
unpolluted, *a.* Incontaminato, puro.
unpopular, *a.* Impopolare. **An — law,** una legge impopolare.
unpopularity, *n.* Impopolarità, *f.*
unpopularly, *adv.* Impopolarmente.
unposted, *a.* Non impostato.
unpractical, *a.* Non pratico.
unpractised, *a.* Inesperto, non pratico, poco provetto.
unprecedented, *a.* Senza precedenti, inaudito.
unprefaced, *a.* Senza prefazione, non preceduto da.
unprejudiced, *a.* Spregiudicato, imparziale.
unpremeditated, *a.* Impremeditato, impensato, improvviso.
unprepared, *a.* Impreparato, improvviso, improvvisato; spontaneo, alla sprovvista. **To be — for,** non aspettare, non esser pronto per; **to be taken —,** esser colto alla sprovvista.
unpreparedness, *n.* Impreparazione, *f.*
unprepossessing, *a.* Poco avvenente, antipatico.
unpresentable, *a.* Impresentabile, indecoroso.
unpresuming, unpresumptuous, *a.* Umile, modesto, non presuntuoso, senza pretese.
unpretending, unpretentious, *a.* Non pretenzioso, senza pretese, naturale, semplice.
unpreventable, *a.* Inevitabile.
unpriced, *a.* Senza prezzo.
unprincely, *a.* Indegno d'un principe.
unprincipled, *a.* Senza principii, immorale.
unprintable, *a.* Non stampabile; impubblicabile, non adatto per la stampa; indecente.
unprivileged, *a.* Senza privilegi, non privilegiato.
unprized, *a.* Non apprezzato.
unprocurable, *a.* Inottenibile, introvabile.
unproductive, *a.* Improduttivo; sterile, infecondo.
unproductiveness, *n.* Sterilità, infecondità, *f.*
unprofessional, *a.* Scorretto, contrario agli usi di una professione. **— conduct,** scorrettezza professionale, *f.*
unprofitable, *a.* Infruttuoso, inutile, poco proficuo, svantaggioso.
unprofitableness, *n.* Infruttuosità, inutilità, *f.*
unprofitably, *adv.* Inutilmente, senza profitti.
unprogressive, *a.* Poco progressivo, retrivo, arretrato.
unprohibited, *a.* Non proibito, permesso.
unpromising, *a.* Poco promettente, che promette poco.
unprompted, *a.* Volontario, spontaneo.
unpronounceable, *a.* Impronunziabile.
unpropitious, *a.* Poco propizio, inopportuno, sfavorevole.
unpropitiously, *adv.* Sfavorevolmente.
unprosperous, *a.* Poco prospero, infelice, sfortunato, sfavorevole.
unprotected, *a.* Indifeso, non protetto, senza protezione.
unprovable, *a.* Indimostrabile.
unproved, *a.* Indimostrato; non provato; non sperimentato.
unprovided, *a.* Sprovvisto, sfornito; impreparato.
unprovoked, *a.* Non provocato; gratuito, ingiusto, immeritato. **An — insult,** un'offesa gratuita, *f.*
unpublished, *a.* Inedito.
unpunctual, *a.* Poco puntuale.
unpunctuality, *n.* Mancanza di puntualità, *f.*
unpunctuated, *a.* Non punteggiato.
unpunished, *a.* Impunito. **To go —,** rimanere impunito, andare impunito.
unpurchased, *a.* Non comprato, inacquistato.
unpurified, *a.* Non purificato, impuro.
unqualified, *a.* Incapace, inabile, incompetente; (*fig.*) senza riserva, pieno, assoluto; (*Law*) senza titoli, senza requisiti; (*of doctors*) non autorizzato.
unquenchable, *a.* Inestinguibile, indomabile, insaziabile.
unquenched, *a.* Insaziato. **His thirst was still —,** non si era dissetato.
unquestionable, *a.* Incontestabile, indubitabile, indiscutibile.
unquestionably, *adv.* Incontestabilmente, indubitabile.
unquestioned, *a.* Incontestato, indubitato; non interrogato.
unquestioning, *a.* Indiscusso, assoluto, pieno, senza discussione. **— obedience,** obbedienza assoluta, *f.*
unquiet, *a.* Inquieto, agitato, turbato, irrequieto.
unquietly, *a.* Inquietamente, agitatamente, turbatamente.
unquietness, *n.* Inquietudine, agitazione, irrequietezza, *f.*
unquotable, *a.* Non citabile.
unravel, *v.t.* Districare, sbrogliare, sciogliere, disfare, dipanare.
unreachable, *a.* Inaccessabile, irraggiungibile.
unread [ʌn'red], *a.* Non letto; incolto, ignorante. **I returned the book —,** ho restituito il libro senza averlo letto.
unreadable [ʌn'ri:dəbl], *a.* Illeggibile.
unreadily [ʌn'redili], *a.* Lentamente, contro voglia, riluttantemente.
unreadiness, *n.* Impreparazione, riluttanza, lentezza, *f.*
unready, *a.* Impreparato, non pronto; non disposto, riluttante; lento, tardo.
unreal, *a.* Irreale, immaginario, fantastico, illusorio.
unreality, *n.* Irrealtà, *f.*; incorporeità, immaterialità, *f.*
unrealizable, *a.* Irrealizzabile.
unreasonable, *a.* Irragionevole, assurdo; stravagante.
unreasonableness, *n.* Irragionevolezza, assurdità, *f.*; stravaganza, *f.*

Unless otherwise indicated, the pronunciation of words prefixed by "un" can be ascertained by reference to the unprefixed words or their derivatives in their alphabetical position in this dictionary.

unreasonably, *adv.* Irragionevolmente, senza ragione.
unreasoned, *a.* Irragionevole.
unreasoning, *a.* Irragionevole.
unrebuked, *a.* Senza biasimo, senza rimprovero.
unreciprocated, *a.* Non contraccambiato.
unreckoned, *a.* Non calcolato, non contato.
unrecognizable, *a.* Irriconoscibile.
unrecognized, *a.* Sconosciuto, non riconosciuto, misconosciuto.
unrecompensed, *a.* Senza compenso, non ricompensato.
unreconciled, *a.* Irriconciliato.
unrecorded, *a.* Non registrato, non segnalato.
unrectified, *a.* Non rettificato.
unredeemable, *a.* Non redimibile, non riscattabile.
unredeemed, *a.* Non riscattato; non ritirato, non rimborsato; non ammortizzato; irredento. (*Hist.*) — **Italy**, Italia irredenta, *f.*
unredressed, *a.* Non riparato.
unreel, *v.t.* Sgomitolare, disfare.
unrefined, *a.* Crudo, greggio, non raffinato; rozzo, sgarbato, grossolano.
unreflecting, *a.* Irriflessivo, sventato, leggiero.
unreformed, *a.* Non mutato, non corretto.
unrefreshed, *a.* Non rinfrescato, non ristorato; affaticato.
unrefuted, *a.* Irrefutato, inconfutato.
unregarded, *a.* Negletto, sprezzato, misconosciuto.
unregenerate, *a.* Non rigenerato.
unregistered, *a.* Non registrato, non iscritto; (*of letters*) non raccomandato.
unregretted, *a.* Incompianto, non lamentato, non rimpianto.
unregulated, *a.* Sregolato, disordinato.
unrehearsed, *a.* Improvviso; inaspettato, imprevisto.
unrelated, *a.* Senza rapporto con; non imparentato.
unrelaxed, *a.* Non rallentato; non diminuito.
unrelenting, *a.* Inesorabile, inflessibile, irremovibile, implacabile.
unrelentingly, *adv.* Inesorabilmente, irremovibilmente, implacabilmente.
unreliable, *a.* Malfido, infido, instabile, da non fidarsene; (*of news*) inattendibile.
unreliableness, unreliability, *n.* Incertezza, instabilità, *f.*; inattendibilità, *f.*
unrelieved, *a.* Non sollevato, non alleviato, non alleggerito; senza soccorso.
unremarked, *a.* Inosservato.
unremedied, *a.* Non rimediato, senza rimedio.
unremembered, *a.* Dimenticato, scordato.
unremitting, *a.* Incessante, continuo, indefesso, assiduo, senza tregua.
unremittingly, *adv.* Incessantemente.
unremunerative, *a.* Poco rimunerativo, infruttifero, poco lucrativo.
unrepealed, *a.* Non revocato, non abrogato.
unrepentant, *a.* Impenitente, indurito, incorreggibile.
unreplenished, *a.* Non riempito, vuoto.
unreported, *a.* Non riportato.
unrepresentative, *a.* Non rappresentativo.
unrepresented, *a.* Non rappresentato.
unreproved, *a.* Senza biasimo, senza rimprovero.
unrequested, *a.* Spontaneo, volontario, non richiesto. || *adv.* Spontaneamente.
unrequited, *a.* Non retribuito, senza compenso; misconosciuto, non corrisposto.
unreserved, *a.* Franco, spontaneo, schietto; assoluto, senza riserva. — **seats**, posti non riservati, *m.pl.*
unreservedly, *adv.* Francamente, schiettamente.
unresisting, *a.* Sottomesso, remissivo.
unresistingly, *adv.* Senza resistenza.
unresolved, *a.* Insoluto, irresoluto, indeciso.
unresponsive, *a.* Che non corrisponde, insensibile, ottuso, inerte, apatico.
unrest, *n.* Inquietudine, agitazione, *f.*; sommossa, rivolta, sedizione, *f.*
unrestful, *a.* Inquieto, agitato.
unresting, *a.* Incessante, continuo, assiduo, senza posa, ininterrotto.
unrestored, *a.* Non restituito, non restaurato; non rimesso.
unrestrained, *a.* Irrefrenabile, sfrenato, non represso.
unrestrainedly, *adv.* Sfrenatamente, senza ritegno.
unrestricted, *a.* Senza restrizione, assoluto, illimitato, libero.
unretarded, *a.* Non ritardato.
unrevealed, *a.* Non rivelato, non scoperto.
unrevenged, *a.* Invendicato.
unrewarded, *a.* Senza ricompensa, irretribuito.
unrhymed, *a.* Non rimato, sciolto.
unrig, *v.t.* (*Naut.*) Disarmare.
unrighteous, *a.* Ingiusto, iniquo, cattivo, malvagio.
unrighteously, *adv.* Ingiustamente, iniquamente.
unrighteousness, *n.* Ingiustizia, iniquità, malvagità, nequizia, *f.*
unripe, *a.* Immaturo; acerbo, verde.
unripeness, *n.* Immaturità, acerbezza, acerbità, *f.*
unrivalled, *a.* Impareggiabile, incomparabile, senza pari.
unrivet, *v.t.* Schiodare.
unrobe, *v.t.* Svestire, spogliare; *v.i.* svestirsi, spogliarsi.
unroll, *v.t.* Svolgere, spiegare, sviluppare; *v.i.* svolgersi, spiegarsi, svilupparsi.
unromantic, *a.* Poco romantico.
unroof, *v.t.* Levare il tetto a, portar via il tetto a.
unruffled, *a.* Tranquillo, calmo, sereno; liscio, non increspato.
unruled, *a.* Senza righe.
unruliness, *n.* Turbolenza, sregoletezza, indisciplina, *f.*
unruly, *a.* Turbolento, facinoroso, sregolato, indisciplinato, insubordinato.
unsaddle, *v.t.* Dissellare, levare la sella da; disarcionare.
unsafe, *a.* Malsicuro; rischioso, pericoloso, arrischiato.
unsaid, *a.* Non detto, taciuto. **To leave —**, tacere, passare sotto silenzio.

Unless otherwise indicated, the pronunciation of words prefixed by "un" can be ascertained by reference to the unprefixed words or their derivatives in their alphabetical position in this dictionary.

unsalable, unsaleable, *a.* Invendibile.
unsalaried, *a.* Non salariato, non pagato, non retribuito.
unsalted, *a.* Non salato.
unsanctified, *a.* Non santificato, profano.
unsanctioned, *a.* Non sanzionato, non sancito.
unsanitary, *a.* Malsano, antigienico.
unsated, *a.* Insaziato, insaziabile, insoddisfatto.
unsatisfactorily, *adv.* Malamente, insufficientemente, difettosamente.
unsatisfactoriness, *n.* Insufficienza, manchevolezza, *f.*
unsatisfactory, *a.* Poco soddisfacente, insufficiente, manchevole, difettoso.
unsatisfied, *a.* Insoddisfatto, scontento.
unsatisfying, *a.* Poco soddisfacente, insufficiente.
unsavouriness, *n.* Insipidità, insipidezza, *f.*; nausea, *f.*, disgusto, *m.*
unsavoury, *a.* Senza sapore, insipido; nauseante, disgustoso.
unsay, *v.t.* Disdire, ritrattare, negare. **To leave unsaid,** tacere.
unscalable, *a.* Inaccessibile.
unscarred, *a.* Non sfregiato, senza cicatrici.
unscathed, *a.* Illeso, intero, incolume, sano e salvo.
unscented, *a.* Inodoro, senza profumo.
unscholarly, *a.* Incolto, indotto.
unschooled, *a.* Ignorante, incolto, poco istruito.
unscientific, *a.* Poco scientifico.
unscientifically, *adv.* Non scientificamente, poco scientificamente.
unscorched, *a.* Non bruciato.
unscreened, *a.* Non riparato, senza difesa; non vagliato.
unscrew, *v.t.* Svitare.
unscriptural, *a.* Contrario alla Sacra Scrittura.
unscrupulous, *a.* Poco scrupoloso, senza scrupoli, disonesto.
unscrupulously, *adv.* Senza scrupoli, disonestamente.
unscrupulousness, *n.* Disonestà, mancanza di scrupoli.
unseal, *v.t.* Dissigillare, aprire, schiudere.
unsealed, *a.* Senza suggello, dissigillato.
unsearchable, *a.* Imperscrutabile, inscrutabile; impenetrabile.
unseasonable, *a.* Intempestivo, inopportuno; mal a proposito. **— weather,** tempo fuori stagione, *m.*
unseasonableness, *n.* Intempestività, inopportunità, *f.*
unseasonably, *adv.* Intempestivamente, male a proposito.
unseasoned, *a.* (*of wood*) Non stagionato; (*unaccustomed*) non indurito, immaturo, non abituato; (*of food*) non condito, insipido.
unseat, *v.t.* (*from horse, etc.*) Far cader di sella; privare della sedia. (*Pol.*) **To be unseated,** perdere il seggio.
unseaworthy, *a.* Che non può navigare, logoro, non atto alla navigazione.
unseconded, *a.* Non appoggiato, non sostenuto.
unsecured, *a.* Non assicurato, non chiuso, non serrato.
unseeing, *a.* Cieco, non veggente.
unseemliness, *n.* Sconvenienza, indecorosità, disdicevolezza, *f.*
unseemly, *a.* Sconveniente, sconvenevole, disdicevole, indecoroso. **— conduct,** comportamento indecoroso.
unseen, *a.* Inosservato, non visto; invisibile. || *n.* Traduzione a prima vista, *f.* **The — world,** il mondo invisibile, *m.*
unselfish, *a.* Disinteressato, altruista, generoso.
unsentimental, *a.* Poco sentimentale, non sentimentale.
unserviceable, *a.* Inutile, inservibile; non servizievole.
unserviceableness, *n.* Inutilità, inservibilità, *f.*
unserviceably, *adv.* Inutilmente.
unsettle, *v.t.* Disordinare, scompaginare, sconvolgere; agitare, commuovere, turbare, sconnettare, sconcertare.
unsettled, *a.* Disordinato, sconvolto, scomposto, instabile; agitato, turbato; indeciso, incerto; (*of weather*) variabile; (*of bills*) non saldato; (*of land*) non colonizzato.
unsettledness, *n.* Instabilità, *f.*; agitazione, *f.*; disordine, turbamento, *m.*; indecisione, incertezza, *f.*
unsex, *v.t.* Privare del sesso.
unsexed, *a.* Senza sesso.
unshackle, *v.t.* Disinceppare, liberare.
unshaded, *a.* Senz'ombra, non ombreggiato; senz'ombreggiatura.
unshaken, *a.* Fermo, irremovibile, incrollabile. **His resolve was —,** continuò a persistere nella sua decisione.
unshapely, *a.* Deforme, sgraziato.
unshaved, unshaven, *a.* Non raso, non sbarbato.
unsheathe, *v.t.* Sguainare, sfoderare. **To — the sword,** sguainare la spada.
unsheltered, *a.* Senza riparo, indifeso, senza difesa, esposto, non protetto.
unship, *v.t.* (*Naut.*) Sbarcare, scaricare; (*rudder*) smontare, togliere; (*oars*) disarmare.
unshod, *a.* Senza scarpe, scalzo; (*of horse*) non ferrato.
unshoe, *v.t.* (*a horse*) Togliere i ferri.
unshorn, *a.* Intonso.
unshrinkable, *a.* Irrestringibile.
unshrinking, *a.* Intrepido, impavido, imperterrito
unshut, *a.* Non chiuso; aperto.
unshuttered, *a.* Senza persiane, senza scuri.
unsightliness, *n.* Bruttezza, *f.*
unsightly, *a* Brutto, spiacevole, poco vistoso.
unsigned, *a.* Senza firma, non firmato.
unsinged, *a.* Non bruciato, non scottato.
unsinkable, *a.* Non affondabile, che non può venir sommerso.
unsinning, *a.* Innocente, senza peccato.
unsisterly, *a.* Non da sorella.
unsized, *a.* (*of paint, etc.*) Senza colla; (*of materials*) senza bozzima.
unskilful, *a.* Inabile, inesperto, maldestro, imperito, malaccorto.
unskilfully, *adv.* Inabilmente, inespertamente.
unskilfulness, *n.* Inabilità, imperizia, *f.*
unskilled, *a.* Inabile, inesperto. **— labour,** lavoro manuale, *m.*

Unless otherwise indicated, the pronunciation of words prefixed by "un" can be ascertained by reference to the unprefixed words or their derivatives in their alphabetical position in this dictionary.

unslacked, unslaked, *a.* Non smorzato; non spento; (*of thirst*) non appagato. **— lime,** calce non estinta, calce viva, *f.*
unsleeping, *a.* Vigilante, sempre desto, guardingo.
unsmoked, *a.* Non fumato; non affumicato.
unsociable, *a.* Insocievole, poco socievole, scontroso.
unsociableness, unsociability, *n.* Insocievolezza, scontrosaggine, insociabilità, *f.*
unsociably, *adv.* Insocievolmente, insociabilmente.
unsocial, *a.* Antisociale.
unsoiled, *a.* Non sporcato; incontaminato, immacolato, puro.
unsold, *a.* Invenduto.
unsoldierly, unsoldierlike, *a.* Indegno d'un soldato, poco militare, non soldatesco.
unsolicited, *a.* Non richiesto, non sollecitato. **An — testimonial,** una testimonianza non richiesta, *f.*
unsolicitous, *a.* Poco desideroso; incurante di.
unsolved, *a.* Insoluto, non risoluto.
unsophisticated, *a.* Semplice, ingenuo, sincero, genuino, schietto; (*unadulterated*) non sofisticato, non adulterato.
unsorted, *a.* Non scelto, non assortito.
unsought, *a.* Non cercato, non ricercato; non richiesto, spontaneo.
unsound, *a.* Difettoso, imperfetto, guasto; (*of health*) infermo, debole; (*fig.*) erroneo, errato, falso, fallace; incerto, instabile. **Of — mind,** non sano di mente, pazzo; **— lungs,** polmoni guasti, *m.pl.*
unsounded, *a.* Inesplorato, non sondato, non scandagliato.
unsoundly, *adv.* Difettosamente, imperfettamente; erroneamente; incertamente; (*of sleep*) agitatamente.
unsoundness, *n.* Infermità, cagionevolezza, debolezza, *f.*; difettosità, imperfezione, *f.*; (*fig.*) erroneità, falsità, fallacia, *f.*; incertezza, instabilità, *f.*
unsparing, *a.* Prodigo, largo, liberale, generoso; spietato, crudele, inesorabile.
unsparingly, *adv.* Prodigalmente, liberalmente; crudelmente.
unsparingness, *n.* Prodigalità, larghezza, liberalità, *f.*; crudeltà, *f.*
unspeakable, *a.* Indicibile, inesprimibile, ineffabile; indescrivibile.
unspeakably, *adv.* Indicibilmente, ineffabilmente, indescrivibilmente.
unspecified, *a.* Non specificato.
unspent, *a.* Non speso; inconsumato, inesausto, non esaurito.
unspillable, *a.* Che non si può rovesciare.
unspoken, *a.* Non detto, taciuto, inespresso.
unsporting, unsportsmanlike, *a.* Non degno d'uno sportivo; ingeneroso, gretto, meschino, vile.
unspotted, *a.* Non macchiato, pulito; (*fig.*) immacolato, senza macchia, puro, incontaminato, illibato.
unstable, *a.* Instabile, incostante, volubile, incerto, malfermo.
unstained, *a.* Non macchiato, non tinto; (*fig.*) immacolato, illibato.
unstamped, *a.* (*of documents*) Senza bollo; (*of letters*) senza francobollo, non affrancato, non timbrato.
unstarched, *a.* Non inamidato, senz'amido.
unstated, *a.* Non dichiarato.
unstatesmanlike, *a.* Impolitico; non da statista.
unsteadfast, *a.* Instabile, incostante.
unsteadfastly, *adv.* Instabilmente.
unsteadily, *adv.* Barcollando; instabilmente, incostantemente; irregolarmente.
unsteadiness, *n.* Titubanza, *f.*; instabilità, variabilità, incertezza, *f.*; irregolarità, dissipazione, *f.*
unsteady, *a.* Malfermo, sconnesso, poco solido; instabile, incostante, traballante, barcollante, vacillante, titubante; irregolare. **To be —,** barcollare, vacillare; titubare; **— winds,** venti variabili, *m.pl.*; **that table is —,** quella tavola è traballante; **an — hand,** una mano malferma, *f.*
unstick, *v.t.* Scollare.
unstinted, *a.* Abbondante, copioso; illimitato, pieno, senza riserve; di tutto cuore.
unstintedly, *adv.* Abbondatamente, copiosamente; pienamente, senza riserve.
unstitch, *v.t.* Scucire, disfare.
unstocked, *a.* Sprovvisto, sfornito.
unstop, *v.t.* Sturare, stasare, stappare, aprire.
unstrained, *a.* Non filtrato; (*fig.*) non sforzato, naturale.
unstraitened, *a.* Non ristretto.
unstressed, *a.* (*Gram.*) Atono, non accentato.
unstring, *v.t.* Togliere le corde a; allentare; sfilare; snervare.
unstudied, *a.* Facile, naturale, spontaneo.
unsubdued, *a.* Indomito, indomato, invitto.
unsubmissive, *a.* Refrattario, indomabile, restio, ribelle.
unsubstantial, *a.* Poco sostanziale, immateriale, poco solido; leggiero.
unsubstantiated, *a.* Non confermato, non comprovato.
unsuccessful, *a.* Non riuscito, inutile, vano, sfortunato, mal riuscito. **To be —,** non riuscire.
unsuccessfully, *adv.* Infruttuosamente, inutilmente, vanamente, senza successo.
unsuccessfulness, *n.* Infruttuosità, inutilità, *f.*
unsuitable, *a.* Disadatto, inadatto, sconveniente; incongruo; intempestivo, inopportuno.
unsuitableness, *n.* Incapacità, inadeguatezza, sconvenienza, *f.*; incongruità, *f.*; inopportunità, *f.*
unsuitably, *adv.* In modo inadeguato, sconvenientemente, inopportunamente.
unsuited, *a.* Disadatto, inadatto, sconvenevole; mal assortito.
unsullied, *a.* Non sporcato; immacolato, puro, senza macchia.
unsummoned, *a.* Non chiamato.
unsung, *a.* Non cantato; non celebrato.
unsupplied, *a.* Sprovvisto.
unsupportable, *a.* Insostenibile.
unsupported, *a.* Non sostenuto, non appoggiato; non comprovato, non confermato.
unsure, *a.* Incerto, non sicuro, malsicuro.

Unless otherwise indicated, the pronunciation of words prefixed by "un" can be ascertained by reference to the unprefixed words or their derivatives in their alphabetical position in this dictionary.

unsurmounted, *a.* Non sormontato, insuperato.
unsurpassed, *a.* Insuperato, imbattibile, invitto.
unsurrendered, *a.* Non restituito.
unsusceptible, *a.* Non suscettibile.
unsuspected, *a.* Insospettato, non sospetto.
unsuspectedly, *adv.* Senza sospetto.
unsuspecting, unsuspicious, *a.* Non sospettoso, senza sospetto.
unsuspectingly, *adv.* Senza sospetto, non sospettando.
unsustained, *a.* Non sostenuto.
unswathe, *v.t.* Sfasciare, sbendare.
unswayed, *a.* Non influenzato, non dominato.
unsweetened, *a.* Non zuccherato, non addolcito; (*of wine*) brusco, asciutto.
unswept, *a.* Non spazzato, non scopato.
unswerving, *a.* Fermo, irremovibile, incrollabile.
unsymmetrical, *a.* Asimmetrico, sproporzionato.
unsymmetrically, *adv.* Senza simmetria.
unsympathetic, *a.* Ostile, poco amichevole; non compassionevole, poco simpatico.
unsympathetically, *adv.* Senza compassione, ostilmente; senza simpatia.
unsystematic, *a.* Poco sistematico, poco metodico.
unsystematically, *adv.* Senza sistema, senza metodo, irregolarmente.
untack, *v.t.* Staccare, disgiungere, scucire.
untainted, *a.* Incorrotto, non guasto; puro, immacolato, illibato.
untalented, *a.* Senza talento, senz'ingegno.
untamable, *a.* Indomabile, ribelle, riottoso.
untamed, *a.* Indomato, indomito, non addomesticato.
untarnished, *a.* Non macchiato; immacolato, senza macchia, puro. **An — reputation,** una reputazione senza macchie.
untasted, *a.* Non assaggiato, non gustato, intatto.
untaught, *a.* Ignorante, poco istruito, senz'istruzione; non studiato.
untaxed, *a.* Esente da imposte.
unteachable, *a.* Non educabile, incapace d'imparare; incorreggibile.
untearable, *a.* Non lacerabile.
untenable, *a.* Insostenibile; non difendibile.
untenantable, *a.* Inabitabile.
untenanted, *a.* Non affittato, sfitto, non occupato, disabitato.
untended, *a.* Non curato, incostudito, non sorvegliato.
unterrified, *a.* Non spaventato.
untested, *a.* Non provato; non collaudato.
untether, *v.t.* Slegare, sciogliere.
unthanked, *a.* Non ringraziato.
unthankful, *a.* Ingrato.
unthankfulness, *n.* Ingratitudine, mancanza di riconoscenza, *f.*
unthinkable, *a.* Impensabile.
unthinking, *a.* Spensierato, irriflessivo, sventato, leggero.
unthinkingly, *adv.* Inconsideratamente, senza pensarci.
unthought-of, *a.* Impensato, improvviso, inaspettato.
unthread, *v.t.* Sfilare.
unthrifty, *a.* Prodigo, scialacquatore, sperperatore.
untidily, *adv.* Disordinatamente, confusamente.
untidiness, *n.* Disordine, *m.*, trascuratezza, confusione, *f.*
untidy, *a.* Disordinato, trascurato, malmesso, malconcio, trasandato.
untie, *v.t.* Slegare, slacciare, snodare; disfare, sciogliere.
until, *prep.* Fino a, sino a, insino a, prima di. || *conj.* Finchè, fino a quando. **Wait — tomorrow,** aspettate fino a domani; **— now,** finora; **— then,** fino allora; **I shall not leave — he comes,** non partirò finchè non sia arrivato lui.
untile, *v.t.* Togliere i tegoli, scoprire, scoperchiare.
untilled, *a.* Incolto, incoltivato.
untimeliness, *n.* Inopportunità, intempestività, *f.*
untimely, *a.* Prematuro; inopportuno, intempestivo. *adv.* Prematuramente; inopportunamente.
untiring, *a.* Infaticabile, instancabile, indefesso.
untiringly, *adv.* Infaticabilmente, instancabilmente.
untitled, *a.* Senza titolo.
unto [cp. **to**]
untold, *a.* Non detto, non raccontato; innumerevole, incalcolabile. **— gold,** mucchi d'oro, monti d'oro, *m.pl.*
untouchable, *n.* (*in India*) Paria, intoccabile, *m.*
untouched, *a.* Non toccato; (*fig.*) imperturbato, non commosso; intatto. **He left his dinner —,** non toccò cibo, lasciò il pranzo intatto.
untoward, *a.* Ritroso, ricalcitrante; sfortunato, disgraziato. **An — event,** un incidente disgraziato, *m.*, una disgrazia, *f.*
untraceable, *a.* Introvabile, irreperibile.
untrained, *a.* Inesperto, novizio; indisciplinato; non allenato; non ammaestrato.
untrammelled, *a.* Non impastoiato, non inceppato, sciolto, libero.
untranslatable, *a.* Intraducibile.
untravelled, *a.* Che non ha viaggiato; inesplorato.
untried, *a.* Non provato; intentato; non processato.
untrimmed, *a.* Non guarnito, non ornato; non regolato, non tagliato.
untrodden, *a.* Non battuto, non frequentato, non calpestrato. **— ways,** sentieri non battuti, *m.pl.*; vie intentate, *f.pl.*; **— snow,** neve intatta, *f.*
untroubled, *a.* Imperturbato, tranquillo, calmo, sereno.
untrue, *a.* Falso, non vero, bugiardo, mendace, menzognero; infedele, perfido, sleale, disonesto.
untruly, *adv.* Falsamente; perfidamente, slealmente.
untrustworthiness, *n.* Falsità, menzogna, *f.*; perfidia, slealtà, *f.*
untrustworthy, *a.* Indegno di fede; falso, menzognero, bugiardo, mendace.

Unless otherwise indicated, the pronunciation of words prefixed by "un" can be ascertained by reference to the unprefixed words or their derivatives in their alphabetical position in this dictionary.

untruth, *n.* Falsità, *f.*; bugia, menzogna, *f.*
untruthful, *a.* Bugiardo, menzognero, falso.
untruthfully, *adv.* Falsamente.
untruthfulness, *n.* Falsità, *f.*
untuck, *v.t.* Disfare una piega.
untuned, *a.*Scordato, stonato.
unturned, *a.* Non voltato, non rivoltato. **To leave no stone —,** non lasciar nulla d'intentato, far fuoco e fiamme.
untutored, *a.* Ignorante, poco istruito; naturale, spontaneo.
untwine, untwist, *v.t.* Districare, sciogliere, spiegare, svolgere; *v.i.* sciogliersi, spiegarsi.
unusable, *a.* Inutilizzabile, inutile, inservibile.
unused, *a.* Non usato, non adoperato, non abituato, non avezzo. **— to,** non abituato a, poco pratico di.
unusual, *a.* Insolito, strano, straordinario, raro, inusitato, eccezionale, non frequente.
unusually, *adv.* Insolitamente; eccezionalmente.
unusualness, *n.* Stranezza, rarità, *f.*; straordinarietà, *f.*
unutterable, *a.* Indicibile, inesprimibile.
unuttered, *a.* Non detto, non espresso, non proferito.
unvalued, *a.* Non valutato, non stimato, disprezzato, negletto.
unvanquished, *a.* Invitto, indomito.
unvaried, *a.* Uniforme, eguale, non variato, monotono.
unvarnished, *a.* Non verniciato; (*fig.*) semplice, schietto, naturale.
unvarying, *a.* Invariabile.
unveil, *v.t.* Svelare; scoprire, palesare; inaugurare.
unveiling, *n.* Inaugurazione, *f.*; scoprimento, *m.*
unventilated, *a.* Non ventilato, senz'aria, non aerato.
unverifiable, *a.* Non verificabile, non controllabile.
unverified, *a.* Non verificato.
unversed, *a.* Poco pratico, inabile. **— in,** poco pratico di, inabile a, inesperto di.
unvisited, *a.* Non visitato, non frequentato.
unvoiced, *a.* Non espresso, non pronunciato; (*Gram.*) muto.
unvouched-for, *a.* Non attestato.
unwakened, *a.* Non sveglio, non svegliato, addormentato.
unwanted, *a.* Non desiderato, non voluto.
unwarily, *adv.* Imprudentemente, incautamente, inconsideratamente.
unwariness, *n.* Imprudenza, sconsideratezza, *f.*
unwarlike, *a.* Pacifico, poco bellicoso, imbelle.
unwarmed, *a.* Non riscaldato.
unwarned, *a.* Non avvertito, non ammonito, non preavvisato.
unwarrantable, *a.* Ingiustificabile, inescusabile, inqualificabile.
unwarrantably, *adv.* Ingiustificabilmente.
unwarranted, *a.* Ingiustificato, infondato; (*Comm.*) senza garanzia; gratuito.
unwary, *a.* Imprudente, incauto, inconsiderato, sventato.
unwashed, *a.* Sporco, sudicio, immondo **The great —,** la plebaglia, *f.*
unwatched, *a.* Non guardato, non sorvegliato.
unwatchful, *a.* Disattento, negligente, sbadato.
unwatered, *a.* Senz'acqua, innaffiato; (*of cattle*) non abbeverato.
unwavering, *a.* Incrollabile, irremovibile, inconcusso, fermo, deciso.
unweakened, *a.*Non infiacchito, non indebolito.
unweaned, *a.* Non svezzato, non slattato, non spoppato.
unwearable, *a.* Fuori uso, non indossabile.
unwearied, *a.* Infaticato, infaticabile, instancabile.
unwedded, *a.* Non sposato; (*of man*) celibe, (*of woman*) nubile, zitella.
unweighed, *a.* Non pesato.
unwelcome, *a.* Male accolto, malaccolto; spiacevole, sgradito, ostico. **To be —,** essere male accolto; riuscir sgradito.
unwell, *a.* Ammalato, indisposto.
unwept, unwept for, *a.* Incompianto, illacrimato.
unwholesome, *a.* Malsano, insalubre; nocivo, guasto, corrotto.
unwholesomeness, *n.* Insalubrità, morbosità, *f.*
unwieldily, *adv.* Con difficoltà, pesantemente.
unwieldiness, *n.* Pesantezza, gravezza, *f.*, impaccio, *m.*
unwieldy, *a.* Poco maneggiabile, impacciante, ingombrante, pesante, grave.
unwilling, *a.* Poco disposto, restio, contrario, avverso, svogliato. **To be — to,** non volere.
unwillingly, *adv.* Malvolentieri, di mala voglia, svogliatamente.
unwillingness, *n.* Malavoglia, svogliatezza, *f.*; ritrosia, *f.*
unwind [ʌnˈwaind], *v.t.* Sgomitolare; svolgere, districare; *v.i.* sgomitolarsi; districarsi, svolgersi.
unwinking, *a.* (*of eye*) Fisso.
unwisdom, *n.* Imprudenza, follia, stoltezza, insensatezza, *f.*
unwise, *a.* Poco savio, insensato, malaccorto, imprudente, incauto; sciocco, balordo.
unwisely, *adv.* Insensatamente, imprudentemente; scioccamente.
unwished-for, *a.* Non desiderato.
unwitnessed, *a.* Senza testimoni.
unwittingly, *adv.* Inconsapevolmente, senza saperlo, per inavvertenza.
unwomanly, *a.* Poco femminile, indegno d'una donna.
unwonted, *a.* Insolito, straordinario, non usato, inusitato.
unwontedly, *adv.* Insolitamente.
unworkable, *a.* Ineseguibile, impraticabile; non lavorabile; incoltivabile.
unworkmanlike, *a.* Inesperto, inabile; malfatto.
unworldliness, *n.* Spiritualità, *f.*, disinteresse, *m.*
unworldly, *a.* Poco mondano, spirituale, disinteressato.
unworn, *a.* Non frusto, non logoro; mai indossato.

Unless otherwise indicated, the pronunciation of words prefixed by "un" can be ascertained by reference to the unprefixed words or their derivatives in their alphabetical position in this dictionary.

unworthily, *adv.* Indegnamente, vilmente, indecorosamente.
unworthiness, *n.* Indegnità, *f.*; viltà, bassezza, *f.*
unworthy, *a.* Indegno, immeritevole; vile, basso, ignobile.
unwound [ʌnˈwaund], *a.* Sgomitolato; districato.
unwounded [ʌnˈwu:ndəd], *a.* Incolume, illeso, non ferito.
unwrap, *v.t.* Disfare, sciogliere, districare, aprire, sfasciare.
unwrinkled, *a.* Senza rughe, liscio, spianato, non corrugato.
unwritten, *a.* Non scritto; tradizionale, orale. **The — law,** la legge dell'onore, la legge non scritta, *f.*
unwrought, *a.* Non lavorato, greggio, crudo.
unyielding, *a.* Inflessibile, inesorabile; rigido, duro, ostinato.
unyieldingness, *n.* Inflessibilità, rigidezza, ostinatezza, *f.*
unyoke, *v.t.* Staccare, liberare dal giogo, togliere il giogo a.
unyouthful, *a.* Poco giovanile.
up [ʌp], *adv.* Su, sopra, in alto, in su; ritto, in piedi; (*of jockey*) in sella. || *prep.* Su, su per. || *a.* Ascendente, in salita. || *inter.* Su! In piedi! All'erta! Levatevi! **What are you doing up there?** Che cosa fate lassù? **a mile further up the river,** un miglio a monte del fiume; **Is he up yet?** È alzato? Non si è ancora levato? **it is all up with him** è finita per lui; **time is up,** il tempo è trascorso, l'ora è passata; **he is not up to the journey,** non è in istato di fare il viaggio; **to be up to date,** essere aggiornato, essere al corrente; **we were up to our knees in mud,** eravamo nel fango fino ai ginocchi; **up to,** fino a, sino a; **to come up with,** raggiungere; **to have someone up,** procedere contro alcuno; **up and down,** su e giù; **up in arms against,** in rivolta contro, infuriato con; **I am going up to town,** vado in città; **he came straight up to me,** venne dritto fino a me; **Stand up!** Alzatevi! Dritto! **I was up late last night,** sono andato a letto tardi la notte scorsa; **his blood is up,** gli ribolle il sangue; **to be well up in,** essere bene istruito in, intendersi di; **What's up?** Che cosa è successo? (*colloq.*) **this book isn't up to much,** questo libro è mediocre; (*colloq.*) **it's up to you to do it,** tocca a voi farlo; (*colloq.*) **he's up against it,** si trova nei guai; è alle prese con; **we climbed up the hill,** salimmo la collina; **he went up the ladder,** salì sulla scala; **he walked up the street,** camminò lungo la strada; (*Rail.*) **the up line,** il binario d'andata; **the ups and downs,** gli alti e i bassi, *m.pl.*, le vicende, *f.pl.*; **up-stream,** a monte; (*Golf*) **three holes up,** tre buche di vantaggio.
upas, upas tree [ˈju:pæs], *n.* Albero del veleno, *m.*
upbear, *v.t.* Sorreggiare, sollevare, sostenere.
upbraid [ʌpˈbreid], *v.t.* Rimproverare, biasimare, riprendere.
upbraiding, *n.* Rimproveri, *m.pl.*
upbringing, *n.* Educazione, *f.*, allevamento, *m.*
upheaval [ʌpˈhi:vəl], *n.* Sollevazione, *f.*, tumulto; sconvolgimento, *m.*, confusione, *f.*; (*Geol.*) sollevamento, *m.*
uphill [ˈʌphil], *a.* In salita, montante; arduo, penoso, duro, difficile. || *adv.* In salita, in su, all'insù. **It's — work,** è un lavoro duro.
uphold [ʌpˈhould], *v.t.* Sostenere, sorreggere, propugnare, appoggiare, mantenere; innalzare, sollevare.
upholder, *n.* Sostenitore, difensore, propugnatore, *m.*
upholster [ʌpˈhoulstəɹ], *v.t.* Tappezzare, imbottire.
upholsterer, *n.* Tappezziere, *m.*
upholstering, upholstery, *n.* Tappezzeria, *f.*
upkeep [ˈʌpki:p], *n.* Mantenimento, *m.*; manutenzione, *f.*
upland [ˈʌplənd], *n.* Altipiano, *m.* || *a.* Montano, alpino.
uplift [ʌpˈlift], *v.t.* Innalzare, elevare, sollevare. || *n.* [ˈʌplift], Edificazione, *f.*
uplifting, *a.* Edificante. || *n.* Innalzamento, *m.*
upon [əˈpɔn], *prep.* Su, sopra; a; di; da; verso [cp. **on**]. **Upon my word,** Perbacco! Caspita!
upper [ˈʌpəɹ], *a.* Superiore, più sopra, più alto. || *n.* (*of shoe*) Tomaio, *m.* (*Theat.*) **Upper circle,** balconata, seconda galleria, *f.*; **the Upper House,** la Camera dei Pari, *f.*; **the — classes,** le classi superiori, *f.pl.*; (*Naut.*) **the — deck,** il ponte di coperta, *m.*; **the — hand,** il vantaggio, *m.*; **the Upper Ten,** l'aristocrazia, *f.*, il gran mondo, *m.*; (*colloq.*) **to keep a stiff — lip,** tenere duro; (*Print.*) **— case,** maiuscole, *f.pl.*; (*colloq.*) **to be on one's uppers,** essere alle strette, essere al verde.
uppermost, *a.* Il più alto, il più elevato; il primo. || *adv.* In alto, su, sopra. **He says whatever comes —,** dice la prima cosa che gli viene in mente; **to be —,** predominare.
uppish, *a.* (*colloq.*) Borioso, superbo, arrogante, altezzoso.
uppishness, *n.* Boria, altezzosità, superbia, arroganza, *f.*
upraise [ʌpˈreiz], *v.t.* Sollevare, elevare, alzare, innalzare.
uprear [ʌpˈriəɹ], *v.t.* Sollevare, innalzare, rialzare.
upright [ˈʌprait], *a.* Diritto, dritto, ritto, eretto; (*fig.*) giusto, integro; perpendicolare. || *adv.* Diritto, ritto, in piedi; a piombo, perpendicolarmente, verticalmente. || *n.* Palo verticale, *m.*, asta verticale, *f.* **To stand —,** stare eretto; **to set —,** mettere in piedi, innalzare; **an — piano,** un pianoforte verticale, *m.*
uprightly, *adv.* Onestamente, rettamente, giustamente.
uprightness, *n.* Rettitudine, onestà, giustizia, *f.*; perpendicolarità, *f.*
uprise [ʌpˈraiz], *v.i.* Levarsi, alzarsi.
uprising, *n.* Sollevamento, tumulto, *m.*, sollevazione, insurrezione, *f.*
uproar [ˈʌprɔ:ɹ], *n.* Baccano, strepito, fracasso, *m.*; tumulto, *m.*, parapiglia, *f.*; scompiglio, *m.*
uproarious, *a.* Tumultuoso, chiassoso, rumoroso.
uproariously, *adv.* Tumultuosamente, rumorosamente.

Unless otherwise indicated, the pronunciation of words prefixed by "un" can be ascertained by reference to the unprefixed words or their derivatives in their alphabetical position in this dictionary.

uproariousness, *n.* Tumultuosità, *f.*; strepito, baccano, scompiglio, *m.*
uproot [ʌpˈruːt], *v.t.* Sradicare, estirpare.
uprooting, *n.* Sradicamento, *m.*, estirpazione, *f.*
upset [ʌpˈset], *v.t.* Sconvolgere, capovolgere, rovesciare; (*fig.*) agitare, turbare, scompigliare, commuovere, emozionare; *v.i.* capovolgersi, rovesciarsi. **— price,** prezzo d'apertura, *m.*
upshot [ˈʌpʃɔt], *n.* Esito, risultato, effetto, *m.*, conclusione, *f.*
upside down [ʌpsaid ˈdaun], *adv.* Sottosopra, sossopra, a catafascio, a rotoli. **To turn — —,** mettere sossopra, capovolgere, rovesciare.
upstanding [ʌpˈstændiŋ], *a.* Dritto, eretto.
upstairs [ʌpˈstɛəɹz], *a.* Di sopra, disopra. || *adv.* Sopra, di sopra. **An — room,** una stanza al piano superiore, *f.*; **to go —,** andar disopra.
upstart [ˈʌpstɑːɹt], *n.* Villano rifatto, arrivista, *m.*, pescecane, *m.*
upstroke [ˈʌpstrouk], *n.* (*handwriting*) Asta, *f.*; (*of piston*) corsa ascendente, salita dello stantuffo, *f.*
uptake [ˈʌpteik], *n.* Presa, *f.*, appiglio, *m.* **Quick in the —,** rapido nel capire.
upthrust [ˈʌpθrʌst], *n.* (*Geol.*) Sollevamento, *m.*
upturn [ʌpˈtəːɹn], *v.t.* Volgere in su, alzare in su. **The crowd stood with upturned faces,** la gente stava colla faccia alzata.
upward, upwards [ˈʌpwəd, ˈʌpwədz], *a.adv.* In su, in alto, all'insù; oltre, più. **— of,** più di, oltre; **children of two years and —,** bambini di due anni e più, *m.pl.*; **an — glance,** uno sguardo in alto, *m.*; **an — movement of prices,** un rialzo dei prezzi, *m.*
Urals [ˈjuːrəlz], *n.pl.* (*Geog.*) Gli Urali, *m.pl.*
uranium [juːˈreiniəm], *n.* (*Min.*) Uranio, *m.*
urban [ˈəːɹbən], *a.* Urbano.
urbane [əːɹˈbein], *a.* Urbano, civile, cortese, educato.
urbanely, *adv.* Urbanamente.
urbanity [əːɹˈbæniti], *n.* Urbanità, gentilezza, *f.*
urchin [ˈəːɹtʃin], *n.* Monello, birichino, bricconcello, *m.* (*Zool.*) **Sea —,** riccio di mare, echino, *m.*
Urdu [ˈuːɹduː], *n.* La lingua indù, *f.*
ureter [juːˈriːtəɹ], *n.* (*Anat.*) Uretere, *m.*
urethra [juːˈriːθrə], *n.* (*Anat.*) Uretra, *f.*
urge [əːɹdʒ], *v.t.* Urgere, spingere, incalzare; incitare, esortare, eccitare, stimolare, sollecitare; insistere in, mettere innanzi, accampare, addurre, far valere. **To — on,** spingere, incalzare, stimolare; **he urged him to take action,** lo spinse ad agire; **the argument was urged in vain,** la questione venne sollevata invano.
urgency, *n.* Urgenza, premura, imminenza, *f.*; bisogno, *m.*, sollecitazione, istanza, *f.*
urgent, *a.* Urgente, incalzante. **To be —,** essere urgente.
urgently, *adv.* Urgentemente, di premura, d'urgenza.
urging, *n.* Sollecitazione, pressione, istigazione, *f.*
uric [ˈjuːrik], *a.* (*Chem.*) Urico.
urinal [ˈjuːrinəl], *n.* Orinale, *m.*; (*public*) orinatoio, vespasiano, *m.*
urinary [ˈjuːrinəri], *a.* Orinario.
urinate, *v.i.* Orinare.
urine [ˈjuːrin], *n.* Orina, *f.*
urn [əːɹn], *n.* Urna, *f.* **Tea- —,** samovar, *m.*; **coffee- —,** caffettiera, *f.*
uroscopy [juːˈrɔskəpi], *n.* Uroscopia, *f.*
ursine [ˈəːɹsain], *a.* Orsino.
Ursula [ˈəːɹsjuːlə], *n.* Orsola, *f.*
Ursuline [ˈəːɹsjuːlain], *n.a.* (*Eccles.*) Orsolina, *f.*
us [ʌs], *pron.* Ci, ce, ne; noi.
usable [ˈjuːzəbl], *a.* Usabile, adoperabile, impiegabile.
usage [ˈjuːzidʒ], *n.* Trattamento, *m.*; uso, *m.*, consuetudine, abitudine, usanza, *f.* **Ill- —,** maltrattamento, *m.*
usance, *n.* (*Comm.*) Usanza, *f.*
use (1) [juːs], *n.* (*custom*) Uso, *m.*, consuetudine, abitudine, usanza, *f.*; (*advantage*) pro, *m.*, utilità, *f.* (*profit*) profitto, frutto, *m.*; (*Law*) usufrutto, *m.* **For the — of,** per uso di; **articles in general —,** articoli d'uso generale, *m.pl.*; **What's the — of doing that?** A che serve fare ciò?; **of —,** utile, giovevole; **it is of no — to . . .,** non vale . . ., è inutile . . .; **of no —,** inutile, vano; **to have no further — for,** non avere più bisogno di; **to make — of,** utilizzare, far uso di; **to put to good —,** usare bene; **it is in daily —,** è usato ogni giorno; **May I have the — of your piano?** Posso servirmi del vostro pianoforte?; **— is second nature,** l'abitudine è una seconda natura.
use (2) [juːz], *v.t.* Usare, servirsi di, adoperare, far uso di; abituare, assuefare, avvezzare; trattare; *v.i.* usare, solere, aver l'uso, avere la consuetudine. **To — ill,** maltrattare; **to — up,** consumare, usare, esaurire, logorare; **I used to read a great deal,** leggevo molto.
used, *a.* Usato, abituato, assuefatto, avvezzo. **Not —,** non usato, insolito, inusitato; **to get — to,** abituarsi a, assuefarsi a, avvezzarsi a; **— up,** esaurito, esausto, logoro, consumato; **as we are — to do,** come siamo soliti fare; **to be badly —,** venir trattato male.
useful [ˈjuːsful], *a.* Utile, giovevole, profittevole, proficuo; servizievole.
usefully, *adv.* Utilmente.
usefulness, *n.* Utilità, *f.*, vantaggio, *m.*
useless, *a.* Inutile, vano.
uselessly, *adv.* Inutilmente.
uselessness, *n.* Inutilità, *f.*
user [ˈjuːzəɹ], *n.* Chi usa, utente, *m.*
Ushant [ˈʌʃənt], *n.* (*Geog.*) Ushanti, *m.*
usher [ˈʌʃəɹ], *n.* (*in court*) Usciere, *m.*; (*at school*) assistente, ripetitore, *m.* || *v.t.* **To — in,** introdurre, fare entrare; annunziare, inaugurare; **to — out,** fare uscire, condurre alla porta.
usual [ˈjuːʒuːəl], *a.* Usuale, solito, ordinario, abituale, consueto, frequente, comune. **As —,** al solito, come al solito; **more than —,** più del solito.
usually, *adv.* Usualmente, di solito, ordinariamente.
usualness, *n.* Frequenza, consuetudine, abitudine, *f.*
usufruct [juːzjuːˈfrʌkt], *n.* Usufrutto, *m.*
usufructuary, *a.* Usufruttuario.
usurer [ˈjuːʒurəɹ], *n.* Usuraio, strozzino, *m.*
usurious [juːˈʒjuːriəs], *a.* Usurario.
usurp [juːˈzəːɹp], *v.t.* Usurpare.
usurpation, *n.* Usurpazione, *f.*
usurper, *n.* Usurpatore, *m.*, usurpatrice, *f.*

usury [ˈjuːʒəri], *n.* Usura, *f.*
ut [ʌt], *n.* (*Mus.*) Do, *m.*
utensil [juːˈtensil], *n.* Utensile, arnese, ordigno, *m.*; vaso, *m.*
uterine [ˈjuːtərain], *a.* Uterino.
uterus [ˈjuːtərəs], *n.* (*Anat.*) Utero, *m.*
utilitarian [juːtiliˈtɛəriən], *n.a.* Utilitario, *m.*
utilitarianism, *n.* Utilitarismo, *m.*
utility [juːˈtiliti], *n.* Utilità, *f.*, vantaggio, profitto, *m.* (*Theat.*) **— -man,** generico, *m.*; **public —,** esercizio pubblico.
utilizable [juːtiˈlaizəbl], *a.* Usabile, adoperabile.
utilization, *n.* Utilizzazione, *f.*
utilize [ˈjuːtilaiz], *v.t.* Utilizzare, servirsi di.
utmost [ˈʌtmoust], *a.* Estremo, massimo, ultimo, sommo. ‖ *n.* L'estremo, l'ultimo, *m.* **At the —,** al più, tutt'al più; **to do one's —,** fare il possibile; **to the —,** fino all'estremo, fino all'ultimo; **with the — speed,** al più presto possibile, a tutta velocità.
Utopia [juːˈtoupiə], *n.* Utopia, *f.*
Utopian, *a.* Utopistico. ‖ *n.* Utopista, *m.*
utricle [ˈjuːtrikl], *n.* (*Bot.*) Follicolo, *m.*
utter (1) [ˈʌtəɹ], *a.* Totale, intiero, completo, assoluto, solenne, matricolato, famigerato. **To my — astonishment,** con mia grande sorpresa; **he is an — stranger to me,** mi è completamente sconosciuto.
utter (2), *v.t.* Dire, proferire, pronunziare; esprimere, manifestare; emettere, metter fuori, passare, mettere in circolazione. **To — a sigh,** sospirare, emettere un sospiro, mandare un sospiro; **to — a cry,** gridare, lanciare un grido; (*Comm.*) **to — notes,** emettere biglietti di banca.
utterance [ˈʌtərəns], *n.* Pronuncia, articolazione, *f.*; detto, espressione, parola, *f.* **To give — to,** esprimere, pronunziare, proferire.
uttering, *n.* (*of coin, etc.*) Emissione, *f.*
utterly, *adv.* Totalmente, intieramente, completamente, assolutamente.
uttermost, *adv.* Estremo, ultimo, massimo. **At the —,** al più, tutt'al più; **to the — ends of the earth,** agli estremi confini della terra.
uvula [ˈjuːvjuːlə], *n.* (*Anat.*) Ugola, *f.*
uvular, *a.* Dell'ugola.
uxoricide [ʌkˈzɔːrisaid], *n.* (*crime*) Uxoricidio, *m.*; (*criminal*) uxoricida, *m.*
uxorious [ʌkˈzɔːriəs], *a.* Attaccato, asservito alla moglie.

V

V, v [viː], *n.* Ventiduesima lettera dell'alfabeto inglese.
vacancy [ˈveikənsi], *n.* Vuoto, spazio, *m.*, vacanza, *f.*; lacuna, *f.*; posto libero, *m.*
vacant [ˈveikənt], *a.* Vuoto, vacante; libero, non occupato; (*of mind*) distratto. **A — air,** un'aria distratta, *f.*; **a — situation,** un impiego vacante, *m.*
vacantly, *adv.* Vacuamente.
vacate [vəˈkeit], *v.t.* Lasciare vuoto, sgombrare; dimettersi da; andarsene da, ritirarsi da, uscire da.
vacation, *n.* Vacanze, *f.pl.*; (*Law*) periodo di ferie, *m.*, vacanze dei tribunali, *f.pl.*
vaccinate [ˈvæksineit], *v.t.* Vaccinare.
vaccinated, *a.* Vaccinato. **To be —,** farsi vaccinare.
vaccination, *n.* Vaccinazione, *f.*
vaccine [ˈvæksiːn], *n.* Vaccino, siero vaccinico, *m.*
vacillate [ˈvæsileit], *v.i.* Vacillare; barcollare; essere incostante.
vacillation, *n.* Vacillazione, *f.*; incostanza, *f.*, vacillamento, *m.*
vacuity [vəˈkjuːiti], *n.* Vacuità, inanità, *f.*; vuoto, *m.*
vacuous [ˈvækjuːəs], *a.* Vacuo, inane; vuoto.
vacuousness, *n.* Vacuità, *f.*
vacuum (pl. **vacua**) [ˈvækjuːəm, ˈvækjuːə], *n.* Vuoto, *m.* **— -cleaner,** aspirapolvere, *m.*; **— flask,** termos, *m.*; **— -brake,** freno pneumatico, *m.*
vade-mecum [veidiˈmiːkəm], *n.* Vademecum, taccuino, libretto, *m.*
vagabond [ˈvægəbɔnd], *n.a.* Vagabondo, *m.*
vagabondage, *n.* Vagabondaggio, *m.*
vagary [vəˈgɛəri], *n.* Capriccio, ghiribizzo, *m.*, divagazione, *f.*
vagina [vəˈdʒainə], *n.* (*Anat.*) Vagina, *f.*; (*Bot.*) guaina, *f.*
vaginal, *a.* Vaginale.
vagrancy [ˈveigrənsi], *n.* Vagabondaggio, accattonaggio, *m.*
vagrant, *n.* Accattone, *m.*, accattona, *f.* ‖ *a.* Vagabondo.
vague [veig], *a.* Vago, impreciso, indeterminato.
vaguely, *adv.* Vagamente, imprecisamente.
vagueness, *n.* Imprecisione, incertezza, indeterminatezza, *f.*
vain [vein], *a.* Vano, inutile; vanitoso.
vainglorious [veinˈglɔːriəs], *a.* Vanaglorioso.
vainglory, *n.* Vanagloria, *f.*
vainly, *adv.* Vanamente, invano, inutilmente; vanitosamente.
vainness, *n.* Inutilità, *f.*; vanità, *f.*
valance [ˈvæləns], *n.* Tenda del letto, *f.*, drappellone, *m.*; balza, *f.* ‖ *v.t.* Decorare, ornare di frangie.
vale [veil], *n.* Valle, vallata, *f.*
valediction [væliˈdikʃən], *n.* Addio, commiato, *m.*
valedictory, *a.* Di addio, di commiato.
valence, valency [ˈveiləns, ˈveilənsi], *n.* (*Chem.*) Valenza, *f.*
Valencia [vəˈlensiə], *n.* (*Geog.*) Valenza, *f.*
valency [cp. **valence** (2)].
Valentine (1) [ˈvæləntain], *n.* Valentino, *m.*
valentine (2), *n.* Lettera amorosa inviata il 14 febbraio, *f.*
valerian [vəˈliəriən], *n.* (*Bot.*) Valeriana, *f.*
valet [ˈvælet, ˈvælei], *n.* Valletto, servitore, cameriere, *m.* ‖ *v.t.* Fare il valletto a, fare il servitore a.
valetudinarian [vælitjuːdiˈnɛəriən], *n.a.* Malaticcio, *m.*
valetudinarianism, *n.* Salute malferma, *f.*
valetudinary, *a.* Malaticcio.
valiant [ˈvæljənt], *a.* Valoroso, prode; robusto.
valiantly, *adv.* Valorosamente, prodemente.
valid [ˈvælid], *a.* Valido, valevole.
validate [ˈvælideit], *v.t.* Rendere valido, convalidare.
validation, *n.* Convalidazione, *f.*
validity, validness, *n.* Validità, *f.*
validly, *adv.* Validamente.
valise [vəˈliːz], *n.* Valigia, *f.*
Valkyrie [vælˈkiri], *n.* (*Myth.*) Valchiria, *f.*

valley ['væli], *n.* Valle, vallata, *f.*, vallone, *m.*; (*of roof*) conversa, *f.* **The entrance of the —,** l'imbocco della valle, *f.*; **the — of the shadow of death,** la valle dell'ombra della morte, *f.*
valorous ['vælərəs], *a.* Valoroso.
valorously, *adv.* Valorosamente, prodemente.
valour, *n.* Coraggio, valore, *m.*, prodezza, *f.*
valuable ['vælju:əbl], *a.* Prezioso, di gran valore.
valuables, *n.pl.* Valori, oggetti di valore, *m.pl.*
valuation [vælju:'eiʃən], *n.* Valutazione, stima, *f.*; apprezzamento, *m.*; perizia, *f.*
value ['vælju:], *n.* Valore, prezzo, *m.*; stima, *f.*; utilità, *f.*; valuta, *f.* || *v.t.* Valutare; apprezzare; stimare, tener conto di. **To — highly,** stimare altamente; **to — a loss,** computare una perdita; **above its real —,** al disopra del valore effettivo.
valued, *a.* Valutato, apprezzato, stimato, pregiato.
valueless, *a.* Senza valore.
valuer, *n.* Stimatore, valutatore, perito, apprezzatore, *m.*
valve [vælv], *n.* Valvola, *f.* **Safety —,** valvola di sicurezza, *f.*; **exhaust —,** valvola di scappamento, *f.*; **suction —,** valvola di aspirazione, *f.*; (*Radio.*) **— set,** apparecchio a valvole, *m.*
valvular, *a.* Valvolare.
vamp [væmp], *n.* (*of shoe*) Tomaio, *m.*; (*colloq.*) donna fatale, *f.* || *v.t.i.* Rimontare le scarpe; improvvisare al pianoforte.
vamper, *n.* Chi improvvisa un accompagnamento al pianoforte.
vampire ['væmpaiɹ], *n.* Vampiro, *m.*
vampirism, *n.* Vampirismo, *m.*
van (1) [væn], *n.* Furgone, carro, *m.*; (*Rail.*) bagagliaio, *m.*
van (2), *n.* Avanguardia, *f.*
vanadium [və'neidiəm], *n.* Vanadio, *m.*
vandal ['vændəl], *n.a.* Vandalo, *m.*
vandalism, *n.* Vandalismo, *m.*
Vandyke [væn'daik], *a.* (*beard*) Pizzo a punta, *m.*; (*collar*) collare alla Vandyke, *m.*
vane [vein], *n.* Banderuola, giretta, *f.*, mostravento, *m.*; pala, *f.*
vanguard ['vængɑ:ɹd], *n.* Avanguardia, *f.*
vanilla [və'nilə], *n.* Vaniglia, *f.* **— ice,** gelato alla vaniglia, *m.*
vanish ['væniʃ], *v.i.* Svanire, scomparire, sparire; dileguarsi; fuggire. **He vanished from sight,** egli sparì.
vanishing, *n.* Sparizione, scomparsa, *f.*
vanity ['væniti], *n.* Vanità, *f.* **— case,** portacipria, *m.*
vanquish ['vænkwiʃ], *v.t.* Vincere.
vanquished, *n.pl.* I vinti, *m.pl.*
vanquisher, *n.* Vincitore, *m.*
vantage ['vɑ:ntidʒ], *n.* (*Tennis*) Vantaggio, *m.* **— in,** vantaggio al battitore, *m.*; **— out,** vantaggio al ribattitore, *m.*; **— -ground,** posizione elevata, posizione superiore, *f.*
vapid ['væpid], *a.* Insipido, scipito, insulso.
vapidity [və'piditi], *n.* Insipidezza, *f.*
vapidly, *adv.* Insipidamente.
vaporable ['veipərəbl], *a.* Evaporabile.
vaporization, *n.* Vaporizzazione, *f.*
vaporize, *v.t.* Vaporizzare; *v.i.* evaporizzare.
vaporizer, *n.* Vaporizzatore, spruzzatore, *m.*
vaporous, *a.* Vaporoso.
vapour, *n.* Vapore, *m.* || *v.i.* Vantarsi, millantare. **— -bath,** bagno a vapore, *m.*
vapouring, *n.* Millanteria, *f.* || *a.* Vanaglorioso.
variability [vɛəriə'biliti], *n.* Variabilità, *f.*; incostanza, *f.*
variable, *a.* Variabile, mutevole, incostante.
variably, *adv.* Variabilmente.
variance ['vɛəriəns], *n.* Disaccordo, dissenso, *m.* **To be at — with,** essere in disaccordo con; **to set at —,** mettere male fra.
variant, *n.* Variante, *f.* || *a.* Variante, diverso, differente.
variation [vɛəri'eiʃən], *n.* Variazione, *f.*; cambiamento, *m.*; modifica, *f.* **— of the compass,** bussola di declinazione.
varicose ['værikouz], *a.* (*Med.*) Varicoso. **— vein,** vena varicosa, *f.*
varied ['vɛərid], *a.* Vario, variato; diversificato. **A — assortment,** un assortimento svariato, *m.*
variegate ['vɛərigeit], *v.t.* Variare; screziare, picchiettare. || *a.* Variegato.
variety, *n.* Varietà, *f.*; variazione; (*Theat.*) spettacoli di varietà, *m.pl.* **— theatre,** teatro di varietà, caffè concerto, *m.*; **— entertainment,** spettacolo di varietà, *m.*; **— performers,** artisti di caffè concerto, *m.pl.*
various ['vɛəriəs], *a.* Vario, diverso; cangiante, variegato; parecchi.
variously, *adv.* Variamente.
variousness, *n.* Varietà, *f.*
varlet ['vɑ:ɹlet], *n.* (*Hist.*) Donzello, paggio, *m.*; furfante, briccone, *m.*
varnish ['vɑ:ɹniʃ], *n.* Vernice, *f.* || *v.t.* Verniciare, inverniciare.
varnisher, *n.* Verniciatore, *m.*
varnishing, *n.* Verniciatura, *f.*
vary ['vɛəri], *v.t.i.* Variare; diversificare; modificare; essere diverso, diversificarsi da. **My watch does not — a minute,** il mio orologio non varia di un minuto.
varying, *a.* Variante, cangiante.
vas [væs], *n.* (*Anat.*) Vaso, *m.*
vascular ['væskju:ləɹ], *a.* Vascolare.
vase [vɑ:z], *n.* Vaso, *m.*
vassal ['væsəl], *n.* (*Hist.*) Vassallo, *m.*, vassalla, *f.* || *a.* Servile.
vassalage, *n.* Vassallaggio, *m.*
vast [vɑ:st], *a.* Vasto, immenso, esteso.
vastly, *adv.* Grandemente, enormemente.
vastness, *n.* Immensità, vastità, *f.*
vasty, *a.* (*Poet.*) Vasto, sconfinato.
vat [væt], *n.* Tino, *m.* || *v.t.* Mettere nel tino.
Vatican ['vætikən], *n.* (*Geog.Pol.*) Vaticano, *m.*
vaticination [vætisi'neiʃən], *n.* Vaticinio, *m.*, predizione, *f.*
Vaucluse ['vouklu:z], *n.* (*Geog.*) Valchiusa, *f.*
vaudeville ['voudvil], *n.* Operetta, canzonetta, *f.*; spettacolo di varietà, *m.*
Vaudois ['voudwɑ:], *n.a.* (*Geog.Eccles.*) Valdese, *m.*
vault (1) [vɔ:lt], *n.* Volta, *f.*; cantina, *f.*; tomba, *f.*; sotterraneo, *m.* || *v.t.* Coprire con una volta, costruire a volta. **Cross —,** volta a crociera, *f.*
vault (2), *v.i.* Saltare, balzare; volteggiare, far capriole. || *n.* Volteggio, salto, *m.* **Vaulting horse,** cavallo di legno per ginnastica, *m.*
vaulted, *a.* Fatto a volta.

vaulting (1), *n.* Volte, *f.pl.*, costruzione a volta, *f.*
vaulting (2), *n.* Volteggiamento, *m.*
vaunt [vɔ:nt], *n.* Vanto, *m.* || *v.t.* Vantare; *v.i.* vantarsi.
vaunting, *n.* Millanteria, *f.* || *a.* Vanitoso, vanaglorioso.
veal [vi:l], *n.* Vitello, *m.*, carne di vitello, *f.* **— cutlet,** costoletta di vitello, *f.*
vector [ˈvektəɹ], *n.* Vettore, *m.*
vedette [veˈdet], *n.* Vedetta, *f.*
veer [viəɹ], *v.i.* (*of wind*) Cambiare direzione; (*Naut.*) virare di bordo; (*of opinion*) mutare di opinione. **To — out,** filare, allentare.
veering, *n.* Mutabilità, *f.*; variabilità, *f.* || *a.* Mutevole, variabile.
vegetable [ˈvedʒetəbl], *n.* Legume, *m.* || *a.* Vegetale. **Vegetables,** legumi, ortaggi, *m.pl.*, verdura, *f.*; **— -dish,** piatto per servire i legumi, *m.*; **— soup,** minestra di verdura, *f.*; **— -marrow,** zucchino, *m.*; **the — kingdom,** il regno vegetale, *m.*; **— oils,** olii vegetali, *m.pl.*
vegetarian [vedʒeˈtεəriən], *n.a.* Vegetariano, *m.*
vegetarianism, *n.* Vegetarianismo, *m.*
vegetate, *v.i.* Vegetare.
vegetation, *n.* Vegetazione, *f.*
vehemence [ˈvi:iməns], *n.* Veemenza, *f.*
vehement, *a.* Veemente.
vehemently, *adv.* Veementemente.
vehicle [ˈvi:ikl], *n.* (*carriage*) Veicolo, *m.*, vettura, *f.*; (*medium*) mezzo, strumento, tramite, *m.*; (*Chem.*) solvente, *m.*
vehicular [veˈhikju:ləɹ], *a.* Veicolare, di veicolo. **— traffic,** circolazione dei veicoli, *f.*
veil [veil], *n.* Velo, *m.*, veletta, *f.*; travestimento, *m.*; apparenza, *f.*; pretesto, *m.* || *v.t.* Velare; celare, nascondere. **To draw a — over,** tirare un velo sopra.
veiled, *a.* Velato; nascosto.
veiling, *n.* Velatura, *f.*
vein [vein], *n.* Vena, *f.*; (*of leaf*) nervatura, *f.* || *v.t.* Venare. **I am in the — for,** sono disposto a, sono in vena di; **poetical —,** vena poetica, *f.*
veining, *n.* Venatura, *f.*
veinous, *a.* Venoso.
vellication [veliˈkeiʃən], *n.* Vellicamento, *m.*
vellum [ˈveləm], *n.* Cartapecora, pergamena fine, *f.* || *a.* Velino.
velocipede [veˈlɔsipi:d], *n.* Velocipede, *m.*
velocity [veˈlɔsiti], *n.* Velocità, *f.*
velours [veˈlu:ɹ], *n.* Feltro floscio, velluto, feltro velluto, *m.*
velum [ˈvi:ləm], *n.* (*Anat.*) Velo, *m.*
velvet [ˈvelvet], *n.* Velluto, *m.* || *a.* Velluto, vellutato; (*fig.*) dolce. **Cotton —,** velluto di cotone, *m.*; **fancy —,** velluto operato, *m.*
velveteen [ˈvelveti:n], *n.* Velluto di cotone, *m.*
velvety, *a.* Di velluto, vellutato; dolce.
venal [ˈvi:nəl], *a.* Venale; (*Anat.*) venoso.
venality [veˈnæliti], *n.* Venalità, *f.*
venally, *adv.* Venalmente.
venation [veˈneiʃən], *n.* (*Bot.*) Nervatura, *f.*; (*Anat.*) venatura, *f.*
vend [vend], *v.t.* (*Law.*) Vendere.
vender, *n.* Mercante, negoziante, *m.*
vendetta [venˈdetə], *n.* Vendetta, *f.*
vendible, *a.* Vendibile.
vendor, *n.* Venditore, *m.*, venditrice, *f.*
veneer [veˈniəɹ], *v.t.* Impiallacciare; (*fig.*) verniciare.
veneer, veneering, *n.* Impiallacciatura, *f.*; (*fig.*) vernice, *f.*
venerability [venərəˈbiliti], *n.* Venerabilità, *f.*
venerable [ˈvenərəbl], *a.* Venerabile.
venerableness, *n.* Venerabilità, *f.*
venerably, *adv.* Venerabilmente.
venerate, *v.t.* Venerare.
veneration, *n.* Venerazione, *f.*
venereal [veˈniəriəl], *a.* Venereo. **— disease,** malattie veneree, *f.pl.*
Venetia [veˈni:ʃə], *n.* (*Geog.*) (*region*) Veneto, *m.*
Venetian, *a.* Veneziano. || *n.* Veneziano, *m.*, Veneziana, *f.* **— blind,** gelosia, persiana, *f.*
vengeance [ˈvendʒəns], *n.* Vendetta, *f.* **To take —,** vendicarsi; (*colloq.*) **with a —,** con veemenza, furiosamente.
vengeful, *a.* Vendicativo.
vengefully, *adv.* Vendicativamente.
venial [ˈvi:niəl], *a.* Veniale. **— sin,** peccato veniale, *m.*
venially, *adv.* Venialmente.
veniality, *n.* Venialità, *f.*
Venice [ˈvenis], *n.* (*Geog.*) Venezia, *f.*
venison [ˈvenzən], *n.* Selvaggina, *f.*; carne di cervo o capriolo, *f.*; cacciagione, *f.*
venom [ˈvenəm], *n.* Veleno, *m.*
venomous, *a.* Velenoso; (*fig.*) malevolo, maldicente, maligno.
venous [ˈvi:nəs], *a.* Venoso.
vent [vent], *n.* Apertura, *f.*, orifizio, *m.*; feritoia, *f.*; forellino, foro, *m.*; spiraglio, *m.*; passaggio, *m.*; ano, *m.* || *v.t.* Dare sfogo a, sfogare; palesare; emettere, esalare. **— pipe,** tubo di scarico, *m.*; **— -hole,** buco di botte, *m.*; **— peg,** zipolo di botte, *m.*; **to give —,** dare sfogo.
ventilate [ˈventileit], *v.t.* Ventilare; (*fig.*) far conoscere, pubblicare, discutere.
ventilation, *n.* Ventilazione, *f.*
ventilator, *n.* Ventilatore, *m.*
ventral, *a.* Ventrale.
ventricle, *n.* Ventricolo, *m.*
ventriloquial [ventriˈloukwiəl], *a.* Ventriloquo.
ventriloquism, ventriloquy [venˈtrilokwizm, venˈtrilokwi], *n.* Ventriloquio, *m.*
ventriloquist, *n.* Ventriloquo, *m.*, ventriloqua, *f.*
venture [ˈventʃəɹ], *n.* Impresa, *f.*; speculazione, *f.*; azzardo rischio, *m.*; caso, *m.* || *v.t.i.* Arrischiare, azzardare; avventurarsi. **At a —,** a caso; **nothing — nothing win,** chi non risica non rosica; **to — to,** osare, permettersi di.
venturesome, *a.* Ardito; avventuroso; azzardoso; avventato.
venturesomeness, *n.* Audacia, arditezza, *f.*, coraggio, *m.*
venue [ˈvenju:], *n.* (*Law*) Sopraluogo, *m.*; (*colloq.*) luogo di oppuntamento, *m.*
Venus [ˈvi:nəs], *n.* (*Myth.Astron.*) Venere, *f.* (*Bot.*) **Venus's flytrap,** dionea, *f.*
veracious [veˈreiʃəs], *a.* Verace, veridico, sincero, genuino.
veraciously, *adv.* Veracemente.
veracity [veˈræsiti], *n.* Veracità, *f.*
veranda, verandah [veˈrændə], *n.* Veranda, *f.*
verb [və:ɹb], *n.* Verbo, *m.*

verbal, *a.* Verbale, orale; letterale.
verbally, *adv.* Verbalmente, oralmente.
verbatim [vəːɹ'beitim], *a.adv.* Parola per parola, alla lettera.
verbena [vəːɹ'biːnə], *n.* (*Bot.*) Verbena, *f.*
verbiage ['vəːɹbiədʒ], *n.* Verbosità, *f.*, sproloquio, *m.*
verbose [vəːɹ'bous], *a.* Verboso.
verbosity [vəːɹ'bɔsiti], *n.* Verbosità, *f.*
verdant ['vəːɹdənt], *a.* Verde, verdeggiante; fresco, vivido.
verderer, *n.* Guardaboschi, *m.*
verdict ['vəːɹdikt], *n.* Verdetto, *m.* **To bring in a — for,** pronunziare un verdetto a favore di.
verdigris ['vəːɹdigris], *n.* Verderame, *m.*
verdure ['vəːɹdjuːɹ], *n.* Verzura, *f.*, il verde, *m.*
verdured, *a.* Verdeggiante.
verge [vəːɹdʒ], *n.* Orlo, bordo, *m.*; limite, *m.*; estremità, *f.*; (*rod*) verga, bacchetta, *f.* || *v.i.* Inclinare verso, tendere verso, avvicinarsi a. **On the — of despair,** al limite della disperazione; **on the — of ruin,** sull'orlo della rovina; **to — on,** essere vicino a.
verger, *n.* Sagrestano, bidello; mazziere, *m.*
veridical [ve'ridikəl], *a.* Veridico; veritiero.
verifiable [veri'faiəbl], *a.* Verificabile.
verification [verifi'keiʃən], *n.* Verifica, *f.*, controllo, *m.*
verify ['verifai], *v.t.* Verificare, confermare, controllare; adempiere. **To — the accounts,** controllare i conti.
verisimilitude [verisi'militjuːd], *n.* Verosimiglianza, *f.*
veritable ['veritəbl], *a.* Vero; reale, genuino.
veritably, *adv.* In verità, veramente.
verity, *n.* Verità, *f.*
verjuice ['vəːɹ'dʒuːs], *n.* Agresto, *m.*
vermicelli [vəːɹmi'seli], *n.* Vermicelli, *m.pl.*
vermicidal [vəːɹmi'saidəl], *a.* Vermicida.
vermiform, *a.* Vermiforme.
vermifuge ['vəːɹmifjuːdʒ], *n.* Vermifugo, *m.*
vermilion [vəːɹ'miljən], *n.a.* Vermiglione, cinabro, *m.*
vermin ['vəːɹmin], *n.* Animali nocivi, *m.pl.*; insetti parassiti, *m.pl.*
verminous, *a.* Verminoso.
vermouth ['vəːɹmuθ], *n.* Vermut, *m.*
vernacular [vəɹ'nækjuːləɹ], *a.* Volgare, vernacolo. || *n.* Vernacolo, *m.*, lingua volgare, *f.*
vernal ['vəːɹnəl], *a.* Primaverile. **— equinox,** equinozio di primavera.
vernier ['vəːɹniəɹ], *n.* Verniere, nonio, *m.*
veronica [ve'rɔnikə], *n.* (*Bot.*) Veronica, *f.*
Versailles [vɛəɹsai, vəːɹ'seilz], *n.* (*Geog.*) Versaglia, *f.*
versatile ['vəːɹsətail], *a.* Versatile.
versatility [vəɹsə'tiliti], *n.* Versatilità, *f.*
verse [vəːɹs], *n.* Verso, *m.*; (*of Bible*) versetto, *m.*; (*of song, poetry, etc.*) strofa, strofetta, stanza, *f.* **In —,** in versi; **blank —,** verso sciolto, *m.*
versed, *a.* Versato, pratico, valente. **— in Latin,** versato nel Latino.
versicle, *n.* Versetto, *m.*
versification [vəɹsifi'keiʃən], *n.* Versificazione, *f.*
versifier ['vəːɹsifaiəɹ], *n.* Versificatore, *m.*, versificatrice, *f.*
versify ['vəːɹsifai], *v.t.* Versificare, ridurre in versi.
version ['vəːɹʃən], *n.* Versione, traduzione, *f.*
verso ['vəːɹsou], *n.* Verso, *m.*; rovescio della medaglia, ecc., *m.*, pagina a sinistra di un libro, *f.*
versus ['vəːɹsəs], *prep.* Contro.
vert [vəːɹt], *n.a.* (*Heraldry*) Verde, *m.*
vertebra (pl. **vertebrae**) ['vəːɹtebrə, 'vəːɹtebriː], *n.* Vertebra, *f.*
vertebral, *a.* Vertebrale.
vertebrata [vəːɹte'breitə], *n.pl.* Vertebrati, *m.pl.*
vertebrate ['vəːɹtebreit], *n.a.* Vertebrato, *m.*
vertex (pl. **vertices**) ['vəːɹteks, 'vəːɹtisiːz], *n.* Vertice, *m.*, cima, sommità, apice, *f.*; zenit, *m.*
vertical ['vəːɹtikəl], *a.* Verticale, perpendicolare.
vertically, *adv.* Verticalmente, perpendicolarmente.
verticality [vəːɹti'kæliti], *n.* Verticalità, *f.*
vertiginous [vəːɹ'tidʒinəs], *a.* Vertiginoso.
vertigo ['vəːɹtigou], *n.* Vertigine, *f.*, capogiro, *m.*
vertu [vəɹ'tuː], *n.* **Article of —,** oggetto d'arte, *m.*
vervain ['vəːɹvein], *n.* (*Bot.*) Verbena, *f.*
verve [vəːɹv], *n.* Brio, entusiasmo, *m.*, vena *f.*; spirito, *m.*
very ['veri], *a.* Stesso; solo; vero; esatto; puro, completo, perfetto. || *adv.* Molto, assai; bene; proprio; tutto; persino. **— good,** buonissimo; **— well,** benissimo; **the — thing,** la cosa stessa, proprio quella cosa, la cosa desiderata, *f.*; **the — thought,** il solo pensiero, *m.*; **the — truth,** la pura verità, *f.*; **this — evening,** questa sera stessa, *f.*; **the — same,** proprio lo stesso, *m.*; **— much,** assai, molto; **— far from,** ben lungi da.
vesica, vesicle, ['vesikə, 'vesikl], *n.* (*Med.*) Vescichetta, pustola, *f.*
vesicant, *a.* Vescicante.
vespers ['vespəɹz], *n.pl.* Vespri, *m.pl.*
vespertine ['vespəɹtain], *a.* Vespertino.
vessel ['vesəl], *n.* Vaso, ricipiente, *m.*; (*ship*) vascello, bastimento, *m.*; (*blood*) vaso, *m.*
vest [vest], *n.* (*man's*) Maglia, *f.*, panciotto, *m.*; sottoveste, *f.*; (*woman's*) camiciola, *f.*; (*infant's*) camicina, *f.* || *v.t.* Investire; affidare; conferire, porre in possesso di; *v.i.* appartenere a. **Vested rights,** diritti acquisiti; **to — with authority,** conferire autorità, investire d'autorità.
vesta ['vestə], *n.* Cerino, *m.*
vestal, *n.* Vestale, *f.* || *a.* Di vestale. **— virgin,** vestale, *f.*
vestiary ['vestiəri], *n.* Vestiario, *m.*
vestibule ['vestibjuːl], *n.* Vestibolo, *m.*
vestige ['vestidʒ], *n.* Vestigio, *m.*; orma, traccia, *f.*
vestigial [ves'tidʒəl], *a.* Di vestigio, d'orma.
vestment ['vestmənt], *n.* Vestimento, abbigliamento, *m.*; (*Eccles.*) paramento sacerdotale, *m.*
vestry, *n.* Sagrestia, *f.*; (*council*) fabbriceria, *f.*, adunanza parrocchiale, *f.*
vestryman, *n.* Fabbriciere, *m.*; membro della assemblea parrocchiale, *m.*
vesture ['vestjuːɹ], *n.* Vestimento, vestito *m.*
Vesuvian [ve'suːviən], *a.* Vesuviano.
Vesuvius, *n.* (*Geog.*) Vesuvio, *m.*

vetch [vetʃ], *n.* (*Bot.*) Veccia, *f.*; cicerchia, *f.*
veteran [ˈvetərən], *n.* Veterano, reduce, *m.* || *a.* Veterano; anziano; vecchio; esperimentato.
veterinary [ˈvetərinəri, ˈvetnəri], *n.a.* Veterinario, *m.*
veto [ˈviːtou], *n.* Veto, *m.* || *v.t.* Vietare, porre il veto a.
vex [veks], *v.t.* Irritare, contrariare; annoiare, inquietare.
vexation, *n.* Irritazione, vessazione, *f.*, dispiacere, *m.*; fastidio, *m.*, noia, *f.*
vexatious [vekˈseiʃəs], *a.* Molesto, fastidioso, noioso, irritante.
vexatiousness, *n.* Contrarietà, noia, *f.*
vexed, *a.* Seccato, annoiato; inquietato. **A — question,** un argomento dibattuto a lungo, una questione noiosa, *f.*
vexing, *a.* Vessatorio, fastidioso.
via [ˈvaiə], *prep.* Per la via di, via.
viability [vaiəˈbiliti], *n.* Viabilità; praticità, *f.*
viable [ˈvaiəbl], *a.* Viabile; pratico.
viaduct [ˈvaiədʌkt], *n.* Viadotto, *m.*
vial [ˈvaiəl], *n.* Fiala, boccetta, *f.* **To pour out the vials of wrath upon someone,** vendicarsi di qualcuno.
viand [ˈvaiənd], *n.* Cibo, piatto, *m.*, vivanda, *f.* **Viands,** vivande, *f.pl.*, commestibili, *m.pl.*
viaticum [vaiˈætikəm], *n.* (*Eccles.*) Viatico, *m.*
vibrant [ˈvaibrənt], *a.* Vibrante, tremante.
vibrate [vaiˈbreit], *v.i.* Vibrare, risonare; oscillare, tremolare.
vibration, *n.* Vibrazione, *f.*; oscillazione, *f.*
vibrator, *n.* Vibratore, *m.*
vicar [ˈvikəɹ], *n.* Vicario, *m.*; pievano, parroco, *m.*
vicarage [ˈvikəridʒ], *n.* Presbiterio, *m.*; vicariato, *m.*
vicariate, *n.* Vicario, *m.*, delegato, *m.*
vicarious, *a.* Vicariale; delegato, sostituto; supplementare.
vicariously, *adv.* Per delega.
vicarship, *n.* Vicariato, *m.*
vice (1) [vais], *n.* Vizio, *m.*; difetto, *m.*, imperfezione, *f.* **Free from —,** senza difetti.
vice (2), *n* Morsa, *f.*, morsetto, *m.*
vice-, *prefix.* Vice-. **—-admiral,** viceammiraglio, *m.*; **—-chairman, —-president,** vicepresidente, *m.*; **—-chancellor,** rettore di università, *m.*; **—-consul,** viceconsole; **—-regal,** di vicerè.
vicegerent [vaisˈdʒerənt], *n.* Vicegerente, *m.*
vicereine [ˈvaisrein], *n.* Viceregina, *f.*
viceroy [ˈvaisrɔi], *n.* Vicerè, *m.*
viceroyalty [vaisˈrɔiəlti], *n.* Dignità di vicerè, *f.*
vice versa [vaisi ˈvəːɹsə], *adv.* Viceversa, reciprocamente.
vicinage [ˈvisinidʒ], *n.* Vicinanza, *f.*, vicinato, *m.*
vicinity [viˈsiniti], *n.* Vicinanza, prossimità, *f.*, vicinato, *m.*
vicious [ˈviʃəs], *a.* Vizioso; cattivo; corrotto; difettoso. **A — circle,** un circolo vizioso, *m.*
viciously, *adv.* Viziosamente.
viciousness, *n.* Viziosità, corruttela, depravazione, *f.*
vicissitude [viˈsisitjuːd], *n.* Vicissitudine, vicenda, *f.*; traversia, *f.*
victim [ˈviktim], *n.* Vittima, *f.* **To be a — to,** essere la vittima di; **to fall a — to,** cadere vittima di.
victimize [ˈviktimaiz], *v.t.* Fare vittima di, immolare; ingannare.
Victor (1) [ˈviktəɹ], *n.* Vittorio, *m.*
victor (2), *n.* Vincitore, *m.*
Victoria (1) [vikˈtɔːriə], *n.* Vittoria, *f.* **— Cross,** croce della Regina Vittoria, *f.*
victoria (2), *n.* (*carriage*) Vittoria, *f.*
Victorian, *a.* Dell'epoca della Regina Vittoria.
victorious, *a.* Vittorioso.
victoriously, *adv.* Vittoriosamente.
victory [ˈviktəri], *n.* Vittoria, *f.* **To gain a —,** riportare una vittoria.
victress, *n.* Vincitrice, *f.*
victual [vitl], *v.t.* Approvvigionare, vettovagliare, rifornire di viveri.
victualler, *n.* Vettovagliatore, *m.*; oste, trattore, *m.*
victualling, *n.* Approvvigionamento, vettovagliamento, *m.*
victuals, *n.pl.* Viveri, *m.pl.*, vettovaglie, *f.pl.*
vicugna, vicuna [viˈkuːnjə], *n.* Vigogna, *f.*
vide [ˈvaidi], *v.imper.* Vedi, vedere.
videlicet, viz. [viˈdiːliset, viz], *conj.* Cioè, è precisamente, vale a dire.
vie [vai], *v.i.* Gareggiare; rivaleggiare. **To — with somebody,** emulare qualcuno.
view [vjuː], *n.* Veduta, vista, *f.*, prospetto, *m.*; prospettiva, *f.*; aspetto, disegno, *m.*; fine, *m.*; intento, *m.*; scopo, *m.* || *v.t.* Guardare, contemplare; considerare, esaminare. **To have in —,** avere in vista, aspirare a; **in —,** in vista; **on —,** esposto; **bird's eye —,** veduta a volo d'uccello, *f.*; **with a — to,** con lo scopo di; **to keep in —,** non perdere di vista; **to support a —,** sostenere un'opinione; **—-finder,** mirino, *m.*; **field of—,** campo visivo, *m.*
viewer, *n.* Spettatore, *m.*; telespettatore, *m.*
viewing, *n.* Esame, *m.*, ispezione, *f.*
vigil [ˈvidʒil], *n.* Vigilia, *f.*; veglia, *f.*
vigilance, *n.* Vigilanza, *f.*
vigilant, *a.* Vigilante, vigile.
vigilantly, *adv.* Vigilantemente, con vigilanza.
vignette [viˈnjet], *n.* Vignetta, *f.* || *v.t.* Fare una vignetta di.
vigorous [ˈvigərəs], *a.* Vigoroso.
vigorously, *adv.* Vigorosamente.
vigorousness, *n.* Vigorosità, *f.*
vigour, *n.* Vigore, *m.*
viking [ˈvaikiŋ], *n.* Vichingo, *m.*
vile [vail], *a.* Vile, abbietto, basso.
vilely, *adv.* Vilmente.
vileness, *n.* Viltà, bassezza, *f.*
vilification [vilifiˈkeiʃən], *n.* Vilipendio, *m.*, diffamazione, *f.*
vilifier, *n.* Diffamatore, denigratore, *m.*, diffamatrice, *f.*
vilify [ˈvilifai], *v.t.* Diffamare, avvilire, denigrare, calunniare.
villa [ˈvilə], *n.* Villino, *m.*, casetta, villa suburbana, *f.*
village [ˈvilidʒ], *n.* Villaggio, paese, *m.*, borgata, *f.* || *a.* Di villaggio.
villager, *n.* Villico, contadino, abitante di villaggio, *m.*
villain [ˈvilən], *n.* Mascalzone, furfante, ribaldo, scellerato, *m.*; (*Hist.*) villano, *m.*
villainous, *a.* Scellerato, infame, vile.
villainously, *adv.* Infamemente, scelleratamente.
villainy, *n.* Scelleratezza, infamia, viltà, *f.*
villein [ˈvilən], *n.* (*Hist.*) Villano, *m.*

villeinage, *n.* Servitù, *f.*
villose ['vilouz], *a.* Villoso.
vim [vim], *n.* Forza, *f.*, vigore, *m.*
vinaigrette [vinei'gret], *n.* Cassettina d'oro o d'argento contenente sali odorosi o profumi vari, *f.*
Vincent ['vinsənt], *n.* Vincenzo, *m.*
vincible [vinsəbl], *a.* Vincibile.
vindicable ['vindikəbl], *a.* Giustificabile, sostenibile.
vindicate ['vindikeit], *v.t.* Giustificare; rivendicare; sostenere.
vindication, *n.* Giustificazione, *f.*; rivendicazione, *f.*
vindictive [vin'diktiv], *a.* Vendicativo; di vendetta.
vindictively, *adv.* Vendicativamente.
vindictiveness, *n.* Carattere vendicativo, *m.*
vine [vain], *n.* Vite, *f.*; vigna, *f.* **—-branch, —-shoot,** sarmento, tralcio, *m.*; **—-dresser,** vignaiolo, *m.*; **—-grower,** viticoltore, *m.*; **—-growing,** viticoltura, *f.*
vinegar ['vinigəɹ], *n.* Aceto, *m.*
vinery ['vainəri], *n.* Serra da viti, *f.*
vineyard ['vinjɑːɹd], *n.* Vigna, *f.*, vigneto, *m.*
vinosity [vi'nɔsiti], *n.* Vinosità, *f.*
vinous ['vainəs], *a.* Vinoso.
vintage ['vintidʒ], *n.* (*season*) Vendemmia, *f.*; (*growth*) raccolto, *m.*, vini, *m.pl.*; (*year*) anno, *m.*, annata, *f.* **— year,** annata di buon raccolto, *f.*
vintager, *n.* Vendemmiatore, *m.*, vendemmiatrice, *f.*
vintner, *n.* Vinaio, mercante di vino, *m.*
viola (1) [vai'oulə, viː'oulə], *n.* (*Mus.*) Viola, *f.*
viola (2) ['vaiolə], *n.* (*Bot.*) Viola, *f.*
violable ['vaioləbl], *a.* Violabile.
violaceae [vaio'leisiː], *n.pl.* (*Bot.*) Violacee, *f.pl.*
violaceous, *a.* Violaceo.
violate ['vaioleit], *v.t.* Violare, profanare; contravvenire a; trasgredire; violentare; rapire.
violation, *n.* Violazione, *f.*; profanazione; ratto, *m.*, violenza carnale, *f.* **— of a secret,** violazione di un segreto, *f.*
violator, *n.* Violatore, *m.*; rapitore, *m.*
violence ['vaiolәns], *n.* Violenza, *f.*; oltraggio, *m.* **To do — to,** violentare, fare violenza a; **the — of the illness,** la violenza della malattia, *f.*; **the — of the storm,** la violenza della tempesta, *f.*
violent, *a.* Violento, estremo. **A — death,** una morte violenta, *f.*; **to lay — hands on,** usare violenza a, maltrattare.
violently, *adv.* Violentemente.
violet ['vaiolet], *n.* (*Bot.*) Violetta, mammola, *f.* || *a.* Colore viola mammola, violetto.
violin [vaio'lin], *n.* Violino, *m.* || *v.t.* Suonare il violino. **—-case,** astuccio per violino, *m.*
violinist, *n.* Violinista, *m.f.*
violoncellist [viːolɔn'tʃelist], *n.* Violoncellista, *m.f.*
violoncello, *n.* Violoncello, *m.*
viper ['vaipəɹ], *n.* (*in all senses*) Vipera, *f.*
viperous, *a.* Viperino, di vipera.
virago [vi'reigou], *n.* Virago, viragine, *f.*; donnaccia, megera, *f.*
Virgil ['vəːɹdʒil], *n.* Virgilio, *m.*
virgin ['vəːɹdʒin], *n.* Vergine, *m.* || *a.* Vergine, di vergine. **The Virgin,** la Vergine Maria, *f.*; **the Blessed Virgin,** la Beatissima Vergine; **— forest,** foresta vergine, *f.*
virginal, *a.* Verginale.
Virginia [vəɹ'dʒiniə], *n.* (*Geog.*) Virginia, *f.* (*Bot.*) **— creeper,** vite del Canada, *f.*
virginity, *n.* Verginità, *f.*
Virgo ['vəːɹgou], *n.* (*Astron.*) Vergine, *f.*
virile [vi'rail], *a.* Virile, maschio.
virility [vi'riliti], *n.* Virilità, *f.*
virtu [cp. **vertu**].
virtual ['vəːɹtjuːəl], *a.* Virtuale.
virtually, *adv.* Virtualmente.
virtue, *n.* Virtù, *f.*, rettitudine, *f.*; efficacia, forza, *f.* **By — of,** in virtù di; **to make a — of necessity,** far di necessità virtù. **The Cardinal Virtues,** le virtù cardinali, *f.pl.*
virtuosity [vəɹtjuː'ɔsiti], *n.* Virtuosità, *f.*
virtuoso (pl. **virtuosi**) [vəɹtjuː'ouzou, vəɹtjuː'ouziː], *n.* Virtuoso, amatore d'arte, *m.*
virtuous ['vəːɹtjuːəs], *a.* Virtuoso; casto; onesto.
virtuously, *adv.* Virtuosamente.
virtuousness, *n.* Virtuosità, *f.*
virulence ['virjuːləns], *n.* Virulenza, *f.*
virulent, *a.* Virulento.
virulently, *adv.* Virulentemente.
virus ['vairəs], *n.* Virus, *m.*
visa ['viːzə], *n.* Visto, *m.*, vidimazione, *f.* || *v.t.* Vistare, vidimare. **To — a passport,** vidimare un passaporto.
visage ['vizidʒ], *n.* Viso, volto, *m.*, faccia, *f.*; aspetto, *m.*
vis-a-vis [viːzɑː'viː], *adv.* Faccia a faccia, di fronte. || *n.* Persona che sta di fronte, *f.*
viscera ['visərə], *n.pl.* Viscere, *f.pl.*, (*Zool. Med.*) visceri, *m.pl.*
visceral, *a.* Viscerale.
viscid ['visid], *a.* Viscido.
viscose ['viskouz], *n.* Viscosa, *f.*
viscosity [vis'kɔsiti], *n.* Viscosità, *f.*
viscount ['vaikaunt], *n.* Visconte, *m.*
viscountess, *n.* Viscontessa, *f.*
viscous ['viskəs], *a.* Viscoso.
visibility [vizi'biliti], *n.* Visibilità, *f.*
visible ['vizibl], *a.* Visibile.
visibly, *adv.* Visibilmente.
Visigoth ['vizigɔθ], *n.* (*Hist.*) Visigoto, *m.*
vision ['viʒən], *n.* Visione, *f.*; apparizione, *f.*; (*faculty*) vista, *f.* **The beatific —,** la visione beatifica, *f.*
visionary, *a.* Visionario. || *n.* Visionario, *m.*, visionaria, *f.*
visit ['vizit], *n.* Visita, *f.* || *v.t.* Visitare, far visita a; andare a vedere; passare da. **To pay a —,** fare una visita; **to return a —,** ricambiare la visita; **a round of visits,** un giro di visite, *m.*; **a flying —,** una visita di sfuggita, *f.*
visitant, *n.* Visitatore, *m.*, visitatrice, *f.*
visitation, *n.* Visita, ispezione, *f.*; (*Eccles.*) visitazione, *f.*; afflizione, *f.*, castigo, *m.* **A — of Providence,** un castigo divino, *m.*; **the Visitation,** la Visitazione di Maria Vergine, *f.*
visiting, *n.* Il visitare, *m.* || *a.* Da visita. **—-card,** biglietto da visita, *m.*
visitor, *n.* Visitatore, *m.*, visitatrice, *f.*, ospite, *m.f.*; turista, *m.f.*; ispettore, *m.*
visor ['vaizəɹ], *n.* Visiera, *f.*
visored, *a.* Con la visiera abbassata.
vista ['vistə], *n.* Vista, prospettiva, *f.*
Vistula ['vistjuːlə], *n.* (*Geog.*) Vistola, *f.*
visual ['viʒjuːəl, 'vizjuːəl], *a.* Visuale, visivo. **— signalling,** telegrafo ottico, *m.*

visualize [ˈviʒjuːəlaiz], *v.t.* Immaginare; vedere coll'occhio della mente.
visually, *adv.* Visualmente.
vital [ˈvaitəl], *a.* Vitale, vivo, essenziale, importantissimo, indispensabile, fondamentale. **A — organ,** una parte vitale, *f.*; **the vitals,** gli organi vitali, *m.pl.*
vitality [vaiˈtæliti], *n.* Vitalità, *f.*
vitalize [ˈvaitəlˈaiz], *v.t.* Dar vita a, vivificare.
vitally, *adv.* Vitalmente. **— important,** importantissimo.
vitamin [ˈvitəmin], *n.* Vitamina, *f.*
vitiate [ˈviʃieit], *v.t.* Viziare, corrompere, guastare.
vitiation, *n.* Guasto, *m.*; corruzione, *f.*
viticultural [vitiˈkʌltjuːrəl], *a.* Viticolo.
viticulture, *n.* Viticultura, *f.*
viticulturist, *n.* Viticultore, *m.*
vitreous [ˈvitriəs], *a.* Vitreo.
vitreousness, *n.* Vetrosità, *f.*
vitrescence [viˈtresəns], *n.* Vitrescenza, *f.*
vitrification [vitrifiˈkeiʃən], *n.* Vetrificazione, *f.*
vitrify [ˈvitrifai] *v.t.* Vetrificare; *v.i.* vetrificarsi.
vitriol [ˈvitriəl], *n.* Vetriolo, *m.*
vitriolic [vitriˈɔlik], *a.* Vetriolico.
vituperate [vaiˈtjuːpəreit], *v.t.* Vituperare; ingiuriare, biasimare.
vituperation, *n.* Vituperazione, *f.*, ingiurie, *f.pl.*, insulti, *m.pl.*
vituperative, *a.* Vituperativo.
Vitus [ˈvaitəs], *n.* Vito. **St. Vitus's dance,** ballo di San Vito, *m.*
vivacious [viˈveiʃəs], *a.* Vivace, vispo; pieno di vita.
vivaciously, *adv.* Vivacemente, con vivacità.
vivaciousness, vivacity, *n.* Vivacità, *f.*
vivarium [vaiˈvɛəriəm], *n.* Vivaio, *m.*; pescheria, *f.*
viva voce [vaivəˈvousi], *adv.* A viva voce. ‖ *a.* Orale. ‖ *n.* Esame orale, *m.*
vivid [ˈvivid], *a.* Vivido, vivo, vivente.
vividly, *adv.* Vividamente.
vividness, *n.* Vividezza, *f.*; vivacità, *f.*
vivification [vivifiˈkeiʃən], *n.* Vivificazione, *f.*
vivify [ˈvivifai], *v.t.* Vivificare.
viviparous [vaiˈvipərəs], *a.* Viviparo.
vivisect [ˈvivisekt], *v.t.* Vivisezionare, fare la vivisezione di.
vivisection, *n.* Vivisezione, *f.*
vivisectionist, *n.* Vivisettore, *m.*
vixen [ˈviksən], *n.* Volpe (femmina), *f.*; (*fig.*) megera, donnaccia, *f.*
vixenish, *a.* Da megera; bisbetico.
viz. [viz], *adv.* Cioè, vale a dire, ossia [cp. **videlicet**].
vizier [viˈziəɹ], *n.* Visir, *m.*
vocable [ˈvoukəbl], *n.* Parola, voce, *f.*, vocabolo, *m.*
vocabulary [vɔˈkæbjuːləri], *n.* Vocabolario, *m.*
vocal [ˈvoukəl], *a.* Vocale. **— cords,** corde vocali, *f.pl.*
vocalist, *n.* Cantante, *m.f.*, cantatore, *m.*, cantatrice, *f.*
vocalization, *n.* Vocalizzazione, *f.*
vocalize, *v.t.i.* Vocalizzare.
vocally, *adv.* Vocalmente, a viva voce.
vocation [voˈkeiʃən], *n.* Vocazione, *f.*; occupazione, *f.*, impiego, *m.*; mestiere, *m.* **To follow one's —,** seguire la propria vocazione; **— for the priesthood,** vocazione sacerdotale.
vocative [ˈvɔkətiv], *n.a.* (*Gram.*) Vocativo, *m.*
vociferant [voˈsifərənt], *a.* Vociferante.
vociferate [voˈsifəreit], *v.t.* Vociferare; gridare, urlare; vociare.
vociferation, *n.* Vociferazione, *f.*
vociferous [voˈsifərəs], *a.* Clamoroso, chiassoso, strepitoso.
vociferously, *adv.* Rumorosamente, chiassosamente.
vogue [voug], *n.* Voga, moda, *f.* **In —,** in voga, di moda; **to come into —,** diventare di moda, venire in voga.
voice [vɔis], *n.* Voce, *f.*; opinione, *f.* ‖ *v.t.* Esprimere; nominare; dar voce a. **In a loud —,** ad alta voce; **a harsh —,** una voce aspra, *f.*; **a hoarse —,** una voce rauca, *f.*; **with one —,** ad una voce, unanimamente; **at the top of one's —,** con tutta la forza della voce, a squarciagola; **to drop one's —,** abbassare la voce; **he replied in a weak —,** rispose con un filo di voce; (*Gram.*) **active, passive —,** voce attiva, passiva, *f.*
voiced, *a.* Espresso; designato, nominato; sonoro.
voiceless, *a.* Senza voce, muto.
void [vɔid], *a.* Vuoto, vano, vacuo; nullo, invalido, senza valore. ‖ *n.* Vuoto, spazio vuoto, *m.*, lacuna, *f.* ‖ *v.t.* Vuotare, espellere, scaricare; annullare; liberare. **To make —,** rendere nullo; **— of reason,** privo della ragione; **to fill a —,** colmare una lacuna; **to — the bowels,** liberare l'intestino.
voidable, *a.* Annullabile; che può essere vuotato.
voidance, *n.* Sgombro, vuotamento, *m.*; stato d'essere vacante, *m.*; evasione, *f.*; invalidamento, *m.*
voile [vɔil], *n.* Velo, *m.*
volatile [ˈvɔlətail], *a.* Volatile; mutevole. **— oils,** olii essenziali, *m.pl.*
volatility, *n.* Volatilità, *f.*; leggerezza, *f.*
volatilization, *n.* Volatilizzazione, *f.*
volatilize, *v.t.* Volatilizzare.
volcanic [vɔlˈkænik], *a.* Vulcanico.
volcano (*pl.* **volcanoes**) [vɔlˈkeinou, vɔlˈkeinouz], *n.* Vulcano, *m.*
vole [voul], *n.* (*Zool.*) Arvicola, *f.*; topo d'acqua, *m.*
volition [vɔˈliʃən], *n.* Volizione, *f.*, atto di volontà, *m.*
volitional, *a.* Relativo alla volizione.
volley [ˈvɔli], *n.* (*Mil.*) Scarica, salve, *f.*; (*Tennis*) volata, *f.*; (*fig.*) carico, torrente, *m.* ‖ *v.t.* Colpire a volo, prendere la battuta a volo; (*Mil.*) tirare a salve.
volleying, *n.* (*Tennis*) Atto che consiste nell'eseguire una volata.
volplane [ˈvɔlplein], *n.* (*Aviat.*) Volo planato, *m.* ‖ *v.i.* Planare, fare un volo planato.
volt [voult], *n.* (*Elect.*) Volta, *m.*; (*horsemanship*) volteggio, *m.*, giravolta, *f.*
voltage, *n.* Voltaggio, *m.*
voltaic [vɔlˈteiik], *a.* Voltaico.
voltmeter [ˈvoultmiːtəɹ], *n.* Voltametro, *m.*
volubility [vɔljuːˈbiliti], *n.* Loquacità, volubilità, *f.*; fluidità, *f.*
voluble, *a.* Loquace; fluente; volubile.
volubleness, *n.* Volubilità, loquacità, *f.*
volubly, *adv.* Loquacemente.
volume [ˈvɔljuːm], *n.* (*quantity*) Volume, *m.*, massa, quantità, *f.*; (*book*) volume, tomo,

m. **Folio —,** volume in-folio, *m.*; **odd —,** volume scompagnato, *m.*; **to speak volumes,** essere molto significativo; **a — of smoke,** un turbine di fumo, *m.*
volumetric [vɔljuːˈmetrik], *a.* Volumetrico.
voluminous [vɔˈljuːminəs], *a.* Voluminoso; copioso, diffuso; ingombrante.
voluminously, *adv.* Voluminosamente.
voluminousness, *n.* Voluminosità, *f.*
voluntarily, *adv.* Volontariamente; spontaneamente.
voluntariness, *n.* Volontarietà, *f.*
voluntary, *a.* Volontario; spontaneo; intenzionale. || *n.* (*Mus.*) Preludio, *m.*
volunteer [vɔlənˈtiəɹ], *n.* (*Mil.*) Volontario, *m.*; uomo di buona volontà, *m.* || *a.* Volontario, spontaneo. || *v.i.* Offrirsi volontariamente; arruolarsi come volontario.
voluptuary [vɔˈlʌptjuːəri], *n.* Epicureo, *m.* epicurea, *f.*; libertino, *m.* || *a.* Voluttuario; di lusso.
voluptuous, *a.* Voluttuoso.
voluptuously, *adv.* Voluttosamente.
voluptuousness, *n.* Voluttà, sensualità *f.*
volute [ˈvɔljuːt], *n.* (*Arch.*) Voluta, *f.*
vomit [ˈvɔmit], *n.* Vomito, *m.* || *v.t.i.* Vomitare.
vomiting, *n* Vomito, *m.*
voracious [vɔˈreiʃəs], *a* Vorace.
voraciously, *adv.* Voracemente.
voraciousness, voracity, *n.* Voracità, *f.*
vortex (pl. **vortices, vortexes**) [ˈvɔːɹteks, ˈvɔːɹtisiːz, ˈvɔːɹteksiz], *n.* Vortice, *m.*; turbine, gorgo, *m.*
vortical [ˈvɔːɹtikəl], *a.* Vorticoso.
vortiginous [vɔːɹˈtidʒinəs], *a.* Vorticoso.
Vosges [vouʒ], *n.pl.* (*Geog.*) Vosgi, *m.pl.*
votaress [ˈvoutəres], *n.* Devota, *f.*, ammiratrice, *f.*
votary [ˈvoutəri], *n.* Devoto, *m.*, devota, *f.*; settario, *m.*, settaria, *f.*; seguace, *m.f.*
vote [vout], *n.* Voto, *m.*; scheda, *f.*; votazione, *f.* || *v.t.i.* Votare, eleggere, nominare; recarsi alle urne. **To — by ballot,** votare a scrutinio segreto; **— by a show of hands,** votazione per alzata e seduta, *f.*; **to carry a —,** approvare una mozione.
voter, *n.* Votante, *m.f*; elettore, *m.*, elettrice, *f.*
voting, *n.* Votazione, *f.*, scrutinio, *m.* **— paper,** scheda di votazione, *f.*
votive, *a.* Votivo; commemorativo.
vouch [vautʃ], *v.t.* Attestare; garantire; provare. **To — for,** rendersi garante di, essere mallevadore di, rispondere di.
vouchee [vautʃˈiː], *n.* Garante, testimone, *m.*
voucher, *n.* Documento giustificativo, *m.*, pezza d'appoggio, *f.*; ricevuta, quietanza, *f.*; buono, scontrino, *m.*
vouchsafe [vautʃˈseif], *v.t.* Accordare, concedere; degnarsi di, accondiscendere.
voussoir [ˈvuːswɑːɹ], *n.* (*Arch.*) Mattone a cuneo, *m.*
vow [vau], *n.* Voto, *m.*; giuramento, *m.* || *v.t.* Giurare, votare, far voto di. **To — and protest,** giurare e spergiurare, giurare su tutti i santi; **to — vengeance,** giurare vendetta; **a — of abstinence,** un voto d'astinenza, *m.*; **to break a —,** infrangere un voto; **to fulfil a —,** adempiere un voto.
vowel [ˈvauəl], *n.* Vocale, *f.* || *a.* Vocalico.
voyage [ˈvɔiədʒ], *n.* Viaggio per mare, passaggio, *m.*, traversata, *f.* || *v.i.* Viaggiare, fare una traversata. **On —,** in viaggio; **on the —,** durante il viaggio.
voyager, *n.* Viaggiatore, *m.*, viaggiatrice, *f.*; passeggiero, *m.*, passeggiera, *f.*
Vulcan [ˈvʌlkən], *n.* (*Myth.Astron.*) Vulcano, *m.*
vulcanite [ˈvʌlkənait], *n.* Gomma vulcanizzata, vulcanite, *f.*
vulcanization, *n.* Vulcanizzazione, *f.*
vulcanize, *v.t.* Vulcanizzare.
vulcanology [vʌlkəˈnɔlədʒi], *n.* Vulcanologia, *f.*
vulgar [ˈvʌlgəɹ], *a.* Volgare, plebeo, popolaresco; comune, triviale; basso, grossolano, meschino. || *n.* Volgo, *m.* **— tongue,** lingua volgare, *f.*; (*Math.*) **— fraction,** frazione propria, *f.*
vulgarian [vʌlˈgɛəriən], *n.* Persona del volgo, *f.*; persona di gusti volgari, *f.*
vulgarism, *n.* Espressione volgare, espressione del volgo, *f.*
vulgarity [ʌvlˈgæriti], *n.* Volgarità, *f.*
vulgarization [vʌlgəraiˈzeiʃən], *n.* Il rendere popolare, *m.*; volgarizzazione, *f.*
vulgarize, *v.t.* Rendere popolare; volgarizzare.
Vulgate [ˈvʌlgeit], *n.* Volgata, *f.*
vulnerability [vʌlnərəˈbiliti], *n.* Vulnerabilità, *f.*
vulnerable [ˈvʌlnərəbl], *a.* Vulnerabile.
vulpine [ˈvʌlpain], *a.* Volpino; astuto.
vulture [ˈvʌltʃəɹ], *n.* (*Zool.*) Avvoltoio, *m.*; (*fig.*) persona rapace, *f.*
vying [ˈvaiiŋ], *a.* Che compete, in competizione, in concorrenza.

W

W, w [ˈdʌbljuː], *n.* Ventitreesima lettera dell'alfabeto inglese, *f.*
wabble [cp. **wobble**].
wad [wɔd], *n.* Borra, *f.*, turacciolo, cuscinetto, *m.*; stoppaccio, *m.* (*Med.*) piumacciolo, *m.* || *v.t.* Tappare.
wadding, *n.* Ovatta, *f.*; bambagia, *f.*, batuffolo, *m.*
waddle [wɔdl], *n.* Dondolamento, *m.* || *v.i.* Camminare dondolandosi, andar barcollando, sculettare.
waddler, *n.* Chi barcolla.
waddling, *n.* Barcollamento, *m.*
wade [weid], *v.t.i.* Guadare; (*through a stream*) passare a guado; (*in the sea*) sguazzare; **to — through a book,** leggere stentatamente.
wader, *n.* (*Zool.*) Trampoliere, *m.*
waders, *n.pl.* Stivaloni impermeabili, *m.pl.*
wafer [ˈweifəɹ], *n.* (*biscuit*) Cialda, *f.*; (*obs.*) (*for seal*) ostia per sigillare, *f.*; (*Eccles.*) ostia, *f.*
waffle [wɔfl], *n.* Cialda, *f.* **— irons,** ferro da cialde, *m.*
waft [wɑːft, wɔft], *v.t.* Portare in aria, spandere, diffondere, portare col vento. || *n.* Soffio, colpo di vento, *m.*
wag (1) [wæg], *n.* Burlone, tipo ameno, uomo faceto, celione, *m.*
wag (2), *v.t.* (*the head*) Scuotere, tentennare, scrollare; (*the tail*) muovere, agitare la coda, scodinzolare.
wage (1) [weidʒ], *n.* Salario, stipendio, *m.*, paga, rimunerazione, *f.*; **—-earner,** salariato, *m.*, salariata, *f.*; **a fair —,** un salario equo, *m.*; **— increase,** aumento dei salari, *m.*

wage (2), *v.t.* Intraprendere; provare, tentare. **To — war,** muovere guerra, guerreggiare.
wager, *n.* Scommessa, *f.*; posta, *f.* || *v.t.* Scommettere. **To lay a —,** fare una scommessa.
waggery [ˈwægəri], *n.* Facezia, *f.*; birichinata, *f.*
waggish, *a.* Faceto, giocoso, scherzevole.
waggishly, *adv.* Facetamente.
waggishness, *n.* Arguzia, *f.*; scherzosità, *f.*
waggle [wægl], *v.t.i.* Tentennare, dimenare, dimenarsi.
waggling, *n.* Scodinzolamento, *m.*
waggon, wagon [ˈwægən], *n.* Carro, furgone, vagone, *m.*; (*Rail.*) vagone, *m.* **—-load,** carrettata, *f.*
wagonage, *n.* Trasporto con carri, *m.*; prezzo di trasporto con carri, *m.*
wagoner, *n.* Carrettiere, *m.*
wagonette, *n.* Carrozzetta, *f.*
wagtail [ˈwægteil], *n.* (*Zool.*) Cutrettola, batticoda, *f.*
waif [weif], *n.* Fanciullo abbandonato, fanciullo derelitto, *m.* **Waifs and strays,** relitti, oggetti smarriti, *m.pl.*; fanciulli abbandonati, *m.pl.*
wail [weil], *n.* Gemito, lamento, *m.* || *v.i.* Gemere, lamentarsi; vagire.
wailing, *n.* Gemito, *m.*
wain [wein], *n.* Carro, *m.* (*Astron.*) **Charles's Wain,** Orsa maggiore, *f.*
wainscot [ˈweinskət], *n.* Intavolato, zoccolo di legno, *m.* || *v.t.* rivestire di legno.
wainscoting, *n.* Intavolatura, *f.*
waist [weist], *n.* Vita, *f.*, busto, *m.*; cintura, cintola, *f.*; parte di mezzo, *f.* **— measurement,** misura della cintola, *f.*; **up to the —,** fino alla cintola.
waistband, *n.* Cintura, *f.*; cinghia, *f.*
waistcoat [ˈweskət, ˈweistkət], *n.* Panciotto, gilè, *m.*
waisted, *a.* Che ha la vita. **Wasp- —,** con una vitina da vespa.
wait [weit], *v.t.i.* Aspettare, attendere; rimanere, indugiare. || *n.* Attesa, *f.*, indugio, *m.*; agguato, *m.*, posta, *f.* **To — upon,** servire; (*visit*) andare a vedere, presentarsi da, presentare i rispetti a; **he did not — to be told,** non attese che glielo dicesse; **he did not — to be told twice,** non se lo fece dire due volte; **to lie in — for,** stare in agguato, essere alla posta.
waiter, *n.* Cameriere, *m.*
waiting, *n.* Attesa, aspettativa, *f.* **—-room,** anticamera, sala d'aspetto, *f.*; **—-maid, —-woman,** cameriera, *f.*; **lady-in- —,** dama d'onore, *f.*
waitress, *n.* Cameriera, *f.*
waits, *n.pl.* Musicanti che suonano per le strade la notte di Natale, *m.pl.*
waive [weiv], *v.t.* Rinunziare a, abbandonare, non insistere su.
wake (1) [weik], *n.* Scia, *f.*; (*fig.*) orma, traccia, *f.* **To follow in the — of,** seguire nella scia di, seguire sulle orme di.
wake (2), **waken,** *v.t.* Svegliare, risvegliare, destare; *v.i.* svegliarsi.
wake (3), *n.* (*funeral*) Veglia, *f.*
wakeful, *a.* Sveglio, insonne; vigile.
wakefulness, *n.* Insonnia, *f.*; vigilanza, *f.*
waken [cp. **wake** (2)].
waking, *a.* Sveglio, vegliante. || *n.* Lo svegliarsi, *m.*
Waldenses [wɔlˈdenzi:z], *n.pl.* Valdesi, *m.pl.*
wale [weil], *n.* Ammaccatura, *f.*; (*Naut.*) cinta, *f.* || *v.t.* Lasciare il segno di un frustamento.
Wales [weilz], *n.* (*Geog.*) Galles, *m.*
walk [wɔ:k], *v.i.* Camminare, andare a piedi, passeggiare, andare a spasso. || *n.* Camminata, passeggiata, *f.*; (*path*) cammino, sentiero, viale, *m.*; (*gait*) andatura, *f.* **To go for a —,** andare a fare due passi; **to — about,** passeggiare; **to — in,** entrare, **to — off,** andarsene, allontanarsi, svignarsela; **to — out,** uscire; **to — on,** procedere oltre; **a — of life,** una carriera, una professione, *f.*; (*Sport*) **a —-over,** una vincita facile, *f.*, una vincita per mancanza di concorrenti, *f.*
walker, *n.* Camminatore, *m.*, camminatrice, *f.*, pedone, *m.f.* (*Theat.*) **—-on,** figurante, *m.*, comparsa, *f.*
walkie-talkie [wɔ:kiˈtɔ:ki], *n.* Radiotelefono da passeggio, *m.*
walking, *n.* Marcia, *f.*, passeggio, *m.*; passeggiata, *f.* || *a.* Ambulante. **— dress,** abito da passeggio, *m.*; **—-stick,** bastone, bastoncino, *m.*; **—-tour,** escursione a piedi, *f.*; (*Theat.*) **— gentleman, lady,** comparsa, *f.*
wall [wɔ:l] *n.* Muro, *m.*; muraglia, *f.*; parete, *f.* || *v.t.* Murare; circondare di muri, immurare. **Retaining —,** muro maestro, *m.*; **—-paper,** carta da parati, *f.*; **—-plate,** trave di bordo, *f.*, piano di posa, *m.*; **the Great Wall of China,** la grande muraglia cinese, *f.*; (*fig.*) **to go to the —,** non riuscire, fallire lo scopo; **walls have ears,** i muri hanno orecchi; **—-fruit,** frutto di spalliera; **—-tree,** albero di spalliera, *m.*
wallet [wɔlit], *n.* Bisaccia, borsa, *f.*, portafoglio, *m.*
wallflower, *n.* (*Bot.*) Violacciocca, *f.* (*fig.*) **To be a —,** fare da comparsa, fare da tappezzeria.
wallop [ˈwɔləp], *v.t.* (*colloq.*) Bastonare. || *n.* Bastonatura, *f.*
walloping, *a.* (*colloq*). Grosso, madornale.
wallow [ˈwɔlou], *v.i.* Voltolarsi, avvoltolarsi, guazzare. || *n.* (*Naut.*) rullio, *m.*
wallowing, *n.* Voltolamento, *m.*
walnut [ˈwɔ:lnʌt], *n.* Noce, *f.* **—-tree, —wood,** noce, *m.*
walrus [ˈwɔ:lrəs, ˈwɔlrəs], *n.* (*Zool.*) Tricheco, *m.*
waltz [wɔ:ls], *n.* Valzer, *m.* || *v.i.* Ballare il valzer, valzare.
waltzer, *n.* Chi balla il valzer, *m.f.*
wampum [ˈwɔmpʌm], *n.* Conchiglie infilate usate come moneta, ecc. dai Pellirosse.
wan [wɔn], *a.* Pallido.
wand [wɔnd], *n.* Bacchetta, verga, *f.*
wander [ˈwɔndəɹ], *v.i.* Vagare, errare, girovagare; deviare, scostarsi, divagare; (*in mind*) delirare. **To — about,** vagolare; **to — from the way,** smarrire la strada.
wanderer, *n.* Vagabondo, girovago, *m.*; giramondo, *m.*
wandering, *n.* Vagabondaggio, *m.*; vagazione, *f.* || *a.* Errante, vagante; (*mental*) distratto, delirante. **The Wandering Jew,** l'Ebreo errante, *m.*

wane [wein], *v.i.* Decrescere, declinare, scemarsi; deperire. || *n.* Declino, decadimento, *m.*; (*of the moon*) il calare, *m.* **On the —,** sul declinare.
waning, *a.* Decadente, declinante; (*of the moon*) calante.
wanly [ˈwɔnli], *adv.* Pallidamente.
wanness, *n.* Pallore, *m.*
want [wɔnt], *v.t.* Avere bisogno di, mancare di; desiderare; *v.i.* mancare, occorrere. || *n.* Bisogno, *m.*, mancanza, deficienza, *f.*; indigenza, *f.*, strettezze, *f.pl.* **I don't know what he wants,** non so che cosa gli occorre; **How much do you — ?** Quanto vi occorre?; **to be in — of,** aver bisogno di; **for — of,** per mancanza di; **to come to —,** cadere nella miseria; **to meet a long-felt —,** colmare una lacuna; **to feel the — of,** sentire il bisogno di; **a — of confidence,** una mancanza di fiducia.
wanted, *a.* Richiesto, ricercato; (*in advertisements*) cercasi, si chiede.
wanting, *a.* Deficiente, mancante. **To be —,** mancare, (*fig.*) essere un po' semplice, essere un po' imbecille.
wanton [ˈwɔntən], *a.* Lascivo, licenzioso; giocoso; perverso; gratuito, senza motivo. || *n.* Lascivo, *m.*; libertino, *m.*, libertina, *f.*; persona frivola, *f.* || *v.i.* Folleggiare, agire a vanvera. **— destruction,** vandalismo, *m.*; **— misconduct,** grave indisciplina, *f.*
wantonly, *adv.* Lascivamente; gratuitamente.
wantonness, *n.* Sregolatezza, licenza, *f.*, libertinaggio, *m.*; gaiezza, *f.* **Out of sheer —,** a cuor leggero.
war [wɔːɹ], *n.* Guerra, *f.* || *v.t.* Guerreggiare, fare la guerra. **To be at —,** essere in guerra; **declaration of —,** dichiarazione di guerra, *f.*; **outbreak of —,** scoppio della guerra, *m.*; **a state of —,** uno stato di guerra, *m.*; **on a — footing,** sul piede di guerra; **— correspondent,** corrispondente di guerra, *m.*; **—-dance,** danza di guerra, *f.*; **—-horse,** cavallo di battaglia, *m.*; **— loan,** prestito di guerra, *m.*; **— memorial,** monumento ai caduti in guerra, *m.*; **War Office,** Ministero della Guerra, *m.*
warble [wɔːɹbl], *v.i.* Gorgheggiare, trillare, canterellare; *v.t.* cantare.
warbler, *n.* (*Zool.*) Capinera, *f.*, beccafico, *m.*
ward [wɔːɹd], *n.* (*minor*) Pupillo, *m.*, pupilla, *f.*, minore, *m.f.*; (*safekeeping*) custodia, tutela, *f.*; (*district*) rione, quartiere, *m.*; (*hospital*) sala, corsia, *f.*; (*Fencing*) guardia, *f.*; (*of lock*) nottolino, mastio, *m.* || *v.t.* Respingere. **To — off,** respingere, parare, tener lontano.
warden, *n.* Custode, guardiano, *m.*; conservatore, *m.*
warder, *n.* Guardiano, *m.*; carceriere, *m.*
wardress, *n.* Carceriera, *f.*
wardrobe [ˈwɔːɹdroub], *n.* Guardaroba, *f.* armadio, *m.*, vestiario, *m.*; abiti, vestiti, *m.pl.* **—-dealer,** mercante di abiti usati, *m.*; (*Theat.*) **— mistress,** vestiarista, *f.*; **— trunk,** baule armadio, *m.*
wardroom, *n.* (*Naut.*) Quadrato degli ufficiali, *m.*
wardship, *n.* Tutela, *f.*; carica di guardiano, *f.*
ware (1) [wɛəɹ], *n.* Articolo, oggetto, *m.* **Gold —,** oreficeria, *f.*; **silver —,** argenteria, *f.*; **earthen —, earthenware,** terraglie, *f.pl.*
ware! (2), *inter.* Attenti; [cp. **beware**].
warehouse, *n.* Magazzino, deposito, *m.* || *v.t.* Immagazzinare, depositare in magazzino. **Bonded —,** magazzino doganale, *m.*; **—-keeper,** magazziniere, *m.*; **—-man,** commerciante all'ingrosso, *m.*, magazziniere, *m.*
warehousing, *n.* Magazzinaggio, deposito, magazzinamento, *m.*
wares, *n.pl.* Merci, *f.pl.*, mercanzia, *f.*; derrate, *f.* **Small —,** mercerie, *f.pl.*
warfare [ˈwɔːɹfɛəɹ], *n.* Guerra, *f.* **Aerial —,** guerra aerea, *f.*
warily [ˈwɛərili], *adv.* Accortamente, con circospezione, a tastoni.
wariness, *n.* Precauzione, accortezza, circospezione, *f.*
warlike [ˈwɔːɹlaik], *a.* Guerriero, guerresco, bellicoso, marziale.
warlock [ˈwɔːɹlɔk], *n.* Stregone, *m.*
warm [wɔːɹm], *a.* Caldo; caloroso, ardente, violento. || *v.t.* Scaldare, riscaldare; *v.i.* scaldarsi. **To — oneself,** riscaldarsi; **to be —,** far caldo; **to feel —,** sentir caldo; **—-blooded,** a sangue caldo; **—-hearted,** di buon cuore, di sentimenti calorosi; **as — as toast,** ben caldo; (*fig.*) **a — man,** un ricco, *m.*
warming, *a.* Riscaldante. || *n.* Riscaldamento, *m.*; (*fig.*) bastonatura, *f.* **—-pan,** scaldino, scaldaletto, *m.*
warmly, *adv.* Caldamente; calorosamente; appassionatamente; violentemente.
warmness, warmth, *n.* Calore, *m.*; ardore, *m.*; zelo, *m.*
warn [wɔːɹn], *v.t.* Avvertire, ammonire, premunire; diffidare. **To — off,** intimare di ritirarsi.
warning, *n.* Avvertimento, ammonimento, *m.*; preavviso, *m.*; allarme, *m.* **To give —,** (*dismissal*) congedare, licenziare, (*to notify*) avvertire.
warp [wɔːɹp], *n.* Ordito, *m.*; contrazione, *f.*; (*Naut.*) cavo da tonnaggio, *m.* || *v.t.* Curvare, storcere; pervertire; ordire; (*Naut.*) tonneggiare; *v.i.* curvarsi, deformarsi; tonneggiarsi.
warping, *n.* Deviamento, *m.*, deformazione, *f.*; (*Naut.*) rimorchiamento, *m.*
warrant [ˈwɔrənt], *n.* Autorizzazione, giustificazione, *f.*; ordine, mandato, *m.*; nota di pegno, *f.*; titolo, *m.* || *v.t.* Garantire; giustificare; attestare; assicurare. **Search —,** ordine di perquisizione domiciliare, *m.*; **— for payment,** mandato di pagamento, *m.*; **— of arrest,** mandato di arresto, *m.*; **— officer,** sott'ufficiale, *m.*
warrantable, *a.* Giustificabile.
warranted, *a.* Garantito; autorizzato.
warranty, *n.* Garanzia, *f.*
warren, *n.* Garenna, *f.*
warrior [ˈwɔriəɹ], *n.* Guerriero, *m.*
Warsaw [ˈwɔːɹsɔː], *n.* (*Geog.*) Varsavia, *f.*
warship [ˈwɔːɹʃip], *n.* Vascello di guerra, *m.*, nave da guerra, *f.*
wart [wɔːɹt], *n.* Verruca, *f.*, porro, neo, *m.*
warty, *a.* Verrucoso, bitorzoluto.
wary [wɛəri], *a.* Circospetto, diffidente; scaltro, accorto; prudente.
wash [wɔʃ], *n.* Lavata, lavatura, *f.*; (*linen*) bucato, *m.*, biancheria da lavarsi, *f.*; (*Art*) acquerello, *m.*; (*of a ship*) onda, *f.* || *v.t.* Lavare; fare il bucato, imbiancare; *v.i.* lavarsi. **To — one's hands,** lavarsi le mani;

I — my hands of it, me ne lavo le mani; to — out, risciacquare; to — away, lavar via; to — up, lavare i piatti; rigettare sulla sponda; to — overboard, spazzare in mare; — -basin, catinella, *f.*, lavabo, *m.*; — -leather, pelle di camoscio, *f.*; — -stand, lavabo, portacatino, *m.*; — -tub, conca del bucato, *f.*; (*colloq.*) — -out, fiasco, *m.*

washable, *a.* Lavabile.

washer, *n.* (*person*) Lavatore, *m.*, lavatrice, *f.*; (*machine*) lavatrice, *f.*; (*for bolt*) rondella, rosetta, *f.*

washerwoman, *n.* Lavandaia, *f.*

washing, *n.* Lavatura, *f.*; bucato, *m.*; toletta, abluzione, *f.* **— -board,** asse per lavare; **— -day,** giorno del bucato, *m.*

washy, *a.* Bagnato; debole, insipido.

wasp [wɔsp], *n.* (*Zool.*) Vespa, *f.* **Wasps' nest,** vespaio, *m.*

waspish, *a.* Di vespa; collerico, irascibile, irritabile, stizzoso.

wassail [wɔsl, wæsl], *n.* Gozzoviglia, *f.* || *v.i.* Gozzovigliare.

wassailer, *n.* Gozzovigliatore, *m.*

wastage [ˈweistidʒ], *n.* Sciupio, *m.*

waste [weist], *a.* Deserto, incolto; perduto; (*of matter*) di scarto. || *n.* Sciupo, scarto, scarico, *m.*; rifiuti, cascami, *m.pl.*; perdita, *f.*; consumo inutile, *m.* || *v.t.* Sciupare, scialacquare, sprecare, dissipare; devastare. **To lay —,** devastare, guastare; **he wastes his time,** sciupa il suo tempo; **he has wasted his substance,** ha dissipato il suo patrimonio; **— not want not,** chi risparmia si arricchisce; **to — away,** consumarsi; **to go to —,** andare in rovina, sciuparsi; **— land,** terra incolta, *f.*; **— matter,** roba di rifiuto, *f.*; **— paper,** carta straccia, *f.*; **— pipe,** tubo di scarico, *m.*; **a wasted life,** una vita mancata, *f.*

wasteful, *a.* Prodigo, spendereccio.

wastefully, *adv.* Prodigamente.

wastefulness, *n.* Prodigalità, *f.*, sciupio, *m.*

waster, *n.* Guastatore, dissipatore, *m.*; fannullone, *m.*

wasting, *n.* Sperpero, *m.*; dissipazione, *f.*; consumo, *m.* || *a.* Che sciupa, che dissipa.

wastrel [ˈweistrəl], *n.* Sprecone, *m.*; libertino, *m.*

watch (1) [wɔtʃ], *n.* Veglia, sorveglianza, *f.*; attenzione, *f.*; guardia, sentinella, *f.*; (*Naut.*) guardia, *f.* || *v.t.i.* Vegliare, sorvegliare, far la guardia a; guardare, osservare; vigiliare. **To be on —,** far la guardia; **— -dog,** cane di guardia, *m.*; **to keep —,** sorvegliare.

watch (2), *n.* Orologio, *m.* **— -chain,** catena da orologio, *f.*; **stop- —,** orologio a scatto, *m.*

watcher, *n.* Vegliatore, *m.*, vegliatrice, *f.*; osservatore, *m.*, osservatrice, *f.*, sorvegliante, *m.f.*

watchful, *a.* Attento, vigilante.

watchfully, *adv.* Vigilantemente.

watchfulness, *n.* Vigilanza, sorveglianza, *f.*; cura, *f.*

watchmaker, *n.* Orologiaio, *m.*

watchman, *n.* Guardia notturna, guardiano, *m.*

watchword, *n.* Parola d'ordine, *f.*

water [wɔːtəɹ], *n.* Acqua, *f.* || *v.t.* (*garden*) Innaffiare; (*a horse*) abbeverare; (*to dilute*) annacquare, diluire, mettere acqua in; (*Comm.*) diluire; (*silk*) marezzare; (*to irrigate*) irrigare; *v.i.* (*of the eyes*) piangere; (*to let in*) fare acqua. **To make one's mouth —,** fare venire l'acquolina in bocca; **to draw —,** attingere acqua; **to take in —,** fare la provvista d'acqua; **drinking —,** acqua potabile, *f.*; **— -bailiff,** guardiano di pesca, *m.*; **— -bottle,** caraffa, *f.*, (*Mil.*) borraccia, *f.*; **— -butt,** botte da acqua, *f.*; **— -borne,** trasportato dall'acqua; **— -cart,** carretto da innaffiare, *m.*; **— -clock,** clessidra, *f.* **— -closet,** gabinetto, cesso, luogo comodo, *m.*; (*Art*) **— -colour,** acquerello, *m.*; **— -colourist** acquerellista, *m.f.*; **— -course,** canale, scolatoio, corso d'acqua, *m.*; **— -cress,** crescione, *m.*; **— -diviner,** rabdomante, *m.*; **— -fowl,** uccello acquatico, *m.*; **— -gauge,** tubo di livello, *m.*; **— -glass,** (*Chem.*) soluzione silicea, *f.*, silicato di potassio, *m.*; (*Golf.*) **— -hazard,** fossatello, *m.*; **— -ice,** sorbetto, *m.*; **— -jacket,** camicia d'acqua, *f.*; **— -jug,** brocca, *f.*; **— -lily,** nenufar, *m.*, ninfea, *f.*; **— -line,** linea d'acqua, *f.*, (*Naut.*) linea di galleggiamento, *m.*; **— -logged,** imbevuto d'acqua, inzuppato; **— -meadow,** prateria irrigabile, *f.*; **— -melon,** cocomero, *m.*; **— -meter,** contatore dell'acqua, *m.*; **— -mill,** mulino ad acqua, *m.*; **— -nymph,** naiade, *f.*; **— -pipe,** condotto d'acqua, *m.*; **— -power,** forza idrica, energia idraulica, *f.*; **— -tower,** castello d'acqua, *m.*; **— -wheel,** ruota idraulica, turbina, idraulica, *f.*; **— on the brain,** idrocefalia, *f.*; **— on the knee,** travaso di sinovia, *m.*; **still waters run deep,** acqua cheta rovina i ponti.

waterage, *n.* Trasporto per via d'acqua, *m.*

waterer, *n.* Innaffiatore, *m.*

waterfall, *n.* Cascata, *f.*

wateriness, *n.* Acquosità, umidità, *f.*; (*Med.*) sierosità, *f.*

watering, *n.* Innaffiamento, abbeveramento, *m.*; irrigazione, *f.*; approvvigionamento d'acqua, *m.* **— -cart,** carro irrigatore, *m.*; **— -place,** stazione balneare, stazione termale, *f.*; (*for animals*) abbeveratoio, *m.*; **— -pot,** innaffiatoio, *m.*

waterless, *a.* Senz'acqua, privo d'acqua, arido.

waterman, *n.* Barcaiuolo, *m.*

watermark, *n.* (*tidal*) Livello dell'acqua, *m.*; (*in paper*) filigrana, *f.*

waterproof, *a.* Impermeabile. || *n.* Impermeabile, *m.* || *v.t.* Rendere impermeabile.

watershed, *n.* Spartiacque, versante, *m.*

waterside, *n.* Sponda, riva, *f.* || *a.* Rivierasco, littoraneo.

waterspout, *n.* Tromba marina, *f.*

watertight [ˈwɔːtəɹtait], *a.* Stagno, impermeabile.

waterway, *n.* Canale navigabile, *m.*

waterworks, *n.pl.* Serbatoio, *m.*; impianto idraulico, *m.*

watery, *a.* Acqueo, acquoso, umido, bagnato; insipido.

watt [wɔt], *n.* (*Elec.*) Watt, *m.*

wattle (1) [wɔtl], *n.* (*of birds*) Bargiglio, *m.*, caruncola, *f.*; (*of fish*) barbetta, *f.*

wattle (2), *n.* Canniccio, graticcio, *m.*, vimini, *f.pl.* || *v.t.* Legare con vimini, intrecciare, ingraticciare.

wattling, *n.* Graticcio, canniccio, *m.*

wave [weiv], *n.* Onda, *f.*, flutto, maroso, cavallone, *m.*; (*with hand*) segno, cenno, *m.*;

(*with wand*) colpo, *m.*; (*of hair*) ondulazione, *f.* || *v.i.* Ondeggiare, fluttuare; far segno; *v.t.* agitare; brandire; (*hair*) ondulare. **To have one's hair waved,** farsi ondulare i capelli; **a permanent —,** una permanente, *f.*; **a — of the hand,** un segno con la mano, *m.*; (*Radio*) **— -length,** lunghezza d'onda, *f.*

waver, *v.i.* Vacillare, esitare, titubare, tentennare.

waverer, *n.* Persona irresoluta, *f.*

wavering, *a.* Esitante, fluttuante.

wavily, *adv.* Con ondulazioni.

wavy, *a.* Ondeggiante, ondulato; serpeggiante.

wax (1) [wæks], *n.* Cera, *f.*; (*cobbler's*) pece, *f.*; (*of ear*) cerume, *m.*; (*colloq.*) stizza, *f.* || *v.t.* Incerare. **Bees' wax,** cera d'api, *f.*; **paraffin —,** cera di paraffina, *f.*; **sealing- —,** ceralacca, *f.*; (*colloq.*) **to get in a —,** montare in collera, arrabbiarsi; **— -works,** museo di figure di cera, *m.*; **— match,** cerino, *m.*

wax (2), *v.i.* Crescere, divenire, farsi.

waxen, *a.* Di cera, ceroso.

waxy, *a.* Cereo, come cera; (*colloq.*) in collera.

way [wei], *n.* Via, strada, *f.*; modo, *m.*, maniera, guisa, *f.*; uso, *m.*, abitudine, usanza, pratica, *f.*; direzione, *f.*; distanza, *f.*; senso, *m.*; (*of ship*) abbrivo, *m.*, invasatura, *f.* **— of living,** modo di vivere, *m.*; **— of thinking,** modo di pensare, *m.*; **in such a way as . . .,** in modo da . . .; **in its —,** nel suo genere; **it is always the — with him,** è sempre così con lui; **the right —,** la maniera giusta, *f.*; **to be in a bad —,** andar male; **to find a — to . . .,** trovare il modo di . . .; **to go the right —,** seguire la via giusta; **to have one's own —,** fare a modo proprio; **by the —,** di passaggio, (*fig.*) a proposito; **in the —,** incomodo, ingombrante, a noia; **over the —,** dall'altra parte della strada, in faccia; **the — in,** l'entrata, *f.*; **the — out,** l'uscita, *f.*; **a good — off,** alquanto discosto; **to clear the —,** aprire la strada; **to give —,** cedere, accondiscendere, (*Naut.*) remare con forza; **to go one's —,** andarsene in pace; **to lead the —,** andare pel primo; **to lose one's —,** smarrirsi; **to make —,** farsi strada, andare; **— -bill,** foglio di rotta, *m.*

wayfarer [ˈweifɛərəɹ], *n.* Viaggiatore, *m.*, viandante, *m.f.*

wayfaring, *a.* Viaggiante.

waylay [weiˈlei], *v.t.* Tendere un agguato a; appostarsi; attendere al passaggio.

wayside, *n.* Margine della strada, *m.* || *a.* Sul bordo della strada. (*Rail.*) **— station,** stazione di campagna, fermata, *f.*

wayward [ˈweiwəd], *a.* Perverso, capriccioso, caparbietto, ostinato.

waywardness, *n.* Ritrosia, *f.*; perversità, *f.*

wayworn, *a.* Stanco di viaggiare.

we [wi:], *pron.* Noi, noi altri, si.

weak [wi:k], *a.* Debole, fiacco, infermo, fievole; (*of tea, etc.*) debole, leggero. **That's my — spot,** ecco il mio lato debole; **to grow —,** indebolirsi; **— -minded,** fiacco, senza anima o forza.

weaken, *v.t.* Indebolire, infiacchire; ammortire; *v.i.* indebolirsi; scemare; attenuare.

weakening, *n.* Indebolimento, *m.*

weakish, *a.* Piuttosto debole.

weakling, *n.* Creatura debole, *f.*, malaticcio, *m.*

weakly, *a.* Debole, infermo, poco robusto. || *adv.* Debolmente.

weakness, *n.* Debolezza, *f.*, fiacchezza, *f.*; (*fig.*) punto debole, *m.*

weal (1) [wi:l], *n.* Ammaccatura, lividura, *f.*

weal (2), *n.* Benessere, bene, *m.* **The common —,** il benessere pubblico, *m.*; **for — or woe,** nella fortuna come nella disgrazia.

weald [wi:ld], *n.* Foresta, *f.*, bosco, *m.*; campagna aperta, *f.*

wealth [welθ], *n.* Ricchezze, *f.pl.*, opulenza, *f.*; beni, *m.pl.*, sostanze, *f.pl.*

wealthily, *adv.* Riccamente.

wealthiness, *n.* Ricchezza, *f.*

wealthy, *a.* Ricco, opulento.

wean [wi:n], *v.t.* Svezzare, spoppare.

weaning, *n.* Spoppamento, divezzamento, *m.*

weapon [ˈwepən], *n.* Arma, arme, *f.*

weaponless, *a.* Senz'armi, disarmato.

wear [wɛəɹ], *n.* Uso, *m.*, durata, *f.*; logorio, logoramento, consumo, *m.*; (*clothes*) abito, abbigliamento, *m.*; (*Mech.*) usura, *f.* || *v.t.i.* (*clothes*) Portare, indossare, avere; (*to last*) durare; usare; (*Naut.*) virare di bordo. **To — off,** sparire lentamente, dissiparsi; **to — away,** consumare, logorare; **to — out,** esaurirsi, spossarsi, logorarsi; **to — well,** avere lunga durata; **the worse for —,** guasto; **— and tear,** logorio, *m.*

wearable, *a.* Portabile, da portarsi, che si può indossare.

wearer, *n.* Indossatore, *m.*, indossatrice, *f.*

weariless [ˈwiɛriles], *a.* Instancabile.

wearily, *adv.* Stancamente, con fatica.

weariness, *n.* Stanchezza, *f.*

wearing [ˈwɛəriŋ], *n.* Uso, *m.*, usura, *f.* || *a.* Esauriente.

wearisome [ˈwiərisəm], *a.* Tedioso, noioso, faticoso.

wearisomely, *adv.* Noiosamente.

wearisomeness, *n.* Noiosità, *f.*, tedio, *m.*; uggia, *f.*

weary [ˈwiəri], *a.* Affaticato, stanco; noioso. || *v.t.* Stancare, affaticare; annoiare, stufare; *v.i.* stancarsi. **To — for,** agognare; languire per.

weasand [ˈwezənd], *n.* Trachea, *f.*

weasel [ˈwi:zəl], *n.* (*Zool.*) Donnola, *f.*

weather [ˈweðəɹ], *n.* Tempo, *m.* || *v.t.* Esporre all'aria; resistere a uscire da; (*a storm*) resistere a; (*a cape*) doppiare, oltrepassare; (*Geol.*) alterare, disgregare. **Exposed to all weathers,** esposto a tutte le intemperie; (*Radio*) **— forecast and news,** giornale radio, *m.*; **fine, bad —,** tempo bello, cattivo, *m.*; **— permitting,** tempo permettendo; **— -beaten,** sbattuto dalla tempesta; **— -board,** riparo contro il vento, *m.*, rabbattitore, *m.*; paraonda, *f.*; **— -boarding,** intavolato di riparo contro le piogge, *m.*; **— side,** lato del vento, *m.*; **— -wise,** esperto del tempo.

weathercock, *n.* Banderuola, *f.*, segnavento, *m.*; ventarola, *f.*; (*fig.*) ventarola, *f.*, arlecchino, *m.*

weathermost, *a.* Il più esposto al vento.

weave [wi:v], *v.t.* Tessere; intrecciare; ordire, inventare. || *n.* Tessuto, *m.*

weaver, *n.* Tessitore, *m.*, tessitrice, *f.*

weaving, *n.* Tessitura, *f.*

weazen [cp. **wizen**].

web [web], *n.* Tela, *f.*, tessuto, *m.*; struttura, *f.*; (*spider's*) ragnatela, *f.*; (*of bird*) membrana, *f.*; (*of key*) ingegno, *m.* **—-footed,** palmipede.
webbed, *a.* Palmato.
webbing, *n.* Tessuto, *m.*, cinghia, *f.*; tela da cigna, *f.*
wed [wed], *v.t.* Sposare, sposarsi; *v.i.* sposarsi, (*of man*) ammogliarsi, (*of woman*) maritarsi.
wedded, *a.* Coniugale; sposato, coniugato; attaccato, legato.
wedding, *n.* Nozze, *f.pl.*, matrimonio, sposalizio, *m.* **—-ring,** anello nuziale, *m.*, fede, *f.*; **golden —,** nozze d'oro, *f.pl.*; **— breakfast,** banchetto nuziale, *m.*; **—-cake,** gateau nuziale, *m.*; **— day,** giorno dello sposalizio, *m.*; **— march,** marcia nuziale, *f.*; **— present,** regalo di nozze, *m.*; **— dress,** veste nuziale, *f.*; **—-guest,** invitato, invitata alle nozze, *m.f.*
wedge [wedʒ], *n.* Cuneo, *m.*, bietta, *f.*; lingotto, *m.* || *v.t.* Incuneare, imbiettare.
wedlock [ˈwedlɔk], *n.* Matrimonio, stato coniugale, *m.* **Child born out of —,** figlio illegittimo, *m.*
Wednesday [ˈwenzdi], *n.* Mercoledì, *m.* **Ash —,** giorno delle ceneri, *m.*
wee [wi:], *a.* Piccolo, piccolino, minuscolo.
weed [wi:d], *n.* Erbaccia, malerba, *f.* || *v.t.* Sarchiare. **Widow's weeds,** bruno di vedova, lutto vedovile, *m.*; **to — out,** estirpare, sradicare.
weeder, *n.* Sarchiatore, *m.*; (*hoe*) sarchio, *m.*
weeding, *n.* Sarchiatura, *f.*
weedy, *a.* Pieno di malerbe; (*fig.*) sparuto, gramo.
week [wi:k], *n.* Settimana, *f.* **Next —,** settimana ventura, *f.*; **this day —,** oggi a otto; **tomorrow —,** domani a otto; **a — ago to-day,** otto giorni fa; **in a week's time,** fra otto giorni; **once a —,** una volta la settimana.
weekday, *n.* Giorno lavorativo, giorno feriale, *m.*
weekend, *n.* Vacanza di fine settimana, *f.* **—-ticket,** biglietto a prezzo ridotto, *m.*; **—-cottage,** villino, *m.*; **a long —,** da venerdì a martedì.
weekly, *a.* Settimanale. || *adv.* Settimanalmente. || *n.* Rivista settimanale, *f.*
ween [wi:n], *v.i.* Immaginarsi, pensare, credere.
weep [wi:p], *v.i.* Piangere, lagrimare. **To — for,** piangere.
weeper, *n.* Chi piange, piagnono, *m.*
weeping, *n.* Pianto, *m.*, lagrime, *f.pl.* || *a.* Piangente. (*Bot.*) **— willow,** salice piangente, *m.*
weevil [ˈwi:vəl], *n.* (*Zool.*) Punteruolo, *m.*
weevily, *a.* Bacato.
weft [weft], *n.* Trama, *f.*
weigh [wei], *v.t.* Pesare; (*anchor*) salpare, levare; (*to ponder*) ponderare, valutare; *v.i.* pesare, avere il peso di. **— bridge,** ponte a basculla, *m.*; **to get under —,** levar l'ancora, salpare, (*fig.*) cominciare; **to — down,** opprimere, aggravare, accasciare.
weigher, *n.* Pesatore, *m.*
weighing, *n.* Pesatura, *f.* **—-machine,** pesatrice, *f.*; **—-in,** pesaggio, *m.*
weight [weit], *n.* Peso, *m.*, pesantezza, *f.*; importanza, *f.* || *v.t.* Caricare di pesi. **Dead —,** peso morto, *m.*; **worth its — in gold,** vale oro quanto pesa; **a person of —,** un pezzo grosso, *m.*
weightily, *adv.* Pesantemente, seriamente.
weightiness, *n.* Pesantezza, *f.*; serietà, importanza, *f.*
weighty, *a.* Pesante, grave, importante.
weir [wiəɹ], *n.* Chiusa, traversa, *f.*; cateratta, *f.*; sbarramento, *m.*
weird, *a.* Fantastico, strano; soprannaturale. || *n.* Destino, *m.*; malia, *f.*, incantesimo, *m.*
weirdness, *n.* Stranezza, *f.*
welcher [cp. **welsher**].
welcome [ˈwelkəm], *a.* Grato, gradito, ben accetto; (*of a person*) benvenuto. || *n.* Benvenuto, *m.*, buona accoglianza, *f.* || *v.t.* Dare il benvenuto a, accogliere cordialmente, far le feste a. **You are —!** Prego!
weld, welding, *n.* Saldatura, *f.* **To weld,** saldare.
welder, *n.* Saldatore, *m.*
welfare [ˈwelfɛəɹ], *n.* Benessere, bene, *m.* **Welfare State,** lo Stato assistenziale, *m.*; **public —,** salute pubblica, *f.*
welkin [ˈwelkin], *n.* Volta celeste, *f.*
well (1) [wel], *n.* Pozzo, *m.*; sorgente, fontana, *f.*; serbatoio, *m.*; (*of boat*) sentina, *f.* **Oil —,** pozzo petrolifero, *m.*; **artesian —,** pozzo artesiano, *m.*; **to bore a —,** forare un pozzo; **to — up,** scaturire, pullulare; **—-spring,** fontana, sorgente, *f.*; **—-head,** sponda, *f.* **— of court,** banco degli avvocati, *m.*
well (2), *a.* Bene, buono, sano, in buona salute. || *adv.* Bene; molto. **To be —, to feel —,** star bene; **to get —,** guarire, guarirsi; **to come — out of a matter,** uscirne bene; **to be — up in,** essere bene informato di; (*colloq.*) **to do oneself —,** godersela; **to live —,** vivere agiatamente; **to be —-to-do, to be —-off,** essere benestante, essere agiato; **all's — that ends —,** è bene tutto ciò che bene finisce; **— and good,** alla buon'ora, sta bene; **that's all very —, but . . .,** tutto ciò sta bene, ma . . .; **—-advised,** ben consigliato; **—-attended,** ben frequentato; **—-appointed,** bene equipaggiato; **—-balanced,** bene equilibrato; **—-being,** benessere; **—-behaved,** ben costumato, che si comporta bene; **—-beloved,** benamato, *m.*, benamata, *f.*; **—-bred,** beneducato; **—-born** bennato; **—-disposed,** ben disposto; **—-favoured,** bello; **—-meaning,** bene intenzionato; **—-done,** ben fatto, (*Cooking*) ben cotto; **Well done!** Bravo! **—-informed,** bene informato; **—-known,** ben noto, ben conosciuto; **—-nigh,** quasi; **—-preserved,** ben portante; **—-timed,** opportuno; **—-read,** istruito, letterato; **—-spoken,** facondo.
wellingtons [ˈweliŋtənz], *n.pl* Stivaloni, *m.pl.*
Welsh [welʃ], *a.* Gallese. || *n.* Lingua gallese, *f.* **— rabbit,** crostino di formaggio fuso, *m.*
welsher, *n.* (*Racing*) Truffatore di somme scommesse, *m.*
Welshman, Welshwoman, *n.* Gallese, *m.f.*
welt [welt], *n.* Trapinta, tramezza, *f.*
welter, *v.i.* Nuotare, avvoltolarsi, essere sballottato. || *n.* Voltolamento, sballottamento, *m.* (*Boxing*) **—-weight,** peso medioleggero, *m.*
wen [wen], *n.* Natta, *f.*, gozzo, *m.*
wench [wentʃ], *n.* Ragazza, giovanetta, zitella, *f.* || *v.i.* Frequentare le prostitute.

wend [wend], *v.i.* Proseguire, continuare. **To — one's way**, proseguire la propria strada, prendere la strada.
went, *p.* of **go**.
were, *p.* of **be**.
we're [ˈwi:əɹ], (*colloq.*) Noi siamo.
werewolf, werwolf [ˈwiəɹwulf], *n.* Lupo mannaro, *m.*
west [west], *n.* Ovest, occidente, ponente, *m.* || *a.* Dell'ovest, d'occidente, di ponente, occidentale. **— wind**, vento di ponente, *m.*; (*colloq.*) **to go —**, morire; **West Africa**, l'Africa Occidentale, *f.*; **West Indies**, le Indie Occidentali, *f.pl.*
westering, *a.* Che va ad occidente.
westerly, *a.* Dell'ovest. ||*adv.* verso l'ovest.
western, *a.* Occidentale, dell'ovest.
westerner, *n.* Che viene dagli Stati occidentali dell'America.
westernmost, *a.* Il più occidentale.
westward, *a.adv.* Verso l'ovest, a ponente.
wet [wet], *a.* Umido, bagnato; fradicio, molle; piovoso; liquido; (*of paint*) fresco. || *n.* Umidità, *f.*; acqua, *f.*; pioggia, *f.* || *v.t.* Bagnare, umettare, inumidire, inzuppare; annaffiare. (*colloq.*) **— blanket**, guastafeste, spegnitoio, *m.*; **— dock**, bacino a chiusa, *m.*, darsena, *f.*; **— nurse**, balia, allattante, *f.*; **to get — through**, farsi tutto bagnato; **out in the —**, alla pioggia.
wether [ˈweðəɹ], *n.* Montone castrato, *m.*
wetness, *n.* Umidità, *f.*
wetting, *n.* Bagnatura, *f.*, inumidimento, *m.*; umettamento, *m.*
wettish, *a.* Alquanto bagnato, umidiccio.
whack [wæk], *n.* Bussa, *f.*, colpo sonoro, *m.* || *v.t.* Bastonare.
whale [weil], *n.* (*Zool.*) Balena, *f.* **—-boat**, baleniera, *f.*; **—-calf**, balenotto, *m.*
whalebone, *n.* Osso di balena, *m.*
whaler, *n.* Baleniere, *m.*, baleniera, *f.*, pescatore di balene, *m.*
whaling, *n.* Pesca della balena, *f.* **—-ship**, **—-vessel**, baleniera, *f.*
wharf [wɔ:ɹf], *n.* Scalo, *m.*, calata, banchina, *f.*; molo, *m.*
wharfage, *n.* Diritto di sosta, *m.*
wharfing, *n.* Ormeggio, *m.*
wharfinger [ˈwɔ:ɹfindʒəɹ], *n.* Padrone di un molo, *m.*; guardiano di molo, *m.*
what [wɔt], *a.pron.adv.* Quale, che; che cosa, ciò che, quel che; quanto; Che cosa? Come? **What for ?** Per che fare? Perchè? **What is the matter ?** Che cosa c'è?; **What is the matter with you ?** Che hai? Che avete? **What do you call this ?** Come si chiama questo? **I do not know what to do**, non so che cosa fare; **What weather it is!** Che tempo fa! **— I feared has happened**, è accaduto ciò che temevo; **call it — you will**, chiamatelo come volete; **— with one thing and another**, sia una cosa sia l'altra; **not but —**, non già che; **I have no doubt but — he will come**, non dubito ch'egli venga.
whatever, whatsoever, *pron.a.* Qualunque, qualunque cosa, qualsiasi cosa, checchessia; tutto ciò che, per quanto. **— he says is true**, qualunque cosa egli dica è vera; **none —**, nessuno, neppure uno solo; **nothing —**, niente del tutto.
whatnot [ˈwɔtnɔt], *n.* Scaffaletto, *m.*
wheat [wi:t], *n.* Frumento, grano, *m.*
wheaten, *a.* Di frumento, di grano, frumentario.
wheedle [wi:dl], *v.t.* Vezzeggiare, accarezzare; blandire; ingannare con moine.
wheedling, *n.* Moine, *f.pl.* || *a.* Carezzevole, lusinghiero.
wheel [wi:l], *n.* Ruota, *f.*; volante, disco, *m.*; rotella, *f.*; (*Naut.*) barra, ruota del timone, *f.*; (*Mil.*) conversione, *f.* || *v.t.* Far rotare; trasportare in un veicolo; (*Mil.*) fare una conversione; (*of birds, etc.*) svolazzare. **Driving- —**, ruota motrice, ruota maestra, *f.*; **fly- —**, volano, *m.*; **spur- —**, ruota dentata, *f.*; **— work, wheels**, meccanismo, ingranaggio, *m.*; **water- —**, ruota idraulica.
wheelbarrow, *n.* Carriola a mano, *f.*
wheeled, *a.* Con ruote, a ruote.
wheeler, *n.* Cavallo del timone, *m.* **Four- —**, veicolo a quattro ruote, *m.*
wheeling, *n.* Giro, giramento, volteggiamento, *m.*; roteamento, *m.*
wheelwright [ˈwi:lrait], *n.* Carraio, *m.*
wheeze [wi:z], *v.i.* Ansimare, soffiare, respirare rumorosamente. || *n.* Respiro affannoso, *m.*; (*colloq.*) nozione, idea, *f.*
wheezing, *n.* Respirazione rumorosa, *f.*
wheezy, *a.* Ansimante, sibilante; asmatico.
whelk [welk], *n.* (*Zool.*) Buccina, bollicina, *f.*
whelp [welp], *n.* Cucciolo, *m.*; lupacchiotto, *m.* || *v.t.* Figliare.
when [wen], *adv.* Quando, allorchè, mentre; qualora; dopo che. **Since — ?** Da quando?; **the day — I saw him**, il giorno in cui lo vidi; **even —**, anche quando; **— all's said and done**, alla fine dei conti.
whence [wens], *adv.* Donde, onde, da dove.
whencesoever, *adv.* Da qualunque luogo, da qualsiasi parte.
whenever, whensoever, *adv.* Ogni volta che, qualora, sempre quando, ogniqualvolta.
where [wɛəɹ], *adv.* Dove, ove. **Where to ?** Dove? **Where are you going ?** Dove va?
whereabout, whereabouts, *adv.* Dove, in che posto. **To know the whereabouts**, conoscere il luogo dove.
whereas [wɛərˈæz], *adv.conj.* Mentre, quando invece; stante che, siccome.
whereat, *adv.conj.* Al che, su di che.
whereby, *adv.conj.* Onde, per mezzo di; per lo che, per cui.
wherefore [ˈwɛəɹfɔ:ɹ], *adv.* Onde, per la qual cosa, perciò. || *n.* Il perchè, *m.*
wherein [wɛərˈin], *adv.conj.* In che, nel quale; Dove?
whereof, *adv.conj.* Di cui, del quale.
whereon, whereupon, *adv.conj.* Al che, su cui, sul quale.
wherever [wɛərˈevəɹ], *adv.* In qualunque luogo, dove che sia.
wherewith, *adv.* Con cui, con che.
wherewithal [ˈwɛəɹwiðɔ:l], *n.* (*colloq.*) I mezzi, *m.pl.*; danaro, *m.*
wherry [ˈweri], *n.* Barchetta, *f.*, barchino, *m.*
wherryman, *n.* Barcaiuolo, *m.*
whet [wet], *v.t.* (*tools*) Affilare, arrotare; (*the appetite*) aguzzare, stimolare. || *n.* (*colloq.*) Aperitivo, *m.*
whether [ˈweðəɹ], *conj.* Se, sia . . . che; sia che . . . che. **— or not he will do it**, se lo farà o no.

whetstone ['wetstoun], *n.* Cote, pietra da affilare, *f.*
whetting, *n.* Affilamento, *m.*
whey [wei], *n.* Siero di latte, *m.*
which [witʃ], *pron.a.* Che, il quale, la quale, i quali, le quali, Quale? **Which way do we go?** Per dove andiamo?
whichever, *pron.a.* Qualunque, qualsisia, sia l'uno sia l'altro.
whiff [wif], *n.* Soffio, alito, sbuffo, *m.*, buffata, *f.* || *v.t.i.* Soffiare, lanciare una buffata di.
whiffler, *n.* Persona incostante, *f.*
whig [wig], *n.a.* (*Hist.*) Liberale, *m.*
while (1) [wail], *n.* Tempo, pezzo, istante, *m.* **A little —,** un breve tempo; **a good — ago,** lungo tempo fa; **after a —,** qualche tempo dopo; **for a —,** per un pezzo; **all the —,** durante tutto il tempo; **once in a —,** occasionalmente; **it is not worth —,** non ne vale la pena; **to — away the time,** far passare il tempo.
while, whilst, *conj.* Mentre, intanto, nel tempo che, intanto che, finchè.
whim [wim], *n.* Capriccio, ghiribizzo, *m.*; (*Mech.*) mulinello, *m.*
whimper, *v.i.* Piagnucolare, pigolare, gemere. || *n.* Piagnucolio, *m.*
whimperer, *n.* Piagnone, *m.*, piagnona, *f.*
whimsical ['wimzikəl], *a.* Capriccioso, bizzarro, fantastico, fantasioso.
whimsicality, *n.* Fantasticheria, *f.*
whimsically, *adv.* Bizzarramente.
whimsy, *n.* Capriccio, *m.*
whin [win], *n.* (*Bot.*) Ginestra gigante, ginestra spinosa, *f.*
whine [wain], *v.i.* Gemere, lamentarsi, piagnucolare; (*of dog*) uggiolare. || *n.* Gemito, lamento, *m.*
whinny ['wini], *v.i.* Nitrire. || *n.* Nitrito, *m.*
whinstone ['winstoun], *n.* (*Geol.*) Basalto, *m.*, diorite, *f.*
whip [wip], *n.* Frusta, sferza, *f.*; (*Mech.*) ghia, *f.*; (*Hunting*) capocaccia, *m.*; (*Pol.*) organizzatore politico, *m.* || *v.t.* Frustare, sferzare; fustigare, flagellare; (*eggs*) sbattere. **To — up,** eccitare; **—-cord,** corda da frusta, *f.*; (*fig.*) **the — hand,** il vantaggio, *m.*
whipper-in, *n.* Capocaccia, *m.*
whipper-snapper ['wipəɹsnæpəɹ], *n.* Vanerello, uomo presuntuoso, *m.*; monello, *m.*
whipping, *n.* Fustigazione, sferzata, *f.*, bastonatura, *f.* **—-top,** paleo, *m.*
whipple-tree ['wipltri:], *n.* Bilancino di carrozza, *m.*
whir, whirr [wə:ɹ], *v.i.* Mugghiare, frusciare, ronzare.
whirl, *v.t.i.* Girare, fare girare, roteare, turbinare. || *n.* Giro rapido, turbine, *m.*
whirligig ['wə:ɹligig], *n.* Girandola, *f.*, girello, *f.*, carosello, *m.*
whirling, *n.* Turbinamento, *m.* || *a.* Turbinante.
whirlpool, *n.* Vortice, *m.*, gorgo, *m.*, mulinello, *m.*
whirlwind, *n.* Turbine, *m.*; tifone, *m.*
whirring, *n.* Sibilo, *m.* || *a.* Sibilante.
whisk [wisk], *n.* (*of broom*) Spolveraccio, *m.*; (*for eggs*) frullino, *m.* || *v.t.* Spolverare, spazzare; (*eggs*) sbattere, frullare.
whiskers ['wiskəɹz], *n.pl.* Fedine, bassette, *f.pl.*, favoriti, *m.pl.*; (*of animal*) baffi, *m.pl.*
whisky ['wiski], *n.* Whisky, *m.*; (*vehicle*) calesse, *m.*
whisper ['wispəɹ], *n.* Bisbiglio, sussurro, mormorio, *m.* || *v.i.* Bisbigliare; sussurrare. **In a —,** sotto voce, a voce bassa.
whisperer, *n.* Bisbiglione, bisbigliatore, *m.*, bisbigliatrice, *f.*
whispering, *n.* Bisbiglio, sussurrio, *m.* || *a.* Sussurrante. **— gallery,** galleria acustica, *f.*
whist [wist], *n.* (*Cards*) Whist, *m.*
whistle [wisl], *n.* (*sound*) Fischio, *m.*; (*instrument*) fischietto, *m.* || *v.t.* Fischiare, fischiettare; sibilare; (*of wind*) muggire, mugghiare. (*fig.*) **To wet one's —,** bere.
whistler, *n.* Fischiatore, *m.*
whistling, *n.* Fischiamento, *m.*
whit [wit], *n.* Ette, iota, *m.* **Not one —,** niente affatto.
white [wait], *a.* Bianco; candido, puro, schietto. || *n.* Bianco, *m.*, bianca, *f.*; (*of egg*) chiaro, *m.* || *v.t.* Imbiancare. **—-faced,** pallido; **—-heat,** incandescenza, *f.*; **—-hot,** incandescente; **to show the — feather,** dar prove di vigliaccheria; **a — lie,** una bugia innocente, *f.*; **a —-elephant,** una cosa inutile e ingombrante, *f.*
whitebait ['waitbeit], *n.* (*Zool.*) Pesciolini, *m.pl.*
whiten, *v.t.i.* Imbiancare; imbiancarsi.
whiteness, *n.* Bianchezza, *f.*; purezza, *f.*, candore, *m.*; (*of face*) pallore, *m.*; (*of hair*) canizie, *f.*
whitethroat, *n.* (*Zool.*) Capinera grigia, *f.*
whitewash, *n.* Calce da imbiancare, *f.* || *v.t.* Imbiancare; (*fig.*) riabilitare, nascondere i difetti di.
whitewasher, *n.* Imbianchino, *m.*
whitewashing, *n.* Imbiancatura. *f.*
whither ['wiðəɹ], *adv.* Dove, per dove; dovunque.
whiting ['waitiŋ], *n.* (*Zool.*) Merluzzo, merlango, *m.*; (*colouring*) bianco di Spagna, *m.*
whitish, *a.* Biancastro, bianchiccio.
whitlow ['witlou], *n.* Panereccio, *m.*
Whitsuntide ['witsəntaid], *n.* Pentecoste, *f.* **Whit Sunday, Whitsunday,** Domenica di Pentecoste.
whittle [witl], *v.t.* Tagliuzzare. **To — down,** attenuare; ridurre, assottigliare.
whiz, whizz [wiz], *n.* Fischio, sibilo, *m.* || *v.t.i.* Fischiare, sibilare.
who [hu:], *pron.* Che, il quale, la quale, i quali, le quali; Chi? **Who's there?** Chi è la? **Who knows!** Chi lo sa!
whoa! [wou], *inter.* Fermo!
whoever [hu:'evəɹ], *pron.* Chiunque, qualunque persona. **— it is,** chiunque sia.
whole [houl], *a.* Tutto; intero; integrale; intatto; totale; pieno; completo. || *n.* Il tutto, il totale, l'insieme, *m.*, somma, *f.* **As a —,** nell'insieme; **on the —,** in fin dei conti; **a — month,** un mese intero, *m.*; **the — world,** tutto il mondo; **—-meal, —-meal bread,** pane integrale, *m.*
wholeness, *n.* Totalità, *f.*; integrità, *f.*
wholesale ['houlseil], *a.* All'ingrosso; vendita all'ingrosso.
wholesome ['houlsəm], *a.* Sano, salubre; salutare.
wholesomely, *adv.* Sanamente, salubremente.

wholesomeness, *n.* Sanità, salubrità, *f.*; qualità di essere salubre, *f.*
wholly, *adv.* Interamente, pienamente, tutto.
whom [huːm], *pron.* Che, chi, il quale, la quale, i quali, le quali.
whomsoever [huːmsouˈevəɹ], *pron.* Qualunque, chiunque, chicchessia.
whoop [huːp], *n.* Urlo, *m.*, urlata, *f.*, grido, *m.* || *v.t.* Urlare, gridare.
whooping, *n.* Urlo, *m.* **—-cough,** tosse canina, pertosse, *f.*
whore [hɔːɹ], *n.* Prostituta, meretrice, *f.*
whorl [wɔːɹl], *n.* Verticillo, *m.*
whortleberry [ˈwəːɹtlberi], *n.* (*Bot.*) Mortella, mora, *f.*
whose [huːz], *pron.* Di cui, il cui, la cui, del quale, della quale, dei quali, delle quali; Di chi? A chi?
whosoever [huːsouˈevəɹ], *pron.* Chiunque.
why [wai], *adv.conj.* Perchè. || *n.* Il perchè, *m.* || *inter.* Ma! Come! Ebbene! **Why not?** Perchè no? **the how and the —,** il come e il perchè, *m.*
wick [wik], *n.* Lucignolo, stoppino, *m.*
wicked [ˈwikid], *a.* Tristo, cattivo, malvagio, scellerato, maligno.
wickedly, *adv.* Cattivamente, criminosamente.
wickedness, *n.* Malvagità, malignità, scelleratezza, *f.*
wicker [ˈwikəɹ], *n.* Vimine, vinco, *m.* **—-work,** viminata, *f.*, lavoro in vimini, *m.*
wicket, *n.* Sportello, *m.*; (*Cricket*) le sbarre, *f.pl.*; (*Croquet*) archetto, *m.*
wide [waid], *a.* Largo, vasto, ampio, esteso, grande. || *adv.* Lontano, lungi, in lontananza. **—-awake,** svegliato, sveglio; (*fig.*) furbo, desto; all'erta; **to be — awake,** essere interamente sveglio; **— open,** spalancato; **— of the mark,** lontano dal vero; **—-spread,** largamente diffuso; **to open —,** aprire del tutto.
widely, *adv.* Largamente, molto. **—-known,** assai conosciuto.
widen, *v.t.* Allargare; dilatare. **To — out,** estendersi.
wideness, *n.* Larghezza, ampiezza, *f.*
widening, *n.* Allargamento, ampiamento, *m.*
widgeon [ˈwidʒən], *n.* Fischione, *m.*, anitra selvatica, *f.*
widow [ˈwidou], *n.* Vedova, *f.* || *v.t.* Vedovare. **Widow's weeds,** abiti da lutto, bruno di vedova; **the widow's mite,** l'obolo di vedova, *m.*
widowed, *a.* Vedovato, vedovo.
widower, *n.* Vedovo, *m.*
widowhood, *n.* Vedovanza, *f.*
width [widθ], *n.* Larghezza, ampiezza, estensione, *f.*; (*of cloth*) altezza, *f.*
wield [wiːld], *v.t.* Maneggiare, brandire; esercitare.
wife (pl. **wives**) [waif, waivz], *n.* Moglie, sposa, *f.*
wifehood, *n.* Condizione di moglie, *f.*
wifelike, wifely, *a.* Da moglie, di moglie, coniugale.
wig [wig], *n.* Parrucca, *f.* **—-maker,** parrucchiere, *m.*
wigging [ˈwigiŋ], *n.* (*colloq.*) Sgridata, ramanzina, *f.*
wight [wait], *n.* Individuo, uomo, *m.*
wild [waild], *a.* Selvaggio; selvatico, incolto; sfrenato, disordinato; tempestoso; furioso, impetuoso; incoerente, pazzo. || *n.* Deserto, luogo selvatico, *m.* **— beast,** fiera, bestia feroce, *f.*; belva, *f.*; **to run —,** vagabondare; **— boar,** cinghiale, cignale, *m.*; **— flowers,** fiori dei prati, *m.pl.*; **— rose,** rosa di macchia, *f.*; **a — shot,** un tiro all'impazzata, *m.*
wilderness [ˈwildəɹnes], *n.* Deserto, *m.*, solitudine, *f.*
wildly, *adv.* Furiosamente, impetuosamente; sfrenatamente.
wildness, *n.* Selvatichezza, *f.*; stato selvaggio, *m.*; (*of look*) smarrimento, *m.*; (*of wind*) impetuosità, *f.*
wile [wail], *n.* Astuzia, furberia, *f.*, artificio, *m.*
wilful [ˈwilfʌl], *a.* Caparbio, ostinato, testardo; intenzionale, premeditato, fatto apposta. **— murder,** omicidio premeditato, *m.*
wilfully, *adv.* Apposta, con premeditazione; da caparbio; maliziosamente.
wilfulness, *n.* Caparbietà, testardaggine, *f.*
wilily [ˈwailili], *adv.* Artificiosamente, astutamente.
wiliness, *n.* Scaltrezza, astuzia, furberia, *f.*
will [wil], *n.* Volontà, *f.*, volere, *m.*; gradimento, piacere, *m.*; desiderio, *m.*; testamento, *m.*, ultima volontà, *f.* || *v.t.* Volere; disporre per testamento; *v.aux.* (*expressed in Italian by future tense*). **Against one's —,** mal volentieri; **at —,** a piacere; **ill- —,** malevolenza, *f.*; **with a —,** con tutto il cuore; **he always has his own —,** fa sempre secondo la sua volontà; **my last — and testament,** la mia volontà, il mio testamento; **a man with a strong —,** un uomo di carattere fermo, *m.*
William [ˈwiljəm], *n.* Guglielmo, *m.*
willing, *a.* Pronto a, disposto a; volontario, compiacente.
willingly, *adv.* Volentieri.
willingness, *n.* Compiacenza, *f.*, consentimento, *m.*; buona volontà, *f.*
will-o'-the-wisp [ˈwiloðəwisp], *n.* Fuoco fatuo, *m.*
willow [ˈwilou], *n.* Salice, *m.* **— bed, — plantation,** salceto, *m.*
willowy, *a.* Plantato a salici; (*fig.*) flessibile.
willynilly [ˈwiliˈnili], *adv.* Buon grado mal grado, volente o nolente.
wilt [wilt], *v.i.* Appassire, avvizzire; languire; *v.t.* far appassire.
wily [ˈwaili], *a.* Astuto, furbo, scaltro.
wimple [wimpl], *n.* Soggolo, *m.*
win [win], *n.* Vincita, vittoria, *f.* || *v.t.* Guadagnare, vincere; cattivarsi, conciliare; acquistare; persuadere; (*colloq.*) rubare. **A — on points,** una vittoria ai punti, *f.*; **to — back,** riguadagnare; **to — over,** persuadere.
wince [wins], *v.i.* Trasalire, fremere; rinculare, indietreggiare.
wincey [ˈwinsi], *n.* Mezzalana, *f.*
winch [wintʃ], *n.* Argano, verricello, *m.* manovella, *f.*, manubrio, *m.*
wind (1) [wind], *n.* Vento, fiato, *m.*; (*Med.*) flatulenza, *f.* || *v.t.* Fare sfiatare, far trafelare. **A gust of —,** raffica, *f.*; **to get — of,** fiutare, scoprire; **a breath of —,** un soffio di vento, *m.*; **a fair —,** un vento favorevole, *m.*; **down- —,** col vento; **trade —,** aliseo, *m.*; **at the mercy of the —,** in balia del vento; (*colloq.*) **to get the — up,** aver paura; to **sow the — and reap the whirlwind,** chi

semina vento raccoglie tempesta; **—-bag,** (*fig.*) chiacchierone, bagolone, *m.* **—-gauge,** anemometro, *m.*

wind (2) [waind], *v.t.* Avvolgere, fare girare, aggomitolare, attorcigliare; rimontare; *v.i.* serpeggiare; girare, fare delle svolte. || *n.* Svoltata, giravolta, *f.*; sinuosità, *f.* **To — up the clock,** caricare l'orologio; **to — up a business,** liquidare un commercio.

windage ['windidʒ], *n.* Forza del vento, *f.*

winded, *a.* Sfiatato.

winder ['waindəɹ], *n.* Arcolaio, *m.*

windfall ['windfɔːl], *n.* Frutto caduto per la forza del vento, *f.*; guadagno inaspettato, *m.*, buona fortuna, *f.*, bazza, *f.*

windiness ['windines], *n.* Ventosità, *f.*

winding ['waindiŋ], *a.* Sinuoso, serpeggiante, tortuoso. **—-sheet,** sudario, lenzuolo mortuario, *m.*; **— staircase,** scala a spirale, *f.*

windlass ['windləs], *n.* Argano, verricello, *m.*

windless ['windles], *a.* Senza vento, calmo.

windmill ['windmil], *n.* Mulino a vento, *m.*

window ['windou], *n.* Finestra, *f.*; (*shop*) vetrina, mostra, *f.*; (*casement*) finestra a gangheri, *f.*; (*carriage*) sportello, *m.*; (*church*) invetriata, *f.* **—-box,** giardino di finestra, *m.*; **—-dresser,** vetrinista, *m.f.*; (*fig.*) **—-dressing,** illusione, *f.*, inganno, *m.*; **—-ledge, —-sill,** davanzale, *m.*; **—-pane,** vetro, *m.*

windpipe ['windpaip], *n.* (*Anat.*) Trachea, *f.*

windrow ['windrou], *n.* (*Agric.*) Falciata, *f.*

windshield ['windʃiːld], *n.* Parabrezza, *m.* **—-wiper,** tergicristallo, *m.*

windward ['windwəd], *n.* Lato del vento, *m.* || *adv.* A sopravvento, contro vento.

windy [windi], *a.* Ventoso, tempestoso. **To be —,** soffiare, tirar vento.

wine [wain], *n.* Vino, *m.* **—-bottle,** bottiglia da vino, *f.*, fiasco, *m.*; **—-glass,** bicchiere da vino, *m.*; **—-cellar,** cantina, *f.*; **—-shop,** bettola, *f.*; **—-merchant,** mercante di vino, *m.*; **—-grower,** viticultore, vignaiolo, *m.*; **sparkling —,** vino spumante, *m.*; **table —,** vino da pasto, *m.*; **—-bibber,** beone, *m.*

wing [wiŋ], *n.* Ala, *f.*; volo, *m.*; (*Theat.*) quinta, *f.* || *v.t.* Traversare volando; ferire nell'ala. **— nut,** dado ad alette, *m.*; **—-span, —-spread,** apertura d'ali, *f.*; **to take —,** prendere il volo; **—-case,** elitra, *f.*

winged, *a.* Alato; ferito nell'ala.

wingless, *a.* Senz'ali.

wink [wiŋk], *n.* Batter d'occhio, ammico, cenno, *m.*; occhiata, *f.* || *v.i.* Ammiccare, batter le palpebre. **To — at,** chiuder un occhio a; (*fig.*) **forty winks,** sonnellino, *m.*; **not to get a — of sleep,** non chiuder occhio.

winkle ['wiŋkəl], *n.* (*Zool.*) Chiocciola di mare, *f.*

winner, *n.* Vincitore, *m.*, vincitrice, *f.*; campione, vincente, *m.*

winning, *a.* Vincitore, vincente; attraente, seducente. **The — game,** la partita decisiva, *f.*; **—-post,** traguardo, *m.*; **winnings,** vincite, *f.pl.*, guadagno, *m.*

winnow ['winou], *v.t.* Vagliare, spulare.

winnowing, *n.* Vagliatura, spulatura, *f.*

winsome ['winsəm], *a.* Amabile, attraente, piacente.

winsomeness, *n.* Attrattività, *f.*

winter ['wintəɹ], *n.* Inverno, *m.* || *v.t.i.* Svernare, passare l'inverno. **In the depth of —,** nel cuore dell'inverno.

wintry, *a.* D'inverno, invernale.

winy ['waini], *a.* Vinoso.

wipe [waip], *v.t.* Strofinare, nettare, pulire, asciugare. || *n.* Strofinata, *f.*, colpo di fazzoletto, *m.* **To — out,** cancellare; **to — off a debt,** liquidare un debito.

wiper, *n.* Strofinaccio, pulitore, *m.*

wire [waiɹ], *n.* Filo, *m.*; corda, *f.*; (*telegram*) telegramma, dispaccio, *m.* || *v.t.* Assicurare con filo; (*Elec.*) montare dei fili in; telegrafare. **Barbed —,** filo spinato, *m.*; **— entanglement,** reticolato, *m.*; **—-cutter,** tagliafili, *m.*; **—-fence,** siepe metallica, *f.*; **—-gauze,** tela metallica, *f.*; **—-netting,** rete metallica, *f.*, reticolato, *m.*; (*fig.*) **—-puller,** intrigante, *m.*

wireless, *a.* Senza fili. || *n.* Radio, *f.* **— telegram,** radiogramma, *m.*; **— telegraphy,** radiotelegrafia, *f.*; **— set,** radio, *f.*, apparecchio radio, *m.*; **— operator,** radiotelegrafista, *m.*

wiriness, *n.* Flessibilità, *f.*; muscolosità, *f.*

wiring, *n.* Montaggio di condutture elettriche, *m.*

wiry, *a.* Magro, secco, nerboruto.

wisdom ['wizdəm], *n.* Saggezza, sapienza, prudenza, *f.* **— tooth,** dente del giudizio, *m.*

wise [waiz], *a.* Saggio, savio, prudente, avveduto. || *n.* Maniera, *f.*, modo, *m.*; guisa, *f.* **In this —,** in questa maniera; **in no —,** in nessuna maniera.

wiseacre ['waizeikəɹ], *n.* Saccentone, saccente, *m.*

wisely, *adv.* Saviamente, saggiamente.

wish [wiʃ], *n.* Voglia, *f.*, desiderio, *m.*; augurio, *m.* || *v.t.i.* Desiderare; bramare; volere; augurare. **To — success,** augurare buona fortuna; **to express a —,** esprimere un desiderio; **to — many happy returns of the day,** augurare mille di questi giorni; **to comply with a —,** uniformarsi ad un desiderio; **—-bone,** forcella, *f.*

wisher, *n.* Chi desidera. **A well- —,** un buon amico, *m.*

wishful, *a.* Desideroso.

wishy-washy ['wiʃiwɔʃi], *a.* Insipido, debole, povero.

wisp [wisp], *n.* Ciuffo, *m.*; (*of hay, straw, etc.*) manciata, manata, *f.*, strofinaccio, *m.*

wistaria [wis'tɛəriə], *n.* (*Bot.*) Glicine, *m.*

wistful ['wistful], *a.* Pensoso, preoccupato; desideroso, pieno di vaghi speranze.

wistfully, *adv.* Desiderosamente, pensosamente, da pensoso.

wistfulness, *n.* Desiderio, *m.*, pensosità, *f.*

wit [wit](1), *n.* Spirito, ingegno, *m.*, intelligenza, *f.*; arguzia, *f.*, sale, *m.*; senso umoristico, *m.*; (*person*) bello spirito, uomo arguto, *m.* **Wits,** Ingegno, cervello, *m.*, testa, *f.*; **at one's wit's end,** non sapere più che cosa fare, essere agli estremi; **to have lost one's wits,** avere perduto la testa; **to have one's wits about one,** sapere ciò che si fa; **to live by one's wits,** viver d'espedienti.

wit (2), *adv.* **To —,** cioè.

witch [witʃ], *n.* Strega, *f.*; vecchiaccia, *f.*

witchcraft ['witʃkrɑːft], *n.* Stregoneria, *f.*, incantesimo, *m.*

witchdoctor [ˈwitʃdɔktəɹ], *n.* Stregone, *m.*
witchery, *n.* Fascino, incanto, *m.*; stregoneria, *f.*
witching, *a.* Magico.
with [wið], *prep.* Con, da, fra, in, a, presso, per, contro, per mezzo di. **Angry —,** adirato contro; **filled —,** pieno di.
withal [wiðˈɔːl], *adv.conj.* Nello stesso tempo, per soprappiù, con tutto ciò, inoltre.
withdraw [wiðˈdrɔː], *v.t.* Ritirare, ritrarre, richiamare, sottrarre; *v.i.* ritirarsi, ritrarsi; rinchiudersi; andarsene; rinunziare a. **To — a charge,** ritirare un'accusa; **to — funds,** prelevare fondi.
withdrawal, *n* (*going away*) Ritiro, *m.*, ritirata, *f.*; (*taking away*) ritiro, *m.* **— of funds,** prelevamento di fondi, *m.*
withdrawn, *a.* Ritirato; stornato; prelevato.
withdrew [wiðˈdruː], *p.* of **withdraw.**
withe [waið], *n.* Vimine, vinco, *m.*
wither [ˈwiðəɹ], *v.t.* Far avvizzire, far deperire, disseccare; *v.i.* disseccarsi, avvizzire, languire; appassire.
withering, *n.* Appassimento, deperimento. || *a.* Fulminante, sprezzante.
withers [ˈwiðəɹz], *n.pl.* Garrese, *m.* **To wring one's —,** fare un appello fortissimo alle emozioni.
withhold [wiðˈhould], *v.t.* Ritenere, rattenere; rifiutare.
within [wiðˈin], *prep.* Entro, in; dentro; nell'interno; in casa; a portata di. **— call,** a portata di voce; **from —,** di dentro; **within a few days,** entro pochi giorni; **— arm's length,** a portata del braccio; **— fire,** a portata di fucile, a tiro.
without [wiðˈaut], *prep.* Senza, senza che; fuori di. **From —,** dall'esterno, di fuori; **to do —,** fare a meno di, fare senza.
withstand [wiðˈstænd], *v.t.* Resistere a, opporsi a; sostenere, appoggiare.
withstander, *n.* Oppositore, *m.*, oppositrice, *f.*; antagonista, *m.f.*
withy [ˈwiði], *n.* Vimine, vinco, *m.*
witless [ˈwitles], *a.* Senza spirito, stupido.
witlessness, *n.* Stupidità, *f.*
witling, *n.* Saccentello, saccentuzzo, *m.*
witness [ˈwitnes], *n.* (*person*) Testimone, *m.f.*, teste, *m.f.*; testimonianza, prova, *f.* || *v.t.* Testimoniare, deporre come testimone; essere testimone di; attestare, sottoscrivere; vedere; essere presente a. **To call to —,** chiamare a testimonio; **— for the defence, prosecution,** teste a discarico, a carico, *m.f.*; **eye- —,** testimone oculare, *m.f.*; **— -box, — -stand,** banco dei testi, *m.*; **to call a —,** indurre un testimone.
witticism [ˈwitisizm], *n.* Spiritosità, *f.*, tratto di spirito, frizzo, *m.*
wittily, *adv.* Spiritosamente.
wittiness, *n.* Spirito, *m.*, spiritosità, *f.*
wittingly, *adv.* Scientemente; apposta, a bello studio, intenzionalmente.
witty [ˈwiti], *a.* Spiritoso, arguto; pungente.
wive [waiv], *v.i.* (*obs.*) Ammogliarsi.
wizard [ˈwizəɹd], *n.* Mago, stregone, *m.* || *a.* Magico; (*colloq.*) buonissimo, bellissimo.
wizardry, *n.* Stregoneria, magia, *f.*
wizened [ˈwizənd], *a.* Raggrinzito, disseccato, magro.
woad [woud], *n.* (*Bot.*) Guado, *m.*
wobble [wɔbl], *v.i.* Vacillare, tentennare.
woe [wou], *n.* Guaio, dolore, *m.*, disgrazia, *f.*; affanno, *m.*; tristezza, *f.*; maledizione, *f.* **Woe betide . . .!** Maledizione a . . .!
woebegone, woeful [ˈwoubigɔn, ˈwouful], *a.* Addolorato, dolente, doloroso; disgraziato.
woefully, *adv.* Dolorosamente, disgraziatamente.
woefulness, *n.* Miseria, afflizione, *f.*
wold [would], *n.* Pianura, *f.*; foresta, *f.*; duna, *f.*
wolf (*pl.* **wolves**) [wulf, wulfz], *n.* (*Zool.*) Lupo, *m.* || *v.t.* (*colloq.*) Mangiare voracemente. **She- —,** lupa, *f.*; **— -cub,** lupacchiotto, *m.*; **— in sheep's clothing,** lupo nella pelle dell'agnello, *m.*; (*Bot.*) **wolf's bane,** aconito, *m.*
wolfish, *a.* Lupesco; (*fig.*) vorace.
wolfishly, *adv.* Da lupo, voracemente.
wolfram [ˈwulfrəm], *n.* Volframio, tungsteno, *m.*
woman (*pl.* **women**) [ˈwumən, ˈwimin], *n.* Donna, femmina, *f.* **— doctor,** medichessa, *f.*; **— driver,** conduttrice, *f.*; **— -hater,** misogino, *m.*; **— suffrage,** suffragio femminile, *m.*; (*Tennis*) **woman's single,** singolare signore, *m.*
womanhood [ˈwumənhud], *n.* Stato di donna, *m.*; qualità di donna, *f.*
womanish, *a.* Effeminato, femminile.
womankind [wumənˈkaind], *n.* Le donne, *f.pl.*
womanlike, *a.* Femmineo, da donna.
womanliness, *n.* Femminilità, *f.*
womanly, *a.* Di donna, degno di donna, femminile.
womb [wuːm], *n.* Grembo; seno, *m.*; (*Anat.*) utero, *m.*
won [wʌn], *p.* of **win.**
wonder [ˈwʌndəɹ], *n.* Meraviglia, *f.*, prodigio, *m.*; sorpresa, *f.* || *v.i.* Meravigliarsi, stupirsi; domandarsi, essere curioso di sapere. **I —,** vorrei sapere; **Need one — ?** C'è di che meravigliarsi? **it is a — that,** è sorprendente che; **much to my —,** con mia grande meraviglia; **— worker,** taumaturgo, *m.*
wonderer, *n.* Chi si stupisce.
wonderful, *a.* Meraviglioso, prodigioso.
wonderfully, *adv.* Meravigliosamente.
wonderland, *n.* Terra delle meraviglie, *f.*
wonderment, *n.* Meraviglia, *f.*, stupore, *m.*
wondrous, *a.* Meraviglioso.
wondrously, *adv.* Meravigliosamente.
won't [wount], *abbrev.* of **will not.**
wont [wount], *n.* Uso, costume, *m.*, abitudine, *f.* **To be — to do,** essere abituato a fare.
wonted, *a.* Solito, abituale.
woo [wuː], *v.t.* Corteggiare, far la corte a; sollecitare.
wood [wud], *n.* (*growing*) Bosco, *m.*, foresta, *f.*; (*material*) legno, legname, *m.*; (*Bowls*) boccino, *m.*; (*cask*) botte, *f.*, fusto, *m.* **— -ash,** ceneri, *f.pl.*; **— -carver,** scultore in legno, *m.*; **wine in the —,** vino del barile, *m.*; **— -louse,** porcellino terrestre, *m.*; **— -nymph,** ninfa dei boschi, driade, *f.*; **— -pigeon,** colombo selvatico, *m.*; **— -spirit,** alcool metilico, *m.*; (*Mus.*) **— -wind,** i legni, *m.pl.*
woodbine [ˈwudbain], *n.* (*Bot.*) Caprifoglio, *m.*
woodcock, *n.* (*Zool.*) Beccaccia, *f.*
woodcut, *n.* Incisione su legno, *f.*

wooded, *a.* Boscoso, coperto di boschi.
wooden, *a.* Di legno, in legno, legnoso; rigido.
woodiness, *n.* Legnosità, *f.*
woodland [ˈwudlənd], *n.* Terreno boscoso, *m.* ‖ *a.* Silvestre.
woodman [ˈwudmən], *n.* Boscaiuolo, guardaboschi, *m.*
woodpecker [ˈwudpekəɹ], *n.* (*Zool.*) Picchio, *m.*
woodshed, *n.* Tettoia da legno, *f.*
woodwork, *n.* Lavoro in legno, *m.*; intavolato, *m.*
woodworker, *n.* Lavoratore del legno, *m.*
woody, *a.* Legnoso; boscoso.
woodyard, *n.* Legnaia, *f.*
wooer [ˈwu:əɹ], *n.* Corteggiatore, pretendente, innamorato, *m.*
woof [wu:f], *n.* Trama, tessitura, *f.*
wooing, *n.* Corte, *f.*, corteggiamento, *m.*
wooingly, *adv.* Amorosamente.
wool [wul], *n.* Lana, *f.* ‖ *a.* Di lana. **—-carder,** cardatore, *m.*
wool-gathering [ˈwulgæðəriŋ], *n.* Distrazione, sbadataggine, *f.* **To go —,** essere distratto, andare almanaccando.
woollen [ˈwulən], *a.* Di lana. ‖ *n.* Tessuto di lana, *m.* **— goods, woollens,** laneria, *f.*, lanerie, *f.pl.*, tessuti di lana, *m.pl.*; **— manufacturer,** lanaiuolo, *m.*; **—-mill,** lanificio, *m.*; **— trade,** industria laniera, *f.*
woollies [ˈwuliz], *n.pl.* Indumenti di lana, *m.pl.*
woolliness, *n.* Lanosità, *f.*; (*fig.*) confusione mentale, *f.*
woolly, *a.* Lanoso; (*of fruit*) cotonoso; (*of hair*) crespo; (*of sound*) morbido. ‖ *n.* Giubbettino di lana, *m.*
word [wəːɹd], *n.* Parola, voce, *f.*; avviso, *m.*, notizia, *f.*; segnale, *m.* ‖ *v.t.* Formulare, redigere, esprimere. **To send out —,** mandare avviso, dare notizia; **by — of mouth,** oralmente, a viva voce; (*Eccles.*) **the Word,** il Verbo, *m.*; **— of command,** parola d'ordine, *f.*; **to keep one's —,** mantenere la parola; **to give one's —,** impegnare la propria parola; **— by —,** parola per parola; **in other words,** in altri termini; **to weigh one's words,** misurare le parole; **to take someone at his —,** prendere uno in parola; **beyond words,** oltre misura.
worded, *a.* Formulato.
wordily, *adv.* Verbosamente.
wordiness, *n.* Verbosità, *f.*
wording, *n.* Espressione, *f.*, modo di dire, *m.*; termini, *m.pl.*
wordy, *a.* Verboso, parolaio.
wore *p.* of **wear.**
work [wəːɹk], *n.* Lavoro, *m.*; opera, *f.*; compito, impiego, daffare, *m.*; azione, *f.*, funzionamento, *m.* ‖ *v.t.* Lavorare, operare; fare, esercire; far funzionare; far correre, mettere in moto; manipolare; ricamare; *v.i.* lavorare, funzionare; operarsi, prodursi; bollire; andare, fare effetto. **To — hard,** lavorare a tutt'uomo; **to — in,** introdurre, insinuare; **to — loose,** sconnettersi; **to — off,** liberarsi di; abbindolare; **to — out,** effettuare; esaurire; risolvere; espiare; pagare col lavoro; calcolare; dare risultati; **to — up,** elaborare; fare uso di; stimolare; eccitarsi; mescolare; preparare; **to — upon,** agire su, commuovere; **piece- —,** lavoro a cottimo; **—-bag, —-basket,** borsetta, *f.*, cestino da lavoro, *m.*; **—-box,** cassetta da lavoro; **works,** (*of art, etc.*) opere, *f.pl.*, (*of machinery*) congegno, meccanismo, movimento, *m.*; (*premises*) fabbrica, officina, *f.*, stabilimento, *m.*
workable, *a.* Eseguibile; che si può lavorare; pratico, praticabile.
worker, *n.* Lavoratore, *m.*, lavoratrice, *f.*; operaio, *m.*, operaia, *f.*, manovale, *m.f.*; operatore, *m.*, operatrice, *f.*
workhouse, *n.* Ospizio, asilo, ricovero, *m.*
working, *n.* Operazione, *f.*, funzionamento, *m.*; attività, *f.*; giuoco, *m.*, manovra, *f.* ‖ *a.* Attivo; occupato; laborioso. **— order,** buon ordine, *m.*, efficienza, *f.*; **— capital,** capitale d'esercizio, capitale circolante, *m.*; **—-classes,** classi operaie, *f.pl.*, classe lavoratrice, *f.*; **—-clothes,** vestiti di lavoro, *m.pl.*; **—-committee,** giunta dei lavoratori, *f.*; **—-day,** giorno di lavoro, giorno lavorativo, *m.*; **—-hours,** ore di lavoro, *f.pl.*; **—-expenses,** spese di gestione, spese d'esercizio, *f.pl.* **—-drawing,** disegno d'officina, piano costruttivo, *m.*
workless, *a.* Senza lavoro, disoccupato.
workman, *n.* Operaio, artigiano, *m.* **workmen's compensation insurance,** assicurazione contro gli infortuni sul lavoro, *f.*
workmanlike, *a.* Ben fatto, ben lavorato, da buon operaio.
workmanship, *n.* Fattura, mano d'opera, esecuzione, *f.*
workroom, *n.* Officina, stanza da lavoro, *f.*
workshop, *n.* Officina, *f.*
workwoman, *n.* Operaia, *f.*
world [wəːɹld], *n.* Mondo, *m.* ‖ *a.* Mondiale, universale. **— without end,** sino alla fine dei secoli; **not for the —,** per nulla al mondo.
worldliness, *n.* Mondanità, *f.*, spirito mondano, *m.*
worldling, *n.* Mondano, *m.*, persona mondana, *f.*
worldly, *a.* Mondano, frivolo. **—-minded,** troppo mondano; **—-wise,** saggio per questo mondo; **all one's — goods,** tutta la propria roba.
worm [wəːɹm], *n.* (*Zool.*) Verme, *m.*; (*of screw*) filetto, *m.*; (*Mech.*) vite senza fine, *f.*; (*of still*) storta, *f.* ‖ *v.t.* Liberare dai vermi; *v.i.* insinuarsi in. **To — one's way in,** insinuarsi presso; **—-eaten,** bacato, tarlato, roso dai vermi; **book- —,** tarma, *f.*, (*fig.*) topo di biblioteca, *m.*; **—-powder,** polvere vermifuga, *f.*; **to — out a secret,** cavar un segreto.
wormwood, *n.* Assenzio, *m.*
wormy, *a.* Verminoso, pieno di vermi, brulicante di vermi.
worn [wɔːɹn], *p.* of **wear.**
worried [ˈwʌrid], *a.* Infastidito, preoccupato, vessato, annoiato.
worriedly, *adv.* Con fastidio.
worrier, *n.* Seccatore, noioso, *m.*; uno che si infastidisce.
worry [ˈwʌri], *n.* Fastidio, dispiacere, cruccio, *m.*; ansietà, *f.*; tormento, *m.* ‖ *v.t.* Disturbare, tormentare, annoiare, seccare; (*of an animal*) dilaniare, sbranare; *v.i.* preoccuparsi, tormentarsi, crucciarsi.

worse [wəːɹs], *a.* Peggio, peggiore. ‖ *adv.* Peggio. **The — for wear,** sgangherato; **to be — than useless,** essere più che inutile; **to be none the — for it,** non trovarsi peggio; **to grow —,** peggiorare; **to make —,** rendere peggiore; **to get — and —,** andare di male in peggio; **to be — off,** star peggio; **so much the —,** tanto peggio.
worship [ˈwəːɹʃip], *v.t.i.* Adorare; venerare. ‖ *n.* Culto, *m.*, adorazione, *f.* **Your Worship,** Signor Giudice, Signor Sindaco; **hero- —,** culto degli eroi, *m.*; **place of —,** chiesa, *f.*
worshipful, *a.* Onorevole.
worshipper, *n.* Adoratore, *m.*, adoratrice, *f.*
worshipping, *n.* Adorazione, *f.*
worst [wəːɹst], *a.* Il peggiore, il peggio, il più cattivo; il più grave. ‖ *v.t.* Vincere, battere. ‖ *n.* Il peggio, *m.*; svantaggio, *m.* **At the —,** alla peggio; **to do one's —,** fare il peggio che si può; **to get the — of it,** averne la peggio; **let the — come to the —,** a peggio andare.
worsted [ˈwustəd], *n.* Lana filata, *f.* ‖ *a.* Di lana filata.
wort [wəːɹt], *n.* (*Bot.*) Erba, pianta, *f.*; (*of beer*) mosto, *m.*
worth [wəːɹθ], *n.* Valore, *m.*; merito, *m.*; pregio, *m.*; (*money's*) per la somma di. ‖ *a.* Del valore di; degno di; che merita, meritevole di. **To be — while,** valer la pena; **to be —,** valere, meritare; **this is — more than that,** questo vale più di quello; **it can't be — much,** non può valere gran cosa; **it's — its weight in gold,** vale tant'oro quanto pesa; **it's not — mentioning,** non vale la pena parlarne.
worthily [ˈwəːɹðili], *adv.* Degnamente.
worthiness, *n.* Merito, *m.*
worthless [ˈwəːɹθles], *a.* Senza valore, di nessun valore, spregevole; (*of a cheque*) senza provvisione.
worthlessness, *n.* Mancanza di valore, *f.*; inutilità, *f.*
worthy [ˈwəːɹði], *a.* Degno, pregevole. ‖ *n.* Uomo illustre, *m.*
would [wud], *v.aux.* Volere; (*also expressed in Italian by the conditional mood*) **Would to God!** Piaccia a Dio! **he — have it that,** voleva assolutamente che; **I — rather,** preferirei.
would-be [ˈwudbiː], *a.* Sedicente, preteso; sperato; mancato.
wound (1) [wuːnd], *n.* Ferita, piaga, *f.* ‖ *v.t.* Ferire; offendere. **To dress a —,** medicare una ferita.
wound (2) [waund], *p.* of **wind** (2).
wounded [ˈwuːnded], *a.* Ferito. ‖ *n.pl.* I feriti, *m.pl.*
wove [wouv], *a.* **— paper,** carta tipo stoffa, *f.*
woven, *a.* Tessuto.
wrack [ræk], *n.* Rifiuti di mare, *m.pl.*; alghe, *f.pl.*
wraith [reiθ], *n.* Spettro, *m.*
wrangle [ræŋgl], *v.i.* Disputare, litigare, bisticciarsi. ‖ *n.* Alterco, *m.*, disputa, rissa, *f.*; litigio, *m.*
wrangler, *n.* Attaccabrighe, *m.*; (*Univ.*) uno di prima classe nella matematica a Cambridge, *m.*; (*American*) domatore di cavalli, *m.*
wrangling, *n.* Disputazione, *f.*, litigio, *m.*
wrap [ræp], *v.t.* Avvolgere, arrotolare; avviluppare; incartare, impaccare. ‖ *n.* Scialle, mantello, *m.*; accappatoio, *m.*; coperta, *f.* **To — oneself up,** avvolgersi, coprirsi.
wrapper, *n.* Involto, *m.*; carta d'involto, *f.*; fascia, fascetta, *f.* **Stamped —,** sottofascia affrancata, *f.*
wrapping, *n.* Involgimento, involto, *m.*
wrath [rɔːθ], *n.* Ira, collera, rabbia, *f.* **The — of God,** la collera di Dio, *f.*
wrathful, *a.* Adirato, sdegnato, incollerito.
wrathfully, *adv.* Collericamente.
wrathfulness, *n.* Rabbia, collera, *f.*
wreak [riːk], *v.t.* Eseguire, sfogare, infliggere. **To — vengeance,** vendicarsi, compiere la propria vendetta.
wreath [riːθ], *n.* Ghirlanda, corona, *f.*; (*of smoke*) turbine, *m.*, nuvola, *f.*
wreathe [riːð], *v.t.* Inghirlandare, intrecciare; intessere.
wreathed, *a.* Inghirlandato; intessuto.
wreck [rek], *n.* Naufragio, *m.*; bastimento naufragato, *m.*; (*fig.*) rovina, *f.* ‖ *v.t.* Fare naufragare; rovinare; sabotare; *v.i.* naufragare; andare in rovina.
wreckage [ˈrekidʒ], *n.* Relitti di mare, resti d'un naufragio, *m.pl.*
wrecker, *n.* Saccheggiatore di nave naufragata, naufragatore, *m.*
wren [ren], *n.* (*Zool.*) Scricciolo, *m.*
wrench [rentʃ], *v.t.* Storcere; strappare; svisare. ‖ *n.* Strappo, *m.*; storcimento, sforzo violento, *m.*; (*Med.*) storta, slogatura, *f.*; (*tool*) chiave, chiave inglese, madrevite, *f.* **To — open,** sforzare.
wrest [rest], *v.t.* Torcere; strappare.
wrestle [resl], *v.i.* Lottare. **To — with,** lottare contro.
wrestler, *n.* Lottatore, *m.*
wrestling, *n.* Lotta, *f.*, combattimento, *m.* **— match,** incontro di lotta, *m.*, partita di lotta, *f.*
wretch [retʃ], *n.* Disgraziato, *m.*, disgraziata, *f.*; sfortunato, *m.*, sfortunata, *f.*; sciagurato, *m.*, sciagurata, *f.*; miserabile, *m.f.* **Poor —!** Povero diavolo!
wretched [ˈretʃid], *a.* Misero, sfortunato, sciagurato; meschino, povero; cattivo.
wretchedly, *adv.* Disgraziatamente, sfortunatamente.
wretchedness, *n.* Miseria, *f.*; meschinità, *f.*; povertà, *f.*
wrick [rik], *v.t.* Storcersi. ‖ *n.* Storta, *f.* **To — one's back,** storcersi il dorso.
wriggle [ˈrigəl], *v.i.* Contorcersi, dimenarsi, dibattersi; (*fig.*) agire subdolamente. **To — out of,** cavarsi da; **to — into,** insinuarsi dentro.
wriggling, *n.* Storcimento, contorcimento, *m.*
wright [rait], *n.* (*obs.*) Operaio, *m.*; costruttore, *m.*
wring [riŋ], *v.t.* Torcere, torcersi; attorcere; estorcere; comprimere; spremere; strappare. **To — one's heart,** strappare il cuore; **to — the washing,** torcere il bucato; **to — one's hands,** torcere le mani; **to — a confession from,** far confessare con la forza.
wringer, *n.* Cilindro da bucato, *m.*; torcitoio, *m.*, torcitrice, *f.*
wringing, *n.* Torsione, *f.* ‖ *a.* **— wet,** da torcersi, inzuppato.

wrinkle [riŋkl], *n.* Ruga, grinza, *f.*; piega, crespa, *f.*; (*advice*) utile avviso, *m.*; informazione speciale, *f.* || *v.t.* Corrugare, raggrinzare, increspare; *v.i.* corrugarsi, divenire rugoso. **To — one's brow,** corrugare la fronte; **here's a — for you,** ecco del nuovo; **that's a — worth knowing,** è bene a sapersi.
wrinkling, *n.* Contrazione, *f.*; raggrinzamento, *m.*
wrist [rist], *n.* Polso, *m.* **— watch,** orologio di polso, orologio braccialetto, *m.*
wristband, *n.* Polsino, manichino, *m.*
wristlet, *n.* Braccialetto, *m.*
writ [rit], *n.* Citazione legale, citazione, *f.*, mandato, ordine, *m.*; breve, *m.*, ordinanza, *f.*; decreto, *m.*; (*Pol.*) avviso di convocazione del Parlamento, *m.* **Holy Writ,** la Sacra Scrittura, *f.*
write [rait] *v.t.i.* Scrivere; inscrivere; tracciare. **To — back,** rispondere; **to — about,** scrivere di; **to — down,** mettere in iscritto; denigrare; **to — for,** scrivere per far venire, scrivere invece di; **to — off a debt,** cancellare un debito; **to — up,** fare la pubblicità di, elogiare; **to — out,** copiare, formulare.
writer, *n.* Scrivente, *m.f.*, scrittore, *m.*, scrittrice, *f.*; autore, *m.*, autrice, *f.* **Writer to the Signet,** avvocato scozzese, *m.*
writhe [raið], *v.i.* Torcersi, contorcersi.
writing, *n.* Scrittura, calligrafia, *f.*; documento, scritto, *m.* **In —,** per iscritto; **— -case,** portafogli; **— -desk,** scrittoio, *m.*, scrivania, *f.*; **— -ink,** inchiostro per scrivere, *m.*; **— -pad,** cartella per scrivere, *f.*; **— -paper,** carta da scrivere, *f.*
written, *a.* Scritto, in iscritto, per iscritto. **— evidence,** prova scritta, *f.*
wrong [rɔŋ], *a.* Inesatto, erroneo, scorretto; improprio, ingiusto; sbagliato; cattivo. || *adv.* Male, malamente, a torto. || *n.* Torto, male, danno, *m.*; ingiuria, *f.* || *v.t.* Far torto a, essere ingiusto con; nuocere, maltrattare. **To be —,** aver torto, esser sbagliato; **to go —,** sbagliare, andare a male; **not to be far —,** non avere tutti i torti; **to be in the —,** essere dalla parte del torto; **to do someone a —,** fare un torto a qualcuno; **— -doer,** autore di un male, cattivo, *m.*; (*of fabric*) **the — side,** il rovescio, *m.*; (*Print.*) **— fount,** refuso, *m.*; **— -headed,** ostinato.
wrongful, *a.* Iniquo, ingiusto, nocivo.
wrongfully, *adv.* A torto, falsamente, ingiustamente.
wrongfulness, *n.* Iniquità, *f.*, torto, *m.*
wrongly, *adv.* Male, a torto, ingiustamente.
wrote [rout], *p.* of **write.**
wroth [rouθ, rɔθ], *a.* Arrabbiato, irritato.
wrought iron [rɔːt ˈaiəɹn], *n.* Ferro battuto, *m.*
wry [rai], *a.* (*neck*) Torto; (*smile, mouth*) storto; obliquo; ironico. **To make a — face,** far boccuccia, contorcere il viso, fare smorfia.
wryneck [ˈrainek], *n.* (*Zool.*) Torcicollo, *m.*
wryness, *n.* Distorsione, contorsione, *f.*
wych-elm [ˈwitʃelm], *n.* (*Bot.*) Olmo di montagna, *m.*

X

X, x [eks], Ventiquattresima lettera dell'alfabeto inglese.
Xantippe, Xanthippe [zænˈtipi], *n.* Santippe, *f.*
Xavier [ˈzeivjəɹ], *n.* Saverio, *m.*
Xenophon [ˈzenofɔn], *n.* Senofonte, *m.*
Xmas [cp. **Christmas**].
X-rays [ˈeksreiz], *n.pl.* Raggi X, *m.pl.*
xylographic [zailoˈgræfik], *a.* Silografico.
xylography [zaiˈlɔgrəfi], *n.* Silografia, *f.*
xylonite [ˈzailənait], *n.* Celluloide, *f.*
xylophone [ˈzailofoun], *n.* (*Mus.*) Silofono, *m.*

Y

Y, y [wai], Venticinquesima lettera dell'alfabeto inglese.
yacht [jɔt], *n.* Yacht, canotto, *m.*; nave da diporto, *f.*, panfilo, *m.* **— race,** gara fra navi da diporto, *f.*
yachting, *n.* Crociera in panfilo, crociera su nave da diporto, *f.*; lo sport nautico, *m.*
yachtsman, *n.* Proprietario di un nave da diporto, *m.*
yahoo [jɑːˈhuː], *n.* Ignorante, zottico, *m.*
yam [jæm], *n.* Igname, *m.*
yank [jæŋk], *v.t.* Strappare. || *n.* Strappata, *f.*
Yankee, Yank [ˈjæŋki, jæŋk], *n.a.* Americano, *m.*
yap [jæp], *v.i.* Abbaiare, guaire.
yard [jɑːɹd], *n.* Cortile, *m.*; (*measure*) iarda, *f.*; (*on mast*) antenna, *f.*, pennone, *m.*; (*shipbuilding*) cantiere, *m.* **Building- —,** cantiere di costruzione, *f.*; **dock- —,** arsenale, *m.*; (*Naut.*) **main —,** pennone di maestra, *m.*; (*Rail.*) **freight —,** scalo merci, *m.*
yarn (1) [jɑːɹn], *n.* Filato, *m.*
yarn (2), *n.* Racconto, *m.*, storia, *f.*; filastrocca, *f.*; bugia, *f.* || *v.i.* Raccontare una storia.
yarrow [ˈjærou], *n.* (*Bot.*) Millefoglie. *m.*
yaw [jɔː], *v.i.* (*Naut.*) Deviare, cambiare rotta. || *n.* Straorzata, deviazione dalla rotta, *f.*
yawl, *n.* (*Naut.*) Iole, *f.*
yawn, *v.i.* Sbadigliare; (*fig.*) spalancarsi. || *n.* Sbadiglio, *m.*
yawning, *a.* Spalancato.
ye [jiː], (*Lit.*) *pron.* Voi.
yea [jei], *adv.* Sì.
yean [jiːn], *v.i.* Partorire.
yeanling, *n.* Agnellino, *m.*; capretto, *m.*
year [jəːɹ, jiəɹ], *n.* Anno, *m.*, annata, *f.*; (*Comm.*) esercizio, periodo di gestione, *m.* **Every —,** tutti gli anni; **every other —,** ogni due anni; **to be five years old,** aver cinque anni; **years of discretion,** età della ragione, *f.*; **a calendar —,** un anno civile, *m.*; **last —,** l'anno passato, *m.*; **by the —,** all'anno, annualmente; **from — to —,** di anno in anno; **New Year's Day,** capodanno, capo d'anno, *m.*; **New Year's gift,** strenna, *f.*; **the financial —,** l'esercizio finanziario, *m.*; **— -book,** annuario, *m.*
yearly, *a.* Annuale, all'anno. || *adv.* Annualmente, ogni anno, tutti gli anni.
yearn [jəːɹn], *v.i.* Struggersi, desiderare vivamente. **To — for,** sospirare, agognare, struggersi di, non veder l'ora di.
yearning, *n.* Desiderio ardente, struggimento, *m.*
yeast [jiːst], *n.* Lievito, *m.*
yeasty, *a.* Fermentante, spumante, schiumoso.

yell [jel], *v.i.* Urlare, strillare. || *n.* Urlo, strillo, *m.*
yelling, *n.* Urli, *m.pl.*, urla, *f.pl.*
yellow ['jelou], *n.a.* Giallo, *m.* **To turn —,** ingiallire; **the — races,** le razze gialle, *f.pl.*
yellowish, *a.* Giallastro, giallognolo.
yellowness, *n.* Giallo, giallore, *m.*
yellowy, *a.* D'una tinta gialla.
yelp [jelp], *v.i.* Guaire, squittire. || *n.* Guaito, *m.*
yen [jen], *n.* (*colloq.*) Desiderio vivissimo, *m.*
yeoman ['joumən], *n.* Piccolo proprietario di terra, *m.*; (*Naut.*) sotto ufficiale, *m.* **— of the guard,** guardia del corpo a piedi, *f.*
yeomanry, *n.* (*Mil.*) Cavalleria nazionale, *f.*
yes [jes], *adv.* Sì, già.
yesterday ['jestəɹdei], *n.* Ieri, *m.* **The day before —,** ieri l'altro, avant'ieri.
yesteryear, *n.* L'anno passato, *m.*
yestreen [jes'tri:n], *n.* (*Poet.*) Iera sera, *f.*
yet [jet], *conj.* Pure, eppure, tuttavia, nondimeno, però, nonostante. || *adv.* Ancora. **As —,** finora; **not —,** non ancora.
yew [ju:], *n.* (*Bot.*) Tasso, *m.*
yield [ji:ld], *v.t.* Rendere, produrre; dare; *v.i.* cedere, arrendersi; acconsentire. || *n.* Raccolto, prodotto, *m.*, rendita, *f.*; frutto, *m.*
yielding, *n.* Sottomissione, *f.*; abbandono, *m.* || *a.* Accomodante; produttivo; cedevole.
yoke [jouk], *v.t.* Aggiogare, mettere il giogo; accoppiare. || *n.* Giogo, *m.*; paio, *m.*, coppia, *f.* **To throw off the —,** scuotere il giogo.
yokel, *n.* Villano, zoticone, *m.*
yolk [jouk], *n.* Giallo d'uovo, torlo d'uovo, *m.*
yon, yonder [jɔn, 'jɔndəɹ], *a.* Quello, quello di là, quello . . . là. || *adv.* Al di là, laggiù, lassù.
yore [jɔ:ɹ], *adv.* **Of —,** Anticamente, altre volte, un tempo.
you [ju:], *pron.* Voi, tu; vi, ve, ti, te; Loro, Ella, Lei. **— Italians,** voi altri italiani; **you fool!** la bestia che sei! **if I were —,** se fossi te, se fossi al vostro posto.
young [jʌŋ], *a.* Giovane, giovanile, piccolo. || *n.* (*persons*) I giovani, *m.pl.*, la gioventù, *f.*; (*animals*) i nati, i piccoli, *m.pl.* **To look —,** avere l'aspetto giovanile; **a — lady,** una signorina, *f.*; **a — girl,** una ragazzina, *f.*; **a — man,** un giovane, un giovanotto, *m.*; (*of animals*) **with —,** incinta; **to bring forth —,** partorire, figliare.
younger ['jʌŋgəɹ], *a.* Più giovane, minore. **— brother, sister,** fratello, sorella minore, *m.f.*
youngish ['jʌŋiʃ], *a.* Piuttosto giovane.
youngster, *n.* Giovanotto, ragazzo, *m.*
your [jɔ:ɹ] *pron.* Vostro, vostra, vostri, vostre; tuo, tua, tuoi, tue; suo, sua, suoi, sue.
yours [jɔ:ɹz], *pron.* Il vostro, la vostra, i vostri, le vostre; a voi, di voi. **— truly, — faithfully,** vostro devotissimo, il Suo devotissimo; **Is this book —?** Questo libro è il vostro? **a friend of —,** un vostro amico, *m.*
yourself (*pl.* **yourselves**), *pron.* Voi stesso, voi stessa, voi stessi, voi stesse; vi.
youth [ju:θ], *n.* Giovinezza, *f.*; gioventù, *f.*; adolescenza, *f.*; giovane, giovanotto, *m.*
youthful, *a.* Giovanile, giovane, di giovinezza.
youthfulness, *n.* Giovinezza, *f.*
Yule, Yuletide [ju:l, 'ju:ltaid], *n.* Natale, *m.*, festa di Natale, *f.* **The Yule log,** il ceppo di Natale, *m.*

Z

Z, z [zed], *n.* Ventesima sesta e ultima lettera dell'alfabeto inglese.
Zachariah [Zækə'raiə], *n.* Zaccaria, *m.*
zany ['zeini], *n.* Zanni, buffone, semplicione, *m.*
zeal [zi:l], *n.* Zelo, *m.*
zealot ['zelət], *n.* Zelatore, *m.*, zelatrice, *f.*, fanatico, *m.*, fanatica, *f.*; partigiano, *m.*, partigiana, *f.*
zealous ['zeləs], *a.* Zelante, premuroso; fanatico.
zealously, *adv.* Con zelo, zelantemente.
zealousness, *n.* Zelo, *m.*
zebra ['zi:brə, 'zebrə], *n.* (*Zool.*) Zebra, *f.*
zenith ['zeniθ], *n.* Zenit, *m.*; (*fig.*) culmine, apogeo, *m.*
zephyr ['zefəɹ], *n.* Zeffiro, *m.*
zero ['ziərou], *n.* Zero, *m.*
zest [zest], *n.* Gusto, ardore, *m.*; sapore piccante, *m.* **To give — to,** accrescere il piacere di.
zigzag ['zigzæg], *n.* Zigzag, *m.* || *v.i.* Andare a zigzag.
zinc [ziŋk], *n.* (*Min.*) Zinco, *m.*
zincography [ziŋ'kɔgrəfi], *n.* Zincografia, *f.*
zip, zip fastener [zip, zip 'fa:sənəɹ], *n.* Chiusura lampo, *f.*
zircon ['zə:ɹkən], *n.* Zirconio, *m.*
zither ['ziθəɹ], *n.* (*Mus.*) Cetra, *f.*
zodiac ['zoudiæk], *n.* Zodiaco. **The Signs of the Zodiac,** i segni dello zodiaco, *m.pl.*
zodiacal [zo'daiəkəl], *a.* Zodiacale, dello zodiaco.
zone [zoun], *n.* Zona, *f.*; cintura, fascia, *f.*
zoo [zu:], *n.* (*colloq.*) Giardino zoologico, *m.*
zoological [zu:o'lɔdʒikəl], *a.* Zoologico.
zoologist [zu:'ɔlodʒist], *n.* Zoologo, *m.*
zoology, *n.* Zoologia, *f.*
zounds! [zaundz], *inter.* (*obs.*) Caspita!
Zulu ['zu:lu:], *n.a.* Zulù, *m.f.*
Zurich ['zju:rik], *n.* (*Geog.*) Zurigo, *m.*

Italian-English Appendix

N.B. The sign † against a word shows that it has already been given in the Dictionary, although not necessarily in the same grammatical form.

A

abbiosciarsi, *v.r.* To collapse; to hang down; to shrink.
†abbozzare, *v.i.* (*Roman dial.*) To put up with it; to resign oneself.
abitificio, *n.m.* Clothes manufacturing company *or* factory.
accapo, *n.m. inv.* New paragraph. **Andare —,** to begin a new paragraph.
accendigas [accEndigas], *n.m.* Gas-lighter.
†accordo, *n.m.* (*fig.*) **— multilaterale, — a pacchetto,** package deal.
aclassista, aclassistico [aclassIstico], *a.* Classless.
aconfessionale, *a.* Undenominational.
acquaplano, *n.m.* Aquaplane.
acritico [acrItico], *a.* Undiscriminating, uncritical.
additivo, *n.m.a.* Additive.
addizionatrice, *n.f.* Adding machine.
Adriatico [adriAtico], *n.m.a.* Adriatic.
aduso, *a.* Accustomed.
aeroassistente, *n.f.* (*Aviat.*) Air hostess.
aerogramma, *n.m.* Air-letter, aerogramme.
aeromodellista, *n.m.* Model aircraft enthusiast.
aeromodello, *n.m.* Model aircraft.
†aeroplano, *n.m.* **— radiocomandato,** radio-controlled aeroplane.
aeroportato, *a.* Airborne. **Truppe aeroportate,** airborne troops.
aeroportuale, *a.* Pertaining to an airport.
aerosiluro, *n.m.* Aerial torpedo.
aerotreno, *n.m.* Convoy of aeroplanes.
aerovia, *n.f.* Air corridor.
afflosciarsi, *v.r.* To collapse, to become flabby.
†affondare, *v.t.* (*Print.*) **— una notizia,** to print a news item at the bottom of the page.
affrancatrice, *n.f.* Franking-machine.
†agenzia, *n.f.* **— ippica,** betting shop.
aggancio [aggAncio], *n.m.* Grasp; approach.
aggeggiare, *v.t.* (*colloq.*) To touch up, to fix up; to arrange.
agrochimica [agrochImica], *n.f.* Chemical study of soil fertility.
†albergo, *n.m.* **— per la gioventù,** youth hostel.
Alfista, *n.m.* Owner *or* driver of an Alfa Romeo.
aliantista, *n.m.* Glider pilot.
aliscafo, *n.m.* Boat with hydrofoils; (*Am.*) seawings.
†allettante, *a.* Attractive.
allibito, *a.* Astonished, thunder-struck.
alloglotto, *n.m.a.* (Person) belonging to a linguistic minority.
allunaggio [allunAggio], *n.m.* Moon landing, landing on the moon.
altoatesino, *n.m.a.* (Person) of the province of Bolzano.
alzabicchieri, *n.m.* Raising of glasses (at a dinner) to drink and toast.
†ambientare, *v.t.* To set, to place (of novels, films, etc.). **Il romanzo è ambientato in Italia,** the novel is set in Italy.
ambrosianità [-à], *n.f.* Quality of being Milanese; Milanese characteristics.
†amen, *n.m.* (*fig.*) **In un —,** in a trice, in a jiffy, in the twinkling of an eye.
amichetta, *n.f.* Girl friend; sweetheart.
ammanigliato, *n.m.* (*colloq.*) One who is well recommended, one who has friends at court.
†ammaraggio, *n.m.* Splashdown (of space capsule).
amministrativista, *n.m.* Specialist in administrative law.
ammortizzatore, *n.m.* Buffer, fender.
ammuffito, *a.* Mouldy; stale.
anabbagliante, *n.m.a.* Anti-dazzle; (*Motor.*) dipped, (*Am.*) low; dipped headlight, (*Am.*) low beam.
†analizzare, *v.t.* (*TV*) Scan.
anariano, *a.* Non-Arian.
anastatico [anastAtico], *a.* (*Print.*) Anastatic.
anazionale, *a.* Anational.
ancheggiare, *v.i.* To sway one's hips.
andazziere, *n.m.* Follower of current fashions.
androcrazia [androcrazIa], *n.f.* Social order in which men are the privileged members.
aneddotica [aneddOtica], *n.f.* (*Lit.*) Collection of anecdotes and curiosities.
aneddotista, *n.m.* Collector *or* teller of anecdotes.
anestesista, *n.m.* (*Med.*) Anaesthetist.
anfetamina, *n.f.* (*Med.*) Amphetamine.
angolista, *n.m.* One who sells (matches, etc.) at the corner of the street.
†angoscia, *n.f.* (*Existentialism*) Angst.
anguilleggiare, *v.i.* (*fig.*) To be as slippery as an eel, to wriggle out of a definite stance.
anta, *n.f.* Window-shutter.
antennista, *n.m.* One who has a radio *or* television set with an outside aerial.
†anteprima, *a.* **— rappresentazione,** private showing (of a play or film) before the official opening.
antiansia [antiAnsia], *a.* Tranquillizing.
antibomba, *a.* Bomb-proof.
anticoncezionale, *a.* Contraceptive.
anticorpo, *n.m.a.* (*Physiol.*) Antibody.
antidivorzista, *n.m.* One who is opposed to divorce.
antifurto, *a.* Anti-theft.

anti-influenzale, *n.m.a.* Anti-influenza (drug etc.).
antimine, *a.* (*Mil.*) Preventing damage by mines, antimine.
antincendio [antincEndio], *a.* Fire-fighting. **Apparati —,** fire-fighting appliances.
antipiega, antipieghe, *a.* Crease-resistant (of cloth).
antischeggia [antischEggia], *a.* Chip-resistant.
antislittante, *a.* (*Motor.*) Anti-skid.
antitarmico [antitArmico], *n.m.a.* Moth-repellent.
†**Antonio,** *n.m.* **Fuoco di Sant' —,** St. Anthony's fire; erysipelas.
apartitico [apartItico], *a.* (*Pol.*) Non-party.
†**apertura,** *n.f.* (*Pol.*) Willingness to collaborate with another political party *or* other parties. **— a sinistra,** an agreement to work together, since 1957, between Italian left-wing Christian Democrats and the Socialists.
aperturismo, *n.m.* (*Pol.*) The movement *or* tendency towards an **apertura** (q.v.).
aperturista, *n.m.* (*Pol.*) A politician who supports an **apertura** (q.v.).
apotropaico, *a.* Acting as an amulet against the evil eye, amuletic, apotropaic.
†**apparato,** *n.m.* (*Pol.*) Political machine of the Communist party, apparat; caucus.
†**appartamento,** *n.m.* (*Am.*) Apartment.
apporto, *n.m.* Contribution; aid.
†**apprendista,** *n.m.* **— stregone,** sorcerer's apprentice.
appuntalapis, *n.m.* [cp. **temperalapis**].
apripista, *n.m.* Bulldozer.
†**aquilotto,** *n.m.* (*fig.*) Young airman.
araucaria [araucAria], *n.f.* (*Bot.*) Monkey-puzzle tree.
arcanista, *n.m.* Writer with an obscure *or* difficult style.
†**arco,** *n.m.* (*colloq.*) **— di tempo,** period of time.
†**arena,** *n.f.* Open-air cinema. **— dei tori,** bull-ring.
†**arrangiarsi,** *v.r.* To resort to expedients; (*colloq.*) to wangle, (*Am.*) to finagle.
arrangista, *n.m.* (*colloq.*) Smart customer; scrounger.
arredatore, arredatrice, *n.m.f.* Interior decorator; (*Theat.*) set decorator.
artigianale, *a.* Pertaining to the artisan class; craftsmanly; made by a craftsman.
†**arzente,** *n.m.* Italian brandy.
ascensionista, *n.m.* Mountain climber.
ascensorista, *n.m.* Liftman, lift boy.
†**asciugamano,** *n.m.* **— a rullo,** roller towel.
asciugatrice, *n.f.* (*Mech.*) Drier. **— centrifuga,** spin-drier.
asciughino, *n.m.* Dish cloth, tea cloth.
ascorbico [ascOrbico], *a.* (*Chem.*) Ascorbic.
asociale, *a.* Asocial.
†**assenteismo,** *n.m.* Indifference.
†**astante,** *n.m.* **(medico) —,** doctor on duty in an out-patients' department of a hospital; doctor in charge of a casualty ward.
†**astanteria,** *n.f.* Out-patients' department (of a hospital); casualty ward.
astatore, *n.m.* Auctioneer.
astenuto, *n.m.* Abstentionist, non-voter.
astista, *n.m.* (*Sport*) Pole-vaulter.
astrattista, *n.m.f.* Abstract artist, abstractionist.
astrodromo, *n.m.* Launching station for space-ships.
astrofisica [astrofIsica], *n.f.* Astrophysics.
astronauta [astronAuta], *n.m.* Astronaut.
astronautica [astronAutica], *n.f.* Astronautics.
astronave, *n.f.* Space-ship.
atipico [atIpico], *a.* Not conforming to type, atypical.
Atlantico (Patto), *n.m.* The Atlantic Pact or Treaty between the U.S.A. and the countries of western Europe; the N.A.T.O. alliance proclaimed in the spring of 1948.
atlantismo, *n.m.* N.A.T.O. policy.
atomica [atOmica], *n.f.* Atom bomb.
†**atomistica,** *n.f.* Atomic energy research, and its practical uses.
atomizzare, *v.t.* To atomize, to vaporize; to destroy with the atomic bomb.
atonale, *a.* (*Mus.*) Atonal.
atout [a'tu:], *n.m.inv.* Trump(s). **Avere degli atout,** to hold trumps, (*fig.*) to have a strong hand.
†**attacco,** *n.m.* (*Football*) Forwards.
attendismo, *n.m.* (*Pol.*) 'Wait-and-see' policy.
†**attivista,** *n.m.* (*Pol.*) Activist.
attivizzare, *v.t.* To start up, to set going.
†**attore,** *n.m.* (*Theat.*) **— promiscuo,** character actor; **— di seconda parte,** supporting actor.
†**attualità,** *n.f.* Actuality; reality; present time. **Un argomento di grande —, di palpitante —,** a subject of great topical interest.
†**attuazione,** *n.f.* **In via d'—,** in the pipeline.
audiola, *n.f.* Wireless set.
audiotreno, *n.m.* Radio train.
audiovisivo, *a.* Audiovisual.
aumentomania [aumentomanIa], *n.f.* The senseless, obsessive urge to increase prices and wages.
ausiliaria [ausiliAria], *n.f.* A woman belonging to the Auxiliary Service of the Army, Navy and Air Force.
australiano, *n.m.a.* Australian.
autarchista, *n.m.* One who believes in economic self-sufficiency or autarchy (esp. during the Fascist period in Italy).
autiere, *n.m.* (*Mil.*) Army driver.
autismo, *n.m.* (*Med.*) Autism.
†**autista,** *a., n.m.f.* Autistic, autistic person.
autobloccante, *a.* Self-locking.
autobotte, *n.f.* Tank-wagon, tanker.
autobruco, *n.m.* (*Mech.*) Caterpillar tractor (*reg. trade name*); (*Mil.*) tank.
autocamion [autocAmion], *n.m.* Lorry, (*Am.*) truck.
autocamionale, *n.f.* Road for heavy traffic.
autocampeggio [autocampEggio], *n.m.* Camping site for motorists.
autocarriera, *n.f.* Long-distance motor bus.
auto-carrozzeria, *n.f.* Workshop *or* factory where car bodies are made *or* repaired.
autocasa, *n.f.* Trailer caravan.
autocingolo, *n.m.* [cp. **autobruco**].
auto-civetta, *n.f.* Private car used by plain-clothes policemen as an observation post.
autocritica [autocrItica], *n.f.* Self-criticism.
autoferrotranviario, *a.* Pertaining to the three main varieties of public transport: buses, railways, trams.
autoferrotranvieri, *n.pl.* (Portmanteau word for) busmen, railwaymen and tramway men,

considered collectively (e.g. in a wage claim, strike, etc.).
autofficina, *n.f.* (*Motor.*) Garage workshop.
autofunebre, *n.m.* (Motor) hearse.
autogassogeno [autogassOgeno], *n.m.* Car running on producer gas.
autogol [Autogol], *n.m.* (*Sport*) Goal scored by player against his own side.
autogrill [Autogrill], *n.m.* Motorway filling station with a grill-room.
autogrù, *n.f. inv.* Crane mounted on a lorry *or* carrier (esp. for removal of cars by police).
autoinaffiatrice, *n.f.* Motor sprinkler; street watering truck.
autolesionismo, *n.m.* (*Mil.*) The practice of malingering by means of self-inflicted injuries; (*fig.*) defeatism.
autolesionista, *n.m.* (*Mil.*) Malingerer with self-inflicted injuries.
autolettiga, *n.f.* (Motor) ambulance.
automaticizzare, automatizzare, *v.t.* To automate.
automobilastro, *n.m.* Road hog.
†**autoparcheggio,** *n.m.* Car park. **— a torre,** multistorey car park.
autoparco, *n.m.* The cars belonging to an army unit, to a firm *or* company; car *or* automobile park.
autopiano, *n.m.* Pianola, player piano.
autopilota, *n.m.* (*Aviat.*) Automatic pilot, robot pilot.
autoplastica [autoplAstica], *n.f.* The plastic surgery operation of transplanting skin from one part of the body to another of the same person.
autoplastico, *a.* Pertaining to the above operation.
autoporto, *n.m.* Large parking and delivery centre for lorries.
autopullman, *n.m.* [cp. **torpedone**].
autoradio [autorAdio], *n.f.* Car radio.
autorete, *n.f.* [cp. **autogol**].
†**autorità,** *n.f.* (*Sport*) **D'—,** in a decisive manner, decisively (of a clear win).
autosilo, *n.m.* (*Motor.*) Multistorey car park.
autoslitta, *n.f.* Snowmobile.
autostazione, *n.f.* (*Motor.*) Service station; bus station.
autosufficienza, *n.f.* Self-sufficiency.
autovaccino, *n.m.* (*Med.*) Vaccination with a culture of germs taken from the patient himself.
avalve, *a.* Valveless.
avancittà [-à], *n.f.* Remotest outskirts of a town.
avanguardista, *n.m.* (*Hist.*) Member of the Fascist youth organization.
avansipario [avansipArio], *n.m.* (*Theat.*) Variety number performed in front of the lowered curtain (often while the scene is being changed).
avanspettacolo [avanspettAcolo], *n.m.* (*Theat.*) Curtain-raiser; live act (in a cinema).
†**avanti,** *adv.* (*Football*) **Gli —,** the forwards.
avantilettera [avantilEttera], *n.f.* (*Print.*) First incision of the metal.
avantilettera, *a., adv.* (*fig.*) Before one's time, *ante litteram.*
†**avere,** *v.t.* **Avercela con qualcuno,** to have a grievance against someone.
aviario, *a.* Avian.
avicoltore, *n.m.* Bird breeder; bird fancier.
aviogetto, *n.m.* Jet-plane, jet.
aviolancio, *n.m.* Parachute drop (men or supplies).
aviopista, *n.f.* Runway.
aviotruppa, *n.f.* Airborne troops.
avveniristico [avvenirIstico], *a.* Futuristic.
azionato, *a.* **— a moneta,** coin-operated.
azzurrabile [azzurrAbile], *a.* (*Sport*) Up to international match standard (esp. footballer).
azzurrabile, *n.m.* Player of international standard.
†**azzurro,** *n.m.* (*Sport*) Italian competitor *or* member of an Italian team in international events.

B

bacissimo [bacIssimo], *n.m.* (*hum.*) Prolonged kiss.
Baffino, *n.m.* Popular nickname for Hitler.
Baffone, *n.m.* Popular nickname for Stalin.
bagarinaggio [bagarinAggio], *n.m.* Forestalling; buying up (esp. of seats in a theatre).
bagarinare, *v.t.* [cp. **accaparrare**].
bagnarola, *n.f.* (*colloq.*) Bath; old car.
bagnasciuga, *n.f.* (*Naut.*) Water-line, Plimsoll line.
Bagnasciuga, *n.m.* Nickname for Mussolini used by anti-Fascists.
bagolone, *n.m.* (*colloq.*) Gas-bag, chinwagger; braggart.
ballista, *n.m.* One who tells fibs, fibber.
balordista, *n.m.* (*slang*) Dealer in forged coins, banknotes *or* travellers' cheques.
†**bambino,** *n.m.* **— prodigio,** infant prodigy.
†**bambola,** *n.f.* (*colloq.*) Girl, (*Am.*) dolly.
bananiero, *a.* Pertaining to bananas. **Nave bananiera,** banana boat; **commercio —,** banana trade.
†**banca,** *n.f.* **— d'affari,** merchant bank.
†**banchiere,** *n.m.* **— d'affari,** merchant banker.
banchisa, *n.f.* Ice-pack.
banchista, *n.m.* [cp. **banconiere**].
†**banco,** *n.m.* **— di negozio,** counter; (*fig.*) **— di prova,** test case; trial, try-out; **— di scuola,** form.
banconiere, banconista, *n.m.* Server at a bar counter; server at a market stall.
†**bandiera,** *n.f.* (*Naut.*) **— ombra, — di comodo,** flag of convenience.
banditismo, *n.m.* Banditry.
†**bar,** *n.m.* **— bianco,** milk bar,
baraccato, *n.m.* Shanty dweller (esp. disaster victim).
baraccopoli, *n.f.* Shanty town.
barattina, *n.f.*, **barattino,** *n.m.* (*slang*) (*used by barrow boys*) Cheating by substituting an inferior article in place of a better one while wrapping up; fraudulent substitution of a worthless parcel for a valuable one.
barbieria [barbierIa], *n.f.* Barber's shop.
barbosità [-à], *n.f.* Tediousness, tiresomeness.
barboso, *a.* (*colloq.*) Tedious, boring.
†**barchino,** *n.m.* (*Naval*) Midget submarine.
barisfera, *n.f.* Barysphere.
†**basco,** *n.m.* **— verde,** man belonging to the Catholic Action movement.
†**base,** *n.f.* (*Pol.*) Rank and file (of a party).
basista, *n.m.* (*colloq.*) 'Caser' (scout for housebreakers and burglars).

†**bastina,** *n.f.* (*colloq.*) Double-lined corset (used by women smugglers to hide contraband goods).
battaglista, *n.m.* Painter whose speciality is depicting battle scenes.
batterista, *n.m.* (*Mus.*) Drummer.
batticarne, *n.m.* Iron *or* wooden pestle (used for tenderizing meat before it is cooked).
battipanni, *n.m.* Carpet-beater.
battitacco, *n.m.* Leather band round the inner side of the turn-up of a trouser leg.
†**battito,** *n.m.* Throb, beat; pulsation; ticking (of a clock).
bavaglino, bavagliuolo, *n.m.* Bib (of a child).
†**bellezza,** *n.f.* (*colloq.*) **Vincere in —,** to win in fine style, to win handsomely.
belligeranza, *n.f.* Belligerency. (*colloq.*) **Non —,** nominal neutrality of a country which is giving aid to one of the belligerents.
†**bene,** *a.* (*colloq.*) Of high social standing; rich, fashionable.
bentoscopio [bentoscOpio], *n.m.* Benthoscope.
benzinaio [benzinAio], **benzinaro,** *n.m.* Filling station attendant.
bestiare, *v.t.* (*Students' slang*) To insult (someone) by calling him a beast.
bianconerista, *n.m.* Artist who specializes in black and white drawings.
bibbiaro, *n.m.* (*in parts of Central Italy*) Itinerant seller of Protestant Bibles.
bibliobus [bIbliobus], *n.m.* Travelling library.
biblioterapia, *n.f.* Repair *or* restoration of books.
bifocale, *a.* Bifocal.
bigodino, *n.m.* Hair-curler.
biliardino, *n.m.* Pin-table, (*Am.*) flipper.
†**biondo,** *n.m.a.* **— cenere,** ash blonde; **— platino,** platinum blonde.
bipolarizzazione, *n.f.* Bipolarization.
bloccasterzo, *n.m.* (*Motor.*) Steering lock.
blocchetto, *n.m.* Pad, note-pad.
bloc(k)-notes, *n.m.* Note-pad.
bocciofilo [bocciOfilo], *n.m.* Bowling enthusiast *or* fan.
boccolo, *n.m.* Curl; ringlet.
†**bolero,** *n.m.* Bolero jacket.
†**bolide,** *n.m.* (*fig.*) Very fast car *or* aeroplane.
†**bomba,** *n.f.* Doughnut; top-hat; 'home', base (in games); bubble gum; (*Sport*) pep pill. **— H** (o **all'idrogeno**), H (*or* hydrogen) bomb; **— illuminante,** flare; **— a mano,** hand grenade; **— a orologeria** o **a tempo,** time bomb; **— plastica,** plastic bomb; **— di profondità,** depth charge; **— radioguidata,** guided missile.
bombaiolo, *n.m.* Fisherman who catches fish illegally by killing them with underwater explosive charges.
bombastico [bombAstico], *a.* Bombastic.
bombolone, *n.m.* Doughnut.
bomboneria [bombonerIa], *n.f.* Assortment of sweets; confectioner's shop.
†**borghesia,** *n.f.* (*Army slang*) Civilian life, 'civvy street'.
borrana, *n.f.* Gully.
†**borsa,** *n.f.* Briefcase.
†**borsista,** *n.m.f.* University student with a scholarship. **— nero,** black marketeer.
†**bossolo,** *n.m.* **— di granata,** shell case.
†**bottiglia,** *n.f.* **— Molotov,** Molotov cocktail.
bozzettistica [bozzettIstica], *n.f.* Art *or* practice of writing sketches.
†**braccio,** *n.m.* (*fig.*) **— di ferro,** trial of strength, tug-of-war.
bradisismo, *n.m.* Bradyseism.
brevettistica [brevettIstica], *n.f.* Regulations governing the issue of patents; bibliography of books on the subject of patents.
†**brodo,** *n.m.* **— secco,** powdered soup.
bruciatore, *n.m.* Burner.
brufolo [brUfolo], *n.m.* Pimple.
buono-libro, *n.m.* Book token.
buono-pasto, *n.m.* Luncheon voucher.
burba, *n.f.* (*Army slang*) Raw recruit.
bustarella, *n.f.* (*colloq.*) Bribe; (*Am.*) payola.

C

†**caccia,** *n.f.* (*fig.*) **— alle streghe,** witch hunt.
cachigrafo [cachIgrafo], *n.m.* Someone with bad *or* illegible handwriting.
cachistocrazia [cachistocrazIa], *n.f.* Kakistocracy.
†**calamitare,** *v.t.* To attract, to draw (esp. publicity, crowds, etc.).
†**calcio,** *n.m.* (*Am.*) Soccer. **— -balilla,** pin-table football.
calciofilo [calciOfilo], *n.m.* Football enthusiast *or* fan.
calcitare, *v.t.* [cp. **calcinare**].
calderone, *n.m.* Cauldron.
†**calmiere,** *n.m.* Price-list.
†**calza,** *n.f.* **Calze-mutande,** pantie-hose, tights.
calzamaglia [calzamAglia], *n.f.* (*Theat.*) Tights.
calziere, *n.m.* Stocking manufacturer, hosier.
camaleontico [camaleOntico], *a.* Chameleon-like; changeable, unstable.
†**cambio,** *n.m.* (*Motor.*) **— automatico,** automatic gear change; **— automatico dei dischi,** automatic record changer.
†**camera,** *n.f.* **— blindata,** strong-room.
campeggista, *n.m.* [cp. **campeggiatore**].
†**canapa,** *n.f.* **— indiana,** Indian hemp.
†**canarino,** *n.m.* A drink made of hot water and lemon peel.
candeggiare, *v.t.* To bleach, to whiten.
†**cane,** *n.m.* **— -poliziotto,** police dog, tracker dog.
†**canguro,** *n.m.* (*colloq.*) One who, thanks to influence, is able to jump ahead of others in the queue for promotion.
†**cannonata,** *n.f.* (*colloq.*) Big success, (*Am.*) wow.
†**cannone,** *n.m.* (*colloq.*) Champion.
†**cannoniere,** *n.m.* (*Football*) Great goal scorer.
canoista, *n.m.* Canoeist.
cantagiro, *n.m.* A singing tour of Italy, in which popular songs are sung in a number of towns.
†**cantare,** *v.t.i.* (*colloq.*) To confess, to come clean, to spill the beans.
†**canzoniere,** *n.m.* Singer (particularly of popular songs).
Canzonissima, *n.f.* Italy's national popular song contest on television.
capellone, *n.m.* (*colloq.*) Long-haired hippie.
†**capillare,** *a.* (*fig.*) With many ramifications; extending everywhere.

†**capitoso,** *a.* (*colloq.*) Heady.
†**capoccia,** *n.f.* (*colloq.*) 'Loaf', 'noddle'.
†**cappa,** *n.f.* **Romanzo di — e spada,** cloak and dagger novel; **— magna,** official robe, ceremonial robe.
†**cappella,** *n.f.* (*Army slang*) Raw recruit.
capriolare, caprioleggiare, *v.i.* To caper, to cut capers.
†**carbone,** *n.m.* (*colloq.*) **— azzurro,** the use of wind-power for industrial purposes; **— rosso,** geothermal energy (geysers, hot springs, etc.) used for industrial purposes.
carboniere, *n.m.* Coal merchant.
carbosiderurgico [carbosiderUrgico], *a.* Pertaining to coal and steel; **Comunità Carbosiderurgica Europea,** the European Coal and Steel Community.
†**carciofo,** *n.m.* Bad actor, ham actor.
carente, *a.* Lacking, deficient.
carestia, *n.f.* Famine; (*fig.*) shortage, dearth.
carismatico [carismAtico], *a.* Charismatic.
†**carnaio,** *n.m.* (*colloq.*) Bathing beach, nudist centre etc. (where there are crowds of naked or near-naked people).
caropane, *n.m.* The high price of bread; an allowance to help people to meet this high price.
carrellista, *n.m.* Seller of food, drinks, *or* newspapers from a trolley on a railway platform.
†**carrello,** *n.m.* **— porta-vivende,** food-trolley.
carrettinista, *n.m.* Itinerant hawker.
carrierista, *n.m.* Careerist, *arriviste.*
†**carro,** *n.m.* **— sonoro,** loud-speaker car *or* van.
carro-botte, *n.m.* Tanker (road *or* railway).
carro-marsupio, *n.m.* (*Rail.*) Car transporter.
carrozza-ristoro, *n.f.* (*Rail.*) Bar (for drinks and snacks on a train).
†**carrozzone,** *n.m.* (*colloq.*) Handsome profit made out of shady transactions; (*Pol.*) batch of ministerial decrees.
†**carruccio,** *n.m.* (Baby's) playpen.
†**carta,** *n.f.* **— oleata,** grease-proof paper; **— pergamenata,** parchment-paper; **— quadrettata, — a quadretti,** squared paper, graph paper.
cartacarbone, *f.* (pl. **cartecarbone**) Carbon paper.
cartellonista, *n.m.f.* Artist who designs and paints posters; commercial artist.
cartellonistica [cartellonIstica], *n.f.* Commercial art, poster designing.
cartolibreria, *n.f.* Stationery and book shop.
†**cartone,** *n.m.* (*Cinema*) **— animato,** animated cartoon.
cartonista, *n.m.* Cartoonist; (*Cinema*) designer of animated cartoons.
cartoteca, *n.f.* Collection of maps (in a library); the room (in a library) where they are kept.
†**casa,** *n.f.* **— chiusa,** brothel; (*colloq.*) **— squillo,** house where call-girls receive their customers.
†**casalingo,** *a.* **Casalinga,** *n.f.* Housewife.
†**casco,** *n.m.* (*colloq.*) Bunch of bananas; (*Motor.*) **— di sicurezza,** crash helmet.
caseario [caseArio], *a.* Of cheese. **Mercato —,** cheese market.
†**casistica,** *n.f.* (*Med.*) Series of cases, case-history.
†**caso,** *n.m.* **— -limite,** border-line case.
†**cassetta,** *n.f.* Cassette. **Video —,** video-cassette.
cassettista, *n.m.* (*Banking*) Bank customer who rents a private safe.
†**castello,** *n.m.* **— aereo,** raised platform on a lorry (from which workmen repair overhead electric wires or cables).
catarifrangente, *n.m.* (*Motor.*) Cat's eye, reflector.
†**catena,** *n.f.* (*Phys.*) **Reazione a —,** chain reaction.
†**catenaccio,** *n.m.* (*fig.*) New tax; (*Football*) strictly defensive game.
†**cattivaccio,** *n.m.* (*colloq.*) Baddy, (*Am.*) Bad Guy.
cauteloso, *a.* Cautious [cp. **cauto**].
cavernicolo [cavernIcolo], *n.m.* Cave dweller.
cecchino, *n.m.* (*Mil.*) Sniper.
†**cella,** *n.f.* (*Phys.*) Cell. **— fotoelettrica,** photo-electric cell.
cementificio, *n.m.* Cement factory.
†**centauro,** *n.m.* (*colloq.*) Motor-cyclist; motor scooterist.
centrocampista, *n.m.* (*Football*) Midfield player.
centrocampo, *n.m.* (*Football*) Midfield.
centralinista, *n.m.* Telephone operator.
†**centro,** *n.m.* **— di rieducazione,** approved school, reformatory.
cercamine, *n.m.* Mine-detector.
cernia [cErnia], *n.f.* (*Zool.*) Gurnard, gurnet.
†**cervello,** *n.m.* **— meccanico, — elettronico,** electronic 'brain'.
†**cestino,** *n.m.* (Baby's) playpen.
†**chicchera,** *n.f.* (*colloq.*) **Parlare in —,** to speak affectedly.
chilometrico [chilomEtrico], *a.* Very long; long-winded.
†**chinotto,** *n.m.* Soft drink made from citron juice.
†**chiodo,** *n.m.* **— fisso,** one-track mind.
chiropodista, *n.m.* [cp. **pedicure**].
chiropratica, chiroterapia, *n.f.* (*Med.*) Chiropractic.
†**chirurgia,** *n.f.* **— estetica,** cosmetic surgery; **— plastica,** plastic surgery.
cibernetica [cibernEtica], *n.f.* Cybernetics.
cicalino, *n.m.* Buzzer (the diminutive kind used instead of door bell).
†**ciclista,** *n.m.* Bicycle repairer; attendant in charge of parked bicycles.
ciclocross, *n.m.* (*Sport*) Cyclocross.
ciclopista, *n.f.* Lane *or* track for cyclists (on a main road).
†**ciglio,** *n.m.* **Ciglia finte,** false eyelashes.
ciglione, *n.m.* Edge, brink.
cinecamera [cinecAmera], *n.f.* Movie camera, cinecamera.
cinecittà [-à], *n.f.* Film-producing centre.
cinematografaio, *n.m.* [cp. **cinematografaro**].
cinematografaro, *n.m.* Film producer; anyone engaged in the cinema industry.
cinemobile [cinemObile], *n.m.* Mobile cinema.
cineparco, cineparcheggio [cineparchEggio] *n.m.* Drive-in cinema.
cineteca, *n.f.* Film library.
†**cinghia,** *n.f.* (*fig.*) **Tirar la —,** to tighten one's belt.
cingolato, *a.* Running on a track. **Veicolo —,** tracked vehicle.

cinodromo, *n.m.* Dog-track.
citodiagnosi, *n.f.* (*Med.*) Rapid diagnosis.
citofono [citOfono], *n.m.* Internal telephone; intercom, interphone.
†**città,** *n.f.* — **aperta,** open city (i.e. a town which in wartime is not used in any way as a military centre).
clacchista, *n.m.* (*Theat.*) Hired clapper.
†**classe,** *n.f.* — **differenziale,** class for backward children.
clergyman, *n.m.* The dress, now more frequently worn, of Catholic priests in place of the traditional soutane: black trousers, coat and vest and 'dog collar'.
club, *n.m.* (*colloq.*) **Il — spaziale,** the space club (nations taking part in space travel); **il — nucleare,** the nuclear club (nations that have nuclear bombs).
coacervo, *n.m.* Accumulation; aggregate; (*Chem.*) coacervate.
cobelligeranza, *n.f.* Cobelligerency.
†**coccodrillo,** *n.m.* (*Journalism*) Obituary notice prepared when the death of a celebrity is expected.
cocktail, *n.m.* Cocktail; cocktail party.
†**coda,** *n.f.* (*Motor.*) **Fanalino di —,** rear light, tail light; (*fig.*) last *or* lowest in a classified list.
†**codice,** *n.m.* — **d'avviamento postale,** postal code.
coeducazione, *n.f.* Coeducation.
colesterina, *n.f.* [cp. **colesterolo**].
colesterolo, *n.m.* (*Med.*) Cholesterol.
colofone, *n.m.* (*Print.*) Colophon.
colonialismo, *n.m.* (*Pol.*) Colonialism.
†**colpo,** *n.m.* (*Boxing*) — **basso,** hit below the belt.
†**comando,** *n.m.* **Al —,** in charge (of), in authority (over); (*Sport*) in the lead.
comareccio [comarEccio], *n.m.* Gossip, tittle-tattle.
combattentismo, *n.m.* Views *or* feelings of ex-servicemen after a war.
†**combinazione,** *n.f.* Combinations (under-garment).
†**compagno,** *n.m.* (*Pol.*) — **di viaggio,** fellow-traveller.
†**complesso,** *n.m.* (*Psych.*) Complex; (*Theat.*) cast.
compravendere, *v.t.* (*Stock Exchange*) To buy and sell.
†**comunella,** *n.f.* Master key.
comunicativa, *n.f.* Ability to communicate or to put over effectively.
comunitario [comunitArio], *a.* Relating to a community; pertaining to the European Economic Community.
concelebrazione, *n.f.* (*R.C.*) Concelebration.
concorrenziale, *a.* Competitive.
concretizzare, *v.t.* To carry out, to realize.
condizionatore, *n.m.* Air-conditioning plant.
conduplex, *n.m.f.* (*Telephone*) Sharer of a party line.
confinferare, *v.i.* (*hum.*) To suit, to please.
confirmatario [confirmatArio], *n.m.* Co-signatory.
conflittualità [-à], *n.f.* State of *or* tendency towards strife *or* conflict.
confortato, *a.* (*Advertising*) Furnished with mod cons (of a house or flat).
congeniale, *a.* Congenial.
coniglicoltura, *n.f.* Rabbit breeding.
†**coniuntura,** *n.f.* Juncture; crisis; economic situation. (*Econ.*) **Alta —,** boom, favourable trend; **bassa —,** slump, recession.
connotazione, *n.f.* Connotation.
consumismo, *n.m.* Consumptionism.
consustanziazione, *n.f.* (*Eccles.*) Consubstantiation.
contaballe, *n.m.* (*colloq.*) Teller of tall stories.
contattare, *v.t.* To contact.
contazione, *n.f.* [cp. **conteggio**].
contenimento, *n.m.* (*Pol.*) Containment.
†**contestare,** *v.i.* To agitate, to demonstrate (of students).
†**contestare,** *v.t.* — **un professore,** to demonstrate against a professor.
contestatore, *n.m.* Demonstrating student; demonstrator.
†**contingenza,** *n.f.* Additional allowance.
†**conto,** *n.m.* — **-spese,** expense account.
contraccettivo, *n.m.a.* Contraceptive.
controfigura, *n.f.* (*Cinema*) Stand-in.
contromano, *adv.* In the wrong direction; in the opposite direction.
contropartita, *n.f.* Counterpart; return, reciprocation.
contropedalare, *v.i.* To back-pedal.
controproducente, *a.* Self-defeating, (*Am.*) counterproductive.
controricorso, *n.m.* (*Leg.*) Counter-appeal.
conurbamento, *n.m.* Conurbation.
convalescenziario [convalescenziArio], *n.m.* Convalescent home.
†**conversazione,** *n.f.* (*Radio*) Talk.
cooptare, *v.t.* To co-opt.
†**coperta,** *n.f.* — **-termofero, — elettrica,** electric blanket.
coppatura, *n.f.* (*colloq.*) The practice of displaying high quality goods on top of a box, sack etc. and those of an inferior quality or rubbish below.
coproduzione, *n.f.* (*Cinema*) Co-production.
corizza [cOrizza], *n.f.* (*Med.*) Cold.
Cornelio Tacito (*hum.*) Complaisant husband [cp. **pappataci**].
†**coronella,** *n.f.* Emergency dike.
†**corsia,** *n.f.* (*Sport*) Lane.
†**cortina,** *n.f.* (*Pol.*) — **di bambù,** Bamboo Curtain.
cortocircuitare, *v.t.* (*Elect.*) To short-circuit.
†**cosa,** *n.f.* (*Am.*) **Cosa Nostra,** American Mafia.
cosmetologia [cosmetologIa], *n.f.* Cosmetology.
cosmonauta [cosmonAuta], *n.m.* Cosmonaut.
costumista, *n.m.* Theatrical costumier.
cratopluto, *n.m.* One who becomes rich through holding an important political office.
cremlinista, cremlinologo [cremlinOlogo], *n.m.* (*Pol.*) Kremlinologist.
cremlinologia [cremlinologIa], *n.f.* (*Pol.*) Kremlinology.
criptocomunista, *n.m.* (*Pol.*) Cryptocommunist.
crocchiolare, *v.i.* [cp. **croccolare**].
croda, *n.f.* Peak, aiguille.
crodaiolo, *n.m.* Rock-climber.
†**cronaca,** *n.f.* — **nera,** crime report *or* news.
cronicario [cronicArio], *n.m.* Hospital *or* home for chronic invalids.

cruciverba, ***n.m.*** Crossword puzzle.
†**cucciolo,** ***n.m.*** (*Motor.*) A kind of autocycle.
cucirino, ***n.m.*** Reel-cotton.
curapipe, ***n.m.inv.*** Pipe cleaner.

D

daidai, ***n.m.*** [cp. **monopattino**].
dantistica [dantIstica], ***n.f.*** The study of Dante and his works.
davantino, ***n.m.*** Crop (of a bird).
decadentismo, ***n.m.*** (*Lit.*) Decadentism.
decapottabile [decapottAbile], ***a.*** (*Motor.*) With a folding hood, convertible.
decelerazione, ***n.f.*** Deceleration.
†**declassare,** ***v.t.*** (*Rail.*) To reduce the class of (a carriage; usu. from first to second).
decodificare, *v.t.* To decode.
decompressione, ***n.f.*** Decompression.
decongestionare, *v.t.* (*Med.*) To decongest; to keep (traffic) moving smoothly.
decontaminare, *v.t.* To decontaminate.
decurtazione, ***n.f.*** Cutting off; curtailment.
deflazionare, *v.t.* (*Comm.*) To deflate.
deidratare, *v.t.* Dehydrate.
deidratazione, ***n.f.*** Dehydration.
demilitarizzare, ***v.t.*** To demilitarize.
†**demografico,** ***a.*** **Incremento —,** population increase; **limitazione demografica,** family planning.
demonismo, ***n.m.*** Demonism.
demuscazione, ***n.f.*** Fly disinfestation.
denatalità [-à], ***n.f.*** Fall in the birth rate.
denazionalizzare, *v.t.* To denationalize.
deputatessa, ***n.f.*** Woman member of Parliament.
derattizzazione, ***n.f.*** Rat *or* mouse disinfestation, deratization.
†**derby,** ***n.m.*** (*Sport*) The Derby. **Il — italiano,** the Italian Derby, started in Rome by king Umberto I in 1884; a football match between two teams belonging to the same town or district.
desegregazione, ***n.f.*** (*Pol.*) Desegregation.
desonorizzare, ***v.t.*** To sound-proof.
deteriore, ***a.*** Bad; worse; depreciatory.
deterrente, ***n.m.a.*** (*Pol.*) Deterrent.
deviazionismo, ***n.m.*** (*Pol.*) Deviationism.
deviazionista, ***n.m.*** (*Pol.*) Deviationist.
dezanzarizzare, ***v.t.*** To rid of mosquitoes (ponds, swamps, towns, etc.).
dialettismo, dialettalismo, ***n.m.*** Dialectal word *or* phrase.
diditizzare, ***v.t.*** To disinfect with D.D.T. (*reg. trade name*).
dietologia [dietologIa], ***n.f.*** Dietology.
†**differenziale,** ***n.m.a.*** (*Comm.*) **Contratto —,** time bargain; **dazio —,** sliding scale duty.
†**diga,** ***n.f.*** **— di ritegno,** retaining dike; **— di sbarramento,** dam, weir.
†**dimostrare,** ***v.i.*** To take part in a demonstration.
diottria [diottrIa], ***n.f.*** (*Med.*) Dioptrics; diopter.
†**dire,** ***v.t.*** (*colloq.*) **A chi lo dici!** You're telling me!
†**direttrice,** ***n.f.*** (*fig.*) The main direction of a military *or* political offensive.
dirigismo, ***n.m.*** State-controlled economic planning; authoritarian kind of government *or* organization.
†**dirimpettaio,** ***n.m.*** Man who lives opposite.
disadattamento, ***n.m.*** Ill-adjustment, maladjustment.
disadattato, ***a.*** (*Psych.*) Ill-adjusted, maladjusted.
disamministrazione, ***n.f.*** Lack of administration; maladministration.
disattitudine, ***n.f.*** Ineptitude; incapacity.
disattivare, *v.t.* To de-activate (bomb etc.).
discatore, ***n.m.*** (*Sport*) Discus thrower.
†**disco,** ***n.m.*** **— microsolco,** long-playing record, (*Am.*) microgroove; (*traffic signal*) **— rosso,** stop; (*fig.*) red light; **— verde,** go; (*fig.*) green light.
discoamatore, discofilo [discOfilo], ***n.m.*** Collector of gramophone records.
discografico [discogrAfico], ***a.*** Of gramophone records.
†**discorso,** ***n.m.*** **— -fiume,** long-winded speech.
diserbare, *v.t.* To weed.
disgenico [disgEnico], ***a.*** Dysgenic.
disinfestare, *v.t.* To disinfest.
disinfestazione, ***n.f.*** Disinfestation.
disinflazione, ***n.f.*** Disinflation.
†**disinnescare,** *v.t.* To defuse.
dissacrazione, ***n.f.*** Deconsecration.
†**distaccare,** *v.t.* (*Administration*) To second.
†**distacco,** ***n.m.*** (*Sport*) **Per —,** easily, decisively.
distensivo, ***a.*** Tending to ease tension. **Politica distensiva,** appeasement.
disturna, ***n.f.*** Backchat, repartee.
divismo, ***n.m.*** Cult of film stars *or* stage celebrities.
divizzare, *v.t.* To give (actor, pop singer etc.) star treatment, to confer star status upon.
documentaristico [documentarIstico], ***a.*** Having the characteristic features of a documentary film.
†**dolce,** ***a.*** (*colloq.*) **La — vita,** a life of pleasure; unbridled hedonism.
dolciario [dolciArio], ***a.*** Pertaining to sweets and confectionery. **L'industria dolciaria,** the confectionery industry.
dolina, ***n.f.*** Cave, cavern (in the Carso).
dopofascismo, ***n.m.*** The post-Fascist period.
doppiaggio [doppiAggio], ***n.m.*** (*Cinema*) Dubbing.
doppiatore, ***n.m.*** (*Cinema*) Actor who dubs (generally in another language) the part of another actor, **dubber.**
†**drenaggio,** ***n.m.*** (*slang*) **Il — dei cervelli,** the 'brain drain'.
dressaggio [dressAggio], ***n.m.*** Training; breaking in (a horse).
drink, ***n.m.*** (Alcoholic) drink; get-together. **Prendere un —,** to have a drink.
drogaggio [drogAggio], ***n.m.*****, drogatura,** ***n.f.*** (*Sport*) Doping.
duplex, ***n.m.*** Party line, shared line.

E

eccipiente, ***n.m.*** (*Med.*) Excipient.
ecometro, ***n.m.*** Echometer, echo sounder.
econometria [econometrIa], ***n.f.*** Econometrics.
ecumenismo, ***n.m.*** (*Eccles.*) Ecumenicism, ecumenism.
edibile [edIbile], ***a.*** Edible.
edicolista, ***n.m.*** Proprietor *or* tenant of a newspaper kiosk.

editorialista, *n.m.* (*Journalism*) Leader writer.
edulcorato, *a.* Sweetened; (*fig.*) sugary.
egalitario [egalitArio], *a.* Egalitarian.
eiezione, *n.f.* Ejection.
elaboratore, *n.m.* One who works out *or* develops in detail. — **elettronico,** electronic computer.
elettrauto, *n.m.* Car electrician; workshop for electrical repairs to motor vehicles.
elettrocardiogramma, *n.m.* Electrocardiogram.
elettrodotto, *n.m.* Electric power lines *or* cables.
elettrofono [elettrOfono], *n.m.* Electronic organ.
elettronica [elettrOnica], *n.f.* Electronics.
elettrotipia [elettrotipIa], *n.f.* Electrotype printing.
elibus [Elibus], *n.m.* Helicopter (used to provide a passenger service).
eliporto, *n.m.* Heliport.
†**elzeviro,** *n.m.* (*Journalism*) Literary *or* topical article printed on the 3rd page of an Italian newspaper.
emoscopia [emoscopIa], *n.f.* (*Med.*) Blood test, blood examination.
emoteca, *n.f.* (*Med.*) Blood bank.
empatia [empatIa], *n.f.* (*Phil.*) Empathy.
encomiastica [encomiAstica], *n.f.* Books and articles in praise of someone.
endovenoso, *a.* (*Med.*) Intravenous.
enoteca, *n.f.* Collection of choice wines (on exhibition).
enucleare, *v.t.* To form the nucleus of (*also fig.*).
ergonomia [ergonomIa], *n.f.* Ergonomics.
esentasse, *a.* Exempt from tax, free of tax.
esodare, *v.i.* To move out, to depart; to emigrate.
esogamia [esogamIa], *n.f.* Exogamy.
esproprio [esprOprio], *n.m.* [cp. **espropriazione**].
esternalizzazione, *n.f.* (*Psych.*) Externalization.
esternato, *n.m.* Day school pupil.
†**esterno,** *a.* (*Cinema*) **Gli esterni,** open-air sequences in a film.
estetista, *n.m.f.* Beautician, beauty specialist.
estivare, *v.i.* To spend the summer, to summer.
estrapolare, *v.t.* To extrapolate.
estromettere [estromEttere], *v.t.* To eject, to throw out, to expel.
estroverso, *n.m.a.* Extrovert; extroverted.
eterosessuale, *a.* Heterosexual.
etruscologia [etruscologIa], *n.f.* (*Hist.*) Etruscology.
euforia [euforIa], *n.f.* Well-being; elation; euphoria.
euforico [eufOrico], *a.* Elated; euphoric.
eupeptico [eupEptico], *a.* (*Med.*) Eupeptic.
eurocrate, *n.m.* Eurocrat.
europeismo, *n.m.* (*Pol.*) A policy that aims at the economic and cultural unity of Europe; a belief in the importance of Europe.
europeista, *n.m.* Scholar interested in European studies; one who believes in the economic and cultural unity of Europe.
eurovisione, *n.f.* (*Television*) Eurovision.
evasionismo, *n.m.* Escapism.
evasore, *n.m.* Evader. — **fiscale,** tax evader, tax dodger.
eversivo, *a.* [cp. **sovversivo**].
evidenziare, *v.t.* To make clear, to show clearly.
ex-libris, *n.m.* Book-plate.
exlibrista, *n.m.* Collector of book-plates.
extraconiugale, *a.* Adulterous, extra-marital.
extraeuropeo, *a.* Non-European.
extrafino, *a.* (*Comm.*) Best-quality, top-grade; very fine, superfine.
extramarginale, *a.* (*Comm.*) Running at a loss.
extrarapido [extrarApido], *a.* High-speed, extra fast.
extrasensoriale, *a.* Extrasensory.
ex-voto, *n.m.* Votive offering.

F

faciloneria [facilonerIa], *n.f.* Tendency to take things lightly; easy-going behaviour; carelessness; amateurishness.
fagocitare, *v.t.* (*fig.*) To devour; to take over, to absorb, to incorporate.
fagottaro, *n.m.* Traveller *or* tourist who carries his own packed provisions (instead of relying on cafés or restaurants).
†**fallo,** *n.m.* (*Football*) Foul.
falloso, *a.* (*Football*) Full of fouls.
fantascientifico [fantascientIfico], *a.* Pertaining to science fiction, (*Am.*) scientifictional.
fantascienza, *n.f.* Science fiction, (*Am.*) scientifiction.
†**fantasma,** *n.m.* (*fig.*) **Scrittore —,** ghost writer.
†**fantino,** *n.m.* Jockey-cap.
faraonico [faraOnico], *a.* (*Hist.*) Pharaonic; (*fig.*) monumental, imposing, impressive.
†**fare,** *v.t.* (*colloq.*) To have an air *or* look. **La sua giacca fa molta inglese,** his jacket has a very English look; (*vulg.*) — **un baffo,** not to matter; (*colloq.*) — **fuori,** to kill.
†**farfalla,** *n.f.* (*hum.*) Bill of exchange, promissory note; (*slang*) letter *or* note smuggled out of *or* into prison; (*Journalism*) literary paragraph, short article.
†**fascia,** *n.f.* — **verde,** green belt (*round town*).
fasullo, *a.* Sham, false, (*Am.*) phoney.
†**fatale,** *a.* **Donna —,** siren, vamp, *femme fatale.*
fatalona, *n.f.* Vamp.
fatalone, *n.m.* Lady-killer.
fatiscente, *a.* Decayed; decrepit.
fatturato, *n.m.* (*Comm.*) Proceeds of sales; invoiced amount; turnover.
fertirrigazione, *n.f.* Irrigation with sprayed water containing fertilizers.
fesseria [fesserIa], *n.f.* (*vulg.*) Blunder; nonsense.
†**festa,** *n.f.* — **della mamma,** Mother's Day (*May 10th in Italy*).
fiabesco, *a.* Pertaining to fairy-tales; fairy-tale like.
fiabista, *n.m.* Writer of fairy tales.
†**fibra,** *n.f.* — **di vetro,** fibreglass.
fidelista, *n.m.* (*Pol.*) Follower of Fidel Castro.
figurinista, *n.m.* Designer of fashion-plates.
filmare, *v.t.* To film; to make a film of.
†**filtro,** *n.m.* Cigarette-tip.
†**finocchio,** *n.m.* (*colloq.*) Homosexual, (*colloq.*) queer, fairy.
floriera, *n.f.* Window-box.

fisarmonicista, *n.m.* Accordion-player, accordionist.
fisiografia [fisiografIa], *n.f.* Physiography.
fissile [fIssile], *a.* Fissile; (*Phys.*) fissionable.
fissione, *n.f.* Fission.
fiumara, *n.f.* Torrent; flood.
focalizzare, *v.t.* (*Phot.*) To focus (*also fig.*).
foiba [fOiba], *n.f.* [cp. **dolina**].
fondista, *n.m.* (*Sport*) Long-distance runner *or* swimmer; (*Journalism*) leader writer.
fonema, *n.m.* Phoneme.
fonometro [fonOmetro], *n.m.* Phonometer, noise meter.
foto, *n.f.* — **robot,** identikit.
fotocellula, fotocella, *n.f.* (*Phys.*) Photo-electric cell.
fotogrammia [fotogrammIa], *n.m.* (*Cinema*) Still.
fotomodella, *n.f.* Model (for press or commercial photographs).
fotomontaggio [fotomontAggio], *n.m.* Photomontage.
fotone, *n.m.* (*Phys.*) Photon.
fotoromanzo, *n.m.* A novel in strip-cartoon form.
fotostatico [fotostAtico], *a.* Photostatic.
fotostato, *n.m.* Photostat.
fototeca, *n.f.* Photographic collection, archive *or* library.
fototipia [fototipIa], *n.f.* Phototypy.
†**frazione,** *n.f.* — **di percorso,** fare stage.
frazionismo, *n.m.* (*Pol.*) The tendency in a party to break up into contending groups or factions.
†**freccia,** *n.f.* (*Motor.*) Trafficator; (*Rail.*) express train.
frigo, *n.m.* [cp. **frigorifero**].
frullato, *n.m.* Shake (drink).
fruttariano, *n.m.a.* Fruitarian.
frutteria [frutterIa], *n.f.* Fruit shop.
fumeria [fumerIa], **fumatoria** [fumatorIa], *n.f.* Smoking-den (for drug addicts).
†**fuoco,** *n.m.* — **di Sant'Elmo,** corposant; **mettere a —,** to consider carefully, to ponder; to state precisely, to evaluate justly.
fuorilegge, *n.m.* Outlaw, bandit.
fuoriserie, *a.* Custom built, purpose made.
†**fusto,** *n.m.* (*colloq.*) Handsome man.
futuribile [futurIbile], *n.m.a.* (Something) possible in the future.
futurologia [futurologIa], *n.f.* Futurology.

G

†**gabinetto,** *n.m.* — **ombra,** shadow cabinet.
gagà [-à], *n.m.* (*colloq.*) Fop, dandy, beau.
gallismo, *n.m.* A crudely gallant and sometimes aggressive male attitude towards women; an excessive male preoccupation with sexuality.
†**gambero,** *n.m.* (*Print.*) Line repeated by mistake.
†**ganga,** *n.f.* Gang.
ganghista, *n.m.* Gangster.
†**gas,** *n.m.* — **di gassogeno,** producer gas.
†**gazzella,** *n.f.* A fast police car (used by **carabinieri**).
gemellaggio [gemellAggio], *n.m.* Twinning.
†**generalizzare,** *v.t.* (*Bureaucracy*) To describe the personal features *or* particulars (of someone).
†**generazione,** *n.f.* (*colloq.*) — **bruciata,** — **perdita,** the lost generation (that which grew up during World War II).
genocidio [genocIdio], *n.m.* Genocide.
geotermico [geotErmico], *a.* (*Geol.*) Geothermic, geothermal.
geriatria [geriatrIa], **geriatrica** [geriAtrica], *n.f.* Geriatrics.
germanistica [germanIstica], *n.f.* Germanic *or* German studies.
gerontologia [gerontologIa], *n.f.* (*Med.*) Gerontology.
†**gerundio,** *n.m.* (*colloq.*) **Dare nei gerundi,** to become furious, to go mad, to go off the deep end.
gestaltismo, *n.m.* Gestalt psychology.
gettonare, *v.t.* (*colloq.*) To ring up; to select, to choose (song on juke-box).
†**gettone,** *n.m.* Metal disk, token (for telephones, juke-boxes, etc.).
ghenga, *n.f.* (*colloq.*) Gang.
†**ghiaccio,** *n.m.* (*Chem.*) — **secco,** — **asciutto,** dry ice.
†**giacca,** *n.f.* — **a vento,** windcheater.
giallista, *n.m.* Connoisseur *or* expert on thrillers.
giardinante, *n.m.* Amateur gardener.
giardinetta, *n.f.* (*Motor.*) Estate car, (*Am.*) station-wagon.
giavellottista, *n.m.* (*Sport*) Javelin-thrower.
†**giavellotto,** *n.m.* (*Sport*) **Tiro del —,** javelin throwing.
gigantismo, *n.m.* The trend towards making *or* constructing excessively large things (blocks of flats, tankers, towns, etc.).
gigione, *n.m.* (*colloq.*) Conceited and broken-winded singer.
gigionismo, *n.m.* (*Theat.*) Ham acting.
ginecocrazia [ginecocrazIa], *n.f.* Matriarchy.
giobba, *n.f.* **giobbo,** *n.m.* (*colloq.*) Job.
†**giocoliere,** *n.m.* (*colloq.*) Acrobatic *or* exhibitionist footballer.
†**giornale,** *n.m.* (*Radio*) — **radio,** — **parlato,** news bulletin, newscast.
†**giornata,** *n.f.* — **tipo,** typical day.
†**gioventù,** *n.f.* (*colloq.*) — **bruciata,** beats, beatniks; angry young men.
giradischi, *n.m.* Turntable (radio or gramophone); record-player.
†**girello,** *n.m.* (Baby's) playpen.
†**giro,** *n.m.* (*fig.*) — **di vite,** turn of the screw; — **d'orizzonte,** general survey.
girone, *n.m.* Great *or* wide bend (in river *or* road); one of Dante's circles (in Hell); (*Sport*) round, lap.
glassa, *n.f.* Icing (on cake).
glassare, *v.t.* To ice (a cake).
godronare, *v.t.* To knurl.
goduria [godurIa], *n.f.* [cp. **godimento**].
goffrare, *v.t.* To emboss.
gommapiuma, *n.f.* Foam rubber, rubber foam.
gommare, *v.t.* To rubberize; to gum; to fit with tyres.
†**gommato,** *a.* Provided with tyres (car etc.).
gommatura, *n.f.* (*Motor.*) Set of tyres.
†**gorilla,** *n.m. inv.* (*colloq.*) Bouncer, chucker-out; muscle man; body-guard.
gradualismo, *n.m.* (*Pol.*) Gradualism, policy of gradual reform.
gradualista, *n.m.* (*Pol.*) Gradualist.

gradualistico [gradualIstico], *a.* Gradualist, gradualistic.
graffa, *n.f.* (*Print.*) Brace; clip, fastener; clamp; double bracket.
Granturco soffiato, *n.m.* (*Am.*) Popcorn.
†grattare, *v.t.* (*colloq.*) **Gratta gratta, at** bottom, after all, when all's said and done.
grattascartoffie, *n.m.* (*hum.*) Bureaucrat.
†gruppo, *n.m.* (*Pol.*) **— di pressione,** pressure group.
gruppuscolo [gruppUscolo], *n.m.* Small group.
†guanto, *n.m.* **Mezzi guanti,** mittens.
†guerra, *n.f.* (*colloq.*) **— calda,** hot war; **— fredda,** cold war; **— lampo,** Blitzkrieg; **— totale,** total war.

H

holding, *n.f.* Holding company.
hostess [ˈostes], *n.f.* (Air) hostess, stewardess.

I

iconoteca, *n.f.* A collection of reproductions of works of art.
†idiotizzare, *v.t.* (*colloq.*) To make idiotic, to render fatuous.
idratante, *a.* Hydrating. **Crema —,** moisturizing cream.
idrobiologia [idrobiologIa], *n.f.* Hydrobiology.
idroponica [idropOnica], *n.f.* Hydroponics.
idrosci, *n.m.* (*Sport*) Water skiing.
idrosoccorso, *n.m.* Air-sea rescue service.
idrovia, *n.f.* Waterway (rivers or canals).
idrovoro, *a.* Water-drawing, water-pumping.
iella, *n.f.* (*dial.*) Bad luck; jinx, hoodoo.
iellato, *a.* Jinxed, hoodooed.
igienomane [igienOmane], *n.m.* [cp. **salutista**].
†illecito, *n.m.* Illicit act, offence.
†imbastitura, *n.f.* (*Sport*) Physical collapse (of an athlete).
†imboccare, *v.i.* (*slang*) To get in without paying.
immobilismo, *n.m.* Inactivity; (*Pol.*) wait-and-see policy; ultra-conservatism.
impatto, *n.m.* Impact.
†impegnato, *a.* (*Lit.*) Committed, engagé.
implosione, *n.f.* Implosion.
†imposta, *n.f.* **— del (o sul) valore aggiunto (IVA),** value added tax (VAT).
imprecisato, *a.* Unspecified.
impresenziato, *a.* (*Rail.*) Unmanned (small stations).
inceneritore, *n.m.* Incinerator.
incentivare, *v.t.* To provide an incentive for; to encourage.
†incidere, *v.t.* (*fig.*) **Per inciso,** by the way, incidentally.
incontenibile [incontenIbile], *a.* Uncontainable.
incontrollabile [incontrollAbile], *a.* Uncontrollable; unverifiable.
incrodarsi, *v.r.* To get stuck in rock-climbing.
indiziato, *n.m.* Suspect; (*Leg.*) person suspected on circumstantial evidence.
indonesiano, *n.m. a.* Indonesian.
indossatore, *n.m.* Male fashion model.
indottrinare, *v.t.* To indoctrinate.
inessenziale, *a.* Inessential.
infarto, *n.m.* (*Med.*) Infarct; heart disease; heart attack.
†influenza, *n.f.* (*colloq.*) **— spaziale,** the 1969-70 influenza epidemic; space-age influenza.
informale, *a.* Informal; (*Art*) non-representational, non-figurative.
infortunistica [infortunIstica], *n.f.* The study of accidents (particularly in industry).
infrasettimanale, *a.* In the middle of the week, midweek.
infrastruttura, *n.f.* Infrastructure.
infrasuono, *n.m.* (*Phys.*) Infrasonic wave.
infravisibile [infravisIbile], *a.* Not visible through the microscope.
infungibile [infungIbile], *a.* (*Leg.*) Non-fungible.
inghippo, *n.m.* Imbroglio; swindle, fraud.
inguaiare, *v.t.* To get (s.o.) into trouble.
innervosire, *v.t.* To make (s.o.) nervous.
inquilinato, *n.m.* Tenancy; tenant's status; tenantry.
insicurezza, *n.f.* Insecurity.
†insolvibile, *a.* Indissoluble.
insonorizzazione, *n.f.* Sound-proofing.
insopprimibile [insopprimIbile], *a.* Irrepressible.
insorgenza, *n.f.* Insurgence; onset, arising.
insostituibile [insostituIbile], *a.* Irreplaceable.
intarmabile [intarmAbile], *a.* Moth-proof.
integralismo, *n.f.* Unitary policy.
†integrazione, *n.f.* (*euphemism*) Annexation; (*Am.*) integration (of white and black citizens).
inteneritore, *n.m.* Tenderizer.
interazione, *n.f.* Interaction.
interbellico [interbEllico], *a.* Interwar.
intercambio, *n.m.* [cp. **interscambio**].
interclassismo, *n.m.* (*Sociology*) A tendency to encourage relationships between the various classes; (*Pol.*) the policy of seeking support among many social classes.
interculturale, *a.* Intercultural (referring to cultural exchanges between one country and another).
interfacoltà [-à], *n.f.* (*University*) Interfaculty students' council, students' representative body.
interfamiliare, *a.* Between two or more families. **Saluti interfamiliari,** greetings between families.
interfonico [interfOnico], *n.m.* Intercom, interphone.
interfono, *n.m.* [cp. **citofono**].
interlinguistica [interlinguIstica], *n.f.* The study of plans for an international language; the study of existing international languages.
internazionalizzare, *v.t.* To internationalize.
internista, *n.m.* (*Med.*) Hospital doctor, house surgeon; specialist in internal diseases.
†interno, *n.m.* (*Cinema*) Indoor *or* studio sequence.
interrazziale, *a.* Interracial.
interscambio, *n.m.* Commercial exchange; (*Motor.*) flyover crossing.
intersesso, *n.m.* (*Biol.*) Intersex.
intersindacale, *a.* Interunion.
interurbano, *a.* Between two or more towns, interurban. **Telefonata interurbana,** trunk call, long-distance call.
interzonale, *a.* Interzonal.
†intonaco, *n.m.* **— a pinocchino, — granuloso,** pebble dash.

intramontabile [intramontAbile], *a.* (*colloq.*) Eternal, undying.
introversione, *n.f.* (*Psych.*) Introversion.
introversità [-à], *n.m.* Introversion, introvertedness.
introverso, *n.m.a.* Introvert; introverted.
inutilizzabile [inutilizzAbile], *a.* Unusable.
invadenza, *n.f.* Tendency to encroach, to interfere *or* to meddle.
invalicabile [invalicAbile], *a.* Impassable; insurmountable.
inverificabile [inverificAbile], *a.* Unverifiable.
†**invertebrato,** *a.* (*fig.*) Spineless.
†**investigatore,** *n.m.* Detective.
ionosfera, *n.f.* Ionosphere.
ipersensibile [ipersensIbile], *a.* Hypersensitive; oversensitive, touchy.
iperspazio, *n.m.* (*Math.*) Hyperspace.
ipertensione, *n.f.* (*Med.*) Hypertension.
ipnopedia, *n.f.* Hypnopedia.
ipotetizzare, *v.t.* [cp. **ipotizzare**].
ipotizzabile [ipotizzAbile], *a.* Admissible as a supposition (or hypothesis); conceivable, possible.
ipotizzare, *v.t.* To consider hypothetically, to consider as a supposition.
iridato, *n.m.* (*Sport*) A world cycling champion (so called from the rainbow striped jersey he is entitled to wear).
irizzare, *v.t.* To bring under the jurisdiction *or* management of the I.R.I. (the Italian Government Industrial Planning Organization).
irrazionalismo, *n.m.* (*Phil.*) Irrationalism.
irre orre (*onomatopoeic*) Hemming and hawing. **Rispondimi senza tanti —,** answer me without all this hemming and hawing.
irreversibile [irreversIbile], *a.* Irreversible.
irriferibile [irriferIbile], *a.* Irreferable; unmentionable.
†**isola,** *n.f.* Island, refuge (in road).
isterotomia [isterotomIa], *n.f.* (*Med.*) Hysterotomy.
istituzionale, *a.* Institutional.
iter, *n.m.* Established legal *or* administrative procedure.

L

labiolettura, *n.f.* Lip-reading.
labronico, *n.m.a.* (*Lit.*) [cp. **livornese**].
lampeggiatore, *n.m.* (*Motor.*) Flashing indicator, winking light, blinker, trafficator.
†**lana,** *n.f.* — **aperta,** open wool; — **arricciata,** crimpy wool, curly wool; — **d'acciaio,** — **metallica,** steel wool; — **dura,** brashy wool, harsh wool; — **filabile,** spinning wool; — **follata,** milled wool; — **lavata,** scoured wool.
lanciamissili [lanciamIssili], *n.m.inv.* Rocket launching; rocket launcher.
†**lancio,** *n.m.* (*Aviat.*) Parachute drop.
†**lasciare,** *v.t.* **Lascia o raddoppia,** double your money (telequiz).
lassismo, *n.m.* Laxity; negligence; carelessness.
†**lastra,** *n.f.* (*Med.*) X-ray slide.
†**latte,** *n.m.* — **crudo,** unpasteurized milk.
lavabiancheria [lavabiancherIa], *n.f.inv.* Washing-machine.
†**lavaggio,** *n.m.* (*fig.*) — **del cervello,** brainwashing.
lavastoviglie, *n.m. inv.* Dishwashing machine, dishwasher.
†**lavatura,** *n.f.* — **dei cervelli,** brainwashing.
lavostireria [lavostirerIa], *n.f.* A laundry where clothes are washed and ironed.
†**legge,** *n.f.* (*colloq.*) — **della giungla,** law of the jungle, jungle law.
†**lente,** *n.f.* **Lenti a contatto,** contact lenses.
†**lettera,** *n.f.* (*fig.*) **Dire in tutte lettere,** to spell out.
letturista, *n.m.* Gas- or electricity-man who reads meters.
liberalizzare, *v.t.* To liberalize.
†**liberista,** *n.m.* (*Sport*) Free-style swimmer.
liceità [-à], *n.f.* Legality, lawfulness.
†**licenziare,** *v.t.* — **in tronco,** to dismiss, to sack without notice.
†**lievitare,** *v.t.i.* (*Comm.*) To rise (of prices).
†**lingua,** *n.f.* (*colloq.*) — **di Menelicche,** blow-out.
†**lista,** *n.f.* (*colloq.*) — **nera,** black list.
locutore, *n.m.* Radio announcer.
†**loggia,** *n.f.* (*Pol.*) Lobby.
†**lucciola,** *n.f.* (*colloq.*) Cinema usherette.
lucciolato, *n.m.* Glow-worm.
ludoterapia [ludoterapIa], *n.f.* (*Med.*) Play therapy.
lumachesco, *a.* Snail-like. **Andatura lumachesca,** snail-like pace *or* progress.
luminista, *n.m.* (*Theat.*) Light-effects man.
luna-park, *n.m.* Funfair, amusement park.
lungimiranza, *n.f.* Far-sightedness.
lungodegente, *n.m.f.* Long-term patient.
lungometraggio [lungometrAggio], *n.m.* Full-length film, long film.
lustrafinestre, *n.m. inv.* Window cleaner.

M

†**macchiato,** *a.* (*colloq.*) With a touch *or* dash (of). **Pasta asciutta macchiata,** boiled macaroni with a touch of tomato sauce; **latte —,** coffee dash.
macinafieno, *n.m.* Hay-cutting machine, hay-cutter.
†**macroscopico,** *a.* On a large scale, extensive.
maglione, *n.m.* Jersey; pullover.
magnetofono [magnetOfono], *n.m.* Tape-recorder.
mah! *inter.* Who knows? I can't make it out!
†**malavita,** *n.f.* (*colloq.*) **Il tam-tam della —,** the underworld grape-vine.
malloppo, *n.m.* (*colloq.*) Bundle, parcel; (*fig.*) wad of bank notes, (*colloq.*) lolly.
mammaiolo, mammaione, *n.m.* Mother's boy.
manageriale, *a.* Managerial.
†**manco,** *adv.* — **a dirlo,** needless to say.
mancolista, *n.f.* List of missing items *or* specimens from a collection.
†**mandato,** *n.m.* (*Pol.*) **Sotto —,** under mandate.
†**manica,** *n.f.* (*Aviat.*) Wind-sock, wind-sleeve. (*fig.*) **Aver l'asso nella —,** to have an ace up one's sleeve.
†**manifestare,** *v.i.* To make a public demonstration, to demonstrate.
manifestino, *n.m.* Leaflet.
†**marsupiale,** *n.m.* (*Aviat.*) A kind of transport plane.

massimizzare, *v.t.* To maximize; to magnify.
massivo, *a.* [cp. **massiccio**].
mattatore, *n.m.* Killer; (*fig.*) champion, star, winner.
†**matto,** *a.* Mat, matt (of colour or surface).
matusa, *n.m.f.* (*colloq.*) Middle-aged *or* old man *or* woman (*vogue word among teenagers. Shortened form of* **Matusalemme**).
maxicappotto, *n.m.* Maxi-coat.
maxigonna, *n.f.* Maxiskirt, maxi.
medicone, *n.m.* [cp. **medicastro**].
†**mela,** *n.f.* **— ruggine, — rugginosa,** russet.
menefreghismo, *n.m.* (*colloq.*) An 'I don't give a damn' attitude.
†**mensilità,** *n.f.* **La tredicesima —,** one month's extra salary *or* wages; **la quattordicesima —,** two months' extra salary; **la quindicesima —,** three months' extra salary.
mercantile, *n.m.* Cargo-boat, merchantman.
mercatistica [mercatIstica], *n.f.* The study of marketing.
†**mercato,** *n.m.* (*Pol.*) **— delle vacche,** political bargaining; (*fig.*) horse-dealing, horse-trading.
mesone, *n.m.* (*Phys.*) Meson.
mesotrone, *n.m.* (*Phys.*) Mesotron.
metalmeccanico, *n.m.a.* Metal worker; pertaining to metal workers *or* their industry.
metanifero [metanIfero], *a.* Methane-producing.
†**metano,** *n.m.* Natural gas.
metanodotto, *n.m.* Methane pipe-line.
†**metodista,** *n.m.* Lottery player who bets according to a 'method' or 'system'.
metronotte, *n.m.* Policeman on night duty.
†**mezzeria,** *n.f.* Centre white line (of a road).
†**mezzo,** *a.* **— servizio,** part-time service (domestic helps, waiters, etc.).
mezzofondista, *n.m.* (*Sport*) Middle distance runner.
microcamera [microcAmera], *n.f.* (*Phot.*) Miniature camera, microcamera.
microcitemia, *n.f.* (*Med.*) Cooley's disease.
microsolco, *n.m.a.* Long-playing record; long-playing.
mieti-legatrice, *n.f.* Binder (for corn harvesting).
militesente, *a.* Exempt from military service.
millefoglie, *n.f.* (*Bot.*) Milfoil, yarrow; cream puff, Genoese pastry.
minigonna, *n.f.* Miniskirt, mini.
minimizzare, *v.t.* To minimize.
minoritario [minoritArio], *a.* Relating to a minority, minority.
miracolato, miracolata, *n.m.f.* Miraculously healed man *or* woman.
missile [mIssile], *n.m.* Missile; rocket.
missilistica [missilIstica], *n.f.* Rocketry.
miticizzare, mitizzare, *v.t.* To create a myth about (someone or something).
mitomane [mitOmane], *n.m.* Mythomaniac.
mnemonismo, *n.m.* An excessive use of *or* stress on memory in teaching.
†**mobile,** *n.f.* (*police*) **La —,** the flying squad.
mobiliere, *n.m.* Cabinet-maker; furnisher.
†**moda,** *n.f.* **Alta —,** haute couture.
modellismo, *n.m.* The hobby of collecting *or* making models of ships, aeroplanes, railways etc.
†**modo,** *n.m.* **Grosso —,** approximately, roughly, more or less.
†**modulazione,** *n.f.* (*Radio*) **— di frequenza** (MF), frequency modulation (VHF).
†**modulo,** *n.m.* **— lunare,** lunar module.
molitorio [molitOrio], *a.* Milling.
mondialismo, *n.m.* (*Pol.*) Global foreign policy.
mondine, *n.f.* Girl *or* woman who works in the rice-fields.
mondovisione, *n.f.* (*Television*) Series of intercontinental telecasts through Telstar.
mongolismo, *n.m.* (*Med.*) Mongolism.
monocolore, *a.* Monochrome; (*Pol.*) of one party. **Governo —,** one-party government.
monocoltura, *n.f.* (*Agric.*) Monoculture.
monologare, *v.i.* To talk to oneself; to recite a monologue.
monopattino, *n.m.* (Child's) scooter.
monopetto, *a. inv.* Single-breasted. **Giacca —,** single-breasted jacket.
monorotaia, *n.f.* (*Rail.*) Monorail.
monotipo, *n.m.* (*Print.*) Monotype.
†**montante,** *n.m.* (*Boxing*) Uppercut.
montgomery, *n.m.* Duffle coat.
†**moralizzazione,** *n.f.* The process of purging *or* cleaning up (Government department etc.).
†**mordente,** *n.m.* Militancy; aggressiveness; (*colloq.*) bite.
†**moretto,** *n.m.* Choc ice.
†**mosca,** *n.f.* **— cocchiera,** horse fly; (*colloq.*) interfering busybody.
†**moscone,** *n.m.* (*Journalism*) Short item of news in Society column; a kind of outboard motor; catamaran.
motocolonna, *n.f.* (*Mil.*) Motorized column of troops.
motodromo, *n.m.* Racing track for motorcycles.
motofalciatrice, *n.f.* Mechanical reaper.
motofracassone, motofragorista, *n.m.* (*colloq.*) Noisy and bad-mannered motorcyclist.
motofurgoncino, *n.m.* Light motor van.
motoleggera, *n.f.* Light motorcycle (below 125 c.c.).
motoleso, *a.* Disabled.
motopompa, *n.f.* Motor pump.
motoretta, *n.f.* Motor scooter; autocycle, moped.
motorismo, *n.m.* Motorized sport.
motovedetta, *n.f.* Motor-patrol vessel.
motuproprio [motuprOprio], *adv.* Of one's own accord.
multirazziale, *a.* Multiracial.
†**muro,** *n.m.* **— del suono,** sound barrier.
museificare, *v.t.* To exhibit in museums and art galleries.
musetta, *n.f.* Nose-bag.
musichiere, *n.m.* Composer who puts a popular song to music.
mutuato, *n.m.* (Italian) National Health patient; insured person (health, accidents etc.).

N

nailon, *n.m.* Nylon.
narcolessia [narcolessIa], *n.f.* (*Med.*) Narcolepsy.
†**nastro,** *n.m.* **— adesivo,** sellotape (*reg. trade name*); **— comico,** comic strip; (*Am.*) **— di telescrivente,** ticker-tape; **— televisivo, video —,** videotape.

nastroteca, *n.f.* Collection *or* library of tape-recordings.
†naturista, *n.m.f.* Naturist, (*used as euphemism for*) nudist.
†negro, *n.m.* (*Journalism*) Ghost. **Fare il —,** to ghost.
neocolonialismo, *n.m.* Neocolonialism.
neofascismo, *n.m.* (*Pol.*) Neofascism.
neofascista, *n.m.* (*Pol.*) Neofascist.
neorealismo, *n.m.* Neorealism.
neorealista, *n.m.* Neorealist.
netturbino, *n.m.* Scavenger; dustman.
neurofisiologia [neurofisiologIa], *n.f.* (*Med.*) Neurophysiology.
neutralismo, *n.m.* Policy of non-intervention.
†nevralgico, *a.* (*fig.*) **Punto —,** the quick, sore point; sensitive spot; vital *or* critical question.
nientepopodimeno, *adv.* (*hum.*) Nothing less, no less.
ninfetta, *n.f.* Nymphet.
nocività [-à], *n.f.* Harmfulness.
Norna, *n.f.* (*Myth.*) Norn.
norreno, *n.m.a.* Norse.
nozionismo, *n.m.* The practice, in education, of imparting a great deal of information, but without adequately stimulating the imagination and critical faculties of students.
†numero, *n.m.* (*colloq.*) **Dare i numeri,** to draw attention to oneself, to show off.
nutrizionista, *n.m.* Nutritionist.
nuzialità [-à], *n.f.* Marriage rate (in a country or population).

O

obiettore, *n.m.* Objector. **— di coscienza,** conscientious objector.
occhiaio, *n.m.* Maker of glass eyes for the blind.
occhiera, *n.f.* (*Med.*) Eye-bath.
occupazionale, *a.* Occupational.
†oceanico, *a.* (*colloq.*) Vast, ocean-like.
odontotecnico [odontotEcnico], *n.m.* Dental technician.
ombretto, *n.m.* Eye-shadow.
omogeneizzare, *v.t.* To homogenize.
†oncologia, *n.f.* (*Med.*) oncology; treatise on tumours.
ondina, *n.f.* (*Myth.*) Undine; (*colloq.*) woman swimmer.
orbitare, *v.i.* To orbit.
†organico, *n.m.* (*Administration*) Permanent staff; establishment.
organigramma, *n.m.* Plan for the organization of a large concern.
†orientamento, *n.m.* **— professionale,** vocational guidance.
ospedalizzare, *v.t.* To put in hospital, (*Am.*) to hospitalize.
ospitante, *n.m.* Host.
†ospite, *n.m.* **— pagante,** paying guest.
†osso, *n.m.* (*fig.*) **Farsi le ossa,** to develop, to grow strong.
ottimale, *a.* Optimal, optimum.
ottimetro, *n.m.* Optometer.
†otto, *a.* **— volante,** switchback railway.

P

†padronato, *n.m.* Employers (taken collectively).
†paga, *n.f.* **— -base,** basic wage.
†pagare, *v.i.* (*colloq.*) To pay, to be *or* prove profitable.
pagliaccetto, *n.m.* (*colloq.*) Combinations (undergarment).
palafitticolo [palafittIcolo), *n.m.* Pile-dweller.
†paletta, *n.f.* (*Rail.*) Italian station-master's departure signal (a green, circular bat with a long handle).
pallanuoto, *n.m.* (*Sport*) Water polo.
pallonetto, *n.m.* (*Tennis*) Lob.
†palo, *n.m.* (*colloq.*) Accomplice, look-out.
†pane, *n.m.* **— a cassetta,** square loaf, tin-loaf, pan-loaf.
†panino, *n.m.* **— toast,** toasted sandwich.
panoramica [panorAmica], *n.f.* Hill *or* mountain road from which fine views can be enjoyed; (*Radio and Journalism*) short survey of a subject *or* situation.
†pantera, *n.f.* A fast police car (used by **squadra volante**).
paparazzo, *n.m.* (*hum.*) Press photographer.
Paperino, *n.m.* Donald Duck.
†pappagallo, *n.m.* (*colloq.*) Man who pesters women, (*Am.*) wolf.
†pappardella, *n.f.* (*colloq.*) A long and boring article *or* book.
paracomunista, *n.m.f.* (*Pol.*) Fellow-traveller.
parastinchi, *n.m.* (*Sport*) Pad (for the legs).
parchimetro [parchImetro], *n.m.* (*Motor.*) Parking meter.
†parola, *n.f.* (*colloq.*) **— -macedonia,** portmanteau word.
paroliere, *n.m.* One who writes the words (of a song).
parrocchialismo, *n.m.* Parochialism.
†partito, *n.m.* (*Pol.*) **Scheggia di —,** splinter party.
pasquetta, *n.f.* Easter Monday.
passamontagna, *n.m.* Balaclava helmet.
passeggiatrice, *n.f.* (*colloq.*) Street-walker.
paternalismo, *n.m.* Paternalism.
pattinatoio, *n.m.* Skating rink.
pattino, *n.m.* Catamaran.
†pedaliera, *n.f.* (*Bicycle*) Cog-wheel.
†pedana, *n.f.* (*Fencing*) Piste.
pediatra, *n.m.* Paediatrician.
pendolare, *a.n.m.* Swinging, oscillating; (*colloq.*) commuting; commuter. **Traffico —,** commuter traffic.
penicilloresistente, *a.* (*Med.*) Resistant *or* refractory to penicillin (of viruses).
pentagramma, *n.m.* (*Mus.*) Stave.
perbenismo, *n.m.* (*colloq.*) Respectability.
percentualizzare, *v.t.* To express in the form of a percentage, to reduce to a percentage.
perentorietà [-a], *n.f.* Peremptory *or* trenchant manner, bluntness.
†perequare, *v.t.* (*Administration*) To distribute equally; to distribute proportionately.
perfezionista, *n.m.* (*Phil.*) Perfectionist.
pernacchio, *n.m.*, **pernacchia,** *n.f.* (*vulg.*) Raspberry, (*Am.*) Bronx cheer.
†personale, *n.f.* **(mostra) —,** One-man show (of artist).
personalizzare, *v.t.* To personalize.
†pesante, *a.* (*Phys.*) **Acqua —,** heavy water.
†pesce, *n.m.* (*fig.*) **Fare il — in barile,** to be indifferent; to pretend to be indifferent; to remain neutral.
†peschereccio, *n.m.* Fishing boat; trawler.
pesista, *n.m.* (*Sport*) Weight-lifter.

petrolchimico [petrolchImico], *a.* Petrochemical.
pianismo, *n.m.* (*Mus.*) Pianism.
pianola, *n.f.* Pianola, player-piano.
piantagrane, *n.m.* Hair-splitter; trouble-maker.
pianuzza, *n.f.* (*Zool.*) Plaice.
†**piazzuola,** *n.f.* (*Mil.*) Emplacement; (*Traffic*) lay-by.
†**picchetto,** *n.m.* Picket (by striking workmen).
picchiatello, *a.* (*colloq.*) Crazy, cracked, touched.
†**piede,** *n.m.* **— di porco,** barbed wire stake; crowbar.
†**pieghevole,** *n.m.* Folder, brochure, leaflet.
†**pieno,** *a.* **— impiego,** full employment.
†**pieno,** *n.m.* (*Motor.*) **Fare il —,** to fill up.
pignolaggine [pignolAggine], **pignoleria** [pignolerIa], *n.f.* (*colloq.*) Strict *or* rigid discipline; pedantic adherence to regulations; meticulousness.
pillolomania [pillolomanIa], *n.f.* Mania *or* craze for taking pills.
†**pilota,** *a.* Serving as a guiding *or* trial device; pilot.
†**pioggia,** *n.f.* **— radioattiva,** radioactive fall-out.
piorrea, *n.f.* (*Med.*) Pyorrhoea.
pirofilo [pirOfilo], *a.* Heat-resistant, fire-proof.
piromane [pirOmane], *n.m.* Pyromaniac, (*Am.*) fire-bug.
†**pizzicare,** *v.t.* (*colloq.*) To catch red-handed; to arrest, (*colloq.*) to pinch.
placebo, *n.m.* (*Med.*) Placebo.
†**plastica,** *n.f.* Plastic (material).
plateresco, *a.* (*Arch.*) Plateresque.
pluridimensionale, *a.* Multi-dimensional.
plurilaterale, *a.* [cp. **multilaterale**].
plurimilionario [plurimilionArio], *n.m.* Multi-millionaire.
pneumogramma, *n.m.* Message sent by pneumatic dispatch.
†**poco,** *a., adv.* (*colloq.*) **Ne punto ne —,** not at all, not in the least; **po' po',** a lot; **roba da —,** rubbish, trash.
poderizzazione, *n.f.* The breaking up of large estates into small *or* smaller holdings.
polentone, *n.m.* Someone who is dull and slow, slow-coach; (*colloq.*) Italian from Northern Italy (because he feeds on **polenta**).
poliambulatorio [poliambulatOrio], *n.m.* Large hospital.
policentrismo, *n.m.* The existence of *or* tendency towards more than one centre (in administration, industry etc.).
poliedrico [poliEdrico], *a.* Polyhedric; (*fig.*) many-sided.
poliestere, *n.m.* (*Chem.*) Polyester.
politene, *n.m.* Polythene.
politicizzare, *v.t.* To make political use of; to make a political issue of.
polivalente, *a.* (*Chem.*) Polyvalent; (*fig.*) uncertain, ambiguous.
†**poliziesco,** *n.m.* Whodunnit.
poliziotta, *n.f.* Woman police constable *or* officer.
†**pollo,** *n.m.* (*hum.*) **— a quattro zampe,** rabbit.
†**polmone,** *n.m.* (*Med.*) **— di acciaio,** iron lung.
†**pomello,** *n.m.* Pommel; knob; ball-grip.
pomiciare, *v.i.* (*colloq.*) To dangle after women; to womanize.
pomicione, *n.m.* (*colloq.*) Womanizer.
pompelmo, *n.m.* Grapefruit.
†**pompiere,** *n.m.* (*colloq.*) Vulgar *or* sensational artist, writer *or* playwright.
pompierismo, *n.m.* Vulgarity; sensationalism.
pompista, *n.m.* (*Motor.*) Filling station attendant.
†**ponte,** *n.m.* (*Dentistry*) Bridge; (*Aviat.*) **— aereo,** airlift.
populismo, *n.m.* (*Pol.*) Populism.
populistico [populIstico], *a.* (*Pol.*) Populist.
portabagagli [portabagAgli], *n.m.* (*Motor.*) Boot, (*Am.*) trunk.
portacipria [portacIpria], *n.f.* Compact.
portanza, *n.f.* Capacity.
portavalori, *n.m.* Bank employee who carries, under guard, cash etc. from one bank to another.
positone, *n.m.* (*Phys.*) Positon.
positrone, *n.m.* (*Phys.*) Positron.
postazione, *n.f.* (*Mil.*) Emplacement.
postdatato, *a.* Post-dated.
†**posteggiatore,** *n.m.* (*Naples and S. Italy*) Itinerant musician (guitar, violin, etc. who has a regular round of places, generally cafés, where he performs).
postfascismo, *n.m.* Post-Fascist period.
postgraduato, *n.m.a.* Postgraduate.
postludio, *n.m.* (*Mus.*) Postlude.
potenziometro, *n.m.* (*Elect.*) Potentiometer.
preallarme, *n.m.* Advance warning (of air raids, etc.).
precisazione, *n.f.* Precise statement; specification.
†**predicare,** *v.t.i.* (*fig.*) **— bene e razzolare male,** not to practise what one preaches.
prefabbricare, *v.t.* To prefabricate. **Casa prefabbricata,** prefab.
preistoria [preistOria], *n.f.* Prehistory.
premorte, *n.f.* [cp. **premorienza**].
†**prendere,** *v.t.i.* (*Football and fig.*) **— in contropiede,** to turn the tables (on).
prepagamento, *n.m.* Prepayment.
†**presa, presina,** *n.f.*, **presino,** *n.m.* (*colloq.*) Kettle-holder.
presalario [presalArio], *n.m.* Government grant to university students.
presentatore, presentatrice, *n.m.f.* (*Radio and Television*) Compère.
pressaforaggio [pressaforAggio], *n.m.* Hay-baler, grain-baler.
pressurizzare, *v.t.* To pressurize.
prestavoce, *n.m.* (*Cinema*) An actor who takes part in a film only with his voice (as in dubbing).
†**prestigioso,** *a.* Conjuring; deceptive; enjoying *or* carrying prestige, prestigious.
†**prete,** *n.m.* **— operaio,** worker priest.
†**primario,** *a.* (*Leg.*) **Delinquente —,** first offender.
†**principe,** *n.m.* (*fig.*) **Principe Azzurro,** Prince Charming.
prioritario [prioritArio], *a.* Having *or* taking priority.
privatizzare, *v.t.* To return to private ownership (nationalized industries etc.).
problematica [problemAtica], *n.f.* Group *or* series of inter-related problems.
professionismo, *n.m.* (*Sport*) Professionalism.
programmatore, *n.m.* (Computer) programmer.

programmista, *n.m.* (*Broadcasting*) Programme deviser *or* planner.
†**proiettile,** *n.m.* (*Mil.*) — **tracciante,** tracer bullet.
promozionale, *a.* Promotional. **Programma** —, promotional programme.
propellere [propEllere], *v.t.* To propel.
prospettore, *n.m.* Prospector.
prospezione, *n.f.* Prospecting.
prossenetismo, *n.m.* (*Leg.*) Procuring, pimping.
protesi, *n.f.* (*Med.*) Prothesis; artificial limb *or* organ.
protostoria [protostOria], *n.f.* Early *or* earliest history.
provveduto, *a.* (*colloq.*) Understanding; well educated.
psicanalizzare, *v.t.* To psychoanalyse.
psichedelico [psichedElico], *a.* Psychedelic.
psico-attivo, *a.* (*Med.*) Having an effect on a patient's mood (of drugs).
psicocinesi, *n.f* Psychokinesis.
psicofarmacologia [psicofarmacologIa], *n.f.* Psychopharmacology.
†**psicosi,** *n.f.* Morbid state of mind; (*colloq.*) craze, obsession.
psicoterapia [psicoterapIa], *n.f.* Psychotherapy.
psicosomatico [psicosomAtico], *a.* Psychosomatic.
pubblicizzare, *v.t.* To publicize; to bring under public ownership.
†**pubblico,** *a.* **Pubbliche relazioni,** public relations.
pulsantiera, *n.f.* Row of push-buttons.
†**punta,** *n.f.* (*Broadcasting*) **Ora di** —, peak hour, (*Am.*) prime time.
puntasecca, *n.f.* (*Art*) Dry-point.
†**punto,** *n.m.* **Fare il — su,** to give up-to-date information, to say how matters stand in regard to (s.o. or s.th.).

Q

†**quadrato,** *n.m.* (*Sport*) Boxing ring.
quadrigetto, *n.m.* (*Aviat.*) Large four-engined jet-plane.
quadripartito, *n.m.* (*Pol.*) Group of four political parties which agree to co-operate in forming and running a government.
quadrireattore, *n.m.* (*Aviat.*) Four-engined jet-plane.
†**quadro,** *n.m.* (*fig.*) **Nel — di,** as part of, within the framework of.
qualunquismo, *n.m.* (*Pol.*) A movement, and later a party, founded in 1945 by G. Giannini to defend the rights of 'the man in the street' (**uomo qualunque).**
quanto, *n.m.* (*Phys.*) Quantum.
†**quattro,** *a.* (*Pol.*) **Le — libertà,** the four freedoms of the Atlantic Charter.
quorum, *n.m.* (*Leg.*) Quorum.
†**quota,** *n.f.* (*fig.*) **Prendere** —, to get off the ground.

R

†**raccomandato,** *n.m.* (*hum.*) — **di ferro,** someone so highly recommended that he is almost bound to get the job.
racchio [rAcchio], *a.* (*slang*) Ugly; plain, (*Am.*) homely.
radicalizzare, *v.t.* (*Pol.*) To make radical (esp. a political struggle *or* contest); to carry to extremes.
†**radio,** *n.f.* **Ponte** —, a radio programme featuring a conversation *or* debate between people in two different countries.
radioascoltatore, *n.m.* (*Radio*) Listener.
radioastronomia [radioastronomIa], *n.f.* Radio astronomy.
radiocafone, *n.m.* (*hum.*) Radio lout (i.e. someone who keeps his set full on, regardless of the feelings of others).
radiocorriere, *n.m.* Radio news broadcast.
radiodisturbo, *n.m.* Interference.
radiofototelegrafia [radiofototelegrafIa], *n.f.* Photoradio.
radiomobile [radiomObile], *n.f.* Radio car (usu. police car).
radiopilota, *n.m.* (*Aviat.*) Radio pilot.
radiopirata, *n.m.* Someone who owns and uses a set without paying for a licence.
radiorario [radiorArio], *n.m.* Weekly magazine corresponding to the *Radio Times.*
radiosbafatore, *n.m.* (*hum.*) [cp. **radiopirata].**
radiosonda, *n.f.* Radiosonde; radio altimeter.
radiotelescopio [radiotelescOpio], *n.m.* Radiotelescope.
radiotelescrivente, *n.f.* Radioteletypewriter; radio telex.
ragade [rAgade], *n.f.* (*Med.*) Fissure.
†**raganella,** *n.f.* (*colloq.*) Machine gun.
†**ragazza,** *n.f.* (*colloq.*) — **-copertina,** cover girl; — **-madre,** unmarried mother.
†**ramo,** *n.m.* (*Rail.*) — **secco,** branch line that no longer pays its way.
ranista, *n.m.* (*Sport*) Breast-stroke swimmer.
rateare, *v.t.* To divide into instalments.
ravina, *n.f.* Ravine.
razzista, *n.m.* Racialist, racist.
†**razzo,** *n.m.* — **pluristadio,** multi-stage rocket; — **telecomandato,** guided missile; — **vettore,** carrier rocket.
†**reattore,** *n.m.* Atomic *or* nuclear reactor.
recessione, *n.f.* Recession.
recintare, *v.t.* [cp. **recingere].**
reclamizzare, *v.t.* To advertise.
redditività [-à], *n.f.* Profitability.
referenziare, *v.t.* To provide with a reference, to give (s.o.) a testimonial.
referire, *v.t.* [cp. **riferire].**
reflazione, *n.f.* (*Economics*) Reflation.
reggicalze, *n.m.* Suspender-belt; (*Am.*) garter belt.
reggilibri, *n.m.* Book-end.
regimare, *v.t.* To regulate the flow of (river, etc.).
reginetta, *n.f.* (*colloq.*) — **di bellezza,** beauty queen.
†**registrare,** *v.t.* To record (on disc, tape etc.).
†**registratore,** *n.m.* Tape recorder.
regolabile [regolAbile], *a.* (*Mech.*) Adjustable.
relax, *n.m.* Complete rest *or* relaxation.
†**relegare,** *v.t.* (*colloq.*) — **in soffitta,** to discard; to consign to oblivion.
repubblichino, *a.* (*Pol.*) A disparaging name for a supporter of the Fascist Salò Republic
†**resa,** *n.f.* — **incondizionata,** unconditional surrender.
†**restituire,** *v.t.* To recondition.
restrizionismo, *n.m.* (*Pol.*) Restrictionist policy.

†**reticolato,** *n.m.* The network of lines and squares of a crossword puzzle.
†**retrocedere,** *v.i.* (*Football*) To be relegated.
†**retrocessione,** *n.f.* (*Sport*) Relegation.
retrovisivo, *a.* Looking back, backward looking. **Specchio —,** driving mirror.
retrovisore, *n.m.* (*Motor.*) Driving mirror.
revanscismo, *n.m.* Revanchism.
revanscista, *n.m.a.* Revanchist.
reversibile [reversIbile], *a.* Reversible.
revisionare, *v.t.* To check, to overhaul.
revisionismo, *n.m.* (*Pol.*) Revisionism.
revisionista, *n.m.* (*Pol.*) Revisionist.
reviviscenza, *n.f.* Revival; reawakening.
riannuncio, *n.m.* (*Broadcasting*) Brief restatement (at the end of a broadcast) of what it was about; summary.
†**ribaltabile,** *n.m.* Tipping lorry, (*Am.*) dumper.
ricetrasmettitore, *n.m.* (*Radio*) Transceiver.
ricognitore, *n.m.* (*Aviat.*) Reconnaissance plane.
†**riconoscimento,** *n.m.* (*Mil.*) **Piastrina di —,** identity disk.
ridimensionare, *v.t.* To adjust; to reorganize; to redeploy.
rieducazione, *n.f.* Re-education; rehabilitation.
†**rientro,** *n.m.* Returning, coming back; (*Comm.*) return on money invested.
riesame, *n.m.* Re-examination.
†**rifarsi,** *v.r.* **— una vita,** to start a new life.
rifasare, *v.t.* (*Elect.*) To correct *or* improve the power factor, to rephase.
†**rifilare,** *v.t.* To deliver; to saddle with; to foist upon.
†**rigenerare,** *v.t.* To restore; to recondition; to repair.
†**rigore,** *n.m.* (*Football*) Penalty kick.
rilanciare, *v.t.i.* To throw again; to throw back; to rebroadcast; (*poker*) to raise; to make a higher bid; to start afresh.
rilancio, *n.m.* Another throw; higher bid; (*fig.*) a new or fresh start; relaunching; revival; new presentation.
riloga, *n.f.* Curtain rail.
†**rimediare,** *v.t.* (*colloq.*) To get; to get hold of.
†**rimessa,** *n.f.* (*Tennis*) Return of service; (*Football*) **— laterale,** throw-in.
rinascimentale, *a.* Of the Renaissance.
riseria [riserIa], *n.f.* Rice mill.
risorgimentale, *a.* Of the Risorgimento.
rispiegamento, *n.m.* (*Mil.*) Redeployment.
rispiegare, *v.t.* (*Mil.*) Redeploy.
ristobar, *n.m.* (Portmanteau word for) restaurant and bar.
ristrutturare, *v.t.* To restructure.
†**risvolto,** *n.m.* (*Journalism*) An article which begins on one page and continues on another.
†**ritorno,** *n.m.* (*Sport*) Come-back.
rivistaio, rivistaiolo, *n.m.* (*Theat.*) Author *or* composer of a musical revue.
robinia [robInia], *n.f.* Locust-tree.
rocambolesco, *a.* (*colloq.*) Cloak-and-dagger.
rodaggio [rodAggio], *n.m.* (*Motor.*) Running-in.
roggia [rOggia], *n.f.* Irrigation channel [cp. **gora**].
romania, *n.f.* Collective word for all the countries in which Latin languages have been and are spoken.
romanistica [romanIstica], *n.f.* (*Leg.*) The study of Roman law; romance philology; the study of Rome.
†**romanzo,** *n.m.* **— d'appendice,** serial story in a newspaper; (*fig.*) sensational *or* melodramatic narrative; (*colloq.*) **— del brivido,** thriller; **— fiume,** roman-fleuve, saga; **— giallo,** thriller, detective novel; **— rosa,** novelette.
ronchiare, *v.i.* To growl.
†**rondò,** *n.m.* (*traffic*) Roundabout.
†**rosa,** *n.f.* Short list (of candidates for a post).
rosaista, rosicoltore, *n.m.* Rose grower.
rotariano, *a.* Rotarian.
rotellista, *n.m.* (*Sport*) Roller-skater.
rotocalco, *n.m.* (*Print.*) Rotogravure; (*colloq.*) glossy magazine.
rotolante, *n.m.f.* Roll-up Venetian blind.
rotonave, *n.f.* (*Naut.*) Rotorship.
rotore, *n.m.* (*Mech.*) Rotor.
rovesciata, *n.f.* (*Football*) Overhead backward kick.
rumorista, *n.m.* (*Theat., cinema*) Sound-effects man; noisy and inconsiderate motorcyclist.
rumorosità [-à], *n.f.* Noisiness.
†**ruota,** *n.f.* (*Mech.*) **— libera,** free wheel.
†**ruspa,** *n.f.* Excavator; bulldozer.

S

†**sabatico, sabbatico,** *a.* (*Univ.*) **Anno —,** sabbatical year.
†**sacca,** *n.f.* (*Aviat.*) **— d'aria,** air pocket.
sadico [sAdico], *a.* Sadistic.
†**saldo,** *n.m.* (*Comm.*) Remainder; remaindered article; article to be disposed of at a sale; (*colloq.*) article at a reduced price, bargain.
salottiere, salottaio, *n.m.* Frequenter of drawing-rooms, lounge-lizard.
salottiero, *a.* Relating to drawing-rooms; gossipy; frivolous; fashionable.
†**salto,** *n.m.* (*Sport*) **— con l'asta,** pole-jumping.
†**salvagente,** *n.m.* (*Naut.*) **— a brache,** breeches-buoy.
samba, *n.f.* Samba (dance).
†**San,** *abbrev.* (*colloq.*) **— Paganino,** pay-day.
sanforizzare, *v.t.* To sanforize.
†**sapere,** *v.t.i.* (*colloq.*) **Saperci fare,** to know how to do (something); (*fig.*) to be clever, to know one's way about.
†**satellite,** *n.m.a.* **Città —,** satellite town.
satelloide [satellOide], *n.m.* (*Rocketry*) Artificial satellite.
sauna, *n.f.* Sauna bath.
†**sbancare,** *v.t.* To break up and level down (uneven ground).
sbancatrice, *n.f.* [cp. **ruspa**].
sbattiuova, *n.m.* Egg-whisk.
sberla, *n.f.* (*vulg.*) Slap (in the face).
sbolognare, *v.t.* To foist, to palm off. **— a,** to foist upon.
sbronza, *n.f.* Drunkenness; drinking bout, booze.
sbruffone, *n.m.* (*colloq.*) Braggart; tell-tale.
sbuccione, *n.m.* (*colloq.*) Layabout; scrimshanker; good-for-nothing.
sbullonare, *v.t.* (*Mech.*) To unbolt.
scacciacani, *n.m.* Blank pistol for frightening dogs away.
†**scala,** *n.f.* **— mobile,** method of allotting

increases in wages and salaries in accordance with the cost-of-living index.
scansabrighe, *n.m.* One who avoids quarrels, peace-loving man.
scapolaggine [scapolAggine], *n.f.* (*hum.*) Bachelorhood.
scaramanzia [scaramanzIa], *n.f.* Evil spell; charm *or* gesture against bad luck.
scassato, *a.* (*colloq.*) Broken down, bust.
scatinare, *v.i.* To skate.
scattista, *n.m.f.* (*Sport*) Sprinter.
†**scatto**, *n.m.* (*Sport*) Sprint.
scavatrice, *n.f.* (*Mech.*) Excavator.
†**scena**, *n.f.* (*Cinema*) — **retrospettiva**, flash-back.
scendibagno, *n.m.* Bath-mat.
scespiriano, *a.* Shakespearian.
schedare, *v.t.* To file; to put on record.
†**scheggia**, *n.f.* (*Pol.*) — **di partito, partito —**, splinter party.
schermare, *v.t.* To screen; to shield.
schiacciapatate, *n.m. inv.* Potato masher.
†**schiacciare**, *v.t.* (*Tennis*) To smash.
schiacciasassi, *n.m. inv.* Steam roller.
schiarita, *n.f.* Brightening up, clearing up; clarification.
†**schifo**, *n.m.* (*colloq.*) **Fa —**, it's lousy, (*Am.*) it stinks.
schizofrenico [schizofrEnico], *n.m.a.* Schizophrenic.
†**sci**, *n.m.* — **nautico**, water ski-ing.
sciabordio [sciabordIo], *n.m.* Splashing; rinsing.
sciangai, *n.m.* (*colloq.*) Spillikins (game).
scientismo, *n.m.* Scientism.
scioccato, *a.* (*Med.*) Suffering from shock; (*fig.*) shocked.
†**sciopero**, *n.m.* (*colloq.*) — **articolata**, staggered *or* phased strike; (*colloq.*) — **a singhiozzo**, intermittent strike, (*Am.*) scattered time strike; — **a scacchiera, — a settori**, strike in turn by various departments of a factory or company; **scioperi a zone**, strikes in succession in different places; **scioperi a catena**, continuous chain of strikes.
sciovia [sciovIa], *n.f.* Ski-lift, ski-tow.
scippo, *n.m.* (*slang*) Bag-snatching.
sci-sci, *a.* Chi-chi.
scissionismo, *n.m.* (*Pol*) [cp. **frazionismo**].
sciuscià [-à], *n.m.* (*colloq.*) Shoe-black.
scombinato, *a.* Disarranged; rambling, inconsequent.
scomparto, *n.m.* Partition; compartment.
scompenso, *n.m.* Imbalance; maladjustment.
scondizionato, *a.* Substandard.
sconfortato, *a.* (*colloq.*) Without modern conveniences.
sconsacrazione, *n.f.* Deconsecration.
†**scontare**, *v.t.* (*colloq.*) To foresee; to expect; to take for granted.
scopiazzare, *v.t.* To copy incorrectly; to plagiarize.
scopofilia [scopofIlia], *n.f.* Voyeurism.
†**scorpione**, *n.m.* (*Mil.*) Flail-tank, scorpion.
†**scotto**, *a.* Overcooked.
scriteriato, *a.* Rash, reckless, thoughtless.
†**scuderia**, *n.f.* (*Motor.*) A group of racing cars under a single ownership or management (e.g. **la scuderia Ferrari**).
†**scudetto**, *n.m.* The Italian equivalent of the British Soccer League Cup.
scuocersi, *v.r.* To get *or* become overcooked.
sdrammatizzare, *v.t.* To take the drama *or* sensationalism out of; to take the heat out of.
sediovia, *n.f.* [cp. **seggiovia**].
sefardita, *n.m.* Sephardi (pl. Sephardim).
sefardito, *a.* Sephardic.
seggiovia [seggiovIa], *n.f.* Chair-lift.
segnaletica [segnalEtica], *n.f.* Code of signals. — **stradale**, traffic signals.
segnalinee, *n.m.* (*Football*) Linesman.
segnaprezzo, *n.m.* Price tag, price card.
segregazionista, *n.m.* (*Pol.*) Segregationist.
†**selezione**, *n.f.* (*Mus.*) Pot-pourri, medley; (*Journalism*) digest.
†**seminario**, *n.m.* (*Univ.*) Seminar.
seminterrato, *n.m.* Basement; semi-basement. **Appartomento al —**, basement flat.
senatrice, *n.f.* Lady Senator *or* member of the Italian Upper House.
†**sensibilizzare**, *v.t.* To bring to public notice, to make aware (of), to publicize.
†**seppia**, *n.f.* (*Schoolboy slang*) Sneak.
serioso, *a.* Affectedly *or* smugly serious.
†**servizio**, *n.m.* (*Journalism*) Series of articles; (*Tennis*) service.
servofreno, *n.m.* (*Mech.*) Servo-brake; brake booster.
servosterzo, *n.m.* (*Motor.*) Power steering gear.
sess(u)ologia [sess(u)ologIa], *n.f.* Sexology.
†**sesto**, *a.* (*Mountaineering*) — **grado**, the highest degree of difficulty in a climb (according to Welzenbach's scale); — **senso**, sixth sense.
sfasato, *a.* (*Elect., Mech.*) Out of phase; (*fig.*) out of step, not in harmony, unco-ordinated; disorganized.
sferragliare, *v.i.* To clank.
sfessare, *v.t.* (*vulg.*) To wear out, to tire.
sfocato, *a.* (*Phot.*) Out of focus (*also fig.*).
†**sfondare**, *v.t.i.* (*colloq.*) To succeed, to be a hit, (*Am.*) to be a wow.
sfondone, *n.m.* Blunder; howler.
†**sformato**, *n.m.* Pie, pudding.
†**sfottere**, *v.t.* (*colloq.*) To take the mickey out of, to make fun of.
sfrecciare, *v.i.* To dart, to flash (by); to rush, to fly, to whizz along.
sfuso, *a.* Loose (not packaged).
†**sicurezza**, *n.f.* — **collectiva**, collective security; — **sociale**, social security; — **di sè**, self-assurance.
†**sigla**, *n.f.* (*Radio*) — **(musicale)**, signature tune.
siglare, *v.t.* To initial (an agreement, a treaty, etc.).
silenziare, *v.t.* (*Mech.*) To make silent, to furnish with a silencer *or* silencers; (*Mil.*) to silence (an enemy gun etc.).
similpelle, *n.f.* Imitation leather.
sincronizzato, *a.* Synchronized. (*Motor.*) **Cambio —**, synchromesh gear.
sincrotrone, *n.m.* (*Phys.*) Synchrotron.
sindromo, *n.m.* (*Med.*) Syndrome.
†**sinistrorso**, *a.* Anti-clockwise.
sinusite, *n.f.* (*Med.*) Sinusitis.
siparietto, *n.m.* (*Theat.*) Drop-curtain; (*Radio*) fill-up.
sistematicità [-à], *n.f.* The quality of being systematic.
sistemista, *n.m.* Someone who gambles *or* bets according to a 'system'.

†**slittare,** *v.i.* (*colloq.*) To lose value, to 'slide' (currencies, shares, etc.).
smontabile [smontAbile], *a.* (*Mech.*) That can be taken to pieces *or* dismantled, demountable.
smorzata, *n.f.* (*Tennis*) Drop shot.
snazionalizzare, *v.t.* To denationalize.
snobbare, *v.t.* (*colloq.*) To snub, to humiliate.
sociolinguistica [sociolinguIstica], *n.f.* Sociolinguistics.
†**soffiare,** *v.t.* (*colloq.*) To steal, to pinch.
soggettista, *n.m.* (*Cinema*) Subject-writer, story-writer, script-writer.
solario [solArio], *n.m.* Sun-bathing terrace, solarium.
soldata, *n.f.* Woman soldier.
solidarizzare, *v.i.* To show *or* express solidarity.
†**sonda,** *n.f.* (*Astrophysics*) **— spaziale,** space probe.
sonico [sOnico], *a.* Sonic. (*Aviat.*) **Barriera sonica,** sound barrier.
sonorista, *n.m.* (*Cinema*) Sound-track technician.
sonorizzatore, *n.m.* (*Radio*) Sound-effects man.
soppressore, *n.m.* (*Radio*) Suppressor.
sopralzo, *n.m.* Floor *or* storey added on top of a building; penthouse.
soprannazionale, *a.* Supranational.
soroptimista, *n.f.* Soroptimist.
sorvolo, *n.m.* (*Aviat.*) [cp. **sorvolata**].
†**sospetto,** *n.m.* Touch, trace, soupçon.
†**sotto,** *adv.* (*colloq.*) **Sotto sotto,** in one's heart of hearts, at the back of one's mind.
sottobanco, *adv.* Secretly, surreptitiously. **Vendere —,** to sell under the counter.
sottobosco, *n.m.* Undergrowth; (*fig.*) groups of people who work together in the shade of official parties to promote their own interests.
sottoccupato, *a.* Underemployed.
sottoccupazione, *n.f.* Underemployment.
sottocipria [sottocIpria], *n.m.* Make-up foundation.
sottocultura, *n.f.* Inferior culture, subculture.
sottofondo, *n.m.* (*Arch.*) Foundation; (*Radio*) background.
sottogoverno, *n.m.* (*Pol.*) Unscrupulous dealings promoting undercover favourites by a political party or a group of parties.
sottomondo, *n.m.* Underworld.
sottosviluppato, *a.* Underdeveloped.
sottosviluppo, *n.m.* Underdevelopment.
sottovalutare, *v.t.* To undervalue, to belittle.
sottovia, *n.f.* Subway, underpass.
sottovita, *n.f.* Life of the underworld.
sovroccupazione, *n.f.* Overmanning.
†**spaccare,** *v.t.* (*of clock or watch*) **— il minuto,** to keep perfect time, to be dead accurate.
sparacchiare, *v.i.* To shoot in a desultory *or* intermittent manner.
†**sparare,** *v.t.i.* (*Mil.*) **— a zero,** to fire point blank.
spartineve, *n.m.* Snow-plough.
spartitraffico [spartitrAffico], *n.m.* Traffic island; (*motorway*) centre reservation, (*Am.*) median strip.
spastico [spAstico], *a.* (*Med.*) Spastic.
†**spazio,** *n.m.* **— aereo,** air space.
spedalizzare, *v.t.* To send to hospital, (*Am.*) to hospitalize.
spersonalizzare, *v.t.* To depersonalize.
spezzoniera, *n.f.* (*Aviat.*) Bomb rack, bomb bay.
spianatrice, *n.f.* Bulldozer.
spider, *n.m. or f.* Sports-car.
spignattare, *v.i.* (*hum.*) To cook, to work in the kitchen.
spintarella, *n.f.* (*colloq.*) Little help *or* 'push' (from s.o. in power or authority).
spiritiera, *n.f.* Spirit-lamp.
spoetizzante, *a.* Disillusioning, disenchanting.
spogliarello, *n.m.* Strip-tease act.
†**spola,** *n.f.* (*colloq.*) **Fare la — tra casa e ufficio,** to commute.
†**spregiudicato,** *a.* (*colloq.*) Unscrupulous, unprincipled.
†**spremere,** *v.t.* (*fig.*) **Spremersi le meningi,** to rack one's brains.
spremifrutta, *n.m.* Fruit-squeezer.
sputtanarsi, *v.r.* To behave like a prostitute; (*fig.*) to demean oneself, to lower oneself.
†**squillo,** *n.m.* (*colloq.*) **Ragazza- —,** call-girl.
†**staccare,** *v.t.i.* (*colloq.*) To stop working; to end the day's work.
†**stampa,** *n.f.* (*colloq.*) **— gialla,** yellow press.
statalismo, *n.m.* (*Pol.*) Excessive State interference *or* control.
statalizzare, *v.t.* To bring under State control.
statunitense, *a.* Relating *or* belonging to the U.S.A.
†**stella,** *n.f.* **— alpina,** edelweiss.
stereofonia [stereofonIa], *n.f.* Stereophony.
stigliaghi, *n.m.pl.* Russian Teddy boys, stilyagi.
storicizzare, *v.t.* To see *or* place against a historical background.
†**stralcio,** *n.m.* (*Leg.*) **Legge —,** a clause or section of a new bill before Parliament, which as a matter of urgency is made enforceable before the bill as a whole has become law.
strappaborse, *n.m. inv.* Bag-snatcher.
strumentalizzare, *v.t.* To make an instrument of; to make use of, to make capital out of.
strutturare, *v.t.* To structure, to structuralize.
subinquilino, *n.m.* Subtenant.
subliminale, *a.* (*Psych.*) Subliminal. **Pubblicità —,** subliminal projection.
†**successo,** *n.m.* **Di —,** successful.
†**suggeritore,** *n.m.* **— televisivo,** teleprompter.
sulfamidici [sulfamIdici], *n.m.pl.* Sulphonamides, sulpha-drugs.
sulfamidico, *n.m.a.* Sulphamidic; sulphonamide.
supercilioso, *a.* Supercilious.
supercongelato, *a.* Deep frozen.
supermercato, *n.m.* Supermarket.
supernazionale, *a.* Supranational.
supersonico [supersOnico], *a.* Supersonic.
supervestito, *a.* Overdressed.
†**surriscaldamento,** *n.m.* Overheating (*also fig.*).
sventagliata, *n.f.* Fanning; (*Mil.*) burst, volley (of machine-gun fire).
†**svettare,** *v.i.* (*of trees, plants*) To wave their tops; (*of mountains*) to loom, to be visible; to be silhouetted.
†**svincolo,** *n.m.* (*Motor.*) Side exit from a motorway.
svio, *n.m.* (*Rail.*) Derailment.

T

†**tacco**, *n.m.* — **a spillo**, stiletto heel.
†**taglio**, *n.m.* (*Tennis*) Spin.
Tailandia, *n.f.* Thailand.
tait, *n.m.* [cp. **tight**].
talassografia [talassografIa], *n.f.* Thalassography, oceanography.
talidomide, *n.m.* (*or f.*) (*Med.*) Thalidomide.
†**tamponamento**, *n.m.* (*Motor.*) Collision; bump, crash.
†**tamponare**, *v.t.* (*Motor.*) To run into, to collide with, to crash into.
tangenziale, *n.m.a.* (*Geom.*) Tangential; (*Motor.*) bypass.
†**tapparella**, *n.f.* Roll-up blind made of matting.
†**tappeto**, *n.m.* (*Aviat.*) **Bombardamento a —**, carpet-bombing.
†**tarare**, *v.t.* To calibrate; to rate.
tardona, *n.f.* (*colloq.*) Old maid, spinster.
†**tastiera**, *n.f.* (*fig.*) Scale; range.
†**tavola**, *n.f.* — **calda**, café in which customers are seated and served at the counter; — **rotonda**, round-table discussion.
tecnicizzato, *a.* Technicalized.
tecnicolore, *n.m.* (*reg. trade name*) Technicolor.
tecnocrate, *n.m.* Technocrat.
telearma, *n.f.* (*Mil.*) Guided weapon; missile.
teleautografo [teleautOgrafo], *n.m.* Teleautograph.
telecamera [telecAmera], *n.f.* Television camera, telecamera.
telecomandato, *a.* Remote-controlled, guided.
telecomando, *n.m.* Remote control, telecontrol.
telecomunicazioni, *n.f.pl.* Telecommunications.
teledramma, *n.m.* Television play.
telefilm, *n.m.* Televised film.
telegenico [telegEnico], *a.* Telegenic.
teleobbiettivo, *n.m.* Telescopic lens.
teleromanzo, *n.m.* Novel serialized on television.
teleselezione, *n.f.* (*Telephone*) Direct dialling system.
telespettatore, *n.m.* Televiewer, viewer.
televisore, *n.m.* Television set.
telo-slitta, *n.f.* Canvas chute (used by firemen).
tematica [temAtica], *n.f.* Characteristic musical themes of a composer; characteristic views of a writer, speaker *or* thinker.
†**tempesta**, *n.f.* (*fig.*) — **in un bicchier d'acqua**, storm in a tea-cup.
†**tempo**, *n.m.* (*Sport*) — **supplementare**, extra time.
tenesmo, *n.m.* (*Med.*) Tenesmus.
teratismo, *n.m.* (*Med.*) Abnormal *or* monstrous growth.
terilene, *n.m.* Terylene (*reg. trade name*).
termalismo, *n.m.* The therapeutic use of thermal waters.
†**terminale**, *n.m.* (*Rail.*) Terminal station, terminus.
termonucleare, *a.* Thermonuclear.
termoterapia [termoterapIa], *n.f.* (*Med.*) Thermotherapy.
ternato, *n.m.* One who is on a short list of three (for an appointment).
†**terra**, *n.f.* (*fig.*) — **bruciata**, scorched earth.
terriero, *n.m.* (*colloq.*) Landlubber.
terrone, *n.m.* (*colloq.*) Southerner (from the south of Italy).
†**testa**, *n.f.* (*Mil.*) — **di sbarco**, bridge-head; (*fig.*) — **di turco**, butt, target; (*colloq.*) Aunt Sally; (*colloq.*) — **d'uovo**, high brow, egghead.
†**testata**, *n.f.* (*Rocketry*) Warhead. — **atomica**, atomic warhead; — **nucleare**, nuclear warhead.
tettarella, *n.f.* Rubber teat (on baby's bottle).
†**tetto**, *n.m.* (*colloq.*) Maximum, 'ceiling'. **Prezzo-** —, ceiling price.
tifare, *v.i.* (*Sport*) To support, to root for.
tight, *n.m.* Tight-fitting coat; morning coat, morning-dress.
tintarella, *n.f.* (*colloq.*) Sunburn, tan.
†**tirare**, *v.t.* (*fig.*) — **per le falde (in)**, to drag into.
†**tiratore**, *n.m.* (*Pol.*) **Franco —**, an M.P. who, in a secret ballot, flouts the acknowledged line of his party or the instructions of its whips.
titolazione, *n.f.* The process of milk skimming.
titolista, *n.m.* (*Journalism*) Sub-editor who provides suitable titles for articles etc.
tombarolo, *n.m.* (*colloq.*) (*Central Italy*) illegal digger of ancient Etruscan tombs.
tombino, *n.m.* Man-hole.
†**topo**, *n.m.* (*fig.*) — **d'auto**, thief who steals from parked cars.
topologia [topologIa], *n.f.* Topology.
toponomastica [toponomAstica], *n.f.* Study of place names, toponymy.
†**torre**, *n.f.* (*fig.*) — **d'avorio**, ivory tower.
tosatrice, *n.f.* Clipper (for sheep shearing). — **per prati**, lawn mower.
tossicomania [tossicomanIa], *n.f.* Drug addiction, toxicomania.
tossicosi, *n.f.* (*Med.*) Toxicosis, toxemia.
tostapane, *n.m.* Electric toaster.
totalizzare, *v.t.* To reach a total of. **Ha totalizzato sei vincite**, he has reached a total of six wins.
tracimare, *v.i.* To overflow.
†**traliccio**, *n.m.* Electricity pylon.
transistore, *n.m.* Transistor.
transumanza, *n.f.* Transhumance.
trapezista, *n.m.* Trapeze artist.
†**trasferta**, *n.f.* (*Sport*) **In —**, away.
†**tratta**, *n.f.* — **delle bianche**, white slave traffic.
traumatologia [traumatologIa], *n.f.* Traumatology.
travestitismo, *n.m.* Transvestism.
travettopoli, *n.f.* (*colloq.*) Rome.
treninista, *n.m.* Toy railways enthusiast; maker of model railways.
†**triangolo**, *n.m.* (*colloq.*) **Il — industriale**, the part of Italy between Turin, Milan and Genoa.
tribale, *a.* Tribal.
tricologia [tricologIa], *n.f.* Trichology.
tricologo [tricOlogo], *n.m.* Trichologist.
tridimensionale, *a.* Three-dimensional.
trionfalismo, *n.m.* Triumphalism.
tropicalista, *n.m.* (*Med.*) Specialist in tropical diseases.
†**tuffatore**, *n.m.* (*Aviat.*) Dive bomber.
tuffistica [tuffIstica], *n.f.* (*Sport*) The art of diving.
turboelica [turboElica], *n.f.* Turbo-prop. **Aeroplano a —**, turbo-prop plane.

turbonave, *n.f.* Turbine-driven ship.
turboreattore, *n.m.* Turbo-jet plane.
turistizzare, *v.t.* To provide with amenities for tourists.

U

ufficialessa, *n.f.* (*Mil.*) Woman officer.
†**ugola**, *n.f.* (*fig.*) — **d'oro**, golden voice.
ultimativo, *a.* In the nature of an ultimatum.
ultracongelamento, *n.m.* Quick-freezing; deep-freezing.
ultrasonico [ultrasOnico], *a.* Supersonic.
ultrasuono, *n.m.* (*Phys.*) Ultra-sound.
†**undici**, *n.m.* (*colloq.*) Soccer team, soccer eleven.
unicamerale, *a.* (*Pol.*) Having a single Chamber *or* House, unicameral.
unifamiliare, *a.* For a single family. **Una casa —**, a single family dwelling.
unpista, *n.m.* Air-raid warden.
uranista, *n.m.* Male homosexual.
urbanista, *n.m.* Town-planning expert *or* specialist.
urbanizzare, *v.t.* To urbanize.
urgenzare, *v.t.* To treat *or* consider as urgent.
uricemia [uricemIa], *n.f.* (*Med.*) Lithaemia.
†**urlatore**, *n.m.* (*colloq.*) Brash singer.
utilitaria [utilitAria], *n.f.* (*Motor.*) Light car; utility car, brake.
uxorio, *a.* Of a wife; wifelike, wifely; uxorious.

V

valutario [valutArio], *a.* Pertaining to money *or* currency.
vanificare, *v.t.* To foil, to baffle; to frustrate.
varietista, *n.m.* (*Theat.*) Variety artist.
vaselina, *n.f.* Vaseline (*reg. trade name*).
†**vedere**, *v.t.* (*colloq.*) **Non lo posso —!** I can't stand him!
†**vedetta**, *n.f.* (*colloq.*) Stage *or* screen star, vedette.
vedutista, *n.m.* Landscape painter.
†**vendere**, *v.t.* (*fig.*) — **la pelle dell'orso prima di prenderlo**, to count one's chickens before they are hatched.
ventisettino, *n.m.* (*hum.*) Employee (esp. whitecollar worker) who anxiously looks forward to the 27th day of the month (i.e. pay day).
verbalismo, *n.m.* Verbiage; empty verbosity.
verdello, *n.m.* A special kind of lemon which ripens between May and September.
†**vero**, *a.* (*colloq.*) — **e proprio**, real, genuine, out and out.
†**vertice**, *n.m.* (*Pol.*) **Incontro, conferenza al —**, summit meeting *or* conference.
†**vessillo**, *n.m.* (*Naut.*) — **di comodo**, flag of convenience.
vetrinista, *n.m.* (*slang*) Shop-lifter.
vetrinistica [vetrinIstica], *n.f.* The art of window dressing.
viabile [viAbile], *a.* Viable, workable.
vibrafono [vibrAfono], *n.m.* (*Mus.*) Vibraphone.
video [vIdeo], *n.m.* Television screen.
videofono [videOfono], *n.m.* Videophone.
virale, *a.* (*Med.*) Viral.
virologia [virologIa], *n.f.* (*Med.*) Virology.
virosi, *n.f.* (*Med.*) Virosis.
visualizzare, *v.t.* To present a clear picture (of); to visualize.
vitaiolo, *n.m.* Viveur.
vitalizzare, *v.t.* To vitalize; to stir up.
vitaminico [vitamInico], *a.* Vitaminic.
vitellone, *n.m.* Idle and pleasure-loving young man, playboy.
vittimismo, *n.m.* Victimization; posing as a victim; persecution complex.
vittimizzare, *v.t.* To victimize.
vivacizzare, *v.t.* To enliven, to make more exciting (or interesting).
vivanderia [vivanderIa], *n.f.* (*Mil.*) Canteen.
vocazionale, *a.* Vocational.
†**volere**, *v.t.i.* (*colloq.*) **Ci vorrà del bello e del buono per**, it will be very difficult to, it will take a lot of doing to; (*colloq.*) **volerne a qualcuno**, to have a down on *or* grudge against s.o.
volino, *n.m.* (*slang*) Theft by snatching and running away.
†**volo**, *n.m.* (*Aviat.*) — **a vela**, gliding.

X

xerografia [xerografIa], *n.f.* Xerography.

Z

zembo, (*Billiards*) Twist, screw (on the ball).
zembo, zembuto, *a.* Distorted; deformed.
†**zero**, *n.m.* (*colloq.*) **Rapare a —**, to cut s.o.'s hair very short, to crop.
zitellismo, zitellonismo, *n.m.* Sour *or* embittered attitude; old-maidishness.
zonale, *a.* Zonal.
zonizzare, *v.t.* To zone.
†**zucchero**, *n.m.* — **filato**, candy floss.

English-Italian Appendix

(containing many new and current Americanisms)

A

abomasum [æbə'meisəm], *n.* Abomaso, *m.*
abrasive [ə'breisiv], *a.* Abrasivo; (*fig.*) ruvido, burbero; scorbutico.
abreaction [æbri'ækʃən], *n.* Abreazione, *f.*
†absorbent, *a.* (*Am.*) **— cotton** [cp. **cotton-wool**].
accessorize [æk'sesəraiz], *v.t.* (*Am.*) Provvedere d'accessori, equipaggiare.
acclimate ['æklimeit], *v.t.* (*Am.*) [cp. **acclimatize**].
†ace, *n.* (*fig.*) **To have an — up one's sleeve,** tenere una grossa carta in riserva.
acrophony [a'krɔfoni], *n.* (*Am.*) Trascrizione fonetica, *f.*
acrotheater ['ækroθiətəɹ], *n.* (*Am.*) Rappresentazioni acrobatiche e drammatiche, *f.pl.*
activation [ækti'veiʃən], *n.* Attivazione, *f.*
activist ['æktivist], *n.* (*Pol.*) Attivista, *m.f.*
†actor, *n.* (*Theat.*) **Supporting —,** attore di seconda parte, *m.*
actualize ['æktjuəlaiz], *v.t.* Realizzare; (*fig.*) far rivivere; (*fig.*) descrivere al vivo.
ad [æd], *n.* Avviso pubblicitario, *m.* (forma abbreviata di **advertisement**).
ad-lib [æd'lib], *v.t.i.* (*colloq.*) Improvvisare (soprattutto nel parlare in pubblico, alla radio, ecc.).
adman ['ædmæn], *n.* Esperto di pubblicità, pubblicitario, *m.*
admass ['ædmæs], *n.* Massa uniforme di uomini, di scarsa intelligenza e originalità, suggestionata dalla propaganda politica o pubblicitaria e dedita agli spettacoli televisivi, *f.*
†adviser, *n.* (*Am.*) [cp. **tutor**].
†aerial, *a.* **— photography,** aerofotografia, *f.*
†after, *prep.* (*Am.*) **Half — two** [cp. **past**]; **— -effect,** effetto ritardato, *m.*; **— -growth,** guaime, *m.* [cp. **aftermath**].
afterburning ['ɑːftəɹbəɹniŋ], *n.* Postcombustione, *f.*
†agate, *n.* (*Am.*) [cp. **ruby**].
†age, *n.* **— -old,** antichissimo, vecchissimo.
aggro ['ægrou], *n.* (*slang*) attacco, *m.*, rissa, *f.* (forse forma abbreviata di **aggression**).
agitpropist ['ædʒitprɔpist], *n.* (*Am.*) [cp. **activist**].
†air, *n.* **— corridor,** aerovia, *f.*; (*Mil.*) **— drop,** atterraggio di paracadutisti, *m.*; **— -minded,** che ama volare; **— -raid shelter,** rifugio antibomba, *m.*; (*Aviat*) **— strip,** pista d'atterraggio temporanea o di fortuna, *f.*; (*Radio*) **on the —,** in onda.
airglow ['ɛəɹglou], *n.* (*Am.*) Chiarore notturno, *m.*
airlift ['ɛəɹlift], *n.* Ponte aereo, *m.*
†aisle, *n.* (*Am.*) [cp. **gangway**]. (*Am.*) **— -sitter,** critico teatrale, *m.*
†alcohol, *n.* (*Am.*) **— -lamp** [cp. **spirit-lamp**].
†alibi, *n.* (*fig.*) **Cast-iron —,** alibi di ferro, *m.*
†all, *adv.* (*colloq.*) **— in —,** tutto sommato, in complesso; **— in,** tutto compreso; stremato, spossato. || *a.* **— -night,** notturno.
allergic [ə'ləːɹdʒik], *a.* Allergico.
allergy ['æləɹdʒi], *n.* Allergia, *f.*
†alp, *v.t.i.* (*Am.*) Scalare; arrampicarsi.
aluminum [ə'ljuːminum], *n.* (*Am.*) [cp. **aluminium**].
alumnus (pl. **alumni**) [ə'lʌmnəs, ə'lʌmni], *n.* (*Am.*) Ex-studente universitario, *m.*
ambiance, *n.* [cp. **ambience**].
ambience ['æmbiəns], *n.* Ambiente, *m.* (morale, sociale, ecc.).
ambivalent [æm'bivələnt], *a.* Ambivalente.
†American, *a.* (*Am.*) **— plan** [cp. **inclusive charge**].
amorist ['æmərist], *n.* (*Lit.*) Uomo o donna galante, *m.f.*
amperage ['æmpəridʒ], *n.* Amperaggio, *m.*
amphoric [æm'fɔrik], *a.* (*Med.*) Anforico.
anabatic [ænə'bætik], *a.* (*Med., Meteor.*) Anabatico.
†angry, *a.* (*colloq.*) **— young man,** giovane arrabbiato contro il mondo, *m.*
animalier [ænimə'liəɹ], *n.* (*Am.*) Pittore o scultore di animali, animalista, *m.*
anodize ['ænədaiz], *v.t.* Anodizzare.
anodizing, *n.* Anodizzazione, *f.*
anorak ['ænəræk], *n.* Pelliccia di stile groenlandese, impermeabile e col cappuccio, *f.*
†answer, *n.* Rimedio, *m.* **The — to a rising crime rate is a larger and better organized police force,** il rimedio a un aumento di delinquenza è una polizia più numerosa e meglio organizzata.
antibiotic [æntibai'ɔtik], *n.a.* (*Med.*) Antibiotico, *m.*
anti-semitism, *n.* Antisemitismo, *m.*
anti-skid, *a.* (*Motor.*) Antisdrucciolevole; antislittante.
apartheid [ə'pɑːɹtait], *n.* Apartheid, *f.*, segregazione, *f.*
†apartment, *n.* (*Am.*) Appartamento, alloggio, *m.*
†appeasement, *n.* (*Pol.*) Politica distensiva, *f.*, distensionismo, *m.*
†apron, *n.* Superficie per parcheggio di aerei, *f.*
†aptitude, *n.* **— test,** esame (*m.*) o prova (*f.*) d'idoneità.
aquacade ['ækwəkeid], *n.* (*Am.*) Spettacolo sportivo acquatico, *m.* (nuoto, tuffo, ecc.).
†armament, *n.* **Armaments race,** corsa agli armamenti, *f.*
†armour, *n.* (*Mil.*) Carri armati, *m.pl.*
arsonist ['ɑːɹsənist], *n.* (*Am.*) Chi causa un incendio doloso, incendiario, *m.*
†aside, *adv.* (*Am.*) **— from,** oltre a, a parte.
assiduate [ə'sidjuːeit], *n.* (*Am.*) Seguace, assiduo, *m.*

astrogator ['æstrəgeitəɹ], *n.* (*Am.*) [cp. **astronaut**].
astronaut ['æstrənɔ:t], *n.* Astronauta, *m.*
astronautics [æstrə'nɔ:tiks], *n.pl.* Astronautica, *f.*
astrophysics [æstro'fisiks], *n.pl.* Astrofisica, *f.*
astroturf ['æstrotə:ɹf], *n.* (*Am.*) Erba finta, erba di plastica, *f.*
†**atomic,** *a.* **— -powered,** atomico.
atomize ['ætəmaiz], *v.t.* Atomizzare.
attaboy! ['ætəbɔi], *inter.* (*Am.*) Bravo! Coraggio!
audiovisual [ɔ:dio'vizjuəl], *a.* Audiovisivo.
authoritarianism [ɔ:θɔri'tɛəriənizm], *n.* (*Pol.*) Autoritarismo, *m.*
autism ['ɔ:tizm], *n.* (*Med.*) Autismo, *m.*
autistic [ɔ:'tistik], *a.* Autista.
autocade ['ɔ:tokeid], *n.* (*Am.*) [cp. **motorcade**].
automat ['ɔ:təmæt], *n.* (*Am.*) Ristorante con distribuzione automatica delle vivande, *f.*
automate ['ɔ:təmeit], *v.t.* Automatizzare.
†**automatic,** *a.* (*Motor.*) **— gear change,** cambio automatico, *m.*; **— record changer,** cambio automatico dei dischi, *m.*
autosled ['ɔ:tosled], *n.* (*Am.*) Autoslitta, *f.*
†**away,** *adv.* (*Sport*) **To play —,** giocare in trasferta.

B

babysit ['beibisit], *v.i.* Accudire ai bambini (in assenza dei genitori).
babysitter ['beibisitəɹ], *n.* Curabimbi, *m.f.*, bambinaio, *m.*, bambinaia, *f.*
†**background,** *a.* Di sfondo; (*Cinema*) **— music,** commento musicale, *m.*
†**backlash,** *n.* (*colloq.*) Reazione esasperata o violenta che segue a un eccesso (politico, sociale, ecc.), *f.*
backlog ['bæklɔg], *n.* Ritardo, *m.*; affari non sbrigati a tempo, *m.pl.*
bafflegab ['bæflgæb], *n.* (*Am.*) Gergo burocratico, *m.*
†**baggage,** *n.* (*Am.*) **— car** [cp. **luggage van**].
†**balcony,** *n.* (*Am.*) [cp. **dress circle**].
†**ball,** *n.* (*Am.*) [cp. **baseball**].
ballistic [bə'listik], *a.* (*Mil.*) Balistico. **— missile,** missile balistico, *m.*
ballyhoo ['bælihu:], *n.* (*Am.*) Propaganda esagerata, *f.*; pubblicità volgare, *f.*
baloney, boloney [bə'louni], *n.* (*Am.*) Balle, sciocchezze, fandonie, *f.pl.*
†**band,** *n.* (*colloq.*) **To climb on the — -wagon,** associarsi a un'impresa che promette bene.
†**bank,** *v.t.* (*colloq.*) **To — on,** contare su, fare assegnamento su.
barbiturate [bɑ:ɹ'bitjurit], *n.* Barbiturico, *m.* **— poisoning,** avvelenamento da barbiturici, *m.*
barkeep ['bɑ:ɹki:p], **barkeeper, bartender,** *n.* (*Am.*) [cp. **barman**].
†**barn,** *n.* (*Am.*) [cp. **stable**].
barney ['bɑ:ɹni], *n.* (*colloq.*) Diverbio, battibecco, *m.*; putiferio, *m.*; baldoria, *f.*
barysphere ['bærisfiəɹ], *n.* Barisfera, *f.*
†**basement,** *n.* **— flat,** appartamento al seminterrato, *m.*
bathyscaphe ['bæθiskeif], *n.* (*Am.*) Batiscafo, *m.*
†**battle,** *n.* (*colloq.*) **— -axe,** donna battagliera, virago, *f.*
beachwear ['bi:tʃwɛəɹ], *n.* Abiti da spiaggia, *m.pl.*
†**beacon,** *n.* **Radio** or **wireless —,** radiofaro, *m.*
†**bean,** *n.* (*Am.*) Testa, *f.*; (*fig.*) quattrino, centesimo, *m.*
beano ['bi:nou], *n.* Festa, *f.*; bagordo, *m.*
†**beat,** *n.*, **beats, beatniks** ['bi:tniks], *n.pl.* Gioventù bruciata, *f.*
beautician [bju:'tiʃən], *n.* (*Am.*) Cosmetista, *m.f.*
†**beef,** *v.i.* (*colloq.*) Lagnarsi, brontolare.
bellhop ['belhɔp] **(boy),** *n.* (*Am.*) [cp. **page**].
†**belt,** *n.* (*Town planning*) **Green —,** fascia verde, *f.* || *v.i.* (*colloq.*) **— up!** taci! smettila!
†**bend,** *n.* (*colloq.*) **Round the —,** fuor di sè, matto, pazzo.
†**benefit,** *n.* **Maternity —,** indennità di maternità, *f.*; **sickness —,** indennità di malattia, *f.*
benthoscope ['benθoskoup], *n.* Specie di batisfera, *f.*
†**bet,** *n.* (*fig.*) **A safe —,** una cosa praticamente sicura, *f.*
†**bid,** *n.* (*colloq.*) Tentativo, *m.*
bifocal [bai'foukəl], *a.* Bifocale. || *n.pl.* (*colloq.*) Lenti bifocali, *f.pl.*
bikini [bi'ki:ni], *n.* Bikini, *m.*
billboard ['bilbɔ:ɹd], *n.* (*Am.*) [cp. **hoarding**].
†**bin,** *n.* Pattumiera, *f.*; **pedal- —,** pattumiera a pedale, *f.*
biogenetic [baiodʒə'netik], *a.* Biogenetico.
biosynthesis [baio'sinθəsis], *n.* Biosintesi, *f.*
bipartisan [baipɑ:ɹti'zæn], *a.* Bipartitico.
†**bird,** *n.* (*colloq.*) Ragazza, *f.*; (*colloq.*) pupa, *f.* (*colloq.*) **A little — told me,** me l'ha detto l'uccellino (quando si vuol tacere la fonte di qualche informazione).
bitchy ['bitʃi], *a.* (*colloq.*) Malizioso, maligno.
bituminize ['bitjuminaiz], *v.t.* Bitumare, bituminare.
blacketeer [blækə'tiəɹ], *n.* (*Am.*) Borsaro nero, borsanerista, *m.*
black-list, *n.* (*fig.*) Lista **nera,** *f.* **To be on the —,** essere nella lista nera. || *v.t.* Mettere sulla lista nera.
blah-blah ['blɑ:blɑ:], *n.* (*Am.*) Paroloni, *m.pl.*; sciocchezze, fesserie, *f.pl.*
†**blanket,** *n.* **Electric —,** coperta-termofero, coperta elettrica, *f.*
blast-off, *n.* Lancio (di un missile), *m.*
blimp [blimp], *n.* (*Pol.*) Conservatore ottuso e retrivo, passatista, *m.*
†**blond, blonde,** *a.* **Ash —,** biondo cenere; **platinum —,** biondo platino.
†**blood,** *n.* (*Med.*) **— bank,** banca del sangue, *f.*; (*fig.*) **— bath,** eccidio, *m.*, ecatombe, *f.*; **— clot,** grumo di sangue, *m.*; **— donor,** donatore di sangue, *m.*; **— group, gruppo** sanguigno, *m.*
†**bloody,** *a.* (*vulg.*) **— -minded,** maldisposto; refrattario.
blooper ['blu:pəɹ], *n.* (*Am.*) Grosso sbaglio, strafalcione, sfrondone, *m.*
†**blot,** *v.t.* (*fig.*) **To — one's copy-book,** fare uno sproposito, fare una topica, farle grosse.
blowhard ['blouhɑ:ɹd], *n.* (*Am.*) Spaccone, fanfarone, *m.*
blowmobile ['bloumobi:l], *n.* (*Am.*) Slitta a motore, *f.* [cp. **autosled**].
†**blue,** *a.* (*colloq.*) Osceno, pornografico. **— film,** film *cochon*, *m.*

blue-pencil, *v.t.* Correggere, fare tagli in o su, radiare.
bo [bou], *n.* (*Am.*) Amico, compare, *m.*
†**body, bod,** *n.* (*colloq.*) Persona qualunque, *f.*; individuo, *m.*; (*fig.*) **over my dead body,** son pronto a farmi ammazzare per impedirlo.
bodywork ['bɔdiwəːɹk], *n.* (*Motor.*) Carrozzeria, *f.*
boffin ['bɔfin], *n.* [cp. **backroom boy**].
boiler-suit, *n.* Tuta, *f.*
boloney, *n.* [cp. **baloney**].
†**bomb,** *n.* **Flying —,** bomba volante, *f.* [cp. **doodle-bug**].
bonanza [bə'nænzə], *n.* (*fig.*) Ricchezza, *f.*; tesoro, *m.*; abbondanza, *f.*
†**bone,** *v.t.* (*Am.*) **— up** [cp. **swot**].
bone-idle, *a.* Pigrone.
boner ['bounəɹ], *n.* (*Am.*) [cp. **howler**].
boob [buːb], *n.* (*Am.*) [cp. **booby**]. || *v.t.i.* (*colloq.*) Sbagliare, fare uno sproposito, prendere una cantonata.
†**book,** *n.* (*colloq.*) **To get one's books,** essere licenziato; **— -plate,** exlibris, *m.*
booksie ['buksi], *a.* (*Am. colloq.*) Versato nella letteratura, amante dei libri.
†**boost,** *v.t.* (*Mech.*) Aumentare, spingere, elevare.
booster ['buːstəɹ], *n.* (*Am.*) Esagerato, scalmanato, *m.*
†**boot,** *n.* **Gum boots,** stivaloni di gomma, *m.pl.*
booze [buːz], *n.* (*colloq.*) Bevanda alcoolica, *f.*; sbevazzata, *f.*
bottle-feeding, *n.* Allattamento artificiale, *m.*
bottleneck ['bɔtlnek], *n.* Collo di bottiglia, *m.*; (*fig.*) ingorgo, intasamento, *m.*
boulevard ['buːləvɑːɹd], *n.* (*Am.*) [cp. **arterial road**].
†**bouncer,** *n.* (*colloq.*) Gorilla, *m. inv.*
†**bouquet,** *n.* (*fig.*) Lode, *f.*; complimento, *m.*
†**boy,** *n.* (*colloq.*) **Backroom —,** scienziato o perito alle dipendenze di un ministero, *m.*; **old —,** vecchio alunno di una scuola, *m.* (soprattutto di una **public school**); (*colloq.*) **the old — network,** il cameratismo e anche il clientelarismo che si verificano frequentemente tra vecchi compagni della stessa scuola; **wide —,** truffatore, trafficante disonesto, *m.*
bra [brɑː], *n.* (*colloq.*) Reggipetto, *m.*
†**brain,** *n.* (*colloq.*) **— -child,** parto del cervello o della mente, *m.*, pensata, *f.*; **— -washing,** lavaggio del cervello, *m.*
†**brake,** *n.* **Band —,** freno a nastro, *m.*; **foot —,** freno a pedale; **hand —,** freno a mano; **lever —,** freno a leva; **screw-spindle —,** freno a vite.
†**bread,** *n.* (*slang*) Denaro, *m.*
†**break,** *n.* (*colloq.*) Successo, *m.*, riuscita, *f.*; bazza, *f.* || *v.i.* **To — even,** pareggiare il bilancio.
breakdown ['breikdaun], *n.* Analisi, *f.*; classificazione, *f.*
breathalyzer ['breθəlaizəɹ], *n.* Apparecchio per controllare il fiato del presunto automobilista ubbriaco, *m.*
breathtaking ['breθteikiŋ], *a.* Che toglie il respiro; meraviglioso, stupendo.
briefcase ['briːfkeis], *n.* Borsa, *f.*
†**brief,** *n.* **briefs,** *n.pl.* Mutandine, *f.pl.*
†**brightness,** *n.* (*TV*) **— control,** controllo della luminosità, *m.*
brinkmanship ['briŋkmənʃip], *n.* (*Pol.*) Equilibrismo, *m.* (*in international crises*).
brisling ['brizliŋ], *n.* (*Ichth.*) Spratto, *m.*
†**broad,** *n.* (*Am. slang*) Ragazza, compagna, *f.*; puttana, *f.*
†**broadcloth,** *n.* (*Am.*) [cp. **poplin**].
broiler ['brɔiləɹ], *n.* Pollastro da arrostire, *m.*
†**brown,** *v.t.* (*colloq.*) **Browned-off,** annoiato, giù, depresso [cp. **fed-up**].
brunch [brʌntʃ], (*contr.* di **breakfast** e **lunch**) Pasto che sostituisce la prima e la seconda colazione, *m.*
†**brush,** *v.t.* (*colloq.*) **— -off,** ripulsa, *f.*; brusco rifiuto, *m.*
†**bubble,** *n.* **— bath,** bagno di schiuma, *m.*; **— -gum,** gomma da masticare che fa le bolle come quelle del sapone, *f.*
†**buck,** *n.* (*Am.*) Dollaro, *m.*; (*fig.*) **to pass the —,** scaricare la responsabilità addosso a un altro.
†**bud,** *n.* **Taste —,** calice gustativo, *m.*, papilla gustativa, *f.*
bud, *n.* (*Am. colloq.*) Amico, compagno, *m.* [cp. **buddy**].
†**budget,** *n.* **To be on a —,** essere costretto a fare economie.
†**bug,** *n.* (*Am. colloq.*) **Fire —,** piromane, *m.*
†**build,** *v.t.* **— -up,** accumulamento, *m.*; preparativi, *m.pl.*; (*Mech.*) **built-in,** incastrato, incorporato.
built-up, *a.* **— area,** agglomerato urbano, centro abitato, *m.*
†**bulletin,** *n.* (*Am.*) **— board** [cp. **notice-board**].
bumf, bumph [bʌmf], *n.* (*slang*) Carta igienica, *f.*; (*fig.*) cartacce, scartoffie, *f.pl.*
†**bunch,** *n.* (*Am.*) Comitiva, *f.*, gruppo, *m.*; combriccola, *f.*
burn-out, *n.* Bruciatura, *f.*
burp [bəːɹp], *v.i.* Ruttare.
†**business,** *n.* (*Am.*) **— suit** [cp. **lounge-suit**]; (*colloq.*) **nobody's —,** inqualificabile, irreferibile (*allusione, generalmente scherzosa, a cose dette o fatte che se considerano scandalose o altrimenti deplorevoli*); **like nobody's —,** eccessivamente, smoderatamente.
businessman, *n.* Uomo d'affari, *m.*; affarista, *m.*
busker ['bʌskəɹ], *n.* Guitto che recita nella strada, *m.*
†**butterfly,** *n.* (*colloq.*) **Butterflies in the stomach,** formicolio (o crampi) allo stomaco, *m.* (*m.pl.*) (per paura o nervosismo).
†**buzz,** *n.* (*Am.*) **— saw** [cp. **circular saw**].

C

†**cab,** *n.* (*colloq.*) Tassì, *m.*
cabette [kæ'bet], *n.* (*Am.*) Donna autista, *f.*
†**cabin,** *n.* **— class,** seconda classe, *f.*
cablese [keib'liːz], *n.* (*Am.*) Cifrario per trasmissioni radiotelegrafiche, *m.*
cahoots [kə'huːts], *n.pl.* **To be in — with,** far lega con.
†**cake,** *n.* **Cheese- —,** torta di formaggio, *f.*; (*fig.*) fotografie di donne nude o seminude (stelle del cinema, ballerine ecc.) in certe riviste illustrate, *f.pl.*; (*colloq.*) **a piece of —,** come bere un bicchier d'acqua.
calibration [kæli'breiʃən], *n.* Calibratura, calibrazione, *f.*

†**call**, *n.* — **-girl**, ragazza-squillo, *f.*; (*Am.*) — **-pay**, paga sindacale, *f.*
†**camp**, *a.* (*slang*) Che è tipico di omosessuali (parole, frasi, gesti, vestiti, ecc.).
campanologist [kæmpə'nɔlədʒist], *n.* Campanologo, *m.*
campanology, *n.* Campanologia, *f.*
campus ['kæmpəs], *n.* (*Am.*) Giardino o recinto intorno a un collegio, *m.*
†**candy**, *n.* (*Am.*) [cp. **sweets**]; — **floss**, zucchero filato, *m.*; (*Am.*) — **-leg**, giovanotto ricco, *m.*; (*Am.*) — **-store** [cp. **sweet-shop**].
cannabis ['kænəbis], *n.* Canapa indiana, cannabis, *f.*
cannibalize ['kænibəlaiz], *v.t.* (*colloq.*) Smantellare una o più macchine difettose allo scopo di adoperarne le parti per costruire una nuova.
canoodle [kə'nu:dl], *v.i.* (*Am. colloq.*) [cp. **neck**, *v.i.*].
can-opener, *n.* (*Am.*) [cp. **tin-opener**].
capacitance [kə'pæsitəns], *n.* (*Elec.*) Capacità, capacitanza, *f.*; **input** —, capacità d'ingresso, *f.*
†**car**, *n.* — **-crash**, scontro, tamponamento automobilistico, *m.*; — **park**, autoparcheggio, *m.*; **Dodgem cars**, autoscontri, *m.pl.*; **vintage** —, vecchia automobile (storicamente interessante), *f.*
†**carbon**, *n.* — **copy**, copia a carbone (di macchina da scrivere), *f.*; (*fig.*) cosa, concreta o astratta, del tutto identica a un'altra, *f.* (progetto, delitto, ecc.).
carborundum [kɑ:ɹbə'rʌndəm], *n.* Carborundo, carborundum, *m.*
cardiogram ['kɑ:ɹdiogræm], *n.* (*Med.*) Cardiogramma, *m.*
cardiograph, *n.* (*Med.*) Cardiografo, *m.*
cardiography [kɑ:ɹdi'ɔgrəfi], *n.* (*Med.*) Cardiografia, *f.*
cardiologist [kɑ:ɹdi'ɔlədʒist], *n.* (*Med.*) Cardiologo, *m.*
cardiology, *n.* (*Med.*) Cardiologia, *f.*
cardiovascular [kɑ:ɹdio'væskjuləɹ], *a.* (*Med.*) Cardiovascolare; — **system**, apparato cardiovascolare, *m.*
†**career**, *n.* — **girl**, carrierista, arrivista, *f.*
carfuffle, curfuffle [kə'fʌfl], *n.* scenata, *f.*, putiferio, *m.*
carom ['kærɔm], *n.* (*Am.*) Carambola (al biliardo), *f.* ‖ *v.i.* Far carambola (al biliardo).
†**carpet**, *n.* — **bombing**, bombardamento a tappeto, *m.*; (*fig.*) **on the** —, rimproverato, sgridato, punito; (*fig.*) **red — treatment**, accoglienza di gala fatta a un personaggio importante, *f.* ‖ *v.t.* (*fig.*) Rimproverare, punire.
carport ['kɑ:ɹpɔ:ɹt], *n.* Autorimessa per una macchina sola, *f.*
†**case**, *n.* — **history**, (*Med.*) cartella clinica, *f.*; (*fig.*) curriculum vitæ, *m.*; (*colloq.*) vita, opera, e miracoli.
†**cash**, *v.t.* (*colloq.*) **To — in on**, lucrare (su), approfittare (di).
cassette [kæ'set], *n.* Cassetta, *f.*
†**cat**, *n.* (*Am.*) — **-nip**, [cp. **cat-mint**].
catabolism [kə'tæbəlizm], *n.* (*Biol.*) Catabolismo, *m.*
catalyst ['kætəlist], *n.* Catalizzatore, *m.*
cataplectic [kætə'plektik], *a.* (*Med.*) Cataplettico.
cataplexy ['kætəpleksi], *n.* (*Med.*) Cataplessia, *f.*
catchment ['kætʃmənt], *n.* — **area** or **basin**, bacino idrografico o imbrifero, *m.*
†**cauliflower**, *n.* (*Boxing*) — **ears**, orecchi sformati dai pugni, *m.pl.*
†**cautionary**, *a.* — **tale**, racconto o fatto che serve da ammonimento, *m.*
cavitation [kævi'teiʃən], *n.* Cavitazione, *f.*
†**central**, *n.* (*Am.*) [cp. **telephone exchange**].
ceramel [sə'ræməl], *n.* (*Am.*) Materiale composto di ceramica e metallo, *m.*
cervix ['sə:ɹviks], *n.* Cervice, *f.*
chair-lift, *n.* Seggiovia, *f.*
†**change**, *n.* (*fig.*) **To get no — out of someone**, non ottenere niente da uno; (*fig.*) **a wind of** —, una ventata di cambiamenti, *f.*, un vento foriero di novità, *m.*
charisma [kə'ri zmə], *n.* Carisma, *m.*; fascino, *m.*
charismatic [kæriz'mætik], *a.* Carismatico.
†**chat**, *v.i.* (*colloq.*) **To — up**, parlare coll'intenzione di flirtare o amoreggiare; **to — up a bird**, parlare con una ragazza coll'idea di 'agganciarla'.
†**check**, *n.* (*Am.*) [cp. **bill, cheque**]; (*Am.*) — **-list**, lista di controllo, *f.*; (*Am.*) — **-up**, controllo, *m.*, verifica, *f.*
checkers ['tʃekəɹz], *n.* (*Am.*) [cp. **draughts**].
checkpoint, *n.* Posto di controllo, *m.*
checkroom, *n.* (*Am.*) Deposito bagagli, *m.*
†**cheer**, *n.* (*Am.*) **Bronx** —, pernacchio, *m.* [cp. **raspberry**].
†**cheese**, *n.* — **biscuit**, salatino, *m.*; — **straws**, bastoncini al formaggio, *m.pl.*; **toasted** —, toast o tosto al formaggio, *m.*
†**chemical**, *a.* — **engineering**, ingegneria chimica, *f.*; — **plant**, impianto chimico, *m.*; — **warfare**, guerra chimica, *f.*
†**chip**, *n.* (*Games*) Gettone, *m.*; (*fig.*) **when the chips are down**, quando si giunge al fatto concreto, alla prova dei fatti, alla resa dei conti; — **-resistant**, antischeggia, *inv.*
chipmunk ['tʃipmʌŋk], *n.* Scoiattolo americano, *m.*
cholesterol [kə'lestərɔl], *n.* Colesterolo, *m.*
choosey ['tʃu:zi], *a.* Di difficile accontentatura, esigente.
chores [tʃɔ:ɹz], *n.pl.* Lavori domestici, compiti della massaia, *m.pl.*
chromogenic [kroumo'dʒenik], *a.* (*Biol.*) Cromogeno.
chromosome ['krouməsoum], *n.* (*Med.*) Cromosomo, *m.*
†**chuck**, *n.* (*Am.*) — **-wagon** [cp. **vehicle**].
chucker-out, *n.* (*colloq.*) Gorilla, *m. inv.*
chute [ʃu:t], *n.* (*Am.*) Paracadute, *m.* [cp. **parachute**].
chutist ['ʃu:tist], *n.* (*Am.*) Paracadutista, *m.* [cp. **parachutist**].
†**cigar**, *n.* (*Am.*) — **store** [cp. **tobacconist's (shop)**].
†**circle**, *n.* (*Naut.*) **Great — sailing**, rotta ortodromica, *f.*; (*fig.*) **to come full** —, tornare al punto di partenza.
clanger ['klæŋgəɹ], *n.* (*colloq.*) **To drop a** —, fare uno sproposito, prendere una cantonata.
classless ['klɑ:slis], *a.* Senza classi.
†**clear**, *a.* (*fig.*) **In the** —, esente da ogni sospetto; uscito da una situazione difficoltosa; solvibile.
†**click**, *v.t.* **To — one's tongue**, schioccare la lingua.

cliffhanger ['klifhæŋəɹ], *n.* (*fig.*) Situazione estremamente rischiosa o drammatica e penosa, incertezza, *f.*
climactic [klai'mæktik], *a.* Arrivato al suo apogeo.
clinicar ['klinikɑ:ɹ], *n.* (*Am.*) Autoambulanza, autolettiga, *f.*
clinician [kli'niʃən], *n.* (*Am.*) Clinico, *m.*
†**cloak,** *n.* (*colloq.*) **— and dagger,** avventuroso, pieno d'intrigo, rocambolesco.
clobber ['klɔbəɹ], *n.* (*slang*) Roba, *f.*, oggetti, *m.pl.* ‖ *v.t.* Battere, bastonare; (*fig.*) dare addosso a; criticare aspramente, stroncare.
†**club,** *n.* (*colloq.*) **Darby and Joan —,** circolo o sodalizio per vecchi e vecchie, *m.*
†**clue,** *n.* (*colloq.*) **I haven't a —,** non ne so niente, non ne ho la minima idea.
†**cocktail,** *n.* **— cabinet,** (mobile) bar, *m.*; **— dress,** abito da cocktail, *m.*; **— party,** cocktail, *m.*
†**code,** *n.* **Postal —,** codice d'avviamento postale (CAP), *m.*
codeine ['koudi:n], *n.* Codeina, *f.*
codswallop ['kɔdzwɔləp], *n.* (*hum.*) Coglionerie, balle, *f.pl.*
co-ed [kou'ed], *n.* (*Am.*) Ragazza che frequenta una scuola o università mista, *f.*
coeducational [kouedju'keiʃənəl], *a.* Maschile e femminile, misto.
†**coffin,** *n.* (*Am. colloq.*) **— -nail,** sigaretta, *f.*
†**coil,** *n.* **— antenna,** antenna a quadro, *f.*; **— ignition,** accensione a spinterogeno, *f.*
†**coin,** *n.* **— operated,** azionato a moneta.
coincidental [kouinsi'dentl], *a.* Dovuto a una coincidenza.
collage [kɔ'lɑ:ʒ], *n.* Collage, *m.*
†**collect,** *v.t.* (*Am.*) **— on delivery** [cp. **cash on delivery**].
colonialism [kə'louniəlizm], *n.* (*Pol.*) Colonialismo, *m.*
†**colour,** *n.* (*Phot.*) **— filter,** filtro colorato, *m.*
colourcast ['kʌləɹkɑ:st], *n.* (*Am.*) Trasmissione televisiva a colori, *f.*
†**come,** *v.i.* (*colloq.*) **To — unstuck,** rompersi, sfasciarsi; sbagliare; fallire [cp. **to — asunder**].
come-back, *n.* (*Sport*) Ritorno, *m.*
†**commencement,** *n.* (*Am.*) **— -day,** giorno del conferimento dei diplomi, *m.*
†**commercial,** *a.* **— artist,** cartellonista, *m.f.* ‖ *n.* (*Rad.*, *TV*) Pubblicità commerciale, *f.*
commercialization, *n.* Commercializzazione, *f.*
†**commit,** *v.t.* (*Lit.*) **Committed,** impegnato, engagé.
†**common,** *a.* **— denominator,** comun denominatore, *m.* (*also fig.*); **— fraction,** frazione semplice, *f.*; **(European) Common Market,** il mercato comune (europeo), il Mec.
†**commutation,** *n.* (*Am.*) **— ticket** [cp. **season ticket**].
†**commute,** *v.i.* Far la spola tra casa e ufficio.
commuter [kə'mju:təɹ], *n.* Chi fa la spola tra casa e ufficio, *m.f.*, pendolare, *m.f.*
†**compact** ['kɔmpækt], *n.* Portacipria, *m.*
†**compensation,** *n.* (*Pysch.*) Compenso psicologico, *m.*
compère ['kɔmpɛəɹ], *n.* Presentatore, *m.*, presentatrice, *f.* ‖ *v.t.* Presentare (uno spettacolo, una teletrasmissione, ecc.).
competitiveness, *n.* (*Comm.*) Competitività, *f.*
†**compulsive,** *a.* (*Psych.*) Soggetto a impulsi irrefrenabili. **A — drinker,** un uomo rotto al bere, *m.*
computer [kəm'pju:təɹ], *n.* Calcolatrice, *f.*
computerization [kɔmpju:tərai'zeiʃən], *n.* Organizzazione di un'azienda o impresa secondo dati forniti da calcolatrici, *f.*; trasferimento del compito di eseguire calcoli computistici e statistici dalle persone alle calcolatrici, *m.*
†**con,** *v.t.* (*slang*) Truffare, frodare, raggirare. ‖ *n.* Truffa, *f.*, imbroglio, raggiro, *m.*
†**concert,** *n.* **— goer,** chi frequenta i concerti; **— grand,** pianoforte a (gran) coda o da concerto, *m.*
concierge [kɔnsi'ɛəɹʒ], *n.* Portinaio, *m.*, portinaia, *f.*
†**concourse,** *n.* Atrio (di una stazione, di un collegio, o di altro pubblico edifizio), *m.*
concrescence [kən'kresəns], *n.* (*Biol.*) Concrescenza, *f.*
†**conditioned,** *a.* **Air- —,** con aria condizionata.
†**conductor,** *n.* (*Am. Rail.*) [cp. **guard**].
conductorette [kəndʌktə'ret], *n.* (*Am.*) Bigliettaia, *f.*
conicity [kə'nisiti], *n.* Conicità, *f.*
conjunctivitis [kəndʒʌŋkti'vaitis], *n.* (*Med.*) Congiuntivite, *f.*
conman ['kɔnmæn], *n.* (*slang*) Truffatore, imbroglione, *m.*
consortium [kən'sɔ:ɹtiəm], *n.* Consorzio, *m.*, associazione, *f.*
†**consumer,** *n.* **— goods,** beni, generi o articoli di consumo, *m.pl.*; **— spending,** spesa su generi o articoli di consumo, *f.*
†**contact** ['kɔntækt], *n.* **— lenses,** lenti a contatto, *f.pl.*
containment [kən'teinmənt], *n.* (*Pol.*) **— (policy),** tattica di arginamento, *f.*
†**continuity,** *n.* (*Cinema*) Sceneggiatura, *f.*
contraption [kən'træpʃən], *n.* (*colloq.*) Ordigno, congegno, aggeggio, *m.*
conurbation [kɔnəɹ'beiʃən], *n.* Agglomeramento urbano, *m.*
†**convention,** *n.* [cp. **conference**].
†**cooker,** *n.* **Pressure- —,** pentola di Papin, *f.*; digestore, *m.*
†**cool,** *n.* Calma, *f.*; disinvoltura, *f.*
coolant ['ku:lənt], *n.* (Liquido) refrigerante, *m.*
copywriter ['kɔpiraitəɹ], *n.* Copywriter, *m.f.*, redattore pubblicitario, *m.*
corm [kɔ:ɹm], *n.* (*Bot.*) Bulbo, *m.*
†**corn,** *n.* (*Am.*) [cp. **Indian corn, maize**].
†**corner,** *n.* (*Am.*) [cp. **turning**].
cornstarch ['kɔ:ɹnstɑ:ɹtʃ], *n.* (*Am.*) [cp. **corn-flour**].
coronary ['kɔrənəri], *a.* Coronario; **— thrombosis,** trombosi coronarica, *f.*
†**corporation,** *n.* Società, *f.*, ente, *m.*
†**corral,** *n.* (*Am.*) Campo cintato, *m.*
†**correspondence,** *n.* **— course,** corso per corrispondenza, *m.*
cortisone ['kɔ:ɹtizoun], *n.* (*Med.*) Cortisone, *m.*
cosh [kɔʃ], *n.* Sfollagente, *m.* [cp. **truncheon**].
cosmonaut ['kɔzmənɔ:t], *n.* Cosmonauta, *m.*
†**cost,** *n.* (*Econ.*) **— effectiveness,** riduzione al minimo necessario del costo di un'impresa (o di una produzione industriale), *f.*, **— -of-living allowance,** indennità di carovita, *f.*;

— -of-living index, indice del costo della vita, *m.* || *v.i.* (*fig.*) **To — the earth,** costare un occhio.
co-star [ˈkoustɑːɹ], *n.* Attore comprimario, *m.*, attrice comprimaria, *f.*
countdown [ˈkauntdaun], *n.* Conto alla rovescia, *m.* (nel lancio di missili, ecc.).
counter-attack, *n.* Contrattacco, *m.* (*also fig.*); controffensiva, *f.* || *v.t.i.* Contrattaccare; muovere al contrattacco; passare al contrattacco o alla controffensiva.
counter-charge, *n.* Contraccusa, *f.*
†counterfeiter, *n.* (*Am.*) [cp. **coiner**].
Counter-Reformation, *n.* Controriforma, *f.*
†county, *n.* (*Am.*) **— seat** [cp. **county town**].
†cover, *v.t.* (*Am.*) [cp. **report**]. || *n.* **— -charge,** prezzo del coperto, *m.*; (*colloq.*) **— - girl,** ragazza-copertina, *f.*
coyp(o)u [ˈkɔipuː], *n.* Miopotamo, *m.*
†crab, *n.* (*Am.*) Guastafeste, *m.*
crackpot [ˈkrækpɔt], *n.* Pazzo, *m.*; persona stravagante, *f.*
†crash, *a.* (*colloq.*) Di estrema urgenza o emergenza. **— programme,** programma che richiede attuazione immediata, *m.*; **— salvage operation,** opera urgentissima di salvataggio, *f.*
crash-helmet, *n.* Casco, elmetto, *m.*
crash-land, *v.i.* Fare un atterraggio di fortuna.
crash-landing, *n.* Atterraggio di fortuna, *m.*
†cream, *n.* **— bun,** pasticcino con crema o con panna, *m.*; **— cake,** torta alla crema, *f.*; (*fig.*) **it's not all — and honey,** non è tutto rose. || *v.t.* (*fig.*) **To — off,** togliere la parte migliore o gli elementi migliori.
crease-resistant, *a.* Antipiega, antipieghe.
creepage [ˈkriːpidʒ], *n.* (*Elec.*) Dispersione, *f.*
†crew, *n.* (*Am.*) [cp. **team**]; **— -cut,** rapata, rapatura, *f.*
cross-check [krɔsˈtʃek], *v.t.* Controllare attentamente.
cross-fertilization, *n.* (*Bot.*) Fecondazione incrociata o indiretta, *f.*
crummy [ˈkrʌmi], *a.* (*slang*) Scadente, scalcinato.
crush-proof, *a.* [cp. **crease-resistant**].
†cub, *n.* (*Am.*) Aereo leggero, *m.*
†cuff, *n.* **Off the —,** a braccio, ex abrupto. **He was speaking off the —,** egli parlava a braccio.
curette [kjuˈret], *n.* (*Med.*) Raschiatoio, *m.* || *v.t.i.* Eseguire un raschiamento (a).
curler [ˈkəːɹləɹ], *n.* Bigodì, bigodino, *m.*
†curtain, *n.* (*Pol.*) **Bamboo —,** cortina di bambù, *f.*; **iron —,** cortina di ferro, *f.*; (*Theat.*) **— -call,** chiamata (alla ribalta), *f.*
curvaceous [kəːɹˈveiʃəs], *a.* Piena di curve (*girl or woman*); (*fig.*) provocante, appetitosa.
†custom, *n.* (*Am.*) [cp. **bespoke**]; (*Am.*) **— -made** [cp. **made-to-measure**].
†cut, *n.* **— -back,** falcidia, riduzione, *f.* (nelle spese, nei programmi, ecc.); (*Am.*) **— -off,** [cp. **by-pass**].
cybernetics [saibəɹˈnetiks], *n.* Cibernetica, *f.*
cyclocross [ˈsaiklokrɔs], *n.* (*Sport*) Ciclocross, *m.*
cyclotron [ˈsaiklotrɔn], *n.* (*Phys.*) Ciclotrone, *m.*
cystotomy [sisˈtɔtəmi], *n.* (*Med.*) Cistotomia, *f.*
cytolysis [saiˈtɔlisis], *n.* Citolisi, *f.*

D

†daddy, *n.* **Sugar —,** amico o amante anziano di giovane ragazza, *m.*
dagwood [ˈdægwud], *n.* (*Am.*) Sandwich con molti ingredienti, *m.*
†dandy, *a.* (*Am.*) [cp. **tip-top**].
data processing, *n.* Esame (*m.*) o disamina (*f.*) dei dati.
†date, *n.* (*Am. colloq.*) Persona con cui si ha un appuntamento.
†day, *n.* **— nursery,** asilo nido, *m.*
de-activate, *v.t.* Disattivare.
deadline [ˈdedlain], *n.* Ultima data o ora possibile, *f.*; l'ora zero, *f.*
dead-pan [ˈdedpæn], *n.* Attore o attrice senza espressione nel viso, *m.f.* || *a.* Impassibile, senza espressione.
deaf-aid, *n.* (*colloq.*) [cp. **hearing-aid**].
decedent [diˈsiːdənt], *n.* (*Am.*) [cp. **deceased**].
deceleration [diːseləˈreiʃən], *n.* Decelerazione, *f.*
decider [diˈsaidəɹ], *n.* (*colloq.*) Spareggio, *m.*
decimalization [desiməlaiˈzeiʃən], *n.* Adozione del (o riduzione al) sistema decimale, *f.*
declivous [diˈklaivəs], *a.* Declive, in pendenza.
decompress [diːkəmˈpres], *v.t.* Decomprimere.
decompression [diːkəmˈpreʃən], *n.* Decompressione, *f.*; **— chamber,** camera di decompressione, *f.*
decongest [diːkənˈdʒest], *v.t.* Decongestionare.
decongestant, *a.n.* Decongestionante, *m.*
decongestion, *n.* Decongestionamento, *m.*
decontaminate [diːkənˈtæmineit], *v.t.* Decontaminare.
decontamination [diːkəntæmiˈneiʃən], *n.* Decontaminazione, *f.*
décor [ˈdeikɔːɹ], *n.* Decorazione, *f.*
decrepitude [diˈkrepitjuːd], *n.* Decrepitezza, *f.*
deep-freeze, *v.t.* Surgelare, supercongelare. || *n.* (Frigorifero per) surgelamento, *m.*
deep-freezer, *n.* Impianto per il surgelamento, *m.*
de-escalate [diːˈeskəleit], *v.t.i.* Restringere, diminuire; restringersi.
defrost [diːˈfrɔst], *v.t.* Disgelare (un frigorifero).
defuse [diːˈfjuːz], *v.t.* Disinnescare.
†degree, *n.* (*Leg.*) **Third —,** interrogatorio martellante e spietato, terzo grado, *m.*
dehydrate [ˈdiːhaidreit], *v.t.* Deidratare.
dehydration [diːhaiˈdreiʃən], *n.* Deidratazione, *f.*
de-ice [diːˈais], *v.t.* Disgelare; (*Aviat.*) liberare (un aereo) dalle incrostazioni di ghiaccio.
†de-icer [diːˈaisəɹ], *n.* Dispositivo antighiaccio, *m.*
dekko [ˈdekou], *n.* (*slang*) Occhiata, guardata, *f.*
delegation [deliˈgeiʃən], *n.* [cp. **deputation**].
delicatessen [delikəˈtesən], *n.* Salumeria, *f.*
deltiology [deltiˈɔlədʒi], *n.* Collezione di cartoline, *f.*
de luxe [diˈluks], *a.* Di lusso.
démarche [deiˈmɑːɹʃ], *n.* Démarche, *f.*
demo [ˈdemou], *n.* (*slang*) Dimostrazione, *f.* (*forma abbreviata di* **demonstration**).
demographic [deməˈgræfik], *a.* Demografico

demography [di'mɔgrəfi], *n.* Demografia, *f.*
demountable [di:'mauntəbl], *a.* (*Am.*) Smontabile.
†**denature,** *v.t.* (*Am.*) **Denatured alcohol** [cp. **methylated spirit**].
denazification [di:nɑ:tsifi'keiʃən], *n.* Denazificazione, *f.*
denazify [di:'nɑ:tsifai], *v.t.* Denazificare.
†**dental,** *a.* — **mechanic,** meccanico dentista, *m.*, odontotecnico, *m.*
deoxidation [di:ɔksi'deiʃən], *n.* Disossidazione, *f.*
†**depot,** *n.* (*Am.*) [cp. **station**].
deprived [di'praivd], *a.* (*Sociology*) Bisognoso, disagiato, svantaggiato [cp. **underprivileged**].
deration [di:'ræʃən], *v.t.* Derazionare.
deratization [di:ræti'zeiʃən], *n.* Derattizzazione, *f.*
derby ['də:ɹbi], *n.* (*Am.*) [cp. **bowler hat**].
derequisition [di:rekwi'ziʃən], *v.t.* Derequisire.
derequisitioning, *n.* Derequisizione, *f.*
†**derivative,** *a.* (*Lit.*) Non originale, imitato.
dermatosis [də:ɹmə'tousis], *n.* Dermatosi, *f.*
desegregation [di:segrə'geiʃən], *n.* (*Pol.*) Desegregazione, *f.*
desensitize [di:'sensitaiz], *v.t.* (*Phot.*, *Med.*) Desensibilizzare.
desensitizer, *n.* (*Phot.*, *Med.*) Desensibilizzatore, *m.*
†**detective,** *n.* **Private —,** agente investigativo privato, *m.*
deterrent [di'terənt], *n.* (*Pol.*) Deterrente, *m.*
devaluate [di:'væljueit], *v.t.* Svalutare.
deviant ['di:viənt], *n.* [cp. **deviationist**].
deviationism [di:vi'eiʃənizm], *n.* (*Pol.*) Deviazionismo, *m.*
deviationist [di:vi'eiʃənist], *n.* (*Pol.*) Deviazionista, *m.f.*
diatomic [daiə'tɔmik], *a.* Biatomico.
dictaphone ['diktəfoun], *n.* Dittafono, *m.*
dietician [daiə'tiʃən], *n.* Dietista, *m.f.*, dietologo, *m.*
dietology [daiə'tɔlədʒi], *n.* Dietologia, *f.*
differentiable [difə'renʃiəbl], *a.* Differenziabile.
†**differential,** *n.* (*Administration*) Differenza di salario tra i diversi gradi di una categoria, *f.*
†**dig,** *v.t.* (*colloq.*) Capire; studiare; interessarsi (a).
†**dim,** *a.* (*colloq.*) **To take a — view of,** disapprovare, condannare.
†**dime,** *n.* (*Am.*) — **-novel** [cp. **penny-dreadful**]; (*Am.*) — **-store,** magazzino che vende a buon mercato, *m.*
dimwit ['dimwit], *n.* Balordo, zuccone, *m.*
dimwitted, *a.* Ottuso, stupido, duro di comprendonio.
dinette [di'net], *n.* (*Am.*) Saletta da pranzo, *f.*; posto per pranzare in una stanza, tinello, *m.*
†**dip,** *v.t.* (*Motor.*) — **-stick,** asta per controllare il livello del carburante, *f.*; — **switch,** commutatore per luce anabbagliante, *m.*
dipole ['daipoul], *n.* Antenna a dipolo, *f.*, dipolo, *m.*
†**dirt,** *n.* (*Am.*) [cp. **earthen**].
disappointing [disə'pɔintiŋ], *a.* Indisponente, contrariante.
disembroil [disim'brɔil], *v.t.* Districare, sbrogliare.
†**dish,** *n.* (*colloq.*) Ragazza o donna appetitosa, *f.*
dishwasher ['diʃwɔʃəɹ], *n.* Lavapiatti elettrico, *m.*
dishy ['diʃi], *a.* (*colloq.*) Attraente, appetitoso.
disinfestation [disinfes'teiʃən], *n.* Disinfestazione, *f.*
†**disk,** *n.* (*Motor.*) — **brake,** freno a disco, *m.*
disorientation [disɔ:rien'teiʃən], *n.* Disorientamento, *m.*
†**district,** *n.* (*Am.*) [cp. **constituency**].
†**diversification,** *n.* Estensione delle attività di una grande compagnia o impresa a nuovi campi, *f.*
†**dock,** *n.* (*Am.*) [cp. **wharf**].
†**dog,** *n.* **Tracker —,** cane-poliziotto, *m.*; (*colloq.*) — **-collar,** colletto clericale, *m.*
doghouse ['dɔghaus], *n.* (*Am.*) Canile, *m.*; (*fig.*) **to be in the —,** essere in disgrazia, essere in penitenza.
do-gooder [du:'gudəɹ], *n.* Umanitario zelante con idee strambe o balzane, *m.*
dogsbody ['dɔgzbɔdi], *n.* (*colloq.*) Giovane ufficiale di Marina, *m.*; (*fig.*) uomo di fatica, *m.*; chi deve sobbarcarsi ai lavori più ingrati.
donkey-work, *n.* (*colloq.*) Lavoro pesante, *m.*, fatica da cane, *f.*
doodads ['du:dædz], *n.pl.* (*Am.*) Sciocchezze, cose da nulla, *f.pl.*
†**doodle,** *v.i.* (*colloq.*) — **bug,** bomba volante, *f.*
†**door,** *n.* — **to —,** porta a porta; — **-stop,** arresto della porta, *m.*
doping ['doupiŋ], *n.* (*Sport*) Drogaggio, *m.*, drogatura, *f.*
†**double,** *a.* (*Motor.*) — **parked,** parcheggiato in seconda fila. || *n.* (*Cinema*) Controfigura, *f.* || *v.t.* (*Cinema*) Doppiare.
double-action, *a.* A doppio effetto.
double-check, *v.t.i.* Controllare una seconda volta.
†**dough,** *n.* (*Am.*) Denaro, *m.*
doughboy ['doubɔi], *n.* (*Am.*) [cp. **dumpling**].
†**dove,** *n.* (*Pol.*) Chi appoggia un atteggiamento conciliante e pacifico; pacifista, *m.*
†**down,** *a.* (*colloq.*) — **and out,** rovinato, ridotto alla miseria.
downtown ['dauntaun], *n.* (*Am.*) Centro commerciale, *m.*
†**draft,** *n.* (*Am.*) [cp. **conscription**].
draftee [drɑ:f'ti:], *n.* (*Am.*) Coscritto, *m.*
†**drag,** *v.t.* **To — one's feet,** camminare di mala voglia, rallentare (*also fig.*).
drag, *n.* (*slang*) Vesti femminili (indossate da un uomo), *f.pl.*
†**drain,** *n.* **The brain —,** l'eccessiva emigrazione di intellettuali da un paese all'altro, *f.* (soprattutto dall'Inghilterra verso gli Stati Uniti), il drenaggio dei cervelli, *m.*
dramatis personae ['dræmətis pəɹ'sounai], *n.pl.* (*Theat.*) Personaggi, *m.pl.*
dramatization, *n.* Drammatizzazione, *f.*
dressage [dre'sɑ:ʒ], *n.* Ammaestramento dei cavalli, *m.*
†**dresser,** *n.* (*Am.*) [cp. **chest of drawers, dressing table**].
†**drier,** *n.* Asciugatrice, *f.* **Spin- —,** asciugatrice centrifuga, *f.*
†**drip,** *v.i.* (*colloq.*) — **-dry,** *a.* che si asciuga da sè, stendi-e-asciuga. || *n.* (*colloq.*) imbecille, *m.*
drive-in ['draivin], *n.* (*Am.*) Ristorante (*m.*), banca (*f.*), ufficio (*m.*) che serve i clienti senza che si muovano dall'auto. || *a.* — **cinema,** cineparco, *m.*

drool [druːl], *v.i.* (*colloq.*) [cp. **drivel**].
†**drop,** *n.* (*colloq.*) **At the — of a hat,** come niente, senza farsi pregare; (*Tennis*) **— shot,** smorzata, *f.*
drop-out, *n.a.* (*colloq.*) Chi si allontana o si ritira dal mondo delle consuetudini borghesi.
†**drug,** *n.* **— -pusher,** spacciatore di droga, *m.*
†**drugstore,** *n.* (*Am.*) Magazzino, emporio, *m.*
†**dry,** *v.i.* (*fig.*) **To — up,** non poter più parlare, trovarsi a corto di parole; **zittirsi.**
†**duck,** *n.* (*Am. colloq.*) Scappatella, evasione, *f.*; (*Mil.*) camionetta anfibia adoperata nelle operazioni di sbarco, *f.*; (*fig.*) **a sitting —,** bersaglio facile, *m.*, preda facile, *f.*
†**due,** *n.* (*Am.*) **dues** [cp. **subscription**].
duffel [ˈdʌfl] **coat,** *n.* Montgomery, *m.*
†**dumb,** *a.* (*Am.*) [cp. **stupid**].
†**dummy,** *n.* (*Sport*) **To sell a —,** fare una finta che inganna l'avversario.
†**dump,** *n.* (*colloq.*) Postaccio, *m.*
dunk [dʌŋk], *v.t.* (*Am.*) Tuffare, bagnare.
durables, *n.pl.* (*Econ.*) Beni stabili o durevoli, *m.pl.*
dust-up [ˈdʌstʌp], *n.* (*colloq.*) Litigio, diverbio, *m.*
†**Dutch,** *a.* (*Am.*) [cp. **German**].
†**dynamite,** *v.t.* Far saltare colla dinamite.
dysgenic [disˈdʒenik], *a.* Disgenico.

E

†**earth,** *n.* (*fig.*) **Scorched- —,** terra bruciata, *f.*
†**easy,** *a.* (*colloq.*) **— on the eye,** avvenente, attraente.
†**eat,** *v.t.* (*colloq.*) Turbare, disturbare; preoccupare. **What's eating him?** Che cosa lo disturba? (*fig.*) **to have someone eating out of one's hand,** mansuefare, una persona difficoltosa, rendere maneggevole una persona.
ecumenicism, ecumenism [iːkjuˈmenisizm, ˈiːkjumənizm], *n.* (*Eccles.*) Ecumenismo, *m.*
†**edit,** *v.t.* **Edited recording** or (*Rad.*) **programme,** fonomontaggio, *m.*
egghead [ˈeghed], *n.* (*colloq.*) Intellettuale, studioso, *m.*
egocentric [egoˈsentrik], *a.* Egocentrico.
egocentricity [egosenˈtrisiti], *n.* Egocentrismo, *m.*, egocentricità, *f.*
†**ejector,** *n.* **— seat,** sedile eiettabile, *m.*
†**election,** *n.* **— campaign,** campagna elettorale, *f.*
electrocardiogram [elektrouˈkɑːɹdiogræm], *n.* Elettrocardiogramma, *m.*
electrocardiograph, *n.* Elettrocardiografo, *m.*
electronic [elekˈtrɔnik], *a.* Elettronico. **— organ,** elettrofono, *m.*
electronics [elekˈtrɔniks], *n.pl.* Elettronica, fisica o tecnica elettronica, *f.*
empathy [ˈempəθi], *n.* (*Phil.*) Empatia, *f.*
encapsulate [inˈkæpsjuleit], *v.t.* Incapsulare.
encapsulation [inkæpsjuˈleiʃən], *n.* Incapsulamento, *m.*
†**end,** *v.t.* **Open-ended,** il cui termine nel tempo non è fissato (di sedute, discussioni, trasmissioni radiofoniche, ecc.).
endogenous [enˈdɔdʒinəs], *a.* Endogeno.
endogeny, *n.* Endogenesi, *f.*
engraftation [engrɑːfteiʃən], *n.* Innesto, *m.*
eniac [ˈeniæk], *n.* (*Am.*) Calcolatrice elettronica, *f.* [cp. **computer**].
†**enlist,** *v.t.i.* (*Am.*) **Enlisted men** [cp. **rank and file**].
†**enough,** *adv.*, *a.* (*colloq.*) **— is —,** quando si dice basta, basta.
en route [ɔnˈruːt], *adv.* In viaggio, in cammino.
entelechy [enˈteləki], *n.* Entelechia, *f.*
†**entertainment,** *n.* **— allowance,** indennità (per spese) di rappresentanza, *f.*; **— tax,** tassa sugli spettacoli, *f.*
entrecôte [ˈɔntrəkɔt], *n.* Entrecôte, *f.*
enucleate [iˈnjuːklieit], *v.t.* Spiegare, enucleare; (*Chem.*) enucleare.
enucleation [injuːkliˈeiʃən], *n.* Spiegazione, enucleazione, *f.*; (*Chem.*) enucleazione, *f.*
enuresis [enjuˈriːsis], *n.* Enuresi, *f.*
epicentre [ˈepisentəɹ], *n.* (*Geol.*) Epicentro, *m.*
epicyclic [epiˈsaiklik], *a.* Epicicloidale.
†**equity,** *n.* (*Comm.*) Valore d'una proprietà al netto d'ipoteche, *m.*; **equities,** azioni e titoli a interesse variabile, *pl.*; **Equity,** sindacato di attori, *m.*
ergonomics [əːɹgoˈnɔmiks], *n.* Ergonomia, *f.*
escalate [ˈeskəleit], *v.t.i.* Estendere, dilatare; estendersi, dilatarsi.
escalation [eskəˈleiʃən], *n.* Estensione, dilatazione, *f.*
†**escape,** *n.* **— literature,** letteratura di evasione, *f.*; **— pipe,** tubo di scappamento, *m.*
escapism [isˈkeipizm], *n.* Desiderio di evadere dalla realtà presente, *m.*; evasione, *f.*
escapist [isˈkeipist], *a.* Di evasione, evasivo. || *n.* Chi cerca di sfuggire alla realtà.
escargot [eskɑːɹˈgou], *n.* Chiocciola, lumaca, *f.*
espresso [esˈpresou], *a.* **— bar,** bar dove si beve caffè espresso, *m.*; **— coffee,** (caffè) espresso, *m.*; **— machine,** macchina espresso, *f.*
†**estate,** *n.* **— car,** giardiniera, giardinetta, *f.*
euphoria [juːˈfɔːriə], *n.* Euforia, *f.*
euphoric [juːˈfɔrik], *a.* Euforico.
ex-directory, *a.* **— telephone number,** numero telefonico privato (non incluso nell'elenco), *m.*
†**executive,** *n.* Capufficio, dirigente, *m.*
exhibitionism [eksiˈbiʃənizm], *n.* Esibizionismo, *m.*
exhibitionist, *n.* Esibizionista, *m.f.*
exogamous [ekˈsɔgəməs], *a.* Esogamo.
exogamy [ekˈsɔgəmi], *n.* Esogamia, *f.*
expellee [ekspeˈliː], *n.* Profugo, profuga, *m.f.*
expendable [eksˈpendəbl], *a.* Che si può spendere o usare senza riguardi; sacrificabile.
expertise [ekspəɹˈtiːz], *n.* Abilità, perizia, *f.*
explicate [ˈeksplikeit], *v.t.* Sviluppare.
exposé [ekspouˈzei], *n.* Smascheramento, *m.*
†**exposure,** *n.* **Indecent —,** oltraggio al pudore, *m.*; (*Phot.*) **— meter,** esposimetro, *m.*
†**express,** *a.* **— telegram,** telegramma lampo, *m.*
†**extension,** *n.* (*Am.*) **— wire** [cp. **flex**].
†**eye,** *n.* **— -catching,** che dà nell'occhio, vivido, chiassoso; (*colloq.*) **private —,** agente investigativo privato, *m.*
†**eyebrow,** *n.* **Pencilled —,** sopracciglio disegnato a matita, *m.*
†**eyelash,** *n.* **Artificial, false eyelashes,** ciglia finte, *f.pl.*
extrasensory [ˈekstrəsensəri], *a.* **— perception,** percezione extrasensoriale, *f.*
extrovert [ˈekstrovəːt], *n.*, **extroverted,** *a.* (*Psych.*) Estroverso, estroversa, *m.f.*

F

†face, *n.* (*colloq.*) Prestigio, *m.* **To lose —**, perdere prestigio, soffrire una *diminutio capitis*.
faceless ['feislis], *a.* Senza faccia; (*fig.*) senza carattere individuale; anonimo.
†faculty, *n.* (*Am.*) [cp. **teaching staff**].
†fair, *n.* **Trade —**, fiera o esposizione campionaria, *f.*
†fall, *v.i.* **To — for**, innamorarsi di, prendere una cotta per; (*fig.*) **to — over backwards**, fare sforzi penosi e ridicoli.
fall-out, *n.* (*atomic bomb*) Pioggia radioattiva, *f.*; ricadute radioattive, *f.pl.*
familial [fə'miliəl], *a.* (*Am.*) Famigliare.
†family, *n.* (*Am.*) **— name** [cp. **surname**].
fanciable ['fænsiəbl], *a.* Attraente, seducente [cp. **attractive**].
†faucet, *n.* (*Am.*) [cp. **tap**].
faze [feiz], *v.t.* (*Am.*) Disturbare, preoccupare.
†feather, *v.t.* (*fig.*) **To — one's nest**, guadagnare illecitamente, 'mangiare'.
featherbed [feθəɹ'bed], *v.t.* Trattare con eccessiva indulgenza; viziare.
fed-up ['fedʌp], *a.* (*colloq.*) stanco; annoiato; depresso.
†feed, *n.* (*colloq.*) **Chicken —**, compenso irrisorio, *m.*
†fender, *n.* (*Am. Motor.*) [cp. **mudguard**]; paraurti, *m.*
fibreboard ['faibəɹbɔːɹd], *n.* Cartone di fibra, *m.*
fibreglass ['faibəɹglɑːs], *n.* Fibra di vetro, *f.*
fibrositis [faibro'saitis], *n.* Fibrosite, *f.*
fictionalize ['fikʃənəlaiz], *v.t.* Romanzare.
†fiddle, *n.* (*colloq.*) Truffa, *f.*, imbroglio, *m.*
†filibuster, *n.* (*Am. Pol.*) Manovra ostruzionistica di un deputato alla Camera, che consiste nel prolungare il proprio discorso oltre il tempo normale.
†fill, *v.t.* (*Motor.*) **To — up**, fare il pieno, rifornirsi.
†film, *n.* (*Dentistry*) Patina, *f.* **Colour —**, film a colori, *m.*; **feature —**, film a soggetto, *m.*; **— library**, cineteca, *f.*; **— music**, cinemusica, *f.*; **— script**, copione, *m.*
finagle [fi'neigl], *v.t.i.* (*Am.*) Manovrare, arrangiarsi, intrallazzare.
finalize ['fainəlaiz], *v.t.* Ultimare, completare.
†finger, *n.* (*colloq.*) **To keep one's fingers crossed**, fare gli scongiuri, fare le corna.
†finishing, *a.* **— -school**, scuola di perfezionamento, *f.*
fink [fiŋk], *n.* (*Am. slang*) Delatore, *m.*, spia, *f.*; crumiro, *m.* || *v.i.* Fare la spia; cantare.
†first, *a.* (*Am.*) **— -floor** [cp. **ground floor**].
†fish, *n.* (*Am.*) **— -dealer** [cp. **fishmonger**].
†fix, *v.t.* (*Am.*) [cp. **do**].
flashback, *n.* (*Cinema*) Scena retrospettiva, *f.*
flashbulb, *n.* (*Phot.*) Lampadina lampo, *f.*, lampada al flash, *f.*
flashlight ['flæʃlait], *n.* (*Am.*) [cp. **electric torch**].
†flight, *n.* **— -deck**, piattaforma di lancio, *f.*; **— path**, traiettoria di volo, *f.*; **test —**, volo di collaudo, *m.*
flivver ['flivəɹ], *n.* (*Am.*) Automobile malandata, *f.* [cp. **jalopy**].
†floor, *n.* **— -show**, spettacolo di varietà sulla pista di un nightclub, *m.*; (*Am.*) **— walker**, ispettore (di un grande magazzino), *m.*
floozie ['fluːzi], *n.* Donna scostumata; puttana, sgualdrina, *f.*
flophouse ['flɔphaus], *n.* (*Am.*) [cp. **doss-house**].
flummox ['flʌməks], *v.t.* Rovinare; (*colloq.*) confondere, turbare, mettere in imbarazzo.
fluoridation [fluɔːri'deiʃən], *n.* L'aggiunta del fluoruro all'acqua potabile, *f.*
fluoridize ['fluɔridaiz], *v.t.* Medicare (l'acqua) con l'aggiunta del fluoruro.
†fly, *v.i.* (*colloq.*) **— -by-night**, chi va in giro di notte, nottambulo; chi taglia la corda di notte per non pagare i debiti.
†flying, *a.* **— club**, aeroclub, *m.*; **— saucer**, disco volante, *m.*
flyover ['flaiouvəɹ], *n.* Passaggio sopraelevato, cavalcavia, *m.*
†foam, *n.* **— rubber**, gommapiuma, *f.*
†folder, *n.* Pieghevole, *m.*
†food, *n.* **— -trolley**, carrello porta-vivande, *m.*
†foot, *n.* (*colloq.*) **My — !** Un corno!
footloose ['futluːs], *a.* (*Am.*) Abituato a muoversi e comportarsi liberamente (spesso in senso non buono); non vincolato; nomade, errante.
footsie, footie ['fut(s)i], *n.* (*Am. slang*) Giuoco di bambini seduti a tavola, che si toccano o si pestano i piedi di nascosto, *m.*; (*fig.*) amoreggiamento fatto di nascosto, *m.* **To play —**, amoreggiare in questo modo.
foreseeable [fɔːɹ'siːəbl], *a.* Prevedibile.
†four, *n.a.* (*Am.*) **— hundred** [cp. **Upper Ten**].
fractionalism ['frækʃənəlizm], *n.* (*Pol.*) Frazionismo, *m.*
†fraternity, *n.* (*Am.*) Associazione studentesca maschile, *f.*
frazzle ['fræzl], *v.t.* Logorare; sfilacciare; stracciare. || *n.* Condizione di cosa o persona logorata o ridotta a uno straccio, *f.* **To be beaten to a —**, essere ridotto a uno straccio.
freeway ['friːwei], *n.* (*Am.*) Strada di circonvallazione esterna, *f.* [cp. **by-pass**].
†freight, *n.* (*Am.*) **— train** [cp. **goods train**].
frenetic [frə'netik], *a.* Frenetico.
fridge [fridʒ], *n.* [cp. **refrigerator**]. Frigo, *m.*
frogman ['frɔgmæn], *n.* Sommozzatore, *m.*
fuddy-duddy ['fʌdidʌdi], *n.* (*colloq.*) Vecchio rimbambito, *m.* [cp. **old fogy**].
fug [fʌg], *n.* (*colloq.*) Aria che sa di rinchiuso, aria stantia, *f.*
†full, *a.* **— face**, di prospetto; **— -time job**, impiego a orario completo, *m.*
funfair ['fʌnfɛəɹ], *n.* Lunapark, *m.*
fungicidal [fʌndʒi'saidl], *a.* Fungicida.
fuzz [fʌz], *n.* (*slang*) **The —**, la polizia.

G

gabby ['gæbi], *n.* (*Am.*) Chiacchierone, *m.*
Gallup-poll ['gæləp poul], *n.* Sondaggio Gallup, *m.*
gangling ['gæŋgliŋ], *a.* (*Am.*) Alto, magro e dinoccolato.
†garbage, *n.* (*Am.*) **— can** [cp. **dustbin**].
†garter, *n.* (*Am.*) [cp. **sock-suspender**].
gastro-enteric [gæstroen'terik], *a.* (*Med.*) Gastroenterico, gastrointestinale.
gastroenteritis [gæstroentə'raitis], *n.* (*Med.*) Gastroenterite, *f.*

gatecrash, *v.t.i.* (*colloq.*) Farsi largo per partecipare a, intromettersi, immischiarsi.
gauche [gouʃ], *a.* Goffo, maldestro, impacciato; senza tatto.
gaucherie ['gouʃəri], *n.* Goffaggine, *f.*
†gay, *a.* (*slang*) Omosessuale.
geezer ['giːzəɹ], *n.* Tipo strano, *m.*; uomo, individuo, *m.*
gelignite ['dʒelignait], *n.* Nitroglicerina, *f.*
gen [dʒen], *n.* (*colloq.*) Informazione, *f.*; ragguaglio, *m.*
†generator, *n.* (*Am. Motor.*) [cp. **dynamo**].
genocide ['dʒenosaid], *n.* Genocidio, *m.*
genotype ['dʒenotaip], *n.* Genotipo, *m.*
geochemistry [dʒiːo'kemistri], *n.* Geochimica, *f.*
geopolitics [dʒiːo'pɔlitiks], *n.* Geopolitica, *f.*
geriatric [dʒeri'ætrik], *a.* Geriatrico.
geriatrics, *n.* Geriatria, geriatrica, *f.*
†germ, *n.* — **warfare,** guerra batteriologica, *f.*
gerontocracy [dʒerɔn'tɔkrəsi], *n.* Gerontocrazia, *f.*
gerontology [dʒerɔn'tɔlədʒi], *n.* Gerontologia, *f.*
gestalt [gə'ʃtælt], *a.* (*Psych.*) Gestaltico. — **psychology,** gestaltismo, *m.*
†get, *v.t.* (*colloq.*) **To — away with it,** saper cavarsela, farla franca; (*colloq.*) **to — cracking,** muoversi, spicciarsi; (*colloq.*) **to — on to,** mettersi in contatto con.
get-together, *n.* Riunione, *f.*, drink, *m.*
†ghost, *n.* — **town,** città abbandonata, *f.*; (*Journalism*) — **(writer),** negro, *m.* || *v.t.i.* scrivere un articolo che viene pubblicato a firma di un altro, fare il negro.
gimmick ['gimik], *n.* Trovata, *f.*, espediente, trucco, *m.*
gimmickry ['gimikri], *n.* Complesso di aggeggi, *m.*
give, *v.t.* (*fig.*) **To — hostages to fortune,** oberarsi con impegni e responsabilità tali da compromettere le proprie iniziative future (*si direbbe, per esempio, di uomo che mette su famiglia*); (*colloq.*) **to — (someone) what-for,** sgridare, rimbrottare.
giveaway ['givəwei], *a.* Che si dà per niente, regalato.
†given, *a.* (*Am.*) — **name** [cp. **Christian name**].
global ['gloubəl], *a.* (*Am.*) Mondiale.
gluteal ['gluːtiəl], *a.* Gluteo.
†go, *v.i.* (*Am.*) — **out** [cp. **come to grief**]; (*Am.*) — **-fog,** apparato per la dispersione della nebbia, *m.*; (*Am.*) — **-getter,** persona avida di denaro o di successo, *f.*, arrivista, *m.f.*
†goggle, *v.i.* (*colloq.*) — **box,** televisore, *m.*
go-go, *a.* (*Am. colloq.*) In piena efficienza; attivo, dinamico; prospero, felice, fiorente.
†gold, *a.* (*Am.*) — **brick** [cp. **fraud**]. || *n.* (*colloq.*) — **-digger,** donna che dà la caccia agli uomini ricchi, *f.*
†golden, *a.* (*fig.*) — **handshake,** cospicua gratificazione a un direttore d'azienda quando si ritira, *f.*
†golf, *n.* — **-trolley,** carrello per i bastoni del golf, *m.*
goner ['gɔnəɹ], *n.* (*colloq.*) Chi è rovinato, finito, o morto.
†gracious, *a.* (*colloq.*) — **living,** vita signorile, *f.*
†grade, *n.* (*Am.*) — **-crossing** [cp. **level-crossing**]; — **school,** scuola elementare, *f.*
†graduate, *n.* (*Am.*) — **school,** corsi universitari di perfezionamento, *m.pl.*
†graduation, *n.* (*Am.*) — **exercises** [cp. **prize-giving**].
†grafter, *n.* (*colloq.*) Imbroglione, *m.*
grapevine ['greipvain], *n.* (*slang*) Fonte segreta di informazione, *f.*
grease-gun, *n.* Pompa per ingrassaggio, *f.*, ingrassatore a pressione, *m.*
gremlin ['gremlin], *n.* Spiritello maligno, *m.*; (*fig.*) iella, scalogna, *f.*
†grind, *v.t.* (*fig.*) **To have an axe to —,** avere una lagnanza da esporre; avere una tesi da propugnare.
†grip, *n.* [cp. **travelling-bag**].
†gripe, *v.t.* (*Am.*) Importunare.
grouch [grautʃ], *v.i.* (*Am.*) Essere imbronciato; lamentarsi. || *n.* Persona imbronciata, *f.*
†ground, *n.* (*fig.*) **To be thick on the —,** essere abbondante, essere numerosi.
†group, *n.* — **-captain,** colonnello d'aviazione, *m.*
†guard, *n.* (*Am.*) [cp. **warder**]; — **-dog,** cane da guardia, *m.*
†gun, *n.* — **-dog,** cane da caccia, *m.*
gyromagnetic [dʒairomæg'netik], *a.* Giromagnetico.
gyrostabilizer [dʒairo'steibilaizəɹ], *n.* Girostabilizzatore, *m.*

H

†hair, *n.* — **weaving,** nuovo rimedio, di origine svedese, alla calvizie: la capigliatura posticcia viene tessuta invece d'essere sovrapposta in una parrucca.
hair-do, *n.* (*colloq.*) Acconciatura, pettinatura, *f.*
†ham, *n.* — **acting,** gigionismo, *m.*; — **actor,** attore da strapazzo,
hamburger ['hæmbəɹgəɹ], *n.* (*Am.*) Panino imbottito di manzo tritato, *m.*
†hand, *n.* (*Am. colloq.*) **A big —,** un grande o caloroso applauso, *m.*; (*colloq.*) **to win hands down,** vincere o battere nettamente; — **-knitted,** lavoratoa maglia o a mano; (*colloq.*) — **-out,** opuscolo, *m.*; regalo, *m.*; — **-picked,** scelto individualmente, selezionato.
†handle-bar, *n.* (*colloq.*) — **moustache,** baffi a manubrio di bicicletta, *m.pl.*; baffi grossi e sporgenti, *m.pl.*
†hang, *v.t.i.* (*Am. colloq.*) **To be hung up,** essere trattenuto, bloccato; **to be hung up on,** essere coinvolto (in), essere preso (da); (*fig.*) **to get the — of something,** scoprire come va o funziona una cosa, scoprirne il *modus operandi.*
hang-nail, *n.* Pipita, *f.*
hang-up, *n.* (*colloq.*) Problema, *m.*
hanky-panky ['hæŋki'pæŋki], *n.* (*colloq.*) Trucco, inganno, inghippo, *m.*
harassment, *n.* Vessazione, molestia, *f.*
†hard, *a.* (*fig.*) — **core,** nucleo, *m.*; (*Pol.*) — **-liner,** uomo politico duro e intransigente, *m.*; (*Am.*) — **liquor** [cp. **spirits**].
†harvester, *n.* **Combine- —,** auto-mietitrice-trebbiatrice, *f.*
†hat, *n.* (*Sport*) — **-trick,** il vincere tre volte di seguito (*also fig.*).

†**hawk**, *n.* (*Pol.*) Chi appoggia un atteggiamento duro e aggressivo; guerrafondaio, *m.*
haywire ['heiwaiəɹ], *a.* (*colloq.*) In disordine, disordinato. **To go —**, disordinarsi, scombussolarsi.
†**he**, *pron.* (*Am.*) **— -man**, uomo forte e virile, *m.*
hearing-aid, *n.* Apparecchio acustico, *m.*
†**heart**, *n.* **— -searching**, angosciosa incertezza, *f.*; penoso esame di coscienza, *m.*; (*colloq.*) **— -throb**, persona amata, *f.*; rubacuori, *m.f.*
†**heaven**, *n.* (*colloq.*) **He was in the seventh —**, gli pareva di toccare il cielo col dito.
heliport ['helipɔːɹt], *n.* Scalo per elicotteri, *m.*
†**help**, *n.* (*Am.*) [cp. **employee**].
hep [hep], *a.* (*Am. colloq.*) Pratico o tifoso dei passatempi della gioventù bruciata americana (jazz, rock and roll, droghe, ecc.).
hermeneutics [həːɹmə'njuːtiks], *n.* Ermeneutica, *f.*
heteromorphic [hetəro'mɔːɹfik], *a.* Eteromorfo.
heterosexual ['hetəroseksjuəl], *n.a.* Eterosessuale, *m.f.*
†**hick**, *n.* (*Am.*) Zotico, *m.*; ignorante, *m.*
hi-fi ['hai'fai], *a.* (*colloq.*) [cp. **high fidelity**].
†**high**, *a.* (*colloq.*) Ubbriaco; drogato; (*colloq.*) **— falutin'**, (*Am.*) **— -hat**, pretenzioso, pomposo; **— -handed**, arbitrario, tirannico, violento; **— -powered**, ad alta potenza.
high-fidelity, *n.* Alta fedeltà, *f.* || *a.* Ad alta fedeltà.
highlight, *n.* Clou, *m.*, culmine, *m.*
hijack ['haidzæk], *v.t.* Togliere la refurtiva (a un ladro); far dirottare (un aereo) a mano armata.
hijacker, *n.* Ladro che a mano armata toglie la refurtiva a un altro ladro, *m.*; [cp. **skyjacker**].
†**hike**, *v.i.* (*Am.*) [cp. **tramp**].
hindsight ['haindsait], *n.* Sguardo retrospettivo su fatti già avvenuti; apprezzamento a ragion veduta, *m.* (*the opposite of* **foresight**).
hippie ['hipi], *n.* (*colloq.*) Membro della gioventù bruciata, *m.*
histogram ['histogræm], *n.* Istogramma, *m.*
†**hive**, *v.t.* (*fig.*) **To — off**, staccare, separare, isolare.
hokum ['houkəm], *n.* (*Am. Theat.*) Sentimentalismo, *m.*; sensazionalismo, *m.*
†**holiday**, *n.* **Holidays with pay**, ferie spesate, *f.pl.*
†**home**, *n.* (*fig.*) **To be — and dry**, essere al sicuro; essere a cavallo, essere a posto; (*Sport*) **— -stretch**, dirittura d'arrivo, *f.*
homework, *n.* Compito o compiti per casa, *m.*(*pl.*) (*fig.*) **To do one's —**, preprararsi coscienziosamente a un compito.
homogenized [hə'mɔdʒənaizd], *a.* Omogeneizzato.
homomorphic [hɔmo'mɔːɹfik], *a.* Omomorfo.
honorific [ɔnə'rifik], *a.* Onorifico.
†**hood**, *n.* (*Am. Motor.*) Cofano, *m.* [cp. **bonnet**].
hoodlum ['huːdləm], *n.* (*Am.*) Giovinastro, *m*; teppista, *m.*
hoodoo ['huːduː], *n.* Disdetta, iella, scalogna, *f.*
hooey ['huːi], *n.* (*Am. slang*) Schiocchezza, *f.*
hoo-ha ['huːhaː], *n.* (*slang*) Confusione, *f.*; chiasso, scalpore, *m.*
†**hook**, *v.t.* (*Radio*) **— -up**, collegamento, *m.*
hookey ['huki], *n.* (*Am.*) **To play —**, marinare la scuola.
hormone ['hɔːɹmoun], *n.* Ormone, *m.*
†**horn**, *v.i.* (*Am.*) **To — in**, intromettersi, interferire.
horrific [hɔ'rifik], *a.* Orribile, orripilante.
horrify ['hɔrifai], *v.t.* Scandalizzare; atterrire; offendere.
hospitalization [hɔspitəlai'zeiʃən], *n.* Ricovero in ospedale, *m.*, ospedalizzazione, *f.*
hospitalize ['hɔspitəlaiz], *v.t.* (*Am.*) Ospedalizzare.
†**hot**, *a.* (*colloq.*) **— line**, filo diretto, *m.*; **— -plate**, piastra riscaldante, *f.*; fornello, *m.*
houseboat, *n.* Casa galleggiante, *f.*
housecoat, *n.* Veste (*f.*) o abito (*m.*) da casa, vestaglia, *f.*
house-hunting, *n.* **To go —**, cercare casa.
housework, *n.* Faccende di casa, *f.pl.*, lavori di casa, *m.pl.*
hovercraft ['hɔvəɹkraːft], *n.* Hovercraft, *m.*
†**how**, *adv.* (*Am.*) **— come?** Come mai?
†**howling**, *a.* (*slang*) Terribile. **A — success**, un successo strepitoso.
hubris ['hjuːbris], *n.* Arroganza intellettuale, *f.* (soprattutto degli scienziati e dei tecnocrati).
†**huckster**, *n.* (*Am.*) Presentatore di pubblicità radio, *m.*
†**huddle**, *n.* (*Am.*) Riunione, assemblea, *f.*
humdinger ['hʌmdiŋəɹ], *n.* (*Am.*) Qualcosa di straordinario, *f.*; una cosa superlativa, *f.*
humidifier [hjuː'midifaiəɹ], *n.* Vaporizzatore, *m.*
humidify [hjuː'midifai], *v.t.* Inumidire.
†**humour**, *n.* (*colloq.*) **Sick —**, umorismo perverso, *m.*; umorismo nero o macabro, *m.*
humus ['hjuːməs], *n.* Humus, *m.*
hunky-dory [hʌŋki'dɔːri], *a.* (*Am.*) In ottimo stato, in perfette condizioni. **Everything is —**, tutto va benone.
†**hunting**, *n.* (*Am.*) [cp. **shooting**].
hush-hush, *a.* Segreto, segretissimo.
huskily ['hʌskili], *adv.* Con voce rauca.
†**husky**, *a.* (*colloq.*) Forte, robusto.
†**hustle**, *v.t.i.* (*Am.*) [cp. **solicit**].
hybridism ['haibridizm], *n.* Ibridismo, *m.*
hybridization [haibridai'zeiʃən], *n.* Ibridazione, *f.*, ibridismo, *m.*
hybridize ['haibridaiz], *v.t.* Ibridare.
†**hydrate**, *v.t.* Idratare.
hydration [hai'dreiʃən], *n.* Idratazione, *f.*
hydrofoil ['haidrofɔil], *n.* Aliscafo, *m.*
†**hydrogen**, *n.* **— bomb**, bomba all'idrogeno, *f.*; **— peroxide**, acqua ossigenata, *f.*
hydrogenate, hydrogenize [hai'drɔdʒineit, -naiz], *v.t.* Idrogenare.
hydrolysis [hai'drɔlisis], *n.* Idrolisi, *f.*
hydrous ['haidrəs], *a.* Acquoso.
†**hygiene**, *n.* **Mental —**, igiene mentale, *f.*; **personal —**, igiene del corpo, igiene individuale o personale, *f.*
hygroscopic [haigro'skɔpik], *a.* Igroscopico.
hypersensitive ['haipəɹsensitiv], *a.* Ipersensibile.
hypertension ['haipəɹtenʃən], *n.* Ipertensione, *f.*
hypnotherapy [hipno'θerəpi], *n.* Cura del sonno, *f.*
hypothesize [hai'pɔθəsaiz], *v.i.* Fare ipotesi..
hysterotomy [histə'rɔtəmi], *n.* (*Med.*) Isterotomia, *f.*

I

†**ice**, *v.t.* (*a cake*) Glassare.
†**icing**, *n.* (*on cake*) Glassa, *f.*

identikit [ai'dentikit], *n.* Identikit, foto robot, *m.*
idioplasm ['idioplæzm], *n.* Idioplasma, *m.*
imbalance [im'bæləns], *n.* Squilibrio, *m.*, sperequazione, *f.*
†**imitation**, *a.* — **jewellery** or **stones**, gioielli falsi, *m.pl.*; — **leather**, finta pelle, *f.*, similcuoio, *m.*, similpelle, *f.*
impermissible [impəɹ'misibl], *a.* Non permissibile.
impersonator [im'pəːɹsəneitəɹ], *n.* Chi personifica o interpreta.
implausible [im'plɔːzibl], *a.* Non plausibile.
implementation [impləmen'teiʃən], *n.* Attuazione, realizzazione, *f.*
implosion [im'plouʒən], *n.* Implosione, *f.*
improviser ['imprəvaizəɹ], *n.* Improvvisatore, *m.*, improvvisatrice, *f.*
†**in**, *adv.* (*colloq.*) Di moda, in voga.
incidentally [insi'dentəli], *adv.* Tra parentesi, per inciso.
incoercible [inko'əːɹsibl], *a.* Incoercibile.
incontrollable [inkən'trouləbl], *a.* Incontrollabile.
incontrollably, *adv.* In modo incontrollabile.
inductility [indʌk'tiliti], *n.* Mancanza di duttilità, *f.*
industrialization [indʌstriəlai'zeiʃən], *n.* Industrializzazione, *f.*
industrialize [in'dʌstriəlaiz], *v.t.* Industrializzare.
infarct, infarction ['infɑːɹkt, in'fɑːɹkʃən], *n.* Infarto, *m.*
inflationary [in'fleiʃənəri], *a.* Inflazionistico.
inflationist [in'fleiʃənist], *n.* Inflazionista, *m.f.*
†**information**, *n.* — **bureau**, ufficio informazioni, *m.*
informative, informatory [in'fɔːɹmətiv, in'fɔːɹmətəri], *a.* Informativo; istruttivo.
infra-red ['infrəred], *a.* (*Phys.*) Infrarosso.
infrastructure ['infrəstrʌktʃəɹ], *n.* Infrastruttura, *f.*
inhalant [in'heilənt], *a.* (*Med.*) Inalante, inalatore. || *n.* Inalatore, apparecchio inalatorio, *m.*
in-laws, *n.pl.* (*colloq.*) Parenti acquisiti, affini, *m.pl.*
innards ['inəɹdz], *n.pl.* (*colloq.*) Interiora, budella, *f.pl.*
insectifuge [in'sektifjuːdʒ], *n.a.* Insettifugo, *m.*
inseminate [in'semineit], *v.t.* (*Biol.*) Inseminare, fecondare.
insemination [insemi'neiʃən], *n.* (*Med.*) Fecondazione, *f.*; **artificial —**, fecondazione artificiale, *f.*
†**inside**, *a.* — **information**, informazioni riservate, *f.pl.*
insomniac [in'sɔmniæk], *n.* (*Med.*) Chi soffre abitualmente d'insonnia.
institutional [insti'tjuːʃənəl], *a.* Istituzionale.
†**insurance**, *n.* **Third-party —**, assicurazione di responsabilità civile, assicurazione a favore di o contro terzi, *f.*
insurgence, insurgency [in'səːɹdʒəns(i)], *n.* Insurrezione, rivolta, *f.*
intercom ['intəɹkɔm], *n.* Citofono, interfono, *m.*
†**interior**, *a.* — **decorator**, arredatore, *m.*, arredatrice, *f.*
interminable [in'təːɹminəbl], *a.* Interminabile.
intermission [intəɹ'miʃən], *n.* (*Theat.*) Intervallo, *m.*
intermittent [intəɹ'mitənt], *a.* Intermittente.
intermix [intəɹ'miks], *v.t.i.* mescolare, frammischiare; mescolarsi, frammischiarsi.
†**intern** ['intəːɹn], *n.* (*Am.*) Medico di ospedale, internista, *m.*
interphone ['intəɹfoun], *n.* Telefono interno, citofono, *m.*
interplay ['intəɹplei], *n.* Azione reciproca, *f.*
interpretership [in'təːɹprətəɹʃip], *n.* Lavoro di interprete, *m.*
interrelationship [intərə'leiʃənʃip], *n.* Interdipendenza, interrelazione, *f.*
†**intersection**, *n.* (*Am.*) [cp. **cross-roads**].
intersex ['intəɹseks], *n.* (*Med.*) Neonato o neonata il cui sesso appare ambiguo, *m.f.*
interwar ['intəɹwɔːɹ], *a.* Interbellico.
intravenous [intrə'viːnəs], *a.* Endovenoso.
inutterable [in'ʌtərəbl], *a.* Inesprimibile; impronunciabile.
†**investment**, *n.* — **trust**, società d'investimento, *f.*
invigilation [invidʒi'leiʃən], *n.* Sorveglianza, assistenza, *f.*
ionosphere [ai'ɔnəsfiəɹ], *n.* Ionosfera, *f.*
Iran [i'rɑːn], *n.* Iran, *m.*
Iraq, Irak [i'rɑːk], *n.* Iraq, Irak, *m.*
Iraqi [i'rɑːki], *n.a.* Iracheno, *m.*, irachena, *f.*
†**iron**, *v.t.* (*fig.*) **To — out**, appianare, risolvere, comporre.
irrepealable [irə'piːləbl], *a.* Inabrogabile.
isobar ['aisobɑːɹ], *n.* (Linea) isobara, *f.*
isochron ['aisokrɔn], *n.* (Linea) isocrona, *f.*
isogamous [ai'sɔgəməs], *a.* (*Biol.*) Isogamo.
isolationism [aisə'leiʃənizm], *n.* (*Pol.*) Isolazionismo, *m.*
isolationist, *a.* Isolazionistico. || *n.* Isolazionista, *m.f.*
isomorphic [aiso'mɔːɹfik], *a.* Isomorfo.
isotope ['aisotoup], *n.* Isotopo, *m.*
Israeli [iz'reili], *n.a.* Israeliano, *m.*
itchiness ['itʃinis], *n.* Prurito, *m.*
itemize ['aitəmaiz], *v.t.* Dettagliare.

J

†**jab**, *n.* (*colloq.*) Iniezione, inoculazione, *f.*
jackpot ['dʒækpɔt], *n.* Massimo premio in una lotteria, m.; (*fig.*) **to hit the —**, **vincere** o guadagnare una forte somma; diventare ricco.
jalopy [dʒə'lɔpi], *n.* (*Am.*) Automobile vecchia o malandata, *f.*
jampacked ['dʒæmpækt], *a.* Pieno zeppo, stipato, pigiato.
jaywalk ['dʒeiwɔːk], *v.i.* (*colloq.*) Attraversare la via distrattamente.
†**jazz**, *n.* — **musician** or **player**, jazzista, *m.f.* || *v.t.* **To — up**, rendere vivace; eccitare, infiammare.
jazzy ['dʒæzi], *a.* (*slang*) Sfarzoso, brillante.
†**jeans**, *n.pl.* (*Am.*) **Blue —**, calzoni da fatica, pantalonacci, *m.pl.*
†**jeep**, *n.* (*Am.*) **Air- —**, elicottero monoposto, *m.*
†**jerk**, *n.* (*Am.*) Mascalzone, cialtrone, *m.*
†**jet**, *n.* (*colloq.*) — **set**, tipico bel mondo contemporaneo di ricchi che si spostano liberamente da un continente all'altro in aviogetti, *m.*; — **setter**, chi fa parte di questo mondo.

jimmy ['dʒimi], *n.* (*Am.*) [cp. **jemmy**].
jodhpurs ['dʒɔdpəɹz], *n.pl.* Calzoni alla cavallerizza, *m.pl.*
†**joint**, *a.* — **account**, conto di partecipazione, *m.*; — **industrial committee**, comitato misto di produzione, *m.* || *n.* (*colloq.*) Impresa, azienda, *f.* (*Mech.*) **Cardan** —, giunto cardanico, *m.*; (*colloq.*) **clip** —, impresa o azienda losca, *f.*
jokingly ['dʒoukiŋli], *adv.* Per scherzo, ridendo.
jotting ['dʒɔtiŋ], *n.* Annotazione, *f.*
†**joy**, *n.* (*colloq.*) — **ride**, gita in automobile (generalmente rubata), *f.*; (*colloq.*) — **stick**, leva di governo (di aeroplano), *f.*
judder ['dʒʌdəɹ], *v.i.* Vibrare. || *n.* Vibrazione, *f.*
juke-box ['dʒu:kbɔks], *n.* Grammofono a gettone, *m.*
jumbo ['dʒʌmbou], *n.* (*hum.*) Elefante, *m.* — **jet**, grosso aviogetto per passeggeri, *m.*
†**junction**, *n.* (*Motor.*) **Clover-leaf** —, incrocio o raccordo a quadrifoglio, *m.*; **road** —, incrocio stradale, *m.*
junkie ['dʒʌŋki], *n.* (*slang*) Persona dedita alla droga, *f.*, tossicomane, *m.*
juvenilia [dʒu:vɔ'ni:liə], *n.pl.* Opere giovanili (di un autore), *f.pl.*

K

kakistocracy [kækis'tɔkrəsi], *n.* Cachistocrazia, *f.*
kaput(t) [kə'put], *a.* (*slang*) Kaputt, finito.
†**keep**, *v.i.* (*colloq.*) **To — up with the Joneses**, emulare, gareggiare con gli amici o con i vicini di casa.
key-man, *n.* Personalità importante, *f.*
†**kick**, *n.* (*colloq.*) Piacere, gusto, *m.* **To get a — out of something**, provarci gusto; **for kicks**, solo per divertimento.
kickback ['kikbæk], *n.* (*Am.*) Somma prelevata o ritenuta sulla paga di un operaio dal datore di lavoro o dal soprastante, *f.*
†**kid**, *n.* (*Am. colloq.*) **Mixed-up** —, ragazzo o giovanotto confuso o perplesso nelle idee o nei sentimenti, *m.*
kike [kaik], *n.* (*Am.*) Ebreo, ebrea, *m.f.*
†**kindred**, *a.* — **spirits**, anime gemelle, *f.pl.*
†**king**, *n.* — **-sized**, molto grande.
kinky ['kiŋki], *a.* Ricciuto; attorcigliato; (*fig.*) tortuoso; perverso; sessualmente capriccioso o anormale.
kip [kip], *v.i.* (*slang*) Andare a letto; dormire.
†**kitchen**, *n.* (*colloq.*) Batteria d'un'orchestra, *f.*; (*Am.*) — **sideboard** [cp. **dresser**].
kitchenette [kitʃi'net], *n.* Cucinino, *m.*, cucinetta, *f.*
kitchenware ['kitʃinwεəɹ], *n.* Utensili da cucina, *m.pl.*
†**kitten**, *n.* (*colloq.*) **Sex** —, ragazza molto giovane, attraente e procace, *f.*
kitty ['kiti], *n.* Gattino, *m.*; posta, *f.*, banco, *m.*
†**knock**, *v.t.* (*colloq.*) **To — back**, sbevazzare.
†**know**, *v.t.* (*colloq.*) **Not to want to** —, non volerne sapere; non voler sentirne parlare; non volersene occupare; (*colloq.*) — **-all**, saccente, saccentone, *m.*; — **-how**, perizia, conoscenza, competenza, *f.*
knowledgeable ['nɔlidʒəbl], *a.* Intelligente; bene informato.
knuckle, *n.* (*fig.*) **Near the** —, che rasenta il lubrico o l'osceno.
koala (bear) [ko'ɑ:lə], *n.* Koala, *m. inv.*
kook [ku:k], *n.* (*Am. colloq.*) Testa matta, *f.*, mattacchione, *m.*
kooky ['kuki], *a.* (*Am. colloq.*) Matterello, pazzerello.
kope(c)k ['koupek], *n.* Copeco, kopeck, *m.*
kotow [kau'tau], *v.i.* Inchinarsi; comportarsi ossequiosamente.
Kremlinologist [kremli'nɔlədʒist], *n.* Cremlinologo, cremlinista, *m.*
Kremlinology, *n.* Cremlinologia, *f.*
kyle [kail], *n.* (*Scottish*) Stretto canale tra due isole, *m.*

L

lambaste ['læmbeist], *v.t.* (*Am.*) Bastonare; (*fig.*) criticare aspramente, stroncare.
land-rover, *n.* (*reg. trade name*) Specie di jeep.
†**landslide**, *n.* (*Pol.*) — **victory**, vittoria schiacciante, *m.*
†**lap**, *v.t.* (*Sport*) Superare (un concorrente) di uno o più giri.
lap-joint, *n.* Giunto a sovrapposizione, *m.*
laprobe ['læproub], *n.* (*Am.*) [cp. **travelling rug**].
laser ['leizəɹ], *n.* Laser, *m.*
lashings, *n.pl.* (*colloq.*) Abbondanza, *f.* (soprattutto del bere e del mangiare).
launching-site, *n.* Pista di lancio, *f.*
launderette [lɔ:ndə'ret], *n.* Lavanderia con lavatrici a disposizione del pubblico, *f.*
layabout ['leiəbaut], *n.* (*colloq.*) Ozioso, fannullone, *m.*
lay-by, *n.* Piazzuola, *f.*
†**layout**, *n.* (*Typ.*) — **man**, impaginatore, *m.*
†**league**, *n.* **The League of Nations**, la Società delle Nazioni.
†**leak**, *n.* (*colloq.*) Notizia ancora privata o segreta che trapela anzi tempo sulla stampa o in un discorso pubblico, *f.* || *v.t.* Rivelare, propalare una notizia di questo genere.
†**left**, *a.* — **wing**, (*Football*) di ala sinistra, (*Pol.*) di estrema sinistra; — **winger**, (*Football*) ala sinistra, *f.*, (*Pol.*) appartenente all'estrema sinistra, *m.f.*
leftist ['leftist], *n.* Membro della sinistra, *m.*; progressista, *m.* || *a.* Sinistrale, appartenente alla sinistra.
†**lens**, *n.* **Telescopic** —, teleobiettivo, *m.*
leprechaun ['leprəkɔ:n], *n.* (*Irish*) Gnomo, folletto, *m.*
†**let**, *v.t. i.* (*colloq.*) **To — up**, diminuire; rallentare.
let-up, *n.* Diminuzione; cessazione, *f.*
leukemia, leucemia [lu:'ki:miə], *n.* (*Med.*) Leucemia, *f.*
†**level**, *n.* (*colloq.*) **On the** —, onesto, genuino.
liberalization, *n.* Liberalizzazione, *f.*
libertarian [libəɹ'tεəriən], *n.* Fautore o fautrice del libero arbitrio, *m.f.*
†**lid**, *n.* (*colloq.*) Cappello, *m.*
lido ['li:dou], *n.* Lido, *m.*
lie-detector, *n.* Macchina della verità, *f.*
†**life**, *n.* **The facts of** —, le realtà della vita, *f.pl.*, (*fig.*) le cose come stanno, *f.pl.*, i dati concreti della situazione, *m.pl.*, (*eufemismo*) le modalità concrete del sesso e della riproduzione, *f.pl.*

†**life-sentence**, *n.* Ergastolo, *m.*
†**lift**, *v.t.* (*Am.*) [cp. **increase**].
lift-off, *n.* Lancio (di un missile), *m.*
†**lightning**, *n.* (*colloq.*) **Like greased —**, come un razzo, in un battibaleno.
liminal [ˈliminəl], *a.* (*Psych.*) Liminare.
†**line**, *n.* (*Am.*) **— is busy** [cp. **engaged**]; **top-—**, di primo rango, di prima qualità. || *v.t.* (*Am.*) **— up** [cp. **queue up**].
linguistician [liŋgwiˈstiʃən], *n.* (*Am.*) Linguista, studioso di lingue, *m.*
†**liqueur**, *n.* **— glass**, bicchierino, *m.*
liquidize [ˈlikwidaiz], *v.t.* Rendere liquido.
†**live**, *v.i.* (*fig.*) **To — in a goldfish bowl**, vivere sotto gli occhi di tutti, vivere soggetti a una pubblicità spietata.
†**loaf**, *n.* **Sliced —**, pagnotta venduta già affettata, *f.*, pan carrè, *m.*
†**local**, *a.* (*Am.*) **— taxes** [cp. **rates**].
locale [louˈkæl], *n.* (*Am.*) Luogo, locale, *m.*
†**locate**, *v.i.* (*Am.*) [cp. **settle**].
lock-out, *n.* Chiusura, serrata, *f.*
lollop [ˈlɔləp], *v.i.* Camminare goffamente.
lolly [ˈlɔli], *n.* (*slang*) Denaro, *m.*; lecca-lecca, *f.*
loner [ˈlounəɹ], *n.* (*Am.*) Solitario, *m.*
†**long**, *a.* (*Telephone*) **— -distance call**, telefonata o chiamata interurbana, *f.*; (*Betting slang*) **— odds**, quota alta, *f.*; **— -range**, a lunga portata; **— -term**, a lunga scadenza.
loo [luː], *n.* (*slang*) Gabinetto, *m.*
†**look**, *n.* (*colloq.*) **The casual —**, trascuratezza elegante, *f.*
loosener [ˈluːsənəɹ], *n.* (*slang*) Lassativo, *m.*
lope [loup], *v.i.* Muoversi a lunghi balzi. || *n.* Lungo balzo, *m.*
†**lot**, *n.* (*colloq.*) **The —**, tutto quanto, tutti quanti.
†**lounge**, *n.* (*Am.*) **Men's —**, gabinetto per uomini, *m.*
†**low**, *a.* **— brow**, (individuo) poco evoluto; **— -necked**, scollato; **— pressure**, bassa pressione, *f.*
low-down, *n.* (*slang*) Fatti nascosti, *m.pl.*; manovre dietro le quinte, *f.pl.*; informazioni segrete, *f.pl.*; **to give the — on**, dare informazione su, dare ragguagli su; rivelare i segreti di.
†**lunar**, *a.* **— module**, modulo lunare, *m.*
lunarnaut [ˈluːnəɹnɔːt], *n.* (*Am.*) Astronauta che viaggia intorno alla luna o vi sbarca, *m.*
†**lunatic**, *a.* (*colloq.*) **— fringe**, elemento marginale nella popolazione la cui eccentricità confina colla pazzia, *m.*
†**lunch**, *n.* (*Am.*) [cp. **snack**].

M

†**machine**, *n.* **Vending —**, venditrice automatica (a moneta), *f.*, distributore automatico, *m.*
maculation [mækjuˈleiʃən], *n.* (*Biol.*) Maculamento, *m.*
†**mad**, *a.* (*Am.*) [cp. **angry**].
†**magazine**, *n.* (*colloq.*) **Glossy —**, rivista mondana illustrata con fotografie e avvisi pubblicitari, *f.*, rotocalco, *m.*
magnification [mægnifiˈkeiʃən], *n.* Ingrandimento, *m.*
†**mail**, *n.* (*Am.*) **— -box** [cp. **letter-box**].
maladjusted [mæləˈdʒʌstid], *a.* (*Psych.*) Moralmente spostato, squilibrato.
malingering, *n.* Simulazione di malattia, *f.*
†**mammoth**, *a.* (*colloq.*) Enorme; gigantesco; mastodontico.
†**man**, *n.* (*colloq.*) **Dirty old —**, vecchio lascivo, vecchio sporcaccione, *m.*; **— hour**, ora lavorativa, *f.*; **— power**, potenziale umano, *m.*; (*fig.*) **— -sized**, di grandezza o qualità adeguata per un uomo; **a — -sized helping**, una porzione sufficiente per un uomo (del mangiare); **a — -sized job**, un lavoro da uomo.
managerial [mænəˈdʒiəriəl], *a.* Manageriale.
†**mandatory**, *a.* (*Am.*) [cp. **obligatory**].
†**maniac**, *n.* (*Am.*) Analizzatore numerico elettronico, *m.*
manicurist [ˈmænikjuːrist], *n.* Manicure, *f.*
marina [məˈriːnə], *n.* Marina, *f.*
†**marker**, *n.* (*Am.*) [cp. **tablet**].
†**market**, *n.* (*Comm.*) **Buyers' —**, mercato favorevole ai compratori (in cui l'offerta supera la domanda), *m.*; **sellers' —**, mercato favorevole alle vendite (in cui la domanda supera l'offerta), *m.*
Marxism [ˈmɑːɹksizm], *n.* Marxismo, *m.*
Marxist, *n.* Marxista, *m.f.*
mascara [mæsˈkɑːrə], *n.* Cosmetico per ciglia, *m.*
†**masher**, *n.* Utensile per schiacciare, *m.*; **potato —**, schiacciapatate, *m. inv.*
mashie [ˈmæʃi], *n.* Tipo di mazza da golf.
†**master**, *n.* **— key**, comunella, *f*; (*Elec.*) **— switch**, interruttore principale, *m.*
†**mastermind** [ˈmɑːstəɹmaind], *n.* Mente che dirige un'impresa, *f.*; caporione, *m.* || *v.t.* Dirigere, sorvegliare.
masturbate [ˈmæstəɹbeit], *v.i.* Masturbarsi.
masturbation, *n.* Masturbazione, *f.*
†**maternity**, *n.* (*colloq.*) **— dress**, **— gown**, veste per gestanti, *f.pl.*, abito pre-maman, *m.*
maverick [ˈmævərik], *n.a.* (*Am.*) Nonconformista, dissidente, *m.f.*
maxi [ˈmæksi], *n.* La maxi, *f.* **— -coat**, maxicappotto, *m.*; **— -skirt**, maxigonna, *f.*
maximise [ˈmæksimaiz], *v.t.* Massimizzare.
†**meal**, *n.* **Meals-on-wheels**, forma di pubblica assistenza (in Inghilterra), che consiste nel provvedere pasti già cotti portati in furgoncini alle case dei vecchi e dei malati, *f.*
†**medium** (pl. **media**), *n.* (*Psych.*) Mezzo di comunicazione, *m.* **Mass media**, mezzi con cui si diffondono informazioni, spettacoli e propaganda alle masse (*e.g.* stampa, radio, televisione).
megaton [ˈmegətʌn], *n.* Megaton, *m.*
megawatt [ˈmegəwɔt], *n.* Megawatt, *m.*
menticide [ˈmentisaid], *n.* [cp. **brain-washing**].
methane [ˈmiːθein], *n.* Metano, *m.*
methodology [meθəˈdɔlədʒi], *n.* Metodologia, *f.*
me-tooism [miːˈtuːizm], *n.* (*Am.*) L'adottare temi politici del partito avverso, *m.*
metrication [metriˈkeiʃən], *n.* Il passaggio (in Inghilterra) dal vecchio sistema di misure a quello metrico decimale, *m.*
microfilm [ˈmaikrofilm], *n.* Microfilm, *m.*
microgroove [ˈmaikrogruːv], *n.a.* (*Am.*) Microsolco, *m.*
micronize [ˈmaikrənaiz], *v.t.* (*Am.*) Frantumare, sbriciolare.
micro-organism, *n.* Microrganismo, *m.*

microwave ['maikroweiv], *n.* (*Phys.*) Microonda, *f.*
midfield ['midfi:ld], *n.* (*Football*) Centrocampo, *m.* — **player**, centrocampista, *m.*
midi ['midi], *n.* La midi, *f.* — **-skirt**, midigonna, *f.*
midweek, *a.* Infrasettimanale.
†**milk**, *n.* — **bar**, bar bianco, *m.*
†**milking**, *a.* — **-machine**, mungitrice, *f.*
milquetoast ['milktoust], *n.* (*Am.*) Persona che non ha stima di sè, *f.*
mimeograph ['mimiogrɑ:f], *v.t.* Ciclostilare. || *n.* Ciclostile, ciclostilo, *m.*
†**mind**, *n.* (*fig.*) **One-track —**, chiodo fisso, *m.*; dirizzone, *m.*
mind-read, *v.i.* Leggere il pensiero.
mind-reading, *n.* Lettura del pensiero, *f.*
mini ['mini], *n.* La mini, *f.* — **-skirt**, minigonna, *f.*
minimization [minimai'zeiʃən], *n.* Riduzione al minimo, *f.*
mish-mash ['miʃmæʃ], *n.* Miscuglio, *m.*; guazzabuglio, *m.*
mistreat [mis'tri:t], *v.t.* Maltrattare.
mistreatment, *n.* Maltrattamento, *m.*
†**mixed**, *a.* — **-grill**, misto di carne ai ferri; (*colloq.*) — **-up**, disorientato, spostato, confuso, perplesso.
mixer ['miksəɹ], *n.* (*colloq.*) Cordialone, amico di tutti, *m.*; (*Arch.*) impastatrice, *f.* **Cement —**, impastatrice di cemento; **concrete —**, impastatrice di calcestruzzo.
mock-up, *n.* Simulacro, *m.*; modello dimostrativo, *m.*
mod [mɔd], *n.* (*slang*) Giovanotto (o ragazza) del popolo, di tipo **hippie** e volgarmente elegante, abituato a gironzolare sulla motocicletta. || *a.* Moderno, di moda.
moisturize ['mɔistjəraiz], *v.t.* Idratare. **Moisturizing cream**, crema idratante, *f.*
moll [mɔl], *n.* (*Am.*) Amica o compagna di un gangster, *f.*
momism ['mɔmizm], *n.* (*Am.*) Eccessivo affetto materno, mammismo, *m.*
†**money**, *n.* (*colloq.*) **For my —**, per me, per conto mio.
†**monitor**, *v.t.* (*TV*, *Rad.*) Controllare.
†**monkey**, *n.* (*colloq.*) — **-business**, imbroglio, pasticcio, *m.*; — **-nut**, arachide, *f.*
moped ['mouped], *n.* Micromotore, *m.*
moppet ['mɔpit], *n.* (*Am.*) Bambino, bambina, *m.f.*; ragazza leggiera, fraschetta, *f.*
moron ['mɔ:rɔn], *n.* Deficiente, frenastenico, *m.*
mortician [mɔ:ɹ'tiʃən], *n.* (*Am.*) Impresario di pompe funebri, *m.*
†**most**, *adv.* (*Am.*) [cp. **almost**].
motelier [mou'teliəɹ], *n.* Proprietario o gerente di autostello, *m.*
moth-balls, *n.pl.* Palline antitarma, *f.pl.*
motorcade ['moutəɹkeid], *n.* (*Am.*) Sfilata o processione di automobili, *f.*
†**movies**, *n.pl.* (*Am.*) **Movie-show** [cp. **film**].
†**muck**, *v.t.* (*colloq.*) **To — up**, impasticciare.
†**muffler**, *n.* (*Am. Motor.*) Silenziatore, *m.* [cp. **silencer**].
†**multi-millionaire**, *n.* Plurimilionario, *m.*
†**multiple**, *a.* — **store**, negozio a catena, *m.*
multi-purpose, *a.* Dai molti usi, usabile in vari modi.
multiracial [mʌlti'reiʃəl], *a.* Multirazziale.
multistorey ['mʌltistɔ:ri], *a.* — **carpark**, autosilo, autoparcheggio a torre, *m.*
Mumbo Jumbo ['mʌmbou'dʒʌmbou], *n.* Dio di certe tribù africane, *m.*; (*fig.*) feticcio, babau, *m.*
musak ['mju:sæk], *n.* (*Am.*) Musica da sfondo (su disco o nastro) e a getto continuo nei luoghi pubblici (alberghi, ristoranti ecc.), *f.*
muscle-bound, *a.* Coi muscoli induriti per eccesso di fatica.
†**muslin**, *n.* (*Am.*) [cp. **calico**].
muss [mʌs], *v.t.* (*Am.*) Arruffare, mettere in disordine.
†**must**, *n.* (*colloq.*) Cosa che si deve fare, *f.*, obbligo, dovere, *m.*
†**mutual**, *a.* (*fig.*) — **admiration society**, società di mutuo incensamento, *f.*
mystique [mis'ti:k], *n.* Fascino, *m.*; ascendente, prestigio, *m.*
myxomatosis [miksəmə'tousis], *n.* Mixomatosi, *f.*

N

nancy-boy ['nænsibɔi], *n.* (*colloq.*) Invertito, (*vulg.*) finocchio, *m.*
†**nap**, *n.* Napoleone, *m.* (*giuoco di carte*); il puntare tutto il denaro in una scommessa. **To go —**, rischiare il tutto per tutto.
narcosis [nɑ:ɹ'kousis], *n.* (*Med.*) Narcosi, *f.*
natter ['nætəɹ], *v.i.* (*colloq.*) Brontolare, mormorare; ciarlare.
†**natural**, *n.* (*colloq.*) **A —**, **persona** fornita per natura di doti richieste per un dato compito o mestiere, *f.* **He is a — for the stage**, è un attore nato. || *a.* — **gas**, metano, *m.*
naturist ['neitʃərist], *n.* Nudista, *m.f.* [cp. **nudist**].
†**neck**, *v.i.* (*colloq.*) Abbracciarsi, accarezzarsi [cp. **cuddle**].
†**needle**, *v.t.i.* Cucire; infilare; (*fig.*) irritare, punzecchiare.
†**neon**, *n.* — **sign**, insegna al neon, *f.*
neurological [njuərə'lɔdʒikəl], *a.* Neurologico.
neutralist ['nju:trəlist], *n.* Neutralista, *m.f.*
neutron ['nju:trɔn], *n.* Neutrone, *m.*
†**news**, *n.* (*Am.*) — **-dealer** [cp. — **-agent**]; — **-item**, notizia, *f.*; (*Am.*) — **stand** [cp. **bookstall, kiosk**].
†**newsagent**, *n.* Edicolista, *m.*
newscaster, newsreader, *n.* Radiocronista, *m.*
newsworthy, *a.* Importante, interessante.
nickelodeon [nikə'loudiən], *n.* (*Am.*) [cp. **juke-box**].
nifty ['nifti], *a.* (*colloq.*) Abile, destro.
†**night**, *n.* (*Am.*) — **stick** [cp. **truncheon**].
†**nightcap**, *n.* (*Am.*) Spettacolo sportivo serale, *m.*
nisei ['ni:sei], *n.* Americano di origine giapponese, *m.*
†**noise**, *n.* — **(level) meter**, fonometro, *m.*
no-man's-land, *n.* Terra di nessuno, *f.*
non-acceptance, *n.* Mancata accettazione, *f.*
non-aligned, *a.* Non allineato. — **countries**, paesi non impegnati, *m.pl.*
non-cooperation, *n.* Rifiuto di cooperare, *m.*
non-delivery, *n.* Mancata consegna, *f.*
non-event, *n.* Avvenimento mancato, *m.*; azione, *f.*, trattenimento, *m.*, manifestazione, *f.*, ecc., che fa fiasco.

non-fading, *a.* Resistente alla luce, solido (di colore).
non-flammable, *a.* Incombustibile, ininfiammabile.
non-member, *n.* **Open to non-members,** aperto al pubblico.
non-white, *n.a.* (Persona) di sangue misto.
normalcy ['nɔːɹməlsi], *n.* (*Am.*) Normalità, *f.*
normality [nɔːɹ'mæliti], *n.* Normalità, *f.*
normalize ['nɔːɹməlaiz], *v.t.* Normalizzare.
normative ['nɔːɹmətiv], *a.* Normativo.
nosey ['nouzi], *a.* Curioso, ficcanaso. **Nosey Parker,** uomo o donna ficcanaso, *m.f.*, persona che ama curiosare, *f.*
nosh [nɔʃ], *v.i.* (*slang*) Mangiare. — **-up,** panciata, scorpacciata, *f.*
no-show ['nouʃou], *n.* (*Am.*) Passeggero che non si presenta alla partenza dell'aereo, *m.*
notelet ['noutlit], *n.* Noterella, *f.*; breve annotazione, *f.*
†**nothing,** *n.* (*colloq.*) — **doing,** nulla da fare, non si combina niente.
†**notion,** *n.* (*Am.*) **Notions** [cp. **haberdashery, fancy goods, novelties**].
nougat ['nuːgɑː], *n.* Torrone, *m.*
†**novelette,** *n.* Romanzo rosa, *m.*
†**novelist,** *n.* (*Am.*) **Dime** —, romanziere dozzinale o banale, *m.*
†**now,** *adv.* (*Am.*) **As of** —, ora, adesso.
nub [nʌb], *n.* (*colloq.*) Nocciolo, punto essenziale, *m.* (*of a question*).
nuclear ['njuːkliəɹ], *a.* Nucleare. — **charge,** carica atomica, *f.*; — **deterrent,** deterrente atomico o nucleare, *m.*; — **energy,** energia nucleare, *f.*; — **physicist,** fisico nucleare, *m.*; — **physics,** fisica nucleare, *f.*; — **power station,** centrale atomica, *f.*; — **reactor,** reattore nucleare, *m.*; — **war(fare),** guerra atomica, *f.*; — **weapons,** armi nucleari, *f.pl.*
nucleonics [njuːkli'ɔniks], *n.pl.* Fisica nucleare, *f.*
nutritionist [njuː'triʃənist], *n.* Dietista, nutrizionista, *m.*
nylon ['nailɔn], *n.* Nailon, *m.* (*colloq.*) **Nylons,** calze di nailon, *f.pl.*
nymphet ['nimfit], *n.* Ninfetta, *f.*

O

oarlock ['ɔːɹlɔk], *n.* (*Am.*) [cp. **rowlock**].
†**oatmeal,** *n.* (*Am.*) [cp. **porridge**].
†**observation,** *n.* — **gallery,** loggia o galleria con veduta panoramica ad uso del pubblico, *f.*
octane ['ɔktein], *n.* Ottano, *m.* **High-octane,** ad alto numero di ottani.
odontologist [ɔdɔn'tɔlədʒist], *n.* Odontoiatra, *m.*
†**of,** *prep.* (*Am.*) **Ten minutes — six** [cp. **to**].
†**off,** *prep.* — **beat,** non convenzionale; eccentrico; (*fig.*) — **the map,** scomparso, sparito; — **the record,** confidenziale, riservato; — **stage,** fra le quinte. || *adv.* — **-white,** quasi bianco.
officialese [ɔfiʃə'liːz], *n.* Linguaggio degli uffici governativi, *m.*; gergo della burocrazia statale, *m.*
†**oil,** *n.* (*Motor.*) — **gauge,** oleometro, *m.*; (*Am.*) — **-pan** [cp. **sump**].
omegatron [o'megətrən], *n.* (*Phys.*) Piccolo ciclotrone, *m.*
†**one,** *n.a.* (*Am.*) — **-way ticket** [cp. **single ticket**].
opencast ['ɔːpənkɑːst], *n.* — **mine,** scavo a cielo, *m.*
†**opera,** *n.* (*Radio, TV*) **Soap** —, dramma radiofonico o televisivo a puntate, di carattere sentimentale o melodrammatico.
†**operating,** *a.* (*Am.*) — **costs** [cp. **working expenses**].
operational [ɔpə'reiʃənəl], *a.* Operante, attivo, in funzione.
opt [ɔpt], *v.i.* Optare; — **for,** optare per; — **out,** ritirarsi.
optometer [ɔp'tɔmitə], *n.* Ottimetro, *m.*
optometrist [ɔp'tɔmətrist], *n.* [cp. **optician**].
orthopaedics [ɔːɹθə'piːdiks], *n.pl.* Ortopedia, *f.*
orthopaedist, *n.* Ortopedico, *m.*
oscillograph ['ɔsilogrɑːf], *n.* Oscillografo, *m.*
osteo-arthritis, *n.* Osteoartrite, *f.*
osteomyelitis [ɔstiomaiə'laitis], *n.* (*Med.*) Osteomielite, *f.*
osteopathy ['ɔstiopæθi], *n.* Osteopatia, *f.*
osteosclerosis [ɔstiosklə'rousis], *n.* Osteosclerosi, *f.*
ouch! [autʃ], *inter.* Ahi!
†**out,** *adv.* (*colloq.*) Fuori moda, non in voga.
outback ['autbæk], *n.* (*Australia*) Paesi dell'interno, *m.pl.*
†**outfit,** *n.* (*Am.*) [cp. **team**].
outsell [aut'sel], *v.i.* Vendere in quantità superiore.
†**outsider,** *n.* Estraneo, refrattario, fuorimondo, *m.*
outworn [aut'wɔːɹn], *a.* Logoro; vecchio; fuori moda.
overman [ouvəɹ'mæn], *v.t.* Impiegare più operai del necessario, sovrabbondare nella manodopera. **We are overmanned,** abbiamo più operai del necessario.
†**overproduction,** *n.* (*Theat.*) Inframmettenza pignola o sofisticheria nella regia di uno spettacolo teatrale, *f.*
overtone ['ouvəɹtoun], *n.* Armonica, *f.*, ipertono, *m.*; (*fig.*) sfumatura, *f.*; sottinteso, *m.*
oxygenize ['ɔksidʒənaiz], *v.t.* Ossigenare.

P

†**package,** *v.t.* Impaccare, involtare (*goods for sale*). || *n.* (*fig.*) — **deal,** accordo multilaterale, accordo a pacchetto, *m.*
†**packed,** *a.* (*colloq.*) Composto di uomini venduti.
†**packet,** *n.* **Pay** —, busta-paga, *f.*
†**paddle,** *v.t.* (*Am.*) [cp. **smack**].
paediatric [piːdi'ætrik], *a.* Pediatrico.
paediatrician [piːdiə'triʃən], *n.* Pediatra, *m.*
paediatrics, *n.pl.* Pediatria, *f.*
†**pain,** *n.* — **-killer,** anodino, *m.*; — **-killing,** — **-relieving,** antidolorifico, anodino, antinevralgico.
†**pan,** *v.t.* (*Am.*) Denigrare, sparlare (di). || *v.i.* (*Cinema, TV*) Panoramicare.
†**panel,** *n.* Gruppo di esperti, *m.* (*Motor.*) **Instrument** —, cruscotto, *m.*
panning ['pæniŋ], *n.* (*Cinema, TV*) — **(shot),** panoramica, *f.*
panties ['pæntiz], *n.pl.* Mutandine aderenti da bambino o da donna, *f.pl.*
paperback ['peipəɹbæk], *n.* Libro in brochure, *m.*, brochure, *f.*

†**parachute,** *v.t.i.* Paracadutare; lanciarsi col paracadute. || *n.* — **drop,** lancio col paracadute, *m.*
†**parade,** *n.* **Fashion —,** sfilata di modelli, *f.*
†**parking,** *n.* (*Am.*) — **-lot** [cp. — **-place**]; — **meter,** parchimetro, *m.*; — **ticket,** multa per sosta vietata, *f.*
part-time, *a.* — **job,** impiego a mezza giornata, *m.*
†**party,** *n.* (*Am.*) **To throw a —,** dare un ricevimento; (*Telephone*) — **line,** duplex, *m.*; — **politics,** politica di partito, *f.*
†**pass,** *n.* **To make a — at,** (*Fencing*) tirare un colpo a, (*fig.*) cercare di amoreggiare con.
†**passenger,** *n.* — **service,** servizio passeggieri, *m.*
pasteurization [pɑ:stjərai'zeiʃən], *n.* Pastorizzazione, *f.*
†**patch,** *n.* — **pocket,** tasca a toppa, tasca applicata, *f.*
pâté ['pætei], *n.* Pâté, *m.*
patrolman [pə'troulmən], *n.* (*Am.*) Agente di polizia, *m.*
†**pay,** *n.* (*Am.*) **Call-back —,** compenso per lavoro straordinario, *m.*; (*Am.*) — **-off,** risultato finale, *m.*
payola [pei'oulə], *n.* (*Am.*) Sbruffo, *m.*; bustarella, *f.*
†**pay-roll,** *n.* **To be on the —, essere sul libro** paga; far parte di una impresa.
†**peak,** *a.* (*Elec.*) — **load,** carico massimo, *m.*, — **season,** alta stagione, *f.*
†**pebble,** *n.* — **dash,** intonaco a pinocchino, intonaco granuloso, *m.*
†**peg,** *n.* (*colloq.*) **Off the —,** confezionato (*clothes*).
†**pen,** *n.* **Ball-point —,** penna a sfera, *f.*, biro, *m.* (*reg. trade name*); — **-friend,** corrispondente, *m.f.*; (*Am.*) — **-point** [cp. **nib**].
penis ['pi:nis], *n.* Pene, *m.*
†**penthouse,** *n.* (*Am.*) Appartamento di lusso all'ultimo piano di una casa, *m.*
perfectionist [pəɹ'fekʃənist], *n.* (*Phil.*) Perfezionista, *m.*; chi cerca o pretende la perfezione nel proprio lavoro o in quello degli altri.
†**permissive,** *a.* (*fig.*) **The Permissive Society,** la società lassista.
permissiveness [pəɹ'misivnis], *n.* Lassismo morale, *m.*
†**period,** *n.* — **furniture,** mobili antichi, *m.pl.*; — **piece,** mobile antico, *m.*; — **play,** commedia di costume, *f.*, dramma storico, *m.*
pernickety [pəɹ'nikəti], *a.* (*colloq.*) Schifiltoso, difficile.
perry ['peri], *n.* Sidro di pere, *m.*
personalize ['pə:ɹsənəlaiz], *v.t.* Rendere personale, personalizzare.
pesky ['peski], *a.* (*Am. colloq.*) Noioso, fastidioso, molesto.
pesticide ['pestisaid], *n.* Insetticida, *m.*
petersham ['pi:təɹʃəm], *n.* Gros-grain, *m.*
petrochemical [petro'kemikəl], *a.* Petrolchimico.
pharyngoscope [fæ'riŋgəskoup], *n.* Faringoscopio, *m.*
†**phase,** *v.t.* Attuare gradualmente, attuare in fasi consecutive. (*colloq.*) **To — out,** abolire, rimuovere gradualmente.
phew! [fju:], *inter.* Auf!
phoney ['founi], *a.* (*Am.*) Fasullo [cp. **sham**].
photocell ['foutousel], *n.* Fotocella, fotocellula, *f.*
photocopy ['foutoukɔpi], *n.* Fotocopia, *f.*
photocopying machine, *n.* Fotocopiatrice, *f.*
photomontage [foutomɔn'tɑ:ʒ], *n.* Fotomontaggio, *m.*
phototypy ['foutotaipi], *n.* Fototipia, *f.*
physiotherapist [fizio'θerəpist], *n.* Fisioterapista, *m.f.*
physiotherapy [fizio'θerəpi], *n.* Fisioterapia, *f.*
†**pick,** *v.t.* (*colloq.*) **To — on,** dare addosso a, prendersela con; dare la colpa a.
pick-up, *n.* (*Gramophone*) Pick-up, *m.*, fonorivelatore, *m.*
pièce de résistance, *n.* Cavallo di battaglia, *m.*
†**pigeon-hole,** *v.t.* Archiviare; registrare; classificare.
†**pilot,** *a.* — **light,** accenditoio, *m.*
pinpoint ['pinpɔint], *v.t.* Individuare, segnalare con precisione.
pin-up ['pinʌp], *n.* (*Am.*) Fotografia (di amico, amica, o personaggio del teatro, del cinema e della televisione ecc.) che viene appesa nelle stanze dei patiti, *f.*; la persona o il personaggio di cui viene appesa la foto, *f.*, *m.*
†**pip,** *v.t.* (*Sport*) Battere, sconfiggere.
†**pipe,** *n.* — **-cleaner,** curapipe, *m. inv.*; (*colloq.*) — **-dream,** sogno, progetto inattuabile, castello in aria, *m.*
†**pipeline,** *n.* (*fig.*) **In the —, in via d'attua**zione.
pivotal ['pivətəl], *a.* (*Am.*) Cardinale, centrale, vitale.
pixilated ['piksileitid], *a.* (*Am.*) Eccentrico, pazzerello, picchiatello.
†**plan,** *n.* **Development —,** piano regolatore, *m.*
†**plastic,** *a.* — **surgery,** chirurgia estetica, chirurgia plastica, *f.*
plasticize ['plæstisaiz], *v.t.i.* Rendere plastico; diventare plastico.
†**play,** *v.t.* (*colloq.*) **To — down,** attenuare, smorzare; sdrammatizzare; **to — up,** esagerare, gonfiare; esasperare.
play-off, *n.* (*Sport*) Spareggio, *m.*
playpen ['pleipen], *n.* Girello, cestino, carruccio, *m.*
†**plough,** *v.t.* (*Comm.*) **To — back profits,** reinvestire i guadagni di un'impresa nell'impresa stessa.
ploy [plɔi], *n.* (*colloq.*) Manovra, *f.*, giuoco, tiro, *m.*
†**plumbing,** *n.* (*Am.*) [cp. **drains**].
†**plummet,** *v.i.* Cadere a piombo, a picco.
†**plush,** *a.* (*colloq.*) Lussuoso, sontuoso.
†**pocket,** *n.* **Out-of- — expenses,** indennità per spese minute, *f.*
po-faced ['poufeist], *a.* (*colloq.*) Con faccia impassibile, senza scomporsi [cp. **deadpan**].
†**point,** *v.t.i.* (*colloq.*) **To — up,** mettere in evidenza, in rilievo; sottolineare.
†**poker,** *n.* — **-faced,** impassibile, senza espressione [cp. **dead-pan**].
†**police,** *n.* — **dog,** cane poliziotto, *m.*; — **force,** corpo di polizia, *m.*
†**polite,** *a.* — **society,** il bel mondo.
polythene ['pɔliθi:n], *n.* Politene, *m.*
pong [pɔŋ], *n.* (*colloq.*) Puzzo, fetore, *m.* [cp. **stink**].
†**pony,** *n.* (*Hairstyle*) — **-tail,** coda di cavallo, *f.*
poolroom ['pu:lru:m], *n.* (*Am.*) [cp. **billiard-room**].

†**pop**, *n.* — **music**, musica popolare, *f.*
popcorn [ˈpɔpkɔːɹn], *n.* (*Am.*) Granturco soffiato, *m.*
pop-eyed, *a.* Dagli occhi sporgenti; dagli occhi spalancati (per stupore).
poppycock [ˈpɔpikɔk], *n.* (*Am.*) Sciocchezze, fesserie, *f.pl.*
†**porch**, *n.* (*Am.*) Veranda, *f.*
†**portmanteau**, *n.* — **word**, parola macedonia, *f.*
†**post**, *v.t.* (*Am.*) — **no bills!** [cp. **stick no bills!**].
postlude [ˈpoustluːd], *n.* (*Mus.*) Posludio, postludio, *m.*
post-operative, *a.* (*Med.*) Che è stato operato (di degente all'ospedale).
†**pot**, *n.* (*slang*) Marijuana, *f.*
†**potato**, *n.* (*Am.*) — **chips** [cp. **crisps**].
†**power**, *n.* — **plant**, impianto di energia elettrica, *m.*; — **station**, centrale elettrica, *f.*
pragmatize [ˈprægmətaiz], *v.t.* Rappresentare come reale.
†**precinct**, *n.* (*Am.*) Ufficio di polizia, *m.*
pre-cooked, *a.* Già cucinato, già cotto (si dice soprattutto di cibi in scatola).
pre-driven, *a.* (*Am.*) Di seconda mano (automobile).
pre-election, *a.* — **promises**, promesse di candidatura, *f.pl.*
†**pre-emption**, *n.* (*Leg.*) Diritto di prelazione, *m.*; acquisto fatto esercitando il diritto di prelazione, *m.*
pre-emptive [priːˈemptiv], *a.* Compiuto esercitando il diritto di prelazione.
prefab [ˈpriːfæb], *n.* (*colloq.*) Casa prefabbricata, *f.*
prelims [ˈpriːlimz], *n.pl.* (*colloq.*) Esami preliminari, *m.pl.*
†**press**, *n.* — **agent**, agente pubblicitario, *m.*; — **campaign**, campagna giornalistica, *f.*; — **conference**, conferenza stampa, *f.*
†**pressure**, *n.* (*Pol.*) — **group**, gruppo di pressione, *m.*
pressurized [ˈpreʃəraizd], *a.* (*Aviat.*) Pressurizzato. — **cabin**, cabina pressurizzata, *f.*
prestigious, *a.* Da prestigiatore; ingannevole; (*colloq.*) prestigioso.
preview [ˈpriːvjuː], *v.t.* Vedere o presentare in anteprima. || *n.* Anteprima, *f.*; (*Am.*) prossimamente (di film), *m.*
†**prime**, *a.* (*Am.*) — **time**, ora o ore di punta, *f.*(*pl.*) [cp. **peak hour**].
†**prince**, *n.* (*colloq.*) — **Charming**, Principe Azzurro, *m.*; (*Am.*) — **Albert** [cp. **frock-coat**].
printable [ˈprintəbl], *a.* Stampabile; imprimibile.
prissy [ˈprisi], *a.* (*colloq.*) Effeminato; schifiltoso.
†**problem**, *n.* — **child**, bambino difficile, *m.*
†**producer**, *n.* — **gas**, gas di gassogeno, *m.* **Car using — gas**, automobile a gassogeno, *m.*
professionalism [prəˈfeʃənəlizm], *n.* (*Sport*) Professionismo, *m.*
†**programme**, *v.t.* Progettare, fare il programma di.
programmer, *n.* Programmatore, *m.*
programming, *n.* Programmazione, *f.*
propane [ˈproupein], *n.* Propano, *m.*
†**proper**, *a.* (*Colloq.*) **A — Charlie**, un vero sciocco, un vero balordo, *m.*
†**pry**, *v.t.* (*Am.*) [cp. **prise**].
psephology [seˈfɔlədʒi], *n.* Scienza che analizza le statistiche delle elezioni politiche, traendone conclusioni sull'andamento dei vari partiti, *f.*
psittacosis [sitəˈkousis], *n.* Psittacosi, *f.*
psychedelic [saikəˈdelik], *a.* Psichedelico.
psychoanalyse [saikouˈænəlaiz], *v.t.* Psicanalizzare.
psychokinesis [saikoukiˈniːsis], *n.* Psicocinesi, *f.*
†**psychological**, *a.* — **warfare**, guerra psicologica, *f.*
psychopath [ˈsaikopæθ], *n.* Psicopatico, *m.*
psychopathic [saikoˈpæθik], *a.* Psicopatico.
psychosomatic [saikosəˈmætik], *a.* Psicosomatico.
†**public**, *a.* (*Admin.*) — **relations**, servizio di stampa e propaganda, *m.*, pubbliche relazioni *f.pl.*; — **relations officer**, propagandista, *m.*
†**pump**, *n.* (*Am.*) **Pumps** [cp. **court-shoe**].
†**punch**, *n.* — **card**, scheda perforata, *f.*; (*colloq.*) — **-drunk**, tramortito; stordito.
†**puppet**, *n.* — **government**, governo fantoccio, *m.*
purée [pjuˈrei], *n.* Purè, *m.*
†**push**, *v.t.i.* (*colloq.*) **To — around**, trattare da padrone a servo, bistrattare, spadroneggiare.
pushover [ˈpuʃouvəɹ], *n.* (*colloq.*) Impresa molto facile, *f.*; avversario che si può vincere senza difficoltà, *m.*
†**puss**, *n.* (*colloq.*) **Sour- —**, persona di umore acido o bisbetico, *f.*
†**put**, *v.t.* (*colloq.*) **To — it across someone**, sonarle a uno, darle sode a uno; abbindolare, ingannare uno. || *n.* (*Econ.*) Diritto di opzione, *m.*, opzione, *f.* — **option**, opzione di vendita, *f.*
pyromaniac [pairoˈmeiniæk], *n.* Piromane, *m.*

Q

†**queen**, *n.* **Beauty —**, reginetta, Miss, *f.*
†**queer**, *a.* Omosessuale (uomo o donna). || *n.* invertito, (*vulg.*) finocchio, *m.*; lesbica, *f.*
†**question**, *n.* (*colloq.*) **The 64,000 dollar —**, la domanda più difficile, il problema più arduo.
†**queue**, *n.* (*colloq.*) — **-jumper**, chi, nel far la coda, cerca di scavalcare quelli che lo precedono, *m.*
quickset [ˈkwikset], *a.* (*Bot.*) Di sempreverdi.
quisling [ˈkwizliŋ], *n.* Collaborazionista, *m.f.*; (*colloq.*) traditore, *m.*
quizmaster [ˈkwizmɑːstəɹ], *n.* Presentatore di quiz alle trasmissioni radio-televisive, *m.*
quiz-show, *n.* Programma di quiz, *m.*

R

†**race**, *n.* (*Am.*) — **-track** [cp. **racecourse**].
racialism [ˈreiʃəlizm], *n.* Razzismo, *m.*
racialist, *n.* Razzista, *m.f.*
racism [ˈreisizm], *n.* Razzismo, *m.*
racist, *n.* Razzista, *m.f.*
†**racket**, *n.* (*Am.*) Attività illegale, *f.*; imbroglio, *m.*, truffa, *f.*
†**racy**, *adj.* (*Am.*) [cp. **salacious**].
radac [ˈreidæk], *n.* (*Am.*) Computo automatico delle impronte digitali, *m.*

radiogenic [reidio'dʒenik], *a.* Radiogenico.
radiologist [reidi'ɔlədʒist], *n.* Radiologo, *m.*
radiology, *n.* Radiologia, *f.*
†**rag,** *n.* (*colloq.*) **The — trade,** l'industria della confezione degli abiti, *f.*
raincoat ['reinkout], *n.* Impermeabile, *m.*
†**raise,** *n.* (*Am.*) [cp. **rise**].
†**rake,** *v.t.* **— -off,** senseria, mediazione, *f.*
†**randy,** *a.* (*colloq.*) Lascivo, impudico.
rangy ['reindʒi], *a.* (*Am.*) Aperto, spazioso; (di uomo) alto, forte, e magro.
†**rap,** *v.t.* (*Journalese*) Rimproverare, riprendere severamente.
†**rape,** *n.* (*fig.*) Atto violento e ingiusto, sopruso, *m.*, soperchieria, *f.*; **the — of Czechoslovakia,** l'invasione russa della Cecoslovacchia, *f.*
rapist ['reipist], *n.* Stupratore, *m.*
rapport [ræ'pɔːɹ], *n.* Rapporto, *m.*, comunicazione, *f.*
†**rat,** *n.* **The — -race,** la corsa affannosa e disperata della vita moderna, *f.*; competizione incessante e spietata, *f.*
ratability [reitə'biliti], *n.* Tassabilità, imponibilità, *f.*
†**rate,** *v.t.* (*Am.*) Classificare; considerare, valutare.
†**reaction,** *n.* **Chain —,** reazione a catena, *f.*
reactor [ri'æktəɹ], *n.* (*Phys.*) Reattore, *m.*
realtor ['riːəltɔːɹ], *n.* (*Am.*) Agente immobiliare [cp. **estate agent**].
reapply [riə'plai], *v.t.* Reapplicare.
reappraisal [riːə'preizəl], *n.* Riesame, *m.*; riconsiderazione, *f.*
rebarbative [ri'bɑːɹbətiv], *a.* Severo; burbero, arcigno.
rebirth ['riːbəːɹθ], *n.* Rinascita, *f.*
recalcitrance [ri'kælsitrəns], *n.* Recalcitrazione, *f.*; ostinata opposizione, *f.*
recap ['riːkæp], *v.t.* (*colloq.*) Riassumere. ‖ *n.* Riassunto, *m.*
receptionist [ri'sepʃənist], *n.* Cerimoniere, *m.*; cerimoniera, *f.*; segretaria, *f.*
recidivism [ri'sidivizm], *n.* Recidività, recidiva, *f.*
recidivist, *n.* Recidivo, *m.*, recidiva, *f.*
recitalist [rə'saitəlist], *n.* (*Mus.*) Concertista, *m.f.*
recondition [riːkən'diʃən], *v.t.* Revisionare; ripristinare.
reconditioned, *a.* **A — car,** una macchina revisionata.
reconversion [riːkən'vəːɹʃən], *n.* Riconversione, *f.*
reconvert [riːkən'vəːɹt], *v.t.* Riconvertire.
†**record,** *n.* **— changer,** cambiadischi automatico, *m.*; (*Sport*) **— holder,** detentore di un primato, *m.*, recordman, *m.inv.*; **— player,** giradischi, *m.inv.*; **world —,** record mondiale, *m.* ‖ *v.t.* **— on tape, registrare su nastro.**
redeploy [riːdə'plɔi], *v.t.* (*Mil.*) rispiegare; riorganizzare, ridimensionare.
redeployment [riːdə'plɔimənt], *n.* (*Mil.*) rispiegamento, *m.*; riorganizzazione, *f.*, ridimensionamento, *m.*
redevelopment [riːdi'veləpmənt], *n.* Ricostruzione; nuova costruzione, *f.*
redundancy [ri'dʌndənsi], *n.* Sovrabbondanza, *f.*; ridondamento, *m.*
†**reefer,** *n.* (*Am.*) Nave frigorifera, *f.*; sigaretta drogata o alla marijuana, *f.*
refashion [riː'fæʃən], *v.t.* Rimodellare; rimodernare.
†**refit** ['riːfit], *n.* (*Naut.*) Raddobbo, *m.*
reformist [ri'fɔːɹmist], *n.* (*Pol.*) Riformista, *m.f.*
†**refresher,** *n.* (*Education*) **— course,** corso di aggiornamento, *m.*
régime [rei'ʒiːm], *n.* Regime, *m.*
†**register,** *v.t.* Mostrare o esprimere **in faccia** una determinata emozione (di attori cinematografici); esprimere, manifestare.
regroup [riː'gruːp], *v.t.* Raggruppare (di nuovo), riordinare.
rehash ['riːhæʃ], *n.* Rimaneggiamento, rifacimento, *m.* *v.t.* [riː'hæʃ], Rimaneggiare, rifare.
rehearing [riː'hiəriŋ], *n.* Nuova udienza, *f.*
reincorporate [riːin'kɔːɹpəreit], *v.t.* Incorporare di nuovo.
rejuvenation [ridʒuːvə'neiʃən], *n.* Ringiovanimento, *m.*
†**relay,** *n.* (*Sport*) **— race,** corsa a staffetta, *f.*
†**relegation,** *n.* (*Football*) Retrocessione, *f.* **To suffer —,** retrocedere.
relocate [riːlou'keit], *v.t.i.* (*Am.*) Cambiare di casa, traslocare.
remarriage [riː'mæridʒ], *n.* Nuovo matrimonio, *m.*; seconde nozze *f.,pl.*
†**remote,** *a.* **— control,** telecomando, *m.*; **— -controlled,** telecomandato, teleguidato.
†**remover,** *n.* **Spot or stain —,** smacchiatore, *m.*
†**rent,** *n.* (*Am.*) **For — [cp. to let].**
rep [rep], *n.* (*colloq.*) [cp. **repertory theatre**].
repaper [riː'peipəɹ], *v.t.* Ritappezzare.
repeatable [ri'piːtəbl], *a.* Ripetibile.
repetitious [repə'tiʃəs], *a.* Che si ripete; (*colloq.*) che si ripete troppo.
rephrase [riː'freiz], *v.t.* Formulare o esprimere di nuovo.
†**replay** ['riːplei], *n.* Partita di spareggio, *f.*, spareggio, *m.*
†**require,** *v.t.* (*Am.*) **Required** [cp. **compulsory**].
†**research,** *n.* (*Psych.*) **Motivational —,** ricerca motivazionale, *f.*; **— work,** lavori di ricerca, *m.pl.*
†**reserve,** *n.* (*Econ.*) **Gold —,** riserva aurea, *f.*
reshape [riː'ʃeip], *v.t.* Dare nuova forma a.
†**residence,** *n.* **— permit,** permesso di soggiorno, *m.*
†**rest,** *v.t.* (*Am. Leg.*) [cp. **conclude**].
restructure [riː'strʌktʃəɹ], *v.t.* Ristrutturare.
†**retread,** *v.t.* (*Motor.*) Ricostruire.
revaluation [rivælju'eiʃən], *n.* Rivalutazione, *f.*
revalue [riː'væljuː], *v.t.* Rivalutare.
revisionism [rə'viʒənizm], *n.* (*Pol.*) Revisionismo, *m.*
revisionist [rə'viʒənist], *n.* Revisionista, *m.f.*
revisory [ri'vaizəri], *a.* Che rivede.
revitalize [riː'vaitəlaiz], *v.t.* Dare nuova vita a.
†**rib,** *v.t.* (*Am. colloq.*) Prendere in giro, sfottere.
riffle ['rifl], *v.i.* Scorrere rapidamente. **To — through a book,** scorrere rapidamente un libro.
†**rig,** *v.t.* (*colloq.*) Manipolare; alterare, falsificare.
†**right,** *a.* **— wing,** (*Football*) di ala destra, (*Pol.*) di estrema destra; **— winger,** (*Football*) ala destra, *f.*, (*Pol.*) appartenente all'estrema

destra, *m.f.* || *adv.* (*Am.*) **— now,** proprio ora, in questo momento.
†ringer, *n.* (*Am.*) Imbroglione, *m.*
ringside [ˈriŋsaid], *n.* (*Boxing*) Spazio intorno al quadrato.
†riot, *n.* **— squad,** (polizia) volante, *f.*
risqué [ˈriskei], *a.* Audace, piccante.
†road, *n.* **— accident,** incidente stradale, *m.*; **— block,** blocco stradale, posto di blocco, *m.*; **— building, construction, making,** costruzione stradale o di strade, *f.*; **— sign,** cartello (stradale), *m.*
†roadster, *n.* (*Am.*) [cp. **two-seater**].
roadworks [ˈroudwəːɹks], *n.pl.* Lavori stradali, *m.pl.*
†rocker, *n.* (*slang*) Tipo di giovane rude e manesco, vestito colla giacca di cuoio e sempre in giro sulla motocicletta.
†rocket, *n.* (*colloq.*) Rimprovero, rabbuffo, *m.*; (*rocketry*) **carrier- —,** razzo vettore, *m.*; **— -launcher,** lanciamissili, lanciarazzi, *m.inv.*
rocketry [ˈrɔkitri], *n.* Missilistica, *f.*
†roller, *n.* Bigodì, bigodino, *m.* (*Am.*) **— coaster** [cp. **scenic railway, switchback**].
romanticize [rəˈmæntisaiz], *v.t.i.* Romanzare; assumere atteggiamenti romantici.
roomer [ˈruːməɹ], *n.* (*Am.*) [cp. **lodger**].
†root, *v.i.* (*Am.*) **To — for,** sostenere, appoggiare; (*Sport*) fare il tifo per.
ropy [ˈroupi], *a.* (*colloq.*) Scadente, scalcinato.
†rot, *v.t.* (*slang*) **— -gut,** liquore cattivo, *m.*; liquore forte, *m.*
rotogravure [routogrəˈvjuəɹ], *n.* (*Am.*) [cp. **intaglio**].
†rough, *a.* (*slang*) **— -house,** rissa, *f.*
roughneck, *n.* (*Am.*) Uomo rozzo o zotico, *m.*
†round, *a.* (*Am.*) **— -trip,** viaggio di andata e ritorno, *m.*
†roundabout, *n.* (*traffic*) Rondò, *m.*, circolazione rotatoria, *f.*
rozzer [ˈrɔzəɹ], *n.* (*slang*) [cp. **policeman**].
†rubber, *a.* (*Am.*) **— -check** [cp. **dud cheque**]; **— gloves,** guanti di gomma, *m.pl.*; **— plant,** albero della gomma, *m.*; **— solution,** mastice, *m.*
rubberize [ˈrʌbəraiz], *v.t.* gommare, coprire di gomma.
rubberneck [ˈrʌbəɹnek], *v.i.* (*Am.*) Allungare o torcere il collo (atto tipico delle comitive di turisti intenti a vedere molte cose in poco tempo).
†rubber-stamp, *v.t.* Timbrare; (*fig.*) approvare.
ruckle [ˈrʌkl], *v.t.i.* **— up,** increspare; incresparsi. || *n.* Piega, *f.*; increspamento, *m.*, increspatura, *f.*
ruckus [ˈrʌkəs], *n.* (*Am. slang*) [cp. **rumpus**].
ruction [ˈrʌkʃən], *n.* Diverbio, *m.*, scenata, *f.*
rumbustious [rʌmˈbʌstʃəs], *a.* Rumoroso, chiassoso.
†run, *n.* (*Am.*) [cp. **ladder**]; (*colloq.*) **— of the mill,** ordinario, regolare; banale.
ruritanian [ruːriˈteiniən], *a.* Fantastico; romantico; irreale.
rutabaga [ruːtəˈbeigə], *n.* (*Am.*) [cp. **swede**].

S

sadism [ˈseidizm], *n.* Sadismo, *m.*
sadist, *n.* Sadista, *m.f.*
sadistic [səˈdistik], *a.* Sadico.
safari [səˈfɑːri], n. viaggio (*m.*) o spedizione (*f.*) di cacciatori; (*colloq.*) viaggio (*m.*) o spedizione (*f.*) in terre remote e selvagge; qualsiasi lungo e fortunoso viaggio, *m.*
†safety, *n.* (*Aer.*) **— factor,** coefficiente di sicurezza, *m.*
†saint, *n.* (*fig.*) **Plaster —,** santo falso, santo di cartapesta, *m.*
salability [seiləˈbiliti], *n.* Facilità di smercio, *f.*
†sale, *n.* **— goods,** merci in liquidazione, *m.pl.*; **— price,** prezzo di liquidazione, *m.*
†saloon, *n.* (*Am.*) [cp. **public-house, pub**].
†salt, *n.* **— dispenser,** spargisale, *m.* [cp. **salt-cellar**].
†same, *a.* (*fig.*) **The — to you with (brass) knobs on,** idem con patate.
sandalled [ˈsændəld], *a.* Calzato di sandali.
†sandwich, *n.* **Toasted —,** panino toast, *m.*
sanforized [ˈsænfəraizd], *a.* (*Reg. trade name*) Irrestringibile.
sassy [ˈsæsi], *a.* (*Am.*) Insolente, impertinente [cp. **saucy**].
†satellite, *n.* **TV —,** satellite spaziale artificiale usato nelle trasmissioni televisive, *m.*, Telstar, *m.*; **— -town,** città-satellite, *f.*
savvy [ˈsævi], *n.* (*colloq.*) Senno, *m.*; comprendonio, *m.*
†scan, *v.t.i.* (*TV*) Analizzare, esplorare.
scanner [ˈskænəɹ], *n.* (*TV*) Analizzatore, *m.*
scarper [ˈskɑːɹpəɹ], *v.i.* (*slang*) Scappare, tagliare la corda, squagliarsi.
scatterbrained, *a.* Scervellato, stordito.
schematize [ˈskiːmətaiz], *v.t.* Schematizzare.
schizoid [ˈskitsɔid], *a.* Schizoide.
†school, *n.* **Comprehensive —,** scuola inglese in cui i vari tipi di scuole secondarie vengono fusi in un solo istituto.
science-fiction, *a.* Fantascientifico. || *n.* Fantascienza, *f.*
scientifiction [saientiˈfikʃən], *n.* (*Am.*) Fantascienza, *f.*
scofflaw [ˈskɔflɔː], *n.* (*Am.*) Trasgressore della legge, *m.*
scram [skræm], *v.i.* (*Am.*) Battersela, filare, scappare.
scrappy [ˈskræpi], *a.* Frammentario.
scrawly [ˈskrɔːli], *a.* Scarabocchiato.
screamingly [ˈskriːmiŋli], *adv.* (*colloq.*) **The farce was — funny,** la farsa era terribilmente buffa.
†screech, *v.i.* (*of brakes*) Stridere. || *n.* **Stridio,** *m.*
screed [skriːd], *n.* Filastrocca, *f.*
†screen, *n.* **— adaptation,** adattamento cinematografico, *m.*
screwball [ˈskruːbɔːl], *n.* (*Am.*) Tipo strambo, eccentrico, pazzoide, *m.*
screwy [ˈskruːi], *a.* (*colloq.*) Pazzo.
†script, *n.* (*Cinema, Radio, TV*) Copione, *m.*
scrubwoman, *n.* (*Am.*) [cp. **char**].
scruffy [ˈskrʌfi], *a.* (*colloq.*) Scadente, malandato, scalcinato.
scuff [skʌf], *v.t.* Strascicare; **sfiorare.**
†sea, *n.* (*colloq.*) **To get one's — legs,** acquistare il piede marino.
sealer [ˈsiːləɹ], *n.* Cacciatore di foche, *m.*; imbarcazione per la caccia alla foca, *f.*
seaport [ˈsiːpɔːɹt], *n.* Porto marittimo, *m.*
†search, *v.t.i.* **To — far and wide,** cercare in lungo e in largo; **to — high and low,** cercare in alto e in basso.

†second [si'kɔnd], *v.t.* Togliere dal posto o lavoro normale e impiegare in un compito speciale.
†second, *a.* (*Pol.*) — **chamber,** camera alta, *f.*; (*Am.*) — **floor** [cp. **first floor**].
†secret, *a.* — **agent,** agente segreto, *m.*; **top —,** riservatissimo.
†section, *v.t.* Sezionare.
sectionalize ['sekʃənəlaiz], *v.t.* Dividere in sezioni.
†security, *n.* **Social —,** previdenza sociale, *f.*
†sedan, *n.* (*Am.*) [cp. **saloon car**].
seeded ['si:did], *a.* (*Sport*) Classificato.
seedless ['si:dlis], *a.* Senza semi (di frutta).
segmental, segmentary [seg'mentəl, 'segməntəri], *a.* Segmentale; a segmenti.
segregationist [segrə'geiʃənist], *n.* (*Pol.*) Segregazionista, *m.*
seismologist [saiz'mɔlədʒist], *n.* Sismologo, *m.*
seismology, *n.* Sismologia, *f.*
selective [si'lektiv], *a.* Selettivo. **Selective Employment Tax (SET),** tassa selettiva sull'impiego, *f.*
self-appointed, *a.* Autonominato.
self-assurance, *n.* Sicurezza di sè, *f.*
self-closing, *a.* — **door,** porta a chiusura automatica, *f.*; — **tap,** rubinetto a pressione, *m.*
†self-determination, *n.* (*Pol.*) **Right of —,** diritto di scegliere il proprio ordinamento, *m.*
self-locking, *a.* A chiusura automatica.
self-regulating, *a.* Autoregolatore.
self-service, *n.* Il servirsi da sè.
†sell, *n.* (*Am.*) Vendita, *f.*; (*colloq.*) **hard —,** vendita effettuata con una pubblicità martellante e aggressiva, *f.*; **soft —,** vendita effettuata mediante suggerimenti e propaganda persuasiva, *f.*
sellotape ['seloteip], *n.* (*reg. trade name*) Nastro adesivo, *m.*
†semen, *n.* — **donor,** donatore di sperma, *m.*
semifurnished, *a.* Semilavorato.
†seminal, *a.* (*fig.*) Originale; creativo; che racchiude in fieri sviluppi importanti; che precorre grandi avvenimenti.
semi-smile, *n.* Mezzo sorriso, *m.*
†send, *v.t.* (*colloq.*) Entusiasmare.
sensationalist, *n.* Chi cerca di far sensazione.
†sense, *n.* **To make —,** essere coerente, essere ragionevole (di azione, di cosa, ecc.).
servery ['sə:ɹvəri], *n.* (*Am.*) Posto dove vengono serviti rinfreschi, bar, *m.*
†service, *n.* (*TV*) — **area,** zona utile, *f.*; — **charge,** servizio compreso, *m.*; (*Motor.*) — **station,** stazione di servizio, *f.*
servo-brake, *n.* (*Motor.*) Servofreno, *m.*
†set, *a.* — **-piece,** rappresentazione (*f.*) o spettacolo (*m.*) di ruolo.
†settle, *v.t.i.* (*colloq.*) **To — for,** accettare come compromesso, accontentarsi di.
sexy ['seksi], *a.* Lubrico, salace.
†shade, *n.* (*Am.*) [cp. **blind**].
†shadow, *a.* Non operante, ma pronto a funzionare in caso di emergenza. (*Pol.*) — **cabinet,** gruppo di capi dell'opposizione nel parlamento britannico che costituirebbe il gabinetto se il loro partito venisse chiamato al potere, gabinetto ombra, *m.* || *n.* (*make-up*) **Eye- —,** ombretto, *m.*
†shambles, *n.* (*colloq.*) Luogo in cui regna disordine o confusione, *m.*; posto rovinato o devastato, *m.*
sheepman ['ʃi:pmən], *n.* (*Am.*) [cp. **sheep-farmer**].
†shellac, *v.t.* (*Am.*) Sconfiggere; sfracellare.
shellfire, *n.* Bombardamento, *m.*
shiftwork ['ʃiftwə:ɹk], *n.* Lavoro a turno, *m.*
†shingle, *n.* (*Am.*) [cp. **(door) plate**].
†ship, *n.* (*Navy*) **Decoy —,** nave civetta, *f.*; **mother —,** nave appoggio, *f.*; **repair —,** nave officina, *f.*
†shipping, *n.* — **company** or **firm,** compagnia o società di navigazione, *f.*
†shock, *n.* — **tactics,** tattica d'urto, *f.*
†shoot, *v.t.* (*fig.*) **To — down in flames,** stroncare; confutare decisamente.
†shop, *v.t.* (*slang*) Far imprigionare.
shopworn, *a.* Scolorito, sciupato.
†short, *a.* — **list,** rosa, *f.*; — **sight,** vista corta, miopia, *f.* || *n.* (*Cinema*) Cortometraggio, *m.*
†short-circuit, *v.t.i.* Cortocircuitare, mettere in corto circuito; andare in corto circuito.
†show, *n.* (*Art*) **One-man —,** mostra personale, *f.*; (*Theat.*) soliloquio, *m.*
show-off, *n.* Esibizionista, *m.f.*
†shrift, *n.* (*fig.*) **To give short — to,** trattare in modo spiccio, trattare bruscamente; liquidare prontamente.
†shut, *v.t.* — **down,** sospendere l'attività (in una fabbrica, ecc.), chiudere.
shutdown, *n.* Chiusura, *f.*; sospensione, *f.*
†shy, *prep.* (*Am.*) [cp. **short of**].
side-effect, *n.* Effetto secondario, *m.*
†sight, *n.* — **-read,** leggere (la musica) a prima vista.
†sign, *v.t.i.* (*fig.*) **To — on the dotted line,** attenersi alle norme vigenti; seguire le istruzioni ricevute. || *n.* — **language,** mimica, *f.*
†signature, *n.* (*Radio*) — **tune,** sigla musicale, *f.*
sinusitis [sainə'saitis], *n.* Sinusite, *f.*
†silent, *a.* (*Am.*) — **partner** [cp. **sleeping partner**].
†ski, *n.* — **jump,** salto (con gli sci), *m.*; — **lift,** sciovia, *f.*
†skin, *n.* — **-diver,** sommozzatore, *m.*; — **-tight,** molto stretto, aderente alla pelle.
skinhead ['skinhed], *n.* (*slang*) Tipo di giovane rude e manesco, il cui nome deriva dai capelli cortissimi che suole portare.
skint [skint], *a.* (*colloq.*) Al verde, alle strette.
†skull, *n.* — **and crossbones,** teschio e tibie incrociate, testa di morto.
†sky, *n.* (*fig.*) (*colloq.*) **Pie in the —,** compenso in cielo, dopo la morte, a chi in terra si trova nei guai, *m.*
skyjacker ['skaidʒækəɹ], *n.* (*Am.*) Chi, a mano armata, fa dirottare un aereo, pirata dell'aria, *m.*
†slam, *v.t.* (*Journalese*) Criticare aspramente, stroncare [cp. **lambaste**].
†slant, *n.* (*Am.*) [cp. **bias**].
sleazy ['sli:zi], *a.* (*colloq.*) Losco, equivoco, sospetto.
†slick, *n.* **Oil —,** chiazza di carburante, *f.* (sul mare, sui fiumi, ecc.). || *v.t.* (*Am.*) — **up** [cp. **tidy up**].
slingshot ['sliŋʃɔt], *n.* (*Am.*) [cp. **catapult**].
†slug, *v.t.* (*Am.*) [cp. **slog**].
smarmy ['smɑ:ɹmi], *a.* (*colloq.*) Untuoso; adulatorio; servile.

†**smart**, *a.* (*colloq.*) — **Alec**, uomo scaltro e spregiudicato, *m.*
smashing [ˈsmæʃiŋ], *a.* (*colloq.*) Meraviglioso, eccellente, coi fiocchi.
smog [smɔg], *n.* (composto di **smoke** e **fog**) Nebbia o caligine impregnata di fumo, *f.*, smog, *m.*
smokescreen, *n.* Cortina di fumo, cortina fumogena, cortina di nebbia, *f.*
smooch [smuːtʃ], *v.i.* [cp. **neck**].
†**snarl**, *v.t.* (*colloq.*) — **up**, intasare, imbottigliare (traffico stradale). ‖ *n.* — **up**, intasamento, imbottigliamento, *m.*
†**sneak**, *v.i.* (*Am.*) — **thief**, ladruncolo, *m.*
snide [snaid], *a.* Falso, contraffatto; disonesto; sottilmente o maliziosamente denigratorio.
†**snigger**, *n.* Risolino malizioso o cinico, *m.*
snoop [snuːp], *v.i.* Ficcare il naso, ficcanasare.
snooper [ˈsnuːpəɹ], *n.* (*slang*) Spia, *f.*, delatore, inquisitore, *m.*
snooty [ˈsnuːti], *a.* (*slang*) Che si dà delle arie, altezzoso.
snorkel [ˈʃnɔːɹkəl], *n.* (*Naval*) Presa d'aria per sommergibili, *f.*
snot [snɔt], *n.* (*vulg.*) Muco, moccio, *m.* — **rag**, fazzoletto, *m.*
snotty [ˈsnɔti], *a.* (*vulg.*) Moccioso; (*slang*) sdegnoso.
snowmobile [ˈsnouməbiːl], *n.* Autoslitta, *f.*
†**sob**, *v.i.* (*Am.*) — **-sister**, scrittrice sentimentale e piagnucolosa, *f.*
soccer [ˈsɔkəɹ], *n.* (*colloq.*) (Termine familiare per Association Football) il giuoco del calcio.
socialite [ˈsouʃəlait], *n.* (*Am.*) Chi appartiene al bel mondo, *m.f.*, membro dell'alta società, *m.*
†**socialize**, *v.t.* Frequentare il bel mondo.
†**sock**, *n.* (*colloq.*) **To pull one's socks up**, scuotersi, darsi da fare; rendersi efficiente.
†**soft**, *a.* — **drinks** [cp. **minerals**].
†**soldier**, *v.i.* Fare il soldato. (*fig.*) **To — on**, continuare, perseverare, durarla.
sonic [ˈsɔnik], *a.* (*Aviat.*) — **boom**, scoppio sonico, boato sonico, *m.*
†**sophisticated**, *a.* (*Am.*) Scaltrito; evoluto, moderno.
†**sound**, *n.* — **-barrier**, muro del suono, *m.*
sozzled [ˈsɔzld], *a.* (*slang*) Brillo, alticcio.
†**space**, *n.* **The — age**, l'era spaziale, l'età spaziale, *f.*; — **-ship**, astronave, *f.*; — **travel**, astronautica, *f.*
spaceman [ˈspeismən], *n.* Astronauta, *m.* [cp. **astronaut**].
spastic [ˈspæstik], *a.* (*Med.*) Spastico.
†**special**, *a.* (*Am.*) — **delivery** [cp. **express delivery**].
speleologist [spiːliˈɔlədʒist], *n.* Speleologo, *m.*
speleology, *n.* Speleologia, *f.*
†**spell**, *v.t.* (*fig.*) **To — out**, chiarire; rendere evidente; sottolineare; dire in tutte lettere; (*Am.*) [cp. **relieve**].
spelunk [speˈlʌŋk], *v.i.* (*Am.*) Esplorare le grotte, dedicarsi alla speleologia.
†**spigot**, *n.* (*Am.*) [cp. **tap**].
†**spiky**, *a.* (*colloq.*) Mordace, aspro, tagliente.
spiv [spiv], *m.* (*slang*) Borsanerista, intrallazzista, *m.*
splashdown [ˈsplæʃdaun], *n.* (*Space capsule*) Ammaraggio al ritorno da un viaggio spaziale, *f.*
†**splinter**, *n.* (*Pol.*) — **party**, scheggia di partito, *f.*, partito scheggia, *m.*
†**split**, *a.* **In a — second**, in una frazione di secondo; (*colloq.*) in un battibaleno.
spoof [spuːf], *n.* Millanteria, *f.*, bluff, *m.*, inganno, *m.*
†**spot**, *n.* — **welding**, saldatura a punti, *f.*
†**spotlight**, *v.t.* (*Theat.*, *Cinema*) Puntare il riflettore su; mettere in evidenza, illuminare.
†**square**, *n.* (*colloq.*) Persona seria e posata, *f.*; uomo di vedute convenzionali, *m.*; filisteo, *m.*
†**squash**, *n.* (*Am.*) [cp. **vegetable marrow**].
squiffy [ˈskwifi], *a.* (*slang*) Brillo, alticcio.
stabilizer, *n.* Stabilizzatore, *m.*
staffer [ˈstɑːfəɹ], *n.* (*Am.*) Membro del personale, *m.*
†**stagger**, *v.t.* (*Administration*) Regolare con turni prestabiliti (traffico, ferie, ore di lavoro, ecc.).
stairway [ˈstɛəɹwei], *n.* (*Am.*) [cp. **staircase**].
stamping-ground, *n.* (*slang*) Luogo di ritrovo molto frequentato, *m.*
stand-in, *n.* (*Cinema*) Controfigura, *f.*
starlet [ˈstɑːɹlit], *n.* (*Cinema*) Stellina, *f.*
stash [stæʃ], *v.t.* (*Am.*) **To — away**, mettere da parte, riporre; accumulare [cp. **stack, stow**].
†**station**, *n.* (*Am.*) **Comfort —**, latrina, *f.*, cesso, gabinetto, *m.*; (*Rail.*) — **manager**, capostazione, *m.*; (*Am.*) — **wagon** [cp. **estate car**].
†**statistics**, *n.pl.* **Vital —**, statistiche demografiche, *f.pl.*; (*hum.*) le tre misure (in una donna o ragazza): intorno al petto, alla vita e alle anche.
†**status**, *n.* (*colloq.*) — **symbol**, indice di classe o di rango, *m.*; **loss of —**, *diminutio capitis.*
†**stave**, *n.* (*Mus.*) Pentagramma, *m.*
steakburger [ˈsteikbəːɹgəɹ], *n.* (*Am.*) Panino imbottito di bistecca, *m.*
†**steering**, *a.* — **committee**, comitato direttivo, *m.*
†**stellar**, *a.* (*Cinema*) Importante.
†**stem**, *v.i.* (*colloq.*) Nascere, derivare.
†**step**, *v.i.* (*colloq.*) **To — on the gas**, accelerare il motore; (*fig.*) fare presto, spicciarsi.
stereo [ˈsteriou], *a.* (*colloq.*) [cp. **stereophonic**].
stereophonic [sterioˈfɔnik], *a.* Stereofonico.
†**stick**, *v.t.* (*fig.*) **To — one's neck out**, esporsi agli attacchi, rendersi vulnerabile.
†**stiletto**, *n.* — **heel**, tacco a spillo, *m.*
†**still**, *n.* (*Cinema*) Fotogrammia *m.*
†**stock**, *n.* — **size**, taglia corrente, *f.*
stockist [ˈstɔkist], *n.* (*Comm.*) Grossista, *m.*; fornitore, *m.*
stockpile, *n.* Riserva di armi, materiali, ecc., *f.* ‖ *v.t.i.* Far riserve (di armi, materiali, ecc.).
stoned [stound], *a.* (*slang*) Ubbriaco fradicio.
stooge [stuːdʒ], *n.* (*Theat.*) Spalla, *f.*; (*fig.*) strumento cieco della volontà altrui, *m.*
†**stop**, *n.* **To pull all the stops out**, tirar fuori tutti i registri (di un organo); (*fig.*) esprimersi o agire in modo esuberante o drammatico; (*Am.*) — **-over**, fermata, sosta, *f.* (durante un viaggio). ‖ *v.i.* (*Am.*) **To — off**, fermarsi, fare un breve soggiorno.
†**stopping**, *n.* (*Motor.*) — **distance**, distanza di arresto, *f.*; — **time**, tempo di arresto, *m.*
†**straight**, *n.* (*Sport*) **Home** or **finishing —**, dirittura d'arrivo, *f.* ‖ *a.* (*Am.*) [cp. **neat**].

stratoliner ['strætolainəɹ], *n.* Apparecchio di linea per volo stratosferico, *m.*
†straw, *n.* (*fig.*) **Straws in the wind,** leggeri indizi, *m.pl.*
†street, *n.* (*Am.*) **— -cleaner** [cp. **street-sweeper**].
†strike, *n.* (*Am.*) **Wildcat —,** sciopero non autorizzato dal sindacato, *m.*
†string, *n.* (*colloq.*) Condizione, limitazione, *f.* (*Am.*) **— bean** [cp. **French bean**]; **without strings,** senza condizioni, senza limitazioni.
stripper ['stripəɹ], *n.* (*slang*) Artista di spogliarello, *f.*
strip-tease, *n.* Strip-tease, spogliarello, *m.*
†strong, *a.* **— -arm,** coercitivo, coattivo, violento.
†student, *n.* (*Am.*) [cp. **schoolboy, schoolgirl**].
†stuff, *v.t.* (*colloq.*) **A stuffed shirt,** un pallone gonfiato. || *n.* **Hard —,** bevanda alcoolica, *f.*; droga forte e pericolosa, *f.*
stuntman ['stʌntmæn], *n.* (*Cinema*) Controfigura, *f.*
stylize ['stailaiz], *v.t.* Stilizzare.
stylus ['stailus], *n.* (*Gramophone*) Puntina, *f.*
†submarine, *n.* (*Am. slang*) Immigrante clandestino, *m.*
†subway, *n.* (*Am.*) [cp. **underground**].
†sugar, *n.* (*Am.*) **— -bowl** [cp. **sugar-basin**].
†suit, *v.t.* (*colloq.*) **To — down to the ground,** andare a fagiolo.
†summit, *n.* (*Pol.*) **— meeting,** incontro (*m.*) o conferenza (*f.*) al vertice.
†sun, *n.* **— -glasses,** occhiali da sole, *m.pl.*; **— (-ray) lamp,** lampada a raggi ultravioletti, *f.*
supermale ['su:pəɹmeil], *n.* (*Med.*) Maschio dotato di un addizionale cromosomo maschile, *m.*
supermarket ['su:pəɹmɑ:ɹkit], *n.* Supermercato, *m.*
supersonic [su:pəɹ'sɔnik], *a.* Supersonico. **— bang** [cp. **sonic boom**].
suppressor [sə'presəɹ], *n.* (*Radio*) Soppressore, *m.*
†surgery, *n.* **Tree —,** termine di origine recente che indica il taglio o la potatura degli alberi nelle vie e nei giardini di una città.
†survival, *n.* (*colloq.*) **Medicated —,** sopravvivenza a furia di cure mediche di chi per estrema vecchiaia o grave infermità è pronto a morire, *f.*
†swallow, *n.* (*fig.*) **One — does not make a summer,** una rondine non fa primavera.
†switch, *v.t.* (*colloq.*) Cambiare; scambiare.
†sweep, *v.t.* (*colloq.*) **To — under the carpet,** far sparire, nascondere, mettere nel dimenticatoio (una magagna).
†swinging, *a.* (*slang*) Vivo, dinamico; in gamba.
†swish, *a.* (*colloq.*) Lussuoso, sontuoso [cp. **plush**].
swizz [swiz], *n.* (*colloq.*) Inganno, *m.*, frode, *f.*
synchromesh ['siŋkromeʃ], *a.* (*Motor.*) **— gear,** cambio sincronizzato, *m.*
syndrome ['sindroum], *n.* (*Med.*) Sindromo, *m.*

T

†tab, *n.* (*colloq.*) **To keep tabs on,** tener d'occhio, sorvegliare.
taffy ['tæfi], *n.* (*Am.*) [cp. **toffee**].
†tail, *v.i.* **To — off,** diminuire, assottigliarsi, perdersi.
†take, *v.t.* (*colloq.*) **What it takes,** i requisiti, i numeri, *m.pl.*; **to — for a ride,** ingannare; liquidare; (*Comm.*) **— -over,** rilevamento, assorbimento (di un'azienda in un'altra più grande), *m.*; **to — the mickey out of,** sbaldanzire, sgonfiare, umiliare; prendere in giro, canzonare, sfottere.
†talk, *v.i.* (*colloq.*) **To — big,** esagerare, smargiassare; (*Am.*) **to — turkey,** dire la verità, parlar chiaro, parlare fuori dei denti.
†talking, *n.* (*colloq.*) **— -point,** argomento di cui si parla, *m.*, questione d'attualità, *f.*
†tape, *n.* **— -recorder,** magnetofono, registratore, *m.*; **— -recording,** registrazione a nastro, *f.*
tatty ['tæti], *a.* (*colloq.*) Scadente, malandato, scalcinato.
†tax, *n.* (*colloq.*) **— dodger,** evasore (fiscale), *m.*; **— evasion,** evasione fiscale, *f.*
†taxi, *n.* (*Am.*) **— -stand** [cp. **cab-rank**].
†teach, *v.t.* (*Am.*) **— in,** discussione in pubblico tra professori, studenti, e altre persone interessate, su qualche importante argomento d'attualità, *f.*
†tear, *n.* (*colloq.*) **A — -jerker,** un dramma lacrimevole, una pellicola lacrimogena.
technocracy [tek'nɔkrəsi], *n.* Governo di tecnici o scienziati, *m.*
technocrat ['teknəkræt], *n.* Tecnocrate, *m.*
technolator ['teknəleitəɹ], *n.* (*Am.*) Studioso di tecnologia, *m.*
technologist, *n.* Tecnico, *m.*
teddy-boy ['tedibɔi], *n.* Giovane del popolo che sfoggia vestiti eleganti, *m.*; giovane teppista, *m.*
teenage ['ti:neidʒ], *a.* Adolescente.
†teething, *n.* (*fig.*) **— troubles, — problems,** crisi di assestamento, *f.*, problema di crescenza, *m.*
teeter ['ti:təɹ], *v.i.* Stare in bilico, tentennare, vacillare.
telecar ['telikɑ:ɹ], *n.* (*Am.*) Motoveicolo per invio e ricezione di telegrammi, *m.*
telecast ['telika:st], *n.* (*Am.*) Teletrasmissione, *f.*
telegenic [teli'dʒenik], *a.* Telegenico.
†telephone, *n.* (*Am.*) **— booth** [cp. **— box**].
teleprompter ['teliprɔmptəɹ], *n.* Suggeritore televisivo, *m.*
teletype ['telitaip], *v.t.i.* Telescrivere. || *n.* Telescrivente, *m.*
teletypesetter, *n.* Telecompositrice, *f.*
†tell, *v.t.* (*colloq.*) **To — someone where he gets off,** sgridare, rabbuffare uno.
telly ['teli], *n.* (*colloq.*) Televisione, *f.*; televisore, *m.*; trasmissione televisiva, *f.*
tenderize ['tendəraiz], *v.t.* (*Am.*) Rendere tenero (carne e altri commestibili).
tenderloin ['tendəɹlɔin], *n.* (*Am.*) [cp. **undercut, fillet**].
tenigue [te'ni:g], *n.* (*Am.*) Stanchezza psicofisica, *f.*
tenpins ['tenpinz], *n.pl.* (*Am.*) [cp. **nine-pins**].
thalidomide [θə'lidəmaid], *n.* (*Med.*) Talidomide, *m.f.*
†theatre, *n.* **— in the round,** teatro col palcoscenico a centro dell'auditorio, *m.*
†therapy, *n.* Terapia, *f.*; **group —,** terapia di gruppo, *f.*

†thing, *n.* (*colloq.*) **It's one of those things!** Son cose che capitano! Cose che capitano ai vivi! (*colloq.*) **to have a — about something or somebody,** avere un'antipatia o mania per qualche cosa o persona.
†think, *v.t.i.* (*Am. colloq.*) **— -tank,** istituto, laboratorio o studio dove scienziati indagano o preparano apprestamenti tecnologici, *m.*; luogo in cui si pensa o studia collegialmente, *m.*
†thrash, *v.t.* **To — about,** dimenarsi, divincolarsi.
throwback [ˈθroubæk], *n.* (*Biol.*) Regresso, *m.*; individuo regredito, *m.*
†thumb, *n.* **— -nail sketch,** disegno o schizzo grossolano e approzzimativo, *m.*, sbozzatura, *f.*; (*fig.*) descrizione orale o scritta dello stesso tipo; (*Am.*) **— -tack** [cp. **drawing-pin**]. || *v.t.* **To — a lift,** chiedere, facendo segnale col pollice, un viaggio gratuito a un' auto che passa, fare l'autostop.
ticker [ˈtikəɹ], *n.* (*colloq.*) Orologio, *m.*; cuore, *m.*; (*Am.*) telegrafo, *m.*; telescrivente, *m.* **— tape,** nastro di telescrivente, *m.*
†ticket-agent [cp. **booking-clerk**].
tiddly [ˈtidli], *a.* (*slang*) Brillo, alticcio.
†tie, *n.* (*fig.*) **The old school —** [cp. **the old boy network**]; (*Am.*) **— -up** [cp. **stoppage**].
†time, *n.* (*Am.*) **Big —,** su vasta scala; in grande stile; **Time,** pubblico servizio telefonico che trasmette oralmente l'ora precisa, *m.*; (*a Roma, a Milano*) L'Ora Esatta, *f.*; (*Sport*) **extra —,** tempo supplementare, *m.*; **— bomb,** bomba a orologeria o a tempo, *f.*; **— -lag,** ritardo, *m.*
†tin, *n.* (*fig.*) **— -god,** idolo di cartapesta, *m.*, persona o idea dappoco portata alle stelle, *f.*
tinter [ˈtintəɹ], *n.* (*Am.*) Film a colori, *m.*
†toffee, *n.* (*colloq.*) **— -nosed,** altezzoso, borioso; vanitoso.
togetherness [təˈgeθəɹnis], *n.* (*Am.*) Lo stare insieme, *m.*; unione, solidarietà, *f.*; socievolezza, *f.*
†token, *n.* **Book —,** buono-libro, *m.*
†top, *n.* (*Am.*) [cp. **hood**].
trainee [treiˈniː] *n.* Apprendista, *m.f.*
†touch, *n.* (*colloq.*) **To be a soft — for,** essere facilmente persuaso a concedere (denaro, favori, ecc.).
†tower, *n.* (*Aviat.*) **Control —,** torre de controllo, *f.*
†trading, *n.* **Horse —,** commercio dei cavalli, *m.*; (*fig.*) mercanteggiare, pattuire, *m.*
†traffic, *n.* **— jam,** ingorgo stradale, *m.*
†trailer, *n.* (*Cinema*) Prossimamente, *m.*
tranquillizer [ˈtræŋkwilaizəɹ], *n.* Calmante, sedativo, *m.*
transceiver [trɑːnˈsiːvəɹ], *n.* (*Radio*) ricetrasmettitore, *m.*
†transfer, *n.* Biglietto di coincidenza tranviario, *m.*
transistor [trɑːnˈzistəɹ], *n.* Transistore, *m.*
†transplant [ˈtrɑːnzplɑːnt], *n.* (*Med.*) Trapianto chirurgico, *m.* (rene, fegato, cuore, ecc.).
transvestism [trɑːnzˈvestizm], *n.* Desiderio o abitudine di adottare le vesti, le maniere, e spesso anche la sessualità dell'altro sesso.
transvestite [trɑːnzˈvestait], *n.* Chi pratica il **transvestism.**
travelogue [ˈtrɑːvəlɔg], *n.* (*Cinema*) Documentario turistico, *m.*
travolator [ˈtrævəleitəɹ], *n.* Specie di rampa mobile per il trasporto di passeggeri nelle stazioni della metropolitana londinese, *f.*
trendy [ˈtrendi], *a.* (*colloq.*) Alla moda, conforme all'andazzo.
trichologist [triˈkɔlədʒist], *n.* Tricologo, *m.*
trichology [triˈkɔlədʒi], *n.* Tricologia, *f.*
†trick, *n.* (*colloq.*) **The whole bag of tricks,** tutt'i trucchi del mestiere, *m.pl.*; tutta la faccenda, *f.*; **— photography,** fotografia truccata, *f.*, trucco fotografico, *m.*
†trigger, *n.* (*Am.*) **— -happy,** che ha voglia di sparare, dal grilletto facile.
†trillion, *n.* (*Am.*) [cp. **billion**].
triumphalism [traiˈʌmfəlizm], *n.* Trionfalismo, *m.*
†trolley, *n.* **Shopping —,** carrello per la spesa, *m.*
†trouble, *n.* **— -shooter,** operaio che scopre e localizza i guasti, *m.*
†truck, *n.* (*Am.*) Autocarro, *m.* (*Am.*) **— farmer** [cp. **market-gardener**].
†trunk, *n.* (*Am. Motor.*) Portabagagli, *m.* [cp. **boot**].
†tube, *n.* (*Am. Radio*) [cp. **valve**].
†tumble, *v.i.* (*colloq.*) **To — to,** accorgersi di, rendersi conto di.
†tune, *v.t.* (*Radio*) **To — in (to),** sintonizzarsi (su).
turbo-prop [ˈtəːɹboprɔp], *n.* (*Aviat.*) Turboelica, *f.* **— plane,** aeroplano a turboelica, *m.*
tuxedo [tʌkˈsiːdou], *n.* (*Am.*) Smoking a doppio petto, *m.*
twerp, twirp [twəːɹp], *n.* (*vulg.*) Cialtrone, mascalzone, *m.*
†twilight, *n.* (*colloq.*) **— housing,** le case più scadenti e derelitte dei quartieri poveri, *f.pl.*
twinning [ˈtwiniŋ], *n.* Associazione fraterna tra due città in paesi diversi, *f.*; gemellaggio, *m.*
twit [twit], *n.* (*colloq.*) Persona insignificante, nullità, *f.*; sciocco, balordo, *m.*
†two, *a.* (*Motor.*) **— -seater,** macchina a due posti, *f.*

U

umpteen [ˈʌmptiːn], *a.* (*colloq.*) Molti, parecchi.
umpteenth, *a.* (*colloq.*) Ennesimo.
†uncle, *n.* (*colloq.*) **Bob's your —,** sei a posto, sei a cavallo.
uncrushable [ʌnˈkrʌʃəbl], *a.* Antipiega.
†undated, *a.* Che non è caduto in disuso; che non ha perduto la sua popolarità; ancora in voga.
†underbelly, *n.* (*colloq.*) Posto (*m.*) o area (*f.*) vulnerabile.
undercover [ˈʌndəɹkʌvəɹ], *a.* Segreto, nascosto, clandestino. **— agent, — man,** agente segreto, *m.*
underdeveloped [ʌndəɹdiˈveləpt], *a.* Sottosviluppato.
underemployed [ʌndəɹimˈplɔid], *a.* Sottoccupato.
†underground, *n.* (*slang*) La musica, la poesia, l'arte, e in genere la coltura del mondo 'sotterraneo' dei **hippies.**
underpass [ˈʌndəɹpaːs], *n.* Sottovia, *f.*
underprivileged [ʌndəɹˈprivilidʒd], *a.* Bisognoso, disagiato, povero.

undershirt ['ʌndəɹʃə:ɹt], *n.* (*Am.*) Maglia, camiciola, *f.*
†**union,** *n.* (*Am.*) **— suit** [cp. **combinations**].
unisex ['ju:niseks], *a.* Che si può usare per ambo i sessi (abitudini, educazione, idee, ecc.).
†**university,** *n.* **The Open University, University of the Air,** università radiofonica e televisiva, *f.*
†**up,** *adv.* (*colloq.*) **To be on the — and —,** essere in continuo aumento; andare a gonfie vele; **to be one — on someone,** aver un vantaggio su uno.
uppity ['ʌpiti], *a.* [cp. **uppish**].
upsurge ['ʌpsə:ɹdʒ], *n.* Insorgenza, *f.*; sollevamento, *m.*
uptight [ʌp'tait], *a.* (*colloq.*) teso, nervoso; preoccupato, turbato.
usherette [ʌʃə'ret], *n.* (*Cinema*) Maschera, *f.*

V

†**value,** *n.* **— added tax (VAT),** imposta del (o sul) valore aggiunto (IVA), *f.*
vaseline ['væsəli:n], *n.* (*Reg. trade name*) Vaselina, *f.*
†**vaudeville,** *n.* (*Am.*) [cp. **variety**]. (*Am.*) **— theater** [cp. **music hall**].
veep [vi:p], *n.* (*Am. colloq.*) Vicepresidente degli Stati Uniti, *m.*
verbalize ['və:ɹbəlaiz], *v.i.* Parlare.
†**vest,** *n.* (*Am.*) [cp. **waistcoat**]. || *v.t.* (*Leg.*) **Vested interest,** diritto acquisito, *m.*; (*fig.*) diritto o interesse posseduto da lungo tempo, *m.*
vet [vet], *n.* (*colloq.*) Veterinario, *m.* [cp. **veterinary surgeon**]. *v.t.* (*fig.*) Esaminare; tagliare, ridurre.
vibraphone ['vaibrəfoun], *n.* (*Mus.*) Vibrafono, *m.*
†**vice,** *n.* **— squad,** squadra del buon costume, *f.*
videologist [vidi'ɔlədʒist], *n.* (*Am.*) Patito della televisione, *m.*
videotape ['vidiouteip], *n.* Nastro televisivo, video nastro, *m.*
†**volcano,** *n.* (*fig.*) **To be sitting on a —,** essere minacciato da un pericolo incombente, trovarsi sotto la spada di Damocle.
†**voucher,** *n.* **Luncheon —,** buono-pasto, *m.*
voyeur [vwɑ:'jə:ɹ], *n.* Voyeur, *m.*
voyeurism ['vwɑ:jərizm], *n.* Scopofilia, *f.*

W

wacky ['wæki], *a.* (*Am.*) Buffo, buffonesco, farsesco.
†**wad,** *n.* (*Am.*) [cp. **sheaf**].
†**waffle,** *v.i.* (*colloq.*) Parlare o agire in modo sconclusionato.
†**wage,** *n.* **Basic —,** paga-base, *f.*
†**waiting,** *n.* **— list,** elenco di candidati, *m.*
†**walk,** *n.* (*colloq.*) **Cake —,** ballo americano di origine negra, *m.*; (*fig.*) impresa (*f.*) o compito (*m.*) facile [cp. **walk-over**].
walkie-peekie [wɔ:ki'pi:ki], *n.* (*Am.*) Stazione teletrasmittente a piccolo raggio, *f.*
wank, whank [waŋk], *v.i.* (*slang*) Masturbarsi.
†**war,** *n.* (*fig.*) **Cold —,** guerra fredda, *f.*; **hot —,** guerra calda, guerra guerreggiata, *f.*
warhead ['wɔ:ɹhed], *n.* (*Rocketry*) Testata, *f.* **Atomic —,** testata atomica, *f.*; **nuclear —,** testata nucleare, *f.*
†**wart,** *n.* (*fig.*) **Warts and all,** con tutt'i difetti.
†**washing,** *n.* **— machine,** lavatrice, *f.*
washroom ['wɔʃru:m], *n.* (*Am.*) [cp. **lavatory**].
†**water,** *n.* **— heater** [cp. **geyser**].
†**week,** *n.* **A five-day —,** una settimana corta.
†**weight,** *n.* (*colloq.*) **To throw one's — about,** spadroneggiare, tiranneggiare.
†**western,** *n.* Film western, *m.*
†**what,** *pron.* (*colloq.*) **And — have you,** e tutto quello che volete, e tutto il resto, eccetera.
whirlybird ['wə:ɹlibə:ɹd], *n.* (*Am. colloq.*) Elicottero, *m.*
whizz-kid, *n.* (*Am. colloq.*) Giovane dirigente o consigliere di grande abilità e successo, *m.*; persona molto abile o brillante, *f.*, un fenomeno, *m.*
whodunit [hu:'dʌnit], *n.* Romanzo poliziesco, romanzo giallo, *m.*
wimpy ['wimpi], *n.* (*Reg. trade name*) Panino imbottito di manzo tritato, *m.*
†**wind,** *n.* (*Am. Motor.*) **— shield,** parabrezza, *m.* [cp. **windscreen**].
windcheater ['windtʃi:təɹ], *n.* Giacca a vento, *f.*
†**wipe,** *v.t.* (*fig.*) **To — the floor with,** sconfiggere, sgominare.
†**witch,** *n.* (*fig.*) **— -hunt,** persecuzione fanatica e crudele di una persona o di un gruppo di persone, *f.*
†**with,** *prep.* (*colloq.*) **— it,** sveglio; in gamba.
†**wolf,** *n.* (*Am.*) Dongiovanni; pappagallo, *m.*; **— -whistle,** fischio ammirativo di un uomo quando vede una bella donna o ragazza, *m.*
womanizer ['wumənaizəɹ], *n.* (*Am.*) Donnaiolo, sottaniere, *m.*
wop [wɔp], *n.* (*Am. colloq.*) Italiano, *m.*
†**word,** *n.* (*colloq.*) **The operative —,** la parola importante o significativa nella frase, *f.*
†**work,** *n.* (*Am.*) **— -out,** prova, *f.*, collaudo, *m.*
†**worker,** *n.* **White-collar —,** impiegato, *m.*; professionista, *m.*
wow [wau], *n.* (*Am. colloq.*) **Successo strepitoso,** successone, *m.*
†**wrapping,** *n.* **— paper,** carta da impacco, *f.*, incarto, *m.*

Y

†**yes,** *adv.* (*Am.*) **— -man,** uomo servile, *m.*; adulatore, *m.*; tirapiedi, *m.*
yob [jɔb], *n.* (*slang*) Giovinastro, ragazzaccio, *m.*
yoghourt ['jɔgəɹt], *n.* Yoghurt, *m.*
†**youth,** *n.* **— hostel,** ostello della gioventù, *m.*

Z

zing [ziŋ], *n.* (*Am.*) Ronzio, *m.*; crepitio, *m.*; (*fig.*) vigoria, vitalità, *f.*
†**zip,** *n.* (*Am.*) **— code,** codice d'avviamento postale (CAP), *m.*
zombie ['zɔmbi], *n.* (*Am. colloq.*) Persona senza volontà o immaginazione, *f.*
†**zone,** *n.* **Smokeless —,** zona di città in cui si possono bruciare soltanto combustibili senza fumo, *f.* || *v.t.* Zonizzare.
zoom [zu:m], *v.i.* Rombare; ronzare (soprattutto di aerei).

ENGLISH IRREGULAR VERBS

* = archaic or poetic. *A = archaic or poetic except as attributive adjective. R = rare. S = slang.

INFINITIVE	PAST INDICATIVE	PAST PARTICIPLE
abide	abode (*sometimes* abided)	abode (*sometimes* abided)
arise	arose	arisen
awake	awoke	awoke *or* awaked
be (*Pres. Ind.* am, are, is)	was, were	been
bear	bore	borne (born[1])
beat	beat	beaten[2]
become	became	become
beget	begot	begotten
begin	began	begun
bend	bent	bent[3]
bereave	bereave *or* bereft	bereaved *or* bereft
beseech	besought	besought
bestride	bestrode	bestridden *or* bestrode *or* bestrid
bid	bade *or* bid	bidden *or* bid
bide	bided *or* bode	bided
bind	bound	bound (*A bounden)
bite	bit	bitten (*sometimes* bit)
bleed	bled	bled
blow	blew	blown (S blowed)
break	broke (*brake)	broken (*sometimes* broke)
breed	bred	bred
bring	brought	brought
build	built	built
burn	burnt (*sometimes* burned)	burnt (*sometimes* burned)
burst	burst	burst
buy	bought	bought
Pres. Ind. can[4]	could	—[5]
cast	cast	cast
catch	caught	caught
chiae	chid	chidden *or* chid
choose	chose	chosen
cleave (*v.a.* = *split*)	cleft *or* clove	cleft *or* cloven[6]
cleave (*v.n.* = *cling*)	cleaved *or* clave	cleaved
cling	clung	clung
clothe	clothed *or* clad	clothed *or* clad
come	came	come
cost	cost	cost
creep	crept	crept
crow	crowed *or* crew	crowed
cut	cut	cut
dare[7]	dared (*sometimes*[8] durst)	dared
deal	dealt	dealt
dig	dug (*digged)	dug (*digged)
do[9]	did[10]	done
draw	drew	drawn

INFINITIVE	PAST INDICATIVE	PAST PARTICIPLE
dream	dreamt *or* dreamed	dreamt *or* dreamed
drink	drank	drunk (*A drunken)
drive	drove	driven
dwell	dwelt	dwelt
eat	ate[11]	eaten
fall	fell	fallen
feed	fed	fed
feel	felt	felt
fight	fought	fought
find	found	found
flee	fled	fled
fling	flung	flung
fly	flew	flown
forbear	forbore	forborne
forbid	forbade *or* forbad	forbidden
forget	forgot	forgotten (*forgot)
forgive	forgave	forgiven
forsake	forsook	forsaken
freeze	froze	frozen
get	got	got (*A *and Amer.* gotten[12])
gird	girded *or* girt	girden *or* girt
give	gave	given
go	went	gone
grind	ground	ground
grow	grew	grown
hang (*v.i.*[13])	hung	hung
have[14]	had	had
hear	heard	heard
heave	heaved *or* hove	heaved *or* hove
hew	hewed	hewn *or* hewed
hide	hid	hidden *or* hid
hit	hit	hit
hold	held	held (*holden)
hurt	hurt	hurt
keep	kept	kept
kneel	knelt	knelt
knit	knitted *or* knit	knitted *or* knit[15]
know	knew	known
lade	laded	laden
lay	laid	laid
lead	led	led
lean	leant *or* leaned	leant *or* leaned
leap	leaped *or* leapt	leaped *or* leapt
learn	learned *or* learnt	learned *or* learnt
leave	left	left
lend	lent	lent
let	let	let
lie (= *recline*[16])	lay	lain
light	lit *or* lighted	lit *or* lighted[17]
lose	lost	lost
make	made	made
Pres. Ind. may[18]	might	—
mean	meant	meant

[1] *Si usa nel passivo parlando di nascita, ed anche come aggettivo.* [2] *Ma* beat *nella forma idiomatica* dead-beat, *stanco morto.* [3] *Ma* bended *nella frase* on bended knee, *in ginocchio.* [4] *Forma negativa:* cannot *o* can't. [5] *Manca il participio passato. In questo e in altri tempi difettivi di* can *supplire con* to be able. [6] *Adoperato generalmente come aggettivo* (*p.e.* cloven hoof, cleft stick). [7] *La terza persona è* dare *se adoperato davanti a un'infinito usato senza* to *o sottinteso; altrimenti sempre* dares *al singolare dell'indicativo* (*3ª persona*). [8] Durst *si usa soltanto davanti a un infinito senza* to; *altrimenti, sempre* dared. [9] *Il negativo* do not *diventa spesso* don't; does not *si abbrevia in* doesn't. [10] Did not *si abbrevia* didn't. [11] *Si pronunzia* [ɛt]. *Amer.* [eit]. [12] *Si usa, per esempio, nella frase* ill-gotten gains, *illeciti guadagni.* [13] *Quando* to hang *è verbo transitivo, nel senso di impiccare, è regolare.* [14] *Nell'uso familiare, il negativo viene abbreviato in* haven't *e* hasn't. [15] *Per esempio:* well-knit. [16] *Quando* to lie *significa mentire è regolare.* [17] *Adoperato per lo più come aggettivo.* [18] *Il negativo può essere* must not *o* cannot *quando* may *indica permesso.*

Infinitive	Past Indicative	Past Participle
meet	met	met
melt	melted	melted (*A molten)
mow	mowed	mown
Pres. Ind. must[1]	—	—
pay	paid	paid
put	put	put (*dial.* putten)
quit	quitted (R quit)	quitted (R quit)
—	quoth[2]	—
read	read[3]	read[3]
rend	rent	rent
rid	rid *or* ridded	rid (R ridded)
ride	rode (*rid)	ridden (*rid)
ring	rang (R rung)	rung
rise	rose	risen
rive	rived	riven (R rived)
run	ran	run
saw	sawed	sawn (R sawed)
say	said	said
see	saw	seen
seek	sought	sought
sell	sold	sold
send	sent	sent
set	set	set
shake	shook	shaken
Pres. Ind. shall[4]	should[5]	—
shape	shaped	shaped (*shapen)
shear	sheared (*shore)	shorn (R sheared)
shed	shed	shed
shine	shone	shone
shoe	shod	shod
shoot	shot	shot
show (shew)	showed (shewed)	shown (shewn) (R showed (shewed))
shrink	shrank	shrunk (*A shrunken)
shut	shut	shut
sing	sang (R sung)	sung
sink	sank (R sunk)	sunk (*A sunken)
sit	sat	sat
slay	slew	slain
sleep	slept	slept
slide	slid	slid
sling	slung	slung
slink	slunk (R slank)	slunk
slit	slit	slit
smell	smelt (R smelled)	smelt (R smelled)
smite	smote (*smit)	smitten (*smit)
sow	sowed	sown *or* sowed
speak	spoke (*spake)	spoken
speed	sped[6] *or* speeded[7]	sped[6] *or* speeded[7]

Infinitive	Past Indicative	Past Participle
spell	spelt *or* spelled	spelt *or* spelled
spend	spent	spent
spill	spilled *or* spilt	spilled *or* spilt
spin	spun *or* span	spun
spit *v.n. & a.* (*= expectorate*[8])	spat (*spit)	spat (*spit)
split	split	split
spread	spread	spread
spring	sprang	sprung
stand	stood	stood
stave	staved *or* stove	staved *or* stove
steal	stole	stolen
stick	stuck	stuck
sting	stung	stung
stink	stank *or* stunk	stunk
strew	strewed	strewed *or* strewn
stride	strode	strided (R stridden *or* strid)
strike	struck	struck (*A stricken[9])
string	strung	strung
strive	strove	striven
*strow	*strowed	*strown *or* strowed
swear	swore (*sware)	sworn
sweep	swept	swept
swell	swelled	swollen (R swelled)
swim	swam	swum
swing	swung (R swang)	swung
take	took	taken
teach	taught	taught
tear	tore	torn
tell	told	told
think	thought	thought
thrive	thrived (R throve)	thrived (R thriven)
throw	threw	thrown
thrust	thrust	thrust
tread	trod (*trode)	trodden
wake	woke *or* waked	waked *or* woken *or* woke
wear	wore	worn
weave	wove	woven (*A wove[10])
weep	wept	wept
will[11]	would[12]	—
win	won	won
wind	wound	wound
work	worked (*wrought[13])	worked (*wrought[13])
wring	wrung	wrung
write	wrote (*writ)	written (*writ)

[1] *Quando* must *significa* to be obliged, *la forma negativa è* need not. [2] *Forma oggi rara, e limitata quasi sempre alla prima e terza persona singolare.* [3] *Si pronunzia* [rɛd]. [4] *Il negativo è* shall not *o* shan't. [5] *Negativo:* should not *o* shouldn't. [6] *Nel senso di andare o far andare presto.* [7] *Nel senso di regolare la velocità di* (*macchine, ecc.*). [8] *Nel senso di schidionare è verbo regolare.* [9] *Per esempio:* stricken with fever. [10] *Usato oggi soprattutto parlando di articoli manifatturati, come p.e.* vellum-wove paper. [11] *Negativo:* will not *o* won't. [12] *Negativo:* would not *o* wouldn't. [13] *Forma arcaica usata oggi soltanto parlando di lavori artigianali in certi materiali, come p.e.* wrought in brass.